OFFICIAL MANUAL
STATE of MISSOURI
2015–2016

JASON KANDER
SECRETARY of STATE

Endsheet images
Front: *Truman Lake*, courtesy of Constance Wyrick
Back: *Weston Bend State Park*, courtesy of Charly M. Brewer

Dear Fellow Missourians,

I am pleased to present the 2015–2016 Official Manual of the State of Missouri, more commonly known to most Missourians as the "Blue Book." For more than 130 years, the Blue Book has stood alone as the most comprehensive source of history and information about our state, and I am honored to continue this great tradition with the publication of the second and final volume from my administration.

Missouri's history and the work of countless public servants, including state employees and elected officials, have been collected in this book every other year since 1878. Within these pages you'll find extensive information on state government, as well as the names and faces of many folks who work day after day, year after year, to make sure our state government runs smoothly and efficiently.

What better way to honor the history of our state and the hard work of so many than by featuring photos from Missouri's many parks. No matter if you live in a small town, big city or can't see a neighbor for miles, you've probably enjoyed an afternoon in one of our 87 state parks, or countless municipal and county parks. Parks, in any incarnation, are part of all Missourians' common heritage and experience.

I'm pleased to dedicate the 2015–2016 "Blue Book" to the many parks that highlight our state's natural beauty or offer a quiet respite on a busy street. I hope you'll enjoy the many photographs of Missouri's parks displayed throughout the following pages, and that they inspire you to visit your favorite park or discover a new one.

Finally, this book represents the work of many talented and dedicated employees in the secretary of state's office. It takes nearly a year to produce the Blue Book, and this edition would not have been possible without the hard work of Julie Stegeman, Michael Douglas-Llyr, Jamie Crockett, Laura Swinford, Daniel Klote and Stephanie Fleming—thank you for this latest edition of Missouri's history.

Sincerely,

Jason Kander
Secretary of State

ISBN: 978-0-8262-2109-4

Table of Contents

Chapter 11—Index

CHAPTER 1
MISSOURI ALMANAC

Guides at Big Spring State Park
photo courtesy of Missouri State Archives

A Day at the Park
by Bill Bryan, Director of Missouri State Parks

Capaha Park, Cape Girardeau
photo courtesy of Missouri State Archives

Missourians love parks. We are blessed to have awesome state parks and historic sites, city parks, ballparks, dog parks, water parks, theme parks and skate parks. Our parks help us live happier and healthier lives, make our communities more beautiful and livable, preserve our cultural and natural heritage, provide opportunities for fun and learning and contribute to our economy. Who among us doesn't enjoy a day at the park?

A day at the park means different things to different people, but despite those differences, there is much common ground when it comes to parks. A park belongs to all of us and each of us. It is a place for friends and families to gather. A park is a place for fun. It is a place like no other.

Missourians have always been leaders when it comes to parks. In 1876, St. Louisans opened their beloved Forest Park, and Kansas Citians followed soon after with the ever-popular Swope Park. After more than 125 years, these Missouri masterpieces are still two of the nation's most outstanding urban parks. Each is nearly twice the size of New York City's famed Central Park and offers many different opportunities for city residents and visitors to enjoy their leisure time. It wasn't until later that Missourians looked outside of cities and saw the potential and need for state parks. When they did, they again helped lead the nascent state park movement in America.

View from the 1,000th Mile Trail at Harry S Truman State Park, named in honor of the state park system's milestone achievement of 1,000 miles of trails.
photo courtesy of Missouri State Parks

Public interest in a state park system first began to blossom in Missouri in 1907. After years of public conversation, state legislators introduced a bill to create a state park system. Although the bill did not pass, interest continued to grow, and seven years later, a committee of six senators travelled four days by train, automobile, wagon and on foot, evaluating proposed sites for parks. One of those special places was the site of what is now Ha Ha Tonka State Park, which was established 60 years later. In 2015, Ha Ha Tonka State Park was recognized as one of the five best state parks in America.

In 1916, U.S. Congress established the National Park Service. On April 9, 1917, the Missouri General Assembly passed legislation creating the state park fund and Missouri had a state park system. In 1924, Missouri established Big Spring State Park, the state's very first. Over the next several years, the park system grew rapidly and Missourians were excited about the movement. When Meramec State Park opened in 1928, the park's dedication drew 10,000 visitors.

> In 1924, Missouri established Big Spring State Park, the state's very first.

In the 1930s, the Missouri state park system went through its most significant period of change and development. Beginning in 1933, under the direction of President Franklin Roosevelt, Con-

Stonemason from Company 1743 of the Civilian Conservation Corps, building a structure at Washington State Park in the 1930s.
photo courtesy of Missouri State Parks

gress authorized many federal public works programs to help alleviate the unemployment problem associated with the Great Depression.

The program that meant the most to Missouri's state park system was the Civilian Conservation Corps (CCC), an organization providing jobs for

Stone structure built by Civilian Conservation Corps, still in use today.
photo courtesy of Missouri State Parks

young men between the ages of 18 and 25. By 1934, some 4,000 men were employed in Missouri to complete both conservation and construction work in national and state forests and state parks. Projects ranged from construction of dining lodges, picnic shelters, cabins and campgrounds, to installation of sewer lines. Today, the legacy of the CCC lives on thanks to State Parks Youth Corps (SPYC), a nationally recognized jobs initiative created by Governor Jay Nixon in 2010 to enhance Missouri's 87 state parks and historical sites. The program challenges young people to "think outside" by working at parks and historic sites throughout the state.

The state park system has continued to grow and represent the major natural and cultural heritage themes of Missouri. As Missouri entered the 1980s, the state's economy declined as the entire nation experienced a recession. This recession led to reduced state revenues and mandatory cuts in the budget for the state park system. At this same time, federal revenue sharing and Land and Water Conservation Funds important to state and local parks also were being greatly reduced. A solution was needed to meet the impending fiscal crisis.

In 1984, Missouri voters again showed their support by approving a sales tax to be used for state parks and soil and water conservation efforts in Missouri. Funds from the one-tenth-of-one-percent sales tax are divided equally between the two programs, both of which are administered by the

2015 Trout Season Opener at Bennet Spring State Park.
photo courtesy of Missouri State Parks

Missouri Department of Natural Resources. The tax has been renewed three times and will expire in 2016 if not re-authorized by voters. The sales tax has made our state park system the envy of the nation.

Today, Missouri's state park system contains 87 state parks and has been repeatedly ranked as one of the top four systems in the nation. With more than 145,000 acres available to the public, the state park system has something to fit everyone's needs. A total of 1,000 miles of trail provide opportunities for hikers, backpackers, bicyclists, equestrians and even kayakers. There are campgrounds, picnic areas, beaches and boat ramps for water access for fishing and boating. Lodging facilities, restaurants, stores and visitor centers make visits more convenient and memorable, and are located in some of Missouri's most spectacular landscapes of deep forests, sunny prairies and refreshing lakes and streams.

In 2015, Governor Nixon announced that Missouri State Parks had record attendance, with more than 18.5 million guests, representing a nearly 25 percent increase since 2008. Parks also noted a 5.1 percent increase in camping occupancy at the 40 state parks and historic sites that offer almost 3,600 campsites. The park system noted an important increase in youth camping. A total of 26 percent of campers who stayed the night in a state park were under 18. This strong growth trend is evidence that people love our parks and that we are doing a good job taking care of these treasures, thanks to inno-

vative programs, a dedicated and talented staff and Governor Nixon's unparalleled support for state parks.

Even with outstanding programs and beautiful facilities, not everyone has the "outdoor bug." Fortunately, our state and local parks also preserve our rich cultural heritage as well as natural landscapes. Historic sites allow people to experience history—not just read about it. There is no better way to understand our culture than to see it firsthand. Visitors learn about prehistory at places like Mastodon State Historic Site, experience the American Indian Cultural Center at Van Meter State Park, better understand the Civil War at places like Battle of Island Mound State Historic Site, explore the Negro Leagues Baseball Museum and learn about a favorite son of Missouri at Thomas Hart Benton Home and Studio State Historic Site. Our culture is diverse, and so is the history interpreted in our state, private and local parks.

> Missouri's state park system contains 87 state parks and has been repeatedly ranked as one of the top four systems in the nation.

Parks aren't just limited to those who enjoy time on land. Many formative memories are created drifting down a river on a canoe or raft. From the Ozark's pristine floating streams, to large, manmade lakes, water recreation is an important part of spending time

Sitting around the campfire.
photo courtesy of Missouri State Parks

outdoors in Missouri. Our crystal-clear waterways provide opportunities for visitors of all ages to paddle, boat, fish and swim.

Missouri's park legacy goes far beyond state parks, and includes nearly every city and town in the Show-Me State. Whether you live in a big city, small town or the country, chances are you've been

Autumn color on the bluffs above the Katy Trail, at Katy Trail State Park.
photo courtesy of Missouri State Parks

to the ballpark. If not to see the Royals or the Cardinals, then to enjoy watching a son, daughter, niece, nephew or grandchild play ball. There's not a bad seat in the house at the local ball diamond.

Long before taking the field, for many of us, the playground at a local park provided opportunities to grow stronger, acquire socialization skills and simply enjoy the day. Parks are more than just a place to play: They are important community elements that help make us better people. No matter your age, a day at the park will make you happier and healthier.

In fact, there is medical evidence that is well-established and convincing—a park a day can help keep the doctor away. Spending time outdoors relieves symptoms of anxiety and depression, improves mood and elevates a person's psychological well-being. A walk in the park increases strength, endurance and agility, reducing problems associated with obesity, such as high blood pressure and diabetes. Parks are essential to a healthy Missouri.

In addition to local and state parks, there are also private parks operated by non-profit foundations and some maintained by businesses. Six Flags, Worlds of Fun and Silver Dollar City provide opportunities for family fun that can't be found anywhere else. While adventure can always be found in a park, it doesn't have to be a roller coaster. If you're looking for excitement, it can be found in parks all over the state. Zip-lines, high ropes courses, archery tag, paintball, skateboarding and moun-

> One of the challenges for parks is to remain relevant as our society evolves: Providing new recreation choices is critical to the future of parks.

tain biking opportunities are increasingly easy to find in Missouri. City, state and county parks, as well as places like the Two Rivers Mountain Bike Park near Ozark, provide many choices for mountain biking for different skill levels. Zip-lines also can be found around the state in local and private parks. The Internet is a great way to find relevant recreation alternatives that may help someone you know enjoy a day in the park, regardless of their interest. One of the challenges for parks is to remain relevant as our society evolves: Providing new recreation choices is critical to the future of parks.

Another challenge is to develop more parks to provide additional opportunities for all Missourians to enjoy the benefits of spending time outdoors. Unlike most states, Missouri does not charge an admission fee to enjoy a state park. This means that our park system is far more accessible to all Missourians than most states. In fact, a park is democracy at its finest. No matter who you are or where you live or work, you are always welcome in Missouri state parks.

There still are obstacles for some, however, and solutions are needed to better ensure social equity and provide access to everyone, regardless of their ability. Building the park estate is one way to provide greater access to these critical public services and the inherent benefits. Programs that provide transportation to a park, teach people how to enjoy parks and encourage visits by people who haven't used parks before are also important strategies to ensure that parks serve all Missourians.

Kayaks at Finger Lakes State Park.
photo courtesy of Missouri State Parks

Since taking office in 2009, Governor Nixon has made increasing access to state parks for Missouri families a priority. This means expanding the state park system. Examples of these efforts range from developing the property formerly known as Camp Zoe into a new state park, to efforts that are on pace to complete the extension of the Katy Trail from Windsor to Pleasant Hill through Rock Island Trail State Park in 2016.

Parks are critical to the future of our state. Parks are a public service, every bit as vital as livable roads and streets, effective wastewater treatment and safe drinking water. Parks add immeasurably to the quality of life we enjoy. Instead of thinking of parks as a luxury or amenity, we need to value them for the multitude of vital public service benefits they provide to us. As our population continues to grow and become increasingly urban, parks become even more important to our general welfare. Most of us do not have the resources to build and maintain our own park system, but collectively, we own the nation's very best system of state and local parks. The benefits we enjoy from parks far outweigh the cost of having parks in our communities. Indeed, we cannot afford life without a day at the park.

Graham Cave State Park.
photo courtesy of Missouri State Parks

Sandy Creek Covered Bridge State Historic Site.
photo courtesy of Missouri State Parks

> **Parks are a public service, every bit as vital as livable roads and streets, effective wastewater treatment, and safe drinking water.**

Creek at Hawn State Park.
photo courtesy of Missouri State Parks

Bison at Prarie State Park.
photo courtesy of Missouri State Parks

2015–16 OFFICIAL MANUAL PHOTO CONTEST

A DAY AT THE PARK!

No matter where you live in Missouri, you've likely visited one of our many state and local parks, explored state historical sites or spent a fun afternoon at a sports or theme park. Some of my favorite memories growing up were spent at local sports parks playing Little League.

In celebration of Missouri's fantastic state and local parks, this year's state-wide photo contest asked amateur and professional photographers alike to capture the beauty and tranquility offered at our many parks. A committee from the secretary of state's office narrowed down hundreds of outstanding entries from all over the state to three photos in each category:

State and Local Parks

Sports and Theme Parks

State Historical Sites

Thousands of Missourians weighed in to choose the final winners. You'll find in the following pages, that this year's strong entries show the amazing diversity and beauty of our state and its residents. Thank you to all the Missourians who submitted photos, and congratulations to those whose entries were selected for printing in this historic volume.

Sincerely,

Jason Kander

State & Local Parks

FIRST PLACE—
Ha Ha Tonka Overlook
Kelly Creech, Jefferson City

SECOND PLACE—
Canoeing at Missouri Conservation Area, Millstream Gardens
Jon Berry, Jefferson City

THIRD PLACE—
Evie and Caroline enjoy the swings at Avery Family Park
Vicki Griffon, Troy

Sports & Theme Parks

FIRST PLACE—
Silver Dollar City entrance at Christmas
Barbara Phifer, Springfield

SECOND PLACE—
St. Louis Cardinals at Busch Stadium
Kelly Creech, Jefferson City

HIRD PLACE—
anny Duffy pitching for the Kansas City Royals at Kauffman Stadium
heryl Sloan, Cameron

State Historical Sites

FIRST PLACE—
Alley Mill and Spring on the Ozark National Scenic Riverways
Barbara Romines, Houston

SECOND PLACE—
A doe wanders Jefferson Barracks National Cemetery
Linda K. Behrens, St. Louis

THIRD PLACE—
Union Covered Bridge at Union Covered Bridge State Park
Janice Poole, Hallsville

State Symbols
of Missouri

THE GREAT SEAL OF MISSOURI

The Great Seal was designed by Judge Robert William Wells and adopted by the Missouri General Assembly on January 11, 1822. The center of the state seal is composed of two parts. On the right is the United States coat-of-arms containing the bald eagle. In its claws are arrows and olive branches, signifying that the power of war and peace lies with the U.S. federal government. On the left side of the shield, the state side, are a grizzly bear and a silver crescent moon. The crescent symbolizes Missouri at the time of the state seal's creation, a state of small population and wealth which would increase like the new or crescent moon; it also symbolizes the "second son," meaning Missouri was the second state formed out of the Louisiana Territory.

This shield is encircled by a belt inscribed with the motto, "United we stand, divided we fall," which indicates Missouri's advantage as a member of the United States. The two grizzlies on either side of the shield symbolize the state's strength and its citizens' bravery. The bears stand atop a scroll bearing the state motto, "Salus Populi Suprema Lex Esto," which means, "The welfare of the people shall be the supreme law." Below this scroll are the Roman numerals for 1820, the year Missouri began its functions as a state.

The helmet above the shield represents state sovereignty, and the large star atop the helmet surrounded by 23 smaller stars signifies Missouri's status as the 24th state. The cloud around the large star indicates the problems Missouri had in becoming a state. The whole state seal is enclosed by a scroll bearing the words, "The Great Seal of the State of Missouri." (RSMo 10.060)

MISSOURI DAY

On March 22, 1915, the 48th General Assembly set aside the first Monday in October each year as "Missouri Day," due to the efforts of Mrs. Anna Brosius Korn, a native Missourian. In 1969, the 75th General Assembly changed the date to the third Wednesday in October. Missouri Day is a time for schools to honor the state and for the people of the state to celebrate the achievements of all Missourians. (RSMo 9.040)

THE STATE FLAG

Nearly 100 years after achieving statehood, Missouri adopted an official flag on March 22, 1913. The flag was designed by the late Mrs. Marie Elizabeth Watkins Oliver, wife of former State Senator R.B. Oliver. The flag consists of three horizontal stripes of red, white and blue. These represent valor, purity, vigilance and justice. In the center white stripe is the Missouri coat-of-arms, circled by a blue band containing 24 stars, denoting that Missouri was the 24th state. The Oliver flag embraced national pride, and at the same time expressed characteristics of Missouri and Missourians.

The three large stripes were symbolic of the people of the state—the blue stripe represented vigilance, permanency and justice, the red represented valor, and the white stripe symbolized purity. The Missouri coat-of-arms appeared in the center of the flag, signifying both Missouri's independence as a state, and its place as a part of the whole United States. Having the coat-of-arms in the center of the national colors represents Missouri, as it is—the geographical center of the nation. By mingling the state coat-of-arms with the national colors of red, white and blue, the flag signified the harmony existing between the two. Twenty-four stars surrounded the coat-of-arms, representative of Missouri's position as the 24th state admitted to the Union. (RSMo 10.020)

THE STATE FLORAL EMBLEM

On March 16, 1923, a bill was signed naming the **white hawthorn blossom** the official state floral emblem of Missouri. Known as the "red haw" or "white haw," the hawthorn (*Crataegus*) is a member of the great rose family, which resembles the apple group. The hawthorn blossoms have greenish-yellow centers and form in white clusters. More than 75 species of the hawthorn grow in Missouri, particularly in the Ozarks. (RSMo 10.030)

THE STATE BIRD

On March 30, 1927, the native **bluebird** (*Sialia Sialis*) became the official state bird of Missouri. The bluebird, considered a symbol of happiness, is usually 6½ to 7 inches long. While its upper parts are covered with light blue plumage, its breast is cinnamon red, turning rust-colored in the fall. The bluebird is common in Missouri from early spring until late November. (RSMo 10.010)

THE STATE TREE

On June 20, 1955, the **flowering dogwood** (*Cornus Florida L.*) became Missouri's official tree. The tree is small in size, rarely growing over 40 feet in height or 18 inches in diameter. The dogwood sprouts tiny greenish-yellow flowers in clusters, with each flower surrounded by four white petals. The paried, oval leaves are olive green above and covered with silvery hairs underneath. In the fall, the upper part of the leaves turn scarlet or orange and bright red fruits grow on the tree. (RSMo 10.040)

THE STATE SONG

The **"Missouri Waltz"** became the state song under an act adopted by the General Assembly on June 30, 1949. The song came from a melody by John V. Eppel and was arranged by Frederic Knight Logan, using lyrics written by J.R. Shannon. First published in 1914, the song did not sell well and was considered a failure. By 1939, the song had gained popularity and six million copies had been sold. Sales increased substantially after Missourian Harry S Truman became president. (RSMo 10.050)

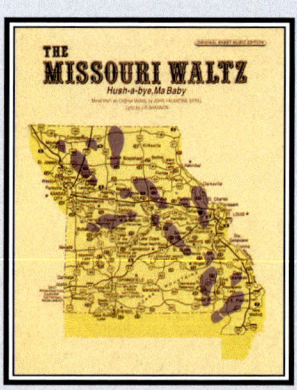

THE STATE MINERAL

On July 21, 1967, the mineral **galena** was adopted as the official mineral of Missouri. Galena is the major source of lead ore, and the recognition of this mineral by the state legislature was to emphasize Missouri's status as the nation's top producer of lead. Galena is dark gray in color and breaks into small cubes. Mining of galena has flourished in the Joplin-Granby area of southwest Missouri, and rich deposits have been located in such places as Crawford, Washington, Iron and Reynolds counties. (RSMo 10.047)

THE STATE ROCK

Mozarkite was adopted as the official state rock on July 21, 1967, by the 74th General Assembly. An attractive rock, mozarkite appears in a variety of colors, most predominantly green, red or purple. The rock's beauty is enhanced by cutting and polishing into ornamental shapes for jewelry. Mozarkite is most commonly found in Benton County. (RSMo 10.045)

THE STATE INSECT

On July 3, 1985, the **honeybee** was designated as Missouri's state insect. The honeybee, (*Apis Mellifera*) yellow or orange and black in color, is a social insect which collects nectar and pollen from flower blossoms in order to produce honey. The honeybee is common to Missouri and is cultivated by beekeepers for honey production. (RSMo 10.070)

THE STATE MUSICAL INSTRUMENT

The **fiddle** became the state's official musical instrument on July 17, 1987. Brought to Missouri in the late 1700s by fur traders and settlers, the fiddle quickly became popular. The instrument was adaptable to many forms of music, could be played without extensive formal training and was light and easy to carry. For generations, the local fiddle player was the sole source of entertainment in many communities and held a position of great respect in the region. (RSMo 10.080)

THE STATE FOSSIL

The **crinoid** became the state's official fossil on June 16, 1989, after a group of Lee's Summit school students worked through the legislative process to promote it as a state symbol. The crinoid (*Delocrinus missouriensis*) is a mineralization of an animal which, because of its plant-like appearance, was called the "sea lily." Related to the starfish, the crinoid which covered Missouri lived in the ocean more than 250 million years ago. (RSMo 10.090)

THE STATE TREE NUT

The nut produced by the black walnut tree (*Juglans Nigra*), known as the **eastern black walnut**, became the state tree nut on July 9, 1990. The nut has a variety of uses. The meat is used in ice cream, baked goods and candies. The shell provides the soft grit abrasive used in metal cleaning and polishing, and oil well drilling. It is also used in paint products and as a filler in dynamite. (RSMo 10.100)

THE STATE ANIMAL

On May 31, 1995, the **Missouri mule** was designated as the official state animal. The mule is a hybrid, the offspring of a mare (female horse) and a jack (male donkey). After its introduction to the state in the 1820s, the mule quickly became popular with farmers and settlers because of its hardy nature. Missouri mules pulled pioneer wagons to the Wild West during the 19th century and played a crucial role in moving troops and supplies in World Wars I and II. For decades, Missouri was the nation's premier mule producer. (RSMo 10.110)

THE STATE AMERICAN FOLK DANCE

The **square dance** was adopted as Missouri's official American folk dance on May 31, 1995. Square dances are derived from folk and courtship dances brought to the United States by European immigrants. Lively music and callers are hallmarks of square dancing. The caller directs the dancers by singing the names of figures and steps to be performed. (RSMo 10.120)

THE STATE AQUATIC ANIMAL

The **paddlefish** (*Polyodon Spathula*) became Missouri's official aquatic animal on May 23, 1997. Only three rivers in Missouri support substantial populations of the paddlefish: the Mississippi, Missouri and the Osage. They are also present in some of the state's larger lakes. The paddlefish is primitive, with a cartilage skeleton, rather than bone. They commonly exceed five feet in length and weights of 60 pounds; 20-year olds are common, and some live 30 years or more. (RSMo 10.130)

The State Fish

On May 23, 1997, the **channel catfish** became the official fish of Missouri. The channel catfish (*Ictalurus Punctatus*) is slender, with a deeply forked tail. Young have spots that disappear with age. The catfish does not rely on sight to find its food; instead, it uses cat-like whiskers to assist in the hunt. The channel cat is the most abundant large catfish in Missouri streams. Its diet includes animal and plant material. Adults are normally 12 to 32 inches long and weigh from a half-pound to 15 pounds. (RSMo 10.135)

The State Horse

On June 4, 2002, the **Missouri fox trotting horse** became Missouri's official state horse. Missouri fox trotters were developed in the rugged Ozark hills of Missouri during the early 19th century. Bloodlines can be traced from early settlers to Missouri from the neighboring states of Kentucky, Illinois, Tennessee and Arkansas. The distinguishing characteristic of the fox trotter is its rhythmic gait, in which the horse walks with the front feet and trots with the hind feet. This gait gives the rider a smooth gentle ride. (RSMo 10.140)

The State Grape

On July 11, 2003, the **Norton/Cynthiana grape** (*Vitis Aestivalis*) was adopted as the official state grape. This adaptable, self-pollinating variety has been cultivated since the 1830s and is likely North America's oldest grape variety still commercially grown. Norton/Cynthiana has long been prized by Missouri vintners for its hardy growth habit and intense flavor characteristics, which produce lush, dry premium red wines of world-class quality and distinction. (RSMo 10.160)

The State Dinosaur

Hypsibema missouriense is a type of dinosaur called a Hadrosaur or "duck billed" dinosaur. It was an herbivore with jaws that contained more than 1,000 teeth. Hypsibema had evolved specialized teeth to handle the tough, fibrous vegetation of the time. Hypsibema lived in Missouri during the Late Cretaceous Period. Hypsibema was first discovered in 1942 by Dan Stewart, near the town of Glen Allen, Mo., and became the state's offical dinosaur on July 9, 2004. (RSMo 10.095)

THE STATE AMPHIBIAN

On June 5, 2005, the **American Bullfrog** (*Rana catesbeiana*) became the official state amphibian. The bullfrog is the largest frog native to Missouri and is found in every county. Most Missourians are familiar with the deep, resonant "jug-of-rum" call, which is typically heard on warm, rainy nights between mid-May and early July. The idea for the bullfrog designation came from a fourth grade class at Chinn Elementary School in Kansas City. (RSMo 10.170)

THE STATE GAME BIRD

The **bobwhite quail** (*Colinus virginianus*), also known as the northern bobwhite, became the official state game bird on July 13, 2007. The northern bobwhite is found throughout Missouri in a variety of habitats. In the fall and winter, northern bobwhites form loose social groups better known as a covey. A covey will generally contain 10 to 12 quail, but can have as many as 20 or 30 birds. The familiar two- or three-note "bobwhite" whistle is made by males in the spring and summer to attract females. (RSMo 10.012).

THE STATE INVERTEBRATE

On June 21, 2007, the **crayfish** (also known as crawfish and crawdad) became the official state invertebrate. Crayfish are an important food source for Missouri fishes. Missouri supports more than 30 species of crayfish (including seven species that occur nowhere else in the world). Crayfish are found in every county of the state and contribute to our unique biodiversity and conservation heritage. The nomination of crayfish for state invertebrate came from Mrs. Janna Elfrink's elementary school class in Reeds Spring, Missouri. (RSMo 10.125)

THE STATE REPTILE

On June 21, 2007, the **three-toed box turtle** (*Terrapene carolina triunguis*) became the official state reptile. Most Missourians are familiar with this land-dwelling turtle. Three-toed box turtles, as their name implies, typically have three hind toes. The hinged bottom shell allows the turtle to retreat inside as if enclosed in a box. Males have red eyes and females have brown eyes. (RSMo 10.175).

The State Grass

Big bluestem (*Andropogon gerardii*) was designated as Missouri's stategrass on June 11, 2007, as a result of efforts by the fourth-grade class at Truman Elementary School in Rolla. Big bluestem is native to Missouri and occurs throughout the state, with the exception of a few southeast-ern-most counties. It is a major component of Missouri's tallgrass prairies where it impressed the first explorers by sometimes growing tall enough to hide a person on horse-back. The name bluestem comes from the bluish-green color of the leaves and stems that turn an attractive reddish-copper color in autumn. (RSMo 10.150).

The State Dessert

The **ice cream cone** became the state of Missouri's offi-cial dessert on August 28, 2008. The 1904 World's Fair in St Louis was the birthplace of the treat and has become a staple at many community events across the state, such as the State Fair. The University of Missouri–Columbia has played a large role in the development of ice cream prod-ucts for over a century. Missouri presently ranks tenth in ice cream production. (RSMo 10.180).

Louise and Omar Putman Collection, photograph by Louise Putman—Missouri State Archives

The State Symbol for Child Abuse Prevention

The **blue ribbon** became the state of Missouri's official symbol for child abuse prevention on August 28, 2012. It is a symbol of efforts to increase awareness of the prevalence and warning signs of child abuse and the prevention meth-ods and measures available to reduce the incidence of child abuse in Missouri. (RSMo 10.185).

The State Exercise

The **jumping jack** exercise was invented by Missouri-born Army General John J. "Black Jack" Pershing as a training drill for cadets when he taught at West Point in the late 1800s. The idea for the jumping jack designation came from students at Pershing Elementary School in St. Joseph. (RSMo 10.115)

Missouri at a Glance

General Information

Entered the Union: August 10, 1821 (24th state).
Capitol: Jefferson City.
Present Constitution adopted: 1945.
Motto: "Salus populi suprema lex esto" which is Latin for "The welfare of the people shall be the supreme law."
Nickname: The Show Me State.
Origin of state name: "Missouri" is most likely a French rendition of the Algonquian word meaning "town of large canoes."
Land area in square miles (national rank): 68,741.52 (18).
Number of counties: 114 with one independent city (St. Louis).
Largest county: Texas—1,177 square miles.
Smallest county: Worth—267 square miles.

Population

Ten largest cities:

Kansas City	465,005
St. Louis	318,727
Springfield	162,333
Independence	117,160
Columbia	113,155
Lee's Summit	92,813
O'Fallon	81,978
St. Joseph	77,040
St. Charles	66,900
St. Peters	54,236

Missouri population 6,028,076
National rank 18
Male/female population (percentage) . . . . 49.0 / 51.0
Ethnic population (by percentage)
White 82.8
Black 11.5
Asian 1.7
Native American 0.4
Native Hawaiian / Pacific Islander 0.1
Other / Two or More Races 2.4
Hispanic (not considering race) 3.8
Urban/rural distribution (by percentage) (2010 census) . . . . 70.4 / 29.6
Resident live births (Missouri Vital Statistics 2013) 75,244
Resident deaths (Missouri Vital Statistics 2013) 57,256
Total personal income and national rank (2014) . . . . $252.4 billion (22)
(U.S. Bureau of Economic Analysis)
Per capita income and national rank (2014) $41,639 (31)
(U.S. Bureau of Economic Analysis)
Median household income and national rank (2014) $48,363 (37)
(American Community Survey)
Real Gross Domestic Product and national rank (2014) . . . . $279.8 billion (22)
(U.S. Bureau of Economic Analysis)

Geography/Climate

Highest point (in feet above sea level: Taum Sauk Mountain, Iron County) 1,722
Lowest point (in feet above sea level: St. Francis River, Bootheel) 230
Approximate mean elevation in feet above sea level (national rank) 800 (32)
Normal daily mean temperature . . . . 54.6°F
Percentage of full sunshine days per year . . . . 30%–est.

CHAPTER 2
EXECUTIVE BRANCH

Trout fishing, Montauk State Park, 1980
Photo courtesy of Missouri State Archives

Jeremiah W. (Jay) Nixon
Governor
Elected November 4, 2008
Term expires January 2017

JAY NIXON (Democrat) is serving his second term as governor of Missouri. After garnering the highest margin of victory for a non-incumbent governor in 44 years when first elected in 2008, Nixon was re-elected by Missourians as their 55th governor in 2012 to continue creating jobs and moving the state forward.

As governor, Jay Nixon has worked to make government more efficient, effective and responsive to the needs of Missouri families. He is committed to maintaining fiscal discipline, creating jobs, growing the economy and investing in public education.

As he did in the state Senate and during four terms as attorney general, Governor Nixon is reaching across the aisle to put Missouri families first. He successfully worked with the legislature to pass several jobs initiatives, including a bill credited with saving Missouri's auto industry and creating thousands of good manufacturing jobs. As a result, Ford, General Motors and automotive suppliers around the state have invested billions of dollars and created thousands of jobs to build next-generation vehicles and parts in the Show-Me State.

Just as Missouri families have to do at home, Governor Nixon has made the tough choices necessary to balance the budget every year without raising taxes. The governor's commitment to fiscal discipline has helped protect Missouri's AAA credit rating, while enabling smart investments to improve education, expand access to mental health services and help communities struck by disasters rebuild and recover.

Governor Nixon has made a strong public education system one of his chief priorities. Under his leadership, Missouri's public elementary and secondary schools have received record funding, and test scores and graduation rates have gone up. Similarly, even as other states were raising tuition by double digits, Missouri has led the nation in holding down tuition increases at public universities.

He has been a strong supporter of the Missouri National Guard and Missourians serving in the military, creating the Show-Me Heroes program to help returning veterans find jobs here at home and enacting a dedicated source of funding for veterans homes. A member of the President's Council of Governors, Governor Nixon has made multiple trips to Iraq and Afghanistan to visit with troops and be briefed on military operations.

Nixon has visited each of Missouri's 87 state parks and historic sites to help promote them as recreational destinations, with a goal of reaching 20 million visitors by 2020. He also began the State Parks Youth Corps to beautify the parks and put young people to work. Governor Nixon is an avid hunter and fisherman, and after Missouri was named the "Best Trails State" in America in 2013, both he and the first lady led the 100 Missouri Miles Challenge to encourage Missourians to spend more time getting active outdoors.

Prior to becoming governor, Jay Nixon was elected to a record four terms as Missouri's attorney general. His settlements with the insurance industry and hospitals led to the formation of two of the largest health care foundations in state history. One of Nixon's most successful programs, Missouri's popular No-Call List, has become a model for states across the nation to stop unwanted telemarketing calls.

A native of De Soto, Nixon was raised in a family of public servants. His mother, the late Betty Nixon, was a teacher and served as president of the local school board. His father, Jerry Nixon, was mayor of De Soto and a municipal judge.

Growing up in a home with these strong examples, Nixon learned at a young age that faith and family come first—and giving back to the community comes next. That philosophy has guided him throughout his career in public service.

After earning his undergraduate and law degrees from the University of Missouri, Nixon returned to De Soto to practice as an attorney. In 1986, he would be elected to the Missouri Senate, where he would represent the people of Jefferson County for six years.

Governor Nixon and his wife, Georganne Wheeler Nixon, have two sons, Jeremiah and Willson. They belong to the First United Methodist Church in Jefferson City.

Office of Governor

State Capitol
Jefferson City 65102
Telephone: (573) 751-3222 / FAX: (573) 751-1588
www.gov.mo.gov

CHRIS PIEPER
Chief of Staff

JUDY MURRAY
Assistant to the Governor

Qualifications

The chief executive officer of the state of Missouri must be at least 30 years old, a U.S. citizen for at least 15 years and a resident of Missouri for at least 10 years before being elected governor.

The governor is elected to a four-year term during the same year as a presidential election and may seek re-election to a second four-year term. No person may hold the office for more than two terms.

EDWARD R. ARDINI
Chief Counsel

JEFF HARRIS
Director of Policy

Responsibilities

The governor appoints the members of all boards and commissions, all department heads in state government and fills all vacancies in public offices unless otherwise provided by law. The board members of Missouri's state universities and colleges are appointed by the governor. The governor also selects the members of the Supreme and Appellate Courts of Missouri from names submitted by the Appellate Judicial Commission. The governor appoints members to certain election boards, the Kansas City police board and the Board of Probation and Parole. Most appointments require the advice and consent of the Senate.

The governor addresses the General Assembly on the state of the State and recommends changes or other actions to be taken. A budget is submitted by the governor to the General Assembly within 30 days after the General Assembly convenes. The budget contains the governor's estimates of available state revenues and an itemized plan for proposed expenditures.

All bills passed by both houses of the legislature are submitted to the governor for consideration. The governor must return the legislation to the house of its inception within 15 days after receiving it. The governor may either approve a bill, making it law, or return it to the legislature with objections. When the legislature is adjourned, the governor has 45 days in which to consider a bill.

The governor may object to one or more items or portions of items of an appropriations bill while approving other items or portions of the ap-

JASON ZAMKUS
Director of Legislative Affairs

propriations bill. Upon signing the appropriations bill, appended to it is a statement of the items or portions of items to which there are objections and such items or portions will not take effect. The governor may control the rate of expenditure in other areas whenever the actual revenues are less than the revenue estimates upon which the appropriations were based.

Additional Duties and Powers

The governor performs many other duties assigned by the constitution, statute or custom. For example, the governor issues writs of election to

KELSEY THOMPSON
Director of Scheduling

A.J. FOX
Director of Boards and
Commissions

MIKE NIETZEL
Senior Policy Advisor

ANDREA SPILLARS
Senior Policy Advisor

WILLIAM L. MILLER, JR.
Senior Policy Advisor &
Legal Counsel

CHANNING ANSLEY
Director of Communications

SCOTT HOLSTE
Press Secretary

SETH BUNDY
Deputy Press Secretary &
Policy Advisor

fill vacancies in either house of the General Assembly. The governor also has the power to grant reprieves, commutations and pardons, but this does not include the power to parole.

In addition to other duties, the governor is a member of a number of boards and commissions, such as the Board of Public Buildings and the State Board of Fund Commissioners.

Moreover, the governor is the conservator of peace throughout Missouri and is commander-in-chief of the state's militia. The militia may be called out to execute laws, suppress threats of danger to the state and prevent and repel invasion.

SHARI CHILDS
Mansion Director

TIFFANY BAYER
Assistant to the First Lady

Executive Department

The executive department consists of all state elective and appointive employees, except those of the legislative and judicial departments.

Missouri's First Lady

Like the governor, First Lady Georganne Wheeler Nixon earned her undergraduate and law degrees from the University of Missouri–Columbia. Her support of Governor Nixon's call for strong public education in Missouri comes naturally: her father, the late Hubert Wheeler, served as Missouri's first commissioner of education; her mother and grandmother were both teachers; and Mrs. Nixon herself has taught in public schools.

Mrs. Nixon is an outdoor enthusiast who has helped lead the Governor's 100 Missouri Miles Challenge, an initiative launched by the governor and the first lady to encourage families to enjoy Missouri's outdoors as part of an active lifestyle. Mrs. Nixon also has actively promoted the state's 85 parks and historic sites as vacation destinations and as a way to learn more about Missouri. She

also gardens, and has planted a vegetable and herb garden on the mansion grounds.

An avid supporter of the arts and literature, the first lady often goes to schools and libraries to read to children as a way of encouraging literacy for both children and adults. Mrs. Nixon also serves as honorary chair for Missouri Citizens for the Arts and presents the Missouri Art Education Association awards to young artists whose artworks are selected to be on display at the Capitol and in the Missouri Governor's Mansion.

Missouri Governor's Mansion

The Missouri Governor's Mansion serves as the official residence of Governor Jay Nixon and First Lady Georganne Nixon. The first family extends an invitation to all Missourians to tour "the people's house," which in 2014 hosted more than 37,000 visitors.

First occupied by Governor G. Gratz Brown and his family in 1872, this stately three-story brick building is one of the oldest and most beautifully restored governors' homes in the United States. Built and finished in the Renaissance Re-

vival style, the entry consists of an imposing portico with four dignified pink granite columns. A Victorian atmosphere greets visitors as they enter the great hall with its 17-foot ceilings, a rare free-flowing staircase of solid walnut and one of the best collections of period furnishings in the country. Missouri first ladies' portraits are featured throughout the mansion, along with loaned works of art created by the world-famous Missouri artist George Caleb Bingham. Designed by George Ingham Barnett of St. Louis, the mansion is listed on the National Register of Historic Places.

Since moving to the mansion, the Nixons have added a vegetable and herb garden. Baker Creek Heirloom Seed Company, of Mansfield, Mo., has provided heirloom seeds for the garden. Food grown in the garden is used in meals served at the mansion, and Mrs. Nixon enjoys encouraging schoolchildren to start their own gardens. The Missouri Botanical Gardens and Powell Gardens provided assistance in planning the garden at the mansion. The mansion grounds also contain apple trees, cherry trees and berry bushes planted in 2014 by Stark Bro's Nurseries in honor of former Gov. Lloyd Stark

Historical Listing, Governors

	Name and (Party)	Term	County	Born	Died
1.	Alexander McNair (D)[1]	1820–24	St. Louis	5/5/1775	3/18/1826
2.	Frederick Bates (D)[1]	1824–25	St. Louis	6/23/1777	8/4/1825
3.	Abraham J. Williams (D)[1]	1825	Boone	2/26/1781	12/30/1839
4.	John Miller (D)[1]	1825–32	Howard	11/25/1781	3/18/1846
5.	Daniel Dunklin (D)	1832–36	Washington	1/14/1790	8/25/1844
6.	Lilburn W. Boggs (D)	1836–40	Jackson	12/14/1792	3/14/1860
7.	Thomas Reynolds (D)	1840–44	Howard	3/12/1796	2/9/1844
8.	Meredith Miles Marmaduke (D)[2]	1844	Saline	8/25/1791	3/26/1864
9.	John Cummins Edwards (D)	1844–48	Cole	6/24/1806	9/17/1888
10.	Austin Augustus King (D)	1848–53	Ray	9/21/1802	4/22/1870
11.	Sterling Price (D)	1853–57	Chariton	9/20/1809	9/29/1867
12.	Trusten Polk (D)[3]	1857	St. Louis	5/29/1811	4/16/1876
13.	Hancock Lee Jackson (D)[4]	1857	Randolph	5/12/1796	3/19/1876
14.	Robert Marcellus Stewart (D)	1857–61	Buchanan	3/12/1815	9/21/1871
15.	Claiborne Fox Jackson (D)	1861	Saline	4/4/1806	12/6/1862
16.	Hamilton Rowan Gamble (U)[5, 6]	1861–64	St. Louis	11/29/1798	1/31/1864
17.	Willard Preble Hall (U)[6]	1864–65	Buchanan	5/9/1820	11/3/1882
18.	Thomas Clement Fletcher (R)[7]	1865–69	St. Louis	1/22/1827	3/25/1899
19.	Joseph Washington McClurg (R)[7]	1869–71	Camden	2/22/1818	12/2/1900
20.	Benjamin Gratz Brown (R)[8]	1871–73	St. Louis	5/28/1826	12/13/1885
21.	Silas Woodson (D)	1873–75	Buchanan	5/18/1819	10/9/1896
22.	Charles Henry Hardin (D)	1875–77	Audrain	7/15/1820	7/29/1892
23.	John Smith Phelps (D)	1877–81	Greene	12/14/1814	11/20/1886
24.	Thomas Theodore Crittenden (D)	1881–85	Johnson	1/1/1832	5/29/1909
25.	John Sappington Marmaduke (D)	1885–87	St. Louis City	3/14/1833	12/28/1887
26.	Albert Pickett Morehouse (D)	1887–89	Nodaway	7/11/1835	9/23/1891
27.	David Rowland Francis (D)	1889–93	St. Louis City	10/1/1850	1/15/1927
28.	William Joel Stone (D)	1893–97	Vernon	5/7/1848	4/14/1918
29.	Lon Vest Stephens (D)[9]	1897–1901	Cooper	12/21/1858	1/10/1923
30.	Alexander Monroe Dockery (D)	1901–05	Daviess	2/11/1845	12/26/1926
31.	Joseph Wingate Folk (D)	1905–09	St. Louis City	10/28/1869	5/28/1923
32.	Herbert Spencer Hadley (R)	1909–13	Jackson	2/20/1872	12/1/1927
33.	Elliott Woolfolk Major (D)	1913–17	Pike	10/20/1864	7/9/1949
34.	Frederick Dozier Gardner (D)	1917–21	St. Louis City	11/6/1869	12/18/1933
35.	Arthur Mastick Hyde (R)	1921–25	Grundy	7/12/1877	10/17/1947
36.	Sam Aaron Baker (R)	1925–29	Cole	11/7/1874	9/16/1933
37.	Henry Stewart Caulfield (R)	1929–33	St. Louis	12/9/1873	5/11/1966
38.	Guy Brasfield Park (D)	1933–37	Platte	6/10/1872	10/1/1946
39.	Lloyd Crow Stark (D)	1937–41	Pike	11/23/1886	9/17/1972
40.	Forrest C. Donnell (R)	1941–45	St. Louis	8/20/1884	3/3/1980
41.	Phil M. Donnelly (D)	1945–49	Laclede	3/6/1891	9/12/1961
42.	Forrest Smith (D)	1949–53	Ray	2/14/1886	3/8/1962
43.	Phil M. Donnelly (D)	1953–57	Laclede	3/6/1891	9/12/1961
44.	James T. Blair Jr. (D)	1957–61	Cole	3/15/1902	7/12/1962
45.	John M. Dalton (D)	1961–65	Dunklin	11/9/1900	7/7/1972
46.	Warren E. Hearnes (D)	1965–73	Mississippi	7/24/1923	8/16/2009
47.	Christopher S. (Kit) Bond (R)	1973–77	Audrain	3/6/1939	
48.	Joseph P. Teasdale (D)	1977–81	Jackson	3/29/1936	5/8/2014
49.	Christopher S. (Kit) Bond (R)	1981–85	Audrain	3/6/1939	
50.	John Ashcroft (R)[10]	1985–93	Greene	5/9/1942	
51.	Mel Carnahan (D)[10]	1993–2000	Phelps	2/11/1934	10/16/2000
52.	Roger Wilson (D)[11]	2000–01	Boone	10/10/1948	
53.	Bob Holden (D)	2001–05	Shannon	8/24/1949	
54.	Matt Blunt (R)	2005–09	Greene	11/20/1970	
55.	Jeremiah W. (Jay) Nixon (D)[10]	2009-	Jefferson	2/13/1956	

[1]At the time of the elections of McNair, Bates and Williams, and of the first election of Miller in 1825, there were no organized political parties in Missouri. Individual popularity prevailed. All called themselves Jeffersonian Republicans, or what now are called Democrats.
[2]Marmaduke was elected Lt. Governor in 1840. Upon the death of Governor Thomas Reynolds in February 1844, Marmaduke became governor. He served the remainder of that year, because John Cummins Edwards was elected.
[3]Soon after Polk was inaugurated, the Legislature convened and elected him by 101 votes to be a U.S. Senator. He resigned to take that office in February 1857. His occupancy of the governor's office was shorter than any other governor of Missouri.
[4]Jackson was Lt. Governor under Polk and became acting governor after Polk resigned in February 1857. He served until October of that year when Robert Stewart took office. Stewart was elected at a special election in August 1857.
[5]Gamble was elected provisional governor by the Missouri State Convention on July 31, 1861. The office had been declared vacated after Governor Claiborne Fox Jackson joined the Confederacy.
[6]Unionist.   [7]Radical.   [8]Liberal.
[9]Gov. Stephens is credited with creating the State Fair in Sedalia.
[10]Some held multiple terms as governor. In consideration of space, some are listed here only once.
[11]Wilson became Missouri's 52nd governor on October 17, 2000, upon the death of Governor Mel Carnahan.

Peter D. Kinder
Lieutenant Governor
Elected November 2, 2004
Term expires January 2017

PETER D. KINDER (Republican) was elected Missouri's 46th lieutenant governor on November 2, 2004. On November 4, 2008, he was re-elected to a second term and on November 6, 2012, he became only the second Missourian in state history to win the office three times, carrying 108 of Missouri's 114 counties.

Prior to his election as lieutenant governor, Kinder served for 12 years in the Missouri Senate, representing the counties of Bollinger, Cape Girardeau, Madison, Mississippi, Perry and Scott. In 2001, Republicans gained a majority in the Senate. As a result, Kinder's colleagues elected him president pro tem, the Senate's top elected official. He was the first Republican to hold that position in 53 years.

As lieutenant governor, Kinder is the official senior advocate for Missouri, and during his Senate service he was known for his work on behalf of the state's senior residents. He sponsored and passed the Elderly Protection Act of 2003, which increased the penalties for elder abuse crimes. With his leadership, Missouri crafted the Missouri Senior Rx plan, providing prescription drug coverage for the poorest seniors. In 2006, Lt. Gov. Kinder was instrumental in passing the Assisted Living Bill, a top priority for many senior advocacy groups. This legislation gives seniors more options and choice in the type of long-term care facility they want to call home.

Kinder has led the fight on issues affecting Missouri's veterans. In 2005, he proposed and helped to pass the Missouri Military Family Relief Fund, which benefits family members of the Missouri National Guard and Reserve personnel who have been called to active duty.

Kinder coordinated the Missouri Mentor Initiative, a program that encourages state employees to mentor children by receiving up to 40 hours a year in paid time off to volunteer. He also ensured funding for the Amachi Program that assists Big Brothers/Big Sisters of Missouri to mentor children whose parents are incarcerated in Missouri prisons.

The lieutenant governor is a member of several boards and commissions including the Missouri Development Finance Board, the Missouri Housing Development Commission, the Board of Public Buildings and the Missouri Tourism Commission.

Born and raised in Cape Girardeau, Kinder attended Cape Girardeau Public Schools and continued his education at Southeast Missouri State University and the University of Missouri–Columbia. He graduated from St. Mary's University School of Law in San Antonio, Texas, in 1979, and was admitted to the Missouri Bar in 1980.

From 1981 to 1983, Kinder was a member of U.S. Rep. Bill Emerson's Washington, D.C. staff and then worked as an attorney and real estate representative for Drury Industries. In 1987, he became associate publisher of the Southeast Missourian newspaper in Cape Girardeau.

Kinder is a member of the United Methodist Church, Beta Theta Pi social fraternity, Missouri Farm Bureau, Cape Girardeau Chamber of Commerce and Lions Club. He is active in many civic causes, including extensive work with United Way, the Nature Conservancy, the American Cancer Society and Boy Scouts of America.

Kinder has been honored by various groups including: Missouri Right to Life, Defender of Life; National Rifle Association; University of Missouri, Presidential Citation Award; National Scouting Association Distinguished Eagle Scout Award; St. Louis Children's Hospital, SSM Cardinal Glennon Hosdpital, and Children's Mercy of K.C.; March of Dimes; Southeast Missouri State University Alumni Association Distinguished Service Award; St. Louis Business Journal Legislative Award; Support Your Troops Committee Award; Missouri Farm Bureau Outstanding Service to Agriculture; St. Louis Regional Commerce and Growth Association Lewis and Clark Statesman Award for Outstanding Leadership; Missouri Restaurant Association Distinguished Service; Associated Industries of Missouri Voice of Missouri Business; Southeast Missouri Alliance for Disability Independence; SSM Cardinal Glennon Hospital Child Advocate Award; National Federation of Independent Businesses, Guardian of Small Business; Missouri State Medical Association; and Missouri Chamber of Commerce and Industry Spirit of Enterprise.

Office of Lieutenant Governor

224 State Capitol, Jefferson City 65101
Telephone: (573) 751-4727 / FAX: (573) 751-9422
www.ltgov.mo.gov
Email: ltgovinfo@ltgov.mo.gov

Qualifications

Missouri's lieutenant governor must be at least 30 years old, a U.S. citizen for at least 15 years and a resident of Missouri for at least 10 years before being elected to the office. The lieutenant governor is elected for a four-year term and is subject to re-election.

Duties

The lieutenant governor is the only statewide elected official that is part of both the executive and legislative branches of state government. Under the constitution, the lieutenant governor is *ex officio* president of the Missouri Senate. The lieutenant governor is elected independently from the governor, and each can be members of different political parties. Upon the governor's death, conviction, impeachment, resignation, absence from the state or other disabilities, the lieutenant governor shall act as governor. By law, the lieutenant governor is a member of the Board of Public Buildings, Board of Fund Commissioners, Missouri Development Finance Board, Missouri Community Service Commission, Missouri Housing Development Commission and the Tourism Commission. The lieutenant governor is an adviser to the Department of Elementary and Secondary Education on early childhood education and the Parents-as-Teachers program and the state's official advocate for senior citizens.

Roles of the Office

In recent years, the lieutenant governor has embraced more responsibilities, especially relating to seniors, veterans, tourism and service. These modern developments have made the lieutenant governor more visible and accessible to Missourians. The many boards and commissions on which the lieutenant governor serves provide numerous opportunities to help Missouri citizens. These boards and commissions cover a wide variety of functions for Missouri's diverse population.

REID FORRESTER
Chief of Staff

LAURIE DAWSON
Director of Administration

JAY EASTLICK
Director of Communications

WILLIS JONES
Director of Constituent Services

MATTHEW BAIN
Staff Assistant

JOSEPH PONDROM
Director
Policy and Legislative Affairs

By statute, the lieutenant governor is the official senior advocate for the State of Missouri. This office investigates problems and issues on behalf of senior citizens. The lieutenant governor's office works very closely with the Department of Health and Senior Services to ensure the safety and well-being of Missouri's senior citizens. The lieutenant governor helps manage the Missouri Rx Prescription Drug Program. More information may be found at www.morx.mo.gov.

Military veterans exemplify the meaning of service. They have answered the call of duty, boldly facing death, injury and uncertainty. Their sacrifice should never be forgotten. The lieutenant governor is proud to advocate for issues vital to our Missouri veterans.

Lt. Gov. Kinder actively promotes the Missouri Military Family Relief Fund, a state-administered fund assisting families of the Missouri National Guard and reservists who have been deployed for the global war on terrorism. Those interested in donating should contact the Missouri Veterans Commission at (573) 522-4220 or make an income tax check-off donation when filing a state income tax return.

As a member of the Missouri Tourism Commission, the lieutenant governor helps market Missouri to the rest of the world. Out-of-state visitors bring new revenue to Missouri businesses and new tax dollars to Missouri. Centrally located in the United States and bordering eight other states, Missouri hosts tens of millions of visitors each year. The Tourism Commission plans campaigns to show visitors all Missouri has to offer.

Lt. Gov. Kinder led the effort to bring the Tour of Missouri, an international professional bicycle race, to Missouri in 2007. Before funding was pulled in 2010, the competition was one of the top five professional cycling events outside of Europe, drawing spectators from across the U.S. and the globe.

As part of the Missouri Community Service Commission, the lieutenant governor is honored to continue a legacy of service to citizens across Missouri. This commission nurtures volunteerism by encouraging an atmosphere that enables citizen service to prosper. By partnering with national service programs, the commission promotes volunteer opportunities to interested citizens. Each year, the Community Service Commission recognizes award winners who have demonstrated exemplary service.

Lt. Gov. Kinder also sponsors the Senior Service Award to promote and highlight the positive accomplishments senior citizens selflessly provide their communities. Bi-annual winners are recognized from every region of the state. More information may be found at *www.ltgov.mo.gov*. The lieutenant governor also serves on the Missouri Housing Development Commission. As such, the lieutenant governor has the opportunity to help ensure quality, affordable housing for Missourians, regardless of income. Other boards and commissions on which the lieutenant governor serves include: Board of Fund Commissioners; Board of Public Buildings; Missouri Development Finance Board; Second State Capitol Commission; and the Special Health, Psychological and Social Needs of Minority Older Individuals Commission. He is also an adviser to the Department of Elementary and Secondary Education on early childhood education.

This compilation of the lieutenant governor's responsibilities demonstrates how the office can assist all Missourians. Citizens are urged to contact the lieutenant governor's office regarding issues that affect seniors by calling (800) 699-2377, or through the website at *www.ltgov.mo.gov*.

Historical Listing, Lieutenant Governors

	Name and (Party)	Term	County	Born	Died
1.	William Henry Ashley (D)	1820–24	St. Louis	1785	3/26/1839
2.	Benjamin Harrison Reeves (D)	1824–28	Howard	3/21/1787	4/16/1849
3.	Daniel Dunklin (D)	1828–32	Washington	1/14/1790	8/25/1844
4.	Lilburn W. Boggs (D)	1832–36	Jackson	12/14/1792	3/14/1860
5.	Franklin Cannon (D)	1836–40	Cape Girardeau	3/12/1794	6/13/1863
6.	Meredith Miles Marmaduke (D)	1840–44	Saline	8/28/1791	3/26/1864
7.	James Young (D)	1844–48	Lafayette	5/11/1800	2/9/1878
8.	Thomas Lawson Price (U)[1]	1848–52	Cole	1/19/1809	7/15/1870
9.	Wilson Brown (D)[2]	1853–57	Cape Girardeau	8/27/1804	8/27/1855
10.	Hancock Lee Jackson (D)	1857–61	Randolph	5/12/1796	3/19/1876
11.	Thomas Caute Reynolds (D)	1860–61	St. Louis	10/11/1821	3/30/1887
12.	William Willard Preble Hall (U)[1, 3]	1861–64	Buchanan	5/ 9/1820	11/3/1882
13.	George Smith (R)	1865–69	Caldwell	2/2/1809	7/14/1881
14.	Edwin Obed Standard (R)[4]	1869–71	St. Louis	1/5/1832	3/12/1914
15.	Joseph Jackson Gravely (R)[5]	1871–73	Cedar	9/25/1828	4/28/1872
16.	Charles Phillip Johnson (R)[5]	1873–75	St. Louis	1/8/1836	5/21/1920
17.	Norman J. Colman (D)	1875–77	St. Louis	3/16/1827	11/3/1911
18.	Henry Clay Brockmeyer (D)	1877–81	St. Louis City	8/12/1828	7/26/1906
19.	Robert Alexander Campbell (D)	1881–85	St. Louis City	9/2/1832	4/2/1926
20.	Albert Pickett Morehouse (D)	1885–89	Nodaway	7/11/1835	9/23/1891
21.	Stephen Hugh Claycomb (D)	1889–93	Jasper	8/11/1847	6/6/1930
22.	John Baptiste O'Meara (D)	1893–97	St. Louis City	6/24/1852	7/22/1926
23.	August Henry Bolte (D)	1897–1901	Franklin	9/3/1854	6/24/1920
24.	John Adams Lee (D)	1901–03	St. Louis City	6/28/1851	10/10/1928
25.	Thomas Lewis Rubey (D)[6]	1903–04	Laclede	9/27/1862	11/2/1928
26.	John C. McKinley (R)	1905–09	Putnam	11/20/1859	5/1/1927
27.	Jacob Friedrich Gmelich (R)	1909–13	Cooper	7/23/1839	2/21/1914
28.	William Rock Painter (D)	1913–17	Carroll	8/27/1863	7/1/1947
29.	Wallace Crossley (D)	1917–21	Johnson	10/4/1874	12/13/1943
30.	Hiram Lloyd (R)	1921–25	St. Louis	7/27/1875	9/10/1942
31.	Phillip Allen Bennett (R)	1925–29	Dallas	3/5/1881	12/7/1942
32.	Edward Henry Winter (R)	1929–33	Cole	4/5/1879	6/29/1941
33.	Frank Gaines Harris (D)[7]	1933–45	Boone	4/25/1871	12/30/1944
34.	Walter Naylor Davis (D)	1945–49	St. Louis	11/29/1876	9/16/1951
35.	James T. Blair Jr. (D)[7]	1949–57	Cole	3/15/1902	7/12/1962
36.	Edward V. Long (D)	1957–61	Pike	7/18/1908	11/6/1972
37.	Hilary A. Bush (D)	1961–65	Jackson	6/21/1905	5/11/1966
38.	Thomas F. Eagleton (D)	1965–69	St. Louis	9/4/1929	3/4/2007
39.	William S. Morris (D)	1969–73	Jackson	11/8/1919	3/5/1975
40.	William C. Phelps (R)[7]	1973–81	Jackson	4/5/1934	
41.	Kenneth J. Rothman (D)	1981–85	St. Louis	10/11/1935	
42.	Harriett Woods (D)	1985–89	St. Louis	6/2/1927	2/8/2007
43.	Mel Carnahan (D)	1989–93	Phelps	2/11/1934	10/16/2000
44.	Roger B. Wilson (D)[7]	1993–2000	Boone	10/10/1948	
45.	Joe Maxwell (D)[8]	2000–05	Audrain	3/17/1957	
46.	Peter D. Kinder (R)[7]	2005-	Cape Girardeau	5/12/1954	

[1]Unionist.
[2]Wilson Brown died in office in August 1855. The office remained vacant until the 1856 election.
[3]Hall was elected provisional lieutenant governor by the Missouri State Convention on July 31, 1861. The office had been declared vacated after Governor Claiborne Fox Jackson joined the Confederacy.
[4]The Constitution of 1865 shortened lieutenant governor. terms to two years. In 1876, terms went back to four years.
[5]Liberal.
[6]Was president pro tem of Senate and served as lieutenant governor following Lee's resignation.
[7]Some held multiple terms as lieutenant governor. In consideration of space, they are listed here only once.
[8]Maxwell became Missouri's 45th lieutenant governor finishing the remaining months of Roger Wilson's term, who became governor on October 17, 2000, upon the death of Mel Carnahan.

Missouri State Capitol

State government in Missouri is centered in the state's beautiful, domed Capitol, dominating the bluffs of the Missouri River in Jefferson City.

The dome, rising 238 feet above ground level and topped by a bronze statue of Ceres, goddess of agriculture, is the first view of Jefferson City for travelers arriving from the north. The structure is Jefferson City's leading tourist attraction and is a mecca for school groups who arrive by busloads, particularly during General Assembly sessions when they fill the galleries to watch the Senate and House of Representatives in action.

In addition to housing the two legislative bodies, the Capitol provides office space for the governor, lieutenant governor, secretary of state, treasurer, state auditor and some administrative agencies. The structure is also notable for its architectural features, including its eight 48-foot columns on the south portico and six 48-foot columns on the north side; its 30-foot-wide grand stairway and its bronze front doors, each 13-by-18 feet, among the largest cast since the Roman era.

The Capitol's first floor features the State Museum. Outstanding paintings, pediments and friezes decorate the Capitol interior. Of historical significance is a series of Thomas Hart Benton murals in the House Lounge.

Statuary is a prominent feature of the Capitol grounds. Heroic bronze figures depicting Missouri's two great rivers, the Mississippi and Missouri, and a 13-foot statue of Thomas Jefferson

dominate the south entrance. A bronze relief depicting the signing of the Louisiana Purchase by Livingston, Monroe and Marbois and the Fountain of the Centaurs are the most outstanding features on the north grounds.

The present Capitol, completed in 1917 and dedicated in 1924, is the fourth Capitol in Jefferson City. Before the seat of government was moved to Jefferson City, the functions of Missouri territorial government were based in the Mansion House, a hotel in St. Louis, and later at the Missouri Hotel, also in St. Louis. The upper story of a mercantile store in St. Charles was designated as temporary capital of the state in 1821 and remained the seat of government until 1826 when Jefferson City became the permanent capital city. The first Capitol in Jefferson City was located on land now occupied by the Governor's Mansion. It burned in 1837, apparently after some hot coals fell out of one of its fireplaces. A second structure, completed in 1840 and expanded in 1887–88 burned when the dome was struck by lightning on February 5, 1911. A temporary Capitol made of lathe and stucco was erected in an area to the east of the present building and was used from 1912 to 1917.

The present Capitol was constructed for $4,215,000, including site and furnishings. It is five stories high, 437 feet long, 300 feet wide in the center and 200 feet wide in the wings. The dome is 238 feet high and the height of the wings is 88 feet. It includes over 650,000 square feet of floor space.

Jason Kander
Secretary of State
Elected November 6, 2012
Term expires January 2017

JASON KANDER (Democrat), 34, was sworn in as Missouri's 39th Secretary of State in January 2013. A former U.S. Army Captain, Kander is a veteran of the war in Afghanistan. Prior to his election as secretary of state, he practiced law, represented Kansas City in the Missouri General Assembly and served on the Missouri Veterans Commission. He is a graduate of American University and Georgetown Law School and is married to his high school sweetheart, Diana. Their son True was born in September 2013.

A fifth generation Missourian, Kander learned early in life about the importance of community service. His mother was a juvenile probation officer and his father was a police officer who later ran a small business.

On September 11, 2001, Kander was a student at American University. Moved by what he saw that day, Kander later enlisted in the Army National Guard and served in an infantry unit. While a law student at Georgetown University, he successfully pursued his commission as a military intelligence officer in the Army Reserve. He volunteered to deploy to Afghanistan in 2006. As an intelligence officer in Afghanistan, he investigated groups and individuals suspected of corruption, espionage, drug trafficking and facilitating Al Qaeda and the Taliban.

In an unclassified evaluation, Kander's commanders praised his willingness to volunteer for dangerous duty, describing him as an "outstanding leader" whose work saved lives. The U.S. director of intelligence in Afghanistan advised the Army to "track this officer's career closely; he is one of the best." After his deployment, Kander was assigned as a combat leadership instructor in the Missouri Army National Guard's Officer Candidate School at Fort Leonard Wood. In 2010, he earned national recognition and was selected as one of 10 finalists for the Army Reserve Junior Officer of the Year Award by the Reserve Officer Association.

In 2008, Kander knocked on 20,000 doors in Kansas City during his first successful campaign for state representative. As a state legislator, Kander worked with both parties to pass ethics reform legislation. As a member of the House Budget Committee, he exposed a no-bid contract and helped balance the budget without raising taxes. He passed legislation to take Missouri's human trafficking laws from some of the weakest to some of the strongest in the nation. He also authored and passed Sam and Lindsey's Law to help authorities prevent kidnapping during custody battles.

In 2009, Kander was appointed to the Missouri Veterans Commission, a nine-member board that oversees all services for our state's veterans. He was also an attorney in private practice representing clients in state and federal courts before assuming statewide office.

As secretary of state, Kander has fought for access to the ballot for eligible voters, protected Missourians from fraud and helped small business owners succeed. He created the Elections Integrity Unit to increase transparency and encourage Missourians to report their concerns regarding elections and voting. Kander was also proud to launch the Military and Overseas Voting Access Portal that allows Missourians serving away from home to receive and return absentee ballots more efficiently. Throughout his tenure in the Missouri General Assembly and now as Secretary of State, Kander continues to fight for campaign finance and ethics reform.

Office of Secretary of State

600 W. Main and 208 State Capitol
PO Box 1767, Jefferson City 65102
Telephone: (573) 751-4936 / FAX: (573) 526-4903
www.sos.mo.gov
Email: sosmain@sos.mo.gov

BARBARA WOOD
Deputy Secretary of State /
General Counsel

CASEY CLARK
Chief of Staff

The secretary of state's office serves Missourians in a number of diverse and important ways. The major divisions within the secretary of state's office are: Business Services, Elections, Securities, State Library, Records Services and Administrative Rules.

At Secretary of State Jason Kander's direction, the office has focused on making state government more accessible and transparent to all Missourians. These efforts include the creation of a 30-day public comment period for initiative petitions, an online voter registration form and the creation of the Elections Integrity Unit. Additionally, Kander launched the *www.TheMissouriChannel.com*, a site dedicated to archiving legislative debate and other proceedings in state government. Kander has also made the adoption of early or no-excuse absentee voting a top legislative priority, and he has consistently advocated for stronger ethics and campaign finance laws.

JOHN SCOTT
Deputy Chief of Staff

STEPHANIE FLEMING
Director of Communications

In the Business Services Division, Kander opened the Business Outreach Office to assist entrepreneurs and small business in navigating the requirements to do business in Missouri. Additionally, Kander launched a new online system that allows nearly every business form that must be filed with his office to be filed on an easy-to-use website. Through the Securities Division, he has protected consumers by cracking down on firms that defraud investors and educated Missourians about responsible investing. As Missouri's chief elections official, Kander has worked to ensure fair, accessible and transparent elections for Missouri voters.

In addition, the office is responsible for compiling, storing and publishing a variety of documents, including many historic records available on *www.MissouriDigitalHeritage.com*. As the keeper of the Great Seal of the State of Missouri, Kander is also responsible for authenticating official acts of the governor. The office also includes the following divisions: Information Technology,

PHYLLIS ALLSBURY
Executive Secretary to the
Secretary of State

JOSE CALDERA
Senior Deputy Counsel

Communications and Publications, Fiscal and Facilities and Human Resources.

Business Services Division

www.sos.mo.gov/business/

The Business Services Division has three units: Notaries and Commissions, Corporations and Uniform Commercial Code. The division oversees regional filing offices in St. Louis, Kansas City and Springfield, and the Safe at Home

ANDREW ADAMS
Deputy Counsel

ELIZABETH ZERR
Director of Governmental and
Legislative Affairs

JOHN GASKIN III
Deputy Director, Legislative and
Governmental Affairs and
Business Outreach

JIM BENOIST
Director of External Operations

JAMIE CROCKETT
Deputy Director of
Communications

JASE CARTER
Director of Business Services /
Senior Advisor

VAL HEET
Director of Fiscal and Facilities

LORI HUGHES
Assistant Director of Fiscal and
Facilities

address confidentiality program. The Business Services Division is committed to making it easier to do business in Missouri.

Notaries and Commissions

The Notaries and Commissions Unit commissions notaries public, maintains the official bonds of over 81,000 Missouri notaries, and is responsible for certifying notaries for foreign documents, elected officials and the State Registrar of Vital Statistics.

The unit also authenticates official acts of the governor. The Great Seal of the State of Missouri is affixed to more than 35,000 documents annually, including all commissions of state and county elected officials; appointments made by the governor; and proclamations, executive orders, extraditions, commutations of sentence and restoration of citizenship issued by the governor. The unit maintains bonds and oaths of office for state officials as required by law and is responsible for the official signature, facsimile signature filings, resident agent filings and trademark and service mark filings.

Corporations

The secretary of state is responsible for the registration of all Missouri and out-of-state businesses operating in Missouri. Businesses file various documents required by law: creation documents, annual reports, amendments, mergers, consolidations, dissolutions, terminations, withdrawals and conversions. There are approximately 600,000 active businesses registered in Missouri. Nearly every registration and filing may be easily filed online at *www.sos.mo.gov/fileonline*, saving businesses time and money.

The Business Outreach Office (*www.sos. mo.gov/business/outreach*) and the Missouri Business Portal (*www.business.mo.gov*) continue to help Missouri businesses navigate state government and help their businesses grow.

Uniform Commercial Code

The secretary of state's office is the centralized office for perfecting personal property liens and other creditor interests under the Uniform Commercial Code (UCC). These liens are perfected by filing a financing statement in the accepted national format indicating the debtor

MICHELE WATLEY
Director
Kansas City Branch Office

MYRA LEWIS
Director
St. Louis Branch Office

DEBBIE EVANS
Director
Springfield Branch Office

JON BARRY
Director of Business Outreach

name and address and the secured party name and address along with a description of the collateral. Once a lien or other interest is filed and perfected, the public is considered "on notice" regarding those liens. These financing statements are effective for five years; they may be continued for an additional five-year term by filing a continuation statement within six months preceding expiration. Ninety percent of the UCC filings with the secretary of state are now completed online. UCC online filings, forms and the fee schedule for filing are available at *www.sos.mo.gov/ucc*.

Safe at Home Address Confidentiality Program

The Safe at Home address confidentiality program was created in 2007 to help protect survivors of domestic violence, rape, sexual assault or stalking through the use of a designated address. Through the Safe at Home program, survivors and their minor children may use the substitute mailing address through the secretary of state's office for all their first class, legal and certified mail. The program also allows survivors to use a substitute address on their government records and public filings to keep their address confidential and out of the hands of potential abusers.

Business Services Offices:

James C. Kirkpatrick State Information Center
600 W. Main, Rm. 322
PO Box 778, Jefferson City, MO 65102-0778
Telephone: (866) 223-6535 / FAX (573) 751-5841

Fletcher Daniels State Office Building
615 E. 13th St., Rm. 513, Kansas City 64106
Telephone: (816) 889-2925 / FAX: (816) 889-2879

U.S. Customs & Post Office Building
815 Olive St., Ste. 150, St. Louis 63101
Telephone: (314) 340-7490 / FAX: (314) 340-7500

LESLEY LUECKENOTTE
Director of Corporations

Springfield State Office Building
149 Park Central Sq., Rm. 624, Springfield 65806
Telephone: (417) 895-6330 / FAX: (417) 895-6537

Safe at Home Address Confidentiality Program
PO Box 1409, Jefferson City, MO 65102-1409
Telephone: (866) 509-1409 / FAX: (573) 522-1525
www.mosafeathome.com

Securities Division
James C. Kirkpatrick State Information Center
600 W. Main, PO Box 1276, Jefferson City 65102
Telephone: (573) 751-4136 / FAX: (573) 526-3124
Investor Protection Hotline: (800) 721-7996
www.sos.mo.gov/securities
www.MissouriSafeSavings.com

For more than 80 years, the secretary of state has been responsible for ensuring compliance with state securities laws through activities of the Securities Division. This responsibility includes enforcement of the law when violations occur and the registration of securities, broker-dealers, agents, investment advisers and investment-adviser representatives. State securities laws are intended to protect investors from unsuitable investment recommendations, dishonest or unethical practices and fraudulent investment schemes. The secretary of state appoints the commissioner of securities, who administers these laws and oversees the Securities Division.

The enforcement section of the Securities Division receives and investigates complaints from Missouri investors. The division maintains a toll-free Investor Protection Hotline, (800) 721-7996, so investors can report complaints or make inquiries about firms or professionals in the securities business. Each year the office fields hundreds of investor complaints that result in the initiation of hundreds of investigations, many of which result in cease and desist orders, licensing revocations, investor restitution, civil penalties or criminal prosecutions. The attorneys and investigators in the enforcement section typically collect millions of dollars in penalties, payments and restitution each year and are leaders in national enforcement actions and task forces.

The examination section regulates the registration of individuals and firms and performs routine and for-cause inspections and pre-registration exams of the offices of broker-dealers and investment advisers to ensure compliance with Missouri securities laws.

As of summer 2015, there were 144,358 agents, 1,658 broker-dealers, 10,395 investment-adviser representatives and 1,720 investment advisers registered in Missouri. Prior to granting each registration, an application review process is conducted to determine if applicants are sufficiently qualified to participate in the securities business.

The registration section reviews proposed securities offerings to ensure Missouri-approved registrations are "fair, just and equitable." The staff receives filings of federally covered securities and reviews requests for exemption from the registration requirements, provides interpretative opinions of the securities laws and assists Missouri issuers seeking to raise funds with securities law compliance. In the 2015 fiscal year, the registration section staff received filings or exemption notices for almost 2,800 securities offerings and collected over $15.9 million in revenues for the State of Missouri.

The Securities Division also oversees the Missouri Investor Protection Center, which creates and promotes investor education initiatives designed to educate and assist both current and future investors. The center also includes a website, accessible at *www.MissouriSafeSavings.com*, and a Senior Investor Protection Unit to help educate and protect Missouri's older investors.

ANDREW HARTNETT
Commissioner of Securities

MARY HOSMER
Assistant Commissioner of Securities

Elections Division

James C. Kirkpatrick State Information Center
600 W. Main, PO Box 1767, Jefferson City 65102
Telephone: (573) 751-2301 / FAX: (573) 526-3242
www.sos.mo.gov/elections/

The secretary of state's office oversees all state elections for candidates, various judges and issues. Candidates for the six constitutional state offices, U.S. Congress, the General Assembly and certain judges file for election with the secretary of state. Statewide ballots for primary, general and certain special elections are also prepared by the secretary of state, and certified copies of those ballots are sent to local election officials. It is the responsibility of the office to canvass, certify and publish state election results.

Missouri has more than 4 million registered voters. In the November 2014 general election, 1.4 million voters went to the polls. Elections are run by Missouri's 116 local election authorities (county clerks or election boards) and the secretary of state provides assistance to the authorities in several ways. This includes maintaining annual election deadline calendars, the secretary of state's website and various training materials and workshops. The secretary of state also promulgates rules governing elections and publishes the Missouri Election Laws for use by the local election authorities. The secretary of state works together with state and local officials, schools and civic organizations to provide materials to support voter registration, civic responsibility and education. This collaboration also extends to oversight of the statewide poll worker recruitment initiative.

The secretary of state's office also assists military and overseas voters by facilitating their voter registration and absentee ballot request process. The Missouri Military and Overseas Portal, created and maintained by the secretary of state's office, is available online for these eligible voters.

The secretary of state also certifies statewide ballot measures proposed by the General Assembly or through the initiative and referendum petition process, including the oversight of signature verification. Before an initiative petition can be circulated, the petition and its summary statement must be approved by the secretary of state and the state attorney general. The secretary of state must certify the summary statement along with the state auditor's fiscal note statement. Those wishing to place an initiative changing state law on the ballot must obtain signatures from registered voters equal to five (5) percent of the total votes cast in the last gubernatorial election in six of Missouri's eight congressional districts. In order to place an initiative changing the state constitution on the ballot, signatures must be obtained from registered voters equal to eight (8) percent of the votes cast in the last gubernatorial election in six of the state's eight congressional districts. The secretary of state is responsible for verifying the number of signatures for each initiative. A ballot issue's full text is published in newspapers around the state, printed for display at polling places and is also available on the secretary of state's website. The secretary of state also oversees the signature verification process for the formation of new political parties and the nomination of independent candidates for offices that file with the secretary of state. In 2014, 67 initiative petitions were approved for circulation. One initiative petition was certified for the November 2014 ballot.

The secretary of state is also responsible for coordinating Missouri's compliance with federal election law, including the Help America Vote Act of 2002, which requires increased training for election officials, poll workers and voters, at least one accessible voting system per polling place for voters with disabilities and the creation of a statewide voter registration list. This interactive, statewide voter registration list has improved the ability of local election officials to manage their voter registration records and keep Missouri's voter list up-to-date and accurate.

Finally, the secretary of state's office upholds the fairness and security of the elections process by investigating concerns received by voters and local election authorities. The Elections Integrity Unit resolves these complaints and publishes their reviews on the secretary of state's website.

Missouri State Library

James C. Kirkpatrick State Information Center
600 W. Main, PO Box 387, Jefferson City 65102
Telephone: (573) 751-3615 / FAX: (573) 751-3612
www.sos.mo.gov/library/

The responsibilities of the Missouri State Library are to provide library and reference servic-

JULIE ALLEN
Director of Elections and
Information Technology

SURESH DESU
Deputy Director
Information Technology

es to Missouri state government, provide library services to the blind and visually impaired and promote the development and improvement of library services throughout the state.

Library Development

Telephone: (800) 325-0131 / (573) 751-0586

The library development section supports libraries through consulting, administration of grant programs, continuing education and statewide programs. The consultant staff works with librarians and library governing boards to improve the quality of library service for all Missouri citizens. Through research, publications and personal contacts, consultants provide assistance on general library issues and needs, promote the organization and development of library services, manage statewide projects and maintain statistics on public library services in the state.

The state library administers several programs to provide funds and services for libraries. State-funded programs include state aid for public libraries to meet a wide variety of local needs. Public library costs for materials are supported through funds appropriated from the income tax on earnings of out-of-state athletes and entertainers. State funds also support summer reading programs in public libraries. The State Library coordinates the funding for the Remote Electronic Access to Libraries (REAL) Program, which provides Internet access for public libraries through MOREnet and database content for public, K–12 and academic libraries. The federal Library Services and Technology Act provides approximately $3 million in funding for grants to libraries and for statewide projects, including training for library staff and trustees, technology infrastructure, summer reading and early literacy programs, and development of library service for underserved populations, such as seniors and persons with disabilities.

Ongoing projects include digitization of primary resource material for www.MissouriDigitalHeritage.com, resource-sharing initiatives including Show Me The World database access and courier delivery service for materials, and providing a resource collection for use by library staff.

The state library also serves as the lead agency for the State Census Data Center program, a cooperative venture with the U.S. Census Bureau.

Secretary's Council on Library Development

www.sos.mo.gov/library/council/sosc.asp.

The Secretary's Council on Library Development advises the secretary of state and the state librarian on matters that relate to the state's libraries and library service to Missouri citizens.

Sanders, Kathryn, chair;
Bacon, Donna, Representing: Library Service Providers;
Buthod, Sharla, Representing: School Libraries;
Cooper, Regina, Representing: Public Libraries;
Dawes, Trevor A., Representing: Academic Libraries;
DePriest, Renee, Representing: Citizens;
Diel, James, Representing: Citizens;
Geerlings, Karla L., Representing: Citizens Using Wolfner Library;
Lundy, Christie, Representing: State Employees;
Nasheed, Sen. Jamilah, Representing: Legislature;
Pennington, Buddy, Representing: Academic Libraries;
Pierson, Rep. Tommie, Representing: Legislature;
Price, Beverly, Representing: Citizens;
Revels, Mary Beth, Representing: Public Libraries;
Riddle, Sen. Jeanie, Representing: Legislature;
Schmitt, Michelle, Representing: School Libraries;
Stierholz, Katrina, Representing: Special Libraries;
Swan, Rep. Kathryn, Representing: Legislature;
Walker, Scotty, Representing: Library Trustees.

Reference Services

Telephone: (573) 751-3615 / FAX: (573) 751-3612

The Reference Services Division supports the research needs of Missouri state government employees with its collections of books, journals, newspapers, and government documents in print and digital formats. It is also a member of MOBIUS, the statewide library consortium of academic and public libraries in Missouri, which provides access to many additional resources.

In-person and online training is offered for Missouri state government employees around the state on topics such as Census statistics, Internet searching, and specific databases.

BARBARA READING
State Librarian

DEBBIE MUSSELMAN
Director of Library Development

WAHEEDAH BILAL
Director of Reference Services

DONNA RIEGEL
Director of Wolfner Library

Reference Services produces Keeping Up, a daily news clipping service that provides current, focused information about Missouri state government from a selection of Missouri digital news sources. It is distributed electronically to the legislature and Missouri state government employees.

Documents from federal and Missouri state agencies are also available through the library. Many Missouri state government documents are available in print onsite and in a digital library at the Internet Archive www.archive.org/details/missouristatepublications. The division has participated in the Federal Depository Library Program since 1963 and has an assortment of print federal government documents, some of which focus on Missouri.

Reference Services hosts the Missouri Department of Transportation library collection as part of a joint agreement between the MoDOT and the State Library. Other special collections in the library include Missouri history, library science, and historical documents about Missouri libraries.

Wolfner Library

James C. Kirkpatrick State Information Center
600 W. Main, PO Box 387, Jefferson City 65102
Telephone: (573) 751-8720 / FAX: (573) 751-3612
Toll free: (800) 392-2614
www.sos.mo.gov/wolfner

Wolfner Talking Book and Braille Library serves as the public library for Missourians unable to use standard print because of a visual or physical disability. The library loans a half million books and magazines in Braille, recorded audio and large print from its collection of more than 300,000 volumes. The library also provides access to locally recorded Missouri titles and to over 60,000 titles via the national Braille and Audio Reading Download (BARD) site. Audio players are also loaned to users of the recorded materials. More than 12,500 individuals and 2,000 institutions, including nursing homes, schools, hospitals and hospices, use the library. Wolfner also provides reference and information services, children's programming, interlibrary loans, a newsletter, catalogs and bibliographies and descriptive DVDs and videos. Access to the collection is available online.

Wolfner services are available to qualified Missourians at no charge. Applications for service are available directly from Wolfner, local Missouri public libraries or on the secretary of state's website. Wolfner is Missouri's regional library in the national network of libraries serving individuals who are blind and disabled, in cooperation with the National Library Service of the Library of Congress.

The Wolfner Talking Book and Braille Library has a rich history of library service, predating the Missouri State Library and the Library of Congress network. Loaning Braille books to a multi-state region in 1924, Wolfner became one of the first 18 regional libraries for the blind designated by the Library of Congress. Named in memory of noted ophthalmologist Henry L. Wolfner and originally administered by the St. Louis Public Library, Wolfner became part of the Missouri State Library in 1977 and physically moved to Jefferson City in 1985.

Wolfner Advisory Council

The Wolfner Advisory Council advises on the services provided by the Wolfner Library and how these services may be improved. Current Council members can be found at *www.sos. mo.gov/wolfner/council.asp.*

Flasar, Dan, chair, Richmond Heights, National Federation of the Blind;
Dingus, Mary, St. Louis, Department Elementary and Secondary Education;

Miller, Zeze, Jefferson City, Washington, Missouri Council of the Blind;
Altschual, Peter, Columbia;
Jaco, Bob, St. Louis;
Ormsby, Andrew A. Jr., Sikeston;
Rogers, Darla J., M.S., Gladstone; and
Tussey, Carolyn Sue, Jefferson City.

Records and Archives

James C. Kirkpatrick State Information Center
600 W. Main St., PO Box 1747, Jefferson City 65102
(573) 751-3280
www.sos.mo.gov/records/

Established as a separate department in 1965, Records and Archives now includes three divisions: the Missouri State Archives, Records Management and Local Records. These divisions are collectively responsible for managing both the current and historical records of the state, ensuring they are preserved and making them accessible to Missouri citizens.

Missouri State Archives

Telephone: (573) 751-3280 / Fax: (573) 526-5327

The Missouri State Archives is the official repository for government records of enduring value. Its mission is to foster an appreciation of Missouri history by preserving and making available the state's permanent records to its citizens and their government.

Records in the Archives date from 1770 to the present. They include executive, legislative and judicial records; records of state departments and agencies; early French and Spanish colonial and U.S. territorial records; military records from the War of 1812 through World War II; records detailing the region's role in the 19th century fur trade and America's westward expansion; trademarks and business records; and records documenting women's and African-American history.

Holdings currently total more than 338 million pages of paper records, 770,000 photographs, 199,000 reels of microfilm and 270,000 microfiche. The Missouri State Archives is one of the most accessed state repositories in the nation and has been formally acknowledged by historical and genealogical organizations for its service to researchers. While thousands visit or write to the Archives each year, the majority turn to the Internet as their preferred research method. In 2014, the Archives website logged 91.6 million hits from 8.3 million visitors.

Over the past few years, the Missouri State Archives has become involved in a number of important initiatives. The African-American History Initiative is designed to stimulate interest in African-American history through educational projects and the promotion of the Archives holdings. The Missouri State Archives also played a leading role in the activities of the Civil War Sesquicentennial Commission and the development of the Missouri Digital Heritage website, an online portal through which the public can access digital collections from institutions across the state.

The Archives is devoted to educating the public about materials in its holdings. Programs are provided for school and civic groups, as are traveling exhibits, tours and monthly educational programs. Archives Alive!, a history based theatrical performance, brings history to life each spring for thousands of Missouri fourth- and fifth-grade students. The Friends of the Missouri State Archives, Inc., promote and support the Archives by underwriting many of the costs associated with these outreach activities. The Archives also hosts student interns and practicum students from Missouri colleges and universities, and sponsors the central Missouri National History Day competition.

Volunteers are an important resource of the Missouri State Archives. They provide invaluable support to staff, helping with records processing across the state as well as assisting with reference and tours in Jefferson City. More novel is the Archives' innovative e-Volunteer program in which volunteers provide indexing and transcription services from their home computers. Completed projects are posted online, providing greater access to collections. In-person access to the Archives is provided through the Alex M. Petrovic Reading Room. Hours are 8 a.m. to 5 p.m. on Monday, Tuesday, Wednesday and Friday, and 8 a.m. to 8 p.m. on Thursday. Saturday hours are from 9 a.m. to 3 p.m.

Missouri Historical Records Advisory Board

The Missouri Historical Records Advisory Board was created by statute in 1989 to be the central advisory body for historical records planning within the state. The board also serves as the state affiliate of the National Historical Publications and Records Commission, the grant-awarding arm of the National Archives and Records Administration and is responsible for reviewing grant proposals submitted to that program from Missouri applicants, as well as applications to the Local Records Preservation Grant Program.

Missouri Historical Records Advisory Board Members

Kander, Jason, chair, state historical records coordinator, secretary of state;

Dougan, John, deputy coordinator, state archivist;

JOHN DOUGAN
State Archivist

SHELLY CROTEAU
Assistant State Archivist

CHRISTINA MILLER
Senior Reference Archivist

Allen, Gregory B., president, Allen Financial Corporation, Kansas City;

Bennett, Marcia L., executive director, St. Joseph Convention and Visitors Bureau, St. Joseph;

Doswell, Raymond, vice president of curatorial services, Negro League Baseball Museum, Kansas City;

Gordon, Christopher A., director of library and archives, Missouri History Museum, St. Louis;

Neumann, Robert P., director, Greene County Archives and Records Center, Springfield;

Offord, Jerome Jr., dean, Library Services and University Archives, Lincoln University, Jefferson City;

Parks, Cynthia L., director of records management, University of Missouri, Columbia;

Richards, David E., head, Special Collections and Archives Department, Meyer Library, Missouri State University, Springfield;

Rhodes, Joel P., associate professor, Southeast Missouri State University, Cape Girardeau;

Sparks, Susan, president, Polk County Genealogical Society, Humansville; and

Kremer, Gary R., executive director, State Historical Society of Missouri, Jefferson City, *ex officio.*

Missouri Board on Geographic Names

The Missouri Board on Geographic Names was created by state statute in 1995 to coordinate place-naming activity among local, state and federal agencies. Additionally, the board provides uniformity in geographic nomenclature throughout the state, while retaining the significance, history and culture associated with the names of Missouri's geographic features. Proposed changes or additions to names of geographic features and places are received and evaluated, and recommendations are made to the U.S. Board on Geographic Names for approval. Members include both interested citizens and professionals.

Missouri Board on Geographic Names Members

Kander, Jason, chair, secretary of state;
Dougan, John, chair designee, state archivist;
Barnett, Christopher J., vice chair, University of Missouri, Columbia;
Carter, Joseph, Missouri Department of Transportation, Jefferson City;
Claspill, Gary, Office of Administration, Jefferson City;
Fisher, John, Kennett;
Foreman, Alan, U.S. Army Corps of Engineers, St. Louis;
Gillman, Joe, Missouri Department of Natural Resources, Rolla;
Greene, Debra F., Lincoln University, Jefferson City;
Kremer, Gary R., State Historical Society of Missouri, Jefferson City;
McCann, Gordon, Springfield;
Moorman, Amy, Missouri State Archives, Jefferson City;
Morrow, Lynn, Jefferson City;
Nickell, Frank, Center for Regional History and Cultural Heritage, Cape Girardeau;
Silch, Shelley, U.S. Geological Survey, Rolla;
Spicci, Tony, Missouri Department of Conservation, Columbia;
Sweets, Henry, Mark Twain Home Foundation, Hannibal;
Turner, Jay, Mark Twain National Forest-Salem Ranger District, Salem;
Vineyard, Jerry, Ozark; and
Weaver, Dwight, Eldon.

Records Management

Telephone: (573) 751-3319 / Fax: (573) 526-5327

The mission of Records Management is to provide state agencies with the necessary instruments to effectively manage information and records, in order to promote the efficiency and continuity of government, document the rights of Missouri citizens and preserve the state's heritage. To achieve this mission, the division is divided into three sections: Records Management Services, Imaging Services and the State Records Center.

Sound records management programs consist of a planned and coordinated set of policies, procedures and activities to manage recorded information in all media. Records Management Services assists state government agencies in identifying and effectively managing their official records. Section records analysts consult with agency officials to develop retention schedules that list the agency's records, specify their retention periods and determine the ultimate disposition of inactive records (those with limited use that do not warrant retention in expensive agency office space). They also advise agencies on cost and technical matters related to microfilm, digital imaging and low-cost storage of inactive and semi-active records.

Imaging Services provides micrographic and digital imaging services to state agencies and local governments. Agencies can reduce the volume of, improve access to, and ensure archival preservation for their long-term and significant records by utilizing these services. Micrographics services include microfilming, processing, quality control and duplication. Digital imaging includes image production from microfilm or original documents. The section also provides ideal storage for original microfilm within a climate-controlled vault.

The State Records Center provides state agencies with an economical storage solution for inactive records. Services provided by the section include pick-up; delivery; reference pulls and re-filing; and destruction of agency records. All records remain in the legal custody of the transferring agency, and access to stored documents is restricted to authorized personnel. The transfer of inactive files to the records center allows agencies to free up office space and equipment, saving Missouri taxpayers millions of dollars over the life of the records. As of October 2015, the State Records Center's two facilities stored 396,871 cubic feet of records.

State Records Commission

The State Records Commission was established by statute in 1965 to guide records management in the determination of retention periods for all records in the executive branch of state government. Currently, more than 800 state agencies, commissions, bureaus and boards operate under approved record retention schedules. Additionally, the commission reviews, approves and recommends guidelines for the management of both paper and electronic records generated by the state of Missouri.

State Records Commission Members

Kander, Jason, chair, secretary of state;
Dougan, John, secretary, state archivist;
Beard, Nathan, state representative;
Dixon, Bob, state senator;
Galloway, Nicole, state auditor;
Koster, Chris, attorney general;
Kremer, Gary R., executive director, State Historical Society of Missouri;
Nelson, Doug, commissioner, Office of Administration; and
Robyn, Tim, chief information officer.

NATHAN TROUP
Assistant Director of Records Management

JOHN KORASICK
Director of Local Records

Local Records

Telephone: (573) 751-9047 / Fax: (573) 526-5327

The Local Records Division works to improve long-term management of local government records by advising, educating and encouraging records custodians in the use of sound records management and archival practices. Local Records archivists provide expertise to local government officials on the retention of records and conducting records preservation projects.

A part-time local records program was started in 1986 with legislation funding the creation of a separate division in 1989. Through Local Records, documents of great historical value have been identified and preserved, revealing long-lost local histories and enhancing the collection of the Missouri State Archives. Consultations, records inventories and preservation projects conducted by division staff make local public records more accessible. Records are properly organized, identified and, in many instances, space in public buildings is freed up for purposes other than storage.

More than 3,500 governmental entities, including all offices in county, municipal and local district government offices, rely on Local Records for assistance in managing records. Field archivists are located around the state to assist this effort. Local officials in every county have received assistance from Local Records.

Local Records also houses the state document conservation lab, where staff provide advice to local government offices on all aspects of record care, preservation and disaster recovery. Conservation treatment is provided on the most historically significant and fragile documents as well.

Local Records Board

The Local Records Board was created by statute in 1972. The Local Records Board, comprised of representatives from all local government classifications, reviews and establishes retention schedules for local governments records.

Local Records Board Members

Barnard, Barbara, Morgan County Historical Society, Versailles;
Chamberlain, Neal, Kirksville County R-III Schools, Kirksville;
Diggs, Chris, Columbia Public Schools, Columbia;
Hall, Crystal, Lincoln County Clerk, Troy;
Harper, Kathryne, Howard County Clerk, Fayette;
Koehn, Casey, Butler City Administrator, Butler;
Littrell, Robin, Riverside City Clerk, Riverside;
Matthews, Karen, Christian County Treasurer, Ozark;
Parsons, Lili, Tri-County Health Department, Stanberry;
Reese, Charles, City of Kansas City Records Manager, Kansas City;
Rogers, Brett, Columbia College, Columbia;
Roof, Jeneen, Putnam County Recorder, Unionville; and
Stokely, David, Ozark.

Administrative Rules Division

James C. Kirkpatrick State Information Center
600 W. Main, PO Box 1767, Jefferson City 65102
Telephone: (573) 751-4015 / FAX: (573) 751-3032

Since 1976, the Administrative Rules Division has been charged by state law with setting uniform standards, procedures and guidelines for the preparation and publishing of rules in the Missouri Register and the Missouri Code of State Regulations. The Administrative Rules Division initially publishes rulemakings proposed by state agencies in the Missouri Register. The rulemakings are published to provide public notice and allow agencies to receive comments and revise the proposed rulemakings based on comments. Agencies then file final versions of orders of rulemaking with the division for final publication in the Missouri Register and subsequently in the Missouri Code of State Regulations. The division provides a user's guide for the proper preparation and filing of agency rules entitled Rulemaking 1-2-3, Drafting and Style Manual, which is available at www.sos.mo.gov/adrules/manual/manual or in hard copy.

The Administrative Rules Division also publishes emergency rules in the Missouri Register. An agency may file an emergency rule if the agency finds an immediate danger to public health, safety or welfare or if the emergency rule is necessary to preserve a compelling governmental interest that requires an early effective date, prior to that allowed by the traditional rulemaking process. An emergency rule is only in effect for a limited period of time and normally has a corresponding proposed rulemaking that allows for public notice and comment. Once an emergency rule is approved and processed, it may be viewed on the secretary of state's website at www.sos.mo.gov/adrules/EmergenciesforInternet/emergency under the Emergency Rules section until it is published in the Missouri Register.

The Missouri Register is published twice a month, and updates to the 15-volume Missouri Code of State Regulations are published once a month. Both the Missouri Register and Missouri Code of State Regulations are available on the secretary of state's website. Additionally, Missourians who are interested in particular rules may sign up on the secretary of state's website at www.sos.mo.gov/adrules/notifications for email notification of rule filings by rule number or subject matter.

WAYLENE HILES
Director of Administrative Rules
and Human Resources

Historical Listing, Secretaries of State

Name and (Party)	Term	County	Born	Died
1. Joshua Barton (D)	1820–21	St. Louis	7/28/1792	6/30/1823
2. William Grymes Pettus (D)[1]	1821–24	St. Charles	12/31/1794	1867
3. Hamilton Rowan Gamble (D)	1824–26	St. Louis	11/29/1789	1/31/1864
4. Spencer Darwin Pettis (D)	1826–28	St. Louis	1802	8/27/1831
5. Priestly Haggin McBride (D)	1829–30	Boone	1796	5/21/1869
6. John Cummins Edwards (D)[5]	1830–35	St. Louis	6/24/1806	9/17/1888
7. Henry Shurlds (D)	1835–37	Washington	11/21/1796	8/2/1852
8. John Cummins Edwards (D)	1837	Cole	6/24/1806	9/17/1888
9. Peter Garland Glover (D)	1837–39	Callaway	1/14/1792	10/27/1851
10. James Lawrence Minor (D)[5]	1839–45	Marion	6/9/1813	6/2/1897
11. Faulkland Heard Martin (D)	1845–49	Jefferson	1804	11/16/1856
12. Ephriam Brevard Ewing (D)	1849–53	Ray	5/1819	6/2/1873
13. John M. Richardson (D)[2]	1853–57	Greene	1820	5/1/1899
14. Benjamin Franklin Massey (D)	1857–61	Jasper	1811	12/18/1879
15. Mordecai Oliver (U)[3,4]	1861–65	Greene	1819	4/25/1898
16. Francis A. Rodman (R)[5]	1865–71	Buchanan	1829	1/1/1888
17. Eugene F. Weigel (D)	1871–75	St. Louis	1844	10/23/1896
18. Michael Knowles McGrath (D)[5]	1875–89	St. Louis	9/23/1833	1/29/1913
19. Alexander A. Lesueur (D)[5]	1889–1901	Lafayette	11/25/1842	1/29/1924
20. Sam Baker Cook (D)	1901–05	Audrain	7/11/1852	2/5/1931
21. John Ephriam Swanger (R)	1905–09	Sullivan	6/22/1864	10/19/1936
22. Cornelius Roach (D)[5]	1909–17	Jasper	8/9/1863	9/3/1934
23. John Leo Sullivan (D)	1917–21	Pettis	10/14/1877	1/11/1936
24. Charles U. Becker (R)[5]	1921–33	Polk	10/21/1868	5/21/1934
25. Dwight H. Brown (D)[5]	1933–44	Butler	1/12/1887	5/8/1944
26. Gregory C. Stockard (R)[6]	1944–45	Cole	8/3/1904	10/14/1993
27. Wilson Bell (D)	1945–47	Washington	5/24/1897	5/20/1947
28. Edgar C. Nelson (D)[7]	1947–49	Cooper	8/17/1883	10/9/1970
29. Walter Hendricks Toberman (D)[5]	1949–60	St. Louis	4/19/1879	2/13/1960
30. Robert W. Crawford (D)[8]	1960–61	Vernon	11/11/1926	2/20/1991
31. Warren E. Hearnes (D)	1961–65	Mississippi	7/24/1923	8/16/2009
32. James C. Kirkpatrick (D)[5]	1965–85	Henry, Barton, Cole	6/15/1905	12/26/1997
33. Roy D. Blunt (R)[5]	1985–93	Greene	1/10/1950	
34. Judith K. Moriarty (D)	1993–94	Pettis	2/2/1942	
35. Richard Hanson (D)[9]	1994	Cole	2/20/1940	
36. Rebecca McDowell Cook (D)[5,10]	1994–2001	Cape Girardeau	7/18/1950	
37. Matt Blunt (R)	2001–05	Greene	11/20/1970	
38. Robin Carnahan (D)[5]	2005–2013	Phelps	8/4/1961	
39. Jason Kander (D)	2013-	Jackson	5/4/1981	

[1]Appointed when Barton resigned to become U.S. District Attorney for Missouri in September 1821.
[2]Richardson was the first secretary of state to be elected to the office. Prior to 1852, secretaries of state were appointed by the governor.
[3]Unionist
[4]Oliver was elected provisional secretary of state by the Missouri State Convention on July 31, 1861. The office had been declared vacated after Governor Jackson joined the Confederacy.
[5]Some held multiple terms as secretary of state. In consideration of space, some are listed here only once.
[6]Appointed upon death of Dwight H. Brown.
[7]Appointed upon death of Wilson Bell.
[8]Appointed upon death of Walter H. Toberman.
[9]Appointed upon impeachment of Judith K. Moriarty.
[10]Appointed upon resignation of Richard Hanson.

Nicole R. Galloway, CPA
State Auditor
Appointed April 27, 2015
Term expires 2019

NICOLE R. GALLOWAY (Democrat) is the 38th State Auditor of Missouri. She is a certified public accountant and certified fraud examiner. She took the oath of office on April 27, 2015.

Auditor Galloway believes government's purpose is to serve the citizens it represents. In her role as state auditor, she serves as the citizen's advocate, making sure government at all levels is efficient, effective and transparent. She brings her expertise to work for Missourians each day to be a strong, independent watchdog, holding government accountable.

Auditor Galloway's office is focused on bringing private-sector best practices to state government, including a focus on cybersecurity. As a mother of two young boys, she understands the benefits and risks of changing technology, and the responsibility governments at all levels owe their citizens to protect private data. As an experienced professional private-sector auditor, she will always shine a light when government fails to safeguard the information families expect to be kept safe and secure.

Prior to becoming state auditor, Galloway was Treasurer of Boone County for four years. She ran for election in 2012, winning unopposed. Galloway put her experience to use as treasurer to manage a $100 million investment portfolio and nearly $200 million in annual cash flows. She was responsible for debt issuance, and protected the county's top-tier bond rating, putting that financial strength to use to consolidate debt and save taxpayers more than $4.6 million. Galloway launched the first online unclaimed property database for any county in the state, allowing citizens to claim their money faster and through a streamlined process. The initiative won the County Excellence Award from the Missouri Association of Counties. Galloway has worked tirelessly to ensure citizens know how their tax dollars are managed. She led the implementation of investment and debt management policies to protect taxpayers and make critical community investments. The debt management policy has become a model for other local governments in the state, providing transparency for the issuance process and the administration of the debt portfolio.

Prior to entering public service, Galloway was a corporate auditor at Shelter Insurance's national headquarters in Columbia. She began her career in public accounting at Brown Smith Wallace, a public accounting firm, headquartered in Creve Coeur. As an auditor in the private sector, Galloway audited Fortune 500 companies domestically and internationally by evaluating business risk, operational processes and internal controls surrounding asset management and revenue recognition. She performed financial statement, compliance and internal control audits of insurance and reinsurance companies throughout the country. She also worked as an actuarial analyst with Allstate Insurance.

A lifelong Missourian, Auditor Galloway is committed to improving the state. Galloway served as Secretary/Treasurer of the Missouri Technology Corporation, a public-private partnership that invests in entrepreneurs and small businesses to help create jobs and expand innovation in Missouri. She also served as Secretary/Treasurer of the Missouri County Employees' Retirement Fund, protecting the retirement benefits of nearly 16,000 participants in 111 counties. While on the retirement fund's board, she led the effort to ensure equal protection for the retirement benefits of county employees in same-sex marriages.

An active member of her local community, Auditor Galloway has served on the board of the Heart of Missouri United Way and on the Columbia Interfaith Resource Center's Finance Committee. She has been involved in Rotary Club and served as a youth mentor for Discovering Options in St. Louis.

Auditor Galloway received a Master of Business Administration from the University of Missouri and degrees in Applied Mathematics and Economics from Missouri University of Science and Technology.

Auditor Galloway was raised in the St. Louis region. She now lives in Columbia with her husband, Jon, and sons, William and Benjamin.

Office of State Auditor

121 State Capitol, Jefferson City 65101
Telephone: (573) 751-4824
Truman State Office Bldg., Room 880
Telephone: (573) 751-4213 / FAX: (573) 751-7984
www.auditor.mo.gov
Email: moaudit@auditor.mo.gov

JOHN LUETKEMEYER, CPA
Deputy Auditor

MICHAEL MOOREFIELD
Chief of Staff

Duties

The Missouri state auditor's office is Missouri's independent watchdog agency, charged with auditing approximately 200 state agencies and programs, including departments, boards, commissions, statewide offices and the General Assembly. The state auditor conducts audits of the state's expenditure of state funds and federal awards, the court system, counties that do not have an elected county auditor and may also audit school districts. Upon receipt of a petition signed by local voters, the state auditor conducts audits of other political subdivisions in the state.

In addition to fulfilling the primary auditing duties of the office, the state auditor reviews all property tax rates set by local political subdivisions and drafts fiscal notes and fiscal note summaries for initiative petitions. The state auditor also examines and registers general obligation bonds issued by political subdivisions of the state to ensure each bond complies with state law.

The powers of the state auditor are derived from Article IV, Section 13 of the Missouri Constitution. Statutory authority and duties are outlined in Chapter 29 of the Revised Statutes of Missouri.

PAUL HARPER
General Counsel

GENA TERLIZZI
Director of Communications

EMILY KALMER
Legislative Director & Policy
Counsel

EMILY WALES
Communications and Policy
Counsel

Audits

Audits are performed to determine how well governmental agencies and elected officials are protecting taxpayers' dollars from fraud, waste and abuse, and whether tax dollars are being spent efficiently, economically and legally. All audits are conducted in an impartial, nonpartisan manner and in accordance with government auditing standards issued by the Comptroller General of the United States.

The state auditor's office performs financial and performance audits, which also include review of management practices. Financial records of auditees are examined to determine how the auditee accounted for funds under its control. The state auditor's office reviews the auditee's systems and controls to ensure taxpayer dollars

are protected. The state auditor's office also reviews the auditee's compliance with constitutional provisions, laws, legislative appropriation levels and administrative rules and the efficiency and accountability of management practices.

Completed financial audits contain a formal opinion from the state auditor regarding the fair presentation of financial statements. A management advisory report listing any management weaknesses discovered during the audit is also included. Findings and recommendations in the management advisory report are reviewed with the auditee at an exit conference prior to the release of the audit so responses from the auditee may be included in the final report.

Follow-Up Reports

Audit follow-up reviews are conducted to increase accountability in government for the taxpayers of Missouri. Audit follow-up reports document whether audit recommendations have been implemented as recommended by the auditor. The state auditor's office works with audited entities to establish a reasonable timeline for the implementation of audit recommendations, with a particular focus on findings requiring immediate action.

Fraud Hotline

The state auditor may take immediate action when there is evidence of fraud; violation of state or federal law, rule or regulation; significant mismanagement or waste of public resources; or significant risk of loss of confidence by the public due to government fiscal abuse or mismanagement. Audit staff, under the guidance of general counsel and chief litigation counsel, may take immediate action, up to and including immediate referral to appropriate authorities, in order to preserve relevant evidence and/or prevent continued harm.

Missouri residents may contact the Auditor's Fraud Hotline with concerns related to fraud or waste in government operations by calling (800) 347-8597, Monday through Friday, from 8 a.m. to 5 p.m.

Cybersecurity Initiative

Advances in technology have led to an increased need for data protection. Auditor Galloway's Cybersecurity Initiative places an emphasis on government data protection practices when interacting with citizens and handling or storing personal or financial data. When information and records can be accessed from anywhere in the world, increased precautions must be taken to ensure criminals are not able to access data within schools or other government bodies. Government must be held accountalbe to keep sensitive information secure and protected for all Missourians.

Public Engagement

Auditor Galloway is dedicated to helping government officials identify best practices and make lasting improvements for the taxpayers of Missouri. The state auditor and her representative staff regularly speak to groups and organizations on matters related to audit processes, financial controls and procedures and the importance of

YAMINI LAKS
Chief Litigation Counsel

REBECCA GORLEY
Public Information Officer

JOHN HAWLES, CPA
Director of Quality Control
& Planning

DOUG PORTING, CPA
Director of State Audits

REGINA PRUITT, CPA
Director of Local
Government Audits

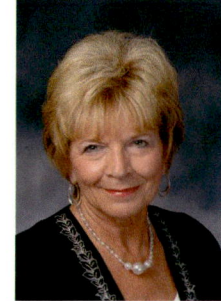

JOAN DOERHOFF
Special Assistant to State Auditor

compliance and transparency in state government.

The state auditor also publicly announces the start of each new audit and requests information from citizens, legislators and government employees to assist in completing the audit process and identifying problems. Citizens are urged to contact the auditor's office if they have information they believe could be useful to audit staff.

Citizens may contact the auditor's office to provide information for an audit, request information on audit practices and priorities or schedule a speaker for an upcoming event by calling (800) 347-8597 or by emailing *moaudit@auditor. mo.gov.*

Commitment to Transparency

All audit reports issued by the state auditor are public documents. Reports are available on the state auditor's website and distributed electronically to the public and members of the media. Citizens may sign up to recieve email alerts when audit reports are issued by visiting the state auditor's website at *www.auditor.mo.gov.*

Historical Listing, State Auditors

	Name and (Party)	Term	County	Born	Died
1.	William Christy (D)	1820–21	St. Louis	1/10/1764	4/3/1837
2.	William V. Rector (D)	1821–23	St. Louis	Unknown	9/16/1829
3.	Elias Barcroft (D)[5]	1823–33	St. Louis	1778	8/26/1851
4.	Henry Shurlds (D)	1833–35	Washington	11/21/1796	8/2/1852
5.	Peter Garland Glover (D)	1835–37	Callaway	1/14/1792	10/27/1851
6.	Hiram H. Baber (D)[5]	1837–45	Cole	9/10/1795	10/23/1873
7.	William Monroe (D)	1845	Morgan	Unknown	4/9/1846
8.	James W. McDearmon (D)	1845–48	St. Charles	8/31/1805	3/20/1848
9.	George W. Miller (D)	1848–49	Cole	Unknown	3/19/1879
10.	Wilson Brown (D)	1849–52	Cape Girardeau	8/27/1804	8/27/1855
11.	Abraham Fulkerson (D)	1852	Cole	Unknown	10/2/1892
12.	William H. Buffington (D)	1853–61	Cole	Unknown	9/26/1899
13.	W.S. Moseley (D)	1861–65	New Madrid	Unknown	1/3/1879
14.	Alonzo Thompson (R)	1865–69	Nodaway	2/22/1832	4/9/1913
15.	Daniel M. Draper (R)	1869–73	Montgomery	1839	5/26/1915
16.	George Boardman Clark (D)	1873–75	Washington	Unknown	12/8/1903
17.	Thomas Holladay (D)[5]	1875–81	Madison	1834	7/31/1904
18.	John Walker (D)[5]	1881–89	Howard	Unknown	9/30/1892
19.	James Monroe Seibert (D)	1889–1901	Cape Girardeau	2/3/1847	1/23/1935
20.	Albert Otis Allen (D)	1901–05	New Madrid	12/12/1842	4/4/1926
21.	William Werner Wilder (R)	1905–09	Ste. Genevieve	12/13/1857	8/26/1930
22.	John Pemberton Gordon (D)[5]	1909–17	Lafayette	4/29/1866	3/5/1949
23.	George Ernst Hackman (R)[5]	1917–25	Warren	8/10/1877	12/29/1954
24.	Lorenzo Dow Thompson (R)[5]	1925–33	Callaway	11/22/1873	10/1/1951
25.	Forrest Smith (D)[5]	1933–49	Ray	12/14/1886	3/8/1962
26.	William Henry Holmes (D)	1949–53	Maries	4/21/1883	3/31/1953
27.	Haskell Holman (D)[1, 5]	1953–71	Randolph	11/29/1908	7/12/1974
28.	Christopher S. (Kit) Bond (R)	1971–73	Audrain	3/6/1939	
29.	John Ashcroft (R)[2]	1973–74	Greene	5/9/1942	
30.	George W. Lehr (D)	1974–77	Jackson	3/10/1937	3/21/1988
31.	Thomas M. Keyes (D)[3]	1977–78	Jackson	2/4/1914	4/3/1987
32.	James Antonio (R)[5]	1978–84	Cole	6/30/1939	
33.	Margaret B. Kelly (R)[4, 5]	1984–99	Cole	9/17/1935	
34.	Claire McCaskill (D)	1999–2007	Jackson	7/24/1953	
35.	Susan Montee (D)[6]	2007–2011	Buchanan	7/06/1959	
36.	Thomas A. Schweich (R)	2011–2015	St. Louis	2/10/1960	2/26/2015
37.	Nicole R. Galloway (D)[7]	2015–	Boone	6/13/1982	

[1]Appointed upon death of W.H. Holmes.
[2]Appointed upon resignation of Christopher S. Bond.
[3]Appointed upon resignation of George W. Lehr.
[4]Appointed upon resignation of James Antonio.
[5]Some held multiple terms as state auditor. In consideration of space, they are listed here only once.
[6]Appointed upon resignation of Claire McCaskill to become U.S. Senator in November 2006.
[7]Appointed upon the death of Thomas Schweich.

Clint Zweifel
State Treasurer
Elected November 4, 2008
Term expires January 2017

CLINT ZWEIFEL (ZWY-ful) (Democrat) was elected Missouri's 45th State Treasurer on Nov. 4, 2008, the youngest in more than a century. He was re-elected to his second and final term as Treasurer on Nov. 6, 2012.

Throughout his administration, Treasurer Zweifel has focused on fiscal accountability, economic growth, and making government work better.

As the state's chief investment officer, Treasurer Zweifel has consistently sought simple yet meaningful reforms to ensure the government remains accountable to the public. He manages Missouri's $3.5 billion portfolio, and through smart, conservative investing, he has protected Missouri's AAA credit rating through the worst economic downturn since the Great Depression.

The Treasurer uses his position as a board member for the Missouri State Employees' Retirement System (MOSERS) to advocate for Missouri taxpayers. In 2014, he successfully fought to make Missouri the first state to ban pension advances, which severely jeopardize public employees' retirement security. He has also worked to create a more transparent state pension fund, pushing for a more complete fee reporting system for taxpayers and retirees. While serving as chair of the pension committee within the National Association of State Treasurers (NAST), he brought awareness of responsible fee disclosures and the danger of pension advances to the national level.

Finally, the Treasurer has overseen several innovations to his Unclaimed Property division, improving Missourians' experience with one of his most popular services. He has returned more than half of all Unclaimed Property in state history, setting return records each year.

In addition to keeping government accountable to Missourians, Treasurer Zweifel has used the scope of his office to enhance economic growth in Missouri from the ground up. Immediately upon taking office, he developed a legislative package that improved and streamlined the Missouri Linked Deposit Program, a low-interest lending program which helps farms and small businesses access low-interest capital, resulting in the approval of nearly $2 billion in loans.

In 2014, Treasurer Zweifel accepted an appointment by Governor Nixon to lead the Missouri Military Partnership's effort to retain and strengthen the military presence in Missouri, which currently contributes $40 billion in economic activity and 275,000 jobs in the state.

As a proponent of good government, the Treasurer has regularly sought creative ways to serve more Missourians. In 2010, as a board member of the Missouri Housing Development Commission, he successfully pushed the board to adopt a policy to provide quality, affordable housing for populations with special needs including individuals who are chronically homeless, mentally ill, veterans, children aging out of foster care, and most recently, survivors of domestic violence. Thanks to his efforts more than 1,000 special needs housing units have been built at no additional cost to taxpayers.

Treasurer Zweifel has also strived to make a college education more affordable for Missouri families. He launched a matching grant program in 2012 for low- and moderate-income families using MOST—Missouri's 529 College Savings Plan, which he chairs. Since then he has partnered with private and nonprofit organizations across the state to implement similar programs which have reached more than 1,000 students in Missouri.

Finally, in recognition of Missouri veterans' service to our state and nation, he championed legislation which forbids the sale of military medals and insignia held in Unclaimed Property. The measures also allow him to work with the public to return those medals. Through this effort he has returned more than 100 medals to the heroes who earned them or their families.

In two terms as State Treasurer, Clint Zweifel has maintained solid fiscal health, overseen economic growth and created more efficient and responsive government for Missourians.

Prior to serving as State Treasurer, Zweifel served in the Missouri House of Representatives for six years.

Born Nov. 3, 1973, in St. Louis, Treasurer Zweifel grew up in nearby Florissant. He graduated from Hazelwood West High School in 1992 and became the first member of his family to attend college. He graduated from the University of Missouri-St. Louis with a Bachelor of Arts in Political Science in 1996 and a Master of Business Administration in 2001. Treasurer Zweifel resides in Columbia with his wife, Janice, and their daughters, Selma and Ellie.

Office of State Treasurer

Office of State Treasurer
Room 229, State Capitol, Jefferson City 65101
Rooms 157, 780, Harry S. Truman State Office Bldg.
PO Box 210, Jefferson City 65102
Telephone: (573) 751-8533
www.treasurer.mo.gov

SARAH SWOBODA
Deputy State Treasurer

NICOLE HACKMANN
Director of Banking

Duties

State Treasurer Clint Zweifel is Missouri's chief financial officer, making all investments for the State of Missouri. He oversees state banking services and its $3.5 billion investment portfolio. Treasurer Zweifel safeguards more than $874 million in unclaimed property, manages a $720 million low-interest loan program and leads the state's 529 College Savings Plan. He also serves on a number of public boards. He is one of six statewide elected officials and serves a term of four years. A person may only serve as state treasurer for two terms.

MEGHAN LEWIS
Director of Communications

SPENCER GIROUARD
Deputy Director of
Communications

Protecting Missouri Taxpayers: Banking and Investments

As Missouri's chief financial officer, Treasurer Zweifel provides management of state revenue and investments that is critical to maintaining the state's AAA bond rating. Operating similarly to an official bank, he must authorize payments and balance accounts. To protect taxpayer money, Treasurer Zweifel maintains a separate accounting system to provide a check and balance on the state accounting system and distributes investment earnings to the proper funds. Treasurer Zweifel contracts with Missouri banks to process state receipts and disbursements; handles money and security transfers; reports on the state's accounts, balances and payment activities; and provides related banking services. Bidding for state banking services contracts is open to all qualifying Missouri banks.

Treasurer Zweifel determines the amount of state funds not needed for current operating expenses and invests those funds in interest-bearing time deposits in Missouri banks, U.S. Treasury and federal agency securities, repurchase agreements, banker's acceptances and top-rated commercial paper. Safety is Treasurer Zweifel's top priority in the investment of public funds. Treasurer Zweifel has an average of $3.5 billion invested daily.

Helping Missouri Farmers and Entrepreneurs: Missouri Linked Deposit Program

The Missouri Linked Deposit Program provides low-interest loans to small businesses and farms through partnerships with qualified Missouri lenders. Loan savings are usually 30 percent to the borrower. The loans can be used by small businesses with fewer than 100 employees, agricultural operations, beginning farmers, businesses adding jobs, entities making alternative energy investments, multi-family housing developments and local governments making community improvements.

Treasurer Zweifel expanded this program through his 2009 jobs and economic development legislative package, which has a $720 million statutory cap. The legislation enhanced program eligibility to incentivize job creation, job retention and community reinvestment. Since taking office in 2009, Treasurer Zweifel has approved nearly $2 billion in loans impacting 34,000 jobs and farmers. Of that, $444 million in loans were approved that would not have been allowed before Treasurer Zweifel developed and worked to pass his 2009 jobs and economic de-

SCOTT HARPER
Director of Unclaimed
Property and General Services

BRUCE RING
Director of Investments

PATRICK MORGAN
General Counsel

DEBBIE SCHERTZER
Executive Assistant

velopment package that allows more farmers and businesses to qualify for loans.

In May 2011, Treasurer Zweifel implemented the Harmed-Area Emergency Loan Priority system, or HELP. HELP provides 24-hour loan approval for counties dealing with disasters. Since its inception, more than $80 million in loans have been approved.

Financial institutions and borrowers should visit www.treasurer.mo.gov to learn more about the program. Borrowers can find a list with more than 130 participating lenders and 350 branches throughout Missouri. The application process has been streamlined and takes about one week to complete.

Returning Missourians' Money: Unclaimed Property

Treasurer Zweifel is responsible for Unclaimed Property: Missouri's Largest Lost and Found. State law requires financial institutions, insurance companies, public agencies and other business entities to turn over assets that belong to a customer, client, employee or other owner if there have been no documented transactions or contact with the owner for five or more years. Treasurer Zweifel operates an aggressive program to return unclaimed assets to the original owners or their legal heirs. He set another unclaimed property record during fiscal year 2015 by returning nearly $42 million to account owners.

Most unclaimed property consists of cash from bank accounts, stocks, bonds and contents of safe deposit boxes that have been abandoned. It also can include uncollected insurance policy proceeds, government refunds, utility deposits and wages from past jobs. Unclaimed property does not include real property such as land or houses, or personal property such as cars or boats.

Treasurer Zweifel is dedicated to protecting the military medals and honors turned over to

KYLE OLMSTEAD
Legislative Liaison and
Special Projects Coordinator

his office in safe deposit boxes. When Treasurer Zweifel took office, he found unclaimed military medals were being sold as part of the statutorily required unclaimed property auctions. He immediately put a stop to this practice and set to work on legislation that would ensure no future treasurer could sell medals either. In June of 2010, the Veterans Medal Bill was signed into law after passing through the House and Senate unanimously.

In June 2011, Treasurer Zweifel placed the first Unclaimed Property military medals on display as part of a partnership with the Missouri State Museum made possible by the Veterans Medal Bill. The Distinguished Service Cross and French Cross of War earned by a World War I doctor represent the hundreds of servicemen and women who have sacrificed for the State of Missouri and the country. Treasurer Zweifel continues to work with veterans' organizations and museums to locate and preserve the medals and to honor those that remain in his care.

Building off of his initial efforts, Treasurer Zweifel worked with the legislature in 2013 to pass the Military Medal Return Act. Passed with strong bipartisan support, this bill allows him to share further information about the owners of the medals on his website and with veterans' organizations.

Treasurer Zweifel currently holds more than $874 million in unclaimed property in nearly five million owner accounts. All unclaimed property is held in trust forever and may be claimed at any time. To recover unclaimed property, claimants must be either the original owner of the property or a legal heir. Treasurer Zweifel provides all services free of charge. Individuals can check to see if Treasurer Zweifel is holding unclaimed property that may belong to them, sign up for email notifications and file paperless claims at *www.showmemoney.com*.

Building Access to an Affordable College Education: MOST–Missouri's 529 College Savings Plan

Treasurer Zweifel chairs the Missouri Higher Education Savings Program Board, which oversees MOST–Missouri's 529 College Savings Plan. Developed in 1999, MOST 529 encourages Missouri families to save for higher education while taking advantage of significant federal and state tax benefits. Accounts can be opened through the do-it-yourself, direct-sold MOST 529 Plan or through the advisor-sold MOST 529 Plan with as little as $25 or $15 through payroll deduction. Contributions of up to $8,000 ($16,000 for married couples) annually can be deducted from Missouri income taxes, and all earnings are free of federal and state income taxes for qualified withdrawals. Funds from MOST 529 accounts can be used to pay for all eligible educational expenses at virtually any two-year or four-year college or university, vocational, technical or professional school anywhere in the country. As of July 2013, MOST 529 had more than $2.2 billion in assets, with more than 150,000 account owners.

To open a direct-sold MOST 529, call toll free at (888) 414-MOST or (800) 414-6678), or visit *www.missourimost.org*. To open a MOST 529 advisor-sold account, contact your financial advisor, call 1-800-617-5097 or visit www.most529advisor.com.

Representing Taxpayers: Boards and Commissions

Treasurer Zweifel serves on the governing boards of four large public entities: the Missouri Housing Development Commission, which assists in the creation of affordable housing for Missourians; the Missouri State Employees' Retirement System, which manages retirement funds for more than 111,000 state employees and retirees; the Board of Fund Commissioners, which issues, redeems and cancels state general obligation bonds and other debt; and the Missouri Higher Education Savings Program Board, which oversees MOST–Missouri's 529 College Savings Plan. Treasurer Zweifel also serves on the Missouri Cultural Trust Board.

Staying Accountable to Missouri Tax Payers

Treasurer Zweifel is committed to a transparent and accountable administration. He maintains an open government portal at *www.treasurer.mo.gov/content/about-the-office/open-government*. Citizens may access investment returns, office policies, meeting minutes and other public information through this portal. Sunshine requests may also be filed electronically through the site.

Historical Listing, State Treasurers

	Name and (Party)	Term	County	Born	Died
1.	John Peter Didier (D)	1820–21	St. Louis	Unknown	8/25/1823
2.	Nathaniel Simonds (D)[1]	1821–29	St. Louis	1775	4/7/1850
3.	James Earickson (D)	1829–33	Howard	1792	1844
4.	John Walker (D)	1833–38	Cole	10/17/1772	5/26/1838
5.	Abraham McClellan (D)	1838–43	Jackson	1775	9/18/1851
6.	Peter Garland Glover (D)[1]	1843–51	Cole	1/14/1792	10/27/1851
7.	Alfred William Morrison (D)[1]	1851–61	Howard	11/25/1802	8/24/1883
8.	George Caleb Bingham (D)[1,2]	1862–65	Jackson	3/20/1811	7/7/1879
9.	William Bishop (R)	1865–69	Clark	1822	5/2/1879
10.	William Quintilis Dallmeyer (R)	1869–71	Gasconade	10/23/1829	3/15/1908
11.	Samuel Hays (R)	1871–73	Buchanan	Unknown	10/8/1897
12.	Harvey Wallis Salmon (D)	1873–75	Henry	2/26/1839	4/27/1927
13.	Joseph Wayne Mercer (D)	1875–77	Jackson	2/25/1846	3/13/1906
14.	Elijah Gates (D)	1877–81	Buchanan	1827	3/4/1915
15.	Phillip Edward Chappel (D)	1881–85	Cole	8/18/1837	2/23/1908
16.	James Monroe Seibert (D)	1885–89	Cape Girardeau	12/3/1847	1/23/1935
17.	Edward T. Noland (D)	1889–90	Cape Girardeau	3/24/1847	6/20/1926
18.	Lon Vest Stephens (D)	1890–97	Cooper	12/1/1855	1/10/1923
19.	Frank Littleton Pitts (D)	1897–1901	Monroe	4/25/1841	2/4/1905
20.	Robert Prewitt Williams (D)	1901–05	Howard	9/8/1841	7/11/1910
21.	Jacob Friedrich Gmelich (R)	1905–09	Cooper	7/23/1839	2/21/1914
22.	James Cowgill (D)	1909–13	Jackson	4/2/1848	1/20/1922
23.	Edwin P. Deal (D)	1913–17	Mississippi	4/19/1859	12/10/1945
24.	George H. Middlekamp (D)	1917–21	Warren	4/20/1880	10/5/1966
25.	Lorenzo Dow Thompson (R)	1921–25	Callaway	11/22/1873	10/1/1951
26.	C. Eugene Stephens (R)	1925–29	St. Louis	12/20/1889	6/25/1970
27.	Larry Brunk (R)	1929–33	Lawrence	2/9/1883	11/22/1956
28.	Richard R. Nacy (D)	1933–37	Cole	11/7/1895	1/10/1961
29.	Robert William Winn (D)	1937–41	Ralls	6/9/1895	8/13/1948
30.	Wilson Bell (D)	1941–45	Washington	5/24/1897	5/20/1947
31.	Robert William Winn (D)	1945–48	Ralls	6/9/1895	8/13/1948
32.	Richard R. Nacy (D)[3]	1948–49	Cole	11/7/1895	1/10/1961
33.	Mount Etna Morris (D)	1949–53	Grundy	9/1/1900	7/8/1988
34.	George Hubert Bates (D)	1953–57	Lafayette	12/8/1884	7/22/1978
35.	Mount Etna Morris (D)	1957–61	Grundy	9/1/1900	7/8/1988
36.	Milton Carpenter (D)	1961–65	St. Louis City	3/4/1905	11/19/1996
37.	Mount Etna Morris (D)	1965–69	Grundy	9/1/1900	7/8/1988
38.	William Edmond Robinson (D)	1969–73	Cole	6/1/1920	10/16/1992
39.	James I. Spainhower (D)[1]	1973–81	Cole	8/3/1928	
40.	Mel Carnahan (D)	1981–85	Phelps	2/11/1934	10/16/2000
41.	Wendell Bailey (R)[1]	1985–93	Howell	7/31/1940	
42.	Bob Holden (D)[1]	1993–2001	Shannon	8/24/1949	
43.	Nancy Farmer (D)	2001–05	St. Louis City	9/11/1956	
44.	Sarah Steelman (R)	2005–09	Phelps	5/3/1958	
45.	Clint Zweifel (D) [1]	2009–	St. Louis	11/3/1973	

[1] Some held multiple terms as state treasurer. In consideration of space, they are listed here only once.
[2] Bingham was appointed state treasurer by provisional Governor Gamble when Morrison refused to take a loyalty oath.
[3] Appointed upon the death of Robert William Winn.

Chris Koster
Attorney General
Elected November 4, 2008
Term expires January 2017

CHRIS KOSTER (Democrat) was sworn in as the 41st attorney general for Missouri on Jan. 12, 2009, and was subsequently re-elected in 2012. Since becoming attorney general, Koster has focused efforts on detecting and prosecuting Medicaid fraud, cracking down on fraudulent auto service contract businesses, using Missouri's legal authority to protect the state's water resources, educating young people about Internet safety and making local public officials aware of their obligations under Missouri's open records laws.

Through the office's Consumer Protection Division, Koster is working to focus efforts on the biggest threats to consumers. Early in his term, as the state and nation were deep in a housing-foreclosure crisis, the attorney general demanded a "zero tolerance" campaign against businesses that promised foreclosure relief without delivering services, as well as against businesses that used deceptive practices to entice consumers to refinance. The attorney general also is aggressively targeting businesses that violate Missouri's no-call list, pursuing substantial penalties against them.

As attorney general, Koster argued before the United States Supreme Court and personally prosecuted two murder cases. Koster has conducted statewide conferences on the issues of domestic violence, public safety and representative policing

Before his election as attorney general, Koster represented the 31st district in the Missouri Senate from 2004 to 2008, which covers Cass, Johnson, Bates and Vernon counties.

During his time in the General Assembly, Koster played key roles in the debates over stem cell research, tort reform and the elimination of Medicaid fraud. Additionally, in 2006, Koster successfully carried legislation in the Senate to dramatically overhaul Missouri's eminent domain laws.

Prior to his election to the Missouri Senate in 2004, Koster served as prosecuting attorney of Cass County for 10 years. He was first elected prosecutor in 1994 and was subsequently re-elected in 1998 and 2002 by wide margins. As prosecutor, Koster supervised a staff of 20 individuals dedicated to enforcing Missouri's criminal laws in Cass County. His office also served as the civil counsel for all non-criminal matters before the county government.

During his tenure, Koster supervised litigation in approximately 20,000 cases. He led investigations into many of Kansas City's most notorious criminal cases, including the investigation and prosecution of serial killer John E. Robinson. He has developed extensive trial experience and has argued and won cases before the Missouri Supreme Court. He played a leading role in the construction of the Cass County Justice Center, which opened in 2002 in Harrisonville.

Koster is active in his community. He has served on the Missouri Sentencing Advisory Commission and the state's Bioterrorism Task Force. Additionally, Koster has served as a director of the Missouri Association of Prosecuting Attorneys, a member of the U.S. Attorney's Anti-Terrorism Task Force and director of the Hope Haven Women's Shelter. In 2002, *Ingram's* magazine named Koster "one of Kansas City's most influential citizens under 40 years old." In 2004, the *Kansas City Business Journal* named Koster to its list of Kansas City's best attorneys. On multiple occasions, he has been included among Missouri's most influential lawyers by *Missouri Lawyers Weekly*.

Prior to becoming prosecuting attorney, Koster practiced law with the Kansas City law firm of Blackwell Sanders from 1993 to 1994. He also served as a Missouri Assistant Attorney General from 1991 to 1993.

Koster was born and raised in St. Louis. After graduating from St. Louis University High School in 1982, he received a liberal arts degree from the University of Missouri–Columbia in 1987 and his law degree from University of Missouri–Columbia School of Law in 1991. Additionally, Koster earned a Master in Business Administration from Washington University in St. Louis in 2002.

Office of Attorney General

Supreme Court Building
PO Box 899, Jefferson City 65102
Telephone: (573) 751-3321 / FAX: (573) 751-0774
www.ago.mo.gov
Email: attorney.general@ag.mo.gov

JOE DANDURAND
Deputy Attorney General

JOAN GUMMELS
General Counsel

The attorney general is the attorney for the state, representing the legal interests of Missouri and its state agencies.

As the state's chief legal officer, the attorney general must prosecute or defend all appeals to which the state is a party, including every felony criminal case appealed to the Missouri Supreme Court and Courts of Appeal. The attorney general also is required to institute, in the name and on behalf of the state, all civil suits and other proceedings that are necessary to protect the state's rights, interests or claims. The attorney general may appear, interplead, answer or defend any proceedings that involve the state's interests or appear on behalf of the state in declaratory judgment proceedings when the constitutionality of a statute is challenged.

The attorney general also renders official opinions to the executive and legislative branches and county prosecuting attorneys on questions of law relating to their duties. The attorney general may institute *quo warranto* proceedings against anyone unlawfully holding office or move to oust any public official for malfeasance in office.

The attorney general's office was created in 1806 when Missouri was part of the Louisiana Territory. The first Missouri Constitution in 1820 provided for an appointed attorney general, but since the 1865 Constitution, the attorney general has been elected.

By law, the attorney general is a member of the Board of Fund Commissioners, the Board of Public Buildings, the Governor's Committee on Interstate Cooperation, the Missouri Highway Reciprocity Commission and the Missouri Housing Development Commission.

To fulfill these and other responsibilities, the attorney general's office is organized into nine divisions.

JIM FARNSWORTH
Chief of Staff

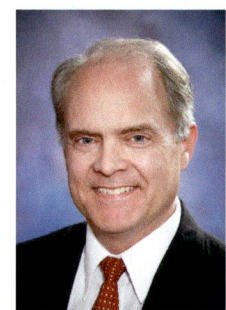

JIM LAYTON
State Solicitor

RHONDA MEYER
Deputy Chief of Staff

BEN BURKEMPER
Legislative Director

Agriculture and Environment Division

The Agriculture and Environment Division aggressively protects Missouri's natural resources and agricultural productivity. The division's attorneys take legal action to stop pollution, seek monetary fines and penalties and, in the most serious cases, to criminally prosecute those who violate Missouri's environmental laws.

The division works to protect and enhance agriculture and the quality of life for rural Missourians by enforcing Missouri's agricultural laws and advocating responsible public policy. The attorney general protects the state's interests in the Missouri River and other valuable resources, including state parks and waterways such as the Meramec River and White River basin.

Division attorneys represent the Department of Natural Resources and its constituent boards and commissions, as well as the Department of Agriculture, in hundreds of active enforcement cases and administrative appeals. The division also cooperates with the U.S. Environmental Protection Agency, the U.S. Department of Justice and the U.S. Attorney's Office to enforce state and federal environmental laws.

Consumer Protection Division

The attorney general is responsibile for protecting the public's interests in an open and honest marketplace. The Consumer Protection Division enforces Missouri's Consumer Protection Act and antitrust laws, and has the responsibility of representing the commissioner of securities of the secretary of state's office. Missouri's consumer protection statutes prohibit deception, fraud, unfair practices and misrepresentation or concealment of material facts in the sale or advertisement of goods or services. These laws authorize the attorney general to take action against such fraud and ensure consumers' rights are protected.

The division also has an active consumer education program. Consumers can file complaints or obtain information by calling the Attorney General's Consumer Hotline at (800) 392-8222 or online at www.ago.mo.gov. The division receives more than 90,000 consumer complaints and inquiries each year.

Under Missouri antitrust laws, the attorney general has the authority to represent the state or any of its political subdivisions, public agencies, school districts or municipalities in actions to prohibit monopolies and trade restraints. The attorney general also may act under federal antitrust statutes to bring civil actions in the name of the state and on behalf of Missouri residents to recover damages for injuries caused by certain antitrust violations.

The attorney general is the state's chief prosecutor for securities fraud, and may initiate legal actions for civil injunctive relief, penalties and restitution under the Missouri Merchandising Practices Law. Attorneys in this division also protect Missourians by enforcing compliance with state laws by trusts, foundations and nonprofit corporations.

The No Call program to reduce unwanted telemarketing calls also is under the Consumer Protection Division. Missourians may register for No Call by calling (866) 662-2551 or online at www.ago.mo.gov.

NANCI GONDER
Press Secretary

JACK McMANUS
Chief Counsel, Agriculture and Environment Division

JOE BINDBEUTEL
Chief Counsel
Consumer Protection Division

SHAUN MACKELPRANG
Chief Counsel
Criminal Division

Criminal Division

The attorney general represents the state in every felony case appealed to the Supreme Court of Missouri and Missouri Court of Appeals. Each year, attorneys in the Criminal Division brief and argue more than 700 cases in the Missouri Court of Appeals and the Missouri Supreme Court. Division attorneys also assist local and state authorities with extraditions to and from Missouri of those charged in criminal cases.

Financial Services Division

The Financial Services Division protects Missourians by recouping money owed to the state or state agencies, including providing collection services to several divisions of the attorney general's office and more than 40 other state agencies. Division attorneys also take legal action to establish, maintain and modify child support obligations and work to recover money owed by inmates to reimburse the state for the cost of their care.

Governmental Affairs Division

The Governmental Affairs Division protects the safety and well-being of Missourians by ensuring regulated professionals adhere to state laws and disciplinary rules by enforcing state ethics and campaign finance laws and enforcing penalties against nursing homes for violating standards of care and removing caregivers who abuse or neglect vulnerable citizens. They also help mentally ill and physically challenged Missourians obtain guardians to help obtain care.

The division provides legal representation to state officers—including the secretary of state, treasurer and auditor—as well as several state agencies, including the departments of health and senior services, mental health and social services; the Missouri Ethics Commission; the Health Facilities Review Committee; and more than 30 professional licensing boards. Division attorneys also defend constitutional challenges to state laws and ballot issues. Division attorneys enforce the provisions of the tobacco Master Settlement Agreement, which has brought in more than $1.5 billion to the state as of April 2009. Attorneys in the division also address questions from the public, from government officials and from the media about Missouri's open meetings and records law, commonly known as the Sunshine Law.

Labor Division

The Labor Division provides general counsel and litigation services for the Missouri Department of Labor and Industrial Relations and its officers and agencies. The division also represents the state in crime victims' claims and workers' compensation cases of state employees, including claims involving the Second Injury Fund.

Litigation Division

Litigation division attorneys handle major and complex litigation for Missouri, providing legal defense to state officials, state agencies and their employees. Cases in the division include damage claims, contract actions, class-action lawsuits, employment issues, constitutional challenges, suits seeking injunctive relief and other types of civil litigation.

The division defends the state in lawsuits brought by inmates of Missouri's correctional facilities. Division attorneys also defend constitutional challenges to state laws and ballot issues. Attorneys in the litigation division defend lawsuits filed against the police boards and the police officers of the cities of St. Louis and Kansas City, Mo.

The division also represents the Missouri Commission on Human Rights in cases before the Administrative Hearing Commission and in all subsequent court actions. The division enforces the Missouri Human Rights Act and takes action on behalf of Missouri citizens in discrimination cases. The division enforces state interests

GREG PERRY
Chief Counsel
Financial Services Division

PATRICIA CHURCHILL
Chief Counsel
Governmental Affairs Division

CARA HARRIS
Chief Counsel
Labor Division

JOEL POOLE
Chief Counsel
Litigation Division

regarding the Americans with Disabilities Act and the Federal Fair Housing Act.

Finally, the division protects and enforces workers' rights in Missouri under the prevailing wage and minimum wage laws, and Missouri's unauthorized workers law.

Medicaid Fraud Control Unit

The Medicaid Fraud Control Unit prosecutes cases involving fraud of the state Medicaid program by health professionals, and prosecute abuse or neglect of Medicaid recipients by caregivers. The unit has obtained more than $278 million in Medicaid fraud judgments and recoveries since 2009.

Public Safety Division

The Public Safety Division is involved in a wide range of criminal prosecutions at the trial level. The division's special prosecution unit prosecutes or assists in the prosecution of cases throughout Missouri, many of them homicide cases. In 2010, division attorneys had more than 483 active special prosecutions throughout the state's 114 counties and the City of St. Louis. The unit also specializes in handling criminal cases involving the manufacture, sale or possession of methamphetamine.

The Workers' Compensation Fraud Unit prosecutes fraud or misconduct involving workers' compensation, and the division's High Technology and Computer Crime Unit assists local law enforcement with investigations and prosecutions of computer and Internet crime cases. The Sexually Violent Predator Unit seeks the civil commitment of sexual predators who suffer from a mental abnormality making them more likely to commit additional predatory acts of sexual violence.

Attorneys in the division also serve as legal counsel for the Department of Public Safety, the Missouri State Highway Patrol, the Missouri State Water Patrol and other state law enforcement agencies, and represent those agencies in all civil litigation to which they are a party. Division attorneys also defend the state in all habeas corpus actions filed by prison inmates in state and fed-

JOANNA TRACHTENBERG
Chief Council
Medicaid Fraud Control Unit

SUSAN BORESI
Chief Council
Public Safety Division

eral courts. Each year, they litigate some 500 federal habeas corpus actions in the federal district courts, the Eighth Circuit Court of Appeals and the U.S. Supreme Court.

Historical Listing, Attorneys General

	Name and (Party)	Term	County	Born	Died
1.	Edward Bates (D)	1820–21	St. Louis	9/4/1793	3/25/1869
2.	Rufus Easton (D)	1821–26	St. Louis	3/4/1774	7/5/1834
3.	Robert William Wells (D)	1826–36	St. Charles	11/29/1795	9/22/1861
4.	William Barclay Napton (D)	1836–39	Howard	1808	1/8/1883
5.	Samuel Mansfield Bay (D)	1839–45	Cole	1810	7/1849
6.	Benjamin F. Stringfellow (D)	1845–49	Chariton	9/3/1816	4/25/1891
7.	William A. Robards (D)	1849–51	Boone	5/3/1817	9/3/1851
8.	James B. Gardenhire (Whig)	1851–57	Buchanan	1821	2/20/1862
9.	Ephraim B. Ewing (D)	1857–58	Ray	5/1819	6/2/1873
10.	J. Proctor Knott (D)	1858–61	Scotland	8/29/1830	6/18/1911
11.	Aikman Welch (D)[1]	1861–64	Johnson	5/25/1827	7/28/1864
12.	Thomas Theodore Crittenden (D)[2]	1864	Johnson	1/22/1832	5/29/1909
13.	Robert Franklin Wingate (D)	1865–69	St. Louis	1/24/1822	11/12/1897
14.	Horace B. Johnson (R)	1869–71	Cole	8/14/1842	3/30/1904
15.	Andrew Jackson Baker (R)[3]	1871–72	Schuyler	6/6/1832	4/23/1911
16.	Henry Clay Ewing (D)	1873–75	Cole	8/15/1828	3/22/1907
17.	John A. Hockaday (D)	1875–77	Callaway	1837	11/20/1903
18.	Jackson Leonidas Smith (D)	1877–81	Cole	1/31/1837	11/13/1908
19.	Daniel Harrison McIntyre (D)	1881–85	Audrain	5/5/1833	1/1/1910
20.	Banton Gallitin Boone (D)	1885–89	Henry	10/23/1838	2/11/1900
21.	John McKee Wood (D)	1889–93	Clark	8/8/1850	1/24/1926
22.	Robert Franklin Walker (D)	1893–97	Morgan	11/29/1850	11/19/1930
23.	Edward Coke Crow (D)	1897–1905	Jasper	12/19/1861	5/9/1945
24.	Herbert Spencer Hadley (R)	1905–09	Jackson	2/20/1872	12/1/1927
25.	Elliott Woolfolk Major (D)	1909–13	Pike	10/20/1864	7/9/1949
26.	John Tull Barker (D)	1913–17	Macon	8/2/1877	12/7/1958
27.	Frank Winton McAllister (D)	1917–21	Monroe	1/26/1873	6/11/1948
28.	Jesse W. Barrett (R)	1921–25	Lewis	3/17/1884	11/12/1953
29.	Robert William Otto (R)[4]	1925	Franklin	12/25/1892	5/5/1977
30.	North Todd Gentry (R)	1925–28	Boone	3/2/1866	9/18/1944
31.	Stratton Shartel (R)	1928–33	Newton	12/25/1895	2/2/1956
32.	Roy M. McKittrick (D)5	1933–45	Chariton	8/24/1888	1/22/1961
33.	Jonathan E. (Buck) Taylor (D)[5]	1945–53	Livingston	11/26/1906	12/27/1981
34.	John M. Dalton (D)	1953–61	Dunklin	11/9/1900	7/7/1972
35.	Thomas F. Eagleton (D)	1961–65	St. Louis City	9/4/1929	3/4/2007
36.	Norman H. Anderson (D)	1965–69	St. Louis	3/24/1924	6/16/1997
37.	John C. Danforth (R)	1969–77	St. Louis, Cole	9/5/1936	
38.	John D. Ashcroft (R)	1977–85	Greene	5/9/1942	
39.	William L. Webster (R)[5]	1985–93	Jasper	9/17/1953	
40.	Jeremiah W. (Jay) Nixon (D)[5]	1993–2009	Jefferson	2/13/1956	
41.	Chris Koster (D)[5]	2009–	Cass	8/31/1964	

[1]Welch was appointed attorney general by provisional Governor Gamble when Knott refused to take a loyalty oath.
[2]Crittenden was appointed to fill the unexpired term of Aikman Welsh, who died in office. Crittenden only served until the end of that year.
[3]Baker ran and was elected as a Liberal Republican.
[4]Otto left office to become a Supreme Court Judge.
[5]Some held multiple terms as attorney general. In consideration of space, some are listed here only once.

Note: Like other state offices, except governor and lieutenant governor, the attorney general's office was filled by appointment from 1820-1852. The offices then became elective for four-year terms. They changed to two-year elective terms in 1868, and changed back to four-year elective terms in 1875.

CHAPTER 3
FEDERAL GOVERNMENT

The "Castle" ruins at Ha Ha Tonka State Park.
Photo courtesy of Missouri State Archives

United States Government

Executive Branch

Barack H. Obama, President of the United States
The White House
1600 Pennsylvania Ave. N.W., Washington, D.C. 20500
Telephone: (202) 456-1414
www.whitehouse.gov

The president and the vice president of the United States are elected every four years by a majority of votes cast in the Electoral College. These votes are cast by delegates from each state who traditionally vote in accordance with the majority of the state's voters. States have as many electoral college votes as they have congressional delegates. Missouri has 10 electoral college votes—one for each of the eight U.S. Congress districts and two for the state's two seats in the U.S. Senate.

The president is the chief executive of the United States, with powers to command the armed forces, control foreign policy, grant reprieves and pardons, make certain appointments, execute all laws passed by Congress and present the administration's budget. The president earns $400,000 annually, with an allowance for expenses.

The vice president is selected by members of each national political committee and runs on the same ticket for the same term as the president. The vice president assumes the presidency if the president dies or resigns from the office, is incapacitated to the extent that he or she cannot exercise presidential duties for an extended period or is impeached. The vice president presides over the functions of the U.S. Senate and acts as emissary of the president. The vice president earns $231,900 annually.

The tradition of the Cabinet dates back to the beginnings of the presidency itself. Established in Article II, Section 2, of the U.S. Constitution, the Cabinet's role is to advise the president on any subject he or she may require relating to the duties of each member's respective office. It is made up of 15 cabinet members (or secretaries) who have the responsibility to operate each department. Secretaries are appointed by the president and serve at his or her pleasure. Cabinet secretaries earn $199,700 annually.

Members, President Obama's Cabinet

Joseph R. Biden, Vice President
www.whitehouse.gov/vicepresident
John Kerry, Secretary of State
www.state.gov
Jack Lew, Secretary, Department of the Treasury
www.treasury.gov
Ashton Carter, Secretary, Department of Defense
www.defense.gov
Loretta E. Lynch, Attorney General, Department of Justice
www.usdoj.gov
Sally Jewell, Secretary, Department of the Interior
www.doi.gov
Thomas J. Vilsack, Secretary, Department of Agriculture
www.usda.gov
Penny Pritzker, Secretary, Department of Commerce
www.commerce.gov
Thomas E. Perez, Secretary, Department of Labor
www.dol.gov
Sylvia Matthews Burwell, Secretary, Department of Health and Human Services
www.hhs.gov
Julián Castro, Secretary, Department of Housing and Urban Development
www.hud.gov
Anthony Foxx, Secretary, Department of Transportation
www.dot.gov
Ernest Moniz, Secretary, Department of Energy
www.energy.gov
Arne Duncan, Secretary, Department of Education
www.ed.gov
Robert McDonald, Secretary, Department of Veterans Affairs
www.va.gov
Jeh Johnson, Secretary, Department of Homeland Security
www.dhs.gov

In addition to secretaries of the cabinet, the president maintains a White House staff of advisers who serve at his pleasure.

President Obama's Executive Officers of Cabinet Rank

Denis McDonough, White House Chief of Staff
www.whitehouse.gov
Gina McCarthy, Administrator, Environmental Protection Agency
www.epa.gov
Shaun L. S. Donovan, Director, Office of Management and Budget
www.whitehouse.gov/omb
Michael Froman, Ambassador, United States Trade Representative
www.ustr.gov

Samantha Power, Ambassador, United States
Mission to the United Nations
www.usun.state.gov
Jason Furman, Chair, Council of Economic
Advisers
www.whitehouse.gov/administration/eop/cea
Maria Contreras-Sweet, Administrator, Small
Business Administration
www.sba.gov

Legislative Branch

www.house.gov / www.senate.gov

The U.S. Constitution provides for two legislative houses, known as the Congress. The Senate
is composed of 100 members; two senators are
elected from each state. The House of Representatives is composed of 435 members; the number of representatives is determined based on the
population of each state.

Senators must be at least 30 years of age and
must be residents of the United States for at least
nine years. They also must reside in the state they
are elected to represent. Senators serve terms
of six years, with one-third of Senate members
elected every two years. Senators earn $174,000
annually, plus expenses.

Representatives must be at least 25 years of
age and must have been residents of the United
States for at least seven years. They also must reside in the state they represent. Representatives
serve two-year terms and earn $174,000 annu-
ally, plus expenses.

Congress is in session for two years, beginning on January 3 of each year unless another
date is specified. The presiding officer of the Senate is the vice president of the United States. The
Senate also elects a president *pro tem* of the Senate to serve in the absence of the vice president.
The president *pro tem* also represents the party in
power and earns $193,400. The presiding officer
of the House is called the speaker. The speaker
traditionally represents the party in majority and
earns $223,500.

Judicial Branch

The U.S. Supreme Court heads the nation's judicial branch of government. The Supreme Court
is composed of nine justices, appointed for life.
Supreme Court justices may only be removed by
impeachment and trial by Congress. Justices re-

ceive $246,800 annually while the chief justice,
who leads the court, earns $258,100.

The Supreme Court concerns itself with national issues or matters concerning the constitutionality of certain laws or findings. Decisions
of the court are binding and overrule any other
court decision.

Members, United States Supreme Court

1 First St. N.E., Washington, D.C. 20543
Telephone: (202) 479-3000
www.supremecourt.gov

John G. Roberts Jr., chief justice;
Antonin Scalia, associate justice;
Anthony M. Kennedy, associate justice;
Clarence Thomas, associate justice;
Ruth Bader Ginsburg, associate justice;
Stephen G. Breyer, associate justice;
Samuel A. Alito Jr., associate justice;
Sonia Sotomayor, associate justice;
Elena Kagan, associate justice.

Other Federal Courts

Immediately below the Supreme Court are
the U.S. Courts of Appeals and the U.S. District
Courts. The Courts of Appeals operate in 11 regions and the District of Columbia. Missouri is
served by the Eighth Circuit. Appeals Court judges earn $213,300 annually.

There are 94 U.S. District Court districts with
federal jurisdiction. Two of these are located in
Missouri: the Eastern Missouri District and the
Western Missouri District. Eastern District courts
are located in St. Louis, Hannibal and Cape
Girardeau, and the Western District courts are
in Kansas City, St. Joseph, Springfield, Jefferson
City and Joplin. Federal charges stemming from
both civil and criminal suits generally begin in
U.S. District Court. Judges in these courts earn
$201,100 annually.

For information on other agencies or programs of the U.S. government operating in Missouri, contact the Federal Information Center,
Rm. 2616 Federal Building, 1520 Market St., St.
Louis 63103, phone (toll free) (800) 333-4636
((800) FED-INFO).

*All salary information provided by the Congres-
sional Research Service.

Barack H. Obama
United States President
Elected November 4, 2008
Term expires January 2017

Barack H. Obama is the 44th President of the United States.

His story is the American story — values from the heartland, a middle-class upbringing in a strong family, hard work and education as the means of getting ahead, and the conviction that a life so blessed should be lived in service to others.

With a father from Kenya and a mother from Kansas, President Obama was born in Hawaii on August 4, 1961. He was raised with help from his grandfather, who served in Patton's army, and his grandmother, who worked her way up from the secretarial pool to middle management at a bank.

After working his way through college with the help of scholarships and student loans, President Obama moved to Chicago, where he worked with a group of churches to help rebuild communities devastated by the closure of local steel plants.

He went on to attend law school, where he became the first African-American president of the *Harvard Law Review*. Upon graduation, he returned to Chicago to help lead a voter registration drive, teach constitutional law at the University of Chicago and remain active in his community.

President Obama's years of public service are based around his unwavering belief in the ability to unite people around a politics of purpose. In the Illinois State Senate, he passed the first major ethics reform in 25 years, cut taxes for working families, and expanded health care for children and their parents. As a United States Senator, he reached across the aisle to pass groundbreaking lobbying reform, lock up the world's most dangerous weapons and bring transparency to government by putting federal spending online.

He was elected the 44th president of the United States on November 4, 2008, and sworn in on January 20, 2009. He and his wife Michelle are the proud parents of two daughters, Malia, 17, and Sasha, 14.

Joseph R. Biden Jr.
United States Vice President
Elected November 4, 2008
Term expires January 2017

Joseph Robinette Biden, Jr., was born November 20, 1942, in Scranton, Pa., the first of four siblings. In 1953, the Biden family moved from Pennsylvania to Claymont, Del. He graduated from the University of Delaware and Syracuse Law School and served on the New Castle County Council. Then, at age 29, he became one of the youngest people ever elected to the United States Senate.

Just weeks after the election, tragedy struck the Biden family, when Biden's wife, Neilia, and their one-year-old daughter, Naomi, were killed and their two young sons critically injured in an auto accident. Vice President Biden was sworn in to the U.S. Senate at his sons' hospital bedsides and began commuting to Washington every day by train, a practice he maintained throughout his career in the Senate.

In 1977, Vice President Biden married Jill Jacobs. Jill Biden, who holds a Ph.D. in education, has been an educator for over two decades and currently teaches at a community college in Northern Virginia. The vice president's son, Beau (1969-2015) was Delaware's attorney general from 2007-2015 and a major in the 261st Signal Brigade of the Delaware National Guard. The vice president's other son, Hunter, is an attorney and chairman of the World Food Program USA. Ashley is a social worker and executive director of the Delaware Center for Justice. Vice President Biden has five grandchildren: Naomi, Finnegan, Roberta Mabel (Maisy), Natalie and Robert Hunter.

As a senator from Delaware for 36 years, Sen. Biden established himself as a leader on some of our nation's most important domestic and international challenges. As chair or ranking Member of the Senate Judiciary Committee for 17 years, then-Sen. Biden was widely recognized for his work on criminal justice issues including the landmark 1994 Crime Bill and the Violence Against Women Act. As chair or ranking member of the Senate Foreign Relations Committee since 1997, then-Sen. Biden played a pivotal role in shaping U.S. foreign policy. He has been at the forefront of issues and legislation related to terrorism, weapons of mass destruction, post-Cold War Europe, the Middle East and Southwest Asia.

Now, as the 47th vice president of the United States, Joe Biden has continued his leadership on important issues facing the nation. The vice president was tasked with implementing the American Recovery and Reinvestment Act, helping to rebuild our economy and lay the foundation for a sustainable economic future. As part of his continued efforts to raise the living standards of middle class Americans across the country, Vice President Biden has also focused on the issues of college affordability and American manufacturing growth, key priorities of the administration.

Vice President Biden continues to draw on his foreign policy experience, advising the president on a multitude of international issues. He helped secure the Senate's approval of the New Strategic Arms Reduction Treaty (START) with Russia, together with significant new funding to maintain our nuclear laboratories. He played a lead role in ending the war in Iraq responsibly, traveling to the country eight times since being elected – most recently in December 2011 to mark the formal end of the war.

In addition, Vice President Biden has supported the administration's effort to reestablish leadership in the Asia Pacific, traveling to China, Japan and Mongolia in August 2011 and completing an exchange of visits with China's then-vice president in February 2012, that country's current leader. He has represented our country in every region of the world, advancing our unprecedented support for Israel's security, securing approval in Europe for the administration's more effective approach to missile defense, working with Latin American leaders to combat drug trafficking and international crime and building relations with key leaders in Africa. He has traveled to more than two dozen countries, including Germany, Belgium, Chile, Costa Rica, Bosnia and Herzegovina, Serbia, Kosovo, Lebanon, Georgia, Ukraine, Iraq, Poland, Romania, the Czech Republic, Israel, the Palestinian Territories, Jordan, Spain, Egypt, Kenya, South Africa, Afghanistan, Pakistan, Finland, Russia, Moldova, Italy, China, Mongolia, Japan, Saudi Arabia, Turkey, Greece, Mexico, Honduras, Brazil, Colombia and Trinidad and Tobago.

Historical Listing, Presidents and Vice Presidents

	President	Political Party	Vice President	Term
1	George Washington	Federalist	John Adams	April 30, 1789–March 4, 1797
2	John Adams	Federalist	Thomas Jefferson	March 4, 1797–March 4, 1801
3	Thomas Jefferson	Democrat-Rep.	Aaron Burr	March 4, 1801–March 4, 1805
	Thomas Jefferson	Democrat-Rep.	George Clinton	March 4, 1805–March 4, 1809
4	James Madison	Democrat-Rep.	George Clinton	March 4, 1809–March 4, 1813
	James Madison	Democrat-Rep.	Elbridge Gerry	March 4, 1813–March 4, 1817
5	James Monroe	Democrat-Rep.	Daniel D. Tompkins	March 4, 1817–March 4, 1825
6	John Quincy Adams	Democrat-Rep.	John C. Calhoun	March 4, 1825–March 4, 1829
7	Andrew Jackson	Democratic	John C. Calhoun	March 4, 1829–March 4, 1833
	Andrew Jackson	Democratic	Martin Van Buren	March 4, 1833–March 4, 1837
8	Martin Van Buren	Democratic	Richard M. Johnson	March 4, 1837–March 4, 1841
9	William Henry Harrison [a]	Whig	John Tyler	March 4, 1841–April 4, 1841
10	John Tyler	Whig	—	April 6, 1841–March 4, 1845
11	James K. Polk	Democratic	George M. Dallas	March 4, 1845–March 4, 1849
12	Zachary Taylor [b]	Whig	Millard Fillmore	March 4, 1849–July 9, 1850
13	Millard Fillmore	Whig	—	July 9, 1850–March 4, 1853
14	Franklin Pierce	Democratic	William R. King	March 4, 1853–March 4, 1857
15	James Buchanan	Democratic	John C. Breckinridge	March 4, 1857–March 4, 1861
16	Abraham Lincoln	Republican	Hannibal Hamlin	March 4, 1861–March 4, 1865
	Abraham Lincoln [c]	Republican	Andrew Johnson	March 4, 1865–April 15, 1865
17	Andrew Johnson	Democratic	—	April 15, 1865–March 4, 1869
18	Ulysses S. Grant	Republican	Schuyler Colfax	March 4, 1869–March 4, 1873
	Ulysses S. Grant	Republican	Henry Wilson	March 4, 1873–March 4, 1877
19	Rutherford B. Hayes	Republican	William A. Wheeler	March 4, 1877–March 4, 1881
20	James A. Garfield [d]	Republican	Chester A. Arthur	March 4, 1881–Sept. 19, 1881
21	Chester A. Arthur	Republican	—	Sept. 20, 1881–March 4, 1885
22	Grover Cleveland	Democratic	Thomas A. Hendricks	March 4, 1885–March 4, 1889
23	Benjamin Harrison	Republican	Levi P. Morton	March 4, 1889–March 4, 1893
24	Grover Cleveland	Democratic	Adlai E. Stevenson	March 4, 1893–March 4, 1897
25	William McKinley	Republican	Garret A. Hobart	March 4, 1897–March 4, 1901
	William McKinley [e]	Republican	Theodore Roosevelt	March 4, 1901–Sept. 14, 1901
26	Theodore Roosevelt	Republican	—	Sept. 14, 1901–March 4, 1905
	Theodore Roosevelt	Republican	Charles W. Fairbanks	March 4, 1905–March 4, 1909
27	William H. Taft	Republican	James S. Sherman	March 4, 1909–March 4, 1913
28	Woodrow Wilson	Democratic	Thomas R. Marshall	March 4, 1913–March 4, 1921
29	Warren G. Harding [f]	Republican	Calvin Coolidge	March 4, 1921–August 2, 1923
30	Calvin Coolidge	Republican	—	August 2, 1923–March 4, 1925
	Calvin Coolidge	Republican	Charles G. Dawes	March 4, 1925–March 4, 1929
31	Herbert Hoover	Republican	Charles Curtis	March 4, 1929–March 4, 1933
32	Franklin D. Roosevelt [g]	Democratic	John N. Garner	March 4, 1933–Jan. 20, 1941
	Franklin D. Roosevelt [h]	Democratic	Henry A. Wallace	Jan. 20, 1941–Jan. 20, 1945
	Franklin D. Roosevelt	Democratic	Harry S. Truman	Jan. 20, 1945–April 12, 1945
33	Harry S. Truman	Democratic	—	April 12, 1945–Jan. 20, 1949
	Harry S. Truman	Democratic	Alben W. Barkley	Jan. 20, 1949–Jan. 20, 1953
34	Dwight D. Eisenhower	Republican	Richard M. Nixon	Jan. 20, 1953–Jan. 20, 1961
35	John F. Kennedy [i]	Democratic	Lyndon B. Johnson	Jan. 20, 1961–Nov. 22, 1963
36	Lyndon B. Johnson	Democratic	—	Nov. 22, 1963–Jan. 20, 1965
	Lyndon B. Johnson	Democratic	Hubert H. Humphrey	Jan. 20, 1965–Jan. 20, 1969
37	Richard M. Nixon [j]	Republican	Spiro T. Agnew	Jan. 20, 1969–August 9, 1974
38	Gerald R. Ford [k]	Republican	Nelson A. Rockefeller	August 9, 1974–Jan. 20, 1977
39	Jimmy Carter	Democratic	Walter Mondale	Jan. 20, 1977–Jan. 20, 1981
40	Ronald Reagan	Republican	George H.W. Bush	Jan. 20, 1981–Jan. 20, 1989
41	George H.W. Bush	Republican	J. Danforth Quayle	Jan. 20, 1989–Jan. 20, 1993
42	William Jefferson Clinton	Democratic	Albert Gore Jr.	Jan. 20, 1993–Jan. 20, 2001
43	George W. Bush	Republican	Richard B. Cheney	Jan. 20, 2001–Jan. 20, 2009
44	Barack H. Obama	Democratic	Joseph R. Biden Jr.	Jan. 20, 2009–

(a) Died April 4, 1841. (b) Died July 9, 1850. (c) Died April 15, 1865. (d) Died September 19, 1881. Chester Arthur wasn't sworn in until Sept. 20, 1881. (e) Died September 14, 1901. (f) Died August 2, 1923. (g) Dates of service changed with 20th Amendment to the U.S. Constitution. (h) Died April 12, 1945. (i) Died November 22, 1963. (j) Vice President Spiro T. Agnew resigned October 10, 1973. His successor was Gerald R. Ford, sworn in December 6, 1973. (k) President Nixon resigned August 9, 1974. Vice President Gerald R. Ford was sworn in as President on August 9, 1974.

Claire McCaskill

United States Senator

Washington Office

730 Hart Senate Office Bldg., Washington, D.C. 20510
Telephone: (202) 224-6154 / FAX: (202) 228-6326
www.mccaskill.senate.gov

District offices

- *555 Independence, Rm. 1600, Cape Girardeau 63703*
  Telephone: (573) 651-0964 / FAX: (573) 334-4278;
- *915 E. Ash St., Columbia 65201*
  Telephone: (573) 442-7130 / FAX: (573) 442-7140;
- *4141 Pennsylvania Ave., Ste. 101, Kansas City 64111*
  Telephone: (816) 421-1639 / FAX: (816) 421-2562;
- *324 Park Central W., Ste. 101, Springfield 65806*
  Telephone: (417) 868-8745 / FAX: (417) 831-1349;
- *5850 Delmar Blvd., Ste. A, St. Louis 63112*
  Telephone: (314) 367-1364 / FAX: (314) 361-8649.

Committees

Committee on Armed Services
Committee on Commerce, Science and Transportation
Committee on Homeland Security and Governmental
Affairs
Special Committee on Aging

CLAIRE McCASKILL (Democrat) The year Harry Truman left the presidency, Claire McCaskill's parents, Bill and Betty Anne, traveled to Rolla for the birth of their daughter. Not long after she was born, the family moved to Lebanon, Mo., where Betty Anne's family ran the corner drug store. Another move shortly thereafter landed Claire in Columbia, Mo., where she attended Hickman High School.

A product of Missouri's public schools, Claire began waiting tables at the Lake of the Ozarks the day after graduating high school, a job she would hold for six years to help pay her way through college and law school at the University of Missouri.

In 1982, McCaskill won a seat in the state legislature. Claire made history in 1992 when she became the first woman elected Jackson County prosecutor. As head of the largest prosecutor's office in the state, she launched one of the nation's first drug courts and established a domestic violence unit—a first-of-its-kind initiative for the region.

Claire won reelection and served as Jackson County prosecutor until 1999 when she was sworn in as state auditor. Her pursuit of accountability included audits of the state's Social Services Foster Care Program and child support enforcement, as well as domestic violence shelters and puppy mills.

In 2006, she became the first woman elected to the U.S. Senate from Missouri, winning the seat once held by Harry Truman.

Making good on a campaign pledge, Claire waged a successful effort to rein in wasteful wartime contracting practices—modeled on Truman's battle

against war profiteering. During the final hours of Claire's first term, her signature legislation implementing historic wartime contracting reforms was signed into law.

Claire drew on her personal commitment to America's veterans, establishing a "secret shopper" program to improve health care services for Missouri's veterans. Following reports of neglect, she successfully pushed for the removal of Army officials managing Walter Reed Army Medical Center, and led the successful effort to reform management of Arlington National Cemetery after disclosures of mismarked gravesites.

When dozens of small towns across rural Missouri were threatened with post office closures, Claire waged a successful battle to protect those post offices, which she called "the lifeblood of rural Missouri."

Following reelection in 2012, her oversight panel was expanded into a permanent subcommittee charged with investigating waste, fraud and abuse at every federal agency. A tech leader with a penchant for communicating with constituents via Twitter, Claire was also named chair of the Subcommittee on Consumer Protection. In the first year of her second term, she launched investigations into areas including robocalls, inaccuracies on credit reports, security clearance background checks and the Pentagon's troubled POW/MIA recovery program.

As a senior member of the Armed Services Committee, Claire drew on her years as a prosecutor in leading efforts to curb sexual assaults in our armed forces.

Claire returns home nearly every weekend to spend time with her nine grandchildren. She and husband Joseph have a blended family of seven children, all but two of whom live in St Louis.

Roy Blunt

United States Senator

Washington Office

260 Russell Senate Office Bldg.,
Washington, D.C. 20510
Telephone: (202) 224-5721 / FAX: (202) 224-8149
www.blunt.senate.gov

District offices

- *911 Main St., Ste. 2224, Kansas City 64105*
  Telephone: (816) 471-7141 / FAX: (816) 471-7338
- *2740 B E. Sunshine, Springfield 65804*
  Telephone: (417) 877-7814 / FAX: (417) 823-9662
- *7700 Bonhomme, #315, Clayton 63105*
  Telephone: (314) 725-4484 / FAX: (314) 727-3548
- *Rush Hudson Limbaugh Sr., United States Courthouse,*
  555 Independence St., Ste. 1500, Cape Girardeau
  63703
  Telephone: (573) 334-7044 / FAX: (573) 334-7352;
- *308 E. High, Ste. 202, Jefferson City 65101*
  Telephone: (573) 634-2488 / FAX: (573) 634-6005
- *1001 Cherry St., Ste. 104, Columbia 65201*
  Telephone: (573) 442-8151 / FAX: (573) 442-8162

Committees

Committee on Appropriations
 Subcommittee on the Departments of Labor, Health
  and Human Services, Education and Related
  Agencies, chair
 Subcommittee on Agriculture, Rural Development,
  Food and Drug Administration and Related
  Agencies
 Subcommittee on Transportation, Housing and
  Urban Development, and Related Agencies
 Subcommittee on Interior, Environment, and Related
  Agencies
 Subcommittee on Department of State, Foreign
  Operations, and Related Programs
 Subcommittee on Defense
Committee on Commerce, Science, and Transportation
Committee on Rules and Administration, chair
Select Committee on Intelligence

ROY BLUNT (Republican) Building on a background as a public servant, university president, and teacher, United States Senator Roy Blunt was elected to the United States Senate in 2010.

Senator Blunt serves as the Vice Chair of the Senate Republican Conference. He also serves on the Senate Appropriations Committee.

The people of Southwest Missouri overwhelmingly elected Senator Blunt seven times to the U.S. House of Representatives. Senator Blunt was elected the Majority Whip earlier in his career than any member of Congress in eight decades, and he was elected to the Senate leadership during his first year in the Senate.

Before serving in Congress, he was a history teacher, a county official, and in 1984 became the first Republican elected as Missouri's Secretary of State in more than 50 years. Senator Blunt also served four years as the president of Southwest Baptist University, his alma mater, in Bolivar, Missouri. Senator Blunt earned an M.A. in history from Missouri State University.

Senator Blunt is a member of the Smithsonian Council for American Art and is a Trustee of the State Historical Society of Missouri. Senator Blunt is also a member of the Kennedy Center Board of Trustees.

The Senator is married to Abigail Blunt and has four children: Matt Blunt, Missouri's 54th Governor; Amy Blunt, an attorney in Columbia, Mo.; Andy Blunt, an attorney in Jefferson City; and Charlie (age 10). Blunt has six grandchildren: Davis Mosby, Ben Blunt, Branch Blunt, Eva Mosby, Allyson Blunt and Brooks Blunt.

Historical Listing, United States Senators

Name	Political Party	Elected
David Barton[1]	Republican, Adams-Clay R.	1820, 1824
Thomas Hart Benton[2]	Democratic	1820–48
Alexander Buckner[3]	Jacksonian	1830
Lewis F. Linn[3, 4]	Jacksonian, Democratic	1834, 1836, 1842
David R. Atchison[4]	Democratic	1843, 1844, 1848
Henry S. Geyer	Whig	1850
James S. Green	Democratic	1856
Trusten Polk[5]	Democratic	1856
Waldo P. Johnson[6]	Democratic	1860
B. Gratz Brown[9]	Unconditional Unionist	1862
John B. Henderson[8]	Unionist	1862
Robert Wilson[7]	Unionist	1862
Charles D. Drake[10]	Republican	1866
Carl Schurz	Republican	1868
Francis P. Blair[12]	Democratic	1870
Daniel F. Jewett[11]	Republican	1870
Lewis V. Bogy[13]	Democratic	1872
Francis M. Cockrell	Democratic	1874, 1880, 1886, 1892, 1898
David H. Armstrong[14]	Democratic	1876
James Shields[15]	Democratic	1878
George Graham Vest	Democratic	1878, 1884, 1890, 1896
William Joe Stone[16]	Democratic	1902, 1908, 1914
William Warner	Republican	1904
James A. Reed	Democratic	1910, 1916, 1922
Seldon Spencer[17, 18]	Republican	1918, 1920
Xenophon P. Wilfley[16]	Democratic	1918
George H. Williams[17]	Republican	1924
Harry B. Hawes[18]	Democratic	1926
Roscoe C. Patterson	Republican	1928
Joel Bennett (Champ) Clark[18, 19]	Democratic	1932, 1938
Harry S. Truman[20]	Democratic	1934, 1940
Forrest Donnell	Republican	1944
Frank P. Briggs[20]	Democratic	1945
James P. Kem	Republican	1946
Thomas C. Hennings Jr.[21]	Democratic	1950, 1956
Stuart Symington[23]	Democratic	1952, 1958, 1964, 1970
Edward V. Long[21, 22]	Democratic	1962
Thomas F. Eagleton[22]	Democratic	1968, 1974, 1980
John C. Danforth[23]	Republican	1976, 1982, 1988
Christopher Samuel (Kit) Bond	Republican	1986, 1992, 1998, 2004
John Ashcroft	Republican	1994
Jean Carnahan[24]	Democratic	2000
James M. Talent	Republican	2002
Claire McCaskill	Democratic	2006, 2012
Roy Blunt	Republican	2010

[1]Admitted to seat, December 1821.   [2]Admitted to seat, December 1821.
[3]Linn was appointed to succeed Alexander Buckner, who died in 1838.
[4]Linn died October 3, 1848, and was succeeded by David R. Atchison, who served until 1855.
[5]Polk was expelled from the Senate on a charge of disloyalty, January 10, 1862.
[6]Johnson was expelled from the Senate on a charge of disloyalty, January 10, 1862.
[7]Wilson was appointed by Provisional Governor Hall in the absence of Governor Gamble.
[8]Henderson was appointed by Provisional Governor Hall in the absence of Governor Gamble.
[9]Brown was elected for a term ending March 4, 1867.
[10]Drake resigned in 1871 to become a judge of the U.S. Court of Claims in Washington D.C.
[11]Jewett was appointed to succeed Charles Drake until the meeting of Congress.
[12]Blair was elected to serve the remainder of Drake's senate term.
[13]Bogy died September 20, 1877.   [14]Armstrong was appointed September 27, 1877, to succeed Bogy until meeting of Congress.
[15]Shields was elected January 21, 1879, to serve the remainder of Bogy's senate term.
[16]Stone died April 14, 1918, and was succeeded by Xenophon P. Wilfley, who served until December 5, 1926.
[17]Spencer died May 16, 1925, and was succeeded by George H. Williams.
[18]Hawes resigned February 3, 1933, and was succeeded by Joel Bennett (Champ) Clark, who was named by Governor Guy B. Clark for the remainder of the term.

[19]Clark was elected November 8, 1932, for a term expiring March 4, 1939.

[20]Briggs was appointed January 18, 1945, to fill the unexpired term of Harry S. Truman, who resigned to become Vice President of the United States and succeeded to the presidency on April 12, 1945, upon the death of Franklin D. Roosevelt.

[21]Hennings died while in office on September 13, 1960, and was succeeded by Edward V. Long, appointed September 23, 1960, then elected at a special election November 8, 1960.

[22]Long resigned December 27, 1968, and was succeeded by Thomas F. Eagleton, appointed December 27, 1968.

[23]Symington resigned December 27, 1976, and was succeeded by John C. Danforth, appointed December 27, 1976.

[24]Carnahan was appointed to serve Mel Carnahan's term until the next general election. Mel Carnahan was elected posthumously on November 7, 2000.

U.S. Representative—District 1

WM. LACY CLAY

Washington office: 2418 Rayburn House Office Bldg., Washington, D.C. 20515; Telephone: (202) 225-2406, FAX: (202) 226-3717.

District offices: Thomas F. Eagleton U.S. Courthouse, 111 S. 10th St., Ste. 24.344, St. Louis 63102, Telephone: (314) 367-1970; FAX: (314) 367-1341; 6830 Gravois, St. Louis 63116, Telephone: (314) 669-9393, FAX: (314) 669-9398.

www.lacyclay.house.gov
www.facebook.com/pages/Congressman-Wm-Lacy-Clay/109135405838588

Committees: Oversight and Gov't. Reform; Financial Services (ranking member, Subcommittee on Financial Institutions).

Biography: A native St. Louisan, he succeeded his father, the Hon. Bill Clay, who served for 32 years and was a founding member of the Congressional Black Caucus. He is a graduate of the University of Maryland and holds honorary degrees from Lincoln University, Harris-Stowe State University and Logan College. Nonprofits: St. Louis Gateway Classic Sports Foundation; Mary Ryder Homes; William L. Clay Scholarship and Research Fund. Clay is the proud father of Carol and Will. He resides in St. Louis and attends St. Nicholas' Catholic Church. Prior to his election to the U.S. House, Clay served for 17 years in both chambers of the Missouri General Assembly. Elected to the U.S. House: 2000–2014. Democrat.

U.S. Representative—District 2

ANN WAGNER

Washington office: 435 Cannon House Office Bldg., Washington, D.C. 20515; Telephone: (202) 225-1621; FAX: (202) 225-2563.

District offices: 301 Sovereign Court, Ste. 201, Ballwin 63011, Telephone: (636) 779-5449.

www.wagner.house.gov

Committee: House Financial Services.

Biography: Attended the University of Missouri–Columbia and received her B.S. in business administration from the business school with an emphasis in logistics. After college, worked in the private sector and held management positions at Hallmark Cards and Ralston Purina. Ann and Ray have three children: Raymond, Stephen and Mary Ruth. Ann served as: local GOP committeewoman; chair of the Missouri Republican Party and co-chair of the Republican National Committee. In 2005, was sworn in as the 19th U.S. ambassador to Luxembourg by Secretary of State Condoleezza Rice. In 2010, was asked to serve as the chair of Roy Blunt's U.S. Senate campaign. Ann announced her first run for public office on April 26, 2011, and won her 2012 congressional race with over 60 percent of the vote. Ann was also selected by the freshman class of the 113th Congress to be their representative on the Elected Leadership Committee. Elected to the U.S. House: 2012, 2014. Republican.

U.S. Representative—District 3

BLAINE LUETKEMEYER

Washington office: 2440 Rayburn House Office Bldg., Washington, D.C. 20515; Telephone: (202) 225-2956; FAX: (202) 225-5712.

District offices: 2117 Missouri Blvd, Jefferson City, 65109, Telephone: (573) 635-7232; 113 E. Pearce, Wentzville, 63385, Telephone: (636) 327-7055; 516 Jefferson St., Washington 63090, Telephone: (636) 239-2276.

www.luetkemeyer.house.gov

Committees: Subcommittee on Housing and Insurance, chair; Financial Services; Subcommittee on Financial Institutions & Consumer Credit; Small Business Committee, vice chair; Subcommittee on Health and Technology and Agriculture; Subcommittee on Energy and Trade

Biography: Born May 7, 1952, in Jefferson City. Educated at Lincoln University, B.A., political science, 1974. He is married to Jackie Luetkemeyer, they have three children: Trevor, Brandy and Nikki. Member: St. Lawrence Catholic Church; Knights of Columbus; Missouri Farm Bureau; Eldon Chamber of Commerce; Missouri House of Representatives, 1999–2005; Missouri Director of Tourism, 2006–2008. Elected to the U.S. House: 2008–2014. Republican.

U.S. Representative—District 4

VICKY HARTZLER

Washington Office: 1023 Longworth House Office Bldg., Washington, D.C. 20515; Telephone: (202) 225-2876, FAX: (202) 225-0148

District Offices: 2415 Carter Ln., Ste. 4, Columbia 65201, Telephone: (573) 442-9311, FAX: (573) 442-9309; 1909 N. Commercial St., Harrisonville 64701, Telephone: (816) 884-3411, FAX: (816) 884-3163; 219 N. Adams St., Lebanon 65536, Telephone: (417) 532-5582, FAX: (417) 532-3886.

www.hartzler.house.gov

Committees: Agriculture, Budget and Armed Services.

Biography: Born October 13, 1960. Raised on a farm in Archie. Graduate of the Univ. of Missouri–Columbia with a B.S. in education and Central Missouri State Univ. (now Univ. of Central Missouri) with a M.S. in education. Taught family and consumer sciences for 11 years. Vicky and her husband Lowell have one daughter, Tiffany. The Hartzlers are small business owners with three farm equipment stores in the fourth district. First elected to office in November 1994 as the state representative from Missouri's 124th district, serving three terms. In 2004, served as spokesperson for the Coalition to Protect Marriage, a state constitutional amendment that passed resoundingly. In 2005, she was appointed chair of the Missouri Women's Council. Elected to the U.S. House: 2010–2014. Republican.

U.S. Representative—District 5

EMANUEL CLEAVER II

Washington office: 2335 Rayburn House Office Bldg., Washington, D.C. 20515; Telephone: (202) 225-4535, FAX: (202) 225-4403.

District offices: 101 W. 31st St., Kansas City 64108, Telephone: (816) 842-4545; 211 W. Maple Ave., Independence 64050, Telephone: (816) 833-4545; 1923 Main St., Higginsville 64037, Telephone: (660) 584-7373, FAX: (660) 584-7227.

www.house.gov/cleaver

Committee: Financial Services (subcommittees: Housing and Insurance; Oversight and Investigations).

Biography: Born in Waxahachie, TX. Graduated high school in Wichita Falls, TX. Attended Prairie View A&M Univ., earned B.S. in sociology; St. Paul's School of Theology, master's in divinity. An ordained Methodist minister, he served as senior pastor at St. James United Methodist Church, Kansas City. He's been married for 30 years to his wife Dianne. They have four children and three grandchildren. He was first elected to public office, 1979 as city council-man in Kansas City, a 12-year tenure during which he served as mayor *pro tem* and chair of the Planning and Zoning Comm.. Elected mayor of Kansas City, and the first African-American elected to that office, served two terms. Served two-terms as pres. of the Nat'l. Conf. of Black Mayors. He was honored by Kansas City designating a major thoroughfare as "Emanuel Cleaver II Blvd." Elected to the U.S. House: 2004–2014. Elected chair of the Congressional Black Caucus, 2011–2012. Democrat.

U.S. Representative—District 6

SAMUEL B. (Sam) GRAVES

Washington office: 1415 Longworth House Office Bldg., Washington, D.C. 20515; Telephone: (202) 225-7041, FAX: (202) 225-8221.

District offices: 11724 N.W. Plaza Cir., Ste. 900, Kansas City 64153, Tele-phone: (816) 792-3976; 411 Jules St., Rm. 111, St. Joseph 64501, Telephone: (816) 749-0800; 906 Broadway, PO Box 364, Hannibal 63401; Telephone: (573) 221-3400.

www.graves.house.gov

Committees: Transportation and Infrastructure; (subcommittees: Aviation; High-ways and Transit, chair; Railroads, Pipelines and Hazardous Materials) and Armed Services.

Biography: Born Nov. 7, 1963, in Tarkio. Graduate of Tarkio High School, 1982. Attended University of Missouri–Columbia, receiving his degree in agron-omy from the School of Agriculture, 1986. Member: First Baptist Church; Alpha Gamma Sigma; Rotary; Jaycees; volunteer fireman and rescue squad; University Extension Council; Farm Bureau; Missouri Historical Society. Awards: National Outstanding Young Farmer; Missouri State Med. Association; Legislative Excellence; Association Industries of Missouri, Voice of Missouri Business; Mo. Chamber of Commerce; Spirit of Enterprise; Eagle Scout. Elected to the U.S. House: 2000–2014. Republican.

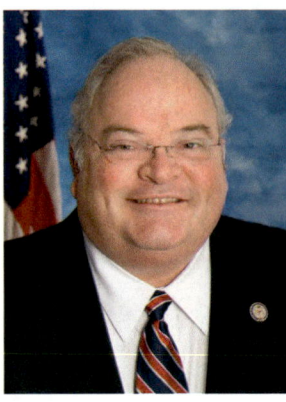

U.S. Representative—District 7

BILLY LONG

Washington Office: 1541 Longworth House Office Bldg., Washington, D.C. 20515; Telephone: (202) 225-6536; FAX: (202) 225-5604.

District Offices: 3232 E. Ridgeview St., Springfield 65804; Telephone: (417) 889-1800, FAX: (417) 889-4915; 2727 E. 32nd St., Ste. 2, Joplin 64804; Telephone: (417) 781-1041, FAX: (417) 781-2832.

www.long.house.gov

Committees: Energy and Commerce (subcommittees: Communications and Technology; Energy and Power; Health).

Biography: Long attended the Univ. of Missouri in Columbia. He graduated from the Missouri Auction School in Kansas City, receiving Certified Auctioneer Institute designation at the Univ. of Indiana–Bloomington. Billy was a real estate broker and owner of Billy Long Auctions, LLC in Springfield. He was also a radio talk show host from 1999–2006 on KWTO AM560. Long was a member of the Nat'l. Assoc. of Realtors, Nat'l. Auctioneers Assoc. and the Missouri Professional Auctioneers' Assoc. Long has been inducted into the Missouri Professional Auctioneers' Hall of Fame. Long also holds memberships in the Nat'l. Rifle Assoc. and the Springfield Area Chamber of Commerce. Long and his wife Barbara married in 1984. They are members of First & Cavalry Presbyterian Church. Elected to the U.S. House: 2010–2014. Republican.

U.S. Representative—District 8

JASON SMITH

Washington office: 2230 Rayburn House Office Bldg., Washington, D.C. 20515; Telephone: (202) 225-4404; FAX: (202) 226-0326.

District offices: 2502 Tanner Dr., Ste. 205, Cape Girardeau 63701, Telephone: (573) 335-0101; 830A S. Bishop, Rolla 65401, Telephone: (573) 364-2455; 22 E. Columbia, Farmington 63640, Telephone: (573) 756-9755; 35 Court Sq., Ste. 300, West Plains 65775, Telephone: (417) 255-1515.

www.jasonsmith.house.gov

Committees: Judiciary (subcommittees: Courts, Intellectual Property and the Internet; Regulatory Reform, Commercial and Antitrust Law; Constitution and Civil Justice); Natural Resources (subcommittees: Fisheries, Wildlife, Oceans and Insular Affairs; Public Lands and Environmental Regulation).

Biography: Born June 16, 1980. Graduate of Salem High School, received B.S. degrees, agricultural economics and business administration with an emphasis in finance, Univ. of Missouri–Columbia. Earned law degree from Oklahoma City Univ. School of Law; also spent summer studying international law, Trinity College, Cambridge, England. He is an attorney, real estate agent, small business owner and fourth generation owner of the family farm. Member: Grace Community Church; NRA; Missouri Bar; numerous local chambers of commerce and Missouri Farm Bureau. Former president, current member of the Salem FFA Alumni Assn., holds an American FFA degree. Elected to the Missouri House: November 2005 (special election), 2006, 2008, 2012. Elected to the U.S. House: June 2013 (special election), 2014. Republican.

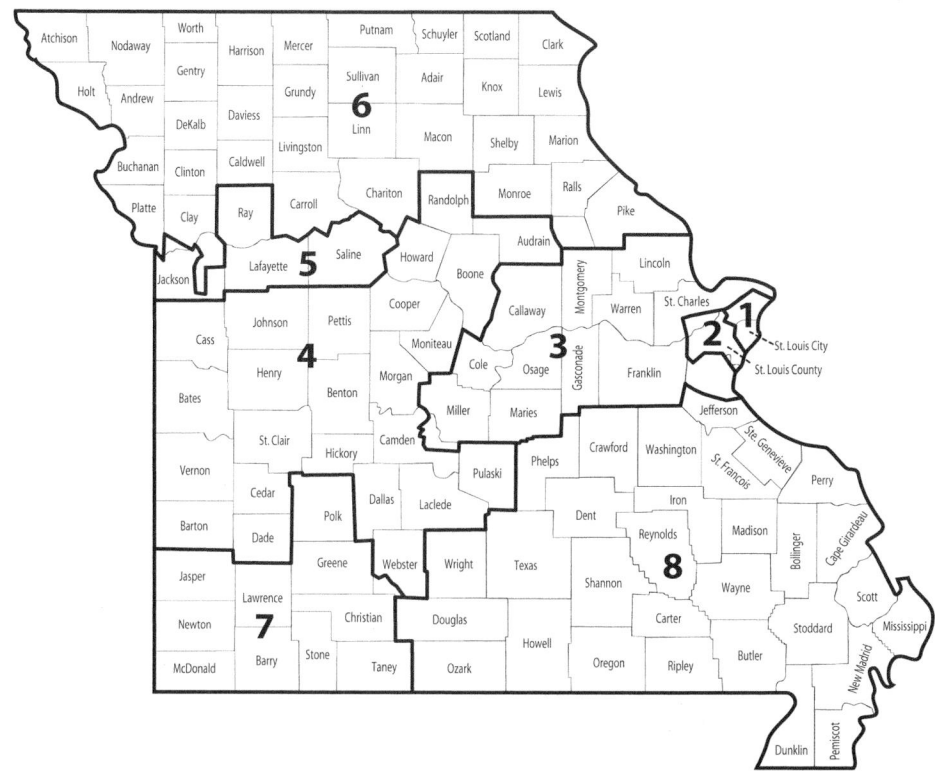

The congressional district bill (H.B. 193), passed over veto by the 96th General Assembly on May 4, 2011, established these district boundaries.

District	Description or boundary	Population
1	Parts of St. Louis County and St. Louis City	748,615
2	St. Charles (part of), St. Louis County (part of), and Jefferson County (part of)	748,615
3	Counties of Lincoln, Warren, Montgomery, Callaway, Cole, Miller, Maries, Osage, Gasconade, Franklin, St. Charles (part of), Camden (part of), and Jefferson (part of)	748,615
4	Counties of Randolph, Boone, Howard, Cooper Moniteau, Morgan, Pulaski, Laclede, Webster, Dallas, Hickory, Benton, Pettis, Johnson, Henry, St. Clair, Cedar, Dade, Barton, Vernon, Bates, Cass and Camden (part of), Audrain (part of)	748,615
5	Saline, Lafayette, Ray, and Jackson (part of)	748,615
6	Counties of Atchison, Nodaway, Worth, Harrison, Mercer, Putnam, Schuyler, Scotland, Clark, Lewis, Knox, Adair, Sullivan, Grundy, Daviess, Gentry, Andrew, Holt, Buchanan DeKalb, Caldwell, Livingston, Linn, Macon, Shelby, Marion, Ralls, Pike, Monroe, Chariton, Caroll, Clay, Platte, Clinton, Jackson (part of), Audrain (part of)	748,615
7	Counties of McDonald, Newton, Jasper, Lawrence, Barry, Stone, Taney, Christian, Greene, Polk, and Webster (part of)	748,615
8	Counties of Ozark, Douglas, Wright, Texas, Phelps, Dent, Crawford, Washington, St. Francois, Ste. Genevieve, Perry, Cape Girardeau, Bollinger, Madison, Iron, Reynolds, Shannon, Howell, Oregon, Ripley, Carter, Butler, Wayne, Stoddard, Scott, Mississippi, New Madrid, Pemiscot, Dunklin, and Jefferson (part of)	748,615

Historical Listing, United States Representatives

Name	District	Political Party	Elected
John Scott		Democratic	1820–24
Edward Bates		Whig	1826
Spencer D. Pettis		Jacksonian	1828, 1831
William H. Ashley		Jacksonian	1831, 1832, 1835
John Bull		Democratic	1833
Albert G. Harrison		Democratic	1835, 1836-1838
John Miller		Democratic	1836–40
John Jameson		Democratic	1839, 1842, 1846
John C. Edwards		Democratic	1840
Gustavus M. Bower		Democratic	1842
James B. Bowlin		Democratic	1842–48
James M. Hughes		Democratic	1842
James H. Relfe		Democratic	1842-1844
John S. Phelps	5, 6	Democratic	1844-60
Sterling Price[1]		Democratic	1844
Leonard H. Sims		Democratic	1844
William McDaniel[1]		Democratic	1846
James S. Green	3	Democratic	1846, 1848, 1856
Willard P. Hall	4	Democratic, Union–D	1846–50
William Van Ness Bay	2	Democratic	1848
John F. Darby	1	Whig	1850
John G. Miller[2]	3	Whig, Opposition	1850–1854
Gilchrist Porter	2	Whig, Opposition	1850, 1854
Thomas Hart Benton	1	Democratic	1852
Alfred W. Lamb	2	Democratic	1852
Mordecai Oliver	4	Whig, Opposition	1852, 1854
Samuel Caruthers	7	Whig, Opposition, Democratic	1853–56
James J. Lindley	3	Whig, Opposition	1853, 1854
Thomas P. Akers[2]	5	American	1856
Luther M. Kennett	1	Opposition	1854
Thomas L. Anderson	2	American, Ind. D	1856-1858
Francis P. Blair[3]	1	Democratic	1856-1862
John B. Clark[4]	3	Democratic	1856–1860
James Craig	4	Democratic	1856-1858
John R. Barret	1	Union–D	1858, 1860
John W. Noell[5]	7, 3	Democratic, Unconditional Unionist	1858, 1860
Samuel H. Woodson	5	American	1856-1858
William A. Hall[4]	3, 8	Democratic, Unionist	1860, 1862
Eligan H. Norton	4	Democratic	1860
Thomas L. Price[6]	5	Democratic	1861
John W. Reid[6]	5	Democratic	1860
James S. Rollins	2, 9	Unionist	1860, 1862
Henry T. Blow	2	Unionist, Republican	1862, 1864
Sempronius H. Boyd	4	Unionist, Republican	1862, 1868
Austin A. King	6	Unionist	1862
Samuel Knox	1	Unionist	1862
Benjamin F. Loan	7	Unionist, Republican	1862–66
Joseph W. McClurg[7]	5	Unionist, Republican	1862–66
John G. Scott[5]	3	Democratic	1862

Name	District	Political Party	Elected
George W. Anderson	9	Republican	1864, 1866
John F. Benjamin	8	Republican	1864–68
John Hogan	1	Democratic	1864
John R. Kelso	4	Indep. Republican	1864
Thomas E. Noell[8]	3	Republican, Democratic	1864, 1866
Robert T. Van Horn	6, 8, 5	Republican	1864–68, 1880, 1894
Joseph J. Gravely	4	Republican	1866
James R. McCormick[8]	3	Democratic	1867–70
Carman A. Newcomb	2	Republican	1866
William A. Pile	1	Republican	1866
John H. Stover[7]	5	Democratic	1866
Joel F. Asper	7	Republican	1868
Samuel S. Burdette	5	Republican	1868-1870
D. Pat Dyer	9	Republican	1868
Gustavus A. Finkelnburg	2	Republican	1868-1870
Erastus Wells	1, 2	Democratic	1868–74, 1878
James G. Blair	8	Liberal Republican	1870
Abram Comingo	6, 8	Democratic	1870-1872
Harrison E. Havens	4, 6	Republican	1870-1872
Andrew King	9	Democratic	1870
Isaac C. Parker	7, 9	Republican	1870-1872
Richard P. Bland[9]	5, 11, 8	Democratic	1872–92, 1896-1898
Aylett H. Buckner	13, 7	Democratic	1872–1882
Thomas T. Crittenden	7	Democratic	1872, 1876
John Montgomery Glover	12	Democratic	1872–76
Robert A. Hatcher	4	Democratic	1872–76
Ira B. Hyde	10	Republican	1872
Edwin O. Stanard	1	Republican	1872
William H. Stone	3	Democratic	1872-1874
John B. Clark Jr.	11	Democratic	1872–1880
Rezin A. DeBolt	10	Democratic	1874
Benjamin J. Franklin	8	Democratic	1874, 1876
Edward C. Kehr	1	Democratic	1874
Charles H. Morgan	6, 12, 15	Democratic	1874, 1876, 1882, 1892, 1908
John F. Philips[10]	7	Democratic	1874, 1879
David Rea	9	Democratic	1874, 1876
Nathan Cole	2	Republican	1876
Anthony F. Ittner	1	Republican	1876
Lyne S. Metcalf	3	Republican	1876
Henry M. Pollard	10	Democratic	1876
Martin L. Clardy	1, 10	Democratic	1878–1886
Lowndes H. Davis	4, 14	Democratic	1878–1882
Nicholas Ford	9	Greenback	1878-1882
R. Graham Frost	3	Democratic	1878-1880
William H. Hatch	12, 1	Democratic	1878–1892
Alfred M. Lay[10]	7	Democratic	1878
Gideon F. Rothwell	10	Democratic	1878
Sam L. Sawyer	8	Democratic	1878
James R. Waddill	6	Democratic	1878
Thomas Allen[11]	2	Democratic	1880
Joseph H. Burrows	10	Greenback	1880
Ira S. Hazeltine	6	Greenback	1880
James H. McLean[11]	2	Democratic	1880

Name	District	Political Party	Elected
Theron M. Rice	7	Greenback	1880
Gustavus Sessinghaus	3	Republican	1880
Armstead M. Alexander	2	Democratic	1882
James O. Broadhead	9	Democratic	1882
James N. Burnes[12]	4	Democratic	1882–86
John Cosgrove	6	Democratic	1882
Alexander M. Dockery	3	Democratic	1882–96
Robert W. Fyan	13	Democratic	1882, 1890, 1892
Alexander Graves	5	Democratic	1882
John J. O'Neil	8	Democratic	1882–86, 1890, 1892
William Dawson	14	Democratic	1884
John B. Hale	2	Democratic	1884
John T. Heard	6, 7	Democratic	1884–92
John E. Hutton	7	Democratic	1884, 1886
William J. Stone	12	Democratic	1884–88
William H. Wade	13	Republican	1884–88
William Warner	5	Republican	1884, 1886
John Milton Glover	9	Democratic	1884-1886
Charles F. Booher[12]	4	Democratic	1889, 1906–1918
Charles H. Mansur	2	Democratic	1886–90
James P. Walker[13]	14	Democratic	1886, 1888
Nathan Frank	9	Republican	1888
William M. Kinsey	10	Republican	1888
F.G. Niedringhaus	8	Republican	1888
Richard H. Norton	7	Democratic	1888, 1890
John C. Tarsney	5	Democratic	1888–92
Robert H. Whitelaw[13]	14	Democratic	1888
Robert P.C. Wilson	4	Democratic	1888, 1890
Marshall Arnold	14	Democratic	1890, 1892
Samuel Byrns	10	Democratic	1890
Seth W. Cobb	9, 12	Democratic	1890–94
David A. DeArmond[14]	12, 6	Democratic	1890–1908
Richard Bartholdt	10	Republican	1892–1912
Daniel D. Burnes	4	Democratic	1892
James B. (Champ) Clark	9	Democratic	1892, 1896–1918
Uriel S. Hall	2	Democratic	1892, 1894
Charles F. Joy	11	Republican	1892–1900
Charles G. Burton	15	Republican	1894
Charles N. Clark	1	Republican	1894
George C. Crowther	4	Republican	1894
Joel D. Hubbard	8	Republican	1894
Norman A. Mozley	14	Republican	1894
John H. Raney	13	Republican	1894
John P. Tracey	7	Republican	1894
William M. Treloar	9	Republican	1894
Maecenas E. Benton	15	Democratic	1896–1902
Robert N. Bodine	2	Democratic	1896
Charles F. Cochran	4	Democratic	1896–1902
James A. Cooney	7	Democratic	1896–1900
William S. Cowherd	5	Democratic	1896–1902
James T. Lloyd	1	Democratic	1897–1914
Charles E. Pearce	12	Republican	1896, 1898
Edward A. Robb	13	Democratic	1896–1902
Willard D. Vandiver	14	Democratic	1896–1902

Name	District	Political Party	Elected
John Dougherty	3	Democratic	1898–1902
William W. Rucker	2	Democratic	1898–1920
Dorsey W. Shackleford[9]	8	Democratic	1899–1916
James J. Butler	12	Democratic	1900, 1902
John T. Hunt	11	Democratic	1902–1904
Robert Lamar	16	Democratic	1902, 1906
Courtney W. Hamlin	7	Democratic	1902, 1906–16
George C.R. Wagoner	12	Republican	1902
Harry M. Coudrey	12	Republican	1904–08
Ernest E. Wood	12	Republican	1904
Edgar C. Ellis	5	Republican	1904, 1906, 1920, 1924, 1928
Frank B. Fulkerson	4	Republican	1904
Frank B. Klepper	3	Republican	1904
Arthur P. Murphy	16	Republican	1904, 1908
Marion E. Rhodes	13	Republican	1904, 1918, 1920
Cassius M. Shartel	15	Republican	1904
William T. Tyndall	14	Republican	1904
John Welborn	7	Republican	1904
Joshua W. Alexander[15]	3	Democratic	1906–18
Henry S. Caulfield	11	Republican	1906
Joseph J. Russell	14	Democratic	1906, 1910–16
Madison R. Smith	13	Democratic	1906
Thomas Hackney	15	Democratic	1906
William P. Borland	5	Democratic	1908–16
Charles A. Crow	14	Republican	1908
Clement C. Dickinson[14]	6, At large	Democratic	1910–18, 1922–26, 1930, 1932*
Politte Elvins	13	Republican	1908
Patrick F. Gill	11	Democratic	1908
Theron E. Catlin	11	Republican	1910
James A. Daugherty	15	Democratic	1910
Leonidas C. Dyer	12	Republican	1910, 1914–30
Walter L. Hensley	13	Democratic	1910–16
Thomas L. Rubey	16	Democratic	1910–18, 1922–26
Perl D. Decker	15	Democratic	1912–16
Michael J. Gill	12	Democratic	1912
William L. Igoe	11	Democratic	1912–18
Jacob E. Meeker[16]	10	Republican	1914, 1916
Frederick Essen[16]	10	Republican	1916
Milton A. Romjue	1, At large	Democratic	1916, 1918, 1922–31*, 1934–40
William T. Bland	5	Democratic	1918
Edward D. Hayes	14	Republican	1918-1920
Isaac V. McPherson	15	Republican	1918-1920
Samuel C. Major	7	Democratic	1918, 1922-1926, 1930
Jacob L. Milligan[15]	3, At large	Democratic	1918, 1922–33*
William L. Nelson	8, 2	Democratic	1918, 1922–30, 1934–40
Cleveland A. Newton	10	Republican	1918–24
William O. Atkeson	6	Republican	1920
Harry B. Hawes[18]	11	Democratic	1920–24
Charles L. Faust[19]	4	Republican	1920–28

Name	District	Political Party	Elected
Theodore W. Hukriede	9	Republican	1920
Henry F. Lawrence	3	Republican	1920
Frank C. Millspaugh	1	Republican	1920
Roscoe C. Patterson	7	Republican	1920
Sid C. Roach	8	Republican	1920, 1922
Samuel A. Shelton	16	Republican	1920
Clarence A. Cannon	9, At large	Democratic	1922–1931*, 1934–1962
James F. Fulbright	14	Democratic	1922, 1926, 1930
Henry L. Jost	5	Democratic	1922
Ralph F. Lozier	2, At large	Democratic	1922–31*
Joe J. Manlove	15	Democratic	1922–30
J. Scott Wolff	13	Democratic	1922
Ralph E. Bailey	14	Republican	1924
John J. Cochran[18]	11, 13, At large	Democratic	1926–32*, 1934–45
Charles Edward Kiefner	13	Republican	1924, 1928
George H. Combs Jr.	5	Democratic	1926
Henry F. Niedringhaus	10	Republican	1926–30
Clyde Williams	13, 8, At large	Democratic	1926, 1930, 1932*, 1934–40
Thomas J. Halsey	6	Republican	1928
David Hopkins[19]	4	Republican	1929-1930
Rowland C. Johnston	16	Republican	1928
John W. Palmer	7	Republican	1928
Dewey J. Short	14, 7	Republican	1928, 1934–54
William E. Barton	16	Democratic	1930
Robert D. Johnson[17]	7	Democratic	1931
Joseph B. Shannon	5, At large	Democratic	1930, 1932*, 1934–40
James R. Claiborne	12, At large	Democratic	1932*, 1934
Richard M. Duncan	3, At large	Democratic	1932*, 1934–40
Frank H. Lee	At large	Democratic	1932*
James E. Ruffin	At large	Democratic	1932*
Reuben T. Wood	6, At large	Democratic	1932*, 1934–38
Charles Jasper Bell	4	Democratic	1934–46
Thomas C. Hennings Jr.	11	Democratic	1934–38
Orville Zimmerman	10	Democratic	1934–46
C. Arthur Anderson	12	Democratic	1936, 1938
Philip A. Bennett	6	Republican	1940
Walter Ploeser	12	Republican	1940–46
John B. Sullivan	11	Democratic	1940, 1944, 1948, 1950
Samuel Washington (Wat) Arnold	1	Republican	1942–46
Marion T. Bennett	6	Republican	1942–46
William C. Cole	3	Republican	1942–46, 1952
William Price Elmer	8	Republican	1942
Louis E. Miller	11	Republican	1942
Max Schwabe	2	Republican	1942–46
Roger C. Slaughter	5	Democratic	1942, 1944
A.S.J. Carnahan	8	Democratic	1944, 1948–58
Claude I. Bakewell	11	Republican	1946, 1951
Park M. Banta	8	Republican	1946
Frank M. Karsten	13, 1	Democratic	1946-1966

Name	District	Political Party	Elected
Albert L. Reeves Jr.	5	Republican	1946
Richard W. Bolling	5	Democratic	1948–80
George H. Christopher	6, 4	Democratic	1948, 1954-1958
Leonard Irving	4	Democratic	1948, 1950
Paul C. Jones	10	Democratic	1948–66
Raymond W. Karst	12	Democratic	1948
Clare Magee	1	Democratic	1948, 1950
Morgan M. Moulder	2	Democratic	1948-1960
Phil J. Welch	3	Democratic	1948-1950
O.K. Armstrong	6	Republican	1950
Thomas B. Curtis	12, 2	Republican	1950–66
Jeffrey P. Hillelson	4	Republican	1952
Leonor K. Sullivan	3	Democratic	1952–74
William R. Hull Jr.	6	Democratic	1954–70
Charles H. Brown	7	Democratic	1956, 1958
William J. Randall	4	Democratic	1959–74
Durward G. Hall	7	Republican	1960–70
Richard H. Ichord	8	Democratic	1960–78
William L. Hungate	9	Democratic	1962–74
Bill D. Burlison	10	Democratic	1968–78
William Lacy Clay Sr.	1	Democratic	1968–98
James W. Symington	2	Democratic	1968–74
Jerry Litton[20]	6	Democratic	1972, 1974
Gene Taylor	7	Republican	1972–86
E. Thomas Coleman[20]	6	Republican	1976–90
Richard A. Gephardt	3	Democratic	1976–2002
Ike Skelton	4	Democratic	1976-2008
Harold L. Volkmer	9	Democratic	1976–94
Robert A. Young III	2	Democratic	1976–84
Wendell Bailey	8	Republican	1980
William (Bill) Emerson[21]	10, 8	Republican	1980–94
Alan D. Wheat	5	Democratic	1982–92
John W. (Jack) Buechner	2	Republican	1986,1988
Melton D. (Mel) Hancock	7	Republican	1988–94
Joan Kelly Horn	2	Democratic	1990
Patsy Ann (Pat) Danner	6	Democratic	1992–98
James M. Talent	2	Republican	1992–98
Karen McCarthy	5	Democratic	1994–2002
Roy D. Blunt	7	Republican	1996–present
Jo Ann Emerson[21, 22]	8	Independent, Republican	1996–2012
Kenny Hulshof	9	Republican	1996–2008
W. Todd Akin	2	Republican	2000–2012
William Lacy Clay Jr.	1	Democratic	2000–present
Sam B. Graves Jr.	6	Republican	2000–present
Russ Carnahan	3	Democratic	2004–2010
Emanuel Cleaver II	5	Democratic	2004–present
Blaine Luetkemeyer	9	Republican	2008–present
Vicky Hartzler	4	Republican	2010–present
Billy Long	7	Republican	2010–present
Ann Wagner	2	Republican	2012–present
Jason Smith[22]	8	Republican	2013–present

[1]Sterling Price resigned, going to the Mexican War, and William McDaniel was elected to fill the vacancy.
[2]John G. Miller died, and Thomas P. Akers was elected to fill the vacancy.
[3]Francis P. Blair resigned.
[4]John B. Clark was expelled and William A. Hall was elected to fill the vacancy.
[5]John W. Noell died and J.G. Scott was elected to fill the vacancy.
[6]John W. Reid was expelled and Thomas L. Price was elected to fill the vacancy.
[7]Joseph W. McClurg was elected Governor and resigned. John H. Stover was elected to fill the vacancy.
[8]Thomas E. Noell died and J.R. McCormick was elected to fill the vacancy.
[9]Richard P. Bland died and Dorsey W. Shackleford was elected to fill the vacancy.
[10]Alfred M. Lay died December 8, 1879 and John F. Philips was elected at a special election January 10, 1880 to fill the vacancy.
[11]Thomas Allen died and James H. McLean was elected to fill the vacancy.
[12]James N. Burnes died in 1889 and Charles F. Booher was elected to fill the vacancy.
[13]James P. Walker died and R.H. Whitelaw was elected to fill the vacancy.
[14]David A. DeArmond died and Clement C. Dickinson was elected to fill the vacancy.
[15]Joshua W. Alexander resigned and Jacob L. Milligan was elected to fill the vacancy.
[16]Jacob E. Meeker died and Frederick Essen was elected to fill the vacancy.
[17]Sam C. Major died and Robert D. Johnson was elected to fill the vacancy.
[18]Harry B. Hawes resigned and John J. Cochran was elected to fill the vacancy.
[19]Charles L. Faust died December 17, 1928, and David Hopkins was elected to fill the vacancy.
[20]Jerry Litton died and E. Thomas Coleman was elected November 2, 1976, to fill the vacancy. He was also elected to a full term beginning January 3, 1977.
[21]Jo Ann Emerson was elected to two terms in the 1996 general election. She ran as a Republican in the special election to serve out the remainder of the term in the seat held by her late husband, U.S. Rep. Bill Emerson, who died in June 1996. With not enough time for her name to be added to the ballot for the next full term in Congress, Jo Ann Emerson ran for the upcoming term as an Independent. She won both elections and began her congressional service during the 104th Congress, representing Missouri's eighth district starting in November 1996.
[22]Jo Ann Emerson resigned and Jason Smith was elected to fill the vacancy.

Historical Note: The election of early Missouri delegates was by general statewide ticket. In 1847, the state was divided into five congressional districts from which representatives were elected. In 1863, the districts were expanded to number nine, and 10 years later in 1873, Missouri was redistricted to allow for 13 congressional districts. By acts approved in 1882 and 1885, Missouri was allowed one additional district and in 1893, the congressional districts numbered 15. Missouri was allowed 16 districts in 1901; these were in place until 1933. In that year, the state was allotted 13 representatives, while the legislature redistricted the state. Those 13 representatives were elected at large (indicated by an asterisk (*) in the listing). The state has been redistricted at various times over the last 40 years, moving from 11 districts in the 1950s, to ten districts in the 1960s, to nine in the 1980s, to the current number of 8 congressional districts in 2011. Because of the redistricting, it may be necessary to check the Revised Statutes of Missouri to determine which Missouri counties were represented by a district during a particular year. Redistricting changes generally occur in the years following the taking of the federal census.

CHAPTER 4
LEGISLATIVE BRANCH

Ha Ha Tonka
Photo courtesy of Missouri State Archives

The Missouri General Assembly

Legislative power in Missouri is vested by Article III, Section 1 of the 1945 Constitution in the General Assembly, composed of the Senate and the House of Representatives. Their website is *www.moga.mo.gov*.

The Senate consists of 34 members elected for four-year terms. Senators from odd-numbered districts are elected in presidential election years. Senators from even-numbered districts are chosen in the midterm elections. Each senator must be at least 30 years of age, a qualified voter of the state for three years and of the district he or she represents for one year. The lieutenant governor is president and presiding officer of the Senate. In the absence of the lieutenant governor, the president *pro tem*, elected by the Senate members, presides.

The House of Representatives consists of 163 members, elected at each general election for a two-year term. A representative must be at least 24 years of age, a qualified voter of the state for two years and of the district he or she represents for one year. The House is presided over by the speaker, chosen by the members, and in the absence of the speaker by the speaker *pro tem*.

Reapportionment of both houses of the Missouri General Assembly following each decennial U.S. census is provided for by the Missouri Constitution.

Senators and representatives receive a salary of $35,904 per year, a weekly allowance for miles traveled going to and returning from their place of meeting and expenses for each day the General Assembly is in session.

Time of Meeting

The General Assembly convenes annually on the first Wednesday after the first Monday of January. Adjournment is midnight on May 30, with no consideration of bills after 6 p.m. on the first Friday after the second Monday in May. The General Assembly reconvenes on the first Wednesday following the second Monday in September for a period not to exceed 10 calendar days to consider vetoed bills.

A special session of the General Assembly may be called by petition of the General Assembly. If three-fourths of the members of the Senate and three-fourths of the members of the House sign the petition calling for a special session, the president *pro tem* of the Senate and the speaker of the House shall, by joint proclamation, convene the General Assembly in special session. The petition and proclamation must specifically state the subjects to be considered during the special session, and the signed petition must be filed with the secretary of state.

The General Assembly shall automatically stand adjourned *sine die* at 6 p.m. on the 30th calendar day after the convening of the special session unless it has adjourned *sine die* before the 30th day. No appropriation bill shall be considered in the special session if the General Assembly has not passed the operating budget in compliance with Article III, Section 25 of the Missouri Constitution.

The governor may convene the General Assembly in extraordinary session for a maximum of 60 calendar days at any time. Only subjects recommended by the governor in his or her call or a special message may be considered.

Organization of the General Assembly

Following the general election in November of even numbered years, the majority and minority members of each house caucus separately nominate candidates for the offices to be elected by each body and organize their parties for the coming session. Nominees of the majority party and minority party are elected. Each party names its floor leader, assistant floor leader, caucus chair and secretary.

Both houses of the General Assembly convene at noon on the opening day of the session. The Senate is called to order by the lieutenant governor. Temporary officers are named and the roll of new and incumbent senators is read. Newly elected senators are then sworn in, usually by a judge of the Supreme Court. The president *pro tem* and other permanent officers are then elected and take an oath of office administered by the president of the Senate.

The House of Representatives is called to order by the secretary of state and the oath is administered to all members. After the swearing-in ceremony, a roll call is taken and a temporary speaker is named. He or she presides for the nomination and election of permanent officers. Temporary rules, usually the rules in force for the preceding session, are adopted.

After each house notifies the other that it is duly organized, a House Resolution is adopted, inviting the Senate to a joint meeting to receive the governor's message. Under the Constitution, the governor, at the beginning of each session, delivers a message concerning state government with any recommendations he or she wishes to make for the enactment of legislation. This message is commonly referred to as the State of the State Address.

Each house determines its own rules. Procedures and rules may not be dispensed with, except by unanimous consent or concurrence by a constitutional majority. Both the Senate and House are required to keep a daily journal of their proceedings. At the end of the session, the journals are bound by the House and Senate. The secretary of state's office maintains microform copies of the journals.

Term Limits

In November 1992, the voters approved an amendment to the Missouri Constitution to limit for the first time the amount of total service in the House and Senate to eight years in each. Total legislative service was limited to sixteen years. In November 2002 voters approved an additional amendment to allow members elected through a special election, after the effective date, to serve the partial term and two full terms for the Senate and four full terms for the House, through a general election.

How Bills Become Laws

General Provisions

Bills may originate in either house and are designated as Senate Bills or House Bills, depending on the house in which they originate. No bill (except general appropriation bills) may contain more than one subject, which is to be expressed clearly in its title. No bill can be amended in its passage through either house so as to change its original purpose. No bill can be introduced in either house after the 60th legislative day of a session unless consented to by a majority of the elected members of each house. No appropriation bill shall be taken up for consideration after 6 p.m. on the first Friday following the first Monday in May of each year.

Introduction of a Bill

Missouri law provides for pre-introduction of bills beginning Dec. 1 preceding the opening of the assembly session and continuing up to, but not including, the first day of session. Bills filed during the pre-introduction period are automatically introduced and read the first time on the opening day of session.

Bills also may be introduced by any senator or representative during session. Bills may be written by the legislator or by staff drafting attorneys at the request of a senator or representative. When introduced, a bill is assigned a number and read for the first time by its title. It then goes on the calendar for second reading and assignment to committee by the speaker of the House or the president *pro tem* of the Senate.

A public hearing before the committee to which a bill is assigned is the next step in the legislative process. Except in the case of unusually controversial, complex or lengthy bills, the bill is presented by its sponsor, and both proponents and opponents are heard in a single hearing. When hearings are concluded, the committee meets to vote and makes its recommendations. The committee may (1) report the bill with the recommendation that it "do pass;" (2) recommend passage with committee amendments, which are attached to the bill; (3) return the bill without recommendation; (4) substitute in lieu of the original bill a new bill to be known as a committee substitute; (5) report the bill with a recommendation that it "do not pass;" or (6) make no report at all.

Perfection of a Bill

If a bill is reported favorably out of committee or a substitute is recommended, it may be placed on the "perfection calendar." When it is brought up for consideration, it is debated on the floor of the originating house. If a substitute is recommended by the committee or if committee amendments are attached to the bill, they are first presented, debated and voted upon. At this point, further amendments can be proposed by other members. When all amendments and substitutes have been considered, a motion is made to declare the bill perfected. Perfection is voted on by a voice vote or, on the request of five members, by roll call. If a majority of members vote to perfect, the bill is reprinted in its original or amended form.

Final Passage of a Bill

After perfection and reprinting, the bill goes on the calendar for third reading and final passage. When the bill is reached in the order of business, any member may speak for or against its passage, but no further amendments can be offered. At the conclusion of debate, a recorded vote is taken. Approval of a constitutional majority of the elected members (18 in the Senate and 82 in the House) is required for final passage.

Passage of the bill is then reported to the other chamber where it is first and second read, referred to committee for hearing, reported by committee, read a third time and offered for final approval. If further amendments or substitutes are approved, these are reported to the originating house with a request that the changes be approved. If the originating house does not approve, a conference may be requested and members from each house are designated as a conference committee. Upon agreement by the conference committee (usually a compromise of differences), each reports to its own house on the committee's recommendation. The originating house acts first on the conference committee version of the bill. If it is approved, it goes to the other house; upon approval there, the bill is declared "truly agreed to and finally passed." If either house rejects the conference committee report, it may be returned to the same or a newly appointed committee for further conferences.

Upon final passage, a bill is ordered enrolled, printed in its final form and the bills are closely compared and proofed for errors.

Signing of the Bill

Bills truly agreed to and finally passed in their printed form are then signed in open session by the House speaker and Senate president or president *pro tem*. At the time of signing, any member may file written objections, which are sent with the bill to the governor.

Governor's Part in Lawmaking

The governor has 15 days to act on a bill if it is sent to him during the legislative session and 45 days if the Legislature has adjourned or has recessed for a 30-day period.

If he or she signs a bill, it is returned to its house of origin with a message of approval, then delivered to the Office of the Secretary of State. The bill is delivered directly to the Office of the Secretary of State if the Legislature is not in session.

If the governor vetoes a bill, it is returned to the house of origin with his or her objections. A two-thirds vote by members of both houses is required to override a governor's veto.

If any bill is not returned by the governor within the time limits prescribed by Article III, Section 31 of the Missouri Constitution, it will become law in the same manner as if the governor had signed it.

Effective Date of Laws

The 1945 Constitution provides that no law passed by the General Assembly shall take effect until 90 days after the end of the session in which it was enacted, except an appropriation act or in case of an emergency, which must be expressed in the preamble or in the body of the act. Some bills specify the exact date when they are to take effect.

Duties of the Secretary of State

The secretary of state preserves and the state archives binds and maintains the finally printed and signed copy of the law. The laws are published annually by the Committee on Legislative Research in a volume titled Laws of Missouri.

The general statute laws are revised, digested and promulgated by the revisor of statutes, in the Office of the Committee on Legislative Research. These are known as the Revised Statutes of Missouri. The Committee on Legislative Research also publishes annual supplements to the statutes to include changes in laws since the last revision.

Ninety-Eighth General Assembly Schedule

First Regular Session

Bill filing opens	Dec. 1, 2014
Session convened	Jan. 7, 2015
Last day for bills to be considered	May 15, 2015
Session adjourned	May 15, 2015
Governor's approval by	July 14, 2015
Effective date of laws*	Aug. 28, 2015

Veto Session

Session convened	Sept. 16, 2015

Second Regular Session

Bill filing opens	Dec. 1, 2015
Session convenes	Jan. 6, 2016
Last day for bills to be considered	May 13, 2016
Session adjourns	May 13, 2016
Governor's approval by	July 14, 2016
Effective date of laws*	Aug. 28, 2016

Veto Session

Session convenes	Sept. 14, 2016

*Unless an emergency date or other date is specified.

The Missouri Senate

Officers of the Senate, Ninety-Eighth General Assembly, First Regular Session, 2015

Peter Kinder, President (Lt. Governor)
Ron Richard, President *Pro Tem*
Mike Kehoe, Majority Floor Leader
Bob Onder, Assistant Majority Floor Leader
Eric Schmitt, Majority Caucus Chair
Jay Wasson, Majority Caucus Secretary
Brian Munzlinger, Majority Caucus Whip
Joseph Keaveny, Minority Floor Leader
Gina Walsh, Assistant Minority Floor Leader
S. Kiki Curls, Minority Caucus Chair
Jason Holsman, Minority Caucus Secretary
Maria Chappelle-Nadal, Minority Caucus Whip
Adriane Crouse, Secretary of Senate
Marga Hoelscher, Senate Administrator
Bill Smith, Sergeant-at-Arms

Committees of the Senate, Ninety-Eighth General Assembly, First Regular Session, 2015

(As of Jan. 31, 2015)

Administration: Dempsey, chair; Richard, vice chair; Keaveny; Kehoe; and Walsh.

Agriculture, Food Production and Outdoor Resources: Munzlinger, chair; Libla, vice chair; Brown; Curls; Hegeman; Holsman; Parson; and Pearce.

Appropriations: Schaefer, chair; Silvey, vice chair; Brown; Curls; Kehoe; Nasheed; Parson; Pearce; Sater; Schaaf; and Walsh.

Commerce, Consumer Protection, Energy and the Environment: Kehoe, chair; Emery, vice chair; Cunningham; Holsman; Keaveny; Kraus; Riddle; Romine; Schatz; Sifton; and Wallingford.

Education: Pearce, chair; Romine, vice chair; Brown; Chappelle-Nadal; Emery; Holsman; Libla; and Onder.

Financial and Governmental Organizations and Elections: Wasson, chair; Cunningham, vice chair; Hegeman; Keaveny; Kraus; Riddle; Sater; Sifton; Wallingford; and Wieland.

General Laws and Pensions: Schaaf, chair; Wieland, vice chair; Hegeman; Keaveny; Onder; Schatz; and Schupp.

Governmental Accountability and Fiscal Oversight: Cunningham, chair; Silvey, vice chair; Kehoe; Nasheed; Riddle; and Wasson.

PETER KINDER
President
Missouri Senate

RON RICHARD
President *Pro Tem*
Missouri Senate

MIKE KEHOE
Majority Floor Leader
Missouri Senate

JOSEPH KEAVENY
Minority Floor Leader
Missouri Senate

Gubernatorial Appointments: Richard, chair; Kehoe, vice chair; Curls; Emery; Munzlinger; Nasheed; Schaaf; Schaefer; Schatz; and Schmitt.

Jobs, Economic Development and Local Government: Schmitt, chair; Hegeman, vice chair; Curls; Dixon; Holsman; Kraus; Nasheed; Romine; Schatz; Wasson; and Wieland.

Judiciary and Civil and Criminal Jurisprudence: Dixon, chair; Onder, vice chair; Emery; Keaveny; Schaefer; Schmitt; and Sifton.

Progress and Development: Keaveny, chair; Walsh, vice chair; Schupp; Silvey; and Wallingford. Contact: Stacy Morse (573) 751-3599

Rules, Joint Rules, Resolutions and Ethics: Kehoe, chair; Richard, vice chair; Dixon; Libla; Wallingford; and Walsh.

Seniors, Families and Children: Sater, chair; Riddle, vice chair; Chappelle-Nadal; Kraus; Libla; Romine; and Schupp.

Small Business, Insurance and Industry: Parson, chair; Libla, vice chair; Curls; Munzlinger; Wallingford; Walsh; Wasson; and Wieland.

Transportation, Infrastructure and Public Safety: Libla, chair; Schatz, vice chair; Chappelle-Nadal; Curls; Dixon; Kehoe; and Munzlinger.

Veterans' Affairs and Health: Brown, chair; Schaaf, vice chair; Chappelle-Nadal; Cunningham; Onder; Sater; Schmitt; Schupp; Sifton; and Silvey.

Ways and Means: Kraus, chair; Wallingford, vice chair; Dixon; Emery; Onder; and Sifton.

ADRIANE D. CROUSE
Senate Secretary

MARGA HOELSCHER
Senate Administrator

BILL SMITH
Sergeant-at-Arms

Alphabetical list of State Senators, 2015

Name	District	Email Address
Brown, Dan W. (R)	16	dan.brown@senate.mo.gov
Chappelle-Nadal, Maria (D)	14	maria.chappellenadal@senate.mo.gov
Cunningham, Mike (R)	33	mike.cunningham@senate.mo.gov
Curls, Shalonn (Kiki) (D)	9	shalonn.curls@senate.mo.gov
Dixon, Bob (R)	30	bob.dixon@senate.mo.gov
Emery, Edgar G.H. (R)	31	ed.emery@senate.mo.gov
Hegeman, Dan (R)	12	dan.hegeman@senate.mo.gov
Holsman, Jason R. (D)	7	jason.holsman@senate.mo.gov
Keaveny, Joseph P. (D)	4	joe.keaveny@senate.mo.gov
Kehoe, Mike (R)	6	mike.kehoe@senate.mo.gov
Kraus, Will (R)	8	will.kraus@senate.mo.gov
Libla, Doug (R)	25	doug.libla@senate.mo.gov
Munzlinger, Brian (R)	18	brian.munzlinger@senate.mo.gov
Nasheed, Jamilah (D)	5	jamilah.nasheed@senate.mo.gov
Onder, Bob (R)	2	bob.onder@senate.mo.gov
Parson, Michael L. (R)	28	mparson@senate.mo.gov
Pearce, David Brent (R)	21	david.pearce@senate.mo.gov
Richard, Ronald F. (R)	32	ronald.richard@senate.mo.gov
Riddle, Jeanie (R)	10	jeanie.riddle@senate.mo.gov
Romine, Gary A. (R)	3	gary.romine@senate.mo.gov
Sater, David (R)	29	david.sater@senate.mo.gov
Schaaf, Rob (R)	34	rob.schaaf@senate.mo.gov
Schaefer, Kurt U. (R)	19	kurt.schaefer@senate.mo.gov
Schatz, Dave (R)	26	dave.schatz@senate.mo.gov
Schmitt, Eric S. (R)	15	eschmitt@senate.mo.gov
Schupp, Jill (D)	24	jill.schupp@senate.mo.gov
Sifton, Scott (D)	1	scott.sifton@senate.mo.gov
Silvey, Ryan A. (R)	17	ryan.silvey@senate.mo.gov
Wallingford, Wayne (R)	27	wayne.wallingford@senate.mo.gov
Walsh, Gina (D)	13	gina.walsh@senate.mo.gov
Wasson, Jay (R)	20	jay.wasson@senate.mo.gov
Wieland, Paul (R)	22	paul.wieland@senate.mo.gov

Number of Senators 34
Republicans 24
Democrats 8
Vacancies 2
Terms expire:
Even-numbered districts, January 2019
Odd-numbered districts, January 2017

District 1—**SCOTT SIFTON**

Capitol office: Room 329; phone (573) 751-0220
Email address: *scott.sifton@senate.mo.gov*
Senate committees: Commerce, Consumer Protection, Energy and the Environment; Financial and Governmental Organizations and Elections; Judiciary and Civil and Criminal Jurisprudence; Ways and Means; Veterans' Affairs and Health.

Biography: Involved in the Affton Chamber of Commerce, Lemay Chamber of Commerce and South County Chamber of Commerce. Served on the Affton Board of Education from 2001–2010. He graduated *cum laude* with a bachelor's degree from Truman State University,1996; Juris Doctor from the University of Michigan Law School, 1999. Sen. Sifton is a partner at the Husch Blackwell Law Firm. He resides in Affton with his son, Stephen, and his daughter, Madelyn. Elected to the House: 2010. Elected to the Senate: 2012. Democrat.

District 2—**ROBERT F. (BOB) ONDER JR.**

Capitol office: Room 226; phone (573) 751-1282
Email address: *bob.onder@senate.mo.gov*
Senate committees: Judiciary and Civil and Criminal Jurisprudence (vice chair); Education; General Laws and Pensions; Veterans' Affairs and Health; Ways and Means.

Biography: Sen. Onder has been a physician and small businessman for more than 20 years. He is board certified in Allergy and Clinical Immunology and Internal Medicine. Sen. Onder is a member of the O'Fallon, Western St. Charles and Greater St. Charles County chambers of commerce, and the Missouri State Medical Association. He is a former board member of Missouri Right to Life and is a life member of the National Rifle Association. He is a graduate of Washington University School of Medicine and St. Louis University Law School. Sen. Onder lives with his wife, Allison, and their six children in Lake St. Louis. Elected to the House: 2006. Elected to the Senate: 2014. Republican.

District 3—**GARY A. ROMINE**

Capitol office: Room 429; phone (573) 751-4008
Email address: *gary.romine@senate.mo.gov*
Senate committees: Education (vice chair); Commerce, Consumer Protection, Energy and the Environment; Jobs, Economic Development and Local Government; Seniors, Family and Children.

Biography: Graduate of Poplar Bluff High School, received associate degree from Three Rivers Community College and bachelor's degree from Central Missouri State University, 1978. He and his wife, Kathy, have five children and 11 grandchildren. In addition to his legislative duties, he currently serves as president of Show-Me-Rent-To-Own, which he founded more than 25 years ago. Board member of MRV Banks. Member: Association of Progressive Rental Organization. He serves on the Missouri Lead Industry Employment, Economic Development and Environmental Remediation Task Force (chair) and the Joint Committee on Education (vice chair). Elected to the Senate: 2012. Republican

District 4—**JOSEPH P. KEAVENY**

Capitol office: Room 333; phone (573) 751-3599
Email address: *joe.keaveny@senate.mo.gov*
Senate committees: Progress and Development (chair); Administration; Commerce, Consumer Protection, Energy and the Environment; Financial and Governmental Organizations and Elections; Judiciary and Civil and Criminal Jurisprudence.

Biography: Minority Floor Leader. Sen. Keaveny practices trust and probate law for Weiss Attorneys at Law, and serves as committeeman for the 28th Ward. Received a B.S. in accounting from the University of Missouri–St. Louis. Master's degree in finance and a law degree, both from St. Louis Univ. For the past 20 years, he managed high-income portfolios and compliance issues with the U.S. Securities and Exchange Commission for U.S. Bank. His legislative agenda includes expanding early childhood education, evaluating the death penalty, improving procedures for child support, reducing wrongful convictions and issues related to trusts and probate, banking and retirement. Serves on Joint Committee on Public Employee Retirement. Elected to Senate: 2009 (special election), 2010, 2014. Democrat.

District 5—**JAMILAH NASHEED**

Capitol office: Room 328; phone (573) 751-4415
Email address: *jamilah.nasheed@senate.mo.gov*
Senate Committees: Appropriations; Governmental Accountability and Fiscal Oversight; Gubernatorial Appointments; Jobs, Economic Development and Local Government.

Biography: Born Oct. 17, 1972, in St. Louis. She and her husband, Fahim Nasheed, reside there with her 15-year-old cousin, Najawah Williams, for whom she is the longtime, primary caretaker. Served as chair of the Urban Issues Committee and as a member of the Budget, Economic Development and Financial Institutions committees. Prior to entering politics, Sen. Nasheed owned an inner-city bookstore and founded an organization to educate youth about electoral processes. Sen. Nasheed has received numerous awards, including awards from the St. Louis Public Schools Role Model Program, the St. Louis Association of Colored Women's Club and the St. Louis Bar Foundation's Spirit of Justice Award. Elected to the House: 2006. Elected to the Senate: 2012. Democrat.

District 6—**MIKE KEHOE**

Capitol office: Room 220; phone (573) 751-2076
Email address: *mike.kehoe@senate.mo.gov*
Senate committees: Commerce, Consumer Protection, Energy and the Environment (chair); Administration; Appropriations, Government Accountability and Fiscal Oversight; Transportation, Infrastructure and Public Safety.

Biography: Assistant Majority Floor Leader. Born Jan. 17, 1962, in St. Louis. He and his wife, Claudia McCormick, have four children: Carol, Michael, Maggie and Claire. Member: Cathedral of St. Joseph; Jefferson City Chamber of Commerce; Missouri Farm Bureau; Central Missouri United Way; National Rifle Association; Missouri Automobile Dealers Association; Sons of the American Legion. Former member: Missouri Highway and Transportation Commission (chair, 2009); MoDOT & Patrol Employees Retirement System (MPRS) Board (chair, 2009); Linn State Technical College Board of Regents; USS Missouri Commissioning Committee; and Jefferson City Diocese Jubilee Committee. Former owner/president of Osage Industries, Linn, and Mike Kehoe Ford, Jefferson City. Inducted into the National Automobile Dealers Hall of Fame, 2001. Elected to the Senate: 2010, 2014. Republican.

District 7—**JASON R. HOLSMAN**

Capitol office: Room 421; phone: (573) 751-6607
Email address: *jason.holsman@senate.mo.gov*
Senate committees: Agriculture, Food Production and Outdoor Resources; Commerce, Consumer Protection, Energy and the Environment; Education; Jobs, Economic Development and Local Government.

Biography: Born March 25, 1976. Graduate of Blue Valley High School; B.A. in political science and U.S. history from University of Kansas, 1999; M.A. in diplomacy and military science from Norwich University, 2003. Taught at Van Horn High School, Kansas City, Mo., while coaching varsity sports. Holsman has been an advocate for legislation that promotes a sustainable economy through energy independence and food security. Holsman and wife, Robyn, are the proud parents of two young children. They live in Kansas City and are active members at John Knox Kirk Presbyterian Church. Holsman also teaches international relations and history of the Constitution at the University of Phoenix. Elected to the House: 2006, 2008, 2010. Elected to the Senate: 2012. Democrat.

District 8—**WILL KRAUS**

Capitol office: Room 418; phone (573) 751-1464
Email address: *will.kraus@senate.mo.gov*
Senate committees: Ways and Means (chair); Commerce, Consumer Protection, Energy and the Environment; Financial and Governmental Organizations and Elections; Jobs, Economic Development and Local Government; Seniors, Families and Children.

Biography: Born March 1973. Graduate of Univ. of Central Mo. He and his wife, Carmen, have two children: Tylor and Tannor. He is an officer in the Mo. Natl. Guard and served in Operation Iraqi Freedom. Member: VFW, American Legion, Lee's Summit Chamber of Commerce, Mo. Farm Bureau, First Baptist Church, and Rotary. Has won awards such as the VFW Legislator of the Year, "A Better Missouri for Children Award" from the Missouri PTA, the Locke and Smith Award and the Missouri Chamber of Commerce Spirit of Enterprise Award. He was named "Guardian of Small Business" by the Missouri Chapter of the National Federation of Independent Businesses. In addition to his legislative duties, he is a small business owner. Elected to the House: 2004, 2006, 2008. Elected to the Senate: 2010, 2014. Republican.

District 9—**SHALONN (KIKI) CURLS**

Capitol office: Room 434; phone (573) 751-3158
Email address: *shalonn.curls@senate.mo.gov*
Senate committees: Agriculture; Appropriations; Gubernatorial Appointments; Jobs, Economic Development and Local Government; Small Business, Insurance and Industry; Transportation, Infrastructure and Public Safety.

Biography: Sen. Shalonn "Kiki" Curls represents the 9th senatorial district in Jackson County. Sen. Curls won a special election to the Missouri Senate in February 2011, after serving two terms in the Missouri House of Representatives. In addition to her legislative duties, she works in real estate development and currently serves as the 14th Ward Democratic committeewoman in Kansas City. She is also a member of St. Monica's Catholic Church. Sen. Curls received her education from St. Teresa's Academy in Kansas City and the University of Missouri–Columbia. She is the proud mother of twins, James and Michaela. Elected to the House: 2007. Elected to the Senate: 2011 (special election), 2012. Democrat.

District 10—**JEANIE RIDDLE**

Capitol office: Room 431; phone (573) 751-2757
Email address: *jeanie.riddle@senate.mo.gov*
Senate committees: Seniors, Families and Children (vice chair); Administration; Commerce, Consumer Protection, Energy and the Environment; Financial and Governmental Organizations and Elections; Governmental Accountability and Fiscal Oversight.

Biography: Born in Joplin, May 27, 1954. Graduate of McCluer High School and Drury University, B.A. in education. Married to Randy Riddle. They have two children, Randee Rae (Riddle) Phelps and Thomas Riddle, and three grandsons. Attends First Baptist Church. Member: Fulton Rotary; Women Legislators of Missouri, treasurer 2009–2010; Missouri Federation of Republican Women; Callaway County Federated Republican Women; life member of National Rifle Association; Callaway County Farm Bureau; Missouri Farm Bureau; Kingdom of Callaway Retired Teachers Association; Fulton Area Development Corporation; Missouri Retired Teachers Association; Missouri Cattlemen's Association; Joint Committee on Education; and Missouri Children's Services Commission. Elected to the House: 2008, 2010, 2012. Elected to the Senate: 2014. Republican.

District 11—**VACANCY**

District 12—**DAN HEGEMAN**

Capitol office: Room 332; phone (573) 751-1415
Email address: *dan.hegeman@senate.mo.gov*
Senate committees: Jobs, Economic Development and Local Government (vice chair); Agriculture, Food Production and Outdoor Resources; Financial and Governmental Organizations and Elections; General Laws and Pensions.

Biography: A lifelong resident of northwest Missouri. He represents the 12th Senatorial District, comprised of 15 counties throughout northwest Missouri. Graduate of Savannah High School, 1981. Graduated of University of Missouri, 1985, where he was a member of the Alpha Gamma Rho agriculture fraternity. He is a lifetime farmer and is part-owner of a six-generation, family-owned row crop and cattle farm in Andrew County. Served as Andrew County Clerk from 2003 to 2008. He and his wife, Fran, live on a farm near Cosby and have four children: Hannah, Joshua, Heidi and Joseph. He is a life-long member of Hope United Church of Christ in Cosby. Elected to the House: 1992–2002. Elected to the Senate: 2014. Republican.

District 13—**GINA WALSH**

Capitol office: Room 427; phone (573) 751-2420
Email address: *gina.walsh@senate.mo.gov*
Senate committees: Progress and Development (vice chair); Administration; Appropriations; Rules, Joint Rules, Resolutions and Ethics; Small Business, Insurance and Industry.

Biography: Minority Caucus Assistant Floor Leader. Born in Spanish Lake, Mo. Graduate of Rosary High School and the International Association of Heat and Frost Insulators Apprenticeship School. Gina and her late husband, Jim, have three children: Michaela, Sarah and Kathleen. Retired construction insulator. Member: Holy Name of Jesus parish in Bellefontaine Neighbors; North County Labor Legislative Club; St. Ferdinand and Spanish Lake Democratic Clubs; North County Incorporated board of directors; Heat and Frost Insulators and Allied Workers Local #1 and Missouri State Building and Construction Trades Council (AFL-CIO), president. Elected to House: 2002–2010; Elected to Senate: 2012. Democrat.

District 14—**MARIA CHAPPELLE-NADAL**

Capitol office: Room 428; phone (573) 751-4106
Email address: *maria.chappellenadal@senate.mo.gov*
Senate committees: Education; Seniors, Families and Children; Transportation, Infrastructure and Public Safety; Veterans' Affairs and Health.

Biography: Born Oct. 3. Graduate of Georgia State University, with a B.A. dual degree in political science and sociology. She is a jewelry-maker. Previously worked as director of communications, director of Boards and Commissions and became Missouri's senior advocate for former Lt. Gov. Joe Maxwell. Member: Democratic Minority Caucus; Women in the Neighborhood; National Organization of Black Elected Legislative Women; National Hispanic Council of State Legislators; Young Elected Officials; and Democratic National Committee 2005–2009. Currently serves on Joint Committee on Public Employee Retirement; Joint Committee on Tax Policy; and Joint Committee on Solid Waste Management District Operations. Elected to the House: 2004, 2006, 2008. Elected to the Senate: 2010, 2014. Democrat.

District 15—**ERIC S. SCHMITT**

Capitol office: Room 320; phone (573) 751-2853
Email address: *eschmitt@senate.mo.gov*
Senate committees: Jobs, Economic Development and Local Government (chair); Judiciary and Civil and Criminal Jurisprudence; Gubernatorial Appointments; Veterans' Affairs and Health.

Biography: Born June 20, 1975. Graduate of Truman State Univ., B.A., *cum laude*, 1997; St. Louis University School of Law, J.D., 2000. He and his wife, Jaime, have three children: Stephen, Sophia and Olivia. He is an attorney. Member: Missouri Bar; Mary Queen of Peace Catholic Church; Habitat for Humanity; Tuberous Sclerosis Alliance; Autism Society; Nurses For Newborns Board; St. Louis Crisis Nursery Advisory Board; Kirkwood Parents as Teachers Advisory Board; Local Chambers of Commerce; and Alderman, Glendale, Mo., 2005–2008. Elected Senate Republican secretary, 2010; Senate Republican caucus chair, 2012; served on and chaired the Joint Committee on Administrative Rules, 2013 and 2015. Elected to the Senate: 2008, 2012. Republican.

District 16—**DAN W. BROWN**

Capitol office: Room 422; phone (573) 751-5713
District address: 407 W. Fourth St., Rolla 65401
Email address: *dan.brown@senate.mo.gov*
Senate committees: Veterans' Affairs and Health (chair); Agriculture, Food Production and Outdoor Resources; Appropriations; Education.

Biography: Born Dec. 22, 1950. Received a B.S. in agriculture from the University of Missouri–Columbia. Graduated *summa cum laude* with a Doctor of Veterinary Medicine degree from the University of Missouri–Columbia. He and his wife, Kathy, have two children, Danette Sherrell and Justin Brown, and five grandchildren. He has practiced veterinary medicine in Rolla for more than 35 years. Member: First Christian Church in Rolla; American Veterinary Medical Association; Mo. Veterinary Medical Association; Mo. Farmers Association; Mo. Farm Bureau; Mid-Missouri Energy; Paseo Biofuel; Rolla Area Chamber of Commerce; Quail Forever and the National Rifle Association. He also served on the Missouri Veterinary Licensing Board. Elected to the House: 2008. Elected to the Senate: 2010, 2014. Republican.

District 17—**RYAN A. SILVEY**

Capitol office: Room 331A; phone (573) 751-5282
Email address: *ryan.silvey@senate.mo.gov*
Senate committees: Appropriations (vice chair); Governmental Accountability and Fiscal Oversight (vice chair); Veterans' Affairs and Health.

Biography: Sen. Silvey was born and raised in Clay County, where he attended Meadowbrook Elementary, Antioch Middle School and Oak Park High School. From 2011–2012, Sen. Silvey was chair of the House Budget Committee, making him the youngest House Budget chair in the nation. He guided the state through the recent recession by balancing Missouri's budget without raising taxes. Under his leadership, Missouri remained one of just seven states to boast a AAA bond rating during that period. Sen. Silvey resides in Kansas City with his wife, Angela, and their two daughters, Taylor Mansker and Kally Silvey. Elected to the House: 2005 (special election)–2012. Elected to the Senate: 2012. Republican.

District 18—**BRIAN MUNZLINGER**

Capitol office: Room 319; phone (573) 751-7985
District address: 15255 200th Ave., Williamstown 63473
Email address: *brian.munzlinger@senate.mo.gov*
Senate committees: Agriculture, Food Production and Outdoor Resources (chair); Gubernatorial Appointments; Small Business, Insurance and Industry; Transportation and Infrastructure.

Biography: Sen. Munzlinger, a lifelong farmer, is a 1978 graduate of the University of Missouri–Columbia with a B.S. in general agriculture and teaching certificate in agriculture. Sen. Munzlinger and his wife, Michele, have two children. They attend Monticello United Methodist Church. Member: Mo. Farm Bureau, Mo. Corn Growers, Mo. Soybean, Mo. Cattlemen's, NFIB, Alpha Gamma Rho Fraternity, State Fair Foundation, 1st Vice President of State Ag and Rural Leaders, life member of University of Mo. Alumni Association, and life member of the National Rifle Association. He serves on the advisory board to the University of Missouri's Greenley Research Center and the board of directors for the NEMO Grain Processors Co-op. Elected to the House: 2002–2008. Elected to the Senate: 2010, 2014. Republican.

District 19—**KURT U. SCHAEFER**

Capitol office: Room 416; phone (573) 751-3931
Email address: *kurt.schaefer@senate.mo.gov*
Senate committees: Appropriations (chair); Gubernatorial Appointments; Judiciary and Civil and Criminal Jurisprudence.

Biography: Born in St. Louis. Received a M.S.L. in environmental law, 1996, and J.D., 1995, from the Vermont Law School, and a B.A., 1990, from University of Missouri–Columbia. Married to Stacia, has three children and resides in Columbia. Member: First Christian Church. Lathrop and Gage LLP, partner. Former general counsel and deputy director of the Mo. Department of Natural Resources, special counsel to the governor, special counsel to the Mo. Dept. of Agriculture, Mo. asst. attorney general and special assistant United States attorney. Has litigated bench and jury trials of all kinds in numerous circuit and federal courts throughout Missouri and elsewhere, including approximately 100 appellate cases before the Missouri Court of Appeals and Missouri Supreme Court. Serves on Joint Committee on Government Accountability (chair) and Joint Committee on Legislative Research—Oversight Subcommittee (chair). Elected to the Senate: 2008, 2012. Republican.

District 20—**JAY WASSON**

Capitol office: Room 323; phone (573) 751-1503
Email address: *jay.wasson@senate.mo.gov*
Senate committees: Financial and Governmental Organizations and Elections (chair); Governmental Accountability and Fiscal Oversight; Jobs, Economic Development and Local Government; Small Business, Insurance and Industry.

Biography: Majority Caucus Secretary. Born Oct. 24, 1956, in Springfield. A 1974 graduate of Nixa High School, he attended Drury University. Married to Retha Wasson. A lifelong resident of Christian County, he has been in real estate development for more than 30 years. Member of First Baptist Church, Nixa. Active in community organizations, he is a charter member of the Nixa Area Chamber of Commerce, a former board member of the Community Foundation and of the Ozark Branch Chapter of the Multiple Sclerosis Society. He was a board member for St. John's Health Systems, Inc. Served as mayor of Nixa, 1997–2002. Elected to the House: 2002–2008. Elected to the Senate: 2010, 2014. Republican.

District 21—**DAVID BRENT PEARCE**

Capitol office: Room 227; Phone (573) 751-2272
Email address: *david.pearce@senate.mo.gov*
Senate committees: Education Committee (chair); Appropriations; Agriculture, Food Production and Outdoor Resources.

Biography: Attended the University of Central Missouri and earned a B.S. in agricultural journalism from the University of Missouri–Columbia. Recipient of the 2012 Henry Geyer Award by the Mizzou Alumni Association; recipient of the Gordon Warren Land Grant Award by the University of Missouri Extension; recipient of the Horace Mann Award by the Missouri National Education Association; and recipient of the Legislator of the Year Award of the Missouri Association of Veterans Organizations. Midwestern Higher Education Compact, chairman 2016. Missouri Veterans Commission, 2009–2014. He and his wife, Teresa, have two children. Elected to the House: 2003–2008. Elected to the Senate: 2008, 2012. Republican.

District 22—**PAUL WIELAND**

Capitol office: Room 334; phone (573) 751-1492
Email address: *paul.wieland@senate.mo.gov*
Senate committees: General Laws and Pensions (vice chair); Financial and Governmental Organizations and Elections; Jobs, Economic Development and Local Government; Small Business, Insurance and Industry.

Biography: Born in St. Louis. He and his wife, Terri, have three children: Coleen, Cathy and Nicole. Graduate of St. Pius X High School, Festus. Member: St. Joseph's Catholic Church in Imperial and Fourth Degree–Knights of Columbus. Serves on Jefferson County Community Partnership Board. He and his wife own Wieland Insurance Group, LLC. They published *The Edition* newspaper and the *Jefferson County Business Journal*. Former chairman of the Jefferson County Health Department Board; former president of St. Joseph School Board; former chair, University of Missouri Extension Council; former member of Mastodon Arts and Sciences Fair Advisory Board; and a founding member of the Jeffco Business Network. He also serves on the Joint Committee on Education. Elected to the House: 1994, 2010, 2012. Elected to the Senate: 2014. Republican.

District 23—**VACANCY**

District 24—**JILL SCHUPP**

Capitol office: Room 425; phone (573) 751-9762
District address: 418 North Mosley Rd., St. Louis 63141
Email address: *jill.schupp@senate.mo.gov*
Senate committees: General Laws and Pensions; Seniors, Families and Children; Progress and Development; Veterans' Affairs and Health.

Biography: While serving in the Missouri House, Schupp founded the Mo. Veterans History Project. She received the 2014 Public Health Assoc. Robert L. Northcutt Award; the United 4 Children Ray of Light Award; and the Mo. Coalition for Community Behavioral Healthcare Leadership Award. She was named Legislator of the Year by the Mo. Assoc. for Community Action and the Mo. Assoc. for Social Welfare; Distinguished Legislator by the Mo. Community College Assoc. and the Mo. Bicycle Assoc.; and Outstanding Legislator by the University of Mo. Graduate Students and the Univ. of Mo. Assoc. of Students. Schupp is a Mizzou graduate. She is married to Mark and they have two grown children, Brandon and Alex. She serves on the Joint Committee on Child Abuse and Neglect. Elected to the House: 2008, 2010, 2012. Elected to the Senate: 2014. Democrat.

District 25—**DOUG LIBLA**

Capitol office: Room 219; phone (573) 751-4843
Email address: *doug.libla@senate.mo.gov*
Senate committees: Transportation, Infrastructure and Public Safety (chair); Agriculture, Food Production and Outdoor Resources (vice chair); Rules, Joint Rules, Resolutions and Ethics; Small Business, Insurance and Industry (vice chair); Education; Seniors, Families and Children.

Biography: Born March 25, in Greenville, Mo. He and his wife, Elaine, have a daughter, son-in-law and three grandchildren. Began his business career on the corner of N. Main and Davis St. in Poplar Bluff on June 9, 1971, as owner and operator of Doug's Sinclair and Tire. Member: First Baptist Church in Poplar Bluff, Board; Fellowship of Christian Athletes (FCA); Three Rivers College Endowment Trust; past president, Charter Member and current Troop E Director Missouri Assoc. of State Troopers Emergency Relief Society (MASTERS). Community Work: Baptist Children's Home, Boys and Girls Club of Poplar Bluff, Haven House and Ozark Family Resource Center. Elected to Senate: 2012. Republican.

District 26—**DAVID SCHATZ**

Capitol office: Room 433; phone (573) 751-3678
Email address: *dave.schatz@senate.mo.gov*
Senate committees: Transportation, Infrastructure and Public Safety (vice chair); Commerce, Consumer Protection, Energy, and the Environment; General Laws and Pensions; Gubernatorial Appointments; Jobs, Economic Development and Local Government.

Biography: Born Nov. 28, 1963, in Sullivan. Graduate of Sullivan High School, 1982. He and his wife, Chara, have five children: David (Stephanie), Daniel, Devon, Dana and Dailee, and one grandchild, Caden. Member: Temple Baptist Church; life member, National Rifle Association. Served on the Spring Bluff School District Board. Volunteered as a coach in youth sports. In addition to his legislative duties, he is vice president of a family-run business, Schatz Underground, Inc. He also serves on the Joint Committee on Transportation Oversight. Elected to the House: 2010–2012. Elected to the Senate: 2014. Republican.

District 27—**WAYNE WALLINGFORD**

Capitol office: Room 225; phone (573) 751-2459
Email address: *wayne.wallingford@senate.mo.gov*
Senate committees: Ways and Means (vice chair); Commerce, Consumer Protection, Energy and the Environment; Financial and Governmental Organizations and Elections; Progress and Development; Rules, Joint Rules, Resolutions and Ethics; Small Business, Insurance and Industry.

Biography: Born July 11, 1946, in Geneva, Ill. A 1964 graduate of Geneva High School. Received B.S. degree in business administration from University of Nebraska, Omaha, 1968, and M.A. degree in management supervision from Central Michigan University, 1983. He lives in Cape Girardeau with his wife, Susan. They have two children, London Jolliff and Brandon Scott Wallingford, and seven grandchildren. He is the chief people officer at McDonald's of Southeast Missouri. A retired Lt. Colonel with the United States Air Force and past Commander of American Legion Post 63. Member: Cape Bible Chapel, United Way of Southeast Missouri, Habitat for Humanity, Young Life, SALT and Boys and Girls Club. Elected to the Senate: 2012. Republican.

District 28—**MICHAEL L. PARSON**

Capitol office: Room 420; phone (573) 751-8793
Email address: *mparson@senate.mo.gov*
Senate committees: Small Business, Insurance and Industry (chair); Agriculture, Food Production and Outdoor Resources; Appropriations.

Biography: Born and raised on a farm in Hickory County. Graduated from Wheatland High School. A third generation farmer who owns and operates a cow and calf operation near Bolivar, and a small business owner. A former Polk County Sheriff and U.S. Veteran. He and his wife, Teresa, live in Bolivar. They have two children, Stephanie and Kelly, and five grandchildren, David, Alicia, Michaela, Benjamin and Isabella. Member: American Legion, Optimist Club, NRA lifetime member, Mo. Farm Bureau, Mo. Cattlemen's Assoc., Mo. Sheriff's Assoc., and National Sheriff's Assoc. Elected to the House: 2004–2010; served as Chair of House Rules Committee. Elected to the Senate: 2010, 2014; served as Majority Whip. Republican.

District 29—**DAVID SATER**

Capitol office: Room 419; phone (573) 751-1480
Email address: *david.sater@senate.mo.gov*
Senate committees: Seniors, Families and Children (chair); Appropriations; Financial and Governmental Organizations and Elections; Veterans' Affairs and Health.

Biography: Born Nov. 7, 1947, in Springfield. Graduate of Greenwood H.S. in Springfield. Received B.S. degrees in biology and chemistry, S.W. Mo. State Univ.; Doctor of Pharmacy, University of Missouri–Kansas City. He owned and operated Sater Pharmacy in Cassville from 1974–2004. Member: Cassville First Baptist Church; Pregnancy Care Center in Aurora, founder; Cassville Chamber of Commerce; Mo. Pharmaceutical Assoc. 2011 UMKC Alumni of the Year Award. Stockholder and board of directors for Security Bank of S.W. Missouri. Pharmacist of the Year, 1983. Served as appropriation chair for Health, Mental Health and Social Services for five years and chair of Health Care Policy in the House of Representatives for two years. He and his wife, Sharon, have two children. Elected to the House: 2004, 2006, 2008, 2010. Elected to the Senate: 2012. Republican.

District 30—**BOB DIXON**

Capitol office: Room 221; phone (573) 751-2583
Email address: *bob.dixon@senate.mo.gov*
Senate committees: Judiciary and Civil and Criminal Jurisprudence (chair); Jobs, Economic Development and Local Government; Rules, Joint Rules, Resolutions and Ethics; Transportation, Infrastructure and Public Safety; Ways and Means.

Biography: Born May 27, 1969. Graduate of Drury University, Springfield, B.S. degree in business administration, 1997, *magna cum laude;* Drury University, Springfield, M.Ed. degree in human services, 2009. He and his family live in historic Midtown. Member: Mo. Children's Trust Fund board. Awards: Dr. John P. Ferguson Award for Child Advocacy, 2014; Mo. CASA Lasting Legacy Award, 2014; MAPA Legislator of the Year, 2014; MCCA Child Welfare Champion, 2013; Mo. Police Chiefs Assoc. Senator of the Year, 2013; MATA Champion of Justice, 2013; and Natl. MS Society Committed Statesperson Award, 2012, 2013. House Majority Caucus Chair, 2004–2008. Elected to the House: 2002–2008. Elected to the Senate: 2010, 2014. Republican.

District 31—**ED EMERY**

Capitol office: Room 431; phone (573) 751-2108
Email address: *ed.emery@senate.mo.gov*
Senate committees: Commerce, Consumer Protection, Energy and the Environment (vice-chair); Education; Gubernatorial Appointments; Judiciary and Civil and Criminal Jurisprudence; Ways and Means.

Biography: Born May 25, 1950, in Nevada. Graduated from Univ. of Mo.–Rolla, B.S., engineering, 1972. Worked in the oil and gas industry until 1994, when he and his family moved back to Missouri. He and his wife, Rebecca, have four children: Elizabeth, Samuel, Daniel and Paul, and one grandchild. He is a member of Lamar First Baptist Church; Mo. Farm Bureau; NRA; Gun Owners of America; VFW Men's Auxiliary; Barton County Excel; and area chambers of commerce. He also served as executive director of Mo. Fair Tax. Awards and Honors: 2006 Legislator of the Year, American Legislative Exchange Council; 2008 Leadership Award, Mo. Telecommunications Industry Assoc.; 2008 Legislator of the Year, Mo. Energy Development Assoc.; 2009 William Wilberforce Award, Concerned Women for America, Missouri Chapter; and 2010 Legislator of the Year, Missouri Republican Assembly. Elected to the House: 2002–2010. Elected to the Senate: 2012. Republican.

District 32—**RONALD F. RICHARD**

Capitol office: Room 321; phone (573) 751-2173
Email address: *ronald.richard@senate.mo.gov*
Senate committees: Administration (vice chair); Gubernatorial Appointments (vice chair); Rules, Joint Rules, Resolutions and Ethics (chair).

Biography: President *Pro Tem*. Born July 4, 1947, in Parsons, Kan. He received a Bachelor of Arts in history with a minor in political science from Missouri Southern State University and a Master of Arts in recent American history from Missouri State University. He and his wife, Patty, have two children, Kara and Chad, and four grandchildren: Natalie, Landon, Molly and Claire. He has full duties with C & N Bowl Corp. He is a member of St. Mary's Catholic Church. Joplin City Council, from 1990 to 1994; mayor of Joplin, from 1994 to 1997. Chair of House Economic Development Committee, 2004–2006; speaker of the House, 2009. He is the first speaker to be elected to the Senate in 100 years. Elected to the House: 2002–2008. Elected to the Senate: 2010, 2014. Republican.

District 33—**MIKE CUNNINGHAM**

Capitol office: Room 331; phone (573) 751-1882
Email address: *mike.cunningham@senate.mo.gov*
Senate committees: Governmental Accountability and Fiscal Oversight (chair); Financial and Governmental Organizations and Elections (vice chair); Commerce, Consumer Protection, Energy and the Environment; Veterans' Affairs and Health.

Biography: Born Jan. 8, 1947, in Columbia, Mo. Graduated from Macon H.S., 1965; attended Jacksonville Univ., Jacksonville, Fla.; received a B.S. in business administration, minor in economics, Truman State Univ., 1972. He has three children: Zach, Seth and Leah (Jeremy). Grandchildren: Baylee, Connor and Blaire. He is a livestock farmer. Retired in 2001 as owner/manager of Cunningham's Fresh Foods, Marshfield. Served in U.S. Army, 1967–1969, honorably discharged, Sgt. E-5, Military Police. Member: River Bluff Fellowship; Marshfield Chamber of Commerce; Industrial Authority; Farm Bureau; American Legion; Mo. Foxtrotter Horse Assoc.; and the A.Q.H.A. Member of Emerging Leaders, Darden University, Va. Elected to the House: 2002–2008. Elected to the Senate: 2012. Republican.

District 34—**ROB SCHAAF**

Capitol office: Room 423; phone (573) 751-2183
District address: 516 Pinewood Dr., St. Joseph, 64506
Email address: *rob.schaaf@senate.mo.gov*
Senate committees: General Laws and Pensions (chair); Veterans' Affairs and Health (vice chair); Appropriations; Gubernatorial Appointments.

Biography: Born Jan. 4, 1957, in St. Louis. A graduate of Central High School, St. Joseph, 1975; Missouri Western State College, B.S., mathematics, 1979; and St. Louis University School of Medicine, M.D., 1983. Married Deborah Schoenlaub, Oct. 1, 1983. They have two children, Robert and Renee. He is a family physician in St. Joseph and board chair of Missouri Doctors Mutual Insurance Co., started April 1, 2004. He is a Christian. Member: Buchanan County Medical Society, past president; Missouri State Medical Assoc., councilor; Missouri State Medical Foundation Board; and MO HealthNet Oversight Committee. Member: Joint Committee on Public Employee Retirement; and the Arts Trust Fund, board of trustees. Elected to the House: 2002–2008. Elected to the Senate: 2010, 2014. Republican.

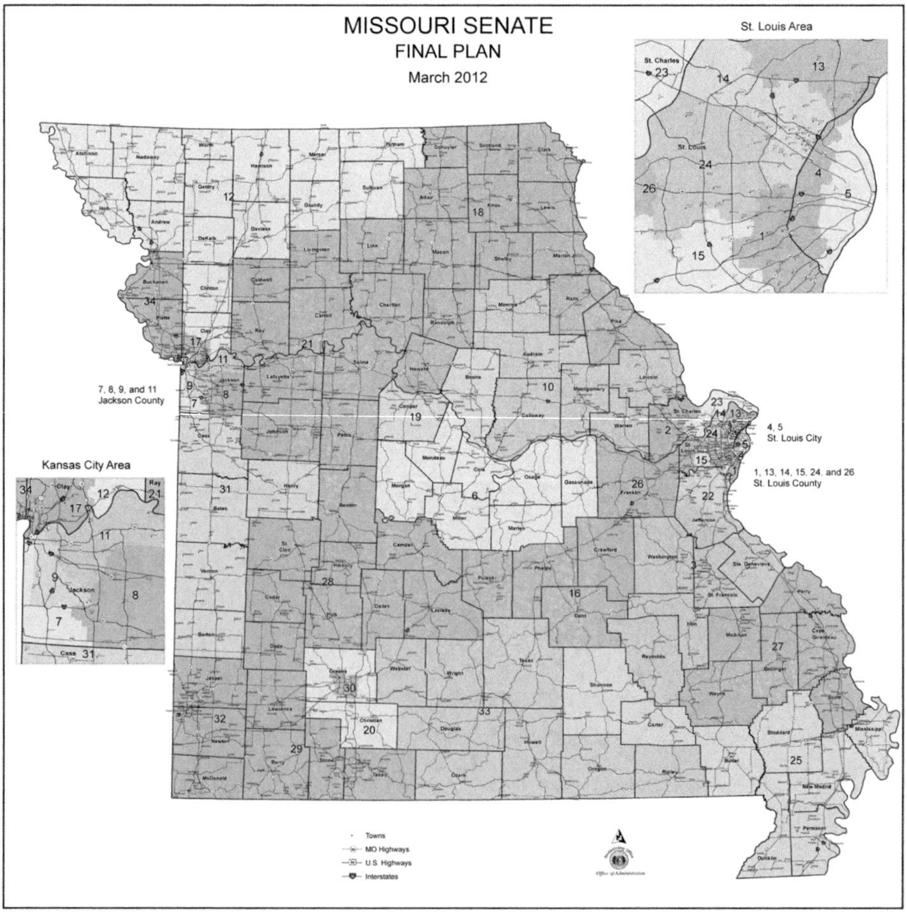

MISSOURI SENATE
FINAL PLAN
March 2012

St. Louis Area

Kansas City Area

7, 8, 9, and 11
Jackson County

4, 5
St. Louis City

1, 13, 14, 15, 24, and 26
St. Louis County

· Towns
MO Highways
U.S. Highways
Interstates

Office of Administration

State Senate Districts

State senate districts as established by the Missouri Appellate Apportionment Commission and filed with the Secretary of State on Nov. 30, 2011.

District	Description or boundary	Population
1	Part of St. Louis County	179,606
2	St. Charles	181,073
3	Iron, Reynolds, Ste. Genevieve, St. Francois, Washington, Jefferson (part of)	173,099
4	Parts of St. Louis County and St. Louis City	176,107
5	Part of St. Louis City	177,016
6	Cole, Gasconade, Maries, Miller, Moniteau, Morgan, Osage	175,186
7	Part of Jackson	168,435
8	Part of Jackson	168,462
9	Part of Jackson	168,649
10	Audrain, Callaway, Lincoln, Monroe, Montgomery, Warren	176,016
11	Part of Jackson	168,612
12	Andrew, Atchison, Clinton, Daviess, DeKalb, Gentry, Grundy, Harrison, Holt, Mercer, Nodaway, Putnam, Sullivan, Worth, Clay (part of)	181,976
13	Part of St. Louis County	171,967
14	Part of St. Louis County	171,753
15	Part of St. Louis County	178,836
16	Camden, Crawford, Dent, Phelps, Pulaski	181,785
17	Part of Clay	176,894
18	Adair, Chariton, Clark, Knox, Lewis, Linn, Macon, Marion, Pike, Ralls, Randolph, Schuyler, Scotland, Shelby	181,771
19	Boone, Cooper	180,243
20	Christian and Greene (part of)	176,274
21	Caldwell, Carroll, Howard, Johnson, Lafayette, Livingston, Ray, Saline	176,898
22	Part of Jefferson	171,659
23	Part of St. Charles	179,412
24	Part of St. Louis County	181,622
25	Butler, Carter, Dunklin, Mississippi, New Madrid, Pemiscot, Shannon, Stoddard	171,031
26	Franklin, St. Louis County (part of)	182,833
27	Bollinger, Cape Girardeau, Madison, Perry, Scott, Wayne	171,946
28	Benton, Cedar, Dallas, Hickory, Laclede, Pettis, Polk, St. Clair	178,156
29	Barry, Lawrence, McDonald, Stone, Taney	181,191
30	Part of Greene	176,322
31	Barton, Bates, Cass, Henry, Vernon	172,360
32	Dade, Jasper, Newton	183,401
33	Douglas, Howell, Oregon, Ozark, Ripley, Texas, Webster, Wright	169,813
34	Buchanan and Platte	178,523

Senatorial Districts by Municipality

Municipality	Senate District	Municipality	Senate District	Municipality	Senate District
Adrian	31	Battlefield	20	Bridgeton	14, 24
Advance	25	Bella Villa	1	Brimson	12
Affton	1	Bell City	25	Bronaugh	31
Agency	34	Belle	6	Brookfield	18
Airport Drive	32	Bellefontaine Neighbors	13	Brooklyn Heights	32
Alba	32	Bellerive	14	Browning	12, 18
Albany	12	Bellflower	10	Brownington	31
Aldrich	28	Bel-Nor	14	Brumley	6
Alexandria	18	Bel-Ridge	14	Brunswick	18
Allendale	12	Belton	31	Bucklin	18
Allenville	27	Bennett Springs	28	Buckner	11
Alma	21	Benton	27	Buffalo	28
Altamont	12	Benton City	10	Bull Creek	29
Altenburg	27	Berger	26	Bunceton	19
Alton	33	Berkeley	14	Bunker	3, 16
Amazonia	12	Bernie	25	Burgess	31
Amity	12	Bertrand	25	Burlington Junction	12
Amoret	31	Bethany	12	Butler	31
Amsterdam	31	Bethel	18	Butterfield	29
Anderson	29	Beverly Hills	14	Byrnes Mill	22
Annada	18	Bevier	18	Cabool	33
Annapolis	3	Biehle	27	Cainsville	12
Anniston	25	Bigelow	12	Cairo	18
Appleton City	28	Big Lake	12	Caledonia	3
Arbela	18	Big Spring	10	Calhoun	31
Arbyrd	25	Billings	20	California	6
Arcadia	3	Birch Tree	25	Callao	18
Archie	31	Birmingham	17	Calverton Park	14
Arcola	32	Bismarck	3	Camden	21
Argyle	6	Blackburn	21	Camden Point	34
Arkoe	12	Black Jack	13	Camdenton	16
Armstrong	21	Blackwater	19	Cameron	12
Arnold	22	Blairstown	31	Campbell	25
Arrow Point	29	Blanchard	12	Canalou	25
Arrow Rock	21	Bland	6	Canton	18
Asbury	32	Blodgett	27	Cape Girardeau	27
Ashburn	18	Bloomfield	25	Cardwell	25
Ash Grove	20	Bloomsdale	3	Carl Junction	32
Ashland	19	Blue Eye	29	Carrollton	21
Ashley	18	Blue Springs	8	Carterville	32
Atlanta	18	Blythedale	12	Carthage	32
Augusta	2	Bogard	21	Caruthersville	25
Aullville	21	Bolckow	12	Carytown	32
Aurora	29	Bolivar	28	Cassville	29
Auxvasse	10	Bonne Terre	3	Castle Point	13
Ava	33	Boonville	19	Catron	25
Avilla	32	Bosworth	21	Cave	10
Avondale	17	Bourbon	16	Cedar Hill	22
Bagnell	6	Bowling Green	18	Cedar Hill Lakes	22
Baker	25	Bragg City	25	Center	18
Bakersfield	33	Brandsville	33	Centertown	6
Baldwin Park	31	Branson	29	Centerview	21
Ballwin	15	Branson West	29	Centerville	3
Ballwin	24, 26	Brashear	18	Centralia	19
Baring	18	Braymer	21	Chaffee	27
Barnard	12	Breckenridge	21	Chain of Rocks	10
Barnett	6	Breckenridge Hills	24	Chain-O-Lakes	29
Barnhart	22	Brentwood	1, 4	Chamois	6
Bates City	21	Brewer	27	Champ	24

Municipality	Senate District	Municipality	Senate District	Municipality	Senate District
Charlack	14	Danville	10	Excello	18
Charlack	24	Dardenne Prairie	2	Excelsior Estates	12, 21
Charleston	25	Darlington	12	Excelsior Springs	12, 21
Cherokee Pass	27	Dawn	21	Exeter	29
Chesapeake	29	Dearborn	34	Fairdealing	25, 33
Chesterfield	15, 24, 26	Deepwater	31	Fairfax	12
Chilhowee	21	Deerfield	31	Fair Grove	20
Chillicothe	21	Defiance	2	Fair Play	28
Chula	21	De Kalb	34	Fairview	32
Clarence	18	Dellwood	13, 14	Farber	10
Clark	18	Delta	27	Farley	34
Clarksburg	6	Dennis Acres	32	Farmington	3
Clarksdale	12	Denver	12	Fayette	21
Clarkson Valley	15, 26	Des Arc	3	Fenton	15
Clarksville	18	Desloge	3	Ferguson	13, 14
Clarkton	25	De Soto	3	Ferrelview	34
Claycomo	17	Des Peres	15	Festus	3, 22
Clayton	4, 14	De Witt	21	Fidelity	32
Clearmont	12	Dexter	25	Fillmore	12
Cleveland	31	Diamond	32	Fisk	25
Clever	20	Diehlstadt	27	Fleming	21
Cliff Village	32	Diggins	33	Flemington	28
Clifton Hill	18	Dixon	16	Flint Hill	2
Climax Springs	16, 28	Doe Run	3	Flordell Hills	14
Clinton	31	Doniphan	33	Florissant	13, 14
Clyde	12	Doolittle	16	Foley	10
Cobalt	27	Dover	21	Fordland	33
Coffey	12	Downing	18	Forest City	12
Cole Camp	28	Drexel	31	Foristell	2, 10
Collins	28	Dudley	25	Forsyth	29
Columbia	19	Duenweg	32	Fortescue	12
Commerce	27	Duquesne	32	Fort Leonard Wood	16
Conception	12	Dutchtown	27	Foster	31
Conception Junction	12	Eagle Rock	29	Fountain N Lakes	10
Concord	1, 15	Eagleville	12	Frankclay	3
Concordia	21	East Lynne	31	Frankford	18
Coney Island	29	Easton	34	Franklin	21
Conway	28	East Prairie	25	Fredericktown	27
Cool Valley	14	Edgar Springs	16	Freeburg	6
Cooter	25	Edgerton	34	Freeman	31
Corder	21	Edina	18	Freistatt	29
Corning	12	Edinburg	12	Fremont	25
Cosby	12	Edmundson	14	Fremont Hills	20
Cottleville	2, 23	Eldon	6	Frohna	27
Country Club	12	El Dorado Springs	28	Frontenac	24
Country Club Hills	14	Ellington	3	Fulton	10
Country Life Acres	24	Ellisville	15, 26	Gainesville	33
Cowgill	21	Ellsinore	25	Galena	29
Craig	12	Elmer	18	Gallatin	12
Crane	29	Elmira	21	Galt	12
Creighton	31	Elmo	12	Garden City	31
Crestwood	1	Elsberry	10	Gasconade	6
Creve Coeur	24	Emerald Beach	29	Gentry	12
Crocker	16	Eminence	25	Gerald	26
Cross Timbers	28	Emma	21	Gerster	28
Crystal City	3, 22	Eolia	18	Gibbs	18
Crystal Lake Park	24	Essex	25	Gideon	25
Crystal Lakes	21	Ethel	18	Gilliam	21
Cuba	16	Eureka	26	Gilman City	12
Curryville	18	Evergreen	28	Ginger Blue	29
Dadeville	32	Everton	32	Gladstone	17
Dalton	18	Ewing	18	Glasgow	18, 21

Municipality	Senate District	Municipality	Senate District	Municipality	Senate District
Glasgow Village	13	Hermann	6	Junction City	27
Glenaire	17	Hermitage	28	Kahoka	18
Glen Allen	27	Higbee	18	Kansas City	7, 9, 11, 12, 17, 31, 34
Glendale	15	Higginsville	21		
Glen Echo Park	14	High Hill	10	Kearney	12
Glenwood	18	Highlandville	20	Kelso	27
Golden	29	High Ridge	22	Kennett	25
Golden City	31	Hillsboro	3	Keytesville	18
Goodman	29	Hillsdale	14	Kidder	21
Goodnight	28	Hoberg	29	Kimberling City	29
Gordonville	27	Holcomb	25	Kimmswick	22
Gower	12	Holden	21	King City	12
Gower	34	Holland	25	Kingdom City	10
Graham	12	Holliday	10	Kingston	21
Grain Valley	8	Hollister	29	Kingsville	21
Granby	32	Holt	12	Kinloch	14
Grand Falls Plaza	32	Holts Summit	10	Kirbyville	29
Grandin	25	Homestead	21	Kirksville	18
Grand Pass	21	Homestown	25	Kirkwood	1, 15
Grandview	7	Hopkins	12	Kissee Mills	29
Granger	18	Horine	22	Knob Noster	21
Grant City	12	Hornersville	25	Knox City	18
Grantwood Village	1	Houston	33	Koshkonong	33
Gravois Mills	6	Houstonia	28	LaBarque Creek	22
Grayhawk	3	Houston Lake	34	La Belle	18
Grayridge	25	Howardville	25	Laclede	18
Gray Summit	26	Hughesville	28	Laddonia	10
Greencastle	12	Humansville	28	La Due	31
Green City	12	Hume	31	Ladue	14, 24
Greendale	14	Humphreys	12	La Grange	18
Greenfield	32	Hunnewell	18	Lake Annette	31
Green Park	1	Hunter	25	Lake Lafayette	21
Green Ridge	28	Huntleigh	24	Lake Lotawana	8
Greentop	18	Huntsdale	19	Lake Mykee Town	10
Greenville	27	Huntsville	18	Lake Ozark	6, 16
Greenwood	8	Hurdland	18	Lake St. Louis	2
Guilford	12	Hurley	29	Lakeshire	1
Gunn City	31	Iatan	34	Lake Tapawingo	8
Hale	21	Iberia	6	Lake Tekakwitha	22
Halfway	28	Imperial	22	Lake Viking	12
Hallsville	19	Independence	8, 11	Lake Waukomis	34
Halltown	29	Indian Point	29	Lake Winnebago	31
Hamilton	21	Innsbrook	10	Lamar	31
Hanley Hills	14	Ionia	28	Lamar Heights	31
Hannibal	18	Irena	12	Lambert	27
Hardin	21	Irondale	3	La Monte	28
Harris	12	Iron Mountain Lake	3	Lanagan	29
Harrisburg	19	Ironton	3	Lancaster	18
Harrisonville	31	Irwin	31	La Plata	18
Hartsburg	19	Jackson	27	Laredo	12
Hartville	33	Jacksonville	18	La Russell	32
Hartwell	31	Jameson	12	Lathrop	12
Harviell	25	Jamesport	12	La Tour	21
Harwood	31	Jamestown	6	Laurie	6, 16
Hawk Point	10	Jasper	32	Lawson	12, 21
Hayti	25	Jefferson City	6, 10	Leadington	3
Hayti Heights	25	Jennings	13	Leadwood	3
Hayward	25	Jennings	14	Leasburg	16
Haywood City	27	Jerico Springs	28	Leawood	32
Hazelwood	13, 14	Jonesburg	10	Lebanon	28
Henrietta	21	Joplin	32	Lees Summit	7, 8, 11, 31
Herculaneum	22	Josephville	2	Leeton	21

Municipality	Senate District	Municipality	Senate District	Municipality	Senate District
Leisure Lake	12	Mehlville	1	New London	18
Lemay	1	Memphis	18	New Madrid	25
Leonard	18	Mendon	18	New Melle	2
Leslie	26	Mercer	12	Newtonia	32
Levasy	11	Merriam Woods	29	Newtown	12
Lewis and Clark Village	34	Merwin	31	Niangua	33
Lewistown	18	Meta	6	Nixa	20
Lexington	21	Metz	31	Noel	29
Liberal	31	Mexico	10	Norborne	21
Liberty	12, 17	Miami	21	Normandy	14
Licking	33	Middletown	10	North Kansas City	17
Lilbourn	25	Milan	12	North Lilbourn	25
Lincoln	28	Milford	31	Northmoor	34
Linn	6	Millard	18	Northwoods	14
Linn Creek	16	Miller	29	Norwood	33
Linneus	18	Mill Spring	27	Norwood Court	14
Lithium	27	Milo	31	Novelty	18
Livonia	12	Mindenmines	31	Novinger	18
Loch Lloyd	31	Mine La Motte	27	Oak Grove	8, 21
Lock Springs	12	Miner	27	Oak Grove Village	26
Lockwood	32	Mineral Point	3	Oakland	1
Lohman	6	Miramiguoa Park	26	Oak Ridge	27
Loma Linda	32	Missouri City	12	Oaks	17
Lone Jack	8	Moberly	18	Oakview	17
Longtown	27	Mokane	10	Oakville	1
Louisburg	28	Moline Acres	13	Oakwood	17
Louisiana	18	Monett	29	Oakwood Park	17
Lowry City	28	Monroe City	10, 18	Odessa	21
Lucerne	12	Montgomery City	10	OFallon	2, 23
Ludlow	21	Monticello	18	Old Appleton	27
Lupus	6	Montier	25	Old Jamestown	13
Luray	18	Montrose	31	Old Monroe	10
McBaine	19	Mooresville	21	Olean	6
McCord Bend	29	Morehouse	25	Olivette	24
McFall	12	Morley	27	Olympian Village	3
Mackenzie	4	Morrison	6	Oran	27
McKittrick	10	Morrisville	28	Oregon	12
Macks Creek	16	Mosby	12	Oronogo	32
Macon	18	Moscow Mills	10	Orrick	21
Madison	10	Mound City	12	Osage Beach	6, 16
Maitland	12	Moundville	31	Osborn	12
Malden	25	Mountain Grove	33	Osceola	28
Malta Bend	21	Mountain View	33	Osgood	12
Manchester	15, 24	Mount Leonard	21	Otterville	19
Mansfield	33	Mount Moriah	12	Overland	24
Maplewood	1, 4	Mount Vernon	29	Owensville	6
Marble Hill	27	Murphy	22	Oxly	33
Marceline	18	Napoleon	21	Ozark	20
Marionville	29	Naylor	33	Ozora	3
Marlborough	1	Neck City	32	Pacific	26
Marquand	27	Neelyville	25	Pagedale	14
Marshall	21	Nelson	21	Palmyra	18
Marshfield	33	Neosho	32	Paris	10
Marston	25	Nevada	31	Parkdale	22
Marthasville	10	Newark	18	Park Hills	3
Martinsburg	10	New Bloomfield	10	Parkville	34
Maryland Heights	24	Newburg	16	Parkway	26
Maryville	12	New Cambria	18	Parma	25
Matthews	25	New Florence	10	Parnell	12
Maysville	12	New Franklin	21	Pasadena Hills	14
Mayview	21	New Hampton	12	Pasadena Park	14
Meadville	18	New Haven	26	Pascola	25

Municipality	Senate District	Municipality	Senate District	Municipality	Senate District
Passaic	31	Renick	18	Scotsdale	22
Pattonsburg	12	Rensselaer	18	Scott City	27
Paynesville	18	Republic	20	Sedalia	28
Peaceful Village	22	Revere	18	Sedgewickville	27
Peculiar	31	Rhineland	10	Seligman	29
Pendleton	10	Richards	31	Senath	25
Penermon	25	Rich Hill	31	Seneca	32
Perry	18	Richland	16, 28	Seymour	33
Perryville	27	Richmond	21	Shelbina	18
Pevely	22	Richmond Heights	4	Shelbyville	18
Phelps City	12	Ridgely	34	Sheldon	31
Phillipsburg	28	Ridgeway	12	Shell Knob	29
Pickering	12	Risco	25	Sheridan	12
Piedmont	27	Ritchey	32	Shoal Creek Drive	32
Pierce City	29	River Bend	11	Shoal Creek Estates	32
Pierpont	19	Riverside	34	Shrewsbury	4
Pilot Grove	19	Riverview	13	Sibley	11
Pilot Knob	3	Riverview Estates	31	Sikeston	25, 27
Pine Lawn	14	Rives	25	Silex	10
Pineville	29	Rocheport	19	Silver Creek	32
Pinhook	25	Rockaway Beach	29	Skidmore	12
Plato	33	Rock Hill	1	Slater	21
Platte City	34	Rock Port	12	Smithton	28
Platte Woods	34	Rockville	31	Smithville	12
Plattsburg	12	Rogersville	20, 33	South Fork	33
Pleasant Hill	8	Rolla	16	South Gifford	18
Pleasant Hill	31	Roscoe	28	South Gorin	18
Pleasant Hope	28	Rosebud	6	South Greenfield	32
Pleasant Valley	17	Rosendale	12	South Lineville	12
Plevna	18	Rothville	18	Southwest City	29
Pocahontas	27	Rush Hill	10	Spanish Lake	13
Pollock	12	Rushville	34	Sparta	20
Polo	21	Russellville	6	Spickard	12
Pomona	33	Rutledge	18	Spokane	20
Pontiac	33	Saddlebrooke	20, 29	Springfield	20, 30
Poplar Bluff	25	Saginaw	32	Stanberry	12
Portage Des Sioux	23	St. Ann	14, 24	Stark City	32
Portageville	25	St. Charles	23	Steele	25
Potosi	3	St. Clair	26	Steelville	16
Powersville	12	St. Clement	18	Stella	32
Prairie Home	19	St. Cloud	16	Stewartsville	12
Prathersville	12	Ste. Genevieve	3	Stockton	28
Preston	28	St. Elizabeth	6	Stotesbury	31
Princeton	12	St. Francisville	18	Stotts City	29
Purcell	32	St. George	1	Stoutland	16, 28
Purdin	18	St. James	16	Stoutsville	10
Purdy	29	St. John	14, 24	Stover	6
Puxico	25	St. Joseph	34	Strafford	20
Queen City	18	St. Louis	4, 5	Strasburg	31
Quitman	12	St. Martins	6	Sturgeon	19
Qulin	25	St. Mary	3	Sugar Creek	11
Randolph	17	St. Paul	2	Sullivan	16
Ravanna	12	St. Peters	2	Sullivan	26
Ravenwood	12	St. Peters	23	Summersville	25, 33
Raymondville	33	St. Robert	16	Sumner	18
Raymore	31	St. Thomas	6	Sundown	33
Raytown	9, 11	Salem	16	Sunrise Beach	6, 16
Rayville	21	Salisbury	18	Sunset Hills	1, 15
Rea	12	Sappington	15	Sweet Springs	21
Redings Mill	32	Sarcoxie	32	Sycamore Hills	24
Reeds	32	Savannah	12	Syracuse	6
Reeds Spring	29	Schell City	31	Tallapoosa	25

Municipality	Senate District	Municipality	Senate District	Municipality	Senate District
Taneyville	29	Velda Village Hills	14	West Alton	23
Taos	6	Verona	29	Westboro	12
Tarkio	12	Versailles	6	West Line	31
Tarrants	18	Viburnum	3	Weston	34
Terre du Lac	3	Vienna	6	Westphalia	6
Thayer	33	Village of Four Seasons	16	West Plains	33
Theodosia	33	Villa Ridge	26	West Sullivan	16
Thomasville	33	Vinita Park	14	Westwood	24
Three Creeks	10	Vinita Terrace	14	Wheatland	28
Tightwad	31	Vista	28	Wheaton	29
Tina	21	Waco	32	Wheeling	21
Tindall	12	Walker	31	Whiteman AFB	21
Tipton	6	Walnut Grove	20	Whiteside	10
Town and Country	24	Wardell	25	Whitewater	27
Tracy	34	Wardsville	6	Wilbur Park	1
Trenton	12	Warrensburg	21	Wildwood	15
Trimble	12	Warrenton	10	Wildwood	26
Triplett	18	Warsaw	28	Willard	20
Troy	10	Warson Woods	24	Williamsville	27
Truesdale	10	Washburn	29	Willow Springs	33
Truxton	10	Washington	26	Wilson City	25
Turney	12	Wasola	33	Winchester	15
Tuscumbia	6	Watson	12	Winchester	24
Twin Oaks	15	Waverly	21	Windsor	28
Umber View Heights	28	Wayland	18	Windsor	31
Union	26	Waynesville	16	Windsor Place	19
Union Star	12	Weatherby	12	Winfield	10
Unionville	12	Weatherby Lake	34	Winigan	12
Unity Village	9	Weaubleau	28	Winona	25
University City	14, 24	Webb City	32	Winston	12
Uplands Park	14	Webster Groves	1	Wood Heights	21
Urbana	28	Webster Groves	4	Woodson Terrace	14
Urich	31	Weingarten	3	Wooldridge	19
Utica	21	Weldon Spring	23	Worth	12
Valley Park	15	Weldon Spring Heights	2	Wortham	3
Van Buren	25	Wellington	21	Worthington	12
Vandalia	10	Wellston	14	Wright City	10
Vandiver	10	Wellsville	10	Wyaconda	18
Vanduser	27	Wentworth	32	Wyatt	25
Velda City	14	Wentzville	2	Zalma	27

Johnson Shut-Ins State Park
Photo courtesy of Missouri State Archives

Missouri House of Representatives

TODO RICHARDSON
Speaker, Missouri House of
Representatives

DENNY HOSKINS
Speaker *Pro Tem*, Missouri
House of Representatives

Officers of the House of Representatives, Ninety-Eighth General Assembly, First Regular Session, 2015

Todd Richardson, Speaker of the House
Denny Hoskins, Speaker *Pro Tem*
Mike Cierpiot, Majority Floor Leader
Kevin Austin, Assistant Majority Floor Leader
Shelley Keeney Taylor, Majority Caucus Chair
Mike Bernskoetter, Majority Caucus Secretary
Delus Johnson, Majority Whip
Jacob Hummel, Minority Floor Leader
Gail McCann Beatty, Assistant Minority Floor Leader
Gina Mitten, Minority Caucus Chair
Jon Carpenter, Minority Caucus Vice Chair
Karla May, Minority Caucus Secretary
John Rizzo, Minority Whip
D. Adam Crumbliss, Chief Clerk
Ralph Robinett, Sergeant-at-Arms
Msgr. Robert A. Kurwicki, Chaplain

MIKE CIERPIOT
Majority Floor Leader
Missouri House of
Representatives

KEVIN AUSTIN
Assistant Majority Floor Leader
Missouri House of
Representatives

Committees of the House, Ninety-Eighth General Assembly, First Regular Session, 2015

(As of March 7, 2015)

Administration and Accounts: Leara, chair; Shumake, vice chair; Cierpiot; Conway (10); Johnson; Keeney; and Kratky.

Agriculture Policy: Houghton, chair; Hurst, vice chair; Black; Eggleston; Entlicher; Harris; Korman; Lavender; Love; McCreery; McGaugh; Muntzel; Peters; Pierson; Pike; Redmon; Rone; and Spencer.

Appropriations – Agriculture and Natural Resources: Redmon, chair; Rone, vice chair; Anderson; Basye; Gardner; Harris; Houghton; McCreery; Moon; and Reiboldt.

Appropriations – Elementary and Secondary Education: Bahr, chair; Gannon, vice chair; Dohrman; Franklin; Kendrick; Lynch; McNeil; Montecillo; Morris; and Pfautsch.

Appropriations – General Administration: Ross, chair; Justus, vice chair; Barnes; Conway (10); Green; Houghton; Love; Mathews; Newman; and Pike.

Appropriations – Health, Mental Health and Social Services: Haefner, chair; Wood, vice chair; Curtis; Frederick; Kirkton; Mims; Neely; Rehder; Ruth; and Wiemann.

Appropriations – Higher Education: Lichtenegger, chair; Lauer, vice chair; Adams; LaFaver; Muntzel; Neely; Parkinson; Pogue; Taylor; and Webber.

Appropriations–Public Safety and Corrections: Conway (104), chair; Wilson, vice chair; Curtman; Ellington; Fitzwater (144); Higdon; Hill; Nichols; Peters; and Roden.

Appropriations–Revenue, Transportation and Economic Development: Hough, chair; Basye, vice chair; Chipman; Dunn; Hicks; Kidd; May; Pace; Rehder; and Shull.

Banking: Crawford, chair; Pogue, vice chair; Bondon; Brown; Gosen; Green; Hinson; Kidd; Nichols; Otto; Redmon; and Shull.

Children and Families: Franklin, chair; Neely, vice chair; Beard; Brattin; Brown; Gannon; Haefner; Lauer; Meredith; Newman; Norr; and Remole.

Civil and Criminal Proceedings: Cornejo, chair; White, vice chair; Andrews; Colona; Corlew; Gardner; Higdon; Marshall; McDaniel; McGaugh; Mitten; and Vescovo.

Conservation and Natural Resources: Anderson, chair; Remole, vice chair; Andrews; Chipman; Cookson; Harris; Kendrick; Meredith; Phillips; Pietzman; Ross; and Rowland.

D. ADAM CRUMBLISS
Chief Clerk

DANA RADEMAN MILLER
Assistant Chief Clerk

DAVID WILLIS
Chief of Staff
Office of the Speaker

KENNY ROSS
Legislative Director
to the Speaker

LEANN HAGER
Executive Assistant
to the Speaker

RALPH ROBINETT
Sergeant-at-Arms

MSGR. ROBERT A. KURWICKI
Chaplain

Consumer Affairs: Parkinson, chair; Brattin, vice chair; Andrews; Barnes; Berry; Brown; Lair; Mitten; Otto; Reiboldt; Taylor; and Webber.

Corrections: Fitzwater (144), chair; Brattin, vice chair; Andrews; Black; Chipman; Gardner; Hill; Hubbard; Mims; Reiboldt; Roden; and Shumake.

Economic Development and Business Attraction and Retention: Rowden, chair; Corlew, vice chair; Austin; Beard; Butler; Dogan; Dunn; Hansen; Johnson; Kratky; Lichtenegger; Pfautsch; and Rizzo.

Elections: Entlicher, chair; Dogan, vice chair; Chipman; Conway (10); Dugger; Kidd; Kolkmeyer; McGaugh; Newman; Shaul; Smith; and Taylor.

Elementary and Secondary Education: Swan, chair; Spencer, vice chair; Anders; Arthur; Burlison; Cierpiot; Cookson; Dogan; Hubrecht; Montecillo; Pierson; Roeber; and Ruth.

Emerging Issues: Haahr, chair; Cross, vice chair; Bondon; Hansen; Hicks; LaFaver; Lant; McDonald; Muntzel; Pace; Rowden; and Zerr.

Emerging Issues in Education: Rowland, chair; Gannon, vice chair; Bahr; Bondon; Butler; Hinson; Koenig; Love; McNeil; Morgan; Shaul; and Wood.

Employment Security: Brown, chair; Spencer, vice chair; Alferman; Allen; Davis; Fitzpatrick; Flanigan; May; Parkinson; Runions; and Wiemann.

Energy and the Environment: Miller, chair; Marshall, vice chair; Basye; Bondon; Colona; Corlew; Ellington; Hubrecht; Kolkmeyer; McNeil; Redmon; Remole; and Runions.

Ethics: Richardson, chair; Mitten, vice chair; Arthur; Barnes; Beard; Bernskoetter; Conway (10); Crawford; Mims; and Newman.

Fiscal Review: Allen, chair; Fitzpatrick, vice chair; Alferman; Anderson; Conway (104); Lavender; Morgan; Rhoads; Walton Gray; and Zerr.

Government Efficiency: Curtman, chair; Kelley, vice chair; Green; Johnson; Koenig; McCreery; Pike; Pogue; Runions; Solon; Vescovo; and Wilson.

Government Oversight and Accountability: Barnes, chair; Hurst, vice chair; Cornejo; Curtis; Fitzpatrick; Haahr; Hubbard; Messenger; Mitten; and Vescovo.

Health and Mental Health Policy: Frederick, chair; Morris, vice chair; Arthur; Entlicher; Haefner; Hubrecht; Kirkton; Pace; Rehder; Ruth; White; and Zerr.

Health Insurance: Hansen, chair; Morris, vice chair; Cornejo; Eggleston; Engler; Hill; Kendrick; McNeil; Mitten; Roeber; White; and Wiemann.

Higher Education: Cookson, chair; Dohrman, vice chair; Arthur; Brown; Fitzwater (144); Hoskins; Lichtenegger; McDaniel; Mims; Pierson; Sommer; and Walker.

Local Government: Hinson, chair; Wilson, vice chair; Adams; Austin; Cross; Engler; Gosen; King; Marshall; Rizzo; and Ruth.

Pensions: Walker, chair; White, vice chair; Anders; Hough; Jones; Justus; Kendrick; Lair; Leara; Morgan; Rhoads; and Rowland.

Professional Registration and Licensing: Burlison, chair; Sommer, vice chair; Austin; Beard; Carpenter; Cornejo; Fraker; Franklin; Frederick; Keeney; Kratky; McCann Beatty; Moon; Peters; Ross; Swan; Walton Gray; and Wiemann.

Property, Casualty, and Life Insurance: Shull, chair; Muntzell, vice chair; Alferman; Burns; Colona; Fitzwater (49); Lant; Marshall; Moon; Otto; Pietzman; and Sommer.

Public Safety and Emergency Preparedness: Rhoads, chair; Higdon, vice chair; Black; Conway (104); Hill; Hubbard; Lauer; McDaniel; Norr; Roden; Walton Gray; and Wilson.

Small Business: McCaherty, chair; Cross, vice chair; Bernskoetter; Butler; Ellington; English; Fraker; Green; Hansen; Harris; King; Lavender; Lynch; Messenger; Neely; Pietzman; Shaul; and Shumake.

Telecommunications: Korman, chair; Hicks, vice chair; Adams; Crawford; Dugger; Flanigan; Kidd; Love; Nichols; Pace; Rone; and Taylor.

Trade and Tourism: Phillips, chair; Justus, vice chair; Berry; Fitzwater (49); Gannon; Hurst; Kratky; McCaherty; McDonald; Miller; Norr; and Wood.

Transportation: Kolkmeyer, chair; Korman, vice chair; Burns; Entlicher; Hough; Jones; Lant; Mathews; May; McDonald; Roeber; and Rone.

Utility Infrastructure: Fraker, chair; Remole, vice chair; Anders; Bernskoetter; Cierpiot; Davis; Dogan; Dugger; Fitzwater (49); Haahr; Hicks; Korman; McCreery; McDonald; Miller; Montecillo; Rehder; Smith; and Spencer.

Veterans: Davis, chair; Lynch, vice chair; Basye; Beard; Burns; Conway (10); Dohrman; McCaherty; Otto; Pike; Roden; Shumake; and Solon.

Ways and Means: Koenig, chair; Moon, vice chair; Carpenter; Cross; Curtis; Curtman; Ellington; Higdon; Hubrecht; Kelley; Pogue; and Shaul.

Workforce Standards and Development: Lant, chair; Dohrman, vice chair; Brattin; Burns; Fraker; Gosen; Hurst; Kelley; Lynch; Smith; Walker; and Webber.

Select House Committees
(As of March 7, 2015)

Select Committee on Agriculture: Reiboldt, chair; Black, vice chair; Anderson; Bernskoetter; Eggleston; Harris; Houghton; McCreery; Meredith; and Shumake.

Select Committee on Budget: Flanigan, chair; Fitzpatrick, vice chair; Alferman; Allen; Bahr; Brown; Burlison; Conway (104); Haefner; Hough; Jones; Keeney; King; Kirkton; LaFaver; Lichtenegger; Mathews; May; McCann Beatty; Messenger; Montecillo; Redmon; Rizzo; Ross; Rowden; Swan; and Webber.

Select Committee on Commerce: Zerr, chair; Lauer, vice chair; Butler, Justus, King, Kratky, McCaherty, Norr, Phillips, Rowden.

Select Committee on Education: Lair, chair; Wood, vice chair; Cookson, Kelley, Lichtenegger, Montecillo, Morgan, Pierson, Rowland, Swan.

Select Committee on Financial Institutions and Taxation: Dugger, chair; Brown, vice chair; Anders; Berry; Carpenter; Crawford; Koenig; Nichols; Pietzman; and Walker.

Select Committee on General Laws: Jones, chair; Mathews, vice chair; Burlison; Carpenter; Curtman; Engler; Haahr; LaFaver; McCreery; and Sommer.

Select Committee on Insurance: Gosen, chair; Roeber, vice chair; Burns; Eggleston; English; Hansen; Lynch; McNeil; Otto; Ruth; and Shull.

Select Committee on Judiciary: Austin, chair; McGaugh, vice chair; Colona; Corlew; Cornejo; Fitzwater (144); Gardner; Keeney; Mitten; and Parkinson.

Select Committee on Labor and Industrial Relations: Rehder, chair; Kelley, vice chair; Brown; Burlison; Lant; Messenger; Smith; Vescovo; and Webber.

Select Committee on Rules: Engler, chair; Pfautsch, vice chair; Gardner; Lair; Lauer; Lavender; Leara; Morris; Phillips; and Rizzo.

Select Committee on Social Services: Allen, chair; Haefner, vice chair; Bahr; Conway (10); Davis; Fitzwater (49); Franklin; Frederick; Kirkton; and Meredith.

Select Committee on State and Local Governments: Solon, chair; Kolkmeyer, vice chair; Alferman; Entlicher; Hinson; McDonald; Newman; Pfautsch; and Rhoads.

Select Committee on Utilities: Berry, chair; Crawford, vice chair; Colona; English; Fraker; Korman; Leara; McDaniel; Miller; Pace; and Smith.

Special Standing House Committees
(As of March 7, 2015)

Special Committee on Security Infrastructure of the Capitol Complex: Higdon, chair; Wilson, vice chair; Conway (10); Ellington; and Phillips.

Special Committee on Urban Issues: Curtis, chair; Ellington, vice chair; Alferman; Austin; Gardner; Hubbard; Marshall; Peters; Roeber; and Rowden.

Alphabetical list of State Representatives, 2015

Name	District	Email Address
Adams, Joe (D)	68	joe.adams@house.mo.gov
Alferman, Justin (R)	61	justin.alferman@house.mo.gov
Allen, Sue J. (R)	100	sue.allen@house.mo.gov
Anders, Ira (D)	21	ira.anders@house.mo.gov
Anderson, Sonya A. (R)	131	sonya.anderson@house.mo.gov
Andrews, Allen (R)	1	allen.andrews@house.mo.gov
Arthur, Lauren A. (D)	18	lauren.arthur@hose.mo.gov
Austin, Kevin L. (R)	136	kevin.austin@house.mo.gov
Bahr, Kurt M. (R)	102	kurt.bahr@house.mo.gov
Barnes, Jason O. (R)	60	jay.barnes@house.mo.gov
Basye, Chuck (R)	47	chuck.basye@house.mo.gov
Beard, Nathan G. (R)	52	nathan.beard@house.mo.gov
Bernskoetter, Mike (R)	59	mike.bernskoetter@house.mo.gov
Berry, T.J. (R)	38	tj.berry@house.mo.gov
Black, Linda R. (D)	117	linda.black@house.mo.gov
Bondon, Jack (R)	56	jack.bondon@house.mo.gov
Brattin, Rick R. Jr. (R)	55	rick.brattin@house.mo.gov
Brown, Cloria (R)	94	cloria.brown@house.mo.gov
Brown, Wanda (R)	57	wanda.brown@house.mo.gov
Burlison, Eric (R)	133	eric.burlison@house.mo.gov
Burns, Bob (D)	93	bob.burns@house.mo.gov
Butler, Michael (D)	79	michael.butler@house.mo.gov
Carpenter, Jon (D)	15	jon.carpenter@house.mo.gov
Chipman, Jason (R)	120	jason.chipman@house.mo.gov
Cierpiot, Mike (R)	30	mike.cierpiot@house.mo.gov
Colona, Michael J. (D)	80	mike.colona@house.mo.gov
Conway, Kathie (R)	104	kathie.conway@house.mo.gov
Conway, Pat (D)	10	pat.conway@house.mo.gov
Cookson, Stephen C. (R)	153	steve.cookson@house.mo.gov
Corlew, Kevin (R)	14	kevin.corlew@house.mo.gov
Cornejo, Robert W. (R)	64	robert.cornejo@house.mo.gov
Crawford, Sandy (R)	129	sandy.crawford@house.mo.gov
Cross, Gary L. (R)	35	gary.cross@house.mo.gov
Curtis, Courtney Allen (D)	73	courtney.curtis@house.mo.gov
Curtman, Paul R. (R)	109	paul.curtman@house.mo.gov
Davis, Charlie E. (R)	162	charlie.davis@house.mo.gov
Dogan, Shamed (R)	98	shamed.dogan@house.mo.gov
Dohrman, Dean (R)	51	dean.dohrman@house.mo.gov
Dugger, Tony (R)	141	tony.dugger@house.mo.gov
Dunn, Randy D. (D)	23	randy.dunn@house.mo.gov
Eggleston, J. (R)	2	j.eggleston@house.mo.gov
Ellington, Brandon R. (D)	22	brandon.ellington@house.mo.gov
Engler, Kevin P. (R)	116	kevin.engler@house.mo.gov
English, Keith (D)	68	keith.english@house.mo.gov
Entlicher, Sue (R)	128	sue.entlicher@house.mo.gov
Fitzpatrick, Scott A. (R)	158	scott.fitzpatrick@house.mo.gov
Fitzwater, Paul (R)	144	paul.fitzwater@house.mo.gov
Fitzwater, Travis (R)	49	travis.fitzwater@house.mo.gov
Flanigan, Thomas Callaway (R)	163	thomas.flanigan@house.mo.gov
Fraker, Lyndall (R)	137	lyndall.fraker@house.mo.gov
Franklin, Diane (R)	123	diane.franklin@house.mo.gov
Frederick, Keith J. (R)	121	keith.frederick@house.mo.gov
Gannon, Elaine Freeman (R)	115	elaine.gannon@house.mo.gov
Gardner, Kimberly (D)	77	kimberly.gardner@house.mo.gov

Gosen, Don (R) . . . . 101. . . . . .don.gosen@house.mo.gov
Green, Alan K. (D) . . . . 67. . . . . alan.green@house.mo.gov
Haahr, Elijah (R) . . . . 134. . . . . .elijah.haahr@house.mo.gov
Haefner, Marsha E. (R) . . . . 95. . . . . marsha.haefner@house.mo.gov
Hansen, James (Jim) E. (R) . . . . 40. . . . . jim.hansen@house.mo.gov
Harris, Ben S. (D) . . . . 118. . . . . ben.harris@house.mo.gov
Hicks, Ronald Lee (R) . . . . 107. . . . . .ron.hicks@house.mo.gov
Higdon, Galen Wayne Jr. (R) . . . . 11. . . . . .galen.higdon@house.mo.gov
Hill, Justin S. (R) . . . . 108. . . . . justin.hill@sos.mo.gov
Hinson, Dave (R). . . . . 119. . . . . dave.hinson@house.mo.gov
Hodges, Steve (D). . . . . 149. . . . . steve.hodges@house.mo.gov
Hoskins, Denny L. (R). . . . . 54. . . . . .denny.hoskins@house.mo.gov
Hough, Lincoln (R). . . . . 135. . . . . lincoln.hough@house.mo.gov
Houghton, Jay D. (R) . . . . 43. . . . . .jay.houghton@house.mo.gov
Hubbard, Penny V. (D) . . . . 78. . . . . penny.hubbard@house.mo.gov
Hubrecht, Tila (R) . . . . 151. . . . . tila.hubrecht@house.mo.gov
Hummel, Jacob W. (D) . . . . 81. . . . . .jake.hummel@house.mo.gov
Hurst, Tom (R) . . . . 62. . . . . .tom.hurst@house.mo.gov
Johnson, Delus (R). . . . . 9. . . . . delus.johnson@house.mo.gov
Jones, Caleb M. (R) . . . . 50. . . . . caleb.jones@house.mo.gov
Justus, Jeff D. (R) . . . . 156. . . . . jeff.justus@house.mo.gov
Keeney Taylor, Shelley (R) . . . . 145. . . . . shelley.keeney@house.mo.gov
Kelley, Mike (R) . . . . 127. . . . . mike.kelley@house.mo.gov
Kendrick, Kip D. (D) . . . . 45. . . . . kip.kendrick@house.mo.gov
Kidd, Bill E. (R) . . . . 20. . . . . bill.kidd@house.mo.gov
King, Nick (R) . . . . 17. . . . . nick.king@house.mo.gov
Kirkton, Jeanne M. (D) . . . . 91. . . . . .jeanne.kirkton@house.mo.gov
Koenig, Andrew P. (R). . . . . 99. . . . . andrew.koenig@house.mo.gov
Kolkmeyer, Glen (R) . . . . 53. . . . . glen.kolkmeyer@house.mo.gov
Korman, Bart (R) . . . . 42. . . . . bart.korman@house.mo.gov
Kratky, Michele R. (D). . . . . 82. . . . . .michele.kratky@house.mo.gov
LaFaver, Jeremy (D) . . . . 25. . . . . .jeremy.lafaver@house.mo.gov
Lair, Mike F. (R) . . . . 7. . . . . mike.lair@house.mo.gov
Lant, Bill (R). . . . . 159. . . . . bill.lant@house.mo.gov
Lauer, Jeanie (R). . . . . 32. . . . . .jeanie.lauer@house.mo.gov
Lavender, Deb (D). . . . . 90. . . . . .deb.lavendar@house.mo.gov
Leara, Mike (R) . . . . 96. . . . . .mike.leara@house.mo.gov
Lichtenegger, Donna (R) . . . . 146. . . . . .donna.lichtenegger@house.mo.gov
Love, Warren D. (R). 125. . . . . .warren.love@house.mo.gov
Lynch, Steven M. (R). . . . . 122. . . . . steve.lynch@house.mo.gov
McCann Beatty, Gail (D). . . . . 26. . . . . .gail.beatty@house.mo.gov
Marshall, Nickolas A. (R). . . . . 13. . . . . .nick.marshall@house.mo.gov
Mathews, Kirk (R) . . . . 110. . . . . .kirk.mathews@house.mo.gov
May, Karla (D) . . . . 84. . . . . karla.may@house.mo.gov
McCaherty, John C. (R) . . . . 97. . . . . .john.mccaherty@house.mo.gov
McCreery, Tracy (D) . . . . 88. . . . . tracy.mccreery@house.mo.gov
McDaniel, Andrew . . . . 150. . . . . andrew.mcdaniel@house.mo.gov
McDonald, Tom (D) . . . . 28. . . . . .tom.mcdonald@house.mo.gov
McGaugh, Joe Don (R) . . . . 39. . . . . .joedon.mcgaugh@house.mo.gov
McNeil, Margo (D) . . . . 69. . . . . margo.mcneil@house.mo.gov
Meredith, Sue (D) . . . . 71. . . . . .sue.meredith@house.mo.gov
Messenger, Jeff L. (R). . . . . 130. . . . . jeff.messenger@house.mo.gov
Miller, Rocky C. (R). 124. . . . . rocky.miller@house.mo.gov
Mims, Bonnaye V. (D) . . . . 27. . . . . bonnaye.mims@house.mo.gov
Mitten, Gina C. (D) . . . . 83. . . . . gina.mitten@house.mo.gov
Montecillo, Genise D. (D) . . . . 92. . . . . genise.montecillo@house.mo.gov
Morgan, Judy (D). . . . . 24. . . . . .judy.morgan@house.mo.gov

Morris, Lynn A. (R) . . . . 140. . . . . lynn.morris@house.mo.gov
Muntzel, Dave E. (R) . . . . 48. . . . . dave.muntzel@house.mo.gov
Neely, Jim (R) . . . . 8. . . . . jim.neely@house.mo.gov
Newman, Stacey G. (D) . . . . 87. . . . . .stacey.newman@house.mo.gov
Nichols, Mary (D) . . . . 72. . . . . mary.nichols@house.mo.gov
Norr, Charlie (D) . . . . 132. . . . . charlie.norr@house.mo.gov
Otto, Bill (D) . . . . 70. . . . . bill.otto@house.mo.gov
Pace, Sharon L. (D) . . . . 74. . . . . sharon.pace@house.mo.gov
Parkinson, Mark A. (R) . . . . 105. . . . . .mark.parkinson@house.mo.gov
Peters, Joshua D. (D) . . . . 76. . . . . joshua.peters@house.mo.gov
Pfautsch, Donna S. (R) . . . . 33. . . . . .donna.pfautsch@house.mo.gov
Phillips, Donald E. (R) . . . . 138. . . . . don.phillips@house.mo.gov
Pierson, Tommie L. (D) . . . . 66. . . . . .tommie.pierson@house.mo.gov
Pietzman, Randy (R) . . . . 41. . . . . .randy.pietzman@house.mo.gov
Pike, Patricia (R) . . . . 126. . . . . randy.pike@house.mo.gov
Pogue, Jeff L. (R) . . . . 143. . . . . jeff.pogue@house.mo.gov
Redmon, Craig (R) . . . . 4. . . . . craig.redmon@house.mo.gov
Rehder, Holly Renee (R) . . . . 148. . . . . .holly.rehder@house.mo.gov
Reiboldt, Bill (R) . . . . 160. . . . . bill.reiboldt@house.mo.gov
Remole, Tim (R) . . . . 6. . . . . .tim.remole@house.mo.gov
Rhoads, Shawn (R) . . . . 154. . . . . .shawn.rhoads@house.mo.gov
Richardson, Todd (R) . . . . 152. . . . . .todd.richardson@house.mo.gov
Rizzo, John J. (D) . . . . 19. . . . . john.rizzo@house.mo.gov
Roden, Shane (R) . . . . 111. . . . . shane.roden@house.mo.gov
Roeber, Rebecca S. (R) . . . . 34. . . . . .rebecca.roeber@house.mo.gov
Ross, Robert (R) . . . . 142. . . . . robert.ross@house.mo.gov
Rowden, Caleb (R) . . . . 44. . . . . caleb.rowden@house.mo.gov
Rowland, Lyle (R) . . . . 155. . . . . lyle.rowland@house.mo.gov
Runions, Joe (D) . . . . 37. . . . . joe.runions@house.mo.gov
Ruth, Becky (R) . . . . 114. . . . . becky.ruth@sos.mo.gov
Shaul, Dan Y. (R) . . . . 113. . . . . dan.shaul@house.mo.gov
Shull, Noel (R) . . . . 16. . . . . noel.shull@house.mo.gov
Shumake, Lindell F. (R) . . . . 5. . . . . .lindell.shumake@house.mo.gov
Smith, Clem (D) . . . . 85. . . . . clem.smith@house.mo.gov
Solon, Sheila (R) . . . . 31. . . . . sheila.solon@house.mo.gov
Sommer, Chrissy (R) . . . . 106. . . . . .chrissy.sommer@house.mo.gov
Spencer, Bryan F. (R) . . . . 63. . . . . .bryan.spencer@house.mo.gov
Swan, Kathryn (R) . . . . 147. . . . . kathryn.swan@house.mo.gov
Taylor, Jared (R) . . . . 139. . . . . jared.taylor@house.mo.gov
Vescovo, Rob (R) . . . . 112. . . . . rob.vescovo@house.mo.gov
Walker, Nate (R) . . . . 3. . . . . .nate.walker@house.mo.gov
Walton Gray, Rochelle (D) . . . . 75. . . . . .rochelle.gray@house.mo.gov
Webber, Stephen D. (D) . . . . 46. . . . . .stephen.webber@house.mo.gov
White, Bill (R) . . . . 161. . . . . bill.white@house.mo.gov
Wiemann, John David (R) . . . . 103. . . . . .john.wiemann@house.mo.gov
Wilson, Kenneth (R) . . . . 12. . . . . kenneth.wilson@house.mo.gov
Wood, David (R) . . . . 58. . . . . david.wood@house.mo.gov
Zerr, Anne (R) . . . . 18. . . . . anne.zerr@house.mo.gov

Number of Representatives 163
Republicans 116
Democrats 43
Independents 1
Vacancy 3
Terms expire: January 2017

District 1—**ALLEN ANDREWS**

Capitol office: Room 135AB; phone (573) 751-9465
District address: PO Box 118, Grant City 64456
Email address: *allen.andrews@house.mo.gov*
House committees: Conservation and Natural Resources; Civil and Criminal Proceedings; Corrections; Consumer Affairs.

Biography: Born Feb. 5, 1967, in St. Joseph, Mo. Graduate of Northwest Missouri State University, B.S. in business management/marketing in 1989. He and his wife, Robin, have three children: Mitchell, Kristen and Luke. Co-owner and president of Andrews Family Corporation (Wool Shop), a family company started in 1983. Member: Missouri Farm Bureau; Missouri Right to Life; National Rifle Association; National Federation of Independent Business; and International Housewares Manufacturers. Elected to the House: 2014. Republican.

District 2—**J. EGGLESTON**

Capitol office: Room 406B; phone (573) 751-4285
Email address: *j.eggleston@house.mo.gov*
House committees: Agriculture Policy; Health Insurance.

Biography: Rep. J. Eggleston was born in DeKalb County and grew up on a farm there. He resides near Maysville with his wife, Cathie. They have two children. He is a 1984 graduate of Maysville High School in Maysville, Mo., and received his Bachelor of Science degree in electronic engineering technology in 1987. In addition to his legislative duties, Rep. Eggleston is a small business owner in his district. He was a software engineer in Silicon Valley from 1987–1992, and currently owns a consumer electronics small business he founded in 1994. He also serves on the Select Committee on Agriculture and the Select Committee on Insurance. Elected to the House: 2014. Republican.

District 3—**NATE WALKER**

Capitol office: Room 405B; phone (573) 751-3647
Email address: *nate.walker@house.mo.gov*
House committees: Pensions (chair); Higher Education; Workforce Standards and Development.

Biography: Rep. Nate Walker resides in Kirksville and is the proud father of two sons: Madison Belt Walker and Samuel Preston Belt Walker. Walker has a diverse professional career working as a licensed realtor; former owner, publisher and editor of the *La Plata Home Press;* a family farmer; and involvement in downtown revitalization, community growth and economic development, as well as work on national, state and regional transportation issues. He holds a Bachelor of Science degree in agricultural journalism, Master of Science degree in regional and community affairs from the University of Missouri–Columbia, and has done post graduate studies at Duke University and the Haus Rissen Institute of International

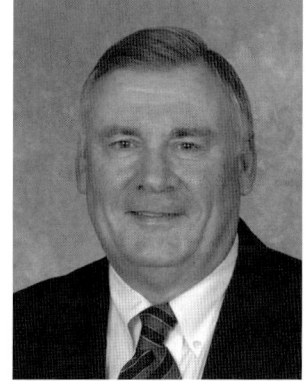

Politics and Economics in Germany. Rep. Walker also serves on the Select Committee on Financial Institutions Taxation, and the Joint Committee on Public Employee Retirement. Elected to the House: 1980, 1982, 2012, 2014. Republican.

District 4—**CRAIG REDMON**

Capitol office: Room 111; phone (573) 751-3644
District office: PO Box 43, Monticello 63457
Email address: *craig.redmon@house.mo.gov*
House committees: Appropriations–Agriculture, Conservation and Natural Resources (chair); Agriculture Policy; Banking; Energy and the Environment.

Biography: Born on Jan. 29, 1959, in Kirksville. Rep. Redmon currently resides in Canton with his wife, Brenda. They are the parents of twins, Andrew and Audrey. In addition to his legislative duties, Rep. Redmon owns a small business in Monticello. He previously owned and operated a convenience store. He is a 1977 graduate of Highland High School. Rep. Redmon received his B.S. from Culver Stockton College in 1982. He also serves on: Select Committee on Agriculture; Select Committee on Budget; Joint Committee on Real Property Tax Increment Allocation Redevelopment; Joint Committee on Solid Waste Management District Operations; Interim Committee on Development and Improvement of Missouri Ports (vice chair); and Conference Committee on Budget. Elected to the House: 2010, 2012, 2014. Republican.

District 5—**LINDELL F. SHUMAKE**

Capitol office: Room 404A; phone (573) 751-3613
District address: 1101 Central Ave., Hannibal 63401
Email address: *lindell.shumake@house.mo.gov*
House committees: Administration and Accounts (vice chair); Corrections; Small Business; Veterans.

Biography: Rep. Shumake's hometown is Hannibal, and he graduated from Hannibal High School in 1968. He served in the U.S. Army from 1969 to 1971, including a tour in Vietnam. He graduated from Hannibal Lagrange College in 1974 and Quincy University in 1976 with a B.A. degree in sociology and obtained a Missouri teaching certificate. Rep. Shumake was employed for the Division of Family Services as a caseworker from 1977 to 1996. He owned and operated a metal recycling business and continues to operate LS Tax Service. He was ordained to the gospel ministry in 1974 and continues to do prison and jail ministry and foreign missions, including trips to the Philippines, Malaysia and Vietnam. He married his wife Lydia in 1975, and they have one child, Johanna, adopted from China in 2001. He also serves on the Select Committee on Agriculture. Elected to the House: 2010, 2012, 2014. Republican.

District 6—**TIM REMOLE**

Capital office: Room 201-G; (573) 751-6566
Email address: *tim.remole@house.mo.gov*
House committees: Agri-Business; Utilities; Tourism and Natural Resources; Children, Families and Persons with Disabilities.

Biography: Born Oct. 2, 1957, in Danville, Ill., Rep. Remole graduated from Westran Senior High School in 1976. In addition to his legislative duties, he has been a small business owner for 23 years, and owns Remole Coatings, LLC. He also has served as a volunteer firefighter for 26 years. Rep. Remole currently resides in Excello with his wife of 34 years, Brenda. They have two children, Nathan and Amy. They have a son-in-law, Travis, and daughter-in-law, KaraLee. They have six grandchildren. He is a member of the Church of Nazarene and was the proud recipient of a 20-year Distinguished Service Award. He is currently a member of Moberly Holiness Independent Church, and a Golden Eagle member of the NRA. Elected to the House: 2012, 2014. Republican.

District 7—**MIKE LAIR**

Capitol office: Room 402; phone (573) 751-2917
Email address: *mike.lair@house.mo.gov*
House committees: Consumer Affairs; Pensions.

Biography: Born Feb. 27, 1946, in Omaha, Neb. A 1964 Creighton Prep Jesuit High School graduate, he played in Nebraska's Shrine Bowl football game and football at Colorado State Univ. He earned a B.S. in history from the University of Nebraska–Omaha in 1970, and an M.S. in education from Central Methodist University in 2003. He and wife, Jeanne, have lived in Chillicothe since 1987 and have two children, Jillian Harris and Trevor Lair, and three grandchildren, Margaux and Jack Harris, and Elsie Lair. He taught and coached in Nebraska, South Dakota and Missouri until his retirement after 38 years in 2008. Member: St. Columban Roman Catholic Church, Missouri Farm Bureau, Chillicothe Chamber of Commerce, Ducks Unlimited, NRA (life member) and the NRA–Institute for Legislative Action. He also serves on the Select Committee on Education (chair); Select Committee on Rules; and the Joint Committee on Education (vice chair). Elected to the House: 2008, 2010, 2012, 2014. Republican.

District 8—**JIM NEELY**

Capitol office: Room 110A; (573) 751-0246
Email address: *jim.neely@house.mo.gov*
House committees: Children and Families (vice chair); Appropriations–Health, Mental Health and Social Services; Appropriations–Higher Education; Small Business.

Biography: Rep. Jim Neely represents Clinton and Caldwell counties and parts of Clay and Ray counties. He was recently selected to serve on the Missouri Children's Services Commission. In addition to his legislative duties, Rep. Neely is a physician at Cameron Regional Medical Center. He also is a veteran of the United States Army. Rep. Neely served on the Cameron School Board from 1996 to 2005. He is a graduate of the University of Missouri–Columbia and received his D.O. from the Kansas City University of Medicine and Biosciences. He and his wife, Sandra, reside in Cameron and have six children: Stephenie, Kristina, Jillian, Chandler and twins John and Warren. Elected to the House: 2014. Republican.

District 9—**DELUS JOHNSON**

Capitol office: Room 302-1; phone (573) 751-3666
Email address: *delus.johnson@house.mo.gov*
House committees: *Ex officio* member of all House committees; Administration and Accounts; Economic Development and Business Attraction and Retention; Government Efficiency.

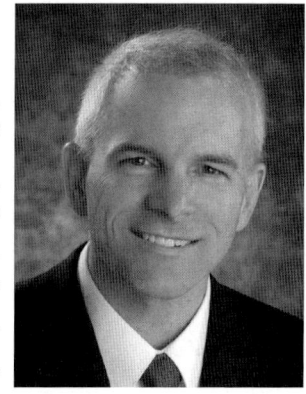

Biography: Majority Whip. Represents parts of Andrew and Buchanan counties. Served nearly 20 years as a captain on the St. Joseph Fire Department. He has received the Fire Chief's Life Saving Award, has been recognized for his perfect attendance and was a former emergency medical technician for the Andrew County Ambulance District. Owned numerous businesses, including a training company, which has helped more than 5,000 Missouri entrepreneurs start their own businesses. He is a member of the National Rifle Association, St. Joseph Metro Chamber of Commerce, Savannah Chamber of Commerce and the International Association of Firefighters. Raised in St. Joseph, Rep. Johnson currently resides there with his wife, Tara, daughter, Julia, and niece, Taylee. Elected to the House: 2010, 2012, 2014. Elected Majority Whip: 2014. Republican.

District 10—**PAT CONWAY**

Capitol office: Room 109-B; phone (573) 751-9755
Email address: *pat.conway@house.mo.gov*
House committees:; Administration and Accounts Appropriations–General Administration; Elections; Ethics; Veterans.

Biography: Born Oct. 8, 1947, in St. Joseph, and currently resides there with his wife, Mary. They have five children: Ritchie, Kenyon, Beth, Regan and Jennisen. He represents part of Buchanan County. He served as county clerk of Buchanan County from 1983 to 2010. A veteran of the Vietnam War, he served with the 2/12th Infantry, 25th Infantry Division in 1969–1970. He attends St. Joseph's Cathedral Catholic Church and belongs to the following organizations: Knights of Columbus, American Legion, Ancient Order of Hibernians, 25th Infantry Division Association, Zeredetha/Charity Lodge and Moila Shrine Temple, and Missouri State Capitol Commission. A 1965 graduate of Christian Brothers High School, Rep. Conway received a bachelor's degree in social science from Missouri Western State University. He also serves on the Select Committee on Social Services, the Special Committee on Security Infrastructure of the Capitol Complex and the Joint Committee on Legislative Research. Elected to the House: 2010, 2012, 2014. Democrat.

District 11—**GALEN WAYNE HIGDON JR.**

Capitol office: Room 412-A; phone (573) 751-3643
Email address: *galen.higdon@house.mo.gov*
House committees: Ways and Means (vice chair); Appropriations–Public Safety and Corrections; Crime Prevention and Public Safety; Judiciary.

Biography: Born May 30, 1954, in St. Joseph, Mo. He attended McKinley Grade School, Spring Garden Middle School and is a graduate of Benton High School, Class of 1973. He attended Missouri Western, 1979. Retired from Buchanan County Sheriff's Department after 30 years of service. Served on the transportation advisory committee; active member of the Knights of Columbus; served as second vice president for the Missouri Deputy Sheriffs Association; and member of the St. Joseph Host Lions Club. He attends St. James Catholic Church in St. Joseph. Married Lou Anne Bravo, 1973. They have three daughters: Monika Ford, Andrea Higdon and Emily Cummingham. They have five grandchildren. Appointed to the Sentencing Advisory Commission in 2013. Elected to the House: 2010, 2012. Republican.

District 12—**KENNETH WILSON**

Capitol office: Room 206A; phone (573) 751-9760
District address: 19507 Diamond Ln., Smithville 64089
Email address: *ken.wilson@house.mo.gov*
House committees: Appropriations–Public Safety and Corrections (vice-chair); Local Government (vice chair); Government Efficiency; Public Safety and Emergency Preparedness.

Biography: Born May 1. Rep. Wilson received a B.A. in criminal justice from Missouri Western State University, and is a graduate of the 210th Class of FBI National Academy, the U.S. Department of Justice Executive Excellence Program and the FBI Central States Law Enforcement Executive Development program. He and his wife have been married for 41 years and have two grown children with families of their own, including two grandchildren and expecting a third in June. He is a board member of Missouri Western Regional Law Enforcement Academy; Farm Bureau; NRA; Missouri Peace Officers Assoc.; Missouri Police Chiefs Assoc.; FBI National Academy Assoc.; International Assoc. of Ethics Trainers and International Assoc. of Chiefs of Police. He also serves on the Special Committee on Security Infrastructure of the Capitol Complex (vice chair); Elected to the House: 2012, 2014. Republican.

District 13—**NICK MARSHALL**

Capitol office: Room 134; phone (573) 751-6593
District address: PO Box 14235, Parkville 64152
Email address: *nick.marshall@house.mo.gov*
House committees: Energy and the Environment (vice chair); Civil and Criminal Proceedings; Property, Casualty and Life Insurance; Local Government; Special Committee on Urban Issues.

Biography: Born Oct. 5, 1972, in Kansas City. Rep. Nickolas A. Marshall represents Platte County. In addition to his legislative duties, he is also a practicing attorney. Rep. Marshall received his B.A. from Bob Jones University in 1995 and his law degree from the University of Missouri–Kansas City in 1999. After his admission to the Missouri Bar, he served the people of Missouri as an assistant prosecuting attorney. He is a three-time recipient, in 2011, 2012 and 2013, of the Locke and Smith Award, and the Champion of Justice Award in 2012 from the Missouri Association of Trial Attorneys. Rep. Marshall is also a member of the NRA, the NWTF and the Missouri Prairie Foundation. Rep. Marshall resides with his family in southern Platte County. Elected to the House: 2010, 2012 and 2014. Republican.

District 14—**KEVIN CORLEW**

Capitol office: Room 201-A; phone (573) 751-3618
Email address: *kevin.corlew@house.mo.gov*
House committees: Economic Development and Business Attraction and Retention (vice chair); Civil and Criminal Proceedings; Energy and the Environment.

Biography: Rep. Kevin Corlew and his wife, Amy, have three children. They live in Kansas City and attend Tiffany Fellowship Church. He graduated from high school in North Platte, Neb. Rep. Corlew received a Bachelor of Arts degree from Columbia College–Chicago, and a Juris Doctor degree from the University of Nebraska College of Law. Following law school, Rep. Corlew worked for two years as a judicial law clerk for a judge on the Nebraska Supreme Court. Before assuming his legislative duties, Rep. Corlew served on the school board for North Kansas City Schools. He also served on the board and as the chair for his homeowners association. He is a member of Rotary and is active in several local chambers of commerce and economic development councils. He is an attorney, and his law practice involves business litigation at a firm in Kansas City. Prior to law school, he worked as a church youth director, where he led ministries for junior and senior high school, and college students. Elected to the House: 2014. Republican.

District 15—**JON CARPENTER**

Capitol office: Room 101-I; phone (573) 751-4787
District address: PO Box 47318, Kansas City 64188
Email address: *jon.carpenter@house.mo.gov*
House committees: Professional Registration and Licensing; Ways and Means.

Biography: Rep. Carpenter is the owner of Carpenter Communications, a marketing and advertising firm that partners with businesses and nonprofit organizations. Member of the Gladstone Area Chamber of Commerce and the Northland Democratic Club. He is a graduate of St. Charles grade school and North Kansas City High School, and was a National Merit Scholar. Graduated *magna cum laude* from the University of Southern California with a B.A. in political science and a minor in international relations. He also serves on the Select Committee on General Laws and the Select Committee on Financial Institutions and Taxation. Rep. Carpenter lives in Gladstone with his wife, Midori. Elected to the House: 2012, 2014. Democrat.

District 16—NOEL J. SHULL

Capitol office: Room 201B; phone (573) 751-9458
District address: PO Box 281, Liberty 64069
Email address: *noel.shull@house.mo.gov*
House committees: Property, Casualty and Life Insurance (chair); Appropriations–Revenue, Transportation and Economic Development; Banking

Biography: Born, May 28, 1942, in Hale, Mo., to loving parents Larkie I. and Lester Gayle Shull. He and his wife Peggy have two sons and six grandchildren. Graduate of Hale High School; B.S. in finance and real estate, University of Missouri–Columbia; Graduate School of Banking, Southern Methodist Univ., Dallas, Texas. Retired UMB Bank, executive vice president. Member: Pleasant Valley Baptist Church, Small Business Administration National Advisory Council, 1978–2001, first male appointed to SBA NAC Women Business Owners Committee, Mid Continent Public Library Bd. of Trustees, Mo. Cattlemen's Foundation Board, Univ. of Mo., Honorary Professors Program, SBA Regional Financial Advocate of the year, 2004 recipient Greater Kansas City UMC Business Alumni Chapter Alumni of the Year Award, licensed real estate broker, and Shoal Creek Living History Museum. Elected to the House: 2012, 2014. Republican.

District 17—STUART NICHOLAS (NICK) KING II

Capitol Office: Room 201-CA; phone (573) 751-1218
Email address: *nick.king@house.mo.gov*
House committees: Local Government; Small Business.

Biography: Born in Springfield, Mass. Graduated from Montana State University, with a bachelor's degree in music education. Served a two-year mission for the Church of Jesus Christ of Latter-Day Saints. Taught in Idaho and Montana, and began career in business-to-business marketing. Moved to Liberty, Mo., in 1990 with his wife, Norma, and five children. Served eight years on the Liberty City council. He also serves on the Select Committee on Budget and the Select Committee on Commerce. Elected to the House: 2014. Republican.

District 18—LAUREN A. ARTHUR

Capitol office: Room 109H; phone (573) 751-2199
Email address: *lauren.arthur@house.mo.gov*
House committees: Ethics; Elementary and Secondary Education; Health and Mental Health Policy; Higher Education.

Biography: Rep. Lauren Arthur was born and raised in Northland. She currently lives in Kansas City, Mo. She is a graduate of the International Baccalaureate Program from North Kansas City High School. She earned her bachelor's degree in history from Smith College in Northampton, Mass., graduating *magna cum laude* and Phi Beta Kappa. While attending Smith College, Rep. Arthur interned at the Smithsonian's American History Museum and the Scottish Parliament. She also received her master's in education from the University of Missouri–St. Louis. In addition to her legislative duties, Rep. Arthur currently works as a project manager at VML, a global advertising agency. She has also worked in Kansas City as a middle school teacher, and teaching English Language Arts at Urban Community Leadership Academy, a charter school in Kansas City. Elected to the House: 2014. Democrat.

District 19—JOHN J. RIZZO

Capitol office: Room 102BB; phone (573) 751-3310
Email address: *john.rizzo@house.mo.gov*
House committees: Economic Development and Business Attraction and Retention; Local Government.

Biography: Born on Oct. 3, 1980, in Kansas City, where he resides with his wife, Lindsay, and daughter, Sofia. He is a 1999 graduate of St. Pius X High School. He received a B.S. in political science and a B.A. in English in 2004 from Rockhurst University. He has served as the 11th Ward Committeeman for Jackson County. He is a former board member for Truman Medical Center and a former member of the Kansas City Planning Commission. He is also a member of the Indian Mound Neighborhood Association. Rep. Rizzo attends Holy Rosary Catholic Church. He was elected by the Democratic Caucus to the position of Minority Whip in 2013 and again in 2015. He serves on the Select Committee on Budget, the Select Committee on Rules and the Joint Committee on Government Accountability. In addition to his legislative duties, Rep. Rizzo is a marketing consultant. Elected to the House: 2010, 2012, 2014. Democrat.

District 20—BILL E. KIDD

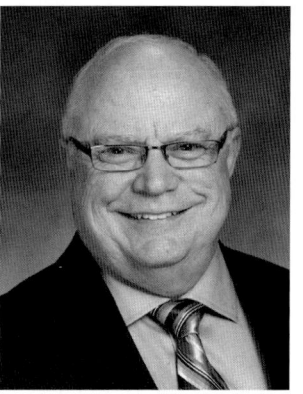

Capitol office: Room 201-E; phone (573) 751-3674
Email address: *bill.kidd@house.mo.gov*
House committees: Appropriations–Revenue, Transportation and Economic Development; Banking; Elections; Telecommunications.

Biography: Rep. Kidd is a 1971 graduate of Yukon Oklahoma High School in Yukon, Okla., and received his Bachelor of Science degree in electrical engineering and technology from Oklahoma State University. Prior to his legislative duties, he held various corporate positions and was a small business owner. He has held the the the following certifications or licenses: life and health insurance broker; real estate broker; Securities and Exchange license Series 6, 63 and 65; registered investment advisor; Johnson County, Kan., Class A contractor license; served as reserve deputy sheriff of Collin County, Texas; and served on the Independence Parks Commission. Rep. Kidd currently volunteers as a member of the command staff for the Emergency Operations Center of Eastern Jackson County and the City of Independence. He resides in Independence and has two adult children. Elected to the House: 2014. Republican.

District 21—IRA ANDERS

Capitol office: Room 101-E; phone (573) 751-5701
Home address: 731 N. Spring, Independence 64050
Email address: *ira.anders@house.mo.gov*
House committees: Elementary and Secondary Education; Pensions; Utility Infrastructure.

Biography: Born April 15, 1942. Graduate of Moundridge H.S., Moundridge, Kan.; Emporia State Univ., Emporia, Kan., B.S. and M.S. in education. Ira and his wife, Nina, have two children, Jon and Amy, and a daughter-in-law, Cindy. Retired elementary teacher, Independence Public Schools. Former member of the Independence Board of Education. Former president Independence NEA. Member: Mo. Historical Society; Jackson County Historical Society; Sierra Club; National Wildlife Federation; Truman Library Institute; United Eastern Democrats; and Mo. NEA Retired. In 2009, Ira and Nina received the Independence Citizens of the Year Award and the Brian and Sharon Snyder Historical Building Preservation Award. Mo. NEA Education awards, 2011 and 2013. He also serves on the Select Committee on Finance Institutions and and Taxation and the Joint Committee on Public Employee Retirement. Elected to House: 2010, 2012, 2014. Democrat.

District 22—**BRANDON ELLINGTON**

Capitol office: Room 101-C; phone (573) 751-3129
Email address: *brandon.ellington@house.mo.gov*
House committees: Appropriations–Public Safety and Corrections; Energy and the Environment; Small Business; Ways and Means.

Biography: Rep. Ellington, who lives in Kansas City, was born on Nov. 18, 1980. He represents part of Jackson County. Rep. Ellington is a 1999 graduate of Paseo High School in Kansas City. He also attended Penn Valley University and the University of Missouri–Kansas City. Rep. Ellington is the co-founder of Voices of the People and serves as president of I Am My Brother's Keeper. He also is a board member of Oak Park Neighborhood Association and a member of Consolidated Social Service Works, Operation Promise Land and G.Y.R.L. Rep. Ellington is chair of the Missouri Legislative Black Caucus. He also serves on the Special Committee on Security Infrastructure of the Capitol Complex, the Special Committee on Urban Issues (vice chair), and the Joint Committee on Corrections. Elected to the House: 2011 (special election), 2012, 2014. Democrat.

District 23—**RANDY D. DUNN**

Capitol office: Room 116-1; phone (573) 751-0538
Email address: *randy.dunn@house.mo.gov*
House committees: Appropriations–Revenue, Transportation, and Economic Development; Economic Development and Business Attraction and Retention.

Biography: Born Nov. 18, 1982, in Kansas City. Rep. Randy Dunn currently resides there. He is a licensed realtor and small business owner. He previously served as a city planner. He attends St. James United Methodist Church. He is involved with the following organizations: Alpha Phi Alpha Fraternity, Inc.; Omicron Xi Lambda Chapter; Construction Committee for Kansas City Habitat for Humanity, member; Steering Committee for Greater Kansas City Food Policy Coalition, member; Kansas City Youth Court, board member; Freedom, Inc.; and Vine Street District Council, board member. A graduate of Raytown South H.S., he obtained his B.A. in urban affairs and his M.P.A. from the Univ. of Mo.–Kansas City, where he was also a HUD Fellow. He is currently in his second year of law school at UMKC. Elected to the House: 2012, 2014. Democrat.

District 24—**JUDY MORGAN**

Capitol office: Room 101-G; phone (573) 751-4485
District address: 3837 Campbell St., Kansas City 64109
Email address: *judy.morgan@house.mo.gov*
House committees: Emerging Issues in Education; Fiscal Review.

Biography: Born Jan. 11, 1948, Kansas City. Graduate of University of Missouri–Kansas City, bachelor's degree in secondary education, and master's degree in guidance and counseling. She and her husband, Gene, have one daughter, a son-in-law and a grandson. Rep. Morgan is a retired Kansas City school teacher and American Federation of Teachers Local Union president. Member: American Federation of Teachers; Missouri Association of Social Welfare board member; and Greater Kansas City Women's Political Caucus, Missouri Legislative chair. She serves on the Select Committee on Education. Elected to the House: 2011, 2012, 2014. Democrat.

District 25—**JEREMY LaFAVER**

Capitol office: Room 105J; phone (573) 751-2437
Email address: *jeremy.lafaver@house.mo.gov*
House committees: Appropriations–Higher Education; Budget; Emerging Issues; General Laws.

Biography: Rep. LaFaver resides with his wife, Stephanie, and daughters, Isabelle and Caroline, in Kansas City. He received his bachelor's degree from Kansas State University before working as a legislative staffer and then an aide to the president of the University of New Mexico. In addition, he served his country overseas in the United States Peace Corps as a community health education volunteer in Turkmenistan. Jeremy spends much of his free time volunteering for local organizations that help children who are survivors of abuse and neglect. Elected to the House: 2012, 2014. Democrat.

District 26—**GAIL McCANN BEATTY**

Capitol office: Room 130-DB; phone (573) 751-2124
District address: PO Box 22333, Kansas City 64113
Email address: *gail.beatty@house.mo.gov*
House committees: *Ex officio* member of all committees of the House. Budget; Professional Registration and Licensing.

Biography: Assistant Minority Floor Leader. Rep. Gail McCann Beatty represents the Kansas City metro area. She is a member of the Missouri Legislative Black Caucus and board member and president of the Missouri Legislative Black Caucus Foundation. She also serves as the 16th Ward Jackson County Democratic Committeewoman and the state 9th Senatorial District Committeewoman. Prior to running for the Legislature, Rep. Beatty served on the Missouri Real Estate Appraisers Commission and the Missouri Tourism Commission. Rep. Beatty is a graduate of Pembroke Hill High School and received her B.A. in political science from Stanford University. She resides in Kansas City with her husband, Bruce, and is a general certified real estate appraiser. Elected to the House: 2010, 2012, 2014. Democrat.

District 27—**BONNAYE MIMS**

Capitol office: Room 103B; phone (573) 751-7639
District address: PO Box 9604, Kansas City 64134
Email address: *bonnaye.mims@house.mo.gov*
House committees: Appropriations–Health, Mental Health and Social Services; Corrections; Ethics; Higher Education.

Biography: Rep. Bonnaye Mims was born in Kansas City and currently resides there. She has four children and eight grandchildren. Graduate of Paseo High School, Kansas City; Park University— associate's degree, liberal arts; bachelor's degree, public administration and political science; M.P.A., business government/labor management. Formerly a forensic coordinator for the Mo. Dept. of Mental Health. Former president, Hickman Mills School Board, 2008 to 2012; president, AFL-CIO AFSCME Local 1812, 1992–1998; and Jackson County Democratic Committee for 20 years, vice chair for six years. Rep. Mims attends St. Paul AME Zion Church. Member: Hickman Mills School Board, 2001 to present; Order of Eastern Star (Lone Star #2 and Golden Circle); Daughters, Allah Court #6; Citizens Association; and South Kansas City Alliance. She also serves on the Joint Committee on Education. Elected to the House: 2012, 2014. Democrat.

District 28—**TOM McDONALD**

Capitol office: Room 109A; phone (573) 751-9851
Home address: 8120 Kentucky Ave., Raytown 64138
Email address: *tom.mcdonald@house.mo.gov*
House committees: Trade and Tourism; Transportation; Utility Infrastructure.

Biography: Born Sept. 17, 1946, in Omaha, Neb. A 1965 graduate of St. Francis High School in Council Bluffs, Iowa. Received undergraduate degree in advertising communication. Resides in Raytown. He and his wife, Lois, have 12 children and eight grandchildren. Retired after 18 years as retail environment and industrial designer for Hallmark Cards Inc. Worked for 13 years as partner with the advertising firm of McDonald, Slater and Associates. Acting committeeman for Jackson Co. Democrats; active member of Raytown Democrats Assoc. and Raytown Chamber of Commerce; and belongs to numerous civic and service organizations. In 2007, he and his wife received a National Angels in Adoption Award from the United States Congress. Rep. McDonald also serves on the Select Committee on State and Local Government, the Select Committee on Legislative Research and the Joint Committee on Transportation Oversight. Elected to the House: 2008, 2010, 2012, 2014. Democrat.

District 29—**VACANCY**

District 30—**MIKE CIERPIOT**

Capitol office: Room 302-A; phone (573) 751-0907
Email address: *mike.cierpiot@house.mo.gov*
House committees: *ex officio* member of all House committees; Ethics (chair); Administration and Accounts.

Biography: Majority Floor Leader. Born Jan. 14, 1953. Graduate of De La Salle High School, 1971. Attended Longview and University of Missouri–Kansas City. He Lives in Lee's Summit, Mo., with his wife of 43 years, Connie. They have two sons and two grandchildren. He is retired from SBC/AT&T, where he worked for 38 years. Mike is a member of the NRA and Missouri Right to Life. He is an avid biker and has run two marathons. Elected to the House: 2010, 2012, 2014. Republican.

District 31—**SHEILA SOLON**

Capitol office: Room 305-B; phone (573) 751-8636
Email address: *sheila.solon@house.mo.gov*
House committees: Government Efficiency; Veterans.

Biography: Rep. Solon lives in Blue Springs with her husband of 29 years, Charlie. They have two children; Lindsey, a first grade school teacher with the Blue Springs School District, and Spencer, who is studying engineering. She is an account coordinator with Parlux Fragrances. Served three years on the Blue Springs City Council and as mayor *pro tem*, and nine years on the Blue Springs Planning Commission. Chair of the Comprehensive Plan Review Commission, Blue Springs; Board of Zoning and Adjustment, Charter Review committees; Capital Improvements committee; Bond Task Force Committee; and the Citizen's Police Academy of Blue Springs. She serves on the Blue Springs School District Citizens Advisory Council and was PTA president at Cordill-Mason Elementary. She attends the First United Methodist Church in Blue Springs. She serves as chair of the Select Committee on State and Local Governments. Elected to the House: 2010, 2012, 2014. Republican.

District 32—**JEANIE LAUER**

Capitol office: Room 413-B; phone (573) 751-1487
Email address: *jeanie.lauer@house.mo.gov*
House committees: Appropriations–Higher Education (vice chair); Children and Families; Public Safety and Emergency Preparedness; Utility Infrastructure.

Biography: Born May 8, 1954, in Cape Girardeau, Rep. Lauer currently resides in Blue Springs. She has a son, Chris. She is a graduate of Perryville High School, and received a B.S. in mathematics from Southeast Missouri University and her M.B.A. from Central Michigan University. In addition to her legislative duties, Rep. Lauer is the founder and owner of The Management Edge, a firm providing mediation, strategic planning and performance improvement services to area enterprises. She also served as the Blue Springs District 1 City Councilwoman. She attends Timothy Lutheran Church in Blue Springs and is a past president of the congregation. Rep. Lauer also serves on the Select Committee on Commerce (vice chair) and the Select Committee on Rules. Elected to the House: 2010, 2012, 2014. Republican.

District 33—**DONNA S. PFAUTSCH**

Capitol office: Room 236-B; phone (573) 751-9766
Email address: *donna.pfautsch@house.mo.gov*
House committees: Appropriations—Elementary and Secondary Education; Economic Development and Business Attraction and Retention.

Biography: Rep. Pfautsch represents parts of Cass, Jackson and Lafayette counties. Prior to being elected, she served as alderwoman and mayor *pro tem* for the city of Harrisonville. A lifelong resident of Cass Co., Rep. Pfautsch grew up on a large crop and dairy farm south of Pleasant Hill. She graduated from Pleasant Hill High School, and received bachelor's and master's degrees from the University of Central Missouri. She retired in 2012 after 40 years as a teacher and gifted-education facilitator in the Harrisonville School District. Rep. Pfautsch and her husband, Larry, own a 110-acre Century Farm southeast of Pleasant Hill. They have two grown children, Tobias Ford and Emily Boyd. She also serves on the Select Committee on Rules (vice chair) and the Select Committee on State and Local Government. Elected to the House: 2012, 2014. Republican.

District 34—**REBECCA ROEBER**

Capitol office: Room 116-3; phone (573) 751-1456
Email address: *rebecca.roeber@house.mo.gov*
House committees: Elementary and Secondary Education; Health Insurance; Transportation

Biography: Born May 25, 1958, in Kansas City. She has a B.S. in elementary education from Avila University, Kansas City, Mo. She is married to Rick and is the mother of two children: Andrea and Nathan. She also has a grandson, Raiden. Rep. Roeber was a classroom teacher in the Raytown school district for 17 years. She taught 6th grade English. Before beginning her teaching career, she was a homemaker for several years while her children were small. Prior to that, she was an office manager at a local car dealership. Rep. Roeber also serves on the Select Committee on Insurance (vice chair) and the Special Committee on Urban Issues. Elected to the House: 2014. Republican.

District 35—**GARY L. CROSS**

Capitol office: Room 112; phone (573) 751-1459
District address: PO Box 1737, Lee's Summit 64063
Email address: *gary.cross@house.mo.gov*
House committees: Emerging Issues (vice-chair); Small Business (vice chair); Local Government; Ways and Means.

Biography: Born in Independence. A graduate of Lee's Summit High School. Received an A.A. in automotive marketing, Northwood University, Midland, Mich;, and a B.S. in business administration, University of Central Missouri, Warrensburg. Lives in Lee's Summit with his wife, Jan; they have two daughters. He is a small business owner. Member: Woods Chapel United Methodist Church; NFIB, 1985–1991; Mid-America Association of Real Estate Investors; Lee's Summit Chamber of Commerce; and an Eagle Scout. Elected to the House: 2010, 2012, 2014. Republican.

District 36—**VACANCY**

District 37—JOE RUNIONS

Capitol office: Room 101F; phone (573) 751-0238
District address: 12336 Norton Ave., Grandview 64030
Email address: *joe.runions@house.mo.gov*
House committees: Employment Security; Energy and the Environment; Government Efficiency.

Biography: Born Nov. 6, 1940, in Kansas City, Mo. Graduated from Ruskin High School in 1958. Currently resides in Grandview with his wife, Janice. They have two children and two grandchildren. Member of St. Thomas More Catholic Church; completed four years of Electrical Apprentice School; electrician for 42 years and is a current member of the International Brotherhood of Electrical Workers, Local 124; former president of the Muscular Dystrophy Association; former grand knight and current member of the O'Hara Council of the Knights of Columbus; served on the Grandview Board of Aldermen for seven years; former advisor for the Kansas City Port Authority; former member of the Grandview Planning Commission; and former member of the Missouri Municipal League and the National League of Cities. Member of the Jackson County Democratic Committee. He also serves on the Joint Committee on Public Employee Retirement. Elected to the House: 2012, 2014. Democrat.

District 38—T.J. BERRY

Capitol office: Room 205; phone (573) 751-2238
District address: PO Box 512, Kearney 64060
Email address: *tj.berry@house.mo.gov*
House committees: Trade and Tourism; Consumer Affairs

Biography: Born Sept. 11, 1965. Rep. Berry is a life-long resident of Clay County and currently resides in Kearney with his wife and two children. He received his Bachelor of Science degree in graphic arts management from Central Missouri State University in 1987. He owned and operated Business Cards, Ltd., for 20 years. Rep. Berry serves as a deacon at First Baptist Church of Kearney and is a member of the Excelsior Springs and Kearney chambers of commerce and Rotary Club. He is also a member of the Missouri Technology Corporation Board, where he sits on the investment board. He chairs the Select Committee on Utilities, as well as the Kansas City Caucus. He also serves on the Select Committee on Financial Institutions and Taxation. Elected to the House: 2010, 2012, 2014. Republican.

District 39—JOE DON MCGAUGH

Capitol office: Room 236-A; phone (573) 522-0439
District address: 11 W. Washington, Carrollton 64633
Email address: *joedon.mcgaugh@house.mo.gov*
House committees: Civil and Criminal Proceedings (chair); Agriculture Policy; Elections.

Biography: Born Nov. 29, 1983, in Carrollton. Graduate of Univ. of Mo.–Columbia, 2006, B.A. in agricultural economics and minor in political science; Univ. of Mo.–K.C., 2010; and Juris Doctorate. Member: Alpha Gamma Rho Fraternity, Mo. Farm Bureau, Mo. Cattleman's Assoc., NRA, Wakanda Lodge #52 AF & AM, Carrollton Lions Club, and Carroll County Univ. of Mo. Extension Council. Attends Carrollton United Methodist Church. Served as counselor and city attorney for the Town of Carrollton. Attorney at McGaugh Law Offices. He resides in Carrollton with his wife, Kassie, and their three daughters, Nora Kate, Vivian and Gemma. Awards: 2014 Farm Bureau Friend of Agriculture; Mo. Association of County Clerks and Election Authorities Legislative award; Missouri Judicial Conference Outstanding Legislative Service; and Mo. Cattlemen's Assoc. 2014 Legislator of the Year. He also serves on the Select Committee on Judiciary (vice chair) and the Joint Committee on Administrative Rules. Elected to the House 2012, 2014. Republican.

District 40—JIM HANSEN

Capitol office: Room 405A; phone (573) 751-4028
Home address: 5877 Hwy. C, Frankford 63441
Email address: *jim.hansen@house.mo.gov*
House committees: Health Insurance (chair); Economic Development and Business Attraction and Retention; Emerging Issues; Small Business.

Biography: Born Jan. 24, 1947, in Hannibal. Rep. Hansen resides in Frankford with his wife, Cindy. They have three children: Erin, Brad and Brett. There is also daughter-in-law Heidi, Brett's wife, and son-in-law, Donald, Erin's husband, and their son, Ty. Rep. Hansen represents Ralls, Monroe, Pike and part of Lincoln counties. He graduated from Hannibal High School in 1965 and earned a Bachelor of Science degree in 1969 from the University of Arizona and a master's in secondary education. He retired in 2002 as vice president of the State Farm Insurance office in Columbia, Mo. He was elected to the Hannibal School Board in 1980. Rep. Hansen is a member of Home Care/Hospice Foundation Board, Pike County Health Department and the Adiel Baptist Church. Additionaly, Rep. Hansen served in the U.S. Army. He also serves on the Select Committee on Insurance. Elected to the House: 2012, 2014. Republican.

District 41—RANDY PIETZMAN

Capitol office: Room 201D; phone (573) 751-9459
Email address: *randy.pietzman@house.mo.gov*
House committees: Conservation and Natural Resources; Property, Casualty, and Life Insurance; Small Business

Biography: Born June 1, 1961, in Troy. Rep. Pietzman graduated from Troy Buchanan High School. Rep. Pietzman has been a small business owner for 29 years, operating Pietzman Concrete. He and his family are members of the Faith Christian Family Church in Warrenton. Rep. Pietzman serves as vice president of the Board of Liberty Christian Academy in Wright City. He is also a member of the advisory board for El Shaddai Ranch. Rep. Pietzman and his wife of 29 years, Faith, are the proud parents of three biological children, Danielle, Erin and Jacob, and one adopted son, Vince. They are also the proud grandparents of three grandsons, Dillon, Gavin and Harrison. Rep. Pietzman serves on the Select Committee on Financial Institutions and Taxation. Elected to the House: 2014. Republican.

District 42—BART KORMAN

Capitol office: Room 113; phone (573) 751-2689
Email address: *bart.korman@house.mo.gov*
House committees: Telecommunications (chair); Transportation (vice-chair); Agriculture Policy; Utility Infrastructure.

Biography: Represents Montgomery County and parts of St. Charles and Warren counties. He is a 1999 University of Missouri–Columbia graduate with a B.S. in agricultural systems management and a B.S. in agricultural engineering. That same year, he also graduated from the Missouri Auction School, joining the family auction business of Korman Auction Service. After graduation, he joined Lewis-Bade, Inc., in Warrenton, Mo., as an engineer and surveyor. He has furthered his professional development with dual certification as a professional land surveyor and a professional engineer. He and his wife, Sarah, have three children: Wyatt, Grant and Alice. He also serves on the Select Committee on Utilities. Elected to the House: 2010, 2012, 2014. Republican.

District 43—**JAY D. HOUGHTON**

Capitol office: Room 236-A, phone (573) 751-3649
Email address: *jay.houghton@house.mo.gov*
House committees: Agriculture Policy (chair); Appropriations—Agriculture, Conservation and Natural Resources; Appropriations—General Administration.

Biography: Born Oct. 27, 1966, in Kansas City, Rep. Houghton was raised near Monticello, Mo., and currently resides in Martinsburg. Rep. Jay D. Houghton represents Audrain and part of Callaway counties. Rep Houghton is a 1984 graduate of Highland High School. He attended the University of Missouri–Columbia. He has two children, Tyler and Hunter. In addition to his legislative duties, Rep. Houghton works in agriculture, Missouri's No. 1 industry. Rep. Houghton is the nephew of Sen. Brian Munzlinger, a former state representative, who currently serves Missouri's 18th Senate District. In addition, Rep. Houghton's great-great-great uncle, and his great-great-great-great grandfather, served as state representatives. He also serves on the Select Committee on Agriculture. Elected to the House: 2010, 2012, 2014. Republican.

District 44—**CALEB ROWDEN**

Capitol office: Room 415-B; phone (573) 751-1169
Email address: *caleb.rowden@house.mo.gov*
House committees: Economic Development and Business Attraction and Retention (chair); Emerging Issues.

Biography: Born Oct. 22, 1982, Rep. Rowden attended Rock Bridge High School and the University of Missouri–Columbia. He owns Clarius Interactive, a media and marketing company. He and his wife, Aubrey, have one son, Willem Keane. They are members of Christian Chapel, in Columbia. Rep. Rowden was named one of Columbia's "20 under 40" by the *Columbia Business Times* in 2014. Member of Rotary Club of Columbia N.W. and the Columbia Chamber of Commerce. Board Member: Missouri Consolidated Health Care Plan Board of Trustees and Love Inc., of Columbia. Rep. Rowden also serves on the Joint Committee on Life Sciences, the Select Committee on Budget, the Select Committee on Commerce and the Special Committee on Urban Issues. Elected to the House: 2012, 2014. Republican.

District 45—**KIP KENDRICK**

Capitol office: Room 106B; phone (573) 751-4189
Email address: *kip.kendrick@house.mo.gov*
House committees: Appropriations–Elementary and Secondary Education; Conservation and Natural Resources; Health Insurance; Pensions.

Biography: Rep. Kip Kendrick represents part of the City of Columbia and Boone County. He is a native of Monroe City and is married to Sarah Kendrick. Graduate of Monroe City H.S. and Columbia College, with an undergraduate degree in psychology. He is pursuing a graduate degree in Higher Education Administration at the Univ. of Mo. Rep. Kendrick currently serves on the board of the Missouri Consolidated Health Care Plan. Member of the Intern Review Program. Named in *Columbia Business Times* "20 under 40," Class of 2015. He has a long history of civic engagement in Columbia. Until assuming his legislative position, he coordinated support services for Boone County Family Resources, assisting children with developmental disabilities and their families. Rep. Kendrick also serves on the Interim Investigative Committee on State Park Creation. Elected to the House: 2014. Democrat.

District 46—**STEPHEN WEBBER**

Capitol office: Room 106-A; phone (573) 751-9753
Email address: *stephen.webber@house.mo.gov*
House committees: Appropriations–Higher Education; Budget; Consumer Affairs; Labor and Industrial Relations; Workforce Standards and Development.

Biography: Born June 8, 1983, in Morgantown, W. Va. A 2001 graduate of Hickman High School; Eagle Scout recipient; graduate of St. Louis University, bachelor's degree in economics, 2006; and a 2013 graduate of the University of Missouri's School of Law. Served two tours in Iraq as a Marine infantryman (2004 and 2007). Previously on staff in the Washington D.C. office of U.S. Sen. Claire McCaskill. Elected to the House: 2008, 2010, 2012, 2014. Democrat.

District 47—**CHUCK BASYE**

Capitol office: Room 201G; phone (573) 751-1501
Email address: *chuck.basye@house.mo.gov*
House committees: Appropriations–Revenue, Transportation, and Economic Development (vice chair); Appropriations–Agriculture, Conservation and Natural Resources; Energy and the Environment; Labor and Insurance; Veterans.

Biography: Represents Boone, Howard, Randolph and Cooper counties. Born June 11, 1958, in Kansas City, he resides in Rocheport with his wife, Rhonda. They have three children: Randy, Robert and Tim, and six grandchildren. He attended St. Charles High School in St. Charles. Graduated from the University of Missouri–Columbia, B.S., agriculture. Rep. Basye served in the U.S. Marine Corps, from 1976–1980, as a field radio operator and parachutist. He retired from the Federal Aviation Administration in 2014, after 31 years of government service. Member: Mizzou Alumni Association; Farm Bureau; Missouri Cattlemen's Association; and Federated Republican Women of Boone County. He is also a lifetime member of the NRA. Elected to the House: 2014. Republican

District 48—**DAVE MUNTZEL**

Capitol office: Room 235BB; phone (573) 751-0169
Email address: *dave.muntzel@house.mo.gov*
House committees: Property, Casualty, and Life Insurance (vice chair); Agriculture Policy; Appropriations–Higher Education; Emerging Issues.

Biography: Born Sept. 30, 1950, in Boonville. Graduate of Central Missouri State University–Warrensburg, bachelor's degree in business administration, major in marketing. He and his wife, Marianne (Ann), have a daughter and a son. He is a fourth generation farmer, past district manager with Ralston Purina Company and Missouri Farm Bureau Insurance Service, Inc., a member of Masonic Wallace Lodge #456 at Bunceton and a past deacon and elder at the Broadway Presbyterian Church in Sedalia. Elected to the House: 2012, 2014. Republican.

District 49—**TRAVIS FITZWATER**

Capitol office: Room 116-A2; phone (573) 751-5226
Email address: *travis.fitzwater@house.mo.gov*
House committees: Property, Casualty and Life Insurance; Trade and Tourism; Utility Insurance.

Biography: Rep. Fitzwater was born in Cleveland, Ohio. He resides in Holts Summit with his wife, Amy. They have two daughters, Sadie and Eliza. He graduated from Presbyterian College in Clinton, S.C., with a B.A. in political science. He has worked in nonprofit management, and as staff in a campus ministry. He also owns Fitzwater Enterprises, LLC. Member: Jefferson City Church of the Nazarene, board member; Jefferson City Young Life, chair; Fulton Area Chamber of Commerce; National Rifle Association; Americans for Prosperity; Missouri Society of Association Executives; Missouri Governor's Student Leadership Forum; Callaway County Young Professionals and Jefferson City Young Republicans; and former member, Holts Summit Fire Protection District Board. Elected to the House: 2014. Republican.

District 50—**CALEB M. JONES**

Capitol office: Room 303-A; phone (573) 751-2134
Email address: *caleb.jones@house.mo.gov*
House committees: Pensions; Transportation.

Biography: Born Jan. 9, 1980. He resides in Columbia. Graduate of California H.S. Received degree in agricultural economics from Univ. of Mo.; J.D. from Univ. of Mo. School of Law. Worked for U.S. Rep. Kenny Hulshof, focusing on agricultural and environmental issues. Worked on 2004 Bush/Cheney presidential campaign. Appointed by President Bush to serve as special assistant in U.S. Dept. of Agriculture. He practices law with his brother, Clayton. Deacon at First Christian Church of California, Mo. Member: Farm Bureau; Moniteau County Cattleman's Assoc.; and California and Boonville chambers of commerce. He is the son of former state Rep. Kenny Jones. He is married to wife, Lindsey, and has one son, Max. Rep. Jones also serves on Select Committee on General Laws (chair); Select Committee on Budget; Joint Committee on Gaming and Wagering; Joint Committee on Legislative Research; and Joint Committee on Tax Policy. Elected to the House: 2010, 2012, 2014. Republican.

District 51—**DEAN A. DOHRMAN**

Capitol office: Room 115-G; phone (573) 751-2204
District address: PO Box 234, La Monte 65337
Email address: *dean.dohrman@house.mo.gov*
House committees: Higher Education (vice chair); Workforce Standards and Development (vice chair); Appropriations–Elementary and Secondary Education; Elementary and Secondary Education; Veterans.

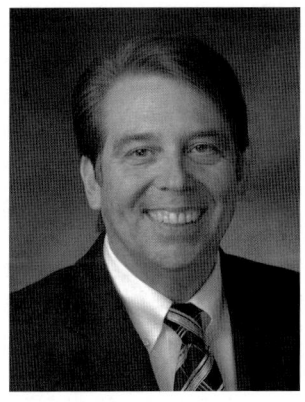

Biography: Graduated from La Monte H.S. Program coordinator and faculty member of Applied Social Sciences and Public Management, Colo. State Univ.–Global Campus; adjunct faculty, Mo. Valley College. Graduate of State Fair Community College, A.A., Alumni of the Year Award, 2013; Univ. of Central Mo., B.A., history/political science, *cum laude*; M.A. history, Univ. of Mo.–K.C. and M.A., political science, and Ph.D. Attends Wesley United Methodist Church. Member: Sedalia Lions Club; Pettis County Historical Society; and Warrensburg Chamber of Commerce. Past president, West Central Mo. Assessors Assoc.; past treasurer, Show-Me Honor Flight; and past presidential management intern. Vice chair, Interim Committee on Mo. Military Impact and Sustainability; Interim Committee on Emerging Issues in Agriculture Policy; Natl. Conference of State Legislators; and Military and Veterans Task Force. Member of Mo. River Caucus and Privacy Caucus. Elected to the House: 2012, 2014. Republican.

District 52—**NATHAN BEARD**

Capitol office: Room 409-A; phone (573) 751-9774
District address: 316 S. Ohio, Sedalia 65301
Email address: *nathan.beard@house.mo.gov*
House committees: Economic Development and Business Attraction and Retention; Ethics, Children and Families; Professional Registration and Licensing.

Biography: Born March 9, 1978. Graduate of Smith-Cotton High School, Sedalia; Brigham Young University; University of Missouri-Kansas City, Juris Doctorate. He and his wife, Elisabeth, have five children: Elinor, Natalie, Gretchen, Andrew and Tennison. Attorney and partner at Beard and Associates Law Firm, LLC, and owns and operates a real estate company with his wife. Member and financial clerk, The Church of Jesus Christ of Latter-Day Saints, Sedalia; served two years as a full time Spanish-speaking missionary for his church in northern California; board member for American Red Cross; and Scout Master of Troop 150 of the Boy Scouts of America. Elected to the House: 2014. Republican.

District 53—**GLEN KOLKMEYER**

Capitol office: Room 400CA; phone (573) 751-1462
Email address: *glen.kolkmeyer@house.mo.gov*
House committees: Transportation (chair); Elections; Energy and the Environment.

Biography: Owner and CEO of Energy Transport Solutions, Inc., for 25 years. He spent 39 years as a volunteer firefighter and EMT with the Wellington-Napoleon Fire Protection District, with 20 years as fire chief. He was a former president of Missouri Propane Gas (Safety) Commission, Missouri Propane Gas Assoc. and Lafayette Co. Firefighters Assoc. He is also the current president of the Lafayette County Law Enforcement Restitution Fund, a member of the National Rifle Association, a past board member of the Wellington-Napoleon Protection District and the Lafayette County 9-1-1 Board. Rep. Kolkmeyer attends Calvary Baptist Church in Odessa. He resides in rural Wellington with his wife, Lisa. They have two children, Eric and Emily, and four grandchildren. Rep. Kolkmeyer also serves on the Select Committee on State and Local Government (vice chair) and the Joint Committee on Transportation Oversight (vice chair). Elected to the House: 2012, 2014. Republican.

District 54—**DENNY L. HOSKINS**

Capitol office: Room 301; phone (573) 751-4302
Email address: *denny.hoskins@house.mo.gov*
House committees: Higher Education; *ex officio* member of all committees of the House.

Biography: Speaker *Pro Tem*. Born Oct. 10, in Jefferson City. Resides in Warrensburg and has two children: Cole and Amelia. Graduated from Fatima High School; Central Missouri State University, *cum laude*, accounting. Specializes in auditing for not-for-profit, governmental and farming entities. Member: Missouri Brotherhood of Elks; American Institute of CPAs; Missouri Society of CPAs; Warrensburg, Holden and Clinton chambers of commerce; and Warrensburg Noon Rotary. Served in the Missouri Army National Guard. Principal with Cochran Head Vick & Co. Outstanding Service Awards: Mo. Humanities, 2014; Mo. Assoc. of Veteran Organizations, 2014; and Mo. Chamber 100% Club, 2014; Capitol Impact Award, 2015 Mo. Grocers Assoc. Elected to the House: 2008, 2010, 2012, 2014. Republican.

District 55—**RICK R. BRATTIN**

Capitol office: Room 114C; phone (573) 751-3783
District address: 22405 Excelsior Rd., Harrisonville 64701
Email address: *rick.brattin@house.mo.gov*
House committees: Corrections (vice chair), Small Business; Children, Families and Persons with Disabilities.

Biography: Born July 22, 1980, in Harrisonville. Rep. Brattin is a 1999 graduate of Lee's Summit High School. He has a lovely wife, Athena, and is a proud father of five children: Mariah, Kayla, Rick III, Garrett and Hannah. He represents central Cass County. In addition to his legislative duties, he owns and operates a small construction company. He also served honorably as a noncommissioned officer in the United States Marine Corps for six years. He is an active member of his church, Abundant Life Baptist Church; a member of the NRA; Chamber of Commerce; and NFIB. Elected to the House: 2010, 2012, 2014. Republican.

District 56—**JACK BONDON**

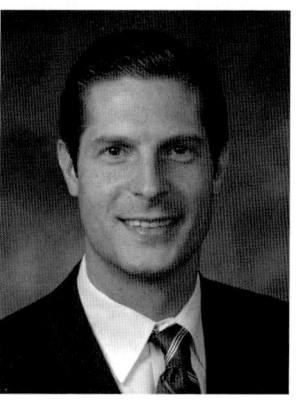

Capitol office: Room 201-F; phone (573) 751-2175
Email address: *jack.bondon@house.mo.gov*
House committees: Banking; Emerging Issues; Emerging Issues in Education; Energy and the Environment.

Biography: Rep. Bondon was born in Kansas City, Mo., and grew up on a cattle ranch in Lee's Summit. He currently resides in Belton with his wife, Melissa. They have one daughter, Cecilia. Rep. Bondon is a 2000 graduate of Rockhurst High School. He earned his bachelor's degree in business administration from Georgetown University in 2004. In addition to his legislative duties, Rep. Bondon is the vice president of Berbiglia Wine & Spirits. He attends St. Sabina Parish in Belton. He is a member of the National Rifle Association. He is also a member of the Belton Chamber of Commerce. Elected to the House: 2014. Republican.

District 57—**WANDA BROWN**

Capitol office: Room 412-C; phone (573) 751-3971
District address: 24515 Taylor Rd., Lincoln 65338
Email address: *wanda.brown@house.mo.gov*
House committees: Employment Security (chair); Banking; Consumer Affairs; Labor and Industrial Relations.

Biography: Wanda Brown represents all of Henry County and parts of Benton, Cass and Bates counties. She is a 1984 graduate of Benton County R-1 schools and attended State Fair Community College in Sedalia. She resides in Cole Camp with her husband, Bob. They have a daughter, Nicole. She formerly owned and operated the Benton County License Office until her election as state representative. Rep. Brown is a member of the NRA; Western Missouri Shooters Alliance; Missouri Cattlemen's Association; and the Missouri Farm Bureau. Elected to the House: 2010, 2012, 2014. Republican.

District 58—DAVID WOOD

Capitol office: Room 115-A; phone (573) 751-2077
District address: 7443 Hwy. 52, Versailles 65084
Email address: *david.wood@house.mo.gov*
House committees: Appropriations–Health, Mental Health and Social Services (vice chair); Emerging Issues in Education; Trade and Tourism.

Biography: Rep. Wood represents Morgan County and parts of Moniteau and Miller counties. Born April 15, 1961, in Jefferson City. Rep. Wood currently resides in Versailles with his wife, Cheryl. They have two sons, Jonathan and Patrick, and a granddaughter, Joanna; and two grandsons, Logan and Grayson. In addition to his legislative duties, he has worked as a telecom administrator for Capital Region Medical Center. He taught mathematics and computer science in Versailles for 25 years and was also a tech coordinator. He is a member of the First Christian Church of Versailles and serves on the board of directors for Quality Industries. A 1979 graduate of Eldon High School, Rep. Wood has a bachelor's degree in education with a specialization in mathematics from University of Central Missouri. Rep. Wood also serves on the Joint Committee on Education (chair) and the Select Committee on Education (vice chair). Elected to the House: 2012, 2014. Republican.

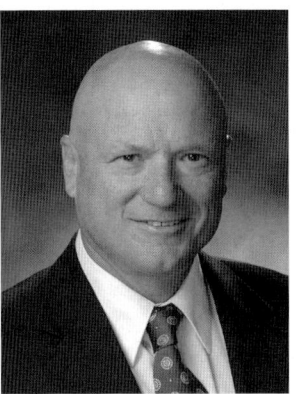

District 59—MIKE BERNSKOETTER

Capitol office: Room 414; phone (573) 751-0665
Email address: *mike.bernskoetter@house.mo.gov*
House committees: Ethics; Small Business; Utility Infrastructure.

Biography: Born Nov. 29, 1959. Graduate of Helias H.S., 1978. He and his wife Jeannette have four children: Brian, Krista, Kyle and Luke, and two grandchildren. They have owned and operated Art's Pest Control for the past 30 years. Member: Immaculate Conception Parish, serves as Eucharistic and hospitality minister; Knights of Columbus; Elks; Eagles; East Side Business Association; West Side Business Assoc.; Jefferson City Chamber of Commerce; Wardsville Lions Club; Home Builders Assoc.; Jefferson City Area Board of Realtors; National Federation of Independent Businesses; Farm Bureau; 2001 Jefferson City Chamber Leadership Class; Capital Region Board of Governors; Natl. Pest Management Assoc.; Mo. Pest Management Assoc., past president; and has received the John Veatch Award and Man of the Year Award for his work in the pest control industry. Rep. Bernskoetter also serves on the Select Committee on Agriculture and the Joint Committee on Public Employee Retirement. Elected to the House: 2010, 2012, 2014. Republican.

District 60—JAY BARNES

Capitol office: Room 306A; phone (573) 751-2412
Email address: *jay.barnes@house.mo.gov*
House committees: Government Oversight and Accountability (chair); Ethics (vice chair); Appropriations–General Administration; Consumer Affairs.

Biography: Married to Jane with four children. Born Dec. 27, 1979, in Jefferson City, Mo. A 1998 Graduate of Helias, 2002 graduate of University of Missouri–Columbia and a 2005 graduate of the University of Missouri School of Law. Attorney with Barnes and Associates. Attends Immaculate Conception Church in Jefferson City. Elected to the House: 2010, 2012. Republican.

District 61—**JUSTIN ALFERMAN**

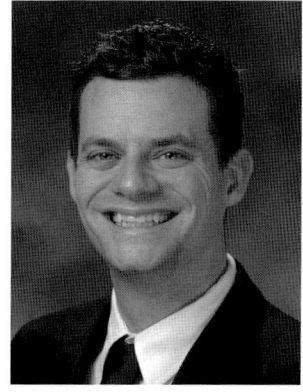

Capitol office: Room 116-2; phone (573) 751-6668
Email address: *justin.alferman@house.mo.gov*
House committees: Employment Security; Fiscal Review; Property, Casualty, and Life Insurance.

Biography: Born Feb. 3, 1986, in Washington, Mo. He resides in Hermann with his wife, Amy, and daughter, Layla. Graduate of St. Francis Borgia H.S., Washington, Mo., 2004;. East Central College, associate's degree in communication, 2006; Univ. of Mo.– Columbia, bachelor's degree in political science, 2008. Prior to his legislative duties, he worked as an executive assistant to Assistant Majority Floor Leader Rep. Mike Cierpiot. He has worked for former Rep. Ed Robb, former Rep. Brian Yates and conducted research and grassroots for the Missouri Republican Party. Member: Hermann Lion's Club; Hermann Regional Economic Development Council (*ad hoc*); Hermann Eagles Club; and Hermann Rod and Gun Club. He and his family attend St. George's Church in Hermann. Rep. Alferman also serves on the Select Committee on Budget, the Select Committee for State and Local Governments and the Special Committee on Urban Issues. Elected to the House: 2014. Republican

District 62—**TOM HURST**

Capitol office: Room 206C; phone (573) 751-1344
Email address: *tom.hurst@house.mo.gov*
House committees: Agriculture Policy (vice chair); Government Oversight and Accountability (vice chair); Trade and Tourism; Workforce Standards and Development.

Biography: Born Feb. 10, 1966, in Jefferson City. He resides in Meta with his wife, Staci. They have three children: Macey, Hayden and Emma. In addition to his legislative duties, he is an accountant, farmer, auctioneer, business owner and landlord. He received the Nat'l. Leadership Award. Honorary co-chair of the Business Council, and member of the Golden Key Natl. Honor Society. Member: St. Cecilia Church in Meta, Mo.; Farm Bureau; Fraternal order of the Eagles; Fraternal order of the Elks; Knights of Columbus; Missouri Cattlemen's Assoc.; Mo. Professional Auctioneers Assoc.; and Osage and Gasconade County 4-H. Served as treasurer of the City of Meta, president of Meta MFA and vice president/volunteer of the Meta Rural Fire Dept. Graduate of Fatima H.S., and received a B.S. in accounting from University of Missouri. Elected to the House: 2012, 2014. Republican.

District 63—**BRYAN SPENCER**

Capitol office: Room 200B; phone (573) 751-1460
District address: PO Box 445, Wentzville 63385
Email address: *bryan.spencer@house.mo.gov*
House committees: Employment Security (vice chair); Agriculture Policy; Utility Infrastructure.

Biography: Born Sept. 25, 1967, Rolla, Mo. Resides in Wentzville. Attended Culver-Stockton College, Canton, Mo.; received a B.S. in social science/education; Harris Stowe College, St. Louis, Mo., behavior disorder/learning disability certification; University of Missouri–St. Louis, M.Ed., administration education; and Truman University +30 Humanizing Education. Teacher, Francis Howell School District, 1990–2013, inducted into the Francis Howell Hall of Fame, 2011. BMH Outstanding Young Teacher, 2008. He has also been employed simultaneously as adaptive daily living instructor at Lighthouse for the Blind–Careers; Alcohol compliance officer/trainer at Aramark Sports and Entertainment Inc.; and education consultant at Metropolitan Psychiatric. Member: Church of Christ (Foristell); Wentzville Junior Chamber of Commerce, president, 2007; St. Charles Community Assistant Board, 2010–2012; and various others. Elected to the House: 2012, 2014. Republican.

District 64—**ROBERT CORNEJO**

Capitol office: Room 115-B; phone (573) 751-1484
District address: P.O. Box 346, St. Peters, MO 63376
Email address: *robert.cornejo@house.mo.gov*
House committees: Civil and Criminal Proceedings (chair); Government Oversight and Accountability; Health Insurance; Judiciary; Professional Registration and Licensing.

Biography: Born March 25, 1983, in St. Louis County. Rep. Cornejo currently lives in St. Peters with his wife Kara. They have a son, Clark, and a one-year old daughter, Nora. A 2001 graduate of Hazelwood Central, Rep. Cornejo graduated from Washington University in St. Louis with a degree in political science, with a second major in international business. In 2008, he earned his J.D. from University of Missouri–School of Law. In addition to his legislative duties, he is an attorney and a member of the law firm Kespohl, McCrary and Cornejo, LLC. In 2004, he interned for U.S. Sen. Jim Talent's St. Louis office. He is an active member in his church, Zion Lutheran Church in Harvester. Elected to the House: 2012, 2014. Republican.

District 65—**ANNE ZERR**

Capitol office: Room 315; phone (573) 751-3717
Email address: *anne.zerr@house.mo.gov*
House committees: Emerging Issues; Fiscal Review; Health and Mental Health Policy; *ex officio* member of Small Business, Trade and Tourism, and Economic Development and Business Attraction and Retention.
Biography: Serves on the Select Committee on Commerce (chair). Political science instructor, Lindenwood Univ., MBA, M.A., Lindenwood Univ. Member: NRA and the St. Charles Pachyderms. Awards: St. Louis Business Journal Legislative Award 2010, 2011, 2012; 2010 Distinguished Legislator Award, Mo. Community College Assoc.; 2010 Friend of Agriculture, Mo. Farm Bureau; 2011 Statesman Award, RCGA; 2011 YMCA Legislative Recognition; 2011 Committed Statesperson, National Multiple Sclerosis Society; 2012 Champion of Small Business, National Coalition for Capital; 2013 Chamber Champion, St. Louis Regional Chamber; 2014 St. Louis Building & Construction Trades Leadership Award; 2014 Champion for Disabilities Service Award, Easter Seals Midwest; 2014 Advocate of the Year, Family Advocacy & Community Training; and 2015 Mo. Assoc. of Rehabilitation Facilities Legislator of the Year Award. Elected to the House: 2008, 2010, 2012, 2014. Republican.

District 66—**TOMMIE PIERSON**

Capitol office: Room 101-H; phone (573) 751-6845
District address: 9950 Glen Owen Dr., St. Louis 63136
Email address: *tommie.pierson@house.mo.gov*
House committees: Appropriations–Education; Elementary and Secondary Education; Government Oversight and Accountability; Higher Education; Ways and Means.

Biography: Born Jan. 29, 1946, in Ripley, Tenn. Rep. Pierson represents part of St. Louis County. In 1965, he graduated from Beaumont High School in St. Louis. In addition to his legislative duties, he is pastor of Greater St. Mark Family Church. He also worked for General Motors as an assembly worker for 32 years. Rep. Pierson served on the Riverview Gardens School Board and is involved with the Citizens for Modern Transit. He resides in Bellefontaine Neighbors with his wife, JoAnn. They have three children: Linell Green, Tommie Pierson Jr. and Lavenia Draper. Elected to the House: 2010, 2012, 2014. Democrat.

District 67—**ALAN K. GREEN**

Capitol office: Room 102BA; phone (573) 751-2135
Email address: *alan.green@house.mo.gov*
House committees: Appropriations–General Administration; Banking; Government Efficiency; Small Business.

Biography: Born Sept. 9, 1960. Rep. Green is a 32-year resident of Florissant. He is the proud father of four children: Tiffany, Alan Jr., Garrett and Trevor. Attended Ecorse H.S., Ecorse, Mich. Graduated from Univ. of Texas at Tyler, B.S. in criminal justice and American diplomacy; National Louis Univ., master's in management and development of human resources; Lindenwood Univ., master's in business administration; United Theological Seminary Survine Bible College of St. Louis, Ph.D. in religious education; and Univ. of Va., Certification, Executive Leadership. Rep. Green worked for St. Louis County Executives Buzz Westfall and Charlie Dooley. He has also worked for Lutheran Family and Children Services as a director and has served as a St. Louis police officer. His work has been recognized by the White House, *Wall Street Journal*, *New York Times*, *St. Louis Post-Dispatch*, HBO and many other awards. He is the CEO of Green & Associates LLC, which specializes in surety bonds, payment bonds, finance, government and business consulting. Elected to the House: 2014 (special election). Democrat.

District 68—**KEITH ENGLISH**

Capitol office: Room 317A; phone (573) 751-9628
Email address: *keith.english@house.mo.gov*
House committees: Small Business.

Biography: Rep. English was born on Nov. 4, 1967, in Saint Louis. He graduated from Hazelwood Central High School in 1986, attended Saint Louis University and graduated from the IBEW Joint Apprenticeship Training Center in 1989. In addition to his legislative duties, Rep. English has been an IBEW electrician, Local 1, for 25 years. He has been a business owner for 10 years and served as a Florissant city councilman from 2007–2012. Rep. English has three children and six grandchildren. He and his wife, Kelly, attend First Christian Church of Florissant. He also serves on the Select Committee on Insurance, the Select Committee on Utilities and the Joint Committee on Gaming and Wagering. Elected to the House: 2012, 2014. Independent.

District 69—**MARGO McNEIL**

Capitol office: Room 130DC; phone (573) 751-5365
District address: 124 St. Stanislaus Ct., Florissant 63031
Email address: *margo.mcneil@house.mo.gov*
House committees: Appropriations–Elementary and Secondary Education; Emerging Issues in Education; Energy and the Environment; Health Insurance.

Biography: Born June 22, 1948, in Cincinnati, Ohio. Graduate of Hannibal High School and University of Cincinnati with a B.A. in fine arts and an M.A. in art education. Rep. McNeil currently lives in Hazelwood with her husband Jim. They have three adult children: Nathan, Stuart and Megan. She served 22 years as an art teacher in the Ferguson Florissant School District. In 2006, was elected to the St. Louis Community College Board of Trustees and served six years. She attends St. Andrew United Methodist Church, Florissant. Member: Missouri NEA Retired; North County Legislative Labor Club; ADK sorority; Greater North County Chamber of Commerce; North County, Inc.; Women's Political Caucus; League of Women Voters; and National Organization for Women. She also serves on the Select Committe on Insurance and the Joint Committee on Life Sciences. Elected to the House: 2008, 2010, 2012, 2014. Democrat.

District 70—**BILL OTTO**

Capitol office: Room 103-BC; phone (573) 751-4163
Email address: *bill.otto@house.mo.gov*
House committees: Banking; Consumer Affairs; Property, Casualty and Life Insurance; Veterans.

Biography: Born Jan. 1, 1956, in St. Louis. Attended Meramec Community College and Embry-Riddle Aeronautical University. He and his wife Kathy have six children and five grandchildren. He worked for 31 years as an air traffic controller. He is a founding member of the National Air Traffic Controllers Association, where he served as president and represented air traffic controllers as U.S. representative on an international committee. He also served on the Bridgeton City Council from 1989–1995; St. Charles Board of Adjustment; St. Peters Green Environmental and Solid Waste Advisory Committee; and a Boy Scout leader, youth baseball coach and Pattonville Team leader. A veteran, he served seven years in the United States Navy. He also serves on the Select Committee on Insurance. Elected to the House: 2012, 2014. Democrat.

District 71—**SUE MEREDITH**

Capitol office: Room 103BB; phone (573) 751-4183
District address: 8 Sunview Ln., St. Louis 63146
Email address: *susan.meredith@house.mo.gov*
House committees: Children and Families; Conservation and Natural Resources.

Biography: Rep. Sue Meredith serves as chair of the Missouri Children's Services Commission. She also serves on the Select Committee on Agriculture, Select Committee on Social Services and the Joint Committee on Neglect and Abuse. She is a volunteer Court Appointed Special Advocate (CASA) for children removed from their homes due to abuse or neglect. A lifelong Missourian, she holds a B.A in political science, an M.A. in legal studies and paralegal certification from Webster University. She served two terms on the Ritenour School District Board of Education. Member: National Council of Jewish Women (NCJW) and serving on the Human Trafficking Task Force. She and her husband Michael have three adult daughters and two granddaughters. Elected to the House: 2012, 2014. Democrat.

District 72—**MARY NICHOLS**

Capitol office: Room 101-A; phone (573) 751-1832
Email address: *mary.nichols@house.mo.gov*
House committees: Appropriations–Public Safety and Corrections; Banking; Financial Institutions; Telecommunications.

Biography: Rep. Nichols received her A.A. from Monticello College in 1969, and her B.S. from Southern Illinois University in 1972. She also received her teaching certificate from the state of Illinois in 1972. She resides in Maryland Heights with her husband, Robert K. Nichols. She is a residential real estate sales person for Coldwell Banker Gundaker in Maryland Heights. She served four terms on the Maryland Heights City Council and two terms as the Maryland Heights Township committeewoman. Rep. Nichols also serves on the Select Committee on Financial Institutions and Taxation, the Joint Committee on Real Property Tax Increment Allocation Redevelopment and the Joint Committee on Solid Waste Management District Operations. Elected to the House: 2010, 2012, 2014. Democrat.

District 73—**COURTNEY CURTIS**

Capitol office: Room 116; phone (573) 751-0855
Email address: *courtney.curtis@house.mo.gov*
House committees: Appropriations–Health, Mental Health, and Social Services; Government Oversight and Accountability; Ways and Means.

Biography: Freshman Democratic Caucus president. Born April 12, 1981, St. Louis, Mo. Graduate of McCluer Senior High School. Attended Columbia College and University of Missouri; studied accounting. Actively involved in various community projects including the Ferguson Youth Initiative. Named the 2013 Legislator of the Year by the Associated Students of the University of Missouri. He has also worked as an entrepeneur in the areas of human resources and information technology, specifically with technology start-ups. He also serves on the Special Committee on Urban Issues (chair) and the Joint Committee on Education. Elected to the House: 2012, 2014. Democrat.

District 74—**SHARON PACE**

Capitol office: Room 105-G; (573) 751-4726
Email address: *sharon.pace@house.mo.gov*
House committees: Appropriations–Revenue, Transportation and Economic Development; Emerging Issues; Health and Mental Health Policy; Telecommunications.

Biography: Minority Chief Deputy Whip. Born in St. Louis; proud parent of three daughters. Administrative experience in the health care industry; Alderwoman, City of Northwoods. Member, First Baptist Church. Attended Forest Park Community College; St. Louis University, emphasis in Business Management/Administration. Awards: 2015 Friend of Transit; 2015 Gutsy Woman; 2014 Veteran Feminists Medal of Honor; 2013 Outstanding Community Service, Lane Tabernacle C.M.E. Church; 2013 Community Service, North County Community Development Corp; Community Action Agency of St. Louis County, Inc., Child & Family Advocate; and Annie Malone Children & Family Services Center. Member: Women's Democratic Caucus, president; Mo. Legislative Black Caucus; Women Legislators of Mo., vice president; Democratic Caucus; NAACP; NBCSL; Community Resource Team: Ferguson, Florissant and Normandy; MOLLI's List; and Emily's List. She also serves on the Select Committee on Utilities. Elected to the House: 2008, 2010, 2012, 2014. Democrat.

District 75—**ROCHELLE WALTON GRAY**

Capitol office: Room 105E; phone (573) 751-5538
District address: 2320 Chambers Rd., St. Louis 63136
Email address: *rochelle.gray@house.mo.gov*
House committees: Fiscal Review; Professional Registration and Licensing; Public Safety and Emergency Preparedness.

Biography: Policy Chair and Deputy Whip. Born in St. Louis. Received a B.S. in public policy administration, Univ. of Mo.–St. Louis; legal administrator. Married to Alan Gray. Two children: Alan II and Alana. Hosted: Energy Assistance Workshops, Town Hall Meetings and Community Fairs. Promotes Sickle Cell and Colon Cancer Awareness. Awards: Annie Malone Child Advocate; National Council of Negro Women's Legacy; Top Ladies; and Community Service and Recognition Awards. Member: Christ Our Redeemer Church; NOBEL/Women; NCSL; NBCSL; Women Legislators of Missouri, pres.; WPC; Women's Democratic Caucus, chair; MLBC, secretary; MLBCF, parliamentarian; WPC; Winning Women Coalition; Molli's List; Emily's List; NOWL/NFWL, state director; WIG; Helping Hands Food Pantry, Board; and Community Action Alliance, 2nd vice; Ferguson Township. Serves on: Mo. Military Impact and Sustainability; Government Accountability; and Mo. Veterans Commission. Elected to the House: 2008, 2010, 2012, 2014. Democrat.

District 76—**JOSHUA D. PETERS**

Capitol office: Room 109-G, phone (573) 751-7605
District address: 3009 Abner Pl., St. Louis 63120-2123
Email address: *joshua.peters@house.mo.gov*
House committees: International Trade; Downsizing State Government; Appropriations–Public Safety and Corrections.

Biography: Born Aug. 25, 1987, in the City of St. Louis. He is a graduate of Lincoln University, where he served as president of the student body and graduated *magna cum laude* with a B.S. degree in political science. He served as a congressional legislative assistant to U.S. Rep. Wm. Lacy Clay for three years and was appointed by President Barack Obama as the confidential assistant to Secretary of Education Arne Duncan. Member: Cathedral Basilica of St. Louis; Rotary International; and Local Board, (Missouri) United States Selective Service System. He is a former board member of the Democratic Youth Council, Missouri. Elected to the House: 2013 (special election). Democrat.

District 77—**KIMBERLY M. GARDNER**

Capitol office: Room 109-I; phone (573) 751-1400
District address: PO Box 24782, St. Louis 63115
Email address: *kimberly.gardner@house.mo.gov*
House committees: Appropriations-Agriculture, Conservation and Natural Resources; Civil and Criminal Proceedings; Corrections.

Biography: Native of St. Louis City. Graduate of Harris Stowe University, B.S., health care administration; Saint Louis University Law School, Juris Doctor; and Saint Louis University School of Nursing, M.S., nursing. She has one daughter, Te'a. She is an attorney at Bell, Kirksey and Associates. Former assistant circuit attorney for the City of St. Louis. Member: Missouri Bar Association and Missouri Funeral Directors Association. She also serves on the Joint Committee on Legislative Research, the Select Committee on Judiciary, Select Committee on Rules and the Special Committee on Urban Issues. Elected to the House: 2012, 2014. Democrat.

District 78—**PENNY V. HUBBARD**

Capitol office: 105-B ; phone: (573) 751-2383
District address: 1017 N. 16th St., St. Louis 63106; phone: (314) 588-9342
Email address: *penny.hubbard@house.mo.gov*
House committees: Corrections; Public Safety and Emergency Preparedness; Government Oversight and Accountability.

Biography: Born Sept. 26, 1953, in St. Louis, Mo. A 1971 graduate of St. Alphonsus "Rock" H.S. Received an associates degree from Forest Park Community College, 1974. She lives in St. Louis, Mo., with her husband, Rodney Hubbard, Sr. They have four children. She was appointed by former Gov. Bob Holden to serve as a commissioner on the Mo. State Board of Probation and Parole from 2004 through 2010. She has more than 30 years of experience with the Department of Corrections, having served there in various capacities. Rep. Hubbard has the distinction of having served as the first female unit manager of the St. Louis Justice Center. She serves on the Mo. Health Facilities Review Committee-Certificate of Need. Awards: Carr Square Community Center Achievement Award, 2014; and the National Council of Negro Women, Distinguished Visionary Leadership Award, 2014. Elected to the House: 2010, 2012, 2014. Democrat.

District 79—MICHAEL BUTLER

Capitol office: Room 109D; phone (573) 751-6800
Email address: *michael.butler@house.mo.gov*
House committees: Economic Development and Business Attraction and Retention; Emerging Issues in Education; Small Business.

Biography: Rep. Michael Butler represents part of St. Louis City. Prior to his legislative duties, Rep. Butler gained experience in the legislature while serving as legislative aide in the office of state Sen. Robin Wright-Jones, and as legislative assistant to state Rep. Mary Wynne Still. During his 2012 campaign, he worked as an educator in the St. Louis Public School System. Rep. Butler has valuable private sector experience gained while employed as a manager at the home office of Wal-Mart Stores, Inc. in Bentonville, Ark. He holds a bachelor's degree in business from Alabama A&M University, where he also served as a board of trustees member. While working in the Legislature, he obtained a master's degree in public affairs from the University of Missouri–Columbia. Born and raised in the 79th district, Rep. Butler's childhood home is near the corner of Shaw Boulevard and South Spring Avenue. His father owns Pelican Printing in Midtown, and his grandfather taught for 20 years at Vashon High School, both in the 79th district. Rep. Butler is married to Erin K. Butler, and they have a one-year-old daughter, Kimber. Elected to the House: 2012, 2014. Democrat.

District 80—MICHAEL J. COLONA

Capitol office: Room 107; phone (573) 751-6736
Email address: *mike.colona@house.mo.gov*
House committees: Civil and Criminal Proceedings; Emerging Issues; Energy and the Environment; Property, Casualty, and Life Insurance.

Biography: Born April 18, 1969, in St. Louis. Graduated from Fox H.S. in Arnold in 1987; received bachelor's degree in political science from Truman State University in 1991; and received his J.D. from St. Louis University Law School in 1994. He is a board member for the St. Louis Effort for AIDS, an *ex officio* board member for the Grand Oak Hills Neighborhood Assoc. and is a member of the Missouri Association of Trial Attorneys. He also served as president of the Truman State University Alumni Association. In addition to his legislative duties, Rep. Colona is an attorney. He also serves on the Select Committee on Judiciary, the Select Committee on Utilities, the Joint Committee on Judiciary and the Joint Committee on Administrative Rules. Elected to the House: 2008, 2010, 2012, 2014. Democrat.

District 81—JACOB W. HUMMEL

Capitol office: Room 204; phone (573) 751-0438
Email address: *jake.hummel@house.mo.gov*
House committees: *Ex officio* member of all committees of the House.

Biography: Minority Floor Leader. Born May 24, 1976, in St. Louis. Rep. Hummel resides in St. Louis City with his wife, Sarah, and his son, Timothy. He is a 1994 graduate of St. Mary's Catholic High School. In addition to his legislative duties, Rep. Hummel is the secretary-treasurer of AFL-CIO. He has 17 years of experience as a union electrician and is a member of the International Brotherhood of Electrical Workers. He is also vice president of the St. Louis City Labor Club. He attends St. Stephen Protomartyr Catholic Church. He also is a member of the Carondelet Community Betterment Federation, Holly Hills Improvement Assoc., Boulevard Heights Neighborhood Assoc. and the Dutchtown South Community Corporation. Elected to the House: 2008, 2010, 2012, 2014. Democrat.

District 82—**MICHELE KRATKY**

Capitol office: Room 109-C; phone (573) 751-4220
Email address: *michele.kratky@house.mo.gov*
House committees: Administration and Accounts; Economic Development and Business Attraction and Retention; Professional Registration and Licensing; Trade and Tourism.

Biography: Born in St. Louis in 1957. Graduate of Southwest High School in St. Louis. Currently resides in St. Louis with her husband Fred Kratky. They have four sons: Anthony, Steven, Nickolas and Mark Mechler, and one granddaughter Hannah Eileen Kratky. Prior to her legislative duties, she served as vice president of governmental affairs for the St. Louis Association of Realtors. She also worked in the field of law for years as a court room clerk, assistant to several judges and a legal secretary. She was an appointed member of the St. Louis City Board of Adjustment and served as chair for two years. Her civic activities have included service on the RCGA Legislative Committee, Mayor's Lead Paint Task Force, Downtown Partnership Legislative Committee and the St. Louis Lead Prevention Coalition Legislative Committee. She also serves on the Select Committee on Commerce. Elected to the House: 2008 (special election), 2010, 2012, 2014. Democrat.

District 83—**GINA C. MITTEN**

Capitol office: Room 101B; phone (573) 751-2883
Email address: *gina.mitten@house.mo.gov*
House committees: Ethics (vice chair); Civil and Criminal Proceedings; Consumer Affairs; Government Oversight and Accountability; Health Insurance.

Biography: Minority Caucus Chair, 2015–2016. Received a B.G.S., *summa cum laude,* UM–St. Louis, minors in philosophy and political science and Juris Doctor, Washington University (primary editor, *Journal of Law and Policy*). Recipient: American Mock Trial Assoc. National All-American Attorney award, 2001 and Don Sommers Prize for Professional Responsibility, 2005. Served on the Richmond Heights City Council, 2004–2012, St. Louis County Municipal League Legislative Affairs Committee, 2005–2010, and Clayton/Richmond Heights Joint Study Committee, 2005–2006. Ms. Mitten has been an active supporter of the Maplewood Richmond Heights School District since 1998, and served on its Building Corporation since 2007. Attorney with St. Louis Lawyers Group, focusing on civil litigation and domestic relations. Member: 2013 Interim Medicaid committees. She also serves on the Select Committee on Judiciary, the Joint Committee on Administrative Rules and the Joint Committee on the Justice System. Elected to House: 2012, 2014. Democrat.

District 84—**KARLA MAY**

Capitol office: Room 101-J; phone (573) 751-2198
District office: PO Box 21339, St. Louis 63115
Email address: *karla.may@house.mo.gov*

House committees: Appropriations–Revenue, Transportation and Economic Development; Transportation; Employment Security.

Biography: Karla May is a lifetime resident of the City of St. Louis first ward, where her mother, City Register Parrie May, served as alderwoman. She is a graduate of St. Louis Univ., where she received her B.S. in business admin., and Lindenwood Univ., where she received her M.A. in teaching. She has been employed for the past 14 years at AT&T, and worked as a union steward with Communication Workers of America 6300. She also served on the legislative committee and lobbied the Legislature for years on issues affecting the lives of working men and women. She is a member of the Coalition of Black Trade Unionists, where she sits on the executive board; St. Louis City Labor Club; and CWA. Karla has been a board member for the St. Louis Philanthropic Board for the past 16 years. This board awards grants to agencies focused on education and programs that benefit residents of the City of St. Louis. She serves on the Select Committee on Budget. Elected to the House: 2010, 2012, 2014. Democrat.

District 85—**CLEM SMITH**

Capitol office: Room 105C; phone (573) 751-4468
District address: PO Box 210851, St. Louis 63121
Email address: *clem.smith@house.mo.gov*
House committees: Elections; Utility Infrastructure; Workforce Standards and Development.

Biography: Minority Whip team. Born in 1977, in St. Louis City. Rep. Smith is a graduate of Clayton High School, and received his bachelor's degree from Columbia College. He currently resides in St. Louis County. Rep. Smith is employed as an aircraft assembly mechanic. He is a member of Albert Holman #179 F&AM-PHA; the International Association of Machinist and Aerospace Workers L.L 837A; Missouri State Workers Union/CWA Local 6355; Multiple Sclerosis Society; and CBTU. Rep. Smith serves on the executive committees of the National Black Caucus of State Legislators and the National Labor Caucus (AFL-CIO). He also serves on the Select Committee on Labor and Industrial Relations, the Select Committee on Utilities and the Joint Committee on Tax Policy. Elected to the House: 2010, 2012, 2014. Democrat.

District 86—**JOE ADAMS**

Capitol office: Room 105-H; phone (573) 751-4265
Email address: *joe.adams@house.mo.gov*
House committees: Appropriations–Higher Education; Local Government; Telecommunications.

Biography: Born Jan. 5, 1944, in Kansas City. Resides in University City with his wife, Nancy. Children: Lee (Rachel) and Patrick (Melissa) Adams; Heather and John Shulze. Grandchildren: Emily, Maxwell, Scarlet and Langston Adams. Graduate of De LaSalle High School, 1962; University of Missouri–Kansas City, B.A., 1970; and M.A., 1971, urban American history. Pursued Ph.D from Washington University, 1977–1980, urban American History. Professor of American history, St. Louis Community College-Meramec, 1971–2003. First African-American City Council Member, 1974–1995, and mayor, 1995–2010. Prior president: St. Louis County Municipal League; Missouri Municipal League; and Mayors of Large Cities of St. Louis County. Awards: Buzz Westfall; St. Louis Legend; University City Gates of Opportunity; University City Meritorious Service; and Royal Vagabonds African-American Trailblazer. Military: U.S. Air Force, 1962–1966. Elected to the House: 2014. Democrat.

District 87—**STACEY NEWMAN**

Capitol office: Room 101-K; phone (573) 751-0100
District address: 6340 Clayton Rd. #206, St. Louis 63117
Email address: *stacey.newman@house.mo.gov*
House committees: Appropriations–General Administration; Children, Families and Persons with Disabilities; Ethics; Elections.

Biography: Minority Whip team, House Progressive Caucus chair. Born Aug. 20, 1954, in Kansas City, Kan. Graduate of Emporia State Univ., B.S., education, and B.F.A., speech/theatre, 1977. Resides in Richmond Heights with husband, Burt Newman; one daughter, Sophie, two sons, Andrew and Ben, and four grandchildren. Retired TWA flight crew member. Taught at the American School in London. Appointed: Missouri Attorney General's Domestic Violence Task Force and the Governor's Task Force on Prevention of Sexual Abuse in Children. Former executive board member: National Women's Legislator Lobby; Central Reform Congregation–St. Louis; Congregation Temple Israel; Institute for Women's and Gender Studies at the Univ. of Mo.–St. Louis; PROMO PAC board; and National Women's Political Caucus of Metropolitan St. Louis. She also serves on the Select Committee on State and Local Governments. Elected to the House: 2009 (special election), 2010, 2012, 2014. Democrat.

District 88—**TRACY McCREERY**

Capitol office: Room 105-E; phone (573) 751-7535
District address: 41 Rye Lane, St. Louis, 63132
Email address: *tracy.mccreery@house.mo.gov*
House committees: Agriculture Policy; Appropriations–Agriculture, Conservation, and Natural Resources; Government Efficiency; Utility Infrastructure.

Biography: Rep. McCreery is a founding member of the Consumers Council of Missouri. She serves her community as a member of the Rescue and Restore (anti-human trafficking) Coalition and the Women's Group on Race Relations. She's on the board of Family Care Health Centers. She has held positions in sales, sales training and management in the pharmaceutical, telecommunications and health care industries. Rep. McCreery was born Dec. 26, 1966, in Norwalk, Ohio. She is a 1985 graduate of Edison High School in Milan, Ohio. She received her B.S.B.A. in marketing in 1989 from Ohio State University. She and her husband, Thom Wham, reside in Olivette. Rep. McCreery also serves on the Select Committee on Agriculture and the Select Committee on General Laws. Elected to the House: 2011 (special election), 2014. Democrat.

District 89—**VACANCY**

District 90—**DEB LAVENDER**

Capitol office: Room 109-F; phone (573) 751-4069
District address: 11247 Manchester Rd., Kirkwood 63122
Email address: *deb.lavender@house.mo.gov*
House committees: Agriculture Policy; Fiscal Review; Small Business.

Biography: Born and raised in New England, Rep. Lavender attended Marquette University in Milwaukee, where she graduated with a Bachelor of Science in Physical Therapy. She has resided in St. Louis for more than 35 years. She owns Des Peres physical therapy. She served as intern to Rep. Barbara Fraser, 2006. She participated in raising her nephew, Griffin, now attending Meramec College. Member: Kirkwood Rotary Club; Steering Committee, Hands on Kirkwood; Kirkwood Area Chamber of Commerce; Kirkwood Historical Soc.; Friends of Kirkwood Public Library; Kirkwood Living Green; Women's Voices Raised for Social Justice; American Physical Therapy Association; and Missouri Physical Therapy Association. She also serves on the board of directors, Mary Culver Home for the Visually Impaired, a 100-year old nursing home in the heart of Kirkwood. Rep. Lavender also serves on the Select Committee on Rules. Elected to the House: 2014. Democrat.

District 91—JEANNE KIRKTON

Capitol office: Room 135-BC; phone (573) 751-1285
Email address: *jeanne.kirkton@house.mo.gov*
House committees: Budget; Appropriations–Health, Mental Health and Social Services; Health and Mental Health Policy.

Biography: Born in October, 1953, in St. Charles, Mo. Graduate of Maryville Univ., A.A., nursing, Barnes Hospital School of Nurse Anesthesia and Webster Univ., B.A., history and political science. She practiced surgical critical-care nursing and anesthesia. She and her husband, Dr. Larry King, have one daughter, a son-in-law and two grandchildren. Member: Jefferson Township Democratic Club; Mo. State Parks Advisory Board, member and chair, 2005–2007; Webster Groves/Shrewsbury Area and Crestwood-Sunset Hills chambers of commerce; National Conference of Environmental Legislators; League of Women Voters of St. Louis; National Organization for Women; Epworth Children and Family Services, Nurses for Newborns, board member; Women Legislators of Mo.; Missouri HealthNet Oversight Committee; and Joint Committee on Child Abuse and Neglect. Elected to the House: 2008, 2010, 2012, 2014. Democrat.

District 92—GENISE D. MONTECILLO

Capitol office: Room 130D-B; phone (573) 751-9472
District address: 7491 Hardscrapple A, St. Louis 63123
Email address: *genise.montecillo@house.mo.gov*
House committees: Appropriations–Education; Budget; Elementary and Secondary Education; *ex officio:* Emerging Issues in Education; Higher Education.

Biography: Minority Caucus Deputy Whip. Born on Jan. 6, 1963, in Kirkwood. She represents St Louis County. She was a special education teacher and has taught in the Special School District for 24 years. She is a 1981 graduate of Northwest House Springs High School. She graduated from the University of Missouri–St. Louis with a B.S. in elementary and special education and earned her M.A. in curriculum and instruction from the University of Phoenix. She is mother to Paul Nappier. Rep. Montecillo serves on the board of the Missouri Women's Council and on the Autism Commission. She also serves on the Select Committee on Education. Elected to the House: 2010, 2012, 2014. Democrat.

District 93—BOB BURNS

Capitol office: Room 109E; phone (573) 751-0211
Email address: *bob.burns@house.mo.gov*
House committees: Transportation; Property, Casualty, and Life Insurance; Veterans; Workforce Standards and Development.

Biography: Prior to his legislative duties, he worked for 33 years in the brewery industry at Grey Eagle Distributors, Inc. He was an alderman for the City of St. George. He served on the Affton School District Board of Education and was inducted into the Affton School District Hall of Fame in 2010. He worked on the congressional staff of U.S. Rep. Richard Gephardt from 1995–1999 and the senatorial staff of U.S. Senator Claire McCaskill from 2007–2010. Member: First Baptist Church of Affton, International Brotherhood of Teamsters, and a former member of the St. Louis Community College Board of Trustees. Appointed trustee by St. Louis County Council to close out business for the disincorporated City of St. George. In 2001, he became co-chair of citizens' advocacy group, Lemay on the Move, which worked to bring River City Casino to the town of Lemay. Elected to the House: 2012, 2014. Democrat.

District 94—**CLORIA BROWN**

Capitol office: Room 135BB; phone (573) 751-3719
Email address: *cloria.brown@house.mo.gov*
House committees: Children and Families; Higher Education.

Biography: Rep. Brown is a graduate of McKinley H.S. and Washington Univ., where she received her B.A. in information systems. She is married, with one adult daughter and one granddaughter. Prior to her legislative duties, Rep. Brown worked for MasterCard International as vice president of Information Systems. She also worked as a software tech manager for Statistical Tabulating Corp. and Wohl Shoe Co. Member: St. Johns Evangelical United Church of God; Lemay, Affton and South County chambers of commerce; Jefferson Barracks Community Council; Reagan Federated Republican Women; Missouri Federation; and Crestwood/Sunset Hills Rotary. She is a former Lemay Township Republican Committeewoman and a 1st Senate District Committeewoman. Rep. Brown is on the Board of Directors of the Lemay Child and Family Center. She also serves on the Select Committee on Financial Institutions and Taxation (vice chair) and the Select Committee on Budget. Elected to the House: 2010, 2014. Republican.

District 95—**MARSHA E. HAEFNER**

Capitol office: Room 305-A; phone (573) 751-3762
Email address: *marsha.haefner@house.mo.gov*
House committees: Appropriations–Health, Mental Health, and Social Services (chair); Children and Families; Health and Mental Health Policy.

Biography: Born July 8, 1951, in St. Louis, Rep. Haefner currently resides in Oakville with her husband Greg. They have three children: Melissa, Mark and Lauren. A 1969 graduate of Webster Groves High School, she attended Meramec Community College and received her B.S. in parks and recreation from the University of Missouri–Columbia. She owns and operates Haefner's Greenhouses. She is a member of St. Paul's United Church of Christ. Rep. Haefner served on the South County Chamber of Commerce board of directors for five years and the executive board for two years. She also serves on the Select Committee on Social Services (vice chair) and the Select Committee on Budget. She is an appointed member of the Governor's Task Force on the Prevention of Sexual Abuse. Elected to the House: 2010, 2012, 2014. Republican.

District 96—**MIKE LEARA**

Capitol office: Room 313-2; phone (573) 751-2150
Email address: *mike.leara@house.mo.gov*
House committees: Administration and Accounts (chair).

Biography: Born March 27, 1960, Rep. Leara currently resides in unincorporated St. Louis County near Sunset Hills. A 1978 graduate of Southwest High School, he attended St. Louis Community College at Meramec and Saint Louis University. Rep. Leara attends Abiding Savior Lutheran Church. He is a member of the Sunset Hills–Crestwood Chamber of Commerce and the Fenton Chamber of Commerce. He also serves on the Joint Committee on Public Employee Retirement (chair), the Select Committee on Rules and the Select Committee on Utilities. Elected to the House: 2008, 2010, 2012, 2014. Republican.

District 97—**JOHN McCAHERTY**

Capitol office: Room 401-B; phone (573) 751-3751
Home address: High Ridge, 63049
Email address: *john.mccaherty@house.mo.gov*
House committees: Small Business (chair); Trade and Tourism; Veterans.

Biography: Born in Mississippi and raised in Louisiana. Graduated *summa cum laude* from Liberty University in 2010. He received a masters degree from Liberty University in 2012. Served in the U.S. Air Force. Lives in High Ridge with his wife, Chris. They have two sons: John B. McCaherty and Joshua D. McCaherty. He is the pastor of First Baptist Church of Murphy. Executive board member, Jefferson Baptist Association. Member: Northwest Jefferson County, Arnold and South County chambers of commerce; Jefferson County and Tesson Ferry Republican Clubs; Hwy. 30 Evangelical Ministerial Alliance; and NRA. He also serves on the Select Committee on Commerce, and the Interim Committee on Missouri Ports. Elected to the House: 2010, 2012, 2014. Republican.

District 98—**SHAMED DOGAN**

Capitol office: Room 201C; phone (573) 751-4392
Email address: *shamed.dogan@house.mo.gov*
House committees: Elections (vice chair); Economic Development and Business Attraction and Retention; Elementary and Secondary Education; Utility Infrastructure.

Biography: Born Aug. 28, 1978, in St. Louis. Rep. Dogan resides in Ballwin with his wife, Sara, and their two children, Natalie and Theo. A 1996 graduate of Mary Institute and St. Louis Country Day School, he received his bachelor's degree from Yale University in 2000 in both political science and philosophy. Prior to his legislative duties, Rep. Dogan served from 2011–2014 as an alderman representing Ballwin's 2nd Ward and worked as a fundraiser for Washington University. He also served for three years as a legislative assistant to Sen. Jim Talent. Elected to the House: 2014. Republican.

District 99—**ANDREW P. KOENIG**

Capitol office: Room 312; phone (573) 751-5568
Email address: *andrew.koenig@house.mo.gov*
House committees: Ways and Means (chair); Emerging Issues in Education; Finance and Taxation; Government Efficiency.

Biography: Rep. Andrew Koenig represents parts of St. Louis County, which includes Manchester, Twin Oaks, Valley Park and parts of Fenton. Born Dec. 21, 1982, in St. Louis. Graduated from Marquette High School in 2001 and from Lindenwood University with a B.A. in business administration in 2005. He resides in Manchester with his wife, Brooke, and their three children: Jeremiah, Isaac and Gideon. Rep. Koenig and his family attend West County Assembly of God and are licensed foster care parents. In addition to his legislative duties, Rep. Koenig is the owner of a construction company that focuses on roofing and painting. He is a licensed insurance adjuster. Rep. Koenig also serves on the Select Committee on Financial Institutions and Taxation and the Joint Committee on Tax Policy. Elected to the House: 2008, 2010, 2012, 2014. Republican.

District 100—**SUE ALLEN**

Capitol office: Room 310; phone (573) 751-9765
District address: PO Box 6123, Town and Country 63006
Email address: *sue.allen@house.mo.gov*
House committees: Fiscal Review (chair); Employment Security.

Biography: After attending Brookfield R-3 High School, Rep. Allen graduated with a degree in physical therapy from the University of Missouri–Columbia and earned her master's degree in physical therapy from Saint Louis University. During her 25 years as a physical therapist, Rep. Allen worked in a variety of clinical and educational settings, co-owning a pediatric therapy practice for a number of years. Rep. Allen resides in Town and Country with her husband. They are proud parents of two children and have four grandchildren. Before being elected in 2008, Rep. Allen lobbied the House of Representatives on issues such as healthcare, children's health and early intervention. Rep Allen also serves on the Select Committee on Social Services (chair), the Select Committee on Budget and the Joint Committee on Legislative Research. Elected to the House: 2008, 2010, 2012, 2014. Republican.

District 101—**DON GOSEN**

Capitol office: Room 311; phone (573) 751-1247
District address: 2448 Taylor Rd., Wildwood 63040
Email address: *don.gosen@house.mo.gov*
House committees: Banking; Local Government; Workforce Standards and Development.

Biography: Born Jan. 16, 1963. Rep. Gosen graduated from Hermann High School and earned his B.S. in business administration from the University of Missouri in 1985, and an MBA from the University of Missouri in 1989. Married Jeanne Kallmeyer; they have three daughters: Anna, Laura and Rachael. He helped found the Tin Mill Brewing Company and earned his Brewing Certificate from the Institute of Brewing and Distilling in London, and his brewing microbiology schooling from the Lallemand Institute in Montreal. A State Farm insurance agent for more than 20 years, Gosen is a member of the West County Chamber of Commerce, Wildwood Business Association, Master Brewers Association of St. Louis and Wildwood Area Lion's Club. Rep. Gosen also serves on and chairs the Select Standing Committee on Insurance. Elected to the House: 2010, 2012, 2014. Republican.

District 102—**KURT M. BAHR**

Capitol office: Room 408B; phone (573) 751-9768
District address: 1001 Boardwalk Springs Ln., Ste. 111, O'Fallon 63368
Email address: *kurt.bahr@house.mo.gov*
House committees: Appropriations–Elementary and Secondary Education (chair); Emerging Issues in Education.

Biography: Raised in O'Fallon, the oldest of eight children. Graduated from homeschool in O'Fallon. Graduated from Oklahoma Wesleyan University in 2001 with a degree in history and political science. Officer in the United States Air Force. Master's degree in public policy from Regent University. He lives in O'Fallon with his wife, Jen. They have six children: Micah, Lydia, Josiah, Judah, Carissa and Isaiah. He is a small business owner. Member: American Legion, Missouri Right to Life, the National Rifle Association, the St. Charles County Pachyderm Club and the St. Charles County Christian Home Educators. Rep. Bahr also serves on the Select Committee on Budget and the Select Committee on Social Services. Elected to the House: 2010, 2012, 2014. Republican.

District 103—**JOHN D. WIEMANN**

Capitol office: Room 135AC, phone (573) 751-2176
District address: 92 Myrtle Wood Ct., O'Fallon, 63368
Email address: *john.wiemann@house.mo.gov*
House committees: Appropriations–Health, Mental Health and Social Services; Employment Security; Health Insurance; Professional Registration and Licensing.

Biography: Born in St. Louis, May 15, 1967. Rep. Wiemann is a graduate of University of Missouri–Columbia, with a bachelor's degree in business administration and master's degree in health administration. He lives in O'Fallon with his wife, Yvette. They have two sons, Blake and Clayton. He has been employed by Midwest Physician Insurance Advisors as president and CEO since 2009. Member: Assumption Catholic Church; assistant scout master for Boy Scout Troop 977; board member, Junior GAC Youth Football League; St. Charles County Lions Club; Knights of Columbus; NRA; immediate past president of the Pachyderm Clubs; and member of O'Fallon Lewis & Clark Pachyderm Club. Elected to the House: 2014. Republican.

District 104—**KATHIE CONWAY**

Capitol office: Room 114B; phone (573) 751-2250
District address: 3904 Cambridge Crossing Dr., St. Charles 63304
Email address: *kathie.conway@house.mo.gov*
House committees: Appropriations–Public Safety and Corrections (chair); Fiscal Review; Public Safety and Emergency Preparedness.

Biography: Born Feb. 8, in Jerseyville, Ill. Rep. Conway is a former criminal and civil investigator in the St. Louis area. She is a 1973 graduate of Alton High School, and a 1977 graduate of Western Illinois University, with a B.S. in law enforcement administration. Rep. Conway currently resides in St. Charles with her husband, Patrick, and son, Ryan. Rep. Conway also serves on the Select Committee on Budget and chairs the Joint Committee on Government Accountability. Elected to the House: 2010, 2012, 2014. Republican.

District 105—**MARK A. PARKINSON**

Capitol office: Room 200A; phone (573) 751-2949
District address: 3429 Indiana Ave., St. Charles 63303
Email address: *mark.parkinson@house.mo.gov*
House committees: Consumer Affairs (chair); Appropriations–Higher Education; Employment Security.

Biography: Born in St. Charles in 1972 and resides there with his wife, Brigit. Rep. Parkinson is a graduate of Francis Howell H.S. and in 2000 earned a B.A. in political science from St. Louis Univ. Former deputy district office director for U.S. Sen. Christopher "Kit" Bond. He conducted Sen. Bond's Listening Post program in 17 counties in northeast Missouri, and worked with the office of former U.S. Sen. John Ashcroft. He received multiple freshman legislator of the year awards between 2008–2010 for his work on immigration, taxpayer issues and Second Amendment rights. He is a member of the NRA, Ducks Unlimited, Mo. Right to Life and National Park Foundation. Mark and his wife are the proud "parents" of a 10-lb. Chihuahua named Penny and a 3-lb. Chihuahua named Fergie; both were rescued from a shelter. Rep. Parkinson also serves on the Select Committee on Judiciary and the Joint Committee on Capital Improvements and Leases Oversight. Elected to the House: 2008 (special election), 2008 (general election), 2010, 2012, 2014. Republican.

District 106—**CHRISSY SOMMER**

Capitol office: Room 401-A; phone (573) 751-1452
Email address: *chrissy.sommer@house.mo.gov*
House committees: Professional Registration and Licensing (vice chair); General Laws; Higher Education; Property, Casualty and Life Insurance.

Biography: Born Oct. 15, 1965, in Kirkwood. Rep Sommer is a graduate of the University of Missouri–St. Louis and St. Louis Community College and has more than 30 years experience in the private sector. Rep. Sommer has more than 35 years of community service experience and is a member of Greater St. Charles County Chamber of Commerce, Five Acres Animal Shelter Advisory Board, St. Charles Jaycees, Boy Scout Troop 911, assistant scoutmaster, St. Charles Republican Central Committee and the St. Charles County Pachyderms. Chrissy is a wife, mother and small business owner. Elected to the House: 2011 (special election), 2012, 2014. Republican.

District 107—**RONALD LEE HICKS**

Capitol office: Room 115E; phone (573) 751-1470
Email address: *ron.hicks@house.mo.gov*
House committees: Telecommunications (vice chair); Appropriations–Revenue; Emerging Issues; Transportation, and Economic Development; Utilities Infrastructure.

Biography: Born May 10, 1972, in La Jolla, Calif. Rep. Hicks graduated from his family's home school in 1990 in Oceanside, Calif., and currently resides in St. Charles County with his wife Katie and their two sons, Hunter and Tyler. In addition to his legislative duties, Rep. Hicks works in the family-owned Kentucky Fried Chicken/Yum Franchises. He is den and pack leader for his son's Cub Scout troop, coaches T-Ball and little league sports and is very active in his family's church community. He is also a professional hunter for Missouri's Ultimate Sportsmen and Eureka Hunting Products. Rep Hicks serves on and is vice chair of the Juvenile Justice Task Force. Elected to the House: 2012, 2014. Republican.

District 108—**JUSTIN HILL**

Capitol office: Room 116-A1; phone (573) 751-3572
Email address: *justin.hill@house.mo.gov*
House committees: Appropriations–Public Safety and Corrections; Corrections; Health Insurance; Public Safety and Emergency Preparedness.

Biography: Born Sept. 26, 1978, in Kirkwood, Rep. Hill resides in Lake St. Louis with his wife, Mandy. They have four children: Ethan, Matthew, Jackson and Gavin. He owns and operates an employee benefits consulting agency. He served with the O'Fallon Police Department for 13 years and was assigned to the St. Charles County Regional Drug Task Force as an undercover detective and to the Drug Enforcement Administration as a Task Force Officer. Rep. Hill finished his law enforcement career as a patrol sergeant in 2014. He attended De Smet Jesuit High School, Creve Coeur; St. Louis Community College, associate's degree in criminal justice, 2000; Bellevue University, bachelor's degree in management, 2010. He attends Immaculate Conception Church of Dardenne, where his children attend school. Member: Knights of Columbus; National Rifle Association; Missouri Right to Life; and former committeeman, National Wild Turkey Federation. Rep. Hill is also a member of the National Association of Health Underwriters. Elected to the House: 2014. Republican.

District 109—**PAUL R. CURTMAN**

Capitol office: Room 306B, phone (573) 751-3776
Email address: *paul.curtman@house.mo.gov*
House committees: Government Efficiency (chair); Appropriations–Public Safety and Corrections; Ways and Means.

Biography: Rep. Rep. Curtman is a 1999 graduate of Pacific High School and received his B.A. in political science from the University of Missouri–St. Louis. After graduating, he became a licensed Series 7 financial advisor. Rep. Curtman served from 1999 to 2003 on active duty as an infantryman in the United States Marine Corps, attaining the rank of sergeant. While on active duty, he participated in operations in support of the Global War on Terror. After leaving active duty, he served as a Marine reservist until 2009. Rep. Curtman is a member of Cornerstone Baptist Church. Rep. Curtman also serves on the Select Committee on General Laws, the Joint Committee on Government Accountability and the Joint Committee on General Laws. Elected to the House: 2010, 2012, 2014. Republican.

District 110—**KIRK MATHEWS**

Capitol office: Room 203A; phone (573) 751-0562
Email address: *kirk.mathews@house.mo.gov*
House committees: Appropriations–General Administration; Transportation.

Biography: Graduate of Northwest Missouri State University, with a bachelor's degree in accounting and an MBA. He and his wife of 34 years have four children and are members of Genesis Church Eureka. Rep. Mathews founded a health care company in 1997 that employed physicians in 19 states. After selling the company in 2011, he launched Schmidt|Mathews executive search firm. He is also an author of a book on recruiting hospitalists and served on the Public Policy Committee of the Society of Hospital Medicine. Rep. Mathews also serves on the Select Committee on General Laws (vice chair) and the Select Committee on Budget. Elected to the House: 2014. Republican.

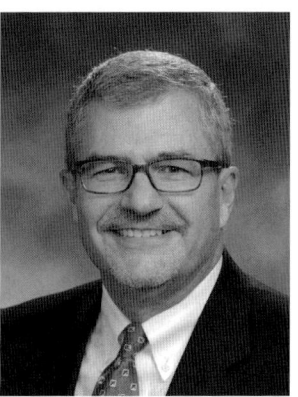

District 111—**SHANE RODEN**

Capitol office: Room 115J; phone (573) 751-4567
Email address: *shane.roden@house.mo.gov*
House committees: Appropriations–Public Safety and Corrections; Corrections; Public Safety and Emergency Preparedness; Veterans.

Biography: Born on March 5, 1983, and raised in Franklin County, Rep. Shane Roden resides with his wife Shannon in Cedar Hill. Rep. Roden is a 2001 graduate from Washington High School. He received his B.S. in fire science management from Lindenwood in 2007. In 2014, he received a master's degree in public administration from Arkansas State University. In addition to his legislative duties, Rep. Roden is a firefighter, paramedic and a reserve deputy sheriff. Rep. Roden is also a life member of the Commemorative Air Force. Elected to the House: 2014. Republican.

District 112—**ROB VESCOVO**

Capitol office: Room 409B; phone (573) 751-3607
Email address: *rob.vescovo@house.mo.gov*
House committees: Civil and Criminal Proceedings (vice chair); Government Efficiency; Government Accountability and Oversight.

Biography: Born Jan. 6, 1977, in St. Louis. Rep. Vescovo currently resides in unincorporated Jefferson County between Arnold and High Ridge with his wife Amanda. They have four children, Robert, Jillian, Nicolas and Peter. He attended Fern Ridge High School and Southeast Missouri State University, where he studied public relations. In addition to his legislative duties, Rep. Vescovo served as a member on the Jefferson County Port Authority from September 2011 to January 2015. He has served as assistant cub master for Troop 830 in Jefferson County and currently serves as its committee chair. Rep. Vescovo is self-employed in business development. Rep. Vescovo also serves on the Select Committee on Labor and Industrial Relations and the Interim Committee on Development and Improvement of Missouri Ports. Elected to the House: 2014. Republican.

District 113—**DAN SHAUL**

Capitol office: Room 116-5; phone (573) 751-2504
Email address: *dan.shaul@house.mo.gov*
House committees: Elections; Emerging Issues in Education; Small Business; Ways and Means.

Biography: Rep. Shaul was born Dec. 13, 1968, in St. Louis. He resides in Imperial with his wife Kim and their three children: Matthew, Emily and Sarah. He is a 1987 graduate of Lindbergh High School in St. Louis. He earned an associate's degree in aviation from Park College in 1992. He has been the state director of the Missouri Grocers Association since 2006. Before becoming the state director, he was the director of Mid-America Grocers Association in St. Louis. He served in the United States Air Force until his honorable discharge from active duty under the troop reduction act of 1990. Rep. Shaul serves as a board member on the Windsor School Board of Education, the Food Marketing Industry Government Relations Committee and the National Grocers Association, where he was recognized with the "Association Leadership Award." He also served as a past chairman of the board for Food Industry Association Executives. Rep. Shaul also serves on the Joint Committee on Legislative Research and Oversight. Elected to the House: 2014. Republican.

District 114—**BECKY RUTH**

Capitol office: Room 115-F; phone (573) 751-4451
Email address: *becky.ruth@house.mo.gov*
House committees: Appropriations–Health, Mental Health, and Social Services; Elementary and Secondary Education; Health and Mental Health Policy; Local Government.

Biography: Born Sept. 27, 1964. Rep. Ruth resides in Festus with her husband Don. They have three children and five grandchildren. Rep. Ruth is a 1982 graduate from Festus R-6 H.S. She received her B.A. with teacher certification from the College of the Ozarks. In addition to her legislative duties, Rep. Ruth works as a real estate agent and serves on the Jefferson County Board of Realtors. A retired teacher, she taught at Festus H.S. Rep. Ruth attends Victory Church in Pevely. Member: Twin City Optimist Club, Jefferson County Growth Association and Mo. State Teachers Association (serves on the State Retired Committee). Awards: Freshman of the Year Award for Children and Education; Jefferson County Region MSTA Friends of Education, 2011; ReMax Best Choice Humanitarian, 2014; and Legislative Award from the Gateway Region YMCA for Social Responsibility, 2015. Elected to the House: 2014. Republican.

District 115—**ELAINE FREEMAN GANNON**

Capitol office: Room 203C; phone (573) 751-7735
District address: 5226 State Rd. H, De Soto 63020
Email address: *elaine.gannon@house.mo.gov*
House committees: Appropriations–Elementary and Secondary Education (vice chair); Emerging Issues in Education (vice chair); Children and Families; Trade and Tourism.

Biography: Born Feb. 2, 1953, in Bonne Terre, Rep. Gannon was raised in Bismarck. She lives in De Soto with her husband Dennis. They have two sons, Andrew and Jason. Rep. Gannon graduated from Bismarck High School in 1971 and earned an associate's degree from Jefferson County Community College, a B.S. in education from Southeast Missouri State University and an M.S. in education from Southwest Missouri Baptist University. In addition to her legislative duties, Rep. Gannon spent 32 years teaching junior high physical education and coaching in the De Soto public schools, as well as serving as the director of the parks program from 1989–2000. She is the chair of the Get Healthy De Soto Christmas Home Tour, a member of the NRA and attends First Baptist Church. She also serves on the Standing Committee on Missouri Ports. Elected to the House: 2012, 2014. Republican.

District 116—**KEVIN P. ENGLER**

Capitol office: Room 411-2; phone (573) 751-3455
Email address: *kevin.engler@house.mo.gov*
House committees: Health Insurance; Local Government.

Biography: Born June 23, 1959, in Festus. Earned degrees in finance/general business and marketing from Southwest Missouri State University. He and his wife Chris have four children: Aimeé, Daniel, Andrew and Joseph; and three grandchildren, Max, Basil and Evelyn. He is a registered representative for Edward Jones, served six years as mayor of Farmington and one year on the city council. Rep. Engler also serves on the Select Committee on Rules (chair), the Select Committee on General Laws, the Joint Committee on Legislative Research (chair) and the Joint Committee on Government Accountability. Elected to the House: 2002. Elected to the Senate 2004, 2008. Senate Majority Floor Leader, 2009-2010. Re-elected to the House: 2012, 2014. Republican.

District 117—**LINDA BLACK**

Capitol office: Room 411-2; phone (573) 751-2317
Email address: *linda.black@house.mo.gov*
House committees: Agriculture Policy; Corrections; Public Safety and Emergency Preparedness.

Biography: Born in Bonne Terre. Rep. Black received an associate's degree from Mineral Area College, a B.S. from Central Missouri University and an M.A. in education from Southwest Baptist University. She taught school for 11 years in St. Francois County. She lives on a working cattle farm near Park Hills and has two children. Member: National Rifle Association; Missouri Farm Bureau; UM Extension Council, board; and *ex officio* member, Backstoppers Org. Member of the Bonne Terre, Desloge, Farmington and Park Hills/Leadington chambers of commerce. Rep. Black is a lifelong member of East Bonne Terre First Baptist Church, where she has served as youth director, treasurer and Sunday school teacher. Rep. Black serves on the executive council of the National Assembly of Sportsmen Caucuses. Rep. Black also serves on the Select Committee on Agriculture as vice chair. Elected to the House: 2008, 2010, 2012, 2014. Republican.

District 118—**BEN S. HARRIS**

Capitol office: Room 105A; phone (573) 751-2398
Email address: *ben.harris@house.mo.gov*
House committees: Agriculture Policy; Appropriations–Agriculture, Conservation and Natural Resources; Conservation and Natural Resources; Small Business.

Biography: Born Oct. 20, 1976, in St. Louis. Rep. Harris currently resides in Hillsboro. In addition to his legislative duties, he works on the family farm that has a cow/calf operation. Rep. Harris is a 1995 graduate of Grandview R-2 High School, and received an associate's degree from Jefferson College in 1997 and a bachelor's degree from Missouri Baptist College in 2000. Rep. Harris is a member of the Morse Mill Baptist Church. He is the son of Ed and Belinda Harris. His mother Belinda served as the state representative for the 110th district from 2002–2010. Rep. Harris also serves on the Select Committee on Agriculture. Elected to the House: 2010, 2012, 2014. Democrat.

District 119—**DAVE HINSON**

Capitol office: Room 411A; phone (573) 751-0549
Email address: *dave.hinson@house.mo.gov*
House committees: Local Government (chair); Banking; Emerging Issues in Education.

Biography: Born Feb. 3, 1972, in Washington, Mo., and represents Franklin County and the northwest corner of Washington County. He was a career firefighter and continues to work as a paramedic. He currently is serving his third term as a member of the St. Clair School Board. Rep. Hinson is a member of the St. Clair Chamber of Commerce, the Missouri Farm Bureau, Missouri Emergency Response Commission, the International Association of Firefighters and First Baptist Church of Arnold, Mo. Rep. Hinson is a 1990 graduate of St. Clair High School. He received a degree in fire science from East Central College. He is also an FFA alumnus. Rep. Hinson currently resides in St. Clair with his wife Heather and his three children: A.J., Adam and Austin. He and his wife are both small business owners. He serves on the Missouri Emergency Response Commission. Rep. Hinson also serves on the Select Committee on State and Local Governments and the Joint Committee on the Justice System. Elected to the House: 2010, 2012, 2014. Republican.

District 120—**JASON CHIPMAN**

Capitol office: Room 115H; phone 751-1688
Email address: *jason.chipman@house.mo.gov*
House committees: Appropriations–Revenue, Transportation and Economic Development; Conservation and Natural Resources; Corrections; Elections.

Biography: Born in St. Charles, Mo., Rep. Chipman resides in Steelville with his wife, Elane. They have four children: Alexander, Konnor, Xavier and Chloe. He is a 1995 graduate of Steelville High School. He received an associate's degree from East Central College in 2007, and his bachelor's degree in organizational leadership from Drury University in 2010. Rep. Chipman served in the U.S. Navy from 1995 to 2000. After an honorable discharge, he began working at Brewer Science in Rolla, and was the inventory manager prior to being elected. Rep. Chipman and his family attend Greentree Christian Church in Rolla. Elected to the House: 2014. Republican.

District 121—**KEITH J. FREDERICK**

Capitol office: Room 403B; phone (573) 751-3834
District address: 716 Oak Knoll Rd., Rolla 65401
Email address: *keith.frederick@house.mo.gov*
House committees: Health and Mental Health Policy (chair); Appropriations–Health, Mental Health, and Social Services; Professional Registration and Licensing.

Biography: Born Nov. 6, 1952, in St. Louis. A 1971 graduate of Cleveland High School in St. Louis. Received a B.S. from St. Louis College of Pharmacy, 1976, and a doctorate of osteopathic medicine from Chicago College of Osteopathic Medicine, 1981. Residency in orthopedic surgery at Normandy Hospital 1981–86, with electives at Alaska Native Medical Center and at University of Missouri–Columbia. He lives in Rolla with his wife Marilyn. Three children: Catherine, Ben and Dorothy. Orthopedic surgeon with PCRMC in Rolla at The Frederick Knee Center. Attends United Methodist Church in Rolla. Member: American Academy of Orthopedic Surgeons, AOAO, AOA, MSMA, MAOP&S and MSOA. He also serves on the Select Committee on Social Services. Elected to the House: 2010, 2012, 2014. Republican.

District 122—**STEVEN M. LYNCH**

Capitol office: Room 203A; phone (573) 751-1446
Email address: *steve.lynch@house.mo.gov*
House committees: Veterans (vice chair); Appropriations–Elementary and Secondary Education; Small Business; Workforce Standards and Development.

Biography: Rep. Lynch was born June 1, 1954, in Waynesville and graduated from Waynesville High School in 1972. He currently lives in Waynesville with his wife, Deborah. They have three children, nine grandchildren and one great granddaughter. Before being elected, Rep. Lynch was a business leader as the third-generation owner of his family's furniture and appliance store for more than 35 years. He has served as a community and church leader most of his life. Rep. Lynch also serves on the Select Committee on Insurance. Elected to the House: 2012, 2014. Republican.

District 123—**DIANE FRANKLIN**

Capitol office: Room 206B; phone (573) 751-1119
Email address: *diane.franklin@house.mo.gov*
House committees: Children and Families (chair); Appropriations–Elementary and Secondary Education; Professional Registration and Licensing.

Biography: Rep. Franklin is a graduate of Camdenton R-III schools and Ozarks Technical Community College. She resides in Camdenton with her husband, Dr. Chris Franklin, and is a fifth-generation farmer. She is the mother of two sons and the proud grandmother of two granddaughters and two grandsons. She served on the Camdenton R-III School Board from 1993 to 1999. Rep. Franklin has served as Lake Masters Area Gardeners' president and vice president. Member: Mo. Youth Sport Shooting Alliance; Mo. National Rifle Association; National Wild Turkey Federation; Mo. Farm Bureau; Amateur and Mo. Trap Shooting Associations; Canopy Church; Lake Area, Camdenton and Lebanon chambers of commerce; Kiwanis International; and Rotary International. She also serves on the Select Committee on Social Services and the Joint Committee on Child Abuse and Neglect. Elected to the House: 2010, 2012, 2014. Republican.

District 124—**ROCKY MILLER**

Capitol office: Room 233B; phone (573) 751-3604
Email address: *rocky.miller@house.mo.gov*
House committees: Energy and the Environment (chair); Conservation and Natural Resources; Utility Infrastructure.

Biography: Born Oct. 22, 1965, in West Palm Beach, Fla. Graduate of Missouri S & T, B.S. in civil engineering, and an MBA. from St. Ambrose University. He and his wife Della have four children. He is a professional engineer and land surveyor with Miller Companies. Involved with the Missouri Society of Professional Engineers, Missouri Society of Professional Surveyors and Rotary. Past president of the School of the Osage School Board and director of MSBA, member of Farm Bureau and the NRA. Rep. Miller also serves on the Select Committee on Utilities. Elected to the House: 2012, 2014. Republican.

District 125—**WARREN D. LOVE**

Capitol office: Room 235BA; phone (573) 751-4065
District address: 8381 N.E. Hwy ZZ, Osceola 64776
Email address: *warren.love@house.mo.gov*
House committees: Agriculture Policy; Appropriations–General Administration; Emerging Issues in Education; Telecommunications.

Biography: Born February 3, 1950, Osceola, Mo. A 1968 graduate of Osceola High School. A attended University of Central Missouri at Warrensburg and Metro Jr. College in Kansas City, Kan. He and his wife Marla have four children and 10 grandchildren. He is a rancher, restaurant owner and carpenter-contractor, and had a 20-year career in sales and sales management with MoorMan Manufacturing Company. He attends Hopewell Baptist Church in Osceola and is a member of several organizations, including Missouri Farm Bureau, Missouri Cattlemen's Association, National Rifle Association, the Masons, Lions Club International and Gideons International. Elected to the House: 2012, 2014. Republican.

District 126—**PATRICIA A. PIKE**

Capitol office: Room 400-CB; phone (573) 751-5388
District address: PO Box 282, Butler 64730
Email address: *patricia.pike@house.mo.gov*
House committees: Agriculture Policy; Appropriations–General Administration; Government Efficiency; Veterans.

Biography: A 1972 graduate of Adrian High School, with a M.S.Ed degree from University of Central Missouri. Family and consumer science teacher, senior high guidance counselor and A+ coordinator from 1976–2013. Dual-credit instructor for Metropolitan Community College. Missouri Teaching Honors. Annual volunteer White House Egg Roll. Member: Chamber of Commerce, Missouri Retired Teachers, United Methodist Women, NRA, Ducks Unlimited, 4-H Judge and Missouri Farm Bureau. She and her husband, former Rep. Randy W. Pike have two children, Dillion and Michelle, and two grandchildren, Isabella Bo and Josephine Harper. Elected to the House: 2014. Republican.

District 127—**MIKE KELLEY**

Capitol office: Room 235; phone (573) 751-2165
E-mail address: *mike.kelley@mo.house.gov*
House committees: Government Efficiency (vice-chair); Ways and Means; Workforce Development.

Biography: Rep. Kelley was born in Lamar and graduated from Lamar High School in 1993. He currently resides in Lamar with his wife, Ann, son, Brenden, and Vera, their exchange daughter (Ukraine). Mike belongs to the NRA and is an NRA certified pistol instructor. He also belongs to the Barton County, Lockwood and Greenfield chambers of commerce. Rep. Kelley is a member of Rotary International and a past local chapter president. He attends Oakton United Methodist Church. Rep. Kelley has been honored with the following awards, among others: Friend of Agriculture, Friend of Manufacturing, ACU Conservative, Administration of Justice and Liberty Standard. Rep. Kelley also serves as vice chair of the Select Committee on Labor and Industrial Relations and on the Select Committee on Education. Elected to the house: 2010, 2012, 2014. Republican.

District 128—**SUE ENTLICHER**

Capitol office: Room 207A; phone (573) 751-1347
Email address: *sue.entlicher@house.mo.gov*
House committees: Elections (chair); Agriculture Policy; Health and Mental Health Policy; Transportation.

Biography: Born Dec. 28, 1950, in Hoisington, Kan. Represents part of Cedar and all of Polk counties. Prior to her legislative duties, she served as the Polk County clerk. Attends Morrisville Assembly of God Church. She is a member of the Polk County Women's Republican Club, Pachyderms and the Polk County Cattleman's Club. Rep. Entlicher is a 1968 graduate of El Dorado Springs High School and attended Southwest Baptist University. She currently resides in Bolivar with her husband, Ronald. They have three children, Natalie Francka, Ronda Stewart and Sheila Walters, and seven grandchildren. Rep. Entlicher also serves on the Select Committee on State and Local Governments. Elected to the House: 2010, 2012, 2014. Republican.

District 129—**SANDY CRAWFORD**

Capitol office: Room 207B; phone (573) 751-1167
District address: PO Box 332, Buffalo 65622
Email address: *sandy.crawford@house.mo.gov*
House committees: Banking (chair); Utilities (vice chair); Ethics; Finance and Taxation; Telecommunications.

Biography: Born Oct. 1, 1957, in Buffalo. She is a 1975 graduate of Buffalo High School. She received a B.S. in finance from Missouri State University in 1995 and graduated from the Graduate School of Banking in Colorado in 1998. She lives in Buffalo with her husband John. Prior to becoming a state representative, she enjoyed a 30-year banking career. She is a member of Tabernacle Baptist Church in Lebanon, where she teaches a third-grade girls Sunday school class. Member/activities: Buffalo Area Chamber of Commerce, Lebanon Area Chamber of Commerce, Dallas County Cattleman, Farm Bureau, NRA and Mo. Cattleman's Association. Elected to the House: 2010, 2012, 2014. Republican.

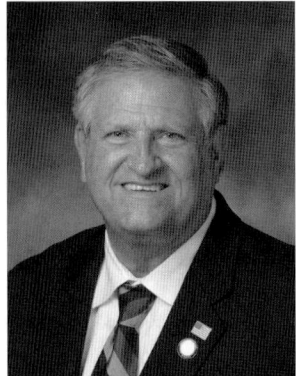

District 130—JEFF L. MESSENGER

Capitol office: Room 407A; phone (573) 751-2381
Email address: *jeff.messenger@house.mo.gov*
House committees: Budget; Ways and Means; Economic Development; Government Oversight and Accountability.

Biography: Rep. Messenger joined the Navy in 1969 and, after completing Naval Aviation Electronics School, was assigned to Naval Air Station, Corpus Christi, Texas. Rep. Messenger served four years in the Navy and received an honorable discharge in 1973. He has been a small business owner since the early 1980s, running a water well–drilling company for more than 22 years. He now owns a prosthetics and orthotics company in Springfield, with facilities in Monett and Joplin. In 2015, he became the owner of a gymnastics facility in Republic, Mo. He and his wife, Wanda, have two sons, Eric and Jeffrey, who help run the family business. Elected to the House: 2012, 2014. Republican.

District 131—SONYA ANDERSON

Capitol office: Room 233A; phone (573) 751-2948
Email address: *sonya.anderson@house.mo.gov*
House committees: Conservation and Natural Resources (chair); Appropriations_Agriculture, Conservation and Natural Resources; Fiscal Review.

Biography: Rep. Anderson is a seventh generation native of Greene County. She is a 1988 graduate from Willard and attended Southwest Missouri State University. She currently resides in Springfield with her husband, Jim. They have two children, Zack and Tyler. She has more than 20 years of experience in small business and management, and currently co-owns and operates Show Me Horses and Farrier Service. Rep. Anderson is an active member of Glidewell Baptist Church and has served on the board of directors for Cross Roads Stock Horse Association, Missouri Equine Council, Greater Ozarks Pachyderm Club and the Missouri Apartment and Housing Association. She also serves on the Select Committee on Agriculture. Elected to the House: 2012, 2014. Republican.

District 132—CHARLIE NORR

Capitol office: Room 105D; phone (573) 751-3795
District address: 533 W Calhoun Springfield 65802
Email address: *charlie.norr@house.mo.gov*
House committees: Children and Families; Public Safety and Emergency Preparedness; Trade and Tourism.

Biography: Born in Baltimore, Md., he attended the Baltimore Polytechnic Institute, University of Maryland and National Fire Academy. Rep. Norr served in the U.S. Navy from 1961 to 1967. After retiring from the Baltimore County Fire Department as captain, he and his wife Peggy moved to Springfield to be near their three sons and two granddaughters. He was awarded the Urban Neighborhood Alliance Outstanding Volunteer Award, Nova Award for exceptional services and the Missouri Family 4 Family Community Service Award. The Springfield Greene County Park Board recently named a building, "The Charlie Norr Community Building" for his exceptional work. Also serves on the Select Committee on Commerce. Elected to the House: 2006, 2008, 2012, 2014. Democrat.

District 133—**ERIC BURLISON**

Capitol office: Room 316; phone (573) 751-0136
District address: 3204 S. Anabranch Blvd., Springfield 65807
Email address: *eric.burlison@house.mo.gov*
House committees: Professional Registration and Licensing (chair); Budget; Elementary and Secondary Education; General Laws; Labor and Industrial Relations.

Biography: Born Oct. 2, 1976, in Springfield. Rep. Burlison resides there with wife Angela and daughters, Reese and Aubrey. After graduating from Parkview High School, he attended Missouri State University, where he received a B.A. in philosophy and an MBA. He currently works for Cerner and attends Destiny Church in Republic, where he is active in supporting campus ministries. He serves on the board of D.R.E.A.M. In 2013, CPAC recognized Rep. Burlison as a top young conservative on its national "10 Under 40" list. He is a member of the National Rifle Association, Missouri Right to Life and the Missouri Chamber of Commerce. Elected to the House: 2008, 2010, 2012, 2014. Republican.

District 134—**ELIJAH HAAHR**

Capitol office: Room 409B; phone (573) 751-2210
District address: 4740 S. Woodpointe, Springfield 65810
Email address: *elijah.haahr@house.mo.gov*
House committees: Emerging Issues (chair); Government Oversight and Accountability; Utility Infrastructure.

Biography: Rep. Haahr grew up in southwest Missouri and was homeschooled through high school. He attended Ozarks Technical Community College and Missouri Western State University, graduating *cum laude* from MWSU in 2005. He attended the MU School of Law and graduated with honors in 2008. He is an attorney with Aaron Sachs and Assoc. He lives in Springfield with his wife Amanda and four children: Jackson, Reagan, Scarlett and Alexandra. He remains active in the local community as a member (and former president) of the Springfield Jaycees; the Springfield Metropolitan Bar Association; and the Springfield Chamber of Commerce, Government Relations Committee. Rep. Haahr also serves on the Select Committee on General Laws and the Joint Committee on Missouri's Promise. He serves as vice chair of the Interim Committee on Missouri High School Activities Association. Elected to the House: 2012, 2014. Republican.

District 135—**LINCOLN P. HOUGH**

Capitol office: Room 411B; phone (573) 751-9809
District address: PO Box 121, Springfield 65803
Email address: *lincoln.hough@house.mo.gov*
House committees: Appropriations–Revenue, Transportation and Economic Devlopment (chair); Pensions; Transportation.

Biography: Born June 17, 1982, in Springfield. A 2001 graduate of Hillcrest High School, Rep. Hough earned a B.S. in political science from Mo. State Univ. in 2005. He is a cattle rancher and has worked in the offices of the Missouri House of Representatives' budget chair, Greene Co. prosecuting attorney and the Greene Co. public defender. He is a past president of the Greene Co. Cattlemen's Assoc. and member of the State Board of the Mo. Cattleman's Assoc. He serves as a member of the Greene Co. Farm Bureau board of directors and the Main Street Missouri Connection Inc. Advisory Board. He attends Mount Comfort Bible Church and lives in Springfield with wife, Sarah, and son, William. He also serves on the Select Committee on Budget, the Joint Committee on Real Property Tax Increment Allocation Redevelopment and the Joint Committee on Solid Waste Management District Operations. Elected to the House: 2010, 2012, 2014. Republican.

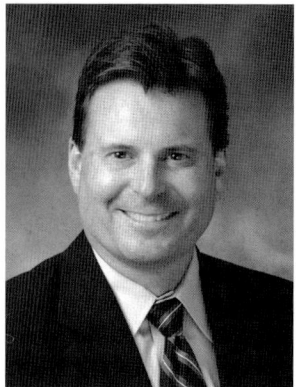

District 136—**KEVIN AUSTIN**

Capitol office: Room 410B; phone (573) 751-0232
Email address: *kevin.austin@house.mo.gov*
House committees: *Ex officio* member of all House committees.

Biography: Assistant Majority Floor Leader. Rep. Austin is a lifelong Springfield resident, graduating from Wilder, Pershing and Glendale schools. He received a B.S. in financial management from Missouri State University, and a J.D. from the University of Missouri. He graduated as a member of the Order of the Coif, a national organization whose members represent the top 10 percent of graduating law students. Rep. Austin is married to his wife, Jody, and they have two sons, Alex and Nick. They attend King's Way United Methodist Church, where he leads the Military Ministries and is a scripture reader for the Sunday services. When not fulfilling his legislative duties, Rep. Austin practices law in Springfield. Elected to the House: 2012, 2014. Republican.

District 137—**LYNDALL D. FRAKER**

Capitol office: Room 110A; phone (573) 751-3819
District address: 202 S. Crittenden, Marshfield 65706
Email address: *lyndall.fraker@house.mo.gov*
House committees: Utility Infrastructure (chair); Professional Registration and Licensing; Small Business; Workforce Standards and Development.

Biography: Born Aug. 9, 1959. A 1977 graduate of Marshfield H.S., Rep. Fraker has lived his entire life in Webster County. He attended MSU in Springfield and graduated from the Walton Institute. He is a small business owner and spent 17 years in management with Wal-Mart Stores and served as Webster County commissioner. He is a building contractor in Marshfield where he lives with his wife Melanie. They have two sons, Landon and Logan; one daughter, Kasey, and son-in-law, Axel; two grandsons, Emmett and Huxley. Lifetime member of Marshfield United Methodist Church. Member: Marshfield Rotary Club, Marshfield Chamber of Commerce and Marshfield Public Schools Foundation Board. Named Marshfieldian of the year, 2002. Awarded Mo. Assoc. of Counties House Legislator of the Year, 2013, and Friend of Agriculture award, 2012 and 2014. Legislator of the Year award from Mo. Assoc. of Electric Cooperatives, 2014. Elected to the House: 2010, 2012, 2014. Republican.

District 138—**DONALD E. (DON) PHILLIPS**

Capitol office: Room 135; phone (573) 751-3851
Email address: *don.phillips@house.mo.gov*
House committees: Trade and Tourism (chair); Conservation and Natural Resources.

Biography: Rep. Phillips was raised on a farm near Salem, and graduated from College of the Ozarks. For four years, he was head basketball and baseball coach at Hollister High School. For eight years, he worked as an actor in the Shepherd of the Hills outdoor drama. Rep. Phillips is a retired seargeant, after serving for 28 years with the the Missouri State Highway Patrol. He has been married to his wife Kathy for 42 years. They have two daughters, two sons-in-law and four grandchildren. He serves on the Missouri Tourism Commission. Rep. Phillips is a member of First Baptist Church of Kimberling City, Rotary and the Gideons. He is a member of the board of directors for Christian Associates. Rep. Phillips serves on the Select Committee on Commerce and the Select Committee on Rules. He also serves on the Interim Committee on the 2011 Missouri Water Patrol Division Merger (vice chair) and the Special Committee on Security Infrastructure of the Capitol Complex. Elected to the House: 2010, 2012, 2014. Republican.

District 139—**JERED TAYLOR**

Capitol office: Room 116-4; phone (573) 751-3833
District address: PO Box 1315, Nixa 65714
Email address: *jered.taylor@house.mo.gov*
House committees: Appropriations–Higher Education; Consumer Affairs; Elections; Telecommunications.

Biography: Rep. Taylor is a lifelong Missourian and graduated with a B.S. in administration of justice from Hannibal LaGrange University. He has experience in corporate America, private sector and government. He and his family are members of Jefferson Avenue Baptist Church in Springfield. He currently resides in Nixa with his wife and two daughters. He also serves on the Joint Committee on Gaming and Wagering. Elected to the House: 2014. Republican.

District 140—**LYNN MORRIS**

Capitol office: Room 200 BC; phone (573) 751-2565
District address: PO Box 949, Ozark 65721
Email address: *lynn.morris@house.mo.gov*
House committees: Health Insurance (vice chair); Health and Mental Health Policy (vice chair); Appropriations–Education; Appropriations–Health, Mental Health and Social Services.

Biography: Born Jan. 22, 1949, Rep. Morris currently resides in Ozark with his wife Janet and represents the eastern part of Christian County. He is a pharmacist and president/owner of Family Pharmacy, Family Pharmacy HealthCare Services and Family Pharmacy Partners LLC. Rep. Morris received his B.S. in pharmacy from University of Missouri–Kansas City and an M.H.A. from Southwest Baptist University. Rep. Morris was selected as U.S. Pharmacist of the Year by U.S. Pharmacists Publications and was awarded the Frist Humanitarian Award in 1997. His company has

been recognized as one of the top 100 U.S. drug store chains by the National Association of Chain Drug Stores from 2000–2013. Rep. Morris also serves on the Select Committee on Rules. Elected to the House: 2012, 2014. Republican.

District 141—**TONY DUGGER**

Capitol office: Room 300; phone (573) 751-2205
District address: PO Box 275, Hartville 65667
Email address: *tony.dugger@house.mo.gov*
House committees: Financial Institutions (chair); Agriculture Policy; Utilities.

Biography: Rep. Dugger lives in Hartville and owns and operates a 243-acre beef cow operation. He is an alumnus of Mountain Grove High School; also attended Southwest Baptist University in Bolivar, earning his B.S. in business administration. Prior to joining the House, he was elected county clerk in 1994 and served in that position for 14 years. Before that, he served as presiding commissioner from 1991–1994. Dugger was president of the Missouri County Clerks Association in 2007, and was a member of the Missouri Association of Counties Board of Directors. He has served on boards of the Wri-Tex 911, Ozark Action, Southwest Solid Waste and Hartville Food Pantry. Member: Union Grove Freewill Baptist

Church, Farm Bureau, National Rifle Association and National Wild Turkey Federation. He enjoys hunting, fishing and collecting antiques. Rep. Dugger chairs the Select Committee on Financial Institutions and Taxation. Elected to the House: 2008, 2010, 2012, 2014. Republican.

District 142—ROBERT ROSS

Capitol office: Room 114A; phone (573) 751-1490
District address: 19420 Evans Rd., Yukon 65589
Email address: *robert.ross@house.mo.gov*
House committees: Appropriations–General Administration (chair); Budget; Conservation and Natural Resources; Professional Registration and Licensing.

Biography: Born in Houston, Mo. Rep. Ross is a graduate of Summersville High School and received a Bachelor of Science degree in cartography with an emphasis in land surveying at Southwest Missouri State University in 2003. He and his wife Chrissy have two boys, Rylan and Carson. They attend Summersville First Christian Church. In addition to his legislative duties, he is a self-employed professional land surveyor and the owner of Midwest Benchrest, which is a nationally sanctioned 600 and 1,000 yard shooting range. He is an active member of the Missouri Society of Professional Surveyors and is involved with the Missouri Cattlemen's Association, Texas County Farm Bureau and the NRA. Elected to the House: 2012, 2014. Republican.

District 143—JEFFREY POGUE

Capitol office: Room 400CC; phone (573) 751-2264
Email address: *jeff.pogue@house.mo.gov*
House committees: Banking (vice chair); Appropriations–Higher Education; Government Efficiency; Ways and Means.

Biography: Born April 23, 1981, in Rolla, Mo. A 1999 graduate of Salem High School, Rep. Pogue earned an associate degree in general studies from Southwest Baptist University. He and his wife Kimberly have three children: Logan, Shelby and Levi. Rep. Pogue runs his own business as a carpenter and general contractor. He still works on the family farm in Salem where he was born and raised. He is also a staff pastor at Living Water Worship Center in Rolla. Rep. Pogue represents the counties of: Dent, Shannon, Oregon and part of Reynolds counties. Elected to the House: 2012, 2014. Republican.

District 144—PAUL FITZWATER

Capitol office: Room 110B; phone (573) 751-2112
District address: 12007 S. State Hwy. 21, Potosi 63664
Email address: *paul.fitzwater@house.mo.gov*
House committees: Corrections (chair); Appropriations–Public Safety and Corrections; Higher Education.

Biography: Rep. Fitzwater lives in Potosi with his wife, Sandy. A 1977 graduate of Potosi High School, he graduated with a B.S. in education from Tarkio College and served in the Potosi R-3 school district for 29 years as a high school health teacher, head track and field coach and football and basketball official. He started his own business, Fitzwater and Son Concrete, which he has owned and operated for more than 25 years. Rep. Fitzwater has been awarded the Missouri Forest Products Association Legislator Appreciation Award; the MASA Friend of Education Award; and the Friend of Agriculture Award, 2012 and 2014. Member: Mo. State Teachers Association; Mo. Retired Teachers Association, NRA and IAABO Officials Association in St. Louis. He also serves on the Select Committee on Judiciary. Elected to the House: 2010, 2012, 2014. Republican.

District 145—**SHELLEY KEENEY TAYLOR**

Capitol office: Room 313-1; phone (573) 751-5912
District address: PO Box 275, Marble Hill 63764
Email address: *shelley.keeney@house.mo.gov*
House committees: Administration and Accounts; Budget; Judiciary; Professional Registration and Licensing.

Biography: Majority Caucus Chair. Born in Cape Girardeau. Graduate of Advance Missouri High School. She received a bachelor's degree in elementary education from Southeast Missouri State University and a master's degree in education administration from William Woods University. Served as district assistant for former House Speaker Rod Jetton and state Sen. Jason Crowell, and was an elementary school teacher with the Leopold School District. Member: Harmony Congregational Methodist Church, Chamber of Commerce, Marble Hill Study Club-GFWC, Missouri Farm Bureau, National Rifle Association, Women in the Outdoors and National Wild Turkey Federation. Elected to the House: 2008, 2010, 2012, 2014. Republican.

District 146—**DONNA LICHTENEGGER**

Capitol office: Room 314; phone (573) 751-6662
District address: 509 Summit Ct., Jackson 63755
Email address: *donna.lichtenegger@house.mo.gov*
House committees: Appropriations–Higher Education (chair); Economic Development and Business Attraction and Retention; Higher Education.

Biography: Born in St. Louis. Rep. Lichtenegger is a graduate of Normandy High School and received an A.S. in dental hygiene from St. Louis Community College. She has 40 years' experience as a dental hygienist. She resides in Jackson with her husband John. They have two children, Brent and Leigh Ann, and five grandchildren. Member: American Dental Hygienist Assoc., Cape Girardeau Boys and Girls Club, Cape County Black and Gold Club, Lutherans for Life and University of Missouri Alumni Assoc. Past public service: Republican Central Committee; Republican State Committeewoman from 1998 to 2010 for the 25th senatorial district; six years chair of the 32nd Judicial District; and 10 years chair for the Eighth Congressional District. She also serves on the Select Committee on Budget and the Select Committee on Education. Elected to the House: 2010, 2012, 2014. Republican.

District 147—**KATHRYN SWAN**

Capitol office: Room 115C; phone (573) 751-1443
Email address: *kathryn.swan@house.mo.gov*
House committees: Elementary and Secondary Education (chair); Professional Registration and Licensing.

Biography: Rep. Swan earned an A.A. and B.S.N. in nursing from Southeast Missouri State University. She and her husband, Reg, along with their two children, Regan and Maria, work in the family business, JCS Wireless. Recipient of the following legislative awards: 2013 Freshman Legislator of the Year, Mo. Chamber of Commerce; 2013 and 2014 100% Voting Record, Mo. Chamber of Commerce; 2013 Music Therapy Advocate Award; 2014 Freedometer Award, Concerned Women of America; 2014 100% Voting Record on Small Business Issues, NFIB; 2014 #KIDSWIN Award, Mo. Children's Leadership Council; 2014 Distinguished Legislator Award, MCCA; and 2014 Friends of the Arts, Sigma Alpha Iota. Rep. Swan also serves on the Select Committee on Budget and the Select Committee on Education. Elected to the House: 2012, 2014. Republican.

District 148—**HOLLY REHDER**

Capitol office: Room 404-B; phone (573) 751-5471
District address: PO Box 1868, Sikeston 63801
Email address: *holly.rehder@house.mo.gov*
House committees: Appropriations–Health, Mental Health and Social Services; Appropriations–Revenue, Transportation and Economic Development; Health and Mental Health Policy; Utility Infrastructure.

Biography: Born Sept. 15, 1969, in Memphis, Tenn., Rep. Rehder received a B.S. in mass communications from Southeast Missouri State University. She and her husband, Ray, are the owners of Integrity Communications and have three children: Raychel Smart, Johnny Griswell Jr. and Christian Rehder, and one grandson, Kayden Talley. She is a former government affairs consultant for the Missouri Cable Telecommunications Assoc.; former director of government affairs for Galaxy Cablevision; and former staffer to Congresswoman Jo Ann Emerson. Her family attends Life Church in Sikeston. Member: NFIB; Sikeston, Charleston, Benton and Scott City chambers of commerce; Rotary Club, Sikeston Historic Downtown Assoc.; Natl. Right to Work Assoc.; ALEC; and NRA. Rep. Rehder currently serves as chair of the Select Committee on Labor and Industrial Relations. Elected to the House: 2012, 2014. Republican.

District 149—**DON RONE**

Capitol office: Room 116-1; phone (573) 751-4085
Email address: *don.rone@house.mo.gov*
House committees: Appropriations–Agriculture, Conservation and Natural Resources (vice chair); Agriculture Policy; Telecommunications; Transportation.

Biography: Born Dec. 21, 1944, Rep. Rone is a graduate of Southeast Missouri State University. He and his wife Myra have two children, two daughters-in-law and six beautiful grandchildren. He currently operates a farm in his hometown of Portageville. Prior to his legislative duties, Rep. Rone was a national accounts manager for FMC Corporation, Agriculture Solutions. He also spent time as a teacher for Matthews and Portageville high schools. Rep. Rone has served as mayor of Portageville Missouri and New Madrid County Public Administrator, as well as serving in the Missouri National Guard. Rep. Rone currently serves on the board of the St. Francis Levee District of Missouri. Elected to the House: 2014. Republican.

District 150—**ANDREW McDANIEL**

Capitol office: 115-I; phone (573) 751-3629
District address: PO Box 234, Deering 63840
Email address: *andrew.mcdaniel@house.mo.gov*
House committees: Civil and Criminal Proceedings; Higher Education; Public Safety and Emergency Preparedness.

Biography: Rep. Andrew McDaniel was born on Jan. 22, 1984, in Blytheville, Ark. He graduated valedictorian of Delta C-7 High School in Derring, Mo., in 2002. After high school, he attended Arkansas Northeastern College and received an Associate of Arts degree in 2005. Representative McDaniel worked as a jailer at Pemiscot County Sheriff Office in 2006 and in 2010 attended SEMO Law Enforcement Academy. While at Pemiscot, he received a Class A license from the Peace Officer Standards and Training Program, and shortly thereafter became a deputy sheriff. He lives in Deering with his wife Jessica and son, Evan. Rep. McDaniel also serves on the Select Committee on Utilities. Elected to the House: 2014. Republican.

District 151—**TILA HUBRECHT**

Capitol office: Room 407C; phone (573) 751-1494
Email address: *tila.hubrecht@house.mo.gov*
House committees: Elementary and Secondary Education; Energy and the Environment; Health and Mental Health Policy; Ways and Means.

Biography: A fourth generation native of Stoddard County, Rep. Hubrecht and her husband, a retired Army veteran, reside in Dexter where they raised two daughters. She is a graduate of Richland High School and has a bachelor's degree in education and a master's degree in nursing. She serves on several House committees with a focus on healthcare and education issues, as well other committees related to energy, taxation and government oversight. Prior to serving in the House, she worked in a variety of healthcare settings as a registered nurse as well as an adjunct nursing instructor, with a prior career in education at the elementary and junior high levels. Rep. Hubrecht is active in her church and in her community through various civic organizations. She also serves on the Joint Committee on Child Abuse and Neglect. Elected to the House: 2014. Republican.

District 152—**TODD RICHARDSON**

Capitol office: Room 308A; phone (573) 751-4039
Email address: *todd.richardson@house.mo.gov*
House committees: *Ex officio* member of all House committees.

Biography: Speaker of the House. Born Dec. 26, 1976, in Cape Girardeau. Rep. Richardson graduated from Poplar Bluff High School in 1995, earned a B.A. in political communication and a J.D. from the University of Memphis in 2004 and 2007, respectively. He lives in Poplar Bluff with wife, Amber, and two children, Sawyer and Briley. A practicing attorney in Poplar Bluff, he previously served as an adjunct instructor at Three Rivers College, teaching business law and national and state government classes. He is an elder and board member of First Christian Church in Poplar Bluff. Elected to the House: 2010, 2012, 2014. Republican.

District 153—**STEVE C. COOKSON**

Capitol office: Room 403A; phone (573) 751-1066
District address: 226 Forest Meadow, Poplar Bluff 63901
Email address: *steve.cookson@house.mo.gov*
House committees: Higher Education (chair); Elementary and Secondary Education; Trade and Tourism.

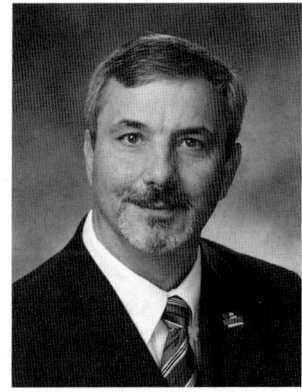

Biography: Rep. Cookson is a former superintendent. He received MASA's "New Superintendent of the Year" in 2013, received the Mo. Community College Association "Distinguished Legislator Award" and is a two-time recipient of the Mo. Farm Bureau Friend of Agriculture Award. Served on: Board of the Mo. Association of Rural Education; MSHSAA Administrative Advisory Committee; and State BETA Clubs Administrative Council. He received an A.A. from Three Rivers Community College and later served as chairman of the Board of Trustees; graduated from College of the Ozarks; and received an M.A. and specialist's degree from Southeast Missouri State University. Member: Missouri Farm Bureau, NRA, NWTF and Ducks Unlimited. Married to Joy Rice Cookson and has a son, Tyler. Rep. Cookson also serves on the Select Committee on Education and the Joint Committee on Education. Elected to the House: 2010, 2012, 2014. Republican.

District 154—**SHAWN RHOADS**

Capitol office: Room 407B; phone (573) 751-1455
Email address: *shawn.rhoads@house.mo.gov*
House committees: Public Safety and Emergency Preparedness (chair); Fiscal Review; Pensions.

Biography: Born in West Plains and raised on a small farm. Rep. Rhoads graduated from West Plains High School in 1995, then attended the Missouri Sheriffs Training Academy and became a certified police officer. He worked for the Howell County Sheriff's Department and West Plains Police Department as an investigator. He also served on the West Plains R-7 School Board for six years. He enjoys going to the lake, hunting and spending time with his wife Jennifer and children, Katie, Kameron and Jillian. Rep. Rhoads is currently a reserve deputy with the Howell County Sheriff's Department. Rep. Rhoads also serves on the Select Committee on State and Local Governments. Elected to the House: 2012, 2014. Republican.

District 155—**LYLE ROWLAND**

Capitol office: Room 413A; phone (573) 751-2042
Email address: *lyle.rowland@house.mo.gov*
House committees: Emerging Issues in Education (chair); Conservation and Natural Resources; Pensions.

Biography: Born Jan. 2, 1954, in Branson. Graduate of Forsyth High School and attended College of the Ozarks. Earned his B.S. and M.Ed. in agriculture education from the University of Missouri in Columbia and his specialist in educational administration from M.S.U. Resides in Cedarcreek with his wife Glenda. They have two daughters, Holly and Laura, and seven grandchildren. A beef cattle farmer, he taught agriculture for 10 years at Forsyth High School, was superintendent at Taneyville R-II and retired after 31 years in education. Recipient of the FFA Blue and Gold Award, Outstanding Rural Administrator, Missouri K-8 School Superintendent of the Year and Outstanding Emeritus Educator. Member: NRA, Missouri Farm Bureau and the Cedarcreek Community Church. Rep. Rowland also serves on the Select Committee on Educaton. Elected to the House: 2010, 2012, 2014. Republican.

District 156—**JEFF D. JUSTUS**

Capitol office: Room 115D; phone (573) 751-1309
Email address: *jeff.justus@house.mo.gov*
House committees: Appropriations–General Administration (vice chair); Trade and Tourism (vice chair); Pensions.

Biography: Born Feb. 18, 1954, in Springfield. Rep. Justus represents part of Taney County. In addition to his legislative duties, Rep. Justus is the president of L and J Plumbing Supply. Rep. Justus has had numerous accomplishments during his time in the Branson area, including: Branson Chamber Small Business of the Year; past chair, Small Business; past president, Branson-Hollister Rotary Club; past president, Downtown Branson Main Street Assoc.; past president, Branson Historic Community Improvement District; Branson Advisory Park Board; and past chair, Table Rock Lake Area Chamber. Rep. Justus attends First Presbyterian Church, where he is a lifelong member. He currently resides in Branson with his wife Glenda. They have two sons, Glenn and Jacob, and a daughter, Rebecca. Rep. Justus also serves on the Select Committee on Commerce. Elected to the House: 2012, 2014. Republican.

District 157—**MIKE MOON**

Capitol office: Room 203B; phone (573) 751-4077
Email address: *mike.moon@house.mo.gov*
House committees: Ways and Means (vice chair); Appropriations–Agriculture, Conservation and Natural Resources; Professional Registration and Licensing; Property, Casualty, and Life Insurance.

Biography: Born Dec. 31, 1958, in Kannapolis, N.C. Rep. Moon lives on his family farm in Ash Grove with his wife Denise and their children. After his 1977 graduation from Western Branch High School in Chesapeake, Va., he relocated to Missouri where he received his bachelor's degree in secondary education from Southwest Missouri State University. Following a 27-year career with Mercy Hospital, he currently works on his cattle ranch. He is a member of High Street Baptist Church, serves on deacon and mission committees and teaches Sunday school. He is a member of the Springfield-Southeast Rotary Club. Elected to the House: April 2013 (special election). Republican.

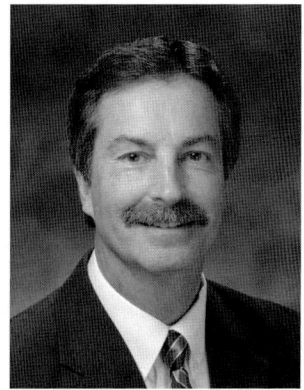

District 158—**SCOTT M. FITZPATRICK**

Capitol office: Room 158; phone (573) 751-1488
District address: PO Box 701, Shell Knob 65747
Email address: *scott.fitzpatrick@house.mo.gov*
House committees: Fiscal Review (vice chair); Employment Security; Government Oversight and Accountability.

Biography: Born Sept. 28, 1987, in Springfield. Rep. Fitzpatrick graduated from Cassville High school in 2006 and the University of Missouri in 2010. He currently lives in Cassville. He and his wife Mallory are members of United Methodist Church in Cassville. In addition to his legislative duties, Rep. Fitzpatrick is the president of MariCorp US., a Shell Knob-based marine manufacturing and construction company. He is a member of Cassville, Shell Knob and Monett chambers of commerce. He has been recognized in *Springfield Business Journal's* "40 under 40." Rep. Fitzpatrick also serves on the Select Committee on Budget (vice chair) and the Joint Committee on Legislative Research. Elected to the House: 2012, 2014. Republican.

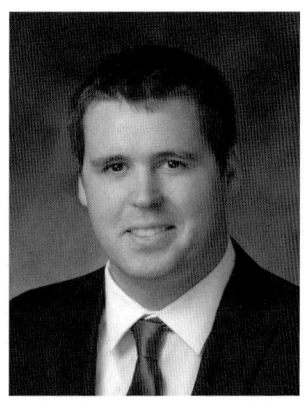

District 159—**BILL LANT**

Capitol office: Room 400; phone (573) 751-9801
Email address: *bill.lant@house.mo.gov*
House committees: Workforce Standards and Development (chair); Emerging Issues; Property, Casualty and Life Insurance; Transportation.

Biography: Born Jan. 18, 1947, in Evansville, Ind. A 1964 graduate of Collinsville High School in Collinsville, Ill. Attended Jasper County Junior College in Joplin, Mo., and Pittsburg State Teachers College in Pittsburg, Kan. He lives in Pineville with his wife Jane. They have three sons: Will, Stephen and Craig, and six grandchildren. He was a salesman for ABF Freight System and owned and operated a farm and feed supply in Seneca, Mo. Member: Racine Christian Church; Missouri Right to Life; Missouri Cattleman's Association; Seneca Area Chamber of Commerce; Life Choices; Masonic Lodge. Rep. Lant also serves on the Select Committee on Labor and Industrial Relations and the Joint Committee on Child Abuse and Neglect (chair). Elected to the House: 2010, 2012, 2014. Republican.

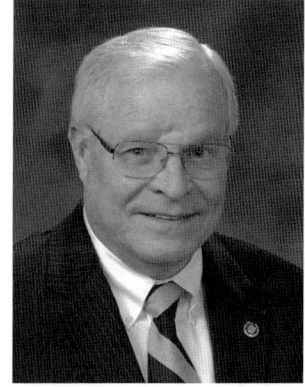

District 160—BILL REIBOLDT

Capitol office: Room 235BB; phone (573) 751-9781
Email address: *bill.reiboldt@house.mo.gov*
House committees: Appropriations–Agriculture and Natural Resources; Consumer Affairs; Corrections.

Biography: Rep. Reiboldt was born in Neosho, where he and his family still own and operate the farm where he grew up. After graduating from Neosho High School, he graduated from Harding University with a degree in business administration. He then served in the United States Army and the Missouri National Guard. He is a member of the Hillcrest Church of Christ, Missouri Farm Bureau, Dairy Farmers of America, Missouri Cattlemen's Association, Missouri Corn Growers, Missouri Soybean Association and the National Federation of Independent Business. He now resides just outside of Neosho with his wife Kathleen. They have three children: Bryan, Beth and Jennifer, and eight grandchildren. Rep. Reiboldt also serves as chair of the Select Committee on Agriculture. Elected to the House: 2010, 2012, 2014. Republican.

District 161—BILL WHITE

Capitol office: Room 408A; phone (573) 751-3791
Email address: *bill.white@house.mo.gov*
House committees: Pensions (vice chair); Civil and Criminal Proceedings; Health and Mental Health Policy; Health Insurance.

Biography: Born June 16, 1953. Represents parts of Jasper and Newton counties. In addition to his legislative duties, he is an attorney who has focused on representing children, the elderly and business law. He previously served as juvenile attorney for Jasper County. He is a member of the Rotary Club, Chamber of Commerce, American Legion, Missouri Bar, NRA and Naval Institute. Received his B.A. from the University of Kansas, his M.A. in Soviet area studies from the University of Chicago and his J.D. from Washburn University. Currently resides in Joplin with his wife, Ellen Nichols. They have four children: Jesse, Brandyn, Amanda and Jera. Rep. White also serves on the Select Committee on Judiciary (vice chair). Elected to the House: 2010, 2012, 2014. Republican.

District 162—CHARLIE E. DAVIS

Capitol office: Room 234; phone (573) 751-7082
Email address: *charlie.davis@house.mo.gov*
House committees: Veterans (chair); Employment Security; Utility Infrastructure.

Biography: Born July 18, 1965, in Fayetteville, N.C. A 1983 graduate of Karlsruhe American High School in Karlsruhe Germany, Rep. Davis studied advertising and marketing. He studied advertising and marketing while serving in the U.S. Navy. He served in the U.S. Navy from 1983 to 1989 aboard the USS Saratoga and USS Independence, honorably discharged in 1989. He lives in Webb City with his wife of 24 years, Laura. They have three children: Jennifer, Timothy and Robert. He owns Software Center in Joplin and attends Wellspring Church in Webb City. Member: Webb City/Carl Junction Rotary Club, Joplin Area Chamber of Commerce, Webb City Chamber of Commerce, NRA, Missouri Right to Life, NFIB, VFW and American Legion. Rep. Davis also serves on the Select Committee on Social Services. Elected to the House: 2010, 2012, 2014. Republican.

District 163—**THOMAS C. FLANIGAN**

Capitol office: Room 309, phone (573) 751-5458
District address: PO Box 1034, Carthage 64836
Email address: *thomas.flanigan@house.mo.gov*
House committees: Budget (chair); Employment Security;
Telecommunications.

Biography: Born in Carthage. Rep. Flanigan is a fifth generation Jasper County resident and graduated from the University of
Missouri–Columbia. He serves in the same legislative seat held
by his great-grandfather, John H. "Fire Alarm" Flanigan, a member
of the 35th General Assembly (1888). Married to Anita, they have
three children: ELizabeth (Jeb) Cook, Kathleen (William) Rhodes
and William C. (Maggie) Flanigan; and twin grandsons, Lincoln
and Barrett Cook, and a granddaughter, Finley Faye Cook. Member:
Kappa Alpha Order; Jasper Co. Farm Bureau; Carthage and Carl
Junction chambers of commerce; Rotary Club of Carthage; Ozark
Trails Council Boy Scouts of America; Mercy McCune-Brooks
Hospital Healthcare Foundation; Carthage City Council, former mayor *pro tem*; and Grace Episcopal
Church. Elected to the House: 2008, 2010, 2012, 2014. Republican.

House Apportionment Plan 2011
Missouri Appellate Apportionment Commission

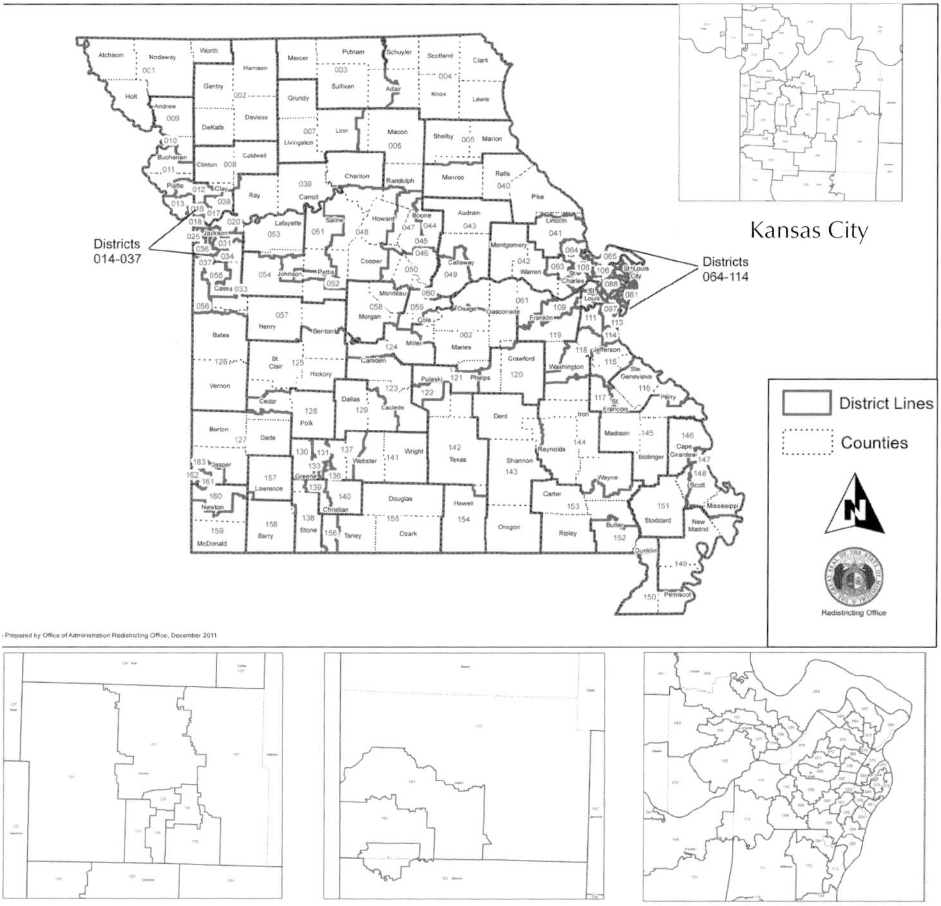

Kansas City

Districts
014-037

Districts
064-114

☐ District Lines

⬜ Counties

Prepared by Office of Administration Redistricting Office, December 2011

Redistricting Office

| Greene County | Jasper County | St. Louis |

State House Districts

State house districts as established by the Missouri Appellate Apportionment Commission and filed with the Secretary of State on Nov. 30, 2011.

District	Description or boundary	Population
1	Counties of Atchison, Holt, Nodaway, Worth	36,138
2	Daviess, DeKalb, Gentry, Harrison	37,020
3	Mercer, Putnam, Sullivan, Adair (part of)	36,537
4	Clark, Knox, Lewis, Schuyler, Scotland, Adair (part of)	35,303
5	Marion, Shelby, Monroe (part of)	37,619
6	Macon, Randolph, Linn (part of)	36,920
7	Grundy, Livingston, Linn (part of)	35,453
8	Caldwell, Clinton, Clay (part of), Ray (part of)	36,798
9	Andrew, Buchanan (part of)	37,119
10	Part of Buchanan	37,035
11	Parts of Buchanan and Platte	32,338
12	Parts of Platte and Clay	38,108
13	Part of Platte	37,018
14	Parts of Clay and Platte	38,142
15	Part of Clay	37,199
16	Part of Clay	37,983
17	Part of Clay	38,012
18	Part of Clay	37,919
19	Part of Jackson	36,335
20	Part of Jackson	37,841
21	Part of Jackson	37,925
22	Part of Jackson	36,168
23	Part of Jackson	35,521
24	Part of Jackson	37,866
25	Part of Jackson	36,857
26	Part of Jackson	36,233
27	Part of Jackson	35,425
28	Part of Jackson	35,873
29	Part of Jackson	36,684
30	Part of Jackson	36,069
31	Part of Jackson	36,827
32	Part of Jackson	36,744
33	Cass (part of), Jackson (part of), Lafayette (part of)	22,610
34	Part of Jackson	35,832
35	Part of Jackson	38,015
36	Part of Jackson	38,040
37	Parts of Cass and Jackson	38,139
38	Part of Clay	37,958
39	Carroll, Chariton (part of), Ray (part of)	35,304
40	Pike, Ralls, Monroe (part of), Lincoln (part of)	35,618
41	Part of Lincoln	38,050
42	Montgomery, St. Charles (part of), Warren (part of)	37,932
43	Audrain, Calloway (part of)	35,434
44	Parts of Boone and Randolph	35,968
45	Part of Boone	35,636
46	Part of Boone	36,530
47	Boone (part of), Cooper (part of), Howard (part of), Randolph (part of)	35,390
48	Chariton (part of), Cooper (part of), Howard (part of), Pettis (part of), Randolph (part of), Saline (part of)	35,428
49	Callaway (part of), Cole (part of)	36,347
50	Boone (part of), Cole (part of), Cooper (part of), Moniteau (part of)	36,823
51	Johnson (part of), Pettis (part of), Saline (part of)	35,439
52	Johnson (part of), Pettis (part of),	36,862
53	Lafayette, Jackson (part of), Johnson (part of)	35,744
54	Johnson (part of), Pettis (part of),	36,083
55	Part of Cass	35,411

District	Description or boundary	Population
56	Bates (part of), Cass (part of), Jackson (part of)	35,829
57	Henry, Bates (part of), Benton (part of), Cass (part of)	35,320
58	Morgan, Miller (part of), Moniteau (part of)	35,311
59	Parts of Cole and Miller	36,332
60	Part of Cole	35,717
61	Franklin (part of), Gasconade (part of), Osage (part of)	36,332
62	Maries, Cole (part of), Crawford (part of), Gasconade (part of), Miller (part of), Osage (part of), Phelps (part of)	35,804
63	Parts of St. Charles and Warren	38,170
64	Parts of Lincoln and St. Charles	37,849
65	Part of St. Charles	37,714
66	Parts of St. Louis City and St. Louis	37,779
67	Part of St. Louis	37,574
68	Part of St. Louis	36,441
69	Part of St. Louis	37,138
70	Parts of St. Charles and St. Louis	35,751
71	Part of St. Louis	35,755
72	Part of St. Louis	36,988
73	Part of St. Louis	36,291
74	Part of St. Louis	37,216
75	Part of St. Louis	36,991
76	Part of St. Louis City	37,443
77	Part of St. Louis City	36,072
78	Part of St. Louis City	37,961
79	Part of St. Louis City	37,280
80	Part of St. Louis City	36,382
81	Part of St. Louis City	37,524
82	Part of St. Louis City	37,144
83	Parts of St. Louis City, St. Louis	36,853
84	Part of St. Louis City	36,036
85	Part of St. Louis	37,891
86	Part of St. Louis	37,549
87	Part of St. Louis	37,710
88	Part of St. Louis	36,377
89	Part of St. Louis	37,799
90	Part of St. Louis	36,703
91	Parts of St. Louis City, St. Louis	36,412
92	Part of St. Louis	36,492
93	Parts of St. Louis City, St. Louis	36,947
94	Part of St. Louis	36,475
95	Part of St. Louis	35,645
96	Part of St. Louis	37,655
97	Part of Jefferson and St. Louis	35,664
98	Part of St. Louis	37,412
99	Part of St. Louis	37,425
100	Part of St. Louis	37,201
101	Part of St. Louis	37,361
102	Part of St. Charles	38,077
103	Part of St. Charles	37,957
104	Part of St. Charles	35,833
105	Part of St. Charles	36,794
106	Part of St. Charles	36,798
107	Part of St. Charles	36,932
108	Part of St. Charles	38,129
109	Part of Franklin	36,036
110	Parts of Franklin and St. Louis	36,609
111	Part of Jefferson	35,423
112	Part of Jefferson	36,574
113	Part of Jefferson	36,333

District	Description or boundary	Population
114	Part of Jefferson	35,794
115	Jefferson (part of), Ste Genevieve (part of), St. Francois (part of)	35,637
116	Perry (part of), Ste Genevieve (part of), St. Francois (part of)	36,688
117	Part of St. Francois	37,100
118	Parts of Jefferson and Washington	36,394
119	Parts of Franklin and Washington	35,343
120	Parts of Crawford and Phelps	36,235
121	Parts of Phelps and Pulaski	36,596
122	Part of Pulaski	36,964
123	Parts of Camden and Laclede	35,343
124	Parts of Camden and Miller	36,858
125	Henry, St. Clair, Benton (part of), Cedar (part of)	36,871
126	Vernon, Bates (part of)	36,682
127	Dade, Barton (part of), Cedar (part of), Jasper (part of)	36,577
128	Polk, Cedar (part of)	37,023
129	Dallas, Laclede (part of)	37,089
130	Part of Greene	36,297
131	Part of Greene	37,674
132	Part of Greene	36,007
133	Part of Greene	37,100
134	Part of Greene	36,518
135	Part of Greene	36,723
136	Part of Greene	36,634
137	Parts of Greene and Webster	36,953
138	Christian (part of), Stone (part of), Taney (part of)	36,984
139	Part of Christian	36,623
140	Part of Christian	36,901
141	Wright, Webster (part of)	36,287
142	Texas, Howell (part of), Phelps (part of), Pulaski (part of)	37,084
143	Dent, Oregon, Shannon, Reynolds (part of)	35,837
144	Iron, Reynolds (part of), Washington (part of), Wayne (part of)	35,775
145	Bollinger, Madison, Perry (part of)	37,354
146	Part of Cape Girardeau	38,063
147	Part of Cape Girardeau	37,611
148	Parts of Mississippi and Scott	36,009
149	New Madrid, Mississippi (part of), Pemiscot (part of), Scott (part of)	36,470
150	Parts of Dunklin and Pemiscot	36,385
151	Stoddard, Scott (part of)	36,271
152	Parts of Butler and Dunklin	37,114
153	Carter, Ripley, Butler (part of), Wayne (part of)	37,051
154	Part of Howell	36,274
155	Douglas, Ozark, Howell (part of), Taney (part of)	36,828
156	Part of Taney	37,066
157	Part of Lawrence	37,325
158	Barry, Lawrence (part of), Stone (part of)	37,210
159	McDonald, Newton (part of)	36,167
160	Part of Newton	37,066
161	Parts of Jasper and Newton	36,886
162	Parts of Jasper and Newton	36,705
163	Part of Jasper	37,042

House of Representatives Districts by Municipality

Municipality	House District	Municipality	House District	Municipality	House District
Adrian	126	Battlefield	133	Breckenridge Hills	72, 85
Advance	151	Bella Villa	93	Brentwood	83, 87
Affton	92	Bell City	151	Brewer	116
Affton	93, 94	Belle	62	Bridgeton	70, 72, 73
Agency	9, 11	Bellefontaine Neighbors	66, 75	Brimson	7
Airport Drive	162	Bellerive	85	Bronaugh	126
Alba	127	Bellflower	42	Brookfield	7
Albany	2	Bel-Nor	85	Brooklyn Heights	163
Aldrich	128	Bel-Ridge	85	Browning	3, 7
Alexandria	4	Belton	56	Brownington	57
Allendale	1	Bennett Springs	129	Brumley	124
Allenville	146	Benton	148	Brunswick	48
Alma	53	Benton City	43	Bucklin	6
Altamont	2	Berger	61	Buckner	20
Altenburg	145	Berkeley	73	Buffalo	129
Alton	143	Berkeley	85	Bull Creek	156
Amazonia	9	Bernie	151	Bunceton	48
Amity	2	Bertrand	148	Bunker	143
Amoret	126	Bethany	2	Burgess	127
Amsterdam	126	Bethel	5	Burlington Junction	1
Anderson	159	Beverly Hills	85	Butler	126
Annada	40	Bevier	6	Butterfield	158
Annapolis	144	Biehle	145	Byrnes Mill	111, 112
Anniston	148	Bigelow	1	Cabool	142
Appleton City	125	Big Lake	1	Cainsville	2
Arbela	4	Big Spring	42	Cairo	6
Arbyrd	150	Billings	138	Caledonia	144
Arcadia	144	Birch Tree	143	Calhoun	57
Archie	57	Birmingham	17	California	50, 58
Arcola	127	Bismarck	117	Callao	6
Argyle	62	Blackburn	51	Calverton Park	74
Arkoe	1	Blackburn	53	Camden	39
Armstrong	48	Black Jack	67, 68, 75	Camden Point	12
Arnold	97, 113	Blackwater	48	Camdenton	123
Arrow Point	158	Blairstown	57	Cameron	2, 8
Arrow Rock	48	Blanchard	1	Campbell	150, 152
Asbury	127	Bland	62	Canalou	149
Ashburn	40	Blodgett	148	Canton	4
Ash Grove	130	Bloomfield	151	Cape Girardeau	146, 147
Ashland	50	Bloomsdale	116	Cardwell	150
Ashley	40	Blue Eye	138	Carl Junction	162
Atlanta	6	Blue Springs	30-33	Carl Junction	163
Augusta	42	Blythedale	2	Carrollton	39
Aullville	53	Bogard	39	Carterville	162, 163
Aurora	157	Bolckow	9	Carthage	127, 163
Auxvasse	43	Bolivar	128	Caruthersville	150
Ava	155	Bonne Terre	115	Carytown	127
Avilla	127	Bonne Terre	117	Cassville	158
Avondale	18	Boonville	48	Castle Point	75
Bagnell	124	Bosworth	39	Catron	149
Baker	151	Bourbon	120	Cave	41
Bakersfield	155	Bowling Green	40	Cedar Hill	111
Baldwin Park	33	Bragg City	149	Cedar Hill Lakes	111
Ballwin	98-101	Brandsville	154	Center	40
Baring	4	Branson	156	Centertown	59
Barnard	1	Branson West	138	Centerview	54
Barnett	58	Brashear	4	Centerville	144
Barnhart	112-114	Braymer	8	Centralia	44
Bates City	53	Breckenridge	8	Chaffee	151

Municipality	House District	Municipality	House District	Municipality	House District
Chain of Rocks	64	Crystal Lakes	39	Ethel	6
Chain-O-Lakes	158	Cuba	120	Eureka	110
Chamois	61	Curryville	40	Evergreen	129
Champ	70	Dadeville	127	Everton	127
Charlack	85	Dalton	48	Ewing	4
Charleston	148	Danville	42	Excello	6
Cherokee Pass	145	Dardenne Prairie	102, 103, 108	Excelsior Estates	38, 39
Chesapeake	157	Darlington	2	Excelsior Springs	38, 39
Chesterfield	70, 71, 88, 89, 100, 101	Dawn	7	Exeter	158
Chilhowee	54	Dearborn	11	Fairdealing	152, 153
Chillicothe	7	Deepwater	57	Fairfax	1
Chula	7	Deerfield	126	Fair Grove	137
Clarence	5	Defiance	102	Fair Play	128
Clark	44	De Kalb	11	Fairview	159
Clarksburg	58	Dellwood	74, 75	Farber	43
Clarksdale	2	Delta	146	Farley	13
Clarkson Valley	101	Dennis Acres	161	Farmington	116, 117
Clarksville	40	Denver	1	Fayette	48
Clarkton	150	Des Arc	144	Fenton	96
Claycomo	17	Desloge	115, 117	Ferguson	73, 74, 75
Clayton	87	De Soto	115, 118	Ferrelview	13
Clearmont	1	Des Peres	89	Festus	114, 115
Cleveland	56	De Witt	39	Fidelity	163
Clever	139	Dexter	151	Fillmore	9
Cliff Village	161	Diamond	160	Fisk	153
Clifton Hill	6	Diehlstadt	148	Fleming	39
Climax Springs	124, 125	Diggins	141	Flemington	128
Clinton	57	Dixon	121	Flint Hill	63, 64
Clyde	1	Doe Run	117	Flordell Hills	74
Cobalt	145	Doniphan	153	Florissant	68, 69, 74
Coffey	2	Doolittle	121	Foley	41
Cole Camp	57	Dover	53	Fordland	141
Collins	125	Downing	4	Forest City	1
Columbia	44	Drexel	56	Foristell	63
Columbia	45, 46, 47, 50	Dudley	151	Forsyth	155
Commerce	148	Duenweg	162, 163	Fortescue	1
Conception	1	Duquesne	161, 162	Fort Leonard Wood	122, 142
Conception Junction	1	Dutchtown	146, 147	Foster	126
Concord	92, 94, 96	Eagle Rock	158	Fountain N Lakes	64
Concordia	53	Eagleville	2	Frankclay	117
Coney Island	138	East Lynne	33	Frankford	40
Conway	129	Easton	9	Franklin	48
Cool Valley	73	East Prairie	149	Fredericktown	145
Cooter	150	Edgar Springs	142	Freeburg	62
Corder	53	Edgerton	11	Freeman	56
Corning	1	Edina	4	Freistatt	157
Cosby	9	Edinburg	7	Fremont	153
Cottleville	102, 103	Edmundson	73	Fremont Hills	140
Country Club	9	Eldon	58, 124	Frohna	145
Country Club Hills	74	El Dorado Springs	125	Frontenac	88, 89
Country Life Acres	89	Ellington	144	Fulton	49
Cowgill	8	Ellisville	98, 101, 110	Gainesville	155
Craig	1	Ellsinore	153	Galena	138
Crane	138	Elmer	6	Gallatin	2
Creighton	57	Elmira	8	Galt	7
Crestwood	91, 92	Elmo	1	Garden City	55, 57
Creve Coeur	71, 88	Elsberry	40, 41	Gasconade	61
Crocker	121	Emerald Beach	158	Gentry	2
Cross Timbers	125	Eminence	143	Gerald	61
Crystal City	114, 115	Emma	51, 53	Gerster	125
Crystal Lake Park	89	Eolia	40	Gibbs	4
		Essex	151	Gideon	149

Municipality	House District	Municipality	House District	Municipality	House District
Gilliam	48	Haywood City	148	Jerico Springs	127
Gilman City	2	Hazelwood	69	Jonesburg	42
Ginger Blue	159	Hazelwood	70, 73, 74	Joplin	160, 161, 162
Gladstone	15	Henrietta	39	Josephville	64
Glasgow	48	Herculaneum	114	Junction City	145
Glasgow Village	66	Hermann	61	Kahoka	4
Glenaire	17	Hermitage	125	Kansas City	12-19, 22-30,
Glen Allen	145	Higbee	47		35-38, 56
Glendale	83, 90	Higginsville	53	Kearney	12, 38
Glen Echo Park	85	High Hill	42	Kelso	148
Glenwood	4	Highlandville	139	Kennett	150
Golden	158	High Ridge	111, 112	Keytesville	39
Golden City	127	Hillsboro	111, 118	Kidder	8
Goodman	159	Hillsdale	85	Kimberling City	138
Goodnight	128	Hoberg	157	Kimmswick	113
Gordonville	146	Holcomb	150	King City	2
Gower	8, 11	Holden	54	Kingdom City	49
Graham	1	Holland	150	Kingston	8
Grain Valley	32, 33	Holliday	40	Kingsville	54
Granby	160	Hollister	156	Kinloch	73
Grand Falls Plaza	161	Holt	8	Kirbyville	155
Grandin	153	Holts Summit	49	Kirksville	3
Grand Pass	51	Homestead	39	Kirkwood	89, 90
Grandview	37	Homestown	149	Kissee Mills	155
Granger	4	Hopkins	1	Knob Noster	52
Grant City	1	Horine	114	Knox City	4
Grantwood Village	92	Hornersville	150	Koshkonong	143
Gravois Mills	58	Houston	142	LaBarque Creek	111
Grayhawk	116	Houstonia	51	La Belle	4
Grayridge	151	Houston Lake	14	Laclede	7
Gray Summit	109, 110	Howardville	149	Laddonia	43
Greencastle	3	Hughesville	51	La Due	57
Green City	3	Humansville	128	Ladue	87-89
Greendale	85	Hume	126	La Grange	4
Greenfield	127	Humphreys	3	Lake Annette	56
Green Park	92, 94	Hunnewell	5	Lake Lafayette	53
Green Ridge	54	Hunter	153	Lake Lotawana	31, 33, 34
Greentop	4	Huntleigh	89	Lake Mykee Town	49
Greenville	144	Huntsdale	47	Lake Ozark	124
Greenwood	34	Huntsville	6	Lake St. Louis	107, 108
Guilford	1	Hurdland	4	Lakeshire	92
Gunn City	33	Hurley	138	Lake Tapawingo	31
Hale	39	Iatan	11	Lake Tekakwitha	111
Halfway	128	Iberia	124	Lake Viking	2
Hallsville	44	Imperial	113	Lake Waukomis	14
Halltown	157	Independence	19-22, 28-32	Lake Winnebago	55
Hamilton	8	Indian Point	138	Lamar	127
Hanley Hills	86	Innsbrook	63	Lamar Heights	127
Hannibal	5, 40	Ionia	54, 57	Lambert	148
Hardin	39	Irena	1	La Monte	51
Harris	3	Irondale	144	Lanagan	159
Harrisburg	47	Iron Mountain Lake	117	Lancaster	4
Harrisonville	33, 55	Ironton	144	La Plata	6
Hartsburg	50	Irwin	127	Laredo	7
Hartville	141	Jackson	146	La Russell	127
Hartwell	57	Jacksonville	6	Lathrop	8
Harviell	152	Jameson	2	La Tour	54
Harwood	126	Jamesport	2	Laurie	58, 124
Hawk Point	41	Jamestown	50	Lawson	8
Hayti	149	Jasper	127	Leadington	117
Hayti Heights	149	Jefferson City	49, 59, 60	Leadwood	117
Hayward	149	Jennings	66, 74, 75, 85	Leasburg	120

Municipality	House District	Municipality	House District	Municipality	House District
Leawood	161	Matthews	149	New Florence	42
Lebanon	123, 129	Maysville	2	New Franklin	48
Lees Summit	30, 34, 35, 37, 55	Mayview	53	New Hampton	2
Leeton	54	Meadville	7	New Haven	61
Leisure Lake	7	Mehlville	93, 94	New London	40
Lemay	93	Memphis	4	New Madrid	149
Leonard	5	Mendon	39	New Melle	42, 63, 102
Leslie	61	Mercer	3	Newtonia	159
Levasy	53	Merriam Woods	156	Newtown	3
Lewis and Clark Village	11	Merwin	126	Niangua	141
Lewistown	4	Meta	62	Nixa	139
Lexington	53	Metz	126	Noel	159
Liberal	127	Mexico	43	Norborne	39
Liberty	16, 17, 38	Miami	48	Normandy	73, 85
Licking	142	Middletown	42	North Kansas City	18
Lilbourn	149	Milan	3	North Lilbourn	149
Lincoln	57	Milford	127	Northmoor	14
Linn	62	Millard	4	Northwoods	85
Linn Creek	123	Miller	157	Norwood	141
Linneus	7	Mill Spring	144	Norwood Court	74
Lithium	116	Milo	126	Novelty	4
Livonia	3	Mindenmines	127	Novinger	3
Loch Lloyd	56	Mine La Motte	145	Oak Grove	32, 33
Lock Springs	2	Miner	148	Oak Grove Village	119
Lockwood	127	Mineral Point	118	Oakland	90
Lohman	59	Miramiguoa Park	119	Oak Ridge	146
Loma Linda	160	Missouri City	38	Oaks	15
Lone Jack	33	Moberly	6, 47	Oakview	15
Longtown	145	Mokane	49	Oakville	94, 95
Louisburg	129	Moline Acres	66, 75	Oakwood	15
Louisiana	40	Monett	157, 158	Oakwood Park	15
Lowry City	125	Monroe City	5, 40	Odessa	53
Lucerne	3	Montgomery City	42	OFallon	63-64, 102-103, 107-108
Ludlow	7	Monticello	4		
Lupus	50	Montier	143	Old Appleton	146
Luray	4	Montrose	57	Old Jamestown	67, 68
McBaine	50	Mooresville	7	Old Monroe	64
McCord Bend	138	Morehouse	149	Olean	59
McFall	2	Morley	148	Olivette	71
Mackenzie	92	Morrison	61	Olivette	88
McKittrick	42	Morrisville	128	Olympian Village	115
Macks Creek	123	Mosby	38	Oran	151
Macon	6	Moscow Mills	64	Oregon	1
Madison	40	Mound City	1	Oronogo	163
Maitland	1	Moundville	126	Orrick	39
Malden	152	Mountain Grove	141, 142	Osage Beach	124
Malta Bend	51	Mountain View	142	Osborn	2, 8
Manchester	99	Mount Leonard	51	Osceola	125
Mansfield	141	Mount Moriah	2	Osgood	3
Maplewood	83	Mount Vernon	157	Otterville	48
Marble Hill	145	Murphy	97	Overland	71, 72, 85
Marceline	6, 7, 39	Napoleon	53	Owensville	62
Marionville	157	Naylor	153	Oxly	153
Marlborough	91, 92	Neck City	127	Ozark	140
Marquand	145	Neelyville	152	Ozora	116
Marshall	51	Nelson	48	Pacific	110, 119
Marshfield	137	Neosho	159, 160	Pagedale	86
Marston	149	Nevada	126	Palmyra	5
Marthasville	42	Newark	4	Paris	40
Martinsburg	43	New Bloomfield	49	Parkdale	111, 112
Maryland Heights	70-72	Newburg	121	Park Hills	115, 117
Maryville	1	New Cambria	6	Parkville	13, 14

Municipality	House District	Municipality	House District	Municipality	House District
Parkway	119	Rayville	39	Sappington	92, 96
Parma	149	Rea	9	Sarcoxie	127
Parnell	1	Redings Mill	161	Savannah	9
Pasadena Hills	85	Reeds	127	Schell City	126
Pasadena Park	85	Reeds Spring	138	Scotsdale	111
Pascola	149	Renick	47	Scott City	148
Passaic	126	Rensselaer	40	Sedalia	48, 52
Pattonsburg	2	Republic	130, 133, 138	Sedgewickville	145
Paynesville	40	Revere	4	Seligman	158
Peaceful Village	111	Rhineland	42	Senath	150
Peculiar	55	Richards	126	Seneca	159
Pendleton	42	Rich Hill	126	Seymour	141
Penermon	151	Richland	121, 123	Shelbina	5
Perry	40	Richmond	39	Shelbyville	5
Perryville	116, 145	Richmond Heights	83, 87	Sheldon	126
Pevely	114	Ridgely	12	Shell Knob	138, 158
Phelps City	1	Ridgeway	2	Sheridan	1
Phillipsburg	129	Risco	149	Shoal Creek Drive	161
Pickering	1	Ritchey	159	Shoal Creek Estates	161
Piedmont	144	River Bend	20	Shrewsbury	91
Pierce City	157, 158	Riverside	14	Sibley	20
Pierpont	50	Riverview	66	Sikeston	148, 149
Pilot Grove	48	Riverview Estates	56	Silex	41
Pilot Knob	144	Rives	150	Silver Creek	160, 161
Pine Lawn	85	Rocheport	47	Skidmore	1
Pineville	159	Rockaway Beach	156	Slater	48
Pinhook	149	Rock Hill	83	Smithton	48
Plato	142	Rock Port	1	Smithville	12
Platte City	12	Rockville	126	South Fork	154
Platte Woods	14	Rogersville	137	South Gifford	6
Plattsburg	8	Rolla	62, 121	South Gorin	4
Pleasant Hill	33, 34	Roscoe	125	South Greenfield	127
Pleasant Hope	128	Rosebud	62	South Lineville	3
Pleasant Valley	17	Rosendale	9	Southwest City	159
Plevna	4	Rothville	39	Spanish Lake	66, 67
Pocahontas	146	Rush Hill	43	Sparta	140
Pollock	3	Rushville	11	Spickard	7
Polo	8	Russellville	59	Spokane	139
Pomona	154	Rutledge	4	Springfield	130-137, 139
Pontiac	155	Saddlebrooke	139, 140, 156	Stanberry	2
Poplar Bluff	152, 153	Saginaw	160	Stark City	159
Portage Des Sioux	65	St. Ann	72, 73	Steele	150
Portageville	149	St. Charles	65, 70, 105, 106	Steelville	120
Potosi	118, 144	St. Clair	119	Stella	159
Powersville	3	St. Clement	40	Stewartsville	2
Prairie Home	50	St. Cloud	120	Stockton	128
Prathersville	38	Ste. Genevieve	116	Stotesbury	126
Preston	125	St. Elizabeth	62	Stotts City	157
Princeton	3	St. Francisville	4	Stoutland	123
Purcell	127	St. George	93	Stoutsville	40
Purdin	7	St. James	120	Stover	58
Purdy	158	St. John	72, 85	Strafford	137
Puxico	151	St. Joseph	9-11	Strasburg	33
Queen City	4	St. Louis	66, 76-84, 91, 93	Sturgeon	44
Quitman	1	St. Martins	59	Sugar Creek	19, 20
Qulin	152	St. Mary	116	Sullivan	119, 120
Randolph	17	St. Paul	64, 107	Summersville	142, 143
Ravanna	3	St. Peters	64, 103-107	Sumner	39
Ravenwood	1	St. Robert	122	Sundown	155
Raymondville	142	St. Thomas	62	Sunrise Beach	58, 124
Raymore	37, 55, 56	Salem	143	Sunset Hills	90, 96
Raytown	27-29, 35	Salisbury	39	Sweet Springs	51

Municipality	House District	Municipality	House District	Municipality	House District
Sycamore Hills	85	Vandiver	43	Wentworth	160
Syracuse	58	Vanduser	151	Wentzville	63, 64, 107, 108
Tallapoosa	149	Velda City	85	West Alton	65
Taneyville	155	Velda Village Hills	85	Westboro	1
Taos	59	Verona	157	West Line	56
Tarkio	1	Versailles	58	Weston	11
Tarrants	40	Viburnum	144	Westphalia	62
Terre du Lac	117	Vienna	62	West Plains	154
Thayer	143	Village of Four Seasons	124	West Sullivan	120
Theodosia	155	Villa Ridge	109	Westwood	88
Thomasville	143	Vinita Park	85, 86	Wheatland	125
Three Creeks	42	Vinita Terrace	86	Wheaton	158
Tightwad	57	Vista	125	Wheeling	7
Tina	39	Waco	127	Whiteman AFB	52
Tindall	7	Walker	126	Whiteside	41
Tipton	58	Walnut Grove	130	Whitewater	146
Town and Country	88, 89, 100	Wardell	149	Wilbur Park	92
Tracy	11	Wardsville	59	Wildwood	98, 101, 110
Trenton	7	Warrensburg	51, 54	Willard	130
Trimble	8	Warrenton	42	Williamsville	153
Triplett	39	Warsaw	125	Willow Springs	154
Troy	41	Warson Woods	87, 90	Wilson City	148
Truesdale	42	Washburn	158	Winchester	100
Truxton	41	Washington	61, 109	Windsor	54
Turney	8	Wasola	155	Windsor	57
Tuscumbia	124	Watson	1	Windsor Place	48
Twin Oaks	99	Waverly	53	Winfield	64
Umber View Heights	127	Wayland	4	Winigan	3
Union	109	Waynesville	122	Winona	143
Union Star	2	Weatherby	2	Winston	2
Unionville	3	Weatherby Lake	13	Wood Heights	39
Unity Village	30	Weaubleau	125	Woodson Terrace	73, 85
University City	86-88	Webb City	162, 163	Wooldridge	47
Uplands Park	85	Webster Groves	83, 90, 91	Worth	1
Urbana	129	Weingarten	116	Wortham	117
Urich	57	Weldon Spring	70, 102, 103	Worthington	3
Utica	7	Weldon Spring Heights	102	Wright City	63
Valley Park	99	Wellington	53	Wyaconda	4
Van Buren	153	Wellston	86	Wyatt	148
Vandalia	43	Wellsville	42	Zalma	145

Legislative historical data

Officers—Missouri Senate and House, 1820–2013

Session	President Pro Tem of Senate	Secretary of Senate	Speaker of House	Chief Clerk of House
1—1820	Silas Bent	Jno. S. Brickey	James Caldwell	John McArthur
1821[a]	Isadore Moore	Arthur Nelson	Hy. S. Geyer	Thompson Douglas
2—1822	Benj. Emmons	Bernard O. Neill	Hy. S. Geyer	Thompson Douglas
3—1824	William Biggs A.J. Williams	William G. Pettus	Hy. S. Geyer	Thompson Douglas
4—1826	Felix Scott	J.S. Langham	Alex. Stuart	Sam'l C. Owen
5—1828	Geo F. Bollinger	Wm. Wright	John Thornton	Jas. H. Birch
1829[a]	Geo F. Bollinger	Wm. Wright	John Thornton	Jas. H. Birch
6—1830	N.S. Burkhartt	Jas. H. Birch	John Thornton	Sam'l C. Owen
7—1832	John Miller	Henry Schurlds	Thos. Reynolds	Alb. G. Harrison
8—1834	Daniel Ashby	Wm. B. Napton	John Jameison	Jas. B. Bowling
9—1836	Daniel Ashby	Jos. B. Wells	John Jameison	Thos. C. Burch
10—1838	Abraham Hunter	Jas. L. Minor	Thos. H. Harvey	M.V. Harrison
11—1840	Owen Rawlins	Jas. S. Watson	Sterling Price	Wm. Gilpin
12—1842	Owen Rawlins	Hampton L. Boone	Sterling Price	Jas. S. Watson
13—1844	Robt. E. Acock	W. Claude Jones	Claib F. Jackson	Wm. Gilpin
14—1846	Ayres Hudspeth	Ephraim B. Ewing	Claib F. Jackson	Benj. F. Massey
15—1848	Ayres Hudspeth	Jas. H. Britton	Alex. M. Robinson	Benj. F. Massey
16—1850	Ayres Hudspeth	Wm. G. Minor Richard R. Rees[b]	Nath. W. Watkins	Geo. W. Huston
17—1852	Extra (no record)	Math. W. Irwin	Reuben Shelby	Geo. W. Huston
17—1852	Regular (no record)	W.D. McCracken[c]	Reuben Shelby	Geo. W. Huston
18—1854	Owen Rawlins	W.D. McCracken	Wm. Newland	Sam'l A. Lowe
1855[a]	Walter B. Morris	W.D. McCracken	Wm. Newland	Sam'l A. Lowe
19—1856	Jno. D. Stevenson	W.D. McCracken	Robt. C. Harrison	Jas. H. Britton
1857[a]	Jno. D. Stevenson	Benj. F. Hesser	James Chiles	Wm. S. Moseley
20—1858	Thos. S. Richardson	Warwick Hough	John T. Coffee	Wm. S. Moseley
1859[a]	B.J. Brown	Warwick Hough	John T. Coffee	Wm. S. Moseley
1860[a]	B.J. Brown	Warwick Hough	Christian Kribben	Wm. S. Moseley
21—1860	B.J. Brown	Warwick Hough	John McAffee	Thos. H. Murray
1861[a]		Nath. C. Claiborne[d]	John McAffee	Thos. H. Murray
1861[e]	Miles Vernon	John T. Crisp	John McAfee	Thos. H. Murray
22—1862	A.C. Marvin	I.V. Pratt	L.C. Marvin	Walter C. Gantt
1863[a]	A.C. Marvin	I.V. Pratt	L.C. Marvin	Walter C. Gantt
23—1864	Geo. R. Smith	T.J.C. Fagg	Walter L. Lovelace	Dam M. Draper
1865[a]	Jewett Norris	T.J.C. Fagg	Andrew J. Harlan	Dam M. Draper
24—1867	David Bonham	David P. Dyer	Andrew J. Harlan	N.T. Doane
1868[a]	David Bonham	David P. Dyer	Andrew J. Harlan	J.C.S. Colby
25—1869	S.W. Headlee	Geo. A. Moser	John C. Orrick	J.C.S. Colby
1870[a]	S.W. Headlee	Geo. A. Moser	John C. Orrick	J.C.S. Colby
26—1871	Louis Gottschalk	Jno. W. Hendricks	Robt. P.C. Wilson	David A. Sutton
1871[a]	Louis Gottschalk	Jno. W. Hendricks	Robt. P.C. Wilson	David A. Sutton
1872[a]	Louis Gottschalk	Jno. W. Hendricks	Robt. P.C. Wilson	David A. Sutton
1872[a]	Louis Gottschalk	Jno. W. Hendricks	Robt. P.C. Wilson	David A. Sutton
27—1873	Thos. Essex	Benj. F. Wallace	Mortimer McIlhaney	John T. Pratt
1874[a]	Thos. Essex	Benj. F. Wallace	Mortimer McIlhaney	John T. Pratt
28—1875	Th. J.O. Morrison	W.W. Protsman	Banton G. Boone	V.M. Hobbs
29—1877	Th. J.O. Morrison	Daniel Able	John F. Williams	Geo. W. Frame
30—1879	Mich. H. Phelan	W.Y. Pemberton	J. Edwin Belch	W.S. Seymour
31—1881	Th. J.O. Morrison	Francis C. Nesbit	Thos. P. Bashaw	J.H. Hawley
1882[a]	Th. J.O. Morrison	Francis C. Nesbit	Thos. P. Bashaw	Jno. A. Hannay
32—1883	Th. J.O. Morrison	Francis C. Nesbit	Jos. F. Richardson	Jno. A. Hannay
33—1885	Alb. H. Edwards	Francis C. Nesbit	John M. Wood	W.P. Bentley
34—1887	David A. Ball	Ashley S. Coker	J.W. Alexander	T.C. Hornbuckle

Session	President Pro Tem of Senate	Secretary of Senate	Speaker of House	Chief Clerk of House
1887[a]	David A. Ball	Ashley S. Coker	J.W. Alexander	T.C. Hornbuckle
35—1889	H.W. Johnson	Henry L. Gray	Jos. J. Russell	Caleb G. Yate
36—1891	N.B. Anderson	Henry L. Gray	Wilbur F. Tuttle	Abner S. Smith
1892[a]	N.B. Anderson	Henry L. Gray	Wilbur F. Tuttle	Abner S. Smith
37—1893	James W. Sebree	Cornelius Roach	Thos. W. Mabrey	John W. Jacks
38—1895	G.T. Dunn	Cornelius Roach	B.F. Russell	Albert Griffin
1895[a]	G.T. Dunn	Cornelius Roach	B.F. Russell	Albert Griffin
39—1897	Chas. E. Peers	Cornelius Roach	John W. Farris	Chas. W. Green
40—1899	W.S. McClintic	Cornelius Roach	Wm. J. Ward	H.W. Newman
41—1901	Frank H. Farris	Cornelius Roach	J.H. Whitecotton	Jos. S. Tall
42—1903	Thos. L. Rubey	Cornelius Roach	J.H. Whitecotton	Jos. S. Tall
43—1905	Emmett B. Fields	Cornelius Roach	David W. Hill	Ben F. Russell
44—1907	Frank M. McDavid	Cornelius Roach	J.M. Atkinson	Frank L. Dawson
1907[a]	Frank M. McDavid	Cornelius Roach	J.M. Atkinson	Frank L. Dawson
45—1909	G.W. Humphrey	R.S. McClintic	Alfred A. Speer	W.C. Goshorn
46—1911	F.W. McAllister	R.S. McClintic	John T. Barker	J. Kelly Pool
47—1913	Francis M. Wilson	R.L. Daniels	James H. Hull	Omar D. Gray
48—1915	Carter M. Buford	W.A. Norman	James P. Boyd	R.E.L. Marrs
49—1917	John F. Morton	Doc Brydon	Drake Watson	R.E.L. Marrs
50—1919	Walter C. Goodson	R.E.L. Marrs	S.F. O'Fallon	W.G. Kitchen
1919[a]	Walter C. Goodson	R.E.L. Marrs	S.F. O'Fallon	W.G. Kitchen
51—1921	Howard Gray	A.S. Zellweger	S.F. O'Fallon	J. Fent Chapin
1921[f]	Howard Gray	A.S. Zellweger	S.F. O'Fallon	J. Fent Chapin
52—1923	Wm. R. Painter	R.E.L. Marrs	Oak Hunter	William Hicks
53—1925	Wm. R. Painter	R.E.L. Marrs	Jones H. Parker	Wm. M. Turbett
54—1927	Nick T. Cave	R.E.L. Marrs	E.H. Winter	Vic. H. Essen
55—1929	M.E. Casey	R.E.L. Marrs	Jones H. Parker	Vic. H. Essen
56—1931	Lon S. Haymes	R.E.L. Marrs	Eugene W. Nelson	Jos. L. Kennedy
57—1933	Michael Kinney	R.E.L. Marrs	Willis H. Meredith	Jos. A. Bauer
1933[a]	Michael Kinney	R.E.L. Marrs	Willis H. Meredith	Jos. A. Bauer
58—1935	Phil M. Donnelly	R.E.L. Marrs	John G. Christy	Jos. A. Bauer
59—1937	Albert M. Clark	R.E.L. Marrs	John G. Christy	Jos. A. Bauer
60—1939	Joseph H. Brogan	R.E.L. Marrs	John G. Christy	Jos. A. Bauer
1940[a]	Phil M. Donnelly	R.E.L. Marrs	John G. Christy	Jos. A. Bauer
61—1941	Frank P. Briggs	R.E.L. Marrs	Morris E. Osborn	Jos. A. Bauer
1941[a]	Frank P. Briggs	R.E.L. Marrs	Morris E. Osborn	Jos. A. Bauer
62—1943	Frank P. Briggs	R.E.L. Marrs	Howard Elliott	Leonard F. Newton
1944[a]	Frank P. Briggs	R.E.L. Marrs	Howard Elliott	Leonard F. Newton
63—1945	M.C. Matthes	Kirk Jones	Howard Elliott	Herold D. Condray
64—1947	M.C. Matthes	Roy D. Miller	Murray E. Thompson	Curtis J. Tindel
65—1949	E.W. Allison	Joseph A. Bauer	Roy Hamlin	J.S. Wallace
66—1951	William M. Quinn	Joseph A. Bauer	Roy Hamlin	Ray Fordham
67—1953	Michael Kinney	Joseph A. Bauer	L.A. Vonderschmidt	W.D. Cruce
1953[a]	Michael Kinney	Joseph A. Bauer	L.A. Vonderschmidt	W.D. Cruce
1954[g]	Michael Kinney	Joseph A. Bauer	L.A. Vonderschmidt Richard M. Webster[g]	W.D. Cruce
68—1955	Edward V. Long	Joseph A. Bauer	Roy Hamlin	Austin Hill
69—1957	Floyd R. Gibson	Joseph A. Bauer	Roy Hamlin	Austin Hill
1957[a]	Floyd R. Gibson	Joseph A. Bauer	Roy Hamlin	Austin Hill
1958[a]	Floyd R. Gibson	Joseph A. Bauer	Roy Hamlin	Austin Hill
70—1959	Floyd R. Gibson	Joseph A. Bauer	Richard H. Ichord	Austin Hill
1960[a]	Floyd R. Gibson	Joseph A. Bauer	Richard H. Ichord	Austin Hill
71—1961	Albert M. Spradling Jr.	Joseph A. Bauer	Thomas D. Graham	Agnes Moore
72—1963	Albert M. Spradling Jr.	Joseph A. Bauer	Thomas D. Graham	Agnes Moore
73—1965	John W. Joynt	Joseph A. Bauer	Thomas D. Graham	Agnes Moore
1965[a]	John W. Joynt	Joseph A. Bauer	Thomas D. Graham	Agnes Moore
74—1967	John W. Joynt	Joseph A. Bauer	James E. Godfrey	Agnes Moore
1968[a]	John W. Joynt	Joseph A. Bauer	James E. Godfrey	Agnes Moore

Session	President Pro Tem of Senate	Secretary of Senate	Speaker of House	Chief Clerk of House
1968[a]	John W. Joynt	Joseph A. Bauer	James E. Godfrey	Agnes Moore
75—1969	Earl R. Blackwell	Joseph A. Bauer	James E. Godfrey	Agnes Moore
1969[a]	Earl R. Blackwell	Joseph A. Bauer	James E. Godfrey	Agnes Moore
1970[a]	Earl R. Blackwell J.F. Patterson[h]	Joseph A. Bauer	James E. Godfrey	Agnes Moore
1970[a]	J.F. Patterson	Joseph A. Bauer	James E. Godfrey	Agnes Moore
1970[a]	J.F. Patterson	Joseph A. Bauer	James E. Godfrey	Agnes Moore
76—1971	J.F. Patterson	Joseph A. Bauer	James E. Godfrey	Agnes Moore
1972[a]	J.F. Patterson	Vinita E. Ramsey	James E. Godfrey	Agnes Moore
77—1973	William J. Cason	Vinita E. Ramsey	Richard J. Rabbitt	Agnes Moore
1973[a]	William J. Cason	Vinita E. Ramsey	Richard J. Rabbitt	Agnes Moore
1974	William J. Cason	Vinita E. Ramsey	Richard J. Rabbitt	Agnes Moore
1974[a]	William J. Cason	Vinita E. Ramsey	Richard J. Rabbitt	Agnes Moore
78—1975	William J. Cason	Vinita E. Ramsey	Richard J. Rabbitt	Agnes Moore
1975[a]	William J. Cason	Vinita E. Ramsey	Richard J. Rabbitt	Agnes Moore
1976	William J. Cason	Vinita E. Ramsey	Richard J. Rabbitt	Agnes Moore
79—1977	Norman L. Merrell	Vinita E. Ramsey	Kenneth J. Rothman	Dwight Fine
1977[a]	Norman L. Merrell	Vinita E. Ramsey	Kenneth J. Rothman	Dwight Fine
1978	Norman L. Merrell	Vinita E. Ramsey	Kenneth J. Rothman	Dwight Fine
80—1979	Norman L. Merrell	Vinita E. Ramsey	Kenneth J. Rothman	Dwight Fine
1979[a]	Norman L. Merrell	Vinita E. Ramsey	Kenneth J. Rothman	Dwight Fine
1980	Norman L. Merrell	Vinita E. Ramsey	Kenneth J. Rothman	Dwight Fine
1980[a]	Norman L. Merrell	Vinita E. Ramsey	Kenneth J. Rothman	Dwight Fine
81—1981	Norman L. Merrell	Vinita E. Ramsey	Bob F. Griffin	Douglas Burnett
1981[a]	Norman L. Merrell	Vinita E. Ramsey	Bob F. Griffin	Douglas Burnett
1982	Norman L. Merrell	Vinita E. Ramsey	Bob F. Griffin	Douglas Burnett
1982[a]	Norman L. Merrell	Terry Spieler	Bob F. Griffin	Douglas Burnett
82—1983	John E. Scott	Terry Spieler	Bob F. Griffin	Douglas Burnett
1984	John E. Scott	Terry Spieler	Bob F. Griffin	Douglas Burnett
1984[a]	John E. Scott	Terry Spieler	Bob F. Griffin	Douglas Burnett
83—1985	John E. Scott	Terry Spieler	Bob F. Griffin	Douglas Burnett
1986	John E. Scott	Terry Spieler	Bob F. Griffin	Douglas Burnett
84—1987	John E. Scott	Terry Spieler	Bob F. Griffin	Douglas Burnett
1988	John E. Scott	Terry Spieler	Bob F. Griffin	Douglas Burnett
85—1989	James L. Mathewson	Terry Spieler	Bob F. Griffin	Douglas Burnett
1990	James L. Mathewson	Terry Spieler	Bob F. Griffin	Douglas Burnett
86—1991	James L. Mathewson	Terry Spieler	Bob F. Griffin	Douglas Burnett
1992	James L. Mathewson	Terry Spieler	Bob F. Griffin	Douglas Burnett
87—1993	James L. Mathewson	Terry Spieler	Bob F. Griffin	Douglas Burnett
1993[a]	James L. Mathewson	Terry Spieler	Bob F. Griffin	Douglas Burnett
1994	James L. Mathewson	Terry Spieler	Bob F. Griffin	Douglas Burnett
1994[a]	James L. Mathewson	Terry Spieler	Bob F. Griffin	Douglas Burnett
88—1995	James L. Mathewson	Terry Spieler	Bob F. Griffin	Douglas Burnett
1996	James L. Mathewson	Terry Spieler	Steve Gaw[j]	Anne C. Walker
1996	James L. Mathewson	Terry Spieler	Steve Gaw	Anne C. Walker
89—1997	Bill McKenna	Terry Spieler	Steve Gaw	Anne C. Walker
1997[i]	Bill McKenna	Terry Spieler	Steve Gaw	Anne C. Walker
1998	Bill McKenna	Terry Spieler	Steve Gaw	Anne C. Walker
90—1999	Ed Quick	Terry Spieler	Steve Gaw	Anne C. Walker
2000	Ed Quick	Terry Spieler	Steve Gaw	Anne C. Walker
91—2001	Peter Kinder	Terry Spieler	Jim Kreider	Ted Wedel
2001[a]	Peter Kinder	Terry Spieler	Jim Kreider	Ted Wedel
2002	Peter Kinder	Terry Spieler	Jim Kreider	Ted Wedel
92—2003	Peter Kinder	Terry Spieler	Catherine Hanaway	Stephen Davis
2004	Peter Kinder	Terry Spieler	Catherine Hanaway	Stephen Davis
93—2005	Michael Gibbons	Terry Spieler	Rod Jetton	Stephen Davis
2006	Michael Gibbons	Terry Spieler	Rod Jetton	D. Adam Crumbliss
94—2007	Michael Gibbons	Terry Spieler	Rod Jetton	D. Adam Crumbliss

Session	President Pro Tem of Senate	Secretary of Senate	Speaker of House	Chief Clerk of House
2008	Michael Gibbons	Terry Spieler	Rod Jetton	D. Adam Crumbliss
95—2009	Charlie Shields	Terry Spieler	Ron Richard	D. Adam Crumbliss
2010	Charlie Shields	Terry Spieler	Ron Richard	D. Adam Crumbliss
96—2011	Robert N. Mayer	Terry Spieler	Steven Tilley	D. Adam Crumbliss
2012	Robert N. Mayer	Terry Spieler	Steven Tilley	D. Adam Crumbliss
97—2013	Tom Dempsey	Terry Spieler	Tim Jones	D. Adam Crumbliss
97—2015	Tom Dempsey	Adriane D. Crouse	John Diehl [k]	D. Adam Crumbliss
—2015	Tom Dempsey	Adriane D. Crouse	Todd Richardson [l]	D. Adam Crumbliss

[a] Indicates extra sessions.
[b] Elected to replace Minor (deceased).
[c] Elected to replace Irwin (resigned).
[d] Elected to replace Hough (resigned).
[e] Secession legislature first met at Neosho and then at Cassville.
[f] Two extra sessions were held in 1921.
[g] Elected to replace Vonderschmidt (deceased).
[h] Elected to replace Blackwell.
[i] Elected to replace Griffin (resigned).
[j] Two extra sessions were held in 1997.
[k] January 7, 2015–May 15, 2015.
[l] Elected May 15, 2015 to replace John Diehl (resigned).

Joint Legislative Committees

Joint Committee on Administrative Rules

Room B-8, State Capitol
Jefferson City 65101
Telephone: (573) 522-7980
www.senate.mo.gov/jcar

The Joint Committee on Administrative Rules (JCAR) was created in 1975 and is a permanent joint committee of the General Assembly as provided in Chapter 536, RSMo. The Committee is comprised of five members of the Senate and five members of the House. In order to provide continuity in the operation of the committee, the statute authorizing the committee provides the appointment of each member shall continue during his or her term of office as a member of the General Assembly.

The Senate members are appointed by the president *pro tem* of the Senate, while the representatives are appointed by the House speaker. No more than three members from each chamber may be of the same political party.

Under state law, the Joint Committee on Administrative Rules is to continuously monitor and review both proposed and existing rules promulgated by the various executive branch departments and divisions of state government. Citizens or interested organizations who have concerns about rules issued by state agencies can contact the committee with their concerns. In its review the committee is authorized to hold public hearings and review rules in question. Actions taken by the committee on rules and regulations of state agencies must be ratified by the full General Assembly through a concurrent resolution, which then must be signed by the governor. The goal of the Committee on Administrative Rules is to ensure a state agency does not exceed its statutory authority and that the agencies effectively accomplish their missions as mandated by the statutes.

The members of the committee are: Senators Schmitt, Silvey, Wallingford, Holsman, Sifton. Representatives Barnes, Burlison, Colona, McGaugh, Mitten.

Joint Committee on Child Abuse and Neglect

www.senate.mo.gov13info/comm/statutory/jccn.htm

The Joint Committee on Child Abuse and Neglect is a statutory committee of the General Assembly. It is composed of seven members of the House of Representatives, appointed by the speaker and the minority floor leader of the House of Representatives; and seven members of the Senate, appointed by the president *pro tem and the* minority floor leader of the Senate. The duties of the committee are set forth in Section 21.771, RSMo.

Members are: Senators Dixon, Schaefer, Riddle, Schaaf, Chappelle-Nadal, Curls, Schupp. Representatives Lant, Franklin, Haefner, Hubrecht, May, Kirkton, Meredith.

Joint Committee on Education

Room 502, State Capitol
Jefferson City 65101
Telephone: (573) 522-7987
www.senate.mo.gov/13info/comm/statutory/jced.htm

The Joint Committee on Education was created in 2004 and is a statutory committee of the General Assembly. It is composed of seven members of the Senate and seven members of the House. The committee meets to review and monitor the progress of education in the state's public schools; receive reports from the commissioner of education concerning the public schools; conduct a study and analysis of the public school system; make recommendations to the General Assembly for legislative action; and conduct an in-depth study concerning all issues relating to the equity and adequacy of the distribution of state school aid, teachers' salaries, funding for school buildings and overall funding levels for schools and any other education funding-related issues the committee deems relevant. Duties of the committee are set forth in Section 160.254, RSMo.

Members are: Senators Romine, Pearce, Riddle, Schaefer, Wieland, Holsman, Nasheed. Representatives Wood, Cookson, Lair, Swan, Allen, Mims, Pierson.

Joint Committee on Government Accountability

www.senate.mo.gov/13info/comm/statutory/jcga.htm

The Joint Committee on Government Accountability was created in 2004 by House Bill 1599. It is composed of seven members each of the House and the Senate. The bill requires continuing studies and analysis of state government; the determination of the appropriate methods to obtain relevant data at least biennially from each state entity in regard to its function, duties, and performance; and recommendations on any needed changes to statutory law, rules or policies.

Members are: Senators Emery, Kraus, Schaefer, Schmitt, Chappelle-Nadal, Nasheed, Walsh. Representatives Conway, Curtman, Engler, Pierson, Richardson, Rizzo, Walton Gray.

Joint Committee on Legislative Research

Research Division
Room 117A State Capitol
Jefferson City 65101
Telephone: (573) 751-4223
www.moga.mo.gov/legres/legreshome.htm

The Committee on Legislative Research is a permanent joint committee as provided by Sof Article III, Section 35 of the Missouri Constitution.

The committee is composed of 20 members of the General Assembly, with 10 members appointed by the leaders of each chamber. No major party may have more than six members appointed as members from either chamber.

The committee is directed by statute to provide a variety of services for the General Assembly and its members. The committee's offices and staff are divided into two divisions, a Research Division and an Oversight Division. The committee itself is not a policy making group and formulates no legislative program. Its staff renders only such technical and professional assistance as may be requested by the General Assembly or any of its members, or as required by statute.

The Research Division provides bill drafting assistance, prepares concurrent and courtesy resolutions, operates a legislative reference library and publishes the Revised Statutes of Missouri and subsequent supplements, and Session Laws of Missouri.

Bills are drawn at the request of any member of the General Assembly, but the fact that a bill has been drafted by a member of the staff does not carry with it the endorsement of the Committee on Legislative Research. All bill requests are treated confidentially by the bill drafter and without comment or criticism of the subject matter.

One need of state government is a modern legislative reference library. The library maintained by the Committee on Legislative Research continuously acquires books, pamphlets, periodicals and reports and the staff works closely with the staff of the Missouri State Library and the Supreme Court Library.

Through its acquisitions, exchanges and loans with other libraries, the legislative library provides much of the material requested by members of the General Assembly for the analysis of public questions and provides a research tool for bill drafting and research services.

Courtesy resolutions continue to be of great importance to members of the General Assembly. More than 600 per month are prepared by the resolution-writers for a variety of observances.

The Oversight Division is supervised by a subcommittee of the Committee on Legislative Research. The Oversight Division is responsible for preparing fiscal notes on all bills pending before the General Assembly with the exception of appropriation bills. Fiscal notes must state the cost of the proposed legislation to the state for the next two fiscal years; whether the proposal would establish a program or agency which would duplicate an existing program or agency; whether the provisions of the proposal were federally mandated; whether the proposal would have significant direct fiscal impact upon any political subdivision of the state; whether any new physical facilities would be required; and whether an impact to small businesses would be expected. The division prepares approximately 3,000 fiscal notes during a regular legislative session.

The Oversight Division is authorized to perform management and program evaluations of state agencies and is assigned work pursuant to a duly adopted concurrent resolution of the General Assembly or a resolution adopted by the Committee on Legislative Research. The division conducts the evaluations in accordance with government auditing standards set forth by the U.S. Government Accountability Office. The management and program evaluations of the division provide the General Assembly with important information regarding the status of programs they have created and the expenditure of funds they have authorized.

In 2003, the Oversight Division was authorized to perform sunset reviews of any new program enacted into law. Each new program that is enacted will have a sunset date period of not more than six years. A program may be re-authorized for a period of up to 12 years. The committee shall issue a report to the General Assembly with recommendations on whether the program should continue, be reorganized, sunset or consolidated within state agencies not under review.

Committee members are: Senators Dixon, Munzlinger, Parson, Schaefer, Silvey, Wallingford, Holsman, Sifton, Walsh. Representatives Engler, Allen, Conway, Flanigan, Jones, Fitzpatrick, Gardner, McDonald, Pierson, Shaul.

Joint Committee on Life Sciences

The Joint Committee on Life Sciences is a statutory committee of the General Assembly. It is composed of seven members of the Senate and seven members of the House of Representatives. The duties of the committee are set forth in Section 21.805.1, RSMo.

Members are: Senators Brown, Munzlinger, Richard, Wasson. Representatives Frederick, Rowden, Zerr, Carpenter, McNeil.

Joint Committee on MO HealthNet

www.senate.mo.gov/13info/comm/statutory/jcmh.htm

The Joint Committee on MO HealthNet was created in 2007 and is a statutory joint committee under Section 208.952, RSMo. Missouri's Medicaid program was renamed "MO HealthNet" and various new provisions pertaining to the program were adopted in that same year. The committee has been charged with the study of the resources needed to continue and improve the MO HealthNet program over time.

The committee consists of ten members of the general assembly, five from the Senate and five from House of Representatives, with no more than three members from each house from the same party. In addition, the committee shall consist of members from the appropriate budget and appropriations committees assigned to MO HealthNet and health related matters.

The committee is tasked with making recommendations in a report to the general assembly by January first each year on anticipated growth in the MO HealthNet program, needed improvements, anticipated appropriations, and suggested strategies on ways to structure the state budget in order to satisfy the future needs of the program.

Members are: Senators Brown, Schmitt, Schaefer, Curls.

Joint Committee on Public Employees Retirement

Room 219A, State Capitol
Jefferson City 65101
Telephone: (573) 522-7990
www.jcper.org

The Joint Committee on Public Employees Retirement (JCPER) was created in 1983 and is a permanent joint committee as provided in Chapter 21, RSMo.

The committee is composed of 12 members of the General Assembly; six appointed from the House of Representatives by the speaker and six appointed from the Senate by the president *pro tem*. No political party may be represented on the committee by more than three members

from the Senate, nor by more than three members from the House of Representatives.

The Joint Committee on Public Employees Retirement is directed by statute to:

1) make a continuing study and analysis of all state and local government retirement systems;

2) devise a standard reporting system to obtain data on each public employee retirement system that will provide information on each system's financial and actuarial status at least biennially;

3) determine from its study and analysis the need for changes in statutory law; and

4) make any other recommendations to the General Assembly necessary to provide adequate retirement benefits to state and local government employees within the ability of taxpayers to support their future costs.

The committee is required to meet at least quarterly and may subpoena witnesses or records and may take testimony under oath in matters pertaining to public employee retirement.

Members are: Senators Kehoe, Schaaf, Chappelle-Nadal, Keaveny, Wallingford, Walsh. Representatives Bernskoetter, Leara, Runions, Anders, Pierson, Walker.

Joint Committee on Tax Increment Financing

The Joint Committee on Tax Increment Financing is a statutory committee of the General Assembly. Established pursuant to Chapter 99, Section 863, RSMo.

Members are: Senators Romine, Kraus. Representatives Allen, Leara.

Joint Committee on Tax Policy

Room 235C, State Capitol
Jefferson City 65101
Telephone: (573) 522-7995
www.senate.mo.gov/taxpolicy/

The Joint Committee on Tax Policy is a statutory committee of the General Assembly. It is composed of five members of the Senate and five members of the House of Representatives. It is the duty of the committee to:

1) make a continuing study and analysis of the current and proposed tax policy of this state;

2) make a continuing study and review of the department of revenue, the department of economic development, the state tax commission, and any other state agency, commission, or state executive office

responsible for the administration of tax policies;

3) study the effects of the coupling or decoupling with the federal income tax code as it relates to the state income tax;

4) make recommendations, as and when the committee deems fit, to the General Assembly for legislative action or to report findings and to the departments, commissions and offices for administrative or procedural changes;

5) study the effects of a sales tax holiday; and

6) examine and assess the public benefit of any tax credit program that is the subject of an audit by the state auditor.

Members are: Senators Kraus, Hegeman, Onder, Chappelle-Nadal, Curls. Representatives Haefner, Jones, Smith.

Joint Committee on Transportation Oversight

www.senate.mo.gov/13info/comm/statutory/jcto.htm

The Joint Committee on Transportation Oversight was created in 1998 and is a permanent, statutory committee of the General Assembly. It is composed of seven members of the House of Representatives, and seven members of the Senate. The duties of the committee are set forth in Section 21.795, RSMo.

Members are: Senators Libla, Dixon, Munzlinger, Romine, Schatz, Chappelle-Nadal, Curls. Representatives Kolkmeyer, Korman, Lant, Rone, Burns., May, McDonald.

Chain of Rocks Park
photo courtesy of Missouri State Archives

CHAPTER 5
JUDICIAL BRANCH

Fishing at Pershing State Park
Photo courtesy of Missouri State Archives

Missouri's Judicial System

From its inception in 1820, Missouri state government constitutionally has been divided into three separate branches—legislative, executive and judicial. The judicial branch's function is not to make the laws of the state or to administer them but to adjudicate the controversies that arise between persons and parties, to determine fairly and justly the guilt or innocence of persons charged with criminal offenses and to interpret the laws of the state as enacted by the legislature and carried out by the executive branch.

The roots of Missouri's judicial branch reach back to the days when Missouri was a part of the Missouri Territory controlled by the French and Spanish. When Missouri officially was organized as a territory in 1812, the judicial power was vested in a superior court, inferior courts and justices of the peace. The Constitution of 1820, the state's first constitution, placed the judicial power in a Supreme Court, chancery courts (later abolished by the General Assembly) and circuit and other courts to be established by the legislature.

Today, Missouri has a three-tier court system. Article V of the constitution, as amended by Missouri voters in 1976, vests the judicial power in a Supreme Court, the state's highest court, with statewide jurisdiction; in a court of appeals consisting of districts established by the General Assembly; and in a system of circuit courts that have original jurisdiction over all cases and matters, civil and criminal.

Effective Jan. 2, 1979, the circuit court system absorbed all former courts of limited jurisdiction and became the state's single trial court. Cases once heard in magistrate and probate courts, in the St. Louis Court of Criminal Corrections, in the Hannibal and Cape Girardeau courts of common pleas, and in municipal and other local courts, now are heard in appropriate divisions of the circuit courts.

All the judges of these former courts have become either circuit, associate circuit or municipal judges. They may hear and determine different classes of cases within their respective circuits. A presiding judge, elected by the other judges in the circuit, has general administrative authority over all judicial personnel in the circuit. He or she may assign other judges throughout the circuit to relieve caseload and administrative backlogs. The Supreme Court and court of appeals have general superintending control over all courts and tribunals within their jurisdictions. Original remedial writs may be issued and determined at each level of the court system. Decisions of the Supreme Court are controlling in all other state courts.

Selection of Judges

In the first 30 years of Missouri's statehood, the judges of the supreme, circuit and chancery courts were appointed by the governor with the advice and consent of the Senate. After much public discussion, the constitution was amended in 1850 to provide for the popular election of judges, and this system remains in effect for most Missouri courts today. In most circuits, the judges are elected by the voters in partisan elections.

In 1940, Missouri voters amended the constitution by adopting the "Nonpartisan Selection of Judges Court Plan," which was placed on the ballot by initiative petition and which provides for the nonpartisan (non-political) appointment of certain judges, rather than having them popularly elected.

The constitution, as amended further in 1976, provides that the Nonpartisan Court Plan applies in the Supreme Court, the court of appeals and the circuit courts within the City of St. Louis and Jackson County. In addition, voters in Clay, Greene, Platte and St. Louis counties have elected to institute the plan, and the Kansas City charter extends a nonpartisan selection plan to Kansas City municipal court judges. While all other judges are elected in partisan elections, other judicial circuits may adopt the plan on approval by a majority of the voters in the circuit.

Under the Missouri Plan, as it often is called nationally, a vacancy on a court to which the plan applies is filled through a nonpartisan judicial commission of lay persons and lawyers. The commission selects three persons from those who apply, based on merit. The governor then appoints one of the three. A judge appointed in this way must stand for retention in office at the first general election occurring after the judge has been in office for 12 months. The judge's name is placed on a separate judicial ballot, without political party designation, and the voters must vote either for or against retention in office. The judge's name again is placed on the ballot for a retention vote at certain intervals if the judge wishes to serve subsequent terms. The Missouri Plan has served as a national model for the selection of judges and has been adopted by a number of other states.

Every supreme, appellate, circuit and associate circuit court judge must be licensed to practice law in Missouri. By constitutional amendment and statute, all judges must retire by age 70.

Supreme Court of Missouri

Supreme Court Bldg.
207 W. High St., PO Box 150, Jefferson City 65102
Telephone: (573) 751-4144
www.courts.mo.gov

History and Organization

The Supreme Court has been the state's highest court since 1820, when the first Missouri Constitution was adopted. The earliest court, consisting of only three members, was required to hold sessions in four different judicial circuits in the state. At various times, the court sat in Boonville, Cape Girardeau, Fayette, Hannibal, Jackson, Lexington, St. Charles, St. Louis and other cities.

The size of the Supreme Court was increased to five judges in 1872 and to its present size—seven judges—in 1890. Because of the court's increasing caseload, commissioners were appointed for a brief period in the 1880s. In 1911, the legislature authorized the court to appoint four commissioners, and in 1927, the number was changed to six. The commissioners were required to possess the same qualifications as judges of the Supreme Court. They received the same compensation and were appointed for four-year terms. The commissioners heard cases along with the judges, and their written opinions, if approved by the court, were issued as opinions of the court.

Under terms of the 1970 constitutional amendment of Article V, the offices of the commissioners ceased to exist when the individuals holding the offices retired, resigned, died or were removed from office.

In 1890, the Supreme Court was divided into two divisions to permit it to handle and decide more cases in a shorter time. Under the present constitution, the court may sit *en banc* (all seven judges together) or in as many divisions as the court determines are needed. Today, cases are assigned to and decided by the court *en banc*.

Supreme Court Jurisdiction

Originally, the Supreme Court had only the traditional powers to decide cases on appeal from the lower courts (either the circuit courts or the court of appeals) and to issue and determine original remedial writs, such as those in *habeas corpus, mandamus* and prohibition. The Constitution of 1945 also authorized the court to establish rules for practice and procedure in the courts and to make temporary transfers of judicial personnel from court to court. Maintaining and updating the rules is a continuous process requiring substantial time. Each year, the Su-

preme Court, through its Office of State Courts Administrator, transfers several hundred court personnel on a temporary basis to assist other courts. This usually is done when a judge has been disqualified by the parties in a case or when a judge's docket has become overly crowded and the judge cannot handle all the cases expeditiously.

The constitutional amendments of 1976 and 1982 defined the jurisdiction of the Supreme Court more narrowly than in the past, resulting in its receiving fewer cases on appeal and directing more appeals to the court of appeals. Now the Supreme Court has exclusive appellate jurisdiction in all cases involving: the validity of a treaty or statute of the United States or of a statute or provision of the Missouri Constitution, the construction of the state's revenue laws, the title to any state office and the death penalty.

Cases do not have to fall within this area of exclusive jurisdiction, however, to reach the Supreme Court. The court may order cases transferred to it from the court of appeals if the cases involve questions of general interest or importance, if the court believes the existing law should be re-examined or for other reasons provided by rule of the court. The court of appeals also may order a case transferred to the Supreme Court either by order of the court of appeals itself or by the dissent of a court of appeals judge, if that judge certifies the court of appeals opinion is contrary to previous decisions of the Supreme Court or of other districts of the court of appeals.

In addition to its decision-making powers, the Supreme Court supervises all lower courts in the state. It is assisted in this task by its Office of State Courts Administrator, established in 1970. The Supreme Court also licenses all lawyers practicing in Missouri and disciplines those found guilty of violating the legal rules of professional conduct.

Qualifications and Terms

Supreme Court judges must be at least 30 years of age, licensed to practice law in Missouri, U.S. citizens for 15 years and qualified Missouri voters for nine years. Supreme Court judges are retained for 12-year terms. They earn $147,591 annually. Compensation is determined by statute (section 476.405, RSMo).

Chief Justice

The seven judges of the Supreme Court select one of their members to be chief justice and preside over the court. The chief justice also handles many of the administrative details for the court. The present practice of the court is to rotate the position of chief justice every two years. The chief justice earns $154,215 annually. Compensation is determined by statute (section 476.405, RSMo).

The court hears oral arguments each month from September through May. Court sessions are open to the public, and oral arguments are broadcast live and are archived through the court's website, *www. courts.mo.gov.*

Supreme Court Building

The Supreme Court Building, a three-story, red brick structure of French Renaissance architecture, was completed in 1907 and stands opposite the Capitol Building. By statute, it houses the attorney general's offices as well as those of the Supreme Court. The building's main features are a massive marble staircase in the lobby and the two-story high library. The building has been refurbished extensively and modernized with the use of monies appropriated by the General Assembly.

BILL L. THOMPSON
Supreme Court Clerk

Clerk's Office

The clerk of the Supreme Court is responsible for a wide range of duties, including the supervision of the internal administrative function of the court itself as well as the planning and administrative direction of the Judicial Conference of Missouri, the organization comprising all of the state judges.

Supreme Court Function

The court's day-to-day administrative duties include handling all inquiries and procedural requests from attorneys throughout the state, arranging the docketing (scheduling) of cases, maintaining files in each case before the court, receiving and disposing of fees related to those cases and distributing opinions of the court. In all of these matters, the clerk reports directly to the chief justice.

Missouri Bar Responsibilities

Telephone: (573) 635-4128
www.mobar.org

The clerk of the Supreme Court has a number of additional duties relating to The Missouri Bar and supervising the admission of new attorneys.

Among the records required to be maintained by the clerk are the official and permanent roll of attorneys for the State of Missouri. The clerk's office also prepares, on request, certificates evidencing admission to The Missouri Bar. By Supreme Court rule, the clerk is treasurer of the state board of law examiners, which conducts bar examinations twice yearly. The clerk also supervises the court's semiannual enrollment ceremonies and prepares all attorney licenses.

By Supreme Court rule, the clerk is *ex officio* treasurer of both The Missouri Bar and the advisory committee and is responsible for collecting the annual attorney enrollment fee and distribut-

ing Missouri Bar membership cards to all attorneys licensed to practice in Missouri. He or she is responsible for maintaining the official records of The Missouri Bar and the bar fund and for preparing annual financial reports for publication in the *Journal of The Missouri Bar*. The clerk is also responsible for conducting annual elections for The Missouri Bar Board of Governors.

Security Administration

The Supreme Court's marshal is under the clerk's supervision. The marshal is responsible for the security of the building and its judges and employees. The marshal also acts as bailiff when the court is in session. In addition, the marshal is responsible for all homeland security matters as they affect the Supreme Court.

Supreme Court Library

Telephone: (573) 751-2636
www.courts.mo.gov

The Supreme Court Library, which is on the second floor of the Supreme Court Building, contains more than 110,000 volumes. These include decisions of state and federal courts as well as state and federal administrative agencies, Missouri-approved jury instructions, state and federal statutes, legal periodicals and treatises. In addition, the library contains computer research services for the use of court personnel.

The library's main responsibility is to meet the research needs of the Supreme Court, the attorney general's office, the General Assembly and the state's executive department agencies, but it also provides resources to members of the bench and bar and the general public. It is open 8 a.m. to 5 p.m., Monday through Friday, throughout the year, excluding state holidays.

Patricia Breckenridge

Chief Justice of the Supreme Court

PATRICIA BRECKENRIDGE was elected chief justice by her colleagues for a two-year term beginning July 1, 2015. She was born and raised in Nevada and was educated in the Nevada public schools. She attended the Univ. of Arkansas–Fayetteville and the Univ. of Mo.–Columbia, where she earned a B.S. and J.D. She was admitted to The Missouri Bar in 1978. Following law school, she practiced law in the firm Russell, Brown, Bickel & Breckenridge. While practicing, she served as an assistant municipal judge for the City of Nevada.

In 1982, she was appointed associate circuit-judge of Vernon County. Chief Justice Breckenridge was elected to that position until 1990, when she was appointed to the Missouri Court of Appeals, Western District. There, she authored more than 900 opinions and participated in more than 2,700 cases. Chief Justice Breckenridge was appointed to the Supreme Court of Missouri, 2007.

She served as chair to the Supreme Court's Judicial Education Coordinating Commission for six years and served as a faculty member at the new judges' orientation for 12 years. She established the Judicial Education's Civic Education Committee in 2011, and served as chair for four years. She is a founding faculty member of Missouri's Court Management Institute program, receiving her certification in Purposes and Responsibilities of Courts from the National Center of State Courts, Williamsburg, Va. Chief Justice Breckenridge also served as liaison to the Family Court Committee and liaison to the Joint Committee on Gender and Justice for six years.

Chief Justice Breckenridge is an Elwood L. Thomas American Inn of Court Master, and also serves as a member of the Missouri Crossover Youth Policy team, American Bar Assoc., The Missouri Bar, the Kansas City Metropolitan Bar Assoc., the National Assoc. of Women Judges, the Assoc. for Women Lawyers of Kansas City, and the Missouri Assoc. of Probate and Associate Circuit Judges. She was a member of the Casey Family Programs' National Impact Outcomes Committee, 2012–2013. She has served on the board of directors of Lawyers Encouraging Economic Performance and the Missouri Institute for Justice. Chief Justice Breckenridge was a member of the Missouri Task Force on Gender and Justice and co-chair of the Missouri Gender Fairness Implementation Joint Committee of the Supreme Court of Missouri and The Missouri Bar.

She has received The Missouri Bar President's Award, the University of Missouri School of Law's Citation of Merit, Association of Women Lawyers of Greater Kansas City's Judicial Recognition Award, Judge of the Year and Special Achievement Award, Daily Record's Legal Leader Award, the Nevada Rotary International Citizen of the Year, Nevada Business and Professional Women Woman of the Year, Soroptimist International of Nevada Women Helping Women and Woman of Distinction and the Ozark Area Girl Scout Council Woman of Distinction. She is a Women Lawyers' Association of Greater St. Louis Honoree, Council of State Government Toll Fellow, an American Bar Foundation Fellow, and a Fellow of the Georgetown University Center for Juvenile Justice Reform.

Chief Justice Breckenridge has served both the Kansas City and Nevada communities through numerous civic and charitable activities. In Kansas City, she was a mentor and tutor for children at St. Vincent's Operation Breakthrough. She served on the board of directors and as president of the Mattie Rhodes Center, and on the board of directors of Cabot West Side Clinic and the University of Health Sciences, College of Osteopathic Medicine. In Nevada, she served as president of Soroptimist International of Nevada and the Business and Professional Women of Nevada, on the board of directors for the Home Health Advisory Board and was a member of Rotary International of Nevada. She is a member of PEO Sisterhood, Chapter DW and the United Methodist Church of Nevada.

She married Bryan C. Breckenridge on May 15, 1976. She and Bryan live in Nevada and maintain a home in Columbia. She was retained by Missouri voters at the November 2008 general election for a term expiring Dec. 31, 2020.

George W. Draper III
Judge of the Supreme Court

GEORGE W. DRAPER III was born Aug. 5, 1953, in St. Louis. He attended Hamilton Elementary School in north St. Louis City until his family moved to Silver Spring, Md., in 1964. In 1977, he graduated from Morehouse College in Atlanta, Ga., with a bachelor's degree in psychology. After earning his law degree in 1981 from Howard University School of Law in Washington, D.C., he served as a law clerk to Judge Shellie Bowers in the Superior Court of the District of Columbia.

Draper worked for the circuit attorney of the City of St. Louis as assistant prosecuting attorney from 1984 to 1994. There he served as assistant prosecutor, then team leader and, finally, as first assistant, for which he handled numerous felony prosecutions.

In 1994, Draper was appointed associate circuit judge in St. Louis County by Gov. Mel Carnahan. While serving on this court, Draper presided over 60 to 200 cases each week and was assigned specially to 12 jury trials. In 1998, he was appointed to circuit judge in St. Louis County by Gov. Carnahan. He presided over the civil, criminal, family court and juvenile division throughout his time as a trial judge.

In 2000, Gov. Carnahan appointed Judge Draper to the Missouri Court of Appeals, Eastern District. Draper served as that court's first African-American chief judge from July 2005 to June 2006. While on that court, he also served by special assignment on the Appellate Apportionment Commission, a constitutional commission created to resolve redistricting disputes, and on the court's rules, security and facilities committees. His October 2011 appointment to the Supreme Court of Missouri by Gov. Jeremiah Nixon makes Draper one of the few judges to have served at every level of Missouri's current court system.

When not on the bench, Draper counsels students interested in legal careers and has served as a mentor to attorneys deferred from practicing.

Draper is a member of the Mound City Bar Association, the Bar Association of Metropolitan St. Louis, the Lawyer's Association of St. Louis, the National Bar Association and the Missouri Asian Bar Association. He is an inaugural member of the Gallery of St. Louis Legal Pioneers within the Bar Association of Metropolitan St. Louis. He is a member and vice president of the board of Covenant Community Church in north St. Louis County. He also is a member of the Prince Hall Free and Accepted Masons.

As an advocate for continuing legal education, Draper has organized and presented numerous programs. He also has served as a panelist on the Mound City Bar Association's program "Mistakes to Avoid" and at the judicial forum hosted by the Missouri Association of Trial Attorneys.

In addition to his service to the court, Draper has taught trial advocacy as an adjunct professor at Saint Louis University School of Law from 1996 to the present.

Draper's wife, Judy Preddy Draper, is an associate circuit judge in St. Louis County and previously served as general counsel for the Missouri Department of Corrections. They have a daughter, Chelsea, who graduated from Amherst College in Amherst, Mass., and is presently a student at Washington University School of Law in St. Louis.

Zel M. Fischer
Judge of the Supreme Court

ZEL M. FISCHER was born in Hamburg, Iowa, on April 28, 1963, and grew up in Watson, Mo.

Judge Fischer was educated in Rock Port public schools. He attended William Jewell College, in Liberty, Mo., and received his B.A. in philosophy and political science in 1985. He is the recipient of the Harry S Truman Most Outstanding Political Science Major for the class of 1985.

He graduated from the University of Missouri–Kansas City School of Law with distinction in 1988. He is the recipient of the Order of the Bench and Robe, the American Jurisprudence Award from the UMKC School of Law and was a member of UMKC Law Review. He is the original author of *Chapter 40, Strict Liability of Product Manufacturers and Sellers — Manufacturing Defect of the Products Liability Handbook*, published by the University of Missouri–Kansas City, Continuing Legal Education.

Judge Fischer was admitted to The Missouri Bar in 1988. Upon graduation, he served for one year as a law clerk for the Honorable Andrew Jackson Higgins of the Supreme Court of Missouri. From 1989–1992, he practiced law in the Law Offices of James D. Boggs in Kansas City. From 1992–2006, he engaged in a solo law practice in northwest Missouri. In November 2006, he was elected associate circuit judge for Atchison County, in the Fourth Judicial Circuit, and served in that capacity until his appointment to the Supreme Court of Missouri in October 2008.

Judge Fischer was selected as an ASTAR Fellow by the board of directors of the Advanced Science and Technology Adjudication Resource Center for his knowledge and ability to preside over complex cases involving science or technology issues. The National Courts and Science Institute (NCSI) is a not-for-profit organization dedicated to training judges in science. Recently, the NCSI board of directors selected him to be the vice president and chair of the executive committee.

Judge Fischer is an active member of his church and community.

Judge Fischer was married July 13, 1985, to the former Julie Ann Moore. They have four children.

Judge Fischer was appointed to the Supreme Court by Gov. Matt Blunt on Oct. 15, 2008, and was retained at the 2010 general election for a 12-year term expiring Dec. 31, 2022.

Mary R. Russell

Judge of the Supreme Court

MARY R. RUSSELL, a seventh-generation Missourian, was raised on a dairy farm in Ralls County, near Hannibal, where she learned the value of hard work. She graduated valedictorian from Hannibal High School and summa cum laude from Truman State University. She received her J.D. from the University of Missouri-Columbia School of Law.

Upon graduation from law school, Judge Russell clerked for the Honorable George Gunn of the Supreme Court of Missouri. She later practiced law in Hannibal with the law firm of Clayton and Rhodes until her appointment to the Missouri Court of Appeals, Eastern District in 1995. At the Court of Appeals, she served as chief judge from 1999–2000.

Judge Russell is active in many professional and legal organizations around the state and country. Always promoting the administration of justice, Judge Russell is currently on the Board of Directors of the National Courts and Science Institute, and a member of the Council of the Section of Legal Education and Admissions to the Bar. She has served as second vice-president of the Conference of Chief Justices; on the Commission on Retirement, Removal and Discipline of Judges; Missouri Lawyers Trust Account Foundation; Young Lawyers Council of The Missouri Bar; numerous Missouri Bar committees; the Supreme Court Civil Rules Committee; and the Appellate Practice Committee. She is a past co-chair of the Appellate Practice Committee of BAMSL and has served as chair on other committees in BAMSL.

She has been a member on a variety of statewide boards and commissions, including the Board of Governors of Truman State Univ. (president, 1996), Missouri State Senate Reapportionment Commission in 1991, the Missouri Council on Women's Economic Development, the Missouri Job Development and Training Council and, in 2009, she was the president of the board of directors of Missouri's Court Appointed Special Advocates (CASA). Currently, she serves on the Missouri Press-Bar Commission and is a trustee of the State Historical Society of Missouri.

Judge Russell is the recipient of numerous awards, including the Women's Justice Award, the Faculty/Alumni Award from the University of Missouri-Columbia, the Citation of Merit Award

from the University of Missouri–Columbia Law School, the Distinguished Alumni Award-Truman State University, the Legal Services of Eastern Missouri Equal Justice Award, the Lasting Legacy award from Missouri CASA, the Soroptomist International Women Helping Women Award, the Jefferson City Rotarian of the Year, Zonta Woman of Achievement in Jefferson City, the Matthews-Dickey Boys & Girls Club Appreciation Award, a Henry Toll Fellow, the Kirkwood Citizen of the Year and she was named in 2015 to the Ingram's 50 Missourians You Should Know. She is a member of the Missouri Academy of Squires and the Rollins Society of the University of Missouri.

Active in many community organizations, Judge Russell is a member of the BackStoppers, Inc., Missouri Women's Forum, Jefferson City Rotary Club (past president), PEO, Grace Episcopal Church and The Tuesday Club. She also volunteers as a truancy court judge at Lewis and Clark Middle School in Jefferson City. She was active in many organizations in Hannibal and Kirkwood prior to her move to Jefferson City.

Judge Russell is easily approachable and devotes much time to mentoring young people. In addition to lecturing to many attorney organizations and continuing education programs, she spends many hours demystifying the court system by speaking to community groups and students.

Judge Russell and her husband, Jim, live in Jefferson City. She was appointed to the Supreme Court in 2004 and was retained by the voters in November 2006 for a 12-year term. She was elected chief justice by her colleagues for a two-year term beginning July 1, 2013, and ending on June 30, 2015.

Laura Denvir Stith

Judge of the Supreme Court

LAURA DENVIR STITH was born in St. Louis on October 30, 1953. She was raised in St. Louis and graduated with honors from the John Burroughs School, 1971. She received a National Merit Scholarship to attend Tufts University in Boston, Mass. While there, she was an Iglauer Fellowship Intern in Washington, DC, for Sen. Thomas Eagleton, 1973. She studied at the University of Madrid through a program administered by the Institute of European Studies. In 1975, she graduated *magna cum laude* from Tufts, receiving her B.A. in political science and social psychology. She then attended the Georgetown University Law Center, distinguishing herself as an editor of the *Law and Policy in International Business Journal*. Judge Stith graduated *magna cum laude* from Georgetown in 1978.

Following her graduation from law school, Judge Stith served for one year as a law clerk to the Honorable Robert E. Seiler of the Missouri Supreme Court. In 1979, she moved to Kansas City and practiced law with the firm of Shook, Hardy & Bacon, becoming a partner of the firm in 1984 and later co-founding the firm's appellate practice group.

In the fall of 1994, Gov. Mel Carnahan appointed Judge Stith to the Missouri Court of Appeals, Western District. She was retained in the November 1996 general election. During her time on the court of appeals, Judge Stith authored over 400 opinions in cases involving nearly every area of state law.

Governor Bob Holden appointed Judge Stith to the Supreme Court of Missouri effective March 7, 2001, and she was retained in the November 2002 general election, and again at the 2014 general election. She is the second woman in Missouri history to serve on the state's Supreme Court. She served as chief justice of the court from July 1, 2007, through June 30, 2009.

Judge Stith has been involved in many organizations in the legal community. She has served as chair of the Gender and Justice Joint Committee of The Missouri Bar and the Missouri Supreme Court. She was a founding director of Lawyers Encouraging Academic Performance (LEAP), an inter-bar lawyers' public service organization. She has served as president and member of the board of directors of the Association for Women Lawyers (AWL) of Greater Kansas City, chair and vice-chair of the Missouri Bar Civil Practice and Procedure Committee, chair of the Appellate Practice Committee and vice-chair of the Tort Law Committee of the Kansas City Metropolitan Bar Association (KCMBA) and is a member of the American Bar Association (ABA).

Judge Stith has served as a speaker on appellate practice at the annual conventions of the ABA, Missouri Bar, Missouri Association of Trial Attorneys (MATA) and Missouri Organization of Defense Lawyers (MODL). She has also served as a speaker or moderator on civil procedure and evidence at The Missouri Bar, KCMBA, AWL, and University of Missouri–Kansas City Continuing Legal Education (CLE) programs and as a speaker on gender bias at the Missouri New Judges School. She has authored many publications, including Stith, *A Contrast of State and Federal Court Authority to Grant Habeas Relief,* 38 *Val. U .L. Rev.* 421 (Spring 2004); *Stith and Root, The Missouri Nonpartisan Court Plan: The Least Political Method of Selecting High Quality Judges,* 74 *Mo. L. Rev.* 711 (2009); and *Stith, Just Because You Can Measure Something, Does it Really Count?,* 58 *Duke L.J.* 1743 (2009).

Judge Stith has been actively involved in many community activities in Kansas City, serving as a mentor and tutor to young students at St. Vincent's Operation Breakthrough and a guest speaker at many local civic organizations, talking about the law, the role of the courts and public service.

Judge Stith is married to fellow attorney Donald G. Scott. Mr. Scott served as a law clerk for Judge Warren D. Welliver of the Supreme Court of Missouri. He is a shareholder in McDowell, Rice, Smith and Buchanan, P.C., in Kansas City. They have three daughters.

Richard B. Teitelman
Judge of the Supreme Court

RICHARD B. TEITELMAN opened a solo law practice after graduating from law school. In 1975, he joined Legal Services of Eastern Missouri, serving for 23 years—18 of those as executive director and general counsel.

Judge Teitelman served on the Missouri Court of Appeals, Eastern District, from 1998 to 2002, when he was appointed to the Supreme Court of Missouri, becoming the first legally blind and the first Jewish member of the court. He was retained in the 2004 general election. He was elected chief justice for a two-year term beginning July 1, 2011 and served on the Executive Council of the Judicial Conference of Missouri. He serves as second vice president of the Conference of Chief Justices.

In his pursuit of equality and access to justice for all, Judge Teitelman is currently a member of the African-American/Jewish Task Force. He served on the board of the American Jewish Congress and is a member of the board of the American Association of Jewish Lawyers and Jurists. He served on the Midwest Board of the American Federation for the Blind; as a board member of the St. Louis Public Library; and is a lifetime member of the Urban League of St. Louis.

Devoted to the administration of justice, Judge Teitelman is a Life Patron Fellow of the American Bar Association (ABA). He served on the executive committee of the ABA Appellate Judicial Conference and the American Judicature Society (AJS) and is an AJS delegate to the ABA House of Delegates. He has served as president of the Bar Association of Metropolitan St. Louis (BAMSL); president of the BAMSL Young Lawyers Section; charter member and president of the St. Louis Bar Foundation; and vice president and president-elect of The Missouri Bar. He was chair of the bar's Delivery of Legal Services Committee. He is a Life Fellow of and serves as ex officio of the Missouri Bar Foundation; trustee of the National Council of Bar Foundations; and served as chair of the ABA Commission on Mental and Physical Disability Law. He served as a member of the ABA Standing Committee on Pro Bono and Public Service.

Judge Teitelman's dedication to the legal services program has earned him many honors, including the prestigious Missouri Bar President's Award, the American Council for the Blind's Durward K. McDaniel Ambassador Award, the Women's Legal Caucus Good Guy Award, the Mound City Bar Association Legal Service Award, the ABA Young Lawyers Division Award of Merit, the ABA Young Lawyers Division Difference Maker Award and the St. Louis Bar Foundation Award. Legal Services of Eastern Missouri has named its pro bono award for legal services the "Richard Teitelman Award."

A strong proponent of legal scholarship, Judge Teitelman is an honorary dean of St. Louis University School of Law's DuBourg Society and an honorary member of Washington University School of Law's Order of the Coif and Eliot Society. He is a member of the Washington University School of Law National Council. He was honored by Washington University School of Law as a Distinguished Alumnus. Judge Teitelman participated in the Toll Fellowship Program of the Council of State Governments.

Other honors Judge Teitelman has received include The Missouri Bar Purcell Award for Professionalism; the American Jewish Congress Democracy in Action Award; the Lawyers Association of St. Louis Award of Honor; the St. Louis Society for the Blind Lifetime Achievement Award; the University of Missouri–Columbia School of Law Distinguished Non-Alumnus Award; the ABA Government and Public Sector Lawyers Division's Hodson Award, ABA Legislative Advocacy Award and its Grassroots Legislative Advocacy Award; the Dr. Martin L. King Jr. State Celebration Committee Distinguished Statesman Award; the Ethical Humanist of the Year (St. Louis); the St. Louis University School of Law Clarence Darrow Award; The Missouri Bar Spurgeon Smithson Award; the Interfaith Legal Service for Immigrants (St. Louis) Lifetime Achievement Award; the BAMSL Access to Justice Award; the Jews United For Justice Heschel-King Lifetime Achievement Award, and the Asian-American Bar Association's 2013 Torch Bearer Award.

Paul C. Wilson
Judge of the Supreme Court

PAUL C. WILSON was born in Jefferson City, and raised in a home dedicated to public service. His father, McCormick Wilson, served as a long-time municipal and associate circuit judge in Cole County. His mother, Lorna Wilson, served as director of the state health department's Division of Maternal, Child and Family Health, as well as the first executive director of the Missouri Association of Local Public Health Agencies.

Judge Wilson earned his undergraduate degree from Drury College in Springfield, Mo., and graduated *cum laude* from the University of Missouri–Columbia School of Law, where he was named to both the Order of the Coif and the Order of the Barristers.

Judge Wilson interned for Judge Edward D. (Chip) Robertson on the Supreme Court of Missouri, and Judge Pasco Bowman on the U.S. Court of Appeals for the Eighth Circuit, while in law school. Upon graduation, Judge Wilson served as a full-time law clerk for then-Chief Justice Robertson and Judge Richard F. Suhrheinrich on the U.S. Court of Appeals for the Sixth Circuit. Judge Wilson then moved to New York City to join the law firm Sullivan & Cromwell as an associate in the firm's litigation practice.

In 1996, Judge Wilson returned to Missouri to work in the state attorney general's office. During his tenure there, he represented the State of Missouri in numerous criminal and civil matters in trial and appellate courts around the state and across the country. He argued dozens of cases in Missouri's Court of Appeals and Supreme Court, as well as in the United States Supreme Court. On Jan. 16, 2010, Judge Wilson was appointed circuit judge in the 19th Judicial Circuit (Cole County).

In 2012, while a member of the Columbia law firm of Van Matre, Harrison, Hollis, Taylor & Bacon, P.C., Judge Wilson was nominated by the Appellate Judicial Commission to fill the vacancy on the Supreme Court of Missouri created by the retirement of his long-time friend and mentor Judge Ray Price. Pursuant to the Missouri Constitution's nonpartisan court plan, he was appointed by Gov. Jeremiah (Jay) Nixon and subsequently retained for a full term by the voters in the 2014 general election.

Before becoming a member of the Supreme Court, Judge Wilson was a member of the board of directors for Legal Services of Mid-Missouri and counsel to the board of directors for a regional child advocacy center, and he remains an Elder in the First Presbyterian Church in Jefferson City.

Judge Wilson is married to Laura O'Kelley Wilson, and they are the proud parents of daughters Meredith and Alice.

Office of State Courts Administrator

2112 Industrial Dr., Jefferson City 65110
Telephone: (573) 751-4377 / FAX: (573) 522-6152
www.courts.mo.gov

The Office of State Courts Administrator (OSCA) is responsible for providing administrative, business and technology support services to the courts. The duties and responsibilities assigned to the state courts administrator's office relate to all levels of the state court system. The first state courts administrator was appointed in 1970.

Some of the ways the office assists the courts include case processing; criminal history reporting; debt collection and judgment enforcement; crime victims' rights; treatment court programming; the implementation of time standards for case disposition; and court improvement projects in the areas of child abuse and neglect, juvenile services and family preservation. The office also provides administrative and technology support, training of judicial personnel and statistical analysis.

KATHY S. LLOYD
State Courts Administrator

EARL KRAUS
Deputy State Courts
Administrator

Office of the Administrator

The administrator is responsible for the overall management of OSCA and the services and support provided. The state courts administrator reports to the Supreme Court about administrative policy developments and initiatives.

SHERRI PASCHAL
Director
Court Business Services Division

PAT BROOKS
Director, Information
Technology Services Division

Administrative Services Division

The administrative services division provides support in the areas of legal services, human resources, budget and fiscal services, sponsored programs and contracts, project management, legislative services, judicial transfers, facilities operations and publications services. The division provides legal advice and prepares legal documents; supports the office and circuit court personnel systems; provides technical assistance related to court security, foreign language court interpreters and the Americans with Disabilities Act; compiles and organizes the judiciary's annual state appropriation request; supports the circuit and appellate court budget committees; processes all monies appropriated to the office and to the circuit courts; manages fund balances; applies for and manages grant funds; prepares and administers contracts for goods and services; provides project management services to all interdivisional and interagency projects; prepares fiscal notes for proposed legislation that affects the judicial system; handles requests for information from the legislature, governor's office, other public officials and the public in general; manages the facilities and fleet; and provides mail and printing services.

Court Business Services Division

The court business services division provides support to the courts in the areas of education, program development, research, statistical analysis and court procedures. The division provides program support to the family, juvenile and treatment court divisions; provides technical support to the courts in the areas of case processing, jury management, videoconferencing and financial management; designs statewide court forms; manages cost collection efforts; prepares transcripts from sound-recorded hearings submitted by the courts; compiles statistical caseload information; prepares workload estimates; provides technical assistance regarding research methods and program evaluations; compiles court performance measures; conducts evaluation and longitudinal studies of court programs and population behaviors; handles issues with criminal and traffic offenses and civil and probate cases and appeals; works with courts and state departments to electronically share juvenile justice information, criminal history, records of conviction and warrants; develops business specifications for, conducts testing of, and delivers training about automated programs and systems for use in the courts; and develops and coordinates courses and certificate programs for judicial employees. The division also works closely with standing committees of the Supreme Court of Missouri and with statutory commissions.

Information Technology Services Division

The information technology services division supports court technology and communication services for the judicial branch. Services provid-ed by the division include software applications development, maintenance of all existing applications, database administration, deployment and support of computer hardware to the courts, maintenance of the statewide judicial network and servers, system security and initial help desk support for judicial branch users and the general public. The division works with the committee that oversees the statewide court automation program and with metropolitan courts that have information technology staff on location.

Judges of the Supreme Court of Missouri: 1821–2015

Name	County	Years Served
Mathias McGirk	Montgomery	1821-1841
John Dillard Cook	Cape Girardeau	1821-1823
John Rice Jones	Washington	1821-1824
Rufus Pettibone	St. Louis	1823-1825
George Tompkins	Howard	1824-1845
Robert Wash	St. Louis	1825-1837
John Cummins Edwards	Cole	1837-1839
William Barclay Napton	Saline	1839–1849; 1857–1861; 1873–1880
William Scott	Cole	1841-1849
Priestly Haggin McBride	Monroe	1845–1849
John Ferguson Ryland	Lafayette	1849
James Harvey Birch	Clinton	1849

Note: In 1849, an amendment to the 1820 Constitution vacated the office of judge of the Supreme Court. See 12 Mo. ii (1849).

Name	County	Years Served
James Harvey Birch	Clinton	1850–1851
John Ferguson Ryland	Lafayette	1850–1857
Hamilton Rowan Gamble	St. Louis	1850–1855
William Scott	Cole	1851–1862
Abiel Leonard	Howard	1855–1857
John Crowley Richardson	St. Louis	1857–1859
Ephraim Brevard Ewing	Ray	1859–1861; 1873

Note: In March 1862, the pre-Civil War judges were purged from the bench for refusing to take the loyalty oath. See "Preface" to 31 Mo. (1862).

Name	County	Years Served
Barton Bates	St. Charles	1862–1865
William Van Ness Bay	St. Louis	1862–1865
John D.S. Dryden	Marion	1862–1865

Note: By "Order" of the State Convention, the office of judge of the Supreme Court became vacant on May 1, 1865. Judge Bates resigned from the Court Feb. 1, 1865; and Judges Bay and Dryden were forcibly removed from the bench for failure to take the new loyalty oath, called the "Ironclad Oath." See 35 Mo. iii, at iv-vi (1865).

Name	County	Years Served
David Wagner	Lewis	1865–1877
Walter L. Lovelace	Montgomery	1865–1866
Nathaniel Holmes	St. Louis	1865–1868
Thomas James Clark Fagg	Pike	1866–1868

Name	County	Years Served
James Baker	Greene	1868
Philemon Bliss	Buchanan	1868–1872
Warren Currier	St. Louis	1868–1872
Washington Adams	Cooper	1871–1874
Henry M. Vories	Buchanan	1873–1876
Thomas Adiel Sherwood	Greene	1873–1902
Edward Augustus Lewis	St. Louis	1874
Warwick Hough	Jackson	1875–1884
Elijah Hise Norton	Platte	1877–1888
John Ward Henry	Macon	1876–1888
Robert D. Ray	Carroll	1881–1890
Francis Marion Black	Jackson	1885–1894
Theodore Brace	Monroe	1887–1907
Shephard Barclay	St. Louis	1889–1898
James Britton Gantt	Henry	1891–1910
John Lilburn Thomas	Jefferson	1890–1892
George Bennett MacFarlane	Audrain	1890–1898
Gavon Drummond Burgess	Linn	1893–1910
Waltour Moss Robinson	Jasper	1895–1904
William Muir Williams	Cooper	1898
William Champe Marshall	St. Louis	1899–1906
Leroy B. Valliant	St. Louis	1899–1912
James David Fox	Madison	1903–1910
Henry Lamm	Pettis	1905–1914
Waller Washington Graves	Bates	1906–1928
Archelaus Marius Woodson	Buchanan	1907–1925
Franklin Ferris	St. Louis	1910–1912
John Kennish	Holt	1910–1913
John Chilton Brown	Carter	1911–1915
Henry Whitelaw Bond	St. Louis	1913–1919
Charles Breckenridge Faris	Pemiscot	1913–1919
Robert Franklin Walker	Morgan	1913–1930
James Thomas Blair	DeKalb	1915–1924
Charles G. Revelle	St. Francois	1915–1916
Fred Lincoln Williams	Jasper	1917–1920
John Isaac Williamson	Jackson	1919–1920
Richard Livingston Goode	St. Louis	1919–1922
Conway Elder	St. Louis	1921–1922
Edward Higbee	Adair	1921–1922
David Elmore Blair	Jasper	1921–1930
William T. Ragland	Monroe	1923–1932
John Turner White	Greene	1923–1932
Frank Ely Atwood	Carroll	1925–1934
Robert William Otto	Franklin	1925–1926
Ernest S. Gantt	Audrain	1927–1946
North Todd Gentry	Boone	1928
William Francis Frank	Adair	1929–1938
Berryman Henwood	Marion	1930–1932
George Robb Ellison	Nodaway	1931–1955
Charles Thomas Hays	Marion	1933–1942
Clarence Alexander Burney	Jackson	1933

Name	County	Years Served
Ernest Moss Tipton	Jackson	1933–1955
Charles A. Leedy Jr.	Jackson	1933–1964
Walter D. Coles	St. Louis	1935
John Caskie Collet	Chariton	1935–1937
James Marsh Douglas	St. Louis	1937–1949
Raymond B. Lucas	Scott	1938
Albert M. Clark	Ray	1939–1950
Laurence Mastick Hyde	Mercer	1943–1966; 1966–1976
Roscoe P. Conkling	Buchanan	1947–1954
Sidna Poage Dalton	Cape Girardeau	1950–1965
Frank Hollingsworth	Audrain	1950–1964
Henry J. Westhues	Howard	1954–1963
Henry I. Eager	Jackson	1955–1968
Clem F. Storckman	City of St. Louis	1955–1970
Lawrence Holman	Randolph	1963–1977
Fred L. Henley	Pemiscot	1964–1978
James A. Finch Jr.	Cape Girardeau	1965–1978
Robert True Donnelly	Laclede	1965–1988
Robert Eldridge Seiler	Jasper	1967–1982
June P. (J.P.) Morgan	Lincoln	1969–1982
John E. Bardgett	St. Louis	1970–1982
Albert L. Rendlen	Marion	1977–1992
Joseph J. Simeone	St. Louis	1978–1979
Warren Dee Welliver	Boone	1979–1989
Andrew Jackson Higgins	Platte	1979–1991
George F. Gunn Jr.	St. Louis	1982–1985
William Howard Billings	Dunklin	1982–1991
Charles Blakey Blackmar	St. Louis	1982–1992
Edward D. Robertson Jr.	Cole	1985–1998
Ann K. Covington	Boone	1989–2001
John C. Holstein	Howell	1989–2002
Duane Benton	Cole	1991–2004
Elwood L. Thomas	Clay	1991–1995
William Ray Price Jr.	Jackson	1992–2012
Stephen N. Limbaugh Jr.	Cape Girardeau	1992–2008
Ronnie L. White	St. Louis	1995–2007
Michael A. Wolff	St. Louis	1998–2011
Laura Denvir Stith	Jackson	2001–Present
Richard B. Teitelman	City of St. Louis	2002–Present
Mary R Russell	Marion	2004–Present
Patricia Breckenridge	Vernon	2007–Present
Zel M. Fischer	Atchison	2008–Present
George W. Draper III	St. Louis	2011–Present
Paul C. Wilson	Cole	2012–Present

Missouri Court of Appeals

The Constitution of 1865 provided for Missouri's first general intermediate courts, known as district courts. There were district courts in Cape Girardeau, Jefferson City, Macon, St. Charles, St. Joseph and Springfield. Each district was composed of three circuits. Appeals were taken from the circuit court to the district court and then to the Supreme Court. The district courts, however, were abolished in 1870 by a constitutional amendment.

Alarmed at the congested docket of the Supreme Court, the St. Louis Bar Association urged the 1875 Constitutional Convention to provide for another appellate court. As a result, the convention created the St. Louis Court of Appeals, consisting of three judges who heard appeals from Lincoln, St. Charles, St. Louis and Warren counties. Its territorial jurisdiction was expanded in 1884 to include several more counties.

Another constitutional amendment in 1884 established the Kansas City Court of Appeals and authorized creation of another appellate court, when necessary, by the General Assembly.

The Springfield Court of Appeals was organized in 1909. Missouri's current appellate structure—a single court of appeals consisting of three geographic districts—was established by a 1970 constitutional amendment.

The Eastern District of the Court of Appeals sits in St. Louis and consists of 14 judges. Eleven judges preside over the Western District in Kansas City, and seven judges sit on the Southern District, meeting either in Springfield or Poplar Bluff. Trained law clerks, who are licensed attorneys, assist each appellate judge with legal research.

The Missouri Court of Appeals may issue and determine original remedial writs and has general appellate jurisdiction in all cases not within the exclusive jurisdiction of the Supreme Court. Cases not within the Supreme Court's exclusive jurisdiction, however, may be transferred from the Court of Appeals to the Supreme Court when it is determined that a case involves a split among the districts of the Court of Appeals or an important issue that should be decided by the state's highest court.

A chief judge is elected for each district of the Missouri Court of Appeals by the judges in the districts and serves for such time as the districts determine. Traditionally, the chief judge in the Eastern District serves for one year, while the chief judges in the Southern and Western districts serve for two years.

The districts are authorized to sit in divisions of three judges if they choose, which all three districts have elected to do.

Missouri Court of Appeals judges must be at least 30 years of age, licensed to practice law in Missouri, residents of their district, U.S. citizens for 15 years and qualified Missouri voters for nine years before their selection. Appeals judges serve 12-year terms. They earn $134,685 annually. Compensation is determined by statute (section 476.405, RSMo).

Missouri's Court of Appeals Districts

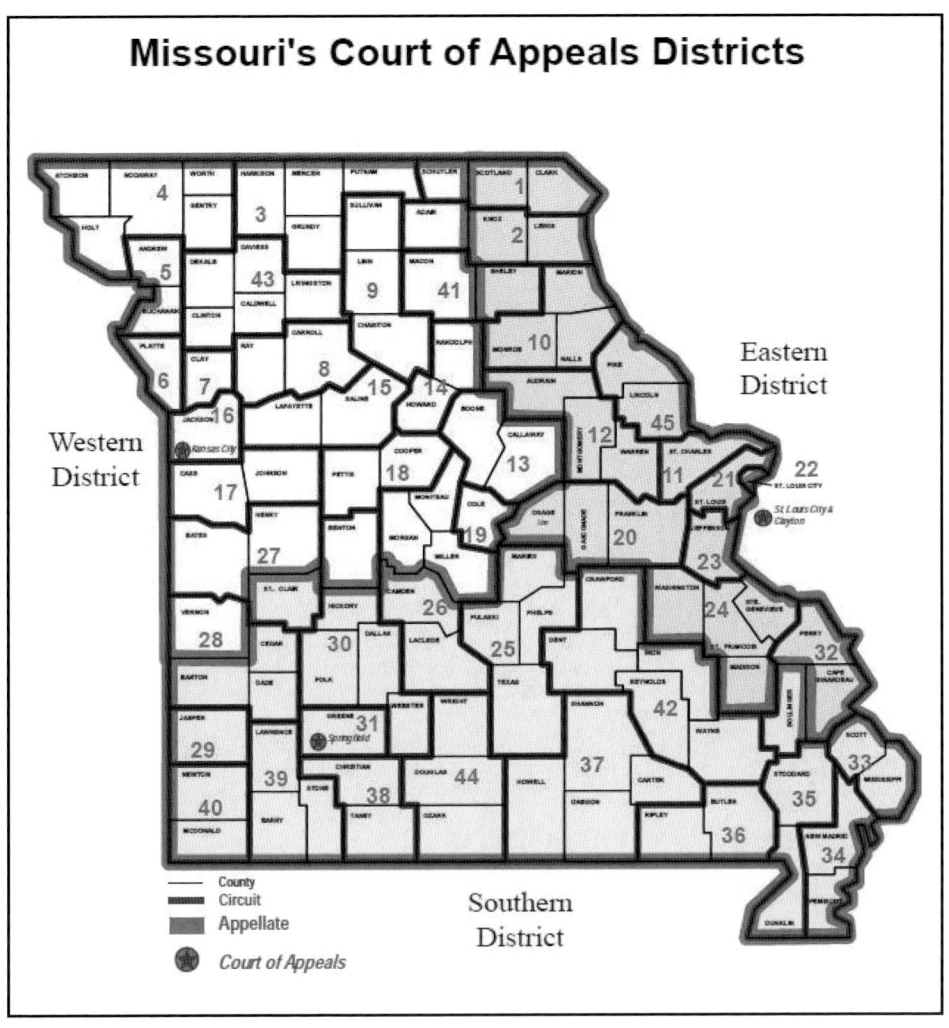

Eastern District

Western District

Southern District

County
Circuit
Appellate
Court of Appeals

Appellate Judges, Eastern District

One Post Office Square
815 Olive St., Rm. 304, St. Louis 63101
Clerk: Laura Roy
Telephone: (314) 539-4300 / FAX: (314) 539-4324
www.courts.mo.gov

The Eastern District Court of Appeals sits in St. Louis. Judges serve 12-year terms under a nonpartisan selection plan set out in the Missouri Constitution. Each of the 14 judges earns an annual salary of $154,176. Members of the court elect one from their number to act as chief judge.

Territorial Jurisdiction:

The City of St. Louis and counties of Audrain, Cape Girardeau, Clark, Franklin, Gasconade, Jefferson, Knox, Lewis, Lincoln, Madison, Marion, Monroe, Montgomery, Osage, Perry, Pike, Ralls, St. Charles, St. Francois, St. Louis, Ste. Genevieve, Scotland, Shelby, Warren and Washington.

LISA VAN AMBERG
Office phone: (314) 539-4391.
Office address: One Post Office Sq.; 815 Olive St., St. Louis 63101.
Biography: Chief judge. Educated at Washington University, B.A. in political science; St. Louis University School of Law, J.D. Practiced law in St. Louis until appointed Circuit Judge. Member: Missouri Bar, Bar Association of Metropolitan St. Louis, Lawyers Association of St. Louis, Women Lawyers' Association; American Bar Association and American Judicature Society. Received President's Award from Women Lawyers' Association, the Robert Walston Chubb Award from Legal Services of Eastern Missouri, the Horace Mann Award from MNEA and the Legal Services to Civil Liberties Award from the American Civil Liberties Union. Appointed circuit judge 2003. Appointed to the Missouri Court of Appeals, Eastern District, Aug. 2012. Retained in 2014. Term expires 2026.

ROBERT M. CLAYTON III
Office phone: (314) 539-4371.
Office address: One Post Office Sq., 815 Olive St., St. Louis 63101.
Biography: Born Aug. 20, 1969, in Hannibal. Sixth-generation Missourian. Educated in Hannibal public schools; Southern Methodist University, Bachelor of Arts, history, 1991; and the University of Missouri–Kansas City, J.D., 1994. Joined family law firm and engaged in private practice as associate and partner, 1994–2003. Elected state representative, 1994–2002. Appointed to Public Service Commission, 2003–2011, chair, 2009–2011. Member: The Missouri Bar; the 10th Circuit Bar, president 2012–2013; the American Bar Association's Section on Public Utilities; Federal Communications Bar Association; BAMSL; St. Louis County Bar; Lawyer's Association of St. Louis; WLA and Mound City Bar. Serves as trustee of the State Historical Society; treasurer, Trinity Episcopal Church; and president of board of Affordable Community Education, Inc. Member: Hannibal YMCA Men's Club. Awards: Missouri Bar President's, 2001 and 2005, KCMBA YLS President's, 1994 and UMKC Law School's Decade, 2004. Married to Erin Lindsay Clayton with two children. Appointed July 18, 2011. Retained Nov. 2012. Chief judge 2013–2014. Term expires Dec. 31, 2024.

PATRICIA L. COHEN

Office phone: (314) 539-4330.

Office address: One Post Office Sq.; 815 Olive St., St. Louis, 63101.

Biography: Born May 24, 1956, in St. Louis. Educated at University of Michigan, B.A., with high honors, 1978; Cornell Law School, J.D., 1982. In private practice from 1982–1997. Member: American and Metropolitan St. Louis bar associations, Women Lawyer's Associations of Greater St. Louis, National Association of Women Judges. Former or present member: Missouri Board of Certified Court Reporters, chair; Supreme Court of Missouri Civil Rules Committee and Legislative Committee; Appellate Judge Education Committee; Brith Sholom Kneseth Israel Congregation, trustee and vice president of administration. Appointed circuit judge for the 22nd judicial circuit on Sept. 26, 1997. Retained in 1998. Appointed to the Court of Appeals, Sept. 29, 2003. Retained in 2004. Chief judge, 2007–2008. Term expires Dec. 31, 2016.

JAMES M. DOWD

Office phone: (314) 539-4367.

Office address: One Post Office Sq.; 815 Olive St., St. Louis 63101.

Biography: Born June 26, 1964 in St. Louis. Educated at St. Louis University–Madrid, Spain and St. Louis, Missouri campuses, B.A.; University of Missouri–Kansas City School of Law, J.D. Married to Angeles Nieto. They have three children. Prior employment: Judicial clerk, Missouri Court of Appeals–Western District, Judge William E. Turnage (1990–1992); associate, Watson & Dameron (1992–1994); partner, Dowd & Dowd (1995–2009); principal, The James M. Dowd Law Firm (2009–2015). Member: The Missouri Bar; The Bar Association of Metropolitan St. Louis; Backstoppers; Mock trial team coach, St. Louis U. High School (2012–2013); Mary Queen of Peace Catholic Church. Appointed to the Missouri Court of Appeals on June 3, 2015.

ROBERT G. DOWD JR.

Office phone: (314) 539-4351.

Office address: One Post Office Sq.; 815 Olive St., St. Louis 63101.

Biography: Born March 6, 1951, in St. Louis. Served as United States Senate page, 1967. Educated at University of Missouri–St. Louis; Quincy College, B.A.; St. Mary's University, J.D. Married in 1982 to Denise Sandoz; they have three children. Engaged in private law practice with Dowd & Dowd P.C. Elected magistrate judge, 1978. Retained as associate circuit judge, 1982. Member: Catholic Church; American, Missouri and Metropolitan St. Louis Bar associations; Lawyers Association; St. Mary's University Alumni Association. Former chair of Judicial Education Committee and the Trial Judge Education Committee; former chair of Judicial Finance Commission. Board of directors: CYC. Past member: Quincy College Alumni Association, Mental Health Association, Daughters of St. Paul, Dismas House. Attended: National Judicial College, Reno, Nev.; American Academy of Judicial Education, Cambridge, Mass. Appointed circuit judge in 1985. Retained in 1986 and 1992. Appointed to the Court of Appeals, Aug. 19, 1994. Retained in 1996 and 2008. Chief judge 1998–1999. Term expires Dec. 31, 2020.

GARY M. GAERTNER JR.

Office phone: (314) 539-4375.

Office address: One Post Office Sq.; 815 Olive St., St. Louis 63101.

Biography: Born Dec. 17, 1964, in St. Louis. Educated at St. Louis University School of Business, Honors Program, B.S., *magna cum laude*; St. Louis University School of Law, J.D., *cum laude*. Married to Julie H. Sauer. They have seven children. Former associate of Bryan Cave; assistant state prosecutor, the Circuit Attorney's Office; assistant federal prosecutor, the U.S. Attorney's Office for the Eastern District of Missouri; and chair, U.S. Department of Justice Insurance Fraud Task Force for the Eastern District. Awarded: Adler-Rosecan, Childress and Thomas J. White Fellowships, Alpha Sigma Nu Honorary Scholastic Society and Law Review, St. Louis University School of Law. Received John C. Shepherd Professionalism Award, Bar Association of Metropolitan St. Louis. Member: Catholic Church; Crusade Against Crime of America (Medal of Valor), board of directors and secretary; and Missouri History Museum, trustee. Appointed circuit judge for the 21st Judicial Circuit, 2000; retained 2002 and 2008. Appointed to the Court of Appeals, Nov. 2009; retained 2012. Chief judge, July 2012–June 2013. Term expires Dec. 31, 2024.

PHILIP M. HESS

Office phone: (314) 539-4386.

Office address: One Post Office Sq.; 815 Olive St., St. Louis 63101.

Biography: Born March 22, 1958. Served as United States Senate Page, summer 1975. Educated in Crystal City Public Schools; Rockhurst University, B.A., 1980 in economics and philosophy; and University of Missouri School of Law, J.D., 1983. Married to Teresa Mayhew Hess with three sons. Engaged in the private practice of law for 30 years, the last 15 as a partner in Larsen & Hess, P.C. Member: St. Catherine Laboure Catholic Church; The Missouri Bar, past chair of its Workers' Compensation Committee; Bar Association of Metropolitan St. Louis, past chair of its Workers' Compensation Committee; Lawyers Association; and Jefferson County Bar Association. Past president, Missouri Association of Trial Attorneys (MATA). Received Outstanding Service Award, MATA, 2012; President's Award, MATA, 2003; elected Fellow, College of Workers' Compensation Attorneys, 2009. Appointed to the Court of Appeals Nov. 2013.

MARY KATHRYN HOFF

Office phone: (314) 539-4356.

Office address: One Post Office Sq.; 815 Olive St., St. Louis 63101.

Biography: Born Jan. 5, 1953, in St. Louis. Married with two children. Educated at University of Missouri–Columbia, B.S., education, and St. Louis University, J.D. Served as assistant public defender, St. Louis City, 1978–1982, and was engaged in private law practice, 1982–1989. Member: Missouri Bar Association; Metropolitan St. Louis Bar Association; Women Lawyers' Association of Greater St. Louis, past president; National Association of Women Judges; Dean's Council, St. Louis University Law School; St. Margaret of Scotland Catholic Church. Former or present member: Judicial Resources Commission, chair; Supreme Court Judicial Records Committee; Missouri Court Automation Committee; Supreme Court Family Court Committee; and Appellate Judicial Education Committee. Appointed circuit judge on May 15, 1989. Retained in 1990. Appointed to the Court of Appeals, Dec. 15, 1995. Retained in 1998 and 2010. Chief judge, 2000–2001. Term expires Dec. 31, 2022.

LAWRENCE E. MOONEY

Office phone: (314) 539-4361.

Office address: One Post Office Sq., 815 Olive St., Ste. 304; St. Louis 63101.

Biography: Born Sept. 3, 1949 in St. Louis. Educated at St. Louis University , A.B., J.D. His husband is Dr. James D. Reid. Engaged in private law practice, 1974–1975; 1977–1978. Served in St. Louis County as Assistant Prosecuting Attorney (1975–1977), First Assistant Prosecuting Attorney, 1979–1990, and Executive Assistant to the County Executive, 1991–1998. Chief Judge for the Missouri Court of Appeals–Eastern District, July, 2002 through June, 2003. Chairman of the Judicial Finance Commission. Member of the Drug Court Coordinating Commission. Member of the American Bar Association, the Missouri Bar Association, the Bar Association of Metropolitan St. Louis, the St. Louis County Bar Association, the Lawyers Association of St. Louis, the International Association of Lesbian and Gay Judges; and Lawyers for Equality. Appointed to the Court of Appeals Aug. 14, 1998. Retained in 2000 and 2012. Term expires Dec. 31, 2024.

KURT S. ODENWALD

Office phone: (314) 539-4341.

Office address: One Post Office Sq., 815 Olive St., St. Louis 63101.

Biography: Born Nov. 17, 1954, in St. Louis. Educated at University of Missouri–St Louis, *magna cum laude*, B.A. in political science; St. Louis University School of Law, *cum laude*, J.D. Recipient of fellowship to study German law through the German Academic Exchange Service and the Ministry of Justice for NordRhein-Westfallen. Former member and chairman of the St. Louis County Council. Married to Sandra M. Odenwald; four children. Previously employed as associate general counsel for Anheuser-Busch, Inc. Served as assistant public defender, City of St. Louis. Partner with Guilfoil, Petzall & Shoemake prior to appointment to the bench. Member: St. Michael the Archangel Catholic Church; Missouri Bar Association; Bar Association of Metropolitan St. Louis. Appointed to the Court of Appeals on Oct. 30, 2007. Retained in 2008. Chief judge, 2011–2012. Term expires Dec. 31, 2020.

ANGELA TURNER QUIGLESS

Office phone: (314) 539-4346.

Office address: One Post Office Sq., 815 Olive St., St. Louis 63101.

Biography: Born Jan. 4, 1960. Married with one child. Educated at University of Missouri–Columbia, B.A.; St. Louis University Law School, J.D. Previously employed at the Missouri Department of Revenue; Missouri Public Service Commission; St. Louis Circuit Attorney's Office; St. Louis City Counselor's Office and the U.S. Attorney's Office for Eastern District of Missouri. Member: Missouri Bar, Bar Association of Metropolitan St. Louis, American Bar Association, National Bar Association of Women Judges, Lawyers Association of St. Louis and the Mound City Bar Association. Appointed associate circuit judge for the 22nd Judicial Circuit, Feb. 1995 and circuit judge, Jan. 2003. Appointed to the Missouri Court of Appeals, April 2012. Chief Judge, 2014–2015. Term expires Dec. 31, 2024.

ROY L. RICHTER

Office phone: (314) 539-4300.

Office address: One Post Office Sq.; 815 Olive St., St. Louis 63101.

Biography: Born in St. Louis. Undergraduate degree from Drury University, Springfield; law degree from the University of Missouri–Columbia. Elected as prosecuting attorney of Montgomery County, 1977–1978. Elected as probate/magistrate judge of Montgomery County, 1979. Became an associate circuit judge on Jan. 2, 1979. Re-elected in 1982–2002. Served 15 years as the juvenile division judge for the 12th Circuit. Past president: Missouri Association of Probate and Associate Circuit Judges, Missouri Council of Juvenile and Family Court Judges and Kiwanis Club of Montgomery City. Served on The Missouri Bar's Judicial Article Review Commission and Missouri Supreme Court committees including: Circuit Court Budget Committee, Judge Transfer Committee, Fine Collection Center and Municipal Judge Education. Appointed to the Court of Appeals, Jan. 6, 2006, by Gov. Matt Blunt. Retained Nov. 2008. Chief judge, 2010–2011. Term expires Dec. 31, 2020.

SHERRI B. SULLIVAN

Office phone: (314) 539-4381.

Office address: One Post Office Sq.; 815 Olive St., St. Louis 63101.

Biography: Born Sept. 20, 1953, in St. Louis. Undergraduate degree from University of Missouri–St. Louis, B.S., administration of justice; law degree, St. Louis University, J.D. Married with two children. Member: American Bar Association, Metropolitan St. Louis Bar Association, Women Lawyers' Association of Greater St. Louis, National Association of Women Judges. Appointed associate circuit judge of the 22nd Judicial Circuit, Feb. 27, 1989. Appointed circuit judge Oct. 17, 1994. Retained in 1996. Appointed to the Court of Appeals, Aug. 5, 1999. Retained in 2000 and 2012. Chief judge 2003–2004. Term expires Dec. 31, 2024.

Appellate Judges, Southern District

300 Hammons Pkwy., Springfield 65806
Telephone: (417) 895-6811 / FAX: (417) 895-6817
Clerk: Sandra L. Skinner
www.courts.mo.gov

The Southern District Court of Appeals meets in Springfield and in Poplar Bluff. Judges are named to 12-year terms under a nonpartisan selection plan set out in the Missouri Constitution. Each of the district's seven judges earns an annual salary of $154,176. Members of the court elect one from their number to act as chief judge.

Territorial jurisdiction:

The counties of Barry, Barton, Bollinger, Butler, Camden, Carter, Cedar, Christian, Crawford.

Dade, Dallas, Dent, Douglas, Dunklin, Greene, Hickory, Howell, Iron, Jasper, Laclede, Lawrence, Maries, McDonald, Mississippi, New Madrid, Newton, Oregon, Ozark, Pemiscot, Phelps, Polk, Pulaski, Reynolds, Ripley, Scott, Shannon, St. Clair, Stoddard, Stone, Taney, Texas, Wayne, Webster and Wright.

Except by different stipulation of the parties, all cases from the counties of Bollinger, Butler, Carter, Crawford, Dent, Dunklin, Iron, Mississippi, New Madrid, Oregon, Pemiscot, Reynolds, Ripley, Scott, Shannon, Stoddard and Wayne will be heard at Poplar Bluff.

MARY W. SHEFFIELD

Office phone: (417) 895-6818
Office address: 300 Hammons Pkwy., Springfield 65806
Biography: Chief judge. Born in Durham, N.C. Educated at North Carolina State University, B.A., 1976; and the University of Miami, J.D., 1980. Editor: *Lawyer of the Americas Journal of International Law.* Married to Dr. W. Kent Wray. Has two daughters, Jennifer Sheffield and Katherine Sheffield; one son Christopher Sheffield. Former president of the National College of Probate Judges and past president of the Blue Ridge Institute for Juvenile and Family Law Judges. Appointed to serve as one of four U.S. International Liaison Network Judges for the Hague Convention on Child Abduction. Co-founded the Russell House in Phelps County and CASA of South Central Missouri. Appointed to the Missouri Task Force on Aging-Out. Appointed by the Supreme Court of Missouri to chair the Missouri Family Court Committee. Received the CASA HOPE Award in 2011. Recipient of the *Missouri Lawyers Weekly's* Women's Justice Awards honoree class of 2012. Involved in her Rotary Club, PEO, the First United Methodist Church and the board for the Community Partnership Program. Elected as associate circuit judge for Phelps County in 1983 and then as presiding circuit judge for the 25th Judicial Circuit in 2004 and 2010. Appointed to the Court of Appeals in Dec. 2012. Retained in 2014. Term expires Dec. 31, 2026.

JEFFREY BATES

Office phone: (417) 895-6824.
Office address: 300 Hammons Pkwy., Springfield 65806.
Biography: Educated at Southwest Missouri State University, B.S., 1979; and the University of Missouri–Columbia, J.D., 1984. Practiced law in Springfield for 19 years prior to being appointed to the bench. Member: Order of the Coif; Phi Delta Phi; Missouri Law Review; Springfield Metropolitan and Missouri Bar Associations. Appointed to the Court of Appeals Nov. 14, 2003, for a term beginning on Dec. 1, 2003. Retained in 2006. Term expires Dec. 31, 2018.

DON E. BURRELL JR.

Office phone: (417) 895-6826.

Office Address: 300 Hammons Pkwy., Springfield 65806.

Biography: Chief judge, 2011–13. Born Dec. 1960 in Springfield. Educated at Missouri State University, formerly Southwest Missouri State University, B.S., 1983; and the University of Missouri–Kansas City, J.D., 1991. Married Denise Campfield in 1983. They have one son, Brooks, and one daughter, Claire. Practiced law in Kansas City and Springfield. Member: UMKC Law Review; Order of Bench and Robe; Springfield Metropolitan and Missouri Bar associations; Judiciary's Legislative Committee; Trial Court Education Committee, chair; Missouri Juvenile Court Improvement Project; Greene County Teen Court and Kids' Court; Victory Trade School Community Advisory Board. Elected circuit judge of the 31st judicial circuit in 1998. Re-elected in 2000 and 2006 (three years as presiding judge). Inaugural recipient of Springfield Metropolitan Bar Association's Judicial Excellence award in 2007. Appointed to the Court of Appeals Jan. 13, 2008. Retained in 2010. Term expires Dec. 31, 2022.

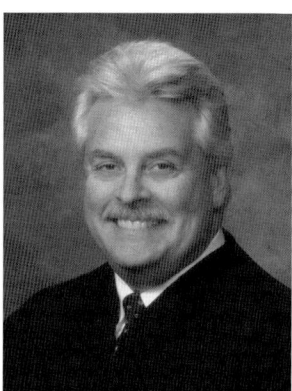

WILLIAM W. FRANCIS JR.

Office phone: (417) 895-6820.

Office Address: 300 Hammons Pkwy., Springfield 65806.

Biography: Born in Springfield. Educated at Southwest Missouri State University, B.S., 1974; and the University of Missouri–Columbia, J.D., 1977. Married Beverly A. Francis; they have three children. Practiced law with Miller, Fairman, Sanford & Carr as an associate, 1977–1982. Partner: Miller & Sanford, 1982–1989, and Placzek & Francis, 1989–2010. Judge Francis is the author of many publications. Member: First & Calvary Presbyterian Church, ordained deacon, elder and former trustee; Founders Club, Missouri State University; American Cancer Society; Missouri Bar, 1977–present; vice chair, Insurance Law Committee, 1979–1988; Workers' Compensation Committee, 1981–2010, chair, 1988–2000, vice chair, 1992–1997, Legislative Review Subcommittee, 2003–2005; Springfield Metropolitan Bar Association, president, 1987; board of directors, 1985–1986, Library Committee, 1984; Charter & Bylaws Committee, 1986; Workers' Compensation Committee, chair, 1991; Medical/Legal Workers' Compensation Committee, 1990–1996; and Bench/Bar Committee, 2007–2010. Appointed to the Court of Appeals, May 2010. Chief Judge, 2013–2015. Retained in 2012. Term expires Dec. 31, 2024.

GARY W. LYNCH

Office phone: (417) 895-6825.

Office Address: 300 Hammons Pkwy., Ste. 300, Springfield 65806.

Biography: Born in St. Petersburg, Fla. Educated at Southwest Baptist University, B.A. in mathematics and elementary education, 1974; and the University of Missouri–Columbia, J.D., 1976. Married Dana J. Cochran on Aug. 17, 1974. They have two sons. Practiced law in Bolivar, 1977–2002. Served as associate circuit judge of Polk County in the 30th judicial circuit, 2003–2006. Member: *Missouri Law Review*; Polk County, Springfield Metropolitan and Missouri Bar associations. Appointed to the Court of Appeals Jan. 6, 2006, for a term beginning on Feb. 1, 2006. Retained in 2008. Term expires Dec. 31, 2020.

NANCY STEFFEN RAHMEYER

Office phone: (417) 895-6823.

Office Address: 300 Hammons Pkwy., Springfield 65806.

Biography: Born in Spencer, Iowa. Educated at Iowa State University, B.S., history; Southwest Missouri State University, M.S., education; University of Arkansas, J.D. Was a clerk in the Federal District Court, 1987–1989; served as part-time municipal judge in Springfield, 1993–2001. Engaged in private law practice in Springfield. Member: Missouri and Springfield Bar Associations; *Arkansas Law Review*. Appointed to the Court of Appeals, Feb. 1, 2001. Retained in 2002 and 2014. Term expires Dec. 31, 2026.

DANIEL E. SCOTT

Office phone: (417) 895-6822.

Office Address: 300 Hammons Pkwy., Springfield 65806.

Biography: Born in Herington, Kan.; grew up in Trenton. Educated at University of Missouri–Rolla, Central Missouri State University, B.S., 1977; and University of Missouri, J.D., 1980. Married Trina Pohle, J.D., (1981); they have two daughters and a son. Practiced law in Joplin and served as assistant county prosecutor and special prosecutor. Order of the Coif; Phi Delta Phi; *Missouri Law Review*; Lon O. Hocker Trial Lawyer Award; Missouri Bar Board of Governors; and YLS chair. Member: The Missouri Bar and Jasper County Bar Association. Appointed to the Court of Appeals Sept. 2006; retained in 2008. Chief judge, 2009–2010. Term expires Dec. 31, 2020.

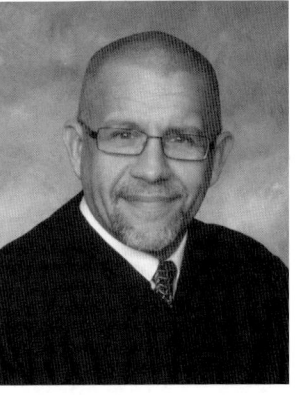

Appellate Judges, Western District

1300 Oak St., Kansas City 64106
Clerk: Terence G. Lord
Telephone: (816) 889-3600 / FAX: (816) 889-3668
www.courts.mo.gov

The Western District Court of Appeals is headquartered in Kansas City. The court primarily hears cases in Kansas City but also sits in locations throughout the district. Judges are named to 12-year terms under a nonpartisan selection plan set out in the Missouri Constitution. Each of the district's 11 judges earns an annual salary of $154,176. The chief judge serves a two-year term by rotation, generally according to seniority.

Territorial Jurisdiction:

The counties of Adair, Andrew, Atchison, Bates, Benton, Boone, Buchanan, Caldwell, Callaway, Carroll, Cass, Chariton, Clay, Clinton, Cole, Cooper, Daviess, DeKalb, Gentry, Grundy, Harrison, Henry, Holt, Howard, Jackson, Johnson, Lafayette, Linn, Livingston, Macon, Mercer, Miller, Moniteau, Morgan, Nodaway, Pettis, Platte, Putnam, Randolph, Ray, Saline, Schuyler, Sullivan, Vernon and Worth.

ALOK AHUJA
Office phone: (816) 889-3601.
Office address: 1300 Oak St., Kansas City 64106.
Biography: Chief judge. Born in Raipur, India. Educated at the University of Kansas, B.A., philosophy and English literature; Yale Law School, J.D. Married to Nina J. Ahuja. They have two daughters. Following graduation from law school, Judge Ahuja served as a law clerk to Judge Richard D. Cudahy on the U.S. Court of Appeals for the Seventh Circuit in Chicago from 1988–1989 and engaged in private practice in Washington, DC, from 1989–1992. He returned to Kansas City in 1992, where he practiced with the Lathrop & Gage law firm as an associate (1992–1997) and member (1997–2007). Appointed to the Court of Appeals Dec. 19, 2007. Retained in 2010. Term expires Dec. 31, 2022.

JOSEPH M. ELLIS
Office phone: (816) 889-3622.
Office address: 1300 Oak St., Kansas City 64106.
Biography: Born Oct. 25, 1946, in St. Louis. Educated at University of Missouri–St. Louis, B.A., history; Washington University, J.D.; managing editor, *Urban Law Annual*. Married Linda Basler June 11, 1966; they have a daughter. Practiced law, 1972–1993. Served in U.S. Air Force, Office of Special Investigations and Judge Advocate General's Corps. Was municipal judge, City of Macon, 1987–1993. Member: Immaculate Conception Church; American, Missouri Young Lawyers Section, 1975–1983, chair, 1981–1982, board of governors, 1982–1990; division of judicial administration, chair, 2004–present; 41st judicial circuit (past president) and Kansas City Metropolitan Bar Associations; 1970 White House Conference on Children, planner; Blue Ribbon Committee, Future of Services to Children, 1987; Industrial Development Authority of Macon, president, 1978–1993; the Bar Plan Foundation, trustee, 1994–1997; Committee on Judicial Independence, 2005. Awards: Outstanding Jaycee, 1973; Missouri Bar President's Award, 2005. Appointed to the Court of Appeals, Aug. 4, 1993. Retained in 1994 and 2006. Chief judge, 2002–2004. Term expires by age on Oct. 25, 2016.

ANTHONY REX GABBERT

Office phone: (816) 889-3605.

Office address: 1300 Oak St., Kansas City 64106.

Biography: Born in Kansas City. Educated University of Missouri–Kansas City, B.A. 1980; Mississippi College School of Law, J.D., 1985. He has two daughters. Private practice, 1986, 1991–1994; assistant prosecuting attorney, Clay County, 1987–91; prosecuting attorney, Gladstone, 1991–1993; municipal judge, North Kansas City, 1993–1994; associate circuit judge, circuit court, Clay County, 1994–2004; circuit judge, circuit court of Clay County, 2004–2013 (served as presiding judge 2008–2010); Member: Missouri Bar, Kansas Bar Association; Clay County Bar Association, past secretary–treasurer), Kansas City Metropolitan Bar Association; American Judges Association. Past member: Circuit Judge, Executive Council of the Missouri Judiciary, board member of the Missouri Judicial Legislative Steering Committee; board member of the Missouri Municipal and Associate Circuit Judges' Association; 6th Congressional District member of the 1993 U.S. Attorney and U.S. Marshall nomination selection committee; board of trustees, Clay–Platte–Ray Mental Health Tax Levy committee; board. of trustees of North Kansas City Hospital, past secretary; and adjunct faculty: Mid-American Nazarene University, Ottawa University, Park University, Penn Valley Community College, Rockhurst University and William Jewell College. Appointed to the Court of Appeals, April 3, 2013. Term expires Dec. 31, 2026.

LISA WHITE HARDWICK

Office phone: (816) 889-3611.

Office address: 1300 Oak St., Kansas City 64106.

Biography: Born Oct. 5, 1960, in Kansas City. Educated at University of Missouri–Columbia, B.J., 1982; Harvard Law School, J.D., 1985. Practiced law with Shook, Hardy & Bacon in Kansas City as associate, 1985–1991, and partner, 1992–2000. Elected to Jackson County Legislature, 1993–2000. Member: St. James United Methodist Church; Jackson County and Kansas City Metropolitan Bar associations; Niles Home for Children, board of directors; Center School District Education Foundation, board of directors; Swope Community Enterprises and Swope Health Services, board of directors; Supreme Court of Missouri Appellate Practice Committee, chair. Appointed circuit judge of Jackson County, 16th Judicial Circuit in 2000. Appointed to the Court of Appeals May 2, 2001; chief judge, 2010–2012. Retained in 2002 and 2014. Term expires Dec. 31, 2026.

VICTOR C. HOWARD

Office phone: (816) 889-3626.

Office address: 1300 Oak St., Kansas City 64106.

Biography: Born July 9, 1952, in Kansas City. Graduate of Central Missouri State University, B.S., 1973; University of Missouri–Kansas City, J.D., 1976. He has three sons. Served: North Kansas City Board of Education, 1977–1993, secretary; law clerk to Judge William Marsh, Jackson County Circuit Court, 1977; Clay County deputy county counselor, 1977–1991; Youth Friends Advisory Board, chair; Adult and Community Education Advisory Committee, board member. Member: Tri County Mental Health Supportive Employment Task Force; Domestic Violence Community Response Team, board; Kansas City Consensus Leadership Task Force; Kansas City Board of Zoning Adjustment, 1991–1993; Clay County Bar Association, president, 1992–1993. Practiced law until his appointment as a Clay County circuit judge in 1993. Retained in 1994. Appointed to the Court of Appeals, Oct. 11, 1996. Retained in 1998 and 2010. Term expires by age on July 9, 2022.

CYNTHIA LYNETTE MARTIN

Office phone: (816) 889-3617.

Office address: 1300 Oak St., Kansas City 64106.

Biography: Born July 1, 1959, in Clinton. Educated at Lee's Summit High School, 1977; William Jewell College, *summa cum laude*, B.A. in communication and B.A. in psychology, 1981; University of Missouri–Kansas City School of Law, Order of the Coif, J.D., 1984. Married to James D. Martin. She has two sons. Engaged in private practice for 25 years, the last 10 years. as a solo practitioner. Member: National Conference of Bar Examiners, board of trustees, 2011; Missouri Board of Law Examiners, 2001–2011; KC Metropolitan Bar Foundation, president, 2002–2003; Kansas City Metropolitan Bar Association, president, 1999; Young Lawyers Section of the KCMBA, president, 1990; 16th Circuit Judicial Nominating Committee, lawyer member, 2004–2009; Association for Women Lawyers; Lee's Summit Educational Foundation, board member, 2006–2009; Southeastern Jackson County Citizens Association, board member, 2002–2009; Lee's Summit North Music Parents Organization, president, 2005–2006. Listed Among the Best of the Bar by *Missouri Lawyer's Weekly* 2003, 2005–2009. Listed as Missouri and Kansas Super Lawyer, 2006–2009. Women's Justice Award, Public Official, 2010. Appointed to the Court of Appeals Oct. 13, 2009. Retained in 2012. Term expires Dec. 31, 2024.

KAREN KING MITCHELL

Office phone: (816) 889-3620.

Office address: 1300 Oak St., Kansas City 64106.

Biography: Born Nov. 28, 1958, in Kansas City. Married to Gregory C. Mitchell, Esq.; they have one son, Samuel H. Mitchell. Educated at the University of Missouri–Columbia, B.A.; and the University of Missouri–Kansas City, J.D. Served as a law clerk to the Hon. Fernando J. Gaitan, Missouri Circuit Court, 16th Judicial Circuit, 1984–1985, and the Hon. Charles B. Blackmar, Supreme Court of Missouri, 1985–1986. Served as an assistant attorney general, office of the Missouri Attorney General, 1987–2009; chief deputy attorney general, 1999–2009; and state solicitor, 1996–1999. Member: Saint Andrews Lutheran Church, ELCA; Missouri Supreme Court Trial Judge Education Committee; Kansas City Association for Women Lawyers Connections Program. Former member: Board of Governors,The Missouri Bar; Elwood L. Thomas Inn of Court; Missouri Supreme Court Committee on Procedure in Criminal Cases; Missouri Supreme Court Appellate Practice Committee; and Judicial Task Force for Gender and Justice. Recipient of the David J. Dixon Award for outstanding appellate advocacy. Appointed to the Court of Appeals July 9, 2009. Retained in 2010. Term expires Dec. 31, 2022.

THOMAS H. NEWTON

Office phone: (816) 889-3629.

Office address: 1300 Oak St., Kansas City 64106.

Biography: Born April 23, 1952, in Washington, DC. Graduate of Howard University, Washington, DC, B.A., J.D. Married to Renee Pryor of Kansas City. They have one daughter. Member: Swope Parkway United Christian Church. Former assistant prosecuting attorney, Jackson County, 1984–1987; former assistant United States attorney, Western District, 1987–1993. Appointed circuit judge on Sept. 7, 1993. Retained in 1994. Appointed to the Court of Appeals, Nov. 1, 1999. Retained in 2000 and 2012. Chief judge, 2008–2010. Term expires by age April 23, 2022.

MARK D. PFEIFFER

Office phone: (816) 889-3614.

Office address: 1300 Oak St., Kansas City 64106.

Biography: Born May 25, 1967. Married to Tracey Wright Pfeiffer; they have two sons, Wilson and Brady. Bachelor of Arts degree from Westminster College. Juris Doctor degree from University of Missouri–Columbia School of Law. Private law practice with Farrington & Curtis, 1992–1995, Springfield, Missouri; and Bley & Pfeiffer, P.C., 1995–2009, Columbia, Mo. The Missouri Bar, member; Kansas City Metropolitan Bar Association, member; Boone County Bar Association, member; Kansas City Metropolitan Bar Association, member; National Board of Trial Advocacy, judicial fellow. The Crossing Evangelical Church, member. Appointed by Gov. Jeremiah Nixon to the Court of Appeals, May 6, 2009. Retained in 2010. Term expires Dec. 31, 2022.

GARY D. WITT

Office phone: (816) 889-3608.

Office address: 1300 Oak St., Kansas City 64106.

Biography: Born Feb. 2, 1965, in Smithville. Graduate of William Jewell College, B.A., 1987; University of Missouri–Columbia, J.D., 1990. Married to Angie LaRose Witt, 1994. Practiced law, Witt, Hicklin and Witt, P.C. until his appointment as a Platte County associate circuit judge, 1998–2010. State representative 29th Dist., 1991–96 (chair, Judiciary and Ethics Committe and Special Committee on Impeachment); assistant city attorney and prosecutor for four cities; Governor's Commission on Driving While Intoxicated and Impaired Driving, 1991; Governor's Task Force on Urban Violence, 1993; Missouri Probate and Associate Circuit Judges Association, past president; Interim Legislative Committee on Judicial Resources, 2003; Chief Justice Advisory Council, 2005–10. Member Platte County Bar Association, president, 2002–03; Eleemosynary Society; Mechanical and Agricultural Society, stockholder; Historical Society, life member. Member: Edward D. Ellison Inn, KCMBA Board of Directors, judicial liaison; Judicial Conference Leg. Comm, chair; Walter Pope Binns Public Service Fellow; William Jewell College, Ten Outstanding Young Missourians, 1993; Missouri Jaycees, 1993. Voted Best Associate Circuit Judge; *Missouri Lawyer's Weekly* newspaper reader's poll 2009. Appointed to the Court of Appeals, Feb. 2010. Term expires Dec. 31, 2024.

JAMES E. WELSH

Office phone: (816) 889-3632.

Office address: 1300 Oak St., Kansas City 64106.

Biography: Born May 26, 1948, in Brookfield. Educated at Parks College of Aeronautical Technology; St. Louis University, B.S., aeronautics, 1969; St. Louis University School of Law, J.D., 1975. Married Theresa M. Kaszko, 1968. They have two daughters. Worked for aeronautics company, 1969–1975; law clerk to Judge Turnage, Missouri Court of Appeals, 1975–1976; a law firm, 1976–1985; Liberty municipal judge, 1983–1985; associate circuit judge, 1985–1988; circuit court judge, 1988–2007. Adjunct professor, University of Missouri–Kansas City Law School. Member St. James Church; Missouri, Clay County and Kansas City Metropolitan Bar associations. Served as vice president and president of Missouri Circuit Judges Association. and Clay and Platte Municipal and Associate Judges Association; Missouri Municipal and Associate Circuit Court Association, treasurer and secretary. Appointed to the Court of Appeals Nov. 5, 2007. Chief judge, 2013–2014. Term expires by age on May 26, 2018.

Missouri's 45 Judicial Circuits

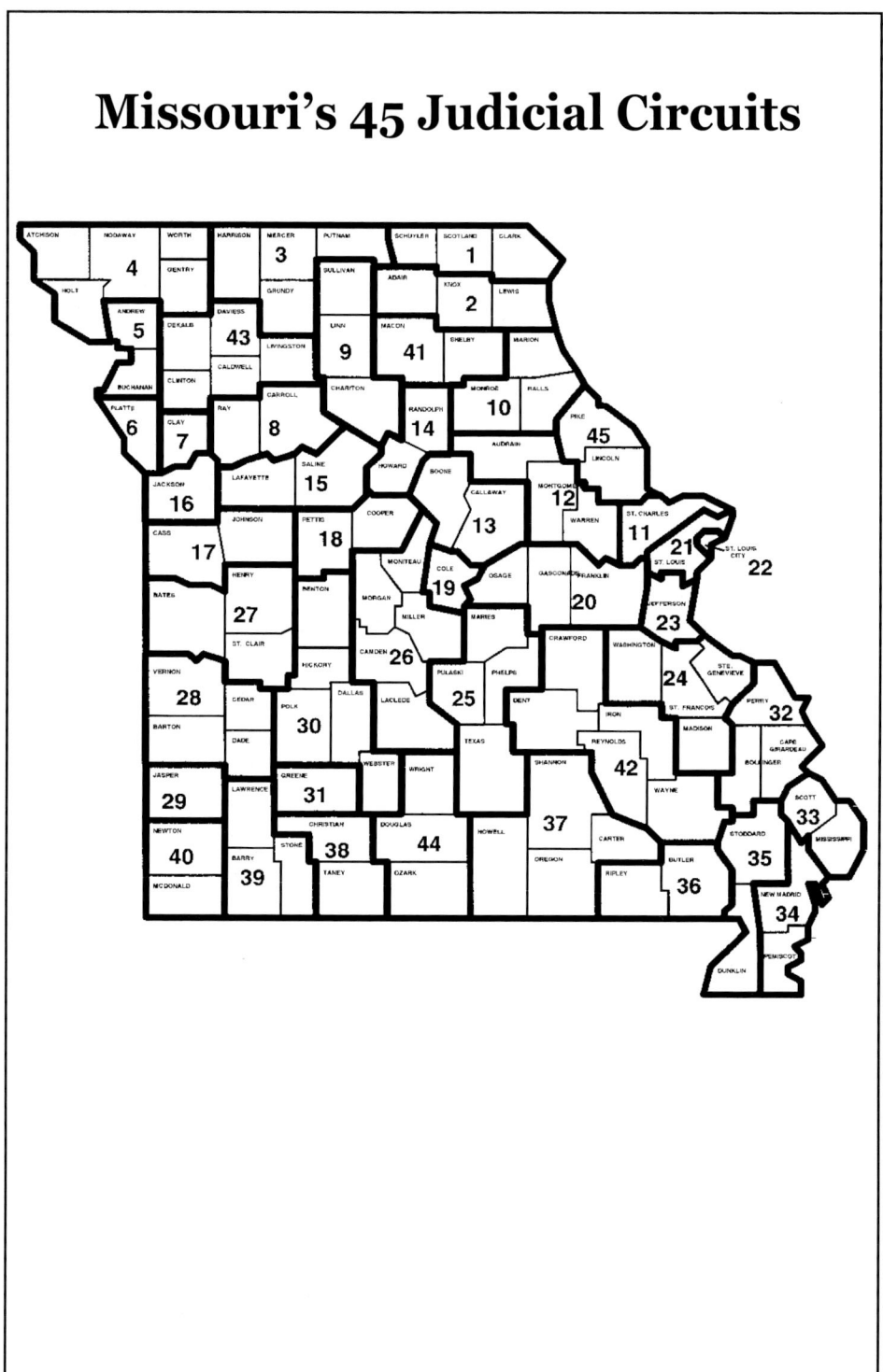

Missouri Circuit Courts

Missouri's first two circuit courts were established in 1815. The 1820 Constitution provided for the creation of four circuits, each containing from four to eight counties. The number of circuits has increased over the years; today, 45 circuits operate in Missouri.

The first circuit judges were appointed by the governor and confirmed by the Senate. The life term of the judges and their method of appointment proved unpopular, however; in 1850, the constitution was amended to provide for popular election. Most circuit judges are elected today, though judges in six circuits—Clay, Greene, Jackson, Platte and St. Louis counties and the City of St. Louis—are selected under provisions of the Nonpartisan Court Plan.

Constitutional amendments approved by Missouri voters in 1976 provide that the circuit courts shall be courts of original civil and criminal jurisdiction. All trials start at this level. Former courts of limited jurisdiction became divisions of the circuit court effective Jan. 2, 1979.

Within the divisions of the circuit court, there are three levels of jurisdiction: circuit, associate and municipal. Circuit judges may act within all circuit jurisdictions.

The number of circuit judges is determined by the General Assembly. The constitution requires at least one circuit judge in each of Missouri's 45 judicial circuits.

Associate circuit judges may hear matters pending in the circuit court or assigned by the Supreme Court. Associate circuit judges hear all cases pursuant to Chapter 517, RSMo, and have concurrent jurisdiction over all cases pending in the circuit court.

The constitution requires at least one resident associate circuit judge in each county. The statutes authorize additional associate circuit judges depending on county populations. Presently, there are 197 associate circuit judges.

Municipalities with 400,000 or more people must establish a municipal division over which a municipal judge presides. Communities of fewer than 400,000 people may establish municipal divisions to hear ordinance violations, or the municipality may request that these matters be heard in the associate division of the circuit court. Municipal judges are paid locally.

By statute, each circuit judge appoints a court reporter, and the court in each circuit appoints a juvenile officer. A circuit clerk in each county is selected according to law, and salaries are set by statute.

Circuit court judges must be at least 30 years old, residents of their circuit, licensed to practice law in Missouri, U.S. citizens for 10 years and Missouri voters for three years. Circuit judges serve six-year terms. Associate circuit judges must be at least 25 years old, Missouri voters and residents of the counties they serve and licensed to practice law in Missouri. Associate circuit judges serve four-year terms.

Circuit court judges each earn $146,803 annually; associate circuit court judges earn $135,059. Compensation is determined by statute (section 476.405, RSMo).

The Fine Collection Center

The Supreme Court of Missouri established the Fine Collection Center pursuant to section 476.385, RSMo. It is a central bureau authorized by statute to process certain traffic, conservation and watercraft violations for the courts. The center began operation July 1, 1999, and all courts now participate in the center's program.

Offenders who receive citations eligible to be processed by the center have the option of pleading guilty by paying their fine and costs directly to the center or by pleading not guilty and having their citations sent to the county or circuit prosecutor. When the offender pleads guilty and pays the fine and costs, the center issues a record of conviction and sends it to the Missouri Department of Revenue and the Missouri State Highway Patrol. All fines and costs are distributed to the local jurisdiction and the appropriate state agencies.

Policy and oversight of the center is provided by a committee consisting of at least seven associate circuit judges appointed by the Supreme Court of Missouri. The committee establishes and maintains the uniform fine schedule in use by the center.

Circuit Court Judges

Circuit 1
GARY DIAL
Office address: Scotland County Courthouse, 117 S. Market, Room 205, Memphis 63555; phone (660) 465-7012.
Counties: Clark, Schuyler and Scotland.
Biography: Presiding judge. Born Oct. 12, 1955, in Kirksville. Graduate of Truman State (formerly known as Northeast Missouri State University), B.A., political science, 1977; University of Missouri–Kansas City, J.D., 1980. Married Lana Porter July 29, 1978. They have two children, Lydia and Brian. Engaged in private practice in Memphis. Served as prosecuting attorney of Scotland County, 1981–1996; city attorney for Memphis. Member: Missouri and American Bar associations. Appointed circuit judge on Jan. 30, 1996; elected November 1996 to fill an unexpired term. Re-elected 1998, 2004 and 2010. Term expires Dec. 31, 2016. Democrat.

Circuit 2
RUSSELL E. STEELE
Office address: Adair County Courthouse, 3rd Fl., 106 W. Washington, Kirksville 63501; phone (660) 665-3145.
Counties: Adair, Knox and Lewis.
Biography: Presiding judge. Born Feb. 27, 1952, in Kirksville. Graduate of University of Missouri–Columbia, A.B., economics, 1974; J.D., 1977. In private law practice, 1977–1997. Member: Missouri, Adair County and American Bar associations. Appointed circuit judge December 1997. Elected: 1998, 2000, 2006 and 2012. Term expires Dec. 31, 2018. Democrat.

Circuit 3
JACK PEACE
Office address: 802 E. Main, Princeton 64673; phone (660) 748-3430.
Counties: Grundy, Harrison, Mercer and Putnam.
Biography: Presiding judge. Born July 20, 1951, in Princeton. Graduate of Northwest Missouri State University, B.S., business administration, 1973; University of Missouri–Kansas City, J.D., 1976. Private practice of law, Andereck, Evans, Milne, Peace & Widger, in Trenton, 1976–2006. Member: Missouri Bar Association Board of Governors and Third Judicial Bar Association. Elected circuit judge November 2006. Term expires Dec. 31, 2018. Republican.

Circuit 4
ROGER M. PROKES

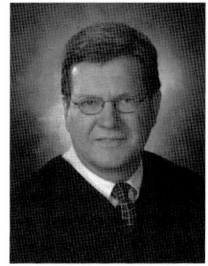

Office address: 305 N. Main, Ste. 204, Maryville 64468; phone (660) 582-4231.

Counties: Atchison, Gentry, Holt, Nodaway and Worth.

Biography: Presiding judge. Born Nov. 10, 1951, in Scottsbluff, Neb. Graduate of University of Nebraska–Lincoln, B.S., business administration, 1973; J.D., 1976. Married Julie A. Willson June 2, 1975. They have five children. Engaged in general law practice in northwest Missouri for 24 years. Former assistant professor of business law and adjunct professor of education law at Northwest Missouri State University. ASTAR trained. Member: Presiding Judges Executive Committee and Circuit Judges Association Executive Committee. Elected circuit judge 2000, 2006 and 2012. Term expires Dec. 31, 2018. Republican.

Circuit 5—Division 3
PATRICK ROBB

Office address: Buchanan County Courthouse, 411 Jules, St. Joseph 64501; phone (816) 271-1511.

Counties: Andrew and Buchanan.

Biography: Presiding judge. Born Nov. 6, 1955. Graduate of Southeast Missouri State University, B.A., political science; University of Missouri–Kansas City, J.D. Married Carol Ganter. They have two children, Nick and Andrea. Served as assistant prosecuting attorney in Buchanan County and practiced law for seven years. Elected associate circuit judge in 1986. Member: St. Joseph Bar Association; American Judicature Society; Missouri Council of Juvenile and Family Court Judges; National Council of Juvenile and Family Court Judges; chair, Supreme Court Committee on Procedure in Criminal Cases; and Presiding Judges' Executive Committee. Elected circuit judge 1988, 1994, 2000, 2006 and 2012. Term expires Dec. 31, 2018. Democrat.

Circuit 5—Division 1
RANDALL R. JACKSON

Office address: Buchanan County Courthouse, 411 Jules, St. Joseph 64501; phone (816) 271-1447.

Counties: Andrew and Buchanan.

Biography: Born July 19, 1949, in St. Joseph. Educated at Missouri Western State College; University of Missouri–Columbia, B.A., political science, 1971; J.D., 1974. Married Vicki Leigh Burton Aug. 22, 1981. They have two sons, Garrett and Tyler. Former assistant city attorney and prosecutor for the City of St. Joseph; engaged in private law practice. Appointed magistrate judge January 1977; served through December 1978. Elected associate circuit judge in 1978, 1982 and 1986. Member: Green Valley Baptist Church, Missouri Western College Department of Criminal Justice Advisory Committee and St. Joseph and Missouri Bar associations. Received W. Oliver Rasch Award for outstanding article in *Journal of Missouri Bar*, 1999. Appointed circuit judge Feb. 8, 1988. Elected 1988, 1994, 2000, 2006 and 2012. Term expires Dec. 31, 2018. Republican.

Circuit 5—Division 2
WELDON C. JUDAH

Office address: Buchanan County Courthouse, 411 Jules, St. Joseph 64501; phone (816) 271-1441.

Counties: Andrew and Buchanan.

Biography: Born July 2, 1949, in St. Joseph. Graduate of Missouri Western State College, B.S., business administration; University of Missouri–Kansas City, J.D., 1980. Married Linda C. Bachman. They have two daughters, Idean and Abigail. Admitted to The Missouri Bar, 1980; in private practice, 1981. Appointed Buchanan County assistant prosecutor, 1982–1986; elected St. Joseph municipal judge, 1986–1988; and Buchanan County associate circuit judge, 1988, 1990 and 1994. Appointed circuit judge 1995. Elected: 1996, 1998, 2004 and 2010. Term expires Dec. 31, 2016. Democrat.

Circuit 5—Division 4
DANIEL F. KELLOGG

Office address: Buchanan County Courthouse, 411 Jules, St. Joseph 64501; phone (816) 271-1477.

Counties: Andrew and Buchanan.

Biography: Born Feb. 1, 1960, in St. Joseph. Graduate of Missouri Western State University, B.S., B.A. 1982; University of Missouri–Columbia, J.D., 1988. Married Jennifer Lang Dec. 30, 1988. They have four children: Xan, Joseph, Annaka and Jomel. Engaged in private practice in Kansas City, 1988–1990. Served as an assistant prosecuting attorney for Buchanan County and practiced law from 1990–1995. Appointed associate circuit judge in 1995 by Gov. Mel Carnahan and retained in 1996 and 1998. Member: Wellspring Community Church; Central Standard Chorus; Robidoux Resident Theatre; St. Joseph Area Chamber of Commerce; Board of Trustees, Natl. Assoc. of Juvenile and Family Court Judges; American, Missouri and St. Joseph Bar associations; board member, Missouri Association of Drug Court Professionals; and Missouri Western Arts Society. Elected circuit judge 2000, 2006 and 2012. Term expires Dec. 31, 2018. Democrat.

Circuit 6—Division 2
JAMES W. VAN AMBURG

Office address: Platte County Courthouse, 415 Third St., Platte City 64079; phone (816) 858-2232.

County: Platte.

Biography: Presiding judge. Born Oct. 23, 1951, in Dayton, Ohio. Graduate of William Jewell College, B.A.; University of Missouri–Kansas City, M.A.; Washburn University School of Law, J.D. Assistant Platte County prosecuting attorney, 1987–1993. Member West Platte R-II School Board, 1986–1992; Missouri Bar Association; Probate and Associate Judges Association; Municipal and Associate Judges Association; and Platte County Bar Association. Appointed associate judge in 1993. Elected 1994, 1998, 2002, 2006 and 2010. Appointed circuit judge in 2013. Elected in 2014. Term expires Dec. 31, 2020. Nonpartisan.

Circuit 6—Division 1
THOMAS C. FINCHAM

Office address: Platte County Courthouse, 415 Third St., Ste. 50, Platte City 64079; phone (816) 858-2232.

County: Platte.

Biography: Born Aug. 21, 1956. Graduate of University of Missouri–Kansas City, B.A. economics, 1977; University of Missouri–Kansas City Law School, J.D. 1981. Engaged in private practice in Kansas City area, 1981–2010. Served as city attorney and city prosecutor, Dearborn, 1997–2003; municipal judge in the following jurisdictions: Oakview, 1995–2010; Richmond, 1999–2010; Ferrelview, 1998–2010; Riverside, 2006–2010; Platte Woods, 2003–2010; and Lawson, 2001–2006. Member: Missouri Municipal and Associate Circuit Judges Association, president, 2011–2012, board member, 1999–present; Missouri, Platte County and Clay County Bar associations; and Missouri Association of Probate and Associate circuit judges, board of directors, 2013–present. Appointed associate circuit judge May 2010. Retained 2012. Appointed circuit judge November 2013 by Gov. Jeremiah (Jay) Nixon. Term expires Dec. 31, 2016. Nonpartisan.

Circuit 7—Division 1
SHANE T. ALEXANDER

Office address: Clay County Courthouse, 11 S. Water, Liberty 64068; phone (816) 407-3910.

County: Clay.

Biography: Presiding judge. Born May 8, 1968, in North Kansas City. Graduate of University of Missouri–Columbia, B.A., history, 1990. Surface Warfare Officer, U.S. Navy, 1990–1994. Graduate of University of Missouri–Kansas City, J.D., 1997. Married Amy Alexander in 1993; they have three children. Assistant prosecuting attorney, Buchanan County, 1997–1999; assistant prosecuting attorney, Clay County, 1999–2004; chief assistant prosecuting attorney, Clay County, 2004–2008; municipal judge, Excelsior Springs, 2004–2008; and municipal prosecutor, Smithville, 2006–2008. Appointed circuit judge Aug. 6, 2008. Elected in 2010. Term expires Dec. 31, 2016. Nonpartisan.

Circuit 7—Division 2
JANET SUTTON

Office address: Clay County Courthouse, 11 S. Water, Liberty 64068; phone (816) 407-3920.

County: Clay.

Biography: Born August 1965, in Kansas City. Graduate of University of Missouri–Kansas City, 1987, B.A., communication studies; J.D., 1990. Lives in Liberty with husband Tim Sutton and son Sam. Assistant prosecutor for Clay County, 1990–2003; chief assistant prosecutor, 2000–2003; municipal prosecutor for Excelsior Springs, May 1994–December 2000. Municipal judge for Excelsior Springs, January 2001–December 2002. Legal counsel to the Clay County Sheriff's Office, 1993–1999. Member: Clay County Bar Association; Association of Women Lawyers of Kansas City, Missouri Associate and Probate Judges Association, Missouri Municipal and Associate Judges Association, and KCMBA. Appointed associate circuit judge in January 2003. Retained 2004, 2008 and 2012. Appointed circuit judge in July 2013. Retained in 2014. Term expires Dec. 31, 2020.

Circuit 7—Division 3
K. ELIZABETH DAVIS

Office address: Clay County Courthouse, 11 S. Water, Liberty 64068; phone (816) 407-3930.

County: Clay.

Biography: Completed undergrad from University of Kansas. Graduated law school from University of Kansas in 1982. Assistant prosecuting attorney for Clay County Non-Support Division from 1982–1997. She is married and has one son. Appointed associate judge of Clay County, Division 5, in February 1997. Appointed circuit judge for Division 3 in January 2007. Retained in 2010. Term expires Dec. 31, 2016. Nonpartisan.

Circuit 7—Division 4
LARRY HARMAN

Office address: Clay County Courthouse, 11 S. Water, Liberty 64068; phone (816) 407-3940.

County: Clay.

Biography: Born Aug. 29, 1953, in St. Joseph. Graduate of William Jewell College, B.A.; University of Missouri–Kansas City, J.D., 1975. Married Debra A. (Perry) Harman. They have three children. Member of Liberty United Methodist Church. Engaged in private practice, 1978; assistant public defender, Clay County; Clay County prosecuting attorney; municipal judge, Claycomo; city attorney, Smithville and Lathrop; prosecuting attorney, Liberty; and special assistant attorney general, 1986–1987. Active with various local service groups and charities. Member: Kansas City Federation of Musicians 34-627; past member, Missouri Masonic Home Board. Appointed circuit judge Aug. 26, 1992. Retained in 1994, 2000, 2006 and 2012. Term expires Dec. 31, 2016. Nonpartisan.

Circuit 8
DAVID H. MILLER

Office address: Ray County Courthouse, 100 W. Main, Ste. 38, Richmond 64085; phone (816) 776-3525.

Counties: Carroll and Ray.

Biography: Presiding judge. Born Oct. 6, 1947, in Springfield. Graduate of University of Missouri–Columbia, B.S., 1969; J.D., 1975. Married to Valerie Miller with two children, Ian and Whitney. Served in the United States Navy, 1969–1972, with rank at discharge of lieutenant, senior grade. General practice, 1975–1989. District public defender, 1989–2008. Served as president of Ray County Ambulance District, 1985–2009. Member: Richmond United Methodist Church; Ray County and Missouri Bar Associations; and Richmond Kiwanis Club, past president. Elected 2010. Term expires Dec. 31, 2018. Republican.

Circuit 9
TERRY TSCHANNEN

Office address: Linn County Courthouse, PO Box 84, Linneus 64653; phone (660) 895-5523.

Counties: Chariton, Linn and Sullivan.

Biography: Presiding judge. Born June 14, 1963, in St. Louis. Graduate of University of Missouri–Columbia, B.S., business administration, 1985; University of South Carolina, J.D., 1988. Married to Barbara Tschannen with four children. Labor/employment law emphasis, 1988–1992; general practice, 1992–2012. Elected 2012. Term expires Dec. 31, 2018.

Circuit 10
RACHEL BRINGER SHEPHERD

Office address: Marion County Courthouse, 906 Broadway, Hannibal 63401; phone (573) 221-0579; FAX (573) 221-0366.

Counties: Marion, Monroe and Ralls.

Biography: Presiding judge. Born Sept. 19, 1971, in Marion County. Married Bobby Shepherd July 21, 2012. Graduate of Palmyra High School; Univ. of Mo.–Columbia, B.A., honors, English, *summa cum laude*; and J.D. Served as asst. prosecutor, 2000–02; law clerk, 1995–1997; state representative, 2002–10; private practice, 1997–2010. Member: Missouri Law Review; South Union Baptist Church, Maywood; Missouri Children's Justice Task Force; Mark Twain Home Foundation Board; Hannibal Arts Council Board; Palmyra Kiwanis; Hannibal Rotary; Palmyra Chamber of Commerce; PEO; King's Daughters; GFWC of Hannibal; and Beth Haven Board. Former board member: Hannibal-LaGrange College and American Red Cross. Honored by the Missouri Judicial Conference, NAACP, UMC School of Law, Missouri Bar, Missouri Farm Bureau, Missouri Association of School Administrators and Palmyra Chamber of Commerce. Appointed circuit judge Dec. 30, 2010. Elected 2012. Term expires Dec. 31, 2018. Democrat.

Circuit 11—Division 2
NANCY L. SCHNEIDER

Office address: St. Charles County Courthouse, 300 N. Second St., Rm. 439, St. Charles 63301; phone (636) 949-7900, ext. 5512.

County: St. Charles.

Biography: Presiding judge. Born in St. Louis. Educated at University of Missouri, Lindenwood College, B.A., business administration, *magna cum laude*, 1978; St. Louis University, J.D., *cum laude*, 1981. She has two daughters, Kristin and Meghan. Practiced law in St. Charles, 1981–1991. Board of governors, Truman State University, 1987–1995; special assistant, Missouri attorney general, 1989–1991; prosecuting attorney, St. Charles County Juvenile Court, 1986–1990; special assistant, St. Charles county counselor, 1986–1987; and appointed St. Charles County associate judge, 1991. Elected in 1992 and 1994. Elected circuit judge 1998, 2004 and 2010. Term expires Dec. 31, 2016. Republican.

Circuit 11—Division 1
TED HOUSE

Office address: St. Charles County Courthouse, 300 N. Second St., Rm. 539, St. Charles 63301; phone (636) 949-3093.

County: St. Charles.

Biography: Born in Kansas City. Graduate of Fayette High School, 1977; Central Methodist University, B.A., 1981; University of Missouri–Kansas City School of Law, J.D., 1984. Married Martha Smith in St. Charles. Children: Benjamin, Catherine and Daniel. Employment: private law practice, St. Charles; asst. professor of business law and political science, Lindenwood University; emergency medical technician; legal intern for Missouri attorney general; field representative for Congressman Ike Skelton. Member: First United Methodist Church of St. Charles. Immediate past president, Missouri Circuit Judges Association. Elected to Missouri House of Representatives 1988, 1990 and 1992; Missouri Senate, 1994 and 1998. Associate circuit judge, 2002; circuit judge, 2004, 2008 and 2014. Term expires December 31, 2020. Democrat.

Circuit 11—Division 3
JACK BANAS

Office address: St. Charles County Courthouse, 300 N. Second St., Rm. 341, St. Charles 63301; phone (636) 949-7900, ext. 5541.

County: St. Charles.

Photo not available

Biography: Born Sept. 3, 1954, Lorain, Ohio. Graduate of Southeast Missouri State University, B.S., criminal justice, 1976; M.S., criminal justice administration, 1982; St. Louis University, J.D., 1991. Married Kathy Banas; they have two sons, John and Jacob. Employment: St. Charles City Police, 1977–1991, 1995–1998; Riezman and Blitz Law Firm, 1991–1992; St. Charles County Prosecuting Attorney's Office, assistant prosecuting attorney, 1992–1994, 1994–1995; and Charlie James Law Firm, 1994–1995. Member: Sts. Joachim and Ann Church; Advisory Board, Crisis Nursery; former president and board member, The Child Center and St. Charles County Bar Association. Elected prosecuting attorney for St. Charles County 1998, 2002, 2006 and 2010. Elected circuit judge, 2013. Term expires 2018. Republican.

Circuit 11—Division 4
RICHARD K. ZERR

Office address: St. Charles County Courthouse, 300 N. Second St., Rm. 535, St. Charles 63301; phone (636) 949-3094.

County: St. Charles.

Biography: Administrative judge of the Family Court. Born April 10, 1949. Graduate of University of Missouri–Columbia, A.B., political science; University of Arkansas–Fayette-ville, J.D. First lieutenant-retired U.S. Air Force. Served in St. Charles County: magistrate judge, 1975–1978; associate circuit judge, 1979–1982; and circuit judge 2007–present. Member: Missouri Bar Association, St. Charles County Bar Association, American Judges Association, Association of Family and Conciliation Courts. Elected November 2006. Elected presiding judge of the 11th Judicial Circuit for 2011–2012. Term expires Dec. 31, 2018. Republican.

Circuit 11—Division 5
JON A. CUNNINGHAM

Office address: St. Charles County Courthouse, 300 N. Second St., Rm. 330, St. Charles 63301; phone (636) 949-3095.

County: St. Charles.

Biography: Born Nov. 8, 1955, in Louisiana. Graduate of Truman State University, B.S., education in history, *magna cum laude*, 1978; University of Missouri–Columbia, J.D., 1982. Married to Sally Cunningham; they have one son, Jonathan. Practiced law in St. Charles, 1982–1990. Past president, St. Charles County Bar Association; member, Missouri Association of Probate and Associate Circuit Judges, 1991–2011; and National Association of Drug Court Professionals. Elected associate circuit judge in 1990, 1994, 1998 and 2002. Elected circuit judge in 2006 and 2012. Elected presiding judge of the 11th Judicial Circuit for 2009–2010. Term expires Dec. 31, 2018. Republican.

Circuit 11—Division 7
DANIEL PELIKAN

Office address: St. Charles County Courthouse, 300 N. Second St., Rm. 333, St. Charles 63301; phone (636) 949-7900, ext. 3026.

County: St. Charles.

Biography: Born Jan. 11, 1958, in St. Louis. Graduate of St. Louis University High School, 1976; University of Missouri, B.J., 1980; St. Louis University Law School, J.D., 1984. Married to Lisa (White) Pelikan. They have two sons, Nicholas and Jake. Practiced law in St. Charles, 1985–1998; St. Charles County assistant county counselor, 1985–1986; and county counselor, 1986–1987. Member: Children's Trust Fund Board, 1988–1993, chair, 1991–1993; Missouri Bar Board of Governors, 2001–2003; United Services for the Handicapped board, 1989–1999, chair, 1995–1996; St. Cletus Catholic Church; St. Charles Rotary Club; Boys and Girls Club Board; and Eagle Scout Association. Appointed to Supreme Court Commission on Alternative Dispute Resolution in Domestic Relations Cases and Supreme Court Automation Committee. Elected associate judge 1998 and 2002. Elected circuit judge 2006 and 2012. Term expires Dec. 31, 2018. Republican.

Circuit 12
WESLEY DALTON

Office address: Warren County Courthouse, 104 W. Main St., Warrenton 63383; phone (636) 456-9705.

Counties: Audrain, Montgomery and Warren.

Biography: Presiding judge. Born Oct. 10, 1958 in St. Charles. Graduate of University of Missouri, B.A., 1982; J.D., 1988. Married. Has eight children: Nicole, Taylor, Michael, Ariel, Allison, Rilee, Madison and Mitchell. Operated solo practice in Warrenton, 1988–2000, and represented Warren County as special counsel. Served as primary Drug Court judge, Warren County, 2003–07, and again in 2011–2013. Elected to the Missouri Association of Probate and Associate Circuit Judges, board of directors, 2005. Appointed by the Missouri Supreme Court as a board member of the Centralized Fine Collection Bureau Committee. Warren County Rotary Club, ast president; City of Warrenton Tourism Committe, past chair; Warrenton Rotary Club and the Missouri Association of Drug Court Professionals, member/past president; Warrenton Boy Scout Troop 22 member and committee chair. Appointed to the Associate Circuit Court by Gov. Wilson, 2001. Elected in 2002. Retained in 2006 and 2010. Elected presiding circuit judge, 2013. Term expires 2018. Republican.

Circuit 13—Division 1
CHRISTINE CARPENTER

Office address: 705 East Walnut, Boone County Courthouse, Columbia 65201; phone (573) 886-4050.

Counties: Boone and Callaway.

Biography: Presiding judge. Born Oct. 20, 1947, in Syracuse, N.Y. Graduate of University of Missouri, B.A, art history and archaeology, 1973; J.D., 1980. Married Joseph Bindbeutel. Four sons: Gabriel, Burke, Nicholas and Duncan. Missouri Supreme Court Committee for Alternative Treatment Courts member since 2007; Advanced Science and Technology Adjudication Resource Center (ASTAR) Fellow since 2009; faculty member, National Drug Court Institute, since 2002; and board member of Missouri Association of Drug Court Professionals since 2008. Appointed Drug Court Commissioner in 1999. Appointed associate circuit judge in 2001. Elected 2002, 2006 and 2010. Appointed circuit judge in 2010 and elected in 2012. Term expires Dec. 31, 2018. Democrat.

Circuit 13—Division 2
GARY OXENHANDLER

Office address: Boone County Courthouse, 705 E. Walnut St., Columbia 65201; phone (573) 886-4050.

Counties: Boone and Callaway.

Biography: Born in St. Louis, 1946. Graduate of University City High School, 1964; University of Missouri, B.A., 1968; and J.D., 1973. Served in the United States Army, 1969–1970. Married for 43 years. Private practice for 29 years with Marvin Tofle. AV Rating Martindale-Hubbel. Member of numerous boards and commissions, including: Columbia Chamber of Commerce, president; Columbia's 1996 Race Relations Task Force, co-chair; Boone County's 1997 Jail Task Force, chair; and 2000 Judicial and Law Enforcement Task Force. Missouri Sentencing Advisory Commission. Supreme Court Education Committee. Interests include competitive handball, golf and reading. Appointed circuit judge in 2002. Elected in 2004 and 2010. Term expires in 2016. Democrat.

Circuit 13—Division 3
KEVIN CRANE

Office address: Boone County Courthouse, 705 E. Walnut St., Columbia 65201.

Counties: Boone and Callaway.

Biography: Born Dec. 29, 1961. Graduate of University of Missouri–Columbia, 1984, speech/communications; University of Missouri–Columbia School of Law, J.D., 1987. Married Lesley Pugh Sept. 16, 2010. They have six children. Missouri assistant attorney general, 1987–1990; assistant Boone County prosecuting attorney, 1990–1993; and Boone County prosecuting attorney, 1993–2006. Elected circuit judge in 2006 and 2012. Term expires Dec. 31, 2018. Republican.

Circuit 13—Division 4
JODIE CAPSHAW ASEL

Office address: Boone County Courthouse, 705 E. Walnut St., Columbia 65201; phone (573) 886-4050.

Counties: Boone and Callaway.

Biography: Born June 9, 1950, in Chaffee. Graduate of Univ. of Mo.–Columbia, B.S., 1972; J.D., 1975. Married to Donald B. Asel; three daughters: Ashley, Toby and Mackenzie. Boone Co. asst. prosecuting attorney, 1976–1978; asst. public defender, 1979–1980; and private practice, 1981–1991. Served on Exec. Council of the Judicial Conf., 1994–2006; Board of Directors, Missouri Association of Probate and Associate Circuit Judges, 1995–2002, president, 2000–2001. Supreme Court committees: Family Court, Case Management; Fine Collection; Legislative Steering; Trial Judge Education, vice chair; Coordinating Commission for Judicial Education; and Presiding Judges' Exec. Comm. Missouri Bar committees: Foresight and the Division of Judicial Administration; Exec. Committee of the Boone Co. Bar, 2003–2006, pres., 2004–2005. Officer of the Mo. Circuit Judges Assoc., 2010–2013, president, 2012-2013. Appointed associate circuit judge 1991. Elected in 1992–2006. Elected circuit judge 2006, 2008 and 2014. Term expires Dec. 31, 2020. Republican.

Circuit 14
SCOTT HAYES

Office Address: Randolph County Justice Center, 372 Hwy. JJ, Ste. C, Huntsville 65259; phone (660) 277-4240.

Counties: Howard and Randolph.

Biography: Presiding judge. Graduate of University of Missouri–Columbia School of Law. United States Air Force veteran. Served as Randolph County associate circuit judge, 2003–2006; assistant public defender, 1998–2002; and Randolph County assistant prosecuting attorney, 1994–1998. Member of Missouri Association of Drug Court Professionals, National Council of Juvenile and Family Court Judges and American Judicature Society. Elected circuit judge 2006 and 2012. Term expires Dec. 31, 2018. Democrat.

Circuit 15
DENNIS A. ROLF

Office address: PO Box 10, Lexington 64067; phone (660) 463-5834.

Counties: Lafayette and Saline.

Biography: Presiding judge. Born Dec. 7, 1958, in Warrensburg. Graduate of Santa Fe High School, Alma, 1977; University of Missouri–Columbia, B.S., agricultural economics, 1980; J.D., 1983. Married Rebecca S. Owens, 1981; they have three children. Practiced law in Carrollton, 1983–1984, and in Concordia, 1984–2000. Assistant prosecutor for Lafayette County; public defender for Lafayette and Saline counties; municipal prosecutor for Alma, Concordia, Corder, Higginsville, Napoleon and Wellington; municipal attorney for Alma, Concordia, Corder, Napoleon and Wellington; and municipal judge for Alma, Higginsville, Lexington, Napoleon, Waverly and Wellington. Member: Trinity Lutheran Church, Alma; Santa Fe R-10 Foundation, Inc.; Missouri, Lafayette and Saline County Bar associations; The Missouri Bar Disciplinary Committee; and active in youth activities. Elected circuit judge 2000, 2006 and 2012. Term expires Dec. 31, 2018. Democrat.

Circuit 16—Division 4
JUSTINE E. DEL MURO

Office address: Jackson County Courthouse, 415 E. 12th St., Kansas City 64106; phone (816) 881-3604.

Home address: Kansas City.

County: Jackson.

Biography: Presiding judge. Born July 15, 1955, in Chicago, Ill. Graduate of the University of Missouri–Kansas City, B.A., speech and hearing sciences/psychology; University of Missouri–Kansas City School of Law, J.D., 1981–1984. Practiced law at Legal Aid, the Jackson County public defender's office and the Popham Law Firm. Adjunct professor at Rockhurst College, 1990–1991. Member: Association of Women Lawyers; Missouri, Hispanic and Kansas City Metropolitan Bar associations. Recipient of the David J. Dixon Appellate Advocacy Award, 1990. Appointed circuit judge July 30, 1993. Retained in 1994, 2000, 2006 and 2012. Term expires Dec. 31, 2018. Nonpartisan.

Circuit 16—Division 1
SANDRA C. MIDKIFF

Office address: Jackson County Courthouse, 415 E. 12th St., Kansas City 64106; phone (816) 881-3601.

County: Jackson.

Biography: Born Aug. 29, 1950, in St. Louis. Graduate of Normandy High School, St. Louis, 1968; Knox College, Galesburg, Ill., B.A., political science, 1972; University of Missouri–Kansas City, J.D., 1975, with honors. Engaged in private practice from 1975 until her appointment to the bench. Member: Kansas City Metropolitan Bar Association; founding member of Association of Women Lawyers; former board member, Legal Aid of Western Missouri (LAWMO); and former board member, Rose Brooks Center. 2008 Recipient of Missouri Association of Criminal Defense Lawyers Benjamin Cardozo Award for Judicial Courage and Excellence. Appointed circuit judge March 8, 2002. Retained in 2004 and 2010. Term expires December 31, 2016. Nonpartisan.

Circuit 16—Division 2
KENNETH R. GARRETT III

Office address: Jackson County Courthouse Annex, 308 W. Kansas, Independence 64050; phone (816) 881-4402.

County: Jackson.

Biography: From Kansas City. Graduate of University of Missouri–Kansas City, B.A., political science; master's, public administration; and J.D. Served as an instructor in strategic business planning and policy at Baker University, Overland Park, Kan. Served as an assistant prosecuting attorney for Jackson County, 2004–2010. Prior to joining the Jackson County prosecuting attorney's office, worked as an assistant attorney general for the state of Missouri, representing various state agencies in civil matters. Member of The Missouri Bar Association; Kansas Bar Association, American Bar Association, Jackson County Bar Association and the Kansas City Metropolitan Bar Association. Appointed associate circuit judge Aug. 26, 2010. Retained in 2012. Appointed circuit judge by Gov. Jay Nixon on Oct. 4, 2013. Retained in 2014. Term expires Dec. 31, 2020. Nonpartisan.

Circuit 16—Division 3
DAVID M. BYRN

Office address: Jackson County Courthouse, 415 E. 12th St., Kansas City 64106; phone (816) 881-3603.

County: Jackson.

Biography: Born April 25, 1957 in Detroit, Mich. Educated at Kirtland High School, Kirtland, Ohio, 1975. Graduate of Graceland University, B.A., *summa cum laude*, economics and social studies, 1978; University of Missouri–Kansas City Law School, J.D., 1981. Married to Pamela, 1983; two children. Practiced law at Jeter, Rains & Byrn, L.C., with emphasis on business, real estate, construction and commercial litigation, 1981–2008. Certified mediator. Member: The Missouri Bar, Kansas City Metropolitan Bar Association and Eastern Jackson County Bar Association (recipient of Community Service Award). Member and ordained minister, Community of Christ. Past or present board member and officer of Habitat for Humanity, Boy Scouts of America local council, Truman Neurological Center, Optimist Club and numerous city and church boards and commissions. Appointed circuit judge September 2008. Retained in 2010. Term expires Dec. 31, 2016. Nonpartisan.

Circuit 16—Division 5
JAMES F. KANATZAR

Office address: Jackson County Courthouse, 415 E. 12th St., Kansas City 64106; phone (816) 881-4405.

County: Jackson.

Biography: Graduate of Creighton Univ., B.A.; Univ. of Mo.–Kansas City, J.D. Assistant prosecuting attorney for Jackson County, 1993–2000, and 2002–2007. During that time, he was a trial team leader, chief trial asst., chief deputy pros. and also served on the homicide committee for the prosecutor's office. Associate for Armstrong Teasdale, Kansas City, 2000–2002. Jackson County prosecutor, 2007, elected i2008. Serves on the Board of Governors and the Criminal Law Committee for The Missouri Bar. Member: Kansas City Metropolitan Bar Association; Eastern Jackson County Bar Association; Kansas Bar Association; and past member, of Missouri Association of Prosecuting Attorneys. Recipient of Louis Lombardo Prosecutor of the Year Award, Distinguished Lifetime Achievement Award from Jackson County and recognized by the U.S. Dept. of Defense with Patriotic Employer Award for support of Guard and Reserve forces. Appointed to the court by Gov. Jay Nixon in 2011. Retained in 2012. Term expires Dec. 31, 2018. Nonpartisan.

Circuit 16—Division 6
J. DALE YOUNGS

Office address: Jackson County Courthouse, 415 E. 12th St., Kansas City 64106; phone (816) 881-3606.

County: Jackson.

Biography: Born Sept. 14, 1964, in Kansas City. Graduate of University of Missouri–Columbia, B.J.; University of Missouri–Kansas City, J.D. Married with two children. Engaged in private practice of law from 1989–1996, and again from 2002–2009. Served as assistant Missouri attorney general from 1996–2002. Served on Kansas City Metropolitan Bar Association board of directors and as president of Missouri Institute for Justice. Served as adjunct professor of trial advocacy, University of Missouri–Kansas City School of Law. Member of board of directors, Sherwood Center. Appointed circuit judge April 30, 2009. Retained in 2010. Term expires Dec. 31, 2016. Nonpartisan.

Circuit 16—Division 7
S. MARGENE BURNETT

Office address: Jackson County Courthouse, 415 E. 12th St., Kansas City 64106; phone (816) 881-3607.

County: Jackson.

Biography: Not available.

Photo not available

Circuit 16—Division 8
BRYAN E. ROUND

Office address: Jackson County Courthouse, 415 E. 12th St., Kansas City 64106; phone (816) 881-3608.

County: Jackson.

Biography: Not available.

Photo not available

Circuit 16—Division 9
JOEL P. FAHNESTOCK

Office address: Jackson County Courthouse, 415 E. 12th St., Kansas City 64106; phone (816) 881-3609.

County: Jackson.

Biography: Born March 1, 1969, in Marshall. Graduate of William Woods College, B.S., English communications, teaching certification secondary schools; University of Missouri–Kansas City, J.D., 1994. Prior to appointment, practiced at the United States attorney's office–civil division. Served as law clerk to the Hon. Scott O. Wright, 1994–1996. Appointed in December 2008. Retained in 2010. Term expires Dec. 31, 2016. Nonpartisan.

Circuit 16—Division 10
PATRICK W. CAMPBELL

Office address: Jackson County Courthouse, 415 E. 12th St., Kansas City 64106; phone (816) 881-3610.

County: Jackson.

Biography: Born Feb. 7, 1961, in Kansas City. Lifelong resident of Jackson County. Graduate of University of Missouri–Kansas City, B.A., administration of justice and political science, 1984; J.D., 1990. In private practice prior to appointment by the 16th Circuit Court as a Family Court Commissioner in December 2006. Appointed circuit judge by Gov. Jay Nixon on May 6, 2013. Term expires Dec. 31, 2020. Nonpartisan.

Circuit 16—Division 11
W. BRENT POWELL

Office address: Jackson County Courthouse, 415 E. 12th St., Kansas City 64106; phone (816) 881-3611.

County: Jackson.

Biography: Born July 21, 1970. Originally from Springfield. Undergraduate degree at William Jewell College; University of Missouri–Columbia School of Law, J.D., 1996. Editor for the *Missouri Law Review*, Student Bar Association president and student law clerk for Missouri Supreme Court Judge Elwood Thomas. Practiced law at Lathrop & Gage in Kansas City. Assistant prosecutor in Platte County prosecutor's office, 1997. Assistant U.S. attorney for the United States attorney's office in 2001. Served as the chief of the General Crimes Unit and executive assistant U.S. attorney. Serves on Missouri Supreme Court Committee on Access to Family Courts and the Trial Judge Education Committee. He and his wife Beth live in Kansas City. Appointed circuit judge in February 2008. Retained in 2010. Term expires Dec. 31, 2016. Nonpartisan.

Circuit 16—Division 12
JENNIFER M. PHILLIPS

Office address: Jackson County Courthouse, 415 E. 12th St., Kansas City 64106; phone (816) 881-3612.

County: Jackson.

Biography: Graduate of Milan C-2 High School, Milan, 1993; University of Missouri–Columbia, B.A., speech communication, 1997; University of Missouri–Columbia, J.D., 2001. Practiced at Missouri Department of Revenue General Counsel's Office, 2001–2002; assistant prosecuting attorney for Jackson County, 2002–2014. During that time, she was an assistant prosecutor in the Community Justice Unit and Major Crimes Unit. She became a trial team leader in the Street Crimes Unit and a chief trial assistant in the Violent Crimes Unit. Member of the Kansas City Metropolitan Bar Association and Association of Women Lawyers. Recipient of Lon O. Hocker Award from Missouri Bar, 2011. Appointed to the court by Gov. Jay Nixon in 2014. Term expires Dec. 31, 2016. Nonpartisan.

Circuit 16—Division 13
CHARLES H. McKENZIE

Office address: Jackson County Courthouse Annex, 308 W. Kansas, Independence 64050; phone (816) 881-3613.

County: Jackson.

Biography: Born April 17, 1963, in Indianapolis, Ind. Graduate of Cardinal Newman College, B.A., business administration; University of Missouri–Kansas City Law School, J.D., 1988. He is married to Jennifer McKenzie; they have four children. He served as assistant prosecuting attorney in the Jackson County prosecutor's office from 1988–1993, and was in private practice from 1993–2011. Member: Missouri Bar Association, Kansas City Metropolitan Bar Association and St. Thomas More Catholic Church. Appointed circuit court judge June 2011. Retained in 2012. Term expires Dec. 31, 2018. Nonpartisan.

Circuit 16—Division 14
JOHN M. TORRENCE

Office address: Jackson County Courthouse, 415 E. 12th St., Kansas City 64106; phone: (816) 881-3614.

County: Jackson.

Biography: Born Dec. 7, 1957, in St. Louis. Educated at University of Missouri–Columbia and St. Louis University, B.A., 1979; University of Missouri–Kansas City School of Law, J.D., 1982. Married Julie Marie Hill June 3, 1989; they have three children. Former assistant public defender, Jackson County, 1982–1988. Engaged in private practice and partner in law firm, 1988–2001. Member: St. Elizabeth Catholic Church. Appointed circuit judge July 12, 2001. Retained in 2002, 2008 and 2014. Term expires Dec. 31, 2020. Nonpartisan.

Circuit 16—Division 15
ROBERT M. SCHIEBER

Office address: Jackson County Courthouse, 415 E. 12th St., Kansas City 64106; phone (816) 881-3615

County: Jackson.

Biography: Born Nov. 15, 1960. Graduate of University of Missouri–Columbia, dual degree, broadcast journalism and advertising, 1983; University of Missouri–Kansas City School of Law, J.D., 1988. He is married and the father of three children. Law clerk for then-Circuit Judge John I. Moran, 1988. Appointed by Jackson County Circuit Court as Family Court commissioner, May 2000. Assistant legal advisor to the Kansas City Police Department, 1998–2000. He was also on contract with the Jackson County Family Court's Office of the Juvenile Officer from 1997 until his appointment as family court commissioner, representing that office in cases on appeal. Has worked in public and private practice, prosecuting and defending criminal cases and has had an extensive civil litigation practice. Appointed circuit judge November 2006. Retained in 2008 and 2014. Term expires Dec. 31, 2020. Nonpartisan.

Circuit 16—Division 16
MARCO A. ROLDAN

Office address: Jackson County Courthouse, 415 E. 12th St., Kansas City 64106; phone (816) 881-4416.

County: Jackson.

Biography: Born June 13, 1957, in Nuevo Laredo, Mexico. Graduate of Central Missouri State University, B.S., 1979; University of Missouri–Kansas City School of Law, J.D., 1983. Married with three children. Appointed circuit judge Sept. 28, 1999. Retained in 2000, 2006 and 2012. Term expires Dec. 31, 2018. Nonpartisan.

Circuit 16—Division 17
JACK R. GRATE

Office address: Jackson County Courthouse, 308 W. Kansas, Independence 64050-3715; phone (816) 881-4417.

County: Jackson.

Biography: Born Oct. 7, 1949, in St. Louis. Graduate of University of Notre Dame, B.A., 1972; University of Missouri–Columbia, J.D., 1976. Married to Joan Canoy; they have four children. Member: Catholic Church. In private practice, 1976–2004; former board member of Legal Aid of Western Missouri, 1987–1996, president, 1994–1995; Eastern Jackson County Bar Association, president, 1999–2000; and member of The Missouri Bar. Appointed circuit judge by Gov. Bob Holden April 2004. Retained in 2006 and 2012. Term expires Dec. 31, 2018. Nonpartisan.

Circuit 16—Division 18
KEVIN D. HARRELL

Office address: Jackson County Courthouse, 415 E. 12th St., Kansas City, 64106; phone (816) 881-3618.

County: Jackson.

Biography: Born April 4, 1970, in Kansas City. Graduate of University of Missouri–Kansas City, B.A., administration of justice, 1993; J.D., 1998. Appointed by Gov. Jay Nixon on July 24, 2012. At the time of his appointment, he was the chief deputy prosecuting attorney for the Jackson County Prosecutor's Office. During his 15-year tenure, he was honored three times by his colleagues as Victim Champion of the Year in 2001 and 2003, and as Trial Attorney of the Year in 2005. Term expires Dec. 31, 2018. Nonpartisan.

Circuit 16—Division 19
KATHLEEN A. FORSYTH

Office address: Jackson County Courthouse, 415 E. 12th St., Kansas City 64106; phone (816) 881-3759.

County: Jackson.

Biography: Graduate of Emporia State University, B.S., business administration; University of Missouri–Kansas City, J.D. Engaged in private law practice, 1980–1994. Appointed Jackson County Probate Court commissioner, 1994. Served as council member, vice chair and chair, Missouri Probate and Trust Law Committee; Kansas City Metro Bar Association Probate and Estate Planning Committee, vice chair and chair; and Association for Women Lawyers of Greater Kansas City, executive committee, board and treasurer. Member: Missouri Bar Gender and Justice Committee; Pets for Life Board, Legal Beagle Chapter. Appointed circuit judge June 19, 2003. Retained in 2004 and 2010. Term expires Dec. 31, 2016. Nonpartisan.

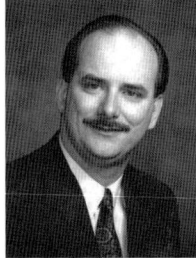

Circuit 17—Division 1
WILLIAM B. COLLINS

Office address: Cass County Juvenile Justice Center, 2501 W. Mechanic, Harrisonville 64701; phone (816) 380-8180.

Counties: Cass and Johnson.

Biography: Presiding judge. Born Dec. 1, 1956 in Kansas City. Graduate of Rockhurst University, 1979, B.S., B.A., accounting; University of Missouri–Kansas City Law School, J.D., 1982. Member of the Missouri Association of Probate and Associate Circuit Judges; Missouri Municipal and Associate Circuit Judges Association; and The Missouri Bar. Resides in Harrisonville. Elected associate circuit judge 1994. Re-elected 1998, 2002, 2006 and 2010. Elected circuit judge Nov. 6, 2012. Term expires Dec. 31, 2018. Republican.

Circuit 17—Division 2
R. MICHAEL WAGNER

Office address: Johnson County Justice Center, 101 W. Market, Warrensburg 64093; phone (660) 422-7407.

Counties: Cass and Johnson.

Biography: Born Sept. 24, 1963. Graduate of Rockhurst College, B.A., 1986; University of Missouri–Kansas City School of Law, J.D., 1990. Married Aug. 7, 1998, to wife, Melody. Engaged in private law practice, 1990–2008. Raymore and Garden City municipal judge, 2006–2008. Board of directors of Casco. Member of Bel-Ray Lions Club and National Rifle Association. Attends Holy Spirit Catholic Church. Elected circuit judge November 2008. Term expires Dec. 31, 2016. Democrat.

Circuit 18
ROBERT L. KOFFMAN

Office address: Pettis County Courthouse, 415 S. Ohio, Sedalia 65301; phone (660) 827-5000, ext. 465.

Counties: Cooper and Pettis.

Biography: Presiding judge. Born Dec. 24, 1953, in Maryville. Educated at Moberly public schools. Graduate of Central Missouri State University, B.S., 1977; St. Mary's University, San Antonio, Texas, J.D., 1980. Married Doris Fry, 1981. Two children, John and Kathryn. Associate circuit judge, Pettis County, 1981–2005. Member: Wesley United Methodist Church; Missouri and Pettis County Bar associations; Sedalia School Foundation; AF & AM Lodge No. 272; Legislative Steering Committee and Executive Council, Missouri Judicial Conference; Sedalia Jaycees, past vice president; Circuit Court Budget Committee member; Missouri Association of Probate and Associate Circuit Judges, past president; Sedalia Symphony Society; Central Missouri State University Alumni Band; and Sedalia Rotary Club. Appointed circuit judge 2005. Elected 2006 and 2012. Term expires Dec. 31, 2018. Republican.

Circuit 19—Division 4
PATRICIA JOYCE

Office address: Cole County Courthouse, 301 E. High St., Jefferson City 65101; phone (573) 634-9178.

County: Cole.

Biography: Presiding judge. Born Sept. 6, 1955, in Cape Girardeau. Graduate of Southeast Missouri State University, B.S., law enforcement, *summa cum laude*, 1976; St. Louis University, J.D., *cum laude*, 1979. Married to Dan Joyce. They have five children. Staff attorney, Mid-Missouri Legal Services, 1980–1983; assistant prosecuting attorney, Cole County, 1983–1994. Member: St. Joseph Cathedral; Chief Justice Advisory Council; State Judicial Records Committee; Circuit Court Budget Committee; and Missouri Association of Drug Court Professionals. Elected associate circuit judge 1994 and 1998. Elected circuit judge 2002, 2008 and 2014. Term expires Dec. 31, 2020. Democrat.

Circuit 19—Division 1
JON E. BEETEM

Office address: Cole County Courthouse, 301 E. High St., Rm. 201, PO Box 1870, Jefferson City 65102-1870; phone (573) 634-9192.

County: Cole.

Biography: Born May 1, 1959. Graduate of University of Kentucky, B.S., pharmacy; University of Missouri–Columbia School of Law, J.D. He is married and has two children. Engaged in the private practice of law, 1992–2006. Member: First Presbyterian Church; Missouri Bar and Cole County Bar associations, past president. Elected circuit judge 2006 and 2012. Term expires Dec. 31, 2018. Republican.

Circuit 19—Division 2
DANIEL R. GREEN

Office Address: Cole County Courthouse, 301 E. High St., Jefferson City 65101; phone (573) 634-9190.

County: Cole.

Biography: Born March 9, 1963. Graduate of Trevecca Nazarene University, B.A., history; Vanderbilt University, M.A. candidate, religion; University of Missouri School of Law, J.D. Married to Samantha Green, with four children. Private practice of law, 1990–2010. Jefferson City prosecuting attorney, 1997–2010. Elected circuit judge 2014. Term expires Dec. 31, 2020. Republican.

Circuit 20—Division 1
GAEL D. WOOD
Office address: Franklin County Judicial Center, 401 E. Main St., Room 100C, Union 63084; phone (636) 583-6306.

Counties: Franklin, Gasconade and Osage.

Biography: Presiding judge. Born Oct. 23, 1947, in Washington. Graduate of University of Missouri, B.A., 1969; University of Missouri–Kansas City, J.D., with distinction, 1975. Married; one daughter, Samantha. In private practice in Washington, 1975–2000. Served as municipal judge for Washington and Owensville. Served as president of 20th Circuit Bar Association; Washington Rotary; Washington Area Chamber of Commerce; and Emmaus Homes, Inc., board of directors. Member: Emmaus Homes, Inc., Property Board. Elected circuit judge in 2000, 2006 and 2012. Term expires Dec. 31, 2018. Republican.

Circuit 20—Division 2
I.I. LAMKE
Office address: Franklin County Judicial Center, 401 E. Main St., Room 100B, Union 63084; phone (636) 583-6309.

Counties: Franklin, Gasconade and Osage.

Biography: Born Dec. 20, 1951, in Washington. Graduate of St. Louis University, B.A., 1974; Washington University School of Law, J.D., 1977. Married Susan J. Schweitzer Nov. 27, 1983. In private practice in Union and Washington, 1977–2010. Elected circuit judge in 2010. Term expires Dec. 31, 2016. Republican.

Circuit 21—Division 2
MAURA McSHANE
Office address: St. Louis County Court Bldg., 104 S. Central Ave., Clayton 63105; phone (314) 615-1502.

County: St. Louis.

Biography: Presiding judge. Born in San Antonio, Texas. Graduate of St. Louis University, B.S.; South Texas College of Law, Houston, Texas, J.D. Private practice, 1982–1984. Served as assistant prosecuting attorney, St. Louis County, 1984–1994. Member: Missouri, Metropolitan St. Louis and St. Louis County Bar associations and Women Lawyers Association. Appointed circuit judge: October 17, 1994. Retained in 1996, 2002, 2008 and 2014. Term expires December 31, 2020. Nonpartisan.

Circuit 21—Division 1
ROBERT S. COHEN
Office address: St. Louis County Court Bldg., 105 Central Ave., Clayton 63105; phone (314) 615-1501.

County: St. Louis.

Biography: Born July 4, 1946, in St. Louis. Educated at University of Missouri–Columbia and Washington University, A.B.; St. Louis University School of Law, J.D. Married Aug. 16, 1970, to Sheila Ann Brin. They have two children. Engaged in private law practice. Elected to two terms as magistrate, Second District, St. Louis County. Served as magistrate and associate circuit judge, 1975–1994. Member: Congregation Shaare Emeth; Missouri and St. Louis County (past president) Bar associations. Appointed circuit judge July 6, 1994, by Gov. Mel Carnahan. Retained in 1996, 2002, 2008 and 2014. Presiding judge, 1998–2000. Term expires Dec. 31, 2020. Nonpartisan.

Circuit 21—Division 3
SANDRA FARRAGUT-HEMPHILL

Office address: St. Louis County Court Bldg., 105 S. Central Ave., Clayton 63105; phone (314) 615-1503.

County: St. Louis.

Biography: Born Dec. 9, 1953, in Tampa, Fla. Graduate of Spelman College in Atlanta, Ga., B.S., political science, *cum laude*; University of Florida School of Law, J.D. Served as associate at Bell, Harris Kirksey and Thomas; staff attorney at Legal Services of Eastern Missouri; assistant county counselor for St. Louis County; and engaged in private practice until appointment to the bench in March 1991. Member: Missouri Bar, Mound City Bar Association, Bar Association of Metropolitan St. Louis, Women Lawyers Association, National Bar Association, Alpha Kappa Alpha Sorority, Inc. and The Links, Inc.. Faculty member of the Trial Judges Education Committee since 2007. Served as associate circuit judge, 1991–2014. Appointed circuit judge November 2015 by Gov. Jeremiah (Jay) Nixon. Term expires Dec. 31, 2016. Nonpartisan.

Circuit 21—Division 4
THOMAS J. PREBIL

Office address: St. Louis County Court Bldg., 105 S. Central Ave., Clayton 63105; phone (314) 615-1504.

County: St. Louis.

Biography: Born Feb. 17, 1946, in St. Louis. Graduate of St. Louis University, B.A., 1968; St. Louis University School of Law, J.D., 1971; Married to Ann M. Fehlig Aug. 20, 1969; they have three children. Served in the U.S. Army Reserves, 1971–1980; served as assistant public defender in the City of St. Louis, 1972–1975; and engaged in private law practice from 1975–2009. Member: Missouri Bar Association, St. Louis County Bar Association, Bar Association of Metropolitan St. Louis, the Lawyers Association, Alpha Sigma Nu Honor Society, Our Lady of Lourdes Catholic Church and Missouri Master Gardeners. Appointed circuit judge June 10, 2009. Retained in 2010. Term expires Dec. 31, 2016. Nonpartisan.

Circuit 21—Division 5
THEA A. SHERRY

Office address: St. Louis County Court Bldg., 105 S. Central Ave., Clayton, Mo 63105; phone: (314) 615-1505.

County: St. Louis.

Biography: Born in London, England. Gradute of University of California–Riverside, B.A.; Washington University in St. Louis, J.D. Married in 1978 and has two children. Law clerk for Honorable Gerald Smith, Missouri Court of Appeals, Eastern District; served as assistant public defender in St. Louis County; and engaged in private practice until appointment to the bench in 1998. Member of Missouri Bar, Metropolitan St. Louis and St. Louis County Bar associations, Lawyers Association and Women Lawyers Association. Adjunct professor of law at Washington University School of Law. Appointed associate circuit judge by Gov. Mel Carnahan July 1998. Retained in 2000, 2004 and 2008. Appointed circuit judge by Gov. Jeremiah (Jay) Nixon February 2011. Retained in 2012. Term expires Dec. 31, 2018. Nonpartisan.

Circuit 21—Division 6
DOUGLAS R. BEACH

Office address: St. Louis County Court Bldg., 105 S. Central Ave., Clayton 63105; phone (314) 615-1506.

County: St. Louis.

Biography: Born Sept. 20, 1948, Kittery, Maine. Undergrad, Central Connecticut State Univ.; J.D., New England School of Law, *cum laude*. Member: Missouri Bar; Mass. Bar; St. Louis County Bar; St. Louis Metropolitan Bar Assoc.; past pres., St. Louis County Bar; chair, Family Law Section, Mo. Bar and Metropolitan Bar associations; past pres., American Academy of Matrimonial Lawyers, Mo. Chapter; fellow, American Academy of Matrimonial Lawyers; Children's Home Society; Kids in the Middle Programs; certified Matrimonial Arbitrator; Outstanding Young Lawyer, St. Louis County Bar. Listed in "The Best Lawyers in America," 1991–2005, and St. Louis "Top Lawyers," *St. Louis Magazine*. Author: *Trial Practice in Domestic Relations and Division of Marital Property in Missouri*; city attorney for Chesterfield 1988–2005; lt. col., U.S. Marine Corps Reserve, retired; and 2011 recipient of Champion of Kids Award. Appointed associate circuit judge 2005. Retained 2008. Appointed circuit judge 2010. Retained in 2012. Term expires Dec. 31, 2018. Nonpartisan.

Circuit 21—Division 7
CAROLYN C. WHITTINGTON

Office address: St. Louis County Court Bldg., 105 S. Central Ave., Clayton 63105; phone (314) 615-1507.

County: St. Louis.

Biography: Born in Chicago, Ill. Graduate of Northwestern University, Evanston, Ill., B.S., journalism; St. Louis University, J.D. Married Joseph M. Whittington Aug. 12, 1972. They have two children. Served as assistant county counselor, 1980–1987. Engaged in private law practice from 1987 until appointment to the bench. Member: Missouri Supreme Court Committee on Procedure in Criminal Cases; Missouri Association of Probate and Associate Circuit Judges, president, 2002. Appointed associate circuit judge October 1992, by Gov. John Ashcroft. Retained in 1994 and 1998. Appointed circuit judge December 2001 by Gov. Bob Holden. She was retained in 2004 and 2010. Term expires Dec. 31, 2016. Nonpartisan.

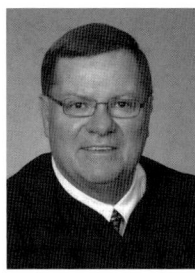

Circuit 21—Division 8
TOM W. DEPRIEST JR.

Office address: St. Louis County Court Bldg., 105 S. Central Ave., Clayton 63105; phone (314) 615-1508.

County: St. Louis.

Biography: Born Oct. 9, 1947, in Poplar Bluff. Educated at Southeast Missouri State University and University of Missouri–Columbia, B.S. and J.D. Married to Mary S. Dreyer. They have three children. Served in the U.S. Army, 1969–1971. Member: Missouri, Metropolitan St. Louis and St. Louis County Bar associations and Lawyers Association of St. Louis. Served as assistant prosecuting attorney and chief warrant officer, St. Louis County, 1975–2000. Appointed circuit judge June 14, 2000. Retained in 2008 and 2014. Term expires Dec. 31, 2020. Nonpartisan.

Circuit 21—Division 9
DAVID LEE VINCENT III

Office address: St. Louis County Court Bldg., 105 S. Central Ave., Clayton 63105 ; phone (314) 615-1509.

County: St. Louis.

Biography: Born July 15, 1958, in Dayton, Ohio. Graduate of Tenn. State Univ.–Nashville, B.S.E.E.; Univ. of Wisconsin–Madison Law School, J.D. Married Marcia Nathelia Thomas June 5, 1982. They have two children. Asst. circuit atty. 1988–93, homicide unit and felony staff supervisor. Actively practiced law until appointment to the bench. Participated in truancy court—Pattonville School Dist. and high school mock trial competition for Pattonville and Marquette High Schools (five state championships). Currently high school mock trial coach, Normandy High School. Member: Missouri Bar, Bar Association of Metro St. Louis and Mound City Bar Association. Elected Missouri Bar Board of Governors, 2008–2010. Appointed to Supreme Court Board of Certified Court Reporter Examiners. Previous appointments and service: Supreme Court Judicial Finance Commission, Supreme Court special judge, 2005, and St. Louis For Kids board member. Appointed circuit judge Nov. 14, 1997. Retained in 2000, 2006 and 2012. Term expires Dec. 31, 2018. Nonpartisan.

Circuit 21—Division 10
MICHAEL T. JAMISON

Office address: St. Louis County Court Bldg., 105 S. Central Ave., Clayton 63105; phone (314) 615-1510.

County: St. Louis.

Biography: Born Dec. 16, 1949, St. Louis. Graduate of O'Fallon Technical High School, 1968; Washington University, B.A., political science, 1976; St. Louis University School of Law, J.D., 1976. Married attorney Gayle C. Williams in St. Louis, 1975. Children: Dorian, Brandon and Brenton. Employment: field attorney, Region 14, National Labor Relations Board 1976–1992; private practice, Lashly & Baer, 1992–1994; and associate general counsel, Anheuser-Busch Companies, 1994–1997. Member of numerous boards and adjunct professor at several colleges. Appointed associate circuit judge May 8, 1997. Appointed circuit judge Oct. 6, 2005. Retained in 2006 and 2012. Term expires Dec. 31, 2018. Nonpartisan.

Circuit 21—Division 11
ELLEN LEVY-SIWAK

Office address: St. Louis County Court Bldg., 501 S. Brentwood, Clayton 63105; phone (314) 615-1511.

County: St. Louis.

Biography: Born Aug. 3, 1963, in St. Louis. Graduate of Washington University, A.B., 1985; J.D., 1988. Married to Jeffrey Siwak; they have two children. Prior to appointment to the bench, actively practiced law as a litigation partner at Rosenblum, Goldenhersh, Silverstein & Zafft. Member: Missouri and Metropolitan St. Louis Bar associations; St. Louis County Bar Association, president, 2005; Missouri Association of Probate and Associate Circuit Judges, president 2006–2007; National Association of Women Judges, director, 2006–2008; and Mound City and Women's Lawyer's Bar associations. Serves on the faculty of the state trial judge education programs. Appointed Family Court commissioner June 9, 1999. Appointed associate circuit judge May 22, 2002. Retained in 2010. Appointed circuit judge Jan. 24, 2008. Retained in 2010. Term expires Dec. 31, 2016. Nonpartisan.

Circuit 21—Division 12
STEVEN H. GOLDMAN

Office address: St. Louis County Court Bldg., 105 S. Central Ave., Clayton 63105; phone (314) 615-1512.

County: St. Louis.

Biography: Born Sept. 26, 1946, in St. Louis. Graduate of Washington University, A.B.; St. Louis University, J.D. Married to Victoria R. Kochner, 1979; they have two children. Served in the U.S. Army Reserve, discharged in 1971. Assistant prosecuting attorney in the St. Louis County Prosecutor's Office, 1972–1988; chief trial attorney, 1977. Member: United Hebrew Temple; Phi Delta Phi; Sigma Alpha Mu; St. Louis County Bar Association; Lawyers Association of St. Louis; Grievance Committee, St. Louis Metropolitan Medicine Society; and *ad hoc* committee to revise Supreme Court criminal rules, chair. Guest lecturer: Metropolitan Police Academy; St. Louis County Police Education Services; and Missouri Office of Prosecution Services. Appointed circuit judge Feb.19, 1988. Retained in 1990, 1996, 2002, 2008 and 2014. Term expires Dec. 31, 2020. Nonpartisan.

Circuit 21—Division 13
BARBARA W. WALLACE

Office address: St. Louis County Court Bldg., 105 S. Central Ave., Clayton 63105; phone (314) 615-1513.

County: St. Louis.

Biography: Born June 9, 1951, in Blue Island, Ill. Gradute of Washington University, A.B., economics; J.D. Married Aug. 21, 1971. Engaged in private law practice, 1976–1995, until appointed to the bench. Member: Missouri, Metropolitan St. Louis and St. Louis County Bar associations; Lawyers Association, president, 1989–1990; Women Lawyers Association, president, 1980–1981; Elected lawyer member, Judicial Nominating Commission, 21st Judicial Circuit, 1988–1994. Awards: Outstanding Young Lawyer, 1985; President's Award, 1988. Appointed circuit judge Nov. 15, 1995. Retained in 1998, 2004 and 2010. Elected presiding judge 2000–2004. Term expires Dec. 31, 2016. Nonpartisan.

Circuit 21—Division 14
KRISTINE ALLEN KERR

Office address: St. Louis County Court Bldg., 105 S. Central Ave., Clayton 63105; phone (314) 615-1514.

County: St. Louis.

Biography: Born 1959, in Philadelphia, Pa. Gradute of Brown University, B.A., economics, 1982; Boston University, J.D., 1985. Clerkship: Missouri Court of Appeals (ED), 1986–87. Engaged in private law practice, 1987–88. Assistant public defender, St. Louis City Trial Office, 1988–99; Capital Division, 1990–93; first assistant public defender, St. Louis City, 1993–2003; and assistant public defender, St. Louis County, 2003–2004. Appointed Family Court Commissioner (Juvenile Division), 2004; retained 2008. Member: St. Louis County Bar Association, the Women Lawyer's Association (President's Award, 2011), the Lawyer's Association, the National Association of Women Judges, the Bar Association of Metropolitan St. Louis and Mound City Bar Association. Elected a Fellow in the Advanced Science and Technology Adjudication Resource Center (ASTAR), Washington, DC, 2009. Appointed circuit court judge 2012. Retained in 2014. Term expires Dec. 31, 2020. Nonpartisan.

Circuit 21—Division 15
JOHN D. WARNER JR.

Office address: 501 W. Brentwood Ave., Clayton 63105; phone (314) 615-1515.

County: St. Louis.

Biography: Born 1951, in St. Louis. Graduate of the University of Missouri–St. Louis, B.A. 1979; St. Louis University School of Law, J.D. 1982. Married Pamela L. Hill, June 1982, and has two children. Engaged in private practice, 1982–2012. Member: Metropolitan St. Louis Bar Association; Lawyers Association of St. Louis; and Missouri Association of Trial Attorneys. Licensed to practice law in Missouri and Illinois, U.S. District Court, Eastern and Western Districts of Missouri, Court of Appeals, 8th Circuit, and Supreme Court of the United States. Appointed circuit judge April 2012. Retained in 2014. Term expires Dec. 31, 2020. Nonpartisan.

Circuit 21—Division 16
MICHAEL D. BURTON

Office address: Family Court Center, 105 S. Central Ave., Clayton 63105; phone (314) 615-1516.

County: St. Louis.

Biography: Born June 20, 1960, in Philadelphia, Pa. Graduate of University of Notre Dame, B.A., government; Washington University, J.D. Married Sheila A. Shunick in 1991. They have three children. Assistant special public defender for St. Louis County and St. Louis City, 1985–1989. Engaged in private law practice, 1989–1999. Member: Mary Queen of Peace Catholic Church; administrative judge of the family court, 2008–present; ADA Committee, chair; Domestic and Family Violence Council, chair; and Metropolitan St. Louis and St. Louis County Bar associations. Adjunct professor of law at St. Louis University and Washington University law schools. Appointed associate circuit judge April 20, 1999. Retained in 2000. Appointed circuit judge Feb. 16, 2004. Retained in 2006 and 2012. Term expires Dec. 31, 2018. Nonpartisan.

Circuit 21—Division 17
JOSEPH L. WALSH III

Office address: Circuit Court of St. Louis County, 105 S. Central Ave., Clayton 63105; phone (314) 615-1517.

County: St. Louis.

Biography: Born Dec. 7, 1954, in St. Louis. Graduate of Loras College, Dubuque, Iowa, B.S., *cum laude*, 1977; St. Mary's University School of Law, San Antonio, Texas, J.D., 1984; and senior associate editor of *Law Review* and *Order of Barristers*. Married Eileen R. Walsh in 1982. They have five children. Private practice, 1984–2010, handling general civil trials and appeals. Served as municipal judge in the City of Creve Coeur, 2003–2010, and the City of Frontenac, 2000–2001. Member: Our Lady of the Pillar Catholic Church; Missouri Bar; Texas Bar; American Board of Trial Advocates; and St. Louis Lawyer's Association. Lectured in the areas of civil trial practice and insurance law. Co-authored *MOBar CLE Tort Law Handbook*, Second Edition, Chap. 1, Intro and Overview; authored *Demonstrative Evidence*, St. Louis Lawyer, November 1992. Appointed circuit judge on May 14, 2010, by Gov. Jeremiah (Jay) Nixon. Sworn in on June 11, 2010. Retained in 2012. Term expires Dec. 31, 2018. Nonpartisan.

Circuit 21—Division 18
ELLEN (NELLIE) HANNIGAN RIBAUDO

Office address: St. Louis County Court Bldg., 105 S. Central Ave., Clayton 63105; phone (314) 615-1518.

County: St. Louis.

Biography: Born in St. Louis on May 7, 1971. Graduate of the University of Dayton, B.A., 1993; St. Louis University School of Law, J.D., 1996. Appointed associate circuit judge July 2009. Retained in 2010 and 2014. Appointed circuit judge on Nov. 5, 2015. Term expires Dec. 31, 2018. Nonpartisan.

Circuit 21—Division 19
GLORIA CLARK RENO

Office address: St. Louis County Court Bldg., 105 S. Central Ave., Clayton 63105; phone (314) 615-1519.

County: St. Louis.

Biography: Born in St. Louis. Graduate of University of Missouri–St. Louis, B.A., English; St. Louis University, J.D. Has one son through marriage. Previously an assistant public defender, 1988–1992; engaged in the private practice of law, 1992–2002; and served as municipal judge for the City of Northwoods, 1994–2002. Member: Women Lawyer's Association; Mound City Bar Association; National Association of Women Judges; Supreme Court Commission on Alternative Dispute Resolution in Domestic Relation Cases; and Cardinal Ritter Senior Services, board member. Appointed associate circuit judge March 8, 2002. Retained 2004 and 2008. Appointed circuit judge April 3, 2009. Retained 2010. Term expires Dec. 31, 2016. Nonpartisan.

Circuit 21—Division 20
COLLEEN DOLAN

Office address: St. Louis County Court Bldg., 105 S. Central Ave., Clayton 63105; phone (314) 615-1520.

County: St. Louis.

Biography: Born in Baltimore, Md. Graduate of University of Missouri–St. Louis, B.S., administration of justice; St. Louis University, J.D. Married to Glenn A. Norton; they have four children. Engaged in private law practice from 1984–1994, when appointed to the bench as an associate circuit judge. Retained in 1996. Member: St. Clare of Assisi Catholic Church; Missouri Municipal and Associate Circuit Judges Association, vice president, 1998, secretary, 1996–1997; Missouri Association of Probate and Associate Circuit Judges; Supreme Court Committees on Alternative Dispute Resolution, Municipal Division Education, 1995–2000, and Family Law, 1997–1999; and ASTAR fellow, 2009. Appointed circuit judge March 30, 1999. Retained in 2000, 2006 and 2012. Term expires Dec. 31, 2018. Nonpartisan.

Circuit 22—Division 1
BRYAN L. HETTENBACH

Office address: Civil Courts Bldg., 10 N. Tucker St., St. Louis 63101; phone (314) 622-4381.

City of St. Louis.

Biography: Presiding judge. Born Feb. 10, 1955, in St. Louis. Graduate of University of Missouri–Columbia, B.A.; University of Michigan, M.A.; and University of Missouri–Columbia School of Law, J.D. Engaged in private practice of law for 23 years. Former staff attorney for Missouri Supreme Court. Former news editor of *Missouri Lawyers Weekly.* Former adjunct professor of legal studies at William Woods College. Recurring service as guardian *ad litem* in family and juvenile law cases. Certified civil law and family court mediator. Frequent speaker and contributor to continuing legal education programs and publications for The Missouri Bar and other legal organizations. Appointed circuit judge April 2, 2008. Term expires Dec. 31, 2016. Nonpartisan.

Circuit 22—Division 2
DAVID L. DOWD

Office address: Civil Courts Bldg., 10 N. Tucker St., St. Louis 63101; phone (314) 622-4372.

City of St. Louis.

Biography: Born Dec. 18, 1953, in St. Louis. Gradute of Quincy College, B.A.; St. Mary's University, J.D. Engaged in private law practice with Dowd and Dowd, P.C., 1983–1984; assistant county counselor, 1984–1988; administrative law judge, 1988–1993; and chief administrative law judge, 1993–2000. Member: St. Raphael's Catholic Church. Board of directors: Saint Louis Crisis Nursery, Dismas House of St. Louis and Catholic Youth Apostolate. Commissioner of the Judge Dowd Soccer League. Chair of Commission on Retirement, Removal and Discipline. Appointed circuit judge Dec. 13, 2000, by Gov. Roger B. Wilson. Retained in 2002, 2008 and 2014. Presiding judge 2009–2010. Term expires Dec. 31, 2020. Nonpartisan.

Circuit 22—Division 3
ELIZABETH B. HOGAN

Office address: Civil Courts Bldg., 10 N. Tucker St., St. Louis 63101; phone (314) 622-4453. **City of St. Louis.**

Biography: Born in St. Louis. Graduate of the Academy of the Visitation,1986; DePauw University, B.A., political science, 1990; Thomas M. Cooley Law School, J.D. Employed as assistant prosecuting attorney in Jefferson County; assistant circuit attorney in City of St. Louis; in private practice; and as an attorney supervisor at St. Louis City CASA from 1996–2005. Member: Missouri Bar Association, Women Lawyers Association, St. Louis Lawyer's Association and St. Roch Catholic Church. Appointed associate circuit judge in 2005 by Gov. Matt Blunt. Retained in 2006 and 2010. Appointed circuit judge in 2012 by Gov. Jeremiah (Jay) Nixon. Retained in 2013. Term expires 2020.

Circuit 22—Division 4
JULIAN L. BUSH

Office address: Civil Courts Bldg., 10 N. Tucker St., St. Louis 63101; phone (314) 622-3668. **City of St. Louis.**

Biography: Graduate of the George Washington University and Washington University School of Law. In 1995, after practicing law for almost 20 years, he was appointed a circuit judge for the City of St. Louis. He is the author of many articles in legal journals and chapters in the Missouri CLE series of books. Appointed circuit judge June 15, 1995. Retained in 1996, 2002, 2008 and 2014. Term expires Dec. 31, 2020. Nonpartisan.

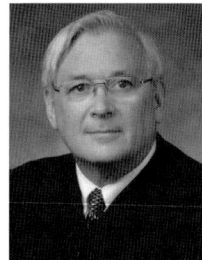

Circuit 22—Division 5
MARK H. NEILL

Office address: Civil Courts Bldg., 10 N. Tucker St., St. Louis 63101; phone (314) 622-4802. **City of St. Louis.**

Biography: Born March 21, 1949, in St. Louis. Graduate of St. Louis University, B.A., history, 1971; J.D., 1974. Married Catherine Kelly Cross Dec. 28, 1973. They have four adult children: Thomas, John, Kevin and Katie. Engaged in private practice in St. Louis. Former attorney for the St. Louis Police Department. Member: Our Lady of Lourdes Catholic Church; Missouri Bar Association; Bar Association of Metropolitan St. Louis; and Lawyers Association of St. Louis. Appointed circuit judge Feb. 15, 2002. Retained in 2004 and 2010. Term expires Dec. 31, 2016. Nonpartisan.

Circuit 22—Division 6
JAMES SULLIVAN

Office address: Civil Courts Bldg., 10 N. Tucker St., St. Louis 63101; phone (314) 622-4827. **City of St. Louis.**

Photo not available

Biography: Not available.

Circuit 22—Division 7
JOHN J. RILEY

Office address: Civil Courts Bldg., 10 N. Tucker St., St. Louis 63101; phone (314) 613-7187.
City of St. Louis.
Biography: Born June 20, 1947, in St. Louis. Graduate of St. Louis University, B.S., 1969; St. Louis University School of Law, J.D., 1972. Married Kathleen Loberg June 7, 1975, in St. Louis. Engaged in private law practice, 1972–1995. Lieutenant colonel, United States Army Reserve, retired. Member: St. Margaret of Scotland Catholic Church, Shaw Neighborhood Improvement Association, Missouri and St. Louis Metropolitan Bar associations and National Conference of Metropolitan Courts. Municipal judge, City of Black Jack, 1983–1995. Appointed circuit judge March 22, 1995. Presiding judge, 2005–2006. Retained in 1996, 2002, 2008 and 2014. Term expires Dec. 31, 2020. Nonpartisan.

Circuit 22—Division 8
MICHAEL F. STELZER

Office address: Civil Courts Bldg., 10 N. Tucker St., St. Louis 63101; phone (314) 622-4476.
St. Louis City
Biography: Born Feb. 11, 1964, St. Louis. Graduate of Augustana College, Rock Island, Ill., 1986; St. Louis University School of Law, J.D., *cum laude*, 1992. Clerked for the Hon. Carl R. Gaertner, Missouri Court of Appeals Eastern District. Assistant and associate city counselor, City of St. Louis, 1993–2004. General counsel to the Board of Police Commissioners, St. Louis City. Appointed to the associate circuit bench, January 2004, by Gov. Bob Holden. Elected in 2006 and 2010. Appointed circuit judge 2012. Term expires Dec. 31, 2020.

Circuit 22—Division 9
MARGARET M. NEILL

Office address: Civil Courts Bldg., 10 N. Tucker St., St. Louis 63101; phone (314) 622-4682.
City of St. Louis.
Biography: Born March 21, 1949, in St. Louis. Graduate of St. Louis University, B.A., J.D.; College of Notre Dame, M.Ed. Engaged in private practice in St. Louis. Past president, Lawyers Association of St. Louis and Missouri Circuit Judges Association. Member: Catholic Church; Missouri Bar Association; Bar Association of Metropolitan St. Louis; Board of Certified Court Reporter Examiners of Missouri, 1994–2006; Missouri Circuit Judges Association, 2009–present; Lawyers Association of St. Louis; Women Lawyer's Association; and National Conference of Metropolitan Courts, board, 1998–2007, executive committee, 1999–2007, president, 2003. Presiding judge, 22nd Judicial Circuit, 2001–2002. Appointed circuit judge Feb. 5, 1993. Retained in 1994, 2000, 2006 and 2012. Term expires Dec. 31, 2018. Nonpartisan.

Circuit 22—Division 10
REX M. BURLISON

Office address: Civil Courts Bldg., 10 N. Tucker St., St. Louis 63101; Phone: (314) 622-4819.
City of St. Louis.
Biography: Not available. Appointed circuit judge Aug. 9, 2011. Term expires Dec. 31, 2018. Nonpartisan.

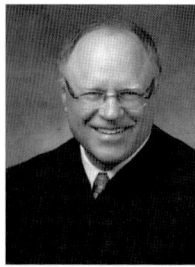

Circuit 22—Division 11
PHILIP D. HEAGNEY

Office address: Civil Courts Bldg., 10 N. Tucker St., St. Louis 63101; phone (314) 622-4491.
City of St. Louis.

Biography: Born Nov. 24, 1947, in Spokane, Wash. Graduate of Johns Hopkins University, B.A., 1970; Harvard Law School, J.D., 1976. Married Barbara Lynn Prosser Oct. 12, 1991. They have two children, Nathaniel Owen and Samuel Joseph. Engaged in private law practice, 1976–1996; general law practice in St. Louis. Member: St. Cronan Catholic Church; Gibson Heights Neighborhood Association; St. Margaret of Scotland Basketball; and Boy Scout Troop 110. Appointed circuit judge Feb. 28, 1996. Retained in 1998, 2004 and 2010. Term expires Dec. 31, 2016. Nonpartisan.

Circuit 22—Division 12
DENNIS M. SCHAUMANN

Office address: Civil Courts Bldg., 10 N. Tucker St., St. Louis 63101; phone (314) 622-4420.
City of St. Louis.

Biography: Born Jan. 7, 1948, in the city of St. Louis. Graduate of Southeast Missouri State University, B.A.; St. Louis University School of Law, J.D. Married Patricia Ann Singrun Aug. 23, 1969. Two children, Michael and Marissa. Two grandsons, Preston and Landon. Legal officer for the Juvenile Division, Circuit Court, City of St. Louis, 1973–1975. Private practice of law, 1975–1994. Appointed Municipal Judge for the City of St. Louis, 1981; reappointed 1985, 1989 and 1993. Served as presiding judge for the St. Louis Municipal Court, 1981–1993. Member: Lawyers Association of St. Louis; St. Louis Metropolitan Bar Association; and Missouri Bar Association. Appointed associate circuit judge Dec. 16, 1994. Retained in 1996. Appointed circuit judge Oct. 16, 1997. Retained in 1998, 2004, 2010 and 2012. Term expires Dec. 31, 2016. Nonpartisan.

Circuit 22—Division 13
STEVEN R. OHMER

Office address: Civil Courts Bldg., 10 N. Tucker St., St. Louis 63101; phone (314) 622-4411.
City of St. Louis.

Biography: Born April 18, 1954, in St. Louis. Graduate of St. Louis Univ. High, 1972; Florida State Univ., B.S., 1975; and Creighton Univ., J.D., 1979. Married to Roberta Marie Ohmer Dec. 29, 1976; two children, Rachel Caroline and Rebecca Anne. Assistant circuit attorney, City of St. Louis, 1979–1983, and 1987–1994; in private practice, 1983–1987, with Ohmer & Ohmer, P.C.; chief warrant officer for the circuit attorney, 1992–1994. Member: Missouri Supreme Court Circuit Court Budget Comm., chair; Missouri Supreme Court Family Court Comm.; American Judges Association; the Bar Association of Metropolitan St. Louis; Lawyers Assoc. of St. Louis; Missouri and Illinois Bar associations. St. Pius V Catholic Church. Former assoc: athletic dir., St. Pius V; chair/member of St. Pius V Parish Council and Parents Council of Truman State Univ. Volunteer judge for Stand Down Project for homeless veterans and Washington Univ. School of Law Moot Court. Judge Ohmer authored and co-authored several articles. Appointed assoc. circuit judge June 16, 1994. Retained in 1996. Appointed circuit judge Aug. 1, 2000. Presiding judge, 2011–2012, and assistant presiding judge, 2009–2010. Retained in 2002, 2008 and 2012. Term expires Dec. 31, 2020. Nonpartisan.

Circuit 22—Division 15
CHRISTOPHER E. McGRAUGH

Office address: Civil Courts Bldg., 10 N. Tucker St., St. Louis 63101; phone (314) 622-4827.
City of St. Louis.

Biography: Born Oct. 18, 1960 in Saint Louis. Graduate of DeSmet Jesuit High School, 1979; St. Louis University, B.A., history, 1983; St. Louis University School of Law, J.D., 1987. Married to Susan Woods; two children. Admitted to Missouri Bar Association, 1987. Assistant public defender, St. Louis County Trial Division, 1987–1990, Lead Counsel for Capital Litigation Unit, Missouri Public Defender Office the Eastern District, 1990–1992. From 1992 to appointment, principal in the law firm of Leritz, Plunkert and Bruning, P.C. Adjunct Professor of Law at St. Louis University School of Law and Washington University School of Law. Member of Missouri Bar Association, Bar Association of Metropolitan St. Louis and St. Louis Lawyer Association. Appointed to the Associate Circuit by Gov. Jeremiah (Jay) Nixon November 2012. Retained in 2014. Appointed to Circuit Court April 2015. Nonpartisan.

Circuit 22—Division 16
MICHAEL K. MULLEN

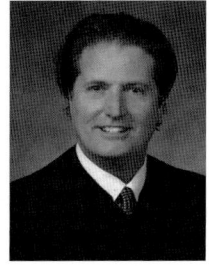

Office address: Carnahan Bldg., 114 Market St., St. Louis 63103; phone (314) 622-3583.
City of St. Louis.
Biography: Born May 8, 1964, in St. Louis. Graduate of University of Missouri–Columbia, A.B.; University of Missouri–Columbia, J.D. Married Joan Heilweck. They have four children: Mary Katherine, Mark, James, and Phillip. Law clerk to James A. Pudlowski, Missouri Court of Appeals Eastern District, 1989–1990; assistant circuit attorney, City of St. Louis 1990–1995; associate, Charles M. Shaw Law Firm, 1995–1996; Partner, Mullen and Fernandez, 1996–2000; and solo practitioner, 2000–2001. Member: St. Gabriel Catholic Church; Bar Association of Missouri, St. Louis; and Lawyers Association. Appointed associate circuit judge May 2001. Retained in 2002 and 2006. Appointed circuit judge July 2008. Retained in 2010. Term expires Dec. 31, 2016. Nonpartisan.

Circuit 22—Division 17
MICHAEL W. NOBLE

Office address: Carnahan Bldg., 1114 Market St., St. Louis 63101; phone (314) 622-4096.
City of St. Louis.
Biography: Born May 21, 1966. Graduate of United States Military Academy, B.S., 1988; St. Louis University School of Law, J.D., 2004. Field artillery officer, patent attorney at Armstrong Teasdale and assistant public defender before becoming Drug Court commissioner in 2007; reappointed by court *en banc* 2011. Married and has two children. Member: The Church of St. Michael and St. George. Appointed associate circuit judge in 2013. Retained in 2014. Appointed circuit judge on Nov. 17, 2015. Term expires Dec. 31, 2018. Nonpartisan.

Circuit 22—Division 18
ROBERT H. DIERKER

Office address: Carnahan Bldg., 1114 Market St., St. Louis 63101; phone (314) 622-4331.
City of St. Louis.
Biography: Born Feb. 24, 1949, in St. Louis. Graduate of St. Louis University, A.B.; University of Missouri–Kansas City, J.D.; and Harvard University, LL.M. Married Dorothy Dreyer July 3, 1982; they have three children. Law clerk to Joseph J. Simeone, Missouri Court of Appeals, summers 1973, 1974; associate with a St. Louis law firm, 1975–1978; and assistant and associate city counselor, City of St. Louis, 1979–1986. Candidate for Missouri House of Representatives, 1978; campaign treasurer for Paul Kiel, Missouri Senate candidate, 1978. Member: Catholic Church; Circuit Bar Committee, Division 1, 22nd Circuit, 1985–1986; Missouri and Metropolitan St. Louis Bar associations; and other legal and fraternal organizations. Appointed circuit judge February 1986. Retained in 1988, 1994, 2000 and 2006. Presiding judge, 1997–1998. Retained in 2006 and 2012. Term expires Dec. 31, 2018. Nonpartisan.

Circuit 22—Division 19
JIMMIE EDWARDS

Office address: Carnahan Bldg., 1114 Market St., St. Louis 63101; phone (314) 622-4376.
City of St. Louis.
Biography: Graduate of St. Louis University, B.A., 1978; J.D., 1982. Married to Stacy Maria. They have three children. He began private practice in a small law firm in St. Louis in 1981. In 1984, he joined Sabreliner Corporation. He then joined Southwestern Bell Telephone Company's legal staff. Serves as chair, Missouri Supreme Court's Records Committee; Missouri Supreme Court Civil Rules Committee, member; served on the executive council for Missouri State Judges; and chief juvenile court judge for the City of St. Louis. Founder, Innovative Concept Academy. In 1992, he was appointed circuit judge for the 22nd Judicial Circuit. Term expires Dec. 31, 2018. Nonpartisan.

Circuit 22—Division 20
EDWARD SWEENEY

Office address: Carnahan Bldg., 1114 Market St., St. Louis 63101; phone (314) 622-4452. **City of St. Louis.**

Biography: Born Sept. 11, 1947, in St. Louis. Graduate of Univ. of Mo.–Columbia, A.B., political science, 1969; J.D., 1974; and St. Louis Univ., M.B.A., 1981. National Judicial College, certificates in trial judge and dispute resolution skills. Admitted to The Missouri Bar, 1974. Field artillery officer, Army, 1969–1971, including service with the 101st Airborne Division, Vietnam, 1970–1971. Democratic Committee, 8th Ward, St. Louis, 1984–1996. Delegate to the 1988 Democratic National Convention. Chair, third congressional district Democratic Committee, 1986–1992. Engaged in private law practice, 1974–1986, and as assistant circuit attorney, City of St. Louis, 1986–1997. Married Mary Myerscough Wiechens May 17, 1986. Father and step-father to four children. Member: Saint Joan of Arc parish, the St. Louis Saint Patrick's Day Parade Committee and veterans and community organizations. Appointed associate circuit judge Dec. 12, 1997. Retained in 2000 and 2004. Appointed circuit judge Jan. 6, 2005. Retained in 2006 and 2012. Term expires Dec. 31, 2018. Nonpartisan.

Circuit 22—Division 21
ROBIN RANSOM VANNOY

Office address: Carnahan Bldg., 1114 Market St., St. Louis 63103; phone (314) 622-4342. **City of St. Louis.**

Biography: Born July 21, 1967, in St. Louis. Graduate of Douglass College–Rutgers University in New Brunswick, N.J., B.A., political science and sociology; University of Missouri–Columbia School of Law, J.D. Married, two children. Served as an assistant public defender in St. Louis County, 1992–1995, and also as an assistant prosecuting attorney in St. Louis County, 1995–1996. Joined the legal department of the St. Louis County Family Court–Juvenile Division in 1996 and remained until December 2002, when appointed as family court commissioner for the 22nd Judicial Circuit. Board member of the Wilson School. Member: Family Court Committee of the Supreme Court; Committee on Access to Family Courts. Appointed circuit judge, 2008. Retained in 2010. Term expires Dec. 31, 2016. Nonpartisan.

Circuit 22—Division 22
THOMAS J. FRAWLEY

Office address: Carnahan Bldg., 1114 Market St., St. Louis 63101; phone (314) 622-3438. **City of St. Louis.**

Biography: Born Feb. 28, 1947, in Rochester, N.Y. Graduate of Hamilton College, B.A.; University of Missouri–Columbia, J.D. Member: National Advisory Board, National Quality Improvement Center on Differential Response; Supreme Court Family Court Comm., chair, 1995–2004; and Supreme Court Comm. on Children's Justice. Awards: Equal Justice, Legal Services of Eastern Missouri; Judge of the Year, Missouri Court Appointed Special Advocates; Person of the Year, Missouri Coalition Against Domestic Violence, St. Louis Metropolitan Region; Champion of Kids, Kids-in-the-Middle, Inc.; President's Advocacy, NBA ECHO Emergency Children's Home; Outstanding Leader for Governmental Leadership, St. Louis Children's Agenda, Vision for Children at Risk; Advocacy, St. Louis Mental Health Board; World of Children Honoree, Progressive Youth Connection; and Family Service Award, Provident, Inc. Appointed circuit judge September 1991. Retained in 1992, 1998, 2004 and 2010. Term expires Dec. 31, 2016. Nonpartisan.

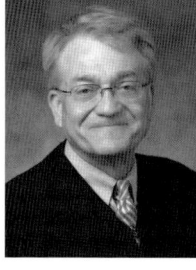

Circuit 22—Division 23
TIMOTHY J. WILSON

Office address: Carnahan Bldg., 1114 Market St., St. Louis 63101; phone (314) 622-4926. **City of St. Louis.**

Biography: Born Dec. 2, 1947, in St. Louis. Educated at St. Louis University College of Arts and Science; St. Louis University Law School, A.B., *cum laude*; J.D. Married Carol A. Newcombe Aug. 24, 1973, in St. Louis. Participated in the United States Department of Justice honors program, trial attorney in Washington, DC, 1973–1978; assistant United States attorney, Eastern District of Missouri, 1978–1989. Member: Catholic Church. Appointed circuit judge May 15, 1989. Retained in 1990, 1996, 2002, 2008 and 2014. Term expires Dec. 31, 2020. Nonpartisan.

Circuit 22—Division 30
DAVID C. MASON

Office address: Carnahan Bldg., 920 N. Vandeventer, St. Louis 63108; phone (314) 552-2025.

City of St. Louis.

Biography: Born March 12, 1956, in Nashville, Tenn. Graduate of Austin Peay State Univ., B.S.; Washington Univ., J.D. Married Taunia L. Allen June 3, 1995. They have two children, William R. and Harrison M. Member: Catholic Church; American, Missouri, Metro and Mound City Bar assocs.; American Law Institute, elected 1996; St. Louis Regional Convention and Sports Complex Authority, vice chair, 1990–1991. Boards: American Judicature Society, 1998–2002; Regional Housing and Community Development Alliance. 1997 Honor Initiate; Order of the Coif, honorary member; American Bd. of Trial Advocates; 1991 Missouri Bar Thomas D. Cochran for Community Service.; 1990 Bar Assn. of Metropolitan St. Louis Merit; 1992 Austin Peay State Univ. Outstanding Alumnus; 1999 Washington Univ. School of Law Outstanding Young Alumnus; *Missouri Lawyers Weekly*; 2009 reader's poll "Best Circuit Judge, Eastern District"; and 16-time recipient of American College of Trial Lawyers Award of Merit. Appointed circuit judge: August 1991. Retained in 1992, 1998, 2004 and 2010. Term expires Dec. 31, 2016. Nonpartisan.

Circuit 22—Division 31
JOAN L. MORIARTY

Office address: Carnahan Bldg., 1114 Market St., St. Louis, 63101; phone (314) 622-4927.

City of St. Louis.

Biography: Born in Brookings, S.D. Graduate of Creighton University School of Pharmacy, Omaha, Neb.; St. Louis School of Law. Law clerk for the Hon. Robert G. Dowd Sr., Missouri Court of Appeals, Eastern District. Served as assistant prosecuting attorney for St. Louis County. Member: Bar Association of Metropolitan St. Louis, St. Louis Lawyer's Association and St. Ambrose Catholic Church. Appointed circuit judge Jan. 1, 1998. Retained 2000, 2006 and 2012. Term expires Dec. 31, 2018. Nonpartisan.

Circuit 23—Division 1
ROBERT WILKINS

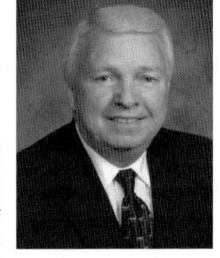

Office address: Jefferson County Courthouse, PO Box 100, Hillsboro 63050; phone (636) 797-5410.

County: Jefferson.

Biography: Presiding judge. Born Sept. 6, 1946, in St. Louis. Graduate of Univ. of Mo.–St. Louis, B.S., *summa cum laude*, 1976; St. Louis Univ. School of Law, J.D., 1979; USDOJ Natl. Law Institute, 1997. Married Sandra L. Blackwell June 1, 1985. United States Marine Corps, 1964–1965; asst. prosecuting attorney, St. Louis County, 1979–1983; and prosecuting attorney, Jefferson County, 1995–2006. Board member: Missouri Assoc. of Prosecuting Attorneys, 2000–2006, president, 2005; Children's Advocacy Center of East Central Missouri, 2000–2006, president, 2000–2006; Mo. Children's Justice Act Task Force, 1998–2004; Community Treatment Inc., 1998–2006; Third Congressional District Task Force on Domestic Violence, 2000–2004; and Natl. District Attorneys' Assoc., 1995–2006. Awards: MADD Prosecutor of the Year, 1999; Child Advocate of the Year, CACECM, 2006. Elected circuit judge in 2006 and 2012. Term expires Dec. 31, 2016. Democrat.

Circuit 23—Division 2
DARRELL E. MISSEY

Office address: Jefferson County Courthouse, PO Box 100, Hillsboro 63050; phone (636) 797-5425.

County: Jefferson.

Biography: Born April 12, 1967, in St. Louis. Graduate of Truman State University, B.A., political science, 1989; St. Louis University, J.D., 1992. Married Andrea Schalk Missey on May 27, 1989; they have three daughters. Member: Missouri Bar Association; Supreme Court Family Court Committee; Children's Services Commission; and the Juvenile Detention Alternative Initiative Replication Team. Elected in 2014. Term expires Dec. 31, 2020. Republican.

Circuit 23—Division 3
NATHAN STEWART

Office address: Jefferson County Courthouse, PO Box 100, Hillsboro 63050; phone (636) 797-5430.

County: Jefferson.

Biography: Born Oct. 27, 1965, in Charlottesville, Va. Graduate of University of Missouri–Columbia, B.S., education, 1988, lifetime certified to teach secondary social studies; J.D., 1992. Married Kimberly A. Stewart June 23, 1990. They have two children. Wegmann Law Firm, 1992–1997. Nathan B. Stewart, P.C., 1997–1999. Appointed first family court commissioner 23rd Circuit, 1999–2005. Established a judges truancy court at Hillsboro Jr. High. Member of Hillsboro Community Civic Club since 1992, Sons of AMVETS and Elks. Appointed associate circuit judge 2005. Elected associate circuit judge, 2006–2010. Elected circuit judge in 2010. Term expires Dec. 31, 2016. Democrat.

Circuit 23—Division 4
MARK T. STOLL

Office address: Jefferson County Courthouse, PO Box 100, Hillsboro 63050; phone (636) 797-5420.

County: Jefferson.

Biography: Born April 11, 1952, in St. Louis. Graduate of University of Missouri–Columbia, B.S., business administration, 1974; J.D., 1977. Married Tanya L. Brotherton, 1992. They have two sons. Partner in Wegmann, Gasaway, Stewart, Schneider, Dieffenbach, Tesreau, Stoll & Sherman, Hillsboro, 1977–1997. Served as mediator, Missouri Bar Dispute Resolution Committee. Associate circuit judge, 1997–2006. Secretary-treasurer, Mo. Association of Probate & Associate Circuit Judges, 2002–2006. Board of Directors, Mo. Municipal & Associate Circuit Judges Association, 1998–2007, President's Advisory Committee, 2007–2013. Legislative Steering Committee, Missouri Judicial Conference, 1998–2006. Member and past president, DeSoto Rotary Club. Served as treasurer, asst. scoutmaster, troop committee chair and unit commissioner for Boy Scouts and Cub Scouts. Elected circuit judge in 2006 and 2012. Presiding judge, 2009–2010. Term expires Dec. 31, 2018. Democrat.

Circuit 23—Division 5
LISA K. PAGE

Office address: Jefferson County Courthouse, PO Box 100, Hillsboro 63050; phone (636) 797-6435.

County: Jefferson.

Biography: Born Sept. 12, 1966, in Festus. Graduate of Southeast Missouri State University, *magna cum laude*, 1988; St. Louis University School of Law. *cum laude*, 1997. Married to Eddie Page since 1988. They have three children: Maggie, Joe and Anna-Lisa. Practiced law from 1997–2005 with a strong emphasis in ADR and domestic relations. Appointed family court commissioner on April 29, 2005, and, when the position was eliminated, was elected Jefferson County's first female circuit judge in 2006 and 2012. Term expires Dec. 31, 2018. Democrat.

Circuit 23—Division 6
TROY CARDONA

Office address: Jefferson County Courthouse, PO Box 100, Hillsboro 63050; phone (636) 797-6461.

County: Jefferson.

Biography: Born Feb. 16, 1963, in St. Louis. Educated at Windsor High School, Imperial, 1981; Hosei University, Tokyo, Japan, 1983; Jefferson College; Truman State (formerly known as Northeast Missouri State University), Kirksville, B.A., 1984, *summa cum laude*, co-salutatorian, third in graduating class; Northeastern University Law School, Boston, Mass., J.D., 1988; Kansai University of Foreign Studies, Osaka, Japan, 1989. Experience: U.S attorney's office–Hawaii, law clerk 1987; Missouri public defender, four years; private practice, three years (Honolulu, Hawaii; and St. Louis-Imperial-Hillsboro); chief warrant attorney and chief trial attorney, Jefferson County; assistant prosecutor, 11 years; and general counsel Union Pacific Railroad, one year. Elected circuit judge in 2006. Term expires Dec. 31, 2018. Democrat.

Circuit 24—Division 1
SANDY MARTINEZ

Office address: St. Francois County Courthouse, 1 N. Washington, Third Fl., Farmington 63640; phone (573) 756-5144.

Counties: Madison, St. Francois, Ste. Genevieve and Washington.

Biography: Presiding judge. Born June 14, 1963. Graduate of University of Texas at El Paso, B.A.; University of Missouri–Columbia, J.D. Married to Michael J. Anderson, an assistant prosecutor for the 42nd Circuit Child Support Enforcement. They have two children, Chris and Amber. Served as assistant public defender, assistant prosecuting attorney and prosecuting attorney for St. Francois County. Elected circuit judge in 2000, 2006 and 2012. Term expires Dec. 31, 2018. Democrat.

Circuit 24—Division 2
WENDY L. WEXLER HORN

Photo not available

Office address: St. Francois County Courthouse, 1 N. Washington, Second Fl., Farmington 63640; phone (573) 756-5144.

Counties: Madison, St. Francois, Ste. Genevieve and Washington.

Biography: Born May 5, 1967. Bachelor of Science, Graduate of University of Illinois at Urbana-Champaign, B.S., May 1989; St. Louis University, J.D., 1992. Former prosecuting attorney, St. Francois County, 2001–2011. Private law practice, 1995–2000. Assistant public defender; 1993–1995. Married to Phillip Horn; one son, Jacob. Former president, Children's Advocacy Center of East Central Missouri Board of Directors; 2005 St. Francois County Citizen of the Year Award; and 2009 St. Francois County Democrat of the Year. Appointed Oct. 24, 2011. Elected 2012 to fill an unexpired term. Term expires Dec. 31, 2014. Democrat.

Circuit 25—Division 1
WILLIAM E. HICKLE

Office address: 200 N. Main St., Rolla, 65401; phone (573) 458-6232.

Counties: Maries, Phelps, Pulaski and Texas.

Biography: Presiding judge. Born Aug. 23, 1957, in Fort Worth, Texas. Graduate of Baylor University, B.A., chemistry, 1979; University of Missouri–Columbia, J.D., 1982. Married to Debbie Nov. 26, 1982. Five children: David, Mark, Nathan, Sarah and Rachel. Practiced law in Rolla 27 years. Served as municipal judge, City of Rolla, 1996–2010. Served as chair of Missouri Head Injury Advisory Council to the Governor; Rolla Public Library Board of Trustees, president; and Rolla Rotary Club, president. Elected associate circuit judge, Division II, 2010. Elected circuit judge, Division I, 2012. Term expires Dec. 31, 2018. Republican.

Circuit 25—Division 2
JOHN D. BEGER

Office address: 200 N. Main St., Rolla 65401; phone (573) 458-6232.

Counties: Maries, Phelps, Pulaski and Texas.

Biography: Born St. Charles, 1954. Attended Orchard Farm High School; University of Missouri–Columbia, School of Business, B.S., B.A., 1976; and Law School, J.D., 1978, Class of 1979). Married Cynthia Morris, 1981; they have two daughters and one grandson. Phelps County assistant prosecuting attorney, 1979–1982; elected Prosecutor, 1991–1994, 2011–2014. Private practice, 1979–2010, including Price & Beger, Salem, and Beger & Bushie, Rolla, 1997–2010; City Counsellor, Rolla, 1995–2010. Certified Trial Advocate, National Board of Trial Advocacy, civil, 1998, criminal, 1999. Board of Trustees, Phelps County Regional Medical Center, 2002–2012, chair, 2011–2012. Member, elder and trustee Ozark Highlands Christian Church, Disciples of Christ. Elected without opposition to partial term that expires Dec. 31, 2016. Republican.

Circuit 26—Division 2
KENNETH M. HAYDEN

Office address: Camden County Courthouse, 1 Court Circle, Ste. 9, Camdenton 65020; phone (573) 346-5160.

Counties: Camden, Laclede, Miller, Moniteau and Morgan.

Biography: Presiding judge. Born March 23, 1962. Graduate of Central Missouri State University, B.S., 1984; University of Missouri–Columbia School of Law, J.D., 1987; admitted to Missouri Bar, 1987. Married to Deborah; they have two children, a daughter and a son. Formerly engaged in private law practice, 1987–2008. Member: The Missouri Bar; the 26th Judicial Circuit Bar Association; Versailles United Methodist Church; and Versailles Lions Club. Appointed circuit judge Sept. 11, 2008, to fill an unexpired term. Elected circuit judge Nov. 4, 2008. Elected circuit judge Nov. 2, 2010. Term expires Dec. 31, 2016. Republican.

Circuit 26—Division 1
STANLEY MOORE

Office address: Camden County Courthouse, 1 Court Circle, Ste. 9, Camdenton 65020; phone (573) 346-5160.

Counties: Camden, Laclede, Miller, Moniteau and Morgan.

Biography: Circuit and juvenile judge. Born Sept. 20, 1947, in Pettis County. Graduate of Central Missouri State College, B.S., B.A.; University of Tulsa, J.D. Admitted to the Oklahoma Bar, 1982; Missouri Bar 1983. Married Paulette M. Moore December 1966. They have two children, a son and a daughter. Engaged in private law practice, 1982–2006. Laclede County assistant prosecuting attorney from January 1991–September 2006. Previously appointed acting interim Laclede County public administrator. Member: First United Methodist Church, Lebanon; Laclede County, 26th Circuit and Missouri Bar associations; and Lebanon Downtown Optimist Club. Appointed circuit judge Sept. 1, 2006, to fill an unexpired term. Elected circuit judge in 2006 and 2012. Term expires Dec. 31, 2018. Republican.

Circuit 27
JAMES K. JOURNEY

Office address: PO Box 487, Clinton 64735; phone (660) 885-7242.

Counties: Bates, Henry and St. Clair.

Biography: Presiding judge. Born Aug. 23, 1951, in Kansas City. Graduate of Clinton High School, 1969; Central Missouri State University, B.A., political science, 1973; and University of Missouri–Columbia Law School, J.D., 1975. Married Rachelle E. Wilkins Nov. 6, 1993. They have three children. Served as law clerk in the Jackson County Circuit Court–Division 10, 1976–1977. Practiced law in Clinton from 1979–2006. Elected circuit judge in 2006 and 2012. Term expires Dec. 31, 2018. Democrat.

Circuit 28
JAMES R. BICKEL

Office address: Office of the Circuit Judge, 100 W. Cherry, Ste. A, Nevada 64772; phone (417) 667-5016; FAX (417) 448-2535.

Counties: Barton, Cedar, Dade and Vernon.

Biography: Presiding judge. Born July 24, 1946, in Lamar. Graduate of University of Missouri–Columbia, B.S., 1968; J.D., 1973. Married to Sherry Culbertson. They have three children. Phi Delta Phi (president, Tiedeman Inn, 1972–1973); Order of the Coif; *Missouri Law Review*; U.S. Army, 1968–1970; and municipal judge, Nevada, 1976–2000. AG's Professional Liability Review Board, 1977–1979; Missouri Bar Fee Dispute Resolution Committee, 1992–2000; Rotary Club, Citizen of the Year, 2004; Nevada United Methodist Church; and Missouri United Methodist Foundation, Inc., board of directors, 1993–2001, executive committee, 1999–2000. Elected circuit judge Nov. 7, 2000. Retained in 2006 and 2012. Term expires Dec. 31, 2016. Republican.

Circuit 29—Division 2
DAVID C. DALLY

Office address: Jasper County Courts Bldg., 601 S. Pearl, Joplin 64801; phone (417) 625-4320.

County: Jasper.

Biography: Presiding judge. Born March 15, 1948, in Ishpeming, Mich. Graduate of the University of Missouri, B.A.; J.D. Married Gaye Ramm Aug. 16, 1969. They have two children and nine grandchildren. Served as assistant prosecuting attorney of Jasper County, 1974–1986; prosecuting attorney of Jasper County, 1987–1998; city attorney of Carthage, 1974–1998; and engaged in the private practice of law in Carthage, 1973–1998. Member: Grace Episcopal Church; Carthage Rotary Club; University of Missouri Alumni Association; and Missouri and Jasper County Bar associations. Past president of Missouri Association of Prosecuting Attorneys, Missouri Association of Municipal Attorneys and Jasper County Bar Association. Elected circuit judge in 1998, 2004 and 2010. Term expires Dec. 31, 2016. Republican.

Circuit 29—Division 1
GAYLE L. CRANE

Office address: Jasper County Courts Bldg., 601 S. Pearl, Rm. 320, Joplin 64801; phone (417) 625-4318.

County: Jasper.

Biography: Born Dec. 10, 1958, in Neosho. Graduate of KU, B.S.W.; University of Missouri–Kansas City School of Law, J.D. Married John Podleski. She has three children. Partner in a law firm, 1985–2006. Member: Saint Paul's United Methodist Church. Elected circuit judge in November 2006 and 2012. Presiding juvenile judge of Jasper County. Term expires Dec. 31, 2018. Republican.

Circuit 29—Division 3
DAVID B. MOUTON

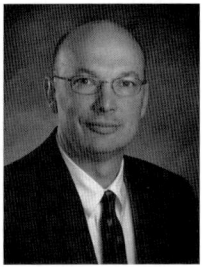

Office address: Jasper County Courts Bldg., 601 S. Pearl, Rm. 216, Joplin 64801; phone (417) 625-4325.

County: Jasper.

Biography: Born March 5, 1958, in Joplin. Graduate of the University of Missouri–Kansas City, B.A.; J.D. Married Beverly Edwards June 28, 1980; they have two children. Engaged in the private practice of law in Carthage, 1986–2006; city attorney of Carthage 1999–2006. Member: Fairview Christian Church; Missouri and Jasper County Bar associations; and Community Foundation of Southwest Missouri board of directors, past member. Jasper County Bar Association, past president; Salvation Army Advisory Board, past member; and Carthage Parks and Recreation Board, former member. Elected circuit judge Nov. 7, 2006. Retained Nov. 6, 2012. Term expires Dec. 31, 2018. Republican.

Circuit 30
MICHAEL O. HENDRICKSON

Office address: PO Box 679, Buffalo 65622; phone (417) 345-6822.

County: Benton, Hickory, Dallas, Polk and Webster.

Biography: Presiding judge. Born Sept. 25, 1963, in Lincoln, Neb. Married with three children. Graduate of University of Nebraska, B.A., 1986; J.D., 1990. Served as special assist. U.S. attorney, assist. Missouri Attorney. general, chief assist. Taney Co. pros., assist. Jefferson Co. pros. and a private practitioner. Member of Missouri, Nebraska, Kansas and Springfield Metro Bar associations; Mo. Assoc. of Probate and Associate Circuit Judges, Legislative and Membership Committees; and Mo. Municipal and Associate Circuit Judges Assoc. Selected as special judge, Southern District Court of Appeals, 2009, and to Applied Science and Technology Adjudication Resource (ASTAR) program, 2010. Member of Prairie Chapel United Methodist Church and Hermitage Lions Club. Served on Pittsburg Community Center Board, Hermitage Visioning Committee and Community Improvement Coalition. Elected Hickory County associate judge in 2006 and 2010. Elected circuit judge of 30th Judicial Circuit in 2012. Term expires Dec. 31, 2018. Republican.

Circuit 31—Division 4
THOMAS MOUNTJOY

Office address: Greene County Courthouse, 1010 Boonville, Springfield 65802; phone (417) 868-4089.

County: Greene.

Biography: Presiding judge. Born in 1953 in Stockton, Calif. Graduate of Central Missouri State Univ., B.S., criminal justice administration; University of Missouri–Kansas City, J.D. Married Donna Newman; they have three daughters. Served as assistant professor, criminal justice administration; Juvenile Court Services, director; assistant Greene County prosecuting attorney; and Greene County prosecuting attorney. Member: East Sunshine Church of Christ; Missouri Association of Prosecuting Attorneys, past president; Governor's Crime Commission; State Task Force on Fatal Child Abuse; Community Alternative Service Program; Child Advocacy Center of Southwest Missouri, co-founder; and Juvenile Court Improvement Project, steering committee. Awards: David B. Woodruff Memorial Community Justice; Child Advocacy Council Friend of Children. Appointed circuit judge Feb. 9, 1996. Elected in 1996, 2000 and 2006. Retained in 2012. Term expires Dec. 31, 2018. Nonpartisan.

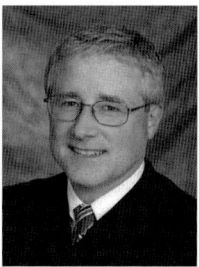

Circuit 31—Division 1
MICHAEL J. CORDONNIER

Office address: Greene County Courthouse, 1010 Boonville, Springfield 65802; phone (417) 868-4078.

County: Greene.

Biography: Born Sept. 6, 1957, in St. Louis, and raised in Springfield. Graduate of University of Missouri, B.S., business administration, 1979; University of Tulsa, College of Law, J.D., 1982. Engaged in private practice as a partner in the firm of Cunningham, Harpool & Cordonnier L.C. until merger and became partner with Lathrop & Gage, L.C., in 2004. Married Martha Love; they have two sons. Member: Christ Episcopal Church, Springfield; included as one of the "Best Lawyers in America," 2007; and named as 417 Top Attorneys 2007. Author, *Automobile Torts,* supplement Mo. Bar CLE. Member of American Bar, Missouri Bar and Springfield Metropolitan Bar associations. Past and present board member of several non profit organizations. Appointed circuit judge in January 2008 and was elected circuit judge in 2008 to fill unexpired term. Retained in 2012. Term expires Dec. 31, 2018. Nonpartisan.

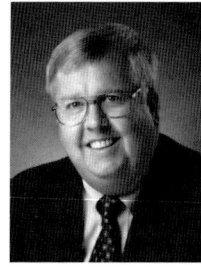

Circuit 31—Division 2
DAVID JONES

Office address: Greene County Courthouse, 1010 Boonville, Springfield 65802; phone (417) 868-4086.

County: Greene.

Biography: Born 1953 in Springfield. Graduate of Albright College, 1975; Delaware Law School, J.D., *magna cum laude,* 1978. Married to Ginger Wagner, with one child. Served as an assistant United States attorney, United States Department of Justice, from 1979–2006. Engaged in private practice and professor at Drury University and Ozark Technical College, from 2006–2008. Elected circuit judge in November 2008. Retained 2014. Term expires Dec. 31, 2020. Nonpartisan.

Circuit 31—Division 3
JASON BROWN

Office address: Greene County Courthouse, 1010 Boonville, Springfield 65802; phone (417) 868-4097.

County: Greene.

Biography: Born January 11, 1963, in St. Louis. Graduate of University of Missouri, B.A., Phi Beta Kappa, 1985; Vanderbilt University, J.D., 1988. Engaged in private practice in Kansas City area and Springfield from 1988–2004. Volunteer Greene County teen court judge; Member: Missouri Bar Professionalism Committee; MAPACJ, board member; Springfield. SE Rotary Club; and Good Samaritan Boys Ranch, past board member and current committee. Appointed January 1, 2005. Elected November 2006, 2010 and 2014. Term expires December 31, 2018. Nonpartisan.

Circuit 31—Division 5
CALVIN HOLDEN

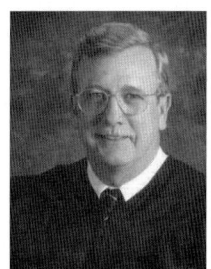

Office address: Greene County Courthouse, 1010 Boonville, Springfield 65802; phone (417) 868-4838.

County: Greene.

Biography: Born Sept. 28, 1953, in Mountain View. Graduate of Southwest Missouri State University, B.S., *cum laude*; Drake University, J.D., 1980. He has four children: Chrysa, Calie, Alexander and Zoe. Engaged in the practice of law, 1980–1996. Administrative law judge, Division of Employment Security, 1980–1981; Greene County assistant prosecuting attorney, 1983. Served in the U.S. Navy, 1972–1974. Member: Phi Kappa Phi; Springfield Metropolitan and Missouri Bar associations. Admitted to U.S. Supreme Court Bar. Missouri Drug Court Commission, commissioner. David B. Woodruff Memorial Community Justice Service Award recipient, 2000; NAMI of Southwest Missouri Governmental Award for Excellence, 2001; and Missouri Association of Drug Court Professionals President's Award, 2002. Appointed circuit judge in 1996. Elected in 1996, 2002 and 2006. Retained in 2012. Term expires Dec. 31, 2018. Nonpartisan.

Circuit 32—Division 2
BENJAMIN F. LEWIS

Office address: Common Pleas Courthouse, 44 N. Lorimier, Cape Girardeau 63701; phone (573) 335-2802.

Counties: Bollinger, Cape Girardeau and Perry.

Biography: Presiding judge. Born March 17, 1955, in Cape Girardeau. Graduate of Southeast Missouri State University, B.A., 1977; University of Missouri–Kansas City, J.D., 1980. Married Debra K. Scholl July 5, 1986. Law clerk, 16th Circuit, 1980–1981. Private practice, 1981–1990. Associate circuit judge, 1991–1994. Member, Layton & Lewis, L.L.C., 1995–2004. Southeast Missouri Hospital Board of Trustees; Hanover Lutheran Church, past president; 32nd Judicial Circuit Bar Association, past president; Cape Girardeau Lions Club, past president; and Shawnee District, B.S.A., past district chair, Award of Merit, Silver Beaver Award. Elected circuit judge 2004, 2006 and 2012. Term expires: Dec. 31, 2018. Republican.

Circuit 32—Division 1
MICHAEL E. GARDNER

Office address: Common Pleas Courthouse, 44 N. Lorimier, Cape Girardeau 63701; phone (573) 335-2802.

Counties: Bollinger, Cape Girardeau and Perry.

Biography: Born in 1979 in St. Louis, and raised in Kelso. Graduate of University of Missouri, B.A., 2001; University of Missouri School of Law, J.D., *cum laude*, 2004. Order of the Coif. Lead Articles Editor, *Missouri Law Review*. Law Clerk to Hon. Stephen N. Limbaugh, Jr., Supreme Court of Missouri, 2004-2005. Private practice, 2005-2014. Missouri Board of Law Examiners, 2013-present. Board of Governors of The Missouri Bar, 2012-2014. Young Lawyers' Section Council, 2010-2014. Member and past-president, Cape West Rotary Club. Knights of Columbus, Fourth Degree. Member: Shawnee District of the Boy Scouts of America, chair; St. Vincent de Paul Catholic Church, Cape Girardeau. Married with four children. Elected Circuit Judge Nov. 4, 2014. Term expires Dec. 31, 2020. Republican.

Circuit 33
DAVID DOLAN

Office address: Scott County Courthouse, PO Box 256, Benton 63736; phone (573) 545-3141.

Counties: Mississippi and Scott.

Biography: Presiding judge. Born June 19, 1954, in Memphis, Tenn. Graduate of Univ. of Memphis, B.B.A.; J.D. Married Julie Crader Aug. 2, 1980. Two children, Win and Claire. Member: St. Francis Xavier Catholic Church; Knights of Columbus, Fourth Degree; Mo. and Tenn. Bar assocs.; Natl. Assoc. of Juvenile and Family Court Judges; Mo. Juvenile Justice Assoc.; Natl. (sec.) and Mo. Assocs. of Drug Court Professionals; Sikeston Youth Soccer, pres.; Sikeston Little League, coach; Rotary Club; Sikeston Jaycees; SMC Pi Kappa Alpha Fraternity; ODK; and Bar Governor Univ. of Memphis School of Law. ASTAR Fellow, 2009; Presiding Judges Exec. Comm. 2006–present; Mo. Supreme Court Leg. Comm., 2008–present; Circuit Judges Leg. Comm., 2008–present; and Mo. Sentencing and Corrections Oversight Comm., 2013–17. Private practice, Crader, Crader, Dolan and Dolan, 1982–90. Asst. pros. atty. Scott Co., 1986–1990; pros. atty., 1991–93. Elected associate circuit judge of Scott County, 1992 and 1994. Appointed circuit judge March 1998. Elected in 1998, 2000, 2006 and 2012. Term expires Dec. 31, 2018. Democrat.

Circuit 34
FRED COPELAND

Office address: New Madrid County Courthouse, 450 Main, New Madrid 63869; phone (573) 748-2669.

Counties: New Madrid and Pemiscot.

Biography: Presiding judge. Born Nov. 13, 1954, in Coronado, Calif. Graduate of University of Missouri–Columbia, B.S., public administration; J.D. Engaged in private law practice in New Madrid. Appointed associate circuit judge, New Madrid County, for a term beginning Jan. 15, 1982. Elected 1982 and 1986. Member: United Methodist Church; Optimist; Eagles; and Phi Delta Phi. Elected circuit judge 1988–2006. Term expires Dec. 31, 2018. Democrat.

Circuit 35
ROBERT N. MAYER

Office address: Dunklin County Courthouse, PO Box 507, Kennett 63857; (573) 888-9133.

Counties: Stoddard and Dunklin.

Biography: Presiding judge. Born Feb. 25, 1957, in Cape Girardeau. Graduate of Southeast Missouri State University, B.S., political science; University of Missouri–Kansas City, J.D. Married Nancy Tuley July 29, 1978. Three sons: Jason, Dustin and Daniel. Member of First Baptist Church, Dexter. Practiced law in Dexter. Elected to the House of Representatives, 2000 and 2002. Served as chair of Crime Prevention and Public Safety Committee, 2003–2004. Elected to the Senate in 2004 and 2008. Served as Education Committee chair, 2008–2009. Served as Appropriations Committee chair, 2010. Served as Senate *president pro tem*, 2011–2012. Elected Presiding Judge 2012. Term expires Dec. 31, 2018. Republican.

Circuit 36
MICHAEL PRITCHETT

Office address: Butler Co. Courthouse, 100 N. Main, Poplar Bluff 63901; phone (573) 686-8080.

Counties: Butler and Ripley.

Biography: Presiding judge. Born Nov. 17, 1953, in Des Moines, Iowa. Graduate of Drury University, B.M.E., *summa cum laude*, 1976; University of Missouri–Columbia Law School, J.D., 1980. Married Nell Hearne Pritchett July 30, 1977. Former Poplar Bluff city attorney and city prosecuting attorney; former Butler County assistant prosecuting attorney; engaged in private practice of law, 1981–2010; former board member of Poplar Bluff Transit Authority; ADAPT; Poplar Bluff Chamber of Commerce; and Poplar Bluff Industries. Member: First Baptist Church. Elected circuit judge in 2010. Term expires Dec. 31, 2020. Republican.

Circuit 37
DAVID EVANS

Office address: 225 Courthouse, West Plains 65775; phone (417) 256-4383.

Counties: Carter, Howell, Oregon and Shannon.

Biography: Presiding judge. Born April 26, 1960, in West Plains. Graduate of Southern Methodist University, B.S., political science, *summa cum laude*, B.B.A., business; Southern Methodist University, J.D., chief counsel Legal Clinic. Married Saundra Kay Hardin Aug. 11, 1979; they have four children. Served in the private practice of law, 1985–1991 (received Missouri Pro Bono Award); city attorney for Thayer; municipal judge for West Plains, Willow Springs and Mountain View; associate circuit judge, 1991–2005; and elected presiding circuit judge, 2006. Member: United Methodist Church; President's Volunteer Service Award; and Missouri Municipal and Associate Circuit Judges Association, past president. Term expires Dec. 31, 2018. Republican.

Circuit 38
LAURA J. JOHNSON

Office address: 110 W. Elm, Rm. 205, Ozark 65721; phone (417) 582-5162.

Counties: Christian and Taney.

Biography: Presiding judge. Graduate of Missouri University, B.S., finance, *magna cum laude*, 1985, National Merit Scholar; Southern Methodist University School of Law, J.D. *cum laude*, 1988; Order of the Coif; and Leading Articles Editor for the *Journal of Air Law & Commerce*. Married to Todd,1987; two children. Clerked from 1988–1990 for the Hon. Elmo B. Hunter, federal district judge on the United States District Court for the Western District of Missouri. Associate for the firm of Stinson, Mag & Fizzell in Kansas City, 1990–1991. Attorney with the firm Ellis, Ellis, Hammons & Johnson, P.C., in Springfield, 1991–2015. Member of the Missouri Bar Association, the Springfield Metropolitan Association and the Christian and Taney County Bar Associations. Past or present board member and officer of Court Appointed Special Advocates, Least of These Food Pantry, Board of Education for the Ozark School District and member of Rotary. Elected November 2014. Term expires Dec. 31, 2018. Republican.

Circuit 39
JACK A. L. GOODMAN

Office address: PO Box 364, Monett 65708; phone (417) 235-8500; FAX (417) 235-8502.

Counties: Barry, Lawrence and Stone.

Biography: Presiding judge. Born 1973, in Aurora. Graduate of Pierce City High School, 1991; University of Mo.–Columbia, bachelor's degree, 1995; and University of Mo.–Columbia School of Law, J.D., 1998. Elected presiding judge, 39th Circuit, 2012. Served in Missouri Senate, 2005–2012; Senate asst. majority leader, 2007–2012; Chair of Senate Committee on the Judiciary and Civil and Criminal Jurisprudence; Senate Committee on General Laws, & Senate Committee on Governmental Accountability and Fiscal Oversight. Served in Missouri House of Representatives, 2003–2005; House asst. majority leader, 2004–2005. Attorney in private practice, 1998–2012; assistant prosecuting attorney, 1997–2002. Former member: Missouri Tourism Commission, Children's Services Commission, Missouri Rural Economic Development Council, Southwest Center Advisory Council and American Lung Association Government Relations Committee. Married to Laura with two sons, Jack and William. Member: Trinity Lutheran Church, Missouri Synod, in Freistatt. Various civic organizations. Elected 2012. Term expires Dec. 31, 2018. Republican.

Circuit 40
TIMOTHY W. PERIGO

Office address: Newton County Courthouse, 101 S. Wood, Ste. 306, Neosho 64850; phone (417) 451-8234, ext. 114.

Counties: McDonald and Newton.

Biography: Presiding judge. A native of Tulsa, Okla. Graduate of University of Tulsa, B.S., 1975; J.D., 1977. Married with three children. Engaged in private practice until June 1, 1985, when appointed as prosecuting attorney. Elected prosecutor for a full term in 1986. Elected associate circuit judge in 1990. Elected circuit judge in 1992. Retained in 1994, 2000, 2006 and 2012. Term expires Dec. 31, 2018. Republican.

Circuit 41
FREDERICK (RICK) TUCKER

Office address: Macon Co. Courthouse, PO Box 368, Macon 63552; phone (660) 385-3713.

Counties: Macon and Shelby.

Biography: Presiding judge. Born Jan. 24, 1961, Independence. Graduate of William Chrisman High School, 1979; Park College, B.A., 1983, Five years carpet cleaner and welder. Married to Karma L. Swoffer, 1987. Graduate of University of Missouri–Kansas City Law School, J.D., 1991 Public Defender, 1991–2004. Four children. Private law practice, 2004–2011. Appointed circuit judge by Gov. Jeremiah "Jay" Nixon 2011. Elected circuit judge 2012. Term expires Dec. 31, 2018. Democrat.

Circuit 42—Division 2
KELLY PARKER

Office address: Dent County Judicial Bldg., PO Box 551, Salem 65560; phone (573) 729-6816.

Counties: Crawford, Dent, Iron, Reynolds and Wayne.

Biography: Presiding judge. Born Feb. 28, 1966, in Rolla. Graduate of Southwest Missouri State University, B.S.; University of Missouri–Columbia School of Law, J.D. Three children: Braxton, Kennison and Slayton. Serves with the Missouri Army National Guard, rank of major, Judge Advocate General's Corps, assigned as the senior defense counsel for the 429th Trial Defense Team (Missouri and Nebraska Army National Guard). Dent County prosecuting attorney, 1995–1997; assistant prosecutor, 1991–1995. State representative, 150th District, 1997–2001. Appointed Iron County associate circuit judge, 2001. Elected Iron County associate circuit judge on Nov. 5, 2002. Elected circuit judge on Nov. 7, 2006. Retained 2008 and 2014. Term expires Dec. 31, 2020. Democrat.

Circuit 42—Division 1
SIDNEY T. PEARSON III

Office address: Dent County Judicial Bldg., PO Box 551, Salem 65560; phone (573) 729-6816; FAX (573) 729-5146.

Photo not available

Counties: Crawford, Dent, Iron, Reynolds and Wayne.

Biography: Born Oct. 17, 1952, in Pleasant Plains, Ark. Graduate of Missouri S&T, B.A., psychology, 1978; University of Missouri–Columbia, J.D., 1981. Married Naomi Haacke 1975. Two children and four grandchildren. U.S. Air Force, 1971–1974, 366 Tactical Fighter Wing RVN service, 1972–1973; private practice, 1982–1990; assistant prosecuting attorney of Crawford County, 1990–1995; executive director Meramec Legal Aid Corporation, 1995–1998; prosecuting attorney of Crawford County, 1998–2011; and prosecuting attorney of Dent County, 2011–2012. Elected circuit judge in 2012. Term expires Dec. 31, 2018. Democrat.

Circuit 43—Division 1
THOMAS N. CHAPMAN

Office address: 700 Webster, Chillicothe 64601; phone (660) 646-8000; FAX (660) 646-2734.

Counties: Caldwell, Clinton, Daviess, DeKalb and Livingston.

Biography: Presiding judge. Born March 23, 1966; lifelong resident of Chillicothe. Graduate of Westminster College, B.S., political science, *summa cum laude*, 1988; University of Virginia School of Law, J.D., 1991; and University of Missouri–Kansas City, LLM tax law, 1995. Elected circuit judge, 43rd Circuit–Division 1, 2010. Term expires Dec. 31, 2016. Republican.

Circuit 43—Division 2
R. BRENT ELLIOTT

Office address: Clinton County Courthouse, Box 275, Plattsburg 64477; phone (816) 539-3732; FAX (816) 539-3893.

Counties: Caldwell, Clinton, Daviess, DeKalb and Livingston.

Biography: Born Aug. 8, 1955, Eagleville. Graduate of North Harrison High School ,1973; Graceland College, B.A., 1977; and University of Missouri, J.D., 1980. Son, Connor MacLeod Elliott, D.V.M., University of Missouri Veterinary Medicine, 2013. Elected prosecuting attorney Livingston County, 1982 and 1986, and maintained private law practice in Chillicothe for 19 years, trying dozens of jury trials without a loss. Appointed DeKalb County associate circuit judge Jan. 1, 2001; elected 2002 and 2006. Governor Jeremiah "Jay" Nixon's first judicial appointment as circuit judge Feb. 1, 2009. Elected 2010 and 2012. Presiding circuit judge, 2010–2012. Term expires Dec. 31, 2018. Democrat.

Circuit 44
R. CRAIG CARTER

Office address: PO Box 489, Ava 65608; phone (417) 683-5556; FAX (417) 683-5557.

County: Douglas, Wright and Ozark

Biography: Presiding judge. Born April 16, 1969, in Springfield. United States Army, second Ranger Battalion, 1989–1991 (Panama, Operation Just Cause 1989); 10th, 12th, 20th Special Forces Groups, 1993–2002. Military decorations include: Purple Heart, Combat Infantryman's Badge, Parachutist Wings with Combat Jump Device, Expeditionary Badge, Kosovo Service Ribbon and Army Commendation Medal. Graduate of Missouri State University, B.S., accounting, 1977; University of Arkansas, J.D., 2000. Private practice of law, 2000–2005. Member: Missouri Bar; Ava and Mansfield Lodges A.F. & A.M.; and Trinity Lutheran Church, Ava. Appointed associate circuit judge by Gov. Matt Blunt, 2005. Elected 2006 and 2010. Elected circuit judge 2012. Term expires Dec. 31, 2018. Republican.

Circuit 45
CHRIS KUNZA MENNEMEYER

Office address: Lincoln County Justice Center, 45 Business Park Dr., Troy 63379; phone (636) 528-6300.

Counties: Lincoln and Pike.

Biography: Presiding judge. Born in Troy. Valedictorian of Troy Buchanan High School, 1990; Bright Flight Scholar and attended University of Missouri–Columbia and earned B.S.Ed in mathematics and science education with certificate to teach K–12, *magna cum laude*, 1993; earned J.D. from University of Missouri–Columbia, 1997. Employment history includes: CB Richard Ellis Commercial Real Estate Corporate Advisory Group; Gray-Bar Electric Company, Legal/Real Estate Department; DESCO Group, Legal/Real Estate Department; Earthgrains/Sara Lee Corporate, Real Estate Department; Lincoln County assistant prosecuting attorney; and operated sole private practice for more than 10 years, representing clients in civil, criminal, family, juvenile, drug court, administrative, probate, landlord/tenant and estate-planning matters. Successfully ran contested campaign and was elected presiding circuit court judge Nov. 6, 2012, for the 45th Judicial Circuit. Took office Jan. 1, 2013. Term expires Dec. 31, 2018. Republican.

Circuit courts by county

Adair	Circuit No. 2
Andrew	Circuit No. 5
Atchison	Circuit No. 4
Audrain	Circuit No. 12
Barry	Circuit No. 39
Barton	Circuit No. 28
Bates	Circuit No. 27
Benton	Circuit No. 30
Bollinger	Circuit No. 32
Boone	Circuit No. 13
Buchanan	Circuit No. 5
Butler	Circuit No. 36
Caldwell	Circuit No. 43
Callaway	Circuit No. 13
Camden	Circuit No. 26
Cape Girardeau	Circuit No. 32
Carroll	Circuit No. 8
Carter	Circuit No. 37
Cass	Circuit No. 17
Cedar	Circuit No. 28
Chariton	Circuit No. 9
Christian	Circuit No. 38
Clark	Circuit No. 1
Clay	Circuit No. 7
Clinton	Circuit No. 43
Cole	Circuit No. 19
Cooper	Circuit No. 18
Crawford	Circuit No. 42
Dade	Circuit No. 28
Dallas	Circuit No. 30
Daviess	Circuit No. 43
DeKalb	Circuit No. 43
Dent	Circuit No. 42
Douglas	Circuit No. 44
Dunklin	Circuit No. 35
Franklin	Circuit No. 20
Gasconade	Circuit No. 20
Gentry	Circuit No. 4
Greene	Circuit No. 31
Grundy	Circuit No. 3
Harrison	Circuit No. 3
Henry	Circuit No. 27
Hickory	Circuit No. 30
Holt	Circuit No. 4
Howard	Circuit No. 14
Howell	Circuit No. 37
Iron	Circuit No. 42
Jackson	Circuit No. 16
Jasper	Circuit No. 29
Jefferson	Circuit No. 23
Johnson	Circuit No. 17
Knox	Circuit No. 2
Laclede	Circuit No. 26
Lafayette	Circuit No. 15
Lawrence	Circuit No. 39
Lewis	Circuit No. 2
Lincoln	Circuit No. 45
Linn	Circuit No. 9
Livingston	Circuit No. 43
Macon	Circuit No. 41
Madison	Circuit No. 24
Maries	Circuit No. 25
Marion	Circuit No. 10
McDonald	Circuit No. 40
Mercer	Circuit No. 3
Miller	Circuit No. 26
Mississippi	Circuit No. 33
Moniteau	Circuit No. 26
Monroe	Circuit No. 10
Montgomery	Circuit No. 12
Morgan	Circuit No. 26
New Madrid	Circuit No. 34
Newton	Circuit No. 40
Nodaway	Circuit No. 4
Oregon	Circuit No. 37
Osage	Circuit No. 20
Ozark	Circuit No. 44
Pemiscot	Circuit No. 34
Perry	Circuit No. 32
Pettis	Circuit No. 18
Phelps	Circuit No. 25
Pike	Circuit No. 45
Platte	Circuit No. 6
Polk	Circuit No. 30
Pulaski	Circuit No. 25
Putnam	Circuit No. 3
Ralls	Circuit No. 10
Randolph	Circuit No. 14
Ray	Circuit No. 8
Reynolds	Circuit No. 42
Ripley	Circuit No. 36
St. Charles	Circuit No. 11
St. Clair	Circuit No. 27
St. Francois	Circuit No. 24
St. Louis Co.	Circuit No. 21
St. Louis City	Circuit No. 22
Ste. Genevieve	Circuit No. 24
Saline	Circuit No. 15
Schuyler	Circuit No. 1
Scotland	Circuit No. 1
Scott	Circuit No. 33
Shannon	Circuit No. 37
Shelby	Circuit No. 41
Stoddard	Circuit No. 35
Stone	Circuit No. 39
Sullivan	Circuit No. 9
Taney	Circuit No. 38
Texas	Circuit No. 25
Vernon	Circuit No. 28
Warren	Circuit No. 12
Washington	Circuit No. 24
Wayne	Circuit No. 42
Webster	Circuit No. 30
Worth	Circuit No. 4
Wright	Circuit No. 44

Circuit 1
RICKEY R. ROBERTS

Office address: 111 E. Court St., Ste. 210, Kahoka 63445; phone (660) 727-2133.
County: Clark.
Biography: Born April 17, 1955, Keokuk, Iowa. United States Air Force, 1973–1977. Graduate of Truman State University (formerly Northeast Missouri State University), B.A. public administration and history, *summa cum laude*, 1980; Univeristy of Missouri–Kansas City, J.D., 1983. Married Diana Hart, Nov. 26, 1986. Engaged in private practice in Kahoka, 1983–2010. Served as city attorney for the cities of Kahoka, Wayland and Alexandria; general counsel for the Second Judicial Circuit Juvenile Division, 1997–2010. Member: Missouri Bar, the Association of Trial Lawyers of America and the Missouri Juvenile Justice Association. Elected associate circuit judge for Clark County November 2010. Appointed by democratic Gov. Jeremiah (Jay) Nixon to fill unexpired term Dec. 2010. Elected November 2014. Term expires Dec. 31, 2018. Republican.

Circuit 1
KELLY L. LOVEKAMP

Office address: Schuyler County Courthouse, PO Box 417, Lancaster 63548; phone (660) 457-3755.
County: Schuyler County.
Biography: Born in Kirksville. Graduate of Truman State University (formerly Northeast Missouri State University), B.S., 1983, business administration and psychology major with a minor in personnel management; University of Missouri–Columbia School of Law, J.D., 1990. Engaged in private practice, 1990–2010. Two children, Tara and Karissa. Received the Family Law Mediation Certificate, University of Missouri, 1999; MACC, Medical Terminology Certificate, 2003; Association of Professional Trainers, Tactual Handgun Certificate, 2006; and University of Denver Tax Program, estate planning, 2007. Elected associate circuit judge 2010. Re-elected in 2014. Term expires Dec. 31, 2018. Democrat.

Circuit 1
KARL A.W. DeMARCE

Office address: Scotland County Courthouse, 117 S. Market, Rm. 200, Memphis 63555; phone (660) 465-2404.
County: Scotland.
Biography: Born August 18, 1968, in Maryville. Graduate of University of Missouri–Columbia, B.S. in agriculture 1989; M.S., 1992; and J.D., 1997. Married Brenda Annette Russell, 1992. Five children: Catherine, Marie, Renée, William and Susannah. State Judicial Records Comm., 2003–present; Exec. Comm. of the Judicial Conference, 2008–present. State representative District 1, 1997–1998. Community development specialist, University of Missouri Extension, Scotland County, 1991–1994. Member: Grace Evangelical Lutheran Church; Missouri Bar; Missouri Association of Probate and Associate Circuit Judges, president, 2012–2013; Scotland County Rotary Club; Scotland County Community Fitness Center, board of directors; Scotland County Association of Music Parents; and Memphis Area Chamber of Commerce. Editor-in-Chief, *Missouri Law Review*, 1996–1997. Elected associate circuit judge 1998. Re-elected 2002, 2006, 2010 and 2014. Term expires Dec. 31, 2018. Democrat.

Circuit 2
KRISTIE J. SWAIM

Office address: Adair County Courthouse, 106 W. Washington, Kirksville 63501; phone (660) 665-3877.
County: Adair.
Biography: Born Sept. 27, 1967. Graduate of University of Iowa, B.A., political science, 1990; University of Missouri–Columbia, J.D., 1993. Board of Advocates, writing director, 1992–1993; University of Missouri–Columbia, teaching assistant in legal research, writing and advocacy, 1992–1993; Order of Barristers, 1993; assistant editor, Missouri Supreme Court Publications, 1991–1993; private law practice, 1993–2002; Kirksville City Council, 1991–2002; and director and member of numerous service groups and organizations. Received West Publishing Award for Excellence in Research and Writing, 1990; Richard J. Chamier Award in Public Speaking, 1991; and Fred L. Howard Prize for Excellence in Appellate Advocacy, 1992–1993. Elected Adair County associate circuit judge in 2002. Re-elected in 2006, 2010 and 2014. Term expires Dec. 31, 2018. Democrat.

Circuit 2
THOMAS P. REDINGTON

Office address: Knox County Courthouse, PO Box 116, Edina 63537; phone (660) 397-3146.

County: Knox.

Biography: Graduate of Quincy University, B.A., 1979; Seattle University, J.D., 1983. Marion County prosecuting attorney, 1996 -2013; adjunct Faculty of the National College of District Attorneys (NDAA), 2008-2013; and Board of Governors, Missouri Association of Trial Attorneys, member, 1984 to 1999. Faculty of the Missouri Office of Prosecution Services Trial School, 2010-2013; Board of Directors of the Missouri Association of Drug Court Professionals, member, 2011-2013. Previously the President of the Holy Family School Board in Hannibal and served as president of the Board of Directors of the Hannibal Council on Alcohol and Drug Abuse. Elected associate circuit judge 2014. Term expires Dec. 31, 2018. Democrat.

Circuit 2
FRED WESTHOFF

Office address: Lewis County Courthouse, PO Box 36, Monticello 63457; phone (573) 767-5352.

County: Lewis.

Biography: Born Dec. 23, 1952, in Quincy, Ill. Graduate of Truman State University, B.A., *magna cum laude*, 1975; University of Missouri Law School, J.D. 1978. Married Reggie DeVerger June 11, 1983; four children. Prosecuting attorney Lewis County 1981–1986. Member of Missouri Bar; Probate and Associate Circuit Judges Association; and Heartland Resources, Inc., and Lewis County Home Health Advisory Board. Elected associate circuit judge for Lewis County in 1986. Re-elected in 1990, 1994, 1998, 2002, 2006, 2010 and 2014. Term expires Dec. 31, 2018. Democrat.

Circuit 3
STEVEN D. HUDSON

Office address: Grundy County Courthouse, 700 Main St., Ste 6, Trenton 64683; phone (660) 359-4040.

County: Grundy.

Biography: Born Sept. 7, 1961 in Trenton. Graduate of William Jewell College, B.S., business administration, *magna cum laude*, 1983; University of Missouri–Kansas City, J.D., 1986. Married to Lora Barnett, with two children. Member: Wesley United Methodist Church; NCMO Fair Board; Trenton High School Vocational Agriculture Advisory Board; and Missouri Sheep Merchandising Council. Served as Grundy County prosecutor, September 1993–December 1998. Elected Grundy County associate circuit judge in November 1998. Re-elected in 2002, 2006, 2010 and 2014. Term expires Dec. 31, 2018. Republican.

Circuit 3
THOMAS R. ALLEY

Office address: Harrison County Courthouse, 1501 Central, PO Box 189, Bethany 64424; phone (660) 425-6432.

County: Harrison.

Biography: Born in Harrison County. Graduate of Missouri Western State Univ., B.S., business administration, accounting, *summa cum laude*; University of Missouri–Kansas City, J.D.; and certified public accountant (active). Wife, Carla, and son, Willoughby. Employment: Missouri State Auditor's Office; Tax Division of Ernst & Whinney (now Ernst & Young); private practice in Clay County; municipal judge, Kearney; adjunct professor, William Jewell College; and city prosecutor, Bethany. Member: Methodist Church, past president; Bethany Rotary Club; Masonic Lodge; Missouri Bar; and Third Circuit Bar. Elected associate circuit judge 1998, 2002, 2006, 2010 and 2014. Term expires Dec. 31, 2018. Republican.

Circuit 3
MATTHEW M. KROHN

Office address: Mercer County Courthouse, 802 E. Main St., Princeton 64673; phone (660) 748-4232.

County: Mercer.

Biography: Not available. Elected November 2014. Term expires Dec. 31, 2018. Republican.

Photo not available

Circuit 3
SAMUEL D. FRANK

Office address: Putnam County Courthouse, 1601 W. Main, Rm. 204, Unionville 63565; phone (660) 947-2117.

County: Putnam.

Biography: Born 1961, in Centerville, Iowa. Graduate of Truman State University, Kirksville, B.A., political science, 1984; M.A., history, 1986; and Oklahoma City University, J.D., 1989. Married Mary Helmken June 12, 1998. Solo practitioner for 20 years. Served as city prosecutor, Unionville, for 10 years. Member: Missouri Bar and American Bar associations since 1990. Elected associate circuit judge 2010. Re-elected in 2014. Term expires Dec. 31, 2018. Democrat.

Circuit 4
COREY K. HERRON

Office address: Atchison County Courthouse, PO Box 280, Rock Port 64482; phone (660) 744-2700.

County: Atchison.

Biography: Born August 16, 1969, in Fairfax. Graduate of University of Missouri–Columbia, B.S., B.A., 1992; J.D. 1996. Married Kristina Kelsall Nov. 24, 2001. They have one son, Phillip. Engaged in private law practice in northern Missouri with Andereck, Evans, Milne, Widger & Johnson, L.L.C. in Trenton, 1996–2008. Admitted to United States District Court, Western District, and United States Court of Appeals, Eighth Circuit. Past president of Third Circuit Bar Association. Member: St. John's Lutheran Church; Missouri Bar Association; Fourth Circuit Bar Association, president 2011–present; Phi Alpha Delta; Missouri Association of Probate and Associate Circuit Judges; and Rotary. Appointed Atchison County associate circuit judge by Gov. Matt Blunt in 2008 to fill unexpired term of the Hon. Zel M. Fischer. Elected in 2010. Re-elected in 2014. Term expires Dec. 31, 2018. Republican.

Circuit 4
EDWARD MANRING

Office address: Gentry County Courthouse, 200 W. Clay St., Albany 64402; phone (660) 726-3411.

County: Gentry.

Biography: Born July 23, 1950, in northwest Missouri. Graduate of University of Missouri, B.S., 1972; J.D., 1975. Married Nancy Stout July 14, 1978. Private practice in Albany, 1975–2006. Worth County prosecuting attorney, 1989–1990. Gentry County prosecuting attorney, 1995–2006. Member: Albany United Methodist Church, Rotary Club and volunteer firemen. Elected associate judge 2006, 2010 and 2014. Term expires Dec. 31, 2018. Republican.

Circuit 4
WILLIAM S. RICHARDS

Office address: Holt County Courthouse, PO Box 173, Oregon 64473; phone (660) 446-3380.

County: Holt.

Biography: Born June 11, 1952, in St. Joseph. Graduate of Loyola University–New Orleans, B.A., philosophy, 1974; University of Missouri–Kansas City, J.D., 1977. Married Katherine Weber August 10, 1996. They have two children. General practice of law from 1977–1990. Elected in 1990, 1994, 1998, 2002, 2006, 2010 and 2014. Term expires Dec. 31, 2018. Republican.

Circuit 4
W. DOUGLAS THOMSON

Office address: Nodaway County Courthouse, 303 N. Market, Maryville 64468; phone (660) 582-2531.

County: Nodaway.

Biography: Born Nov. 8, 1962 in Kansas City. Graduate of Maryville High School, 1981; Missouri State University, B.S., finance, 1985; University of Missouri–Kansas City Law School, J.D., 1989. Assoc. with Krebbs & Holdsworth, Liberty, 1989–1993; assoc. and then partner with Zahnd, Ross & Thomson and it's successors, Maryville, 1995–2013; and solo practice in Maryville, 2014. *Pro Bono* service recognition, 2013 and 2014. Serves on the Bd. of Governors of the Missouri Bar, 2011–present; chair of Finance Comm., 2013–present. Missouri Judiciary's Civic Education Comm. member. Past pres. and current member of the 4th Judicial Circuit Bar Assoc.. Past or present member of Kansas City Bar Assoc. and Missouri Municipal Attorney's Assoc.. Past or present bd. member or officer of Boy Scouts of America, Maryville Host Lions Club, Liberty Sertoma Club and numerous church committees. Former Cub Scout Leader and youth sports coach. Elected associate circuit judge November 2014. Term expires Dec. 31, 2018.

Circuit 4
JOEL MILLER

Office address: Worth County Courthouse, PO Box 350, Grant City 64456; phone (660) 564-2152.

County: Worth.

Biography: Born August 22, 1970, in Albany. Graduate of the University of Missouri–Columbia, B.A., political science; Missouri State University, M.A., public administration; and Drake University Law School, Des Moines, Iowa, J.D. Assistant prosecuting attorney of Gentry County. Private practice in the law office of Edward M. Manring, P.C. Member: Missouri Supreme Court's State Judicial Records Committee; Fourth Circuit Bar Association; First Christian Church of Grant City; Worth County Education Foundation; Allensville and Grant City lodges; and Allendale Fourth of July Breakfast Club. Appointed Sept. 1, 2006. Elected Nov. 7, 2006. Re-elected in 2010 and 2014. Term expires Dec. 31, 2018. Republican.

Circuit 5
MICHAEL J. ORDNUNG

Office address: Andrew County Courthouse, PO Box 318, Savannah 64485; phone (816) 324-3921.

County: Andrew.

Biography: Not available. Took office Jan. 1, 1999. Term expires Dec. 31, 2018. Republican.

Circuit 5–Division 5
KEITH MARQUART

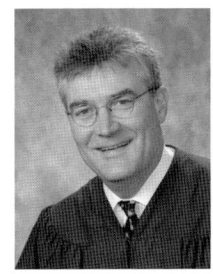

Office address: Buchanan County Courthouse, 411 Jules, St. Joseph 64501; phone (816) 271-1454.

County: Buchanan.

Biography: Born Jan. 6, 1954, in Washington, Missouri. Graduated from Benedictine College, Atchison, Kan., B.A. in political science; University of Missouri–Kansas City School of Law, J.D. Married to Corky and has two children, Blake and Brooke. Was appointed to fill an unexpired term in 1988. Elected in 1990, 1994. 1998, 2002, 2006, 2010 and 2014. Term expires Dec. 31, 2018. Republican.

Circuit 5
REBECCA L. SPENCER

Office address: Buchanan County Courthouse, 411 Jules, Rm. 331, St. Joseph 64501; phone (816) 271-1448.

County: Buchanan.

Biography: Graduate of University of Wisconsin–Milwaukee, B.A., English and political science, 1996; University of Missouri–Kansas City, J.D., 1999. Assistant Prosecuting Attorney in Buchanan County until May of 2001. Prosecuting Attorney for the City of St. Joseph until December of 2014. Served as the Municipal Judge for the City of Easton for seven years. Served as the president of the St. Joseph Bar Association, 2012. Elected Associate Circuit Judge in 2015. Judge Spencer presides over a variety of civil cases, including cases where the amount of controversy is $25,000 or less, small claims actions and landlord tenant cases. In addition, she presides over felony and misdemeanor charges of non-support and misdemeanor criminal cases in Buchanan County. She also presides over preliminary hearings in Buchanan County on criminal felony complaints. She currently resides in St. Joseph, with her three children. Elected November 2014. Term expires Dec. 31, 2018. Republican.

Circuit 6—Division 3
ABE (QUINT) SHAFER V

Office address: 415 Third St., Ste. 50, Platte City 64079; phone (816) 858-2232.

County: Platte.

Biography: Born Oct. 19, 1968, in Kansas City. Graduate of West Platte R-II School District, Weston, 1987; University of Colorado, B.A., 1991; Mississippi College School of Law, J.D., 1995; and Graduate School of Banking, University of Wisconsin–Madison, 2013. Formerly: Member/Manager of Shafer Law Office, LC (later, Shafer & Welch, LC); city attorney for City of Weston; general counsel, Bank of Weston; special prosecutor, Platte County; adjunct professor, Benedictine College; attorney for numerous boards and political subdivisions; and served as director/officer/attorney for numerous philanthropic and charitable organizations. Member: Missouri Bar, Kansas City Metropolitan Bar Association, Platte County Bar Association, and Weston Christian Church. Married to Christy Shafer, 1995, with two children. Appointed associate circuit judge by Gov. Jeremiah (Jay) Nixon on April 1, 2014. Term expires Dec. 31, 2016. Nonpartisan.

Circuit 6—Division 4
W. ANN HANSBROUGH

Office address: 415 Third St., Ste. 50, Platte City 64079; phone (816) 858-2232.

County: Platte.

Biography: Born July 7, 1960 in Poplar Bluff. Graduate of Poplar Bluff High School, 1978; University of Missouri–Columbia, Bachelor in journalism, 1982; University of Missouri-Columbia School of Law, J.D., 1985. Bar Register of Preeminent Women Lawyers (Peer Review selected Top 5% of Women Lawyers - 2011-2013); selected as "Super Lawyer" for Missouri, 2008-2011; selected as "Super Lawyer" for Kansas, 2008-2011; and board member for "Meritas Law Firms Worldwide," 2003-2003. Practiced at Swanson, Midgley LLC, from 1985 to 2004; selected as the firm's first woman partner in firm's 112 year history; Management Committee, 1999-2003; founder and director of firm's Volunteer Attorney Project; awarded Volunteer Service Award from Kansas City Metropolitan Bar Association. Member: Platte County Bar Association, Association of Women Lawyers and Missouri Bar Association. Married to David Stout, 1987; two children: Courtney and Mackenzie Stout. Appointed Jan. 21, 2014. Term expires Dec. 31, 2018. Nonpartisan.

Circuit 6—Division 5
DENNIS C. ECKOLD

Office address: Platte County Courthouse, 415 Third St., Ste. 50, Platte City 64079; phone (816) 858-2232.

County: Platte.

Biography: Born Oct. 8, 1956. Graduate of University of Michigan–Ann Arbor, B.A., psychology, 1979; University of Missouri–Columbia, J.D., 1983. Married to Lisa D. Eckold; they have four children. Engaged in private practice in Kansas City, 1983–2010. Member: Gloria Dei Lutheran Church and Missouri and Platte County Bar associations. Served as a member of the Kansas City Board of Police Commissioners, former board president, 1998–2003. Appointed associate circuit judge May 2010. Retained 2012. Term expires Dec. 31, 2016. Nonpartisan.

Circuit 7—Division 5
DAVID CHAMBERLAIN

Office address: Clay County Courthouse, 11 S. Water, Liberty 64068; phone (816) 407-3950.

Photo not available

County: Clay.

Biography: Born Dec. 13, 1962 in Cambridge, Neb. Graduate of Southwest Missouri State (now Missouri State University), 1985, B.S., economics; University of Missouri–Kansas City School of Law, 1989. Married Roberta L. Block Jan. 4, 1986; they have two children, Amanda and Hannah. Member: Missouri Bar, Clay County Bar and Kansas City Missouri Bar associations. Appointed associate circuit judge April 10, 2008. Retained in 2010 and 2014. Term expires Dec. 31, 2018. Nonpartisan.

Circuit 7—Division 6
KAREN L. KRAUSER

Office address: Clay County Courthouse, 11 S. Water, Liberty 64068; phone (816) 407-3960.

County: Clay.

Biography: Born Dec. 10, 1976, in Fort Leavenworth, Kan. Graduate of Park College (now Park University), 1999, B.A., criminal justice and psychology; University of Missouri–Kansas City School of Law, 2002. Lives in Liberty with her daughter, Alexandria. Assistant prosecutor for Clay County, 2002–2012; deputy chief prosecutor, 2008–2012; municipal judge for Excelsior Springs, 2008–2012; and municipal judge for Platte Woods, 2010–2012. Member: Missouri Bar; Clay County Bar Association; Kansas City Metropolitan Bar Association; Association for Women Lawyers of Kansas City; Missouri Probate and Associate Circuit Judges Association; Missouri Municipal and Associate Circuit Judges Association; and American Judges Association Appointed associate circuit judge on Jan. 10, 2012. Retained in 2014. Term expires Dec. 31, 2018. Nonpartisan.

Circuit 7—Division 7
LOUIS ANGLES

Office address: Clay County Courthouse, 11 S. Water St., Liberty 64068; phone (816) 407-3970.

County: Clay.

Biography: Born Sept. 18, 1957 in Havana, Cuba. Graduate of Shawnee Mission East High School, Prairie Village, Kan., 1976; University of Missouri-Kansas City School of Pharmacy, B.S., pharmacy, 1983; and Washburn University School of Law, J.D, 1988. Engaged in private law practice, 1988 until appointment to the bench in 2013. Member: Kansas City Metropolitan Bar Association, Clay County Bar Association and Missouri Bar. Former member: Missouri Association of Trial Attorneys. Appointed Associate Circuit Judge Oct. 18, 2013. Term expires Dec. 31, 2016. Nonpartisan.

Circuit 8
KEVIN L. WALDEN

Office address: Carroll County Courthouse, 8 S. Main, Ste. 1, Carrollton 64633; phone (660) 542-1818.

County: Carroll.

Biography: Born Oct. 9, 1961, in Carrollton. Graduate of Carrollton High School, 1980; Truman State (formerly Northeast Missouri State University), B.S.E., history, *cum laude*, 1984; University of Iowa College of Law, J.D., with high distinction, 1989; and Order of the Coif. Married Linda Miller Jan. 6, 1996. Taught high school social studies, 1984–1985. Engaged in private practice, 1989–2004. Served as Carroll County prosecuting attorney, 1997–2004; city attorney for Carrollton, Bogard, Bosworth, DeWitt, Hale and Tina; and special assistant attorney general. Member: First Christian Church, Disciples of Christ; The Missouri Bar; Carroll County Bar Association, president 1995–present; Wakanda Masonic Lodge #52; A.F. & A.M.; Lions Club, past president; *Iowa Law Review*; Chamber of Commerce; and Farm Bureau. Elected associate circuit judge 2004, 2006, 2010 and 2014. Term expires Dec. 31, 2018. Republican.

Circuit 8
LORI J. BASKINS

Office address: Ray County Courthouse, 100 Main St., Second Fl., Richmond 64085; phone (816) 776-2335.

County: Ray.

Biography: Born in 1964, in Windsor. Graduate of Fort Osage High School, Independence, 1983; Southwest Missouri State University, B.A., economics and mathematics, *summa cum laude*, 1987; Washington University School of Law, J.D., 1990; and Order of the Coif. Engaged in private practice, Kohn, Shands, Elbert, Gianoulakis & Giljum, St. Louis, 1990-1997; deputy state supervisor, Missouri Department of Public Safety, Division of Alcohol & Tobacco Control, 1997-2005; and private practice, 2005-2014, Richmond. Elected November 2014, for term beginning Jan.1, 2015. Term expires Dec. 31, 2018. Democrat.

Circuit 9
ANDREA RAVENS VANDELOECHT

Office address: Chariton County Courthouse, 306 S. Cherry, Keytesville 65261; phone (660) 288-3271.

County: Chariton.

Biography: Born Sept. 23, 1976. Graduate of Westminster College, B.A.; University of Missouri–Columbia School of Law, J.D. Married to Brent Vandeloecht; they have two children. General practice with Chapman, Cowherd, Turner and Tschannen, P.C., 2001–2010. Elected November 2010. Re-elected in 2014. Term expires Dec. 31, 2018. Democrat.

Circuit 9
SCOT T. OTHIC

Office address: Linn County Courthouse, PO Box 84, Linneus 64653; phone (660) 895-5212.

County: Linn.

Biography: Not available. Elected November 2014. Term expires Dec. 31, 2018. Democrat.

Photo not available

Circuit 9
TRACEY A. MASON-WHITE

Office address: Sullivan County Courthouse, 109 N. Main, Ste. 20, Milan, 63556; phone (660) 265-3303.

County: Sullivan.

Biography: Graduate of University of Missouri–Kansas City, B.S., business administration, 1999; University of Denver College of Law, J.D., 2004. Elected associate circuit judge in 2010 and 2014. Term expires Dec. 31, 2018. Republican.

Circuit 10
JOHN J. JACKSON

Office address: Marion County Courthouse, 906 Broadway, Hannibal 63401; phone (573) 221-0288.

County: Marion.

Biography: Born March 16, 1960. Graduate of University of Missouri–Columbia, B.A., 1982; J.D., 1985. Member and past president, 10th Circuit Bar Association. Elected Marion County prosecuting attorney, 1990 and 1994. Appointed associate circuit judge 1996. Elected 1998, 2002, 2006, 2010 and 2014. Term expires Dec. 31, 2018. Democrat.

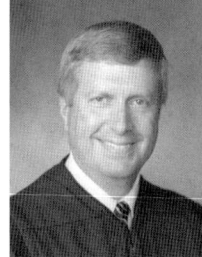

Circuit 10
MICHAEL P. WILSON

Office address: Monroe County Courthouse, 300 N. Main, Paris 65275; phone (660) 327-5220.

County: Monroe.

Biography: Born Nov. 18, 1951, in Tucson, Ariz. Graduate of University of Missouri–Columbia, A.B., B.J., 1973; J.D., 1980. Married Kathleen Roegge August 19, 1973. Commissioned U.S. Air Force, 1973, became JAG in 1980. Retired as Lieutenant colonel, 1993. Recipient of five meritorious service medals. Prosecuting attorney, Monroe County, 1995–2004. Kansas City Arson Task Force Prosecutor of Year, 2000. Member: Lutheran Church–Missouri Synod, Rotary and American Legion. Appointed associate circuit judge 2004. Elected 2006, 2010 and 2014. Term expires Dec. 31, 2018. Democrat.

Circuit 10
DAVID MOBLEY

Office address: Ralls County Courthouse, PO Box 466, New London 63459; phone (573) 985-5641.

County: Ralls.

Biography: Born Sept. 25, 1961. Graduate of Culver-Stockton College, B.A; University of Missouri–Columbia, J.D. Married Sherre Lubker June 16, 1984; they have three children. Served in private practice of law, 1986–2001. Appointed by Supreme Court to Family Court Committee and reappointed in 2009. Member: First Christian Church; Rotary Club; Mark Twain Home Foundation board; Culver-Stockton College Board of Trustees; Great River Honor Flight Board of Directors; and Hannibal Pirate Family Foundation board of directors. Past president and campaign chair of Mark Twain Area United Way. Past district chairman of Mark Twain District Great Rivers Council, B.S.A. Received District Award of Merit, Great Rivers Counsel, B.S.A. Former member: Missouri Bar Complaint Resolution program. Term expires Dec. 31, 2018. Democrat.

Circuit 11—Division 6
TERRY R. CUNDIFF

Office address: St. Charles County Courthouse, 300 N. Second St., Rm. 436, St. Charles 63301; phone (636) 949-3096.
County: St. Charles County.
Biography: Not available. Took office Jan. 1, 1995. Term expires Dec. 31, 2018. Republican.

Circuit 11—Division 8
ERIN S. BURLISON

Photo not
available

Office address: St. Charles County Courthouse, 300 N. Second St., Rm. 431, St. Charles 63301; phone (636) 949-7496.
County: St. Charles.
Biography: Born in St. Charles. Graduate of University of Missouri–Columbia, B.A., psychology, 2004; St. Louis University, J.D., 2007. Resides in St. Louis with her husband and daughter. Member: Missouri Bar Association, St. Charles County Bar Association, and Young Lawyers Association of St. Charles County, past president. Boards: Missouri Consolidated Health Care Plan, 2011–2013; St. Charles County Boys and Girls Club, 2010–present; and Enterprise Bank and Trust, 2012–present. Appointed associate circuit judge 2013. Republican.

Circuit 11—Division 9
ELIZABETH SWANN

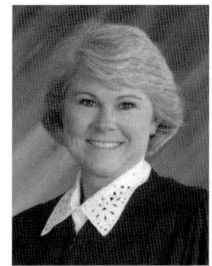

Office address: St. Charles County Courthouse, 300 N. Second St., St. Charles 63367; phone (636) 949-7900, ext. 7497.
County: St. Charles.
Biography: Born in Magnolia, Ark., on Oct. 16, 1956. Graduate of Southeast Missouri State University, B.S., education; University of Missouri–Columbia, J.D. Admitted to the Missouri Bar, 1982. Served as a family court commissioner in St. Charles County, 1997–2006, and has served as an associate circuit judge, 2007–present. A member of the Family Court Committee and is currently serving as co-chair of a sub-committee reviewing guardian *ad litem* standards. Recently completed service on the Ad Hoc Committee for Videoconferencing. Member: St. Charles County and Missouri Bar associations. Resides in Lake St. Louis with her husband and son. Term expires Dec. 31, 2018. Republican.

Circuit 11—Division 10
NORMAN C. STEIMEL III

Office address: St. Charles County Courthouse, 300 N. Second St., Rm. 335, St. Charles 63301; phone (636) 949-7900, ext. 3064.
County: St. Charles.
Biography: Born Dec. 30, 1953, in Spokane, Wash. Graduate of Washington University, A.B., 1975; J.D., 1978. Appellate law clerk for the Hon. Douglas W. Greene, Missouri Court of Appeals, Southern District, 1979–1980. Married Libby C. Toney June 17, 1978. They have nine children. Member: Christ Presbyterian Church; The Missouri Bar; Illinois State Bar Association; Bar Association of Metropolitan St. Louis; St. Charles County Bar Association; Association of Family and Conciliation Courts, Missouri Chapter president, 2008–2010; and Christian Legal Society. Appointed family court commissioner, 1995. Reappointed 1999 and 2003. Elected associate circuit judge 2006. Re-elected 2010 and 2014. Term expires Dec. 31, 2018. Republican.

Circuit 11—Division 11
PHILLIP OHLMS

Office address: St. Charles County Courthouse, 300 N. Second St., Rm. 429, St. Charles 63301; phone (636) 949-7462.

County: St. Charles.

Biography: Born August 12, 1955, in St. Charles County. Graduate of St. Mary's Junior College, A.A., 1975; University of Missouri–Columbia, B.S., B.A., 1977; J.D., 1980. Married Diana Mueller March 24, 1984. They have four children: Grant, Mark, Paul and Abigail. Attends Assumption BVM Church in O'Fallon. Appointed drug court commissioner, 2000. Elected associate circuit judge 2006, 2010 and 2014. Term expires Dec. 31, 2018. Republican.

Circuit 11—Division 12
MATTHEW E.P. THORNHILL

Office address: St. Charles County Courthouse, 300 N. Second St., Rm. 429, St. Charles 63301; phone (636) 949-7486.

County: St. Charles.

Biography: Born May 20, 1968, in St. Charles. Married Heather Denise Thornhill in 1997. They have four children: Martha June Kelly, Sophia Axie Mae, Calvin Daniel Cornelius and Phoebe Noelle Serene. Graduate of Rockhurst College, Kansas City, B.S., B.A., 1990; Notre Dame Law School, Notre Dame, Ind., J.D., 1993. Served as an assistant prosecutor for St. Charles County, 1993–2006. Member of Harvester Christian Church, St. Charles. Term expires Dec. 31, 2018. Republican.

Circuit 12
LINDA R. HAMLETT

Office address: Audrain County Courthouse, 101 N. Jefferson., Rm. 205, Mexico 65265; phone (573) 473-5850.

County: Audrain.

Biography: Not available. Took office Jan. 1, 1991. Term expires Dec. 31, 2018. Democrat.

Circuit 12
KELLY C. BRONIEC

Office address: Montgomery County Courthouse, 211 E. Third St., Ste. 301, Montgomery City 63361; phone (573) 564-3348.

County: Montgomery.

Biography: Born in St. Louis. Graduate of William Woods College, B.A., business administration, *summa cum laude*; University of Missouri–Columbia School of Law, J.D. Married Mark Broniec April 29, 2000; they have 2 children. Served as Montgomery County prosecuting attorney, 1999–2006; assistant prosecuting attorney in Warren County, 1996–1998; and assistant prosecutor in Lincoln County, 1998–1999. Member: Grace Lutheran Church; Montgomery City Kiwanis Club, past president; Montgomery County Rotary Club; GFWC-Montgomery Study Club; Montgomery City Chamber of Commerce; and founding board member of The Child Center, Inc., 2000–2006. Elected 2006, 2010 and 2014. Term expires Dec. 31, 2018. Republican.

Circuit 12
RICHARD L. SCHEIBE

Office address: Warren County Courthouse, 104 W. Main St., Warrenton 63383; phone (636) 456-3375.

County: Warren.

Biography: Born July 28, 1970. Served in the U.S. Army Infantry during Desert Storm. Graduate of University of Missouri, B.G.S.; J.D., 1997; and M.A., 2006. Public defender, 1997–2013. Appointed associate circuit judge by Gov. Jeremiah (Jay) Nixon in 2013. Term expires Dec. 31, 2018. Democrat.

Circuit 12
MICHAEL S. WRIGHT

Office address: Warren County Courthouse, 104 W. Main St., Warrenton 63383; phone (636) 456-3375.

County: Warren.

Photo not available

Biography: Not available. Elected November 2014. Term expires Dec. 31, 2018. Republican.

Circuit 13—Division 5
KIMBERLY J. SHAW

Office address: Boone County Courthouse, 705 E. Walnut St., Columbia 65201; phone (573) 886-4050.

County: Boone.

Biography: Born November 24, 1960 in Louisiana, Missouri. Graduate of David H. Hickman High School, Columbia, Missouri; Columbia College B.A., Business Administration, 1986; University of Missouri–Columbia School of Law, J.D., 1986. Began her legal career at Cape Girardeau County Public Defender Trial Office. Returned to Columbia with the Central Capital Division where she was the District Defender prior to leaving in 2000 to go into private practice. The five years prior to taking the bench she worked at the Boone County Public Defender's Trial Office. Member: Missouri Bar Association, Boone County Bar Association, Missouri Municipal and Associate Circuit Judges Association, Missouri Association of Probate and Associate Circuit Judges, Married to Charles "Chuck" Brown (2009) and we have a blended family of four children. Elected November 2014. Term expires Dec. 31, 2018. Democrat.

Circuit 13–Division 6
CAROL ENGLAND

Office address: Callaway County Courthouse, 10 E. Fifth St., Fulton 65251; phone (573) 642-0777.

County: Callaway.

Biography: Born in Kewanee, Ill. Graduate of Columbia College, B.A.; Lincoln University, M.A.; and University of Missouri School of Law, J.D. Employed as a police officer before and while attending law school, then worked as an assistant prosecuting attorney for the Callaway County prosecutor's office immediately after law school. Member: Missouri Bar Association; Callaway County Bar Association, treasurer; Ebenezer Baptist Church in Fulton; Fulton Rotary Club; and Callaway County Chapter of the American Red Cross, board member. Elected associate circuit judge in 2006, 2010 and 2014. Term expires Dec. 31, 2018. Democrat.

Circuit 13–Division 7
SUE M. CRANE

Office address: Callaway County Courthouse, 10 E. Fifth St., Fulton 65251; phone (573) 642-0777.

County: Callaway.

Biography: Graduate of Rock Bridge High School, Columbia; University of Missouri, B.S., animal science; and University of Missouri J.D. 1989. Assistant public defender, 1989 - 1993. Engaged in private practice from 1993 until elected. Partner in Brady & Crane LLC. During that time, served on the Callaway County Drug Court Team, Certified Mediator. Founder and director of CrossWind Ranch, a non-profit organization for kids. Past member of various boards. Currently president of the Callaway County Bar Association. Elected November 2014. Term expires Dec. 31, 2018. Republican.

Circuit 13—Division 9
MICHAEL W. BRADLEY

Office address: Boone County Courthouse, 705 E. Walnut St., Columbia 65201; phone (573) 886-4050.

County: Boone

Biography: Born March 11, 1952, at George Air Force Base, Victorville, Calif. Graduate of the University of Missouri–Columbia, B.A., 1974; J.D., 1978. Appellate law clerk to Hon. George Flanigan, Missouri Court of Appeals, Southern District, 1978–79. Assistant city attorney, Kansas City, 1979–1984. Private law practice, 1984–1995. Prosecuting attorney, Carroll County, 1991–1994. Associate circuit judge, Carroll County, 2004. Assistant attorney general, 1995–2004, 2005–2009. Member of the Supreme Court Committee on Procedure in Criminal Cases, 2005–2008. Counsel to the Missouri Department of Public Safety and the Missouri State Highway Patrol, 2009–2010. Chief counsel to the Missouri Gaming Commission, 2010–2011. Member: Roman Catholic Church, Boone County Bar Association, Mizzou Alumni Association, Jefferson Club and Columbia Chamber of Commerce. Lives in Columbia with wife, Katie. Appointed associate circuit judge April 2011. Elected associate circuit judge 2012 and 2014. Term expires Dec. 31, 2018. Democrat.

Circuit 13—Division 10
LESLIE SCHNEIDER

Office address: Boone County Courthouse, 705 E. Walnut St., Columbia 65201; phone (573) 886-4050.

County: Boone.

Biography: Born in 1955 in Ames, Iowa. Graduated from Kirksville High School, 1973; University of Missouri–Columbia, B.A., 1976; and J.D., 1979. Married Thomas Schneider 1979, and they have two children, Julia and Scott. Assistant attorney general, 1979–1983; municipal judge, City of Columbia, 1987–1996, private practice, 1983–2006. Supreme Court Access to Family Courts Committee. Member: Family Court committee. Adjunct professor, University of Missouri–Columbia School of Law. Elected 2006, 2010 and 2014. Term expires Dec. 31, 2018. Democrat.

Circuit 13–Division 11
DEBORAH DANIELS

Office Address: Boone County Courthouse, 705 E. Walnut St., Columbia 65201; phone (573) 886-4050.

County: Boone.

Biography: Born June 14, 1950, Fayette. Graduate of Univ. of Missouri–Columbia, B.A., B.S., 1972; J.D., 1977. Honorary Order of the Coif, 2004. Fellow of the American Bar Assoc. Three children: Ian, Sydney Brette and Paige Harrison. Law clerk on the Missouri Supreme Court, 1977–78 for Hon. Fred Henley; director of Missouri Supreme Court research staff, 1979–1982; adjunct prof. of law at UMC, 1984–2010; reporter for the Comm. on Procedure in Criminal Cases, 1982–2007; asst. pros. atty., Boone Co., 1999–2004; chief counsel, Criminal Div., Missouri Attorney General's Office, 2004–2006. Missouri Supreme Court Comm. on Procedure in Criminal Cases, 2007–present; and Court's Automation Comm., 2011–present. Appointed Mo. Bar Special Task Force Comm. on the Public Defender's Office, 2004–2006. Advanced Science and Technology Adjudication Resource Program (ASTAR), 2007–present; ASTAR Fellow, 2009–present; editorial board for the ASTAR Journal, 2012–present. Faculty: Missouri Judicial College, 2005–2012. Elected associate circuit judge in 2006, 2010 and 2014. Term expires Dec. 31, 2018. Democrat.

Circuit 14
MASON R. GEBHARDT

Office address: Howard County Courthouse, PO Box 370, Fayette 65248; phone (660) 248-3326.

County: Howard.

Biography: Born Sept. 12, 1969, at Keller Hospital, Fayette. Graduate of University of Missouri–Columbia, bachelor's degree, 1992; University of Missouri–Kansas City School of Law, J.D., 1996. Married Lisa Kauffman on Nov. 25, 2000. They have three daughters: Kaleigh, Kassidy and Olivia. Private practice in Fayette, 1977–2010. Howard County prosecuting attorney, 1999–2010. Elected associate circuit judge in Howard County 2010 and 2014. Term expires Dec. 31, 2018. Republican.

Circuit 14
CYNTHIA A. SUTER

Office address: Randolph County Justice Center, 372 HWY JJ, Ste. D., Huntsville 65259; phone (660) 277-4601.

County: Randolph.

Biography: Born Dec. 17, 1947, in Ft. Madison, Iowa. Graduate of Moberly Senior High School; Moberly Area Junior College; Truman State University; and University of Missouri–Kansas City School of Law. Engaged in private practice from 1971–2006. Member: Trinity United Methodist Church, Rotary Club and VFW Ladies Auxiliary. Appointed to Supreme Court Intervention Committee. Former board member of the Missouri State Board of Nursing, NECAC, Community Day Care, Safe Passage, Missouri Lawyers Trust Fund, Missouri Bar Lawyers Assistance Committee and Mid-Mo Legal Services. Elected 2006, 2010 and 2014. Term expires Dec. 31, 2018. Democrat.

Circuit 15
KELLY HALFORD ROSE

Office address: Lafayette County Courthouse - Lafayette Hall, 116 S. 10th St., PO Box 10, Lexington 64067; phone (660) 259-6101.

Photo not available

County: Lafayette.

Biography: Not available. Elected November 2014. Term expires Dec. 31, 2018.

Circuit 15
RUSSELL J. KRUSE

Office address: Lafayette County Courthouse - Lafayette Hall, 116 S. 10th St., PO Box 10, Lexington 64067; phone (660) 259-2324.

County: Lafayette.

Biography: Born 1962, IA. Married Beth Anne McKinney, has 6 children. Education: St. Paul's College, Concordia, A.A. degree, 1981; Univ. of Mo.–Col., B.A., pol. science, 1983, J.D., 1986. Law & bus. prac., 1986–2005; solo prac., 2005–14; Broker-Partner, Show-Me Realty, 1992–2008; co-owner/agent, title Ins. Co., 1992–2005; owner-agent, 2005–08. Member: Lafayette Co. Bar, 2004–15, sec., 2015; 10th Jud. Cir. Bar, 1986–2015, past pres., 2006; Mo. Bar, 1986–pres.; Ill. Bar, 1987–2014 (inactive 2015–pres.); U.S. Dist. Crts & bankruptcy crts., 1986–2014; Central U.S. Dist. Crt. & bankruptcy crt., Ill., 1990–2014; Eighth Cir. Crt. of Appeals, 1991–2014; U.S. Supreme Ct., 1999–2014; Mo. Assoc. of Probate & Assoc. Cir. Judges, 2015–pres.; Legal Svcs., NE Mo. bd., 1987–89, MATA, 1988–93. LCMS Mo. Dist. bd., 2012–pres.; St. Paul Lutheran High bd., 2013–pres.; Concordia Lion's Club, 2004–pres.; Children's Svcs. bd., 2004–pres.; Enterprises Inc., 2005–14, vp, 2012–13, chair, 2014; I-70 Med. Center Fndn., 2012–14; Luther Manor Nursing Home bd., 1991–93 & 2002–04, Nutrition Center bd., 1987–89; Kiwanis, 1988–93. Civics teacher, 1987–2014. Member & elder, St. Paul's Lutheran Church, Missouri Synod. Elected Nov. 2014. Term expires Dec. 31, 2018. Republican.

Circuit 15
HUCH C. HARVEY

Office address: Saline County Courthouse, 101 E. Arrow, Rm. 302, Marshall 65340; phone (660) 886-8808.

County: Saline.

Biography: Graduate of Oral Roberts University, B.S., in business management, 1977–1981; Drake University, 1982–1985, J.D./MBA. Saline County prosecuting attorney, 1987–1998. Saline County associate circuit judge, 2000–present. Term expires Dec. 31, 2018. Democrat.

Circuit 15
JAMES T. BELLAMY

Office address: Saline County Courthouse, PO Box 751, Marshall 65340; phone (660) 886-6988.

County: Saline.

Biography: Born March 2, 1953, in Marshall. Graduate of Westminster College, B.A.; University of Missouri–Kansas City, J.D. Member: First Presbyterian Church; Lions Club; Masonic Lodge; and Saline County Bar Association. Appointed to associate circuit court 2000. Elected 2000, 2002, 2006, 2010 and 2014. Term expires Dec. 31, 2018. Democrat.

Circuit 16—Division 25
RICHARD T. STANDRIDGE

Office address: Jackson County Courthouse, 415 E. 12th St., Kansas City 64106; phone (816) 881-3678.

County: Jackson.

Biography: Born Jan. 28, 1953, at Camp Chaffee, Ark. Graduate of Southwest Missouri State University, 1976, B.S. political science; and the University of Missouri–Kansas City, J.D., 1980. Married to Melissa T. Standridge; they have five children. Member: Congregation Beth Torah. Appointed associate circuit judge June 1993 by Gov. Mel Carnahan. Retained in 1994, 1998, 2002, 2006, 2010 and 2014. Term expires Dec. 31, 2018. Nonpartisan.

Circuit 16—Division 26
JALILAH OTTO

Office address: Jackson County Courthouse, 415 E. 12th St., Kansas City 64106; phone (816) 881-3685.

County: Jackson.

Biography: Born in Kansas City. Graduate of Lincoln College Preparatory Academy, Kansas City; Tulane University, New Orleans, La., B.A., communication and political science; University of Missouri-Columbia, J.D. Served as a law clerk to the Hon. Lisa White Hardwick, Missouri Court of Appeals, 2002-2005; assistant prosecuting attorney for Jackson County, 2005-2010; and special assistant U.S. attorney for the Western District of Missouri, 2010-2013. Simultaneously served as special assistant U.S. attorney and chief trial assistant for Jackson County, 2013. Recipient of the Louis Lombardo Prosecutor of the Year Award. Member: the Missouri Bar, Missouri Probate and Associate Circuit Court Judge Association, Jackson County and Kansas City Metropolitan Bar Associations, and Association of Women Lawyers. Appointed by the Missouri Supreme Court to serve on the Joint Commission on Women in the Profession, Joint Task Force on the Future of the Profession and the Racial and Ethnic Fairness Commission. Appointed associate circuit judge by Gov. Jeremiah (Jay) Nixon on Jan. 7, 2014. Term expires Dec. 31, 2018. Nonpartisan.

Circuit 16—Division 27
GREGORY B. GILLIS

Office address: Jackson County Courthouse, 415 E. 12th St., Kansas City 64106; phone (816) 881-3691.
County: Jackson.
Biography: Lifelong resident of Kansas City. Graduate of the University of Missouri–Columbia, 1981; University of Missouri–Columbia School of Law, 1984. Married to Joyce Gillis since 1985. Served as the drug court commissioner and as assistant prosecuting attorney for 12 years in Jackson County. Member: KC Metropolitan Bar Association and the Jackson County Bar Association. Serves as historian and board member of the Missouri Association of Probate and Associate Circuit Judges, and served on the advisory board of Operation Breakthrough. Appointed by Gov. Bob Holden in April 2001. Retained in 2002, 2006, 2010 and 2014. Term expires Dec. 31, 2018. Nonpartisan.

Circuit 16—Division 28
JEFFREY C. KEAL

Office address: Jackson County Courthouse, 308 W. Kansas, Independence 64050; phone (816) 881-4606.
County: Jackson.
Biography: Born/raised in Independence. Graduate of Univ. of Mo.–Kansas City, B.A., bus. admin., 1982; Univ. of Mo.–Kansas City, J.D., 1986. Solo practitioner, 1986-1988. Associate with Crews, Smart, Whitehead & Waits,1988–1991. Jackson County Prosecutor's Office, 1991–2013; chief warrant officer, trial team leader and handled wide variety of cases within office including assaults, robberies, white collar and property crimes. Warrant officer of the year and received certificate of appreciation from U.S. Secret Service for collaborative work in white collar crime prosecutions. Member: Missouri Bar, Kansas City Metropolitan Bar, and Eastern Jackson County Bar associations; Association for Women Lawyers. Involved with the community and spent many years coaching youth sports, including softball, basketball and baseball. Member of Firefighters Local Number 42 and the Kansas City Curling Club. Proud graduate of Van Horn High School in Independence and a lifetime member of BCAS. Appointed in 2013. Term expires Dec. 31, 2016.

Circuit 16—Division 29
JANETTE K. RODECAP

Office address: Jackson County Courthouse, 415 E. 12th St., Kansas City 64106; phone (816) 881-3735.
County: Jackson.
Biography: Born Sept. 24, 1974, in Decorah, Iowa. Graduate of Northwestern University, Evanston, Ill., B.A.; University of Iowa College of Law, J.D., 2001. Served as a law clerk for the Hon. Nanette K. Laughrey, U.S. District Court Judge for the Western District of Missouri, 2001-2003. Court Counsel for the Palau Supreme Court in Koror, Palau, 2003-2004. Assistant state attorney in Fort Myers, Fla., 2005-2006. Assistant prosecuting attorney in Jackson County, 2006-2014. Member: Missouri Bar Association, Kansas City Metropolitan Bar Association and Association of Women Lawyers. Married with two children. Appointed associate circuit judge May 28, 2014. Term expires Dec. 31, 2016. Nonpartisan.

Circuit 16—Division 30
TWILA K. RIGBY

Office address: Jackson County Courthouse Annex, 308 W. Kansas, Independence 64050; phone (816) 881-4506.
County: Jackson.
Biography: Born in Urbana. Graduate of Missouri State University, B.S., education, *magna cum laude*, 1975; M.Ed.; and University of Missouri–Kansas City Law School, J.D., 1988. Married Robert Rigby May 17, 1987. They have three children. Member of Faith United Methodist Church, Grain Valley. Jackson County prosecutor's office, 1987–1997. Appointed associate circuit judge 1997. Retained in 1998, 2002, 2006, 2010 and 2014. Term expires Dec. 31, 2018. Nonpartisan.

Circuit 16—Division 31
MARY F. WEIR

Office address: Jackson County Courthouse, 415 E. 12th St., Kansas City 64106; phone (816) 881-3544.

County: Jackson.

Biography: Born Sept. 30, 1961, in Buffalo, N.Y. Graduate of Mount Mercy Academy, Buffalo, N.Y., 1979; Univ. of Mo.–Kansas City, B.A., pol. science, 1991; Washburn School of Law, Topeka, Kan, J.D., 1995. Worked as a law clerk, div. 31 of the 16th Judicial Circuit Court for the Hon. Christine Sill-Rogers, Sept. 1995–April 1998. Assistant Missouri state public defender, Kansas City office, 1998–2001. Began working as a contract attorney in 2001 with Hope House, Inc., providing representation to victims of domestic violence and their children until her appointment to the bench. Also represented juveniles and parents in the Jackson County Family Court through her work as of counsel with the Raith Law Firm until her appointment. Adjunct professor of law at the Univ. of Mo.–Kansas City School of Law since 2004. Appointed associate circuit judge in May 2013. Retained in 2014. Term expires in Dec. 31, 2018. Nonpartisan.

Circuit 16—Division 32
ROBERT L. TROUT

Office address: Jackson County Courthouse Annex, 308 W. Kansas, Independence 64050; phone (816) 881-4518.

County: Jackson.

Biography: Born Sept. 4, 1949, in Clarinda, Iowa. Graduate of William Jewell College, B.A., 1971; University of Missouri–Kansas City School of Law, J.D., 1975. Married with two children. Practiced law in Blue Springs and Odessa. Appointed associate circuit judge Oct. 5, 1987. Retained in 1988, 1992, 1996, 2000, 2004, 2008 and 2012. Term expires Dec. 31, 2016. Nonpartisan.

Circuit 16—Division 33
JEFFREY L. BUSHUR

Office address: Jackson County Courthouse Annex, 308 W. Kansas, Independence 64050; phone (816) 881-1783.

County: Jackson.

Biography: Graduate of University of Missouri–Kansas City, B.A., philosophy and communication students, 1983; J.D., 1986. U.S. Army, 1975–1978. Married with two children. Served as an assistant prosecutor in the Jackson County Prosecuting Attorney's Office, 1985–2000. Named Jackson County Prosecutor of the Year, 1991 and 1995. CLE lecturer for Missouri Office of Prosecution Services, 1990–1999; lecturer for Central Missouri State University law enforcement program, 1986–2000. Member of Trial Judge Education Committee; ASTAR Judge Program; and Trial Judge Education lecturer. Appointed June 2000. Retained in 2002, 2006, 2010 and 2014. Term expires Dec. 31, 2018. Nonpartisan.

Circuit 17
J. MICHAEL RUMLEY

Office address: Cass County Justice Center, 2501 W. Mechanic, Harrisonville 64701; phone (816) 380-8217.

County: Cass.

Biography: Born April 30, 1953, in Kansas City, Kan. Graduate of Park University, B.A., public administration, 1980; and University of Missouri–Kansas City, J.D., 1984. Engaged in private law practice, 1984–2010. Adjunct professor of law, Uuniversity of Missouri–Kansas City, 1985–2000. Raymore Municipal Judge, December 2008–December 2010. Member: Cass County Bar Association; The Order of Barristers; Missouri Farm Bureau; Ray-Pec Optimist Club; and Raymore, Belton, Peculiar and Pleasant Hill chambers of commerce. Elected 2010. Re-elected in 2014. Term expires Dec. 31, 2018. Republican.

Circuit 17
STACEY JO LETT

Office address: Cass County Justice Center, 2501 W. Mechanic, Harrisonville 64701; phone (816) 380-8216.

County: Cass.

Biography: Not available. Elected November 2014. Term expires Dec. 31, 2018. Republican

Photo not available

Circuit 17
DAN OLSEN

Office address: Cass County Justice Center, 2501 W. Wall St., Harrisonville 64701; phone (816) 380-8701.

County: Cass.

Biography: Born August 28, 1952, in El Dorado, Kan. Graduate of Kansas State University, B.S., animal science; Washburn University of Topeka, J.D. Married Margaret C. Eisenmayer Feb. 9, 1985; two sons, Alex and Ian. Engaged in private law practice, 1979–April 2006; Raymore municipal judge, April 1980–April 2006; Lake Winnebago municipal judge, Jan. 1982–April 2006; and Garden City municipal judge, July 2004–April 2006. Member: Bel-Ray Lions Club, Ray-Pec Optimist Club, Elks Lodge #2791 and Cass County Bar Association. Appointed to the associate circuit court judge April 2006. Elected 2010. Re-elected in 2014. Term expires Dec. 31, 2018. Republican.

Circuit 17
CHAD N. PFISTER

Office address: Johnson County Justice Center, 101 W. Market, Warrensburg 64093; phone (660) 422-7405.

County: Johnson.

Biography: Born Chanute AFB, Ill. Graduate of University of Missouri-Columbia, B.A., political science; Valparaiso University, J.D., *cum laude*. Wife, Marci, and sons, Adrian and Hayden. Employment: University of Missouri-Columbia; private practice in Johnson County Missouri. Member: The Missouri Bar, Johnson County Bar Association, Warrensburg Noon Rotary Club, Elks Lodge #673 and Beta Sigma Psi (27th National President). Elected associate circuit judge 2014. Term expires Dec. 31, 2018. Republican.

Circuit 17
SUE DODSON

Office address: Johnson County Justice Center, 101 W. Market, Warrensburg 64093; phone (660) 422-7410.

County: Johnson.

Biography: Born May 24, 1955, in Kansas City. Graduate of University of Central Missouri., B.S.; University of Missouri–Kansas City, J.D. Member: *UMKC Law Review*, Warrensburg and Holden chambers of commerce, Missouri and Johnson County Bar associations, Missouri Farm Bureau and Whiteman Base Community Council and Military Affairs Committee. Elected 2006, 2010 and 2014. Term expires Dec. 31, 2018. Democrat.

Circuit 18
KEITH M. BAIL

Office address: Cooper County Courthouse, 200 Main, Rm. 31, Boonville 65233; phone (660) 882-5604.

County: Cooper.

Biography: Born August 26, 1963, in Boonville. Graduate of the University of Missouri College of Agriculture, agricultural economics, 1984; University of Missouri School of Law, J.D., 1993. Married Catherine Reynolds March 23, 1996. They have two sons. Law clerk to late Judge Robert W. Berrey III, Missouri Court of Appeals, Western District, 1993–1995; private practice, 1995–1996; and assistant prosecuting attorney, Boone County, 1996–2006. Member: United Church of Christ; Masonic Lodge; Shriners; Chamber of Commerce; and Rotary Club. Elected 2006, 2010 and 2014. Term expires Dec. 31, 2018. Republican.

Circuit 18
JEFF A. MITTELHAUSER

Office address: Pettis County Courthouse, 415 S. Ohio, Sedalia 65301; phone (660) 826-5000, ext. 924.

Photo not available

County: Pettis.

Biography: Born 1956 in Sedalia. Graduate of Smith-Cotton High School, Sedalia, 1975; Central Missouri State University, 1978; and University of Missouri-Columbia School of Law, 1981. Married to Maria; two children. Served as public defender for Pettis, Cooper, Morgan and Moniteau Counties, 1981-82; assistant prosecutor for Pettis County, 1982-1986; and Pettis County Prosecuting Attorney, 1987-2014. Member: Georgetown United Methodist Church, Sedalia Runners Club and Sedalia School District Foundation. Past board member of Child Safe of Central Missouri and State Fair Area Community Service Agency. Elected associate judge 2014, term beginning 2015. Term expires Dec. 31, 2018. Republican.

Circuit 18
R. PAUL BEARD

Office address: Pettis County Courthouse, 415 S. Ohio, Sedalia 65301; phone (660) 826-5000, ext. 924.

County: Pettis.

Biography: Born in Missouri in 1969. Graduate of Brigham Young University, B.A., 1993; University of Missouri–Columbia, J.D., 1997. Partner in the law firm of Beard & Associates, LLP, 1997–2005. Appointed associate circuit judge, Pettis County, 2005. Elected to the same position, 2006 and 2010. Married Stacey Hill, 1993; they have six children. Member: Church of Jesus Christ of Latter-Day Saints, Rotary, Red Cross, Boy Scouts of America, Pettis County Ministerial Alliance, United Way, Paul Klover Soccer Association, PTA and Bothwell Hospital Volunteer Chaplins. Term expires Dec. 31, 2018. Republican.

Circuit 19
THOMAS L. SODERGREN

Office address: Cole County Courthouse, PO Box 1870, Jefferson City 65102; phone (573) 634-9170.

County: Cole.

Biography: Born Dec. 17, 1952. Graduate of the University of Missouri–Columbia, B.S., English education; University of Missouri–Columbia School of Law, J.D., 1978. Widowed with two children. Private practice of law, 1978–1994. Jefferson City municipal judge, 1990–1994. Former president, Cole County Bar. Former member, Missouri Bar Young Lawyers Section Council. Former counsel to Missouri Police Chief's Association. 2004 recipient of Mothers Against Drunk Driving Judicial Officer of the Year. Former board member of the Missouri Probate and Associate Circuit Judges Association. Elected associate circuit judge 1994, 1998, 2002, 2006, 2010 and 2014. Term expires Dec. 31, 2018. Republican.

Circuit 20
DAVID B. TOBBEN

Office address: Franklin County Judicial Center, 401 E. Main, Rm. 100C, Union 63084; phone (636) 583-6316.

County: Franklin.

Biography: Born Nov. 20, 1950, in Washington. Graduate of University of Notre Dame, B.A., economics, 1973; University of Missouri–Columbia, J.D., 1976. Married Lucille Struckhoff August 2, 1975. Six children: Laura, Eric, Ellen, Brian, Emily and Andrew. Assistant prosecuting attorney, Franklin County, 1976–1981, 1984–1988; city attorney, City of Washington, 1978–1982; municipal judge, City of Washington, 1984–1990; and Franklin County prosecuting attorney, 1991–1995. Elected associate circuit judge 2006, 2010 and 2014. Term expires Dec. 31, 2018. Republican.

Circuit 20
DAVID L. HOVEN

Office address: Franklin Judicial Center, 401 E. Main St., Rm. 100B, Union 63084; phone (636) 583-7332.

County: Franklin.

Biography: Born March 12, 1952, Scott Air Force Base, Belleville, Ill. Married Janet Jones Sept. 8, 1979; they have two children. Graduate of St. Joseph's College (Ind.), B.A., 1974; Pepperdine University School of Law, J.D., 1977. Engaged in private practice, 1978–2005. Member: Chamber of Commerce; Lions Club; California Bar Association; and Our Lady of Lourdes parish, Washington. Appointed Jan. 2005. Elected 2006, 2010 and 2014. Term expires Dec. 31, 2018. Democrat.

Circuit 20
STANLEY D. WILLIAMS

Office address: Franklin County Judicial Center, 401 E. Main, Rm. 100C, Union 63084; phone (636) 583-6330.

County: Franklin.

Biography: Born Oct. 9, 1957, in Cuba. Educated at East Central College, Union; University of Missouri–Columbia, A.B., *cum laude*, 1978; UCLA Law School, J.D., 1981. Married to Debbie Williams. Engaged in private practice, Franklin County, 1981–1996. Past municipal judge, St. Clair. Member: Pacific Presbyterian Church, Missouri Bar Association and 20th Judicial Circuit Bar. Serves as Franklin County drug court judge. Appointed associate circuit judge 1996. Elected 1996, 1998, 2002, 2006, 2010 and 2014. Term expires Dec. 31, 2018. Democrat.

Circuit 20
ADA BREHE-KRUEGER

Office address: Gasconade County Courthouse, 119 E. First St., Rm. 3, Hermann 65041; phone (573) 486-2321.

County: Gasconade.

Biography: Not available. Elected November 2014. Term expires Dec. 31, 2018. Republican.

Photo not available

Circuit 20
ROBERT D. SCHOLLMEYER

Office address: Osage County Courthouse, PO Box 825, Linn 65051; phone (573) 897-2136.

County: Osage.

Biography: Born Nov. 27, 1962, in Jefferson City. Graduate of the University of Missouri–Columbia, A.B., with honors; Washington University in St. Louis, J.D. Married Kathi O. Jones. Member: St. Mary's Parish, Chamois. Served as public defender, Hannibal, 1989–1991; and as prosecuting attorney, Osage County, 1991–2002. Appointed associate circuit judge, 2002. Elected 2002, 2006, 2010 and 2014. Term expires Dec. 31, 2018. Democrat.

Circuit 21—Division 31
MARY E. OTT

Photo not
available

Office address: St. Louis County Court Bldg., 105 S. Central Ave., Clayton 64050; phone (314) 615-1531.

County: St. Louis.

Biography: Born Sept. 25, 1960 in St. Louis. Graduate of St. Mary's College, B.A., 1982; St. Louis University School of Law, J.D., 1985. Appointed May 30, 2008. Retained 2010 and 2014. Term expires Dec. 31, 2018. Nonpartisan.

Circuit 21—Division 32
MARY BRUNTRAGER SCHROEDER

Office address: Clayton Courthouse, 105 S. Central Ave., Clayton 63105; phone (314) 615-1532.

County: St. Louis.

Biography: Graduate of St. Louis University, B.A.; St. Mary's University in San Antonio, Texas, J.D. Resides in St. Louis County with her family. Circuit attorney for the City of St. Louis, 1980–1982. Engaged in private law practice, 1983–1999, until she was appointed to the bench. Involved with the St. Louis County Truancy Court Program in the Valley Park School District. Active in community and youth activities, including UMSL Community Chorus and church groups. Member: Missouri Bar; Bar Association of Metropolitan St. Louis; St. Louis County Bar Association; Lawyers Association; the Women Lawyers Association; Missouri Association of Associate Circuit and Probate Judges, past president. Appointed associate circuit judge on May 11, 1999. Retained in 2000, 2004, 2008 and 2012. Term expires Dec. 31, 2016. Nonpartisan.

Circuit 21—Division 33
NANCY M. WATKINS

Office address: St. Louis County Court Bldg., 105 S. Central Ave., St. Louis 63105; phone (314) 615-8717.

County: St. Louis.

Biography: Lifelong resident of St. Louis County. Graduate of Washington University, B.A. history, 1978; University of Missouri–Columbia, J.D., 1981. Served as law clerk to the Hon. David J. Dixon, Missouri Court of Appeals, Western District, 1981-1982; served on Missouri Public Defender Commission and Missouri Sentencing Advisory Commission and engaged in private practice prior to appointment to the Bench. Appointed Associate Circuit Judge by Gov. Jeremiah (Jay) Nixon in 2014. Term expires Dec. 31, 2018. Nonpartisan.

Circuit 21—Division 34
DALE W. HOOD

Office address: St. Louis County Court Bldg., 105 S. Central Ave., Clayton 63105; phone (314) 615-1534.

County: St. Louis.

Biography: Born Dec. 9, 1950, in Washington. Graduate of University of Missouri–Columbia, B.S. and M.S.; St. Louis University, J.D.; U.S. Army Command and General Staff College, Fort Leavenworth, Kan. Career Army officer, 1973–1990. Assistant prosecuting attorney, St. Louis County, 1999–2005. Member: University of Missouri–Columbia Alumni Association; Association of U.S. Army; 101st Airborne Division Association; and First Presbyterian Church, Kirkwood. Appointed associate circuit judge 2005. Elected in 2008 and 2012. Term expires Dec. 31, 2016. Nonpartisan.

Circuit 21—Division 35
JOHN N. BORBONUS

Office address: St. Louis County Court Bldg., 105 S. Central Ave., Clayton 63105; phone (314) 615-1535.

County: St. Louis.

Biography: Graduate of George Mason University, B.A. government and politics, 1988; St. Louis University School of Law, J.D., 1994. Married with three daughters, and resides in St. Louis County. Principal with law firm of King, Krehbiel, Hellmich & Borbonus, L.L.C.; served for several years as assistant attorney general, State of Missouri. Appointed in 2003 by Gov. Bob Holden to serve as board member on the Missouri Humanities Council until 2010. In 2005, appointed as commissioner Board of Planning and Zoning for the City of Des Peres, until judicial appointment. In 2011, he was appointed to serve as a commissioner on the Missouri Senate Appointment Commission. Member: Leadership St. Louis, Class of 2008–2009. Appointed August 2011 by Gov. Jeremiah (Jay) Nixon. Retained in 2012. Term expires Dec. 31, 2016. Nonpartisan.

Circuit 21—Division 36
VACANCY

Circuit 21—Division 37
JOHN R. ESSNER

Office address: St. Louis County Court Bldg., 105 S. Central Ave., Clayton 63105; phone (314) 615-1537.

County: St. Louis.

Biography: Born on March 12, 1951, in southeast Missouri. Graduate of UCLA, political science, 1973; St. Louis University School of Law, J.D., *cum laude*, 1976. Married with two children. Clerked for the Hon. Theodore McMillian. Worked for Legal Services of Eastern Missouri, from 1978 until being appointed to the bench in July 1999. Handled family court docket. Member: Bar Association of Metropolitan St. Louis; the St. Louis County Bar Association; The Lawyers' Association; The Women Lawyers' Association; the Association of Family and Conciliation Courts; and the National Council of Juvenile and Family Court Judges. Retained in 2012. Term expires Dec. 31, 2016. Nonpartisan.

Circuit 21—Division 38
LAWRENCE J. PERMUTTER

Office address: St. Louis County Court Bldg., 105 S. Central Ave., Clayton 63105; phone (314) 615-1538.

County: St. Louis.

Biography: Born Feb. 14, 1947, in St. Louis. Graduate of University of Missouri–St. Louis, B.A.; Washington University, J.D. Married Darlene Permuter Feb. 28, 1982.Served in U.S. Army Reserve, 1968–1974. Member: Missouri Bar; St. Louis County Bar Association, Rules Committee. Appointed to the associate circuit court 2009. Elected 2010. Re-elected in 2014. Term expires Dec. 31, 2018. Nonpartisan.

Circuit 21—Division 39
PATRICK CLIFFORD

Office address: St. Louis County Court Bldg., 105 S. Central Ave., Clayton 63105; phone (314) 615-1539.

County: St. Louis.

Biography: Graduate of St. Louis University, B.A.; J.D. Elected magistrate judge of St. Louis County, 1978. Engaged in private practice from 1973–1975, specializing in labor relations, federal and general civil practice. Served as an assistant prosecuting attorney for St. Louis County, 1975–1978. Member: The Missouri Bar Association, the St. Louis County Bar Association, the Missouri Association of Probate and Associate Circuit Judges, the Missouri Municipal and Associate Circuit Judges Association, the American Academy of Forensic Sciences, the 94th Infantry Division Alliance and a board member of the American Board of Medicolegal Death Investigators. He has served as a guest lecturer for the Medical/Legal Death Investigators Course at the St. Louis University School of Medicine since 1989. Appointed associate circuit judge in 1982. Elected 1978–2014. Term expires Dec. 31, 2018. Nonpartisan.

Circuit 21—Division 40
DENNIS SMITH

Office address: St. Louis County Court Bldg., 105 S. Central Ave., Clayton 63105; phone (314) 615-1540.

County: St. Louis.

Biography: Born April 19, 1949, in St. Louis. Graduate of Washington University, St. Louis, B.S., applied math and computer science, 1971; Duke University School of Law, Durham, N.C., 1974. Married and has four children. Assistant public defender, St. Louis County, 1975–1977; assistant public defender, St. Charles County, 1977–1978. Private practice of law, 1977–1994. Mayor of Ellisville, 1992–1994. Appointed family court commissioner, St. Louis County, 1994. Co-chair, Missouri Supreme Court Committee on Access to Family Courts, 2008–2009. Appointed associate circuit judge, 1995. Retained in 1998, 2002, 2006, 2010 and 2014. Term expires Dec. 31, 2018. Nonpartisan.

Circuit 21—Division 41
JUDY P. DRAPER

Office address: St. Louis County Court Bldg., 100 S. Central Ave., Clayton 63105; phone (314) 615-1541.

County: St. Louis.

Biography: Graduate of University of North Carolina–Chapel Hill, B.S., labor relations, 1977; Howard University Law School, J.D.; and *Law Journal*, 1980. Former prosecutor for City of St. Louis (assistant circuit attorney); law clerk to Hon. Clyde S. Cahill, federal district court judge. First female general counsel for the Missouri Dept. of Corrections. Engaged in private practice, criminal and civil; adjunct professor of pre-trial practice at Washington University School of Law; municipal judge for the cities of Northwoods and Berkley. Member: Missouri Asian American Bar Association, founding member; Women Lawyer's Association; the Bar Association of Metropolitan St. Louis; St. Louis County Bar Association; National Association of Women Judges; and National Bar Association. Appointed by the Missouri Supreme Court to sit on the Education Committee for the Missouri Municipal and Associate Circuit Judges Association. Former member of the Congressional Committee for Americans with Disabilities. Appointed associate circuit judge 2004. Retained 2006, 2010 and 2014. Term expires Dec. 31, 2018. Nonpartisan.

Circuit 21—Division 42
ROBERT M. HEGGIE

Office address: St. Louis County Court Bldg., 105 S. Central Ave., Clayton 63105; phone (314) 615-1538.

County: St. Louis.

Biography: Born Feb. 3, 1963 in St. Louis. Graduate of Unversity of Missouri–Columbia, B.S., accountancy, 1985; St. Louis University School of Law, J.D., 1991. Married to Jean, 1999. Engaged in private practice from 1991 until his appointment to the bench by Gov. Jeremiah (Jay) Nixon in 2015. City attorney for Chesterfield, 2005-2015. General counsel, The Children's Home Society of Missouri, 1994-2015. Member: Mary Queen of Peace Parish. Term Appointed March 2015. Term expires Dec. 31, 2016. Nonpartisan.

Circuit 21—Division 43
JOSEPH S. DUEKER

Office address: St. Louis County Court Bldg., 105 S. Central Ave., Clayton 63105; phone (314) 615-1543.

County: St. Louis.

Biography: Born Nov. 10, 1966, in St. Louis County. Graduate of the University of Richmond, B.A., *cum laude*; St. Louis University School of Law, J.D. Married to Jane E. Eilermann. They have two children. Engaged in private practice, 1992–1993. Served as assistant prosecuting attorney, St. Louis County, 1993–2010; associate chief trial attorney, St. Louis County, 2008–2010. Member: Christ, Prince of Peace Catholic Church. Appointed associate circuit judge August 13, 2010. Retained in 2012. Term expires Dec. 31, 2016. Nonpartisan.

Circuit 22—Division 14
NICOLE COLBERT-BOTCHWAY

Office address: Civil Courts Building, 10 N. Tucker Blvd., St. Louis 63101; phone (314) 622-4278.

City of Saint Louis.

Biography: Born Sept. 29, in St. Louis City. Graduate of Rosati-Kain High School; St. Louis University, B.A.; St. Louis University School of Law, J.D.; University of Missouri–St. Louis, M.B.A. Served as an Administrative Hearing Commissioner for the State of Missouri when appointed to the Associate Circuit bench by Gov. Jeremiah (Jay) Nixon on July 2, 2015. Assistant circuit attorney for the St. Louis City Circuit Attorney's Office. Elected to the Missouri Bar Board of Governors and has served in several bar and community leadership roles. Membership/Associations: Saint Alphonsus Liguori; "Rock" Catholic Church; American Bar Association; Missouri Bar Association; National Bar Association–Judicial Council; Mound City Bar Association; Women Lawyer's Association of Greater St. Louis; Bar Association of Metropolitan St. Louis; and Lawyers Association of St. Louis. Appointed July 2, 2015. Term expires Dec. 31, 2016.

Circuit 22—Division 24
PAULA P. BRYANT

Office address: Civil Courts Bldg., 10 N. Tucker St., St. Louis 63103; phone (314) 622-4788.

City of St. Louis.

Biography: Born Dec. 2, 1956, in St. Louis. Graduate of the University of Missouri–St. Louis, B.S., 1981; St. Louis University School of Law, J.D., 1983. Married and has two children. Adjunct professor for Webster University, St. Louis. Assistant circuit attorney, 1993–2004; assigned to the Specialized Homicide Unit, later a team leader; and recipient of the Outstanding Trial Attorney award, 2004. Engaged in private practice in St. Louis, 1991–1993; public defender, 1987–1991; and staff attorney for the 22nd Judicial Circuit Court. Active with several bar associations, a member of the Catholic Church and is affiliated with other community and educational organizations. Appointed associate circuit judge 2004. Elected in 2006, 2010 and 2014. Term expires Dec. 31, 2018. Nonpartisan.

Circuit 22—Division 25
VACANCY

Circuit 22—Division 26
CALEA STOVALL-REID

Office address: Carnahan Bldg., 1114 Market, St. Louis 63101; phone (314) 622-4536.

City of St. Louis.

Biography: Born Springfield, Mass. Married and has two children. Graduate of Howard University, Washington, DC, B.A., 1982. Washington University School of Law, J.D., 1990. Corporate counsel to the St. Louis Housing Authority, 1997–2003; litigation associate with the law firm of Peoples and Hale, 1995–1997; assistant circuit attorney with the circuit attorney's office, City of St. Louis, 1993–1995 and an assistant public defender with the Missouri Public Defender's Office St. Louis City litigation office, 1991–1993. Member: Imani A.M.E. Church; Missouri Association of Probate and Associate Judges; the Women Lawyers Association of Greater St. Louis; Mound City Bar Association and the South City YMCA, Volunteer Advisory Board. Teaches part-time at St. Louis Community College. Served as a volunteer judge with truancy court for St. Louis City Public Schools. Appointed associate circuit judge March 2003. Retained in 2012. Term expires Dec. 31, 2016. Nonpartisan.

Circuit 22—Division 27
BARBARA PEEBLES

Office address: Civil Courts Building, 10 N. Tucker St, St. Louis 63101; phone (314) 641-3573.

City of St. Louis.

Biography: Born July 14, 1960, in St. Louis. Graduate of Washington University, B.A, 1982; American University Washington College of Law, J.D., 1986. Previously an assistant city counselor, City of St. Louis; assistant circuit attorney, City of St. Louis; and drug court commissioner, 22nd Judicial Circuit. Member: St. Alphonsus Liguori Rock Catholic Church; National Association of Women Judges; Women Lawyers' Association of Greater St. Louis; and Mound City Bar Association. Appointed associate circuit judge September 2000. Elected in 2002, 2006, 2010 and 2014. Term expires Dec. 31, 2018. Nonpartisan.

Circuit 22—Division 28
THERESA COUNTS BURKE

Office address: Civil Courts Building, 10 N. Tucker St., St. Louis 63101; phone (314) 622-4282.

City of St. Louis.

Biography: Born Oct. 11, 1965, in Granite City, Ill. Graduate of Southern Illinois University at Edwardsville, Ill., B.A., political science, 1985; St. Louis University School of Law, J.D., 1988. Engaged in private practice for 20 years; provisional judge for the Municipal Court of St. Louis City, 2001–2008; and adjunct professor for Fontbonne University OPTIONS program since 2007. Member: Missouri Supreme Court's Committee on Access to Family Courts, 2011; Missouri Association of Probate and Associate Circuit Judges (MAPACJ); Missouri Municipal and Associate Circuit Judges Association (MMACJA); Lawyers for Kids, *ex officio* board member; and Women Lawyers' Association. Appointed as an associate circuit judge Nov. 25, 2008. Retained in 2010 and 2014. Term expires Dec. 31, 2018. Nonpartisan.

Circuit 22—Division 29
THOMAS C. CLARK II

Office address: Carnahan Bldg., 1114 Market St., St. Louis 63101; phone (314) 622-4798.

City of St. Louis.

Biography: Born Dec. 12, 1966, in Kansas City. Graduate of University of Kansas, B.S. history and journalism, 1990; St. Louis University, M.A. public administration, 1993; J.D., 1998. Served as assistant circuit attorney, 1998–2006, City of St. Louis; elected to the young lawyers section of The Missouri Bar Association; and participated in Leadership St. Louis/FOCUS. Member: Missouri Bar Association; St. James the Greater Catholic Church, St. Louis; St. Louis Zoo; and Boy Scouts of America, merit badge counselor. Appointed associate circuit judge Jan. 17, 2006, to fill an unexpired term. Retained in 2008 and 2012. Term expires Dec. 31, 2016. Nonpartisan.

Circuit 23—Division 10
JEFFREY T. COLEMAN

Office address: Jefferson County Courthouse, PO Box 100, Hillsboro 63050; phone (636) 797-5365.

County: Jefferson.

Biography: Not available. Elected November 2014. Term expires Dec. 31, 2018. Republican.

Photo not
available

Circuit 23—Division 11
BRENDA STACEY

Office address: Jefferson County Courthouse, PO Box 100, Hillsboro 63050; phone (636) 797-5453.

County: Jefferson.

Biography: Not available. Elected November 2014. Term expires Dec. 31, 2014. Republican.

Photo not
available

Circuit 23—Division 12
ANTONIO (TONY) MANANSALA

Office address: Jefferson County Courthouse, PO Box 100, Hillsboro 63050; phone (636) 797-5375.

County: Jefferson.

Biography: Born July 1, 1959 in Pueblo, Colo. Graduate of DeSmet High School, St. Louis, 1977; University of Maryland–Far East Division, B.A., business management, 1982; and Washburn University, Topeka, Kan., J.D., 1985. Engaged in private practice, 1985–1993. Employed with the Missouri State Public Defender System from March 1993, to December 2014; as an assistant public defender, district defender, Hillsboro Trial Office; Capital PCR attorney; and district defender, Columbia Trial Office. Recipient of the Defender of Distinction award in 2004. Member: Jefferson County Bar Association. Elected associate circuit judge Nov. 4, 2014. Term expires Dec. 31, 2018. Republican.

Circuit 23—Division 13
PATRICIA RIEHL

Office address: Jefferson County Courthouse, PO Box 100, Hillsboro 63050; phone (636) 797-6020.

County: Jefferson.

Photo not available

Biography: Born August 29, 1957, in St. Louis. Graduate of Southeast Missouri State University, B.S., education; University of Missouri–Kansas City, J.D. Engaged in private practice, 1982–2003. Served as municipal judge for DeSoto and Crystal City, board of directors; Missouri Municipal and Associate Circuit Judge's Association, past president; Jefferson County Bar Association, Disciplinary Hearing officer; and Circuit Bar Committee, member. Member: Missouri Bar Association and Jefferson County Bar Association. Appointed to the bench as drug court commissioner in 2003. Elected associate circuit judge in 2006, 2010 and 2014. Term expires Dec. 31, 2018. Democrat.

Circuit 23—Division 14
TIMOTHY S. MILLER

Office address: Jefferson County Courthouse, PO Box 100, Hillsboro 63050; phone (636) 797-6045.

County: Jefferson.

Biography: Born Oct. 7, 1964, in Festus. Graduate of Festus High School; Southeast Missouri State University, B.S., education, 1989; and Washington University, St. Louis, J.D., 1993. Missouri Army National Guard, 1983–1991. Marrried Christina (Jackson) Miller in 1986; they have two children, Anna and Dylan, and two grandchildren, Emma (2006–2009) and Cameron. Private law practice, 1993–2011. Member: Kiwanis, Elks, MMACJA, Jefferson County Bar Association and Missouri Bar Association. Elected associate circuit judge 2010. Re-elected 2014. Term expires 2018. Democrat.

Circuit 23—Division 15
SHANNON DOUGHERTY

Office address: Jefferson County Courthouse, PO Box 100, Hillsboro 63050; phone (636) 797-6442.

County: Jefferson.

Biography: Born Jan. 11, 1973, in St. Louis. Graduate of Grandview R-2 High School, 1991; University of Missouri, B.A., psychology, *summa cum laude,* 1995; Universite Stendhal, France, summer 1992; and St. Louis University School of Law, J.D., 2002. Married to Christopher Moenster. Mother of one daughter. Probation and parole officer for the State of Missouri, 1995–2001; Jefferson County prosecuting attorney's office, 2001–2006 (assistant prosecuting attorney, 2002–2006). Elected associate circuit judge 2006, 2010 and 2014. Term expires Dec. 31, 2018. Democrat.

Circuit 24
ROBIN EDWARD FULTON

Office address: Madison County Courthouse, PO Box 470, Fredericktown 63645; phone (573) 783-3105.

County: Madison.

Biography: Born July 27, 1953, in Ft. Leonard Wood. Graduate of Southeast Missouri State University, B.A., 1978; University of South Carolina, J.D., 1981. Research editor, *South Carolina Law Review,* 1980. Married Karen Sylvester June 7, 1975; two children, Jacob Fulton (deceased 1997) and Jennifer Detwiler; and one granddaughter, Morgan Detwiler. Served in the private practice of law, 1981–2006. Member: Chamber of Commerce; Rotary Club; Elks Club; 24th Circuit Bar Association; and Missouri Association of Probate and Associate Circuit Judges. Elected associate circuit judge 2006, 2010 and 2014. Term expires Dec. 31, 2018. Democrat.

Circuit 24
JOSEPH L. GOFF JR.
Office address: St. Francois County Courthouse, 1 N. Washington, Ste. 300, Farmington 63640; phone (573) 756-5755.

County: St. Francois.

Photo not available

Biography: Born June 18, 1986, in St. Louis. Graduate of Farmington High School 2004; Southeast Missouri State University, B.S., political science, 2007; St. Louis University, J.D., 2011. Prior to appointment, served as an assistant prosecuting attorney for St. Francois County. Prior practice also includes the Governmental Affairs Division of the Missouri Attorney General's Office in Jefferson City and private practice at the firm of Reeves & Goff, P.C., in Farmington. Appointed in 2015. Term expires Dec. 31, 2016.

Circuit 24
SHAWN R. McCARVER

Office address: St. Francois County Courthouse, 1 N. Washington, Ste. 201, Farmington 63640; phone (573) 756-6601.

County: St. Francois.

Biography: Born May 12, 1960, in Bonne Terre. Graduate of Natl. Honor Society, Central R-3 High School, Park Hills, 1978; Central Missouri State Univ., B.S., *summa cum laude*, 1981; J.D.; *Mo. Law Review*, Univ. of Mo.–Columbia School of Law, 1984. Admitted to Missouri Bar, 1984. Married to Julie Huffman McCarver; one child, Dagny Elizabeth McCarver. Practiced law, 1984–2010. Municipal judge for more than 25 years in Park Hills, Desloge, Bismarck, Bonne Terre and Leadwood. Member: St. Joseph Catholic Church; 24th Circuit Bar Assoc.; Missouri Bar; Missouri Assoc. of Probate and Associate Circuit Judges; and Missouri Municipal and Assoc. Circuit Judges Association, past pres. Serves on the Supreme Court Municipal Judge Education Comm. Served on the faculty of the Judicial College since 1988 and various other commissions and committees. Appointed and serves as tech. advisor to the Supreme Court's Commission on Children's Justice. Authored numerous articles, books and given many presentations on juvenile, family law and adoptions. Elected 2010 and 2014. Term expires Dec. 31, 2018. Democrat.

Circuit 24
TIMOTHY W. INMAN

Office Address: Ste. Genevieve County Courthouse, 55 S. Third St., Ste. Genevieve 63670; phone (573) 883-2265.

County: Ste. Genevieve.

Biography: Born Oct. 7, 1964, in Vinita, Okla. Graduate of Southeast Missouri State University, B.S., business and accounting, 1987; University of Missouri–Kansas City School of Law, J.D., 1990. Private practice, 1990–2010; Ste. Genevieve County prosecuting attorney, 1997–2010. Elected associate circuit judge 2010 and 2014. Term expires Dec. 31, 2018. Democrat.

Circuit 24
TROY HYDE

Office address: Washington County Courthouse, 102 N. Missouri St., Potosi 63664; phone (573) 438-3691.

County: Washington.

Biography: Born Nov. 2, 1962, in St. Louis. Graduate of University of Missouri–St. Louis, B.A., political science; Ohio Northern University, Claude W. Petit College of Law, J.D., 1990. Married Sonya Lawson June 12, 1998. Member: *Ohio Northern Law Review*, lead article research editor; Benevolent Protective Order of Elks, Lodge 2218. Served as assistant public defender, 24th Judicial Circuit, 1990–1992; assistant prosecuting attorney, Washington County, 1993–1995; and private practice of law, 1993–1996. Elected associate circuit judge, 1997. Term expires Dec. 31, 2018. Democrat.

Circuit 25
MARK D. CALVERT

Office address: Phelps County Courthouse, 200 N. Main, Ste. 201, Rolla 65401; phone (573) 458-6246, FAX (573) 458-6224.

County: Phelps.

Biography: Born Oct. 25, 1965 in Norfolk, Va Married to Lisa, 1989; three children. Graduate of Central Methodist College, B.A., English 1988; University of Missouri-Columbia School of Law, J.D., 1991. Engaged in private practice, 1991-2014, with an emphasis in Family Law. Certified Family Law Mediator. Former Board Member, MARCH Mediation, CASA. Member: Missouri Bar Association, Phelps County Bar Association and Optimist Club of Rolla. Elected associate circuit judge 2014. Term expires Dec. 31, 2018. Republican.

Circuit 25
RONALD D. WHITE

Office address: Phelps County Courthouse, 200 N. Main, Ste. 201, Rolla 65401; phone (573) 458-6233.

County: Phelps.

Biography: Born Sept. 10, 1954, at Scott Air Force Base, Ill. Graduate of University of Missouri–Rolla (now Missouri S&T), B.S., economics, 1975; University of Missouri–Columbia School of Law, J.D., 1978. Married to Clarissa since April 7, 1979. Two sons, Aaron and Adam. Engaged in private practice in Rolla for 26 years. Phelps County prosecuting attorney, 1979–1983. Assistant Phelps County prosecuting attorney, 1983–1986. Member: Christ Episcopal Church. Appointed associate circuit judge, Probate Division, Jan. 1, 2005, to fill an unexpired two-year term. Elected associate circuit judge, Probate Division, 2006, 2010 and 2014. Term expires Dec. 31, 2018. Democrat.

Circuit 25
COLIN LONG

Office address: Pulaski County Courthouse, 301 Historic Rt. 66, Ste. 314, Waynesville 65583; phone (573) 774-4786.

County: Pulaski.

Biography: Born Nov. 14, 1969, in Waynesville. Graduate of University of Missouri–Rolla; Oklahoma City University, J.D. Married Courtney Lawson July 27, 2002. They have two children, Connor and Cate. Former partner with Smith, Turley, Long. Member: St. Robert Church of God; Waynesville-St. Robert Chamber of Commerce; former vice chair, Regional Commerce and Growth Association; and Waynesville Masonic Lodge #375 A.F. & A.M. Appointed November 2004. Elected November 2006, 2010 and 2014. Term expires Dec. 31, 2018. Democrat.

Circuit 25
MICHAEL V. HEADRICK

Office address: Pulaski County Courthouse, 301 Historic Rt. 66, Ste. 316, Waynesville 65583; phone (573) 774-4784.

County: Pulaski.

Biography: Born Oct. 22, 1967 in Rolla. Graduate of Waynesville High School, 1986; University of Missouri-Columbia, B.A., political science, 1990; University of Missouri-Kansas City, J.D., 1993. Married to Tammy (1998). Pulaski County prosecutor, elected 1994 and 1998. Associate circuit judge, Probate Division. Elected November 2014. Term expires Dec. 31, 2018. Republican.

Circuit 25
KERRY G. ROWDEN

Office address: Maries County Courthouse, PO Box 490, Vienna 65582; phone (573) 422-3303.

County: Maries.

Biography: Born Dec. 3, 1964. Graduate of Maries R-1 in Vienna, 1983; Lincoln University, 1985, B.A., history; and University of Missouri–Columbia, J.D., 1989. Elected prosecuting atttorney for Miller County, 1990; served four years. Married Wendy Hensley Dec. 29, 1984; they have six children. Elected associate circuit judge November 2010 and 2014. Term expires Dec. 31, 2018. Republican.

Circuit 25
DOUGLAS D. GASTON

Office address: Texas County Courthouse, 519 N. Grand, Ste. 203, Houston 65483; phone (417) 967-3663.

County: Texas.

Biography: Born August 11, 1967, in Houston. Graduate of Houston High School; Southwest Baptist University, B.S.; and University of Arkansas, Little Rock, J.D. Private law practice, 1995–2002; state representative, 1997–98. Texas County prosecuting attorney, 1999–2002. Special assistant, U.S. attorney, 2003–2004. Chief of staff/general counsel, Missouri Senate president *pro tem*, 2004. Missouri deputy state treasurer, 2005–2008. Appointed associate circuit judge 2009. Term expires Dec. 31, 2018. Republican.

Circuit 26—Division 3
AARON G. KOEPPEN

Office address: #1 Court Circle, Ste. 9, Camdenton 65020; (573) 346-4440.

County: Camden.

Biography: Born April 1, 1976, in Anchorage, Alaska; raised in Neosho. Graduate of Utah State University, B.A., 2000; Creighton University, J.D., 2004. Married Nancy Tarbet, 1999. Missouri State Public Defender's Office, 2004–2006. Iberia city prosecutor, 2006–2010. Special prosecutor, Village of Four Seasons, 2009–2010. Camden County assistant prosecuting attorney, 2006–2010. Adjunct professor at Ozark Technical College. Member: The Church of Jesus Christ of Latter-Day Saints and Lake Ozark Rotary. Elected associate circuit judge 2010 and 2014. Term expires Dec. 31, 2018. Republican.

Circuit 26—Division 4
MATTHEW P. HAMNER

Office address: Camden County Courthouse, 1 Court Circle, Ste. 9, Camdenton 65020; phone (573) 346-5160.

County: Camden.

Biography: Born Nov. 18, 1976 in Chesterfield. Graduate of Camdenton High School, 1994; University of Missouri-Columbia, B.A., communications, *cum laude* and Phi Beta Kappa, 1998; University of Missouri-Columbia School of Law, J.D., 2001, Order of the Coif and Order of the Barristers. Law clerk for the Hon. William Ray Price, Jr., Missouri Supreme Court, 2001-2002. Associate with the firm of Rouse, Hendricks, German, May P.C., Kansas City, 2002-2007. Associate and shareholder with the firm of Phillips, McElyea, Carpenter & Welch, P.C., Camdenton, 2007-2014, until election to the bench.
Member: Missouri Bar Association; Kansas Bar Association; 26th Judicial Circuit Bar Association, president; Board of Directors for Camdenton Rotary Club; and Camdenton R-III Education Foundation and Camdenton Laker Athletic Boosters. Elected associate circuit judge for Camden County in 2014. Term expires Dec. 31, 2018. Republican..

Circuit 26
STEVEN JACKSON

Office address: Laclede County Courthouse, 200 N. Adams, Lebanon 65536; phone (417) 532-9196.

County: Laclede.

Biography: Born Dec. 12, 1963. Graduate of Lebanon High School; Missouri State University, B.S.; and University of Arkansas at Little Rock, J.D. Served in private practice of law for more than 19 years, 1991–2010. Past Laclede County Bar president. Began service in the judiciary Jan.1, 2011. Married Angie Wampler on August16, 1994; has two daughters, Pavin and Payne, born in 1995 and 2000. Passions include Laclede County, family and being outdoors. Attends First Baptist Church in Lebanon. Elected associate circuit judge 2010 and 2014. Term expires Dec. 31, 2018. Republican.

Circuit 26
LARRY WINFREY

Office address: Laclede County Courthouse, 200 N. Adams, Lebanon 65536; phone (417) 532-7451.

County: Laclede.

Biography: Born May 4, 1967, in Lebanon. Graduate of the University of Missouri–Columbia, B.S., B.A., 1989; J.D, 1992. Married Sharon Smith on June 21, 1986. Private law practice, 1992–2002. President, Laclede County C-5 Board of Education, 1995–2002. Laclede Early Education Program Board of Directors, 1994–2002. Past president of Laclede County Bar. Adjunct instructor at Ozark Technical Community College. Member: First Baptist Church, Rotary, Laclede Lodge #83 AF & AM and Laclede County Shriners Club. Elected associate circuit judge for Laclede County in 2002, 2006, 2010 and 2014. Term expires: Dec. 31, 2018. Republican.

Circuit 26
JON A. KALTENBRONN

Office address: Miller County Courthouse, 2001 Hwy. 52, Tuscumbia 65082; phone (573) 369-1970.

Photo not available

County: Miller.

Biography: Not available. Elected November 2014. Term expires Dec. 31, 2018. Republican.

Circuit 26
PEGGY RICHARDSON

Office address: Moniteau County Courthouse, 200 E. Main, California 65018; phone (573) 796-4671.

County: Moniteau.

Biography: Born Oct. 8, 1957, in Versailles. Graduate of State Fair Community College, A.S.; University of Central Missouri, B.A.; and University of Missouri–Columbia, J.D. Engaged in private law practice, 1983–1998; former assistant prosecuting attorney, Morgan County. Member: First Baptist Church, Tipton. Municipal judge for Tipton, Clarksburg and Jamestown. Elected associate circuit judge 1998, 2002, 2006, 2010 and 2014. Term expires Dec. 31, 2018. Republican.

Circuit 26
KEVIN SCHEHR

Office address: Morgan County Courthouse, 211 E. Newton, Versailles 65084; phone (573) 378-4235.

County: Morgan.

Biography: Born August 22, 1954, in Cincinnati, Ohio. Graduate of Wabash College, B.A., 1976; master's degree in English from the University of Missouri–Columbia, 1978; and J.D., 1985. Engaged in private practice in Versailles, 1985–2002. Elected associate circuit judge 2002, 2006, 2010 and 2014. Term expires Dec. 31, 2018. Republican.

Circuit 27
DEBRA A. HOPKINS

Office address: Bates County Courthouse, 1 N. Delaware, Butler 64730; phone (660) 679-3311.

County: Bates.

Biography: Born June 19, 1950, in Ft. Worth, Texas. Graduate UMKC, B.A. in History, 1990. UMKC School of Law, 1992, *Urban Lawyer*, publications editor, 1991. Member St. Patrick Catholic Church; Bates County Bar Assoc.; American Bar Assoc., 1992–2000; Probation and Parole CAB, 2000–2004. Married David Hopkins on August 23, 1969; they have four children and ten grandchildren. Appointed April 2009. Elected 2010. Re-elected in 2014. Term expires Dec. 31, 2018. Democrat.

Circuit 27
WAYNE STOTHMANN

Office address: Henry County Courthouse, 100 W. Franklin, Room 212, Clinton 64735; phone (660) 885-7231.

County: Henry.

Biography: Born March 21, 1954, Washington. Graduate of University of Missouri–Columbia, B.S., B.A., *summa cum laude*, 1976; University of Missouri–Columbia School of Law, J.D., 1979. Married Denise Ann Soucie on June 10, 1973; they have three children and four grandchildren. Practiced law in Clinton, 1979–1994. Assistant prosecuting attorney, Henry County, 1979–1980, 1984–1986. Prosecuting attorney, Henry County, 1987–1990. Member: Missouri and Henry County Bar associations; Missouri Association of Probate and Associate Circuit Judges, board of directors, 2007–2011; Missouri Municipal and Associate Circuit Judges' Association, board of directors, 2007–present; Missouri Commission on Judicial Resources 1998–2000; Clinton Area Chamber of Commerce, past member, board of directors; and Clinton Mid-Day Optimist Club, past president and director. Elected 1994, re-elected 1998, 2002, 2006, 2010 and 2014. Term expires Dec. 31, 2018. Democrat.

Circuit 27
JERRY J. RELLIHAN

Office address: St. Clair County Courthouse, 655 Second St., Osceola 64776; phone (417) 646-2421.

County: St. Clair.

Biography: Graduate of Benediction College, Atchison Kan., B.A. in sociology, 1981; University Missouri–Kansas City, J.D., 1984. Principal at Jerry J. Rellinhan PC, general practice, 1984–2014. Past member of MATA, Missouri & Municipal Circuit Judges Association and MMACJA. Elected November 2014. Term expires Dec. 31, 2018. Republican.

Photo not available

Circuit 28
JAMES V. NICHOLS

Photo not available

Office address: Barton County Courthouse, 1004 Gulf, Ste. 204, Lamar 64759; phone (417) 682-2444.

County: Barton.

Biography: Born 1957, Lamar. Graduated Golden City High School, 1976. Missouri State, B.A., economics; University of Missouri–Kansas City School of Law, J.D., 1985, law review. Private practice in Lamar from 1985 to 2014; Barton County prosecuting attorney, 1987–1994; Municipal Judge, City of Lamar, 1994–2014. Elected November 2014. Term expires Dec. 31, 2018.

Circuit 28
THOMAS G. PYLE

Office address: Cedar County Courthouse, P.O. Box 665, Stockton, MO 65785; phone (417) 276-6700, ext. 234.

County: Cedar.

Biography: Eagle Scout, Troop 80, St. Louis. Graduate of Stockton High School, 1974. United States Army enlisted, 1975-78; Honors Graduate Defense Language Institute, Korean language. Graduate Missouri State University, B.A., (major, economics; minor, political science), 1981; University of Missouri-Columbia, J.D., 1983; and University of Denver, LL.M Degree in Natural Resources/Environmental Law, 2005. Outstanding Scholar Award; 2005 graduate of Air War College. Retired USAF Reserve Lt. Col., with more than 30 years military service. Awards include the 2009 AFMC JAG Reservist of the year; the Defense Meritorious Service Medal issued by the Secretary of Defense; and seven Meritorious Service Medals. Elected Associate Circuit Judge for Cedar County in 2014 and took office Jan. 2015. Term expires Dec. 31, 2018. Partisan position.

Circuit 28
DAVID MUNTON

Office address: Dade County Courthouse, 300 W. Water, Greenfield 65661; phone (417) 637-2741.

County: Dade.

Biography: Born March 19, 1958, in Kirkwood. Graduate of Southwest Baptist College, B.S., political science, 1979; University of Missouri–Columbia, J.D., 1982. Married Jeanne Kingland on August 10, 1985. They have three sons and one daughter. Member: Main Street Baptist Church. Clerked for the Hon. George Fannigan, Southern District, 1982–1983. Engaged in private practice in Springfield and Bolivar, 1983–1994. Elected associate circuit judge of Dade County November 1994, 1998, 2002, 2006, 2010 and 2014. Term expires Dec. 31, 2018. Republican.

Circuit 28
NEAL R. QUITNO

Office address: Vernon County Courthouse, 100 W. Cherry, Ste. A, Nevada 64772; phone (417) 667-5016.

County: Vernon.

Biography: Born Jan. 19, 1957, in Houlton, Maine. Graduate of University of Kansas. Bachelor's degree, 1979; J.D., 1982. Married Nora Foster on April 17, 1993; four children. Prosecuting attorney, Vernon County, 1987–1998. Member: St. Mary's Catholic Church. Elected 2006, 2010 and 2014. Term expires Dec. 31, 2018. Democrat.

Circuit 29
JOHN A. NICHOLAS

Office address: Jasper County Courthouse, 302 S. Main, Carthage 64836; phone (417) 358-0450.

County: Jasper.

Biography: Born Dec. 28, 1970 in Oklahoma City, OK. Graduate, University of Oklahoma, B.A. in Economics, 1993. University of Oklahoma, College of Law, J.D., with distinction, 1996. Private practice of law, 1996-2007 with Blanchard, Robertson, Mitchell & Carter, P.C in Joplin, and The Law office of Hensley & Nicholas, LLC, and Assistant Prosecution Attorney, Jasper County Missouri, 2007-2014. Member of Missouri and Oklahoma Bar Associations, and the Jasper County Bar Association, President 2001. Wife Greta and two children, Joseph and Benjamin. Elected November 2014. Term expires Dec. 31, 2018. Republican.

Circuit 29
JOSEPH L. HENSLEY

Office address: Jasper County Courts Bldg., 601 S. Pearl, Rm. 211, Joplin 64801; phone (417) 625-4316.

County: Jasper.

Biography: Born Feb. 4, 1973 in Joplin. Graduate of Webb City High School, 1991; Univ. of Mo.–Columbia, B.A., psychology, *summa cum laude*, 1995; J.D. 1998. Married to Dina, 2000; two children. Practiced law at Neale & Newman, L.L.P., 1998 – 2002; The Hensley Law Firm, LLC , 2002–2007; Chief Legal Counsel for the Jasper County Juvenile Office, 2003–2007; and Law Office of Hensley & Nicholas, LLC, 2007–2014. Adjunct professor at Drury University, 2000-2002. Chair of the Springfield Bar Association's Young Lawyer's Committee, 2000-2002. Missouri Bar Leadership Academy, 2002-2003; and former vice-chair of the Missouri Bar Juvenile Courts and Laws Committee. Certified Mediator by the AAA; Certified Guardian ad Litem. Member: Missouri Bar and Jasper County Bar Association; American Academy of Adoption Attorneys (AAAA); andCarterville Christian Church. Elected Nov. 4, 2014. Term expires Dec. 31, 2018. Republican.

Circuit 29
STEPHEN P. CARLTON

Office address: Jasper County Courthouse., 302 S. Main, Carthage 64836; phone (417) 237-1096.

County: Jasper.

Biography: Graduate of Missouri Southern State University, B.S., 1976; University of Arkansas, J.D., 1979. Married and has three children. Law clerk for the Hon. James Prewitt, Missouri Court of Appeals, Southern District, 1979; assistant public defender, 1980–1986; and private practice, 1980–2002. Member: Jasper County Bar Assoc., past president and secretary; Missouri Southern State University Board of Regents, past president and member, 1993–2003; board of directors, St. John's Regional Medical Center, past chair and member, 1995–2004; board of directors, Arvest Bank, 2000–present; and Missouri Association of Probate and Associate Circuit Judges, 2007–present, president, 2013. Elected associate circuit judge 2002, 2006, 2010 and 2014. Term expires Dec. 31, 2018. Republican.

Circuit 30
MARK B. PILLEY

Office address: Benton County Courthouse, PO Box 37, Warsaw 65355; phone (660) 438-6231.

County: Benton.

Biography: Born Sept. 23, 1952, in Kansas City, Kan. Graduate of the University of Kansas, B.G.S.; Washburn University, J.D., 1978. Married Judy A. Jones on June 3, 1977; they have three children. Engaged in private law practice, 1979–2008. Member: Benton County and Missouri Bar associations, 1992–present; Kansas Bar Association, 1979–2008. Assistant prosecuting attorney of Benton County, 1993–1994. Former city attorney and municipal judge. Former board member of the Warsaw Fire District, TLC Sheltered Workshop, Nelson Rolf Animal Shelter, Lions Club, Free University and library board. Real estate law and wills and estate planning instructor. Appointed associate circuit judge November 2008. Elected 2010 and 2014. Term expires Dec. 31, 2018. Republican.

Circuit 30
LISA HENDERSON

Office address: Dallas County Courthouse, PO Box 1910, Buffalo 65622; phone (417) 345-2243.

County: Dallas.

Biography: Born 1961 in Springfield. Graduate of Central Missouri State University, B.S.; University of Missouri–Columbia School of Law, J.D., 1989. Private law practice, 1989–2010. Member of the Dallas County Bar Association and Missouri Bar Association. Former prosecuting attorney for Hickory County. Former city attorney, Buffalo. Elected in 2010. Re-elected in 2014. Term expires Dec. 31, 2018. Republican.

Circuit 30
JAMES A. HACKETT

Office address: Hickory County Courthouse, PO Box 305, Hermitage 65668; phone (417) 745-6421.

County: Hickory.

Biography: Not available. Appointed 2013. Term expires Dec. 31, 2018. Democrat.

Circuit 30
JOHN PORTER

Office address: Polk County Courthouse, 102 E. Broadway, Rm. 14, Bolivar 65613; phone (417) 326-4912.

County: Polk.

Biography: Born March 21, 1969, in Nevada, Mo. Graduate of Southwest Baptist University, B.S., English; Oklahoma City University, J.D., 1995. Married Jill Thomeczek Dec. 31, 2007. Two daughters: Abbi and Alex. Prosecuting attorney for Polk County 1999–2006. Member: United Methodist Church of Bolivar; Polk County Bar Association. Appointed associate circuit judge 2006. Re-elected 2006, 2010 and 2014. Term expires Dec. 31, 2018. Republican.

Circuit 30
DAVID T. TUNNELL

Office address: Webster County Courthouse, PO Box B, Marshfield 65706; phone (417) 326-2041.

County: Webster.

Biography: Born Nov. 13, 1976, in Springfield. Graduate of Marshfield High School,1994; University of Missouri-Columbia, B.A.,1997; and J.D., 2001. Married Rebecca Floyd Oct. 28, 2006; they have two children, Luke and Lily. Served in private practice at Corbett Law Firm, P.C., 1999-2014. Served on Board of Directors of Web-Co Custom Industries (sheltered workshop), 2002-2008. Member: Missouri, Webster County and Springfield Metropolitan Bar associations. Municipal judge for Marshfield and Rogersville. Member of the Mt. Sinai Christian Church in rural Marshfield. Elected associate circuit judge on Nov. 4, 2014. Term expires Dec. 31, 2018. Republican.

Circuit 30
KENNETH THOMPSON

Office address: Webster County Courthouse, PO Box B, Marshfield 65706; phone (417) 859-2041.

County: Webster.

Biography: Born May 24, 1951, in Louisville, Ky. Graduate of Drury University, B.A.; University of Missouri–Columbia, J.D. Married to Joy Chapman on March 21, 1992. Served in private practice from 1976–2001. Municipal judge for Marshfield, Seymour, Rogersville, Fordland and Niangua. Member of the Marshfield United Methodist Church. Appointed associate circuit judge in 2001 and elected in 2002, 2006, 2010 and 2014. Term expires Dec. 31, 2018. Democrat.

Circuit 31—Division 21
DAN IMHOF

Office address: Judicial Courts Facility, 1010 Boonville, Springfield 65802; phone (417) 868-4097.

County: Greene.

Biography: Born June 19, 1954, in St. Louis. Graduate of Southwest Missouri State University (now Missouri State University), B.S.; University of Missouri–Kansas City, J.D. Married Virginia S. Ratliff May 26, 1991. They have two daughters, Nichole and Megan. Law Clerk for the Hon. Douglas Greene at Missouri Court of Appeals, Southern District; assistant Greene County prosecuting attorney; assistant public defender; and 25 years in private practice. Member: Campbell United Methodist Church; Rotary; Solomon Lodge #271 AF & AM; Scottish Rite; Abou Ben Adhem Shrine Temple; former board member, Easter Seals; Friends of the Zoo, board member; Greene County Republican Central Committee, chair. Elected associate circuit judge in 2006. Retained 2010 and 2014. Term expires: Dec. 31, 2018. Nonpartisan.

Circuit 31—Division 22
MARGARET HOLDEN

Office address: Greene County Courthouse, 1010 Boonville, Springfield 65802; phone (417) 868-4097.

County: Greene.

Photo not available

Biography: Not available. Appointed November 2015. Term expires Dec. 31, 2018. Nonpartisan.

Circuit 31—Division 23
D. ANDREW HOSMER

Office address: Greene County Courthouse, 1010 Boonville, Springfield 65802; phone (417) 868-4095.

County: Greene.

Biography: Born April 2, 1964, in Marshfield. Graduate of University of Missouri-Columbia, B.A., psychology, Phi Beta Kappa, 1986; New York University School of Law, J.D., 1989. Worked as assistant public defender and assistant prosecuting attorney in Greene County; and as assistant Attorney General. Engaged in private practice in Tampa, Fla., 1989-1992; New York, N.Y., 1993-1995; and Springfield, 2000-2014. Appointed associate circuit judge November 2014. Term expires Dec. 31, 2016. Nonpartisan.

Circuit 31—Division 24
MARK POWELL

Office address: Greene County Courthouse, 1010 Boonville, Springfield 65802; phone (417) 829-6546.

County: Greene.

Biography: Born May 10, 1960, in Springfield. Graduate of Missouri State University, B.A., psychology, *cum laude*, 1982; Drake University, J.D., with honors, 1985. Engaged in the practice of law with Miller and Sanford P.C., 1985–2000. Member: First and Calvary Presbyterian Church. Established Truancy Court Program at Reed Middle School. Recipient: Red Cross Everyday Hero Award; Council of Churches Gift of Time Award; and O. Franklin Kenworthy Award for Outstanding Leadership. Circuit Court Budget Committee. Appointed associate circuit judge 2000. Elected: 2000, 2002, 2006, 2010 and 2014. Term expires Dec. 31, 2018. Nonpartisan.

Circuit 31—Division 26
JAMES RONALD CARRIER

Office address: Greene County Courthouse, 1010 Boonville, Springfield 65802; phone (417) 829-6005.

County: Greene.

Biography: Graduate of Mt. Vernon High School, 1982; Drury University, B.A., political science, *magna cum laude*, 1986; and University of Missouri-Columbia School of Law, J.D., 1988. Private practice of law, 1989-1990. Served as assistant prosecuting attorney and prosecuting attorney, Greene County, 1990-1998. Served as assistant Attorney General and Southwest Regional Chief Counsel, Missouri Attorney General's Office, 1999-2013. Member: Springfield Metropolitan Bar Association. Recipient of Dr. John P. Ferguson Award for Child Advocacy. Recognized by U. S. Department of Justice for legal training provided in Republic of Kosovo. Appointed associate circuit judge by Gov. Jeremiah (Jay) Nixon in 2013. Term expires Dec. 31, 2016. Nonpartisan.

Circuit 32
SCOTT E. THOMSEN

Office address: Bollinger County Courthouse, 204 High St., Ste. 4, Marble Hill 63764; phone (573) 238-2730.

County: Bollinger.

Biography: Born June 10, 1964, in Cumberland, Md. Graduate of Brigham Young University, B.S., accounting, 1988; J.D., 1991. Married Joanna Chamberlain March 28, 1992. They have six children. Worked as assistant public defender, 32nd Judicial District. Member: The Church of Jesus Christ of Latter-Day Saints; Missouri, Utah and Nevada Bar associations; Bollinger County Chamber of Commerce; Bollinger County Optimist Club; and The General Society of Mayflower Descendants. Elected associate circuit judge 1994. Re-elected in 1998, 2002, 2006, 2010 and 2014. Term expires Dec. 31, 2018. Republican.

Circuit 32
GARY KAMP

Office address: Cape Girardeau County Courthouse, 100 Court St., Jackson 63755; phone (573) 243-8446.

County: Cape Girardeau.

Biography: Born April 9, 1952, in Cape Girardeau. Graduate of Jackson High School, 1970; Southeast Missouri State University, 1975, B.A.; University of Missouri– Columbia, 1978, J.D. Married Gail Friedrich Sept. 21, 1985. Member of Missouri National Guard, 1970–76. Assistant prosecuting attorney, Bollinger County, 1978–1989; Cape Girardeau County, 1989. Member: St. Paul Lutheran Church; Jackson Chamber of Commerce; American Legion Post 158, life member, former commander and second vice commander; Cape Girardeau County Bar Association, former president; United States Jaycees; Cape Area Friends of the NRA, president, endowed life member; Missouri Association of Probate and Associate Judges, past board of directors, member and presently chair of the Legislative Committee; and Missouri Municipal and Associate Circuit Judges Association, presently a member of the board of directors. Elected as judge, 1994, 1998, 2002, 2006, 2010 and 2014. Term expires Dec. 31, 2018. Republican.

Circuit 32
SCOTT A. LIPKE

Office address: Common Pleas Courthouse, 44 N. Lorimier, Cape Girardeau 63701; phone (573) 334-6249.

County: Cape Girardeau.

Biography: Born March 28, 1969. Graduate of Murray State University, B.S., political science; Valparaiso University School of Law, J.D. Married to Ashley Hobbs. They have three children. Previously engaged in private practice and also served as assistant prosecuting attorney, Cape Girardeau County. Elected state representative, 2002–2008. Chair, Crime Prevention Committee. Elected associate circuit judge 2010. Re-elected in 2014. Term expires Dec. 31, 2018. Republican.

Circuit 32
CRAIG D. BREWER

Office address: Perry County Courthouse, 15 W. Ste. Marie, Ste. 2, Perryville 63775; phone (573) 547-7861.

County: Perry.

Biography: Born Oct. 22, 1971, in Perryville. Graduate of St. Vincent High School, 1990; University of Missouri-Columbia, B.A., political science and English, 1994; University of Missouri-Columbia, J.D., 1998. Married A. Lauren Brazel July 27, 1996; they have three children, Grace, Kate and Max. Practiced law at Eng & Woods in Columbia, 1998-1999; The Brewer Law Firm, P.C., 1999-2013; and Arbeiter & Brewer, 2013-2014, in Perryville. Member: St. Vincent de Paul Catholic Church; Perryville Chamber of Commerce, 1999-present; Perry County Economic Development Authority, 2000-present; Perryville Development Corporation, 2001-present; Knights of Columbus, Fourth Degree; St. Vincent Alumni Association , president, 2010-2015. Elected associate circuit judge 2014. Term expires Dec. 31, 2018. Independent.

Circuit 33
ROB BARKER

Office address: Mississippi County Courthouse, PO Box 369, Charleston 63834; phone (573) 638-2146.

County: Mississippi.

Biography: Graduate of East Prairie High School, 1986; Missouri Southern State University, B.S., criminal justice administration, 1993; Southern Illinois University, J.D., 2004. Twelve years experience as a law enforcement officer. Worked in Missouri Public Defender's Office, 2004-2006; engaged in private general practice, 2006-2014; appointed as Municipal Judge for the City of East Prairie, 2012; and member and current president of Mississippi County Bar Association. Elected Mississippi County associate circuit judge, 2015. Term expires Dec. 31, 2018. Democrat.

Circuit 33
SCOTT HORMAN

Office address: Scott County Judicial Bldg., PO Box 587, Benton 63736; phone (573) 545-3576.

County: Scott.

Biography: Born Sept. 2, 1975, in southeast Missouri. Graduate of Central Methodist University, B.S., *summa cum laude*; University of Missouri–Columbia, J.D. Married Leslie Garner June 7, 1997. They have two sons, Garner and Griffin. Engaged in private law practice in Oct. 2000. Member: St. Augustine Catholic Church; Chaffee Chamber of Commerce; Knights of Columbus; Elks; and Chaffee Youth League. Elected associate circuit judge 2006, 2010 and 2014. Term Expires Dec. 31, 2018. Republican.

Circuit 33
W.H. WINCHESTER III

Office address: Scott County Courthouse, 131 S. Winchester St., PO Box 587, Benton 63736; phone (573) 545-3511.

County: Scott.

Biography: Born Oct. 27, 1946. Graduate of the University of Missouri, B.S.; University of Missouri Law School, J.D. Engaged in the private practice of law, 1973–1998. Member: Missouri and Scott County Bar associations. Served for five years as secretary-treasurer of the Missouri Association of Probate and Associate Circuit Judges, serving on the state fine collection committee. Elected associate circuit judge 1998–2014. Term expires Dec. 31, 2018. Democrat.

Circuit 34
JOSHUA D. UNDERWOOD

Office address: New Madrid County Courthouse, 450 Main St., New Madrid 63869; phone (573) 748-5556.

Photo not available

County: New Madrid.

Biography: Born Feb. 10, 1981, in Sikeston. Graduate of Portageville High School; Mississippi State University, B.B.A.; and Mississippi College School of Law, J.D. Married Lou Oliver August 11, 2007. They have one daughter, Emmaline, and one son, J. Douglas. Engaged in the private practice of law in Caruthersville, 2007–2010, and New Madrid, 2010–2013. Member: The Missouri Bar, 34th Judicial Circuit Bar Association and Missouri Association of Probate and Associate Circuit Judges. Appointed by Gov. Jeremiah (Jay) Nixon in 2013. Elected November 2014. Term expires Dec. 31, 2018. Democrat.

Circuit 34
W. KEITH CURRIE

Office address: Pemiscot County Courthouse, 610 Ward Ave., Ste. 2E, Caruthersville 63830; phone (573) 333-0152.

County: Pemiscot.

Biography: Born Dec. 20, 1964, in Hayti. Graduate of Caruthersville High School; Mississippi State University, B.B.A.; University of Missouri, J.D. Married Deborah Cybulski May 9, 1992. They have two daughters, Anne Marie and Ellen. Engaged in the private practice of law in Jefferson City, 1990–1992, and Hayti, 1992–2003. Elder at First Presbyterian Church of Caruthersville. Member: The Missouri Bar; 34th Judicial Circuit Bar Association; and Missouri Association of Probate and Associate Circuit Judges. Elected in 2002, 2006, 2010 and 2014. Term expires Dec. 31, 2018. Democrat.

Circuit 34
WILLIAM W. CARTER

Office address: Pemiscot County Justice Center, PO Box 228, Caruthersville 63830; phone (573) 333-2784.

Photo not available

County: Pemiscot.

Biography: Not available. Elected November 2014. Term expires Dec. 31, 2018. Democrat.

Circuit 35
H. MARK PREYER

Office address: Dunklin County Courthouse, PO Box 466, Kennett 63857; phone (573) 888-3272.

County: Dunklin.

Photo not available

Biography: Born Feb. 24, 1958, in Poplar Bluff. Graduate of the University of Missouri–Columbia, College of Agriculture, B.S., agricultural economics, 1980; University of Missouri–Columbia School of Law, J.D., 1983. Married Amy Phillips July 7, 2007. They share five children: Erin Preyer, Eric Preyer, Jake Phillips, Emma Phillips and Audrey Phillips. Previously served on Missouri Public Defender Commission and on the Missouri Highway and Transportation Commission. Member: Kennett Chamber of Commerce, Kiwanis Club, Farmers and Merchants Club of Holcomb and of Homersville. Engaged in the practice of law in Kennett, 1983–2010. Elected associate circuit judge in 2010 and 2014. Term expires Dec. 31, 2018. Democrat.

Circuit 35
JOHN SPIELMAN

Office address: Dunklin County Courthouse, Rm. 103, Kennett 63857; phone (573) 888-3378.

County: Dunklin.

Biography: Born May 11, 1972, in Missouri. Graduate of Wichita State University, B.A. political science, 1990; St. Louis University, J.D., 1997. Married Julie Bartlett April 28, 2001. They have two children, Barbara (Ara) Gray and Meagan Grace. Member: First United Methodist Church of Kennett, Kiwanis Club of Kennett, Farmers & Merchants Club of Holcomb and Masonic Lodge, A.F. & A.M. of Kennett. Elected 2006, 2010 and 2014. Term expires Dec. 31, 2018. Democrat.

Circuit 35
JOE Z. SATTERFIELD

Office address: Stoddard County Courthouse, P.O. Box 30 Bloomfield 63825; phone (573) 568-4671.

County: Stoddard.

Biography: Born in Dexter. Graduate of Southeast Missouri State University, B.S., business administration; University of Missouri–Columbia, J.D. Engaged in private law practice in Dexter at Parsons, Mitchell, Wilson and Satterfield, 1982–1995. Appointed associate circuit judge 1995. Elected 1996, 1998, 2002, 2006, 2010 and 2014. Term expires Dec. 31, 2018. Democrat.

Circuit 35
STEPHEN R. MITCHELL

Office address: Stoddard County Justice Center, PO Box 30, Bloomfield 63825; phone (573) 568 2181.

County: Stoddard.

Biography: Born in Poplar Bluff. Undergraduate and law degree from University of Missouri–Columbia. Practiced law in Dexter. Former director Missouri Association of Probate and Associate Circuit Judges. Judicial Conference Executive Council, 2002–present. Missouri Supreme Court Trial Judge Education Committee, 1999–present. Elected associate circuit judge in Stoddard County, serving from 1995–present. Term expires Dec. 31, 2018. Democrat.

Circuit 36
JOHN BLOODWORTH

Office address: Butler County Courthouse, 100 S. Main, Poplar Bluff 63901; phone (573) 686-8087.

County: Butler.

Biography: Born May 29, 1954, in Poplar Bluff. Recipient of B.S.E. in social studies from Arkansas State Univ., Jonesboro, 1976; and J.D. from Univ. of Arkansas, Fayetteville, 1980. Married Dr. Dorothy M. Munch in 1993, with one child born of the marriage. Practiced law for 17 years prior to being elected as an associate circuit judge in 1998. Past/present member of the Commerce Bank Board of Directors; Kenny Roger's Children's Foundation; Poplar Bluff Chamber of Commerce; Missouri Bar Association; Member and past president of the Butler County Bar Association; board member of the Claudia Foundation; Academic Assistance Group and Veteran's Tour. Awarded Elk's Officer of the Year, 2008, for the Butler/Ripley County Drug Court Programs. Term expires Dec. 31, 2018. Democrat.

Circuit 36
JOHN H. SHOCK

Office address: Butler County Courthouse, 100 N. Main, Poplar Bluff 63901; phone (573) 686-8073.

Photo not
available

County: Butler.

Biography: Not available. Elected November 2014. Term expires Dec. 31, 2018. Republican.

Circuit 36
THOMAS SWINDLE

Office address: Ripley County Courthouse, 100 Court Sq., Doniphan 63935; phone (573) 996-2013.

County: Ripley.

Biography: Born in Wood River, Ill., August 12, 1956. Graduate of Southeast Missouri State University, B.A., 1978, legal education; Salmon P. Chase College of Law, Northern Kentucky University, J.D., 1981. Admitted to the Bar in 1983. Assistant prosecuting attorney, Ripley County, 1983–1984. Elected associate circuit judge November 2006, 2010 and 2014. Term expires Dec. 31, 2018. Republican.

Circuit 37
MICHAEL LIGONS

Office address: PO Box 578, Van Buren 63965; phone (573) 323-4344.

Photo not
available

County: Carter.

Biography: Not available. Took office Jan. 1, 2007. Term expires Dec. 31, 2018. Republican.

Circuit 37
DON M. HENRY

Office address: Howell County Courthouse, 222 Courthouse, West Plains 65755; phone (417) 256-4050.

County: Howell.

Biography: Born Oct. 28, 1949, in Springfield. Graduate of the University of Missouri, B.S., 1971; and University of Arkansas, J.D., 1973. Married with two children. Member: First United Methodist Church; Rotary; Chamber of Commerce; 37th Judicial Circuit Bar Association, former president; and Missouri Bar Association. Former member of Pro Se Commission, Missouri Association of Trial Attorneys and American Trial Lawyers Association. Associate circuit judge since June 2002. Term expires Dec. 31, 2018. Democrat.

Circuit 37
TRUMAN WILES

Office address: Howell County Courthouse, 222 Courthouse, West Plains 65755; phone (417) 256-4050.

County: Howell.

Biography: Born June 18, 1958, in Jonesboro, Ark. Graduate of University of Missouri–Columbia, B.S., with honors; University of Illinois–Champaign Urbana, J.D., 1983. Married Pamela Lynne Reagan May 17, 1980. They have one daughter. Member: Pomona Christian Church and Rotary Club. City attorney for West Plains, 1985–1987. Elected associate circuit judge in 2006, 2010 and 2014. Term expires Dec. 31, 2018. Republican.

Circuit 37
HARVEY S. ALLEN

Photo not available

Office address: Oregon County Courthouse, P.O. Box 406, Alton 65606; phone (417) 778-7461.

County: Oregon.

Biography: Born Dec. 20, 1960, in Mammoth Spring, Ark. Graduate of Southwest Missouri State University, B.S., 1983; University of Missouri–Kansas City, J.D., 1985. Married Marcia Cozort in 1982. Thayer Church of Christ deacon. Member: Missouri Association of Probate and Associate Circuit Judges, Thayer Area Chamber of Commerce and Thayer-Mammoth Spring Rotary Club. Thayer city attorney, 1991–2003. Elected associate circuit judge November 2010 and 2014. Term expires Dec. 31, 2018. Republican.

Circuit 37
SANDRA WEST

Office address: Shannon County Courthouse, PO Box 148, Eminence 65466; phone (573) 226-3315.

County: Shannon.

Biography: Born March 6, 1974. Graduate of Drury University, B.A.; University of Missouri–Kansas City School of Law, J.D. Married to Vance West. Engaged in private practice in Eminence, 2000–2006. Served as prosecuting attorney of Shannon County, 2004–2006. City attorney for Eminence, Winona and Birch Tree. Member of Missouri Association of Probate and Associate Circuit Judges. Elected 2006, 2010 and 2014. Term expires Dec. 31, 2018. Democrat.

Circuit 38
LARRY LUNA

Office address: Christian County Judicial Center, 110 W. Elm, Rm. 203, Ozark 65721; phone (417) 582-5140.

County: Christian.

Biography: Born June 28, 1948, in Gainesville. Graduate of University of Missouri–Columbia, B.S., 1970; University of Missouri–Kansas City, J.D., 1973. Married to Laurie M. Dale; they have 3 children and reside in Christian County. Prosecuting attorney of Ozark County, 1974–1980. General law practice and worked in private sector in southwest Missouri, 1980–2006. Recognition from Legal Services of Southwest Missouri for his volunteer work. Member: Missouri Association of Associate and Probate Judges, Juvenile Courts & Laws Committee and the Family Law Section of The Missouri Bar. Elected associate circuit judge in 2006, 2010 and 2014. Term expires Dec. 31, 2018. Republican.

Circuit 38
DOUGLAS P. BACON

Office address: Christian County Courthouse, 110 W. Elm, Rm. 105, Ozark 65721; phone (417) 582-5160.

Photo not available

County: Christian.

Biography: Not available. Elected November 2014. Term expires Dec. 31, 2018. Republican.

Circuit 38
TONY WILLIAMS

Office address: Taney County Courthouse, PO Box 129, Forsyth 65653; phone (417) 546-7212.

County: Taney.

Biography: Not available. Elected November 2000. Re-elected 2002, 2006, 2010 and 2014. Term expires Dec. 31, 2018. Republican.

Circuit 38
ERIC D. EIGHMY

Office address: Taney County Courthouse, PO Box 1030, Forsyth 65653; phone (417) 546-7206.

Photo not available

County: Taney.

Biography: Not available. Elected November 2014. Term expires Dec. 31, 2018. Republican.

Circuit 39
JOHNNIE E. COX

Office address: Barry County Judicial Center, 102 W. St., Ste. 2, Cassville 65625; phone (417) 847-3133.

County: Barry.

Biography: Born August 12, 1974 in Cassville. Attended Cassville High School; Missouri Southern State College, 1997, B.S. Criminal Justice Admin.; University of Missouri-Kansas City, J.D., 2000. Assistant prosecuting attorney for Taney County 2000-02. Elected Barry County Prosecuting Attorney in 2002, re-elected in 2006 and 2010. Member of the SVP prosecuting attorney review committee, Monett Children's Center Advisory Board, Cassville Rotary Club, Missouri Farm Bureau. Married Megan Gibson in 2004 and they have 3 children. Member of the Cassville First Baptist Church and also attends Cassville United Methodist Church. Elected associate circuit judge in 2014. Term expires Dec. 31, 2018. Republican.

Circuit 39
ROBERT J. FOULKE

Office address: 102 West St., Ste. 2, Cassville 65625; phone (417) 847-3133.

County: Barry.

Biography: Born Oct. 14, 1966 in Winnebago, Minn. Graduate of Southwest Missouri State University (now Missouri State University), B.S., 1990; University of Missouri–Kansas City, J.D., 1999. Married Nancy Lawrence March 3, 1998. One son, Evan. Assistant prosecuting attorney of Barry County. Private practice of law, Cassville. Current 39th Circuit Bar Association president and 2002 39th Circuit Bar Association president. Served YMCA board. Member: First Baptist Church, Cassville. Elected associate circuit judge of Barry County, 2010 and 2014. Term expires, Dec. 31, 2018. Republican.

Circuit 39
SCOTT S. SIFFERMAN

Office address: Lawrence County Courthouse, 240 N. Main St., Ste. 110, Mt. Vernon 65712; phone (417) 466-2471.

County: Lawrence.

Biography: Graduate of the University of Missouri–Columbia, B.S. and M.S.; University of Missouri–Kansas City, J.D. Prosecuting attorney for Lawrence County, 1982–1989. Engaged in the private practice of law, 1980–1989. Past president of the 39th Judicial Circuit and a past board member of the Missouri Association of Probate and Associate Circuit Judges. Associate circuit judge for Lawrence County since 1989. Term expires Dec. 31, 2018. Republican.

Circuit 39
ROBERT E. GEORGE

Office address: Lawrence County Justice Center, 240 N. Main St., Suite 110, Mount Vernon 65712; phone 417-466-2471.

County: Lawrence.

Biography: Born Kirksville. Graduate of Mt. Vernon High School; Missouri Southern State College, A.S., law enforcement; B.S., criminal justice; and Tulsa University College of Law, J.D., 1986. Private practice in Aurora, 1989-2000. Elected prosecuting attorney Lawrence County, 1989-2010. Married to Sherrie; two daughters, Heather and Holly; grandchildren Conner and Chloe. Past President of Missouri Association of Prosecuting Attorneys; Missouri Office of Prosecution Services, past president; Children's Center, past president and board member; Drury College, past adjunct professor; PACARS retirement board, chairman; Mt. Vernon Rotary, past president. Certified trial advocacy instructor vehicle homicide. Trial advocacy instructor Missouri Association of Prosecuting Attorney. Aurora city attorney, 1992-95. Served on the Supreme Court Committee dealing with court consolidation issues. Member: Aurora United Methodist Church. Elected November 2014. Term expires Dec. 31, 2018. Republican.

Circuit 39
ALAN BLANKENSHIP

Office address: Stone County Courthouse, 110 S. Maple, Ste. F, Galena 65656; phone (417) 357-6511.

County: Stone.

Biography: Born June 14, 1961, in Neosho. Graduate of University of Arkansas and Missouri Southern State University, B.S., B.A., accounting; University of Missouri, J.D.; and certified public accountant, 1987. Married Dee Ann Casey June 27, 1987; they have three children. Served on the professional audit staff with the Missouri State Auditor's Office, 1984–1987. Served in private law practice, 1991–2002. Served as municipal judge for Kimberling City and Branson West. Member: Judicial Weighted Workload Steering Committee; Trial Judge Education Committee; Living Word Church; and American Legion Missouri Boys State Executive Committee. Elected associate circuit judge 2002, 2006, 2010 and 2014. Term expires Dec. 31, 2018. Republican.

Circuit 39
MARK A. STEPHENS

Office address: Stone County Courthouse, PO Box 18, Galena 65656; phone (417) 357-6114.

County: Stone.

Biography: Born Oct. 29, 1956, Wichita, Kan. Served in U.S. Army Military Police Corps, 1978–1985. Graduate of WSU, B.S., administration of justice, *cum laude*; University of Missouri–Columbia, J.D., 1994. Married to Monica H. Stephens; they have four children and five grandchildren. He lives in the Ozarks, near Crane. Member: Hurley Community Baptist Church; Missouri Bar Association; Missouri Association of Probate and Associate Judges; Southern Gospel Music Association; private practice, Van Matre & Harrison, Columbia, 1994–1999; and solo general practice, Aurora, 1999–2009. Elected as associate circuit judge, 2009. Term expires Dec. 31, 2018. Republican.

Circuit 40
JOHN LEPAGE

Office address: McDonald County Courthouse, PO Box 157, Pineville 64856; phone (417) 223-4487.

County: McDonald.

Biography: Born in Jefferson City, Oct. 3, 1957. Graduate of Bemidji State University, B.A., 1980; University of Missouri–Columbia, J.D., 1983. Married to Marci G. McNeill; they have two children, Melodi Gerstner and Trista LePage, and two grandchildren. Member: Anderson United Methodist Church. Former board member and past president of Missouri Association of Probate and Associate Judges. Judicial Records Committee , 2005–present. Elected 1998, 2002, 2006, 2010 and 2014. Term expires Dec. 31, 2018. Republican.

Circuit 40
KEVIN SELBY

Office address: Newton County Courthouse, 101 S. Wood St., Ste. 204, Neosho 64850; phone (417) 451-8231.

Counties: Newton and McDonald.

Biography: Born June 10, 1965, in Joplin. Graduate of Webb City High School, 1983; University of Kansas, 1988; and McGeorge School of Law, Sacramento, Calif., 1992. Elected associate circuit judge, Division 3, Nov. 2002, 2006, 2010 and 2014. Term expires Dec. 31, 2018. Republican.

Circuit 40
GREGORY N. STREMEL

Office address: Newton County Courthouse, 101 S. Wood, Neosho 64850; phone (417) 451-8212.

County: Newton.

Biography: Born July 1, 1954, in Joplin. Graduate of McAuley High School in Joplin; Missouri Southern State College, A.S., computer programming, and B.S., B.A., general business, 1980; and University of Missouri–Columbia, 1983 J.D. Engaged in private practice from 1983–1992. Appointed by Gov. John Ashcroft as associate circuit judge Dec. 8, 1992. Elected 1994, 1998, 2002, 2006, 2010 and 2014. Term expires Dec. 31, 2018. Republican

Circuit 41
PHILLIP E. PREWITT

Office address: Macon County Courthouse, 100 East Washington Street, Macon 63552; phone (660) 385-4631.

County: Macon.

Biography: Born August 24, 1967, in Moberly. Graduate of Washington University, B.A., 1989; J.D., 1992; U.S. Army Armor School, Ft. Knox, Ky., 1993; and U.S. Army Transportation School, Ft. Eustis, Va., 1995. Married with two children. Engaged in private practice, 1993–2010. Also served as city attorney for Atlanta and Bevier. Awarded the Conspicuous Service Medal by the State of Missouri in 2005 for pro bono legal work on behalf of military service members and their families. Former commissioner, Missouri Veterans Commission. Elected associate circuit judge 2010. Re-elected 2014. Term expires Dec. 31, 2018. Republican.

Circuit 41
MIKE GREENWELL

Office address: Shelby County Courthouse, PO Box 206, Shelbyville 63469; phone (573) 633-2251.

County: Shelby.

Biography: Born Nov. 8, 1959, in Hannibal. Graduate of South Shelby High School, 1978; Northeast Missouri State University (now Truman State University), B.S., agriculture, 1983; University of Dayton, J.D., 1986. Married Marcia Love August 4, 1984. Engaged in the private practice of law in Shelbina, 1986–2010. Member: Missouri Ethics Commission, 1998–2002, chair 2001–2002; Missouri Bar Association Board of Governors, 2001–2008; Truman State University Board of Governors, 2008–2011; American Bar Association; Missouri Bar Association; 41st Circuit Bar Association; Shelbina Lions Club; Knights of Columbus; and St. Mary's Catholic Church. Elected associate circuit judge 2010. Re-elected in 2014. Term expires Dec. 31, 2018. Democrat.

Circuit 42
SCOTT BERNSTEIN

Office address: Crawford County Courthouse, PO Box 1550, Steelville 65565; phone (573) 775-2149.

County: Crawford.

Biography: Born May 15, 1961, in St. Louis. Graduate of Clayton High School, 1979; University of Missouri–Columbia, B.S., Honors College, 1984; College of William & Mary, M.B.A., 1988; St. Louis University, J.D., *cum laude*, *Pubic Law Review*, 1992. Judicial clerkships at Missouri Court of Appeals, Eastern District, for Albert Stephen Jr. and Clifford Ahrens, and U.S. District Court, Clyde Cahill. Associate with Brown and James, P.C. Sole practitioner, 1998–2006. Assistant prosecutor for Crawford and Dent counties. Member: A & A Free Mason and Scottish Rite, Quad County volunteer firefighter and EMT. Elected associate circuit judge 2006, 2010 and 2014. Term expires Dec. 31, 2018. Democrat.

Circuit 42
BRANDI L. BAIRD

Office address: Dent County Judicial Building, 112 East Fifth Street, Salem 65560; phone (573)729-3134.

County: Dent

Biography: Born Oct. 26, 1972, in Rolla. Graduate of John F. Hodge High School, St. James, 1990; Central Missouri State University, B.S., 1996; University of Missouri–Kansas City, J.D., 2000. Married Brandon D. Schloemer; they have two sons, Maxton and Madden. Legislative and constituent director to the Missouri Speaker of the House, 2001–2003. Engaged in private practice, 2004–2010. Dent County prosecuting attorney, 2010–2011. Member: the Salem Lutheran Church. Term expires Dec. 31, 2018. Democrat.

Circuit 42
RANDALL HEAD

Office address: Iron County Courthouse, 250 S. Main St., Ste. 220, Ironton 63650; phone (573) 546-2511.

County: Iron.

Biography: Born Sept. 24, 1951, in Clayton. Graduate of Southeast Missouri State University, B.A.; University of Missouri–Columbia, J.D. Married to Paula Head. Member of St. Paul's Lutheran Church, Ironton. Served in United States Marine Corps, 1969–1971; Vietnam veteran; Veterans of Foreign Wars, life member. Prosecuting attorney for Iron County, 1981–1990. Member of Life Endowment, NRA; NRA basic handgun instructor; P.O.S.T.-certified law enforcement handgun and shotgun instructor; and Missouri concealed carry instructor. Term expires Dec. 31, 2018. Democrat.

Circuit 42
EDITH R. RUTTER

Office address: Reynolds County Courthouse, PO Box 39, Centerville 63633; phone (573) 648-2494.

County: Reynolds.

Biography: Born August 18, 1953, in Leitchfield, Ky. Graduate of Western Kentucky University, B.S., accounting; University of Louisville, J.D. Clerked for Kentucky Supreme Court 1989–1990. Elected associate circuit judge in Reynolds County 1998, 2002, 2006, 2010 and 2014. Term expires Dec. 31, 2018. Democrat.

Circuit 42
RANDY P. SCHULLER

Office address: Wayne County Courthouse, PO Box 78, Greenville 63944; phone (573) 224-5600.

County: Wayne.

Biography: Born May 23, 1955, in St. Louis. Graduate of Drake University, B.S., business administration, *cum laude*, 1977; University of Missouri, J.D., 1980. Prosecuting attorney, Wayne County, 1983–1986. Member: Trinity United Methodist Church; Piedmont Rotary Club; 42nd Circuit Bar Association; Missouri Bar Association; and Eastern and Western Districts of U.S. District Court of Missouri. Elected Wayne County associate circuit judge 1990. Re-elected 1994, 1998, 2002, 2006, 2010 and 2014. Term expires Dec. 31, 2018. Democrat.

Circuit 43
JASON KANOY

Office address: Caldwell County Courthouse, PO Box 68, Kingston 64650; phone (816) 586-2771.

County: Caldwell.

Biography: Not available. Took office Jan. 1, 2007. Term expires Dec. 31, 2018. Independent.

Circuit 43
TERESA L. BINGHAM

Office address: Clinton County Courthouse, PO Box 275, Plattsburg 64477; phone (816) 539-3755.

County: Clinton.

Photo not available

Biography: Born in St. Louis. Graduate of Washburn University, B.A., *cum laude*; University of Kansas School of Law, J.D. She began practicing law with the law firm of Morrison, Frost and Olsen in Manhattan, Kan. She then returned to Kansas City and practiced law with the Jackson County Public Administrator for 12 years. Before being elected as Clinton County Associate Judge, she practiced with UAW Legal Services plan, doing most of the estate planning and probate work. She is married with two adult children. She has been involved with a Science Olympiad coach, Girl Scouts as a Leader and is also a part time youth leader for two rural churches. Elected November 2014. Term expires Dec. 31, 2018.

Circuit 43
DAREN L. ADKINS

Office address: Daviess County Courthouse, PO Box 233, Gallatin 64640; phone (660) 663-2532.

County: Daviess.

Biography: Born Nov. 13, 1967, in Bethany. Graduate of Baylor University, B.A., 1990; University of Tulsa School of Law; University of Missouri–Kansas City, J.D. Miller, Seidel, & Havens associate, 1994–1997. Miller, Seidel, Havens, & Adkins, LLP, 1997–1999. Member: Gallatin Rotary Club, past president; Gallatin Area Revitalization Alliance, vice president; Daviess County Fair Board; Gallatin United Methodist Church; Gallatin R-V School Board, 1996–1999; and Daviess County Library Board, vice president, 2000–present. Associate circuit judge, Daviess County, 1999–present. Term expires Dec. 31, 2018. Democrat.

Circuit 43
BART SPEAR

Office address: DeKalb County Courthouse, 109 West Main Street, P.O. Box 248, Maysville, 64469; phone (816) 449-2602

County: DeKalb.

Biography: Born Dec. 18, 1958. Graduate of Central Methodist College, B.A., 1981; University of Missouri–Columbia School of Law, J.D., 1984. Engaged in private practice in Cameron, 1984–2009; assistant prosecuting attorney, DeKalb County, 1990–1994; appointed DeKalb County prosecuting attorney by Gov. Mel Carnahan, 1994; assistant child support enforcement prosecuting attorney, 43rd Judicial Circuit, 1995; and elected DeKalb County prosecuting attorney, 1998, 2002 and 2006. Serves on Clinco Sheltered Industries board of directors. Member: Cameron Elks Lodge No. 2615, Cameron United Methodist Church, Maysville Area Chamber of Commerce and Fairport Lions Club. Appointed associate circuit judge by Gov. Jeremiah (Jay) Nixon, 2009. Elected associate circuit judge 2010. Re-elected in 2014. Term expires Dec. 31, 2018. Democrat.

Circuit 43
JAMES P. VALBRACHT

Office address: Livingston County Courthouse, 700 Webster, Chillicothe 64601; phone (660) 646-8000.

County: Livingston.

Biography: Born Sept. 23, 1953, in Carrollton. Graduate of Central Missouri State University, B.S., 1977; University of Missouri–Columbia, J.D., 1977. Member: Missouri Bar; Livingston County Bar; United Methodist Church; and Chillicothe Elks Lodge 656. Engaged in private practice of law, 1978–2006. Elected associate circuit judge 2006, 2010 and 2014. Term expires Dec. 31, 2018. Republican.

Circuit 44
ELIZABETH BOCK

Office address: Douglas County Courthouse, 203 SE Second Ave., PO Box 249, Ava 65608; phone (417) 683-2114.

Photo not available

County: Douglas.

Biography: Born Dec. 20, 1961, in St. Louis, raised in New Madrid. Graduate of William Woods College, B.A., history and English, 1983, with honors; University of Missouri–Kansas City School of Law, J.D., 1986. Served as an assistant public defender, 1986–1995; Greene County assistant prosecuting attorney, 1995–1999; and assistant attorney general, 1999–2013, in Public Safety Division, handling special prosecutions. Member: St. Leo the Great Parish, Ava, and Ava Kiwanis Club. Appointed associate circuit judge in Jan. 2013 by Gov. Jeremiah (Jay) Nixon. Elected Nov. 2014. Term expires Dec. 31, 2018. Democrat.

Circuit 44
CYNTHIA MacPHERSON

Office address: Ozark County Courthouse, PO Box 278, Gainesville 65655; phone (417) 679-4611.

Photo not available

County: Ozark.

Biography: Not available. Elected November 2014. Term expires Dec. 31, 2018. Republican.

Circuit 44
LYNETTE B. VEENSTRA

Office address: Wright County Courthouse, 125 Courthouse Sq., PO Box 58, Hartville 65667; phone (417) 741-6505.

County: Wright.

Biography: Born March 21, 1968, in Luverne, Minn. Graduate of Southwest Missouri State Univ., B.S., economics, *summa cum laude,* 1990; Vanderbilt University, J.D., 1993, Order of the Coif. Married Leon Veenstra Dec. 19, 1992; they have three children. Member: Mansfield Cumberland Presbyterian Church. Served in private practice, 1993–2002. Licensed in Missouri and California. Elected associate circuit judge in 2002, 2006, 2010 and 2014. Term expires Dec. 31, 2018. Republican.

Circuit 45
JAMES D. BECK

Office address: Lincoln County Justice Center, 45 Business Park Drive, Troy, 63379; phone (636) 528-6300.

County: Lincoln.

Biography: Born Sept. 3, 1968, in Troy. Graduate of Lindenwood College, B.S., 1990; Washington University School of Law, J.D., 1993. Married to Kendra Beck July 17, 1999; three children. Missouri assistant public defender, 1993–94; Missouri district public defender for the 45th Judicial Circuit, 1994–1997; began private practice, 1997, with Mueller & Suddarth, and continued in private practice with Mueller, Beck & Meyer until taking the bench on Jan. 1, 2011. Member: Missouri Bar Assoc.; Missouri Assoc. of Probate and Associate Circuit Judges; Missouri Municipal and Associate Circuit Judges; Troy Bible Holiness Church; Troy Area Chamber of Commerce, past president; Troy Kiwanis Club, past president; Troy Rotary Club, past president; Troy Elks Lodge; Lincoln County Bar Assoc., past president; Lincoln County Habitat for Humanity, board member; Elsberry Chamber of Commerce; and Moscow Mills Chamber of Commerce. Elected 2010. Re-elected 2014. Term expires Dec. 31, 2018. Republican.

Circuit 45
GREGORY K. ALLSBERRY

Office address: Lincoln County Justice Center, 45 Business Park Dr., Troy 63379; phone (636) 528-0329.

County: Lincoln.

Biography: Graduate of Concordia University Chicago, 1979; Washington University School of Law, 1984. Articles Editor, *Journal of Urban and Contemporary Law*, 1982-1984. Former prosecuting attorney, City of Frontenac and City of Pagedale. Engaged in private practice of law from 1984-2014. Associate at Bill T. Walker & Associates, 1984–1987. Associate and partner, Susman, Schermer, Rimmel & Shifrin, 1987–1999. Gregory K. Allsberry, L.C, 1999-2014. Elected associate circuit judge November 2014, for a term beginning Jan. 1, 2015. Term expires Dec. 31, 2018.

Circuit 45—Division 4
DAVID ASH

Office address: Pike County Courthouse, 115 W. Main, Rm. 24, Bowling Green 63334; phone (573) 324-5582.

County: Pike.

Biography: Born June 13, 1950 in Boston, Mass. Attended Columbia public schools until ninth grade. Graduate of Univ. City HS, 1968; Univ. of Mo.–Col., 1972, B.A., pol. science; J.D., 1976. Married Denise M. Jansen Sept. 3, 1977; they have two children. Employed in priv. pract. of law, 1976–2003. Served as asst. prosecutor, Pike Co., 1976–1981. City attorney, Wellsville, Farber and Laddonia, and prosecutor, City of New Florence. Served on bd. of dir. for Legal Svcs., Northeast Missouri, and as drug court judge, 45th Circuit, 2004–2009. Prior to taking the bench, served as municipal judge, Louisiana, Clarksville and Eolia. Currently is municipal judge, City of Bowling Green. Member: Bowling Green Lions Club; St. Clement Catholic Church; Knights of Columbus Council 1928; St. Isidore 4th Degree Assembly; Twin Pike YMCA, bd. of dir.. Past member: Bowling Green R-1 School Bd., 1999–2005; and Twin Pike Family YMCA, bd. of dir., 2004–2010. Elected 2002, 2006, 2010 and 2014. Term expires Dec. 31 2018. Democrat.

Alphabetical list of Missouri Judges

Judicial Organizations

Commission on Retirement, Removal and Discipline

2190 S. Mason Rd., Ste. 201, St. Louis 63131
Telephone: (314) 966-1007 / FAX: (314) 966-0076
www.courts.mo.gov/page.jsp?id=230

The Commission on Retirement, Removal and Discipline of Judges was created by a constitutional amendment in 1970. It began operating Jan. 1, 1972, and is governed by Supreme Court Rule 12.

The commission is responsible for receiving and investigating all requests and suggestions for the retirement of judges because of disability and all complaints concerning the alleged misconduct of judges and members of judicial commissions. It is composed of six members who serve six-year terms. Two non-lawyers are appointed by the governor, two lawyers are appointed by The Missouri Bar's governing body, one court of appeals judge is selected by court of appeals judges and one circuit judge is selected by the state's circuit judges.

The members are: Chairman Mr. Skip Walther, attorney, Columbia; Mr. Barry Aycock, lay member, Parma; Rev. Dr. Carlton R. Caldwell, lay member, St. Louis County; Mr. Arthur S. Margulis, attorney, St. Louis County; Hon. Sandra C. Midkiff, circuit judge, 16th Judicial Circuit (Jackson County-Kansas City); and Hon. Nancy Steffen Rahmeyer, appellate judge, Missouri Court of Appeals, Southern District.

On receiving a complaint against a judge or member of a judicial commission, the commission conducts an investigation. If at least four members of the commission find there is probable cause to believe the person may be guilty of misconduct, incompetency or other action constituting grounds for discipline as listed in Rule 12.08, a formal hearing is conducted. If at least four members find the person investigated should be disciplined, a report containing findings of fact and conclusions of law is made to the Supreme Court with recommendations for discipline (removal from office, suspension or reprimand). The court then makes a final ruling based on the commission's record and transcript.

A similar procedure is followed in cases involving retirements because of disability.

The Chief Disciplinary Counsel, The Advisory Committee and Legal Ethics Counsel

Office of Chief Disciplinary Counsel
3327 American Ave., Jefferson City 65109
Telephone: (573) 635-7400 / FAX: (573) 635-2240

Advisory Committee and Legal Ethics Counsel
3335 American Ave., Jefferson City 65109
Telephone: (573) 638-2263/ FAX: (573) 635-8806
www.mo-legal-ethics.org

To protect the public from persons unqualified or unauthorized to practice law, the Supreme Court of Missouri has established an attorney discipline system. The Supreme Court appoints a chief disciplinary counsel to investigate allegations of professional misconduct, incompetence and incapacity of lawyers. The Court also has established an Advisory Committee, which oversees the disciplinary hearings process. Complaints filed against attorneys are reviewed by the Office of Chief Disciplinary Counsel. Regional disciplinary committees located in Kansas City, Springfield and St. Louis—composed of at least four lawyers and two nonlawyers—also may investigate complaints referred to them by the chief disciplinary counsel or the Advisory Committee.

If the chief disciplinary counsel or a majority of a regional disciplinary committee finds there is probable cause to believe a lawyer is guilty of professional misconduct, they may issue a written admonition to the attorney or file information making specific allegations of the lawyer's violations of the Rules of Professional Conduct. The lawyer may request a hearing to be held before a disciplinary hearing panel composed of two lawyers and one nonlawyer, all of whom are appointed as disciplinary hearing officers by the Supreme Court. If the disciplinary hearing panel finds, by a preponderance of the evidence, that the lawyer is guilty of misconduct, it makes findings of fact, conclusions of law and recommendations for discipline, which then are filed in the Supreme Court. It is the Supreme Court's responsibility to impose any warranted discipline. If a lawyer who has been suspended or disbarred later seeks reinstatement, the chief disciplinary counsel investigates the application. The chief disciplinary counsel also investigates the unauthorized practice of law and takes appropriate action to stop such practices. The chief disciplinary counsel is Alan Pratzel.

In addition to providing oversight of the disciplinary hearing process, the Advisory Committee reviews complaint files that have been closed after investigation, at the request of the complainant. It also may issue formal ethics opinions, interpreting Supreme Court Rules 4, 5 and 6. Members of the Advisory Committee, appointed by the Supreme Court are: Jennifer Gille Bacon, Kansas City, chair; Susan Appelquist, Springfield; Richard E. Banks, St. Louis; John Briscoe, New London; Al Brooks, Kansas City; Doreen D. Dodson, St. Louis; Sidney Dulle, Jefferson City; Hon. John C. Holstein, Springfield; David P. Macoubrie, Chillicothe; Richard N. Priest, St. Louis; Susan Ford Robertson, Kansas City; and Dorothy White-Coleman, St. Louis.

The legal ethics counsel, who serves as counsel to the Advisory Committee, may give nonbinding informal advisory opinions, interpreting Supreme Court Rules 4, 5 and 6 to members of the Bar. The legal ethics counsel is Melinda Bentley.

Missouri Board of Law Examiners

Supreme Court Clerk's Office
PO Box 104236, Jefferson City 65110-4236
Telephone: (573) 751-9814
www.mble.org
E-mail: mble@courts.mo.gov

The Supreme Court of Missouri regulates admission to the Bar. The Missouri Board of Law Examiners is authorized by Supreme Court Rule 8 to conduct the bar examination and to determine the character and fitness and eligibility of applicants for admission to The Missouri Bar. Application forms and information about the bar examination, the character and fitness process and the requirements for admission are available online at *www.mble.org*. In addition, pass/fail statistics for the bar examination are published on the website.

The Missouri Board of Law Examiners is comprised of six members who are lawyers appointed by the Supreme Court of Missouri to serve a nine-year term. The current members of the board are: Patricia A. Sexton, Kansas City, president; James G. Nowogrocki, St. Louis, vice president; Jennifer K. Huckfeldt, Springfield; Karen M. Jordan, St. Louis; and Sandra L. Schermerhorn, Kansas City.

The Missouri Bar

326 Monroe St., PO Box 119, Jefferson City 65102
Telephone: (573) 635-4128 / FAX: (573) 635-2811
www.mobar.org
E-mail: mobar@mobar.org

The Missouri Bar is the official organization of all Missouri lawyers and judges. Established by rule of the Supreme Court of Missouri in 1944, it is the successor of the original Missouri Bar Association, a voluntary organization of lawyers founded in 1880. Its executive director is Sebrina Barrett.

Membership in The Missouri Bar is required of every lawyer who practices in Missouri and of every judge of a state court. To qualify for membership, a person must have completed an approved law school leading to a juris doctor degree. Those seeking membership in The Missouri Bar also must pass a comprehensive bar examination and character and fitness investigation and make application for admission to the Bar with the Supreme Court of Missouri.

Committees

There are numerous standing committees of The Missouri Bar, plus a number of special project committees. Committees of The Missouri Bar meet at least twice each year to discuss particular areas of the law and, in some cases, draft potential legislation in those areas. Committee members, as well as officers and other members of The Missouri Bar, are available to testify before the General Assembly in support of those bills. In addition, the Bar's Board of Governors often votes to support or oppose other bills pending before the legislature and the Bar's legislative services are directed accordingly. Because of its status as a mandatory organization for those practicing law in Missouri, the Bar's legislative efforts are confined to bills affecting the administration of justice.

Education

The Missouri Bar's Continuing Legal Education Department (MoBarCLE) has taken the lead in keeping Bar members informed of the latest developments in the law. Each year, the CLE department organizes and presents a number of programs—live, videotaped, webinars and by telephone—to keep lawyers abreast of changes in state and federal laws. These sessions are regularly accompanied by detailed course materials designed to supplement the programs themselves. In addition, the department's renowned deskbook series (the "black books"), supplements and guidebooks provide attorneys with valuable reference materials they can make use of in their own law libraries.

Publications/Public Information

The Journal of The Missouri Bar, offering valuable perspectives about the law from its lawyer-authors, is published six times per year as the official publication of the legal profession in Missouri. Also available to members are the *Legislative Digest*, published during and after each year's session of the General Assembly; *Precedent*, a quarterly publication featuring practice-oriented articles and columns; and *The Courts Bulletin*, a monthly update on recent court decisions in pertinent areas of the law.

For more than 50 years, The Missouri Bar has conducted a broad program of public information and education. Thousands of informative pamphlets and other educational materials about the law are distributed annually, including materials from an extensive law-related education audio-visual lending library. Copies of the Bar's brochures are also available on the Internet at *www.mobar.org*. The growth of the Bar's public information programs has been aided by cooperative ventures with the Extension Division of the University of Missouri, the Missouri Department of Elementary and Secondary Education, the Missouri Press Association, the Missouri Broadcasters Association, various state colleges and other groups and associations.

Other Activities

Other prominent programs and services offered by The Missouri Bar include: a client security fund that considers partial financial reimbursement to eligible clients who have been harmed by the unethical conduct of a lawyer; a lawyer referral service that links attorneys with Missourians in need of legal assistance; a lawyers assistance program that offers help to lawyers hindered by impairment issues; a complaint resolution program that offers an alternative to the formal lawyer disciplinary system for matters considered to be less serious in nature; a fee-dispute resolution program that works to resolve disputes between a lawyer and a client over fees charged for services; and many more.

Through the years, The Missouri Bar has gained recognition on the national and international level. It has been cited many times by the American Bar Association as the most outstanding bar organization in the nation. Its programs have won Freedom Foundation awards, the American Bar Association Award of Merit and the American Judicature Society's Justice Award. Similarly, staff members and officers serve on many important national committees and work with various national groups on problems of national scope.

Officers, The Missouri Bar, 2015–2016

Bergmanis, Erik, Camdenton, president;
Tippin Cutler, Dana, Kansas City, president elect;
Mogab, Nancy R., St. Louis, vice president.

Judicial Conference of Missouri

Supreme Court Bldg.
PO Box 150, Jefferson City 65102
Telephone: (573) 751-4144

In 1943, the General Assembly established the Judicial Conference of Missouri, which is composed of all state judges. The conference is charged by statute (section 476.350, RSMo) with studying the organization and administration of the state's judicial system, compiling data about the work of various courts and making biennial reports to the General Assembly, including any recommendations the conference may have for improving the laws. Since 1974, the chief justice of the Supreme Court, who is the conference's presiding officer, has presented an annual State of the Judiciary address to a joint session of the General Assembly, reviewing the problems, needs and goals of the judicial branch.

The statute also requires the conference to hold an annual meeting to be attended by all judges. At this meeting, the judges discuss the problems of court administration and invite experts in various fields to speak about matters of particular concern.

The clerk of the Supreme Court provides administrative and staff assistance and also serves as secretary to the executive council and the conference.

Nonpartisan Judicial Nominating Commissions

Under provisions of Article V of the Missouri Constitution, any vacancy occurring in the office of judge of the Supreme Court, the court of appeals or the circuit courts within St. Louis City or Jackson County is filled through the "Nonpartisan Selection of Judges Court Plan," adopted through initiative petition at the November 1940 general election, which provides for the governor to appoint one of three qualified persons nominated by a nonpartisan judicial commission. This method of selecting judges was adopted by the voters of the 21st Judicial Circuit (St. Louis County) in 1970; by the voters of the Sixth Judicial Circuit (Platte County) and the Seventh Judicial Circuit (Clay County) in 1973; and by the voters of the 31st Judicial Circuit (Greene County) in November 2008.

Under the Missouri Plan, as it often is called nationally, a vacancy on a court to which the plan applies is filled in the following way. A nonpartisan judicial commission of lay persons, lawyers and a judge selects three persons from those who apply, based on merit. The governor appoints one of the three. A judge appointed in this way must stand for retention in office at the first general election occurring after the judge has been in office for 12 months. The judge's name is placed on a separate judicial ballot, without political party designation, and the voters must vote either for or against retention in office. The judge's name again is placed on the ballot for a retention vote at certain intervals if the judge wishes to serve subsequent terms. The Missouri Plan has served as a national model for the selection of judges and has been adopted by a number of other states.

Appellate Judicial Commission

Nominations for judges of the Supreme Court and the Court of Appeals are made by a seven-member Appellate Judicial Commission. It consists of a judge of the Supreme Court selected by the members of the Court and two resident citizens from each of the three court of appeals districts. One lawyer is elected from each district by members of The Missouri Bar residing in that district, and one non-lawyer is appointed from each district by the governor. The judge member serves a two-year term, while the other members serve staggered terms of six years each.

Members: Mary R. Russell, chief justice, Supreme Court of Missouri, chair, term expires June 30, 2015.

From the Missouri Court of Appeals, Eastern District: Thomas M. Burke, lawyer member, term expires Dec. 31, 2017; Edward "Nick" Robinson, lay member, term expires Dec. 31, 2018.

From the Missouri Court of Appeals, Southern District: Michelle Beckler, lay member, term expires Dec. 31, 2020; Donald E. Woody, lawyer member, term expires Dec. 31, 2019.

From the Missouri Court of Appeals, Western District: Cheryl M. Darrough, lay member, term expires Dec. 31, 2016; James R. Hobbs, lawyer member, term expires Dec. 31, 2015.

Circuit Judicial Commissions

Nominations for judges of circuit courts are made by a five-member circuit judicial commission consisting of the chief judge of the district of the Court of Appeals in which the circuit or the major portion of its population lies, two lawyers elected by other members of The Missouri Bar residing in the circuit and two non-lawyer residents of the circuit appointed by the governor.

Sixth Circuit (Platte County) Judicial Commission: Chair: Alok Ahuja, chief judge, Missouri Court of Appeals, Western District, term expires June 30, 2014. Members: Keith Hicklin, Platte City, lawyer member; John W. Pepper, Kansas City, lay member; Staci L. Petrillo, Kansas City, lay member; Robert Shaw, Platte City, lawyer member.

Seventh Circuit (Clay County) Judicial Commission: Chair: Alok Ahuja, chief judge, Missouri Court of Appeals, Western District, term expires June 30, 2014. Members: Dr. Lancer G. Gates, Kansas City, lay member; Ben T. Schmitt, Kansas City, lawyer member; Jason Starr, Liberty, lay member; James H. Thompson Jr., Kansas City, lawyer member.

Sixteenth Circuit (Jackson County) Judicial Commission: Chair: James E. Welsh, chief judge, Missouri Court of Appeals, Western District,

term expires June 30, 2014. Members: Scott Bethune, Kansas City, lawyer member, term expires Dec. 31, 2015; Byron G. Thompson, Kansas City, lay member, term expires Dec. 31, 2012; Rev. Eric D. Williams, Kansas City, lay member, term expires Dec. 31, 2016; and Teresa Woody, Kansas City, lawyer member, term expires Dec. 31, 2017.

Twenty-first Circuit (St. Louis County) Judicial Commission: Chair: Lisa Van Amburg, chief judge, Missouri Court of Appeals, Eastern District, term expires June 30, 2014. Members: Christine Bertelson, Webster Groves, lay member; Matthew Rossiter, St. Louis, lawyer member; Rev. Anthony Witherspoon, Florissant, lay member; Richard Wuestling IV, St. Louis, lawyer member.

Twenty-second Circuit (St. Louis) Judicial Commission: Chair: Lisa Van Amburg, chief judge, Missouri Court of Appeals, Eastern District, term expires June 30, 2014. Members: Rita Burlison, St. Louis, lay member; Tiffany Franklin, St. Louis, lay member; Steven L. Groves, St. Louis, lawyer member; Thomas Neill, St. Louis, lawyer member..

Thirty-first Circuit (Greene County) Judicial Commission: Chair: Mary W. Sheffield, chief judge, Missouri Court of Appeals, Southern District, term expires June 30, 2015. Members: Andrew K. Bennett, Springfield, lawyer member; Steven B. Garner, Springfield, lawyer member; Joann Hosmer, Springfield, lay member; Steven Stepp, Springfield, lawyer member.

Office of State Public Defender

231 E. Capitol Ave., Jefferson City 65101
Telephone: (573) 526-5210 / FAX: (573) 526-5213
www.publicdefender.mo.gov
Email: public.defender@mspd.mo.gov

The Office of State Public Defender is created by Section 600.019.1., RSMo as an independent department within the judicial branch of state government.

The Missouri State Public Defender System (MSPD) is the state agency created to fulfill the state's constitutional obligation to ensure that all persons facing criminal prosecution in its courts have the assistance of counsel in their defense. MSPD's lawyers provide legal representation to persons who are charged with or challenging convictions for state criminal offenses but do not have the means available to hire defense counsel.

Public Defender Commission

State law (Chapter 600, RSMo) provides for a seven-member Public Defender Commission to oversee the State Public Defender System. The members of the commission are appointed by the governor with consent of the Senate and serve

DOUGLAS COPELAND
Chair
Public Defender Commission

H. RILEY BOCK
Commissioner
Public Defender Commission

CRAIG CHVAL
Commissioner
Public Defender Commission

CRISTA HOGAN
Commissioner
Public Defender Commission

CHARLES JACKSON
Commissioner
Public Defender Commission

JOEL ELMER
Deputy State Public Defender

MICHAEL BARRETT
State Public Defender

without compensation for six-year terms. Four members must be lawyers, and no more than four members may be of the same political party.

Members, Public Defender Commission

Copeland, Douglas, chair;
Bock, H. Riley, commissioner;
Chval, Craig, commissioner;
Hogan, Crista, commissioner;
Jackson, Charles, commissioner.

MSPD is a statewide department primarily comprised of three legal service divisions: the Trial Division, the Capital Division and the Appellate/Post-Conviction Division. Attorneys in district offices within each division provide direct representation to indigent clients.

Trial Division

The Trial Division employs close to 300 full-time attorneys as well as investigators, paralegals and legal assistants. Trial Division attorneys represent both adult and juvenile indigent clients

charged with crimes at the state trial court level throughout Missouri.

The Commitment Defense Unit represents indigent people throughout the state of Missouri against whom the government has initiated civil commitment proceedings based on the allegation that the citizen is a "sexually violent predator" (SVP). The unit was created in 1999 in response to Missouri's sexually violent predator legislation. This legislation enables the state to incarcerate individuals after they have completed their sentences for eligible sex offenses, and allows for indefinite civil commitment upon a jury finding that an individual meets the legislative criteria of a SVP.

Capital Division

The Capital Division of MSPD was established in 1989 to handle the complex litigation involved when the state seeks the death penalty. The purpose of this division is to provide the highest-quality representation to individuals against whom the state of Missouri is seeking the death penalty in the State Trial Court, the State Supreme Court and the United States Supreme Court.

Missouri State Public Defender Trial Division District Map

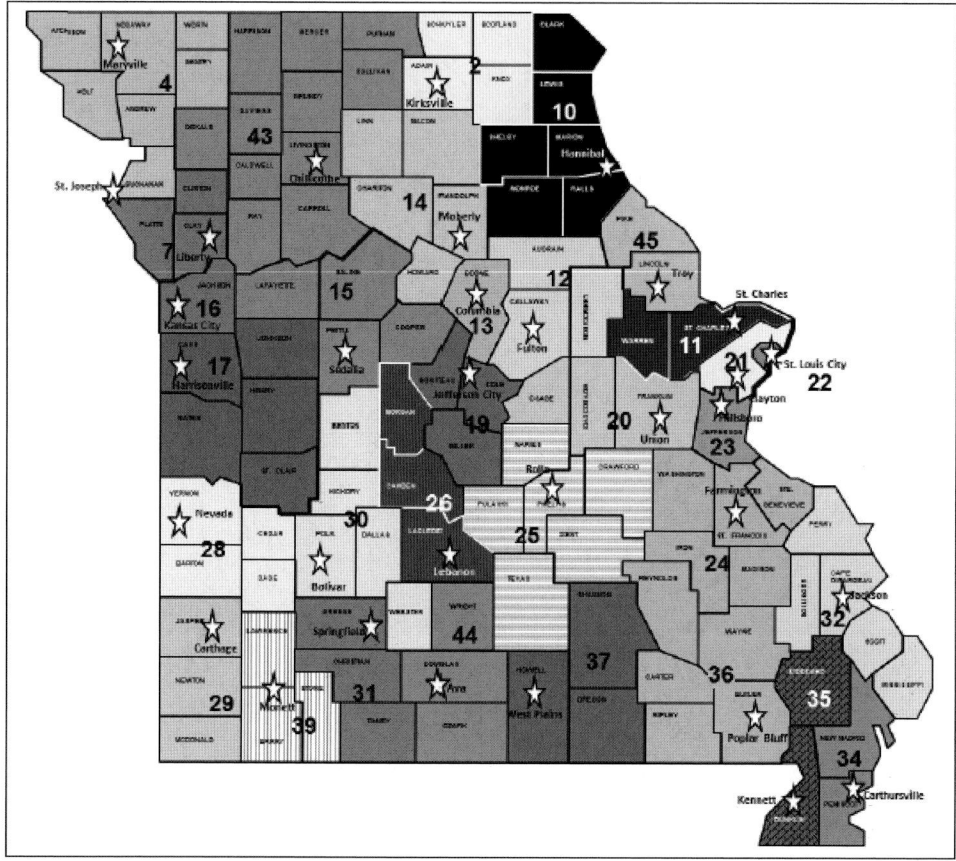

The division employs experienced attorneys who excel as litigators to handle the initial trial of the case. The division also employs experienced attorneys with exceptional appellate advocacy skills to handle the direct appeal of cases following a trial and sentence of death.

There are three Capital Division district offices within the state, located in St. Louis, Kansas City and Columbia. Trial attorneys in the division have the opportunity to try cases in both the urban and rural areas of Missouri.

Division of Appellate/Post Conviction Relief

This division ensures that the constitutional rights of citizens are preserved and protected, and that the trial or guilty-plea process was fair and legal. In essence, the division monitors and provides quality-control for the criminal judicial process.

There are six district offices in this division. The offices are located in St. Louis, Kansas City and Columbia in close proximity to most of Missouri's appellate courts.

Attorneys in this division provide representation to indigent citizens who have been convicted of felony offenses, after either a trial or a guilty plea. These attorneys handle direct appeals from non-capital felony convictions, post-conviction trial court challenges and appeals from post-conviction proceedings. The post-conviction practice includes providing aggressive representation to death-row clients at the trial-court level, and in the Supreme Courts of Missouri and the United States.

CHAPTER 6
EXECUTIVE DEPARTMENTS

Trout Catch, Bennet Springs State Park
Photo courtesy of Missouri State Archives

Executive Departments

Government exists to serve, and a broad network of government organizations has been created to accomplish the purpose. The Missouri Constitution (Article II, Section 1) states: "The powers of government shall be divided into three distinct departments—the legislative, executive and judicial." This section also prohibits persons within each branch from exercising powers of the other branches. From these three branches spring the variety of organizations which deliver services of state government.

The many different names used by these groups—departments, divisions, agencies, boards, commissions, bureaus, units, sections, programs and others—can make it difficult to determine which area of government is responsible for certain services, and sorting out responsibilities or relationships within the governmental framework.

It is through the executive branch that the greatest proportion of state services are delivered. The Constitution (Article IV, Section 12) and the Reorganization Act of 1974 have established a number of "executive departments" to deal with specific areas of interest. A chart showing the present state departments is shown on the following page.

The Missouri Constitution provides for 16 specific departments: the Office of Administration and the departments of Agriculture, Conservation, Corrections, Economic Development, Elementary and Secondary Education, Health and Senior Services, Higher Education, Insurance, Financial Institutions and Professional Registration, Labor and Industrial Relations, Mental Health, Natural Resources, Public Safety, Revenue, Social Services and Transportation.

Within each executive department exists a variety of offices of varying size and scope which deal with specific services. Traditionally, "divisions" are the next-largest organizations within departments and function to bring together smaller-sized groups, such as "bureaus," "sections" or "units." Divisions may be governed by a "board" or "commission" composed of members who are either appointed by the governor, made members by law or appointed by a department official. State agencies may administer certain sections of state law as defined by the Revised Statutes of Missouri, may develop their own rules and regulations as promulgated in the Missouri Register and Code of State Regulations or may institute programs and policies which address the needs of their areas of service.

Generally speaking, the legislative and judicial branches rely on committees or other small, appointed groups to perform research, develop policy, provide advocacy services or handle administrative duties. In these two branches services are delivered through the offices of the elected officials themselves and not by related agencies.

The Missouri Constitution

Since achieving statehood and joining the union on August 10, 1821, Missouri has operated under four Constitutions. The first was adopted in 1820 and was presented to Congress before Missouri was allowed to enter the union of states. The state's second Constitution, born in the bitterness and strife of the Civil War, was drafted and adopted in 1865. It was replaced by a third Constitution only ten years later, in 1875. Missourians approved their current Constitution in 1945, and it has been amended a number of times in order to meet the changing needs of our state and its people.

The Constitution of the State of Missouri is published by the Office of Secretary of State pursuant to the *Revised Statutes of Missouri* (RSMo 2.110). Copies of the Missouri Constitution, which also includes the text of the U.S. Constitution, are available without charge by contacting:

Secretary of State Jason Kander
Division of Publications
PO Box 1767
Jefferson City, MO 65102
Phone: (573) 751-4218 or (866) 716-0237
www.sos.mo.gov/pubs
Email: publications@sos.mo.gov

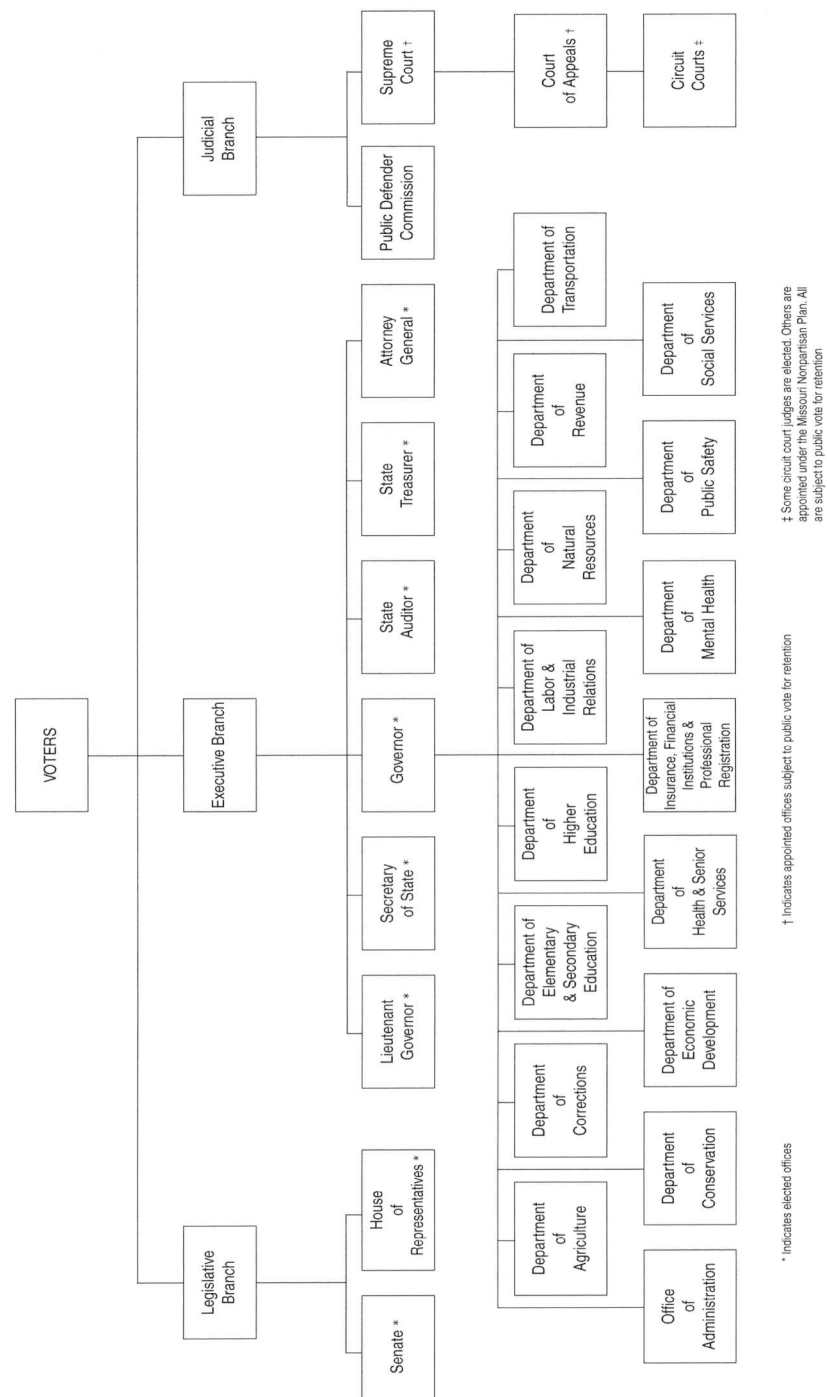

VOTERS

Legislative Branch
- Senate *
- House of Representatives *

Executive Branch
- Lieutenant Governor *
- Secretary of State *
- Governor *
- State Auditor *
- State Treasurer *
- Attorney General *

Judicial Branch
- Public Defender Commission
- Supreme Court †
  - Court of Appeals †
  - Circuit Courts ‡

Office of Administration
Department of Agriculture
Department of Conservation
Department of Corrections
Department of Economic Development
Department of Elementary & Secondary Education
Department of Higher Education
Department of Health & Senior Services
Department of Insurance, Financial Institutions & Professional Registration
Department of Labor & Industrial Relations
Department of Mental Health
Department of Natural Resources
Department of Public Safety
Department of Revenue
Department of Social Services
Department of Transportation

* Indicates elected offices

† Indicates appointed offices subject to public vote for retention

‡ Some circuit court judges are elected. Others are appointed under the Missouri Nonpartisan Plan. All are subject to public vote for retention

Office of Administration

State Capitol, Rm. 125
PO Box 809, Jefferson City 65102
Telephone: (573) 751-1851 / FAX: (573) 751-1212
www.oa.mo.gov

The Office of Administration is the state's service and administrative control agency. Created by the General Assembly on Jan. 15, 1973, it combines and coordinates the central management functions of state government. Its responsibilities were clarified and amended by the *Omnibus State Reorganization Act of 1974*.

The chief administrative officer is the Commissioner of Administration, who is appointed by the governor with the advice and consent of the Senate. The commissioner appoints the deputy commissioner, assistant commissioner, chief counsel and the directors of the divisions who report directly to him. The divisions are: Accounting; Budget and Planning; Facilities Management, Design and Construction; General Services; Information Technology Services; Personnel; and Purchasing and Materials Management.

The Office of Equal Opportunity (OEO) is a program within the Office of Administration. The OEO assists and monitors state agencies in promoting and ensuring equal opportunity within state government through employment, provision of services and operation of facilities. The director of the OEO reports to the Assistant Commissioner of Administration.

Division of Accounting

Truman State Office Bldg., Rm. 570
Telephone: (573) 751-2971 / FAX: (573) 526-9810
www.oa.mo.gov/acct
Email: acctmail@oa.mo.gov

The Division of Accounting (ACCT) provides central accounting and central payroll system services for state government, producing checks and electronic payments for state vendors and state employees. The ACCT publishes annual financial reports, administers bond sales for the Board of Fund Commissioners, Board of Public Buildings and Board of Unemployment Fund Financing and administers the Social Security coverage for all employees of the state and its political subdivisions.

DOUG NELSON
Commissioner

RENEE SLUSHER
Deputy Commissioner /
General Counsel

WALTER PEARSON
Assistant Commissioner

EMILY KRAFT
Special Assistant to the
Commissioner

STACY NEAL
Director
Division of Accounting

DAN HAUG
Director, Division of Budget
and Planning

Division of Budget and Planning

State Capitol, Rm. 124
Telephone: (573) 751-2345 / FAX: (573) 526-4811
www.oa.mo.gov/bp
Email: bpmail@oa.mo.gov

The Division of Budget and Planning (B&P) analyzes budget policy issues and provides information to the commissioner, the governor's office, the General Assembly, Missouri's congressional delegation and state, local and fed-

SHERRECE R. SMITH
Executive Assistant

KRISTEN PAULSMEYER
Legal Counsel

MARK TUCKER
Legislative Liaison

WANDA SEENEY
Public Information Officer /
Community Outreach and
Marketing Director

eral agencies. The division prepares the budget instructions, reviews agency budget requests, prepares the annual executive budget, analyzes economic and demographic conditions, forecasts state revenues and conducts technical policy and program analyses. To assist in state government management, the division controls appropriation allotments, manages the automated state budget system, prepares legislative fiscal notes, reviews legislation, tracks agency performance measures, analyzes and develops policy options and reviews federal issues and their impact on Missouri. The division coordinates preparations for, and assistance during, elected-official transitions. The division compiles population estimates and projections, provides technical assistance during decennial reapportionment and is Missouri's liaison to the U.S. Bureau of the Census.

RYAN BURNS
Public Information Officer

SARA VANDERFELTZ
Administrative Assistant

Division of Facilities Management, Design and Construction

Truman State Office Bldg., Rms. 730, 740, 780 and 840
Telephone: (573) 751-3339 / FAX: (573) 751-7277
www.oa.mo.gov/fmdc
Email: fmdcmail@oa.mo.gov

The Division of Facilities Management, Design and Construction (FMDC) operates, maintains and manages state-owned office buildings and other structures at the seat of government and other locations within the state. The FMDC oversees leased property for agencies statewide and is also responsible for design, construction, renovation and repair of state facilities. Review of all requests for appropriations for capital improvements also falls under the responsibilities of the FMDC.

The division's **Administrative/Legal Unit** consists of the following sections: Legal, Contracts and Fiscal/Accounting. This unit has oversight of the division's overall administrative and fiscal issues. The Real Estate Services fiscal section is

CATHY BROWN
Director, Division of Facilities
Management, Design and
Construction

also a part of this unit. This unit provides budgeting and payment processing for an approximate $150 million annual budget for state-owned, institutional and leased facilities.

The division's **Operations Unit** maintains state-owned buildings and grounds for agencies that are tenants in state-owned office buildings, as well as buildings for the Department of Elementary and Secondary Education, Mental

Health, Division of Youth Services and the Missouri Highway Patrol. The division manages 22 structures in the Capitol complex, comprising approximately 1.75 million square feet of usable space, including the state Capitol and the executive mansion. In addition, the unit operates state office buildings in St. Joseph, Kansas City, Springfield and St. Louis. These facilities contain approximately 535,000 square feet of usable office space. Institutional operations include providing maintenance management services for mental health, highway patrol, youth services and state school facilities. These services include providing the maintenance management staff and the authorization and administration of maintenance funding. This division is responsible for the maintenance of approximately 8 million square feet of institutional buildings. The unit also has oversight of the state's ID Badge Security System.

In addition, this Project Management Unit is responsible for the oversight of maintenance and repair, as well as new construction projects at state facilities (excluding higher education, conservation and transportation projects). The unit implements, contracts, reviews and has oversight of plans and specifications for statewide construction, selects architectural/engineering consultants and oversees expenditures of capital improvement appropriations statewide.

The division's **Energy Unit** is responsible for monitoring energy consumption in state-owned buildings and continues to develop and implement programs to help departments comply with the governor's *Executive Order 09-18*, mandating a reduction of energy consumption in state-owned buildings. This unit also assists the State Emergency Management Agency (SEMA) in providing emergency services during disaster relief efforts.

The division's **Real Estate Services Unit** coordinates real estate transactions on behalf of the state to include conveyance of state-owned property, purchase of property and granting easements. The unit also oversees leases within state-owned and leased space for state agencies throughout Missouri. The real estate services unit oversees approximately 520 separate contracts, providing 3.24 million square feet of leased space, with an annual rent of approximately $31 million.

The **Capital Improvement Planning/Asset Management Unit** is responsible for the CI budget, which includes the maintenance and repair budget, new construction budget and the reappropriation budget. In addition, it maintains the condition of all assets in a comprehensive database. Within this unit is an accounting section that provides payment processing for all CI projects.

MARK S. KAISER
Director
Division of General Services

Division of General Services

Truman State Office Bldg., Rm. 760
Telephone: (573) 751-0929 / FAX: (573) 751-7819
www.oa.mo.gov/gs
Email: gsmail@oa.mo.gov

The Division of General Services provides essential support services to state departments and to the Office of Administration.

State Printing provides comprehensive reproduction services including design, printing, finishing, and quick copy services.

Central Mail Services advises agencies on efficient mailing practices and provides comprehensive mailing services to most state agencies operating within the Jefferson City area.

Risk Management administers the Legal Expense Fund and the workers' compensation program for state employees, purchases insurance as required, and advises state agencies on risk management issues.

Vehicle Maintenance operates a centralized maintenance facility to provide mechanical repairs and body shop services for state vehicles based in the Mid-Missouri area.

Fleet Management establishes statewide policies governing state vehicle operations and management; coordinates a centralized fleet information system; operates a consolidated car pool serving agencies in the Jefferson City area; and serves as a resource for fleet management issues.

Surplus Property transfers and disposes of state surplus property and distribution of excess federal property to eligible entities.

State Recycling coordinates statewide recycling efforts and serves as a resource for recycling issues.

General Services also provides administrative support and staffing to operate the Missouri Public Entity Risk Management Fund (MOPERM) program and coordinates the Missouri State Employees Charitable Campaign.

The materials management section, the **State Agency for Surplus Property (SASP)**, is responsible for transfers and disposal of state surplus property to obtain the maximum return on investment. SASP acquires property declared excess by federal government agencies to distribute to eligible Missouri entities. SASP is also responsible for the statewide in-house recycling program.

Information Technology Services Division

Truman State Office Bldg., Rm. 280
Telephone: (573) 751-3290 / FAX: (573) 751-3299
www.oa.mo.gov/itsd

The mission of the Information Technology Services Division (ITSD) is to provide technology and communication services and solutions to the state's departments and agencies so they can efficiently and effectively serve the citizens of Missouri.

Under the leadership of the chief information officer, the ITSD offers centralized staff and resources in a single unified entity, and supports 14 executive branch departments. The new organizational model allows for enterprise standards and guidance in the common areas of security, networking, data management, server administration, end user support, technical architecture and application management, while maintaining a department-focused perspective on service delivery.

In collaboration with other state agencies, the ITSD aims to deliver reliable and accessible IT systems and services in an environment striving for optimization, collaboration, productivity and cost savings.

Division of Personnel

Truman State Office Bldg., Rm. 430
Telephone: (573) 751-4162 / FAX: (573) 751-8641
www.oa.mo.gov/pers
Email: persmail@oa.mo.gov

The Division of Personnel is responsible for the Uniform Classification and Pay System, as established in the State Personnel Law (Chapter 36, RSMo) and also assists all agencies and branches of state government with various human resources functions.

The Missouri Merit System is based on the principles of merit and fitness as determined by competitive examinations for employment, as well as objective and consistent human resource management policies and procedures. The system also grants employees the ability to appeal

RICH KLIETHERMES
Interim Chief Information Officer
Information Technology
Services Division

NANCY JOHNSTON
Director
Division of Personnel

disciplinary actions. Approximately 32,100 state employees in six state departments and sections of three other departments comprise the Missouri Merit System.

The Uniform Classification and Pay (UCP) system is designed to promote equity in pay among state employees in most executive branch agencies and to provide coordinated compensation policies. The UCP system covers approximately 35,750 employees of merit system agencies and employees from several other departments. The Division of Personnel is also responsible for the oversight of the statewide performance appraisal system.

The Division of Personnel is composed of four sections:

Employee services reviews applications for employment; ensures employees are assigned to appropriate job classes; develops and administers position classifications for agencies covered by the UCP; and develops, updates and administers merit system examinations.

Pay, leave and reporting provides information on the UCP system pay plan; interprets policies on pay, leave and hours of work; provides workforce reports and assistance with the SAM II HR/Payroll System; maintains lists of individuals from which agencies can select for merit system jobs; and ensures personnel transactions are in compliance with state personnel law.

The Center for Management and Professional Development develops and delivers management and supervisory training programs, as well as computer and technical training programs; administers statewide recognition programs; and coordinates the WeSave Employee Discount Program.

The Human Resources Service Center (HRSC) provides administration of human resources by providing a single point of contact for Office of Administration management and employees to

KAREN BOEGER
Director, Division of Purchasing
and Materials Management

MAIDA COLEMAN
Director, Office of Community
Engagement

AUDREY HANSON MCINTOSH
Presiding Commissioner
Administrative Hearing
Commission

obtain consistent responses to human resources situations and issues. Within this section, the state operators provide responses to questions from the general public.

Division of Purchasing and Materials Management

Truman State Office Bldg., Rm. 630
Telephone: (573) 751-2387 / FAX: (573) 526-9815
www.oa.mo.gov/purch
Email: purchmail@oa.mo.gov

The Division of Purchasing (Purchasing) is responsible for the procurement of all state-required supplies, materials, equipment and professional or general services, except for those agencies exempted by law. Purchasing executes procurement functions in accordance with applicable statutes by maximizing competition in the procurement process, conducting evaluations and negotiations as appropriate, and awarding contracts to the "lowest and best" bidders.

Office of Equal Opportunity

Truman State Office Bldg., Rm. 630
Telephone: (573) 751-8130 or (877) 259-2963
FAX: (573) 522-8078
www.oeo.mo.gov

The Office of Equal Opportunity, governed by Executive Order 10-24, assists and monitors state agencies in promoting and ensuring equal opportunity within state government through employment, provision of services, and operation of facilities. The OEO is also responsible for assisting state agencies in promoting contracting and procurement opportunities for minority- and women-owned businesses. In addition, the OEO continues to monitor the implementation of state employment practices to ensure that Missouri has a diversified and well-balanced state workforce.

The OEO director reports to the Assistant Commissioner of Administration.

Office of Community Engagement

Truman State Office Bldg., Rm. 560
Telephone: (573) 751-1637
www.oce.mo.gov

The Office of Community Engagement (OCE) was created in 2014 by Gov. Nixon's Executive Order 14-11. OCE is responsible for facilitating and encouraging meaningful communication between all Missouri citizens and state and local governments. OCE is also responsible for assisting the development of policy solutions and strategies that foster greater prosperity and opportunity for low-income individuals and minority communities. OCE is no longer in existence as of July 1, 2015.

Administrative Hearing Commission

Truman State Office Bldg., Rm. 640
PO Box 1557, Jefferson City 65102
Telephone: (573) 751-2422 / FAX: (573) 751-5018
www.oa.mo.gov/ahc

The Administrative Hearing Commission (AHC) is a neutral, independent administrative tribunal that decides disputes between a state agency and another party. The AHC typically decides the cases after a trial-type hearing in which it takes evidence. Any party may seek review of an AHC decision by the judicial branch.

By law, the AHC has jurisdiction over many types of disputes. Chief among them are disputes involving the director of the Department of Revenue's tax decisions; professional licensing decisions of many boards of the Department of Insurance, Financial Institutions and Professional Registration and the Department of Social Services' decisions on payments to Medicaid service providers; personnel matters arising under the state's merit system; and most recently added, due-process complaints under the Individuals with Disabilities Education Act. The AHC opens over 2,300 cases per year.

The AHC currently consists of five commissioners, appointed by the governor and confirmed by the Senate, who serve six-year terms.

Commissioners, Administrative Hearing Commission

Hanson McIntosh, Audrey, presiding commissioner;
Colbert-Botchway, Nicole J.;
Dandamudi, Sreenivaso Rao;
Vacancy (1);
Winn, Karen.

Board of Fund Commissioners

The Board of Fund Commissioners issues, redeems and cancels state general obligation bonds and performs other administrative activities related to state general obligation debt as assigned by law.

The board is composed of the governor, lieutenant governor, attorney general, state treasurer and commissioner of administration. The governor is president of the board, and the state treasurer is secretary. An executive secretary performs staff functions for the board.

Board of Public Buildings

The Board of Public Buildings (BPB) is composed of the governor, lieutenant governor and attorney general. The governor serves as the chair, and the lieutenant governor the secretary. The speaker of the House of Representatives and the president *pro tempore* of the Senate serve as *ex officio* members of the BPB but do not have the power to vote.

Missouri law provides the BPB has general supervision and charge of state facilities at the seat of government. The BPB also has the authority to issue revenue bonds for the construction of state office buildings and certain other facilities.

The board works with the Division of Facilities Management, Design and Construction and the Division of Accounting in carrying out its responsibilities.

Board of Unemployment Fund Financing

The Board of Unemployment Fund Financing is composed of the governor, lieutenant governor, attorney general, director of the Department of Labor and Industrial Relations and the commis-

KIRK SCHREIBER
Director
Children's Trust Fund

sioner of administration. The governor serves as chair, the lieutenant governor serves as vice chair and the commissioner of administration serves as secretary. Staff support is provided by the Division of Accounting.

The board is authorized to issue debt or credit instruments to provide funds for the payment of unemployment benefits or maintaining an adequate fund balance in the unemployment fund, and as an alternative to borrowing or obtaining advances from the federal unemployment trust fund or for refinancing these loans or advances.

Children's Trust Fund

Truman State Office Bldg., Rm. 860
PO Box 1641, Jefferson City 65102-1641
Telephone: (573) 751-5147 / FAX: (573) 751-0254
ctf4kids.org

The Children's Trust Fund (CTF) works to prevent child abuse and neglect through grant distribution, education and awareness. Established in 1983, the CTF is a nonprofit public/private partnership located within state government and governed by a 21-member board of directors. Funding is obtained from dedicated fees on marriage licenses and vital records, voluntary contributions designated on state income tax returns, sales of the CTF specialty license plates, general donations, interest income from the fund and other grants.

Children's Trust Fund Board of Directors

Krokstrom, M. Peggy, chair, Chesterfield, Sept. 15, 2016;
Heskett, John, Ed.D., chair-elect, Chersterfield, Sept. 15, 2017;
Beechner-McCarthy, Amy, Rolla;
Beetem, Nela, Holts Summit, Sept. 15, 2012;
Block, Susan E., University City, Sept. 15, 2012;
Bobrow, Nanci A., Ph.D., St. Louis, Sept. 15, 2013;
Bryan, Rev. Andy, Springfield;
Clay, Paula E., Columbia, Sept. 15, 2009;

Crockett, Michelle, Carthage, Sept. 15, 2015;
Dalen, Kathleen Boyle, Ph.D., Kansas City, Sept. 15, 2011;
Dixon, Sen. Bob, Springfield;
Huss, Stephen F., Ph.D., Hillsboro, Sept. 15, 2010;
LaFaver, Rep. Jeremy;
Lant, Rep. Bill, Pineville;
Mugg, Patrice, Kirkwood, Sept. 15, 2010;
Peterson, Martina L., Kansas City, Sept. 15, 2012;
Schupp, Sen. Jill, Creve Coeur;
Smith, Charmaine, St. Louis;
Staves, Regina M., Ph.D., Kansas City, July 23, 2012;
Wright, Jeffrey M., Turney, Sept. 15, 2015;
Vacancy (1).

Citizens' Commission on Compensation for Elected Officials

State Capitol, Rm. 125
Telephone: (573) 751-1851 / FAX: (573) 751-1212

In 1994, Missouri voters approved the creation of the Missouri Citizens' Commission on Compensation for Elected Officials. This commission was established to ensure the power to control the rate of compensation of elected officials of this state is retained and exercised by tax-paying citizens of the state.

Beginning in 1996 and every two years thereafter, the commission reviews the relationship of compensation to the duties of all elected state officials. The commission's recommendation of a salary schedule becomes effective unless disapproved by the General Assembly. The 22-member commission serves four-year terms.

Members, Citizens' Commission on Compensation for Elected Officials

Alexander, Kristin, Independence;
Anderson, Jim, Springfield;
Clemens, Dan;
Daughtrey, Tamara, Bolivar;
Forkner, Larry;
Gray, Jon;
Hawk, Gwenda, Parkville;
Jones, Gary;
Linza, Daniel;
Murphy, Gary III;
Newland, Neal, Union;
Perry, Bob, Bowling Green;
Ponder, Mike;
Roeder, Carol, Ballwin;
Schlottach, Charlie;
Shaw, Booker, Clayton;
Smith, Ralph, Amsterdam;
Vacancy (1);
Wallis, Lynn, Cuba;
Warren, Kathleen, Valles Mines;
Whipple, Katherine, St. Louis;
Wright, Judy.

ROBERT HONAN
Executive Director, Governor's Council on Disability

SHEILA FORREST
Chair, Missouri Minority Business Advocacy Commission

Governor's Council on Disability

Truman State Office Bldg., Rm. 840
PO Box 1668, Jefferson City 65102
Telephone: (573) 751-2600 / FAX: (573) 526-4109
Toll-free: (800) 877-8249
www.mo.gov/disability/gcd

The Governor's Council on Disability (GCD) serves as the voice and advocate in state policy-making for 949,000 Missourians with disabilities. The GCD educates people with disabilities about their rights and responsibilities; increases employment opportunities for job seekers with disabilities; and expands access to equal and full participation for all individuals with disabilities in their communities at the local, state and federal levels. The GCD provides youth leadership programming for young people with disabilities.

In 1947, President Harry S. Truman issued an executive order establishing the President's Committee on Employment of the Handicapped. This federal agency was created to assist disabled World War II veterans with re-entry into the civilian workforce. Following President Truman's lead, Missouri established the Governor's Committee in 1949 after it became obvious that a local network was needed to disseminate information about work-related problems facing people with disabilities.

The mission of the GCD has naturally evolved from strictly promoting employment to addressing all of the barriers to employment and full participation in community life. To more accurately reflect the mission, the 1994 General Assembly renamed this agency the Governor's Council on Disability. The GCD was transferred by executive order in 2004 from the Department of Labor and Industrial Relations (DOLIR) to the Office of Administration (OA) to better meet its mission.

The GCD consists of 21 council members, including the chair and one member from each state congressional district, as well as the executive director. The majority of the GCD is composed of people with disabilities representing various disability groups. Family members of people with disabilities, persons who represent other disability-related groups and other advocates fill the remaining positions.

The governor appoints the chair with the advice and consent of the Senate. The governor also appoints the 20 members-at-large. The GCD meets at least quarterly to act as an advisory body to its staff and to discuss and suggest ways to address current issues affecting persons with disabilities in Missouri.

In the administration of its duties, the GCD also offers assistance to help the various departments, divisions and branches of government to comply with all laws regarding persons with disabilities. To further that goal, the director of each state department designates at least one employee to act as a liaison with the council. The assistance offered includes educational programming and consultation on the rights of persons with disabilities.

Missouri Minority Business Advocacy Commission

State Capitol, Rm. 125
Telephone: (573) 751-1851 / FAX: (573) 751-1212

The Missouri Minority Business Advocacy Commission (MBAC) identifies and assesses the needs of minority businesses throughout the state; initiates aggressive programs to assist minority businesses in obtaining state and federal procurement; makes recommendations regarding state policies, programs and procedures; and provides a focal point to assist and counsel minority small businesses in their dealing with federal, state and local governments. The MMBAC also initiates and encourages minority business education programs; analyzes current legislation and regulations as they affect minority businesses; and receives complaints and recommendations concerning policies and activities of federal, state and local governmental agencies that affect minority small businesses. The purpose of the MMBAC is to increase economic opportunity for minority businesses to improve the overall business climate of the state of Missouri; and to develop and establish the inclusionary process for state departments so that they can meet or exceed the goals and objectives of the legislation and executive order designed to increase minority participation in state procurement.

Missouri Minority Business Advocacy Commission Board Members

Forrest, Sheila, (D), chair, St. Louis;
Kennedy, Michael, (D), Wildwood;

THOMAS GEORGE
Chair, Health and Educational
Facilities Authority

Shariff, Dr. Adam R., (R), Ballwin;
Downing, Mike, director, Department of Economic Development;
Neslon, Doug, (D), commissioner, Office of Administration;
Vacancies (4).

Missouri Health and Educational Facilities Authority

15450 S. Outer Forty Rd., Ste. 230, Chesterfield 63017
Telephone: (636) 519-0700 / FAX: (636) 519-0792

The Health and Educational Facilities Authority of the State of Missouri was created in 1975 by an act of the Missouri General Assembly. It is empowered to make loans to qualified health or educational institutions and to refund outstanding obligations, mortgages or advances previously issued, made or given for the cost of such facilities and to do all things necessary to carry out the purposes of the act. The authority consists of seven members appointed by the governor with the advice and consent of the Senate. Each member must be a resident of the state and no more than four members may be of the same political party.

The mission of the authority is to provide access to the capital markets in an effort to lower the cost of health and educational services in Missouri by providing high quality, readily available, low cost financing alternatives for Missouri public and private, nonprofit health and educational institutions.

Missouri Health and Educational Facilities Authority Board Members

George, Thomas, (D), chair, Florissant, July 30, 2015;
Scott, Judith W., (R), vice chair, Poplar Bluff, July 30, 2011;

Thompson, Kevin, (R), treasurer, St. Louis, July 30, 2009;

Maguffee, Sarah R., (D), member, Columbia, July 30, 2013;

Cavato, Joseph, (D), member, University City, July 30, 2013;

Vacancies (2).

Jackson County Sports Complex Authority

Harry S. Truman Sports Complex
8501 Stadium Dr., Kansas City 64129
Telephone: (816) 921-3600 / FAX: (816) 921-3677

This bipartisan authority consists of five commissioners who are qualified voters of the state of Missouri and residents of Jackson County. The Jackson County Legislature submits a list of candidates to the governor to replace members of the authority whose terms have expired. The governor then appoints the succeeding members from that list of candidates. The commissioners serve staggered terms of five years and hold office until a successor has been appointed and qualified. No more than three members may be of the same political party. The authority is empowered to issue bonds.

The Jackson County Sports Complex Authority is authorized under the constitution and laws of the State of Missouri to plan, construct, operate and maintain a sports stadium fieldhouse, indoor and outdoor recreational facilities center, playing fields, parking facilities and other concessions within Jackson County; negotiate and perform its obligations as landlord under lease agreements with the Kansas City Royals Baseball Corporation and the Kansas City Chiefs Football Club, Inc.; oversee the maintenance and operation of the Harry S. Truman Sports Complex in a fiscally responsible manner, which will allow it to maintain its stature as a premier sports facility in the nation; administer funds received from the State of Missouri, Jackson County and the City of Kansas City, Mo., or any other sources that are to be used for furtherance of its statutory duties; develop a land-use plan for potential development of the sports complex and recommend to the county appropriate long-term leasing arrangements for the sports complex facilities; and to work with other political subdivisions, agencies and commissions for the furtherance of all types of sports, either professional or amateur, commercial or private, within Jackson County.

Members, Jackson County Sports Complex Authority

Cherry, Deron, (R), chair, Greenwood, July 15, 2016;

Gromowsky, Aimee, (D), first vice chair, Kansas City, July 15, 2017;

Kratofil, Gregory, (R), second vice chair, Lee's Summit, July 15, 2019;

Miles, Rev. John, (D), secretary, Kansas City, July 15, 2018;

Kemp, Garry, (D), treasurer, Lee's Summit, July 15, 2015.

Missouri Ethics Commission

3411-A Knipp Dr., Jefferson City 65109
Telephone: (573) 751-2020 / FAX: (573) 526-4506
www.mec.mo.gov

The Missouri Ethics Commission (MEC) was created by the *Missouri Ethics Law of 1991* (Section 105.955, RSMo). The commission is charged with enforcement of conflicts of interest and lobbying laws (Section 105.450-498, RSMo) and campaign finance disclosure laws (Chapter 130, RSMo).

The MEC is composed of six members, not more than three of whom may be from the same political party. These members must be from different congressional districts, and no more than three can be from an odd- or even-numbered congressional district. The governor appoints the members of the commission with the advice and consent of the Senate. The commission elects a biennial chair and is assigned to the Office of Administration for budgeting purposes only.

The MEC receives and reviews complaints alleging violations of the conflict of interest and lobbying statutes and the campaign finance disclosure statute. After investigation of these complaints, the commission refers the complaints to the appropriate prosecuting authority or disciplinary authority along with recommendations for sanctions. The commission may also initiate judicial proceedings on its own.

The MEC reviews and audits reports required by the campaign finance disclosure law, the financial interest disclosure laws and the lobbying registration and reporting laws. The MEC acts as the public repository for such reports. The MEC provides information and assistance to lobbyists, elected and appointed officials, employees of the state, political subdivisions and the general public.

Members, Missouri Ethics Commission*

Weedman, Charles E., (R), chair, Congressional District 4, March 15, 2016;

Munich, John R., (D), vice chair, Congressional District 2, March 15, 2016;

Stoltz, William, (R), Congressional District 8, March 15, 2016;

Deeken, Bill, (R), Congressional District 3, March 15, 2018;

Hagan, Nancy, (D), Congressional District 7, March 15, 2018;

Vacancy (1), (D), Congressional District 5, March 15, 2018.

*\$100 per diem.

Missouri Public Entity Risk Management Fund (MOPERM)

PO Box 7110, Jefferson City 65109-7110
Telephone: (888) 389-8198 / FAX: (573) 751-8276
www.moperm.com

The MOPERM board of trustees operates a shared-risk program offering tort liability, property and other coverages for participating public entities of the state.

Membership of the board consists of the attorney general, the commissioner of administration and four members appointed by the governor with the advice and consent of the Senate, who are officers or employees of those public entities participating in the fund. No more than two members appointed by the governor shall be of the same political affiliation. Members appointed by the governor serve four-year terms. Members serve without compensation.

MOPERM Board of Trustees

Spence, Larry, (R), chair, Willow Springs, July 15, 2012;
Rodenberg, Thomas D., (D), vice chair, Blue Springs, July 15, 2017;
Bodenhamer, Steven D., (R), Strafford, July 15, 2015;
Koster, Attorney General Chris, (D);
Milam, Rita, (D), Benton, July 15, 2014;
Nelson, Doug, (D), Office of Administration Commissioner, Jefferson City.

Missouri State Penitentiary Redevelopment Commission

Truman State Office Bldg., Rm. 730
Telephone: (573) 751-4174

The Missouri State Penitentiary Redevelopment Commission was established in 2000, by authority of House Bill 621 of the 91st General Assembly.

The commission is composed of 10 members. Three commissioners, no more than two of whom shall belong to the same political party, are residents of Jefferson City and are appointed by the mayor, with the advice and consent of the governing body of that city; three commissioners, no more than two of whom shall belong to the same political party, are residents of Cole County but not of Jefferson City and are appointed by the

LARRY SPENCE
Chair, Missouri Public Entity
Risk Management Fund

LARRY WEBER
Executive Director
Missouri Public Entity Risk
Management Fund

county commission; and four commissioners, no more than three of whom shall belong to the same political party, none of whom shall be residents of Cole County or of Jefferson City, are appointed by the governor with the advice and consent of the Senate. The governor appoints one of the commissioners who is not a resident of Cole County or Jefferson City as chair of the commission. No elected official of the State of Missouri or of any city or county in this state is appointed to the commission.

The director of the Division of Facilities Management, Design and Construction provides staff support for this commission. The commission may also employ staff or secure the services of consultants through contract for the purpose of conducting the business of the commission.

The purpose of the commission is to redevelop the real property that encompassed the grounds of the Missouri State Penitentiary for more than 150 years, so as to maintain its historic value for present and future generations of Missourians, and to provide new uses for the property that will benefit the citizens of the City of Jefferson, the County of Cole and the State of Missouri as a whole.

To accomplish its purpose, the commission may perform the following functions:

- Acquire and hold title to the property historically utilized as the Missouri State Penitentiary;
- To acquire by gift or bequest from public or private sources property adjacent to the Penitentiary property and necessary or appropriate to the successful redevelopment;
- To lease or sell real property to developers who will utilize the property consistently with the master plan for the property;
- To hire employees necessary to perform the commission's work;

- To enter into contracts with private or governmental entities in connection with the acquisition by gift or bequest and in connection with the planning, construction, financing, leasing, subleasing, operation and maintenance of any real property or facility and for any other lawful purpose;

- To sue and be sued;

- To receive any rentals, or proceeds from the sale of real estate, contributions or moneys provided by any governmental entity and to apply for grants and other funding;

- To disburse funds for its lawful activities and fix salaries and wages of its employees;

- To borrow money for the acquisition, construction, equipping, operation, maintenance repair, remediation or improvement of any facility or real property to which the commission holds title and for any other property purpose and to issue negotiable notes, bonds and other instruments in writing as evidence of sums borrowed;

- To perform all other necessary and incidental functions, and to exercise such additional powers as shall be conferred by the General Assembly; and

- To purchase insurance, including self-insurance, of any property or operations of the commission or its members, director, officers and employees, against any risk or hazard, and to indemnify its members, agents, independent contractors, directors, officers and employees against any risk or hazard.

MSP Redevelopment Commissioners

Berry, Michael, vice chair (acting chair), Jefferson City, May 18, 2014;
Burkhead, Frank, Cole County, March 31, 2014;
Bushmann, Gene, Jefferson City, May 18, 2014;
Meyer, Bob, Cole County, March 31, 2012;
Jones, Bob, Jefferson City, May 18, 2014.
Vacancies (5).

Office of Child Advocate

PO Box 809, Jefferson City 65102-0809
Telephone: (573) 522-8680 / FAX: (573) 522-6870
Toll-free: (866) 457-2302
www.oca.mo.gov

The Office of Child Advocate provides families and citizens an avenue through which they can obtain an independent and impartial review of the decisions and/or actions made by the Department of Social Services, Children's Division.

The main duties of the Office of Child Advocate are: (1) review foster care case management;

GARY O'BANNON
Chair
Personnel Advisory Board

(2) review unsubstantiated hotline investigations; (3) mediate between parents and schools regarding abuse allegations that occur in a school setting; (4) review child fatalities when there is a history of child abuse and neglect or involvement with the Children's Division; and (5) provide information and referrals for families needing resources.

Personnel Advisory Board

Truman State Office Bldg., Rm. 430
Telephone: (573) 751-3053 / FAX: (573) 522-8462

Within the Office of Administration, the State Personnel Law (Chapter 36, RSMo) provides for a Personnel Advisory Board (PAB) of seven members, six of whom are appointed by the governor with the advice and consent of the Senate. Four members are appointed from the public at large, one is a member of executive management in state government and one is a non-management state employee. The seventh member is the person designated as the state equal opportunity officer.

The board has oversight responsibility for the Missouri Merit System and the Uniform Classification and pay system, and has broad policy making authority in various areas of human resources administration. Responsibilities also include meeting with appointing authorities regarding human resource management needs and making recommendations to the governor and the General Assembly regarding the state's compensation policy.

Personnel Advisory Board* Members

O'Bannon, Gary, chair, Kansas City, July 31, 2014;
Bloch, Paul, California, July 31, 2010;
Ferguson, Karen, Holts Summit, July 31, 2006;
Kincheloe, Duncan, Jefferson City, July 31, 2010;
Vacancies (3).

*Public members receive $99.66 per diem.

Missouri State Capitol Commission

Truman State Office Bldg., Rm. 730
Telephone: (573) 751-1034
www.friendsofmsa.org/sscc

The Missouri State Capitol Commission (MSCC) was established by the 91st General Assembly in 2001 by Senate Bill 470.

The purpose of the MSCC is to assure the future preservation and integrity of the Capitol and to preserve its historical significance. The commission evaluates and recommends courses of action on the restoration and preservation of the Capitol and its history, as well as evaluates and recommends courses of action to ensure accessibility to the Capitol.

The commission works with the Office of Administration, the Archives Division of the Office of the Secretary of State, the historic program within the Department of Natural Resources, the Division of Tourism within the Department of Economic Development and the Historical Society of Missouri.

Commission Members

Miller, Dana, chair, House staff, appointed by Speaker of the House;

Conway, Rep. Pat, House member, minority;

Curls, Sen. Shalonn (Kiki), Senate member, minority.

Davis, Steve, gubernatorial appointment, April 18, 2010;

Flannigan, Rep. Tom, House member, majority;

Hearnes, Betty Cooper, gubernatorial appointment, April 18, 2008;

Hoelscher, Marga, Senate staff, appointed by the Senate President *pro tempore*;

Kehoe, Sen. Mike, Senate member, majority;

Nelson, Doug, Commissioner of Administration;

Kinder, Lt. Gov. Peter, ex *officio*;

Vacancies (2).

Department of Agriculture

1616 Missouri Blvd., PO Box 630, Jefferson City 65102
Telephone: (573) 751-4211
agriculture.mo.gov
Email: aginfo@mda.mo.gov

Promoting and Protecting Missouri Agriculture

Established in 1933 by the General Assembly, the Department of Agriculture promotes and protects Missouri's multi-billion dollar agriculture and agribusiness industry. The department also enforces state laws that regulate and market the agricultural industry.

The department's divisions include Agriculture Business Development, Animal Health, Grain Inspection and Warehousing, Plant Industries and Weights, Measures and Consumer Protection. The department also houses the Missouri Agricultural and Small Business Development Authority, the Missouri State Fair, the State Milk Board and the Missouri Wine and Grape Board.

Office of the Director

The Missouri Department of Agriculture is managed by a director who is appointed by the governor and confirmed by the Senate. The director determines department policy, oversees the department's five divisions and serves as a liaison to the governor, state legislators, the agriculture community and the public.

The director is a standing member of the State Milk Board, the State Fair Commission, the Missouri Soil and Water Districts Commission, the Missouri Development Finance Board, the Missouri Petroleum Storage Tank Insurance Fund and the Missouri Agricultural and Small Business Development Authority.

Agriculture Business Development Division

The Agriculture Business Development Division creates opportunities for success for Missouri's farmers and agribusinesses. Division staff help facilitate growth in Missouri's agriculture-based businesses by providing business counseling and information and training on a sector-by-sector basis.

RICHARD FORDYCE
Director of Agriculture

DARRYL CHATMAN
Deputy Director

CHRISTA MOODY
Executive Assistant to the
Director and Deputy Director

MICHAEL WARRICK
General Counsel

Areas of specialization include capitalization, business planning, marketing, industry development, product and brand development and organizational structures. The division also helps facilitate growth in Missouri's agriculture-based industries by working with key players such as universities, associations, private sector partners and federal and state agencies.

AgriMissouri

AgriMissouri is a branded program designed to grow the production of and demand for agricultural products grown and made in Missouri. The program works with farmers, agribusinesses and retail outlets statewide to increase consumer recognition of Missouri's agricultural products in the marketplace.

International and Business Development Programs

The International and Business Development Programs focus on both domestic and international marketing. Department specialists work with specific industry representatives or groups to establish marketing opportunities and promote Missouri commodities here and abroad. Through

LOYD WILSON
Senior Policy Advisor

TONY BENZ
Director
Legislative Affairs

ROBIN PERSO
Director
Budget and Planning

ALAN CLEMENTS
Fiscal and Administrative
Manager

MISTI PRESTON
Director
Strategic Initiatives

SARAH ALSAGER
Public Information Officer

KEN STRUEMPH
Director, Agriculture
Business Development

DR. LINDA HICKAM
State Veterinarian / Director
Animal Health Division

providing one-on-one assistance to producers interested in marketing, production and processing their commodities in new ways, the marketing personnel enhance farm profitability in Missouri through innovations in technology and marketing and promotions of value-added agriculture. With an international office in Taiwan, international marketing specialists are able to work worldwide to promote and sell Missouri agriculture products.

The division's staff also works with Missouri youth, encouraging them to pursue agricultural degrees and careers through the Missouri Agri-Business Academy, the Missouri Livestock Grading and Judging Contest, Building Our American Communities grants and working with state FFA and 4-H Chapters.

Farmers' Markets/Specialty Crops

Consumers demand high quality and fresh products at more than 270 farmers' markets as well as traditional retail outlets. To increase awareness for Missouri markets, this program works one-on-one with farmers' markets to ensure safe and abundant fresh products. Farmers marketing fresh products require knowledge of food safety, manufacturing, distribution and general market and business regulations. This program assists both markets and growers in efforts to increase the production, consumption and sales of specialty crops.

Market News

Market News provides an unbiased, reliable, accurate and timely source for livestock and grain market news to remain competitive and assist them in making wise and profitable marketing decisions. It also guides producers in production planning and provides a more even playing field in the marketplace. Market News staff report prices from 25 livestock auctions and 28 grain markets in Missouri. Daily market figures are published online and through the Weekly Market Summary.

Animal Health Division

The Division of Animal Health, under the direction of the state veterinarian, promotes and protects Missouri's diverse and dynamic livestock industry. The assistance and oversight provided by the division's programs ensures greater market access for Missouri's livestock and companion animal industries.

Animal agriculture accounts for about one-half of Missouri's annual agriculture cash receipts. The division administers laws and programs designed to control and eradicate livestock disease and maintain and enhance the integrity of the state's animal industries. This includes both mandatory and voluntary regulatory programs for beef and dairy cattle, horses, swine, poultry, sheep, goats, and exotic and companion animals.

The state's progress in national disease control and eradication is due to the cooperative efforts of livestock producers, markets, practicing veterinarians, other agencies and division staff. Through these efforts, Missouri has achieved Bovine Tuberculosis and Brucellosis Free status, Swine Pseudorabies stage V status and Avian Pullorum-Typhoid Clean status. In addition, the division operates two state-of-the-art diagnostic laboratories, located in Jefferson City and Springfield.

Agri-Security

The Animal Health Division works to safeguard the livestock industry and the public against the threat of bioterrorist attacks. In addition, the division informs cattle producers of quality assurance, targeting breeding and cow-herd management; increases awareness and understanding of environmental issues affecting production; presents marketing and food safety programs to small poultry producers; and inspects Missouri meat processors to supplement existing U.S. Department of Agriculture (USDA) inspections.

Animal Care Facilities

The Animal Care Facilities Act (ACFA) became law to ensure dogs and cats, specifically those under the care of breeders, dealers, animal shelters, rescue operations and municipal pounds, receive adequate health care, shelter and proper socialization. The ACFA law, designed to benefit both the animals and the pet industry, requires any animal shelters, pounds or dog pounds, boarding kennels, commercial kennels, contract kennels, pet shops, exhibition facilities, dealers and commercial breeders be licensed and inspected annually.

Branding Cattle

Branding is one of the oldest and best ways to permanently identify livestock. It serves as an excellent safeguard against livestock theft, loss or dispute. Legislation passed in 1971 made the Department of Agriculture responsible for registering livestock brands. Brands must be recorded as required by Missouri's Marks and Brands of Animals Law to prove ownership and be considered legal evidence in a court of law.

Livestock Markets and Dealers

Missouri has a livestock inventory of 4.25 million cattle, three million hogs and pigs, 73,000 sheep and 200,000 equine. To help livestock producers obtain the maximum return on their investment, Missouri is fortunate to have a number of livestock market/sales throughout the state. To operate a livestock market/sale in the state, the operator must have a license issued by the Division of Animal Health. This license shall entitle the applicant to conduct business for one calendar year, January through December. All livestock markets must be licensed and provide a satisfactory bond (with a minimum bond amount of $10,000), determined by business volume. Missouri Livestock Dealer Registration is required for those who buy, sell or exchange livestock.

Missouri Meat and Poultry Inspection Program

The Missouri Meat and Poultry Inspection Program is dedicated to ensuring that the commercial supply of meat and poultry products within the state are safe, wholesome, accurately labeled and secure, as required by state/federal meat and poultry inspection laws. By providing inspection service and guidance to Missouri processors, the program continues to endorse the mission of the Missouri Department of Agriculture — to serve, promote and protect the agricultural producers, processors and consumers of Missouri's food, fuel and fiber products. In cooperation with USDA-Food Safety Inspection Service (FSIS), the Missouri Meat and Poultry Inspection Program (MMPIP) offers equal inspection authority and service within the state of Missouri. As a result, any meat processed under MMPIP inspection and sold within the state of Missouri is offered the same privileges and exemptions as USDA inspected meat products.

Grain Inspection and Warehousing Division

The Grain Inspection and Warehousing Division is composed of two programs that administer the Missouri Grain Warehouse Law: the Missouri Grain Dealer Law and the United States Grain Standards Act. These laws promote and protect commerce in the interest of grain producers, merchandisers, warehousemen, processors and consumers. They also promote a uniform, official inspection system for the orderly marketing of grain. This division also collects and disburses funds for nine commodity merchandising programs.

Commodity Services Program

The Commodity Services Program provides commodity councils with an organized procedure for collection and distribution of commodity checkoff funds for nine Missouri commodities (beef, corn, soybeans, rice, sheep and wool, wine, aquaculture, peaches and apples). The program is also responsible for conducting seven annual merchandising council elections and administers the Missouri Hay Directory, an online hay listing service.

Grain Inspection Services Program

The Grain Inspection Services Program is designated to officially inspect, grade and weigh all grains that have standards established under the United States Grain Standards. The program provides four primary services: official sampling to take a representative sample of grain from a particular lot; official inspection to determine and certify the type, class, quality or condition of grain; weighing certification to supervise the loading, unloading and weighing of grain containers; and chemical analysis to determine the protein or oil content of grain and the existence of mycotoxins in grain.

Services are provided at inspection offices in Marshall, New Madrid and St. Joseph. The program is self-supporting and operates entirely on fees charged for inspection services performed.

Grain Regulatory Services Program

The Grain Regulatory Services Program protects the public interest by auditing grain warehouses and grain dealers to determine grain obligations and financial solvency. The program enforces the Missouri Grain Warehouse Law, the Missouri Grain Dealer Law and the United States Grain Standards Act, so producers are assured of storing or merchandising their grain with licensed, bonded, reputable and financially stable grain businesses. The program annually licenses approximately 200 warehouses and 400 grain dealers and conducts more than 900 audits and investigations.

Plant Industries Division

The Plant Industries Division comprises four bureaus, which together administer state and federal laws. These laws facilitate agricultural production and marketing, and provide consumer and environmental protection for Missouri citizens by regulating animal feeds, seeds and treated timber; providing necessary certifications for interstate and international shipment of agricultural and forest products; ensuring plant pest protection for crops and forests; inspecting for

CHRIS KLENKLEN
Director, Grain Inspection and
Warehousing Division

JUDY GRUNDLER
Director
Plant Industries Division

conformance to USDA grades for fresh fruits and vegetables; and regulating the use of pesticides.

Bureau of Feed, Seed and Treated Timber

The bureau administers the Missouri Commercial Feed Law, Missouri Seed Law and the Missouri Treated Timber Law. The feed law regulates the manufacturing, distribution and labeling of commercial feed products to ensure that livestock producers and pet owners receive the feed product guaranteed. In partnership with the USDA, the bureau provides inspection reports and regulation involved with preventing Bovine Spongiform Encephalopathy (BSE), provides labeling assistance and investigates complaints related to animal feed.

The bureau regulates seed products through inspecting, sampling, testing and labeling. Products are reviewed to ensure they meet the label guarantees and comply with the USDA Seed Regulatory and Testing branch in regulating the interstate movement of seed.

The bureau is responsible for the licensure of all treated timber producers and dealers doing business within the state of Missouri and for regulations governing the quality and distribution of treated wood products.

Laboratories are maintained for analytical support to the seed, treated timber and commercial feed and other programs.

Bureau of Pesticide Control

The bureau administers laws for registration, distribution and use of pesticides. All pesticides sold and used in Missouri are regulated by the Missouri Pesticide Registration Act and the Missouri Pesticide Use Act. Bureau personnel inspect pesticides for proper labeling and registration and investigate claims of pesticide misuse. The Missouri Pesticide Use Act allows the bureau to certify commercial, noncommercial and private applicators and public operators. The act also provides for licensing pesticide dealers and pesticide technicians.

Bureau of Plant Pest Control

The bureau administers laws to control the introduction and spread of insect and disease pests of plants, and administers the Missouri Plant Law, which mandates controlling harmful insect pests and plant pathogens through early detection surveys, quarantines, nursery and greenhouse inspections and certification. The law also enables interstate and international shipments of Missouri plants and plant products. Additionally, the bureau works to diminish the threat of exotic, invasive plant pests through outreach and education efforts.

As a service to Missouri beekeepers, the bureau works under the Missouri Apiculture Law to inspect and certify honeybee colonies. These procedures are required for interstate shipment of honeybees.

Bureau of Integrated Pest Management

The Integrated Pest Management (IPM) Bureau includes the Fresh Fruit and Vegetable Inspection, Noxious Weed and IPM in Missouri Schools programs. IPM strategies anticipate pest problems and prevent them from reaching economically damaging levels. The goal of the IPM program is to assist in reducing pesticide use through pest identification and surveys; increasing adoption of improved cultural management practices and strategic control methods; and overseeing the use of biological control agents. The program administers the noxious weed statutes as well as the appointment of Johnson Grass Control Board members in their respective counties. The bureau provides oversight for Missouri DriftWatch, a tool to enhance communications between specialty crop producers and pesticide applicators.

The Fresh Fruit and Vegetable Inspection Program assures buyers and sellers of this highly perishable product that commodities are graded and packed to comply to established USDA standards. Terminal market inspections confirm quality and grade of produce received by Missouri wholesale purchasers for distribution to retail outlets. Shipping-point inspections determine the quality and grade of Missouri-grown produce. Both types of inspections are provided upon request and at the expense of growers, shippers or wholesale purchasers. The program is a cooperative effort between the state and the USDA Agricultural Marketing Service.

RONALD HAYES
Director, Weights, Measures and
Consumer Protection Division

Weights, Measures and Consumer Protection Division

As the chief consumer protection agency in the state, the Weights, Measures and Consumer Protection Division maintains surveillance of commercial weighing and measuring devices. The division promotes uniformity in laws, regulations and standards to achieve equity between buyers and sellers. Sales of products and services impacted by weights and measure laws represent more than 50 percent of U.S. gross national product, totaling over $4.5 trillion.

The Missouri Weights, Measures and Consumer Protection programs are operated in accordance with the National Institute of Standards and Technology. The division is also a member of the National Conference on Weights and Measures, American Society for Testing Materials International and the National Fire Protection Association.

Land Survey Program

The division's Land Survey Program provides information and resources for the accurate location of all private and public boundaries in Missouri. The program is responsible for the restoration and preservation of the original corner monuments established by the General Land Office for the U.S. Public Land Survey System. The division also maintains a records storage and retrieval system for all land survey records and geodetic data.

Device and Commodity Inspection Program

As required by Missouri statutes, device and commodity field personnel inspect large and small scales; grain hopper scales; taxicab meters; devices that measure time, fabric and grain moisture; milk for quantity determination; prepackaged merchandise; and method of sale of commodities. The program enforces the Missouri Egg Law and the Missouri Unfair Milk Sales Practices Law.

LOWELL MOHLER
Chair
State Fair Commission

KEVIN ROBERTS
Vice Chair
State Fair Commission

JANET CRAFTON
Member
State Fair Commission

BARBARA HAYDEN
Member
State Fair Commission

SHERRY JONES
Member
State Fair Commission

DR. JACK MAGRUDER
Member
State Fair Commission

TED SHEPPARD
Member
State Fair Commission

RICHARD FORDYCE
Director of Agriculture
State Fair Commission

Petroleum/Propane/Anhydrous Ammonia Program

The program combines a variety of services. Under the program, petroleum dispensers, petroleum terminal meters and metered fuel delivery trucks are tested for accuracy. Service station pumps are also inspected for accuracy and safety. Metered propane delivery trucks are checked, and the storage and handling of anhydrous ammonia are monitored for safety.

Metrology Program

The metrology program conducts tests, calibrates and certifies field standards for state agencies and private institutions. The state metrologist is the official keeper of Missouri's primary standards of mass, volume and length.

Fuel Quality Program

Fuel samples are collected by field personnel and submitted for testing. The petroleum laboratory analyzes gasoline, kerosene, heating oils and diesel fuel to ensure they meet state quality and safety standards.

DON McQUITTY
Commissioner
Missouri State Fair

MARK WOLFE
Director
Missouri State Fair

Missouri State Fair

2503 W. 16th St., Sedalia 65301
Telephone: (660) 530-5600
www.mostatefair.com

Established in 1899, the Missouri State Fair is one of the oldest in the nation. The fairgrounds, which cover 396 acres in Sedalia (Pettis County), are open year-round, providing facilities for horse and livestock shows, art and craft festivals, camping, rallies and other events. During the annual fair held in August, visitors enjoy educational and recreational activities, a carnival midway and musical entertainment.

The Missouri State Fair continues to be the state's largest agricultural and tourism event, with exhibits showcasing livestock, row crops, horticulture and floriculture. The State Fair plays an important role in shaping Missouri agriculture, contributing to the state's economy and educating the public about the importance and necessity of agriculture. It features agribusiness exhibits and displays of Missouri-produced commodities.

The State Fair Commission, whose members are appointed by the governor, oversees the fair's operations.

State Fair Commission

Mohler, Lowell, (R), chair, Jefferson City, Dec. 29, 2013;

Roberts, Kevin, (D), vice chair, Hillsboro, Dec. 29, 2014;

Crafton, Janet, (D), St. James, Dec. 29, 2015;

Hayden, Barbara, (R), Sedalia, Dec. 29, 2009;

Jones, Sherry, (R), Dawn, Dec. 29, 2014;

Magruder, Dr. Jack, (D), Kirksville, Dec. 29, 2012;

McQuitty, Don, (D), Sunrise Beach, Dec. 29, 2015;

Sheppard, Teddy (Ted) E., (R), Cabool, Dec. 29, 2012;

Fordyce, Richard, director, Department of Agriculture.

Missouri Agricultural and Small Business Development Authority

The Missouri Agricultural and Small Business Development Authority promotes the development of agriculture and small business and works to reduce, control and prevent environmental damage in Missouri.

Available loans and grants include: Alternative Loan Program, Missouri Agribusiness Revolving Loan, Beginning Farmer Loan Program, Animal Waste Treatment System Loan, Single-Purpose Animal Facilities Loan Guarantee, Missouri Value-Added Grant, Missouri Value-Added Loan Guarantee, New Generation Cooperative Incentive Tax Credit, Agricultural Products Utilization Contributor Tax Credit, Family Farm Breeding Livestock Tax Credit, Qualified Beef Tax Credit Program, Livestock Feed and Crop Input Loan Guarantee.

The authority is administered by a seven-member commission, which is appointed by the governor and confirmed by the Senate. The director of agriculture serves as an *ex officio* member.

Howerton, John, (R), chair, Chilhowee, June 30, 2008;

DAVID MEYER
Executive Director
Missouri Agriculture and Small
Business Development Authority

JIM ANDERSON
Executive Director
Missouri Wine and Grape Board

Culler, Robert, (D), vice chair, Hayti, June 30, 2014;

Forck, Kelly, (D), Jefferson City, June 30, 2011;

Jones, Sherry, (R), Dawn, June 30, 2011;

Heitman, Morris, (R), Mound City, June 30, 2015;

Devlin, Karisha, (R), Edina, June 30, 2015;

Fordyce, Richard, director, Department of Agriculture, *ex officio* member.

Missouri Wine & Grape Board

The Missouri Wine and Grape Board is responsible for researching, developing and promoting Missouri grapes, juices and wine. The board is funded by a tax on all wine sold in Missouri.

Missouri wineries continue to refine their grape-growing and winemaking skills to offer distinct, quality wines. The Wine and Grape Board sponsors research and advisory programs at the Grape & Wine Institute.

Missouri has more than 1,700 acres of grapes. Missouri wineries produce more than 950,000 gallons of wine with an overall economic impact of $1.6 billion. Many of the state's 120 plus wineries consistently take top honors in prestigious domestic and international competitions.

Hofherr, Peter, chair, St. James, Oct. 28, 2012;

Bomgaars, Cory, vice chair, Rocheport, president, Missouri Vintner's Association;

Dressel, Charles, Ladue, Oct. 28, 2012;

Gerke, Jason, Platte City, president, Missouri Grape Growers Association;

Held, John, Hermann, Oct. 28, 2011;

Kirby, Matthew K., Higbee, Oct. 10, 2010;

Schmidt, Sarah, Baltimore Bend, president, Wine Marketing & Research Council;

Meyer, Ken E., Springfield, Oct. 28, 2012;

Ostmann, Barbara Gibbs, Gerald, Oct. 28, 2011;

Fordyce, Richard, director, Department of Agriculture.

State Milk Board

The State Milk Board consists of 12 members, 10 of whom are nominated by the director of agriculture, appointed by the governor and confirmed by the Senate. The two remaining members of the board are from the state Department of Health and Senior Services and the Department of Agriculture.

Four of the appointed members of the board must be Grade A dairy farmers representing recognized producer organizations. Four appointees are active members of local health departments in the state. The two remaining appointees represent processor and consumer interests. No more than six of the 12 board members can be from the same political party.

The board administers milk inspection in relation to Grade A milk and milk supplies to ensure uniformity of procedures and interpretation of milk inspection regulations. The Grade A or fluid milk activities of the state are supported by revenue from inspection fees.

The Manufacturing Grade Dairy Program enforces sanitation and quality standards for manufactured dairy products and provides market testing of all milk at the first point of sale. Milk procurers, manufacturing plants, field superintendents, testers, graders, samplers and bulk milk truck operators are licensed by the State Milk Board.

GENE WISEMAN
Executive Director
State Milk Board

Brandt, Alfred J., (R), Linn, Sept. 28, 2010;
Helbig, Gregory, (R), Springfield, Sept. 28, 2013;
Hickam, Dr. Linda, Department of Agriculture representative;
Mahoney, Patricia, (D), St. Louis City Health representative, Sept. 28, 2010;
Mooney, Randy, (R), Rogersville, Sept. 28, 2011;
Owen, Thomas, (R), St. Louis County Health Department representative, Sept. 28, 2013;
Prescott, Karen M., (D), Springfield Health Department representative, Sept. 28, 2011;
Shannon, Pat, Health Department representative;
Siebenborn, William, (D), Trenton, Sept. 28, 2009;
Vacancies (3).

Department of Conservation

2901 W. Truman Blvd., Jefferson City 65109
Telephone: (573) 751-4115 / FAX: (573) 751-4467
www.mdc.mo.gov

The Missouri Department of Conservation (MDC), authorized in 1937 by an initiative process and statewide vote to amend the Missouri Constitution, was created by public demand for better management of the state's forest, fish and wildlife resources. The department is headed by the Conservation Commission, whose four members, no more than two of whom may belong to the same political party, are appointed by the governor with the advice and consent of the Senate. They serve with no compensation for staggered six-year terms.

The department's principal sources of revenue are receipts from the sale of hunting and fishing permits and the one-eighth of one percent conservation sales tax. The conservation sales tax was approved as a constitutional amendment through a citizen initiative process and statewide vote in 1976. Funds are also received, primarily on a matching basis, from federal aid provisions of the Wildlife Restoration, Sport Fish Restoration Act and Cooperative Forestry Assistance Act. The department receives no state general revenue funds.

The department's mission is to protect and manage the forest, fish and wildlife resources of the state; and to facilitate and provide opportunities for all citizens to use, enjoy and learn about these resources. The vision is that the department shall be a forward-looking agency, implementing solid core values that ensure integrity and trust; using adaptive learning and creative thinking; embracing technology; and providing superior public service. The department seeks to be the national leader in forest, fish and wildlife management, proactively advancing its mission through understanding natural resource and social landscapes.

The mission and vision are accomplished using a set of values that include: excellent public service; believing all citizens are important; providing open communication; offering opportunities for Missourians to partner; ensuring fairness, objectivity, sound science, integrity and accountability to guide actions; and knowing employees are the department's most important asset. The department works to advance conservation by being results-driven, working as a team, serving

DON C. BEDELL
Member
Conservation Commission

JAMES T. BLAIR IV
Member
Conservation Commission

MARILYNN J. BRADFORD
Member
Conservation Commission

DAVID W. MURPHY
Member
Conservation Commission

as ambassadors for conservation and living out the conservation ethic through actions.

Conservation Commission

Bedell, Don C., (R), Sikeston, July 1, 2021;
Blair, James T. IV, (R), St. Louis, July 1, 2017;
Bradford, Marilynn J., (I), Jefferson City, July 1, 2019;
Murphy, David W., (D), Columbia, July 1, 2019.

Director's Office

The Conservation Commission appoints the department director who, along with two deputy directors, directs programs and activities through the divisions of administrative services, design and development, fisheries, forestry, human resources, outreach and education, private land services, protection, resource science and wildlife. In addition to division assignments, the deputy directors provide leadership for projects and initiatives through partnerships, federal aid coordination, the policy coordination unit and the information technology unit. The Policy Coordination Unit serves the director's office, divisions and regions by providing technology planning, systems research and design, customer technical

BOB ZIEHMER
Director

TOM DRAPER
Deputy Director

TIM RIPPERGER
Deputy Director

AARON JEFFRIES
Assistant to Director

RHONDA MAPLES
Executive Assistant to the
Director / Commission Secretary

JENNIFER FRAZIER
General Counsel

LISA WEHMEYER
Internal Auditor

support and administers voice and data network operations. The director also supervises the general counsel, internal auditor and an assistant to the director for government relations.

General Counsel

The general counsel is appointed by the director of the Department of Conservation, with the consent of the Conservation Commission, to provide legal advice and representation to the commission and the department. The Office of General Counsel handles litigation, works with prosecutors and staff to enforce statutes and regulations, provides legal advice and opinions, drafts and reviews documents, oversees real estate transactions and reviews administrative regulations.

Internal Auditor

The internal auditor assists the commission and director by independently analyzing department operations, policies, procedures, records and compliance with laws and regulations to ensure effectiveness and accountability. The internal auditor also serves the Department of Conservation as a custodian of records and the hearing officer for revocation of hunting and fishing privileges.

Regional Offices

The department has two administrative units and eight regions. The Missouri River Unit includes the Central, Kansas City, Northeast and Northwest regions. The Ozark Unit includes Ozark, St. Louis, Southeast and Southwest regions. A regional service center in each region, in addition to other offices, nature centers, staffed shooting ranges and interpretive centers, provides close-to-home opportunities for Missourians to participate in conservation programs and services. Regional offices are located in Columbia, Lee's Summit, St. Joseph, Kirksville, West Plains, St. Charles, Cape Girardeau and Springfield.

Administrative Services Division

The administrative services division provides administrative support through five units: financial services, permit services, fleet services, flight services and general services.

The financial services unit administers all financial activities of the department. It maintains a liaison with the state treasurer, state auditor, Office of Administration and Department of Revenue. It is responsible for revenue collection, accounts payable, accounting, budget and payroll. Revenue from the conservation sales tax, hunting and fishing permits, federal reimbursement, timber sales, publications and surplus property is received and deposited in the state treasury for department programs.

The other units are responsible for: management, operation and purchasing of the department's fleet; management of aircraft operations; inventory control; repair and disposition of vehicles, marine and other mechanical equipment; operation of a distribution center and warehouse for publications, products and media loan services; operation of printing, mailing and sign production services; the distribution of hunting and fishing permits statewide for sale to the public; and purchasing services.

Design and Development Division

The design and development division provides engineering, architecture, land surveying, construction, quality control and facility maintenance services to develop, maintain and manage the department's infrastructure and to implement and administer capital improvement projects.

Infrastructure and capital improvement projects include boat accesses, docks, roads, parking areas, office and storage buildings, fish hatcheries, fishing lakes and ponds, nature centers, shooting ranges, trails, wetlands and other projects. The division provides engineering and architectural designs that apply sound engineering principles to the design of conservation projects and public-use facilities that are in harmony with the environment and enhance the enjoyment of Missouri's natural resources. The division provides: land surveying; ongoing renovation, repair and maintenance; facility maintenance, including grounds maintenance, grading of parking areas and entry roads, cleaning boat ramps and maintenance of privies, boat docks and other infrastructure; and coordinates and obtains regulatory environmental permits and cultural clearances for construction and management activities involving soil disturbance on public lands owned and managed by the department.

The division also administers the department's County Aid Road Trust Fund (CART) program that assists county and other governmental units with road maintenance to ensure public access is available to department areas.

Fisheries Division

The fisheries division provides fisheries and aquatic resource expertise and management efforts. Responsibilities include four warm water and five cold water hatcheries; administering a Stream Unit program that includes over 4,196 active "Stream Team" citizen groups; monitoring and maintaining the quality of Missouri's aquatic

MARGIE MUELLER
Administrative Services
Chief Financial Officer

JACOB CAREAGA
Design and Development
Division Chief

BRIAN CANADAY
Fisheries Division Chief

LISA ALLEN
Forestry Division Chief

resources; managing public fisheries resources for quality fishing; providing technical stream and lake management advice to private landowners and other public agencies; and providing and assisting with public information and education programs.

The four warm water hatcheries rear and coordinate the stocking of about 8 million fish in public waters, suitable private lakes and waters used for special fishing events and aquatic resources education. Methods are also developed for rearing endangered species. The five cold water hatcheries (Bennett Spring, Maramec Spring, Montauk, Roaring River and Shepherd of the Hills) rear and coordinate the stocking of about 2 million trout in public waters.

The division directs and administers fisheries programs, develops and refines regulations, works on the acquisition and development of public fishing and boat access areas, administers the Community Assistance Program and Corporate and Agency Partnership Program, administers federal aid grants, coordinates angler recognition programs, develops and revises technical and popular written materials and distributes a weekly fishing report during the fishing season.

Missouri has more than 975 public lakes with approximately 281,450 acres of surface water,

486 miles of the Mississippi River, 553 miles of the Missouri River, about 110,000 miles of permanent and intermittent streams, and 500,000 private impoundments. These waters support rich and diverse aquatic communities that are used, enjoyed and appreciated by millions of people each year. Fishing is one of the most popular and economically important uses of these waters. Each year, nearly 1.1 million anglers in Missouri generate more than $1 billion of economic impact in the state.

Forestry Division

The forestry division provides management and protection of the state's forest resources to have healthy and sustainable forest and woodland communities on both public and private land. Forestry programs assist forest landowners and forest industries with practices designed to: ensure healthy and sustainable forests; ensure the proper management and sustainability of public forest lands; control and reduce the impact from major infestations of forest insects and diseases; work with communities to develop sustainable community forestry programs; and improve rural fire protection throughout the state.

Each year, technical assistance is provided by the division to private woodland owners. These services are available statewide and include tree selection and planting advice, forest management plans and recommendations, forest products utilization and marketing assistance and wildlife management recommendations. The forest health protection program ensures the continuing health of forest resources through survey and detection, pest and control evaluations and public information. The division also provides training for loggers to encourage the sustainable harvest of Missouri's forests.

The division manages more than 440,000 acres of public forest land. Forest management benefits include biodiversity, watershed protection, wildlife habitat, forest products and recreational opportunities. To encourage forest and wildlife plantings, 3 million seedlings of more than 60 different tree and shrub species are produced at the George O. White State Forest Nursery each year to fill requests from Missourians. Every fourth-grade student in the state receives an Arbor Day seedling produced at the nursery.

The division provides assistance to communities through the Tree Resource Improvement and Management (TRIM) program, which provides funds to implement community forestry programs, including tree establishment, maintenance and care. Special consideration has been given to communities that have sustained significant damage from natural disasters and invasive pests.

In addition, the division assists more than 776 volunteer rural fire departments to suppress approximately 3,000 wildfires annually, which burn forest and grassland. Technical assistance, training and federal excess equipment are available at no cost to cooperating rural fire departments. Grants, supported in part by the U.S. Forest Service (USFS), are available to rural fire departments on a competitive basis. A rural forest fire equipment center is located in Lebanon. The center acquires and distributes federal excess property to rural fire departments for use in fire suppression activities. "Operation Forest Arson" is a program to combat the high number of arson-caused wildfires. This program is combined with the Smokey Bear wildfire prevention campaign to educate school children.

In Missouri, there are about 15.5 million acres of forests, or 35 percent of the land area. Approximately 80 percent of the forested land is the oak-hickory type, 6 percent is shortleaf pine and oak-pine types and the remainder is in cedar and bottomland hardwoods. Over 83 percent of forests are privately owned by about 350,000 individual owners. Missouri's forests support a large forest products industry with about 1,000 manufacturing plants producing lumber, railroad ties, cooperage, cedar and walnut items (including gunstocks and veneer), charcoal and other products. Missouri leads the nation in the production of charcoal, cooperage barrels, cedar novelties, gunstocks, walnut bowls and walnut nutmeats. The economic impact of the forest industry and wood products in Missouri is $8 billion annually.

Human Resources Division

The Human Resources Division provides services that help the department attract and retain a diverse and dynamic workforce, including recruitment and selection; administering salary and fringe benefits programs; overseeing a comprehensive group life, medical, accidental death and dismemberment and dependent life insurance program; maintaining official employee documents and records through a human resources information system; and managing a safety program, including worker's compensation. The division also monitors compliance with employment practices relating to affirmative action, American's with Disabilities Act (ADA) and drug testing; provides employee training and development programs; administers employee assistance and wellness activities; and assists with disciplinary and grievance processes. A workforce council implements programs to increase the department's efforts to experience the benefits of a diverse workforce.

Outreach and Education Division

The Outreach and Education Division helps Missourians learn to conserve and enjoy Missouri's forests, fish and wildlife resources through focused education, interpretation and outreach efforts. The division develops, coordinates and implements education curriculum, materials and programs; public relations, news and marketing; hunter education; print, image and digital media; exhibits; nature and interpretive centers; shooting ranges; hands-on and indirect learning opportunities; and volunteer programs.

The *Missouri Conservationist* magazine is published monthly and is free to adult Missourians. The magazine has been published since 1938. The monthly circulation is about 500,000. A children's magazine, *Xplor*, is published every other month. The division coordinates the department webpage information, *www.missouri conservation.org*, which includes an online Conservation Atlas with maps and information about department areas. Other information includes tips for getting outdoors, hunting and fishing reports, conservation videos, the *Missouri Conservationist* magazine and news online, a calendar of events, links to special programs such as "Grow Native!" and "No MOre Trash!" and the ability to purchase hunting and fishing permits online. Through many free publications, Missourians can also learn about subjects as diverse as how to fish, hunting regulations or animal identification. A Natural Events Calendar, books and DVDs are available at nature centers, through a catalog or online.

There are nature and education centers in Blue Springs, Jefferson City, Kirkwood, Springfield, Cape Girardeau and Winona, and visitor centers in Taney, St. Charles and St. Louis counties that offer unique nature exploration programs. The Discovery Center, located in the heart of Kansas City, features workshops offering hands-on instruction to school groups and individuals in a building that highlights energy-efficient design.

The division develops and makes available conservation education programs, including "Discover Nature–Schools," which helps students get outside to experience hands-on learning in nature close to home. Instructional units are provided at no cost, which meet testing needs and are combined with grants for field trips and instructional materials to complement the national "No Child Left Inside" effort. Additional units provide focused conservation information for other grade levels. The division delivers conservation education to public, private and parochial schools and colleges, as well as youth leaders and community leaders.

TOM NEUBAUER
Human Resources
Division Chief

JOANIE STRAUB
Outreach and Education
Division Chief

Opportunities for citizen involvement include "Missouri Master Naturalists," which is a community-based, adult natural resource education and volunteer program sponsored by the Department of Conservation, the University of Missouri Extension program and the University of Missouri College of Agriculture, Food and Natural Resources.

The division also teaches Missourians skills to enjoy the outdoors safely and responsibly. Outdoor skills specialists work to give Missourians of all ages direct experience in nature-based activities such as fishing, hunting and archery. The "Missouri National Archery in the Schools Program (MoNASP)" is supported by the department with the help of the Missouri Conservation Federation to bring archery to schools statewide. Other programs called "Discover Nature–Families" and "Discover Nature–Women" help Missourians learn a variety of skills to enjoy the outdoors. The division coordinates a team of volunteers to provide hunter education training, which is mandatory for all persons born on or after Jan. 1, 1967, as a prerequisite to the purchase of firearms hunting permits; about 25,000 students receive training each year.

Shooting ranges administered by the division provide hunters a safe place to practice and develop outdoor skills. Five staffed shooting range and outdoor education centers and more than 75 unstaffed ranges (including both firearms and archery ranges) provide Missourians with opportunities to practice firearm and archery skills. Programs offered at the staffed ranges help educate new hunters.

Private Land Services Division

The private land services division helps Missouri landowners achieve their land use objectives in ways that enhance forest, fish and wildlife conservation. Private landowners own about 93 percent of the land in Missouri. The division promotes the wise use of forests, fish, wildlife and natural communities through voluntary participation, information, financial assistance and partnerships.

The health of Missouri's forest, fish and wildlife resources depends on the stewardship of Missouri landowners. The division provides technical assistance and tailors management recommendations to the goals of the landowner and site-specific natural resource needs. Assistance is provided to communities, including urban developers, homeowners, city and county planners and others to address natural resource protection and management in developed areas, as well as in areas under development. Wildlife damage control biologists provide assistance to landowners experiencing damage to their property caused by wildlife.

The division develops partnerships with state and federal agencies, commodity groups, agribusinesses and conservation organizations. Partnerships with the Natural Resources Conservation Service and Farm Service Agency integrate forest, fish and wildlife considerations into implementation of Farm Bill programs. To complement funding available through federal programs, the department offers cost-share to landowners for implementation of select natural resource management practices.

Protection Division

The protection division is responsible for enforcement of the Wildlife Code of Missouri and related statutes on both private and public lands. Uniformed Conservation Agents are assigned to each county in Missouri and represent the department in a wide variety of programs.

Agents are licensed as peace officers to enforce all state laws on lands owned, managed or leased by the department. Agents are also commissioned by the U.S. Department of the Interior to enforce federal fish and wildlife laws. Agents administer the hunter education program in their local area. Agents provide conservation information and education through newspaper articles, adult and youth meetings, exhibits, clinics, radio and television programs and other media. The division helps to provide basic information on forest, fish and wildlife management, assists with landowner assistance programs and conducts surveys and special field studies.

Agents are the primary contact for landowners with poaching or trespassing problems and are often contacted about nuisance wildlife issues.

The division works with the Conservation Federation of Missouri to administer the Operation Game Thief, Operation Forest Arson and Share the Harvest programs. Operation Game Thief provides an avenue for concerned citizens to report poaching through a centralized toll-free

BILL WHITE
Private Land Services
Division Chief

LARRY YAMNITZ
Protection Division Chief

hotline: (800) 392-1111. Rewards for information leading to the arrest of violators are available. Since the inception of this program in 1982, over 7,600 arrests have been made with information supplied by concerned citizens. This program has been shown to be an effective means of public awareness and involvement in protecting the natural resources of Missouri.

Share the Harvest, a program where hunters donate deer meat to those less fortunate through established charitable organizations, has received over 3.2 million pounds of deer meat for Missouri citizens. Hunters who donate their entire deer receive a reduction in the price of processing, which is paid to the processor by the Missouri Conservation Federation, a private citizen's organization. In some cases, local organizations provide additional funds for processing so there is no cost to hunters who wish to donate deer.

Resource Science Division

The resource science division provides the science-based information needed to conserve, appreciate and effectively manage the living natural resources of Missouri. The division is organized around systems and functions, rather than traditional disciplines, and delivers management assistance through a series of field stations. The systems include terrestrial systems, aquatic and wetland systems, science technology and policy support, geographic information systems (GIS), environmental health and the Heritage Program. Field stations include a grasslands systems field station in Clinton, a forest systems field station in West Plains, a big rivers and wetlands systems field station in Jackson, an agricultural systems field station in Kirksville and the Missouri River field station in Chillicothe. A Conservation Research Center is located in Columbia.

The terrestrial systems work includes evaluating plant and animal habitat relationships, monitoring population status and developing harvest and species management recommendations for statewide populations of deer, furbearers, turkey and migratory birds. Specialized projects monitor wildlife and plant diversity, population changes and forest silviculture.

Aquatic and wetland systems work includes evaluating fisheries, wetland and waterfowl management, fish communities, watersheds, stream systems, interactions among predators and prey and species of concern.

Science technology and policy support work includes post-harvest hunter and angler surveys, attitude surveys and public-use surveys to understand the opinions and attitudes of Missourians. This information, combined with biological information and natural resource economics data, informs management decisions. The GIS program uses geospatial technology and products to support natural resource decisions, archive the processes, evaluate results and train users. Biometricians ensure statistically sound study designs and the use of appropriate statistical techniques to analyze and interpret complex natural resource questions.

Environmental health work includes evaluating aquatic biodiversity, such as mussel conservation and genetics research, water quality and provides responsive service to the department, the public and other agencies and entities. Issues involving pollution, fish kills and contaminants are coordinated with other agencies. Wildlife Health work provides expertise for management and research of wildlife health-related issues.

The Heritage Program provides expertise for management and research on high-priority taxa and maintains the Heritage Database. The Natural Heritage program tracks the status and location of 1,252 species and natural communities of conservation concern, with ongoing documentation and mapping. These data are used in the department and by federal and state agencies for recovery efforts, environmental reviews and management efforts.

Wildlife Division

The wildlife division actively manages and restores Missouri's plants, animals and habitats for the use and enjoyment of present and future generations. The division manages over 538,000 acres, which is about one-half of department-managed lands. The division provides technical advice for wildlife and habitat management to other agencies, organizations, communities, industries and private landowners.

MIKE HUBBARD
Resource Science Division Chief

JENNIFER BATTSON WARREN
Wildlife Division Chief

The division administers the department's endangered species, invasive species, natural community management, Natural Areas, Missouri Comprehensive Conservation Strategy and other state and national wildlife initiatives. The division assists with the development of regulations for public use of department-managed lands and statewide wildlife management. The division assists with research and monitoring projects that inform regulation changes and improve wildlife and habitat management practices. The division promotes active citizen involvement in conservation and outdoor recreation and connects urban and rural citizens with opportunities to appreciate and enjoy Missouri's wildlife and their habitats.

The division's public land management activities accommodate public recreation opportunities through the active management of wildlife and their habitats. The division maintains more than 285 miles of trails and administers numerous managed hunts, including special opportunities for youth and hunters with disabilities. Wildlife habitat management on public lands provides environmental benefits for all citizens by maintaining the ecological health of Missouri forests, prairies, glades, wetlands and streams. Healthy ecosystems are necessary to produce healthy and sustainable forest, fish and wildlife resources. They also contribute to high water quality, groundwater recharge, air quality, soil erosion control, watershed protection and the economy. In Missouri, approximately 576,000 individuals hunt and 1.7 million view wildlife. Missourians and non-residents spend more than $2.6 billion dollars annually related to fish and wildlife recreation. These expenditures generate $4.7 billion dollars annually in economic impacts in Missouri.

Department of Corrections

PO Box 236, Jefferson City 65102
Telephone: (573) 751-2389 / FAX: (573) 751-4099
TTD: (573) 751-5984
www.doc.mo.gov

GEORGE A. LOMBARDI
Director

DAVID ROST
Deputy Director

The Department of Corrections is an agency dedicated to public safety through the successful management and supervision of offenders on probation, in prison and on parole. The department's responsibility is to administer the sentence set by the court in ways that promote public safety at the lowest cost to taxpayers. Offenders assigned to the department are successfully managed by ensuring they are supervised at the correct custody or supervision level. A cadre of over 11,000 well-trained correctional professionals committed to the vision, mission, values and professional principles of the department assess each offender's criminal history, evaluate community and institutional conduct and enforce court orders and department rules. This mixture of ongoing assessment, classification, referral-to-supervision strategies and assignment to basic habilitation interventions are several of the key methods used to promote sober, responsible, productive and law-abiding behavior. When offenders are held accountable for their behavior and responsible for their actions, the public's safety is enhanced.

In all, the department is responsible for the care, custody and supervision of approximately 94,371 adult offenders in Missouri. On Dec. 31, 2014, there were 31,942 offenders confined in Missouri's 20 correctional facilities, and the department was supervising 16,599 parolees and 45,830 probationers across the state. In addition to the correctional facilities, the department operates two community release centers and seven community supervision centers.

There are four divisions within the department. The management of felons and selected misdemeanants committed by the court are divided between the Division of Probation and Parole and the Division of Adult Institutions. The Division of Offender Rehabilitative Services provides program services to felons assigned to probation, parole or prison. All staff-related activities and special program services are provided through the Division of Human Services.

The department utilizes strategic planning to promote continuous improvement and excellent customer service at all levels of the organization.

JOE EDDY
Director, Budget, Research and Evaluation

DENA SIKOUTRIS
Reentry Services

This commitment to continuous improvement ensures offenders under the supervision of the Department of Corrections are assigned to the correct custody classification and receive those services that reduce criminal behavior and promote long lasting public safety through a measurable reduction in recidivism and revocation.

The strength of the Department of Corrections is found in the women and men who serve around the clock to ensure that offenders are supervised at the most appropriate level with the greatest care for public safety. To assist staff in their challenging work, the department has developed policies and procedures based on statutes, case law and the best practices in the field.

Sometimes overlooked are the line staff and supervisors dedicated to providing quality correctional supervision to offenders. Working together, these units of probation and parole officers, correctional officers, clerical staff, cooks, substance abuse counselors, caseworkers, maintenance workers, teachers, treatment staff and others blend into a team that holds offenders accountable for their behavior and responsible for their actions. Through a combination of supervision strategies and classification criteria, offenders are supervised in ways that address public safety concerns while meeting the needs of the offender.

Supervision levels in the community range from intensive to minimum supervision of offenders, to community corrections programs, such as electronic monitoring and residential facilities. Community supervision centers provide additional supervision and treatment for at-risk offenders. In the prisons, there are three custody levels: minimum, medium and maximum. Using objective criteria to establish supervision and custody levels ensures offenders with corresponding need and disposition are supervised and confined safely and securely with appropriate programming.

The employees of the Missouri Department of Corrections are among the finest in the field of corrections. They are active in their local communities both in developing professional relationships with citizen groups and maintaining their role as citizens building strong communities. The department takes its responsibilities seriously and is committed to making Missouri a safe and secure place for its citizens and visitors.

Offender Management

Risk management is the process of classifying offenders according to the risk they currently present to the public so as to assign them to the institutional custody or community supervision level that best monitors their conduct. Department staff assess, evaluate and intervene as necessary to ensure offenders are managed in ways that best promote public safety in accordance with the sentence of the court.

Risk management is accomplished in a variety of ways. Sentencing assessment reports assist the court in determining sentencing options. Individualized institutional treatment programs for substance abusers, sex offenders and others who experience mental health or other special problems provide offenders with the necessary skills for successful reintegration into society. Supervision strategies such as intensive specialized programming, electronic monitoring, community supervision centers, day reporting centers and residential facilities provide offenders with a structured environment for increased supervision. Restorative justice programming in institutions and field offices allow offenders an opportunity to repair the harm their crimes have caused individual victims and their communities. The institutional classification system ensures felons in prison are confined at custody levels that maintain facility security and public safety.

Office of the Director

The director of the Missouri Department of Corrections is charged with shaping legislation, formulating policies and procedures and keeping the public informed in order to effectively and efficiently guide and implement objectives and goals that increase the public's safety. The Office of the Inspector General is also charged with the oversight of the Prison Rape Elimination Act (PREA) standards for the department to ensure compliance needs are met. Included in the Office of the Director are units that participate in these endeavors, notably Victim Services, Inspector General, Legal Services, Budget and Research, Reentry and Women Offender Programs, Emergency Preparedness/Workplace Violence, Legislative/Constituent Services and Public Information.

Budget, Research and Evaluation

The Budget Unit is responsible for developing, preparing and presenting the department's annual budget request. Budget staff coordinate with the department's operating divisions to determine the resources required to implement agency programs and strategies. The unit then develops funding requests that accurately reflect the department's strategic planning goals and objectives. Through analysis of research data on program outcomes and population trends, the unit provides guidance on ways to use department resources more effectively and efficiently. The Budget Unit presents the budget request to the governor's office and then works closely with the General Assembly to provide information during the appropriations process. This unit also coordinates fiscal note responses for the department.

The Federal Grants Unit is responsible for obtaining, monitoring, managing and disbursing all federal funds obtained through grants to the department. This section pays all bills and salaries for federal programs in which the department participates. The Federal Grants Unit prepares financial and progress reports for all department grants.

The Research and Evaluation Unit is responsible for providing research data and analysis to support the entire Department of Corrections. The unit tracks population growth of all offenders and maintains statistical data required for the evaluation of department programs and trends. The unit provides research information required to support the strategic planning process and all departmental decision-making. The unit also provides research and survey data to agencies within and outside state government and reviews outside research requests.

Reentry, Restorative Justice and Women Offender Programs

Missouri was chosen as one of the first two states to implement a model created by the National Institute of Corrections called the Transition from Prison to Community Initiative (TPCI). This initiative was the impetus for the development of the Missouri Reentry Process (MRP), which is a system of resources, programs and partnerships designed to decrease offender risk and enhance offender self-sufficiency to improve public safety. The Reentry Unit manages a number of programs and initiatives related to the MRP and provides offender reentry assistance and direction to divisions within the Department of Corrections, partnering agencies and the community. The purpose of this assistance is to empower professionals and community members to better assist the offender population with their reintegration to the community. The Women Offender Program was established to ensure accountability, reliability and continuous improvement in meeting the department's commitment to provide gender-specific resources and interventions to women incarcerated or under probation or parole supervision. The Department of Corrections understands the value of partnership and works closely with the state level MRP Steering Team, the 40 local MRP Steering Teams and various other state and community agencies, organizations and faith-based groups.

The Reentry Unit also provides oversight and support to the Department of Corrections' restorative justice efforts. Through restorative justice initiatives, offenders assist victims and victimized communities as part of their sentence to prison. Restorative justice holds the offender accountable and provides a means for them to repay their debt to the victim and the community. These initiatives also provide the offender an opportunity to leave the system with an improved attitude and sense of belonging, as well as strengthened social bonds that serve as the foundation of communities. Through the efforts of offender volunteers, not-for-profit agencies and victims statewide receive reparative products and services. Examples include donation of quilts, fruits and vegetables harvested from inmate gardens, wooden toys, refurbished bicycles, etc. to organizations such as the Salvation Army, children's hospitals, senior citizen homes, schools, KidSmart, Newborns in Need, Head Start, Boys and Girls Club, Veterans Administration hospitals, homeless shelters and many more. In addition, many offenders attend Impact of Crime on Victims classes (ICVC), which help offenders develop sensitivity and respect toward victims that helps prevent further victimization.

Inspector General

The Office of Inspector General is charged with objectively examining department operations through the Investigations Unit and the Intelligence Unit. The Investigations Unit is the investigative arm of the department and conducts investigations in response to reports of suspected

AMY RODERICK
Inspector General

KIMBERLY EVANS
Victim Services Coordinator

violations of policy and procedure, statute and events that might endanger the safety and security of offenders, staff, facilities, employees or the public. The Intelligence Unit is responsible for developing and filtering intelligence information.

Emergency Preparedness/Workplace Violence

This section is responsible for writing, reviewing and revising departmental policies and procedures related to emergency preparedness, disaster planning and response. This includes the oversight of department emergency preparedness with mitigation planning, monitoring training programs and evaluating emergency exercises at worksites to prepare all staff to respond to emergencies efficiently and effectively.

This section also serves as the liaison to the State Emergency Management Agency (SEMA), which includes responding to SEMA when an emergency dictates an activation. Participation in SEMA sponsored committees and training sessions representing the Department of Corrections and participation in statewide emergency exercises is expected as well.

Coordinating the Department Workplace Violence Program, including development and review of department procedures for program management and Peer Action Care Teams (PACT), is also handled by this section. Additional responsibilities include: developing, revising and coordinating training for PACT members (peer responders); mobilizing PACT when appropriate; receiving and responding to calls regarding workplace violence and critical incidents; assisting with Employee Assistance Program (EAP) referrals; and critical incident stress debriefing at worksites.

Legislative/Constituent Services, Public Information and Victim Services

These three sections of the Office of the Director provide and coordinate information to specific audiences concerning the department and its divisions.

The Legislative/Constituent Services Office processes offender-related inquiries from legislative offices, offender families and the public. Through a customer-focused approach, the office provides information about specific offenders and education about the department's policies, procedures and practices. This office also responds to inquiries from legislators and other interested parties about the department's operations and the potential impact of proposed legislation.

The department's Public Information Office responds to inquiries from the news media and the general public. The office responds to dozens of media calls and inquiries each week. The office also produces department publications and videos. It promotes activities and handles updates to the department website. The unit develops organizational plans to improve internal communication and has implemented a media outreach plan for interviews designed to promote department programs and activities.

The department's Office of Victim Services (OVS) was established to ensure core services and accurate and timely information are provided to Missouri's crime victims. The OVS provides notification of changes in an offender's status to victims of crime in accordance with 595.209, RSMo. The OVS enhances accessibility to department operations including parole hearings, victim impact statements for the Parole Board's consideration and reasonable protection from offenders or others acting on behalf of the offender. The OVS provides services including notification, crisis intervention, support and referrals to approximately 16,000 victims of crime. Upon the request of the victim, OVS staff will provide accompaniment to parole hearings and provide support to families of homicide victims during an execution.

Division of Human Services

The Division of Human Services consists of Human Resource Management, Training and Employee Development, Employee Health/Wellness/Safety, Religious/Spiritual Services, Volunteer/Intern Programs, Planning, Fiscal Management, Offender Financial Services and General Services. This division provides support to the other divisions of the department. A professionally trained workforce, where safety and wellness is practiced as a part of the job, is essential to carrying out the vision, mission, values and professional principles of the department. The Division of Human Services is tasked with recruiting a diverse professional workforce, maintaining that qualified workforce, improving the work environment of employees and communication be-

JEFF EARL
Legislative / Constituent Services

RICHARD WILLIAMS
General Counsel

CARI COLLINS
Director
Division of Human Services

tween management and staff. Strategic planning and fiscal management are essential to support the operation of the department. Additionally, the division has oversight of the institutional food operations, major new construction and maintenance projects, the management of the vehicle fleet and the Central Region's business office and warehouse functions.

Fiscal Management Unit

The Fiscal Management Unit oversees the implementation and maintenance of a variety of complex accounting systems that provide essential fiscal oversight, support and assistance to correctional institutions, probation and parole district offices and Missouri Vocational Enterprises. The unit's primary responsibility is to ensure the accountability and transparency of the state resources entrusted to the department. This is accomplished through the efforts of skilled and experienced staff in the areas of Purchasing, Accounting and Internal Auditing. The unit also serves as the department liaison with the Office of Administration, the state auditor's office, the state treasurer's office and the Department of Revenue.

Offender Financial Services

Offender Financial Services provides fiscal oversight, support and assistance to the offender population by managing the offender canteen and offender banking system. The offender banking system is used to maintain offenders' personal funds, savings accounts, savings bonds and liabilities owed to other entities. The system is also used to process offender payroll and accounts receivable. Each institution operates an offender canteen offering approved products for sale to offenders with revenues used for the benefit of offenders in the areas of recreation, religion or educational services.

Planning Section

The Planning Section provides organizational development assistance in the preparation of the department's strategic plan and oversees the monitoring of strategies and performance measures associated with the strategic plan to ensure success. The Planning Section also facilitates departmental teams that work on process improvement, problem-solving and customer satisfaction projects.

Training Academy

The Training Academy develops, coordinates and delivers pre-service, in-service and management/supervisory training to staff in each of the department's divisions. The academy consists of 53 full-time staff and a cadre of part-time volunteer trainers who perform their duties in one of the department's three regions: Central, Eastern and Western. The academy promotes personal growth, professional development and imparts the departmental vision to all staff members to help them achieve the short- and long-term goals of the agency. To this end, the regions conduct pre-service basic training courses for all new corrections officers, non-custody staff and probation and parole officers. In addition, more than 1,000 in-service and management courses are presented annually. The academy is also responsible for probation and parole safety training and a variety of other certification programs. The academy designs and develops all departmental curricula.

Employee Health and Safety

This section addresses job-related health and safety concerns with a focus on control of infectious diseases. It also oversees and implements occupational safety concerns, coordinates the department's "Early Return to Work Program" and promotes employee wellness activities. The department's Employee Drug Testing Program is coordinated through this unit.

SUSAN WOOD
Offender Finance Officer

COLLEEN DOWD
Planning Section Manager

JIM WISEMAN
Chief of Staff Training

GALE BAILEY
Employee Health and Safety

JENNIFER ZAMKUS
Human Resouces Director

Human Resources Section

The Human Resources Section provides technical assistance on all human resource functions. This section is responsible for the timely and accurate processing of payroll, maintenance and updating of official personnel records for all departmental staff, testing and hiring of corrections officers, reviewing and coordinating classification actions, ensuring the department recruits a qualified and diverse workforce and ensuring that all merit guidelines are followed. The Human Resources Section assists employees in their career development and employee conflict resolution.

Religious/Spiritual Programming

Religious programming opportunities and pastoral care services are provided for inmates in correctional centers. Department chaplains assigned to every institution work with volunteers from various faith-groups to ensure constitutional rights of inmates to practice the religion of their choice are facilitated within the limitations of a secure setting. Religious and spiritual services are used as a restorative and transforming tool for inmate change, growth and social reintegration. Chaplains partner with the outside faith community to provide effective service delivery for the offenders, both in the institution and relative to community reentry. Raising public awareness of offender spiritual needs and volunteer recruitment are essential tasks in which chaplains regularly engage.

The impact of religious and spiritual services for inmates has been shown to decrease conduct violations and promote inmate institutional adjustment. Inmates attending religious and spiritual programming are more likely to engage in activities that promote positive attitudes and behaviors needed to take advantage of other inmate programs.

Volunteers/Interns

Volunteers serve throughout the department and are recognized as non-salaried staff. They receive an orientation to the department, training and supervision by department staff. Volunteers provide a variety of services and programs in areas such as substance abuse, recovery support, literacy, tutoring, parenting, anger management, employability skills and religion. Volunteers provide incarcerated offenders the opportunity to participate in community organizations including: NAACP, Vietnam Veterans, Kiwanis, Toastmasters, American Legion and other such organizations.

This section also coordinates student internships from various educational institutions and colleges around the state. The Volunteer Section coordinates the involvement of representatives from other state agencies, community organizations and individuals in providing reentry services and programs to incarcerated offenders.

General Services

General Services is responsible for the purchasing, storage and distribution of commodity food items to the department's institutions statewide from two regional warehouses. This section also oversees the operations of institutional food service, including regional cook-chill facilities, major new construction and maintenance projects within the department and management of

DOUG WORSHAM
Supervisor, Religious / Spiritual Programming

DORIS FALKENRATH
Coordinator
Volunteer Services

JAY EDWARDS
Manager
General Services

the statewide departmental vehicle fleet. The General Services Unit also oversees the central business office, telecommunications and warehouse functions.

Division of Offender Rehabilitative Services

The Division of Offender Rehabilitative Services is responsible for developing and delivering interventions and services necessary for offenders to correct their criminal behavior at each point in the department's supervision continuum and prepare for successful reintegration into the community upon release. These services and interventions include: academic and vocational education, medical services, mental health services, Missouri Sexual Offender Program, Missouri Vocational Enterprises, toxicology and substance abuse services. These program services allow corrections professionals throughout the department to fully utilize the supervision continuum to better resolve offender issues such as literacy, sobriety and employability. Without remediation, these factors would impede their return to the community as law-abiding and productive citizens. The public's safety is best served by creating increased offender accountability.

MATT STURM
Director, Division of Offender
Rehabilitative Services

JOAN REINKEMEYER
Assistant Division Director
Education Services, Division of
Offender Rehabilitative Services

SCOTT O'KELLEY
Assistant Division Director
Mental Health Services,
Division of Offender
Rehabilitative Services

JOHN SCOTT
Assistant Division Director
Missouri Vocational Enterprises,
Division of Offender
Rehabilitative Services

DELOISE WILLIAMS
Assistant Division Director
Health Services, Division of
Offender Rehabilitative Services

MARTA NOLIN, Ph.D.
Assistant Division Director
Substance Abuse Services
Division of Offender
Rehabilitative Services

CINDY STEUBER
Warden, Cremer Therapeutic
Community Center, Division of
Offender Rehabilitative Services

Adult Basic Education

In order to prepare inmates for successful reintegration into society and to reduce recidivism, offenders without a high school diploma or equivalent are required by statute to participate in Adult Basic Education classes. The educational program provides offenders an opportunity to obtain a high school equivalency certificate and make measurable progress in academic education. The Department of Corrections offers:

- Assessment: Intake centers screen and diagnose offenders prior to school assignments.

- Adult Education: Classes assist the offender in working toward a high school equivalency certification.

- Literacy: Courses provide specific instruction for those with limited English proficiency and reading skills.

- Title I: Supplemental instructional services are offered for educationally disadvantaged students under age 21.

- Special Education: Education for offenders with learning disabilities through the age of 22.

- Library: Library services are provided and focus on leisure, legal and informational needs. Each library is composed of a general collection and maintains a collection of legal resources and online law library services to provide offender "access to courts," per the U.S. Supreme Court's *Bounds v Smith* decision.

The Missouri Department of Elementary and Secondary Education certifies all department teachers and administrators.

The Mandatory Academic Education Statute, Section 217.690.10 RSMo establishes that offenders must earn their high school equivalency certificate or exhibit a continuous honest, good-faith effort toward academic success to be eligible for parole.

Academic education can serve more than 5,000 eligible offenders daily and during the past two fiscal years, approximately 3,300 inmates have earned high school equivalency certificates. More than 80 percent of the inmates who take the equivalency test pass. This rate exceeds both the state and national average.

Career and Technical Education

Current programs include vocational training programs throughout the prison system. These programs include web design, simulated commercial vehicle driving, applied computer technology, automotive mechanics, basic welding, building trades, business technology, electrical wiring, residential plumbing, diesel mechanics, modern woodworking, culinary arts, cosmetology, professional gardening, small engines mechanics and certified nursing assistant. The department also partners with local community colleges to offer technical literacy and certified production technician training programs. All of the vocational programs provide offenders with a Department of Labor certificate upon completion. In addition, offenders obtain the following certifications and/or licenses upon completion of the applicable coursework: ServSafe (culinary arts), National Center for Construction Education and Research (welding, plumbing, electrical and building trades), Certiport (computer technology), State Board of Cosmetology License (cosmetology) and Certified Nursing Assistant License (certified nursing assistant).

Missouri Vocational Enterprises

Missouri Vocational Enterprises (MVE) is responsible for 23 different industries in 13 correctional institutions throughout the state. At any one time, MVE employs approximately 1,350 offenders who provide a variety of products and services for sale to state agencies, city and county governments, political subdivisions, state employees and not-for-profit organizations. MVE's goal is to increase work and training opportunities for offenders. Profits generated by MVE sales are used to develop new products and create expanded vocational training opportunities. More than 50 MVE jobs now qualify as federally certified apprenticeships by the U.S. Department of Labor.

Work-based programs are delivered via apprenticeships and on-the-job training delivered by MVE and through institutional jobs. MVE also provides skilled training programs such as computer-aided drafting and similar software to assist the offender to secure and retain meaningful employment upon release.

Medical Services

Health care for offenders is required by Missouri law (217.230, RSMo). It was also determined that the 8th and 14th amendments of the U.S. Con-

stitution further established this right. The Missouri Department of Corrections is responsible for the health care of offenders in its custody. The Medical Services Unit oversees medical care, which has been provided on a contractual basis since Dec. 1, 1992. This health care system stresses education, disease prevention, immediate identification of health problems and early intervention to prevent more debilitating, chronic health problems. Medical units are located in 21 correctional centers. Depending upon institutional size, the level of care provided to offenders ranges from daily, routine medical and dental sick-call services to 24-hour care infirmaries. Many sites have X-ray equipment, laboratory services, physical therapy and minor surgical procedures. Chronic care clinics ensure those with chronic conditions are regularly assessed and provided continuous medical care by licensed nurses and physicians.

All facilities utilize community hospitals and clinics for emergency care, consultation and in-patient treatment. Consultation agreements are also in place with community specialists. The Division of Offender Rehabilitative Services' contract-monitoring staff ensures offenders receive medical care equivalent to the community standard, and that all mandates of the contract are fulfilled. The goal is to return offenders to the community as medically stable as possible, so they may become productive citizens of the state.

Mental Health

When offenders are sentenced to prison, their mental health needs are assessed at the reception and diagnostic centers. All offenders receive a mental health screening and psychological testing. While in the corrections system, mentally ill offenders receive individualized treatment to stabilize their mental illness and help with institutional adjustment.

The department works closely with the Department of Mental Health. A specialized treatment program, the Correctional Treatment Center, offers programming for seriously mentally ill offenders at Farmington Correctional Center. Both departments also work together coordinating treatment for mentally ill offenders being released from incarceration.

The department also has other specialized mental health treatment programs at Farmington Correctional Center (Social Rehabilitation Unit); Jefferson City Correctional Center (Secure Social Rehabilitation Unit); Potosi Correctional Center (Potosi Reintegration Unit); and Women's Eastern Reception, Diagnostic and Correctional Center (Women's Social Rehabilitation Unit).

The department also has the Special Needs Unit for developmentally disabled offenders. This is located at the Potosi Correctional Center.

DAVE DORMIRE
Director
Division of Adult Institutions

CYNDI PRUDDEN
Deputy Director
Zone 1

DWAYNE KEMPKER
Deputy Director
Zone II

ALAN EARLS
Deputy Director
Zone III

Mental health services are available at all institutions. Services are provided by teams of psychiatrists, psychologists, advanced nurse practitioners, social workers, professional counselors, psychiatric nurses and activity therapists.

Missouri Sexual Offender Program (MoSOP)

Missouri law (589.040, RSMo) mandates the director of the Department of Corrections to develop a program of treatment, education and rehabilitation for sexual assault offenders. By statute, the successful completion of MoSOP is mandatory for a release prior to an offender's sentence completion time. The MoSOP program generally takes 9 to 12 months to complete and is provided at the Farmington Correctional Center for males and at the Women's Eastern Reception, Diagnostic and Correctional Center in Vandalia for females. Programming for handicapped offenders and those in protective custody, is offered at the Eastern Reception Diagnostic and Correctional Center in Bonne Terre. During the fiscal year of 2014, 354 offenders completed the MoSOP program.

The Sex Offender Assessment Process (SOAP) at the Farmington Correctional Center is a 120-day, pre-sentencing residential process established in fiscal year 1994. SOAP assesses risk to the community and sex offender treatment needs. Information is shared with the court for sentencing considerations.

The Department of Corrections is responsible for assessing sex offenders prior to their release from incarceration to determine whether any qualify for civil commitment as sexually violent predators (632.480, RSMo). After careful examination by highly specialized staff, 26 out of 510 offenders reviewed (5 percent) from fiscal year 2014 were referred for possible civil commitment to the Department of Mental Health.

CINDY WANSING
Assistant to the Division of
Adult Institutions Director

JOHN GIBBS
Security Coordinator

Institutional Substance Abuse Treatment and Toxicology Services

Substance use problems and disorders are well-documented criminogenic factors with a direct impact on offender recidivism. Substance use disorders are progressive and the need for treatment and recovery management usually recurs throughout an offender's life span. In fiscal year 2014, approximately 40 percent of new admissions to prison were alcohol- or drug-related offenders.

An array of treatment services for substance use disorders are provided to offenders incarcerated in Missouri's prisons who have been sentenced by the courts or stipulated by the Board of Probation and Parole for substance abuse treatment. In fiscal year 2014, 2,987 beds were designated for institutional treatment. Approximately 92 percent of offenders who were discharged from institutional treatment successfully completed their programs.

The Department of Corrections provided the following services in correctional institutions in fiscal year 2014:

- Substance Use Assessment services.

- Long-Term Institutional Treatment programs of one year or longer.
- Offenders Under Treatment (OUT) programs for 180-day treatment.
- Partial-Day Treatment programs for parole violators.
- Short-Term Treatment programs for offenders ordered by the court or board to serve 84 to 120 days of treatment.
- Treatment programs for offenders with special needs who are mandated substance use treatment and face health, cognitive or mobility problems that prevent them from attending other facilities.
- Toxicology Services for the department are a critical aspect of the drug interdiction approach of Department of Corrections. The department conducts both random and targeted urinalysis at every correctional institution for offenders and district office staff.

Cremer Therapeutic Community Center

The Cremer Therapeautic Center (CTCC) is a minimum-security facility located in Fulton, in which all offenders receive substance use treatment. The facility has a capacity of 180 beds.

Division of Adult Institutions

The Division of Adult Institutions is responsible for supervision and management of the state's 20 adult correctional institutions. The division operates safe, secure and humane institutions for the confinement of individuals committed by the courts to serve a prison sentence. By Missouri law, a felon must be 17 years of age or older or certified as an adult by a circuit court and have a sentence of not less than one year to be committed to the division.

Incarcerated inmates are accountable for civil conduct and compliance with institutional rules. Inmates are also required to make payments from their individual inmate accounts for court-ordered fines or judgments to the Crime Victims Compensation Fund. In addition, each inmate is required to engage in work, school or treatment on a full-time basis throughout their period of confinement in order to prepare them to be productive, law-abiding citizens upon their release. Inmates are encouraged to make positive contributions to society and take responsibility for repairing the harm caused by their past criminal actions by participating in community service, restorative justice activities and impact-of-crime-on-victims programs. Over 97 percent of all offenders committed to the division to serve a sentence are released at some point. Preparing inmates to transition successfully from prison to

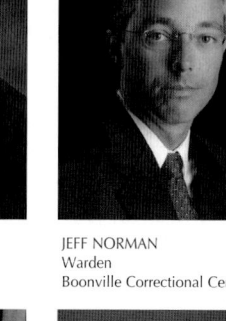

SCOTT LAWRENCE
Warden
Algoa Correctional Center

JEFF NORMAN
Warden
Boonville Correctional Center

ALANA BOYLES
Warden
Chillicothe Correctional Center

RONDA PASH
Warden
Crossroads Correctional Center

the community is an investment in public safety and reduces future victimization.

Citizens Advisory Committee

The department utilizes a Citizens Advisory Committee (CAC) composed of nine private citizens appointed by the governor to evaluate grievances filed by inmates and referred to the director of the department. The CAC makes recommendations to the director for the resolution of those grievances as specified in the department Inmate Grievance Procedure. The CAC meets on a regular basis at different correctional institutions.

Algoa Correctional Center

The Algoa Correctional Center (ACC) is a minimum-security institution located in Jefferson City. The institution maintains a capacity of 1,537 male offenders.

Boonville Correctional Center

The Boonville Correctional Center (BCC) is a minimum-security institution located in Boonville. The institution maintains a capacity of 1,346 male offenders.

TROY STEELE
Warden, Eastern Reception
Diagnostic and Correctional Center

TOM VILLMER
Warden, Farmington
Correctional Center

BILL HARRIS
Warden, Fulton Reception and
Diagnostic Center

JAY CASSADY
Warden, Jefferson City
Correctional Center

SONNY COLLINS
Warden, Maryville
Treatment Center

JENNIFER SACHSE
Warden, Missouri Eastern
Correctional Center

DEAN MINOR
Warden, Moberly
Correctional Center

JAMES HURLEY
Warden, Northeast
Correctional Center

Central Missouri Correctional Center

The Central Missouri Correctional Center (CMCC) is an institution located in Jefferson City. The institution closed in June 2005 due to budget cuts in state fiscal year 2006. The institution had a capacity of 1,000 male offenders.

Chillicothe Correctional Center

The Chillicothe Correctional Center (CCC) is an all-custody level institution located in Chillicothe. The institution has a capacity of 1,636 female offenders.

Crossroads Correctional Center

The Crossroads Correctional Center (CRCC) is a maximum-medium institution located in Cameron. The institution maintains a capacity of 1,455 male offenders.

Eastern Reception, Diagnostic and Correctional Center

The Eastern Reception, Diagnostic and Correctional Center (ERDCC) is a maximum-medium

security institution located in Bonne Terre. The institution has a total capacity of 2,721 male offenders.

Farmington Correctional Center

The Farmington Correctional Center (FCC) is a medium-minimum security institution located in Farmington. The institution maintains a capacity of 2,655 male offenders.

Fulton Reception and Diagnostic Center

The Fulton Reception and Diagnostic Center (FRDC) is a diagnostic and medium-security institution located in Fulton. The institution maintains a capacity of 1,302 male offenders.

Jefferson City Correctional Center

The Jefferson City Correctional Center (JCCC) is a maximum-medium institution located in Jefferson City. The institution maintains a capacity of 1,956 male offenders.

BRIAN O'CONNELL
Warden, Ozark
Correctional Center

CINDY GRIFFIN
Warden
Potosi Correctional Center

MICHAEL BOWERSOX
Warden, South Central
Correctional Center

IAN WALLACE
Warden
Southeast Correctional Center

DOUG PRUDDEN
Warden
Tipton Correctional Center

HEATH SPACKLER
Warden, Western Missouri
Correctional Center

RYAN CREWS
Warden, Western Reception
Diagnostic and Correctional
Center

ANGELA MESMER
Warden, Women's Eastern
Reception Diagnostic and
Correctional Center

Maryville Treatment Center

The Maryville Treatment Center (MTC) is a treatment facility located in Maryville. The institution maintains a capacity of 561 male offenders.

Missouri Eastern Correctional Center

The Missouri Eastern Correctional Center (MECC) is a medium-minimum security institution located in Pacific. The institution maintains a capacity of 1,100 male offenders.

Moberly Correctional Center

The Moberly Correctional Center (MCC) is a medium-minimum security institution located in Moberly. The institution maintains a capacity of 1,800 male offenders.

Northeast Correctional Center

The Northeast Correctional Center (NECC) is a medium-minimum security institution located in Bowling Green. The institution maintains a capacity of 2,106 male offenders.

Ozark Correctional Center

The Ozark Correctional Center (OCC) is a treatment facility located in Fordland. The institution maintains a capacity of 738 male offenders.

Potosi Correctional Center

The Potosi Correctional Center (PCC) is a maximum-medium security institution located in Mineral Point. The institution maintains a capacity of 912 male offenders.

South Central Correctional Center

The South Central Correctional Center (SCCC) is a maximum-medium security institution located in Licking. The institution maintains a capacity of 1,643 male offenders.

Southeast Correctional Center

The Southeast Correctional Center (SECC) is a maximum-medium security institution located in Charleston. The institution maintains a capacity of 1,643 male offenders.

ELLIS McSWAIN JR.
Chair, Board of Probation and
Parole

KENNETH C. JONES
Member, Board of
Probation and Parole

MARTIN RUCKER
Member, Board of
Probation and Parole

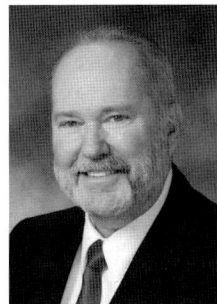

DON RUZICKA
Member, Board of
Probation and Parole

Tipton Correctional Center

The Tipton Correctional Center (TCC) is a minimum security institution located in Tipton. The institution maintains a capacity of 1,222 male offenders.

Western Missouri Correctional Center

The Western Missouri Correctional Center (WMCC) is a medium-minimum security institution located in Cameron. The institution currently maintains a capacity of 1,958 male offenders.

Western Reception, Diagnostic and Correctional Center

The Western Reception, Diagnostic and Correctional Center (WRDCC) is a diagnostic and minimum-security institution located in St. Joseph. The institution maintains a capacity of 1,968 male offenders.

Women's Eastern Reception, Diagnostic and Correctional Center

The Women's Eastern Reception, Diagnostic and Correctional Center (WERDCC) is an all custody level institution located in Vandalia. The institution maintains a capacity of 1,560 female offenders.

Board of Probation and Parole

The Missouri Board of Probation and Parole is composed of seven full-time members appointed by the governor, subject to the advice and consent of the Senate. During their six-year terms, members determine the release of individuals from confinement in the Division of Adult Institutions through parole or conditional release. Parole hearings are held at each correctional center monthly. If a release date is set, the Parole Board determines whether release strategies,

JIM WELLS
Member, Board of
Probation and Parole

KELLY DILLS
Director of Board Operations

such as electronic monitoring, residential facility and community release center, are appropriate. The Parole Board stipulates special conditions in order to address specific offender needs and improve the opportunity for success under supervision. They also monitor the supervision of offenders in the community and return those offenders to prison who pose a risk to the community. The Parole Board also investigates and reports to the governor on all applications for pardons, commutations of sentence, reprieves or restorations of citizenship. The Parole Board may include information relating to the applicant along with appropriate recommendations.

The chair of the Board of Probation and Parole is designated by the governor and is the chief administrative officer in charge of operations, expenditures, Interstate Compact Services for supervision of parolees and probationers and chief spokesperson for the Parole Board. The members of the Parole Board are:

McSwain, Ellis Jr., (D), chair, Jefferson City;
Jones, Kenneth C., (R), Clarksburg;
Rucker, Martin, (D), St. Joseph;
Ruzicka, Don, (R), Mt. Vernon;
Wells, Jim, (D), Bowling Green.

JULIE KEMPKER
Chief State Supervisor

PEG McCLURE
Assistant Division Director

NANCY McCARTHY
Regional Administrator
Eastern Region

BRENT MORRIS
Regional Administrator
Western Region

DARDI SMITH
Regional Administrator
Southwest Region

SHARON DERRINGTON
Regional Administrator
Southeast Region

LISA SCHULZE
Regional Administrator
North Region

MICHELLE KASAK
Regional Administrator
Institutional Region

Division of Probation and Parole

The Division of Probation and Parole supports the operations of the Board of Probation and Parole and is responsible for field and institutional services for probationers, parolees and conditional releases, as well as community corrections programming, two community release centers and seven community supervision centers. The Division of Probation and Parole assesses and supervises criminal offenders assigned to the division by the circuit courts of Missouri, the Parole Board or under the terms of the Interstate Compact.

The division is divided statewide into six regions for the effective management of the offenders assigned to it. Regions are made up of a network of local district offices, institutional parole offices and residential facilities, and, in some instances, are supported by satellite offices. The chief state supervisor reports directly to the chair of the Parole Board and oversees the daily operations of the division. An assistant division director is responsible for managing the division's support staff, including the Command Center. The assistant division director reports directly to the chief state supervisor.

Eastern Region consists of 11 district field offices in St. Louis City, St. Louis County, St. Charles County and the St. Louis Community Release Center.

Western Region encompasses district field offices in Kansas City (4), St. Joseph (satellite in Maryville), Cameron, Lexington (satellite in Marshall), Trenton (satellite in Brookfield), Independence, Belton, Warrensburg, Liberty and the Kansas City Community Release Center.

Southwest Region consists of two field district offices in Springfield and other district offices in Joplin, Neosho, Branson, Nixa, Aurora, West Plains, Lebanon and Nevada.

Southeast Region has district field offices in Hillsboro, Cape Girardeau (satellite in Perryville), Farmington, Sikeston, Kennett (satellite in New Madrid), Caruthersville, Potosi, Dexter, Union, Poplar Bluff and Charleston.

North Central Region has district field offices in Hannibal, Columbia, Fulton, Jefferson City, Sedalia, Moberly (satellites in Macon and Kirksville) Lake Ozark, Troy (satellite in Warrenton), Rolla and Camdenton.

Institutional Region consists of the institutional parole offices in Jefferson City (2), Fordland,

Licking, Fulton, Vandalia, Tipton, Bowling Green, Bonne Terre, Farmington, Charleston, Pacific, Chillicothe, Maryville, Cameron (2), Moberly and St. Joseph.

Institutional Services

The institutional probation and parole officers are responsible for the assessment of incarcerated offenders and the tracking of their progress for the Parole Board or the court. The institutional parole officers report their findings to the Parole Board, prior to an offender's parole hearing and to the court, when the offender is being considered for release to probation supervision. The institutional parole staff and parole analyst assist the Parole Board as they conduct hearings. The officers work with the offenders to develop supervision plans as they prepare for their release from confinement.

Institutional parole offices are located at the following correctional centers: Algoa, Boonville, Chillicothe, Crossroads, Farmington, Potosi, Jefferson City, Maryville, Missouri Eastern, Moberly, Northeast, Western, Ozark, South Central, Southeast and Tipton. Parole offices are also located at diagnostic and reception centers in Bonne Terre, St. Joseph, Vandalia and Fulton (satellite at Cremer Therapeutic Community Center).

Field Services

Field services encompass the supervision of probationers in the community assigned to the division by the courts, offenders released under supervision by the Parole Board and offenders from other states through the Interstate Compact. There were approximately 66,500 offenders under the supervision of the division in the community at the end of calendar year 2014, including parole and conditional release cases received from the Parole Board and probationers.

In order to reduce recidivism, field probation and parole officers continuously assess and evaluate offenders assigned to them and supervise the offenders at a level consistent with their risk to re-offend. The probation and parole officer effectively balances treatment and supervision strategies necessary to manage offender risk with the needs and interests of victims and the community. This supervision process consists of a number of critical activities including:

- accurate and ongoing assessment of offender risk and need;
- development of effective supervision and treatment plans;
- restorative justice practices; and

- use of appropriate sanctions and strategies to minimize risk and maximize the potential for successful outcomes.

Offenders may be ordered to perform community service hours by the court as part of their reparation to the community. They may also be required to compensate victims of crime, pay court costs and make restitution to individual victims.

Probation and Parole staff is engaged with local communities to assist in the coordination of service delivery and activities to improve public safety. Across the state, Citizen Advisory Boards (CABs) provide valuable assistance to their communities. CABs promote an environment for offenders to gain the skills they need to be productive, law-abiding citizens. To this end, CABs fund special programs, such as financial management, providing transportation and assistance and substance abuse education and training.

In addition to CABs, Probation and Parole staff participates in more than 30 local Missouri Reentry Process Teams. The goal of the teams is to improve the transition process of offenders leaving prison and returning to their communities and to enhance options for offenders sentenced to probation within those communities. This creative approach has led to strong partnerships from which new and innovative interventions and supervision approaches have emerged.

Community Supervision Strategies

Probation and Parole staff coordinates and manages a continuum of community based programs and employ a variety of supervision services to improve public safety and offender success. These facilities, programs and services assist with the supervision of probationers assigned by the courts and with the reintegration of parolees upon release from prison. The following programs are designed to provide additional treatment, intervention, sanctions and structure for offenders:

- cognitive skills development classes;
- community reentry contracts;
- community sex offender treatment and registration;
- contract residential facilities;
- day report centers;
- domestic violence supervision;
- electronic monitoring;
- employment services;
- mental health treatment; and
- outpatient substance abuse treatment.

Community Release and Supervision Centers

Community Release Centers and Community Supervision Centers provide the Parole Board and courts with a structured, residential program to better assist and supervise offenders transitioning from prison to the community or offenders at risk of revocation from community supervision. Offenders assigned to these facilities are required to accept personal responsibility in finding and maintaining employment, obtaining substance abuse and medical care and obtaining educational or vocational opportunities. Assessment and treatment sessions are scheduled to coincide with the offenders' off-hours from work.

LILLY ANGELO
Superintendent
Kansas City Community
Release Center

JOHN YOUNG
Superintendent
St. Louis Community Release
Center

Kansas City Community Release Center

The Kansas City Community Release Center (KCCRC) opened in May 1978 and is located in the downtown area of Kansas City. KCCRC has a capacity to house 350 offenders.

St. Louis Community Release Center

The St. Louis Community Release Center (SL-CRC) is located just north of downtown St. Louis and has been in operation since April 1978. SL-CRC has a capacity to house 550 offenders.

Community Supervision Centers

The division has seven community supervision centers. Each center includes an administrative area to accommodate the existing probation and parole district office located in that area, as well as sufficient program/classroom areas and dormitory housing space for 30 offenders in need of structured, residential supervision. Each center provides short-term residential services for offenders who otherwise would have to be housed within the department's correctional centers or local jails. The centers are located in St. Joseph, Farmington, Hannibal, Kennett, Poplar Bluff, Fulton and Kansas City.

Command Center

The department's Command Center is a 24/7 communication center whose staff tracks offenders in the community on electronic monitoring, in community release centers and residential centers. This unit was established to ensure that offenders assigned to community corrections programs maintain their curfews and adhere to other restrictions as required around the clock. Command Center staff conduct investigations for every serious rule violation. They issue arrest warrants should offenders fail to return to their assigned residence at the appointed time. Command Center staff also maintain regular contact with state and local law enforcement to develop leads and ensure absconders are apprehended and returned to department custody without delay.

Finance

The state of Missouri has a variety of tools to assist in the financing of a variety of economic development projects. Tax credits, grants and loans are available in the areas of business development, community development, redevelopment and infrastructure development. The finance team houses professionals that oversee the programs including application and program creation, application review, evaluation, coordination with the sales team, recommendation and reporting. The team also provides professional technical assistance and training to businesses, communities, nonprofits and developers.

LEWIS MILLS
Director
Division of Energy

BILL ANDERSON
Acting Director, Missouri
Technology Corporation

Compliance

The compliance team monitors the finance and incentive programs administered by the department to ensure efficiency and compliance. The monitoring process includes both internal file reviews and on-site visits. The professional staff strives to ensure the stated purpose of each program is being achieved, funds have been used in a manner consistent with the statute and that there is adequate source documentation indicating compliance. The compliance team provides feedback and suggestions to both the sales and finance teams to ensure programs are efficient and effective.

Division of Energy

Telephone: (573) 751-2254 / FAX: 573-526-7553

The Division of Energy helps Missourians meet their energy needs through education and assistance, and encourages Missourians to advance the efficient use of diverse energy resources to provide for a healthier environment and to achieve greater energy security for future generations.

The division provides technical and financial assistance for energy efficiency and renewable energy improvements; supports market development and demonstration projects promoting clean energy sources and technologies; provides energy data, information and research on energy issues, including supplies and prices, to all Missourians; and promotes policies that support energy efficiency.

Employees work with residential, agricultural, educational, local government, business and industrial clients to develop energy-efficiency programs and measures that pay back the initial investment within a reasonable time frame. Staff consults with the Office of Administration and other state agencies to integrate energy efficiency into state buildings and purchases.

The division monitors energy supplies and prices, works with state decision-makers to help ensure adequate energy supplies for Missouri and reviews policy issues relevant to Missouri energy needs.

Staff trains other state agencies to use alternative fuel vehicles in compliance with state laws. The division also partners with the federal Clean Cities programs in Missouri's metropolitan areas to strive for cleaner air and water through alternative transportation fuels and technologies. Staff assists the Missouri Department of Transportation with the Mid-Missouri Rideshare Program and connects Missouri commuters to the carpooling program nearest them.

The division provides financial assistance for energy efficiency projects and administers the Weatherization Assistance Program, which serves Missouri citizens through 19 local agencies. The weatherization program has provided cost-effective, energy-efficient home improvements to more than 182,000 homes since the inception of the program in 1977. The department's energy revolving loan fund helps schools, colleges, universities, hospitals and local governments finance energy-efficiency projects so money saved can be used for other needs related to the mission of the entity.

Missouri Weatherization Policy Advisory Council

The council provides policy review and recommendations for delivery of the Weatherization Assistance Program in Missouri. Federal regulations require that a policy advisory council be formed to advise the department on weatherization program issues and distribution of financial assistance. The council reviews and makes recommendations to the department pertaining to the Missouri Weatherization State Plan, federal grant application and programmatic policies.

Sanders, Terry, chair;
Steinmann, Todd, vice chair;
Boustead, Kory, member;
Dean, Shaylyn, member;
Hunter, Charity, member;
Miller, David, member;

Patterson, Bonnie, member;
Poston, Marc, member;
Rohlfing, Chris, member;
Vacancy (1), member.

Missouri Technology Corporation

Truman State Office Bldg., Rm. 680
PO Box 2137, Jefferson City 65102
Telephone: (573) 526-0470 / FAX: (573) 526-8202
www.missouritechnology.com
Email: info@missouritechnology.com

The Missouri Technology Corporation (MTC) is a public-private partnership created by the Missouri General Assembly to promote entrepreneurship and foster the growth of new and emerging high-tech companies. MTC focuses on 21st century bioscience industries that build on Missouri's rich history in agriculture. It is governed by a 15-member board of directors appointed by the governor, speaker of the House, and president *pro tem* of the Senate. The president of the University of Missouri System and the director of the Department of Economic Development are *ex officio* members of the board.

Missouri Technology Corporation Board of Directors

Bannister, Joseph G., chair, St. Louis;
Baker, Jim, vice chair, Jefferson City;
Vacancy, secretary/treasurer, Springfield;
Canuteson, Elizabeth, Liberty;
Gonzalez, Victoria, Manchester;
Kemp, Garry, Lee's Summit;
Kerr, David D., Ballwin;
O'Connel, Michael J., St. Louis;
Rubin, Donn, St. Louis;
Steinhoff, Gregory A., Columbia;
Wetle, Michael D., St. Louis;
Silvey, Senator Ryan, Missouri Senate;
Berry, Rep. T.J., member, Missouri House of Representatives;
Downing, Mike, Department of Economic Development, *ex officio*;
Williams, Col. Charles A., Fort Leonard Wood, *ex officio*;
Tate, Raymond, Ph.D., St. Louis, *ex officio*;
Arshadi, Nasser, Ph.D., St. Louis, *ex officio*;
Anderson, Bill, acting executive director.

Research Alliance of Missouri

Truman State Office Bldg., Rm. 680
PO Box 2137, Jefferson City 65102
Telephone: (573) 526-0470 / FAX: (573) 526-8202
www.missouritechnology.com/ram/

The Research Alliance of Missouri (RAM) was founded on January 15, 2003, as a "new alliance between business and universities to coordinate research and provide more access to technology for Missouri businesses." RAM provides expertise and guidance in linking education and business, working together to coordinate research, pool resources, boost commercialization opportunities and provide Missouri businesses with greater access to technology. The Research Alliance of Missouri is composed of chief research officers from universities and research institutions throughout the state.

Research Alliance of Missouri Members

Tait, Raymond, Ph.D., chair, St. Louis University, St. Louis;
Kunkel, Allen, vice chair, Missouri State University, Springfield;
Arshadi, Nasser, Ph.D., treasurer, University of Missouri–St. Louis, St. Louis;
Di Stefano, Maria C., Ph.D., Truman State University, Kirksville;
Duncan, Robert V., Ph.D., University of Missouri, Columbia;
Glaros, Alan G., Ph.D., Kansas City University of Medicine and Biosciences, Kansas City;
Johnson, Jane C., A.T. Still University, Kirksville;
Kharasch, Evan, M.D., Ph.D., Washington University, St. Louis;
Knous, Ted R., Ph.D., University of Missouri–Kansas City, Kansas City;
Krishnamurthy, K., Ph.D., chair, Missouri University of Science and Technology, Rolla;
Goldstein, Karla, director of Public/Governmental Affairs, Donald Danforth Plant Sciences Center, St. Louis;
Nichols, Michael F., Ph.D., University of Missouri System, Columbia;
Kiel, Cindy, assistant vice chancellor for Research Services, Washington University, St. Louis;
Anderson, Bill, acting executive director.

Missouri Community Service Commission

Truman State Office Bldg., Rm. 770
PO Box 118, Jefferson City 65102
Telephone: (573) 751-7488 / FAX: (573) 526-0463
Email: americorps@ded.mo.gov or mcsc@ded.mo.gov
www.movolunteers.org

The Missouri Community Service Commission (MCSC) is dedicated to creating opportunities to enable all citizens to serve their communities. The MCSC connects Missourians of all ages and backgrounds in an effort to improve unmet community service needs through direct and tangible service. The MCSC serves as the administrator for AmeriCorps*State funding in Missouri by awarding monetary grants and providing technical assistance and support to its grantees. By col-

RUSSELL UNGER
Chair, Missouri Community
Service Commission

JOHN R. ALBRIGHT
Vice Chair, Missouri Community
Service Commission

JANICE K. VANMETER
Member, Missouri Community
Service Commission

NINA NORTH MURPHY
Member, Missouri Community
Service Commission

DR. MARGIE VANDEVEN
Member, Missouri Community
Service Commission

REENA HAJAT CARROLL
Member, Missouri Community
Service Commission

LT. GOV. PETER KINDER
Member, Missouri Community
Service Commission

RANDALL J. McARTHUR
Member, Missouri Community
Service Commission

FORREST MILLER JR.
Member, Missouri Community
Service Commission

NICOLE ROACH
Member, Missouri Community
Service Commission

MOLLY TURNER
Ex officio Member, Missouri
Community Service Commission

DON STAMPER
Executive Director, Missouri
Community Service Commission

laborating with volunteer organizations and state agencies and continuing to effectively administer National Service initiatives, the MCSC makes it possible for Missourians to serve their communities.

The MCSC was established by an act of the Missouri Legislature in 1994 as a direct response to the National and Community Service Trust Act of 1993. Its 15 to 25 members are appointed by the governor and meet quarterly. The Missouri Legislature passed a measure in 1998 allowing the commission to raise private contributions to assist in its work, thus enabling the commission to broaden its impact on the service and volunteer communities. The MCSC receives federal funding from the Corporation for National and Community Service (CNCS) to administer the AmeriCorps*State and Education Awards programs in Missouri, making federal funds more responsive to state and local needs and providing greater assistance to educational, nonprofit, secular and faith-based community organizations.

Overseeing the AmeriCorps program is the MCSC's primary responsibility. AmeriCorps is a national service network supported by the Corporation for National and Community Service (CNCS) of Washington, D.C. AmeriCorps members may serve full-time or part-time. The participants are often referred to as "members." These members, through the MCSC and CNCS, are provided opportunities to serve their communities and build capacity to meet local needs.

AmeriCorps, often referred to as the "domestic Peace Corps," engages citizens of all ages in projects ranging from tutoring, youth mentoring, public safety, housing rehabilitation, health care, environmental issues, disaster relief and other human needs. It provides communities and neighborhoods with valuable human resources for addressing their most pressing civic issues and gives individuals a way to serve their country by reaching out to others. Since 1994, more than 10,000 Missouri residents have served more than 14 million hours and have qualified for Segal AmeriCorps Education Awards totaling more than $29,900,000. In 2011–2012, 389 AmeriCorps Members recruited 77,568 volunteers who served 612,484.5 hours. Based on the Independent Sector's Value of Volunteer Time, the National Value of Volunteer Time for 2011 was $21.79 per hour. This equates to $13,346,037. Also in 2011–2012, AmeriCorps Members tutored and/or mentored 46,734 individuals. Of these, 168 were children of incarcerated parents. 167 AmeriCorps members participated in disaster response and relief and 263 were certified in disaster preparedness and response.

Most not-for-profit organizations with 501(c)(3) status in the state of Missouri, local or state governments, school districts or institutions of higher education may sponsor an AmeriCorps program. An AmeriCorps member's term of service for one year on a full-time basis is a minimum of 1,700 hours. Part-time can consist of 900, 675, 450 or 300 hours. At the successful completion of their service commitment, they may be eligible to receive up to a $5,550 education award (less for part-time service) that may be redeemed at a Title IV university, college or trade school. Most AmeriCorps members receive a living allowance while serving, though it varies with the type of program. In 2011–2012, a full-time minimum living allowance equaled $12,100. The living allowance is optional for part-time members.

Missouri Community Service Commission

Unger, Russell, (D), chair, Columbia, Dec. 15, 2014;
Albright, John R., (R), vice chair, Sunrise Beach, Dec. 15, 2013;

Carroll, Reena Hajat, (D), Jefferson City, Dec. 15, 2015;
Hibbeler, Cheryl, (D), O'Fallon, Dec. 15, 2013;
Kinder, Lt. Gov. Peter, (R), Jefferson City;
McArthur, Randall J., (R), Maryland Heights, April 5, 2012;
Miller, Forrest Jr., (R), Crestwood, Dec. 15, 2014;
Murphy, Nina North, (D), St. Louis, Dec. 15, 2012;
Roach, Nicole, (D), St. Louis, March 26, 2015;
Turner, Molly, CNCS ex officio, Corporation for National Service, Kansas City;
VanDeven, Dr. Margie, O'Fallon, Dec. 17, 2014;
VanMeter, Janis K., (D), Lewistown, Dec. 15, 2014;
Don Stamper, executive director.

Missouri Housing Development Commission

3435 Broadway, Kansas City 64111-2459
Telephone: (816) 759-6600 / FAX: (816) 759-6828
Toll free: (866) 605-7467
www.mhdc.com
Email: information@mhdc.com

The Missouri Housing Development Commission (MHDC), created by the 75th General Assembly, has invested and loaned in excess of $4 billion to construct, renovate and preserve affordable housing. MHDC functions as a bank, providing financing directly to developers of affordable rental properties.

The commission also provides funding for home loans to qualified, first-time buyers through a network of certified, private mortgage lenders.

The funds for mortgage financing are provided through the sale of tax-exempt notes and bonds that the commission is authorized to issue.

The commission administers the federal and Missouri Low Income Housing Tax Credit (LIHTC) programs, federal HOME funds, U.S. Department of Housing and Urban Development (HUD) Project-Based Section 8 rental assistance contracts, Affordable Housing Assistance tax credit and several housing assistance programs funded directly by MHDC. Additionally, the commission administers the Missouri Housing Trust Fund, a program designed to prevent homelessness and provide emergency housing assistance for very low-income Missourians.

The commission participates with the Department of Economic Development in preparing the state's Consolidated Plan for HUD.

The commission includes the governor, lieutenant governor, attorney general, treasurer and six persons appointed by the governor with the advice and consent of the Senate.

Missouri Housing Development Commission

Bay, Jeffrey S., (D), chair, Kansas City, Oct. 13, 2012;

Nash, Troy, (D), vice chair, Kansas City, Oct. 13, 2012;

Roberts, Greg L., (D), secretary/treasurer, Chesterfield, Oct. 13, 2015;

Miller, William, (D), commissioner, Oct. 13, 2017;

Kinder, Lt. Gov. Peter, (R), *ex officio*;

Koster, Attorney General Chris, (D), *ex officio;*

Nixon, Governor Jay, (D), *ex officio;*

Zweifel, State Treasurer Clint, (D), *ex officio;*

Vacancy (1).

Missouri State Council on the Arts

815 Olive St., Ste. 16, St. Louis 63101-1503
Telephone: (314) 340-6845 / FAX: (314) 340-7215
TDD: (800) 735-2966 / Toll free: (866) 407-4752
www.missouriartscouncil.org
Email: moarts@ded.mo.gov

The Missouri Arts Council (MAC)—as a public leader, partner and catalyst—is dedicated to broadening the appreciation and availability of the arts in the state and fostering the diversity, vitality and excellence of Missouri's communities, economy and cultural heritage.

Created by an act of the 73rd General Assembly, the MAC acts as the state's arts grant-making division, providing financial assistance to nonprofit organizations across the state to encourage and stimulate economic and community growth and development through the arts. A division of the Missouri Department of Economic Development, MAC is the second oldest state-funded arts agency in the country, providing vital support and leadership to bring the arts to all the people of Missouri. The Missouri Arts Council board consists of 15 volunteer citizens from across the state who are appointed by the director of the Department of Economic Development. The governor designates a chair and a vice chair. The board meets regularly to provide direction in policy making and programmatic oversight.

Through funds from the Missouri General Assembly and the National Endowment for the Arts, MAC provides funding for quality arts programming in both large and small communities. Funding areas include: discipline program assistance (music, dance, theater, literature, electronic media, visual arts, multidiscipline, festivals), community arts, established institutions and mid-sized organizations, folk arts, arts education, minority arts, touring, monthly strategic grants and capacity building.

MAC allocates every program dollar based on the recommendations of Missouri citizens who review grant applications from organizations

NOLA RUTH
Chair
Missouri Arts Council

DR. REYNALDO ANDERSON
Member
Missouri Arts Council

SHARON BESHORE
Member
Missouri Arts Council

MICHAEL BURKE
Member
Missouri Arts Council

throughout the state. The panel's recommendations are based on established criteria, including artistic excellence, education and outreach, community support, administrative ability and diversity of audience served.

The Missouri Arts Council Trust Fund is an invested fund created by the state legislature in 1993. Income from the trust is dedicated to supporting the arts in Missouri. A portion of the income tax revenue generated by Missouri's nonresident professional athletes and entertainers is the funding source for the Missouri Arts Council Trust Fund. The trust is administered by a board of trustees, consisting of the state treasurer, two members of the Senate appointed by the president *pro tem* of the Senate, two members of the House of Representatives appointed by the speaker of the House, and the members of the Missouri Arts Council.

Missouri Arts Council

Ruth, Nola, chair, Columbia;
Anderson, Dr. Reynaldo S., St. Louis;
Beshore, Sharon, Joplin;
Burke, Michael, Kansas City;
Cartwright, Cynthia Laing, Kansas City;
Hunter, Marie Nau, Columbia;
Kilroy, Marianne, Kansas City;

MARIE NAU HUNTER
Member
Missouri Arts Council

MARIANNE KILROY
Member
Missouri Arts Council

DR. DAVID C. NICHOLS
Member
Missouri Arts Council

DR. JOEL W. RAY
Member
Missouri Arts Council

LINDA BROWN REED
Member
Missouri Arts Council

MARK SAPPINGTON
Member
Missouri Arts Council

PATT ANN SHARP
Member
Missouri Arts Council

DAVID CARL WILSON
Member
Missouri Arts Council

McAuliffe, Robert E., St. Louis;
Nichols, Dr. David C., Kirksville;
Ray, Dr. Joel W., Cape Girardeau;
Reed, Linda Brown, St. Louis;
Sappington, Mark, Kansas City;
Sharp, Patt Ann, Kennett;
Wilson, David Carl, St. Louis.

Missouri Cultural Trust Board

Ruth, Nola, chair, Columbia;
Anderson, Dr. Reynaldo S., St. Louis;
Beshore, Sharon, Joplin;
Burke, Michael, Kansas City;
Cartwright, Cynthia Laing, Kansas City;
Hunter, Marie Nau, Columbia;
Kilroy, Marianne, Kansas City;
McAuliffe, Robert E., St. Louis;
Nichols, Dr. David C., Kirksville;
Ray, Dr. Joel W., Cape Girardeau;
Reed, Linda Brown, St. Louis;
Sappington, Mark, Kansas City;
Sharp, Patt Ann, Kennett;
Wilson, David Carl, St. Louis;
Flanigan, Rep. Thomas, Carthage;
Peters, Rep. Joshua, St. Louis;
Keaveny, Sen. Joe, St. Louis;
Schaaf, Sen. Rob, Platte and Buchanan Counties;
Zweifel, Clint, State Treasurer.

MICHAEL DONOVAN
Executive Director
Missouri Arts Council

Division of Workforce Development

421 E. Dunklin St., PO Box 1087, Jefferson City 65102
Telephone: (573) 751-3349 / FAX: (573) 751-8162
www.jobs.mo.gov
Email: wfd@ded.mo.gov

As the employment and training arm of the Department of Economic Development, the Division of Workforce Development (DWD) provides a robust menu of vital re-employment services, including access to skill-building training, career connections for job seekers and human resources assistance for businesses. These services are provided through a statewide network of Missouri Career Centers and the *jobs.mo.gov* web portal. Missouri's workforce system is a collaborative partnership that includes the Missouri Department of Labor and Industrial Relations' Division of Employment Security, 14 local workforce investment boards and 12 community college districts and other local educational agencies across the state.

With the assistance of trained, professional staff, Missouri's Next Generation Career Centers streamline customer flow to provide an expanded product box of valuable career assistance services, like specialized workshops, skills assessments, résumé-writing assistance and more. These services equip the state's workforce with the training and skills needed by employers to compete in this 21st century economy. Career Centers offer job seekers use of supportive equipment, such as computers, telephones, fax machines and copiers. Businesses may use Career Centers to seek or interview potential employees, test applicants' occupational skills or gain access to labor market information.

DWD also provides several innovative, targeted skill-building programs, such as the WorkReadyMissouri program for unemployment insurance claimants, the Show-Me Heroes program for veterans; a nationally recognized On-the-Job Training (OJT) Program, the National Career Readiness Certificate, as well as a summer youth program in partnership with the Department of Natural Resources' State Parks Youth Division.

Because Missouri's businesses are critical to the success of a long-term healthy economy, DWD provides industry training programs, cost-saving financial incentives, hiring assistance and other business services. The division's state-funded industry training programs provide funding to assist eligible companies in training their workers for the purpose of creating or retaining jobs in Missouri. These programs are operated locally by educational agencies, such as community colleges.

The division also provides staff to the governor-appointed Missouri Workforce Investment Board (MoWIB). This board sets workforce policy for Missouri's local workforce areas and strengthens ties among state workforce, education and economic development agencies. MoWIB is currently a 37-member board, a majority of whom represent high-level management from Missouri's most progressive and successful companies. The board meets quarterly and engages the directors and commissioners of six state agencies to meet the objective of strengthening Missouri's workforce system.

By fostering a skilled workforce, DWD helps our businesses to be more competitive—both regionally and globally—and helps Missouri citizens become more competitive and successful as they seek jobs and advance up the career ladder.

AMY SUBLETT
Acting Director, Division of
Workforce Development

MARK BAUER
Director, Missouri Workforce
Investment Board

LISA ALTHOFF
Director, Women's Council

Missouri Women's Council

The Missouri Women's Council was established in 1985 by the state's 83rd General Assembly. For over 20 years, the council has been meeting its mandate to identify and address the issues affecting the economic and employment status of Missouri women. The council serves as a resource and referral center connecting women to information on all aspects of women, work and family life.

The Women's Council promotes women's economic and employment opportunities through education and training programs, conferences and referral consultations and by providing free resources for Missouri citizens including: a website that provides timely information on women's economic issues with links to various resources; the Women's Resource Guide; the Missouri Family Affirming Wage Guide; current statistics and fact sheets on economic issues affecting women; and the Outstanding Women of Missouri Traveling History Exhibit featuring Missouri women recognized in their disciplines throughout our state's history. The council consists of 15 members. The governor, with the advice and consent of the Senate, appoints 11 members for staggered terms. The remaining four members of the council consist of two senators and two representa-

MICHELLE J. WORD
Chair, Women's Council

JANET BANDERA
Member, Women's Council

NICOLE COLBERT-BOTCHWAY,
J.D., M.B.A.
Member, Women's Council

JACKIE COLEMAN
Member, Women's Council

SEN. KIKI CURLS
Member, Women's Council

REP. MARSHA HAEFNER
Member, Women's Council

MELODEE COLBERT KEAN
Member, Women's Council

REP. GENISE MONTECILLO
Member, Women's Council

NORMA NISBET
Member, Women's Council

KAREN THORNTON
Member, Women's Council

VALERIE WHITE
Member, Women's Council

DONAYLE WHITMORE-SMITH
Member, Women's Council

tives, who are appointed by their respective bodies in the same manner as members of the standing committees. An executive director serves at the pleasure of the council.

Missouri Women's Council

Word, Michelle J., chair, (D), Kansas City, Dec. 6, 2012;

Bandera, Janet, (R), O'Fallon, Dec. 6, 2010;

Colbert-Botchway, Nicole, J.D., M.B.A., (D), St. Louis, Dec. 6, 2013;

Coleman, Jackie, (D), Jefferson City, Dec. 6, 2011;

Crum Thompson, Catherine, (I), Jefferson City, Dec. 6, 2013;

Curls, Sen. Kiki, (D), Kansas City;

Haefner, Rep. Marsha, (R), St. Louis;

Kean, Melodee Colbert, (D), Joplin, Dec. 6, 2011;

Montecillo, Rep. Genise, (D), St. Louis;

Nisbet, Norma, (I), St. Louis, Dec. 6, 2011;

Thornton, Karen, (R), Sunrise Beach, Dec. 6, 2009;

White, Valerie, (R), St. Charles, Dec. 6, 2007;

Whitmore-Smith, Donayle, (D), St. Louis, Dec. 6, 2006;

Vacancy (1);

Althoff, Lisa, executive director.

MARIE CARMICHAEL
Chair, Missouri
Development Finance Board

REUBEN A. SHELTON
Vice Chair, Missouri
Development Finance Board

LARRY D. NEFF
Secretary, Missouri
Development Finance Board

JOHN E. MEHNER
Treasurer, Missouri
Development Finance Board

MATTHEW L. DAMERON
Member, Missouri
Development Finance Board

BRADLEY G. GREGORY
Member, Missouri
Development Finance Board

PATRICK J. LAMPING
Member, Missouri
Development Finance Board

KELLEY M. MARTIN
Member, Missouri
Development Finance Board

LT. GOVERNOR PETER KINDER
Ex Officio Member, Missouri
Development Finance Board

MIKE DOWNING
Ex Officio Member, Missouri
Development Finance Board

RICHARD FORDYCE
Ex Officio Member, Missouri
Development Finance Board

SARA PARKER PAULEY
Ex Officio Member, Missouri
Development Finance Board

Missouri Development Finance Board

Governor Office Bldg.
200 Madison St., Ste. 1000, PO Box 567,
Jefferson City 65102
Telephone: (573) 751-8479 / FAX: (573) 526-4418
www.mdfb.org
Email: mdfb@ded.mo.gov

The Missouri Development Finance Board (MDFB) administers several financing programs for public infrastructure and private economic development capital projects of all sizes through-

out Missouri. Additionally, the board provides technical consulting services that support Missouri business export activities in partnership with Ex-Im Bank, the Small Business Administration and small cities' downtown development efforts. The board manages many of these programs in partnership with the Missouri DED.

The board was originally created in 1982 as a separate body corporate and politic of the state within DED as the Missouri Industrial Development Board. Its primary mission was to finance small- to medium-sized new and expanding manufacturing businesses. The board's name and mission have evolved at various times since its inception based upon subsequent legislation that expanded its business financing authority and added authority to fund local and state public infrastructure improvements and nonprofit facilities.

The board funds its loans and investments through the issuance of project-specific conduit revenue bond debt, limited authorization to approve tax credits and fee income earned. Borrowers participating in the board's programs are responsible for debt repayment. The state of Missouri does not incur any costs, nor does it bear any obligation for repaying conduit loans, bonds or notes issued by the board for private or local government borrowers. The board sustains its staffing and operational costs from fee income paid by applicants to its programs and other general operating revenues.

Membership on the board is composed of eight private Missouri residents appointed by the governor with the advice and consent of the Senate to four-year terms. These volunteer members must have been residents of the state for not less than five years prior to their appointment. Remaining membership consists of the lieutenant governor and directors of the departments of economic development, agriculture and natural resources. Seven members constitute a quorum. Not more than five appointed members may be of the same political party. Appointed members serve staggered terms to provide continuity and enhance program development.

Missouri Development Finance Board

Carmichael, Marie, (D), chair, Springfield, Sept. 14, 2012;

Shelton, Reuben A., (D), vice chair, St. Louis, Sept. 14, 2014;

Neff, Larry D., (D), secretary, Neosho, Sept. 14, 2010;

Mehner, John E., (R), treasurer, Cape Girardeau, Sept. 14, 2011;

Dameron, Matthew L., (D), Kansas City, Sept. 14, 2015;

Gregory, Bradley G., (R), Bolivar, Sept. 14, 2015;

Lamping, Patrick J., (D), Barnhart, Sept. 14, 2012;

Martin, Kelley M., (R), Kansas City, Sept. 14, 2012;

Downing, Mike, Department of Economic Development, *ex officio*;

Kinder, Lt. Gov. Peter, *ex officio*;

Fordyce, Richard, director, Department of Agriculture, *ex officio*;

Parker Pauley, Sara, Department of Natural Resources, *ex officio*.

ROBERT V. MISEREZ
Executive Director, Missouri
Development Finance Board

Missouri Division of Tourism

Tourism continues to rank as one of the most important revenue- and job-producing industries in Missouri, creating more than 290,000 jobs. Missouri's 6 million residents welcome more than 39 million visitors annually. With a $15.3 billion dollar economic impact, tourism is a dynamic component of economic development. The travel industry has a broad footprint in Missouri because it is composed of a diverse group of businesses found in every county in the state. The money visitors spend while in Missouri produces business receipts at these firms, in turn employing Missouri residents and paying their wages and salaries.

State and local government units benefit from travel as well. The state government collects taxes on the gross receipts of businesses operating in the state, as well as sales and use taxes levied on the sale of goods and services to travelers. Local governments also collect sales and use taxes generated from traveler purchases.

The 74th General Assembly recognized the importance of tourism when it created the Missouri Tourism Commission in 1967. In collaboration with the Missouri Department of Transportation, the Division of Tourism operates nine welcome centers at key locations around the state, providing interaction with visitors, many of whom extend their stay after learning about the opportunities to be found in the state.

As the official destination marketing organization charged with promoting Missouri as a leisure travel destination, the Missouri Division of Tourism (MDT) plans and implements a wide variety of marketing and strategic sales initiatives. The division's award-winning marketing program includes print, television, radio, online, outdoor, search text and mobile advertising focusing on the experiences Missouri offers and tourists' perceptions of Missouri as a scenic destination with cultural, historical and family activities. A major component of the division is its website: *VisitMO. com.*

SCOTT HOVIS
Chair
Missouri Tourism Commission

BRENDA TINNEN
Vice Chair
Missouri Tourism Commission

JOHN JOSLYN
Member
Missouri Tourism Commission

BENNETT KELLER
Member
Missouri Tourism Commission

LT. GOV. PETER KINDER
Member
Missouri Tourism Commission

REP. MICHELLE KRATKY
Member
Missouri Tourism Commission

REP. DON PHILLIPS
Member
Missouri Tourism Commission

ERIC RHONE
Member
Missouri Tourism Commission

In 1993, HB 188 was signed into law as section 620.467, RSMo. This legislation included a performance-based funding formula for the Missouri Division of Tourism.

Tourism Commission

The commission consists of 10 members: the lieutenant governor, two members of the Senate of different political parties appointed by the president *pro tem* of the Senate, two members of the House of Representatives of different political parties appointed by the speaker of the House, and five other persons appointed by the governor, which may include but are not limited to persons engaged in tourism-oriented operations. No more than three of the governor's appointees shall be of the same political party.

Commission members appointed by the governor serve staggered four-year terms and may be reappointed at the end of their terms. All serve without compensation but are reimbursed for necessary expenses incurred in the performance of their duties.

The commission elects a chairman and meets at least four times in a calendar year, at the call of the chairman, to determine all matters relating to

SEN. DAVID SATER
Member
Missouri Tourism Commission

WILLIAM DANFORTH (DAN)
LENNON
Director
Missouri Tourism Commission

the tourism policies of the state of Missouri and the administration of the Division of Tourism.

The commission reports to each regular session of the General Assembly the results of its marketing program and any recommendations for legislation in the field of tourism promotion.

The budget of the Division of Tourism is contained within the annual submittal of the Department of Economic Development to the Missouri General Assembly for approval.

The Tourism Commission employs a director of the Division of Tourism, qualified by education and experience in public administration with a background in the use of the various news media. The director employs a staff of professional, technical and clerical personnel.

Tourism Commission

Hovis, Scott, (D), chair, Jefferson City;
Tinnen, Brenda, (I), vice chair, Kansas City;
Joslyn, John, (R), Branson;
Keller, Bennett, (D), Ballwin;
Kinder, Lt. Gov. Peter, (R), Cape Girardeau;
Kratky, Rep. Michelle, (D), St. Louis;
Phillips, Rep. Don, (R), Kimberling City;
Rhone, Eric, (D), St. Louis;
Sater, Sen. David, (R), Cassville;
Vacancy (Senate position);
Lennon, William Danforth (Dan), director, Jefferson City.

Advertising and Promotion

The division's primary activities are in the areas of advertising and promotion. The goal is to deliver the right message, through the right medium, to the right audience, at the right time, in order to maximize the economic impact of travel to the Show-Me State.

The strategic marketing plan is the roadmap that guides all marketing efforts of MDT and has been designed to highlight the benefits that mean the most to the largest potential universe of customers. The goal is to implement a competitively funded program providing the required manpower and marketing resources to achieve success. Among the promotional tools is the annual *Missouri Travel Guide.* News releases and a monthly newsletter, *The Tourism Monitor,* are distributed to the news media, travel writers and others interested in Missouri tourism. MDT also engages with thousands of potential travelers, all of whom have expressed an interest in travel in Missouri through its twice-monthly email marketing campaign and via social media outlets.

Through a paid-advertising program, the division promotes Missouri's vacation opportunities. MDT's advertising is designed to create a positive image of Missouri and to generate travel to the state. The majority of MDT marketing efforts are focused on the domestic leisure traveler, which includes visits to friends and relatives as well as trips taken for cultural, arts, outdoor recreation and entertainment purposes. A person-trip is defined as one person on a trip away from home overnight in paid accommodations, or on a day or overnight trip to places 50 miles or more, one-way, away from home.

Research plays a vital and necessary role in measuring the effectiveness of the division's efforts to increase tourism spending and stimulate economic and market-share growth at the state and local level. MDT's research measures past efforts and offers insights as to how, where, when and to whom the state should direct promotional efforts to increase the number of visitors, the length of stay and their expenditures. Research projects are conducted on a continual basis to determine the size, growth and impact of these marketing efforts.

The division works with independent research firms to assess the effect of travel spending on the state's economy, tax revenue derived from travel spending and employment generated through tourism.

In 1993, the Missouri Division of Tourism initiated the Cooperative Marketing Program designed to leverage division marketing resources through participation in strategic marketing partnerships.

For travelers to the Show-Me State, the division's nine Official State Welcome Centers are at the following locations:

- Joplin Welcome Center—Interstate 44 at Mile Marker 2 Rest Area, west of Joplin;
- St. Louis Welcome Center—Interstate 270 and Riverview Drive;
- Hayti Welcome Center—Interstate 55 at Mile Marker 20;
- The Hardin C. Cox Welcome Center at Rock Port—Interstate 29 S. at Mile Marker 109;
- Hannibal Welcome Center—Hwy. 61 N.;
- Kansas City Welcome Center—Interstate 70 at Blue Ridge Cutoff;
- Eagleville Welcome Center—Interstate 35 at Eagleville;
- Conway Welcome Center East—110620 Interstate 44 East;
- Conway Welcome Center West—110619 Interstate 44 West.

These centers welcome more than a half-million visitors each year.

Close relationships with others in the travel promotion field are vital. The division maintains these relationships through memberships, with organizations such as the U.S. Travel Association, National Tour Association and American Bus Association.

The division also works to reach international markets, with a marketing representative assigned to oversee the growth of these important markets.

The division works in collaboration with Brand USA to market Missouri to the international traveler.

The division also oversees work of the Missouri Film Office, which works to attract film, television and video productions to Missouri and to promote the growth of the film and video-production industry in the Show-Me State.

Regulatory Groups

Through its regulatory agencies, the Department of Economic Development works to safeguard the public interest by ensuring safe and sound financial institutions, just and reasonable utility rates and ethical services by licensed professionals. These agencies include the Office of the Public Counsel and the Missouri Public Service Commission.

Office of the Public Counsel

Governor Office Bldg.
200 Madison St., Ste. 650, PO Box 2230
Jefferson City 65102
Telephone: (573) 751-4857 / FAX: (573) 751-5562
www.mo-opc.org
Email: mopco@ded.mo.gov

The Office of the Public Counsel is Missouri's consumer advocate in the area of utility regulation. The public counsel must be an attorney licensed to practice in Missouri and is appointed by the director of the Department of Economic Development. The Office of the Public Counsel was established in 1974 as an independent agency to represent the interests of utility customers in proceedings before and appeals from the Missouri Public Service Commission (PSC) and the courts. The PSC regulates the rates and services of investor-owned electric, natural gas, telephone, water, sewer and steam heat utilities and manufactured housing. The public counsel's participation in PSC cases and its power to appeal PSC decisions has resulted in important victories for utility consumers. While keeping abreast of the rapid changes currently occurring in the utility sector, the Office of the Public Counsel advocates for safe and adequate utility services at just and reasonable rates. By statute, the Office of the Public Counsel represents all customers and focuses its representation on residential and small business customers who otherwise would not have their point of view presented or their interests protected. The public counsel's representation gives these consumers an essential voice in the regulation of life-sustaining public utility services. The public counsel educates and communicates with consumers about their rights and responsibilities. These efforts are especially important to guard against consumer fraud. The office consists of attorneys, technical experts and administrative staff. The attorneys represent the public interest in proceedings before the PSC and the state and federal courts, as well as before the Federal Communi-

DUSTIN ALLISON
Acting Public Counsel
Office of the Public Counsel

cations Commission and Federal Energy Regulatory Commission. Accountants and economists are the backbone of the technical staff. These experts offer the public counsel's testimony on the reasonableness, feasibility and affordability of utility proposals and practices. The public counsel attempts to focus on the most significant cases for utility consumers and cases that have broad public policy effects. The office also consults and works with other public utility consumer advocates in the other states to keep current on issues vital to the consumer and to address national and regional issues of interest to Missouri consumers. In addition, through the property rights ombudsman, the Office of the Public Counsel provides assistance to citizens seeking guidance about condemnation process and procedures.

Missouri Public Service Commission

Governor Office Bldg.
200 Madison St., PO Box 360, Jefferson City 65102
Telephone: (573) 751-3234; Toll free: (800) 392-4211
www.psc.mo.gov
Email: pscinfo@psc.mo.gov

The Missouri Public Service Commission is charged with the statutory responsibility of ensuring public utility consumers receive safe and adequate services at just and reasonable rates that will provide the utility companies' shareholders the opportunity to earn a reasonable return on their investment.

The commission consists of five commissioners who are appointed by the governor to six-year terms with the advice and consent of the Missouri Senate. The terms are staggered so no more than two terms expire in any one year. The governor designates one member as chair, who serves in that capacity at the pleasure of the governor.

The commission regulates utility rates, service and safety for investor-owned electric, natural gas, sewer and water companies. The commission also monitors the construction and set-up of manufactured homes to ensure compliance with state and federal law. While the rates charged by rural electric cooperatives and municipally owned utilities are determined by their respective governing bodies, the commission has jurisdiction regarding matters of safety over the electric cooperatives and municipal electric and natural gas systems. The commission has limited authority over telecommunications services. The commission also oversees service territory issues involving investor-owned electric utilities, rural electric cooperatives and municipally owned electric utilities, as well as those involving privately owned water and sewer utilities and public water supply districts.

The commission has a staff of professional accountants, engineers, economists, attorneys, financial analysts and management specialists who evaluate utility requests for commission approval. These requests deal with matters such as tariff changes regarding rates and business operations, financing proposals, business reorganizations, asset transfers and mergers. The staff will provide the results of its evaluation and recommend actions that satisfy the agency's statutory requirements.

The staff conducts routine and special investigations to ensure compliance with commission statutes, rules and orders, including standards for safety and quality of service. Staff will initiate or implement actions to enforce these laws when necessary. Enforcement actions for injunctive relief or monetary penalties are prosecuted in state court by the commission's general counsel.

The traditional rate case is the process through which the commission ultimately determines what customers will pay for their utility services. The process is commenced in one of two ways: a utility company files a tariff for authority to change its rates, or a complaint is filed by the commission, the PSC staff, the Office of the Public Counsel or others challenging the reasonableness of the utility's rates.

The general public is formally represented before the commission by the Office of the Public Counsel, which is a separate state agency under the Department of Economic Development.

Under both the tariff method and the complaint case method, the commission normally will conduct hearings for the purpose of addressing the reasonableness of the proposed tariff or the rates being challenged. In many tariff filing cases, by law, the commission has up to 11 months from the time a tariff is filed to reach its decision, or the rates will go into effect as filed. Many of these cases are resolved in accord with a settlement between the parties and processed in a shorter time frame.

Special rules apply for water and sewer companies with fewer than 8,000 customers in Mis-

DANIEL Y. HALL
Chair, Missouri Public Service Commission

MAIDA J. COLEMAN
Commissioner, Missouri Public Service Commission

WILLIAM P. KENNEY
Commissioner, Missouri Public Service Commission

SCOTT T. RUPP
Commissioner, Missouri Public Service Commission

STEPHEN M. STOLL
Commissioner, Missouri Public Service Commission

souri. They can pursue changes in rates without the necessity of filing a formal rate case (called an informal rate case). Water and sewer companies with over 8,000 customers are subject to filing a traditional rate case.

The commission staff conducts an independent, on-site investigation of the company's books and records to provide the commission with a recommendation as to what increase or decrease, if any, should be ordered. This investigation can take from two weeks to several months and re-sults in the pre-filing of written testimony. Other parties such as the Office of the Public Counsel, consumer groups, commercial and industrial in-terests and municipalities are given an opportu-nity to provide written testimony.

In addition to holding formal evidentiary hear-ings, the commission may hold local public hear-ings, which allow customers to express their views on the proposed increase or the utility's service.

Once the formal hearings are completed, the commission reviews the evidence submitted, de-liberates and then issues a decision. That decision is subject to court appeal.

The commission is also engaged in a variety of activities reflecting changes in state and federal law regarding the telecommunications and ener-gy sectors of the utility industry. As federal regu-lators make decisions that directly affect Missouri utility consumers, the commission participates in proceedings before the Federal Energy Regu-latory Commission (FERC) and the Federal Com-munications Commission (FCC). Commissioners and staff members have submitted comments or testified on numerous occasions before these agencies and the commission has taken appeals from decisions adverse to Missouri rate-payers to the federal courts.

Regular meetings of the commission are each week. As with other state agencies, commission meetings are subject to the state's open meetings law.

The Data Center keeps a record of all filings and proceedings of the commission. These re-cords are available for public inspection from 8 a.m. to 5 p.m., Monday through Friday, except legal holidays. Many of these records are also available via the commission's website: *www.psc.mo.gov*.

A consumer with questions about specific matters relating to utility service should first call the utility company. If the consumer is not satis-fied with the company response, he or she may call the commission's consumer services depart-ment. Consumers may also file formal, written complaints. The commission's main consumer services office is located in Jefferson City. The commission's toll-free hotline number for com-plaints is (800) 392-4211.

Under the commission's procedure, each in-formal complaint is assigned a specialist who acts as an intermediary between the consumer and the utility in an attempt to resolve the complaint. Through investigations of consumer complaints, the consumer services department works to en-sure that utilities comply with their approved tar-iffs and commission regulations.

The Missouri Public Service Commission was established in 1913 by the 47th General Assem-bly. The 1974 State Reorganization Act placed the commission within the Department of Con-sumer Affairs, Regulation and Licensing, which in 1984 was renamed the Department of Economic Development.

Missouri Public Service Commission

Hall, Daniel Y., (R), chair, Jefferson City, Sept. 27, 2019;

Coleman, Maida J., (D), commissioner, St. Louis;

Kenney, William P., (R), commissioner, Lee's Summit, Jan. 9, 2019;

Rupp, Scott T., (R), commissioner;

Stoll, Stephen M., (D), commissioner, Festus, Dec. 13, 2017.

Department of Elementary and Secondary Education

Jefferson State Office Bldg.
205 Jefferson St., PO Box 480, Jefferson City 65102
Telephone: (573) 751-4212
www.dese.mo.gov

State Board of Education

Under the Missouri Constitution (Article IX), the State Board of Education has general authority for "supervision of instruction in the public schools." Today, this responsibility includes the oversight of educational programs and services that serve Missourians from preschool through the adult levels.

The State Board of Education is composed of eight lay citizens, appointed by the governor and confirmed by the Senate to serve eight-year terms. The terms are staggered so that one term expires each year. No more than four members may belong to the same political party. No more than one member of the board may live in the same county or congressional district.

The board appoints the commissioner of education to serve as its chief executive officer and as director of the Department of Elementary and Secondary Education.

The primary role of the board is to provide leadership and advocacy for the improvement of Missouri's public education system. The board also establishes policies and regulations needed to carry out state and federal laws related to public education. The board's major duties include:

- Setting performance indicators that determine accreditation for local school districts through the Missouri School Improvement Program (MSIP). The indicators define basic requirements regarding performance on assessments, both in aggregate as well as subgroups; high school graduation and/or dropout; advanced coursework; post-secondary and career preparedness; and other areas of student achievement;

- Establishing academic performance standards for the public schools;

- Setting education and certification requirements for all professional personnel (teachers, administrators, librarians, counselors, etc.) in public schools;

- Approving public and private educator preparation programs in the state;

- Establishing regulations and administrative requirements for the distribution of state and federal funds to school districts and other agencies;

- Monitoring school districts' compliance with state and federal laws and regulations. This includes the administration of federally supported programs in the areas of special education, career-technical education and child nutrition (the school lunch and breakfast programs);

- Administering the State Board Operated School Systems—Missouri School for the Blind (St. Louis), Missouri School for the Deaf (Fulton) and Missouri Schools for Severely Disabled; and

- Administering adult learning and rehabilitation services for adult citizens.

State Board of Education

Shields, Charlie, (R), president, St. Joseph, Congressional District 6;

Lenz, O. Victor Jr., (R), vice president, St. Louis, Congressional District 2;

Driskill, Joseph, (D), Jefferson City, Congressional District 3;

Herschend, Peter F., (R), Branson, Congressional District 7;

Jones, Michael, (D), St. Louis, Congressional District 1;

Martin, John, (D), Kansas City, Congressional District 5;

Still, Russell, (D), Columbia, Congressional District 4;

Wallace, Maynard, (R), Thornfield, Congressional District 8.

Department of Elementary and Secondary Education

Article IX of the Missouri Constitution reads, in part: "A general diffusion of knowledge and intelligence being essential to the preservation of the rights and liberties of the people, the General Assembly shall establish and maintain free public schools for the gratuitous instruction of all persons in this state within ages not in excess of twenty-one years as prescribed by law."

To help carry out this mandate, the legislature first established a state office of education, with an elected state superintendent, in 1839. The office went through several transformations until the current constitution, adopted in 1945, established the State Board of Education in its pres-

CHARLIE SHIELDS
President
State Board of Education

O. VICTOR LENZ JR.
Vice President
State Board of Education

JOSEPH DRISKILL
Member
State Board of Education

PETER F. HERSCHEND
Member
State Board of Education

MICHAEL JONES
Member
State Board of Education

JOHN MARTIN
Member
State Board of Education

RUSSELL STILL
Member
State Board of Education

MAYNARD WALLACE
Member
State Board of Education

ent form and created a department of education, headed by an appointed commissioner.

The Department of Elementary and Secondary Education (DESE) was reorganized and established in its present form by the Omnibus State Reorganization Act of 1974.

The department is primarily a service agency that works with educators, legislators, government agencies, community leaders and citizens to maintain a strong public education system. Through its statewide school-improvement initiatives and its regulatory functions, the department strives to ensure all citizens have access to high-quality public education.

The Department of Elementary and Secondary Education is the administrative arm of the State Board of Education. In addition to the commissioner of education, the department organization reflects functions under two divisions—Financial and Administrative Services and Learning Services.

Office of the Commissioner of Education

The commissioner of education directs the Department of Elementary and Secondary Edu-

cation and fulfills other duties as prescribed by law (161.122, RSMo). These duties include: supervising schools and directing the process by which school districts are accredited; suggesting ways to upgrade curriculum and instruction in public schools; working with state and local officials to ensure efficient management of public schools; advising local school officials, teachers and patrons about education-related issues and laws; and seeking "in every way to elevate the standards and efficiency of the instruction given in the public schools of the state." The commissioner is appointed by, and serves at the pleasure of, the State Board of Education.

Division of Financial and Administrative Services

This division is responsible for distributing all federal and state funds to local school districts and other agencies that provide education-related services. The division assists local school officials with budgeting, audits and the reporting of financial statistics, both state and federal. The division also provides assistance with school administrative and governance issues. Other personnel in this division administer the federally funded school lunch and breakfast programs. This

MARGIE VANDEVEN
Commissioner of Education

RONALD LANKFORD
Deputy Commissioner
Division of Financial and
Administrative Services

STACEY PREIS
Deputy Commissioner
Division of Learning Services

ROBIN COFFMAN
Chief of Staff

C. JEANNE LOYD
Assistant Commissioner
Adult Learning and
Rehabilitation Services

CHRIS NEALE
Assistant Commissioner
Quality Schools

PAUL KATNIK
Assistant Commissioner
Educator Quality

WILLIAM THORTON
General Counsel

division also manages the department's internal business operations, such as accounting and procurement, budget and human resources.

Division of Learning Services

This division is composed of offices that manage adult learning and rehabilitation services; college and career readiness; data system management; educator quality; quality schools, which includes early childhood and extended learning; and special education.

The Office of Adult Learning and Rehabilitation Services administers statewide adult education services, including adult education and literacy, the high school equivalency testing program and veterans education, including the Troops to Teachers program.

Rehabilitation Services provide specialized services to adult citizens with disabilities to help them achieve employment and independence. Offices are maintained across the state to provide convenient services to clients. Rehabilitation Services personnel provide individualized counseling, training and other services to help clients achieve gainful employment or independent liv-

STEPHEN BARR
Assistant Commissioner
Special Education

SARAH POTTER
Communications Coordinator

ing. Rehabilitation Services is supported primarily with federal funds.

Independent Living Centers (ILC) are located throughout the state. ILC personnel provide counseling, advocacy, personal care and training in independent living skills for adults with disabilities.

The Disability Determinations Program is part of this office and operates under regulations of the Social Security Administration. Located in offices across the state, Disability Determinations personnel adjudicate claims from Missouri residents seeking federal disability benefits.

The Office of College and Career Readiness provides technical assistance to local school personnel in the adoption and adaptation of the state's performance standards, and curriculum development/adoption of all content areas — math, science, social studies, English/language arts, health/physical education, fine arts and the career-technical content areas. The office assists schools and career centers with the monitoring and approving of Perkins programming.

The development and oversight of the Missouri Assessment Program, consisting of the annual, grade-level assessments for grades 3 through 8 and high school end-of-course assessments, as well as the administration of the National Assessment of Educational Progress (NAEP), are also responsibilities of this office.

The Office of Data System Management is responsible for the development and implementation of the Missouri Comprehensive Data System (MCDS), which includes the student-level record system, the Missouri Student Information System (MOSIS) and Core Data, a web-based data collection system of education-related statistics. This office collects and generates data to meet federal reporting requirements and compliance, as well as provide data utilized in research and analysis that impacts policy decision-making.

The Office of Educator Quality is responsible for approving public and private educator preparation programs. The Office of Educator Quality also issues certificates (licenses) to all professional personnel who work in the state's public school systems, as well as assisting with the review of certificate-holders who are charged with misconduct.

This office is responsible for implementation of teacher, principal and administrator standards, as well as implementation of Missouri's Educator Evaluation System.

A primary function of the Office of Quality Schools is to manage the Missouri School Improvement Program (MSIP), the accreditation/ accountability system for public school districts. This office also administers a wide range of state and federally funded programs that assist local schools (Title I, Title III and other federal programs), charter and other innovative schools, as well as developing and implementing a statewide system of support for schools, communities and families. Schools are also provided assistance on federally and state-developed improvement initiatives that are coordinated with other state and regional services.

The Office of Quality Schools is also responsible for the oversight of the department's efforts to expand and improve early learning opportunities for children and providing support for teachers, programs, parents and families of young children. Staff administers the Missouri Preschool Program and the Child Care Development Fund Grant. The office is also responsible for the development of early learning goals.

Extended learning (after school) programs, under the Office of Quality Schools, provide a safe, caring and nurturing place for extended learning, social, recreational and personal life-skills development for students outside school hours. Grant programs administered by this section include the 21st Century Community Learning Centers grants and School Age Community grants. The programs foster partnerships among the schools, parents/families and communities.

The Office of Special Education administers state and federal funds to support services for students and adults with disabilities. This office works with other state and local agencies to coordinate the Missouri First Steps program, which provides early intervention services for infants and toddlers with disabilities and their families. The office works with local school districts in developing and improving special education services for students (ages 3–21) with disabilities. It also provides financial and technical support for all approved sheltered workshops in the state. Sheltered workshops provide employment for adults with disabilities.

This office also oversees the operation of three school systems administered by the State Board of Education. These are the Missouri School for the Blind, the Missouri School for the Deaf and the Missouri Schools for Severely Disabled. In addition to providing direct services to eligible students with disabilities, these school systems, through their outreach programs and consulting services, assist local school personnel and families throughout the state in meeting the needs of children with disabilities.

Missouri Commission for the Deaf and Hard of Hearing

The Missouri Commission for the Deaf and Hard of Hearing was created in 1988 to improve the quality of life for all Missourians with hearing loss. It advocates for public policies, regulations and programs to improve the quality and coordination of existing services for deaf and hard-of-hearing persons and promotes new services whenever necessary.

The commission promotes deaf awareness to the general public and serves as a consultant to any public agency needing information regarding deafness; develops a system of state certification for those individuals serving as interpreters of the deaf; maintains the quality of interpreting services statewide; maintains a census of persons with a hearing loss in Missouri; promotes the development of a plan that advocates the initiation of improved physical and mental health services for deaf Missourians; conducts or makes available workshops or seminars as needed for educating non-deaf individuals of the problems associated with deafness and ways by which these groups or agencies can more effectively interact with those who are deaf; promotes the development of services for deaf adults, such as shelter homes, independent living skill training facilities and post-school educational training that will help provide for those deaf individuals requiring such services an opportunity to live independently; and establishes a network for effective communication among the deaf adult community and promotes the establishment of TDD relay services where needed.

Missouri Assistive Technology Advisory Council

The Missouri Assistive Technology Advisory Council was established in 1993. The mission of Missouri Assistive Technology is to increase access to assistive technology for Missourians with all types of disabilities, of all ages.

The council is charged to serve as an advocate for policies, regulations and programs to establish a consumer-responsive, comprehensive, assistive technology service delivery system. The council meets at least four times a year, reports annually to the governor and the General Assembly on council activities to increase access to assistive technology, and provides programmatic direction for all activities and services.

Missouri Charter Public School Commission

The Missouri Charter Public School Commission was established by state statute in 2012 with the authority to sponsor higher-quality charter schools throughout the State of Missouri.

The commission shall consist of nine members and shall collectively possess strong experience and expertise in governance, management and finance, school leadership, assessment, curriculum and instruction and education law. All members of the commission shall have demonstrated understanding of and commitment to charter schooling as a strategy for strengthening public education.

Department of Health and Senior Services

PO Box 570, Jefferson City 65102
Telephone: (573) 751-6400
www.health.mo.gov
Email: info@health.mo.gov

The Department of Health and Senior Services was created by the passage of House Bill 603 in May 2001. The bill transferred the roles and responsibilities of the Division of Aging in the Department of Social Services to the Department of Health, creating the Department of Health and Senior Services (DHSS). The department's mission is to promote, protect and partner for better health for all Missourians. This is accomplished through disease prevention, control and surveillance activities; regulation and licensure of health and child care facilities; and programs designed to create safeguards and health resources for seniors and the state's vulnerable populations. The department strives to provide all Missourians with information and tools to improve their own health and well-being and the health of their communities.

State Board of Health

The State Board of Health serves as an advisory body for activities of the Department of Health and Senior Services. It consists of seven members appointed by the governor with the advice and consent of the Senate. Members serve four-year terms and may serve a maximum of two terms. Missouri law (191.400, RSMo) specifies that three members shall be licensed physicians; one member shall be a licensed dentist; one member shall be a licensed chiropractic physician; and the other two members shall be persons other than those licensed by the State Board of Registration for the Healing Arts, the Missouri Dental Board or the Missouri State Board of Chiropractic Examiners, and shall be representative of those persons, professions and businesses that are regulated and supervised by the Department of Health and Senior Services and the State Board of Health. The State Board of Health advises the director operating the department and acts in an advisory capacity regarding rules promulgated by the department.

State Board of Senior Services

The State Board of Senior Services serves as an advisory body for activities of the Department of Health and Senior Services. It consists of seven members appointed by the governor with the advice and consent of the Senate. Members serve four-year terms and may serve a maximum of two terms. Missouri law (660.062, RSMo) specifies that board members shall currently be working in the fields of gerontology, geriatrics, mental health issues, nutrition and rehabilitation services of persons with disabilities. Four of the seven members appointed must belong to the Governor's Advisory Council on Aging. The State Board of Senior Services advises the director in operating the department and acts in an advisory capacity regarding rules promulgated by the department.

Office of the Director

The governor, with the advice and consent of the Senate, appoints the director of the Department of Health and Senior Services. The department director is responsible for the management of the department and the administration of its programs and services. The department deputy director assists the director and acts in his or her absence. Under the director, the department is organized into four divisions: Administration; Community and Public Health; Licensure and Regulation; and Senior and Disability Services. The offices of General Counsel, Governmental Policy and Legislation, Human Resources and Public Information also report to the director. In addition, the director's office oversees the Office of Minority Health, the Office on Women's Health, the Office of Primary Care and Rural Health and the State Public Health Laboratory.

Office of General Counsel (OGC)

The office provides legal counsel to all departmental divisions, programs and offices. The office represents the department in regulatory and licensure cases before departmental hearing officers, the Administrative Hearing Commission and circuit courts. It pursues guardianships for eligible adults and represents the department in Employee Disqualification List appeals. It provides legal assistance in the promulgation of regulations. The **Employee Disqualification List Unit** is also maintained within the Office of General Counsel.

Office of Governmental Policy and Legislation

This office coordinates the development, review and tracking of legislation related to matters involving the department. The legislative liaison serves as the department's point of contact for

PETER LYSKOWSKI
Acting Director

BRET FISCHER
Deputy Director
Division of Administration

BILL WHITMAR
Director, Missouri State Public
Health Laboratory

STEVE RAMSEY
Governmental Policy and
Legislation

NIKKI LOETHEN
General Counsel

RYAN HOBART
Communications Director

CARRIE HALEY
Human Resources

DEBORAH MEBRUER
Executive Assistant to Director

elected officials, other state agencies and constituent groups.

Office of Human Resources (OHR)

The Office of Human Resources ensures the department's compliance with state personnel law and serves as a liaison with the state Office of Administration's Division of Personnel. Staff administer personnel functions of employment, promotion, compensation (including payroll preparation), performance appraisal, discipline, termination, personnel records maintenance and related personnel activities. The office also provides assistance to managers and supervisors in those areas. The OHR investigates and monitors complaints and grievances, maintains DHSS' administrative policies and coordinates and conducts professional development opportunities for DHSS staff.

Office of Public Information (OPI)

The Office of Public Information coordinates all public information released by the department, including media contacts and information, in response to inquiries from other agencies and the public. OPI staff design department publications, including newsletters, brochures and

pamphlets, for programs and divisions within the department. This office also oversees the department's website and maintains the department's social media presence.

Office of Minority Health

The Office of Minority Health seeks to eliminate minority health disparities through monitoring departmental policies and programs, providing technical assistance and developing culturally sensitive health education initiatives. The office also works collaboratively with community-based organizations and leaders to identify and implement specialized strategies that address the health needs of minority populations in Missouri.

Office on Women's Health

The Office on Women's Health provides recommendations to the director on issues affecting the health of women and assists the department in developing priority initiatives and policies to address health inequities. The Sexual Violence Primary Prevention and Education program provides community-based, sexual violence primary prevention education to the citizens of Missouri. The Public Health and Health Services Sexual Assault Victims Services grant provides funding for direct services for victims of sexual assault.

Office of Primary Care and Rural Health

The Office of Primary Care and Rural Health (OPCRH) is composed of the Oral Health Program (OHP), the Primary Care Office (PCO) and the State Office of Rural Health (SORH).

- The **Oral Health Program** provides a broad range of core public health activities, including surveillance education and support for the provision of preventive services, to improve the oral health of Missourians. The initiatives under this program include the Preventive Services Program, which provides oral health surveillance, education and preventive services to children in Missouri under the age of 18.

- The **Primary Care Office** works to ensure access to and the availability of primary health care services for all of Missouri's populations. This includes the Health Professional Loan Repayment Program, which provides financial incentives for primary care physicians and general practice dentists, the Primary Care Resource Initiative for Missouri (PRIMO) Student Loan Program and the Professional and Practical Nursing Student Loan and Loan Repayment programs.

- The **State Office of Rural Health** provides leadership in the development of rural health initiatives; a central resource for information and education related to rural health; and coordination for rural health initiatives to support, strengthen and improve rural health care. This includes the Medicare Rural Hospital Flexibility Program, which provides quality and financial support to Critical Access Hospitals as well as the Small Rural Hospital Improvement Program, which provides financial and technical assistance to small rural hospitals.

Missouri State Public Health Laboratory

The **Missouri State Public Health Laboratory** provides a wide range of diagnostic and analytical services for individuals, health care providers and local public health authorities. These services include quality-assurance measures for laboratory functions and laboratory testing for infectious diseases, genetic disorders and environmental health concerns, both in support of public health

JOSEPH PALM
Office of Minority Health

TUCK VANDYNE
Office on Women's Health

BEN HARVEY
Office of Primary Care and Rural Health

programs and as a reference laboratory performing unique or specialized procedures.

The laboratory provides specimen courier service, scientific expertise, biosafety training and consultation and managerial leadership in meeting the rapidly changing challenges in the clinical and environmental laboratory disciplines and in the development of public health policy.

About 5 million analyses are performed in the State Public Health Laboratory. Approximately 350,000 test kits are assembled and distributed each year for specimens from hospitals and private laboratories, as well as city, county and district health offices.

The State Public Health Laboratory also functions as an emergency response laboratory for biological and chemical events, as well as serving as the main reference laboratory for clinical laboratories in the state by confirming results or completing organism identification.

Division of Administration

The **Division of Administration** provides a wide array of support functions to help programmatic divisions deliver services to Missourians in a cost-effective manner that assures fiscal accountability.

Division Director's Office

- Develops and submits the department's indirect cost plan.
- Evaluates administrative, management and fiscal controls of departmental operations.
- Provides technical assistance to programs concerning contract monitoring and granting requirements.
- Reviews and evaluates contractors' financial management systems and audit reports for financial and administrative compliance.

Budget Services and Analysis Bureau

- Prepares and tracks the department's operating and leasing budget requests.
- Administers the budget after passage.
- Monitors department expenditures.
- Coordinates department efforts to review legislative proposals and prepare fiscal notes.

Financial Services Bureau

- Coordinates department-wide financial activities.
- Oversees the receipt of funds and ensures timely deposit of funds.
- Reviews department expenditures to ensure appropriate fund disbursement, including vendor payments and employee expense accounts.
- Develops, reviews and approves all department contracts.
- Oversees procurement of all supplies, materials, equipment and services.
- Provides technical assistance and support in the development of grant applications.
- Maintains and prepares financial status reports on all federal grants.
- Administers the fixed assets accounting system.

General Services Bureau

- Manages leased property occupied by department staff.
- Manages department-owned vehicles.
- Provides warehouse services.
- Supports telecommunications needs.
- Controls building security access.
- Provides mail service.
- Provides forms management.

- Oversees office moves and space reconfigurations.
- Handles surplus equipment.

Division of Community and Public Health

The **Division of Community and Public Health** coordinates public health resources to protect and promote the public's health and prevent diseases. The programs in this division provide a broad range of services to Missourians of all ages, incomes, races and ethnicities. These programs are in turn supported by the division on specific issues including epidemiology and local public health systems.

The **Emergency Response Center** serves as the coordination point for all department responses to emergencies. It operates at a non-threat level and can quickly be activated as a command and control center in an emergency. It monitors the public health and allied systems' day-to-day emergency preparedness and also serves as part of the Health Alert Network to rapidly receive and disperse communications among public health and health care partners at the local, regional, state and federal levels, and to assign and track follow-up activities. The hotline, (800) 392-0272, is the primary contact point for the general public and emergency response partners.

The **Center for Local Public Health Services** (CLPHS) works to strengthen Missouri's public health system composed of the state department and 115 local public health agencies. The CLPHS is responsible for managing 333 contracts that support local public health efforts including Aid to Local Public Health, Maternal Child Health improvement services and Child Care Health Consultation. Technical assistance is provided by the CLPHS to the Council for Public Health Nursing, Heartland Learning Management System and numerous agencies applying for public health grants. The CLPHS staff provides leadership, training and technical assistance to local public health agencies, communities, not-for-profit organizations and other health-related key stakeholders regarding the development of processes that improve community-based public health systems.

The **Section for Healthy Families and Youth** promotes optimal health by providing leadership to both the public and private sectors in assessing health care needs of families and communities and ensuring the health system responds appropriately. The section is composed of the following:

- **Bureau of Genetics and Healthy Childhood:** utilizes multiple programs that promote and protect the health and safety of individuals and families based on their unique conditions, needs and situations. This is achieved by implementing prevention and intervention strategies to optimize an individual's health and environment from pre-pregnancy through adulthood. Related activities of the bureau encompass public and professional education, screening and follow-up services, surveillance, needs assessment and resource identification and/or development. The bureau accomplishes its mission in collaboration with families, health care providers and other community, state and national partners.

- **Genetics Services Program:** expands existing programs and develops new ones, to reduce the morbidity and mortality associated with genetic disorders. Information is provided to the public and medical professionals regarding genetic disorders and the availability of genetic services in Missouri. A referral network is maintained for individuals in need of diagnostic services, treatment, counseling and other genetic-related services.

- **Adult Genetics Program:** provides limited assistance with health care costs for Missouri adults (21 years of age and older) with cystic fibrosis, hemophilia and sickle cell disease. The program provides applicants who meet financial and medical guidelines with limited financial assistance for inpatient and outpatient services, medication and blood factor products, emergency care and home equipment. Service coordination is provided for those who meet the medical eligibility requirements.

- **Metabolic Formula Distribution Program:** provides prescribed dietary formulas to individuals with covered metabolic disorders such as phenylketonuria and maple syrup urine disease. Use of the dietary formula combined with a medically supervised diet eliminates or reduces the adverse consequences of the disorders.

- **Sickle Cell Anemia Program:** provides information to the public and health professionals about sickle cell disease and sickle cell traits and promotes and provides screening, testing, referral, education, counseling, follow-up and outreach services for individuals and families with sickle cell conditions.

- **Newborn Health Program:** promotes healthy birth outcomes and healthy infants by increasing awareness of rec-

HAROLD KIRBEY
Director, Division of Community
and Public Health

ommended best practices through educational activities and materials, including *text4baby*. Messages and activities promote the importance of preconception care; early entry into prenatal care; use of folic acid to prevent birth defects; avoidance of smoking, alcohol and other drugs; promotion of breast-feeding; safe infant sleep practices; and other healthy behaviors.

- **Newborn Blood Spot Screening Program:** provides early identification and follow-up of galactosemia, congenital hypothyroidism, congenital adrenal hyperplasia, hemoglobinopathies, organic acid disorders, fatty acid oxidation disorders, amino acid disorders (including phenylketonuria), cystic fibrosis, biotinidase deficiency and lysosomal storage disorders. Newborn screening can indicate the presence of disease in affected yet asymptomatic infants. Infants found to be positive are referred to a system of health care for confirmation of diagnosis and management.

- **Newborn Hearing Screening Program:** develops, promotes and supports systems to ensure all babies born in Missouri receive hearing screenings, audiologic evaluations and early intervention, as appropriate. The hearing screening program is dedicated to providing unbiased support to families of children who are deaf or hard of hearing.

- **Folic Acid Program:** endeavors to increase the number of Missourians who are aware of the importance of folic acid intake in helping to prevent certain birth defects, diseases and health conditions.

- **Fetal and Infant Mortality Review:** analyzes infant and fetal death records to develop recommendations for community change, if appropriate, to reduce fetal and infant mortality. The communities then determine and implement interventions based upon recommendations received that may improve outcomes for future families.

- **Building Blocks Program:** is an evidence-based prenatal and early childhood nurse home-visiting program based on the David Olds Model. Participants in the program are low-income, first-time mothers who enter the program prior to the 28th week of pregnancy. Nurses make home visits to work with the women and their families during pregnancy and the first two years of the child's life to improve pregnancy outcomes, child health and development and family economic self-sufficiency.

- **Healthy Families Missouri Home Visiting (HFMoHV) Program:** is founded on the Healthy Familes of America evidence-based home visitation model. The HFMoHV provides intensive, sustained home visits to include health assessments and education during the prenatal period; parenting education both prenatally and postnatally; newborn and infant assessments, including developmental screenigns; and referral information based on health, social and financial assessments. Services are provided through registered nurses, social workers and paraprofessionals to the target population of at-risk, low-income pregnant and postpartum women and their children up to five years of age. Services are offered for a minimum of three years. The goals of this program are to increase healthy pregnancies and positive birth outcomes, as well as decrease child abuse and neglect through home-based services.

- **Maternal, Infant and Early Childhood Home Visiting Program:** is a voluntary program that delivers high-quality, evidence-based, early childhood home-visitation services to ensure more children have the opportunity to grow up healthy, safe, ready to learn and able to become productive members of society. In Missouri, this is accomplished utilizing three evidence-based home visiting models (Nurse Family Partnership, Early Head Start—Home Based Option and Parents as Teachers)　and one promising approach model (Nurses for Newborns) serving pregnant women and children up to kindergarten entry. Home visitors work with the women and their families to improve maternal and new-

born health; reduce child injuries, child abuse, neglect or maltreatment and emergency department visits; improve school readiness and achievement; reduce prevalence of domestic violence; improve family economic self-sufficiency; and improve coordination and referrals for other community resources and support for families.

- **Early Childhood Comprehensive System:** improving early chilhood comes by providing opportunities for implementation of the Missouri Early Childhood Strategic Plan for Missouri's children and their families. The plan is organized around five critical components for helping young children be healthy and ready to learn at school entry. The five components are: health, mental health and social-emotional development, early childhood programs, parenting education and family support. Within the focus of each of the five critical components are the outcomes and strategies for supporting Missouri's young children. In addition to these components, there is an added focus on the mitigation of toxic stress and trauma in infants and young children by partnering with the Department of Mental Health to bring training and technical assistance to early childhood professionals across the state.

- **TEL-LINK:** is the department's toll-free telephone line for maternal, child and family health services. The purpose of TEL-LINK is to provide information and referrals to Missourians concerning a wide range of health services. TEL-LINK can connect callers to services for: WIC (women, infants and children), MO HealthNet, pregnancy assistance, home visiting services, prenatal drug abuse treatment, immunizations, child care, social services, down syndrome helpline services, First Steps, genetics services, audiology services, parenting, special health care needs, alcohol and drug abuse treatment, mental health treatment, family violence services, nonemergency medical transportation, etc. The toll-free telephone number is (800) 835-5465.

- **Sexual Assault Forensic Examination – Child Abuse Resource and Education (SAFE-CARE) Program:** provides education and support to medical providers who evaluate children suspected of being abused or neglected. SAFE-CARE providers (physicians, nurse practitioners and physician assistants) receive

Missouri-based initial training and annual update training on the medical evaluation of child maltreatment. Collaboration and mentoring are provided through Missouri's Child Abuse Medical Resource Centers (St. Louis Children's Hospital, Cardinal Glennon Children's Medical Center and Children's Mercy Hospital).

- **Safe Cribs for Missouri:** provides portable cribs to low-income families who have no other resources for obtaining a safe crib. Local public health agencies distribute the cribs and provide one-on-one safe sleep education to each family before the crib is taken home. A follow-up home visit is conducted four to six weeks later to assess the family's use of safe-sleep practices.

- **Bureau of Immunization Assessment and Assurance:** The Bureau of Immunization Assessment and Assurance supports efforts to plan, develop and maintain a public health infrastructure that helps assure high immunization coverage levels and low incidence of vaccine-preventable diseases for all ages throughout the state. Every effort is made to provide children, adolescents and adults with information on all vaccines recommended by the Advisory Committee on Immunization Practices (ACIP).

  - **Vaccines for Children (VFC) Program**: is a federally funded program that provides vaccines at no cost to children who might not otherwise be vaccinated because of inability to pay. Children who are eligible for VFC vaccines are entitled to receive those vaccines recommended by the ACIP.

  - **ShowMeVax:** is an immunization registry that offers medical providers an opportunity to track vaccine inventory, input immunization records and verify immunization status of clients. Schools and child care providers have the ability to review the immunization status of children to verify compliance with state regulation.

  - **School and Child Care Program:** uses data from annual surveys and validation visits to analyze trends in meeting Missouri's child care attendance requirements and school immunization requirements.

  - **Quality Improvement Program:** uses data from Assessment, Feedback, Incentive and Exchange (AFIX) visits at providers enrolled in Vaccines for Children to offer guidance and technical assistance

to assist providers in increasing immunization rates.

- **Influenza Program:** actively reaches communities across the state through outreach efforts promoting influenza awareness.

- **Adult Immunization Program:** utilizes Section 317 federal funding to offer selected vaccines at no cost to uninsured or underinsured adults.

The **Section for Special Health Services** is responsible for developing policy, planning systems of care and designing, implementing and evaluating programs to meet the special health care needs of families in the state. The section is composed of the following:

- **Bureau of Special Health Care Needs (SHCN):** provides statewide health care support services, including service coordination, for children and adults with disabilities, chronic illness and birth defects. State and federal funding supports SHCN services. To be eligible for SHCN services, individuals must be a Missouri resident, have a special health care need and meet medical and financial eligibility when required. There is no application fee for these services. Service coordination, an essential service for people with complex conditions and needs, is provided to all bureau program participants, regardless of financial status.

- **Children and Youth with Special Health Care Needs Program (CYSHCN):** provides assistance statewide for individuals from birth to age 21 who have, or are at increased risk for, a disease, defect or medical condition that may hinder their normal physical growth and development, and who require more medical services than children and youth generally. The program focuses on early identification and service coordination for individuals who meet medical eligibility guidelines. The CYSHCN Program provides limited funding for medically necessary diagnostic and treatment services for individuals whose families also meet financial eligibility guidelines.

- **Healthy Children and Youth-Administrative Case Management**: provides home- and community-based services for children under the age of 21 who are enrolled in MO HealthNet (Medicaid). Public health nurses provide service coordination and authorization for medically necessary in-home services. Service coordination includes assessment through home visits and links to services and resources that enable participants to remain safely in their homes with their families. Authorized services may include in-home personal care, in-home nursing care, case management and skilled nursing visits.

- **Medically Fragile Adult Waiver:** provides home- and community-based services for individuals with serious and complex medical needs who have reached the age of 21 and are no longer eligible for home care services available through the Healthy Children and Youth Program in Missouri. This waiver is designed to provide a cost-effective alternative to placement in an intermediate care facility for individuals with intellectual disabilities (ICF/IID). Public health nurses provide service coordination and authorization for medically necessary services. Service coordination includes assessment through home visits and links to services and resources that enable participants to remain safely in their homes with their families. Authorized services may include in-home personal care, in-home nursing care and medical supplies.

- **Adult Brain Injury Program:** assists Missouri residents, ages 21 to 65, who are living with a traumatic brain injury (TBI). Through service coordination, the program links individuals to resources to enable each person to obtain goals of independent living, community participation and employment. Individuals who meet financial eligibility requirements may also receive community-based rehabilitation services to help achieve identified goals. Rehabilitation services include counseling, vocational training, employment support and home- and community-based support training.

The **Section for Community Health and Chronic Disease Prevention** (CHCDP) is engaged in activities to reduce risk factors for the prevention and control of chronic diseases. The section is composed of the following:

- **Bureau of Community Health and Wellness (CHW):** focuses on promotion and delivery of primary prevention strategies to address optimum health across a citizen's lifespan and prevention of chronic conditions through interventions to reduce tobacco use and obesity.

  - **Chronic Disease Primary Prevention Program:** works to reduce the primary risk factors for chronic diseases—tobacco use and exposure to secondhand smoke, as well as physical inactivity and unhealthy eating—that lead to obesity. Contracts are established with 16 local public health departments in a multi-county collaborative. Emphasis is placed on making environmental, policy and system changes to support healthy behaviors for schools, worksites and communities.

  - **Comprehensive Tobacco Use Prevention Program:** works to prevent youth from tobacco-use initiation, promote quitting among youth and adults, eliminate exposure to secondhand smoke and reduce the impact on populations disproportionately affected by tobacco. The program collaborates with youth advocacy groups, community-based coalitions, volunteer organizations and partners to educate the public about the health effects of tobacco use and exposure to secondhand smoke. The program advocates for policies prohibiting tobacco use on school property and eliminating exposure to secondhand smoke in public places. To increase quitting among tobacco users, the Missouri Tobacco Quitline (1-800-QUIT-NOW) provides free cessation counseling services and referrals for local assistance.

  - **Team Nutrition Program:** activities are designed to reduce rates of overweight children and create healthier school and child care nutrition and physical activity environments.

  - **Adolescent Health Program:** addresses various adolescent, teen and young adult issues of Missourians age 10 to 24 years old. The program provides consultation, education, technical assistance and resources for health professionals, school personnel, parents, adolescents and state and community organizations. The Council for Adolescent and School Health assists the department in promoting a multi-level approach to achieve healthy adolescent development.

  - **School Health Program:** provides technical support to public school districts and local public health agencies to establish or expand preventive, population-based health services educational programs in school settings. Technical assistance and consultation are provided. The program is a collaborative effort of Missouri's departments of Health and Senior Services, Elementary and Secondary Education and Social Services.

- **Injury and Violence Prevention (IVP) Program:** provides targeted unintentional injury prevention services to children zero to 14 years old through local Safe Kids coalitions. The IVP Program, through the local Safe Kids coalitions, provides safety education on child passenger safety, bicycle safety, fire safety, crib safety, water safety, poisoning and other prevention activities based on community needs. The Missouri Injury and Violence Prevention Advisory Committee (MIVPAC) provides advice, expertise and guidance to the IVP Program. The committee also identifies and mobilizes the state, regional and community resources and networks needed to support and implement state injury prevention initiatives.

- **Physical Activity and Nutrition Program to Prevent Obesity:** works to increase access to healthy food and safe places to be physically active in order to prevent obesity and other chronic diseases. Program goals are reached through policy and environmental changes. The program collaborates with other stakeholders to advocate for statewide policy changes, provide training and technical assistance to local communities and provide support for local initiatives. Major initiatives include Missouri Livable Streets, healthy corner stores and worksite wellness, including support for nursing mothers in the workplace.

- **The Abstinence Education Grant Program:** is funded by the Administration for Children and Families at the Department of Health and Human Services. Funding is provided for communities to deliver Abstinence Education to high-risk youth, ages 10 to 17, based on criteria identified by the funding source. The main goals of the program are to reduce teen pregnancy, decrease the rate of sexually transmitted disease, expand foster parent/youth communication and increase the percentage of high school graduates.

- **Faith-Based Initiatives:** is a developing initiatives targeted to harness efforts of the faith-based community to deliver public health messages to a hard-to-reach/hard-to-convince segment of the population. Initial efforts for this initiative are to gather information regarding current faith-based efforts within the Department of Health and Senior Services (i.e., disaster preparedness, heart disease, cancer, obesity and nutrition).

- **Bureau of Cancer and Chronic Disease Control (CCDC):** administers services and programs to assist individuals who have a noncommunicable, chronic disease or disability, and promotes recognition of signs and symptoms, screenings and other early intervention strategies (including Chronic Disease Self-Management programs) to lessen the impact of the disease and disability.

  - **Comprehensive Cancer Control Program:** partners with individuals, professionals and cancer survivors who share expertise, resources and ideas to develop a statewide cancer plan. The program and its partners support healthy lifestyles, recommend cancer screenings, educate people about cancer symptoms, increase access to quality cancer care and enhance cancer survivors' quality of life.

  - **Show Me Healthy Women (SMHW):** provides free breast and cervical cancer screening and diagnostic services to low-income, uninsured or underinsured women aged 35 years and older to reduce the mortality rate of breast and cervical cancer in Missouri women. The program is funded by the Centers for Disease Control and Prevention, general revenue and donations. Most women diagnosed with breast or cervical cancer through the program are eligible for free treatment under the Breast and Cervical Cancer Treatment Act (Medicaid).

  - **Arthritis and Osteoporosis Control Program:** promotes optimal health and quality of life for all Missourians affected by arthritis, osteoporosis, lupus, rheumatic diseases and related musculoskeletal conditions.

  - **Asthma Prevention and Control Program:** works to improve the capacity of Missouri's public health system to define and reduce the burden of asthma. Program services include linking existing resources and partners, maintaining comprehensive surveillance and evaluation and providing technical assistance for local control efforts.

  - **Diabetes Prevention and Control Program:** addresses diabetes prevention and diabetes complications by influencing change at the policy, environmental, health systems and community levels.

  - **Heart Disease and Stroke Prevention Program:** addresses the ABC's of heart disease and stroke prevention, with the main focus on preventing and controlling high blood pressure and reducing sodium intake. The ABCs include: Aspirin, (increase low-dose aspirin therapy according to recognized guidelines); blood pressure, (prevent and control high blood pressure, reduce sodium intake); cholesterol (prevent and control high blood cholesterol) and smoking (increase the number of smokers counseled to quit and increase availability of no or low-cost cessation products).

- **Organ and Tissue Donor Program:** works to maintain a statewide, confidential registry of potential organ and tissue donors that is available to procurement agencies and individual registrants 24/7. The program works with state and national partners to develop and implement initiatives to increase awareness about the benefits of donation and how to enroll in the registry. An advisory committee makes recommendations related to priorities, development and implementation of program activities, registry management and strategic planning. The program works with the Department of Revenue to aid program reach and registry operations.

- **WISEWOMAN Program:** provides services for low-income, underinsured women age 40 and older who are clients of the Show Me Healthy Women Program. Services include health screenings for heart disease risk factors, such as high cholesterol, high blood pressure, obesity and diabetes. In addition, WISEWOMAN risk counseling and lifestyle education helps women eat healthier, be more physically active and quit smoking to reduce their risk for heart disease.

- **Bureau of WIC and Nutrition Services:** is a short-term intervention program designed to influence lifetime nutrition and health behavior in a targeted, at-risk population. WIC provides specific nutrition education to pregnant, breast-feeding and postpartum women, as well as infants and children under the age of 5 who are at-risk and meet financial eligibility requirements. This serves to meet enhanced dietary needs during periods of crucial physiological development. WIC also administers breast-feeding support programs, such as the Breastfeeding Peer Counseling Program, and initiatives to increase breastfeeding duration rates, such as making breast pumps available to WIC participants returning to work or school. The statewide breastfeeding coordinator also promotes initiatives to increase breastfeeding initiation and duration rates among the general public through Missouri Breastfeeding Month activities and the Missouri Show Me 5 Hospital initiative.

- **Bureau of Community Food and Nutrition Assistance Programs:** provides meal subsidies to eligible organizations that feed infants, children and youth, and provides food packages for low-income elderly persons.

  - **Child and Adult Care Food Program:** is a federal entitlement program to improve the nutrient intake of participants in licensed childcare centers, licensed family child care homes, licensed adult day care centers, emergency homeless shelters and after-school programs.

  - **Summer Food Service Program:** serves to improve the nutrient intake of low-income children when school is not in session, which reduces the risk for health problems, enhances children's learning capabilities and helps them succeed in school. The program also improves the quality of the summer programs offered in low-income areas and provides summer employment opportunities in local communities.

  - **Commodity Supplemental Food Program:** works to improve the nutrient intake of low-income elderly adults by providing commodity food packages specially formulated to provide additional sources of iron, calcium, protein and vitamins A and C.

The **Section of Epidemiology for Public Health Practice** serves as the scientific authority on issues related to the control and prevention of diseases and health risk behaviors in the state of Missouri. It houses the resources necessary to operate and maintain major public health information systems, the state's vital records and statistics, community health information and medical and public health epidemiology resources necessary to prevent, intervene and control diseases and conditions impacting the health of Missourians. The section is composed of the following:

- **Office of Epidemiology:** uses science to guide and develop public health practices; monitors health status and health risk behaviors through effective use of public health surveillance systems; promotes evidence-based public health interventions; and provides epidemiologic consultation for maternal and child health communicable disease/environmental health, and chronic disease and nutritional health initiatives.

- **Information Support Unit:** is responsible for communication of health information to support public health activities and initiatives. The staff serves as an integral part of preventive health care programs, such as the smoking cessation campaign, cancer detection programs, treatment and management of obesity programs, genetics and healthy childhood and child nutrition assistance and education services.

- **Bureau of Vital Records:** maintains the central registry of births, deaths, fetal deaths (after 20 weeks gestation, but before birth) and reports of marriages and dissolutions of marriages for the state of Missouri. The registry of births and deaths extends back to 1910, while the registry of marriages and dissolution of marriages extends back to 1948. The bureau also corrects vital records as authorized by law; files and issues certified copies of births, deaths and fetal reports; issues statements relating to marriages and dissolution of marriages; and prepares new certificates for adoptions and legitimating.

- **Bureau of Health Care Analysis and Data Dissemination:** collects, analyzes and distributes health-related information that promotes the understanding of health problems and needs in Missouri. Data generated by the bureau aid and guide the planning, development and evaluation of programs and services of the department, as well as the health-related activities of other agencies, institutions and organizations. The bureau provides data analysis and statistical support to health programs and local public health agencies; prepares, edits and publishes other statistical reports for the department; disseminates health data via the Internet and other media; and provides health data and statistics as requested by researchers, public health professionals, legislators, media, educators and the public. The bureau is responsible for maintaining and enhancing Internet-based data and statistical resources such as the Community Data Profiles, the Missouri Information for Community Assessment and the Missouri Health Care Associated Infection Reporting System.

- **Bureau of Vital Statistics:** analyzes and distributes vital statistics and related information to promote the understanding of health problems and needs in Missouri, and also spotlights improvements and progress in the general health status of Missourians. The bureau also maintains the needed vital statistics infrastructure; provides data analysis and statistical support to health programs and local public health agencies; prepares, edits and publishes other statistical reports

for the department; disseminates aggregated health data and statistical reports via the Internet and other media; and provides vital statistics data and oversight to meet data needs of researchers, public health professionals, legislators, media, educators and the public. The bureau is also responsible for quality control of the statistical information on vital records (i.e. births, deaths, fetal deaths, marriages, dissolution of marriages) and induced terminations of pregnancy; ensures compliance with the National Center for Health Statistics, Vital Statistics Cooperative Agreement; analyzes data on vital events and other health status measures; publishes monthly, annual and periodic special statistics; develops and updates various linked data systems used for surveillance of health problems and the evaluation of public health programs; and prepares vital statistics data and maternal and child health indicator data for the Web-based Community Data Profiles and the Missouri Information for Community Assessment data query system.

The **Section for Environmental Public Health** is involved in ensuring environmental hazards that pose unnecessary health risks to the public are identified and appropriate steps are taken to protect the public's health. The section provides services and activities that include food safety, food recalls, general safety and sanitation inspections, evaluation of health risks due to exposure to hazardous substances and guidance involving environmentally related health hazards. The section contributes to the Department of Health and Senior Services' emergency response to public health emergencies and natural disasters, including chemical and radiological terrorism. The section is composed of the following:

- **Bureau of Environmental Health Services:** protects the health of all Missourians and visitors to the state by ensuring healthy environments. There are four unique environmental sanitation programs in the bureau: the Food Safety Program, the Environmental Child Care Program, the Lodging Program and the On-site Wastewater Treatment System Program.

- **Retail Food Safety and Food Processing Program:** is responsible for oversight of all retail food establishments (including restaurants, school food service, temporary food events and grocery and convenience stores), frozen desserts and food processing/storage facilities throughout the state. There are approximately 28,000 retail food establishments, 2,150 frozen dessert facilities and 1,654 food processing/storage facilities statewide.

The program minimizes the potential risk of foodborne illness and injury and provides food safety training to both industry and regulatory personnel. The program responds to complaints and emergencies involving regulated products.

- **Lodging Program:** licenses approximately 1,600 lodging establishments (hotels, motels, bed and breakfasts and resorts) statewide. The program issues licenses after determining compliance with applicable rules and regulations, provides training to local public health agencies and responds to complaints and emergencies involving lodging establishments.

- **Environmental Child Care Program:** serves approximately 180,000 children statewide. The program oversees annual sanitation inspections of more than 4,200 regulated child care providers to ensure sanitary and safe practices are utilized when caring for children and provides training to local public health agencies. In addition, the program responds to complaints and emergencies regarding environmental childcare issues.

- **On-site Wastewater Treatment System Program:** establishes sanitation standards and ensures the applicable onsite systems are in compliance with these standards. In addition, the program trains and provides licensure for approximately 1,970 professionals who install, inspect and repair on-site systems in accordance with sanitation standards set forth by law. The program assists the public and local public health agencies with questions and concerns, and responds to emergency situations.

- **Bureau of Environmental Epidemiology:** is involved in the investigation and prevention of diseases related to the environment. The bureau's efforts focus on diseases associated with exposure to chemical and physical agents in our environment. Services include:

  - Performing health assessments and quantitative risk assessments of hazardous waste sites;

  - Providing public health consultation and toxicological consultation for emergencies involving chemicals and pesticides;

  - Implementing the state Childhood Lead Poisoning Prevention Program;

  - Providing consultation, technical assistance and responding to issues affecting private water supplies;

  - Providing professional and public information on radon and other indoor air-quality issues;

  - Providing technical assistance to local public health agencies and communities on environmental public health issues;

  - Regulating and licensing professionals who remove lead hazards from buildings and providing accreditation training to providers; and

  - Conducting environmental investigations and assessments.

The **Section for Disease Prevention** principal unit investigates the cause, origin and method of transmission of communicable diseases. The interrelated services of this section focus on disease surveillance, prevention and control. This section focuses on communicable diseases, tuberculosis, zoonoses, sexually transmitted diseases (STDs) and HIV/AIDS. The section is integral to the Department of Health and Senior Services' response to public health emergencies, natural and biological disasters and terrorism. The section ensures rapid detection and response through a comprehensive surveillance system operated by public health staff who are prepared through expertise and training to detect diseases/conditions that may indicate an emergency/bioterrorism event. The Section is composed of the following:

- **Bureau of Communicable Disease Control and Prevention:** provides prevention, and intervention programs related to 91 reportable communicable (or infectious) diseases and conditions of public health significance in Missouri. Many of these diseases are emerging infections (such as Multi-drug Resistant Tuberculosis, Cryptosporidiosis, Paragonimiasis and Novel Influenza).

- **Bureau of HIV, STD and Hepatitis:** provides comprehensive prevention, intervention and care programs targeting HIV/AIDS, syphilis, gonorrhea, chlamydia, hepatitis B (including perinatal HBV) and hepatitis C. Services include:

  - Providing guidelines, recommendations, training and technical assistance or consultation to practicing physicians, local public health agencies and community-based providers on HIV disease, certain STDs and hepatitis B and C; coordination of disease outbreak investigations; disease investigation control activities; and analysis of data.

  - Providing HIV counseling, testing and referral.

- Providing HIV/STD/hepatitis outreach, health education and risk-reduction programs statewide.
- Collaborating with community members, community-based organizations and other stakeholders throughout the state who serve on the HIV/STD Prevention Community Planning Group and various other advisory bodies.
- Collaborating with local, state and federal agencies as well as community-based organizations to ensure comprehensive health care and supportive services to individuals living with HIV/AIDS through a statewide case management system.
- Administering the AIDS Drug Assistance Program, Ryan White Title II, Housing Opportunities for People With AIDS and Medicaid AIDS Waiver services to eligible low-income Missourians living with HIV who have no other access to health care and support services.
- Coordinating the perinatal hepatitis B program, in which pregnant women with the virus are followed through delivery to prevent transmission of the disease to their newborns.
- **Bureau of Reportable Disease Informatics:** provides surveillance programs for 91 reportable diseases in Missouri. Services include:
  - Conducting epidemiological studies, identifying communicable disease surveillance data needs, designing data collection processes/systems, developing and maintaining data systems and datasets, analyzing and interpreting data at regular intervals to track trends and providing regular reports on these analyses.
  - Maintaining a statewide surveillance system (WebSurv) and analysis of morbidity to identify trends and risk factors.
  - Maintains the Electronic Surveillance System for Early Notification of Community-Based Epidemics (ESSENCE), a statewide syndromic surveillance system that analyzes chief complaints from hospitals, emergency rooms, over-the-counter drug sales and poison control center data.
- **Office of Veterinary Public Health:** conducts activities related to the prevention and control of zoonotic diseases that might be transmitted from animals native to Missouri, or accidentally through normal trade, commerce or an act of bioterrorism.

- Acts as a liaison with other agencies such as the Missouri departments of Agriculture and Conservation to maintain current knowledge of diseases occurring in animal populations that could affect humans.
- Conducts specific disease prevention programs, including the Rabies Program, which focus on consultations with medical providers to assess patient risk factors, education of the public, vaccination of animals and other preventive measures.
- Coordinates seasonal mosquito surveys to examine the prevalence of mosquito-borne pathogens (like West Nile virus) by contracting with local health agencies and publishes the results on the DHSS website and a national database.
- Monitors the worldwide occurrence of vector-borne disease agents that could be used in a bioterrorism attack or introduced accidentally into North America and assists the department in developing response plans to address these situations.
- Facilitates local public health agencies' capacity to conduct tick- and mosquito-borne disease prevention activities by providing educational materials and developing locally based outreach strategies.

Division of Regulation and Licensure

The **Division of Regulation and Licensure (DRL)** oversees licensure and regulation activities for child care facilities, long-term care facilities and health care facilities. In addition, the division oversees the Certificate of Need Program, the Board of Nursing Home Administrators and the Family Care Safety Registry. The division enforces statutory and regulatory requirements to ensure the safety, health, welfare and rights of children and residents to long-term care and other health care facilities.

The **Family Care Safety Registry** serves as a resource for background screening information maintained by various state agencies. Information accessed by the registry includes Missouri open criminal records, the sex offender registry, the child abuse/neglect registry, the department's employee disqualification registry, child care license revocations and foster parent license denials, revocations and suspensions. In addition to the needs of families selecting an individual for a private employment arrangement, many employers of child care, elder-care and personal-care workers are required to obtain background screening information for staff in order to obtain or maintain licensure or to be in compliance with state regulations. The registry maintains a toll-free call center (866) 422-6872; is staffed from 8 a.m. to 3 p.m., Monday through Friday; and a website *health.mo.gov/safety/fcsr/*.

The **Missouri Board of Nursing Home Administrators:** establishes minimum standards for licensing nursing home administrators and residential care and assisted living administrators; provides testing opportunities for qualified applicants; approves and monitors continuing education programs designed for licensed administrators; renews the licenses of qualified licensees; and conducts licensee disciplinary hearings.

The **Certificate of Need Program (CONP):** The Missouri Health Facilities Review Committee (MHFRC), with the assistance of the CONP staff, carries out its responsibilities as set out in the CON statute to address issues of community need, accessibility, cost containment and other community health services factors. The MHFRC reviews substantial health capital expenditures and expenditures for major medical equipment. The board is made up of members from the legislature and the public sector appointed by the governor.

The **Section for Health Standards and Licensure (HSL):** is responsible for licensing and regulating a wide variety of health care entities, investigating complaints levied against these entities, performing inspection activities for numerous Medicare-certification programs and also ensuring the safe and legal handling and distribution of controlled substances in Missouri. The section consists of six bureaus: Ambulatory Care; Emergency Medical Services; Home Care and Rehabilitative Standards; Hospital Standards; Narcotics and Dangerous Drugs; and Outpatient Healthcare.

- **Bureau of Ambulatory Care:** administers the state licensing program, federal survey activities and complaint investigations for all Missouri freestanding ambulatory surgical centers, birthing centers, abortion facilities, mammography providers and medical facilities that use ionizing radiation.

- **Bureau of Emergency Medical Services:** licenses, inspects and investigates complaints involving Emergency Medical Technicians (Basic, Intermediate and Paramedic) and ground and air ambulance services.

- **Bureau of Home Care and Rehabilitative Standards:** conducts on-site surveys and complaint investigations for compliance with state and federal regulations involving home-health agencies, hospices, comprehensive outpatient rehabilitation facilities and outpatient physical therapy providers.

JEANNE SERRA
Director, Division of Regulation and Licensure

- **Bureau of Hospital Standards:** licenses all applicable Missouri hospitals in the areas of fire safety, sanitation, nursing service, dietary service, organization and administration, and conducts federal hospital survey and complaint investigation activities related to certification of providers of services participating in the Title XVIII (Medicare) and Title XIX (Medicaid) programs. The bureau also performs the review and designation of hospitals seeking to be recognized as a stroke center, a STEMI center or a trauma center as part of the Time Critical Diagnosis System.

- **Bureau of Narcotics and Dangerous Drugs:** maintains a registry of the individuals and firms who prescribe, dispense or otherwise conduct activities that involve controlled substances and inspects and investigates firms and individuals who lawfully manufacture, distribute or dispense controlled substances.

- **Bureau of Outpatient Healthcare:** conducts survey and complaint investigation activities related to certification of providers, including laboratories participating in the CLIA program, end-stage renal disease facilities and rural health clinics.

The **Section for Child Care Regulation (SCCR)** is responsible for ensuring the safety and health of children while in the care of licensed and regulated child care facilities. The section has the statutory authority to discipline licensed child care facilities. The section:

- Conducts twice-yearly inspections of family child care homes, group child care homes and child care centers.

- Conducts annual health and safety inspections of license-exempt child care facilities.

- Conducts renewal inspections for licensed child care facilities every two years.

- Investigates complaints of child care regulations and/or statute violations in child care facilities.

- Provides technical assistance, blue print reviews and facility review conferences with licensed and regulated child care facilities.

- Reviews children's health records for appropriate immunization for communicable vaccine preventable childhood diseases.

- Ensures fire safety requirement for licensed and regulated child care facilities are maintained.

- Ensures sanitation standards for licensed and regulated child care facilities are maintained.

The **Section for Long-Term Care Regulation** (SLCR) is responsible for ensuring the safety, health, welfare and rights of persons residing in long-term care facilities. The section:

- Inspects and licenses adult day care centers, adult residential care, assisted living, intermediate care and skilled nursing facilities.

- Investigates complaints of abuse or neglect at long-term care facilities.

- Reviews and approves plans for proposed health care facilities.

- Investigates complaints for any allegation of failure to comply with all rules and regulations.

- Investigates complaints of misuse of resident funds in long-term care facilities.

- Reviews applications for licenses to operate a long-term care facility.

- Inspects and conducts utilization reviews, and determines client eligibility for intermediate care facilities for persons with mental disabilities.

- Implements appropriate rules and regulations in accordance with the Omnibus Nursing Home Act and the U.S. Department of Health and Human Services, and determines compliance with Medicaid/Medicare requirements in intermediate care and skilled nursing facilities.

Division of Senior and Disability Services

The **Division of Senior and Disability Services** serves as the state agency charged with protecting seniors and adults with disabilities from abuse, neglect and financial exploitation. Additionally, the division serves as the State Unit on Aging, carrying out the mandates for the state of Missouri regarding programs and services for seniors and adults with disabilites. The division is responsible for oversight and implementation of programs designed to maximize independence and health/safety for seniors and adults with disabilities who choose to remain independent in the community by administering state and federally funded home and community-based programs.

The **Long-Term Care Ombudsman Program** advocates for the rights of residents in long-term care facilities. An ombudsman is someone who "speaks on behalf of another." Through the work of regional ombudsman coordinators (who are employees or contractors of the Area Agencies on Aging) and many volunteers, residents and their families receive assistance with questions and are empowered to resolve complaints. The program also provides educational forums and information to the public regarding issues dealing with long-term care facilities.

The **Bureau of Central Registry Unit (CRU)/ Adult Abuse and Neglect Hotline and Home and Community Based Services (HCBS) Call Center** maintains the statewide toll-free number (800-392-0210) for reporting alleged abuse, neglect and financial exploitation of persons age 60 and older and adults with disabilities between the ages of 18 and 59. All information obtained during investigations is confidential. The hotline operates from 7 a.m to midnight, seven days a week, 365 days a year. The number to call to make a referral for Medicaid HCBS Services is (866) 835-3505.

Reports of abuse, neglect or exploitation registered at CRU include those of individuals living in a community setting (such as a private residence or apartment), as well as those residing in state-licensed, long-term care facilities (such as a nursing home or residential care facility). The CRU also registers reports from other care settings, such as hospitals, home health agencies, hospice programs, other entities and certain state programs serving eligible adults.

The Missouri Share Care Tax Credit Registry is maintained at the CRU. Shared Care provides a state tax credit to help qualifying familes offset the costs of caring for an elderly person age 60 or older.

The Home and Community Based Services Call Center serves as the statewide, centralized intake point for Medicaid (TXIX) funded in-home services authorized through the Division of Senior Disability Services. Referrals are initially screened at the call center for preliminary eligibility.

The **Bureau of Senior Programs** is responsible for statewide implementation of the federal Older Americans Act. For the act, states must designate planning and service areas to develop and implement programs and services for older persons at the local level. Missouri has ten Area Agencies on Aging (AAAs), each responsible for providing services and overseeing programs within specifically defined geographic boundaries. Within the mandates of the act, priority is given to serving older adults with the greatest social and economic need with a focus on serving low-income and minority seniors. Under the direction of the bureau chief, staff:

- Conducts periodic monitoring reviews of the local programs to verify compliance with state and federal guidelines, and to validate program and service effectiveness, and
- Provides training and technical assistance to AAA staff members and their boards as requested, keeping them apprised of new developments in the field of aging and federal and state policies and procedures.

Each AAA is allowed flexibility in providing the services most needed within its planning and service area. Each AAA:

- Is required to submit an area plan for review and approval in order to receive funding to carry out various provisions of the Older Americans Act at the local level;
- Administers the nutrition program—both congregate and home-delivered meals—and nutrition education activities;
- Provides services to support family caregivers, ombudsman services, information about the prevention of abuse, neglect and exploitation of seniors and issues relating to elder justice; and
- Provides funding for access services, legal services and in-home services. Access services include transportation and Information and Assistance (I&A) and general outreach and advocacy activities. (In-home services include homemaker chore, personal care and respite.)
- AAAs may also provide one or more of the following services: minor home modification, counseling, adult day care, telephone reassurance, friendly visiting, case management and volunteer recruitment.
- **Special Investigations Unit:** investigates cases of elder abuse/neglect and financial exploitation that may result in referrals to local prosecutors for prosecution. The unit provides assistance to the divisions in the department by conducting training on investigation techniques, consulting for ongoing investigations and assisting to carry out the department's mission. The unit also provides educational outreach programs, informational training seminars and other related program activities to senior citizen

CELESTA HARTGRAVES
Director, Division of Senior and
Disability Services

groups, law enforcement agencies, prosecuting attorney personnel and other governmental entities and community groups in an effort to increase awareness of the threat of exploitation and abuse of elderly citizens.

- **Bureau of Systems and Staff Development:** is composed of two units: the Adult Protective Services (APS) Systems and Staff Development Unit, and the Home-and-Community-Based Services (HCBS) Systems and Data Reporting Unit.

The bureau supports the section by gathering and analyzing data elements to ensure accurate, secure and consistent data. The unit is the central point of contact for coordination with internal and external partners regarding computer data systems. The unit also provides education and training for division staff and external partners.

- **Bureau of Program Integrity:** is responsible for the interpretation, development, implementation and maintenance of Missouri home-and-community-based services and case management policies. Policy interpretation and technical assistance is provided to field staff, management, supervisors, aging network partners and other interested individuals. Policies are developed in compliance with the Medicaid and Division of Senior and Disability Services' *Code of State Regulations*, state and federal statutes, guidelines and rules.

- **Bureau of Home and Community Services:** is responsible for services and programs directly administered by the division involving eligible persons 60 years of age or older and adults with disabilities between the ages of 18 and 59. Through a comprehensive investigative or assessment process, the division determines the intervention and/or services necessary to meet the needs of each eligible adult. Under the direction of the home and community services bureau chief, field staff:

- Investigates all reports of senior abuse, neglect and exploitation of non-institutionalized elderly.

- Intervenes on behalf of eligible adults believed to be at risk of injury or harm, including preparing cases for litigation based on investigative findings.

- Informs individuals considering long-term care about options to ensure individuals have the ability to make a decision about care and care settings.

- Authorizes temporary or short-term home and community-based services funded through Social Service Block Grant/general revenue for persons who need them.

- Authorizes in-home provider and/or consumer-directed services in the home or community through state and federal funding, which includes basic and advanced personal care, homemaker, chore, authorized nursing visits, counseling, basic and advanced respite, home-delivered meals and adult day health care.

- Oversees care plans developed in conjunction with seniors and persons with disabilities in their homes who are screened and determined to be medically eligible for nursing facility care and Medicaid-eligible (or potentially Medicaid-eligible).

Department of Higher Education

205 Jefferson St., Jefferson City 65101-2901
Telephone: (573) 751-2361 / FAX: (573) 751-6635
www.dhe.mo.gov
Email: info@dhe.mo.gov

The Coordinating Board for Higher Education (CBHE) was authorized by an amendment to the Missouri Constitution in 1972 and established by statute in the Omnibus State Reorganization Act of 1974. The nine board members are appointed by the governor and confirmed by the Senate. The term of appointment is six years. No more than five of the nine members may be affiliated with the same political party, and all members serve without compensation. The CBHE has statutory responsibilities relating to higher education programs and policies and oversees the activities of the Missouri Department of Higher Education (MDHE), which serves as the administrative arm of the CBHE.

The CBHE appoints the commissioner of higher education to head the MDHE and carry out administrative responsibilities to achieve the CBHE's desired goals for the state system of higher education, which serves more than 450,000 students through 13 public four-year universities, 13 public two-year colleges, one public two-year technical college, 26 independent colleges and universities, 150 proprietary and private career schools and 27 specialized nonprofit colleges.

The MDHE's primary responsibilities include identification of statewide planning for higher education, evaluation of institutional performance, review of institutional missions, development of specialization among institutions, submission of a unified budget request for public higher education to the governor and the General Assembly, establishment of guidelines to promote student transfer among institutions, approval of new degree programs offered by public colleges and universities, administration of the Proprietary School Certification Program and policy setting for and administration of student financial assistance programs.

The MDHE administers the following state student financial assistance programs: Access Missouri Financial Assistance Program; Missouri Higher Education Academic "Bright Flight" Scholarship Program; A+ Scholarship Program;

BETTY SIMS
Chair, Coordinating Board for Higher Education

BRIAN FOGLE
Vice Chair, Coordinating Board for Higher Education

CAROLYN MAHONEY
Member, Coordinating Board for Higher Education

DALTON WRIGHT
Member, Coordinating Board for Higher Education

DOUGLAS KENNEDY
Member, Coordinating Board for Higher Education

DR. DAVID R. RUSSELL
Commissioner, Coordinating Board for Higher Education

Advantage Missouri Program; Marguerite Ross Barnett Memorial Scholarship Program; Vietnam Veteran's Survivor Grant Program; Public Service Officer or Employee's Child Survivor Grant Program; Wartime Veteran's Survivors Grant Program; Minority Teaching Scholarship; and the Minority and Underrepresented Environmental Literacy Program. During the state fiscal year 2014, the MDHE administered approximately $107 million in state-based student financial assistance to more than 70,000 students.

The MDHE also administers the Missouri Student Loan Program, the state-designated guaranty agency for the Federal Family Education Loan Program (FFELP). The Healthcare and Education Affordability Reconciliation Act went into effect July 1, 2010, eliminating FFELP and mandating that new federal student loans would be disbursed through the Federal Direct Loan Program. As a result, the MDHE maintains its existing $2.1 billion loan guarantee portfolio but will not guarantee new loans issued from the federal government.

In addition, the MDHE works to increase awareness among Missourians regarding postsecondary education and student financial assistance opportunities. Through its student loan default prevention initiatives, the MDHE strives to help students avoid loan default and credit card debt.

The MDHE also has administrative responsibility for several grants as well as organizational responsibility for the Missouri State Anatomical Board.

Missouri Coordinating Board for Higher Education

Sims, Betty, (R), chair, St. Louis, June 2016;
Fogle, Brian, (D), vice chair, Springfield, June 2018;
Mahoney, Carolyn, (D), secretary, Jefferson City, June 2018;
Wright, Dalton (R), member, Lebanon, June 2014;
Kennedy, Douglas (D), member, Poplar Bluff, June 2016;
Vacancies (4).

Missouri State Anatomical Board

Department of Pathology and Anatomical Sciences
M263 Medical Sciences Building., University of
Missouri Columbia
Telephone: (573) 882-2288 / FAX: (573) 884-4612

Established in 1887, the Missouri State Anatomical Board functions to receive "unclaimed" human bodies requiring burial at public expense and to distribute them for scientific study to certain qualified schools. The board, which operates under state law (194.120–180, RSMo), was transferred to the Department of Higher Education by the Ominibus State Reorganization Act of 1974.

In 1969, the board was designated a recipient for bodies donated under the Uniform Anatomical Gift Act (194.230, RSMo).

The day-to-day business of the anatomical board is handled through local anatomical boards or secretaries in Columbia, Kansas City, Kirksville and St. Louis. The annual meeting of

the entire board is held in July in Columbia. Officers are elected for two-year terms.

Officers, Missouri State Anatomical Board

Thomas, Dr. Pamela P., president, Department of Anatomy, Kansas City University of Medicine and Biosciences, Kansas City 64106, Telephone: (816) 654-7533, pthomas@kcumb.edu;
Martin, Dr. John, vice-president, Center for Anatomical Sciences and Education, Department of Surgery, St. Louis University School of Medicine, St. Louis 63104, Telephone: (314) 977-8045, martinj2@slu.edu;
Maddux, Dr. Scott, Secretary/Treasurer, Department of Pathology and Anatomical Sciences, University of Missouri School of Medicine, Columbia 65212, Telephone: (573) 884-7303, madduxs@health.missouri.edu.

University of Missouri System

www.umsystem.edu

The University of Missouri has provided teaching, research and service to Missouri since 1839 and added economic development as its fourth mission in 2004. With campuses in Columbia, Kansas City, Rolla and St. Louis, plus a statewide Extension program and a comprehensive health care system, the university serves more than 77,000 students, more than 37,000 employees, and nearly a half million alumni worldwide.

The mission of the University of Missouri, as a land-grant university and Missouri's only public research and doctoral-level institution, is to discover, disseminate, preserve and apply knowledge.

The University of Missouri awards more than 17,000 degrees annually. The university offers doctoral degree programs as well as professional

DONALD L. CUPPS
Chair, University of
Missouri Board of Curators

PAMELA QUIGG HENRICKSON
Vice Chair, University of
Missouri Board of Curators

MAURICE B. GRAHAM
Member, University of
Missouri Board of Curators

JOHN R. PHILLIPS
Member, University of
Missouri Board of Curators

PHILLIP SNOWDEN
Member, University of
Missouri Board of Curators

YVONNE SPARKS
Member, University of
Missouri Board of Curators

DAVID L. STEELMAN
Member, University of
Missouri Board of Curators

DAVID L. STEWARD
Member, University of
Missouri Board of Curators

degrees in law, medicine, optometry, pharmacy, dentistry and veterinary medicine.

The university attracts more than $304 million annually in grants and contracts for research in a wide range of disciplines, including medicine, agriculture, engineering and life sciences. The university's seed funding programs help develop and move university technologies to the marketplace, and its network of research parks and incubators encourage economic growth across the state.

The University of Missouri is governed by a nine-member Board of Curators appointed by the governor and confirmed by the Senate.

The board also has a non-voting position for a student representative.

The university's chief administrative officer is the president. Each campus is directed by a chancellor.

Members, Board of Curators

Cupps, Donald L., (D), chair, Cassville, Jan. 1, 2017;

Henrickson, Pamela Quigg, (R), vice chair, Jefferson City, Jan. 1, 2017;

Graham, Maurice B., (D), Clayton, Jan. 1, 2021;

TRACY MULDERIG
Student Representative
University of Missouri
Board of Curators

MICHAEL MIDDLETON
Interim President
University of Missouri System

Phillips, John R., (D), Kansas City, Jan. 1, 2019;

Snowden, Phillip H., (D), Kansas City, Jan. 1, 2021;

Sparks, Yvonne S., (D), St. Louis, Jan. 1, 2021;

Steelman, David L., (R), Rolla, Jan. 1, 2021;

Steward, David L., (R), St. Louis, Jan. 1, 2017;

Mulderig, Tracy, student representative, non-voting, St. Louis, Jan. 1, 2016.

University of Missouri

Telephone: (573) 882-2121
missouri.edu
Email: mu4u@missouri.edu

The University of Missouri was founded in 1839 in Columbia as the first public university west of the Mississippi River. Today, with a record enrollment of more than 35,000 students, 13,000 full-time employees and 296,000 alumni worldwide, Missouri's flagship university is a $2.1 billion enterprise and an important investment for the state and nation.

Based on quality of teaching, research and scholarship, MU is one of only 34 public U.S. universities to be selected for membership in the prestigious Association of American Universities (AAU).

Missouri's largest and most comprehensive university, MU has more than 300 degree programs through 18 colleges and schools, and is one of only six public institutions nationwide that can claim a medical school, college of veterinary medicine and a law school on the same campus.

Mizzou students earn 27 percent of all bachelor's degrees, 23 percent of master's degrees and 62 percent of doctoral degrees granted by the state's public universities. Roughly one-third of degrees awarded (more than 3,200 annually) are in science, technology, engineering, mathematics or health fields.

MU spends about $240 million a year on scientific research, accounting for 70 percent, on average, of the research dollars flowing to Missouri's public universities. Known for a collaborative, interdisciplinary culture, Mizzou has incomparable expertise and resources on a global scale in four areas: Food for the Future, One Health/One Medicine, Media of the Future and Sustainable Energy.

As a land-grant institution, MU serves and unifies the state via extension programs, a comprehensive health system, two museums and an NCAA Division I athletic program that competes in the Southeastern Conference.

The historic 1,265-acre campus is a botanic garden, offering visitors 42,000 plants and trees in numerous thematic and special collection settings.

College of Agriculture, Food and Natural Resources (CAFNR)

cafnr.missouri.edu

The College of Agriculture, Food and Natural Resources is at the center of ensuring sustainability for future generations by infusing research, collaboration and science-based technology with confidence, creativity, conscience and commitment.

HENRY (Hank) FOLEY
Interim Chancellor
University of Missouri-Columbia

CAFNR, established in 1870 under the Morrill Act, offers bachelor and graduate degrees in agriculture; agribusiness management; agricultural economics; agricultural education; science and agricultural journalism; agricultural systems management; animal sciences; biochemistry; fisheries and wildlife; food science and nutrition; forestry; hospitality management; parks, recreation and tourism; plant science; and soil, environmental and atmospheric sciences.

Research strengths include agricultural policy, biotechnology, plant and animal genomics, animal reproductive biology, nutrition, production and pest management, agroforestry and environmental sciences. Research is conducted in a system of Agricultural Research Centers located throughout the state to address unique regional needs. This is geared to making the most effective use possible of the state's natural resource base, including people resources.

Through extension, CAFNR conducts educational activities through agriculture and natural resources and community development programs in agribusiness management, integrated crop management, livestock production systems, horticulture and forestry, environmental quality, rural policy and community economic and entrepreneurial development.

College of Arts and Science

coas.missouri.edu

Established in 1841, the College of Arts and Science is the oldest and largest division of the university. The college provides its more than 10,000 undergraduate and graduate students with liberal-education programs in fine and performing arts, humanities and social and natural sciences.

The College of Arts and Science offers undergraduate and graduate programs ranging from art to religious studies, biology to political science, geology to theater. Graduates of the college include a Golden Globe Award-winning actor, an Academy Award-winning actor, a former deputy director of the CIA, a physicist/astronaut, Missouri's first poet laureate, a legendary cartoonist and three current United States senators.

The Undergraduate Research Mentorship Program encourages students to collaborate on research with faculty members. Administered by a faculty committee, the program is an opportunity for rising juniors to cooperate actively with faculty mentors, learning firsthand about the natural integration of research and teaching. Other programs include the Summer Repertory Theatre program and a summer field camp in Wyoming for geology students.

The renowned faculty supplement their achievements in the classroom with significant research, scholarly interpretation, writing and creative production. Faculty include three members of the National Academy of Sciences and one member of the Royal Society of Canada; a recipient of the National Medal of Science; internationally recognized mathematicians; top experts in psychology; winners of the American Book Award and the American Academy of Arts and Letters' Academy Award in Literature; a former astronaut; physics researchers working to reduce the nation's dependence on foreign oil; and a finalist for a national teaching prize.

The college boasts two museums: The Museum of Art and Archaeology, which possesses the third-most extensive art collection in Missouri, and the Museum of Anthropology, which is the only one of its kind in the state.

The Brain Imaging Center accommodates researchers from across the campus and is accessible to other academic institutions as well as technological, scientific and pharmaceutical industries that need imaging of the body and brain. The accessibility to the magnetic resonance imaging technology solely for research sets MU apart from other universities that have restricted access to hospital equipment.

Trulaske College of Business

business.missouri.edu

The Trulaske College of Business, founded in 1914, today enrolls more than 5,000 students. The college has four academic units – accountancy, finance, management, and marketing.

The college offers an undergraduate degree in business administration, a full-time MBA and an execMBA for working professionals, a 150-hour program that confers both undergraduate and master's degrees in accountancy, and Ph.D. programs in accountancy and business administration. These programs are nationally ranked and are fully accredited by the Association to Advance Collegiate Schools of Business (AACSB) International.

For more than a century, the Trulaske College of Business has maintained a proud tradition of outstanding instruction, an experiential learning and impactful research. The college houses internationally known scholars in every academic unit. In addition, several faculty members hold editorial positions with academic journals, and others serve as officers in professional associations.

Student development and preparation is at the core of the college's 3D Learning Model. The Professional Development Program prepares students through workshops and a required internship, while Business Career Services provides placement assistance to graduating students. Other hallmark programs such as the Allen Angel Capital Education Program, the Entrepreneurship Alliance and MBA Consulting provide experiential learning opportunities in addition to rigorous coursework.

With approval by the Board of Curators, the University of Missouri's business school was named the Robert J. Trulaske, Sr. College of Business in October 2007. The naming recognizes the business and personal achievements of alumnus Bob Trulaske and the unprecedented support of the college by the late Mr. and Mrs. Trulaske. More than 32,000 alumni of the college are contributing their expertise to the private and public sectors in every state and in a host of foreign countries.

College of Education

education.missouri.edu

In 1868, MU became the first public university in the nation to open a college specifically for the development of teachers. Today, the MU College of Education offers 24 undergraduate program areas and 20 graduate programs serving more than 1,200 undergraduates and 1,500 graduate students each year. The college consistently ranks among the best education colleges in the nation and has more than 40,000 living alumni.

The college offers bachelor's, master's, specialist and doctoral degrees in a wide range of programs. Graduates work in the private and public sectors as teachers, principals, superintendents, school counselors, special educators, researchers, policymakers, library specialists and in many other roles that support the education field.

In addition, the college collaborates with the MU Partnership for Educational Renewal (MPER). MPER is the largest school partnership in the nation and includes 365 designated schools in 22 districts across Missouri.

College of Engineering

engineering.missouri.edu

MU Engineering was the first college of engineering west of the Mississippi River. The college offers Bachelor of Science, Master of Science and doctoral degrees. Its departments and programs include bioengineering, chemical engineering, civil and environmental engineering, computer science, electrical and computer engineering, industrial and manufacturing systems engineering, mechanical and aerospace engineering and nuclear and information technology programs.

Engineering supports its educational programs with extracurricular and research opportunities for undergraduates. The college has approximately 3,220 undergraduates, with an average freshman ACT score of 28.2. There are more than 50 engineering student organizations that encourage the development of leadership, business, collaboration and social skills as well as an undergraduate honors research program. Faculty are entrepreneurial and interdisciplinary.

MU Engineering currently boasts 15 National Science Foundation CAREER Grant recipients among its faculty members. Faculty have established five college centers of expertise and success and seven signature programs.

Research at the centers is focused on technology that will help the elderly manage their health and remain independent; processing images vital to national security; seeking informatics solutions to biological and medical problems; and more. Signature programs include environmental engineering, supply chain management, production and manufacturing energy efficiency and computer security, among others.

Harry S Truman School of Public Affairs

truman.missouri.edu

The mission of the Harry S Truman School of Public Affairs is to advance the knowledge and practice of governance in Missouri, the nation and beyond by informing public policy, educating for ethical leadership in public service and fostering democratic discourse among citizens, policymakers and scholars.

The Truman School grew out of MU's well-regarded Department of Public Administration and builds on its 40-year history of professional education for public service careers.

The school offers Ph.D. and M.P.A. degrees, a joint M.P.A./J.D. with the MU Law School and a joint M.P.A./M.P.H. with MU's Public Health Program. Through affiliated centers and institutes, faculty conduct cutting-edge research, provide consulting services to public and nonprofit organizations, deliver leadership training to public officials and bring academic expertise directly to policymakers.

Policy forums, roundtables with policymakers, lectures by distinguished visiting scholars and research symposia make for an exciting and highly relevant learning environment.

College of Human Environmental Sciences

hes.missouri.edu

The college's mission touches the heart of humanity: to improve the quality of life for individuals and families where they live and work. Beginning with the basics—food, clothing, shelter, finances, family and community—Human Environmental Sciences (HES) concentrates on providing scientific solutions for contemporary challenges in human lives.

Rooted in the university since 1900 and established as a separate division in 1973, the college offers bachelor's and master's degrees in five departments: human development and family science, focusing on child development and education, family studies, child life and human development; textile and apparel management, focusing on apparel marketing and merchandising, international studies, product development and management; personal financial planning, with options in personal financial management services and personal financial planning; architectural studies, including interior design; and nutrition and exercise physiology, with emphases in dietetics, nutrition and fitness and nutritional sciences.

The MU School of Social Work educates leaders who meet challenges facing individuals and society in the areas of military social work, child welfare, community organization, criminal justice, domestic violence, employee assistance, family and children services, gerontology, homeless, hospice, juvenile justice, mental health, physical health, public welfare, schools, substance abuse and victim assistance.

The School of Social Work joined the College of Human Environmental Sciences in 1988. Bachelor of Social Work, Master of Social Work and a Doctorate of Philosophy in social work degrees are offered in the School of Social Work. MU's School of Social Work provides the only doctoral program for social work at a public institution in Missouri.

Through University of Missouri Extension, educational activities are transmitted to citizens of the state. Human Environmental Sciences' programs prepare students for professional positions in business, industry, government, education, human services and research. Accreditation has been earned within specializations.

Recognized as a leading human sciences program in the United States, Human Environmental Sciences is unique among professional peers in its comprehensive use of advisory boards composed of industry experts to provide guidance and support for each department and the School of Social Work.

Missouri School of Journalism
journalism.missouri.edu

The Missouri School of Journalism is committed to improving democracy through the practice of journalism. The first school of its type in the world, the Missouri School of Journalism educates students for careers in journalism, advertising, public relations and related news and strategic communication fields by combining a strong liberal arts education with hands-on, experiential training in professional media.

The school offers the Bachelor of Journalism degree in six areas of emphasis. Advanced graduate studies lead to the Master of Arts degree and the Doctor of Philosophy degree in journalism. The Donald W. Reynolds Journalism Institute (RJI), a 50,000 square-foot facility on historic Francis Quadrangle dedicated in 2008, is committed to developing solutions for 21st-century journalism. RJI engages students, journalists, researchers and other citizens in programs to test new technologies and experiments with new approaches to producing, designing and delivering news, information and advertising.

School of Law
law.missouri.edu

The School of Law, established in 1872, has a collegial environment, reinforced by a small student body and a low faculty-student ratio. The intimacy of this setting, coupled with reasonable cost, consistently high bar passage rates, a network of alumni around the globe and access to top scholars in the legal world, make the School of Law one of the best values in the nation.

Students receive a traditional legal education paired with practical experience in such areas as trial practice and advocacy, negotiation and client interviewing and counseling. The School of Law offers a Juris Doctor degree, as well as a master's degree in dispute resolution, developed in 1999 as the first such program in the nation. In addition, the school offers ten dual degree programs with other departments on the University of Missouri campus in areas such as journalism, business and public affairs. The curriculum pro-

vides a solid foundation for graduates to take the bar examination and practice in any jurisdiction.

Students at the School of Law publish the highly regarded Missouri Law Review, Journal of Dispute Resolution and Journal of Environmental and Sustainability Law; represent the school on regional and national mock trial teams; organize a variety of philanthropic activities in honor of the school's emphasis on service; and hold a wide array of social activities focused on alleviating the stress of law school and enhancing the strong sense of community for which the law school is known.

School of Medicine
medicine.missouri.edu

The origin of medical education at MU can be traced to 1841, when the university affiliated with Kemper College in St. Louis. After offering a two-year preclinical sciences degree for much of the 1900s, the School of Medicine expanded to a comprehensive four-year medical degree program in 1955. Since awarding its first medical degrees more than 165 years ago, the University of Missouri has developed one of the nation's most progressive medical education programs and created a foundation for biomedical research growth. This is in keeping with the MU School of Medicine's tripartite mission of teaching, health and discovery.

MU is the number one provider of physicians for Missouri. Through the medical school's Rural Track Pipeline Program and other initiatives, many MU physician graduates practice in underserved areas throughout the state. The medical school's patient-based learning curriculum offers patient-centered learning in small-group settings and provides a number of opportunities for students to gain practical experience at clinics and hospitals.

MU physicians treat patients from every county in the state. The School of Medicine's more than 650 faculty physicians and scientists educate more than 1,000 medical students, resident physicians, fellows and others seeking advanced degrees. Their research is focused on lifesaving discoveries that address the most prevalent health problems.

Sinclair School of Nursing
nursing.missouri.edu

The MU Sinclair School of Nursing (SSON) offers a full range of programs at the baccalaureate, master's and doctoral levels. The school is nationally accredited by the Commission of Collegiate Nursing Education and approved by the Missouri State Board of Nursing.

The undergraduate program prepares graduates to practice in a variety of health care settings. Undergraduate program options include a four-year Bachelor of Science in Nursing (B.S.N.), a distance mediated R.N. to B.S.N. degree and an accelerated B.S.N. for individuals with a baccalaureate degree in another area.

Students are prepared at the master's level in nursing education and nursing leadership. The Doctor of Nursing Practice (D.N.P.) prepares nurse administrators and advanced practice nurses as adult-gerontology and pediatric clinical nurse specialists as well as family, pediatric and family mental health nurse practitioners. The D.N.P. prepares nurse executives and clinical scholars to perform direct clinical practice, translate, disseminate and integrate evidence-based research into clinical practice and improve quality care and health outcomes.

The Ph.D. program prepares nurse scholars to assume leadership positions in research and educational settings. The Ph.D.-prepared nurse advances the discipline, conducts research and contributes to the development of social and health policy.

MU SSON graduates of the doctoral programs are prepared for a variety of leadership and scientific roles to advance health care and discover new knowledge.

Major categories of research within the school include: aging, living with chronic conditions and promoting healthy behavior/avoiding health risks. The MU SSON is committed to multi-disciplinary and interdisciplinary collaborations as a means of solving some of the most important health care dilemmas.

School of Health Professions

shp.missouri.edu

The School of Health Professions educates highly qualified health care professionals committed to improving society and the health and well-being of individuals and communities through education, service and discovery in health, diagnostic and rehabilitation sciences. The school is credited with establishing the nation's first baccalaureate degree in respiratory therapy and, to the university's knowledge, has the nation's only master's program in diagnostic medical ultrasound. It is the nation's only health professions school to sponsor an adult day health care facility.

The school's six departments and nine accredited academic programs have a distinguished history, producing many well-respected internationally and nationally recognized professionals. Graduates of the departments of clinical and diagnostic sciences, communication science and disorders, health psychology, health science, occupational therapy and physical therapy fill critical health care roles.

The school offers undergraduate degrees in athletic training, communication science and disorders, diagnostic medical ultrasound, health science, medical technology, occupational therapy, nuclear medicine, radiography and respiratory therapy. Graduate degrees are offered in communication science and disorders, diagnostic medical ultrasound, occupational therapy and physical therapy and post-doctoral training in health psychology.

Students gain valuable experience in the school's service and outreach centers, including The Adult Day Connection, MU Speech and Hearing Clinic, Robert G. Combs Language Preschool, neuropsychology clinics, adult and pediatric occupational therapy clinics, PhysZOU pro-bono physical therapy clinic and more than 800 fieldwork sites. At least 60 percent of the school's graduates remain in Missouri to practice, many of them filling critical roles in rural and underserved areas.

College of Veterinary Medicine

cvm.missouri.edu

The MU College of Veterinary Medicine has graduated more than 3,000 doctors of veterinary medicine (D.V.M.) in its history. The College of Veterinary Medicine's mission encompasses teaching, healing discovery and service. It is the only Missouri institution that awards the Doctor of Veterinary Medicine degree, graduating approximately 115 new veterinarians each year. The college also offers post-graduate specialty training to interns, residents and graduate students.

Most graduates enter private clinical practice, but others choose careers in government, industry and academia.

The college's teaching hospital is a state-of-the-art facility with 140,000 square feet of floor space spread over three clinics for companion animals, horses and farm animals. Clinical faculty provide both primary care and various sophisticated diagnostic procedures and treatment options not available in most private practices. Examples include magnetic resonance imaging, PET scans, hip replacement surgery, a treadmill for evaluation of lameness in horses and herd-health consultation for farmers. Each year, the hospital cares for approximately 17,000 hospitalized animals and thousands more on farms.

Through its research mission, the college fulfills a solemn obligation to advance the understanding of diseases affecting animals and people. People and animals share the same environment and are exposed to the same infectious organisms and environmental pollutants. It should come as no surprise, therefore, that animals and their owners develop many of the same diseases. This is the One Health/One Medicine concept. To pursue the causes of these conditions and develop treatments, faculty of the College of Veterinary Medicine collaborate extensively with colleagues in human medicine, agriculture, engineering and other scientific disciplines.

Libraries

The MU Libraries include Ellis Library, the main library, and eight branch libraries: Columbia Missourian newspaper, engineering, geology, health sciences, journalism, mathematics, University Archives and veterinary medical. The MU Libraries have a collection of 3.2 million print volumes, including 49,000 journal titles.

Some library materials are housed in two off-campus storage facilities that contain more than one million volumes from all of the University of Missouri campus libraries. The libraries' website, library.missouri.edu, provides access to online resources, including the MERLIN (MU system) and MOBIUS (statewide) catalogs and over 195 online databases.

The university collections are frequently reinforced by gifts of friends and alumni. Outstanding gifts include an unpublished manuscript of Charlotte Bronte; the library of John G. Neihardt; the library and manuscripts of Mary Lago; the V.T. Hamlin "Alley Oop" collection; and the libraries of the late Dr. Frank Luther Mott (dean and professor of journalism), manuscripts of deputy minority counsel for the Senate Watergate Committee, Don Sanders and Pulitzer Prize winning playwright Lanford Wilson. Two other libraries, the Western Historical Manuscripts Collection and the library of the State Historical Society of Missouri, are open to faculty, students and the public for study and research. Most of the papers in the Western Historical Manuscripts Collection relate to the area of the Missouri River and Great Plains and include interesting correspondence, account books and diaries representing early and recent business, professional, political and social life.

The library of the State Historical Society of Missouri has an extensive collection of Missouriana and the early West and a painting collection including the works of George Caleb Bingham.

University of Missouri Extension

extension.missouri.edu

University of Missouri Extension has its roots in federal acts, including the Morrill Land Grant Act of 1862 and the Smith-Lever Act of 1914, which enabled the university to deliver the practical benefits of education and scientific research to the people to improve their economic prospects and quality of life.

As early as 1911, MU was reaching out to farmers and families and providing distance education courses for teachers across the state. In 1955, state legislation established county extension councils to advise the university on educational programs. Each year, some 2,000 citizens volunteer on these councils to assess local educational needs and to work with extension faculty in delivering and evaluating programs. A partnership of local, state and federal government forms the basis for supporting these efforts.

Today, MU Extension continues to translate university-generated research and knowledge to meet the practical needs of Missourians. Working with faculty on the four UM System campuses and jointly with Lincoln University Cooperative Extension, specialists serve every county and the City of St. Louis. They reach audiences diverse in age, race and income with educational programs, publications, informative websites and one-on-one consultations.

Programs in community development, agriculture and natural resources, 4-H youth development, human environmental sciences, business development and continuing education build the capacity for success in individuals and communities, and create a foundation for locally and regionally based economic development. Every year, more than 1.3 million Missourians participate in MU Extension programs.

MU Research Reactor

murr.missouri.edu

Lifesaving medical treatments are available every day for patients fighting cancer because of the research mission, facilities and capabilities of the University of Missouri Research Reactor Center (MURR®) and its world-class team of scientists, engineers and professionals. MU is the only university to have brought three FDA-approved radiopharmaceuticals to market, from initial research and development to licensing and commercialization, and MURR and its team were central throughout the process. With medical isotope shelf-lives ranging from a few days to a few weeks, a safe and reliable supply is critical for patient health and MURR is the only U.S. supplier for many of these vital active ingredients.

MURR is a unique international resource and the most powerful university research reactor in the world. The reactor provides an invaluable tool for promoting research, education and economic development providing innovative products and

EXECUTIVE DEPARTMENTS — HIGHER EDUCATION

services including cancer drugs and diagnostic agents. The reactor is online 52 weeks per year supplying critical radioisotopes for patients in Missouri and around the world while supporting ongoing educational and research activities at the university.

MURR is a critical hub for multidisciplinary research on the MU campus, integrating the resources of a major teaching hospital, a respected cancer center and a leading college of veterinary medicine, as well as distinguished university programs in the biosciences, chemistry and engineering, into an unparalleled research environment. Research programs at MURR encompass three major areas including biomedical science and nuclear medicine, materials science, and trace element analysis. The biomedical science program focuses on the development of radiopharmaceuticals for cancer research, including both diagnostic and therapeutic applications. The trace element analysis program utilizes neutron activation analysis and other sophisticated analytical techniques to determine the composition of biological, archaeological and geological samples. The materials sciences program focuses on the use of neutron scattering techniques to define and characterize materials at the molecular or atomic level.

Educational opportunities abound at MURR with students arriving from around the globe to take advantage of this unique resource. Students at both graduate and undergraduate levels participate in research projects from diverse disciplines including anthropology, archaeology, chemistry, engineering (chemical, electrical, mechanical and nuclear), geology, materials science, medical, life sciences (including cancer diagnostics, treatment and prevention), nutrition, physics and veterinary medicine. In addition, MURR conducts numerous extracurricular educational programs for high school students, visiting scholars, science teachers, nuclear workers and professionals in the community and around the world.

University of Missouri Health Care

muhealth.org

As part of the state's premier academic medical center, University of Missouri Health Care offers a full spectrum of care, ranging from primary care to highly specialized, multidisciplinary treatment for patients with the most severe illnesses and injuries. Patients from each of Missouri's 114 counties are served by approximately 6,000 physicians, nurses and health care professionals at MU Health Care.

MU's comprehensive health care system began when University Hospital opened in Columbia in 1956. Today, MU Health Care consists of

Ellis Fischel Cancer Center, the Missouri Orthopaedic Institute, the Missouri Psychiatric Center, University Hospital and Women's and Children's Hospital – all based in Columbia. More than 50 MU Health Care clinics in central Missouri receive outpatient visits exceeding 500,000 annually. Affiliated organizations include Capital Region Medical Center in Jefferson City, Fulton Medical Center and Rusk Rehabilitation Center in Columbia.

MU Health Care offers the region's only Level I trauma center, named for pioneering MU trauma surgeon Frank L. Mitchell Jr. M.D. MU Health is a founding member of the Health Network of Missouri, a regional collaborative network to improve access and better coordinate health care for patients, and MPact, a multi-state collaborative.

Clinical specialties include comprehensive care for patients with cancer; cardiovascular, neurological and gastrointestinal diseases; orthopaedic surgery; primary care; behavioral health; trauma and acute-care surgery; women's health; neurosurgery; and pediatric and neonatal intensive care. MU Health Care is a part of University of Missouri Health, which also includes the MU School of Health Professions, the MU School of Medicine, the Sinclair School of Nursing and University Physicians practice plan.

Admissions

The Office of Admissions serves as the initial contact between students and MU. Information is available at *missouri.edu*.

University of Missouri–Kansas City

Telephone: (816) 235-1000
www.umkc.edu
Email: admit@umkc.edu

The history of the University of Missouri–Kansas City (UMKC) has always been tied to that of its namesake city, conceived and executed as the means to meet the city's need for a major university to drive growth, development and progress.

UMKC's roots run back to the 1880s. Three of the professional schools now a part of the university were founded in the 19th century: the School of Dentistry, 1881; the School of Pharmacy, 1895; and the School of Law, 1895. At the same time the Conservatory of Music was founded in 1906, community leaders began discussing the need for a university in Kansas City.

By the 1920s, two groups had plans for such a university. One group proposed Lincoln and Lee University, a Methodist-affiliated school. The other group wanted a private university.

The two groups eventually united and, in 1929, the University of Kansas City was chartered. In 1930, William Volker, Kansas City manufacturer and philanthropist, started the campus with a donation of 40 acres from the William Rockhill Nelson estate.

Despite the ravages of the Great Depression, civic leaders stayed the course, believing that a university was critical to efforts to reverse the economic doldrums. In 1931, Volker donated funds to purchase the Walter S. Dickey mansion and grounds. It was in this remodeled building that the University of Kansas City began its first academic year on Oct. 2, 1933, with 264 students and 17 faculty members. The first commencement at the University of Kansas City was June 9, 1936, with 80 graduates.

In 1963, the University of Kansas City merged with the University of Missouri System, becoming the University of Missouri–Kansas City. In 1963, the enrollment was 4,394; more than 16,000 now study at UMKC.

The campus has been experiencing a major growth spurt in recent years. Two major new buildings opened in 2013: the $32 million, 68,000-square foot Henry W. Bloch Executive Hall for Entrepreneurship and Innovation, and the 1,000-seat Miller Nichols Learning Center classroom building. Projects breaking ground in 2015 include the $14.8 million Robert W. Plaster Free Enterprise Center, a prototyping and product development hub for entrepreneurs, local industry, and high school and college students; a project at 51st and Oak streets that will include a Whole Foods Market, six floors of 170 market rate apartments and a new home for the UMKC Student Health and Counseling Center; and a $21 million state-funded modernization and upgrade project for the university's biology and chemistry laboratories.

College of Arts and Sciences

cas.umkc.edu

The College of Arts and Sciences is the largest academic unit of UMKC. It provides a broad liberal arts education as well as graduate and doctoral preparation, preparing students as specialists in a number of chosen fields.

The major areas of study are architecture, urban planning and design, art and art history, chemistry, communication studies, criminal justice and criminology, economics, English language and literature, foreign languages and literatures, geosciences, history, mathematics and statistics, philosophy, physics and astronomy, political science, psychology, sociology, social work and theatre.

LEO E. MORTON
Chancellor, University of
Missouri–Kansas City

Nearly all of the college's departments offer graduate work at the master's level. Doctoral studies are available in psychology. Some departments also participate in the Interdisciplinary Doctor of Philosophy (Ph.D.) program offered through the School of Graduate Studies.

The college's students and faculty have earned an array of academic recognitions, including multiple Guggenheim Fellowships, Fulbright and DAAD scholarships, NATIONAL Endowment for the Arts and National Endowment for the Humanities Fellowships, the Benjamin A. Gilman International Scholarship and the Association of Writers and Writing Programs award. Two graduates of the college have won the Pulitzer Prize.

The College of Arts and Sciences is the home base of the Honors College, which seeks exceptionally motivated and academically talented undergraduates to study in an environment that encourages excellence. It is designed to enrich the collegiate experience of the most outstanding students. Traditional and non-traditional undergraduates from every school and college at the university are provided with the opportunity to develop their academic and leadership skills within the context of a broad, interdisciplinary education, which will ultimately prepare them for graduate studies and professional careers.

School of Biological Sciences

sbs.umkc.edu

The School of Biological Sciences seeks to provide quality education, to expand knowledge through scientific research and to apply the latest scientific information for the advancement of human welfare. The school plays a key role in Kansas City's emergence as a center for research and development in the life sciences.

Created in 1985, the school serves to advance the missions of the campus and those programs that have a foundation in the life sciences. It is closely tied to and supports academic programs in the schools of dentistry, nursing, pharmacy and the College of Arts and Sciences. It also offers bachelor's, master's and Interdisciplinary Ph.D. degrees.

In 1999, the School of Biological Sciences announced its membership in an exclusive national consortium to conduct research at the prestigious Argonne National Laboratory in Chicago.

Today, the School of Biological Sciences is home to students seeking bachelor's, master's and doctoral degrees in all areas of cellular and molecular biology. Programs at the School of Biological Sciences train students to further their education in health professional programs, graduate and doctoral degree programs or to directly enter the biotechnology workforce of Kansas City and the Midwest region.

Henry W. Bloch School of Management

bloch.umkc.edu

World-class programs at the renowned Henry W. Bloch School of Management provide present and future associates of for-profit, public and nonprofit enterprises the opportunity to gain or enhance their knowledge and skills for effective leadership locally, nationally and globally.

Degree programs include Bachelor of Business Administration and Bachelor of Science in accounting, as well as a menu of graduate and executive graduate programs, including Master of Business Administration, Master of Science in accounting, Master of Science in finance and Master of Entrepreneurial Real Estate. The Bloch School also offers an Interdisciplinary Ph.D. in public administration, a Ph.D. in global entrepreneurship and innovation and non-degree executive education.

The school actively engages in research that applies to the business community, Kansas City's urban core and government agencies.

The Bloch School differentiates itself by integrating business management with public administration, along with a strong emphasis on entrepreneurial and innovative thinking across all disciplines. Bloch programs in executive MBA and nonprofit management have been ranked among the best in the nation.

School of Computing and Engineering

sce.umkc.edu

The mission of the School of Computing and Engineering is to provide competitive educational opportunities and focused research in computing and engineering, which generates the technical workforce and research vital to economic development, particularly in a city that is home to four of the nation's top 50 engineering firms and eight of the top 200. Undergraduate degree offerings include ABET, Inc.-accredited degrees in computer science, information technology, civil engineering, electrical and computer engineering and mechanical engineering. Master of Science degree programs are offered in civil engineering, computer science, electrical engineering and mechanical engineering. Thesis and non-thesis options are available.

The school also participates in UMKC's Interdisciplinary Ph.D. program through four disciplines: computer science, electrical and computer engineering, engineering and telecommunications and computer networking. Computer science and electrical engineering research strengths cover a wide range of specialties, including networking and telecommunications, software engineering and systems, bio-informatics, communications, computer engineering and algorithms.

Civil and mechanical engineering research strengths include transportation, bioengineering, engineering education, materials, structures, refrigeration and river engineering. All programs are designed to prepare graduates for successful careers in computer science and engineering.

School of Dentistry

dentistry.umkc.edu

What began in 1881 as the Kansas City Dental College is today the UMKC School of Dentistry, which annually admits approximately 100 students into its four-year Doctor of Dental Surgery (D.D.S.) degree program, 30 dental graduates into specialty programs and 30 students into dental hygiene. The school serves 15,000 patients of record, providing the students with more than 61,000 patient visits annually, while providing $650,000 in uncompensated care to indigent, underserved Missouri residents. About two-thirds of the state's dentists are graduates of the UMKC School of Dentistry.

The school offers continuing education programs and supports or participates in dozens of outreach programs. Faculty and students provide oral health screenings to disadvantaged children and others in underserved, rural areas of Missouri and abroad.

UMKC was the first U.S. dental school to develop and implement a fully electronic patient record-keeping system with digital radiography, and the Department of Oral and Craniofacial Sciences has been named an area of eminence by the University of Missouri System in recognition of its interdisciplinary research programs in the areas of biomaterials engineering, mineralized tissue biology and translational and clinical research. Private businesses contract with the Clinical Research Center to perform clinical trials and efficacy testing on dental products and procedures; research funding averages over $5 million annually.

Philanthropic support from the school's 7,500 living alumni has endowed more than 60 scholarships, providing assistance to a significant number of the school's 500 dental, dental hygiene and graduate students.

School of Education

education.umkc.edu

The overall goal of the School of Education is the development of broadly educated, competent practitioners who are able to engage in critical and cooperative inquiry in order to provide for an increasing diversity of educational specialists who are grounded in both theory and practice and can deal effectively with the problems and needs of a culturally, socially and politically diverse society. A national leader in culturally responsive teaching and urban education, the school prepares teachers, counselors and administrators to work with today's diverse youth.

The School of Education is fully accredited, offering degrees through a diverse array of undergraduate, graduate and continuing education classes. For practicing teachers, course offerings include stand-alone programs and courses delivered in conjunction with partner school districts.

Doctoral degrees are available in counseling psychology from the Division of Counseling and Educational Psychology and PK–12 administration from the Division of Educational Leadership, Policy and Foundations. The School of Education also participates in the Interdisciplinary Ph.D. program, offering a combined degree with many other discipline areas.

The School of Education offers undergraduate programs that lead to the Bachelor of Arts degrees in early childhood, elementary, middle school and secondary education. The school recommends students for certification in a variety of content areas. School of Education faculty work closely with local school districts to give future teachers not only a foundation in theory, but also classroom practice through field work, practica and internships.

School of Graduate Studies

sgs.umkc.edu

Programs for advanced degrees in the liberal arts were introduced by the University of Kansas City in 1939. Graduate degree programs are of-fered in a variety of fields in the humanities, social sciences and natural sciences. Several are of special interest to students preparing for careers in the health sciences, performing arts and urban affairs.

Master's degree programs are offered in accounting, anesthesia, art history, bioinformatics, biology, business administration, cellular and molecular biology, chemistry, civil engineering, computer science, counseling and guidance, criminal justice and criminology, dental hygiene, economics, education, English, engineering, history, law, mathematics, music, oral biology, nursing, pharmaceutical sciences, physics, political science, psychology, public administration, romance languages, psychology, social work, sociology, studio art, theater and urban environmental geology. The education specialist degrees, Master of Fine Arts, Master of Laws and Doctor of Musical Arts, are also available.

The Interdisciplinary Ph.D. program offers students a range of doctoral options. Support is available to qualified graduate students through scholarships, assistantships and fellowships.

Honors College

The Honors College, UMKC's newest academic unit, seeks exceptionally motivated and academically talented undergraduates to study in an environment that encourages excellence. It is designed to enrich the collegiate experience of the most outstanding students. Traditional and non-traditional undergraduates from every school and college at the university are provided with the opportunity to develop their academic and leadership skills within the context of a broad, interdisciplinary education, which will ultimately prepare them for graduate studies and professional careers.

School of Law

law.umkc.edu

The Kansas City School of Law, founded in 1895, merged with the University of Kansas City (UKC) in 1938. When UKC joined the UM system in 1963, the school became known as the UMKC School of Law. The school is one of only six in the nation to have educated both a U.S. President and a Supreme Court Justice.

The law school is housed in a modern facility, which includes courtrooms with up-to-date technology that allow actual court proceedings to be held at the school and observed by students and faculty from a sound-proof viewing theater. The building houses the Leon E. Bloch Law Library, which provides both books and online materials and contains an innovative, collaborative teaching classroom for research and writing instruction. A unique feature of the building is the placement of student offices and study carrels in suites shared by faculty.

The law school focuses on the integration of high-level theory with practical skills to educate lawyers with strong problem-solving ability and the foundation for sound judgment. The school is recognized for its strengths in advocacy, family law and entrepreneurship, as well as for its innovative solo and small firm practice program. Students have opportunities for writing and scholarly activity through the three journals edited at the school.

The location of the School of Law on an urban university campus provides abundant opportunities for student participation in externships and clinics that provide excellent skills training while serving community legal needs. It also provides for interdisciplinary collaboration, especially with the Bloch School of Management and the Institute for Entrepreneurship and Innovation.

School of Medicine

med.umkc.edu

In 1971, the UMKC School of Medicine accepted its first class in the six-year medical program. The year-round program, involving 48 weeks of study each year, offers students the opportunity to earn both their Doctor of Medicine (M.D.) degree and a bachelor's degree from either the College of Arts and Sciences or the School of Biological Sciences. It is designed primarily for highly-qualified high school seniors.

The curriculum of the School of Medicine provides early exposure to clinical medicine and basic science education, as well as a liberal arts education that is fully integrated into the six-year program. Admission to this program as a freshman gives the student the opportunity to complete requirements for the Doctor of Medicine degree without a second admission process. A unique feature of the school is the docent system, which assigns a full-time faculty member to 12 students for a four-year period, creating an opportunity for the student to interact with a faculty member who serves as a teacher, role model, counselor and mentor.

Nearby are the medical school's major affiliate hospitals: Truman Medical Center, Children's Mercy Hospital, St. Luke's Hospital, Western Missouri Mental Health Center and the Kansas City Veterans Affairs Medical Center. In addition, the School of Medicine utilizes a number of outstanding private community hospitals in the Kansas City area for education in clinical medicine.

Conservatory of Music and Dance

conservatory.umkc.edu

The Conservatory of Music and Dance has earned national and international recognition through performance, composition, teaching and scholarship. One of the most comprehensive music and dance educational centers in the Midwest since 1906, the conservatory has more than 80 faculty who are highly regarded as scholars, artists, teachers and leaders in their fields.

The conservatory offers the degrees of Bachelor of Music, Bachelor of Arts, Bachelor of Fine Arts, Master of Music Education and Doctor of Musical Arts. It offers the community hundreds of music and dance programs annually by faculty, students and visiting artists, including those in its acclaimed Signature Series. The conservatory also offers students the opportunity to participate in a variety of ensembles that perform throughout the year.

More than 20 ensembles are open by audition to all UMKC students who qualify. Ensembles include the Conservatory Orchestra, Chamber Orchestra, Percussion Ensemble, Wind Symphony, Wind Ensemble, Musica Nova (a contemporary music ensemble), 11 O'Clock Jazz Band and numerous vocal and jazz groups.

School of Pharmacy

pharmacy.umkc.edu

The origin of pharmacy education in Kansas City began in 1885 and evolved into the "Kansas City College of Pharmacy and Natural Science." This college operated independently until 1943, when it merged with the University of Kansas City. For the last 125 years, the School of Pharmacy has maintained its mission to educate students, health care professionals and scientists; conduct research; and serve the public and the pharmacy profession in order to meet pharmaceutical needs and advance the standard of health care.

The UMKC School of Pharmacy is the only public pharmacy school in Missouri, offering professional, post-graduate and graduate programs in the pharmaceutical sciences, including pharmaceutics, pharmacology, biopharmaceutics, pharmacokinetics and toxicology; pharmacy administration; and pharmacy practice. The primary professional degree offered is the doctor of pharmacy (Pharm.D.).

Pharmacy faculty conduct interdisciplinary research and engage in community service. Students are active in various outreach projects, including community health fairs and education of school children about inappropriate use of medication.

The pharmacy program includes significant patient contact and provides an interprofessional approach to patient care. Experiential components of the curriculum are conducted at several area health facilities throughout Kansas City, Columbia and Springfield, as well as at various pharmacy and health care settings throughout the state in rural and metropolitan areas.

In 2005, the School of Pharmacy expanded the Pharm.D. program to the University of Missouri–Columbia campus using distance education and UMKC pharmacy faculty. This program was created in part to help with the shortage of pharmacists statewide and to meet the need for pharmacists in Missouri's rural communities. A similar program was expanded to the Missouri State University campus in Springfield in 2014.

Libraries

library.umkc.edu

UMKC Libraries are an essential partner in intellectual discovery, knowledge creation and empowerment, while serving as the hub of learning activities for UMKC and its urban neighbors. Located on the Volker Campus, the Miller Nichols Library is the largest of UMKC's libraries and houses the general collection, Music/Media Library, LaBudde Special Collections and Marr Sound Archives. The Dental Library and Health Sciences Library are located on the Health Sciences Campus and serve users in those disciplines.

UMKC Libraries' collections contain more than 2 million books, government publications and audiovisual items, as well as more than 2 million microforms supporting the programs of the university. In addition to the physical collections, the libraries provide online access to over 65,000 journals, 250,000 books and 300 research databases. Partnerships with the UMKC School of Law's Leon E. Bloch Law Library and the privately funded Linda Hall Library of Science, Engineering and Technology further extend UMKC's physical and virtual library resources. Reciprocal borrowing agreements and the Community Information Program share UMKC's library resources globally and provides local users access to materials from libraries and repositories located throughout Missouri and around the world. These arrangements assist students, researchers, businesses and all levels of government agencies.

Many rare and priceless collections are part of UMKC Libraries' Kenneth L. LaBudde Special Collections. These include papers and manuscripts of music composers, sheet music and Americana, and British literature. The Marr Sound Archives hold over 330,000 recordings of music and spoken word, documenting the American experience in sound. The libraries have been the recipient of grants from the Andrew W. Mellon Foundation and the National Endowment for the Humanities to catalog and preserve unique library collections.

Through the libraries' website, Missourians and researchers worldwide can access a variety of material, from online exhibits highlighting the musical heritage of the Kansas City region, to a comprehensive catalog of library holdings at all four campuses to historic digital audio recordings. Visitors to UMKC can observe the recently installed high-density automated storage and retrieval system—dubbed by student vote "RooBot"—and experience the new collaborative study spaces made possible by the new system.

School of Nursing and Health Studies

sonhs.umkc.edu

The UMKC School of Nursing and Health Studies prepares students to excel in the delivery and improvement of health care, now and in the future. Approval for establishment of a School of Nursing was granted by the University of Missouri's Board of Curators in 1979, at which time the Master of Science in Nursing (MSN) program was offered. The school accepted its first class of registered nurse undergraduates (RN-BSN) into its baccalaureate program in fall 1981.

Today, the UMKC School of Nursing and Health Studies offers a full range of education programs including a bachelor's degree in Health Science, a four-year bachelor's degree in nursing (B.S.N.), an R.N.-B.S.N., a Master of Science in Nursing (M.S.N.) degree and a Doctor of Nursing Practice (D.N.P.) degree—all fully accredited by the Commission on Collegiate Nursing Education. Options for MSN study include the nurse educator, neonatal and family psychiatric mental health nurse practitioner programs. Options for the DNP include the adult, family, women and pediatric nurse practitioner programs. The Ph.D. in Nursing is an inter-campus Ph.D., offered in cooperation with the University of Missouri–St. Louis and Columbia campuses. Many of the programs are approved by the Higher Learning Commission for distance education using both online and interactive telecommunication technologies.

The school presents students with excellent learning opportunities, such as clinical experiences in settings that provide care to patient populations of diverse backgrounds and state-of-the-art simulation technology. Students benefit from the school's long-standing community partnerships, a commitment to a diverse student body and specialized recruitment and retention strategies. The School of Nursing's program of research is focused on community-based research for underserved and under-represented populations and provides educational, practice, service and research opportunities in the provision of health care and education in this area, emphasizing urban health care and wellness.

Continuing Education

The university's schools and colleges, with responsibility for their respective continuing education programs, extend the university's educational reach beyond the traditional campus degree programs. Through credit courses, noncredit courses, conferences and institutes, the people of the greater Kansas City community have an opportunity to continue their education in a manner suited to the adult learner.

Noncredit continuing education activities involve an academic department and a group from business, industry, government or the general public. Citizens throughout the state are served through UMKC's relationship with the University Extension. Offerings include liberal arts lectures and seminars; professional, refresher, remedial and post-graduate courses; and problem-oriented educational programs designed for the analysis and study of major social and urban problems.

Formal education also may be continued through credit courses offered off campus or by enrollment in correspondence courses for academic credit. Frequently, public forums concerned with vital issues of the day are offered in order to increase both the number and effectiveness of people who work toward solutions of community problems. While responding to the broad and varied needs of the community and state, the university is at the same time placing increased emphasis on the development of specific program areas identified as important to large professional, economic and other specialized audiences within the community.

Admission

umkc.edu/admissions/

The Office of Admissions serves as the initial contact between the student and UMKC. This office conducts the registration of students in cooperation with the various schools and colleges within UMKC and maintains student academic records.

Missouri University of Science and Technology

Telephone: (573) 341-4111
www.mst.edu
Email: admissions@mst.edu

Missouri University of Science and Technology (Missouri S&T) was founded in 1870 as the

DR. CHERYL B. SCHRADER
Chancellor, Missouri University
of Science and Technology

University of Missouri School of Mines and Metallurgy (MSM). MSM was the first technological institution west of the Mississippi River and one of the first in the nation. The campus was renamed the University of Missouri–Rolla (UMR) in 1964. On Jan. 1, 2008, UMR became Missouri University of Science and Technology, or Missouri S&T, to more accurately reflect the university's mission as one of the nation's leading technological research universities.

A product of the land-grant movement of the late 19th century, the campus was Missouri's response to the acute need for scientific and practical education in the developing nation. Early academic programs focused on the mining and metallurgical industries, but the campus broadened its mission over time as the need for engineering and scientific education grew.

Graduate education and research began to assume a greater emphasis on the campus in the 1950s. In 1964, Missouri S&T became one of the four campuses of the reorganized University of Missouri. Today, as a nationally respected research university, Missouri S&T has evolved and expanded its heritage as a science and technology-focused institution to inspire and prepare students of all majors to solve the world's great challenges.

The change from "school" to "university" in the 1960s involved three major shifts in emphasis:

• expanded curricula designed to encompass the full range of engineering and scientific subjects, including nuclear engineering, biological sciences and computer science;

• new degree programs in the liberal arts, humanities and social sciences, with an appropriate growth in the number and quality of faculty and courses; and

• new graduate programs to strengthen the science and engineering disciplines and solidify the commitment to research in all areas.

These changes better enabled the campus to respond to Missouri's needs. Originally a mining school, Missouri University of Science and Technology has become a research university of national distinction.

Missouri University of Science and Technology offers bachelor of arts and bachelor of science degrees in 30 fields of engineering, science, humanities, business and social sciences. Master of science degrees are offered in 27 disciplines, doctor of philosophy in 20 and doctor of engineering in nine.

Academic Programs
futurestudents.mst.edu/degrees/

College of Arts, Sciences and Business
casb.mst.edu

Missouri S&T's College of Arts, Sciences and Business (CASB) is committed to enriching student development and enhancing Missouri S&T's traditional technological disciplines, as well as developing new programmatic areas within the college. The College of Arts, Sciences and Business also plays a vital role in fulfilling Missouri S&T's mission of integrating education, research and application to create and convey knowledge that serves the state and helps solve the world's great challenges.

In order to fulfill this mission, CASB offers a unique mix of traditional liberal arts and humanities, natural and physical sciences, education, business and military science disciplines. The college includes the departments of applied mathematics; arts, languages and philosophy; biological sciences; business and information technology; chemistry; economics; English and technical communication; history and political science; physics; and psychological science. CASB also includes S&T's Air Force ROTC, Army ROTC and teacher certification programs.

The college offers 13 undergraduate degree programs in applied mathematics, biological sciences, business and management systems, chemistry, economics, English, history, information science and technology, multidisciplinary studies, philosophy, physics, psychology, and technical communication. More than 52 minors are offered, and students may specialize in one of more than 27 emphasis areas within these degree programs. CASB also delivers the majority of academic offerings in the general education curriculum.

CASB offers master's degrees in the departments of biological sciences; business and information technology; chemistry; English and technical communication; mathematics and statistics; physics; and psychological science. Online M.S. degrees are offered in business administration, industrial-organizational psychology, information technology and technical communication. In addition, doctoral degrees are offered in the departments of chemistry, mathematics and statistics, and physics.

CASB's academic departments provide course work for students majoring in those fields (about 20 percent of the student body) as well as the science, mathematics and liberal arts courses to students majoring in engineering and computing.

College of Engineering and Computing
cec.mst.edu

Approximately 80 percent of Missouri S&T's students are enrolled in the College of Engineering and Computing (CEC). The college includes the departments of chemical and biochemical engineering; civil, architectural and environmental engineering; computer science; electrical and computer engineering; engineering management and systems engineering; geosciences and geological and petroleum engineering; materials science and engineering; mechanical and aerospace engineering; and mining and nuclear engineering. More than 6,200 students are enrolled in those nine academic departments. More than 5,200 are undergraduate students and more than 1,000 are graduate students, of which 400-plus are in the Ph.D. program. Nearly 900 students in the college are enrolled as distance learning students.

The CEC offers 18 engineering and computing undergraduate degree programs. Sixteen of these programs are ABET-accredited – more than three times the average of U.S. universities. This is complemented by 19 master's degree and Ph.D. programs in engineering and computing, of which 17 have an online presence. Missouri S&T is home to the one of the oldest computer science programs in the country, the nation's first engineering management program and the nation's only Ph.D. program in explosives engineering. The computer science program also is home to Missouri's only National Center of Academic Excellence in Information Assurance and Cyber Defense Research. Missouri S&T is one of only 56 universities in the nation to hold this accreditation.

Missouri S&T recently was ranked the No. 3 engineering school in the nation by College Factual and USA Today (August 2014) and was ranked 15th in the nation and first in the state of Missouri in terms of engineering bachelor's degrees awarded, according to the American Society for Engineering Education (ASEE, 2014). Missouri S&T's commitment to diversity in engineering and computing is also recognized by ASEE, which ranked Missouri S&T 19th in the nation for the number of bachelor's degrees awarded to African Americans and 26th for the number of bachelor's degrees in engineering awarded to women. The same publication also ranked Missouri S&T 22nd in the nation for number of engineering master's degrees awarded. Missouri S&T's online graduate programs in engineering and computing are ranked among the nation's best, according to U.S. News & World Report (January 2015).

As with all students at Missouri S&T, students in the CEC experience a wealth of out-of-class-room learning opportunities that apply knowledge to real-world problems, such as the Experimental Mine – ranked one of the nation's most "Awesome College Labs" by Popular Science.

Bachelor of science (B.S.), master of science (M.S.) and doctor of philosophy (Ph.D.) programs are offered in computer science and all engineering disciplines. The doctor of engineering (D.E.) is offered in ceramic, chemical, civil, electrical, geological, mechanical, mining, nuclear and petroleum engineering. Online M.S. degrees are offered in aerospace engineering, civil engineering, computer engineering, computer science, electrical engineering, engineering management, environmental engineering, explosives engineering, geotechnics, manufacturing engineering, mechanical engineering, mining engineering and systems engineering. Online Ph.D. and D.E. programs are available for certain disciplines on a case-by-case basis.

Since 2006, Missouri S&T has also offered bachelor of science degrees in civil engineering and electrical engineering through the Missouri S&T-Missouri State University Cooperative Engineering Program. The program is located on the Missouri State University campus in Springfield and is available to students from a 16-county area in southwest Missouri.

Graduate Study

grad.mst.edu

Graduate study has been offered at Missouri S&T since about 1900, when the first master of science degree programs were established. The first doctor of philosophy degree for work done on the Rolla campus was granted in 1926. M.S. and Ph.D. degrees are now granted by all engineering and science departments except biological sciences, which offers an M.S. only. Nine disciplines offer the doctor of engineering (D.E.) degree.

Missouri S&T Engineering Education Center

eec.mst.edu

The Missouri S&T Engineering Education Center, located in St. Louis County, was established in 1964 as part of the continuing education program of the Missouri S&T Extension Division. It offers evening courses leading to master's degrees in aerospace, chemical, civil, electrical, mechanical, metallurgical, environmental and planning engineering; engineering management; engineering mechanics; and computer science.

Courses are taught by Missouri S&T faculty and selected engineers and scientists from industry. More than 2,000 degrees have been granted through the center over its 51-year history.

Missouri S&T Global Learning

global.mst.edu

In response to growing national trends, Missouri S&T's Global Learning has expanded its distance and continuing education course offerings to better meet the needs of many of today's students, as well as professionals who want to continue their education but are not able to attend on-campus classes.

Students enrolled in distance courses at Missouri S&T may attend class online from their office, home or while away on business. Courses are broadcast live on the Internet and archived for students unavailable at the scheduled class time. The distance courses are identical to their on-campus versions. In fact, most classes consist of both on- and off-campus students. Students can also learn through mailed CD-ROMs and DVDs and face-to-face communication.

Missouri S&T's distance education offerings have expanded from a few courses at Fort Leonard Wood and the Engineering Education Center in St. Louis to offering 16 online graduate degree programs. The department offers an online M.B.A. degree as well as M.S. and M.E. degrees in aerospace engineering, civil engineering, computer engineering, computer science, electrical engineering, engineering management, environmental engineering, explosives engineering, geotechnics, information science and technology, manufacturing engineering, mechanical engineering, mining engineering, systems engineering and technical communication. S&T Global Learning also offers more than 50 certificate programs.

In 2001, Missouri S&T partnered with Boeing to offer its employees a degree in systems engineering. The program began with 30 students in its first year and has grown to more than 260 students.

Research

research.mst.edu

As a national research university, Missouri S&T's research enterprise primarily supports education and service in science, technology, engineering and mathematics (STEM) and related disciplines. Research activity at Missouri S&T not only contributes to the further understanding of scientific phenomena in nature and designed environments, but also provides applied knowledge to strengthen the state's economy and meet critical societal needs while furthering the education of faculty and students.

Research projects are conducted in every academic department in nearly every phase of engineering and science and in many areas of business, the liberal arts, social sciences and humanities. Much of it is directly related to the needs of the people and industries of Missouri and to national problems such as energy, mineral resources and the environment.

In 2014, Missouri S&T established four "signature areas" to concentrate key research initiatives in areas of national need. The areas are:

• **Advanced Manufacturing**, where faculty and students conduct research to advance areas such as additive manufacturing; micro- and nano-scale manufacturing; network-centric and cloud manufacturing; advanced materials for manufacturing; and intelligent, sensor-enabled manufacturing.

• **Advanced Materials for Sustainable Infrastructure**, where researchers focus on the rehabilitation of urban mass-transportation centers, including highways, bridges, tunnels, rail, airports and port and water navigation channels, as well as utility infrastructure. Researchers from four S&T research centers and six academic departments are working on projects such as a study of high-performance concrete. They are adding new materials, like old concrete, fly ash, ground-up tires and glass and fibers, to traditional concrete and testing how well the mixtures perform in bridges, airports, rail systems and port and harbor facilities.

• **Enabling Materials for Extreme Environments**, where researchers focus on developing new materials for applications involving extreme temperatures, heat fluxes, neutron radiation levels and other stresses. With expertise in chemistry, materials science and engineering, mechanical engineering, nuclear engineering and physics, researchers in this area are developing the ultra-high-temperature ceramic materials that may one day form the leading and trailing edges of future hypersonic aircraft.

• **Smart Living**, through which researchers from the social sciences and humanities work with engineering and science researchers on issues related to developing a more secure and sustainable society. Smart Living draws on expertise in cyber security, sustainable energy research, big data analytics, architectural design, behavioral and environmental psychology, the history of technology, and transportation and infrastructure. Current projects include an experimental microgrid that joins the houses in Missouri S&T's Solar Village and allows them to manage and store renewable energy.

In addition to these signature area initiatives, Missouri S&T continues to focus research in the areas of cyber security, energy, the environment, manufacturing, materials and infrastructure. Among the notable research occurring at Missouri S&T is a multidisciplinary effort to develop bioactive glasses for bone and tissue repair and regeneration; testing and development of new lightweight composite materials for use in bridges, buildings and other infrastructure; investigations into the effects of aircraft, space shuttle and rocket exhaust on the ozone layer; and the development of more environmentally friendly methods for removing paint from aircraft.

Other projects are as diverse as basic investigations in cloud physics, the study of the gases in meteorites and moon rocks, research on lightweight structural steel and earthquake structures, robotics, flexible manufacturing, smart materials and glass beads used in the treatment of cancer and arthritis.

Missouri S&T's research centers carry out interdisciplinary investigations that involve different fields of engineering and science. Missouri S&T's research centers include the Biochemical Processing Institute, Center for Aerospace Manufacturing Technology, Center for Biomedical Sciences and Engineering, Center for Cold-Formed Steel Structures, Center for Infrastructure Engineering Studies, Cloud and Aerosol Sciences Laboratory, Design Engineering Center, Electronics Materials Processing and Characterization Institute, Energy Research and Development Center, Environmental Research Center for Emerging Contaminants, Experimental Mine, Experimental Combustion Laboratory, High Pressure Waterjet Laboratory, Institute for Applied Mathematics, Institute of Applied Chemistry, Institute for Artificial Intelligence, Institute for Chemical and Extractive Metallurgy, Institute of River Studies, Institute of Thin Film Processing, Intelligent Systems Center, International Institute of River and Lake Systems, Laboratory for Atomic and Molecular Research, Materials Research Center, Missouri Mining and Mineral Resources Research Institute, Missouri Transportation Institute, Electromagnetic Compatibility Laboratory, Applied Microwave Nondestructive Testing Laboratory, Nuclear Reactor and the Rock Mechanics and Explosives Research Center.

Admission

futurestudents.mst.edu

Interested students may obtain information on admission and enrollment upon request, in person, online or by mail, from the Office of Admissions at Missouri S&T. Prospective students and their parents are encouraged to visit the campus or call the toll-free number (800) 522-0938 dedicated to inquiries about admissions, financial aid and enrollment procedures. Students also may contact the admissions office by email at *admissions@mst.edu* or by visiting the Missouri S&T web site *www.mst.edu*.

University of Missouri–St. Louis

Telephone: (314) 516-5000 / FAX: (314) 516-6767
www.umsl.edu

St. Louis is more than a college town. It's an exciting metropolitan region with 2.8 million people, 18 Fortune 1000 companies and some of the largest private firms in the U.S. Among those industry leaders that maintain significant operations in St. Louis are Ameren, Anheuser-Busch InBev, Boeing, BJC Healthcare, Centene, Edward Jones, Emerson, Enterprise, Express Scripts, General Motors, Maritz, MasterCard, Monsanto, Olin, Peabody Energy and Sigma Aldrich.

St. Louis also is home to numerous small and mid-sized companies that find the region's know-your-neighbor Midwest vibe refreshingly supportive – perhaps that's why Popular Mechanics magazine named St. Louis one of the nation's best places to start a business.

With a central location, infrastructure capacity, favorable cost structure and high-quality educational institutions, St. Louis' $137 billion regional economy is broad and growing. It all adds up to a great location to live, learn and work.

No university is a better conduit of that energy than the University of Missouri–St. Louis.

With more than 17,000 students, UMSL is the largest public research university in eastern Missouri. It provides excellent learning experiences and leadership opportunities to a diverse student body whose influence on the region upon graduation is immense.

Founded in 1963, UMSL is spread across 470 acres in suburban St. Louis County. It has a mix of modern and historic academic buildings as well as a variety of student residence halls, condominiums and apartments. It's the perfect setting for students to gain unique insights from outstanding faculty and work experience from internships at companies and organizations found only in this world-class metropolitan region.

UMSL graduates can be found in all 50 states and 63 countries. But, their greatest impact is felt right here in St. Louis. More than 65,000 of UMSL's 91,000 alumni call St. Louis home. They drive the region's economy and contribute mightily to its social wellbeing.

DR. THOMAS F. GEORGE
Chancellor
University of Missouri–St. Louis

College of Arts and Sciences

As the largest of the colleges at UMSL, the College of Arts and Sciences offers a curriculum linking the arts, humanities and sciences with the metropolitan area and serves as the institution's academic core. It is composed of 16 departments and the School of Social Work.

Majors include anthropology, biology, biotechnology, chemistry and biochemistry, criminology and criminal justice, economics, English, foreign languages and cultural studies, history, liberal studies, mathematics and computer science, philosophy, physics and astronomy, political science, psychology, social work and sociology. In addition, several interdisciplinary minors and certificates are offered, such as military and veteran studies, American studies, gender studies, neuroscience, history and philosophy of science and technology and child advocacy studies.

The college offers master's degrees in biology, computer science, creative writing, criminology and criminal justice, chemistry, economics, English, gerontology, history, mathematics, physics, physiological optics, political science, psychology, public policy administration, social work and sociology. It also offers graduate certificates in biotechnology, forensic economics, international studies, museum studies, trauma studies, tropical biology and conservation, women's and gender studies and writing.

Doctoral programs within the College of Arts and Sciences include applied mathematics, biology, chemistry, criminology and criminal justice, physics, political science and psychology. The college is also the home of clinical psychology centers including the Children's Advocacy Center of Greater St. Louis, Community Psychological Service and the Center for Trauma Recovery.

Through academic programs offered on and off campus, the College of Arts and Sciences educates diverse, talented, traditional and nontraditional students who will supply knowledge, skills and intellectual leadership in both the private and public sectors.

College of Business Administration

At the undergraduate level, the College of Business Administration offers the bachelor of science degree in business administration with emphases in finance, international business, logistics and operations management, management and marketing.

Bachelor's degrees in accounting and information systems also are offered to undergraduate students. These programs provide students with a high-quality business education that prepares them to become productive contributors in both private and public-sector organizations.

The college offers three master's degree programs. The master of business administration program is designed to fully prepare students for administrative positions. The master of science in information systems program includes a specialized program in computer-based management information systems. The master of accounting program is intended for students preparing to enter the accounting profession or furthering existing accountant careers.

The college also offers a doctoral degree in logistics and supply chain management. All of the college's programs are accredited by the Association to Advance Collegiate Schools of Business (AACSB), the authorized professional accrediting body in collegiate business education.

The Center for Transportation Studies (CTS), initiated in 2000, has been supported through endowments created by the St. Louis Mercantile Library and the John W. Barriger III Railroad Library. Research opportunities are offered through the center to qualified UMSL graduate students. Through the center and the logistics and supply chain program, students have performed several research and network analyses for companies throughout the United States.

College of Education

The College of Education provides undergraduate, graduate and doctoral degree programs to prepare and sustain educational leaders for a variety of school and non-school settings.

The college is consistently one of the top three institutions in the state in the production of educators. The faculty, including a number of nationally recognized endowed professors, is committed to a continuous exchange between research and practice that improves the learning environment of diverse learners.

Bachelor's degrees are offered in general education, early childhood, counseling, fine arts, music, science, biology, physical education, math, languages and English.

In addition to numerous undergraduate degree programs, the college offers master's degrees in counseling, educational administration, elementary education, secondary education and special education. Within these programs, a number of emphasis areas are available, including community education, elementary and secondary school administration, elementary and secondary reading, general and school counseling and secondary curriculum and instruction. The college also offers both doctor of education and doctor of philosophy in education degree programs.

College of Fine Arts and Communication

Founded in 2001, the College of Fine Arts and Communication includes the departments of art and art history, communication, dance, music, media studies and theater. Undergraduates may pursue degrees in art history, communication, music, studio art and theater and dance. The college offers master's degree programs in communication and music.

The college is distinguished by its collaboration with the community. Four endowed professorships through the Des Lee Vision Collaborative link UMSL to the St. Louis Symphony, Saint Louis Art Museum, Opera Theatre of Saint Louis, Laumeier Sculpture Park and other cultural institutions.

University students and faculty, as well as visiting artists, have access to the Blanche M. Touhill Performing Arts Center. Artwork exhibitions are housed in Gallery 210, Gallery FAB and Gallery Visio.

College of Nursing

The College of Nursing was established as a School of Nursing in 1981 and graduated its first class in May 1983. College status was achieved in 1994. Degrees in nursing studies are offered at the undergraduate and graduate levels.

The pre-licensure bachelor's degree in nursing teaches the material and skills to complete the professional licensure examination required to become a registered nurse. The BSN offers three degree completion routes: traditional full-time, traditional part-time and accelerated.

UMSL's College of Nursing also offers the RN to BSN program for registered nurses who already have their associate degree or diploma in nursing but would like to earn their bachelor's degree. The RN to BSN program can be completed on campus, online or off campus.

The master's degree in nursing at UMSL helps propel nursing careers forward. The program offers two curricula, preparing students as nurse educators and nurse practitioners. MSN graduates go into advanced practice, often as primary care providers. The master's level of study also offers a post-MSN certificate program, which provides preparation for certification in additional advanced practice areas.

For serious students seeking the highest academic preparation in nursing, the college has two doctoral programs: a doctorate of nurse practicing and the doctorate of philosophy in nursing. The DNP program focuses on preparing nurses for either clinical or translational analysis for improved practice outcomes. The Ph.D. in nursing concentrates on original research and developing nursing knowledge.

UMSL's College of Nursing is fully accredited by The North Central Association of Colleges and Schools. The BSN, MSN and DNP programs are accredited by the Commission on Collegiate Nursing Education, and the PNP program is approved by The Pediatric Nursing Certificate Board. The pre-licensure program is fully approved by the Missouri State Board of Nursing.

College of Optometry

After more than 10 years of study and planning, the College of Optometry came into existence on June 1, 1980. The first class of 36 students graduated in May 1984. This college offers the only opportunity to study optometry in Missouri.

Doctors of optometry are primary health-care professionals who examine, diagnose, treat and manage diseases and disorders of the visual system, the eye and associated structures, as well as diagnose related systemic conditions. They prescribe glasses, contact lenses, low vision rehabilitation and medications, as well as perform certain surgical procedures as regulated by state law.

Optometric education is a four-year professional degree program accredited by the Accreditation Council on Optometric Education through the authority granted by the U.S. Department of Education. Upon graduation and following successful completion of the three-part examination given by the National Board of Examiners in Optometry, graduates are eligible for licensure in all 50 states plus the District of Columbia.

Entering students must have completed at least 90 credit hours of undergraduate work, including core courses in the sciences (biology, chemistry and physics), mathematics (including calculus), English and the liberal arts. Applicants also must complete the Optometry Admission Test, which is designed to measure general academic ability and comprehension of scientific information. Ninety-eight percent of those admitted hold a bachelor's degree, most from a scientific discipline.

The curriculum leading to the doctor of optometry degree is a four-year, year-round program. The program prepares graduates to deliver compassionate patient care while instilling a sound background in the biomedical, optical, behavioral and clinical sciences, including an understanding of the health-care delivery system.

Graduate School

The Graduate School, which is responsibile for all graduate degree programs in the various schools and colleges of UMSL, promotes scholarship and creativity through graduate programs that inspire in students a passion for discovery.

In addition to participating in graduate level courses, many graduate students work with faculty mentors on advanced research projects. These graduate research projects address problems of local, regional, national and global significance, and they make a critical contribution to the university's mission as a public metropolitan research university.

Graduate students make up roughly a fifth of the UMSL student body. They pursue advanced degrees and certificates in 30 master's, 12 doctoral and two education specialist programs, as well as a variety of graduate certificate programs.

Pierre Laclede Honors College

The Pierre Laclede Honors College was established in 1989 and has grown to include its own campus, complete with instructional, residential and recreational facilities.

Students may pursue degrees in any undergraduate division of UMSL. In addition, students must undertake a personal writing program and pursue independent study through research, internships, public service projects and guided reading.

The college features a student-faculty ratio of 15:1, a scholar development program, a writing program and 11 honors classes. It offers academic excellence comparable to expensive private colleges, but at public institution rates.

The four-year program has a highly selective student body of about 600. The college's teachers are among the university's leading research and teaching faculty.

UMSL/Washington University Joint Undergraduate Engineering Program

The UMSL/Washington University Joint Undergraduate Engineering Program was established in 1993 and offers bachelor's degrees in civil, mechanical and electrical engineering. All three bachelor's degrees are accredited by the Engineering Accreditation Commission of the Accreditation Board for Engineering and Technology.

The Joint Program is designed for both full- and part-time students. The first half of coursework, common to all three degrees, is completed at UMSL as part of the pre-engineering program. The remaining half of the coursework, consisting of upper-division engineering courses and laboratories, is completed on the campus of Washington University in St. Louis. Upper-division courses are offered in the evenings and on Saturdays to accommodate part-time students, but also to encourage all students to take advantage of the parallel cooperative education program. The co-op program allows upper-division students to work part time during the day at local engineering firms and technology-based businesses with which the Joint Program has established connections.

Students register for all their courses at UMSL, pay UMSL tuition rates with a small surcharge fee and receive their degrees from UMSL and WUSTL. The Joint Program allows Missouri to make the most efficient use of public funds while meeting the needs of both traditional and non-traditional students.

School of Public Policy and Administration

The School of Public Policy and Administration provides graduate education, professional development and applied research. The master's degree in public policy administration is accredited by the Network of Schools of Public Policy, Affairs and Administration. The program offers four emphasis areas in which students may concentrate their advanced studies: managing human resources and organizations, policy research and analysis, local government management and nonprofit organization management and leadership.

In addition, the School of Public Policy and Administration offers graduate certificates in nonprofit management and leadership, in local government management and in policy and program evaluation. Credit and noncredit courses and training offered by the Nonprofit Management & Leadership Program and Local Government Partnership provide professional development opportunities to enhance the skills of elected and appointed officials and public administrators in the civic, government and nonprofit sectors.

UMSL's long-standing commitment to applied policy research, community engagement and training programs is enhanced by coordinating the school's Center for Ethics in Public Life, Center for Excellence in Financial Counseling, Public Policy Research Center and Sue Shear Institute for Women in Public Life.

The school's Des Lee Endowed Professor of Community Collaboration and Public Policy Administration serves to integrate public policy research, disseminate research findings, and develop applications and implement plans with community partners in metropolitan St. Louis.

School of Social Work

The School of Social Work offers a bachelor's degree in social work and a master's degree in three general areas: family practice, social work leadership and management and gerontology. The school works with various organizations and agencies throughout the region to provide students with hands-on, real-world experience.

Libraries

UMSL Libraries support the educational objectives of the university, meet the informational needs of the campus community and provide users near and far with broad access to research collections. The UMSL library system includes the Thomas Jefferson Library and the St. Louis Mercantile Library.

The latter is housed on the first two floors of the Thomas Jefferson Library building, a busy campus hub, beneath its signature glass pyramid. Founded in 1846, the Mercantile is the oldest cultural institution west of the Mississippi River. The library moved to the UMSL campus in 1998 with collections that concentrate on Western Expansion and the history and growth of the St. Louis region as well as the development of rail and river transportation in the United States.

Together, the two UMSL libraries house more than one million volumes, 300,000 photographs, one million government documents and one million microforms. They provide access to more than 50,000 full-text online periodicals. The libraries are open more than 80 hours per week during regular academic sessions, and students, faculty and other users make use of library resources 24 hours a day online.

Admissions

Information on admission and enrollment is available in person, by mail or online (umsl.edu). Prospective students and their parents are encouraged to visit the UMSL campus (1 University Blvd. St. Louis, MO 63121-4400).

State Historical Society of Missouri

1020 Lowry St., Columbia 65201-7298
Telephone: (573) 882-7083 / FAX: (573) 884-4950
http://shs.umsystem.edu
Email: shsofmo@umsystem.edu

Organized in 1898 by the Missouri Press Association and a trustee of the state since 1899, the State Historical Society collects, preserves, makes available and publishes materials that enhance research and support learning opportunities in Missouri studies and the history of the Midwest. For more than 100 years, the State Historical Society has been the center for research into every aspect of the society and government of Missouri and the lives of its residents.

DR. GARY R. KREMER
Executive Director
State Historical Society
of Missouri

JUDGE STEPHEN N. LIMBAUGH JR.
President
State Historical Society
of Missouri

Society Research Centers

The society comprises six research centers. The administrative offices, art galleries and one center are located on the ground floor of the University of Missouri–Columbia Ellis Library. The other research centers are located in Pacific Hall, Southeast Missouri State University; Newcomb Hall, University of Missouri–Kansas City; Curtis Laws Wilson Library, Missouri University of Science and Technology; Thomas Jefferson Library, University of Missouri–St. Louis; and Duane G. Meyer Library, Missouri State University.

Research Collections

Researchers, officials, scholars and students interested in Missouri history, biography and genealogy find in the society's research centers unsurpassed collections of books and pamphlets, official state records, newspapers, maps, photographs and manuscripts. Over the years, the society has acquired a number of rare or specialized book collections that have given it added recognition as a research center. These collections include the Mahan Memorial Mark Twain Collection, the Eugene Field Collection, the J. Christian Bay Collection of Middle Western Americana, the Francis A. Sampson Collection and the Paul D. Higday Civil War Collection.

The society's Missouri newspaper collection, which includes more than 3,500 titles and extends from 1808 to the present, is one of the largest state newspaper collections in the nation. Two hundred seventy current newspapers from every Missouri county arrive weekly and are microfilmed to ensure their preservation. The lives of famous and typical Missourians and the history of Missouri communities and local, state and national events can be traced and documented in the collection.

The map collection consists of more than 4,000 rare and old maps of the state as well as modern ones. In addition, the collection contains county atlases, gazetteers, statistical maps, official topographical maps and early state guidebooks. For genealogical research, the society's microfilm file of United States census reports is one of the largest in the Midwest. A pictorial collection contains more than six million photographs and images of individuals and subjects dating from the 19th century to the present. Views of buildings, cityscapes and rural areas throughout the state are also found in the collection.

The society's manuscript collection contains letters, diaries, journals, business and organizational records, oral histories, architectural drawings and official state papers. Research materials of this type furnish most of the intimate day-to-day accounts of Missouri history and lend vitality to historical writing.

Art Collection

The society's collection of Missouri regional and westward expansion art records celebrates Missouri's heritage through works by past and contemporary artists. The art collection includes masterworks by George Caleb Bingham and Thomas Hart Benton as well as paintings, drawings and prints by other Missouri and Missouri-related artists. An extensive editorial cartoon collection is national in scope. Exhibitions in the art galleries showcase the society's diverse holdings.

Missouri History Online

The society's website reflects a commitment to making research sources and the history of Missouri and its residents widely available to learners of all ages. More than one million pages of newspapers are accessible online through the Missouri Digital Newspaper Project. The Historic Missourians pages feature more than 100 biographies and images of men and women who are well-known for their contributions in such fields as literature, politics, sports, education and journalism. Other resources on the website include photographs, Civil War documents, editorial cartoons and artworks, as well as the Missouri Historical Review, catalogs and finding aids to society collections and other materials.

Publications

The *Missouri Historical Review* has served as the cornerstone of the society's publication program since 1906. A benefit of membership, the journal features scholarly articles on diverse topics in Missouri history, book reviews and notes. In addition to the journal, the society has published more than 50 volumes of edited documents, narrative and pictorial history, catalogs, directories and indexes. *Missouri Times*, a quarterly newsletter, informs members about society activities.

Public Programming

To bring the state's history to its residents, the society sponsors educational outreach programs, including genealogy workshops, tours for elementary and secondary school students and adults and presentations on Missouri history and art.

The society sponsors National History Day in Missouri, the statewide component of National History Day, a competition for students in grades 6 through 12. More than 2,500 students participate annually in regional contests held throughout the state.

Additionally, "Show Me Missouri: Conversations about Missouri's Past, Present and Future" is a speakers' bureau program jointly organized and managed by the Missouri Humanities Council and the society.

Officers of the Society

Officers of the State Historical Society, 2013–2016: **Stephen N. Limbaugh Jr.**, Cape Girardeau, president; **Virginia J. Laas**, Joplin, first vice president; **Bob Priddy**, Jefferson City, second vice president; **Roy Blunt**, Springfield, third vice president; **Brent Schondelmeyer**, Independence, fourth vice president; **Henry J. Waters III**, Columbia, fifth vice president; **Albert M. Price**, Columbia, sixth vice president; **Edward W. Scavone**, Columbia, treasurer; **Gary R. Kremer**, Jefferson City, executive director, secretary and librarian.

Trustees of the Society

Permanent trustees, former presidents of the society, are: **Bruce H. Beckett,** Columbia; **H. Riley Bock**, New Madrid; **Lawrence O. Christensen**, Rolla; **Doug Crews**, Columbia; **Richard Franklin**, Independence; **Robert C. Smith**, Columbia.

Trustees elected for three-year terms: **Rodney Boyd**, St. Louis; **David R. Bradley**, St. Joseph; **Robert M. Clayton III**, Hannibal; **James Leon Combs**, Bradleyville; **Bryan Cook**, Clayton; **Don Downing**, St. Louis; **George W. Draper III**, St. Louis; **Steve Ehlmann**, St. Charles; **Michael R. Gibbons**, Kirkwood; **Edward C. Matthews III**, Sikeston; **Kenneth B. McClain**, Independence; **Larry L. McMullen**, Shawnee Mission, Kan.; **Robert J. Mueller**, Ste. Genevieve; **James R. Reinhard**, Hannibal; **Mary R. Russell**, Jefferson City; **William W. Sellers**, Lexington; **Beatrice B. Smith**, Columbia; **Jeffrey E. Smith**, Columbia; **Brian K. Snyder**, Independence; and **Blanche M. Touhill**, St. Louis.

In addition to the elected trustees and officers of the society, the governor, secretary of state, state treasurer, president of the University of Missouri and chancellor of the University of Missouri–Columbia serve as ex *officio* members of the board of trustees.

Executive committee (composed of the president, the treasurer and eight members of the board of trustees): **Stephen N. Limbaugh Jr.**, Cape Girardeau; **H. Riley Bock**, New Madrid; **Robert M. Clayton III**, Hannibal; **Doug Crews**, Columbia; **Steve Ehlmann**, St. Charles; **Virginia J. Laas**, Joplin; **Robert J. Mueller**, Ste. Genevieve; **Bob Priddy**, Jefferson City; **Edward W. Scavone**, Columbia; and **Brent Schondelmeyer**, Independence.

Lincoln University

Jefferson City 65101
Telephone: (573) 681-5000
www.lincolnu.edu
Email: enroll@lincolnu.edu

Lincoln Institute was founded in 1866 by the enlisted men of the 62nd and 65th U.S. Colored Infantry Regiments. The men, who learned to read and write on the battlefields of the Civil War in Texas, dreamed of a school to educate African Americans in their home state of Missouri. In 1890, Lincoln Institute became a land-grant institution. The school was renamed Lincoln University in 1921. In the fall of 1954, Lincoln University expanded its historical mission to serve a broader population from varied social, economic, educational and cultural backgrounds. Today, Lincoln University is a public, comprehensive institution that provides excellent educational opportunities including theoretical and applied learning experiences to a diverse population within a nurturing, student-centered environment.

In 2016, Lincoln University will celebrate 150 years of providing a quality education to those

DON W. COOK SR.
President, Board of Curators
Lincoln University

DANA T. CUTLER
Vice President, Board of
Curators, Lincoln University

GREG S. GAFFKE
Secretary, Board of
Curators, Lincoln University

WINSTON J. RUTLEDGE
Treasurer, Board of Curators
Lincoln University

HERBERT E. HARDWICK
Member, Board of
Curators, Lincoln University

FRANK J. LOGAN
Member, Board of Curators
Lincoln University

MARVIN O. TEER
Member, Board of
Curators, Lincoln University

DR. KEVIN D. ROME
President
Lincoln University

who seek it. The majority of the university's more than 3,000 students are residents of Missouri or one of nine nearby states. The international student population comes from 35 countries.

Lincoln University offers six undergraduate degrees in more than 50 programs of study. Lincoln University also offers non-credit and continuing education courses for those seeking professional or personal development.

The main Lincoln University campus is composed of nearly 158 acres, centrally located in Jefferson City. In addition, the university properties include two agricultural research facilities and extension offices in St. Louis, Kansas City and southeast Missouri. In addition, a satellite nursing program is housed at Fort Leonard Wood.

Members, Board of Curators

Cook, Don W., (D), president, St. Louis, Jan. 1, 2018;

Cutler, Dana T., (R), vice president, Kansas City, Jan. 1, 2012;

Gaffke, Greg S., (D), secretary, Jefferson City, Jan. 1, 2014;

Rutledge, Winston J., (I), treasurer, Jefferson City, Jan. 1, 2016;

Hardwick, Herbert E., (D), member, Kansas City, Jan. 1, 2016;

Logan, Frank J., (D), member, St. Louis, Jan. 1, 2017;

Teer, Marvin O., (D), member, St. Louis, Jan. 1, 2012.

Harris-Stowe State University

St. Louis 63103
Telephone: (314) 340-3366 / FAX: (314) 340-3322
www.hssu.edu
Email: admissions@hssu.edu

Harris-Stowe State University, (HSSU) traces its origin back to 1857 when its first predecessor institution was founded by the St. Louis Board of Education as a normal school for the preparation of white elementary school teachers. It thus became the first public teacher education institution west of the Mississippi River and the 12th such institution in the United States. Its second predecessor institution, Stowe Teachers College, was also a normal school founded by the same public schools in 1890 to prepare African-American el-

RONALD A. NORWOOD
Chair, Harris-Stowe State
University

CHRISTINE A. CHADWICK
Member, Harris-Stowe State
University

VANESSA F. COOKSEY
Member, Harris-Stowe State
University

REGINALD D. DICKSON
Member, Harris-Stowe State
University

ementary school teachers. Both normal schools later became four-year teachers colleges—Harris Teachers College and Stowe Teachers College. The former was named after William Torrey Harris, U.S. Commissioner of Education and former Superintendent of the St. Louis Public Schools. The latter was named after Harriet Beecher Stowe, the famed slavery abolitionist and author of *Uncle Tom's Cabin*. These two colleges merged in 1954, forming Harris-Teachers College and in 1977 became Harris-Stowe College. In 1979, the college became a Missouri public college, with the name Harris-Stowe State College. The university designation and current name occurred in 2005.

In 2014, Harris-Stowe ranked No. 1 in the state of Missouri and No. 47 in the nation in granting degrees in mathematics and statistics to African-Americans according to Missouri Department of Higher Education and *Diverse: Issues In Higher Education*, a newsmagazine that has ranked institutions conferring the most degrees to minority students for the past 30 years. In 2015, the governor signed a law broadening degree-granting authority to Harris-Stowe, which allows the university to offer graduate programs and achieve parity with Missouri's other 12 state universities. Harris-Stowe offers the most affordable bachelor's degree in the state of Missouri.

Over the past decade, Harris-Stowe has greatly expanded its degree programs and offers on-campus housing. Currently, the university offers 31 majors, minors and certificate programs in education, business and arts & sciences – including two fully online degree programs in criminal justice and healthcare management.

Members, Board of Regents

Norwood, Ronald A. , chairman;
Chadwick, Christine A., member;
Cooksey, Vanessa F., member;
Dickson, Reginald D., member;
Hollingsworth, Debra A., member.

DEBRA HOLLINGSWORTH
Member, Harris-Stowe State
University

DWAUN WARMACK
President, Harris-Stowe State
University

State Technical College of Missouri

One Technology Dr., Linn, MO 65051
Telephone: (573) 897-5000 / FAX: (573) 897-4656
www.statetechmo.edu
Email: admissions@statetechmo.edu

State Technical College of Missouri (STC), founded in 1961, is Missouri's only two-year public technical college with a statewide mission. Originating as Linn Technical Junior College, the college became a part of the public higher education system in Missouri in 1996 as a result of legislation by the 88th General Assembly.

The original educational institution was established with funding from the National Defense Education Act as a public postsecondary residential technical institution. The philosophy of the original institution was "to provide two-year vocational/technical programs to all students who wish to prepare themselves for employment."

The college has a longstanding reputation for producing graduates with the valued technical and interpersonal skills needed for career advancement. With a state mandate and college mission to "prepare students for profitable em-

JOHN A. KLEBBA
President, Sttate
Technical College of Missouri
Board of Regents

J. SCOTT CHRISTIANSON
Vice President, State
Technical College of Missouri
Board of Regents

BRUCE DARROUGH
Member, State Technical
College of Missouri Board of
Regents

ERICK V. KERN
Member, State Technical
College of Missouri Board of
Regents

ployment and a life of learning," the college has been responsive to workplace needs.

State Technical College of Missouri offers more than 35 technical programs at the Associate of Applied Science degree and certificate levels. In addition, customized and contract training is offered to Missouri businesses and industry. In each program, the curriculum includes an integration of theory with hands-on application and experience. Such integration ensures the development of functional troubleshooting skills with traditional and innovative techniques, approaches and equipment. Also emphasized are teamwork, interpersonal skills and work ethic. The general education core contributes to the high level of critical thinking, problem-solving and communication abilities of graduates. As part of their education, many students gain on-the-job experience through internships and clinicals.

State Technical College of Missouri monitors the economic, industrial and technological needs of the state as new programs are proposed for development. In response to industry demand over the last decade, State Technical College of Missouri has started or modified over 19 degree and certificate programs. Programs recently developed include: Welding Technology; High Performance and Electric/Hybrid Vehicle options in Automotive Technology; three new health occupations programs - Dental Assisting Technology, Medical Radiologic Technology, and Practical Nursing Technology; and expansion of the Physical Therapist Assistant program through the Missouri Health Professions Consortium, which includes five Missouri community colleges and the School of Health Professions in the University of Missouri Health System.

The faculty has a combination of higher education credentials and industry experience in their professional areas of expertise. In addition, they are continually updating their skills through industry training and workshops.

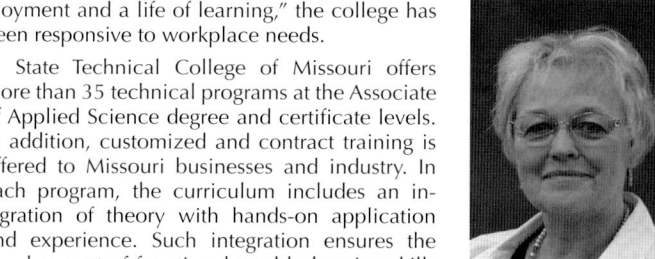

TONI R. SCHWARTZ
Member, State Technical
College of Missouri Board of
Regents

DR. DONALD CLAYCOMB
President
State Technical College of
Missouri

In keeping with preparing students for profitable employment, students are evaluated through a one-of-a-kind system that provides potential employers with a student's track record of success in academic achievement, job readiness work ethic and attendance (AJA@™STC).

State Technical College of Missouri is accredited by The Higher Learning Commission (HLC); for more information contact the HLC at hlccommision.org or (800) 621-7440. Seventeen programs are accredited by the Association of Technology, Management and Applied Engineering (ATMAE). In addition, 16 other program-level professional accreditations and certifications have been obtained by programs at the college. Many instructors hold individual certifications related to their respective teaching fields.

The main campus is located along Highway 50 on 360 acres one mile east of Linn and includes a public airport. The Physical Therapist Assistant program is offered from locations in Jefferson City, Trenton and Poplar Bluff. The Nuclear Technology program is offered in Mexico at the Advanced Technology Center, a cooperative higher education technology center. The Dental Assisting Technology, Medical Radiologic Technology and Practical Nursing Technology programs are located in Jefferson City at Nichols Career Center. The Automation and Robotics - Advanced Manufacturing Technician program is offered in Saint Charles at the Lewis and Clark Career Center.

Members, Board of Regents

Klebba, John A., (R), president, Linn, Dec. 29, 2007;
Christianson, J. Scott, (D), vice president, Columbia, Dec. 29, 2015;
Collom, Mark J., (D), Saint Peters, Dec. 29, 2009;
Darrough, Bruce, (D), Florissant, Dec. 29, 2013;
Kern, Erick V., (R), Chesterfield, Dec. 29, 2011;
Schwartz, Toni R., (R), Jonesburg, Dec. 29, 2013.

Truman State University

100 E. Normal, Kirksville 63501
Telephone: (660) 785-4016
www.truman.edu

Truman State University, founded in 1867, is a vibrant community of teacher and student scholars with the distinction of being Missouri's only statewide public liberal arts and sciences university and the only public university in the state with highly selective admission standards as defined by the Coordinating Board for Higher Education (CBHE). Truman is a residential university focused on providing its 6,200 students with broad liberal arts experiences and depth of study in 48 undergraduate majors and eight graduate programs.

For 18 consecutive years, U.S. News and World Report has recognized Truman as the No. 1 public university in the Midwest Regional Category. They also gave Truman a No. 1 ranking for its "Strong Commitment to Teaching." Other accolades include Washington Monthly, which listed Truman as the No. 2 master's university nationwide in its "2014 College Rankings." Truman was the only Missouri school ranked in the entire Top 100 Master's Universities list. Truman was ranked as the No. 1 value in the nation among public colleges and universities in the May/June 2015 issue of Consumers Digest while Kiplinger's Personal Finance February 2015 magazine ranked Truman as No. 19 on their list of the 100 Best Public College Values in the nation. Both magazines feature schools that combine outstanding academics with affordable costs.

Truman has a long history of being recognized nationally by higher education experts for its assessment program and its commitment to providing a high-quality, liberal arts and sciences education at an affordable price. Truman's program of assessment allows the university to measure the re-

sults of the teaching-learning process and to gather critical information on student growth and development to ensure that graduates are prepared for future success. Truman's curriculum provides each student with a foundation of knowledge appropriate to a traditional liberal arts and sciences education. It also requires specialization in a major, providing each student with in-depth knowledge and mastery of a discipline. This exemplary undergraduate education provides graduates with the knowledge and skills necessary to be successful upon graduation. Truman has the highest public college graduation rate in Missouri as calculated by the CBHE. More than 50 percent of Truman's graduates enter graduate and professional schools within six months of their graduation, while the remainder directly enter the workforce or engage in full-time service, such as the Peace Corps.

Truman's students are among the brightest and the best in their high school graduating classes. Eighty-three percent of Truman's 2014 entering freshman class scored 24 or higher on the ACT examination, with 29 percent scoring above the 95th percentile. In addition, 80 percent ranked in the top quarter of their high school graduating class and more than 98 percent of the class demonstrated leadership through high school and community activities.

Truman emphasizes high-quality teaching as its top priority. Truman students' benefit from a low student-to-faculty ratio, which allows for greater student-teacher interaction and a more personalized educational experience. Truman strongly supports undergraduate research with approximately 1,100 students annually doing structured research with faculty both in and outside the classroom. The Higher Learning Commission of the North Central Association of Colleges and Schools has accredited Truman since 1914. Truman is also accredited by AACSB International–The Association to Advance Collegiate Schools of Business, American Chemical Society, American Speech-Language-Hearing Association, Commission on Accreditation of Athletic Training, National Association of Schools of Music, National Council for Accreditation of Teacher Education, Commission on Collegiate Nursing Education and the Missouri Department of Elementary and Secondary Education.

Truman also has one of the top National Collegiate Athletic Association (NCAA) Division II athletic programs in the country. Truman has produced the highest number of academic All-Americans in Division II athletics in the history of the program. Truman fields 20 intercollegiate sports, which is the largest number in the state. Truman is a member of the Great Lakes Valley Conference. Information on all of Truman's intercollegiate athletics programs may be found online at *www.trumanbulldogs.com.*

JAMES J. O'DONNELL
Chair
Truman Board of Curators

SARAH BURKEMPER
Vice Chair
Truman Board of Curators

MICHAEL J. LaBETH
Secretary
Truman Board of Curators

CHERYL J. COZETTE
Member
Truman Board of Curators

KAREN S. HABER
Member
Truman Board of Curators

SUSAN PLASSMEYER
Member
Truman Board of Curators

MATTHEW W. POTTER
Member
Truman Board of Curators

DAVID L. BONNER
Out-of-State/Non-Voting Member
Truman Board of Curators

MICHAEL A. ZITO
Out-of-State/Non-voting Member
Truman Board of Curators

KELLY KOCHANSKI
Student Representative/Non-voting
Truman Board of Curators

DR. TROY D. PAINO
President
Truman State University

The mission of Truman State University is to offer an exemplary undergraduate education to well-prepared students, grounded in the liberal arts and sciences, in the context of a public institution of higher education. To that end, the University offers affordable undergraduate studies in the traditional arts and sciences, as well as selected pre-professional, professional, and master's level programs that grow naturally out of the philosophy, values, content and desired outcomes of a liberal arts education.

Members, Board of Governors

O'Donnell, James J., (D), chair, Hannibal, Jan. 1, 2017;

Burkemper, Sarah, (D), vice chair, Troy, Jan. 1, 2017;

LaBeth, Michael J., (R), secretary, Kirksville, Jan. 1, 2019;

Cozette, Cheryl J., (R), Columbia, Jan. 1, 2012;

Haber, Karen S., (I), Kansas City, Jan. 1, 2014;

Plassmeyer, Susan, (D), St. Louis, Jan. 1, 2018;

Potter, Matthew W., (D), St. Louis, Jan. 1, 2013;

Bonner, David L., out-of-state/non-voting, Jan. 1, 2019;

Zito, Michael A., out-of-state/non-voting, Jan. 1, 2016;

Kochanski, Kelly, student representative/non-voting, Jan. 1, 2016.

Northwest Missouri State University

Maryville 64468-6001
www.nwmissouri.edu
Email: admissions@nwmissouri.edu

Northwest Missouri State University is a coeducational, primarily residential four-year university offering a broad range of undergraduate and selected graduate programs. Founded as a state normal school in 1905, the university has evolved into a vibrant and diverse learning community with an enrollment of more than 6,700 students hailing from 46 states and 31 countries. More than 700 faculty and staff are employed by the university, which offers classes on its Maryville campus, at centers in Kansas City and St. Joseph, online and through instructional television.

Northwest offers more than 120 undergraduate majors with cutting-edge programs in areas such as education, business, agriculture, fine and performing arts, communications and mass media, behavioral sciences, health and human services, humanities and social sciences, English and modern languages, computer science and natural sciences. Northwest also offers 40 master's programs, certificate programs and a cooperative doctorate in educational leadership.

With its emphasis on student success — every student, every day — the university is focused on providing an exceptional student experience that places high value on scholarship and life-long learning, intercultural competence, collaboration, respect and integrity, strategic thinking and excellence.

Profession-based learning experiences are widely available to Northwest students in a variety of fields. The 448-acre R.T. Wright Farm is a living, hands-on laboratory for agriculture students; while the Horace Mann Laboratory School and the Phyllis and Richard Leet Center for Children and Families, which is located in the center of campus and serves children in preschool through sixth grade, provides hands-on practical classroom experience for students in education and related fields. Northwest's internationally benchmarked student employment program also offers some 1,200 opportunities for students to gain professional development and specialized training in administrative, communications, environmental and other areas throughout the university.

The emphasis on Northwest's values and hands-on experiences is reflected in the university's high success and graduation rates. Northwest boasts a freshman retention rate of 71 percent and a graduation rate of 59 percent, which are considerably higher than the national averages. Additionally, 98 percent of Northwest graduates report finding employment or continuing their education within six months of graduation. Furthermore, Northwest student-athletes have an academic success rate of 74 percent, compared to a rate of 73 percent nationally. Northwest has earned a reputation as a university of champions both on and off the field. In addition to boasting competitive athletics teams, including its four-time NCAA Division II national champion football team and its three-time UCA national champion cheerleading squad, Northwest students compete nationally and excel in fields such as agricultural sciences, forensics and debate and student media.

The first public university in the nation to implement an electronic campus, in 1987, Northwest provides fully-loaded notebook computers for all students. The university also offers an innovative textbook rental program that dates back to the early days of the institution and saves students nearly $1,200 each year.

Recognizing the importance of needs-based financial support for students, Northwest created the American Dream Grant in 2004, a first-of-its-kind program at a public university in the United States. Qualified students meet Northwest admissions criteria and come from the neediest families, based on their applications for federal aid. First-time freshmen are responsible for contributing a portion of their tuition, room and board, which may include private, federal, state and institutional scholarships and grants, and the American Dream Grant fills the remaining gap.

The Missouri Academy of Science, Mathematics and Computing was founded at Northwest in 2000. The rigorous program is an accelerated, two-year residential program for high school juniors and seniors academically talented in science, mathematics or technology. Students are challenged by college coursework tailored to individual abilities and taught by Northwest faculty. Students who complete the program earn both a high school diploma and associate of science degree.

Northwest also provides valuable resources to its community and region that support economic development. The state-of-the-art, 46,679-square-foot Dean L. Hubbard Center for Innovation and Entrepreneurship (CIE), which opened on the campus in 2009, is a mixed-use business incubator and an academic facility that fuels high-tech enterprise and creates jobs while providing academic opportunities and career

DR. MARK H. HARGENS
Chair
Northwest Board of Regents

JOSEPH B. BOSSE
Vice Chair
Northwest Board of Regents

FRANCIS (Gene) DORREL
Member
Northwest Board of Regents

DR. PATRICK B. HARR
Member
Northwest Board of Regents

paths for students. Additionally, the facility houses the university's undergraduate nanoscale science program and serves as the home of Northwest's Small Business and Technology Development Center.

In addition to being a four-time winner of the Missouri Quality Award, Northwest is the only university in Missouri to receive the prestigious Christa McAuliffe Award for Excellence in Teacher Education from the American Association of State Colleges and Universities. Northwest's innovative Alternative Energy program burns wood chips, paper products and pelletized livestock waste to produce most of the thermal energy needed to heat and cool campus buildings, and the university's sustainability efforts earned it the Missouri State Recycling Program Annual Award in 2011, 2013 and 2014. The Northwest campus also is designated the Missouri Arboretum with more than 1,700 trees and 130 species.

JOHN W. RICHMOND
Member
Northwest Board of Regents

VE'SHAWN DIXON
Student Regent
Northwest Board of Regents

Northwest Board of Regents

Hargens, Dr. Mark H., (D), chair, St. Joseph, Jan. 2015;

Bosse, Joseph B., (R), vice chair, St. Louis, Jan. 2016;

Dorrel, Francis (Gene), (R), Maryville, Jan. 2017;

Harr, Dr. Patrick B., (R), Maryville, Jan. 2019;

Richmond, John W., (D), Albany, Jan. 2019;

Dixon, Ve'Shawn, student regent, Kansas City, Kan., Dec. 2015.

DR. JOHN JASINSKI
President, Northwest
Missouri State University

Southeast Missouri State University

Cape Girardeau 63701
Telephone: (573) 651-2000 / FAX: (573) 651-5061
www.semo.edu
Email: admissions@semo.edu

Southeast Missouri State University provides a comprehensive education grounded in the liberal arts and sciences and in practical experience. The University, through teaching and scholarship, challenges students to extend their intellectual capacities, interests and creative abilities; develop their talents; and acquire a lifelong enthusiasm for learning. Students benefit from a relevant, extensive and thorough general education with a global perspective; professional and liberal arts and sciences curricula; co-curricular opportunities; and real-world experiences. By emphasizing student-centered and experiential learning, the University, in collaboration with other entities as appropriate, prepares individuals to participate responsibly in a diverse and technologically advanced world, and in this and other ways contributes to the development of the social, cultural and economic life of the region, state and nation.

With an enrollment of more than 12,000 students, Southeast is an ideal size to take advantage of critical learning and extracurricular opportunities. Class sizes are small with a student/faculty ratio of 21:1. Students come from all 50 states and from more than 50 countries around the world.

Southeast offers more than 200 areas of study and more than 1,500 courses in business, education, the health professions, liberal arts, science, technology and the visual and performing arts. A variety of affordable short-term, spring break and full-semester study abroad programs enhance the academic experience.

Southeast is a leader when it comes to preparing students for careers. Internships and experiential learning are strongly emphasized with all majors having an internship or clinical experience built into the curriculum.

Southeast offers academic programs on five campuses, as well as at other locations and online. Two of the campuses are in Cape Girardeau – the original site founded in 1873 and the River Campus, which opened in 2007. Regional campuses are located in Sikeston, Malden, and Kennett.

Donald L. Harrison College of Business

The Donald L. Harrison College of Business is accredited by the Association to Advance Collegiate Schools of Business (AACSB) International — the gold standard of business school accreditation — an honor held by only five percent of institutions offering business degrees worldwide. Graduates of the college enjoy a job placement rate exceeding 90 percent within the first year after graduation. Princeton Review has included Southeast's Harrison College of Business on its list of "Best Business Schools" for the past nine years.

The Harrison College of Business entrepreneurial studies program is Missouri's most comprehensive, offering options for both B.S., B.A. and M.B.A. degrees. Recognizing that students in any discipline can benefit from knowledge of entrepreneurial processes, Southeast offers seven interdisciplinary minors in entrepreneurship. Combined with a series of annual co-curricular events and services offered by the Douglas C. Greene Center for Innovation and Entrepreneurship, students have the tools to become successful entrepreneurs.

More than 50 Southeast senior business students annually participate in the St. Louis Interview Days recruiting event that attracts more than 35 employers from the greater St. Louis region.

Southeast also offers a mechanism to drive the entrepreneurial mindset of today's students with Catapult Creative House, a groundbreaking creative arts and industries incubator. Catapult is a commercial learning laboratory where creativity, innovation and entrepreneurship converge, bringing novel products and services with a sustainable twist and local connection to market in a modern commercial marketplace.

College of Education

Southeast's education program holds national accreditation in addition to state of Missouri accreditation. Southeast teacher education students get first-hand experience in the classroom beginning their freshman year and concluding with a semester-long student teaching experience. Areas of study in the college include secondary education, elementary education and middle school education. Programs include a wide variety of undergraduate and graduate programs along with a cooperative doctorate with the University of Missouri.

The college offers highly integrated field or clinical experiences across programs to provide real world application of effective practice. The university also provides students a technology rich learning environment with our EDvolution iPad integration for all undergraduate students. The Instructional Resource Technology Center creates flexible space to create lessons, share tools for teaching and practice the art of teaching. Our education is at the forefront of innovation, resulting in graduates who are in demand.

College of Health and Human Services

With health care at the center of national concern, programs in this area are in demand. Health management, communication disorders, nursing and social work are examples of the variety of options available. Even recreation and athletic training focus on healthy living.

Nursing students pass their licensure exams at consistently high rates. Nursing also offers an RN-to-BSN program online and a popular master's degree.

Criminal justice majors also enjoy high rates of employment. The Law Enforcement Academy is dedicated to meeting the training needs of all law enforcement officers and agencies in the region. Our graduates have gone on to work for agencies at all levels of law enforcement, including the FBI, DEA, ATF and the U.S. Marshal's Service.

College of Science, Technology and Agriculture

The College of Science, Technology and Agriculture's engineering physics program is nationally accredited by the Accrediting Board of Engineering and Technology (ABET). Southeast is a designated Center of Excellence in Advanced Manufacturing Technology and all of the bachelor's degree programs in the Department of Polytechnic Studies are nationally accredited. Cybersecurity graduates are in demand to combat computer and Internet crime. Southeast was the first university in Missouri to offer a bachelor's degree in this demanding field.

Pre-med remains a popular major and graduates are accepted to medical schools at a rate higher than the national average. Students in many of the science disciplines enjoy a nearly 100 percent placement rate.

The Department of Mathematics offers a program in actuarial science.

Students learn about the latest in beef production technology and row crop research at the 252-acre David M. Barton Agriculture Research Center. In addition, there is a 110-acre rice research station, an irrigated turf plot facility, a modern soil fertility laboratory and 11,000-square-foot climate-controlled Charles Hutson Horticulture Greenhouse.

College of Liberal Arts

The College of Liberal Arts features the Earl and Margie Holland School of Visual and Performing Arts, which houses the departments of Art, Music and Theatre and Dance at the River Campus.

Blending classic beauty and modern technology, the River Campus is composed of the beautifully restored 19th century St. Vincent's Seminary building and newly constructed facilities including a 950-seat performance hall, black box theatre, dance studio, regional museum and convocation center. The restored seminary buildings are on the National Register of Historic Places. An intimate recital hall seating 200 has been created in the seminary chapel, and the historic buildings also house classrooms, faculty offices, rehearsal rooms, art studios, computer laboratories and other academic and student service rooms. Southeast is the only university in Missouri to have a separate campus dedicated to art, dance, music and theatre.

The newest addition to the River Campus is the Kenneth and Jeanine Dobbins River Campus Center, a 90,000-square-foot building combining academic and living spaces on the same property and creating an environment in which talented students live and learn together. The new facility is just north of the original Convocation Center and Seminary Building, forming the completion of a River Campus quad. The first floor includes a directing/acting black box studio; a dance studio; a spacious choral rehearsal room; sectional practice rooms; and St. Vincent's Commons, a 120-seat dining facility overlooking the majestic Mississippi River complemented with an outdoor seating area. An art education classroom is located on the mezzanine, and the second floor houses faculty offices.

The building also provides a 180-bed living area housing many music, art, theatre and dance majors who are now living close to the academic facilities they frequent. The majority of the second and all of the third floor are four-person student suites, along with practice rooms, laundry facilities and spacious lounges. A fitness center also is located on the third floor.

In addition to the School of Visual and Performing Arts, the College of Liberal Arts consists of academic departments that are key contributors to the university mission of "providing professional education grounded in the liberal arts and sciences." These seven departments are: Communication Studies; English; Global Cultures and Languages; History; Mass Media; Political Science, Philosophy and Religion; and Psychology. In addition to promoting the University-wide goal of enhancing critical thinking skills in our students, faculty in the College of Liberal Arts provide students with an understanding of various cultures, languages, and worldviews, all of which are designed to prepare graduates for effective functioning in a world increasingly characterized by diversity and globalization. This is accomplished not only through formal classroom instruction, but also by providing students with opportunities for study abroad and experiential learning in their major field of study. Southeast mass media students receive the full complement of multi-media experiences – print production through The Arrow and the Southeast Missourian, television production through KFVS12 and radio production through KRCU Radio, Southeast's National Public Radio station. The University recently forged a partnership with Rust Communications and KFVS12 to develop an innovation laboratory in downtown Cape Girardeau. It will house the University's television and video production program and The Arrow student newspaper in the new Center for Excellence in Mass Media.

The College of Liberal Arts public relations program is one of only 20 institutions that hold certification by the Public Relations Society of America (PRSA). The Accrediting Council on Education in Journalism and Mass Communications (ACEJMC) accredits the mass communication program. Only one other institution in Missouri has this elite accreditation. Only nine other institutions in the world have recognition from both ACEJMC and PRSA for their mass communication program.

The college provides other services for the university and the community. The Center for Regional History documents and preserves various aspects of the area's architecture, history and archaeology and supports the activities of faculty and students in history, archaeology, and related fields. The Center for Faulkner Studies is an internationally renowned repository for materials collected by Faulkner scholars and biographers and regularly hosts visiting international scholars. KRCU at Southeast Missouri State University is the University-operated National Public Radio (NPR) affiliate, which broadcasts news, classical music, jazz, folk music and nationally syndicated programs to the Cape Girardeau community and surrounding areas. The Southeast Missouri State University Press benefits the university, community and region by providing regional scholarly publications, operating as a working laboratory for students, and sponsoring events including nationally known writers' visits to the campus.

School of Graduate Studies

Through its graduate faculty, curricula and research programs, the University offers to its more than 1,500 graduate students 35 master's degree programs; specialist degrees in Educational Administration, Educational Leadership and Counseling Education; a certificate program in Applied Behavior Analysis; and a cooperative doctoral degree in Educational Leadership. The School of Graduate Studies is strongly committed to fostering a successful learning environment by maintaining small classes and individualized research experiences for its students.

Jane Stephens Honors Program

By offering educational opportunities tailored to the special needs, aspirations and motivation of students whose intellectual and creative abilities are outstanding, the Jane Stephens Honors Program underscores Southeast Missouri State University's commitment to quality and excellence in matters of knowledge, creativity and leadership. The goals of the Jane Stephens Honors Program reflect this basic commitment. These goals are:

• To address the special needs of outstanding students by providing a center of identity for formulating personal goals, developing self-esteem and increasing the desire for self-directed learning;

• To contribute to the general advancement of learning by encouraging the active pursuit of academic goals, as exemplified by research, scholarly activity and creative endeavor; and

• To encourage an intellectual perspective by providing a model of academic endeavor which emphasizes analytical thought, insight into the methodologies of different disciplines and cross-disciplinary synthesis.

Kent Library

Kent Library is well positioned to support the needs of the 21st century learner. Kent Library's Information Commons combines state of the art technology with traditional library resources and services in one centralized, comfortable academic environment. Student needs in the areas of electronic research, media production, information access and collaborative and individual study space are met with the assistance of librarians.

Traditional library resources and services are folded into the new technologies to form a solid platform for assisting students' individual needs. The library's general stack collection, approximately 500,000 volumes, is supplemented through the statewide MOBIUS consortium and interlibrary loan services. In addition the library also provides more than 30,000 journals, 120,000 books and 12,000 videos online. Kent Library is also an Official Government Depository. The library's Special Collections and Archives preserves and makes accessible research material that document the historical, literary and cultural experience of Southeast Missouri State University and provides access to a world-class literary collection on William Faulkner.

Blending current technologies with traditional library services and resources, further combined with personalized assistance from trained staff and faculty, form the basis for this 21st century academic library.

Athletics

Southeast participates in NCAA Division I athletics as a member of the Ohio Valley Conference. Men's sports include baseball, basketball, cross country, football and indoor and outdoor track. Women's sports include basketball, cross country, gymnastics, soccer, softball, tennis, volleyball and indoor and outdoor track.

Redhawk student-athletes maintained a 3.15 cumulative GPA as a group in 2014-15, while also winning eight conference championships between the start of 2014 and May 2015. Athletics facilities have undergone more than $10 million of renovations since the start of 2014.

JAY B. KNUDTSON
President
Southeast Board of Regents

KENDRA NEELY-MARTIN
Vice President
Southeast Board of Regents

DOYLE L. PRIVETT
Member
Southeast Board of Regents

THOMAS M. MEYER
Member
Southeast Board of Regents

DAREN K. TODD
Member
Southeast Board of Regents

DONALD G. LaFERLA
Member
Southeast Board of Regents

AUSTIN K. CORDELL
Student Representative
Southeast Board of Regents

CARLOS VARGAS-ABURTO
President, Southeast
Missouri State University

Members, Board of Regents

Knudtson, Jay B., president, Cape Girardeau, Jan. 1, 2019;

Neely-Martin, Kendra, vice president, St. Louis, Jan. 1, 2018;

Privett, Doyle L., Kennett, Jan. 1, 2015;

Meyer, Thomas M., Cape Girardeau, Jan. 1, 2018;

Todd, Daren K., Kennett, Jan. 1, 2015;

LaFerla, Donald G., Carthage, Jan. 1, 2019;

Cordell, Austin K., student representative, Festus;

Vargas-Aburto, Carlos, president of the university.

Missouri State University

Springfield 65897
Telephone: (417) 836-5000
www.missouristate.edu
Email: info@missouristate.edu

Missouri State University is a public, comprehensive metropolitan system with a statewide mission in public affairs, whose purpose is to develop educated persons. The university's identity is distinguished by its public affairs mission, which entails a campus-wide commitment to foster expertise and responsibility in ethical leadership, cultural competence and community engagement.

The academic experience is grounded in a general education curriculum that draws heavily from the liberal arts and sciences. This foundation provides the basis for mastery of disciplinary and professional studies. It also provides essential forums in which students develop the capacity to make well-informed, independent critical judgments about the cultures, values and institutions in society.

The task of developing educated persons obligates the university to expand the store of human understanding through research, scholarship and creative endeavor, and, drawing from that store of understanding, to provide service to the communities that support it. In all of its programs, the university uses the most effective methods of discovering and imparting knowledge and the appropriate use of technology in support of these activities.

The Missouri State University campuses are structured to address the special needs of the urban and rural populations they serve. Missouri State University–Springfield is a selective admissions, graduate-level teaching and research institution. Missouri State University–West Plains is a separately accredited open-admissions campus primarily serving seven counties in south central Missouri. Missouri State University–Mountain Grove serves Missouri's fruit industry through operation of the State Fruit Experiment Station. Missouri State Outreach provides anytime, any-place learning opportunities through telecourses, Internet-based instruction, iTunes U and through its interactive video network.

The university also operates various other special facilities, such as the Darr Agricultural Center in southwest Springfield, the Journagan Ranch in Douglas County, the Jordan Valley Innovation Center in downtown Springfield, the Bull Shoals Field Station near Forsyth, Baker's Acres and Observatory near Marshfield, the Missouri State University Graduate Center in Joplin and a branch campus at Liaoning Normal University (LNU) in Dalian, China. In addition, Missouri State has the operations and program offerings of one entire academic department, its Department of Defense and Strategic Studies, located near Washington, D.C., in Fairfax, Va.

Public Affairs: Approved in 1995, Missouri State University's statewide mission in public affairs is maturing. With an emphasis on three specific components in the undergraduate curriculum that reflects the public affairs mission—ethical leadership, cultural competence and community engagement—the university will provide enhanced educational experiences to 21st century students.

Missouri State is the host campus for the Missouri Campus Compact, a statewide coalition of university and college presidents dedicated "to helping students develop the values and skills of civic participation through involvement in public service." Missouri State also hosts a Public Affairs Conference, which brings a variety of noteworthy speakers from around the country to the Springfield campus. During the conference, panels and keynote speakers present discussions that offer perspectives from business, entertainment, education, politics, religion, health and other subject areas.

History: Missouri State University was founded as the Missouri State Normal School, Fourth District, by legislative action on March 17, 1905. Missouri State first opened its doors in June 1906. After 108 years and four name changes, Missouri State is a comprehensive state university system offering a wide variety of programs and services to its students and the citizens of the state.

During the 1995 session of the Missouri General Assembly, Missouri State received a statewide mission in public affairs, making it the only Missouri university emphasizing the development of aware, committed and active participants in tomorrow's society.

In a campus ceremony on March 17, 2005, the 100th anniversary of Founders' Day, Gov. Matt Blunt signed Senate Bill 98, which included changing Southwest Missouri State University's name to Missouri State University, the fifth and final name for the university. The institution was founded as the Normal School in 1905, then changed to Southwest Missouri State Teachers College in 1919, Southwest Missouri State College in 1946 and Southwest Missouri State University in 1972. Each new name has reflected the changed nature of the institution.

Facilities: Missouri State University's main campus is located on 225 acres in the heart of Springfield. The 90-acre William H. Darr Agricultural Center exists in the southwest area of the city. Missouri State's main campus has 19 classroom buildings, an administrative building, a library, 12 residence halls, a multipurpose recreational facility, a sports complex, a health center, a welcome center and a campus-wide transit facility. The Juanita K. Hammons Hall for the Performing Arts hosts a variety of musical, dance and theatrical presentations.

The late Springfield-based hotelier and philanthropist John Q. Hammons gifted $30 million to Missouri State toward the construction of the JQH Arena—a world-class sports facility that features more than 11,000 seats, a grand entrance, 24 private suites, more than 100 loge seats, 55 "Jack Nicholson courtside seats," a Hall of Fame, team souvenir store, ticket office and a 4,500-square-foot club. The new arena is home to the Bears and Lady Bears basketball teams.

Enrollment: In the fall of 2014, Missouri State University's official head-count enrollment total was 24,489, with 22,385 students on the Springfield campus and 2,193 on the West Plains campus. Some 90 students are enrolled on both campuses; these students were only counted once in the system total.

Academic programs: Missouri State offers more than 190 undergraduate and 50 graduate degree options, including four doctoral programs. Missouri State also offers a cooperative doctorate (Ed.D.) through the University of Missouri–Columbia, as well as a cooperative Doctor of Pharmacy program with the University of Missouri–Kansas City. Many of these programs are the state's strongest and largest of their kind. The university is accredited by the North Central Association of Colleges and Secondary Schools, as well as by 23 professional associations, including the National Council for Accreditation of Teacher Education (NCATE), National Association of Schools of Music, National Association of Schools for Public Affairs and Administration, the National Collegiate Athletic Association, the American Chemical Society, the Council on Social Work Education and the American Assembly of Collegiate Schools of Business. The university's academic programs are organized within seven colleges: Arts and Letters, Business Administration, Education, Health and Human Services, Humanities and Public Affairs, Natural and Applied Sciences and the Graduate College.

International programs: Missouri State has established a branch campus at Liaoning Normal University (LNU) in Dalian, China. The LNU-MSU College of International Business has over 775 students, including over 100 international students from numerous countries including Africa, Korea, Hong Kong, Indonesia, Mongolia, the U.S. and more. LNU and Missouri State University also have agreed to collaborate on the basis of their plant science programs and established an Articulation Agreement for Dual Master's Degrees in Plant Science. The articulation terms will accommodate LNU students in obtaining master's degrees in Plant Science from both Missouri State University and LNU.

The university has a wide variety of international education programs available to students, including programs in England, Costa Rica, Chile, Brazil, India and China. Missouri State also is a member of the International Student Exchange Consortium, which provides for reciprocal exchanges to programs in more than 30 countries. In addition, Missouri State's Continuing Education and the Extended Campus offers a wide variety of programs, both credit and non-credit, for adult students who are returning to college. Numerous courses tailored to meet the needs of area employers are offered as well. Missouri State has the largest cooperative program in the state, with more than 1,200 students participating in internships in the public and private sectors.

Academic excellence: The average ACT score for Missouri State's incoming freshmen in the fall of 2014 was 24.1, significantly higher than the average for Missouri high school graduates. Further evidence of academic excellence at Missouri State has been the recognition that student teams have received in regional and national student competitions in a number of areas, including debate, advertising, construction, industrial management and media, journalism and film. The Honors College at Missouri State offers extraordinary opportunities for outstanding students.

Faculty and staff: Missouri State University employs 3,886 full-time and part-time faculty and staff, making it the fifth largest employer in Springfield. The student to faculty ratio is approximately 19:1.

Research: Missouri State University accounts for millions of dollars of grant-funded research each year. Faculty and student research conducted throughout the university system ranges in scope from the studies of grape genomics

and meteor impacts to early childhood development and juvenile crime, and has the potential to positively affect local communities, Missouri, the nation and ultimately the world. In all, Missouri State University received more than $21.9 million from a total of 289 grants and contracts awarded to faculty and staff during 2013–2014. The principal focus of the university is applied research geared to serving the needs of diverse constituencies in the public and private sectors. Faculty members are encouraged to pursue their individual and scholarly activities.

The Roy Blunt Jordan Valley Innovation Center (JVIC) is made up of five separate buildings, covering around 75,000 square feet. What was once a dilapidated MFA mill in downtown Springfield is now the home of leading-edge research and state-of-the-art technology. The capabilities of the center include applied research in nanotechnology, bio-materials, advanced technologies, genomics/proteomics, bio-systems, software engineering and medical material device and instrument technologies. JVIC breaks from a traditional approach to provide a more interdisciplinary experience aimed at serving the technical, commercial and educational needs of industry. JVIC emphasizes the application of theory to practice, including hands-on instruction with advanced technology industrial instruments.

Libraries: The Missouri State University library system is composed of the Duane G. Meyer Library, the Music Library, the Horace and "Pete" Haseltine Library in the Greenwood Laboratory School and the Paul G. Evans Library of Fruit Science on the Mountain Grove campus. These four libraries have collections of more than three million items, including more than 866,000 accessioned volumes; current subscriptions to more than 3,300 periodicals, newspapers and other serials; and extensive back files of journals and newspapers, many on microfilm, microcard and microfiche. More than 20,000 journals are available online with full-text. Total microform holdings amount to more than one million items. More than 930,000 state, federal and United Nations (UN) documents are held as a result of Meyer Library being a designated depository library for each of those areas. Meyer Library is the only UN depository library in the state of Missouri. A large collection of audio CDs is fully cataloged and available in the Music Library. Special collections and archives house a number of special groups of materials: the William J. Jones collections of Rimbaud and Butor French Literature are internationally recognized and the Rimbaud portion comprises the largest collection of this type in the United States; the Ozarks Labor Union Archives document regional labor history; and the University Archives is a growing collection and will be further developed as a $130,000 grant for

STEPHEN B. HOVEN
Chair, Missouri State Board of
Governors

PETER HOFHERR
Vice Chair, Missouri State Board
of Governors

JOE CARMICHAEL
Member, Missouri State Board of
Governors

VIRGINIA FRY
Member, Missouri State Board of
Governors

ORVIN KIMBROUGH
Member, Missouri State Board of
Governors

BEVERLY MILLER
Member, Missouri State Board of
Governors

KENDALL SEAL
Member, Missouri State Board of
Governors

CARRIE TERGIN
Member, Missouri State Board of
Governors

organizing and processing these materials is utilized. Another department in Meyer Library, the Curriculum Resource Center, features a children's literature collection, a textbook collection, curriculum guides and special learning materials.

Innovation and the use of new technologies are evident in the Missouri State University libraries. Most of the bibliographic data for SWAN, the libraries' online catalog, is created as materials are cataloged using the Online Computer Library Center, Inc. (OCLC), a database with more than 73 million bibliographic records. OCLC is also utilized for interlibrary loan and reference, with links to over 41,555 libraries in 112 countries. Electronic document delivery is commonly used to acquire interlibrary loan materials in a timely fashion. The statewide MOBIUS consortium, with a membership of 60 academic libraries, is simplifying access to regional holdings. The MOBIUS database of more than 19 million items utilizing the same interface can be used by faculty, students and staff to borrow items with a two-day delivery time from anywhere in the state.

A central feature of the library and of the campus is the Jane A. Meyer Carillon with its complement of 48 bronze bells.

CALEB DOYLE
Student Representative, Missouri
State Board of Governors

CLIFTON M. SMART III
President
Missouri State University

Campus Technology: Missouri State University offers faculty, staff and students free use of its computing services and facilities for class assignments and research. The campus networks provide high-speed, reliable services to client computers and file server systems in academic, administrative and housing facilities at all Missouri State locations, including Springfield, West Plains, Mountain Grove, Lebanon and Branson. Network access in the residence halls allows students to utilize the online resources of Meyer

Library, various campus computing services and the Internet from their rooms. High-speed Internet, wireless and virtual private network services are all supported, while dial-up access to campus computing resources is provided for those needing free local access. Three centrally managed computer labs located in Glass Hall, Cheek Hall and Strong Hall, plus dozens of discipline-specific computer classrooms and labs, offer substantial access and support for campus computing resources.

Members, Board of Governors

Hoven, Stephen B., (R), chair, Ballwin, Jan. 1, 2017;
Hofherr, Peter, (D), vice chair, St. James, Jan. 1, 2017;
Carmichael, Joe, (D), Springfield, Jan. 1, 2017;
Fry, Virginia, (R), Springfield, Jan. 1, 2019;
Kimbrough, Orvin, (I), St. Louis, Jan. 1, 2015;
Miller, Beverly, (D), Lebanon, Jan. 1, 2015;
Seal, Kendall, (D), Kansas City, Jan. 1, 2019;
Tergin, Carrie, (R), Jefferson City, Jan. 1, 2015;
Doyle, Caleb, student member, Barnhart, Dec. 31, 2015.

Missouri State University–Mountain Grove Campus

The Mountain Grove campus is primarily known for research in agriculture and fruit science and sits on 192 acres in south-central Missouri. The 12-acre campus is located just north and east of the intersection of Highway 60 and State Highway 95 and is home to the State Fruit Experiment Station, the Center for Grapevine Biotechnology and Mountain Grove Cellars. The 180-acre field and research area is located on the west side of State Highway 95. Journagan Ranch is located just 10 miles from campus. The station, center, cellars and ranch are units of the William H. Darr School of Agriculture. The Missouri State Mountain Grove Extended Campus is located at Shannon Hall just south of the Hwy. 60/St. Hwy. 95 intersection and is administered though Missouri State–West Plains.

Facilities: The State Fruit Experiment Station is located on the 192-acre campus just north of Mountain Grove, 65 miles east of Springfield. On the 12 acres east of State Highway 95 are Shepard Hall, housing laboratories, offices and a sales area for fruit and wine; Faurot Hall, home to the Paul Evans Library of Fruit Science, classrooms, a plant science laboratory and offices; a fruit processing laboratory housing the Mountain Grove Cellars; a community building; and three greenhouses. The 180-acre area west of State Highway 95 includes a United States Weather Bureau substation, equipment storage buildings, a shop, several miscellaneous buildings, fruit and horti-

cultural crop research and demonstration plants and hay fields and horse pastures.

The **State Fruit Experiment Station** is the oldest identifiable segment of Missouri State University. The State Fruit Experiment Station was established by a legislative act in 1899. The station was operated as a state agency under a board of trustees appointed by the governor until 1974 when the Omnibus State Reorganization Act transferred administrative responsibility for the State Fruit Experiment Station to the Board of Governors of Missouri State.

Research is conducted in pomology, enology, viticulture, plant pathology, entomology, molecular genetics and plant physiology. Fruit crops under investigation include apples, grapes, blueberries, peaches, strawberries, blackberries, raspberries, elderberries and other fruit species. Research results are disseminated to the scientific community via presentations at professional conferences and peer-reviewed publications and to fruit growers, processors and the public through outreach programs via a variety of events and media.

A U.S. Department of Agriculture (USDA) quarantine facility for the introduction and virus testing of grapes from outside the United States is located at the station. The station's research and advisory programs have been instrumental in the revival of the Missouri grape and wine industry after Prohibition. Today, special emphasis is given to research on the American and hybrid grape varieties and their wines.

The **Center for Grapevine Biotechnology** explores the genetic resources of diverse grapevine species to secure the ecological and economic sustainability of the grape and wine industry and to improve human health. This work includes developing new, improved grape varieties by genome-enabled breeding, conducting molecular analysis of grapevine genes and viruses for the management of major diseases, providing clean and virus-tested grapevines to the industry, exploring and identifying health-promoting compounds in native grapevine species and creating a challenging academic environment to train students in plant biotechnology.

Mountain Grove Cellars is licensed for wine sales and includes a commercially licensed distillery. This facility supports research conducted on specific winemaking problems and offers educational opportunities for Missouri State agriculture students who are interested in enology. Public educational events for artisan distillers, home winemakers and consumers are offered annually. Mountain Grove Cellars produces wine and fruit brandy exclusively from fruit grown in the State Fruit Experiment Station research and demonstration vineyards and orchards.

Journagan Ranch is a working ranch complete with buildings, equipment and cattle. The ranch, given by Leo Journagan and his family, is located about 10 miles from the Mountain Grove campus proper and is the second-largest single gift in the university's history. The 3,300-plus acres stretch over approximately seven miles with barns, buildings, vehicles and machinery. Journagan Ranch has some crossbred cattle, but the main focus of the operation is purebred Polled Herefords, a variation of Hereford cattle without horns. Journagan Ranch has the 15th largest herd of Polled Herefords in the United States. Herefords are known for being docile and for their ability to thrive in any environment.

The ranch offers a potential site for research and teaching in beef genetics and management, agroforestry, soils, water quality and wildlife conservation. The ranch also offers opportunities for hiking and horseback riding. Students working at Journagan Ranch may be housed on the Mountain Grove campus while enrolled in Springfield classes through distance-education technology.

Extended Campus at Mountain Grove offers classes to area students earning an associate degree at Shannon Hall through Missouri State–West Plains. Shannon Hall includes several classrooms, a computer classroom, distance learning classroom and science lab.

Missouri State University–West Plains

West Plains 65775
Telephone: (417) 255-7255
www.wp.missouristate.edu
Email: wpadmissions@missouristate.edu

Missouri State University–West Plains is one of three campuses within the Missouri State University System. The West Plains campus is a teaching and learning institution of higher education offering two-year Associate of Arts, Associate of Science and Associate of Applied Science degrees, certificates and other courses as needed by employers and citizens of the area served. The college provides a liberal arts transfer curriculum at the freshman and sophomore levels, selected occupational programs and a variety of continuing education courses.

A full college experience with quality instruction in a relaxed, personal atmosphere is the hallmark of Missouri State–West Plains. The campus promotes academic and personal success for students through small classes, personalized attention, educational support services and numerous opportunities to participate in extracurricular activities.

History and setting: Missouri State–West Plains was founded in 1963 as the West Plains Residence Center. In 1977, the Southwest Mis-

souri State University Board of Regents and the General Assembly designated the name West Plains Campus of Southwest Missouri State University to replace Residence Center. The legislature enacted a permanent status bill for the campus in 1981 then passed House Bill 51 in 1991, giving the campus the authority to offer "one-year certificates, two-year associate degrees and credit and non-credit courses." The passage of Senate Bill 98 in 2005 changed the university system's name to Missouri State University.

Facilities: The campus consists of five classroom and administrative buildings—Kellett Hall, M.O. Looney Hall, Emory L. Melton Hall, Michael J. Lybyer Technology Center and Garfield Hall. In addition, the campus includes the Garnett Library, the 60-person Grizzly House residence hall, the Putnam Student Center, the V.H. Drago College Store and Cass Hall, a one-stop shop for student services. Maintenance and custodial operations are located in the Broadway Building, and the Richards House serves as the residence for the Missouri State–West Plains chancellor. Gohn Hall houses Missouri State University's Outreach program.

Enrollment: The fall 2014 enrollment was 2,193 students, with the majority of students coming from a seven-county area of the south-central Missouri Ozarks region and from adjacent areas in north Arkansas.

Academic Programs: The campus offers associate degrees designed for transfer into bachelor's degree programs and for immediate employment after two years of study. They include Associate of Arts degrees in general studies and teaching; Associate of Science degrees in agriculture, business and nursing; and Associate of Applied Science degrees in allied health, business, child and family development, computer graphics and programming, enology, entrepreneurship, general agriculture, law enforcement, respiratory therapy, technology and viticulture. Some bachelor's and master's degree programs also are available at the West Plains campus through Missouri State University's Outreach program.

Missouri State–West Plains also offers the Associate of Arts degree in general studies at its extended campus in Mountain Grove.

The college is accredited by the Higher Learning Commission and is a member of the North Central Association. The nursing program is fully approved by the Missouri State Board of Nursing and is accredited by the Accreditation Commission for Education in Nursing. The respiratory therapy program holds provisional accreditation from the Commission on Accreditation for Respiratory Care.

JAMES B. FLEISCHAKER
Chair, Missouri Southern Board
of Governors

GLENN M. (Mitch) McCUMBER
Vice Chair, Missouri Southern
Board of Governors

LYNN M. EWING III
Member, Missouri Southern
Board of Governors

TRACY C. FLANIGAN
Member, Missouri
Southern Board of Governors

ROD ANDERSON
Member, Missouri Southern
Board of Governors

KEITH C. HANKINS
Member, Missouri Southern
Board of Governors

WILLIAM (Bill) GIPSON
Member, Missouri Southern
Board of Governors

ALISON R. HERSHEWE
Member, Missouri Southern
Board of Governors

Missouri Southern State University

Joplin 64801-1595
Telephone: (417) 625-9300 / FAX: (417) 625-9781
www.mssu.edu
Email: admissions@mssu.edu or info@mssu.edu

DR. ALAN D. MARBLE
President, Missouri
Southern State University

Founded in 1937 as Joplin Junior College, Missouri Southern State University (MSSU) was established by the General Assembly in 1965 as a two-year, upper-division state college to be operated in conjunction with the Junior College District of Jasper County. Missouri Southern operated under this arrangement through June 30, 1977, when the state assumed the responsibility of funding and operating the four-year program. Missouri Southern State College (MSSC) became Missouri Southern State University after Gov. Bob Holden signed Senate Bill 55 on July 12, 2003. The legislation also allowed MSSU to enter into cooperative agreements with other state universities to provide graduate programs.

MSSU is committed to the success of its students through a First-Year Experience program, an emphasis on strong academic advising and a campus committed to service-learning, engaging student organizations and intramural activities. MSSU also offers highly competitive NCAA Division II athletic programs in the Mid-America Intercollegiate Athletics Association (MIAA). In June 1990, MSSU's board approved a change in the university mission to include an international emphasis in undergraduate education. This change is intended to help students compete in the global environment.

The following degrees are offered: Bachelor of Arts, Bachelor of Fine Arts, Bachelor of Science, Bachelor of Science in Business Administration, Bachelor of Science in Education, Bachelor of General Studies and Associate of Science. The university offers bachelor's degrees in nearly 150 major areas in liberal arts, teacher education, business and technology. In addition to the four-year programs, the curriculum offers pre-medicine, pre-engineering and other pre-professional programs, as well as two-year associate degrees in dental hygiene, computer information science, law enforcement, radiological technology, drafting and design engineering technology, manufacturing engineering technology and respiratory therapy.

The university is also working to expand its graduate programs. Offerings currently include Master of Science in Education-Curriculum & Instruction, Master of Accountancy and Master of Arts-Teaching degrees.

The university is organized into four schools: Arts and Sciences, Education, Health Sciences and the Robert W. Plaster School of Business and Health Sciences. The university mission statement stresses a liberal arts-based core curriculum designed to provide every graduate with knowledge in the basic areas of learning. Under a revised and moderately selective admission policy, the university encourages high-school students to be better prepared for college study by following the core curriculum requirements outlined by the Missouri Coordinating Board for Higher Education.

The administration of the university is vested in an eight-member Board of Governors appointed by the governor with Senate consent. The 373-acre university campus is located in Joplin, a southwest Missouri city with a population of nearly 50,000 and a regional retail hub serving about 400,000. The MSSU campus presently consists of 30 major buildings, including the 65,000-square-foot Beimdiek Recreation Center and an 85,000-square-foot health sciences building, as well as a performing arts center, an artificial turf football field, a 3,200-seat athletic center with a 200-meter indoor track and a modern library with access to the latest online and electronic databases. In 2015, the university completed work on a six-building residence hall complex featuring 51 student apartments; an 11,000-square-foot FEMA shelter; a new baseball stadium; and a fieldhouse at the north end of the football stadium.

The university is accredited by the Higher Learning Commission and is a member of the North Central Association, the National Council for the Accreditation of Teacher Education, Missouri Department of Elementary and Secondary Education, Association of American Colleges & Universities, Accreditation Board of Engineering and Technology, Association of Collegiate Business Schools and Programs, Commission on Dental Accreditation, American Dental Association, Committee on Accreditation for Respiratory Care, Joint Review Committee on Education in Radiologic Technology, Missouri Department of Health and Senior Services Bureau, Missouri State Board of Nursing, National Accrediting Agency for Clinical Laboratory Science, National League of Nursing Accrediting Commission, National Environmental Health Science and Protection Accreditation Council and Peace Officer Standards and Training (POST).

Members, Board of Governors

Fleischaker, James B., (D), chair, Joplin, 2017;
McCumber, Glenn M. (Mitch), (R), vice chair, Noel, 2018;
Ewing, Lynn M. III, (D), Nevada, 2015;
Flanigan, Tracy, (R), Carthage, 2019;
Anderson, Rod, (D), Monett, 2009;
Hankins, Keith C., (R), Stockton, 2016;
Gipson, William L. (Bill), (R), Shell Knob, 2017;
Hershewe, Alison R., (D), Joplin, 2020.

Missouri Western State University

St. Joseph 64507
Telephone: (816) 271-4200
www.missouriwestern.edu
Email: admission@missouriwestern.edu

Missouri Western State University offers students at all stages of life the opportunity to achieve excellence in the classroom and beyond as they prepare to be leaders in their communities. Providing a blend of traditional liberal arts and career-oriented degree programs, Missouri Western is strongly committed to the educational, economic, cultural and social development of the people it serves, setting the standard for excellence in student development and community leadership.

Founded as St. Joseph Junior College in 1915, Missouri Western transformed into a four-year institution in 1969, became a full member of the State of Missouri system in 1977, and earned university designation in 2005. The university designation legislation also made Missouri Western a statewide institution of applied learning. The university encourages students to engage in learning that occurs outside the classroom, applying the theory of the classroom to practical situations. Nearly 90 percent of Missouri Western graduates participate in an internship, undergraduate research, service-learning, study away or other applied learning experience. The legislation also authorized Missouri Western to offer graduate degrees, and the university has developed several master's degree programs emphasizing applied research and practical experiences. Two of the master's programs have been recognized as professional science master's degrees for allowing students to pursue advanced science training

DIRCK CLARK
Chair, Missouri Western Board
of Governors

GREGORY MASON
Vice Chair, Missouri Western
Board of Governors

LEO BLAKLEY
Member, Missouri Western
Board of Governors

LESLEY GRAVES
Member, Missouri Western
Board of Governors

DAVID LIECHTI
Member, Missouri Western
Board of Governors

ALFRED PURCELL
Member, Missouri Western
Board of Governors

DEBORAH SMITH
Member, Missouri Western
Board of Governors

ATTAWIA LIONEL
Student Governor, Missouri
Western Board of Governors

while developing valuable workplace skills, a designation shared by fewer than 400 programs around the country.

Missouri Western offers more than 100 undergraduate majors, 14 master's degrees and five graduate certificates. The student to faculty ratio is approximately 17:1, and 87 percent of full-time faculty hold the highest degree in their field. The institution is accredited by the Higher Learning Commission, a commission of the North Central Association of Colleges and Schools. Program accreditations include the Association to Advance Collegiate Schools of Business (AACSB) International, Technology Accreditation Commission of the Accreditation Board for Engineering and Technology, American Bar Association, American Chemical Society, Commission on Accreditation for Health Informatics and Information Management Education, Commission on Accreditation in Physical Therapy Education, Commission on Collegiate Nursing Education, Council on Social Work Education, National Accrediting Agency for Clinical Laboratory Science, National Association of Schools of Music and National Council for Accreditation of Teacher Education.

Missouri Western's 723-acre campus features a large nature study area, walking trails and nine ponds. In 2010, Missouri Western became the

DR. ROBERT A. VARTABEDIAN
President, Missouri Western
State University

summer training camp home of the Kansas City Chiefs. In 2013, Missouri Western dedicated the 5,000-square-foot Walter Cronkite Memorial in honor of the legendary journalist who was born in St. Joseph. The university also operates a site in Kansas City's Northland.

Members, Board of Governors

Clark, Dirck, (R), chair, Parkville, Oct. 29, 2015; **Mason, Gregory,** (D), vice chair, Lee's Summit, Oct. 29, 2018;

Blakley, Leo, (D), St. Joseph, Oct. 29, 2016;
Graves, Lesley, (R), Tarkio, Oct. 29, 2011;
Liechti, David, (D), St. Joseph, Oct. 29, 2019;
Purcell, Alfred, (R), Easton, Oct. 29, 2018;
Smith, Deborah, (D), Country Club Village, Oct. 29, 2014;
Lionel Attawia, student governor, Kansas City, Dec. 31, 2015.

University of Central Missouri

Warrensburg 64093
Telephone (660) 543-4111
www.ucmo.edu
Email: admit@ucmo.edu

Founded in 1871, the University of Central Missouri (UCM) has a long history of meeting the higher education needs of Missourians. A new chapter in the institution's development took place Sept. 20, 2006, with a name change to reflect a new vision.

The Missouri Coordinating Board for Higher Education approved the university's statewide mission in professional applied sciences and technology Oct. 10, 1996. This enhanced mission reflects an overall commitment to academic excellence and career preparation that includes the integration of the latest technologies throughout UCM's comprehensive liberal arts curriculum. This is having far-reaching impact on more than 13,000 students from nearly all 50 states and over 50 foreign countries who attend UCM and engage in 150 areas of study tailored to meet individual needs.

Beyond Missouri, UCM offers onsite and on-line learning opportunities to students in other parts of the United States and the world. UCM's international programs include exchange opportunities, internships and student teaching programs that are all among the most challenging and affordable anywhere. Degrees conferred by the university include the Bachelor of Arts, Bachelor of Fine Arts, Bachelor of Music, Bachelor of Music Education, Bachelor of Science, Bachelor of Science in business administration, Bachelor of Science in education and Bachelor of Science in social work. At the graduate level, UCM offers excellent programs leading to Master of Arts, Master of Science, Master of Science in Education, Master of Business Administration and Education Specialist degrees. In addition, a cooperative doctoral program in educational leadership exists in conjunction with the University of Missouri (MU), and a cooperative doctoral program in technology management is available in conjunction with Indiana State University (ISU). MU and ISU serve as the degree-granting institutions.

Administratively, the university's academic affairs division is divided into four core academic colleges, the Honors College and the School of Graduate and Extended Studies. The academic colleges are:

• The Adrian and Margaret Harmon College of Business and Professional Studies, which offers a school of business administration with programs in accounting, marketing and legal studies, public relations, economics, finance, computer information systems and management; and the School of Professional Studies, which has programs in aviation, criminal justice, communication disorders and social work and military science and leadership.

• The College of Arts, Humanities, and Social Sciences, which provides a comprehensive liberal arts foundation in support of the entire university curriculum, while also preparing graduates in areas such as art and design; communication, sociology, history and anthropology; government, international studies and languages; music, theatre and dance; and many other fields.

• The College of Education, which prepares teachers for all grade levels, as well as professionals in career and technology education, counselor education, educational leadership and human development and educational foundations and literacy.

• The College of Health, Science and Technology, with the School of Health and Human Performance; School of Environmental, Physical and Applied Sciences; School of Technology; Department of Mathematics and Computer Science; and Department of Psychological Science.

All UCM coursework is fully accredited by the North Central Association's Higher Learning Commission. UCM also is a state leader in program-specific accreditations, which have been granted by national organizations. This includes business administration degrees, which are accredited by the Association to Advance Collegiate Schools of Business (AACSB).

The main campus—with its instructional buildings, Elliott Student Union, 18 conveniently located residence halls and modern family housing—is the center of university life. However, the complete physical plant comprises more than 1,300 acres, including the Prussing Farm, the 300-acre Pertle Springs recreational and biological research area and Max B. Swisher Skyhaven Airport. Completed in 1999, the James C. Kirkpatrick Library is a leader in developing two-way interactive television, information technologies and Internet training facilities and providing access to electronic information resources to the state's citizens. New initiatives include the The Crossing-South at Holden, a new 325-bed housing-retail facility to be completed in 2015; recent renovation of the Morrow-Garrison buildings; construction of a new Student Recreation and Wellness Center; and a $36 million campus-wide

MARVIN (Bunky) WRIGHT
President
UCM Board of Governors

GUS WETZEL II
Vice President
UCM Board of Governors

MARY DANDURAND
Secretary
UCM Board of Governors

WELDON R. BRADY
Member
UCM Board of Governors

JOHN COLLIER
Member
UCM Board of Governors

WALTER R. HICKLIN
Member
UCM Board of Governors

MARY A. LONG
Member
UCM Board of Governors

DR. CHARLES AMBROSE
President
UCM

energy efficiency project completed in 2011. In fall 2012, UCM also launched in cooperation with the Lee's Summit R-VII School District, Metropolitan Community College and a number of business and community partners, the Missouri Innovation Campus (MIC), located at the school district's Summit Technology Academy. The school district is planning to build a new facility, housing the MIC by 2017 that will also include space for UCM's off-campus courses.

UCM students are valued members of the university family, and their successes—both in the classroom and in life—are the highest priority. Through its strategic positioning initiative known as learning to a greater degree, UCM promises students an education that promotes a culture of service, opportunities for engaged learning, future-focused academics and a worldly perspective.

Members, Board of Governors

Wright, Marvin (Bunky), (D), president, Columbia, Dec. 31, 2015;

Wetzel, Gus II, vice president, Clinton, Jan. 1, 2017;

Dandurand, Mary, (D), secretary, Warrensburg, Dec. 31, 2015;

Brady, Weldon R., (R), Warrensburg, Jan. 1, 2012;

Collier, John, (R), Weston, Jan. 1, 2019;

Hicklin, Walter R., (D), Gravois Mills, Jan. 1, 2013;

Long, Mary A., (D), Kansas City, Jan. 1, 2011;

Vacancy (1), student member.

Missouri's Public Four-Year Institutions

Institution	Location	Year Founded	Fall 2014 Enrollment	Highest Degree Offered
Four-year Institutions				
Harris–Stowe State University	St. Louis	1857	1,280	Baccalaureate
Lincoln University	Jefferson City	1866	3,205	Master's
Missouri Southern State University	Joplin	1965	5,613	Master's
Missouri State University	Springfield	1905	22,385	Doctorate
Missouri Western State University	St. Joseph	1915	5,863	Master's
Northwest Missouri State University	Maryville	1905	6,718	Master's
Southeast Missouri State University	Cape Girardeau	1873	12,039	Master's
Truman State University	Kirksville	1867	6,241	Master's
University of Central Missouri	Warrensburg	1871	13,379	Master's
University of Missouri System				
University of Missouri–Columbia	Columbia	1839	35,425	Doctorate
University of Missouri–Kansas City	Kansas City	1933	16,146	Doctorate
Missouri University of Science and Technology	Rolla	1870	7,644	Doctorate
University of Missouri–St. Louis	St. Louis	1963	17,072	Doctorate
Total enrollment, public four–year institutions			153,010	

Source: *Enhanced Missouri Student Achievement Study*

Missouri's Public Two-Year Colleges

Institution	Location	Year Founded	Fall 2014 Enrollment	Highest Degree Offered
Community colleges				
Crowder College	Neosho	1963	5,710	Associate
East Central College	Union	1968	3,606	Associate
Jefferson College	Hillsboro	1963	4,883	Associate
Metropolitan Community College	Kansas City	1915	18,202	Associate
Mineral Area College	Park Hills	1922	4,632	Associate
Missouri State University-West Plains	West Plains	1927	2,161	Associate
Moberly Area Community College	Moberly	1927	5,444	Associate
North Central Missouri College Ozarks	Trenton	1925	1,720	Associate
Technical Community College	Springfield	1990	14,393	Associate
St. Charles Community College	St. Peters	1986	7,153	Associate
St. Louis Community College	St. Louis City and County	1962	21,218	Associate
State Fair Community College	Sedalia	1966	4,981	Associate
Three Rivers Community College	Poplar Bluff	1966	4,201	Associate
Technical college				
State Technical College of Missouri	Linn	1996*	1,259	Associate
Total enrollment, public two–year colleges			99,563	

Source: *Enhanced Missouri Student Achievement Study*
State Technical College joined the state system of higher education in 1996.
Each public community college is governed by a locally elected board of trustees.
Funding for these colleges is provided by local district levies, student fees and state aid.

Department of Insurance, Financial Institutions & Professional Registration

Truman State Office Bldg., Rm. 530
PO Box 690, Jefferson City 65102
Telephone: (573) 751-4126 / FAX: (573) 751-1165
Insurance Consumer Hotline: (800) 726-7390
TT: (573) 526-4536
www.difp.mo.gov / www.insurance.mo.gov

The Department of Insurance, Financial Institutions and Professional Registration regulates the consumer service industries in Missouri by encouraging a fair and open market; establishing coherent and evolving policies that balance the interest of consumers, professionals and industry; and enforcing state laws and regulations governing business to protect consumers from unfair and inequitable treatment. The department is funded through fees and assessments from the industries and professionals regulated by the department rather than state general revenue.

Office of the Director

The director's office includes the department director, deputy director, general counsel, chief counsel, communications team, legislative coordinator and support team. The director's office also includes receivership activities. When a judge orders an insurance company into receivership, the director is responsible for either rehabilitating the company or liquidating it.

Division of Consumer Affairs

The Division of Consumer Affairs assists the general public in resolving complaints against insurance companies and agents and provides information to consumers regarding policies. Consumers can file complaints using the Insurance Consumer Hotline, (800) 726-7390, or visiting the department's website, *www.insurance. mo.gov*, which has a broad array of consumer and industry information available.

JOHN M. HUFF
Department Director

JAMES R. McADAMS
Deputy Director and
General Counsel

CHRIS CLINE
Director
Communications

RICH LAMB
Legislative Coordinator

KIM GERLT
Special Assistant to the Director

CARRIE COUCH
Director, Insurance
Consumer Affairs Division

In 2014, the division responded to 4,263 complaints and 9,290 inquiries and opened 756 investigations, recovering $11.7 million for consumers. The division accepts complaints for all types of insurance, as well as motor vehicle extended service contracts, public adjusters, bail bond agents and healthcare discount plans. Besides handling complaints, the division provides consumer outreach and educational resources throughout the state at various community events, including those following storms.

The division also investigates unlicensed insurance activities and reviews license applications referred from the Insurance Licensing Section. Department investigations may result in license denials, revocations or suspensions, cease and desist orders, injunctions and referrals for criminal prosecution.

Division of Insurance Company Regulation

The Division of Insurance Company Regulation monitors the financial condition of insurance companies operating in Missouri.

The division works to identify financially troubled companies so that action may be taken to prevent insolvencies. The division conducts financial examinations of 244 domestic insurance companies at least every five years. The department director can call for an examination of a licensed insurer at any time. Between onsite examinations, the financial condition of insurers is monitored through ongoing financial analysis. Besides traditional insurers, the division also licenses and regulates captive insurance companies, which are formalized self-insurance programs that provide risk management benefits for the owner, which is also the insured. Captive insurers paid $2 million in taxes and fees in 2014. The division is also tasked with the regulation of hundreds of insurance-related entities such as third party administrators, managing general agents, reinsurance intermediaries and surplus line insurers. Policies placed with surplus lines insurers in the non-admitted market are taxed at a rate of five percent of premium. Surplus lines tax collections for 2014 totaled $28.7 million.

Division of Insurance Market Regulation

The Division of Insurance Market Regulation protects Missouri consumers by examining insurance company practices for compliance with state law. Most insurance policies and rates must be filed with the division so they can be reviewed for compliance with state law.

Policies and rates are filed with two sections of the division: Life and Healthcare Section and Property and Casualty Section (which includes auto, homeowners, workers' compensation and various types of malpractice insurance).

The division's Market Conduct Section examines insurance companies' past treatment of policyholders through their marketing, rates and claims handling. If violations of the law are detected, the director can order an insurer to pay restitution to consumers, either through re-processing of claims or re-evaluation of the premium

JOHN REHAGEN
Director, Insurance Company
Regulation Division

LESLIE NEHRING
Chief Financial Examiner
Insurance Company Regulation
Division

ANGELA NELSON
Director, Insurance
Market Regulation Division

JIM MEALER
Chief Market Conduct Examiner

GRADY MARTIN
Director
Administration

BRENDA OTTO
Licensing Manager

charged for the policy, as well as penalties. In 2014, consumer recoveries totaled $12.7 million and fines totaled $1.4 million. The division also has a Statistics Section, which analyzes and publishes industry and market data as well as industry trends.

Division of Administration

The Division of Administration is responsible for the general operation and support within

DEBRA J. HARDMAN
Acting Commissioner
Division of Finance

DAVID A. DOERING
Chief Examiner
Division of Finance

CHRISTIE KINCANNON
Acting Deputy Commissioner
and Chief Counsel
Division of Finance

MICK CAMPBELL
Supervisor of Mortgage
Licensing, Division of Finance

the department. The division also includes the Licensing Section, which handles licensing and renewals of nearly 160,800 insurance producers (agents), bail bond agents, public adjusters, surplus lines, navigators, protable electronics, organizational credit business entity producers and motor vehicle extended service contract producers in Missouri.

Other services provided by the division include accounting, budget, grants management, human resources and information technology coordination.

Division of Finance

Truman State Office Bldg., Rm. 630
PO Box 716, Jefferson City 65102
Telephone: (573) 751-3242 / FAX: (573) 751-9192
www.finance.mo.gov

The Division of Finance regulates state-chartered banks, trust companies and savings and loan associations. The division is headed by the commissioner of finance, who is appointed by the governor with the advice and consent of the Senate.

The division has 26 administrative and clerical employees in the Jefferson City office and 88 field examiners in Kansas City, St. Louis, Jefferson City, Springfield and Sikeston.

The division is funded through assessments and fees paid by banks and licensees.

Banking in Missouri

Missouri ranks fifth in the nation in the number of state-chartered banks. As of June 30, 2015, the Division of Finance supervised 261 banks and trust companies with combined assets of $106.9 billion. The deposits in all Missouri state-chartered banks and trust companies are insured by the FDIC; savings and loan associations are also federally insured.

JOE CRIDER
Supervisor of Consumer Credit
Division of Finance

Savings and Loan Supervision

The Division of Savings and Loan Supervision, created in 1895, was merged into the Division of Finance in 1994, giving the division supervision of state-chartered savings and loan associations.

As of June 30, 2015, there were five savings and loan associations with total assets of $197 million.

Mortgage Licensing

The division has 434 licensed mortgage broker companies and 4,269 mortgage originators. The section investigates license applicants for character including criminal history, general fitness, experience and financial responsibility. A five-member Residential Mortgage Board approves regulations and hears appeals from the commissioner's licensing decisions.

Consumer Credit

The Consumer Credit Section supervises 2,871 institutions licensed for consumer lending, payday lending, automobile title lending, retail credit

GLEN (Brad) WILLIAMS
Chair, State Banking and Savings
and Loan Board

ROBERT M. ROBUCK
Secretary, State Banking and
Savings and Loan Board

MARK P. GORMAN
Member
Residential Mortgage Board

GEORGE B. LOPEZ
Member
Residential Mortgage Board

financing of motor vehicles and other goods and the financing of insurance premiums. The section also enforces the Sale of Checks Law, which provides for the licensing of companies that issue money orders or electronically transmitted funds. The section also licenses financial service organizations engaged in credit repair and coordinates enforcement of the Missouri residential real estate anti-discrimination (redlining) laws.

State Banking and Savings and Loan Board*

Williams, Glen (Brad), (D), chair, banker, Eminence, Aug. 29, 2009;
Robuck, Robert M., (D), secretary, banker, Jefferson City, Aug. 28, 2007;
Vacancies (3)

---

*$100 per diem.

Residential Mortgage Board*

Gorman, Mark P., (R), St. Louis, Oct. 10, 2011;
Lopez, George B., (D), Kansas City, Oct. 10, 2013;
Lucas, Gregory C., (R), St. Joseph, Oct. 10, 2010;
Smith, Richard L., (D), St. Louis, Oct. 10, 2009;
Vacancy (1).

---

*$100 per diem

Division of Credit Unions

Truman State Office Bldg., Rm. 720
PO Box 1607, Jefferson City 65102
Telephone: (573) 751-3419 / FAX: (573) 751-6834
www.cu.mo.gov

The Division of Credit Unions regulates and examines state-chartered credit unions for solvency to protect depositors. The division also responds to consumer inquiries and complaints about credit unions.

The division director is appointed by the governor with the advice and consent of the Senate.

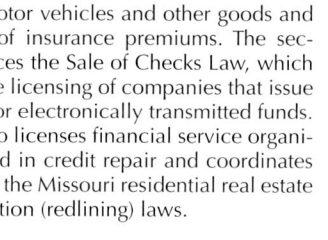

GREGORY C. LUCAS
Member
Residential Mortgage Board

RICHARD L. SMITH
Member
Residential Mortgage Board

A director, deputy director/general counsel, chief examiner, 10 examiners and three administrative personnel staff the division. Examiners are located in Kansas City, St. Louis and Jefferson City. The agency is funded through fees and assessments paid by state-chartered credit unions.

The National Credit Union Administration, an agency of the federal government, insures all member deposits.

As of Dec. 31, 2014, Missouri ranked eighth in the nation in the number of state-chartered credit unions. The Division of Credit Unions currently regulates 112 credit unions with assets of $11.9 billion. There are more than 1.3 million members of Missouri credit unions.

The Credit Union Commission hears appeals from decisions of the division director, approves regulations proposed by the director and advises the director on matters pertaining to the supervision of credit unions.

Credit Union Commission*

Hanneke, John C., (D), president, St. Louis, Jan. 1, 2015;

JOHN C. HANNEKE
President
Credit Union Commission

SUSAN VENABLE
Secretary
Credit Union Commission

HAL JAMES
Member
Credit Union Commission

PAT DANNER MEYER
Member
Credit Union Commission

RICHARD ORR
Member
Credit Union Commission

CATHY STROUD
Member
Credit Union Commission

LAURA VERHULST
Member
Credit Union Commission

KEN BONNOT
Director
Division of Credit Unions

JOE MARTIN
Deputy Director and
General Counsel
Division of Credit Unions

KEVIN WEAVER
Chief Examiner
Division of Credit Unions

KATHLEEN (Katie) STEELE DANNER
Director, Division of
Professional Registration

Venable, Susan, (D), secretary, Kansas City, Jan. 11, 2015;

James, Hal, (R), Columbia, Jan. 1, 2013;

Meyer, Pat Danner, (D), Kansas City, Jan. 1, 2021;

Orr, Richard, (D), Warrensburg, Jan. 1, 2017;

Stroud, Cathy, (R), Springfield, Jan. 1, 2013;

Verhulst, Laura, (R), Ballwin, Jan. 1, 2017.

---

*$100 per diem.

Division of Professional Registration

3605 Missouri Blvd., PO Box 1335
Jefferson City 65102
Telephone: (573) 751-0293 / FAX: (573) 751-0878
TT: (800) 735-2966 / Voice Relay: (800) 735-2466
www.pr.mo.gov
Email: profreg@pr.mo.gov

The Division of Professional Registration protects the public by licensing qualified professionals, enforcing standards of discipline and main-

BOB HELM, CPA
President
Missouri Board of Accountancy

RYAN COOK, CPA
Vice President
Missouri Board of Accountancy

JEANNE DEE, CPA
Secretary
Missouri Board of Accountancy

JAMES MINTERT, CPA
Treasurer
Missouri Board of Accountancy

SANDRA WEDEWER, CPA
Member
Missouri Board of Accountancy

TRAVIS FORD
Public Member
Missouri Board of Accountancy

JOHN SHEEHAN, CPA, J.D.
Public Member
Missouri Board of Accountancy

THOMAS DeGROODT, CPA
Executive Director
Missouri Board of Accountancy

taining an open communication network with more than 434,000 licensees in Missouri. The division director and members of the boards and commissions are appointed by the governor with the advice and consent of the Senate.

The division's 40 boards license 243 professions and are charged with safeguarding the public interest.

The division is funded by licenses, permits, registrations and other fees paid by individuals and entities regulated by the various boards and commissions.

Missouri State Board of Accountancy

3605 Missouri Blvd., PO Box 613
Jefferson City 65102-0613
Telephone: (573) 751-0012 / FAX: (573) 751-0890
TT: (800) 735-2966 / Voice Relay: (800) 735-2466
www.pr.mo.gov/accountancy
Email: mosba@pr.mo.gov

The Missouri State Board of Accountancy was created in 1909 to enforce Chapter 326, RSMo, and regulate individuals, sole proprietors, limited liability companies, partnerships and professional corporations engaged in the practice of public accounting.

Mission: The board regulates the practice of accounting to assure users of financial and economic data of an independent, objective and uniform product based on generally accepted accounting principles and auditing standards. It also ensures services are provided by competent and ethical practitioners. Certified public accountants (CPAs) receive this designation from the board.

Duties of board: Examine; license, regulate, investigate consumer complaints and discipline those subject to board supervision; investigate complaints about those practicing without a license.

Number of certificate holders, licensed professionals and entities (2015): 21,946.

Board composition: Seven members (serving five-year terms); six certified public accountants; and one public member.

Associations: National Association of State Boards of Accountancy; Federation of Associations of Regulatory Boards (FARB); Council on Licensure, Enforcement and Regulation (CLEAR).

Missouri State Board of Accountancy*

Helm, Bob, CPA, president, Springfield, July 1, 2016;

ROBERT N. HARTNETT, P.L.A.,
Board Chair
APEPLSPLA

JAMES C. REARDEN, A.I.A., CSI
Chair
Architectural Division

MICHAEL C. FREEMAN, P.L.S.
Chair, Professional Land
Surveying Division

KEVIN C. SKIBISKI, P.E., P.L.S.
Chair, Professional Engineering
Division

ROBERT S. SHOTTS, P.L.A., P.L.S.
Chair, Professional Landscape
Architectural Division

ABIODUN (Abe) ADEWALE, P.E.
Member, Professional
Engineering Division

KELLEY P. CRAMM, P.E.
Member, Professional
Engineering Division

NOEL T. FEHR, P.L.A.
Member, Professional Landscape
Architectural Division

Cook, Ryan, CPA, vice president, Clinton, July 1, 2015;

Dee, Jeanne, CPA, secretary, St. Louis, July 1, 2013;

Mintert, James, CPA, treasurer, St. Louis, July 1, 2016;

Wedewer, Sandra, CPA, member, St. Charles, July 1, 2018;

Ford, Travis, public member, Jefferson City, July 1, 2017;

Sheehan, John, CPA, J.D., public member, Jefferson City, July 1, 2017;

DeGroodt, Thomas, CPA, executive director.

---

*$70 per diem.

Missouri Board for Architects, Professional Engineers, Professional Land Surveyors and Professional Landscape Architects

3605 Missouri Blvd., PO Box 184, Jefferson City 65102
Telephone: (573) 751-0047 / FAX: (573) 751-8046
TT: (800) 735-2966 / Voice Relay: (800) 735-2466
www.pr.mo.gov/apelsla
Email: moapeplspla@pr.mo.gov

The Missouri Board for Architects, Professional Engineers, Professional Land Surveyors and Professional Landscape Architects (APEPLSPLA) was created in 1941 to enforce Chapter 327, RSMo, and regulate individuals practicing architecture, engineering, land surveying or landscape architecture and corporations rendering or offering architectural, engineering, land surveying or landscape architectural services.

Mission: Protect the health, safety and welfare of the citizens of Missouri against the danger of collapse of structures erected for public use; safeguard Missouri residents and their property from damages that might result from illegal and incompetent architectural, engineering, land surveying and landscape architectural practices.

Duties of board: License, regulate, investigate consumer complaints and discipline those subject to board supervision; investigate complaints about those practicing without a license.

Number of licensed professionals and entities (2015): 28,024.

Number of interns enrolled (2014): 30,054.

Board composition: 15 members (serving four-year terms): one public member, 14 members licensed under Missouri law, residents of Missouri for at least five years and actively en-

JOHN MICHAEL FLOWERS, P.L.S.
Member, Professional Land
Surveying Division

DANIEL L. GOVERO, P.L.S.
Member, Professional Land
Surveying Division

MARTHA K. JOHN, A.I.A.
Member
Architectural Division

CRAIG M. LUCAS, P.E.. CCM
Member, Professional Engineer-
ing Division

MICHAEL L. POPP, A.I.A., CSI
Member
Architectural Division

SHERRY L. COOPER
Public Member
APEPLSPLA Board

JUDY A. KEMPKER
Executive Director
APEPLSPLA Board

gaged in the practice of their profession for 10 consecutive years prior to appointment.

Associations: National Council of Architectural Registration Boards (NCARB); National Council of Examiners for Engineering and Surveying (NCEES); Council for Landscape Architectural Registration Boards (CLARB).

Missouri Board for Architects, Professional Engineers, Professional Land Surveyors and Professional Landscape Architects*

Hartnett, Robert N., P.L.A., board chair, Lee's Summit, Feb. 10, 2019.

Rearden, James C., A.I.A., CSI, division chair, Architectural Division, Barnhart, Sept. 30, 2013;

Freeman, Michael C., P.L.S., division chair, Professional Land Surveying Division, Hermitage, Sept. 28, 2010;

Skibiski, Kevin C., P.E., PLS, division chair, Professional Engineering Division, Ozark, Sept. 30, 2011;

Shotts, Robert S., P.L.A., P.L.S., division chair, Professional Landscape Architectural Division, Lebanon, Sept. 30, 2014;

Adewale, Abiodun (Abe), P.E., member, Professional Engineering Division, St. Louis, Sept. 30, 2013;

Cramm, Kelley P., P.E., member, Professional Engineering Division, Kansas City, Sept. 30, 2012;

Fehr, Noel T., P.L.A., member, Professional Landscape Architectural Division, University City, April 16, 2018;

Flowers, John Michael, P.L.S., member, Professional Land Surveying Division, Rolla, Sept. 30, 2012;

Govero, Daniel L., P.L.S., member, Professional Land Surveying Division, Festus, Sept. 30, 2013;

John, Martha K., A.I.A., member, Architectural Division, Columbia, Sept. 30, 2016;

Lucas, Craig M., P.E., CCM, member, Professional Engineering Division, St. Louis, May 31, 2016;

Popp, Michael L., A.I.A, CSI, member, Architectural Division, Kansas City, Sept. 30, 2015;

Cooper, Sherry L., public member, Chesterfield, Aug. 18, 2018;

Vacancy (1);

Kempker, Judy A., executive director.

---

*$75 per diem.

Office of Athlete Agents

3605 Missouri Blvd., PO Box 1335, Jefferson City 65102
Telephone: (573) 751-0243 / FAX: (573) 751-5649
TT: (800) 735-2966 / Voice Relay: (800) 735-2466
www.pr.mo.gov/athleteagents
Email: athleteagents@pr.mo.gov

The Office of Athlete Agents was created in 2004 to enforce sections 436.215–436.272, RSMo, and regulate athlete agents who enter into an agency contract with student athletes or directly or indirectly recruit or solicit student athletes to enter into agency contracts.

Mission: Protect the rights of and act in the best interest of student athletes who enter in to contracts with athlete agents.

Duties of office: License, regulate, investigate consumer complaints and discipline those subject to board supervision; investigate complaints about those practicing without a license.

Number of licensed professionals (2015): 83.

About the office: The office is staffed by an executive director and clerical staff. Rather than an oversight board or commission, the office is overseen by the director of professional registration.

Associations: Council on Licensure, Enforcement and Regulation (CLEAR).

Lueckenhoff, Timothy J., executive director.

Office of Athletics

3605 Missouri Blvd., PO Box 1335, Jefferson City 65102
Telephone: (573) 751-0243 / FAX: (573) 751-5649
TT: (800) 735-2966 / Voice Relay: (800) 735-2466
www.pr.mo.gov/athletics
Email: athletic@pr.mo.gov

The Office of Athletics was created to enforce Chapter 317, RSMo, and regulate promoters, contestants, matchmakers, managers, referees, judges, timekeepers, announcers, seconds and physicians. A permit is granted for each event allowing the contest to be held under the supervision of the Office of Athletics rules and regulations.

Mission: To protect the health and safety of participants in professional boxing, sparring, professional wrestling, professional kickboxing, professional mixed martial arts and professional full-contact karate contests.

Duties of office: License, regulate, investigate consumer complaints and discipline those subject to board supervision; investigate complaints about those practicing without a license or in violation of statutory and regulatory authority; collect permit and license fees and assesses a tax of 5 percent of the gross receipts on all contests.

TIMOTHY J. LUECKENHOFF
Executive Director, Office
of Athletic Agents, Office of
Atheltics

BRIAN McINTYRE, D.C.
President, Board of
Chiropractic Examiners

GARY CARVER, D.C.
Member, Board of
Chiropractic Examiners

MARGARET FREIHAUT, D.C.
Member, Board of
Chiropractic Examiners

JACK D. RUSHIN, D.C.
Member, Board of
Chiropractic Examiners

Office staff attends every professional boxing and professional mixed martial arts event to monitor and inspect weigh-ins, physicals and safety equipment such as gloves, rings and cages and ensure the venue meets requirements and the rules of the ring are followed. An inspector attends every professional wrestling match to ensure the event meets state requirements. The office has authority to suspend a contestant's license for 180 days as a medical precaution.

LOREE KESSLER, M.P.A.
Executive Director
Board of Chiropractic
Examiners, Acupuncturist
Advisory Committee

JANE L. VANSANT
Chair, Acupuncturist Advisory
Committee

KATHLEEN A. COLETON
Member, Acupuncturist Advisory
Committee

Number of licensed professionals (2015): 1,475.

Number of event permits issued (2014): 112.

About the office: The office is staffed by an executive director and a clerical staff. Rather than an oversight board or commission, the office is overseen by the director of professional registration.

Associations: Association of Boxing Commissions (ABC); Council on Licensure, Enforcement and Regulation (CLEAR).

Lueckenhoff, Timothy J., executive director.

State Board of Chiropractic Examiners

3605 Missouri Blvd., PO Box 672
Jefferson City 65102-0672
Telephone: (573) 751-2104 / FAX: (573) 751-0735
TT: (800) 735-2966 / Voice Relay: (800) 735-2466
www.pr.mo.gov/chiropractors
Email: chiropractic@pr.mo.gov

The State Board of Chiropractic Examiners was created in 1927 to enforce Chapter 331, RSMo, and regulate chiropractic physicians (chiropractors). The board also certifies qualified chiropractic physicians to perform meridian therapy, acupuncture or acupressure (MTAA) and certifies insurance consultants. As an insurance consultant, a chiropractic physician advises health insurance providers on issues pertaining to coverage of chiropractic treatment.

Duties of board: License, regulate, investigate consumer complaints and discipline those subject to licensure requirements; investigate complaints about those practicing without a license.

Associations: Federation of Chiropractic Licensing Boards (FCLB).

Number of licensed professionals (2015): 2,272.

Board composition: Six members (serving four-year terms): five licensed chiropractic physicians and one public member.

Advisory Committee assigned to the State Board of Chiropractic Examiners (responsible for advising the board on the regulation of this profession): Acupuncturist Advisory Committee (created 1998).

State Board of Chiropractic Examiners*

McIntyre, Brian, D.C., president, St. Louis, Feb. 5, 2017

Carver, Gary, D.C., member, Kansas City, March 14, 2012;

Freihaut, Margaret, D.C., member, Fenton, June 1, 2015;

Rushin, Jack D., D.C., member, Poplar Bluff, Jan. 1, 2007;

Vacancies (2);

Kessler, Loree, M.P.A., executive director.

---

*$50 per diem.

Acupuncturist Advisory Committee

3605 Missouri Blvd., PO Box 1335, Jefferson City 65102
Telephone: (573) 526-1555 / FAX: (573) 751-0735
TT: (800) 735-2966 / Voice Relay: (800) 735-2466
www.pr.mo.gov/acupuncturist
Email: acupuncture@pr.mo.gov

The Acupuncturist Advisory Committee was established in 1998 and adopts and revises rules, issues licenses, reviews all complaints and/or investigations and advises the State Board of Chiropractic Examiners on all matters pertaining to the licensing of acupuncturists.

The committee is composed of three acupuncturists, one chiropractic physician duly licensed by the Missouri State Board of Chiroprac-

WAYNE L. KINDLE
President, Board of Cosmetology
and Barber Examiners

JACKLYN J. CROW
Vice President, Board of
Cosmetology and Barber
Examiners

LINDA M. BRAMBLETT
Member, Board of
Cosmetology and Barber
Examiners

LEATA PRICE-LAND
Member, Board of Cosmetology
and Barber Examiners

tic Examiners and a member of the board and one public member.

Number of licensed professionals (2015): 139.

Acupuncturist Advisory Committee

VanSant, Jane L., chair/public member, Leeton, Dec. 10, 2007;

Coleton, Kathleen A., member, Lee's Summit, Dec. 10, 2010;

Hackler, Jason, member, St. Louis, Dec. 10, 2008;

Vacancies (2);

Kessler, Loree, M.P.A., executive director.

State Board of Cosmetology and Barber Examiners

3605 Missouri Blvd., PO Box 1062, Jefferson City 65102
Telephone: (866) 762-9432 or (573) 751-1053
FAX: (573) 751-8167
TT: (800) 735-2966 / Voice Relay: (800) 735-2466
www.pr.mo.gov/cosbar
Email: cosbar@pr.mo.gov

The State Board of Cosmetology and Barber Examiners was created in 2005, merging the State Board of Barber Examiners and the State Board of Cosmetology. The licensing of barbers and the barber board was created in 1899, the licensing of cosmetologists began in 1929 and the State Board of Cosmetology was created in 1956. The board enforces Chapters 328 and 329, RSMo, and regulates barbers, cosmetologists, manicurists, estheticians, instructors, salons, barbershops and cosmetology and barber schools.

Mission: Protect the public's health, safety and welfare by ensuring that only qualified persons are examined and licensed to practice barbering and cosmetology, as well as to strive to reduce the number of instances of incompetent, negligent, fraudulent or dishonest services provided by licensees. Also, conduct inspections of the establishments and schools.

CHRISTIE L. RODRIQUEZ
Member, Board of Cosmetology
and Barber Examiners

EMILY R. CARROLL
Executive Director, Board of
Cosmetology and Barber
Examiners

Duties of board: License, regulate, investigate consumer complaints and discipline those subject to board supervision; investigate complaints about those practicing without a license.

Number of licensed professionals and entities (2015): 82,169.

Board composition: 11 board members (serving five-year terms): four licensed cosmetologists (three with Class-CA licenses and one with any type of cosmetology classification), two cosmetology school owners, three licensed barbers and two public members.

Associations: National Interstate Council of State Boards of Cosmetology; National Association of Barber Boards of America.

State Board of Cosmetology and Barber Examiners*

Kindle, Wayne L., president, Kansas City, May 1, 2011;

Crow, Jacklyn J., vice president, Mexico, May 1, 2014;

Bramblett, Linda M., member, Hannibal, May 1, 2017;

MARK COMENSKY, Ph.D.
Member, Committee for
Professional Counselors

GREGG ROEBACK
Member, Committee for
Professional Counselors

RHONDA WOOD, Ph.D.
Member, Committee for
Professional Counselors

LOREE KESSLER, M.P.A.
Executive Director, Committee
for Professional Counselors

Nicholson, Joseph A., member, Linn Creek, May 1, 2012;

Price-Land, Leata, member, St. Louis, May 1, 2013;

Price, Leo D., member, St. Charles, May 1, 2018;

Rodriquez, Christie L., member, Nevada, May 1, 2016;

Bossert, Lori L., public member, Jefferson City, July 1, 2013;

Vacancies (3);

Carroll, Emily R., executive director.

———
*$70 per diem.

Committee for Professional Counselors

3605 Missouri Blvd., PO Box 1335, Jefferson City 65102
Telephone: (573) 751-0018 / FAX: (573) 526-0735
TT: (800) 735-2966 / Voice Relay: (800) 735-2466
www.pr.mo.gov/counselors
Email: profcounselor@pr.mo.gov

The Committee for Professional Counselors was created in 1985 to enforce portions of Chapter 337, RSMo, and regulate licensed professional counselors (LPCs).

Duties of committee: License, regulate, investigate consumer complaints and discipline those subject to licensure requirements; investigate complaints about those practicing without a license.

Number of licensed professionals (2015): 5,873.

Committee composition: Six members (serving four-year terms): five licensed professional counselors (LPCs) and one public member.

Associations: American Association of State Counseling Boards (AASCB); American Counseling Association (ACA); Missouri Mental Health Counselors Association (MMHCA).

Committee for Professional Counselors*

Pigg, Margaret (Margo), chair, Herculaneum, Aug. 23, 2011;

Comensky, Mark, Ph.D., member, Nevada, Aug. 28, 2001;

Roeback, Gregg, member, Washington, Aug. 28, 2011;

Staves, Regina, Ph.D., member, Kansas City, Aug. 28, 2016;

Wood, Rhonda, Ph.D., member, Jefferson City, Aug. 28, 2013;

Vacancy (1);

Kessler, Loree, M.P.A., executive director.

———
*$50 per diem.

Missouri Dental Board

3605 Missouri Blvd., PO Box 1367, Jefferson City 65102
Telephone: (573) 751-0040 / FAX: (573) 751-8216
TT: (800) 735-2966 / Voice Relay: (800) 735-2466
www.pr.mo.gov/dental
Email: dental@pr.mo.gov

The Missouri Dental Board was created in 1897 to enforce Chapter 332, RSMo, and regulate dentists, specialists and dental hygienists.

Duties of board: License, regulate, investigate consumer complaints and discipline those subject to board supervision; investigate complaints about those practicing without a license.

Number of licensed professionals (2015): 13,786.

Board composition: Seven members (serving five-year terms): five dentists, one public member and one dental hygiene member.

Advisory commissions within the Missouri Dental Board (responsible for advising the board on the regulation of these professions): Advisory Commission for Dental Hygienists (created 2001).

KEVIN D. WALLACE, D.M.D.
President
Missouri Dental Board

BRYAN CHAPMAN, D.M.D.
Secretary, Missouri Dental Board
Member, Dental Hygiene

ERIC AUBERT, D.M.D.
Member
Missouri Dental Board

NANCY S. MAUS
Member, Missouri Dental Board,
Dental Hygienists

RANDALL RELFORD
Public Member
Missouri Dental Board

BRIAN BARNETT
Executive Director
Missouri Dental Board

LORI A. BRUCE, R.D.H.
Member, Advisory Commission
for Dental Hygienists

Associations: American Association of Dental Examiners (AADE); Western Regional Examining Board; Central Regional Dental Testing Service Inc.

Missouri Dental Board*

Wallace, Kevin D., D.M.D., president, Rogersville, Oct. 16, 2010;

Chapman, Bryan, D.M.D., secretary, Farmington, Oct. 16, 2018;

Aubert, Eric, D.M.D., member, St. Louis, Oct. 16, 2011;

Maus, Nancy S., R.D.H., dental hygiene member, Republic, Jan. 10, 2019;

Relford, Randall, public member, Cameron, Oct. 16, 2012;

Vacancies (2);

Barnett, Brian, executive director.

———

*$50 per diem.

Advisory Commission for Dental Hygienists*

Bruce, Lori A., R.D.H., member, Jefferson City, March 22, 2017;

Frank, Ashton, R.D.H., member, Jefferson City, March 22, 2019;

Henderson, Marsha, R.D.H., member, Jefferson City, March 22, 2020;

Maus, Nancy S., R.D.H., member, Republic, Jan. 10, 2019;

O'Malley, Erika, R.D.H., member, Carthage, March 22, 2016;

Barnett, Brian, executive director.

———

*$50 per diem.

State Committee of Dietitians

3605 Missouri Blvd., PO Box 1335, Jefferson City 65102
Telephone: (573) 522-3438 / FAX: (573) 526-3489
TT: (800) 735-2966 / Voice Relay: (800) 735-2466
www.pr.mo.gov/dietitians
Email: diet@pr.mo.gov

The State Committee of Dietitians was created in 1998 to enforce portions of Chapter 324, RSMo, and regulate licensed dietitians (L.D.). Licensees must be registered dieticians (R.D.) with the American Dietetic Association.

Duties of committee: License, regulate, investigate consumer complaints and discipline those

JEAN HOWARD, R.D., L.D.
Chair
State Committee of Dietitians

TERRI POWELL, R.D., L.D.
Secretary
State Committee of Dietitians

LeGRETA HUDSON, R.D., L.D.
Member
State Committee of Dietitians

TOM REICHARD
Executive Director
State Committee of Dietitians

COLLIN FOLLIS
Chair, State Board of Embalmers
and Funeral Directors

JERALD DICKEY
Secretary, State Board of
Embalmers and Funeral Directors

GARY FRAKER
Member, State Board of
Embalmers and Funeral Directors

ERIC PITMAN
Member, State Board of
Embalmers and Funeral Directors

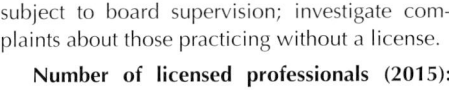

subject to board supervision; investigate complaints about those practicing without a license.

Number of licensed professionals (2015): 2,022.

Committee composition: Six members (serving four-year terms): five dietitians and one public member.

State Committee of Dietitians*

Howard, Jean, R.D., L.D., chair, Auxvasse, June 11, 2011;

Powell, Terri, R.D., L.D., secretary, St. Louis, June 11, 2007;

Brown, Mary Anne, Ph.D., R.D., L.D., member, Lee's Summit, June 11, 2018;

Brody, Nancy J., M.S., R.D., L.D., member, Chesterfield, June 11, 2018;

Hudson, LeGreta, R.D., L.D., member, Columbia, June 11, 2013;

Cartwright, Eric D., public member, Kingdom City, June 11, 2017;

Reichard, Tom, executive director.

*$50 per diem.

ARCHIE CAMDEN
Public Member, State Board of
Embalmers and Funeral Directors

SANDY SEBASTIAN
Executive Director, State Board of
Embalmers and Funeral Directors

State Board of Embalmers and Funeral Directors

3605 Missouri Blvd., PO Box 423, Jefferson City 65102
Telephone: (573) 751-0813 / FAX: (573) 751-1155
TT: (800) 735-2966 / Voice Relay: (800) 735-2466
www.pr.mo.gov/embalmers
Email: embalm@pr.mo.gov

The State Board of Embalmers and Funeral Directors was created in 1965 as an expansion of the board created in 1895 for embalmers only.

This board enforces Chapter 333 and portions of Chapter 436, RSMo, and regulates funeral directors, embalmers, funeral establishments (funeral homes) and the preneed funeral industry.

Mission: To ensure safety, hygiene and fair treatment of consumers in the disposition of the human body.

Duties of board: License, regulate, investigate consumer complaints and discipline those subject to board supervision; investigate complaints about those practicing without a license; conduct inspections of establishments and conduct financial examinations of preneed sellers.

Number of licensed professionals and entities (2015): 6,243.

Board composition: Six members (serving five-year terms): five licensed embalmers or funeral directors and one public member. No more than three members can belong to the same political party.

Associations: International Conference of Funeral Service Examining Boards (Conference); Federations of Associations of Regulatory Boards (FARB); National Funeral Directors Association (NFDA); Missouri Funeral Directors and Embalmers Association (MFDEA); Council on Licensure, Enforcement and Regulation (CLEAR).

State Board of Embalmers and Funeral Directors*

Follis, Collin, chair, Fredericktown, April 1, 2017;
Dickey, Jerald, secretary, Harrisonville, April 1, 2018;
Fraker, Gary, member, Marshfield, April 1, 2011;
McGhee, Kenneth, member, Florissant, April 1, 2019;
Pitman, Eric, member, Wentzville, April 1, 2015;
Camden, Archie, public member, Bonne Terre, Sept. 1, 2016;
Sebastian, Sandy, executive director.

———
*$50 per diem.

Office of Endowed Care Cemeteries

3605 Missouri Blvd., PO Box 1335, Jefferson City 65102
Telephone: (573) 751-0849 / FAX: (573) 526-3489
TT: (800) 735-2966 / Voice Relay: (800) 735-2466
www.pr.mo.gov/endowedcare
Email: endcare@pr.mo.gov

The Office of Endowed Care Cemeteries was created in 1990 to enforce portions of Chapter 214, RSMo, and regulate endowed care cemeteries with a trust fund set aside for maintenance, care and upkeep. Most cemeteries owned by nonprofit organizations (such as churches, governments, fraternal organizations, cemetery associations) are exempt from state regulation.

TOM REICHARD
Executive Director, Office of
Endowed Care Cemeteries

Mission: To ensure that trust funds of endowed care cemeteries are properly managed.

Duties of office: License, regulate, investigate consumer complaints and discipline those subject to regulation; audits cemetery trust funds. In addition to funding from registered cemeteries, the office is also funded by fees generated from the issuance of vital records, such as birth and death certificates.

Number of licensed cemeteries (2015): 129.

Composition of Endowed Care Cemetery Advisory Committee: Five members (serving four-year terms): Three registered endowed cemetery owners or managers and two public members. All members appointed by the director of professional registration.

Reichard, Tom, executive director.

Missouri Board of Geologist Registration

3605 Missouri Blvd., PO Box 1335, Jefferson City 65102
Telephone: (573) 526-7625 / FAX: (573) 526-0661
TT: (800) 735-2966 / Voice Relay: (800) 735-2466
www.pr.mo.gov/geologists
Email: geology@pr.mo.gov

The Missouri Board of Geologist Registration was created in 1994 to enforce Chapter 256,

RSMo, and regulate geologists and geologist registrants in training.

Duties of board: License, regulate, investigate consumer complaints and discipline those subject to board supervision; investigate complaints about those practicing without a license.

Number of licensed professionals (2015): 840.

Board composition: Eight members (serving three-year terms): Five practitioners, with four members representing different geologic specialties and the fifth practitioner employed by the state or a city or county; two public members;

JOHN SZTURO, R.G.
Chair, Missouri Board of
Geologist Registration

JOHN L. BOGNAR, R.G.
Vice Chair, Missouri Board of
Geologist Registration

KENNETH MARKWELL, R.G.
Member, Missouri Board of
Geologist Registration

GARY PENDERGRASS, R.G.
Member, Missouri Board of
Geologist Registration

JOSEPH GILLMAN, R.G.
Ex Officio, State Geologist
Missouri Geological Survey

JOSEPH GULINO, Ph.D.
Public Member, Missouri Board
of Geologist Registration

PAMELA GROOSE
Executive Director, Missouri
Board of Geologist Registration

and the state geologist (also appointed by the governor) who serves as an *ex officio* member.

Associations: Association of State Board of Geology (ASBOG); Council on Licensure, Enforcement and Regulation (CLEAR); Federation of Associations of Regulator Boards (FARB).

Missouri Board of Geologist Registration*

Szturo, John, R.G., chair, Independence, April 11, 2016;

Bognar, John L., R.G., vice chair, St. Louis, April 11, 2010;

Markwell, Kenneth, R.G., member, Jefferson City, April 11, 2014;

Pendergrass, Gary, R.G., member, Springfield, April 11, 2010;

Gillman, Joseph, R.G., ex officio, state geologist;

Gulino, Joseph, Ph.D., public member, Hartsburg, April 11, 2008;

Vacancies (2);

Groose, Pamela, executive director.

_____
*$50 per diem.

State Board of Registration for the Healing Arts

3605 Missouri Blvd., PO Box 4, Jefferson City 65102
Telephone: (573) 751-0098 / FAX: (573) 751-3166
TT: (800) 735-2966 / Voice Relay: (800) 735-2466
www.pr.mo.gov/healingarts
Email: healingarts@pr.mo.gov

The State Board of Registration for the Healing Arts was created in 1939 to enforce sections 334.002–334.749, RSMo, and regulate physicians, physician assistants, physical therapists, physical therapist assistants, speech-language pathologists, speech-language pathology aides, speech-language pathology assistants, audiologists (specialists in hearing disorders), audiology aides, athletic trainers, clinical perfusionists (defined as an individual who operates a heart-and-lung machine during surgery) and anesthesiologist assistants.

Duties of board: License, regulate, investigate consumer complaints and discipline those subject to board supervision; investigate complaints about those practicing without a license.

Number of licensed professionals (2015): 42,614.

BENJAMIN A. LAMPERT, M.D.
President, State Board of
Registration for the Healing Arts

JEFFREY D. CARTER, M.D.
Secretary, State Board of
Registration for the Healing Arts

JAMES A. DiRENNA, D.O.
Member, State Board of
Registration for the Healing Arts

BRADLEY FREEMAN, M.D.
Member, State Board of
Registration for the Healing Arts

JADE D. JAMES, M.D.
Member, State Board of
Registration for the Healing Arts

JOHN LYSKOWSKI, M.D.
Member, State Board of
Registration for the Healing Arts

DAVID A. POGGEMEIER, M.D.
Member, State Board of
Registration for the Healing Arts

DAVID E. TANNEHILL, D.D.
Member, State Board of
Registration for the Healing Arts

Board composition: Nine members (serving four-year terms): at least five doctors of medicine (M.D.), at least two doctors of osteopathy (D.O.) and one public member. Any time there is a vacancy on the board, Missouri law requires the president of the Missouri State Medical Association, for all medical physician appointments, or the president of the Missouri Association of Osteopathic Physicians and Surgeons, for all osteopathic physician appointments, to submit the names of five candidates to the director of professional registration.

Advisory commissions within the Board of Registration for the Healing Arts (responsible for advising the board on the regulation of these professions):

- Advisory Commission for Anesthesiologist Assistants (created 2003).
- Advisory Commission for Physical Therapists (created 1989).
- Athletic Trainers Advisory Committee (created 1983).
- Advisory Commission for Physician Assistants (created 1996).
- Advisory Commission for Speech-Language Pathologists and Audiologists (created 1986).

CONNIE CLARKSTON
Executive Director
State Board of Registration for
the Healing Arts

- Advisory Commission for Clinical Perfusionists (created 1997).

State Board of Registration for the Healing Arts*

Lampert, Benjamin A., M.D., president, Springfield, Sept. 3, 2012;
Carter, Jeffrey D., M.D., secretary, St. Louis, Sept. 3, 2010;

WILLIAM P. HOPFINGER, P.T., Chair, Advisory Commission for Physical Therapists

JUDITH PASTORINO, P.T.A. Secretary, Advisory Commission for Physical Therapists

TAMARA BURLIS, P.T. Member, Advisory Commission for Physical Therapists

JAMES DRONBERGER, D.P.T. Member, Advisory Commission for Physical Therapists

JOHN R. DONNELL, A.T.C. Chairman, Athletic Trainers Advisory Committee

KELLY L. QUINLIN, A.T.C. Member, Athletic Trainers Advisory Committee

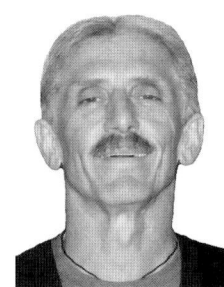

JOHN T. YETTER, M.D. Physician Member, Athletic Trainers Advisory Committee

JAMES B. KELLY, M.D. Chair, Advisory Commission for Anesthesiologists Assistants

MELANIE J. GUTHRIE, A.A. Member, Advisory Commission for Anesthesiologists Assistants

BENJAMIN LAMPERT, M.D. Member, Advisory Commission for Anesthesiologists Assistants

CHRISTOPHER YOUNG, M.D. Member, Advisory Commission for Anesthesiologists Assistants

THOMAS J. FRITZLEN JR. Public Member, Advisory Commission for Anesthesiologists Assistants

DiRenna, James A., D.O., member, St. Joseph, Sept. 3, 2012;

Freeman, Bradley, M.D., member, St. Louis, Sept. 3, 2011;

James, Jade D., M.D., member, Florissant, Sept. 3, 2016;

Lyskowski, John, M.D., member, Jefferson City, Sept. 3, 2015;

Poggemeier, David A., M.D., member, St. Charles, Sept. 3, 2010;

Tannehill, David E., D.O., member, Fenton, Sept. 3, 2014;

Vacancy (1);

Clarkston, Connie, executive director.

_____

*$50 per diem.

DEBORAH GALLEY, M.S.
Member, Advisory Commission
for Speech-Language Pathologists
and Clinical Audiologists

CHARLES HARE, M.S.
Member, Advisory Commission
for Speech-Language Pathologists
and Clinical Audiologists

ANDREW SCHUETTE, AUD.
Member, Advisory Commission
for Speech-Language Pathologists
and Clinical Audiologists

VALERIE HEMING
Public Member, Advisory
Commission for Speech-
Language Pathologists and
Clinical Audiologists

Advisory Commission for Physical Therapists*

Hopfinger, William P., P.T., chair, St. Louis, May 9, 2012;

Pastorino, Judith, P.T.A., secretary, Columbia, Oct. 1, 2010;

Burlis, Tamara, P.T., member, Chesterfield, Oct. 1, 2013;

Dronberger, James, D.P.T., member, Kansas City, Oct. 1, 2015;

Vacancy (1).

---

*$50 per diem.

Athletic Trainers Advisory Committee*

Donnell, John R., A.T.C., chairman, Lee's Summit, July 22, 2017;

Dempsey, Mark, A.T.C., member, Columbia, July 24, 2014;

Quinlin, Kelly L., A.T.C., member, Maryville, April 16, 2016;

Freeman, Ryan, public member, Jefferson City, Sept. 27, 2017;

Yetter, John T., M.D., physician member, Bridgeton, April 1, 2012.

---

*$50 per diem.

Advisory Commission for Anesthesiologists Assistants*

Kelly, James B., M.D., chair, Kansas City, July 1, 2008;

Guthrie, Melanie J., A.A., member, Kansas City, July 1, 2011;

Lampert, Benjamin, M.D., member, Springfield, July 1, 2012;

Young, Christopher, M.D., member, Ballwin, July 1, 2013;

STACEY L. KARNS, P.A.-C.
Chair, Advisory Commission for
Physicians Assistants

JAMES A. DiRENNA, D.O.
Member, Advisory Commission
for Physicians Assistants

Fritzlen, Thomas J. Jr., public member, Kansas City, July 1, 2008.

---

*$50 per diem.

Advisory Commission for Speech-Language Pathologists and Audiologists*

Jaffe, Russell, chair, Manchester, Dec. 4, 2014;

Kimble, Carlotta, secretary, Clinton, April 10, 2016;

Galley, Deborah, M.S., member, Warrensburg, Aug. 28, 2012;

Gilbert, Phon, PhD., member, Chesterfield, Sept. 7, 2017;

Hare, Charles, M.S., member, Independence, Oct. 21, 2014;

Martien, Brenda, M.S., member, Ozark, Sept. 7, 2017;

Schuette, Andrew, Aud., member, St. Louis, Oct. 22, 2017;

Heming, Valerie, public member, Warrensburg, April 14, 2013.

---

*$50 per diem.

MARY LOU HART, C.C.P.
Member, Advisory Commission
for Clinical Perfusionists

JEANNE R. RHOADES, C.C.P.
Member, Advisory Commission
for Clinical Perfusionists

MARGARET RUSSELL, C.C.P.
Member, Advisory Commission
for Clinical Perfusionists

RUSSEL E. DAYTON
Public Member, Advisory
Commission for Clinical
Perfusionists

LINDA ENGLEMANN
Chair, Board of Examiners for
Hearing Instrument Specialists

JANETTE CALL
Vice Chair, Board of Examiners
for Hearing Instrument Specialists

BRIAN VESELY
Member, Board of Examiners for
Hearing Instrument Specialists

SHARLENE RIMILLER
Public Member, Board of
Examiners for Hearing
Instrument Specialists

Advisory Commission for Physician Assistants*

Karns, Stacey L., P.A.-C., chair, New Hampton, June 1, 2017;

DiRenna, James A., D.O., member, St. Joseph, Sept. 3, 2012;

Gatto, David, public member, St. Louis, March 27, 2015;

Vacancies (2).

———

*$50 per diem.

DANA K. FENNEWALD
Executive Director, Board of
Examiners for Hearing
Instrument Specialists

Advisory Commission for Clinical Perfusionists*

Phillips, Michael, C.C.P., chair, Columbia, Feb. 13, 2011;

Hart, Mary Lou, C.C.P., member, Lake Lotawana, Feb. 13, 2008;

Rhoades, Jeanne R., C.C.P., member, St. Louis, Feb. 13, 2007;

Russell, Margaret, C.C.P., member, Kansas City, Feb. 13, 2009;

Steffen-Drake, Judith, C.C.P., member, Springfield, Feb. 13, 2005.

Dayton, Russell E., public member, Cameron, Feb. 13, 2009;

Vacancy (1).

———

*$50 per diem.

Board of Examiners for Hearing Instrument Specialists

3605 Missouri Blvd., PO Box 1335, Jefferson City 65102
Telephone: (573) 751-0240 / FAX: (573) 526-3856
TT: (800) 735-2966 / Voice Relay: (800) 735-2466
www.pr.mo.gov/hearing
Email: behis@pr.mo.gov

The Board of Examiners for Hearing Instrument Specialists was created in 1995 to enforce Chapter 346, RSMo, and regulate individuals selling and fitting hearing instruments (hearing aids).

Duties of board: License, regulate, investigate consumer complaints and discipline of those subject to board supervision; investigate complaints about those practicing without a license.

Number of licensed professionals (2015): 294.

Board composition: Eight members (serving four-year terms): five hearing-instrument specialists, one otolaryngologist (an ear, nose and throat (ENT) physician licensed by the Board of Healing Arts), one public member and one licensed audiologist holding a certificate of clinical competence.

Associations: Council on Licensure, Enforcement and Regulation (CLEAR).

Board of Examiners for Hearing Instrument Specialists*

Engelmann, Linda, chair, Liberty, Jan. 11, 2011;
Call, Janette, vice chair, Perryville, Jan. 11, 2013;
Vesely, Brian, member, Ozark, Jan. 11, 2016;
Rimiller, Sharlene, public member, Jefferson City, Jan. 1, 2012;
Vacancies (4);
Fennewald, Dana K., executive director.

---

*$50 per diem.

Interior Design Council

3605 Missouri Blvd., PO Box 1335, Jefferson City 65102
Telephone: (573) 522-4683 / FAX: (573) 526-3489
TT: (800) 635-2966 / Voice Relay: (800) 735-2466
www.pr.mo.gov/interior
Email: intdesn@pr.mo.gov

The Interior Design Council was created in 1998 to enforce portions of Chapter 324, RSMo, and regulate individuals using the title "Registered Interior Designer."

Duties of council: License, regulate, investigate consumer complaints and discipline those subject to board supervision; investigate complaints about those practicing without a license.

Number of licensed professionals (2015): 77.

Council composition: Five members (serving four-year terms): four interior designers and one public member.

DONALD R. ENGLAND
Chair
Interior Design Council

CYNTHIA CURNUTTE
Vice Chair
Interior Design Council

JEANINE BEQUETTE
Member
Interior Design Council

MICHAEL HODGES
Member
Interior Design Council

TOM REICHARD
Executive Director
Interior Design Council

Interior Design Council*

England, Donald R., chair, Columbia, April 6, 2009;
Curnutte, Cynthia, vice chair, Rocheport, April 6, 2016;
Bequette, Jeanine, member, St. Louis, April 6, 2002;
Hodges, Michael, member, St. Louis, April 6, 2016;
Vacancy (1);
Reichard, Tom, executive director.

---

*$50 per diem.

JOHN ADAMS
Chair
State Committee of Interpreters

KATHLEEN ALEXANDER
Secretary
State Committee of Interpreters

TIM ECK
Member
State Committee of Interpreters

CARRIE McCRAY
Member
State Committee of Interpreters

State Committee of Interpreters

3605 Missouri Blvd., PO Box 1335, Jefferson City 65102
Telephone: (573) 526-7787 / FAX: (573) 526-0661
TT: (800) 735-2966 / Voice Relay: (800) 735-2466
www.pr.mo.gov/interpreters
Email: interpreters@pr.mo.gov

The State Committee of Interpreters was created in 1994 to enforce portions of Chapter 209,
RSMo, and regulate sign language interpreters for
the deaf and hard of hearing. These professionals
provide services in courtrooms, hospitals, elementary and secondary schools as well as institutions of higher education and many other settings.

Duties of committee: License, regulate, investigate consumer complaints and discipline of
those subject to board supervision; investigate
complaints about those practicing without a license; serve as a liaison to the Missouri Commission for the Deaf and Hard of Hearing.

Number of licensed professionals (2015): 719.

Committee composition: Seven members
(serving four-year terms): Five interpreters and
two public members. One of the public members
must be hearing impaired.

Associations: Federation of Associations of
Regulatory Boards (FARB); Council on Licensure,
Enforcement and Regulation (CLEAR).

ANDREA SEGURA
Secretary
State Committee of Interpreters

LISA BETZLER
Public Member
State Committee of Interpreters

PAMELA GROOSE
Executive Director
State Committee of Interpreters

State Committee of Interpreters*

Adams, John, chair, St. Louis, Oct. 9, 2007;
Alexander, Kathleen, secretary, Rocheport, Oct.
9, 2008;
Eck, Tim, member, St. Louis, Oct. 30, 2007;
McCray, Carrie, member, Fulton, Oct. 9, 2009;
Segura, Andrea, member, Liberty, Oct. 9, 2010;
Betzler, Lisa, public member, St. Louis, Dec. 11, 2006;
Harris, Rochelle, public member, Kansas City,
Oct. 9, 2017;
Groose, Pamela, executive director.

*$50 per diem.

State Committee of Marital and Family Therapists

3605 Missouri Blvd., PO Box 1335, Jefferson City 65102
Telephone: (573) 751-0870 / FAX: (573) 526-0735
TT: (800) 735-2966 / Voice Relay: (800) 735-2466
www.pr.mo.gov/marital
Email: maritalfam@pr.mo.gov

The State Committee of Marital and Family
Therapists was created in 1995 to enforce portions of Chapter 337, RSMo, and regulate marital
and family therapists.

Duties of committee: License, regulate, investigate consumer complaints and discipline those subject to license requirements; investigate complaints about those practicing without a license.

Number of licensed professionals (2015): 283.

Committee composition: Six members (serving five-year terms): four marital and family therapists and two public members.

Associations: Association of Marital and Family Therapy Regulatory Boards (AMFTRB).

State Committee of Marital and Family Therapists*

Loney, Teresa, Psy.D., chair, Nevada, Jan. 26, 2005;
Estes, Robert, M.S., secretary, Carthage, Jan. 26, 2009;
Smith, Craig, Ph.D., member, Eureka, Jan. 26, 2016;
Michael, Sara, public member, Jefferson City, Jan. 26, 2014;
Modrell, Dianne, public member, St. Louis, Oct. 8, 2015;
Vacancy (1);
Kessler, Loree, M.P.A., executive director.

Board of Therapeutic Massage

3605 Missouri Blvd., PO Box 1335, Jefferson City 65102
Telephone: (573) 522-6277 / FAX: (573) 751-0735
TT: (800) 735-2966 / Voice Relay: (800) 735-2466
www.pr.mo.gov/massage
Email: massagether@pr.mo.gov

The Board of Therapeutic Massage was created in 1998 to enforce portions of Chapter 324, RSMo, and regulate individuals practicing massage therapy or operating a massage therapy business. Individuals must be licensed to use the terms "massage," "body work" or any of their synonyms on any sign or other form of advertising.

Duties of board: License, regulate, investigate consumer complaints and discipline those subject to license requirements; approve instructors of massage therapy schools/programs; investigate complaints about those practicing without a license; conduct inspections of the massage therapy businesses.

Number of licensed professionals and entities (2015): 6,317.

Board composition: Eight members (serving four-year terms): six massage therapists, one non-voting member from the massage education community and one public member.

Associations: Federation of State Massage Therapy Boards (FSMTB).

Board of Therapeutic Massage*

Brodecker, Renate, chair, Eldon, June 17, 2011;

TERESA LONEY, Psy.D.
Chair, State Committee
of Marital and Family Therapists

ROBERT ESTES, M.S.
Secretary, State Committee
of Marital and Family Therapists

SARA MICHAEL
Public Member, State Committee
of Marital and Family Therapists

LOREE KESSLER, M.P.A.
Executive Director
State Committee of Marital and
Family Therapists / Board of
Therapeutic Massage

JENNIFER MORGAN
Member
Board of Therapeutic Massage

BRANDY MOUSER
Member
Board of Therapeutic Massage

Morgan, Jennifer, member, Independence, June 17, 2018;
Mouser, Brandy, member, Dexter, June 17, 2017;
Nelson, Carl, member, St. Joseph, June 17, 2010;
Griffin, Jennifer, public member, Jefferson City, June 17, 2019;
Vacancies (3);
Kessler, Loree, M.P.A., executive director.

*$50 per diem.

RHONDA SHIMMENS, RN-C,
B.S.N., MBA
President
Missouri State Board of Nursing

LISA GREEN, Ph.D.(c), RN
Secretary
Missouri State Board of Nursing

ROXANNE McDANIEL, Ph.D., RN
Member
Missouri State Board of Nursing

LAURA NOREN, M.B.A., B.S.N.,
RN, NE-BC
Member
Missouri State Board of Nursing

MARIEA SNELL, D.N.P., M.S.N.,
RN, FNP-BC
Member
Missouri State Board of Nursing

ALYSON SPEED, LPN
Member
Missouri State Board of Nursing

ADRIENNE ANDERSON FLY, J.D.
Public Member
Missouri State Board of Nursing

LORI SCHEIDT, MBA-HCM
Executive Director
Missouri State Board of Nursing

Missouri State Board of Nursing

3605 Missouri Blvd., PO Box 656, Jefferson City 65102
Telephone: (573) 751-0681 / FAX: (573) 751-0075
TT: (800) 735-2966 / Voice Relay: (800) 735-2466
www.pr.mo.gov/nursing
Email: nursing@pr.mo.gov

The Missouri State Board of Nursing was created in 1909 to enforce Chapter 335, RSMo, and regulate registered nurses, licensed practical nurses and advanced practice registered nurses.

Duties of board: License, regulate, investigate consumer complaints and discipline those subject to board supervision; investigate complaints about those practicing without a license. The board also prescribes minimum standards for nursing education programs, provides surveys of nursing programs and accredits nursing programs.

Number of licensed professionals (2015): 130,379.

Board composition: Nine members (serving four-year terms): five registered professional nurses (RN), two licensed practical nurses (LPN), one other nurse and one public member.

Associations: National Council of State Boards of Nursing (NCSBN).

Missouri Board of Nursing*

Shimmens, Rhonda, RN-C., B.S.N., MBA, president, Jefferson City, June 1, 2016;

Green, Lisa A., Ph.D.(c), RN, secretary, St. Louis, June 1, 2016;

Heyen, Anne, D.N.P., RN, member, Ashland, June 1, 2018;

McDaniel, Roxanne, Ph.D., RN, member, Columbia, June 1, 2013;

Noren, Laura, M.B.A., B.S.N., RN, NE-BC, member, Columbia, June 1, 2016;

Snell, Mariea, D.N.P., M.S.N., B.S.N., RN, FNP-BC, member, St. Louis, June 1, 2017;

Speed, Alyson, LPN, member, Columbia, June 1, 2016;

Fly, Adrienne Anderson, J.D., public member, St. Louis, June 1, 2011;

Vacancy (1);

Scheidt, Lori, MBA-HCM, executive director.

_____
*$50 per diem.

PEGGY GETTEMEIER, O.T.A.
Member, Missouri Board of
Occupational Therapy

VANESSA BEAUCHAMP
Executive Director, Missouri
Board of Occupational Therapy

KURT FINKLANG, O.D.
President
State Board of Optometry

DONALD VANDERFELTZ, O.D.
Vice President
State Board of Optometry

Missouri Board of Occupational Therapy

3605 Missouri Blvd., PO Box 1335, Jefferson City 65102
Telephone: (573) 751-0877 / FAX: (573) 526-3489
TT: (800) 735-2966 / Voice Relay: (800) 735-2466
www.pr.mo.gov/octherapy
Email: ot@pr.mo.gov

The Missouri Board of Occupational Therapy was created in 1997 to enforce portions of Chapter 324, RSMo, and regulate individuals engaged in the practice of occupational therapy (occupational therapists, occupational therapy assistants).

Duties of board: License, regulate, investigate consumer complaints and discipline those subject to board supervision; investigate complaints about those practicing without a license.

Number of licensed professionals (2015): 5,167.

Board composition: Six members (serving three-year terms): three occupational therapists, one occupational therapy assistant and two public members.

Missouri Board of Occupational Therapy*

Allen, Stephanie, O.T., member, Jefferson City, Dec. 11, 2015;
Dallas, Jeanenne, O.T., member, Maplewood, Dec. 11, 2015;
Gettemeier, Peggy, O.T.A., member, Ferguson, Dec. 11, 2009;
Koch, Heather, O.T.R/L, member, Columbia, Dec. 11, 2016;
Gerdine, Michael, public member, St. Louis, Dec. 11, 2017;
Vacancy (1);
Beauchamp, Vanessa, executive director.

_____
*$50 per diem.

 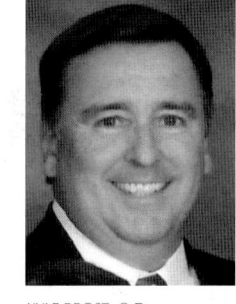

CARRIE T. HRUZA, O.D.
Secretary
State Board of Optometry

KYLE BROST, O.D.
Member
State Board of Optometry

JAMES E. BUREMAN, O.D.
Member
State Board of Optometry

BRIAN BARNETT
Executive Director
State Board of Optometry

State Board of Optometry

3605 Missouri Blvd., PO Box 1335, Jefferson City 65102
Telephone: (573) 751-0814 / FAX: (573) 751-8216
TT: (800) 735-2966 / Voice Relay: (800) 735-2466
www.pr.mo.gov/optometrists
Email: optometry@pr.mo.gov

The State Board of Optometry was created in 1921 to enforce Chapter 336, RSMo, and regulate optometrists.

Duties of board: License, regulate, investigate consumer complaints and discipline those subject to board supervision; investigate complaints about those practicing without a license.

Number of licensed professionals (2015): 1,304.

Board composition: Six members (serving five-year terms): five doctors of optometry and one public member.

Associations: Associations of Regulatory Boards of Optometry (ARBO).

State Board of Optometry*

Finklang, Kurt, O.D., president, Troy, June 30, 2012;
Vanderfeltz, Donald, O.D., vice president, California, June 20, 2013;
Hruza, Carrie T., O.D., secretary, St. Louis, June 30, 2014;
Brost, Kyle, O.D., member, Cape Girardeau, June 30, 2015;
Bureman, James E., O.D., member, Springfield, June 30, 2011;
Vacancy (1);
Barnett, Brian, executive director.

*$50 per diem.

Board of Pharmacy

3605 Missouri Blvd., PO Box 625, Jefferson City 65102
Telephone: (573) 751-0091 / FAX: (573) 526-3464
TT: (800) 735-2966 / Voice Relay: (800) 735-2466
www.pr.mo.gov/pharmacists
Email: missouriBOP@pr.mo.gov

The Board of Pharmacy was created in 1909 to enforce Chapter 338, RSMo, and regulate pharmacists, pharmacy interns, pharmacies, drug distributors and pharmacy technicians.

Duties of board: License, regulate, investigate consumer complaints and discipline those subject to board supervision; investigate complaints about those practicing without a license; conduct inspections of establishments.

Number of licensed professionals and entities (2015): 33,568.

Board composition: Seven members (serving five-year terms): six licensed pharmacists and one public member.

Associations: National Association of Boards of Pharmacy (NABP); Missouri Pharmacy Association (MPA); Council on Licensure, Enforcement and Regulation (CLEAR).

Board of Pharmacy*

Marshall, Pamela, R.Ph., vice president, St. Louis, Sept. 24, 2015;
Bilek, Barbara A., Pharm. D., member, St. Joseph, June 1, 2012;

PAMELA MARSHALL, R.Ph.
Vice President
Missouri Board of Pharmacy

CHRISTINA M. LINDSAY,
Pharm.D., Member, Missouri
Board of Pharmacy

BARBARA A. BILEK, Pharm.D.,
Member, Missouri Board of
Pharmacy

ANITA K. PARRAN
Public Member
Missouri Board of Pharmacy

KIMBERLY GRINSTON
Executive Director
Missouri Board of Pharmacy

Lang, Douglas, R.Ph., member, St. Louis, July 20, 2020;
Lindsay, Christina M., Pharm. D., member, Kansas City, Dec. 3, 2019;
Parran, Anita K., public member, Kansas City, April 27, 2010;
Tadrus, Christian, Pharm. D., R.Ph., member, Moberly, June 10, 2020;
Vacancy (1);
Grinston, Kimberly, executive director.

*$50 per diem.

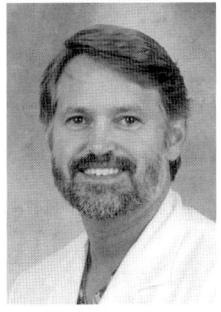   

TERRENCE G. KLAMET, D.P.M.
President, State Board of
Podiatric Medicine

HARRY JOHN VISSER, D.P.M.,
Vice President, State Board of
Podiatric Medicine

JEFFERY APPLEMAN, D.P.M.
Secretary, State Board of
Podiatric Medicine

KAREN POHLMAN HESS
Public Member, State Board of
Podiatric Medicine

State Board of Podiatric Medicine

3605 Missouri Blvd., PO Box 423, Jefferson City 65102
Telephone: (573) 751-0873 / FAX: (573) 751-1155
TT: (800) 735-2966 / Voice Relay: (800) 735-2466
www.pr.mo.gov/podiatrists
Email: podiatry@pr.mo.gov

The State Board of Podiatric Medicine was created in 1945 to enforce Chapter 330, RSMo, and regulate podiatrists.

Mission: To ensure safety, hygiene and fair treatment of consumers in the practice of podiatric medicine.

Duties of board: License, regulate, investigate consumer complaints and discipline those subject to board supervision; investigate complaints about those practicing without a license.

Number of licensed professionals (2015): 356.

Board composition: Five members (serving four-year terms): four licensed doctors of surgical podiatric medicine and one public member.

Associations: Federation of Podiatric Medical Examiners; Missouri Podiatric Medical Association; Federation of Associations of Regulatory Boards (FARB); Council on Licensure, Enforcement and Regulation (CLEAR).

State Board of Podiatric Medicine*

Klamet, Terrence G., D.P.M., president, Wildwood, July 1, 2017;
Visser, Harry John, D.P.M., vice president, Town and Country, July 1, 2016;
Appleman, Jeffery, D.P.M., secretary, Jackson, July 1, 2018;
Hess, Karen Pohlman, public member, Hartsburg, July 1, 2014;
Vacancy (1);
Sebastian, Sandy, executive director.

———
*$70 per diem.

SANDY SEBASTIAN
Executive Director, State Board
of Podiatric Medicine

State Board of Private Investigator and Private Fire Investigator Examiners

3605 Missouri Blvd., PO Box 1335, Jefferson City 65102
Telephone: (573) 522-7744 / FAX: (573) 526-0661
TT: (800) 735-2966 / Voice Relay: (800) 735-2466
www.pr.mo.gov/pi
Email: pi@pr.mo.gov

The Board of Private Investigator Examiners was created in 2007 to enforce portions of Chapter 324, RSMo, and regulate private investigators and private investigator agencies. In 2011 the regulation of private fire investigators was added.

Duties of board: License, regulate, investigate consumer complaints and discipline those subject to board supervision; investigate complaints about those practicing without a license.

Number of licensed professionals (2015): 917.

Board composition: Seven members (serving two-year terms): three licensed private investigators, two public members and two licensed private fire investigators.

Associations: International Association of Security & Investigative Regulators (IASIR); Coun-

DWIGHT McNEIL
Chair, Board of Private
Investigator Examiners

DOUGLAS MITCHELL
Vice Chair, Board of Private
Investigator Examiners

TIMOTHY FLORA
Member, Board of Private
Investigator Examiners

CHARLES GIESSING
Member, Board of Private
Investigator Examiners

KENNETH McGHEE
Public Member, Board of
Private Investigator Examiners

PAMELA GROOSE
Executive Director, Board of
Private Investigator Examiners

MARK SKRADE, Psy.D.
Chair
State Committee of Psychologists

PATRICK MALONEY, Ph.D.
Secretary
State Committee of Psychologists

MARIANN ATWELL, Psy.D.
Member
State Committee of Psychologists

SHARON LIGHTFOOT, Ph.D.
Member
State Committee of Psychologists

NANCY O'REILLY, Psy.D.
Member
State Committee of Psychologists

RENEE STUCKY, Ph.D.
Member
State Committee of Psychologists

cil on Licensure, Enforcement and Regulation (CLEAR); Federation of Associations of Regulatory Boards (FARB).

State Board of Private Investigator Examiners*

McNeil, Dwight, chair, Ozark, March 4, 2012;

Mitchell, Douglas, vice chair, Warrensburg, March 4, 2011;

Flora, Timothy, member, St. Louis, March 4, 2016;

Giessing, Charles, member, Farmington, Dec. 20, 2014;

McGhee, Kenneth, public member, Hazelwood, March 4, 2011;

Vacancies (2);

Groose, Pamela, executive director.

---

*$50 per diem.

JENNY FRISBEE, BCBA
Member, Behavior Analyst
Advisory Board

KAREN GREINER, BCBA
Member, Behavior Analyst
Advisory Board

TERESA RODGERS, Ph.D., BCBA
Member, Behavior Analyst
Advisory Board

MARK SKRADE, Psy.D.
Member, Behavior Analyst
Advisory Board

State Committee of Psychologists

3605 Missouri Blvd., PO Box 1335, Jefferson City 65102
Telephone: (573) 751-0099 / FAX: (573) 526-0661
TT: (800) 735-2966 / Voice Relay: (800) 735-2466
www.pr.mo.gov/psychologists
Email: scop@pr.mo.gov

The State Committee of Psychologists was created in 1977 to enforce portions of Chapter 337, RSMo, and regulate psychologists and provisional licensed psychologists.

Duties of committee: License, regulate, investigate consumer complaints and discipline those subject to board supervision; investigate complaints about those practicing without a license.

TODD STREFF, BCBA
Member, Behavior Analyst
Advisory Board

PAMELA GROOSE
Executive Director, State
Committee of Psychologists /
Behavior Analyst Advisory Board

Number of licensed professionals (2015): 2,154.

Committee composition: Eight members (serving five-year terms): seven psychologists and one public member.

Associations: Association of State and Provincial Psychology Boards (ASPPB); Federation of Associations of Regulatory Boards (FARB); Council on Licensure, Enforcement and Regulation (CLEAR).

Advisory board within the State Committee of Psychologists (responsible for advising the committee on the regulation of this profession):
Behavior Analyst Advisory Board (created 2010).

Number of licensed professionals (2015): 320.

State Committee of Psychologists*

Skrade, Mark, Psy.D., chair, Rogersville, Aug. 28, 2012;
Maloney, Patrick, Ph.D., secretary, St. Louis, Aug. 28, 2012;

Atwell, Mariann, Psy.D., member, Jefferson City, Aug. 24, 2018;
Lightfoot, Sharon, Ph.D., member, St. Louis, Aug. 28, 2013;
O'Reilly, Nancy, Psy.D., member, Rogersville, Aug. 28, 2011;
Stucky, Renee, Ph.D., member, Columbia, Aug. 28, 2017;
Vacancies (2);
Groose, Pamela, executive director.

*$50 per diem.

Behavior Analyst Advisory Board

3605 Missouri Blvd., PO Box 1335, Jefferson City 65102
Telephone: (573) 526-5804 / FAX: (573) 526-0661
TT: (800) 735-2966 / Voice Relay: (800) 735-2466
www.pr.mo.gov/ba.asp
Email: ba@pr.mo.gov

Behavior Analyst Advisory Board*

Frisbee, Jenny, BCBA, member, St. Louis, Jan. 4, 2019;
Greiner, Karen, BCBA, member, St. Louis, Jan. 4, 2014;

SHARON KEATING
Chair
Missouri Real Estate Commission

CHARLES MISKO
Vice Chair/Public Member
Missouri Real Estate Commission

CHARLES DAVIS
Member
Missouri Real Estate Commission

STEVE KENNY
Member
Missouri Real Estate Commission

ROSEMARY VITALE
Member
Missouri Real Estate Commission

JOSEPH DENKLER
Executive Director
Missouri Real Estate Commission

CASH GILL
Member, Missouri Real Estate
Appraisers Commission

BOYD HARRIS
Member, Missouri Real Estate
Appraisers Commission

DARRYL (Skip) KNOPF
Member, Missouri Real Estate
Appraisers Commission

JULIE MOLENDORP
Member, Missouri Real Estate
Appraisers Commission

ANN NUNN-JONES
Member, Missouri Real Estate
Appraisers Commission

VANESSA BEAUCHAMP
Executive Director, Missouri
Real Estate Appraisers Commission

Rodgers, Teresa, Ph.D., BCBA, member, Jefferson City, Jan. 4, 2015;

Skrade, Mark, Psy.D., professional psychology member, Rogersville, Aug. 28, 2012;

Streff, Todd, BCBA, member, Foristell, Jan. 4, 2015;

Vacancies (2).

**$50 per diem.

Missouri Real Estate Commission

3605 Missouri Blvd., PO Box 1339, Jefferson City 65102
Telephone: (573) 751-2628 / FAX: (573) 751-2777
TT: (800) 735-2966 / Voice Relay: (800) 735-2466
www.pr.mo.gov/realestate
Email: realestate@pr.mo.gov

The Missouri Real Estate Commission was created in 1941 to enforce portions of Chapter 339, RSMo, and regulate real estate brokers and salespeople.

FERNANDO McGREGOR, R.R.T.
Chair, Missouri Board for Respiratory Care

CINDY SEYER, R.R.T.
Secretary, Missouri Board for Respiratory Care

ROBERT CRAWFORD, R.R.T.
Member, Missouri Board for Respiratory Care

ROSEMARY HOGAN, R.R.T.
Member, Missouri Board for Respiratory Care

Duties of commission: License and regulate those subject to board supervision, investigate complaints regarding the activities of licensees, audit real estate brokers to verify proper conduct and investigate those practicing real estate without a license.

Number of licensed professionals (2015): 39,030.

Commission composition: Seven members (serving five-year terms): six with at least 10 years' experience as a real estate broker and one public member.

Missouri Real Estate Commission*

Keating, Sharon, chair, Jefferson City, Oct. 16, 2012;
Misko, Charles, vice chair/public member, Creve Coeur, Oct. 16, 2012;
Davis, Charles, member, Chesterfield, Oct. 16, 2010;
Gratz, William, member, Jefferson City, Oct. 16, 2015;
Huntsman, Judith, member, Springfield, Oct. 16, 2016;
Kenny, Steve, member, Neosho, Oct. 16, 2013;
Vitale, Rosemary, member, Kansas City, Oct. 16, 2010;
Denkler, Joseph, executive director.

_____

*$75 per diem.

Missouri Real Estate Appraisers Commission*

3605 Missouri Blvd., PO Box 1335, Jefferson City 65102
Telephone: (573) 751-0038 / FAX: (573) 526-3489
TT: (800) 735-2966 / Voice Relay: (800) 735-2466
www.pr.mo.gov/appraisers
Email: reacom@pr.mo.gov

The Missouri Real Estate Appraisers Commission was created in 1990 to enforce Sections 339.500–339.549, RSMo, and regulate real estate appraisers.

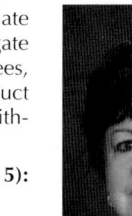

ARLENE HOGUE
Vice Chair / Public Member
Missouri Board for Respiratory Care

VANESSA BEAUCHAMP
Executive Director, Missouri Board for Repiratory Care

Duties of commission: License, regulate, investigate consumer complaints and discipline those subject to board supervision; investigate complaints about those practicing without a license.

Number of licensed professionals (2015): 2,600.

Commission composition: Seven members (serving three-year terms): six licensed appraisers and one public member.

Missouri Real Estate Appraisers Commission*

Gill, Cash, member, Dexter, Sept. 12, 2013;
Harris, Boyd, member, Centralia, Sept. 12, 2011;
Knopf, Darryl (Skip), member, St. Louis, Sept. 12, 2006;
Molendorp, Julie, member, Belton, Sept. 12, 2014;
Nunn-Jones, Ann, member, Jefferson City, Sept. 12, 2015;
Curls, Melba, public member, Kansas City, Sept. 12, 2017;
Vacancy (1);
Beauchamp, Vanessa, executive director.

_____

*$50 per diem.

JENISE COMER, LCSW
Chair, State Committee for
Social Workers

TERRI MARTY, ACSW, LCSW
Secretary, State Committee for
Social Workers

ELLEN BURKEMPER, Ph.D.,
LCSW, FT, RN
Member, State Committee for
Social Workers

KATHIE MILLER, M.S.W.,
LCSW, Member, State
Committee for Social Workers

LAURA NEAL, M.S.W., M.Ph.,
LCSW
Member, State Committee for
Social Workers

SHARON SORRELL, LCSW
Member, State Committee for
Social Workers

TOM REICHARD
Executive Director, State
Committee for Social Workers

Missouri Board for Respiratory Care

3605 Missouri Blvd., PO Box 1335, Jefferson City 65102
Telephone: (573) 522-5864 / FAX: (573) 526-3469
TT: (800) 735-2966 / Voice Relay: (800) 735-2466
www.pr.mo.gov/respiratorycare
Email: rcp@pr.mo.gov

The Missouri Board for Respiratory Care was created in 1989 to enforce Sections 334.800–334.930, RSMo, and regulate individuals engaged in the practice of respiratory care (respiratory therapists).

Duties of board: License, regulate, investigate consumer complaints and discipline those subject to board supervision; investigate complaints about those practicing without a license.

Number of licensed professionals (2015): 4,417.

Board composition: Seven members (serving three-year terms): four respiratory care practitioners, one physician, one hospital administrator and one public member.

Missouri Board for Respiratory Care*

McGregor, Fernando, R.R.T., chair, Independence, April 3, 2007;
Seyer, Cindy, R.R.T., member, Jackson, April 3, 2007;
Crawford, Robert, R.R.T., member, Hannibal, April 3, 2008;
Hogan, Rosemary, R.R.T., member, Columbia, April 3, 2006;
Hogue, Arlene, public member, St. Charles, April 3, 2010;
Vacancies (1);
Beauchamp, Vanessa, executive director.

---

*$50 per diem.

State Committee for Social Workers

3605 Missouri Blvd., PO Box 1335, Jefferson City 65102
Telephone: (573) 751-0885 / FAX: (573) 526-3489
TT: (800) 735-2966 / Voice Relay: (800) 735-2466
www.pr.mo.gov/socialworkers
Email: lcsw@pr.mo.gov

The State Committee for Social Workers was created in 1990 to enforce portions of Chapter 337, RSMo, and regulate licensed clinical social

VANESSA BEAUCHAMP
Executive Director
Office of Tattooing, Body
Piercing and Branding

DAVID GOURLEY, D.V.M.
Chair, Missouri Veterinary
Medical Board

CAROL RYAN, D.V.M.
Vice Chair, Missouri Veterinary
Medical Board

MICHAEL PFANDER, D.V.M.
Member, Missouri Veterinary
Medical Board

VINCIL M. WILT, D.V.M
Member, Missouri
Veterinary Medical Board

CHRISTOPHER ROHLFING
Public Member, Missouri
Veterinary Medical Board

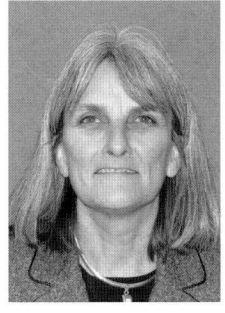

LINDA HICKMAN-FOUNTAIN,
D.V.M., *Ex officio* Member
Missouri Veterinary Medical
Board

DANA FENNEWALD
Executive Director, Missouri
Veterinary Medical Board

workers, licensed master social workers, licensed advanced macro social workers and licensed baccalaureate social workers.

Duties of committee: License, regulate, investigate consumer complaints and discipline those subject to board supervision; investigate complaints about those practicing without a license.

Number of licensed professionals (2015): 7,740.

Committee composition: Ten members (serving four-year terms): six licensed clinical social workers, one licensed master social worker, one licensed baccalaureate social worker, one licensed advanced macro social worker and one public member. Any time there is a vacancy on the board, Missouri law requires the president of the National Association of Social Workers, Missouri chapter, to submit the names of five candidates to the director of professional registration.

State Committee for Social Workers*

Comer, Jenise, LCSW, chair, Kansas City, Oct. 23, 2007;

Marty, Terri, LCSW, secretary, Fulton, Oct. 28, 2016;

Burkemper, Ellen, Ph.D., LCSW, FT, RN, member, Troy, Oct. 23, 2014;

Miller, Kathie, M.S.W., LCSW, member, Dexter, Oct. 23, 2016;

Neal, Laura, M.S.W., M.Ph., LCSW, member, Columbia, Oct. 23, 2009;

Sorrell, Sharon, LCSW, member, Poplar Bluff, Oct. 23, 2015;

Vacancies (4);

Reichard, Tom, executive director.

---

*$70 per diem.

Office of Tattooing, Body Piercing and Branding

3605 Missouri Blvd., PO Box 1335, Jefferson City 65102
Telephone: (573) 526-8288 / FAX: (573) 526-3489
TT: (800) 735-2966 / Voice Relay: (800) 735-2466
www.pr.mo.gov/tattooing
Email: tattoo@pr.mo.gov

The Office of Tattooing, Body Piercing and Branding was created in 1998 to enforce Sections 324.520–324.526, RSMo, and regulate tattooists, body piercers and branders and their establishments.

Mission: Ensure hygienic, safe and sanitary conditions are used by these professionals and their establishments.

Duties of office: License, regulate, investigate consumer complaints and discipline those subject to board supervision; investigate complaints about those practicing without a license; conduct inspections of establishments.

Number of licensed professionals and entities (2015): 1,632.

About the office: The office is staffed by an executive director and licensing technician. Rather than an oversight board or commission, the office is overseen by the director of professional registration.

Beauchamp, Vanessa, executive director.

Missouri Veterinary Medical Board

3605 Missouri Blvd., PO Box 633, Jefferson City 65102
Telephone: (573) 751-0031 / FAX: (573) 526-3856
TT: (800) 735-2966 / Voice Relay: (800) 735-2466
www.pr.mo.gov/veterinarian
Email: vets@pr.mo.gov

The Missouri Veterinary Medical Board was created in 1904 to enforce Chapter 340, RSMo, and regulate doctors of veterinary medicine and veterinary technicians.

Duties of board: License, regulate, investigate consumer complaints and discipline those subject to board supervision; investigate complaints about those practicing without a license.

Number of licensed professionals (2015): 5,287.

Board composition: Six members (serving four-year terms): five licensed veterinarians, one of whom is the state veterinarian (an employee of the Missouri Department of Agriculture), who serves as an *ex officio* member of the board, and one public member. No more than three members of the board may belong to the same political party.

Associations: American Association of Veterinary State Boards; Federation of Associations of Regulatory Boards (FARB); Council on Licensure, Enforcement and Regulation (CLEAR).

Missouri Veterinary Medical Board*

Gourley, David, D.V.M., chair, Mountain Grove, Aug. 29, 2014;

Ryan, Carol, D.V.M., vice chair, Troy, Aug. 29, 2009;

Pfander, Michael, D.V.M., member, Springfield, Aug. 29, 2012;

Wilt, Vincil, M., D.V.M., member, Paris, Aug. 29, 2014;

Rohlfing, Christopher, public member, Columbia, April 29, 2017;

Hickam-Fountain, Linda, D.V.M., *ex officio* member, Thompson, Aug. 29, 2010;

Fennewald, Dana, executive director.

---

*$50 per diem.

Department of Labor & Industrial Relations

421 E. Dunklin St., PO Box 504
Jefferson City 65102-0504
Telephone: (573) 751-4091 / FAX: (573) 751-4135
www.labor.mo.gov

JOHN J. LARSEN JR.
Chair, Labor and Industrial
Relations Commission

JAMES AVERY JR.
Commissioner, Labor and
Industrial Relations Commission

The Missouri Department of Labor and Industrial Relations was created by Article IX section 49 of the Missouri Constitution. The department is composed of the Labor and Industrial Relations Commission and five divisions: the Division of Employment Security adjudicates unemployment claims benefits to employees who become unemployed through no fault of their own; the Division of Workers' Compensation ensures that workers injured on the job receive the benefits they deserve and investigates allegations of workers' compensation fraud and noncompliance; the State Board of Mediation determines the appropriate bargaining unit for public employees and regulates utility labor relations; the Division of Labor Standards regulates wages and wage rates and promotes safe working environments; and the Missouri Human Rights Commission enforces and adjudicates Missouri's anti-discriminatory, fair housing, employment and public accommodation statutes.

CURTIS E. CHICK JR.
Commissioner, Labor and
Industrial Relations Commission

PAMELA M. HOFMANN
Secretary, Labor and Industrial
Relations Commission

Labor and Industrial Relations Commission

3315 W. Truman Blvd., PO Box 599
Jefferson City 65102-0599
Telephone: (573) 751-2461 / FAX: (573) 751-7806
www.labor.mo.gov/lirc
Email: lirc@labor.mo.gov

The Labor and Industrial Relations Commission is composed of three commissioners. Each commissioner is appointed to a staggered six-year term by the governor with the advice and consent of the Senate. One member of the commission, a licensed Missouri attorney, represents the public. The other two members represent employers and employees, respectively. The governor designates one member as chair. The commission hears appeals from administrative decisions in workers' compensation, unemployment compensation, crime victims' compensation and tort victims' compensation cases. The commission also hears objections to prevailing wage disputes and challenges to determinations by public bodies to enter into project labor agreements. In addition, the commission is charged with the statutory authority to approve or disapprove all rules or regulations declared by the divisions within the department. The Labor and Industrial Relations Commission nominates, and the governor appoints, a director to be chief executive officer of the department with the advice and consent of the Senate.

Commissioners

Larsen, John J. Jr., (D), chair;
Chick, Curtis E. Jr., (D), employee representative, July 27, 2014;
Avery, James Jr., (R), employer representative, July 27, 2016.

Office of the Director

The director of the Department of Labor and Industrial Relations is responsible for the supervision of the divisions. The director's office staff provides administrative support, human resource services and financial management.

Office of the General Counsel

The Office of General Counsel provides legal advice regarding the operations of the department and labor-related matters to the director and to the executive staff of the department and its divisions. The largest portion of the work of the General Counsel's Office relates to cases concerning the payment of unemployment benefits and the assessment and collection of unemployment taxes. The General Counsel's Office also represents the department in a variety of other litigation in trial courts, in administrative tribunals and before arbitrators; provides advice on internal administrative and personnel matters; prepares and reviews contracts, leases and other legal documents; responds to requests under the open records law; provides training to departmental personnel; and assists in responding to comments and inquiries from private citizens and public officials.

Division of Employment Security

421 E. Dunklin St., PO Box 59
Jefferson City 65104-0059
Telephone: (573) 751-3215 / FAX: (573) 751-4945
www.labor.mo.gov/des

The Division of Employment Security (DES) was established in 1946 to administer the Missouri Unemployment Compensation Law. The division collects tax contributions from employers and pays unemployment benefits to individuals who are determined eligible under the law. State unemployment contributions paid by Missouri employers into the Missouri Trust Fund are set aside for the sole purpose of providing for the payment of weekly unemployment benefits to qualified claimants. The division consists of six sections: benefits, unemployment insurance tax, unemployment insurance programs, appeals, quality control and unemployment insurance modernization.

Unemployment Insurance

The unemployment benefits paid to insured workers help maintain the economy of the state during periods of economic downturn by helping preserve the level of consumer purchasing power. Payments of benefits under the regular program are made from a trust fund, financed by the aforementioned employer tax contributions. No part of the contribution is deducted from worker wages. Eligible claimants can qualify for up to 20 weeks of unemployment compensation under the state's benefit program. The average weekly wage for FY 2015 was $842.93. The average weekly benefit amount in FY 2015 was $245.49, and the maximum benefit amount of $320.

RYAN MCKENNA
Department Director

KEN JACOB
Department Deputy Director

TAMMY CAVENDER
Director of Administration

CHASTITY YOUNG
Director of Legislative and
Public Affairs

LAUREN SCHAD
Director of Communications

MICHAEL PRITCHETT
General Counsel

Employer Contributions

The division's Contributions Section ensures employers are properly classifying their workers, reporting their workers' wages and paying the correct tax contributions on wages. Correct reporting helps ensure the prompt payment of unemployment benefits to insured workers during periods of unemployment. Employment security law includes an experience rating provision as an incentive for employers to maintain stable employment, review claims and reduce unemployment. The law allows employers that are eligible for rate calculations to submit voluntary payments for the purpose of reducing their contribution rates. Employers file quarterly contribution and wage reports with the division to report their workers' earnings. Reports may be filed online at *www.ustar.labor.mo.gov*.

Payment of Benefits

One of the main objectives of the division is the prompt payment of unemployment benefits to eligible claimants. Through four claims centers located in Jefferson City, St. Louis, Kansas City and Springfield, unemployed Missouri workers file initial and weekly claims for unemployment compensation by telephone. The division also offers filing of unemployment claims online at *www.moclaim.mo.gov*. A person must have worked in employment covered under the Missouri Employment Security Law and earned enough qualifying wages in order to establish a claim for unemployment benefits. Detailed wage records are kept on every worker reported by employers on the quarterly contribution and wage report in order to calculate benefits.

Fraud Efforts

The division continues its efforts to combat fraud by identifying worker misclassification, an act where employers improperly classify their employees to avoid paying employment taxes. The division's worker misclassification taskforce focuses resources to target industries likely to violate worker classification laws. In 2015, 7,276 misclassified workers were identified, associated with more than $1.8 million in unpaid unemployment taxes.

Through numerous cross-match systems, including the federal and state new-hire databases, the division also identifies claimants committing unemployment fraud. During FY 2015, the DES recovered $19.1 million of improperly paid benfits and more than $5.2 million in fraud penalties.

Division of Workers' Compensation

3315 W. Truman Blvd., PO Box 58
Jefferson City 65102-0058
Telephone: (573) 751-4231 / FAX: (573) 751-2012
Toll free: (800) 775-2667
Toll free: (800) 592-6003 (Report Fraud & Noncompliance)
www.labor.mo.gov/dwc
Email: workerscomp@labor.mo.gov

The Missouri Division of Workers' Compensation administers the programs that provide for Missouri workers who are injured on the job or develop occupational diseases. The division focuses on making sure that those who can return to work do so as soon as possible, having re-

JOHN HICKEY
Director, Division of
Workers' Compensatation

ceived adequate treatment and benefits. For those who cannot return to work because of their injury or injuries, permanent disability benefits are allowed by Missouri law.

Missouri employers are required to either obtain workers' compensation insurance or obtain approval from the division to self-insure their workers' compensation liability, paying claims out-of-pocket as they arise. Self-insured employers must provide a bond or letter of credit to the division to secure their promise to compensate employees' for their work-related injuries.

Benefits available through the workers' compensation system include medical treatment, temporary disability benefits while in treatment and permanent disability benefits when treatment is complete. Injured workers can also qualify for benefits from the Second Injury Fund, which was created by the General Assembly during World War II to ease the workers' compensation burden on employers by compensating for employees' preexisting injuries.

Most workers' compensation cases are resolved without lengthy proceedings, as was the intent of the workers' compensation system approved by Missouri voters in 1926. For those cases not resolved voluntarily, the division's administrative law judges conduct hearings and make determinations on what, if any, benefits are owed the injured worker. If a worker or employer disagrees with the administrative law judge's ruling, an appeal may be made with the Labor and Industrial Relations Commission.

The division's Fraud and Noncompliance Unit conducts investigations of all allegations of fraud and noncompliance. Fraud occurs when employers, insurance carriers, physicians, attorneys or employees claim or deny benefits based on assertions they know to be false. Fraudulently making or denying a workers' compensation claim is a criminal offense. Additionally, employers that do not insure their workers' compensation liability as required by law are committing the criminal offense of noncompliance.

All insurance carriers writing workers' compensation insurance in Missouri must provide comprehensive safety engineering and management services to employers. The Workers's Safety Program certifies and audits these services, investigates complaints of inadequate loss control services, monitors the impact of those services on Missouri employers and offers additional safety assistance when needed. The Workers' Safety Program maintains a registry of certified safety consultants and engineers who can offer independent safety services to Missouri employers.

BUTCH ALBERT
Chair
State Board of Mediation

State Board of Mediation

3315 W. Truman Blvd., Ste. 211, PO Box 2071
Jefferson City 65102-2071
Telephone: (573) 751-3614 / FAX: (573) 751-0083
www.labor.mo.gov/sbm
Email: sbm@labor.mo.gov

The State Board of Mediation is a quasi-judicial board created by the General Assembly in 1947 to assist in the resolution of labor disputes in the public utility industry. The Board's primary activity, however, changed in 1965 with the passage of the Public Sector Labor Law, sections 105.500 to 105.530 of the Missouri Revised Statutes. This law authorizes the board to determine appropriate bargaining units of public employees based on their community of interests and to conduct secret ballot elections to determine whether a majority of the employees in a bargaining unit agree to be represented by a petitioning labor organization.

The board consists of five members appointed by the governor. Two members are employers or selected from an association representing employers, two members hold membership in a *bona fide* trade or labor union and the fifth member is a neutral party who serves as full-time chairman and administrator of the agency.

If a public employer and a petitioning labor organization cannot agree on which employees should be included in an appropriate bargaining unit or on the manner of conducting the election, the board will hold a formal hearing at which the parties may present evidence and legal arguments in support of their positions on the disputed questions. After considering the evidence and legal arguments, the board issues a written decision resolving the disputes.

If a majority of the members of a bargaining unit vote for the labor organization in a board-conducted election, the board certifies it as the exclusive bargaining representative for all the unit members for the purposes of collective bargaining. The labor organization will then negotiate with the public employer of the unit members

over salaries and other conditions of employment with the goal of reaching a written agreement governing these matters. The labor organization will also represent unit members with regard to individual employment issues that may arise, such as disciplinary charges.

The board's jurisdiction under the Public Sector Labor Law to determine appropriate bargaining units and to certify exclusive bargaining representatives extends to almost all public employees, including those employed by the state and its agencies, counties, cities, school districts, fire departments and other special districts. The board, however, does not have jurisdiction to resolve such matters for police officers, deputy sheriffs, Missouri Highway Patrol officers, Missouri National Guard members or teachers at schools, colleges and universities. These types of employees still have the right to organize and bargain collectively, but the board has no authority to play a role when they are engaged in such activities.

In FY 2015, the board received 33 petitions and conducted 17 representation elections, affecting 833 employees.

Division of Labor Standards

3315 W. Truman Blvd., PO Box 449
Jefferson City 65102-0449
Telephone: (573) 751-3403 / FAX: (573) 751-3721
www.labor.mo.gov/dls
Email: laborstandards@labor.mo.gov

The Division of Labor Standards currently consists of three sections: Wage and Hour, On-Site Safety and Health Consultation Service, and Mine and Cave Safety.

Wage and Hour Section

The Wage and Hour Section determines and enforces the prevailing wage. Prevailing wage survey information for construction projects is solicited for all applicable construction projects on an ongoing basis. The survey information is used to determine the prevailing wage rates for workers employed on public works construction projects. Communication with contractors, labor unions, public bodies, employees and other interested parties occurs daily to assist in achieving voluntary compliance. Site inspections are performed to assure compliance with prevailing wage rates and to investigate complaints. The prevailing wage not only ensures that in tough economic times wages do not decline, but also supports worker health and pension benefits, increases sales tax revenue and corporate sales taxes, supports apprenticeship training, lowers occupational injuries, and increases the productivity of the construction workforce.

The Wage and Hour Section administers and enforces Missouri's child labor laws. The law ensures that no child younger than 16 years of age is employed in an occupation that is detrimental to the child's safety, health, morals, educational processes or general well-being. No child under the age of 14 may work in any occupation, unless specifically allowed. The exception is entertainment industry employment. The law restricts work hours for youth under 16. A child 14 or 15 years old may not be employed during the regular school term unless the public school superintendent or designee of the district where the youth lives has issued a work certificate. Youth under 16 may work in the entertainment industry if the division issues the youth a work permit.

The Wage and Hour Section is also responsible for the administration and enforcement of Missouri's minimum wage law. The minimum wage rate increased from $7.50 to $7.65 per hour on Jan. 1, 2015.

The Wage and Hour Section provides information for Missouri's labor laws, including allowable breaks, lunches, vacations, hiring, wage levels, dismissals and discipline, among other topics.

On-Site Safety and Health Section

The On-Site Safety and Health Section offers a free, confidential consultation service to employers to ensure they comply with federal Occupational Safety and Health Administration (OSHA) regulations. This program reduces workplace injuries and illnesses. At the employer's request, a consultant visits the workplace and informs the employer of problems found and recommends solutions to eliminate hazards and provides safety and health training. In FY 2015, the On-Site Program helped employers avoid more than $10.8 million in OSHA fines by eliminating hazards within the workplace.

The Safety and Health Achievement Recognition Program (SHARP) is for small businesses that

JOHN LINDSEY
Director
Division of Labor Standards

operate effective safety and health management programs. Participants in SHARP can receive up to a two-year exemption from certain OSHA inspections.

Mine and Cave Inspection Program

The Mine and Cave Inspection Program is mandated by Chapter 293, RSMo. Inspectors travel to the mine or cave site on a regular basis to inspect the property for safety and health hazards, including unsafe processes or work procedures that could cause accidents, injuries or fatalities. All safety and health conditions of the site are inspected, and if any hazards are found, the company is required to abate the problem in a prescribed period of time. Cost-effective recommendations on how to abate any safety or health problem are offered and consultations on any condition are available to the operator to bring them into compliance with state and federal laws.

Show caves must be equipped with necessary safety features, such as guard rails, bridges, ladders, entrances, platforms, walkways, safety barriers, rails, paths and electrical guards. The program also assists with coordinating cave rescue efforts. A listing of the caves inspected by the program can be found online at *www.labor.mo.gov/DLS/WorkplaceSafety/minecave/cave_inspection.asp*.

The Mine and Cave Safety and Health Section trains and retrains miners in the practice of implementing safe and healthy working habits in the mining workplace. This training is partially funded by a grant through the U.S. Department of Labor, Mine Safety and Health Administration (MSHA). Each miner must receive an initial safety and health training and annual retraining. Instructors conduct safety and health audits, prepare site-specific lesson plans corresponding to the training plan of the company, then present innovative training topics to the miners.

SARA NELL LAMPE
Chair, Missouri
Commission on Human Rights

MICHAEL DIERKES
Commissioner, Missouri
Commission on Human Rights

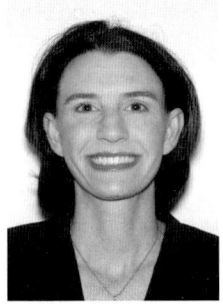

JENIFER PLACZEK
Commissioner, Missouri
Commission on Human Rights

DONNA LYNN BIRKS
Commissioner, Missouri
Commission on Human Rights

Missouri Commission on Human Rights

3315 W. Truman Blvd., PO Box 1129
Jefferson City 65102-1129
Telephone: (573) 751-3325 / FAX: (573) 751-2905
www.labor.mo.gov/mohumanrights
Email: mchr@labor.mo.gov

MELODY SMITH
Commissioner, Missouri
Commission on Human Rights

ALISA WARREN
Executive Director, Missouri
Commission on Human Rights

The mission of the Missouri Commission on Human Rights (MCHR) is to prevent and eliminate discrimination. The MCHR investigates complaints of discrimination in housing, employment and places of public accommodations based on race, color, religion, national origin, ancestry, sex, disability, age (in employment only) and familial status (in housing only). The MCHR also provides training to inform people of their rights and responsibilities under the Missouri Human Rights Act.

The Missouri Commission on Human Rights was created by the 69th General Assembly in 1957 and became a permanent agency in 1959. In 1961 the Fair Employment Practices Act was passed, in 1965 the Public Accommodations Act was passed and in 1972 the Fair Housing Act was passed. In 1986, these three laws were consolidated under Chapter 213, RSMo, as the Missouri Human Rights Act.

The commission staff handles more than 1,000 cases annually. In addition to the enforcement mechanisms in the Missouri Human Rights Act, the statute also empowers the commission to certify local commissions, establish relationships with federal and local civil and human rights agencies, implement educational or research programs and develop ways to prevent discrimination. Commission members are nominated by the director of the Department of Labor and Industrial Relations and appointed by the governor with advice and consent of the Senate. The governor appoints at least one member from each of Missouri's eight congressional districts, two members-at-large and one member as chairperson. The commissioners serve for six years without compensation. The commission meets quarterly, and commission meetings are open to the public.

Missouri Commission on Human Rights

Lampe, Sara Nell, (D), chairperson, Springfield, at-large commissioner, April 1, 2017;

Dierkes, Michael, (R), commissioner, St. Louis, 2nd District, April 1, 2015;

Birks, Donna Lynn, (D), commissioner, Kansas City, 5th District, April 1, 2018;

Placzek, Jenifer, (D), commissioner, Springfield, 7th District, April 1, 2015;

Smith, Melody, (R), commissioner, St. Joseph, 6th District, April 1, 2018;

Vacancies (5).

Martin Luther King Jr. State Celebration Commission

3026 Laclede Ave., St. Louis 63103
Telephone: (314) 340-3380 / FAX: (314) 340-3399

The commission considers and recommends to individuals and organizations appropriate activities for the recognition and celebration of Martin Luther King Day in Missouri. Created by executive order on Dec. 2, 1985, the commission consists of 20 members who serve at the pleasure of the governor.

The Martin Luther King Jr. State Celebration Commission is a continuing commission and meets at the call of the chair.

Members, Martin Luther King Jr. State Celebration Commission

Gully, Constance, chair, St. Louis;
Banks, Anita, St. Louis;
Buford, James, St. Louis;
Cleaver II, Rep. Emanuel, Kansas City;
Gates, Ollie, Kansas City;
Givens, Dr. Henry Jr., St. Louis;
Hardin, Charlotte, Springfield;
Jones, Rev. Dr. Sammie, Florissant;
McBride, Jack, Fulton;
Mensey-Symonds, Myrle, St. Louis;
Middleton, Dr. Michael, Columbia;
Nance, Rev. Earl, St. Louis;
Slay, Mayor Francis, St. Louis;
Smith, Ruth A., Florissant;
Thomas, Bertha, Kirksville;
Thompson, Betty, St. Louis;
Thompson, Lessie, Lee's Summit;
Vacancies (5).

CONSTANCE GULLY
Chair, Martin Luther King Jr.
State Celebration Commission

Department of Mental Health

1706 E. Elm, PO Box 687, Jefferson City 65102
Telephone: (573) 751-4122 / Toll-free: (800) 364-9687
FAX: (573) 751-8224
www.dmh.mo.gov
Email: dmhmail@dmh.mo.gov

STEVE ROLING
Chair
Mental Health Commission

KATHY CARTER
Mental Health Commission

The Department of Mental Health (DMH) was officially established on July 1, 1974, as a cabinet-level state agency by the Omnibus State Government Reorganization Act; however, its functions date back to 1847. The department serves as the state's mental health authority, establishing philosophy, policy and standards of care.

State law provides three principal missions for the department: the prevention of mental disorders, developmental disabilities, substance abuse and compulsive gambling; the treatment, habilitation and rehabilitation of Missourians who have those conditions; and the improvement of public understanding and attitudes about mental disorders, developmental disabilities, substance abuse and compulsive gambling.

KENNETH DOBBINS, Ph.D.
Mental Health Commission

DENNIS TESREAU
Mental Health Commission

The vision for the Missouri Department of Mental Health is that "Missourians receiving mental health services will have the opportunity to pursue their dreams and live their lives as valued members of their communities."

Missourians must know mental illness is treatable, persons with substance abuse problems can triumph over their addictions and persons with developmental disabilities can be productive citizens and good neighbors in their communities.

Mental Health Commission

The commission, composed of seven members, appoints the director of the Department of Mental Health with confirmation of the Senate. Commissioners are appointed to four-year terms by the governor, again with the confirmation of the Senate. The commissioners serve as policy advisors to the department director. The commission, by law, must include an advocate of community mental health centers, a physician who is an expert in the treatment of mental illness, a physician concerned with developmental disabilities, a member with business expertise, an advocate of substance abuse treatment, a citizen who represents the interests of consumers of psychiatric services and a citizen who represents the interests of consumers of developmental disabilities services.

KARL WILSON, Ph.D.
Mental Health Commission

Commissioners*

Rolling, Steve, chair, Jefferson City;
Carter, Kathy, member, Four Seasons;
Dobbins, Kenneth, Ph.D., member, Lake St. Louis;
Seigfred, Mary Patrick, member, Mexico;
Tesreau, Dennis, member, Herculaneum;
Wilson, Karl, Ph.D., member, St. Louis;
Vacancy (1).

---

*$100 per diem.

MARK STRINGER
Department Director

BOB BAX
Acting Deputy Director

HEIDI DiBIASO
Administrative Assistant to the
Director

LAINE YOUNG-WALKER, M.D.
Chief Medical Diretor
Children's Division

ANGELINE STANISLAUS, M.D.
Chief Medical Officer
Adult Services

DEBRA WALKER
Director of Public and
Legislative Affairs

SUSAN FLANIGAN
Legislative Liason

GAIL VASTERLING
General Counsel

Office of the Director

The seven-member Missouri Mental Health Commission serves as the principal policy advisory body to the department director. The director's duties include planning, supervising and evaluating the provision of services for Missourians with mental illness, developmental disabilities and addiction disorders. The department is composed of three divisions: the Division of Behavioral Health, the Division of Developmental Disabilities and the Division of Administration Services, as well as seven support offices.

DMH serves approximately 170,000 Missourians annually through state-operated facilities and contracts with private organizations and individuals. The eight state-operated psychiatric facilities include inpatient psychiatric care for adults and children, as well as sex offender rehabilitation and treatment services. In addition, five habilitation centers, one community support agency, five regional offices and six satellite offices serve individuals with developmental disabilities. Other services are purchased from a variety of privately operated programs statewide through approximately 1,500 contracts managed annually by the DMH.

Deputy Director

The Office of the Deputy Director provides the leadership and direction for a variety of department-wide and statewide functions that support program operations and services to DMH consumers. These include supervisory responsibility for the Office of Deaf Services, Office of General Counsel, Office of Consumer Safety and the DMH investigations units, well as other special projects at the director's discretion.

Chief Medical Directors' Office

The Chief Medical Directors' Office offers senior clinical leadership to the Department of Mental Health. It provides advice and counsel to the department director regarding a broad range of clinical, programmatic and strategic issues, as well as clinical policy. It also provides leadership and mentoring to the department's clinical staff statewide, by establishing and promoting professional, clinical and ethical values and standards to which all clinical staff are expected to adhere. The Chief Medical Directors' Office upholds quality of care, and is responsible for establishing and maintaining the department's standards of care on both clinical and programmatic levels.

Office of Public and Legislative Affairs (OPLA)

The Office of Public and Legislative Affairs provides information internally and externally regarding mental health programs and services and helps promote the people, programs and services of the department through publications and media. The office also provides support services, technical assistance and training to the department's divisions, offices and facilities. The OPLA works with legislators, state office holders and stakeholders regarding legislation related to the department, as well as serves as the liaison to the Mental Health Commission and provides oversight to the Office of Disaster Services.

LYNNE FULKS
Acting Director, Division of
Administrative Services

RICHARD GOWDY, Ph.D.
Director, Division of
Behavioral Health

General Counsel

The Office of the General Counsel is responsible for providing legal advice and assistance for the department, its facilities and division offices in a variety of areas, including: personnel and forensic litigation; rules and policy development; compliance with privacy, administration and coordination under the Health Insurance Portability and Accountability Act; and ensuring the provision of administrative due process hearings before the department hearings administrator

RIKKI WRIGHT
Deputy Director, Division of
Behavioral Health

Division of Administrative Services

The Division of Administrative Services provides administrative and financial services to help the department achieve effective results. The Division of Administrative Services includes the following units: budget and finance, which develops and monitors the annual budget, oversees the legislative fiscal note process, provides expenditure oversight and analyzes and compiles financial and other related reports; accounting, which oversees and monitors all funds, manages expenditures, administers grant funds and produces fiscal summaries, analyses and reports; purchasing and general services, which establishes and administers contracts with private agencies or individuals to provide services in the community and is also responsible for various general services functions in the central office; and Medicaid and reimbursements, which serves as the primary liaison with MO HealthNet on mental health issues and provides Medicaid guidance and support to all three program divisions and collects payments from private insurance, Medicaid and Medicare, and private pay for department services and coordinates revenue maximization activities.

Division of Behavioral Health

The Division of Behavioral Health (DBH), formerly the Divisions of Alcohol and Drug Abuse and Comprehensive Psychiatric Services, provides comprehensive mental health and substance use disorder prevention, treatment and recovery services in Missouri. The division is responsible for seven adult psychiatric facilities, two children's facilities and a statewide network of contracted community providers. Approximately 140,000 people receive behavioral health services each year from programs operated or contracted by the division.

The division oversees seven state-operated facilities for people with serious mental illnesses and children with severe emotional disturbances. All are fully accredited by The Joint Commission (TJC) and certified by the Centers for Medicare and Medicaid Services (CMS) to provide Medicaid services. The facilities include Fulton State Hospital; St. Louis Psychiatric Rehabilitation Center; Metropolitan St. Louis Psychiatric Center; Hawthorn Children's Psychiatric Hospital, St. Louis; Center for Behavioral Medicine, Kansas City; Northwest Missouri Psychiatric Rehabilitation Center, St. Joseph; and Southeast Missouri Mental Health Center, Farmington. The sexually violent predator treatment program operates in secure facilities in both Farmington and Fulton.

Forensic services are provided for evaluation, treatment and community monitoring of individuals with mental illness and developmental disabilities who are involved in the criminal justice system and under the order and direction of circuit courts. The division supervises about 460 forensic clients on conditional release statewide and conducts an average of 500 pretrial evaluations each year.

Community-based treatment is provided through contracted, certified agencies that serve children, youth and adults. Administrative agents are designated by state law as entry points into the mental health system for people with serious mental illness. Services provided by division contractors include the Community Psychiatric Rehabilitation Program (CPRP) for adults with serious mental illness and youth with serious emotional disturbances, and the Comprehensive Substance Treatment and Rehabilitation (CSTAR) Program, which provides general adult treatment as well as specialized services for pregnant and postpartum women, women with children, adolescents and individuals who are addicted to heroin or prescription opiates. Other statewide programs include the Disease Management project, the Health Home initiative and the Substance Abuse Traffic Offender Program (SATOP). Outpatient treatment for compulsive gamblers and their families is provided by contracted agencies that employ specially trained counselors.

Specialized services for children and youth with severe emotional disturbances are provided in a variety of settings, including schools, state-operated facilities and community-based programs.

Recovery services support individuals in recovery from serious mental illness or severe substance use disorders. They include employment programs and affordable housing options, as well as Consumer Operated Service Programs (CO-SPs) and other evidence-based peer services.

Substance abuse prevention and mental health promotion are offered through community- and school-based providers that target individuals, families and communities. Emphasis is placed on evidence-based programs and practices. There is a network of community coalitions, a statewide training resource center, regional support centers, direct service programs for high-risk youth, college-based services and school-based prevention and intervention programs, as well as other statewide initiatives, including suicide prevention, crisis intervention team training for law enforcement, tobacco cessation and Mental Health First Aid.

ROBERT RIETZ, Ph.D.
Deputy Director of Psychiatric Facilities & Central Region Executive Officer

LAURENT JAVOIS
Eastern Regional Executive Officer

JULIE INMAN
Southeast Regional Executive Officer

DENISE NORBURY
West/Southwest Regional Executive Officer

Missouri Advisory Council on Alcohol and Drug Abuse

The Missouri Advisory Council for Alcohol and Drug Abuse (ADA) serves as an advisory body to the Division of Behavioral Health (DBH) and the division director in the areas of substance abuse policy, prevention, treatment and recovery in the state of Missouri. The council was created and empowered through section 631.020 of the Missouri Revised Statutes.

The ADA council is composed of up to 25 members appointed by the director of DBH. Members have professional, research and/or personal interests in the division's purpose. At least one half of the members must be consumers and one member must represent veterans and military affairs. Additional representation has included individuals from state agencies such as corrections, vocational rehabilitation, health and senior services and education. The remainder of the council is made up of private and state-contracted providers, including the Missouri Substance Abuse Professional Credentialing Board, Missouri Recovery Network and other advocacy groups. Each member is appointed for an initial term of one, two or three years to allow for a rotation of one-third of the members each year. Further, each appointed member may be re-appointed to one additional three-year term. Each member serves until a successor has been appointed.

Members

Flowers, Ladell, Kansas City;
Carter, Michael, Springfield;
Czuba, John, Macon;
Hagens, Edgar, Springfield;
Hahne, Joseph, Springfield;
Harris, Diana, St. Louis;
Jackson, Sandra, Poplar Bluff;
Johnson, Nancy K., St. Louis;
McKerrow, Kelly, Perryville;
Menzies, Percy, St. Louis;
Steuber, Cynthia, Fulton;
Waddle, Karah, Wentzville;
Washington, Stephanie, Jefferson City;
Doyle, Lisa, St. Joseph;
McDonald, Christine, St. Charles;
Metcalf, Rosanna, Essex;
Nepote, Gloria, Lee's Summit;
Page, Liz, Jefferson City.

Missouri Advisory Council on Comprehensive Psychiatric Services

The Missouri Advisory Council on Comprehensive Psychiatric Services (CPS) was first established in 1977 by a governor's executive order. Similar councils exist in every state and U.S. territory because of the passage of federal law 99–660 in 1986, continuing through public law 101–639 and public law 102–321 in 1992. These federal laws require states and territories to perform mental health planning to receive federal Mental Health Block Grant funds. These laws further require that stakeholders, including mental health consumers, family members and parents of children with serious emotional disturbances, must be involved in these planning efforts through membership on the council. Members are appointed by the director of DBH.

The council is composed of 25 members who advise and make recommendations to improve the system of care in mental health. Through public education and advocacy efforts, consumers and family members have become an integral part of defining priorities for the division on issues surrounding housing, employment, recovery-oriented community services, crisis intervention and children's system of care. The council membership is required by federal law to have a majority of mental health consumers, including parents of children receiving services and family members. In addition, representation is required from the following state agencies: social services, medicaid, corrections, vocational rehabilitation,

JEANETTE SIMMONS, Ph.D.
Chief Operating Officer
Center for Behavioral Medicine

health and senior services, education, housing and mental health. The remainder of the council is made up of private and state-contracted providers, Missouri Protection and Advocacy and other advocacy groups.

Members

McDowell, Mickie, chair, Southern Region;
Charles, Bruce, vice chair, Central Region;
Chase, Stewart, Western Region;
Cushing, Heather, Eastern Region;
Earll, Sarah, Eastern Region;
Giovanetti, Scott, Dept. of Mental Health;
Greening, Andrew, Eastern Region;
Hagar-Mace, Liz, Housing;
Harper, John, Vocational Rehabilitation;
Hawkins, Robert, Eastern Region;
Johnson, Jessica, Central Region;
Jordan, Jessica, Central Region;
Murph, Rene, Eastern Region;
Scott, Susan, Southern Region;
Thomas, Tish, Person-Centered Planning;
Cayou, Daniel, MO P & A;
Gilkey, Stacey, Western Region;
Horn, Mary, Western Region;
Jordan, Toni, Eastern Region;
Martin, Eric, Dept of Social Services;
Mills, Denise, Western Region;
Myers, Linda, Western Region;
O'Kelley, Scott, Criminal Justice;
Scheidegger, Barb, Central Region;
Ulstad, Mindy, Dept of Health & Senior Services.

Center for Behavioral Medicine

Health Sciences Center for Psychiatry
1000 E. 24th St., Kansas City 64108
Telephone: (816) 512-7000
www.dmh.mo.gov/cbm

Center for Behavioral Medicine (CBM), formerly Western Missouri Mental Health Center (WMMHC), operates 65 adult acute beds, 68 adult residential beds, five group homes and an apartment program in the community. The facility is located on Hospital Hill in the heart of Kansas City and provides comprehensive psychiatric care to patients from Kansas City and the seven surrounding counties. CBM serves as the University of Missouri–Kansas City's Department of Psychiatry, fulfilling academic and research needs. The Center serves the Greater Kansas City, Mo., area and surrounding counties with intensive and specialized behavioral health treatments and services for individuals who require in-patient care after a short-term, acute hospital stay at another inpatient setting. The center focuses its new services on bridging the gap between physical and behavioral medicine with an emphasis on wellness. Students, residents and post-doctoral fellows are trained at the center to deliver integrated physical and behavioral health care. The center provides a therapeutic approach to recovery that assists individuals to progress regardless of their limitations or symptoms. This approach incorporates evidence-based treatment models, including illness management and recovery (IM and R) and dialectical behavioral therapy (DBT).

Fulton State Hospital

600 E. Fifth St., Fulton 65251
Telephone: (573) 592-4100
www.dmh.mo.gov/fulton

Fulton State Hospital, authorized in 1847 and opened in 1851, is the oldest public mental health facility west of the Mississippi River. The 376-bed hospital provides inpatient adult psychiatric services, including treatment and psychosocial rehabilitation for forensic patients and other patients requiring long-term inpatient care. The term "forensic" is used to describe individuals who are charged with a crime and have been committed to the Department of Mental Health by a circuit court for either a pretrial or presentence evaluation, for restoration of competence to stand trial or as a result of an adjudication of Not Guilty by Reason of Mental Disease or Defect (NGRI). Specifically, the hospital serves patients from the entire state who require hospitalization in maximum- and intermediate-security settings, individuals who have been committed to the Department of Mental Health as sexually violent predators and forensic patients with developmental disabilities who require a minimum-security setting.

Fulton has Missouri's only maximum- and intermediate-security units. The 186-bed Biggs Forensic Center provides treatment for individuals who have committed major offenses or those whose behavior in other settings demonstrates a need for a maximum-security setting. Included is a program run in cooperation with the Department of Corrections (DOC) to provide acute men-

MARTY MARTIN-FORMAN
Chief Operating Officer
Fulton State Hospital

MARCIA FORD
Chief Operating Officer
Hawthorn Children's
Psychiatric Hospital

tal health services for inmates from DOC and for jail detainees across the state whose charges or behavior require maximum security.

The 91-bed Guhleman Forensic Center offers an intermediate-security environment for former Biggs patients to progress toward increased liberty and responsibility. In addition, it provides a security setting for individuals whose charges or behaviors do not require maximum security, but are nonetheless in need of a higher level of security than is available in other inpatient settings.

A 75-bed Sexual Offender Rehabilitation and Treatment Services program serves individuals committed to the Department of Mental Health as sexually violent predators. Another 24-bed program serves developmentally disabled patients on forensic commitments who can be safely treated within a minimum-security setting.

The hospital has a training affiliation with the University of Missouri's Department of Psychiatry. In addition, it provides training experience to students from various clinical disciplines, including nursing, social work and occupational therapy and an internship and fellowship program in psychology.

Hawthorn Children's Psychiatric Hospital

1901 Pennsylvania Ave., St. Louis 63133
Telephone: (314) 512-7800 / FAX: (314) 512-7812
www.dmh.mo.gov/hcph/

Hawthorn Children's Psychiatric Hospital provides inpatient and residential psychiatric treatment services for severely emotionally disturbed children and adolescents, ages 6 to 17. The hospital serves residents of Missouri.

Hawthorn has been a freestanding child psychiatric facility in St. Louis County since 1989. The 26-acre campus consists of a main building and five cottages. There are 28 inpatient and 16 residential treatment beds.

Youth admitted to Hawthorn are provided comprehensive mental health treatment services designed to address their psychiatric, psychological, social, educational, vocational and recreational needs. The treatment programs rely on evidence-based practices and deliver services in a trauma-informed milieu. As a service to the community, Hawthorn also provides mental health information and consultation regarding the treatment of children and adolescents. The hospital serves as a training facility for a wide range of mental health professionals. Hawthorn also participates fully with other community agencies in the planning and development of mental health services for the children in the community.

Metropolitan St. Louis Psychiatric Center

5351 Delmar Blvd., St. Louis 63112
Telephone: (314) 877-0500 / FAX: (314) 877-0553
TT: (314) 877-0775
www.dmh.mo.gov/mpc

Metropolitan St. Louis Psychiatric Center (MPC) is a 50-bed facility that provides forensic evaluations and inpatient competency restoration services to residents of the 61 counties of the eastern half of Missouri. The Forensic Pretrial Program at MPC is composed of two units: the inpatient Competency Restoration Service and the Forensic Evaluation Service.

The purpose of the inpatient Competency Restoration Service is to restore competency for those individuals who have been committed by the courts to the Department of Mental Health as incompetent to stand trial. Criminal defendants are found incompetent to stand trial when a major mental illness, cognitive disorder or developmental disability causes the defendant to lack the capacity to understand the legal proceedings against him/her or to be unable to assist the attorney in his/her defense. The Competency Restoration Service provides state-of-the-art psychiatric treatment and psychosocial interventions to restore defendants to competency to proceed to trial. Interventions include: stabilization of mental disorders that result in the defendant being found incompetent to stand trial; in-depth education regarding court-related terminology and procedures; modification of faulty beliefs about the legal system and the individual's mental illness; and individualized interventions to assist the defendant in applying what is learned to that person's case. For those defendants who return to the community, thorough discharge planning takes into account the client's treatment needs and the public safety.

MICHAEL ANDERSON, Ph.D.
Chief Operating Officer
Metropolitan St. Louis
Psychiatric Center

MARY SANDERS
Chief Operating Officer
Northwest Missouri Psychiatric
Rehabilitation Center

The Forensic Evaluation Service serves the courts of Missouri by providing comprehensive, court-ordered evaluations regarding various legal issues. The most common court-ordered evaluation addresses competency to stand trial. Questions of the mental state of a defendant at the time of an alleged crime are evaluated, including criminal responsibility (insanity), diminished capacity and battered spouse syndrome. Risk assessments and other evaluations are conducted on defendants whose probation has been revoked to assist the courts in determining the best sentencing options. Finally, persons detained under sexual predator laws are evaluated to determine if they meet the definition of a sexually violent predator. Most evaluations are done on an outpatient basis either at MPC or at a jail, while some are conducted on an inpatient basis to gather additional data when challenging diagnostic questions or malingering of mental illness are raised. The Forensic Evaluation Service conducts between 180 and 200 evaluations per year.

Northwest Missouri Psychiatric Rehabilitation Center

3505 Frederick Ave., St. Joseph 64506
Telephone: (816) 387-2300 / FAX: (816) 387-2329
TT: (816) 387-2300
www.dmh.mo.gov/nmprc

Northwest Missouri Psychiatric Rehabilitation Center (NMPRC) provides inpatient psychiatric treatment and rehabilitation to adults who are considered to have a persistent mental illness and are in need of hospital-based treatment and rehabilitation.

The hospital opened as State Lunatic Asylum No. 2 in November 1874 on land east of St. Joseph. The capacity ranged from 250 beds to nearly 3,000 in the 1950s, and the name was changed to St. Joseph State Hospital. Over the years, downsizing occurred with the advent of better treatment options and emphasis on returning patients to the community.

In 1997, St. Joseph State Hospital was replaced with the current facility and renamed Northwest Missouri Psychiatric Rehabilitation Center. NMPRC currently provides 108 beds for adult psychiatric patients. Three wings have 20 beds each and are designated as minimum security. Six cottages with eight beds each are designated as open-campus security.

Within NMPRC there are three 20-bed, coed wings and six eight-bed cottages for a combined total of 108 beds. All three wings serve as the entry point for patients transferring from a jail setting and other DMH psychiatric hospitals for psychiatric treatment and rehabilitation. Included are individuals who are committed under Chapter 552, RSMo, for pretrial evaluation and restoration to competency to stand trial as Not Guilty by Reason of Mental Disease or Defect (NGRI), transfers from other psychiatric facilities and forensic patients returning from conditional release, either voluntarily or by revocation. Six eight-bed, coed cottages are designed to prepare patients for a community-living type environment in which individuals learn and practice those critical skills necessary to be successful in their community. Patients are expected to take responsibility for their own actions and recovery as they make more choices in their lives while living in a structured, secure and supportive setting.

St. Louis Psychiatric Rehabilitation Center

5300 Arsenal St., St. Louis 63139
Telephone: (314) 877-6500 / FAX: (314) 877-5982
www.dmh.mo.gov/slprc

St. Louis Psychiatric Rehabilitation Center (formerly known as St. Louis State Hospital), was originally opened in 1869 and is currently a 180-bed, minimum-security hospital, providing long-term inpatient psychiatric treatment and recovery-based psychosocial rehabilitation services. The majority of the clients served have been committed to the Department of Mental Health by a criminal court under the mental health provisions of Chapter 552, RSMo, either upon their adjudication as Not Guilty by Reason of Mental Disease or Defect (NGRI) or a finding of Permanent Incompetence to Stand Trial (PIST). In addition, SLPRC serves a smaller cohort of adults with severe and persistent mental illness, whose admission status is voluntary by guardian, but who are extremely difficult to treat. Finally, the facility recently began operating an eight-bed unit for individuals who are deaf and have a serious mental illness, requiring long-term inpatient treatment.

FELIX VINCENZ, Ph.D.
Chief Operating Officer
St. Louis Psychiatric
Rehabilitation Center

DAVID SCHMITT
Chief Operating Officer
Southeast Missouri Mental
Health Center

Each of these populations typically presents substantial deficits in the management of the symptoms of mental illness, a predilection to high risk behaviors associated with a significant probability for psychiatric relapse and criminal offense and/or a general inability to comport themselves without substantial risk to their safety or that of the community. Co-morbid substance abuse and/or personality disorders are common complications, as is clear evidence of impairment in social role functioning and daily living skills. Many of the patients, particularly those not adjudicated NGRI, are likely to have required multiple inpatient admissions with a demonstrable inability to be successful in the community, even with enhanced community-based services and residential supports. All clients admitted require intensive inpatient services to develop an adequate relapse prevention plan and to achieve the psychiatric stability necessary for discharge from hospital-based care and for safe and successful reintegration into the community.

Southeast Missouri Mental Health Center

1010 W. Columbia, Farmington 63640
Telephone: (573) 218-6792 / FAX: (573) 218-6703
www.dmh.mo.gov/southeast

Southeast Missouri Mental Health Center began in 1903 as Farmington State Hospital. In 1984, the Missouri General Assembly approved the conversion of the hospital grounds into a medium-security prison, operated by the Department of Corrections. Subsequently in 1987, the state hospital was converted into a mental health center and moved into buildings adjacent to the prison. Southeast Missouri Mental Health Center consists of Adult Psychiatric Services and Sexual Offender Rehabilitation and Treatment Services.

The Adult Psychiatric Services division (APS) operates 170 longer-stay inpatient beds for persons demonstrating persistently dangerous behaviors and ongoing impairment in social functioning in daily living skills due to mental illness. Many of these persons are admitted under the criminal court statute as Not Guilty by Reason of Mental Disease or Defect (NGRI).

By cooperative agreement between the departments of corrections and mental health, the Corrections Treatment Center (CTC) operates on the grounds of Farmington Correctional Center. Within the CTC unit, the mental health center staffs a small, medium-security ward for inmates with psychiatric needs.

The Sexual Offender Rehabilitation and Treatment Service, formerly known as Missouri Sexual Offender Treatment Center, provides treatment, care, security and custody for those persons adjudicated as sexually violent predators. With the passage of the Sexually Violent Predator Act, which was effective Jan. 1, 1999, the Missouri General Assembly mandated that individuals adjudicated by the court as sexually violent predators be committed indefinitely to the custody of the director of the Department of Mental Health for "control, care and treatment until such time that the person is safe to be at large." In order for such commitments to pass constitutional scrutiny, the department provides care and treatment consistent with existing professional standards and practice. The law also requires individuals committed for treatment as sexually violent predators be kept in a secure facility and housed separately from Department of Corrections' inmates and from persons served by the Department of Mental Health who have not been found to be sexually violent predators.

In addition to the treatment and custody of sexually violent predators, the department is required to provide staff to participate in the multidisciplinary team to assist the prosecutor's review committee in determining whether an individual may meet the definition of a sexually violent predator. Further, the department is required to evaluate each individual for whom the court finds probable cause to believe the person is a sexually violent predator. Finally, the department must annually provide the committing court an annual report regarding the committed person's mental condition.

VALERIE HUHN
Director, Division of
Developmental Disabilities

VICKI McCARRELL
Deputy Director, Division of
Developmental Disabilities

TONYA PIEPOFF
Chief Operating Officer
Division of Developmental
Disabilities

APRIL MAXWELL
Director of State Operated
Programs, Division of
Developmental Disabilities

MARCY VOLNER
Assistant Director, Division of
Developmental Disabilities

Division of Developmental Disabilities

The Division of Developmental Disabilities (DD), established in 1974, serves persons with developmental disabilities such as cerebral palsy, head injuries, autism, epilepsy and certain learning disabilities. Such conditions must have occurred before age 22 with the expectation that they will continue. To be eligible for services from the division, persons with these disabilities must have substantial functional limitations in two or more of the following six areas of major life activities: self-care, receptive and expressive language development and use, learning, self-direction, capacity for independent living or economic self-sufficiency and mobility.

The division's focus is on improving the lives of persons with developmental disabilities and their families through programs, support and services to enable persons with developmental dis-

REBECCA POST
Superintendent
Bellefontaine Habilitation Center

GEORGE FIZER
Superintendent
Higginsville Habilitation Center

SUSAN BISHOP
Superintendent
Marshall Habilitation Center

BRADLEY MILLER
Superintendent, Southeast
Missouri Residential Services

LAURA WAYER
Superintendent, St. Louis
Developmental Disabilities
Treatment Centers

CHRIS BAKER
Director
Southwest Community Services

JODI MANVILLE
Assistant Director
Albany Satellite Office

WENDY DAVIS
Director, Central Missouri
Regional Office

abilities to live independently and productively. In 1988, the division began participation in the Medicaid home- and community-based waiver program designed to help expand needed services throughout the state.

Specialized services are either provided directly or purchased through contracts by 17 entities operated by the division. The division's regional and satellite offices are the primary points of entry into and exit from the system. These offices determine eligibility, work with individuals and families and contract with SB40 boards (local county boards for the developmentally disabled) and private providers for the provision of a comprehensive array of services in the following areas: Albany, central Missouri, Hannibal, Joplin, Kansas City, Kirksville, Poplar Bluff, Rolla, Sikeston, Springfield and St. Louis. There are also six state-operated programs: Bellefontaine Habilitation Center, Higginsville Habilitation Center, Marshall Habilitation Center, Southeast Missouri Residential Services, St. Louis Developmental Disabilities Treatment Center and Southwest Community Services, which primarily provide residential care and habilitation services to persons who are medically and behaviorally challenged or court-committed. All habilitation cen-

ters are Title XIX-certified as Intermediate Care Facilities for the Mentally Retarded (ICF/MR).

Missouri Developmental Disabilities Council

The Missouri Developmental Disabilities Council was created in 1971 under federal legislation. The council's federal mandate is to plan, advocate for and give advice concerning programs and services for persons with developmental disabilities that will increase their opportunities for independence, productivity and integration into communities. The council also serves, under Missouri statute, as the Missouri Advisory Council on Developmental Disabilities, providing advice to the division and the division director. The council has 23 members, appointed by the governor.

Members

Ohrenberg, Mark, chair, Columbia;
Briscoe, Stephanie, Lathrop;
Blackwell, Brent, Carrollton;
Brewer, Michael, Jefferson City;
Crandall, Lisa, Jefferson City;

TENA GOTTMAN
Assistant Director
Hannibal Satellite Regional Office

JULIE LILLICH
Assistant Director
Joplin Satellite Office

TIM WHOLF
Director
Kansas City Regional Office

MATT SHANNON
Assistant Director
Kirksville Satellite Office

JULIE THARP
Assistant Director
Poplar Bluff Satellite Office

JENNIFER O'DAY
Assistant Director
Rolla Satellite Office

LISA WILLIAMSON
Director
Sikeston Regional Office

KATHLEEN FEATHERSTONE
Director
Springfield Regional Office

Davis, Wendy, Columbia;
Dowell, Dale, Mexico;
Eckles, Susan, St. Louis;
Enfield, Cathy, Independence;
Gilpin, Barb, Jefferson City;
Haas, Allen, Jefferson City;
Harper, John, Jefferson City;
Hoffmeister, Michelle, Farmington;
McVeigh, Tom, Kansas City;
Nelson, Allen, Bolivar;
Niemeyer, Brenda, Edina;
Stahlberg, Kit, Fredericktown;
Swinnie, Jackie, Baldwin;
Willard, Diana, Joplin;
Williams, Sharon, Lee's Summit;
Vacancies (3).

Habilitation Centers

www.dmh.mo.gov/dd/facilities/habcenters.htm

Bellefontaine Habilitation Center
10695 Bellefontaine Rd., St. Louis 63137
Telephone: (314) 340-6000

Higginsville Habilitation Center
100 W. First St., Higginsville 64037
Telephone: (660) 584-2142

LOIS WARREN
Director
St. Louis County Regional Office

JULIA HILLYER
Director, St. Louis Regional
Tri-County Office

Marshall Habilitation Center
PO Box 190, Marshall 65340
Telephone: (660) 886-2201

Southeast Missouri Residential Services:

Poplar Bluff Office
2351 Kanell Blvd., Poplar Bluff 63901
Telephone: (573) 840-9370

Sikeston Office
PO Box 966, 112 Plaza Dr., Sikeston 63801
Telephone: (573) 472-5305

St. Louis Developmental Disabilities Treatment Centers:

South County Habilitation Center
2312 Lemay Ferry Rd., St. Louis 63125
Telephone: (314) 894-5400

St. Charles Habilitation Center
22 Marr Ln., St. Charles 63303
Telephone: (636) 926-1300

Southwest Community Services:

2323 N. Ash, Nevada 64772
Telephone: (417) 667-7833

Regional Offices

dmh.mo.gov/dd/facilities/

Albany Satellite Regional Office
809 N. 13th St., Albany 64402
Telephone: (660) 726-5246

Central Missouri Regional Office
1500 Vandiver Dr., Ste. 100, Columbia 65202
Telephone: (573) 882-9835

Hannibal Satellite Regional Office
805 Clinic Rd., PO Box 1108, Hannibal 63401
Telephone: (573) 248-2400

Joplin Satellite Regional Office
3600 E. Newman Rd., Joplin 64802
Telephone: (417) 629-3020

Kansas City Regional Office
821 E. Admiral Blvd., Kansas City 64106
Telephone: (816) 889-3400

Kirksville Satellite Regional Office
1702 E. LaHarpe, Kirksville 63501
Telephone: (660) 785-2500

Poplar Bluff Satellite Regional Office
2351 Kanell Blvd., Poplar Bluff 63901
Telephone: (573) 840-9300

Rolla Satellite Regional Office
105 Fairgrounds Rd., PO Box 1098, Rolla 65402
Telephone: (573) 368-2200

Sikeston Regional Office
112 Plaza Dr., Sikeston 63801
Telephone: (573) 472-5300

Springfield Regional Office
1515 E. Pythian, Springfield 65801
Telephone: (417) 895-7400

St. Louis County Regional Office
9900 Page Ave., Ste. 106, St. Louis 63132
Telephone: (314) 587-4800

St. Louis Tri-County Regional Office
Wainwright Bldg., 111 N. Seventh St., Sixth Fl.
St. Louis 63101
Telephone: (314) 244-8800

Department of Natural Resources

1101 Riverside Dr., PO Box 176
Jefferson City 65102-0176
Telephone: (573) 751-3443
Toll-free: (800) 361-4827
www.dnr.mo.gov
Email: contact@dnr.mo.gov

SARA PARKER PAULEY
Director

TODD SAMPSELL
Deputy Director

The mission of the Missouri Department of Natural Resources' is to protect our air, land and water; preserve our unique natural and historic places; and provide recreational and learning opportunities for everyone. The department was created under state reorganization on July 1, 1974.

Missouri's air, land and water resources play an important role in our quality of life and health and are essential to the environmental and economic vitality of our state. Staff works to ensure Missouri's citizens enjoy clean air to breathe, clean water for drinking and recreation and land that sustains a diversity of life. Staff also works to preserve the state's historic and natural heritage through state parks and state historic sites. The department continues to learn how to improve environmental protection by using new technologies and fostering better understanding.

VALERIE EVERS
Executive Assistant to Director

MARY MULHEARN
Legislative Liaison

The department accomplishes this work through the Division of Administrative Support, Division of Environmental Quality, Missouri Geological Survey and Missouri State Parks. A number of boards and commissions also support and facilitate the department's roles and responsibilities. In addition, the State Environmental Improvement and Energy Resources Authority and the Petroleum Storage Tank Insurance Fund are connected administratively to the department through the Office of the Director.

Stakeholder and public engagement plays a critical role in helping the department protect and improve Missouri's natural resources. By working together, the Department of Natural Resources ensures a healthy environment in which to live, work and enjoy the great outdoors today and for generations to come.

MARTY MILLER
Acting General Counsel

TOM BASTIAN
Communications Director

Office of the Director

The director of the Department of Natural Resources is appointed by the governor and confirmed by the senate. The director and the Office

RENEE BUNGART
Deputy Communications Director

of the Director staff manage the policy and operations of the department through its four divisions, improve efficiencies through strategic planning and ensure public participation through the decision-making process to ensure the department follows federal and state regulations. The office includes communication, education, general counsel, legislative, Missouri and Mississippi rivers coordination and policy and planning.

The director serves as the trustee for natural resource damages in Missouri, state historic preservation officer, chair of the State Interagency Council for Outdoor Recreation. The director also serves as a member of the Soil and Water Districts Commission, the Petroleum Storage Tank Insurance Fund Board of Trustees and the Unmarked Human Burial Consultation Committee. The department director represents Missouri on three interstate river organizations: the Missouri River Basin Commission, the Arkansas-White-Red Basins Interagency Committee and the Upper Mississippi River Basin Commission.

Environmental Improvement and Energy Resources Authority

Telephone: (573) 751-4919 / FAX: (573) 635-3486
eiera.mo.gov

The Environmental Improvement and Energy Resources Authority (EIERA) is a quasi-governmental environmental finance agency administratively assigned to the Missouri Department of Natural Resources. The authority was established by the Missouri General Assembly in 1972, and EIERA board members are appointed by the governor. EIERA is committed to provide solutions that help Missourians and the environment thrive through finance, research and technical assistance to preserve or foster the responsible management of our air, land, water and energy resources for the well-being of our citizens and Missouri's economy.

As the state's primary energy and environmental bond issuing authority, the EIERA promotes Missouri's environment and economy by providing a broad range of financial support and services. To date, the EIERA has assisted Missouri communities, utilities, schools, organizations and businesses by providing almost $6 billion in bond financing and more than $30 million in project financing that have supported infrastructure upgrades, energy efficiency, pollution prevention, technical assistance, research and environmental education.

Cherry, Deron, (R), member;
Dalton, Andy, (D), member;
DeFreece, LaRee, (D), member;
Massey, Karen, director.

KAREN MASSEY
Director, EIERA

Petroleum Storage Tank Insurance Fund Board of Trustees

The Petroleum Storage Tank Insurance Fund Board of Trustees administers the Petroleum Storage Tank Insurance Fund, which insures tank owners and operators for risks associated with leaks of petroleum products from their tanks or piping. It also provides funding to clean up certain properties where historic tank operations have contaminated the environment, restoring those properties to economic viability.

The 11-member board includes the commissioner of administration and the directors of the departments of agriculture and natural resources. The governor appoints and the Senate approves eight citizens who each serve a four-year term. The citizens represent tank owners, financial institutions, industrial and commercial users of petroleum, the insurance industry and the public.

McNutt, Donald, chair, large owner/operator of petroleum storage tanks representative;
Ford, James P., vice chair, insurance underwriting industry representative;
Greer, James, owner/operator of aboveground storage tanks representative;
Kolb, Thomas, small owner/operator of petroleum storage tanks representative;
Mariea, Schuyler J., financial institutions representative;
Opie, Danny, industrial and commercial users of petroleum representative;
Pfeiffer, Thomas J., public member;
Slusher, Renee, Office of Administration designee;
Albert, John, Department of Agriculture designee;
Miller, Marty, Department of Natural Resources designee;
Vacancy (1), public member;
Eighmey, Carol R., executive director.

DONALD McNUTT
Chair, Petroleum Storage Tank
Insurance Fund

JAMES P. FORD
Vice Chair, Petroleum Storage
Tank Insurance Fund

JAMES GREER
Trustee, Petroleum Storage Tank
Insurance Fund

THOMAS KOLB
Trustee, Petroleum Storage Tank
Insurance Fund

SCHUYLER J. MARIEA
Trustee, Petroleum Storage Tank
Insurance Fund

DANNY OPIE
Trustee, Petroleum Storage Tank
Insurance Fund

THOMAS J. PFEIFFER
Trustee, Petroleum Storage Tank
Insurance Fund

RENEE SLUSHER
Offie of Administration
designee, Petroleum Storage
Tank Insurance Fund

JOHN ALBERT
Dept. of Agriculture designee,
Petroleum Storage Tank
Insurance Fund

MARTY MILLER
Dept. of Natural Resources-
designee, Petroleum Storage
Tank Insurance Fund

CAROL R. EIGHMEY
Executive Director, Petroleum
Tank Insurance Fund

Division of Administrative Support

Telephone: (573) 751-7961 / FAX: (573) 751-7749

The Division of Administrative Support provides the department with administrative and management support. Budget development, internal audit, accounting, human resources, procurement, grants management and general services are functions performed by the division.

The division reviews proposed policies, regulations and legislation to determine fiscal or procedural impacts on the department. Procedures are developed to implement the approved policies, regulations and legislation.

The Budget Program is responsible for developing the department's annual operating and capital improvement budgets as well as the preparation of management and legislative reports.

The Internal Audit Program performs audits of departmental activities to evaluate internal controls and compliance with laws, regulations and policies, as well as efficiencies and effectiveness of meeting department goals and objectives.

The Accounting Program is responsible for purchasing, fixed assets, accounts payable and maintenance; grant, project and fund accounting; reporting and monitoring; grant and fund fiscal management; receipt processing; special projects; and analyses.

The Human Resources Program is responsible for administering the human resources function for the department. This program assists all divisions with position classification, implements the provisions of the state personnel law, interprets employee benefits, conducts personnel research, coordinates training, provides career counseling and maintains personnel records for all employees of the department.

The General Services Program is responsible for maintenance and operation of the agency's motor pool, maintenance and operation of a centralized mailroom and supply center, surplus of departmental property and coordination of telecommunications. The program acts as liaison with the Office of Administration and the Division of Facilities Management, Design and Construction.

Division of Environmental Quality

Telephone: (573) 751-0763 / FAX: (573) 751-9277
dnr.mo.gov/env

Protecting and enhancing the quality of Missouri's environment is the responsibility of the department's Division of Environmental Quality. The division assists Missourians with these goals through the traditional roles of permitting, inspections and proactive efforts to revitalize contaminated sites for redevelopment. Through its regional offices, the department provides compliance assistance, permitting, inspections and other environmental expertise closest to where Missourians live and work. This division is responsible for protecting and enhancing Missouri's water quality. The division certifies and tracks the required continuing education of all operators of public drinking water systems, wastewater systems and concentrated animal feeding operation waste management systems. The division works to ensure clean air, land and water by cleaning up pollution from the past, addressing pollution problems of today and identifying potential pollution issues of the future. The division administers six technical programs: air pollution control, environmental services, hazardous waste management, soil and water conservation, solid waste management and water protection.

LORI GORDON
Director, Division of
Administrative Support

LEANNE TIPPETT MOSBY
Director, Division of
Environmental Quality

Air Pollution Control Program

The Air Pollution Control Program works to maintain the purity of Missouri's air to protect the health, general welfare and property of citizens. The program researches, develops and implements control strategies that help Missouri improve air quality and implement the federal Clean Air Act.

The program evaluates industries wanting to operate in Missouri, predicting their emissions and their impact on the state's air quality and requiring restrictions on emissions where necessary. The program issues construction and operating permits, selects locations for air monitoring equipment and analyzes data collected from these monitors. The program also surveys and inspects sources of air pollution. If a source consistently violates the state's air pollution control regulations, it is subject to enforcement action to return the facility to compliance.

Under the state's federally required plan, the Air Pollution Control Program implements a vehicle emissions testing program in the St. Louis ozone nonattainment area. Ozone is a respiratory irritant that can cause health problems, especially for children, the elderly and people with heart and lung diseases. Through this program, all 1996 and newer gas-powered vehicles and 1997 and newer diesel-powered vehicles 8,500 pounds or less registered in the St. Louis ozone nonattainment area are tested to ensure emissions systems are working properly. This program is a key component of the ongoing effort to improve air quality in the St. Louis region.

This program is a key component of the ongoing effort to improve air quality in the St. Louis region.

The Air Pollution Control Program works with stakeholders, the general public and regulated facilities to comply with local, state and federal air quality regulations. The program carries out the policies established by the Air Conservation Commission.

Air Conservation Commission

The Missouri Air Conservation Commission carries out the Missouri Air Conservation Law. The commission's activities are directed toward achieving and maintaining the National Ambient (outdoor) Air Quality Standards. When air quality in an area meets all standards, the area is considered to be in attainment. If air monitors detect too much of a pollutant, the area is labeled as nonattainment for that pollutant.

The commission adopts, amends and rescinds rules related to air quality and assigns duties to local air pollution control agencies. The commission, through a program involving four delegated local governments and citizens' input, develops strategies for bringing pollutants down to safe levels in nonattainment areas. The commission makes decisions on appeals from enforcement orders and permit conditions. When necessary, the commission also begins legal actions to ensure compliance with Missouri Air Conservation Law and rules.

Zimmermann, David, (D), chair, labor representative;
Pendergrass, Gary J., (R), vice chair, public member;
Baker, Jack C., (D), agriculture representative;
Garnett, Mark S., (D), public member;
Moore, Kyra, staff director, Air Conservation Commission; director, Air Pollution Control Program;
Vacancies (3).

Small Business Compliance Advisory Committee

The Small Business Compliance Advisory Committee and Small Business Ombudsman are supported by the Air Pollution Control Program. The Clean Air Amendments require states to implement a three-component program to assist small businesses in their efforts to comply with air regulations: the Small Business Ombudsman, technical assistance to small businesses and the compliance advisory committee.

Cole, T. Robin III, chair;
Holsman, Gale, vice chair;
Potterfield, Randy L., member;
Cain, Pam, member;
Flowers, Carlton, staff contact, Small Business Compliance Advisory Committee;
Vacancies (3).

Environmental Services Program

The Environmental Services Program provides analytical information and scientific data that supports the department. The program also provides direct assistance to local communities and emergency responders throughout Missouri.

DAVID ZIMMERMANN
Chair
Air Conservation Commission

GARY J. PENDERGRASS
Vice Chair / Public Member
Air Conservation Commission

JACK C. BAKER
Agriculture Representative
Air Conservation Commission

MARK S. GARNETT
Public Member
Air Conservation Commission

KYRA MOORE
Staff Director
Air Conservation Commission

The Environmental Emergency Response Section provides 24/7 support and response capability for hazardous substance releases, radiological incidents, homeland security events, and natural disasters. The section also supports law enforcement in managing hazardous wastes associated with drug labs. In FY 2014, nearly 2,200 incidents were reported via the statewide emergency response line (573) 634-2436.

The program houses the state's environmental laboratory. The laboratory is accredited by the

U.S. Environmental Protection Agency to perform chemical analyses of public drinking water samples. This service is provided to all public drinking water systems statewide. The laboratory also analyzes air, soil and other water samples. In FY 2014, chemists conducted more than 64,800 tests on approximately 24,800 samples.

The program operates about 190 air-monitoring instruments at 51 locations statewide. These instruments monitor air pollutants known to affect people's health. This data may determine whether an area meets federal standards for ozone, carbon monoxide and other pollutants. The data also helps department staff identify air pollution trends, investigate citizen complaints, determine sources of air pollution and keep Missourians posted on current air quality.

The water quality monitoring section performs monitoring to assess the health of lakes, rivers and streams. This section collects water and sediment samples throughout the state of Missouri and performs biological monitoring, stream surveys, monitoring of fish tissues, and bacterial analyses of surface waters as well as other sampling events and special studies.

Hazardous Waste Program

The department's Hazardous Waste Program protects public health and the environment by protecting Missouri's water, soil and air from hazardous wastes and hazardous substances. In addition to enforcing state and federal laws to ensure proper management of hazardous wastes being generated today, the program also oversees the cleanup of problem sites resulting from poor waste management in the past.

The Hazardous Waste Program reviews permit applications and provides oversight on hazardous waste treatment, storage and disposal facilities as well as shipments of radioactive waste transported through Missouri.

The department's Hazardous Waste Management Program facilitates long-term stewardship of sites where management of contaminated environmental media is necessary to protect human health and the environment. The program maintains an easy-to-use online source for site-specific information about long-term stewardship sites so developers, planners and others can learn about use restrictions tied to the land and ensure property is being used safely.

The program's compliance and enforcement staff assist the department's regional offices with inspections of hazardous waste generators and treatment, storage and disposal facilities.

The program oversees cleanup activities at federal facilities in Missouri, including those owned or operated by the U.S. Department of En-

ELIZABETH B. AULL
Vice Chair, Waste Management
Industry Representative,
Hazardous Waste Management
Commission

ANDREW J. BRACKER
Public Member
Hazardous Waste Management
Commission

JAMES T. (Jamie) FRAKES
Public Member
Hazardous Waste Management
Commission

DAVID LAMB
Staff Director
Hazardous Waste Management
Commission

ergy, U.S. Department of Defense, other federal agencies and, in some cases, companies that have a contractual tie with one of the federal agencies.

The program's Superfund Section investigates and oversees cleanups of contaminated property where a release of a hazardous substance has occurred, including sites on the federal National Priorities List and those on the Missouri Registry of Confirmed Abandoned or Uncontrolled Hazardous Waste Disposal Sites. This section also manages the Natural Resources Damages Program, which evaluates injuries to natural resources, negotiates legal settlements and then uses recovered funds to conduct restoration of injured resources.

The program's voluntary cleanup initiative puts properties contaminated by hazardous waste back into productive use by allowing landowners to pay voluntarily for state oversight of cleanups. Landowners receive certification, reducing their environmental liability and increasing economic development in distressed areas.

The program's tanks section provides environmental oversight of leaking underground storage tanks and technical guidance for their closure.

The Hazardous Waste Program carries out the policies of the Missouri Hazardous Waste Management Commission.

Hazardous Waste Management Commission

The Hazardous Waste Management Commission encourages efforts to recycle, incinerate, properly dispose of or otherwise treat hazardous waste. The commission is responsible for categorizing hazardous waste by disposal method and determines fees to be paid by owners or operators of hazardous waste facilities that must obtain a permit. The commission establishes regulations for the generation, transportation, treatment, storage, cleanup and disposal of hazardous waste and hazardous substances, as well as for the operation and cleanup of petroleum underground storage tanks. The commission also hears appeals and rules on requests for variances.

All members represent the general interest of the public and have an interest in and knowledge of waste management and the effects of improper waste management on the health of the public and the environment.

Adams, Charles, (D), chair, agriculture representative;

Aull, Elizabeth B., (R), vice chair, waste management industry representative;

Bracker, Andrew J., (D), public member;

Foresman, Michael R., (R), waste generating industry representative;

Frakes, James T. (Jamie), (R), public member;

Jordan, Mark, (R), retail petroleum industry representative;

Lamb, David, staff director, Hazardous Waste Management Commission; director Hazardous Waste Program;

Vacancy (1);.

Regional and Satellite Offices

The regional offices and satellite offices assist with local environmental matters. Regional offices in St. Louis, Kansas City, Springfield, Poplar Bluff and Macon provide the department closer contact with the public through field inspections of regulated facilities, complaint investigation, front-line troubleshooting and technical assistance, as well as local environmental emergency response.

Soil and Water Conservation Program

The Soil and Water Conservation Program administers the policies and general programs for agricultural lands developed by the Soil and Water Districts Commission. The primary responsibility of the program is to assist local soil and water

conservation districts as they promote voluntary soil and water conservation to their constituents. The districts provide financial incentives and technical assistance working with state and federal conservation partners to agricultural landowners.

Other program activities include administering statewide cost-share assistance and providing educational programs on soil and water conservation. The program provides direct assistance to the 114 county soil and water conservation districts through grants and training to support district staff and other administrative expenses. The program also provides each district with a website at *swcd.mo.gov* as well as software and training to further assist constituents.

Missouri citizens have shown strong support for soil and water conservation and state parks by passing a one-tenth-of-one percent Parks, Soils and Water Sales Tax in 1984, 1988, 1996 and 2006 to fund these efforts. In 2006, the tax passed with more than 70 percent voting in favor of continuing the tax. Half of the sales tax is deposited in the Soil and Water Conservation Sales Tax Fund to support programs within the Department of Natural Resources used for saving soil and protecting the water resources of the state of Missouri.

Soil and Water Districts Commission

Vandiver, Gary, (D), chair; Resident north of Missouri River;

Gaw, H. Ralph, (D), vice chair; resident south of Missouri River;

Ausfahl, Charlie, (D), member; resident north of Missouri River;

Bradley, Thomas, (D), member; resident south of Missouri River;

Lance, Jeff, (R), member; resident north of Missouri River;

Fordyce, Richard, ex *officio* member, director, Department of Agriculture;

Parker Pauley, Sara, ex *officio* member, director, Department of Natural Resources;

Payne, Thomas, ex *officio* member, dean, University of Missouri, College of Agriculture, Food and Natural Resources;

Ziehmer, Robert L., ex *officio* member, director, Department of Conservation;

Meredith, Colleen, staff director, Soil and Water Districts Commission and director, Soil and Water Conservation Program;

Vacancy (1), resident south of Missouri River.

Solid Waste Management Program

The department's Solid Waste Management Program works to help Missourians and Missouri businesses properly manage their solid waste to protect public health and the environment. Per capita, each Missourian generates 1.29 tons of waste each year.

GARY VANDIVER
Chair, Soil and Water
Conservation Program

H. RALPH GAW
Vice Chair, Soil and Water
Conservation Commission

CHARLIE AUSFAHL
Member, Soil and Water
Conservation Commission

THOMAS BRADLEY
Member, Soil and Water
Conservation Commission

JEFF LANCE
Member, Soil and Water
Conservation Commission

RICHARD FORDYCE
Ex Officio Member, Soil and
Water Conservation Program

SARA PARKER PAULY
Ex Officio Member, Soil and
Water Conservation Commission

THOMAS PAYNE
Ex Officio Member, Soil and
Water Conservation Commission

The Solid Waste Management Program issues permits and permit modifications for solid waste disposal and processing facilities. Staff review proposed permits for facility design, construction, operations and proper monitoring controls. Program staff inspect permitted facilities quarterly and oversee the operations of these facilities. In addition, staff investigate reports of illegal dumping across Missouri and teach state regulations to landfill operators. Enforcement activities are conducted when necessary to ensure proper solid waste management.

The program oversees the cleanup of illegal tire dumpsites and the Tire Dump Roundup Program, which provides funding to nonprofit groups to clean up dumpsites with less than 500 scrap tires. The cleanups are funded by a 50-cent fee assessed on each new tire purchased in Missouri. Other focuses of the program include planning, financial and technical assistance and educational activities that inform the public of the relationship between individual consumption and solid waste management.

The Solid Waste Management Program works with stakeholders, the general public and regulated facilities to comply with state and federal solid waste regulations.

ROBERT L. ZIEHMER
Ex Officio Member, Soil and
Water Conservation Commission

COLLEEN MEREDITH
Staff Director, Soil and Water
Conservation Commission

Solid Waste Advisory Board

The Solid Waste Advisory Board advises the department about the effectiveness of its technical assistance and challenges experienced by the solid waste management districts in developing and implementing solid waste management plans. The board advises the department and develops improved methods of solid waste minimization, recycling and resource recovery.

The membership of this board consists of the chair of the executive board of each of Missouri's 20 recognized solid waste management districts; two public members; two representatives from the solid waste industry; and one representative from the recycling or composting industry appointed by the director of the Missouri Department of Natural Resources.

Roach, Debbie, chair, Region A;
Heil, Nelson, chair, Region B;
Thompson, Mark, chair, Region C;
Bontrager, Drew, chair, Region D;
Bussen, Chris, chair, Region E;
Crooks, Susan, chair, Region F;
Wyatt, Alan, chair, Region G;
Henry, Lauren, chair, Region H;
Little, Lon, chair, Region I;
True, Brad, chair, Region J;
Wilson, Brady, chair, Region K;
Haasis, John, chair, Region L;
Honey, Jim, chair, Region M;
Lomax, Gary, chair, Region N;
Smith, Tim, chair, Region O;
Collins, Gary L., chair, Region P;
Dement, Darrell, chair, Region Q;
Heaps, Patrick, chair, Region R;
Herbst, Jeannie, chair, Region S;
Wright, Tom, chair, Region T;
Beal, David, EPC Inc., recycling/composting industry representative;
Curry, Tim, Advanced Disposal, solid waste industry representative;
Powers, Casey, Republic Services Inc., solid waste industry representative; and
Wisecarver, Carolyn, public member.

Water Protection Program

The department's Water Protection Program administers clean water and drinking water responsibilities for Missouri. The program is delegated by the U.S. Environmental Protection Agency to conduct duties for the federal Clean Water Act and Safe Drinking Water Act, and also carries out state responsibilities, such as operator certification and construction permitting. The Water Protection Program works with stakeholders, the general public and regulated facilities to comply with state and federal water regulations.

For clean water, the program regulates pollutants entering the state's waters by issuing permits for the construction and operation of wastewater and stormwater discharges. Permits set wastewater treatment levels necessary to protect water quality. These treatment levels are included in permits issued to municipal, industrial and other dischargers. The program evaluates discharge-monitoring and other data to determine whether facilities comply with applicable laws and whether permits are sufficient to protect water quality. The program, with the Division of Environmental Quality's regional offices, is responsible for the inspection and monitoring of water contaminant sources and investigates complaints from the public. If a source violates the Missouri Clean Water Law, the program works with the facility to correct the problem and may assess penalties if necessary.

Water quality standards protect beneficial uses of water such as swimming, maintaining fish and other aquatic life and providing drinking water for people, livestock and wildlife. The program, with the Clean Water Commission, develops water quality standards that provide clear expectations for Missouri water quality and conducts monitoring to determine if the standards are met. Waters that do not meet these standards are placed on the impaired waters (303(d)) list, which provides a focus for special attention to restore water quality in the lakes, streams and rivers. Once a waterway is added to the 303(d) list, the department develops and implements a study to correct the water impairments. Generally, this study takes the form of a total maximum daily load document. It describes the maximum amount of a pollutant that may enter a water body without violating water quality standards.

For drinking water, the program reviews plans and issues permits for the construction and operation of public drinking water systems and requires these systems to monitor for contaminants and take corrective action if any health-based standards are exceeded. The program performs monitoring of drinking water and conducts periodic inspections and provides compliance assistance on water supply problems to cities, water districts, subdivisions, mobile home parks and other facilities.

Financial assistance is provided through grants and low-interest loans to local governments to assist in the construction of wastewater, drinking water and storm water facilities. The program also provides financial and technical assistance for the control of nonpoint source pollution caused by agriculture, mining, transportation and other activities.

Clean Water Commission

The Clean Water Commission brings together and coordinates all aspects of water quality in an effort to ensure the state's progress toward protecting, preserving and improving water quality in Missouri. The commission implements the federal Clean Water Law through rules and policies, and hears appeals based on those permit decisions. When necessary, the commission will take enforcement action against those who violate the Missouri Clean Water Law and related regulations. The commission also establishes funding

JOHN COWHERD
Public Member
Clean Water Commission

BUDDY BENNETT
Wastewater Treatment
Representative
Clean Water Commission

SAM LEAKE
Agriculture, Industry or Mining
Representative
Clean Water Commission

ASHLEY McCARTY
Agriculture, Industry or Mining
Representative
Clean Water Commission

BEN A. (Todd) PARNELL
Public Member
Clean Water Commission

WALLIS WARREN
Public Member
Clean Water Commission

DENNIS WOOD
Public Member
Clean Water Commission

JOHN MADRAS
Staff Director
Clean Water Commission

priorities and oversees financial assistance to protect and preserve water quality.

All commission members represent the general interest of the public and shall have an interest in and knowledge of conservation and the effects and control of water contaminants.

Cowherd, John, (R), public member;

Bennett, Buddy, (I), wastewater treatment representative;

Leake, Sam, (D), agriculture, industry or mining representative;

McCarty, Ashley, (D), agriculture, industry or mining representative;

Parnell, Ben A. (Todd), (D), public member;

Warren, Wallis, (D), public member;

Wood, Dennis, (R), public member;

Madras, John, staff director, Clean Water Commission and director, Water Protection Program.

Safe Drinking Water Commission

The purpose of the Safe Drinking Water Commission is to ensure all 2,800 public water systems in Missouri provide safe drinking water. The commission adopts rules to carry out the requirements of the Missouri Safe Drinking Water Law and Federal Safe Drinking Water Act. The commission establishes criteria and procedures for administering the Drinking Water State Revolving Fund, which makes federal and state loan funds available to communities to upgrade and improve their drinking water systems.

All members of the commission represent the general interest of the public or public water systems.

Grove, Elizabeth K., chair, represents water systems of 75 to 2,500;

Bockenkamp, D. Scott, vice chair, public representative;

Armstrong, Susan McCray, public representative;

Hazelwood, Susan, public representative;

Ledgerwood, Charli Jo, represents a water system of 2,500 to 100,000;

Manning, Bruce, public representative;

Owens, Rodger D., represents water systems 75 or less;

Skouby, Curtis, represents water systems 100,000 or more;

Vacancy (1), public representative;

Sturgess, Steven W., staff director, Safe Drinking Water Commission and director Public Drinking Water Branch.

ELIZABETH K. GROVE
Chair
Safe Drinking Water Commission

D. SCOTT BOCKENKAMP
Vice Chair
Safe Drinking Water Commission

CHARLI JO LEDGERWOOD
Public Representative
Safe Drinking Water Commission

BRUCE MANNING
Public Representative
Safe Drinking Water Commission

SUSAN HAZELWOOD
Public Representative
Safe Drinking Water Commission

RODGER D. OWENS
Safe Drinking Water Commission

CURTIS SKOUBY
Safe Drinking Water Commission

STEVEN W. STURGESS
Staff Director
Safe Drinking Water Commission

Missouri Geological Survey

Telephone: (573) 368-2100 / FAX: (573) 368-2111
dnr.mo.gov/geology

The Missouri Geological Survey provides technical assistance, education and guidance in the use and protection of Missouri's natural resources, interprets the state's geological setting, helps determine the availability of its energy and mineral resources, evaluates and interprets geological hazards and regulates well drillers. The division investigates and reports on the state's geological resources and defines hazardous areas, such as those subject to earthquake or catastrophic collapse. Staff members work to ensure clean air, land and water by working with the mining industry and Missouri communities to minimize the environmental and health impacts of mining activities in Missouri. The department, through the division's Water Resources Center, has statutory authority for water quantity issues such as statewide water use and availability, water resources monitoring and planning, drought assessment, flood and hydrology studies, wetland studies and dam and reservoir safety. The division addresses the development, conservation and utilization of the state's water resources.

The division maintains GeoSTRAT, a Web application that enables users to easily visualize and explore geospatial data using an interactive map. Data such as geology, water wells, sinkholes, historic mine locations, caves, springs, water traces, well logs, aquifers, groundwater information can be viewed to aid in site assessments.

The division cooperates with the U.S. Geological Survey on numerous projects, including the National Cooperative Geologic Mapping Program. The division also performs work under contract for other state agencies through grants and agreements.

The Missouri Geological Survey administers three technical programs: geological survey, land reclamation and water resources.

Division Director and State Geologist

The division director serves as the state geologist and is responsible for ensuring statutory obligations are met. The state geologist is the administrator of the State Oil and Gas Council; serves on the Well Installation Board, Missouri Mining Commission, Dam and Reservoir Safety County and Industrial Minerals Advisory Council; serves as ex officio member on the Board of Geologist

Registration; and is a Missouri representative to the Central United States Earthquake Consortium and the Association of American State Geologists.

Geological Survey Program

The Geological Survey Program uses geologic information and knowledge to assist Missouri citizens in the management of natural resources for a higher standard of living and healthy natural environment. The program gathers and publishes data that describes and interprets Missouri's vast geological resources, which includes geologic maps, reports of investigations and other print and online publications that can be important in making land-use decisions. This information is necessary for locating mineral deposits, managing groundwater resources, selecting waste disposal facilities and evaluating geologic hazards. The program receives thousands of requests for geological assistance each year.

Staff also conduct geologic field investigations that provide technical assistance to the public and government agencies. These services include determining the environmental hazards posed by waste disposal sites and spills of hazardous materials. Geological principles are applied to minimize the impact of chemical releases or spills.

The Geological Survey Program works to protect groundwater from contamination through regulation of the construction of wells, plugging of abandoned wells and licenses well drillers and pump installers conducting business in Missouri. In addition to assistance provided in siting waste disposal facilities, the program also implements the Oil and Gas Act and the Underground Injection Control Program of the Safe Drinking Water Act.

Industrial Minerals Advisory Council

The Industrial Minerals Advisory Council is composed of eight representatives of the industrial minerals industry who are appointed by the director of the department. The representatives include three from limestone producers and one each from industries involved in mining clay, sandstone, sand and gravel, barite and granite. Other members include the director (or designee) of the Department of Transportation and the director (or designee) of the Department of Natural Resources, who acts as chairperson of the council.

The primary duty of the council is to advise the department on the collection, processing, management and distribution of geologic and hydrologic information to assist the industrial mineral industry. Expenditures from the geologic resources fund, which was created to complete these activities, are reviewed by the council, and

JOE GILLMAN
State Geologist, Director
Missouri Geological Survey

the council advises the department on appropriate fees to support the fund.

Gillman, Joe, chair, department designee, director and state geologist, Missouri Geological Survey;

Ahlvers, David, state construction and materials engineer, Department of Transportation;

Carlson, Mikel, limestone, Gredell Engineering Resources Inc.;

Keller, David, clay, Harbison Walker Refractories;

Rowe, Dan, sandstone, Unimin Corporation;

Tucker, Diane, limestone, APAC;

Upp, Chris, limestone, Conco Quarries Inc.;

Winter, Ryan, sand and gravel, Winter Brothers Materials;

Vacancy, barite;

Vacancy, granite;

Vacancy, sandstone.

Land Reclamation Program

The Land Reclamation Program works with the mining industry and Missouri communities to minimize the environmental and health impacts of mining activities in Missouri.

The program carries out Missouri's Abandoned Mine Land program to reclaim abandoned coal mine sites within Missouri that have safety hazards or environmental problems. The program also regulates mining and reclamation activities and issues permits. Reclamation bonds ensure sites are properly graded, replanted and maintained after mining ceases. After the mining company completes all required reclamation, the commission releases these financial assurances and relieves the responsible company of any further reclamation liabilities.

The program works with stakeholders, the general public and regulated facilities to comply with state and federal mining and land reclamation regulations.

DR. GREGORY HADDOCK
Chair
Mining Commission

MIKE LARSEN
Vice Chair
Mining Commission

DR. LESLIE GERTSCH
Public Member
Mining Commission

JOE GILLMAN
Statutory Member
Mining Commission

JOHN MADRAS
Statutory Member
Mining Commission

AARON JEFFERIES
Ex Officio Member
Mining Commission

KEVIN MOHAMMADI
Staff Director / Statutory Member
Mining Commission

Missouri Mining Commission

The Missouri Mining Commission governs Missouri's mining requirements as set forth in three state statutes. These statutes protect public health, safety and the environment from adverse effects of mining and ensure beneficial restoration of mined lands.

The Missouri Mining Commission is responsible for issuing mining permits and oversees Missouri's Abandoned Mine Land program. The commission establishes rules and regulations for mining activities and oversees investigations and inspections necessary to ensure compliance. The commission conducts hearings and when necessary may revoke a permit, order a forfeiture of bonds or cease operations at a facility for failure to comply.

The eight-member commission includes four statutory and four public members. The statutory members include the state geologist, staff director, director of the Missouri Department of Conservation and staff director of the Clean Water Commission. The four public members must have an interest in and knowledge of conservation and land reclamation, and one must have training and experience in surface mining. Only one member of the commission may have a direct link with the mining industry. With Senate approval, the governor appoints four public members. All members serve a four-year term and continue until their successors are appointed.

Haddock, Dr. Gregory, (R), chair, public member;

Larsen, Mike, (D), vice chair, public member; Photo Attached

Gertsch, Dr. Leslie, (I), public member;

Gillman, Joe, statutory member, director and state geologist, Missouri Geological Survey;

Madras, John, statutory member, staff director of Clean Water Commission;

Vacancy, (1), public member;

Jeffries, Aaron, ex officio member, designee, Department of Conservation;

Mohammadi, Kevin, staff director, statutory member, Missouri Mining Commission.

State Oil and Gas Council

The State Oil and Gas Council promotes the economic development and production of Missouri's oil and gas resources, works to ensure that wastes generated by oil and gas wells are managed properly and protects groundwater aquifers that may be affected by oil and gas well drilling.

Madras, John, council chair and director, staff director, Clean Water Commission; director, Water Protection Program;

Dunn-Norman, Shari Ph.D., vice chair and professor, Petroleum Engineering, Missouri University of Science & Technology, Rolla;

Bleakley, David, industry member, Colt Energy Inc.;

Gillman, Joe, statutory member, director and state geologist, Missouri Geological Survey;

Hall, Daniel, chair, Missouri Public Service Commission;

Luebbert, William J., public member;

Ransdall, Bill L., specialist, Community Planning and Development, Department of Economic Development;

Vacancy (1), public member.

Well Installation Board

The Well Installation Board adopts and amends rules governing well construction and the well drilling industry to protect Missouri's groundwater resources. The board also oversees the examination and licensing of all well drillers and pump installers and takes actions against those who violate the Water Well Driller's Act and Well Construction Rules. The board sets fees by establishing rules that do not substantially exceed the cost and expense of administering the law. The board acts as an appeal board by sustaining, reversing or modifying enforcement orders issued by Missouri Geological Survey after an appeal has been made by an affected person.

All members of the board are conversant in well drilling, completion and plugging methods and techniques.

Flynn, Danny, chair, well installation contractor representative;

Schoen, Fred, vice chair, heat pump installation contractor representative;

Broz, Robert, public member;

Lawrence, Robert, well installation contractor representative;

Morgan, M. Sharlene, public member;

St. Clair, Annetta, private well user representative;

Gillman, Joe, statutory member, director and state geologist, Missouri Geological Survey;

Vacancy, public water user representative;

Vacancy, monitoring well installation permit representative.

Water Resources Center

The Water Resources Center addresses the development, conservation and utilization of the state's water resources. To assist communities, public entities and state and federal agencies, the center provides technical assistance through drought assessment, planning and water resource monitoring. Areas of expertise within the center include interstate waters, groundwater, surface water, dam and reservoir safety, wetland studies and water resource planning.

The interstate waters staff coordinates issues relating to major river basins that affect Missouri and provides technical support for negotiations and litigation actions to protect the state's rights to these waters. The groundwater section operates and maintains a groundwater-level observation well network for monitoring Missouri's aquifers. Collection and analysis of groundwater data provides knowledge of available water quantity, aquifer response to water use, groundwater recharge and aquifer characteristics. The surface water section provides technical support by performing water supply analyses, in-stream flow assessments and flood inundation studies. This section also administers the collection and analysis of statewide water use data in accordance with the Major Water User Law. The Dam and Reservoir Safety staff and the Dam and Reservoir Safety Council are responsible for ensuring all new and existing non-agricultural, non-federal dams 35 feet or more in height meet minimum safety standards as established by the Dam and Reservoir Safety Law. The center also provides technical support to the Missouri Drought Assessment Committee and leadership and coordination of regional water resources planning initiatives and wetland activities.

Dam and Reservoir Safety Council

Boehler, Pat, (D), public member;

Buxton, Dan, PE, (D), professional engineer representing public;

Cawlfield, Jeffrey D., PE, (D), engineering geologist;

Dickerson, Kim, (R), industry;

Drury, Kyle, PE, (R), industry representing earthmoving;

Waddell, Tom, (R), owner of dam or reservoir;

Clay, Robert, department designee, chief engineer, Missouri Geological Survey;

Vacancy (1), professional engineer.

Missouri State Parks

Telephone: (573) 751-2479 / FAX: 573-751-8656
Toll free: (800) 334-6946
www.Mostateparks.com

Missouri State Parks, a division of the Missouri Department of Natural Resources, works to protect and interpret the state's most outstanding natural and cultural resources while providing recreational opportunities compatible with those resources. The Missouri State Park system was established in 1917 and includes 87 state parks and historic sites totaling more than 140,000 acres and the Roger Pryor Pioneer Backcountry.

The primary source of funding for the state park system is half of the dedicated constitutional tax of one-tenth-of-one-percent parks, soils and water sales tax. All additional funding comes from revenues generated in the state park system and some federal funds. The parks, soils and water tax was created through a constitutional amendment and earmarked specifically for the state park system and efforts to stop soil erosion. The tax was first approved by voters in 1984, and has since been reapproved by voters three times in 1988, 1996 and 2006. Two-thirds of voters approved the tax the last three times, showing how much Missouri voters support their state park system.

Approximately 18 million people visit the state park system annually to hike, camp, fish, discover the past and explore nature. The state's most outstanding landscapes are preserved for everyone's enjoyment–deep forests, glades, prairies and blue streams and lakes. State historic sites commemorate events or structures of statewide historical importance and honor people of state and national importance. The system includes homes of famous Missourians, Civil War battlefields and reminders of yesterday, such as gristmills and covered bridges.

Missouri State Park Advisory Board

The governor-appointed board was created in 1986 to advise the department on matters relating to state parks and historic sites.

Grant Management

Missouri State Parks is responsible for administering federal grant programs that provide financial assistance to individuals, groups and public entities for a variety of purposes.

The division administers funds from the Recreational Trails Program, which provides federal money for the development of trails. The Missouri Trails Advisory Board views and scores the grant applications and makes recommendations on grant awards.

The division also administers and monitors projects funded through the federal Land and Water Conservation Fund program, which provides federal funds for local outdoor recreation projects.

State Historic Preservation Office

Missouri was one of the first in the nation to establish the State Historic Preservation Office in 1968 following the Historic Preservation Act of 1966. The office helps facilitate the process of identifying properties significant to the citizens,

BILL BRYAN
Director
Missouri State Parks

state and nation, and planning for their preservation.

The department coordinates surveys statewide to identify historic, architectural and archaeological resources. Significant properties identified in the surveys may be nominated to the National Register of Historic Places. Missouri has more than 2,300 listings on the National Register, representing more than 44,000 historic buildings, sites, structures and objects. The Missouri Cultural Resource Inventory is being built from information gathered from the survey and nomination process.

As part of its federally mandated responsibilities, the department reviews all federally funded or licensed projects in Missouri to ensure compliance with related federal legislation. The department also administers federal Historic Preservation Fund matching grants from the U.S. Department of the Interior's National Park Service. These funds are used to help identify, evaluate and protect Missouri's cultural resources. Through Missouri's Certified Local Government program, the department trains municipalities in local preservation techniques and awards federal matching grants to help accomplish local preservation goals.

Since 1976, federal tax incentives and related legislation have promoted interest in rehabilitating historic buildings. In 1998, that interest was augmented with the authorization of state tax credits, administered by the Missouri Department of Economic Development. The federal tax credits are available to private investors who rehabilitate historic buildings for uses that produce income, such as office buildings and apartments. The Department of Natural Resources reviews both federal and state tax credit applications for historic eligibility and conformity with preservation guidelines.

The State Historic Preservation Office also administers the Missouri Heritage Properties Program using funds from the Missouri's Historic Preservation Revolving Fund. The program provides assistance to help preserve endangered publicly owned historic buildings.

Missouri Advisory Council on Historic Preservation

This council reviews all Missouri nominations to the National Register of Historic Places and advises the state's historic preservation officer.

Crittenden, Brent, architect;
Garner, Martha (Kacky), public member;
Hibbeler, Cheryl, public member;
Holland, Antonio, Ph.D., historian;
Kuypers, Thomas, public member;
Shirley, Allen R., economic and community development;
Stepenoff, Bonnie, Ph.D., architectural historian;
Stiritz, Mary (Mimi), historian;
Wiegers, Robert, Ph.D., historic and prehistoric archaeologist;
Wyatt, Dwight E., architect;
Vacancies (2), public members.

Unmarked Human Burial Consultation Committee

This committee was established under provisions of Missouri's Unmarked Human Burial Act, which governs the disposition of unmarked human burial remains uncovered during ground-disturbing activities.

Appointed by the governor, the seven-member committee, which includes an archaeologist, an anthropologist and representatives of minority and Native American groups, makes final decisions as to the respectful treatment and appropriate reburial of all recovered unmarked human remains.

State Parks and State Historic Sites

Central Region

Arrow Rock State Historic Site, Saline County, 15 miles east of Marshall on Missouri 41.
Boone's Lick State Historic Site, Howard County, MM from Missouri 87, 19 miles northwest of Boonville.
Bothwell Lodge State Historic Site, Pettis County, 5 miles north of Sedalia on U.S. 65.
Clark's Hill/Norton State Historic Site, Cole County near Osage City.
Finger Lakes State Park, Boone County, 10 miles north of Columbia on U.S. 63.
Jefferson Landing State Historic Site/Missouri State Museum, Jefferson City, between State Capitol and Governor's Mansion.
Jewell Cemetery State Historic Site, Boone County, near Columbia.

Katy Trail State Park, the 240-mile trail has been developed between Clinton and Machens.
Rock Bridge Memorial State Park, Boone County, 7 miles south of Columbia on Missouri 163.
Sappington Cemetery State Historic Site, Saline County, 4.5 miles southwest of Arrow Rock on County AA Spur.
Van Meter State Park, Saline County, 12 miles northwest of Marshall on Missouri 122.

Kansas City Region

Battle of Island Mound State Historic Site, near Butler in Bates County.
Battle of Lexington State Historic Site, Lafayette County, in Lexington on U.S. 24.
Thomas Hart Benton Home and Studio State Historic Site, Jackson County, 3616 Belleview, Kansas City.
Big Lake State Park, Holt County, 11 miles southwest of Mound City on Missouri 118 and Missouri 159.
Confederate Memorial State Historic Site, Lafayette County, 1 mile north of Higginsville on Missouri 20 and Missouri 13.
Knob Noster State Park, Johnson County, Knob Noster on U.S. 50.
Lewis and Clark State Park, Buchanan County, 20 miles southwest of St. Joseph on Missouri 45.
Rock Island Trail State Park, from Pleasant Hill to Windsor (under development).
Wallace State Park, Clinton County, 6 miles south of Cameron on Missouri 121.
Watkins Woolen Mill State Park and Historic Site, Clay County, 6.5 miles north of Excelsior Springs on U.S. 69.
Weston Bend State Park, Platte County, 1 mile south of Weston on Missouri 45.

Lakes Region

Battle of Carthage State Historic Site, Jasper County, East Chestnut St., Carthage.
Bennett Spring State Park, Dallas County, 12 miles west of Lebanon on Missouri 64.
Big Sugar Creek State Park, McDonald County, 5 miles east of Pineville on County Road S.E. W24.
Nathan Boone Homestead State Historic Site, Greene County, north of Ash Grove on Missouri V.
Ha Ha Tonka State Park, Camden County, 5 miles southwest of Camdenton.
Harry S Truman Birthplace State Historic Site, Barton County, in Lamar on U.S. 160.
Harry S Truman State Park, Benton County, west of Warsaw.
Lake of the Ozarks State Park, Camden County, near Osage Beach on Missouri 42.
Osage Village State Historic Site, Vernon County, near Schell City, 9 miles north of U.S. 54 off Vernon County C.

Pomme de Terre State Park, Hickory County, 4 miles north of Pittsburg on Missouri 64.

Prairie State Park, Barton County, 25 miles north of Joplin on Barton County P and K, off Missouri 43.

Roaring River State Park, Barry County, 7 miles south of Cassville on Missouri 112.

Stockton State Park, Cedar County, at Stockton on Missouri 215.

Table Rock State Park, Stone County, 5 miles west of Branson on Missouri 165.

Northeast Region

Battle of Athens State Historic Site, Clark County, near Revere.

Crowder State Park, Grundy County, 2 miles west of Trenton on Missouri 128.

Cuivre River State Park, Lincoln County, 5 miles east of Troy on Missouri 47.

Gen. John J. Pershing Boyhood Home State Historic Site, Linn County, in Laclede on Missouri 139.

Graham Cave State Park, Montgomery County, 2 miles west of Danville on County TT.

Iliniwek Village State Historic Site, Clark County, southeast of St. Francoisville.

Locust Creek Covered Bridge State Historic Site, Linn County, 3 miles west of Laclede on U.S. 36.

Long Branch State Park, Macon County, 5 miles west of Macon on U.S. 36.

Mark Twain Birthplace State Historic Site, Monroe County, near Paris on Missouri 107.

Mark Twain State Park, Monroe County, at Florida on Missouri 107.

Pershing State Park, Linn County, 2 miles southwest of Laclede off U.S. 36.

Thousand Hills State Park, Adair County, 4 miles west of Kirksville on Missouri 157.

Union Covered Bridge State Historic Site, Monroe County, 8 miles southwest of Paris on County C.

Wakonda State Park, Lewis County, 3 miles south of LaGrange on U.S. 61.

Southeast Region

Big Oak Tree State Park, Mississippi County, 10 miles south of East Prairie on County A to Missouri 102.

Bollinger Mill State Historic Site and Burfordville Covered Bridge State Historic Site, Cape Girardeau County, in Burfordville on Missouri 34.

Current River State Park, north of Eminence in Shannon County (under development).

Dillard Mill State Historic Site, Crawford County, 12 miles southeast of Steelville near Missouri 49 at Dillard.

Elephant Rocks State Park, Iron County, northeast edge of Graniteville on Missouri 21.

Fort Davidson State Historic Site, Iron County, in Pilot Knob on Missouri 21.

Grand Gulf State Park, Oregon County, 6 miles west of Thayer.

Hunter-Dawson State Historic Site, New Madrid County, in New Madrid on U.S. 61.

Johnson's Shut-Ins State Park, Reynolds County, 8 miles north of Lesterville on County N.

Lake Wappapello State Park, Wayne County, 12 miles north of Poplar Bluff on U.S. 67 and nine miles east on Missouri 172.

Montauk State Park, Dent County, 21 miles southwest of Salem on Missouri 119.

Morris State Park, Dunklin County, southwest of Malden.

Onondaga Cave State Park, Crawford County, 3 miles south of Leasburg on County H.

Roger Pryor Pioneer Backcountry, Shannon County, off State Route P from Hwy. 72.

Sam A. Baker State Park, Wayne County, 3 miles north of Patterson on Missouri 143.

Taum Sauk Mountain State Park, Iron County, 9 miles southwest of Ironton.

Towosahgy State Historic Site, Mississippi County, east of East Prairie on County FF.

Trail of Tears State Park, Cape Girardeau County, 10 miles north of Cape Girardeau on Missouri 177.

St. Louis Region

Castlewood State Park, St. Louis County, near Ballwin.

Deutschheim State Historic Site, Gasconade County, 109 W. Second St., Hermann.

Dr. Edmund A. Babler Memorial State Park, St. Louis County, 20 miles west of St. Louis on Missouri 109 off St. Louis County CC.

Don Robinson State Park, Jefferson County, southeast of Pacific (under development).

Edward "Ted" and Pat Jones-Confluence Point State Park, St. Charles County, in West Alton.

Felix Valle State Historic Site, Ste. Genevieve County, Merchant at Second St., Ste. Genevieve.

First Missouri State Capitol State Historic Site, St. Charles County, in St. Charles on Main St.

Gov. Daniel Dunklin's Grave State Historic Site, Jefferson County, in Herculaneum on U.S. 61.

Hawn State Park, Ste. Genevieve County, 13 miles east of Farmington on Missouri 32.

Mastodon State Historic Site, Jefferson County, near Imperial, off I-55.

Meramec State Park, Franklin County, 4 miles east of Sullivan on Missouri 185.

Missouri Mines State Historic Site, St. Francois County, in Park Hills on Hwy. 32.

Robertsville State Park, Franklin County, 8 miles east of I-44 on Rt. O.

Route 66 State Park, St. Louis County, 2 miles east of Eureka off I-44.

St. Francois State Park, St. Francois County, 4 miles north of Bonne Terre on U.S. 67.

St. Joe State Park, St. Francois County, in Park Hills.

Sandy Creek Covered Bridge State Historic Site, Jefferson County, 5 miles north of Hillsboro, off Missouri 21.

Scott Joplin House State Historic Site, St. Louis County, 2658-A Delmar, St. Louis.

Washington State Park, Washington County, 14 miles northwest of Potosi on Missouri 21.

Department of Public Safety

Lewis and Clark State Office Bldg.
PO Box 749, Jefferson City 65102
Telephone: (573) 751-4905 / FAX: (573) 751-5399
www.dps.mo.gov
Email: dpsinfo@dps.mo.gov

Mission

Established in 1974, the Department of Public Safety (DPS) coordinates statewide law enforcement, criminal justice and public safety efforts to ensure a safe environment for Missourians. The department's mission is to "provide a safe and secure environment for all individuals through efficient and effective law enforcement, national defense, disaster preparedness, service to veterans and education." The department is organized into nine separate agencies: Office of the Director, Missouri Capitol Police, Division of Fire Safety, Division of Alcohol and Tobacco Control, Missouri State Highway Patrol, Missouri National Guard (Office of the Adjutant General), State Emergency Management Agency, Missouri Veterans Commission and Missouri Gaming Commission.

Office of the Director

The director of public safety is appointed to this cabinet-level position by the governor, with the advice and consent of the Senate. The director is responsible for developing public safety programs, peace officer training and licensing and providing legislative guidance on criminal justice issues. Additionally, the director is responsible for overseeing distribution of state and federal resources and funds in contracts for narcotics control, Internet sex crime elimination, victims' assistance, crime prevention, interoperable communications, juvenile justice, substance abuse treatment and student loan repayment for prosecutors and public defenders. As the department's central management unit, the director's office coordinates departmental budget, personnel, legislative matters and related financial and administrative activities. The director's office is also responsible for the administration of specific programs conferred upon it by the legislature or governor. These programs are:

The **Juvenile Justice Unit** administers the federal **Juvenile Justice and Delinquency Prevention Act Formula Grant Program (Title II)** and **Juvenile Accountability Block Grant Program (JABG)**

from the U.S. Department of Justice, Office of Juvenile Justice and Delinquency Prevention for projects to improve juvenile justice in Missouri and provides staff support for the state **Juvenile Justice Advisory Group (JJAG)**.

Missouri Juvenile Justice Advisory Group (JJAG)

Morris, Edwin F., chair, Clark;
Allen, Carolyn, Columbia;
Esserman, Joan M., Webster Groves;
Heard Days, Rita, St. Louis;
Heberle, Bill, Jefferson City;
Ifland, Jordan Ashley*, Columbia;
Kissock, Suzanne, St. Joseph;
Koochel, Erin*, Kearney;
Lee, Donald, Independence;
Lowenstein, Hon. Hal, Kansas City;
Maddox, Larry, Springfield;
Nelson, David, Jefferson City;
Parrish, Hon. John, Lee's Summit;
Ponce, Lindsay*, O'Fallon;
Robinson, Dr. Pili, Florissant;
Wood, Keith, Maryville Department of Public Safety.

―――――――
*Youth Member.

The **Criminal Justice/Law Enforcement (CJ/LE) Unit** administers the following federal grant programs from the U.S. Department of Justice: **Edward Byrne Memorial Justice Assistance Grant (JAG); Local Law Enforcement Block Grant (LLEBG); Residential Substance Abuse Treatment (RSAT); John R. Justice (JRJ); and Paul Coverdell National Forensic Sciences (PCNFS)** and the following state grant programs: **Missouri Crime Lab Upgrade Program (MCLUP), State Cyber Crime Grant (SCCG), and Deputy Sheriff Salary Supplementation Fund (DSSSF)**, and coordinates the **Department of Defense 1033 Excess Property Program.** The **JAG** program makes funds available for law enforcement, drug enforcement, Drug Abuse Resistance Program (DARE) and school resources officers, drug treatment, information sharing/technology and other prevention initiatives that strengthen the criminal justice system. The **LLEBG** program awards funds to law enforcement agencies to purchase equipment directly related to basic law enforcement functions and officer safety. The **RSAT** program assists state and local governments in developing and implementing substance abuse treatment programs in correctional and detention facilities. The **JRJ** program provides student loan repayment assistance for state and federal public defenders and state prosecutors. The **PCNFS** program makes funds available to help improve the quality and timeliness of forensic sciences within crime labo-

LANE J. ROBERTS
Director

STEPHEN P. SOKOLOFF
Deputy Director

DARLA IVEN
Administrative Assistant

TRACY McGINNIS
General Counsel

MICHAEL O'CONNELL
Director of Communications

HEATHER HASLAG
Criminal Justice/Law
Enforcement Program Manager

TYLER RIEKE
Crime Victim Services Unit
Program Manager

SUSAN SUDDUTH
Crime Victims Compensation
Program Manager

ratories. The **MCLUP** program provides financial assistance to defray expenses of crime laboratories. The **SCCG** program makes funds available for law enforcement to combat Internet sex crimes against children. The **DSSSF** program provides funding to supplement deputy sheriffs' salaries. The **1033** program provides excess military equipment to civilian law enforcement agencies for use in counter-narcotics and counterterrorism operations and officer safety. The CJ/LE Unit also provides staff support for the **Missouri Sheriff Methamphetamine Relief Taskforce (MoSMART)** and the **Missouri Crime Laboratory Review Commission (MCLRC).**

JEREMY SPRATT
Peace Officer Standards and
Training Program Manager

Missouri Sheriff Methamphetamine Relief Taskforce (MoSMART)

Petty, Jim, Morgan County sheriff;
Hughes, Christopher, Chariton County sheriff;
Bond, Kevin, Pettis County sheriff;
Hardwick, Robert, Adair County sheriff;
Underwood, George, Oregon County sheriff.

Missouri Crime Laboratory Review Commission

Sokoloff, Stephen, DPS designee;
Hunt, Ted, prosecuting attorney;

Cisar, Tim, criminal defense attorney;
Hampton, Bryan, crime laboratory senior manager;
Williams, Paul, law enforcement officer.

The **Missouri Crime Victim Services Unit (CVSU)** administers the federal **Victims of Crime Act (VOCA)**; federal **STOP Violence Against Women Act (VAWA); Sexual Assault Services Program (SASP);** and the **State Services to Victims Fund (SSVF)** and oversees the **Missouri Of-**

fice for Victims of Crime, which maintains the statewide automated crime victim notification system (**MOVANS**) and provides guidance to not-for-profit, local and state agencies on practices and policies that impact crime victims. **VOCA, VAWA, SASP** and **SSVF** provide grants that fund local victim service providers, law enforcement agencies, prosecutors and other public and private nonprofit agencies to assist crime victims in Missouri. The unit strives to ensure that people affected by crime are treated with fairness, dignity and respect, and to facilitate communication between victim organizations and the government.

Crime Victims' Compensation Program (CVC)

The **Crime Victims' Compensation Program (CVC)** financially assists victims of violent crime in paying for reasonable medical expenses, counseling expenses, funeral expenses, lost wages and loss of support. In the case of death, the program can help the victim's dependents with loss of support if the victim was gainfully employed. As a payer of last resort, the program considers out-of-pocket expenses only after all collateral sources have been exhausted. A maximum benefit of $25,000 may be awarded on eligible claims.

Sexual Assault Forensic Examination Program (SAFE)

The **Sexual Assault Forensic Examination Program (SAFE)** provides payments to cover the cost of gathering evidence during the forensic examination for victims of sexual crimes in Missouri. The medical provider is required to bill the SAFE Program for reasonable charges incurred during the forensic examination. The patient may not be billed for any forensic examination charges.

Child Physical Abuse Forensic Examinations (CPAFE)

Child Physical Abuse Forensic Examination (CPAFE) program provides payments to cover the cost of gathering evidence during the forensic examination for victims of child physical abuse in Missouri. The medical provider is required to bill the CPAFE program for reasonable charges incurred during the forensic examination. The patient may not be billed for any forensic examination charges.

Peace Officer Standards and Training Program (POST)

The **Peace Officer Standards and Training Program (POST)** is a regulatory program with responsibility for licensing peace officers, ensuring

BRYAN COURTNEY
Director, Missouri Statewide
Interoperability Network

compliance with peace officer continuing education requirements, and conducting investigations for disciplining the licenses of peace officers as specified by Chapter 590, RSMo. The POST Program also licenses corporate security advisors, law enforcement basic training centers, basic training instructors, approves law enforcement training curricula and provides staff support for the POST Commission.

Peace Officer Standards and Training Commission

Johnson, Capt. Ron S., chair, state law enforcement member;
Cleaver, Dr. Emanuel III, public member;
Boyer, Sheriff Oliver Glenn, sheriff member;
Cox, Sheriff Stephen V., sheriff member;
Diehl, Sheriff Dwight, sheriff member;
Clark, Sergeant Edward, law enforcement member;
Williams, Chief Paul F., chief of police member;
Mills, Chief Gregory P., chief of police member;
Juden, Chief Charles, chief of police member;
Scanga, Chief Diane, training center director member;
Hughley, Sergeant Jeffery A., law enforcement member.

Office of Homeland Security

The overall responsibility for Missouri's homeland security program falls under the Department of Public Safety. The director of public safety is the governor's designated homeland security advisor. DPS agencies, including the National Guard, Highway Patrol, Division of Fire Safety, State Emergency Management Agency and Capitol Police all support and are considered key to keeping Missouri safe and secure.

The Missouri Office of Homeland Security (OHS) is the designated State Administrative Agency (SAA) and responsible for applying for and administering the Homeland Security suite of grants and the Emergency Management Performance Grant for the state. Responsibilities for homeland security-related training and exercises are a collaborative effort of OHS and SEMA. OHS works closely with other stakeholders to ensure a "one state, one strategy" program. The governor's Homeland Security Advisory Council (HSAC) and the Regional Homeland Security Oversight Committees (RHSOC) work with OHS to ensure seamless engagement and shared ownership of Missouri's homeland security program down to the local level.

Missouri Statewide Interoperability Network (MoSWIN)

In 2009, the Department of Public Safety, in conjunction with its public safety partners, began construction of Missouri's statewide interoperable radio network. The MoSWIN system, which uses the VHF High Band (150MHz) radio spectrum, became operational in 2012 and provides the infrastructure for interoperable communications throughout Missouri for local and state agencies, including the Missouri State Highway Patrol, which also utilize MoSWIN for intra-agency communications. There are two levels of communication for local jurisdictions. As of May 2015, 134 Level 1 agencies utilized MoSWIN for full-time, day-to-day communications, in addition to interoperable communications. As of May 2015, 862 Level 2 agencies utilized MoSWIN to achieve interoperability with local and state agencies but retained their internal radio communications system for day-to-day operations. MoSWIN system administration and operations headquarters is at the **Missouri Interoperability Center (MIC)** in Jefferson City. The MIC also provides training and technical assistance.

Advisory Committee for 9-1-1 Service Oversight

The Missouri General Assembly, through state statute (section 650.330, RSMo), established a committee on 9-1-1 service oversight, with the director of public safety designated to be the chair of the committee. Coordinated through the Office of Administration in the 1990s, these duties were transferred to the Office of Homeland Security in 2009. OHS serves as the state contact for 9-1-1 issues and is the state administrative agent for related grant administration purposes.

The Advisory Committee for 9-1-1 Service Oversight assists and advises the key policymakers in regard to the challenges, availability, implementation and enhancement of the emergency communication access number 9-1-1 common to all jurisdictions throughout the state. The following subcommittees have been identified to provide ongoing strategic planning to support Missouri's 9-1-1 program: legislative, professional standards, technical and educational/outreach.

The advisory committee members are:

Berry, Mary M., Maysville;
Hall, Michael, Hannibal;
Head, Mark D., Leslie;
Hasheider, Mark, Cape Girardeau;
Herring, Rodney, Trenton;
Jarrett, Terry M., Public Service Commission, Jefferson City;
Knight, Betty, Platte City;
Person, James, Belton;
Pierson, Elizabeth M., Norborne;
Preston, Nathan, Richmond;
Robb, Dr. Brian, Liberty;
Roberts, Lane J., Department of Public Safety, Jefferson City;
Rowden, Danny, Wright City;
Stenger, Debra, St. Paul;
Wells, Alan, Farmington;
Representative of Municipalities.

Missouri Capitol Police

630 W. Main St., Jefferson City 65101
Telephone: (573) 751-2764 / FAX: (573) 526-3898
Email: cpinfo@dps.mo.gov
www.mcp.dps.mo.gov

Since 1983, Missouri Capitol Police has been the primary law enforcement agency for the 72-acre state office building campus known as the Capitol Complex. Located within that area are: the state Capitol Building, Jefferson Building, Transportation Building, Supreme Court, James C. Kirkpatrick State Information Center, Broadway Building, Truman Building, Governor's Mansion, Jefferson Landing historic site and associated parking facilities and grounds. Capitol Police also provide services to state agencies and facilities in other areas of Jefferson City. Capitol Police has statutory authority on all state-owned/leased property in Cole County. Capitol Police oversees a computerized, centrally monitored, fire/life safety/after-hours entry control system in the Capitol Complex buildings.

Field Operations

Missouri Capitol Police officers patrol the buildings and grounds in their jurisdiction 24 hours a day, seven days a week. Patrols are made on foot, by vehicle and on bicycle. Criminal investigations, medical emergencies, traffic accidents, security and fire alarms and security escorts are only a few of the many incidents and calls for service officers provide to over 15,000 state employees and over 200,000 annual visitors to the seat of government.

Special Services

Capitol Police officers regularly provide specialized safety training and personal safety instruction for Capitol and other state employees and conduct site security surveys at Jefferson City state facilities.

Executive Protection

Since 1978, officers have staffed the Missouri Governor's Mansion. A team of specially trained officers is assigned on a full-time basis to the Missouri Governor's Mansion, providing residential security for the state's first family 24 hours a day.

Communications Operations

In addition to radio and telephone communications with the public and other agencies, communications operators are responsible for management of a fire/life safety monitoring system, which includes fire, intrusion and duress alarms and after-hours building access.

Missouri Division of Fire Safety

Office of the State Fire Marshal
205 Jefferson St., 13th Fl.; PO Box 844
Jefferson City 65102
Telephone: (573) 751-2930 / FAX: (573) 751-5710
www.dfs.dps.mo.gov
Email: firesafe@dfs.dps.mo.gov

The Missouri State Fire Marshal's Office was established by the 76th Missouri General Assembly in 1973. Effective September 1985, the office was renamed the Division of Fire Safety and was housed within the Missouri Department of Public Safety.

The division is charged with the oversight and enforcement of programs that maintain the safety and well-being of the general public. Responsibilities include: providing fire safety standards and inspections for all state-licensed facilities; investigating fires and explosions in the state upon request; regulating the use and sale of fireworks and licensing fireworks operators; training and certification of firefighters and emergency response personnel; inspecting and licensing nonexempt boilers and pressure vessels; inspecting and issuing operating permits for elevator-related equipment; inspecting and issuing operating permits for amusement rides; monitoring of fire emergencies and assisting local, area and regional fire authorities through the State Fire Mutual Aid System; overseeing the rules and regulations relating to the licensing of explosive blasters and the registration of explosive users; and overseeing the fire standard compliant cigarette program.

TODD HURT
Chief
Capitol Police

PAUL MINZE
Captain, Operations
Commander, Capitol Police

KENT WALKER
Lieutenant, Executive Protection
Commander, Capitol Police

ERIC CLEMONS
Lieutenant, Support Services
Commander, Capitol Police

Fire Service Training/Certification

The Division of Fire Safety's Training and Certification Unit is responsible for the training and certification of over 25,000 firefighters in the state of Missouri. In addition, the unit's customers include representatives from fire service, law enforcement, private industry and other state agencies. The division offers 16 different courses and 22 levels of state certification. The Missouri Division of Fire Safety is accredited through the International Fire Service Accreditation Congress, National Board of Fire Service Professional Qualifications and the Peace Officer Standards and Training Commission.

State Fire Mutual Aid

The Division of Fire Safety coordinates activation and deployment of local resources when interregional mutual aid assistance is requested. When an incident occurs within any one of the nine mutual aid regions and all local resources become exhausted, the regional coordinator contacts the Division of Fire Safety's state mutual aid coordinator to request mutual aid assistance of specific resources. The state coordinator in turn

GREG CARRELL
State Fire Marshal
Division of Fire Safety

SHERRY HOELSCHER
Fiscal/Administrative Manager,
Division of Fire Safety

LARRY WATSON
Public Safety Manager–Elevators
and Amusement Rides Program,
Division of Fire Safety

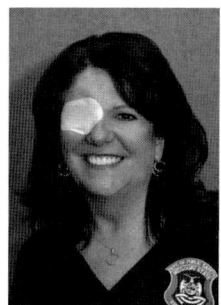

KIM BECKER
Public Safety Manager–Training
and Certification Program
Division of Fire Safety

contacts mutual aid coordinators within unaffected regions to locate and deploy the needed resources to the impacted region. With information gathered from the annual Fire Department Registration program and continued input and support from all fire service agencies, the system stands ready to mitigate the effects of small or large scale emergencies. The state mutual aid coordinator also administers the National Fire Incident Reporting System.

Fire Safety Education/Advisory Commission

The Division of Fire Safety addresses the fire service training needs of our state through contracts in cooperation with community colleges, colleges, regional training facilities, fire and emergency services training entities and universities as appropriated. The Missouri Fire Safety Education/Advisory Commission reviews and determines appropriate programs and activities for which funds may be expended and advises the division accordingly.

Fire Safety Inspection

Fire safety inspectors conduct inspections of facilities and locations licensed or certified by state agencies including the Department of Health and Senior Services, the Department of Mental Health, the Department of Social Services and senior citizens nutrition centers. These inspections, based upon nationally recognized codes and standards, are designed to eliminate fire safety hazards for occupants of childcare homes and centers, facilities and homes providing care for the mentally challenged, foster care providers and facilities housing at-risk youth.

State statute requires the Division of Fire Safety to oversee fire protection sprinkler systems, fire alarm systems, and smoke sections in residential care facilities and assisted living facilities.

WILLIAM ZIERES
Law Enforcement Manager
Division of Fire Safety

JOE BROCKMAN
Public Safety Manager–
Boiler and Pressure Vessel Safety
Program, Division of Fire Safety

ERIC LEWIS
Public Safety Manager–Fire
Safety Inspection Program
Division of Fire Safety

Approximately 600 existing facilities require annual inspections by the Division of Fire Safety in coordination with the Department of Health and Senior Services.

Fire Investigation

The Fire Investigation Unit provides fire- and explosive-related investigative services to Missouri's fire service and law enforcement agencies. Under section 320.230, RSMo, the state fire marshal and the appointed investigators are responsible for investigating incidents involving the possibility of arson, explosion or related offenses as requested by the fire service, law enforcement or prosecuting attorneys within the state. Investigators are trained in several fields of expertise, including insurance fraud, explosive recognition, weapons of mass destruction and post-blast investigations.

Fire Investigators are Peace Officer Standards and Training (POST)-licensed law enforcement officers with the power of arrest for criminal offenses when investigating the cause, origin or circumstances of fires, explosions or similar occurrences involving the possibility of arson or related offenses. Investigators also have arrest powers when aiding and assisting the sheriff or the chief of police of any county or designated representative upon request.

Fireworks Enforcement

The Division of Fire Safety is charged with enforcing section 320.106, RSMo, involving the investigation, permission and inspection of the fireworks industry in Missouri. This statute requires prospective manufacturers, distributors, jobbers, wholesalers, seasonal retailers and persons requesting special fireworks displays to apply to the Division of Fire Safety for permits to do business in Missouri. Applicants must meet certain requirements, follow safety procedures and acquire a fireworks license.

The scope of this program was broadened by the 2004 legislature with the addition of testing and licensing of individuals who shoot fireworks for public displays. This includes proximate (indoor) fireworks shows.

The division's inspection and investigation staff conduct inspections of facilities selling, manufacturing or distributing fireworks.

Blasting Safety Act

The Blasting Safety Act was created in 2007 when the General Assembly enacted House Bill 298. This act established the Blasting Safety Board to develop and adopt a code of rules and regulations relating to the licensing of blasters and the registration of explosives users. The act also requires the division to investigate complaints involving blasting operations throughout the state.

The Blasting Safety Board continues to advise the division on rules and regulations governing the program.

Boiler and Pressure Vessel Rules

The Missouri Boiler and Pressure Vessel Act, per sections 650.200–650.295, RSMo, was passed in 1984 and became mandatory on Nov. 12, 1986. The purpose of the law is to ensure the safety of the general public and those who work in the vicinity of boilers and pressure vessels and to protect property.

The act requires periodic inspections of boilers and pressure vessels and the issuance of state operating certificates. Inspections are performed by certified inspectors in accordance with nationally recognized standards. Vessels found to have violations in relation to these standards are required to be repaired prior to the issuance of the state operating certificate. Accidents involving boilers or pressure vessels are investigated by the Boiler and Pressure Vessel Safety Unit.

The Board of Boiler and Pressure Vessel Rules advises the division on rules and regulations governing the program.

Elevator Safety Act

In 1994, the 86th General Assembly enacted House Bill 1035 creating the Elevator Safety Act. This act established an Elevator Safety Board to develop and adopt a code of rules and regulations relating to the construction, maintenance, testing and inspection of all elevators and similar devices, as well as the evaluation of variance requests.

The legislation requires annual safety inspections of every elevator and similar devices as specified in the statute. Upon an approved inspection, a state operating certificate is issued.

Amusement Ride Safety Act

In 1997, House Bill 276 was enacted relating to amusement ride safety. It requires annual safety inspections of all amusement rides and mandates each ride have a state operating permit before operating in the state. Additionally, the division staff has the authority to conduct spot inspections on any ride operating in the state.

If a serious injury or death occurs as the result of the operation of an amusement ride the Division of Fire Safety initiates an investigation into the cause of the accident.

The legislation also places certain restrictions on the riders of amusement rides. A violation of any restriction may result in criminal prosecution.

Staff of the elevator safety program perform the duties required to support the *Amusement Ride Safety Act*. This program is overseen by a nine-member Amusement Ride Safety Board, which advises the division on rules and regulations governing the program.

LAFAYETTE E. (GENE) LACY
State Supervisor
Division of Alcohol and
Tobacco Control

KAREN GAUT
Administrative Manager
Division of Alcohol and
Tobacco Control

DIANE MARKWAY
Licensing and Collections
Manager, Division of Alcohol
and Tobacco Control

KEITH HENDRICKSON
Chief of Enforcement
Division of Alcohol and
Tobacco Control

Fire Standard Compliant Cigarette Act

This act, passed in 2009, requires the Division of Fire Safety to oversee a program regulating the the sale of reduced ignition propensity cigarettes. Cigarettes sold in Missouri after Dec. 31, 2010, must be fire-safe compliant (FSC).

Division responsibilities include verification of individual cigarette brand styles based upon nationally recognized testing standards to ensure compliance with state law. The division maintains a listing of cigarettes meeting the established performance standard, and this list is also provided to the state Attorney General's Office and Missouri Department of Revenue.

The division recertifies the cigarettes every three years, approves cigarette pack FSC labeling and manages the Cigarette Fire Safety and Fire Fighter Protection Act Fund used to support fire prevention and safety programs.

Missouri Division of Alcohol and Tobacco Control

1738 E. Elm St., Lower Level, Jefferson City 65101
Telephone: (573) 751-2333 / FAX: (573) 526-4540
www.atc.dps.mo.gov

The Department of Liquor Control was established by the Liquor Control Act in 1934 and was restructured as a division within the Department of Public Safety in 1974. The Division of Liquor Control's name was changed to the Division of Alcohol and Tobacco Control (ATC) in 2003. The division's responsibilities are to enforce the liquor control laws under Chapter 311, RSMo, the youth access to tobacco law under Chapter 407, RSMo, and the rules and regulations of the state supervisor of Alcohol and Tobacco Control. The agency's responsibilities are primarily threefold: revenue collection, liquor licensing and regulatory compliance. The liquor control laws and the state's system of alcoholic beverage regulations are designed to ensure the public health and safety as

AMANDA BRANDT
Administrative Assistant
Division of Alcohol and
Tobacco Control

affected by intoxicating beverages. Alcohol and Tobacco Control supervises the state's revenue derived from the collection of excise taxes on alcoholic beverages and license fees. Additionally, state statute mandates the division protect the consumer from tainted alcoholic products and the liquor industry from infiltration and exploitation by the criminal element.

The Division of Alcohol and Tobacco Control is headed by the state supervisor. The state supervisor has the authority under Chapter 311, RSMo, to promulgate regulations, issue liquor licenses and suspend, revoke or fine liquor licenses for liquor control law violations. The supervisor also has the authority under Chapter 407, RSMo, to issue citations prohibiting outlets from selling tobacco products for violations of the youth access to tobacco law.

Licensing and Revenue Collection Section

The main function of the licensing and revenue collection section is to ensure general compliance with liquor control laws requiring the collection of excise taxes on all alcoholic beverages brought into the state of Missouri. Approximately $35 million is collected annually from liquor, wine and beer taxes for deposit into the general revenue fund. This is achieved by regularly conducting audits of licensed manufacturers, wineries, breweries and wholesalers.

This section is responsible for overseeing compliance regarding primary American source of supply, product testing and brand registration, which provides assurances to Missouri citizens that products are safe for consumption, and all excise taxes due have been paid. The licensing section, with assistance from the regulatory compliance section, annually collects and processes almost $5 million in license fees and processes over 30,000 license applications. This section is also responsible for retention of the division's records.

Regulatory Compliance Section

Alcohol and Tobacco Control's regulatory compliance section consists of five districts. The regulatory compliance section is supervised by the chief of enforcement and staffed with POST-licensed special agents. Special agents are assigned to a district. Each district is responsible for licensing, responding to citizen and industry complaints, working with local law enforcement agencies and educating licensees on liquor control laws, tobacco laws and regulations.

Educational Programs

ATC takes a proactive stance by providing industry education, server training and law enforcement education programs. Seminars for thousands of retail servers across the state have been conducted to reduce underage drinking, over-serving alcohol to customers and the sale of tobacco products to minors. Informational pamphlets are also provided to assist liquor licensees and tobacco outlets in complying with liquor control laws and tobacco laws. Alcohol and Tobacco Control also has an educational program to train law enforcement on the liquor control laws.

Summary

ATC has streamlined the liquor renewal process, utilized grants to provide more services and modernized revenue collection. Greater information is provided to the public, liquor industry and tobacco merchants and local law enforcement to achieve an unprecedented level of efficiency and cost-effectiveness for Missourians.

Missouri State Highway Patrol

General Headquarters, Hugh H. Waggoner Building
1510 E. Elm St., Jefferson City 65101
Telephone: (573) 751-3313

Since its inception in 1931, the Missouri State Highway Patrol has served and protected those living and visiting this great state. The Patrol has evolved into a full-service, professional law enforcement agency, yet its primary emphasis is traffic and water safety. The Patrol is responsible not only for law enforcement on our state's highways and waterways, but also motor vehicle and commercial vehicle inspection programs, driver license examinations, criminal investigations, crime laboratory analysis, related research and statistics, public education on safety issues, etc. The Patrol has been an accredited law enforcement agency since 1992.

The Missouri State Highway Patrol utilizes enforcement and education in its approach to traffic and boating safety. Sobriety checkpoints and saturations, hazardous moving violation projects, SAFETE commercial vehicle checks, and Click It or Ticket operations are some examples of enforcement projects aimed at making Missouri's roadways safer. In 2014, the two-week Click It or Ticket enforcement operations resulted in 1,283 citations and 1,557 warnings being issued. Marine enforcement troopers schedule sobriety checkpoints, saturations and equipment spot-checks on Missouri's lakes and rivers. During the last weekend in June, the Patrol participates in Operation Dry Water, a national campaign to detect and apprehend intoxicated watercraft operators. Marine enforcement troopers arrested eight people for boating while intoxicated and issued 72 boating violation summonses and 390 warnings on Missouri's waterways during Operation Dry Water 2014. In addition, troopers ensure safety during large scale marine events. News releases, public service announcements and safety programs educate the public about a variety of traffic and water safety topics throughout the year.

The Patrol's Major Crash Investigation Units provide a higher level of expertise and reporting in the field of traffic crash investigation. Teams are located in Higginsville, Jackson, Wentzville and Rogersville to serve the main population of the state. In 2014, approximately 125 Level IV reconstructions (fatalities involving commercial vehicles, school buses, with felony charges against a driver, etc.) were completed. Additionally, these teams answered 447 calls for service to assist Patrol members and other agencies with mapping of homicide scenes, crash data retrieval system downloads, photography of crash scenes, mapping and crash scene expertise.

The Patrol's four fully equipped Special Weapons and Tactics Teams (SWAT) are located in

COL. J. BRET JOHNSON
Superintendent
Missouri State Highway Patrol

LT. COL. SANDRA K. KARSTEN
Assistant Superintendent
Missouri State Highway Patrol

CAPT. JOHN J. HOTZ
Public Information and
Education Division
Missouri State Highway Patrol

CAPT. COREY J. SCHOENEBERG
Professional Standards Division
Missouri State Highway Patrol

Troop A, Troop C, Troop D and Troop F. The teams comprise troopers assigned to regular road duty. In 2014, the SWAT teams responded to a total of 30 incidents. The activations included barricaded subjects, high-risk search and arrest warrants, manhunts and security details.

The Missouri State Highway Patrol is nationally known for the success of its criminal interdiction program. Because of its central location in the United States and its major interstates, Missouri has become a crossroad for the distribution of drugs. Operation Cash Crop, the methamphetamine hotline, and the trained canine units make the Patrol's criminal interdiction program a success. In 2014, the Patrol's interdiction program resulted in the seizure of over 1,715 pounds of marijuana, 104 pounds of cocaine, 81 pounds of methamphetamine, 14 ounces of heroin and six pounds of psilocybin mushrooms, in addition to quantities of other illegal drugs. In connection with the drug interdiction program, 140 criminal arrests were made, and $1,745,166 in currency and 32 weapons were seized. In 2014, methamphetamine laboratory incidents totaled 1,045.

In accordance with Missouri statutes, DNA collection includes all felons. The Crime Laboratory Division's Combined DNA Index System aided 932 investigations in 2014.

Missouri's Automated Fingerprint Identification System (AFIS) is maintained and operated at the Patrol's Criminal Justice Information Services Division. AFIS houses over 3 million tenprint cards and compares sets of fingerprints in a matter of minutes. AFIS has proven to be an exceptional identification tool for law enforcement agencies throughout the state in identifying and tracking criminals, identifying persons assuming another's identity, identifying persons who were at a crime scene and identifying deceased persons found without identification. Law enforcement agencies are able to submit tenprints electronically via livescan devices and check fingerprints on scene using a handheld FAST ID device.

MAJ. GREGORY K. SMITH
Field Operations Bureau
Missouri State Highway Patrol

CAPT. NORMAN A. MURPHY
FOB - Assistant Bureau
Commander
Missouri State Highway Patro

The superintendent commands the Patrol, with the help of an assistant superintendent who is second-in-command, and six majors, all of whom are uniformed members. A captain commands each of the nine troops and answers to the major assigned to the Field Operations Bureau. Twenty-one divisions are organized under the assistant superintendent and six bureaus, all lending administrative support to the troops and fulfilling additional duties of the Patrol. Chapter 43 RSMo. established the Patrol's original force of 55 officers and a handful of civilians. Today, the Patrol's authorized strength is 1,295 uniformed members, 128 of whom are assigned to the Gaming Division, and 1,184 civilians in the Missouri State Highway Patrol.

Assistant Superintendent

The **Professional Standards Division** ensures integrity and fairness in the Patrol's dealings with the citizens it serves and with its employees. It conducts and reviews internal investigations to ensure the integrity of the Patrol is maintained.

The **Public Information and Education Division** prepares news releases, arranges press con-

CAPT. SCOTT A. SHIPERS
Troop A
Missouri State Highway Patrol

CAPT. JAMES E. WILT
Troop B
Missouri State Highway Patrol

CAPT. RONALD S. JOHNSON
Troop C
Missouri State Highway Patrol

CAPT. JUAN O. VILLANUEVA
Troop D
Missouri State Highway Patrol

CAPT. GEORGE E. RIDENS
Troop E
Missouri State Highway Patrol

CAPT. MICHAEL A. TURNER
Troop F
Missouri State Highway Patrol

CAPT. M.G.INMAN
Troop G
Missouri State Highway Patrol

CAPT. JAMES E. MCDONALD
Troop H
Missouri State Highway Patrol

ferences, creates brochures and disseminates information to the news media and the general public. The division coordinates the Patrol's statewide traffic safety education programs and is a resource for the 13 public information and education officers assigned throughout the state. This division is also responsible for the Colonel Alvin R. Lubker Memorial Safety and Education Center (museum) open to the public Monday–Friday (except holidays) from 8 a.m.–5 p.m.

Field Operations Bureau

The state of Missouri is divided into nine troops with headquarters in Lee's Summit, Macon, Weldon Spring, Springfield, Poplar Bluff, Jefferson City, Willow Springs, St. Joseph and Rolla. The Field Operations Bureau supervises all field activities and has oversight of the Major Crash Investigation Units, SWAT teams, K-9 teams, Dive Team and motorcycle officers.

The **Aircraft Division** assists in all phases of traffic law enforcement, manhunts, searches for lost or missing persons, and transportation for state business. During major disasters, such as floods, tornadoes or major fires, the Aircraft Division provides an aerial observation platform and provides rescue assistance. Division personnel

CAPT. JAMES W. REMILLARD
Troop I
Missouri State Highway Patrol

are qualified in fire suppression techniques and short haul rescues.

The **Water Patrol Division** is responsible for enforcement, registration and inspection as it pertains to boating and other water-related activities, and water safety education.

Criminal Investigation Bureau

The **Crime Laboratory Division** analyzes evidence found at the scene of crimes throughout

CAPT. DAVID K. STRIEGEL
Aircraft Division
Missouri State Highway Patrol

CAPT. MARK E. RICHERSON
Water Patrol Division
Missouri State Highway Patrol

MAJ. KEMP A. SHOUN
Executive Services Bureau
Missouri State Highway Patrol

MAJ. LUKE VISLAY
Criminal Investigation Bureau,
Missouri State Highway Patrol

the state. The division is composed of eight laboratories: two full-service laboratories located in Jefferson City and Springfield, and satellite laboratories located in St. Joseph, Macon, Park Hills, Cape Girardeau, Willow Springs and Carthage. Services are provided to local law enforcement agencies at no cost. Initially, the American Society of Crime Laboratory Directors Laboratory Accreditation Board accredited the Crime Laboratory in 1984. It has been re-accredited every five years since. The accreditation community has since moved its focus toward international accrediting criteria. The Crime Laboratory Division achieved this international accreditation based on ISO 17025 standards through ASCLD/LAB in 2011. The Patrol crime laboratory is responsible for managing Missouri's Combined DNA Index System (CODIS) database.

The **Division of Drug and Crime Control** provides criminal investigators specializing in the investigation of narcotics, criminal intelligence, rural crimes, digital forensics, explosives disposal, field investigations, lottery enforcement, missing persons and motor vehicle theft. The division's criminal investigators assist various criminal justice agencies—federal, state and local—throughout the state.

Gaming Division members perform background investigations on gaming boat operators and upper-level management, and enforce Gaming Commission rules/regulations and state laws on Missouri riverboats. Each operating riverboat must have at least one Gaming Division officer on board during all operating hours. The division also regulates bingo in Missouri.

The **Missouri Information Analysis Center** was formed to collect, evaluate, analyze and disseminate information to local, state and federal agencies tasked with homeland security responsibilities.

CAPT. KYLE D. MARQUART
Criminal Investigation Bureau–
Assistant Bureau Commander
Missouri State Highway Patrol

CAPT. ROBERT F. WOLF
Governor's Security Division
Missouri State Highway Patrol

Executive Services Bureau

The **Budget and Procurement Division** prepares the budget, maintains records of all federal and state purchases and expenditures for the Patrol, maintains a perpetual inventory of all equipment and supplies, coordinates the leasing program and prepares the payroll. Division personnel administer federal grants and fulfill all associated reporting requirements.

The **Governor's Security Division** provides protection for the governor and the governor's family. The division may provide security to the lieutenant governor, upon request when acting as governor, as well as to visiting governors and other dignitaries.

Technical Services Bureau

The Patrol's **Criminal Justice Information Services Division (CJISD)** is the central repository of criminal history records for Missouri. Section 43.500, RSMo., mandated reporting criminal history actions to the central repository for all police officers, prosecutors, court clerks and corrections facilities in Missouri. The CJISD dis-

WILLIAM E. MARBAKER
Crime Laboratory Division
Missouri State Highway Patrol

CAPT. ERIC T. OLSON
Drug and Crime Control
Division
Missouri State Highway Patrol

CAPT. CHRISTOPHER S. JOLLY
Gaming Division
Missouri State Highway Patrol

CAPT. DAVID. A. HALL
Missouri Information Analysis
Center
Missouri State Highway Patrol

MAJ. SARAH L. EBERHARD
Technical Services Bureau
Missouri State Highway Patrol

CAPT. LARRY W. PLUNKETT, JR.
Criminal Justice information
Services Division
Missouri State Highway Patrol

CAPT. VERNON C. DOUGAN
Information & Communications
Technology Division
Missouri State Highway Patrol

seminates criminal history record information through the Missouri Uniform Law Enforcement System (MULES) for criminal justice agencies and disseminates criminal record information to the public. The central repository is the single point of contact for criminal history information exchanged between Missouri and the Federal Bureau of Investigation (FBI). The CJISD also maintains the sex offender registry for Missouri, which can be accessed online at *www.mshp. dps.mo.gov/CJ38/SearchRegistry.jsp* or by calling the Missouri Sex Offender Registry hotline (888-SOR-MSHP). This division also manages the Uniform Crime Reporting program.

The **Information & Communications Technology Division (ICTD)** develops, builds, maintains and provides the services and infrastructure for communications and information systems to the Missouri State Highway Patrol and to criminal justice agencies throughout the state. Communications personnel communicate critical and often time-sensitive information to troopers on patrol on the state's roadways and waterways, as well as coordinate activities with other law enforcement jurisdictions. ICTD operates and maintains a sophisticated statewide voice and data commu-

nications network that provides access to these services on a 365-day/24-hour basis. The division is responsible for the Patrol's state highway emergency hotline (800) 525-5555 and wireless (*55) emergency hotline numbers and Missouri's portion of the America's Missing Broadcast Emergency Response (AMBER) Alert system broadcasts.

ICTD maintains the computer systems that house the state of Missouri's central data repositories for wanted/missing persons, stolen property, criminal records, traffic crash and arrest records, drug and alcohol offender records, and other related criminal justice information. ICTD supports connections to the National Crime Information Center, the National Law Enforcement Telecommunications System, the National Crime Information Bureau, the Missouri Department of Revenue and other regional justice systems. The division consists of highly trained information systems personnel, network engineers, communications technicians and technical field engineers who are located at the General Headquarters in Jefferson City and at troop locations around the state. Division personnel maintain a 24/7, 365-days-per-year call center to provide support to Patrol staff and criminal justice agencies throughout the state.

The **Patrol Records Division** serves as the data repository for statewide motor vehicle and boating crash reports, alcohol- and drug-related traffic offenses, dispositions on Patrol traffic and marine arrests and statewide assignment of unique numbers for inclusion on uniform citations. The division maintains Missouri's Fatality Analysis Reporting System (FARS) for the National Highway Traffic Safety Administration. The fatality analysis reporting system performs in-depth research on causes of fatality traffic crashes and forwards this information to a computerized database in Washington, D.C. The Traffic Arrest Records Section maintains a computerized listing of driving-while-intoxicated offenses occurring in Missouri. The Patrol's Custodian of Records function is administered by PRD.

Support Services Bureau

The **Commercial Vehicle Enforcement Division** operates 23 fixed weigh stations and 57 mobile commercial vehicle units. These are operated by commercial vehicle enforcement inspectors, commercial vehicle officers and commercial vehicle enforcement troopers, who provide uniform enforcement of the laws and regulations governing the operations of commercial motor vehicles. Commercial vehicle enforcement troopers assigned to each troop are responsible for enforcing commercial vehicle and special mobile equipment hazardous laws, inspecting radioactive shipments and have completed homeland security training.

The **Driver Examination Division** develops standards, policies, procedures and written tests for the driver examination program, including commercial driver licensing. Division representatives also aid in the preparation of the Missouri Driver's Guide.

The **Fleet and Facilities Division** directs the procurement, assignment, maintenance, repair and eventual sale of the Patrol's fleet of vehicles and vessels. It is responsible for policies controlling the expenses for fleet operation. The division supports building and grounds maintenance and housekeeping functions throughout the state, and works with the Office of Administration on statewide capital improvements and maintenance projects.

The **Motor Vehicle Inspection Division** collects fees and monitors the activities of mechanics and stations that have been licensed to inspect vehicles in the state. This division also manages the vehicle identification number (VIN)/salvage title inspection program, coordinates Patrol involvement in school bus inspections and administers an emission inspection program in the St. Louis area.

CAPT. REX M. SCISM
Research and Development Division
Missouri State Highway Patrol

CAPT. PAUL D. KERPERIN
Patrol Records Division
Missouri State Highway Patrol

MAJ. GREGORY D. KINDLE
Support Services Bureau
Missouri State Highway Patrol

CAPT. DAVID E. EARNEY
Commercial Vehicle Enforcement Division
Missouri State Highway Patrol

Administrative Services Bureau

The **Career Recruitment Division** recruits civilian and uniformed employees. The division employees cultivate partnerships with diverse groups and organizations, building long-term relationships with young people in order to provide them with information regarding the wide range of career opportunities within the Patrol.

The **Human Resources Division** tests and selects civilian and uniformed employees; maintains records of civilian and uniformed employees; monitors agency personnel policies and actions to ensure compliance with federal and state laws and regulations; and coordinates the Patrol's retirement, evaluation and promotional systems. The division also administers the Patrol's insurance program.

Research and Development Division (RDD) responsibilities include management of organizational policy, strategic planning and the accreditation process. RDD is also responsible for management of organizational forms, staff inspections, external assessments and oversight for the statewide property control system. Monitoring

CAPT. DAVID P. PERKINS
Driver Examination Division
Missouri State Highway Patrol

LARRY G. RAINS
Fleet and Facilities Division
Missouri State Highway Patrol

CAPT. LESTER D. ELDER
Motor Vehicle Inspection
Division
Missouri State Highway Patrol

MAJ. MALIK A. HENDERSON
Administrative Services Bureau
Missouri State Highway Patrol

CAPT. L.M. MACLAUGHLIN
Budget and Procurement
Division
Missouri State Highway Patrol

CAPT. ROGER D. WHITTLER
Career Recruitment Division
Missouri State Highway Patrol

CAPT. DAVID A. FLANNIGAN
Human Resources Division
Missouri State Highway Patrol

CAPT. VINCE S. RICE
Training Division
Missouri State Highway Patrol

legislation and coordinating fiscal note preparation on any initiatives that could have an impact on agency operations falls within the division's purview. RDD includes the Missouri Statistical Analysis Center, which provides research, technical and statistical analytical support to myriad authorities, policymakers and the citizens of Missouri.

The **Training Division** provides centralized training programs at the Law Enforcement Academy in Jefferson City, as well as prepares, conducts and coordinates continuing education, management training rule, in-service, and recertification courses in decentralized locations throughout the state. The Patrol's Law Enforcement Academy is an approved peace officer training center under Chapter 590, RSMo. As such, the Training Division is responsible for comprehensive recruit training for the position of trooper. The division provides certified basic and career enhancement courses to any law enforcement officer upon proper application and payment of appropriate fees.

Office of the Adjutant General

Headquarters, Missouri National Guard
Ike Skelton Training Site
2302 Militia Dr., Jefferson City 65101-1203
Telephone: (573) 638-9500 / FAX: (573) 638-9722
www.moguard.com

The Missouri National Guard is your hometown guard, working to serve Missourians and the United States. The Missouri National Guard is a leader in emergency management and response for the state and routinely deploys forces worldwide to perform federal missions as a partner in the U.S. Army and U.S. Air Force, including combat missions and operations other than war.

The Missouri National Guard claims a military lineage that dates back to units organized in the St. Louis area under French and Spanish colonial rule in the 18th century. Since then, guard units have performed state emergency duty hundreds of times along with their federal role. Missouri National Guard units and members saw active service in World Wars I and II, Korea, the Berlin Crisis, Vietnam, Operation Just Cause in Panama, Operation Desert Shield and Operation

Desert Storm, Somalia, Haiti, Joint Endeavor/Joint Guard in the Balkans, Operation Enduring Freedom, Operation Iraqi Freedom, Operation New Dawn and Operation Odyssey Dawn.

People: Approximately 12,000 men and women serve in Army and Air National Guard armories based in approximately 65 communities across the state; they are trained in hundreds of specific skills, most with direct application to civilian work and professions.

Roles and Missions: Unique among all the nation's armed forces, the National Guard has a dual state and federal role under the U.S. Constitution.

The guard is Missouri's force in times of disaster and emergency. Missions have included response to flooding, blizzards, extreme heat, tornadoes and civil unrest.

State duty is performed under the orders of the governor, the guard's peacetime commander in chief. The governor appoints the adjutant general, who wears the two stars of a major general and oversees the Army and Air National Guard units assigned to the state by the federal government. He is advised by a state military council of senior leaders of the Army and Air National Guard, including commanders of each unit in the state.

The guard is also a federal operational reserve force, fully accessible to the president for short-notice duty in times of national emergency. Federal missions have kept Missouri Army and Air National Guard units very busy since the terrorist attacks on our nation on Sept. 11, 2001. The Missouri National Guard deployed the first Agri-Business Development Team to Nangarhar Province in 2007 and continued that pilot program for five successful years.

The Missouri National Guard also has a Homeland Response Force (HRF) that may be called to respond to both federal and state emergencies within FEMA Region VII. The team's mission is to act as the military response to a chemical, biological, radiological, nuclear or high-yield explosive event. In addition to adding a response asset, the team created several full-time jobs for guard members.

The Missouri National Guard works with community groups in drug demand reduction programs while also supporting local, state and federal agencies in drug supply reduction efforts. Other innovative readiness training projects let Guard units train by working on projects benefiting their communities.

35th Engineer Brigade: The 35th Engineer Brigade, based at Fort Leonard Wood, undertakes plans, integrates and directs the execution of engineer missions conducted by the 1140th Engi-

MG STEPHEN DANNER
Adjutant General, Office of
Adjutant General

neer Battalion in Cape Girardeau and the 203rd Engineer Battalion in Joplin with their respective subordinate units. When federalized, the brigade mobilizes with three to five mission tailored engineer battalions and augments engineer units organic to corps and division. The 35th Engineer Brigade provides technical and tactical guidance and command and control to its teams, companies and battalions.

110th Maneuver Enhancement Brigade: The 110th Maneuver Enhancement Brigade, based in Kansas City, is a mission-tailored force that conducts support area operations, maneuver support operations and support to consequence-management and stability operations in order to ensure the mobility, protection and freedom-of-action of the supported force.

70th Troop Command: The mission of the 70th Troop Command, based in Jefferson Barracks, is to provide command and control, training, guidance, assistance and administrative and logistical support to its subordinate commands. This command serves as the Federal Emergency Management Agency Region VII Homeland Response Force.

35th Combat Aviation Brigade: The 35th Combat Aviation Brigade deploys to an area of responsibility to provide command, control, staff planning and supervision of combat aviation brigade operations. The brigade's units fly a combination of AH-64A Apache attack helicopters, LUH-72 Lakota, observation helicopters and UH-60 Blackhawk utility helicopters, as well as a C-12 transport airplane. The brigade's units are capable of performing unit- and intermediate-level aviation maintenance.

1107th Aviation Group: The 1107th Aviation Group supports the Missouri National Guard by way of its mission to provide a fixed-base theater of operations dedicated to sustainment/depot capability maintenance of rotary-wing aircraft.

One of the largest Missouri Guard units, the 487-member group supports a headquarters division and subordinate companies A and B, as well as the 135th Army Band, all based in Springfield.

35th Infantry Division (Mo.): The 35th Infantry Division is assigned in two states, Missouri and Kansas. The 35th Infantry Division (Mo.) specifically provides command and control of all divisional soldiers from within the Missouri Army National Guard.

131st Bomb Wing: The 131st Bomb Wing continued the total force integration as a classic associate unit with the active duty Air Force 509th Bomb Wing at Whiteman Air Force Base. The 131st Bomb Wing's primary operational mission is to provide full-spectrum, expeditionary, B-2 global strike and combat support capabilities. Wing manpower is also dedicated to providing for the unit's overall combat readiness, base operating support functions for tenant and attached units and for performing combat and emergency duty in support of federal and state missions. Detachment 1, Cannon Range is the state's only aerial bombing and gunnery range, serving all services.

139th Airlift Wing: The 139th Airlift Wing, based in St. Joseph, remains globally engaged in continuing operations by providing the state and nation with immediately deployable, combat-ready C-130 H-model aircraft. The unit performs a variety of roles including airlift and airdrop in peace and wartime missions.

Mission Support: The Missouri National Guard has several important initiatives in place to help support the needs of our guard members and their families.

Missouri National Guard Adjutant General Major General Steve Danner has developed a robust, nationally recognized Resiliency Program, focusing effort on the six dimensions of strength: physical, spiritual, family, emotional, social and financial well-being of soldiers, airmen and their families.

Our **Family Readiness Program** provides support to the families left in Missouri when the citizen-soldiers and airmen mobilize away from home and help them remain ready at all times.

The National Guard's **Yellow Ribbon Reintegration Program** helps soldiers, airmen and families prepare for a deployment and understand the benefits that are available during and after a deployment.

The **Military Family Relief Fund** is chaired by the lieutenant governor and provides financial assistance to families who have been affected by a mobilization.

The **Missouri Committee for Employer Support of the Guard and Reserves** works closely with employers and reserve military members across the state, helping them understand their roles and responsibilities.

The **Show Me Heroes Program**, a program pioneered by Gov. Jay Nixon and Maj. Gen. Steve Danner, works to find jobs for Missouri National Guard members and other veterans.

The Missouri National Guard **Military Funeral Honors Program** coordinates approximately 25 funerals for veterans across the state every day. The program began in July 1999 and coordinates funeral honors for every Missouri veteran. Anyone interested in funeral honors for their family member should inform their funeral home director.

The Missouri National Guard also honors our living veterans with the **Veterans Awards Program**. The Missouri Legislature approved this program providing a medal and certificate to veterans of the Vietnam War, World War II and the Korean War. Veterans or their family members wishing more information can contact the program director at (573) 638-9838.

Federal: The National Guard Bureau, a joint agency of the U.S. Army and Air Force, provides peacetime federal oversight of National Guard units. While the governor commands the guard on a day-to-day basis, most costs are paid with federal funds. That includes the regular pay for soldiers and airmen, except when they are on a state emergency mission. The federal funding and a force of full-time, federally paid employees ensure the readiness of the guard for federal missions or state duty if called on by the governor. The federal government pays approximately 95 percent of the annual cost of the guard.

With its ability to perform federal duties or state duties as the need arises, the guard is the most capable and cost-effective of all the components of the nation's armed forces. While the National Guard units and members can perform federal duty in the same manner as members of the Army, Air Force, Navy and Marine Corps Reserves, only National Guard units have the constitutional responsibility to serve at home during emergencies.

The guard offers additional benefits. It provides Missouri communities with citizens whose military experiences pay off at home. Its men and women receive training in skills, work ethic, physical fitness and leadership that benefits their communities and civilian employers. They earn GI Bill and other educational benefits, including state-funded educational support and matching scholarships provided by many Missouri colleges and universities, unique to the National Guard.

To learn more about the Missouri National Guard, visit our website at *www.moguard.com* or our social media sites at:

- *www.facebook.com/Missouri.National. Guard*
- *www.twitter.com/Missouri_NG*
- *www.youtube.com/MoNationalGuard*
- *www.myspace.com/missouri_ng*
- *www.flickr.com/photos/missouriguard.*

Missouri Military Council

The Missouri Military Council (section 41.220, RSMo) acts in an advisory capacity to the commander in chief on all matters placed before it by the governor, the adjutant general, who also serves as council president, or any member of the council. The council submits recommendations to the governor, which shall become effective only upon his approval. The council meets quarterly in Jefferson City, and special meetings may be called by the governor or the president of the council at any time or place designated.

State Emergency Management Agency

The Missouri Army National Guard
Ike Skelton Training Site
2302 Militia Dr., Jefferson City 65101-9051
Telephone: (573) 526-9100 / FAX: (573) 634-7966
sema.dps.mo.gov

The State Emergency Management Agency's (SEMA) mission is to protect the lives and property of all Missourians when major disasters threaten anywhere in the state. Disasters include major ice storms and blizzards, floods, tornadoes, severe weather, earthquakes, hazardous material and nuclear power plant accidents, radiological and biological events and terrorism. SEMA's program is nationally accredited.

To meet this mission, SEMA coordinates and develops the State Emergency Operations Plan, which directs the actions of Missouri state departments and agencies to aid requesting local jurisdictions. SEMA oversees Missouri's disaster preparedness, floodplain management, hazard mitigation and disaster public assistance programs, and coordinates the state's response operations for all types of large scale emergencies. SEMA is organized into four divisions: Preparedness, Response, Recovery and Finance.

State Emergency Operations Center

SEMA and the State Emergency Operations Center (SEOC) are located at the Missouri Army National Guard Ike Skelton Training Site, east of Jefferson City. SEOC enables state agencies to gather situational awareness and direct Missouri's

RON WALKER
Director
SEMA

DAWN WARREN
Deputy Director
SEMA

RON BROXTON
Recovery Division Manager
SEMA

MELISSA FRIEL
Preparedness Division Manager
SEMA

TERRY CASSIL
Response Division Manager
SEMA

disaster emergency response and recovery operations.

Coordination of Preparedness Activities

Preparedness is a joint responsibility of local, state and federal governments. SEMA coordinates preparedness activities and administers a number of federally funded programs. These programs include disaster planning, earthquake preparedness, radiological protection, public warning, training and education. SEMA offers free classes to local emergency management agencies, local officials, first responders, schools and volunteers.

State and Federal Disaster Assistance

When a disaster exceeds the ability of local communities to respond and/or recover, the governor may declare a state of emergency for the impacted area. This action allows state resources to augment the needs of local governments.

Based on the impact of the disaster and the results of joint damage assessments, the governor may request a federal disaster declaration in accordance with Public Law 93–288. If approved by the president, such a declaration can make a wide variety of federal assistance programs available to Missouri, local governments, individuals, families and businesses adversely affected by the disaster. SEOC coordinates emergency life safety response and recovery actions to the declared areas. SEMA personnel administer federal/state disaster grants to jurisdictions and provide oversight of federal assistance for individuals in declared counties. Disaster assistance includes the Individuals and Households Program (IHP), which helps victims with disaster-related needs. The Small Business Administration (SBA) offers low-interest loans. Federal Disaster Public Assistance helps reimburse local governments repair disaster damaged roads, bridges and critical infrastructure. Communities may be eligible for cost-effective mitigation projects, which help prevent similar damages in the future.

Federal Disaster Declarations for Missouri Since January 2011

- January 2011 severe winter storm and blizzard (direct federal assistance and public assistance)
- April, May and June 2011 severe storms and tornadoes (individual and public assistance)
- June 2011 severe storms and flooding (direct federal assistance, individual assistance and public assistance)
- SBA physical and economic declaration for June 2011 flooding.
- SBA physical and economic declaration for prolonged heat and drought in 2012.
- SBA physical and economic declaration for May 2013 flooding.
- May and June 2013 severe storms and tornadoes (public assistance)
- SBA physical and economic declaration for may and June 2013 severe storms

- Aug. 2013 severe storms and flooding (public assistance)
- SBA physical and economic declaration for Oct. 2013
- SBA economic declaration for Sept. 2014
- Oct. 2014 severe storms and flooding (public assistance)
- SBA economic declaration for Nov. 2014

Preparedness Division

The Preparedness Division works to create coordinated statewide response plans and training for local and state personnel so Missouri can effectively respond to emergencies and disasters. The division is composed of the planning and preparedness sections. It has responsibility for medical counter-measures, Training and Exercises, Emergency Human Services and Radiological Emergency Program (REP). Examples of division work products include preparation and updates of comprehensive disaster assistance plans, standard operating guides (SOGs) to execute responsibilities in state plans and emergency management seminars for local elected officials. Emergency Human Services includes the volunteer coordinator, who works with state agencies, faith-based and volunteer organizations to coordinate assistance during disasters. During recovery, the coordinator provides technical assistance to long-term recovery committees. The coordinator is the point of contact for the Governor's Faith-Based and Community Service Partnership for Disaster Recovery and Missouri Voluntary Organizations Active in Disasters.

Response Division

The Response Division is responsible for disaster management operations. When Missouri is affected by an emergency or disaster, beyond the capabilities of local governments, the Response Division includes the readiness section, regional coordinators, and logistics and resource sections. Once a State of Emergency (SOE) has been declared by the governor, the Response Division coordinates disaster response with local governments, state agencies and the Federal Emergency Management Agency (FEMA). The Logistics and Resources Section coordinates the acquisition and delivery of critical emergency equipment. Along with services and supplies to disaster areas, and may include generators, pumps, technical assistance teams, food, water, ice and temporary facilities. The Logistics and Resources Section, along with the Missouri Public/Private Partnership (MOP3), also co-manages the Missouri Business Emergency Operation Center (BEOC). This helps facilitate both business community recovery and charitable disaster assistance from the business community. The regional coordinators are the state's liaisons to local jurisdictions for emergency management activities. The Response Division also develops and maintains the State of Missouri Emergency Operations Plan.

Recovery Division

The Recovery Division is responsible for requesting and distributing federal and state funds for all presidentially declared disasters. This division works to assist Missouri communities with recovery and to mitigate against disasters. It includes the Public Assistance, Mitigation and Floodplain sections. The Public Assistance Sections' responsibilities include: state damage assessments, assistance in revising state Administrative Plans for Public Assistance, along with the Individuals and Households Program. The Mitigation Section works with local communities to reduce the adverse impacts disasters have on Missourians and has the responsibility for the State Hazard Analysis. This section administers five federal mitigation grant programs and has helped over 1,000 Missouri communities write mitigation plans to qualify for these grants. Community mitigation projects include voluntary flood buyouts, building community tornado safe rooms, replacing bridges and low water crossings, bank stabilization and burying public electric utilities. The Floodplain Management Section, within the Recovery Division, is also the state coordinating agency responsible for Missouri's participation in the National Flood Insurance Program (NFIP). All three sections under the Recovery Division are responsible for the training of state personnel in disaster recovery, mitigation and floodplain management.

Finance and Administrative Division

The Finance Division includes the Fiscal Administration and Emergency Management Performance Grant sections. The Fiscal Administration Section provides administrative services such as accounting, budgeting, grant administration, procurement, fleet management, human resources, payroll and general office services. It coordinates and administers federal, state and local grant requests. The Emergency Management Performance Grant Section (EMPG) administers federal assistance to SEMA and local government emergency management agencies in support of all-hazard emergency management capabilities. An all-hazard approach to emergency response, including the development of a comprehensive program of planning, training and exercises, means there can be an effective and consistent response to disasters and emergencies, regardless of the cause.

Missouri Emergency Response Commission (MERC)

The Missouri Emergency Response Commission implements the federal Emergency Planning and Community Right-to-Know Act (EPCRA) and related Missouri laws pertaining to hazardous chemicals storage. The commission supports Local Emergency Planning Committees (LEPC), reviews hazardous chemical contingency plans, provides chemical emergency training, collects information on toxic and hazardous storage and makes this information available to the public. MERC administers the Hazardous Material Emergency Preparedness (HMEP) for hazardous material (HAZMAT) training to local public sector employees and the Chemical Emergency Preparedness Funds (CEPF) for planning and training for LEPCs.

MERC Members

Brinton, William C., St. Joseph;
Cardone, Lisa A., Ava;
Derickson, Bob, O'Fallon;
Dixon, Sen. Bob, Springfield;
Downing, Mike, director, Department of Economic Development, Jefferson City;
Halmich, Bill, Washington;
Hinson, Rep. Dave, St. Clair;
Moriarty, Bill, Warsaw;
Munzlinger, Sen. Brian, Williamstown;
Pauley, Sara Parker, director, Department of Natural Resources, Jefferson City;
Riddle, Rep. Jeannie, Mokane, Earthquake Preparedness Activities;
Roberts, Lane, director, Department of Public Safety, Jefferson City;
Vasterling, Gail, director, Department of Health and Senior Services, Jefferson City.

Earthquake Program

SEMA's earthquake program provides operational oversight and administrative support to the 1,000-member Structural Assessment Visual Evaluation (SAVE) Coalition authorized by section 44.023, RSMo. This statue establishes a volunteer cadre for post-disaster building inspections to determine if damaged buildings are safe for occupation. The SAVE Coalition members are architects, engineers, building inspectors and construction industry professionals.

Missouri Seismic Safety Commission (MSSC)

SEMA provides administrative support to the Missouri Seismic Safety Commission (MSSC), which was established by section 44.227, RSMo, to initiate a comprehensive program to help Missouri prepare for and respond to a major earthquake. The commission prepares and updates a strategic plan for reducing earthquake hazards in the state. Members also help organize Earthquake Awareness Month (February) activities.

Missouri Seismic Safety Commission Members

Bailey, Raymond, St. Charles;
Bond, Art, St. Louis;
Evans, Joel, Sikeston;
Gould, Phillip, Richmond Heights;
Green, Miles (Joe), Boonville;
Hempen, Gregory L., St. Louis;
Koehler, Jamie, Cape Girardeau;
Mallott, John, Kennett;
Palmer, James, Kansas City;
Rosenblad, Brent, Columbia;
Sandvol, Eric, Columbia;
Shaw, Donald, Jefferson City.

Missouri Veterans Commission

205 Jefferson St., 12th Fl., PO Drawer 147
Jefferson City 65102-0147
Telephone: (573) 751-3779 / FAX: (573) 751-6836

The Missouri Veterans Commission is vested with the responsibility of representing all Missouri veterans, ensuring their needs are met and defending the entitlements of those who have served their country with honor and distinction.

This is accomplished through programs and services funded by the state and federal government as well as private and corporate contributions.

Our Mission

In recognition of the sacrifices made by veterans in service to our country, the Missouri Veterans Commission will provide our veterans with timely benefits assistance, skilled nursing care and a final resting place with honor.

Our History

The State Federal Soldier's Home was established in 1896 by the Women's Relief Corps Soldiers' Home Association and was deeded to the state of Missouri in 1897. Its original purpose was to provide care to aging Missourians who had fought for the Union in the Civil War. In 1931, the state legislature, at the request of organized veterans groups, created the Office of State Service Officer for the purpose of counseling and assisting veterans of World War I (WWI) and earlier conflicts whose service-connected disabilities were becoming manifest and for whom numer-

LARRY KAY
Executive Director
Missouri Veterans Commission

BRYAN HUNT
Deputy Director
Missouri Veterans Commission

ous benefits were being made available through the newly established Veterans Administration.

In 1974, the Omnibus Reorganization Act placed the Division of Veterans Affairs within the Department of Social Services. The State Federal Soldier's Home and Office of State Service Officer remained separate entities until the Omnibus State Reorganization Act of 1974 combined the two, renaming the home and establishing the Division of Veterans Affairs within the Department of Social Services.

As defined in the act, the Division of Veterans Affairs, as provided in Chapter 42, RSMo, in 1978 was transferred from the Department of Social Services to the Department of Public Safety, Office of the Adjutant General, by a type I transfer.

Executive order 81-18 (February 1981) passed at the first regular session of the 81st General Assembly and put this law into effect in September of 1981.

On Aug. 28, 1989, the Division of Veterans Affairs was replaced by the establishment of the Missouri Veterans Commission as a type III transfer. Chapter 42, RSMo, governs the commission's operation as a state agency. The commission shall be composed of nine members. In addition, the chair of the Missouri military preparedness and enhancement commission or the chair's designee shall be an *ex officio* member of the commission.

The commissioners then appoint an executive director, who implements commission policies and is responsible for statewide management of veterans programs. The executive director reports regularly to the commission concerning all aspects of program operations through quarterly commission meetings.

Administrative offices are located in Jefferson City at 205 Jefferson St., 12th Floor. This location also houses the local Veteran Service Office. Services and benefits provided to veterans by the Missouri Commission are:

Veterans Services Program

Through the Veterans Service Program, the Missouri Veterans Commission provides counseling and assistance to veterans throughout the state in filing claims for benefits from the U.S. Department of Veterans Affairs. Veterans service officers are located in almost every county of the state to make services available to veterans close to their homes.

Information concerning locations and phone numbers of veterans service officers may be found on the commission's website *www.mvc. dps.mo.gov.*

Veterans service officers are thoroughly trained and knowledgeable in all areas of veterans benefits, including compensation, pension, education, burial and widow's benefits. Information and counseling regarding medical eligibility, VA Home Loan Guaranty and other benefits, including those offered by the state, may also be obtained from the veterans service officers as well.

Veterans service officers are available to give presentations and instruction regarding the benefits for which veterans are eligible as a result of honorable military service in the U.S. Armed Forces.

Veterans Home Program

The Missouri Veterans Commission currently operates and maintains seven long-term skilled nursing care facilities with a total of 1,350 available beds.

Veterans in need of nursing home care may seek admission to a Missouri veterans home by filling an application with the home of their choice. Prospective residents may obtain application forms from any Missouri veterans home, from a Missouri veterans service officer or by contacting the Missouri Veterans Commission Headquarters at (573) 751-3779. Home applications may also be downloaded from the commission's web site, *www.mvc.dps.mo.gov.*

Eligibility

- Applicant must be an honorably discharged veteran of the U.S. Armed Forces;
- Applicant must have resided in the state of Missouri for at least 180 days during his/her lifetime;
- Applicant must have been determined to require nursing home care.

Funding/Costs

- State general revenue;
- Federal funding, through the U.S. Department of Veterans Affairs Per Diem Grant Program;
- Charges to the veterans themselves, based on the individual's ability to pay.

The maximum amount that a veteran may be charged currently is $2,050 per month. Ability to pay is based upon the veteran's (and his or her spouse's) total income and assets.

Missouri veterans homes are inspected at least annually by the Department of Veterans Affairs for the continuance of per diem payments. Policies for health care administration are centrally managed by the commission's superintendent of homes, who routinely reviews management practice and clinical outcomes. Therapeutic modalities of physical, psychosocial and rehabilitative origin are provided in each facility.

Missouri Veterans Homes

St. James

620 N. Jefferson, St. James 65559
Telephone: (573) 265-3271 / FAX: (573) 265-5771
Cathy.haynes@mvc.dps.mo.gov

Cathy Haynes, Administrator

St. James is the site of the first state veterans home. It was originally opened in 1896 by the Women's Relief Corps Soldiers' Home Association and was deeded to the state of Missouri in 1897. A new, 150-bed facility was dedicated and opened on the original campus in 1996, in conjunction with the 100-year anniversary of the home. St. James is proud of its continuous 100-year tradition of providing care for veterans.

Mt. Vernon

1600 S. Hickory, Mt. Vernon 65712
Telephone: (417) 466-7103 / FAX: (417) 466-4040
james.dennis@mvc.dps.mo.gov

James Dennis, Administrator

In June 2004, a new, state-of-the-art, 200-bed facility opened on Hickory Street in Mt. Vernon. The Missouri veterans home at Mt. Vernon was established April 1, 1983, in a wing of the Missouri Rehabilitation Center. The home is operated by the Missouri Veterans Commission to provide quality rehabilitative nursing care to Missouri's disabled veterans.

Mexico

1 Veterans Dr., Mexico 65265
Telephone: (573) 581-1088 / FAX: (573) 581-5356
brenda.ezell@mvc.dps.mo.gov

Brenda Ezell, Administrator

As the state's third veterans home, the Mexico facility was opened in 1985 and serves the north central area of the state. The 150-bed home features a large, open mall containing dining rooms, lounges, a library, recreation and therapy areas, a general store and medical and administrative officers. An outdoor walking trail among the trees and flowers on the grounds provides much enjoyment and physical exercise for veterans at the Mexico home.

Cape Girardeau

2400 Veterans Memorial Dr., Cape Girardeau 63701
Telephone: (573) 290-5870 / FAX: (573) 290-5909
viviane.markle@mvc.dps.mo.gov

Viviane Markle, Administrator

Serving veterans in southeastern Missouri, the 150-bed veterans home at Cape Girardeau was opened in 1990. It is designed to resemble a small village, with cluster design features consisting of three, 50-bed living units surrounding a central administration building. The home affords residents many amenities, including a lovely chapel adjacent to the lobby, made possible by a fundraising drive led by the American Legion and its auxiliaries.

St. Louis

10600 Lewis and Clark Blvd., St. Louis 63136
Telephone: (314) 340-6389 / FAX: (314) 340-6379
mark.fontana@mvc.dps.mo.gov

Mark Fontana, Administrator

Missouri's fifth veterans home, a 300-bed facility, is located in Bellefontaine Neighbors, off highways I-270 and 367 in St. Louis County. The home opened in November 1993. On the grounds of this veterans home are reminders of the military service and sacrifice by veterans, including the display of a U.S. Army M60A3 tank, made possible by the St. Louis Veterans Home Committee (Assistance League).

Cameron

1111 Euclid, Cameron 64429
Telephone: (816) 632-6010 / FAX: (816) 632-1361
bradley.haggard@mvc.dps.mo.gov

Brad Haggard, Administrator

This 200-bed facility is the commission's sixth veterans home and is located on a 20-acre site donated by the City of Cameron. It was dedicated Feb. 4, 2000, and admitted the first resident on April 3, 2000.

Warrensburg

1300 Veterans Rd., Warrensburg 64093
Telephone: (660) 543-5064 / FAX: (660) 543-5075
eric.endsley@mvc.dps.mo.gov

Eric Endsley, Administrator

This 200-bed facility was dedicated July 14, 2000, as the commission's seventh veterans home. The first resident was admitted Sept. 26, 2000. The design for the Cameron and Warrensburg facilities is identical. They are divided into five sections: sections A, B and C are each 50-bed, long-term skilled nursing care units; section D is a 50-bed dementia unit that contains its own dining room, activity area and enclosed courtyard; and section E houses the administrative offices and ancillary services such as the recreation area, barbershop and rehabilitation area.

State Veterans Cemetery Program

Signed into law in 1996, this program gives the Missouri Veterans Commission statutory responsibility to establish, operate and maintain cemeteries for veterans in Missouri.

The vision and goal of the State Veterans Cemetery System is to locate cemeteries strategically throughout the state, making it possible for veterans and their families to have access within a 75-mile radius of their homes. The mission is to provide interment for veterans and their eligible dependents in a dignified, efficient and compassionate manner.

State Veterans Cemeteries

Springfield

5201 S. Southwood Rd., Springfield 65804
Telephone: (417) 823-3944 / FAX: (417) 823-0252
david.maggard@mvc.dps.mo.gov

David Maggard, Director

The cemetery is located on a 60-acre site and can contain approximately 30,000 burial sites. Groundbreaking occurred July 7, 1998. The cemetery was dedicated Nov. 6, 1999, and the first burial was conducted Jan. 21, 2000.

Higginsville

20109 Business Hwy. 13, Higginsville 64037
Telephone: (660) 584-5252 / FAX: (660) 584-9525
teddie.velleri@mvc.dps.mo.gov

Teddie Velleri, Director

The cemetery is located on a 54-acre site and can contain approximately 21,000 burial sites. Groundbreaking occurred June 6, 1998. The cemetery was dedicated Nov. 13, 1999, and the first burial was conducted Jan. 22, 2000.

Bloomfield

17357 Stars and Stripes Way, Bloomfield 63825
Telephone: (573) 568-3871
ken.swearengin@mvc.dps.mo.gov

Ken Swearengin, Director

The Missouri Veterans Cemetery at Bloomfield was established Oct. 12, 2003. Interments began Sept. 29, 2003. The cemetery is built on 64.21 acres of land, which was donated to the state of Missouri by the people of Stoddard County.

Jacksonville

1479 County Rd. 1675, Jacksonville 65260
Telephone: (660) 295-4237 / FAX: (660) 295-4259
jim.nugent@mvc.dps.mo.gov

Jim Nugent, Director

The Missouri Veterans Cemetery at Jacksonville was established Oct. 25, 2003. It occupies 117.4 acres of majestic green land and includes a lake. The land for the cemetery was donated by Associated Electric.

Fort Leonard Wood

25350 Hwy. H, Waynesville 65583
Telephone: (573) 774-3496
charles.baxter@mvc.dps.mo.gov

Charles Baxter, Director

The Missouri State Veterans Cemetery at Fort Leonard Wood is the result of a partnership between the Department of Veterans Affairs and the Missouri Veterans Commission. The groundbreaking ceremony was held on Nov. 7, 2008, and the cemetery was formally dedicated on Sept. 13, 2010. The cemetery property was donated by the U.S. Army Maneuver Support Center and Fort Leonard Wood and is situated on 229 beautiful acres. Currently the cemetery consists of 25 developed acres in phase 1 with space estimated to last 25 to 30 years.

Eligibility Criteria:

Eligibility criteria for burial in state veterans cemeteries will be the same as that for burial in national cemeteries, as stated in Missouri statute, signed into law in 1998: ". . .solely for the burial of veterans and eligible dependents as defined by the Department of Veterans Affairs. . ." Veterans interested in burial should contact the individual cemetery for a predetermination of eligibility.

Benefits

- burial space;
- grave liner;
- opening and closing of the grave;
- perpetual care;

- placement of cremation remains in either columbarium niche or inground burial;
- upright granite headstone.

Veterans Trust Fund

The Veterans Trust Fund was established in 1989 and is a means by which individuals and corporations may donate money to expand and improve services to veterans in Missouri. Appropriations from the fund are being used to improve training of service officers to expand capabilities in meeting the special needs of residents of state veterans homes and to promote public awareness of the program, benefits and services available to Missouri's veterans.

All contributions to the Veterans Trust Fund are tax deductible. Individuals and corporations can donate any amount over two dollars of their tax refund on their Missouri tax return, or by sending their contributions directly to the commission at any time. Monies from the fund are used to enhance, not replace, existing programs.

Ombudsman

The Missouri Veterans Commission ombudsman assists veterans, service members and their families with extraordinary needs that are not being met by other agencies or organizations. The ombudsman acts as a referral source to local, state and national resources available to address these needs.

Minority Veterans Initiative

The Minority Veterans Initiative was established to encourage minority veterans and dependents to visit local veterans service officers to ascertain benefits they might be legally entitled to through the Federal Department of Veterans Affairs. The program's goals include:

- increase benefit awareness among minority veterans;
- increase benefit awareness among widows of deceased veterans;
- increase Missouri Veterans Commission visibility among community agencies;
- collaboration with other veterans agencies to increase awareness of veterans programs;
- co-brand with businesses to promote veterans benefits awareness.

Women Veterans Initiative

The Missouri Veterans Commission is dedicated to finding all women veterans, past, present and future. They have appointed a women veterans coordinator, and her mission is to ensure that Missouri women veterans have equitable access to federal and state veteran services and to ensure women veterans are aware of their VA benefits, whom to contact and how to apply for these benefits.

The mission of the Women Veterans Initiative is to facilitate proactive leadership and services for women veterans, their dependents and survivors in Missouri.

Incarcerated Veterans Initiative

In February 2007, the Missouri Veterans Commission and the Department of Corrections signed a formalized agreement to provide direct services to Missouri incarcerated veterans. The Incarcerated Veterans Initiative works to facilitate the transition of veteran offenders to a productive life in the community. The program serves veteran offenders and their families as a principal advocate in ensuring they receive appropriate services and empower the offenders with hope and new direction.

Veterans Commission Members

Englund, Scott, chair;
Boyer, Oliver Glen, member;
Mowrer, J. Michael (Mike), member;
Nelson, Nancy M., member;
Wooten, Charles R. (Chuck), member;
Brown, Sen. Dan, member;
Sifton, Sen. Scott, member;
Hoskins, Rep. Denny, member;
Walton Gray, Rep. Rochelle, member.

Missouri Gaming Commission

3417 Knipp Dr., PO Box 1847, Jefferson City 65102
Telephone: (573) 526-4080 / FAX: (573) 526-1999
www.mgc.dps.mo.gov

The Missouri Gaming Commission was established in 1993 by the 87th General Assembly as specified by Chapter 313, RSMo. The commission assumed the responsibility for regulating riverboat and charitable gaming on July 1, 1994.

The commission is composed of five members, no more than three of whom may be members of the same political party. Commission members are appointed by the governor, with the advice and consent of the Senate, for a term of three years. Pursuant to statute, the overall membership of the commission reflects experience in law enforcement, civil and criminal investigation and financial principles.

The commission's role is to monitor gaming-related activities to ensure criminal elements do not infiltrate licensed gaming operations. In addition, the commission works to protect the public

by ensuring games are conducted fairly, according to their rules and with full disclosure.

As a state regulatory agency, the commission and its staff hold themselves to the highest ethical and professional standards and strive to conduct all business in a manner that is in the public interest and maintains the public trust. Pursuant to statute, a strict code of ethics has been adopted prohibiting conflicts of interest and certain *ex parte* communications.

The key regulatory responsibilities of the commission are:

- to conduct thorough background investigations on all key persons involved in gaming operations, including substantial owners, management personnel, key operational employees and suppliers;

- to thoroughly investigate the finances of applicants and their key persons to determine if they have the financial resources and responsibility to meet their proposed obligations;

- to investigate the background of all occupational licensees, including dealers, slot attendants, food and beverage servers, security and surveillance personnel and all other employees who have access to the gaming area to ensure the personnel operating the casino are of sufficient character to maintain the integrity of Missouri gaming;

- to photograph and fingerprint each employee so as to maintain a complete and accurate database of gaming personnel;

- to assign appropriate staff to each gaming operation to be present at all times when gaming is conducted. Enforcement agents are charged with ensuring that gaming is conducted in accordance with the Missouri gaming statutes, the rules and regulations of the commission and the licensee's own internal controls;

- to ensure that the safety of the passengers is guarded, to conduct investigations of suspected wrongdoing and to receive complaints from customers;

- to review and audit the finances and compliance of the gaming operation through the combined use of commission staff, independent public accounting firms and internal casino audit staff that are retained by the licensee and approved by the commission;

- to monitor the financial integrity of gaming operators to ensure that Missouri's financial interests are protected;

- to ensure charitable, fraternal, religious, service, social and veteran organizations

WILLIAM K. SEIBERT, JR.
Executive Director
Missouri Gaming Commission

LELAND M. SHURIN
Chair
Missouri Gaming Commission

LARRY D. HALE
Commissioner
Missouri Gaming Commission

DIANE C. HOWARD
Commissioner
Missouri Gaming Commission

are eligible to hold licenses to conduct charity bingo games in the state. Regular bingo licenses, special bingo licenses, abbreviated pull-tab licenses, supplier licenses, manufacturer licenses and bingo hall provider licenses are all issued by the bingo division. Missouri Gaming Commission staff will assess qualifications of organizations applying for a charitable bingo gaming license, conduct required background investigations, audits, collect taxes and maintain all records related to charitable bingo.

Office of the Executive Director

The Office of the Executive Director is responsible for the day-to-day operations of the commission. The director supervises all staff activities, reports to the commission and is responsible for organizing and distributing all public documents and reports. The director oversees the Administration, Corporate Securities and Finance, Enforcement, Legal and Charitable Bingo sections of the Missouri Gaming Commission.

Pursuant to statute, the executive director has entered into a memorandum of understanding with the Missouri State Highway Patrol to perform background investigations and to provide enforcement personnel.

Missouri Gaming Commission

Shurin, Leland M., chair, Kansas City, April 2017;
Hale, Larry D., St. Louis, April 2016;

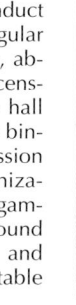

BRIAN JAMISON
Commissioner
Missouri Gaming Commission

THOMAS NEER
Commissioner
Missouri Gaming Commission

Howard, Diane C., Cape Girardeau, April 2015;
Jamison, Brian, Columbia, April 2016;
Neer, Thomas, St. Charles, April 2017.

Satellite Offices

St. Louis
9900 Page Ave., Ste. 107, St. Louis 63132
Telephone: (314) 877-4370 / FAX: (314) 877-4384

Kansas City
1321 Burlington St., Ste. 100
North Kansas City 64116
Telephone: (816) 482-5700 / FAX: (816) 482-5704.

Department of Revenue

Truman State Office Bldg.
PO Box 311, Jefferson City 65105-0311
Telephone: (573) 751-4450 / FAX: (573) 751-7150
www.dor.mo.gov
Email: dormail@dor.mo.gov

The Department of Revenue is one of the largest and most comprehensive of Missouri's state departments. It was established in 1945 and plays a key role in state government by efficiently collecting billions of dollars in state revenue each year. The department also collects local sales and use taxes, and distributes them back to local governments.

The department also enhances public safety by administering the state's motor vehicle and driver licensing laws, including the titling and registration of motor vehicles and the licensing of Missouri's drivers. The duties involved with the oversight of driver licensing include the suspension or revocation of licenses of drunk drivers and other drivers who have committed other motor vehicle transgressions.

Office of the Director

The Office of the Director, which includes the director and other key staff, is responsible for overall guidance and setting policy for the department. The office includes a legislative director, who manages the department's relationships with the legislature and other governmental branches, and a communications director, who works with the news media, coordinates public awareness of department activities and acts as the department's spokesperson. In addition, the office includes the Internal Audit function, reviewing performance of the department and the privately contracted license offices.

Taxation Division

The Taxation Division collects Missouri's taxes and administers the state's tax laws, annually processing more than 5 million tax returns, responding to hundreds of thousands of phone calls and working with Missouri businesses and citizens to ensure they are paying the taxes owed to the state and local entities.

The **Business Tax Bureau** processes and administers the state's business taxes. These include the corporate income tax, local and state sales

NIA RAY
Director

JOHN MOLLENKAMP
Deputy Director

JULIE SCHEPPERS
Executive Assistant to the Director

ELIZABETH WHALEY
Executive Assistant

MICHELLE GLEBA
Communications Director

TODD IVESON
Director, Taxation Division

and use taxes, the state motor fuel tax, excise taxes and employee withholding taxes.

The **Personal Tax Bureau** oversees processing and administration of the state's personal income tax, the Property Tax Credit and fiduciary tax. This bureau also administers business and individual tax non-compliance programs to identify taxes due from those not filing or under-reporting their tax obligations.

The **Collections and Tax Assistance Bureau** helps citizens who need assistance in filling out tax returns or have other questions. The bureau also actively pursues collection of unpaid taxes.

The **Field Compliance Bureau** audits in-state and out-of-state taxpayers to ensure compliance with Missouri's tax laws.

Motor Vehicle and Driver Licensing Division

The Motor Vehicle and Driver Licensing Division provides a variety of services to owners of cars, trucks, motorcycles, trailers and boats. It also helps keep Missouri roads safer by maintaining records of serious violations of Missouri's traffic laws. In FY 2014, the division issued more than 238,000 new driver licenses and renewed more than 607,000 licenses. In calendar year 2014, it issued more than 1.94 million motor vehicle, trailer and boat titles, and oversaw the issuance and renewal of about 4.06 million vehicle registrations.

The **Driver License Bureau** helps citizens obtain or renew their driver licenses. It also processes records relating to traffic violation point assessments and uninsured motorists. The bureau also tracks administrative alcohol violations and those who fail to appear in court for a variety of traffic-related offenses.

The **License Offices Bureau** manages the operations of the 178 contract offices throughout the state. The offices provide many of the most common driver license and motor vehicle services for Missourians. The management of the offices is no longer awarded on a patronage basis, and is now bid out to independent contractors.

The **Motor Vehicle Bureau** provides services for motor vehicle owners, such as issuing or renewing license plates or obtaining owner titles. The bureau also works with new and used automobile dealers, and also helps salvage dealers and leasing companies acquire registration certificates.

Legal Services Division

The Legal Services Division ensures the department's compliance with state and federal law and internal policies.

The **General Counsel's Office** advises the director and Department divisions on all legal matters. It helps keep Missouri drivers safer by defending the state's drunk driving laws in administrative hearings and court proceedings. It also provides training concerning DWI laws to law enforcement officers, judges and other court personnel. The office represents the state in legal cases that involve taxation, bankruptcies and motor vehicle fraud.

The **Criminal Tax Investigation Bureau** investigates and develops information leading to local prosecution of individuals and businesses sus-

JACKIE BEMBOOM
Director, Motor Vehicle and
Driver Licensing Division

WOOD MILLER
Director, Legal Services and
Acting General Counsel

LYNN BEXTEN
Director
Administration Division

pected of violating state statutes related to sales, withholding and income taxes.

The **Compliance and Investigation Bureau** investigates illegal motor vehicle titling and registration, odometer fraud and tax fraud involving motor fuel sales tax and the state cigarette tax. The bureau also ensures the compliance of motor vehicle dealers, salvage businesses and marine dealers with statutes and licensure regulations.

Administration Division

The Administration Division provides professional, innovative and efficient personnel, financial and general services support that allows the department's divisions to carry out their core responsibilities, including safeguarding assets, disseminate information and apply efficient personnel practices. This division also manages employee wellness events and initiatives.

The **Financial and General Services Bureau** provides fiscal services to the department and other governmental agencies in the area of finance, accounting, depositing and cashiering of state and non-state revenues and investing and collateralizing non-state revenue collections. This bureau also provides support in the areas of procurement, child support contract oversight, mail processing, archiving, stores, vehicle pool maintenance, delivery services and facility leasing.

The **Personnel Services Bureau** is in charge of personnel and payroll issues, training, compliance with state and federal employment laws, and the department's affirmative action and diversity programs. The Communications and Training section within this bureau works with all of the department's divisions to update the department's Internet and Intranet websites, train department personnel to be more efficient and update department forms and publications to be more customer-friendly and effective.

State Lottery Commission

PO Box 1603, 1823 Southridge Dr.
Jefferson City 65102-1603
Telephone: (573) 751-4050 / FAX: (573) 751-5188
www.molottery.com

On Nov. 6, 1984, Missouri voters authorized the Missouri General Assembly to establish a Missouri state lottery.

The State Lottery Commission supervises the lottery by issuing rules and appointing a director. The commission is also guided by laws, approved by the General Assembly, that deal with the lottery. These laws cover topics such as distribution of lottery funds, conflicts of interest, who may play the lottery, criminal penalties and taxation of lottery winnings. The director runs the day-to-day business of the lottery, including hiring employees, issuing licenses and negotiating contracts with vendors. The governor, with the advice and consent of the Senate, appoints the five-member commission. No more than three members may be of the same political party. Commissioners receive no salary and serve three-year terms.

The attorney general provides legal services for the lottery, and the state auditor reviews operations by conducting audits.

State Tax Commission

Truman State Office Bldg.
PO Box 146, Jefferson City 65102-0146
Telephone: (573) 751-2414 / FAX: (573) 751-1341
www.stc.mo.gov
Email: stc@stc.mo.gov

The present State Tax Commission was created by an act of the 63rd General Assembly, identified in section 138.190, RSMo.

The commission is composed of three members who are chosen from the two major political parties. The members are appointed by the governor with the advice and consent of the Senate.

MAY SCHEVE REARDON
Executive Director
Missouri Lottery

BRUCE E. DAVIS
Chair
State Tax Commission

VICTOR CALLAHAN
Commissioner
State Tax Commission

RANDY B. HOLMAN
Commissioner
State Tax Commission

SANDY WANKUM
Administrative Secretary
State Tax Commission

The authority and responsibilities of the State Tax Commission are further defined and articulated in the landmark Supreme Court decision of State ex. rel. Cassilly v. Riney, which provided the genesis for the statewide equalization of assessments. The State Tax Commission was created to perform five basic functions. These functions are:

1. Equalize assessments;

2. Conduct *de novo* judicial hearings regarding valuation and classification appeals

from local boards of equalization in individual assessment cases;

3. Formulate and implement statewide assessment policies and procedures to comply with statutory and constitutional mandates;

4. Supervise local assessing officials and local assessment programs to ensure compliance with statewide policy requirements; and

5. Assess the distributable property of railroads and public utilities.

State Tax Commission

Davis, Bruce E., (R), chair, Columbia, Jan. 23, 2010;

Callahan, Victor, (D), member, Independence, Jan. 23, 2018;

Holman, Randy B., (D), member, Festus, Jan. 23, 2014.

Department of Social Services

Broadway State Office Bldg.
PO Box 1527, Jefferson City, 65102
Telephone: (573) 751-4815 / FAX: (573) 751-3203
www.dss.mo.gov

The Missouri Department of Social Services (DSS) was constitutionally established in 1974 because "the health and general welfare of the people are matters of primary public concern." The department is charged with administering programs to promote, safeguard and protect the general welfare of children; to maintain and strengthen family life; and to aid people in need as they strive to achieve their highest level of independence.

The department is organized into four program divisions: Children's Division, Family Support Division, MO HealthNet Division and the Division of Youth Services. The Division of Finance and Administrative Services and the Division of Legal Services provide department-wide administrative and support services.

The department cooperates and partners with many private organizations, businesses and individuals to extend the outreach of human services to Missouri citizens.

Office of the Director

The director of the Department of Social Services is responsible for the overall administration of programs within the department except as otherwise provided by law. The director determines priorities for program implementation and has final approval for uses of state and federal funds appropriated to the department.

Missouri's State Technical Assistant Team (STAT) provides comprehensive, integrated services to the entire child protection community. From data collection and interpretation of the causes of child fatalities to all types of child related criminal investigations, STAT provides training, support and expertise to professionals responsible for the protection of children.

The Human Resource Center (HRC) guides the overall human resources management for the department's 7,000+ employees. The center is responsible for ensuring compliance with merit system rules and coordinating personnel activities in areas such as labor relations, union negotiations, recruitment, selection, classification,

BRIAN KINKADE
Director

JENNIFER TIDBALL
Deputy Director

STEPHAN TOMLINSON
Legislative Liason

REBECCA WOELFEL
Communications Director

DONNA SYBOUTS
Executive Assistant

PATRICK LUEBBERING
Director of Division of Finance
and Administrative Services

compensation, discipline, performance evaluation, personnel records maintenance, civil rights, investigations and compliance, employee grievance procedure and training.

Administration Divisions

The **Division of Finance and Administrative Services** provides budgeting, financial and support services to all divisions within the department. Responsibilities include accounts payable, payroll, purchasing, receipts, audits, grants management, budget, research and data management, mail processing, telecommunications, inventory and warehouse management, homeland security and safety.

The **Division of Legal Services (DLS)** provides comprehensive legal support to all programs and support divisions in DSS. The division represents the department, its divisions and the state. Responsibilities include representing DSS before administrative tribunals; circuit court and appellate courts on child abuse and neglect; licensure and revocation of foster homes, guardianships and permanency planning; establishing, enforcing and modifying child support orders; hearings for public assistance applicants/recipients related to denial or termination of benefits; and investigating fraud and abuse by public assistance recipients, along with establishing claims and tracking collections.

Children's Division

205 Jefferson St., PO Box 88, Jefferson City 65103
Telephone: (573) 522-8024 / FAX: (573) 526-3971
www.dss.mo.gov/CD
Email: AskCD@dss.mo.gov

Child welfare services are provided under federal and state laws to help children and families function at their maximum potential, both personally and socially.

The division has a legal mandate to provide services in three primary areas: child abuse and neglect investigations and family assessments, treatment and placement services to children and families and provision of child care.

Organization

The Children's Division (CD) is administered by a director appointed by the director of the Department of Social Services. The division maintains a presence in each county and the city of St. Louis and supports each of the 45 judicial circuits in the state.

Child Abuse and Neglect Investigations and Assessments

The division is responsible for receiving reports of alleged child abuse or neglect. Once a report is received, the division responds to assure safety of the child(ren). The goals of child abuse or neglect investigations and assessments are to assess the level of risk to the child(ren), protect the child(ren) from harm, determine if abuse or neglect occurred as reported and provide services to the family.

Under the provisions of the Child Abuse and Neglect Law (sections 210.110 and 210.167,

JOEL ANDERSON
Director
Division of Legal Services

TIM DECKER
Director
Children's Division

RSMo): a "child" is any person under 18 years of age; "abuse" includes both actual and threatened physical injury, sexual or emotional abuse inflicted on a child other than by accidental means by those responsible for his or her care, custody and control, except that discipline, including spanking, administered in a reasonable manner, shall not be construed to be abuse; "neglect" is failure to provide, by those responsible for the care, custody and control of the child, the proper or necessary support and education as required by law, or medical, surgical or any other care necessary for the child's well-being; and "persons responsible for the care, custody and control of the child" include, but are not limited to, the parents or guardians of the child, other members of the child's household or those people exercising supervision over a child for any part of a 24-hour day.

All reports of suspected child abuse and neglect are made to a centralized hotline unit of the division, which is required to provide toll-free statewide telephone service 24 hours a day, 7 days a week for reporting purposes (1-800-392-3738).

Family-Centered Services

The overriding goal of family-centered services is to prevent child abuse or neglect, and the removal of the child from the home, by stabilizing the family and improving family functioning.

Treatment services, referred to as "family-centered services," are provided in preventive and protective capacities. Protective family-centered services are case management services provided to families when a finding of child abuse and neglect has been determined by a preponderance of evidence at the conclusion of an investigation. Preventive family-centered services are offered when an investigation of abuse or neglect is unsubstantiated or when a family assessment detects concerns that might be mitigated by services to help prevent abuse or neglect. Preventive services are contingent on the family's willingness to accept services. Families may also self-refer for services. Services may be provided by CD staff and/or purchased on behalf of the family.

Federal law mandates that the division provide services to children and families of children in alternative care. These services are geared toward permanency for the child(ren), either by reunification with his or her biological parent(s) or permanency through adoption or guardianship. The goals of these services are to prevent further child abuse or neglect, mitigate family factors that could lead to further child abuse or neglect, reunite children with their families when possible and obtain permanent homes for children who cannot safely return home through adoption or guardianship.

To achieve these goals, the division employs staff to provide services to eligible children and families. These services are provided through direct services and contracted services.

Direct Services

Children's Division staff provides direct services to families in treatment and families whose children are in alternative care settings. Children's Division staff works with families in assessing service needs and case planning. Actual services may be provided by CD staff, through contractors or both.

Alternative care services (family-centered, out-of-home services) are provided to children who are determined by the juvenile court to need care in a setting other than their biological family homes. These children are cared for in substitute family care or non-familial group care. Any one of three types of licensed settings provides alternative care: foster family homes, group facilities and residential treatment facilities. Transitional living services and independent living may also be utilized for older youth who might not return home and for whom adoption or guardianship is not deemed appropriate.

Child safety and permanency for children is the overriding goal of all services and integrates the principles of permanency planning — reuniting the child with the biological family when possible and, when necessary, finding other permanent family relationships for children.

Families who wish to adopt children unable to reunite with their families may, in some instances, receive an adoption subsidy payment. This is a statewide program developed to provide financial benefits, in the form of a subsidy, to encourage potential adoptive parents to adopt and to finance the cost of adopting "special needs" children.

Contracted Services

Contracted services are available to individuals and families who are receiving family-centered services, or in efforts to recruit and maintain resources for permanency. These services are usually provided as a result of a child abuse/neglect report with a "preponderance of evidence" finding, but may also be authorized for children in alternative care, children in adoptive placements, and family members receiving preventive treatment services or foster and adoptive services. Services are provided through contracts with both public and private community agencies and play a major role in extending services throughout the state.

Licensing Program

The division inspects and licenses foster care facilities, residential care facilities and child-placing agencies. In addition, the licensing staff monitors licensed facilities to ensure the facilities maintain requisite standards, conducts public education programs and consults with facility personnel in the development and implementation of services to the children being served, as well as residential program development.

Early Childhood and Prevention Services

The Early Childhood and Prevention Services section administers early childhood/child care and child abuse prevention programs and services. These programs provide child care subsidies to low-income families and quality improvement and professional development activities for child care programs and their staff. Staff also administer a portion of the state Early Childhood Development Education and Care Fund, which provides grants to community-based organizations and individuals for early childhood and child abuse/neglect prevention services.

Family Support Division

615 Howerton Ct., PO Box 2320
Jefferson City 65102-2320
Telephone: (573) 751-3221 / FAX: (573) 751-8949
Toll-free: (800) 735-2466
www.dss.mo.gov/fsd

The **Family Support Division (FSD)** is responsible for the administration of these programs and services: Food Stamps, Temporary Assistance, Child Support, Medical Assistance, Rehabilitation Services for the Blind and Visually Impaired, Low-Income Home Energy Assistance, Supplemental Nursing Care and Community Services Block Grant.

Organization

The Family Support Division is administered by a director appointed by the director of the Department of Social Services. The division has at least one location in each county and in the City of St. Louis to provide customers with access to the Income Maintenance Programs. The division maintains offices across the state for the administration of the Child Support Program. Administration of the Rehabilitation Services for the Blind is managed by seven offices throughout Missouri.

Income Maintenance Programs

The determination of an individual's financial need is basic to the granting of Temporary Assistance, Food Stamps, child care, blind pension, Supplemental Aid to the Blind, medical assistance and nursing care benefits. The division has a legal requirement to consider all facts and circumstances in determining eligibility for public assistance, including the applicant's earning capacity, income and resources from whatever source received. The amount of benefits, when added to all other income, resources, support, and maintenance, shall provide such person with reasonable subsistence. If the applicant is not found to be in need, assistance is denied.

Temporary Assistance

Temporary Assistance (TA) makes cash grants on behalf of needy children who are living in homes maintained by parents or close relatives. This program provides temporary financial assistance while the adult transitions to self-sufficiency.

MO HealthNet

The Family Support Division determines participant eligibility for MO HealthNet services. MO HealthNet refers to the statewide medical assistance programs for elderly, disabled and blind individuals; low-income families; pregnant women; and children who meet certain eligibility requirements. In order to qualify for the MO HealthNet program, individuals must be a resident of the state of Missouri, a U.S. national citizen, permanent resident or legal alien in need of health care/insurance assistance. Family income is compared to the applicable percentage of the federal poverty guidelines. The applicable income limit for children is dependent on the age of the child(ren). The goals of the MO HealthNet program are to promote good health, prevent illness and premature death, correct or limit disability, treat illness and provide rehabilitation to persons with disabilities. Eligible persons receive a MO HealthNet identification card. There is no cash assistance with this program, although the

JULIE GIBSON
Director
Family Support Division

program does pay for Medicare premiums for eligible individuals.

Supplemental Aid to the Blind and Blind Pension

The division administers two separate programs for the blind: Supplemental Aid to the Blind (SAB) and the Blind Pension Program. Under the SAB program, the amount of the monthly grant is $718 minus any Supplemental Security Income (SSI) payment received. Under the Blind Pension Program, a flat monthly payment of $718 per person is made. The programs differ slightly in eligibility requirements. Funds are provided from a Missouri constitutionally established blind pension fund with no matching federal funds.

Supplemental Nursing Care

The Supplemental Nursing Care Program in Missouri provides cash assistance and medical services coverage to eligible aged, blind or disabled individuals who reside in non-Medicaid, licensed skilled nursing, intermediate care, assisted living or residential care facilities. Individuals who reside in licensed, skilled nursing facilities or intermediate care facilities may receive monthly cash benefits of up to a maximum of $390. If they live in a licensed assisted living facility, they may be eligible for monthly cash benefits of up to $292, or if in a licensed residential care facility, they may receive monthly cash benefits of up to $156.

Food Stamp and Food Distribution Programs

The Supplemental Nutrition Assistance Program (SNAP), known as the Food Stamp Program in Missouri, is designed to help low-income families increase their purchasing power for buying nutritious food for their families. Depending upon the adjusted income and the number of persons in the household, a family receives a monthly benefit amount. The division is responsible for determining the eligibility of Food Stamp applicants according to guidelines established by the U.S. Department of Agriculture (USDA).

The division also administers a number of food distribution programs providing USDA-donated foods to Charitable Institutions, Summer Food Service Programs for Children, The Emergency Food Assistance Program (TEFAP) and Disaster Relief Organizations.

Low Income Home Energy Assistance Program

Low Income Home Energy Assistance Program (LIHEAP) provides assistance to low-income individuals to help pay for heating and cooling. Eligibility for assistance is based on household income and the number of persons residing in the household. Benefit amounts vary based on income, family size and type of fuel utilized. Missouri provides two programs with the LIHEAP grant: Energy Assistance/Regular Heating (EA) and Energy Crisis Intervention Program (ECIP).

Community Services Block Grant Program

The Community Services Block Grant Program (CSBG) makes funds available to support efforts that reduce poverty, revitalize low-income communities and empower low-income families and individuals to become fully self-sufficient. Most CSBG programs are operated locally by community action agencies that provide direct services to individuals and families whose income falls within the federal poverty guidelines, as well as mobilize communities to identify and address the causes and conditions of poverty in their geographic area.

Emergency Solutions Grant Program

The Emergency Solutions Grant Program is designed to provide funding for emergency homeless shelters and street outreach to the homeless. It also provides homelessness prevention and rapid re-housing services to homeless individuals, their families and those at risk of becoming homeless. The overall goal of the ESG program is to move participants to, and help them retain, permanent housing.

Blind and Visually Impaired Services Program

The Rehabilitation Services for the Blind administers six service programs to blind and visually impaired persons: vocational rehabilitation, prevention of blindness, independent living rehabilitation to adults, Older Blind Services (OBS), children services and the Blind Enterprise Program (BEP).

Vocational rehabilitation services are supported by both federal and state funds. Services include diagnosis and evaluation, counseling and guidance, physical and mental restoration, college and other types of vocational training, job placement, and services after employment when needed. Vocational rehabilitation services are to enable a person with visual disabilities to obtain or retain suitable employment.

Prevention of blindness services are funded with state funds and Blindness Education, Screening and Treatment (BEST) funds. Services are for the purpose of early detection of eye disease that may lead to blindness and, when indicated, providing treatment to eligible persons. Services include diagnostic examinations, surgery, hospitalization, glasses, prostheses and medications that are not available through other sources. These services are conditional upon the financial need of the individual. Free vision screening clinics are conducted in conjunction with schools of ophthalmology in Missouri. Free glaucoma screening clinics are conducted throughout the state.

Independent living rehabilitation services—including services for adults, children and the OBS program for seniors over age 55— are supported by both federal and state funds. Services are for the purposes of enabling that person to function independently in the home and community and/or to succeed in appropriate educational settings. Services include diagnosis and evaluation; adjustment to blindness services; alternative techniques in the areas of daily living activities; counseling and families supportive services; physical restoration; homemaking; communication; and orientation to, and travel within, the home and community.

The federal/state Randolph-Sheppard Blind Enterprise Program provides employment opportunities for legally blind persons who have participated in special training and are licensed by the division to manage a vending facility located in federal, state and private industry. Vending facilities range from full food service cafeterias to banks of vending machines.

The Children's Services Program focuses on blind and visually impaired children and their families, providing assistance with education and advocacy. Services include early identification and intervention, fostering a positive sense of self, regardless of vision loss, facilitating access to community services specific to the individual needs of the child, and helping families find information about blindness and its impact on their child's education and future.

Child Support Program

Missouri's Child Support Program operates pursuant to Title IV-D of the federal Social Security Act and Chapter 454, RSMo.

Child Support Program responsibilities include location of parents, paternity establishment, establishing child and medical support orders, enforcing support orders, reviewing support orders for modification and distributing child support collections.

The Family Support Division collects child support on behalf of families receiving public assistance. In addition, individuals not receiving public assistance benefits may apply for child support services.

Currently, the federal government funds the program at the rate of 66 percent. In addition to federal funds, the state is entitled to retain approximately 34 percent of the collections it receives for families that receive temporary assistance.

The program partners with county prosecuting attorneys through cooperative agreements to assist with child support activities. Additionally, the program partners with the state attorney general through a cooperative agreement to assist with child support enforcement and modification activities.

Pursuant to section 454.530, RSMo, the FSD, together with the Missouri Department of Revenue, operates the state disbursement unit known as the Family Support Payment Center (FSPC), which receives and disburses support on behalf of families. FSD collected $683.8 million in State Fiscal Year 2014.

MO HealthNet Division

615 Howerton Ct., PO Box 6500
Jefferson City 65102
Telephone: (573) 751-3425 / FAX: (573) 751-6564
www.dss.mo.gov/mhd
Email: ask.MHD@dss.mo.gov

The MO HealthNet (Missouri Medicaid) program provides medical services to eligible participants within defined program benefits in a similar way insurance companies provide coverage for their policy holders.

Organization

The MO HealthNet Division (MHD) is administered by a director appointed by the director of the Department of Social Services. The division maintains administrative offices in Jefferson City, and contracts with health care providers and managed care organizations for the provision of health care.

JOSEPH PARKS, M.D.
Director
MO HealthNet Division

MO HealthNet Program

The services provided include those required by the federal government, such as hospital and physician services. Also included are optional services, such as pharmaceutical and personal care services authorized by the Missouri General Assembly and identified in section 208.152, RSMo.

The MO HealthNet Division administers a mandatory Medicaid managed care program for eligible participants in the eastern, central and western areas of the state. Children, pregnant women, Temporary Assistance for Needy Families (TANF) recipients and children in state custody receive their medical care through managed care organizations, allowing the state to ensure access to health care and control costs at the same time. The MO HealthNet program is jointly funded by state and federal funds.

The MO HealthNet Pharmacy Program oversees outpatient prescription drug reimbursement. The pharmacy benefit includes reimbursement for all drug products of manufacturers who have entered into a rebate agreement with the Federal Department of Health and Human Services (HHS) and are dispensed by qualified providers, with few therapeutic category exclusions. In addition, MHD is responsible for program development, benefit design and clinical policy decision-making with activities oriented towards wellness and continuum of care.

The MO HealthNet program includes specialized services for specific populations within the state by receiving waiver authority from the federal government. Home and community-based waivers for the elderly, certain developmentally disabled participants, as well as patients with AIDS, were obtained and allow the MO HealthNet program to pay for home care not otherwise covered as an alternative to more expensive institutional care. These services are restricted to those participants who would otherwise require, and whose home care is no more expensive than, institutionalization.

Division of Youth Services

3418 Knipp Dr., Ste. A-1, PO Box 447
Jefferson City 65102
Telephone: (573) 751-3324 / FAX: (573) 526-4494
www.dss.mo.gov/dys/
Email: ASKDYS@dss.mo.gov

The Omnibus Reorganization Act of 1974 created the Division of Youth Services (DYS) and placed it within the Department of Social Services.

Youth judged to be delinquent and in need of rehabilitation and education are committed to the division by the state's juvenile (circuit) courts until approved for return to the community under supervision or discharged.

The division provides an array of services including residential care, nonresidential and community-based services, and after-care supervision. Chapter 219, RSMo, outlines the division's responsibility to also include prevention of delinquency, incentive subsidy to juvenile courts, consultative and information services and technical assistance to local communities.

Organization

The division is administered by the director, who is appointed by the director of the Department of Social Services. The division operates structured residential programs providing youth rehabilitation, treatment, and education services through a continuum of secure and moderate care centers and community-based group homes. Nonresidential programs include case management, day treatment, family therapy and youth employment. Five regional administrators are responsible for the programs in their geographical areas. Central office personnel, together with the regional administrators, aid the director in planning, monitoring, and ongoing quality improvement of all agency services.

Goals and Objectives

The vision of Missouri DYS is that every young person served will become a productive citizen and lead a fulfilling life. The mission is to enable youth to fulfill their needs in a responsible manner within the context of and with respect for the needs of the family and community. This balanced approach relies on community partnerships for the development and enhancement of services for the prevention of delinquency.

PHYLLIS BECKER
Director
Division of Youth Services

Methods of Treatment

Each division facility creates a structured environment designed to contribute to positive changes in the student's behavior and attitudes through the provision of group and individualized treatment services, recreation, academic and vocational training. The ultimate goal is to return each youth to his or her home community as a productive, responsible member of society. The division operates as a fully accredited school program, providing high school credits and High School Equivalency Test (HiSET) coursework.

Case Management

A case management system has been developed to provide assessment, treatment planning, coordination of services, monitoring and evaluation of the services for youths and their families. A needs and risk assessment helps the case manager determine the most appropriate services for each youth. The assessment takes into account all pertinent factors involving the youth's delinquent history while identifying the general treatment needs.

Community-Based Services

Focusing on more individualized services and delivering programs at the community level, the division has expanded its program design to include more community-based options. Nonresidential services are provided to low-risk youth as a diversion to residential care and as a supplement to after-care.

Intensive Case Monitoring

This service is provided by employees who monitor a youth's behavior and activities. Community mentors also provide support and counseling to the youth when needed. Great effort is made to ensure the matching of similar personalities and interests of youth and the mentor.

Day Treatment

This service provides a structured alternative educational program that includes traditional academic courses, GED classes, career planning, job placement and community service supported by individual, group and family therapy.

Family Therapy

Family specialists provide counseling to DYS youth and their families. In addition, the family therapy unit accepts referrals from juvenile courts, child welfare agencies, mental health agencies, schools and other sources. DYS family specialists also provide training to other state agency staff and court personnel.

Group Home Programs

Group homes provide the least restrictive residential environment. Staff provide 24-hour supervision in a home-like setting with a capacity for 10 youths. Youth follow a daily schedule with time allowed for interaction with the community (school, jobs and community projects) as well as treatment services within the facility (group, individual and family counseling).

Moderate Care Residential Facilities

Residential facilities provide a structured environment for DYS youth. The residential programs target youth who cannot function well in the community and require a more structured setting. Many of these youth have participated in repeat property offenses and require continuous structure to mature.

The program divides youth into groups of 10 with 24-hour staff supervision. A rigorous school program is provided on-site by full-time teachers offering basic education, GED programming and various remedial/special education activities.

Secure Care Residential Facilities

For those youth who have a history of offenses and require a more structured setting, the division offers programs in secured facilities. Five highly structured, secure-care programs provide on-site educational classes, vocational training and recreational activities. These programs target youth with longer offense records that might include crimes against people. The offenders tend to be older and might include youth who have been unsuccessful in community-based programs. Scheduled outings into the community serve the purpose of involving the youth in community support projects.

An individual education plan, including both youth goals and staff strategies, is developed for each youth. Parents are encouraged to attend these planning meetings.

Dual Jurisdiction

The division also serves youth in secure care programs in Montgomery City, St. Louis and St. Joseph, sentenced under the dual jurisdiction provisions in section 211.073, RSMo. This alternative sentencing provision allows certified youth to receive an adult and juvenile sentence with a suspended execution of the adult sentence. Treatment and educational services are provided to youth whose length of stay is significantly longer than that of other DYS students.

Aftercare

When youth are ready to return to their communities, the division provides services to help them make a smooth transition. Virtually all youth under DYS care enter the aftercare program upon their return to the community. An assigned case manager ensures support services are provided to help each youth enter and re-adjust to community living including referral, supervision and counseling. The primary goal of aftercare is to support youth in becoming law-abiding and productive citizens.

Division of Youth Services Advisory Board

Established in 1974, the DYS Advisory Board is charged with the responsibility to advise the director, the legislature and the general public on all matters pertaining to the operation of the division. The 15-member board consists of citizens from across the state who are dedicated to the prevention of delinquency and the rehabilitation of juvenile offenders.

Stein, Cindy, chair, Springfield;
Abrams, Doug, vice chair, Columbia;
Bruning, Lauren, member, St. Louis;
Days, Rita Heard, member, St. Louis;
Dobbs, Bill, member, Noel;
Flowers, Tyrone, member, Kansas City;
Gant, Judge Jack E., member, Independence;
Gray, Judge Jon R., member, Kansas City;
Greenlaw, Johnnie, member, St. Louis;
Kehm, Judge Dennis J., member, Festus;
Lowenstein, Judge Harold L., member, Kansas City;
Parrish, Sue, member, Sedalia;
Payne, Sharron, member, Poplar Bluff;
Rust, Rex K., member, Cape Girardeau; and
Smith, William B., member, Monticello.

Department of Transportation

Transportation Office Bldg.
105 W. Capitol Ave., PO Box 270, Jefferson City 65102
Telephone: (573) 751-2551
Customer services telephone: (888) 275-6636
(888-ASK MoDOT)
www.modot.org

The Missouri Department of Transportation (MoDOT), under the guidance of the Missouri Highways and Transportation Commission, is committed to providing the public with a safe and modern transportation system. MoDOT is responsible for maintaining 33,895 miles of highways and 10,376 bridges throughout the state. In addition to designing, building and maintaining roads and bridges, MoDOT works to improve airports, river ports, railroads, public transit systems and pedestrian and bicycle travel. The agency also administers motor carrier and highway safety programs.

State Highways and Transportation Commission

The Missouri Highways and Transportation Commission is a six-member bipartisan board that guides the Missouri Department of Transportation and is responsible for planning, maintaining and improving the state's transportation systems.

Commission members are appointed by the governor and confirmed by the Missouri Senate. No more than three commission members may be of the same political party. State law requires six-year terms, with two members replaced every two years.

The commission appoints the Missouri Department of Transportation's director and secretary to the commission.

State Highways and Transportation Commission*

Miller, Stephen R., (R), chair, Kansas City, March 2011;

Briscoe, John W., (D), New London, March 1, 2021;

Nelson, Mary E., (D), St. Louis, March 2017;

Pace, Michael B., (I), West Plains, March 2019;

Smith, Gregg C., (D), Clinton, March 2019;

STEPHEN R. MILLER
Chair, Highways and
Transportation Commission

MARY E. NELSON
Member, Highways and
Transportation Commission

MICHAEL B. PACE
Member, Highways and
Transportation Commission

GREGG C. SMITH
Member, Highways and
Transportation Commission

MICHAEL T. WATERS JR.
Member, Highways and
Transportation Commission

PAM HARLAN
Secretary to the Commission

Waters, Michael T. Jr., (R), Orrick, March 2021.

*$25 per diem

Commission Secretary's Office

The Highways and Transportation Commission appoints a commission secretary to provide operational support, clerical assistance and record keeping.

PATRICK McKENNA
Director

ED HASSINGER
Chief Engineer

ROBERTA BROEKER, C.P.A.
Chief Financial Officer

RICH TIEMEYER
Chief Counsel

KATHY HARVEY
Assistant Chief Engineer

BILL ROGERS
Director
Audits and Investigations

JAY WUNDERLICH
Director
Governmental Relations

FAY FLEMING
Director
Communications

Director's Office

MoDOT's daily operations are under the direction and supervision of the director, who is appointed by the commission. The MoDOT director is assisted by a chief engineer and an assistant chief engineer, who are in charge of MoDOT's road and bridge design, construction and maintenance activities statewide and a chief financial officer, who is responsible for the financial and administrative operations. The directors of the Chief Counsel's Office, Audits and Investigations, Governmental Relations and Communications also report directly to the department director.

Chief Counsel's Office

The chief counsel is appointed by the MoDOT director with the consent of the Highways and Transportation Commission to handle legal responsibilities for the department and the commission.

Audits and Investigations

The Audits and Investigations Division performs audits of department operations, external contracts, grant agreements and motor carrier fuel tax returns, and apportioned registrations. The division also investigates fraud, waste and abuse; handles employee grievances and Equal Employment Opportunity complaints; and analyzes competitive bidding practices.

Governmental Relations

The role of Governmental Relations is to work with federal, state and local officials, the public and department staff to advocate the department's objectives by advancing legislative initiatives designed to develop sound public policies relating to all modes of transportation.

Communications

The Communications Division provides information about the commission and the department's projects, programs and services to the public, its partners and MoDOT employees.

District Offices

To facilitate providing the state highways and transportation program, the department divides the state into seven geographical districts: northwest, northeast, Kansas City, central, St. Louis,

DON WICHERN
Northwest, St. Joseph

PAULA GOUGH
Northeast, Hannibal

DANIEL C. NIEC
Kansas City, Lee's Summit

DAVID SILVESTER
Central, Jefferson City

southwest and southeast. A district engineer administers the department's work within each district.

Northwest District — headquarters, St. Joseph. The district consists of Andrew, Atchison, Buchanan, Caldwell, Carroll, Chariton, Clinton, Daviess, DeKalb, Gentry, Grundy, Harrison, Holt, Linn, Livingston, Mercer, Nodaway, Putnam, Sullivan and Worth counties. The counties cover a land area of about 10,769 square miles and have a total population of about 280,638 and a total of 5,281 miles of state highways.

Northeast District — headquarters, Hannibal. The district consists of Adair, Audrain, Clark, Knox, Lewis, Lincoln, Macon, Marion, Monroe, Montgomery, Pike, Ralls, Randolph, Schuyler, Scotland, Shelby and Warren counties. The counties cover a land area of about 9,246 square miles, and have a total population of about 292,863 and a total of 4,526 miles of state highways.

Kansas City District — headquarters, Lee's Summit. The district consists of Cass, Clay, Jackson, Johnson, Lafayette, Pettis, Platte, Ray and Saline counties. The counties cover a land area of about 5,650 square miles, and have a total population of about 1,259,938 and a total of 3,042 miles of state highways.

Central District — headquarters, Jefferson City. The district consists of Boone, Callaway, Camden, Cole, Cooper, Crawford, Dent, Gasconade, Howard, Laclede, Maries, Miller, Moniteau, Morgan, Osage, Phelps, Pulaski and Washington counties. The counties cover a land area of about 11,234 square miles, and have a total population of about 652,456 and a total of 5,242 miles of state highways.

St. Louis District — headquarters, Chesterfield. The district consists of the city of St. Louis and Franklin, Jefferson, St. Charles and St. Louis counties. The district covers a land area of more than 2,700 square miles and has a total population of approximately 2,000,000 and a total of 1,677 miles of state highways.

REBECCA J. BALTZ
Southwest, Springfield

MARK SHELTON
Southeast, Sikeston

Southwest District — headquarters, Springfield. The district consists of Barry, Barton, Bates, Benton, Cedar, Christian, Dade, Dallas, Greene, Henry, Hickory, Jasper, Lawrence, McDonald, Newton, Polk, St. Clair, Stone, Taney, Vernon and Webster counties. The counties cover a land area of about 13,274 square miles and have a total population of about 926,656 and a total of 6,533 miles of state highways.

Southeast District — headquarters, Sikeston. The district consists of Bollinger, Butler, Cape Girardeau, Carter, Douglas, Dunklin, Howell, Iron, Madison, Mississippi, New Madrid, Oregon, Ozark, Pemiscot, Perry, Reynolds, Ripley, Scott, Shannon, St. Francois, Ste. Genevieve, Stoddard, Texas, Wayne and Wright counties. The counties cover a land area of about 16,730 square miles and have a total population of about 577,418 and a total of 7,404 miles of state highways.

Bridge

The Bridge Division produces structural designs and detailed plans for state highway bridges, including cost estimates and site-specific job provisions. The division also oversees the inspection of all state, city and county bridges as well as provides weight limits for all bridges.

DENNIS HECKMAN
State Bridge Engineer

DAVE AHLVERS
State Construction and Materials
Engineer

MACHELLE WATKINS
Transportation Planning Director

LESTER WOODS JR.
External Civil Rights
Director

Design

Design prepares roadway plans and advertises projects for bids. Included in plan preparation are determination of state and/or federal funding for projects; ground surveys and aerial photography; public involvement meetings; consideration of social, environmental and economic factors; detailed plan design and the development of specifications; and cost estimates for highway projects prior to advertising for bids.

The division also acquires realty rights for constructing and improving state highways and related facilities. It also disposes of real estate no longer needed for Missouri's transportation system and regulates outdoor advertising and salvage yards.

Construction and Materials

Construction and Materials administers contracts and performs material testing to ensure projects are of high quality, completed on time and within budget. Pavement selection and geotechnical information are provided for the design of roads and bridges. The division also performs research on products and processes to implement innovations for Missouri's transportation system.

Transportation Planning

Transportation Planning is responsible for long-range planning, data administration, road and bridge systems analysis, and planning and programming. The division also develops and tracks the five-year Statewide Transportation Improvement Program, the department's highway and bridge construction program. The division also works to improve MoDOT's efficiency through performance management and to implement the processes, plans and programs to streamline the agency's operations.

EILEEN RACKERS
State Traffic and Highway Safety
Engineer

BECKY ALLMEROTH
State Maintenance Engineer

External Civil Rights

The External Civil Rights Division is responsible for directing the department's external affirmative action, equal opportunity and nondiscrimination programs, which includes the Disadvantaged Business Enterprise Program (DBE), On-the-Job Training Program (OJT), Equal Employment Opportunity, Title VI, Americans with Disability Act (ADA) compliance and all other nondiscrimination or affirmative action programs related to federal-aid contracting activities. The division facilitates all DBE and OJT Supportive Services programs statewide, which includes business assistance centers and pre-apprenticeship training programs in Kansas City, Columbia and St. Louis.

Traffic and Highway Safety

The Traffic and Highway Safety Division is responsible for working with safety partners to implement education, enforcement, engineering, emergency medical services strategies and public policies that are proven effective in preventing deaths and injuries from motor vehicle crashes. The division also provides statewide coordination of traffic incident management activities, work

MICHELLE TEEL
Director
Multimodal Operations

BRENDA MORRIS
Director
Financial Services

MICKI KNUDSEN
Director
Human Resources

zone management, traveler information programs and policy to support signing, striping, traffic signal operations, lighting and roadway access programs throughout the state. These programs provide for the safe and efficient movement of people and goods on the state highway system.

Maintenance

Maintaining state highways and bridges is the primary function of the Maintenance Division. Responsibilities include preservation, upkeep, operation and restoration of roadways, bridges, signs, traffic control equipment and all appropriate facilities so they remain safe and usable.

Multimodal Operations

The Multimodal Operations Division is responsible for administering a number of state and federal programs that fund and support aviation, railroads, transit, waterways and freight development.

Aviation

The aviation section administers federal and state grant programs that help local governments in planning, maintaining and developing existing airports and establishing new facilities.

Railroads

The railroad section is responsible for freight rail regulation, passenger rail support, light rail safety regulation, highway-rail crossing safety, rail/highway construction issues, inspection of railroad employee facilities and railroad safety inspection and outreach.

Transit

The transit section assists in the financial and technical support of the state's public transit and specialized paratransit systems. This function is carried out through the administration of state

and federal programs relating to general public transportation and specific programs for nonprofit agencies serving the mobility needs of senior citizens and people with disabilities.

Waterways

The waterways section helps port authorities develop commerce and foster local economic development. The section also promotes the use of Missouri's navigable rivers, assists in capital and administrative funding, acts as an information clearinghouse, provides technical assistance and represents port interests within industry and government.

Motor Carrier Services

Motor Carrier Services administers registration, fuel tax, permit and safety programs for Missouri's motor carrier companies. It collects millions of dollars in revenue to fund transportation statewide, while helping carriers remain economically successful.

Financial Services Division

The Financial Services Division is responsible for the department's budgeting, accounting, financial reporting and financial policy development. The division produces the department's annual comprehensive financial report, which includes the audited financial statements required by statutes. The Financial Services Division is also responsible for managing the department's state and federal funding and facilitating the efficient and accountable use of fiscal resources.

Human Resources

The Human Resources Division develops and administers the department's statewide personnel program. The division conducts recruiting for civil engineering positions and manages statewide efforts related to employment; work-life support; classification, pay and employee training; development; and assessment. Human Resources also develops personnel policy, maintains personnel records for employees and provides support for all personnel activities within the central office location.

Information Systems

The Information Systems Division provides information technology products, services and support to the department and coordinates its information technology activities. The division develops a comprehensive information technology improvement plan based on department needs and technology research and evaluations.

BETH RING
Director
Information Systems

RUDY NICKENS
Director
Equal Opportunity and Diversity

Equal Opportunity and Diversity

The Equal Opportunity and Diversity Division administers the department's workforce diversity program. This includes outreach, cultural education, cooperative education, mentoring and exit interviews. Additionally, the division coordinates the affirmative action program to comply with federal regulations and state statutes.

General Services

The General Services Division provides support in the management of fleet and facilities and the procurement of goods and services.

DEBBIE RICKARD
Director
General Services

JEFF PADGETT
Director
Risk and Benefits Management

Risk and Benefits Management

The Risk and Benefits Management Division oversees MoDOT's medical and life insurance plan and administers the department's insurance operations in the areas of workers' compensation, general liability and fleet vehicle liability.

The division also provides collection services for property damage, works to provide a safe and healthful work environment for all MoDOT employees and administers the department's pre-employment/post-offer physical program, and the drug and alcohol-testing program.

Missouri Government Resources on the Web

Executive Branch

Governor
www.gov.mo.gov

Lt. Governor
www.ltgov.mo.gov

Secretary of State
www.sos.mo.gov

State Auditor
www.auditor.mo.gov

State Treasurer
www.treasurer.mo.gov

Attorney General
www.ago.mo.gov

Judicial Branch

Missouri Judiciary
www.courts.mo.gov

Missouri Supreme Court
www.courts.mo.gov/page.jsp?id=27

Missouri Appellate Courts
www.courts.mo.gov/page.jsp?id=261

Missouri Circuit Courts
www.courts.mo.gov/page.jsp?id=321

Office of State Courts Administrator
www.courts.mo.gov/page.jsp?id=233

Missouri State Courts Automated Case
Management System
www.courts.mo.gov/casenet

Legislative Branch

Missouri General Assembly
www.moga.mo.gov

Missouri House
www.house.mo.gov

Missouri Senate
www.senate.mo.gov

Executive Departments

Missouri Government Web
www.mo.gov

Office of Administration
www.oa.mo.gov

Agriculture
www.mda.mo.gov

Conservation
www.mdc.mo.gov

Corrections
www.doc.mo.gov

Economic Development
www.ded.mo.gov

Elementary and Secondary Education
www.dese.mo.gov

Health and Senior Services
www.health.mo.gov

Higher Education
www.dhe.mo.gov

Insurance, Financial Institutions and Professional
Registration
www.difp.mo.gov / www.insurance.mo.gov

Labor and Industrial Relations
www.labor.mo.gov

Mental Health
www.dmh.mo.gov

Natural Resources
www.dnr.mo.gov

Public Safety
www.dps.mo.gov

Alcohol & Tobacco Control
www.atc.dps.mo.gov

Capitol Police
www.mcp.dps.mo.gov

Fire Safety
www.dfs.dps.mo.gov

Gaming Commission
www.mgc.dps.mo.gov

Missouri State Highway Patrol
www.mshp.dps.mo.gov

Missouri National Guard
www.moguard.com

State Emergency Agency
www.sema.dps.mo.gov

Veterans Commission
www.mvc.dps.mo.gov

Revenue
www.dor.mo.gov

Social Services
www.dss.mo.gov

Transportation
www.modot.org

Census Information

Missouri Census Data Center
mcdc.missouri.edu

Family & Community History
www.sos.mo.gov/archives/pubs/archweb/history.asp

Missouri Veterans' Commission
www.mvc.dps.mo.gov

Health/Social Services

Missouri Monthly Vital Statistics
www.health.mo.gov/data/vitalstatistics

Missouri Birth/Death Records
www.sos.mo.gov/archives/resources/bdrecords.asp

Missouri Adoption Services
www.dss.mo.gov/cd/adopt.htm

Child Support Enforcement
www.dss.mo.gov/cse

Laws/Regulations

Missouri Constitution
www.moga.mo.gov/const/moconstn.htm

Missouri Revised Statutes
www.moga.mo.gov/statutes/statutes.htm

Code of State Regulations
www.sos.mo.gov/adrules/csr/csr.asp

Missouri Taxes
www.dor.mo.gov

Professional Registration
www.pr.mo.gov

Missouri Drivers' Guide
www.dor.mo.gov/mvdl/drivers

Education

Missouri School Directory
dese.mo.gov/directory

Missouri Colleges & Universities
collegesearch.mo.gov

Missouri Libraries
www.sos.mo.gov/library/libdir.asp

Elections Information

www.govotemissouri.com

Employment/Business

Business Services (SOS)
www.sos.mo.gov/business

Missouri Career Source
www.jobs.mo.gov/

Missouri Women's Council
www.womenscouncil.org

Missouri Insurance Guides: Securities Information
www.sos.mo.gov/securities

Consumer Services
www.insurance.mo.gov/consumers/

Economic Development Research and Planning (MERIC)
www.missourieconomy.org

Missouri Business Portal
www.business.mo.gov

Federal Government Resources on the Web

Executive Branch

The White House
www.whitehouse.gov

U.S. Department of State
www.state.gov

Judicial Branch

Federal Judicial Center
www.fjc.gov

Geography/Environment

Missouri Highway Map Request
www.modot.mo.gov/asp/request_information. shtml?map

Missouri Discover Nature
www.mdc.mo.gov/discover-nature

Legislative Branch

House of Representatives
www.house.gov

Senate
www.senate.gov

Local Information/Contacts

Online Missouri Newspapers
www.mopress.com/

Missouri Chambers of Commerce
mochamber.com

County Clerks
www.sos.mo.gov/elections/countyclerks.asp

Miscellaneous

EASe Job Application System
www.ease.mo.gov

Missouri Digital Heritage
www.sos.mo.gov/mdh/

Missouri Historical Documents
libraryguides.missouri.edu/govdocs

Missouri Investor Protection Center
www.sos.mo.gov/securities/mipc

Missouri Lottery
www.molottery.com

Missouri's Online Services
www.mo.gov/my-government/online-services/

Missouri State Archives Death Records Database
www.sos.mo.gov/archives/resources/ deathcertificates/

Safe At Home Address Confidentiality Program
www.sos.mo.gov/safeathome

Unclaimed Property
www.treasurer.mo.gov/mainucp.aspx

Other Important Federal Resources

General Government Information
www.usa.gov/directory/federal/index.shtml

Library of Congress
www.loc.gov

Federal Blue Pages
www.usa.gov/Contact/Directories.shtml

Government Toll-Free Numbers

Office of Secretary of State
Elections Division 800-669-8683
Securities 800-721-7996
State Library...800-325-0131
State Library–Wolfner Library (Voice) 800-392-2614

Office of State Auditor
Hotline (Voice/TDD)...800-347-8597
Fraud, Waste and Abuse in State Government..800-347-8597

Office of State Treasurer
MOST College Savings Plan..888-414-6678

Office of Attorney General
Consumer Protection/Welfare Fraud 800-392-8222
No Call Registration and Complaints 866-662-2551
Medicaid Fraud Hotline..800-286-3932

Office of Administration
Central Accident Reporting Office (CARO)/Workers Compensation/
    State Employees..888-622-7694
Governor's Council on Disabilities 800-877-8249
State Leasing/Facilities Management 800-225-9138

Department of Agriculture
AgriMissouri Program 866-466-8283
Grape and Wine Program...800-392-WINE (800-392-9463)
Guide to Buying Local in Missouri...866-466-8283
State Fair..800-422-3247
USDA Agricultural Statistics..800-551-1014

Department of Conservation
Operation Game Thief/Operation Forest Arson...800-392-1111

Department of Economic Development
Business and Community Services Division 800-523-1434
Division of Tourism 800-519-2100
Division of Workforce Development 800-877-8698
Public Service Commission ConsumerHotline 800-392-4211

Department of Health and Senior Services
Emergency and Disease Reporting (24/7)...800-392-0272
Elderly Abuse and Neglect Hotline 800-392-0210
Family Care Safety Registry..866-422-6872
Long-Term Care Ombudsman...800-309-3282
Missouri Seniors' Legal Helpline..800-235-5503
Missouri Tobacco Quitline..800-QUIT-NOW (800-784-8669)
Organ Donor Registry 888-497-4564
TEL-LINK..800-835-5465

Department of Higher Education
Information Center..800-473-6757

Department of Insurance, Financial Institutions and Professional Registration
Consumer Hotline..800-726-7390
CLAIM (Medicare Counseling 800-390-3330

Department of Labor and Industrial Relations
Workers' Compensation..800-775-2667
Unemployment Claim Filing...800-320-2519
Fraud and Noncompliance Unit 800-592-6003
Discrimination Complaint...877-781-4236

Department of Mental Health
Main Switchboard/Constituent Services 800-364-9687

Alcohol and Drug Abuse 800-575-7480
Developmental Disabilities 800-207-9329

Department of Natural Resources
Department toll free.. 800-361-4827
State Parks 800-334-6946
TDD / Relay Missouri 800-735-2966
Voice 800-735-2466

Department of Public Safety
Crime Victims Compensation.. 800-347-6881
Arson Hotline 800-392-7766
Missouri Veterans Commission/Veteran Service Officer 888-838-4636
Filling a VOID (DWI Victims Assistance) 888-773-1800
Highway Emergency .... 800-525-5555 or *55 (cell)
Highway Patrol Recruiting 800-796-7000
Methamphetamine Laboratory 800-823-6384
Marijuana 800-223-9333
Rural Crimes Investigation Unit 888-484-8477
Sex Offender Registry.. 888-767-6747

Department of Revenue
Form's Order 800-877-6881

Department of Social Services (DSS)
Adoption/Foster Care 800-554-2222
   Child Abuse/Neglect Hotline 800-392-3738
Child Support Information.. 800-859-7999
   or Enforcement only 866-313-9960
Child Support Payment Center.. 800-225-0530
Civil Rights 800-776-8014
DSS/Division of Legal Services.. 800-568-4931
Employer Help Line / General Information About Child Support 800-585-9234
Food Stamp / Temporary Assistance Case Information 800-392-1261
Missouri Rx Plan... 800-375-1406
MO HealthNet Service Center 800-275-5908
Office of The Child Advocate 866-457-2302
Rehabilitation Services for the Blind 800-592-6004
State Technical Assistance Team... 800-487-1626
School Violence Hotline 866-748-7047

DSS/Division of Medical Services
MO HealthNet Exception Process.. 800-392-8030
MC+ For Kids Eligibility (Family Support Division) 888-275-5908
MC+ Managed Care Enrollment Broker Helpline..................... 800-348-6627
MO Healthnet Participant Services 800-392-2161
Non-Emergency Medical Transportation 866-269-5927
MO HealthNet Premium Collections 877-888-2811
Family Services Division Information Line 855-373-4636

Department of Transportation
Customer Service Center.. 888-275-6636
Highway Safety... 800-800-BELT (800-800-2358)
Motor Carrier Services 866-831-6277

Other
Abuse and Rape Crisis Service.. 800-303-0013
Cafeteria Plan, State Employees 800-659-3035
Crime Victims' Assistance 800-347-6881
Deferred Compensation/CitiStreet 800-392-0925
Environmental Emergency Spills, Hazardous Materials, etc.
   National Response Center... 800-424-8802
Federal Information/Product Safety Unit–Consumer Product Safety Commission....... 800-638-2772
Highway Emergency 800-525-5555

CHAPTER 7
MISSOURI ELECTIONS

Johnson Shut Ins
Photo courtesy of Missouri State Archives

Missouri Voting and Elections

Who registers to vote in Missouri?

Citizens living in Missouri must register in order to vote. Any U.S. citizen 17 years and 6 months of age or older, if a Missouri resident, may register to vote in any election held on or after his or her 18th birthday, except:

A person who is adjudged incapacitated;

A person who is confined under sentence of imprisonment;

A person who is on probation or parole after conviction of a felony until finally discharged; or

A person who has been convicted of a felony or misdemeanor connected with the right of suffrage. (Section 115.133, RSMo.)

How do Missourians register?

Qualified citizens may register in person at the office of their local election authority, by mail, at the driver's license fee office or at participating state agencies. Registration in person is accomplished by filling out registration forms with information on identity, residence and qualifications which are signed and sworn to, then witnessed by the election authority or a designee. (Section 115.155, RSMo.)

Registration by mail, at the driver's license fee office or at the participating state agencies requires submission of an application stating qualifications. A verification or rejection of registration is sent by the election authority within seven working days. (Sections 115.155 and 115.159, RSMo.)

When do Missourians register?

An unregistered citizen may register to vote whenever local election officials' places of business are open, by requesting an application by mail from the election authority, when renewing a Missouri driver's license or when receiving services from a participating state agency. Special registration sites and dates may be utilized prior to major elections.

The deadline for registration is the fourth Wednesday prior to an election. New Missouri residents may register immediately. (Section 115.135, RSMo.)

When do Missourians vote?

In addition to certain special and emergency dates, there are six official election dates in Missouri:

The statutes require all public elections be held on the general election day, the primary election day, the general municipal election day, the first Tuesday after the first Monday in November, or on another day expressly provided by city or county charter, and in nonprimary years on the first Tuesday after the first Monday in August. (Section 115.123.1, RSMo.)

The general election day is the first Tuesday after the first Monday in November in even-numbered years. The primary election day is the first Tuesday after the first Monday in August in even-numbered years. (Sections 115.121 (1 & 2), RSMo.)

Elections for cities, towns, villages, school boards and special district officers are held the first Tuesday after the first Monday in April each year, known as "general municipal election day." (Section 115.121.3, RSMo.)

A statewide presidential preference primary shall be held on the second Tuesday after the first Monday in March of each presidential election year. (Section 115.755 RSMo.)

Who conducts registration and elections?

Voter registration and the conduct of elections are the responsibilities of boards of election commissioners in the counties of Clay, Jackson, Platte and St. Louis; in the cities of Kansas City and St. Louis; and of the election authority in St. Charles County. The county clerk serves as the election authority in all other counties of the state.

Special voting provisions

Disabled voters and persons prevented from voting at the polls because of absence or illness may vote absentee. Persons with permanent disabilities may apply for permanent absentee ballot status by applying with the local election authority. (Section 115.284, RSMo.) Curbside voting is permitted in Missouri, or voters may be transferred to more accessible precincts. Local election officials should be contacted about absentee federal service balloting or "new resident" ballots for residents who arrive after the registration deadline.

When voting, Missourians must show an approved form of identification. (Section 115.427 RSMo.)

Elections and political parties

Missourians do not register under party affiliation. Hence, at primary elections, voters may choose which "established party" they vote within. Party nominees—and independent candidates—are then listed on the general election ballot.

There are presently four "established political parties" statewide—the Democratic, Republican, Libertarian and Constitution parties. Persons may seek the nomination of these parties for any elective office from the county level and above. In order to become "established," a party must have received more than 2 percent of the votes cast statewide for at least one of its candidates. New parties are formed by petition and may exist on the county, district or state level. They must meet the same standard as any other party to remain "established."

At the time of primary elections, voters select county committee members of established parties in Missouri. Those committee people, thus elected, have certain duties and responsibilities. They serve, as appropriate, as members of legislative, senatorial, judicial and congressional district committees. County, district or state committee members may be called on to fill candidate vacancies on party ballots or to select nominees for special elections from time to time. The state committees are selected, indirectly, by local committee persons. The state committees become especially important when delegates to presidential nominating (national) conventions are being selected.

Registered voters in Missouri, 2006–2014

*This is the number of registered voters from the Missouri Centralized Voter Registration list as of the November 4, 2014, General Election. This number is subject to change as the local election authorities continue to conduct their ongoing list maintenance activities.

COUNTY	2006	2008	2010	2012	2014
Adair	14,744	17,427	17,032	15,873	14,676
Andrew	11,400	11,648	12,050	12,308	11,842
Atchison	4,677	4,726	4,291	4,222	3,935
Audrain	16,476	16,397	16,384	16,734	15,442
Barry	19,777	20,794	20,847	20,665	20,292
Barton	9,022	9,015	8,536	8,712	8,686
Bates	12,292	12,091	11,806	11,913	11,218
Benton	12,900	13,670	13,722	13,770	13,525
Bollinger	7,916	8,259	8,611	8,600	8,170
Boone	105,897	121,319	118,350	125,339	116,074
Buchanan	52,561	56,750	54,790	52,390	54,108
Butler	25,779	32,908	33,259	29,999	29,486
Caldwell	6,205	6,248	6,226	6,201	6,043
Callaway	28,177	29,454	30,533	28,307	28,070
Camden	27,689	30,229	30,444	30,680	29,795
Cape Girardeau	49,745	51,205	51,611	52,928	52,628
Carroll	6,730	7,091	6,632	6,473	6,269
Carter	4,789	4,727	4,497	4,518	4,591
Cass	69,129	70,475	69,104	73,146	71,524
Cedar	8,491	8,609	8,597	8,450	8,194
Chariton	5,931	5,957	5,864	5,708	5,630
Christian	53,007	50,033	52,674	54,116	54,721
Clark	5,299	5,384	5,458	5,025	4,957
Clay	137,215	151,042	153,054	156,591	155,779
Clinton	13,663	14,455	13,817	14,395	14,250
Cole	51,285	52,878	52,022	53,249	52,775
Cooper	11,367	11,494	11,202	11,436	11,432
Crawford	17,338	17,337	17,270	16,154	15,908
Dade	5,422	5,510	5,784	5,889	5,909
Dallas	10,438	10,939	11,045	11,092	10,884
Daviess	5,440	5,434	5,389	5,285	5,028

COUNTY	2006	2008	2010	2012	2014
DeKalb	6,664	6,530	6,541	6,678	6,549
Dent	9,991	9,596	9,477	9,676	9,731
Douglas	10,621	10,758	10,147	10,236	9,924
Dunklin	21,236	21,560	20,466	19,117	17,754
Franklin	65,619	67,505	68,812	69,647	69,219
Gasconade	10,263	10,579	10,663	10,723	10,498
Gentry	5,218	5,181	4,914	4,840	4,709
Greene	184,050	190,417	197,379	197,500	189,229
Grundy	6,509	6,862	6,693	6,763	6,751
Harrison	5,959	6,050	5,593	5,583	5,281
Henry	15,868	16,106	16,285	15,937	15,774
Hickory	6,751	7,030	7,138	6,714	6,584
Holt	3,990	3,830	3,841	3,577	3,475
Howard	8,435	8,052	7,805	7,886	7,075
Howell	25,787	25,673	26,229	26,801	26,486
Iron	6,773	7,180	7,143	7,035	6,893
Jackson	228,673	244,570	245,295	246,737	245,782
Jasper	75,549	78,612	76,247	78,268	78,973
Jefferson	141,066	146,316	143,343	148,086	138,097
Johnson	28,739	31,290	32,747	33,224	32,070
Kansas City	235,459	230,897	227,649	221,355	214,871
Knox	2,955	2,926	2,843	2,879	2,610
Laclede	21,733	22,935	23,560	23,376	22,879
Lafayette	22,773	22,986	23,655	24,140	23,322
Lawrence	22,937	23,964	24,134	24,058	23,803
Lewis	6,790	6,793	6,920	6,659	6,680
Lincoln	30,494	33,411	34,090	34,780	34,854
Linn	9,023	8,943	9,079	8,896	8,639
Livingston	9,000	9,582	9,591	9,597	9,456
Macon	10,581	10,871	10,627	7,616	10,331
Madison	8,364	8,377	7,729	6,595	7,549
Maries	6,838	6,622	6,449	19,247	6,214
Marion	19,056	19,005	18,883	12,993	19,207
McDonald	14,725	13,140	13,617	10,659	12,532
Mercer	2,669	2,768	2,764	2,565	2,540
Miller	16,527	17,514	17,279	17,654	17,134
Mississippi	8,144	8,691	8,454	8,677	8,900
Moniteau	9,281	9,404	9,397	9,469	9,268
Monroe	6,275	6,238	6,087	5,972	5,856
Montgomery	8,129	8,457	8,190	8,259	8,143
Morgan	12,703	12,936	12,941	12,836	12,503
New Madrid	11,883	12,660	13,249	13,119	12,388
Newton	38,250	38,791	38,877	40,092	39,286
Nodaway	12,714	14,127	14,098	13,807	13,481
Oregon	6,660	7,045	7,458	7,356	7,307
Osage	9,011	9,215	9,382	9,552	9,407
Ozark	7,817	7,476	7,482	7,011	6,942
Pemiscot	12,214	12,275	13,376	12,013	11,538
Perry	12,016	12,446	12,803	12,398	12,071
Pettis	27,059	28,137	25,420	25,909	25,993
Phelps	25,861	27,387	27,617	28,576	28,401
Pike	11,675	11,724	11,481	11,396	11,085
Platte	58,513	62,658	62,570	64,619	64,285
Polk	18,142	19,899	19,450	20,090	19,561
Pulaski	18,581	20,800	22,782	22,265	21,255

COUNTY	2006	2008	2010	2012	2014
Putnam	3,858	3,936	4,038	3,728	3,724
Ralls	7,969	7,942	7,509	7,413	7,043
Randolph	14,518	15,485	15,617	15,753	15,834
Ray	17,896	16,226	14,539	17,826	17,804
Reynolds	6,620	6,223	6,170	5,375	5,008
Ripley	9,055	9,080	9,259	9,349	9,126
Saline	15,212	15,321	15,590	15,811	14,582
Schuyler	3,262	3,226	3,260	2,913	2,857
Scotland	3,098	3,144	3,138	3,165	3,061
Scott	25,170	27,325	26,850	27,187	26,355
Shannon	5,370	5,274	5,395	5,401	5,145
Shelby	4,900	4,830	4,864	4,673	4,606
St. Charles	224,241	244,155	243,382	256,606	255,582
St. Clair	7,127	7,026	6,755	6,843	6,661
St. Francois	38,442	37,343	38,381	39,517	37,170
St. Louis City	246,473	257,442	239,247	232,850	218,635
St. Louis County	738,775	796,979	748,526	763,992	748,126
Ste. Genevieve	11,864	12,588	12,698	12,994	12,918
Stoddard	20,202	20,923	20,002	20,237	20,390
Stone	23,107	23,955	22,776	23,437	22,973
Sullivan	4,981	5,017	4,838	4,957	4,596
Taney	31,834	33,367	34,811	35,129	34,876
Texas	14,836	15,275	15,785	16,059	15,941
Vernon	13,240	13,056	13,379	13,520	13,167
Warren	19,427	21,492	21,623	22,332	21,874
Washington	16,638	14,684	15,342	14,948	14,495
Wayne	9,140	9,407	9,254	9,315	9,156
Webster	21,825	22,124	22,325	22,908	22,605
Worth	1,683	1,687	1,644	1,573	1,513
Wright	12,997	12,940	12,906	13,140	12,450
TOTAL	**4,007,174**	**4,205,774**	**4,137,545**	**4,180,659**	**4,081,259**

2016 Missouri Election Calendar

Official Election Day	Style of Election	Last Day to Register to Vote	First Day for Candidate Filing	Last Day for Candidate Filing	Final Certification Date
February 2, 2016	Bond elections may be held on the first Tuesday after the first Monday in February but no other issue shall be included on the ballot for such election.	January 6, 2016	October 13, 2015 [Jurisdictions in Kansas City begin filing October 20, 2015]	November 17, 2015	November 24, 2015
March 8, 2016 (see local charter)	Charter cities and charter counties ONLY	February 10, 2016	November 17, 2015 [Jurisdictions in Kansas City begin filing November 24, 2015]	December 22, 2015	December 29, 2015
March 15, 2016	Presidential Preference Primary	February 17, 2016	December 1, 2015	December 29, 2015	January 5, 2016
April 5, 2016	General Municipal Election	March 9, 2016	December 15, 2015 [Candidates for offices in Kansas City, contact the Kansas City Board of Elections, Platte County Board of Elections, Cass County Clerk, or Clay County Board of Elections for filling dates]	January 19, 2016	January 26, 2016
August 2, 2016	Primary Election	July 6, 2016	February 23, 2016	March 29, 2016	May 24, 2016
November 8, 2016	General Election	October 12, 2016	July 19, 2016* [Jurisdictions in Kansas City begin filing July 26, 2016]	August 23, 2016*	August 30, 2016

The final date for new party and independent candidates to submit their petitions to the Secretary of State is 5:00 p.m., August 1, 2016. Independent candidates for county offices and those wishing to form a new party within a county must submit their petition to the local election authority (county clerk or election board) by 5:00 p.m., August 1, 2016. (Section 115.329.1, RSMo.).

1. Official Election Day—Sections 115.121, 115.123, RSMo.
2. Style of Election—Sections 115.121, 115.123, RSMo.
3. Last Day to Register—Sections 115.135.1, RSMo.
4. First Day to File—Sections 115.127.5, 115.329.1, 115.349.2, 115.761, RSMo.
5. Last Day to File—Sections 115.127.5, 115.329.1, 115.349.1, 115.761, RSMo.
6. Final Certification Date—Sections 115.125, 115.387, 115.401, 116.240, RSMo.

*Opening and closing of filing for jurisdictions authorized to elect directors in November, such as 911 & Emergency Services directors.

[Bracketed dates apply to any jurisdiction partially or wholly located in Kansas City, Missouri.]

General Election Results
November 4, 2014

U.S. Representative District 1

	Democratic	Republican	Libertarian
	Lacy Clay	Daniel J. Elder	Robb E Cunningham
St. Louis	74,807	24,676	5,243
St. Louis City	44,508	10,597	3,663
TOTAL	**119,315**	**35,273**	**8,906**

U.S. Representative District 2

	Democratic	Republican	Libertarian
	Arthur Lieber	Ann Wagner	Bill Slantz
Jefferson	3,247	5,988	437
St. Charles	9,913	24,266	1,534
St. Louis	62,224	117,937	5,571
TOTAL	**75,384**	**148,191**	**7,542**

U.S. Representative District 3

	Democratic	Republican	Libertarian	Write-in
	Courtney Denton	Blaine Luetkemeyer	Steven Hedrick	Harold Davis
Callaway	2,750	7,518	530	3
Camden	1,181	4,826	233	-
Cole	5,491	16,401	851	1
Franklin	6,487	17,797	1,268	48
Gasconade	783	3,083	125	-
Jefferson	9,637	16,558	1,345	2
Lincoln	3,473	8,804	635	2
Maries	601	2,036	80	1
Miller	732	4,436	193	-
Montgomery	677	2,426	129	-
Osage	596	3,435	111	3
St. Charles	17,756	38,033	2,794	6
Warren	1,857	5,587	299	-
TOTAL	**52,021**	**130,940**	**8,593**	**66**

U.S. Representative District 4

	Democratic	Republican	Libertarian	Write-in
	Nate Irvin	Vicky Hartzler	Herschel L. Young	Gregory A. Cowan
Audrain	931	3,068	221	-
Barton	400	2,472	142	-
Bates	1,088	2,943	270	1
Benton	10,06	3,566	227	-
Boone	16,762	21,089	2,411	-
Camden	890	3,409	174	-
Cass	6,396	17,869	1,400	-
Cedar	573	2,670	148	-
Cooper	835	2,813	277	-
Dade	337	1,773	98	-
Dallas	589	2,875	185	6
Henry	1,452	3,630	264	-
Hickoy	571	1,778	101	1
Howard	826	1,833	190	-
Johnson	2,950	7,770	745	-
Laclede	1,000	5,654	320	6
Moniteau	629	2,596	200	-
Morgan	1,048	3,964	248	-
Pettis	2,092	6,718	522	-
Pulaski	1,282	5,333	351	-
Randolph	1,507	4,636	400	1
St. Clair	692	2,278	136	-
Vernon	1,292	3,970	226	-
Webster	1,316	5,307	537	-
TOTAL	**46,464**	**120,014**	**9,793**	**15**

U.S. Representative District 5

	Democratic	Republican	Libertarian
	Emanuel Clever II	Jacob Turk	Roy Welborn
Clay	6,711	7,631	838
Jackson	25,206	34,538	2,109
Kansas City	39,738	14,144	1,550
Lafayette	3,153	6,128	298
Ray	2,506	3,535	321
Saline	1,942	3,095	192
TOTAL	**79,256**	**69,071**	**5,308**

U.S. Representative District 6

	Democratic	Republican	Libertarian
	W. A. (Bill) Hedge	Sam Graves	Russ Monchil
Adair	1,711	3,899	211
Andrew	1,421	3,328	167
Atchison	407	1,313	78
Audrain	296	771	33
Buchanan	8,996	11,344	785
Caldwell	468	1,624	164
Carroll	320	1,708	60
Chariton	588	1,643	96
Clark	522	1,464	63
Clay	11,311	23,092	1,599
Clinton	1,794	3,529	271
Daviess	408	1,319	91
DeKalb	615	1,957	131
Gentry	397	1,098	87
Grunday	406	2,000	119
Harrison	381	1,859	110
Holt	224	982	55
Jackson	6,028	13,420	764
Knox	282	971	34
Lewis	697	1,882	68
Linn	797	2,496	130
Livingston	764	3,038	122
Macon	1,197	3,679	136
Marion	1,610	5,008	135
Mercer	176	992	55
Monroe	529	1,592	50
Nodaway	1,558	3,878	191
Pike	1,125	2,696	129
Platte	7,483	13,780	951
Putnam	162	1,032	42
Ralls	884	2,144	66
Schuyler	275	1,108	54
Scotland	329	1,090	38
Shelby	454	1,212	23
Sullivan	336	1,172	38
Worth	206	496	51
TOTAL	**55,157**	**124,616**	**7,197**

U.S. Representative District 7

	Democratic	Republican	Libertarian	Write-in	Write-in	Write-in
	Jim Evans	Billy Long	Kevin Craig	John C. Hagerty	Martin Lindstedt	Nikolas Bruce
Barry	1,677	4,984	488	-	-	-
Christian	4,959	12,261	1,910	1	-	-
Greene	23,624	33,738	5,323	-	1	21
Jasper	4,819	15,989	1,193	2	-	7
Lawrence	2,583	5,078	1,014	-	-	-
McDonald	685	2,970	177	-	-	-
Newton	2,782	9,646	600	-	1	4
Polk	1,527	4,442	537	-	-	-
Stone	1,854	6,087	578	-	-	-
Taney	2,251	7,709	575	-	-	-
Webster	521	1,150	189	-	-	-
TOTAL	**47,282**	**104,054**	**12,584**	**3**	**2**	**32**

U.S. Representative District 8

	Democratic	Republican	Libertarian	Constitution	Independent
	Barbara Stocker	Jason Smith	Rick Vandeven	Doug Enyart	Terry Hampton
Bollinger	520	2,218	129	73	51
Butler	1,624	6,167	163	152	209
Cape Girardeau	3,430	12,276	678	340	290
Carter	358	1,176	44	29	152
Crawford	1,121	4,294	89	74	103
Dent	532	3,445	45	36	57
Douglas	449	2,133	71	64	144
Dunklin	1,414	3,222	93	108	383
Howell	879	4,742	119	163	1,854
Iron	755	1,345	35	76	83
Jefferson	5,826	8,060	436	544	567
Madison	708	1,817	50	96	58
Mississippi	625	1,643	28	45	55
New Madrid	1,161	2,145	65	78	117
Oregon	584	1,458	40	76	254
Ozark	454	1,833	57	33	223
Pemiscot	1,013	1,695	43	47	140
Perry	896	3,387	124	124	170
Phelps	2,585	7,387	191	133	212
Reynolds	415	1,024	20	54	53
Ripley	547	1,842	39	48	127
Scott	1,755	5,305	294	115	145
Shannon	362	1,131	27	43	88
St. Francois	3,798	7,317	288	465	461
Ste. Genevieve	1,461	1,983	98	137	139
Stoddard	1,412	5,159	164	116	177
Texas	997	3,877	97	89	196
Washington	1,668	2,990	109	113	156
Wayne	734	1,896	30	272	61
Wright	638	3,157	93	56	96
TOTAL	**38,721**	**106,124**	**3,759**	**3,799**	**6,821**

State Auditor—General Election: November 4, 2014

	Republican	Libertarian	Constitution
	Tom Schweich	Sean O'Toole	Rodney Farthing
Adair	3,816	927	246
Andrew	3,416	720	303
Atchison	1,274	264	89
Audrain	3,962	746	280
Barry	5,548	892	332
Barton	2,341	336	157
Bates	2,650	752	324
Benton	3,514	680	289
Bollinger	2,269	272	139
Boone	25,900	7,736	1,842
Buchanan	12,701	4,115	1,787
Butler	6,428	948	337
Caldwell	1,512	407	157
Callaway	8,091	1,553	466
Camden	8,354	1,351	449
Cape Girardeau	13,230	1,988	659
Carroll	1,624	240	64
Carter	1,242	226	90
Cass	17,591	4,707	1,493
Cedar	2,679	374	142
Chariton	1,545	370	138
Christian	14,928	2,399	908
Clark	1,339	337	131
Clay	30,696	12,457	3,299
Clinton	3,527	1,193	409
Cole	17,916	2,780	709
Cooper	3,029	537	142
Crawford	4,285	714	253
Dade	1,731	232	123
Dallas	2,794	398	278
Daviess	1,218	317	114
DeKalb	1,870	433	164
Dent	2,696	350	647
Douglas	2,307	301	133
Dunklin	3,507	765	373
Franklin	18,829	3,938	1,386
Gasconade	3,148	423	139
Gentry	1,053	241	99
Greene	45,241	10,712	2,684
Grundy	1,856	300	172
Harrison	1,733	278	134
Henry	3,442	919	360
Hickory	1,827	334	120
Holt	975	137	49
Howard	2,009	459	158
Howell	6,026	868	357
Iron	1,505	368	194
Jackson	49,786	16,449	6,182
Jasper	16,878	3,037	1,044
Jefferson	35,543	9,867	3,772
Johnson	7,710	2,120	826
Kansas City	17,837	18,530	6,419
Knox	819	212	67
Laclede	5,768	722	232
Lafayette	6,554	1,703	463
Lawrence	6,789	1,106	409
Lewis	1,813	364	160
Lincoln	9,144	1,988	947
Linn	1,989	884	178

	Republican	Libertarian	Constitution
	Tom Schweich	Sean O' loole	Rodney Farthing
Livingston	2,781	495	153
Macon	3,623	636	293
Madison	1,875	398	189
Maries	2,174	249	90
Marion	4,685	983	395
McDonald	2,883	461	209
Mercer	870	113	76
Miller	4,316	507	246
Mississippi	1,627	258	208
Moniteau	2,720	400	97
Monroe	1,519	332	111
Montgomery	2,483	414	146
Morgan	3,994	697	275
New Madrid	2,197	614	323
Newton	10,295	1,557	539
Nodaway	3,943	838	266
Oregon	1,654	300	154
Osage	3,453	342	112
Ozark	2,032	303	125
Pemiscot	1,910	420	239
Perry	3,280	654	285
Pettis	6,630	1,555	489
Phelps	7,730	1,349	499
Pike	2,764	624	250
Platte	14,116	4,972	1,071
Polk	5,150	781	260
Pulaski	5,202	937	345
Putnam	908	170	49
Ralls	2,028	501	215
Randolph	4,772	1,024	396
Ray	3,739	1,401	478
Reynolds	1,032	218	106
Ripley	1,829	366	163
Saline	3,216	1,050	358
Schuyler	847	261	124
Scotland	938	218	98
Scott	5,740	844	363
Shannon	1,105	208	132
Shelby	1,183	193	82
St. Charles	67,225	16,218	4,501
St. Clair	2,279	459	140
St. Francois	8,533	1,949	863
St. Louis	181,710	50,343	18,617
St. Louis City	20,819	17,942	7,348
Ste. Genevieve	2,493	647	288
Stoddard	5,409	768	308
Stone	6,896	944	336
Sullivan	1,041	194	116
Taney	8,320	1,277	455
Texas	4,127	558	247
Vernon	3,889	838	297
Warren	5,826	1,106	360
Washington	3,522	744	323
Wayne	2,048	383	176
Webster	6,937	1,075	472
Worth	531	107	35
Wright	3,309	380	172
TOTAL	**937,961**	**252,351**	**89,080**

State Senator—General Election: November 4, 2014

State Senator District 2

	Republican
	Bob Onder
St. Charles	37,607
TOTAL	**37,607**

State Senator District 4

	Democratic	Republican
	Joseph (Joe) Keaveny	Courtney Blunt
St. Louis	5,904	4,423
St. Louis City	23,137	6,783
TOTAL	**29,041**	**11,206**

State Senator District 6

	Democratic	Republican
	Mollie Kristen Freebairn	Mike Kehoe
Cole	5,526	17,157
Gasconade	851	3,105
Maries	512	2,201
Miller	779	4,547
Moniteau	624	2,796
Morgan	1,051	4,214
Osage	594	3,541
TOTAL	**9,937**	**37,561**

State Senator District 8

	Republican
	Will Kraus
Jackson	31,432
TOTAL	**31,432**

State Senator District 10

	Democratic	Republican
	Ed Schieffer	Jeanie Riddle
Audrain	1,484	3,878
Callaway	2,858	7,993
Lincoln	5,801	7,542
Monroe	620	1,559
Montgomery	833	2,424
Warren	2,260	5,475
TOTAL	**13,856**	**28,871**

State Senator District 12

	Republican
	Dan Hegeman
Andrew	4,228
Atchison	1,601
Clay	9,718
Clinton	4,430
Daviess	1,460
DeKalb	2,300
Gentry	1,322
Grundy	2,166
Harrison	2,051
Holt	1,120
Mercer	986
Nodaway	4,743
Putnam	1,036
Sullivan	1,227
Worth	618
TOTAL	**39,006**

State Senator District 14

	Democratic	Write-in
	Maria N. Chappelle-Nadal	Christine LaPorta
St. Louis	30,203	1,869
TOTAL	**30,203**	**1,869**

State Senator District 16

	Republican
	Dan Brown
Camden	8,760
Crawford	4,741
Dent	3,297
Phelps	9,043
Pulaski	5,988
TOTAL	**31,829**

State Senator - District 18

	Republican
	Brian Munzlinger
Adair	4,699
Chariton	1,781
Clark	1,837
Knox	1,174
Lewis	2,363
Linn	2,648
Macon	4,221
Marion	5,630
Pike	3,287
Ralls	2,498
Randolph	5,479
Schuyler	1,224
Scotland	1,244
Shelby	1,375
TOTAL	39,460

State Senator District 20

	Republican
	Jay Wasson
Christian	16,395
Greene	23,796
TOTAL	40,191

State Senator District 22

	Democratic	Republican
	Jeff Roorda	Paul Wieland
Jefferson	18,774	22,208
TOTAL	18,774	22,208

State Senator District 24

	Democratic	Republican	Libertarian
	Jill Schupp	John R. Ashcroft	Jim Higgins
St. Louis	28,022	26,196	1,727
TOTAL	28,022	26,196	1,727

State Senator District 26

	Democratic	Republican
	Lloyd Klinedinst	Dave Schatz
Franklin	6,714	18,752
St. Louis	7,094	18,467
TOTAL	13,808	37,219

State Senator District 28

	Republican
	Mike Parson
Benton	3,956
Cedar	2,969
Dallas	3,132
Hickory	2,075
Laclede	6,050
Pettis	7,943
Polk	5,832
St. Clair	2,616
TOTAL	34,573

State Senator District 30

	Republican
	Bob Dixon
Greene	27,207
Total	27,207

State Senator District 32

	Republican
	Ron Richard
Dade	1,799
Jasper	19,362
Newton	11,397
Total	32,558

State Senator District 34

	Democratic	Republican
	Robert Stuber	Rob Schaaf
Buchanan	9,936	11,068
Platte	8,987	13,071
Total	18,923	24,139

State Representative—General Election: November 4, 2014

State Representative District 1

	Democratic	Republican
	Robert Ritterbusch	Allen Andrews
Atchison	308	1,472
Holt	184	1,075
Nodaway	1,315	4,292
Worth	122	640
TOTAL	**1,929**	**7,479**

State Representative District 2

	Democratic	Republican
	Mike Waltemath	J. Eggleston
Daviess	499	1,275
DeKalb	784	1,899
Gentry	758	844
Harrison	539	1,767
TOTAL	**2,580**	**5,785**

State Representative District 3

	Republican
	Nate Walker
Adair	3,646
Mercer	1,018
Putnam	1,059
Sullivan	1,300
TOTAL	**7,023**

State Representative District 4

	Republican
	Craig Redmon
Adair	1,165
Clark	1,794
Knox	1,144
Lewis	2,450
Schuyler	1,201
Scotland	1,276
TOTAL	**9,030**

State Representative District 5

	Democratic	Republican
	C. LeRoy Deichman	Lindell Shumake
Marion	1,729	5,089
Monroe	165	367
Shelby	543	1,149
TOTAL	**2,437**	**6,605**

State Representative District 6

	Democratic	Republican
	Robert Harrington	Tim Remole
Linn	404	441
Macon	1,435	3,706
Randolph	1,447	3,584
TOTAL	**3,286**	**7,731**

State Representative District 7

	Republican
	Mike Lair
Grundy	2,196
Linn	2,032
Livingston	3,442
TOTAL	**7,670**

State Representative District 8

	Democratic	Republican
	Ted Rights	James W. (Jim) Neely
Caldwell	581	1,668
Clay	235	686
Clinton	1,716	3,824
Ray	265	548
TOTAL	**2,797**	**6,726**

State Representative District 9

	Republican
	Delus Johnson
Andrew	4,188
Buchanan	5,165
TOTAL	**9,353**

State Representative District 10

	Democratic
	Pat Conway
Buchanan	5,590
TOTAL	**5,590**

State Representative District 11

	Republican
	Galen Higdon, Jr.
Buchanan	6,062
Platte	1,298
TOTAL	**7,360**

State Representative District 12

	Democratic	Republican
	Sandy Van Wagner	Kenneth Wilson
Clay	2,651	5,077
Platte	864	1,666
TOTAL	**3,515**	**6,743**

State Representative District 13

	Republican
	Nick Marshall
Platte	7,539
TOTAL	**7,539**

State Representative District 14

	Democratic	Republican
	Stephanie Isaacson	Kevin Corlew
Clay	88	92
Platte	3,749	4,812
TOTAL	**3,837**	**4,904**

State Representative District 15

	Democratic
	Jon Carpenter
Clay	5,541
TOTAL	**5,541**

State Representative District 16

	Republican
	Noel J Shull
Clay	7,010
TOTAL	**7,010**

State Representative District 17

	Democratic	Republican
	Mark Ellebracht	S Nick King
Clay	4,504	4,576
TOTAL	**4,504**	**4,576**

State Representative District 18

	Democratic	Republican
	Lauren Arthur	Robert (Bob) Rowland
Clay	4,284	3,339
TOTAL	**4,284**	**3,339**

State Representative District 19

	Democratic
	John Joseph Rizzo
Jackson	785
Kansas City	1,330
TOTAL	**2,115**

State Representative District 20

	Democratic	Republican
	John A. Mayfield	Bill E. Kidd
Jackson	3,412	4,082
TOTAL	**3,412**	**4,082**

State Representative District 21

	Democratic
	Ira Anders
Jackson	4,889
TOTAL	**4,889**

State Representative District 22

	Democratic
	Brandon Ellington
Jackson	546
Kansas City	4,020
TOTAL	**4,566**

State Representative District 23

	Democratic
	Randy D. Dunn
Kansas City	3,254
TOTAL	**3,254**

State Representative District 24

	Democratic
	Judy Morgan
Kansas City	5,928
TOTAL	**5,928**

State Representative District 25

	Democratic
	Jeremy LaFaver
Kansas City	7,963
TOTAL	**7,963**

State Representative District 26

	Democratic
	Gail McCann Beatty
Kansas City	5,917
TOTAL	**5,917**

State Representative District 27

	Democratic
	Bonnaye V. Mims
Jackson	230
Kansas City	4,411
TOTAL	**4,641**

State Representative District 28

	Democratic
	Tom McDonald
Jackson	4,082
Kansas City	877
TOTAL	**4,959**

State Representative District 29

	Democratic	Republican
	John B. Sutton	Noel Torpey
Jackson	2,416	4,230
Kansas City	1,222	1,468
TOTAL	**3,638**	**5,698**

State Representative District 30

	Republican
	Mike Cierpiot
Jackson	6,960
Kansas City	369
TOTAL	**7,329**

State Representative District 31

	Republican
	Sheila Solon
Jackson	6,287
TOTAL	**6,287**

State Representative District 32

	Democratic	Republican
	Andrew (Andy) Herman	Jeanie Lauer
Jackson	2,361	5,526
TOTAL	**2,361**	**5,526**

State Representative District 33

	Democratic	Republican	Libertarian
	Syed Asif	Donna Pfautsch	Matthew (Matt) Stephens
Cass	769	3,767	727
Jackson	686	2,639	319
Lafayette	3	28	6
TOTAL	**1,458**	**6,434**	**1,052**

State Representative District 34

	Democratic	Republican
	Dale Mercer	Rebecca Roeber
Jackson	3,022	5,583
TOTAL	**3,022**	**5,583**

State Representative District 35

	Democratic	Republican
	Ken Duvall	Gary Cross
Jackson	4,064	5,023
Kansas City	656	213
TOTAL	**4,720**	**5,236**

State Representative District 36

	Democratic	Republican
	Kevin McManus	Nola Wood
Kansas City	4,715	3,146
TOTAL	**4,715**	**3,146**

State Representative District 37

	Democratic
	Joe Runions
Cass	748
Jackson	3,874
Kansas City	867
TOTAL	**5,489**

State Representative District 38

	Republican
	T. J. Berry
Clay	7,044
TOTAL	**7,044**

State Representative District 39

	Republican
	Joe Don McGaugh
Carroll	1,844
Chariton	1,420
Ray	4,583
TOTAL	**7,847**

State Representative District 40

	Democratic	Republican
	Lowell Jackson	Jim Hansen
Lincoln	39	125
Monroe	447	1,208
Pike	976	3,091
Ralls	962	2,223
TOTAL	**2,424**	**6,647**

State Representative District 41

	Democratic	Republican
	Dan Dildine	Randy Pietzman
Lincoln	3,861	6,243
TOTAL	**3,861**	**6,243**

State Representative District 42

	Democratic	Republican
	Rod Sturgeon	Bart Korman
Montgomery	933	2,316
St. Charles	175	528
Warren	1,459	4,210
TOTAL	**2,567**	**7,054**

State Representative District 43

	Democratic	Republican
	Ed Lockwood	Jay Houghton
Audrain	1,419	3,915
Callaway	705	1,816
TOTAL	**2,124**	**5,731**

State Representative District 44

	Democratic	Republican
	Thomas (Tom) Pauley	Caleb Rowden
Boone	3,012	5,107
Randolph	46	142
TOTAL	**3,058**	**5,249**

State Representative District 45

	Democratic
	Kip Kendrick
Boone	3,889
TOTAL	**3,889**

State Representative District 46

	Democratic
	Stephen Webber
Boone	7,948
TOTAL	**7,948**

State Representative District 47

	Democratic	Republican
	John Wright	Charles (Chuck) Basye
Boone	4,020	3,902
Cooper	64	139
Howard	191	330
Randolph	471	636
TOTAL	**4,746**	**5,007**

State Representative District 48

	Republican
	Dave Muntzel
Carroll	-
Chariton	401
Cooper	2,980
Howard	1,962
Pettis	751
Randolph	303
Saline	1,021
TOTAL	**7,418**

State Representative District 49

	Democratic	Republican
	Gracia Yancey Backer	Travis Fitzwater
Callaway	3,171	5,126
Cole	245	442
TOTAL	**3,416**	**5,568**

State Representative District 50

	Republican
	Caleb Jones
Boone	5,600
Cole	426
Cooper	336
Moniteau	1,470
TOTAL	**7,832**

State Representative District 51

	Democratic	Republican	Libertarian
	Gary Grigsby	Dean A. Dohrman	Bill Wayne
Johnson	1,358	1,792	195
Pettis	172	781	47
Saline	1,577	2,154	189
TOTAL	**3,107**	**4,727**	**431**

State Representative District 52

	Republican
	Nathan Beard
Johnson	711
Pettis	5,200
TOTAL	**5,911**

State Representative District 53

	Democratic	Republican
	Henry Grubb	Glen Kolkmeyer
Jackson	117	284
Johnson	123	235
Lafayette	3,709	5,818
TOTAL	**3,949**	**6,337**

State Representative District 54

	Republican	Constitution
	Denny Hoskins	Daniel Plemons
Johnson	5,279	1,479
Pettis	1,142	173
TOTAL	**6,421**	**1,652**

State Representative District 55

	Republican
	Rick Brattin
Cass	8,362
TOTAL	**8,362**

State Representative District 56

	Democratic	Republican
	Patty Johnson	Jack Bondon
Bates	62	111
Cass	2,674	5,259
Kansas City	135	155
TOTAL	**2,871**	**5,525**

State Representative District 57

	Democratic	Republican	Constitution
	William A. Grimes	Wanda Brown	Butch Page
Bates	57	96	16
Benton	410	1,672	109
Cass	350	622	150
Henry	1,807	3,348	212
TOTAL	**2,624**	**5,738**	**487**

State Representative District 58

	Republican
	David Wood
Miller	1,021
Moniteau	1,537
Morgan	4,559
TOTAL	**7,117**

State Representative District 59

	Republican	Constitution
	Mike Bernskoetter	Michael Eberle
Cole	8,396	1,081
Miller	428	65
TOTAL	**8,824**	**1,146**

State Representative District 60

	Republican
	Jason (Jay) Barnes
Cole	9,041
TOTAL	**9,041**

State Representative District 61

	Democratic	Republican
	Tom Smith	Justin Alferman
Franklin	1,950	5,109
Gasconade	439	1,341
Osage	436	1,198
TOTAL	**2,825**	**7,648**

State Representative District 62

	Republican
	Tom Hurst
Cole	592
Crawford	152
Gasconade	1,953
Maries	2,424
Miller	450
Osage	2,195
Phelps	1,093
TOTAL	**8,859**

State Representative District 63

	Democratic	Republican
	Bryan Pinette	Bryan Spencer
St. Charles	2,621	5,734
Warren	616	1,423
TOTAL	**3,237**	**7,157**

State Representative District 64

	Democratic	Republican
	Laura K. Castaneda	Robert Cornejo
Lincoln	912	2,080
St. Charles	2,035	4,280
TOTAL	**2,947**	**6,360**

State Representative District 65

	Republican
	Anne Zerr
St. Charles	7,668
TOTAL	**7,668**

State Representative District 66

	Democratic	Republican
	Tommie Pierson	John Saxton
St. Louis	5,720	980
St. Louis City	602	43
TOTAL	**6,322**	**1,023**

State Representative District 67

	Democratic	Republican	Libertarian
	Alan Green	Dwayne A Strickland	Jeff Coleman
St. Louis	9,616	2,241	296
TOTAL	**9,616**	**2,241**	**296**

State Representative District 68

	Democratic	Republican	Write-in
	Keith English	Rekha (Becky) Sharma	Mickelle L. Adkins
St. Louis	6,758	3,435	3
TOTAL	**6,758**	**3,435**	**3**

State Representative District 69

	Democratic	Republican
	Margo McNeil	John Vahey
St. Louis	6,501	3,414
TOTAL	**6,501**	**3,414**

State Representative District 70

	Democratic	Republican
	Bill Otto	Joe Corica
St. Charles	813	1,511
St. Louis	4,496	3,644
TOTAL	**5,309**	**5,155**

State Representative District 71

	Democratic	Republican
	Sue Meredith	Jim Cain
St. Louis	6,004	4,142
TOTAL	**6,004**	**4,142**

State Representative District 72

	Democratic	Republican
	Mary Nichols	Paul Berry
St. Louis	5,588	3,017
TOTAL	**5,588**	**3,017**

State Representative District 73

	Democratic
	Courtney Allen Curtis
St. Louis	6,055
TOTAL	**6,055**

State Representative District 74

	Democratic
	Sharon L. Pace
St. Louis	6,756
TOTAL	**6,756**

State Representative District 75

	Democratic
	Rochelle Walton Gray
St. Louis	8,077
TOTAL	**8,077**

State Representative District 76

	Democratic
	Joshua Peters
St. Louis City	7,006
TOTAL	**7,006**

State Representative District 77

	Democratic
	Kimberly M. Gardner
St. Louis City	5,829
TOTAL	**5,829**

State Representative District 78

	Democratic	Republican
	Penny V. Hubbard	John Hubb
St. Louis City	4,222	822
TOTAL	**4,222**	**822**

State Representative District 79

	Democratic	Republican
	Michael Butler	Robert Vroman
St. Louis City	6,222	732
TOTAL	**6,222**	**732**

State Representative District 80

	Democratic	Republican
	Mike Colona	Michael Huett
St. Louis City	6,148	1,164
TOTAL	**6,148**	**1,164**

State Representative District 81

	Democratic	Libertarian
	Jacob W. Hummel	Lisa F. Schaper
St. Louis City	4,298	1,144
TOTAL	**4,298**	**1,144**

State Representative District 82

	Democratic	Republican
	Michele Kratky	Jake Koehr
St. Louis City	6,204	2,375
TOTAL	**6,204**	**2,375**

State Representative District 83

	Democratic	Republican	Libertarian
	Gina Mitten	Jeremy Buckingham	Andrew Bolin
St. Louis	4,880	2,358	329
St. Louis City	1,649	632	145
TOTAL	**6,529**	**2,990**	**474**

State Representative District 84

	Democratic
	Karla May
St. Louis City	6,499
TOTAL	**6,499**

State Representative District 85

	Democratic
	Clem Smith
St. Louis	7,319
TOTAL	**7,319**

State Representative District 86

	Democratic
	Joe Adams
St. Louis	8,201
TOTAL	**8,201**

State Representative District 87

	Democratic
	Stacey Newman
St. Louis	8,064
TOTAL	**8,064**

State Representative District 88

	Democratic	Republican
	Tracy McCreery	Raymond Chandler
St. Louis	6,920	5,784
TOTAL	**6,920**	**5,784**

State Representative District 89

	Democratic	Republican
	Al Gerber	John J. Diehl, Jr.
St. Louis	5,114	10,181
TOTAL	**5,114**	**10,181**

State Representative District 90

	Democratic	Republican
	Deb Lavender	Gina Jaksetic
St. Louis	7,597	7,153
TOTAL	**7,597**	**7,153**

State Representative District 91

	Democratic	Republican
	Jeanne Kirkton	Michael Peters
St. Louis	7,667	5,157
St. Louis City	153	92
TOTAL	**7,820**	**5,249**

State Representative District 92

	Democratic	Republican
	Genise Montecillo	Al Faulstich
St. Louis	6,033	4,169
TOTAL	**6,033**	**4,169**

State Representative District 93

	Democratic	Republican
	Bob Burns	Garrett Mees
St. Louis	3,426	2,482
St. Louis City	697	364
TOTAL	**4,123**	**2,846**

State Representative District 94

	Democratic	Republican
	Vicki Lorenz Englund	Cloria Brown
St. Louis	4,240	5,334
TOTAL	**4,240**	**5,334**

State Representative District 95

	Republican
	Marsha Haefner
St. Louis	10,150
TOTAL	**10,150**

State Representative District 96

	Republican	Constitution
	Mike Leara	Cynthia (Cindy) Redburn
St. Louis	10,111	2,380
TOTAL	**10,111**	**2,380**

State Representative District 97

	Democratic	Republican
	Tom Dohack	John McCaherty
Jefferson	2,308	4,681
St. Louis	329	663
TOTAL	**2,637**	**5,344**

State Representative District 98

	Republican
	Shamed Dogan
St. Louis	8,653
TOTAL	**8,653**

State Representative District 99

	Democratic	Republican
	William H. (Bill) Pinkston	Andrew Koenig
St. Louis	3,996	6,961
TOTAL	**3,996**	**6,961**

State Representative District 100

	Republican
	Sue Allen
St. Louis	10,835
TOTAL	**10,835**

State Representative District 101

	Democratic	Republican
	Candace Farmer	Don Gosen
St. Louis	2,872	8,621
TOTAL	**2,872**	**8,621**

State Representative District 102

	Democratic	Republican
	John Callahan	Kurt Bahr
St. Charles	2,944	6,809
TOTAL	**2,944**	**6,809**

State Representative District 103

	Republican	Libertarian
	John D. Wiemann	Dean (Draig) Hodge
St. Charles	7,308	1,980
TOTAL	**7,308**	**1,980**

State Representative District 104

	Democratic	Republican
	Terry Lesinski	Kathie Conway
St. Charles	3,417	5,852
TOTAL	**3,417**	**5,852**

State Representative District 105

	Democratic	Republican
	Matt Judkins	Mark Parkinson
St. Charles	4,152	6,729
TOTAL	**4,152**	**6,729**

State Representative District 106

	Democratic	Republican
	Ken Tucker	Chrissy Sommer
St. Charles	3,107	5,452
TOTAL	**3,107**	**5,452**

State Representative District 107

	Republican	Write-in
	Ron Hicks	AC (Arnie C.) Dienoff
St. Charles	6,861	12
TOTAL	**6,861**	**12**

State Representative District 108

	Democratic	Republican
	Marlon Williams	Justin S. Hill
St. Charles	2,775	7,402
TOTAL	**2,775**	**7,402**

State Representative District 109

	Democratic	Republican
	Barbara (Bobbie) Bollmann	Paul Curtman
Franklin	2,693	6,720
TOTAL	**2,693**	**6,720**

State Representative District 110

	Republican
	Kirk Mathews
Franklin	1,284
St. Louis	6,878
TOTAL	**8,162**

State Representative District 111

	Democratic	Republican
	Michael Frame	Shane Roden
Jefferson	4,291	4,834
TOTAL	**4,291**	**4,834**

State Representative District 112

	Democratic	Republican
	Robert W Butler	Rob Vescovo
Jefferson	3,611	5,432
TOTAL	**3,611**	**5,432**

State Representative District 113

	Democratic	Republican	Constitution
	Sean Fauss	Dan Shaul	Donna Ivanovich
Jefferson	3,168	4,749	427
TOTAL	**3,168**	**4,749**	**427**

State Representative District 114

	Democratic	Republican
	T.J. McKenna	Becky Ruth
Jefferson	4,204	4,791
TOTAL	**4,204**	**4,791**

State Representative District 115

	Democratic	Republican	Constitution
	Dan Darian	Elaine Freeman Gannon	Jerry Dollar Jr.
Jefferson	1,621	3,285	256
St. Francois	689	1,486	103
Ste. Genevieve	163	284	25
TOTAL	**2,473**	**5,055**	**384**

State Representative District 116

	Republican
	Kevin Engler
Perry	1,288
St. Francois	2,826
Ste. Genevieve	2,649
TOTAL	**6,763**

State Representative District 117

	Democratic
	Linda Black
St. Francois	5,081
TOTAL	**5,081**

State Representative District 118

	Democratic	Republican
	Ben Harris	Michael P. McGirl
Jefferson	3,239	2,604
Washington	1,316	1,542
TOTAL	**4,555**	**4,146**

State Representative District 119

	Democratic	Republican
	Susan J. Cunningham	Dave Hinson
Franklin	2,376	5,152
Washington	101	193
TOTAL	**2,477**	**5,345**

State Representative District 120

	Democratic	Republican
	Zechariah (Zech) Hockersmith	Jason Chipman
Crawford	1,248	4,158
Phelps	1,031	2,553
TOTAL	**2,279**	**6,711**

State Representative District 121

	Republican
	Keith Frederick
Phelps	4,075
Pulaski	2,144
TOTAL	**6,219**

State Representative District 122

	Republican
	Steve Lynch
Pulaski	3,580
TOTAL	**3,580**

State Representative District 123

	Republican
	Diane Franklin
Camden	4,173
Laclede	2,659
TOTAL	**6,832**

State Representative District 124

	Republican
	Rocky Miller
Camden	4,853
Miller	2,842
TOTAL	**7,695**

State Representative District 125

	Republican
	Warren D. Love
Benton	2,069
Cedar	1,303
Hickory	2,006
St. Clair	2,447
TOTAL	**7,825**

State Representative District 126

	Democratic	Republican	Constitution
	Sam Foursha	Patricia Pike	William M. Gilmore
Bates	1,119	2,534	367
Vernon	2,398	2,960	170
TOTAL	**3,517**	**5,494**	**537**

State Representative District 127

	Republican
	Mike Kelley
Barton	2,732
Cedar	302
Dade	1,886
Jasper	3,034
Polk	-
TOTAL	**7,954**

State Representative District 128

	Republican
	Sue Entlicher
Cedar	1,303
Polk	5,903
TOTAL	**7,206**

State Representative District 129

	Democratic	Republican
	John L. Wilson	Sandy Crawford
Dallas	648	3,003
Laclede	634	3,281
TOTAL	**1,282**	**6,284**

State Representative District 130

	Republican
	Jeff Messenger
Greene	7,598
TOTAL	**7,598**

State Representative District 131

	Democratic	Republican
	Marlee Yant	Sonya Murray Anderson
Greene	2,072	5,578
TOTAL	**2,072**	**5,578**

State Representative District 132

	Democratic	Republican
	Charlie Norr	Fred Ellison
Greene	2,100	1,635
TOTAL	**2,100**	**1,635**

State Representative District 133

	Republican
	Eric W. Burlison
Greene	7,047
TOTAL	**7,047**

State Representative District 134

	Democratic	Republican
	Kevin Knox	Elijah Haahr
Greene	2,909	5,214
TOTAL	**2,909**	**5,214**

State Representative District 135

	Democratic	Republican
	Angie Filbeck	Lincoln Hough
Greene	3,413	4,698
TOTAL	**3,413**	**4,698**

State Representative District 136

	Republican
	Kevin Austin
Greene	9,808
TOTAL	**9,808**

State Representative District 137

	Democratic	Republican	Libertarian
	Sandy Grogan	Lyndall Fraker	Bill Boone
Greene	1,418	3,876	255
Webster	961	3,935	224
TOTAL	**2,379**	**7,811**	**479**

State Representative District 138

	Republican
	Don Phillips
Christian	856
Stone	7,514
Taney	298
TOTAL	**8,668**

State Representative District 139

	Republican
	Jered Taylor
Christian	7,528
TOTAL	**7,528**

State Representative District 140

	Democratic	Republican
	Jim Billedo	Lynn Morris
Christian	1,872	7,151
TOTAL	**1,872**	**7,151**

State Representative District 141

	Republican
	Tony Dugger
Webster	3,303
Wright	3,591
TOTAL	**6,894**

State Representative District 142

	Republican
	Robert Ross
Howell	589
Phelps	460
Pulaski	390
Texas	4,541
TOTAL	**5,980**

State Representative District 143

	Republican
	Jeff Pogue
Dent	3,430
Oregon	1,948
Reynolds	161
Shannon	1,240
TOTAL	6,779

State Representative District 144

	Republican
	Paul Fitzwater
Iron	2,068
Reynolds	1,167
Washington	1,837
Wayne	1,987
TOTAL	7,059

State Representative District 145

	Democratic	Republican
	Charles Elrod	Shelley (White) Keeney
Bollinger	567	2,447
Madison	899	1,903
Perry	645	2,451
TOTAL	2,111	6,801

State Representative District 146

	Republican
	Donna Lichtenegger
Cape Girardeau	7,933
TOTAL	7,933

State Representative District 147

	Democratic	Republican	Libertarian
	Gary L. Gaines	Kathy Swan	Greg Tlapek
Cape Girardeau	1,676	5,214	615
TOTAL	1,676	5,214	615

State Representative District 148

	Republican
	Holly Rehder
Mississippi	1,255
Scott	4,660
TOTAL	5,915

State Representative District 149

	Democratic	Republican
	Bill Burlison	Don Rone
Mississippi	390	522
New Madrid	1,353	2,334
Pemiscot	574	522
Scott	453	424
TOTAL	2,770	3,802

State Representative District 150

	Democratic	Republican
	Walter Dearing	Andrew McDaniel
Dunklin	2,127	1,934
Pemiscot	766	1,186
TOTAL	2,893	3,120

State Representative District 151

	Democratic	Republican
	Ryan Wm. Holder	Tila Rowland Hubrecht
Scott	403	761
Stoddard	2,103	4,991
TOTAL	2,506	5,752

State Representative District 152

	Republican
	Todd Richardson
Butler	4,646
Dunklin	1,144
TOTAL	5,790

State Representative District 153

	Republican	Libertarian
	Steve Cookson	Ginny Keirns
Butler	2,664	393
Carter	1,332	363
Ripley	2,007	536
Wayne	480	114
TOTAL	6,483	1,406

State Representative District 154

	Republican
	Shawn Rhoads
Howell	5,933
TOTAL	5,933

State Representative District 155

	Republican
	Lyle Rowland
Douglas	2,424
Ozark	2,257
Taney	2,586
TOTAL	**7,267**

State Representative District 156

	Republican
	Jeff Justus
Taney	6,492
TOTAL	**6,492**

State Representative District 157

	Democratic	Republican
	Vince Jennings	Mike Moon
Lawrence	2,011	6,407
TOTAL	**2,011**	**6,407**

State Representative District 158

	Republican
	Scott Fitzpatrick
Barry	6,290
Lawrence	246
Stone	47
TOTAL	**6,583**

State Representative District 159

	Republican
	Bill Lant
McDonald	3,346
Newton	2,362
TOTAL	**5,708**

State Representative District 160

	Republican
	Bill Reiboldt
Newton	7,434
TOTAL	**7,434**

State Representative District 161

	Democratic	Republican
	Charles (Hugh) Shields	William (Bill) White
Jasper	1,176	3,092
Newton	451	1,501
TOTAL	**1,627**	**4,593**

State Representative District 162

	Republican
	Charlie Davis
Jasper	6,263
Newton	5
TOTAL	**6,268**

State Representative District 163

	Democratic	Republican
	Michael Jarrett	Tom Flanigan
Jasper	1,256	5,850
TOTAL	**1,256**	**5,850**

Missouri Supreme Court—General Election: November 4, 2014

Laura Denvir Stith	YES	NO	Laura Denvir Stith	YES	NO
Adair	3,117	1,624	Livingston	2,121	1,152
Andrew	3,017	1,339	Macon	2,719	1,507
Atchison	1,096	480	Madison	1,364	1,078
Audrain	3,153	1,624	Maries	1,394	921
Barry	4,356	1,900	Marion	4,123	1,642
Barton	1,621	1,041	McDonald	1,971	1,259
Bates	2,060	1,604	Mercer	623	407
Benton	2,699	1,572	Miller	3,000	1,708
Bollinger	1,448	1,109	Mississippi	1,258	859
Boone	22,233	8,079	Moniteau	1,854	1,063
Buchanan	13,850	4,793	Monroe	1,263	631
Butler	4,302	2,738	Montgomery	1,755	1,197
Caldwell	1,190	820	Morgan	2,826	1,794
Callaway	6,104	3,204	New Madrid	2,036	1,055
Camden	6,123	3,218	Newton	7,178	4,086
Cape Girardeau	9,637	5,209	Nodaway	3,277	1,564
Carroll	1,184	606	Oregon	1,321	672
Carter	769	665	Osage	1,995	1,627
Cass	13,848	8,510	Ozark	1,450	787
Cedar	1,879	1,066	Pemiscot	1,566	886
Chariton	1,271	725	Perry	2,609	1,338
Christian	11,781	4,704	Pettis	5,497	2,799
Clark	1,231	615	Phelps	6,041	2,922
Clay	28,447	17,220	Pike	2,104	1,367
Clinton	3,082	1,920	Platte	13,114	6,733
Cole	13,777	6,379	Polk	3,798	1,928
Cooper	2,319	1,124	Pulaski	4,372	1,830
Crawford	2,654	2,183	Putnam	675	384
Dade	1,292	622	Ralls	1,788	891
Dallas	2,154	1,061	Randolph	3,974	2,047
Daviess	994	583	Ray	3,520	2,118
DeKalb	1,543	863	Reynolds	779	509
Dent	1,846	1,459	Ripley	1,387	798
Douglas	1,604	943	Saline	3,152	1,452
Dunklin	3,054	1,460	Schuyler	716	516
Franklin	13,001	9,344	Scotland	829	436
Gasconade	1,893	1,472	Scott	4,253	2,382
Gentry	910	483	Shannon	768	552
Greene	38,194	15,324	Shelby	858	543
Grundy	1,474	752	St. Charles	48,773	29,570
Harrison	1,427	580	St. Clair	1,678	1,091
Henry	2,708	1,913	St. Francois	6,441	4,613
Hickory	1,325	827	St. Louis	153,646	97,756
Holt	709	392	St. Louis City	35,684	16,165
Howard	1,683	825	Ste. Genevieve	1,826	1,536
Howell	4,577	2,070	Stoddard	3,997	2,355
Iron	1,178	831	Stone	5,284	2,133
Jackson	43,207	28,188	Sullivan	786	545
Jasper	13,098	5,948	Taney	6,340	2,902
Jefferson	25,661	20,401	Texas	2,846	1,541
Johnson	6,893	3,417	Vernon	3,032	1,765
Kansas City	35,153	12,989	Warren	3,860	2,826
Knox	675	390	Washington	2,294	2,078
Laclede	4,299	2,004	Wayne	1,231	1,188
Lafayette	5,458	2,985	Webster	5,175	2,593
Lawrence	5,169	2,529	Worth	387	269
Lewis	1,691	623	Wright	2,079	1,285
Lincoln	6,758	4,787	**TOTAL**	**790,408**	**442,916**
Linn	1,845	1,129			

Missouri Supreme Court—General Election: November 4, 2014

Paul Campbell Wilson	YES	NO	Paul Campbell Wilson	YES	NO
Adair	3,067	1,560	Livingston	2,096	1,117
Andrew	2,974	1,345	Macon	2,766	1,480
Atchison	1,092	479	Madison	1,343	1,068
Audrain	3,191	1,525	Maries	1,400	898
Barry	4,321	1,897	Marion	4,146	1,537
Barton	1,630	996	McDonald	2,010	1,197
Bates	2,030	1,592	Mercer	609	410
Benton	2,665	1,562	Miller	3,062	1,640
Bollinger	1,409	1,093	Mississippi	1,310	782
Boone	21,760	8,029	Moniteau	1,887	990
Buchanan	13,583	4,828	Monroe	1,284	589
Butler	4,282	2,634	Montgomery	1,647	1,160
Caldwell	1,155	830	Morgan	2,775	1,768
Callaway	6,195	3,096	New Madrid	2,020	1,024
Camden	6,097	3,121	Newton	7,270	3,812
Cape Girardeau	9,546	5,120	Nodaway	3,286	1,542
Carroll	1,161	617	Oregon	1,307	670
Carter	742	659	Osage	2,029	1,557
Cass	13,719	8,446	Ozark	1,442	772
Cedar	1,875	1,049	Pemiscot	1,544	882
Chariton	1,258	712	Perry	2,566	1,294
Christian	11,826	4,479	Pettis	5,437	2,753
Clark	1,221	601	Phelps	6,096	2,716
Clay	27,537	17,769	Pike	2,122	1,321
Clinton	3,001	1,959	Platte	12,886	6,839
Cole	14,262	5,797	Polk	3,824	1,791
Cooper	2,345	1,084	Pulaski	4,394	1,677
Crawford	2,681	2,138	Putnam	681	366
Dade	1,296	598	Ralls	1,803	843
Dallas	2,199	995	Randolph	3,983	1,987
Daviess	990	582	Ray	3,465	2,134
DeKalb	1,538	850	Reynolds	763	511
Dent	1,849	1,403	Ripley	1,385	774
Douglas	1,630	890	Saline	3,083	1,469
Dunklin	3,017	1,461	Schuyler	704	501
Franklin	12,776	9,305	Scotland	870	394
Gasconade	1,891	1,446	Scott	4,166	2,376
Gentry	903	471	Shannon	786	521
Greene	37,715	15,079	Shelby	848	525
Grundy	1,464	726	St. Charles	47,423	30,154
Harrison	1,428	575	St. Clair	1,668	1,086
Henry	2,647	1,924	St. Francois	6,324	4,616
Hickory	1,323	814	St. Louis	143,304	103,916
Holt	726	369	St. Louis City	32,829	18,284
Howard	1,681	807	Ste. Genevieve	1,784	1,527
Howell	4,614	1,959	Stoddard	4,000	2,293
Iron	1,171	813	Stone	5,269	2,065
Jackson	41,677	28,896	Sullivan	777	539
Jasper	13,165	5,794	Taney	6,443	2,776
Jefferson	25,001	20,540	Texas	2,862	1,486
Johnson	6,848	3,369	Vernon	2,990	1,787
Kansas City	33,196	14,112	Warren	3,793	2,777
Knox	682	363	Washington	2,288	2,066
Laclede	4,288	1,973	Wayne	1,249	1,114
Lafayette	5,431	2,966	Webster	5,291	2,414
Lawrence	5,209	2,416	Worth	393	261
Lewis	1,664	619	Wright	2,071	1,203
Lincoln	6,686	4,828	**TOTAL**	**769,033**	**449,128**
Linn	1,850	1,117			

Court of Appeals—General Election: November 4, 2014

Eastern District

	Angela Turner Quigless	Angela Turner Quigless	Lisa S. Van Amburg	Lisa S. Van Amburg
	YES	NO	YES	NO
Audrain	3,166	1,559	3,162	1,558
Cape Girardeau	9,491	5,205	9,606	5,082
Clark	1,194	619	1,198	616
Franklin	12,649	9,435	12,710	9,315
Gasconade	1,819	1,450	1,816	1,440
Jefferson	24,912	20,668	25,179	20,330
Knox	669	369	662	375
Lewis	1,643	641	1,663	619
Lincoln	6,494	4,795	6,479	4,752
Madison	1,342	1,079	1,349	1,070
Marion	4,071	1,608	4,079	1,610
Monroe	1,265	597	1,258	591
Montgomery	1,618	1,200	1,652	1,365
Osage	1,941	1,629	1,940	1,621
Perry	2,566	1,297	2,583	1,270
Pike	2,108	1,340	2,119	1,326
Ralls	1,796	860	1,782	866
Scotland	796	441	808	427
Shelby	826	563	828	553
St. Charles	47,787	29,463	47,395	28,752
St. Francois	6,338	4,628	6,344	4,591
St. Louis	150,355	98,656	150,608	97,938
St. Louis City	36,840	15,199	34,875	16,171
Ste. Genevieve	1,797	1,512	1,785	1,514
Warren	3,791	2,802	3,825	2,762
Washington	2,272	2,014	2,247	2,038
TOTAL	**329,546**	**209,629**	**327,952**	**208,552**

Southern District

	Mary W. Sheffield	Mary W. Sheffield	Nancy Steffen Rahmeyer	Nancy Steffen Rahmeyer
	YES	NO	YES	NO
Barry	4,429	1,805	4,347	1,886
Barton	1,661	983	1,655	989
Bollinger	1,442	1,102	1,434	1,113
Butler	4,338	2,591	4,289	2,650
Camden	6,198	3,060	6,157	3,084
Carter	761	632	762	646
Cedar	1,869	1,034	1,839	1,047
Christian	11,940	4,388	11,904	4,380
Crawford	2,731	2,047	2,638	2,106
Dade	1,307	589	1,301	592
Dallas	2,202	991	2,171	1,018
Dent	2,005	1,342	1,857	1,417
Douglas	1,631	889	1,634	882
Dunklin	3,061	1,399	2,960	1,426
Greene	39,622	13,645	38,996	13,643
Hickory	1,350	784	1,338	794
Howell	4,650	1,974	4,574	2,019
Iron	1,205	776	1,151	830
Jasper	13,236	5,537	13,123	5,590
Laclede	4,345	1,933	4,290	1,976
Lawrence	5,257	2,401	5,194	2,450
Maries	1,573	759	1,386	846
McDonald	2,013	1,194	1,938	1,240
Mississippi	1,321	767	1,341	755
New Madrid	2,054	993	2,019	1,020
Newton	7,343	3,767	7,240	3,840
Oregon	1,330	636	1,281	664
Ozark	1,475	755	1,458	769
Pemiscot	1,588	792	1,549	812
Phelps	7,722	1,965	6,172	2,565
Polk	3,899	1,724	3,888	1,750
Pulaski	4,744	1,525	4,336	1,692
Reynolds	784	496	772	503
Ripley	1,391	766	1,373	777
Scott	4,212	2,345	4,186	2,371
Shannon	804	511	778	508
St. Clair	1,664	1,092	1,673	1,084
Stoddard	4,037	2,270	4,034	2,266
Stone	5,364	1,985	5,319	2,027
Taney	6,507	2,662	6,447	2,651
Texas	3,160	1,337	2,866	1,458
Wayne	1,239	1,124	1,219	1,156
Webster	5,306	2,406	5,235	2,462
Wright	2,089	1,227	2,047	1,202
TOTAL	**186,859**	**83,000**	**182,171**	**84,956**

Western District

	Lisa White Hardwick	Lisa White Hardwick	Anthony Rex Gabbert	Anthony Rex Gabbert
	YES	NO	YES	NO
Adair	3,142	1,515	3,019	1,586
Andrew	3,022	1,297	2,959	1,328
Atchison	1,084	471	1,080	464
Bates	2,099	1,538	2,029	1,563
Benton	2,751	1,496	2,665	1,556
Boone	22,069	7,713	21,203	8,081
Buchanan	13,695	4,639	13,399	4,811
Caldwell	1,192	803	1,162	829
Callaway	6,100	3,027	6,003	3,084
Carroll	1,192	574	1,155	603
Cass	14,058	8,141	13,690	8,437
Chariton	1,301	692	1,290	685
Clay	28,531	16,829	28,286	17,160
Clinton	3,089	1,892	3,026	1,943
Cole	13,874	6,015	13,695	6,090
Cooper	2,311	1,066	2,278	1,089
Daviess	977	576	975	574
DeKalb	1,547	832	1,520	841
Gentry	918	457	907	457
Grundy	1,475	740	1,463	730
Harrison	1,426	582	1,409	581
Henry	2,721	1,861	2,662	1,911
Holt	712	383	725	369
Howard	1,706	789	1,713	780
Jackson	43,162	27,583	41,084	28,840
Johnson	7,003	3,251	6,888	3,325
Kansas City	36,167	12,192	32,754	14,201
Lafayette	5,509	2,849	5,403	2,972
Linn	1,892	1,054	1,835	1,074
Livingston	2,108	1,110	2,097	1,124
Macon	2,776	1,450	2,727	1,507
Mercer	621	402	602	406
Miller	2,978	1,680	2,978	1,635
Moniteau	1,879	1,002	1,855	1,017
Morgan	2,852	1,717	2,768	1,770
Nodaway	3,311	1,466	3,274	1,497
Pettis	5,551	2,664	5,390	2,793
Platte	13,201	6,570	12,965	6,706
Putnam	678	368	677	366
Randolph	4,036	1,942	4,007	1,957
Ray	3,599	2,011	3,469	2,078
Saline	3,137	1,426	3,066	1,480
Schuyler	720	501	695	510
Sullivan	794	526	764	541
Vernon	3,043	1,700	2,990	1,743
Worth	391	262	412	242
TOTAL	**276,400**	**137,654**	**267,013**	**143,336**

Circuit Judges (Partisan)—General Election: November 4, 2014

Circuit 11–Division 1

	Democratic
	Ted House
St. Charles	60,395
TOTAL	**60,395**

Circuit 13 - Division 4

	Republican
	Jodie C. Asel
Boone	27,606
Callaway	8,780
TOTAL	**36,386**

Circuit 19–Division 2

	Republican
	Daniel Green
Cole	18,719
TOTAL	**18,719**

Circuit 19–Division 4

	Democratic	Republican
	Pat Joyce	Brian Stumpe
Cole	12,063	10,722
TOTAL	**12,063**	**10,722**

Circuit 23–Division 2

	Republican
	Darrell Missey
Jefferson	41,703
TOTAL	**41,703**

Circuit 25–Division 2

	Republican
	John Beger
Maries	2,210
Phelps	9,050
Pulaski	5,741
Texas	4,320
TOTAL	**21,321**

Circuit 32–Division 1

	Republican
	Michael Gardner
Bollinger	2,557
Cape Girardeau	14,011
Perry	3,705
TOTAL	**20,273**

Circuit 36

	Republican
	Michael Pritchett
Butler	7,380
Ripley	2,107
TOTAL	**9,487**

Circuit 38

	Republican
	Laura Johnson
Christian	15,875
Taney	9,039
TOTAL	**24,914**

Circuit 42–Division 2

	Democratic
	Kelly Parker
Crawford	3,652
Dent	2,882
Iron	1,908
Reynolds	1,198
Wayne	1,798
TOTAL	**11,438**

Circuit Judges (Nonpartisan)—General Election: November 4, 2014

Circuit 6–Division 2

	James W. Van Amburg	James W. Van Amburg
	YES	NO
Platte	13,370	6,489
TOTAL	**13,370**	**6,489**

Circuit 7–Division 2

	Janet Lee Sutton	Janet Lee Sutton
	YES	NO
Clay	28,626	16,674
TOTAL	**28,626**	**16,674**

Circuit 16–Division 2

	Kenneth R. Garrett, III	Kenneth R. Garrett, III
	YES	NO
Jackson	41,916	28,227
Kansas City	34,161	13,328
TOTAL	**76,077**	**41,555**

Circuit 16–Division 10

	Patrick W. Campbell	Patrick W. Campbell
	YES	NO
Jackson	41,735	28,281
Kansas City	33,442	13,625
TOTAL	**75,177**	**41,906**

Circuit 16–Division 14

	John M. Torrence	John M. Torrence
	YES	NO
Jackson	41,555	28,708
Kansas City	33,058	13,866
TOTAL	**74,613**	**42,574**

Circuit 16–Division 15

	Robert M. Schieber	Robert M. Schieber
	YES	NO
Jackson	41,868	27,910
Kansas City	32,816	13,828
TOTAL	**74,684**	**41,738**

Circuit 16–Division 18

	Kevin Duane Harrell	Kevin Duane Harrell
	YES	NO
Jackson	40,754	28,460
Kansas City	33,214	13,182
TOTAL	**73,968**	**41,642**

Circuit 21–Division 1

	Robert S. Cohen	Robert S. Cohen
	YES	NO
St. Louis	143,829	101,093
TOTAL	**143,829**	**101,093**

Circuit 21–Division 2

	Maura B. McShane	Maura B. McShane
	YES	NO
St. Louis	146,149	96,785
TOTAL	**146,149**	**96,785**

Circuit 21–Division 8

	Tom Depriest, Jr.	Tom Depriest, Jr.
	YES	NO
St. Louis	140,258	101,912
TOTAL	**140,258**	**101,912**

Circuit 21–Division 12

	Steven H. Goldman	Steven H. Goldman
	YES	NO
St. Louis	140,577	101,975
TOTAL	**140,577**	**101,975**

Circuit 21–Division 14

	Kristine Allen Kerr	Kristine Allen Kerr
	YES	NO
St. Louis	147,331	95,067
TOTAL	**147,331**	**95,067**

Circuit 21–Division 15

	John D. Warner, Jr.	John D. Warner, Jr.
	YES	NO
St. Louis	139,352	101,633
TOTAL	**139,352**	**101,633**

Circuit 22–Division 2

	David L. Dowd	David L. Dowd
	YES	NO
St. Louis City	34,814	16,662
TOTAL	**34,814**	**16,662**

Circuit 22–Division 4

	Julian L. Bush	Julian L. Bush
	YES	NO
St. Louis City	32,532	17,828
TOTAL	**32,532**	**17,828**

Circuit 22–Division 7

	John J. Riley	John J. Riley
	YES	NO
St. Louis City	32,682	17,378
TOTAL	**32,682**	**17,378**

Circuit 22–Division 8

	Michael F. Stelzer	Michael F. Stelzer
	YES	NO
St. Louis City	31,884	18,198
TOTAL	**31,884**	**18,198**

Circuit 22–Division 13

	Steven R. Ohmer	Steven R. Ohmer
	YES	NO
St. Louis City	32,365	17,733
TOTAL	**32,365**	**17,733**

Circuit 22–Division 15

	Elizabeth Bryne Hogan	Elizabeth Bryne Hogan
	YES	NO
St. Louis City	34,681	15,510
TOTAL	**34,681**	**15,510**

Circuit 22–Division 23

	Timothy J. Wilson	Timothy J. Wilson
	YES	NO
St. Louis City	33,230	16,772
TOTAL	**33,230**	**16,772**

Circuit 31–Division 2

	David C. Jones	David C. Jones
	YES	NO
Greene	40,276	12,910
TOTAL	**40,276**	**12,910**

Associate Circuit Judges (Nonpartisan)—General Election: November 4, 2014

Circuit 7–Division 5

	David P. Chamberlain	David P. Chamberlain
	YES	NO
Clay	28,418	16,739
TOTAL	**28,418**	**16,739**

Circuit 7–Division 6

	Karen Lee Krauser	Karen Lee Krauser
	YES	NO
Clay	28,067	16,974
TOTAL	**28,067**	**16,974**

Circuit 16–Division 25

	Richard T. Standridge	Richard T. Standridge
	YES	NO
Jackson	41,085	28,381
Kansas City	32,791	14,013
TOTAL	**73,876**	**42,394**

Circuit 16–Division 27

	Gregory Burnett Gillis	Gregory Burnett Gillis
	YES	NO
Jackson	40,838	28,456
Kansas City	33,251	13,535
TOTAL	**74,089**	**41,991**

Circuit 16–Division 30

	Twila Kay Rigby	Twila Kay Rigby
	YES	NO
Jackson	42,006	27,827
Kansas City	33,958	12,868
TOTAL	**75,964**	**40,695**

Circuit 16–Division 31

	Mary Frances Weir	Mary Frances Weir
	YES	NO
Jackson	42,884	27,283
Kansas City	34,387	12,531
TOTAL	**77,271**	**39,814**

Circuit 16–Division 33

	Jeffrey L. Bushur	Jeffrey L. Bushur
	YES	NO
Jackson	41,514	28,409
Kansas City	32,561	14,069
TOTAL	**74,075**	**42,478**

Circuit 21–Division 31

	Mary Elizabeth Ott	Mary Elizabeth Ott
	YES	NO
St. Louis	151,135	90,755
TOTAL	**151,135**	**90,755**

Circuit 21–Division 36

	Ellen Hannigan Ribaudo	Ellen Hannigan Ribaudo
	YES	NO
St. Louis	146,471	94,708
TOTAL	**146,471**	**94,708**

Circuit 21–Division 38

	Lawrence J. Permuter	Lawrence J. Permuter
	YES	NO
St. Louis	138,034	102,443
TOTAL	**138,034**	**102,443**

Circuit 21–Division 39

	Patrick Clifford	Patrick Clifford
	YES	NO
St. Louis	136,401	102,281
TOTAL	**136,401**	**102,281**

Circuit 21–Division 40

	Dennis N. Smith	Dennis N. Smith
	YES	NO
St. Louis	135,965	101,960
TOTAL	**135,965**	**101,960**

Circuit 21–Division 41

	Judy Preddy Draper	Judy Preddy Draper
	YES	NO
St. Louis	138,984	100,746
TOTAL	**138,984**	**100,746**

Circuit 22–Division 14

	Paula Perkins Bryant	Paula Perkins Bryant
	YES	NO
St. Louis City	35,284	15,095
TOTAL	**35,284**	**15,095**

Circuit 22–Division 29

	Christopher E. McGraugh	Christopher E. McGraugh
	YES	NO
St. Louis City	31,802	17,804
TOTAL	**31,802**	**17,804**

Circuit 22–Division 24

	Michael W. Noble	Michael W. Noble
	YES	NO
St. Louis City	32,910	16,813
TOTAL	**32,910**	**16,813**

Circuit 31–Division 21

	Dan Imhof	Dan Imhof
	YES	NO
Greene	41,267	12,521
TOTAL	**41,267**	**12,521**

Circuit 22–Division 25

	Theresa Counts Burke	Theresa Counts Burke
	YES	NO
St. Louis City	34,501	15,702
TOTAL	**34,501**	**15,702**

Circuit 31–Division 22

	Jason Brown	Jason Brown
	YES	NO
Greene	40,723	12,473
TOTAL	**40,723**	**12,473**

Circuit 22–Division 28

	Barbara Tina Peebles	Barbara Tina Peebles
	YES	NO
St. Louis City	33,759	17,056
TOTAL	**33,759**	**17,056**

Circuit 31–Division 24

	Mark A. Powell	Mark A. Powell
	YES	NO
Greene	41,696	12,294
TOTAL	**41,696**	**12,294**

Constitutional Amendment 2—General Election: November 4, 2014

	YES	NO		YES	NO
Adair	3,676	2,021	Maries	1,741	934
Andrew	3,761	1,073	Marion	4,953	1,718
Atchison	1,303	452	McDonald	2,802	959
Audrain	3,489	1,832	Mercer	854	337
Barry	5,529	1,563	Miller	3,701	1,547
Barton	2,188	802	Mississippi	1,805	520
Bates	3,230	1,020	Moniteau	2,176	1,215
Benton	3,619	1,093	Monroe	1,476	682
Bollinger	2,014	888	Montgomery	2,067	1,211
Boone	24,074	16,506	Morgan	3,666	1,562
Buchanan	16,202	4,546	New Madrid	2,658	866
Butler	6,014	1,930	Newton	8,974	3,895
Caldwell	1,637	614	Nodaway	3,644	1,823
Callaway	6,959	3,693	Oregon	1,687	683
Camden	8,380	2,315	Osage	2,682	1,367
Cape Girardeau	12,608	4,201	Ozark	1,962	637
Carroll	1,463	580	Pemiscot	2,060	804
Carter	1,155	516	Perry	3,368	1,299
Cass	20,131	5,242	Pettis	7,029	2,179
Cedar	2,497	847	Phelps	7,203	3,169
Chariton	1,403	906	Pike	2,818	1,183
Christian	14,286	4,697	Platte	17,633	4,544
Clark	1,454	596	Polk	4,722	1,688
Clay	40,415	10,485	Pulaski	5,317	1,538
Clinton	4,215	1,337	Putnam	917	299
Cole	14,656	7,878	Ralls	2,238	844
Cooper	2,601	1,302	Randolph	4,283	2,296
Crawford	3,833	1,679	Ray	4,613	1,648
Dade	1,596	596	Reynolds	1,047	501
Dallas	2,538	1,089	Ripley	1,914	625
Daviess	1,328	467	Saline	3,644	1,477
DeKalb	2,001	697	Schuyler	924	486
Dent	2,743	1,218	Scotland	933	539
Douglas	2,043	852	Scott	5,733	1,810
Dunklin	4,088	1,174	Shannon	1,130	518
Franklin	18,340	7,033	Shelby	1,143	511
Gasconade	2,761	1,128	St. Charles	72,889	22,208
Gentry	1,157	401	St. Clair	2,320	732
Greene	46,613	15,411	St. Francois	9,392	3,080
Grundy	1,849	644	St. Louis	200,126	86,684
Harrison	1,920	428	St. Louis City	34,261	24,126
Henry	3,948	1,306	Ste. Genevieve	2,729	1,119
Hickory	1,764	641	Stoddard	5,079	1,877
Holt	941	287	Stone	6,849	1,596
Howard	1,668	1,205	Sullivan	921	586
Howell	5,684	1,928	Taney	8,229	2,180
Iron	1,522	770	Texas	3,809	1,342
Jackson	64,910	17,423	Vernon	3,400	1,936
Jasper	15,093	6,789	Warren	5,372	2,245
Jefferson	38,756	14,593	Washington	3,369	1,663
Johnson	8,644	2,774	Wayne	1,913	927
Kansas City	35,865	18,630	Webster	6,668	2,254
Knox	835	432	Worth	506	220
Laclede	5,327	1,593	Wright	2,808	1,132
Lafayette	7,081	2,315	**TOTAL**	**1,018,773**	**396,519**
Lawrence	6,463	2,173			
Lewis	1,904	719			
Lincoln	9,956	3,114			
Linn	2,391	952			
Livingston	2,679	1,077			
Macon	3,519	1,409			
Madison	1,897	816			

For official ballot title, see page 626

Constitutional Amendment 3—General Election: November 4, 2014

	YES	NO		YES	NO
Adair	1,073	4,825	Maries	586	2,152
Andrew	936	3,984	Marion	1,426	5,459
Atchison	336	1,466	McDonald	1,176	2,651
Audrain	891	4,551	Mercer	237	1,003
Barry	1,810	5,379	Miller	1,261	4,104
Barton	544	2,503	Mississippi	594	1,793
Bates	784	3,594	Moniteau	603	2,870
Benton	1,142	3,661	Monroe	422	1,801
Bollinger	626	2,387	Montgomery	644	2,451
Boone	7,528	33,643	Morgan	1,316	3,992
Buchanan	4,832	16,254	New Madrid	901	2,715
Butler	2,259	5,963	Newton	3,112	9,940
Caldwell	429	1,866	Nodaway	956	4,645
Callaway	2,301	8,512	Oregon	582	1,891
Camden	3,177	7,636	Osage	745	3,409
Cape Girardeau	3,488	13,697	Ozark	658	2,016
Carroll	371	1,757	Pemiscot	788	2,206
Carter	450	1,282	Perry	899	4,050
Cass	6,815	18,804	Pettis	1,898	7,512
Cedar	763	2,674	Phelps	2,126	8,433
Chariton	348	2,034	Pike	718	3,384
Christian	4,295	14,994	Platte	6,238	16,036
Clark	546	1,582	Polk	1,182	5,373
Clay	13,189	38,383	Pulaski	1,681	5,303
Clinton	1,318	4,300	Putnam	312	944
Cole	4,921	17,881	Ralls	749	2,425
Cooper	760	3,206	Randolph	1,368	5,320
Crawford	1,184	4,485	Ray	1,529	4,852
Dade	489	1,747	Reynolds	346	1,257
Dallas	854	2,831	Ripley	660	1,963
Daviess	348	1,494	Saline	1,000	4,248
DeKalb	552	2,161	Schuyler	413	1,040
Dent	893	3,181	Scotland	402	1,124
Douglas	613	2,321	Scott	1,668	6,021
Dunklin	1,120	4,342	Shannon	309	1,389
Franklin	5,225	20,721	Shelby	341	1,366
Gasconade	884	3,118	St. Charles	22,951	74,695
Gentry	327	1,286	St. Clair	729	2,366
Greene	13,169	49,753	St. Francois	2,582	10,198
Grundy	317	2,239	St. Louis	77,603	213,398
Harrison	581	1,824	St. Louis City	14,721	44,429
Henry	1,331	4,044	Ste. Genevieve	664	3,382
Hickory	603	1,853	Stoddard	1,457	5,686
Holt	192	1,060	Stone	2,503	6,023
Howard	465	2,484	Sullivan	286	1,283
Howell	1,593	6,174	Taney	2,837	7,685
Iron	439	1,949	Texas	1,171	4,111
Jackson	21,357	61,774	Vernon	1,214	4,246
Jasper	4,667	17,579	Warren	1,719	6,052
Jefferson	12,160	42,126	Washington	919	4,281
Johnson	2,263	9,310	Wayne	726	2,241
Kansas City	14,501	40,255	Webster	2,340	6,744
Knox	285	1,076	Worth	206	541
Laclede	1,710	5,293	Wright	919	3,178
Lafayette	1,913	7,659	**TOTAL**	**339,422**	**1,100,628**
Lawrence	1,891	6,877			
Lewis	627	2,077			
Lincoln	2,692	10,686			
Linn	613	2,844			
Livingston	649	3,259			
Macon	1,110	3,932			
Madison	480	2,319			

For official ballot title, see page 626

Constitutional Amendment 6—General Election: November 4, 2014

	YES	NO		YES	NO
Adair	1,671	3,932	Maries	614	2,045
Andrew	1,280	3,463	Marion	1,629	4,995
Atchison	484	1,253	McDonald	1,109	2,621
Audrain	1,290	3,976	Mercer	296	864
Barry	1,730	5,298	Miller	1,328	3,867
Barton	844	2,129	Mississippi	641	1,662
Bates	1,018	3,152	Moniteau	782	2,576
Benton	1,229	3,450	Monroe	502	1,632
Bollinger	681	2,210	Montgomery	651	2,412
Boone	9,719	30,534	Morgan	1,133	4,035
Buchanan	5,917	14,539	New Madrid	996	2,498
Butler	2,411	5,393	Newton	3,439	9,366
Caldwell	461	1,778	Nodaway	1,347	4,077
Callaway	2,633	7,932	Oregon	529	1,797
Camden	2,667	7,971	Osage	808	3,243
Cape Girardeau	4,391	12,336	Ozark	646	1,905
Carroll	556	1,461	Pemiscot	965	1,809
Carter	465	1,167	Perry	1,191	3,407
Cass	7,255	17,944	Pettis	2,323	6,851
Cedar	839	2,475	Phelps	2,504	7,760
Chariton	487	1,795	Pike	885	3,111
Christian	4,509	14,322	Platte	7,170	14,834
Clark	604	1,408	Polk	1,562	4,805
Clay	16,267	34,285	Pulaski	2,036	4,760
Clinton	1,563	3,952	Putnam	308	897
Cole	5,677	16,770	Ralls	785	2,275
Cooper	879	2,990	Randolph	1,540	4,979
Crawford	1,286	4,153	Ray	1,805	4,338
Dade	532	1,639	Reynolds	320	1,219
Dallas	986	2,608	Ripley	675	1,801
Daviess	414	1,357	Saline	1,375	3,694
DeKalb	705	1,940	Schuyler	386	992
Dent	813	3,089	Scotland	379	1,069
Douglas	688	2,169	Scott	1,825	5,656
Dunklin	1,520	3,666	Shannon	353	1,264
Franklin	5,454	19,746	Shelby	371	1,281
Gasconade	917	2,930	St. Charles	27,944	66,227
Gentry	381	1,185	St. Clair	753	2,251
Greene	16,802	44,642	St. Francois	3,222	9,058
Grundy	637	1,841	St. Louis	100,731	184,392
Harrison	763	1,537	St. Louis City	22,855	35,053
Henry	1,293	3,895	Ste. Genevieve	891	2,937
Hickory	682	1,708	Stoddard	1,704	5,259
Holt	334	878	Stone	2,225	6,139
Howard	629	2,212	Sullivan	345	1,143
Howell	1,829	5,724	Taney	3,054	7,209
Iron	537	1,732	Texas	1,304	3,803
Jackson	27,115	53,413	Vernon	1,357	3,939
Jasper	6,078	15,587	Warren	1,834	5,744
Jefferson	12,923	40,029	Washington	1,048	3,924
Johnson	2,844	8,501	Wayne	644	2,158
Kansas City	19,960	34,377	Webster	2,181	6,607
Knox	352	900	Worth	183	534
Laclede	1,779	5,071	Wright	1,019	2,923
Lafayette	2,686	6,608	**TOTAL**	**416,447**	**985,966**
Lawrence	1,966	6,633			
Lewis	713	1,885	For official ballot title, see page 626		
Lincoln	3,156	9,791			
Linn	873	2,445			
Livingston	953	2,743			
Macon	1,180	3,682			
Madison	638	2,038			

For official ballot title, see page 626

Constitutional Amendment 10—General Election: November 4, 2014

	YES	NO		YES	NO
Adair	2,912	2,689	Maries	1,541	1,108
Andrew	2,728	2,011	Marion	4,144	2,511
Atchison	961	744	McDonald	2,515	1,190
Audrain	2,863	2,393	Mercer	731	428
Barry	4,622	2,441	Miller	3,157	2,064
Barton	1,999	983	Mississippi	1,564	771
Bates	2,429	1,714	Moniteau	1,849	1,503
Benton	2,884	1,814	Monroe	1,287	862
Bollinger	1,897	1,026	Montgomery	1,786	1,266
Boone	18,580	20,978	Morgan	3,137	2,048
Buchanan	11,829	8,524	New Madrid	2,194	1,341
Butler	5,358	2,508	Newton	8,537	4,204
Caldwell	1,352	860	Nodaway	2,727	2,592
Callaway	5,614	4,865	Oregon	1,301	1,065
Camden	6,681	3,944	Osage	2,319	1,735
Cape Girardeau	10,964	5,841	Ozark	1,644	943
Carroll	1,226	793	Pemiscot	1,650	1,089
Carter	890	749	Perry	2,983	1,668
Cass	15,729	9,332	Pettis	5,292	3,828
Cedar	2,042	1,286	Phelps	5,927	4,267
Chariton	1,255	1,015	Pike	2,370	1,607
Christian	11,589	7,177	Platte	12,718	9,093
Clark	1,243	784	Polk	3,830	2,515
Clay	29,245	20,817	Pulaski	4,505	2,313
Clinton	3,280	2,206	Putnam	839	367
Cole	10,965	11,264	Ralls	1,882	1,148
Cooper	2,138	1,690	Randolph	3,752	2,723
Crawford	3,131	2,283	Ray	3,525	2,555
Dade	1,399	780	Reynolds	825	716
Dallas	2,413	1,211	Ripley	1,654	878
Daviess	1,021	743	Saline	2,897	2,157
DeKalb	1566	1066	Schuyler	766	609
Dent	2,330	1,587	Scotland	732	710
Douglas	1,916	960	Scott	5,068	2,512
Dunklin	3,113	2,149	Shannon	939	695
Franklin	14,911	10,230	Shelby	942	718
Gasconade	2,248	1,581	St. Charles	58,520	33,879
Gentry	919	632	St. Clair	1,872	1,150
Greene	33,907	27,008	St. Francois	7,134	5,097
Grundy	1,439	1,019	St. Louis	150,530	131,656
Harrison	1,426	840	St. Louis City	26,171	31,753
Henry	3,010	2,157	Ste. Genevieve	2,036	1,779
Hickory	1,457	941	Stoddard	4,210	2,784
Holt	713	497	Stone	5,451	2,931
Howard	1,486	1,342	Sullivan	749	755
Howell	4,474	3,124	Taney	6,624	3,658
Iron	1,228	1,045	Texas	3,260	1,826
Jackson	45,923	33,951	Vernon	2,972	2,274
Jasper	13,912	7,552	Warren	4,371	3,130
Jefferson	30,373	22,198	Washington	2,731	2,210
Johnson	6,169	5,133	Wayne	1,627	1,201
Kansas City	22,918	30,754	Webster	5,479	3,329
Knox	708	559	Worth	368	305
Laclede	4,614	2,253	Wright	2,603	1,326
Lafayette	5,460	3,762	**TOTAL**	**791,099**	**601,699**
Lawrence	5,535	3,057			
Lewis	1,602	998			
Lincoln	7,699	5,084			
Linn	1,945	1,372			
Livingston	2,070	1,536			
Macon	2,842	1,982			
Madison	1,710	1,023			

For official ballot title, see page 626

CONSTITUTIONAL AMENDMENT NO. 2

Proposed by the 97th General Assembly
(First Regular Session) SCS HJR No. 16

OFFICIAL BALLOT TITLE:

Shall the Missouri Constitution be amended so that it will be permissible to allow relevant evidence of prior criminal acts to be admissible in prosecutions for crimes of a sexual nature involving a victim under eighteen years of age?

If more resources are needed to defend increased prosecutions additional costs to governmental entities could be at least $1.4 million annually, otherwise the fiscal impact is expected to be limited.

CONSTITUTIONAL AMENDMENT NO. 3

Proposed by Initiative Petition

Shall the Missouri Constitution be amended to:
• require teachers to be evaluated by a standards based performance evaluation system for which each local school district must receive state approval to continue receiving state and local funding;
• require teachers to be dismissed, retained, demoted, promoted and paid primarily using quantifiable student performance data as part of the evaluation system;
• require teachers to enter into contracts of three years or fewer with public school districts; and
• prohibit teachers from organizing or collectively bargaining regarding the design and implementation of the teacher evaluation system?

Decisions by school districts regarding provisions allowed or required by this proposal and their implementation will influence the potential costs or savings impacting each district. Significant potential costs may be incurred by the state and/or the districts if new/additional evaluation instruments must be developed to satisfy the proposal's performance evaluation requirements.

CONSTITUTIONAL AMENDMENT NO. 6

Proposed by the 97th General Assembly
(Second Regular Session) SS SCS HCS HJR No. 90

OFFICIAL BALLOT TITLE:

Shall the Missouri Constitution be amended to permit voting in person or by mail for a period of six business days prior to and including the Wednesday before the election day in general elections, but only if the legislature and the governor appropriate and disburse funds to pay for the increased costs of such voting?

State governmental entities estimated startup costs of about $2 million and costs to reimburse local election authorities of at least $100,000 per election. Local election authorities estimated higher reimbursable costs per election. Those costs will depend on the compensation, staffing, and, planning decisions of election authorities with the total costs being unknown.

CONSTITUTIONAL AMENDMENT NO. 10

Proposed by the 97th General Assembly
(Second Regular Session) HJR No. 72

Shall the Missouri Constitution be amended to require the governor to pay the public debt, to prohibit the governor from relying on revenue from legislation not yet passed when proposing a budget, and to provide a legislative check on the governor's decisions to restrict funding for education and other state services?

State governmental entities expect no direct costs or savings. Local governmental entities expect an unknown fiscal impact.

Primary Election Results
August 5, 2014

U.S. Representative District 1

	Democratic	Republican	Republican	Republican	Libertarian
	Lacy Clay	Martin D. Baker	Daniel J. Elder	David Koehr	Robb E Cunningham
St. Louis	44,477	2,750	3,199	2,005	311
St. Louis City	25,173	909	997	828	154
TOTAL	**69,650**	**3,659**	**4,196**	**2,833**	**465**

U.S. Representative District 2

	Democratic	Republican	Libertarian
	Arthur Lieber	Ann Wagner	Bill Slantz
Jefferson	1,904	2,286	29
St. Charles	3,907	12,559	100
St. Louis	48,746	40,477	591
TOTAL	**54,557**	**55,322**	**720**

U.S. Representative District 3

	Democratic	Democratic	Republican	Republican	Republican
	Velma Steinman	Courtney Denton	Leonard Steinman	Blaine Luetkemeyer	John Morris
Callaway	759	905	390	3,559	425
Camden	226	337	278	3,313	489
Cole	1,055	1,894	849	9,492	1,146
Franklin	1,682	2,210	1,355	11,129	1,397
Gasconade	209	187	211	2,533	176
Jefferson	2,337	3,359	943	5,136	1,247
Lincoln	1,208	1,259	589	4,118	591
Maries	274	175	163	1,286	102
Miller	144	160	269	3,755	315
Montgomery	221	259	121	1,547	107
Osage	286	241	216	2,595	151
St. Charles	3,268	4,569	2,662	17,845	3,065
Warren	319	432	534	4,722	575
TOTAL	**11,988**	**15,987**	**8,580**	**71,030**	**9,786**

U.S. Representative District 4

	Democratic	Republican	Republican	Libertarian	Libertarian
	Nate Irvin	Vicky Hartzler	John Webb	Randall (Randy) Langkraehr	Herschel L. Young
Audrain	730	1,199	439	14	16
Barton	149	1,378	310	6	5
Bates	749	1,475	415	2	11
Benton	503	2,505	814	6	9
Boone	9,650	6,926	2,742	226	255
Camden	409	2,401	853	12	4
Cass	3,456	8,834	3,251	64	106
Cedar	209	2,107	653	5	6
Cooper	365	2,094	948	11	11
Dade	171	1,219	363	1	3
Dallas	191	2,884	864	3	4
Henry	1,698	1,167	376	8	9
Hickory	336	1,190	426	3	5
Howard	901	419	186	5	9
Johnson	1,343	4,321	1,644	53	35
Laclede	467	4,944	1,187	7	19
Moniteau	264	2,097	630	0	5
Morgan	518	2,624	782	17	11
Pettis	602	4,450	1,900	16	8
Pulaski	701	2,879	894	5	5
Randolph	1,172	1,557	500	16	16
St. Clair	459	1,426	481	2	3
Vernon	1,136	1,327	311	10	1
Webster	652	3,981	1,162	11	11
TOTAL	**26,831**	**65,404**	**22,131**	**503**	**567**

U.S. Representative District 5

	Democratic	Democratic	Democratic	Democratic	Democratic	Republican	Republican	Republican	Republican	Libertarian
	Mark S Memoly	Emanuel Cleaver II	Bob Gough	Eric Holmes	Charles Lindsey	Bill Lindsey	Berton A. Knox	Michael Burris	Jacob Turk	Roy Welborn
Clay	243	3,104	123	375	332	843	265	803	2,140	55
Jackson	1,350	11,914	539	794	893	2,392	651	1,763	13,352	369
Kansas City	765	24,376	436	835	689	637	219	1,450	4,580	323
Lafayette	259	1,994	112	271	269	556	133	342	2,486	34
Ray	183	1,552	161	167	270	282	85	234	957	23
Saline	188	1,356	67	142	234	310	100	205	1,100	9
TOTAL	**2,988**	**44,296**	**1,438**	**2,584**	**2,687**	**5,020**	**1,453**	**4,797**	**24,615**	**813**

U.S. Representative District 6

	Democratic	Democratic	Democratic	Republican	Republican	Republican	Republican	Libertarian
	W. A. (Bill) Hedge	Edward Dwayne Fields	Gary Lynn Crose	Kyle Reid	Brian L. Tharp	Sam Graves	Christopher Ryan	Russ Monchil
Adair	268	136	84	168	138	2,338	266	15
Andrew	348	188	110	193	204	2,093	325	14
Atchison	86	56	43	49	152	863	117	3
Audrain	118	86	25	41	22	283	50	9
Buchanan	4,720	1,078	789	376	442	4,841	682	65
Caldwell	111	100	59	130	83	1,059	165	19
Carroll	74	52	79	98	30	1,461	130	6
Chariton	472	324	401	31	8	460	50	7
Clark	94	69	39	83	38	747	208	3
Clay	2,521	1,754	1,248	615	579	8,748	1,674	96
Clinton	612	340	279	191	168	1,938	314	25
Daviess	269	185	188	39	26	522	55	15
DeKalb	219	128	110	70	139	961	119	11
Gentry	166	114	71	41	37	603	99	5
Holt	56	37	18	48	134	834	99	4
Jackson	1,350	878	773	486	421	5,035	923	105
Knox	199	147	115	19	7	216	23	7
Lewis	275	161	83	65	24	720	96	9
Linn	266	187	187	62	33	1,210	121	10
Livingston	145	92	96	94	83	1,780	178	8
Macon	414	333	186	111	50	1,721	243	6
Marion	1,058	564	407	85	72	1,230	161	10
Mercer	16	16	14	31	21	728	88	1
Monroe	423	467	155	33	29	389	61	6
Nodaway	300	190	147	204	388	2,367	386	7
Pike	623	336	230	129	54	645	227	17
Platte	1,502	911	722	459	499	6,306	1,135	82
Putnam	22	20	27	53	28	839	79	3
Ralls	526	242	176	37	31	495	78	3
Schuyler	86	92	65	8	17	327	31	8
Scotland	126	85	68	23	16	338	36	3
Shelby	420	223	145	27	19	343	33	3
Sullivan	76	36	14	22	24	725	72	0
Worth	64	20	26	50	41	377	57	0
TOTAL	**18,109**	**9,706**	**7,241**	**4,364**	**4,244**	**56,789**	**8,745**	**591**

U.S. Representative District 7

	Democratic	Democratic	Republican	Republican	Libertarian
	Genevieve Williams	Jim Evans	Marshall Works	Billy Long	Kevin Craig
Barry	315	283	1,677	3,482	19
Christian	643	717	4,747	6,081	75
Greene	3,571	5,020	11,859	14,914	423
Jasper	785	593	3,379	8,800	82
Lawrence	337	348	2,792	3,246	24
McDonald	108	111	495	1,778	14
Newton	800	735	1,698	4,686	54
Polk	242	212	1,747	3,607	27
Stone	266	261	2,076	3,325	19
Taney	291	264	2,578	4,982	21
Webster	99	127	450	604	6
TOTAL	**7,457**	**8,671**	**33,498**	**55,505**	**764**

U.S. Representative District 8

	Democratic	Republican	Libertarian	Constitution
	Barbara Stocker	Jason Smith	Rick Vandeven	Doug Enyart
Bollinger	155	2,061	3	8
Butler	482	4,820	8	5
Cape Girardeau	1,151	11,103	83	21
Carter	313	1,003	1	0
Crawford	546	2,704	16	4
Dent	472	1,568	18	14
Douglas	92	2,699	4	3
Dunklin	2,010	576	13	5
Howell	779	3,397	61	61
Iron	1,195	399	6	1
Jefferson	3,914	3,721	54	42
Madison	402	1,099	2	2
Mississippi	1,257	384	0	2
New Madrid	1,488	697	1	2
Oregon	732	458	3	15
Ozark	129	1,765	8	2
Pemiscot	1,240	157	1	0
Perry	110	3,569	4	1
Phelps	1,296	5,013	33	9
Reynolds	995	267	0	3
Ripley	286	1,045	8	10
Scott	1,679	3,235	23	9
Shannon	404	546	5	23
St. Francois	1,927	2,557	39	33
Ste. Genevieve	1,969	548	3	5
Stoddard	462	2,803	12	9
Texas	663	3,295	27	31
Washington	1,046	1,361	11	16
Wayne	896	822	4	16
Wright	213	2,839	11	16
TOTAL	**28,303**	**66,511**	**462**	**368**

State Auditor—Primary Election: August 5, 2014

	Republican	Libertarian	Constitution		Republican	Libertarian	Constitution
	Tom Schweich	Sean O'Toole	Rodney Farthing		Tom Schweich	Sean O'Toole	Rodney Farthing
Adair	2,314	16	0	Maries	1,252	6	1
Andrew	2,352	15	12	Marion	1,254	10	4
Atchison	962	3	1	McDonald	1,814	13	7
Audrain	1,736	38	12	Mercer	630	1	0
Barry	4,351	19	14	Miller	3,608	13	8
Barton	1,303	8	6	Mississippi	322	0	1
Bates	1,311	11	20	Moniteau	2,229	7	0
Benton	2,697	14	6	Monroe	408	6	3
Bollinger	1,883	3	7	Montgomery	1,522	19	8
Boone	8,467	505	87	Morgan	2,764	25	6
Buchanan	5,189	64	25	New Madrid	617	2	2
Butler	4,365	5	5	Newton	5,541	52	19
Caldwell	1,174	18	5	Nodaway	2,596	9	8
Callaway	3,725	66	24	Oregon	433	3	13
Camden	6,059	32	5	Osage	2,512	1	5
Cape Girardeau	10,602	77	20	Ozark	1,731	8	3
Carroll	1,345	4	1	Pemiscot	145	1	0
Carter	856	1	0	Perry	3,334	4	1
Cass	9,643	166	58	Pettis	5,264	23	9
Cedar	2,251	10	6	Phelps	4,492	32	10
Chariton	467	7	2	Pike	994	17	5
Christian	8,941	76	37	Platte	7,161	86	24
Clark	758	3	5	Polk	4,604	22	8
Clay	13,314	157	44	Pulaski	3,034	10	3
Clinton	2,155	24	12	Putnam	841	3	1
Cole	9,862	136	26	Ralls	546	3	6
Cooper	2,577	22	3	Randolph	1,761	30	9
Crawford	2,203	16	4	Ray	1,479	24	17
Dade	1,308	2	1	Reynolds	217	1	2
Dallas	3,178	8	7	Ripley	961	8	8
Daviess	489	15	2	Saline	1,566	8	5
DeKalb	989	13	14	Schuyler	291	8	4
Dent	1,216	18	18	Scotland	292	3	2
Douglas	2,662	4	2	Scott	3,041	22	10
Dunklin	516	12	5	Shannon	454	4	23
Franklin	11,789	116	67	Shelby	358	3	1
Gasconade	2,348	5	1	St. Charles	32,824	319	88
Gentry	579	5	3	St. Clair	1,588	5	9
Greene	22,913	412	93	St. Francois	2,406	38	34
Grundy	1,600	4	1	St. Louis	44,748	903	215
Harrison	1,649	2	2	St. Louis City	2,850	153	16
Henry	1,251	16	22	Ste. Genevieve	531	3	5
Hickory	1,360	8	6	Stoddard	2,372	10	8
Holt	928	3	0	Stone	4,562	19	10
Howard	522	14	1	Sullivan	650	0	2
Howell	3,286	61	58	Taney	6,341	21	7
Iron	389	6	1	Texas	3,095	26	29
Jackson	13,938	482	163	Vernon	1,239	13	1
Jasper	10,425	83	17	Warren	4,859	24	13
Jefferson	12,589	201	155	Washington	1,278	10	16
Johnson	5,048	90	43	Wayne	725	5	16
Kansas City	5,487	325	65	Webster	5,109	27	9
Knox	200	7	0	Worth	396	0	1
Laclede	5,137	27	10	Wright	2,659	10	13
Lafayette	2,956	36	7	**TOTAL**	**431,778**	**5,674**	**2,003**
Lawrence	5,025	24	17				
Lewis	735	9	5				
Lincoln	4,723	51	30				
Linn	1,079	10	5				
Livingston	1,491	8	1				
Macon	1,816	6	3				
Madison	995	2	3				

State Senator—Primary Election: August 5, 2014

State Senator District 2

	Republican	Republican	Republican
	Bob Onder	Vicki Schneider	Chuck Gatschenberger
St. Charles	14,305	4,561	3,635
TOTAL	**14,305**	**4,561**	**3,635**

State Senator District 4

	Democratic	Democratic	Republican
	Joseph (Joe) Keaveny	Bonnie Lynn Green	Courtney Blunt
St. Louis	2,000	1,782	1,106
St. Louis City	9,078	4,624	1,857
TOTAL	**11,078**	**6,406**	**2,963**

State Senator District 6

	Democratic	Republican
	Mollie Kristen Freebairn	Mike Kehoe
Cole	2,801	9,882
Gasconade	371	2,422
Maries	408	1,293
Miller	268	3,700
Moniteau	263	2,348
Morgan	527	2,931
Osage	501	2,566
TOTAL	**5,139**	**25,142**

State Senator District 8

	Republican
	Will Kraus
Jackson	11,552
TOTAL	**11,552**

State Senator District 10

	Democratic	Republican
	Ed Schieffer	Jeanie Riddle
Audrain	997	1,797
Callaway	1,590	4,056
Lincoln	2,758	4,697
Monroe	1,049	429
Montgomery	485	1,625
Warren	727	4,899
TOTAL	**7,606**	**17,503**

State Senator District 12

	Republican
	Dan Hegeman
Andrew	2,565
Atchison	987
Clay	3,740
Clinton	2,134
Daviess	513
De Kalb	1,074
Gentry	664
Grundy	1,557
Harrison	1,718
Holt	1,004
Mercer	612
Nodaway	2,637
Putnam	787
Sullivan	647
Worth	427
TOTAL	**21,066**

State Senator District 14

	Democratic
	Maria N. Chappelle-Nadal
St. Louis	14,388
TOTAL	**14,388**

State Senator District 16

	Republican	Republican
	Bernard (Bernie) Mowinski	Dan Brown
Camden	1,172	5,866
Crawford	359	2,318
Dent	171	1,419
Phelps	585	5,052
Pulaski	516	3,119
TOTAL	**2,803**	**17,774**

State Senator District 18

	Republican
	Brian Munzlinger
Adair	2,609
Chariton	461
Clark	1,064
Knox	284
Lewis	896
Linn	1,081
Macon	1,913
Marion	1,448
Pike	1,032
Ralls	601
Randolph	1,784
Schuyler	348
Scotland	389
Shelby	403
TOTAL	**14,313**

State Senator District 20

	Republican
	Jay Wasson
Christian	9,339
Greene	11,322
TOTAL	**20,661**

State Senator District 22

	Democratic	Republican
	Jeff Roorda	Paul Wieland
Jefferson	8,478	9,681
TOTAL	**8,478**	**9,681**

State Senator District 24

	Democratic	Republican	Republican	Republican	Libertarian
	Jill Schupp	Robb Hicks	Jack Spooner	John R. Ashcroft	Jim Higgins
St. Louis	16,294	1,163	4,209	6,382	194
TOTAL	**16,294**	**1,163**	**4,209**	**6,382**	**194**

State Senator District 26

	Democratic	Republican
	Lloyd Klinedinst	Dave Schatz
Franklin	3,662	12,126
St. Louis	4,412	5,517
TOTAL	**8,074**	**17,643**

State Senator District 28

	Republican
	Mike Parson
Benton	2,746
Cedar	2,419
Dallas	3,295
Hickory	1,422
Laclede	5,096
Pettis	5,296
Polk	5,076
St. Clair	1,664
TOTAL	**27,014**

State Senator District 30

	Republican
	Bob Dixon
Greene	11,684
TOTAL	**11,684**

State Senator District 32

	Republican
	Ron Richard
Dade	1,274
Jasper	10,890
Newton	5,621
TOTAL	**17,785**

State Senator District 34

	Democratic	Republican
	Robert Stuber	Rob Schaaf
Buchanan	5,946	5,430
Platte	3,158	7,199
TOTAL	**9,104**	**12,629**

State Representative—Primary Election: August 5, 2014

State Representative District 1

	Democratic	Republican	Republican	Republican	Republican
	Robert Ritterbusch	Stan Sportsman	Roger Parshall	Kathy DeVault	Allen Andrews
Atchison	184	32	401	83	595
Holt	109	75	189	123	751
Nodaway	627	348	515	411	2,202
Worth	105	13	62	25	476
TOTAL	**1,025**	**468**	**1,167**	**642**	**4,024**

State Representative District 2

	Democratic	Republican
	Mike Waltemath	J. Eggleston
Daviess	598	517
DeKalb	475	1,076
Gentry	405	612
Harrison	92	1,701
TOTAL	**1,570**	**3,906**

State Representative District 3

	Republican	Republican
	Nate Walker	John Bailey
Adair	1,639	1,109
Mercer	536	318
Putnam	502	544
Sullivan	579	319
TOTAL	**3,256**	**2,290**

State Representative District 4

	Republican
	Craig Redmon
Adair	513
Clark	977
Knox	255
Lewis	930
Schuyler	332
Scotland	383
TOTAL	**3,390**

State Representative District 5

	Democratic	Republican
	C. LeRoy Deichman	Lindell Shumake
Marion	1,974	1,465
Monroe	181	135
Shelby	788	392
TOTAL	**2,943**	**1,992**

State Representative District 6

	Democratic	Republican
	Robert Harrington	Tim Remole
Linn	171	226
Macon	982	2,057
Randolph	853	1,496
TOTAL	**2,006**	**3,779**

State Representative District 7

	Republican	Republican
	Mike Lair	Dennis McDonald
Grundy	792	1,219
Linn	571	611
Livingston	1,461	812
TOTAL	**2,824**	**2,642**

State Representative District 8

	Democratic	Republican
	Ted Rights	James W. (Jim) Neely
Caldwell	269	1,266
Clay	166	364
Clinton	1,201	2,261
Ray	182	210
TOTAL	**1,818**	**4,101**

State Representative District 9

	Republican
	Delus Johnson
Andrew	2,541
Buchanan	2,071
TOTAL	**4,612**

State Representative District 10

	Democratic
	Pat Conway
Buchanan	2,188
TOTAL	**2,188**

State Representative District 11

	Republican
	Galen Higdon, Jr.
Buchanan	1,963
Platte	612
TOTAL	**2,575**

State Representative District 12

	Democratic	Republican
	Sandy Van Wagner	Kenneth Wilson
Clay	966	2,127
Platte	303	848
TOTAL	**1,269**	**2,975**

State Representative District 13

	Republican
	Nick Marshall
Platte	3,107
TOTAL	**3,107**

State Representative District 14

	Democratic	Republican	Republican
	Stephanie Isaacson	Josh Catton	Kevin Corlew
Clay	40	1	39
Platte	1,426	797	2,103
TOTAL	**1,466**	**798**	**2,142**

State Representative District 15

	Democratic
	Jon Carpenter
Clay	1,618
TOTAL	**1,618**

State Representative District 16

	Republican
	Noel J Shull
Clay	2,562
TOTAL	**2,562**

State Representative District 17

	Democratic	Republican
	Mark Ellebracht	S Nick King
Clay	1,485	2,098
TOTAL	**1,485**	**2,098**

State Representative District 18

	Democratic	Democratic	Republican
	Kevin Garner	Lauren Arthur	Robert (Bob) Rowland
Clay	699	1,936	1,732
TOTAL	**699**	**1,936**	**1,732**

State Representative District 19

	Democratic
	John Joseph Rizzo
Jackson	284
Kansas City	711
TOTAL	**995**

State Representative District 20

	Democratic	Republican	Republican
	John A. Mayfield	Bill E. Kidd	Brent Lasater
Jackson	1,610	1,757	688
TOTAL	**1,610**	**1,757**	**688**

State Representative District 21

	Democratic
	Ira Anders
Jackson	1,440
TOTAL	**1,440**

State Representative District 22

	Democratic	Democratic
	Brandon Ellington	Daniel R. Edwards
Jackson	162	122
Kansas City	2,130	414
TOTAL	**2,292**	**536**

State Representative District 23

	Democratic
	Randy D. Dunn
Kansas City	1,890
TOTAL	**1,890**

State Representative District 24

	Democratic
	Judy Morgan
Kansas City	3,397
TOTAL	**3,397**

State Representative District 25

	Democratic
	Jeremy LaFaver
Kansas City	4,183
TOTAL	**4,183**

State Representative District 26

	Democratic
	Gail McCann Beatty
Kansas City	3,171
TOTAL	**3,171**

State Representative District 27

	Democratic	Democratic
	Bonnaye V. Mims	India Williams
Jackson	56	32
Kansas City	1,377	1,389
TOTAL	**1,433**	**1,421**

State Representative District 28

| | Democratic | Democratic |
	Tom McDonald	Ryan Meyer
Jackson	1,334	357
Kansas City	344	111
TOTAL	1,678	468

State Representative District 29

| | Democratic | Democratic | Republican |
	John B. Sutton	Winston Apple	Noel Torpey
Jackson	837	1,101	1,705
Kansas City	539	254	626
TOTAL	1,376	1,355	2,331

State Representative District 30

| | Republican |
	Mike Cierpiot
Jackson	2,655
Kansas City	113
TOTAL	2,768

State Representative District 31

| | Republican |
	Sheila Solon
Jackson	2,123
TOTAL	2,123

State Representative District 32

| | Democratic | Republican |
	Andrew (Andy) Herman	Jeanie Lauer
Jackson	1,155	2,125
TOTAL	1,155	2,125

State Representative District 33

| | Democratic | Republican | Libertarian |
	Syed Asif	Donna Pfautsch	Matthew (Matt) Stephens
Cass	705	2,040	56
Jackson	385	1,093	32
Lafayette	3	12	7
TOTAL	1,093	3,145	95

State Representative District 34

| | Democratic | Republican | Republican | Republican |
	Dale Mercer	Justin Kalwei	Rebecca Roeber	Robert Thane (Bob) Johnson
Jackson	989	507	2,161	966
TOTAL	989	507	2,161	966

State Representative District 35

| | Democratic | Republican |
	Ken Duvall	Gary Cross
Jackson	1,288	2,444
Kansas City	240	87
TOTAL	1,528	2,531

State Representative District 36

| | Democratic | Republican |
	Kevin McManus	Nola Wood
Kansas City	2,350	1,277
TOTAL	2,350	1,277

State Representative District 37

| | Democratic |
	Joe Runions
Cass	172
Jackson	1,017
Kansas City	417
TOTAL	1,606

State Representative District 38

| | Republican |
	T. J. Berry
Clay	2,720
TOTAL	2,720

State Representative District 39

| | Republican |
	Joe Don McGaugh
Carroll	1,622
Chariton	377
Ray	1,314
TOTAL	3,313

State Representative District 40

| | Democratic | Republican |
	Lowell Jackson	Jim Hansen
Lincoln	36	70
Monroe	829	322
Pike	1,218	1,072
Ralls	1,021	613
TOTAL	3,104	2,077

State Representative District 41

| | Democratic | Republican | Republican |
	Dan Dildine	Alexandra Salsman	Randy Pietzman
Lincoln	2,014	1,952	2,511
TOTAL	2,014	1,952	2,511

State Representative District 42

	Democratic	Republican
	Rod Sturgeon	Bart Korman
Montgomery	499	1,617
St. Charles	79	320
Warren	455	4,124
TOTAL	**1,033**	**6,061**

State Representative District 43

	Democratic	Republican
	Ed Lockwood	Jay Houghton
Audrain	955	1,840
Callaway	422	965
TOTAL	**1,377**	**2,805**

State Representative District 44

	Democratic	Republican
	Thomas (Tom) Pauley	Caleb Rowden
Boone	1,706	2,095
Randolph	39	49
TOTAL	**1,745**	**2,144**

State Representative District 45

	Democratic
	Kip Kendrick
Boone	1,354
TOTAL	**1,354**

State Representative District 46

	Democratic
	Stephen Webber
Boone	3,736
TOTAL	**3,736**

State Representative District 47

	Democratic	Republican	Republican
	John Wright	Charles (Chuck) Basye	Elizabeth (Betsy) Phillips
Boone	1,927	1,331	564
Cooper	23	113	36
Howard	173	122	36
Randolph	258	188	82
TOTAL	**2,381**	**1,754**	**718**

State Representative District 48

	Republican
	Dave Muntzel
Carroll	0
Chariton	98
Cooper	2,414
Howard	393
Pettis	539
Randolph	115
Saline	370
TOTAL	**3,929**

State Representative District 49

	Democratic	Republican
	Gracia Yancey Backer	Travis Fitzwater
Callaway	1,295	2,789
Cole	99	266
TOTAL	**1,394**	**3,055**

State Representative District 50

	Republican
	Caleb Jones
Boone	2,017
Cole	220
Cooper	247
Moniteau	1,257
TOTAL	**3,741**

State Representative District 51

	Democratic	Republican	Libertarian
	Gary Grigsby	Dean A. Dohrman	Bill Wayne
Johnson	438	1,505	32
Pettis	61	604	5
Saline	1,285	1,271	7
TOTAL	**1,784**	**3,380**	**44**

State Representative District 52

	Republican
	Nathan Beard
Johnson	294
Pettis	3,362
TOTAL	**3,656**

State Representative District 53

	Democratic	Republican
	Henry Grubb	Glen Kolkmeyer
Jackson	44	171
Johnson	46	170
Lafayette	2,527	3,378
TOTAL	**2,617**	**3,719**

State Representative District 54

	Republican	Constitution
	Denny Hoskins	Daniel Plemons
Johnson	3,230	31
Pettis	858	0
TOTAL	**4,088**	**31**

State Representative District 55

	Republican
	Rick Brattin
Cass	3,983
TOTAL	**3,983**

State Representative District 56

	Democratic	Republican
	Patty Johnson	Jack Bondon
Bates	24	49
Cass	1,076	2,905
Kansas City	65	72
TOTAL	1,165	3,026

State Representative District 57

	Democratic	Republican	Constitution
	William A. Grimes	Wanda Brown	Butch Page
Bates	22	59	1
Benton	154	1,457	3
Cass	180	517	13
Henry	1,717	1,338	22
TOTAL	2,073	3,371	39

State Representative District 58

	Republican
	David Wood
Miller	775
Moniteau	1,156
Morgan	2,987
TOTAL	4,918

State Representative District 59

	Republican	Constitution
	Mike Bernskoetter	Michael Eberle
Cole	4,987	6
Miller	334	1
TOTAL	5,321	7

State Representative District 60

	Republican
	Jason (Jay) Barnes
Cole	4,356
TOTAL	4,356

State Representative District 61

	Democratic	Republican
	Tom Smith	Justin Alferman
Franklin	957	3,729
Gasconade	156	1,161
Osage	223	871
TOTAL	1,336	5,761

State Representative District 62

	Republican	Republican
	Bruce Sassmann	Tom Hurst
Cole	79	338
Crawford	35	70
Gasconade	630	955
Maries	518	1,092
Miller	112	370
Osage	485	1,352
Phelps	323	386
TOTAL	2,182	4,563

State Representative District 63

	Democratic	Republican
	Bryan Pinette	Bryan Spencer
St. Charles	985	3,053
Warren	239	1,056
TOTAL	1,224	4,109

State Representative District 64

	Democratic	Republican
	Laura K. Castaneda	Robert Cornejo
Lincoln	562	1,009
St. Charles	795	2,374
TOTAL	1,357	3,383

State Representative District 65

	Republican
	Anne Zerr
St. Charles	3,651
TOTAL	3,651

State Representative District 66

	Democratic	Republican
	Tommie Pierson	John Saxton
St. Louis	2,499	279
St. Louis City	249	7
TOTAL	2,748	286

State Representative District 67

	Democratic	Democratic	Democratic	Democratic	Republican	Libertarian
	Alan Green	Sylvester Taylor, II	Larry Davis Jr.	Tony Weaver	Dwayne A. Strickland	Jeff Coleman
St. Louis	3,031	1,830	512	1,141	618	18
TOTAL	3,031	1,830	512	1,141	618	18

State Representative District 68

	Democratic	Republican
	Keith English	Rekha (Becky) Sharma
St. Louis	4,130	1,045
TOTAL	**4,130**	**1,045**

State Representative District 69

	Democratic	Republican
	Margo McNeil	John Vahey
St. Louis	3,860	1,254
TOTAL	**3,860**	**1,254**

State Representative District 70

	Democratic	Republican
	Bill Otto	Joe Corica
St. Charles	254	729
St. Louis	2,415	1,345
TOTAL	**2,669**	**2,074**

State Representative District 71

	Democratic	Republican
	Sue Meredith	Jim Cain
St. Louis	3,001	1,626
TOTAL	**3,001**	**1,626**

State Representative District 72

	Democratic	Republican
	Mary Nichols	Paul Berry
St. Louis	2,918	1,315
TOTAL	**2,918**	**1,315**

State Representative District 73

	Democratic
	Courtney Allen Curtis
St. Louis	2,291
TOTAL	**2,291**

State Representative District 74

	Democratic	Democratic
	Sharon L. Pace	Don Houston
St. Louis	2,781	762
TOTAL	**2,781**	**762**

State Representative District 75

	Democratic
	Rochelle Walton Gray
St. Louis	3,432
TOTAL	**3,432**

State Representative District 76

	Democratic	Democratic
	Chris Carter	Joshua Peters
St. Louis City	1,823	2,210
TOTAL	**1,823**	**2,210**

State Representative District 77

	Democratic	Democratic
	Bill Haas	Kimberly M. Gardner
St. Louis City	754	2,437
TOTAL	**754**	**2,437**

State Representative District 78

	Democratic	Democratic	Republican
	Penny V. Hubbard	Natalie A. Vowell	John Hubb
St. Louis City	1,699	671	132
TOTAL	**1,699**	**671**	**132**

State Representative District 79

	Democratic	Republican
	Michael Butler	Robert Vroman
St. Louis City	2,578	150
TOTAL	**2,578**	**150**

State Representative District 80

	Democratic	Republican
	Mike Colona	Michael Huett
St. Louis City	3,155	300
TOTAL	**3,155**	**300**

State Representative District 81

	Democratic	Libertarian
	Jacob W. Hummel	Lisa F. Schaper
St. Louis City	2,195	23
TOTAL	**2,195**	**23**

State Representative District 82

	Democratic	Republican
	Michele Kratky	Jake Koehr
St. Louis City	3,675	889
TOTAL	**3,675**	**889**

State Representative District 83

	Democratic	Republican	Libertarian
	Gina Mitten	Jeremy Buckingham	Andrew Bolin
St. Louis	2,745	721	30
St. Louis City	959	224	14
TOTAL	**3,704**	**945**	**44**

State Representative District 84

	Democratic
	Karla May
St. Louis City	3,208
TOTAL	**3,208**

State Representative District 85

	Democratic
	Clem Smith
St. Louis	3,401
TOTAL	**3,401**

State Representative District 86

	Democratic	Democratic	Democratic	Democratic
	Fareedah S. Sidqui	Joe Adams	Dawn Price	Mary Ann Merz
St. Louis	349	2,392	480	1,728
TOTAL	**349**	**2,392**	**480**	**1,728**

State Representative District 87

	Democratic
	Stacey Newman
St. Louis	4,062
TOTAL	**4,062**

State Representative District 88

	Democratic	Republican
	Tracy McCreery	Raymond Chandler
St. Louis	3,431	2,005
TOTAL	**3,431**	**2,005**

State Representative District 89

	Democratic	Republican
	Al Gerber	John J. Diehl, Jr.
St. Louis	2,929	3,446
TOTAL	**2,929**	**3,446**

State Representative District 90

	Democratic	Republican
	Deb Lavender	Gina Jaksetic
St. Louis	4,943	2,815
TOTAL	**4,943**	**2,815**

State Representative District 91

	Democratic	Republican
	Jeanne Kirkton	Michael Peters
St. Louis	5,079	1,963
St. Louis City	104	25
TOTAL	**5,183**	**1,988**

State Representative District 92

	Democratic	Republican
	Genise Montecillo	Al Faulstich
St. Louis	3,901	1,452
TOTAL	**3,901**	**1,452**

State Representative District 93

	Democratic	Republican
	Bob Burns	Garrett Mees
St. Louis	2,546	799
St. Louis City	425	132
TOTAL	**2,971**	**931**

State Representative District 94

	Democratic	Republican
	Vicki Lorenz Englund	Cloria Brown
St. Louis	3,553	1,692
TOTAL	**3,553**	**1,692**

State Representative District 95

	Republican
	Marsha Haefner
St. Louis	2,219
TOTAL	**2,219**

State Representative District 96

	Republican	Constitution
	Mike Leara	Cynthia (Cindy) Redburn
St. Louis	2,698	11
TOTAL	**2,698**	**11**

State Representative District 97

	Democratic	Republican
	Tom Dohack	John McCaherty
Jefferson	1,333	1,646
St. Louis	358	174
TOTAL	**1,691**	**1,820**

State Representative District 98

	Republican	Republican	Republican
	Carol Veillette	Shamed Dogan	Rea Scharnhorst
St. Louis	942	1,690	716
TOTAL	**942**	**1,690**	**716**

State Representative District 99

	Democratic	Republican
	William H. (Bill) Pinkston	Andrew Koenig
St. Louis	2,478	2,198
TOTAL	**2,478**	**2,198**

State Representative District 100

	Republican
	Sue Allen
St. Louis	3,129
TOTAL	**3,129**

State Representative District 101

	Democratic	Republican
	Candace Farmer	Don Gosen
St. Louis	1,839	2,832
TOTAL	**1,839**	**2,832**

State Representative District 102

	Democratic	Republican	Republican
	John Callahan	Kurt Bahr	Michael Swyers
St. Charles	943	2,755	1,408
TOTAL	**943**	**2,755**	**1,408**

State Representative District 103

	Republican	Republican	Republican	Libertarian
	Kyle Schlereth	Alexander McArthy	John D. Wiemann	Dean (Draig) Hodge
St. Charles	872	1,362	2,158	27
TOTAL	**872**	**1,362**	**2,158**	**27**

State Representative District 104

	Democratic	Republican
	Terry Lesinski	Kathie Conway
St. Charles	1,182	2,665
TOTAL	**1,182**	**2,665**

State Representative District 105

	Democratic	Republican
	Matt Judkins	Mark Parkinson
St. Charles	1,339	3,360
TOTAL	**1,339**	**3,360**

State Representative District 106

	Democratic	Republican	Republican
	Ken Tucker	Chrissy Sommer	Erin Schulte
St. Charles	1,259	2,693	712
TOTAL	**1,259**	**2,693**	**712**

State Representative District 107

	Republican
	Ron Hicks
St. Charles	3,081
TOTAL	**3,081**

State Representative District 108

	Democratic	Republican	Republican	Republican
	Marlon Williams	John J. Haman, Jr.	Nina Dean	Justin S. Hill
St. Charles	982	469	1,374	2,622
TOTAL	**982**	**469**	**1,374**	**2,622**

State Representative District 109

	Democratic	Republican
	Barbara (Bobbie) Bollmann	Paul Curtman
Franklin	1,216	4,775
TOTAL	**1,216**	**4,775**

State Representative District 110

	Republican
	Kirk Mathews
Franklin	481
St. Louis	1,889
TOTAL	**2,370**

State Representative District 111

	Democratic	Republican	Republican
	Michael Frame	Shane Roden	Jason Jarvis
Jefferson	2,004	1,505	1,070
TOTAL	**2,004**	**1,505**	**1,070**

State Representative District 112

	Democratic	Democratic	Republican	Republican	Republican
	Larry D. Steinkamp	Robert W Butler	Rob Vescovo	Charles Groeteke	Avery Fortenberry
Jefferson	687	1,182	1,159	1,151	213
TOTAL	**687**	**1,182**	**1,159**	**1,151**	**213**

State Representative District 113

	Democratic	Republican	Republican	Constitution
	Sean Fauss	Jason Fulbright	Dan Shaul	Donna Ivanovich
Jefferson	1,558	910	1,212	25
TOTAL	**1,558**	**910**	**1,212**	**25**

State Representative District 114

	Democratic	Republican
	T.J. McKenna	Becky Ruth
Jefferson	2,260	2,007
TOTAL	**2,260**	**2,007**

State Representative District 117

	Democratic
	Linda Black
St. Francois	1,220
TOTAL	**1,220**

State Representative District 115

	Democratic	Republican	Constitution
	Dan Darian	Elaine Freeman Gannon	Jerry Dollar Jr.
Jefferson	1,274	1,303	10
St. Francois	390	433	5
Ste. Genevieve	146	86	
TOTAL	**1,810**	**1,822**	**15**

State Representative District 118

	Democratic	Republican
	Ben Harris	Michael P. McGirl
Jefferson	1,790	1,292
Washington	822	571
TOTAL	**2,612**	**1,863**

State Representative District 116

	Republican
	Kevin Engler
Perry	1,150
St. Francois	951
Ste. Genevieve	481
TOTAL	**2,582**

State Representative District 119

	Democratic	Republican
	Susan J. Cunningham	Dave Hinson
Franklin	1,285	2,942
Washington	59	86
TOTAL	**1,344**	**3,028**

State Representative District 120

	Democratic	Democratic	Republican	Republican
	Robert Mesger	Zechariah (Zech) Hockersmith	Jason Chipman	Shawn Sisco
Crawford	284	265	1,568	1,135
Phelps	194	282	834	1,128
TOTAL	**478**	**547**	**2,402**	**2,263**

State Representative District 121

	Republican
	Keith Frederick
Phelps	2,207
Pulaski	1,261
TOTAL	**3,468**

State Representative District 123

	Republican
	Diane Franklin
Camden	3,452
Laclede	2,339
TOTAL	**5,791**

State Representative District 122

	Republican
	Steve Lynch
Pulaski	1,904
TOTAL	**1,904**

State Representative District 124

	Republican
	Rocky Miller
Camden	3,128
Miller	2,284
TOTAL	**5,412**

State Representative District 125

	Republican	Republican
	Ethan Newman	Warren D. Love
Benton	736	952
Cedar	327	802
Hickory	491	1,123
St. Clair	663	1,300
TOTAL	**2,217**	**4,177**

State Representative District 126

	Democratic	Republican	Republican	Constitution
	Sam Foursha	Bill Yarberry	Randy Pike	William M. Gilmore
Bates	742	390	1,349	22
Vernon	1,356	395	1,185	2
TOTAL	**2,098**	**785**	**2,534**	**24**

State Representative District 127

	Republican
	Mike Kelley
Barton	1,506
Cedar	257
Dade	1,406
Jasper	2,134
Polk	0
TOTAL	**5,303**

State Representative District 128

	Republican
	Sue Entlicher
Cedar	1,089
Polk	5,075
TOTAL	**6,164**

State Representative District 129

	Democratic	Republican
	John L. Wilson	Sandy Crawford
Dallas	201	3,485
Laclede	284	2,977
TOTAL	**485**	**6,462**

State Representative District 130

	Republican	Republican
	Jeff Messenger	Loren Hunt
Greene	2,273	2,126
TOTAL	**2,273**	**2,126**

State Representative District 131

	Democratic	Republican
	Marlee Yant	Sonya Murray Anderson
Greene	970	2,921
TOTAL	**970**	**2,921**

State Representative District 132

	Democratic	Republican	Republican
	Charlie Norr	Fred Ellison	Shar Lawless
Greene	776	679	297
TOTAL	**776**	**679**	**297**

State Representative District 133

	Republican
	Eric W. Burlison
Greene	2,904
TOTAL	**2,904**

State Representative District 134

	Democratic	Republican
	Kevin Knox	Elijah Haahr
Greene	1,146	2,781
TOTAL	**1,146**	**2,781**

State Representative District 135

	Democratic	Republican
	Angie Filbeck	Lincoln Hough
Greene	1,453	2,586
TOTAL	**1,453**	**2,586**

State Representative District 136

	Republican
	Kevin Austin
Greene	4,700
TOTAL	**4,700**

State Representative District 137

	Democratic	Republican	Libertarian
	Sandy Grogan	Lyndall Fraker	Bill Boone
Greene	626	2,345	30
Webster	526	3,013	17
TOTAL	**1,152**	**5,358**	**47**

State Representative District 138

	Republican
	Don Phillips
Christian	520
Stone	4,754
Taney	1666
TOTAL	**5,440**

State Representative District 139

	Republican	Republican	Republican
	Clayton Jones	Michael Hope	Jered Taylor
Christian	1,371	1,195	2,234
TOTAL	**1,371**	**1,195**	**2,234**

State Representative District 140

	Democratic	Republican
	Jim Billedo	Lynn Morris
Christian	515	4,485
TOTAL	**515**	**4,485**

State Representative District 141

	Republican
	Tony Dugger
Webster	2,366
Wright	2,939
TOTAL	**5,305**

State Representative District 142

	Republican
	Robert Ross
Howell	278
Phelps	239
Pulaski	212
Texas	3,303
TOTAL	**4,032**

State Representative District 143

	Republican
	Jeff Pogue
Dent	1,475
Oregon	460
Reynolds	300
Shannon	502
TOTAL	**2,467**

State Representative District 144

	Republican	Republican
	Paul Fitzwater	Ron Bohn
Iron	393	113
Reynolds	228	36
Washington	706	164
Wayne	569	193
TOTAL	**1,896**	**506**

State Representative District 145

	Democratic	Republican
	Charles Elrod	Shelley (White) Keeney
Bollinger	143	2,169
Madison	395	1,127
Perry	72	2,270
TOTAL	**610**	**5,566**

State Representative District 146

	Republican
	Donna Lichtenegger
Cape Girardeau	6,342
TOTAL	**6,342**

State Representative District 147

	Democratic	Democratic	Republican	Libertarian
	Gary L. Gaines	Blake Hopper	Kathy Swan	Greg Tlapek
Cape Girardeau	375	257	4,569	52
TOTAL	**375**	**257**	**4,569**	**52**

State Representative District 148

	Republican	Republican
	Duston Y. Stone	Holly Rehder
Mississippi	76	295
Scott	1,229	2,031
TOTAL	**1,305**	**2,326**

State Representative District 149

	Democratic	Democratic	Republican	Republican
	Bill Burlison	Diedra Ashley Freeman	Don Rone	Neal E. Boyd
Mississippi	454	289	61	19
New Madrid	1,040	1,149	772	172
Pemiscot	396	189	100	16
Scott	153	74	130	137
TOTAL	**2,043**	**1,701**	**1,063**	**344**

State Representative District 150

	Democratic	Republican
	Walter Dearing	Andrew McDaniel
Dunklin	2,080	289
Pemiscot	833	63
TOTAL	**2,913**	**352**

State Representative District 151

	Democratic	Republican	Republican
	Ryan Wm. Holder	Tila Rowland Hubrecht	Brandon A. Cooper
Scott	370	274	84
Stoddard	785	2,685	855
TOTAL	**1,155**	**2,959**	**939**

State Representative District 152

	Republican
	Todd Richardson
Butler	3,252
Dunklin	260
TOTAL	**3,512**

State Representative District 153

	Republican	Libertarian
	Steve Cookson	Ginny Keirns
Butler	1,801	1
Carter	955	1
Ripley	1,052	7
Wayne	182	1
TOTAL	**3,990**	**10**

State Representative District 154

	Republican
	Shawn Rhoads
Howell	3,128
TOTAL	**3,128**

State Representative District 155

	Republican	Republican	Republican
	Lyle Rowland	Mike Lind	Jason Frodge
Douglas	1,836	329	1,157
Ozark	1,115	252	864
Taney	1,960	228	826
TOTAL	**4,911**	**809**	**2,847**

State Representative District 156

	Republican	Republican
	Ron Herschend	Jeff Justus
Taney	1,278	3,337
TOTAL	**1,278**	**3,337**

State Representative District 157

	Democratic	Republican	Republican
	Vince Jennings	Julie Ruzicka	Mike Moon
Lawrence	576	2,696	3,308
TOTAL	**576**	**2,696**	**3,308**

State Representative District 158

	Republican
	Scott Fitzpatrick
Barry	4,651
Lawrence	155
Stone	42
TOTAL	**4,848**

State Representative District 159

	Republican
	Bill Lant
McDonald	2,068
Newton	1,160
TOTAL	**3,228**

State Representative District 160

	Republican
	Bill Reiboldt
Newton	3,955
TOTAL	**3,955**

State Representative District 161

	Democratic	Republican
	Charles (Hugh) Shields	William (Bill) White
Jasper	382	1,787
Newton	183	816
TOTAL	**565**	**2,603**

State Representative District 162

	Republican
	Charlie Davis
Jasper	3,145
Newton	4
TOTAL	**3,149**

State Representative District 163

	Democratic	Republican
	Michael Jarrett	Tom Flanigan
Jasper	311	3,892
TOTAL	**311**	**3,892**

Circuit Judges (Partisan)—Primary Election: August 5, 2014

Circuit 11–Division 1

	Democratic
	Ted House
St. Charles	11,833
TOTAL	**11,833**

Circuit 13–Division 4

	Republican
	Jodie C. Asel
Boone	8,004
Callaway	3,542
TOTAL	**11,546**

Circuit 19–Division 2

	Republican
	Daniel Green
Cole	9,449
TOTAL	**9,449**

Circuit 19–Division 4

	Democratic	Republican
	Pat Joyce	Brian Stumpe
Cole	3,000	9,480
TOTAL	**3,000**	**9,480**

Circuit 23–Division 2

	Republican
	Darrell Missey
Jefferson	12,274
TOTAL	**12,274**

Circuit 25–Division 2

	Republican
	John Beger
Maries	1,177
Phelps	4,980
Pulaski	2,998
Texas	2,944
TOTAL	**12,099**

Circuit 32–Division 1

	Republican	Republican	Republican
	Allen Moss	Michael Gardner	Trae Bertrand
Bollinger	866	1,040	659
Cape Girardeau	4,001	4,476	5,089
Perry	1,316	1,842	1,540
TOTAL	**6,183**	**7,358**	**7,288**

Circuit 36

	Republican
	Michael Pritchett
Butler	4,845
Ripley	978
TOTAL	**5,823**

Circuit 42–Division 2

	Democratic
	Kelly Parker
Crawford	484
Dent	619
Iron	1,393
Reynolds	1,146
Wayne	983
TOTAL	**4,625**

Constitutional Amendment 1—Primary Election: August 5, 2014

	YES	NO		YES	NO
Adair	2,204	1,820	Maries	1,653	581
Andrew	2,307	1,486	Marion	2,797	2,005
Atchison	1,039	473	McDonald	2,082	651
Audrain	2,496	1,526	Mercer	860	132
Barry	4,154	2,083	Miller	3,471	1,460
Barton	1,557	525	Mississippi	1,888	685
Bates	2,331	871	Moniteau	2,471	868
Benton	2,818	1,452	Monroe	1,302	813
Bollinger	2,212	660	Montgomery	1,879	704
Boone	8,960	18,471	Morgan	2,913	1,514
Buchanan	7,240	6,892	New Madrid	1,923	1,293
Butler	3,962	2,840	Newton	5,860	3,032
Caldwell	1,407	536	Nodaway	2,704	1,662
Callaway	3,548	3,601	Oregon	990	795
Camden	5,255	4,047	Osage	2,878	825
Cape Girardeau	10,340	5,190	Ozark	1,346	1,187
Carroll	1,779	390	Pemiscot	1,321	808
Carter	931	846	Perry	3,783	1,274
Cass	9,603	7,891	Pettis	4,970	2,546
Cedar	2,155	1,078	Phelps	4,778	2,830
Chariton	1,744	680	Pike	1,997	1,058
Christian	5,798	7,456	Platte	6,344	7,218
Clark	1,169	424	Polk	4,754	1,614
Clay	13,408	16,435	Pulaski	3,261	1,617
Clinton	2,501	1,840	Putnam	990	195
Cole	8,978	7,294	Ralls	1,251	895
Cooper	2,585	1,207	Randolph	2,386	1,590
Crawford	2,339	1,486	Ray	2,848	1,660
Dade	1,251	688	Reynolds	1,132	689
Dallas	3,200	1,050	Ripley	1,161	543
Daviess	1,207	394	Saline	3,061	1,227
DeKalb	1,547	506	Schuyler	500	344
Dent	1,721	838	Scotland	435	550
Douglas	2,005	1,716	Scott	4,313	2,061
Dunklin	2,535	1,648	Shannon	700	644
Franklin	11,898	8,588	Shelby	1,237	451
Gasconade	2,585	1,075	St. Charles	29,037	32,082
Gentry	955	349	St. Clair	1,957	690
Greene	14,640	24,622	St. Francois	3,651	2,794
Grundy	1,714	437	St. Louis	65,700	122,317
Harrison	1,808	487	St. Louis City	9,082	25,179
Henry	2,769	1,548	Ste. Genevieve	2,401	1,395
Hickory	1,577	656	Stoddard	2,955	1,907
Holt	942	343	Stone	3,157	3,179
Howard	1,228	972	Sullivan	905	249
Howell	2,887	2,574	Taney	4,374	4,295
Iron	1,173	1,084	Texas	3,105	1,797
Jackson	22,137	28,042	Vernon	2,554	811
Jasper	8,936	5,721	Warren	4,574	2,732
Jefferson	14,383	17,570	Washington	2,068	1,114
Johnson	4,803	3,661	Wayne	1,347	1,124
Kansas City	14,500	23,271	Webster	4,578	3,286
Knox	775	439	Worth	406	309
Laclede	5,015	2,103	Wright	2,852	1,088
Lafayette	4,954	2,261	**TOTAL**	**499,581**	**497,091**
Lawrence	4,688	2,699			
Lewis	1,185	609			
Lincoln	6,072	3,280			
Linn	1,486	970			
Livingston	1,702	1,053			
Macon	2,323	1,304			
Madison	1,218	664			

For official ballot title, see page 652

Constitutional Amendment 5—Primary Election: August 5, 2014

	YES	NO		YES	NO
Adair	2,630	1,458	Maries	1,725	457
Andrew	2,741	1,033	Marion	3,531	1,202
Atchison	1,147	319	McDonald	2,260	422
Audrain	2,858	1,108	Mercer	794	148
Barry	4,882	1,295	Miller	3,726	1,099
Barton	1,664	390	Mississippi	1,873	614
Bates	2,450	669	Moniteau	2,497	702
Benton	3,329	902	Monroe	1,536	526
Bollinger	2,239	543	Montgomery	1,960	582
Boone	12,750	14,553	Morgan	3,372	973
Buchanan	8,768	5,360	New Madrid	2,322	850
Butler	5,265	1,421	Newton	6,780	2,101
Caldwell	1,501	415	Nodaway	2,959	1,358
Callaway	4,766	2,306	Oregon	1,281	486
Camden	6,711	2,546	Osage	2,811	809
Cape Girardeau	11,212	4,122	Ozark	1,847	630
Carroll	1,761	357	Pemiscot	1,637	473
Carter	1,159	578	Perry	3,598	1,205
Cass	12,239	5,178	Pettis	5,656	1,768
Cedar	2,537	633	Phelps	5,450	2,110
Chariton	1,802	570	Pike	2,218	779
Christian	9,253	3,889	Platte	7,907	5,634
Clark	1,286	280	Polk	5,045	1,192
Clay	17,500	12,269	Pulaski	3,902	897
Clinton	3,040	1,285	Putnam	1,007	151
Cole	10,016	6,094	Ralls	1,651	468
Cooper	2,745	982	Randolph	2,928	1,026
Crawford	2,880	869	Ray	3,287	1,165
Dade	1,499	401	Reynolds	1,338	469
Dallas	3,417	751	Ripley	1,351	336
Daviess	1,248	337	Saline	3,078	1,105
DeKalb	1,630	405	Schuyler	616	216
Dent	1,935	598	Scotland	711	250
Douglas	2,735	926	Scott	4,830	1,469
Dunklin	3,084	1,040	Shannon	977	358
Franklin	13,868	6,440	Shelby	1,273	360
Gasconade	2,704	848	St. Charles	36,951	23,813
Gentry	942	345	St. Clair	2,103	497
Greene	24,338	14,711	St. Francois	4,528	1,856
Grundy	1,678	434	St. Louis	77,211	110,295
Harrison	1,834	403	St. Louis City	10,028	24,296
Henry	3,097	1,135	Ste. Genevieve	2,462	1,209
Hickory	1,762	448	Stoddard	3,667	1,147
Holt	1,053	214	Stone	4,848	1,451
Howard	1,429	752	Sullivan	894	232
Howell	3,894	1,503	Taney	6,492	2,119
Iron	1,483	727	Texas	3,893	968
Jackson	30,643	19,331	Vernon	2,585	746
Jasper	10,954	3,716	Warren	5,142	2,083
Jefferson	20,175	11,566	Washington	2,498	659
Johnson	5,840	2,609	Wayne	1,818	660
Kansas City	12,360	25,546	Webster	5,861	1,929
Knox	896	264	Worth	487	205
Laclede	5,790	1,239	Wright	3,227	631
Lafayette	5,256	1,894	**TOTAL**	**602,863**	**386,308**
Lawrence	5,728	1,584			
Lewis	1,372	370			
Lincoln	6,764	2,510			
Linn	1,806	624			
Livingston	1,981	713			
Macon	2,721	849			
Madison	1,387	465			

For official ballot title, see page 652

Constitutional Amendment 7—Primary Election: August 5, 2014

	YES	NO		YES	NO
Adair	1,866	2,270	Maries	982	1,238
Andrew	1,503	2,250	Marion	2,548	2,284
Atchison	822	659	McDonald	1,215	1,471
Audrain	1,793	2,215	Mercer	481	485
Barry	2,581	3,636	Miller	2,215	2,645
Barton	850	1,206	Mississippi	1,221	1,340
Bates	1,624	1,558	Moniteau	1,596	1,714
Benton	2,008	2,259	Monroe	1,065	1,047
Bollinger	1,035	1,815	Montgomery	1,402	1,159
Boone	12,375	15,135	Morgan	2,135	2,274
Buchanan	6,207	8,128	New Madrid	1,424	1,794
Butler	2,814	3,987	Newton	4,125	4,771
Caldwell	865	1,075	Nodaway	1,913	2,451
Callaway	3,425	3,735	Oregon	547	1,239
Camden	3,995	5,288	Osage	1,754	1,910
Cape Girardeau	5,873	9,600	Ozark	759	1,742
Carroll	1,187	968	Pemiscot	1,231	945
Carter	584	1,168	Perry	2,024	2,956
Cass	7,314	10,238	Pettis	3,822	3,633
Cedar	1,501	1,708	Phelps	3,058	4,567
Chariton	1,216	1,151	Pike	1,556	1,460
Christian	5,015	8,207	Platte	5,317	8,317
Clark	922	643	Polk	2,791	3,549
Clay	12,310	17,657	Pulaski	2,217	2,599
Clinton	1,841	2,492	Putnam	560	572
Cole	7,695	8,683	Ralls	1,018	1,133
Cooper	2,029	1,756	Randolph	1,799	2,185
Crawford	1,282	2,521	Ray	2,036	2,408
Dade	799	1,130	Reynolds	661	1,123
Dallas	1,821	2,371	Ripley	762	923
Daviess	703	885	Saline	2,380	1,824
DeKalb	903	1,147	Schuyler	365	474
Dent	881	1,669	Scotland	470	511
Douglas	1,292	2,359	Scott	2,604	3,777
Dunklin	2,385	1,831	Shannon	499	853
Franklin	7,887	12,739	Shelby	777	859
Gasconade	1,623	2,004	St. Charles	23,104	38,463
Gentry	593	716	St. Clair	1,288	1,344
Greene	17,208	22,249	St. Francois	2,730	3,737
Grundy	1,073	1,070	St. Louis	62,901	127,190
Harrison	1,258	1,026	St. Louis City	11,128	23,599
Henry	2,010	2,305	Ste. Genevieve	1,634	2,178
Hickory	891	1,336	Stoddard	2,141	2,656
Holt	594	673	Stone	2,893	3,410
Howard	945	1,254	Sullivan	522	659
Howell	1,713	3,709	Taney	3,864	4,799
Iron	802	1,409	Texas	1,717	3,191
Jackson	20,810	29,725	Vernon	1,617	1,719
Jasper	6,417	8,320	Warren	3,072	4,284
Jefferson	12,128	19,953	Washington	1,282	1,925
Johnson	4,223	4,279	Wayne	1,008	1,507
Kansas City	19,256	18,997	Webster	3,398	4,490
Knox	659	531	Worth	282	371
Laclede	3,009	4,063	Wright	1,537	2,388
Lafayette	3,426	3,826	**TOTAL**	**408,288**	**591,932**
Lawrence	3,251	4,146			
Lewis	875	882			
Lincoln	3,808	5,597			
Linn	1,257	1,184			
Livingston	1,404	1,328			
Macon	1,658	1,941			
Madison	747	1,128			

For official ballot title, see page 652

Constitutional Amendment 8—Primary Election: August 5, 2014

	YES	NO		YES	NO
Adair	2,008	2,053	Maries	1,106	1,063
Andrew	1,670	2,052	Marion	2,346	2,328
Atchison	805	646	McDonald	1,423	1,232
Audrain	1,979	1,973	Mercer	514	353
Barry	2,938	3,192	Miller	2,531	2,234
Barton	852	1,189	Mississippi	1,388	1,064
Bates	1,554	1,542	Moniteau	1,547	1,629
Benton	2,194	1,983	Monroe	1,087	914
Bollinger	1,321	1,447	Montgomery	1,418	1,099
Boone	9,585	17,540	Morgan	2,410	1,891
Buchanan	6,939	7,053	New Madrid	1,660	1,433
Butler	3,499	3,096	Newton	4,287	4,533
Caldwell	894	1,000	Nodaway	1,842	2,458
Callaway	3,463	3,576	Oregon	697	1,063
Camden	4,545	4,643	Osage	1,908	1,693
Cape Girardeau	7,407	7,822	Ozark	1,111	1,334
Carroll	1,131	964	Pemiscot	1,377	720
Carter	723	993	Perry	2,643	2,184
Cass	8,290	9,056	Pettis	3,987	3,394
Cedar	1,554	1,595	Phelps	3,580	3,949
Chariton	1,206	1,114	Pike	1,539	1,372
Christian	5,411	7,666	Platte	5,965	7,546
Clark	914	601	Polk	2,852	3,351
Clay	13,444	16,218	Pulaski	2,598	2,169
Clinton	2,046	2,121	Putnam	613	501
Cole	7,501	8,605	Ralls	1,001	1,058
Cooper	2,062	1,647	Randolph	1,979	1,891
Crawford	1,775	1,956	Ray	2,263	2,113
Dade	890	979	Reynolds	869	882
Dallas	2,174	1,930	Ripley	842	799
Daviess	767	802	Saline	2,205	1,919
DeKalb	999	1,032	Schuyler	436	344
Dent	1,000	1,511	Scotland	497	463
Douglas	1,554	2,042	Scott	3,104	3,134
Dunklin	2,162	1,952	Shannon	516	815
Franklin	9,645	10,666	Shelby	726	852
Gasconade	1,710	1,821	St. Charles	27,091	33,100
Gentry	600	685	St. Clair	1,258	1,324
Greene	15,480	23,498	St. Francois	3,123	3,213
Grundy	1,030	1,027	St. Louis	70,588	114,683
Harrison	1,044	1,187	St. Louis City	12,640	21,682
Henry	1,988	2,000	Ste. Genevieve	1,958	1,613
Hickory	1,096	1,094	Stoddard	2,192	2,523
Holt	582	667	Stone	3,035	3,200
Howard	1,021	1,143	Sullivan	546	561
Howell	2,005	3,359	Taney	3,838	4,715
Iron	949	1,217	Texas	2,155	2,709
Jackson	23,014	26,802	Vernon	1,741	1,574
Jasper	7,117	7,503	Warren	3,695	3,508
Jefferson	14,840	16,805	Washington	1,649	1,486
Johnson	4,054	4,344	Wayne	1,092	1,369
Kansas City	17,543	20,222	Webster	3,454	4,319
Knox	567	579	Worth	272	342
Laclede	3,194	3,784	Wright	1,806	2,016
Lafayette	3,717	3,411	**TOTAL**	**441,520**	**539,519**
Lawrence	3,406	3,835			
Lewis	937	778			
Lincoln	4,615	4,440			
Linn	1,111	1,299			
Livingston	1,324	1,344			
Macon	1,817	1,725			
Madison	858	979			

For official ballot title, see page 652

Constitutional Amendment 9—Primary Election: August 5, 2014

	YES	NO		YES	NO
Adair	3,116	927	Maries	1,706	461
Andrew	2,866	838	Marion	3,826	779
Atchison	1,187	256	McDonald	2,229	406
Audrain	2,770	793	Mercer	753	116
Barry	4,989	1,129	Miller	3,755	977
Barton	1,683	317	Mississippi	1,874	586
Bates	2,538	524	Moniteau	2,481	676
Benton	3,393	775	Monroe	1,557	440
Bollinger	2,158	606	Montgomery	1,980	532
Boone	18,718	8,386	Morgan	3,519	762
Buchanan	10,848	3,143	New Madrid	2,354	736
Butler	5,338	1,266	Newton	7,373	1,438
Caldwell	1,529	354	Nodaway	3,175	1,113
Callaway	5,343	1,681	Oregon	1,242	445
Camden	7,345	1,864	Osage	2,811	751
Cape Girardeau	12,291	2,929	Ozark	1,900	541
Carroll	1,744	352	Pemiscot	1,614	468
Carter	1,110	608	Perry	3,753	1,014
Cass	14,311	3,069	Pettis	6,047	1,315
Cedar	2,549	586	Phelps	5,942	1,585
Chariton	1,802	489	Pike	2,287	615
Christian	10,422	2,684	Platte	10,668	2,865
Clark	1,218	284	Polk	5,166	1,021
Clay	23,018	6,699	Pulaski	3,960	794
Clinton	3,260	907	Putnam	928	182
Cole	11,793	4,219	Ralls	1,687	335
Cooper	3,009	701	Randolph	3,050	715
Crawford	2,911	814	Ray	3,493	886
Dade	1,494	378	Reynolds	1,249	483
Dallas	3,425	657	Ripley	1,308	341
Daviess	1,224	231	Saline	3,329	768
DeKalb	1,652	330	Schuyler	587	190
Dent	1,892	520	Scotland	715	211
Douglas	2,789	800	Scott	4,968	1,138
Dunklin	3,106	760	Shannon	965	326
Franklin	15,828	4,456	Shelby	1,222	350
Gasconade	2,693	804	St. Charles	45,163	14,980
Gentry	929	302	St. Clair	2,092	493
Greene	30,978	8,021	St. Francois	4,897	1,356
Grundy	1,662	406	St. Louis	115,999	68,735
Harrison	1,788	430	St. Louis City	21,377	12,951
Henry	3,172	830	Ste. Genevieve	2,617	883
Hickory	1,721	467	Stoddard	3,758	959
Holt	1,027	218	Stone	5,100	1,119
Howard	1,536	590	Sullivan	852	247
Howell	3,986	1,351	Taney	6,962	1,582
Iron	1,522	634	Texas	3,865	983
Jackson	38,610	10,101	Vernon	2,677	636
Jasper	11,930	2,659	Warren	5,591	1,591
Jefferson	23,668	7,980	Washington	2,474	652
Johnson	6,759	1,630	Wayne	1,788	637
Kansas City	27,438	10,056	Webster	6,152	1,521
Knox	883	231	Worth	542	143
Laclede	5,761	1,184	Wright	3,121	703
Lafayette	5,858	1,261	**TOTAL**	**729,750**	**246,515**
Lawrence	6,064	1,168			
Lewis	1,387	322			
Lincoln	7,144	1,884			
Linn	1,836	459			
Livingston	2,034	638			
Macon	2,818	655			
Madison	1,377	370			

For official ballot title, see page 652

CONSTITUTIONAL AMENDMENT NO. 1
Proposed by the 97th General Assembly
(First Regular Session)
CCS No. 2 SS HCS HJR Nos. 11 & 7

Shall the Missouri Constitution be amended to ensure that the right of Missouri citizens to engage in agricultural production and ranching practices shall not be infringed?

The potential costs or savings to governmental entities are unknown, but likely limited unless the resolution leads to increased litigation costs and/or the loss of federal funding.

CONSTITUTIONAL AMENDMENT NO. 5
Proposed by the 97th General Assembly
(Second Regular Session)
SCS SJR No. 36

Shall the Missouri Constitution be amended to include a declaration that the right to keep and bear arms is a unalienable right and that the state government is obligated to uphold that right?

State and local governmental entities should have no direct costs or savings from this proposal. However, the proposal's passage will likely lead to increased litigation and criminal justice related costs. The total potential costs are unknown, but could be significant.

CONSTITUTIONAL AMENDMENT NO. 7
Proposed by the 97th General Assembly
(Second Regular Session)
SS HJR No. 68

Should the Missouri Constitution be changed to enact a temporary sales tax of three-quarters of one percent to be used solely to fund state and local highways, roads, bridges and transportation projects for ten years, with priority given to repairing unsafe roads and bridges?

This change is expected to produce $480 million annually to the state's Transportation Safety and Job Creation Fund and $54 million for local governments. Increases in the gas tax will be prohibited. This revenue shall only be used for transportation purposes and cannot be diverted for other uses.

CONSTITUTIONAL AMENDMENT NO. 8
Proposed by the 97th General Assembly
(Second Regular Session)
HJR No. 48

Shall the Missouri Constitution be amended to create a "Veterans Lottery Ticket" and to use the revenue from the sale of these tickets for projects and services related to veterans?

The annual cost or savings to state and local governmental entities is unknown, but likely minimal. If sales of a veterans lottery ticket game decrease existing lottery ticket sales, the profits of which fund education, there could be a small annual shift in funding from education to veterans' programs.

CONSTITUTIONAL AMENDMENT NO. 9
Proposed by the 97th General Assembly
(Second Regular Session)
SCS SJR No. 27

Shall the Missouri Constitution be amended so that the people shall be secure in their electronic communications and data from unreasonable searches and seizures as they are now likewise secure in their persons, homes, papers and effects?

State and local governmental entities expect no significant costs or savings.

Special Election Results
August 5, 2014

State Representative District 67, unexpired

	Democratic	Republican	Libertarian	Independent
	Alan Green	Dwayne A Strickland	Jeff Coleman	Tony Weaver
St. Louis	4,989	1,109	144	1,130
TOTAL	**4,989**	**1,109**	**144**	**1,130**

State Representative District 120, unexpired

	Democratic	Republican
	Zechariah (Zech) Hockersmith	Shawn Sisco
Crawford	1,632	4,053
TOTAL	**1,632**	**4,053**

State Representative District 151, unexpired

	Democratic	Republican
	Ryan Wm. Holder	Tila Rowland Hubrecht
Stoddard	1,977	3,579
TOTAL	**1,977**	**3,579**

Officers of Democratic Party

Democratic National Committee, 2015–2016

National Democratic Headquarters
430 S. Capitol St. SE, Washington, D.C. 20003
Telephone: (202) 863-8000 / FAX: (202) 863-8174
www.democrats.org

Officers, Democratic National Committee

Rep. Debbie Wasserman Schultz, chair;
Donna Brazile, vice chair of voter registration & participation;
Linda Chavez-Thompson, vice chair;
Rep. Mike Honda, vice chair;
Raymond Buckley, vice chair, ASDC president;
Alice Germond, secretary;
Andrew Tobias, treasurer;
Jane Stetson, national finance chair.

Democratic State Organization of Missouri

Democratic State Committee Headquarters
208 Madison St., Jefferson City 65102
Telephone: (573) 636-5241 / FAX: (573) 634-8176
www.missouridems.org

NOTE: Information is received from county clerks and the Missouri Democratic Party

Missouri members, Democratic National Committee

Doug Brooks, 3734 Chipmunk, Joplin 64804;
Melba Curls, 3832 Myrtle Ave., Kansas City 64128;
Sandra Querry, 1416 N. Charlton Rd., Independence 64056;
Matt Robinson, 723 Bellflower, Hazelwood 63042;
Brian Wahby, 2914 Milton, St. Louis 63104.

Officers, Democratic State Committee

Roy Temple, chair, 208 Madison St., Jefferson City 65101;
Darlene Greene, vice chair, 5703 Enright Ave., St. Louis 63112;

DOUG BROOKS
National Committeeman

MELBA CURLS
National Committeewoman

SANDRA QUERRY
National Committeewoman

MATT ROBINSON
National Committeeman

BRIAN WAHBY
National Committeeman

Susan Rubino, secretary, 2051 N. Carriage Dr., Nixa 65714;
Airick West, treasurer, 3239 Wabash Ave., Kansas City 64109.

Members, Democratic State Committee

First district: Jim Barrett, 6029 Saddleridge Farm Ct., St. Louis 63129; Joan Barry, 5050 Lampglow Ct., St. Louis 63129.
Second district: David Hurst, 28 Cognac Dr., Lake St. Louis 63129; Shelly Hoffman, 812 Brookwood Bend Tr., St. Peters 63376.
Third district: Clay Copeland, 605 Tyler St., Deslodge 63601; Kathy Renee Murphey, 601 Tyler St., Deslodge 63061.

Fourth district: Joseph Keaveny, 6219 Westminister, St. Louis 63130; Sharon Tyus, 4968 Maffitt Pl., St. Louis 63113.

Fifth district: Bob Hilgemann, 4131 Blaine Ave., St. Louis 63110; Sen. Jamilah Nasheed, 4710 Lee Ave., St. Louis 63115.

Sixth district: Larry Hunt, 13 CR 420, Linn 65051; Sandi Schwartz, 27128 Marina Ln., Barnett 65011.

Seventh district: John Comstock, 4019 Clark, Kansas City 64111; Hila (Dutch) Newman, 4122 Mercier, Kansas City 64111.

Eighth district: Joe Becker, 638 NW Rosaceae Dr., Blue Springs 64015; Chere Chaney, 1933 SW Second St., Lee's Summit 64081.

Ninth district: Keith Thomas, 1832 E. 49th St., Kansas City 64130; Rep. Gail McCann Beatty, 6012 Woodland Ave., Kansas City 64110.

Tenth district: Mike Backer, 2885 State Rd. TT, New Bloomfield 65063; Rita Adams, 1844 Country Rd. 360, Fulton 65251.

Eleventh district: Phil LeVota, 16000 Ess Rd., Kansas City 64136; Meghan LeVota, 4316 S. Avon Dr., Independence 64055.

Twelfth district: Joe Gangon, 600 East St., Lathrop 64465; Linda Shumate, 15222 Old Quarry Rd., Excelsior Springs 64024.

Thirteenth district: Benjamin Broadnax, 1259 Bakewell Dr., St. Louis 63137; Mary Elizabeth, Dorsey, 8 St. Thomas Ct., Florissant 63031.

Fourteenth district: Matt Robinson, 723 Bellflower, Hazelwood 63670; Karen Pierre, 7541 Hillsdale, St. Louis 63121.

Fifteenth district: Dennis Roach, 825 Marco Dr., Kirkwood 63122; Alexis (Lexie) Miller, 1305 D Crossings, Manchester 63021.

Sixteenth district: William Seay, 429 Hwy. M, Steelville 65565; Clara Ichord, 1508 Hull Valley Dr., Waynesville 65583.

Seventeenth district: Bill Skaggs, 3509 N. Park Ave., Kansas City 64116; Sandy Skaggs, 3509 N. Park Ave., Kansas City 64116.

Eighteenth district: Jerry Caldwell, 25305 Eagle Ln., Kirksville 63501; Diana Scott, 33146 St. Hwy. 156, La Plata 63549.

Nineteenth district: Greg Ahrens, 1504 Sylvan Ln., Columbia 65202; Barbara Schneider, 807 Forest Hills Ct., Columbia 65203.

Twentieth district: Wes Zongker, 803 W. Farm Rd. 68, Springfield 65803; Kristine (Tina) Ballhorn, 2354 E. Allison Ln., Springfield 65803.

Twenty-first district: Terrence Messonnier, 407 E. Chestnut, Odessa 64076; Mildred Connor, 15045 Hwy. 20, Malta Bend 65339.

Twenty-second district: Sean Fauss, 2231 Summit Dr., Arnold 63010; Tammy Vent, 684 S. Old Hwy. 141, Apt. 302, Fenton 63026.

Twenty-third district: Morton Todd, 2813 Droste, St. Charles 63301; Amanda Kelley, 2 Preston Ct., St. Charles 63303.

ROY TEMPLE
State Chair

DARLENE GREEN
State Vice Chair

SUSAN RUBINO
State Secretary

AIRICK WEST
State Treasurer

Twenty-fourth district: Bob Levine, 2 Troll Ct., Manchester 63011; Marianne Solari, 3427 St. Mark Ln., St. Ann 63074.

Twenty-fifth district: Michael Moroni, PO Box 24, Bloomfield 63825; Dorothy Adams, PO Box 328, Senath 63876.

Twenty-sixth district: Dennis Lavallee, 412 Still Creek Pass, Wildwood 63011; Candace Farmer, 2371 W. Club Terrace Dr., Wildwood 63011.

Twenty-seventh district: Chuck Banks, HC 1, Box 1550, Silva 63964; Fonda Davis, 2305 Sherwood Dr., Cape Girardeau 63701.

Twenty-eighth district: Fred Higginbotham, 4431 S. 157th Rd., Bolivar 65613; Vanessa Hardy, 780 E. Hwy. BB, Eldorado Springs 64744.

Twenty-ninth district: Rod Anderson, 800 Central Ave., Monett 65708; Sherie Snider, 278 Lakefront Cir., Kimberling City 65686.

Thirtieth district: David Trippe, 616 E. Loren, Springfield 65807; Vicky Trippe, 616 E. Loren, Springfield 65807.

Thirty-first district: Phyllis Sprenkle, 29540 S. 1850 Rd., Sheldon 64772.

Thirty-second district: Doug Brooks, 3734 Chipmunk Dr., Joplin 64804; Genevieve Williams, 11110 Mulberry Rd., Neosho 64850.

Thirty-third district: Perry Jenks, HC 1, Box 693, Fairdealing 63955; Cindy Jenks, HC 1, Box 693, Fairdealing 63955.

Thirty-fourth district: Bill Caldwell, 17227 S.E. Y Hwy., Dearborn 64439; Paula Willmarth, 5967 N. London Ave., Kansas City 64151.

Officers, Democratic Congressional District Committees

First district: Hazel Erby, chair, 8340 Fullerton, St. Louis 63132; Nathan Boyd, vice chair, 5642 Pamplin Pl., St. Louis 63136; Marianne Solari, secretary, 3427 St. Mark Ln., St. Ann 63074; Robert Hilgemann, treasurer, 4131 Blaine, St. Louis 63110.

Second district: Alexis Miller, chair, 1305 D Crossings Ct., Manchester 63021; Dennis Lavalee, vice chair, 412 Still Creek Pass, Wildwood 63011; Candace Farmer, secretary, 2371 W. Club Terrace, Wildwood 63011; Bob Levine, treasurer, 2 Troll Ct., Manchester 63011.

Third district: Clyde Voelkerding, chair, 1529 Biecker Rd., Washington 63090; Amanda Kelley, vice chair, 2 Preston Ct., St. Charles 63303; Laura Adams, secretary, 25740 Bethlehem Valley Rd., Marthasville 63357; Jackson Tompson, treasurer, 59 Verdant View Manor Ct., Wentzville 63385.

Fourth district: JC Owsley, chair, RR 91, Box 1894, Cross Timbers 65634; Clara Ichord, vice chair, 1508 Hull Valley Dr., Waynesville 65583; Peg Miller, secretary, 102 E. Green Meadows Rd. 6, Columbia 65203; Randy Huggins, treasurer, 207 N. Moulton, Leeton 64761.

Fifth district: Cathy Spainhower, chair, 3512 Bridge Manor Dr., Kansas City 64137; Chris Whiting, vice chair, 2933 Sweet Briar D, Independence 64057; Donna Cushman, secretary, 3615 NE 49th St., Kansas City 64119; Bob Cecil, treasurer, 31710 W. 157th St., Excelsior Springs 64024.

Sixth district: Bob Saunders, chair, 1542 Merit Ln., Liberty 64068; Charli Seitz, vice chair, 8616 NE 73rd Ct., Kansas City 64158; Karen LaVaver, secretary, 5678 Leslie Rd., Green City 63545; Keivan Moghadam, treasurer, 8616 NE 73rd Ct., Kansas City 64158.

Seventh district: Krista Stark, chair, 514 W. Third St., Webb City 64870; Jack Hembree, vice chair, 2323 E. Rosebriar St., Springfield 65804; Matthew Patterson, secretary, 225 E. Commercial St., Springfield 65803; Vicki Trippe, treasurer, 616 E. Loren, Springfield 65807.

Eighth district: Jim Scaggs, chair, 3743 Hwy. F, Annapolis 63640; Cindy Jenks, vice chair, HC 1, Box 693, Fairdealing 63939; Deborah Sallings, secretary, RR 72, Box 2578, Alton 65606; vacancy, treasurer.

Officers, Democratic Senatorial Districts

First district: Paul Wrabec, chair, 11227 Thompson, Sugar Creek 64054; Ingrid Burnett, vice chair, 3418 Gladstone, Kansas City 64123; John Burnett, secretary, 3418 Gladstone, Kansas City 64123; Virginia Evens, treasurer, 2548 W. Paseo Blvd., Kansas City 64108.

Second district: David Turney, chair, 665 Falconcrest Dr., Lake St. Louis 63367; Laura Castaneda, vice chair, 19 Lippizan Rd., St. Peters 63376; Julie Biermann, secretary, 3308 Apple Dr., St. Charles 63301; Fred Banks, treasurer, 6 Oak Post Rd., Wentzville 63385.

Fifth district: Bob Hilgemann, chair, 4131 Blaine Ave., St. Louis 63110; Jesse Todd, vice chair, 4250 Enright Ave., St. Louis 63108; vacancy, secretary; vacancy, treasurer.

Seventh district: Joe Runions, chair, 12336 Norton, Grandview 64030; Michele Newby, vice chair, 11522 Wornall Rd., Kansas City 64114; Mike Damico, secretary, 21 E. 54th Terr., Kansas City 64112; Elaine Brewer, treasurer, 6131 E. 127th St., Grandview 64040.

Eighth district: Lanna Ultican, chair, 1204 SW 18th St., Blue Springs 64015; Robert Clarke, vice chair, 908 NE Third St., Blue Springs 64014; Roxann Thorley, secretary, 21200 E. 50th Terrace Dr. S., Blue Springs 64015; Joe Becker, treasurer, 638 NW Rosaceae Dr., Blue Springs 64015.

Ninth district: Keith Thomas, chair, 1832 E. 49th St., Kansas City 64130; Virginia Evans, vice chair, 2548 W. Paseo Blvd., Kansas City 64108; Mike Downing, secretary, 9300 E. 65th St., Raytown 64133; Vacancy, treasurer.

Eleventh district: Chris Whiting, chair, 2933 Sweet Briar Dr., Independence 64057; Meghan LeVota, vice chair, 4316 S. Avon, Independence 64055; Sam LeVota, secretary, 2613 Santa Fe Rd., Independence 64052; DeAun Young, treasurer, 107 E. Jefferson, Buckner 64016.

Twelfth district: Linda Shumate, chair, 15222 Old Quarry Rd., Excelsior Springs 64024; John Bless, vice chair, 1824 SW Hwy. 169, Gower 64454; Mylissa Stutesman, secretary, 3695 Hwy. 33 N., Plattsburg 64477; Jim Banks, treasurer, 408 W. Locust St., Plattsburg 64477.

Thirteenth district: Jeff Caputa, chair, 655 Lilac Dr., Florissant 63031; Leslie Broadnax, vice chair, 1259 Bakewell, St. Louis 63137; Gwen Reed, secretary, 301 Behlman Meadows Way, Florissant 63034; Tim Jones, treasurer, 865 Daniel Boone, Florissant 63031.

Fourteenth district: Charlie Dooley, chair, 4408 Mathew, St. Louis 63121; Hazel Erby, vice chair, 8340 Fullerton, St. Louis 63132; Karen Pierre, secretary, 7541 Hillsdale Dr., St. Louis 63121; Matthew Robinson, treasurer, 723 Bellflower, Hazelwood 63042.

Sixteenth district: Rick Pope, chair; vacancy, vice chair; vacancy, secretary; vacancy, treasurer.

Seventeenth district: Charles Myers, chair, 505 NW 43rd Terr., Kansas City 64116; Charli Seitz, vice chair, 8616 NE 73rd Ct., Kansas City 64158; Cathy Spears, secretary, 6928 N. Mercier St., Kansas City 64118; Tom Gant, treasurer, 403 Sunset Dr., Smithville 64068.

Eighteenth district: Matthew Eichor, chair, 23942 Buck Creek Rd., Greentop 63546; Janice McGinnis, vice chair, RR 3, Box 95A, Edina 63537; Paul Parsons, secretary, 901 E. Morgan St., Edina 63537; Melanie McAuley, treasurer, 31318 State Hwy. A, Greentop 63546.

Nineteenth district: Peg Miller, chair, 102 E. Green Meadows 6, Columbia 65203; Homer Page, vice chair, 503 N. Brookline, Columbia 65203; Kathleen Weinschenk, secretary, 1504 Sylvan Ln., Columbia 65202; Greg Ahrens, treasurer, 1504 Sylvan Ln., Columbia 65202.

Twenty-first district: Gary Grigsby, chair, 303 S. Mitchell St., Warrensburg 64093; Cindy Schroer, vice chair, 919 Main St., Higginsville 64037; Mildred Connor, secretary, 15045 Hwy. 20, Malta Bend 65339; Don Gage, treasurer, 1243 S. Highland Ct., Marshall 65340.

Twenty-second district: Tammy Vent, chair, 684 S. Old Hwy. 141, Apt. 302, Fenton 63026; Carl Hayes, vice chair, 2512 Skyline Dr., High Ridge 63114; Frank Newkirk, secretary, 36 Huntleigh Woods, Barnhart 63012; Helge Puchalla, treasurer, 101 Winter Lake Blvd., Fenton 63026.

Twenty-third district: Morton Todd, chair, 2813 Droste, St. Charles 63301; Carolyn Landry, vice chair, 2725 Stone Wall Station, St. Charles 63303; Kelly Hoffman, secretary, 10124 Jeffleigh Ln., St. Louis 63123; Fred Banks, treasurer, 6 Oak Post Rd., Wentzville 63385.

Twenty-fourth district: Burton Boxerman, chair, 9622 Old Bonhomme, St. Louis 63132; Suzanne Jackson, vice chair, 10312 Lackland Rd., St. Louis 63114; Marianne Solari, secretary, 3427 St. Mark Ln., St. Ann 63074; Bob Levine, treasurer, 2 Troll Ct., Manchester 63011.

Twenty-fifth district: Art Cole, chair, 2211 Orr Rd., Poplar Bluff 63901; Danielle Chidester, vice chair; Tabitha Johnson-Thurman, secretary, 235 Sandy Ln., East Prairie 63845; David Greene, treasurer, 3185 State Hwy. E 61, Steele 63877.

Twenty-sixth district: Dennis Lavallee, chair, 412 St. Creek Pass, Wildwood 63011; Carol Johnson, vice chair, 1515 W. Pacific St., Apt. 203, Pacific 63069; Candace Farmer, secretary, 2371 W. Club Terrace Dr., Wildwood 63011; Brian Legate, treasurer, 220 Vonbehren Dr., Chesterfield 63005.

Twenty-eighth district: Don Fohn, chair, 15960 Hwy. E, Eldridge 65463; Gerda Fitts, vice chair, 101 Pace Circle, Hermitage 65668; Vanessa Hardy, secretary, 780 E. Hwy. BB, El Dorado Springs 64744; Will Westmoreland, treasurer, PO Box 983, Bolivar 65613.

Thirtieth district: Matthew Patterson, chair, 225 E. Commercial, Unit D, Springfield 65803; Debbie Hopkins, vice chair, 1905 S. Dollison Ave., Apt. A, Springfield 65807; Zach Allen, secretary, 413 E. Seminole St., Springfield 65807; Carolyn Hembree, treasurer, 2323 E. Rosebrier St., Springfield 65804.

Thirty-first district: Charlie Burton, chair, 30501 Fox Tail Dr., Drexel 64742; Debbi Lehr, vice chair, 2105 E. Ann Terr., Harrisonville 64701; Phyllis Sprenkle, secretary, 29540 S. 1850 Rd., Sheldon 64772; Jim Switzer, treasurer, 136 S. Main St., Clinton 64735.

Thirty-second district: Doug Brooks, chair, 3734 Chipmunk Dr., Joplin 64804; Sherry Buchanan, vice chair, 4702 S. Jackson Ave., Joplin 64804; Lindsey Brooks-Cade, secretary, 1631 Count Rd. 120, Carthage 64836; James Fleischaker, treasurer, 2402 Indiana Ave., Joplin 64801.

Thirty-third district: RA Pendergrass, chair, 772 CR 7320, Bakersfield 65609; Cindy Jenks, vice chair, HC 1, Box 693, Fairdealing 63939; Deborah Sallings, secretary, RR 72, Box 2578, Alton 65606; Perry Jenks, treasurer, HC 1, Box 693, Fairdealing 63939.

Thirty-fourth district: Patrick Squires, chair, 2649 Fredrick Ave., St. Joseph 64506; Melba Nicolaisen, vice chair, 6802 N. Fisk Ave., Kansas City 64151; Dee Dee Squires, secretary, 2649 Fredrick Ave., St. Joseph 64056; Ken Hunt, treasurer, 8202 NW Tadwa, Kansas City 64152.

Democratic County Committees, 2015–2016

(Township, ward or precinct precedes name of committee members. Vacancies not published. County Committee lists are provided by county clerks, election officials from each county and the State Democratic Party.)

Adair County

Chair, Matt Eichor, 23942 Buck Creek Rd., Greentop 63546

Vice Chair, Melanie McAuley, 31318 State Hwy. A, Greentop 63546

Secretary, Claudia Minor, 904 E. Randolph, Kirksville 63501
Treasurer, Donnie Parish, 30086 State Hwy. E, La Plata 63549

Andrew County

Chair, M. Scott Howell, 12040 CR 323, Savannah 64485
Vice Chair, Brooke Schweizer, 646 State Rt. K, Amazonia 64421
Secretary, Hanh Dudley, 604 Clark, Bolckow 64427
Treasurer, Gene Bales, 1000 W. Main St., Savannah 64485

Audrain County

Chair, Molly Shellabarger, 12271 Hwy. M, Mexico 65265
Vice Chair, Lewis Brooks, 1333 Lexington St., Mexico 65265

Barton County

Chair, Roger Seeley, 773 S. M Hwy., Asbury 64832
Vice Chair, Sandy Harris, 405 W. 10th St., Lamar 64759

Bates County

Chair, Larry Berry, RR 1, Box 170, Hume 64752
Vice Chair, Edith Dilley, 201 Colonial Dr., Butler 64730

Benton County

Chair, Joe McDowell, 30489 Hastain Ave., Edwards 65326
Vice Chair, Melissa McDowell, 30489 Hastain Ave., Edwards 65326

Boone County

Chair, Homer Page, 503 N. Brookline Dr., Columbia 65203
Vice Chair, Phyllis Fugit, PO Box 70, Rocheport 65279
Secretary, Greg Ahrens, 1504 Sylvan Ln., Columbia 65202
Treasurer, Kay Callison, 600 Crestland Ave., Columbia 65203
Columbia Ward 2, James Givens, 4182 N. Riviera Dr., Columbia 65202
Missouri, Diana E. Rickard, 4308 W. South Pinebrook Ln., Columbia 65203
Perche, John Schultz, 1301 W. Colchester Rd., Columbia 65202
Three Creeks, Greg Rennier, 10900 S. Hardwick Ln., Columbia 65201

Buchanan County

Chair, Randy Adams, 6810 SE 110th Rd., Easton 64443
Vice Chair, Jacqueline Ross, 4111 Miller Rd., St. Joseph 64505
Secretary, Heather Thornton, 6810 SE 110th Rd., Easton 64443
Treasurer, Mike Veale, 13 Summerhill Dr., St. Joseph 64507
St. Joseph
    Ward 1, Les Beattie, 1223 N. Second St., St. Joseph 64501
    Ward 1, Joyce Edwards, 3215 N. Third St., St. Joseph 64505
    Ward 2, Sharon Kosek, 2 Wishbone Rd., St. Joseph 64506

Ward 4, DeeDee Squires, 2649 Frederick Ave., St. Joseph 64506
Ward 4, Patrick Squires, 2649 Frederick Ave., St. Joseph 64506
Ward 5, Ray Allen, 2702 Mitchell Ave., Apt. 1, St. Joseph 64507
Ward 6, Jerome Williams, 2411 Angelique St., St. Joseph 64501
Ward 6, Nancy Reed, 2602 Francis St., St. Joseph 64501
Ward 10, Deborah Borchers, 5302 S. 22nd St., St. Joseph 64503
Ward 11, Jacqueline Ross, 4111 Miller Rd., St. Joseph 64505
Ward 12, David Lichliter, 3312 N. 35th Pl., St. Joseph 64506
Ward 12, Sharon Womach, 4902 Ashbey Dr., St. Joseph 64506
Ward 15, Richard Lewin, 4615 Stonecrest Terr., St. Joseph 64506
Ward 15, Sheila Murray, 5211 Mockingbird Ln., St. Joseph 64506
Crawford, Dale Morgan, 113 Fifth St., Faucett 64448
Crawford, Gail Tyler, 4798 SE Tillery Rd., Faucett 64448
Jackson, Bill Caldwell, 17227 SE State Rt. Y, Dearborn 64439
Jackson, Marie Caldwell, 17227 SE State Rt. Y, Dearborn 64439
Tremont, Randy Adams, 6810 SE 110th Rd., Easton 64443
Tremont, Heather Thornton, 6810 SE 110th Rd., Easton 64443
Washington, Mike Veale, 13 SE Summerhill Dr., St. Joseph 64507
Washington, Donna Miller, 3008 SW Lakefront Ln. W, St. Joseph 64504
Wayne, Sharon Hicks, 3103 SW Pettet Rd., St. Joseph 64504

Butler County

Chair, Shirley Langley Hindman, 2045 Hwy. F, Harviell 63945
Vice Chair, Ken Michel, 2033 Schweizer Dr., Poplar Bluff 63901
Secretary, Thelma Brannum
Treasurer, Levell Hinton, Hwy. 158, Harviell 63945
Ash Hill, Joe Janes, 14863 Hwy. 51, Qulin 63961
Ash Hill, Barbara Snider, 6524 CR 654, Broseley 63932
Beaver Dam, Levell Hinton, Hwy. 158, Harviell 63945
Beaver Dam, Shirley Hindman, 2045 Hwy. F, Harviell 63945
Black River, Doug Kennedy, 626 Pine Cone Rd., Poplar Bluff 63901
Black River, Sheri Kennedy, 626 Pine Cone Rd., Poplar Bluff 63901
Cane Creek, Mark Kennedy, 490 Moccasin Ln., Poplar Bluff 63901
Epps, Mac West, 5449 Hwy. PP, Poplar Bluff 63901
Epps, Marion West, 5449 Hwy. PP, Poplar Bluff 63901
Poplar Bluff
    Poplar Bluff at Large, Bob Brannum, 565 CR 304, Poplar Bluff 63901
    Poplar Bluff at Large, Irma Brannum, 565 CR 304, Poplar Bluff 63901
    Ward 1, Gene Brannum
    Ward 1, Thelma Brannum
    Ward 2, Ken Michel, 2033 Schweizer Dr., Poplar Bluff 63901

Ward 2, Gloria Michel, 2033 Schweitzer Dr., Poplar Bluff 63901
Ward 3, Ryan Nely, 1602 Sanders, Poplar Bluff 63901
Ward 4, Art Cole, 2211 Orr Rd., Poplar Bluff 63901
Ward 4, Dorthy Credille, 1983 Greenwood, Poplar Bluff 63901
Ward 5, Keith Frye
Ward 5, Helen Frye

Caldwell County

Chair, Dori Creekmore, 510 E. Arthur, Hamilton 64644
Vice Chair, Donnie Cox, 3275 SE Sunnyvale Rd., Braymer 64624
Secretary, William Lewin, 10121 SW Price Dr., Lawson 64062
Treasurer, Gayle Toms, 5670 SW State Rt. T, Polo 64671

Callaway County

Chair, Mike Backer, 2885 State Rd. TT, New Bloomfield 65063
Vice Chair, Melody Craighead, 3940 Tara Ridge Rd., Fulton 65251
Secretary, Sharon Fischer, 3547 State Rd. KK, Fulton 65251
Treasurer, Lee Fritz, 6894 State Rd. C, Fulton 65251

Camden County

Chair, Rick Pope, 97 Kingsrow Dr., Camdenton 65020
Vice Chair, Marcia Crandall, 60 Cedar Crest, Linn Creek 65052
Secretary, Martha Driskel, 2895 State Rd. V, Linn Creek 65052
Treasurer, Joe Bodziony, 1555 Buckingham Dr., Unit 4, Camdenton 65020

Cape Girardeau County

Chair, Michael Davis, 2305 Sherwood Dr., Cape Girardeau 63701
Vice Chair, Don Smith, 1726 Westridge, Cape Girardeau 63701
Secretary, Linda Sanders, 3401 CR 618, Jackson 63755
Treasurer, John Heisserer, 160 S. Broadview, Cape Girardeau 63701
Cape Girardeau
    Cape Precinct 9, Robert Harris Jr., 628 S. Benton St., Cape Girardeau 65703
    Cape Precinct 13, Fonda Davis, 2305 Sherwood Dr., Cape Girardeau 63701
    Cape Precinct 13, Michael Davis, 2305 Sherwood Dr., Cape Girardeau 63701
    Cape Precinct 16, Debby Brewer, 2030 Perryville Rd., Cape Girardeau 63701
    Cape Precinct 17, Michael Masterson, 3413 Glenview, Cape Girardeau 63701
    Cape Precinct 17, Nancy Caldwell Ayers, 1006 Oak Ridge Ct., Cape Girardeau 63701
    Cape Precinct 18, John P. Heisserer, 1198 Wolf Ln., Cape Girardeau 63701
Gordonville, Bill Harshaw, 205 Albert Ln., Gordonville 63701
Gordonville, Carol Harshaw, 205 Albert Ln., Gordonville 63701
Hanover, Linda M. Sanders, 3401 CR 618, Jackson 63755

Carroll County

Chair, Michael Decker, 19474 CR 185, Bogard 64622
Vice Chair, Terre Franken, 1400 N. Jefferson, Carrollton 64633
Secretary, Don White, PO Box 85, Hale 64643
Treasurer, John C. Franken, 1400 N. Jefferson, Carrollton 64633
Carrollton
    Ward I, John C. Franken, 1400 N. Jefferson, Carrollton 64633
    Ward I, Terre A. Franken, 1400 N. Jefferson, Carrollton 64633
    Ward III, Parley (Jim) Veach, 312 Santa Fe, Carrollton 64633
    Ward III, June Newman, 209 Santa Fe, Carrollton 64633
    Ward IV, David Sugg, 903 N. Main, Carrollton 64633
    Ward IV, Sharon Sugg, 903 N. Main, Carrollton 64633
Combs, Dinah Storm, 31346 CR 230, Bosworth 64623
DeWitt, Stephany Link, 36902 CR 230, Bosworth 64623
Egypt I, Cassandra Brown, 100 E. Fourth, Norborne 64668
Egypt I, Kenneth Brown, 100 E. Fourth, Norborne 64668
Hurricane, Carl R. White, PO Box 85, Hale 64643
Hurricane, Donna Funk, 518 Elm, Hale 64643
Leslie, Ron Hundley, 16791 CR 201, Bogard 64622
Leslie, Janice Hundley, 16791 CR 201, Bogard 64622
Moss Creek, Deborah L. Lueders, 21434 CR 316, Carrollton 64633
Rockford, Loren Esten Wright, 18303 CR 351, Bosworth 64623
Rockford, Pat M. Wright, 18303 CR 351, Bosworth 64623
Wakenda, Hubert Carter, 22497 CR 280, Carrollton 64633
Wakenda, Norene R. Carter, 22497 CR 280, Carrollton 64633

Carter County

Chair, Eugene Oakley, PO Box 249, Van Buren 63965
Vice Chair, Vicki Smart, HC 2, Box 2277, Van Buren 63965
Secretary, Betty Smith, PO Box 162, Ellsinore 63937
Treasurer, Doral Rymer, HC 2, Box 2663A, Van Buren 63965
Eugene (Gene) Oakley, PO Box 249, Van Buren 63965
Vicki Smart, HC 2, Box 2277, Van Buren 63965
Jackson, Doral Rymer, HC 2, Box 2663A, Van Buren 63965
Johnson, Betty Smith, PO Box 1562, Ellsinore 63937

Cass County

Chair, Charles Burton, 30501 S. Fox Tail Dr., Drexel 64742
Vice Chair, Pam Scrudder, 20718 S. State Rt. CC, Pleasant Hill 64080
Secretary, Meryline Kramer, 2601 Meadowlark Dr., Harrisonville 64701
Treasurer, Marc Gagne, 302 Catron, Belton 64012
Belton
    Ward 1, Joe Cooper, 7314 Tennisen Ct., Belton 64012
    Ward 1, Dawn Elmore-Fricke, 15719 Richmond Ave., Belton 64012
    Ward 1, Bobby L. Davidson, 16315 Springvalley Rd., Belton 64012
    Ward 1, Patty Johnson, 16404 Rebecca Ln., Belton 64012
    Ward 3, Charles L. Foland, 205 Eldorado Dr., Belton 64012
    Ward 3, Connie Hubbard, 404 Colbern St., Belton 64012

Ward 4, Jerry Duvall, 803 Commercial St., Belton 64012

Ward 4, Nancy Duvall, 803 Commercial St., Belton 64012

Dolan, Sharon Marshall, 12702 E. State Rt. 2, Freeman 64746

Dolan, Tom Marshall, 12702 E. State Rt. 2, Freeman 64746

East Creek, Fred H. Olinger, 5801 E. 187th St., Lot 13, Belton 64012

East Creek, Rebecca K. (Becky) Ivers, 18805 S. Lakeside Dr., Belton 64012

Grand River Rural, Levi Eugene Long, 26511 S. Timberlake Rd., Harrisonville 64701

Grand River Rural, Sharon M. Long, 26511 S. Timberlake Rd., Harrisonville 64701

Harrisonville

Ward 1, J. Chase Linder, 401 S. James, Harrisonville 64701

Ward 2, Kelly R. Mangan, 703 N. Patton St., Harrisonville 64071

Ward 2, Christie K. Gray Mangan, 703 N. Patton St., Harrisonville 64071

Ward 4, Debra (Debbi) Lehr, 2105 E. Ann Terr., Harrisonville 64701

Ward 4, Phil Lehr, 2105 E. Ann Terr., Harrisonville 64701

Lake Winnebago, Kenneth C. Hensley, PO Box 245, Raymore 64083

Lake Winnebago, Ashley Beard Fosnow, 905 Eve Orchid Dr., Greenwood 64034

Polk, Jim White, 21921 S. Walnut Bluff Rd., Pleasant Hill 64080

Polk, Pamela A. (Pam) Scrudder, 20718 S. State Rt. CC, Pleasant Hill 64080

Pleasant Hill, Kirk Powell, 1918 Hidden Valley Dr., Pleasant Hill 64080

Pleasant Hill, Joan Smith, 806 Wildwood Dr., Pleasant Hill 64080

Peculiar Rural, Cindy Kalwei, 24802 Twin Pines Dr., Harrisonville 64701

Peculiar Rural, Larry Kalwei, 24802 Twin Pines Dr., Harrisonville 64701

Raymore

Ward 1, Karen McKinney, 315 N. Fox Ridge Dr., Apt. 104, Raymore 64083

Ward 1, JoAnna Dale, 1315 W. John Blvd., Raymore 64083

Ward 3, Donald L. Davis, 1100 E. Hubach Hill Rd., Raymore 64083

Ward 3, Donna J. Davis, 1100 E. Hubach Hill Rd., Raymore 64083

Raymore Rural, Mary Dobson, PO Box 347, Raymore 64083

Raymore Rural, Larry L. Dobson, PO Box 347, Raymore 64083

West Dolan, Charles A. Burton, 30501 Foxtail Dr., Drexel 64742

West Dolan, Debra J. Burton, 30501 Foxtail Dr., Drexel 64742

West Peculiar Rural, Bob Sherrick, 10807 E. 205th St., Peculiar 64078

West Peculiar Rural, Doris Sherrick, 10807 E. 205th St., Peculiar 64078

West Peculiar City, G.C. Shores, PO Box 545, Peculiar 64078

West Peculiar City, Sharon A. Shores, PO Box 545, Peculiar 64078

Cedar County

Chair, Vanessa Hardy, 780 E. Hwy. BB, El Dorado Springs 64744

Vice Chair, Dean Stansbury, 7899 S. Hwy. J, Humansville 65674

Secretary, Darrel Martin, El Dorado Springs 64744

Treasurer, Dorathey Veble

Chariton County

Chair, Walter S. Iman, PO Box 182, Salisbury 65281

Vice Chair, Clarice Gladbach, 18065 Marquette Ave., Mendon 64660

Secretary, Barbara McKenzie, 33812 Hwy. WW, Salisbury 65281

Treasurer, Larry Peters, 27612 Settlers Ave., Keytesville 65261

Bee Branch, Jim Bruner, 32838 Peden Chapel Rd., Marceline 64658

Bee Branch, Barbara Bruner, 32838 Peden Chapel Rd., Marceline 64658

Brunswick, Wayne Fletcher, 23092 Hickory Grove Rd., Brunswick 65236

Brunswick, Mary Frances Fox, 23945 Rodeo Ave., Brunswick 65236

Cunningham, Wayne Foster, 16890 Hog Ridge Ave., Sumner 64681

Cunningham, Theresa Foster, 16890 Hog Ridge Ave., Sumner 64681

Keytesville, Larry Peters, 27612 Settlers Ave., Keytesville 65261

Keytesville, Barbara McKenzie, 33812 Hwy. WW, Salisbury 65281

Mendon, Kenny Mauzey, 18641 Vernon Kennedy Ave., Mendon 64660

Mendon, Monica Graves, 18031 Mike Rd., Mendon 64660

Musselfork, Brian Butler, 1005 Canoe Ln., Keytesville 65261

Musselfork, Bonnie Clark, 21552 Prather Ave., Keytesville 65261

Salisbury, Walter S. Iman, PO Box 182, Salisbury 65281

Salisbury, Donna M. Morrison, 40502 Pleasant Woods Rd., Salisbury 65281

Salt Creek, Tom Gladbach, 18065 Marquette Ave., Mendon 64660

Salt Creek, Clarice Gladbach, 18065 Marquette Ave., Mendon 64660

Triplett, Carolyn S. Sanders, 14820 Ohio Rd., Triplett 65286

Christian County

Chair, Jim Billedo, 224 Hedgerow Dr., Ozark 65721

Vice Chair, Anita Jones, 1761 W. Willow Wood Dr., Nixa 65714

Secretary, David Lee, 1491 W. Craig Hollow Rd., Nixa 65714

Treasurer, Susan Billedo, 224 Hedgerow Dr., Ozark 65721

Bruner, Dick Wilson, 16448 State Hwy. 14 E, Bruner 65620

Cassidy, Sue Denner, 3305 Olympic Cir., Nixa 65714

East Finley, Robert Snook, 269 Kansas Dr., Ozark 65721

Garden Grove, Lin, Shawgo, 317 S. Market, Nixa 65714

Garden Grove, Ron Shawgo, 317 S. Market, Nixa 65714

Lincoln, David Stokely, 1141 Davis Bridge Rd., Republic 65731

Lincoln, Sandra Asher, 126 Lilly Ln., Clever 65631

North Galloway, David M. Lee, 1491 Craig Hollow Rd, Nixa 65714

North Galloway, Polly C. Dross, 1491 Craig Hollow Rd, Nixa 65714

North Linn, Kelly Hall, 135 Serenity Ridge Rd., Ozark 65721

Polk, Aurthur Steinbaugh Jr., 349 Drier Rd., Billings 65610

Polk, Juanita Steinbaugh, 349 Drier Rd., Billings 65610

Riverside, James Billedo, 224 Hedgerow Dr., Ozark 65721

Riverside, Susan Billedo, 224 Hedgerow Dr., Ozark 65721

Rosedale, Anita Jones, 1716 W. Willow Wood Dr., Nixa 65714

Sparta, Violet Roller, 8915 State Hwy. 14 E., Sparta 65753

Sparta, Wesley Roller, 8915 State Hwy. 14 E., Sparta 65753

South Galloway, Chris A. Guise, 1030 Opal Ln., Walnut Shade 65771

South Galloway, Christine Guise, 1030 Opal Ln., Walnut Shade 65771

Union Chapel, Betty Maples, 2621 W. Wild West Rd., Nixa 65714

Union Chapel, Eddie Maples, 2621 W. Wild West Rd., Nixa 65714

Clay County

Chair, Charles Myers, 505 NW 43rd Terr., Kansas City 64116

Vice Chair, Linda Shumate, 15222 Old Quarry Rd., Excelsior Springs 64024

Secretary, Gail Goeke, 18703 Plattsburg Rd., Holt 64048

Treasurer, Don Hanks, 2115 N. Bridge St., Smithville 64068

Clinton County

Chair, Joe Gagnon, 504 Center St., Lathrop 64465

Vice Chair, Mylissa Stutesman, 3695 Hwy. 33 N., Plattsburg 64477

Secretary, Tiffany Kirkland, 1104 Oak St., Lathrop 64465

Treasurer, Mike Shryock, 305 Third St., Trimble 64492

Cole County

Chair, Stephen R. Waters, 1909 Tanner Bridge Rd., Jefferson City 65101

Vice Chair, Charmaine Owens, 315 Eastwood Dr., Jefferson City 65101

Secretary, Susan Cook, 2909 Sue Dr., Jefferson City 65101

Treasurer, Ken Menges, 3617 Schott Rd., Jefferson City 65101

Jefferson City

    Ward 1, Ken Wenzel, 1725 Del Cerro Dr., Jefferson City 65101

    Ward 1, Charmaine Owens, 315 Eastwood Dr., Jefferson City 65101

    Ward 2, Liz Lehmann, 138 E. Circle Dr., Jefferson City 65109

    Ward 2, Kevin Thompson, 138 E. Circle Dr., Jefferson City 65109

    Ward 3, Luana Gifford, 344 Old Gibler Rd., Jefferson City 65109

    Ward 3, Susan Cook, 2909 Sue Dr., Jefferson City 65109

    Ward 4, Susan Vaughn, 1907 Woodcliff Dr., Jefferson City 65109

    Ward 5, Stephen R. Waters, 1909 Tanner Bridge Rd., Jefferson City 65101

    Ward 5, Sherrie Koechling-Burnett, 1103 Lee St., Jefferson City 65101

Jefferson, Carol Menges, 3617 Schott Rd., Jefferson City 65101

Jefferson, Ken Menges, 3617 Schott Rd., Jefferson City 65101

Osage, Kathy J. Quick, 3415 Wardsville Rd., Jefferson City 65101

Marion, Robert Haslag, 10513 Bryant Rd., Centertown 65023

Cooper County

Chair, Richard (Jack) Bell, 1406 El Dorado Tr., Boonville 65233

Dade County

Chair, Sue Jay, 951 W. Dade 22, Lamar 64759

Vice Chair, Don Jay, 951 W. Dade 22, Lamar 64759

Secretary, Velma Wood

Dallas County

Chair, Dewon Rankin, 340 State Rd. C, Buffalo 65622

Vice Chair, Dortha Hill, 659 S. Oak, Buffalo 65622

Secretary, Vickie Stepp, 54 Cascade Ln., Buffalo 65622

Daviess County

Chair, Teresa Eaton, 28143 State Hwy. CC, Gallatin 64640

Vice Chair, Ronnie Mann, 29477 Harbor Ave., Jamesport 64648

Secretary, Pam Howard, 512 S. Wilow St., Gallatin 64640

Treasurer, Mark Corwin, 26348 242nd St., Gallatin 64640

Douglas County

Chair, Teresa Tost, PO Box 863, Ava 65608

Vice Chair, Sandy Hylton, PO Box 490, Ava 65608

Secretary, Tanya Williams, HC 71, Box 222, Ava 65608

Treasurer, Chaz Franzke, PO Box 266, Ava 65608

Franklin County

Chair, Clyde Voelkerding Jr., 1929 Bieker Rd., Washington 63090

Vice Chair, Robin Stewart, 819 Camp St., Washington 63090

Secretary, Becky Russell, 513 S. Washington, Union 63084

Treasurer, William Stewart, 819 Camp St., Washington 63090

Boles, N J Shacklette, 125 American Inn Rd., Villa Ridge 63089

Boone, Donald F. Hess, 210 Broadway, Leslie 63056

Central, Jeff Maune, 7564 Hwy. 47, Union 63084

Lyon, Norman Kloeppel, 4429 Hwy. C, Gerald 63037

Meramec, Tod DeVeydt, 217 East & West Rd., Sullivan 63080

Meramec, Juanita (Stuesse) Abernathy, 7338 Hwy. 185, Leslie 63056

Pacific 2, Carol Johnson, 1515 W. Pacific, Apt. 203, Pacific 63069

Union Ward 1, Daniel J. Kloeppel, 15 Georgetown Ct., Union 63084

Union Ward 2, Mary Jo Straatmann, 622 S. Lincoln Ave., Union 63084

Union, Clyde Voelkerding Jr., 1929 Bieker Rd., Washington 63090

Union, Rebecca Voelkerding, 1929 Bieker Rd., Wasington 63090

Washington Ward 1, Bill Stewart, 819 Camp St., Washington 63090

Washington Ward 1, Robin Stewart, 819 Camp St., Washington 63090

Washington Ward 2, Tom W. Smith, 4 Scenic Dr., Washington 63090

Washington Ward 2, Ruth Ann Smith, 4 Scenic Dr., Washington 63090

Gentry County

Chair, Angela McQuinn, PO Box 81, Stanberry 64489
Vice Chair, John Scirotino, 3327 520th Rd., Albany 64402
Secretary, Linda Bounds, 2616 State Hwy. N., Albany 64401
Huggins, John Sciortino
Huggins, Rose Sciortino

Greene County

Chair, Chris Brown, 1314 E. University St., Springfield 65804
Vice Chair, Mary Faucett, 1334 E. Harrison St., Springfield 65804
Secretary, Marla Marantz, 2445 E. Montclair Ct., Springfield 65804
Treasurer, Wes Zongker, 803 W. Farm Rd. 68, Springfield 65803
Battlefield AB, Jon (Art) Kessler, 4830 W. Elm St., Brookline Station 65619
Battlefield AB, Jo Behlmann, 3402 W. Vincent Dr., Springfield 65810
Campbell
    2nd, Mike Swan, 3771 W. Morningside, Springfield 65807
    1st North, Gale Clithero, 4479 E. Summerfield Dr., Springfield 65802
    1st Nort, Susan Hawkins, 4479 E. Summerfield Dr., Springfield 65802
Cherokee, Catherine Gilpin, 4757 S. Holland Ave., Springfield 65810
Clay
    East (A, B, C), Jeff Munzinger, 2010 S. Shady Hill Ln., Springfield 65809
    East (A, B, C), Linda Palmisano, 3387 E. Farm Rd. 186, Rogersville 65742
Franklin
    1st, David Curtis, 8445 N. Farm Rd. 197, Fair Grove 65648
    2nd, David Peery, 944 E. Farm Rd. 48, Pleasant Hope 65725
    2nd, Kristine Ballhorn, 2354 E. Allison Ln., Springfield 65803
Jackson
    1st, Roy Planchon, 7346 N. Farm Rd. 209, Strafford 65757
    1st, Brenda Planchon, 7346 N. Farm Rd. 209, Strafford 65757
    2nd, Richard Hopper, 4589 N. Farm Rd. 205, Strafford 65757
    2nd, Lanae Gillespie, 6478 N. Farm Rd. 227, Strafford 65757
Murray, Janet Adams, 9695 W. Farm Rd. 76, Willard 65781
Republic
    East, Patricia Hutton, 144 S. Redbud, Republic 65738
    West, Jim Gwaltney, 198 N. Tierra Dr., Republic 65738
    West, Carolyn Gwaltney, 198 N. Tierra Dr., Republic 65738

Robberson
    2nd, Wes Zongker, 803 W. Farm Rd. 68, Springfield 65803
Springfield
    Ward 1 ABC, Craig Hosmer, 1655 E. Delmar, Springfield 65804
    Ward 1 ABC, Jeanie Carver, 1115 S. Weller Ave., Springfield 65804
    Ward 2 AB, Chris Brown, 1314 E. University, Springfield 65804
    Ward 2 AB, Mary Faucett, 1334 E. Harrison, Springfield 65804
    Ward 3 AB, David Trippe, 616 E. Loren, Springfield 65807
    Ward 3 AB, Vicky Trippe, 616 E. Loren, Springfield 65807
    Ward 4 AB, Robert Drake, 1451 S. Roanoke, Springfield 65807
    Ward 4 AB, Kay Mills, 1016 S. Roanoke, Springfield 65807
    Ward 6 AB, Len Eagleburger, 923 S. Missouri, Springfield 65806
    Ward 6 AB, Phyllis Netzer, 845 S. Missouri, Springfield 65806
    Ward 7 ABC, Virgil Hill, 2013 W. Water, Springfield 65802
    Ward 11, Stephen Losh, 1601 S. Ranch Dr. , Springfield 65809
    Ward 11, Violet Losh, 1601 S. Ranch Dr. , Springfield 65809
    Ward 12 AB, Lois Brown, 1231 E. Walnut, Springfield 65802
    Ward 16 ABC, Richard Napieralski, 800 W. Calhoun, Springfield 65802
    Ward 20 AB, Matthew Patterson, 225 E. Commercial Unit D, Springfield 65803
    Ward 22 ABC, Crystal Quade-Waterland, 1612 N. Jefferson Ave., Springfield 65803
    Ward 26 ABC, Charlie Norr, 533 W. Calhoun St., Apt. B, Springfield 65802
    Ward 26 ABC, Janetta Tracy, 2113 N. Douglas, Springfield 65803
    Ward 27 ABC, Brian Madden, 2244 N. Grace, Springfield 65803
    Ward 27 ABC, Anita Kuhns, 1108 W. Hovey, Springfield 65802
    Ward 29 ABC, Floyd Dillabough, 809 E. Hill, Springfield 65803
    Ward 29 ABC, Theresa Armstrong, 2273 E. Nora St., Springfield 65803
    Ward 30 AB, George Burrows, 1610 E. Central St, Springfield 65802
    Ward 30 AB, Linda Powell Bossi, 1201 N. Cooper Blvd., Springfield 65802
    Ward 31 ABC, Chris Albert, 2747 E. McDaniel #B, Springfield 65802
    Ward 31 ABC, Laura Entwisle, 203 N. Burton Ave., Springfield 65802
    Ward 32 ABC, Jack Hembree, 2323 E. Rosebrier, Springfield 65804
    Ward 32 ABC, Carolyn Hembree, 2323 E. Rosebrier, Springfield 65804
    Ward 33 AB, Zachary Allen, 413 E. Seminole St., Springfield 65807
    Ward 33 AB, Debbie Hopkins, 1905-A S. Dollison, Springfield 65807
    Ward 34 ABC, Neil Duvall, 1711 W. Crestview, Springfield 65807

Ward 37 ABC, Gerald Clary, 1650 S. Estate Ave., Springfield 65804

Ward 37 ABC, Shirley Clary, 1650 S. Estate Ave., Springfield 65804

Ward 38 AB, Wayne Bartee, 3033 E. Carlisle, Springfield 65804

Ward 38 AB, Laura Gwin, 1963 S. Mayfair, Springfield 65804

Ward 39 ABC, Jon Moran, 4649 S. Kelly, Springfield 65804

Ward 39 ABC, Jenelle Buxton, 4548 S. Pratt, Springfield 65804

Ward 40 AB, Bob Detherow, 3318 S. Elmira, Springfield 65807

Ward 40 AB, Mary Detherow, 3318 S. Elmira, Springfield 65807

Ward 41 AB, Mark Nelson, 1372 E. Gretna, Springfield 65804

Ward 41 AB, Julia Nelson, 1372 E. Gretna, Springfield 65804

Ward 42 ABC, Terry Bond, 3462 S. Pinehurst Ct, Springfield 65807

Ward 42 ABC, Gwendolyn Jones, 1132 W. Swan, Springfield 65807

Ward 45 AB, Allan Gillihan, 2510 S. Wallis Smith Blvd., Springfield 65804

Taylor, Jim MacLachlan, 5975 E. Farm Rd. 142, Springfield 65809

Taylor, Sandy Grogan, 877 S. Lloyd Dr., Rogersville 65742

Wilson (A,C,CW), Larry Pitts, 4693 S. Forest, Springfield 65810

Wilson (A,C,CW), Frances Pitts, 4693 S. Forest, Springfield 65810

Grundy County

Chair, Marie Gladbach Dolan, 625 SE 10th Ave., Trenton 64683

Vice Chair, Ed Arnold, 500 Hanh, Brimson 64642

Secretary, Beverly Whorton, 1801 Crestview Terr., Trenton 64683

Treasurer, Dan Dennis, 1795 Park Lane Dr., Trenton 64683

Harrison, Jerry Patridge, 592 NW Hwy. A, Trenton 64683

Harrison, Faye Patridge, 592 NW Hwy. A, Trenton 64683

Jackson, Terry Dolan, 625 SE 10th Ave., Trenton 64683

Jackson, Marie Gladback Dolan, 625 SE 10th Ave., Trenton 64683

Liberty, Betty Grambling, 404 S. Elm St., Galt 64641

Madison, Thomas Kenady, 60202 NW Hwy. 146, Trenton 64683

Madison, Patricia Koon, 60205 NW Hwy. 146, Trenton 64683

Myers, Jake Batson, 1168 NE Hwy. J, Galt 64641

Trenton Ward 2, Marilyn Davidson, 1707 Tower St., Trenton 64683

Trenton Ward 3, Dan Dennis, 1795 Parklane Dr., Trenton 64683

Trenton Ward 3, Beverly Whorton, 1801 Crestview Terr, Trenton 64683

Trenton Ward 4, John Dolan, 4002 Manor Dr., Trenton 64683

Trenton Ward 4, Barb Pfaff, 435 SE Hwy. Z, Trenton 64683

Washington, Jack Clark, 994 NW Hwy. A, Spickard 64679

Henry County

Chair, James Switzler, 283 SE 200 Rd., Clinton 64735

Vice Chair, Karen Switzler, 283 SE 200 Rd., Clinton 64735

Treasurer, Harold Dump, 200 S. High, Calhoun 65323

Hickory County

Chair, Henry Garcia, RR 2, Box 1557, Wheatland 65779

Vice Chair, Gerda Fitts, 101 Pace Circle, Hermitage 65668

Secretary, Don Parks, RR 81, Box 544, Flemington 65650

Treasurer, John Parks, RR 81, Box 544, Flemington 65650

Howard County

Chair, Mary Markland Jarboe, PO Box 127, Armstrong 65230

Vice Chair, Henry B. Graham, 3160 Hwy. 240, Fayette 65248

Secretary, Mark Jarboe, PO Box 127, Armstrong 65248

Treasurer, Charles (Steve) Frevert, 683 State Rt. AA, Glasglow 65254

Howell County

Chair, Greta Myers, 1027 Sassafrass St., Willow Springs 65793

Vice Chair, Travis Morrison, PO Box 30, West Plains 65775

Secretary, Connie Pendergrass, 772 CR 6320, Bakersfield 65609

Treasurer, RA Pendergrass, 772 CR 6320, Bakersfield 65609

Iron County

Chair, Jim Scaggs, 3743 Hwy. F, Annapolis 63620

Vice Chair, Vivian Adams, 106 Fairlane, Ironton 63650

Secretary, Shelley Bishop, 3014 Hwy. A, Belleview 63623

Treasurer, Ralph Trask, 22725 Hwy. 32, Belleview 63623

Arcadia, Jack Adams, 106 Fairlane, Ironton 63650

Arcadia, Vivian A. Adams, 106 Fairlane, Ironton 63650

Dent, Lance Mayfield, 20 Meadowcrest Dr., Viburnum 65566

Iron, William McKinney Sr., 2850 Hwy. 21, Belleview 63623

Iron, Paula McKinney, 2846 Hwy. 21, Belleview 63623

Kaolin, Ralph Trask, 22725 Hwy. 32, Belleview 63623

Kaolin, Shelley Bishop, 2014 Hwy. A, Belleview 63623

Union, Jim Scaggs, 3743 Hwy. F, Annapolis 63620

Jackson County

Chair, Tom Wyrsch, 9815 Cherry St., Apt. 4, Kansas City 64131

Vice Chair, Dee Evans, 2548 Paseo Blvd., Kansas City 64108

Secretary, Judy Briggs, 2424 S.W. 12th Ct., Lee's Summit 64081

Treasurer, John Comstock, 4019 Clark Ave., Kansas City 64111

Blue

Sub-District 1, Goldie Troutwine, 9850 E. Winner Rd., Independence 64052

Sub-District 1, Paul J. Wrabec, 11227 Thompson Ave., Sugar Creek 64054

Sub-District 2, Curt Dougherty, 16003 E. Cogan Ln., Independence 64050

Sub-District 2, Susan Dougherty, 16003 E. Cogan Ln., Independence 64050

Sub-District 3, Diane Egger, 1814 Ashley Dr., Independence 64058

Sub-District 3, John A. Mayfield, 18926 Powahatan Ct. E, Independence 64056

Sub-District 4, Caroline Gnefkow, 610 N. River Blvd., Independence 64050

Sub-District 4, Travis Richey, 127 E. Kansas Ave., Independence 64050

Sub-District 5, Sam LeVota, 2613 Santa Fe Rd., Independence 64052

Sub-District 5, Sheri Tindle, 9714 E. 27th St. S., Independence 64052

Sub-District 6, Christopher R. Whiting, 2933 Sweet Briar Dr., Independence 64057

Sub-District 6, Jaqueline Whiting, 3000 Iva Dr., Independence 64057

Sub-District 7, Meghan LeVota, 4316 S. Avon Dr., Independence 64055

Sub-District 7, Paul LeVota, 4316 S. Avon Dr., Independence 64055

Sub-District 8, Jeffrey Walker, 4901 S. Kendall Dr., Independence 64055

Sub-District 8, Nicki Cardwell, 16617 Cogan Rd., Independence 64055

Brooking, Kimberly, Clause Luaces, 11411 E. 83rd St., Raytown 64138

Brooking, Michael N. Downing, 9300 E. 65th St., Raytown 64133

Brooking, Fred H. Hartwell, 10901 E. 82nd St., Raytown 64138

Brooking, Sandra A. Hartwell, 10901 E. 82nd St., Raytown 64138

Fort Osage, B. DeAun Young, 107 E. Jefferson St., Buckner 64016

Fort Osage, Jeff M. Jones, 36106 E. Steinhauser Rd., Buckner 64016

Fort Osage, Keith Querry, 1516 N. Charlton Rd., Independence 64056

Fort Osage, Sandra A. Querry, 1516 N. Charlton Rd., Independence 64056

Prairie, Chere Chaney, 1933 SW Second St., Lee's Summit 64081

Prairie, Martin Kerr, 4802 NE Pebble Beach, Lee's Summit 64064

Prairie, Michael A. LeVota, 400 NE Brockton Dr., Lee's Summit 64064

Prairie, Judy Briggs, 2424 SW 12th Ct., Lee's Summit 64081

Prairie, Jerry L. Briggs, 2424 SW 12th Ct., Lee's Summit 64081

Prairie, Karen Conrad, 2449 SW Lilly Dr., Lee's Summit 64081

Sni-A-Bar, Joe Becker, 638 NW Rosaceae Dr., Blue Springs 64015

Sni-A-Bar, Lanna Ultican, 1204 SW 18th St., Blue Springs 64015

Sni-A-Bar, Robert Alton Clarke, 908 NE Third St., Blue Springs 64014

Sni-A-Bar, Michael J. Bellinghausen, 26 Anchor Dr., Lake Tapawingo 64015

Sni-A-Bar, Tomi R. Bellinghausen, 26 Anchor Dr., Lake Tapawingo 64015

Sni-A-Bar, Roxann Thorley, 21200 E. 50th Terr. Dr. S., Independence 64015

Van Buren, Ron Harvey, 33811 E. 50 Hwy., Lee's Summit 64086

Van Buren, Renee Paluka-White, 10219 S. Munro Rd., Lone Jack 64070

Kansas City

Ward 1, Norma A. Raya, 2940 Holly St., Kansas City 64108

Ward 1, Porfirio Raya Sr., 2940 Holly St., Kansas City 64108

Ward 2, Shaheer Akhtab, 2535 Campbell St., Apt. G, Kansas City 64108

Ward 2, Virginia Dee Evans, 2548 W. Paseo Blvd., Kansas City 64108

Ward 3, Pat Clarke, 4010 S. Benton, Kansas City 64130

Ward 3, LeShyeka Roland, 3114 Agnes #2, Kansas City 64128

Ward 4, Gene Morgan, 3837 Campbell, Kansas City 64109

Ward 4, Lali Garcia, 915 W. 32nd, Kansas City 64111

Ward 5, Hila (Dutch) Newman, 4122 Mercier, Kansas City 64111

Ward 5, John (Coach) Comstock, 4019 Clark Ave., Kansas City 64111

Ward 6, Michael J. Damico, 21 E. 54th Terr., Kansas City 64112

Ward 6, Beth Low, 5930 Cherry St., Kansas City 64110

Ward 7, Keith Martin Thomas, 1832 E. 49th St., Kansas City 64130

Ward 7, Rosa James, 4207 Benton Blvd., Kansas City 64130

Ward 8, Philip Glynn, 6537 Summit St., Kansas City 64113

Ward 8, Lori Ann Lewellen, 1007 W. 70th St., Kansas City 64113

Ward 9, Janet Lillis, 7301 Jarboe, Kansas City 64114

Ward 9, John Lillis, 7301 Jarboe, Kansas City 64114

Ward 10, India Williams, 9925 Locust St., Apt 3205, Kansas City 64131

Ward 10, Tom Wyrsch, 9815 Cherry St., Apt. 4, Kansas City 64131

Ward 11, Ingrid Burnett, 3418 Gladstone Blvd., Kansas City 64123

Ward 11, John P. Burnett, 3418 Gladstone Blvd., Kansas City 64123

Ward 12, Sam Crowley, 4246 E. Eighth St., Kansas City 64124

Ward 12, Tracy L. Marriott, 320 S. Colorado, Kansas City 64124

Ward 13, Crispin Rea Jr., 1611 Topping, Kansas City 64126

Ward 13, Sayra Amelia Gordillo, 5821 E. Ninth St., Kansas City 64125

Ward 14, Shalonn (Kiki) Curls, 1909 Myrtle Ave., Kansas City 64127

Ward 14, James D. Tindall Sr., 1904 Mersington Ct., Kansas City 64127

Ward 15, Thurman Michael Davis Jr., 4508 Chelsea Ave., Kansas City 64130

Ward 15, Norma Bredemeier, 3544 Fremont Ave., Kansas City 64129

Ward 16, Darren L. Smith, 5629 Tracy Ave., Kansas City 64110

Ward 16, Gail McCann Beatty, 6012 Woodland Ave., Kansas City 64110

Ward 17, Alicia Bland, 7125 E. 69th St., Kansas City 64133

Ward 17, Craig Bland, 7125 E. 69th St., Kansas City 64133

Ward 18, Janice Dunn, 7600 E. 75th Terr., Kansas City 64138

Ward 18, Kenneth E. Ray, 7560 Wabash Ave., Kansas City 64132

Ward 19, Kristi D. Whitaker, 6307 Fairlane Dr., Kansas City 64134

Ward 20, Cathy Spainhower, 3512 Bridge Manor Dr., Kansas City 64137

Ward 20, Scott Taylor, 632 E. 108th St., Kansas City 64131

Ward 22, Michele A. Newby, 11522 Wornall Rd., Kansas City 64114

Ward 22, Vincent P. Accurso, 322 W. Minor Dr., Kansas City 64114

Ward 23, Dean T. Moulder, 4300 Ditzler Ave., Kansas City 64133

Ward 23, Phyllis Woodson, 10417 E. 43rd St., Apt. 141, Kansas City 64133

Ward 24, Lanette LeVota, 16000 Ess Rd., Kansas City 64136

Ward 24, Terry M. Riley, 9414 E. Pleasant Ave., Kansas City 64138

Ward 25, Vanessa Claborn-Welch, 10530 Wallace Ave., Kansas City 64134-2166

Ward 25, Darrell Curls, 8006 E. 117th Terr., Kansas City 64134

Ward 26, Breman Anderson Jr., 8303 E. 92nd Terr., Kansas City 64138

Ward 26, Carol Graves, 9619 Manning, Kansas City 64134

Washington, Dorothy M. Kennedy, 8031 E. 130th Ct., Grandview 64030

Washington, Elaine Brewer, 13306 Crystal Ave., Grandview 64030

Washington, Joe Runions, 12336 Norton, Grandview 64030

Washington, Patrick J. Oxler, 13209 Winchester, Grandview 64030

Jasper County

Chair, Jospeh Cowen, 3040 S. Woodland Dr., Joplin 64804
Vice Chair, Don Evans, 5941 CL 184, Joplin 64801
Secretary, Steve Daniels, 202 Timberlane, Carl Junction 64834
Treasurer, Sue Cowen, 3040 S. Woodland Dr., Joplin 64804

Jefferson County

Chair, Linda Schilly, 313 Jefferson Ave., Crystal City 63019
Vice Chair, Wayne Stanley, 4200 Hillsboro Hematite Rd., Hillsboro 63050
Secretary, William (Bill) Matzker, 6921 Old Lemay Ferry Rd., Imperial 63052
Treasurer, Frances Newkirk, 36 Huntleigh Woods, Barnhart 63012

Johnson County

Chair, Randy Huggins, 207 N. Moulton, Leeton 64761
Vice Chair, Myrna Clifford, 575 N.E. 200, Knob Noster
Secretary, Jewell James
Treasurer, Bob Yates

Knox County

Chair, Paul Parsons, 901 E. Morgan, Edina 63537
Vice Chair, Janice McGennis, Hwy. 6 East, Edina 63537
Secretary, Jeanne Mayfield, RR 1, Box 185, Edina 63531
Treasurer, Patsy Parsons, 901 E. Morgan, Edina 63537
Bourbon, Ann Greenley, RR 1, Box 284, Novelty 63460
Bourbon, Quentin Greenley, RR 1, Box 284, Novelty 63460
Center–East, Patsy Parsons, 901 E. Morgan, Edina 63537
Center–East, Paul Parsons, 901 E. Morgan, Edina 63537
Fabius, Evelyn Johnston, RR 1, Box 78D, Newark 63458
Greensburg, Jeanne Mayfield, RR 1, Box 185, Baring 63531
Greensburg, L.P. Mayfield, RR 1, Box 185, Baring 63531

Jeddo, Mark Greenley, RR 1, Box 159, Knox City 63446
Jeddo, Kathy Greenley, RR 1, Box 159, Knox City 63446
Lyon, Maurine Mayer, RR 2, Box 177, Hurdland 63547
Salt River, Billy Wilkerson, RR 1, Box 197, Novelty 63460
Shelton, Joe Mayor, RR 2, Box 51, Hurdland 63547

Laclede County

Chair, Don Fohn, 15960 Hwy. E, Eldridge 65463
Vice Chair, Laura L. Valenti, 25698 Misty View, Lebanon 65536

Lafayette County

Chair, Cindy Schroer, 919 N. Main, Higginsville 64037
Vice Chair, Jack Bainbridge, 7750 Bass Rd., Odessa 64076
Secretary, Terrence Messonnier, 407 E. Chestnut, Odessa 64076
Treasurer, Janet Ritzinger, 1408 N. Main, Higginsville 64037

Lewis County

Chair, John Campen, 24359 200th St., Monticello 63457
Vice Chair, Karen Veatch, 306 S. Water St., Monticello 63457
Secretary, Keri Cottrell, 602 Woodman Cir., Canton 63435
Treasurer, Larry Arnold, 110 White St., Canton 63435

Linn County

Chair, Philip Fay, 22418 Grant Rd., Brookfield 64628
Vice Chair, Lela Groes, 232 S. Pine, Brookfield 64628
Secretary, Eudora Fitzpatrick, 18717 Bow Dr., Linneus 64653
Treasurer, Tracy Carlson, 200 W. Hayden, Marceline 64658
Brookfield 1, Joey R. Enyeart, 414 N. Monroe St., Brookfield 64628
Brookfield 1, Mary S. Enyeart, 414 N. Monroe St., Brookfield 64628
Brookfield 3, Joshua Fay, 764 Tomahawk Dr., Brookfield 64628
Brookfield 3, Patty Gooch, 402 Hunt St., Brookfield 64628
Brookfield 4, Jean F. Teeter, 207 Markham Ct., Brookfield 64628
Brookfield 4, Lela Groes, PO Box 156, Brookfield 64628
Bucklin, Galen Switzer, 32782 Little Rd., Bucklin 64631
Bucklin, Donna Switzer, 32782 Little Rd., Bucklin 64631
Clay, Eudora Fitzpatrick, 18718 Bow Dr., Linneus 64653
Enterprise, Jerome L. Ward, 25179 Ivory Rd., Browning 64630
Enterprise, Peggy Ward, 25179 Ivory Rd., Browning 64630
Jefferson, Philip H. Fay, 22418 Grant Rd., Brookfield 64628
Locust Creek, James M. Libby, 23884 Falcon Dr., Linneus 64653
Locust Creek, Anna Barker, PO Box 103, Linneus 64653
Marceline 1, Tracy L. Carlson, 325 E. Santa Fe Ave., Marceline 64658
North Benton, John W. Grice, 13420 Fawn Rd., Browning 64630
North Benton, Mary E. Grice, 13420 Fawn Rd., Browning 64630
South Benton, Kenny Creason, 20728 Hwy. C, Purdin 64674
South Benton, Rhonda Creason, 20728 Hwy. C, Purdin 64674

Livingston County

Chair, Kelly Christopher, 10128 LIV 529, Chillicothe 64601
Vice Chair, Steve Ripley, 12276 LIV 222, Chillicothe 64601
Secretary, Brian Donath, PO Box 756, Chillicothe 64601
Treasurer, Amy Hobbs, 400 Grandview, Chillicothe 64601
Chillicothe
 Ward 1, Kenneth Lauhoff, 1203 Miller Ave., Chillicothe 64601
 Ward 1, Brenda Lauhoff, 1203 Miller Ave., Chillicothe 64601
 Ward 2, Martha Peery, 75 12th St., Chillicothe 64601
 Ward 3, Jack Kelly, 203 Calhoun St., Chillicothe 64601
 Ward 3, Teresa Kelly, 203 Calhoun St., Chillicothe 64601
 Ward 4, Amy Hobbs, 400 Grandview Ave., Chillicothe 64601
Chillicothe, Brenda Wright, 12707 LIV 224, Chillicothe 64601
Chillicothe, Steve Ripley, 12276 LIV 222, Chillicothe 64601
Grand River, James Figg, 23342 LIV 377, Hale 64643
Jackson, Todd Rodenberg, 9604 LIV 529, Chillicothe 64601
Jackson, Kelly Christopher, 10128 LIV 529, Chillicothe 64601
Mooresville, Robert Donoho, 18855 LIV 405, Mooresville 64664

Macon County

Chair, Glenda Schroeder, 24791 State Hwy. J, Atlanta 63530
Vice Chair, Frankie Wright, 37587 State Hwy. Y, Jacksonville 65260
Secretary, Diana Scott, 33146 State Hwy. 156, La Plata 63549
Treasurer, Gary Roberts, 29946 Macon Lake Rd., Macon 63552

Madison County

Chair, Ronald Pember, 11288 Hwy. 67, Fredericktown 63645
Vice Chair, Patricia Pember, 11288 Hwy. 67, Fredericktown 63645
Secretary, Donal Firebaugh, 1022 Madison 9252, Fredericktown 63645
Treasurer, Paula Francis, 1117 Madison 507, Fredericktown 63645

Marion County

Chair, Nancy Goellner, 6618 CR 318, Palmyra 63461
Vice Chair, John E. Yancey, 7 Sunnyslope, Hannibal 63401
Secretary, Crystal Stephens, 2713 Chestnut, Hannibal 63461
Treasurer, David Klassen, 271 Meadowridge Dr., Hannibal 63401
Fabius, Nancy E. Goellner, 6618 CR 318, Palmyra 63461
Fabius, Richard W. Goellner, 6618 CR 318, Palmyra 63461
Liberty, Marti Myers, 5067 Hwy. C, Palmyra 63461

Liberty, Larry D. Myers, 5067 Hwy. C, Palmyra 63461
Liberty, James M. Ragar, 4801 Hwy. 61, Palmyra 63461
Liberty, Betty M. Ragar, 4801 Hwy. 61, Palmyra 63461
Mason Ward 1, Diane Kocher, 69 Saturn, Hannibal 63401
Mason Ward 1, John S. Hark, 3310 Arapaho, Hannibal 63401
Mason Ward 2, Deborah S. (Debbie) Jackson, 8 Hamlin Heights, Hannibal 63401
Mason Ward 2, John E. Yancey, 7 Sunny Slope, Hannibal 63401
Mason Ward 3, Joseph R, Frese, 212 N. Eighth St., Hannibal 63401
Mason Ward 3, Dian Volkmer, 2107 Crescent Dr., Hannibal 63401
Mason Ward 4, Melanie Powell, 720 Hickory, Hannibal 63401
Mason Ward 5, Crystal Stephens, 2713 Chestnut St., Hannibal 63401
Mason Ward 6, Joyce J. Kesner, 25 Settlers Tr., Hannibal 63401
Mason Ward 6, David H. Klassen, 271 Meadowridge Dr., Hannibal 63401
Miller, Doris Beatty, 8130 Hwy. MM, Hannibal 63401
Miller, David Griffith, 8715 CR 414, Hannibal 63401
Round Grove, Loretta L. Bringer, 4125 CR 118, Maywood 63454
Round Grove, Marvin W. Bringer, 4125 CR 118, Maywood 63454
South River, Teya Stice, 5875 Wisteria Ln., Palmyra 63461
South River, Lyndon Bode, 6950 CR 263, Palmyra 63461
Union, Hazel Kesner, PO Box 84, Philadelphia 63463
Warren, Lowell Schachtsiek, 6938 CR 249, Palmyra 63461
Warren, Valerie A. Dornberger, 5836 CR 253, Palmyra 63461

Moniteau County

Chair, Gail Hughes, 1005 Pamela Dr., California 65018
Vice Chair, Dorothy Hughes, 1005 Pamela Dr., California 65018
Secretary, Teresa (Resa) Dudley, 902 S. Oak St., California 65018
Treasurer, Ralph Gaw, PO Box 240, Tipton 65081

Monroe County

Chair, Jane Akers, 108 Main, Holliday 65258
Vice Chair, Floyd Lawson, 203 Fair St., PO Box 36, Paris 65275
Secretary, Becky Vanlandingham, 30825 RR D, Paris 65275
Treasurer, Eddy Mitchell, 10359 Monroe Rd. 971, Stoutsville 65283
Indian Creek, Floyd J. Buckman, 36627 Monroe Rd. 580, Stoutsville 65283
Jackson, Floyd E. Lawson, 203 Fair, PO Box 36, Paris 65275
Jackson, Dian Lawson, 203 Fair, PO Box 36, Paris 65275
Jefferson, James P. Hunt, 34119 Rt. U, Stoutsville 65283
Jefferson, Lisa Minor, 35744 Monroe Rd. 460, Stoutsville 65283
Marion, Eddy Mitchell, 19349 Monroe Rd. 971, Holliday 65258
Monroe, Joe Ralph Buckman, 30038 Monroe Rd. 381, Monroe City 63456
Monroe, Susie Buckman, 30038 Monroe Rd. 381, Monroe City 63456
South Fork, Linden L. Vanlandingham, 30825 Rt. D, Paris 65275

South Fork, Becky B. Vanlandingham, 30825 Rt. D, Paris 65275

Union, Mike O'Bannon, 12481 Hwy. 151, Madison 65263

Union, Twana Hulen, 19268 Rt. AA, Madison 65263

Woodlawn, Wesley J. Shoemyer, 16350 Monroe Rd. 184, Clarence 63437

Woodlawn, Cheryl L. Shoemyer, 16350 Monroe Rd. 184, Clarence 63437

Montgomery County

Chair, Joan Andrews, 2123 Hwy. 161, Montgomery City 63361

Vice Chair, Walter McQuie Jr., 420 Hensley St., Montgomery City 63361

Secretary, Ann Scarlet, 628 N. Sturgeon, Montgomery City 63361

Treasurer, Rod Sturgeon, 66 Haflinger Rd., Montgomery City 63361

Morgan County

Chair, Sandra Schwartz, 27128 Mari Ln., Barnett 65011

Vice Chair, Harold Schwartz, 27128 Mari Ln., Barnett 65011

Secretary, Beverly Ricker, 31385 Beal Rd., Stover 65078

Treasurer, James Fowler, 12583 Akin Dr., Fortuna 65034

Buffalo, William Ricker, 31385 Beal Rd., Stover 65078

Buffalo, Beverly Ricker, 31385 Beal Rd., Stover 65078

Haw Creek, M.B. Jones, 11276 Fairgrounds Rd., Versailles 65084

Haw Creek, Carol Jones, 11276 Fairgrounds Rd., Versailles 65084

Mill Creek, James Fowler, 12583 Akin Dr., Fortuna 65034

Mill Creek, Norvetta Johnson, 5519 Hwy. D, Syracuse 65354

Moreau, David Francis, 12888 Graystone Rd., Versailles 65084

Moreau, Kathy Francis, 12888 Graystone Rd., Versailles 65084

Osage, Harold Schwartz, 27128 Marina Ln., Barnett 65011

Osage, Sandra Schwartz, 27128 Marina Ln., Barnett 65011

New Madrid County

Chair, Hal Hunter III, 545 Virginia, New Madrid 63869

Vice Chair, Gail Duke, 833 County Hwy. 635, New Madrid 63869

Secretary, Michael Pyles, PO Box 54, Matthews 63867

Treasurer, Wanda Underwood, 200 Clover Ln., Portageville 63873

Newton County

Chair, Sharon Palmer, 8171 W. Hwy. 86, Joplin 64804

Vice Chair, Pat Kelly, 517 W. Neosho St., Granby 64844

Secretary, Doug Brooks, 3734 Chipmunk Dr., Joplin 64801

Treasurer, Karen Croft, 8171 W. Hwy. 86, Joplin 64804

Crowder, Jim Hight, 1192 Industrial Dr., Neosho 64850

Diamond, Alice Black, 174 Reindeer Dr., Sarcoxie 64862

East Neosho, Bill Horton, 15662 Monark Dr., Neosho 64850

East Neosho, Margaret Tracy, 589 Cemetery Rd., Neosho 64850

Granby, Harry Gardner, 1132 S. Main St, Granby 64844

Granby, Janice Reed, 126 E. Neosho, Granby 64844

Hornet, James Iwan, 2111 S. Loma Linda Dr, Loma Linda 64804

Hornet, Dorothy Iwan, 2111 S. Loma Linda Dr, Loma Linda 64804

Neosho 2, Wes Nall, 1205 Northwest Blvd., Neosho 64850

Neosho 2, Vera Nall, 1205 Northwest Blvd., Neosho 64850

Neosho 3, Jim Hight, 1192 Industrial Dr., Neosho 64850

Neosho 4, John Felder, 1807 Rachel Dr., Neosho 64850

Neosho 4, Valerie A. Kirby, 329 Park St., Neosho 64850

Ritchey, Betty Shepherd, 31117 Hwy. 60, Pierce City 65723

Seneca, Skyler Jones, 1904 Cherry Rd, Seneca 64865

Staples West, Doug Brooks, 3734 Chipmunk Dr., Joplin 64804

Thurman, Charles A. Compton, 4410 Old Hwy. 71, Joplin 64804

West Neosho, Robert Brumback, 12070 Wildlife Rd, Neosho 64850

Nodaway County

Chair, Joe Baumli, 30707 U.S. Hwy. 71, Maryville 64468

Vice Chair, Beth Walker, 30650 U.S. Hwy. 71, Burlington Junction 64428

Secretary, Robert A. Steins, 37973 282nd St., Ravenwood 64479

Treasurer, Marilyn K. Jenkins, 122 S. Clayton, Maryville 64468

Grant, Marvin Harper, 202 McCandles, Barnard 64423

Green, Robert L. Ritterbusch, 11554 State Hwy. 46, Skidmore 64487

Green, Mary M. Porter, 12515 215th St., Burlington Junction 64428

Hopkins, Donald R. Crane, 12102 State Hwy. FF, Hopkins 64461

Hopkins, Judith L. Crane, 12012 State Hwy. FF, Hopkins 64461

Jackson, Robert A. Stiens, 37975 282nd St., Ravenwood 64479

Jackson, Joyce E. Stiens, 37975 282nd St., Ravenwood 64479

Jefferson, Ed Holtman, 37009 North St., Conception 64433

Jefferson, Judy Holtman, 37009 North St., Conception 64433

Lincoln, Larry M. Ecker, 14678 120th St., Elmo 64445

Lincoln, Sharron Ecker, 14678 120th St., Elmo 64445

Monroe, Rana Killingsworth, 309 W. Elm, Skidmore 64487

Nodaway, Beth Walker, 20650 U.S. Hwy. 71, Burlington Junction 64428

Nodaway, Mike Walker, 20650 U.S. Hwy. 71, Burlington Junction 64428

Polk, Joe Baumli, 30707 U.S. Hwy. 71, Maryville 64468

Polk, Marilyn K. Jenkins, 122 S. Clayton, Maryville 64468

Union, Larry Dew, 101 S. Harmon, Pickering 64476

Union, Carolyn Dew, 101 S. Harmon, Pickering 64476

Washington, Julie K. Farnan, 37111 Mercury Rd., Guilford 64457

White Cloud, Robert Lager, 33251 U.S. Hwy. 71, Maryville 64468

White Cloud, Terri Lager, 33251 U.S. Hwy. 71, Maryville 64468

Oregon County

Chair, Ronald McNear, RR 81, Box 149, Koshkonong 65692

Vice Chair, Debbie Sallings, RR 72, Box 2578, Alton 65606

Secretary, Mike Luster, RR 2, Box 2147, Thayer 65791

Treasurer, Ramo Roberts, RR 73, Box 1692, Couch 65690

Osage County

Chair, Larry Hunt, 13 Country Rd. 420, Linn 65051
Vice Chair, Judy Tripp, 3157 Hwy. W, Bonnots Mill 65016
Secretary, Lorriane Rehagen, 390 Bozi Valley Tr., Freeburg 65035
Treasurer, Bob Schmitz, 122 Samson Century Ln., Bonnots Mill 65016

Ozark County

Dawt, Jerry F. Lash, HC 2, Box 2390, Tecumseh 65760
Dawt, Jerry Ann Lash, HC 2, Box 2390, Tecumseh 65760
Noble, Don Pinckney, HC 2, Box 11, Wasola 65773
West Bridges, Dennis Lawson, HC 2, Box 810, Gainesville 65655

Pemiscot County

Chair, Lanice Samford, 308 Coil St., Steele 63877
Vice Chair, David Wilkerson, 2739 W. State Hwy. 84, Bragg City 63827
Secretary, Jacqueline McGee, 312 N. Ash, Hayti 63851
Treasurer, Randy McDaniel, 158 Locust, Steele 63877

Pettis County

Chair, Michael G. Franklin, 1103 E. 17th St., Sedalia 65301
Vice Chair, Janice Klenke, 10203 Rangeline Rd., Houstonia 65333
Secretary, Fred Melvin Ream III, 107 W. Hwy. B, Green Ridge 65332
Treasurer, Charli Ackerman, 23280 Hwy. B, Sedalia 65301
Dresden, James R. DeMotte, 22375 Buckeye Rd., Sedalia 65301
Dresden, Mary DeMotte, 22375 Buckeye Rd., Sedalia 65301
Flat Creek, Jesse Blankenship, 22285 Hwy. F, Sedalia 65301
Flat Creek, Sharon Blankenship, 22285 Hwy. F, Sedalia 65301
Green Ridge, Fred Melvin Ream III, 107 W. Hwy. B, Green Ridge 65332
Green Ridge, Pam Doane, 204 W. Cooper St., Green Ridge 65332
Heath Creek, Robert Leftwich, 16099 Woodland Rd., Hughesville 65334
Houstonia, Dennis H. Klenke, 10203 Rangeline Rd., Houstonia 65333
Houstonia, Janice Klenke, 10203 Rangeline Rd., Houstonia 65333
Prairie, Phyllis Domann, 1410 Timber Ridge Dr., Sedalia 65301
Sedalia East, Dianne Lynn Fluty, 3144 Elsie Dr., Sedalia 65301
Sedalia West, Charli Ackerman, 23280 Hwy. B, Sedalia 65301
Sedalia West, Michael Ackerman, 23280 Hwy. B, Sedalia 65301
Smithton W Brooking, James Ellis, 6125 McVey Rd., Sedalia 65301
Smithton W Brooking, Marguerite Ellis, 6125 McVey Rd., Sedalia 65301
Sedalia
  Ward 1, Precinct 3, Jack Arnold, 960 Mitchell Rd., Apt. 18, Sedalia 65301
  Ward 2, Precinct 1, Arwilda Poole, 210 E. Henry, Sedalia 65301
  Ward 2, Precinct 1, Noah Poole, 210 E. Henry, Sedalia 65301
  Ward 2, Precinct 2, Thomas Martin, 1409 Cedar Dr., Sedalia 65301
  Ward 2, Precinct 3, William E. Jeffries Jr., 731 E. Fifth St., Sedalia 65301
  Ward 3, Precinct 1, Janet Kresse, 1700 E. 22nd St., Sedalia 65301
  Ward 3, Precinct 1, George T. Crafton, 2305 S. Ohio, Sedalia 65301
  Ward 3, Precinct 3, Michael E. Franklin, 1103 E. 17th St., Sedalia 65301
  Ward 3, Precinct 3, Donna Sue Franklin, 1103 E. 17th St., Sedalia 65301
  Ward 4, Precinct 1, Oliver T. Bridges, 2417 S. Grand, Sedalia 65301
  Ward 4, Precinct 1, Sharon Bridges, 2417 S. Grand, Sedalia 65301
  Ward 4, Precinct 2, Rachell Finnell, 1516 Honeysuckle, Sedalia 65301
  Ward 4, Precinct 3, Matt Musslin, 1424 S. Sneed, Sedalia 65301
  Ward 4, Precinct 3, Charlene Egbert, 900 S. Carr, Sedalia 65301

Phelps County

Chair, Brad Neckermann, 303 Christy Dr., Rolla 65401
Vice Chair, Katie Croker, 2441 Lanes End Rd., Apt. D, Rolla 65401
Secretary, Kathleen Fox, 1623 Yale, Rolla 65401
Treasurer, Lance Thurman, 1613 Lincoln Ln., Rolla 65401
Cold Springs West, Norma G. Harris, 14504 CR 7240, Newburg 65550
Meramec, Henry E. (Ed) Skaggs, 19900 Hwy. 8, St. James 65559
Meramec, Brenda J. Skaggs, 19900 Hwy. 8, St. James 65559
Miller, Carol J. Bennett, 14211 CR 8050, Rolla 65401
Rolla Ward 1, Bill Lindgren, 702 E. Sixth St., Rolla 65401
Rolla Ward 2, Lance Thurman, 1613 Lincoln Ln., Rolla 65401
Rolla Ward 4, Adrienne Neckermann, 303 Christy Dr., Rolla 65401
Rolla Ward 4, Brad Neckermann, 303 Christy Dr., Rolla 65401
Rolla Ward 5, Nathan Atkinson, 704 S. Rolla, Rolla 65401
Rolla Ward 6, Katie Croker, 2441 Lanes End, Rolla 65401
St. James Ward 2, Pat Lizotte, 524 St. James Ave., St. James 65559

Pike County

Chair, John (Buzz) Lovell, 801 River Ridge Rd., Louisiana 63353
Vice Chair, Barbara Ann Husler, 12876 Pike 103, New London 63439
Secretary, Dold Stewart, 15850 Pike 114, Louisiana 63353
Treasurer, Mary Ann Lovell, 801 River Ridge Rd., Louisiana 63353

Platte County

Chair, Pauli Kendrick, 9308 NW 80th Terr., Weatherby Lake 64152
Vice Chair, Ken Hunt, 8202 NW Cakwallader, Kansas City 64152
Secretary, Melba Nicolaisen, 6802 N. Fisk Ave., Kansas City 64151
Treasurer, Robert Dixon, 1024 West St., Parkville 64152

Polk County

Chair, Will Westmoreland, 1548 E. 432nd Rd., Bolivar 65613
Vice Chair, Patricia Zumwalt, 865 Redel Pl., Bolivar 65613
Secretary, Fred Melvin Higginbotham, 4431 S. 157th Rd., Bolivar 65613
Treasurer, Anita Grant, 4244 S. 205th Rd., Bolivar 65613

Pulaski County

Chair, Clara Ichord, 1508 Hull Valley Dr., Waynesville 65583
Vice Chair, Kyle Bomar, 1500 Hwy. 17, Crocker 65452

Ralls County

Chair, Lucia Hamill, 1117 E. Main St., Perry 63462
Vice Chair, John Briscoe, 209 College, New London 63459
Secretary, Mary Lane, 49506 Hwy. JJ, Center 63436
Treasurer, Wiley Hibbard, 43764 Adams Trl., Perry 63462
Center, Donna Evans, 21895 Coyote Hills Dr., Center 63436
Center, John Palmer, 302 E. Hawkins, Center 63436
Clay, Sheila M. Foster, 13546 Cheyenne Dr., New London 63459
Clay, Willard St. Clair, 3915 New London Gravel Rd., Hannibal 63401
Jasper, George E. Lane, 49506 Hwy. JJ, Center 63436
Jasper, Mary Lane, 49506 Hwy. JJ, Center 63436
Saline, Debbie Durbin, 11834 Mulberry Rd, Monroe City 63456
Saline, Kaleb Thompson, 13946 Gentry Rd., Monroe City 63456
Salt River, Lucia Hamill, 1117 E. Main, Perry 63462
Salt River, Wiley Hibbard, 43764 Adams Trl, Perry 63462
Saverton, Alvina Dotson, 17063 Bailey Bridge Rd., New London 63459
Saverton, John E. Stone, 65146 Red Barn Rd., New London 63459
Spencer, Bobbie G. Winders, 17732 Eastside Dr., New London 63459
Spencer, John Briscoe, 209 College, Box 446, New London 63459

Randolph County

Chair, Sue Fennel, 1739 Country Rd. 2365, Moberly 65270
Vice Chair, Donald Martin, 1716 CR 1170, Huntsville 65259
Secretary, Ann Martin, 1716 CR 1170, Huntsville 65259
Treasurer, Gary Smith, 1881 Hwy. 3, Clifton Hill 65244

Ray County

Chair, Bob Cecil
Vice Chair, Gwen Weate

Ripley County

Chair, Mary (Cindy) Jenks, HC 1, Box 693, Fairdealing 63939
Vice Chair, Perry Jenks, HC 1, Box 693, Fairdealing 63939
Secretary, Dalia (Dee) Garrison, RR 8, Box 2461, Doniphan 63935
Treasurer, Chris Miller, RR 3, Box 10899, Doniphan 63035

Saline County

Chair, Dee Friel, 207 Virginia St., Sweet Spring 65351
Vice Chair, Jim Bridges, 22433 265th Tr., Marshall 65340
Secretary, Tonya Chapin, 926 Bolte St., Slater 65349
Treasurer, Don Gage, 12435 Highland Ct., Marshall 65340
Arrow Rock, Loyd French, 35364 E. Hwy. 41, Marshall 65430
Cambridge Rural, Howard H. Jones, 34944 Hwy. F, Slater 65349
Cambridge Rural, Mary Vale Jones, 34944 Hwy. F, 65349
Elmwood, Mildred G. Conner, 15045 Hwy. 20, Malta Blend 65339
Elmwood, Seth H. Conner, 21048 Saline 127 Hwy., Box 85, Malta Blend 65339
Liberty/Herndon, Jim Bridges, 22433 165th Trail, Marshall 65340
Marshall
    Marshall Rural, Frank Swisher, 22689 N. 65 Hwy., Marshall 65340
    Marshall Rural, Carol Pemberton, 30521 E. Hwy. 41, Marshall 65340
    Ward 1, Donald L. Gage, 1243 S. Highland Ct., Marshall 65340-3056
    Ward 2, Roy Hunter, 1211 E. Watermill Rd., Marshall 65340
    Ward 2, Susan Hunter, 1211 Watermill Rd., Marshall 65340
    Ward 3, Mary Kay Peterson, 503 E. Eastwood, Marshall 65340
    Ward 3, Robert E. Martin, 217 E. Yerby 4, Marshall 65340
Miami, Dorothy M. Clements, 37309 Koala Ave., Marshall 65340
Slater 3, Ginger Burks, 721 Elm St., Slater 65349
Slater 4, Tonya Chapin, 926 Bolte St., Slater 65349
Sweet Springs 2, Dee Friel, 207 Virginia St., Sweet Springs 65351
Sweet Springs 2, David Friel, 207 Virginia St., Sweet Springs 65351

Scott County

Chair, Larry Tetley, 141 Greenbrier, Sikeston 63801
Vice Chair, Deborah Gunter, PO Box 81, Benton 63736
Secretary, Jim Marshall, PO Box 24, Blodgett 63824
Treasurer, Susan Hester, 161 State Hwy. Ra, Chaffee 63740

Shannon County

Chair, Melany Williams, PO Box 148, Eminence 65466
Vice Chair, Anthony Nichols, PO Box 191, Winona 65588
Secretary, Donald Johnson, Rt. 1, Box 1237, Winona 65588
Treasurer, Shelly McAfee, PO Box 187, Eminence 65466
Bartlett, Verlon Thompson, RR 1, Box 106-A, Birch Tree 65438
Bartlett, Shelly McAfee, PO Box 187, Eminence 65466
Birch Tree, Clinton Sanders, Rt. 1, Box 205, Birch Tree 65438
Birch Tree, Lois Sanders, Rt. 1, Box 205, Birch Tree 65438
Delaware, James Orchard, HCR 4, Box 130, Birch Tree 65438
Delaware, Lucille Orchard, HCR 4, Box 130, Birch Tree 65438
Eminence, Dale Counts, PO Box 482, Eminence 65466
Eminence, Melany Williams, PO Box 119, Eminence 65466
Montier I, Earl Bottoms, Rt. 2, Box 2655, Birch Tree 65438

Montier I, Susan Bottoms, Rt. 2, Box 2655, Birch Tree 65438
Montier II, Earl Chowning, Rt. 2, Box 2738, Birch Tree 65438
Montier II, Dorene Chowning, Rt. 2, Box 2738, Birch Tree 65438
Moore, Scott Lanham, Rt. 1, Box 107-B, Bunker 63629
Moore, Gail Lanham, Rt. 1, Box 107-B, Bunker 63629
Newton, Billy Bland, HCR 62, Box 434, Salem 65560
Newton, Irma Baker, HCR 62, Box 515, Salem 65560
Spring Creek, Tommy Rutledge, HCR 3, Box 19A, Birch Tree 65438
Spring Creek, Missy Rutledge, HCR 3, Box 19A, Birch Tree 65438
Spring Valley, Merle Lowell, HC 68, Box 76, Summersville 65571
Spring Valley, Carol Lowell, HC 68, Box 76, Summersville 65571
Winona, Anthony Nichols, PO Box 191, Winona 65588
Winona, Rita Johnson, Rt. 1, Box 1237, Winona 65588

Shelby County

Chair, Maurice Shuck, 8855 Shelby 484, Hunnewell 63443
Vice Chair, Ardith Simpson, 176 Shelby 302, Clarence 63437
Secretary, Jan Beach, 144 Hwy. B, Leonard 63451
Treasurer, Jesse Burton, 5101 Shelby 330, Shelbyville 63469
Bethel, Walter Spilker, 5586 Shelby 1540, Bethel 63434
Black Creek, M. G. (Max) Conrad, 2422 Hwy. K, Shelbyville 63469
Black Creek, Sharon Winn, 503 E. Main, Shelbyville 63469
Clay, Ardith Simpson, 176 Shelby 302, Clarence 63473
Clay, Larry Roberts, 511 W. College, Clarence 63437
Jackson, Maurice Shuck, 8855 Shelby 484, Hunnewell 63443
Jackson, Rose Shuck, 8855 Shelby 484, Hunnewell 63443
Jefferson, Brent Wood, 559 Shelby 410, Clarence 63437
Jefferson, Rachelle Wood, 559 Shelby 410, Clarence 63437
Lentner, Ellen Adams, 7803 Shelby 415, Lentner 63450
Lentner, Leroy Adams, 7803 Shelby 415, Lentner 63450
North River, Donnie Parsons, 8498 Hwy. 168, Shelbyville 63469
North River, Laura Parsons, 8498 Hwy. 168, Shelbyville 63469
Salt River East, James McConnell, 205 E. Spruce, Shelbina 63468
Salt River East, Leslie Thompson, 612 Ridge St., Shelbina 63468
Salt River West, Jesse Burton, 5101 Shelby 330, Shelbyville 63469
Salt River West, Joan Bierly, 211 W. Wood, Shelbina 63468
Taylor, Harold Beach, 144 Hwy. B, Leonard 63451
Taylor, Jan Beach, 144 Hwy. B, Leonard 63451
Tiger Fork, Don Lindsey, 1201 Hwy. W, Bethel 63434

St. Charles County

Chair, Morton Todd, 2813 Droste, St. Charles 63301
Vice Chair, Shelley Hoffman, 812 Brookwood Bend Tr., St. Peters 63376
Treasurer, Larry Laughlin

St. Clair County

Chair, Pat Terry, 385 SE 200 Rd., Osceola 64776
Vice Chair, Gary Mitchell, 1090 SE 651 Rd., Osceola 64776
Secretary, Gladys Smith, 5290 NE 50th Rd., Osceola 64776
Treasurer, Thomas Johnson, 220 Main, Osceola 64776

St. Francois County

Chair, Frank G. Mack, PO Box 135, Ironton 63650
Vice Chair, Mary Mack, PO Box 135, Ironton 63650
Secretary, Sheila Blackwell, 2750 Blomeier Rd., Farmington 63640
Treasurer, Judy Prichett, 1 W. Libert St., Ste. 300, Farmington 63640
Iron, Frank G. Mack, PO Box 135, Ironton 63650
Iron, Mary Mack, PO Box 135, Ironton 63650
Marion, Albert E. Jones, 8616 Snowdell Rd., French Village 63036
Marion, Barbara K. Jones, 8616 Snowdell Rd., French Village 63036
Pendleton, Sheila Blackwell, 2750 Blomeier Rd., Farmington 63640
Perry, Archie Camden, 322 Rue Terre Bonne, Bonne Terre 63628
Perry, Sonja Camden, 322 Rue Terre Bonne, Bonne Terre 63628
Randolph, Clay W. Copeland, 605 Tyler St., Desloge 63601
Randolph, Sandra L. Copeland, 605 Tyler St., Desloge 63601
St. Francois, Ron Bockenkamp, 3808 Hwy. O, Farmington 63640
St. Francois, Emily Firebaugh, 1830 Lakeshore Dr., Farmington 63640

St. Louis City

Chair, Robert Hilgemann, 4131 Blaine Ave., St. Louis 63110
Vice Chair, Lucinda Frazier, 1515 Bremen Ave., St. Louis
Secretary, Kathleen Gamache, 4914 Michigan, St. Louis 63111
Treasurer, Jessie Todd, 4250 Enright, St. Louis 63108

St. Louis County

Chair, Matthew Robinson, 723 Bellflower, Hazelwood 63042
Vice Chair, Mary Elizabeth Dorsey, 8 St. Thomas Ct., Florissant 63031
Secretary, Marianne Solari, 3427 St. Mark Ln., St. Ann 63074
Treasurer, Bob Levine, 2 Troll Ct., Manchester 63011

St. Genevieve County

Chair, Melvin Frelix, 481 Church St., St. Mary 63673
Vice Chair, Renee Murphy
Secretary, Joan Wiln

Stoddard County

Chair, Michael Moroni, PO Box 24, Bloomfield 63825
Vice Chair, Janice Barney, PO Box 397, Dexter 63841
Secretary, Peggy Barks, 1 N. Walnut, Dexter 63841
Treasurer, Briney Welborn, 600 S. Prairie St., Bloomfield 63825

Stone County

Chair, Kathrine Gordon, 336 Grandview Hills Cir., Branson West 65737
Vice Chair, Craig Hodges, 7088 State Hwy. BB, Crane 65633
Secretary, Sally Richardson, 393 Summer Rd., Kimberling City 65686
Treasurer, William Huseby, 336 Grandview Hills Circle, Branson West 65737
Flat Creek B, Al Warzecha, 62 Overlook Rd., Galena 65656
Flat Creek B, Bonnie Warzecha, 62 Overlook Rd., Galena 65656
Pine B, Cathy Tollefson, 1024 Pokeberry Ln., Lampe 65681
Pine B, Duane Tollefson, 1024 Pokeberry Ln., Lampe 65681
Ruth A, R.C. Hopper, 1584 Wilson Creek Rd., Galena 65656
Ruth B Rural, Delores Wright, 264 Fox Fire Knoll, Kimberling City 65686
Ruth B Rural, Sherie Snider, 393 Summer Rd., Kimberling City 65686
Ruth C, Mike Harris, 101 Hidden Shores Dr., Reeds Spring 65737
Ruth C, Cynthia Huhs, 1074 Gobblers Mtn. Rd., Branson West 65737
Union, Chris Daugherty, 1477 Silverlake Rd., Billings 65610
Union, Nicole Daugherty, 1477 Silverlake Rd., Billings 65610

Texas County

Chair, Paul Meier
Vice Chair, Janis Mayberry
Secretary, Rose Ward
Treasurer, James Gagen

Vernon County

Chair, Paul Sprenkle, PO Box 505, Sheldon 64784
Vice Chair, Barbara Labitska, 1001 W. Floral St, Nevada 64772
Secretary, Phyllis Sprenkle, 29540 S. 1850 Rd, Sheldon 64784
Treasurer, Wesley Johnson, 16299 S. 1100 Rd, Nevada 64772
Blue Mound, Cherie Roberts, 24001 E. Earhart Rd, Walker 64790
Blue Mound, Neal Gerster, 22711 E. C Hwy., Walker 64790
Nevada
Center Ward 1, Phyllis Baucom, 821 W. Walnut, PO Box 130, Nevada 64772
Center Ward 1, Winnie Baucom, 821 W. Walnut, PO Box 130, Nevada 64772
Center Ward 2, Dick Peckman, 1205 N Lynn, Nevada 64772
Center Ward 4, Harold Moore, 1112 S. Elizabeth St, Nevada 64772
Center Ward 6, Gary Herstein, 406 N Perkins St, Nevada 64772
Center Ward 6, Mary Herstein, 406 N Perkins St, Nevada 64772
Center Ward 7, Jim Labitska, 1001 W. Floral St, Nevada 64772
Center Ward 7, Barbara Labitska, 1001 W. Floral St, Nevada 64772

Center Outside, James Earll, 19160 S. 1463 Rd., PO Box 837, Nevada 64772
Center Outside, Twila Earll, 19160 S. 1463 Rd., PO Box 837, Nevada 64772
Deerfield, Jill Couch, 10944 E. Stockade Rd, Moundville 64771
Deerfield, Wes Johnson, 16299 S. 1100 Rd, Nevada 64772
Drywood, Paul Sprenkle, 29540 S. 1850 Rd, Sheldon 64784
Drywood, Phyllis Sprenkle, 29540 S. 1850 Rd, Sheldon 64784
Harrison, Carol Holland, 26578 S. 575 Rd, Bronaugh 64728
Harrison, Linn Holland, 26578 S. 575 Rd, Bronaugh 64728
Montevallo, Robert Mitchell, 28080 E. Waldo Rd, Sheldon 64784
Montevallo, Linda Mitchell, 28080 E. Waldo Rd, Sheldon 64784
Moundville, Norman Noel, 26167 S. 43 Hwy., Bronaugh 64728
Moundville, Rosemary Noel, 26167 S. 43 Hwy., Bronaugh 64728
Virgil, Scott Watkins, RR 1, Box 98A, El Dorado Springs 64744
Washington, Tom Pyle, 14400 S. 1700 Rd., Nevada 64772
Washington, Virginia Pyle, 14400 S. 1700 Rd., Nevada 64772
Washington Ward 8, Wanda Arthur, 225 E. Atlantic St., PO Box 571, Nevada 64772

Warren County

Chair, Betty Redecker, 27250 State Hwy. U, Warrenton 63383
Vice Chair, Walter Bittle, 21296 W. Spruce Dr., Warrenton 63383
Secretary, Laura Adams, 25740 Bethlehem Valley Rd., Marthasville 63357
Treasurer, Charles Redecker, 27250 State Hwy. U, Warrenton 63383
Elkhorn North, Walter Bittle, 21296 W. Spruce Dr., Warrenton 63383
Elkhorn South, Charles Redecker, 27250 State Hwy. U, Warrenton 63383
Elkhorn South, Betty Redecker, 27250 State Hwy. U, Warrenton 63383
Pinckney, Paul Adams, 25740 Bethlehem Valley Rd., Marthasville 63357
Pinckney, Laura Adams, 25740 Bethlehem Valley Rd., Marthasville 63357

Washington County

Chair, Micka Sue Jarvis, PO Box 64, Belgrade 63622
Vice Chair, Chad Walton, 1002 Hunter Ct., Potosi 63664
Secretary, Marie Edgar, 10205 Weber Ln., Potosi 63664
Treasurer, Patty Boyer, 313 Lilac Dr., Potosi 63664
Belgrade, Leo David Dickey, 13414 Council Bluff Rd., Belgrade 63622
Belgrade, Micka Sue Jarvis, PO Box 64, Belgrade 63622
Bellevue, Loretta Neier, 10741 Drew Rd., Caledonia 63631
Breton, Marie L. Edgar, 10205 Weber Ln., Potosi 63664
Breton, Chad Walton, 1002 Hunter Ct., Potosi 63664
Concord, Charles Cole, 17656 S. State Hwy. 21, Potosi 63664

672   OFFICIAL MANUAL

Concord, Wilma Cole, 17656 S. State Hwy. 21, Potosi 63664
Kingston, Lois White, 10042 Kayak Rd., Cadet 63630
Kingston, James Ronald, White, 10042 Kayak Rd., Cadet 63630
Liberty, Dorothy Pashia, 10782 Pashia Rd., Potosi 63664
Liberty, Oscar Pashia, 10782 Pashia Rd., Potosi 63664
Union, Joan M. Karsch, 16042 N State Hwy. 21, Cadet 63630
Union, Karl M. Koch, 10120 Juliette Rd., Cadet 63630
Walton, Kathryn Hicks, 22499 W. State Hwy. 8, Potosi 63664
Walton, Steve Hicks, 22499 W. State Hwy. 8, Potosi 63664

Wayne County

Chair, Robert Carter, Rt. 4, Box 4470, Piedmont 63957
Vice Chair, Laura Belmar, HCR 68 Box 75A, Des Arc 63636
Secretary, Mary Sue Dildine, Rt. 1, Box 18880, Patterson 63956
Treasurer, Charles Banks, HC 1 Box 1550, Silva 63964
Benton, Robert Carter, Rt. 4, Box 4470, Piedmont 63957
Benton, Barbara Decker, 410 Ridgeview Dr., Piedmont 63957
Black River, Paul Reynolds, HC 2, Box 114A, Williamsville 63967
Black River, Helen Reynolds, HC 2, Box 114A, Williamsville 63967
Cedar Creek, Ron Belmar, HC 68, Box 75A, Des Arc 63636
Cedar Creek, Laura Belmar, HC 68, Box 75A, Des Arc 63636
Logan, Michael Jackson, Rt. 1, Box 18010, Patterson 63956
Logan, Mary Sue Dildine, Rt. 1, Box 18880, Patterson 63956
Mill Spring, Scott Chadbourne, Rt. 3, Box 3444, Piedmont 63957

Webster County

Chair, John Shaughnessy, 158 Oak Tree Ct., Niangua 65713
Vice Chair, Patty Schroiner, 522 N. Walnut, Marshfield 65706
Secretary, Beverly Whipple, 602 N. Pine St., Marshfield 65706
Treasurer, Gary Price, 7757 State Hwy. W, Elkland 65644
Benton, Harry Harmes, 416 Ozark Church Ln., Rogersville 65742
Diggins, Tom Byrd, 8101 State Hwy. A., Marshfield 65706
Diggins, Connie Byrd, 8101 State Hwy. A., Marshfield 65706

East Ozark, Dan Knust, 4069 Old Seymour Rd., Marshfield 65706
East Ozark, Susie Knust, 4069 Old Seymour Rd., Marshfield 65706
Grant, Kathleen (Kathy) Muckala, 726 Black Walnut Rd., Marshfield 65706
Finley, Fred Farthing, 5393 State Hwy. K, Seymour 65746
Finley, Judy Farthing, 5393 State Hwy. K, Seymour 65746
Fordland, Reggie Bumgarner, 4000 New Hope Rd., Fordland 65652
Fordland, Leesa Bumgarner, 4000 New Hope Rd., Fordland 65652
Hazelwood, Bill Leonard, 523 Severs Rd., Marshfield 65706
Hazelwood, Carolyn Leonard, 523 Severs Rd., Marshfield 65706
Jackson, Doug Owen, 2469 Whitetail Rd., Elkland 65644
Jackson, Marcia Owen, 2469 Whitetail Rd., Elkland 65644
Marshfield East, David Young, 207 Crestwood, Marshfield 65706
Marshfield East, Debbie Young, 207 Crestwood, Marshfield 65706
Marshfield West, Tom Blumberg, 212 Ash Dr., Marshfield 65706
Marshfield West, Connie Clark, 180 N. Blair St., Marshfield 65706
Niangua, John Shaughnessy, 158 Oak Tree Ct., Niangua 65713
Niangua, Susan Keene, 1030 Bowen Creek Rd., Niangua 65713
Northview, Lynn Minor, 12857 State Hwy. KK, Marshfield 65706
Northview, Judy Minor, 12857 State Hwy. KK, Marshfield 65706
Union, Larry Deckard, 598 Marble Rd., Conway 65632
Union, Brenda Deckard, 598 Marble Rd., Conway 65632
Washington, Joe Bill Day, 820 S. Dallas County Line Rd., Conway 65632
Washington, June Day, 820 S. Dallas Count Line Rd., Conway 65632

Wright County

Chair, James Wright, 1011 E. Ninth St., Mtn Grove 65711
Vice Chair, Wanda Cope, PO Box 92, Hartville 65667
Secretary, Judith Sprague-Anderson, 2607 E. 26th St., Mountain Grove 65711
Treasurer, Darrell Cope, PO Box 92, Hartville 65667

Officers of Republican Party

Republican National Committee, 2015–2016

Republican National Committee Headquarters
310 First St., S.E., Washington, D.C. 20003
Telephone: (202) 863-8500
www.gop.com

Officers, Republican National Committee

Reince Priebus, chair, Wisconsin;
Sharon Day, co-chair, Florida;
Susie Hudson, secretary, Vermont;
Tony Parker, treasurer, District of Columbia.

Republican State Organization of Missouri

Republican Party Headquarters
105 E. High St., PO Box 73, Jefferson City 65102
Telephone: (573) 636-3146
www.mogop.org

NOTE: Information is received from county clerks and the Missouri Republican Party

Missouri members, Republican National Committee

Lance Beshore, 1340 Northridge Terr., Joplin 64801;
Susan Eckelkamp, PO Box 330, St. Albans 63073.

Officers, Republican State Committee

John Hancock, chair, 1561 Candish Ln., St. Louis 63017;
Valinda Freed, vice chair, 2662 CR 1310, Moberly 65270;
Patricia Thomas, secretary, 3444 Hobbs Ln., Jefferson City 65109;
Richard C. Peerson, treasurer, 211 Marshal, Jefferson City 65101.

Members, Republican State Committee

First district: Tony Pousosa, 9700 Antigo Dr., Green Park 63123; Jennifer Bird, 9204 Medallion Ct., St. Louis 63126.

LANCE BESHORE
National Committeeman

SUSAN ECKELKAMP
National Committeewoman

JOHN HANCOCK
State Chair

VALINDA FREED
State Vice Chair

PATRICIA THOMAS
State Secretary

RICHARD C. PEERSON
State Treasurer

Second district: Dave Evans, 5 Conestoga Ct., O'Fallon 63368; Cindy Evans, 5 Conestoga Ct., O'Fallon 63368.

Third district: David Courtway, 3303 Piney Knot Dr., Festus 63028; Chris Dinkins, 18217 Hwy. K, Annapolis 63620.

Fourth district: Phil Chrsitofanelli, 2118 Edwards, St. Louis 63118; Courtney Blunt, 4605 Milentz Ave., First Fl., St. Louis 63116.

Fifth district: Robert Vroman, 3867 Shaw 3E, St. Louis 63110; Heather Coil, 2300 S. 10th St., Unit C, St. Louis 63104.

Sixth district: Richard Peerson, 211 Marshall, Jefferson City 65101; Carol Ellinger, 5003 Henwick Ln., Jefferson City 65109.

Seventh district: Mark Anthony Jones, 4029 Warwick Blvd., Kansas City 64111; Sally Miller, 835 W. 55th St., Kansas City 64113.

Eighth district: Paul Trask, 210 E. Whispering Hills Blvd., Lone Jack 64070; Erin Dunn, 1405 SW 25th St., Blue Springs 64015.

Ninth district: Leonard Snow, 8401 E. 47th Terrace, Kansas City 64129; Jennifer Finch, 407 Benton Blvd., Kansas City 64124.

Tenth district: Mike West, 1740 Ashley Ct., Fulton 65251; Carol Wessel Boyer, 248 E. Hwy. U, Troy 63379.

Eleventh district: Job Howen, 1527 E. Hayward Ave., Independence 64050; Joy Freeland, 4009 S. Crysler Ave. 2, Independence 64055.

Twelfth district: Ron Crider, 506 Macadee, Maysville 64469; Dixie Crider, 506 Macadee, Maysville 64469.

Thirteenth district: Bryan Koen, 1345 Willowbrook Dr., Florissant 63033; Kim Benz, 640 Jamaica Pl., Florissant 63033.

Fourteenth district: Ted Engler, 1236 Dielman Ind. Ct., St Louis 63132; Sarah Davoli, 7378 Milan Ave., St Louis 63130.

Fifteenth district: Chris Howard, 222 Blue Sage Dr., Ballwin 63011; Jaci Winship, 38 Provincial Ct., St. Louis 63122.

Sixteenth district: Mike Gosnell, 1815 Ashwood Dr., Rolla 65401; Joyce Karnes, 177 Country Rd. 2110, Lecoma 65401.

Seventeenth district: Tom Brown, 1306 NW 47th St., Kansas City 64116; Amy Corlew, 5317 N. Pennsylvania Ave., Kansas City 64118.

Eighteenth district: Larry Craig, 4025 Edgewood Rd., Hannibal 63401; Valinda Freed, 2662 CR 1310, Moberly 65270.

Nineteenth district: Gary Harris, 13267 B Hwy., Boonville 65233; Sara Walsh, 6676 American Setter Dr., Ashland 65010.

Twentieth district: Gordon Kinne, 4500 E. Farm Rd. 148, Springfield 65809; Patsy Wilcox, 2699 E. Clearview Dr., Republic 65738.

Twenty-first district: Steve Solomon, 10360 Skelton Rd., Odessa 64076; Kay Hoflander, PO Box 603, Higginsville 64037.

Twenty-second district: Jim Berberich, 2840 E. Springview Dr., Imperial 63052; Janet Engelbach, 3489 Linhorst Rd., Hillsboro 63050.

Twenty-third district: Fred Henke, 770 Meadow Cliff Dr., St. Charles 63303; Penny Henke, 770 Meadow Cliff Dr., St. Charles 63303.

Twenty-fourth district: Bruce Buwalda, 95 Grand Circle Dr., Maryland Heights 63043; Maryann Rober, 14 Blaytonn Ln., Ladue 63124.

Twenty-fifth district: Hardy Billington, 80 E. Outer Rd., Poplar Bluff, 63901; Gail Cox, HCR Box 2124, Van Buren 63965.

Twenty-sixth district: Anthony Hough, 2384 Gross Point Ln., Wildwood 63011; Robbie Brouk, 1073 Cedar Gulch, Robertsville 63072.

Twenty-seventh district: Scott Clark, 1010 Greensferry, Jackson 63755; Sandy Haertling, 539 PCR 212, Perryville 63775.

Twenty-eighth district: Craig Westfall, 4671 Hwy. H, Halfway 65663; Shirley Burris, 19901 Providence Dr., Lebanon 65536.

Twenty-ninth district: David Cole, 1002 Chinaquapin Woods, Cassville 65625; Lea Ann Coffelt, PO Box 1497, Forsyth 65653.

Thirtieth district: Darrell Proctor, PO Box 548, Willard 65781; Danette Proctor, PO Box 548, Willard 65781.

Thirty-first district: David Kelsay, 901 Willow, Clinton 64735; Debbie Rector, 23400 College Ln., Harrisonville 64701.

Thirty-second district: Nick Myers, PO Box 2523, Joplin 64803; Lorri Wycuff, PO Box 398, Ash Grove 65604.

Thirty-third district: Charlie Dickinson, 6276 Hwy. 5, Hartville 65667; Jan Kelly, PO Box 10, Norwood 65717.

Thirty-fourth district: Jim Rooney, 306 Summerset Dr., Weston 64098; Rebecca Rooney, 306 Summerset Dr., Weston 64098.

Officers, Republican Congressional District Committees

First district: Shaun O'Hara, chair, 5072 Mardel Ave., Apt. A, St. Louis 63109; Theresa Cummings, vice chair, 3414 Juniata Ave., St. Louis 63118; Rebecca Buwalda, secretary, 95 Grand Circle, Maryland Heights 63043; Bryan Koen, treasurer, 1345 Willowbrook Dr., Florissant 63033.

Second district: Mark Harder, chair, 542 Lering Ct., Ballwin 63011; Penny Henke, vice chair, 770 Meadow Cliff Dr., St. Charles 63303; Anne Gassel, secretary, 16309 Autumn Crest Ct., Ellisville 63011; John Judd, treasurer, 4769 Cactus Wren Ct., St. Louis 63128.

Third district: Ron Fitzwater, chair, 916 Nob Hill Rd., Jefferson City 65101; Roberta (Robbie) Brouk, vice chair, 1073 Cedar Gulch, Robertsville 63072; Romona Wilkinson, secretary, 135 Brookstone Dr., Holts Summit 65043; Derek Goode, treasurer, 6185 Regina Rd., Cedar Hill 63016.

Fourth district: Carla Young, chair, 809 W. Broadway, Sedalia 65301; Lewis Melahn, vice chair, 1453 Briarwood Pl., Mexico 65265; Lorri Wycuff, secretary, PO Box 398, Ash Grove 65604; Dean Dohrman, treasurer, 16695 Wood Rd., PO Box 234, LaMonte 65337.

Fifth district: Jennifer Finch, chair, 407 Benton Blvd., Kansas City 64124; Chris Lievsay, vice chair, 201 NW Third St., Blue Springs 64014; Joy Freeland, secretary, 4009 S. Crysler Ave., Condo 2, Independence 64055; Tom Lehman, treasurer, 2903 SW Scherer Rd., Lee's Summit 64086.

Sixth district: Dixie Crider, chair, 506 Macadee, Maysville 64469; vacancy, vice chair; vacancy, secretary; vacancy, treasurer.

Seventh district: Gordon Kinne, chair, 4500 E. Farm Rd. 148, Springfield 65809; Vacancy, vice chair; vacancy, secretary; vacancy, treasurer.

Eighth district: Eddy Justice, chair, 379 Remington Pl., Poplar Bluff 63901; Holly Lintner, vice chair, 978 CR 546, Jackson 63755; Christy Roberts, secretary, PO Box 790, Ellington 63638; John Bailiff, treasurer.

Officers, Republican Senatorial Districts

First district: Alan Leaderbrand, chair, 3918 Jacinto, St. Louis 63125; Frieda Keough, vice chair, 411 S. Sappington, St. Louis 63122; Teresa Douglas, treasurer, 8208 Weimar, St. Louis 63123; John Judd, secretary, 4769 Cactus Wren Ct., St. Louis 63128.

Second district: Frank Eggering, chair, 204 Dauphine Dr., Lake St. Louis 63367; Sandy Garber, vice chair, 7 Vienna Ct., Lake St. Louis 63367.

Third district: David Courtway, chair, 3303 Piney Knot Dr., Festus 63028; Chris Dinkins, vice chair, 18217 Hwy. K, Annapolis 63620; Carol Gamble, secretary, 5120 Westmeyer Rd., Farmington 63640; Dustin Layton, treasurer, 17 McClanahan Rd., Farmington 63640.

Fourth district: Michael Chance, chair, 4180 Cleveland, St. Louis 63110; Jennifer Bird, vice chair, 9204 Medallion Ct., St. Louis 63126; Caitlin Hartsell, secretary, 4949 W. Pine, Apt. 110, St. Louis 63108; Shaun O'Hara, treasurer, 5072 Mardel Ave., Apt. A, St. Louis 63109.

Fifth district: Mark Ogier, chair, 1621 N. Seventh, St. Louis 63102; Thea Cummings, vice chair, 3414 Juniata Ave., St. Louis 63118; Robert Vroman, treasurer, 715 N. 21st 301, St. Louis 63103.

Sixth district: Penelope Quigg, chair, 612A Blair Dr., Jefferson City 65109; Kevin Harvey, vice chair, 17 CR 603, Loose Creek 65054; Pat Thomas, secretary, 3444 Hobbs Ln., Jefferson City 65109; Joe Maybrier-Moore, treasurer, 150 Hwy. 42 W., Vienna 65582.

Seventh district: Sarah Miller, chair, 5801 CR 135, Rosendale 64483; Ralph Munyan, vice chair, 6423 Wyandotte, Kansas City 64113; Matthew Dale Quinn, secretary, 9401 Jarboe, Kansas City 64114.

Eighth district: Robert Hertzog, chair, 24800 Milton Thompson Rd., Lee's Summit 64086; Donna Turk, vice chair, 417 SE Annette St.,

Lee's Summit 64063; Job Howen, secretary, 1527 E. Hayward Ave., Independence 64050.

Ninth district: Tom Lehman, chair, 2903 SW Scherer Rd., Lee's Summit 64082; Jamie Gidman, vice chair, 3308 E. 10th St., Kansas City 64127.

Tenth district: Bev Ehlen, chair, 19335 Primrose Ridge, Warrenton 63383; Gary Grunick, vice chair, 541 Harmony Grove Rd., Troy 63379.

Eleventh district: Mary Jane Van Buskirk, chair, 7812 Woodson Rd., Raytown 64138; Dan Stacy, vice chair, 1215 SW Hillcrest Dr., Blue Springs 64015.

Twelfth district: Mark Schneider, chair, 20257 CR 302, Cosby 64436; Wanda Shupe, vice chair, 3622 U.S. Hwy. 169, Stanberry 64489; Dixie Crider, secretary, 506 Macadee, Maysville 64469; Dennis McDonald, treasurer, 410 NE Hwy. J, Galt 64841.

Thirteenth district: Bryan Koen, chair, 1345 Willowbrook Dr., Florissant 63033; June Schmidt, vice chair, 1470 Estes Dr., Florissant 63031; Jim Rowe, secretary, 1283 Chambers Rd., St. Louis 63137; Becky Buwalda, treasurer, 95 Grand Circle Dr., Maryland Heights 63043.

Fourteenth district: Ted Engler, chair, 857 Berick Dr., St. Louis 63132; DeAnn Deimeke, vice chair, 3081 Lake Ave., Maryland Heights 63043; Sarah Davoli, secretary, 7378 Milan Ave., St. Louis 63130; Dan O'Sullivan, treasurer, 7365 Arlington, St. Louis 63117.

Fifteenth district: Tony Pousosa, chair, 9700 Antigo Dr., Green Park 63123; Renne Artman, vice chair, 1530 Winter Chase Dr., Fenton 63026.

Sixteenth district: John Taylor, chair, 140 Farr View Dr., Steelville 65565; Mary Pat Luebbering, vice chair, 164 Sycamore Ln., St. Thomas 65076; Pamela K. Grow, secretary, 10385 Southwood Dr., Rolla 65401; Michael Gosnell, treasurer, 1815 Ashwood Dr., Rolla 65402.

Seventeenth district: Craig Porter, chair, 9504 N. Arlington Ave., Kansas City 64157; Elnora Overman, vice chair, 4046 N. Askew Ave., Kansas City 64117.

Eighteenth district: Jim Willis, chair, 24377 State Hwy. OO, Bevier 63532; Dorothy Sisson, vice chair, 400 S. Cuivre, Bowling Green 63334; Aaron Baker, secretary, 18192 Old Hwy. 63, Atlanta 63530; Cindy O'Laughlin, treasurer, 6584 Frances Ln., Shelbina 63468.

Nineteenth district: Gary Harris, chair, 13267 B Hwy., Boonville 65233; Cheri Toalson Reisch, vice chair, 115 East St., Hallsville 65255.

Twentieth district: Bill Owen, chair, 5115 N. Farm Rd. 185, Springfield 65803; Ginny Wade, vice chair, 1970 Spring Hill Rd., Sparta 65753; Terri Merritt, secretary, 1455 N. 14th

St., Ozark 65721; Ron Mark, treasurer, 1567 N. Farm Rd. 97, Springfield 65802.

Twenty-first district: Linda Leabo, chair, 122 S. Maple St., Norborne 64668; Chris Lievsay, vice chair, 201 NW Third St., Blue Springs 64014; Steve Solomon, secretary, 10360 Skelton Rd., Odessa 64076; Toni Houx, treasurer, PO Box 115, Warrensburg 64093.

Twenty-second district: Bill Alter, chair, 1800 Gravois Rd., High Ridge 63049; Jim Berberich, vice chair, 2840 E. Springview Dr., Imperial 63052; Jim Berberich, secretary, 2840 E. Springview, Imperial 63052; Diane Berberich, treasurer, 2840 E. Springview, Imperial 63052.

Twenty-third district: Joe Smith, chair, 4137 Stonecraft Dr., St. Charles 63304; Cindy Carpenter, vice chair, 12 Lippizan Rd., St. Peters 63376; Joan Gettemeyer, secretary, 52 S. Hillview, St. Peters 63376; David Hoffman, treasurer, 30 Oakshire Ct., St. Peters 63376.

Twenty-fourth district: Patrick Walker, chair, 300 Babler Dr., St. Louis 63141; Jeanne Gosen, vice chair, 2765 Kehrs Mill Rd., Chesterfield 63017; Becky Buwalda, secretary, 95 Grand Circle Dr., Maryland Heights 63043; JB Richman, treasurer, 2931 Sprucewood, Maryland Heights 63043.

Twenty-fifth district: Eddy Justice, chair, 379 Remington Pl., Poplar Bluff 63901; Etheleen Montgomery, vice chair, 714 S. State Hwy. 25, Dexter 63841; Gail Cox, secretary, HCR Box 2124, Van Buren 63965.

Twenty-sixth district: Roberta (Robbie) Brouk, chair, 1073 Cedar Gulch, Robertsville 63072; Mark Harder, vice chair, 542 Lering Ct., Ballwin 63011; Anne Gassel, secretary, 16309 Autumn Crest Ct., Ellisville 63011; Todd Rio, treasurer, 363 Covey Ct., Union 63084.

Twenty-seventh district: Holly Lintner, chair, 978 CR 546, Jackson 63755; John McMillen, vice chair, 810 Glenn Dr., Sikeston 63801; Cynthia Hazelwood, secretary, 1010 CR 516, New Wells 63732; Alan Beussink, treasurer, RR 1, Box 3, Leopold 63760.

Twenty-eighth district: Jack Dill, chair, 638 State Rd. M, Conway 65632; Angie Wright, vice chair, 18145 Hwy. 64, Lebanon 65536; Michelle Morgan, secretary; Gary Noakes, treasurer, 3170 NW Hwy. A, Lowry City 64763.

Twenty-ninth district: Cherry Warren, chair, 11866 Farm Rd. 1045, Purdy 65734.

Thirtieth district: M. Lloyd Wright, chair, 1443 S. Delaware, Springfield 65804; Jennifer McClure, vice chair, 1219 E. Catalpa, Springfield 65804; Melanie Bach, secretary, 3734 S. Elmview Ave., Springfield 65804; Ron Mark, treasurer, 1567 N. Farm Rd 97, Springfield 65802.

Thirty-first district: Maxine Rader, chair, 300 E. Hwy. EE, Lamar 64759; Gerald Wadel, vice chair, 7511 E. D Hwy., Richards 64778.

Thirty-second district: Jerry Carter, chair, 6623 Hwy. E, Granby 64844; Nick Myers, vice chair, 5873 Riverside Dr., Joplin 64804; Lorri Wycuff, secretary, PO Box 398, Ash Grove 65604.

Thirty-third district: Jan Kelly, chair, PO Box 10, Norwood 65717; Ross McElvain, vice chair, PO Box 71, Ava 65608; Leann Green, secretary, PO Box 597, Licking 65542; Charlie Dickinson, treasurer, 6276 Hwy. 5, Hartville 65667.

Thirty-fourth district: Jim Rooney, chair, 306 Summerset Dr., Weston 64098; Joanna Boyer, vice chair, 6300 NW Old Tiffany Springs Rd., Kansas City 64154.

Missouri Republican County Committees, 2015–2016

(Township, ward or precinct precedes name of committee members. Vacancies not published. County Committee lists are provided by the county clerks, election officials from each county and the State Republican Party.)

Adair County

Chair, Brian Noe, PO Box 306, Kirksville 63501
Vice Chair, Janet Waybill, 20205 State Hwy. 149, Green Castle 63544

Andrew County

Chair, Mark Schneider, 20257 CR 302, Cosby 64436
Vice Chair, Shirley Ford, 17647 CR 283, Cosby 64436
Benton, Dustin Schneider, 3660 CR 136, Blockow 64427
Benton, Sarah Miller, 5801 CR 135, Rosendale 64483
Clay, Dick Townsend, 7122 CR 54, Rosendale 64483
Jackson, Jim Paxton, 5013 CR 71, Savannah 64485
Jackson, Carole Paxton, 5013 CR 71, Savannah 64485
Jefferson, Chris Anderson, 18 Ridgeland Rd., Country Club 64505
Jefferson, Janice Goforth, 7124 Lundeen Dr., Country Club 64505
Lincoln, Mike Miller, 15025 CR 410, Amazonia 64421
Lincoln, Ruth Miller, 15025 CR 410, Amazonia 64421
Monroe, Mark Schneider, 20257 CR 302, Cosby 64436
Monroe, Shirley Ford, 17647 CR 283, Cosby 64436
Nodaway, Bob Caldwell, 10750 CR 464, Savannah 64485
Nodaway, Rose Lancey, 1000 W. Price, Savannah 64485
Platte, Larry Atkins, 1511 Hwy. 48, Rea 64480
Platte, Carlene Miller, 16689 Hwy. 48, Rea 64480
Rochester, Ron Christmas, 11642 State Rt. D, Savannah 64485
Rochester, Janice Christmas, 11642 State Rt. D, Savannah 64485
Cyndee Merritt, 505 S. 12th Terr., Savannah 64485
Keith Ferguson, PO Box 212, Cosby 64436

Atchison County

Chair, Larry Morrison, 16265 St. Hwy. O, Tarkio 64491
Vice Chair, Janet Morrison, 16256 St. Hwy. O, Tarkio 64491

Audrain County

Chair, Lewis Melahn, 1453 Briarwood Pl., Mexico 65265
Vice Chair, Linda Rice, 1014 E. Love, Mexico 65265
Secretary, Jane Webster, 28198 Audrain Rd. 376, Laddonia 63352
Treasurer, Tim Taylor, 7888 ACR 355, Mexico 65265

Barry County

Chair, David Cole, 1002 Chinaquapin Woods, Cassville 65625
Vice Chair, Barbara White, 10010 Farm Rd. 1085, Purdy 65734
Secretary, Gary Schad, 7017 Farm Rd. 2070, Purdy 65734
Treasurer, Lois Lowe, 20145 State Hwy. 86, Cassville 65625
Ash, Gary VanZandt, 29448 State Hwy. NN, Seligman 65745
Ash, Narissa VanZandt, 29448 State Hwy. NN, Seligman 65745
Butterfield, Cherry Warren, 11866 Farm Rd. 1045, Purdy 65734
Butterfield, Ann Warren, 11866 Farm Rd. 1045, Purdy 65734
Capps Creek, Terry Hunt, 2350 Farm Rd. 2040, Pierce City 65723
Capps Creek, Robin Terry, 6001 State Hwy. 97, Monett 65708
Flat Creek
    City, David Cole, 1002 Chinaquapin Woods, Cassville 65625
    City, Frances Nicoll, 1007 Hickory, Cassville 65625
    Rural, Derek Couch, 13125 Farm Rd. 2165, Cassville 65625
    Rural, Lana Couch, 13125 Farm Rd. 2165, Cassville 65625
Jenkins, Doyle Russell, 11830 Farm Rd. 1195, Aurora 65605
Jenkins, Vivian Wilson, 11421 State Hwy. 39, Aurora 65605
Liberty, Mike Cole, 3712 Farm Rd. 2190, Exeter 65647
Liberty, Amy Cole, 3712 Farm Rd. 2190, Exeter 65647
McDonald, Tyler Smith, 11566 Farm Rd. 1112, Purdy 65734
McDonald, Leslie Smith, 11566 Farm Rd. 1112, Purdy 65734
McDowell, William Dummitt, 7569 Dummitt Ranch Rd., Verona 65769
McDowell, Queeta Crawford, 7512 Dummitt Ranch Rd., Verona 65769
Monett
    1, Melvin Casper, 812 Lincoln, Monett 65708
    1, Terry Casper, 812 Lincoln, Monett 65708
    2, John Woodard, 2910 Farm Rd. 1063, Monett 65708
    2, Sarah Woodard, 2910 Farm Rd. 1063, Monett 65708
    4, Becky Head, 301 N. Belaire Dr., Monett 65708
Ozark, Glen Cope, 2508 Farm Rd. 1180, Aurora 65605
Ozark, Leanne Cope, 2508 Farm Rd. 1180, Aurora 65605
Mineral, Brent Herrin, 13039 Farm Rd. 1157, Aurora 65605
Mineral, Lois Lowe, 20145 State Hwy. 86, Cassville 65625
Pleasant Ridge, Jerry Laney, 4529 Farm Rd. 1135, Verona 65769
Pleasant Ridge, Betty Laney, 4529 Farm Rd. 1135, Verona 65769
Purdy, Jerry White, 10010 Farm Rd. 1085, Purdy 65734
Purdy, Barbara White, 10010 Farm Rd. 1085, Purdy 65734
Roaring River, John Lewright, PO Box 70, Eagle Rock 65641
Roaring River, Kima Lewright, PO Box 70, Eagle Rock 65641
Shell Knob, Frank Herbert, 23445 Green Shores Dr., Shell Knob 65747
Shell Knob, Luanna Urie, 23445 Green Shores Dr., Shell Knob 65747
Washburn, Jerry Varner, 24818 Farm Rd. 1045, Washburn 65772
Washburn, Janice Varner, 330 E. Pineville Rd., Washburn 65772
Wheaton, Jack England, 114 Kelly Ave., Wheaton 64874
Wheaton, Donna England, 13374 Farm Rd. 1005, Exeter 65647
White River
    1, Jimmy Williams, 29129 Farm Rd. 1215, Eagle Rock 65641
    1, June Jones, 28979 Farm Rd. 1247, Golden 65658
    2, William Schliem, 26003 Ledger Dr., Shell Knob 65747
    2, Janet Schliem, 26003 Ledger Dr., Shell Knob 65747

Barton County

Chair, Maxine Rader, 300 E. Hwy. EE, Lamar 64759
Vice Chair, Ed Patterson, 471 SE 10th Rd., Lamar 64759
Secretary, Sterling Martin, 777 NE 100th Ln., Lamar 64759
Treasurer, Marno Patterson, 471 SE 10th Rd., Lamar 64759
Central, Doug McKibben, 53 SW 40th Ln., Lamar 64759
Central, Cathy McKibben, 53 SW 40th Ln., Lamar 64759
City, Meredith Chapman, 1805 Hagny St., Lamar 64759
City, Sharron Chapman, 1805 Hagny St., Lamar 64759
Doylesport, Frank Rader, 300 E. Hwy. EE, Lamar 64759
Doylesport, Maxine Rader, 300 E. Hwy. EE, Lamar 64759
Lamar, Ed Patterson, 471 SE 10th Rd., Lamar 64759
Lamar, Marno Patterson, 471 SE 10th Rd., Lamar 64759
Milford, Mildred Martin, 777 NE 100th Ln., Lamar 64759
Milford, Sterling Martin, 777 NE 100th Ln., Lamar 64759
Nashville, Todd Robertson, 621 SW 70th Ln., Liberal 64762
Nashville, Amanda Robertson, 621 SW 70th Ln., Liberal 64762
North Fork, Rick Morgan, 432 SW 50th Ln., Lamar 64759
North Fork, Melinda Morgan, 432 SW 50th Ln., Lamar 64759
Ozark, James McClendon, 321 NW 130th Ln., Liberal 64762
Ozark, Leota McClendon, 321 NW 130th Ln., Liberal 64762
Richland, Gray Fast, 587 E. Hwy. U, Lamar 64759
Richland, Jill Fast, 587 E. Hwy. U, Lamar 64759
Southwest, Howard Overman, 475 SW 110th Ln., Liberal 64762
Southwest, Tracy Overman, 475 SW 110th Ln., Liberal 64762
Union, Charles Lathrop, 116 NW 80th Rd., Lamar 64759
Union, Ange Lathrop, 116 NW 80th Rd., Lamar 64759

Bates County

Chair, Winifred Gaston, 706 Parkview, Butler 64730
Vice Chair, Felix Salazar, RR 1, Butler 64730
Secretary, Floyd Gaston, 706 Parkview, Butler 64730
Treasurer, Sheila Fischer, RR 3, Appleton 64724

Benton County

Chair, Cole, Mark Nolte, 22641 Hwy. BB, Warsaw 65355
Vice Chair, Marilyn Drake, PO Box 1511, Warsaw 65355

Secretary, Barbara Hammond, 320 Lacey Ave., Lincoln 65338
Treasurer, Roger Reedy
Cole, Mark Nolte, 22641 Hwy. BB, Warsaw 65355
Cole, Donna Hart-Nolte, 22641 Hwy. BB, Warsaw 65355
Fristoe, Jack White, 30143 MM Hwy., Warsaw 65355
Lindsey, Gerry Smith, 1510 Roxanne St., Warsaw 65355
Lindsey, Marlene Meyer, 801 Hickory Dr., Warsaw 65355
Tom, Richard Bacon, 11315 Ulysses Rd., Warsaw 65355
Tom, Marilyn Drake, PO Box 1511, Warsaw 65355
Union, Ted Markham, 30637 Robinson Dr., Edwards 65326
Union, Lynne Markham, 30637 Robinson Dr., Edwards 65326
White, Rick Renno, Lincoln 65338
White, Barbara Hammond, 320 Lacey Ave., Lincoln 65338
Williams, Bob Brown, 24515 Taylor Rd., Lincoln 65338
Williams, Wanda Brown, 24515 Taylor Rd., Lincoln 65338

Bollinger County

Chair, Beverly Peters, PO Box 530, Marble Hill 63764
Vice Chair, Alan Beussink, HC 01, Box 3, Leopold 63760
Secretary, Wanda Rhodes, HC 64, Box 4330, Marble Hill 63764
Treasurer, Brian Collier, RR 3, Box 3702, Marble Hill 63764
Crooked Creek, Wanda Rhodes, HC 64, Box 4330, Marble Hill 63764
Liberty, Heath Robins, RR 81, Box 1881A, Advance 63730
Liberty, Beverly Peters, PO Box 530, Marble Hill 63764
Lorance, Alan Beussink, HC 01, Box 3, Leopold 63760
Lorance, Dana Beussink, HC 01, Box 3, Leopold 63760
Wayne, Roger Vangennip, HC 01, Box 150, Zalma 63787
Wayne, Betsy Vangennip, HC 01, Box 150, Zalma 63787
Whitewater, Patrick Johnson, RR 2, Box 2588, Sedgewickville 63781
Whitewater, Emily Johnson, RR 2, Box 2588, Sedgewickville 63781

Boone County

Chair, Rick Rowden, 1401 Berwick Ct., Columbia 65203
Vice Chair, Rosa Robb, 4105 Blue Hollow Dr., Columbia 65203
Cedar, James D. Green, 7701 E. Zumwalt Rd., Hartsburg 65239
Cedar, Marylou Green, 7701 E. Zumwalt Rd., Hartsburg 65239
Columbia, Russ Walker, 8101 Dusty Rhodes Ln., Columbia 65202
Columbia, Stacy Summers, 6231 N. Gregory Dr., Columbia 65202
Columbia
Ward 1, Mitch Richards, 119 Bicknell, Columbia 65201
Ward 1, Laurien Rose, 707 Washington Ave., Apt. A, Columbia 65201
Ward 2, Dale Parmer, 3712 Galland Fox Dr., Columbia 65202
Ward 2, Joanne Basye, 3812 Ivanhoe Blvd., Columbia 65203
Ward 3, Eric Albert, 803 N. Ann St., Columbia 65201
Ward 4, Daniel Anderson, 503 Edgewood Ave., Columbia 65203
Ward 4, Kristen B. Anderson, 503 Edgewood Ave., Columbia 65203

Ward 5, Rick Rowden, 1401 Berwick Ct., Columbia 65203
Ward 5, Rosa Robb, 4105 Blue Hollow Dr., Columbia 65203
Ward 6, Cory McMahon, 1506 Anthony St., Columbia 65201
Ward 6, Amy R. Bremer, 2301 Silver Leaf Ct., Columbia 65201
Hallsville
Ward 1, Cheri Reisch, 115 East St., Hallsville 65255
Katy, Charles Basye, 15000 W. Hwy. 40, Rocheport 65279
Katy, Rhonda Basye, 15000 W. Hwy. 40, Rocheport 65279
Missouri, Mike Zweifel, 520 Sackets Rd., Columbia 65203
Perche, Dan C. Judy, 7300 N. Bell Rd., Columbia 65202
Perche, Peggy L. Eskew, 2550 W. Oak Ridge Dr., Columbia 65202
Rock Bridge, Thomas C. Mendenhall, 7300 S. Quantirlls Pass, Columbia 65203
Rock Bridge, Carolyn Fresenburg, 9320 S. Constien Rd., Columbia 65203
Rocky Fork, Steven Spellman, 9701 E. Mt. Zion Church Rd., Hallsville 65255
Rocky Fork, Elizabeth Phillips, 2670 Buffalo Dr., Columbia 65202
Sturgeon
Ward 2, Elba J. Roark, 410 S. Ogden St., Sturgeon 65284
Three Creeks, Terry Spickert, 7925 Bennett Dr., Columbia 65201
Three Creeks, Lynn Acton, 8002 S. Barry Rd., Columbia 65201

Buchanan County

Chair, David Jones
Vice Chair, Noel Cross
Agency, John Dunlap
Agency, Becky Dunlap
Center, John Tapia
Center, Denise Bartles
Crawford, David McMahan
Tremont, Patricia Brunell Dyer
Buchanan
Ward 1, David Rich
Ward 2, David Jones
Ward 4, Noel Cross
Ward 4, Ellis Cross
Ward 7, Sherrie Ott
Ward 12, Judith Hausman
Ward 15, Noah Green
Ward 15, Kristi Green
Washington, Jim Hausman

Butler County

Chair, Eddy Justice, 379 Remington Pl., Poplar Bluff 63901
Secretary, Joe Leahy, 5806 Melissa Ln., Poplar Bluff 63901
Treasurer, Emily Hogg, 2521 Lee St., Poplar Bluff 63901
Ash Hill, Irvin Mansbridge, 1204 Hwy. DD, Fisk 63940
Ash Hill, Karen Buttrey, 2220 CR 640, Fisk 63940
Beaver Dam, Charles Hampton, 570 Roxy Lake Estates, Poplar Bluff 63901
Black River, John Scott, 14110 Christy Ln., Poplar Bluff 63901
Black River, Danielle Berry, 608 River Rd., Williamsville 63967
Epps, Eddy Justice, 379 Remington Pl., Poplar Bluff 63901
Kinyon, Hardy Billington, 80 E. Outer Rd., Poplar Bluff 63901

Kinyon, Gayle Robison, 361 Stonecreek Dr., Poplar Bluff 63901

Lake Road, Emily Thurman, 1340 CR 543, Poplar Bluff 63901

Neely, Carrie Jones, 684 CR 260, Neeleyville 63954

Oak Grove, Scott Lundstrom, 1589 CR 523, Poplar Bluff 63901

Oak Grove, Debby Lundstrom, 1589 CR. 523, Poplar Bluff 63901

Sale Barn, Dustin Midyett, 2487 CR 309, Poplar Bluff 63901

St. Francis, Natasha Sentell, 111 Old Hwy. T, Poplar Bluff 63901

Poplar Bluff

Ward 1, Freda Ballard, 2001 Wasson Dr., Poplar Bluff 63901

Ward 2, Steve Whitworth, 1411 Yarber St., Poplar Bluff 63901

Ward 2, Cindy Fuller, 1700 Sylvan Dr., Poplar Bluff 63901

Ward 3, Jeff Shawan, 513 Poplar St., Poplar Bluff 63901

Ward 3, Kami Ortego, 939 Poplar St., Poplar Bluff 63901

Ward 4, Eric Schalk, 2737 10th St., Poplar Bluff 63901

Ward 4, June Rigby, 3620 Tanglewood Rd., Poplar Bluff 63901

Ward 5, Peter Tinsley, 2722 N. Main, Poplar Bluff 63901

Caldwell County

Chair, Richard Lee, 408 N. Ewing St., Hamilton 64644

Vice Chair, Julie Feil, 7489 SE Tobin Vallley Dr., Cowgill 64637

Secretary, Jill Kopek, 200 N. Burruss St., Hamilton 64644

Treasurer, Leanard Feil, 7489 SE Tobin Valley Dr., Cowgill 64637

Hamilton, Richard Lee, 408 N. Ewing St., Hamilton 64644

Hamilton, Jill Kopek, 200 N. Burruss St., Hamilton 64644

Kingston, Gerald McBrayer, 875 NW Carter Rd., Kingston 64650

Lincoln, Leanard Feil, 7489 SE Tobin Valley Dr., Cowgill 64637

Lincoln, Julie Feil, 7489 SE Tobin Valley Dr., Cowgill 64637

Callaway County

Chair, Dean Powell, 2651 Country Club Dr., New Bloomfield 65063

Vice Chair, Christine Kleindienst, 3621 CR 121, Fulton 65251

Secretary, Michael West, 1740 Ashley Ct., Fulton 65251

Treasurer, Leona Powell, 2651 Country Club Dr., New Bloomfield 65063

Fulton

West, Donald Kritzer, 5055 Pendergras, Fulton 65251

Ward 1, Michael West, 1740 Ashley Ct., Fulton 65251

Ward 3, Chris Wilson, 1211 Randall Ln., Fulton 65251

Ward 3, Betty Clevenger, 515 Bluff St., Fulton 65251

Ward 4, Mitchell Hubbard, 704 Jefferson St., Fulton 65251

Guthrie, Tom Suttles, 8603 State Rd. J, New Bloomfield 65063

Holts Summit Co - Cedar City, Thomas Woods, 367 CR 394, Hartsburg 65039

Holts Summit Co - Cedar City, Roselee Hogan, 441 Julie Ln., Holts Summit 65043

Holts Summit

Ward 1, Karey Wilkinson, 135 Brookstone Dr., Holts Summit 65043

Ward 1, Romona Wilkinson, 135 Brookstone Dr., Holts Summit 65043

McCredie, Christine Kleindienst, 3621 CR 121, Fulton 65251

Millersburg, Bob Jones, 1198 State Rd. WW, Fulton 65251

Millersburg, Eva Jones, 1198 State Rd. WW, Fulton 65251

Mokane, Earl Williamson, 9610 CR 455, Mokane 65059

New Bloomfield, Dean Powell, 2651 Country Club Dr., New Bloomfield 65063

New Bloomfield, Leona Powell, 2651 Country Club Dr., New Bloomfield 65063

Readsville, Gary Jungermann, 7472 State Rd. D, Portland 65067

Williamsburg, James Zerr, 9262 CR 164, Williamsburg 63388

Williamsburg, Alyce Zerr, 9262 CR 164, Williamsburg 63388

Camden County

Chair, Brent Salsman, 7439 S. State Hwy. 7, Montreal 65591

Vice Chair, Judy Taylor, 6293 Chapel Bluff Rd., Macks Creek 65789

Adair, James Jackson, 669 N. Hwy. 7, Camdenton 65020

Adair, Katherine Benton-Black, 379 El Tampa Rd., Camdenton 65020

Auglaize, Brent Salsman, 7439 S. State Hwy. 7, Montreal 65591

Auglaize, Melissa Salsman, 7439 S. State Hwy. 7, Montreal 65591

Jackson, Morgan Morris, 8877 State Rd. A, Montreal 65591

Jackson, Lori Morris, 8877 State Rd. A, Montreal 65591

Jasper, Jim Halloran, 574 Liahona Ln., Sunrise Beach 65079

Jasper, Nancy Osborn, 228 Hi Way Cove Cir., Sunrise Beach 65079

Ki He Ka, David Edwards, PO Box 82, Camdenton 65020

Ki He Ka, Lisa Simpson, 516 Timberlake Terr., Linn Creek 65052

Niangua, Michael Lloyd, 3433 Old Route 5, Camdenton 65020

Niangua, Eunice Jeffries, 1503 Resorts Rd., Camdenton 65020

Osage, John Farrell, PO Box 364, Osage Beach 65065

Osage, Lynn Farrell, PO Box 364, Osage Beach 65065

Osceola, John Beckett, 169 Viewpoint Dr., Camdenton 65020

Osceola, Abbey Beckett, 169 Viewpoint Dr., Camdenton 65020

Pawhuska, Doug Olauson, PO Box 46, Lake Ozark 65049

Russell, Kelly Luttrell, 860 W. Branch Rd., Macks Creek 65786

Russell, Judy Taylor, 6293 Chapel Bluff Rd., Macks Creek 65789

Warren, Ernie Calvert, 998 Dry Hollow Rd., Camdenton 65020

Warren, Christina Calvert, 998 Dry Hollow Rd., Camdenton 65020

Cape Girardeau County

Chair, Holly M. Lintner, 978 CR 546, Jackson 63755

Vice Chair, James C. Roche, 3137 CR 349, Jackson 63755

Secretary, Kristi King, 868 Bella Vista Dr., Jackson 63755

Treasurer, Jerry Keele, 217 N. West End Blvd., Cape Girardeau 63701

Friedheim, Glenn Wilke, 544 CR 406, Friedheim 63747

Friedheim, Karen Wilke, 544 CR 406, Friedheim 63747

Oak Ridge, Bill Freeman, 4683 State Hwy. E, Oak Ridge 63769

Oak Ridge, Linda K. Freeman, 4683 State Hwy. E, Oak Ridge 63769

Bryd

1, Allen Moss, 1034 Trail Ridge Dr., Jackson 63755

1, Kathryn Moss, 1034 Trail Ridge Dr., Jackson 63755

2, Leonard F. Sander Jr., 1131 Shady Ln., Jackson 63755

2, Marsha D. Sander, 1131 Shady Ln., Jackson 63755

3, Jon Abernathy, 620 Randy Dr., Jackson 63755

3, Janet Boston, 1201 Greenleaf, Jackson 63755

4, Scott R. Clark, 1010 Greensferry, Jackson 63755

5, Larry Bock, 2572 CR 324, Gordonville 63701

6, Fred Barnard, 243 CR 438, Jackson 63755

6, Barb Barnard, 243 CR 438, Jackson 63755

Brown Owl, Bill Garner, 3283 CR 318, Cape Girardeau 63701

Brown Owl, Linda Garner, 3283 CR 318, Cape Girardeau 63701

Campster / Pecan Grove, Paul R. Summers, 6005 State Highway K, Cape Girardeau 63701

Campster / Pecan Grove, Debra Jenkins, 239 Mockingbird Ln., Cape Girardeau 63701

Cape Girardeau

Precinct 2, Kenneth R. Gullett, 1408 Stoddard St., Cape Girardeau 63701

Precinct 4, Peter Kinder, 1220 Rockwood, Cape Girardeau 63701

Precinct 4, Gail Hoffman, 10 N. Ellis, Cape Girardeau 63701

Precinct 7, Doug Austin, 758 Woodbine Pl., Cape Girardeau 63701

Precinct 7, Fran Austin, 758 Woodbine Pl., Cape Girardeau 63701

Precinct 8, Mark Slinkard, 1126 N. Fountain, Cape Girardeau 63701

Precinct 8, Robin Slinkard, 1126 N. Fountain, Cape Girardeau 63701

Precinct 13, Matt Henson, 2521 Allendale Dr., Cape Girardeau 63701

Precinct 13, Cindie Yanow, 2140 West Cape Rock Dr., Cape Girardeau 63701

Precinct 14, Wayne Wallingford, 2405 Terrie Hill Rd., Cape Girardeau 63701

Precinct 14, Susan Wallingford, 2405 Terrie Hill Rd., Cape Girardeau 63701

Precinct 15, Evan Trump, 2503 Fairlane Dr., Cape Girardeau 63701

Precinct 15, Lori Trump, 2503 Fairlane Dr., Cape Girardeau 63701

Precinct 16, Mark Welker, 2912 Cuesta Dr., Cape Girardeau 63701

Precinct 16, Loretta Schneider, 3215 Lakewood Dr., Cape Girardeau 63701

Precinct 17, Reg Swan, 3926 Annwood, Cape Girardeau 63701

Precinct 17, Kathy Swan, 3926 Annwood, Cape Girardeau 63701

Precinct 18, Wayne Bowen, 2577 Cobblestone Ct., Cape Girardeau 63701

Delta, Mark Reitzel, 7349 State Hwy. N, Whitewater 63785

Delta, Lisa Reitzel, 7349 State Hwy. N, Whitewater 63785

Fruitland, Jon Lintner, 978 CR 546, Jackson 63755

Fruitland, Holly M. Lintner, 978 CR 546, Jackson 63755

Gordonville, Wavis Jordan, PO Box 907, Cape Girardeau 63702

Gordonville, Melissa Miller, 4501 State Hwy. Z, Cape Girardeau 63701

Hanover, Chris Weiss, 6933 Hwy. W., Jackson 63755

Hanover, Diane Diebold, 4490 E. Jackson Blvd., Jackson 63755

Millersville, James C. Roche, 3137 CR 349, Jackson 63755

Millersville, Cindy Grothman, 2058 CR 349, Jackson 63755

Nell Holcomb, Dave Heise, 432 Wind River Ln., Cape Girardeau 63701

Nell Holcomb, Jeanne Heise, 432 Wind River Ln., Cape Girardeau 63701

New Wells, Cynthia Hazelwood, 1010 CR 516, New Wells 63732

Pocahontas, Don Bogenpohl, 314 State Highway E, Jackson 63755

Whitewater, John Helderman, 2974 CR 389, Whitewater 63785

Whitewater, Jan Farrar, 4886 State Hwy. A, Gordonville 63701

Carroll County

Chair, Linda Leabo, 122 S. Maple, Norborne 64668

Vice Chair, Robert Pavlu, 1103 Hillcrest Dr., Carrollton 64633

Secretary, Earlene Martin, 20518 Hwy. 65, Bogard 64622

Treasurer, William D. Placke, 716 W. Sixth, Carrollton 64633

Carrollton

Ward 1, Ken Warren, 24326 CR 271, Carrollton 64633

Ward 1, Beth Warren, 24326 CR 271, Carrollton 64633

Ward 2, Linda Thurlo, 102 S. Maple, Carrollton 64633

Ward 2, Gail Thurlo, 102 S. Maple, Carrollton 64633

Ward 3, Bill Boelsen, 616 Pearl St., Carrollton 64633

Ward 4, Robert Pavlu, 1103 Hillcrest Dr., Carrollton 64633

Ward 4, Cynthia Pavlu, 1103 Hillcrest Dr., Carrollton 64633

Cherry Valley, David Durham, 35355 CR 109, Hardin 64035

Cherry Valley, Karen Durham, 35355 CR 109, Hardin 64035

Combs, Eugene Audsley, 26396 CR 337, DeWitt 64639

Combs, Lillie Audsley, 26396 CR 337, DeWitt 64639

DeWitt, Dean Miller, 25097 CR 381, DeWitt 64639

DeWitt, Ruth Miller, 25097 CR 381, DeWitt 64639

Egypt

1, Nelson Heil, 229 E. Fifth, Norborne 64668

1, Bonnie Waits, 518 E.Third, Norborne 64668

2, Roger Leabo, 122 S. Maple, Norborne 64668

2, Linda Leabo, 122 S. Maple, Norborne 64668

Eugene, Roy Staton, 29378 CR 317, Carrollton 64633

Eugene, Nancy Staton, 29378 CR 317, Carrollton 64633

Farfield, Ricky Newport, 20799 CR 151, Carrollton 64633

Farfield, Fern Green, 20459 CR 141, Norborne 64668

Hurricane, Robert Deatherage, 118 E. 3rd, Hale 64643

Hurricane, Nancy Deatherage, 118 E. 3rd, Hale 64643

Leslie, Darrell Dorner, 19079 CR 171, Bogard 64622

Leslie, Renae McMullin, 19649 CR 171, Bogard 64622

Moss Creek, Rick Pierson, 17806 CR 320, Norborne 64668

Moss Creek, Elizabeth Pierson, 17806 CR 320, Norborne 64668

Sugartree, Annette Smith, 21239 CR 366, Carrollton 64633

Sugartree, Nick Ahnefeld, 34008 CR 183, Carrollton 64633

Trotter, Roy Ritchhart, 27532 CR 191, Carrollton 64633

Trotter, Sue Ritchhart, 27532 CR 191, Carrollton 64633

Prairie, Ricky Lee Miller, 22170 CR 111, Norborne 64668

Prairie, Staci Wood, 26251 CR 111, Norborne 64668

Van Horn, David Martin, 20518 Hwy. 65, Bogard 64622

Van Horn, G. Earlene Martin, 20518 Hwy. 65, Bogard 64622

Wakenda, Ron Linneman, 30989 CR 257, Carrollton 64633

Wakenda, Karen Linneman, 30989 CR 257, Carrollton 64633

Carter County

Chair, Tom Cox, HCR Box 2124, Van Buren 63965

Vice Chair, Gail D. Cox, HCR Box 2124, Van Buren 63965

Colemansville, Kevin Burkhart, RR 2 Box 4432, Elliforne 63937

Colemansville, Marrine Burkhart, RR 2 Box 4432, Elliforne 63937

Van Buren, Tom Cox, HCR Box 2124-A, Van Buren 63965

Van Buren, Gail Cox, HCR Box 2124-A, Van Buren 63965

Cass County

Chair, Bill Kartsonis, 218 N. Winnebago Dr., Lake Winnebago 64034

Vice Chair, Erica O'Hanlon, 606 Lacy Ln., Belton 64012

Secretary, John Webb, 23906 S. State Rt. D, Cleveland 64734

Treasurer, Janice Patterson, 22119 South St. Rt. 291, Harrisonville 64701

Belton

    Ward 2A, Jack Bondon, 16507 Fairway Rd., Belton 64012

    Ward 2A, Melissa Bondon, 16507 Fairway Rd., Belton 64012

    Ward 3A, Ryan O'Hanlon, 606 Lacy Ln., Belton 64012

    Ward 3A, Erica O'Hanlon, 606 Lacy Ln., Belton 64012

    Ward 3B, Steven Breshears, 521 London Way, Belton 64012

    Ward 3B, Betty Breshears, 521 London Way, Belton 64012

Dolan, Jim Danner, 26501 S. Redbud Rd., Freeman 64746

Dolan, Nancy Danner, 26501 S. Redbud Rd., Freeman 64746

Grand River Rural, C. Ted Turney, 13506 E. 277th St., Freeman 64746

Harrisonville

    Ward 1, Steve Cheslik, 1601 E. Mechanic St., Harrisonville 64701

    Ward 3, William M. Day, 701 S. Highland Dr., Harrisonville 64701

    Ward 3, Bonnie Werner, 201 N. Commercial, Harrisonville 64701

    Ward 4, Jaret Jensen, 1501 S. Independence St., Harrisonville 64701

Mt. Pleasant Rural, Jack Bondon, 16680 Country Club Ct., Village of Loch Lloyd 64012

Mt. Pleasant Rural, Peggy Bondon, 16680 Country Club Ct., Village of Loch Lloyd 64012

Peculiar Rural, Rex Rector, 23400 Cottage Ln., Harrisonville 64701

Peculiar Rural, Deborah Rector, 23400 Cottage Ln., Harrisonville 64701

Raymore

    Ward 1B, Kevin Kellogg, 1605 Stasi Ave., Raymore 64083

    Ward 1B, Lisa Vinck, 1613 Christi Ln., Raymore 64083

    Ward 2, Ryan Johnson, 815 S. Park Dr., Raymore 64083

    Ward 2, Rebecca Shephard Johnson, 815 S. Park Dr., Raymore 64083

    Ward 4, Kim York, 604 Horizon Pkwy., Raymore 64083

Union, John Webb, 23906 S. State Rt. D, Cleveland 64734

Union, Mary Webb, 23906 S. State Rt. D, Cleveland 64734

West Dolan, Gail Alston, 404 E. 289th St., Cleveland 64734

West Peculiar City, Charles M. Chaffin, 813 S. Morgan Dr., Peculiar 64078

West Peculiar City, Barbie Chaffin, 813 S. Morgan Dr., Peculiar 64078

West Peculiar Rural, Jeremy Long, 10508 E. 243rd St., Peculiar 64078

West Peculiar Rural, Tonya Long, 10508 E. 243rd St., Peculiar 64078

Winnebago, Peggy Patterson, 5051 SW Raintree Pkwy, Lee's Summit 64082

Winnebago, Bill Kartsonis, 218 N. Winnebago Dr., Lake Winnebago 64034

Cedar County

Chair, Marlon Collins, 507 S. Cherry St., Linn 65785

Vice Chair, Sarah Turner, 19373 S. Hwy. M, Jefferson 65785

Secretary, Kenneth Turner, 19373 S. Hwy. M, Jefferson 65785

Treasurer, Carol Stubock, 16998 S. Hwy. O, Benton 65785

Benton, Frank Stubock, 16998 S. Hwy. O, Benton 65785

Benton, Carol Stubock, 16998 S. Hwy. O, Benton 65785

Jefferson, Kenneth Turner, 19373 S. Hwy. M, Jefferson 65785

Jefferson, Sarah Turner, 19373 S. Hwy. M, Jefferson 65785

Linn, Marlon Collins, 507 S. Cherry St., Linn 65785

Washington, Peggy Konney, 9505 S. 1471 Rd., Washington 65785

Chariton County

Chair, Evan Emmerich, 304 W. Sixth St., Salisbury 65281

Vice Chair, Audrey Stephenson, 608 Second St., Mendon 64660

Secretary, Genny Wright, 33833 Birch St., Marceline 64658

Treasurer, Fred Carpenter, 10639 Hwy. YY, Sumner 64681

Bee Branch, Warren Ross, 15688 Hwy. 129, Salisbury 65281

Bee Branch, Genny Wright, 33833 Birch St., Marceline 64658

Bowling Green, Bob Littleton, 23999 Hwy. 24, Brunswick 65246

Bowling Green, Norman Grotjan, 24918 King Hill Rd., Dalton 65246

Brunswick, Kathy Manson, 22848 Hwy. 24, Brunswick 65246

Clark, Kevin Allen, 30862 Peden Chapel Rd., Marceline 64658
Clark, Brenda Allen, 30862 Peden Chapel Rd., Marceline 64658
Cunningham, Fred Carpenter, 10639 Hwy. YY, Sumner 64681
Cunningham, Dorothy Kaye, 12499 Kaye Rd., Sumner 64681
Keytesville, Darin Byrd, 25481 Settlers Ave., Keytesville 65261
Keytesville, Lisa Byrd, 25481 Settlers Ave., Keytesville 65261
Mendon, Kenny Stephenson, 608 Second St., Mendon 64660
Mendon, Audrey Stephenson, 608 Second St., Mendon 64660
Mussel Fork, Harry Wolfe, 1008 Whitecap Cir., Keytesville 65261
Mussel Fork, Rita Wolfe, 1008 Whitecap Circle, Keytesville 65261
Salisbury, Evan Emmerich, 304 W. Sixth St., Salisbury 65281
Salisbury, Jamie Haines, 33911 N. Lake Ln., Salisbury 65281
Salt Creek, Harry Holderieath, 25572 Hwy. C, Mendon 64660
Salt Creek, Hilda Sayler, 21205 Rodeo Ave., Mendon 64660
Triplett, Matt Reichert, 19640 Iowas Rd., Keytesville 65261
Triplett, Tina Reichert, 19640 Iowas Rd., Keytesville 65261
Wayland, Josh Boeger, 34308 McDonald Rd., Salisbury 65281
Wayland, Katie Boeger, 34308 McDonald Rd., Salisbury 65281
Yellow Creek, Valerie Gladbach, 19625 Hwy. E, Mendon 64660

Christian County

Chair, Alec Wade, 1970 Spring Hill Rd., Sparta 65733
Vice Chair, West Finley, Sandy Worley, 1208 W. Robin St., Ozark 65721
Bruner, Joan Heinline
Bruner, Plethcer Rogers
Cassidy, Ed Merritt
Cassidy, Terri Merritt
Benton
    East, Robert Palmer
    East, Bonne Palmer
    West, Alec Wade, 1970 Spring Hill Rd., Sparta 65733
    West, Ginny Wade
Finley
    East, Steve Maples
    East, Julia Maples
    West, Michael Phillips
    West, Sandy Worley, 1208 W. Robin St., Ozark 65721
Galloway
    North, Gerald Yarnell
    North, Dorothy Doenning
    South, Margaret Dollarhite
Garden Grove, Bill Elmer
Garden Grove, Helen Elmer
Lincoln, Rann Coffman
Lincoln, Jennifer Coffman
Linden, Ken Spangler
Linden, Christina Tonsing
Linn–North, Walter Martens
Linn–North, Wanda Martens
McCracken, George Burns

McCracken, Patsy Wilcox
Northview, John Dollarhite
Northview, Merilyn Anne Master, 122 E. Peachtree Dr., Nixa 65714
Oldfield, Donny Gardner
Oldfield, Jeanna Gardner
Polk, Steven Darryl Sipes
Polk, Carolyn Sue Sipes
Riverside, Josh Lenz
Riverside, Glenda Nichols
Rosedale, Jim Bowen
Rosedale, Pam Bowen
Sparta, Dale Roller
Sparta, Catherine Roller
Union Chapel, Thomas Taylor
Union Chapel, Lacey Hart

Clark County

Chair, Henry Dienst, RR 3, Box 48A, Kahoka 63445
Vice Chair, Gloria Hodges, RR 2, Box 2215, Wyaconda 63474
Secretary, Michelle Allen, RR 1, Box 113, Luray 63453
Treasurer, Roberta McAfee, RR 3, Box 26, Kahoka 63445
Clark, Michael Phillips
Clark, Jill McAfee, RR 1, Box 90AAA, Luray 63453
Clay, Henry Dienst, RR 3, Box 48A, Kahoka 63445
Clay, Deborah Dienst, RR 3, Box 48A, Kahoka 63445
Folker, Judith Gaston, RR 2, Box 34A, Farmington, IA, 52626
Jackson, Ron Brewer, PO Box 108, Kahoka 63445
Lincoln, Charles Kerner, 289 Garfield, Kahoka 65355
Lincoln, Michelle Allen, RR 1, Box 113, Luray 63453
Madison, Paul Allen, 15 Edgewood Estates, Kahoka 63445
Madison, Roberta McAfee, RR 3, Box 26, Kahoka
Union, Stuart Strickler, RR 1, Box 67A, Williamstown 63473
Union, Julie Kattelmann, RR 1, Box 48, Kahoka 63445
Washington, Gloria Hodges, RR 2, Box 2215, Wyaconda 63474
Wyaconda, Rodney Smith, PO Box 115, Wyaconda 63474
Wyaconda, Phyllis Smith, PO Box 115, Wyaconda 63474

Clay County

Chair, Benjamin Wierzbicki, 113 Delores St., Excelsior Springs 64024
Vice Chair, Elnora Overman, 4046 N. Askew Ave., Kansas City 64117
08-2, Dawn Holterman, 19600 N. 69 Hwy., Lawson 64062
12-1, Joshua Hurlbert, 19400 Diamond Ln., Smithville 64089
12-1, Lynda Fullmer, 18003 Rollins Dr., Smithville 64089
12-3, William Doores, 17108 Quinn Rd., Kearney 64060
12-3, Sandra Doores, 17108 Quinn Rd., Kearney 64060
12-4, Ryan Silvey, 11231 N. Pennsylvania Ave., Kansas City 64155
12-4, Angela Silvey, 11231 N. Pennsylvania Ave., Kansas City 64155
12-5, Shawna Searcy, 801 Susan St., Kearney 64060
14-1, Kevin Corlew, 5317 N. Pennsylvania Ave., Kansas City 64118
14-1, Amy Corlew, 5317 N. Pennsylvania Ave., Kansas City 64118
15-1, Brad Werth, 1701 NE 76th St.
15-2, Brent Arant, 4039 NE 60th St., Gladstone 64119

15-2, Jean Eleanor, Swofford, 3005 NE 68th Terr., Gladstone 64119

15-3, Jerry Nolte, 1304 NE Shady Lane Dr., Gladstone 64118

15-4, Anthony Tetzlaff, 5730 N. Tracy Ave., Gladstone 64118

15-4, Jeana Tetzlaff, 5730 N. Tracy Ave., Gladstone 64118

15-5, Jeffrey Henak, 405 NW 53rd St., Gladstone 64118

15-5, Lisa Henak, 405 NW 53rd St., Gladstone 64118

16-1, Kevin McEvoy, 1409 NE 102nd Terr., Kansas City 64155

16-1, Pamela Mason, 9701 N. Kenwood Ct., Kansas City 64155

16-2, Mina Jo Brown, 2 NE 90th Terr., Kansas City 64155

16-3, Victor Hurlbert, 4305 NE 73rd St., Kansas City 64119

16-3, Trish Martin, 3400 NE 78th, Kansas City 64119

16-4, Craig Porter, 9504 N. Arlington Ave., Kansas City 64157

16-4, Katee Porter, 9504 N. Arlington Ave., Kansas City 64157

16-5, Jeff Mason, 10304 N. Spruce Ct., Kansas City 64156

16-5, Veronika McDonald, 10402 N. Spruce Ct., Kansas City 64156

17-1, Adam Cross, 7315 N. Donnelly Ave., Kansas City 64158

17-1, Mary Hill, 1354 Wildbrier Dr., Liberty 64068

17-2, Matthew Thompson, 419 E. Arthur, Liberty 64068

17-3, Sarah Olson, 1233 Westboro Cir., Liberty 64068

17-4, Paul Evans, 8106 NE 53rd St., Kansas City 64119

17-4, Pamela Evans, 8106 NE 53rd St., Kansas City 64119

18-1, Ronald Thiewes, 4513 N. Baltimore Dr., Kansas City 64116

18-1, Beverly Sims, 4242 N. Grand Ave., Kansas City 64116

18-3, Thomas Salisbury, 4105 NE 58th Terr., Kansas City 64119

18-3, Karen Salisbury, 4105 NE 58th Terr., Kansas City 64119

18-4, Elnora Overman, 4046 N. Askew Ave., Kansas City 64117

18-5, Jim Welsh, 4851 N. Wabash Ave., Kansas City 64118

18-5, Virginia Mason, 3232 N. Forest, Kansas City 64116

38-1, Michael Ebernroth, 12613 Ridgeview Rd., Kearney 64060

38-2, John Sanderford, 9915 N. Ash Ave., Kansas City 64157

38-2, Vicki Lynn Dunning, 992 Ellis, Liberty 64068

38-3, Stephen Hemphill, 424 Wilson St., Liberty 64068

38-3, Valerie Jo Furrow, 211 N. Water St., Apt. B, Liberty 64068

38-4, Bradley Fisher, 19616 NE 102 St., Liberty 64068

38-4, Mary Jilka, 18015 Hwy. H, Liberty 64068

38-5, Benjamin Wierzbicki, 113 Delores St., Excelsior Springs 64024

Clinton County

Chair, Dan Snodgrass, 3491 SE Powell Rd., Lathrop 64465

Vice Chair, Ann Mowry, 8031 SW 227th St., Trimble 64492

Atchison, Jayson Watkins, 506 Andrew Ct., Gower 64454

Clinton, Mike Larkin, 1975 SW J Hwy., Plattsburg 64477

Hardin, Steve Mowry, 8031 SW 227th St., Trimble 64492

Hardin, Ann Mowry, 8031 SW 227th St., Trimble 64492

Jackson, Dan Snodgrass, 3491 SE Powell Rd., Lathrop 64465

Lathrop, Ed Shrewsbury, 400 South St., Lathrop 64465

Shoal, Wade Wilken, 6150 NE 312th St., Turney 64493

Cole County

Chair, Ron L. Fitzwater, 916 Nob Hill Rd., Jefferson City 65109

Vice Chair, Penelope Z. Quigg, 612 Blair Dr., Apt. A, Jefferson City 65109

Secretary, Bonnie Linhardt, 7408 Scrivner Rd., Jefferson City 65109

Treasurer, Jeff Ahlers, 2024 Scenic Dr., Jefferson City 65109

Clark, Bonnie Linhardt, 7408 Scrivner Rd., Jefferson City 65109

Clark, Todd Linhardt, 7408 Scrivner Rd., Jefferson City 65109

Cole

Ward 1, Kristina Bernskoetter, 1015 Las Brisas Ct., Jefferson City 65101

Ward 1, Jeff Ahlers, 2024 Scenic Dr., Jefferson City 65101

Ward 2, Carolyn McDowell, 1222 Carter St., Jefferson City 65109

Ward 2, Mark Rehagen, 1104 Swifts Hwy., Jefferson City 65109

Ward 3, Doug Thomas, 3444 Hobbs Ln., Jefferson City 65109

Ward 3, Patricia Thomas, 3444 Hobbs Ln., Jefferson City 65109

Ward 4, Penelope Z. Quigg, 612 Blair Dr., Apt. A, Jefferson City 65109

Ward 4, Ron Fitzwater, 916 Nob Hill Rd., Jefferson City 65109

Ward 5, Patricia (Trish) Vincent, 1422 Edgevale Rd., Jefferson City 65101

Jefferson, Carol T. Ellinger, 5003 Henwick Ln., Jefferson City 65109

Liberty, Ronald E. Ahlers, 6320 Village Rd., Jefferson City 65101

Marion, Katherine Peerson, 820 Lazy Brook Ln., Jefferson City 65109

Marion, Mark C. Schepers, 7223 Henwick Ln., Jefferson City 65109

Osage, Stephen Cearlock, 1203 Somerset Ln., Jefferson City 65101

Cooper County

Chair, Gary Harris, 13267 Hwy. B, Boonville 65233

Vice Chair, Billie Litton, 19251 Hwy. CC, Blackwater 65322

Secretary, Mary Klenklen, 302 Highland Dr., Boonville 65233

Treasurer, Dean Barker, 110 W. College St., Bunceton 65237

Blackwater, Mark Danner, 18600 Wildcliff, Blackwater 65322

Blackwater, Lisa Danner, 18600 Wildcliff, Blackwater 65322

Boonville

Ward 1, Paul Davis, 19367 Hwy. 98, Boonville 65233

Ward 1, Elizabeth Thomas, 18533 Hunters Ridge Rd., Boonville 65233

Ward 3, Mary Klenklen, 302 Highland Dr., Boonville 65233

Clarks Fork, Gary Harris, 13267 Hwy. B, Boonville 65233

Clarks Fork, Janet Harris, 13267 Hwy. B, Boonville 65233

Kelly, Dean Barker, 110 W. College St., Bunceton 65237

Kelly, Ruth Young, 11819 Wallace Rd., Bunceton 65237

Lamine, Theodore Smith, 8205 White Oak Rd., Blackwater 65322

Lamine, Billie Litton, 19251 Hwy. CC, Blackwater 65322
Lebanon, Bobby Thomas, 6749 Roberts Dr., Bunceton 65237
Moniteau
    North, Eddie Brickner, 19671 Hwy. J, Bunceton 65237
    North, Karen Brickner, 19671 Hwy. J, Bunceton 65237
    South, Dale Hodges, 19863 Oakland Church Rd., Clarksburg 65025
    South, Carol Hodges, 19863 Oakland Church Rd., Clarksburg 65025
Palestine, Larry Grissum, 14316 Hwy. F, Boonville 65233
Palestine, Linda Grissum, 14316 Hwy. F, Boonville 65233
Pilot Grove, James Schuster, 14200 Hwy. 135, Pilot Grove 65276
Pilot Grove, Mary Booker, 12387 Hwy. 135, Pilot Grove 65276
Prairie Home, Dennis Schilb, 27108 Hwy. EE, Prairie Home 65068
Prairie Home, Jeanie Lachner, 206 Carey St., Prairie Home 65068
Saline, Kent Friedrich, 26034 Big Lick Rd., Prairie Home 65068

Crawford County

Chair, John Taylor, 140 Farr View Dr., Steelville 65565
Vice Chair, Jean Stubblefield, 4995 I Hwy. F, Cuba 65453
Secretary, Edward Harman, 95 Merrihills Dr., Cuba 65453
Treasurer, Patricia Elders, 10863 Hwy. 19, Cuba 65453
Benton, Edward Harman, 95 Merrihills Dr., Cuba 65453
Benton, Catherine Lange, 4060 Cotton Dodd Rd., Cuba 65453
Boone, Kenneth Crowder, 190 Hwy. WW, Sullivan 63080
Courtois, Kent Howald, 298 Hwy. BB, Steelville 65565
Courtois, Betty Ann Howald, 298 Hwy. BB, Steelville 65565
Knobview, Jean Stubblefield, 4995 Hwy. F, Cuba 65453
Liberty, Paul Hutson, 310 Liberty Rd., Steelville 65565
Liberty, Pamela Hutson, 310 Liberty Rd., Steelville 65565
Meramec, John Taylor, 140 Farr View Dr., Steelville 65565
Meramec, Patricia Elders, 10863 Hwy. 19, Cuba 65453
Osage, William Thomas, 1835 Iron CR 3, Viburnum 65566
Osage, Judy Bass, 1835 Iron CR 3, Viburnum 65566
Taylor, John Cowling, 96 Shelly Branch Ln., Cuba 65453
Taylor, Loretta Cowling, 96 Shelly Branch Ln., Cuba 65453
Union, Kimberly Gibbs, 21435 Hwy. 19, Cherryville 65446

Dade County

Chair, Wendell Wycuff, PO Box 398, Ash Grove 65604
Vice Chair, Lori Wycuff, PO Box 398, Ash Grove 65604
Cedar, Mr. & Mrs. John McArthur, 829 N. Dade 51, Lockwood 65682
Center, Mr. & Mrs. Larry McGuire, 350 Route BB, Greenfield 65661
Earnest, Mr. & Mrs. Afton McGuire, 509 N. Dade 85, Lockwood 65682
Grant, Ivan Davis, 1152 W. Dade 152, Golden City 64748
Grant, Dorothy Davis, 1152 W. Dade 152, Golden City 64748
Lockwood, Willie Stefan, 658 W. Dade 122, Lockwood 65682
Lockwood, LaRue Lemons, PO Box 1, Lockwood 65682
Marion, Jerry Schnelle, 613 Route VV, Golden City 64748
Marion, Tina Schnelle, 613 Route VV, Golden City 64748

Morgan
    North, Ransom Proctor, 716 N. Dade 231, Aldrich 65601
    North, Crystal Proctor, 716 N. Dade 231, Aldrich 65601
    South, Carl Speight, PO Box 217, Dadeville 65635
    South, Loretta Speight, PO Box 217, Dadeville 65635
North, Mr. & Mrs. Jerry McGuire, 558 N. State Hwy. 39, Greenfield 65661
Pilgrim, Mr. & Mrs. Rick Jones, 365 E. Dade 162, Everton 65646
Polk, John Long, 619 E. Hwy. 160, Everton 65646
Polk, Judy Long, 619 E. Hwy. 160, Everton 65646
Rock Prarie, Wendell Wycuff, PO Box 398, Ash Grove 65604
Rock Prarie, Lori Wycuff, PO Box 398, Ash Grove 65604
Sac, Robert Jackson, 729 College St., Greenfield 65661
Sac, Jackie Montgomery, 832 N. Dade 177, Dadeville 65635
Smith, Wayne West, 463 S. Dade 103, South Greenfield 65752
Smith, Lisa West, 463 S. Dade 103, South Greenfield 65752
South, Mr. & Mrs. Dwain Hughes, 812 S. Dade 141, South Greenfield 65752
Washington, David Hughes, 155 E. Dade 152, South Greenfield 65752
Washington, Betty Hughes, 155 E. Dade 152, South Greenfield 65752

Dallas County

Chair, Jack Dill, 638 State Rd. M, Conway 65632
Vice Chair, Becky Schofield, PO Box 605, Buffalo 65622
Benton
    North, Charles Nimmo, 44 State Rd. DD, Buffalo 65622
    North, Becky Schofield, PO Box 605, Buffalo 65622
    South, Bill Cahow, 66 Chicago Rd., Elkland 65644
Grant, Derrick Enloe, 583 State Rd. U, Louisburg 65685
Grant, Audrey Enloe, 583 State Rd. U, Louisburg 65685
Jackson, Thelbert Gott, 54 Stever Branch Rd., Elkland 65644
Jackson, Janice Uchtman, 70 State Rd. TT, Buffalo 65622
Jasper, Wayne Randleman, 62 Hackler Ford Trl., Buffalo 65622
Jasper, JoAnn Bramwell, 225 Aurora Ln., Windyville 65783
Lincoln, George Bruce, 42 Dixie Rd., Urbana 65767
Lincoln, Marie Bruce, 42 Dixie Rd., Urbana 65767
Miller, Hosea Clemmons, 260 State Rd. YY, Tunas 65764
Miller, Marion Clemmons, 260 State Rd. YY, Tunas 65764
Sheridan, Jeff Avers, 59 Panhandle Rd., Fair Grove 65648
Sheridan, Leah Avers, 59 Panhandle Rd., Fair Grove 65648
Sherman, Jerry Duff, 2746 State Hwy. 73, Tunas 65764
Sherman, Starr Duff, 2746 State Hwy. 73, Tunas 65764
Washington, Jack Dill, 638 State Rd. M, Conway 65632
Washington, Patty Dill, 638 State Rd. M, Conway 65632
Wilson, Bryce Bradley, 121 State Rd. FF, Long Lane 65590

Daviess County

Chair, Larry McNeely, 401 S. Fifth St., Pattonsburg 64670

DeKalb County

Chair, Dixie Crider, 506 Macadee St., Maysville 64469
Vice Chair, Ronald Crider, 506 Macadee St., Maysville 64469

Secretary, Harold Allison, 4925 NE Route W, Weatherby 64469
Treasurer, Pauline Hindman, 2574 W. Hwy. 6, Maysville 64469
Adams, Kenneth Bray, 3545 SE Harris Rd., Cameron 64429
Adams, Margaret Bray, 3545 SE Harris Rd., Cameron 64429
Camden, Ronald Crider, 506 Macadee St., Maysville 64469
Camden, Dixie Crider, 506 Macadee St., Maysville 64469
Colfax, Greg Robinson, 544 SE Grindstone, Maysville 64469
Colfax, Melissa Robinson, 544 SE Grindstone, Maysville 64469
Dallas, Raymond Sweiger, 6958 NE State Rt. E, Weatherby 64497
Dallas, Judy Sweiger, 6958 NE State Rt. E, Weatherby 64497
Grant, Gayle Vessar, 4320 NW Maple Rd., Maysville 64469
Grant, Juanita Vessar, 4320 NW Maple Rd., Maysville 64469
Polk, Jake Carlson, 7235 NW Gospel Rd., Amity 64422
Polk, Petrea Carlson, 7235 NW Gospel Rd., Amity 64422
Sherman, Glenn Dyer, 4715 Ogle Rd., Stewartsville 64490
Sherman, Leslie Dyer, 4715 Ogle Rd., Stewartsville 64490
Washington, Kyle White, 6380 SW Highway 6, Clarksdale 64430
Washington, Dawn Sellers, Bay 125, Stewartsville 64490

Dent County

Chair, Joyce Karne, 177 CR 2110, Lacoma 65401
Vice Chair, Michael Homeyer, 702 N. Warfel St., Salem 65560
Norman, Bill Smith
Norman, Mary Smith
Shortbend, Ralph Shook
Shortbend, Evelyn Shook
Spring Creek East, Michael Homeyer
Spring Creek East, Jamie Homeyer
Watkins, Jim Karnes
Watkins, Joyce Karnes

Douglas County

Chair, Ross McElvain, PO Box 71, Ava 65608
Vice Chair, Susie Griswold, RR 72, Box 362, Norwood 65717
Benton, David Fleagle, RR 6, Box 6008, Ava 65608
Benton, Pat Davis, RR 2, Box 64, Ava 65608
Boone, Jack Charchol, PO Box 1296, Ava 65608
Boone, Peggy Charchol, PO Box 1296, Ava 65608
Bryan, Gregory Griswold, RR 1, Box 615, Vanzant 65768
Bryan, Tamara Griswold, RR 1, Box 615, Vanzant 65768
Campbell, James Hathcock, RR 3, Box 241-A, Ava 65608
Cass, Archie Daily, RR 72, Box 224, Norwood 65717
Cass, Christina Daily, RR 72, Box 224, Norwood 65717
Champion, Doug Hurchinson, RR 72, Box 270, Norwood 65717
Champion, Patricia Smith, RR 72, Box 266, Norwood 65717
Clay, Donald Potter, RR 71, Box 48, Norwood 65717
Clay, Portia Potter, RR 71, Box 48, Norwood 65717
Clinton, Patrick Moorhead, RR 61, Box 90, Cabool 65689
Clinton, Elizabeth Moorhead, RR 61, Box 90, Cabool 65689
Findley, Ross McElvain, PO Box 71, Ava 65608

Findley, Beth McElvain, PO Box 71, Ava 65608
Jackson, Fred Follis, RR 5, Box 790 , Ava 65608
Jackson, Joan Follis, RR 5, Box 790 , Ava 65608
McMurtrey, Wayne Griswold, RR 72, Box 362, Norwood 65717
McMurtrey, Susie Griswold, RR 72, Box 362, Norwood 65717
Miller, Bobby Watterson, RR 62, Box 59, Mansfield 65704
Miller, Wilda Watterson, RR 62, Box 59, Mansfield 65704
Springcreek, Luther Jackson, HC 17, Box 178, Ava 65608
Springcreek, Hazel Jackson, HC 17, Box 178, Ava 65608
Walls, Leon Potter, RR 7, Box 71348, Ava 65608
Washington, Charles Berger, RR 3, Box 101-C, Ava 65608
Washington, Lesa Berger, RR 3, Box 101-C, Ava 65608

Dunklin County

Chair, Tammy Gibson, PO Box 759, Senath 63876
Vice Chair, Joe Droke, PO Box 336, Senath 63876

Franklin County

Chair, Paul Curtman, 4 Josie Dr., Apt. D, Union 63084
Vice Chair, Roberta (Robbie) Brouk, 1073 Cedar Gulch, Robertsville 63072
Secretary, Alisha Allison, 519 Stafford St., Washington 63090
Treasurer, Tim Millerick, 956 St. Mary's Rd., Villa Ridge 63089
Boles Township, Tim Millerick, 956 St. Mary's Rd., Villa Ridge 63089
Boles Township, Sue Luedde, 518 Hwy. M, Villa Ridge 63089
Boone Township, Chad Johnston, 235 Purple Martin Ln., Sullivan 63080
Boone Township, Virginia J. Froelker, 4496 Big Creek Rd., Gerald 63037
Calvey Township, James P. Deniston, 2696 Wild Plum Valley, Pacific 63069
Calvey Township, Roberta (Robbie) Brouk, 1073 Cedar Gulch, Robertsville 63072
Central Township, Dennis Hartmann, 598 Wing Dr., St. Clair 63077
Central Township, Wendy Hartmann, 598 Wing Dr., St. Clair 63077
Lyon Township, Jerry Breihan, 612 Horseshoe Trail Ln., New Haven 63068
Lyon Township, Joan Breihan, 612 Horseshoe Trail Ln., New Haven 63068
Meramec Township, Stanley Laubinger, 5151 Hwy. K, Sullivan 63080
Sullivan Ward 2, Sandra K. Davidson, 542 Manion St., Sullivan 63080
St. Johns Township, Sue Hellebusch, 143 Country Ridge Ln., Washington 63090
Union Township, Todd Rio, 363 Covey Ct., Union 63084
Union Township, Pam Heitzmann, 895 Coyote Ridge Rd., Beaufort,
Union
    Ward 3, Carolyn Sansone-Webb, 618 W. State St., Union 63084
    Ward 3, Paul Curtman, 4 Josie Dr. Apt. D, Union 63084
Washington
    Ward 1, Joy Gerstein, 820 Camp St., Washington 63090
    Ward 3, Scott D. Dieckhaus, 402 Michelle Dr., Washington 63091

Ward 4, Nick Kotakis, 611 Fremont St., Washington 63089

Ward 4, Alisha Allison, 519 Stafford St., Washington 63090

Gasconade County

Chair, Ronald Hardeke, 3944 Blocks Branch Rd., Owensville 65066

Vice Chair, Sharon Fennewald, 1954 Hwy. NN, Hermann 65041

Boeuf, Sharon Fennewald, 1954 Hwy. NN, Hermann 65041

Boulware, Rilla Klein, 2275 Hwy. K, Hermann 65041

Brush Creek, Ronald Hardeke, 3944 Blocks Branch Rd., Owensville 65066

Brush Creek, Krista Hardeke, 3944 Blocks Branch Rd., Owensville 65066

Gentry County

Chair, Wanda Shoupe, 3622 U.S. Hwy. 169, Stanberry 64489

Vice Chair, Larry Hopkins, 2795 507 Rd., Gentry 64453

Secretary, Donald Grantham, 4326 257 St., Ravenwood 64479

Treasurer, Norma Beauchamp, 1501 E. Clark St., Albany 64402

Athens, Shelby Beauchamp, 1501 E. Clark St., Albany 64402

Athens, Norma Beauchamp, 1501 E. Clark St., Albany 64402

Bogle, Larry Hopkins, 2795 507 Rd., Gentry 64453

Bogle, Sue Hopkins, 2795 507 Rd., Gentry 64453

Cooper, Milton Sager, 4815 State Hwy. E, Stanberry 64489

Cooper, Wanda Shoupe, 3622 U.S. Hwy. 169, Stanberry 64489

Wilson, Donald Grantham, 4326 257 St., Ravenwood 64479

Wilson, Margaret Grantham, 4326 257 St., Ravenwood 64479

Greene County

Chair, Danette Proctor, 3802 W. Riverbend Ln., Springfield 65803

Vice Chair, Bill Owen, 5115 N. Farm Rd. 185, Springfield 65803

Secretary, Mavis Busiek, 1325 S. Jones Mill Ln., Springfield, 65809

Treasurer, Justin Hill, 6804 N. State Hwy. HH, Willard 65781

Battlefield, Marc Cerce, 4226 W. Seirra, Battlefield 65619

Battlefield, Leigh Anne Garren, 3562 W. Cardinal, Springfield 65810

Campbell

1st, Paul Nahon, PO Box 10074, Springfield 65808

1st, Sharon Nahon, PO Box 10074, Springfield 65808

2nd, John Compton, 4427 W. Sunshine, Springfield 65807

2nd, Ann Compton, 4427 W. Sunshine, Springfield 65807

2nd North, Dennis Hobbs, 1841 Stoneridge, Springfield 65803

2nd North, Joyce Jones, 3839 N. Kenna Ct., Springfield 65803

3rd North, Clate Baker, 4152 N. Farm Rd. 103, Springfield 65803

Cass, Norm Nothnagel, PO Box 145, Willard 65781

Cass, Janet Nothnagel, PO Box 145, Willard 65781

Center

1st, Ron Mark, 1567 N. Farm Rd. 97, Springfield 65802

1st, Phyllis Mark, 1567 N. Farm Rd. 97, Springfield 65802

3rd, Shelley Washam, 2222 N. Mya Ln., Springfield 65802

Cherokee, Scott Magill, 4650 S. Hampton, Springfield 65810

Cherokee, Jan Murphy, 5601 S. Kimbrough, Springfield 65810

Clay, Gordon Kinne, 4500 E. Farm Rd. 148, Springfield 65809

Clay, Cindy Stein, 4140 S. Gastonbery, Springfield 65809

Franklin

2nd, Bill Owen, 5115 N. Farm Rd. 185, Springfield 65803

2nd, Lisa Loftis, 4364 N. Shirley, Springfield 65803

Jackson

1st, Dennis Frame, 233 W. Saddle Club Rd., Fair Grove 65648

1st, Susan Frame, 233 W. Saddle Club Rd., Fair Grove 65648

Republic

East, Dave O'Dell, 563 E. Ritter, Republic 65738

East, Jane Cox, 318 E. Elm, Republic 65738

North, Michael Tull, 717 N. Hillside, Republic 65738

North, Renee Tull, 717 N. Hillside, Republic 65738

Murray, Will Bird, 805 Saratoga, Willard 65781

Murray, Marie Bird, 805 Saratoga, Willard 65781

Pond Creek, Jim Viebrock, PO Box 176, Republic 65610

Robberson

1st, Micah Burks, 10146 N. Farm Rd. 141, Brighton 65617

2nd, Darrell Proctor, 3802 W. Riverbend Ln., Springfield 65803

2nd, Danette Proctor, 3802 W. Riverbend Ln., Springfield 65803

Springfield

Ward 1, M. Lloyd Wright, 1443 S. Delaware, Springfield 65804

Ward 1, Roseann Bentley, 1500 E. Meadowmere, Springfield 65804

Ward 6, Fred Ellison, 1045 S. New, Springfield 65807

Ward 6, Janice Ellison, 1045 S. New, Springfield 65807

Ward 7, Jared Tucker, 3140 W. Madison, Springfield 65802

Ward 7, Diane Tucker, 3140 W. Madison, Springfield 65802

Ward 12, Nancy Lewis, 621 S. Grandview, Springfield 65802

Ward 22, Amanda Dixon, 1434 N. Benton, Springfield 65802

Ward 27, Randy Wimmer, 2722 N. Oakland, Springfield 65803

Ward 27, Connie DeGeere, 2601 N. Oakland, Springfield 65803

Ward 29, Jim Tygrett, 3320 N. Stewart, Springfield 65803

Ward 29, Sharon Tygrett, 3320 N. Stewart, Springfield 65803

Ward 30, Mark Maynard, 1504 E. Pythian, Springfield 65803

Ward 30, Anna Mobley, 3528 E. Sheffield Way, Springfield 65802

Ward 31, Teddy Fleck, 231 S. Burton, Springfield 65802

Ward 31, Thelma Neff, 802 N. Fairfax, Springfield 65802

Ward 32, Brooke Hobbs, 1954 E. Cambridge, Springfield 65807

Ward 35, Rick Kessinger, 326 S. Troy, Springfield 65802

Ward 35, Jane Kessinger, 326 S. Troy, Springfield 65802

Ward 34, David Schultz, 2560 S. Ferguson, Springfield 65807

Ward 34, Helen Schultz, 2560 S. Ferguson, Springfield 65807

Ward 38, Kyle Theobald, 3156 E. Latoka St., Springfield 65804

Ward 39, David Jones, 1811 E. Holiday, Springfield 65804

Ward 39, Melanie Bach, 3734 S. Elmview Ave., Springfield 65804

Ward 40, Ann Russell, 3348 S. Kings Ave., Springfield 65807

Ward 41, LoVene Claypole, 1351 E. Walnut Lawn, Springfield 65804

Ward 42, Jerry Carrol, 4428 S. Quail Creek, Springfield 65810

Ward 42, Diana Clarke, 1211 W. Westview, Springfield 65807

Ward 45, Steve Helms, 2261 E. Kirkwood, Springfield 65804

Ward 45, Marilyn Huffman, 2445 E. Latoka, Springfield 65804

Wilson, Paul Sherman, 1772 W. Farm Rd. 186, Springfield 65810

Wilson, Dee Kugler, 2316 W. Alta, Springfield 65810

Taylor, Frank Gillham, 2098 S. Hillside, Springfield 65809

Taylor, Georjene Tilton, 6348 E. Ridgeline, Springfield 65809

Washington, Scott Bonacker, 6775 E. Farm Rd. 186, Rogersville 65742

Washington, Malissa Shawley, 4106 Tipperary, Rogersville 65742

Grundy County

Chair, Gary Black, 729 W. 15th St., Trenton 64683
Vice Chair, Becky McDonald, 410 NE Hwy. J, Galt 64641
Secretary, Diane Lowrey, 227 Town & Country, Trenton 64684
Treasurer, L.D. Gibson, 1124 NW Hwy. NN, Spickard 64679
Franklin, Brandon Spencer, 286 NW Hwy. C, Spickard 64679
Franklin, Tammie Spencer, 286 NW Hwy. C, Spickard 64679
Harrison, Phillip Thomas, 460 NW 40th St., Trenton 64683
Harrison, Carol Thomas, 460 NW 40th St., Trenton 64683
Jackson, David Meservey, 134 SE 61st St., Trenton 64683
Jackson, Marcy Meservey, 134 SE 61st St., Trenton 64683
Liberty, Dennis McDonald, 410 NE Hwy. J, Galt 64641
Liberty, Becky McDonald, 410 NE Hwy. J, Galt 64641
Lincoln, Matt Gibson, 378 N. Hwy. 65, Trenton 64683
Lincoln, Martha Roberts, 783 NE 35th Ave., Trenton 64683
Madison, Robert Kincade, 455 W. Hwy. 6, Trenton 64683
Madison, Alida Kincade, 455 W. Hwy. 6, Trenton 64683
Marion, Brian Peterson, 55 SE 75th Ave., Trenton 64683
Marion, Barbara Peterson, 55 SE 75th Ave., Trenton 64683
Myers, L.D. Gibson, 1124 NW Hwy. NN, Spickard 64679
Myers, Sara Gibson, 1124 NW Hwy. NN, Spickard 64679

Taylor, Lucille Smith, 568 NW Hwy. CC, Brimson 64624
Trenton
Ward 1, Eric Hoffman, 139 S. Main St., Trenton 64683
Ward 1, Diane Lowrey, 227 Town & Country, Trenton 64683
Ward 2, Gary Black, 729 W. 15th St., Trenton 64683
Ward 2, Meredith Black, 729 W. 15th St., Trenton 64683
Ward 3, Joe Brinser, 265 NE Hwy. Y, Trenton 64683
Ward 4, Tom Eads, 3999 Littlewoods Dr., Trenton 64683
Ward 4, Linda Eads, 3999 Littlewoods Dr., Trenton 64683
Wilson, Donald Reeter, 630 SE 72nd Ave., Laredo 64652
Wilson, Nora Reeter, 630 SE 72nd Ave., Laredo 64652

Harrison County

Chair, Rick Smith, 16588 W. 310th St., Bethany 64424
Vice Chair, Cathy Smith, 16588 W. 310th St., Bethany 64424
Adams, Michael Klindt
Adams, Laura Klindt
Butler, Barbara Gates
Cypress, Jim Holcomb
Cypress, Barbara Holcomb
Grant, Bill Thomas
Grant, Virginia Thomas
Jefferson, Rand Slama
Jefferson, Jane Slama
Madison, Edward Kellner
Madison, Louise Kellner
Sherman, John Fordyce
Sherman, Stefani Fordyce
Sugar Creek, Carl McDaniel
Sugar Creek, Sandra McDaniel
Union, Lila Craig
White Oak, Rick Smith
White Oak, Cathy Smith

Henry County

Chair, David Kelsay, 901 Willow, Clinton 64735
Vice Chair, Jamie Perry, 101 Kristine Ave., Clinton 64735
Secretary, Ray Noland, 164 NW Private Rd., Clinton 64740
Treasurer, Gail Perryman, 129 NW 1301 Rd., Urich 64788
Bear Creek, Michael Henzlik, 680 SW 900 Rd., Montrose 64770
Bear Creek, Michelle Henzlik, 680 SW 900 Rd., Montrose 64770
Clinton, David Kelsay, 901 Willow, Clinton 64735
Clinton, Jamie Perry, 101 Kristine Ave., Clinton 64735
Deer Creek, Ray Noland, 164 NE 116 Private Rd., Clinton 64735
Fields Creek, Lori Watson, 329 NW 61 Rd., Clinton 64735
Osage, Bill Houk, 878 SE 421 Private Rd., Deepwater 64740
White Oak, Robert E. Perryman Jr., 129 NW 1301 Rd., Urich 64788
White Oak, Gail Perryman, 129 NW 1301 Rd., Urich 64788

Hickory County

Chair, William Jung, RR 1, Box 2099, Wheatland 65779
Vice Chair, Mary Glor, RR 71, Box 830, Urbana 65767
Secretary, Brad Turner, PO Box 34, Hermitage 65668
Treasurer, Karen Nelson, RR 71, Box 2325, Urbana 65767

Center, Brad Turner, PO Box 34, Hermitage 65668
Center, Trisha Turner, PO Box 34, Hermitage 65668
Green, James Nelson, RR 71, Box 2325, Urbana 65767
Green, Karen Nelson, RR 71, Box 2325, Urbana 65767
Hermitage, Nancy Johnson, HCR 1, Box 40, Hermitage 65668
Jordan, James Mackie, RR 91, Box 1550, Cross Timbers 65634
Jordan, Peggy Mackie, RR 91, Box 1550, Cross Timbers 65634
Stark, Keith Glor, RR 71, Box 830, Urbana 65767
Stark, Mary Glor, RR 71, Box 830, Urbana 65767
Tyler, William Jung, RR 1, Box 2099, Wheatland 65779
Tyler, Ramona Jung, RR 1, Box 2099, Wheatland 65779
Weaubleau, Kenny Ratliff, RR 1, Box 10-20, Weaubleau 65774
Weaubleau, Renae Ratliff, RR 1, Box 10-20, Weaubleau 65774

Holt County

Chair, Connie Gordon, 28233 Holt 280, Forest City 64451
Vice Chair, Mick Derr, 32371 Holt 110, Maitland 64466
Benton, Maurice Smith
Benton, Phyllis Smith
Clay, Mick Derr, 32371 Holt 110, Maitland 64466
Clay, Val Derr
Forbes, Edward Kurtz
Forbes, Darlyne Kurtz
Forest, Jerry Kneale
Forest, Billie Jo Ripley
Hickory, Michael Freeman
Lewis, Aaron Luce
Lewis, Connie Gordon, 28233 Holt 280, Forest City 64451
Lincoln, Nancy Peters
Nodaway, Ronnie Stephenson
Nodaway, Deborah Mueller

Howard County

Chair, Cord Harper, 707 N. Church St., Fayette 65248
Vice Chair, Shawna Rye, 1005 W. Davis, Fayette 65248
Franklin, Jason Davidson, 805 Clifton Heights Cir., New Franklin 65274
Richmond, Cord Harper, 707 N. Church St., Fayette 65248
Richmond, Shawna Rye, 1005 W. Davis, Fayette 65248

Howell County

Chair, Ward Franz, 8938 CR 9090, West Plains 65775
Vice Chair, Nancy Heavrin, PO Box 328, Pomona 65789
Secretary, Roxanne Rupar
Treasurer, Michael Hutchings, 300 Turner Dr., Willow Springs 65793
Benton, Melvin Giles, 12042 CR 7690, Caulfield 65626
Benton, Charm Eagleman, 13952 State Rt. FF, Caulfield 65626
Dry Creek, Ray Fine, 5171 CR 1540, West Plains 65775
Howell, Ward Franz, 8938 CR 9090, West Plains 65775
Howell, Judy Von Allmen, 2811 Paula Dr., West Plains 65775
Hutton, Lou Wehmer, 5104 CR 2660, Willow Springs 65793
Myatt, Missy Gastineau, 14700 CR 9290, Koskonong 65692
Sisson, Nick Heavrin, 4105 State Rt. 17, Pomona 65789
Sisson, Nancy Heavrin, 4105 State Rt. 17, Pomona 65789
South Fork, Roy Chapin, 5752 CR 9720, West Plains 65775

South Fork, Regina Eades, 11274 State Rt. JJ, West Plains 65775
Spring Creek, Leon Brassfield, 2578 CR 6420, West Plains 65775
Spring Creek, Freda Brassfield, 2578 CR 6420, West Plains 65775
Willow Springs, Michael Hutchings, 300 Turner Dr., Willow Springs 65793
Willow Springs, JoAnn Bailey Russell, 800 Ln., Willow Springs 65793

Iron County

Chair, Tony Harbison, 12696 Hwy. E, Arcadia 63621
Vice Chair, Shanyn Nelson, 744 Hwy. O, Belleview 63623
Secretary, Norma Owens, 18149 Hwy. C, Annapolis 63620
Treasurer, Randy Matthiesen, 125 E. Walnut, Arcadia 63621
Arcadia, Randy Matthiesen, 125 E. Walnut, Arcadia 63621
Arcadia, Margie Matthiesen, 125 E. Walnut, Arcadia 63621
Iron, Joshua Campbell, 1005 Hwy. O, Belleview 63623
Iron, Shanyn Nelson, 744 Hwy. O, Belleview 63623
Liberty, Tony Harbison, 12696 Hwy. E, Arcadia 63621
Liberty, Janice Harbison, 12696 Hwy. E, Arcadia 63621
Union, Marc Renicke, 501 E. Second St., Annapolis 63620
Union, Christina Dinkins, 18217 Hwy. K, Annapolis 63620

Jackson County

Chair, Mark Anthony Jones, 4029 Warwick Blvd., Kansas City 64111
Vice Chair, Jennifer Finch, 407 Benton Blvd., Kansas City 64124
Secretary, Rose Teer, 5908 E. 84th St., Kansas City 64138
Treasurer, Job Howen, 1527 E. Hayward Ave., Independence 64050
Blue
   Subdistrict 1, James Kersey, 11418 E. 16th St. S, Independence 64052
   Subdistrict 1, Debra Earley, 1609 S. Harris Ave., Independence 64052
   Subdistrict 2, Kyle Davidson, 1103 N. Swope Dr., Independence 64056
   Subdistrict 2, Sharon Wilson, 3608 N. Osage St., Independence 64050
   Subdistrict 3, Michelle Scherer, 1820 N. Ashley Dr., Independence 64058
   Subdistrict 3, Nathan Scherer, 1820 N. Ashley Dr., Independence 64058
   Subdistrict 4, Albert W.L. Moore Jr., 311 S. Osage St., Independence 64052
   Subdistrict 4, Cynthia Hulett, 1827 Harold Ave., Independence 64052
   Subdistrict 5, Gary Hisch, 15820 E. 29th St., Independence 64055
   Subdistrict 5, Julie Torpey, 821 E. Manor Rd., Independence 64055
   Subdistrict 6, Job Howen, 1527 E. Hayward Ave., Independence 64050
   Subdistrict 6, Terry Howen, 1527 E. Hayward Ave., Independence 64050
   Subdistrict 7, Bob Holliger, 14706 E. 43rd St., Independence 64055
   Subdistrict 7, Joy Freeland, 4009 S. Crysler Ave., Unit 2, Independence 64055

Subdistrict 8, Rod Walsh, 3111 S. Arrowhead Ct., Independence 64057

Subdistrict 8, Pat Walsh, 3111 S. Arrowhead Ct., Independence 64057

Brooking, Jason Greene, 6325 Ralston Ave., Raytown 64133

Brooking, Bill Van Buskirk, 7812 Woodson Rd., Raytown 64138

Brooking, Mary Jane Van Buskirk, 7812 Woodson Rd., Raytown 64138

Brooking, Lisa Emerson, 10920 E. 57th Terr., Raytown 64133

Fort Osage, Tom Mershon, 33404 E. Old Lexington Rd., Buckner 64016

Fort Osage, Janet A. Mershon, 33404 E. Old Lexington Rd., Buckner 64016

Fort Osage, Tim Mershon, 209 N. Sibley St., Buckner 64016

Fort Osage, Nikki Mershon, 209 N. Sibley St., Buckner 64016

Kansas City

Ward 1, Joanne Collins, 128 W. 13th St., Kansas City 64105

Ward 1, Jonathan Sternberg, 2015 Grand Blvd., Apt. 523, Kansas City 64108

Ward 2, Dan Gidman, 3308 E. 10th St., Kansas City 64127

Ward 2, Jamie Gidman, 3308 E. 10th St., Kansas City 64127

Ward 3, Edward Lee Stoll Jr., 3747 Indiana Ave., Kansas City 64128

Ward 3, Randi Weber, 3530 Forest Ave., Kansas City 64109

Ward 4, Mark Anthony Jones, 4029 Warwick Blvd., Kansas City 64111

Ward 4, Jamie Barker Landes, 4310 Charlotte St., Kansas City 64110

Ward 5, Dennis Owens, 1115 Valentine Rd., Kansas City 64111

Ward 5, Cathy Owens, 1115 Valentine Rd., Kansas City 64111

Ward 6, Steve Drake, 4901 Bell St., Kansas City 64112

Ward 6, Sarah (Sally) Miller, 835 W. 55th St., Kansas City 64113

Ward 8, Ralph Munyan, 6423 Wyandotte St., Kansas City 64113

Ward 9, Lucas Staus, 8430 Ward Parkway Plaza, Kansas City 64114

Ward 9, Francesca Saxer, 7531 Walnut St., Kansas City 64114

Ward 10, Matthew Dale Quinn, 9401 Jarboe St., Kansas City 64114

Ward 10, Mary Harkins Quinn, 9401 Jarboe St., Kansas City 64114

Ward 11, Jennifer Finch, 407 Benton Blvd., Kansas City 64124

Ward 11, Steve, Stockman, 411 Benton Blvd., Kansas City 64124

Ward 12, Michael Donnici, 4410 Sunrise Dr., Kansas City 64123

Ward 13, Josh Urness, 1737 Newton Ave., Kansas City 64126

Ward 14, Derron Black, 2505 College Ave., Kansas City 64127

Ward 15, Marvin Bredemeier, 3544 Fremont, Kansas City 64129

Ward 15, Karen Spalding, 3009 Ashland Ridge Rd., Kansas City 64129

Ward 17, Jerry Vanalst, 7245 College Ave., Kansas City 64132

Ward 18, Ivan Griffin, 1828 E. 76th Terr., Kansas City 64132

Ward 19, Joel Bangen, 4412 E. 107th St., Kansas City 64137

Ward 19, Deborah Palmer-Dean, 10408 Hillcrest Rd. Apt. 16, Kansas City 64134

Ward 20, Joseph C. Berry, 3710 Birchwood Dr., Kansas City 64137

Ward 20, Nola Wood, 11301 Kensington Ave., Kansas City 64137

Ward 22, Jose Leon, Martinez, 109 E. 117th St., Kansas City 64114

Ward 22, Raquel Martinez, 109 E. 117th St., Kansas City 64114

Ward 23, Leonard Snow, 8401 E. 47th Terr., Kansas City 64129

Ward 24, Celine Porrevecchio, 13111 E. 75th St., Kansas City 64138

Ward 25, Galen Verhulst, 10512 Oakland Ave., Kansas City 64134

Ward 25, Deloris Verhulst, 11200 Applewood Dr., Kansas City 64134

Ward 26, Michael Ort, 6504 E. 110th St., Kansas City 64134

Ward 26, Sandy Sexton

Prairie, Dan Stacy, 1215 SW Hillcrest Dr., Blue Springs 64015

Prairie, Tom Lehman, 2903 SW Scherer Rd., Lee's Summit 64082

Prairie, Robert (Bud) Hertzog, 24800 Milton Thompson Rd., Lee's Summit 64086

Prairie, Betty Hertzog, 24800 Milton Thompson Rd., Lee's Summit 64086

Prairie, Donna Turk, 417 SE Annette St., Lee's Summit 64063

Prairie, Amy Fox, 1432 NE Whitestone Dr., Lee's Summit 64086

Sni-A-Bar, Gary Dusenberg, 1608 NW Willow Brook Dr., Blue Springs 64015

Sni-A-Bar, Michael Freeman, 513 SE Alger Dr., Blue Springs 64014

Sni-A-Bar, Chris Lievsay, 201 NW Third St., Blue Springs 64014

Sni-A-Bar, Erin Dunn, 1405 SW 25th St., Blue Springs 64015

Sni-A-Bar, Donna Dusenberg, 1608 NW Willow Brook Dr., Blue Springs 64015

Sni-A-Bar, Mary Potter, 2319 NE Third St., Blue Springs 64014

Van Buren, Paul Trask, 210 E. Whispering Hills Blvd., Lone Jack 64070

Van Buren, Andrew Dawson, 217 E. Whispering Hills Blvd., Lone Jack 64070

Van Buren, Leslie Trask, 210 E. Whispering Hills Blvd., Lone Jack 64070

Van Buren, Shelley Holsten, 102 S. Rosehill Rd., Lone Jack 64070

Washington, Ronald Hess, 13015 13th St., Grandview 64030

Washington, Jim Dougan, 6724 E. 127th St., Grandview 64030

Washington, Jan Martinette, 6601 E. 129th St., Grandview 64030

Washington, Ellen Dougan, 6724 E. 127th St., Grandview 64030

Jasper County

Chair, Jimmy Morris, 1715 S. Porter Ave., Joplin 64804
Vice Chair, Gwen, Wadell, 300 N. Van Hoorebeke Rd., Joplin 64801
Secretary, Holly Snow, 1110 Euclid Blvd., Carthage 64836
Treasurer, Charlie Davis, 1624 Lakeview Dr., Webb City 64870
Alba, Nathan Moss, 19120 Locust Ln., Carthage 64836
Alba, Margaret Thompson, PO Box 484, Alba 64830
Carl Junction
  Jim Shember, 124 Concord Ln., Carl Junction 64834
  Jim Moffett, 25874 Hawthorne Rd.
  Carlene Shember
  John Evans, 1010 Southgate Cir., Carl Junction 64834
  Darlene Fairchilds, 7494 Quince Ln., Webb City 64870
Carterville, David Comstock, 706 N. Kentucky, Carterville 64835
Carterville, Bill Birkes, 502 Timber Hill Rd., Joplin 64801
Carthage
  Alan Snow, 1110 Euclid Blvd., Carthage 64836
  Holly Snow, 1110 Euclid Blvd., Carthage 64836
  Tom Flanigan, 1513 S. Main St., Carthage 64836
Centennial, Bob Sonntag, 6652 County Ln. 96, Carthage 64836
Centennial, Gwen Wadell, 300 N. Van Hoorebeke Rd., Joplin 64801
Gem, John Putnam, 1239 CR 110, Carthage 64836
Gem, Diane Hutchins, 9960 Bluff Rd., Carthage 64836
Jackson West, Richard Volk, PO Box 487, Duenweg 64841
Jackson West, Diane Volk, PO Box 487, Duenweg 64841
Jasper, Dale Flenniken, 19347 CR 130, Jasper 64755
Jasper, Karalyle Flenniken, 19347 CR 130, Jasper 64755
Joplin
  Jim Morris, 716 Central, Joplin 64801
  Rebekah Morris, 716 Central, Joplin 64801
  Terry Publow, 2114 Quincy St., Joplin 64801
  Roxanne Publow, 2114 Quincy St., Joplin 64801
  Jimmy, Morris, 1715 S. Porter Ave., Joplin 64804
  Megan Morris, 1715 S. Porter Ave., Joplin 64804
  Ivan Obert, 2927 S. Minnesota Ave., Joplin 64804
  Jane Obert, 2927 S. Minnesota Ave., Joplin 64804
  Duane Eberhardt, 1037 Campbell Pkwy., Joplin 64801
  Victoria Myers, 843 S. Patterson, Joplin 64801
  Rodney Noran, 2301 S. Florida, Joplin 64804
Lakeside, Danny, Fanning, 21245 Hawthorne Rd., Joplin 64801
Lakeside, Lila Fanning, 21245 Hawthorne Rd., Joplin 64801
Madison South, Gene Morris, 7111 CR 110, Carthage 64836
Madison South, Joyce Morris, 7111 CR 110, Carthage 64836
Oronogo, Rene Jones, 756 N. Prairie Meadow Ln., Oronogo 64855
Oronogo, John Greenlaw, 117 Jason Blvd., Webb City 64870
Oronogo, Kimberly Kuhns, 348 Sadie Ln., Webb City 64870
Pine, Mike Moss, 19761 Oak Rd., Japser 64755
Pine, Louise Ott, 15794 CR 200, Jasper 64755
Prairie Star, Mark Russell, 20500 Redbud Rd., Jasper 64755
Prairie Star, Suzanne Russell, 20500 Redbud Rd., Jasper 64755
Rex, Ray Schell, 4677 E. 24th, Joplin 64804
Rex, Kay Schell, 4677 E. 24th, Joplin 64804
Sarcoxie, Racine Palmer, 2356 CR 15, Sarcoxie 64862
Sarcoxie, Doug Pickering, 1617 Franklin, Sarcoxie 64862
Sarcoxie, Charlotte Pickering, 1617 Franklin, Sarcoxie 64862
Sheridan, Tyler Rush, 19508 CR 100, Jasper 64755
Sheridan, Margaret Weldy, 11354 Thorn Rd., Jasper 64755
Tuckahoe, Bill Ward, 6525 Park Cir., Joplin 64801
Webb City, Charlie Davis, 1624 Lakeview Dr., Webb City 64870
Webb City, Laura Davis, 1624 Lakeview Dr., Webb City 64870
Webb City, Linda Uselmann, 1115 W. Austin St., Webb City 64870
Zincite, Steve Hunter, 7105 W. Emerald Rd., Joplin 64801

Jefferson County

Chair, Teresa Kreitler, 55 Castle Bluff Acres Rd., Festus 63028
Vice Chair, George Engelbach, 3489 Linhorst Rd., Hillsboro 63050
Secretary, David Hoouser, 4243 Sonshine Ln., Hillsboro 63050
Treasurer, Kathy Vierling, 9435 Bluebird Ln., Hillsboro 63050
Arnold, Jason Fulbright, 3443 Tenbrook Rd., Arnold 63010
Arnold, Tammy Fulbright, 3443 Tenbrook Rd., Arnold 63010
Big River, Ken Waters, 6220 Hwy. Y, Hillsboro 63050
Big River, Debbie Dunnegan-Waters, 6220 Hwy. Y, Hillsboro 63050
Central, John Gebel, 5114 Tishomingo Rd., Hillsboro 63050
Central, Kathy Vierling, 9435 Bluebird Ln., Hillsboro 63050
High Ridge, Roy Sims, 2812 Moravec Dr., High Ridge 63049
High Ridge, Donna Sims, 2812 Moravec Dr., High Ridge 63049
Imperial, Mark Paul, 5461 Regency Woods Manor, Imperial 63052
Imperial, Michelle Paul, 5461 Regency Woods Manor, Imperial 63052
Joachim, George Engelbach, 3489 Linhorst Rd., Hillsboro 63050
Joachim, Janet Engelbach, 3489 Linhorst Rd., Hillsboro 63050
Meramec, Ken Hollenberg, 5300 Robin Rd., House Springs 63051
Meramec, Wendi Good, 6185 Regina Rd., Cedar Hill 63016
Plattin, David Courtway, 3303 Pineyknot Dr., Festus 63028
Plattin, Teresa Kreitler, 55 Castle Bluff Acres Rd., Festus 63028
Riverview, Gerald Bollinger, 108 Summerset Ln., Festus 63028
Riverview, Jane Bollinger, 108 Summerset Ln., Festus 63028
Rock, Bill Alter, 1800 Gravois Rd., High Ridge 63049
Rock, Carol Soppeland, 55 W. Lakewood Dr., Fenton 63026
Valle, Daniel Stallman, 5201 Hwy. H, DeSoto 63020
Valle, Paulette Northcutt, 12728 Williamson Dr., DeSoto 63052
Windsor, Sam Goodrum, 5023 Scenic View Acres Dr., Imperial 63052
Windsor, Denise Lutes, 2721 Cindy Dr., Imperial 63052

Johnson County

Chair, Violet J. Corbett, 1127 NE 175, Knob Noster 65336
Vice Chair, Dan Houx, 214 NW 21st Rd., Warrensburg 64093
Chilhowee, Nancy Jo Jennings, 906 SW 600th Rd., Holden 64040
Grover-Lowland, Amanda Strobel, 1221 NE 1075th Rd., Warrensburg 64093
Hazel Hill, Mason Wirsig, 163 NW 700th Rd., Warrensburg 64093
Jackson-Pittsville, Jason C. Davis, 1359 NW 275th Rd., Holden 64040
Madison-North Holden, Mary Ellen Young, 123 SW 1201st Rd., Holden 64040
Montserrat, Mark Reynolds, 22 SE 501st Rd., Warrensburg 64093
Montserrat, Gretchen Reynolds, 22 SE 501st Rd., Warrensburg 64093
Post Oak, Bobbie Grainger, 890 SW 151st Rd., Chilhowee 64733
Post Oak, Norma Jean Grainger, 890 SW 151st Rd., Chilhowee 64733
Rose Hill, Kevin Buckstead, 905 SW 1301st Rd., Holden 64040
Rose Hill, Darlene Buckstead, 905 SW 1301st Rd., Holden 64040
Simpson, Tom Fitzpatrick, 275 NE 875th Rd., Warrensburg 64093
Simpson, Heather Myers-Reynolds, 774 NE 361st Rd., Warrensburg 64093
Warrensburg
  Northeast, Gary Waner, 1427 Grandview Dr., Warrensburg 64093
  Northeast, Karen Waner, 1427 Grandview Dr., Warrensburg 64093
  Northwest, Dan Houx, 214 NW 21st Rd., Warrensburg 64093
  Northwest, Laurie Larson, 32 NW 225th Rd., Warrensburg 64093
  Southeast 1, Natalie Halpin, 504 Hurricane Hill, Warrensburg 64093
  Southwest, B. Lindel Jones, 701 W. Hale Lake Rd., Warrensburg 64093
  Southwest, Jan Jones, W. Hale Lake Rd., Warrensburg 64093
Washington-Knob Noster, Joe Corbett, 225 NE 1201, Knob Noster 65336
Washington-Knob Noster, Violet J. Corbett, 1127 NE 175, Knob Noster 65336

Knox County

Chair, Rhett Hunziker, RR 1, Box 183, Knox City 63446
Vice Chair, Barb Hunziker, RR 1, Box 183, Knox City 63446
East Center, Brenton Karhoff
Greensberg, Leon James

Laclede County

Chair, Robert Smith, 20879 Dove Rd., Lebanon 65722
Vice Chair, Angie Wright, 18145 Hwy. 64, Lebanon 65536
Secretary, Richard Hobbs, 20392 Kingsbrook Rd., Lebanon 65536
Treasurer, Yolanda Hobbs, 20392 Kingsbrook Rd., Lebanon 65536
Auglaize, Howard Fuller, 25100 Ironstone Rd., Lebanon 65536
Auglaize, Joan Fuller, 25100 Ironstone Rd., Lebanon 65536
Gasconade, Don Myers, 40000 Hwy. U, Falcon 65470
Gasconade, Wanda Myers, 40000 Hwy. U, Falcon 65470
Lebanon
  East, Steve Hall Murrell, 22213 Falcon Rd., Lebanon 65536
  East, Richard Hobbs, 20392 Kingsbrook Rd., Lebanon 65536
  East, Yolanda Hobbs, 20392 Kingsbrook Rd., Lebanon 65536
  West, Jim Hall, 19376 Hazel Rd., Lebanon 65536
  West, Gayle Hall, 19376 Hazel Rd., Lebanon 65536
May/Smith, Robert, Mooney, 33800 Kensington Ln., Richland 65566
May/Smith, Dawne, Mooney, 33800 Kensington Ln., Richland 65566
Osage, Tina Howerton, 25129 Evanston Rd., Lebanon 65536
Phillipsburg, Frank Rinehart, 16398 Hwy. C, Phillipsburg 65722
Spring Hollow, Matt Wright, 18145 Hwy. 64, Lebanon 65536
Spring Hollow, Angie Wright, 18145 Hwy. 64, Lebanon 65536
Union, Steve Hall, 11858 Ottawa Dr., Conway 65632
Union, Linda Hall, 11858 Ottawa Dr., Conway 65632
Washington, Robert Smith, 20879 Dove Rd., Lebanon 65722
Washington, Jennifer Powell, 14455 Hwy. B, Lebanon 65722

Lafayette County

Chair, Kay Hoflander, PO Box 603, Higginsville 64037
Vice Chair, Mark Schroer, PO Box 285, Wellington 64097
Secretary, Steve Solomon, 10360 Skelton Rd., Odessa 64076
Treasurer, Heidi Kolkmeyer, PO Box 56, Wellington 64097
Clay, Mark Schroer, PO Box 285, Wellington 64097
Clay, Heidi Kolkmeyer, PO Box 56, Wellington 64097
Davis, Bill Kolas, 905 W. 36th St. 14, Higginsville 64037
Davis, Kay Hoflander, PO Box 603, Higginsville 64037
Dover, Ted Traczewski, 21389 Hwy. 24, Dover 64022
Dover, Diane Traczewski, 21389 Hwy. 24, Dover 64022
Freedom, Daniel Janik, 209 SE Fifth St., Concordia 64020
Freedom, Beth Kruse, 548 S. Main, Concordia 64020
Lexington, Earl Stricker, 104 Francis, Lexington 64067
Lexington, Doris Stricker, 105 Francis, Lexington 64067
Middleton, David Lueck, 15553 Hwy. 23, Alma 64001
Middleton, Sherry Drunert, 901 Broad, Waverly 64096
Sni-A-Bar, Tracy Dyer, 561 Hwy. OO, Odessa 64076
Sni-A-Bar, Sharon Dyer, 561 Hwy. OO, Odessa 64076
Washington, Olin Struchtemeyer, 10677 Hwy. O, Odessa 64076
Washington, Virginia Bertz, 10595 Hwy. E, Mayview 64076

Lawrence County

Chair, Dane Roaseau, 2070 Ash Grove, Lawrence 65604
Vice Chair, Pat Tracy, 1106, Mt. Vernon, Lawrence 65712
Aurora
  North, Paul Donley, 18896 Lawrence 2164, Aurora 65605
  Southeast, Steve Kahre, 1206 S. Hudson, Aurora 65605
  Southeast, Sherri George, PO Box 466, Aurora 65605

Southwest, Kelli McVey, 1147 L.C. Cowan Dr., Aurora 65605

Buck Prairie, William Reed, 23155 Lawrence 2160, Marionville 65705

Buck Prairie, Amy Reed, 23155 Lawrence 2160, Marionville 65705

Forest Park, Bruce McAlexander, 1301 Seventh St., Monett 65708

Freistatt, Fred Schoen, 17187 Hwy. H, Monett 65708

Freistatt, Pamela Schoen, 17187 Hwy. H, Monett 65708

Green, Paul Hood, 827 E. Sunshine, Springfield 65807

Green, J. Hood, 827 E. Sunshine, Springfield 65807

Hoberg, Joe Patton, PO Box 175, Mt. Vernon 65712

Hoberg, Sandi Feith, 8142 Lawrence 2130, Stotts City 65756

Mount Pleasant, Eric Vought, 14280 Lawrence 1050, Stotts City 65756

Mount Pleasant, Carole Kleiboeker, 14579 Lawrence 1060, Stotts City 65756

Mount Vernon

    North, Jason Haymes, 721 Tracy Ln., Mt. Vernon 65712

    North, Pat Tracy, 11998 Lawrence 1106, Mt. Vernon 65712

    Southeast, Phillip Trokey, 1377 Quail Run, Mt. Vernon 65712

    Southeast, Julia Ruzicka, 1328 Deer Ln., Mt Vernon 65712

    Southwest, Curtis Barrett, 1206 Parkway Dr., Mt. Vernon 65712

    Southwest, Dee Barrett, 211 W. Alice, Mt. Vernon 65712

Ozark, James Young, 5634 Hwy. M, Miller 65707

Ozark, Denise Moon, 6935 Lawrence 1222, Ash Grove 65604

Pierce City, Nathan Fisher, 21935 Hwy. 97, Pierce City 65723

Pierce City, Dana Stanphill, 813 N. Walnut, Pierce City 65723

Red Oak, Boyd Arthur, 5924 Lawrence 1025, La Russell 64848

Red Oak, Retah Arthur, 5924 Lawrence 1025, La Russell 64848

Turnback, Dane Roaseau, 20381 Lawrence 2070, Ash Grove 65604

Turnback, Sharree Trout, 20445 Lawrence 2070, Ash Grove 65604

Vineyard, Steven Shields, 4607 Lawrence 2100, Stotts City 65756

Vineyard, Angela Shields, 4607 Lawrence 2100, Stotts City 65756

Lewis County

Chair, Nancy Berhorst, 17295 Hwy. 81, Canton 63435

Vice Chair, Dennis McCutchan, 22596 140th St., Monticello 63457

Secretary, Dan Musholt, 31884 State Hwy. C, LaGrange 63448

Treasurer, Judy Klingele, PO Box 24, Monticello 63457

Canton, Brad Davis, 801 Lewis St., Canton 63435

Canton, Nancy Berhorst, 17295 Hwy. 81, Canton 63435

Dickerson, Emery Geisendorfer, 21082 State Hwy. Y, Lewistown 63452

Dickerson, Arminta Geisendorfer, 21082 State Hwy. Y, Lewistown 63452

Highland, Greg Sharpe, 22364 Hwy. 156, Ewing 63440

Highland, Linda Schmitz, 20413 State Hwy. 156, Ewing 63440

LaBelle, Francis Richmond, 22395 State Hwy. J, Lewistown 63452

Labelle, Teresa Rush, 10665 Ash St., LaBelle 63447

Lyon, Dennis McCutchan, 22596 140th St., Monticello 63457

Lyon, Judy Klingele, PO Box 24, Monticello 63457

Reddish, William Steffen, 16797 128th Ave., LaBelle 63447

Reddish, Helen Steffen, 16797 128th Ave., LaBelle 63447

Salem, Joe Schroeder, 28508 180th Ave., Ewing 63440

Union, Dan Musholt, 31884 State Hwy. C, LaGrange 63448

Union, Loretta Musholt, 31884 State Hwy. C, LaGrange 63448

Lincoln County

Chair, Gary Grunick, 541 Harmony Grove Rd., Troy 63379

Vice Chair, Kathlyn Fares, 5 Bethel Woods Ct., Hawk Point 63349

Secretary, Renee Clark, 58 Hall Rd., Eolia 63344

Treasurer, Wade Grimes, 303 David St., Elsberry 63343

Bedford, David Cluster, 740 Cap Au Gris St., Troy 63379

Bedford, Alexandra Salsman, 150 E. Pershing St., Troy 63379

Birkhead, David Walker, 224 Red Hawk Ridge Dr., Troy 63379

Birkhead, Jackie Walker, 224 Red Hawk Ridge Dr., Troy 63379

Burr Oak, Robert Padella, 158 Lone Dove Ln., Winfield 63389

Burr Oak, Norma Padella, 158 Lone Dove Ln., Winfield 63389

Clark, David Henke, 90 Kinkade Ln., Moscow Mills 63362

Clark, Tracey Creech, 3045 Scott Rd., Moscow Mills 63362

Hawk Point, Clatyon Duff, PO Box 187, Hawk Point 63349

Hawk Point, Kathlyn Fares, 5 Bethel Woods Ct., Hawk Point 63349

Hurricane, Wade Grimes, 303 David St., Elsberry 63343

Hurricane, Renee Clark, 58 Hall Rd., Eolia 63344

Millwood, Fred Pickering, 290 Tagg Rd., Silex 63377

Millwood, Joyce Pickering, 290 Tagg Rd., Silex 63377

Monroe, Dennis Folwarczny, 101 Flowarczny Ln., Winfield 63389

Monroe, Deann Prange, 101 Flowarczny Ln., Winfield 63389

Snow Hill, Gary Grunick, 541 Harmony Grove Rd., Troy 63379

Snow Hill, Elizabeth Grunick, 541 Harmony Grove Rd., Troy 63379

Linn County

Chair, Shelly Milford, 130 W. Lake St., Marceline 64658

Vice Chair, Harold Turner, PO Box 149, Linneus 64653

Secretary, Elaine Duncan, 19875 Expo Rd., Purdin 64674

Treasurer, Jim Schrader, 26425 Image Rd., Brookfield 64628

Baker, Ryan Montgomery, 30463 Kale Rd., Brookfield 64628

Baker, Valerie Montgomery, 30463 Kale Rd., Brookfield 64658

Benton

    North, Jeff Morelock, 11106 Field Dr., Browning 64630

    North, Robin Morelock, 11106 Field Dr., Browning 64630

South, Terrance D. Oertwig, 15994 Hwy. 5, Purdin 64674

South, Cherry Oertwig, 15994 Hwy. 5, Purdin 64674

Brookfield

Ward 1, Martha Beach, 722 N. Main, Brookfield 64628

Ward 2, Randy Fay, 1109 Sunset Hill Rd., Brookfield 64628

Ward 3, Jon Mendenhall, 26153 Image Rd., Brookfield 64628

Ward 4, Farrel Hahn, 700 S. Main, Brookfield 64628

Ward 4, Jane Hahn, 700 S. Main, Brookfield 64628

Bucklin, Vernon Robertson, 609 Oak St., Bucklin 64631

Bucklin, Karmen Robertson, 609 Oak St., Bucklin 64631

Clay, Rex Wood, 15129 Balkan Rd., Meadville 64659

Clay, Pat Wood, 15129 Balkan Rd., Meadville 64659

Grantsville, Kay Baum, 20746 Gaton Dr., Linneus 64653

Jackson, Amy Creason, 10645 Delton Dr., Browning 64630

Jefferson, Mike Brown, PO Box 35, Laclede 64651

Jefferson, Alicyn Ehrich, 28211 Felton Dr., Laclede 64651

Locust Creek, Harold Turner, PO Box 149, Linneus 64653

Locust Creek, Connie Turner, PO Box 149, Linneus 64653

Marceline

Ward I, Shane Cavanah, PO Box 304, Marceline 64658

Ward I, Cheryl Cavanah, PO Box 304, Marceline 64658

Ward 3, Lewis Evans, 409 S. Fairview Dr., Marceline 64658

Ward 3, Shelly Milford, 130 W. Lake St., Marceline 64658

North Salem, Jim Fitzgerald, 11545 Hwy. CC, New Boston 63557

North Salem, Becky Fitzgerald, 11545 Hwy. CC, New Boston 63557

Parson Creek, John Schmitz, 605 E. Crandall, Meadville 64659

Parson Creek, Jane Schmitz, 605 E. Crandall, Meadville 64659

Yellow Creek, Terell Lane, 31023 London Rd., Brookfield 64628

Yellow Creek, Dana Lane, 31023 London Rd., Brookfield 64628

Livingston County

Chair, James Black, 9083 LIV 529, Chillicothe 64601

Vice Chair, Mary Quinn, 10485 LIV 511, Chillicothe 64601

Blue Mound, Sherry Jones, 20841 LIV 431, Dawn 64638

Chillicothe, Robert Reasoner, 9573 Hwy. 65, Chillicothe 64601

Chillicothe, Wilma Reasoner, 9573 Hwy. 65, Chillicothe 64601

Chillicothe

Ward 1, Earle Teegarden, 1720 Country Club Dr., Chillicothe 64601

Ward 2, Nancy Anderson, 1504 Morningside Dr., Chillicothe 64601

Ward 3, Adam Warren, 711 Washington St., Chillicothe 64601

Ward 4, Clifford Harlow, 1405 Jackson St., Chillicothe 64601

Ward 4, Kathryn Harlow, 1405 Jackson St., Chillicothe 64601

Cream Ridge, James Meservey, 17002 LIV 204, Chula 64635

Cream Ridge, Ann Meservey, 17002 LIV 204, Chula 64635

Fairview, Dale Whiteside, 20401 LIV 447, Chillicothe 64601

Fairview, Mary Pat Whiteside, 20599 Hwy. 65, Chillicothe 64601

Grand River, Raymond Quinn, 21452 Hwy. J, Hale 64643

Grand River, Robin Quinn, 21452 Hwy. J, Hale 64643

Green, Marion Harter, 16266 LIV 425, Mooresville 64664

Green, Sue Rose Harter, 16266 LIV 425, Mooresville 64664

Jackson, James Black, 9083 LIV 529, Chillicothe 64601

Jackson, Karie Black, 9083 LIV 529, Chillicothe 64601

Medicine, Orville Jacobs, 2617 LIV 277, Chula 64635

Medicine, Rita Jacobs, 2617 LIV 277, Chula 64635

Mooresville, Claude Bevelle, 18005 LIV 403, Mooresville 64664

Rich Hill, Dave Beck, 15201 Hwy. M, Chillicothe 64601

Rich Hill, Suzi Beck, 15201 Hwy. M, Chillicothe 64601

Sampsel, John Quinn, 10485 LIV 511, Chillicothe 64601

Sampsel, Mary Quinn, 10485 LIV 511, Chillicothe 64601

Wheeling, Jerry Norman, 11125 Hwy. B, Wheeling 64688

Wheeling, Nicolette Norman, 11125 Hwy. B, Wheeling 64688

Macon County

Chair, Kathy Austin, 22421 State Hwy. 149, Ethel 63539

Vice Chair, Jim Willis, 24377 State Hwy. OO, Bevier 63532

Secretary, Aaron Baker, 18192 Old Hwy. 63, Atlanta 63530

Treasurer, Jane Thompson, 1103 E. Briggs, Macon 63552

Bevier City, Rick Shoemaker, 29601 State Hwy. C, Bevier 63532

Bevier Township, Larry Stacy, 24421 Hickory St., Bevier 63532

Bevier Township, Jane Ann Stacy, 24421 Hickory St., Bevier 63532

Hudson, David Doctorian, 28728 Kellogg Ave., Macon 63552

Hudson, Phyllis Doctorian, 28728 Kellogg Ave., Macon 63552

Independence, Matt Halley, 24542 Impala St., Atlanta 63530

Independence, Twila Halley, 24542 Impala St., Atlanta 63530

La Plata Township, Lee Moots, 14876 Laredo Ave., La Plata 63549

La Plata Township, Linda Moots, 14876 Laredo Ave., La Plata 63549

Liberty, Jim Willis, 24377 State Hwy. OO, Bevier 63532

Liberty, Rowena Young, 24377 State Hwy. OO, Bevier 63532

Lyda, Aaron Baker, 18192 Old Hwy. 63, Atlanta 63530

Lyda, Louise Gaughan, 31793 Landmark St., Atlanta 63530

Macon

Ward 1, Dale Brown, 903 Remington Pl., Macon 63552

Ward 1, Bonnie Morris, 1201 Highland St., Macon 63552

Ward 2, Jon Dwiggins, 101 Bennett St., Macon 63552

Ward 2, Sue Williams, 504 Pine Crest Dr., Macon 63552

Ward 3, Charlotte Neeson, PO Box 93, Macon 63552

Middle Fork, Dean Sandner, 35492 Marshall Rd., Excello 65247
Morrow, Bill Hoke, 39075 State Hwy. 3, Callao 63534
Morrow, Velda Hoke, 39075 State Hwy. 3, Callao 63534
Narrows, Harold Smith, 34474 Lion Ave., Macon 65247
Narrows, Virginia Smith, 34474 Lion Ave., Macon 65247
Russell, Bruce Harding, 22872 Bayport, Ethel 63539
Russell, Elna Williams, 25803 State Hwy. TT, New Cambria 63558
Ten Mile, Drew Belt, 35089 State Hwy. DD, Macon 63552
Ten Mile, Sally Weber, 37897 State Hwy. KK, Anabel 63431
Valley, Benjamin Williams, 22526 State Hwy. 149, Ethel 63539
Valley, Kathy Austin, 22421 State Hwy. 149, Ethel 63539

Madison County

Chair, Larry Kemp, 2135 W. Hwy. 72, Fredericktown 63645
Vice Chair, Cherly Mooney, 1100 Madison 9216, Fredericktown 63645
Secretary, Athony E. Walker Jr., 202 Williams St., Fredericktown 63645
Treasurer, Kathy L. Walker, 202 Williams St., Fredericktown 63645
Castor, Sheldon J. Combs, 3602 Madison 208, Fredicktown 63645
Central, William Jud, 3429 Madison 423, Fredricktown 63645
Central, Judy Jud, 3429 Madison 423, Fredricktown 63645
Mine LaMotte, Bill Rice, 7514 W. Hwy. 72, Fredicktown 63650
Mine LaMotte, Nadean Rice, 7514 W. Hwy. 72, Fredicktown 63650
Polk, Cora L. Stephens, 1048 Madison 9314, Fredricktown 63645
St. Michael, Kenneth E. Lee, 1807 Madison 208, Fredericktown 63645
St. Michael, Kelsey Skaggs, 1704 Hwy. OO, Fredericktown 63645

Maries County

Chair, Joe Maybrier-Moore, 313 Third St., Vienna 65582
Vice Chair, Anita Martin, 18423 Maries Rd. 505, Dixon 65459
Boone, John French, 11011 Maries Rd. 611, Brinktown 65443
Boone, Linda French, 11011 Maries Rd. 611, Brinktown 65443
Dry Creek, Roger Schulte, 13051 Hwy. 133, Brinktown 65443
Dry Creek, Melanie Yoakum, 12455 Maries Rd. 605, Dixon 65459
Jackson, Joe Maybrier Moore, 313 Third St., Vienna 65582
Jackson, Roberta Juergens, 14003 Maries Rd. 617, Vienna 65582
Jefferson, Jason Comstock, 706 Tebbets Ave., Belle 65013
Jefferson, Jillian Comstock, 706 Tebbets Ave., Belle 65013
Johnson, Roger Wegner, 26997 CR 429, St. James 65559
Johnson, Kim Nisbett, 26503 CR 432, St. James 65559
Miller, Ed Martin, 18508 Maries Rd. 505, Dixon 65459
Miller, Anita Martin, 18423 Maries Rd. 505, Dixon 65459
Spring Creek, Lynn Davis, 12457 Maries Rd. 324, Vienna 65582
Spring Creek, Denise Davis, 12457 Maries Rd. 324, Vienna 65582

Marion County

Chair, Larry B. Craig, 4025 Edgewood Rd., Hannibal 63401
Vice Chair, Geri Graves, 4156 Woodridge Dr., Hannibal 63401
Secretary, Sandy Cox, 2425 Chestnut St., Hannibal 63401
Treasurer, Harry Graves, 4025 Edgewood Rd., Hannibal 63401
Mason
   Ward 1, Louis Riggs, 42 Holiday Dr., Hannibal 63401
   Ward 1, Geraldine Graves, 4156 Woodridge Dr., Hannibal 63401
   Ward 2, Larry B., Craig, 4025 Edgewood Rd., Hannibal 63401
   Ward 2, Lydia Shumake, 1101 Central Ave., Hannibal 63401
   Ward 3, Earl Dean Cox, 2425 Chestnut St., Hannibal 63401
   Ward 3, Sandra Cox, 2425 Chestnut St., Hannibal 63401
   Ward 4, Michelle Beck, 217 O'Fallon, Hannibal 63401
   Ward 4, Richard Cerretti, 1206 Tyrone, Hannibal 63401
   Ward 5, Joan Thompson, 1525 Frank St., Hannibal 63401
   Ward 5, Everette Lee Vedenhaupt, 3213 Market St., Hannibal 63401
   Ward 6, Steve Lane, 75 Heritage, Hannibal 63401
   Ward 6, Kathy Lane, 75 Heritage, Hannibal 63401
Miller, Cheryl Rawlings, 9218 CR 404, Hannibal 63401
Miller, Chris Hull, 8640 CR 404, Hannibal 63401
Liberty, Michele Nunemacher, 5159 CR 254, Palmyra 63461
Liberty, Thomas B. Lockett, 511 N. Lane St., Palmyra 63461
South River, Frank Burch, 6361 CR 262, Hannibal 63401
South River, Michelle Lehenbauer, 6624 CR 262, Hannibal 63401
Union, James Yarbrough, 4042 Hwy. 168, Palmyra 63461
Union, Mary Yarbrough, 4042 Hwy. 168, Palmyra 63461
Round Grove, Jessica Yoder, 2061 CR 110, Ewing 63440
Round Grove, Herman Yoder, 2061 CR 110, Ewing 63440

McDonald County

Chair, Janice Pratt, 702 Moss Church, Andeson 64831
Vice Chair, Bill Wilson

Mercer County

Harrison, Marilyn Sponsler, 15576 Elder St., Princeton 64673
Madison, Edward Evans, 27015 Hwy. A, Princeton 64673
Madison, Susan Moore, 25861 Hamilton Rd., Princeton 64673
Ravanna, Carolyn Sealine, 21057 Hwy. C, Princeton 64673

Miller County

Chair, Donald Pittrich, 202 Lynn Ave., Eldon 65206
Vice Chair, Ruby Bunch, 82 Frazier Oaks, Eldon 65206
Secretary, Colleen Abbott, 51 Whiteoak Rd., Tuscumbia 65082
Treasurer, Paul Ritter, PO Box 62, St. Elizabeth 65075
Equality, Bill Abbott, 47 Whiteoak Rd., Tuscumbia 65082
Equality, Colleen Abbott, 51 Whiteoak Rd., Tuscumbia 65082

Franklin, Darnell Bunch, 82 Frazier Oaks, Eldon 65206
Franklin, Ruby Bunch, 82 Frazier Oaks, Eldon 65206
Glaize, Brian Duncan, 320 Bentown Ridge Rd., Brumley 65017
Glaize, Ragenia Duncan, 320 Bentown Ridge Rd., Brumley 65017
Jim Henry, Aaron Wood, 20 Lage Ln., Henley 65040
Jim Henry, Roselyn Wood, 20 Lage Ln., Henley 65040
Osage, Paul Ritter, PO Box 62, St. Elizabeth 65075
Richwood, Norman DeVore, 40 Tavern Creek Rd., Eldon 65206
Richwood, Carolyn DeVore, 40 Tavern Creek Rd., Eldon 65206
Saline, Donald Pittrich, 202 Lynn Ave., Eldon 65206
Saline, Billie Pittrich, 202 Lynn Ave., Eldon 65206

Mississppi County

Chair, Kevin Mainord, 116 S. Center, East Prairie 63845
Vice Chair, Pat Helms, 423 Miller Rd., East Prairie 63845

Moniteau County

Chair, Darrel King, 905 Debie St., California 65018
Vice Chair, Judy Wittenberger, 21785 Cave Spring Rd., Jamestown 65046

Monroe County

Chair, Cyril Penner, 13217 Monroe Rd. 1050, Madison 65263
Vice Chair, Sharon Penner, 13217 Monroe Rd., Madison 65263
Secretary, Pat Kendrick, 27574 Monroe Rd. 533, Monroe City 63456
Treasurer, John Kendrick, 39549 Monroe Rd. 588, Monroe City 63456
Indian Creek, Sam Smith, 37357 Monroe Rd. 370, Monroe City 63456
Indian Creek, Pat Kendrick, 27574 Monroe Rd. 533, Monroe City 63456
Jackson, Tal Henderson, 306 Farview Ave., Paris 65275
Jackson, Wanda Boggs, 31037 Route U, Stoutsville 65283
Marion, Phil Blakemore, PO Box 7116, Holliday 65258
Marion, Jane Wilsdorf, 19829 Route JJ, Holliday 65358
Monroe, John Kendrick, 39549 Monroe Rd. 588, Monroe City 63456
Monroe, Phyllis Campbell, 743 S. Main St., Monroe City 63456
Union, Cyril Penner, 13217 Monroe Rd. 1050, Madison 65263
Union, Sharon Penner, 13217 Monroe Rd. 1050, Madison 65263

Montgomery County

Chair, Brent Speight, 301 N. Coulmbus, Montgomery City 63361
Vice Chair, Toni Schwartz, 315 Cedar Ave., Jonesburg 63351
Secretary, Donna Viehmann, 183 Sunbeam Rd., New Florence 63363
Treasurer, Paul Korman, 720 Hwy. K, Rhineland 65069
Bear Creek, Bart Korman, PO Box 33, High Hill 63350
Bear Creek, Toni Schwartz, 315 Cedar Ave., Jonesburg 63351
Danville, Allen Sullivan, 84 Oak Ridge Rd., Montgomery City 63361

Danville, Anita Sullivan, 146 Oak Ridge Rd., Montgomery City 63361
Loutre, John Noltensmeyer, 6 Hwy. EE, Rhineland 65069
Loutre, Brenda Korman, 720 Hwy. K, Rhineland 65069
Montgomery, Brent Speight, 301 N. Coulmbus, Montgomery City 63361
Montgomery, Donna Viehmann, 183 Sunbeam Rd., New Florence 63363
Prairie, Richard Hollywood, 54 Floyd Rd., Middletown 63359
Prairie, Pam Hollywood, 54 Floyd Rd., Middletown 63359
Upper Loutre, Rich Daniel, 256 E. Locust St., Wellsville 63384
Upper Loutre, Amanda Daniels, 256 E. Locust St., Wellsville 63384

Morgan County

Chair, A. Wayne Kanenbley, 2253 Wildlife Dr., Syracuse 65354
Vice Chair, Rita Kananbley. 2253 Wildlife Dr., Syracuse 65354
Secretary, Cheryl Morris, 19393 Old Five Rd., Versailles 65084
Treasurer, Kimberly Ingersoll, 12547 Hwy. 135, Stover 65078
Haw Creek, Joseph Berkstresser, PO Box 885, Stover 65078
Haw Creek, Deborah Berkstresser, PO Box 885, Stover 65354
Mill Creek, A. Wayne Kanenbley, 2253 Wildlife Dr., Syracuse 65354
Mill Creek, Rita Kanenbley, 2253 Wildlife Dr., Syracuse 65354
Moreau, Kenneth Welker, 18285 Hwy. W., Versailles 65084
Moreau, Cherly Morris, 19393 Old Five Rd., Versailles 65084
Richland, Jeffrey Nolting, 3675 Jay Hawk Rd., Florence 65329
Richland, Jill Nolting, 3675 Jay Hawk Rd., Florence 65329

New Madrid County

Chair, Sharon Medlin
Portage, William Holland, 2101 E. State Hwy. 62, Portageville 63783

Newton County

Chair, Nick Myers, 5873 Riverside Dr., Joplin 64804
Vice Chair, Susan Taylor, Neosho 64850
Crowder, Patsy Loncarich, 20726 Kodiak Rd., Goodman 64843
Diamond, Tommy Eaves, 1681 Jaguar Rd., Joplin 64804
Diamond, Marolyn Beaver, 19655 Newton Rd., Diamond 64840
East Neosho, Bryan Reiboldt, 15947 Business 60, Neosho 64850
East Neosho, Heather Reiboldt, 15947 Business 60, Neosho 64850
Granby, Jerry Carter, 6623 Hwy. E, Granby 64844
Granby, Judy Carter, 6623 Hwy. E, Granby 64844
Hornet, John Dorman, 7036 Beef Branch Rd., Joplin 64804
Hornet, Anita Ketchum, 8699 Akron Ln., Seneca 64865
Neosho
    1, Scott Wade, 718 Laurel Cir., Neosho 64850
    1, Chris Wade, 718 Laurel Cir., Neosho 64850
    2, James Link, 704 Baxter St., Neosho 64850

2, Linda Goodman, 1224 Skyline Dr., Neosho 64850
3, Jim Taylor, 2110 Dixie Land Ln., Neosho 64850
3, Susan Taylor, Neosho 64850
4, Rodney Griffin, 517 Joplin St., Neosho 64850
4, Cheryle Perkins, 1429 Hearell St., Neosho 64850
Newtonia, Lee Allphin, 27644 Nylen Ln., Stark City 64866
Reding, Bryan Stevenson, 203 Eagle Ridge Rd., Joplin 64804
Reding, Regina Stevenson, 203 Eagle Ridge Rd., Joplin 64804
Ritchey, Duane Linch, 27176 Howard Ln., Stark City 64866
Ritchey, Lacinda Linch, 27176 Howard Ln., Stark City 64866
Staples
  East, Robert Lawry, 2 Timber Run, Joplin 64804
  East, Mary Stoll Lawry, 2 Timber Run, Joplin 64804
  West, Nick Myers, 5873 Riverside Dr., Joplin 64804
  West, Marilyn Ruestman, 5562 Riverside Dr., Joplin 64804
  21, Hicklin, 3811 Spring Hill, Joplin 64804
  21, Nancy Koester, 4312 S. Pearl Ave., Joplin 64804
  27, Allen Shirley, 3520 S. Alabama Ave., Joplin 64804
  27, Gwen Delano, 3417 Connecticut, Joplin 64804
Stella, Klint Guinn, 26524 Hwy. A , Stella 64867
Stella, Vickie Guinn, 26524 Hwy. A , Stella 64867
West Neosho, Jonathan Russell, 11285 Mulberry Rd., Neosho 64850
West Neosho, Tami Owens, 10402 Holly Rd., Neosho 64850
Westview, Bill Thogmartin, 17249 Grizzly Dr., Neosho 64850
Westview, Tammy Thogmartin, 17249 Grizzly Dr., Neosho 64850

Nodaway County

Chair, Stan Sportsman, 36803 Galaxy Rd., Graham 64455
Vice Chair, Monica Patton, 1925 S. Main, Maryville 64468
Secretary, Cheryl Chestnut, 20136 State Hwy. 113, Skidmore 64487
Treasurer, Jessie Smith, 511 W. 16th St., Maryville 64468
Atchison, Bryon Clark, 224 W. Third, Clearmont 64431
Atchison, Hazel Hester, 16910 U.S. Hwy. 71, Burlington Jct. 64428
Green, Randy McCollam, 23703 Hwy. PP, Burlington Jct. 64428
Green, Belva Dawson, 26289 Hwy. 113, Skidmore 64487
Grant, Sandra Wilmes, 33702 St. Hwy. N, Barnard 64423
Hopkins, Stan Alexander, 14979 Katy Rd., Hopkins 64461
Hopkins, Lindsey Alexander, 14979 Katy Rd., Hopkins 64461
Hughes, Stan Sportsman, 36803 Galaxy Rd., Graham 64455
Hughes, Kathy DeVault, 37757 Galaxy Rd., Graham 64455
Jackson, Lowell Dean Adwell, 24963 Olympic Rd., Ravenwood 64479
Jackson, Monica Patton, 1925 S. Main, Maryville 64468
Jefferson, Gerald E. Nelson, 33357 Noble Rd., Conception Jct. 64434
Jefferson, Dottie Nelson, 33357 Noble Rd., Conception Jct. 64434
Lincoln, Terry Ecker, 11334 Bobcat Rd., Elmo 64445
Monroe, Delbert Chestnut, 20136 State Hwy. 113, Skidmore 64487
Monroe, Cheryl Chestnut, 20136 State Hwy. 113, Skidmore 64487

Nodaway, James Rasmussen, 221 E. Seventh, Burlington Jct. 64428
Nodaway, Suzanne Rasmussen, 221 E. Seventh, Burlington Jct. 64428
Polk, Richard Smith, 511 W. 16th St., Maryville 64468
Polk, Jessie Smith, 511 W. 16th St., Maryville 64468

Oregon County

Chair, Laird B. Kelly, RR 9, Box 460, Gatewood 63942
Vice Chair, Genevieve Kelly, RR 9, Box 460, Gatewood 63942
Secretary, Sarah Crowder, RR 73, Box 165701, Couch 65690
Treasurer, Bill D. Williams, 304 Caroline St., Thayer 6579
Big Apple, Charles T. Pease, RR 81, Box 144-A, Koshkonong 65692
Big Apple, Mary Lee Pease, RR 81, Box 144-A, Koshkonong 65692
Cedar Bluff, Laird B. Kelly, RR 9, Box 460, Gatewood 63942
Cedar Bluff, Genevieve Kelly, RR 9, Box 460, Gatewood 63942
Couch, Bob Crowder, RR 73, Box 165701, Couch 65690
Couch, Sarah Crowder, RR 73, Box 165701, Couch 65690
Jeff, Michael Don Slack, RR 1, Box 1232, Thayer 65791
Jobe-Billmore, Sandy Crews, RR 73, Box 1820, Alton 65606
King, John H. Cook, HC 67, Box 61, Fremont 63941
King, Val Cook, HC 67, Box 61, Fremont 63941
Moore-Blackpond, Mike Sullivan, HC 3, Box 156, Birch Tree 65438
Moore-Blackpond, Betty Sullivan, HC 3, Box 156, Birch Tree 65438
Piney 1, Dale Me Adrain, RR 73, Box 3536, Alton 65606
Piney 1, Beverly Adrain, RR 73, Box 3536, Alton 65606
Thayer
  1, Gene Boren, 1112 Lacy Ave., Thayer 65791
  1, Brenda J. Ledgerwood, HCR 64, Box 25-A, Alton 65606
  2, Bill D. Williams, 304 Caroline St., Thayer 65791
  2, Carlene Williams, 304 Caroline St., Thayer 65791

Osage County

Chair, Kevin Harvey, 17 CR 603, Loose Creek 65054
Vice Chair, Christal Jones, 416 Honey Creek Dr., Linn 65051
Osage, Christal Jones, 416 Honey Creek Dr., Linn 65051

Ozark County

Chair, Roger W. Pittaway, 17075 CR 522, Gainesville 65655
Vice Chair, Dawn Pittaway, 17075 CR 522, Gainesville 65655
Secretary, Barbara Luna, 56 Oakwood Dr., Gainesville 65655
Treasurer, Billy D. Hambelton III, PO Box 855, Gainesville 65655
Barren Fork, Layne Nance, HC 72, Box 317, Wasola 65773
Barren Fork, Lisa Hawkins, 740 State Hwy. Z, Noble 65715
Bayou 1, Gary Orf, PO Box 112, Bakersfield 65609
Bayou 1, Verlene Halford, PO Box 67, Bakersfield 65609

West Bridges, Don Luna, 56 Oakwood Dr., Gainesville 65655

Dawt, Raymond Pace, 29005 U.S. Hwy. 160, Tecumseh 65760

Dawt, Irene Corp, 32580 U.S. Hwy. 160, Tecumseh 65760

Jackson, Steve Thomas, 72 ABC Ln., Wasola 65773

Jackson, Sheila Thomas, 72 ABC Ln., Wasola 65773

Lick Creek, Roger W. Pittaway, 17075 CR 522, Gainesville 65655

Lick Creek, Dawn Pittaway, 17075 CR 522, Gainesville 65655

Longrun, Boyd Garrison, 383 CR 879, Theodosia 65761

Longrun, Freeda Garrison, 383 CR 879, Theodosia 65761

Noble, Larry Warrick, 354 Warrick Way, Wasola 65773

Pontiac, Jason Frodge, 383 Day Spring Farm Ln., Gainesville 6655

Pontiac, Ashley Frodge, 383 Day Spring Farm Ln., Gainesville 6655

Richland, Gary Lee Collins, 123 C Ridge Dr., Dora 65637

Richland, Nancy Collins, 123 C Ridge Dr., Dora 65637

Thornfield, Maynard Wallace, 303 Wallace Ln., Thornfield 65762

Thornfield, Linda Wallace, 303 Wallace Ln., Thornfield 65762

West Bridges, Barbara Luna, 56 Oakwood Dr., Gainesville 65655

Perry County

Chair, Sandra Haertling, 539 PCR 212, Perryville 63775

Vice Chair, Mark Renaud, 807 PCR 508, Perryville 63775

Secretary, Moriah Rose Renaud, 807 PCR 508, Perryville 63775

Treasurer, Chad Unterreiner, 507 Grand Ave., Perryville 63775

Bois Brule, Sandra Haertling, 539 PCR 212, Perryville 63775

Central, Chad Unterreiner, 507 Grand Ave., Perryville 63775

Cinque Hommes, Mark Renaud, 807 PCR 508, Perryville 63775

Cinque Hommes, Moriah Rose Renaud, 807 PCR 508, Perryville 63775

Pettis County

Chair, Carla Young, 809 W. Broadway, Sedalia 65301

Vice Chair, Kevin Bond, 4130 Apple Ridge Rd., Sedalia 65301

Ward 2, Precinct 3, Kirk Holman, 1118 E. 3rd , Sedalia 65301

Ward 2, Precinct 3, Judy Petrie, 915 E. Broadway, Sedalia 65301

Phelps County

Chair, Michael P. Monaldi, 16976 CR 8200, Newburg 65550

Vice Chair, Pamela K. Grow, PO Box 1171, Rolla 65402

Secretary, Jennifer Riegel, 513 Ashley Dr., Rolla 65401

Treasurer, William (Bill) W. Aaron Jr., PO Box 1528, Rolla 65402

Arlington, Michael P. Monaldi, 16976 CR 8200, Newburg 65550

Cold Springs, Gary Cizek, 16890 Hwy. 72, Rolla 65401

Dillon, David Grow, PO Box 1171, Rolla 65402

Dillon, Pamela K. Grow, PO Box 1171, Rolla 65402

Doolittle

Ward 1, Joseph E. Osborne III, 118 Eisenhower, Doolittle 65401

Ward 3, Ruth Ellen Sturgeon, 402 Eisenhower, Doolittle 65401

Miller, Robert May, PO Box 465, Rolla 65401

Miller, Carlene May, PO Box 465, Rolla 65401

Rolla

Outside, William (Bill) W. Aaron Jr., PO Box 1528, Rolla 65402

Outside, Susan Aaron Kellems, 15761 Private Dr. 7106, Rolla 65402

Ward 1, Jonathan Hines, 621 Salem Ave., Rolla 65401

Ward 1, Melinda Hines, 621 Salem Ave., Rolla 65401

Ward 2, Matthew R. Miller, 603 Wakefield Dr., Rolla 65401

Ward 3, George Karr, 1906 Kensington Pkwy., Rolla 65401

Ward 3, Jenni Riegel, 513 Ashley Dr., Rolla 65401

Ward 4, Russel O. Schmidt, 702 Lariat Ln., Rolla 65401

Ward 4, Judith H. Jepsen, 702 Lariat Ln., Rolla 65401

Ward 5, Karen A. Morgan, 107 Adrian Ave., Rolla 65401

St. James, Gene DeLuca, 22385 State Rt. KK, St. James 65559

St. James

Ward 1, Clark Harrison, 121 W. James Blvd., St. James 65559

Ward 2, Greg E. Edwards, 524 Walters St., St. James 65559

Ward 4, Paul Goddard, 501 E. Eldon St., St. James 65559

Ward 4, Kathy Lewis, 21 Kathryn Dr., St. James 65559

Pike County

Chair, Jim Garrison, 717 S. Court St., Bowling Green 63334

Vice Chair, Dorothy Sisson, 400 S. Cuivre St., Bowling Green 63334

Treasurer, John Baker, 23954 Pike 262, Clarksville 63336

Buffalo, Jim York, 410 Cottonwood Dr., Louisiana 63353

Calumet, John Baker, 23954 Pike 262, Clarksville 63336

Cuivre, Dorothy Sisson, 400 S. Cuivre St., Bowling Green 63334

Cuivre, Jim Garrison, 717 S. Court St., Bowling Green 63334

Indian, Leo Brueggen, 9504 Pike 410, Middletown 63364

Indian, Mary Nell Brueggen, 9504 Pike 410, Middletown 63364

Peno, Bob Griffith, 511 Water St., Frankford 63441

Peno, Gale Frolos, 500 Water St., Frankford 63441

Prairieville, Cecil Hupper, 2265 Pike 300, Bowling Green 63334

Prairieville, Bonnie Stone, 22976 Hwy. WW, Clarksville 63336

Platte County

Chair, Chris Seufert, 6140 Union Chapel Rd., Parkville 64152

Vice Chair, Janet Stark, 15755 NW 130th St., Platte City 64079

Secretary, Rebecca Rooney, 306 Summerset Dr., Weston 64098

Treasurer, Russell Hollander, Kansas City 64151

12-2, Kirby Holden, 14890 Interurban Rd., Platte City 64079

13-1, Joe Vanover, 15755 Timber Park Ct., Platte City 64079
13-1, Janet Stark, 15755 NW 130th St., Platte City 64079
13-3, Bert Godding, 6720 NW Willowick Ln., Kansas City 64152
13-4, Chris Seufert, 6140 Union Chapel Rd., Parkville 64152
13-4, Theresa Emerson, 14255 NW 65th Pl., Parkville 64152
13-5, Justin Teiwes, 8147 Clearwater Dr., Parkville 64152
13-5, Jacque Cox, 6200 S. National Dr., Parkville 64152
14-2, Ryan Cashatt, 7207 NW Maple Ln., Platte Woods 64151
14-2, Tracy Zahnd, 6406 NW Crystal Pool Dr., Platte Woods 64151
14-3, Russell Hollander, Kansas City 64151
14-4, Larry Womack, 7921 NW 73rd St., Kansas City 64152
14-5, Russell Wojtkiewicz, 5014 NW Woody Creek Ln., Kansas City 64151

Polk County

Chair, Melinda Robertson, 4507 S. 160 Rd., Bolivar 65613
Vice Chair, Trent Drake, 848 Hwy. 32, Bolivar 65613
Secretary, Becky Legan, 1901 E. 487 Rd., Halfway 65663
Treasurer, Craig Westfall, 4671 Hwy. H, Halfway 65663
Benton
  North, Gary Drake, 2039 E. 415 Rd., Halfway 65663
  North, Janet Drake, 2039 E. 415 Rd., Halfway 65663
  South, Craig Westfall, 4671 Hwy. H, Halfway 65633
  South, Becky Legan, 1901 E. 487 Rd., Halfway 65633
Cliquot, David Scott, 3999 Hwy. O, Dunnegan 65640
Cliquot, Revonda Scott, 3999 Hwy. O, Dunnegan 65640
East Looney, Leland Jones, 1566 E. 565th Rd., Brighton 65617
East Looney, Kimberly Jones, 1566 E. 565th Rd., Brighton 65617
Flemington, Brian Allison, 3380 Hwy. O, Flemington 65650
Flemington, Tracey Allison, 3380 Hwy. O, Flemington 65650
Greene–South, Jimmy Greer, 3653 Hwy. P, Goodson 65663
Greene–South, Amy Greer, 3653 Hwy. P, Goodson 65663
Jefferson, Bob Pitts, 3134 S. 95th Rd., Flemington 65650
Jefferson, Kay Pitts, 3134 S. 95th Rd., Flemington 65650
Johnson, Bobby McAntire, 601 N. Pine, Humansville 65674
Johnson, Arlene Lear, PO Box 167, Humansville 65674
Madison
  East, Tiffany Phillips, 4176 S. 33 Rd., Fair Play 65649
  West, Danny Morrison, 165 E. 405 Rd., Dunnegan 65640
  West, Rebecca Morrison, 165 E. 405 Rd., Dunnegan 65640
Marion
  Northeast, Gene Rice, 4113 S. 135 Rd., Bolivar 65613
  Northeast, Linda Rice, 4113 S. 135 Rd., Bolivar 65613
  Northwest, Bill Bob Kallenbach, 4153 Hwy. 83, Bolivar 65613
  Northwest, Sandra Jones, 610 W. Summit St., Bolivar 65613
  Southeast, Bill Little, 301 S. Denver Pl., Bolivar 65613
  Southeast, Melinda Robertson, 4507 S. 160 Rd., Bolivar 65613
  Southwest, Trent Drake, 848 Hwy. 32, Bolivar 65613
  Southwest, Linda Porter, 438 N. Williams Ave., Bolivar 65613

McKinley, Denzil Roberts, 3438 Hwy. RB, Bolivar 65613
McKinley, Donna Roberts, 3438 Hwy. RB, Bolivar 65613
Mooney, Shirley Allison, 5616 S. 222 Rd., Fair Grove 65648
Union, Bill Dryer, 626 E. 505 Rd., Aldrich 65601
Union, Kay Dryer, 626 E. 505 Rd., Aldrich 65601
Wishart, Donald Mitchell, 5114 E. 405 Rd., Dunnegan 65640
Wishart, Wilma Mitchell, 5114 E. 405 Rd., Dunnegan 65640

Pulaski County

Chair, Kristine Stone, 20999 Bangor Rd., Crocker 65452
Vice Chair, Dennis Thornsberry, 12265 Belle Rd., Crocker 65452
Secretary, David Dickie, 28176 Hwy. AB, Richland 65583
Treasurer, Melissa Whittle, 10612 Hwy. 17N, Crocker 65452
Cullen, David Dickie, 28176 Hwy. AB, Richland 65583
Cullen, Terri Mitchell, PO Box 741, Richland 65583
Liberty, David Ernst, 19775 Salina Rd., Waynesville 65583
Liberty, Sherry Ernst, 19775 Salina Rd., Waynesville 65583
Tavern, Dennis Thornsberry, 12265 Belle Rd., Crocker 65452
Tavern, Kristine Stone, 20999 Bangor Rd., Crocker 65452
Union, April Marshall, 16892 Woodcrest Ln., Plato 65552

Putnam County

Chair, Donna Oakley, PO Box 66, Lucerne 64655
Vice Chair, Don Summers, 15783 State Hwy. Y, Unionville 63565
Secretary, Sheryl Riley, 15730 300th Rd., Unionville 63565
Treasurer, Evelyn Morgan, 23157 Gambel Trl., Pollock 63560
Elm, Richard Cullum, 18953 State Hwy. FF, Livonia 63551
Grant, Craig Vestal, 15441 State Hwy. N, Livonia 63551
Grant, Shayla Vestal, 15441 State Hwy. N, Livonia 63551
Jackson, Evelyn Morgan, 23157 Gambel Trl., Pollock 63560
Liberty, Lowell Brown, 37044 120th St., Unionville 63565
Liberty, Mary Bartram, 13333 Palm Trl., Unionville 63565
Lincoln, Don Summers, 15783 State Hwy. Y, Unionville 63565
Lincoln, Nancy Summers, 15783 State Hwy. Y, Unionville 63565
Medicine, Ora Williams, 502 W. Main St., Lucerne 64655
Medicine, Donna Oakley, PO Box 66, Lucerne 64655
Richland, Robert Puffer, 25808 U.S. Hwy. 136, Unionville 63565
Richland, Melanie Robbins, 34743 U.S. Hwy. 136, Unionville 63565
Sherman, Dwight Alley, 11653 Grand Fir Trl., Powersville 64672
Sherman, Judith Alley, 11653 Grand Fir Trl., Powersville 64672
Union, Thomas Keedy, 1802 Lincoln St., Unionville 63565
Union, Sheryl Riley, 15730 300th Rd., Unionville 63565
Wilson, David Noel, 20505 267th Rd., Unionville 63565
Wilson, Sharon Parks, 18110 State Hwy. 5, Unionville 63565
York, Larry Rollins, 16885 State Hwy. E, Powersville 64672
York, Lois Jane Rollins, 16885 State Hwy. E, Powersville 64672

Ralls County

Chair, Linda Laird, 55272 Buffalo Ln., New London 63459
Vice Chair, Michial Bacon, 13336 New London Gravel Rd., New London 63459
Secretary, Gerald Miner, 23009 Buckrun Pl., Perry 63462
Treasurer, Ruth Tucker, 501 E. Hawkins, Center 63436
Center, Mark Tucker, 501 E. Hawkins, Center 63436
Center, Ruth Tucker, 501 E. Hawkins, Center 63436
Clay, Michial Bacon, 13336 New London Gravel Rd., New London 63459
Clay, Judy Swank, 49177 Rensselaer Ln., Hannibal 63401
Jasper, Dave Shrader, 53007 Bridgewater Ln., Center 63462
Jasper, Deb Shrader, 53007 Bridgewater Ln., Center 63462
Saline, Jonathon McClellan, 43155 Deerview Dr., Apt. 4, Monroe 63456
Salt River, Gerald Miner, 23009 Buckrun Pl., Perry 63462
Salt River, Helen, Miner, 23009 Buckrun Pl., Perry 63462
Saverton, Gary, Carlisle, 61366 Crooked Creek Pl., New London 63459
Saverton, Tanya Carlisle, 61366 Crooked Creek Pl., New London 63459
Spencer, Alan, Laird, 55272 Buffalo Ln., New London 63459
Spencer, Linda Laird, 55272 Buffalo Ln., New London 63459

Randolph County

Chair, Valinda Freed, 2662 CR 1310, Moberly 65270
Cairo, Valinda Freed, 2662 CR 1310, Moberly 65270
Moberly
    Ward 1, Glenda Winkler, 405 Madison Ave., Moberly 65270
    Ward 2, Edward Haynes, 604 Harrison Ave., Moberly 65270
    Ward 2, Linda Berry, 1113 Bradford Cir., Moberly 65270
    Ward 3, Sam Richardson, 816 Gilman, Moberly 65270
    Ward 3, Lori Miller, 4 Fair Oaks, Moberly 65270
Sugar Creek
    North, Ted Sander, 2457 CR 1330, Moberly 65270
    North, Theresa Sander, 2457 CR 1330, Moberly 65270
    South, James Myles, 1583 CR 2275, Moberly 65270
    South, Patsy Myles, 1583 CR 2275, Moberly 65270
Prairie, Paul Courture, 1348 Private Rd. 2632, Higbee 65257
Prairie, Elizabeth Courture, 1348 Private Rd. 2532, Higbee 65257
Salt River, Gerald Luntsford, 8654 Hwy. J, Jacksonville 65260
Salt River, Wanda Luntsford, 8654 Hwy. J, Jacksonville 65260
Salt Springs, Harry Hall, 2837 CR 1205, Moberly 65270
Salt Springs, Judy Hall, 2837 CR 1205, Moberly 65270
Silver Creek, Tony Sloan, 77565 Hwy. 3, Armstrong 65230
Union, Charles Coatney, 4691 E. Hwy. 24, Moberly 65270
Union, Mary Ann Coatney, 4691 E. Hwy. 24, Moberly 65270

Ray County

Chair, Steven W. Mynatt, 21754 Shelton Rd., Polo 64671
Vice Chair, Marianne Mynatt, 500 W. Medbury, Richmond 64085
Secretary, Steven M. Mynatt, 500 W. Medbury, Richmond 64085
Knoxville, Steven W. Mynatt, 21754 Shelton Rd., Polo 64671
Richmond, Steven M. Mynatt, 500 W. Medbury, Richmond 64085
Richmond, Marianne Mynatt, 500 W. Medbury, Richmond 64085

Reynolds County

Chair, Christy Roberts, PO Box 790, Ellington 63638
Vice Chair, Phillip Roberts, PO Box 790, Ellington 63638
Secretary, Susan Summers, 34101 Hwy. 21, Lesterville 63654
Treasurer, Joseph Moore, 2715 A Hwy., PO Box 838, Belleview 63623
Black, Joseph Moore, 2715 A Hwy., PO Box 838, Belleview 63623
Lesterville, Susan Summers, 34101 Hwy. 21, Lesterville 63654
Logan, Phillip Roberts, PO Box 790, Ellington 63638
Logan, Christy Roberts, PO Box 790, Ellington 63638

Ripley County

Chair, Donna Kirby, PO Box 54, Doniphan 63935
Vice Chair, James Daniel, HC 4, Box 410, Doniphan 63935
Current River, Dennis Braschler, HC 4, Box 672, Doniphan 63935
Current River, Beverly Braschler, HC 4, Box 672, Doniphan 63935
Doniphan, J.W. Burford, HC 5, Box 65, Doniphan 63935
Doniphan, Donna Kirby, PO Box 54, Doniphan 63935
Gatewood, J.B. Newton, PO Box 211, Doniphan 63935
Gatewood, Lavonne Newton, PO Box 211, Doniphan 63935
Harris, Dalton March, RR 1, Box 2585, Doniphan 63935
Harris, Deborah March, RR 1, Box 2585, Doniphan 63935
Johnson, Timothy Slayton, HC 1, Box 240-M, Fairdealing 63939
Johnson, Kathy Slayton, HC 1, Box 239-S, Fairdealing 63939
Jordan, Ray Lassen, RR 2, Box 5012, Doniphan 63935
Jordan, Beverly Williamson, RR2, Box 5012, Doniphan 63935
Poynor, James Daniel, HC 4, Box 410, Doniphan 63935
Poynor, Tammy Daniel, HC 4, Box 410, Doniphan 63935
Shirely, Judy Stone, HC 7, Box 203, Doniphan 63935
Shirley, Charles Hudson, HC 7, Box 356, Doniphan 63935
Thomas, Betty Slayton, RR 62, BOx 296, Naylor 63953
Varner, Rick Powell, HC 1, Box 3726, Oxly 63955
Varner, Marilyn Woolard, HC 1, Box 3565, Oxly 63955
Washington, Roy LeGrand, HC 1, Box 3820, Oxly 63955
Washington, Stacey Roach, RR 61, Box 2820, Naylor 63953

St. Charles County

Chair, Joe Brazil, 1436 Boone Valley Ridge, Augusta 63332
Vice Chair, Cindy Evans, 5 Conestoga Ct., O'Fallon 63368
Secretary, Sandy Garber, 7 Vienna Ct., Lake St. Louis 63367
Treasurer, Mike Sommer, 6 Williamsburg Ct., St. Charles 63303
Boone, Joe Brazil, 1436 Boone Valley Ridge, Augusta 63332
Boone, Marcia Behr, 601 Stone Ridge Ln., Augusta 63332
Cottleville, John Strick, 52 S. Hillview, St. Peters 63376

Cottleville, Joan Gettemeyer, 827 Nancy Ln., Weldon Spring 63304

Dardenne, Mark Tiefenthaler, 34 Harris Horth, St. Peters 63376

Dardenne, Carole Paul, 76 Huckleberry Ct., O'Fallon 63368

First Capitol, Joe Wetter, 3255 Janton Ln., St. Charles 63301

First Capitol, Brenda Webb, 2216 W. Adams, St. Charles 63301

Frontier, Fred Henke, 770 Meadow Cliff Dr., St. Charles 63303

Frontier, Penny Henke, 770 Meadow Cliff Dr., St. Charles 63303

Harvester, Joe Smith, 4643 Shoshone Trl., St. Charles 63304

Harvester, Cheryl Bates, 4137 Stonecroft Dr., St. Charles 63304

Lake St. Louis, Frank Eggering, 204 Dauphine, Lake St. Louis 63367

Lake St. Louis, Sandy Garber, 7 Vienna Ct., Lake St. Louis 63367

Muegge, Mike Sommer, 6 Williamsburg Ct., St. Charles 63303

Muegge, Chrissy Sommer, 6 Williamsburg Ct., St. Charles 63303

O'Fallon, Dave Evans, 5 Conestoga Ct., O'Fallon 63368

O'Fallon, Cindy Evans, 5 Conestoga Ct., O'Fallon 63368

Rivers, Bryce Steinhoff, 3396 Cottonwood Dr., St. Charles 63301

Rivers, Barbara Hall, 2944 Thrush Dr., St. Charles 63301

Spencer Creek, David Hoffman, 12 Lippizan Rd., St. Peters 63376

Spencer Creek, Cindy Carpenter, 30 Oakshire Ct., St. Peters 63376

St. Paul, Bill Gardner, 1139 Water View Ln., O'Fallon 63366

St. Paul, Amy Belt, 1122 St. Matthew, O'Fallon 63368

St. Peters, David Zucker, 2032 Hanley Rd., Ste. 232, Dardenne Prairie 63368

St. Peters, Linda Klingerman, 706 Knollshire Way Ct., Dardenne Prairie 63368

Wentzville, Justin Brewer, 206 Preserve Park Pl., O'Fallon 63366

Wentzville, Kathy Chesher, 162 Old Williamsburg Pkwy., Wentzville 63385

St. Clair County

Chair, Gary Noakes, 3170 NW Hwy. A, Lowry City 64763

Vice Chair, Frances Trainer, 12350 NE Hwy. 82, Osceola 64776

Secretary, Alan Cole, 10195 NE 1281 Private Rd., Osceola 64766

Treasurer, Rhonda Shelby, 4415 SE 731 Rd., Osceola 64766

Appleton II, Leroy Strope, 9900 NW Hwy. AA , Appleton City 64724

Appleton II, Ronda Strope, 9900 NW Hwy. AA, Appleton City 64724

Butler East, Keith Carmichael, 3760 NE 1000 Rd., Lowry City 64763

Butler East, Laurie Stinnett, 4480 NE 1270 Rd., Deepwater 64740

Butler West, Marley McLerran, 9150 NE 201 Rd., Lowry City 64763

Butler West, Sharon McLerran, 9150 NE 201 Rd., Lowry City 64763

Dallas, Charlene Wisner, 12580 SE Hwy. T, Osceola 64766

Doyal, Scott Keeler, 2629 SE 450 Rd., Osceola 64766

Doyal, Rhonda Shelby, 4415 SE 731 Rd., Osceola 64766

Jackson, Alan Cole, 10195 NE 1281 Private Rd., Osceola 64766

Jackson, Georgia Cole, 10195 NE 1281 Private Rd., Osceola 64766

Monegaw, Gary Noakes, 3170 NW Hwy. A, Lowry City 64763

Monegaw, Joyce Noakes, 3170 NW Hwy. A, Lowry City 64763

Osage, Harold Rosbrugh, 430 NW 775 Rd., Rockville 64780

Osage, Betty Rosbrugh, 430 NW 775 Rd., Rockville 64780

Osceola East, Vernon Putnam, 460 SE Hwy. WW, Osceola 64776

Osceola East, Janice Putnam, 460 SE Hwy. WW, Osceola 64776

Osceola West, Charles Bourland, 1105 NE 450 Rd., Osceola 64776

Polk, John Trainer, 12350 NE Hwy. 82, Osceola 64776

Polk, Frances Trainer, 12350 NE Hwy. 82, Osceola 64776

Speedwell, Rusty Norval, 1000 SW 900 Rd., El Dorado Springs 64744

Taber, Craig Siegismund, 1485 NW Hwy. H, Rockville 64780

Taber, Margie Siegismund, 1485 NW Hwy. H, Rockville 64780

St. Francois County

Chair, Gary Matheny, 4615 Quail Run, Farmington 63640

Vice Chair, Carolyn Foster, 406 Rue Bergerac, Bonne Terre 63628

St. Louis City

Chair, Robert Vroman, 715 N. 21st 301, St. Louis 63103

Vice Chair, Caitlin Hartsell, 4949 West Pine, Apt. 110, St. Louis 63108

Ward 2, John Saxton, 2 Chambers Rd., St. Louis 63137

Ward 5, Mark Ogier, 1621 N. Seventh St., St. Louis 63102

Ward 6, John Hubb, 1917 Park Ave., No. 3, St. Louis 63104

Ward 7, Peter Wiegert, 2028 Hickory St., St. Louis 63104

Ward 8, Thea Cummings, 3414 Juniata Ave., St. Louis 63118

Ward 8, Michael Chance, 4180 Cleveland Ave., St. Louis 63110

Ward 9, Shirley DeMay, 2020 Cherokee St., St. Louis 63118

Ward 9, Christopher Rowley, 2130 Victor St., St. Louis 63104

Ward 10, Rhonda Christofanelli, 2118 Edwards, St. Louis 63118

Ward 10, Shaun O'Hara, 5072 Mardel Ave., Apt. A, St. Louis 63109

Ward 13, Courtney Blunt, 4605 Milentz Ave., St. Louis 63116

Ward 14, Tyson Lauby, 4424 Neosho Ave., St. Louis 63116

Ward 15, Michael Huett, 3954 Miami St., Apt. 1E, St. Louis 63116

Ward 16, Kimberley Mathis, 5322 Tamm Ave., St. Louis 63109

Ward 16, Fred Hodes, 6490 Kinsey Pl., St. Louis 63109

Ward 17, Caitlin Hartsell, 4949 West Pine, Apt. 110, St. Louis 63108

Ward 18, Charles Grumbach, 4253 Maryland, St. Louis 63108

Ward 19, Robert Vroman, 715 N. 21st 301, St. Louis 63103

Ward 23, Robert Crump, 3955 Jamieson, Apt. 1E, St. Louis 63109

Ward 23, Patricia Luna, 5739 Pernod Ave., St. Louis 63139

Ward 24, Tristan Walker, 6622 Wise Ave., St. Louis 63139

St. Louis County

Chair, Bruce Buwalda, 95 Grand Circle Dr., Maryland Heights 63043

Vice Chair, Rene Artman, 1530 Winterchase Dr., Fenton 63026

Treasurer, Jim Rowe, 1283 Chambers Rd., St. Louis 63137

Secretary, Judy Hon, 19073 Bear Trail Rd., Wildwood 63038

Airport, Bruce Buwalda, 95 Grand Circle Dr., Maryland Heights 63043

Airport, Becky Buwalda, 95 Grand Circle Dr., Maryland Heights 63043

Bonhomme, Alan Wheeler, 728 Evans, Kirkwood 63122

Bonhomme, Janice Perdue DeWeese, 307 Dart Ln., Fenton 63026

Creve Coeur, Michael Burr, 472 Magna Carta Dr., St. Louis 63141

Creve Coeur, Julia McQueen, 883 Somerton Ridge Dr., St. Louis 63146

Chesterfield, Norm Baxter, 1879 Stenton Path, Chesterfield 63005

Clayton, David Stokes, 7450 Washington Ave., St. Louis 63130

Clayton, Maryann Rober, 14 Blaytonn Ln., Ladue 63124

Concord, Anthony Pousosa, 9700 Antigo Dr., Green Park 63123

Concord, Joann Raisch, 10608 E. Grantview Dr., St. Louis 63123

Ferguson, Tim Dreste, 234 Argent Ave., St. Louis 63135

Ferguson, Lisa Kaliski, 15641 Moonlight Dr., Ferguson 63135

Florissant, Bryan Koen, 1345 Willowbrook Dr., Florissant 63033

Florissant, Teresa Stone, 260 Brightmoor Dr., Florissant 63033

Gravois, John Winston, 8510 Skyline, St. Louis 63123

Gravois, Jennifer Bird, 9204 Medallion Ct., St. Louis 63126

Hadley, Dan O'Sullivan, 7715 Lindbergh Dr., St. Louis 63143

Hadley, Jackie Coleman, 6633 Alamo Ave., Unit 1E, St. Louis 63105

Jefferson, Rich Magee, 725 Glenway Dr., Glendale 63122

Jefferson, Frieda Keough, 411 S. Sappington, St. Louis 63122

Lafayette, Mark Harder, 542 Lering ct, Ballwin 63011

Lafayette, Jeanne Gosen, 2765 Kehrs Mill Rd., Chesterfield 63017

Lewis & Clark, David Blanke, 1811 Charleston Estates Dr., Florissant 63031

Lewis & Clark, June Schmidt, 1470 Estes Dr., Florissant 63031

Lemay, Alan Leaderbrand, 3918 Jacinto Dr., St. Louis 63125

Lemay, Teresa Douglas, 8208 Weimar Dr., St. Louis 63123

Meramec, Byron Keelin, 1423 Piedras Parkway, Fenton 63026

Meramec, Rene Artman, 1530 Winterchase Dr., Fenton 63026

Maryland Heights, Patrick Walker, 300 Babler Dr., St. Louis 63141

Maryland Heights, Margaret Walker, 300 Babler Dr., St. Louis 63141

Midland, Mark Hanses, 2460 Oakland Ave., St. Louis 63114

Midland, Carol Downen, 3365 Marmary Ln., St. Ann 63074

Missouri River, Mark Dunn, 13321 N. Outer Forty Rd., Town & Country 63017

Missouri River, Mary Jane Jokerst, 2314 Clifton Forge Dr., St. Louis 63131

Normandy, Thomas Harner, 8807 Alva Ave., St. Louis 63121

Normandy, Maggie Jost, 2853 moniteau Dr., St. Louis 63121

Northwest, Dave Powell, 3128 Edwards Pl., Apt. 101, Maryland Heights 63043

Northwest, DeAnn Deimeke, 3081 Lake Ave., Maryland Heights 63043

Norwood, Jennifer Krupp, 410 Jehling Dr., Fergson 63135

Oakville, Kurt Witzel, 3116 Southridge Park Ln., St. Louis 63129

Oakville, Celeste Witzel, 3116 Southridge Park Ln., St. Louis 63129

Queeny, Jonatha Taylor, 636 Vest Ave., Valley Park 63088

Queeny, Peggy Koch, 1139 Arbor Place Dr., Valley Park 63088

St. Ferdinand, Jim Rowe, 1283 Chambers Rd., St. Louis 63137

Spanish Lake, Bobby Koch, 2763 Aberdeen Dr., Florissant 63033

Spanish Lake, Edna Ditto, 3580 Dwyer Ln., Florissant 63033

Tesson Ferry, John Judd, 4769 Cactus Wren Ct., St. Louis 63128

Tesson Ferry, Anita Zolman, 4854 Towne S. Rd., St. Louis 63128

University, Ted Engler, 857 Berick Dr., St. Louis 63132

University, Sarah Davoli, 7378 Milan Blvd., St. Louis 63130

Wild Horse, Ken Newhouse, 321 Carmel Woods Dr., Ellsville 63021

Wild Horse, Anne Gassel, 16309 Autumn Crest Ct., Ellisville 63011

Ste. Genevieve County

Chair, Kenneth Williams, 21726 Palmer Ln., Sainte Mary 63673

Vice Chair, Donna Williams, 21726 Palmer Ln., Sainte Mary 63673

Secretary, Robin Naeger, 10635 State Rt. O, Sainte Genevieve 63670

Treasurer, Wendell Johnson, 22276 State Rt. N, St. Mary 63673

Beauvais, Kenneth Williams, 21726 Palmer Ln., Sainte Mary 63673

Beauvais, Donna Williams, 21726 Palmer Ln., Sainte Mary 63673

Jackson, Kerry Messer, 6336 State Rt. DD, Festus 63627

Saline, Mike Naeger, 21894 State Rt. B, Ste. Genevieve 63670

Ste. Genevieve, Carl Ritter Jr., 700 La Porte, Sainte Genevieve 63670

Ste. Genevieve, Diana Wall, 823 N. Sixth, Ste. Genevieve 63670

Union, Jeremy Brooks, 3832 Frye Rd., Farmington 63640

Saline County

Chair, Richard Clemens, 23999 Marigold Ave., Marshall 65340
Vice Chair, Patricia Edwards, 1016 S. Ann, Marshall 65340
Secretary, Lee Hamilton, 1414 E. Eastwood, Marshall 65340
Treasurer, Arthur Madden, 16989 N. Saline 65, Malta Bend 65339
Arrow Rock, Robert Doty, 14366 Oleander, Nelson 65347
Arrow Rock, Joyce Doty, 14366 Oleander, Nelson 65347
Elmwood, Mary S. Borchers, 615 N. Main, Blackburn 65321
Grand Pass, Arthur Madden, 16989 N. Saline 65, Malta Bend 65339
Miami, Bernice Sporleder, 26447 295th Ln., Marshall 65340
Marshall
    1, Kenneth Donnell, 820 S. Miami, Apt. 6, Marshall 65340
    1, Melda Lingel, 911 S. Apache Dr., Apt. 3, Marshall 65340
    2, Thomas Purta, 1716 S. Odell, Marshall 65340
    2, Patricia Edwards, 1016 S. Ann, Marshall 65340
    3, Michael Mills, 1124 E. Eastwood, Marshall 65340
    3, Lee Hamilton, 1414 E. Eastwood, Marshall 65340
Marshall Rural, Richard Clemens, 23999 Marigold Ave., Marshall 65340
Marshall Rural, Nellie Clemens, 23999 Marigold Ave., Marshall 65340
Cambridge Rural, Betty Potts, 33595 Hwy. M, Gillam 65330
Sweet Springs 2, Ken Hughson, 109 Main St., Sweet Springs 65351
Sweet Springs Rural, Ryan Sims, 16001 146 Trl., Sweet Springs 65351
Sweet Springs Rural, Cindi Sims, 16001 146 Trl., Sweet Springs 65351

Schuyler County

Chair, Judy Wilson, 825 Second St., Glenwood 63541
Vice Chair, Herb Austin, RR 1, Box 171B, Queen City 63561
Secretary, Berkley Barton, RR 2, Box 26, Lancaster 63584
Treasurer, Luetta Barton, RR 2, Box 26, Lancaster 63584
Fabius, Royce Jeffries, RR 2, Box 18, Downing 63536
Glenwood, Allen Wilson, 825 Second St., Glenwood 63541
Glenwood, Judy Wilson, 825 Second St., Glenwood 63541
Liberty, Berkley Barton, RR 2, Box 26, Lancaster 63584
Liberty, Luetta Barton, RR 2, Box 26, Lancaster 63584
Prairie, Herb Austin, RR 1, Box 171B, Queen City 63561
Prairie, Lorraine Austin, RR 1, Box 171B, Queen City 63561

Scotland County

Chair, Dwayne Ebeling, RR1 Box 1765, Wyaconda 63474
Vice Chair, Patty Freeberg, R2 Box 55, Memphis 63555
Secretary, Sandra Ebeling
Treasurer, Bill Kiddoo

Scott

Chair, John McMillen, 810 Glenn Dr., Sikeston 63801
Vice Chair, Ann Rolwing, 102 State Hwy. NN, Charleston 63834

Diehlstadt, Ann Rolwing, 102 State Hwy. NN, Charleston 63834
New Hamburg, Roger Record, 26274 U.S. Hwy. 61, Benton 63736
New Hamburg, Connie Record, 26274 U.S. Hwy. 61, Benton 63736
Scott City, Shirley Young, 414 Grand Ave., Scott City 63780
Sikeston
    Ward 1, Perry Waltrip, 309 W. Salcedo Rd., Sikeston 63801
    Ward 1, Susan Werner, 938 N. West, Sikeston 63801
    Ward 2, Clifton Shirrell, 1204 Fairfield, Sikeston 63801
    Ward 2, Lynette Shirrell, 1204 Fairfield, Sikeston 63801
    Ward 3, John McMillen, 810 Glenn Dr., Sikeston 63801

Shannon County

Chair, Jerry King, RR 1, Box 150B, Summersville 65571
Vice Chair, Suzie Needels, PO Box 636, Winona 65588
Birch Tree, Clinton Reeves
Birch Tree, Joyce McAfee
Bunker, Robert Skrunkrud
Bunker, Mindy Gallaway
Eminence, J.C. Ray
Eminence, Mickey Schad
Montier, Barbara Shepherd
Montier, Charles Shepherd
Newton, Robert Graham
Summersville, Jerry King, RR 1, Box 150B, Summersville 65571
Summersville, Mary Lou Beasley
Winona, Hunter Fears
Winona, Sharon Davis

Shelby County

Chair, Kathleen Wilham, 2 Sharon Dr., Shelbina 63468
Vice Chair, Keith Gardner, 304 S. Center, Shelbina 63468
Secretary, Donna Myers, 302 S. Cleveland, Shelbyville 63469
Treasurer, Jim Gingrich, 4118 Hwy. 151, Clarence 63437
Bethel, Joan Rains, 6084 Shelby 240, Bethel 63434
Bethel, Joe Rains, 6084 Shelby 240, Bethel 63434
Black Creek, Donna Myers, 302 S. Cleveland, Shelbyville 63469
Black Creek, Jerry Myers, 302 S. Cleveland, Shelbyville 63469
Clay, Nancy Gingrich, 4118 Hwy. 151, Clarence 63437
Clay, Jim Gingrich, 4118 Hwy. 151, Clarence 63437
Jackson, Frances Snider, 7696 Hwy. PP, Shelbina 63468
Jackson, Bob Snider, 7696 Hwy. PP, Shelbina 63468
Jefferson, Virginia Baker, 1564 Hwy. DD, Clarence 63437
Jefferson, LaRue Baker, 1564 Hwy. DD, Clarence 63437
Lentner, Michele Collins, 3309 Shelby 432, Lentner 63450
Lentner, Jay Collins, 3309 Shelby 432, Lentner 63450
North River, Janet White, 8826 Shelby 368, Emden 63439
North River, Gary White, 8826 Shelby 368, Emden 63439
Salt River East, Kathleen Wilham, 2 Sharon Dr., Shelbina 63468
Salt River East, Darrell Wilham, 2 Sharon Dr., Shelbina 63468
Salt River West, Alice Gardner, 304 S. Center, Shelbina 63468
Salt River West, Keith Gardner, 304 S. Center, Shelbina 63468

Taylor, Betty McCoy, 120 E. Hwy. 151, Leonard 63451
Taylor, Jesse Schwanke, 288 Shelby 106, Leonard 63451
Tiger Fork, Debbie Coonrod, 1362 J Spur, Bethel 63434
Tiger Fork, Kevin Sisson, 1363 J Spur, Bethel 63434

Stoddard County

Chair, Wayne Jean, 814 Whitman St., Dexter 63841
Vice Chair, E. Montgomery, 714 S. State Hwy. 25, Dexter 63841
Secretary, Danny Talkington, PO Box 70, Grayridge 63850
Treasurer, Christy Edwards, 13861 CR 284, Bloomfield 63825
Castor, Gerald Griffin, 19875 Griffin Ln., Bloomfield 63825
Castor, Evelyn Griffin, 19875 Griffin Ln., Bloomfield 63825
Duck Creek, James Graham, 8438 State Hwy. J, Puxico 63960
Liberty, Wayne Jean, 106 W. Stoddard St., Dexter 63841
Liberty, E. Montgomery, 714 S. State Hwy. 25, Dexter 63841
New Lisbon, Christy Edwards, 13861 CR 284, Bloomfield 63825
Richland, Danny Talkington, PO Box 70, Grayridge 63850
Richland, Dana McCormick, 26115 State Hwy. 114, Essex 63846

Stone County

Chair, Tom Martin, 345 Briar Cliff Rd., Lampe 65681
Vice Chair, Connie Johnson, 574 Horse Creek Tree Farm Rd., Galena 65656
Secretary, Richard Nierman, 168 Nier Ln., Shell Knob 65747
Treasurer, Cynthia Patrick, 125 Rockyview Ln., Shell Knob 65747
Alpine, Richard Nierman, 168 Nier Ln., Shell Knob 65747
Grant, Judy Berkstresser, 551 Billy Joe Rd., Crane 65633
Pierce, Kent Brosseau, 1008 Dodge Hollow Rd., Crane 65633
Pierce, Leasa Brosseau, 1008 Dodge Hollow Rd., Crane 65633
Pine B, Tom Martin, 345 Briar Cliff Rd., Lampe 65681
Pine B, Nancy Martin, 345 Briar Cliff Rd., Lampe 65681
Ruth
  A, Tim Gideon, 651 E. State Hwy. 248, Reeds Spring 65737
  A, Samantha Phillips, 34 Sams Ln., Reeds Spring 65737
  B City, Layne Morrill, 75 Port Holiday Ln. 2, Kimberling City 65686
  C, Gary Clark, 39 Secluded Cir., Reeds Spring 65737
  C, Kathy Clark, 39 Secluded Cir., Reeds Spring 65737
Washington, John Johnson, 574 Horse Creek Tree Farm Rd., Galena 65656
Washington, Connie Johnson, 574 Horse Creek Tree Farm Rd., Galena 65656
Williams, Charles Patrick, 125 Rockyview Ln., Shell Knob 65747
Williams, Cynthia Patrick, 125 Rockyview Ln., Shell Knob 65747

Sullivan County

Chair, Danny Beusick, 10975 Acordn Dr., Newtown 64667
Vice Chair, Phyllis Blondefield, 606 Second St., Pollock 63560

Taney County

Chair, Buddy Roberts, PO Box 958, Forsyth 65653
Vice Chair, Lea Ann Coffelt, P. O. Box 1497, Forsyth 65653
Secretary, Nathan Easley, 989 Beaver Creek Ranch Rd., Bradleyville 65614
Treasurer, Crystal Rodgers, 425 Deer Run Rd., Branson 65616
Beaver, Nathan Easley, 989 Beaver Creek Ranch Rd., Bradleyville 65614
Beaver, Lyn Wieneke, 136 State Hwy. DD, Bradleyville 65614
Big Creek, Frank Baxter, 1523 Coker Rd., Protem 65733
Big Creek, Ellamae Baxter, 1523 Coker Rd., Protem 65733
Branson, Jeff Justus, 880 Wilshire, Branson 65616
Branson, Donna Watson, 117 Stoneridge Dr., Branson 65616
Cedar Creek, Lyle Rowland, 2333 Moores Bend Rd., Cedar Creek 65627
Cedar Creek, Glenda Rowland, 2333 Moores Bend Rd., Cedar Creek 65627
Oliver, Marc Beede, 137 Blue Waters Ct., Hollister 65672
Oliver, Lea Ann Coffelt, PO Box 1497, Forsyth 65653
Scott, Scott Rodgers, 425 Deer Run Rd., Branson 65616
Scott, Crystal Rodgers, 425 Deer Run Rd., Branson 65616
Swan, Buddy Roberts, PO Box 958, Forsyth 65653

Texas County

Chair, Robert (Bob) Green, PO Box 597, Licking 65542
Vice Chair, Treena Heiney, 22599 Midvale Rd., Summersville 65571
Secretary, Connie Thompson, 3547 Stultz Rd., Cabool 65689
Treasurer, Melvin & Georgia Adey, 8707 Hwy. E, Houston 65483
Swan, Linda Stillings, 135 Swan Valley Dr., Forsyth 65653
Boone, Robert (Bob) Green, PO Box 597, Licking 65542
Boone, Leann Green, PO Box 597, Licking 65542
Carroll, Doyle Heiney, 22599 Midvale Rd., Summersville 65571
Carroll, Treena Heiney, 22599 Midvale Rd., Summersville 65571
Current, Frankie Shoults, 6647 Hwy. KK, Hartshorn 65479
Current, Heather DeWitt, 22600 Birchen Rd., Hartshorn 65479
Date, Ron Tuggle, 2108 Hwy. W, Summersville 65571
Date, Heather Tuggle, 2108 Hwy. W, Summersville 65571
Lynch, Linda Garrett, 10949 Prescott Rd., Licking 65542
Morris, Bill Ewan, 13438 Hwy. Y Y, Cabool 65689
Morris, Faye Ewan, 13438 Hwy. Y Y, Cabool 65689
Piney, Robert Krantz, 5886 Hogan Rd., Houston 65483
Piney, Diane Krantz, 5886 Hogan Rd., Houston 65483
Roubidoux, Bill R. Reece, 12565 Hwy. AP, Success 65570
Roubidoux, Kathy Reece, 12565 Hwy. AP, Success 65570
Sargent, Jack Hines, 16540 Varvel Rd., Willow Springs 65793
Sargent, Ann Hines, 16540 Varvel Rd., Willow Springs 65793
Sherrill, Brad North, 14786 Hwy. 63, Licking 65542
Sherrill, Betty Sue Crow, 18946 Hwy. V V, Licking 65542

Vernon County

Chair, Gerald Wadel, 7511 E. D Hwy., Richards 64778
Vice Chair, Valo Jones, 1015 S. Adams, Nevada 64772
Secretary, Theodore Koller, 609 S. Cedar St., Nevada 64772
Treasurer, Frieda Hickman, 22635 S. 2525 Rd., Milo 64767
Center
  Ward 3, Theodore Koller, 609 S. Cedar St., Nevada 64772
  Ward 3, Adriel Koller, 609 S. Cedar St., Nevada 64772
  Ward 4, Robert Jones, 1015 S. Adams, Nevada 64772
  Ward 4, Valo Jones, 1015 S. Adams, Nevada 64772
  Ward 6, Gregory Kepler, 1518 W. Allison St., Nevada 64772
  Ward 7, April Mosher, 1233 N. Olive, Nevada 64772
Dover, Darrell Hickman, 22635 S. 2525 Rd., Milo 64767
Dover, Frieda Hickman, 22635 S. 2525 Rd., Milo 64767
Metz, Gerald Wadel, 7511 E. D Hwy., Richards 64778
Moundville, Michael Morris, 12358 E. Hwy. F, Moundville 64771
Osage, Clay Lyons, 16256 E. Artillery Rd., Rich Hill 64779
Osage, Priscilla Lyons, 16256 E. Artillery Rd., Rich Hill 64779
Virgil, Jay Bowmaster, 26066 E. Rebel Rd., Milo 64767
Virgil, Barbara York, 17150 S. Hwy. HH, El Dorado Springs 64744
Washington, Scott Buerge, 14383 S. 1532 Rd., Nevada 64772
Washington, Charlotte Buerge, 14383 S. 1532 Rd., Nevada 64772
Deerfield, Rob Selsor, 18853 S. 1256 Rd., Nevada 64772

Warren County

Chair, Cathy Engelage, 21201 Howard Branch, Warrenton 63383
Vice Chair, Ted Schneider, 33745 State Rd. W, Warrenton 63383
Secretary, Bev Ehlen, 19335 Primrose Rdg., Warrenton 63383
Treasurer, Jeff Thomsen, 2143 Meadow Valley Dr., Innsbrook 63390
Bridgeport, Karen Shafferkoetter, 29421 Red School House Rd., Jonesburg 63351
Camp Branch, Ted Schneider, 33745 State Rd. W, Warrenton 63383
Camp Branch, Kathryn Fischer, 37499 Pin Oak Church Rd., Truxton 63381
Charrette, Al Bayliss, 21434 S. State Hwy. 47, Warrenton 63383
Charrette, Cathy Engelage, 21201 Howard Branch, Warrenton 63383
Elkhorn
  North, Wendy Nordwald, 28789 N. Spoede Ln., Warrenton 63383
  South, Gilbert Nordwald, 19644 Durango Dr., Warrenton 63383
  South, Sherry Nordwald, 19644 Durango Dr., Warrenton 63383
Hickory Grove
  North, Fred Heberer, 1100 James, Wright City 63390

North, Mary Massey, 11903 Henke Ln., Foristell 63348
South, Jeff Thomsen, 2143 Meadow Valley Dr., Innsbrook 63390
South, Jean Briggs, 532 Amber Glen Dr., Wright City 63390
Pinckney, Clif Ehlen, 19335 Primrose Ridge, Warrenton 63383
Pinckney, Bev Ehlen, 19335 Primrose Ridge, Warrenton 63383
Warrenton
  Ward 1, Wallace Grant, 917 Pine Ave., Warrenton 63383
  Ward 1, Alouise Marschel, 903 Pine Ave., Warrenton 63383
  Ward 2, Gary Foland, 1410 Robin Ave., Warrenton 63383
  Ward 2, Diane Foland, 1410 Robin Ave., Warrenton 63383
  Ward 3, Ray Kehoe, 1022 Pin Oak Dr., Warrenton 63383
  Ward 3, Carol LeGrand, 1009 Arlington Way, Warrenton 63383

Washington County

Chair, John Robinson III, 1125 Alexander St., Caledonia 63631
Vice Chair, Phyllis Hochstatter, 10200 Bates Creek Rd., Potosi 63664
Secretary, MaryAnn Pankhurst, 108 S. Hickory St., Irondale 63648
Treasurer, Carl Pankhurst, 10216 Shut-in Rd., Irondale 63648
Belgrade, Curt Friese, 14353 Council Bluff Rd., Belgrade 63622
Belgrade, Abby Friese, 14353 Council Bluff Rd., Belgrade 63622
Belview, John Robinson III, 1125 Alexander St., Caledonia 63631
Breton, Robert Yount, 10923 State Hwy. 185, Potosi 63664
Breton, Phyllis Hochstatter, 10200 Bates Creek Rd., Potosi 63664
Concord, Carl Pankhurst, 10216 Shut-in Rd., Irondale 63648
Concord, MaryAnn Pankhurst, 108 S. Hickory St., Irondale 63648
Liberty, Edward Pashia, 10924 Pashia Rd., Putosi 63664
Liberty, Linda Pashia, 10924 Pashia Rd., Putosi 63664
Union, David Pratt, 10208 Roubidoux Springs Rd., Cadet 63630

Wayne County

Chair, Bill Hovis, HCR 2, Box 5670, Greenville 63944
Vice Chair, Linda Scowden, PO Box 513, Greenville 63944
Secretary, Donna Eads, HC 3, Box 3015, Wappapello 63966
Treasurer, Don Scowden, PO Box 513, Greenville 63944
Benton, Cindy Stout, 915 Northwood Dr., Piedmont 63957
Cowan, Bill Hovis, HCR 2, Box 5670, Greenville 63944
Lost Creek, Mike Eads, HC 3, Box 3015, Wappapello 63966
Lost Creek, Donna Eads, HC 3, Box 3015, Wappapello 63966
St. Francis, Don Scowden, PO Box 513, Greenville 63944
St. Francis, Linda Scowden, PO Box 513, Greenville 63944

Webster County

Chair, Terry Blakenship, 26676 State Hwy. 38, Marshfield 65706
Vice Chair, Kay Fleming, 28 Whippoorwill Rd., Seymour 65746
Secretary, Francis Spain, 86 Prospect Rd., Marshfield 65706
Treasurer, Mike Vinehout, 1457 River Rd., Marshfield 65706
Diggins, Paul Ipock, 2864 State Hwy. O, Seymour 65746
Finley, Denzil Young, 1273 Walnut Ridge Rd., Seymour 65746
Fordland, James Fleming, 28 Whippoorwill Rd., Seymour 65746
Fordland, Kay Fleming, 28 Whippoorwill Rd., Seymour 65746
Grant, Gregory W. Linn, 367 Indian Hills Ln., Strafford 65757
Grant, Donna Burks, 953 Fellowship Rd., Marhsfield 65706
Hazelwood, Paul Vliestra, 3549 State Hwy. V, Seymour 65746
Hazelwood, Casey Peck, 1652 Teagues Rd., Seymour 65746
High Prairie, Terry Blakenship, 26676 State Hwy. 38, Marshfield 65706
High Prairie, Francis Spain, 86 Prospect Rd., Marshfield 65706
Jackson, Don Hartwell, 411 Shady Grove Rd., Elkland 65644
Jackson, Charlene Hartwell, 411 Shady Grove Rd., Elkland 65644
Marshfield
    East, Ward Jones, 243 N. Pitts St., Marshfield 65706
    West, Randy Clair, PO Box 182, Marshfield 65706
Niangua, Gary Don Letterman, 1430 Valley View Rd., Niangua 65713
Northview, Terry Wrinkle, 714 Lakewood Loop, Marshfield 65706
Northview, Cheryl Wrinkle, 714 Lakewood Loop, Marshfield 65706
Ozark East, Mike Vinehout, 1457 River Rd., Marshfield 65706
Ozark East, Joyce Harmon, 110 Shewanano Loop, Marshfield 65706
Union, John Geltemeyer, 2448 Amity Rd., Niangua 65713
Washington, Aaron Bixler, 1041 W. College St., Springfield 65806
Washington, Nikki Whitehead, Conway 65632

Worth County

Chair, Ben Abplanalp, 14701 Indigio Ave., Grant City 64456
Vice Chair, Nancy Burns, 20213 Holly Trail, Grant City 64456
Russell Burns
Nancy Burns
Dawn Brown
Will Brown
Robert Hull
Eric Hunt
Les New
Sharon Nonneman
Don Null
Lois Null
Lloyd Ridge
Deb Thummel
Chuck Warner

Wright County

Chair, Charles Dickinson, 6276 Hwy. 5, Hartville 65667
Vice Chair, Janis Kelly, 229 W. Outer Rd., Norwood 65717
Secretary, Barbara Graham, 6898 Turkey Tail Dr., Hartville 65667
Treasurer, Norman Virtue, 6029 Clark Creek Rd., Hartville 65667
Boone, Charles Dickinson, 6276 Hwy. 5, Hartville 65667
Boone, Patricia Clifton, 2225 Akers Dr., Hartville 65667
Brush Creek, Nelda Masner, 4652 Hwy. E, Hartville 65667
Clark, Houston Kelly, 6190 Dake Rd., Norwood 65717
Clark, Janis Kelly, 229 W. Outer Rd., Norwood 65717
Elk Creek, Donald Long, 5602 Cope Dr., Hartville
Elk Creek, Cathern Long, 5602 Cope Dr., Hartville
Hart, Norman Virtue, 6029 Clark Creed Rd., Hartville 65667
Montgomery, Larry Graham, 6898 Turkey Trail Dr., Hartville
Montgomery, Barbara Graham, 6898 Turkey Tail Dr., Hartville 65667
Mountain Grove, John Kelly, 6743 Outer Rd., Norwood 65717
Mountain Grove, Heidi Kelly, 6743 Outer Rd., Norwood 65717
Union, Vincent Finelli, 8777 Hunters Creek Rd., Hartville 65662
Union, Sandra Finelli, 8777 Hunters Creek Rd., Hartville 65662
Wood, Tony Dugger, 4975 Bull Frog Rd., Hartville 65667
Wood, Judy Chadwell, 3896 S. Hwy. E, Norwood 65717

Officers of Libertarian Party

Libertarian National Committee, 2015–2016

National Libertarian Headquarters
2600 Virginia Ave. NW, Ste. 100
Washington, D.C. 20037
Telephone: (800)-ELECT-US (800-353-2887)
www.lp.org

Officers, Libertarian National Committee

Nicholas Sarwark, chair;
Arvin Vohra, vice chair;
Alicia Mattson, secretary;
Tim Hagan, treasurer.

Libertarian State Organization of Missouri

Missouri Libertarian Party
PO Box 78623, St. Louis 63178
Telephone: (877)-Vote 4 Us (877-868-3487)
www.lpmo.org

NOTE: Information is received from county clerks and the Missouri Libertarian Party

Officers, Libertarian State Committee

Bill Slantz, chair, chair@lpmo.org;
Rick Vandeven, vice chair, vicechair@lpmo.org;
Randy Langkraehr, secretary, secretary@lpmo.org;
Sean O'Toole, treasurer, treasurer@lpmo.org;
Greg Tlapek, executive director, director@lpmo.org.

Members, Libertarian State Committee

Fourth district: Robb Cunningham, PO Box 102, St. Ann 63074.
Eighth district: Ron Bream, 649 NE Newport Dr., Lee's Summit 64064.
Ninth district: Sean O'Toole, 3425 Gladstone Blvd., Kansas City 64123; Cisse Spragins, 3425 Gladstone Blvd., Kansas City 64123.
Twelfth district: Russ Monchil, 8940 SW Duroc Dr., Cameron 64429.
Thirteenth district: Eric Harris, 1848 High Sun Dr., Florissant 63031; Julie Stone, 269 Habecking Dr., St. Louis 63137.

BILL SLANTZ
State Chair

RICK VANDEVEN
State Vice Chair

RANDY LANGKRAEHR
State Secretary

SEAN O'TOOLE
State Treasurer

GREG TLAPEK
Executive Director

Fifteenth district: Raymond Harbert, 359 Village Creek Dr., Ballwin 63021.
Seventeenth district: Matthew Copple, 4037 NE 50th Terr., Gladstone 64119.
Nineteenth district: Jim Givens, 4182 N. Riviera Dr., Columbia 65202; John Schultz, 1301 W. Colchester Rd., Columbia 65202.
Twentieth district: Bill Boone, 4230 E. FR 132, Springfield 65802; Mark (Majic) Jones, 1515 N. Grant, Springfield 65803.
Twenty-first district: Randy Langkraehr, 618 N. Maguire, PO Box 1099, Warrensburg 64093; Bill Wayne, 431 SE CR Y, Warrensburg 64093.
Twenty-third district: Bill Slantz, 1620 Congress Way, St. Charles 63303.

Twenty-fourth district: Jim Higgins, 11944 Craig View Dr., St. Louis 63146.

Twenty-seventh district: Greg Tlapek, 1569 Cape Rock Dr., Cape Girardeau 63701; Rick Vandeven, 724 Helen Ave., Chaffee 63740.

Twenty-eighty district: Bill Lower, 21010 S. Hwy. 245, Fair Play 65649.

Thirty-first district: Herschel Young, 17100 E. 2 Hwy., Harrisonville 64701.

Thirty-fourth district: Mike Bozarth, 5207 Swift Ave., St. Joseph 64504; Rick Reynolds, 11350 SE 32nd Rd., St. Joseph 64507.

Libertarian County Committees

(Township, ward or precinct precedes name of committee members. Vacancies not published. County Committee lists are provided by the county clerks, election officials from each county and the State Libertarian Party.)

Boone County

Chair, John Schultz, 1301 W. Colchester Rd., Columbia 65202
Vice Chair, Diana Rickard, 4308 W. South Pinebrook Ln., Columbia 65202
Secretary, Jim Givens, 4182 N. Riviera Dr., Columbia 65202
Treasurer, Greg Rennier, 10900 S. Hardwick Ln., Columbia 65201
Columbia Ward 2, Jim Givens, 4182 N. Riviera Dr., Columbia 65202
Perche, John Schultz, 1301 W. Colchester Rd., Columbia 65202
Missouri, Diana Rickard, 4308 W. South Pinebrook Ln., Columbia 65202
Three Creeks, Greg Rennier, 10900 S. Hardwick Ln., Columbia 65201

Buchanan County

Chair, Mike A. Bozarth, 5207 Swift Ave., St. Joseph 64504
Vice Chair, Kristen Larabee, RR 1, Rushville 64484
Secretary, Cindy Summerford, 1626 Savannah Ave., St. Joseph 64505
Treasurer, Kevin Wisneski, 903 W. Valley St., St. Joseph 64504
Rush, Kristen Larabee, RR 1, Rushville 64484
Ward 10, Mike A. Bozarth, 5207 Swift Ave., St. Joseph 64504
Ward 10, Kevin Wisneski, 903 W. Valley St., St. Joseph 64504

Caldwell County

Chair, Russ Monchil, 8940 SW Duroc Dr., Cameron 64429

Cape Girardeau County

Chair, Pete Kerr, 1908 Huntington Dr., Cape Girardeau 63701
Vice Chair, Tim Doubledee, 660 Sandy Dr., Altenburg 63732 Treasurer,
Cape Girardeau, Greg Tlapek, 1569 N. Cape Rock, Cape Girardeau 63701

Cape Girardeau 2, Peter (Pete) M. Kerr, 1908 Huntington Dr., Cape Girardeau 63701
Cape Girardeau 13, Greg Tlapek, 1569 N. Cape Rock Rd., Cape Girardeau 63701
New Wells, Tim Doubledee, 660 Sandy Dr., Altenburg 63732

Cass County

Chair, Herschel Young, 17100 E. State Rt. 2, Harrisonville 64701
Precinct 12–Ward 2, Matt Stephens, 1101 N. Independence, Harrisonville 64701
Precinct 12–Ward 2, Theresa Stephens, 1101 N. Independence, Harrisonville 64701

Cedar County

Chair, Bill Lower, 21010 S. Hwy. 245, Fair Play 65649
Madison Township, Bill Lower, 21010 S. Hwy. 245, Fair Play 65649

Christian County

Cassidy, Lauren Bostian, 4347 S. Weller Ave., Apt. G, Springfield 65804
E Finley, Nathanial Light, 1006 E. Diane St., Ozark 65721

Clay County

Chair, Matt Copple, 37 NE 59th Terr., Gladstone 64119
Vice Chair, Erik Buck, 764 Hillside Ave., Liberty 64068
Secretary, Heidi Johnson, 501 NW 78th Terr., Kansas City 64118
Treasurer, Benjamin Casebolt, 1404 NE 68th St., Gladstone 64118
Ward 15/1, Benjamin Casebolt, 1404 NE 68th St., Gladstone 64118
Ward 17/1, Erik Buck, 764 Hillside Ave., Liberty 64068

Cole County

Chair, Janine Steck, 7125 St. Martins Blvd., Jefferson City 65109

Cooper County

Chair, Marvin J. Utterback, 1525 W. Monroe St., Mexico
Booneville, Marvin J. Utterback, 1525 W. Monroe St., Mexico

Gasconade County

Chair, Robert Kormeier, 705 E. Jefferson Ave., Owensville 65066
Canaan, Robert Kormeier, 705 E. Jefferson Ave., Owensville 65066

Greene County

Chair, Bill Boone, 4230 E. Farm Rd. 132, Springfield 65802
Vice Chair, Karinda Thompson, 1431 S. Briar Ave., Springfield 65809
Secretary, Daniel Redden, 815 N. Lexington, Springfield 65804
Treasurer, Ben Brixey, 103 W. Kennedy, Springfield 65803
Campbell 1, Karinda Thompson, 1431 S. Briar Ave., Springfield 65809

Campbell 1, Bill Boone, 4230 E. Farm Rd. 132, Springfield 65802

Robberson 2, Mark Jones, 4203 W. Arbor Hill Ln., Springfield 65803

Howell County

Willow Springs, Sean Hill, 414 E. Seventh St., Mountain View 65548

Jackson County

Chair, Sean O'Toole, 3425 Gladstone Blvd., Kansas City 64123

Vice Chair, Ronald Bream, 649 NE Newport Dr., Lees' Summit 64064

Secretary / Treasurer, Cisse W. Spragins, 3425 Gladstone Blvd., Kansas City 64123

Ward 11, Cisse W. Spragins, 3425 Gladstone Blvd., Kansas City 64123

Ward 11, Sean O'Toole, 3425 Gladstone Blvd., Kansas City 64123

Ward 16, Robert Tolbert, 3421 E. 62nd St., Kansas City 64130

Blue Sub-District, David H Schwensen, 9417 E. 18th St. S., Independence 64052

Johnson County

Chair, Bill Wayne, 431 SE CR Y, Warrensburg 64093

Vice Chair, Randall D. Langkraehr, PO Box 1099, Warrensburg 64093

Secretary, Thomas Holbrook II, 708 N. Warren St., Apt. 1, Warrensburg 64093

Treasurer, Steve Daugherty, 708 N. Warren St., Apt. 1, Warrensburg 64093

Warrensburg NE, Randall D. Langkraehr, PO Box 1099, Warrensburg 64093

Montserrat, 431 SE CR Y, Warrensburg 64093

Laclede County

Chair, Greg Cowan, 20224 Kenyon Ln., Lebanon 65536

Union, Curtis Everett, 19250 Hwy. J, Conway 65632

New Madrid County

Chair, Raymond A. Nabors, 1612 Hwy. 162, Portageville 63873

Newton County

Neosho 4, Jonas Yost, 415 E. Glenview Pl., Neosho 64850

Gramby, Martin Lindstedt

Pemiscot County

Steele 2, William Berry, 343 S. Walnut, Steele 63877

Pettis County

Chair, John Hansen, 1106 W. Third St., Sedalia 65301

Platte County

Chair, John Diment, 18377 Pleasantview Dr., Weston 64098

Polk County

SE Marion, Keith Cook, 910 E. Drake St., Bolivar 65613

Ripley County

Doniphan Township, Ginny Keirns, RR 3, Box 7588, Doniphan 63935

Scott County

Chair, Rick Vandeven, 724 Helen Ave., Chaffee 63740

Chaffee, Rick Vandeven, 724 Helen Ave., Chaffee 63740

St. Charles County

Chair, Bill Slantz, 1620 Congress Way, St. Charles 63303

Vice Chair, Allen Underdown, 4136 Towers Rd., St. Charles 63304

Township 3, Bill Slantz, 1620 Congress Way, St. Charles 63303

Township 5, Ryan Traughber, 408 Glengate Estates Dr., St. Charles 63366

Township 6, Allen Underdown, 4136 Towers Rd., St. Charles 63304

St. Louis County

Chair, Ladonna Higgins, 11944 Craig View Dr., St. Louis 63146

Vice Chair, Jeff Coleman, 4643 Robbins Grove Dr., Florissant 63031

Secretary, Eric Harris, 1848 High Sun Dr., Florissant 63031

Treasurer, Ray Harbert, 359 Village Creek Dr., Baldwin 63021

Sergeant-at-Arms, Theodis (Ted) Brown Sr., 9901 Lilac, Riverview 63137

Parliamentarian, Arnold Trembley, 12066 Charter House Ln., Apt. E, St. Louis 63146

Bonhomme, Beverly Bartlett, 2300 Timberview Rd., Kirkwood 63122

Bonhomme, Tim Thorndike, 2300 Timberview Rd., Kirkwood 63122

Chesterfield, James McCoy, 18846 Highwood Estates Dr. Wildwood 63069

Clayton, Sam Stufflebam, 8160 Whitburn Dr., Clayton 63105

Concord, Don Keil, 10561 Stephenson Dr., St. Louis 63128

Creve Coeur, Ladonna Higgins, 11944 Craig View Dr., St. Louis 63146

Creve Coeur, Arnold Trembley, 12066 Charter House Ln., Apt. E, St. Louis 63146

Ferguson, Nick Kasoff, 125 Royal Ave., Ferguson 63135

Hadley, Andrew Bolin, 2639 Sutton Blvd., Maplewood 63143

Maryland Heights, Shawn McDonald, 1857 Strathearn Ct., St. Louis 63146

Meramec, Ray Harbert, 359 Village Creek Dr., Baldwin 63021

Northwest, Eric Harris, 1848 High Sun Dr., Florissant 63031

Northwest, Sally Harris, 1848 High Sun Dr., Florissant 63031

Oakville, Joan Werner, 2674 Lido Ln., St. Louis 63129

Oakville, Walter Werner, 2674 Lido Ln., St. Louis 63129

Spanish Lake, Jeff Coleman, 4643 Robbins Grove Dr., Florissant 63031

St. Ferdinand, Theodis (Ted) Brown Sr., 9901 Lilac, Riverview 63137

St. Ferdinand, Julie Stone, 269 Habecking Dr., St. Louis 63137

Officers of the Constitution Party

DOUG ENYART
State Chair

CINDY REDBURN
State Vice Chair

Constitution Party National Committee, 2015–2016

Constitution Party National Headquarters
PO Box 1782, Lancaster, PA 17608
Telephone: (800) 2-VETO-IRS (800-283-8647)
www.constitutionparty.com

Officers, Constitution Party National Committee

Frank Fluckiger, chair, Utah;
Randall Stufflebeam, vice chair, Illinois;
Cindy Redburn, secretary, Missouri;
James Headings, treasurer, Tennessee;
Dr. Curtis Caine, parliamentarian, Mississippi.

At Large Members, Constitution Party National Committee

James Clymer, Pennsylvania;
Darrell Castle, Tennessee;
Peter Gemma, Florida;
Virgil Goode, Virginia;
Karen Murray, Washington;
Steven Walker, Indiana.

Members, Constitution Party Regional Area Chairs

Nicholas Sumbles, Massachusetts;
Don Shrader, Ohio;
Wayne Zimmerschied, Minnesota;
Ricardo Davis, Georgia;
Janine Hansen, Nevada;
Sam Pew, Utah.

Constitution Party State Organization of Missouri

Constitution Party State Committee Headquarters
PO Box 176, Peidmont 63957
Telephone: (573) 429-7800
www.cpmo.us

NOTE: Information is received from county clerks and the Missouri Constitution Party

FRANCES HOXSEY
State Secretary

MICHAEL EBERLE
State Treasurer

Missouri Members National Committee

Michael Eberle, 5509 Scherr Dr., Jefferson City 65109;
Doug Enyart, PO Box 176, Piedmont 63957;
Donna Ivanovich, 3775 Cindy Ct., Arnold 63010;
Ray Kish, 122 Airport Rd., Buffalo 65622;
Dan Plemons, 178 NW 187, First Rd., Kingsville 64061;
Alan Redburn, 5266 Brass Lantern Pl., St. Louis 63128;
Cindy Redburn, 5266 Brass Lantern Pl., St. Louis 63128.

Officers, Constitution Party State Executive Committee

Doug Enyart, chair, PO Box 176, Piedmont 63957;
Cindy Redburn, vice chair and education director, 5266 Brass Lantern Pl., St. Louis 63128;
Frances Hoxsey, secretary, 12947 NE CR 1754, Butler 64730;
Michael Eberle, treasurer, 5509 Scherr Dr., Jefferson City 65109.

At Large Members–Constitution Party State Executive Committee

Raymond Kish, immediate past chair, 122 Airport Rd., Buffalo 65622;

William Gilmore, field director, RR 3, Box 191A, Montrose 64770;

Donna Ivanovich, communications director, 3775 Cindy Ct., Arnold 63010;

Harold Thompson, legislative advisor, 5611 Elmira Ave., Springfield 65810;

Cynthia Davis, social and moral concerns advisor, 1008 Hwy. K, O'Fallon 63366.

Members, Constitution Party Congressional District Committees

Fourth district: Frances Hoxsey, chair, 12947 NE CR 1754, Butler 64730.

Eighth district: Doug Enyart, chair, PO Box 176, Piedmont 63957.

Members, Constitution Party State Committee

Sixth district: Michael Eberle, 5509 Scherr Dr., Jefferson City 65109.

Eleventh district: Richard McKie, 3804 S. Haden Dr., Independence 64055.

Fifteenth district: Alan Redburn, 5266 Brass Lantern Pl., St. Louis 63128; Cindy Redburn, 5266 Brass Lantern Pl., St. Louis 63128.

Nineteenth district: Dan Howell, 2312 Katy Ln., Columbia 65203.

Twentieth district: Harold Thompson, 5611 S. Elmira Ave., Springfield 65810.

Twenty-first district: Connie Plemons, 178 NW 187 First Rd., Kingsville 64061; Dan Plemons, 178 NW 187 First Rd., Kingsville 64061.

Twenty-second district: Donna Ivanovich, 3775 Cindy Ct., Arnold 63010.

Twenty-seventh district: Doug Enyart, PO Box 176, Piedmont 63957.

Twenty-eighth district: Laurie Kish, 122 Airport Rd., Buffalo 65622; Ray Kish, 122 Airport Rd., Buffalo 65622.

Thirty-first district: Frances Hoxsey, 12947 NE CR 1754, Butler 64730; William Gilmore, RR 3, Box 191A, Montrose 64770.

Thirty-third district: Chris Tomlinson, HC Box 63, Wasola 65773; Marianne Eberle, 14286 Hwy. AW, Plato 65552.

Thirty-fourth district: Stanley Jaggars, 11100 SE 90th St., Agency 64401; Susy Jaggars, 11100 SE 90th St., Agency 64401.

Constitution County Committees

(Township, ward or precinct precedes name of committee members. Vacancies not published. County Committee lists are provided by the county clerks, election officials from each county and the State Constitution Party.)

Bates County

Chair, William Gilmore, RR 3, Box 191A, Montrose 64770

Boone County

Chair, Dan Howell, 2312 Katy Ln., Columbia 65203;

Buchanan County

Chair, Stanley Jaggars, 11100 SE 90th Rd., Agency, 64401

Dallas County

Chair, Laurie Kish, 122 Airport Rd., Buffalo 65622

Dent County

Co-Chairs, Rodney and Jan Farthing, 3127 Hwy. K, Salem 65560

Franklin, Rodney Farthing, 3127 Hwy. K, Salem 65560

Franklin, Jan Farthing, 3127 Hwy. K, Salem 65560

Franklin County

Chair, Keith Mueller, 2251 Hwy. TT, St. Clair 63077

Jackson County

Chair, Richard McKie, 3804 S. Haden Dr, Independence 64055

Blue Sub-District 7, Richard McKie, 3804 S. Haden Dr., Independence 64055

Johnson County

Co-Chairs, Dan and Connie Plemons, 178 NW 187 First Rd., Kingsville 64061

Warrensburg, Dan Plemons, 178 NW 187 First Rd., Kingsville 64061

Warrensburg, Connie Plemons, 178 NW 187 First Rd., Kingsville 64061

Ozark County

Chair, Chris Tomlinson, HC Box 63, Wasola 65773

Wayne County

Chair, Linda Cravens, HC 2 Box 5380, Hiram 63944

Cowan, Linda Cravens, HC 2 Box 5380, Hiram 63944

Logan, Bruce Purdom, RR 4, Box 1171, Piedmont 63957

Madison County

St. Michael, Tim Rutherford, PO Box 145, Fredericktown 63645

St. Michael, Linda Rutherford, PO Box 145, Fredericktown 63645

CHAPTER 8
CITIES AND COUNTIES

Wallace State Park
Photo courtesy of Missouri State Archives

Missouri County Officials

The following list of officials for 2015–2016 was furnished by county clerks, the Jackson County executive, St. Louis County executive and St. Louis City Register. Listed are the officials' names, political affiliation, office addresses and telephone numbers. Population for each county is furnished by the U.S. Census (2014 County Population Estimates). Assessed valuation is furnished by the Missouri State Tax Commission. Assessed value is for 2014 taxable properties. County official positions are listed in alphabetical order.

Adair County

County seat and zip code: Kirksville 63501. **County population:** 25,602. **Classification:** Third Class. **Assessed valuation:** $271,848,440. **Square miles:** 567. **Organized:** January 29, 1841. **Named for:** John Adair, Governor of Kentucky.

Assessor, Donnie Waybill, (R), Adair County Courthouse, 106 W. Washington St., Kirksville 63501; (660) 665-4423; FAX (660) 665-0349; dwaybill@adaircomo.com

Clerk Circuit Court, Linda Decker, (D), Adair County Circuit Clerk, PO Box 690, Kirksville 63501; (660) 665-2552; FAX (660) 665-3420

Clerk County Commission, Sandra Collop, (D), Adair County Courthouse, 106 W. Washington St., Kirksville 63501; (660) 665-3350; FAX (660) 785-3233; scollop@adaircomo.com

Collector of Revenue, Sonja Harden, (D), Adair County Courthouse, 106 W. Washington St., Kirksville 63501; (660) 665-3481; FAX (660) 785-3200

Commissioner, First District, Carson Adams, (D), Adair County Courthouse, 106 W. Washington St., Kirksville 63501; (660) 234-7926; FAX (660) 665-8406; cadams@adaircomo.com

Commissioner, Second District, Mark Thompson, (R), Adair County Courthouse, 106 W. Washington St., Kirksville 63501; (660) 234-7927; FAX (660) 665-8406; mthompson@adaircomo.com

Coroner, Brian C. Noe, (R), 1008 N. Potter Ave., Kirksville 63501; (660) 665-1300; FAX (660) 665-3223

County Health Department Administrator*, Jim LeBaron, 1001 S. Jamison St., Kirksville 63501; (660) 665-8491; FAX (660) 627-2913; lebarj@lpha.mopublic.org

County Road and Bridge Supervisor*, Isaiah Curtis, 23016 Potter Tr., Kirksville 63501; (660) 665-6767; FAX (660) 785-3227; adaircountyrandb@cableone.net

County Surveyor*, David W. Borden, 21611 State Hwy. T, Callao 63534; (660) 346-8214

Emergency Management Director, Robert T. Hardwick, 215 N. Franklin, Kirksville 63501; (660) 665-4644; FAX (660) 785-3224; rhardwick@adaircoso.com

Presiding Commissioner, Stan Pickens, (R), Adair County Courthouse, 106 W. Washington St., Kirksville 63501; (660) 665-2283; FAX (660) 665-8406; spickens@adaircomo.com

Prosecuting Attorney, Matt Wilson, (D), 300 N. Franklin St., PO Box 314, Kirksville 63501; (660) 627-3625; FAX (660) 627-3835; adairprosecutor@gmail.com

Public Administrator, Rhonda Noe, (R), Adair County Annex, 300 N. Franklin St., Kirksville 63501; (660) 785-3211; FAX (660) 785-3229; rnoe@adaircomo.com

Recorder of Deeds, Pat Shoush, (R), Adair County Courthouse, 106 W. Washington St., Kirksville 63501; (660) 665-3890; FAX (660) 785-3212

Sheriff, Robert T. Hardwick, (R), 215 N. Franklin, Kirksville 63501; (660) 665-4644; FAX (660) 785-3224; rhardwick@adaircoso.com

Treasurer, Lori J. Smith, (R), Adair County Courthouse, 106 W. Washington St., Kirksville 63501; (660) 665-6755; FAX (573) 234-7002; lsmith@adaircomo.com

*Appointed

Andrew County

County seat and zip code: Savannah 64485. **County population:** 17,379. **Classification:** Third class. **Assessed valuation:** $240,312,084. **Square miles:** 436. **Organized:** January 29, 1841. **Named for:** Andrew Jackson Davis, a prominent citizen of St. Louis.

Assessor, Paul Garrison, (R), Andrew County Courthouse, PO Box 149, Savannah 64485; (816) 324-3023; FAX (816) 324-6154; assessor@andrewcounty.org

Clerk Circuit Court, Tena Christmas, (R), PO Box 318, Savannah 64485; (816) 324-3921;

FAX (816) 324-3191; tena.christmas@courts. mo.gov

Clerk County Commission, Sarah Miller, (R), Andrew County Courthouse, PO Box 206, Savannah 64485; (816) 324-3624; FAX (816) 324-6154; clerk@andrewcounty.org

Collector of Revenue, Phil Rogers, (R), Andrew County Courthouse, PO Box 47, Savannah 64485; (816) 324-3914; FAX (816) 324-6154; collector@andrewcounty.org

Commissioner, Eastern District, Ray Furst, (R), Andrew County Courthouse, PO Box 206, Savannah 64485; (816) 324-5716; FAX (816) 324-6154; clerk@andrewcounty.org

Commissioner, Western District, Darryl Howard, (D), Andrew County Courthouse, PO Box 206, Savannah 64485; (816) 324-5716; FAX (816) 324-6154; andrewcounty@hotmail.com

Coroner, Doug Johnson, (R), 10701 State Rt. H, Savannah 64485; (816) 487-2100

County Health Department Director, Andrew Hoffman, PO Box 271, Savannah 64485; (816) 324-3139

County Surveyor, F. Shane Terhune, (R), 13433 County Rd. 191, Savannah 64485; (816) 324-5320

Emergency Management Director, Roger Latham, PO Box 206, Savannah 64485; (816) 324-5023

Presiding Commissioner, Bob Caldwell, (R), Andrew County Courthouse, PO Box 206, Savannah 64485; (816) 324-5716; FAX (816) 324-6154; clerk@andrewcounty.org

Prosecuting Attorney, Steven Stevenson, (R), Andrew County Courthouse, PO Box 377, Savannah 64485; (816) 324-3535; FAX (816) 324-6015; prosecutor@andrewcounty.org

Public Administrator, Janet Rosenauer, (D), Andrew County Courthouse, PO Box 347, Savannah 64485; (816) 432-4349; FAX (816) 324-5056

Recorder of Deeds, Rosa Lea Lancey, (R), Andrew County Courthouse, PO Box 208, Savannah 64485; (816) 324-4221; FAX (816) 324-5667; lanceyrl@andrewcounty.org

Road and Bridge Supervisor, Jim Galbraith, 15950 County Rd. 322, Savannah 64485; (816) 324-4012; FAX (816) 324-6527; achwydept@bbwi.net

Sheriff, Bryan Atkins, (R), Andrew County Jail, 402 W. Market, Savannah 64485; (816) 324-4114; FAX (816) 324-5110; bryan.atkins@andrewcounty.org

Treasurer, Cindy Esely, (R), Andrew County Courthouse, PO Box 122, Savannah 64485; (816) 324-3614; treasurer@andrewcounty.org

Atchison County

County seat and zip code: Rock Port 64482. **County population:** 5,382. **Classification:** Third class. **Assessed valuation:** $126,839,398. **Square miles:** 560. **Organized:** February 14, 1845. **Named for:** David Rice Atchison, United States Senator.

Assessor, Lori Brown Jones, (D), Atchison County Courthouse, PO Box 280, Rock Port 64482; (660) 744-2948; atchcoassessor@rpt.coop

Clerk Circuit Court, Lori Hall, (R), Atchison County Courthouse, PO Box 280, Rock Port 64482; (660) 744-2700; FAX (660) 744-5705; acrecorder@rpt.coop

Clerk County Commission, Susette M. Taylor, (R), Atchison County Courthouse, 400 S. Washington, PO Box 280, Rock Port 64482; (660) 744-6214; FAX (660) 744-5499; acclerk@rpt.coop

Collector of Revenue, Diane Livengood, (R), Atchison County Courthouse, PO Box 280, Rock Port 64482; (660) 744-2770; FAX (660) 744-5499; accollector@rpt.coop

Commissioner, Northern District, David P. Chapin, (R), Atchison County Courthouse, PO Box 280, Rock Port 64482; (660) 744-6214; FAX (660) 744-5499; dchapin@rpt.coop

Commissioner, Southern District, Richard C. Burke, (D), Atchison County Courthouse, PO Box 280, Rock Port 64482; (660) 744-6214; FAX (660) 744-5499; rcburke@rpt.coop

Coroner, Shawn Minter Jr., (R), 217 N. Main, Rock Port 64482; (660) 744-2215; minterfuneral @rpt.coop

County Health Department Director, Jo Blackney, 421 Main St., Tarkio 64491; (660) 736-4121; FAX (660) 736-5533; blacke@lpha.dhss.mo.gov

Emergency Management Director/911 Director, Rhonda Wiley, 472 Rainbow, Rock Port 64482; (660) 744-6606; ac911@rpt.coop

Presiding Commissioner, Curtis Livengood, (R), Atchison County Courthouse, PO Box 280, Rock Port 64482; (660) 744-6214; FAX (660) 744-5499; livengoods@rpt.coop

Prosecuting Attorney, Brett Hurst, (I), Atchison County Courthouse, PO Box 280, Rock Port 64482; (660) 744-5440; FAX (660) 744-5480; atchisonpa@rpt.coop

Public Administrator, Teresa Jayne Scott, (R), 1006 Chestnut St., Tarkio 64491; (660) 623-9900; acpubadmin@rpt.coop

Recorder of Deeds, Eliza Beasing, (R), Atchison County Courthouse, PO Box 280, Rock Port 64482; (660) 744-2707; FAX (660) 744-5705; acrecorder@rpt.coop

Sheriff, Dennis D. Martin, (D), Atchison County Jail, 511 W. Clay, Rock Port 64482; (660) 744-6271; FAX (660) 744-6274; countybear@rpt.coop

Treasurer, Debbie True, (R), Atchison County Courthouse, PO Box 280, Rock Port 64482; (660) 744-2800; FAX (660) 744-5499; dtrueac treasurer@yahoo.com

Audrain County

County seat and zip code: Mexico 65265. **County population:** 25,887. **Classification:** Third class. **Assessed valuation:** $364,240,904. **Square miles:** 692. **Organized:** December 17, 1836. **Named for:** James H. Audrain, Missouri legislator.

Assessor, Melissa Maupin, (D), Audrain County Courthouse, 101 N. Jefferson, Rm. 106, Mexico 65265; (573) 473-5827; FAX (573) 581-2380; mmaupin@audraincounty.org

Clerk Circuit Court, Penny J. Creed Craghead, (D), Audrain County Courthouse, 101 N. Jefferson, Rm. 204, Mexico 65265; (573) 473-5840; FAX (573) 581-3237; penny.creed@courts.mo.gov

Clerk County Commission, Shelley Harvey, (D), Audrain County Courthouse, 101 N. Jefferson, Rm. 101, Mexico 65265; (573) 473-5820; FAX (573) 581-2380; sharvey@audraincounty.org

Collector of Revenue, Kate Becker, (R), Audrain County Courthouse, 101 N. Jefferson, Rm. 103, Mexico 65265; (573) 473-5824; FAX (573) 582-7221

Commissioner, Eastern District, Roger Young, (D), Audrain County Courthouse, 101 N. Jefferson, Rm. 102, Mexico 65265; (573) 473-5822; FAX (573) 581-2380; ryoung@audrain county.org

Commissioner, Western District, Thomas Groves, (D), Audrain County Courthouse, 101 N. Jefferson, Rm. 102, Mexico 65265; (573) 473-5822; FAX (573) 581-2380; tgroves@audrain county.org

Coroner, Todd Yager, (R), 425 S. Jefferson, Mexico 65265; (573) 581-5330

Presiding Commissioner, Steve Hobbs, (R), Audrain County Courthouse, 101 N. Jefferson, Rm. 102, Mexico 65265; (573) 473-5823; FAX (573) 581-2380; shobbs@audraincounty.org

Prosecuting Attorney, Jacob Shellabarger, (D), Audrain County Courthouse, 101 N. Jefferson, Rm. 306, Mexico 65265; (573) 473-5860; FAX (573) 473-5865; jshellabarger@audraincounty.org

Public Administrator, Connie J. Hagan, (D), Audrain County Courthouse, 101 N. Jefferson, Rm. 305, Mexico 65265; (573) 473-5891; chagan@audraincounty.org

Recorder of Deeds, Janis Deimeke, (R), Audrain County Courthouse, 101 N. Jefferson, Rm. 105, Mexico 65265; (573) 473-5830; FAX (573) 581-8087; jdeimeke@audraincounty.org

Sheriff, Stuart D. Miller, (D), Audrain County Jail, 1100 Littleby Rd., Mexico 65265; (573) 473-5801; FAX (573) 581-2924; stuart@audrain sheriff.org

Treasurer, Patty Meyers, (D), Audrain County Courthouse, 101 N. Jefferson, Rm. 104, Mexico 65265; (573) 473-5826; FAX (573) 581-2380; pmeyers@audraincounty.org

Barry County

County seat and zip code: Cassville 65625. **County population:** 35,662. **Classification:** Third class. **Assessed valuation:** $461,251,852. **Square miles:** 773. **Organized:** January 5, 1835. **Named for:** William T. Barry, U.S. Postmaster General.

Assessor, Sherry Sears, (R), Barry County Courthouse, 700 Main, Ste. 7, Cassville 65625; (417) 847-4589; FAX (417) 847-2377

Clerk Circuit Court and ex officio Recorder of Deeds, Craig Williams, (R), Barry County Judicial Center, 102 West St., Ste. 1, Cassville 65625; (417) 847-3133; FAX (417) 847-6298

Clerk County Commission, Gary Youngblood, (R), Barry County Courthouse, 700 Main, Ste. 2, Cassville 65625; (417) 847-2561; FAX (417) 847-5311; barrycountyclerk@centurytel.net

Collector of Revenue, Janice Varner, (R), Barry County Courthouse, 700 Main, Ste. 3, Cassville 65625; (417) 847-2113; FAX (417) 847-5045; barrycountycollector@centurytel.net

Commissioner, Northern District, Gary Schad, (R), Barry County Courthouse, 700 Main, Ste. 2, Cassville 65625; (417) 847-4628; FAX (417) 847-5311

Commissioner, Southern District, Wayne Hendrix, (D), Barry County Courthouse, 700 Main, Ste. 2, Cassville 65625; (417) 847-4628; FAX (417) 847-5311

Coroner, Jim Fohn, (R), PO Box 250, Cassville 65625; (417) 847-2141

County Health Department Director*, Roger Brock, PO Box 207, Cassville 65625; (417) 847-2114

County Surveyor*, Sam Goodman, (R), 3215 Lawrence 2217, Pierce City 65723; (417) 476-2206

Emergency Management Director*, David Compton, PO Box 34, Purdy 65734; (417) 737-1142

Presiding Commissioner, Cherry Warren, (R), Barry County Courthouse, 700 Main, Ste. 2, Cassville 65625; (417) 847-4628; FAX (417) 847-5311

Prosecuting Attorney, Amy Boxx, (R), Barry County Judicial Center, 102 West St., Ste. 4, Cassville 65625; (417) 847-3133; FAX (417) 847-5760

Public Administrator, Pam Modlin, (R), 102 West St., Ste. 5, Cassville 65625; (417) 847-2005; FAX (417) 847-2006

Sheriff, Mick Epperly, (R), 600 Mill St., Cassville 65625; (417) 847-6556; FAX (417) 847-6422

Treasurer, Lois Lowe, (R), Barry County Courthouse, 700 Main St., Ste. 5, Cassville 65625; (417) 847-2019; FAX (417) 847-2019

---

*Appointed

Barton County

County seat and zip code: Lamar 64759. **County population:** 12,057. **Classification:** Third class. **Assessed valuation:** $172,319,215. **Square miles:** 597. **Organized:** December 12, 1855. **Named for:** David Barton, United States Senator.

Assessor, Ivan Frieden, (R), Barton County Courthouse, 1004 Gulf, Rm. 109, Lamar 64759; (417) 682-3553; FAX (417) 681-0176

Clerk Circuit Court, Janet B. Maupin, (R), Barton County Courthouse, 1004 Gulf, Rm. 204, Lamar 64759; (417) 682-2444; FAX (417) 682-2960

Clerk County Commission, Kristina Crockett, (R), Barton County Courthouse, 1004 Gulf, Rm. 103, Lamar 64759; (417) 682-3529; FAX (417) 682-4100; bartoncountyclerk@ sbcglobal.net

Collector/Treasurer, Barba Parrish, (R), Barton County Courthouse, 1004 Gulf, Rm. 101, Lamar 64759; (417) 682-5881; FAX (417) 682-4136

Commissioner, District One, Dennis Wilson, (R), Barton County Courthouse, 1004 Gulf, Rm. 102, Lamar 64759; (417) 682-4110; FAX (417) 682-4100

Commissioner, District Two, Jeff Tucker, (R), Barton County Courthouse, 1004 Gulf, Rm. 102, Lamar 64759; (417) 682-4110; FAX (417) 682-4100

Coroner, C. Tucker Joustra, D.O., (R), 116 SE First Ln., Lamar 64759; (417) 682-5508

County Health Department Director, Linda Talbott, 1301 E. 12th, Lamar 64759; (417) 682-3363

Emergency Management Director, Tom Ryan, Barton County Courthouse, 1004 Gulf, Lamar 64759; (417) 682-1279

Presiding Commissioner, Mike Davis, (R), Barton County Courthouse, 1004 Gulf, Rm. 102, Lamar 64759; (417) 682-4110; FAX (417) 682-4100

Prosecuting Attorney, Steven H. Kaderly, (D), 114 W. Tenth, Lamar 64759; (417) 682-6061; FAX (417) 682-6063

Public Administrator, Teresa E. Moore, (R), Barton County Courthouse, 1004 Gulf, Rm. 201, Lamar 64759; (417) 682-5060; FAX (417) 682-4109

Recorder of Deeds, Kathleen Dimond, (R), Barton County Courthouse, 1004 Gulf, Rm. 107, Lamar 64759; (417) 682-2110; FAX (417) 682-4102

Sheriff, Mitchell (Mitch) Shaw, (R), 1010 Cherry St., Lamar 64759; (417) 682-5541; FAX (417) 682-5805

Bates County

County seat and zip code: Butler 64730. **County population:** 16,584. **Classification:** Third class. **Assessed valuation:** $212,745,689. **Square miles:** 849. **Organized:** January 29, 1841. **Named for:** Frederick Bates, Governor of Missouri.

Assessor, Roger Pruden, (D), Bates County Courthouse, 1 N. Delaware, Butler 64730; (660) 679-3157; FAX (660) 679-4935

Clerk Circuit Court, Diana L. Rich, (D), Bates County Courthouse, 1 N. Delaware, Butler 64730; (660) 679-5171; FAX (660) 679-4446

Clerk County Commission, Marlene Wainscott, (D), Bates County Courthouse, 1 N. Delaware, Butler 64730; (660) 679-3371; FAX (660) 679-9922; bates@sos.mo.gov

Collector/Treasurer, Jimmy Platt, (D), Bates County Courthouse, 1 N. Delaware, Butler 64730; (660) 679-3341; FAX (660) 679-9922

Commissioner, Northern District, Jim Scott, (D), Bates County Courthouse, 1 N. Delaware, Butler 64730; (660) 679-3371; FAX (660) 679-9922

Commissioner, Southern District, Larry Hacker, (D), Bates County Courthouse, 1 N. Delaware, Butler 64730; (660) 679-3371; FAX (660) 679-9922

Coroner, Gary Schowengerdt, (D), 1301 N. Orange, Butler 64730; (660) 679-6555; FAX (660) 679-5819

County Health Department Director, Jody Welston, 501 N. Orange, PO Box 208, Butler 64730; (660) 679-6108; FAX (660) 679-6022

County Surveyor and Engineer, W.C. Bill Lethcho, (D), Bates County Courthouse, 1 N. Delaware, Butler 64730; (660) 679-4031; FAX (660) 679-9922

Emergency Management Director, Ron Nissen, 108 E. Fort Scott, Butler 64730; (660) 200-2034; FAX (660) 200-2035

Presiding Commissioner, Jim Wheatley, (R), Bates County Courthouse, 1 N. Delaware, Butler 64730; (660) 679-3371; FAX (660) 679-9922

Prosecuting Attorney, Hugh C. Jenkins, (D), 1 N. Delaware, Butler 64730; (660) 679-4030; FAX (660) 679-4246

Public Administrator, Sharon Cumpton, (D), 108 E. Fort Scott, Butler 64730; (660) 220-7225

Recorder of Deeds, Lucille Mundey, (D), Bates County Courthouse, 1 N. Delaware, PO Box 186, Butler 64730; (660) 679-3611; FAX (660) 679-4935; mundeyrecorder@hotmail.com

Sheriff, Chad Anderson, (D), 6 W. Fort Scott, Butler 64730; (660) 679-3232; FAX (660) 679-4147

Benton County

County seat and zip code: Warsaw 65355. **County population:** 18,806. **Classification:** Third class. **Assessed valuation:** $247,067,804. **Square miles:** 729. **Organized:** January 3, 1835. **Named for:** Thomas Hart Benton, United States Senator.

Assessor, Rodger L. Reedy, (R), Benton County Courthouse, PO Box 40, Warsaw 65355; FAX (660) 438-5323; county.assessor@bentoncomo.com

Clerk Circuit Court, Cheryl Lutjen-Schultz, (R), Benton County Courthouse, PO Box 37, Warsaw 65355; (660) 438-7712; FAX (660) 438-5755

Clerk County Commission, Susan Porterfield, (R), Benton County Courthouse, 316 Van Buren St., PO Box 1238, Warsaw 65355; (660) 438-7326; FAX (660) 438-3275; county.clerk@bentoncomo.com

Collector of Revenue, Donna Hart, (D), Benton County Courthouse, PO Box 428, Warsaw 65355; (660) 438-7721; FAX (660) 438-2062; county.collector@bentoncomo.com

Commissioner, Northern District, Jim Hansen, (R), Benton County Courthouse, PO Box 1238, Warsaw 65355; (660) 438-7406; FAX (660) 438-3275; jim.hansen@bentoncomo.com

Commissioner, Southern District, Steve Daleske, (R), Benton County Courthouse, PO Box 1238, Warsaw 65355; (660) 438-7406; FAX (660) 438-3275; steve.daleske@bentoncomo.com

Coroner, J. Weston Miller, (R), PO Box 910, Warsaw 65355

County Health Department Director, Linda Viebrock, PO Box 935, Warsaw 65355; (660) 438-2876; FAX (660) 438-5476

County Surveyor, Jesse Wininger, (R), PO Box 790, Warsaw 65355; (660) 438-9473; FAX (660) 438-9574

Emergency Management Director, Bill Gant, 1231 Hirsch Pkwy., PO Box 852, Warsaw 65355; (660) 438-8412; FAX (660) 438-8413; bencoemd@bentoncomo.com

Presiding Commissioner, Michelle McLerran-Morgan, (R), Benton County Courthouse, PO Box 1238, Warsaw 65355; (660) 438-7406; FAX (660) 438-3275; county.commissioner@bentoncomo.com

Prosecuting Attorney, Karen Coffey Woodley, (R), Benton County Courthouse, PO Box 937, Warsaw 65355; (660) 438-5022; FAX (660) 438-9506; prosecutor@bentoncomo.com

Public Administrator, Lori Dunkin, (R), Benton County Courthouse, PO Box 219, Lincoln 65338; (660) 547-3041; FAX (660) 547-3719; public.admin@bentoncomo.com

Recorder of Deeds, Beverly Burnett, (R), Benton County Courthouse, PO Box 1147, Warsaw 65355; (660) 438-5732; FAX (660) 438-3652; county.recorder@bentoncomo.com

Sheriff, Rick Fajen, (R), Benton County Sheriff's Office, PO Box 67, Warsaw 65355; (660) 438-6135; FAX (660) 438-3053; county.sheriff@bentoncomo.com

Treasurer, Rick Renno, (R), Benton County Courthouse, PO Box 684, Warsaw 65355; (660) 438-6313; FAX (660) 438-3275; county.treasurer@bentoncomo.com

Bollinger County

County seat and zip code: Marble Hill 63764. **County population:** 12,394. **Classification:** Third class. **Assessed valuation:** $121,900,307. **Square miles:** 621. **Organized:** March 1, 1851. **Named for:** George F. Bollinger, pioneer settler and Missouri legislator.

Assessor, Ronda Elfrink, (R), Bollinger County Courthouse, 204 High St., Ste. 1, Marble Hill 63764; (573) 238-1900, ext. 1; FAX (573) 238-3275; bocoassessor@bocogov.com

Clerk Circuit Court, Jeaneal Vandeven, (R), Bollinger County Courthouse, 204 High St., Ste. 6, Marble Hill 63764; (573) 238-1900; FAX (573) 238-2773; janeal.vandeven@courts.mo.gov

Clerk County Commission, Brittany Hovis, (R), Bollinger County Courthouse, 204 High St., Ste. 5, Marble Hill 63764; (573) 238-1900; FAX (573) 238-3275; bollinger@sos.mo.gov

Collector of Revenue, Sonya Fulton, (R), Bollinger County Courthouse, 204 High St., Ste. 2, Marble Hill 63764; (573) 238-1900; FAX (573) 238-3275; bococollector@sbcglobal.net

Commissioner, First District, James Null, (R), Bollinger County Courthouse, 204 High St., Ste. 5, Marble Hill 63764; (573) 238-1900; FAX (573) 238-3275; bollinger@sos.mo.gov

Commissioner, Second District, Steve Jordan, (R), Bollinger County Courthouse, 204 High St., Ste. 5, Marble Hill 63764; (573) 238-1900; FAX (573) 238-3275; bollinger@sos.mo.gov

Coroner, Charles Hutchings, (R), 203 Bass St., Marble Hill 63764; (573) 238-3644

County Health Department Director, Juanita Welker, PO Box 409, Marble Hill 63764; (573) 238-2817; piepeb@lpha.dhss.mo.gov

County Surveyor, (Vacancy)

Emergency Management Director*, James D. Bollinger, PO Box 175, Marble Hill 63764; (573) 238-2600; jbllngr@clas.net

Presiding Commissioner, Travis M. Elfrink, (R), Bollinger County Courthouse, 204 High St., Ste. 5, Marble Hill 63764; (573) 238-1900; FAX (573) 238-3275; tmelfrink@hotmail.com

Prosecuting Attorney, Heath Robins, (R), 300 High St., PO Box 140, Marble Hill 63764; (573) 238-3223; FAX (573) 238-0433

Public Administrator, Larry L. Welker, (R), PO Box 38, Marble Hill 63764; (573) 238-3538

Recorder of Deeds, Dana Fulbright, (R), Bollinger County Courthouse, 204 High St., Ste. 7, Marble Hill 63764; (573) 238-1900; FAX (573) 238-3275

Sheriff, Darin Shell, (R), Bollinger County Sheriff's Dept., 202 High St., Marble Hill 63764; (573) 238-2633; FAX (573) 238-3095; sheriffdarinwshell@gmail.com

Treasurer, Naomi Null, (R), Bollinger County Courthouse, 204 High St., Ste. 8, Marble Hill 63764; (573) 238-1900; FAX (573) 238-3275; bcocot@hotmail.com

*Appointed

Boone County

County seat and zip code: Columbia 65201. **County population:** 172,717. **Classification:** First class. **Assessed valuation:** $2,548,292,445. **Square miles:** 687. **Organized:** November 16, 1820. **Named for:** Daniel Boone.

Assessor, Tom Schauwecker, (D), Boone County Government Center, 801 E. Walnut, Rm. 143, Columbia 65201; (573) 886-4270; FAX (573) 886-4254

Auditor, June E. Pitchford, (D), Boone County Government Center, 801 E. Walnut, Rm. 304, Columbia 65201; (573) 886-4275; FAX (573) 886-4280; jpitchford@boonecountymo.org

Clerk Circuit Court, Christy Blakemore, (D), Boone County Courthouse, 705 E. Walnut, Columbia 65201; (573) 886-4000; FAX (573) 886-4044; christy.blakemore@courts.mo.gov

Clerk County Commission, Wendy S. Noren, (D), Boone County Government Center, 801 E. Walnut, Rm. 236, Columbia 65201; (573) 886-4295; FAX (573) 886-4300; wnoren@boonecountymo.org

Collector of Revenue, Brian C. McCollum, (D), Boone County Government Center, 801 E. Walnut, Rm. 118, Columbia 65201; (573) 886-4285; FAX (573) 886-4294; bmccollum@boonecountymo.org

Commissioner, District I, Karen M. Miller, (D), Boone County Government Center, 801 E. Walnut, Rm. 333, Columbia 65201; (573) 886-4305; FAX (573) 886-4311; kmiller@boonecountymo.org

Commissioner, District II, Janet M. Thompson, (D), Boone County Government Center, 801 E. Walnut, Rm. 333, Columbia 65201; (573) 886-4305; FAX (573) 886-4311; jthompson@boonecountymo.org

Presiding Commissioner, Daniel Atwill, (D), Boone County Government Center, 801 E. Walnut, Rm. 333, Columbia 65201; (573) 886-4305; FAX (573) 886-4311; datwill@boonecounty.org

Prosecuting Attorney, Dan Knight, (D), Boone County Courthouse, 705 E. Walnut, Columbia 65201; (573) 886-4100; FAX (573) 886-4148; dknight@boonecountymo.org

Public Administrator, Cathy D. Richards, (D), Boone County Courthouse, 705 E. Walnut, PO Box 1307, Columbia 65201; (573) 886-4190; FAX (573) 886-4193; crichards@boonecountymo.org

Public Health and Human Services Director*, Stephanie Browning, 1005 W. Worley, PO Box 6015, Columbia 65205; (573) 874-7345; FAX (573) 874-7756; skbrowni@gocolumbiamo.org

Recorder of Deeds, Nora Dietzel, (D), Boone County Government Center, 801 E. Walnut, Rm. 132, Columbia 65201; (573) 886-4345; FAX (573) 886-4359; ndietzel@boonecounty mo.org

Sheriff, Robert Dwayne Carey, (D), 2121 County Dr., Columbia 65201; (573) 875-1111; FAX (573) 874-8953; dcarey@boone countymo.org

Treasurer*, Thomas D. Darrough, (D), 801 E. Walnut, Rm. 205, Columbia 65201; (573) 886-4365; FAX (573) 886-4369

*Appointed

Buchanan County

County seat and zip code: St. Joseph 64501. **County population:** 89,486. **Classification:** First class. **Assessed valuation:** $1,260,377,946. **Square miles:** 409. **Organized:** December 31, 1838. **Named for:** James Buchanan, senator from Pennsylvania and later U.S. President.

Assessor, Scot W. Van Meter, (D), Buchanan County Courthouse, 411 Jules, Rm. 222, St. Joseph 64501; (816) 271-1469; FAX (816) 271-1410; svanmeter@co.buchanan.mo.us

Auditor, Tara Horn, (R), Buchanan County Courthouse, 411 Jules, Rm. 133, St. Joseph 64501; (816) 271-1408; FAX (816) 271-1434; nnash@co.buchanan.mo.us

Clerk Circuit Court, Mary Beattie, (D), Buchanan County Courthouse, 411 Jules, Rm. 331, St. Joseph 64501; (816) 271-1462; FAX (816) 271-1538; mary.beattie@courts.mo.gov

Clerk County Commission, Mary Baack Garvey, (R), Buchanan County Courthouse, 411 Jules, Rm. 121, St. Joseph 64501; (816) 271-1411; FAX (816) 271-1535; mgarvey@co.buchanan. mo.us

Collector of Revenue, Peggy Campbell, (D), Buchanan County Courthouse, 411 Jules, Rm. 123, St. Joseph 64501; (816) 271-1401; FAX (816) 271-1584; pcampbell@co.buchanan. mo.us

Commissioner, Eastern District, Dan Hausman, (R), Buchanan County Courthouse, 411 Jules, Rm. 101, St. Joseph 64501; (816) 271-1501; FAX (816) 271-1569; dhausman@ co.buchanan.mo.us

Commissioner, Western District, Ron Hook, (D), Buchanan County Courthouse, 411 Jules, Rm. 101, St. Joseph 64501; (816) 271-1501; FAX (816) 271-1569; rhook@co.buchanan.mo.us

Emergency Management Director*, Bill Brinton, Buchanan County Courthouse, 411 Jules, Rm. 102, St. Joseph 64501; (816) 271-1574; FAX (816) 901-1604; bbrinton@co.buchanan. mo.us

Medical Examiner*, Adam Wineinger, Med Clinic, 401 Illinois Ave., St. Joseph 64504; (816) 238-9355

Presiding Commissioner, Harry Roberts, (R), Buchanan County Courthouse, 411 Jules, Rm. 101, St. Joseph 64501; (816) 271-1503; FAX (816) 271-1569; turner@co.buchanan.mo.us

Prosecuting Attorney, Dwight K. Scroggins Jr., (D), Buchanan County Courthouse, 411 Jules, Rm. 132, St. Joseph 64501; (816) 271-1480; FAX (816) 271-1521; dscroggins@ co.buchanan.mo.us

Public Administrator, Bill McMurray, (D), 310 N. Fourth St., Ste. A, St. Joseph 64501; (816) 271-1442; FAX (816) 271-1563; bmcmurray@ co.buchanan.mo.us

Purchasing Agent*, Kim Hartman, Buchanan County Courthouse, 411 Jules, Rm. 101-B, St. Joseph 64501; (816) 271-1512; FAX (816) 271-1569; khartman@co.buchanan.mo.us

Recorder of Deeds, Ed Wildberger, (D), Buchanan County Courthouse, 411 Jules, Rm. 103, St. Joseph 64501; (816) 271-1437; FAX (816) 271-1582; ewildberger@co.buchanan.mo.us

Sheriff, Mike Strong, (D), Buchanan County Law Enforcement Center, 501 Faraon St., St. Joseph 64501; (816) 236-8812; FAX (816) 901-1758; mstrong@co.buchanan.mo.us

Treasurer, John D. Nash, (D), Buchanan County Courthouse, 411 Jules, Rm. 112, St. Joseph 64501; (816) 271-1432; FAX (816) 271-1543; jnash@co.buchanan.mo.us

*Appointed

Butler County

County seat and zip code: Poplar Bluff 63901. **County population:** 42,972. **Classification:** Third class. **Assessed valuation:** $544,049,869. **Square miles:** 698. **Organized:** February 27, 1849. **Named for:** William O. Butler, a Kentucky congressman.

Assessor, Marion Tibbs, (R), Butler County Courthouse, 100 N. Main, Rm. 201, Poplar Bluff 63901; (573) 686-8084

Clerk Circuit Court*, Cindi Bowman, (R), Butler County Courthouse, 100 N. Main, Rm. 301 A, Poplar Bluff 63901; (573) 686-8082; FAX (573) 686-8094

Clerk County Commission, Tonyi Deffendall, (R), Butler County Courthouse, 100 N. Main, Rm. 202, Poplar Bluff 63901; (573) 686-8050; FAX (573) 686-8066; tdbutler@tcmax.net

Collector of Revenue, Emily Clark-Parks, (R), Butler County Courthouse, 100 N. Main, Poplar Bluff 63901; (573) 686-8088

Commissioner, Eastern District, Don Anderson, (R), Butler County Courthouse, 100 N. Main, Rm. 203, Poplar Bluff 63901; (573) 686-8081; FAX (573) 686-8066; butch@tcmax.net

Commissioner, Western District, Jeffrey Darnell, (R), Butler County Courthouse, 100 N. Main, Rm. 203, Poplar Bluff 63901; (573) 686-8081; FAX (573) 686-8066

Coroner, Jim Akers, (R), Butler County Courthouse, 100 N. Main St., Poplar Bluff 63901; (573) 686-7884

County Health Department Director, Robert Hudson, 1619 N. Main, Poplar Bluff 63901; (573) 785-8478

Emergency Management Director, Jeff Shawan, 218C N. Broadway, Poplar Bluff 63901; (573) 686-8686

Presiding Commissioner, Vince Lampe, (R), Butler County Courthouse, 100 N. Main, Rm. 203, Poplar Bluff 63901; (573) 686-8081; FAX (573) 686-8066

Prosecuting Attorney, Kevin Barbour, (R), Office of the Prosecuting Attorney, 106 S. Second St., Poplar Bluff 63901; (573) 686-8060; FAX (573) 686-8077

Public Administrator, Sharron Payne, (R), Butler County Courthouse, 100 N. Main, Poplar Bluff 63901; (573) 686-8078

Recorder of Deeds, Debby Lundstrom, (R), Butler County Courthouse, 100 N. Main, Poplar Bluff 63901; (573) 686-8086

Sheriff, Mark L. Dobbs, (R), Butler County Justice Center, 200 Oak St., Poplar Bluff 63901; (573) 785-8444; (573) 686-8058

Treasurer, Joe Humphrey, (R), Butler County Courthouse, 100 N. Main, Poplar Bluff 63901; (573) 686-8083

*Appointed

Caldwell County

County seat and zip code: Kingston 64650. **County population:** 9,034. **Classification:** Third class. **Assessed valuation:** $141,166,233. **Square miles:** 431. **Organized:** December 29, 1836. **Named for:** John Caldwell, Indian scout.

Assessor, Beverly Alden, (R), Caldwell County Courthouse, 49 E. Main St., PO Box 85, Kingston 64650; (816) 586-5261; FAX (816) 586-3600; cassessor@centurytel.net

Clerk Circuit Court, Carrie Miller, (D), Caldwell County Courthouse, 49 E. Main St., PO Box 68, Kingston 64650; (816) 586-2581; FAX (816) 586-2333; carrie.miller@courts.mo.gov

Clerk County Commission, Beverly Bryant, (D), Caldwell County Courthouse, 49 E. Main St., PO Box 67, Kingston 64650; (816) 586-2571; FAX (816) 586-3001; countyclerk@centurytel.net

Commissioner, Eastern District, Donald Raymond Cox, (D), Caldwell County Courthouse, 49 E. Main St., PO Box 67, Kingston 64650; (816) 586-2571; FAX (816) 586-3001; county clerk@centurytel.net

Commissioner, Western District, Gerald McBrayer, (R), Caldwell County Courthouse, 49 E. Main St., PO Box 67, Kingston 64650; (816) 586-2571; FAX (816) 586-3001; county clerk@centurytel.net

Coroner, Dana Brown, (R), 208 E. School, Hamilton 64644; (816) 583-7405

County Health Department Director, Shelley Reed, (R), 275 S. Washington, PO Box 66, Kingston 64650; (816) 586-2311; FAX (816) 586-2603

Emergency Management Director, George Pease, 200 E. Walnut, Hamilton 64644; (816) 583-2456

Presiding Commissioner, C.R. (Bud) Motsinger, (R), Caldwell County Courthouse, 49 E. Main St., PO Box 67, Kingston 64650; (816) 586-2571; FAX (816) 586-3001; countyclerk@centurytel.net

Prosecuting Attorney, Brady C. Kopek, (R), Caldwell County Courthouse, 49 E. Main St., PO Box 8, Kingston 64650; (816) 586-2511; FAX (816) 586-3084

Public Administrator, Richard Lee, (R), 408 N. Ewing, Hamilton 64644; (816) 583-2086

Recorder of Deeds, Julie Hill, (R), Caldwell County Courthouse, 49 E. Main St., PO Box 65, Kingston 64650; (816) 586-3080; FAX (816) 586-1252; corecorder@centurytel.net

Sheriff, Jerry Galloway, (R), Caldwell County Sheriff's Office, 54 N. Franklin, PO Box 156, Kingston 64650; (816) 586-2681 or (816) 586-2751; FAX (816) 586-2103

Treasurer and ex *officio* Collector of Revenue, June Grooms, (R), Caldwell County Courthouse, 49 E. Main St., PO Box 127, Kingston 64650; (816) 586-2781; FAX (816) 586-1260; cctreasurer@centurytel.net

Callaway County

County seat and zip code: Fulton 65251. **County population:** 44,750. **Classification:** First class. **Assessed valuation:** $802,701,708. **Square miles:** 842. **Organized:** November 25, 1820.

Named for: James Callaway, Missouri ranger killed by Indians in the War of 1812.

Assessor, Jodie Paschal, (R), Callaway County Courthouse, 10 E. Fifth St., Fulton 65251; (573) 642-0766; FAX (573) 642-7929; assessor.gis@callawaycounty.org

Auditor, Karen Rentschler, (R), Callaway County Courthouse, 10 E. Fifth St., Fulton 65251; (573) 642-0727; FAX (573) 642-0744; krentschler@callawaycounty.org

Clerk Circuit Court, Judy O. Groner, (R), Callaway County Courthouse, 10 E. Fifth St., Fulton 65251; (573) 642-0780 or (573) 642-0777; FAX (573) 642-0700; judy.groner@courts.mo.gov

Clerk County Commission, Denise Hubbard, (R), Callaway County Courthouse, 10 E. Fifth St., Fulton 65251; (573) 642-0730; FAX (573) 642-7181; deniseh@callawaycounty.org

Collector of Revenue, Pam J. Oestreich, (D), Callaway County Courthouse, 10 E. Fifth St., Fulton 65251; (573) 642-0747; FAX (573) 642-7929; calltaxs@callawaycounty.org

Commissioner, Eastern District, Randall L. Kleindienst, (R), Callaway County Courthouse, 10 E. Fifth St., Fulton 65251; (573) 642-0737; FAX (573) 642-1032; comish@callawaycounty.org

Commissioner, Western District, Donald (Doc) Kritzer, (R), Callaway County Courthouse, 10 E. Fifth St., Fulton 65251; (573) 642-0737; FAX (573) 642-1032; comish@callawaycounty.org

County Health Department Director, Sharon Lynch, 4950 County Rd. 304, Fulton 65251; (573) 642-6881; FAX (573) 642-2098; lynch@lpha.mopublic.org

Emergency Management Director, Michelle Kidwell, 1201 State Rd. O, Fulton 65251; (573) 592-2480; FAX (573) 592-2481; michelle kidwell@cceoc.org

Medical Examiner, Carl C. Stacy, 1 Hospital Dr., Medical Science Bldg., Rm. M236, Columbia 65212; (573) 474-2700; FAX (573) 474-2764

Presiding Commissioner, Gary Jungermann, (R), Callaway County Courthouse, 10 E. Fifth St., Fulton 65251; (573) 642-0737; FAX (573) 642-1032; comish@callawaycounty.org

Prosecuting Attorney, Christopher Wilson, (R), Callaway County Courthouse, 10 E. Fifth St., Fulton 65251; (573) 642-0714; FAX (573) 642-5725; calpacw@callawaycounty.org

Public Administrator, Karen Digh, (D), 10 W. Sixth St., Fulton 65251; (573) 642-0720

Recorder of Deeds, Christine Kleindienst, (R), Callaway County Courthouse, 10 E. Fifth St., PO Box 406, Fulton 65251; (573) 642-0787; FAX (573) 642-1491; christinek@callawaycounty.org

Sheriff, Dennis Crane, (D), Callaway County Law Enforcement Center, PO Box 817, 1201 State Rd. O, Fulton 65251; (573) 592-2454; FAX (573) 592-2440; denniscrane@cceoc.org

Treasurer, Debbie Zerr, (R), Callaway County Courthouse, 10 E. Fifth St., Fulton 65251; (573) 642-0770; dzerr@callawaycounty.org

Camden County

County seat and zip code: Camdenton 65020. **County population:** 44,021. **Classification:** First class. **Assessed valuation:** $1,603,679,878. **Square miles:** 641. **Organized:** January 29, 1841. **Named for:** Charles Pratt, Earl of Camden.

Assessor, Edward Whitworth, (D), 1 Court Circle NW, Ste. 6, Camdenton 65020; (573) 317-3820; FAX (573) 317-3964; eddie_whitworth@camdenmo.org

Auditor, Ronald Capps, (R), 1 Court Circle NW, Ste. 7, Camdenton 65020; (573) 317-3825; FAX (573) 346-2399; ronnie_capps@camdenmo.org

Clerk Circuit Court, Jo McElwee, (R), 1 Court Circle NW, Ste. 8, Camdenton 65020; (573) 317-3900; FAX (573) 346-5422; jo.mcelwee@courts.mo.gov

Clerk County Commission, Rowland Todd, (R), 1 Court Circle NW, Ste. 2, Camdenton 65020; (573) 317-3890; FAX (573) 346-8445; rowland_todd@camdenmo.org

Collector of Revenue, Vicky Burns, (R), 1 Court Circle NW, Ste. 4, Camdenton 65020; (573) 317-3800; FAX (573) 346-4263; vicky_burns@camdenmo.org

Commissioner, First District, Beverly Thomas, (R), 1 Court Circle NW, Ste. 1, Camdenton 65020; (573) 317-3850; FAX (573) 346-5181; beverly_thomas@camdenmo.org

Commissioner, Second District, Cliff Luber, (R), 1 Court Circle NW, Ste. 1, Camdenton 65020; (573) 317-3850; FAX (573) 346-5181; cliff_luber@camdenmo.org

County Health Department Director, Bryant Burton, 1976 N. State Hwy. 5, Camdenton 65020; (573) 346-5479; FAX (573) 346-0173; burtob@lpha.dhss.mo.gov

Emergency Management Director, Denise Russell, 1 Court Circle NW, Ste. 1, Camdenton 65020; (573) 346-7108; FAX (573) 346-5736; denise.russell@camdencomoema.org

Presiding Commissioner, Greg Hasty, (R), 1 Court Circle NW, Ste. 1, Camdenton 65020; (573) 317-3850; FAX (573) 346-5181; greg_hasty@camdenmo.org

Prosecuting Attorney, Michael J. Gilley, (R), 1 Court Circle NW, Ste. 10, Camdenton 65020; (573) 317-3910; FAX (573) 346-0823; michael_gilley@camdenmo.org

Public Administrator, Nancy A. Douglas, (R), 1 Court Circle NW, Ste. 11, Camdenton 65020; (573) 317-3930; FAX (573) 346-6029; nancy_douglas@camdenmo.org

Recorder of Deeds, Donnie Snelling, (R), 1 Court Circle NW, Ste. 5, Camdenton 65020; (573) 317-3880; FAX (573) 346-8367; donnie_snelling@camdenmo.org

Sheriff, Dwight Franklin, (R), 1 Court Circle NW, Ste. 13, Camdenton 65020; (573) 346-2243; FAX (573) 346-2513; d_franklin@camdenmo.org

Treasurer, Elaine Gilley, (R), 1 Court Circle NW, Ste. 3, Camdenton 65020; (573) 317-3870; FAX (573) 346-2399; elaine_gilley@camdenmo.org

Cape Girardeau County

County seat and zip code: Jackson 63755. **County population:** 78,043. **Classification:** First class. **Assessed valuation:** $1,211,114,411. **Square miles:** 577. **Organized:** October 1, 1812. **Named for:** Sieur de Girardot, a French officer.

Assessor, Bob Adams, (R), Cape Girardeau County Administration Bldg., 1 Barton Sq., Ste. 201, Jackson 63755; (573) 243-2468; FAX (573) 204-2525; badams@capecounty.us

Auditor, Eugene (Pete) Frazier III, (R), Cape Girardeau County Administration Bldg., 1 Barton Sq., Ste. 304, Jackson 63755; (573) 243-2184; FAX (573) 204-2465; pfrazier@capecounty.us

Clerk Circuit Court, Patti Wibbenmeyer, (R), Jackson Courthouse, 100 Court St., Ste. 301, Jackson 63755; (573) 243-1755; FAX (573) 204-2405; patti.wibbenmeyer@courts.mo.gov

Clerk County Commission, Kara Clark Summers, (R), Cape Girardeau County Administration Bldg., 1 Barton Sq., Ste. 301, Jackson 63755; (573) 243-3547; FAX (573) 204-2418; kclark@capecounty.us

Collector of Revenue, Diane Diebold, (R), Cape Girardeau County Administration Bldg., 1 Barton Sq., Ste. 303, Jackson 63755; (573) 243-4476; FAX (573) 204-2444; collector@capecounty.us

Commissioner, First District, Paul Koeper, (R), Cape Girardeau County Administration Bldg., 1 Barton Sq., Jackson 63755; (573) 243-1052; FAX (573) 204-2493; commish@capecounty.us

Commissioner, Second District, Charles J. Herbst III, (R), Cape Girardeau County Administration Bldg., 1 Barton Sq., Jackson 63755; (573) 243-1052; FAX (573) 204-2493; commish@capecounty.us

Coroner, John Clifton, (R), PO Box 1773, Cape Girardeau 63702; (573) 270-8558 or (573) 243-3551; FAX (573) 332-8592; jaclifton@charter.net

County Health Department Director*, Jane Wernsman, 1121 Linden, PO Box 1839, Cape Girardeau 63702; (573) 335-7846; FAX (573) 335-5909; wernsp@lpha.mopublic.org

Emergency Management/911 Director*, Richard Knaup, Cape Girardeau County Administration Bldg., 1 Barton Sq., Ste. 102, Jackson 63755; (573) 204-0911; FAX (573) 204-2949; rknaup@capecounty.us

Highway Administrator*, Scott Bechtold, Cape Girardeau County Administration Bldg., 1 Barton Sq., Jackson 63755; (573) 243-5270; FAX (573) 204-2552; msbechtold@capecounty.us

Information Technology Director*, Eric McGowen, Cape Girardeau County Administration Bldg., 1 Barton Sq., Jackson 63755; (573) 243-5303; FAX (573) 204-2949; emcgowen@capecounty.us

Park Department*, Superintendent, Bryan Sander, 2400 County Park Dr., Cape Girardeau 63701; (573) 335-4146; FAX (573) 334-7529; countypark@capecounty.us

Presiding Commissioner, Clint Tracy, (R), Cape Girardeau County Administration Bldg., 1 Barton Sq., Jackson 63755; (573) 243-1052; FAX (573) 204-2493; commish@capecounty.us

Prosecuting Attorney, Christopher K. Limbaugh, (R), 100 Court St., Jackson 63755; (573) 243-2430; FAX (573) 204-2318; cklimbaugh@capecounty.us

Public Administrator, Lisa Reitzel, (R), Cape Girardeau County Administration Bldg., 1 Barton Sq., Ste. 301, Jackson 63755; (573) 204-2340; FAX (573) 243-5011; ljreitzel@capecounty.us

Public Works Director*, Don McQuay, Cape Girardeau County Administration Bldg., 1 Barton Sq., Jackson 63755; (573) 243-8619; FAX (573) 204-2418;

Recorder of Deeds, Andrew David Blattner, (R), Cape Girardeau County Administration Bldg., 1 Barton Sq., Ste. 203, Jackson 63755; (573) 243-8123; FAX (573) 204-2477; adblattner@capecounty.us

Sheriff, John D. Jordan, (R), Cape Girardeau County Sheriff's Office, 216 N. Missouri St.,

Jackson 63755; (573) 243-3551; FAX (573) 204-2927; sjjs01@clas.net

Treasurer, Roger L. Hudson, (R), Cape Girardeau County Administration Bldg., 1 Barton Sq., Ste. 302, Jackson 63755; (573) 243-3720; FAX (573) 204-2465; rlhudson@capecounty.us

---

*Appointed

Carroll County

County seat and zip code: Carrollton 64633. **County population:** 9,043. **Classification:** Third class Township. **Assessed valuation:** $212,785,668. **Square miles:** 695. **Organized:** January 2, 1833. **Named for:** Charles Carroll of Carrollton.

Assessor, Devin Rae Frazier, (R), Carroll County Courthouse, 8 S. Main, Ste. 4, Carrollton 64633; (660) 542-2184; FAX (660) 542-3491; assessor@carrollcomo.org

Clerk Circuit Court and *ex officio* Recorder of Deeds, Cheryl A. Mansur, (R), Carroll County Courthouse, 8 S. Main, Ste. 3, PO Box 245, Carrollton 64633; (660) 542-1466; FAX (660) 542-1444; cheryl.mansur@courts.mo.gov

Clerk County Commission, Peggy McGaugh, (R), Carroll County Courthouse, 8 S. Main, Ste. 6, Carrollton 64633; (660) 542-0615; FAX (660) 542-0621; countyclerk@carrollcomo.org

Collector-Treasurer, Alta M. O'Neal, (D), Carroll County Courthouse, 8 S. Main, Ste. 2, Carrollton 64633; (660) 542-1977; FAX (660) 542-0895; treascollector@carrollcomo.org

Commissioner, District 1, Bill Boelsen, (R), Carroll County Courthouse, 8 S. Main, Ste. 6, Carrollton 64633; (660) 542-0615; FAX (660) 542-0621; countyclerk@carrollcomo.org

Commissioner, District 2, David Martin, (R), Carroll County Courthouse, 8 S. Main, Ste. 6, Carrollton 64633; (660) 542-0615; FAX (660) 542-0621; countyclerk@carrollcomo.org

Coroner, Steven W. Bittiker, (R), PO Box 223, Carrollton 64633; (660) 542-2011; FAX (660) 542-2014; bittikerfuneralhomes@mediacombb.net

County Health Department Director, Roberta Hartwig, 5 N. Ely, Carrollton 64633; (660) 542-3247; harwr@ltha.mopublic.com

County Surveyor, Marcus J. Magee, (R), Carroll County Courthouse, 8 S. Main, Carrollton 64633; (660) 542-3310; msurveyllc@sbcglobal.net

Emergency Management Director Assistant, Chrissy Aldredge, 106 S. Folger, Carrollton 64633; (660) 542-1121; FAX (660) 542-1539; chrissya4@hotmail.com

Presiding Commissioner, Nelson Heil, (R), Carroll County Courthouse, 8 S. Main, Ste. 6, Carrollton 64633; (660) 542-0615; FAX (660) 542-0621; countyclerk@carrollcomo.org

Prosecuting Attorney, Cassandra Brown, (D), Carroll County Courthouse, 8 S. Main, Ste. 5, Carrollton 64633; (660) 542-0323; FAX (660) 542-0464; ccpa@carrollcomo.org

Public Administrator, Linda Leabo, (R), Carroll County Courthouse, 8 S. Main, Ste. 7, Carrollton 64633; (660) 542-3276; rleabo@greenhill.net

Sheriff, Troy Hofstetter, (R), 106 S. Folger, Carrollton 64633; (660) 542-2828 or (660) 542-1121; FAX (660) 542-1539; sheriff@carrollcountyso.org

Carter County

County seat and zip code: Van Buren 63965. **County population:** 6,258. **Classification:** Third class. **Assessed valuation:** $60,684,148. **Square miles:** 509. **Organized:** March 10, 1859. **Named for:** Zimri A. Carter, pioneer settler.

Assessor, George Meyers, (D), Carter County Courthouse, 105 Main St., PO Box 429, Van Buren 63965; (573) 323-4709; FAX (573) 323-4527

Clerk Circuit Court, Mary Godsy, (R), Carter County Courthouse, 105 Main St., PO Box 578, Van Buren 63965; (573) 323-4513; FAX (573) 323-4885

Clerk County Commission, Leona Stephens, (R), Carter County Courthouse, 105 Main St., PO Box 517, Van Buren 63965; (573) 323-4527; FAX (573) 323-4527; carter@sos.mo.gov

Collector of Revenue*, Lisa Goodwin, (D), Carter County Courthouse, 105 Main St., PO Box 445, Van Buren 63965; (573) 323-4708; FAX (573) 323-4527

Commissioner, Eastern District, Eddie Ballard, (D), Carter County Courthouse, 105 Main St., RR 1, Box 125, Ellsinore 63937; (573) 323-4527; FAX (573) 323-4527

Commissioner, Western District, Lynn Murdick, (D), Carter County Courthouse, 105 Main St., PO Box 876, Van Buren 63965; (573) 323-4527; FAX (573) 323-4527

Coroner, Erik McSpadden, (D), PO Box 298, Van Buren 63965; (573) 323-4222

County Health Department Director*, Debbie Sandarciero, PO Box 70, Van Buren 63965; (573) 323-4413; FAX (573) 323-8703

Emergency Management Director*, Justin Eudaley, PO Box 817, Van Buren 63965; (573) 323-4510

Presiding Commissioner, Donald Black, (R), Carter County Courthouse, 105 Main St., PO Box 117, Van Buren 63965; (573) 323-4527; FAX (573) 323-4527

Prosecuting Attorney, Ernie Richardson, (D), 504 Main St., PO Box 456, Van Buren 63965; (573) 323-8933; FAX (573) 323-8933; cartercountypa@gmail.com

Public Administrator, Mary Jo Sanders, (D), PO Box 514, Van Buren 63965; (573) 323-4650

Recorder of Deeds, Pauline Peterman, (D), Carter County Courthouse, 105 Main St., PO Box 1107, Van Buren 63965; (573) 323-9656; FAX (573) 323-4885

Sheriff, Richard Stephens, (R), Carter County Ustice Center, 15 Syamore St., PO Box 817, Van Buren 63965; (573) 323-4510; FAX (573) 323-8271

Treasurer, Velvet Ricker, (R), Carter County Courthouse, 105 Main St., PO Box 32, Van Buren 63965; (573) 323-8271

---

*Appointed

Cass County

County seat and zip code: Harrisonville 64701. **County population:** 100,889. **Classification:** First class. **Assessed valuation:** $1,426,288,925. **Square miles:** 702. **Organized:** March 3, 1835. **Named for:** Lewis Cass, Michigan senator and presidential candidate.

Assessor, Bob Huston, (R), 2733 Cantrell Rd., Harrisonville 64701; (816) 380-8154; FAX (816) 380-8171; bobh@casscounty.com

Associate Commissioner, District 1, Luke Scavuzzo, (D), Cass County Courthouse, 102 E. Wall St., Harrisonville 64701; (816) 380-8158; FAX (816) 380-8156; lukes@casscounty.com

Associate Commissioner, District 2, Jimmy Odom, (R), Cass County Courthouse, 102 E. Wall St., Harrisonville 64701; (816) 380-8159; FAX (816) 380-8156; jimmyo@casscounty.com

Auditor, Ryan Wescoat, (R), Cass County Courthouse, 102 E. Wall St., Harrisonville 64701; (816) 380-8213; FAX (816) 380-8191; ryanw@casscounty.com

Clerk Circuit Court, Kim York, (R), Cass County Justice Center, 2501 W. Mechanic St., Harrisonville 64701; (816) 380-8234; FAX (816) 380-8225; kim.york@courts.mo.gov

Clerk County Commission, Michael Vinck, (R), Cass County Courthouse, 102 E. Wall St., Harrisonville 64701; (816) 380-8109; FAX (816) 380-8101; mikev@casscounty.com

Collector of Revenue, Pam Shipley, (D), 2725 Cantrell Rd., Harrisonville 64701; (816) 380-8376; FAX (816) 380-8375; pams@casscounty.com

County Health Department Administrator, Tiffany Klassen, 300 S. Main St., Harrisonville 64701; (816) 380-8427; FAX (816) 380-8450; klasst@lpha.mopublic.org

Emergency Management Director, Stan Swaggart, Cass County Courthouse, 2501 W. Mechanic St., Harrisonville 64701; (816) 380-8125; stans@casscounty.com

Medical Examiner*, Dr. Mary Dudley, 660 E. 24th St., Hospital Hill, Kansas City 64108; (816) 881-6600; FAX (816) 881-6641; medexaminer@jacksongov.org

Presiding Commissioner, Jeff Cox, (R), Cass County Courthouse, 102 E. Wall St., Harrisonville 64701; (816) 380-8160; FAX (816) 380-8156; jeffc@casscounty.com

Prosecuting Attorney, Ben Butler, (R), Cass County Justice Center, 2501 W. Wall St., Harrisonville 64701; (816) 380-8260; FAX (816) 380-8252; benb@casscounty.com

Public Administrator, Melody Folsom, (R), Cass County Justice Center, 2501 W. Wall St., Harrisonville 64701; (816) 380-8787; FAX (816) 380-8785; casspub@casscounty.com

Recorder of Deeds, Mike Medsker, (R), Cass County Courthouse, 102 E. Wall St., Harrisonville 64701; (816) 380-8120; FAX (816) 380-4086; mikem@casscounty.com

Sheriff, Dwight E. Diehl, (R), Cass County Sheriff's Office, 2501 W. Wall St., Harrisonville 64701; (816) 380-8305; FAX (816) 380-8558; 600@casscounty.com

Treasurer, Steve Cheslik, (R), Cass County Courthouse, 102 E. Wall St., Harrisonville 64701; (816) 380-8105; FAX (816) 380-8101; stevec@casscounty.com

---

*Appointed

Cedar County

County seat and zip code: Stockton 65785. **County population:** 13,952. **Classification:** Third class. **Assessed valuation:** $161,773,519. **Square miles:** 471. **Organized:** February 14, 1845. **Named for:** Its abundance of cedar trees. **Website:** www.cedarcountymo.gov

Assessor, Chad E. Pyle, (R), Cedar County Courthouse, 113 South St., PO Box 580, Stockton 65785; (417) 276-6700, ext. 259; FAX (417) 276-2207; assessor@cedarcountymo.gov

Clerk Circuit Court, Melinda Gumm, (R), Cedar County Courthouse, 113 South St., PO Box 665, Stockton 65785; (417) 276-6700, ext. 230; (417) 276-5001; melindagumm@courts.mo.gov

Clerk County Commission, Peggy Kenney, (R), Cedar County Courthouse, 113 South St., Stockton 65785; (417) 276-6700, ext. 221; FAX (417) 276-3461; peggykclerk@yahoo.com

Collector of Revenue, Joan Haines, (R), Cedar County Courthouse, 113 South St., PO Box 280, Stockton 65785; (417) 276-6700, ext. 224; FAX (417) 276-4658; joanhaines@windstream.net

Commissioner, Northern District, Don Boultinghouse, (R), Cedar County Courthouse, 113 South St., Stockton 65785; (417) 276-6700, ext. 221; FAX (417) 276-3461; commission@cedarcountymo.gov

Commissioner, Southern District, John A. Fox, (R), Cedar County Courthouse, 113 South St., Stockton 65785; (417) 276-6700, ext. 221; FAX (417) 276-3461; commission@cedarcountymo.gov

Coroner, C. W. Bill Neale, (R), PO Box 327, El Dorado Springs 64744; (417) 876-4124

County Health Department Director, Linda Mann, Community Services, 1317 S. Hwy. 32, El Dorado Springs 64744; (417) 876-5477; FAX (417) 876-5017

Emergency Management Director*, Arlo Rupke, PO Box 235, Stockton 65785; (417) 276-1134; FAX (417) 276-3461; cedarcountyoem@live.com

Presiding Commissioner, Marlon Collins, (R), Cedar County Courthouse, 113 South St., Stockton 65785; (417) 276-6700, ext. 221; FAX (417) 276-3461; commission@cedarcountymo.gov

Prosecuting Attorney, Ty Gaither, (R), Cedar County Courthouse, 113 South St., Stockton 65785; (417) 276-6700, ext. 236; FAX (417) 276-7739

Public Administrator*, Charlotte Haden, (D), Cedar County Courthouse, 113 South St., Stockton 65785; (417) 276-6700, ext. 265; FAX (417) 276-4588; publicadmin@cedarcountymo.gov

Recorder of Deeds, Carole Wilkerson, (R), Cedar County Courthouse, 113 South St., Stockton 65785; (417) 276-6700, ext. 246; FAX (417) 276-5499; recorder@cedarcountymo.gov

Sheriff, Leon Dwerlkotte, (R), Cedar County Law Enforcement Facility, 202 S. High St., Stockton 65785; (417) 276-5133; FAX (417) 276-5135; ldwerlkotte@cedarcountysheriff.com

Surveyor, Charles (Mark) Francis, Cedar County Courthouse, 113 South St., Stockton 65785; (417) 276-6700, ext. 261; FAX (417) 276-3461

Treasurer, Ronnie Miller, (R), Cedar County Courthouse, 113 South St., Stockton 65785; (417) 276-6700, ext. 245; cecotreasurer@windstream.net

---

*Appointed

Chariton County

County seat and zip code: Keytesville 65261. **County population:** 7,694. **Classification:** Third class. **Assessed valuation:** $224,983,871. **Square miles:** 758. **Organized:** November 16, 1820. **Named for:** The Chariton River.

Assessor, Darrin E. Gladbach, (D), Chariton County Courthouse, 306 S. Cherry St., Keytesville 65261; (660) 288-3873; FAX (660) 288-1503; countyassessor@centurytel.net

Clerk Circuit Court and ex officio Recorder of Deeds, Eric Stallo, (D), Chariton County Courthouse, 306 S. Cherry St., Keytesville 65261; (660) 288-3602; FAX (660) 288-3763; eric.stallo@courts.mo.gov

Clerk County Commission, Susan Littleton, (D), Chariton County Courthouse, 306 S. Cherry St., Keytesville 65261; (660) 288-3273; FAX (660) 288-3403; charitonclerk@centurytel.net

Collector/Treasurer, Darlene Shipp, (D), Chariton County Courthouse, 306 S. Cherry St., Keytesville 65261; (660) 288-3789; FAX (660) 288-2041; countytreasurer@centurytel.net

Commissioner, Eastern District, Steve Atkinson, (D), Chariton County Courthouse, 306 S. Cherry St., Keytesville 65261; (660) 288-3200; FAX (660) 288-3403

Commissioner, Western District, Danny Price, (D), Chariton County Courthouse, 306 S. Cherry St., Keytesville 65261; (660) 288-3200; FAX (660) 288-3403

Coroner, Larry Breshears, (D), 207 W. Broadway, Brunswick 65236; (660) 548-3222; FAX (660) 548-3224

County Health Department Administrator, Carrie Scheid, 206 State St., PO Box 214, Keytesville 65261; (660) 288-3675; FAX (660) 288-3725; schelc@lpha.mopublic.org

Emergency 911 Director, Chris Brown, PO Box 15, Keytesville 65261; (660) 288-3460; FAX (660) 288-3462

Emergency Management Director, Eric McKenzie, 306 S. Cherry St., Keytesville 65261; (660) 973-0353; FAX (660) 288-3403; eric_mckenzie 86@hotmail.com

Presiding Commissioner, Tony McCollum, (D), Chariton County Courthouse, 306 S. Cherry St., Keytesville 65261; (660) 288-3200; FAX (660) 288-3403

Prosecuting Attorney, Robert W. Wheeler, (I), Chariton County Courthouse, 306 S. Cherry St., Keytesville 65261; (660) 288-3275; FAX (660) 288-1415; charitoncopa1@gmail.com

Public Administrator*, Sherry Hershey, (D), Chariton County Courthouse, 306 S. Cherry St., Keytesville 65261; (660) 288-3336; FAX (660) 288-3403; charitoncopa@yahoo.com

Sheriff, Chris Hughes, (D), Chariton County Courthouse, 307 S. Cherry St., Keytesville 65261; (660) 288-3277; FAX (660) 288-3612

*Appointed

Christian County

County seat and zip code: Ozark 65721. **County population:** 82,101. **Classification:** First class. **Assessed valuation:** $1,066,547,443. **Square miles:** 564. **Organized:** March 8, 1859. **Named for:** William Christian, Kentucky Revolutionary War soldier.

Assessor, Danny Gray, (R), Christian County Courthouse, 100 W. Church, Rm. 301, Ozark 65721; (417) 582-4310; FAX (417) 581-3029; assessor@christiancountymo.gov

Clerk Circuit Court, Barb Stillings, (R), Christian County Judicial Center, 110 W. Elm, Rm. 202, Ozark 65721; (417) 581-5120; FAX (417) 581-0391; barb.stillings@courts.mo.gov

Clerk County Commission, Kay Brown, (R), Christian County Courthouse, 100 W. Church, Rm. 206, Ozark 65721; (417) 582-4340; FAX (417) 581-8331; kaybrown@christian countymo.gov

Collector of Revenue, Ted Nichols, (R), Christian County Courthouse, 100 W. Church, Rm. 206, Ozark 65721; (417) 582-4330; FAX (417) 582-1463; tnichols@christiancounty mo.gov

Commissioner, Eastern District*, Sue Ann Childers, (R), Christian County Courthouse, 100 W. Church, Rm. 100, Ozark 65721; (417) 582-4300; FAX (417) 581-5924; countycommission @christiancountymo.gov

Commissioner, Western District, Bill Barnett, (R), Christian County Courthouse, 100 W. Church, Rm. 100, Ozark 65721; (417) 582-4300; FAX (417) 581-5924; countycommission@ christiancountymo.gov

Coroner*, Amanda M. Armitage, (R), Christian County Courthouse, 100 W. Church, Rm. 100, Ozark 65721; (417) 840-2950; FAX (417) 724-3206; coronerchristiancounty@ hotmail.com

County Auditor, Lacey Hart, (R), Christian County Courthouse, 100 W. Church, Rm. 209, Ozark 65721; (417) 582-4368; FAX (417) 581-9948; lhart@christiancounty mo.gov

County Health Department Director*, Cindy Bilyeu, 301 E. Brick St., PO Box 340, Ozark 65721; (417) 581-7285; FAX (417) 581-6130; bilyeuc@lpha.mopublic.org

County Surveyor, Loyd E. Todd, (R), PO Box 365, Ozark 65721; (417) 581-2187; FAX (417) 581-4085; toddsurveying@msn.com

Emergency Management Director*, Phil Amtower, Christian County Courthouse, 100 W. Church, Rm. 100, Ozark 65721; (417) 582-5400; FAX (417) 582-5420; phila69682@ aol.com

Presiding Commissioner, Ray Weter, (R), Christian County Courthouse, 100 W. Church, Rm. 100, Ozark 65721; (417) 582-4300; FAX (417) 581-5924; countycommission @christiancountymo.gov

Prosecuting Attorney, Amy Fite, (R), Christian County Judicial Center, 110 W. Elm, Rm. 109, Ozark 65721; (417) 582-5180; FAX (417) 581-7918; afite@christiancountymo.gov

Public Administrator, Ken Davis, (R), Christian County Courthouse, 100 W. Church, Rm. 207, Ozark 65721; (417) 582-4370; FAX (417) 581-3254; kendavis@christiancounty mo.gov

Recorder of Deeds, Kelly Hall, (R), Christian County Courthouse, 100 W. Church, Rm. 104, Ozark 65721; (417) 582-4360; FAX (417) 581-9943; khallrecorder@christian countymo.gov

Interim Sheriff, Dwight McNeil, Christian County Judicial Center, 110 W. Elm, Rm. 70, Ozark 65721; (417) 582-5330; FAX (417) 581-1641; jkyle@christiancountymo.gov

Treasurer, Karen Matthews, (R), Christian County Courthouse, 100 W. Church, Rm. 209, Ozark 65721; (417) 582-4348; FAX (417) 581-1191; karenmatthews@christiancountymo.gov

*Appointed

Clark County

County seat and zip code: Kahoka 63445. **County population:** 6,917. **Classification:** Third class. **Assessed valuation:** $102,991,927. **Square miles:** 507. **Organized:** December 16, 1836. **Named for:** William Clark, Governor of the Missouri Territory.

Assessor*, Anthony R. Daniel, (D), 111 E. Court St., Ste. 120, Kahoka 63445; (660) 727-3023; FAX (660) 727-2544

Clerk Circuit Court, Kimberly Schantz, (R), 111 E. Court St., Ste. 210, Kahoka 63445; (660) 727-3292; FAX (660) 727-1051

Clerk County Commission, Jena Church, (R), 111 E. Court St., Ste. 110, Kahoka 63445; (660) 727-3282; FAX (660) 727-1088; clark@sos. mo.gov

Collector of Revenue, Michelle Allen, (R), 111 E. Court St., Ste. 140, Kahoka 63445; (660) 727-3787; FAX (660) 727-3788

Commissioner, Eastern District, Henry W. Dienst, (R), 111 E. Court St., Ste. 110, Kahoka 63445; (660) 727-3283; FAX (660) 727-1088

Commissioner, Western District, Paul V. Brotherton, (D), 111 E. Court St., Ste. 110, Kahoka 63445; (660) 727-3283; FAX (660) 727-1088

Coroner, Edwin Wilson, (R), 975 E. Main, Kahoka 63445; (660) 727-2117; FAX (660) 727-3743

Presiding Commissioner, Buddy Kattelmann, (R), 111 E. Court St., Ste. 110, Kahoka 63445; (660) 727-8241

Prosecuting Attorney, Holly Conger, (R), 111 E. Court St., Ste. 20, Kahoka 63445; (660) 727-2616; FAX (660) 727-2617

Public Administrator, Gloria Hodges, (R), RR 2, Box 2215, Wyaconda 63474; (660) 341-0160

Recorder of Deeds, Melissa Bevans, (R), 111 E. Court St., Ste. 130, Kahoka 63445; (660) 727-8261

Sheriff, Paul Gaudette, (R), 518 N. Lincoln, Ste. 1, Kahoka 63445; (660) 341-0160

Treasurer, Roberta McAfee, (R), 111 E. Court St., Ste. 150, Kahoka 63445; (660) 727-3272; FAX (660) 727-1088

*Appointed

Clay County

County seat and zip code: Liberty 64068. **County population:** 233,682. **Classification:** First class. **Assessed valuation:** $3,810,273,656. **Square miles:** 403. **Organized:** January 2, 1822. **Named for:** Henry Clay, Kentucky congressman.

Airport Transportation Manager, Duane Jackson, 13106 Rhodus Rd., Excelsior Springs 64024; (816)628-2286;FAX(816)628-2204;djackson@ claycountymo.gov

Assessor, Cathy Rinehart, (D), 1 Courthouse Sq., Liberty 64068; (816) 407-3502; FAX (816) 407-3501; crinehart@claycountymo.gov

Auditor, Carol McCaslin, (R), 1 Courthouse Sq., Liberty 64068; (816) 407-3592; FAX (816) 407-3591; cmccaslin@claycountymo.gov

Clerk Circuit Court, Stephen Haymes, Clay County Courthouse, 11 S. Water St., Liberty 64068; (816) 407-3901; FAX (816) 407-3888; stephen.haymes@courts.mo.gov

Clerk County Commission, Megan Thompson, (R), 1 Courthouse Sq., Liberty 64068; (816) 407-3572; FAX (816) 407-3571; megan. thompson@claycountymo.gov

Collector of Revenue, Lydia McEvoy, (R), 1 Courthouse Sq., Liberty 64068; (816) 407-3202; FAX (816) 407-3201; lmcevoy@ claycountymo.gov

Commissioner, Eastern District, Luann Ridgeway, (R), 1 Courthouse Sq., Liberty 64068; (816) 407-3613; FAX (816) 407-3601; lridgeway@claycountymo.gov

Commissioner, Western District, Gene Owen, (D), 1 Courthouse Sq., Liberty 64068; (816) 407-3612; FAX (816) 407-3601; gowen@ claycountymo.gov

County Administrator, Dean Brookshier, 1 Courthouse Sq., Liberty 64068; (816) 407-3622; FAX (816) 407-3601; dbrookshier@ claycountymo.gov

County Counselor, Kevin Graham, 11 E. Kansas St., Liberty 64068; (816) 792-0500; FAX (816) 781-6843; kevin@flookandgraham.com

County Counselor Assistant, Timothy Flook, 11 E. Kansas St., Liberty 64068; (816) 792-0500; FAX (816) 781-6843; tim@flookandgraham. com

Emergency Management Director, Eric Ramsey, Clay County Courthouse, 11 S. Water St., Liberty 64068; (816) 407-3732; FAX (816) 407-3731; eramsey@claycountymo.gov

Facilities Director, Donna Koontz, 115 S. Main, Liberty 64068; (816) 407-3333; FAX (816) 407-3321; dkoontz@claycountymo.gov

Highway Administrator, Karl Walters, 16616 N.E. 116th St., Kearney 64060; (816) 407-3306; FAX (816) 407-3301; kwalters@ claycountymo.gov

Human Resources Director, Laurie Bonk, 1 Courthouse Sq., Liberty 64068; (816) 407-3662; FAX (816) 407-3661; lbonk@ claycountymo.gov

Information Technology Director, Kevin Shaw, 34 W. Shrader, Ste. B, Kansas City 64068; (816) 407-3340; FAX (816) 407-3351; kshaw@ claycountymo.gov

Medical Examiner, Mary H. Dudley, M.D., 660 E. 24th St., Kansas City 64108; (816) 881-6608; FAX (816) 404-1345; mdudley@jackson gov.org

Parks and Recreation, *Assistant County Administrator-Facilities,* Donna Koontz, One Courthouse Square, Liberty, 64068; dkoontz@claycountymo.gov. *Assistant County Administrator-Operations,* Karl Walters, One Courthouse Square, Liberty, 64068; kwalters@claycountymo.gov

Planning and Zoning Director, Matt Tapp, 234 W. Shrader, Ste. C, Liberty 64068; (816) 407-3382; FAX (816) 407-3381; mtapp@ claycountymo.gov

Presiding Commissioner, Jerry Nolte, (R), 1 Courthouse Sq., Liberty 64068; (816) 407-3611; FAX (816) 407-3601; jnolte@ claycountymo.gov

Prosecuting Attorney, Dan White, (D), Clay County Courthouse, 11 S. Water St., Liberty 64068; (816) 407-8302; FAX (816) 407-8301; daniel_white@claycopa.com

Public Administrator, Debbie L. Gwin, (D), Clay County Courthouse, 11 S. Water St., Liberty 64068; (816) 407-3252; FAX (816) 407-3251; dgwin@circuit7.net

Public Health Center Director, Gary Zaborac, 800 Haynes Dr., Liberty 64068; (816) 595-4200; FAX (816) 792-1285; gzaborac@clay health.com

Recorder of Deeds, Katee Porter, (R), 1 Courthouse Sq., Liberty 64068; (816) 407-3552; FAX (816) 407-3601; kporter@claycountymo.gov

Sheriff, Paul Vescovo, (R), Clay County Courthouse, 11 S. Water St., Liberty 64068; (816) 407-3752; FAX (816) 407-3751; pvescovo@ sheriffclayco.com

Treasurer, Ted Graves, (R), 1 Courthouse Sq., Liberty 64068; (816) 407-3542; FAX (816) 407-3541; tgraves@claycountymo.gov

Clinton County

County seat and zip code: Plattsburg 64477. **County population:** 20,299. **Classification:** Third class. **Assessed valuation:** $281,663,056. **Square miles:** 423. **Organized:** January 2, 1833. **Named for:** DeWitt Clinton, Governor of New York.

Assessor, Jerry Howard, (D), Clinton County Courthouse, 207 N. Main, PO Box 436, Plattsburg 64477; (816) 539-3716; FAX (816) 539-3097

Clerk Circuit Court and *ex officio* Recorder of Deeds, Molly Livingston, (D), Clinton County Courthouse, 207 N. Main, PO Box 275, Plattsburg 64477; (816) 539-3731; FAX (816) 539-3893; molly.livingston@courts.mo.gov

Clerk County Commission, Mary Blanton, (D), Clinton County Courthouse, 207 N. Main, Rm. 103, Plattsburg 64477; (816) 539-3713; FAX (816) 539-3072; mblanton@centurytel. net

Collector of Revenue, Michele Wells, (R), Clinton County Courthouse, 207 N. Main, PO Box 334, Plattsburg 64477; (816) 539-3726; FAX (816) 539-2240

Commissioner, First District, Charles Dawson, (R), Clinton County Courthouse, 207 N. Main, Rm. 102, Plattsburg 64477; (816) 539-2536; FAX (816) 539-3072

Commissioner, Second District, Larry King, (D), Clinton County Courthouse, 207 N. Main, Rm. 102, Plattsburg 64477; (816) 539-2536; FAX (816) 539-3072

Coroner, Kathleen M. Little, (R), 118 Lakeview Dr., Plattsburg 64477; (816) 632-9362

County Health Department Director*, Blair Shock, 106 Bush Hwy., Plattsburg 64477; (816) 539-2144; FAX (816) 539-3306; shockb@lpha.mopublic.org

County Highway Engineer*, Doug Williams, Clinton County Courthouse, 207 N. Main, Plattsburg 64477; (816) 539-2932; FAX (816) 539-3622

Emergency Management Director*, Blair Shock, Clinton County Courthouse, 207 N. Main, Plattsburg 64477; (816) 244-8925; FAX (816) 539-3072; blair.shock@clintoncomo.org

Presiding Commissioner, Wade Wilken Jr., (R), Clinton County Courthouse, 207 N. Main, Rm. 102, Plattsburg 64477; (816) 539-2536; FAX (816) 539-3072; cccomm@centurytel.net

Prosecuting Attorney, Joe Gagnon, (D), Clinton County Courthouse, 207 N. Main, PO Box 285, Plattsburg 64477; (816) 539-3711; FAX (816) 539-3026

Public Administrator, Nancy D. Wingate, (D), 6437 NE Crouch Rd., Turney 64493; (816) 592-0177

Sheriff, K. Porter Hensen, (D), Clinton County Courthouse, 207 N. Main, Rm. 106, Plattsburg 64477; (816) 539-3777; FAX (816) 539-2346

Treasurer, Leann Gump, (D), Clinton County Courthouse, 207 N. Main, Rm. 113, Plattsburg 64477; (816) 539-3724; FAX (816) 539-2240; clcotreas@centurytel.net

---

*Appointed

Cole County

County seat and zip code: Jefferson City 65101. **County population:** 76,699. **Classification:** First class. **Assessed valuation:** $1,346,326,600. **Square miles:** 400. **Organized:** November 16, 1820. **Named for:** Stephen Cole, pioneer settler and Indian fighter.

Assessor, Chris Estes, (R), Carnegie Bldg., 210 Adams St., Jefferson City 65101; (573) 634-9131; FAX (573) 634-9139

Auditor, Kristen Berhorst, (R), Cole County Courthouse Annex, 311 E. High St., Rm. 301, Jefferson City 65101; (573) 634-9123; FAX (573) 634-7797

Clerk Circuit Court, Dawnel Davidson, (R), Cole County Courthouse, 301 E. High St., Rm. 200, PO Box 1870, Jefferson City 65101; (573) 634-9150; FAX (573) 635-0796

Clerk County Commission, Steve Korsmeyer, (R), Cole County Courthouse Annex, 311 E. High St., Rm. 201, Jefferson City 65101; (573) 635-2542; FAX (573) 681-9678; skorsmeyer@colecounty.org

Collector of Revenue, Larry Vincent, (R), Cole County Courthouse Annex, 311 E. High St., Rm. 100, Jefferson City 65101; (573) 634-9124; FAX (573) 634-9060

Commissioner, Eastern District, Jeff Hoelscher, (R), Cole County Courthouse Annex, 311 E. High St., Rm. 200, Jefferson City 65101; (573) 634-9112; FAX (573) 634-8031

Commissioner, Western District, Kris Scheperle, (R), Cole County Courthouse Annex, 311 E. High St., Rm. 200, Jefferson City 65101; (573) 634-9111; FAX (573) 634-8031

Coroner, Carl R. Doerhoff, M.D., 1705 Christy Dr., Jefferson City 65101; (573) 659-5500

County Health Department Director*, Kristi Campbell, 1616 Industrial Dr., Jefferson City 65109; (573) 636-2181; FAX (573) 636-3851

County Highway Engineer*, Eric Landwehr, 5055 Monticello Rd., Jefferson City 65109; (573) 636-3614; FAX (573) 636-8389

Director of Public Works*, Larry Benz, 5055 Monticello Rd., Jefferson City 65109; (573) 636-3614; FAX (573) 636-8389

Emergency Management Director*, Bill Farr, 1736 Southridge Dr., Jefferson City 65109; (573) 634-9146; FAX (573) 634-5666

Presiding Commissioner, Sam Bushman, (R), Cole County Courthouse Annex, 311 E. High St., Rm. 200, Jefferson City 65101; (573) 634-9113; FAX (573) 634-8031

Prosecuting Attorney, Mark Richardson, (R), Cole County Courthouse Annex, 311 E. High St.,

Rm. 300, Jefferson City 65101; (573) 634-9180; FAX (573) 634-7797

Public Administrator, Marilyn Schmutzler, (D), 301 E. High St., Rm. 404, Jefferson City 65101; (573) 634-9199; (573) 634-6275

Recorder of Deeds, Ralph Bray, (R), Cole County Courthouse Annex, 311 E. High St., Rm. 101, Jefferson City 65101; (573) 634-9115; FAX (573) 634-4631

Sheriff, Greg White, (R), 350 E. High St., PO Box 426, Jefferson City 65102; (573) 634-9160; FAX (573) 634-2336

Treasurer, Eric Peters, (R), 301 E. High St., Rm. 306, Jefferson City 65101; (573) 634-9121; FAX (573) 634-8257

---

*Appointed

Cooper County

County seat and zip code: Boonville 65233. **County population:** 17,585. **Classification:** Third class. **Assessed valuation:** $235,108,160. **Square miles:** 566. **Organized:** December 17, 1818. **Named for:** Sarshal and Benjamin Cooper, pioneer settlers.

Assessor, James R. Lachner, (R), Cooper County Courthouse, 200 Main St., Rm. 22, Boonville 65233; (660) 882-2646; FAX (660) 882-2640; assessor@coopercountymo.gov

Clerk Circuit Court and *ex officio* **Recorder of Deeds*,** Nancy Fisher, (R), Cooper County Courthouse, 200 Main St., Rm. 26, Boonville 65233; (660) 882-2232; FAX (660) 882-2043; nancy.fisher@courts.mo.gov; Recorder's office: (660) 882-2161; FAX (660) 882-2155

Clerk County Commission, Darryl Kempf, (D), Cooper County Courthouse, 200 Main St., Rm. 23, Boonville 65233; (660) 882-2114; FAX (660) 882-5645; darryl.k@coopercountymo.gov

Collector of Revenue*, Diana Thomas, (D), Cooper County Courthouse, 200 Main St., Rm. 27, Boonville 65233; (660) 882-2584; FAX (660) 882-9058; collector@coopercountymo.gov

Commissioner, Eastern District, Paul Davis, (R), Cooper County Courthouse, 200 Main St., Rm. 24, Boonville 65233; (660) 882-2228; FAX (660) 882-5645; paul.davis@coopercountymo.gov

Commissioner, Western District, David Booker, (R), Cooper County Courthouse, 200 Main St., Rm. 24, Boonville 65233; (660) 882-2228; FAX (660) 882-5645; david.booker@coopercountymo.gov

Coroner, James Hurt, (R), 220 Mohawk, Boonville 65233; (660) 882-7532; jameshurt31@yahoo.com

County Health Department Director, Melanie Hutton, 17040 Klinton Dr., Boonville 65233; (660) 882-2626; FAX (660) 882-2586

Emergency Management Director, Tom White, 200 Main St., Ste. 911, Boonville 65233; (660) 882-2614; FAX (660) 882-7908; ema@classicnet.net

Presiding Commissioner, Don Baragary, (R), Cooper County Courthouse, 200 Main St., Rm. 24, Boonville 65233; (660) 882-2228; FAX (660) 882-5645; don.baragary@coopercountymo.gov

Prosecuting Attorney, Douglas Abele, (R), United Missouri Bank Bldg., 422 E. Spring St., Boonville 65233; (660) 882-7577; FAX (660) 882-6621; douglasabele@gmail.com

Public Administrator, Stephanie Young, (R), 200 Main St., Rm. 25, Boonville 65233; (660) 882-5022; FAX (660) 882-6675; publicadministrator@coopercountymo.gov

Sheriff, Jerry Wolfe, (R), Cooper County Courthouse, 200 Main St., Rm. 33, Boonville 65233; (660) 882-2771; FAX (660) 882-7075; jerry.wolfe@coopercountymo.gov

Treasurer, Marcia Imhoff, (R), Cooper County Courthouse, 200 Main St., Rm. 21, Boonville 65233; (660) 882-0451; FAX (660) 882-5645; marcia.imhoff@coopercountymo.gov

---

*Appointed

Crawford County

County seat and zip code: Steelville 65565. **County population:** 24,696. **Classification:** Third class. **Assessed valuation:** $269,702,812. **Square miles:** 744. **Organized:** January 23, 1829. **Named for:** William H. Crawford, Secretary of War.

Assessor, Kerry Summers Sr., (R), 101 Third St., PO Box 149, Steelville 65565; (573) 775-2065; crawassr@misn.com

Clerk Circuit Court, Karen R. Harlan, (R), Crawford County Courthouse, 302 W. Main St., PO Box 1550, Steelville 65565; (573) 775-2866; FAX (573) 775-2452

Clerk County Commission, John G. Martin, (R), Crawford County Courthouse, 302 W. Main St., PO Box AS, Steelville 65565; (573) 775-2376; FAX (573) 775-3066; crawford@sos.mo.gov

Collector of Revenue, Pat Schwent, (R), 101 Third St., PO Box 250, Steelville 65565; (573) 775-2845; FAX (573) 775-4295; collector@misn.com

Commissioner, First District, Paul Watson, (R), Crawford County Courthouse, 302 W. Main St., PO Box AS, Steelville 65565; (573) 775-3539; FAX (573) 775-3066; crawford@sos.mo.gov

Commissioner, Second District, Kenny Killeen, (R), Crawford County Courthouse, 302 W. Main St., PO Box AS, Steelville 65565; (573) 775-3539; FAX (573) 775-3066; crawford@sos.mo.gov

Coroner, Paul Hutson, (R), PO Box 306, Steelville 65565; (573) 775-4250; FAX (573) 775-3339; pkhutson@misn.com

County Health Department Director, Kimberly Smith, PO Box 367, Steelville 65565; (573) 775-2555

County Surveyor, Mark Mueller, (R), 140 Merrihills Dr., Cuba 65453; (573) 885-6811; FAX (573) 885-2593; mueller01@centurytel.net

Emergency Management Director, Scott Cason, 61 E. Hwy. 8, Steelville 65565; (573) 775-4911

Presiding Commissioner, Leo Sanders, (R), Crawford County Courthouse, 302 W. Main St., PO Box AS, Steelville 65565; (573) 775-3539; FAX (573) 775-3066; crawford@sos.mo.gov

Prosecuting Attorney, J. Kent Howald, (R), Crawford County Courthouse, 302 W. Main St., PO Box 486, Steelville 65565; (573) 775-2326; ccpa@misn.com

Public Administrator, Franky Todd, (R), Crawford County Courthouse, 302 W. Main St., PO Box 1429, Steelville 65565; (573) 775-3440; FAX (573) 775-4177; crawfordcopa@hotmail.com

Recorder of Deeds, Kimberly A. Cook, (R), Crawford County Courthouse, 302 W. Main St., PO Box 236, Steelville 65565; (573) 775-5048; FAX (573) 775-3365; recorder@misn.com

Sheriff, Randy Martin, (R), 212 Third St., PO Box BE, Steelville 65565; (573) 775-2125; FAX (573) 775-2126; ccsd@misn.com

Treasurer, Catie Ringeisen, (R), Crawford County Courthouse, 302 W. Main St., PO Box 484, Steelville 65565; (573) 775-2897; treasurer@misn.com

Dade County

County seat and zip code: Greenfield 65661. **County population:** 7,628. **Classification:** Third class. **Assessed valuation:** $109,071,372. **Square**

miles: 491. **Organized:** January 29, 1841. **Named for:** Francis L. Dade, pioneer settler.

Assessor, Annette Black, (R), Dade County Courthouse, 300 W. Water St., Greenfield 65661; (417) 637-2224; FAX (417) 637-2224

Clerk Circuit Court, Mary McGee, (R), Dade County Courthouse, 300 W. Water St., Greenfield 65661; (417) 637-2271; FAX (417) 637-5055

Clerk County Commission, Melinda Wright, (R), Dade County Courthouse, 300 W. Water St., Greenfield 65661; (417) 637-2724; FAX (417) 637-1006; dade@sos.mo.gov

Commissioner, Eastern District, Dallas Maxwell, (R), Dade County Courthouse, 300 W. Water St., Greenfield 65661; (417) 637-2724; FAX (417) 637-1006

Commissioner, Western District, David Rusch, (R), Dade County Courthouse, 300 W. Water St., Greenfield 65661; (417) 637-2724; FAX (417) 637-1006

Coroner, Gary Banta, (I), 520 S. Main, Greenfield 65661; (417) 637-2071

County Health Department Director*, Pamela Allen, 413 W. Water St., Greenfield 65661; (417) 637-2345; FAX (417) 637-2507

Emergency Management Director*, Bob Kitsmiller, 300 W. Water St., Greenfield 65661; (417) 637-5322

Presiding Commissioner, Randy Daniel, (R), Dade County Courthouse, 300 W. Water St., Greenfield 65661; (417) 637-2724; FAX (417) 637-1006

Prosecuting Attorney*, Gary Troxell, (R), 8 S. Main, PO Box 126, Greenfield 65661; (417) 637-2121

Public Administrator, Chrissy Welch, (R), 300 W. Water, Greenfield 65661; (417) 637-6076

Recorder of Deeds, Carolyn Kile, (R), Dade County Courthouse, 300 W. Water St., Greenfield 65661; (417) 637-5373

Sheriff, Max Huffman, (R), 201 E. Water, Greenfield 65661; (417) 637-2312; FAX (417) 637-2508

Surveyor*, Justin Hunt, (R), 300 W. Water St., Greenfield 65661; FAX (417) 637-2724

Treasurer and Collector of Revenue, Rod O'Connor, (R), Dade County Courthouse, 300 W. Water St., Greenfield 65661; (417) 637-2732

---

*Appointed

Dallas County

County seat and zip code: Buffalo 65622. **County population:** 16,389. **Classification:** Third class. **Assessed valuation:** $157,621,569. **Square miles:** 543. **Organized:** January 29, 1841. **Named for:** George M. Dallas, diplomat and later vice president.

Assessor, Sue Doty, (R), Dallas County Administration Bldg., 102 S. Cedar, PO Box 263, Buffalo 65622; (417) 345-8774; FAX (417) 345-1752; dcassess1@centurytel.net

Clerk Circuit Court, Susan Potter, (R), Dallas County Courthouse, PO Box 373, Buffalo 65622; (417) 345-2243; FAX (417) 345-5539; susan.potter@courts.mo.gov

Clerk County Commission, Stephanie Hendricks, (R), Dallas County Administration Bldg., 102 S. Cedar, PO Box 436, Buffalo 65622; (417) 345-2632; FAX (417) 345-5321; dallas@sos.mo.gov

Collector of Revenue, Sheryl Ferrell, (R), Dallas County Administration Bldg., 102 S. Cedar, PO Box 529, Buffalo 65622; (417) 345-7836; FAX (417) 345-4997; dccoll1@centurytel.net

Commissioner, Northern District, Rex (Pete) Barclay, (R), Dallas County Administration Bldg., 102 S. Cedar, PO Box 436, Buffalo 65622; (417) 345-2632; FAX (417) 345-5321

Commissioner, Southern District, Owen Kjar, (R), Dallas County Administration Bldg., 102 S. Cedar, PO Box 436, Buffalo 65622; (417) 345-2632; FAX (417) 345-5321

Coroner, Lamont Swanson, (R), 112 W. Kennedy Blvd., Buffalo 65622; (417) 345-8785

County Health Department Director*, Cheryl Eversole, 1001 W. Main St., PO Box 199, Buffalo 65622; (417) 345-2332; FAX (417) 345-2025

County Surveyor, Greg Maynard, (R), 193 Bison Rd., Buffalo 65622; (417) 345-7623

Emergency Management Director*, Jason Wendlandt, PO Box 436, Buffalo 65622; (417) 752-3203; FAX (417) 345-5321; jasewend19@live.com

Presiding Commissioner, Kevin D. Sharpe, (R), Dallas County Administration Bldg., 102 S. Cedar, PO Box 436, Buffalo 65622; (417) 345-2632; FAX (417) 345-5321

Prosecuting Attorney, Barbara J. Viets, (R), 119 E. Main St., PO Box 20, Buffalo 65622; (417) 345-5644; FAX (417) 345-5561; bviets@positech.net

Public Administrator, Carol Johnson, (R), PO Box 1497, Buffalo 65622; (417) 345-5899; FAX (417) 345-5899; dallascopubad@yahoo.com

Recorder of Deeds, Stacy Satterfield, (R), Dallas County Courthouse, PO Box 406, Buffalo 65622; (417) 345-2242; FAX (417) 345-2230; ddallas000@centurytel.net

Sheriff, Mike Rackley, (R), Dallas County Detention Center, 204 S. Poplar St., PO Box 405, Buffalo 65622; (417) 345-2441

Treasurer, Becky Schofield, (R), Dallas County Administration Bldg., 102 S. Cedar, PO Box 605, Buffalo 65622; (417) 345-2020; FAX (417) 345-5321; dallas024@centurytel.net

---

*Appointed

Daviess County

County seat and zip code: Gallatin 64640. **County population:** 8,297. **Classification:** Third class. **Assessed valuation:** $121,735,069. **Square miles:** 568. **Organized:** December 29, 1836. **Named for:** Joseph H. Daviess, Kentucky soldier in the War of 1812.

Assessor, Betty Harmison, (R), Daviess County Courthouse, 102 N. Main, First Fl., Gallatin 64640; (660) 663-3300

Clerk Circuit Court, Pam Howard, (D), Daviess County Courthouse, 102 N. Main, PO Box 337, Gallatin 64640; (660) 663-2532; FAX (660) 663-2646; pam.howard@courts.mo.gov

Clerk County Commission, Vicki J. Corwin, (D), Daviess County Courthouse, 102 N. Main, Ste. 5, Gallatin 64640; (660) 663-2641; FAX (660) 663-3075; daviess@sos.mo.gov

Collector/Treasurer, Reta J. Rains, (D), Daviess County Courthouse, 102 N. Main, Ste. 1, Gallatin 64640; (660) 663-2432; FAX (660) 663-9270; daviesscocoltreas@windstream.net

Commissioner, District 1, David Cox, (D), Daviess County Courthouse, 102 N. Main, Gallatin 64640; (660) 663-2641; daviesscounty@windstream.net

Commissioner, District 2, Carl Carder, (D), Daviess County Courthouse, 102 N. Main, Gallatin 64640; (660) 663-2641; daviesscounty@windstream.net

Coroner, David W. McWilliams, (D), 1329 W. Grand St., Gallatin 64640; (660) 663-2117

County Health Department Director, Cheryl Alexander, 609 S. Main St., Gallatin 64640; (660) 663-2414

Emergency Management Director, Randy Sims, Daviess County Courthouse, 102 N. Main, Ste. 4, Gallatin 64640; (660) 749-5856; daviesscounty@windstream.net

Presiding Commissioner, Randy Sims, (R), Daviess County Courthouse, 102 N. Main, Gallatin 64640; (660) 663-2641; daviesscounty@windstream.net

Prosecuting Attorney, Andrea (Annie) Gibson, (D), Daviess County Courthouse, 102 N. Main, Gallatin 64640; (660) 663-4129; FAX (660) 663-3374; daviesscountypa@gmail.com

Public Administrator, Linda S. Houghton, Daviess County Courthouse, 102 N. Main, Gallatin 64640; (660) 663-4160

Recorder of Deeds, Jane McKinsey, (D), 102 N. Main, PO Box 132, Gallatin 64640; (660) 663-3183; FAX (660) 663-3376; dcrecorder@windstream.net

Sheriff, Ben Becerra, (D), Daviess County Courthouse, 102 N. Main, Rm. 2, Gallatin 64640; (660) 663-2031; FAX (660) 663-2149; daviess@windstream.net

DeKalb County

County seat and zip code: Maysville 64469. **County population:** 12,692. **Classification:** Third class. **Assessed valuation:** $150,626,478. **Square miles:** 425. **Organized:** February 25, 1845. **Named for:** Johann Kalb, Baron de Kalb.

Assessor, Ruth A. Ross, (D), DeKalb County Courthouse, PO Box 248, Maysville 64469; (816) 449-2212

Clerk Circuit Court and *ex officio* **Recorder of Deeds,** Julie Whitsell, (R), DeKalb County Courthouse, PO Box 248, Maysville 64469; (816) 449-2602

Clerk County Commission, Melissa (Missy) Meek, (R), DeKalb County Courthouse, PO Box 248, Maysville 64469; (816) 449-5402; FAX (816) 449-2440; dekctyclk@centurytel.net

Collector/Treasurer, Joan (Jody) Pearl, (D), DeKalb County Courthouse, PO Box 248, Maysville 64469; (816) 449-5810; FAX (816) 449-2440

Commissioner, Eastern District, Garry McFee, (R), DeKalb County Courthouse, PO Box 248, Maysville 64469; (816) 449-5402

Commissioner, Western District, Joe Kagay, (R), DeKalb County Courthouse, PO Box 248, Maysville 64469; (816) 449-5402

Coroner, Heath Turner, (R), 603 S. Sloan, Maysville 64469; (816) 449-2126

Emergency Management Director, Harold O. Allison, (R), PO Box 248, Maysville 64469; (816) 449-5545

Presiding Commissioner, Harold O. Allison, (R), DeKalb County Courthouse, PO Box 248, Maysville 64469; (816) 449-5402

Prosecuting Attorney, Erik C. Tate, (D), DeKalb County Courthouse, PO Box 248, Maysville 64469; (816) 449-2279

Public Administrator, Connie Bray, (R), 4095 N.E. Cook Rd., Weatherby 64497; (816) 449-5724

Recorder of Deeds, JoAnn Marshall, (D), DeKalb County Courthouse, PO Box 248, Maysville 64469; (816) 449-2602

Sheriff, Wes Raines, (R), DeKalb County Courthouse, PO Box 317, Maysville 64469; (816) 449-5802

Dent County

County seat and zip code: Salem 65560. County population: 15,655. Classification: Third class. Assessed valuation: $155,034,382. Square miles: 755. Organized: February 10, 1851. Named for: Lewis Dent, pioneer settler.

Assessor, Tina Whitaker, (D), Dent County Courthouse, 400 N. Main St., Salem 65560; (573) 729-6010; FAX (573) 729-6106; dentcounty@embarqmail.com

Clerk Circuit Court, Becky Goforth Swiney, (D), Dent County Judicial Bldg., 112 E. Fifth St., Salem 65560; (573) 729-3931; FAX (573) 729-9414; becky.swiney@courts.mo.gov

Clerk County Commission, Angie Curley, (D), Dent County Courthouse, 400 N. Main St., Salem 65560; (573) 729-4144; FAX (573) 729-3350; dent@sos.mo.gov

Collector of Revenue, Dennis O. Medlock, (D), Dent County Courthouse, 400 N. Main St., Salem 65560; (573) 729-3911; FAX (573) 729-5278; dentcounty1@embarqmail.com

Commissioner, First District, Dennis Purcell, (R), Dent County Courthouse, 400 N. Main St., Salem 65560; (573) 729-3350; dpurcell@centurylink.net

Commissioner, Second District, Gary Larson, (R), Dent County Courthouse, 400 N. Main St., Salem 65560; (573) 729-3044; FAX (573) 729-3350; dent@sos.mo.gov

Coroner, Gina White, (D), 205 E. Fourth St., Salem 65560; (573) 729-2381; FAX (573) 729-2391; coroner_dc617@live.com

County Health Department Director, Jane Jadwin, Dent County Health Center, 501 S. McArthur, Salem 65560; (573) 729-3106; FAX (573) 729-3546; jadwij@lpha.mopublic.org

County Surveyor, Craig Ruble, (D), 201 N. Hwy. 19, Salem 65560; (573) 729-8740

Emergency Management Director, Brad Nash, Dent County Fire District, Salem 65560; (573) 247-2578; FAX (573) 729-6650; dcfpd801@embarqmail.com

Presiding Commissioner, Darrell Skiles, (R), Dent County Courthouse, 400 N. Main St., Salem 65560; (573) 729-3044; darrellskiles@hotmail.com

Prosecuting Attorney, Andrew M. Curley, (R), Dent County Judicial Bldg., 112 E. Fifth St., Salem 65560; (573) 729-3406; FAX (573) 729-3728; pa@dentcountypa.com

Public Administrator, James Kotschedoff, (R), Dent County Judicial Bldg., 112 E. Fifth St., Salem 65560; (573) 729-6088; FAX (573) 729-9414; dentpublicadmin@hotmail.com

Recorder of Deeds, Cindy Ard, (R), Dent County Judicial Bldg., 112 E. Fifth St., Salem 65560; (573) 729-2198; FAX (573) 729-9414; dentcodeeds@embarqmail.com

Sheriff, Rick Stallings, (D), Dent County Judicial Bldg., 112 E. Fifth St., Ste. 7, Salem 65560; (573) 729-3241; FAX (573) 729-3058; info@dentcountysheriff.org

Treasurer, Denita Williams, (R), Dent County Courthouse, 400 N. Main St., Salem 65560; (573) 729-8260; FAX (573) 729-6106; denitakay_w@yahoo.com

Douglas County

County seat and zip code: Ava 65608. County population: 13,546. Classification: Third class. Assessed valuation: $134,069,690. Square miles: 814. Organized: October 29, 1857. Named for: Stephen A. Douglas, Illinois senator and later presidential candidate.

Assessor, Alicia Degase, (R), Douglas County Courthouse, 203 SE Second Ave., PO Box 92, Ava 65608; (417) 683-2829; FAX (417) 683-4003

Clerk Circuit Court and ex officio Recorder of Deeds, Kim Hathcock, (R), Douglas County Courthouse, 203 SE Second Ave., PO Box 249, Ava 65608; (417) 683-4713; FAX (417) 683-2794 or (417) 683-3121; kim.hathcock@courts.mo.gov

Clerk County Commission, Karry Davis, (R), Douglas County Courthouse, PO Box 398, Ava 65608; (417) 683-4714; FAX (417) 683-1017; douglas@sos.mo.gov

Collector of Revenue, Laura Stillings, (R), Douglas County Courthouse, 203 SE Second Ave., PO Box 1330, Ava 65608; (417) 683-4314; FAX (417) 683-4246; dccollectr@gmail.com

Commissioner, District 1, Craig Cunningham, (R), Douglas County Courthouse, 203 SE Second Ave., PO Box 398, Ava 65608; (417) 683-6080; FAX (417) 683-1017; dccom01@yahoo.com

Commissioner, District 2, Leon Potter, (R), Douglas County Courthouse, 203 SE Second Ave., PO Box 398, Ava 65608; (417) 683-6080; FAX (417) 683-1017; dccom01@yahoo.com

Coroner*, Rick Miller, (R), PO Box 63, Ava 65608; FAX (417) 543-0208; rickmiller5061@yahoo.com

County Health Department Director*, Valerie Reese, PO Box 940, Ava 65608; (417) 683-4174; FAX (417) 683-4111; valerier@dchd.org

County Surveyor*, W. Andrew Daniel, 102 W. Cleveland St., PO Box 71, West Plains 65775; (417) 683-6831; FAX (417) 256-6971; adaniel32@hotmail.com

Emergency Management Director, Bill Long, PO Box 398, Ava 65608; (417) 683-3315; FAX (417) 683-1864; avadouglasema@gmail.com

Presiding Commissioner, Lance Stillings, (R), Douglas County Courthouse, 203 SE Second Ave., PO Box 398, Ava 65608; (417) 683-6080; FAX (417) 683-1017; dccom01@yahoo.com

Prosecuting Attorney, Christopher Wade, (R), PO Box 245, Ava 65608; (417) 683-2919; FAX (417) 683-0138; douglascountypa@centurylink.net

Public Administrator, Linda Coonts, (R), Douglas County Courthouse, 203 SE Second Ave., PO Box 308, Ava 65608; (417) 683-3499

Recorder of Deeds, Jacinda Sheppard, (R), 203 S.E. Second Ave., PO Box 1528, Ava 65608; (417) 683-1219; FAX (417) 683-1275; douglascountyrecorder@centurytel.net

Sheriff, Chris Degase, (R), Douglas County Courthouse, 203 SE Second Ave., PO Box 907, Ava 65608; (417) 683-1020; FAX (417) 683-3100; chris@dcsosheriff.com

Treasurer, Theresa Miller, (R), Douglas County Courthouse, 203 SE Second Ave., PO Box 203, Ava 65608; (417) 683-2183; FAX (417) 683-2092; theresamiller63@yahoo.com

---

*Appointed

Dunklin County

County seat and zip code: Kennett 63857.
County population: 31,344. **Classification:** Third class. **Assessed valuation:** $311,677,290. **Square miles:** 547. **Organized:** February 14, 1845. **Named for:** Daniel Dunklin, Governor of Missouri.

Assessor, Karen Vandiver, (D), Dunklin County Courthouse, PO Box 727, Kennett 63857; (573) 888-1409; FAX (573) 888-4711

Clerk Circuit Court, Paula Gargus, (D), Dunklin County Courthouse, Kennett 63857; (573) 888-2456; FAX (573) 888-0754

Clerk County Commission, Kent Hampton, (R), Dunklin County Courthouse, PO Box 188, Kennett 63857; (573) 888-1374; FAX (573) 888-2832; dunklin@sos.mo.gov

Collector/Treasurer, Kathy Rasberry, (D), Dunklin County Courthouse, PO Box 445, Kennett 63857; (573) 888-2180; FAX (573) 888-2180

Commissioner, First District, Jeanie Herbst, (D), Dunklin County Courthouse, PO Box 188, Kennett 63857; (573) 888-4460; FAX (573) 888-2832

Commissioner, Second District, Patrick McHaney, (D), Dunklin County Courthouse, PO Box 188, Kennett 63857; (573) 888-4460; FAX (573) 888-2832

Coroner, James B. Powell, (D), 22882 State Hwy. AB, Malden 63863; (573) 276-7939

County Health Department Director, Steve Neal, 1051 Jones St., Kennett 63857; (573) 717-7317

Emergency Management Director*, Larry Kelley, 1175 Floyd St., Kennett 63857; (573) 344-5545; FAX (573) 888-2604

Presiding Commissioner, Don Collins, (D), Dunklin County Courthouse, PO Box 188, Kennett 63857; (573) 888-4460; FAX (573) 888-2832; don@rsc-cpa.com

Prosecuting Attorney, Jeff McCormick, (D), Dunklin County Justice Center, PO Box 864, Kennett 63857; (573) 888-6676; FAX (573) 888-6677

Public Administrator, Shawnee L. Trowbridge, (D), PO Box 62, Kennett 63857; (573) 888-1433; FAX (573) 888-6781; s_trowbridge@yahoo.com

Recorder of Deeds, Susan Luce, (D), Dunklin County Courthouse, PO Box 389, Kennett 63857; (573) 888-3468; FAX (573) 888-8956; slucerecorder@yahoo.com

Sheriff, Bob Holder, (D), PO Box 801, Kennett 63857; (573) 888-2424; FAX (573) 888-2604; dccourthouse@yahoo.com

---

*Appointed

Franklin County

County seat and zip code: Union 63084.
County population: 102,084. **Classification:** First class. **Assessed valuation:** $1,818,870,265.

Square miles: 922. **Organized:** December 11, 1818. **Named for:** Benjamin Franklin.

Assessor, Tom Copeland, (R), Franklin County Administration Bldg., 400 E. Locust, Rm. 105, Union 63084; (636) 583-6346; FAX (636) 583-6383; tcopeland@franklinmo.net

Auditor, Tambra L. Vemmer, (R), Franklin County Administration Bldg., 400 E. Locust, Rm. 203, Union 63084; (636) 583-6350; FAX (636) 583-7355; tvemmer@franklinmo.net

Clerk Circuit Court, Bill D. Miller, (R), Franklin County Judicial Center, 401 E. Main, Union 63084; (636) 583-7378; bill.miller@courts.mo.gov

Clerk County Commission, Debbie Door, (R), Franklin County Administration Bldg., 400 E. Locust, Rm. 201, Union 63084; (636) 583-6355; FAX (636) 583-7320; ddoor@franklinmo.net

Collector of Revenue, Linda Emmons, (R), Franklin County Administration Bldg., 400 E. Locust, Rm. 103, Union 63084; (636) 583-6353; FAX (636) 583-6398; collector@franklinmo.net

Commissioner, First District, Tim Brinker, (R), Franklin County Administration Bldg., 400 E. Locust, Rm. 206, Union 63084; (636) 583-6358; FAX (636) 583-6399; tbrinker@franklinmo.net

Commissioner, Second District*, Jeffrey A. Maune, (D), Franklin County Administration Bldg., 400 E. Locust, Rm. 206, Union 63084; (636) 583-6358; FAX (636) 583-6399; mschatz@franklinmo.net

County Health Department Director*, Angie Hittson, 414 E. Main St., Union 63084; (636) 583-7300; FAX (636) 583-7305; hittsa@lpha.mopublic.org

Emergency Management Director*, Abraham Cook, 401 E. Springfield Ave., Union 63084; (636) 583-1679; FAX (636) 583-4146; fcema@franklinmo.net

Presiding Commissioner, John Griesheimer, (R), Franklin County Administration Bldg., 400 E. Locust, Rm. 206, Union 63084; (636) 583-6358; FAX (636) 583-6399; jgriesheimer@franklinmo.net

Prosecuting Attorney, Robert E. Parks, (R), 15 S. Church, Rm. 204, Union 63084; (636) 583-6370; FAX (636) 583-7343; rparks@franklinmo.net

Public Administrator, Mary Jo Strattmann, (D), 15 S. Church, Rm. 110, Union 63084; (636) 583-7377; FAX (636) 583-7386; publicadmin@franklinmo.net

Public Works Director*, Eva Gadcke, Franklin County Administration Bldg., 400 E. Locust,

Rm. 003, Union 63084; (636) 583-6361; FAX (636) 584-0902

Recorder of Deeds, Jennifer L. Metcalf, (R), Franklin County Administration Bldg., 400 E. Locust, Rm. 102, Union 63084; (636) 583-6367; FAX (636) 583-7330; recorder@franklinmo.net

Sheriff, Gary F. Toelke, (R), 1 Bruns Dr., Union 63084; (636) 583-2560; FAX (636) 584-6877; gtoelke@franklinmo.net

Treasurer, Debbie Aholt, (R), Franklin County Administration Bldg., 400 E. Locust, Rm. 204, Union 63084; (636) 583-6311; treasurer@franklinmo.net

---

*Appointed

Gasconade County

County seat and zip code: Hermann 65041. **County population:** 14,866. **Classification:** Third class. **Assessed valuation:** $220,975,761. **Square miles:** 521. **Organized:** November 25, 1820. **Named for:** The Gasconade River.

Assessor, Joseph M. Mundwiller, (D), Gasconade County Courthouse, 119 E. First St., Ste. 23, Hermann 65041; (573) 486-3100; FAX (573) 486-3693; gassessor@centurytel.net

Clerk Circuit Court and ex officio Recorder of Deeds, Pamela R. Greunke, (R), Gasconade County Courthouse, 119 E. First St., Ste. 6, Hermann 65041; (573) 486-2632; FAX (573) 486-5812; pam.gruenke@courts.mo.gov

Clerk County Commission, Lesa Lietzow, (R), Gasconade County Courthouse, 119 E. First St., Ste. 2, Hermann 65041; (573) 486-5427; FAX (573) 486-8893; gasconade@sos.mo.gov

Collector of Revenue, Shawn Schlottach, (R), Gasconade County Courthouse, 119 E. First St., Rm. 4, Hermann 65041; (573) 486-2711; FAX (573) 486-4052

Commissioner, Northern District, Jim Holland, (D), Gasconade County Courthouse, 119 E. First St., Ste. 2, Hermann 65041; (573) 486-5427; FAX (573) 486-8893; jtsubs@hotmail.com

Commissioner, Southern District, Jerry D. Lairmore, (R), Gasconade County Courthouse, 119 E. First St., Ste. 2, Hermann 65041; (573) 486-5427; FAX (573) 486-8893; jdlcommish@yahoo.com

Coroner, Benjamin D. Grosse, (R), 1221 Washington St., Hermann 65041; (573) 486-5429; FAX (573) 486-2243

County Health Department Director*, Sara Michie, Gasconade County Health Dept.,

300 Schiller St., Hermann 65041; (573) 486-3129; FAX (573) 486-3745

County Surveyor, Paul Dopuch, (R), PO Box 101, Hermann 65041; (573) 486-2879; FAX (573) 486-5222

Emergency Management Director, Kristopher Bayless, Gasconade County Courthouse, 119 E. First St., Rm. 2, Hermann 65041; (573) 486-3621; FAX (573) 486-8996; gascoemd@ktis.net

Presiding Commissioner, Larry Miskel, (R), Gasconade County Courthouse, 119 E. First St., Ste. 2, Hermann 65041; (573) 486-5427; FAX (573) 486-8893; lnl94@centurytel.net

Prosecuting Attorney*, Mary E. Weston, (R), Gasconade County Courthouse, 119 E. First St., Ste. 24, Hermann 65041; (573) 486-2173; FAX (573) 486-1426; gaspa@centurytel.net

Public Administrator, Fay Owsley, (R), 3287 Hwy. 19, Owensville 65066; (573) 437-7390; FAX (573) 437-6497

Sheriff, Randy Esphorst, (R), Gasconade County Courthouse, 119 E. First St., Rm. 22, Hermann 65041; (573) 486-3880; FAX (573) 486-3693; gcsd700@centurytel.net

Treasurer, Michael Feagan, (R), Gasconade County Courthouse, 119 E. First St., Rm. 5, Hermann 65041; (573) 486-2411; FAX (573) 486-8893; feagan4treas@gmail.com

---

*Appointed

Gentry County

County seat and zip code: Albany 64402. **County population:** 6,826. **Classification:** Third class. **Assessed valuation:** $91,949,050. **Square miles:** 493. **Organized:** February 14, 1845. **Named for:** Richard Gentry, Seminole War general.

Assessor, Penny Woods, (R), Gentry County Courthouse, 200 W. Clay, Albany 64402; (660) 726-5289; FAX (660) 726-5810; gcassessor@windstream.net

Clerk Circuit Court and *ex officio* Recorder of Deeds, Janet Parsons, (R), Gentry County Courthouse, 200 W. Clay, Albany 64402; (660) 726-3618; FAX (660) 726-4102; janet.parsons@courts.mo.gov

Clerk County Commission, Carol Reidlinger, (D), Gentry County Courthouse, 200 W. Clay, Albany 64402; (660) 726-3525; FAX (660) 726-4478; gencoclerk@windstream.net

Collector/Treasurer, Linda Combs, (D), Gentry County Courthouse Annex, 104 N. Polk,

Albany 64402; (660) 726-3319; FAX (660) 726-5769

Commissioner, First District, Larry B. Wilson, (D), Gentry County Courthouse, 200 W. Clay, Albany 64402; (660) 726-3525; FAX (660) 726-4478; gencoclerk@windstream.net

Commissioner, Second District, Gary Carlson, (R), Gentry County Courthouse, 200 W. Clay, Albany 64402; (660) 726-3525; FAX (660) 726-4478; gary@kingcitymotors.com

Coroner, Andrew Lindner, 712 N. Elm St., Stanberry 64489; (660) 783-2869; alindner84@msn.com

County Health Department Director, Lillie Parsons, 302 N. Park St., Stanberry 64489; (660) 783-2707; FAX (660) 783-2775

Emergency Management Director, James D. Boothe, 308 N. Olive, Albany 64402; (660) 562-8933; FAX (660) 726-4478; gentrycoemd@windstream.net

Presiding Commissioner, Rod Dollars, (R), Gentry County Courthouse, 200 W. Clay, Albany 64402; (660) 726-3525; FAX (660) 726-4478; gencoclerk@windstream.net

Prosecuting Attorney, David B. Parman, (D), Gentry County Courthouse, 200 W. Clay, Albany 64402; (660) 726-3844; FAX (660) 726-3323; gencopa@windstream.net

Public Administrator*, Jody Barnes-Novak, (D), 103 E. South, Albany 64402; (660) 726-5242; FAX (660) 726-3200; jnovak@windstream.net

Sheriff, Tim Davis, (D), Gentry County Courthouse Annex, 104 N. Polk, PO Box 37, Albany 64402; (660) 726-3721; FAX (660) 726-3665; gcsheriff@alltel.net

---

*Appointed

Greene County

County seat and zip code: Springfield 65802. **County population:** 283,870. **Classification:** First class. **Assessed valuation:** $4,441,512,657. **Square miles:** 678. **Organized:** January 2, 1833. **Named for:** Nathaniel Greene, Revolutionary War general.

Assessor, Rick Kessinger, (R), Greene County Courthouse, 940 Boonville, Springfield 65802; (417) 868-4101; FAX (417) 868-4844; rkessinger@greenecountymo.org

Auditor, Cindy S. Stein, (R), Greene County Courthouse, 940 Boonville, Rm. 211, Springfield 65802; (417) 868-4120; cstein@greenecountymo.org

Clerk Circuit Court, Thomas R. Barr, (R), Circuit Clerk, 1010 Boonville, Springfield 65802;

(417) 868-4074; FAX (417) 868-4186; tom.barr@courts.mo.gov

Clerk County Commission, Shane Schoeller, (R), Greene County Courthouse, 940 Boonville, Rm. 113, Springfield 65802; (417) 868-4055; FAX (417) 868-4170; sschoeller@greenecountymo.org

Collector of Revenue, Leah Betts, (R), Greene County Courthouse, 940 Boonville, Springfield 65802; (417) 868-4036; FAX (417) 868-4854; lbetts@greenecountymo.org

Commissioner, First District, Harold Bengsch, (R), 933 N. Robberson, Springfield 65802; (417) 868-4112; FAX (417) 868-4818; hbengsch@greenecountymo.org

Commissioner, Second District, Roseann Bentley, (R), 933 N. Robberson, Springfield 65802; (417) 868-4112; FAX (417) 868-4818; rbentley@greenecountymo.org

County Health Department Director*, Kevin Gipson, Springfield-Greene County Health Department, 227 E. Chestnut Expressway, Springfield 65802; (417) 864-1657; FAX (417) 864-1125; kgipson@springfieldmo.gov

County Highway Administrator*, Rick Artman, 2065 N. Clifton, Springfield 65803; (417) 831-3591; FAX (417) 831-5216; rartman@greenecountymo.org

Emergency Management Director*, Chet Hunter, 330 W. Scott, Springfield 65802; (417) 869-6040; FAX (417) 869-6654; chunter@greenecountymo.org

Medical Examiner*, Dr. Jeff Harkey, 916 N. Campbell, Springfield 65802; (417) 868-4822; FAX (417) 868-4823; jharkey@greenecountymo.org

Presiding Commissioner, Bob Cirtin, (R), 933 N. Robberson, Springfield 65802; (417) 868-4112; FAX (417) 868-4818; bcirtin@greenecountymo.org

Prosecuting Attorney, Dan Patterson, (R), Greene County Courthouse, 1010 Boonville, Springfield 65802; (417) 868-4061; FAX (417) 868-4160; dpatterson@greenecountymo.org

Public Administrator, David Yancey, (R), 917 Boonville, Springfield 65802; (417) 868-4022; FAX (417) 868-4840; dyancey@greenecountymo.org

Recorder of Deeds, Cheryl Dawson-Spaulding, (R), Greene County Courthouse, 940 Boonville, Springfield 65802; (417) 868-4068; FAX (417) 868-4807; cdawson@greenecountymo.org

Sheriff, Jim Arnott, (R), Sheriff's Department, 1000 N. Boonville, Springfield 65802; (417) 868-4040; FAX (417) 868-4830; jarnott@greenecountymo.org

Treasurer*, Justin Hill, (R), Greene County Courthouse, 940 Boonville, Rm. 112, Springfield 65802; (417) 868-4051; jrhill@greenecountymo.org

---

*Appointed

Grundy County

County seat and zip code: Trenton 64683. **County population:** 10,197. **Classification:** Third class. **Assessed valuation:** $122,055,336. **Square miles:** 437. **Organized:** January 29, 1841. **Named for:** Felix Grundy, Tennessee senator and United States attorney general.

Assessor, Kathy Veatch, (R), Grundy County Courthouse, 700 Main, First Fl., Trenton 64683; (660) 359-4040, ext. 2; FAX (660) 339-7637; assessor@grundycountymo.com

Clerk Circuit Court and ex officio Recorder of Deeds, Becky Stanturf, (R), Grundy County Courthouse, 700 Main, Second Fl., Trenton 64683; (660) 359-4040, ext. 1; FAX (660) 359-6604; recorder@grundycountymo.com

Clerk County Commission, Betty Spickard, (R), Grundy County Courthouse, 700 Main St., Second Fl., Trenton 64683; (660) 359-4040, ext. 4; FAX (660) 359-6786; countyclerk@grundycountymo.com

Collector/Treasurer, Barbara Harris, (R), Grundy County Courthouse, 700 Main, Second Fl., Trenton 64683; (660) 359-4040, ext. 3; FAX (660) 339-7180; treasurer@grundycountymo.com

Commissioner, First District, Gene Wyant, (R), Grundy County Courthouse, 700 Main, Second Fl., Trenton 64683; (660) 359-4040, ext. 5; FAX (660) 359-6786; commissioners@grundycountymo.com

Commissioner, Second District, Joe Brinser, (R), Grundy County Courthouse, 700 Main, Second Fl., Trenton 64683; (660) 359-4040, ext. 5; FAX (660) 359-6786; commissioners@grundycountymo.com

Coroner, Dewayne Slater, (R), 412 E. Ninth St., Trenton 64683; (660) 359-3954

County Health Department Director, Derek Nelson, 1716 Lincoln St., Trenton 64683; (660) 359-4196; FAX (660) 359-5470; nelsodl@lpha.mopublic.org

Emergency Management Director, Glen Briggs, 705 E. Fifth St., Trenton 64683; (660) 635-0706

Presiding Commissioner, Rick Hull, (R), Grundy County Courthouse, 700 Main, Second Fl., Trenton 64683; (660) 359-4040, ext. 5; FAX

(660) 359-6786; commissioners@grundy
countymo.com

Prosecuting Attorney, Carrie Lamm-Clark, (R),
115 E. Eighth St., Trenton 64683; (660) 359-
4888; lammclarklegal@gmail.com

Public Administrator, Jill Eaton, (R), Grundy
County Courthouse, 700 Main, First
Fl., Trenton 64683; (660) 359-3177;
publicadmin@grundycountymo.com

Sheriff, Rodney Herring, (R), Grundy County
Detention Center, 610 Main St., Trenton 64683;
(660) 359-2828; FAX (660) 359-3761; gruco
so@grundycountymo.com

Harrison County

County seat and zip code: Bethany 64424.
County population: 8,639. **Classification:**
Third class. **Assessed valuation:** $104,769,162.
Square miles: 725. **Organized:** February 14,
1845. **Named for:** Albert G. Harrison, Missouri
congressman.

Assessor, Lila Mae Craig, (R), Harrison County
Courthouse, 1505 Main, PO Box 525,
Bethany 64424; (660) 425-2313; FAX (660)
425-0127; harco@grm.net

**Clerk Circuit Court and ex officio Recorder
of Deeds,** C. Sherece Eivins, (R), Harrison
County Courthouse, 1505 Main, PO Box 525,
Bethany 64424; (660) 425-6425; FAX (660)
425-6390

Clerk County Commission, Jackie Deskins, (R),
Harrison County Courthouse, 1505 Main, PO
Box 525, Bethany 64424; (660) 425-6424;
FAX (660) 425-3772; harrison@sos.mo.gov

Collector/Treasurer, Cheryl Coleman, (R),
Harrison County Courthouse, 1505 Main, PO
Box 525, Bethany 64424; (660) 425-6442;
FAX (660) 425-0125; hctreas@grm.net

Commissioner, Northern District, Rick J. Smith,
(R), Harrison County Courthouse, 1505 Main,
Bethany 64424; (660) 425-6424; FAX (660)
425-3772; harrisoncounty@ymail.com

Commissioner, Southern District, Jim Holcomb,
(R), Harrison County Courthouse, 1505 Main,
PO Box 525, Bethany 64424; (660) 425-
6424; FAX (660) 425-3772; harrisoncounty@
ymail.com

Coroner, Jeremy Eivins, (R), Box 283, Bethany
64424; (660) 425-8686

County Health Department Director*, Courtney
Cross, 1700 Bethany Ave., Bethany 64424;
(660) 425-6324; FAX (660) 425-7642; onealm
@lpha.dhss.mo.gov

Emergency Management Director*, Phillip G.
Martz, PO Box 93, Bethany 64424; (660)

425-6790; FAX (660) 425-6806; gjmartz@
grm.net

Presiding Commissioner, Jack W. Hodge, (R),
Harrison County Courthouse, 1505 Main, PO
Box 525, Bethany 64424; (660) 425-6424;
FAX (660) 425-3772; harrisoncounty@ymail.
com

Prosecuting Attorney, R. Cristine Stallings, (D),
Harrison County Courthouse, 1505 Main, PO
Box 87, Bethany 64424; (660) 425-6423; FAX
(660) 425-7765; hcpa@grm.net

Public Administrator, Kimberly King, (R),
Harrison County Courthouse, 1505 Main, PO
Box 525, Bethany 64424; (660) 425-6460;
FAX (660) 425-3772

Sheriff, Josh Eckerson, (R), Harrison County Law
Enforcement Center, 1501 Central St., PO Box
169, Bethany 64424; (660) 425-3199; FAX
(660) 425-7906; harco778@grm.net

---

*Appointed

Henry County

County seat and zip code: Clinton 64735.
County population: 22,059. **Classification:** Third
class. **Assessed valuation:** $321,697,439. **Square
miles:** 729. **Organized:** December 13, 1834.
Named for: Patrick Henry, revolutionary patriot.
Website: www.henrycomo.com

Assessor, Scott Largent, (R), Henry County
Courthouse, 100 W. Franklin St., Clinton
64735; (660) 885-7214; FAX (660) 885-6972;
hcassessors@embarqmail.com

Clerk Circuit Court, Marsha A. Abbott, (D),
Henry County Courthouse, 100 W. Franklin
St., Clinton 64735; (660) 885-7230; FAX
(660) 885-8247; mabbott@courts.mo.gov

Clerk County Commission, Rick Watson, (R),
Henry County Courthouse, 100 W. Franklin
St., Clinton 64735; (660) 885-7204; FAX
(660) 890-2963; henrycoclerk1@yahoo.com

Collector/Treasurer, Maggie Stoddard, (D),
Henry County Courthouse, 100 W. Franklin
St., Clinton 64735; (660) 885-7207; FAX
(660) 885-7259

Commissioner, Northern District, Daniel L.
Doll, (D), Henry County Courthouse, 100 W.
Franklin St., Clinton 64735; (660) 885-7202;
FAX (660) 890-2963

Commissioner, Southern District, Jim Talley, (D),
Henry County Courthouse, 100 W. Franklin
St., Clinton 64735; (660) 885-7202; FAX
(660) 890-2963

Coroner, Dain Sisk, (R), Henry County Courthouse, 100 W. Franklin, Clinton 64735; (660) 525-2275; FAX (660) 890-2963

County Health Department Director*, Bonnie Glass, 306 S. Second St., Clinton 64735; FAX (660) 885-8193

County Surveyor, Jacob Hann, (D), 114 N. Main, Clinton 64735; (660) 885-8311; FAX (660) 885-8447

Emergency Management Director*, John Gover, 100 W. Franklin, Clinton 64735; (660) 885-7217; henrycomoemd@gmail.com

Presiding Commissioner, Jim Stone, (D), Henry County Courthouse, 100 W. Franklin St., Clinton 64735; (660) 885-7201; FAX (660) 890-2963

Prosecuting Attorney, Richard Shields, (D), Henry County Courthouse, 100 W. Franklin St., Clinton 64735; (660) 885-7221; FAX (660) 885-2027

Public Administrator, Kay Holt, (D), Henry County Courthouse, 100 W. Franklin St., Clinton 64735; (660) 885-7245; FAX (660) 885-7258

Recorder of Deeds, Ronda Ake, (R), Henry County Courthouse, 100 W. Franklin St., Clinton 64735; (660) 885-7209; FAX (660) 885-2264; rakerecorder11@hotmail.com

Sheriff, J. Kent Oberkrom, (R), 200 N. Main, Clinton 64735; (660) 885-7300; FAX (660) 885-3173; henrysheriff@embarqmail.com

*Appointed

Hickory County

County seat and zip code: Hermitage 65668. **County population:** 9,219. **Classification:** Third class. **Assessed valuation:** $116,611,940. **Square miles:** 411. **Organized:** February 14, 1845. **Named for:** Andrew Jackson, "Old Hickory."

Assessor, Clint D. Baker, (R), Hickory County Courthouse, Spring & Polk, PO Box 97, Hermitage 65668; (417) 745-6346; FAX (417) 745-6715; assessor@hickorycountymo.org

Clerk Circuit Court, Cee Cee Smith, (R), Hickory County Courthouse, Spring & Polk, PO Box 345, Hermitage 65668; (417) 745-6421; FAX (417) 745-6670

Clerk County Commission, Jeanne Lindsey, (R), Hickory County Courthouse, Spring & Polk, PO Box 3, Hermitage 65668; (417) 745-6450; FAX (417) 745-6057; hickory@sos.mo.gov

Collector of Revenue, Karen Stokes, (R), Hickory County Courthouse, Spring & Polk, PO Box 92, Hermitage 65668; (417) 745-6713; FAX (417) 745-2516

Commissioner, Eastern District, Robert Breshears, (R), Hickory County Courthouse, Spring & Polk, PO Box 3, Hermitage 65668; (417) 745-6450; FAX (417) 745-6057

Commissioner, Western District, Rick Pearson, (R), Hickory County Courthouse, Spring & Polk, PO Box 3, Hermitage 65668; (417) 745-6450; FAX (417) 745-6057

Coroner, Connie Boller, (R), PO Box 342, Hermitage 65668; (417) 745-6682; FAX (417) 745-2327; connie@hctitle.com

County Health Department Director, Dawn Vader, PO Box 21, Hermitage 65668; (417) 745-6628; FAX (417) 745-2400; acarter@hickorycounty.net

Emergency Management Director, Carolyn Ream, PO Box 3, Hermitage 65668; (417) 745-0095 or (417) 224-5012; carolyn.ream.emd@gmail.com

Presiding Commissioner, Robert Sawyer, (R), Hickory County Courthouse, Spring & Polk, PO Box 3, Hermitage 65668; (417) 745-6450; FAX (417) 745-6057

Prosecuting Attorney, J. Michael Brown, (R), Hickory County Courthouse, Spring & Polk, PO Box 154, Hermitage 65668; (417) 745-6413; FAX (417) 745-6732; hickorycopa@hotmail.com

Public Administrator, Venessa Prettyman, (R), RR 71, Box 78-1, Weaubleau 65774; (417) 745-6626; FAX (417) 745-6160; nessa2u2002@yahoo.com

Recorder of Deeds, Pamela Hutton, (R), Hickory County Courthouse, Spring & Polk, PO Box 101, Hermitage 65668; (417) 745-6833; FAX (417) 745-0199

Sheriff, Raymond S. Tipton, (R), Hickory County Courthouse, 254 Dallas, Rt. 2, Box 2805, Hermitage 65668; (417) 745-6415; FAX (417) 745-6205; hhickory@centurytel.net

Treasurer, Kenny Ratliff, (R), Hickory County Courthouse, Spring & Polk, PO Box 17, Hermitage 65668; (417) 745-6310; FAX (417) 745-6057; treasurer@hickorycountymo.org

Holt County

County seat and zip code: Oregon 64473. **County population:** 4,516. **Classification:** Third class. **Assessed valuation:** $122,326,999. **Square miles:** 456. **Organized:** January 29, 1841. **Named for:** David Rice Holt, Missouri legislator from Platte County.

Assessor, LaDonna Jones, (R), Holt County Courthouse, PO Box 366, Oregon 64473; (660) 446-3329; FAX (660) 446-3092

Clerk Circuit Court and ex officio Recorder of Deeds, Vicki Book, (R), Holt County Courthouse, PO Box 318, Oregon 64473; (660) 446-3301

Clerk County Commission, Kathy J. Holstine, (R), Holt County Courthouse, 102 W. Nodaway St., PO Box 437, Oregon 64473; (660) 446-3303; FAX (660) 446-3353; holtcoclerk@ofmlive.net

Collector of Revenue, Donna Cotton, (R), Holt County Courthouse, PO Box 572, Oregon 64473; (660) 446-3384; FAX (660) 446-3346

Commissioner, First District, Bill Gordon, (R), Holt County Courthouse, PO Box 437, Oregon 64473; (660) 446-3304

Commissioner, Second District, David Carroll, (D), Holt County Courthouse, PO Box 437, Oregon 64473; (660) 446-3304

Coroner, Susan Lentz, (R), 24130 Squirrel Rd., Oregon 64473; (660) 446-2046; FAX (660) 446-3353 or (660) 446-2020

County Health Department Director, Brenda Nelson, RN, 108 S. Main, Oregon 64473; (660) 446-2909; FAX (660) 446-2921; nelsob@lpha.mopublic.org

Emergency Management Director, Mark Sitherwood, 102 W. Nodaway St., PO Box 437, Oregon 64473; (660) 446-3304; FAX (660) 446-3353

Presiding Commissioner, Mark Sitherwood, (R), Holt County Courthouse, PO Box 437, Oregon 64473; (660) 446-3304; FAX (660) 446-3353

Prosecuting Attorney, Robert Shepherd, (R), 102 W. Nodaway, PO Box 467, Oregon 64473; (660) 446-3326; FAX (660) 446-3585; holtcountypa@ofmlive.net

Public Administrator, Edward Meng, (R), 30094 Holt 300, Oregon 64473; (660) 491-2863; FAX (660) 491-2863; edmeng@semapplications.com

Sheriff, Scott Wedlock, (R), 107 S. Main, PO Box 229, Oregon 64473; (660) 446-3300; FAX (660) 446-2020; swedlock@holtcountysheriffoffice.org

Treasurer, Gay Quick, (R), Holt County Courthouse, PO Box 291, Oregon 64473; (660) 446-3397

Howard County

County seat and zip code: Fayette 65248. **County population:** 10,159. **Classification:** Third class. **Assessed valuation:** $117,780,935. **Square miles:** 464. **Organized:** January 23, 1816. **Named for:** Benjamin Howard, Governor of the Missouri Territory.

Assessor, John (Woody) McCutcheon, (D), Howard County Courthouse, 1 Courthouse Sq., Fayette 65248; (660) 248-3400; FAX (660) 248-1765

Clerk Circuit Court and ex officio Recorder of Deeds, Charles J. Flaspohler, (D), Howard County Courthouse, 1 Courthouse Sq., Fayette 65248; (660) 248-2194

Clerk County Commission, Kathyrne Harper, (R), Howard County Courthouse, 1 Courthouse Sq., Fayette 65248; (660) 248-2284; FAX (660) 248-9810; howard@sos.mo.gov

Collector of Revenue, Jinger Felten, (R), Howard County Courthouse, 1 Courthouse Sq., Fayette 65248; (660) 248-2195

Commissioner, Eastern District, Richard Conrow, (D), Howard County Courthouse, 1 Courthouse Sq., Fayette 65248; (660) 248-2193; hococomm@yahoo.com

Commissioner, Western District, Howard McMillan, (D), Howard County Courthouse, 1 Courthouse Sq., Fayette 65248; (660) 248-2193

Coroner, Frank Flaspohler, (D), Howard County Ambulance Service, Fayette 65248; (660) 248-2229

County Health Department Director, Sheila Wallace, 600 W. Morrison, Fayette 65248; (660) 248-3100

County Surveyor, Nathanael Kohl, (D), 1080 State Route Y, Harrisburg 65256; (573) 499-1241

Emergency Management Directors, Bryan Kunze and Bill John, 600 W. Morrison, Fayette 65248; (660) 248-1111

Presiding Commissioner, Sam Stroupe, (D), Howard County Courthouse, 1 Courthouse Sq., Fayette 65248; (660) 248-2193

Prosecuting Attorney, Stephen Murrell, (D), 124 E. Morrison, Fayette 65254; (660) 248-3005; FAX (660) 248-3007; stephenmurrell@sbcglobal.net

Public Administrator, Lisa Asbury, (D), Howard County Courthouse, 1 Courthouse Sq., Fayette 65248; (660) 248-5161

Sheriff, Mike Neal, (I), Howard County Courthouse, 1 Courthouse Sq., Fayette 65248; (660) 248-2477

Treasurer, Susan Keyton, (D), Howard County Courthouse, 1 Courthouse Sq., Fayette 65248; (660) 248-2196

Howell County

County seat and zip code: West Plains 65775. **County population:** 40,173. **Classification:** Third class. **Assessed valuation:** $444,921,066. **Square miles:** 927. **Organized:** March 2, 1857. **Named for:** Josiah Howell, pioneer settler.

Assessor, Daniel Franks, (R), 101 Courthouse, West Plains 65775; (417) 256-8284; FAX (417) 256-8266

Clerk Circuit Court, Cindy Weeks, (R), 106 Courthouse, PO Box 967, West Plains 65775; (417) 256-3741; FAX (417) 256-4650

Clerk County Commission, Dennis K. Von Allmen, (R), 35 Court Sq., Rm. 200, West Plains 65775; (417) 256-2591; FAX (417) 256-2512; howell@sos.mo.gov

Collector of Revenue, Larry Spence, (R), 104 Courthouse, West Plains 65775; (417) 256-4001; FAX (417) 257-0589

Commissioner, Northern District, Bill Lovelace, (R), 35 Court Sq., Rm. 302, West Plains 65775; (417) 256-3872; FAX (417) 256-2512

Commissioner, Southern District*, Billy Sexton, (R), 35 Court Sq., Rm. 302, West Plains 65775; (417) 256-3872; FAX (417) 256-2512

Coroner, James T. Tim Cherry, (R), 211 W. Main, West Plains 65775; (417) 256-2121; FAX (417) 256-2124

County Health Department Director*, Chris Gilliam, 180 S. Kentucky, West Plains 65775; (417) 256-7078; FAX (417) 256-1179

County Surveyor, Ralph Riggs, (R), 102 W. Trish Knight, PO Box 71, West Plains 65775; (417) 256-8125; FAX (417) 256-2899

Emergency Management Director*, Mike Coldiron, 1106 Missouri Ave., West Plains 65775; (417) 256-2544; FAX (417) 256-6464

Presiding Commissioner, Mark B. Collins, (R), 35 Court Sq., Rm. 302, West Plains 65775; (417) 256-3872; FAX (417) 256-2512

Prosecuting Attorney, Michael P. Hutchings, (R), 326 Courthouse, West Plains 65775; (417) 256-2317; FAX (417) 256-6756

Public Administrator, John Pruett, (R), 35 Court Sq., Rm. 303, West Plains 65775; (417) 255-0350; FAX (417) 255-0352

Recorder of Deeds, Sharon Trowbridge, (R), 107 Courthouse, West Plains 65775; (417) 256-3750

Sheriff, James M. (Mike) Shannon, (R), Howell County Detention Center, 1106 Missouri Ave., West Plains 65775; (417) 256-2544; FAX (417) 256-6464

Treasurer, Nancy Franz, (R), 35 Court Sq., Rm. 301, West Plains 65775; (417) 256-4261; FAX (417) 256-2512

---

*Appointed

Iron County

County seat and zip code: Ironton 63650. **County population:** 10,267. **Classification:** Third class. **Assessed valuation:** $212,110,157. **Square miles:** 552. **Organized:** February 17, 1857. **Named for:** Abundant iron ore.

Assessor, David L. Huff, (D), Iron County Courthouse, 202 S. Shepherd St., Ironton 63650; (573) 546-7319; FAX (573) 546-4129; ironassessor@centurytel.net

Clerk Circuit Court, Sammye Gail White, (D), Iron County Circuit Court, 250 S. Main St., Ste. 220, Ironton 63650; (573) 546-2511; FAX (573) 546-6006

Clerk County Commission, Virginia Queen, (D), Iron County Courthouse, 250 S. Main, PO Box 42, Ironton 63650; (573) 546-2912; FAX (573) 546-6499; iron@sos.mo.gov

Collector of Revenue, Linda Kemp, (D), Iron County Courthouse, 202 S. Shepherd St., Ironton 63650; (573) 546-2911; FAX (573) 546-4129; ironcollector@centurytel.net

Commissioner, Southern District, Dwayne Warncke, (D), Iron County Courthouse, 250 S. Main St., PO Box 42, Ironton 63650; (573) 546-2915; FAX (573) 546-6499

Commissioner, Western District, Mark Yates, (D), Iron County Courthouse, 250 S. Main St., PO Box 42, Ironton 63650; (573) 546-2915; FAX (573) 546-6499

Coroner, Anthony N. Cole, (D), 265 Karina, Arcadia 63621; (573) 546-3682; tcole001@centurytel.net

County Health Department Director, Heidi Wharton, 606 W. Russell St., Ironton 63650; (573) 546-7121

Emergency Management Director, (Vacancy)

Presiding Commissioner, Jim Scaggs, (D), Iron County Courthouse, 250 S. Main St., PO Box 42, Ironton 63650; (573) 546-2915; FAX (573) 546-6499; jscaggs@windstream.net

Prosecuting Attorney, Brian Parker, (D), 222 S. Shepherd St., PO Box 81, Ironton 63650; (573) 546-2333; FAX (573) 546-7499

Public Administrator, Sandra Trask, (D), 127 County Rd. 39E, Ironton 63650; (573) 546-7555; FAX (573) 546-7555; sandra308@centurytel.net

Recorder of Deeds, Karen K. Reagan, (D), Iron County Courthouse, 250 S. Main St., PO Box 24, Ironton 63650; (573) 546-2811; FAX (573) 546-2166

Sheriff, Roger D. Medley, (D), Office of Sheriff, 220 S. Shepherd, Ironton 63650; (573) 546-7051; FAX (573) 546-7139; rmedley@icsomo.org

Treasurer, Carol Hardy, (D), Iron County Courthouse, 250 S. Main St., PO Box 216, Ironton 63650; (573) 546-7611, irontreasurer.chardy@gmail.com

Jackson County

County seat and zip code: Independence 64050. **County population:** 683,191. **Classification:** First class. **Assessed valuation:** $9,688,012,600. **Square miles:** 611. **Organized:** December 15, 1826. **Named for:** Andrew Jackson.

Chief Administrative Officer*, Mary Lou Brown, Jackson County Courthouse, 415 E. 12th St., Ste. 200, Kansas City 64106; (816) 881-3064; FAX (816) 881-3133; mbrown@jacksongov.org

Chief Operating Officer*, Gary Panethiere, Jackson County Courthouse, 415 E. 12th St., Ste. 200, Kansas City 64106; (816) 881-3333; FAX (816) 881-3133; gpanethiere@jacksongov.org

Chief of Staff/Chief of Inter-Governmental Relations and Taxation*, Calvin Williford, Jackson County Courthouse, 415 E. 12th St., Ste. 200, Kansas City 64106; (816) 881-3333; FAX (816) 881-3133; cwilliford@jacksongov.org

Circuit Court Administrator*, Jeff Eisenbeis, Jackson County Courthouse, Third Fl., 415 E. 12th St., Kansas City 64106; (816) 881-3658; FAX (816) 881-3719; jeff.eisenbeis@courts.mo.gov

Clerk County Legislature*, Mary Jo Spino, Jackson County Courthouse, 415 E. 12th St., Ste. 201, Kansas City 64106; (816) 881-3242; FAX (816) 881-3234; mspino@jacksongov.org

County Counselor*, W. Stephen Nixon, Jackson County Courthouse, Second Fl., 415 E. 12th St., Kansas City 64106; (816) 881-3355; FAX (816) 881-3398; counselor@jacksongov.org

County Executive, Michael D. Sanders, (D), Jackson County Courthouse, 415 E. 12th St., Ste. 200, Kansas City 64106; (816) 881-3333; FAX (816) 881-3133; msanders@jacksongov.org

County Health Department Director, Jim Kelly, 313 S. Liberty, Independence 64050; (816) 404-6415; FAX (816) 404-6418; jim.kelly@tmcmed.org

County Legislature, First District at Large, Frank White Jr., (D), 201 W. Lexington, Ste. 201, Independence 64050; (816) 881-4477; FAX (816) 881-4473; fwhite@jacksongov.org

County Legislature, Second District at Large, Crystal Williams, (D), Jackson County Courthouse, 415 E. 12th St., Ste. 201, Kansas City 64106; (816) 881-3464; FAX (816) 881-3340; cwilliams@jacksongov.org

County Legislature, Third District at Large, Tony Miller, (D), Jackson County Legislature, 201 W. Lexington, Ste. 201, Independence 64050; (816) 881-4423; FAX (816) 881-4473; tmiller@jacksongov.org

County Legislature, First District, Scott Burnett, (D), Jackson County Courthouse, 415 E. 12th St., Ste. 201, Kansas City 64106; (816) 881-3076; FAX (816) 881-3340; sburnett@jacksongov.org

County Legislature, Second District, Alfred Jordan, (D), Jackson County Courthouse, 415 E. 12th St., Ste. 201, Kansas City 64106; (816) 881-3806; FAX (816) 881-3340; ajordan@jacksongov.org

County Legislature, Third District, Dennis Waits, (D), Jackson County Legislature, 201 W. Lexington, Ste. 201, Independence 64050; (816) 881-4441; FAX (816) 881-4473; dwaits@jacksongov.org

County Legislature, Fourth District, Dan Tarwater III, (D), Jackson County Courthouse, 415 E. 12th St., Ste. 201, Kansas City 64106; (816) 881-3362; FAX (816) 881-3340; dtarwater@jacksongov.org

County Legislature, Fifth District, Greg Grounds, (R), Jackson County Courthouse, 201 W. Lexington, Ste. 201, Independence 64050; (816) 881-4476; FAX (816) 881-4473; ggrounds@jacksongov.org

County Legislature, Sixth District, Theresa Galvin, (R), Jackson County Courthouse, 415 E. 12th St., Ste. 201, Kansas City 64106; (816) 881-3132; FAX (816) 881-3340; tlgalvin@jacksongov.org

Deputy Chief Administrative Officer*, V. Edwin Stoll, Jackson County Courthouse, 415 E. 12th St., Ste. 100, Kansas City 64106; (816) 881-3187; FAX (816) 881-3200; estoll@jacksongov.org

Deputy Director of Assessment*, Jeff Burroughs Scanlon, Jackson County Courthouse, First Fl., 415 E. 12th St., Ste. 100M, Kansas City 64106; (816) 881-3256; FAX (816) 881-1388; jbs@jacksongov.org

Director of Human Resources*, Dennis Dumovich, Jackson County Courthouse, First Fl., 415 E. 12th St., Kansas City 64106; (816) 881-3135; FAX (816) 881-3474; ddumovich@jackson gov.org

Acting Director of Public Works*, Earl Newill, Jackson County Public Works, 303 W. Walnut, Independence 64050; (816) 881-4538; FAX (816) 881-4448; enewill@jacksongov.org

Director Emergency Preparedness and Homeland Security, Michael Curry, 201 W. Lexington, Ste. 201, Independence 64050; (816) 881-4625; FAX (816) 881-1625; mcurry@jacksongov.org

Legislative Auditor*, Crissy Wooderson, Jackson County Courthouse, 415 E. 12th St., Kansas City 64106; (816) 881-3310; FAX (816) 881-3340; auditor@jacksongov.org

Medical Examiner*, Dr. Mary Dudley, 660 E. 24th St., Hospital Hill, Kansas City 64108; (816) 881-6600; FAX (816) 881-6641; medexaminer@jacksongov.org

Prosecuting Attorney, Jean Peters-Baker, (D), Jackson County Courthouse, 11th Fl., 415 E. 12th St., Kansas City 64106; (816) 881-3555; FAX (816) 881-3821; jpetersbaker@jackson gov.org

Public Administrator*, Rebecca Lake Wood, Jackson County Courthouse, Fourth Fl., 415 E. 12th St., Rm. 400, Kansas City 64106; (816) 881-3775; FAX (816) 881-3783; rwood@jackson gov.org

Recorder of Deeds*, Robert Kelly, Jackson County Courthouse, First Fl., 415 E. 12th St., Kansas City 64106; (816) 881-3191; FAX (816) 881-3719; records@jacksongov.org

Sheriff, Mike Sharp, (D), 3310 N.E. Rennau Dr., Lee's Summit 64064; (816) 524-4302; FAX (816) 524-4340; msharp@jacksongov.org

*Appointed

Jasper County

County seat and zip code: Carthage 64836. **County population:** 117,543. **Classification:** First class. **Assessed valuation:** $1,642,932,703. **Square miles:** 641. **Organized:** January 29, 1841. **Named for:** William Jasper, revolutionary soldier.

Assessor, Connie Hoover, (R), Jasper County Courthouse, 302 S. Main St., Rm. 201, Carthage 64836; (417) 358-0440; FAX (417) 237-0036; jasperassessor@ecarthage.com

Auditor, Richard M. Webster Jr., (R), Jasper County Courthouse, 302 S. Main St., Rm. 108, Carthage 64836; (417) 358-0406; FAX (417) 237-1097; jascoauditor@ecarthage. com

Clerk Circuit Court, Melissa Holcomb, (R), Jasper County Courthouse, 302 S. Main St., Rm. 304, Carthage 64836; (417) 358-0441; FAX (417) 358-0460; melissa.holcomb@courts. mo.gov

Clerk County Commission, Marilyn S. Baugh, (R), Jasper County Courthouse, 302 S. Main St., Rm. 102, Carthage 64836; (417) 358-0416; FAX (417) 358-0415; countyclerk@ ecarthage.com

Collector of Revenue, Stephen H. Holt, (R), Jasper County Courthouse, 302 S. Main St., Rm. 107, Carthage 64836; (417) 358-0409; FAX (417) 358-0495; shholt@ecarthage.com

Commissioner, Eastern District, Jim Honey, (R), Jasper County Courthouse, 302 S. Main St., Rm. 101, Carthage 64836; (417) 358-0421; FAX (417) 358-0483; honeyjim@ecarthage. com

Commissioner, Western District, Darieus K. Adams, (R), Jasper County Courthouse, 302 S. Main St., Rm. 101, Carthage 64836; (417) 358-0421; FAX (417) 358-0483; dadams@ ecarthage.com

Coroner, Rob Chappel, (R), 506 Ware St., Webb City 64870; (417) 673-7020; FAX (417) 673-0082; rwchappel@hotmail.com

County Health Department Director*, Tony Moehr, 105 Lincoln, Carthage 64836; (417) 358-3111; FAX (417) 358-0494; moehra@ lpha.mopublic.org

Emergency Management Director*, Keith Stammer, 303 E. Third St., Joplin 64801; (417) 624-0820, ext. 260; (417) 625-4737; kstammer@joplinmo.org

Presiding Commissioner, John Bartosh, (R), Jasper County Courthouse, 302 S. Main St., Rm. 101, Carthage 64836; (417) 358-0421; FAX (417) 358-0483; john.bartosh@ecarthage.com

Prosecuting Attorney, Dean G. Dankelson, (R), Jasper County Courts Bldg., 601 Pearl, Rm. 100, Joplin 64801; (417) 625-4314; FAX (417) 625-4315; dank@jaspercopa.org

Public Administrator, Angela Casavecchia, (R), Jasper County Annex II, 116 W. Second St., Ste. 203, Carthage 64836; (417) 358-4271 or (417) 358-4268; FAX (417) 358-4349; angiec@ ecarthage.com

Recorder of Deeds, Charlotte Pickering, (R), Jasper County Annex II, PO Box 387, Carthage 64836; (417) 358-0431; FAX (417) 359-1200; recorder@jaspercounty.org

Sheriff, Randee Kaiser, (R), Jasper County Sheriff's Office, 231 S. Main St., Carthage 64836; (417)

358-8177; FAX (417) 359-8620; rkaiser@
jaspercountysheriff.org

Treasurer, Denise Rohr, (R), Jasper County Annex
II, 116 W. Second St., Ste. 202, Carthage
64836; (417) 358-0448; FAX (417) 359-1105;
jascotreas@ecarthage.com

*Appointed

Jefferson County

County seat and zip code: Hillsboro 63050.
County population: 218,733. **Classification:**
First class. **Assessed valuation:** $3,000,739,371.
Square miles: 668. **Organized:** December 8,
1818. **Named for:** Thomas Jefferson. **Website:**
www.jeffcomo.org

Assessor, Terry Roesch, (D), PO Box 100,
Hillsboro 63050; (636) 797-5466; troesch@
jeffcomo.org

Auditor, Richard Carter III, (R), PO Box 100,
Hillsboro 63050; (636) 797-6427; rcarter@
jeffcomo.org

Clerk Circuit Court, Michael Reuter, (R), PO Box
100, Hillsboro 63050; (636) 797-5443; mike.
reuter@courts.mo.gov

Collector of Revenue, Beth Mahn, (D), PO Box
100, Hillsboro 63050; (636) 797-5406;
bmahn@jeffcomo.org

Council Member, First District, Don Bickowski,
(R), Jefferson County Justice Center, Third Fl.,
Rm. 301, 400 First St., Hillsboro 63050; (636)
797-5312; FAX (636) 797-5542; dbickowski@
jeffcomo.org

Council Member, Second District, Renee Reuter,
(R), Jefferson County Justice Center, Third Fl.,
Rm. 302, 400 First St., Hillsboro 63050; (636)
797-5345; FAX (636) 797-5542; rreuter@
jeffcomo.org

Council Member, Third District, Bob Boyer, (R),
Jefferson County Justice Center, Third Fl., Rm.
303, 400 First St., Hillsboro, 63050; (636)
797-5351; FAX (636) 797-5542; rboyer@
jeffcomo.org

Council Member, Fourth District, George
Engelbach, (R), Jefferson County Justice
Center, Third Fl., Rm. 304, 400 First St.,
Hillsboro 63050; (636) 797-5352; FAX (636)
797-5542; gengelbach@jeffcomo.org

Council Member, Fifth District, Oscar J. (Jim)
Kasten, (D), Jefferson County Justice Center,
Third Fl., Rm. 305, 400 First St., Hillsboro
63050; (636) 797-5353; FAX (636) 797-5542;
jkasten@jeffcomo.org

Council Member, Sixth District, Cliff Lane, (D),
Jefferson County Justice Center, Third Fl., Rm.

306, 400 First St., Hillsboro 63050; (636)
797-5377; FAX (636) 797-5542; clane@
jeffcomo.org

Council Member, Seventh District, Jim Terry,
(R), Jefferson County Justice Center, Third
Fl., Rm. 307, 400 First St., Hillsboro 63050;
(636) 797-5384; FAX (636) 797-5542; jterry@
jeffcomo.org

County Clerk, Wes Wagner, (D), PO Box
100, Hillsboro 63050; (636) 797-5486;
countyclerk@jeffcomo.org

County Counselor*, Carl W. Yates III, (R), PO Box
100, Hillsboro 63050-0100; (636) 797-5072;
wyates@jeffcomo.org

County Executive, Ken Waller, (R), PO Box 100,
Hillsboro 63050; (636) 797-5514; kwaller@
jeffcomo.org

County Health Department Director, Douglas
Dodson, PO Box 437, Hillsboro 63050; (636)
797-3737; FAX (636) 797-4631; douglas.
dodson@jeffcohealth.org

County Municipal Judge*, Joe Rathert, PO Box
100, Hillsboro 63050-0100; (636) 797-5398

Director of Administration*, David Courtway,
PO Box 100, Hillsboro 63050-0100; (636)
797-6487; dcourtway@jeffcomo.org

Director of Parks*, Mike Ginger, PO Box 100,
Hillsboro 63050-0100; (636) 797-5037;
mginger@jeffcomo.org

Emergency Management Director*, Warren
Robinson, PO Box 100, Hillsboro 63050;
(636) 797-5381; wrobinson@jeffcomo.org

Medical Examiner*, Mary F. Case, M.D., PO Box
100, Hillsboro 63050; (636) 977-7841

Prosecuting Attorney, Forrest Wegge, (D), PO
Box 100, Hillsboro 63050; (636) 797-5321;
fwegge@jeffcomo.org

Public Administrator, Steve Farmer, (R), PO
Box 100, Hillsboro 63050; (636) 797-5385;
sfarmer@jeffcomo.org

Public Works Director*, Jason Jonas, PO Box
100, Hillsboro 63050; (636) 797-5369;
jjonas@jeffcomo.org

Recorder of Deeds, Debbie Dunnegan, (R), PO
Box 100, Hillsboro 63050; (636) 797-5414;
ddunnegan@jeffcomo.org

Sheriff, Oliver Glenn Boyer, (D), PO Box 100,
Hillsboro 63050; (636) 797-5000; oboyer@
jeffcomo.org

Treasurer, Linda Nees, (D), PO Box 100, Hillsboro 63050; (636) 797-5368; lindanees@
jeffcomo.org

*Appointed

Johnson County

County seat and zip code: Warrensburg 64093. **County population:** 54,362. **Classification:** Second class. **Assessed valuation:** $592,272,375. **Square miles:** 834. **Organized:** December 13, 1834. **Named for:** Richard M. Johnson, Kentucky senator and later vice president.

Assessor, Mark Reynolds, (R), Johnson County Courthouse, 300 N. Holden, Warrensburg 64093; (660) 747-9822; markreynolds@joco courthouse.com

Auditor, Chad Davis, (R), Johnson County Courthouse, 300 N. Holden, Warrensburg 64093; (660) 747-2633; FAX (660) 747-9355; jocoauditor@earthlink.net

Clerk Circuit Court, Stephanie Elkins, (D), Johnson County Justice Center, 101 W. Market, Warrensburg 64093; (660) 422-7413; FAX (660) 422-7417

Clerk County Commission, Diane Thompson, (R), Johnson County Courthouse, 300 N. Holden, Warrensburg 64093; (660) 747-6161; FAX (660) 747-9332; dthompson@joco courthouse.com

Collector of Revenue, Ruthane Small, (D), Johnson County Courthouse, 300 N. Holden, Warrensburg 64093; (660) 747-5531; rsmall@ jcmtax.com

Commissioner, Eastern District, Scott Sader, (R), Johnson County Courthouse, 300 N. Holden, Warrensburg 64093; (660) 747-2112; FAX (660) 747-9332; ssader@jococourthouse.com

Commissioner, Western District, Destry Hough, (D), Johnson County Courthouse, 300 N. Holden, Warrensburg 64093; (660) 747-2112; FAX (660) 747-9332; dhough@joco courthouse.com

Coroner, C. L. Holdren, (R), 617 N. Maguire, Warrensburg 64093; (660) 747-9114; FAX (660) 429-2245

County Health Department Director*, Deborah Haller, 429 Burkarth Rd., Warrensburg 64093; (660) 747-6121

County Surveyor, Sam King, (R), 425 N. Holden, Warrensburg 64093; (660) 747-9512; FAX (660) 747-9592

Emergency Management Director*, Gloria Michalski, 122 Hout St., Ste. A, Warrensburg 64093; (660) 747-2666; FAX (660) 747-2316; gloria@warrensburgjocoema.com

Presiding Commissioner, William H. Gabel, (R), Johnson County Courthouse, 300 N. Holden, Warrensburg 64093; (660) 747-2112; FAX (660) 747-9332; wgabel@jococourthouse. com

Prosecuting Attorney, Rob Russell, (R), Johnson County Justice Center, 101 W. Market, Ste. 301, Warrensburg 64093; (660) 422-7400; FAX (660) 422-7404

Public Administrator, Nancy Jo Jennings, (R), Johnson County Courthouse, 300 N. Holden, Warrensburg 64093; (660) 747-5327; FAX (660) 747-5361; njennings@jocopublic admin.com

Recorder of Deeds, Jan Jones, (R), Johnson County Courthouse, 300 N. Holden, Ste. 305, Warrensburg 64093; (660) 747-6811; FAX (660) 747-0062

Road Supervisor*, Gary Bell, 335 E. North, Warrensburg 64093; (660) 747-6821; FAX (660) 747-5304; jocobarn@embarqmail.com

Sheriff, Scott Munsterman, (R), 278 SW 871, Centerview 64019; (660) 747-6469; FAX (816) 732-6382

Treasurer, Heather Reynolds, (R), Johnson County Courthouse, 300 N. Holden, Warrensburg 64093; (660) 747-7411; jocotreas1@ earthlink.net

---

*Appointed

Knox County

County seat and zip code: Edina 63537. **County population:** 4,000. **Classification:** Third class. **Assessed valuation:** $76,590,240. **Square miles:** 507. **Organized:** February 14, 1845. **Named for:** Henry Knox, Revolutionary War general.

Assessor, Anita James, (R), Knox County Courthouse, Edina 63537; (660) 397-4002; FAX (660) 397-3331; assessor@marktwain. net

Clerk Circuit Court, Roma March, (D), 107 N. Fourth St., Ste. I, Edina 63537; (660) 397-2305; FAX (660) 397-3331; roma.march@ courts.mo.gov

Clerk County Commission, Marlene Spory, (R), Knox County Courthouse, 107 N. Fourth St., Edina 63537; (660) 397-2184; FAX (660) 397-2642; knox@sos.mo.gov

Collector of Revenue, Brent Karhoff, (R), Knox County Courthouse, Edina 63537; (660) 397-2349; FAX (660) 397-3331; knoxcoll@mark twain.net

Commissioner, Eastern District, Michael R. Fox, (D), Knox County Courthouse, 107 N. Fourth St., Ste. F, Edina 63537; (660) 397-2688; FAX (660) 397-2642; knoxcomm@marktwain.net

Commissioner, Western District, Roger Parton, (D), Knox County Courthouse, 107 N. Fourth

St., Edina 63537; (660) 397-2688; FAX (660) 397-2642; knox@sos.mo.gov

Coroner, Jeffrey Doss, (D), RR 1, Box 172, Edina 63537; (660) 397-2212; FAX (660) 397-3308; jgdoss@marktwain.net

County Health Department Director, Lori Moots-Clair, 217 N. First, Edina 63537; (660) 397-3396; FAX (660) 397-3579; mootsl@lpha.mopublic.org

Emergency Management Director, Keith Gudehus, 107 N. Fourth, Edina 63537; (660) 341-2896; gudehus6@earthlink.net

Presiding Commissioner, Evan Glasgow, (R), Knox County Courthouse, 107 N. Fourth St., Edina 63537; (660) 397-2688; FAX (660) 397-2642; knox@sos.mo.gov

Prosecuting Attorney, Jo Fortney, (R), 207 N. Second St., Edina 63537; (660) 397-2644; FAX (660) 397-2646; fortneylawoffice@gmail.com

Public Administrator, Theresa L. Hamlin, (R), PO Box 206, Edina 63537; (660) 341-8272; FAX (660) 397-2234; knoxcomopubadm@gmail.com

Recorder of Deeds, Sandy Woods, (D), 107 N. Fourth, Edina 63537; (660) 397-4005; FAX (660) 397-3331; knoxrec@marktwain.net

Sheriff, Allen Gudehus, (D), Knox County Courthouse, 107 N. Fourth St., Edina 63537; (660) 397-2186; FAX (660) 397-3432; knoxcountysheriff@hotmail.com

Treasurer*, Donnie L. Davis, (D), Knox County Courthouse, 107 N. Fourth St., Edina 63537; (660) 397-3364; FAX (660) 397-3331; knox trea@marktwain.net

---

*Appointed

Laclede County

County seat and zip code: Lebanon 65536. **County population:** 35,571. **Classification:** Third class. **Assessed valuation:** $404,211,761. **Square miles:** 770. **Organized:** February 24, 1849. **Named for:** Pierre Laclede Liquest, founder of St. Louis.

Assessor, Johnny North, (R), Laclede County Government Center, 200 N. Adams Ave., Lebanon 65536; (417) 532-7163; FAX (417) 533-7417; jnorth.assessor@gmail.com

Clerk Circuit Court, Wanda Tyre, (R), Laclede County Government Center, 200 N. Adams Ave., Lebanon 65536; (417) 532-2471; FAX (417) 532-3683; wanda.tyre@courts.mo.gov

Clerk County Commission, Glenda Mott, (R), Laclede County Government Center, 200 N. Adams Ave., Lebanon 65536; (417) 532-5471; FAX (417) 588-9288; clerk@lacledecountymissouri.org

Collector of Revenue, Steve Pickering, (R), Laclede County Government Center, 200 N. Adams Ave., Lebanon 65536; (417) 532-4301; FAX (417) 533-7420; collector@lacledecountymissouri.org

Commissioner, Eastern District, Joe Pickering, (R), Laclede County Government Center, 200 N. Adams Ave., Lebanon 65536; (417) 532-4897; FAX (417) 588-9288; commission@lacledecountymissouri.org

Commissioner, Western District*, Jack Glendenning, (R), Laclede County Government Center, 200 N. Adams Ave., Lebanon 65536; (417) 532-4897; FAX (417) 588-9288; commission@lacledecountymissouri.org

Coroner, Steve Murrell, (R), Laclede County Government Center, 200 N. Adams Ave., Lebanon 65536; (417) 532-9086; FAX (417) 588-7976; farmedic@hotmail.com

County Health Department Director, Charla Baker, 405 Harwood Ave., Lebanon 65536; (417) 532-2134; FAX (417) 532-6095; bakerc@lpha.mopublic.org

County Surveyor, Robert Shotts, (R), PO Box 83, Lebanon 65536; (417) 588-7877; FAX (417) 588-7832; surveyor@lacledecountymissouri.org

Emergency Management Director, Randy Rowe, 200 N. Adams Ave., Lebanon 65536; (417) 532-6992; FAX (417) 588-7976; rrowe@lacledeoem.net

Presiding Commissioner, Danny Rhoades, (R), Laclede County Government Center, 200 N. Adams Ave., Lebanon 65536; (417) 532-4897; FAX (417) 588-9288; commission@lacledecountymissouri.org

Prosecuting Attorney, Jon Morris, (R), Laclede County Government Center, 200 N. Adams Ave., Lebanon 65536; (417) 532-5401; FAX (417) 532-3140

Public Administrator, Sherry Shamel, (D), Laclede County Government Center, 200 N. Adams Ave., Lebanon 65536; (417) 532-2416; FAX (417) 532-7886; publicadmin@lacledecountymissouri.org

Recorder of Deeds, Lynn Stowe, (R), Laclede County Government Center, 200 N. Adams Ave., Lebanon 65536; (417) 532-4011; FAX (417) 532-3852; recorder@lacledecountymissouri.org

Sheriff, Wayne Merritt, (D), Laclede County Government Center, 200 N. Adams Ave., Lebanon 65536; (417) 532-2311; FAX (417) 532-6719; sheriff265@lacledecountymissouri.org

Treasurer, Jean Cook, (R), Laclede County Government Center, 200 N. Adams Ave., Lebanon 65536; (417) 532-4741; treasurer@laclede countymissouri.org

---

*Appointed

Lafayette County

County seat and zip code: Lexington 64067. **County population:** 32,688. **Classification:** Fourth class. **Assessed valuation:** $423,103,427. **Square miles:** 632. **Organized:** November 16, 1820. **Named for:** Marquis de La Fayette.

Assessor*, Chip Langman, (D), Lafayette County Courthouse, 1001 Main St., Rm. 109, Lexington 64067; (660) 259-6158; FAX (660) 259-4482; dobson@lafayettecountymo.com

Auditor, Cherie Mason, (R), Lafayette County Courthouse, 1001 Main St., Rm. 107, Lexington 64067; (660) 259-6168; FAX (660) 259-6109; mason@lafayettecountymo.com

Clerk Circuit Court, Deana Aversman, (R), Lafayette County Courthouse, PO Box 10, Lexington 64067; (660) 259-6101; FAX (660) 259-6148

Clerk County Commission, Linda Niendick, (R), Lafayette County Courthouse, 1001 Main St., Lexington 64067; (660) 259-4315; FAX (660) 259-6109; niendick@lafayettecountymo.com

Collector of Revenue, Lori Fiegenbaum, (D), Lafayette County Courthouse, 1001 Main St., Rm. 100, Lexington 64067; (660) 259-6171; FAX (660) 259-4268; lfiegenbaum@lafayette countymo.com

Commissioner, Northern District, Gil Rector, (D), Lafayette County Courthouse, 1001 Main St., Lexington 64067; (660) 259-4315; FAX (660) 259-6109

Commissioner, Southern District, Tracy Dyer, (R), Lafayette County Courthouse, 1001 Main St., Rm. 104, Lexington 64067; (660) 259-4315; FAX (660) 259-6109

Coroner, Daljeet Singh, (D), Higginsville Medical Clinic, 3401 Pine St., Higginsville 64037; (660) 584-2192

County Health Department Director, Tom Emmerson, 547 S. 13 Hwy., Lexington 64067; (660) 259-4371; FAX (660) 259-6250

County Surveyor, Mark Nolte, (R), 1001 Main St., Lexington 64067; (660) 259-4315

Emergency Management Director, Robert (Bob) Florence, 1106 Main St., Lexington 64067; (660) 259-6551; (660) 259-6675

Presiding Commissioner, Harold Hoflander, (R), Lafayette County Courthouse, 1001 Main St.,

Rm. 104, Lexington 64067; (660) 259-4315; FAX (660) 259-6109; hchoflan@yahoo.com

Prosecuting Attorney, Kristen Ellis, (D), Lafayette County Courthouse Annex, 116 S. Tenth, Lexington 64067; (660) 259-6181; FAX (660) 259-2884

Public Administrator, Barb Copenhaver, (R), 1108 Main St., Ste. B, Lexington 64067; (660) 259-4520; FAX (660) 259-2159

Recorder of Deeds, JoAnn Swartz, (R), Lafayette County Courthouse, 1001 Main St., Rm. 206, Lexington 64067; (660) 259-6178; FAX (660) 259-2918

Sheriff, Kerrick Alumbaugh, (D), 107 S. 11th St., Lexington 64067; (660) 259-7724; FAX (660) 259-2545

Treasurer, Jennifer Jellum, (D), Lafayette County Courthouse, 1001 Main St., Rm. 108, Lexington 64067; (660) 259-3711; FAX (660) 259-6109

---

*Appointed

Lawrence County

County seat and zip code: Mt. Vernon 65712. **County population:** 38,023. **Classification:** Third class. **Assessed valuation:** $430,043,195. **Square miles:** 614. **Organized:** February 14, 1845. **Named for:** James Lawrence, naval hero of the War of 1812.

Assessor, Doug Bowerman, (R), Lawrence County Courthouse, 1 E. Courthouse Sq., PO Box 188, Mt. Vernon 65712; (417) 466-2831; FAX (417) 466-3931; lcmoassessor@sofnet.com

Clerk Circuit Court, Steven W. Kahre, (R), Lawrence County Justice Center, 240 N. Main, Ste. 110, Mt. Vernon 65712; (417) 466-2471; FAX (417) 466-7899; steven.kahre@ courts.mo.gov

Clerk County Commission, Gary Emerson, (R), Lawrence County Courthouse, 1 E. Courthouse Sq., Ste. 101, Mt. Vernon 65712; (417) 466-2638; FAX (417) 466-4348; lawrence@ sos.mo.gov

Collector of Revenue, Kelli McVey, (R), Lawrence County Courthouse, 1 E. Courthouse Sq., PO Box 29, Mt. Vernon 65712; (417) 466-2410; FAX (417) 466-2065

Commissioner, Eastern District, Joe Ruscha, (R), Lawrence County Courthouse, 1 E. Courthouse Sq., Ste. 101, Mt. Vernon 65712; (417) 466-3666; FAX (417) 466-4348; lawrence@ sos.mo.gov

Commissioner, Western District, David Botts, (R), Lawrence County Courthouse, 1 E. Courthouse Sq., Ste. 101, Mt. Vernon 65712;

(417) 466-3666; FAX (417) 466-4348; lawrence@sos.mo.gov

Coroner, Scott Lakin, (R), 501 Elm St., Pierce City 65723; (417) 476-2626

County Health Department Director, Janella Spencer, 105 W. North, Mt. Vernon 65712; (417) 466-2201; FAX (417) 466-7485; spencj@lpha.mopublic.org

Emergency Management Director*, Bonnie Witt-Schulte, 1901 E. Cleveland Ave., Monett 65708; (417) 235-4241; emd@cityofmonett. com

Presiding Commissioner, Sam Goodman, (R), Lawrence County Courthouse, 1 E. Courthouse Sq., Ste. 101, Mt. Vernon 65712; (417) 466-3666; FAX (417) 466-4348; lawrence@ sos.mo.gov

Prosecuting Attorney, Don Trotter, (R), Lawrence County Justice Center, 240 N. Main, PO Box 69, Mt. Vernon 65712; (417) 466-2846; FAX (417) 466-3697

Public Administrator, Pam Fobair, (R), Lawrence County Justice Center, 240 N. Main, PO Box 431, Mt. Vernon 65712; (417) 466-2273; FAX (417) 466-1108; pamfobair@hotmail.com

Recorder of Deeds, Pam Robertson, (R), Lawrence County Courthouse, 1 E. Courthouse Sq., PO Box 449, Mt. Vernon 65712; (417) 466-2670; FAX (417) 466-4995

Sheriff, Brad DeLay, (R), Lawrence County Justice Center, 240 N. Main, PO Box 107, Mt. Vernon 65712; (417) 466-2131; FAX (417) 466-4222; lawrenceco@sofnet.com

Surveyor*, Aaron Austin, PO Box 451, Mt. Vernon 65712; (417) 471-1628

Treasurer, Kathy S. Fairchild, (R), Lawrence County Courthouse, 1 E. Courthouse Sq., PO Box 46, Mt. Vernon 65712; (417) 466-2662; FAX (417) 466-2666; lawrencecountytreasurer@ yahoo.com

---

*Appointed

Lewis County

County seat and zip code: Monticello 63457. **County population:** 10,138. **Classification:** Third class. **Assessed valuation:** $122,023,311. **Square miles:** 508. **Organized:** January 2, 1833. **Named for:** Captain Meriwether Lewis, Governor of the Missouri Territory.

Assessor, Craig Myers, (D), Lewis County Courthouse Annex, PO Box 14, Monticello 63457; (573) 767-5209; FAX (573) 767-8305; lca@ marktwain.net

Clerk Circuit Court, Jan E. Geisendorfer, (D), Lewis County Courthouse, PO Box 8, Monticello 63457; (573) 767-5352; FAX (573) 767-5342

Clerk County Commission, Regina Dredge, (D), Lewis County Courthouse, 100 E. Lafayette, PO Box 67, Monticello 63457; (573) 767-5205; FAX (573) 767-8245; lewis@sos. mo.gov

Collector of Revenue, Denise Goodwin, (D), Lewis County Courthouse, PO Box 7, Monticello 63457; (573) 767-5438; FAX (573) 767-5392; lewiscol@marktwain.net

Commissioner, Northern District, John Campen, (D), Lewis County Courthouse, PO Box 67, Monticello 63457; (573) 767-5476; FAX (573) 767-8245; lewis@sos.mo.gov

Commissioner, Southern District, Jesse Roberts, (D), Lewis County Courthouse, PO Box 67, Monticello 63457; (573) 767-5476; FAX (573) 767-8245; lewis@sos.mo.gov

Coroner, Larry Arnold, (D), 1100 White, Canton 63435; (573) 288-4488

County Health Department Administrator, Diane Lay, 101 State Hwy. A, PO Box 96, Monticello 63457; (573) 767-5312; FAX (573) 767-5301; layd@lpha.mopublic.org

County Surveyor, Carson W. Lay, (R), 19016 100th Ave., LaBelle 63447; (660) 341-5556; carsonl@psba.com.com

Emergency Management Director*, David L. Keith, 200 N. Highland, Ewing 63440; (573) 248-4789; FAX (573) 209-5391; klelec@ marktwain.net

Presiding Commissioner, Wayne Murphy Jr., (R), Lewis County Courthouse, 100 E. Lafayette, PO Box 67, Monticello 63457; (573) 767-5476; FAX (573) 767-8245; waynemurphyjr@ gmail.com or lewis@sos.mo.gov

Prosecuting Attorney, Jules V. (Jake) DeCoster, (D), Lewis County Courthouse, PO Box 11, Monticello 63457; (573) 767-5478; FAX (573) 767-5470

Public Administrator, Brett B. Bozarth, (D), PO Box 270, Canton 63435; (573) 288-1111; FAX (573) 288-1110

Recorder of Deeds, Amy Parrish, (D), Lewis County Courthouse, PO Box 97, Monticello 63457; (573) 767-5440; FAX (573) 767-5378

Sheriff, David T. Parrish, (D), 107 S. Washington St., Monticello 63457; (573) 767-5287; FAX (573) 767-5412; lcso@marktwain.net

Treasurer, Bonnie Roberson, (D), Lewis County Courthouse, PO Box 33, Monticello 63457; (573) 767-5446; FAX (573) 767-8245; lewtreas@marktwain.net

---

*Appointed

Lincoln County

County seat and zip code: Troy 63379. **County population:** 54,249. **Classification:** Second class. **Assessed valuation:** $689,361,122. **Square miles:** 627. **Organized:** December 14, 1818. **Named for:** Benjamin Lincoln, Revolutionary War general.

Assessor, Kevin L. Bishop, (R), Lincoln County Courthouse, 201 Main St., Troy 63379; (636) 528-6300, ext. 232

Auditor, Barb Wehde, (R), Lincoln County Courthouse, 201 Main St., Troy 63379; (636) 528-2865

Clerk Circuit Court, Grace Sinclair, (D), Lincoln County Justice Center, 45 Business Park Dr., Troy 63379; (636) 528-6300, ext. 253

Clerk County Commission, Crystal Hall, (D), Lincoln County Courthouse, 201 Main St., Troy 63379; (636) 528-0311; FAX (636) 528-5528

Collector of Revenue, Jerry Fox, (D), Lincoln County Courthouse, 201 Main St., Troy 63379; (636) 528-6300, ext. 275

Commissioner, First District, Eugene Galloway, (D), Lincoln County Courthouse, 201 Main St., Troy 63379; (636) 528-6300, ext. 223

Commissioner, Second District, Matt Bass, (R), Lincoln County Courthouse, 201 Main St., Troy 63379; (636) 528-6300, ext. 224

Coroner, Kelly Walters, (D), 250 W. College, Troy 63379; (636) 528-5087

County Health Department Director*, Brett Seifert, 5 Health Dept. Dr., Troy 63379; (636) 528-6117

County Surveyor, Donald (Tec) Parr, (D), Lincoln County Courthouse, Oak St., PO Box 182, Troy 63379; (636) 528-7110

Emergency Management Director, Jerry Daugherty, 250 W. College St., Troy 63379; (636) 528-6300, ext. 2248

Presiding Commissioner, Daniel H. Colbert, (R), Lincoln County Courthouse, 201 Main St., Troy 63379; (636) 528-0311

Prosecuting Attorney, Leah Askey, (D), PO Box 319, 45 Business Park Dr., Troy 63379; (636) 528-8571

Public Administrator, Betty Cox, (D), 201 Main St., Troy 63379; (636) 528-8287

Recorder of Deeds, Dottie D. Crenshaw, (D), Lincoln County Courthouse, 201 Main St., Troy 63379; (636) 528-6300, ext. 249

Sheriff, John Cottle, (R), 65 Business Park, Troy 63379; (636) 528-8546

Treasurer, Kristen Burkemper, (R), Lincoln County Courthouse, 201 Main St., Troy 63379; (636) 528-6300, ext. 268

———

*Appointed

Linn County

County seat and zip code: Linneus 64653. **County population:** 12,311. **Classification:** Third class. **Assessed valuation:** $144,986,446. **Square miles:** 620. **Organized:** January 6, 1837. **Named for:** Lewis F. Linn, United States Senator.

Assessor, Marlene Graves, (D), Linn County Courthouse, Rm. 106, Linneus 64653; (660) 895-5387

Clerk Circuit Court*, Mary S. Enyeart, (D), PO Box 84, Linneus 64653; (660) 895-5212

Clerk County Commission, Suzan Stephenson, (R), Linn County Courthouse, 108 N. High, Rm. 102, PO Box 92, Linneus 64653; (660) 895-5417; FAX (660) 895-5527; linn@sos.mo.gov

Collector/Treasurer, Pamela S. Reed, (D), Linn County Courthouse, Rm. 104, Linneus 64653; (660) 895-5410

Commissioner, District 1, Bill Dorsey, (D), Linn County Courthouse, Rm. 103, Linneus 64653; (660) 895-5547

Commissioner, District 2, Jim Libby, (D), Linn County Courthouse, Rm. 103, Linneus 64653; (660) 895-5547

Coroner, Kenny F. Creason, (D), 20728 Hwy. C, Purdin 64674; (660) 375-2127; FAX (660) 244-3201

County Health Department Director, Vanessa Lincoln, 635 S. Main, Brookfield 64628; (660) 258-7251

Emergency Management Director, Justin Griffin, 116 W. Brooks, Brookfield 64628; (660) 258-3332

Presiding Commissioner, Dick King, (R), Linn County Courthouse, Rm. 103, Linneus 64653; (660) 895-5547

Prosecuting Attorney, Tracy L. Carlson, (D), Courthouse Annex, PO Box 77, Linneus 64653; (660) 895-5589

Public Administrator, Kay Cunningham, (R), 521 N. Main, Brookfield 64628; (660) 258-7825

Recorder of Deeds, Loretta Brookshier, (D), Linn County Courthouse, Rm. 204, PO Box 151, Linneus 64653; (660) 895-5216

Sheriff, Tom Parks, (D), 115 W. Jackson St., Linneus 64653; (660) 895-5312

---

*Appointed

Livingston County

County seat and zip code: Chillicothe 64601. **County population:** 15,053. **Classification:** Third class. **Assessed valuation:** $172,994,026. **Square miles:** 537. **Organized:** January 6, 1837. **Named for:** Edward Livingston, former Secretary of State.

Assessor, Steve Ripley, (D), Livingston County Courthouse, 700 Webster St., Chillicothe 64601; (660) 646-8000, ext. 2; FAX (660) 646-8005; assessor@livingstoncountymo.com

Clerk Circuit Court, Brenda Wright, (D), Livingston County Courthouse, 700 Webster St., Chillicothe 64601; (660) 646-8000; FAX (660) 646-2734; brenda.wright@courts.mo.gov

Clerk County Commission, Sherry Parks, (D), Livingston County Courthouse, 700 Webster St., Ste. 10, Chillicothe 64601; (660) 646-8000, ext. 3; FAX (660) 646-8010; countyclerk@livingstoncountymo.com

Collector/Treasurer, Paula McCoy, (D), Livingston County Courthouse, 700 Webster St., Chillicothe 64601; (660) 646-8000, ext. 7; FAX (660) 646-8015; treasurer@livingstoncountymo.com

Commissioner, Eastern District, Ken Lauhoff, (D), Livingston County Courthouse, 700 Webster St., Chillicothe 64601; (660) 646-8000, ext. 209; FAX (660) 646-8010; countycommission@livingstoncountymo.com

Commissioner, Western District, Todd Rodenberg, (D), Livingston County Courthouse, 700 Webster St., Chillicothe 64601; (660) 646-8000, ext. 218; FAX (660) 646-8010; countycommission@livingstoncountymo.com

Coroner, J. Scott Lindley, (D), 910 Washington, Chillicothe 64601; (660) 646-4857

County Health Department Director, Sherry Weldon, 800 Adam Dr., Chillicothe 64601; (660) 646-5506; FAX (660) 646-4485; weldos@lpha.mopublic.org

Emergency Management Director, Darrel Wright, 700 Second St., Chillicothe 64601; (660) 646-2139

Presiding Commissioner, Ed Douglas, (D), Livingston County Courthouse, 700 Webster St., Chillicothe 64601; (660) 646-8000, ext. 202; FAX (660) 646-8010; countycommission@livingstoncountymo.com

Prosecuting Attorney, Adam L. Warren, (R), Livingston County Courthouse, 700 Webster St., Ste. 7, Chillicothe 64601; (660) 646-8000, ext. 5; FAX (660) 646-1819; prosecutor2@livingstoncountymo.com

Public Administrator, Sherry Parks, (D), 700 Webster St., Chillicothe 64601; (660) 646-8000, ext. 8; FAX (660) 646-8021; parkssherry66@yahoo.com

Recorder of Deeds, Kelly Christopher, (D), 700 Webster St., Chillicothe 64601; (660) 646-8000, ext. 6; FAX (660) 646-5402; recorder@livingstoncountymo.com

Sheriff, Steve Cox, (R), Livingston County Jail, 901 Webster St., Chillicothe 64601; (660) 646-0515; FAX (660) 646-0520; scox@livcoso.org

Macon County

County seat and zip code: Macon 63552. **County population:** 15,566. **Classification:** Third class. **Assessed valuation:** $183,408,093. **Square miles:** 797. **Organized:** January 6, 1837. **Named for:** Nathaniel Macon, revolutionary soldier and North Carolina congressman.

Assessor, Alan Spencer, (D), Macon County Courthouse, 101 E. Washington, Ste. 301, Macon 63552; (660) 385-2416; FAX (660) 385-3140; assessor@cvalley.net

Clerk Circuit Court, Twila Halley, (R), Macon County Courthouse, 101 E. Washington, Bldg. 2, Ste. 1, Macon 63552; (660) 385-4631; FAX (660) 385-4235; twila.halley@courts.mo.gov

Clerk County Commission, Shirley Sims, (R), Macon County Courthouse, 101 E. Washington, Ste. B, Macon 63552; (660) 385-2913; FAX (660) 385-7203; macon@sos.mo.gov

Collector of Revenue, Jeanette Powell, (D), Macon County Courthouse, 101 E. Washington, Ste. 302, Macon 63552; (660) 385-3214; FAX (660) 385-4085; jrcollector@cvalley.net

Commissioner, District 1, Drew Belt, (R), Macon County Courthouse, 101 E. Washington, Ste. B, Macon 63552; (660) 385-2913; FAX (660) 385-7203; macon.district1@gmail.com

Commissioner, District 2, Jon Dwiggins, (R), Macon County Courthouse, 101 E. Washington, Ste. B, Macon 63552; (660) 385-2913; FAX (660) 385-7203; macon.district2@gmail.com

Coroner, Brian Hayes, (D), 402 Pearl St., Macon 63552; (660) 385-5721

County Health Department Director, Judy R. Rushton, 503 N. Missouri St., Macon 63552; (660) 385-4711; FAX (660) 385-2014; rushtj@lpha.mo.public.org

County Surveyor, John H. Schaefer, (R), 30638 Kenbrook Pl., Macon 63552; (660) 395-5942; jschaefer@cvalley.net

Emergency Management Director, Michael J. Shively, PO Box 471, Macon 63552; (660) 591-2900; director@maconcountyoem.net

Presiding Commissioner, Alan R. Wyatt, (R), Macon County Courthouse, 101 E. Washington, Ste. B, Macon 63552; (660) 385-2913; FAX (660) 385-7203; macon.presiding@gmail.com

Prosecuting Attorney, Josh Meisner, (D), 101 E. Washington St., Ste. A, Macon 63552; (660) 385-2175; FAX (660) 385-6800; mcpa@cvalley.net

Public Administrator, Lois Noland, (D), 101 E. Washington St., Ste. E, Macon 63552; (660) 385-6173; FAX (660) 385-1720; nolandlois@gmail.com

Recorder of Deeds, Sherry Muncy, (R), Macon County Courthouse, 101 E. Washington, Ste. 300, Macon 63552; (660) 385-2732; FAX (660) 395-4022; maconrecorder@cvalley.net; maconrecorder2@cvalley.net

Sheriff, Kevin Shoemaker, (D), Macon County Jail, 101 W. Sheridan, PO Box 522, Macon 63552; (660) 385-2062; FAX (660) 385-5308; mcso@cvalley.net

Treasurer, Krista Bruno, (R), Macon County Courthouse, 101 E. Washington, Ste. D, Macon 63552; (660) 385-2713; FAX (660) 385-7203; mct@cvalley.net

Madison County

County seat and zip code: Fredericktown 63645. **County population:** 12,368. **Classification:** Third class. **Assessed valuation:** $109,482,472. **Square miles:** 497. **Organized:** December 14, 1818. **Named for:** James Madison.

Assessor, Dennis Bradford, (R), Madison County Courthouse, 1 Courthouse Sq., Fredericktown 63645; (573) 783-3325; FAX (573) 783-8482; assessor@madisoncountymo.us

Clerk Circuit Court, Eileen Provow, (D), Madison County Courthouse, 1 Courthouse Sq., Fredericktown 63645; (573) 783-2102; FAX (573) 783-5920

Clerk County Commission, Donal E. Firebaugh, (D), Madison County Courthouse, 1 Courthouse Sq., Fredericktown 63645; (573) 783-2176; FAX (573) 783-5351; countyclerk@madisoncountymo.us

Collector of Revenue, Debby Boone, (R), Madison County Courthouse, 1 Courthouse Sq., Fredericktown 63645; (573) 783-6544; FAX (573) 783-2274; collector@madisoncountymo.us

Commissioner, First District, Tom Stephens, (R), Madison County Courthouse, 1 Courthouse Sq., Fredericktown 63645; (573) 783-2176

Commissioner, Second District, Jim Thompson, (R), Madison County Courthouse, 1 Courthouse Sq., Fredericktown 63645; (573) 783-2176

Coroner, Collin L. Follis, (D), 700 Madison Plaza Dr., Fredericktown 63645; (573) 783-8336; FAX (573) 783-7729

County Health Department Director, Becky Hunt, 806 W. College, Fredericktown 63645; (573) 783-2746; FAX (573) 783-8039

County Surveyor, William Douglas McFarland, (D), 1095 Madison 214, Fredericktown 63645; (573) 783-6345

Emergency Management Director/County Health Department Director, Becky Hunt, 806 W. College, Fredericktown 63645; (573) 783-2746; FAX (573) 783-8039

Presiding Commissioner, Robert Mooney, (R), Madison County Courthouse, 1 Courthouse Sq., Fredericktown 63645; (573) 783-2176; FAX (573) 783-5351; bobmooney2003@yahoo.com

Prosecuting Attorney, M. Dwight Robbins, (R), PO Box 207, Fredericktown 63645; (573) 783-7212; FAX (573) 783-2473

Public Administrator*, Carol Lachance, (R), 1519 Madison 209, Fredericktown 63645; (573) 783-5372

Recorder of Deeds, Paula Francis, (D), Madison County Courthouse, 1 Courthouse Sq., Fredericktown 63645; (573) 783-3410; FAX (573) 783-2715

Sheriff, Robert (Bobby) Spain, (R), Madison County Jail, 124 N. Main St., Fredericktown 63645; (573) 783-2234

Treasurer, Nadean Rice, (R), Madison County Courthouse, 1 Courthouse Sq., Fredericktown 63645; (573) 783-7847; FAX (573) 783-2274; treasurer@madisoncountymo.us

*Appointed

Maries County

County seat and zip code: Vienna 65582. **County population:** 9,013. **Classification:** Third class. **Assessed valuation:** $120,510,832. **Square miles:** 528. **Organized:** March 2, 1855. **Named for:** The Maries Rivers.

Assessor, Dana Simmons, (D), Maries County Courthouse, PO Box 188, Vienna 65582;

(573) 422-3540; FAX (573) 422-3859; danas@mariesco.org

Clerk Circuit Court and ex officio Recorder of Deeds, Mark Buschmann, (D), Maries County Courthouse, PO Box 213, Vienna 65582; (573) 422-3338; FAX (573) 422-3976; mark. buschmann@courts.mo.gov

Clerk County Commission, Rhonda Brewer, (D), Maries County Courthouse, PO Box 205, Vienna 65582; (573) 422-3388; FAX (573) 422-3269; rhonda@mariesco.org

Collector of Revenue, Jayne Helton, (D), Maries County Courthouse, PO Box 71, Vienna 65582; (573) 422-3343; FAX (573) 422-6884; jayne@mariesco.org

Commissioner, Eastern District, Douglas Drewel, (R), Maries County Courthouse, PO Box 205, Vienna 65582; (573) 422-3388; FAX (573) 422-3269

Commissioner, Western District, Ed Fagre, (D), Maries County Courthouse, PO Box 205, Vienna 65582; (573) 422-3388; FAX (573) 422-3269

Coroner, David H. Martin, (D), PO Box 210, Vienna 65582; (573) 422-3331; FAX (573) 422-3145; birminghammartin@att.net

Emergency Management Director*, Ken Ramsey, Maries County Courthouse, PO Box 205, Vienna 65582; (573) 422-3388; FAX (573) 422-3269

Presiding Commissioner, Ray Schwartze, (R), Maries County Courthouse, PO Box 205, Vienna 65582; (573) 422-3388; FAX (573) 422-3269

Prosecuting Attorney, Terry D. Schwartze, (D), Maries County Courthouse, PO Box 212, Vienna 65582; (573) 422-3396; FAX (573) 422-3829; terry@mariesco.org

Public Administrator, Eugene J. Meyer, (D), PO Box 186, Vienna 65582; (573) 422-6151; FAX (573) 422-3156; ej@mariesco.org

Sheriff, Harold Chris Heitman, (R), Maries County Courthouse, PO Box 23, Vienna 65582; (573) 422-3381; FAX (573) 422-3100; cheitman@ mariesco.org

Treasurer, Rhonda Slone, (D), Maries County Courthouse, PO Box 104, Vienna 65582; (573) 422-3311; FAX (573) 422-3269; rhondas@ mariesco.org

---

*Appointed

Marion County

County seat and zip code: Palmyra 63461. **County population:** 28,920. **Classification:** Third

class. **Assessed valuation:** $386,873,256. **Square miles:** 438. **Organized:** December 23, 1826. **Named for:** Francis Marion, Revolutionary War hero.

Assessor, Mark Novak, (D), Marion County Assessor, 906 Broadway, Hannibal 63401; (573) 221-0589; FAX (573) 221-4250

Clerk Circuit Court, Division I, Valerie Munzlinger, (D), Marion County Courthouse, 100 S. Main, Rm. 207, PO Box 431, Palmyra 63461; (573) 769-2550; FAX (573) 769-4558

Clerk Circuit Court, Division II, Carolyn Conners, (D), Marion County Courthouse, 906 Broadway, Rm. 105, Hannibal 63401; (573) 221-0198

Clerk County Commission, Valerie Dornberger, (D), Marion County Courthouse, 100 S. Main, Palmyra 63461; (573) 769-2549; FAX (573) 769-4312; val@mcco.mo.com

Collector of Revenue, Harry Graves, (R), Marion County Courthouse, 100 S. Main, Palmyra 63461; (573) 769-3282; 906 Broadway, Hannibal 63401; (573) 221-0727

Commissioner, Eastern District, Larry Welch, (R), 5 Pioneer Tr., Hannibal 63401; (573) 769-2549

Commissioner, Western District, Randy Spratt, (R), 2404 CR 169, Philadelphia 63463; (573) 769-2549

Coroner*, Darrell McCoy, (D), 5 Village Rd., Hannibal 63401; (573) 231-6484

County Health Department Director, Olivia Jean McBride, 3105 Rt. W, PO Box 1378, Hannibal 63401; (573) 221-1166

County Surveyor, John D. Janes, (I), 5497 County Rd. 409, Hannibal 63401; (573) 769-7020

Emergency Management Director, John Hark, 3310 Arapaho, Hannibal 63461; (573) 221-5346; FAX (573) 221-3772; hark203@ mywdo.com

Land Use and Capitol Improvements Coordinator, Teya Stice, Marion County Courthouse, 100 S. Main, Palmyra 63461; (573) 769-5545; FAX (573) 769-5545; mccoordinator@ centurytel.net

Presiding Commissioner, Lyndon Bode, (D), 6950 County Rd. 263, Palmyra 63461; (573) 769-2549; FAX (573) 221-6796

Prosecuting Attorney, David Clayton, (D), Marion County Courthouse, 906 Broadway, Hannibal 63401; (573) 221-0146

Public Administrator*, Wendy Howe, (D), Marion County Courthouse, 906 Broadway, Rm. 104, Hannibal 63401; (573) 221-9149; FAX (573) 221-2645

Recorder of Deeds, Harla Friesz, (D), Marion County Courthouse, 100 S. Main, Rm. 103, PO Box 392, Palmyra 63461; (573) 769-7001; FAX (573) 769-6012

Sheriff, Jimmy Shinn, (D), 1703 Marion City Rd., Palmyra 63461; (573) 769-2077

Treasurer, Joelle Fohey, (D), Marion County Courthouse, 100 S. Main, Palmyra 63461; (573) 769-2552; FAX (573) 769-2552; marioncotreas@hotmail.com

---

*Appointed

McDonald County

County seat and zip code: Pineville 64856. **County population:** 22,800. **Classification:** Third class. **Assessed valuation:** $263,460,877. **Square miles:** 541. **Organized:** March 3, 1849. **Named for:** Alexander McDonald, Revolutionary War soldier.

Assessor, Laura Pope, (R), PO Box 726, Pineville 64856; (417) 223-4361; lspope@olemac.net

Clerk Circuit Court, Jennifer Mikeska, (R), PO Box 157, Pineville 64856; (417) 223-7512; jennifer.mikeska@courts.mo.gov

Clerk County Commission, Kimberly Bell, (R), PO Box 665, Pineville 64856; (417) 223-4662; mcdonald@sos.mo.gov

Collector of Revenue, Jennifer Weber, (R), PO Box 725, Pineville 64856; (417) 223-7408; mcdonaldcountycollector@yahoo.com

Commissioner, Eastern District, John Bunch, (R), PO Box 665, Pineville 64856; (417) 223-7516; commission@olemac.net

Commissioner, Western District, David Hollaway, (R), PO Box 665, Pineville 64856; (417) 223-2842; commission@olemac.net

Coroner, B.J. Goodwin III, (R), PO Box 520, Anderson64831;(417)845-3393;ozarkfh@olemac.net

County Health Department Administrator*, Paige Behm, PO Box 366, Pineville 64856; (417) 223-4351; behmp@lpha.mopublic.org

County Surveyor, Travis Green, (R), PO Box 816, Pineville 64856; (417) 436-3900; t_green@netins.net

Emergency Management Director*, Gregg Sweeten, PO Box 665, Pineville 64856; (417) 223-7575; mcdema@olemac.net

Presiding Commissioner, Keith Lindquist, (R), PO Box 665, Pineville 64856; (417) 223-2842; commission@olemac.net

Prosecuting Attorney, Bill Dobbs, (R), PO Box 566, Pineville 64856; (417) 223-4142; bdobbs@mcprosecutor.org

Public Administrator, Donna Underwood, (R), PO Box 758, Pineville 64856; (417) 223-7333; donnau@olemac.net

Recorder of Deeds, Kenny Underwood, (R), PO Box 606, Pineville 64856; (417) 223-7523; recorder@olemac.net

Sheriff, Mike Hall, (R), PO Box 68, Pineville 64856; (417) 223-4319; m.hall@mcdonaldcountysheriff.com

Treasurer, Joye Helm, (R), PO Box 654, Pineville 64856; (417) 223-7514; mctreasurer@olemac.net

---

*Appointed

Mercer County

County seat and zip code: Princeton 64673. **County population:** 3,719. **Classification:** Third class. **Assessed valuation:** $63,978,122. **Square miles:** 454. **Organized:** February 14, 1845. **Named for:** Hugh Mercer, Revolutionary War general.

Assessor, Diana J. Blunk, (R), Mercer County Courthouse, 802 E. Main St., Princeton 64673; (660) 748-3511; FAX (660) 748-3007; assessor@grm.net

Clerk Circuit Court and ex officio **Recorder of Deeds,** Tammy Crouse, (R), Mercer County Courthouse, 802 E. Main St., Princeton 64673; (660) 748-4335; FAX (660) 748-4539; tammy.crouse@courts.mo.gov

Clerk County Commission, Judy Hamilton, (R), Mercer County Courthouse, 802 E. Main St., Princeton 64673; (660) 748-3425; FAX (660) 748-3445; mcclerk@grm.net

Collector/Treasurer, Susan Moore, (R), Mercer County Courthouse, 802 E. Main St., Princeton 64673; (660) 748-3435; FAX (660) 748-3135; smoorecoll_treas@yahoo.com

Commissioner, First District, Thomas Shane Grooms, (R), Mercer County Courthouse, 802 E. Main St., Princeton 64673; (660) 748-3425; FAX (660) 748-3445

Commissioner, Second District, Zachary W. Martin, (D), Mercer County Courthouse, 802 E. Main St., Princeton 64673; (660) 748-3425; FAX (660) 748-3445

Coroner, Michael Greenlee, (D), 305 Broadway, 802 E. Main St., Princeton 64673; (660) 748-3319

County Health Department Director*, Phyllis Johnson, 305 W. Main St., Princeton 64673; (660) 748-3693

Emergency Management Director*, Mark Thompson, 27272 US Hwy. 65, Princeton 64673; (660) 748-3247

Presiding Commissioner, James Mason, (R), Mercer County Courthouse, 802 E. Main St., Princeton 64673; (660) 748-3425; FAX (660) 748-3445; mcclerk@grm.net

Prosecuting Attorney, John L. Young, (R), 712 Main St., Princeton 64673; (660) 748-3332; FAX (660) 748-4707; younglaw@grm.net

Public Administrator, Kelli Judd, (R), Mercer County Courthouse, 802 E. Main St., Princeton 64673; (660) 748-3640; FAX (660) 748-3411

Sheriff, Steve Stockman, (R), Mercer County Courthouse, 802 E. Main St., Princeton 64673; (660) 748-3165; FAX (660) 748-3180; mercoso@grm.net

*Appointed

Miller County

County seat and zip code: Tuscumbia 65082. **County population:** 25,141. **Classification:** Third class. **Assessed valuation:** $415,509,044. **Square miles:** 593. **Organized:** February 6, 1837. **Named for:** John Miller, Governor of Missouri.

Assessor, Joseph Cochran, (R), Miller County Courthouse, PO Box 12, Tuscumbia 65082; (573) 369-1960

Clerk Circuit Court, Genise L. Buechter, (R), Miller County Courthouse, PO Box 12, Tuscumbia 65082; (573) 369-1970

Clerk County Commission, Clinton Jenkins, (R), Miller County Courthouse, PO Box 12, Tuscumbia 65082; (573) 369-1910; FAX (573) 369-1905; clayton@millercountymo.org

Collector of Revenue*, William Harvey, (R), Miller County Courthouse, PO Box 12, Tuscumbia 65082; (573) 369-1925

Commissioner, First District, Darrell Bunch, (R), Miller County Courthouse, PO Box 12, Tuscumbia 65082; (573) 369-1900

Commissioner, Second District, Brian Duncan, (R), Miller County Courthouse, PO Box 12, Tuscumbia 65082; (573) 369-1900

Coroner, Rick Callahan, (R), 201 N. Maple, Eldon 65026; (573) 392-3351

County Health Department Director*, Bruce Jenkins, PO Box 2, Tuscumbia 65082; (573) 369-2359

County Highway Engineer*, Darren Evers, (R), Miller County Courthouse, PO Box 12, Tuscumbia 65082; (573) 369-1900

County Surveyor, Gerard J. Harms Sr., (R), 2105 S. Oak, Eldon 65026; (573) 392-3312

Emergency Management Director*, Barlow Biggers, PO Box 12, Tuscumbia 65082; (573) 369-1880

Presiding Commissioner, Tom Wright, (R), Miller County Courthouse, PO Box 12, Tuscumbia 65082; (573) 369-1900

Prosecuting Attorney, Benjamin Winfrey, (R), Miller County Courthouse, PO Box 12, Tuscumbia 65082; (573) 369-1940

Public Administrator, Theresa Lupardus, (R), Miller County Courthouse, PO Box 12, Tuscumbia 65082; (573) 369-1955

Recorder of Deeds, Deb Wiles, (R), Miller County Courthouse, PO Box 12, Tuscumbia 65082; (573) 369-1935

Sheriff, William Abbott, (R), Miller County Courthouse, PO Box 13, Tuscumbia 65082; (573) 369-2341

Treasurer, Phil Lawson, (R), Miller County Courthouse, PO Box 24, Tuscumbia 65082; (573) 369-1920

*Appointed

Mississippi County

County seat and zip code: Charleston 63834. **County population:** 14,232. **Classification:** Third class. **Assessed valuation:** $159,689,429. **Square miles:** 410. **Organized:** February 14, 1845. **Named for:** The Mississippi River.

Assessor, Lisa Finley-Norton, (D), Mississippi County Courthouse, PO Box 369, Charleston 63834; (573) 683-2146, ext. 237; FAX (573) 683-7548; lnorton@misscomo.net

Clerk Circuit Court, Dottie McKenzie, (D), Mississippi County Courthouse, PO Box 369, Charleston 63834; (573) 683-2146, ext. 225; FAX (573) 683-7696; dottie.mckenzie@courts.mo.gov

Clerk County Commission, Hubert DeLay Jr., (D), Mississippi County Courthouse, PO Box 369, Charleston 63834; (573) 683-2146, ext. 221; FAX (573) 683-6071; jrdelay@misscomo.net

Collector of Revenue, Ann McCuiston, (D), Mississippi County Courthouse, PO Box 369, Charleston 63834; (573) 683-2146, ext. 231; FAX (573) 683-6217; am@misscomo.net

Commissioner, First District, Mitch Pullen, (D), Mississippi County Courthouse, PO Box 369, Charleston 63834; (573) 683-2146, ext. 221;

FAX (573) 683-6071; mitchpullen@yahoo.com

Commissioner, Second District, Darrell Jones, (D), Mississippi County Courthouse, PO Box 369, Charleston 63834; (573) 683-2146, ext. 221; FAX (573) 683-6071; mbjdad499@yahoo.com

Coroner, Terry A. Parker, (D), 802 E. Cypress St., Charleston 63834; (573) 683-3773; taparker71@yahoo.com

County Health Department Director, Rachlle Johnson, 1200 E. Marshall, Charleston 63834; (573) 683-2191; johnsr1@lpha.mopublic.org

County Highway Engineer, Richard Wallace, (D), Mississippi County Courthouse, PO Box 369, Charleston 63834; (573) 683-6428; FAX (573) 683-2069

County Surveyor, (Vacancy)

Emergency Management Director, Danny Harris, Mississippi County Courthouse, PO Box 369, Charleston 63834; (573) 683-1782

Presiding Commissioner, Carlin Bennett, (R), Mississippi County Courthouse, PO Box 369, Charleston 63834; (573) 683-2146, ext. 221; FAX (573) 683-6071; carlin@creativeschoolzone.com

Prosecuting Attorney, Darren Cann, (D), Mississippi County Courthouse, PO Box 435, Charleston 63834; (573) 683-2146, ext. 245; FAX (573) 683-6228; dcann@misscomo.net

Public Administrator, Julie Summers-Day, (R), Mississippi County Courthouse, PO Box 369, Charleston 63834; (573) 683-2146, ext. 256; FAX (573) 683-6071; jsummersday@misscomo.net

Recorder of Deeds, George Bays, (D), Mississippi County Courthouse, PO Box 369, Charleston 63834; (573) 683-2146, ext. 226; FAX (573) 683-7696; gbays@misscomo.net

Sheriff, Keith Moore, (D), Mississippi County Courthouse, PO Box 369, Charleston 63834; (573) 683-2111; FAX (573) 683-2113

Treasurer, Sandra B. Morrow, (D), Mississippi County Courthouse, PO Box 369, Charleston 63834; (573) 683-2146, ext. 235; FAX (573) 683-6071; sbmorrow@misscomo.net

Moniteau County

County seat and zip code: California 65018. **County population:** 15,856. **Classification:** Third class. **Assessed valuation:** $191,795,318. **Square miles:** 417. **Organized:** February 14, 1845. **Named for:** The Moniteau Creek.

Assessor, Melissa Hentges, (R), Moniteau County Courthouse, Rm. 105, California 65018; (573) 796-4637; FAX (573) 796-3082

Clerk Circuit Court and *ex officio* Recorder of Deeds, Michele A. Higgins, (R), Moniteau County Courthouse, Rm. 102, 200 E. Main St., California 65018; (573) 796-2071

Clerk County Commission, Roberta Elliott, (R), Moniteau County Courthouse, 200 E. Main St., California 65018; (573) 796-4661; FAX (573) 796-3082; monitcoclk@yahoo.com

Collector of Revenue, Cheryl K. Duvall, (D), Moniteau County Courthouse, Rm. 101, California 65018; (573) 796-4521; FAX (573) 796-3851

Commissioner, First District, Tony Barry, (R), Moniteau County Courthouse, 200 E. Main St., California 65018; (573) 796-2213; FAX (573) 796-3082; monitcocmm@yahoo.com

Commissioner, Second District, Kim F. Roll, (D), Moniteau County Courthouse, 200 E. Main St., California 65018; (573) 796-2213; FAX (573) 796-3082; monitcocmm@yahoo.com

Coroner, Loyd Fulks, (R), 600 Dave Dr., California 65018; (573) 796-3855

County Health Department Director, Andrea Kincaid, 401-A Francis St., California 65018; (573) 796-3412; FAX (573) 796-8364

Emergency Management Director, William R. Roll, 200 N. Main St., California 65018; (573) 796-2213

Presiding Commissioner, Kenneth Kunze, (R), Moniteau County Courthouse, 200 E. Main St., California 65018; (573) 796-2213; FAX (573) 796-3082; monitcocmm@yahoo.com

Prosecuting Attorney, Shayne W. Healea, (R), 410 N. East St., California 65018; (573) 796-3220; FAX (573) 796-2793

Public Administrator, Cher King Caudel, (R), Moniteau County Courthouse, 200 E. Main St., California 65018; (573) 796-4704

Sheriff, Jay Gump, (R), Moniteau County Jail, 101 E. North St., California 65018; (573) 796-2525

Treasurer, Sarah B. Jones, (R), 200 E. Main, California 65018; (573) 796-4608

Monroe County

County seat and zip code: Paris 65275-1399. **County population:** 8,707. **Classification:** Third class. **Assessed valuation:** $118,723,364. **Square miles:** 670. **Organized:** January 6, 1831. **Named for:** James Monroe.

Assessor, Judy Harmon, (D), Monroe County Courthouse, 300 N. Main, Rm. 107, Paris 65275; (660) 327-5607; FAX (660) 327-5119; mocoassessor@centurytel.net

Clerk Circuit Court, Heather D. Wheeler, (D), Monroe County Courthouse, 300 N. Main, Rm. 201, Paris 65275; (660) 327-5220; FAX (660) 327-5651; heather.wheeler@courts.mo.gov

Clerk County Commission, Christina Buie, (D), Monroe County Courthouse, 300 N. Main, Rm. 204, Paris 65275; (660) 327-5106; FAX (660) 327-1019; monroecountyclk@centurytel.net

Collector of Revenue, Anita Dunkle, (D), Monroe County Courthouse, 300 N. Main, Rm. 101, Paris 65275; (660) 327-4320; FAX (660) 327-5063; monroecountycollector@centurytel.net

Commissioner, Eastern District, Mike Whelan, (D), Monroe County Courthouse, 300 N. Main, Rm. 203, Paris 65275; (660) 327-5107; FAX (660) 327-1019

Commissioner, Western District, Glenn E. Turner, (D), Monroe County Courthouse, 300 N. Main, Rm. 203, Paris 65275; (660) 327-5107; FAX (660) 327-1019

Coroner, James K. Reinhard, (D), 128 W. Caldwell, Paris 65275; (660) 327-4168; FAX (660) 327-4169

County Health Department Director, Paula Delaney, 310 Market St., Paris 65275; (660) 327-4653; FAX (660) 327-4533

Emergency Management Director, Steve Jones, Monroe County Courthouse, 300 N. Main, Rm. 203, Paris 65275; (660) 327-4173; FAX (660) 327-1019; parisfirechief@yahoo.com

Presiding Commissioner, Michael Minor, (D), Monroe County Courthouse, 300 N. Main, Rm. 203, Paris 65275; (660) 327-5107; FAX (660) 327-1019

Prosecuting Attorney, Talley Kendrick, (D), Monroe County Courthouse, 300 N. Main, Third Fl., Paris 65275; (660) 327-4484; FAX (660) 327-4990

Public Administrator, Marguerite Jones, (D), 15049 Rt. Z, Paris 65275; (660) 327-4615; FAX (660) 327-1019

Recorder of Deeds, Merry Sue Meals, (D), Monroe County Courthouse, 300 N. Main, Rm. 103, Paris 65275; (660) 327-1131; FAX (660) 327-1130

Sheriff, J. David Hoffman, (D), Monroe County Courthouse, 300 N. Main, Rm. 205, Paris 65275; (660) 327-4060; FAX (660) 327-5188

Treasurer, Rita C. Wilkerson, (D), Monroe County Courthouse, 300 N. Main, Rm. 102, Paris 65275; (660) 327-4711; FAX (660) 327-5063

Montgomery County

County seat and zip code: Montgomery City 63361. **County population:** 11,841. **Classification:** Third class. **Assessed valuation:** $221,946,259. **Square miles:** 540. **Organized:** December 14, 1818. **Named for:** Richard Montgomery, Revolutionary War general.

Assessor, Jerome P. Overkamp, (R), 310 Salisbury St., Ste. B, Montgomery City 63361; (573) 564-2445; assessor@mcmo.us

Clerk Circuit Court, Robyn Schmidt, (R), 211 E. Third St., Ste. 301, Montgomery City 63361; (573) 564-3341; FAX (573) 564-3914

Clerk County Commission, Pamela A. Cartee, (R), 211 E. Third St., Ste. 205, Montgomery City 63361; (573) 564-3357; FAX (573) 564-8088; coclerk@mcmo.us

Collector of Revenue, Anita L. Sullivan, (R), 310 Salisbury St., Ste. C, Montgomery City 63361; (573) 564-2389; FAX (573) 564-1406; collector@mcmo.us

Commissioner, First District, Rich Daniels, (R), 211 E. Third St., Ste. 205, Montgomery City 63361; (573) 564-3357; FAX (573) 564-8088; commission@mcmo.us

Commissioner, Second District, John W. Noltensmeyer, (R), 211 E. Third St., Ste. 205, Montgomery City 63361; (573) 564-3357; FAX (573) 564-8088; commission@mcmo.us

Coroner, David Colbert, (R), 109 Salisbury St., Montgomery City 63361; (573) 564-2340

County Health Department Director, Linda Harman, 400 Salisbury St., Montgomery City 63361; (573) 564-2495; FAX (573) 564-5059; harmal@lpha.mopublic.org

County Surveyor, Larry P. Bade, (R), 471 Hwy. FF, Jonesburg 63351; (636) 456-2615; FAX (636) 456-7252; lewis_bade@hotmail.com

Emergency Management Director, Bob Bishop, 211 E. Third St., Ste. 103, Montgomery City 63361; (573) 564-2284; FAX (573) 564-3942; montemd@mcmo.us

Presiding Commissioner, Ryan D. Poston, (R), 211 E. Third St., Ste. 205, Montgomery City 63361; (573) 564-3357; FAX (573) 564-8088; commission@mcmo.us

Prosecuting Attorney, Nathan Carroz, (R), 211 E. Third St., Montgomery City 63361, (573) 564-2252; nathan.carroz@mcmo.us

Public Administrator, Ann Scarlet, (D), 628 N. Sturgeon St., Montgomery City 63361; (573) 564-3362; FAX (573) 564-3141

Recorder of Deeds, Sheila See, (R), 310 Salisbury St., Ste. A, Montgomery City 63361; (573) 564-3157

Sheriff, Robert (Bob) Davis, (R), 211 E. Third St., Ste. 209, Montgomery City 63361; (573) 564-8084; FAX (573) 564-8083

Treasurer, Donna Huenefeld, (R), 211 E. Third St., Ste. 204, Montgomery City 63361; (573) 564-2319; FAX (573) 564-8088

Morgan County

County seat and zip code: Versailles 65084. **County population:** 20,240. **Classification:** Third class. **Assessed valuation:** $480,964,580. **Square miles:** 594. **Organized:** January 5, 1833. **Named for:** Daniel Morgan, Revolutionary War general.

Assessor, Jim Anderson, (R), Morgan County Courthouse, 100 E. Newton St., Versailles 65084; (573) 378-5459; FAX (573) 378-5453; janderson@morgan-county.org

Clerk Circuit Court, Lori Moon, (R), Morgan County Justice Center, 211 E. Newton St., Versailles 65084; (573) 378-4413; FAX (573) 378-5356; lori.moon@courts.mo.gov

Clerk County Commission, Cathy Daniels, (D), Morgan County Courthouse, 100 E. Newton St., Versailles 65084; (573) 378-5436; FAX (573) 378-5991; cathydaniels63@yahoo.com

Collector of Revenue, Kathy Francis, (D), Morgan County Courthouse, 100 E. Newton St., PO Box 315, Versailles 65084; (573) 378-5370; FAX (573) 378-1987; kfrancis@morgan-county.org

Commissioner, Eastern District, Rodney Schad, (R), Morgan County Courthouse, 100 E. Newton St., Versailles 65084; (573) 378-4643; FAX (573) 378-5790; rschad@morgan-county.org

Commissioner, Western District, Wayne Kroeschen Jr., (R), Morgan County Courthouse, 100 E. Newton St., Versailles 65084; (573) 378-4643; FAX (573) 378-5790

Coroner, Maynard B. Jones, (D), 11276 Fairground Rd., Versailles 65084; (573) 378-4430; FAX (573) 378-5790

County Health Department Director, Shawn Brantley, 104 W. Lafayette St., Versailles 65084; (573) 378-5438; FAX (573) 378-7375

Emergency Management Director*, Rick Bias, Morgan County Justice Center, 211 E. Newton St., Versailles 65084; (573) 378-2453; FAX (573) 378-4045; rbias@morgan-county.org

Presiding Commissioner, James Bryant, (R), Morgan County Courthouse, 100 E. Newton St., Versailles 65084; (573) 378-4643; FAX (573) 378-5790; jbryant@morgan-county.org

Prosecuting Attorney, Dustin Dunklee, (D), Morgan County Justice Center, 211 E. Newton

St., Versailles 65084; (573) 378-4694; FAX (573) 378-5984; ddunklee@morgan-county.org

Public Administrator, Amanda Huffman, (R), Morgan County Courthouse, 100 E. Newton St., PO Box 11, Versailles 65084; (573) 378-4011; FAX (573) 378-0601; ahuffman@morgan-county.org

Recorder of Deeds, Nancy Boles, (R), Morgan County Courthouse, 100 E. Newton St., Versailles 65084; (573) 378-4029; FAX (573) 378-6431; nboles@morgan-county.org

Sheriff, Jim Petty, (D), Morgan County Justice Center, 211 E. Newton St., Versailles 65084; (573) 378-5481; FAX (573) 378-7171

Treasurer, Kimberly Ingersoll, (R), Morgan County Courthouse, 100 E. Newton St., Versailles 65084; (573) 378-4404; FAX (573) 378-5991; kingersoll@morgan-county.org

---

*Appointed

New Madrid County

County seat and zip code: New Madrid 63869. **County population:** 18,272. **Classification:** Third class. **Assessed valuation:** $446,659,513. **Square miles:** 679. **Organized:** October 1, 1812. **Named for:** Madrid, Spain.

Assessor, Ronnie Simmons, (D), New Madrid County Courthouse, PO Box 247, New Madrid 63869; (573) 748-5441; FAX (573) 748-7219

Clerk Circuit Court, Marsha Meatte Holiman, (D), New Madrid County Courthouse, Second Fl., 450 Main St., New Madrid 63869; (573) 748-2228; FAX (573) 748-5409; marsha.holiman@courts.mo.gov

Clerk County Commission, Clement Cravens, (D), New Madrid County Courthouse, PO Box 68, New Madrid 63869; (573) 748-2524; FAX (573) 748-9269; clemcravens@newmadridcounty.net

Collector of Revenue, Dewayne Nowlin, (D), New Madrid County Courthouse, PO Box 249, New Madrid 63869; (573) 748-2127; FAX (573) 748-9271; dewaynenowlin@newmadridcounty.net

Commissioner, First District, Tom Bradley, (D), New Madrid County Courthouse, PO Box 68, New Madrid 63869; (573) 748-2524

Commissioner, Second District, Don Day, (D), New Madrid County Courthouse, PO Box 68, New Madrid 63869; (573) 748-2524

Coroner, George DeLisle, (D), 501 W. Tenth St., Portageville 63873; (573) 379-5486; delisle@semo.net

County Health Department Director, Jayne Dees, 406 Hwy. 61, New Madrid 63869; (573) 748-5541

County Highway Engineer, Donnie Brown, 379 Bloomfield Rd., New Madrid 63869; (573) 748-2080

Emergency Management Director, David McClarty, PO Box 602, Lilbourn 63862; (573) 688-2942

Presiding Commissioner, Mark Baker, (D), New Madrid County Courthouse, PO Box 68, New Madrid 63869; (573) 748-2524

Prosecuting Attorney, Andrew Lawson, (D), New Madrid County Courthouse, Second Fl., 450 Main St., New Madrid 63869; (573) 748-5144; FAX (573) 748-5409; nmpa@newmadrid county.net

Public Administrator, Paula Scobey, (D), 450 Main St., New Madrid 63869; (573) 748-9275; paulascobey@newmadridcounty.net

Recorder of Deeds, Kim St. Mary Hall, (D), New Madrid County Courthouse, PO Box 217, New Madrid 63869; (573) 748-5146; recorder@ newmadridcounty.net

Sheriff, Terry M. Stevens, (D), New Madrid County Jail, Courthouse Sq., New Madrid 63869; (573) 748-2516; FAX (573) 748-2540; nmcos@yahoo.com

Treasurer, Steve Riley, (D), PO Box 68, New Madrid 63869; (573) 748-2329; steveriley@ newmadridcounty.net

Newton County

County seat and zip code: Neosho 64850. **County population:** 58,845. **Classification:** Second class. **Assessed valuation:** $789,338,796. **Square miles:** 627. **Organized:** December 31, 1838. **Named for:** John Newton, Revolutionary War soldier.

Assessor, Gloria Gourley, (R), Newton County Courthouse, 101 S. Wood St., Neosho 64850; (417) 451-8228; FAX (417) 451-8259, glorianca@yahoo.com

Auditor, Charlotte Ward, (R), Newton County Courthouse, 101 S. Wood St., Neosho 64850; (417) 451-8379; FAX (417) 455-0810; auditor @swbell.net

Clerk Circuit Court, Patty Krueger, (R), Newton County Courthouse, 101 S. Wood St., PO Box 130, Neosho 64850; (417) 451-8210; FAX (417) 451-8298; patty.krueger@courts. mo.gov

Clerk County Commission, Kay Baum, (R), Newton County Courthouse, 101 S. Wood St., PO Box 488, Neosho 64850; (417) 451-8221; FAX (417) 451-7434; newton@sos.mo.gov

Collector of Revenue, James Otey, (R), Newton County Courthouse, 101 S. Wood St., PO Box 296, Neosho 64850; (417) 451-8216; FAX (417) 451-8205; nccollector@swbell.net

Commissioner, First District, Alan Cook, (R), Newton County Courthouse, 101 S. Wood St., Neosho 64850; (417) 451-8223; FAX (417) 451-8289; commission@swbell.net

Commissioner, Second District, Jim Jackson, (R), Newton County Courthouse, 101 S. Wood St., Neosho 64850; (417) 451-8223; FAX (417) 451-8289; commission@swbell.net

Coroner, Mark Bridges, (R), Newton County Courthouse Annex, 107 N. Jefferson, PO Box 97, Neosho 64850; (417) 451-8333; coroner@swbell.net

County Health Department Administrator, Bob Kulp, 812 W. Harmony, PO Box 447, Neosho 64850; (417) 451-3743; kulpb@ newtoncountyhealth.org

County Surveyor, James Loncarich, (R), 125 S. Washington, Neosho 64850; (417) 451-2727; jloncarich@hurst-rosche.com

Emergency Operations Director, Gary Roark, Newton County Armory, 202 W. Brook, Neosho 64850; (417) 451-8255; FAX (417) 451-8260; groark@nc-em.org

Presiding Commissioner, Marilyn Ruestman, (R), Newton County Courthouse, 101 S. Wood St., Neosho 64850; (417) 451-8223; FAX (417) 451-8289; commission@swbell.net

Prosecuting Attorney, Jacob Skouby, (R), Newton County Courthouse, 101 S. Wood St., Neosho 64850; (417) 451-8242; FAX (417) 451-8243; jskouby@newtoncopa.com

Public Administrator, JeAnna McGarrah, (R), Newton County Courthouse Annex, 107 N. Jefferson, Neosho 64850; (417) 451-8271; FAX (417) 451-8371, jeanna.mcgarrah@ gmail.com

Recorder of Deeds, Lenora Hyder, (R), Newton County Courthouse, 101 S. Wood St., PO Box 604, Neosho 64850; (417) 451-8224; FAX (417) 451-8273; lhyder@ncrecorder.org

Sheriff, Ken Copeland, (R), Newton County Sheriffs Dept., 208 W. Coler, Neosho 64850; (417) 451-8300; FAX (417) 451-8352; kencopeland@nc-so.org

Treasurer, Gina Rodriguez, (R), Newton County Courthouse, 101 S. Wood St., Neosho 64850; (417) 451-8226; FAX (417) 451-8219; nctreasurer@swbell.net

Nodaway County

County seat and zip code: Maryville 64468. **County population:** 23,081. **Classification:** Third class. **Assessed valuation:** $314,611,450. **Square miles:** 875. **Organized:** February 14, 1845. **Named for:** The Nodaway River.

Assessor, Rex Wallace, (D), 403 N. Market, Maryville 64468; (660) 582-7633; FAX (660) 562-8175; nodassessor@gmail.com

Clerk Circuit Court, Elaine Wilson, (R), Nodaway County Courthouse, 305 N. Main, Maryville 64468; (660) 582-5431; FAX (660) 582-5499; elaine.wilson@courts.mo.gov

Clerk County Commission*, Karen K. Leader, (D), 403 N. Market, Maryville 64468; (660) 582-2251; FAX (660) 582-5282; nodclerk@gmail.com

Commissioner, Northern District, Bob Westfall, (R), 403 N. Market, Maryville 64468; (660) 582-5541; FAX (660) 582-5282; nodawaycom@gmail.com

Commissioner, Southern District, Bob Stiens, (D), 403 N. Market, Maryville 64468; (660) 582-5541; FAX (660) 582-5282; nodawaycom@gmail.com

Coroner, Vince Shelby, (R), 23001 State Hwy. AB, Skidmore 64487; (660) 582-4722; doctorv@ludicrouspeed.net

Emergency Management Director*, Christy Forney, 403 N. Market, Maryville 64468; (660) 562-3209; cf235@maryvilledps.com

Presiding Commissioner, Bill Walker, (R), 403 N. Market, 305 N. Main, Maryville 64468; (660) 582-5541; (660) 582-5282; nodawaycom@gmail.com

Prosecuting Attorney, Robert Rice, (R), Nodaway County Courthouse, 305 N. Main, Maryville 64468; (660) 582-8285; FAX (660) 582-5282; prosatty@embarqmail.com

Public Administrator, Diane Thomsen, (D), PO Box 660, Maryville 64468; (660) 582-3134; thomsen@suddenlink.net

Recorder of Deeds, Sandra L. (Sandy) Smail, (D), 403 N. Market, Maryville 64468; (660) 582-5711; FAX (660) 582-5711; recorder@nodawaycountyrecorder.com

Sheriff, Darren White, (D), Nodaway County Jail, 404 N. Vine, Maryville 64468; (660) 582-7451; sheriffwhite@embarqmail.com

Surveyor, Troy Hayes, (D), 27230 Cedar Ridge Dr., Maryville 64468; (660) 562-3509

Treasurer and *ex officio* Collector of Revenue, Marilyn Jenkins, (D), 403 N. Market, Maryville 64468; (660) 582-4302; FAX (660) 582-5282; nctreas@embarqmail.com

---

Oregon County

County seat and zip code: Alton 65606. **County population:** 10,911. **Classification:** Third class. **Assessed valuation:** $89,569,404. **Square miles:** 792. **Organized:** February 14, 1845. **Named for:** The Territory of Oregon.

Assessor, Charles Lon Alford, (D), Oregon County Courthouse, First Fl., Rm. 4, PO Box 361, Alton 65606; (417) 778-7471; FAX (417) 778-7441

Clerk Circuit Court, Rosemary Romans, (D), Oregon County Courthouse, Second Fl., Rm. 10, PO Box 406, Alton 65606; (417) 778-7460; FAX (417) 778-7206

Clerk County Commission*, Tracy J. Bridges, (D), Oregon County Courthouse, PO Box 324, Alton 65606; (417) 778-7475; FAX (417) 778-7488; oregoncounty@sos.mo.gov

Collector of Revenue, Jerry Richardson, (D), Oregon County Courthouse, First Fl., Rm. 2, PO Box 352, Alton 65606; (417) 778-7495; FAX (417) 778-6700

Commissioner, First District, Johnny D. Wrenfrow, (D), Oregon County Courthouse, First Fl., Rm. 1, PO Box 324, Alton 65606; (417) 778-7475; FAX (417) 778-7488

Commissioner, Second District, Edward Casey, (R), Oregon County Courthouse, First Fl., Rm. 1, PO Box 324, Alton 65606; (417) 778-7475; FAX (417) 778-7488

Coroner, Tom Clary, (D), Clary Funeral Home, PO Box 305, Alton 65606; (417) 778-7221

County Health Department Director, Shiela Russell, PO Box 189, 4 Market, Alton 65606; (417) 778-7450; FAX (417) 778-6826; russes@lpha.dhss.mo.gov

County Surveyor, Scott Simer, (D), Rt. 2, Box 2104-A, Thayer 65791; (417) 264-7255

Emergency Management Director, Eric King, Third Fl., PO Box 265, Alton 65606; (417) 778-7888; FAX (417) 778-6641

Presiding Commissioner, Patrick Ledgerwood, (R), Oregon County Courthouse, First Fl., Rm. 1, PO Box 324, Alton 65606; (417) 778-7475; FAX (417) 778-7488

Prosecuting Attorney, Jennifer Hyde Crask, (D), Oregon County Courthouse, Second Fl., Rm. 10, PO Box 393, Alton 65606; (417) 778-7616; FAX (417) 778-7615

Public Administrator, Mike Crawford, (R), PO Box 483, Alton 65606; (417) 778-7780; FAX (417) 778-7206

Recorder of Deeds*, Dawn Holman, (D), Oregon County Courthouse, First Fl., Rm. 10, PO Box

86, Alton 65606; (417) 778-1827; FAX (417) 778-2007

Sheriff, George R. Underwood, (D), Oregon County Courthouse, Third Fl., PO Box 265, Alton 65606; (417) 778-7888; FAX (417) 778-6641

Treasurer, Kim Hollis, (D), Oregon County Courthouse, First Fl., Rm. 11, PO Box 371, Alton 65606; (417) 778-6303; FAX (417) 778-7488

*Appointed

Osage County

County seat and zip code: Linn 65051. **County population:** 13,703. **Classification:** Third class. **Assessed valuation:** $200,275,835. **Square miles:** 606. **Organized:** January 29, 1841. **Named for:** The Osage River.

Assessor, Ross Seals, (R), Osage County Administration Bldg., 205 E. Main, PO Box 409, Linn 65051; (573) 897-2217, ext. 135; FAX (573) 897-3851

Clerk Circuit Court, Charlene J. Eisterhold, (D), Osage County Courthouse, PO Box 825, Linn 65051; (573) 897-3114

Clerk County Commission, Patrick Steele, (R), Osage County Courthouse, PO Box 826, Linn 65051; (573) 897-2139; FAX (573) 897-4741; osage@sos.mo.gov

Collector of Revenue, Doris J. Keilholz, (D), Osage County Administration Bldg., 205 E. Main, PO Box 616, Linn 65051; (573) 897-2135, ext. 120; FAX (573) 897-3706; doris@osagecollector.com

Commissioner, First District, John Glavin, (R), Osage County Courthouse, PO Box 826, Linn 65051; (573) 897-2139

Commissioner, Second District, Larry Kliethermes, (R), Osage County Courthouse, PO Box 826, Linn 65051; (573) 897-2139; larrykliet@gmail.com

Coroner, Lois Jaegers, (D) 1099 County Rd. 602, Loose Creek 65054; (573) 897-3858; jaegersl@lincolnu.edu

County Health Department Director, April Schubert, PO Box 533, Linn 65051; (573) 897-4915

County Surveyor, Ralph P. Kliethermes, (D), Linn 65051; (573) 897-3644

Emergency Management Director, Andi Rice, Osage County Administration Bldg., PO Box 192, Linn 65051; (573) 897-2139, ext. 220; FAX (573) 897-0379; director911@midamerica.net

Presiding Commissioner, Dave Dudenhoeffer, (D), Osage County Courthouse, PO Box 826, Linn 65051; (573) 897-2139; FAX (573) 897-4741

Prosecuting Attorney, Amanda L. Grellner, (D), Osage County Courthouse, PO Box 378, Linn 65051; (573) 897-3101; FAX (573) 897-9951; agrellner@sbcglobal.net

Public Administrator, Paul G. Stratman, (R), PO Box 1128, Linn 65051; (573) 455-2379; osagecountypa@yahoo.com

Recorder of Deeds, Cindy Hoffman, (D), Osage County Administration Bldg., PO Box 110, Linn 65051; (573) 897-3095, ext. 145; FAX (573) 897-2864; cindyhoffman2009@yahoo.com

Sheriff, Michael Dixon, (R), Osage County Courthouse, PO Box 619, Linn 65051; (573) 897-3927; FAX (573) 897-4383

Treasurer, Tim G. Neuner, (R), Osage County Courthouse, PO Box 573, Linn 65051; (573) 897-3095

Ozark County

County seat and zip code: Gainesville 65655. **County population:** 9,492. **Classification:** Third class. **Assessed valuation:** $105,087,561. **Square miles:** 731. **Organized:** January 29, 1841. **Named for:** The Ozark Mountains.

Assessor, Jama M. Berry, (R), Ozark County Courthouse, PO Box 81, Gainesville 65655; (417) 679-4705

Clerk Circuit Court and *ex officio* **Recorder of Deeds,** Becki Strong, (R), Ozark County Courthouse, PO Box 36, Gainesville 65655; (417) 679-4232

Clerk County Commission, Brian Wise, (R), Ozark County Courthouse, PO Box 416, Gainesville 65655; (417) 679-3516; FAX (417) 679-3209; ozark@sos.mo.gov

Collector of Revenue, Billy D. Hambelton II, (R), Ozark County Courthouse, PO Box 25, Gainesville 65655; (417) 679-4448

Commissioner, Eastern District, Gary Collins, (R), Ozark County Courthouse, PO Box 247, Gainesville 65655; (417) 679-4096

Commissioner, Western District, Greg Donley (D), Ozark County Courthouse, PO Box 247, Gainesville 65655; (417) 679-4096

Coroner, Shane Ledbetter, (R), PO Box 65, Gainesville 65655; (417) 679-3315

County Health Department Director, Rhonda Suter, PO Box 180, Gainesville 65655; (417) 679-3334

County Surveyor, Matt Wade, (R), 52 Parrothead Ln., Pontiac 65729; (417) 679-0129

Emergency Management Director, Wendy Bales, 594 State Rt. 142, Bakersfield 65609; (417) 274-3760

Presiding Commissioner, Johnnie M. Turner, (R), Ozark County Courthouse, PO Box 247, Gainesville 65655; (417) 679-4096

Prosecuting Attorney, Thomas W. Cline, (R), PO Box 67, Gainesville 65655; (417) 679-4648

Public Administrator, Melinda Abraham, (R), Ozark County Courthouse, PO Box 688, Gainesville 65655; (417) 679-3809

Sheriff, Darrin Reed, (R), Ozark County Law Enforcement Center, HC 1, Box 8-1, Gainesville 65655; (417) 679-4633

Treasurer, Phyllis Gaulding Turner, (R), Ozark County Courthouse, PO Box 525, Gainesville 65655; (417) 679-3553

Pemiscot County

County seat and zip code: Caruthersville 63830. **County population:** 17,650. **Classification:** Third class. **Assessed valuation:** $193,388,498. **Square miles:** 517. **Organized:** February 19, 1851. **Named for:** The Indian word meaning "liquid mud."

Assessor, Patsy Hinklin, (D), Pemiscot County Courthouse, 610 Ward Ave., Ste. 2-D, Caruthersville 63830; (573) 333-1390; FAX (573) 333-0440

Clerk Circuit Court, Kelly Cagle Maners, (D), Pemiscot County Courthouse, 610 Ward Ave., Ste. 3-A, Caruthersville 63830; (573) 333-0182; FAX (573) 333-1272

Clerk County Commission, Pam Treece, (D), Pemiscot County Courthouse, 610 Ward Ave., Ste. 2-A, Caruthersville 63830; (573) 333-4203; FAX (573) 333-0440; pemcoclerk@sbcglobal.net

Collector of Revenue, Rhonda Parkinson Price, (D), Pemiscot County Courthouse, 610 Ward Ave., Ste. 1-C, Caruthersville 63830; (573) 333-0224; FAX (573) 333-0225

Commissioner, First District, Steve Watkins, (D), Pemiscot County Courthouse, 610 Ward Ave., Ste. 1-B, Caruthersville 63830; (573) 333-5811; FAX (573) 333-0440

Commissioner, Second District, Ben H. Baker, (D), Pemiscot County Courthouse, 610 Ward Ave., Ste. 1-B, Caruthersville 63830; (573) 333-5811; FAX (573) 333-0440

Coroner, James Brimhall, (D), 103 E. Washington, Hayti 63851; (573) 359-2085

County Health Department Director, Karen Malin, 810 E. Reed, Hayti 63851; (573) 359-1656; FAX (573) 359-0159

Emergency Management Director, Jess Cagle, (D), 800 Ward Ave., Caruthersville 63830; (537) 333-4101, ext. 3043; FAX (573) 333-0713; jess.cagle@pemcosheriff.org

Presiding Commissioner, Mark Cartee, (D), Pemiscot County Courthouse, 610 Ward Ave., Ste. 1-B, Caruthersville 63830; (573) 333-5811; FAX (573) 333-0440; hhamc@att.net

Prosecuting Attorney, Jereme Lytle, (D), Pemiscot County Justice Center, 800 Ward Ave., PO Box 1117, Caruthersville 63830; (573) 333-2738; FAX (573) 333-2531; prosecutor@pemcopa.com

Public Administrator, Carol DeRousse Miller, (D), Pemiscot County Courthouse, 610 Ward Ave., Ste. 2-B, Caruthersville 63830; (573) 333-2812; FAX (573) 333-0440

Recorder of Deeds, Pam Strawbridge, (D), Pemiscot County Courthouse, 610 Ward Ave., Ste. 1-A, Caruthersville 63830; (573) 333-2204; FAX (573) 333-0440

Sheriff, Tommy Greenwell, (D), Pemiscot County Justice Center, 800 Ward Ave., PO Box 1031, Caruthersville 63830; (573) 333-4101; FAX (573) 333-0713

Treasurer, Frankie R. Stewart, (D), Pemiscot County Courthouse, 610 Ward Ave., Ste. 2-C, Caruthersville 63830; (573) 333-4171; FAX (573) 333-0440

Perry County

County seat and zip code: Perryville 63775. **County population:** 19,202. **Classification:** Third class. **Assessed valuation:** $324,045,500. **Square miles:** 473. **Organized:** November 16, 1820. **Named for:** Oliver H. Perry, naval hero of the War of 1812.

Assessor, Charles Triller, (R), Perry County Administration Bldg., 321 N. Main St., No. 5, Perryville 63775; (573) 547-5211; FAX (573) 547-5297; ctriller1@sbcglobal.net

Clerk Circuit Court, Becky A. Paulus, (R), Perry County Courthouse, 15 W. St. Maries St., Perryville 63775; (573) 547-6581, ext. 305; FAX (573) 547-9323; becky.paulus@courts.mo.gov

Clerk County Commission, Jared W. Kutz, (R), Perry County Administration Bldg., 321 N. Main St., No. 2, Perryville 63775; (573) 547-4242; FAX (573) 547-7367; jaredkutz@perrycountymo.net

Collector of Revenue, Rodney J. Richardet, (R), Perry County Administration Bldg., 321 N. Main St., No. 4, Perryville 63775; (573)

547-4422; FAX (573) 547-2055; colperry@sbcglobal.net

Commissioner, First District, Patrick Heaps, (D), Perry County Administration Bldg., 321 N. Main St., Ste. 2, Perryville 63775; (573) 547-4242; FAX (573) 547-7367; perryco commission@sbcglobal.net

Commissioner, Second District, Jim Sutterer, (R), Perry County Administration Bldg., 321 N. Main St., Ste. 2, Perryville 63775; (573) 547-4242; FAX (573) 547-7367; perryco commission@sbcglobal.net

Coroner, Herbert E. Miller, (D), 829 W. St. Joseph, Perryville 63775; (573) 547-6511; FAX (573) 547-6512; millerfuneral@powrup.net

County Health Department Director*, Judy Laurentius, 406 N. Spring St., Ste. 1, Perryville 63775; (573) 547-6564; FAX (573) 547-3908; laurej@lpha.mopublic.org

County Surveyor, Tim Baer, (R), 313 N. Jackson St., Perryville 63775; (573) 547-2310; FAX (573) 547-6175; tbaer@baerengineering.com

Emergency Management Director*, Hank Voelker, 406 N. Spring St., Ste. 3, Perryville 63775; (573) 547-4000; FAX (573) 547-2104; perrycountyema911@gmail.com

Presiding Commissioner, Carl Lueckel Jr., (R), Perry County Administration Bldg., 321 N. Main St., Ste. 2, Perryville 63775; (573) 547-4242; FAX (573) 547-7367; perryco commission@sbcglobal.net

Prosecuting Attorney, Thomas L. Hoeh, (R), 17 E. St. Joseph St., Perryville 63775; (573) 547-1023; FAX (573) 547-4718; t.hoeh@sbc global.net

Public Administrator, Tamara M. Tarrillion, (R), Perry County Courthouse, 15 W. St. Maries St., Ste. 7, Perryville 63775; (573) 547-8207; FAX (573) 517-0147; pcpa2010@att.net

Recorder of Deeds, Dana Pritchard, (R), Perry County Courthouse, 15 W. St. Maries St., Ste. 1, Perryville 63775; (573) 547-1611; FAX (573) 547-3879; perrycorecorder@gmail.com

Sheriff, Gary J. Schaaf, (R), Perry County Sheriff's Dept., 710 S. Kingshighway, Perryville 63775; (573) 547-4576; FAX (573) 547-7461; sheriff@powrup.net

Treasurer, Kathy A. Shumer, (R), Perry County Administration Bldg., 321 N. Main St., No. 3, Perryville 63775; (573) 547-4502; FAX (573) 517-7024; perrycotreasurer@gmail.com

---

*Appointed

Pettis County

County seat and zip code: Sedalia 65301. **County population:** 42,225. **Classification:** Second class. **Assessed valuation:** $571,091,925. **Square miles:** 686. **Organized:** January 24, 1833. **Named for:** Spencer Pettis, Missouri congressman.

Assessor, Karissa Logan, (R), Pettis County Courthouse, 415 S. Ohio, Ste. 218, Sedalia 65301; (660) 826-5000, ext. 412; FAX (660) 829-2492; logank@pettiscomo.com

Auditor, Beverly Dillon, (R), Pettis County Courthouse, 415 S. Ohio, Ste. 210A, Sedalia 65301; (660) 826-5000, ext. 931; FAX (660) 827-8637; dillonb@pettiscomo.com

Circuit Court Clerk, Susan Sadler, (R), Pettis County Courthouse, 415 S. Ohio, Ste. 324, Sedalia 65301; (660) 826-5000, ext. 926; FAX (660) 826-4520; susan.sadler@courts.mo.gov

County Clerk/Election Authority, Nick La Strada, (R), Pettis County Courthouse, 415 S. Ohio, Ste. 214, Sedalia 65301; (660) 826-5000, ext. 918; FAX (660) 829-0717; nick@pettiscomo.com

Collector of Revenue, Marsha L. Boeschen, (R), Pettis County Courthouse, 415 S. Ohio, Ste. 216, Sedalia 65301; (660) 826-5000, ext. 921; FAX (660) 826-6254; boeschenm@pettiscomo.com

Commissioner, Presiding, David Dick, (R), Pettis County Courthouse, 415 S. Ohio, Ste. 212-A, Sedalia 65301; (660) 826-5000, ext. 405; FAX (660) 826-4953; davidd@pettiscomo.com

Commissioner, Western District, Jim Marcum, (R), Pettis County Courthouse, 415 S. Ohio, Ste. 212-B, Sedalia 65301; (660) 826-5000, ext. 407; FAX (660) 829-4953; jmarcum@pettiscomo.com

Commissioner, Eastern District, D. Brent Hampy, (R), Pettis County Courthouse, 415 S. Ohio, Ste. 212-C, Sedalia 65301; (660) 826-5000, ext. 406; FAX (660) 829-4953; hampyb@pettiscomo.com

Coroner, Robert (Skip) Smith Jr., (R), Pettis County Sheriff's Office, 319 S. Lamine, Sedalia 65301; (660) 827-0052; smiths@pettiscomo.com

County Health Department Director*, JoAnn Martin, 911 E. 16th St., Sedalia 65301; (660) 827-1130; FAX (660) 827-1141; martij@lpha.mopublic.org

County Surveyor, Kerry Turpin, (D), 23670 Sacajawea Rd., Sedalia 65301; (660) 829-1949; FAX (660) 827-3672; ls1993@iland.net

Emergency Management Director, Dave Clippert, Pettis County Courthouse, 415 S. Ohio, Ste.

B-10, Sedalia 65301; (660) 827-4800, ext. 1; FAX (660) 826-7288; ema@pettiscomo.com

Prosecuting Attorney, Phillip Sawyer, (R), Pettis County Courthouse, 415 S. Ohio, Ste. 320, Sedalia 65301; (660) 826-5000 ext. 925; FAX (660) 827-8633; psawyer@pettiscomo.com

Public Administrator, Charli Ackerman, (D), Pettis County Courthouse, 415 S. Ohio, Ste. 104, Sedalia 65301; (660) 826-5000, ext. 923; FAX (660) 829-4087; pettispubadmin@pettiscomo.com

Recorder of Deeds, Barbara Clevenger, (R), Pettis County Courthouse, 415 S. Ohio, Ste. 106, Sedalia 65301; (660) 826-5000, ext. 922; FAX (660) 829-4479; clevengerb@pettiscomo.com

Sheriff, Kevin Bond, (R), Pettis County Sheriff's Office, 319 S. Lamine, Sedalia 65301; (660) 827-0052; FAX (660) 826-5254; sheriff@pettiscomo.com

Treasurer, Kim Lyne, (R), Pettis County Courthouse, 415 S. Ohio, Ste. 210B, Sedalia 65301; (660) 826-5000, ext. 408; FAX (660) 827-8637; lynek@pettiscomo.com

---

*Appointed

Phelps County

County seat and zip code: Rolla 65401. **County population:** 44,847. **Classification:** Third class. **Assessed valuation:** $561,611,059. **Square miles:** 674. **Organized:** November 13, 1857. **Named for:** John F. Phelps, congressman and governor of Missouri.

Assessor, Bill Wiggins, (R), Phelps County Courthouse, 200 N. Main St., Ste. 126, Rolla 65401; (573) 458-6145; FAX (573) 458-6149; bill.wiggins@phelpscounty.org

Clerk Circuit Court, Sue Brown, (R), Phelps County Courthouse, 200 N. Main St., Ste. 201, Rolla 65401; (573) 458-6201; FAX (573) 458-6224; sue.brown@courts.mo.gov

Clerk County Commission, Pamela K. Grow, (R), Phelps County Courthouse, 200 N. Main St., Ste. 102, Rolla 65401; (573) 458-6101; FAX (573) 458-6119; pam.grow@phelpscounty.org

Collector of Revenue, Davis R. Haas, (D), Phelps County Courthouse, 200 N. Main St., Ste. 129, Rolla 65401; (573) 458-6151; FAX (573) 458-6159; davis.haas@phelpscounty.org

Commissioner, District 1, Larry J. Stratman, (R), Phelps County Courthouse, 200 N. Main St., Ste. 105, Rolla 65401; (573) 458-6121; FAX (573) 458-6119; larry.stratman@phelpscounty.org

Commissioner, District 2, Gary W. Hicks, (R), Phelps County Courthouse, 200 N. Main St., Ste. 105, Rolla 65401; (573) 458-6122; FAX (573) 458-6119; gary.hicks@phelpscounty.org

Coroner, Larry Swinfard, (D), Phelps County Courthouse, 200 N. Main St., Rolla 65401; (573) 465-2947; larry.swinfard@phelpscountysheriff.org

County Health Department Director*, Jodi Waltman, 200 N. Main St., Ste. G51, Rolla 65401; (573) 458-6020; FAX (573) 458-6060; waltmj@lpha.mopublic.org

County Surveyor, Louis Gilbert, (R), PO Box 700, Rolla 65402, 1714 E. Tenth St., Rolla 65401; (573) 341-2100

Emergency Management Director*, Sandy North, 500 W. Second St., Rolla 65401; (573) 426-3830; FAX (573) 426-3857

Presiding Commissioner, Randy Verkamp, (D), Phelps County Courthouse, 200 N. Main St., Ste. 105, Rolla 65401; (573) 458-6120; FAX (573) 458-6119; randy.verkamp@phelpscounty.org

Prosecuting Attorney, Brendon Fox, (R), Phelps County Courthouse, 200 N. Main St., Ste. G-69, Rolla 65401; (573) 458-6170; FAX (573) 458-6179; brendon.fox@phelpscounty-pa.org

Public Administrator, Kathleen S. Oliver, (R), Phelps County Courthouse, 200 N. Main St., Ste. 122, Rolla 65401; (573) 458-6080; FAX (573) 458-6081; kathy.oliver@phelpscounty.org

Recorder of Deeds, Robin Kordes, (R), Phelps County Courthouse, 200 N. Main St., Ste. 133, Rolla 65401; (573) 458-6090; FAX (573) 458-6098; robin.kordes@phelpscounty.org

Sheriff, Richard Lisenbe, (D), Phelps County Sheriff's Department, 500 W. Second St., Rolla 65401; (573) 426-3860; FAX (573) 426-3857; rick.lisenbe@phelpscountysheriff.org

Treasurer, Carol Green, (R), Phelps County Courthouse, 200 N. Main St., Ste. 125, Rolla 65401; (573) 458-6130; FAX (573) 458-6134; carol.green@phelpscounty.org

---

*Appointed

Pike County

County seat and zip code: Bowling Green 63334. **County population:** 18,541. **Classification:** Third class. **Assessed valuation:** $270,432,395. **Square miles:** 673. **Organized:** December 4, 1818. **Named for:** Zebulon Montgomery Pike, explorer.

Assessor, Donna Prior, (D), Pike County Courthouse, 115 W. Main, Bowling Green 63334; (573) 324-3261; FAX (573) 324-5919; dsp@pikecounty-mo.gov

Circuit Clerk, Jerri Harrelson, (D), 115 W. Main, Bowling Green 63334; (573) 324-5582; FAX (573) 324-3150; jerri.harrelson@courts.mo.gov

Clerk County Commission, Melissa Kempke, (D), Pike County Courthouse, 115 W. Main, Bowling Green 63334; (573) 324-2412; FAX (573) 324-5154; pike@sos.mo.gov

Collector of Revenue, Marty J. Morrison, (D), Pike County Courthouse, 115 W. Main, Bowling Green 63334; (573) 324-3281; FAX (573) 324-6708; martym@pikecounty-mo.gov

Commissioner, Eastern District, Curt Mitchell, (D), Pike County Courthouse, 115 W. Main, Bowling Green 63334; (573) 324-2412; FAX (573) 324-5154; pike@sos.mo.gov

Commissioner, Western District, Jim Luebrecht, (D), Pike County Courthouse, 115 W. Main, Bowling Green 63334; (573) 324-2412; FAX (573) 324-5154; jimluebrecht.pike. commish@gmail.com

Coroner, Jim Turner, (D), 115 W. Main St., Bowling Green 63334; (573) 785-5420; FAX (573) 324-2374; jim_turner_1998@yahoo. com

County Surveyor, Marty Wasson, 14374 Fort Mason Tr., New London 63459; (573) 221-5413

Emergency Management Director, Al Murry, 13055 Pike 133, Louisiana 63353; (573) 754-0151; murrya@louisiana.k12.mo.us

Presiding Commissioner, Chris Gamm, (R), Pike County Courthouse, 115 W. Main, Bowling Green 63334; (573) 324-2412; FAX (573) 324-5154; gamm.chris72@gmail.com

Prosecuting Attorney, Mark Fisher, (D), Pike County Courthouse, 115 W. Main, Bowling Green 63334; (573) 324-2201; pikepa@sbcglobal.net

Public Administrator, Nina K. Long, (D), 15140 Pike 138, Bowling Green 63334; (573) 324-2382

Recorder of Deeds, Sherry McCarty, (D), Pike County Courthouse, 115 W. Main, Bowling Green 63334; (573) 324-5567; FAX (573) 324-5210; pikecountyrecorder@sbcglobal. net

Sheriff, Stephen Korte, (R), 1600 Business Hwy. 54 W., Bowling Green 63334; (573) 324-3202; FAX (573) 324-3972; pcskorte@sbcglobal.net

Treasurer, Patti Crane, (D), Pike County Courthouse, 115 W. Main, Bowling Green 63334; (573) 324-2102; pcrane24@sbcglobal.net

Platte County

County seat and zip code: Platte City 64079. **County population:** 93,310. **Classification:** First class. **Assessed valuation:** $2,284,217,209. **Square miles:** 421. **Organized:** December 31, 1838. **Named for:** The Platte River.

Assessor, David Cox, (R), Platte County Administration Bldg., 415 Third St., Rms. 114 and 115, Platte City 64079; (816) 858-3301; FAX (816) 858-3314

Auditor, Kevin Robinson, (R), Platte County Administration Bldg., 415 Third St., Rm. 112, Platte City 64079; (816) 858-3327; FAX (816) 858-1929; krobinson@co.platte.mo.us

Clerk Circuit Court*, Sandra L. Dowd, (D), Platte County Courthouse, 415 Third St., Ste. 5, Platte City 64079; (816) 858-3481; FAX (816) 858-3392; sandy.dowd@courts.mo.gov

Clerk County Commission, Nancy Armstrong, (R), Platte County Administration Bldg., 415 Third St., Rm. 116, Platte City 64079; (816) 858-3343; FAX (816) 858-3363; nancy. armstrong@co.platte.mo.us

Collector of Revenue, Sheila Palmer, (R), Platte County Administration Bldg., 415 Third St., Rm. 212, Platte City 64079; (816) 858-3355; FAX (816) 858-3357; spalmer@co.platte. mo.us

Commissioner, First District, Beverlee Roper, (R), Platte County Administration Bldg., 415 Third St., Rm. 210, Platte City 64079; (816) 858-3330; FAX (816) 858-3329; beverlee.roper@co.platte.mo.us

Commissioner, Second District, Duane Soper, (R), Platte County Administration Bldg., 415 Third St., Rm. 210, Platte City 64079; (816) 858-3333; FAX (816) 858-3329; duane. soper@co.platte.mo.us

County Health Department Director, Mary Jo Vernon, 212 Marshall, Platte City 64079; (816) 858-2412; FAX (816) 858-2087; maryjo. vernon@plattehealth.com

County Surveyor, Rob Young, PO Box 14069, Parkville 64152; (816) 741-6152; FAX (816) 741-6198; rob@rlbuford.com

Emergency Management Coordinator, Capt. Anthony Avery, Tom Thomas Law Enforcement Center, 415 Third St., Ste. 10, Platte City 64079; (816) 858-3521; FAX (816) 858-3230; anthony.avery@plattesheriff.org

Medical Examiner*, Mary Helen Dudley, M.D., Jackson County Medical Examiner, 660 E.

24th St., Kansas City 64108; (816) 881-6600; FAX (816) 404-1345; mdudley@jacksongov. org

Presiding Commissioner, Ron Schieber, (R), Platte County Administration Bldg., 415 Third St., Rm. 210, Platte City 64079; (816) 858-3331; FAX (816) 858-3329; ron.schieber@ co.platte.mo.us

Prosecuting Attorney, Eric Zahnd, (R), Platte County Courthouse, 328 Main St., Ste. 60, Platte City 64079; (816) 858-2232; FAX (816) 858-3472; ezahnd@co.platte.mo.us

Public Administrator, Toni Clemens, (D), Platte County Courthouse, 415 Third St., Ste. 90, Platte City 64079; (816) 858-2232; FAX (816) 858-3447; tclemens@co.platte.mo.us

Recorder of Deeds, Gloria Boyer, (R), Platte County Administration Bldg., 415 Third St., Rm. 110, Platte City 64079; (816) 858-1832; FAX (816) 858-2379; gboyer@co.platte.mo.us

Sheriff, Mark S. Owen, (R), Platte County Courthouse, 415 Third St., Ste. 10, Platte City 64079; (816) 858-2424; FAX (816) 858-3053; mark.owen@plattesheriff.org

Treasurer, Rob Willard, (R), Platte County Administration Bldg., 415 Third St., Rm. 117, Platte City 64079; (816) 858-3318; FAX (816) 858-3393; rob.willard@co.platte.mo.us

---

*Appointed

Polk County

County seat and zip code: Bolivar 65613. **County population:** 31,054. **Classification:** Third class. **Assessed valuation:** $289,871,898. **Square miles:** 642. **Organized:** January 5, 1835. **Named for:** James K. Polk.

Assessor, Carolyn Page, (R), Polk County Courthouse, 102 E. Broadway, Rm. 9, Bolivar 65613; (417) 326-4643; FAX (417) 326-3131; assessor@polkcountymo.org

Clerk Circuit Court, Tiffany Phillips, (R), Polk County Courthouse, 102 E. Broadway, Rm. 14, Bolivar 65613; (417) 326-4912; FAX (417) 326-4194; tiffany.phillips@courts.mo.gov

Clerk County Commission, Melinda Robertson, (R), Polk County Courthouse, 102 E. Broadway, Rm. 11, Bolivar 65613; (417) 326-4031; FAX (417) 326-3525; clerk@ polkcountymo.org

Collector of Revenue, Debbi R. McGinnis, (R), Polk County Courthouse, 102 E. Broadway, Rm. 6, Bolivar 65613; (417) 326-4032; FAX (417) 777-8693; collector@polkcountymo. org

Commissioner, Northern District, Kyle Legan, (R), Polk County Courthouse, 102 E. Broadway, Rm. 12, Bolivar 65613; (417) 326-2922; FAX (417) 326-3525; commissioners@polk countymo.org

Commissioner, Southern District, Rex Austin, (R), Polk County Courthouse, 102 E. Broadway, Rm. 12, Bolivar 65613; (417) 326-2922; FAX (417) 326-3525; commissioners@polk countymo.org

Coroner, Roy Harms, (R), 102 E. Broadway, Rm. 10, Bolivar 65613; (417) 298-3213 or (417) 326-6195; FAX (417) 326-3525

County Health Department Director*, Michelle Morris, PO Box 124, 1317 W. Broadway, Bolivar 65613; (417) 326-7250; FAX (417) 326-2766; morrim@lpha.mopublic.org

County Highway Engineer*, Dean Smith, (R), Polk County Courthouse, 102 E. Broadway, Rm. 12, Bolivar 65613; (417) 326-4022; FAX (417) 326-3525

County Surveyor, Michael Shuler, (R), Polk County Courthouse, 102 E. Broadway, Rm. 3, Bolivar 65613; (417) 326-4010; FAX (417) 326-4010; mikeshuler@shulerlandsurvey. com

Emergency Management Director*, Robert Dickson, 1705 S. Lillian, Ste. B, Bolivar 65613; (417) 326-6610; FAX (417) 777-8175; emadirector@polkcountymo.org

Presiding Commissioner, Shannon Hancock, (R), Polk County Courthouse, 102 E. Broadway, Rm. 12, Bolivar 65613; (417) 326-2922; FAX (417) 326-3525; commissioners@ polkcountymo.org

Prosecuting Attorney, Kenneth R. Ashlock, (R), Polk County Courthouse, 102 E. Broadway, Rm. 4, Bolivar 65613; (417) 326-5756; FAX (417) 326-3030; pa@polkcountymo.org

Public Administrator, Barbara Davolt, (R), Polk County Courthouse, 102 E. Broadway, Box 5, Bolivar 65613; (417) 777-4053; FAX (417) 777-5789; publicadmin@polkcountymo.org

Recorder of Deeds, Carol Poindexter, (R), Polk County Courthouse, 102 E. Broadway, Rm. 8, Bolivar 65613; (417) 326-4924; FAX (417) 326-6898; recorder@polkcountymo.org

Sheriff, Kay Williams, (R), 113 E. Jackson, Bolivar 65613; (417) 777-9020; FAX (417) 777-7684; kwilliams@polkcountymosheriff.org

Treasurer, Vonna Bauer, (R), Polk County Courthouse, 102 E. Broadway, Rm. 1, Bolivar 65613; (417) 326-4913; FAX (417) 326-3615; treasurer@polkcountymo.org

---

*Appointed

Pulaski County

County seat and zip code: Waynesville 65583. **County population:** 53,436. **Classification:** Third class. **Assessed valuation:** $462,627,173. **Square miles:** 551. **Organized:** January 19, 1833. **Named for:** Casmir Pulaski, Revolutionary War general from Poland.

Assessor, Daniel Whittle, (R), Pulaski County Courthouse, Waynesville 65583; (573) 774-4717; FAX (573) 774-4722; pulaskiassessor@leblink.com

Clerk Circuit Court and ex officio Recorder of Deeds, Rachelle Beasley, (D), Pulaski County Courthouse, 301 Historic Rte. 66 E., Ste. 202, Waynesville 65583; (573) 774-4755; FAX (573) 774-6967; rachelle.beasley@courts.mo.gov

Clerk County Commission, Brent Bassett, (R), Pulaski County Courthouse, 301 Historic Rt. 66 E., Waynesville 65583; (573) 774-4701; FAX (573) 774-5601; pcclerk@fidnet.com

Collector of Revenue, Terri Mitchell, (R), Pulaski County Courthouse, 301 Historic Rte. 66 E., Waynesville 65583; (573) 774-4711; FAX (573) 774-4722; pulaskicollector@leblink.com

Commissioner, Eastern District, Lynn Sharp, (R), Pulaski County Courthouse, 301 Historic Rte. 66 E., Waynesville 65583; (573) 774-4701; FAX (573) 774-5601; pcclerk@fidnet.com

Commissioner, Western District, Rickey Zweerink, (R), Pulaski County Courthouse, Waynesville 65583; (573) 774-4701; FAX (573) 774-5601; pcclerk@fidnet.com

Coroner, Mikel Hartness, (D), 310 Historic Rte. 66 E., Waynesville 65583; (573) 774-5413; FAX (573) 774-2748

County Health Department Director, Deborah Baker, 101 12th St., Crocker 65452; (573) 736-2217; FAX (573) 736-5370; bakerd1@lpha.mopublic.org

County Surveyor, Don Mayhew, (R), Pulaski County Courthouse, 301 Historic Rte. 66 E., Waynesville 65583; (573) 774-6777; FAX (573) 774-5601

Emergency Management Director*, Lawson Smith, 301 Historic Rte. 66 E., Waynesville 65583; (573) 774-4701; FAX (573) 774-5601; react32@yahoo.com

Presiding Commissioner, Gene Newkirk, (R), Pulaski County Courthouse, 301 Historic Rte. 66 E., Waynesville 65583; (573) 774-4701; FAX (573) 774-5601; genenewkirk@cablemo.net

Prosecuting Attorney, Kevin Hillman, (R), Pulaski County Courthouse, 301 Historic Rte. 66 E., Ste. 300, Waynesville 65583; (573) 774-4770; FAX (573) 774-4779; kevin@pulaskicountymopa.com

Public Administrator, Loretta Rouse, (R), Pulaski County Courthouse, 301 Historic Rte. 66 E., Waynesville 65583; (573) 774-4741; FAX (573) 774-4743; pulaskicountypubadm@hotmail.com

Sheriff, Ron Long, (R), Pulaski County Jail, 301 Historic Rte. 66 E., Waynesville 65583; (573) 774-4790; FAX (573) 774-4795; ronlong@pcsheriff2.com

Treasurer, Sue Rapone, (R), Pulaski County Courthouse, 301 Historic Rte. 66 E., Ste. 124, Waynesville 65583; (573) 774-4724; FAX (573) 774-5601; suerapone@gmail.com

---

*Appointed

Putnam County

County seat and zip code: Unionville 63565. **County population:** 4,829. **Classification:** Third class. **Assessed valuation:** $80,613,988. **Square miles:** 520. **Organized:** February 28, 1845. **Named for:** Israel Putnam, Revolutionary War general.

Assessor, Chrissy Gillis, (D), Putnam County Courthouse, Rm. 201, Unionville 63565; (660) 947-3900; FAX (660) 947-3902; assessor@nemr.net

Clerk Circuit Court, Mitzi D. Shipley, (R), Putnam County Courthouse, Rm. 204, Unionville 63565; (660) 947-2071; FAX (660) 947-2320; mitzi.shipley@courts.mo.gov

Clerk County Commission*, Chrystal Perkins, (R), Putnam County Courthouse, Rm. 101, Unionville 63565; (660) 947-2674; FAX (660) 947-4214; putclerk@nemr.net

Collector/Treasurer, Sharon Thompson Parks, (R), Putnam County Courthouse, Rm. 200, Unionville 63565; (660) 947-2095; FAX (660) 947-7774

Commissioner, Eastern District, Shane Bradshaw, (R), 1601 Main St., Rm. 101, Unionville 63565; (660) 947-2674; FAX (660) 947-4214

Commissioner, Western District, Gerald Owings, (R), 1601 Main St., Rm. 101, Unionville 63565; (660) 947-2674; FAX (660) 947-4214

Coroner*, Anna Watt, 32113 Falcon Dr., Unionville 63565; (660) 947-3803

County Health Department Director, Erica Klingner, 103 N. 18th St., Unionville 63565; (660) 947-2429

Emergency Management Director, Paul Andrew, 1601 Main St., Rm. 101, Unionville 63565; (660) 292-2274; pclepcemd@gmail.com

Presiding Commissioner, Randy Sands, (R), 1601 Main St., Rm. 101, Unionville 63565; (660) 947-2674; FAX (660) 947-4214; rasands@nemr.net

Prosecuting Attorney, Tom Keedy, (R), 1802 Lincoln St., PO Box 205, Unionville 63565; (660) 947-7301; (660) 947-3845; tkeedy@nemr.net

Public Administrator, Peggy Wood, 1601 Main St., Third Fl. Courthouse, Unionville 63565; (660) 947-2461; FAX (660) 947-2462

Recorder of Deeds, Jeneen Roof, (R), Putnam County Courthouse, Rm. 202, Unionville 63565; (660) 947-3295; FAX (660) 947-7348; ejr@nemr.net

Sheriff, Jason Knight, (R), Putnam County Courthouse, Rm. 0101, Unionville 63565; (660) 947-3200; FAX (660) 947-3700; sheriff@nemr.net

———

*Appointed

Ralls County

County seat and zip code: New London 63459. **County population:** 10,192. **Classification:** Third class. **Assessed valuation:** $204,479,025. **Square miles:** 481. **Organized:** November 16, 1820. **Named for:** Daniel Ralls, Missouri legislator.

Assessor, Thomas E. Ruhl, (D), Ralls County Courthouse, PO Box 339 New London 63459; (573) 985-5671; FAX (573) 985-3251; rallsasor@missouricom.com

Clerk Circuit Court and ex officio Recorder of Deeds, Gina Jameson, (D), Ralls County Courthouse, PO Box 466, New London 63459; (573) 985-5631; FAX (573) 985-5630; gina.jameson@courts.mo.gov

County Clerk, Sandy Lanier, (D), Ralls County Courthouse, 311 S. Main, PO Box 400, New London 63459; (573) 985-7111; FAX (573) 985-6100; rcclerk@missouricom.com

Collector of Revenue, Connie L. Berry, (D), Ralls County Courthouse, PO Box 340, New London 63459; (573) 985-5621; FAX (573) 985-3251; rallscoll@missouricom.com

Commissioner, Eastern District, R.C. Harlow, (D), Ralls County Courthouse, PO Box 400, New London 63459; (573) 985-7111; FAX (573) 985-6100; rallsclerk@missouricom.com

Commissioner, Western District, Steven H. Whitaker, (D), Ralls County Courthouse, PO Box 400, New London 63459; (573)

985-7111; FAX (573) 985-6100; rallsclerk@missouricom.com

Coroner, Denise Goodwin, (D), 22341 Coyote Hills, Center 63436; (573) 822-9692; FAX (573) 985-6100; denisegoodwincoroner@gmail.com

County Health Department Director, Tanya M. Taylor, 405 W. First St., New London 63459, (573) 985-7121; FAX (573) 985-1531; taylor2@lpha.mopublic.org

Emergency Management Director, Assistant Manager Brian Reed, 18758 Hwy. 19, New London MO 63459; (573) 719-7347

Presiding Commissioner, Wiley Hibbard, (D), Ralls County Courthouse, PO Box 400, New London 63459; (573) 985-7111; FAX (573) 985-6111; rallsclerk@missouricom.com

Prosecuting Attorney, Rodney J. Rodenbaugh, (D), Ralls County Courthouse, PO Box 427, New London 63459; (573) 985-5681; FAX (573) 985-5682; rallspa@missouricom.com

Public Administrator, Paula Evans, (D), PO Box 87, Center 63436; (573) 822-8698; FAX (573) 267-9809; paula3800@att.net

Sheriff, Gerry Dinwiddie, (R), PO Box 309, 209 E. Fourth St, New London 63459; (573) 985-5611; FAX (573) 985-3100; 475@rallscountysheriff.com

Surveyor, Marty Wasson, (D), 14374 Fort Mason Dr., New London 63459; (573) 406-0637

Treasurer, Jena L. Epperson, (D), Ralls County Courthouse, PO Box 247, New London 63459; (573) 985-7151; rallstreas@missouricom.com

Randolph County

County seat and zip code: Huntsville 65259. **County population:** 25,414. **Classification:** Third class. **Assessed valuation:** $459,145,057. **Square miles:** 473. **Organized:** January 22, 1829. **Named for:** John Randolph of Virginia.

Assessor, Richard Tregnago, (D), Randolph County Courthouse, 110 S. Main St., Ste. E, Huntsville 65259; (660) 277-4716; richard.tregnago@randolphcounty-mo.gov

Clerk Circuit Court, Michelle Chapman, (R), Randolph County Justice Center, 372 Hwy. JJ, Huntsville 65259; (660) 277-4601; FAX (660) 277-4611; michelle.chapman@courts.mo.gov

Clerk County Commission, Will Ellis, (R), Randolph County Courthouse, 110 S. Main St., Ste. A, Huntsville 65259; (660) 277-4717; FAX (660) 277-3246; will.ellis@randolphcounty-mo.gov

Collector of Revenue, Shiela Miller, (D), Randolph County Courthouse, 110 S. Main, Huntsville 65259; (660) 277-4713; FAX (660) 277-4834; shiela.miller@randolph county-mo.gov

Commissioner, Eastern District, Robert Wayne Wilcox, (R), Randolph County Courthouse, 110 S. Main, Huntsville 65259; (660) 277-4722; FAX (660) 277-3246; wayne.wilcox@randolphcounty-mo.gov

Commissioner, Western District, Jerry Crutchfield, (D), Randolph County Courthouse, 110 S. Main, Huntsville 65259; (660) 277-4722; FAX (660) 277-3246; jcrutchfield@randolph county-mo.gov

Coroner, Gerald A. Luntsford, (R), 8654 Hwy. J, Jacksonville 65260; (660) 670-1461

County Health Department Director, Debra Laird, PO Box 488, 423 E. Logan St., Moberly 65270; (660) 263-6643; FAX (660) 263-0333; lairdd@lpha.mopublic.org

Emergency Management Director*, Robert L. Creed, 310 N. Clark St., Moberly 65270; (660) 269-8705; FAX (660) 263-8540; rcreed@moberlyfd.com

Presiding Commissioner, John Truesdell, (R), Randolph County Courthouse, 110 S. Main, Huntsville 65259; (660) 277-4722; FAX (660) 277-3246; john.truesdell@randolphcounty-mo.gov

Prosecuting Attorney, Michael Fusselman, (R), 200-B E. Rollins St., Moberly 65270; (660) 263-6390; FAX (660) 263-9203; fuss@mcmsys.com

Public Administrator, Mary Jo Colley, (R), 1005 County Rd. 2460, Huntsville, 65259; (660) 263-1216; FAX (660) 263-1296; maryjo.colley@randolphcounty-mo.gov

Recorder of Deeds, Mark Price, (D), Randolph County Courthouse, 110 S. Main, Ste. B, Huntsville 65259; (660) 277-4718; FAX (660) 277-4273; mprice@rcao.com

Sheriff, Mark Nichols, (D), 372 Hwy. JJ, #B, Huntsville 65259; (660) 277-5095; FAX (660) 277-5084; randcosheriff2@randolphcounty-mo.gov

Treasurer, Penny Henry, (R), Randolph County Courthouse, 110 S. Main, Huntsville 65259; (660) 277-4714; penny.henry@randolphcounty-mo.gov

---

*Appointed

Ray County

County seat and zip code: Richmond 64085. **County population:** 22,949. **Classification:** Third class. **Assessed valuation:** $293,812,570. **Square miles:** 568. **Organized:** November 16, 1820. **Named for:** John Ray, member of the first state Constitutional Convention.

Assessor, Kent Wollard, (D), Ray County Courthouse, Richmond 64085; (816) 776-4511; FAX (816) 776-4521

Clerk Circuit Court, Carolyne Conner, (D), Ray County Courthouse, Richmond 64085; (816) 776-3377; FAX (816) 776-6016

Clerk County Commission, Glenda Powell, (R), Ray County Courthouse, 100 W. Main, Ste. 23, Richmond 64085; (816) 776-4502; FAX (816) 776-4512; ray@sos.mo.gov

Collector of Revenue, Julie Chowning, (D), Ray County Courthouse, 100 W. Main, Ste. 12, Richmond 64085; (816) 776-2187; FAX (816) 776-2740; raycountycollectormo.com

Commissioner, Eastern District, Allen Dale, (D), Ray County Courthouse, Richmond 64085; (816) 776-4507; FAX (816) 776-4512

Commissioner, Western District, Michael Twyman, (D), 35565 W. 108th St., Richmond 64085; (816) 516-5885

Coroner*, Bartley J. Willim, (D), PO Box 271, Excelsior Springs 64024

County Surveyor, Thomas Sisco, (D), 39724 E. 172nd St., Richmond 64085; (816) 470-7231

Emergency Management Director, Gary Wilhite, (R), Ray County Courthouse, 100 W. Main, Richmond 64085; (816) 776-4507; FAX (816) 776-4512; raycountycommissioners@yahoo.com

Presiding Commissioner, Gary Wilhite, (R), Ray County Courthouse, 100 W. Main, Richmond 64085; (816) 776-4507; FAX (816) 776-4512; raycountycommissioners@yahoo.com

Prosecuting Attorney, Camille Johnston, (R), Ray County Courthouse, 112 W. North Main, PO Box 535, Richmond 64085; (816) 776-2882; FAX (816) 776-6802

Public Administrator, Kenneth A. Nolker, (D), 219 S. College St., Richmond 64085; (816) 776-8612; FAX (816) 776-5077

Recorder of Deeds, Shirley O'Dell, (D), Ray County Courthouse, Richmond 64085; (816) 776-4500; FAX (816) 776-4512

Sheriff, Garry Bush, (D), 200 W. Ninth St., Henrietta 64036; (816) 290-5631 or (816) 290-5323; FAX (816) 290-5548

Treasurer, Melissa Holloway, (I), Ray County Courthouse, 100 W. Main, Ste. 24, Richmond 64085; (816) 776-4504; FAX (816) 776-4512

---

*Appointed

Reynolds County

County seat and zip code: Centerville 63633. **County population:** 6,565. **Classification:** Third class. **Assessed valuation:** $181,492,548. **Square miles:** 808. **Organized:** February 25, 1845. **Named for:** Thomas Reynolds, Governor of Missouri.

Assessor, Rick Parker, (D), Reynolds County Courthouse, PO Box 57, Centerville 63633; (573) 648-2494, ext. 18; FAX (573) 648-2530; 081assessor@centurytel.net

Clerk Circuit Court, Randy L. Cowin, (D), Reynolds County Courthouse, PO Box 39, Centerville 63633; (573) 648-2494, ext. 34; FAX (573) 648-1002

Clerk County Commission, Mike Harper, (D), Reynolds County Courthouse, PO Box 10, Centerville 63633; (573) 648-2494, ext. 12; FAX (573) 648-2449; reynolds@sos.mo.gov

Collector of Revenue, Kathy Hoffman, (D), Reynolds County Courthouse, PO Box 17, Centerville 63633; (573) 648-2494, ext. 33; FAX (573) 648-2061

Commissioner, First District, Doug Warren, (D), Reynolds County Courthouse, PO Box 10, Centerville 63633; (573) 648-2494, ext. 14; FAX (573) 648-2449

Commissioner, Second District, Eddie Williams, (D), Reynolds County Courthouse, PO Box 10, Centerville 63633; (573) 648-2494, ext. 14; FAX (573) 648-2449; reynolds@sos.mo.gov

Coroner, Jeffrey N. McSpadden, (D), 610 S. Main St., Ellington 63638; (573) 663-7111

County Health Department Director, Frances Vermillion, Reynolds County Heath Center, PO Box 40, Centerville 63633; (573) 648-2498; FAX (573) 648-2510

Emergency Management Director*, Renee Horn, PO Box 10, Centerville 63633; (573) 648-2494; FAX (573) 648-2449; runts33@hotmail.com

Presiding Commissioner, Joe Loyd, (D), Reynolds County Courthouse, PO Box 10, Centerville 63633; (573) 648-2494, ext. 14; FAX (573) 648-2449; rccloyd@live.com

Prosecuting Attorney, Benjamin Thompson, (D), Reynolds County Courthouse, PO Box 78, Centerville 63633; (573) 648-2494, ext. 26; FAX (573) 648-2265

Public Administrator*, Robyn Gray, (D), Reynolds County Courthouse, PO Box 44, Centerville 63633; (573) 648-2494, ext. 22; FAX (573) 648-2061

Recorder of Deeds, Myra Turner, (D), Reynolds County Courthouse, PO Box 76, Centerville 63633; (573) 648-2494; FAX (573) 648-1002

Sheriff, Tom Volner, (D), Reynolds County Courthouse, PO Box 16, Centerville 63633; (573) 648-2491, ext. 20; FAX (573) 648-2296; rcsheriff@gmail.com

Treasurer, Wanda Corder, (D), Reynolds County Courthouse, PO Box 68, Centerville 63633; (573) 648-2494, ext. 37; FAX (573) 648-2061

---

*Appointed

Ripley County

County seat and zip code: Doniphan 63935. **County population:** 13,969. **Classification:** Third class. **Assessed valuation:** $96,728,519. **Square miles:** 632. **Organized:** January 5, 1833. **Named for:** Eleazar W. Ripley, soldier in the War of 1812.

Assessor, Jan Spencer, (D), Ripley County Courthouse, 100 Courthouse Sq., Doniphan 63935; (573) 996-7113 or (573) 996-7112; FAX (573) 996-5187; ripcoassess@windstream.net

Clerk Circuit Court, Sharon R. Richmond, (R), Ripley County Courthouse, Doniphan 63935; (573) 996-2818; FAX (573) 996-5014; sharon.richmond@courts.mo.gov

Clerk County Commission, Becky York, (D), Ripley County Courthouse, 100 Courthouse Sq., Ste. 2, Doniphan 63935; (573) 996-3215; FAX (573) 996-9774; ripley@sos.mo.gov

Collector of Revenue, Marcia L. Tackett, (R), Ripley County Courthouse, 100 Courthouse Sq., Ste. 1, Doniphan 63935; (573) 996-4707; FAX (573) 996-5786

Commissioner, Eastern District, David Johnson, (D), Ripley County Courthouse, 100 Courthouse Sq., Doniphan 63935; (573) 996-3215; FAX (573) 996-9774; ripley@sos.mo.gov

Commissioner, Western District*, Jerry W. Halley, (D), Ripley County Courthouse, 100 Courthouse Sq., Doniphan 63935; (573) 996-3215; FAX (573) 996-9774; ripley@sos.mo.gov

Coroner, Mike Jackson, (D), c/o Edwards Funeral Home, 606 Walnut St., Doniphan 63935; (573) 996-2121; FAX (573) 996-2225; mikejackson1969@gmail.com

County Health Department Director, Jan Morrow, 1003 E. Locust, Doniphan 63935; (573) 996-2181; FAX (573) 996-7632; jmorrow@semo.net

County Surveyor, William Troy Ayers, (R), HC 6, Box 244, Gatewood 63942; (573) 255-3746

Emergency Management Director, Lance Pigg, 124 W. Jefferson, Doniphan 63935; (573) 996-7146; FAX (573) 996-7877; doniphanfd@windstream.net

Presiding Commissioner, William D. Kennon Jr., (R), Ripley County Courthouse, 100 Courthouse Sq., Doniphan 63935; (573) 996-3215; FAX (573) 996-9774; ripley@sos.mo.gov

Prosecuting Attorney, Christopher J. Miller, (D), Ripley County Courthouse, 100 Courthouse Sq., Ste. 8, Doniphan 63935; (573) 996-2138; FAX (573) 996-7762; ripleycopa@windstream.net

Public Administrator, Diane Knight Moore, (R), 100 Courthouse Sq., Doniphan 63935; (573) 996-5254

Recorder of Deeds, June Watson, (D), Ripley County Courthouse, 100 Courthouse Sq., Doniphan 63935; (573) 996-7941; FAX (573) 996-9706; jwatsonrecorder@windstream.net

Sheriff, Ron Barnett, (R), 301 Lafayette St., Doniphan 63935; (573) 996-5555; FAX (573) 996-4318; ripleyco510@windstream.net

Treasurer, Terry L. Slayton, (R), Ripley County Courthouse, 100 Courthouse Sq., Ste. 6, Doniphan 63935; (573) 996-3903; FAX (573) 996-5004; tlfarms@hotmail.com

---

*Appointed

St. Charles County

County seat and zip code: St. Charles 63301. **County population:** 379,493. **Classification:** First class charter. **Assessed valuation:** $7,208,852,679. **Square miles:** 558. **Organized:** October 1, 1812. **Named for:** St. Charles Borromeo, Italian Cardinal.

Assessor, Scott Shipman, (R), Administration Bldg., 201 N. Second St., Rm. 250, St. Charles 63301; (636) 949-7425; FAX (636) 949-7435; cyassess@sccmo.org

Auditor*, Brent Statler, Administration Bldg., 201 N. Second St., Rm. 526, St. Charles 63301; (636)949-7455; FAX (636)949-7467; auditor@sccmo.org

Clerk Circuit Court*, Judy Zerr, (R), Courts Administration Bldg., 300 N. Second St., Rm. 541, St. Charles 63301; (636) 949-3098; FAX (636) 949-7390

Collector of Revenue, Michelle McBride, (R), Administration Bldg., 201 N. Second St., Rm. 134, St. Charles 63301; (636) 949-7470; FAX (636) 949-7471; collector@sccmo.org

Council Member, First District, Joe Cronin, (R), Executive Office Bldg., 100 N. Third St., Ste. 124, St. Charles 63301; (636) 949-7530; FAX (636) 949-7532; council@sccmo.org

Council Member, Second District, Joseph Brazil, (R), Executive Office Bldg., 100 N. Third St.,

Ste. 124, St. Charles 63301; (636) 949-7530; FAX (636) 949-7532; council@sccmo.org

Council Member, Third District, Mike Elam, (R), Executive Office Bldg., 100 N. Third St., Ste. 124, St. Charles 63301; (636) 949-7530; FAX (636) 949-7532; council@sccmo.org

Council Member, Fourth District, Dave Hammond, (R), Executive Office Bldg., 100 N. Third St., Ste. 124, St. Charles 63301; (636) 949-7530; FAX (636) 949-7532; council@sccmo.org

Council Member, Fifth District, Terry Hollander, (R), Executive Office Bldg., 100 N. Third St., Ste. 124, St. Charles 63301; (636) 949-7530; FAX (636) 949-7532; council@sccmo.org

Council Member, Sixth District, Mike Klinghammer, (R), Executive Office Bldg., 100 N. Third St., Ste. 124, St. Charles 63301; (636) 949-7530; FAX (636) 949-7532; council@sccmo.org

Council Member, Seventh District, John W. White, (R), Executive Office Bldg., 100 N. Third St., Ste. 124, St. Charles 63301; (636) 949-7530; FAX (636) 949-7532; council@sccmo.org

County Executive, Steve Ehlmann, (R), Executive Office Bldg., 100 N. Third St., Ste. 318, St. Charles 63301; (636) 949-7520; FAX (636) 949-7521; executive@sccmo.org

County Health Department Interim Director*, Hope Woodson, 1650 Boone's Lick Rd., St. Charles 63301; (636) 949-7400; comhealth@sccmo.org

County Highway Engineer*, Craig Tajkowski, Administration Bldg., 201 N. Second St., Rm. 429, St. Charles 63301; (636) 949-7305; FAX (636) 949-7307; highway@sccmo.org

County Registrar*, Ruth Miller, County Administration Bldg., 201 N. Second St., Ste. 541, St. Charles 63301; (636) 949-7560; FAX (636) 949-7562

Director of Elections, Rich Chrismer, (R), St. Charles County Election Authority, 397 Turner Blvd., St. Peters 63376; (636) 949-7550; FAX (636) 949-7552; election@sccmo.org

Director of Finance*, Bob Schnur, Administration Bldg., 201 N. Second St., Ste. 541, St. Charles 63301; (636) 949-7465; (636) 949-7456; finance@sccmo.org

Emergency Management Director*, (Vacancy), 301 N. Second St., Rm. 280, St. Charles 63301; (636) 949-3023; FAX (636) 949-3021; ema@sccmo.org

Medical Examiner*, Mary F. Case, M.D., 3556 Caroline, Rm. C-305, St. Louis 63104; (314) 977-7841

Prosecuting Attorney, Tim Lohmar, (R), Courts Administration Bldg., 300 N. Second St., Ste. 601, St. Charles 63301; (636) 949-7355; FAX (636) 949-7360; pa@sccmo.org

Public Administrator*, Deborah J. Lanham, (D), 300 N. Second, Ste. 233-A, St. Charles 63301; (636) 949-7315; FAX (636) 949-7317; publicadmin@sccmo.org

Recorder of Deeds, Barbara J. Hall, (R), Administration Bldg., 201 N. Second St., Ste. 338, St. Charles 63301; (636) 949-7505; FAX (636) 949-7512; recorder@sccmo.org

Sheriff, Scott Lewis, (R), Administration Bldg., 201 N. Second St., Rm. 429, St. Charles 63301; (636) 949-3010; FAX (636) 949-7372; sheriff@sccmo.org

Police Chief, Dave Todd, 101 Sheriff Dierker Ct., O'Fallon 63366; (636) 949-4540; FAX (636) 949-3077; dtodd@sscmo.org

---

*Appointed

St. Clair County

County seat and zip code: Osceola 64776. **County population:** 9,457. **Classification:** Third class. **Assessed valuation:** $108,875,857. **Square miles:** 698. **Organized:** January 29, 1841. **Named for:** Arthur St. Clair, Revolutionary War general.

Assessor, Gladys J. Smith, (D), St. Clair County Courthouse, PO Box 95, Osceola 64776; (417) 646-2449; FAX (417) 646-5523; glad@centurytel.net.

Clerk Circuit Court, Karen Hubbard, (D), St. Clair County Courthouse, PO Box 493, Osceola 64776; (417) 646-2226; FAX (417) 646-2401

Clerk County Commission, Debbie Peden, (D), St. Clair County Courthouse, PO Box 525, Osceola 64776; (417) 646-2315; FAX (417) 646-8080; stclair@sos.mo.gov

Collector of Revenue, Pamela Guffey, (R), St. Clair County Courthouse, PO Box 505, Osceola 64776; (417) 646-2486; FAX (417) 646-5556

Commissioner, Northern District, Leroy D. Strope, (R), St. Clair County Courthouse, PO Box 525, Osceola 64776; (417) 646-8003; FAX (417) 646-8080; stclair@sos.mo.gov

Commissioner, Southern District, Gerald R. Williams, (R), St. Clair County Courthouse, PO Box 525, Osceola 64776; (417) 646-8003; FAX (417) 646-8080; stclair@sos.mo.gov

Coroner, C. Randy Sheldon, (R), PO Box 384, Osceola 64776; (417) 646-8135

County Health Department Director, Nancy Stephan, 530 Arduser Dr., Osceola 64776; (417) 646-8332; FAX (417) 646-8159; stephn@lpha.dhss.mo.gov

Emergency Management Director, John Christiansen, 14390 NE 500 Rd., Osceola 64776; (417) 777-1234; FAX (913) 322-7173; jchristi@cccjdc.com

Presiding Commissioner, Robert Salmon, (R), St. Clair County Courthouse, PO Box 525, Osceola 64776; (417) 646-8003; FAX (417) 646-8080; stclair@sos.mo.gov

Prosecuting Attorney, Josh Jones, (R), St. Clair County Courthouse, PO Box 494, 655 Second St., Osceola 64776; (417) 646-2512; FAX (417) 646-2836

Public Administrator, Laurie Stinnett, (R), PO Box 362, Lowry City 64763; (660) 492-3182; FAX (417) 644-7324

Recorder of Deeds, Pat Speight Terry, (D), St. Clair County Courthouse, PO Box 323, Osceola 64776; (417) 646-2950; FAX (417) 646-2951

Sheriff, Scott Keeler, (D), St. Clair County Jail, PO Box 546, Osceola 64776; (414) 646-2565; FAX (417) 646-2852

Treasurer, Rhonda Shelby, (R), St. Clair County Courthouse, PO Box 216, Osceola 64776; (417) 646-8068; FAX (417) 646-8787

St. Francois County

County seat and zip code: Farmington 63640. **County population:** 65,960. **Classification:** First class. **Assessed valuation:** $699,722,326. **Square miles:** 451. **Organized:** December 19, 1821. **Named for:** The St. Francois River.

Assessor, Dan Ward, (D), St. Francois County Courthouse Annex, 1 W. Liberty, Ste. 200, Farmington 63640; (573) 756-1878; FAX (573) 756-5687; assessor@sfcgov.org

Auditor, Bret Burgess, (R), St. Francois County Courthouse Annex, 1 W. Liberty, Ste. 302, Farmington 63640; (573) 756-6892, ext. 250; FAX (573) 760-9610; bburgess@sfcgov.org

Clerk Circuit Court, Vicki J. Weible, (D), St. Francois County Courthouse, 1 N. Washington, Ste. 303, Farmington 63640; (573) 756-4551, ext. 317; FAX (573) 756-3733; ciclerk@sfcgov.org

Clerk County Commission, Mark L. Hedrick, (D), St. Francois County Courthouse Annex, 1 W. Liberty, Ste. 300, Farmington 63640; (573) 756-5411; FAX (573) 431-6967; coclerk@sfcgov.org

Collector of Revenue, Pamela J. Williams, (D), St. Francois County Courthouse Annex, 1 W. Liberty, Ste. 201, Farmington 63640; (573)

756-2645, ext. 134; FAX (573) 760-1292; collector@sfcgov.org

Commissioner, First District, Gay Wilkinson, (R), St. Francois County Courthouse Annex, 1 W. Liberty, Ste. 301, Farmington 63640; (573) 756-3623, ext. 231; FAX (573) 454-2040; gwilkinson@sfcgov.org

Commissioner, Second District, Patrick Mullins, (D), St. Francois County Courthouse Annex, 1 W. Liberty, Ste. 301, Farmington 63640; (573) 756-3623, ext. 232; FAX (573) 454-2040; pmullins@sfcgov.org

Coroner*, James Coplin, (D), 910 Taylor Ave., PO Box 702, Park Hills 63601; (573) 431-4273; FAX (573) 431-7553; coplin@smols.com

County Health Department Director*, Debra Hoehn, 1025 W. Main St., PO Box Q, Park Hills 63601; (573) 431-1947

County Highway Engineer*, Taylor Engineering, LLC, 518 Sequoia Ct. Farmington 63640; (573) 756-9226

County Surveyor, Terry Effan, (D), 3138 Pimville Rd., Park Hills 63601

Emergency Management Director*, Alan Wells, 102 Industrial Dr., Park Hills 63601; (573) 431-3131; FAX (573) 431-4110

Highway Administrator, Wendell Jarvis, St. Francois County Couthouse Annex, 1 W. Liberty, Ste. 301, Farmington 63640; FAX (573) 756-3623, ext. 235

Presiding Commissioner, Harold Gallaher, (R), St. Francois County Courthouse Annex, 1 W. Liberty, Ste. 301, Farmington 63640; (573) 756-3623, ext. 231; FAX (573) 454-2040; hgallaher@sfcgov.org

Prosecuting Attorney, Jerrod Mahurin, (D), St. Francois County Courthouse, 1 N. Washington, Ste. 301, Farmington 63640; (573) 756-6666, ext. 322; FAX (573) 756-5192; prosecutor@sfcgov.org

Public Administrator, V. Kenneth Rohrer, (D), 202 W. Columbia, Farmington 63640; (573) 756-6435

Recorder of Deeds, Steve Grider, (D), St. Francois County Courthouse Annex, 1 W. Liberty, Ste. 100, Farmington 63640; (573) 756-2323, ext. 140; recorder@sfcgov.org

Sheriff, Daniel R. Bullock, (D), 1550 Doubet Rd., Farmington 63640; (573) 756-3252; FAX (573) 756-9622; sheriff@sfcsd.org

Treasurer, Kerry Glore, (D), St. Francois County Courthouse Annex, 1 W. Liberty, Ste. 303, Farmington 63640; (573) 756-3349, ext. 240; FAX (573) 756-3940; treasurer@sfcgov.org

*Appointed

Ste. Genevieve County

County seat and zip code: Ste. Genevieve 63670. **County population:** 17,914. **Classification:** Third class. **Assessed valuation:** $422,792,832. **Square miles:** 504. **Organized:** October 1, 1812. **Named for:** Saint Genevieve, French saint, patroness of Paris.

Assessor, Linda Wagner, (D), Ste. Genevieve County Courthouse, 55 S. Third St., PO Box 26, Ste. Genevieve 63670; (573) 883-2333; FAX (573) 883-5312; sgassessor@yahoo.com

Clerk Circuit Court, Diana Grass, (D), Ste. Genevieve County Courthouse, 55 S. Third St., Ste. Genevieve 63670; (573) 883-2705; FAX (573) 883-9351; diana.grass@courts.mo.gov

Clerk County Commission, Sue Wolk, (D), Ste. Genevieve County Courthouse, 55 S. Third St., Rm. 2, Ste. Genevieve 63670; (573) 883-5589; FAX (573) 883-7202; swolkcoclerk@yahoo.com

Collector of Revenue, Phyllis A. Vessell, (D), Ste. Genevieve County Courthouse, 55 S. Third St., Ste. Genevieve 63670; (573) 883-5492; FAX (573) 883-5312; sgcollect@yahoo.com

Commissioner, First District*, Randal Bahr, (D), Ste. Genevieve County Courthouse, 55 S. Third St., Ste. Genevieve 63670; (573) 883-5589; FAX (573) 883-7202; sgcocomm2008@yahoo.com

Commissioner, Second District*, Joe Gettinger, (D), Ste. Genevieve County Courthouse, 55 S. Third St., Ste. Genevieve 63670; (573) 883-5589; FAX (573) 883-7202; sgcocomm2008@yahoo.com

Coroner, Eric Basler, (D), 21791 Siebert Rd., Ste. Genevieve 63670; (573) 883-3558; FAX (573) 883-3559; eric@baslerfuneralhome.com

County Health Department Director*, Sandra Bell, 115 Basler Dr., Ste. Genevieve 63670; (573) 883-7411; FAX (573) 883-5857; bells@lpha.mopublic.org

County Surveyor, Gerald Bader, (D), 16255 Sugar Bottom Rd., Ste. Genevieve 63670; (573) 483-2777; FAX (573) 483-2777; baderls@brick.net

Emergency Management Director, Felix Meyer, 295 Brooks Dr., Ste. Genevieve 63670; (573) 883-3866; FAX (573) 883-7209; sgcsd911@gmail.com

Presiding Commissioner*, Garry Nelson, (D), Ste. Genevieve County Courthouse, 55 S. Third St., Ste. Genevieve 63670; (573) 883-5589; FAX (573) 883-7202; sgcocomm2008@yahoo.com

Prosecuting Attorney, Carl Kinsky, (D), Ste. Genevieve County Courthouse, 55 S. Third

St., Rm. 7, Ste. Genevieve 63670; (573) 883-2791; FAX (573) 883-9636; ckinsky@ stegenpa.com

Public Administrator, Mary Jo Ramer, (D), 55 S. Third St., Ste. Genevieve 63670; (573) 883-7560; FAX (573) 883-3692; tramer3692@ hotmail.com

Recorder of Deeds, Peggy Yamnitz, (D), Ste. Genevieve County Courthouse, 55 S.Third St., Rm. 3, Ste. Genevieve 63670; (573) 883-2706; FAX (573) 883-5312; pyamrecorder@ yahoo.com

Sheriff, Gary Stolzer, (D), Ste. Genevieve County Jail, 5 Basler Dr., Ste. Genevieve 63670; (573) 883-5820; FAX (573) 883-5315; gstolzer@ sgcso.com

Treasurer, Judy E. Thomas, (D), Ste. Genevieve County Courthouse, 55 S. Third St., Ste. Genevieve 63670; (573) 883-3000; FAX (573) 883-5312; sgcotreasurer@yahoo.com

---

*Appointed

St. Louis City

St. Louis. Population: 317,419. **Classification:** First class city. **Assessed valuation:** $4,302,085,108. **Square miles:** 61. **Organized:** April 1764. **Named for:** St. Louis (King Louis IX of France), patron saint of King Louis XV.

Assessor*, Freddie Dunlap, (D), City Hall, 1200 Market St., Rm. 120, St. Louis 63103; (314) 622-4050; FAX (314) 622-3619

Circuit Attorney, Jennifer M. Joyce, (D), Carnahan Courthouse, 1114 Market St., Rm. 401, St. Louis 63101; (314) 622-4941; FAX (314) 622-3369

Circuit Clerk, Thomas Kloeppinger, (D), Civil Courts Bldg., 10 N. Tucker Blvd., First Fl., St. Louis 63101; (314) 622-4433; FAX (314) 622-4537

City Register*, Parrie L. May, City Hall, 1200 Market St., Rm. 118, St. Louis 63103; (314) 622-4145; FAX (314) 622-4247

Collector of Revenue, Gregory F.X. Daly, (D), City Hall, 1200 Market St., Rm. 110, St. Louis 63103; (314) 622-4111; FAX (314) 622-4413

Comptroller, Darlene Green, (D), City Hall, 1200 Market St., Rm. 212, St. Louis 63103; (314) 622-4389; FAX (314) 622-4026

License Collector, Mavis T. Thompson, Esq., City Hall, 1200 Market St., Rm. 102, St. Louis 63103; (314) 622-4528; FAX (314) 622-3275; licensecollectorsoffice@stlouiscity.com

Mayor, Francis G. Slay, (D), City Hall, 1200 Market St., Rm. 200, St. Louis 63103; (314) 622-3201; FAX (314) 622-4061

Medical Examiner*, Michael A. Graham, M.D., 1300 Clark Ave., St. Louis 63103; (314) 622-4971

President of the Board of Aldermen, Lewis E. Reed, (D), City Hall, 1200 Market. Rm. 230, St. Louis, 63103; (314) 622-4114; FAX (314) 589-6921

Public Administrator, Gerard A. Nester, (D), Civil Courts Bldg., 10 N. Tucker Blvd., Rm. 101, St. Louis 63101; (314) 622-4394; FAX (314) 621-7189

Recorder of Deeds, Sharon Quigley Carpenter, (D), City Hall, 1200 Market St., Rm. 126, St. Louis 63103; (314) 622-4610; FAX (314) 622-4175; info@stlouisrecorder.org

Sheriff, James W. Murphy, (D), Civil Courts Bldg., 10 N. Tucker Blvd., Eighth Fl., St. Louis 63101; (314) 622-4851; FAX (314) 622-3414

Treasurer, Tishaura O. Jones, (D), City Hall, 1200 Market St., Rm. 220, St. Louis 63103; (314) 622-4700; FAX (314) 622-4246

---

*Appointed

St. Louis County

County seat and zip code: Clayton 63105. **County population:** 1,001,876. **Classification:** First class. **Assessed valuation:** $22,065,919,467. **Square miles:** 505. **Organized:** October 1, 1812. **Named for:** St. Louis (King Louis IX of France), patron saint of King Louis XV.

Assessor, Jake Zimmerman, (D), Lawrence K. Roos County Government Center, 41 S. Central Ave., Clayton 63105; (314) 615-5124; assessor@stlouisco.com

Auditor*, David Makarewicz, Lawrence K. Roos County Government Center, 41 S. Central Ave., Clayton 63105; (314) 615-5491; FAX (314) 615-7890; auditor@stlouisco.com

Chief Accounting Officer*, Don Rode, Lawrence K. Roos County Government Center, 41 S. Central Ave., Eighth Fl., Clayton 63105; (314) 615-5062; FAX (314) 615-3707; drode@ stlouisco.com

Chief Information Officer*, Michael Duncan, County Government Center, 121 S. Meramec, Second Fl., Clayton 63105; (314) 615-7805; FAX (314) 615-7743; mduncan@stlouisco. com

Chief Medical Examiner*, Mary E. Case, M.D., Gantner Bldg., 6039 Helen Ave., First Fl., St. Louis 63134; (314) 522-3262; FAX (314) 522-0955; mcase@stlouisco.com

Chief of Police*, Jon Belmar, County Government Center, 7900 Forsyth Blvd., First Fl., Clayton

63105; (314) 615-4260; FAX (314) 615-7065; jbelmar@stlouisco.com

Clerk of Circuit Court*, Joan M. Gilmer, County Government Center, 7900 Carondelet Ave., Fifth Fl., Clayton 63105; (314) 615-8006; jgilmer@stlouisco.com

Collector of Revenue, Mark Devore, Lawrence K. Roos County Government Center, 41 S. Central Ave., Street Level, Clayton 63105; (314) 615-7191; mdevore@stlouisco.com

Council Member, First District, Hazel Erby, (D), Lawrence K. Roos County Government Center, 41 S. Central Ave. First Fl., Clayton 63105; (314) 615-5436; FAX (314) 615-7890; herby@stlouisco.com

Council Member, Second District, Sam Page, (D), Lawrence K. Roos County Government Center, 41 S. Central Ave. First Fl., Clayton 63105; (314) 615-5437; FAX (314) 615-7890; spage@stlouisco.com

Council Member, Third District, Colleen Wasinger, (R), Lawrence K. Roos County Government Center, 41 S. Central Ave. First Fl., Clayton 63105; (314) 615-5438; FAX (314) 615-7890; cwasinger@stlouisco.com

Council Member, Fourth District, Michael E. O'Mara, (D), Lawrence K. Roos County Government Center, 41 S. Central Ave. First Fl., Clayton 63105; (314) 615-5439; FAX (314) 615-7890; momara@stlouisco.com

Council Member, Fifth District, Patrick Dolan, (D), Lawrence K. Roos County Government Center, 41 S. Central Ave. First Fl., Clayton 63105; (314) 615-5441; FAX (314) 615-7890; pdolan@stlouisco.com

Council Member, Sixth District, Kevin O'Leary, (D), Lawrence K. Roos County Government Center, 41 S. Central Ave. First Fl., Clayton 63105; (314) 615-5442; FAX (314) 615-7890; koleary@stlouisco.com

Council Member, Seventh District, Mark Harder, (R), Lawrence K. Roos County Government Center, 41 S. Central Ave. First Fl., Clayton 63105; (314) 615-5443; FAX (314) 615-7890; mharder@stlouisco.com

County Clerk and Council Administrative Director*, Genevieve M. Frank, Lawrence K. Roos County Government Center, 41 S. Central Ave. First Fl., Clayton 63105; (314) 615-5440; FAX (314) 615-7890; gfrank@stlouisco.com

County Counselor*, Peter Krane, Lawrence K. Roos County Government Center, 41 S. Central Ave., Clayton 63105; (314) 615-7025; FAX (314) 615-3732; pkrane@stlouisco.com

County Executive, Steve Stenger, (D), Lawrence K. Roos County Government Center, 41 S.

Central Ave., Ninth Fl., Clayton 63105; (314) 615-7016; FAX (314) 615-2727; sstenger@stlouisco.com

Director of Administration*, Pamela Reitz, Lawrence K. Roos County Government Center, 41 S. Central Ave., Eighth Fl., Clayton 63105; (314) 615-7046; FAX (314) 615-3707; preitz@stlouisco.com

Director of Health*, Faisal Khan, M.D., New Health Camplus, 6121 N. Hanley Rd., Second Fl., Berkeley 63134; (314) 615-1680; fkhan@stlouisco.com

Acting Director of Highways and Traffic*, Stephanie Leon Streeter, 1050 N. Lindbergh, St. Louis 63132; (314) 615-8501; FAX (314) 615-8194; sleonstreeter@stlouisco.com

Director of Human Services*, Andrea Jackson, County Government Center, 121 S. Meramec, Third Fl., Clayton 63105; (314) 615-4485; FAX (314) 615-4416; ajackson@stlouisco.com

Director of Judicial Administration*, Paul Fox, Circuit Court of St. Louis County, 7900 Carondelet Ave., Third Fl., Clayton 63105; (314) 615-2666; pfox@stlouisco.com

Director of Justice Services*, Herbert Bernsen, Buzz Westfall Justice Center, 100 S. Central Ave., Third Fl., Clayton 63105; (314) 615-4763; FAX (314) 615-4329; hbernsen@stlouisco.com

Director of Parks and Recreation*, Gary Bess, Lawrence K. Roos County Government Center, 41 S. Central Ave., Seventh Fl., Clayton 63105; (314) 615-7642; FAX (314) 615-4696

Director of Personnel*, Kirk McCarley, Lawrence K. Roos County Government Center, 41 S. Central Ave., Seventh Fl., Clayton 63105; (314) 615-5410; FAX (314) 615-7703; kmccarley@stlouisco.com

Director of Planning*, Glenn Powers, Lawrence K. Roos County Government Center, 41 S. Central Ave., Fifth Fl., Clayton 63105; (314) 615-2515; FAX (314) 615-3729; gpowers@stlouisco.com

Director of Procurement*, Toreen Parker, Lawrence K. Roos County Government Center, 41 S. Central Ave., Eighth Fl., Clayton 63105; (314) 615-2530; FAX (314) 615-0197; tparker@stlouisco.com

Director of Transportation and Public Works*, Nichalos Gardner, 1050 N. Lindbergh, Creve Coeur 63132; (314) 615-8501; FAX (314) 615-8194; ngardner@stlouisco.com

Director of Revenue*, Greg Quinn, (R), Lawrence K. Roos County Government Center, 41 S. Central Ave., Fourth Fl., Clayton 63105; (314)

615-7179; FAX (314) 615-7121; gquinn@stlouisco.com

Emergency Management Director*, Michael Smiley, 14847 Ladue Bluffs Crossing Dr., Chesterfield 63017; (314) 628-5400; FAX (314) 628-5403; msmiley@stlouisco.com

President and CEO, St. Louis County Economic Council*, Dennis Coleman, County Government Center, 121 S. Meramec, First Fl., Clayton 63105; (314) 615-7663; FAX (314) 615-7666; dcoleman@slcec.com

Prosecuting Attorney, Robert P. McCulloch, (D), 100 S. Central Ave., Second Fl., Clayton 63105; (314) 615-2600; FAX (314) 615-2611; pa@stlouisco.com

Public Administrator*, Thomas Arras, County Government Center, 7900 Carondelet Ave., Rm. 535, Clayton 63105; (314) 615-2663; FAX (314) 615-8738

Recorder of Deeds, Gerald Smith, Lawrence K. Roos County Government Center, 41 S. Central Ave., Fourth Fl., Clayton 63105; (314) 615-7178; gsmith4@stlouisco.com

Sheriff*, Jim Buckles, County Government Center, 7900 Carondelet Ave., Rm. 551, Clayton 63105; (314) 615-4724; jbuckles2@stlouisco.com

---

*Appointed

Saline County

County seat and zip code: Marshall 65340. **County population:** 23,347. **Classification:** Fourth class. **Assessed valuation:** $331,171,015. **Square miles:** 755. **Organized:** November 25, 1820. **Named for:** Its numerous salt springs.

Assessor, Margaret Pond, (D), Saline County Courthouse, 19 E. Arrow, Rm. 203, Marshall 65340; (660) 886-3111; FAX (660) 886-2644

Auditor, Tara Vogelsmeier, (D), Saline County Courthouse, 19 E. Arrow, Rm. 105, Marshall 65340; (660) 886-8582; FAX (660) 886-2603; scauditor@mmuonline.net

Clerk Circuit Court, Sharon D. Crawford, (D), Saline County Courthouse, 19 E. Arrow, Rm. 205, Marshall 65340; (660) 886-2300; FAX (660) 831-5360; sharond.crawford@courts.mo.gov

Clerk County Commission, Debbie Russell, (D), Saline County Courthouse, 19 E. Arrow, Rm. 202, Marshall 65340; (660) 886-3331; FAX (660) 886-2603; derussell@mmuonline.net

Collector of Revenue, Cindi Sims, (R), Saline County Courthouse, 19 E. Arrow, Rm. 201, Marshall 65340; (660) 886-5104; FAX (660) 886-2644; csimscollector@mmuonline.net

Commissioner, Northern District, Charlie Guthrie, (D), Saline County Courthouse, 19 E. Arrow, Rm. 101, Marshall 65340; (660) 886-7777; FAX (660) 886-2603; salcocom@mmuonline.net

Commissioner, Southern District, Monte Fenner, (D), Saline County Courthouse, 19 E. Arrow, Rm. 101, Marshall 65340; (660) 886-7777; FAX (660) 886-2603; salcocom@mmuonline.net

Coroner, William (Wilie) Harlow, (I), 226 S. Odell, Marshall 65340; (660) 831-5700

County Surveyor, Robert Robinson, (I), Saline County Courthouse, 19 E. Arrow, Rm. 102, Marshall 65340; (660) 886-9117; FAX (660) 886-2603

Presiding Commissioner, Kile Guthrey Jr., (D), Saline County Courthouse, 19 E. Arrow, Rm. 101, Marshall 65340; (660) 886-7777; FAX (660) 886-2603; salcocom@mmuonline.net

Prosecuting Attorney, Donald G. Stouffer, (D), Saline County Courthouse, 19 E. Arrow, Rm. 100, Marshall 65340; (660) 886-9608; FAX (660) 886-4884

Public Administrator*, Paula Barr, (D), 19 E. Arrow St., Rm. 301, Marshall 65340; (660) 886-8699; FAX (660) 866-4834

Recorder of Deeds, Jamie Nichols, (D), Saline County Courthouse, 19 E. Arrow, Rm. 206, Marshall 65340; (660) 886-2677; FAX (660) 831-0649

Sheriff, Wally George, (D), 1915 W. Arrow, PO Box 366, Marshall 65340; (660) 886-5511; FAX (660) 886-5513

Treasurer, Marty Smith, (R), Saline County Courthouse, 19 E. Arrow, Rm. 200, Marshall 65340; (660) 886-3636; FAX (660) 886-2603

---

*Appointed

Schuyler County

County seat and zip code: Lancaster 63548. **County population:** 4,370. **Classification:** Third class. **Assessed valuation:** $43,785,480. **Square miles:** 308. **Organized:** February 14, 1845. **Named for:** Philip Schuyler, a Revolutionary War general.

Assessor, Gary Stump, (D), Schuyler County Courthouse, PO Box 418, Lancaster 63548; (660) 457-3211; FAX (660) 457-2295

Clerk Circuit Court, Judy Keim, (D), Schuyler County Courthouse, PO Box 417, Lancaster 63548; (660) 457-3784; FAX (660) 457-3016

Clerk County Commission, Bree Shaw, (D), Schuyler County Courthouse, PO Box 187,

Lancaster 63548; (660) 457-3842; FAX (660) 457-2295; schuyler@sos.mo.gov

Collector of Revenue, Tammy R. Steele, (D), Schuyler County Courthouse, PO Box 65, Lancaster 63548; (660) 457-3825; FAX (660) 457-3124

Commissioner, Northern District, Jim Werner, (D), Schuyler County Courthouse, PO Box 187, Lancaster 63548; (660) 457-3842; FAX (660) 457-2295

Commissioner, Southern District, Jeff Lindquist, (R), Schuyler County Courthouse, PO Box 187, Lancaster 63548; (660) 457-3842; FAX (660) 457-2295

Coroner, Douglas B. Norman, (D), PO Box 176, Lancaster 63548; (660) 457-3137

County Health Department, PO Box 387, Lancaster 63548; (660) 457-3721

County Road Supervisor, Rex Kelsey, Schuyler County Courthouse, PO Box 187, Lancaster 63548; (660) 457-3842; FAX (660) 457-2295

Emergency Management Director, Phil Beeler, Schuyler County Courthouse, PO Box 187, Lancaster 63548; (660) 457-3842; FAX (660) 457-2295

Presiding Commissioner, Rodney Cooper, (R), Schuyler County Courthouse, PO Box 187, Lancaster 63548; (660) 457-3842; FAX (660) 457-2295

Prosecuting Attorney, Lindsay Gravett, (D), Schuyler County Courthouse, PO Box 277, Lancaster 63548; (660) 457-2262

Public Administrator, Ronald L. Morgan, (D), PO Box 302, Lancaster 63548; (660) 457-3282

Recorder of Deeds, Linda Blessing, (R), Schuyler County Courthouse, PO Box 417, Lancaster 63548; (660) 457-2251

Sheriff, Joe Wuebker, (D), Schuyler County Courthouse, PO Box 355, Lancaster 63548; (660) 457-3436

Treasurer, Karmen Burt, (D), Schuyler County Courthouse, PO Box 206, Lancaster 63548; (660) 457-3825; FAX (660) 457-3124

Scotland County

County seat and zip code: Memphis 63555. **County population:** 4,863. **Classification:** Third class. **Assessed valuation:** $67,966,614. **Square miles:** 439. **Organized:** January 29, 1841. **Named for:** Scotland.

Assessor, James Ward, (R), Scotland County Courthouse, 117 S. Market St., Ste. 2, Memphis 63555; (660) 465-2269; FAX (660) 465-2408; scasses@nemr.net

Clerk Circuit Court, Anita Watkins, (D), Scotland County Courthouse, 117 S. Market St., Ste. 200, Memphis 63555; (660) 465-8605; FAX (660) 465-8673

Clerk County Commission, Batina Dodge, (D), Scotland County Courthouse, 117 S. Market St., Ste. 100, Memphis 63555; (660) 465-7027; FAX (660) 465-7785; scotland@sos.mo.gov

Collector of Revenue, Kathy Becraft, (D), Scotland County Courthouse, 117 S. Market St., Ste. 103, Memphis 63555; (660) 465-7705; FAX (660) 465-7785; sccoll@nemr.net

Commissioner, Eastern District, Danette Clatt, (R), 117 S. Market St., Ste. 100, Memphis 63555; (660) 465-7027; FAX (660) 465-7785

Commissioner, Western District, David Wiggins, (R), Scotland County Courthouse, 117 S. Market St., Ste. 100, Memphis 63555; (660) 465-7027; FAX (660) 465-7785

Coroner*, Jeffrey Davis, DO, 117 S. Market St., Ste. 100, Memphis 63555; (660) 465-2106

County Health Department Director, Margaret Curry, 450-B E. Sigler, Memphis 63555; (660) 465-7275

Emergency Management Director, Duane Ebeling, (R), Scotland County Courthouse, 117 S. Market St., Ste. 100, Memphis 63555; (660) 465-7027; FAX (660) 465-7785

Presiding Commissioner, Duane Ebeling, (R), Scotland County Courthouse, 117 S. Market St., Ste. 100, Memphis 63555; (660) 465-7027; FAX (660) 465-7785

Prosecuting Attorney, Kimberly J. Nicoli, (D), 133 S. Main St., Memphis 63555; (660) 465-7753; FAX (660) 465-7723

Public Administrator, Patty Freburg, (R), RR 2, Box 55, Memphis 63555; (660) 328-6305

Recorder of Deeds, Dana Glasscock, (D), Scotland County Courthouse, 117 S. Market, Ste. 106, Memphis 63555; (660) 465-2284; FAX (660) 465-2408

Sheriff, Wayne Winn, (R), Scotland County Courthouse, 117 S. Market St., Ste. 3, Memphis 63555; (660) 465-2106; FAX (660) 465-7005

Treasurer, Kathy Kiddoo, (R), Scotland County Courthouse, 117 S. Market St., Ste. 104, Memphis 63555; (660) 465-2529; FAX (660) 465-7785; sctreas@nemr.net

---

*Appointed

Scott County

County seat and zip code: Benton 63736. **County population:** 38,903. **Classification:** Third class. **Assessed valuation:** $450,954,047. **Square miles:** 423. **Organized:** December 28, 1821. **Named for:** John Scott, Missouri congressman.

Assessor, Teresa Houchin, (D), Scott County Courthouse, PO Box 245, Benton 63736; (573) 545-3535; FAX (573) 545-3536; thsca@hotmail.com

Clerk Circuit Court, Christy Hency, (D), Scott County Courthouse, PO Box 587, Benton 63736; (573) 545-3596; FAX (573) 545-3597; circuitclerk@scottcountymo.com

Clerk County Commission, Rita Milam, (D), Scott County Courthouse, PO Box 188, Benton 63736; (573) 545-3549; FAX (573) 545-3540; scottcoclerk@scottcomo.com

Collector of Revenue, Mark Hensley, (D), Scott County Courthouse, PO Box 128, Benton 63736; (573) 545-3548; FAX (574) 545-3450; mhcollector@hotmail.com

Commissioner, First District, Dennis Ziegenhorn, (D), Scott County Courthouse, PO Box 188, Benton 63736; (573) 545-3549; FAX (573) 545-3540; dziegenhorn@hotmail.com

Commissioner, Second District, Donnie Kiefer, (D), Scott County Courthouse, PO Box 188, Benton 63736; (573) 545-3549; FAX (573) 545-3540; donkiefer77@outlook.com

Coroner, Scott C. Amick, (D), 115 E. Hickory, Scott City 63780; (573) 264-2111; FAX (573) 264-4539; scotcham57@hotmail.com

County Health Department Director*, Barry Cook, Scott County Health Department, 102 Grove Estates Ct., PO Box 129, Sikeston 63801; (573) 471-4044; FAX (573) 471-7348; cookb@lpha.dhss.mo.gov

Emergency Management Director*, Tom Beardslee, Scott County Courthouse, PO Box 431, Benton 63736; (573) 545-3549; FAX (573) 545-3540; ema@scottcountymo.com

Presiding Commissioner, Jamie Burger, (D), Scott County Courthouse, PO Box 188, Benton 63736; (573) 545-3549; FAX (573) 545-3540; jamieburger@hotmail.com

Prosecuting Attorney, Paul R. Boyd, (D), Scott County Courthouse, PO Box 160, 131 W. Winchester, Benton 63736; (573) 545-3562; FAX (573) 545-3563

Public Administrator*, Julia C. Dolan, (D), PO Box 70, Benton 63736; (573) 545-3084; FAX (573) 545-3095; scott-pa@hotmail.com

Recorder of Deeds, Tara L. Mason, (D), Scott County Courthouse, PO Box 78, Benton 63736; (573) 545-3551; FAX (573) 545-3551; scottcorecorder@scottcomo.com

Sheriff, Rick Walter, (D), Scott County Courthouse, PO Box 279, Benton 63736; (573) 545-3525; FAX (573) 545-3527; scsd@charter.net

Treasurer, Glenda Enderle, (D), Scott County Courthouse, PO Box 278, Benton 63736; (573) 545-3543; FAX (573) 545-7043; getreasurer@yahoo.com

---

*Appointed

Shannon County

County seat and zip code: Eminence 65466. **County population:** 8,329. **Classification:** Third class. **Assessed valuation:** $72,311,770. **Square miles:** 1,004. **Organized:** January 29, 1841. **Named for:** George Shannon of the Lewis and Clark Expedition.

Assessor, Summer J. Crider, (D), Shannon County Courthouse, PO Box 416, Eminence 65466; (573) 226-5539; FAX (573) 226-3103; assessor@shannon-county.com

Clerk Circuit Court and *ex officio* **Recorder of Deeds,** Melany Williams, (D), Shannon County Courthouse, PO Box 148, Eminence 65466; (573) 226-3315; FAX (573) 226-5321; melany.williams@courts.mo.gov

Clerk County Commission, Shelly McAfee, (D), Shannon County Courthouse, PO Box 187, Eminence 65466; (573) 226-3414; FAX (573) 226-5325; shannon@sos.mo.gov

Collector of Revenue, Susie Needels, (R), Shannon County Courthouse, PO Box 459, Eminence 65466; (573) 226-3416; FAX (573) 226-3103; collector@shannon-county.com

Commissioner, Northern District, Dale Counts, (D), Shannon County Courthouse, PO Box 187, Eminence 65466; (573) 226-3965; FAX (573) 226-5325; shannon@sos.mo.gov

Commissioner, Southern District, Herman Kelly, (R), Shannon County Courthouse, PO Box 187, Eminence 65466; (573) 226-3965; FAX (573) 226-5325; shannon@sos.mo.gov

Coroner, Tim Denton, (D), PO Box 639, Winona 65588; (417) 372-2319; FAX (573) 325-4646; pax564@hotmail.com

County Health Department Administrator, Kandra Counts, PO Box 788, Eminence 65466; (573) 226-3914; FAX (573) 226-3240; countk@lpha.mopublic.org

Emergency Management Director, Jeff Cowen, (D), PO Box 187, Eminence 65466; (573) 226-3965; FAX (573) 226-5325; jeffcowen@yahoo.com

Presiding Commissioner, Jeff Cowen, (D), Shannon County Courthouse, PO Box 187, Eminence 65466; (573) 226-3965; FAX (573) 226-5325; jeffcowen@yahoo.com

Prosecuting Attorney, Jodie R. Brumble, (D), Shannon County Courthouse, PO Box 429, Eminence 65466; (573) 226-3714; FAX (573) 226-5552; shannon_pa@hotmail.com

Public Administrator, Linda Wolff-Brewer, (D), HCR 2, Box 169M, Eminence 65466; (573) 996-8917; ljbshannoncounty@yahoo.com

Sheriff, Steven Blunkall, (D), Shannon County Jail, PO Box 880, Eminence 65466; (573) 226-3615; FAX (573) 226-5561; shanso@semo.net

Treasurer, Michelle Shedd, (R), Shannon County Courthouse, PO Box 218, Eminence 65466; (573) 226-3051; FAX (573) 226-5321; mshedd@centurytel.net

Shelby County

County seat and zip code: Shelbyville 63469. **County population:** 6,108. **Classification:** Third class. **Assessed valuation:** $123,741,887. **Square miles:** 501. **Organized:** January 2, 1835. **Named for:** Isaac Shelby, Kentucky governor and Revolutionary War soldier.

Assessor, Liz Miles, (R), Shelby County Courthouse, PO Box 165, Shelbyville 63469; (573) 633-2521; FAX (573) 633-1004; shelbyassessor@marktwain.net

Clerk Circuit Court, Rosalie (Rose) Shively, (D), Shelby County Courthouse, PO Box 176, Shelbyville 63469; (573) 633-2151; FAX (573) 633-2142; rose.shively@courts.mo.gov

Clerk County Commission, Tracy Smith, (D), Shelby County Courthouse, 100 E. Main, PO Box 186, Shelbyville 63469; (573) 633-2181; FAX (573) 633-1004; shelby@sos.mo.gov

Collector of Revenue, John Chinn, (D), Shelby County Courthouse, PO Box 148, Shelbyville 63469; (573) 633-2271; (573) 633-2552; shometax@marktwain.net

Commissioner, Eastern District, Maurice Shuck, (D), Shelby County Courthouse, PO Box 186, Shelbyville 63469; (573) 633-2181; FAX (573) 633-1004

Commissioner, Western District, Kerry McCarty, (D), Shelby County Courthouse, PO Box 186, Shelbyville 63469; (573) 633-2181; FAX (573) 633-1004; shelbycommission@yahoo.com

Coroner, Ralph Eagan, (D), 501 E. Mill, Shelbina 63468; (573) 588-7526

County Health Department Director, Audrey Gough, PO Box 240, 700 E. Main, Shelbyville 63469; (573) 633-2353; FAX (573) 633-2323; gougha@lpha.dhss.mo.gov

County Surveyor*, Martin T. Wasson, (D), 108 N. Third, Hannibal 63401; (573) 221-8443

Emergency Management Director, Glenn Eagan, (D), PO Box 186, Shelbyville 63469; (573) 633-2181; geagan@centurytel.net

Presiding Commissioner, Glenn Eagan, (D), Shelby County Courthouse, PO Box 186, Shelbyville 63469; (573) 633-2181; FAX (573) 633-1004; geagan@centurytel.net

Prosecuting Attorney, Jordan Rogers, (D), Shelby County Courthouse, PO Box 177, Shelbyville 63469; (573) 633-2131; FAX (573) 633-2609; shelbypa@marktwain.net

Public Administrator, Susan C. Wilt, (R), 410 S. Center, Shelbina 63468; (573) 588-1910; rswilt@yahoo.com

Recorder of Deeds, Audrey Grawe Buzzard, (D), Shelby County Courthouse, PO Box 188, Shelbyville 63469; (573) 633-2821; FAX (573) 633-1004; shelbyrecorder@marktwain.net

Sheriff, Dennis Perrigo, (D), Shelby County Courthouse, PO Box 128, Shelbyville 63469; (573) 633-2161; FAX (573) 633-2493; schrf@marktwain.net

Treasurer, Jesse C. Burton, (D), Shelby County Courthouse, PO Box 71, Shelbyville 63469; (573) 633-2574; FAX (573) 633-1004; shelbytr@marktwain.net

*Appointed

Stoddard County

County seat and zip code: Bloomfield 63825. **County population:** 29,867. **Classification:** Third class. **Assessed valuation:** $429,257,415. **Square miles:** 815. **Organized:** January 2, 1835. **Named for:** Amos Stoddard, first American Civil Commandant of Upper Louisiana.

Assessor, Jody Lemmon, (D), 401 S. Prairie St., PO Box 307, Bloomfield 63825; (573) 568-3163

Clerk Circuit Court, Paula Yancey, (R), Stoddard County Justice Center, PO Box 30, Bloomfield 63825; (573) 568-4640

Clerk County Commission, Joe Watson, (R), 401 S. Prairie St., PO Box 110, Bloomfield 63825; (573) 568-3339; FAX (573) 568-2194; stoddcoclk@newwavecomm.net or jwatson@nwcable.net

Commissioner, First District, Danny K. Talkington, (R), 401 S. Prairie St., PO Box 110, Bloomfield 63825; (573) 568-3339; FAX (573) 568-2194

Commissioner, Second District, Carol Jarrell, (R), 401 S. Prairie St., PO Box 110, Bloomfield 63825; (573) 568-3339; FAX (573) 568-2194

Coroner, Kenny Pope, (D), 125 W. Stoddard St., Dexter 63841; (573) 624-4533

County Surveyor, Joseph Pulliam, (I), 407A Medler, Bernie 63822; (573) 785-9621

Emergency Management Director, Kent Polsgrove, 512 Cooper St., PO Box 519, Dexter 63841; (573) 624-8332; kpolsgrove@ stoddems.com

Presiding Commissioner, Greg Mathis, (D), 401 S. Prairie St., PO Box 110, Bloomfield 63825; (573) 568-3339; FAX (573) 568-2194

Prosecuting Attorney, Russell Oliver, (R), 401 S. Prairie St., PO Box 140, Bloomfield 63825; (573) 568-4640

Public Administrator, Pamela Lape, (R), PO Box 347, Bloomfield 63825; (573) 563-3830; FAX (573) 568-2374

Recorder of Deeds, Kay Asbell, (D), 401 S. Prairie St., PO Box 217, Bloomfield 63825; (573) 568-3444; FAX (573) 568-2545

Sheriff, Carl Hefner, (D), Stoddard County Jail, PO Box 336, Bloomfield 63825; (573) 568-4654

Treasurer and ex officio Collector of Revenue, Carla Moore, (D), 401 S. Prairie St., PO Box 80, Bloomfield 63825; (573) 568-3327

Stone County

County seat and zip code: Galena 65656. **County population:** 31,104. **Classification:** Third class. **Assessed valuation:** $565,754,013. **Square miles:** 451. **Organized:** February 10, 1851. **Named for:** William Stone, pioneer judge of Taney County. **Website:** www.stonecomo.us

Assessor, Brad Hudson, (R), Stone County Courthouse, PO Box 135, Galena 65656; (417) 357-6141; FAX (417) 357-6369; scahudson@ centurytel.net

Clerk Circuit Court, Deborah Scobee, (R), Stone County Law Enforcement Bldg., PO Box 18, Galena 65656; (417) 357-6115; FAX (417) 357-6163; deborahjean.scobee@courts. mo.gov

Clerk County Commission, Cindy Elmore, (R), Stone County Courthouse, PO Box 45, Galena 65656; (417) 357-6127; FAX (417) 357-8087; scocelmore@gmail.com

Collector of Revenue, Vicki A. May, (R), Stone County Courthouse, PO Box 256, Galena 65656; (417) 357-6124; FAX (417) 357-1404; stonevickimay@aol.com

Commissioner, Northern District, Mark W. Maples, (R), PO Box 19, Galena 65656; (417) 357-8141; FAX (417) 357-3098; markmaples@gmail.com

Commissioner, Southern District, Jerry Dodd, (R), PO Box 19, Galena 65656; (417) 357-8141; FAX (417) 357-3098; countycommishdodd@ yahoo.com

Coroner, Rick Stumpff, (R), 1343 Hideaway Rd., Galena 65656; (417) 538-2116; FAX (417) 739-4151; rdstumpff@gmail.com

County Health Department Director, Angela Ford, PO Box 125, Galena 65656; (417) 357-6134; FAX (417) 357-6031; forda@lpha. mopublic.org

County Surveyor, Rick Kemp, (R), PO Box 623, Hollister 65673; (417) 334-5195; FAX (417) 337-9285; rdkemp.jmark@yahoo.com

Emergency Management Director, Tom Martin, 2 James River Rd., Kimberling City 65686; (417) 739-2181; FAX (417) 739-2181; protector@ centurytel.net

Northern Road Commissioner, District A, James Gold, (R), PO Box 19, Galena 65656; (417) 357-8141; (417) 357-3098

Presiding Commissioner, Dennis Wood, (R), PO Box 19, Galena 65656; (417) 357-8141; FAX (417) 357-3098; prescomm@centurytel.net

Prosecuting Attorney, Matt Selby, (R), Stone County Law Enforcement Bldg., PO Box 95, Galena 65656; (417) 357-6137; FAX (417) 357-6090; mselby.pros@gmail.com

Public Administrator, Glenda Wendy Metcalf, (R), Stone County Law Enforcement Bldg., PO Box 126, Galena 65656; (417) 357-8404; FAX (417) 357-1447; stonecopa@yahoo.com

Recorder of Deeds, Amy Jo Larson, (R), Stone County Courthouse, PO Box 186, Galena 65656; (417) 357-6362; FAX (417) 357-8131; scramyl@gmail.com

Sheriff, Doug Rader, (R), Stone County Law Enforcement Bldg., PO Box 245, Galena 65656; (417) 357-6117; FAX (417) 357-6079; sheriffrader@stonecountymosheriff.com

Southern Road Commissioner, District B, Stanley Potter, (R), PO Box 19, Galena 65656; (417) 357-8141; FAX (417) 357-3098; sordcommpotter@gmail.com

Treasurer, Kristi Stephens, (R), Stone County Courthouse, PO Box 207, Galena 65656; (417) 357-6131; FAX (417) 357-8273; sctlady2@yahoo.com

Sullivan County

County seat and zip code: Milan 63556. **County population:** 6,411. **Classification:** Third class. **Assessed valuation:** $87,033,026. **Square miles:** 651. **Organized:** February 14, 1845. **Named for:** James Sullivan, Revolutionary War general.

Assessor, Karen LaFaver, (D), Sullivan County Assessor, 109 N. Main St., Ste. 36, Milan 63556; (660) 265-4474; FAX (660) 265-4037

Clerk Circuit Court, Sherry Brinkley, (D), Sullivan County Courthouse, 109 N. Main St., Ste. 20, Milan 63556; (660) 265-4717

Clerk County Commission, Jackie Morris, (D), Sullivan County Courthouse, 109 N. Main St, Ste. 5, Milan 63556; (660) 265-3786; FAX (660) 265-3724; eclerk@windstream.net

Collector/Treasurer, Jennifer Hollon-Russell, (R), Sullivan County Courthouse, 109 N. Main St., Ste. 4, Milan 63556; (660) 265-4514

Commissioner, First District, John Watt, (R), Sullivan County Courthouse, 109 N. Main St., Ste. 7, Milan 63556; (660) 265-3434

Commissioner, Second District, Danny Busick, (R), Sullivan County Courthouse, 109 N. Main St., Ste. 7, Milan 63556; (660) 265-3434

Coroner, Paul Ruschmeier, (D), 120 W. Fourth St., Milan 63556; (660) 265-4456

County Health Department Director, Brok Johnson, Sullivan County Health Department, PO Box 129, Milan 63556; (660) 265-4141

Emergency Management Director, Dennis Goldsmith, 16785 Bear Dr., Harris 64645; (660) 794-5678

Presiding Commissioner, Chris May, (R), Sullivan County Courthouse, 109 N. Main St., Ste. 7, Milan 63556; (660) 265-3434

Prosecuting Attorney, Brian Keedy, (R), Sullivan County Courthouse, 109 N. Main St., Ste. 31, Milan 63556; (660) 265-4712

Public Administrator, Joan Brummitt, (D), Sullivan County Courthouse, 109 N. Main St., Ste. 1, Milan 63556; (660) 265-5333

Recorder of Deeds, Peggy Sloan, (R), Sullivan County Courthouse, 109 N. Main St., Ste. 20, Milan 63556; (660) 265-3630

Sheriff, Roger Smiley, (R), Sullivan County Courthouse, 109 N. Main St., Ste. 9, Milan 63556; (660) 265-3313

Taney County

County seat and zip code: Forsyth 65653. **County population:** 54,230. **Classification:** First class. **Assessed valuation:** $1,034,481,596. **Square miles:** 608. **Organized:** January 4, 1837. **Named for:** Roger B. Taney, Chief Justice of the United States Supreme Court.

Assessor, Chuck Pennel, (R), 132 David St., PO Box 612, Forsyth 65653; (417) 546-7240; FAX (417) 546-6840; chuckp@co.taney.mo.us

Auditor, Rick C. Findley, (R), Taney County Courthouse, 132 David St., PO Box 1407, Forsyth 65653; (417) 546-7201; FAX (417) 546-4908; rickf@co.taney.mo.us

Clerk Circuit Court, Beth Wyman, (R), 266 Main St., PO Box 335, Forsyth 65653; (417) 546-7230; FAX (417) 546-6133; beth.wyman@courts.mo.gov

Clerk County Commission, Donna Neeley, (R), 132 David St., PO Box 156, Forsyth 65653; (417) 546-7200; FAX (417) 546-2519; donnan@co.taney.mo.us

Collector of Revenue, Sheila L. Wyatt, (R), 132 David St., PO Box 278, Forsyth 65653; (417) 546-7216; FAX (417) 546-3525; swyatt@co.taney.mo.us

Commissioner, Eastern District, Danny Strahan, (R), 132 David St., PO Box 1086, Forsyth 65653; (417) 546-7204; FAX (417) 546-3931; dannys@co.taney.mo.us

Commissioner, Western District, Brandon Williams, (R), 132 David St., PO Box 1086, Forsyth 65653; (417) 546-7204; FAX (417) 546-3931; jim@co.taney.mo.us

Coroner, Kevin Tweedy, (R), 125 Kurt Ln., Branson 65616; (417) 334-5201; FAX (417) 546-7218; tcad603@aol.com

County Health Department Director, James Berry, 15479 Hwy. 160, PO Box 369, Forsyth 65653; (417) 546-4725; FAX (417) 546-4727; berryj@lpha.mopublic.org

Emergency Management Director, Chris Berndt, 132 David St., Forsyth 65653; (417) 546-7233; FAX (417) 546-7218; melissad@co.taney.mo.us

Presiding Commissioner, Mike Scofield, (R), 132 David St., PO Box 1086, Forsyth 65653; (417) 546-7204; FAX (417) 546-3931; mikes@co.taney.mo.us

Prosecuting Attorney, Jeffrey M. Merrell, (R), 266 Main St., PO Box 849, Forsyth 65653; (417) 546-7260; FAX (417) 546-2376; jeffm@co.taney.mo.us

Public Administrator, Carol S. Davis, (R), 266 Main St., PO Box 637, Forsyth 65653; (417) 546-7208; FAX (417) 546-3170; pubadmin@co.taney.mo.us

Recorder of Deeds, Robert A. Dixon, (R), 132 David St., PO Box 428, Forsyth 65653; (417) 546-7234; FAX (417) 546-9021; recorder@co.taney.mo.us

Sheriff, Jimmie Russell, (R), 266 Main St., PO Box 1005, Forsyth 65653; (417) 546-7250; FAX (417) 546-8933; jimmier@co.taney.mo.us

Treasurer, Melanie Smith, (R), Taney County Courthouse, 132 David St., PO Box 576, Forsyth 65653; (417) 546-7207; FAX (417) 546-6213; helens@co.taney.mo.us

Texas County

County seat and zip code: Houston 65483. **County population:** 25,642. **Classification:** Third class. **Assessed valuation:** $209,185,734. **Square miles:** 1,180. **Organized:** February 14, 1845. **Named for:** The Republic of Texas.

Assessor, Debbie James, (R), Texas County Administrative Center, 210 N. Grand, Ste. 201, Houston 65483; (417) 967-4709; FAX (417) 967-2091; assessor@texascountymissouri. gov

Clerk County Commission*, Krista N. Neal, (D), Texas County Administrative Center, 210 N. Grand, Ste. 311, Houston 65483; (417) 967-2112; FAX (417) 967-3837; txcomo@ centurytel.net

Clerk Circuit Court, Marci Mosley, (R), Texas County Circuit Court, 519 N. Grand, Ste. 202, Houston 65483; (417) 967-3742; FAX (417) 967-4220; marci.mosley@courts.mo.gov

Collector/Treasurer, Tammy Cantrell, (D), Texas County Administrative Center, 210 N. Grand, Ste. 101, Houston 65483; (417) 967-2580; FAX (417) 967-1439; collector@ texascountymissouri.gov

Commissioner, First District, John Casey, (R), Texas County Administrative Center, 210 N. Grand, Ste. 301, Houston 65483; (417) 967-3222; FAX (417) 967-8040; commission@ texascountymissouri.gov

Commissioner, Second District, Linda Garrett, (R), Texas County Administrative Center, 210 N. Grand, Ste. 301, Houston 65483; (417) 967-3222; FAX (417) 967-8040; commission @texascountymissouri.gov

Coroner, Thomas Whittaker, (D), PO Box 132, Cabool 65483; (417) 962-4889 or (417) 254-0171; FAX (417) 962-4225; tcwhit@centurytel. net

County Health Department Director, Jackie Smith, 950 N. Hwy. 63, Ste. 500, Houston 65483; (417) 967-4131; FAX (417) 967-5700; smithj3@lpha.mopublic.org

County Surveyor, Charles Manier, (R), PO Box 110, Houston 65483; (417) 260-5037; FAX (417) 967-3026; maniersurvey@yahoo.com

Emergency Management Director/Presiding Commissioner, Fred W. Stenger, (R), Texas County Administrative Center, 210 N. Grand, Ste. 301, Houston 65483; (417) 967-3222; FAX (417) 967-8040; commission@ texascountymissouri.gov

Prosecuting Attorney, Parke J. Stevens Jr., (R), Texas County Justice Center, 519 N. Grand, Ste. 102, Houston 65483; (417) 967-2029; FAX (417) 967-4874; prosecutor@ texascountymissouri.gov

Public Administrator, Connie E. Thompson, (R), 519 N. Grand Ave., Ste. 205, Houston 65483; (417) 967-2669; publicadministrator@texas countymissouri.gov

Recorder of Deeds*, Lindsay Koch, (R), Texas County Administrative Center, 210 N. Grand, Ste. 209, Houston 65483; (417) 967-8438; FAX (417) 967-8760; recorder@texascounty missouri.gov

Sheriff, James L. Sigman, (R), Texas County Justice Center, 519 N. Grand, Ste. 101, Houston 65483; (417) 967-4165; FAX (417) 967-5575; sheriff@texascountymissouri.gov

---

*Appointed

Vernon County

County seat and zip code: Nevada 64772. **County population:** 21,159. **Classification:** Third class. **Assessed valuation:** $223,200,061. **Square miles:** 837. **Organized:** February 27, 1855. **Named for:** Miles Vernon, Missouri legislator.

Assessor, Cherie K. Roberts, (D), Vernon County Courthouse, 100 W. Cherry, Ste. 1, Nevada 64772; (417) 448-2530; FAX (417) 667-8360; assessor@vernoncountymo.org

Clerk Circuit Court, Carrie Poe, (D), Vernon County Courthouse, 100 W. Cherry, Ste. 15, Nevada 64772; (417) 448-2525; FAX (417) 448-2525; carrie.poe@courts.mo.gov

Clerk County Commission, Sean M. Buehler, (D), Vernon County Courthouse, 100 W. Cherry, Ste. 6, Nevada 64772; (417) 448-2500; FAX (417) 667-6035, clerk@vernoncountymo.org

Collector/Treasurer, Phil Couch, (D), Vernon County Courthouse, 100 W. Cherry, Ste. 10, Nevada 64772; (417) 448-2510; FAX (417) 448-2510; treasurer@vernoncountymo.org or collector@vernoncountymo.org

Commissioner, Northern District, Neal F. Gerster, (D), Vernon County Courthouse, 100 W. Cherry, Ste. 6, Nevada 64772; (417) 448-2500; FAX (417) 667-6035; commission@ vernoncountymo.org

Commissioner, Southern District, Everett Wolfe, (R), Vernon County Courthouse, 100 W. Cherry, Ste. 6, Nevada 64772; (417) 448-2500; FAX (417) 667-6035; commission@ vernoncountymo.org

Coroner, David L. Ferry, (D), 301 S. Washington, Nevada 64772; (417) 667-3322; FAX (417) 667-4944; davfer@neighborlink.us

County Health Department Administrator, Beth Swopes, 301 N. Washington, Nevada 64772; (417) 667-7418; FAX (417) 667-4131; swopel@lpha.mopublic.org

County Surveyor, (Vacancy)

Emergency Management Director, Dennis Kimrey, Vernon County Courthouse, 100 W. Cherry, Ste. 6, Nevada 64772; (417) 667-8236; FAX (417) 667-2786; vcemd@vernoncountymo.org

Presiding Commissioner, Joe Hardin, (D), Vernon County Courthouse, 100 W. Cherry, Ste. 6, Nevada 64772; (417) 448- 2500; FAX (417) 667-6035; commission@ vernoncountymo.org

Prosecuting Attorney, Brandi McInroy, (D), Vernon County Courthouse, 100 W. Cherry, Ste. 13, Nevada 64772; (417) 667-4862; FAX (417) 448-2529; prosecutor@vernoncountymo.org

Public Administrator, Tammy Bond, (D), Vernon County Courthouse, 100 W. Cherry, Ste. 3, Nevada 64772; (417) 448-2570; FAX (417) 448-8952; pubadmin@vernoncountymo.org

Recorder of Deeds, Doug Shupe, (R), Vernon County Courthouse, 100 W. Cherry, Ste. 11, Nevada 64772; (417) 448-2520; FAX (417) 448-2524; recorder@vernoncountymo.org

Sheriff, Jason M. Mosher, (R), 2040 E. Hunter, Nevada 64772; (417) 667-6042; FAX (417) 448-2580; sheriff@vernoncountymo.org

Warren County

County seat and zip code: Warrenton 63383. **County population:** 33,253. **Classification:** Third class. **Assessed valuation:** $543,764,810. **Square miles:** 429. **Organized:** January 5, 1833. **Named for:** Joseph Warren, Revolutionary War general.

Assessor, Wendy Nordwald, (R), 101 Mockingbird Ln., Ste. 204, Warrenton 63383; (636) 456-8885; FAX (636) 456-9024; wnordwald@warrencountymo.org

Clerk Circuit Court, Brenda Eggering, (R), 104 W. Main St., Warrenton 63383; (636) 456-3363; FAX (636) 456-2422; brenda.eggering@courts.mo.gov

Clerk County Commission, Barbara Daly, (R), 101 Mockingbird Ln., Ste. 302, Warrenton 63383; (636) 456-3331; FAX (636) 456-1801; bdaly@warrencountymo.org

Collector of Revenue, Julie Schaumberg, (R), 101 Mockingbird Ln., Ste. 200, Warrenton 63383; (636) 456-3330; FAX (636) 456-5052; jschaumberg@warrencountymo.org

Commissioner, Northern District, Daniel Hampson, (R), 101 Mockingbird Ln., Ste. 300, Warrenton 63383; (636) 456-3045; FAX (636) 456-1801; dhampson@warrencountymo.org

Commissioner, Southern District, Hubert Kluesner, (R), 101 Mockingbird Ln., Ste. 300, Warrenton 63383; (636) 456-3045; FAX (636) 456-1801; hkluesner@warrencountymo.org

Coroner, (Vacancy)

County Health Department Director, Ruth Walters, 101 Mockingbird Ln. Ste. 100, Warrenton 63383; (636) 456-7474; FAX (636) 456-4966; rwalters@warrencountymo.org

County Surveyor, Robert L. Lewis, (R), 101 Mockingbird Ln., Ste. 205, Warrenton 63383; (636) 456-3332

Emergency Management Director, Michael Daniels, 101 Mockingbird Ln. Ste. 101, Warrenton 63383; (636) 456-3786; FAX (636) 456-1801; mdaniels@warrencountymo.org

Presiding Commissioner, Roger Mauzy, (R), 101 Mockingbird Ln., Ste. 300, Warrenton 63383; (636) 456-3045; FAX (636) 456-1801; rmauzy@warrencountymo.org

Prosecuting Attorney, Kelly King, (R), 104 W. Main St., Ste. E, Warrenton 63383; (636) 456-7024; FAX (636) 456-5285; kking@warrencountymo.org

Public Administrator, Eugene Buxton, (R), 104 W. Main St., Ste. G, Warrenton 63383; (636) 297-5256; ebuxton@warrencountymo.org

Recorder of Deeds, Deborah Engemann, (R), 101 Mockingbird Ln., Ste. 303, Warrenton 63383; (636) 456-9800; FAX (636) 456-1724; dengemann@warrencountymo.org

Sheriff, Kevin Harrison, (R), 104 W. Main St., Ste. A, Warrenton 63383; (636) 456-4332; FAX (636) 456-1811; kharrison@warrencountymo.org

Treasurer, Jeffrey Hoelscher, (R), 101 Mockingbird Ln., Ste. 308, Warrenton 63383; (636) 456-3389; FAX (636) 456-1801; jhoelscher@warrencountymo.org

Washington County

County seat and zip code: Potosi 63664. **County population:** 25,077. **Classification:** Third class. **Assessed valuation:** $244,201,661. **Square miles:** 762. **Organized:** August 21, 1813. **Named for:** George Washington.

Assessor, Tina Litton, (D), Washington County Courthouse, 102 N. Missouri St., Potosi 63664; (573) 438-6111, ext. 252; FAX (573) 436-0014

Clerk Circuit Court, Patti Coleman Boyer, (D), Washington County Courthouse, 102 N. Missouri St., Potosi 63664; (573) 438-6111, ext. 228; FAX (573) 438-7900

Clerk County Commission, Jeanette Allen, (R), Washington County Courthouse, 102 N. Missouri St., Potosi 63664; (573) 438-6111,

ext. 221; FAX (573) 438-4038; washcoclerk@
yahoo.com

Collector of Revenue, Carla Zettler, (R),
Washington County Courthouse, 102 N.
Missouri St., Potosi 63664; (573) 438-6111,
ext. 241; FAX (573) 438-2009

Commissioner, First District, Mike Riddle, (D),
Washington County Courthouse, 102 N.
Missouri St., Potosi 63664; (573) 438-6111,
ext. 227; FAX (573) 438-4038

Commissioner, Second District, Cody Brinley,
(R), Washington County Courthouse, 102 N.
Missouri St., Potosi 63664; (573) 438-6111,
ext. 227; FAX (573) 438-4038;

Coroner, Brian DeClue, (D), 303 E. High, Potosi
63664; (573) 438-1438

County Health Department Director, Nicholas
Hughey, 520 Purcell Dr., Potosi 63664; (573)
438-2164, ext. 237; FAX (573) 438-4759

County Surveyor, R. Timothy Daugherty, (D),
112-A E. High St., Potosi 63664; (573) 438-
6489

Emergency Management Director, Doris
Coffman, 1105 Evans St., Potosi 63664; (573)
438-6851

Presiding Commissioner, Marvin Wright, (R),
Washington County Courthouse, 102 N.
Missouri St., Potosi 63664; (573) 438-6111,
ext. 227; FAX (573) 438-4038

Prosecuting Attorney*, Joshua E. Hedgecorth,
(D), Washington County Courthouse, 102 N.
Missouri St., Potosi 63664; (573) 438-6111,
ext. 261

Public Administrator, Kathy O'Neail, (D), 10157
Prior Rd., Mineral Point 63660; (573) 562-
7727

Recorder of Deeds, Judy Cresswell Moyers, (D),
102 N. Missouri St., Potosi 63664; (573) 438-
6111, ext. 247

Sheriff, Andy Skiles, (D), 116 W. High St., Potosi
63664; (573) 438-5478

Treasurer, Phyllis Long, (R), Washington County
Courthouse, 102 N. Missouri St., Potosi
63664; (573) 438-6111, ext. 245; FAX (573)
438-4038

Wayne County

County seat and zip code: Greenville 63944.
County population: 13,452. **Classification:** Third
class. **Assessed valuation:** $134,430,628. **Square
miles:** 763. **Organized:** December 11, 1818.
Named for: Anthony Wayne, Revolutionary War
general.

Assessor, Frances K. Huitt, (D), Wayne County
Courthouse, PO Box 54, Greenville 63944;
(573) 224-5600, ext. 5; FAX (573) 224-3446

Clerk Circuit Court, Darren T. Garrison, (D),
Wayne County Courthouse, PO Box 78,
Greenville 63944; (573) 224-5600, ext. 1;
FAX (573) 224-3225

Clerk County Commission, Brenda L. Seal, (R),
Wayne County Courthouse, 109 Walnut St.,
PO Box 48, Greenville 63944; (573) 224-
5600, ext. 4; FAX (573) 224-5609; wayne@
sos.mo.gov

Collector of Revenue, Mary Hampton, (D),
Wayne County Courthouse, PO Box 77,
Greenville 63944; (573) 224-5600, ext. 6;
FAX (573) 224-5693

Commissioner, Eastern District, Bill Hovis, (R),
Wayne County Courthouse, PO Box 48,
Greenville 63944; (573) 224-5600, ext. 4;
FAX (573) 224-5609

Commissioner, Western District, Chad Henson,
(R), Wayne County Courthouse, PO Box 48,
Greenville 63944; (573) 224-5600, ext. 4;
FAX (573) 224-5609

Coroner, Gary Umfleet, (D), Rt. 2, Box 2589,
Piedmont 63957; (573) 223-7744; FAX (573)
223-2571

County Health Department Director*,
Raejean Crutchfield, Wayne County Health
Department, PO Box 259, Greenville 63944;
FAX (573) 224-3218

County Road Overseer, Eastern District*, David
Richman, Wayne County Shed, Greenville
63944; (573) 224-3771

County Road Overseer, Western District, Brian
Million, Wayne County Western Shed, Rt.
3, Box 32726, Piedmont 63957; (573) 223-
7513; FAX (573) 224-5609

Emergency Management Director*, Eric Fuchs,
Wayne County Emergency Management, PO
Box 259, Greenville 63944; (573) 224-3218

Presiding Commissioner, Brian M. Polk, (D),
Wayne County Courthouse, PO Box 48,
Greenville 63944; (573) 224-5600, ext. 4;
FAX (573) 224-5609

Prosecuting Attorney, Michael L. Jackson, (D),
Wayne County Courthouse, PO Box 533,
Greenville 63944; (573) 224-5600, ext. 2;
FAX (573) 224-3904

Public Administrator, Donna Eads, (R), HC 3,
Box 3015, Wappapello 63966; (573) 222-
8937; FAX (573) 222-8937

Recorder of Deeds, Cindy Stout, (R), PO Box 47,
Greenville 63944; (573) 224-5600, ext. 7;
FAX (573) 224-3225

Sheriff, Dean Finch, (D), Wayne County Courthouse, PO Box 109, Greenville 63944; (573) 224-3090; FAX (573) 224-3904

Treasurer, Carol Hale, (D), Wayne County Courthouse, PO Box 134, Greenville 63944; (573) 224-5600, ext. 7

---

*Appointed

Webster County

County seat and zip code: Marshfield 65706. **County population:** 36,888. **Classification:** Third class. **Assessed valuation:** $362,093,432. **Square miles:** 594. **Organized:** March 3, 1855. **Named for:** Daniel Webster.

Assessor*, Kathy Galbraith, (D), 101 S. Crittenden St., Rm. 19, Marshfield 65706; (417) 859-2169; FAX (417) 859-0373; assessor@webstercountymo.gov

Clerk Circuit Court, Jill Peck, (R), PO Box B, Marshfield 65706; (417) 859-2041; FAX (417) 468-6265; jill.peck@courts.mo.gov

Clerk County Commission, Stanley D. Whitehurst, (R), 101 S. Crittenden St., Rm. 12, Marshfield 65706; (417) 859-VOTE (8683); FAX (417) 468-5307; clerk@webstercountymo.gov

Collector of Revenue, Kevin Farr, (R), 101 S. Crittenden St., Rm. 15, PO Box 288, Marshfield 65706; (417) 859-2683; FAX (417) 859-0094; collector@webstercountymo.gov

Commissioner, Northern District, Ward Jones, (R), 101 S. Crittenden St., Rm. 11, Marshfield 65706; (417) 859-4250; FAX (417) 468-5307; commission@webstercountymo.gov

Commissioner, Southern District, Denzil Young, (R), 101 S. Crittenden St., Rm. 11, Marshfield 65706; (417) 859-4250; FAX (417) 468-5307; commission@webstercountymo.gov

Coroner, Michael Taylor, (R), PO Box 218, Marshfield 65706; (417) 859-4270; FAX (417) 859-4270; wc720@mchsi.com

County Health Department Director, Terre Banks, 233 E. Washington, Marshfield 65706; (417) 859-2532; FAX (417) 859-6192; tbanks@webstercohealth.com

County Surveyor, Dennis D. Amsinger, (R), 101 S. Crittenden St., Rm. B-3, Marshfield 65706; (417) 859-5516; FAX (417) 859-3923; adsedda@aol.com

Emergency Management Director, William Sexton, 433 E. Commercial St., Marshfield 65706; (417) 859-7959; FAX (417) 859-2782; wsexton@webstercountymo.gov

Presiding Commissioner, Paul Ipock, (R), 101 S. Crittenden St., Rm. 11, Marshfield 65706; (417) 859-4250; FAX (417) 468-5307; commission@webstercountymo.gov

Prosecuting Attorney, Benjamin (Ben) Berkstresser, (R), PO Box 7, Marshfield 65706; (417) 859-0214; FAX (417) 859-3186; prosecutor@webstercountymo.gov

Public Administrator, Danielle Boggs, (R), 101 S. Crittenden St., Rm. B-5, Marshfield 65706; (417) 468-2135; FAX (417) 468-2135; publicadministrator@webstercountymo.gov

Recorder of Deeds, Gary Don Letterman, (R), PO Box 546, Marshfield 65706; (417) 859-5882; FAX (417) 468-3843; recorder@webstercountymo.gov

Sheriff, Roye Cole, (R), 101 S. Crittenden, Rm. 32, Marshfield 65706; (417) 859-2247; FAX (417) 859-3614; sheriff@webstercountymo.gov

Treasurer, Mary P. Clair, (R), 101 S. Crittenden St., Rm. 13, Marshfield 65706; (417) 468-2108; FAX (417) 468-2108; treasurer@webstercountymo.gov

Worth County

County seat and zip code: Grant City 64456. **County population:** 2,073. **Classification:** Third class. **Assessed valuation:** $30,594,403. **Square miles:** 266. **Organized:** February 8, 1861. **Named for:** William Jenkins Worth, soldier in the Florida and Mexican wars.

Assessor, Carolyn J. Hardy, (R), Worth County Courthouse, PO Box 18, Grant City 64456; (660) 564-2153; FAX (660) 564-2153; assesswoco@grantcity.net

Circuit Court, Jana Findley, (D), Worth County Courthouse, PO Box 450, Grant City 64456; (660) 564-2210; FAX (660) 564-3394; jana.findley@courts.mo.gov

Clerk County Commission, Roberta Owens, (R), Worth County Courthouse, 11 W. Fourth St., Grant City 64456; (660) 564-2219; FAX (660) 564-2432; cclerkwoco@grantcity.net

Collector of Revenue, Julie Tracy, (R), Worth County Courthouse, PO Box 217, Grant City 64456; (660) 564-2221; FAX (660) 564-2432; collectorwoco@grantcity.net

Commissioner, Eastern District, Regan Nonneman, (R), Worth County Courthouse, PO Box 450, Grant City 64456; (660) 786-2213; FAX (660) 564-2432; leveractions@grantcity.net

Commissioner, Western District, Chevy Davidson, (R), Worth County Courthouse, PO Box 450, Grant City 64456; (660) 986-3351; FAX (660) 564-2432; davidson@unitedwb.coop

Coroner, Sharon Supinger, (D), 1 W. Third, Box 70, Grant City 64456; (660) 564-3582; FAX (66) 564-2432; cclerkwoco@ grantcity.net

Emergency Management Director, Patricia Kobbe, Grant City 64456; (660) 564-3544; patkobbe@grantcity.net

Presiding Commissioner*, Ted Findley, (D), Worth County Courthouse, PO Box 450, Grant City 64456; (660) 564-2219; FAX (660) 564-2432; cclerkwoco@grantcity.net

Prosecuting Attorney*, David A. Baird, (D), Worth County Courthouse, 9 W. Third St., Grant City 64456; (660) 564-3535 FAX (660) 564-2272; worthpa@grantcity.net

Public Administrator, Patsy A. Worthington, (R), Box 38, Grant City 64456; (660) 786-2229

Recorder of Deeds, Barbara Foland, (D), Worth County Courthouse, PO Box 14, Grant City 64456; (660) 564-2484; FAX (660) 564-2432; recorderwoco@grantcity.net

Sheriff, Terry Sheddrick, (D), Worth County Court house, PO Box 36, Grant City 64456; (660) 564-2222; FAX (660) 564-2225; wcsd@ policeone.com

Treasurer, Linda L. Brown, (R), Worth County Courthouse, Box 122, Grant City 64456; (660) 564-2154; FAX (660) 564-2432; treasurerwoco@grantcity.net

---

*Appointed

Wright County

County seat and zip code: Hartville 65667. **County population:** 18,291. **Classification:** Third class. **Assessed valuation:** $172,009,004. **Square miles:** 682. **Organized:** January 29, 1841. **Named for:** Silas Wright, New York senator.

Assessor, Brenda Day, (R), Wright County Courthouse, PO Box 399, Hartville 65667; (417) 741-6400; FAX (417) 741-6334; wcabkd@getgoin.net

Clerk Circuit Court, Joe Chadwell, (R), Wright County Courthouse, PO Box 39, Hartville 65667; (417) 741-7121; FAX (417) 741-7504; joe.chadwell@courts.mo.gov

Clerk County Commission, Nelda Masner, (R), Wright County Courthouse, PO Box 98, Hartville 65667; (417) 741-6661; FAX (417) 741-6142; neldam@hotmail.com

Collector of Revenue, Cindy Cottengim, (R), Wright County Courthouse, PO Box 9, Hartville 65667; (417) 741-7225; FAX (417) 741-7919; wrightcountycollector@hotmail.com

Commissioner, Eastern District, Randy Pamperien, (R), Wright County Courthouse, PO Box 98, Hartville 65667; (417) 741-6113; FAX (417) 741-6142

Commissioner, Western District, Mike Sherman, (R), Wright County Courthouse, PO Box 98, Hartville 65667; (417) 741-6113; FAX (417) 741-6142

Coroner, Ben Hurtt, (R), 315 N. Main, Mountain Grove 65711; (417) 926-4111; FAX (417) 926-5727; benhurtt@craighurtt.com

County Health Department Director, Tracy Hardcastle, Wright County Health Department, PO Box 97, Hartville 65667; (417) 741-7791; FAX (417) 741-7108; hardct@lpha.mopublic.org

Emergency Management Director, Rick Thompson, Wright County Courthouse, PO Box 300, Hartville 65667; (417) 259-0412; FAX (417) 741-6142; kcoros@dishmail.net

Recorder of Deeds, Kathy Garrison, (R), PO Box 370, Hartville 65667; (417) 741-7322; FAX (417) 741-6016; wrcorecorder@hotmail.com

Presiding Commissioner, Zach Williams, (R), Wright County Courthouse, PO Box 98, Hartville 65667; (417) 741-6113; FAX (417) 741-6142

Prosecuting Attorney, Jason W. MacPherson, (R), Wright County Courthouse, PO Box 395, Hartville 65667; (417) 741-6166; FAX (417) 741-7376; jmac_wcpa@yahoo.com

Public Administrator, John T. Miller, (R), PO Box 169, Mansfield 65704; (417) 924-3233; jtmillerpa@yahoo.com

Sheriff, Glenn Adler, (R), Wright County Court-house, PO Box 250, Hartville 65667; (417) 741-7576; FAX (417) 741-6780; wcsheriff@ hotmail.com

Treasurer, Naomi Gray, (R), Wright County Courthouse, PO Box 25, Hartville 65667; (417) 741-7256

Classification of Municipalities

Missouri statutes classify municipalities on the basis of population and limit the form of government options of each classification. The statutes provide that a community may incorporate as a city of the third class, fourth class or village on the basis of the population at the time of incorporation. [1]Once a community is incorporated under a given classification, the municipality does not automatically change classification with a gain or loss of population. A municipality may change classification only when the change is approved by a majority vote of the people.

There are certain forms of government permitted for each classification of municipality. Villages are permitted only one form of government—an elected board of trustees, five in number if the village has less than 2,500 population and nine if more than 2,500 population. Fourth-class cities are permitted to have either a mayor/board of aldermen form or a mayor/city administrator/aldermen form. The board of aldermen may adopt a city administrator form by ordinance, without a vote of the people. Third-class cities are granted greater flexibility with the authority to establish a mayor/council form, a council/manager form, a commission form or a mayor/city administrator/council form. Finally, constitutional charter cities may adopt any form of government that the people approve in the charter.

---

[1]From 1821 to 1875, the Missouri General Assembly passed special charters for specific cities, until the 1875 Constitution prohibited further granting and amending of special charters. However, eight Missouri municipalities are still operating under special charters granted before 1875. They are Augusta, Carrollton, Chillicothe, LaGrange, Liberty, Miami, Missouri City and Pleasant Hill. If the voters of these municipalities decide to relinquish their special charters, they will be governed by the appropriate sections of the statutes relevant to their population classification.

Class	Population Requirement	Form of Government
Village	less than 500	Board of trustees
4th Class	500-2,999	Mayor/board of aldermen Mayor/city administrator/alderman
3rd Class	3,000-29,999	Mayor/council Mayor/city administrator/council Council/Manager Commission
Constitutional Charter / Home Rule	more than 5,000	To be decided by the people
Special Charter	no requirement	As set forth in the individual special charter

CDP: Census designated places (CDP's) are delineated for the decennial census as the statistical counterparts of incorporated places.

—Annual Estimates of the Resident Population: April 1, 2010 and July 1, 2013
Source: U.S. Census Bureau, Population Division

CITY	COUNTY	DATE OF INCORP.	CLASS	2010 CENSUS	2013 POP. EST.	MAIN PO ZIP
Adrian	Bates	1880	4th	1,677	2,227	64720
Advance	Stoddard	1883	4th	1,347	1,661	63730
Affton	St. Louis	-	CDP	20,307	21,359	63123
Agency	Buchanan	1903	Village	684	798	64401
Airport Drive	Jasper	1947	Village	698	629	64802
Alba	Jasper	1902	4th	555	486	64830
Albany	Gentry	1845	4th	1,730	2,046	64402
Aldrich	Polk	1889	Village	80	81	65601
Alexandria	Clark	1970	4th	159	190	63430
Allendale	Worth	1928	3rd	53	99	64420
Allenton	St. Louis	-	-	-	-	63001
Allenville	Cape Girardeau	-	-	116	62	63741
Alma	Lafayette	1878	4th	402	385	64001
Altamont	Daviess	1896	Village	204	204	64620

CITY	COUNTY	DATE OF INCORP.	CLASS	2010 CENSUS	2013 POP. EST.	MAIN PO ZIP
Altenburg	Perry	1870	4th	352	426	63732
Alton	Oregon	1992	4th	871	1,281	65606
Amazonia	Andrew	1857	4th	312	284	64421
Amity	De Kalb	1907	Village	54	56	64422
Amoret	Bates	1930	4th	190	186	64722
Amsterdam	Bates	1971	4th	242	265	64723
Anabel	Macon	-	-	-	-	63431
Anderson	McDonald	1901	4th	1,961	2,537	64831
Annada	Pike	1912	Village	29	47	63330
Annapolis	Iron	1961	4th	345	477	63620
Anniston	Mississippi	1913	4th	232	244	63820
Appleton City	St. Clair	1871	4th	1,127	1,216	64724
Arbela	Scotland	1877	Village	41	20	63432
Arbyrd	Dunklin	1919	4th	509	561	63821
Arcadia	Iron	1923	4th	608	819	63621
Archie	Cass	1952	4th	1,170	1,256	64725
Arcola	Dade	1967	Village	55	41	65603
Argyle	Maries-Osage	1908	Village	162	146	65001
Arkoe	Nodaway	1905	Village	68	76	64468
Armstrong	Howard	1953	4th	284	304	65230
Arnold	Jefferson	1972	3rd	20,808	20,945	63010
Arrow Point	Barry	1987	Village	86	148	65658
Arrow Rock	Saline	1820	Village	56	37	65320
Asbury	Jasper	1900	4th	207	188	64832
Ash Grove	Greene	1871	4th	1,472	1,339	65604
Ashburn	Pike	-	-	52	31	63433
Ashland	Boone	1877	4th	3,707	3,742	65010
Ashley	Pike	-	CDP	90	103	63334
Atlanta	Macon	1858	4th	385	400	63530
Augusta	St. Charles	1855	Special Charter / Home Rule	253	316	63332
Aullville	Lafayette	1905	Village	100	100	64037
Aurora	Lawrence	1870	3rd	7,508	7,508	65605
Auxvasse	Callaway	1873	4th	983	1,031	65231
Ava	Douglas	1908	4th	2,993	2,999	65608
Avilla	Jasper	1858	Village	125	102	64833
Avondale	Clay	1916	4th	440	530	64117
Bagnell	Miller	1926	4th	93	119	65026
Baker	Stoddard	-	-	3	-	63846
Bakersfield	Ozark	1967	Village	246	246	65609
Baldwin Park	Cass	1972	Village	92	71	64080
Ballwin	St. Louis	1950	4th	30,404	30,427	63011
Baring	Knox	1959	4th	132	133	63531
Barnard	Nodaway	1881	4th	221	265	64423
Barnett	Morgan	1961	4th	203	262	65011
Barnhart	Jefferson	-	CDP	5,682	5,895	63012
Bates City	Lafayette	1904	4th	219	260	64011
Battlefield	Greene	1971	4th	5,590	5,647	65619
Beaufort	Franklin	-	-	-	-	63013
Belgrade	Washington	-	-	-	-	63622
Bell City	Stoddard	1955	4th	448	435	63735
Bella Villa	St. Louis	1947	4th	729	765	63125
Belle	Maries-Osage	1901	4th	1,545	1,864	65013
Bellefontaine Neighbors	St. Louis	1950	4th	10,860	10,849	63137
Bellerive	St. Louis	1939	Village	188	215	63121
Belleview	Iron	-	-	-	-	63623
Bellflower	Montgomery	1905	4th	393	390	63333
Bel-Nor	St. Louis	1937	Village	1,499	1,438	63121

CITY	COUNTY	DATE OF INCORP.	CLASS	2010 CENSUS	2013 POP. EST.	MAIN PO ZIP
Bel-Ridge	St. Louis	1947	Village	2,737	2,737	63121
Belton	Cass	1871	Home Rule	23,116	23,163	64012
Bendavis	Texas	-	-			65433
Bennett Springs	Dallas-Laclede	-	CDP	130	174	65536
Benton	Scott	1953	4th	863	842	63736
Benton City	Audrain	1887	Village	104	111	65232
Berger	Franklin	1928	4th	221	187	63014
Berkeley	St. Louis	1937	Home Rule	8,978	9,106	63134
Bernie	Stoddard	1889	4th	1,958	2,101	63822
Bertrand	Mississippi	1962	4th	821	735	63823
Bethany	Harrison	1860	4th	3,292	3,168	64424
Bethel	Shelby	1883	Village	122	129	63434
Beulah	Phelps	-	-			65436
Beverly Hills	St. Louis	1935	4th	574	396	63121
Bevier	Macon	1881	4th	718	614	63532
Biehle	Perry	-	CDP	48	-	63775
Big Lake	Holt	1983	Village	159	161	64437
Big Spring	Montgomery	-	CDP	167	51	63363
Bigelow	Holt	1868	Village	27	24	64425
Billings	Christian	1871	4th	1,035	909	65610
Birch Tree	Shannon	1908	4th	679	728	65438
Birmingham	Clay	1889	Village	183	266	64161
Bismarck	St. Francois	1877	4th	1,546	1,436	63624
Bixby	Iron	-	-			65439
Black	Reynolds	-	-			63625
Black Jack	St. Louis	1970	3rd	6,929	6,913	63033
Blackburn	Lafayette-Saline	1880	4th	249	256	65321
Blackwater	Cooper	1946	4th	162	145	65322
Blackwell	St. Francois	-	-			63626
Blairstown	Henry	1959	4th	97	103	64726
Blanchard	Atchison	-	CDP	22	23	-
Bland	Gasconade	1902	4th	539	537	65014
Blodgett	Scott	1900	Village	213	200	63824
Bloomfield	Stoddard	1835	4th	1,933	1,988	63825
Bloomsdale	Ste. Genevieve	1963	4th	521	531	63627
Blue Eye	Stone	1946	Village	167	150	65611
Blue Springs	Jackson	1904	Home Rule	52,575	52,776	64015
Blythedale	Harrison	1891	Village	193	221	64426
Bogard	Carroll	1961	4th	164	143	64622
Bois D'Arc	Greene	-	-			65612
Bolckow	Andrew	1982	4th	187	236	64427
Bolivar	Polk	1835	4th	10,325	10,398	65613
Bonne Terre	St. Francois	1917	3rd	6,864	6,975	63628
Bonnots Mill	Osage	-	-			65016
Boonville	Cooper	1839	3rd	8,319	8,317	65233
Boss	Dent	-	-			65440
Bosworth	Carroll	1895	4th	305	247	64623
Bourbon	Crawford	1907	4th	1,632	1,513	65441
Bowling Green	Pike	1823	4th	5,334	5,393	63334
Bradleyville	Taney	-	-			65614
Bragg City	Pemiscot	1919	4th	149	248	63827
Braggadocio	Pemiscot	-	-			63826
Brandsville	Howell	1917	4th	161	110	65688
Branson	Taney/Stone	1912	4th	10,520	10,741	65615
Branson West	Stone	1974	4th	478	639	65737
Brashear	Adair	1956	4th	273	233	63533
Braymer	Caldwell	1888	4th	878	841	64624
Brazeau	Perry	-	-			63737
Breckenridge	Caldwell	1865	4th	383	269	64625

CITY	COUNTY	DATE OF INCORP.	CLASS	2010 CENSUS	2013 POP. EST.	MAIN PO ZIP
Breckenridge Hills	St. Louis	1950	3rd	4,746	4,736	63114
Brentwood	St. Louis	1919	4th	8,055	8,031	63144
Brewer	Perry	-	CDP	374	324	-
Briar	Ripley	-	-	-	-	63931
Bridgeton	St. Louis	1843	Home Rule	11,550	11,661	63044
Brighton	Polk	-	-	-	-	65617
Brimson	Grundy	1906	Village	63	49	64642
Brinktown	Maries	-	-	-	-	65443
Brixey	Ozark	-	-	-	-	65618
Bronaugh	Vernon	1887	4th	249	240	64728
Brookfield	Linn	1859	3rd	4,542	4,350	64628
Brooklyn Heights	Jasper	1967	Village	100	130	64836
Broseley	Butler	-	-	-	-	63932
Browning	Linn-Sullivan	1891	4th	265	265	64630
Brownington	Henry	1870	Village	107	89	64740
Brownwood	Stoddard	-	-	-	-	63738
Brumley	Miller	1926	Village	91	208	65017
Bruner	Christian	-	-	-	-	65620
Brunswick	Chariton	1836	4th	858	999	65236
Bucklin	Linn	1866	4th	467	483	64631
Buckner	Jackson	1930	4th	3,076	3,070	64016
Bucyrus	Texas	-	-	-	-	65444
Buffalo	Dallas	1892	4th	3,084	3,099	65622
Bull Creek	Taney	1993	Village	603	452	65616
Bunceton	Cooper	1868	4th	354	421	65237
Bunker	Dent-Reynolds	1908	4th	407	527	63629
Burfordville	Cape Girardeau	-	-	-	-	63739
Burgess	Barton	1893	Village	57	84	66756
Burlington Junction	Nodaway	1879	4th	537	549	64428
Butler	Bates	1858	3rd	4,219	4,137	64730
Butterfield	Barry	1966	4th	470	584	65623
Byrnes Mill	Jefferson	1986	4th	2,781	2,775	63051
Cabool	Texas	1884	4th	2,146	2,500	65689
Cadet	Washington	-	-	-	-	63630
Cainsville	Harrison	1875	4th	290	259	64632
Cairo	Randolph	1886	Village	292	262	65239
Caledonia	Washington	1819	Village	130	166	63631
Calhoun	Henry	1870	4th	469	406	65323
California	Moniteau	1857	4th	4,278	4,319	65018
Callao	Macon	1858	4th	292	301	63534
Calverton Park	St. Louis	1940	Village	1,293	1,360	63135
Camden	Ray	1846	4th	191	231	64017
Camden Point	Platte	1962	4th	474	435	64018
Camdenton	Camden	1931	4th	3,718	3,767	65020
Cameron	Clinton-DeKalb	1867	3rd	9,933	10,136	64429
Campbell	Dunklin	1892	4th	1,992	2,028	63933
Canalou	New Madrid	1910	4th	338	289	63828
Canton	Lewis	1967	4th	2,377	2,539	63435
Cape Fair	Stone	-	-	-	-	65624
Cape Girardeau	Cape Girardeau	1793	Home Rule	37,941	38,296	63701
Caplinger Mills	Cedar	-	-	-	-	65607
Cardwell	Dunklin	1895	4th	713	639	63829
Carl Junction	Jasper	1884	4th	7,445	7,446	64834
Carrollton	Carroll	1833	Special Charter	3,784	3,671	64633
Carterville	Jasper	1882	3rd	1,891	1,777	64835
Carthage	Jasper	1868	Home Rule	14,378	14,301	64836
Caruthersville	Pemiscot	1857	3rd	6,168	6,128	63830
Carytown	Jasper	1971	Village	271	245	64836

CITY	COUNTY	DATE OF INCORP.	CLASS	2010 CENSUS	2013 POP. EST.	MAIN PO ZIP
Cascade	Wayne	-	-	-	-	63632
Cassville	Barry	1846	4th	3,266	3,272	65625
Castle Point	St. Louis	-	CDP	3,962	3,710	63136
Catawissa	Franklin	-	-	-	-	63015
Catron	New Madrid	1924	4th	67	83	63833
Caulfield	Howell	-	-	-	-	65626
Cave	Lincoln	-	-	5	-	-
Cedar Hill	Jefferson	-	CDP	1,721	1,695	63016
Cedar Hill Lakes	Jefferson	1973	Village	237	190	63016
Cedarcreek	Taney	-	-	-	-	65627
Center	Ralls	1882	4th	508	398	63436
Centertown	Cole	1901	Village	278	264	65023
Centerview	Johnson	1960	4th	267	247	64019
Centerville	Reynolds	1976	4th	191	293	63633
Centralia	Boone	1867	4th	4,027	4,088	65240
Chadwick	Christian	-	-	-	-	65629
Chaffee	Scott	1905	3rd	2,955	2,956	63740
Chain of Rocks	Lincoln	-	-	93	128	63369
Chain-O-Lakes	Barry	1975	Village	126	147	65641
Chamois	Osage	1856	4th	396	389	65024
Champ	St. Louis	1959	Village	13	4	63042
Charlack	St. Louis	1945	4th	1,363	1,440	63114
Charleston	Mississippi	1872	3rd	5,947	5,886	63834
Cherokee Pass	Madison	-	CDP	235	214	63645
Cherryville	Crawford	-	-	-	-	65446
Chesapeake	Lawrence	-	CDP	49	61	65712
Chesterfield	St. Louis	1988	3rd	47,484	47,568	63017
Chestnutridge	Christian	-	-	-	-	65630
Chilhowee	Johnson	1907	4th	325	208	64733
Chillicothe	Livingston	1855	Special Charter	9,515	8,708	64601
Chula	Livingston	1885	4th	210	221	64635
Circle City	Stoddard	-	Village	-	-	63846
Clarence	Shelby	1866	4th	813	876	63437
Clark	Randolph	1928	4th	298	353	65243
Clarksburg	Moniteau	1930	4th	334	256	65025
Clarksdale	DeKalb	1886	4th	271	280	64430
Clarkson Valley	St. Louis	1989	4th	2,632	2,636	63006
Clarksville	Pike	1887	4th	442	419	63336
Clarkton	Dunklin	1885	4th	1,288	1,137	63837
Claycomo	Clay	1946	Village	1,430	1,374	64119
Clayton	St. Louis	1913	Home Rule	15,939	15,862	63105
Clearmont	Nodaway	1964	4th	170	203	64431
Cleveland	Cass	1958	4th	661	772	64734
Clever	Christian	1909	4th	2,139	2,103	65631
Cliff Village	Newton	1959	Village	40	31	64804
Clifton Hill	Randolph	1960	4th	114	88	65244
Climax Springs	Benton-Camden	1882	CDP	124	117	65324
Clinton	Henry	1886	3rd	9,008	9,048	64735
Clyde	Nodaway	1882	Village	82	114	64432
Coatsville	Schuyler	-	-	-	-	63535
Cobalt	Madison	1952	Village	226	340	63645
Coffey	Daviess	1965	4th	166	127	64636
Cole Camp	Benton	1897	4th	1,121	1,691	65325
Collins	St. Clair	1885	Village	159	122	64738
Columbia	Boone	1826	Home Rule	108,500	111,145	65205
Commerce	Scott	1834	4th	67	56	63742
Conception	Nodaway	-	-	210	246	64433
Conception Junction	Nodaway	1915	3rd	198	204	64434

CITY	COUNTY	DATE OF INCORP.	CLASS	2010 CENSUS	2013 POP. EST.	MAIN PO ZIP
Concord	St. Louis	-	CDP	16,421	16,750	63128
Concordia	Lafayette	1877	4th	2,450	2,322	64020
Coney Island	Stone	1993	Village	75	71	65737
Conran	New Madrid	-	-	-	-	63838
Conway	Laclede	1927	4th	788	1,061	65632
Cook Station	Crawford	-	-	-	-	65449
Cool Valley	St. Louis	1951	4th	1,196	1,159	63121
Cooter	Pemiscot	1964	4th	469	464	63839
Corder	Lafayette	1908	4th	404	402	64021
Corning	Holt	1868	Village	15	18	64435
Cosby	Andrew	1905	Village	124	123	64436
Cottleville	St. Charles	1853	4th	3,075	3,329	63338
Couch	Oregon	-	-	-	-	65690
Country Club	Andrew	1954	Village	2,449	2,874	64506
Country Club Hills	St. Louis	1943	4th	1,274	1,444	63136
Country Life Acres	St. Louis	1946	Village	74	122	63131
Courtois	Washington	-	-	-	-	65565
Cowgill	Caldwell	1890	4th	188	185	64637
Craig	Holt	1869	4th	248	205	64437
Crane	Stone	1906	4th	1,462	1,840	65633
Creighton	Cass	1885	4th	349	400	64739
Crestwood	St. Louis	1949	Home Rule	11,912	11,937	63126
Creve Coeur	St. Louis	1949	Home Rule	17,833	17,817	63141
Crocker	Pulaski	1912	4th	1,110	1,113	65452
Cross Timbers	Hickory	1948	4th	216	277	65634
Crystal City	Jefferson	1911	3rd	4,855	4,855	63019
Crystal Lake Park	St. Louis	1957	4th	470	587	63131
Crystal Lakes	Ray	1986	4th	358	461	64024
Cuba	Crawford	1857	4th	3,356	3,370	65453
Curryville	Pike	1874	4th	225	245	63339
Dadeville	Dade	1865	Village	234	298	65635
Daisy	Cape Girardeau	-	-	-	-	63743
Dalton	Chariton	1872	Village	17	19	65246
Danville	Montgomery	-	CDP	34	39	63361
Dardenne Prairie	St. Charles	1981	4th	11,494	11,746	63366
Darlington	Gentry	1892	4th	121	124	64438
Davisville	Crawford	-	-	-	-	65456
Dawn	Livingston	-	-	128	63	64638
De Kalb	Buchanan	1850	4th	220	524	64440
De Soto	Jefferson	1869	3rd	6,400	6,451	63020
De Witt	Carroll	1910	4th	124	54	64639
Dearborn	Platte	1882	4th	496	524	64439
Deepwater	Henry	1885	4th	433	366	64740
Deerfield	Vernon	1963	Village	81	71	64741
Deering	Pemiscot	-	-	-	-	63840
Defiance	St. Charles	-	-	155	154	63341
Dellwood	St. Louis	1951	4th	5,025	5,016	63135
Delta	Cape Girardeau	1967	4th	438	523	63744
Dennis Acres	Newton	1956	Village	76	62	64804
Denver	Worth	1945	Village	39	71	64441
Des Arc	Iron	1890	4th	177	238	63636
Des Peres	St. Louis	1934	4th	8,373	8,403	63131
Desloge	St. Francois	1941	4th	5,054	5,013	63601
Devils Elbow	Pulaski	-	-	-	-	65457
Dexter	Stoddard	1873	4th	7,864	7,869	63841
Diamond	Newton	1950	4th	902	839	64840
Diehlstadt	Scott	1901	Village	161	174	63834
Diggins	Webster	1926	Village	299	487	65636
Dittmer	Jefferson	-	-	-	-	63023

CITY	COUNTY	DATE OF INCORP.	CLASS	2010 CENSUS	2013 POP. EST.	MAIN PO ZIP
Dixon	Pulaski	1889	4th	1,549	1,412	65459
Doe Run	St. Francois	-	-	915	944	63637
Doniphan	Ripley	1891	4th	1,997	2,537	63935
Doolittle	Phelps	1944	4th	630	645	65401
Dora	Ozark	-	-	-		65637
Dover	Lafayette	1900	Village	103	90	64022
Downing	Schuyler	1896	4th	335	281	63536
Drexel	Bates-Cass	1890	4th	965	1,134	64742
Drury	Douglas	-	-	-		65631
Dudley	Stoddard	1915	4th	232	170	63936
Duenweg	Jasper	1959	4th	1,121	1,158	64841
Duke	Phelps	-	-	-		65461
Dunlap	Grundy	1953	Village	-		64683
Dunnegan	Polk	-	-	-		65640
Duquesne	Jasper	1959	4th	1,763	1,724	64801
Durham	Lewis	-	-	-		63438
Dutchtown	Cape Girardeau	-	-	94	42	63745
Dutzow	Warren	-	-	-		63342
Eagle Rock	Barry	-	CDP	199	153	65641
Eagleville	Harrison	1877	Village	316	250	64442
East Fenway	Lewis	1981	Village	-		63435
East Lynne	Cass	1871	4th	303	271	64743
East Prairie	Mississippi	1883	4th	3,176	3,185	63845
Easton	Buchanan	1963	4th	234	215	64443
Edgar Springs	Phelps	1974	4th	208	324	65462
Edgerton	Platte	1883	4th	546	768	64444
Edina	Knox	1879	4th	1,176	1,200	63537
Edinburg	Grundy	-	CDP	92	131	63555
Edmundson	St. Louis	1948	4th	834	982	63134
Edwards	Benton	-	-	-		65326
El Dorado Springs	Cedar	1881	3rd	3,593	3,575	64744
Eldon	Miller	1904	4th	4,567	4,607	65026
Eldridge	Laclede	-	-	-		65463
Elk Creek	Texas	-	-	-		65464
Elkland	Webster	-	-	-		65644
Ellington	Reynolds	1911	4th	987	973	63638
Ellisville	St. Louis	1932	Home Rule	9,133	9,153	63011
Ellsinore	Carter	1913	4th	446	548	63937
Elmer	Macon	1960	4th	80	82	63538
Elmira	Ray	1921	Village	50	54	64062
Elmo	Nodaway	1879	4th	168	165	64445
Elsberry	Lincoln	1883	4th	1,934	2,172	63343
Elvins	St. Francois	1902	4th	-		63601
Emden	Shelby	-	-	-		63439
Emerald Beach	Barry	1981	Village	228	208	65658
Eminence	Shannon	1948	4th	600	605	65466
Emma	Lafayette-Saline	1958	4th	233	246	65327
Eolia	Pike	1964	Village	522	607	63344
Essex	Stoddard	1876	4th	472	533	63846
Esther	St. Francois	1952	4th	-		63601
Ethel	Macon	1962	4th	62	50	63539
Etterville	Miller	-	-	-		65031
Eugene	Cole	1904	Village	-		65032
Eunice	Texas	-	-	-		65468
Eureka	St. Louis	1954	4th	10,189	10,270	63025
Evergreen	Laclede	-	Village	28	48	65536
Everton	Dade	1892	4th	319	370	65646
Ewing	Lewis	1970	4th	456	426	63440
Excello	Macon	-	-	49	113	65247

CITY	COUNTY	DATE OF INCORP.	CLASS	2010 CENSUS	2013 POP. EST.	MAIN PO ZIP
Excelsior Estates	Clay-Ray	1986	4th	147	170	64062
Excelsior Springs	Clay-Ray	1881	3rd	11,084	11,308	64024
Exeter	Barry	1942	4th	772	895	65647
Fair Grove	Greene	1973	4th	1,393	1,666	65648
Fair Play	Polk	1898	4th	475	486	65649
Fairdealing	Butler-Ripley	-	CDP	676	808	63939
Fairfax	Atchison	1908	4th	638	651	64446
Fairview	Newton	1907	4th	383	416	64842
Falcon	Laclede	-	-			65470
Farber	Audrain	1955	4th	322	377	63345
Farley	Platte	1850	Village	269	349	64028
Farmington	St. Francois	1836	3rd	16,240	16,886	63640
Farrar	Perry	-	-			63746
Faucett	Buchanan	-	-			64448
Fayette	Howard	1855	4th	2,688	2,701	65248
Fenton	St. Louis	1837	4th	4,022	4,035	63026
Fenway Landing	Lewis	1974	Village			63435
Ferguson	St. Louis	1894	Home Rule	21,203	21,164	63135
Ferrelview	Platte	1928	Village	451	594	64163
Festus	Jefferson	1887	3rd	11,602	11,662	63028
Fidelity	Jasper	1965	Village	257	250	64836
Fillmore	Andrew	1873	4th	184	221	64449
Fisk	Butler	1954	4th	342	344	63940
Flat River	St. Francois	1934	3rd			63601
Fleming	Ray	1962	4th	128	104	64077
Flemington	Polk	1945	Village	148	83	65650
Fletcher	Jefferson	-	-			63030
Flint Hill	St. Charles	1976	4th	525	598	63346
Flordell Hills	St. Louis	1946	4th	822	702	63136
Florence	Morgan	-	-			65329
Florida	Monroe	-	-			65283
Florissant	St. Louis	1786	Home Rule	52,158	52,335	63031
Foley	Lincoln	1900	4th	161	169	63347
Ford City	Gentry	-	-			64463
Fordland	Webster	1953	4th	800	844	65652
Forest City	Holt	1857	4th	268	290	64451
Foristell	St. Charles-Warren	1980	4th	505	563	63348
Forsyth	Taney	1928	4th	2,255	1,945	65653
Fort Leonard Wood	Pulaski	-	CDP	15,061	16,963	65473
Fortescue	Holt	1918	Village	32	17	64437
Fortuna	Moniteau	-	-			65034
Foster	Bates	1885	Village	117	113	64745
Fountain & Lakes	Lincoln		Village	165	237	63362
Four Seasons	Camden	1986	Village			65049
Frankclay	St. Francois	-	-	221	276	63601
Frankford	Pike	1889	4th	323	347	63441
Franklin	Howard	1894	4th	95	92	65250
Fredericktown	Madison	1827	4th	3,985	4,034	63645
Freeburg	Osage	1909	Village	437	368	65035
Freeman	Cass	1958	4th	482	664	64746
Freistatt	Lawrence	1916	Village	163	166	65654
Fremont	Carter	-	-	129	30	63941
Fremont Hills	Christian	-	4th	826	698	65714
French Village	St. Francois	-	-			63036
Frohna	Perry	1946	4th	254	316	63748
Frontenac	St. Louis	1947	4th	3,482	3,498	63131
Fulton	Callaway	1859	Home Rule	12,790	12,750	65251
Gainesville	Ozark	1896	4th	773	755	65655
Galena	Stone	1903	4th	440	631	65656

CITY	COUNTY	DATE OF INCORP.	CLASS	2010 CENSUS	2013 POP. EST.	MAIN PO ZIP
Gallatin	Daviess	1856	4th	1,786	1,722	64640
Galt	Grundy	1890	4th	253	265	64641
Garden City	Cass	1898	4th	1,642	1,636	64747
Garrison	Christian	-	-			65657
Gasconade	Gasconade	1926	4th	223	218	65036
Gatewood	Ripley	-	-			63942
Gentry	Gentry	1900	Village	72	48	64453
Gerald	Franklin	1907	4th	1,345	1,427	63037
Gerster	St. Clair	1966	Village	25	12	64776
Gibbs	Adair	1887	Village	107	131	63540
Gibson	Dunklin	-	-			63847
Gideon	New Madrid	1909	4th	1,093	897	63848
Gilliam	Saline	1899	4th	197	243	65330
Gilman City	Harrison	1897	4th	383	395	64642
Ginger Blue	McDonald	-	Village	61	73	64854
Gipsy	Bollinger	-	-			63750
Gladstone	Clay	1952	3rd	25,410	25,755	64118
Glasgow	Chariton-Howard	1836	4th	1,103	1,352	65254
Glasgow Village	St. Louis	-	CDP	5,429	5,171	63137
Glen Allen	Bollinger	1906	Village	85	94	63751
Glen Echo Park	St. Louis	1938	Village	160	148	63121
Glenaire	Clay	1950	4th	545	543	64068
Glencoe	St. Louis	-	Village			63038
Glendale	St. Louis	1912	4th	5,925	5,913	63122
Glenwood	Schuyler	1869	Village	196	224	63541
Glover	Iron	-	-			63646
Gobler	Pemiscot	-	-			63849
Golden	Barry	-	-	280	524	65658
Golden City	Barton	1881	4th	765	714	64748
Goodman	McDonald	1956	4th	1,248	1,626	64843
Goodnight	Polk	-	Village	18	7	65659
Goodson	Polk	-	-			65659
Gordonville	Cape Girardeau	1894	Village	391	366	63752
Gorin	Scotland	1889	4th			63543
Gower	Buchanan-Clinton	1946	4th	1,526	1,597	64454
Graff	Wright	-	-			65660
Graham	Nodaway	1929	4th	171	175	64455
Grain Valley	Jackson	1945	4th	12,854	12,843	64029
Granby	Newton	1875	4th	2,134	2,362	64844
Grand Falls Plaza	Newton	1993	Village	114	132	64804
Grand Pass	Saline	1889	Village	66	29	65339
Grandin	Carter	1963	4th	243	207	63943
Grandview	Jackson	1912	4th	24,475	24,673	64030
Granger	Scotland	1914	Village	34	7	63442
Grant City	Worth	1863	4th	859	848	64456
Grantwood	St. Louis	1937	Village	863	801	63123
Grassy	Bollinger	-	-			63753
Gravois Mills	Morgan	1956	Village	144	128	65037
Gray Summit	Franklin	-	CDP	2,701	3,393	63039
Grayhawk	Ste. Genevieve	-	CDP	525	568	63670
Grayridge	Stoddard	-	-	127	66	63850
Grayson	Clinton	1925	Village			64492
Green City	Sullivan	1880	4th	657	650	63545
Green Park	St. Louis	-	4th	2,622	2,623	63123
Green Ridge	Pettis	1903	4th	476	558	65332
Greencastle	Sullivan	-	-	275	295	63544
Greendale	St. Louis	1950	4th	651	661	63121
Greenfield	Dade	1876	4th	1,371	1,394	65661
Greentop	Adair-Schuyler	1870	4th	442	380	63546

CITY	COUNTY	DATE OF INCORP.	CLASS	2010 CENSUS	2013 POP. EST.	MAIN PO ZIP
Greenville	Wayne	1819	4th	511	514	63944
Greenwood	Jackson	1963	4th	5,221	5,249	64034
Grover	St. Louis	-	-	-	-	63040
Grovespring	Wright	-	-	-	-	65662
Grubville	Jefferson	-	-	-	-	63041
Guilford	Nodaway	1880	Village	85	46	64457
Gunn City	Cass	1880	Village	118	84	64760
Hale	Carroll	1884	4th	419	378	64643
Halfway	Polk	1967	Village	173	188	65663
Hallsville	Boone	1957	4th	1,491	1,762	65255
Halltown	Lawrence	1972	Village	173	134	65664
Hamilton	Caldwell	1868	4th	1,809	1,999	64644
Hanley Hills	St. Louis	1948	Village	2,101	2,185	63133
Hannibal	Marion-Ralls	1845	Home Rule	17,916	17,844	63401
Hardenville	Ozark	-	-	-	-	65666
Hardin	Ray	1888	4th	569	696	64035
Harris	Sullivan	1887	4th	61	53	64645
Harrisburg	Boone	1897	Village	266	275	65256
Harrisonville	Cass	1856	4th	10,019	10,012	64701
Hartsburg	Boone	1902	Village	103	107	65039
Hartshorn	Texas	-	-	-	-	65479
Hartville	Wright	1905	4th	613	870	65667
Hartwell	Henry	-	-	16	-	64788
Harviell	Butler	-	-	106	298	63945
Harwood	Vernon	1822	Village	47	61	64750
Hawk Point	Lincoln	1908	4th	669	607	63349
Hayti	Pemiscot	1896	4th	2,939	2,914	63851
Hayti Heights	Pemiscot	1972	4th	626	490	63851
Hayward	Pemiscot	-	CDP	131	97	63873
Haywood City	Scott	1960	Village	206	179	63771
Hazelwood	St. Louis	1949	Home Rule	25,703	25,691	63042
Helena	Andrew	-	-	-	-	64459
Hematite	Jefferson	-	-	-	-	63047
Henley	Cole	-	-	-	-	65040
Henrietta	Ray	1874	4th	369	338	64036
Herculaneum	Jefferson	1972	4th	3,468	3,594	63048
Hermann	Gasconade	1845	4th	2,431	2,507	65041
Hermitage	Hickory	1957	4th	467	496	65668
Higbee	Randolph	1891	4th	568	551	65257
Higginsville	Lafayette	1880	4th	4,797	4,761	64037
High Hill	Montgomery	1947	4th	195	250	63350
High Ridge	Jefferson	-	CDP	4,305	3,891	63049
Highlandville	Christian	1993	4th	911	1,143	65669
Highley Heights	St. Francois	-	-	-	-	63601
Hillsboro	Jefferson	1839	4th	2,821	2,895	63050
Hillsdale	St. Louis	1947	Village	1,478	1,286	63121
Hiram	Wayne	-	-	-	-	63947
Hoberg	Lawrence	1927	Village	56	33	65712
Holcomb	Dunklin	1891	4th	635	802	63852
Holden	Johnson	1861	3rd	2,252	2,253	64040
Holland	Pemiscot	1903	4th	229	266	63853
Holliday	Monroe	1890	Village	137	141	65258
Hollister	Taney	1910	4th	4,426	4,421	65673
Holt	Clay-Clinton	1867	4th	447	483	64048
Holts Summit	Callaway	1973	4th	3,247	3,317	65043
Homestead	Ray	-	-	185	134	64024
Homestown	Pemiscot	1946	4th	151	134	63879
Hopkins	Nodaway	1872	4th	532	446	64461
Horine	Jefferson	-	CDP	821	1,358	63070

CITY	COUNTY	DATE OF INCORP.	CLASS	2010 CENSUS	2013 POP. EST.	MAIN PO ZIP
Hornersville	Dunklin	1840	4th	663	966	63855
Horton	Vernon	-	-	-	-	64751
House Springs	Jefferson	-	-	-	-	63051
Houston	Texas	1893	4th	2,081	2,241	65483
Houston Lake	Platte	1960	4th	235	273	64151
Houstonia	Pettis	1879	4th	220	202	65333
Howardville	New Madrid	1953	4th	383	412	63869
Huggins	Texas	-	-	-	-	65484
Hughesville	Pettis	1905	Village	183	169	65334
Humansville	Polk	1872	4th	1,048	1,013	65674
Hume	Bates	1881	4th	336	332	64752
Humphreys	Sullivan	1880	Village	118	112	64646
Hunnewell	Shelby	1869	4th	184	144	63443
Hunter	Carter	-	CDP	168	156	-
Huntleigh	St. Louis	1929	4th	334	417	63101
Huntsdale	Boone	-	Village	31	27	65203
Huntsville	Randolph	1831	3rd	1,564	1,619	65259
Hurdland	Knox	1872	4th	163	209	63547
Hurley	Stone	1956	4th	178	326	65675
Iatan	Platte	1973	Village	45	49	64098
Iberia	Miller	1875	4th	736	809	65486
Illmo	Scott	-	-	-	-	63754
Imperial	Jefferson	-	CDP	4,709	4,491	63052
Independence	Jackson	1849	Home Rule	116,830	116,881	64051
Indian Point	Stone	1989	Village	528	743	65616
Innsbrook	Warren	-	Village	552	567	63390
Ionia	Benton-Pettis	1904	Village	88	96	65335
Irena	Worth	-	-	18	8	64499
Iron Gates	Jasper	1956	Village	-	-	64801
Iron Mountain Lake	St. Francois	1983	4th	737	794	63624
Irondale	Washington	1910	4th	445	597	63648
Ironton	Iron	1859	4th	1,460	1,600	63650
Irwin	Barton	-	CDP	69	64	64759
Isabella	Ozark	-	-	-	-	65676
Jackson	Cape Girardeau	1885	4th	13,758	13,999	63755
Jacksonville	Randolph	1865	Village	151	193	65260
Jadwin	Dent	-	-	-	-	65501
Jameson	Daviess	1876	Village	133	156	64647
Jamesport	Daviess	1872	4th	524	540	64648
Jamestown	Moniteau	1837	4th	386	396	65046
Jane	McDonald	2005	-	301	543	64856
Jasper	Jasper	1881	4th	931	1,045	64755
Jefferson City	Callaway-Cole	1825	Home Rule	43,079	43,202	65101
Jennings	St. Louis	1946	3rd	14,712	14,755	63136
Jerico Springs	Cedar	-	Village	228	231	64756
Jerome	Phelps	-	-	-	-	65529
Jonesburg	Montgomery	1955	4th	768	765	63351
Joplin	Jasper-Newton	1873	Home Rule	50,150	50,766	64802
Josephville	St. Charles	-	Village	376	386	63385
Junction City	Madison	1952	Village	327	545	63645
Kahoka	Clark	1836	4th	2,078	1,988	63445
Kaiser	Miller	-	-	-	-	65047
Kansas City	Cass-Clay-Jackson-Platte	1850	Home Rule	459,787	462,378	64106
Kearney	Clay	1883	4th	8,381	8,637	64060
Kelso	Scott	1905	Village	586	426	63758
Kennett	Dunklin	1873	3rd	10,932	11,138	63857
Kewanee	New Madrid	-	-	-	-	63860
Keytesville	Chariton	1869	4th	471	548	65261

CITY	COUNTY	DATE OF INCORP.	CLASS	2010 CENSUS	2013 POP. EST.	MAIN PO ZIP
Kidder	Caldwell	1976	4th	323	284	64649
Kimberling City	Stone	1973	4th	2,400	2,739	65686
Kimmswick	Jefferson	1871	4th	157	141	63053
King City	Gentry	1881	4th	1,013	958	64463
Kingdom City	Callaway	1967	Village	128	114	65262
Kingston	Caldwell	1857	4th	348	321	64650
Kingsville	Johnson	1885	4th	269	327	64061
Kinloch	St. Louis	1948	4th	298	253	63140
Kirbyville	Taney	-	Village	207	292	65679
Kirksville	Adair	1857	3rd	17,505	17,520	63501
Kirkwood	St. Louis	1865	Home Rule	27,540	27,541	63122
Kissee Mills	Taney	-	CDP	1,109	1,175	65680
Knob Lick	St. Francois	-	-	-	-	63651
Knob Noster	Johnson	1890	4th	2,709	2,747	65336
Knox City	Knox	1959	4th	216	244	63446
Koeltztown	Osage	-	-	-	-	65048
Koshkonong	Oregon	1899	4th	212	262	65692
La Belle	Lewis	1892	4th	660	576	63447
La Due	Henry	-	Village	28	21	-
La Grange	Lewis	1832	Special Charter	931	1,019	63448
La Monte	Pettis	1880	4th	1,140	1,262	65337
La Plata	Macon	1881	4th	1,366	1,373	63549
La Russell	Jasper	1904	Village	114	244	64848
La Tour	Johnson	-	CDP	62	64	-
LaBarque Creek	Jefferson	-	CDP	1,558	1,493	-
Labadie	Franklin	-	-	-	-	63055
Laclede	Linn	1866	4th	345	278	64651
Laddonia	Audrain	1871	4th	513	523	63352
Ladue	St. Louis	1936	4th	8,521	8,519	63124
Lake Annette	Cass	1982	4th	100	93	64746
Lake Lafayette	Lafayette	1994	4th	327	408	64076
Lake Lotawana	Jackson	1958	4th	1,939	2,030	64086
Lake Mykee	Callaway	1978	4th	350	409	65043
Lake Ozark	Camden-Miller	1966	4th	1,586	1,759	65049
Lake Spring	Dent	-	-	-	-	65532
Lake St. Louis	St. Charles	1975	4th	14,545	14,618	63367
Lake Tapawingo	Jackson	1963	4th	730	676	64015
Lake Tekakwitha	Jefferson	-	Village	254	247	-
Lake Viking	Daviess	-	CDP	483	481	-
Lake Waukomis	Platte	1956	4th	870	1,009	64151
Lake Winnebago	Cass	1975	4th	1,131	1,393	64034
Lakeland	Miller	1963	Village	-	-	65049
Lakeshire	St. Louis	1951	4th	1,432	1,576	63123
Lakeside	Miller	1981	4th	-	-	65026
Lakeview	Miller	1964	Village	-	-	65026
Lakeview Heights	Benton	1930	-	-	-	65338
Lamar	Barton	1867	4th	4,532	4,523	64759
Lamar Heights	Barton	1951	4th	178	151	64759
Lambert	Scott	-	-	34	-	63736
Lampe	Stone	-	-	-	-	65681
Lanagan	McDonald	1963	4th	419	549	64847
Lancaster	Schuyler	1889	4th	728	729	63548
Laquey	Pulaski	-	-	-	-	65534
Laredo	Grundy	1948	4th	198	257	64652
Latham	Moniteau	-	-	-	-	65050
Lathrop	Clinton	1881	4th	2,086	2,033	64465
LaTour	Johnson	1912	Village	-	64	64760
Laurie	Camden-Morgan	1966	4th	945	852	65038

CITY	COUNTY	DATE OF INCORP.	CLASS	2010 CENSUS	2013 POP. EST.	MAIN PO ZIP
Lawson	Clay-Ray	1871	4th	2,473	2,351	64062
Leadington	St. Francois	1976	4th	422	471	63601
Leadwood	St. Francois	1964	4th	1,282	1,537	63653
Leasburg	Crawford	1919	Village	338	657	65535
Leawood	Newton	1956	Village	682	710	64804
Lebanon	Laclede	1959	3rd	14,474	14,558	65536
Lecoma	Dent	-	-	-	-	65540
Lee's Summit	Cass-Jackson	1868	Home Rule	91,364	91,758	64063
Leeton	Johnson	1946	4th	566	676	64761
Leisure Lake	Grundy	-	CDP	160	160	64683
Lemay	St. Louis	-	CDP	16,645	16,521	63125
Lenox	Dent	-	-	-	-	65541
Lentner	Shelby	-	-	-	-	63450
Leonard	Shelby	1913	Village	61	61	63451
Leopold	Bollinger	-	-	-	-	63760
Leslie	Franklin	1912	Village	171	143	63056
Lesterville	Reynolds	-	-	-	-	63654
Levasy	Jackson	1901	4th	83	85	64066
Lewis and Clark	Buchanan	1971	Village	132	97	64484
Lewistown	Lewis	1924	4th	534	466	63452
Lexington	Lafayette	1845	3rd	4,726	4,702	64067
Liberal	Barton	1882	4th	759	726	64762
Liberty	Clay	1861	Special Charter	29,149	29,533	64068
Licking	Texas	1935	4th	3,124	3,104	65542
Liguori	Jefferson	-	-	-	-	63057
Lilbourn	New Madrid	1910	4th	1,190	1,060	63862
Lincoln	Benton	1869	4th	1,190	1,206	65338
Linn	Osage	1911	4th	1,459	1,748	65051
Linn Creek	Camden	1932	4th	244	535	65052
Linneus	Linn	1859	4th	278	328	64653
Lithium	Perry	-	-	89	118	63775
Livonia	Putnam	1911	Village	74	95	63551
Loch Lloyd	Cass	-	Village	600	683	64012
Lock Springs	Daviess	1872	Village	57	57	64654
Lockwood	Dade	1883	4th	936	1,046	65682
Lodi	Wayne	-	-	-	-	63950
Lohman	Cole	1906	4th	163	180	65053
Loma Linda	Newton	1995	Village	725	820	64804
Lone Jack	Jackson	1980	4th	1,050	1,066	64070
Lonedell	Franklin	-	-	-	-	63060
Long Lane	Dallas	-	-	-	-	65590
Longtown	Perry	1871	Village	102	147	63775
Loose Creek	Osage	-	-	-	-	65054
Louisburg	Dallas	1969	Village	122	110	65685
Louisiana	Pike	1848	3rd	3,364	3,369	63353
Lowndes	Wayne	-	-	-	-	63951
Lowry City	St. Clair	1897	4th	640	485	64763
Lucerne	Putnam	1905	Village	85	79	64655
Ludlow	Livingston	1922	Village	137	134	64656
Luebbering	Franklin	-	-	-	-	63061
Lupus	Moniteau	1901	4th	33	37	65046
Luray	Clark	1886	Village	99	58	63453
Lutesville	Bollinger	-	-	-	-	63762
Lynchburg	Laclede	-	-	-	-	65543
Mackenzie	St. Louis	1946	Village	134	114	63123
Macks Creek	Camden	-	CDP	244	399	65786
Macomb	Wright	-	-	-	-	65702
Macon	Macon	1859	3rd	5,471	5,484	63552

CITY	COUNTY	DATE OF INCORP.	CLASS	2010 CENSUS	2013 POP. EST.	MAIN PO ZIP
Madison	Monroe	1894	4th	554	720	65263
Maitland	Holt	1881	4th	343	371	64466
Malden	Dunklin	1878	3rd	4,275	4,285	63863
Malta Bend	Saline	1956	4th	250	358	65339
Manchester	St. Louis	1959	4th	18,094	18,152	63011
Mansfield	Wright	1900	4th	1,296	1,093	65704
Mapaville	Jefferson	-	-	-	-	63065
Maplewood	St. Louis	1908	Home Rule	8,046	8,015	63143
Marble Hill	Bollinger	1947	4th	1,477	1,824	63764
Marceline	Chariton-Linn	1888	3rd	2,233	2,306	64658
Marionville	Lawrence	1885	4th	2,225	2,277	65705
Marlborough	St. Louis	1944	Village	2,179	2,167	63119
Marquand	Madison	1967	4th	203	356	63655
Marshall	Saline	1839	3rd	13,065	13,039	65340
Marshfield	Webster	1869	4th	6,633	6,714	65706
Marston	New Madrid	1898	4th	503	483	63866
Marthasville	Warren	1920	4th	1,136	1,352	63357
Martinsburg	Audrain	1857	4th	304	326	65264
Martinsville	Harrison	1892	Village	-	-	64467
Maryland Heights	St. Louis	1985	3rd	27,472	27,432	63043
Maryville	Nodaway	1854	3rd	11,972	12,000	64468
Matthews	New Madrid	1943	4th	628	775	63867
Maysville	DeKalb	1845	4th	1,114	1,158	64469
Mayview	Lafayette	1957	4th	212	289	64071
Maywood	Lewis	-	-	-	-	63454
McBaine	Boone	-	-	10	4	65203
McClurg	Taney	-	-	-	-	65701
McCord Bend	Stone	1992	Village	297	372	65656
McFall	Gentry	1852	Village	93	168	64657
McGee	Wayne	-	-	-	-	63763
McGirk	Moniteau	-	-	-	-	65055
McKittrick	Montgomery	1909	4th	61	68	65056
Meadville	Linn	1859	4th	462	450	64659
Mehlville	St. Louis	-	CDP	28,380	28,454	63125
Memphis	Scotland	1883	4th	1,822	1,903	63555
Mendon	Chariton	1890	4th	171	161	64660
Menfro	Perry	-	-	-	-	63765
Mercer	Mercer	1886	4th	318	429	64661
Merriam Woods	Taney	1986	Village	1,761	1,945	65740
Merwin	Bates	1894	Village	58	37	64723
Meta	Osage	1959	4th	229	254	65058
Metz	Vernon	1907	Village	49	71	64765
Mexico	Audrain	1857	3rd	11,543	11,533	65265
Miami	Saline	1838	Special Charter	175	184	65344
Middle Brook	Iron	-	-	-	-	63656
Middletown	Montgomery	1962	4th	167	199	63359
Milan	Sullivan	1877	4th	1,960	2,201	63556
Milford	Barton	1964	Village	26	27	64766
Mill Spring	Wayne	1957	Village	189	159	63952
Millard	Adair	1976	Village	89	122	63501
Miller	Lawrence	1915	4th	699	675	65707
Millersville	Cape Girardeau	-	-	-	-	63766
Milo	Vernon	1884	Village	90	93	64767
Mindenmines	Barton	1903	4th	365	257	64769
Mine La Motte	Madison	-	CDP	348	350	63645
Miner	Scott	1951	4th	984	891	63801
Mineral Point	Washington	1905	Village	351	307	63660
Miramiguoa Park	Franklin	1997	Village	120	123	63080

CITY	COUNTY	DATE OF INCORP.	CLASS	2010 CENSUS	2013 POP. EST.	MAIN PO ZIP
Missouri City	Clay	1859	4th	267	251	64072
Moberly	Randolph	1868	3rd	13,974	13,925	65270
Mokane	Callaway	1979	4th	185	211	65059
Moline Acres	St. Louis	1949	4th	2,442	2,614	63136
Monett	Barry-Lawrence	1888	3rd	8,873	8,904	65708
Monroe City	Marion-Monroe-Ralls	1869	4th	2,531	2,368	63456
Montevallo	Vernon	1868	Village	-	-	64767
Montgomery City	Montgomery	1859	4th	2,834	2,811	63361
Monticello	Lewis	1833	Village	98	100	63457
Montier	Shannon	-	CDP	98	31	65546
Montreal	Camden	-	-	-	-	65591
Montrose	Henry	1871	4th	384	449	64770
Moody	Howell	-	-	-	-	65777
Mooresville	Livingston	1874	Village	91	51	64664
Mora	Benton	-	-	-	-	65345
Morehouse	New Madrid	1905	4th	973	832	63868
Morley	Scott	1868	4th	697	734	63767
Morrison	Gasconade	1899	4th	139	97	65061
Morrisville	Polk	1906	4th	388	450	65710
Morse Mill	Jefferson	-	-	-	-	63066
Mosby	Clay	1956	4th	190	280	64073
Moscow Mills	Lincoln	1821	4th	2,509	2,505	63362
Mound City	Holt	1857	4th	1,159	1,133	64470
Moundville	Vernon	1882	Village	124	140	64771
Mount Leonard	Saline	1881	Village	87	49	65339
Mount Moriah	Harrison	1897	Village	87	109	64665
Mount Vernon	Lawrence	1848	4th	4,575	4,565	65712
Mountain Grove	Texas-Wright	1894	4th	4,789	4,839	65711
Mountain View	Howell	1917	4th	2,719	2,719	65548
Murphy	Jefferson	-	CDP	8,690	8,587	63026
Myrtle	Oregon	-	-	-	-	65778
Napoleon	Lafayette	1887	4th	222	218	64074
Naylor	Ripley	1909	4th	632	660	63953
Neck City	Jasper	1899	4th	186	218	64849
Neelyville	Butler	1883	4th	483	472	63954
Nelson	Saline	1892	4th	192	261	65347
Neosho	Newton	1878	Home Rule	11,835	11,990	64850
Nevada	Vernon	1880	Home Rule	8,386	8,653	64772
New Bloomfield	Callaway	1971	4th	669	719	65063
New Boston	Linn	-	-	-	-	63557
New Cambria	Macon	1869	4th	195	191	63558
New Florence	Montgomery	1869	4th	769	847	63363
New Franklin	Howard	1835	4th	1,089	1,191	65274
New Hampton	Harrison	1882	4th	291	319	64471
New Hartford	Pike	-	-	-	-	-
New Haven	Franklin	1858	4th	2,089	2,011	63068
New London	Ralls	1870	4th	974	1,055	63459
New Madrid	New Madrid	1803	4th	3,116	3,083	63869
New Melle	St. Charles	1978	4th	475	379	63365
New Offenburg	Ste. Genevieve	-	-	-	-	63661
New Wells	Cape Girardeau	-	-	-	-	63768
Newark	Knox	1872	Village	94	84	63458
Newburg	Phelps	1888	4th	470	558	65550
Newtonia	Newton	1968	Village	199	185	64853
Newtown	Sullivan	1961	4th	183	208	64667
Niangua	Webster	1964	4th	405	465	65713
Nixa	Christian	1946	4th	19,022	19,461	65714
Noble	Ozark	-	-	-	-	65715

CITY	COUNTY	DATE OF INCORP.	CLASS	2010 CENSUS	2013 POP. EST.	MAIN PO ZIP
Noel	McDonald	1946	4th	1,832	2,113	64854
Norborne	Carroll	1874	4th	708	716	64668
Normandy	St. Louis	1945	3rd	5,008	4,993	63121
North Kansas City	Clay	1912	3rd	4,208	4,269	64116
North Lilbourn	New Madrid	1954	Village	49	90	63862
North Wardell	Pemiscot	1946	Village	-	-	63879
Northmoor	Platte	1954	4th	325	408	64151
Northwoods	St. Louis	1940	4th	4,227	4,220	63121
Northwye	Phelps	-	-	-	-	65401
Norwood	Wright	1927	4th	665	753	65717
Norwood Court	St. Louis	1949	Village	959	906	63121
Nottinghill	Ozark	-	-	-	-	65718
Novelty	Knox	1856	4th	139	118	63460
Novinger	Adair	1879	4th	456	488	63559
O'Fallon	St. Charles	1912	Home Rule	74,976	80,617	63366
Oak Grove	Jackson-Lafayette	1881	4th	7,795	7,745	64075
Oak Grove Village	Franklin	1955	Village	509	592	63080
Oak Ridge	Cape Girardeau	1869	Village	243	274	63769
Oakland	St. Louis	1920	4th	1,381	1,348	63122
Oaks	Clay	1952	Village	129	119	64118
Oakview	Clay	1949	Village	375	498	64118
Oakville	St. Louis	-	CDP	36,143	36,197	63129
Oakwood	Clay	1952	Village	185	173	64118
Oakwood Park	Clay	1949	Village	188	170	64118
Odessa	Lafayette	1880	4th	5,300	5,249	64076
Old Appleton	Cape Girardeau	1824	Village	85	14	63770
Old Jamestown	St. Louis	-	CDP	19,184	19,745	-
Old Monroe	Lincoln	1960	4th	265	325	63369
Oldfield	Christian	-	-	-	-	65720
Olean	Miller	1900	Village	128	154	65064
Olivette	St. Louis	1930	Home Rule	7,737	7,767	63132
Olney	Lincoln	-	-	-	-	63370
Olympian Village	Jefferson	1965	4th	774	654	63020
Oran	Scott	1869	4th	1,294	1,146	63771
Oregon	Holt	1841	4th	857	878	64473
Oronogo	Jasper	1873	4th	2,381	2,692	64855
Orrick	Ray	1872	4th	837	756	64077
Osage Beach	Camden-Miller	1959	4th	4,351	4,563	65065
Osborn	Clinton-DeKalb	1887	4th	423	478	64474
Osceola	St. Clair	1883	4th	947	910	64776
Osgood	Sullivan	1886	Village	48	4	64641
Otterville	Cooper	1878	4th	454	479	65348
Overland	St. Louis	1939	3rd	16,062	16,041	63114
Owensville	Gasconade	1911	4th	2,676	2,653	65066
Oxly	Ripley	-	CDP	200	65	63955
Ozark	Christian	1888	4th	17,820	18,092	65721
Ozora	Ste. Genevieve	-	CDP	183	131	63673
Pacific	Franklin-St. Louis	1859	4th	7,002	6,046	63069
Pagedale	St. Louis	1950	4th	3,304	3,309	63155
Painton	Stoddard	-	-	-	-	63772
Palmyra	Marion	1855	Home Rule	3,595	3,614	63461
Paris	Monroe	1842	4th	1,220	1,247	65275
Park Hills	St. Francois	-	3rd	8,759	8,721	63653
Parkdale	Jefferson	1959	Village	170	186	63049
Parkville	Platte	1858	4th	5,554	5,682	64152
Parkway	Franklin	1943	Village	439	341	63077
Parma	New Madrid	1903	4th	713	744	63870
Parnell	Nodaway	1888	4th	191	110	64475
Pasadena Hills	St. Louis	1935	4th	930	962	63121

CITY	COUNTY	DATE OF INCORP.	CLASS	2010 CENSUS	2013 POP. EST.	MAIN PO ZIP
Pasadena Park	St. Louis	1935	Village	470	497	63121
Pascola	Pemiscot	1893	Village	108	76	63871
Passaic	Bates	1965	Village	34	30	64777
Patterson	Wayne	-	-	-	-	63956
Patton	Bollinger	-	-	-	-	63662
Pattonsburg	Daviess	1906	4th	348	248	64670
Paynesville	Pike	1965	Village	77	57	63371
Peace Valley	Howell	-	-	-	-	65788
Peaceful Village	Jefferson	-	Vilalge	9	3	-
Peculiar	Cass	1953	4th	4,608	4,687	64078
Pendleton	Warren	-	Village	43	22	-
Penermon	Stoddard	-	Village	64	68	63846
Perkins	Scott	-	-	-	-	63774
Perry	Ralls	1891	4th	693	783	63462
Perryville	Perry	1856	4th	8,225	8,264	63775
Pevely	Jefferson	1953	4th	5,484	5,505	63070
Phelps City	Atchison	1874	Village	24	22	64482
Philadelphia	Marion	-	-	-	-	63463
Phillipsburg	Laclede	1912	Village	202	162	65722
Pickering	Nodaway	-	Village	160	229	64476
Piedmont	Wayne	1873	4th	1,977	2,447	63957
Pierce City	Lawrence	1870	4th	1,292	1,259	65723
Pierpont	Boone	2004	Village	76	81	65203
Pilot Grove	Cooper	1880	4th	768	842	65276
Pilot Knob	Iron	1946	4th	746	775	63663
Pine Lawn	St. Louis	1947	4th	3,275	3,320	63121
Pineville	McDonald	1919	4th	791	845	64856
Pinhook	Mississippi	1994	Village	30	21	63845
Pittsburg	Hickory	-	-	-	-	65724
Plato	Texas	-	Village	109	118	65552
Platte City	Platte	1882	4th	4,691	4,729	64079
Platte Woods	Platte	1946	4th	385	403	64151
Plattsburg	Clinton	1861	4th	2,319	2,461	64477
Pleasant Hill	Cass-Jackson	1859	Special Charter	8,113	8,122	64080
Pleasant Hope	Polk	1980	4th	614	527	65725
Pleasant Valley	Clay	1962	4th	2,961	3,001	64068
Plevna	Knox	-	CDP	21	43	63464
Pocahontas	Cape Girardeau	1893	Village	114	131	63779
Point Lookout	Taney	-	-	-	-	65726
Pollock	Sullivan	-	-	89	110	63560
Polo	Caldwell	1953	4th	575	573	64671
Pomona	Howell	-	-	511	338	65789
Ponce DeLeon	Stone	-	-	-	-	65728
Pontiac	Ozark	-	-	175	236	65729
Poplar Bluff	Butler	1870	3rd	17,023	17,172	63901
Portage Des Sioux	St. Charles	1854	4th	328	299	63373
Portageville	New Madrid	1900	4th	3,228	3,200	63873
Portland	Callaway	-	-	-	-	65067
Potosi	Washington	1826	4th	2,660	2,666	63664
Pottersville	Howell	-	-	-	-	65790
Powell	McDonald	-	-	-	-	65730
Powersite	Taney	-	-	-	-	65731
Powersville	Putnam	1911	4th	60	60	64672
Prairie Home	Cooper	1954	4th	280	265	65068
Prathersville	Clay	1957	Village	124	145	64024
Preston	Hickory	1947	Village	223	224	65732
Princeton	Mercer	1891	4th	1,166	1,107	64673
Protem	Taney	-	-	-	-	65733

CITY	COUNTY	DATE OF INCORP.	CLASS	2010 CENSUS	2013 POP. EST.	MAIN PO ZIP
Purcell	Jasper	1904	4th	408	481	64857
Purdin	Linn	1968	4th	190	238	64674
Purdy	Barry	1904	4th	1,098	1,338	65734
Puxico	Stoddard	1884	4th	881	772	63960
Queen City	Schuyler	1863	4th	598	695	63561
Quincy	Hickory	-	-	-	-	65735
Qulin	Butler	1952	4th	458	694	63961
Racine	Newton	-	-	-	-	64858
Randolph	Clay	-	4th	52	31	64161
Ravanna	Mercer	-	CDP	98	74	64673
Ravenwood	Nodaway	1898	4th	440	408	64479
Raymondville	Texas	1942	Village	363	388	65555
Raymore	Cass	1872	Home Rule	19,206	19,330	64083
Raytown	Jackson	1950	4th	29,526	29,513	64133
Rayville	Ray	-	Village	223	223	64084
Rea	Andrew	1914	Village	50	44	64480
Redford	Reynolds	-	-	-	-	63665
Redings Mill	Newton	1955	Village	151	180	64801
Reeds	Jasper	1872	Village	95	104	64859
Reeds Spring	Stone	1947	4th	913	1,231	65737
Renick	Randolph	1866	Village	172	173	65278
Rensselaer	Ralls	-	Village	228	195	63401
Republic	Christian-Greene	1871	Home Rule	14,751	15,002	65738
Revere	Clark	1898	4th	79	58	63465
Reynolds	Reynolds	-	-	-	-	63666
Rhineland	Montgomery	1896	Village	142	250	65069
Rich Hill	Bates	1880	4th	1,396	1,326	64779
Rich Woods	Washington	-	-	-	-	63071
Richards	Vernon	1894	Village	96	82	64778
Richland	Camden-Laclede-Pulaski	1884	4th	1,863	1,756	65556
Richmond	Ray	1827	3rd	5,797	5,746	64085
Richmond Heights	St. Louis	1913	Home Rule	8,603	8,569	63117
Ridgedale	Taney	-	-	-	-	65739
Ridgely	Platte	1867	Village	104	103	64444
Ridgeway	Harrison	1884	4th	464	500	64481
Risco	New Madrid	1934	4th	346	389	63874
Ritchey	Newton	1871	Village	82	55	64844
River Bend	Jackson	1993	Village	10	25	64058
Rivermines	St. Francois	1911	Village	-	-	63601
Riverside	Platte	1951	4th	2,937	2,981	64168
Riverview	St. Louis	1950	Village	2,856	2,854	63137
Riverview Estates	Cass	-	Village	82	118	-
Rives	Dunklin	1991	-	63	74	63875
Roach	Camden	-	-	-	-	65787
Robertsville	Jefferson	-	-	-	-	63072
Roby	Texas	-	-	-	-	65557
Rocheport	Boone	1835	4th	239	215	65279
Rock Hill	St. Louis	1929	4th	4,635	4,644	63119
Rock Port	Atchison	1878	4th	1,318	1,363	64482
Rockaway Beach	Taney	1934	4th	841	924	65740
Rockbridge	Ozark	-	-	-	-	65741
Rockville	Bates	1884	4th	166	169	64780
Rocky Comfort	McDonald	-	-	-	-	64861
Rocky Ridge	Ste. Genevieve	1987	4th	-	-	63670
Rogersville	Greene-Webster	1945	4th	3,073	3,458	65742
Rolla	Phelps	1861	3rd	19,559	19,672	65402
Rombauer	Butler	-	-	-	-	63962
Roscoe	St. Clair	1869	Village	124	161	64781

CITY	COUNTY	DATE OF INCORP.	CLASS	2010 CENSUS	2013 POP. EST.	MAIN PO ZIP
Rosebud	Gasconade	1911	4th	409	392	63091
Rosendale	Andrew	1963	4th	143	153	64483
Rothville	Chariton	1907	Village	99	105	64676
Rueter	Taney	-	-	-	-	65744
Rush Hill	Audrain	1881	Village	151	148	65280
Rushville	Buchanan	1851	Village	303	274	64484
Russellville	Cole	1895	4th	807	882	65074
Rutledge	Scotland	1892	Village	109	169	63563
Saddlebrooke	Christian-Taney		Village	202	286	-
Saginaw	Newton	1957	Village	297	344	64864
Salem	Dent	1881	4th	4,950	4,969	65560
Salisbury	Chariton	1882	4th	1,618	1,579	65281
Santa Fe	Monroe	-	-	-	-	65282
Sappington	St. Louis	-	CDP	7,580	7,426	63126
Sarcoxie	Jasper	1868	4th	1,330	1,244	64862
Savannah	Andrew	1842	4th	5,057	5,076	64485
Saverton	Ralls	-	-	-	-	63467
Schell City	Vernon	1879	4th	249	188	64783
Scotsdale	Jefferson	-	-	222	281	63049
Scott City	Scott	1980	3rd	4,565	4,556	63780
Sedalia	Pettis	1864	3rd	21,387	21,402	65301
Sedgewickville	Bollinger	1898	Village	173	243	63781
Seligman	Barry	1952	4th	851	1,054	65745
Senath	Dunklin	1882	4th	1,767	1,813	63876
Seneca	Newton	1868	4th	2,336	2,173	64865
Seymour	Webster	1895	4th	1,921	1,581	65746
Shelbina	Shelby	1867	4th	1,704	1,595	63468
Shelbyville	Shelby	1867	4th	552	553	63469
Sheldon	Vernon	1883	4th	543	807	64784
Shell Knob	Barry-Stone	-	CDP	1,379	1,423	65747
Sheridan	Worth	1899	4th	195	313	64486
Shoal Creek Drive	Newton	1958	Village	337	303	64803
Shoal Creek Estates	Newton	1977	Village	96	190	64804
Shook	Wayne	-	-	-	-	63963
Shrewsbury	St. Louis	1913	4th	6,254	6,232	63119
Sibley	Jackson	1957	Village	357	356	64088
Sikeston	New Madrid-Scott	1874	Home Rule	16,318	16,511	63801
Silex	Lincoln	1886	4th	187	92	63377
Silva	Wayne	-	-	-	-	63964
Silver Creek	Newton	1955	Village	623		64804
Skidmore	Nodaway	1880	4th	284	322	64487
Slater	Saline	1878	3rd	1,856	2,024	65349
Smithton	Pettis	1955	4th	570	506	65350
Smithville	Clay	1867	4th	8,425	8,602	64089
Solo	Texas	-	-	-	-	65564
Souder	Ozark	-	-	-	-	65751
South Fork	Howell	-	CDP	241	139	65775
South Gifford	Macon	1905	Village	50	47	63549
South Gorin	Scotland	1889	4th	91	113	63543
South Greenfield	Dade	1884	Village	90	79	65752
South Lineville	Mercer	1905	Village	28	45	64661
Southwest City	McDonald	1886	4th	970	1,092	64863
Spanish Lake	St. Louis	-	CDP	19,650	19,959	63138
Sparta	Christian	1885	4th	1,756	1,822	65753
Spickard	Grundy	1871	4th	254	285	64679
Spokane	Christian	-	CDP	177	475	65754
Springfield	Christian-Greene	1838	Home Rule	159,498	161,189	65801
Squires	Douglas	-	-	-	-	65755
St. Albins	Franklin	-	-	-	-	63073

CITY	COUNTY	DATE OF INCORP.	CLASS	2010 CENSUS	2013 POP. EST.	MAIN PO ZIP
St. Ann	St. Louis	1948	4th	13,020	13,011	63074
St. Catherine	Linn	-	-	-	-	64677
St. Charles	St. Charles	1809	Home Rule	65,794	66,361	63301
St. Clair	Franklin	1882	4th	4,724	4,732	63077
St. Clement	Pike	-	CDP	78	56	63334
St. Cloud	Crawford	-	-	41	53	65441
St. Elizabeth	Miller	1948	Village	336	391	65075
St. Francisville	Clark	-	CDP	179	123	63472
St. James	Phelps	1892	3rd	4,216	4,182	65559
St. John	St. Louis	1945	Home Rule	6,517	6,500	63114
St. Joseph	Buchanan	1845	Home Rule	76,780	76,984	64501
St. Louis	-	1809	Home Rule	319,294	318,955	63101
St. Martins	Cole	1972	4th	1,140	1,111	65109
St. Mary	Ste. Genevieve	1867	4th	360	384	63673
St. Patrick	Clark	-	-	-	-	63466
St. Paul	St. Charles	1976	4th	1,829	2,291	63366
St. Peters	St. Charles	1910	4th	52,575	53,589	63376
St. Robert	Pulaski	1953	4th	4,340	4,569	65584
St. Thomas	Cole	1962	4th	263	219	65076
Stanberry	Gentry	1879	4th	1,185	1,206	64489
Stanton	Franklin	-	-	-	-	63079
Stark City	Newton	1910	Village	139	132	64866
Ste. Genevieve	Ste. Genevieve	1805	4th	4,410	4,394	63670
Steedman	Callaway	-	-	-	-	65077
Steele	Pemiscot	1901	4th	2,172	2,054	63877
Steelville	Crawford	1850	4th	1,642	1,851	65565
Steffenville	Lewis	-	-	-	-	63470
Stella	Newton	1952	Village	158	159	64867
Stewartsville	DeKalb	1869	4th	750	794	64490
Stockton	Cedar	1846	4th	1,819	1,814	65785
Stotesbury	Vernon	1894	Village	18	16	64752
Stotts City	Lawrence	1895	4th	220	206	65756
Stoutland	Camden-Laclede	1910	4th	192	214	65567
Stoutsville	Monroe	1871	Village	36	30	65283
Stover	Morgan	1903	4th	1,094	932	65078
Strafford	Greene	1968	4th	2,358	2,360	65757
Strasburg	Cass	1966	4th	141	112	64090
Sturdivant	Bollinger	-	-	-	-	63782
Sturgeon	Boone	1856	4th	872	798	65284
Success	Texas	-	-	-	-	65570
Sugar Creek	Jackson	1920	4th	3,345	3,345	64054
Sullivan	Crawford-Franklin	1883	4th	7,081	7,625	63080
Sulphur Springs	Jefferson	-	-	-	-	63083
Summersville	Shannon-Texas	1936	4th	502	430	65571
Sumner	Chariton	1882	4th	102	108	64681
Sundown	Ozark	1976	Village	48	33	65761
Sunrise Beach	Camden-Morgan	1956	Village	431	468	65079
Sunset Hills	St. Louis	1957	4th	8,496	8,497	63127
Swedeborg	Pulaski	-	-	-	-	65572
Sweet Springs	Saline	1870	4th	1,484	1,438	65351
Sycamore Hills	St. Louis	1941	Village	668	645	63114
Syracuse	Morgan	1894	4th	172	205	65354
Tallapoosa	New Madrid	1965	Village	168	168	63878
Taneyville	Taney	1900	Village	396	365	65759
Taos	Cole	1972	4th	878	1,198	65101
Tarkio	Atchison	1881	4th	1,583	1,553	64491
Tarrants	Pike	1964	Village	22	18	63334
Taylor	Marion	-	-	-	-	63471
Tebbetts	Callaway	-	-	-	-	65080

CITY	COUNTY	DATE OF INCORP.	CLASS	2010 CENSUS	2013 POP. EST.	MAIN PO ZIP
Tecumseh	Ozark	-	-	-	-	65760
Teresita	Shannon	-	-	-	-	65573
Terre du Lac	Oregon	-	CDP	2,320	2,130	63628
Thayer	Oregon	1890	4th	2,243	2,565	65791
The Landing	Ralls	-	-	-	-	-
Theodosia	Ozark	1976	Village	243	202	65761
Thomasville	Oregon	-	CDP	68	40	65438
Thompson	Audrain	-	-	-	-	65285
Thornfield	Ozark	-	-	-	-	65762
Three Creeks	Warren	-	Village	6	4	-
Tiff	Washington	-	-	-	-	63674
Tiff City	McDonald	-	-	-	-	64868
Tightwad	Henry	1984	Village	69	71	64735
Tina	Carroll	1882	Village	157	82	64682
Tindall	Grundy	1920	4th	77	65	64683
Tipton	Moniteau	1858	4th	3,262	3,266	65081
Town and Country	St. Louis	1950	4th	10,815	10,876	63131
Tracy	Platte	1883	4th	219	181	64079
Treloar	Warren	-	-	-	-	63378
Trenton	Grundy	1857	3rd	6,006	6,057	64683
Trimble	Clinton	1909	4th	470	698	64492
Triplett	Chariton	1881	4th	58	15	65286
Troy	Lincoln	1819	4th	12,386	10,833	63379
Truesdale	Warren	1927	4th	668	828	63383
Truxton	Lincoln	1864	Village	120	66	63381
Tunas	Dallas	-	-	-	-	65764
Turners	Greene	-	-	-	-	65765
Turney	Clinton	1879	Village	156	158	64493
Tuscumbia	Miller	1857	Village	223	250	65082
Twin Bridges	Laclede	1988	Village	-	-	65536
Twin Oaks	St. Louis	1938	Village	343	338	63021
Udall	Ozark	-	-	-	-	65766
Ulman	Miller	-	-	-	-	65083
Umber View Heights	Cedar	1975	Village	56	49	65785
Union	Franklin	1851	4th	9,741	10,347	63084
Union Star	DeKalb	1935	4th	397	368	64494
Unionville	Putnam	1857	4th	1,821	1,867	63565
Unity Village	Jackson	1953	Village	117	113	64065
University City	St. Louis	1906	Home Rule	36,262	35,305	63130
Uplands Park	St. Louis	1941	Village	437	403	63121
Urbana	Dallas	1960	4th	428	400	65767
Urich	Henry	1885	4th	501	611	64788
Utica	Livingston	1985	Village	263	266	64686
Valles Mines	Jefferson	-	-	-	-	63087
Valley Park	St. Louis	1917	4th	6,282	6,968	63088
Van Buren	Carter	1927	4th	809	942	63965
Vandalia	Audrain	1874	4th	4,331	3,992	63382
Vandiver	Audrain	1956	Village	82	94	65265
Vanduser	Scott	1903	Village	212	313	63784
Vanzant	Douglas	-	-	-	-	65768
Velda City	St. Louis	1938	4th	1,495	1,165	63121
Velda Village Hills	St. Louis	1945	Village	1,034	1,013	63121
Verona	Lawrence	1916	4th	722	612	65769
Versailles	Morgan	1878	4th	2,663	2,356	65084
Viburnum	Iron	1959	4th	786	807	65566
Vichy	Maries	-	-	-	-	65580
Vienna	Maries	1953	4th	629	777	65582
Villa Ridge	Franklin	-	CDP	-	2,697	63089
Village of Four Seasons	Camden	-	Village	1,601	2,060	65049

CITY	COUNTY	DATE OF INCORP.	CLASS	2010 CENSUS	2013 POP. EST.	MAIN PO ZIP
Vinita Park	St. Louis	1950	4th	1,785	1,686	63114
Vinita Terrace	St. Louis	1940	Village	278	216	63114
Vista	St. Clair	1952	Village	52	49	64789
Vulcan	Iron	-	-	-	-	63675
Waco	Jasper	1919	4th	94	62	64869
Wakenda	Carroll	1869	Village	-	-	64687
Waldron	Platte	-	-	-	-	64092
Walker	Vernon	1870	4th	274	368	64790
Walnut Grove	Greene	1934	4th	667	722	65770
Walnut Shade	Taney	-	-	-	-	65771
Wappapello	Wayne	-	-	-	-	63966
Wardell	Pemiscot	1912	4th	393	449	63879
Wardsville	Cole	1965	Village	1,001	1,708	65101
Warrensburg	Johnson	1855	3rd	19,203	19,332	64093
Warrenton	Warren	1864	4th	7,518	7,934	63383
Warsaw	Benton	1861	4th	2,227	2,138	65355
Warson Woods	St. Louis	1936	4th	1,840	1,742	63122
Washburn	Barry	1962	4th	476	531	65772
Washington	Franklin	1841	3rd	14,356	13,994	63090
Wasola	Ozark	-	-	-	74	65773
Watson	Atchison	1874	Village	115	98	64496
Waverly	Lafayette	1882	4th	779	931	64096
Wayland	Clark	1962	4th	415	499	63472
Waynesville	Pulaski	1931	3rd	4,287	5,017	65583
Weatherby	DeKalb	1887	Village	117	106	64497
Weatherby Lake	Platte	1959	4th	1,923	1,845	64152
Weaubleau	Hickory	1899	4th	513	364	65774
Webb City	Jasper	1876	3rd	11,676	10,983	64870
Webster Groves	St. Louis	1896	Home Rule	22,345	23,022	63119
Weingarten	Ste. Genevieve	-	CDP	-	110	63670
Weldon Spring	St. Charles	1984	4th	5,340	5,482	63304
Weldon Spring Heights	St. Charles	1950	Village	73	63	63304
Wellington	Lafayette	1891	4th	752	902	64097
Wellston	St. Louis	1949	3rd	2,314	2,298	63133
Wellsville	Montgomery	1891	4th	1,308	1,086	63384
Wentworth	Newton	1895	Village	148	100	64873
Wentzville	St. Charles	1872	4th	24,407	30,334	63385
Wesco	Crawford	-	-	-	-	65586
West Alton	St. Charles	-	-	722	572	63386
West Line	Cass	1975	Village	133	75	64791
West Plains	Howell	1883	3rd	12,003	12,125	65775
West Sullivan	Crawford	-	-	91	60	-
Westboro	Atchison	1882	4th	156	179	64498
Weston	Platte	1842	4th	1,723	1,713	64098
Westphalia	Osage	1905	4th	330	329	65085
Westwood	St. Louis	1951	Village	289	349	63131
Wheatland	Hickory	1964	4th	385	424	65779
Wheaton	Barry	1935	4th	746	805	64874
Wheeling	Livingston	1964	4th	256	366	64688
Whiteman AFB	Johnson	-	CDP	-	3,843	65305
Whiteoak	Dunklin	-	-	-	-	63880
Whiteside	Lincoln	1907	Village	85	74	63387
Whitewater	Cape Girardeau	1908	Village	118	196	63785
Wilbur Park	St. Louis	1941	Village	454	472	63123
Wildwood	St. Louis	1995	Home Rule	34,209	35,568	63040
Willard	Greene	1949	4th	3,378	5,333	65781
Williamsburg	Callaway	-	-	-	-	63388
Williamstown	Lewis	-	-	-	-	63473
Williamsville	Wayne	1887	4th	352	411	63967

CITY	COUNTY	DATE OF INCORP.	CLASS	2010 CENSUS	2013 POP. EST.	MAIN PO ZIP
Willow Springs	Howell	1888	4th	2,165	2,300	65793
Wilson City	Mississippi	1954	Village	158	66	63882
Winchester	St. Louis	1935	4th	1,544	1,522	63021
Windsor	Henry-Pettis	1873	4th	3,171	2,821	65360
Windsor Place	Cooper	-	Village	221	424	65233
Windyville	Dallas	-	-	-	-	65783
Winfield	Lincoln	1882	4th	1,134	1,489	63389
Winigan	Sullivan	-	-	-	45	63566
Winona	Shannon	1888	4th	1,315	1,552	65588
Winston	Daviess	1878	Village	251	190	64689
Wittenberg	Perry	-	-	-	-	63786
Wolf Island	Mississippi	-	-	-	-	63881
Wood Heights	Ray	1978	4th	743	745	64024
Woodson Terrace	St. Louis	1954	4th	4,008	4,056	63134
Wooldridge	Cooper	1902	Village	42	20	65287
Worth	Worth	1911	Village	80	74	64499
Wortham	St. Francois	-	CDP	-	388	63601
Worthington	Putnam	-	-	82	209	63567
Wright City	Warren	1869	4th	3,089	3,228	63390
Wyaconda	Clark	1899	4th	289	257	63474
Wyatt	Mississippi	1954	4th	332	396	63882
Yukon	Texas	-	-	-	-	65589
Zalma	Bollinger	1910	Village	93	114	63787
Zanoni	Ozark	-	-	-	-	65784

Map of Missouri Counties

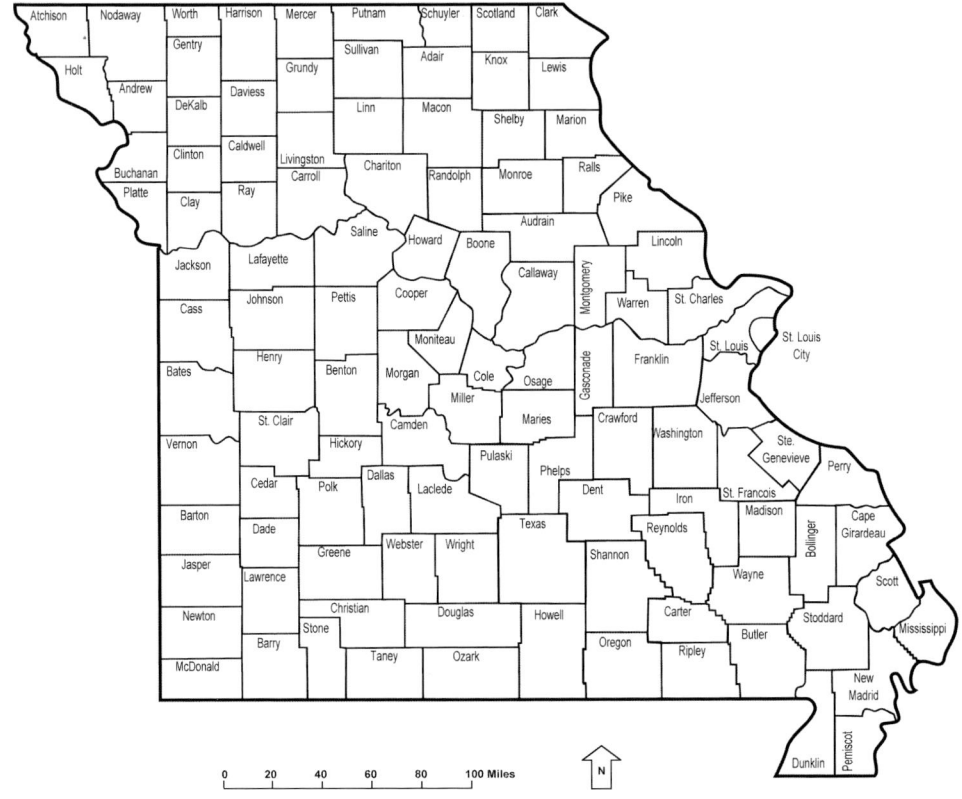

CHAPTER 9
MISSOURI INFORMATION

Elephant Rocks
Photo courtesy of Missouri State Archives

Newspaper Organizations

802 Locust St., Columbia 65201
Telephone: (573) 449-4167 / FAX: (573) 874-5894
www.mopress.com

DOUG CREWS
Executive Director
Missouri Press Association

The Missouri Press Association is an organization of newspapers in the state.

Organized May 17, 1867, as the Editors and Publishers Association of Missouri, the name was changed in 1877 to the Missouri Press Association (MPA). In 1922, the association became a nonprofit corporation, and a central office was opened under a field manager whose job it was to travel the state and help newspapers with problems.

The association, located in Columbia, became the fifth press association in the nation to finance its headquarters through member contributions. The MPA's building was purchased in 1969.

As a founder of institutions, the Missouri Press Association aided in the establishment of the Confederate Soldiers' Home, the upbuilding of the normal schools, support of the public school system and advancement of the University of Missouri.

The association founded the State Historical Society of Missouri in 1898 and today several of its members serve on the board of trustees. Greatest among its achievements is the establishment of the first school of journalism in the world in 1908. The Missouri School of Journalism at the University of Missouri in Columbia continues as the largest and foremost school of its kind. It celebrated its centennial in September 2008. The association led the drive to fund the chair in Community Newspaper Management at the School of Journalism and its donations helped fund the student lounge in the school's Lee Hills Hall.

Through their association, the publishers in Missouri have worked to keep the press free and alert, as well as responsible; to keep it financially independent so it can render impartial public service; and to understand changing trends in business and in reader needs. Activities of the association include setting up workshops, seminars, conventions, publishing of a magazine, The Missouri Press News, supplying information to members, helping newspapers find skilled personnel and assisting with the placement of students.

On the occasion of its 100th anniversary in 1966, the association re-established the old Saline County Herald newspaper office in historic Arrow Rock and maintains a newspaper equipment museum in connection with it.

The Missouri Press Foundation administers and funds seminars and workshops for newspaper people, supports Newspapers In Education programs, and funds scholarships and internships for Missouri students studying community journalism in college.

Membership in the association is voluntary. All daily newspapers in the state are members and 99 percent of the weekly newspapers are members. In 2015, there were 249 weekly and daily newspaper members. The association also has 180 associate and sustaining members. It is supported wholly by dues paid by these members.

The central office in Columbia has nine employees. Doug Crews serves as executive director by appointment of the board of directors.

Officers, Missouri Press Association, 2015

President: Jim Robertson, Columbia Daily Tribune;

First vice president: Dennis Warden, Owensville, Gasconade County Republican;

Second vice president: Bill Miller, Jr., Washington Missourian;

Secretary: Jacob Brower, Monett Times/Cassville Democrat;

Directors: Dennis Ellsworth, St. Joseph News-Press, St. Joseph; Donna Bischoff, St. Louis Post-Dispatch, St. Louis; Jack Miles, The Daily Star-Journal, Warrensburg; Joe Spaar, The Odessan, Odessa; Trevor Vernon, Eldon Advertiser, Eldon; Jeff Schrag, Springfield Daily Events, Springfield; Carol Stark, The Joplin Globe; James White, Benton County Enterprise, Warsaw.

National Newspaper Association Representative: Tianna Brooks, Mountain View Standard News.

Executive Director: Doug Crews.
Advertising director: Mark Nienhueser.
Editor: Bryan Jones.

Past Presidents, Missouri Press Association

1867—J.W. Barrett*, Canton Press
1868—J.W. Barrett*, Canton Press
1869—J.W. Barrett*, Canton Press
1870—N.J. Colman*, Rural World
1871—N.J. Colman*, Rural World
1872—C.B. Wilkinson*, St. Joseph Herald
1873—A.Y. Hull*, Sedalia Democrat
1874—W.F. Switzler*, Columbia Statesman
1875—L.J. Eastin*, Glasgow Journal
1876—Milo Blair*, Boonville Eagle
1877—T.W. Park*, Platte City Landmark
1878—J.E. Hutton*, Mexico Intelligencer
1879—J.E. Hutton*, Mexico Intelligencer
1880—J.H. Turner*, Carrollton Record
1881—J.T. Childs*, Richmond Conservator
1882—A.A. Lesueur*, Lexington Intelligencer
1883—J.B. Thompson*, La Plata Home Press
1884—R.B. Speed*, Nevada Mail
1885—R.M. White*, Mexico Ledger
1886—J.A. Hudson*, Macon Times
1887—W.D. Crandall*, Brookfield Gazette
1888—I.H. Kinley*, Brunswick Brunswicker
1889—Walter Williams*, Boonville Advertiser
1890—E.W. Stephens*, Columbia Herald
1891—J. West Goodwin*, Sedalia Bazoo
1892—W.O.L. Jewett*, Shelbina Democrat
1893—J.C. Kerby*, West Plains Gazette
1894—John Knott*, Hannibal Journal
1895—John W. Jacks*, Montgomery Standard
1896—H.E. Robinson*, Maryville Republican
1897—Henry W. Ewing*, Jefferson City Tribune
1898—George H. Trigg*, Richmond Conservator
1899—H.J. Groves*, Independence Sentinel
1900—W.R. Painter*, Carrollton Democrat
1901—Wes L. Robertson*, Gallatin Democrat
1902—E.P. Caruthers*, Kennett Democrat
1903—Howard Ellis*, New Florence Leader
1904—T.T. Wilson*, Tarkio Avalanche
1905—William Southern Jr.*, Jackson Examiner
1906—William Southern Jr.*, Jackson Examiner
1907—Phillip Ganz*, Macon Republican
1908—Omar D. Gray*, Sturgeon Leader
1909—Henry F. Childers*, Troy Free Press
1910—C.M. Harrison*, Gallatin North Missourian
1911—J.R. Lowell*, Moberly Democrat
1912—E.L. Purcell*, Fredericktown News
1913—Ovid Bell*, Fulton Gazette
1914—Fred Naeter*, Cape Girardeau Republican
1915—H.S. Sturgis*, Neosho Times
1916—J. Kelly Pool*, Centralia Courier
1917—H.J. Blanton*, Paris Appeal
1918—J.P. Tucker*, Parkville Gazette
1919—J.N. Stonebraker*, Carrollton Republican
1920—Will H. Zorn*, West Plains Gazette
1921—Mitchell White*, Mexico Ledger
1922—Fred Hull*, Maryville Tribune
1923—Dwight H. Brown*, Poplar Bluff American
1924—Asa W. Butler*, Albany Capital
1925—Eugene B. Roach*, Carthage Democrat
1926—E.H. Winter*, Warrenton Banner
1927—C.L. Hobart*, Holden Progress
1928—Harry Denman*, Farmington News
1929—Charles L. Woods*, Rolla Herald
1930—E.E. Swain*, Kirksville Express
1931—Frank H. Sosey*, Palmyra Spectator
1932—W.J. Sewall*, Carthage Press
1933—Wallace Crossley*, Warrensburg Star-Journal
1934—Fred M. Harrison*, Gallatin North Missourian
1935—W.L. Bouchard*, Flat River Lead Belt News
1936—Robert C. Goshorn*, Jefferson City Post-Tribune
1937—John C. Stapel*, Rock Port Atchison County Mail
1938—George B. Harlan*, Boonville Cooper County Record
1939—James Todd*, Moberly Monitor-Index
1940—Clint H. Denman*, Sikeston Herald
1941—C.E. Watkins*, Chillicothe Constitution-Tribune
1942—W.E. Freeland*, Forsyth Taney County Republican
1943—O.J. Ferguson*, Fredericktown Democrat-News
1944—Frank H. Hollmann*, Warrenton Banner
1945—W.C. Hewitt*, Shelbyville Shelby County Herald
1946—T. Ballard Watters*, Marshfield Mail
1947—George P. Johnston*, Fulton Sun Gazette
1948—Meredith Garten*, Pierce City Leader Journal
1949—Stanley R. Fike*, Fairmount Inter-City News
1950—T.J. Clark*, Carrollton Republican-Record
1951—L.N. Bowman*, King City Tri-County News
1952—George H. Scruton*, Sedalia Democrat
1953—Mack F. Denman*, Farmington News
1954—A.A. Steinbeck*, Union Franklin County Tribune
1955—C.L. Blanton Jr.*, Sikeston Standard
1956—Joe M. Roberts*, Maysville Record-Herald
1957—W.L. Simpson*, Holden Progress
1958—E.J. Melton*, Boonville Record
1959—James C. Kirkpatrick*, Windsor Review
1960—E.L. Dale*, Carthage Press
1961—Victor Gierke*, Louisiana Press-Journal
1962—Harry E. Guth Sr.*, Perryville Republic
1963—J.W. Brown Jr.*, Harrisonville, Cass County Democrat-Missourian
1964—Jac Zimmerman*, Willow Springs News
1965—Ben F. Weir Sr.*, Nevada Daily Mail
1966—J.J. Graf*, Hermann Advertiser-Courier
1967—Oliver B. Ferguson*, Fredericktown Democrat-News
1968—Lucius B. Morse*, St. Louis Daily Record
1969—Marion O. Ridings*, Hamilton Advocate-Hamiltonian

1970—Robert L. Vickery*, Salem News and Post
1971—J. Porter Fisher*, New London Ralls County Record
1972—Harry Naeter*, Cape Girardeau Southeast Missourian
1973—Wallace G. Vernon, Eldon Advertiser
1974—Bill D. Williams, Thayer News
1975—Joseph Snyder, Gallatin North Missourian
1976—Robert Blosser*, Jefferson City News and Tribune
1977—Charles L. Blanton III*, Sikeston Standard
1978—Weldon H. (Pete) Steiner*, Vandalia Leader-Press
1979—John Henry Cox, Rock Port Atchison County Mail
1980—Rogers Hewitt, Shelbyville Shelby County Herald
1981—William O. Lenhart*, Trenton Republican Times
1982—Mrs. Avis Tucker*, Warrensburg Daily Star-Journal
1983—Ralph E. Clayton*, Caruthersville Democrat-Argus
1984—Robert M. White II*, Mexico Ledger
1985—James C. Sterling, Bolivar Herald-Free Press
1986—Dalton Wright, Lebanon Daily Record
1987—Charles Hedberg, Centralia Fireside Guard
1988—Betty Simpson Spaar, The Odessa Odessan
1989—Kenneth W. Cope, Neosho Daily News
1990—W. Ray Vickery*, Salem News
1991—R.B. (Bob) Smith III, Lebanon Daily Record
1992—Thomas L. Miller Sr., Washington Missourian
1993—Donald Warden, Owensville Gasconade County Republican
1994—F. Kirk Powell, Pleasant Hill Times
1995—Charles E. Haney, Chillicothe Constitution Tribune
1996—Harold Ellinghouse, Piedmont Wayne County Journal-Banner
1997—David Lipman*, St. Louis Post-Dispatch
1998—William E. James, Harrisonville Cass County Democrat–Missourian
1999—Robert W. Wilson*, Milan Standard
2000—William L. Miller Sr., Washington Missourian
2001—Wendell J. Lenhart, Trenton Republican-Times
2002—Dane Vernon, Eldon Advertiser
2003—David Berry, Bolivar Herald-Free Press
2004—Gary Sosniecki, Vandalia Leader
2005—John Spaar, The Odessa Odessan
2006—Steve Oldfield, The Adrian Journal
2007—David Bradley Jr., St. Joseph News-Press
2008—Jack Whitaker, Hannibal Courier-Post
2009—Vicki Russell, Columbia Daily Tribune
2010—Kevin Jones, St. Louis American
2011—Joe A. May, Mexico Ledger
2012—Phil Conger, Bethany Republican-Clipper
2013—Mark Maassen, The Kansas City Star

2014—Richard Gard, St. Louis Missouri Lawyers Media
2015—Jim Robertson, Columbia Daily Tribune.
_____
*Deceased.

Show-Me Press Association

The Show-Me Press Association was formed in June 1995 at Lake Ozark when members of the Central Missouri Press and Northeast Missouri Press associations voted to combine their organizations with one board of directors.

The Central Missouri Press Association was organized Feb. 27, 1925 in Jefferson City with 30 charter members. Edgar C. Nelson, then owner and publisher of the Boonville Advertiser, was elected the first president. The district extended from St. Louis County on the east to Jackson, Cass and Bates counties on the west and included all 28 counties through the central part of the state bordering the Missouri River on both sides. In these counties are located the State Capitol, University of Missouri, State Fair Grounds and the University of Central Missouri. The first organizational meeting of Northeast Missouri Publishers was held in Hannibal in November 1889. Meetings of this group were held up to and including 1896, after which the organization disintegrated and was succeeded by the Northeast Missouri Press Association, organized in 1920 in Kirksville with Charles H. Weisenborn, editor of the Macon Daily Chronicle-Herald, as its first president.

Officers elected in June 2015:

President: Buck Collier, Hermann;
Vice president: Vacancy;
Secretary/Treasurer: Sandy Nelson, News-Press & Gazette Co.;
Directors: Dennis Warden, Owensville; Carolyn Trower, New London; John Spaar, Odessa; and Bruce Wallace, Ashland.

Missouri Advertising Managers' Association, Inc.

The Missouri Advertising Managers' Association, Inc., was formed in May 1948. Thomas F. Briggs of the Macon Chronicle-Herald was the first president. The organization was formed not only to help advertising managers, but, through the use of clinics, courses and exchanges of ideas, to benefit the buying public and merchants who purchase advertising space. The organization is concerned with the honesty, truth and equality of advertising in newspapers.

Officers elected in April 2015:

President: Mark Maassen, Kansas City;
First vice president: Adam Letterman, Ozark;
Second vice president: Les Borgmeyer, Columbia;
Secretary: Suzie Wilson, Milan;

Treasurer: Kristie Williams, Columbia;
Past president: Jeanine York, Washington;
Directors: Jacob Warden, Owensville; Curtis Simmons, Eldon; James White, Warsaw.

Missouri Associated Press Managing Editors Association

The Missouri Associated Press Managing Editors Association is an organization of editors of state AP member newspapers that provides the AP with working-level input on its coverage of Missouri and the rest of the world. The association provides an opportunity for member editors to better understand the functions of the news service and to assist the cooperative in gathering and distributing news and photos in Missouri. It was organized in 1950 as the Missouri AP Wire Editors Association, when C.W. Johnson of the Springfield Newspapers, Inc. called a meeting at Sedalia. He was named the group's first chair. It became the Missouri APME in 1985. It has sponsored an annual news writing contest for member newspapers, held in the spring; an annual Jobs Fair to help Missouri editors recruit from Missouri universities and colleges, held in the fall; and periodically critiques the Missouri AP report.

Chair: Jacob Brower, Monett;
Past chair: Carol Stark, Joplin.

Missouri Circulation Management Association

The Missouri Circulation Management Association was formed in June 1948. Francis Pike, circulation manager of the Columbia Daily Tribune, was the first president. The purpose of the organization is to improve the profession of journalism through courses, clinics and exchanges of ideas related to newspaper distribution in order to benefit the buying public who subscribe to newspapers of the state.

Officers:

President: Brenda Carney, Harrisonville;
First vice president: Jack Kaminsky, Joplin;
Second vice president: Steve Edwards, St. Joseph;
Secretary: David Pine, Kansas City;
Treasurer: Doug Crews, Columbia;
Directors: Jim Kennedy, Bolivar; Mike Johns, Jefferson City.

Missouri Professional Communicators, National Federation of Press Women

Missouri Press Women (MPW) was organized in Columbia, May 5, 1937. The original purpose of the group, as set forth in its constitution, is to secure the benefits of organized efforts; to foster mutual improvement through association; and to promote the highest ideals of journalism. Anyone residing or working in Missouri who qualifies as a professional communicator actively engaged in any aspect of the field of communications for remuneration, for at least one year immediately prior to application, may be eligible for active membership.

Missouri Press Women became a charter member of the National Federation of Press Women, established in Chicago, Ill., in 1937, on the date of the Missouri group's founding. Three Missouri members have served as national presidents: Bertha Bless, Weston, founding president of Missouri Press Women; Mattie Dykes, Maryville; and Mildred Planthold Michie, St. Clair.

In April 1999, the St. Louis Chapter became the Missouri Affiliate, taking responsibility for state functions. Members throughout the state may participate in professional workshops, seminars, programs and field trips planned by the Missouri Affiliate. The state group sponsors a Communicator of Achievement who is honored at the National Federation of Press Women meeting biennially. Each May, the Press Women gives the Virginia Betts White Quest Awards to professional communicators who excel and continuously represent the quest of the highest standards of professional ethics and excellence in the field of communications.

The Missouri Affiliate sponsors annual contests for members and high school journalism students. Categories are specified in all fields of communication. First place winners in the state contest are entered automatically in the national contest. In 1971, MPW received the Sweepstakes Award for earning the most points in the national competition.

In 1999, the St. Louis Chapter, now the Missouri Affiliate, established an educational scholarship fund for a mature woman pursuing a career in journalism, with matching funds provided by the Press Club of Metropolitan St. Louis and administered through the Journalism Foundation of Metropolitan St. Louis.

Officers:

Co-Presidents: Linda Jarrett and Linda Briggs-Harty;
Secretary: Peggy Koch, Barnhart;
Online Editor: Fran Mannino, Kirkwood;
Past president: Colene McEntee, St. Charles;
Archivist: Dee Rabey, Granite City, Ill.;
Contest director: Janice Denham, Kirkwood.

Northwest Missouri Press Association

The Northwest Missouri Press Association was organized in St. Joseph on Nov. 20, 1891. There were 56 charter members. The association totals more than 150 members. The association initiated the movement to secure a field secretary for the Missouri Press Association and started the plan to advertise Missouri, which led to the founding of the Greater Missouri Association.

In 1962, the association dedicated a student lounge in Neff Hall at the University of Missouri School of Journalism, which it completely equipped and furnished.

Officers elected in June 2014:

President: Mike Farmer, Rock Port;
Vice President: Vacancy;
Secretary: Kathy Conger, Bethany;
Treasurer: W.C. Farmer, Rock Port;
Past President: Adam Johnson, Mound City;
Directors: Jim Fall, Maryville; Dennis Ellsworth, St. Joseph; Jim McPherson, Weston; Chuck Haney, Chillicothe; Steve Tinnen, Plattsburg; Kay Wilson, Maryville; Steve Booher, St. Joseph.

Ozark Press Association

The Ozark Press Association was organized in Springfield on Nov. 30, 1889, as the Southwest Missouri Press Association, with an original membership of 30 owners and editors of newspapers in Southwest Missouri. The name was changed to the Ozark Press Association in November 1911. The membership had then passed the 50 mark. The constitution had been changed to admit reporters, writers of news and others connected with newspapers in Southwest Missouri. Now, there are more than 100 members. At one time, the group met twice each year. One was a social gathering, usually in the fall at some resort in the area. The business meeting was held during the spring, at which time members and their families discussed newspaper problems and trends, saw exhibits by newspaper supply companies and heard speakers prominent in journalism and other fields. Today, Ozark Press meets in the spring for its annual convention, and has sponsored several one-day workshops around the region.

Officers elected in July 2014:

President: Adam Letterman, Springfield;
Vice president: Matthew Barba, Bolivar;
Secretary/Treasurer: Emily Letterman, Springfield;
Past President: Roger Dillon, Eminence;
Directors: Dala Whittaker, Cabool; Jody Porter, Ava; David Burton, Springfield; Sharon Vaughn, Summersville; Terry Hampton, West Plains; Keith Moore, Ava; Norene Prososki, Gainesville.

Southeast Missouri Press Association

The Southeast Missouri Press Association was organized at Poplar Bluff in the spring of 1893. E. Hoag, publisher of the Poplar Bluff Citizen, was the first president. For many years, the Association's historian was Mildred Wallhausen of the Charleston Enterprise-Courier until her death in February 2009.

Officers elected in July 2014:

President: Amanda Layton, Perryville;
First vice president: Scott Seal, Portageville;
Second vice president: Toby Carrig, Ste. Genevieve;
Secretary/Treasurer: Michelle Friedrich, Poplar Bluff;
Executive secretary: Ann Hayes, Southeast Missouri State University;
Historian: Peggy Scott, Festus;
Directors: Kim Combs, Piedmont; H. Scott Seal, Portageville; Ed Thomason, New Madrid; Gary Rust, Cape Girardeau; Teresa Ressel, Park Hills.

Missouri Press Foundation, Inc.

The Missouri Press Foundation, Inc. was organized in April 1984. Robert M. White II of the Mexico Ledger was the first president. Among its activities, the foundation was formed to provide newspaper journalism scholarships and fund internships, conduct newspaper journalism seminars, support Newspapers In Education programs, conduct an annual Better Newspaper Contest, collect and preserve old newspaper printing equipment and operate a historical museum at Arrow Rock and help support the Missouri Photojournalism Hall of Fame in Washington, Mo.

Officers:

President: Vicki Russell, Columbia;
First vice president: Wendell Lenhart, Trenton;
Second vice president: Kirk Powell, Pleasant Hill;
Secretary/treasurer: Doug Crews, Columbia;
Directors: James Sterling, Columbia; Dane Vernon, Eldon; Bill Miller Sr., Washington; Chuck Haney, Chillicothe; Dave Berry, Bolivar; Brian Brooks, Columbia; Kathy Conger, Bethany; Jean Snider, Harrisonville; Betty Spaar, Odessa; Paul Stevens, Lenexa, Kan.; Dalton Wright, Lebanon.
Directors emeritus: Mrs. Wanda Brown, Raymore; Rogers Hewitt, Shelbyville; Wallace Vernon, Eldon; Edward Steele, Corvallis, Ore.; R.B. (Bob) Smith III, Lebanon; Tom Miller, Washington.

Newspapers of Missouri

This information is provided through cooperation with individual newspaper publishers and the Missouri Press Association. Listings include: name of city; name of newspaper; website (if available); physical address; name of publisher; name of editor or other personnel; publishing frequency (W–Weekly, D–Daily, M–Monthly); and political affiliation (Rep.–Republican, Dem.–Democrat, Lib.–Libertarian, Ind.–Independent, NP–Nonpartisan). Not all papers listed are legal newspapers as defined by Missouri law.

Albany
ALBANY LEDGER
www.aledger.net
Editorial Email: *news@aledger.net*
213 W. Clay St., PO Box 247, Albany 64402
Telephone: (660) 726-3998 / FAX: (660) 726-3997
Publisher: Matthew Pear
W, Wed. (Ind.)

Alma/Waverly
THE SANTA FE TIMES
Editorial Email: *safetnews@yahoo.com*
106 Third St., Ste. A, PO Box 76, Alma 64001
Telephone: (660) 674-2250 / FAX: (660) 674-2250
Publisher: Colby Gordon
Editor: Klarissa A . Olvera
W, Fri. (NP)

Appleton City
APPLETON CITY JOURNAL
Editorial Email: *sacosagenews@centurytel.net*
285 Pine, PO Box 580, Osceola 64776
Telephone: (660) 476-5566 / FAX: (417) 646-8015
Publisher: Michael Crawford
Editor: April Collins
W, Fri. (NP)

Arnold
ARNOLD-IMPERIAL LEADER
www.MyLeaderPaper.com
Editorial Email: *nvrweakly@aol.com*
503 N. Second St., PO Box 159, Festus 63028
Telephone: (636) 931-7560 / FAX: (636) 931-2226
Publisher: Pam LaPlant
Editor: Peggy Bess
W, Thurs. (NP)

Ash Grove
THE COMMONWEALTH
www.ashgrovecommonwealth.com
Editorial Email: *editor@crosscountrytimes.com*
102 E. Jackson, PO Box 216, Willard 65781
Telephone: (417) 685-4229 / FAX: (417) 685-4145
Publisher: Ryan Squibb
Editor: Ryan Squibb
W, Wed. (Dem.)

Ashland
BOONE COUNTY JOURNAL
www.bocojo.com
Editorial Email: *bruce@bocojo.com*
201 S. Henry Clay, PO Box 197, Ashland 65010
Telephone: (573) 657-2334 / FAX: (573) 657-2002
Publishers: Bruce Wallace
Editor: Bruce Wallace
W, Wed. (Dem.)

Aurora
THE AURORA ADVERTISER
www.auroraadvertiser.net
Editorial Email: *news@auroaadvertiser.net*
33 W. Olive, PO Box 509, Aurora 65605
Telephone: (417) 678-2115 / FAX: (417) 678-2117
Publisher: Matt Guthrie
Editor: Judy Dingman
W, Fri. (NP)

Ava
DOUGLAS COUNTY HERALD
www.douglascountyherald.com
Editorial Email: *scurry@douglascountyherald.com*
302 E. Washington, PO Box 577, Ava 65608
Telephone: (417) 683-4181 / FAX: (417) 683-4102
Publisher: Sue Curry Jones
Managing Editor: Keith Moore
W, Thurs. (Rep.)

Belle
THE BELLE BANNER
Editorial Email: *tricountynewspapers@yahoo.com*
217 S. Alvarado Ave., PO Box 711, Belle 65013
Telephone: (573) 859-3328 / FAX: (573) 859-6274
Publisher: Kurt J. Lewis
Editor: Nichole Snodgrass
W, Wed. (Rep.)

Bethany
BETHANY REPUBLICAN-CLIPPER
www.bethanyclipper.com
Editorial Email: *rclipper@grm.net*
202 N. 16th, PO Box 351, Bethany 64424
Telephone: (660) 425-6325 / FAX: (660) 425-3441
Publisher: Philip G. Conger
Editor: Philip G. Conger
W, Wed. (Rep.)

Bland
THE BLAND COURIER
Editorial Email: *tricountynewspapers@yahoo.com*
217 S. Alvarado Ave., PO Box 711, Belle 65013
Telephone: (573) 859-3328 / FAX: (573) 859-6274
Publisher: Kurt J. Lewis
Editor: Ron J. Lewis
W, Wed. (Dem.)

Bloomfield
NORTH STODDARD COUNTIAN
www.dailystatesman.com/NSC
Editorial Email: *cnoles@dailystatesman.com*
109 S. Prairie St., PO Box 680, Bloomfield 63825
Telephone: (573) 624-4545 / FAX: (573) 624-7449
Publisher: Ernest H. (Bud) Hunt
Editor: Corey Noles
W, Wed. (NP)

Bolivar

BOLIVAR HERALD-FREE PRESS
www.bolivarmonews.com
Editorial Email: *news@bolivarmonews.com*
335 S. Springfield Ave., PO Box 330, Bolivar 65613
Telephone: (417) 725-3745 / FAX: (417) 725-3683
Publisher: Dave Berry
Editor: Matthew Barba
Semi-W, Wed. & Fri (NP)

Boonville

THE BOONVILLE DAILY NEWS
www.boonvilledailynews.com
Editorial Email: *news@boonvilledailynews.com*
412 High St., PO Box 47, Boonville 65233
Telephone: (660) 882-5335 / FAX: (660) 882-2256
Publisher: Marlene Ridgway
Tri-W, Tue., Thur., Fri. (NP)

THE BOONSLICK WEEKLY
www.boonvilledailynews.com
Editorial Email: *news@boonvilledailynews.com*
412 High St., PO Box 47, Boonville 65233
Telephone: (660) 882-5335 / FAX: (660) 882-2256
Publisher: Marlene Ridgway
Editor: Eric Berger
W, Wed. (NP)

Bowling Green

BOWLING GREEN TIMES
www.bowlinggreentimes.com
Editorial Email: *bgted@lcs.net*
106 W. Main St., PO Box 110, Bowling Green 63334
Telephone: (573) 324-2222 / FAX: (573) 324-3991
Publisher: Linda Luebrecht
Editor: Amy Patterson
W, Wed. (NP)

Branson

BRANSON TRI-LAKES NEWS
www.bransontrilakesnews.com
Editorial Email: *editor@bransontrilakesnews.com*
PO Box 1600, Branson 65672
Telephone: (417) 334-3161 / FAX: (417) 335-3933
Publisher: Michael Schuver
Semi-W, Wed. & Sat., (Rep.)

Brentwood

BRENTWOOD SPIRIT
www.thebrentwoodspirit.com
Editorial Email: *toni.bowman@sbcglobal.net*
8901 Bridgeport Ave., Brentwood 63144
Telephone: (314) 475-5086
Publishers: Steve and Toni Bowman
W, Wed., (Rep.)

Brookfield

LINN COUNTY LEADER
www.linncountyleader.com
Editorial Email: *dwatson@linncountyleader.com*
107 N. Main, PO Box 40, Brookfield 64628
Telephone: (660) 258-7237 / FAX: (660) 258-7238
Publisher: Andrea Graves
Editor: Dustin Watson
Tri-W, Mon., Wed., Fri. (NP)

Buffalo

BUFFALO REFLEX
www.buffaloreflex.com
Editorial Email: *paulc@buffaloreflex.com*
114 E. Lincoln St., PO Box 770, Buffalo 65622

Telephone: (417) 315-2224 / FAX: (417) 345-2235
Publisher: Dave Berry
Editor: Paul Campbell
W, Wed. (NP)

Butler

NEWS-XPRESS
www.yourxgroup.com
Editorial Email: *butlernewsxpress@gmail.com*
5 N. Main St., PO Box 210, Butler 64730
Telephone: (660) 679-6127 / FAX: (660) 679-4905
Publisher: Jon Peters
Editor: Jon Peters
W, Fri. (Rep.)

THE MESSENGER
www.messengerweekly.net
Editorial Email: *news@messengerweekly.net*
15 N. Main St., Butler 64730
Telephone: (660) 679-3030
Publisher: LeeAnna Schowengerdt
Editor: Paula Schowengerdt
W, Fri. (Ind.)

Cabool

CABOOL ENTERPRISE
www.thecaboolenterprise.com
Editorial Email: *news@thecaboolenterprise.com*
525 Main St., PO Box 40, Cabool 65689
Telephone: (417) 962-4411 / FAX: (417) 962-4455
Publishers: Dala and Tom Whittaker
W, Thurs. (Rep.)

California

CALIFORNIA DEMOCRAT
www.californiademocrat.com
Editorial Email: *editor@californiademocrat.com*
319 S. High St., PO Box 126, California 65018
Telephone: (573) 796-2135 / FAX: (573) 796-4220
Publisher: Terri Leifeste
Editor: Paula Earls
W, Wed. (NP)

Camdenton

THE CAMDEN COUNTY REPORTER
www.theccreporter.com
Editorial Email: *thereporter@socket.net*
551 Old South 5, PO Box 1265, Camdenton 65020
Telephone: (573) 346-5222 / FAX: (573) 346-6242
Publisher: Dale Johnson
Editor: Dale Johnson
W, Wed. (NP)

LAKE SUN
www.lakenewsonline.com
Editorial Email: *newsroom@lakesunonline.com*
918 N. Bus. Rt. 5, Camdenton 65020
Telephone: (573) 346-2132/ FAX: (573) 346-4508
Publisher: Tom Bookstaver
Editor: Joyce Miller
D, (ex. Sat. & Sun.) (NP)

Cameron

CAMERON CITIZEN-OBSERVER
www.mycameronnews.com
Editorial Email: *editor@mycameronnews.com*
403 E. Evergreen, Hwy. BB, PO Box 498, Cameron 64429
Telephone: (816) 632-6543 / FAX: (816) 632-4508
Publisher: Wally Gallian
Editor: Chris Johnson
W, Thurs. (Ind.)

Canton

THE PRESS NEWS-JOURNAL
www.lewispnj.com
Editorial Email: *news@lewispnj.com*
Physical address: 109 N. Fourth St., LaGrange 63448
Mailing address: PO Box 227, Canton 63435
Telephone: (573) 288-5668 / FAX: (573) 288-0000
Publisher: Rita Cox
Editor: Karen Althof
W, Thurs. (NP)

Cape Girardeau

SOUTHEAST MISSOURIAN
www.semissourian.com
Editorial Email: *bmiller@semissourian.com*
301 Broadway, PO Box 699, Cape Girardeau 63702
Telephone: (573) 335-6611 / FAX: (573) 339-0815
Publisher: Jon Rust
Editor: Bob Miller
D, (ex. Sat.) (NP)

Carl Junction

JASPER COUNTY CITIZEN
Editorial Email: *fstop@centurytel.net*
101 N. Sixth, PO Box 400, Sarcoxie 64862
Telephone: (417) 548-3311 / FAX: (417) 548-3312
Publisher: Paul E. Donley
Editor: Paul E. Donley
W, Wed. (Rep.)

Carrollton

THE CARROLLTON DEMOCRAT
Editorial Email: *democrat@carolnet.com*
102 E. Benton St., PO Box 69, Carrollton 64633
Telephone: (660) 542-0881 / FAX: (660) 542-2580
Publisher: Colby Gordon
Editor: Janet Zullig
Semi-W, Wed. & Fri. (NP)

Carthage

THE CARTHAGE PRESS
www.carthagepress.com
Editorial Email: *jhacker@carthagepress.com*
800 W. Central, PO Box 678, Carthage 64836
Telephone: (417) 358-2191 / FAX: (417) 358-7428
Publisher: Matt Guthrie
Editor: John Hacker
D, (ex. Sat., Sun. & Mon.) (NP)

Caruthersville

DEMOCRAT-ARGUS
www.democratargus.com
Editorial Email: *news@democratargus.com*
1011 Truman Ave., Ste. C, PO Box 1059, Caruthersville
63830
Telephone: (573) 333-4336 / FAX: (573) 333-2307
Publisher: David Tennyson
Editor: Herb Smith
W, Thur. (NP)

Cassville

BARRY COUNTY ADVERTISER
www.4bcaonline.com
Editorial Email: *editor@4bca.com*
904 West St., PO Box 488, Cassville 65625
Telephone: (417) 847-4475 / FAX: (417) 847-4523
Publisher: Emory Melton
General Manager: Marty Jenkins
Editor: Charlea Mills
W, Wed. (Rep.)

CASSVILLE DEMOCRAT
www.cassville-democrat.com
Editorial Email: *editor@cassville-democrat.com*
600 Main St., PO Box 486, Cassville 65625
Telephone: (417) 847-2610 / FAX: (417) 847-3092
Publisher: Jacob Brower
Editor: Kyle Troutman
W, Wed. (NP)

Centralia

CENTRALIA FIRESIDE GUARD
www.firesideguard.com
Editorial Email: *cfged@lcs.net*
123 N. Allen, PO Box 7, Centralia 65240
Telephone: (573) 682-2133 / FAX: (573) 682-3361
Publisher: Walt Gilbert
Editor: James Smith
W, Wed. (Rep.)

Chaffee

SCOTT COUNTY SIGNAL
www.scottcountysignal.com
Editorial Email: *bmiller@semissourian.com*
301 Broadway, PO Box 699, Cape Girardeau 63702
Telephone: (573) 887-3636 / FAX: (573) 887-3637
Publisher: Jon Rust
Editor: Bob Miller
W, Sun. (NP)

Charleston

THE CHARLESTON ENTERPRISE-COURIER
www.enterprisecourier.com
Editorial Email: *news@enterprisecourier.com*
101 E. Main St., East Prairie 63845
Telephone: (573) 683-3351 / FAX: (573) 649-9530
Publisher: Carlin Bennett
Editor: Kevin Pritchett
W, Tue. (NP)

THE MISSISSIPPI COUNTY TIMES
www.misscotimes.com
Editorial Email: *countytimes@sbcglobal.net*
207 S. Main St., PO Box 443, Charleston 63834
Telephone: (573) 683-6689 / FAX: (573) 683-4291
Publisher: Richard Scheffer
Editor: Richard Scheffer
W, Tues. (NP)

Chesterfield

WEST NEWSMAGAZINE
www.newsmagazinenetwork.com
754 Spirit 40 Park Dr., Chesterfield 63005
Telephone: (636) 591-0010 / FAX: (636) 778-9785
Publisher: Sharon Huber
Editor: Kate Uptergrove
W, Wed. (NP)

Chillicothe

CONSTITUTION-TRIBUNE
www.chillicothenews.com
Editorial Email: *ctnews@chillicothenews.com*
818 Washington St., PO Box 707, Chillicothe 64601
Telephone: (660) 646-2411 / FAX: (660) 646-2028
General Manager: Andrea Graves
Editor: Catherine S. Ripley
D, (ex. Sat & Sun.) (NP)

Clarence

THE CLARENCE COURIER
www.clarencecourier.com
Editorial Email: *clarencecourier@centurytel.net*

106 E. Maple St., PO Box 10, Clarence 63437
Telephone: (660) 699-2344 / FAX: (660) 699-2194
Publisher: Dennis W. Williams
Editor: Dennis W. Williams
W, Wed. (Dem.)

Clinton

CLINTON DAILY DEMOCRAT
Editorial Email: ddem.news@embarqmail.com
212 S. Washington St., PO Box 586, Clinton 64735
Telephone: (660) 885-2281 / FAX: (660) 885-2265
Publisher: Daniel B. Miles Jr.
Editor: Daniel B. Miles Jr.
D, (ex. Sat & Sun.) (Dem.)

THE CLINTON EYE
Editorial Email: ddem.news@embarqmail.com
212 S. Washington St., PO Box 586, Clinton 64735
Telephone: (660) 885-2281 / FAX: (660) 885-2265
Publisher: Daniel B. Miles Jr.
Editor: Daniel B. Miles Jr.
W, Thurs. (Dem.)

Cole Camp

COLE CAMP COURIER
Editorial Email: news@ovpinc.com
203 E. Junge, PO Box 280, Cole Camp 65325
Telephone: (660) 668-4418 / FAX: (660) 668-4418
Publisher: Colby Gordon
Editor: Colby Gordon
W, Fri. (NP)

Columbia

COLUMBIA DAILY TRIBUNE
www.columbiatribune.com
Editorial Email: editor@columbiatribune.com
101 N. Fourth St., PO Box 798, Columbia 65201
Telephone: (573) 815-1800 / FAX: (573) 815-1801
Publisher: Vicki Russell
General Manager: Andy Waters
Editor: Jim Robertson
D, (Ind.)

COLUMBIA MISSOURIAN
www.columbiamissourian.com
Editorial Email: news@columbiamissourian.com
221 S. Eighth St., PO Box 917, Columbia 65211
Telephone: (573) 882-5714 / FAX: (573) 884-5293
Publisher: David Kurpius
Managing Editor: Tom Warhover
D, (ex. Sat. & Mon.) (NP)

Concordia

THE CONCORDIAN
www.theconcordianonline.com
Editorial Email: concordian@centurytel.net
714 S. Main St., PO Box 999, Concordia 64020
Telephone: (660) 463-7522 / FAX: (660) 463-7942
Publisher: Dave Phillips
Editor: Sarah Reed
W, Wed. (NP)

Crane

THE CRANE CHRONICLE/STONE COUNTY REPUBLICAN
www.cc-scrnews.com
Editorial Email: srceditor@centurylink.net
114 Main St., PO Box 401, Crane 65633
Telephone: (417) 723-5248 / FAX: (417) 723-8490
Publisher: Emory Melton
General Manager: Marty Jenkins
W, Thurs. (Rep.)

Cuba

THE CUBA FREE PRESS
www.threeriverspublishing.com
Editorial Email: news@cubafreepress.com
501 E. Washington, PO Box 568, Cuba 65453
Telephone: (573) 885-7460 / FAX: (573) 885-3803
Publisher: Rob Viehman
Editor: Chris Case
W, Thurs. (NP)

Dexter

THE DAILY STATESMAN
www.dailystatesman.com
Editorial Email: nhyslop@dailystatesman.com
133 S. Walnut St., PO Box 579, Dexter 63841
Telephone: (573) 624-4545 / FAX: (573) 624-7449
Publisher: Shelia Rouse
Editor: Noreen Hyslop
D, (ex. Mon. & Sat.) (NP)

Dixon

THE DIXON PILOT
www.dixonpilot.com
Editorial Email: dixonpilotnews@yahoo.com
302 Locust St., PO Drawer V, Dixon 65459
Telephone: (573) 759-2127 / FAX: (573) 759-6226
Publishers: Rick Blackburn and Connie Erisman
Editor: Connie Erisman
W, Wed. (NP)

Doniphan

THE PROSPECT-NEWS
Editorial Email: pnpaper@windstream.net
110 Washington St., PO Box 367, Doniphan 63935
Telephone: (573) 996-2103 / FAX: (573) 996-2217
Publisher: Don Schrieber
Editor: Barbie Rogers
W, Wed. (Ind.)

East Prairie

THE EAST PRAIRIE EAGLE
www.enterprisecourier.com
Editorial Email: news@enterprisecourier.com
101 E. Main St., PO Box 10, East Prairie 63845
Telephone: (573) 683-3351 / FAX: (573) 649-9530
Publisher: Carlin Bennett
Editor: Kevin Pritchett
W, Tue. (NP)

Edina

THE EDINA SENTINEL
www.nemonews.net
Editorial Email: edinasentinel@att.net
207 N. Main, PO Box 270, Edina 63537
Telephone: (660) 397-2226 / FAX: (660) 397-3558
Publishers: Mike and Sue Scott
Editor: Mike Scott
W, Wed. (NP)

El Dorado Springs

THE STAR
Editorial Email: thestar@socket.net
105 S. Main St., PO Box 269, El Dorado Springs 64744
Telephone: (417) 876-2500 / FAX: (417) 876-5986
Publisher: Patsy Brownlee
Editor: Mae McNeece
W, Thurs. (Rep.)

EL DORADO SPRINGS SUN
www.eldoradospringsmo.com
Editorial Email: *klong@centurylink.net*
125 N. Main St., PO Box 71, El Dorado Springs 64744
Telephone: (417) 876-3841 / FAX: (417) 876-3848
Publisher: Kimball S. Long
Editor: Kenneth W. Long
W, Thurs. (NP)

Eldon

ELDON ADVERTISER
www.vernonpublishing.com/advertiser
Editorial Email: *advertiser@vernonpublishing.com*
415 S. Maple St., PO Box 315, Eldon 65026
Telephone: (573) 392-5658 / FAX: (573) 392-7755
Publisher: Trevor Vernon
Editor: Tim Flora
W, Thurs. (Dem.)

Ellington

REYNOLDS COUNTY COURIER
www.reynoldscountycourier.com
Editorial Email: *rcc@waynecojournalbanner.com*
370 Main St., PO Box 130, Ellington 63638
Telephone: (573) 663-2243 / FAX: (573) 663-2763
Publishers: Harold and Brenda Ellinghouse
W, Thurs. (NP)

Elsberry

THE ELSBERRY DEMOCRAT
www.elsberrydemocrat.com
Editorial Email: *edgenmgr@lcs.net*
106 A N. Third St., PO Box 105, Elsberry 63343
Telephone: (573) 898-2318 / FAX: (573) 898-2170
Publisher: Walt Gilbert
General Manager: Michael Short
W, Wed. (NP)

Eminence

SHANNON COUNTY CURRENT WAVE
www.shannoncountycurrentwave.com
Editorial Email: *cwave128@gmail.com*
102 Plum St., PO Box 728, Eminence 65466
Telephone: (573) 226-5229 / FAX: (573) 226-3335
Publisher: Roger Dillon
Editor: Roger Dillon
W, Wed. (NP)

Excelsior Springs

EXCELSIOR SPRINGS STANDARD
www.esstandard.com
Editorial Email: *editor@leaderpress.com*
417 Thompson Ave., PO Box 70, Excelsior Springs 64024
Telephone: (816) 637-6155 / FAX: (816) 637-8411
Publisher: Brian Rice
Editor: Eric Copeland
Semi-W, Tue. & Fri. (NP)

Fairfax

FAIRFAX FORUM
Editorial Email: *avalanche@rpt.coop*
521 E. Main St., PO Box 228, Tarkio 64491
Telephone: (660) 686-2741
Publisher: Mike Farmer
Editor: Mike Farmer
W, Thurs. (Dem.)

Fayette

FAYETTE ADVERTISER/THE DEMOCRAT LEADER
www.fayettenewspapers.com
Editorial Email: *news@fayettenews.com*
203 N. Main St., PO Box 32, Fayette 65248
Telephone: (660) 248-2235 / FAX: (660) 248-1200
Publisher: Patrick Roll
Editor: Patrick Roll
W, Advertiser Wed.; Leader Sat. (NP)

Festus

JEFFERSON COUNTY LEADER
www.myleaderpaper.com
Editorial Email: *nvrweakly@aol.com*
503 N. Second St., PO Box 159, Festus 63028
Telephone: (636) 931-7560 / FAX: (636) 931-2226
Publisher: Pam LaPlant
Editor: Peggy Bess
W, Thurs. (NP)

Fort Leonard Wood

GUIDON
www.myguidon.com
Editorial Email: *guidoneditor@myguidon.com*
4079 Illinois Ave., Bldg. 3320, Fort Leonard Wood 65473
Editorial Telephone: (573) 563-5014 / FAX: (573) 329-4359
Advertising Telephone: (417) 837-1904
Publisher: Daniel Norselli
Editor: Mike Bowers
W, Thurs. (NP)

Forsyth

TANEY COUNTY TIMES
Editorial Email: *tcteditor@yahoo.com*
704 Veterans Blvd., PO Box 6670, Branson 65615
Telephone: (417) 334-2285 / FAX: (417) 334-4789
Publisher: Kurt J. Lewis
Editor: Craig Donze
W, Wed. (Dem.)

Fredericktown

DEMOCRAT-NEWS
www.dailyjournalonline.com/democrat-news
Editorial Email: *dn@democratnewsonline.com*
131 S. Main St., PO Box 471, Fredericktown 63645
Telephone: (573) 783-3366 / FAX: (573) 783-6890
Publisher: Gary Berblinger
Editor: Alan Kopitsky
W, Wed. (NP)

Fulton

FULTON SUN
www.fultonsun.com
Editorial Email: *news@fultonsun.com*
115 E. Fifth St., PO Box 550, Fulton 65251
Telephone: (573) 642-7272 / FAX: (573) 642-0656
Publisher: Terri Leifeste
Editor: Rick Kennedy
D, (ex. Mon. & Sat.) (NP)

Gainesville

OZARK COUNTY TIMES
www.ozarkcountytimes.com
Editorial Email: *editor@ozarkcountytimes.com*
504 Court St., PO Box 188, Gainesville 65655
Telephone: (417) 679-4641 / FAX: (417) 679-3423
Publisher: Norene Prososki
Editor: Sue Ann Jones
W, Wed. (Rep.)

Gallatin

NORTH MISSOURIAN
www.gallatinnorthmissourian.com
Editorial Email: *news@gpcink.com*
609 B S. Main St., PO Box 37, Gallatin 64640
Telephone: (660) 663-2154 / FAX: (660) 663-2498
Publisher: Darryl Wilkinson
Editor: Darryl Wilkinson
W, Wed. (Dem.)

Glasgow

THE GLASGOW MISSOURIAN
www.mainstreetmedia.us
Editorial Email: *glasgow@mcmsys.com*
109 Market St., PO Box 248, Glasgow 65254
Telephone: (660) 338-2195 / FAX: (660) 338-2494
Publisher: Colby Gordon
Editor: Michael Heying
W, Fri. (NP)

Grandview

JACKSON COUNTY ADVOCATE
www.jcadvocate.com
Editorial Email: *mwilson@jcadvocate.com*
1102 A Main St., PO Box 620, Grandview 64030
Telephone: (816) 761-6200 / FAX: (816) 761-8215
Publisher: Becky Davis
Editor: Mary Wilson
W, Thurs. (NP)

Grant City

THE TIMES TRIBUNE
Editorial Email: *newsdesk@grantcity.net*
1 E. Third St., PO Box 130, Grant City 64456
Telephone: (660) 564-3603 / FAX: (660) 564-3603
Publishers: Reid and Bridget Gibson
Editor: Bridget Gibson
W, Wed. (NP)

Greenfield

THE VEDETTE
www.greenfieldvedette.com
Editorial Email: *greenfieldvedettegraphics@mchsi.com*
7 N. Main, PO Box 216, Greenfield 65661
Telephone: (417) 637-2712 / FAX: (417) 637-2232
Publisher: Marlene DeClue
Editor: Marlene DeClue
W, Thurs. (NP)

Hale

HALE HORIZONS
Editorial Email: *halehorizons@cvalley.net*
29236 Hwy. J, Hale 65643
Telephone: (660) 565-2555 FAX: (660) 565-2556
Publisher: Cindy Thompson
W, Wed. (NP)

Hamilton

CALDWELL COUNTY NEWS
www.mycaldwellcounty.com
Editorial Email: *news@mycaldwellcounty.com*
101 S. Davis, PO Box 187, Hamilton 64644
Telephone: (816) 583-2116 / FAX: (816) 583-2118
Publisher: Stephanie Henry
Editor: Deb Rankin
W, Mon. (NP)

Hannibal

HANNIBAL COURIER-POST
www.hannibal.net
Editorial Email: *eric.dundon@courierpost.com*
200 N. Third St., PO Box A, Hannibal 63401
Telephone: (573) 221-2800 / FAX: (573) 221-1568
General Manager: Mike Murphy
Editor: Eric Dundon
D, (ex. Sun. & Mon.) (NP)

Harrisonville

CASS COUNTY DEMOCRAT-MISSOURIAN
www.demo-mo.com
Editorial Email: *editor@demo-mo.com*
301 S. Lexington, PO Box 329, Harrisonville 64701
Telephone: (816) 380-3228 / FAX: (816) 380-7650
W, Fri. (NP)

Hermann

HERMANN ADVERTISER-COURIER
www.hermannadvertisercourier.com
Editorial Email: *hacmgr@lcs.net*
136 E. Fourth St., PO Box 350, Hermann 65041
Telephone: (573) 486-5418 / FAX: (573) 486-5524
Publisher: Cathi Utley
Editor: Buck Collier
W, Wed. (Rep.)

Hermitage

THE INDEX
www.vernonpublishing.com/index
Editorial Email: *theindex@positech.net*
109 W. Polk St., PO Box 127, Hermitage 65668
Telephone: (417) 745-6404 / FAX: (417) 745-2222
Publisher: Trevor Vernon
Editor: Charley Dryer
W, Wed. (Rep.)

Higginsville

HIGGINSVILLE ADVANCE
Editorial Email: *Andrew.wp.rounds@gmail.com*
3002 Hwy. 13, PO Box 422, Higginsville 64037
Telephone: (660) 584-3611 / FAX: (660) 584-7966
Publisher: Colby Gordon
Editor: Andrew Rounds
Semi-W, Wed. & Fri. (Ind.)

Hillsboro

THE COUNTIAN
www.molawyersmedia.com
Editorial Email: *edit@molawyersmedia.com*
638 First St., PO Box 498, Hillsboro 63050
Telephone: (636) 789-5853 / FAX: (636) 789-5843
Publisher: Liz Irwin
W, Fri. (NP)

Holden

THE HOLDEN IMAGE
www.holdenimage.com
Editorial Email: *holdenimage@embarqmail.com*
117 E. Second St., PO Box 8, Holden 64040
Telephone: (816) 732-5552 / FAX: (816) 732-4696
Publishers: John and Sandy Roberts
Editor: Dana Raker
W, Thurs. (Dem.)

Hopkins

THE HOPKINS JOURNAL
Editorial Email: *hopkinsjournal@embarqmail.com*
411 E. Barnard St., PO Box 170, Hopkins 64461
Telephone: (660) 778-3205 / FAX: (660) 778-3205
Publisher: Darla Thompson
Editor: Darla Thompson
W, Thurs. (NP)

Houston

HOUSTON HERALD
www.houstonherald.com
Editorial Email: *news@houstonherald.com*
113 N. Grand Ave., PO Box 170, Houston 65483
Telephone: (417) 967-2000 / FAX: (417) 967-2096
Publisher: Bradley G. Gentry
Editor: Jeffrey S. McNiell
W, Thurs. (Dem.)

Humansville

HUMANSVILLE STAR-LEADER
Editorial Email: sacosagenews@centurytel.net
Ohio St., PO Box 40, Humansville 65674
Telephone: (417) 754-2228 / FAX: (417) 646-8015
Publisher: Michael Crawford
Editor: Deborah Nasalroad
W, Fri. (NP)

Independence

THE EXAMINER
www.examiner.net
Editorial Email: *localnews@examiner.net*
410 S. Liberty, PO Box 459, Independence 64050
Telephone: (816) 254-8600 / FAX: (816) 836-3805
Publisher: Julie Moreno
Editor: Sheila Davis
D, (ex. Sun. & Mon.) (NP)

Ironton

THE MOUNTAIN ECHO
www.myironcountynews.com
Editorial Email: *randy@myironcountynews.com*
110 N. Main St., PO Box 25, Ironton 63650
Telephone: (573) 546-3917 / FAX: (573) 546-3919
Publisher: Randall Pribble
Editor: Randall Pribble
W, Wed. (NP)

Jackson

THE CASH-BOOK JOURNAL
www.thecash-book.com
Editorial Email: *cbjeditspo@socket.net*
210 W. Main St., PO Box 369, Jackson 63755
Telephone: (573) 243-3515 / FAX: (573) 243-3517
Publisher: Gina Raffety
Editor: David Bloom
W, Wed. (Dem.)

Jamesport

TRI-COUNTY WEEKLY
www.jamsportweekly.com
Editorial Email: *tcw@grm.net*
103 S. Broadway, PO Box 137, Jamesport 64648
Telephone: (660) 684-6718 / FAX: (660) 684-6515
Publisher: Natha McAllister
Editor: Natha McAllister
W, Thurs. (NP)

Jefferson City

NEWS TRIBUNE
www.newstribune.com
Editorial Email: *editor@newstribune.com*
210 Monroe St., PO Box 420, Jefferson City 65102
Telephone: (573) 636-3131 / FAX: (573) 636-7035
Publisher: Walter E. Hussman
General Manager: Terri Leifeste
Editor: Gary Castor
D (NP)

Joplin

THE JOPLIN GLOBE
www.joplinglobe.com
Editorial Email: *cstark@joplinglobe.com*
117 E. Fourth St., Joplin 64801
Telephone: (417) 623-3480 / FAX: (417) 623-8450
Publisher: Michael Beatty
Editor: Carol Stark
D (Ind.)

Kahoka

HOMETOWN JOURNAL
Editorial Email: *htjournal@yahoo.com*
258 W. Main St., Kahoka 63445
Telephone: (660) 727-3383 / FAX: (660) 727-3522
Publishers: Joe and Lisa Roberts
Editor: Joe Roberts
W, Tues. (Dem.)

THE MEDIA
www.NEMONews.net
Editorial Email: *themedia@centurytel.net*
178 W. Main St., PO Box 230, Kahoka 63445
Telephone: (660) 727-3395 / FAX: (660) 727-2475
Publishers: Mike and Sue Scott
Editor: Mike Scott
W, Wed. (Rep.)

Kansas City

KANSAS CITY DAILY RECORD
www.mlmcounties.com
Editorial Email: *kansascity@molawyersmedia.com*
405 E. 13th St., Ste. 101, Kansas City 64106
Telephone: (816) 931-2002 / FAX: (816) 561-6675
Publisher: Liz Irwin
D (NP)

THE KANSAS CITY STAR
www.kansascity.com
Editorial Email: *mfannin@kcstar.com*
1729 Grand Ave., Kansas City 64108
Telephone: (816) 234-4131 / FAX: (816) 234-4102
Publisher: Mi-Ai Parrish
Editor: Mike Fannin
D (NP)

THE NORTHEAST NEWS
www.northeastnews.net
Editorial Email: *northeastnews@socket.net*
5715 St. John Ave., Kansas City 64123
Telephone: (816) 241-0765 / FAX: (816) 241-3255
Publisher: Michael Bushnell
Editor: Joe Jarosz
W, Wed. (Rep.)

THE PITCH
www.pitch.com
Editorial Email: *editor@pitch.com*
1701 Main St., Kansas City 64108
Telephone: (816) 561-6061 / FAX: (816) 960-1538
Publisher: Chris Sexson
Editor: Scott Wilson
W, Thur. (NP)

THE PULSE LEGAL PUBLICATION
www.pulselegal.com
Editorial Email: *bob@pulselegal.com*
501 E. Armour Blvd., Kansas City 64109
Telephone: (816) 221-2552 / FAX: (816) 221-5096
Publisher: Pamela Weaver
Editor: Will Connaghan
D (Dem.)

Kearney

THE KEARNEY COURIER
www.kearneycourier.com
Editorial Email: *kearneynews@npgco.com*
102 W. Washington, PO Box 140, Kearney 64060
Telephone: (816) 628-6010 / FAX: (816) 628-4422
Publisher: Sandy Nelson
Editor: Dave Hon
W, Thurs. (NP)

Kennett

DAILY DUNKLIN DEMOCRAT
www.dddnews.com
Editorial Email: *spatton@dddnews.com*
203 First St., PO Box 669, Kennett 63857
Telephone: (573) 888-4505 / FAX: (573) 888-5114
Publisher: Shelia Rouse
Editor: Steve Patton
D, (ex. Mon. & Sat.) (NP)

Kimberling City

STONE COUNTY GAZETTE
Editorial Email: *stonegazette@lvbw.net*
110 Kimberling Center, PO Box 1150, Kimberling City 65686
Telephone: (417) 739-3237 / FAX: (417) 739-9417
Publisher: Kurt Lewis
Editor: Dave Abner
W, Thurs. (NP)

King City

THE TRI-COUNTY NEWS
Editorial Email: *news@tricountynews.net*
300 N. Connecticut St., PO Box 428, King City 64463
Telephone: (660) 535-4313 / FAX: (660) 535-6133
Publishers: Matthew and Emily Pearl
Editor: Matthew Pearl
W, Fri. (NP)

Kirksville

DAILY EXPRESS & NEWS
www.kirksvilledailyexpress.com
Editorial Email: *dailyexpresseditor@gmail.com*
110 E. McPherson, PO Box 809, Kirksville 63501
Telephone: (660) 665-2808 / FAX: (660) 665-2608
Publisher: George Wriedt
Editor: Jason Hunsicker
D, (ex. Sat.) (NP)

Knob Noster

THE KNOB NOSTER ITEM
Editorial Email: *knobnosteritem@sbcglobal.net*
111 N. Jackson, PO Box 188, Knob Noster 65336
Telephone: (660) 563-3606
Publisher: Stan Hall
Editor: Stan Hall
W, Thurs. (Dem.)

Lake Ozark/Osage Beach

THE LAKE TODAY
www.thelaketoday.com
Editorial Email: *news@thelaketoday.com*
101 Crossings W., Ste. 203, PO Box 1387, Lake Ozark 65049
Telephone: (573) 365-2827 / FAX: (573) 365-2344
Publisher: Terri Leifeste
Editor: Samantha Edmonds
W, Wed. (NP)

Lamar

LAMAR DEMOCRAT
www.lamardemocrat.com
Editorial Email: *melodymetzger@lamardemocrat.com*
100 E. 11th St., PO Box 458, Lamar 64759
Telephone: (417) 682-5529 / FAX: (417) 214-5266
Publisher: Lewis County Press LLC
Editor: Melody Metzger
Semi-W, Wed. & Sat. (NP)

La Plata

THE HOME PRESS
www.maconhomepress.com
Editorial Email: *news.homepress@gmail.com*
215 S. Gex St., PO Box 57, La Plata 63549
Telephone: (660) 332-4431 / FAX: (660) 332-7561
Publisher: Shon Coram
Editor: Shon Coram
W, Wed. (NP)

Lawson

THE LAWSON REVIEW
Editorial Email: *disneeman@aol.com*
405 N. Pennsylvania St., PO Box 125, Lawson 64062
Telephone: (816) 296-3412 / FAX: (816) 296-3412
Publisher: R. Cress Hewitt
Editor: David Blyth
W, Wed. (Rep.)

Lebanon

THE LEBANON DAILY RECORD
www.lebanondailyrecord.com
Editorial Email: *jturner@lebanondailyrecord.com*
100 E. Commercial, PO Box 192, Lebanon 65536
Telephone: (417) 532-9131 / FAX: (417) 532-8140
Publisher: Matt Wright
Editor: Ken York
D, (ex. Sat.) (NP)

Lee's Summit

LEE'S SUMMIT JOURNAL
www.lsjournal.com
Editorial Email: *editor@lsjournal.com*
415 S.E. Douglas, PO Box 387, Lee's Summit 64063
Telephone: (816) 524-2345 / FAX: (816) 524-5736
Semi-W, Wed & Fri (NP)

LEE'S SUMMIT TRIBUNE
www.lstribune.net
Editorial Email: *editor@lstribune.com*
219 S.E. Douglas St., Lee's Summit 64063
Telephone: (816) 524-0061 / FAX: (816) 600-6102
Publisher: Linda Ahern
W, Sat. (NP)

Lexington

THE LEXINGTON NEWS
Editorial Email: *lexingtonnews@embarqmail.com*
1009 Franklin Ave., PO Box 279, Lexington 64067

Telephone: (660) 259-2266 / FAX: (660) 259-4870
Publisher: Colby Gordon
Editor: Joe Parmon
W, Wed (NP)

Liberal

THE LIBERAL NEWS
106 S. Main St., PO Box 6, Liberal 64762
Telephone: (417) 843-5315 / FAX: (417) 843-5315
Publishers: Darvin E. and Ruth Ann Weaver
Editors: Darvin E. and Ruth Ann Weaver
W, Thurs. (NP)

Liberty

LIBERTY TRIBUNE
www.libertytribune.com
Editorial Email: libtrib@libertytribune.com
104 N. Main St., Liberty 64068
Telephone: (816) 781-4941 / FAX: (816) 781-0909
Publisher: Sandy Nelson
Editor: Stacey Burt
W, Thurs. (NP)

Licking

THE LICKING NEWS
www.thelickingnews.com
Editorial Email: news_ads@thelickingnews.com
115 S. Main St., PO Box 297, Licking 65542
Telephone: (573) 674-2412 / FAX: (573) 674-4892
Publisher: Donald Dodd
Editor: Debbie Dakin
W, Thurs. (NP)

Lincoln

LINCOLN NEW ERA
Editorial Email: news@ovpinc.com
205 S. Main, PO Box 23, Windsor 65360
Telephone: (660) 647-2121 / FAX: (660) 647-2122
Publisher: Colby Gordon
Editor: Colby Gordon
W, Fri. (NP)

Linn

LINN UNTERRIFIED DEMOCRAT
Editorial Email: udenews@socket.net
300 E. Main St., PO Box 109, Linn 65051
Telephone: (573) 897-3150 / FAX: (573) 897-0076
Publisher: Jerrilynn S. Voss
Editor: Neal Johnson
W, Wed. (Rep.)

Louisiana

PRESS-JOURNAL
www.louisianapressjournal.com
Editorial Email: lpjed@lcs.net
3408 Georgia St., PO Box 466, Louisiana 63353
Telephone: (573) 754-5566 / FAX: (573) 754-4749
Publisher: Linda Luebrecht
Editor: Dave Moller
W, Wed. (NP)

Malden

DELTA NEWS-CITIZEN
www.dddnews.com/dnc
Editorial Email: cluke@dddnews.com
127 W. Main St., PO Box 701, Malden 63863
Telephone: (573) 276-5148 / FAX: (573) 276-3687
Publisher: Shelia Rouse
Editor: Noreen Hyslop
W, Wed. (NP)

Mansfield

THE MANSFIELD MIRROR
www.mansfieldmirror.com
Editorial Email: larry@mansfieldmirror.com
300 E. Commercial, PO Box 197, Mansfield 65704
Telephone: (417) 924-3226 / FAX: (417) 924-3227
Publisher: Larry Dennis
Editor: Larry Dennis
W, Thurs. (Rep.)

Marble Hill

THE BANNER PRESS
Editorial Email: bmiller@semissourian.com
103 Walnut, PO Box 109, Marble Hill 63764
Telephone: (573) 238-2821 / FAX: (573) 238-0020
Publisher: Jon Rust
Editor: Linda Redeffer
W, Wed. (NP)

Marshall

MARSHALL DEMOCRAT-NEWS
www.marshallnews.com
Editorial Email: sreed@marshallnews.com
121 N. Lafayette, PO Box 100, Marshall 65340
Telephone: (660) 886-2233 / FAX: (660) 886-8544
Publisher: Dave Phillips
Editor: Sarah Reed
D, (ex. Sat. & Sun.) (NP)

Marshfield

THE MARSHFIELD MAIL
Editorial Email: news@marshfieldmail.com
224 N. Clay, PO Box A, Marshfield 65706
Telephone: (417) 725-3745 / FAX: (417) 725-3683
Publisher: Dave Berry
Editor: Scott Kerber
W, Wed. (NP)

Maryville

MARYVILLE DAILY FORUM
www.maryvilledailyforum.com
Editorial Email: tbrown@maryvilledailyforum.com
111 E. Jenkins, PO Box 188, Maryville 6448
Telephone: (660) 562-2424 / FAX: (660) 562-7863
Publisher: Phil Cobb
Editor: Tony Brown
D, (ex. Sat. & Sun.) (NP)

NODAWAY NEWS LEADER
www.nodawaynews.com
Editorial Email: nodawaynews@socket.net
116 E. Third, PO Box 373, Maryville 64468
Telephone: (660) 562-4747 / FAX: (660) 562-3607
Publisher: Kay Wilson
Editor: Kay Wilson
W, Thurs. (Rep.)

Maysville

DEKALB COUNTY RECORD-HERALD
Editorial Email: pearlterry@gmail.com
508 N. Polk St., PO Box 98, Maysville 64469
Telephone: (816) 449-2121 / FAX: (816) 449-2808
Publisher: Terry Pearl
Editor: Chrissy Stefano
W, Thurs. (NP)

Memphis

MEMPHIS DEMOCRAT
www.memphisdemocrat.com
Editorial Email: memdemoc@nemr.net
121 S. Main St., Memphis 63555

Telephone: (660) 465-7016 / FAX: (660) 465-2803
Publisher: Chris Feeney
Editor: Chris Feeney
W, Thurs. (Rep.)

Mercer

MERCER COUNTY MIRROR
Editorial Email: *mirror@grm.net*
101 S. Square St., PO Box 557, Mercer 64661
Telephone: (800) 373-0256 / FAX: (660) 382-4205
Publisher: Bob Lee Martin
Editor: Bob Lee Martin
W, Wed. (NP)

Mexico

THE MEXICO LEDGER
www.mexicoledger.com
Editorial Email: *news@mexicoledger.com*
300 N. Washington, PO Box 8, Mexico 65265
Telephone: (573) 581-1111 / FAX: (573) 581-2029
Publisher: Martin Keller
Editor: Brenda Fike
D, (ex. Sat. & Sun.) (NP)

Milan

THE MILAN STANDARD
Editorial Email: *milanstd@nemr.net*
105 S. Market St., PO Box 276, Milan 63556
Telephone: (660) 265-4244 / FAX: (660) 265-3180
Publisher: Suzie Wilson
Editor: Suzie Wilson
W, Thurs. (NP)

Moberly

MOBERLY MONITOR-INDEX
www.moberlymonitor.com
Editorial Email: *dvandyke@moberlymonitor.com*
218 N. Williams, PO Box 697, Moberly 65270
Telephone: (660) 263-4123 / FAX: (660) 263-3626
Publisher: Marsha Hargus
General Manager: Drew Vandyke
D, (ex. Sat.) (NP)

Monett

THE MONETT TIMES
www.monett-times.com
Editorial Email: *jbrower@monett-times.com*
505 Broadway, PO Box 40, Monett 65708
Telephone: (417) 235-3135 / FAX: (417) 235-8852
Publisher: Jacob Brower
D, (ex. Tue., Wed., Fri. & Sat.) (NP)

Monroe City

LAKE GAZETTE
www.lakegazette.net
Editorial Email: *lgeditor@lakegazette.net*
304 S. Main St., PO Box 187, Monroe City 63456
Telephone: (573) 735-3300 / FAX: (573) 735-3261
Publisher: Walt Gilbert
General Manager: Adriana Orsini
W, Wed. (NP)

Montgomery City

MONTGOMERY STANDARD
Editorial Email: *standard@socket.net*
115 W. Second St., PO Box 190, Montgomery City 63361
Telephone: (573) 564-2339 / FAX: (573) 564-2313
Publisher: John Fisher Jr.
Editor: Donna Fisher
W, Wed. (Dem.)

Mound City

MOUND CITY NEWS
www.moundcitynews.com
Editorial Email: *moundcitynews@socket.net*
511 State St., PO Box 175, Mound City 64470
Telephone: (660) 442-5423 / FAX: (660) 442-5423
Publisher: Adam Johnson
Editor: Pam Kent
W, Thurs. (NP)

Mount Vernon

LAWRENCE COUNTY RECORD
www.lawrencecountyrecord.com
Editorial Email: *thepaper@lawrencecountyrecord.com*
312 S. Hickory St., PO Box 348, Mount Vernon 65712
Telephone: (417) 466-2185 / FAX: (417) 466-7865
Publisher: Ryan Squibb
Editor: Ryan Squibb
W, Wed. (Dem.)

Mountain Grove

NEWS-JOURNAL
www.news-journal.net
Editorial Email: *doug@news-journal.net*
150 E. First St., PO Box 530, Mountain Grove 65711
Telephone: (417) 926-5148 / FAX: (417) 926-6648
Publisher: Sandy Anderson
Editor: Doub Berger
W, Wed. (NP)

Mountain View

STANDARD NEWS
Editorial Email: *standardnewspub@centurytel.net*
1004 E. Hwy. 60, PO Box 79, Mountain View 65548
Telephone: (417) 934-2025 / FAX: (417) 934-1591
Publisher: Tianna Brooks
Editor: Tianna Brooks
W, Wed. (Rep.)

Neosho

NEOSHO DAILY NEWS
www.neoshodailynews.com
Editorial Email: *jford@neoshodailynews.com*
1006 W. Harmony, PO Box 848, Neosho 64850
Telephone: (417) 451-1520 / FAX: (417) 451-6408
Publisher: Matt Guthrie
Editor: John Ford
D, (ex. Mon., & Sat.) (Ind.)

NEWTON COUNTY NEWS
Editorial Email: *news@newconnews.com*
200 S. Jefferson, Neosho 648850
Telephone: (417) 455-9390 / FAX: (417) 455-9390
Publisher: Jennifer Hayworth
Editor: Chad Hayworth
W, Wed. (NP)

THE NEWS-DISPATCH
www.thenewsdispatch.net
Editorial Email: *jimmy@thenewsdispatch.net*
212 E. Main St., Neosho 64850
Telephone: (417) 451-3798 / FAX: (417) 451-5188
Publisher: Jimmy Sexton
Editor: Jimmy Sexton
W, Thurs. (NP)

Nevada

NEVADA DAILY MAIL
www.nevadadailymail.com
Editorial Email: *editor@nevadadailymail.com*
131 S. Cedar St., PO Box 247, Nevada 64772
Telephone: (417) 667-3344 / FAX: (417) 667-8384

Publisher: Floyd Jernigan, Jr.
Editor: Ralph Pokorny
D, (ex. Mon. & Sun.) (NP)

New London

RALLS COUNTY HERALD
www.rallshe.com
Editorial Email: *news@rallshe.com*
318 S. Main, PO Box 426, New London 63459
Telephone: (573) 985-3420 / FAX: (660) 327-4847
Publisher: Lewis County Press LLC
Editor: Carolyn Trower
W, Thurs. (NP)

New Madrid

WEEKLY RECORD
www.weeklyrecord.net
Editorial Email: *ed@weeklyrecord.net*
218 Main St., New Madrid 63869
Telephone: (573) 748-2120 / FAX: (573) 748-5435
Publisher: Edward Thomason
Editor: Edward Thomason
W, Fri. (NP)

Nixa

NIXA ENTERPRISE
www.nixaenterprise.com
Editorial Email: *news@nixaenterprise.com*
123 Sherman Way, Ste. 101, PO Box 594, Nixa 65714
Telephone: (417) 725-3745 / FAX: (417) 725-3683
Publisher: Dave Berry
General Manager: Tricia Chapman
W, Fri. (NP)

Norborne

NORBORNE DEMOCRAT-LEADER
Editorial Email: *leader@greenhills.net*
208 A S. Pine St., Norborne 64668
Telephone: (660) 593-3712 / FAX: (660) 593-3712
Publisher: Colby Gordon
Editor: Colby Gordon
W, Thurs. (Dem.)

Oak Grove

FOCUS ON OAK GROVE
www.theodessan.net
Editorial Email: *focus@iland.net*
103 S.E. 12th St., Oak Grove 64075
Telephone: (816) 690-7218 / FAX: (816) 690-7219
Publisher: Betty S. Spaar
Editor: Hannah Spaar
W, Thurs. (Dem.)

Odessa

THE ODESSAN
www.theodessan.net
Editorial Email: *spaar@iland.net*
212 Mason St., PO Box 80, Odessa 64076
Telephone: (816) 230-5311 / FAX: (816) 633-8430
Publisher: Betty S. Spaar
Editor: Betty S. Spaar
W, Thurs. (Dem.)

Oregon

TIMES OBSERVER
Editorial Email: *brlogos@ofmlive.net*
119 W. Nodaway, PO Box 317, Oregon 64473
Telephone: (660) 446-3331 / FAX: (660) 446-3077
Publisher: Robert Ripley
Editor: Robert Ripley
W, Thurs. (Rep.)

Osceola

ST. CLAIR COUNTY COURIER
Editorial Email: *sacosagenews@centurytel.net*
285 Pine, PO Box 580, Osceola 64776
Telephone: (417) 646-2211 / FAX: (417) 646-8015
Publisher: Michael Crawford
Editor: Michael Crawford
W, Fri. (NP)

Owensville

GASCONADE COUNTY REPUBLICAN
www.gasconadecountyrepublican.com
Editorial Email: *rmurphy@wardpub.com*
106 E. Washington St., PO Box 540, Owensville 65066
Telephone: (573) 437-2323 / FAX: (573) 437-3033
Publisher: Dennis Warden
Editor: Dave Marner
W, Wed. (Rep.)

Ozark

CHRISTIAN COUNTY HEADLINER-NEWS
www.ccheadliner.com
Editorial Email: *news@ccheadliner.com*
114 N. Second Ave., PO Box 490, Ozark 65721
Telephone: (417) 581-3541 / FAX: (417) 581-3577
Publisher: Dave Berry
General Manager: Tricia Chapman
Editor: Amelia Wigton
W, Wed. (NP)

Palmyra

THE PALMYRA SPECTATOR
www.palmyra-spectator.com
Editorial Email: *editorial@palmyra-spectator.com*
304 S. Main St., PO Box 391, Palmyra 63461
Telephone: (573) 769-3111 / FAX: (573) 769-3554
Publisher: Mark Cheffey
Editor: Mark Cheffey
W, Wed. (Dem.)

Paris

MONROE COUNTY APPEAL
www.monroecountyappeal.com
Editorial Email: *appeal@parismo.net*
230 N. Main St., PO Box 207, Paris 65275
Telephone: (660) 327-4192 / FAX: (660) 327-4847
Publisher: Lewis County Press LLC
W, Thurs. (NP)

Park Hills

DAILY JOURNAL
www.dailyjournalonline.com
Editorial Email: *editorial@dailyjournalonline.com*
1513 St. Joe Dr., PO Box 9, Park Hills 63601
Telephone: (573) 431-2010 / FAX: (573) 431-7640
Publisher: Gary Berblinger
Editor: Doug Smith
D, (ex. Sun.) (NP)

Perryville

MIDAMERICA FARMER-GROWER
www.mafg.net
Editorial Email: *editor@mafg.net*
19 N. Main St., PO Box 323, Perryville 63775
Telephone: (573) 547-2244 / FAX: (573) 547-5663
Publisher: John M. LaRose Sr.
Editor: Barb Galeski
W, Fri. (Ind.)

PERRY COUNTY REPUBLIC-MONITOR
www.perryvillenews.com
Editorial Email: bchism@perryvillenews.com
10 W. Sainte Maries St., PO Box 367, Perryville 63775
Telephone: (573) 547-4567 / FAX: (573) 547-1643
Publisher: Beth Chism
Editor: Beth Chism
Semi-W, Tue. & Thur. (NP)

Piedmont
WAYNE COUNTY JOURNAL-BANNER
www.waynecojournalbanner.com
Editorial Email: kimg@waynecojournalbanner.com
101 W. Elm St., PO Box 97, Piedmont 63957
Telephone: (573) 223-7122 / FAX: (573) 223-7871
Publisher: Harold Ellinghouse
Editor: Harold Ellinghouse
W, Wed. (Ind.)

Pierce City
PIERCE CITY LEADER JOURNAL
Editorial Email: fstop@centurytel.net
101 N. Sixth St., PO Box 400, Sarcoxie 64862
Telephone: (417) 548-3311 / FAX: (417) 548-3312
Publisher: Paul E. Donley
Editors: Paul E. Donley
W, Wed. (Rep.)

Pineville
MCDONALD COUNTY PRESS
www.mdcp.nwaonline.com
Editorial email: rpeck@nwaonline.net
3353 S. Bus. Hwy. 71, PO Box 266, Pineville 64856
Telephone: (417) 223-4657 / FAX: (417) 223-4049
Publisher: Kent Marts
Editor: Rick Peck
W, Thur. (NP)

Platte City
THE PLATTE COUNTY CITIZEN
www.plattecountycitizen.com
Editorial Email: editor@plattecountycitizen.com
1100 Branch St., PO Box 888, Platte City 64079
Telephone: (816) 858-5154 / FAX: (816) 858-2154
Publisher: Ross Martin
Editor: Ross Martin
W, Wed. (NP)

PLATTE COUNTY LANDMARK
www.plattecountylandmark.com
Editorial Email: Ivan@plattecountylandmark.com
252 Main St., PO Box 410, Platte City 64079
Telephone: (816) 858-0363 / FAX: (816) 858-2313
Publisher: Ivan Foley
Editor: Ivan Foley
W, Wed. (Rep.)

Plattsburg
CLINTON COUNTY LEADER
www.clintoncountyleader.com
Editorial Email: leader@clintoncountyleader.com
102 E. Maple, Plattsburg 64477
Telephone: (816) 539-2111 / FAX: (816) 539-3530
Publisher: Steve Tinnen
Editor: Becky Black
W, Thurs. (Ind.)

Pleasant Hill
PLEASANT HILL TIMES
www.phtimes.net
Editorial Email: kirk.phtimes@comcast.net
126 First St., Pleasant Hill 64080

Telephone: (816) 540-3500 / FAX: (816) 987-2939
Publisher: Kirk Powell
Editors: Kirk Powell
W, Wed. (Dem.)

Poplar Bluff
DAILY AMERICAN REPUBLIC
www.darnews.com
208 Poplar St., PO Box 7, Poplar Bluff 63901
Telephone: (573) 785-1414 / FAX: (573) 785-2706
Publisher: Don Schrieber
Editor: Stan Berry
D, (ex. Sat.) (NP)

Portageville
PORTAGEVILLE MISSOURIAN NEWS
www.pvmonews.com
Editorial Email: sseal@dddnews.com
413 E. Main, PO Box 456, Portageville 63873
Telephone: (573) 379-5355 / FAX: (573) 379-5488
Publisher: Sheila Rouse
Editor: H. Scott Seal
W, Thurs. (Rep.)

Potosi
THE INDEPENDENT-JOURNAL
www.theijnews.com
Editorial Email: ijnews@centurytel.com
119 E. High St., PO Box 340, Potosi 63664
Telephone: (573) 438-5141 / FAX: (573) 438-4472
Publishers: Neil and Kris Richards
Editor: Neil Richards
W, Thurs. (NP)

Princeton
PRINCETON POST-TELEGRAPH
Editorial Email: posttele@grm.net
704 Main St., PO Box 286, Princeton 64673
Telephone: (660) 748-3266 / FAX: (660) 748-3267
Publisher: Ron Kinzler
Editor: Preston Cole
W, Thurs. (Rep.)

Puxico
PUXICO PRESS
Editorial Email: puxpress@sbcglobal.net
PO Box 277, Puxico 63960
Telephone: (573) 222-3243 / FAX: (573) 222-6327
Publisher: Don Schrieber
Editor: Christy Pierce
W, Wed. (NP)

Queen City
SCHUYLER COUNTY TIMES
www.schuylercountytimes.com
Editorial Email: news@schuylercountytimes.com
RR 1, Box 171B, Queen City 63561
Telephone: (660) 457-8555 / FAX: (660) 457-8556
Publisher: Herb Austin
Editor: Lorraine Austin
W, Thurs. (Ind.)

Raymore
THE JOURNAL
www.raymorejournal.com
Editorial Email: theraymorejournal@gmail.com
108 N. Madison, PO Box 1391, Raymore 64083
Telephone: (816) 322-6002 / FAX: (816) 322-6009
Publisher: Kansas Chief Publishing and Printing, LLC
Editor: Jennifer Reed
W, Thurs. (NP)

Republic

THE REPUBLIC MONITOR
www.RepublicMoNews.com
Editorial Email: *thepaper@lawrencecountyrecord.com*
249 W. Hwy. 60, Republic 65738
Telephone: (417) 725-3745 / FAX: (417) 725-3683
Publisher: Ryan Squibb
Editor: Ryan Squibb
W, Wed. (NP)

Rich Hill

RICH HILL MINING REVIEW
Editorial Email: *sacosagenews@centurytel.net*
602 E. Park, PO Box 49, Rich Hill 64779
Telephone: (417) 395-4131 / FAX: (417) 646-8015
Publisher: Michael Crawford
Editor: Michael Crawford
W, Fri. (NP)

Richmond

RICHMOND NEWS
www.richmond-dailynews.com
Editorial Email: *editor@richmond-dailynews.com*
204 W. North Main, PO Box 100, Richmond 64085
Telephone: (816) 776-5454 / FAX: (816) 470-6397
Publisher: JoEllen Black
Editor: David Knopf
Semi-W, Mon. & Thur. (Dem.)

Rock Port

ATCHISON COUNTY MAIL
www.farmerpublishing.com
Editorial Email: *amail@rpt.coop*
300 S. Main St., PO Box 40, Rock Port 64482
Telephone: (660) 744-6245 / FAX: (660) 744-2645
Publishers: William C. and Mike Farmer
Editor: William C. Farmer
W, Thurs. (Dem.)

Rolla

ROLLA DAILY NEWS
www.therolladailynews.com
Editorial Email: *rdnnews@gmail.com*
101 W. Seventh St., PO Box 808, Rolla 65401
Telephone: (573) 364-2468 / FAX: (573) 341-5847
Publisher: Tom Bookstaver
Editor: Paul Hackbarth
D, (ex. Sun.) (NP)

Salem

THE SALEM NEWS
www.thesalemnewsonline.com
Editorial Email: *salemnews@thesalemnewsonline.com*
500 N. Washington, PO Box 798, Salem 65560
Telephone: (573) 729-4126 / FAX: (573) 729-4920
Publisher: Donald Dodd
Editor: Catherine Wynn
W, Tue. (NP)

Salisbury

CHARITON VALLEY NEWS PRESS
Editorial Email: *charitonvalleynewspress@gmail.com*
216 S. Boradway, PO Box 185, Salisbury 65281
Telephone: (660) 388-6397 / FAX: (660) 388-7007
Publisher: Patrick Roll
Editor: Alexandra Rash
W, Tue. (NP)

CHARITON COUNTY JOURNAL
Editorial Email: *ps@cvalley.net*
111 S. Broadway, PO Box 313, Salisbury 65281
Telephone: (660) 388-6131 / FAX: (660) 388-6688
Publisher: Susan Baxley
Editor: Glenda Weiseman
W, Thur. (NP)

Sarcoxie

THE SARCOXIE RECORD
Editorial Email: *fstopads@socket.net*
101 N. Sixth St., PO Box 400, Sarcoxie 64862
Telephone: (417) 548-3311 / FAX: (417) 548-3312
Publisher: Paul E. Donley
Editor: Paul E. Donley
W, Wed. (Rep.)

Savannah

SAVANNAH REPORTER
www.thesavannahreporter.com
Editorial Email: *editor@stjoelive.com*
107 W. Hwy. 71, Ste. E, PO Box 299, Savannah 64485
Telephone: (816) 324-3149 / FAX: (816) 324-3632
Publisher: Guy Speckman
Editor: Leslie Speckman
W, Thurs. (Rep.)

Sedalia

SEDALIA DEMOCRAT
www.sedaliademocrat.com
Editorial Email: *tpepperson@civitasmedia.com*
700 S. Massachusetts St., PO Box 848, Sedalia 65301
Telephone: (660) 826-1000 / FAX: (660) 826-2413
Publisher: Denny Koenders
Editor: Tim Epperson
D, (ex. Sun.) (Dem.)

THE SEDALIA OBSERVER
www.sedalianewsjournal.com
Editorial Email: *sedaliaweeklynews2@gmail.com*
2700 W. Broadway, Ste. 10, Sedalia 65301
Telephone: (660) 827-2425/ FAX: (660) 473-4700
Publisher: Michael Agee
W, Thurs. (Rep.)

Seneth

THE TOWN CRIER
www.thetowncrier.com
Editorial Email: *towncrier@centurytel.net*
100 W. Lake St., PO Box 1326, Manila, AR 72447
Telephone: (870) 561-4634 / FAX: (870) 561-3602
Publisher: Ronald Kemp
Editor: Nancy Kemp
W, Wed. (NP)

Seymour

WEBSTER COUNTY CITIZEN
www.webstercountycitizen.com
Editorial Email: *citizen@webstercountycitizen.com*
221 S. Commercial, PO Box 190, Seymour 65746
Telephone: (417) 935-2257 / FAX: (417) 935-2487
Publisher: Dan Wehmer
Editor: Dan Wehmer
W, Wed. (Rep.)

Shelbina

THE SHELBINA WEEKLY
www.shelbinaweekly.com
Editorial Email: *thadweekly@centurytel.net*
217 E. Maple, PO Box 248, Shelbina 63468

Telephone: (573) 588-0051 / FAX: (573) 588-0052
Publishers: Mark and Thad Requet
Editors: Mark and Thad Requet
W, Wed. (NP)

Shelbyville

SHELBY COUNTY HERALD
www.shelbycountyherald.com
Editorial Email: *news@shelbycountyherald.com*
109 E. Main St., PO Box 225, Shelbyville 63469
Telephone: (573) 633-2261 / FAX: (573) 633-2133
Publisher: Dennis W. Williams
Editor: Martha Jane East
W, Wed. (Dem.)

Sheridan

SHERIDAN EXPRESS
www.sheridanexpress.blogspot.com
Editorial Email: *express@grm.net*
106 N. Second, PO Box 136, Sheridan 64486
Telephone: (660) 294-2161 / FAX: (314) 558-8431
Publisher: Jesse Stark
Editor: Jesse Stark
W, Wed. (Ind.)

Sikeston

STANDARD-DEMOCRAT
www.standard-democrat.com
Editorial Email: *news@standard-democrat.com*
205 S. New Madrid, Sikeston 63801
Telephone: (573) 471-1137 / FAX: (573) 471-6277
Publisher: Michael Jensen
Editor: Jill Bock
D, (ex. Sat.) (NP)

Slater

SLATER MAIN STREET NEWS
Editorial Email: *slaternews@socket.net*
222 N. Main St., Slater 65349
Telephone: (660) 529-2249 / FAX: (660) 529-2474
Publisher: Jean E. Black
Editor: Jean E. Black
W, Thurs. (NP)

Smithville

THE SMITHVILLE HERALD
www.smithvilleherald.com
Editorial Email: *smithvillenews@smithvillehearld.com*
1001 S. Commercial Ave., PO Box 1076, Smithville 64089
Telephone: (816) 532-4444 / FAX: (816) 532-4918
Publisher: Jim Card
Editor: Mark Johnson
W, Wed. (NP)

Springfield

THE DAILY EVENTS
www.thedailyevents.com
Editorial Email: *info@thedailyevents.com*
310 W. Walnut St., PO Box 1, Springfield 65801
Telephone: (417) 866-1401 / FAX: (417) 866-1491
Publisher: Jeff Schrag
Editor: Wendy Behlke-Greyowl
D, (Rep.)

SPRINGFIELD NEWS-LEADER
www.news-leader.com
Editorial Email: *webeditor@news-leader.com*
651 Boonville Ave., Springfield 65806
Telephone: (417) 836-1100 / FAX: (417) 831-0891
Publisher: Daniel Norselli
Editor: Paul Berry
D, (NP)

SPRINGFIELD BUSINESS JOURNAL
www.sbj.net
Editorial Email: *news@sbj.net*
313 Park Central W., PO Box 1365, Springfield 65806
Telephone: (417) 831-3238 / FAX: (417) 864-4901
Publisher: Jennifer Jackson
Editor: Eric Olson
W, Mon. (NP)

St. Charles

ST. CHARLES COUNTY BUSINESS RECORD
www.mlmcounties.com
Editorial Email: *stcharles@molawyersmedia.com*
125 N. Main St., Ste. 100, St. Charles 63301
Telephone: (636)-949-6928 / FAX: (636)-949-6973
Publisher: Liz Irwin
Editor: Liz Irwin
D, (NP)

St. Clair

ST. CLAIR MISSOURIAN
www.emissourian.com
Editorial Email: *domkek@emissourian.com*
395 S. Main St., St. Clair 63077
Telephone: (636) 629-2810 / FAX: (636) 629-1027
Publisher: Bill Miller Sr.
Editor: Bill Miller Sr.
Semi-W, Wed. & Sat. (NP)

St. James

ST. JAMES LEADER-JOURNAL
www.leaderjournal.com
Editorial Email: *leaderjournalnews@gmail.com*
104 N. Jefferson, St. James 65559
Telephone: (573) 265-3321
Publisher: Tom Bookstaver
Editor/Manager: Aaron Hadlow
W, Wed. (NP)

ST. JAMES PRESS
www.threeriverspublishing.com
Editorial Email: *news@saintjamespress.com*
120 S. Jefferson, Ste. 107, PO Box 428, St. James 65559
Telephone: (573) 899-2345 / FAX: (573) 899-2346
Publisher: Rob Viehman
Editor: Chris Daniels
W, Thurs. (Ind.)

St. Joseph

THE ST. JOSEPH TELEGRAPH
www.stjtelegraph.org
Editorial Email: *news@stjtelegraph.com*
202 Blake St., St. Joseph 64504
Telephone: (816) 754-6462
Publisher: Mike A. Bozarth
Editor: Mike A. Bozarth
W, Thurs. (Lib.)

ST. JOSEPH NEWS-PRESS
www.newspressnow.com
Editorial Email: *dennisellsworth@newspressnow.com*
825 Edmond St., PO Box 29, St. Joseph 64502
Telephone: (816) 271-8500 / FAX: (816) 271-8692
Publisher: David R. Bradley Jr.
Editor: Dennis Ellsworth
D, (NP)

St. Louis

ST. LOUIS AMERICAN
www.stlamerican.com
Editorial Email: *news@stlamerican.com*
2315 Pine St., St. Louis 63103

Telephone: (314) 533-8000 / FAX: (314) 533-2332
Publisher: Dr. Donald Suggs
Editor: Chris King
COO: Kevin Jones
W, Thurs. (Dem.)

ST. LOUIS BUSINESS JOURNAL
www.stlouis.bizjournals.com/stlouis
Editorial Email: tmiller@bizjournals.com
815 Olive St., Ste. 100, St. Louis 63101
Telephone: (314) 421-6200 / FAX: (314) 621-5031
Publisher: Ellen Sherberg
Editor: Patricia Miller
W, Fri. (NP)

CALL NEWSPAPERS
www.callnewspapers.com
Concord Call • Oakville Call • SunCrest Call • Green
    Park Call • Mail Call
Editorial Email: news1@callnewspapers.com
9977 LinFerry Dr., St. Louis 63123
Telephone: (314) 843-0102 / FAX: (314) 843-0508
Publisher: Deborah Baker
Editor: Mike Anthony
W, Thur. (Ind.)

COMMUNITY NEWS
www.mycnews.com
St. Louis County • St. Charles County
Editorial Email: editor@mycnews.com
2139 Bryan Valley Commercial Dr., O'Fallon 63366
Telephone: (636) 379-1775 / FAX: (636) 379-1632
Publisher: Robert J. Huneke Jr.
Editor: Matthew Dekinder
W, Wed. (NP)

ST. LOUIS DAILY RECORD
www.molawyersmedia.com
Editorial Email: edit@molawyersmedia.com
319 N. Fourth St., Fifth Fl., St. Louis 63102
Telephone: (314) 421-1880 / FAX: (314) 421-0436
Publisher: Liz Irwin
Editor: Richard Jackoway
D, (NP)

MISSOURI LAWYERS WEEKLY
www.mlmcounties.com
Editorial Email: edit@molawyersmedia.com
319 N. Fourth St., Fifth Fl., St. Louis 63102
Telephone: (314) 421-1880 / FAX: (314) 421-0436
Publisher: Liz Irwin
Editor: Liz Irwin
W, Mon. (NP)

ST. LOUIS POST-DISPATCH
www.stltoday.com
Editorial Email: interact.stltoday.com/pr/
900 N. Tucker Blvd., St. Louis 63101
Telephone: (314) 569-9944 / FAX: (314) 569-9942
Publisher: Ray Farris
Editor: Gilbert Bailon
D, (NP)

ST. LOUIS RIVERFRONT TIMES
www.riverfronttimes.com
Editorial Email: sarahfenske@riverfronttimes.com
6358 Delmar Blvd., Ste. 200, St. Louis 63130
Telephone: (816) 234-4047 / FAX: (816) 234-4636
Publisher: Jeff Keller
Managing Editor: Sarah Fenske
W, Thurs. (NP)

ST. LOUIS REVIEW
Editorial Email: teakphillips@stlouisreview.com
20 Archbishop May Dr., St. Louis 63119
Telephone: (314) 792-7500 / FAX: (314) 792-7534
Editor: Teak Phillips
W, Mon. (NP)

SOUTH COUNTY TIMES
www.southcountytimes.com
Editorial Email: newsroom@timesnewspapers.com
122 W. Lockwood Ave., Second Fl., St. Louis 63119
Telephone: (314) 968-2699 / FAX: (314) 968-2961
Publisher: Dwight Bitikofer
Editor: Don Corrigan
W, Fri. (NP)

THE BEACON
www.news.stlpublicradio.org
Editorial Email: freivogelm@umsl.edu
3651 Olive St., St. Louis 63108
Telephone: (314) 616-7479
Publisher: Margaret Wolf Freivogel
D, (NP)

ST. LOUIS LABOR TRIBUNE
www.labortribune.com
Editorial Email: tim@labortribune.com
505 S. Ewing Ave., St. Louis 63103
Telephone: (314) 256-4136 / FAX: (314) 531-6131
Publisher: Edward M. Finkelstein
Editor: Tim Rowden
W, Thurs. (Dem.)

WEBSTER-KIRKWOOD TIMES
www.websterkirkwoodtimes.com
Editorial Email: newsroom@timesnewspapers.com
122 W. Lockwood Ave., Second Fl., St. Louis 63119
Telephone: (314) 968-2699 / FAX: (314) 968-2961
Publisher: Dwight Bitikofer
Editor: Don Corrigan
W, Fri. (NP)

St. Robert
THE PULASKI COUNTY MIRROR
www.pulaskicountymirror.com
Editorial Email: mirror@pulaskicountymirror.com
555 Marshall Dr., St. Robert 65584
Telephone: (573) 336-5359 / FAX: (573) 336-7619
Publisher: Gail Gilbert
Editor: Randy Scruggs
W, Wed. (NP)

Ste. Genevieve
STE. GENEVIEVE HERALD
www.stegenherald.com
Editorial Email: news@stegenherald.com
330 Market St., PO Box 447, Ste. Genevieve 63670
Telephone: (573) 883-2222 / FAX: (573) 883-2833
Publisher: Toby Carrig
Editor: Toby Carrig
W, Wed. (NP)

Steele
STEELE ENTERPRISE
www.steelemoenterprise.com
Editorial Email: steelenews@steelemoenterprise.com
227 W. Main St., PO Box 60, Steele 63877
Telephone: (573) 695-3415 / FAX: (573) 695-2114
Publisher: David Tennyson
Editor: Lisa Rhodes
W, Thurs. (Dem.)

Steelville
STEELVILLE STAR-CRAWFORD MIRROR
www.threeriverspublishing.com
Editorial Email: news@steelvillestar.com
103 W. Main St., PO Box BG, Steelville 65565
Telephone: (573) 775-5454 / FAX: (573) 775-2668
Publisher: Rob Viehman
Editor: Amy England
W, Wed. (Ind.)

Stockton

CEDAR COUNTY REPUBLICAN
www.cedarrepublican.com
Editorial Email: news@cedarrepublican.com
#26 Public Sq., PO Box 1018, Stockton 65785
Telephone: (417) 276-4211
Publisher: Dave Berry
Editor: Becky Groff
W, Wed. (Rep.)

Stover

MORGAN COUNTY PRESS
www.vernonpublishing.com/press
Editorial Email: press@vernonpublishing.com
PO Box 348, Versailles 65804
Telephone: (573) 377-4616 / FAX: (573) 377-4512
Publisher: Dane Vernon
Editor: R.D. Fish
W, Wed. (Ind.)

Sullivan

SULLIVAN INDEPENDENT NEWS
www.mysullivannews.com
Editorial Email: nuz4u@fidnet.com
411 Scottsdale, PO Box 268, Sullivan 63080
Telephone: (573) 468-6511 / FAX: (573) 468-4046
Publishers: James Bartle and Jennifer Manion
Editor: James B. Bartle
W, Wed. (Ind.)

Summersville

THE SUMMERSVILLE BEACON
www.mysummersvillenews.com
Editorial Email: sbeaconnews@centurytel.net
205 Richards Ave., PO Box 272, Summersville 65571
Telephone: (417) 932-4700 / FAX: (417) 932-4707
Publisher: Sharon Vaughn
Editor: Sharon Vaughn
W, Wed. (NP)

Sweet Springs

SWEET SPRINGS HERALD
Editorial Email: ssherald@embarqmail.com
238 W. Main St., Sweet Springs 65351
Telephone: (660) 335-6366 / FAX: (660) 335-6962
Publisher: Kathy Dohrman
Editor: Kathy Dohrman
W, Wed. (Rep.)

Tarkio

THE TARKIO AVALANCHE
www.avalanche-forum.com
Editorial Email: avalanche@rpt.coop
521 Main St., PO Box 278, Tarkio 64491
Telephone: (660) 736-4111 / FAX: (660) 736-5700
Publisher: Mike Farmer
Editor: Mike Farmer
W, Thurs. (Rep.)

Thayer

SOUTH MISSOURIAN NEWS
www.areawidenews.com
Editorial Email: news@areawidenews.com
109 Chestnut St., Thayer 65791
Telephone: (417) 264-3085 / FAX: (417) 264-3814
Publisher: Janie Flynn
Editor: Tammy Curtis
W, Thurs. (NP)

Tipton

THE TIPTON TIMES
www.vernonpublishing.com/times
Editorial Email: times@vernonpublishing.com
113 E. Morgan St., PO Box U, Tipton 65081
Telephone: (660) 433-5721 / FAX: (660) 433-2222
Publisher: Dane Vernon
Editor: Becky Holloway
W, Thurs. (Dem.)

Trenton

TRENTON REPUBLICAN-TIMES
www.republican-times.com
Editorial Email: rtimes@lyn.net
122 E. Eighth St., PO Box 548, Trenton 64683
Telephone: (660) 359-2212 / FAX: (660) 359-4414
Publisher: Wendell J. Lenhart
Editor: Diane Lowery
D, (ex. Sat. & Sun.) (NP)

Troy

TROY FREE PRESS
www.troyfreepress.com
Editorial Email: lcjeditor@lcs.net
20 Business Park Dr., Troy 63379
Telephone: (636) 528-9550 / FAX: (636) 528-6694
Publisher: Kathy Colbert
Editor: Kathy Colbert
W, Wed. (NP)

THE LINCOLN COUNTY JOURNAL
www.lincolncountyjournal.com
Editorial Email: lcjeditor@lcs.net
20 Business Park Dr., Troy 63379
Telephone: (636) 528-9550 / FAX: (636) 528-6694
Publisher: Kathy Colbert
Editor: Kathy Colbert
W, Tues. (NP)

Union

UNION MISSOURIAN
www.emissourian.com
Editorial Email: jonesg@emissourian.com
312 E. Locust, Union 63090
Telephone: (636) 583-7701 / FAX: (636) 239-0915
Publisher: William L. Miller Sr.
Editor: William L. Miller Sr.
Semi-W, Wed. & Sat. (NP)

Unionville

THE UNIONVILLE REPUBLICAN
unionvillerepublicanonline.com
Editorial Email: urep@nemr.net
111 S. 16th St., PO Box 365, Unionville 63565
Telephone: (660) 947-2222 / FAX: (660) 947-2223
Publisher: Ron Kinzler
Editors: Ron Kinzler
W, Wed. (NP)

Van Buren

THE CURRENT LOCAL
Editorial Email: currentlocal@centurytel.net
511 Main St., PO Box 100, Van Buren 63965
Telephone: (573) 323-4515 / FAX: (573) 323-4515
Publisher: Ryan VanWinkle
Editor: Steve Turley
W, Thurs. (Dem.)

Vandalia

THE VANDALIA LEADER
www.vandalialeader.com
Editorial Email: vandalialeader@lcs.net

108 W. State St., PO Box 239, Vandalia 63382
Telephone: (573) 594-2222 / FAX: (573) 594-6741
Publisher: Ron Schott
Editor: Ron Schott
W, Wed. (NP)

Versailles

VERSAILLES LEADER-STATESMAN
www.vernonpublishing.com/leader
Editorial Email: leader-statesman@vernonpublishing.com
104 W. Jasper St., PO Box 348, Versailles 65084
Telephone: (573) 378-5441 / FAX: (573) 378-4292
Publisher: Dane Vernon
Editor: Robin Fish
W, Thurs. (Dem.)

Viburnum

QUAD COUNTY STAR
Editorial Email: quadstar@misn.com
3 Missouri Ave., PO Box 347, Viburnum 65566
Telephone: (573) 244-5206 / FAX: (573) 244-5207
Publisher: Gary R. Dickens
Editor: Marlene Dickens
W, Wed. (Ind.)

Vienna

MARIES COUNTY GAZETTE
Editorial Email: tricountynewspapers@yahoo.com
218 S. Main, PO Box 202, Vienna 65582
Telephone: (573) 422-9997 / FAX: (573) 859-6274
Publisher: Kurt J. Lewis
Editor: Laura Schiermeier
W, Wed. (Dem.)

Warrensburg

THE DAILY STAR-JOURNAL
www.dailystarjournal.com
Editorial Email: jack.miles@npgco.com
135 E. Market St., PO Box 68, Warrensburg 64093
Telephone: (660) 747-8123 / FAX: (660) 747-8741
Publisher: Joe Warren
Editor: Jack Miles
D, (ex. Sat. & Sun.) (NP)

Warrenton

WARREN COUNTY RECORD
www.warrencountyrecord.com
Editorial Email: tschmidt@warrencountyrecord.com
103 E. Booneslick, Warrenton 63383
Telephone: (636) 456-6397 / FAX: (636) 456-6150
Publisher: William L. Miller Jr.
Editor: Tim Schmidt
W, Thurs. (NP)

Warsaw

BENTON COUNTY ENTERPRISE
www.bentoncountyenterprise.com
Editorial Email: jameswhite@bentoncountyenterprise.com
107 E. Main St., PO Box 128, Warsaw 65355
Telephone: (660) 438-6312 / FAX: (660) 438-3464
Publisher: James Mahlon White
W, Thurs. (NP)

Washington

WASHINGTON MISSOURIAN
www.emissourian.com
Editorial Email: washnews@emissourian.com
14 W. Main St., PO Box 336, Washington 63090
Telephone: (636) 239-7701 / FAX: (636) 239-0915

Publisher: William L. Miller Sr.
Editor: William L. Miller Sr.
Semi-W, Wed., Sat. & Sun. (NP)

Waynesville

DAILY GUIDE
www.waynesvilledailyguide.com
Editorial Email: editor@waynesvilledailyguide.com
108 Holly Dr., PO Box 578, Waynesville 65583
Telephone: (573) 364-2468 / FAX: (573) 341-5847
Publisher: Tom Bookstaver
Editor: Mandy Matney
D, (ex. Sun. & Mon.) (NP)

Webb City

WEBB CITY SENTINEL
www.webbcity.net
Editorial Email: news@webbcity.net
8 S. Main St., PO Box 150, Webb City 64870
Telephone: (417) 673-2421 / FAX: (417) 673-5308
Publisher: Robert H. Foos
Editor: Robert H. Foos
W, Fri. (NP)

Wellsville

WELLSVILLE OPTIC-NEWS
Editorial Email: opticnews@socket.net
123 W. Hudson St., PO Box 73, Wellsville 63384
Telephone: (573) 684-2929 / FAX: (573) 684-2929
Publisher: John P. Fisher Jr.
Editor: Tracy L. Hoffman
W, Wed. (NP)

West Plains

WEST PLAINS DAILY QUILL
www.westplainsdailyquill.net
Editorial Email: news@wpdailyquill.net
125 Jefferson St., PO Box 110, West Plains 65775
Telephone: (417) 256-9191 / FAX: (417) 256-9196
Publisher: Jim Perry
D, (ex. Sat. & Sun.) (Dem.)

Weston

THE WESTON CHRONICLE
www.plattechronicle.com
Editorial Email: wcnews@embarqmail.com
18275 Hwy. 45 N., PO Box 6, Weston 64098
Telephone: (816) 640-2251 / FAX: (816) 386-2251
Publishers: Jim and Beth McPherson
Editor: Beth McPherson
W, Wed. (Dem.)

Willow Springs

HOWELL COUNTY NEWS
www.howellcountynews.com
Editorial Email: editor@howellcountynews.com
125 E. Main St., PO Box 249, Willow Springs 65793
Telephone: (417) 469-1167 / FAX: (417) 469-1521
Publisher: Kim Wehmer
Editor: Kim Wehmer
W, Wed. (Rep.)

Windsor

THE WINDSOR REVIEW
Editorial Email: news@ovpinc.com
205 S. Main, PO Box 23, Windsor 65360
Telephone: (660) 647-2121 / FAX: (660) 647-2122
Publisher: Colby Gordon
Editor: Colby Gordon
W, Fri. (NP)

Missouri Broadcasters

Missouri Broadcasters Association

1025 Northeast Dr., Jefferson City 65109
Telephone: (573) 636-6692 / FAX: (573) 634-8258
www.mbaweb.org
Email: mba@mbaweb.org

MARK GORDON
President/CEO
Missouri Broadcasters Association

The first radio stations to begin operations in Missouri were KMBC-AM (now KMBZ) in Kansas City and WEW-AM in St. Louis. Both signed on the air in 1921. In the following years, the number of radio operations steadily increased as the first FM stations began broadcasting in 1948. Today, there are approximately 400 radio stations serving listeners in Missouri.

Television broadcasting began in 1947 when KSD-TV (now KSDK) in St. Louis signed on the air, followed in 1949 by WDAF-TV in Kansas City. Federal policy suspended the granting of any further licenses until 1953. Shortly after licensing resumed, many additional television stations began operations. There are now approximately 60 commercial and public television stations broadcasting a variety of news, information and entertainment programs each day.

The Missouri Broadcasters Association (MBA) was formed Aug. 15, 1948, in Kansas City. Missouri was the second state to have a full-time broadcast association. North Carolina's association was formed earlier that same year. From its offices in Jefferson City, the MBA works for the broadcasters of Missouri, as well as allied organizations, to provide a variety of services.

The MBA is governed by a four-person executive committee and a 10-person board of directors representing radio and television broadcasters. Board members are elected for two-year terms and may seek re-election for one additional term. In addition, there are four standing committees, each responsible for a specific area of service. The committees have three roles: to represent member interests in state and federal legislative and regulatory processes; maintain the MBA office as a resource center for training, revenue expansion, cost control and information; and encourage the highest standards in broadcasting.

Since 1968, the Missouri Broadcasters Association has maintained a communications center on the first floor of the state Capitol. These facilities are available to radio and television broadcast-

ers to aid in their coverage of state news. These facilities are also available to state officials and legislators for the recording of information to be sent to radio and television stations in Missouri.

Executive Committee, 2015-2016

Chair: John Kijowski, Hubbard Radio, St. Louis;
Chair-Elect: Rick Lambers, Withers Broadcasting, Cape Girardeau;
Treasurer: Carla Leible, Zimmer Radio Group of Mid-MO, Columbia/Jefferson City;
Immediate Past Chair: Danny Thomas, KOAMTV, Joplin;
President/CEO: Mark Gordon, Jefferson City, Email: *mgordon@mbaweb.org*;
Assistant to the President: Victoria Sabatino, Jefferson City, Email: *vsabatino@mbaweb.org*.

Board of Directors

District I–Radio: John Beck, Emmis Communications, St. Louis;
District I–TV: Marv Danielski, KSDK-TV, St. Louis;
District II–Radio: Chad Boeger, Union Broadcasting, Kansas City;
District II–TV: Sarah Smith, Hearst Television, Kansas City;
District III: Phillip Lewis, Cumulus, Columbia/Jefferson City;
District IV: Steve Lloyd, KIRX, Inc., Kirksville;
District V: Mike Edwards, Digity Media, Lebanon/Waynesville;
District VI: Brian McDonough, KY-3 Inc., Springfield;
District VII: Dave Thomason, KFVS-TV, Cape Girardeau;
Associate Member: Mark Sableman, Thompson Coburn, St. Louis.
Staff: Frank Forgey, Director of MO-PEP;
Vicotria Sabatino, Business Manager;
Terry Harper, Director of Member services; Email: *tharper@mbaweb.org*

Broadcast Stations

Radio stations in Missouri

Aurora

KQMO/FM
Frequency 97.7
Format: Regional Mexican
126 S. Jefferson, Aurora 65605
Phone: (417) 678-0416 / FAX: (417) 678-4111
Website: *www.radiotalon.com*
General Manager: Janet Gandy

KSWM/AM
Frequency 940
Format: Boomer Radio
126 S. Jefferson, Aurora 65605
Phone: (417) 678-0416 / FAX: (417) 678-4111
Website: *www.radiotalon.com*
General Manager: Bill Lewis

Bethany

KAAN/AM/FM2
Frequency 870 & 103.7
Format: Classic Hits/Farm
1212 S. 25th St., Bethany 64424
Phone: (660) 425-6380 / FAX: (660) 425-8148
Website: *www.NorthwestMoInfo.com*
General Manager: Doug Schmitz

KAAN/FM
Frequency 95.5
Format: Country
1212 S. 25th St., Bethany 64424
Phone: (660) 425-6380 / FAX: (660) 425-8148
General Manager: Doug Schmitz

KMWC/FM
Frequency 91.3
Format: Christian
170 Main St., Bethany 64424
Phone: (660) 425-4494
Website: *www.kmwcradio.com*
General Manager: Scott Jones

Boonville

KWJK/FM
Frequency 93.1
Format: Classic Rock
1600 Radio Hill Rd., Boonville 65233
Phone: (660) 882-6686 / FAX: (660) 882-6688
Website: *www.931jack.fm*
General Manager: Matt Billings

KWRT/AM
Frequency 1370
Format: Classic Country
1600 Radio Hill Rd., Boonville 65233
Phone: (660) 882-6686 / FAX: (660) 882-6688
Website: *www.1370kwrt.com*
General Manager: Matt Billings

Branson

KBCV/AM
Frequency 1570
Format: Christian Talk, News & Information (Bott)
500 W. Main, Branson 65616
Phone: (417) 336-1570 / FAX: (417) 336-2097
Website: *www.bottradionetwork.com*
General Manager: Richard Bott

KBPB/FM
Frequency 91.9
Format: Christian (New Life)
1411 Locust St., St. Louis 63101
Phone: (314) 421-3020 / FAX: (314) 421-1702
Website: *www.hereshelpnet.com*
General Manager: Nathan First

KOMC/AM
Frequency 1220
Format: Southern Gospel
202 Courtney St., Branson 65616
Phone: (417) 334-6003 / FAX: (417) 334-7141
Website: *www.hometowndailynews.com*
General Manager: Scottie Earls

KOMC/FM
Frequency 100.1
Format: Adult Standards
202 Courtney St., Branson 65616
Phone: (417) 334-6003 / FAX: (417) 334-7141
Website: *www.hometowndailynews.com*
General Manager: Scottie Earls

KRZK/FM
Frequency 106.3
Format: News/Talk
202 Courtney St., Branson 65616
Phone: (417) 334-6003 / FAX: (417) 334-7141
Website: *www.hometowndailynews.com*
General Manager: Scottie Earls

KSMS/FM
Frequency 90.5
Format: NPR/News/Classical Music
901 S. National, Springfield 65897
Phone: (417) 836-5878 / FAX: (417) 836-5889
Website: *www.ksmu.org*
General Manager: Tammy Wiley

Brookfield

KZBK-FM/KFMZ-AM
Frequency 96.9 & 1470
Format: Hot AC (Simulcast)
107 S. Main, Brookfield 64628
Phone: (660) 258-3383 / FAX: (660) 258-7307
Website: *www.kzbkradio.com*
General Manager: Dale Palmer

Butler

KMOE-FM/KMAM-AM
Frequency 92.1 & 1530
Format: Country (Simulcast)
800 E. Nursery St., Butler 64730
Phone: (660) 679-4191 / FAX: (660) 679-4193
Website: *www.921news.com*
General Manager: Melody Thornton

Cabool

KOZX/FM
Frequency 98.1
Format: Rock/Classic Rock
800 N. Hubbard St., Mountain Grove 65711
Phone: (417) 926-4650 / FAX: (417) 926-7604
General Manager: Tracy O'Quinn

California

KRLL/AM
Frequency 1420
Format: Country/ABC
PO Box 307, 100-A E. Buchanan, California 65018
Phone: (573) 796-3139 / FAX: (573) 796-4131
General Manager: Jeff Shackleford

Camdenton

KCLQ/FM
Frequency 107.9
Format: Hot Country
42 Camden Ct. SE, Camdenton 65020
Phone: (573) 317-8000 / FAX: (573) 346-3717
Website: *www.107thecoyote.com*
General Manager: Dan Caldwell

Cameron

KKWK/FM
Frequency 100.1
Format: Classic Rock
607 E. Platte Clay Way, Cameron 64429
Phone: (816) 632-6661 / FAX: (816) 632-1334
Website: *www.NorthwestMoInfo.com*
General Manager: Doug Schmitz

KMRN/AM
Frequency 1360
Format: Classic Country
607 E. Platte Clay Way, Cameron 64429
Phone: (816) 632-6661 / FAX: (816) 632-1334
Website: *www.NorthwestMoInfo.com*
General Manager: Doug Schmitz

Cape Girardeau

KAPE/AM/FM
Frequency 1550 & 100.3
Format: News/Talk (SIMULCAST)
PO Box 558, 901 S. Kingshighway, Cape Girardeau 63702
Phone: (573) 339-7000 / FAX: (573) 651-4100
Website: *www.kaperadio1550.com*
General Manager: Rick Lambert

KCGQ/FM
Frequency 99.3
Format: Rock
324 Broadway, Cape Girardeau 63701
Phone: (573) 335-8291 / FAX: (573) 335-4806
Website: *www.realrock993.com*

KEZS/FM
Frequency 102.9
Format: Country
324 Broadway, Cape Girardeau 63701
Phone: (573) 335-8291 / FAX: (573) 335-4806
Website: *www.k103.com*

KGIR/AM
Frequency 1220
Format: ESPN Sports
324 Broadway, Cape Girardeau 63701
Phone: (573) 335-8291 / FAX: (573) 335-4806
Website: *www.espn1220.com*

KGKS/FM
Frequency 93.9
Format: Classic Hits
324 Broadway, Cape Girardeau 63701
Phone: (573) 335-8291 / Fax: (573) 335-4806
Website: *www.939river.com*

KGMO/FM
Frequency 100.7
Format: Classic Rock
PO Box 558, 901 S. Kingshighway, Cape Girardeau 63702
Phone: (573) 339-7000 / FAX: (573) 651-4100
Website: *www.kgmo.com*
General Manager: Rick Lambert

KLSC-FM/KMAL-AM
Frequency 92.9 & 1470
Format: ESPN Sports (Simulcast)
324 Broadway, Cape Girardeau 63701
Phone: (573) 335-8291 / FAX: (573) 335-4806
Website: *www.semoespn.com*

KRCU/FM
Frequency 90.9
Format: NPR News/Classical (Simulcast)
One University Plaza, MSO300, Cape Girardeau 63701
Phone: (573) 651-5070 / FAX: (573) 651-5071
Website: *www.krcu.org*
General Manager: Danny Woods

KREZ/FM
Frequency 104.7
Format: Adult Contemporary
PO Box 558, 901 S. Kingshighway, Cape Girardeau 63702
Phone: (573) 339-7000 / FAX: (573) 651-4100
General Manager: Rick Lambert

KWKZ/FM
Frequency 106.1
Format: Country Music
753 Enterprise St., Cape Girardeau 63703
Phone: (573) 334-7800 / FAX: (573) 334-7440
Website: *www.kwkz.com*
General Manager: Susan Bell

KYRX/FM
Frequency 97.3
Format: Classic County
PO Box 558, 901 S. Kingshighway, Cape Girardeau 63702
Phone: (573) 339-7000 / FAX: (573) 651-4100
Website: *www.hank973.com*
General Manager: Rick Lambert

KZIM/KSIM-AM
Frequency 960 & 1400
Format: News/Talk
324 Broadway, Cape Girardeau 63701
Phone: (573) 335-8291 / FAX: (573) 335-4806
Website: *www.kzimksim.com*

WKIB/FM
Frequency 96.5
Format: Hot AC
PO Box 558, 901 S. Kingshighway, Cape Girardeau 63702
Phone: (573) 339-7000 / FAX: (573) 651-4100
Website: *www.mix965.net*
General Manager: Rick Lambert

Carrollton

KAOL/AM/FM
Frequency 1430 & 101.3
Format: Contemporary Hit Radio
102 N. Mason, Carrollton 64633
Phone: (660) 542-0404 / FAX: (660) 542-3152
Website: *www.1013thegrenade.com*
General Manager: Miles Carter

KMZU/FM
Frequency 100.7
Format: Country
102 N. Mason St., Carrollton 64633
Phone: (660) 542-0404 / FAX: (660) 542-3152
Website: *www.kmzu.com*
General Manager: Miles Carter

Caruthersville

KCRV/AM
Frequency 1370
Format: Classic Country
PO Box 909, 717 State Hwy. 84, Caruthersville 63830
Phone: (573) 333-1370 / FAX: (573) 333-1371
Website: *www.kcrvradio.com*
General Manager: Perry Jones

KCRV/FM
Frequency 105.1
Format: Classic Hits
PO Box 909, Caruthersville 63830
Phone: (573) 333-1370 / FAX: (573) 333-1371
Website: *www.kcrvradio.com*
General Manager: Perry Jones

Cedar Hill

KNLH/FM
Frequency 89.5
Format: Christian (New Life)
5091 Tower Rd., House Springs 63051
Phone: (314) 881-3200 / FAX: (314) 436-2434
Website: *www.hereshelpnet.org*
General Manager: Nathan First

Centralia

KSDQ/FM
Frequency 88.7
Format: Christian
6837 Audrain Rd., 9139 Centralia 65240
Phone: (573) 682-5587
Email: *ksdqradio@sunnydale.org*
Chief Operator: Leland (Micky) Burkett

Chillicothe

KCHI/AM/FM
Frequency 1010 & 102.5
Format: Classic Hits (Simulcast)
PO Box 227, 421 Washington, Chillicothe 64601
Phone: (660) 646-4173 / FAX: (660) 646-2868
Website: *www.kchi.com*
General Manager: Dan Leatherman

KULH/FM
Frequency 105.9
Format: Christian
802 Calhoun St., Chillicothe 64601
Phone: (660) 646-2255 / FAX: (660) 646-2242
Website: *www.1059thewave.com*
General Manager: Ean Leppin

Clinton

KDKD/AM
Frequency 1280
Format: Oldies
PO Box 448, 2201 N. Antioch Rd., Clinton 64735
Phone: (660) 885-6141 / FAX: (816) 885-4801
Website: *www.WestCentralMoInfo.com*
General Manager: Jim Keck

KDKD/FM
Frequency 95.3
Format: New Country / NASCAR
PO Box 448, 2201 N. Antioch Rd., Clinton 64735
Phone: (660) 885-6141 / FAX: (816) 885-4801
Website: *www.WestCentralMoInfo.com*
General Manager: Jim Keck

KXEA/FM
Frequency 104.9.
Format: Classic Hits/70s and 80s
PO Box 448, Clinton 64735
Phone: (660) 885-6141 / FAX: (660) 885-4801
General Manager: Jim Keck

Columbia

KBBM/FM
Frequency 100.1
Format: Country
503 Old Hwy. 63 N., Columbia 65201
Phone: (573) 449-4141 / FAX: (573) 449-7770
Website: *www.nashfm100.com*
General Manager: Phillip Lewis

KBIA/FM
Frequency 91.3
Format: NPR
409 Jesse Hall, Columbia 65211
Phone: (573) 882-3431 / FAX: (573) 882-2636
Website: *www.kbia.org*
General Manager: Dr. Michael Dunn

KBXR/FM
Frequency 102.3
Format: Adult Album Alternative
503 Old Hwy. 63 N., Columbia 65201
Phone: (573) 449-4141 / FAX: (573) 449-7770
Website: *www.bxr.com*
General Manager: Phillip Lewis

KCLR/FM
Frequency 99.3
Format: Country
3215 Lemone Industrial Blvd., Columbia 65201
Phone: (573) 875-1099 / FAX: (573) 875-2439
Website: *www.clear99.com*
General Manager: Carla Leible

KCMQ/FM
Frequency 96.7
Format: Classic Rock
3215 Lemone Industrial Blvd., Columbia 65201
Phone: (573) 875-1099 / FAX: (573) 875-2439
Website: *www.kcmq.com*
General Manager: Carla Leible

KCOU/FM
Frequency 88.1
Format: College Music - Unversity of Missouri
2500 MU Student Center, Columbia 65211
Phone: (573) 882-3780 / FAX: (573) 884-7348
Website: *http://kcou.fm*
Student Media Coordinator: Mark Johnson

KFRU/AM
Frequency 1400
Format: News/Talk
503 Old Hwy. 63 N., Columbia 65201
Phone: (573) 449-4141 / FAX: (573) 449-7770
Website: *www.kfru.com*
General Manager: Phillip Lewis

KOQL/FM
Frequency 106.1
Format: Rhythmic CHR/Dance
503 Old Hwy. 63 N., Columbia 65201
Phone: (573) 449-4141 / FAX: (573) 449-7770
Website: *www.q1061.com*
General Manager: Phillip Lewis

KPLA/FM
Frequency 101.5
Format: Adult Contemporary
503 Old Hwy. 63 N., Columbia 65201
Phone: (573) 449-4141 / FAX: (573) 449-7770
Website: *www.kpla.com*
General Manager: Phillip Lewis

KSSZ/FM
Frequency 93.9
Format: News Talk
3215 Lemone Industrial Blvd., Columbia 65201
Phone: (573) 875-1099 / FAX: (573) 875-2439
Website: *www.939theeagle.com*
General Manager: Carla Leible

KTGR/AM/FM
Frequency 1580 & 103.1
Format: ESPN
3215 Lemone Industrial Blvd., Columbia 65201
Phone: (573) 875-1099 / FAX: (573) 875-2439
Website: *www.ktgr.com*
General Manager: Carla Leible

KTXY/FM
Frequency 106.9
Format: #1 Hit Music
3215 Lemone Industrial Blvd., Columbia 65201
Phone: (573) 875-1099 / FAX: (573) 875-2439
Website: *www.y107.com*
General Manager: Carla Leible

Cuba

KNLQ/FM
Frequency 91.9
Format: Christian (New Life)
1411 Locust St., St. Louis 63101
Phone: (314) 421-3020 / FAX: (314) 421-1702
Website: *www.hereshelpnet.org*
General Manager: Nathan First

Dexter

KDEX/AM/FM
Frequency 1590 & 102.3
Format: Country/ABC (Simulcast)
20487 State Hwy. 114 E., Dexter 63841
Phone: (573) 624-3545 / FAX: (573) 624-9926
General Manager: Walt Turner

Doniphan

KOEA/FM
Frequency 97.5
Format: Classic Country
932 County Rd. 448, Poplar Bluff 63901
Phone: (573) 686-3700 / FAX: (573) 686-6116
Website: *www.foxradionetwork.com*
General Manager: Steven Fuchs

KDFN/AM
Frequency 1500
Format: Talk
932 County Rd. 448, Poplar Bluff 63901
Phone: (573) 686-3700 / FAX: (573) 686-6116
Website: *www.foxradionetwork.com*
General Manager: Steven Fuchs

El Dorado Springs

KESM/AM/FM
Frequency 1580 & 105.5
Format: Country/Oldies (Simulcast)
200 Radio Ln., El Dorado Springs 64744
Phone: (417) 876-2741 / FAX: (417) 876-2743
Website: *www.kesmradio.com*
General Manager: Donald L. Kohn

Ellington

KDKN/FM
Frequency 106.7
Format: Alternative Rock
900 E. Karsch Blvd., Farmington 63640
Phone: (573) 701-9590 / FAX: (573) 701-9696
General Manager: Fred Dockins

Farmington

KLMZ/FM
Frequency 107.1
Format: Alternative Rock
900 E. Karsch Blvd., Farmington 63640
Phone: (573) 701-9590 / FAX: (573) 701-9696
General Manager: Fred Dockins

KREI/AM
Frequency 800
Format: News/Talk/ABC
PO Box 461, 1401 KREI Blvd., Farmington 63640
Phone: (573) 756-6476 / FAX: (573) 756-1110
Website: *www.myMoInfo.com*
General Manager: Les Tuttle

KTJJ/FM
Frequency 98.5
Format: Country /ABC
PO Box 461, 1401 KREI Blvd., Farmington 63640
Phone: (573) 756-6476 / FAX: (573) 756-1110
Website: *www.myMoInfo.com*
General Manager: Les Tuttle

KYLS/FM
Frequency 95.9
Format: Country
900 E. Karsch, Farmington 63640
Phone: (573) 701-9590 / FAX: (573) 701-9696
General Manager: Fred Dockins

KYLS-AM/KTNX-FM
Frequency 1450 & 103.9
Format: Oldies (Simulcast)
900 E. Karsh, Farmington 63640
Phone: (573) 701-9590 / FAX: (573) 701-9696
General Manager: Fred Dockins

Festus

KJFF/AM
Frequency 1400
Format: News/Talk
PO Box 368, 1026 Scenic Dr., Festus 63028
Phone: (636) 937-7642 / FAX: (636) 937-3636
Website: *www.myMoInfo.com*
General Manager: Les Tuttle

Fulton

KFAL/AM
Frequency 900
Format: Country
1805 Westminster Ave., Fulton 65251
Phone: (573) 642-3341 / FAX: (573) 642-3343
Website: *www.kfalthebig900.com*
General Manager: Carla Leible

KTGR/FM
Frequency 100.5
Format: ESPN
3215 Lemone Industrial Blvd., Columbia 65201
Phone: (573) 642-3341 / FAX: (573) 642-3343
Website: *www.ktgr.com*
General Manager: Carla Leible

Gideon

KMIS/FM
Frequency 103.9
Format: Sports
PO Box 509, Kennett 63857
Phone: (573) 888-4616 / FAX: (573) 888-4890
Website: *www.sportsradiokmis.com*
General Manager: Perry Jones

Hannibal

KGRC/FM
Frequency 92.9
Format: Top 40
329 Maine St., Quincy, IL 62301
Phone: (217) 224-4102 / FAX: (217) 224-4133
Website: *www.real929.com*
General Manager: Mike Moyers

KHMO/AM
Frequency 1070
Format: News/Talk/Sports
PO Box 711, 119 N. Third, Hannibal 63401
Phone: (573) 221-3450 / FAX: (573) 221-5331
General Manager: Dave Greene

KICK/FM
Frequency 97.9
Format: Hot Country
PO Box 711, 119 N. Third, Hannibal 63401
Phone: (573) 221-3450 / FAX: (573) 221-5331
General Manager: Dave Greene

KRRY/FM
Frequency 100.9
Format: Hot AC
PO Box 711, 119 N. Third, Hannibal 63401
Phone: (573) 221-3450 / FAX: (573) 221-5331
General Manager: Dave Greene

KZZK/FM
Frequency 105.9
Format: New Rock
329 Maine St., Quincy, IL 62301
Phone: (217) 224-4102 / FAX: (217) 224-4133
Website: www.kzzk.com
General Manager: Mike Moyers

WCOY/FM
Frequency 99.5
Format: Country
329 Maine St., Quincy, IL 62301
Phone: (217) 224-4102 / FAX: (217) 224-4133
Website: www.wcoy.com
General Manager: Mike Moyers

WGEM/AM
Frequency 1440
Format: Sports/ESPN
513 Hampshire, Quincy, IL 62301
Phone: (217) 228-6600 / FAX: (217) 228-6670
Website: www.wgem.com
General Manager: Carlos Fernandez

WGEM/FM
Frequency 105.1
Format: News/ABC
513 Hampshire, Quincy, IL 62301
Phone: (217) 228-6600 / FAX: (217) 228-6670
Website: www.wgem.com
General Manager: Carlos Fernandez

WLIQ/AM
Frequency 1530
Format: Classic Country
PO Box 711, 119 N. Third, Hannibal 63401
Phone: (573) 221-3450 / FAX: (573) 221-5331
General Manager: Dave Greene

WQCY/FM
Frequency 103.9
Format: Classic Rock / Blues
329 Maine St., Quincy, IL 62301
Phone: (217) 224-4102 / FAX: (217) 224-4133
Website: www.1039thfox.com
General Manager: Mike Moyers

WTAD/AM
Frequency 930
Format: News/Talk
329 Maine St., Quincy, IL 62301
Phone: (217) 224-4102 / FAX: (217) 224-4133
Website: www.wtad.com
General Manager: Mike Moyers

Hollister
KTRI/FM
Frequency 95.9
Format: Branson Info/Talk
118 State Dr., Hollister 65672
Phone: (417) 332-1099 / FAX: (417) 339-4072
General Manager: Larry Pittmann

Jackson
KJXX/AM/FM
Frequency 1170 & 92.3
Format: Adult Standards (Simulcast)
PO Box 558, 901 S. Kingshighway, Cape Girardeau 63702
Phone: (573) 339-7000 / FAX: (573) 651-4100
General Manager: Rick Lambert

Jefferson City
KATI/FM
Frequency 94.3
Format: Country
3109 S. Ten Mile Dr., Jefferson City 65109
Phone: (573) 893-5696 / FAX: (573) 893-4137
Website: www.kat943.com
General Manager: Carla Leible

KJLU/FM
Frequency 88.9
Format: Jazz - Lincoln University
1004 E. Dunklin St., Jefferson City 65101
Phone: (573) 681-5301 / FAX: (573) 681-5299
General Manager: Mike Downey

KJMO/FM
Frequency 97.5
Format: Oldies
1002 Diamondridge, Ste. 400, Jefferson City 65109
Phone: (573) 893-5100 / FAX: (573) 893-8330
General Manager: Phillip Lewis

KLIK/AM
Frequency 1240
Format: News/Talk
1002 Diamondridge, Ste. 400, Jefferson City 65109
Phone: (573) 893-5100 / FAX: (573) 893-8330
General Manager: Phillip Lewis

KMCV/FM
Frequency 89.9, 1590, 106.3, 104.3
Format: Christian Talk, News & Information (Bott)
10550 Barkley, Overland Park, KS 66212
Phone: (913) 642-7770 / FAX: (913) 642-1319
Website: www.bottradionetwork.com
General Manager: Richard Bott

KWOS/AM/FM
Frequency 950 & 100.9
Format: News/Talk
3109 S. Ten Mile Dr., Jefferson City 65109
Phone: (573) 893-5696 / FAX: (573) 893-4137
Website: www.kwos.com
General Manager: Carla Leible

KZJF/FM
Frequency 104.1
Format: Sports
1002 Diamondridge, Ste. 400, Jefferson City 65109
Phone: (573) 893-5100 / FAX: (573) 893-8330
General Manager: Phillip Lewis

Joplin
KBTN/AM/FM
Frequency 1420 & 99.7
Format: Classic Country
2510 W. 20th, Joplin 64804
Phone: (417) 781-1313 / FAX: (417) 781-1316
Website: www.kbtnradio.com
General Manager: George DeMarco

KCAR/FM
Frequency 104.3
Format: Hot AC
2510 W. 20th, Joplin 64804
Phone: (417) 781-1313 / FAX: (417) 781-1316
Website: *www.star1043joplin.com*
General Manager: George DeMarco

KDMO/AM
Frequency 1490
Format: Nostalgia
PO Box 426, 221 E. Fourth, Carthage 64836
Phone: (417) 358-2648 / FAX: (417) 358-1278
Website: *www.951mikefm.com*
General Manager: Ronald L. Petersen Sr.

KIXQ/FM
Frequency 102.5
Format: Rock
2702 E. 32nd St., Joplin 64804
Phone: (417) 624-1025 / FAX: (417) 781-6842
Website: *www.kix1025.com*
General Manager: Larry Boyd

KJMK/FM
Frequency 93.9
Format: Classic Hits
2702 E. 32nd St., Joplin 64804
Phone: (417) 624-1025 / FAX: (417) 781-6842
General Manager: Larry Boyd

KJML/FM
Frequency 107.1
Format: Rock
2510 W. 20th, Joplin 64804
Phone: (417) 781-1313 / FAX: (417) 781-1316
Website: *www.rock1071.com*
General Manager: George DeMarco

KKLL/AM
Frequency 1100
Format: Country Gospel/Christian (New Life)
831 Moffet, Joplin 64804
Phone: (314) 421-3020 / FAX: (314) 421-1702
Website: *www.hereshelpnet.org*
General Manager: Nathan First

KMOQ/FM
Frequency 105.3
Format: Christian Contemporary
2510 W. 20th, Joplin 64804
Phone: (417) 781-1313 / FAX: (417) 781-1316
Website: *www.mynewliferadio.com*
General Manager: George DeMarco

KMXL/FM
Frequency 95.1
Format: Adult Hits
PO Box 426, 221 E. Fourth, Carthage 64836
Phone: (417) 358-2648 / FAX: (417) 358-1278
Website: *www.951mikefm.com*
General Manager: Ronald L. Petersen Sr.

KQYX/AM
Frequency 1450
Format: Gospel
2510 W. 20th, Joplin 64804
Phone: (417) 781-1313 / FAX: (417) 781-1316
General Manager: George DeMarco

KRPS/FM
Frequency 89.9
Format: Variety (Pittsburg State)
PO Box 599, Pittsburg, KS 66762
Phone: (620) 235-4288
General Manager: Missi Kelly

KSYN/FM
Frequency 92.5
Format: CHR/Top 40
2702 E. 32nd St., Joplin 64804
Phone: (417) 624-1025 / FAX: (417) 781-6842
Website: *www.ksyn925.com*
General Manager: Larry Boyd

KXDG/FM
Frequency 97.9
Format: Classic Rock
2702 E. 32nd St., Joplin 64804
Phone: (417) 624-1025 / FAX: (417) 781-6842
Website: *www.bigdog979.com*
General Manager: Larry Boyd

KXMS/FM
Frequency 88.7
Format: Classical/BSN
3950 E. Newman Rd., Joplin 64801-1595
Phone: (417) 625-9678
General Manager: Jeff Skibbe

KZRG/AM/FM
Frequency 1310 & 102.9
Format: News/Talk
2702 E. 32nd St., Joplin 64804
Phone: (417) 624-1025 / FAX: (417) 781-6842
Website: *www.newstalkkzrg.com*
General Manager: Larry Boyd

KZYM/AM
Frequency 1230
Format: News/Talk
2702 E. 32nd St., Joplin 64804
Phone: (417) 624-1025 / FAX: (417) 781-6842
General Manager: Larry Boyd

Kansas City

KBEQ/FM
Frequency 104.3
Format: Country
508 Westport Rd., Ste. 202, Kansas City 64111
Phone: (816) 753-4000 / FAX: (816) 531-2250
Website: *www.q104kc.com*
General Manager: Marc Harrell

KCCV/AM/FM
Frequency 760 & 92.3
Format: Christian Talk, News & Information (Bott)
10550 Barkley, Overland Park, KS 66212
Phone: (913) 642-7770 / FAX: (913) 642-1319
Website: *www.bottradionetwork.com*
General Manager: Richard Bott

KCFX/FM
Frequency 101.1
Format: Classic Rock
5800 Foxridge Dr. #600, Mission, KS 66202
Phone: (913) 514-3000 / FAX: (913) 514-3002
Website: *www.cumulus.com / www.101thefox.net*
General Manager: Donna Baker

KCHZ/FM
Frequency 95.7
Format: Rhythmic CHR
5800 Foxridge Dr. #600, Mission, KS 66202
Phone: (913) 514-3000 / FAX: (913) 514-3002
Website: *www.cumulus.com / www.957thevibe.com*
General Manager: Donna Baker

KCJK/FM
Frequency 105.1
Format: AC
5800 Foxridge Dr. #600, Mission, KS 66202
Phone: (913) 514-3000 / FAX: (913) 514-3002
Website: *www.cumulus.com / www.1051jackfm.com*
General Manager: Donna Baker

KCKC/FM
Frequency 102.1
Format: Adult Hits
508 Westport Rd., Ste. 202, Kansas City 64111
Phone: (816) 753-4000 / FAX: (816) 531-2250
Website: *www.kc1021.com*
General Manager: Marc Harrell

KCMO/AM/FM
Frequency 710 & 103.7
Format: News/Talk (Simulcast)
5800 Foxridge Dr. #600, Mission, KS 66202
Phone: (913) 514-3000 / FAX: (913) 514-3002
General Manager: Donna Baker

KCMO/FM
Frequency 94.9
Format: Greatest Hits
5800 Foxridge Dr. #600, Mission, KS 66202
Phone: (913) 514-3000 / FAX: (913) 514-3002
Website: *www.cumulus.com / www.949kcmo.com*
General Manager: Donna Baker

KCMO/FM-HD2
Frequency 102.5
Format: Country
5800 Foxridge Dr. #600, Mission, KS 66202
Phone: (913) 514-3000 / FAX: (913) 514-3002
General Manager: Donna Baker

KCSP/AM
Frequency 610
Format: Sports/Talk
7000 Squibb Rd., Mission, KS 66219
Phone: (913) 744-3600 / FAX: (913) 744-3700
Website: *www.610sports.com*
General Manager: Dave Alpert

KCTE/AM
Frequency 1510
Format: ESPN
6721 W. 121st St., Leawood, KS 66209
Phone: (913) 344-1500 / FAX: (913) 344-1599
Website: *www.1510.com*
General Manager: Chad Boeger

KCUR/FM
Frequency 89.3
Format: Public Radio
4825 Troost #202, Kansas City 64114
Phone: (816) 235-1551 / FAX: (816) 235-2864
Website: *www.kcur.org*
General Manager: Nico Leone

KCWJ/AM
Frequency 1030
Format: Religious
18920 E. Valleyview Parkway, Independence 64055
Phone: (816) 795-6826 / FAX: (816) 795- 8565
Website: *www.kcwj.com*
General Manager: Ken Ball

KCZZ/AM
Frequency 1480
Format: Hispanic Christian
1701 S. 55th St., Kansas City 66106
Phone: (913) 287-1480 / FAX: (913) 287-5881
General Manager: Diana Reyes Raymer

KDTD/AM
Frequency 1340
Format: Regional Mexican
1701 S. 55th St., Kansas City 66106
Phone: (913) 287-1480 / FAX: (913) 287-5881
Website: *www.lagrand1340kc.com*
General Manager: Diana Reyes Raymer

KFKF/FM
Frequency 94.1
Format: Country
508 Westport Rd., Ste. 202, Kansas City 64111
Phone: (816) 753-4000 / FAX: (816) 531-2250
Website: *www.kfkf.com*
General Manager: Marc Harrell

KJNW-FM
Frequency 88.5
Format: Contemporary Christian
8717 W. 110th St., #480, Overland Park, KS 66210
Phone: (913) 451-8850 / FAX: (913) 451-5733
Website: *www.life885.com*
General Manager: Dave Gordon

KKFI/FM
Frequency 90.1
Format: Community/Jazz/Blues
3901 Main St., Kansas City 64108
Phone: (816) 931-3122 / FAX: (816) 931-7078
General Manager: Barry Lee

KKLO/AM
Frequency 1410
Format: News/Talk
6481 Muncie Rd., Leavenworth, KS 66048
Phone: (913) 651-1410
General Manager: R.C. Amer

KMBZ/AM/FM
Frequency 980 & 98.1
Format: News/Talk
7000 Squibb Rd., Mission, KS 66219
Phone: (913) 744-3600 / FAX: (913) 744-3700
Website: *www.kmbz.com*
General Manager: Dave Alpert

KMJK/FM
Frequency 107.3
Format: Urban AC
5800 Foxridge Dr. #600, Mission, KS 66202
Phone: (913) 514-3000 / FAX: (913) 514-3002
Website: *www.magic1703.com*
General Manager: Donna Baker

KMXV/FM
Frequency 93.3
Format: Top 40
508 Westport Rd., Ste. 202, Kansas City 64111
Phone: (816) 753-4000 / FAX: (816) 531-2250
Website: *www.mix93.com*
General Manager: Marc Harrell

KPRS/FM
Frequency 103.3
Format: Urban
11131 Colorado Ave., Kansas City 64137
Phone: (816) 763-2040 / FAX: (816) 966-1055
Website: *www.kprs.com*
General Manager: Michael Carter

KPRT/AM
Frequency 1590
Format: Gospel
11131 Colorado Ave., Kansas City 64137
Phone: (816) 763-2040 / FAX: (816) 966-1055
Website: *www.kprt.com*
General Manager: Michael Carter

KQRC/FM
Frequency 98.9
Format: Active Rock
7000 Squibb Rd., Mission, KS 66219
Phone: (913) 744-3600 / FAX: (913) 744-3700
Website: *www.989therock.com*
General Manager: Dave Alpert

KRBZ/FM
Frequency 96.5
Format: Alternative
7000 Squibb Rd., Mission, KS 66219
Phone: (913) 744-3600 / FAX: (913) 744-3700
Website: *www.965thebuzz.com*
General Manager: Dave Alpert

KWOD/AM
Frequency 1660
Format: Business/Talk
7000 Squibb Rd., Mission, KS 66219
Phone: (913) 744-3600 / FAX: (913) 744-3700
General Manager: Dave Alpert

KYYS/AM
Frequency 1480
Format: Mexican Hit
1701 S. 55th St., Kansas City 66106
Phone: (913) 287-1480 / FAX: (913) 287-5881
General Manager: Diana Reyes Raymer

KZPT/FM
Frequency 99.7
Format: Adult Hits
7000 Squibb Rd., Mission, KS 66219
Phone: (913) 744-3600 / FAX: (913) 744-3700
Website: www.997thepoint.com
General Manager: Dave Alpert

WDAF/FM
Frequency 106.5
Format: Country
7000 Squibb Rd., Mission, KS 66219
Phone: (913) 744-3600 / FAX: (913) 744-3700
Website: www.1065thewolf.com
General Manager: Dave Alpert

WHB/AM
Frequency 810
Format: Sports
6721 W. 121st St., Overland Park, KS 66209
Phone: (913) 344-1500 / FAX: (913) 314-1599
Website: www.810whb.com
General Manager: Chad Boeger

Kennett

KBOA/AM
Frequency 1540 & 105.5
Format: CNN News & Adult Standards
PO Box 509, 1303 Southwest Dr., Kennett 63857
Phone: (573) 888-4616 / FAX: (573) 888-4890
Website: www.kboaradio.com
General Manager: Perry Jones

KBOA/FM
Frequency 105.5
Format: AC
PO Box 509, Kennett 63857
Phone: (573) 888-4616 / FAX: (573) 888-4890
Website: www.kboaradio.com
General Manager: Perry Jones

KCJS/FM
Frequency 102.5.
Format: Christian
113 S. Side Square, Kennett 63857
Phone: (573) 888-4616
Website: www.calvarychapelkennett.com
General Manager: Dr. Brian Shearer

KTMO/FM
Frequency 106.5
Format: Country
PO Box 509, 1303 Southwest Dr., Kennett 63857
Phone: (573) 888-4616 / FAX: (573) 888-4890
Website: www.ktmoradio.com
General Manager: Perry Jones

KXOQ/FM
Frequency 104.3
Format: Classic Rock
932 County Rd. 448, Poplar Bluff 63901
Phone: (573) 686-3700 / FAX: (573) 686-6116
Website: www.foxradionetwork.com
General Manager: Steven Fuchs

Kirksville

KIRX/AM/FM
Frequency 1450 & 99.7
Format: Oldies/News/Talk (Simulcast)
PO Box 130, 1308 N. Baltimore, Kirksville 63501
Phone: (660) 665-9841 / FAX: (660) 665-0711
Website: www.1450kirx.com
General Manager: Steven Lloyd

KLTE/FM
Frequency 107.9
Format: Christian Talk, News & Information (Bott)
3 Crown Dr., Ste. 100, Kirksville 63501
Phone: (913) 642-7770 / FAX: (913) 642-1319
Website: www.bottradionetwork.com
General Manager: Richard Bott

KRXL/FM
Frequency 94.5
Format: Classic Rock
PO Box 130, 1308 N. Baltimore, Kirksville 63501
Phone: (660) 665-9841 / FAX: (660) 665-0711
Website: www.945thex.com
General Manager: Steven Lloyd

KTRM/FM
Frequency 88.7
Format: Alternative Rock
1217 Barnett Hall, Truman State University, Kirksville 63501
Phone: (660) 785-5876
General Manager: Mark Smith

KTUF/FM
Frequency 93.7
Format: Country
PO Box 130, 1308 N. Baltimore, Kirksville 63501
Phone: (660) 665-9841 / FAX: (660) 665-0711
Website: www.937ktuf.com
General Manager: Steven Lloyd

Lake of the Ozarks

KZWV/FM
Frequency 101.9
Format: Adult Contemporary
1081 Osage Beach Rd., Osage Beach 65065
Phone: (573) 746-7873 / FAX: (573) 746-7874
Website: www.1019thewave.com
General Manager: Carla Leible

Lebanon

KBNN/AM
Frequency 750
Format: Talk
PO Box 1112, 18553 Gentry Rd., Lebanon 65536
Phone: (417) 532-9111 / FAX: (417) 588-4191
Website: www.myozarksonline.com
General Manager: Mike Edwards

KJEL/FM
Frequency 103.7
Format: Country
PO Box 1112, 18553 Gentry Rd., Lebanon 65536
Phone: (417) 532-9111 / FAX: (417) 588-4191
Website: www.myozarksonline.com
General Manager: Mike Edwards

Liberty

KCXL/AM/FM
Frequency 1140 & 102.9
Format: Talk/Oldies
PO Box 620, Liberty 64069-0620
Phone: (816) 792-1140 / FAX: (816) 792-8258
Website: www.kcxl.com
General Manager: Pete Schartel

KCTO/AM
Frequency 1160
Format: Hispanic
PO Box 620, Liberty 64069-0620
Phone: (816) 792-1140 / FAX: (816) 792-8258
General Manager: Pete Schartel

KJFM/FM
Frequency 102.1
Format: Country/Sports
PO Box 438, 615 Georgia St., Lousiana 63353
Phone: (816) 792-1140 / FAX: (816) 792-8258
Website: *www.kjfmeagle102.net*
General Manager: Thom Sanders

Macon

KLTI/AM/FM
Frequency 1560 & 93.3
Format: Classic Country (Simulcast)
32968 U.S. Hwy. 63 S., Macon 63552
Phone: (660) 385-1560 / FAX: (660) 385-7090
Website: *www.kltiradio.com*
General Manager: Dale Palmer

Marble Hill

KMHM/FM
Frequency 104.1
Format: Gospel
Rt. 1, Box 266E, Marble Hill 63764
Phone: (573) 238-1041 / FAX: (573) 238-0104
Website: *www.mysoutherngospel.net*
General Manager: Will Stephens

Marceline

KDWD/FM
Frequency 99.1
Format: Country
109 S. Main St., Marceline 64658
Phone: (660) 376-4991
Website: *www.mycountry991.com*
General Manager: Phillip Malone

Marshall

KMMO/AM/FM
Frequency 1300 & 102.9
Format: Country/CBS (Simulcast)
PO Box 128, Marshall 65340
Phone: (660) 886-7422 / FAX: (660) 886-6291
General Manager: John A. Wilson

KMVC/FM
Frequency 91.7
Format: Alternative
500 E. College St., Missouri Valley College, Marshall 65340
Phone: (660) 831-4193
General Manager: Ken Kujawa

KRLI/FM
Frequency 103.9
Format: Classic Country
102 N. Mason St., Carrollton 64633
Phone: (660) 542-0404 / FAX: (660) 542-0420
General Manager: Miles Carter

Marshfield

KMRF/AM
Frequency 1510
Format: Country Gospel/Christian (New Life)
3208 State St., Hwy. 00, Marshfield 65706
Phone: (417) 468-6188 / FAX: (417) 859-2916
Website: *www.hereshelpnet.org*
General Manager: Nathan First

Maryville

KNIM/AM/FM
Frequency 1580 & 95.9
Format: Country (Simulcast)
PO Box 278, Maryville 64448
Phone: (660) 582-2151 / FAX: (660) 582-3211
Website: *www.nodawaybroadcasting.com*
General Manager: Jim Cronin

KVVL/FM
Frequency 97.1
Format: Rock
PO Box 278, Maryville 64448
Phone: (660) 582-2151 / FAX: (660) 582-3211
Website: *www.nodawaybroadcasting.com*
General Manager: Jim Cronin

KXCV/FM - KRNW/FM
Frequency 90.5 & 88.9 (Chillicothe)
Format: NPR/Classical/Jazz
NWMSU-Wells Hall, 800 University Dr., Maryville 64448
Phone: (660) 562-1163 / FAX: (660) 562-1832
Website: *www.kxcv.org*
General Manager: Rodney Harris

Mexico

KJAB/FM
Frequency 88.3
Format: Southern Gospel
621 W. Monroe, Mexico 65265
Phone: (573) 581-8606 / FAX: (573) 581-9655
Website: *www.kjab.com*
General Manager: Gilbert Humphrey

KWWR/FM
Frequency 95.7
Format: Country
PO Box 475, 1705 E. Liberty St., Mexico 65265-0475
Phone: (573) 581-5500 / FAX: (573) 581-1801
Website: *www.kwwr.com*
General Manager: Michael Daugherty

KXEO/AM
Frequency 1340
Format: News/Info/Soft Rock
PO Box 475, 1705 E. Liberty St., Mexico 65265-0475
Phone: (573) 581-5500 / FAX: (573) 581-1801
Website: *www.kxeo.com*
General Manager: Michael Daugherty

Moberly

KIRK/FM (Macon)
Frequency 99.9
Format: Oldies
300 W. Reed St., Moberly 65270
Phone: (660) 263-1500 / FAX: (660) 263-2300
Website: *www.CentralMoInfo.com*
General Manager: Les Tuttle

KRES/FM
Frequency 104.7
Format: Country
300 W. Reed St., Moberly 65270
Phone: (660) 263-1500 / FAX: (660) 263-2300
Website: *www.CentralMoInfo.com*
General Manager: Les Tuttle

KTCM/FM (Madison)
Frequency 97.3
Format: Christian
300 W. Reed St., Moberly 65270
Phone: (660) 263-1500 / FAX: (660) 263-2300
General Manager: Les Tuttle

KWIX/AM
Frequency 1230
Format: News/Talk
300 W. Reed St., Moberly 65270
Phone: (660) 263-1500 / FAX: (660) 263-2300
Website: *www.CentralMoInfo.com*
General Manager: Les Tuttle

KZZT/FM
Frequency 105.5
Format: Classic Hits
PO Box 128, 1037 County Rd., Moberly 65270
Phone: (660) 263-9390 / FAX: (660) 263-8800
Website: *www.kzztradio.com*
General Manager: Dale Palmer

Monett

KKBL/FM
Frequency 95.9
Format: AC
PO Box 109, 1569 N. Central Ave., Monett 65708
Phone: (800) 928-5253 / FAX: (417) 235-6388
General Manager: Janet Gandy

KRMO/AM
Frequency 990
Format: Agriculture/Sports
PO Box 109, 1569 N. Central Ave., Monett 65708
Phone: (417) 235-6041 / FAX: (417) 235-6388
General Manager: Janet Gandy

Montgomery City

KMCR/FM
Frequency 103.9
Format: AC
205 E. Norman, Montgomery City 63361
Phone: (573) 564-2275 / FAX: (573) 564-8087
Website: *www.kmcrradio.com*
General Manager: Dale Palmer

Mountain Grove

KELE/AM
Frequency 1360
Format: Talk/Westwood One
800 N. Hubbard, Mountain Grove 65711
Phone: (417) 926-4650 / FAX: (417) 926-7604
Website: *www.925thegrove.com*
General Manager: Tracy O'Quinn

KELE/FM
Frequency 92.5
Format: Country
800 N. Hubbard, Mountain Grove 65711
Phone: (417) 926-4650 / FAX: (417) 926-7604
Website: *www.925thegrove.com*
General Manager: Tracy O'Quinn

Neosho

KNEO/FM
Frequency 91.7
Format: Preaching/Teaching
10827 E. Hwy. 86, Neosho 64850
Phone: (417) 451-5636
Website: *www.kneo.org*
General Manager: Mark Taylor

Nevada

KNEM-AM/KNMO-FM
Frequency 1240 & 97.5
Format: Country (Simulcast)
414 E. Walnut, Nevada 64772
Phone: (417) 667-3113 / FAX: (417) 667-9797
Website: *www.knemknmo.com*
General Manager: Mike Harbit

New Bloomfield

KNLG/FM
Frequency 90.3
Format: Country Gospel/Christian (New Life)
9810 State Rd. AE, New Bloomfield 65063
Phone: (314) 421-3020
Website: *www.hereshelpnet.org*
General Manager: Nathan First

Oran

KCGR/FM
Frequency 103.3
Format: Christian Talk, News & Information (Bott)
10550 Barkley, Overland Park, KS 66212
Phone: (913) 642-7770 / FAX: (913) 642-1319
Website: *www.bottradionetwork.com*
General Manager: Richard Bott

Park Hills

KDBB/FM
Frequency 104.3
Format: Rock
PO Box 36, 804 St. Joe Dr., Park Hills 63601
Phone: (573) 431-2000 / FAX: (573) 431-0850
Website: *www.b104fm.com*
General Manager: Larry Joseph

KFMO/AM
Frequency 1240
Format: News/Sports/Talk
PO Box 36, 804 St. Joe Dr., Park Hills 63601
Phone: (573) 431-2000 / FAX: (573) 431-0850
Website: *www.kfmo.com*
General Manager: Larry Joseph

Piedmont

KPWB/AM/FM
Frequency 1140 & 104.9
Format: Country (Simulcast)
900 E. Karsh Blvd., Farmington
Phone: (573) 701-9590 / FAX: (573) 701-9696
General Manager: Fred Dockins

Poplar Bluff

KAHR/FM
Frequency 96.7
Format: Adult Hits
932 County Rd. 448, Poplar Bluff 63901
Phone: (573) 686-3700 / FAX: (573) 686-6116
Website: *www.foxradionetwork.com*
General Manager: Steven Fuchs

KFEB/FM
Frequency 107.5
Format: CHR
932 County Rd. 448, Poplar Bluff 63901
Phone: (573) 686-3700 / FAX: (573) 686-6116
Website: *www.foxradionetwork.com*
General Manager: Steven Fuchs

KJEZ/FM
Frequency 95.5
Format: Rock
1015 W. Pine St., Poplar Bluff 63901
Phone: (573) 785-0881 / FAX: (573) 785-0646
General Manager: John Rice

KKLR/FM
Frequency 94.5
Format: Hot New Country
1015 W. Pine St., Poplar Bluff 63901
Phone: (573) 785-0881 / FAX: (573) 785-0646
General Manager: John Rice

KLID/AM
Frequency 1340
Format: Oldies/Talk
102 N. 11th St., Poplar Bluff 63901
Phone: (573) 686-1600 / FAX: (573) 686-2560
Website: *www.klidradio.com*
General Manager: Dolores (Sunny) Skidmore

KLUH/FM
Frequency 90.3
Format: Contemporary Christian
PO Box 1313, 1165 County Rd. 307, Poplar Bluff 63902
Phone: (573) 686-1663 / FAX: (573) 686-7703
Website: *www.dcmliferadio.org*
General Manager: David Craig

KPPL/FM
Frequency 92.5
Format: Hot Country
932 County Rd. 448, Poplar Bluff 63901
Phone: (573) 686-3700 / FAX: (573) 686-6116
Website: *www.foxradionetwork.com*
General Manager: Steven Fuchs

KWOC/AM
Frequency 930
Format: News/Talk
1015 W. Pine St., Poplar Bluff 63901
Phone: (573) 785-0881 / FAX: (573) 785-0646
General Manager: John Rice

Portageville

KMIS/AM
Frequency 1050
Format: Fox Sports
PO Box 509, 1303 Southwest Dr., Kennett 63857
Phone: (573) 888-4616 / FAX: (573) 888-4890
Website: *www.sportsradiokmis.com*
General Manager: Perry Jones

Potosi

KNLP/FM
Frequency 89.7
Format: Country Gospel/Christian (New Life)
10057 Jagar Rd., Mineral Point 63660
Phone: (573) 438-8201 / FAX: (573) 438-6267
Website: *www.hereshelpnet.org*
General Manager: Nathan First

Richmond

KAYX-FM/KLEX-AM
Frequency 92.5 & 1570
Format: Christian Talk, News & Info (Bott) (Simulcast)
10550 Barkley, Overland Park, KS 66212
Phone: (913) 642-7770 / FAX: (913) 642-1319
Website: *www.bottradionetwork.com*
General Manager: Richard Bott

Rolla

KDAA/FM
Frequency 103.1
Format: Classic Hits
PO Box 727, Rolla 65402
Phone: (573) 364-2525 / FAX: (573) 364-5161
General Manager: Mike Thompson

KMNR/FM
Frequency 89.7
Format: Free Format
218 Havner Center, University Dr., Rolla 65049-1440
Phone: (573) 341-4272
Website: *www.kmnr.org*
General Manager: Dr. Jeff Schramm

KTTR/AM/FM
Frequency 1490 & 99.7
Format: News/Talk/Sports (Simulcast)
PO Box 727, Rolla 65402
Phone: (573) 364-2525 / FAX: (573) 364-5161
General Manager: Mike Thompson

KUMR/FM
Frequency 104.5
Format: Adult Contemporary
1051 Kingshighway, Ste. 5, Rolla 65401
Phone: (573) 308-1045 / FAX: (573) 341-3443
General Manager: Kerri Glensky

KXMO/FM
Frequency 95.3
Format: Oldies
PO Box 727, Rolla 65402
Phone: (573) 364-2525 / FAX: (573) 364-5161
General Manager: Mike Thompson

KZNN/FM
Frequency 105.3
Format: Country
PO Box 727, Rolla 65402
Phone: (573) 364-2525 / FAX: (573) 364-5161
General Manager: Mike Thompson

KMST/FM
Frequency 88.5 & 96.3
Format: Public Radio (Simulcast)
400 W. 14th St., G-6 Library, Rolla 65409
Phone: (573) 341-4386 / FAX: (573) 341-4889
Website: *www.kmst.org*
General Manager: Wayne Bledsoe

Salem

KSMO/AM
Frequency 1340
Format: News/Sports/Country
800 S. Main, Salem 65560
Phone: (573) 729-6117 / FAX: (573) 729-7337
Website: *www.ksmoradio.com*
General Manager: Stanley M. Podorski

Sedalia

KSDL/FM
Frequency 92.3
Format: (BOB) Waitt Radio
2209 S. Limit, Sedalia 65301
Phone: (660) 826-1050 / FAX: (660) 827-5072
Website: *www.923bobfm.com*
General Manager: Mike Jenkins

KSIS/AM
Frequency 1050
Format: News/Talk
2209 S. Limit, Sedalia 65301
Phone: (660) 826-1050 / FAX: (660) 827-5072
Website: *www.ksisradio.com*
General Manager: Mike Jenkins

KXKX/FM
Frequency 105.7
Format: Country
2209 S. Limit, Sedalia 65301
Phone: (660) 826-1050 / FAX: (660) 827-5072
Website: *www.kxkx.com*
General Manager: Mike Jenkins

Sikeston

KBHI/FM
Frequency 107.1
Format: Variety
125 S. Kingshighway, Sikeston 63801
Phone: (573) 471-2000 / FAX: (573) 471-8525
General Manager: Rick Lambert

KBXB/FM
Frequency 97.9
Format: Country
125 S. Kingshighway, Sikeston 63801
Phone: (573) 471-2000 / FAX: (573) 471-8525
General Manager: Rick Lambert

KRHW/AM/FM
Frequency 1520
Format: Classic Country (Simulcast)
125 S. Kingshighway, Sikeston 63801
Phone: (573) 471-2000 / FAX: (573) 471-8525
General Manager: Rick Lambert

Springfield

KADI/AM
Frequency 1340
Format: News/Talk
5431 W. Sunshine, Brookline Station 65619
Phone: (417) 831-0995 / FAX: (417) 831-4026
Website: *www.1340bigtalker.com/contact*
General Manager: R.C. Amer

KADI/FM
Frequency 99.5
Format: Contemporary Christian
5431 W. Sunshine, Brookline Station 65619
Phone: (417) 831-0995 / FAX: (417) 831-4026
Website: *www.99hitfm.com*
General Manager: R.C. Amer

KBFL/AM/FM
Frequency 1060 & 99.9
Format: Music Of Your Life & Smooth Jazz
3000 E. Chestnut Expressway, Springfield 65802
Phone: (417) 862-3990 / FAX: (417) 869-7675
Website: *www.radiospringfield.com*
General Manager: Kenneth E. Meyer

KGBX/FM
Frequency 105.9
Format: AC
1856 S. Glenstone, Springfield 65804
Phone: (417) 890-5555 / FAX: (417) 890-5050
Website: *www.kgbx.com*
General Manager: Keith Liesmann

KGMY/AM
Frequency 1400
Format: Fox Sports
1856 S. Glenstone, Springfield 65804
Phone: (417) 890-5555 / FAX: (417) 890-5050
Website: *www.espn1400.com*
General Manager: Keith Liesmann

KKLH/FM
Frequency 104.7
Format: Classic Rock
2453 E. Elm St., Springfield 65802
Phone: (417) 886-5677 / FAX: (417) 886-2155
Website: *www.1047thecave.com*
General Manager: Jason McCutchin

KOMG/FM
Frequency 105.1
Format: Classic Country
2453 E. Elm St., Springfield 65802
Phone: (417) 886-5677 / FAX: (417) 886-2155
Website: *www.105bobfm.com*
General Manager: Jason McCutchin

KOSP/FM
Frequency 92.9
Format: Rhythmic Top 40
2453 E. Elm St., Springfield 65802
Phone: (417) 886-5677 / FAX: (417) 886-2155
Website: *www.929thebeat.com*
General Manager: Jason McCutchin

KQRA/FM
Frequency 102.1
Format: New Rock
2453 E. Elm St., Springfield 65802
Phone: (417) 886-5677 / FAX: (417) 886-2155
Website: *www.q1021.fm*
General Manager: Jason McCutchin

KRVI/FM
Frequency 106.7
Format: AC/Variety
2330 W. Grand, Springfield 65802
Phone: (417) 865-6614 / FAX: (417) 865-9643
Website: *www.journalbroadcastgroup.com*
General Manager: Rex Hansen

KSCV/FM
Frequency 90.1, 92.3, 94.1, 103.9, 104.5, 107.3, 95.7, 103.3, 104.9, 103.3, 104.7, 98.3
Format: Christian Talk, News & Information (Bott)
1111 S. Glenstone Ave., Ste. 3-102, Springfield 65804
Phone: (417) 864-0901 / FAX: (417) 862-7263
Website: *www.bottradionetwork.com*
General Manager: Paul Schneider

KSGF/AM/FM
Frequency 1260 & 104.1
Format: News / Talk (Simulcast) (Journal)
2330 W. Grand, Springfield 65802
Phone: (417) 865-6614 / FAX: (417) 865-9643
Website: *www.ksgf.com*
General Manager: Rex Hansen

KSMU/FM
Frequency 91.1
Format: NPR/News/Classical Music
901 S. National, Springfield 65897
Phone: (417) 836-5878 / FAX: (417) 836-5889
Website: *www.ksmu.org*
General Manager: Tammy Wiley

KSPW/FM
Frequency 96.5
Format: CHR
2330 W. Grand, Springfield 65802
Phone: (417) 865-6614 / FAX: (417) 865-9643
Website: *www.power965.com*
General Manager: Rex Hansen

KSWF/FM
Frequency 100.5
Format: Country
1856 S. Glenstone, Springfield 65804
Phone: (417) 890-5555 / FAX: (417) 890-5050
Website: *www.1005thewolf.com*
General Manager: Kieth Liesmann

KTOZ/FM
Frequency 95.5
Format: Adult Hits
1856 S. Glenstone, Springfield 65804
Phone: (417) 890-5555 / FAX: (417) 890-5050
Website: *www.alice955.com*
General Manager: Keith Liesmann

KTTS/FM
Frequency 94.7
Format: Today's Country
2330 W. Grand, Springfield 65802
Phone: (417) 865-6614 / FAX: (417) 865-9643
Website: *www.ktts.com*
General Manager: Rex Hansen

KTXR/FM
Frequency 101.3
Format: Greatest Hits
3000 E. Chestnut Expressway, Springfield 65802
Phone: (417) 862-3751 / FAX: (417) 869-7675
Website: *www.ktxrfm.com*
General Manager: Kenneth E. Meyer

KWFC/FM
Frequency 89.1
Format: Southern Gospel
2550-100 S. Campbell, Springfield 65807
Phone: (417) 889-0883 / FAX: (417) 866-8656
Website: *www.kwfc.org*
General Manager: Chalmer Harper

KWND/FM
Frequency 88.3
Format: Contemporary Christian
2550-100 S. Campbell, Springfield 65807
Phone: (417) 819-0883 / FAX: (417) 886-8656
Website: *www.88.3thewindfm.com*
General Manager: Chalmer Harper

KWTO/AM
Frequency 560
Format: ESPN
3000 E. Chestnut Expressway, Springfield 65802
Phone: (417) 862-3990 / FAX: (417) 869-7675
Website: *www.jock987.com*
General Manager: Kenneth E. Meyer

KWTO/FM
Frequency 98.7
Format: Sports/Talk
3000 E. Chestnut Expressway, Springfield 65802
Phone: (417) 862-3751 / FAX: (417) 869-7675
Website: *www.radiospringfield.com*
General Manager: Kenneth E. Meyer

KXUS/FM
Frequency 97.3
Format: Classic Rock
1856 S. Glenstone, Springfield 65804
Phone: (417) 890-5555 / FAX: (417) 890-5050
Website: *www.us97.com*
General Manager: Keith Liesmann

St. Joseph

KESJ/AM
Frequency 1550
Format: ESPN
PO Box 8550, 4104 Country Ln., St. Joseph 64506
Phone: (816) 233-8881 / FAX: (816) 279-8280
General Manager: Gary Exline

KFEQ/AM
Frequency 680
Format: News/Talk/Agriculture
PO Box 8550, 4104 Country Ln., St. Joseph 64506
Phone: (816) 233-8881 / FAX: (816) 279-8280
General Manager: Gary Exline

KJCV/FM
Frequency 89.7, 88.9 & 101.5
Format: Christian Talk, News & Information (Bott)
3401 42nd St., St. Joseph 64501
Phone: (913) 642-7600 / FAX: (913) 642-2424
Website: *www.bottradionetwork.com*
General Manager: Richard Bott

KKJO/FM
Frequency 105.5
Format: Adult Top 40
PO Box 8550, 4104 Country Ln., St. Joseph 64506
Phone: (816) 233-8881 / FAX: (816) 279-8280
General Manager: Gary Exline

KSJQ/FM
Frequency 92.7
Format: Modern Country
PO Box 8550, 4104 Country Ln., St. Joseph 64506
Phone: (816) 233-8881 / FAX: (816) 279-8280
General Manager: Gary Exline

St. Louis

KATZ/AM
Frequency 1600
Format: Contemporary/Traditional Gospel
1001 Highlands Plaza Dr. W., Ste. 100, St. Louis 63110
Phone: (314) 333-8000 / FAX: (314) 333-8100
Website: *www.hallelujah1600.com*
General Manager: Beth Davis

KBWX/FM
Frequency 100.3
Format: Rhythmic CHR
1001 Highlands Plaza Dr. W., Ste. 100, St. Louis 63110
Phone: (314) 333-8000 / FAX: (314) 333-8100
Website: *www.wild1049stl.com*
General Manager: Beth Davis

KCFV/FM
Frequency 89.5
Format: Rhythmic - STLCC @ Florrisant Valley
3400 Pershall Rd., St. Louis 63135
Phone: (314) 513-4463 / FAX: (314) 513-4217
Website: *www.stlcc.edu/fv/kcfv*
General Manager: Steve Bai

KEZK/FM
Frequency 102.5
Format: AC
1220 Olive St., Third Fl., St. Louis 63103
Phone: (314) 621-2345 / FAX: (314) 444-3298
Website: *www.fresh1025.cbslocal.com*
General Manager: John Sheehan

KFTK/FM
Frequency 97.1
Format: FM Talk
401 S. 18th St., Ste. 100, St. Louis 63103
Phone: (314) 621-0400 / FAX: (314) 621-3000
Website: *www.971talk.com*
General Manager: John Beck

KFUO/AM
Frequency 850
Format: Religious
1333 S. Kirkwood, St. Louis 63122
Phone: (314) 965-9000 / FAX: (314) 996-1123
Website: *www.kfuo.com*
General Manager: Gary Duncan

KLOU/FM
Frequency 103.3
Format: Classic Hits
1001 Highlands Plaza Dr. W., Ste. 100, St. Louis 63110
Phone: (314) 333-8000 / FAX: (314) 333-8100
Website: *www.klou.com*
General Manager: Beth Davis

KMJM/FM
Frequency 104.9
Format: Hip Hop/R&B
1001 Highlands Plaza Dr. W., Ste. 100, St. Louis 63110
Phone: (314) 333-8000 / FAX: (314) 333-8100
Website: *www.kmjm.com*
General Manager: Beth Davis

KMOX/AM
Frequency 1120
Format: News/Talk/Sports
1220 Olive St., St. Louis 63103
Phone: (314) 621-2345 / FAX: (314) 444-3298
Website: *www.kmox.com*
General Manager: John Sheehan

KNOU/FM
Frequency 96.3
Format: Classic Hits
401 S. 18th St., Ste. 100, St. Louis 63103
Phone: (314) 621-0400 / FAX: (314) 621-3000
Website: *www.k-hits.com*
General Manager: John Beck

KPNT/FM
Frequency 105.7
Format: Alternative Rock
401 S. 18th St., Ste. 100, St. Louis 63103
Phone: (314) 231-1057 / FAX: (314) 621-3000
Website: www.1057thepoint.com
General Manager: John Beck

KSD/FM
Frequency 93.7
Format: Country
1001 Highlands Plaza Dr. W., Ste. 100, St. Louis 63110
Phone: (314) 333-8000 / FAX: (314) 333-8300
Website: www.937thebull.com
General Manager: Beth Davis

KSHE/FM
Frequency 94.7
Format: AOR / Rock
401 S. 18th St., Ste. 100, St. Louis 63103
Phone: (314) 621-0400 / FAX: (314) 621-3000
Website: www.kshe95.com
General Manager: John Beck

KSIV/AM/FM
Frequency 1320 & 91.5
Format: Christian Talk, News & Information (Bott)
1750 S. Brentwood Blvd., Ste. 811, St. Louis 63144
Phone: (314) 961-1320 / FAX: (314) 961-7562
Website: www.bottradionetwork.com
General Manager: Fred Zielonko

KSLZ/FM
Frequency 107.7
Format: CHR
1001 Highlands Plaza Dr. W., Ste. 100, St. Louis 63110
Phone: (314) 333-8000 / FAX: (314) 333-8300
Website: www.z1077.com
General Manager: Beth Davis

KTRS/AM
Frequency 550
Format: Talk/ABC
638 W. Port Plaza, St. Louis 63146
Phone: (314) 453-5500 / FAX: (314) 453-9704
Website: www.ktrs.com
General Manager: Mark Dorsey

KWMU/FM
Frequency 90.7
Format: NPR
3651 Olive St., St. Louis 63108
Phone: (314) 516-5968 / FAX: (314) 516-5993
Website: www.stlpublicradio.org
General Manager: Tim Eby

KXEN/AM
Frequency 1010
Format: Religious Talk
5615 Pershing Ave., Ste. 12, St. Louis 63112
Phone: (314) 454-0400 / FAX: (314) 448-4999
Website: www.kxen1010am.com
General Manager: Dirk Hallemeier

KYKY/FM
Frequency 98.1
Format: Hot AC
1200 Olive St., Third Fl., St. Louis 63103
Website: www.y98.com
Phone: (314) 621-2345 / FAX: (314) 444-3298
General Manager: John Sheehan

WARH/FM
Frequency 106.5
Format: Adult Hits
11647 Olive Blvd., St. Louis 63141
Phone: (314) 983-6000 / FAX: (314) 994-9447
Website: www.1065thearch.com
General Manager: John Kijowski

WFUN/FM
Frequency 95.5
Format: R&B
9666 Olive Blvd., Ste. 610, St. Louis 63132
Phone: (314) 989-9550 / FAX: (314) 989-9551
Website: www.oldschool955.net
General Manager: Gary Gunter

WGNU/AM
Frequency 920
Format: Sports
5615 Pershing Ave., Ste. 12, St. Louis 63112
Phone: (314) 454-0400 / FAX: (314) 448-4999
Website: www.wgnu920am.com
General Manager: Dirk Hallemeier

WHHL/FM
Frequency 104.1
Format: Hip Hop / R&B
9666 Olive Blvd., Ste. 610, St. Louis 63132
Phone: (314) 989-9550 / FAX: (314) 989-9551
Website: www.hot104stl.com
General Manager: Gary Gunter

WIL/FM
Frequency 92.3
Format: Country
11647 Olive Blvd., St. Louis 63141
Phone: (314) 983-6000 / FAX: (314) 994-9447
Website: www.wil92.com
General Manager: John Kijowski

WXOS/FM
Frequency 101.1
Format: Sports
11647 Olive Blvd., St. Louis 63141
Phone: (314) 983-6000 / FAX: (314) 994-9447
Website: www.101sports.com
General Manager: John Kijowski

St. Robert

KFLW/FM
Frequency 98.9
Format: Hot AC
555 Marshall Dr., St. Robert 65584
Phone: (573) 336-5359 / FAX: (573) 336-7619
Website: www.kflw989.com
General Manager: Tracy O'Quinn

Stockton

KRWP/FM
Frequency 107.7
Format: Classic Hit Country
PO Box 1070, 1225 South St., Ste. B, Stockton 65785
Phone: (417) 276-5253 / FAX: (417) 276-2255
Website: www.krwp1077.com

Thayer

KALM/AM
Frequency 1290
Format: Today's Christian / Solid Gospel
PO Box 15, N. Hwy 63, Thayer 65791
Phone: (417) 264-7211 / FAX: (417) 264-7212
Website: www.am1290thegift.com
General Manager: Robert (Bob) Eckman

KAMS/FM
Frequency 95.1
Format: True Country
PO Box 15, N. Hwy 63, Thayer 65791
Phone: (417) 264-7211 / FAX: (417) 264-7212
Website: www.kkountry.com
General Manager: Robert (Bob) Eckman

Trenton

KGOZ/FM
Frequency 101.7
Format: Hot Country
804 Main, Trenton 64683
Phone: (660) 359-2261 / FAX: (660) 359-4126
Website: *www.kgozfm.com*
General Manager: John Anthony

KTTN/AM
Frequency 1600
Format: Classic Rock
804 Main, Trenton 64683
Phone: (660) 359-2261 / FAX: (660) 359-4126
Website: *www.kttn.com*
General Manager: John Anthony

KTTN/FM
Frequency 92.3
Format: Classic Country
804 Main, Trenton 64683
Phone: (660) 359-2261 / FAX: (660) 359-4126
Website: *www.kttn.com*
General Manager: John Anthony

Van Buren

KBIY/FM
Frequency 91.3
Format: Country Gospel/Christian (New Life)
Rt. 1, Box 92, Van Buren 63965
Phone: (573) 323-8867 / FAX: (573) 323-8041
Website: *www.hereshelpnet.org*
General Manager: Nathan First

Vienna

KNLN/FM
Frequency 90.9
Format: Country Gospel/Christian (New Life)
1411 Locust St., St. Louis 63103
Phone: (314) 881-3200 / FAX: (314) 436-2434
Website: *www.hereshelpnet.org*
General Manager: Nathan First

Warrensburg

KOKO/AM
Frequency 1450
Format: Oldies/Jones
PO Box 398, Warrensburg 64093
Phone: (660) 747-9191 / FAX: (660) 747-5611
Website: *www.warrensburgradio.com*
General Manager: Greg Hassler

KWKJ/FM
Frequency 98.5
Format: Country/Waitt
PO Box 398, Warrensburg 64093
Phone: (660) 747-9191 / FAX: (660) 747-5611
Website: *www.warrensburgradio.com*
General Manager: Greg Hassler

Warrenton

KFAV/FM
Frequency 99.9
Format: Today's Hot Country
1217 N. Hwy. 47, Warrenton 63383
Phone: (636) 377-2300 / FAX: (636) 456-8767
Website: *www.kfav.com*
General Manager: Vern Kaspar

KWRE/AM
Frequency 730
Format: Traditional Country
1217 N. Hwy. 47, Warrenton 63383
Phone: (636) 377-2300 / FAX: (636) 456-8767
Website: *www.kwre.com*
General Manager: Vern Kaspar

Washington

KLPW/AM
Frequency 1220
Format: All Talk
PO Box 623, 6501 Hwy. BB, Washington 63090
Phone: (636) 583-5155 / FAX: (636) 583-1644
Website: *www.klpw.com*
General Manager: Buzze Eckelkamp

Waynesville

KFBD/FM
Frequency 97.9
Format: AC
PO Box D, Waynesville 65583
Phone: (573) 336-4913 / FAX: (573) 336-2222
Website: *www.myozarksonline.com*
General Manager: Mike Edwards

KIIK/FM
Frequency 1270
Format: Sports
PO Box D, Waynesville 65583
Phone: (573) 336-4913 / FAX: (573) 336-2222
Website: *www.myozarksonline.com*
General Manager: Mike Edwards

KJPW/AM
Frequency 1390
Format: News/Talk
PO Box D, Waynesville 65583
Phone: (573) 336-4913 / FAX: (573) 336-2222
Website: *www.myozarksonline.com*
General Manager: Mike Edwards

KOZQ/FM
Frequency 102.3
Format: Classic Rock
PO Box D, Waynesville 65583
Phone: (573) 336-4913 / FAX: (573) 336-2222
General Manager: Mike Edwards

West Plains

KBMV/FM
Frequency 107.1
Format: Contemporary Christian
PO Box 107, #10 Court Square, West Plains 65775
Phone: (417) 255-2548 / FAX: (417) 255-2907
General Manager: Tim Eckman

KHOM/FM
Frequency 100.9
Format: Greatest Hits 60s/70s/80s
PO Box 107, #10 Court Sq., West Plains 65775
Phone: (417) 255-2548 / FAX: (417) 255-2907
General Manager: Tim Eckman

KKDY/FM
Frequency 102.5
Format: Hot Country
983 E. Hwy. 160, West Plains 65775
Phone: (417) 256-1025 / FAX: (417) 256-2208
Website: *www.kkdy.com*
General Manager: Tom Marhefka

KSMW/FM
Frequency 90.3
Format: NPR News/Classical Music
901 S. National, Springfield 65897
Phone: (417) 836-5878 / FAX: (417) 836-5889
Website: *www.ksmu.org*
General Manager: Tammy Wiley

KSPQ/FM
Frequency 93.9
Format: Classic Rock
983 E. Hwy. 160, West Plains 65775
Phone: (417) 256-1025 / FAX: (417) 256-2208
Website: *www.kspq.com*
General Manager: Tom Marhefka

KUKU/FM
Frequency 100.3
Format: Classic Country
983 E. Hwy. 160, West Plains 65755
Phone: (417) 256-1025 / FAX: (417) 256-2208
Website: *www.kuku.com*
General Manager: Tom Marhefka

KUPH/FM
Frequency 96.9
Format: Bright AC
983 E. Hwy. 160, West Plains 65755
Phone: (417) 256-1025 / FAX: (417) 256-2208
Website: *www.thefox969.com*
General Manager: Tom Marhefka

KWPM/AM
Frequency 1330 & 1450
Format: News/Talk
983 E. Hwy. 160, West Plains 65755
Phone: (417) 256-1025 / FAX: (417) 256-2208
Website: *www.ozarknewstalkradio.com*
General Manager: Tom Marhefka

Television Stations

Branson

KBNS-CD (Vacation-Channel)
Channel 38
Affiliate: Visitor/Local Info
225 Violyn St., Branson 65616
Phone: (417) 334-1200 / FAX: (417) 334-5209
Website: *www.tvcbranson.com*
General Manager: Scott Earls

Cape Girardeau

KBSI-TV
Channel 23
Affiliate: FOX
806 Enterprise, Cape Girardeau 63703
Phone: (573) 334-1223 / FAX: (573) 334-1208
Website: *www.kbsi23.com*
General Manager: Ed Groves

KFVS-TV/WQWQ-TV
Channel 12.1, 12.2, 12.3
Affiliate: CBS, CW/MeTV/GRITtv
310 Broadway, Cape Girardeau 6370
Phone: (573) 335-1212 / FAX: (573) 335-6306
Website: *www.kfvs12.com*
General Manager: Dave Thomason

WDKA-TV
Channel 49
Affiliate: myTV
806 Enterprise, Cape Girardeau 63703
Phone: (573) 334-1223 / FAX: (573) 334-1208
General Manager: Ed Groves

Columbia

KMIZ-TV/KZOU-TV
Channel 17.1, 17.2, 17.3, 17.4
Affiliate: ABC, MeTV/myTV/FOX
501 Bus. Loop 70 E., Columbia 65201
Phone: (573) 449-0917 / FAX: (573) 875-7078
Website: *www.abc17news.com*
General Manager: Curtis Varns

KOMU-TV
Channel 8.1, 8.3
Affiliate: NBC, CW
5550 Hwy. 63 S., Columbia 65201
Phone: (573) 882-8888 / FAX: (573) 884-8888
Website: *www.komu.com*
General Manager: Martin (Marty) Siddall

KQFX-TV
Channel 22
Affiliate: FOX
501 Bus. Loop 70 E., Columbia 65201
Phone: (573) 449-0917 / FAX: (573) 875-7078
Website: *www.abc17news.com*
General Manager: Curtis Varns

Hannibal

KHQA-TV
Channel 7.1, 7.2
Affiliate: CBS, ABC
301 S. 36th St., Quincy, IL 62301
Phone: (217) 222-6200 / FAX: (217) 228-4909
Website: *www.ConnectTriStates.com*
General Manager: Laura Wolf

WGEM-TV
Channel 10.1, 10.2, 10.3
Affiliate: NBC, CW, FOX
513 Hampshire St., Quincy, IL 62301
Phone: (217) 228-6600 / FAX: (217) 228-6670
Website: *www.wgem.com*
General Manager: Carlos Fernandez

Jefferson City

KRCG-TV
Channel 13.1, 13.2, 13.3
Affiliate: CBS, GetTV, GritTV
10188 Old U.S. Hwy. 54, New Bloomfield 65063
Phone: (573) 896-5144 / FAX: (573) 896-5193
Website: *www.connectmidmissouri.com*
General Manager: Beth Worsham

Joplin

KFJX-TV
Channel 14
Affiliate: FOX
PO Box 659, 2950 NE Hwy. 69, Pittsburg, KS 66762
Phone: (417) 782-1414 / FAX: (417) 624-3115
Website: *www.fox14tv.com*
General Manager: Darren Dishman

KGCS-TV
Channel 22
Affiliate: Independent
3950 E. Newman Rd., Joplin 64801
Phone: (417) 625-9375 / FAX: (417) 625-9742
Website: *www.mssu.edu/kgcs*
General Manager: Judy Stiles

KOAM-TV
Channel 7
Affiliate: CBS
PO Box 659, 2950 NE Hwy. 69, Pittsburg, KS 66762
Phone: (417) 624-0233 / FAX: (417) 624-3115
Website: *www.koamtv.com*
General Manager: Danny Thomas

KODE-TV
Channel 12
Affiliate: ABC
1502 Cleveland St., Joplin 64802
Phone: (417) 781-2345 / FAX: (417) 782-2417
Website: *www.fourstateshomepage.com*
General Manager: Shirley Morton

KOZJ-TV
Channel 26
Affiliate: PBS
901 S. National, Springfield 65897
Phone: (417) 836-3500 / FAX: (417) 836-3569
Website: *www.optv.org*
General Manager: Tammy Wiley

KSNF-TV
Channel 16
Affiliate: NBC
1502 Cleveland, Joplin 64801
Phone: (417) 781-2345 / FAX: (417) 782-2417
Website: *www.fourstateshomepage.com*
General Manager: John Hoffman

Kansas City

KCPT-TV
Channel 19
Affiliate: PBS
125 E. 31st St., Kansas City 64108
Phone: (816) 756-3580 / FAX: (816) 931-2500
Website: *www.kcpt.org*
General Manager: Kliff Kuehl

KCTV
Channel 5
Affiliate: CBS
4500 Shawnee Mission Parkway, Fairway, KS 66205
Phone: (913) 677-5555 / FAX: (913) 677-7298
Website: *www.kctv5.com*
General Manager: Paul Karpowicz

KCWE-TV
Channel 29.1, 29.2
Affiliate: CW, Movies!
6455 Winchester Ave., Kansas City 64133
Phone: (816) 221.2900 / FAX: (816) 760.9149
Website: *www.kcwe.com*
General Manager: Sarah Smith

KMBC-TV
Channel 9.1, 9.2
Affiliate: ABC, MeTV
6455 Winchester Ave., Kansas City 64133
Phone: (816) 221-9999 / FAX: (816) 221-3633
General Manager: Sarah Smith

KMCI-TV
Channel 38.1, 38.2
Affiliate: Independent, Bounce
4720 Oak St., Kansas City 64112
Phone: (816) 753-4141 / FAX: (816) 932-0761
Website: *www.38thespot.com*
General Manager: Brian Bracco

Kirksville

KTVO-TV
Channel 3.1, 3.2
Affiliate: ABC, CBS
PO Box 949, 15518 U.S. Hwy. 63 N., Kirksville 63501
Phone: (660) 627-3333 / FAX: (660) 627-1885
Website: *www.heartlandconnection.com*
General Manager: Carol Kellum

Poplar Bluff

KPOB-TV
Channel 15
Affiliate: ABC (Satellite of WSIL-TV)
1416 Country Aire Rd., Carterville, IL 62918
Phone: (618) 985-2333 / FAX: (618) 985-3709
General Manager: Steve Wheeler

Springfield

KCZ-TV
Channel 15
Affiliate: CW
999 W. Sunshine, Springfield 65807
Phone: (417) 268-3000 / FAX: (417) 268-3100
Website: *www.ky3.com*
General Manager: Brian McDonough

KOLR-TV
Channel 10
Affiliate: CBS
2650 E. Division St., Springfield 65803
Phone: (417) 862-1010 / FAX: (417) 862-6439
Website: *www.ozarksfirst.com*
General Manager: Leo Henning

KOZK-TV
Channel 21.1, 21.2, 21.3
Affiliate: Ozarks Public Television, PBS, CreateTV
901 S. National, Springfield 65897
Phone: (417) 836-3500 / FAX: (417) 836-3569
Website: *www.optv.org*
General Manager: Tammy Wiley

KOZL-TV
Channel 27
Affiliate: MyNetwork
2650 E. Division St., Springfield 65803
Phone: (417) 862-2727 / FAX: (417) 862-6439
General Manager: Leo Henning

KRBK-TV
Channel 49.1, 49.2
Affiliate: FOX, MeTV
1701 S. Enterprise Dr., Springfield 65804
Phone: (314) 522-0020
General Manager: Paul Windisch

KSPR-TV
Channel 33.1, 33.2
Affiliate: ABC, CW
999 W. Sunshine, Springfield 65807
Phone: (417) 268-3000 / FAX: (417) 268-3100
Website: *www.kspr.com*
General Manager: Brian McDonough

KYTV
Channel 3.1, 3.2, 3.3
Affiliate: NBC, WeatherNation, COZI TV
999 W. Sunshine, Springfield 65807
Phone: (417) 268-3000 / FAX: (417) 268-3360
Website: *www.ky3.com*
General Manager: Brian McDonough

St. Joseph

KBJO-TV
Channel 21
Affiliate: CW
825 Edmonds St., St. Joseph 64501
Phone: (816) 689-2626
General Manager: Eric Bradley

KNPG-TV
Channel 30
Affiliate: Telemundo
825 Edmonds St., St. Joseph 64501
Phone: (816) 689-2626
General Manager: Eric Bradley

KNPN-TV
Channel 26.1, 26.2
Affiliate: FOX, NOW
825 Edmonds St., St. Joseph 64501
Phone: (816) 689-2626
General Manager: Eric Bradley

KQTV
Channel 2
Affiliate: ABC
4000 Faron St., St. Joseph 64508
Phone: (816) 364-2222 / FAX: (816) 364-3787
Website: *www.thestjoechannel.com*
General Manager: Heather Shearin

St. Louis

KETC-TV
Channel 9.1, 9.2, 9.3 & 9.4
Affiliate: PBS, Nine Kids, Nine World, Nine Create
3655 Olive St., St. Louis 63108
Phone: (314) 512-9000 / FAX: (314) 512-9005
Website: *www.ninenet.org*
General Manager: John (Jack) Galamiche III

KMOV-TV
Channel 4.1, 4.2
Affiliate: CBS, MeTV
One S. Memorial Dr., St. Louis 63102
Phone: (314) 621-4444 / FAX: (314) 444-6393
Website: *www.kmov.com*
General Manager: Mike Murphy

KNLC-DT
Channel 24.1, 24.2
Affiliate: New Life
1411 Locust St., St. Louis 63103
Phone: (314) 436-2424 / FAX: (314) 436-2434
Website: *www.knlc.tv*
General Manager: Nathan First

KPLR-TV
Channel 11
Affiliate: CW
2250 Ball Dr., St. Louis 63146
Phone: (314) 213-2222 / FAX: (314) 213-7440
General Manager: Spencer Koch

KSDK-TV
Channel 5.1, 5.2
Affiliate: NBC, Bounce Network
1000 Market St., St. Louis 63101
Phone: (314) 421-5055 / FAX: (314) 444-5263
Website: *www.ksdk.com*
General Manager: Marv Danielski

KTVI-TV
Channel 2
Affiliate: FOX
2250 Ball Dr., St. Louis 63146
Phone: (314) 213-2222 / FAX: (314) 213-7440
Website: *www.fox2now.com*
General Manager: Spencer Koch

WARRENSBURG

KMOS-TV
Channel 6.1, 6.2, 6.3
Affiliate: PBS, Create, MHz Worldview
Wood 11, University of Central Missouri,
Warrensburg 64093
Phone: (660) 543-4155 / FAX: (660) 543-8863
Website: *www.kmos.org*
General Manager: Dr. Phil Hoffman

Capitol Correspondents

These newspaper, radio and television correspondents report on Missouri government from the Capitol. Other media representatives are also assigned by these and other news organizations for special reports.

Associated Press
David Lieb and Summer Ballentine
PO Box 272, Jefferson City 65102
(573) 636-9415
Email: *dlieb@ap.org* and *sballentine@ap.org*

Columbia Daily Tribune
Rudi Keller
101 N. Fourth St., Columbia 65201
(573) 815-1708
Email: *rjkeller@columbiatribune.com*

Jefferson City News Tribune
Bob Watson
PO Box 420, Jefferson City 65102-0420
(573) 761-0245
Email: *bwatson@newstribune.com*

Kansas City Star
Jason Hancock and Steve Kraske
1729 Grand Blvd., Kansas City 64108
(573) 634-3565
Email: *jhancock@kcstar.com* and *skraske@kcstar.com*

KMIZ–TV
Business Loop 70 E., Columbia 65201
(573) 449-1700
Email: *news@kmiz.com*

KOMU–TV
5550 Highway 63 S., Columbia 65211-1200
(573) 884-6397
Email: *news@komu.com*

KRCG–TV
Kermit Miller, Anchor/Reporter
PO Box 659, Jefferson City 65102
(573) 896-5144
Email: *kmiller@krcg.com*

MissouriNet
Mike Lear and Alisa Nelson
505 Hobbs Rd., Jefferson City 65109
(573) 893-2829
Email: *mikelear@missourinet.com* and *anelson@missourinet.com*

Missouri Digital News and KMOX Radio
Phill Brooks
State Capitol Room 118-C, Jefferson City 65101
(573) 882-3619
Email: *prb@mdn.org*

Missouri Times
Scott Faughn and Travis Zimpfer
(573) 429-5770
Email: *scott@themissouritimes.com* and *rachael@themissouritimes.com*

St. Louis Post Dispatch
Alex Stuckey
PO Box 266, Jefferson City 65102
(573) 635-6178
Email: *astuckey@postdispatch.com*

St. Louis Public Radio
Jo Mannies and Jason Rosenbaum
(314) 952-9660 and (573) 356-1755
Email: *jomannies@sbcglobal.net* and *rosenbaumj@umsl.edu*

KWMU
Marshall Griffin
(314) 803-6270
Email: *mgriffin@kwmu.org*

Springfield News-Leader
Jon Swedien
651 Boonville, Springfield 65806
(417) 837-1308
Email: *jswedien@gannet.com*

Libraries in Missouri

A full, searchable library directory is located online at www.sos.mo.gov/MOLLI/home.aspx. Web addresses are listed where available.

Academic Libraries

Aquinas Institute of Theology Library
St. Louis
*http://ai.connectingmembers.com/
resources/aquinaslibrary.aspx*

Assemblies of God Theological Seminary
Cordas C. Burnett Library
Springfield
www.agts.edu/lib/index.html

Avila University
Hooley-Bundschu Library
Kansas City
www.avila.edu/hbl/

Baptist Bible College
G.B. Vick Memorial Library
Springfield
http://library.gobbc.edu/

Barnes-Jewish College of Nursing and Allied Health
Allied Health Library
St. Louis
*www.barnesjewishcollege.edu/
?id=5485&sid=1*

Calvary Bible College & Theological Seminary
Hilda Kroeker Library
St. Louis
*www.calvary.edu/college/under
graduate-academics/library/*

Central Bible College
Pearlman Memorial Library
Springfield
www.cbcag.edu/page.aspx?pid=1013

Central Christian College Library
Reese Resource Center
Moberly
www.cccb.edu/academics/library

Central Methodist University
George M. Smiley Memorial Library
Fayette
*www.centralmethodist.edu/library/
index.php*

Cleveland Chiropractic College
Ruth Cleveland Memorial Library
Kansas City
www.cleveland.edu/library/

College of the Ozarks
Lyons Memorial Library
St. Louis
www.cofo.edu/library/

Columbia College
J.W. and Lois Stafford Library
Columbia
*http://web.ccis.edu/en/offices/
library.aspx*

Conception Abbey
Conception Abbey Library
Conception
http://library.conception.edu

Concordia Seminary
Ludwig E. Fuerbringer Library
Louisiana
www.csl.edu/library/

Cottey College
Blanche Skiff Ross Memorial Library
Nevada

Covenant Theological Seminary
J. Oliver Buswell Jr. Library
St. Louis
*www.covenantseminary.edu/
academics/library/*

Crowder College
Bill & Margot Lee Library
Neosho

Culver-Stockton College
Carl Johann Memorial Library
Canton

DeVry Institute of Technology
James E. Lovan Library
Kansas City
www.kc.devry.edu/Library.html

Drury University
F.W. Olin Library
Springfield
http://library.drury.edu/

East Central College
East Central College Library
Union
www.eastcentral.edu/library/

Eden Theological Seminary
Luhr Library
St. Louis
http://library.webster.edu/luhr_library/

Evangel University
Klaude Kendrick Library
Kirkwood
*https://www.evangel.edu/offices/
academic-affairs/library-and-media-
services/*

Fontbonne University
Jack C. Taylor
St. Louis
www.library.fontbonne.edu/home

Forest Institute of Professional Psychology
Learning Resource Center
St. Louis
www.forestinstitute.org/lib-top.aspx

Graceland University
Dr. Charles F. Grabske Sr. Library
Independence

Hannibal-LaGrange University
L.A. Foster Library
Hannibal
www.hlg.edu/library/index.php

Harris-Stowe State University
AT&T Library and Technology Resources Center
St. Louis
*www.hssu.edu/sp_index.
cfm?wid=20*

Jefferson College
Jefferson College Library
Hillsboro
www.jeffco.edu/library/

Kansas City Art Institute
Jannes Library
Kansas City
www.kcai.edu/academics/library

Kansas City University of Medicine and Biosciences
D'Angelo Library
Kansas City
www.kcumb.edu/library/

Kenrick-Glennon Seminary
Charles L. Souvay Library
St. Louis

Kirksville College of Osteopathic Medicine
A.T. Still Memorial Library
Kirksville
www.atsu.edu/library/index.htm

Lincoln University
Inman E. Page Library
Jefferson City
www.lincolnu.edu/web/library/library

Lindenwood University
Margaret Leggat Butler Library
St. Charles
http://library.lindenwood.edu/

**Linn State Technical College
Information Technology Center**
Linn

**Logan College of Chiropractic
Learning Resources Center**
Chesterfield
www.logan.edu/content/215/
Learning-Resources-Center

**Maryville University
Maryville University Library**
St. Louis
www.maryville.edu/library

**Metropolitan Community College
Blue River Library**
Blue Springs
http://mcckc.edu/services/libraries/
blueriver_lib/generalinfo.asp

**Metropolitan Community College
Longview Library**
Lockwood
http://mcckc.edu/services/libraries/
longview_lib/generalinfo.asp

**Metropolitan Community College
Maple Woods Library**
St. Louis
http://mcckc.edu/services/libraries/
maplewoods_lib/generalinfo.asp

**Metropolitan Community College
Penn Valley Library**
Kansas City
http://mcckc.edu/services/libraries/
pennvalley_lib/pv_lib.asp

**Midwestern Baptist Theological
Seminary Library**
Kansas City
www.mbts.edu/library/

**Mineral Area College
C.H. Cozean Library**
Park Hills
www.mineralarea.edu/library/

**Missouri Baptist University
Jung-Kellogg Library**
Creve Coeur
www.mobap.edu/library/

**Missouri Southern State University
George A. Spiva Library**
Joplin
www.mssu.edu/library

**Missouri State University
Duane G. Meyer Library**
Springfield
http://library.missouristate.edu

**Missouri State University
Garnett Library**
West Plains
http://library.missouristate.edu/garnett/

**Missouri State University
Barbe Evans Library**
Mountain Grove

**Missouri University of Science &
Technology
Curtis Laws Wilson Library**
Rolla
http://library.mst.edu/

**Missouri Valley College
Murrell Memorial Library**
Marshall
www.moval.edu/library/

**Missouri Western State University
Hearnes Learning Resources Center**
St. Joseph
www.library.missouriwestern.edu/

**Moberly Area Community College
Kate Stamper Wilhite Library**
Moberly
www.macc.edu/index.php/services/
libraries

**Nazarene Theological Seminary
William Broadhurst Library**
Kansas City
www.nts.edu/library

**North Central Missouri College
Library**
Trenton
www.ncmissouri.edu/library/

**Northwest Missouri State University
B.D. Owens Library**
Maryville
www.nwmissouri.edu/library/

**Ozark Christian College
Seth Wilson Library**
Joplin
http://occ.edu/students/default.
aspx?id=88

**Ozark Technical Community College
Learning Resources Center**
Springfield
www.otc.edu/currentstudents/
library.php

**Park University
McAfee Memorial Library**
Parkville
www.park.edu/library/

**Rockhurst University
Greenlease Library**
Kansas City
www.rockhurst.edu/library/home/

**Southeast Missouri Hospital
Education Services Library**
Cape Girardeau
http://sehealth.adam.com/content.
aspx?productId=127

**Southeast Missouri State University
Kent Library**
Dexter
www.semo.edu/library/

**Southwest Baptist University
Harriett K. Hutchens Library**
Bolivar
https://library.sbuniv.edu/

**Springfield College
Babson Library**
Springfield
www3.spfldcol.edu/homepage/
library.nsf/home

**St. Charles Community College
Paul and Helen Schnare Library**
Cottleville
www.stchas.edu/library/

**St. Louis Christian College
McCaslin Library**
Florissant
www.slcconline.edu/academics/
library_resources

**St. Louis College of Pharmacy
O.J. Cloughly Alumni Library**
St. Louis
www.stlcop.edu/library/

**St. Louis Community College
Florissant Valley Campus Library**
St. Louis

**St. Louis Community College
Forest Park Campus Library**
St. Louis

**St. Louis Community College
Meramec Campus Library**
St. Louis

**St. Louis Community College
Wildwood Campus Library**
Wildwood

**St. Louis University
Medical Center Library**
St. Louis

**St. Louis University
Vincent C. Immel Law Library**
St. Louis

**St. Louis University
Pius XII Memorial Library**
St. Louis
http://lib.slu.edu

**St. Paul School of Theology
Dana Dawson Library**
Kansas City
www.spst.edu/library-main

**State Fair Community College
Donald C. Proctor Library**
Sedalia
www.sfccmo.edu/pages/251.asp

**Stephens College
Hugh Stephens Library**
Columbia
www.stephens.edu/library/

**Three Rivers Community College
Rutland Library**
Poplar Bluff
www.trcc.edu/arc/

State of Missouri
Tax-Supported Public Library Districts

No Tax-Supported Library
Municipal
City-County
County
Regional
Consolidated
County Boundary

Prepared by the Geographic Resources Center
Department of Geography - University of Missouri Columbia
A partner in the Missouri Census Data Center Program
sponsored by the Missouri State Library.
Office of the Secretary of State

Data Source:
Library District Correspondence File
Geographic Resources Center

Truman State University
Pickler Memorial Library
Kirksville
http://library.truman.edu/

University of Central Missouri
James C. Kirkpatrick Library
Warrensburg
http://library.ucmo.edu/

University of Missouri-Columbia
Ellis Library
Columbia
http://mulibraries.missouri.edu/

Missouri-Columbia
J. Otto Lottes Health Sciences Library
Columbia
http://library.muhealth.org/

University of Missouri–Kansas City
Health Sciences Library
Kansas City

University of Missouri–Kansas City
Leon E. Bloch Law Library
Kansas City
www1.law.umkc.edu/Library/

University of Missouri–Kansas City
Miller Nichols Library
Kansas City
http://library.umkc.edu/node

University of Missouri–Kansas City
School of Dentistry Library
Kansas City
http://library.umkc.edu/dentalhome

University of Missouri–St. Louis
Thomas Jefferson Library
St. Louis
www.umsl.edu/services/library/

University of Missouri–St. Louis
Ward E. Barnes Library
St. Louis
www.umsl.edu/services/library/
about-the-libraries/index.html

Urshan Graduate School of Theology
Urshan Gateway Library
Florissant
http://urshan.ccsct.com/page.
cfm?p=160

Washington University
Bernard Becker Medical Library
St. Louis
https://becker.wustl.edu

Washington University
Law Library-Anheuser Busch Hall
St. Louis
http://law.wustl.edu/library/

Washington University
Olin Library
St. Louis
http://library.wustl.edu/about/olin
library.html

Webster University
Emerson Library
St. Louis
http://library.webster.edu/

Wentworth Military Academy Junior
College
Sellers-Coombs Library
Lexington
http://wma.edu/college/

Westminster College
Reeves Library
Fulton
www.westminster-mo.edu/academics/
resources/library/

William Jewell College
Charles F. Curry Library
Liberty
*www.jewell.edu/gen/william_and_*
*jewell_generated_pages/Library_*
Home_p7123.html

William Woods University
Dulany Library
Fulton

Public Libraries

Adair County Public Library
Kirksville
www.youseemore.com/adaircpl

Advance Community Library
Advance

Albany Carnegie Public Library
Albany
http://carnegie.lib.mo.us

Appleton City Public Library
Appleton City

**Atchison County Library
Main Library**
Rock Port
http://acl.tlcdelivers.com

**Atchison County Library
Fairfax Branch**
Fairfax

**Atchison County Library Tarkio
Branch**
Tarkio

**Barry-Lawrence Regional Library
Main Library**
Monett

**Barry-Lawrence Regional Library
Aurora Branch**
Aurora

**Barry-Lawrence Regional Library
Cassville Branch**
Cassville

**Barry-Lawrence Regional Library
Eagle Rock Branch**
Eagle Rock

**Barry-Lawrence Regional Library
Marionville Branch**
Marionville

**Barry-Lawrence Regional Library
Miller Branch**
Miller

**Barry-Lawrence Regional Library
Mt. Vernon Branch**
Mt. Vernon

**Barry-Lawrence Regional Library
Pierce City Branch**
Pierce City

**Barry-Lawrence Regional Library
Purdy Branch**
Purdy

**Barry-Lawrence Regional Library
Shell Knob Branch**
Shell Knob

**Barton County Library
Mary K. Finley Library (Main Library)**
Lamar
www.bartoncountylibrary.com

**Barton County Library
Hylton Library**
Golden City

**Barton County Library
Happy and Mary Curless Library**
Liberal

Bernie Public Library
Bernie
www.cityofbernie.com/library.htm

Bethany Public Library
Bethany
*www.bethanymo.com/pview.
aspx?id=1949&catID=25*

Bloomfield Public Library
Bloomfield
*www.facebook.com/
groups/101918763299920*

Bollinger County Library
Marble Hill
www.bocolib.com

Bonne Terre Memorial Library
Bonne Terre
http://bonneterrelibrary.com

**Boonslick Regional Library
Sedalia Branch**
Sedalia
www.boonslickregionallibrary.com

**Boonslick Regional Library
Boonville Branch**
Boonville

**Boonslick Regional Library
Cole Camp Branch**
Cole Camp

**Boonslick Regional Library
Warsaw Branch**
Warsaw

Bowling Green Public Library
Bowling Green
www.bgmopl.org

Brentwood Public Library
Brentwood
http://brentwood.lib.mo.us

Brookfield Public Library
Brookfield
http://brookfield.lib.mo.us/

Caldwell County Library
Kingston
http://caldwellcountylibrary.webs.com

**Camden County Library District
Main Library**
Camdenton
www.ccld.us

**Camden County Library District
Climax Springs Library**
Climax Springs

**Camden County Library District
Macks Creek Library**
Macks Creek

**Camden County Library District
Osage Beach Library**
Osage Beach

**Camden County Library District
Stoutland Library**
Stoutland

**Camden County Library District
Sunrise Beach Library**
Sunrise Beach

Cameron Public Library
Cameron
www.cameronlibrary.org

Canton Public Library
Canton

Cape Girardeau Public Library
Cape Girardeau
www.capelibrary.org

Carnegie Public Library
Shelbina
http://shelbinacarnegie.lib.mo.us

Carrollton Public Library
Carrollton
www.carrolltonlibrary.com

Carter County Library Main Library
Van Buren
*http://cartercountylibrarydistrict.
com/*

**Carter County Library
Ellsinore Branch**
Ellsinore

**Carter County Library
Grandin Branch**
Grandin

Carthage Public Library
Carthage
http://carthage.lib.mo.us

Caruthersville Public Library
Caruthersville

**Cass County Library
Harrisonville Branch**
Harrisonville
http://casscolibrary.org

**Cass County Library
Archie Branch**
Archie

**Cass County Library
Drexel Branch**
Drexel

**Cass County Library
Garden City Branch**
Garden City

**Cass County Library
Genealogy Branch**
Harrisonville

Cass County Library
Northern Resource Center
Belton

Cass County Library
Pleasant Hill Branch
Pleasant Hill

Cedar County Library
John D. Smith Library
El Dorado Springs
www.cedarcountylibrary.org

Cedar County Library
Geneva Sharp Library
Stockton

Centralia Public Library
Centralia
www.centraliapubliclibrary.com

Chaffee Public Library
Chaffee
www.cityofchaffee.com/library

Christian County Library
Main Library
Ozark
http://christiancounty.lib.mo.us

Christian County Library
Clever Public Library
Clever

Clarence Public Library
Clarence

Conran Memorial Library
Hayti

Crystal City Public Library
Crystal City
http://jeffersoncountyonline.org/
libraries/crystalcity/crystalcitylibrary.
htm

Dade County Library
Greenfield

Dallas County Library
Buffalo
www.dallascountylibrary.missouri.org

Daniel Boone Regional Library
Columbia Public Library
Columbia
www.dbrl.org

Daniel Boone Regional Library
Callaway County Public Library
Fulton

Daniel Boone Regional Library
Southern Boone County Public Library
Ashland

Daviess County Library
Main Library
Gallatin

Daviess County Library
Jamesport Branch
Jamesport

De Soto Public Library
De Soto
http://desotopubliclibrary.lib.mo.us

Desloge Public Library
Desloge
www.desloge.com/publiclibrary.htm

Doniphan-Ripley County Library
Main Library
Doniphan
www.ripleyco.lib.mo.us

Doniphan-Ripley County Library
Naylor Branch
Naylor

Douglas County Library
Ava
http://douglascountylibrary.lib.mo.us/

Dulany Memorial Library
Salisbury
http://dulanylibrary.org

Dunklin County Library
Main Library
Kennett
http://dunklin-co.lib.mo.us/

Dunklin County Library
Campbell Branch
Campbell

Dunklin County Library
Cardwell Branch
Cardwell

Dunklin County Library
Clarkton Branch
Clarkton

Dunklin County Library
Holcomb Branch
Holcomb

Dunklin County Library
Hornersville Branch
Hornersville

Dunklin County Library
Malden Branch
Malden

Dunklin County Library
Senath Branch
Senath

Farmington Public Library
Farmington
www.farmington-mo.gov/library

Ferguson Municipal Public Library
Ferguson
www.ferguson.lib.mo.us

Festus Public Library
Festus

Fisk Community Library
Fisk

Gentry County Library
Stanberry
www.gentrycountylibrary.org

Grundy County-Jewett Norris
Library
Trenton
www.grundycountylibrary.org

Hamilton Public Library
Hamilton

Hannibal Free Public Library
Hannibal
www.hannibal.lib.mo.us

Heartland Regional Library System
Miller County Library Service
Center–Iberia Library
Iberia
http://heartland.lib.mo.us

Heartland Regional Library System
Maries County Library Service Center
– Belle Library
Belle

Heartland Regional Library System
Maries County Library Service Center
– Vienna Library
Vienna

Heartland Regional Library System
Miller County Library Service
Center–Eldon Public Library
Eldon

Henry County Library
Main Library
Clinton
www.henrycolib.org

Henry County Library
Lenora Blackmore Branch
Windsor

Hickory County Library
Hermitage
www.hickorylibrary.org

Howard County Library
www.hocopub.lib.mo.us

Jefferson County Library
Northwest Branch
High Ridge
www.jeffersoncountylibrary.org

Jefferson County Library
Arnold Branch
Arnold

Jefferson County Library
Windsor Branch
Barnhart

Joplin Public Library
Joplin
www.joplinpubliclibrary.org

Kansas City Public Library
Central Library
Kansas City
www.kclibrary.org

Kansas City Public Library
Irene H. Ruiz Biblioteca de las Americas
Kansas City

Kansas City Public Library
Lucile H. Bluford Branch
Kansas City

Kansas City Public Library
North-East Branch
Kansas City

Kansas City Public Library
Plaza Branch
Kansas City

Kansas City Public Library
Southeast Branch
Kansas City

Kansas City Public Library
Sugar Creek Branch
Sugar Creek

Kansas City Public Library
Trails West Branch
Independence

Kansas City Public Library
Waldo Branch
Kansas City

Kansas City Public Library
Westport Branch
Kansas City

Keller Public Library
Dexter
www.kellerpl.org

Kirkwood Public Library
Kirkwood
http://kirkwoodpubliclibrary.org

La Plata Public Library
La Plata
www.facebook.com/pages/
La-Plata-Public-Library/
245178998494?fref=ts

Lebanon-Laclede County Library
Lebanon
www.lebanon-laclede.lib.mo.us

Lewis Library
Glasgow

Lilbourn Memorial Library
Lilbourn

Little Dixie Regional Libraries
Main Library
Moberly

Little Dixie Regional Libraries
Atterbury Memorial Library
Madison

Little Dixie Regional Libraries
Dulany Memorial Library
Paris

Little Dixie Regional Libraries
Huntsville Library
Huntsville

Livingston County Library
Chillicothe
www.livingstoncountylibrary.org

Lockwood Public Library
Lockwood

Louisiana Public Library
Louisiana

Macon Public Library
Macon
www.maconlibrary.org

Maplewood Public Library
Maplewood
www.maplewood.lib.mo.us

Marceline Carnegie Library
Marceline
www.marcelinelibrary.org

Marion County Library
Palmyra
http://marioncounty1.lib.mo.us

Marshall Public Library
Marshall
www.marshallmolibrary.org

Maryville Public Library
Maryville
www.maryvillepubliclibrary.lib.mo.us

McDonald County Library
Main Library
Pineville
www.librarymail.org

McDonald County Library
Anne Croxdale Memorial Library
Southwest City

McDonald County Library
Noel Library
Noel

Mercer County Library
Princeton
www.mcl.lib.mo.us

Mexico-Audrain County Library
Main Library
Mexico
http://mexico-audrain.lib.mo.us

Mexico-Audrain County Library
Farber Branch
Farber

Mexico-Audrain County Library
Ed French Memorial Library
Laddonia

Mexico-Audrain County Library
Martinsburg Branch
Martinsburg

Mexico-Audrain County Library
Vandalia Branch
Vandalia

Mid-Continent Public Library
Administrative Office
Independence
www.mymcpl.org

Mid-Continent Public Library
Antioch Branch
Gladstone

Mid-Continent Public Library
Blue Ridge Branch
Kansas City

Mid-Continent Public Library
Blue Springs North Branch
Blue Springs

Mid-Continent Public Library
Blue Springs South Branch
Blue Springs

Mid-Continent Public Library
Boardwalk Branch
Kansas City

Mid-Continent Public Library
Buckner Branch
Buckner

Mid-Continent Public Library
Camden Point Branch
Camden Point

Mid-Continent Public Library
Claycomo Branch
Claycomo

Mid-Continent Public Library
Colbern Road Branch
Lee's Summit

Mid-Continent Public Library
Dearborn Branch
Dearborn

Mid-Continent Public Library
Edgerton Branch
Edgerton

Mid-Continent Public Library
Excelsior Springs Branch
Excelsior Springs

Mid-Continent Public Library
Grain Valley Branch
Grain Valley

Mid-Continent Public Library
Grandview Branch
Grandview

Mid-Continent Public Library
Kearney Branch
Kearney

Mid-Continent Public Library
Lee's Summit Branch
Lee's Summit

Mid-Continent Public Library
Liberty Branch
Liberty

Mid-Continent Public Library
Lone Jack Branch
Lone Jack

Mid-Continent Public Library
Midwest Genealogy Center
Independence

Mid-Continent Public Library
North Independence Branch
Independence

Mid-Continent Public Library
North Oak Branch
Kansas City

Mid-Continent Public Library
Oak Grove Branch
Oak Grove

Mid-Continent Public Library
Parkville Branch
Parkville

Mid-Continent Public Library
Platte City Branch
Platte City

Mid-Continent Public Library
Joe Herndorn Branch
Raytown

Mid-Continent Public Library
Red Bridge Branch
Kansas City

Mid-Continent Public Library
Riverside Branch
Riverside

Mid-Continent Public Library
Smithville Branch
Smithville

Mid-Continent Public Library
South Independence Branch
Independence

Mid-Continent Public Library
Weston Branch
Weston

Mississippi County Library
Clara Drinkwater Newnam Library
Charleston

Mississippi County Library
Mitchell Memorial Library
East Prairie

Missouri River Regional Library
Main Library
Jefferson City
www.mrrl.org

Missouri River Regional Library
Osage County Library
Linn

Moniteau County Library
Wood Place Public Library
California

Monroe City Public Library
Monroe City
www.monroecitymo.org/City_
Services/library/library.htm

Montgomery City Public Library
Montgomery City
www.montgomerycitymo.org/library

Morgan County Library
Versailles
www.morgancountylibrary.org

Mound City Public Library
Mound City

Mountain View Public Library
Mountain View
http://mvpubliclibrary.webs.com

Neosho/Newton County Library
Main Library
Neosho
www.neosholibrary.org

Neosho/Newton County Library
Seneca Branch
Seneca

Nevada Public Library
Nevada
www.nevadapubliclibrary.com

New Madrid County Library
Headquarters
Portageville
www.newmadridcountylibrary.com

New Madrid County Library
Matthews Service Center
Matthews

New Madrid County Library
Morehouse Service Center
Morehouse

New Madrid County Library
New Madrid Memorial Library
New Madrid

New Madrid County Library
Parma Service Center
Parma

New Madrid County Library
Rhodes Memorial Library
Gideon

New Madrid County Library
Risco Service Center
Risco

Norborne Public Library
Norborne

North Kansas City Public Library &
High School Media Center
North Kansas City

Northeast Missouri Library Service
H.E. Sever Memorial Library
Kahoka
www.nemolibrary.lib.mo.us

Northeast Missouri Library Service
Knox County Library
Edina

Northeast Missouri Library Service
LaBelle Library
LaBelle

Northeast Missouri Library Service
LaGrange Library
LaGrange

Oregon County Library
Alton Public Library
Alton

Oregon County Library
Koshkonong Public Library
Koshkonong

Oregon County Library
Myrtle Public Library
Myrtle

Oregon County Library
Thayer Public Library
Thayer

Oregon County Library
Thomasville Public Library
Thomasville

Oregon Public Library
Oregon
www.facebook.com/
pages/Oregon-Public-
Library/171111009605245?fref=ts

Ozark Regional Library
Ironton Headquarters
Ironton
http://ozarkregionallibrary.lib.mo.us

Ozark Regional Library
Annapolis Branch
Annapolis

Ozark Regional Library
Bourbon Branch
Bourbon

Ozark Regional Library
Fredericktown Branch
Fredericktown

Ozark Regional Library
Recklein Memorial Library
Cuba

Ozark Regional Library
Ste. Genevieve Branch
Ste. Genevieve

Ozark Regional Library
Steelville Branch
Steelville

Ozark Regional Library
Viburnum Branch
Viburnum

Park Hills Public Library
Park Hills
www.parkhillsmo.net/recreation/Library

Piedmont Public Library
Piedmont

Polk County Library
Main Library
Bolivar
www.polkcolibrary.org

Polk County Library
Humansville Branch
Humansville

Poplar Bluff Municipal Library
Poplar Bluff

Pulaski County Library
Richland Branch
Richland
www.pulaskicounty.lib.mo.us

Pulaski County Library
Crocker Branch
Crocker

Pulaski County Library
Waynesville Branch
Waynesville

Putnam County Public Library
Unionville
http://putnamcl.lib.mo.us

Puxico Public Library
Puxico

Ralls County Library
Center
www.rallscounty.org/library.html

Ray County Library
Richmond
http://raycountylibrary.homestead.com

Reynolds County Library
Centerville Branch Library
Centerville
http://reynoldscountylibrarydistrict.
webs.com

Reynolds County Library
Bunker Branch Library
Bunker

Reynolds County Library
Ellington Branch Library
Ellington

Reynolds County Library
Lesterville Branch Library
Lesterville

Reynolds County Library
Oates Branch Library
Black

Rich Hill Memorial Library
Rich Hill
www.facebook.com/
richhillmemoriallibrary?fref=ts

Richmond Heights Memorial Library
Richmond Heights
http://rhml.lib.mo.us

Riverside Regional Library
Main Library
Jackson
www.riversideregionallibrary.org/

Riverside Regional Library
Altenburg Branch
Altenburg

Riverside Regional Library
Benton Branch
Benton

Riverside Regional Library
Oran Branch
Oran

Riverside Regional Library
Perryville Branch
Perryville

Riverside Regional Library
Scott City Branch
Scott City

Robertson Memorial Library
Higginsville
http://higginsvillelibrary.org/

Rock Hill Public Library
Rock Hill
www.rockhill.lib.mo.us

Rolla Public Library
Rolla
www.rollapubliclibrary.org

Rolling Hills Consolidated Library
Belt Branch
St. Joseph
http://rhcl.org/

Rolling Hills Consolidated Library
Savannah Branch
Savannah

Salem Public Library
Salem
www.salempubliclibrary.lib.mo.us

Sarcoxie Public Library
Sarcoxie

Scenic Regional Library
Union Branch
Union
http://scenicregional.org

Scenic Regional Library
Hermann Branch
Hermann

Scenic Regional Library
New Haven Branch
New Haven

Scenic Regional Library
Owensville Branch
Owensville

Scenic Regional Library
Pacific Branch
Pacific

Scenic Regional Library
St. Clair Branch
St. Clair

Scenic Regional Library
Warren County Branch
Warrenton

Schuyler County Library
Lancaster

Scotland County Memorial Library
Memphis
http://scotland.lib.mo.us

Sedalia Public Library
Sedalia
www.sedalialibrary.com

Seymour Community Library
Seymour

Sikeston Public Library
Sikeston
www.sikeston.lib.mo.us

Slater Public Library
Slater

Springfield-Greene County Library
The Library Center
Springfield
http://thelibrary.org

Springfield-Greene County Library
Ash Grove Branch Library
Ash Grove

Springfield-Greene County Library
Brentwood Branch Library
Springfield

Springfield-Greene County Library
Fair Grove Branch Library
Fair Grove

Springfield-Greene County Library
The Library Station
Springfield

Springfield-Greene County Library
Midtown Carnegie Branch Library
Springfield

Springfield-Greene County Library
Park Central Branch Library
Springfield

Springfield-Greene County Library
Republic Branch Library
Republic

Springfield-Greene County Library
Strafford Branch Library
Strafford

Springfield-Greene County Library
Willard Branch Library
Willard

St. Charles City-County Library
Administrative Offices
St. Peters
www.youranswerplace.org

St. Charles City-County Library
Boone's Trail Branch
New Melle

St. Charles City-County Library
Corporate Parkway Branch
Wentzville

St. Charles City-County Library
Deer Run Branch
O'Fallon

St. Charles City-County Library
Kathryn Linnemann Branch
St. Charles

St. Charles City-County Library
Kisker Road Branch
St. Charles

St. Charles City-County Library
Library Express at Discovery Village
Wentzville

St. Charles City-County Library
Library Express at Winghaven
O'Fallon

St. Charles City-County Library
McClay Branch
St. Charles

St. Charles City-County Library
Middendorf-Kredell Branch
O'Fallon

St. Charles City-County Library
North County Branch
Portage Des Sioux

St. Charles City-County Library
South County Branch
Augusta

St. Charles City-County Library
Spencer Road Branch
St. Peters

St. Clair County Library
Main Library
Osceola
http://mostclair.lib.mo.us

St. Clair County Library
Lowry City Branch
Lowry City

St. Joseph Public Library
Downtown Library
St. Joseph
http://sjpl.lib.mo.us/

St. Joseph Public Library
Carnegie Library
St. Joseph

St. Joseph Public Library
East Hills Library
St. Joseph

St. Joseph Public Library
Washington Park Library
St. Joseph

St. Louis County Library
Headquarters
St. Louis
www.slcl.org

St. Louis County Library
Bridgeton Trails Branch
Bridgeton

St. Louis County Library
Cliff Cave Branch
St. Louis

St. Louis County Library
Daniel Boone Branch
Ellisville

St. Louis County Library
Eureka Hills Branch
Eureka

St. Louis County Library
Florissant Valley Branch
Florissant

St. Louis County Library
Grand Glaize Branch
Manchester

St. Louis County Library
Indian Trails Branch
St. Louis

St. Louis County Library
Jamestown Bluffs Branch
Florissant

St. Louis County Library
Lewis and Clark Branch
St. Louis

St. Louis County Library
Meramec Valley Branch
Fenton

St. Louis County Library
Mid-County Branch
St. Louis

St. Louis County Library
Natural Bridge Branch
St. Louis

St. Louis County Library
Oak Bend Branch
St. Louis

St. Louis County Library
Prairie Commons Branch
Hazelwood

St. Louis County Library
Rock Road Branch
St. Ann

St. Louis County Library
Samuel C. Sachs Branch
Chesterfield

St. Louis County Library
Tesson Ferry Branch
St. Louis

St. Louis County Library
Thornhill Branch
St. Louis

St. Louis District Library
Weber Road Branch
St. Louis

St. Louis Public Library
Central Library
St. Louis
www.slpl.org/

St. Louis Public Library
Baden Branch
St. Louis

St. Louis Public Library
Barr Branch
St. Louis

St. Louis Public Library
Buder Branch
St. Louis

St. Louis Public Library
Cabanne Branch
St. Louis

St. Louis Public Library
Carondelet Branch
St. Louis

St. Louis Public Library
Carpenter Branch
St. Louis

St. Louis Public Library
Central Express
St. Louis

St. Louis Public Library
Charing Cross Branch
St. Louis

St. Louis Public Library
Compton Branch
St. Louis

St. Louis Public Library
Divoll Branch
St. Louis

St. Louis Public Library
Julia Davis Branch
St. Louis

St. Louis Public Library
Kingshighway Branch
St. Louis

St. Louis Public Library
Machacek Branch
St. Louis

St. Louis Public Library
Marketplace Branch
St. Louis

St. Louis Public Library
Schlafly Branch
St. Louis

St. Louis Public Library
Walnut Park Branch
St. Louis

Steele Public Library
Steele

Stone County Library
Galena Area Library
Galena
www.stonecountylibrary.org

Stone County Library
Blue Eye Library
Blue Eye

Stone County Library
Crane Area Library
Crane

Sullivan County Public Library
Milan

Sullivan Public Library
Sullivan
www.sullivan.lib.mo.us

Sweet Springs Public Library
Sweet Springs

Texas County Library
Main Library
Houston
http://texascountylibrary.lib.mo.us

Texas County Library
Cabool Branch
Cabool

Texas County Library
Licking Branch
Licking

Texas County Library
Summersville Branch
Summersville

Trails Regional Library
Holden Branch
Holden
http://trailslibrary.org

Trails Regional Library
Concordia Branch
Concordia

Trails Regional Library
Corder Branch
Corder

Trails Regional Library
Knob Noster Branch
Knob Noster

Trails Regional Library
Lexington Branch
Lexington

Trails Regional Library
Odessa Branch
Odessa

Trails Regional Library
Warrensburg Branch
Warrensburg

Trails Regional Library
Waverly Branch
Waverly

University City Public Library
University City
www.ucitylibrary.org

Valley Park Community Library
Valley Park
www.valleyparklibrary.org

Washington County Library
Potosi
www.thewashingtoncountylibrary.com

Washington Public Library
Washington
www.washmolib.org

Webb City Public Library
Webb City
www.webbcitylibrary.org

Webster County Library
Garst Memorial Library
Marshfield
www.webstercounty.lib.mo.us

Webster County Library
Rogersville Branch
Rogersville

Webster Groves Public Library
Webster Groves

Wellsville Public Library
Wellsville
http://wellsvillelibrary.lib.mo.us

West Plains Public Library
West Plains

Willow Springs Public Library
Willow Springs
http://wslibrary.webs.com

Winona Public Library
Winona

Worth County Library
Grant City
http://worthcountylibrary.lib.mo.us

Wright County Library
Hartville Library
Hartville
www.wrightcountylibrary.org

Wright County Library
Laura Ingalls Wilder Library
Mansfield

Wright County Library
Mountain Grove Library
Mountain Grove

Special Libraries

Betty Golde Smith Memorial Library
St. Louis Psychoanalytic Institute
St. Louis
www.stlpi.org/services/library/

Boone Hospital Center Medical Library
Columbia

Burns & McDonnell Library
Kansas City
www.burnsmcd.com

Business Research Library
Hallmark Cards, Inc.
Kansas City
www.hallmark.com

Midwest Research Institute
Kansas City
www.mriglobal.org/

Research Medical Library
Carl R. Ferris Medical Library
Kansas City
http://researchmedicalcenter.com/
your-health/index.dot

Center for Innovations in Education
(CISE) Library
Columbia
http://education.missouri.edu/ESCP/

Center for Reformation Research
Library
Clayton
www.csl.edu/library/the-center-for-
reformation-resources-collection/

Central Region Headquarters Library
National Weather Service
Kansas City
www.lib.ncep.noaa.gov/info

Christian Hospital Northeast Library
St. Louis
www.christianhospital.org/
healthlibrary/hlhome.aspx?sid=45

National Association of Insurance
Commissioners Library
Kansas City
http://naic.softlinkliberty.net/liberty/
libraryHome.do

Bruce C. Clarke Library
General Leonard Wood Army
Fort Leonard Wood
www.wood.army.mil/library/

Cox Health Systems Libraries
Springfield
www.coxhealth.com/body.cfm?id=
2039

Donald Danforth Plant Science
Center Library
St. Louis
www.danforthcenter.org

Eastern District Law Library
Missouri Court of Appeals
St. Louis
www.courts.mo.gov/page.jsp?id=218

Edward D. Jones Business Library
St. Louis
www.edwardjones.com/en_US/index.html

Eighth Circuit Library
U.S. Court of Appeals
St. Louis
www.lb8.uscourts.gov

Emerson Electric Library
St. Louis
www.gotoemerson.com/

Federal Reserve Library
Federal Reserve Bank of St.Louis
St. Louis
www.stlouisfed.org/education_resources/

St. Alexius Hospital Library
St. Louis
www.stalexiushospital.com

Freeman Health System Library
Joplin
www.freemanhealth.com

Community Hospital Library
General Leonard Wood Army
Ft. Leonard Wood
http://glwach.amedd.army.mil/staff_info/staff_tools/med_library.htm

Greensfelder, Hamker and Gale Law
Library
St. Louis
www.greensfelder.com

Health Sciences Library
St. Luke's Hospital
Kansas City
www.stlukesonline.org/medlib/

Heartland Regional Medical Center
Library
St. Joseph

Hi-Tech Charities
Main Library
Hermitage
http://htchar.org/education/components/faq/faq.php?section detailid=6&

International Association of
Assessing Officers Library
Kansas City
www.iaao.org/library/

Information & Library Services St.
Louis
U.S. Army Corps of Engineers St.
Louis District, TILS
St. Louis
www.mvs.usace.army.mil/Library.aspx

Instructional Materials Laboratory
Columbia
http://arc.missouri.edu/content/iml.aspx

International Institute Library
St. Louis
www.iistl.org

Jackson County Historical Society
Independence
www.jchs.org/

Jackson County Law Library, Inc.
Kansas City
www.jcll.org

Jefferson National Expansion
Memorial Library
St. Louis
www.nps.gov/jeff/historyculture/library.htm

Kansas City Star Library
Kansas City
www.kansascity.com/

Lashly and Baer Law Library
St. Louis
www.lashlybaer.com/

Laumeier Sculpture Park Library
St. Louis
www.laumeiersculpturepark.org/visit/hours_directions

Law Library Association of St. Louis
St. Louis

Legislative Library
Jefferson City

Liberty Memorial Museum and
Archives
Liberty
www.theworldwar.org/

Library and Information Services
Nestle Purina Petcare Company
Kansas City
www.nestle.com/aboutus/mediadocuments

Library and Archives
Community of Christ
Independence
www.cofchrist.org/library

Library Archives & Museum of
Optometrics
American Optometric Association
International
St. Louis
www.optometrycharity.org/archives-museum-of-optometry

Library Services S290-1200
Boeing Company
St. Louis
www.boeing.com/

Linda Hall Library of Science,
Engineering and Technology
Kansas City
www.lindahall.org

Mallinckrodt Pharmaceutical and
Chemical Library
St. Louis
www.mallinckrodt.com

Medical and Consumer Health Library
St. John's Regional Medical Center
Joplin
www.mercy.net/st-johns-hospital/medical-library-services

Louise Kraus-Ament Memorial Library
Lutheran Medical Center School of
Nursing
St. Louis
www.nursingschoollmc.com/library.php

Medical Center Library
Veterans Administration
Kansas City
www.kansascity.va.gov

Medical Library
Veterans Affairs Medical Center
Poplar Bluff
www.poplarbluff.va.gov

Medical Library
Veterans Administration Hospital
Columbia
www.columbiamo.va.gov/

Medical Center Library
Truman Medical Center Library
Kansas City
www.trumed.org/truweb/corporate/healthlibrary/health_library.aspx

Midwest Jesuit Archives
St. Louis
www.jesuitsmissouri.org/arch/index.cfm

Medical Library
North Kansas City Hospital
North Kansas City
www.nkch.org

Missouri Botanical Garden Library
East Prairie
www.missouribotanicalgarden.org/plant-science/plant-science/resources/raven-library.aspx

Missouri Historical Society Library
St. Louis
www.mohistory.org/lrc-home/

Library Research Center
Missouri History Museum
St. Louis
www.mohistory.org/lrc-home/

Missouri State Archives
Office of the Secretary of State
Jefferson City
www.sos.mo.gov/archives/

Missouri State Library
Office of the Secretary of State
Jefferson City
www.sos.mo.gov/library/

Missouri State Supreme Court Library
Jefferson City
www.courts.mo.gov/page.jsp?id=218

ParentLink Library
Columbia
www.parentlink.missouri.edu

Polsinelli White Library
Kansas City
www.polsinelli.com/kansascity/

Post Memorial Art Reference Library
Joplin
www.postlibrary.org

Quintiles Library & Information Center
Kansas City
www.quintiles.com/information-library/

Reference Branch
National Imagery and Mapping Agency
Arnold
www1.nga.mil

Reference Library
Springfield Art Museum
Springfield
www.springfieldmo.gov/art

Research Library
Federal Reserve Bank of Kansas City
Kansas City

Sigma Chemical Company Research
Library
Rolla
www.sigmaaldrich.com/united-states.html

Kauffman Foundation Resource
Library
Kansas City
www.kauffman.org

Richardson Memorial Library
St. Louis Art Museum
St. Louis
www.slam.org

Saul Brodsky Jewish Community Library
St. Louis
www.brodskylibrary.org

Solutia, Inc., Library
St. Louis

Sonnenschein, Nath and Rosenthal
Library
St. Louis
www.dentons.com/

Spencer Art Reference Library
Nelson-Atkins Museum of Art
Kansas City
www.nelson-atkins.org/

St. Joseph Museum Library
St. Joseph

St. Louis Children's Hospital Library
St. Louis
http://healthlibrary.stlouischildrens.org/Library/

St. Louis Mercantile at UMSL
St. Louis
www.umsl.edu/mercantile

St. Louis Post-Dispatch Reference
Department
St. Louis
www.stltoday.com

St. Louis Zoo Library
St. Louis
www.stlzoo.org/education/libraryandteacherresourcec/

St. Mary's Health Center Library
St. Louis
www.ssmhealth.com/stmarys

State Historical Society of Missouri
Columbia
http://shs.umsystem.edu/index.shtml

Stinson Leonard Street Law Library
Main Library
Kansas City
www.stinson.com/meet_us/offices/locations/kansas_city.aspx

Stowers Institute for Medical Research
Library
Kansas City
www.stowers.org/

Thomas F. Frawley Medical Center
Library
Mercy Hospital St. Louis
St. Louis
www.mercy.net/services/

Thompson Coburn Library
St. Louis
www.thompsoncoburn.com

Truman Presidential Museum and
Library
Independence
www.trumanlibrary.org

Tyco Healthcare Mallinckrodt
St. Louis
www.mallinckrodt.com

Unity Library
Unity School of Christianity
Unity Village
http://content.unity.org/education/libraryarchives/

Van K. Smith Community Health
Library
Mercy St. Johns
Springfield
www.mercy.net/practice/van-k-smith-community-health-library

Western District Law Library
Missouri Court of Appeals
Kansas City
www.courts.mo.gov/page.jsp?id=227

Western District of Missouri
U.S. Attorney Office Library
Kansas City
www.justice.gov/usao/mow/index.html

Western Historical Manuscript
Collection
Columbia
http://shs.umsystem.edu/manuscripts/index.shtml

Wilson's Creek National Battlefield
Library
National Park Service
Republic
www.nps.gov/wicr/index.htm

Winston Churchill Memorial and
Library
Fulton
www.nationalchurchillmuseum.org/

Wolfner Talking Book and Braille
Library
Office of the Secretary of State
Jefferson City
www.sos.mo.gov/wolfner

Institutional Libraries

Algoa Correctional Center Library
Jefferson City
http://doc.mo.gov/Facilities.php

Boonville Treatment Center Library
Boonville
www.valleyhope.com/missouri/drug-rehab-centers-boonville.aspx

Camp Library
Watkins Mill State Park
Lawson
www.librarytechnology.org/lwc-displaylibrary.pl?RC=126617

Speech, Hearing and Education
Library
Central Institute for the Deaf
St. Louis
www.cid.edu

Chillicothe Correctional Center Library
Chillicothe
http://doc.mo.gov/Facilities.php

Community Resource Library
Springfield Regional Center
Springfield
http://dmh.mo.gov/springfield/

Crossroads Correctional Center Library
Cameron
http://doc.mo.gov/Facilities.php

Division of Youth Services
Missouri Hills Campus
St. Louis
http://dss.mo.gov/dys/

Eastern Reception and Diagnostic Correctional Center Library
Bonne Terre
http://doc.mo.gov/Facilities.php

Farmington Correctional Center Library
Farmington
http://doc.mo.gov/Facilities.php

Fulton Reception and Diagnostic Center Library
Fulton
http://doc.mo.gov/Facilities.php

Green Gables Lodge Library
Macks Creek

Hawthorne Children's Psychiatric Hospital
Student Library
St. Louis
http://dmh.mo.gov/hcph/

Joplin Regional Center for the Developmentally Disabled
Joplin
http://dmh.mo.gov/joplin/

Learning Resource Center
Missouri School for the Blind
St. Louis
http://msb.dese.mo.gov/

Maryville Treatment Center
Maryville
http://doc.mo.gov/Documents/rehab/DORS_ITC.pdf

Mineral Area Regional Medical Center Library
Kansas City
www.mineralarearegional.com/

Missouri Department of Mental Health
Jefferson City
http://dmh.mo.gov/

Missouri Division of Corrections
Division of Adult Institutions
Jefferson City
http://doc.mo.gov/DAI/

Grover C. Farquhar Library
Missouri School for the Deaf
Fulton
573) 592-2513
www.msd.k12.mo.us/rcd

Missouri Veterans Home Library
Cameron
http://mvc.dps.mo.gov/

Missouri Veterans Home Library
Mexico
http://mvc.dps.mo.gov/

Missouri Veterans Home Library
Mount Vernon
http://mvc.dps.mo.gov/

Missouri Veterans Home Library
St. Louis
http://mvc.dps.mo.gov/

Missouri Veterans Home Library
Warrensburg
http://mvc.dps.mo.gov/

Moberly Correctional Center Library
Moberly
http://doc.mo.gov/Facilities.php

Northeast Correctional Center Library
Bowling Green
http://doc.mo.gov/DAI/Institutional_Facilities.php

Northeast Missouri Area Health Education Center Library
Macon
http://www.nemoahec.org/

Northwest Missouri Psychiatric Rehabilitation Center
Anthony Library
St. Joseph
http://dmh.mo.gov/nmprc/

Ozark Correctional Center Library
Fordland
http://doc.mo.gov/DAI/Institutional_Facilities.php

Potosi Correctional Center Library
Mineral Point
http://doc.mo.gov/Facilities.php

Rolla Regional Center Resource Library
Rolla
http://dmh.mo.gov/rolla/resources.htm

Sikeston Regional Center for the Developmentally Disabled
Sikeston

South Central Correctional Center Library
Licking
http://doc.mo.gov/Facilities.php

Southeast Correctional Center Library
Charleston
http://doc.mo.gov/DAI/Institutional_Facilities.php

St. Louis Psychiatric Rehabilitation Center Library
St. Louis
http://dmh.mo.gov/slprc/

Tipton Correctional Center Library
Tipton
http://doc.mo.gov/Facilities.php

Inmate Law Library
U.S. Medical Center for Federal Prisoners
Springfield
www.bop.gov/locations/institutions/spg/

Western Missouri Correctional Center Library
Cameron
http://doc.mo.gov/Facilities.php

Western Reception and Diagnostic Center Library
St. Joseph
http://doc.mo.gov/DORS/

Women's Eastern Rehabilitation Diagnostic Correctional Center
Vandalia
http://doc.mo.gov/DORS/

W.E. Sears Youth Center
Sollars Library
Poplar Bluff
www.dss.mo.gov/dys/

Whiteman Air Force Base Library
Whiteman Air Force Base
www.whiteman.af.mil/library/index.asp

Academy of Missouri Squires

An organization unique among the states, the Academy of Missouri Squires was founded in the fall of 1960 by Governor James T. Blair Jr., who established it with a ceiling of 100 members. Governor Blair's purpose was to establish an organization to honor Missourians for their accomplishments at all levels—community, state or nation.

Governor Blair appointed the first class of 10 Squires after consulting leaders in every section of the state. Each succeeding class has been elected by the membership of the Academy, after receiving nominations from the public as well as from the membership of the Academy. The governor and former governors of Missouri are automatically members.

Squires are listed by class. Present addresses are noted in parentheses when different from address at time of election.

Class of 1960

Thomas Hart Benton, Kansas City*
James T. Blair Jr., Jefferson City*
Clarence Cannon, Elsberry*
Tilghman R. Cloud, Pleasant Hill*
Michael Kinney, St. Louis*
Stan Musial, St. Louis**
Miss Adah Peckenpaugh, Clinton*
Roy Roberts, Kansas City*
Francis Smith, St. Joseph*
Ethan A.H. Shepley Jr., St. Louis*
Harry S Truman, Independence*

Class of 1961

William L. Bradshaw, Columbia*
Arthur V. Burrowes, St. Joseph*
August A. Busch Jr., St. Louis*
John M. Dalton, Jefferson City*
Russell L. Dearmont, St. Louis*
Elmer Ellis, Columbia*
Don Faurot, Columbia*
Gerald R. Massie, Jefferson City*
Albert L. Reeves, Kansas City*
Floyd C. Shoemaker, Columbia*
Stuart Symington, Clayton*

Class of 1962

Richard H. Amberg, St. Louis*
David R. Calhoun, St. Louis*

James G. Conzelman, St. Louis*
E.L. Dale, Carthage*
True Davis, Washington, D.C.*
Joyce C. Hall, Kansas City*
Charles N. Kimball, Kansas City*
Samuel S. Mayerberg, Kansas City*
James S. McDonnell Jr., St. Louis*
Sterling Price Reynolds, Caruthersville*

Special class of 1962

Henry S. Caulfield, St. Louis*
Forrest C. Donnell, St. Louis*
Lloyd C. Stark, Louisiana*

Class of 1963

Edwin M. Clark, St. Louis*
Howard Cook, Jefferson City*
James A. Finch Jr., Jefferson City*
Robert M. Good, Point Lookout*
James M. Kemper, Kansas City*
Dillard A. Mallory, Buffalo*
John I. Rollings, St. Louis*
Ruth Seevers, Osceola*
Leif J. Sverdrup, St. Louis*
Roy D. Williams, Boonville*

Class of 1964

Mrs. G. Baird Fisher, Osgood*
James P. Hickok, St. Louis*
Laurance M. Hyde, Jefferson City*
Edward V. Long, Bowling Green*
Morton D. May, St. Louis*
J. Wesley McAfee, St. Louis*
Frederick A. Middlebush, Columbia*
L. Mitchell White, Mexico*
Rex M. Whitton, Jefferson City*
Mrs. Virginia Garton Young, Columbia*

Class of 1965

William Howard Adams, Shenandoah Junction, WV
Omar N. Bradley, Los Angeles, CA*
Frank P. Briggs, Macon*
Lester E. Cox, Springfield*
Warren E. Hearnes, Charleston*
William B. Massey, Bonne Terre*
Franc L. McClure, St. Charles*
William A. McDonnell, St. Louis*
Mrs. Holton R. Price Jr., Ladue*
Charles Allen Thomas, St. Louis*
Homer C. Wadsworth, Cleveland, OH*

Class of 1966

Sam C. Blair, Jefferson City*
Thomas H. Eliot, St. Louis (Cambridge, MA)*
Fred V. Heinkel, Columbia*

William F. James, Lohman*
Lue C. Lozier, Moberly*
Arthur Mag, Kansas City*
Paul C. Reinert, St. Louis*
Sidney Salomon Jr., St. Louis*
Clem F. Storckman, Jefferson City*
Jacqueline Wexler, Tenafly, NJ (New York City)*

Class of 1967

Henry D. Bradley, St. Joseph*
Ernest R. Breech, Detroit, MI*
Richard S. Brownlee, Columbia*
Stanley R. Fike, Independence*
Leonard Hall, Caledonia*
Edmund I. (Mike) Hockaday, Jefferson City*
Paul C. Jones, Kennett*
Theodore D. McNeal, St. Louis*
Arthur Clay Magill, Cape Girardeau*
Raymond R. Tucker, St. Louis*

Class of 1968

Proctor N. Carter, Rolla (Joplin)*
Edward Pope Coleman Jr., Sikeston*
Richard M. Duncan, Kansas City*
Oliver B. Ferguson, Fredericktown*
Henry C. Haskell, Kansas City*
James C. Kirkpatrick, Warrensburg*
Isaac A. Long, St. Louis*
Lewis E. Meador, Springfield*
Howard A. Rusk, New York City*
Sidney E. Souers, St. Louis*

Class of 1969

Maurice R. Chambers, St. Louis*
Earl E. Dawson, Jefferson City*
Thomas F. Eagleton, St. Louis*
Harry F. Harrington, St. Louis*
Robert Hyland, St. Louis*
James H. Meredith, St. Louis*
H. Lang Rogers, Joplin*
John W. Schwada, Tempe, AZ*
Charles W. Schwartz, Jefferson City*
Joseph C. Welman, Kennett*

Class of 1970

Charles L. Bacon, Kansas City*
H. Roe Bartle, Kansas City*
G. Duncan Bauman, St. Louis*
Dan Devine, Phoenix, AZ*
A.J. Drinkwater Jr., Charleston*
Richard H. Ichord, Houston*
Earle B. Jewell, Forsyth*
Jack Matthews, Columbia*
Lewis M. Means, Fayette*
Jack Stapleton Sr., Stanberry*
Elliot H. Stein, St. Louis*

Class of 1971

John R. Cauley, Washington, D.C.*
D. Howard Doane, Point Lookout*
D.W. Gilmore, Kansas City*
C. Brice Ratchford, Columbia*
Jane Froman Smith, Columbia*
Leonor K. Sullivan-Archibald, St. Louis*
Robert M. White II, Mexico*

Class of 1972

Howard F. Baer, St. Louis**
William H. Danforth, St. Louis
Betty Cooper Hearnes, Charleston
Everett Keith, Columbia*
M.C. Matthes, St. Louis*
Fred R. Weber Jr., St. Louis*

Special class of 1973

Christopher S. Bond, Mexico (Washington, D.C.)

Class of 1974

John C. Danforth, St. Louis
Floyd R. Gibson, Kansas City*
Roy W. Harper, St. Louis*
Clarence M. Kelley, Kansas City*
Maurice E. VanAckeren, Kansas City*

Class of 1975

George H. Capps, St. Louis*
Ilus W. Davis, Kansas City*
Donald J. Hall, Kansas City*
John A. Morgan, Kansas City*
John R. Opel, New York, NY (Ft. Myers, FL)*
Mrs. Kenneth A. Spencer, Kansas City*
Harold E. Thayer, St. Louis*

Class of 1976

No election held

Class of 1977

M. Graham Clark, Point Lookout*
William R. Clarkson, Kansas City
Charles E. Curry, Key Largo, FL*
Elmo B. Hunter, Kansas City*
Louis B. Susman, Chicago, IL

Special class of 1977

Joseph P. Teasdale, Kansas City*

Class of 1978

W. Robert Aylward, Kansas City
James L. McHugh, St. Louis
James C. Olson, Kansas City*
Albert M. Spradling Jr., Cape Girardeau*
William L. Hungate, St. Louis*

Class of 1979

No election held

Class of 1980

No election held

Class of 1981

Clarence C. Barksdale, St. Louis
August A. Busch III, St. Louis**
Jay B. Dillingham, Kansas City*
Charles F. Knight, St. Louis
Dr. Herbert Schooling, Columbia*
Dr. James I. Spainhower, St. Charles (Raymore)
Avis Green Tucker, Warrensburg*
William H. Webster, Bethesda, MD
  (Washington, DC)

Class of 1982

No election held

Class of 1983

Lucile H. Bluford, Kansas City*
Flavius B. Freeman, Springfield*
James M. Kemper Jr., Kansas City
Sanford N. McDonnell, St. Louis**
Marlin Perkins, St. Louis*
James W. Stephens, Lee's Summit*
Gene Taylor, Sarcoxie*
Robert Ellis Young, Carthage*

Special class of 1984

John Ashcroft, Springfield (Washington, D.C.)

Class of 1985

William N. Deramus III, Kansas City*
Douglas Ensminger, Columbia*
Rosemary L. Ginn, Columbia*
Lawrence K. Roos, St. Louis*
Thomas G. Watson, Kansas City (Westwood, KS)
Murray L. Weidenbaum, St. Louis*

Class of 1986

No election held

Class of 1987

Sam B. Cook, Jefferson City
John Q. Hammons, Springfield*
Robert N. Hunter, Jefferson City*
John E. Moore, Springfield
Morton I. Sosland, Kansas City

Class of 1988

No election held

Class of 1989

W.H. Bert Bates, Kansas City
Henry Bloch, Kansas City
Ann Covington, Columbia (Jefferson City)
Richard Gephardt, St. Louis (Washington, D.C.)
Ewing Kauffman, Kansas City*
Ben Parnell, Springfield
Charles Price, Kansas City*
Ike Skelton, Lexington (Washington, D.C.)*
Joseph Stevens, Kansas City*
Ted Wetterau, St. Louis*

Class of 1990

Dr. J. Robert Ashcroft, Springfield*
Robert L. Hawkins Jr., Jefferson City
Lee Liberman, St. Louis*
Veryl Riddle, St. Louis*
George Russell, Kansas City*
Michael Shanahan, St. Louis

Class of 1991

No election held

Class of 1992

No election held

Class of 1993

Mel Carnahan, Rolla*
Andrew B. Craig III, St. Louis
Anita B. Gorman, Kansas City
Thomas J. Guilfoil, St. Louis*
Andrew Jackson Higgins, Jefferson City*
R. Crosby Kemper Jr., Kansas City*
Richard J. Mahoney, St. Louis
William E. Maritz, St. Louis*

Class of 1994

Jack Buck, St. Louis*
Lynn M. Ewing Jr., Nevada*
Ollie Gates, Kansas City
Webb Gilmore, Kansas City
Herman Johnson, Kansas City*
Landon Rowland, Kansas City
Norm Stewart, Columbia
Harry Wiggins, Kansas City*

Class of 1995

No election held

Class of 1996

William H. Dunn Sr., Kansas City
James L. Mathewson, Sedalia
Walter L. Metcalfe Jr., St. Louis
James B. Nutter Sr., Kansas City
Betty Goshorn Weldon, Jefferson City*

Class of 1997

William J. Cason, Clinton
Emanuel Cleaver II, Kansas City
Thomas R. Green, Frontenac
Edward L Dowd Sr., St. Louis*
John L. Morris, Springfield
Michael Pulitzer, St. Louis

Class of 1998

No election held

Class of 1999

Richard Berkley, Kansas City
Lawrence Biondi, St. Louis
William B. Bondeson, Columbia
John Jordan (Buck) O'Neil, Kansas City*
Peter R. Raven, St. Louis
Frank P. Sebree, Kansas City

Special Class of 2000

Roger Wilson, Columbia
Bob Holden, Jefferson City

Class of 2001

No election held

Class of 2002

Kay Barnes, Kansas City
Lou Brock, St. Louis (St. Charles)
Jean Carnahan, St. Louis (Rolla)
S. Lee Kling, St. Louis*
Edward T. Matheny Jr., Kansas City
Mary Rhodes Russell, St. Louis
Jim Stowers, Kansas City*
Jack Taylor, St. Louis

Class of 2003

No election held

Class of 2004

Sheryl Crow, Kennett
John Dillingham, Kansas City
Richard (Dick) Dunn, Jefferson City (Springfield)*
Terrence (Terry) Dunn, Kansas City
Rafaela (Lali) Garcia, Kansas City
Henry Givens Jr., St. Louis
Sam F. Hamra Jr., Springfield
Charles McClain, Columbia*
Daniel (Duke) McVey, Jefferson City
Alan Wheat, Kansas City (Arlington, VA)

Special class of 2005

Matthew R. Blunt, Springfield

Class of 2006

No election held

Class of 2007

Roy Blunt, Springfield
Stephen C. Bradford, Cape Girardeau
Camilla Brauer, St. Louis
William H.T. Bush, St. Louis
Ann Dickinson, Kansas City
Charlie Dooley, St. Louis
Sr. Antona Ebo, St. Louis
L.B. Eckelkamp, Jr., Washington
Ethelmae Humphreys, Joplin
James Talent, St. Louis
Ann Wagner, Ballwin

Class of 2008

James B. Anderson, Springfield
Rudolph E. Farber, Neosho
Rex Sinquefield, St. Louis

Class of 2009

Frankie M. Freeman, St. Louis
Peter Herschend, Branson
Jack Magruder, Kirksville
Mike Shannon, St. Louis

Special Class of 2009

Jeremiah W. (Jay) Nixon, Jefferson City

Class of 2010

No election held

*Deceased
**Resigned

Foreign Consulates in Missouri

Consulates are the offices established by countries for their representatives (consuls) living in certain foreign cities and serving the country's citizens and business interests there. The Missouri Consular Corps is compromised of foreign service officers from nations maintaining friendly relations with the United States. These officials are recognized by the U.S. State Department. They perform trade and diplomatic services for their own citizens and for United States citizens. This information was obtained from: Foreign Consular Offices in the United States by the United States Department of State (Revised Feb. 5, 2014).

Source: *www.state.gov/documents/organization/221620.pdf*

Key: CG – Consulate General; C – Consulate; VC – Vice Consulate; CA – Consular Agency; H – Honorary Consular Status.

Albania

Blue Springs, Mr. Joseph Dale Patterson, HC, 1916 N.W. Fawn Dr., Blue Springs 64015, (816) 228-6321.

Austria

Kansas City, Mr. Dennis James Campbell Owens, HCG, 1111 Main St., Seventh Fl., Kansas City 64105, (816) 474-3000, FAX (816) 474-5533.

St. Louis, Mr. Dieter Karl Ungerboeck, HC, 100 Ungerboeck Park, O'Fallon 63368, (636) 300-5606, FAX (636) 300-5607.

Belgium

Kansas City, Mr. David Barber, HC, 1411 E. 104th St., Kansas City 66208, (816) 898-5147, FAX (816) 942-0006.

Chile

Kansas City, Mr. Robert William Evans, HC, 1101 Walnut St., Ste. 102A, Kansas City 64106, (816) 221-0299.

Czech Republic

Kansas City, Ms. Sharon Kay Valasek, HC, 105 W. 113th St., Kansas City 64114, (816) 363-6827.

Finland

St. Louis, Mr. Peter Brabson Mackeith II, HC, 1 Brookings Dr., Rm. 105, St. Louis 63130, (314) 935-7125.

France

St. Louis, Mr. James Francis Mauze Jr., HCA, 112 S. Hanley Rd., Second Fl., St. Louis 63105, (314) 862-3222, FAX (314) 862-3228.

Germany, Fed. Rep. of

St. Louis, Mr. Lansing Gervig Hecker, HC, 330 Wenneker Dr., St. Louis 63124, (314) 567-4601, FAX (314) 567-1101.

Guatemala

Kansas City, Dr. Joseph Peter Spalitto, HC, 400 E. Red Bridge Rd., Ste. 107, Kansas City 64131, (816) 942-6990, FAX (816) 942-4301.

Hungary

St. Louis, Mr. Julius Joe Adorjan, HCG, 230 S. Bemiston Ave., Ste. 1470, St. Louis 63105, FAX (314) 725-7299.

Iceland

Grandview, Mrs. Vigdis Adalsteinsdottir Taylor, HC, 7100 E. 131st St., Grandview 64030, (816) 763-2046.

Ireland

St. Louis, Mr. Joseph Bernard McGlynn, HCG, 1015 Locust St., Ste. 710, St. Louis 63101, (314) 727-1000.

Italy

St. Louis, Mr. Joseph Colagiovanni Jr., HVC, 190 Carondelet Pz., Ste. 1690, St. Louis 63105, (314) 505-8835, FAX (314) 259-5985.

Japan

St. Louis, Mr. Bruce S. Buckland, HCG, 46 Briarcliff St., St. Louis 63124, (314) 994-1133, FAX (314) 994-1133.

Korea

St. Louis, Ms. Judy Preddy Draper, (HC), 2070 Meadowbrook, Chesterfield 63017, (314) 615-3234, FAX (314) 615-2689.

Luxembourg

Liberty, Mr. Robert F. Schaeffer, HCG, 325 Westwoods Circle, Liberty 64068, (816) 792-0841, FAX (816) 792-4999.

Mexico

Kansas City, Mrs. Alicia Guadalupe Kerber Palma, (C), Miss Maria De Lourdes Orestano Robledo, (C), Mrs. Erica Pardo Rodriguez, (C), Mr. Roberto Ascencion Caldera Arroyo, Deputy Consul, 1617 Baltimore Ave., Kansas City 64108, (816) 556-0800.

Netherlands

St. Louis, Mr. Richard William Lodge, HC, 562 N. Woodlawn, St. Louis 63122, (314) 965-3533, FAX (314) 965-3533.

Pakistan

St. Louis, Dr. Azfar Malik, HC, 5000 Cedar Plaza Parkway, Ste. 350, St. Louis 63128, (314) 843-4333. FAX (636) 441-7300.

Peru

St. Louis, Mr. Francisco Matarazzo Benavides, HC, 10123 Corporate Square Dr., St. Louis 63132.

Poland

St. Louis, Mr. Robert V. Ogrodnik, HC, 121 S. Meramec Ave., Ste. 1140, St. Louis 63105, (314) 822-6266, FAX (314) 965-3728.

Senegal

Clayton, Mr. John Aaron Wright Sr., HC, 7102 Stanford Ave., St. Louis 63130, (314) 726-5612, FAX (314) 726-5612.

Slovak Republic

Kansas City, Mr. Ross Paul Marine, HC, 11729 Central St., Kansas City 64114, (816) 943-0515.

Spain

Kansas City, Dr. Antonio Artigues Serra, HC, 729 W. 121st St., Kansas City 64145.

St. Louis, Mr. Jose Leopoldo Molina Jr., HC, 5715 Manchester Ave., St. Louis 63110, (314) 781-1500, FAX (314) 781-1507.

Sweden

St. Louis, Ms. Liselotte Marie Fox, HC, 7701 Forsyth Blvd., Ste. 600, St. Louis 63105, (314) 540-6532.

Switzerland

Kansas City, Mr. Marcel Bollier, HC, 5018 Main St., Kansas City 64112, (816) 561-3441, FAX (816) 561-2922.

Turkey

St. Joseph, Mr. Emru Ahmet Erten, HCG, 6000 Industrial Rd., St. Joseph 64504, (816) 238-6646, FAX (816) 238-6295.

Boards Assigned to the Governor

Clay County Board of Election Commissioners

100 W. Mississippi St., Liberty 64068-1623
Telephone: (816) 415-8683 / FAX: (816) 792-5334
www.claycoelections.com

Chair: Anthony Bologna (D);
Secretary: Angela Beshears (R);
Members: Thelma Crawford (D); James B. Chappell (R);
Directors of Elections: Patty Evans (D); Vacancy.

Jackson County Board of Election Commissioners

215 N. Liberty, PO Box 296, Independence 64050
Telephone: (816) 325-4600 / FAX: (816) 325-4609

Chair: Mary Ellen Miller (D);
Secretary: Colleen M. Scott (R);
Members: Vacancy; Michael K. Whitehead (R);
Directors of Elections: Robert C. Nichols Jr. (D); Tammy L. Brown (R).

Kansas City Board of Election Commissioners

30 W. Pershing Rd., Union Station, Ste. 610 & Ste. 2800
*   Kansas City 64108*
Telephone: (816) 842-4820 / FAX: (816) 472-4960

Chair: Megan C. Thornberry (D);
Secretary: Melodie Powell (R);
Members: Quinton Jennings (D); Blake Heath (R);
Directors of Elections: Shelley McThomas (D); Shawn Kieffer (R).

Platte County Board of Election Commissioners

2600 NW Prairie View Rd., PO Box 560, Platte City 64079
Telephone: (816) 858-4400 / FAX: (816) 858-3387
www.plattemovotes.org

Chair: James Everett (D);
Secretary: Marvin Ferguson (R);
Members: Diane Pepper (D); Betty Knight (R);
Directors of Elections: Chris Hershey (D); Wendy M. Flanigan (R).

St. Louis City Board of Election Commissioners

300 N. Tucker Blvd., St. Louis 63101
Telephone: (314) 622-4336 / FAX: (314) 589-3587

Chair: Joan Burger (D);
Secretary: Jack Lary (R);
Members: Benjamin Phillips (D); Andrew Schwartz (R); Paul Maloney (R)
Directors of Election: Mary Wheeler-Jones (D); Leo (Gary) Stoff Jr. (R).

St. Louis County Board of Election Commissioners

12 Sunnen Dr., Maplewood 63143
Telephone: (314) 615-1800 / FAX: (314) 622-3587

Chair: Richard Kellett (D);
Secretary: John Maupin (R)
Members: Trudi McCollum Foushee; John King (R);
Directors of Elections: Eric Fey (D); Gary Fuhr (R).

Kansas City Board of Police Commissioners

1125 Locust St., Kansas City 64106
Telephone: (816) 234-5055

President: Alvin Brooks;
Vice President: Michael Rader;
Secretary/Attorney: David V. Kenner;
Treasurer: Angela Wasson-Hunt;
Member: Vacancy;
Member: Mayor Sylvester (Sly) James, Mayor's Office, City Hall, 414 E. 12th St., Kansas City 64106.

Unassigned Boards and Commissions

Missouri Local Government Employees' Retirement System

701 W. Main St., PO Box 1665, Jefferson City 65102
Telephone:(573) 636-9455 / Toll free: (800) 447-4334
www.molagers.org

The Missouri Local Government Employees' Retirement System (LAGERS) was established under legislation that became effective Aug. 13, 1967, to provide retirement, disability and survivor benefits for employees of local government employers. More than 58,000 employees and retirees of more than 660 political subdivisions presently participate in the system. The system is governed by a board of trustees, which includes three members elected by governing bodies of participating subdivisions; three members elected by employee members and one public member appointed by the governor.

LAGERS Board of Trustees

Ashcroft, J. Robert, chair, Platte County, Dec. 31, 2017;
Buck, Frank, vice chair, DeKalb County, Dec. 31, 2016;
Todd, Arby, Lee's Summit, Dec. 31, 2017;
Barszczak, Kathy, Independence, Dec. 31, 2016;
Jadali, Joan, Webster Groves, Dec. 31, 2018;
McCullough, Barry, Gladstone, Dec. 31, 2018;
Hughes, Keith, executive secretary.

Public School Retirement System of Missouri

3210 W. Truman Blvd., PO Box 268, Jefferson City 65102
Telephone: (573) 634-5290 / Toll free: (800) 392-6848
FAX (573) 634-5375
www.psrs-peers.org

The Public School Retirement System of Missouri includes the public school districts of Missouri, except St. Louis and Kansas City; public junior community colleges in Missouri; and certificated members and employees of the board of the system. The system began operations on July 1, 1946, and as of June 30, 2014, the system had 93,419 active members and 54,486 retirees.

The system is financed by contributions of members and the employing school districts in equal amounts and by interest earned on investment of contributions. Administering the program is a seven-member board of trustees. Three members are appointed by the governor, and four are elected for four-year terms by the members and retirees.

Public Education Employee Retirement System of Missouri

The Public Education Employee Retirement System of Missouri (formerly Non-Teacher School Employee Retirement System of Missouri) began operations in 1965. As of June 30, 2014, it included 76,989 active employees and 25,029 retirees of public school districts, except those in St. Louis and Kansas City. Financing of the two systems is similar and the same board administers both programs.

Board of Trustees

Zalis, Aaron, chair, Rolla, June 30, 2016;
Hoffman, Jason, vice chair, Columbia, June 30, 2018;
Wheeler, Wayne, Kimberling City, June 30, 2012;
Heath, Yvonne, Bois D'Arc, June 30, 2016;
Hunt, Scott, St. Louis, June 30, 2013;
Yoakum, M. Steve, executive director.

Missouri Consolidated Health Care Plan

832 Weathered Rock Ct., PO Box 104355
Jefferson City 65110-4355
Telephone: (573) 751-8881 / FAX: (886) 346-8785
www.mchcp.org

The Missouri Consolidated Health Care Plan (MCHCP) provides medical coverage to employees and retirees of most state agencies and to employee and retiree dependents. Public entities such as school districts, cities and counties may also join MCHCP. Nearly 100,000 state and public entity members are covered through two types of medical plans: preferred provider organization (PPO) plan and high deductible health plan (HDHP) with health savings account (HSA). MCHCP also offers dental and vision coverage.

Established Jan. 1, 1994, MCHCP is a statutorily created body corporate and organized under the direction of a 13-member board of trustees including: three *ex officio* members (the director of the Department of Insurance, Financial Institutions and Professional Registration; the director of the Department of Health and Senior Services; and the commissioner of the Office of Administration); two members from the House of Representatives (one from each party); two members from the Senate (one from each party); and six members appointed by the governor (three of the six are members of the plan and the remaining three are not members of the plan).

MCHCP Board of Trustees

Langworthy, Mark A., vice chair, governor-appointed member;

Huff, John M., *ex officio* member, director, Department of Insurance, Financial Institutions and Professional Registration;

Kendrick, Kip, (D), House member;

Luebbering, Linda, governor-appointed member;

Lyskowski, Peter, *ex officio* member, acting director, Department of Health and Senior Services;

Nelson, Doug, *ex officio* member, commissioner, Office of Administration;

Rowden, Caleb, (R), House member;

Sater, David, (R), Senate member;

Schaefer, Viola, governor appointed member;

Sifton, Scott, (D), Senate member;

Warrick, Michael, governor-appointed member.

Missouri State Employees' Retirement System

PO Box 209, Jefferson City 65102
Telephone: (573) 632-6100 / Toll-free: (800) 827-1063
FAX: (573) 632-6103
www.mosers.org

The Missouri State Employees' Retirement System (MOSERS) was established by law in 1957. The system is responsible for administration of the retirement program for all state employees (other than employees of the Highway Commission, the Highway Patrol and the University of Missouri). Effective Sept. 1, 1972, the program became noncontributory for members with the state becoming the sole contributor, except for members employed for the first time on or after Jan. 1, 2011. The system also provides life insurance coverage of one time annual pay for active members and $5,000 for retired members, with optional group life insurance coverage available at the expense of the members. The system is also responsible for administration of the state's long-term disability program for most state employees and the State of Missouri Deferred Compensation Plan. The system operates under the direction and control of an 11-member board of trustees made up of the state treasurer, commissioner of administration, two members each of the House and Senate, two members appointed by the governor, two active members elected by the active members and one retired member elected by the retired members.

MOSERS Board of Trustees

Smith, Antwaun, chair, governor-appointed member;

Carmichael, Lloyd J. (Joe), governor-appointed member, Columbia;

Keaveny, Joe, Senate member, St. Louis;

Leara, Mike, House member; St. Louis;

Jones, Caleb, House member; Columbia;

Martin, Don, elected retired member;

Nelson, Doug, *ex officio* member, commissioner, Office of Administration, Jefferson City;

Owens, Shannon, elected active member, Office of State Courts Administrator, Jefferson City;

Wallingford, Wayne, Senate member, Cape Girardeau;

Wessing, Crystal, elected active member, Office of Administration; California;

Zweifel, Clint, *ex officio* member, state treasurer, Jefferson City;

Watson, John, executive director.

Missouri Department of Transportation and Highway Patrol Employees' Retirement System

1913 William St., PO Box 1930, Jefferson City 65102
Telephone: (573) 298-6080

The Missouri Department of Transportation and Highway Patrol Employees' Retirement System was established under legislation, which became effective in 1955, to provide retirement benefits for employees of the Missouri Department of Transportation and the State Highway Patrol. The system has approximately 18,003 members. Financing of the system is generally from highway funds and investment income. The system is governed by an 11-member board of trustees made up of three members of the Highways and Transportation Commission, the director of the Department of Transportation, the superintendent of the Highway Patrol, one member of the Senate, one member of the House of Representatives, one active member of the Department of Transportation, one active member of the State Highway Patrol, one retired member of the Department of Transportation and one retired member of the State Highway Patrol.

Board of Trustees

Carmichael, Lloyd (Joe), chair, Springfield, Highways and Transportation Commission member, March 1, 2015;

Johnson, Colonel J. Bret, vice chair, Jefferson City, superintendent, Highway Patrol;

Broeker, Roberta, Jefferson City, interim director, Department of Transportation;

Cox, Sue, Jefferson City, MoDOT retiree member, July 1, 2018;

Pace, Mike, West Plains, Highways and Transportation Commission member, March 1, 2019;

Rhoads, Shawn, West Plains, House of Representatives member;

Schatz, Dave, Sullivan, Senate member;

Seibert, William, Jefferson City, Highway Patrol retiree member, July 1, 2018;

Shoun, Major Kemp, Jefferson City, Highway Patrol active member, July 1, 2018;

Tyler, Todd Neosho, MoDOT active member, July 1, 2018;

Vacancy, Highways and Transportation Commission member;

Simon, Scott, executive director.

Missouri Statistics

Agriculture

Number of farms..99,700
Total farm acreages...28,300,000
Total agriculture value..$9,164,886
Farm segment/national rank
Hay production (excluding alfalfa)... Second
Beef cows .... Second
Hog production .... Seventh
Broilers ....Thirteenth
Horses ....Twentieth
Turkeys raised .... Fourth
Corn production ....Seventh
Rice production .... Fourth
Cotton production .... Eighth
Soybean production... Sixth
Milk production .... Twenty-fifth
Winter wheat production ....Thirteenth
Farm segment annual production
Grapes.. 8.1 million pounds
Watermelons .... 837,000 cwt.
Grain sorghum.. 7.3 million bushels
Apples .... 21 million pounds
Peaches .... 8.1 million pounds
Timberland acreage .... 15.4 million acres
Annual value of forestry products.. $7.3 billion
Agritourism and recreational services .... 696 locations
Farmers' Markets.. 293
Wineries..122
Energy
Number of power plants 110
Nuclear plant... 1

Conservation

State conservation acreage (areas/acreage) 1,197/ 998,526.82
Owned (areas/acreage) .... 810 / 794,458.57
Leased acreage (areas/acreage) .... 387 / 204,068.25
Crop land acreage 66,900
Fishing lakes/ponds acreage... 26,970
Forest land acreage 603,050
Grassland/old-fields/prairie acreage 170,130
Wetland acreage... 52,275
Facilities on Conservation Areas
Archery ranges (owned and leased)... 38
Areas with concrete boat ramps... 320
Areas with camping at designated sites 199
Firearm ranges (owned and leased) 52
Fire lookout towers 47
Fish hatcheries... 9
Fishing docks, jetties and platforms.. 367
Forest seedling nursery.. 1
Hunting blinds... 259
Nature centers 7
Parking lots 2,874

Trails (miles).. 852
Viewing blinds, & decks 63
Visitor centers... 9

Education

Public schools (2014–2015)
Elementary...1,233
Junior High 54
Middle..284
High schools...613
Other...108
Charter schools
Elementary 36
Junior High 0
Middle..13
High schools...13
Charter LEA's...37
Six-Director Elementary..72
Districts maintaining high schools 448
Public school districts..520
Public school buildings 2,354
Public school enrollment (2013-2014)..887,641
Elementary (K–8)..618,594
Secondary (9–12)..269,047
Public high school graduation rate (2013–2014) 4 year graduation rate................... 87.3%
Nonpublic schools (2014–2015)
Elementary..464
Secondary...51
Ungraded 4
Nonpublic school districts 519
Nonpublic school enrollment 75,967
Elementary (K-8) 59,130
Secondary (9-12) 16,730
Ungraded 107
Nonpublic high school graduation (2013–2014)...6,705
Area career centers (attached to school ditricts) 57
Colleges and universities
Public four-year colleges and universities...13
Public two-year community colleges 20
Technical College 1
Independent four-year colleges and universities 24
Independent two-year colleges 1
Independent technical, professional and theological schools 30
Private career schools 150
Area public vocational technical schools...38

Employment

Total nonfarm 2,734,000
Total private...2,302,000
Goods producing..370,100
Mining & logging..4,000
Construction..109,800
Manufacturing 256,200
Durable goods 152,400
Non-durable goods 103,800
Service-providing...2,363,900
Private service-providing..1,931,900
Trade, transportation and utilities 522,600
Wholesale trade 120,900

Retail trade	304,300
Transportation, warehousing and utilities	97,500
Information	57, 200
Financial activities	164,200
Professional and business services	353,700
Education and health services	435,000
Educational services	54,600
Health care and social assistance	380,400
Leisure and hospitality	285,600
Arts, entertainment and recreation	43,400
Accommodation and food services	242,200
Other services	113,600
Government	432,000
Federal	53,300
State	99,500
Local	279,200

Unemployment rate
Missouri: 2014.. 5.9%
United States: 2014 .... 6.2%
Cost of living:
Missouri/United States (1st quarter, 2015) 91.5% / 11th lowest

Natural Resources

State Parks and Historic Sites
Parks 52
Historic sites 35
State park acreage... 148,445
State parks and historic sites with bordering lakes... 30
Facilities in state parks and state historic sites
Camping 40
Lodging 14
Beaches 18
Boat ramps on lakes and streams 27
Hiking trails 57
Equestrian trails... 16
Mountain biking trails 14
All-terrain vehicle trails... 2
Interpretive centers/museums.. 25
Guided historic site tours 23
Guided cave tours... 4

Professions/occupations

Missouri State Board of Accountancy 21,946
Acupuncturist Advisory Committee Acupuncturist 139
Missouri Board for Architects, Professional Engineers, Professional Land Surveyors and Landscape
Architects 28,024
Office of Athlete Agents Athlete Agents.. 83
Office of Athletics.. 1,475
Behavior Analyst Advisory Board 320
Board of Cosmetology and Barber Examiners 82,169
State Board of Chiropractic Examiners 2,272
Missouri Dental Board.. 13,786
State Committee of Dietitians 2,022
State Board of Embalmers and Funeral Directors 6,243
Office of Endowed Care Cemetries 129
Missouri Board of Geologist Registration 840
State Board of Registration for the Healing Arts....................................... 42,614
Board of Examiners for Hearing Instrument Specialists.................................. 294
Interior Design Council 77

Missouri State Committee of Interpreters.. 719
State Committee of Marital & Family Therapists 283
Board of Therapeutic Massage 6,317
State Board of Nursing... 130,379
Missouri Board of Occupational Therapy 5,167
State Board of Optometry 1,304
State Board of Pharmacy.. 33,568
State Board of Podiatric Medicine... 356
Board of Private Investigator and Private Fire Investigator Examiners.................... 917
Committee for Professional Counselors... 5,873
State Committee of Psychologists.. 2,154
Real Estate Appraisers Commission... 2,600
Missouri Real Estate Commission... 39,030
Missouri Board for Respiratory Care 4,417
State Committee for Social Workers... 7,740
Office of Tattooing, Body Piercing & Branding.. 1,632
Missouri Veterinary Medical Board 5,287
Insurance
   Insurance agents.. 141,385
   Insurance agencies.. 13,412
   Licensed insurance companies... 1,980
   Bail bond agents 949
   Surety recovery agents 28
   Public adjusters 186
   Registered entities... 1,157
   Surplus lines 1,624
   Navigators 889
   Portable electronics 22
   Organizational credit business entity producers 203
   Motor vehicle extended service contract producers 2,091
Business information
Financial services
   State-chartered commercial banks 261
    Branches 1,537
   Credit unions 115
   Licensed mortgage brokers 417
   Licensed consumer credit outlets 2,930
   Savings and loans 5

Revenue

New driver's licenses and renewals issued... 238,975
Motor vehicle, trailer and boat titles issued... 1.94 million
Vehicle registrations issued... 4.06 million
License offices... 178
Fraudulent individual income tax refunds thwarted .... $39.9 million

Tourism

Tourism's economic impact (FY2014)..$15.3 billion
    (Source: Kaylen Economics/Univ. of Missouri)
Taxable sales from tourism-related industries (FY2014)..$11.62 billion
    (Source: Dept. of Revenue)
Tourism-related Employment in Missouri (FY2014) 290,734

Transportation

Public airports 124
Airline passengers...11.6 million
Highway miles (on the state system) 33,895
Bridges—number of major river bridges ....53 (most in the nation)
Number of MoDOT bridges..10,376
Public transit, miles of light rail (MetroLink in Missouri) 25
Public transportation providers 35
Annual transit trips ....63 million
Miles of mainline railroad track 3,719
Operating railroads...19
Amtrak ridership...536,958
Waterways (navigable)...1,050
Number port authorities 14
Tri-state port commission...1

Crime Statistics

2014 statistics
    Murder 403
    Rape...2,268
    Robbery 5,590
Aggravated assault..18,476
    Burglary...35,223
    Theft 124,518
Motor vehicle theft 16,348
    Arson...1,405

Index of Historical Features in the Official Manual

Flag Etiquette

The following are some of the rules of flag etiquette regarding the time and manner of display and disposal of the flag of the United States of America pursuant to Title 4, Chapter 1 of the United States Code.

It is the universal custom to display the flag only from sunrise to sunset on buildings and on stationary flagstaffs in the open. However, when a patriotic effect is desired, the flag may be displayed 24 hours a day if properly illuminated during the hours of darkness.

No other flag or pennant should be placed above or, if on the same level, to the right of the flag of the United States of America, except during church services conducted by naval chaplains at sea, when the church pennant may be flown above the flag during services for the personnel of the Navy.

No person shall display the flag of the United Nations or any other national or international flag equal, above, or in a position of superior prominence or honor to, or in place of, the flag of the United States at any place within the United States or any territory or possession thereof; provided, that nothing in this section shall make unlawful the continuance of the practice heretofore followed of displaying the flag of the United Nations in a position of superior prominence or honor, and other national flags in positions of equal prominence or honor, with that of the flag of the United States at the headquarters of the United Nations.

When flags of states, cities or localities, or pennants of societies are flown on the same halyard with the flag of the United States, the latter should always be at the peak. When the flags are flown from adjacent staffs, the flag of the United States should be hoisted first and lowered last. No such flag or pennant may be placed above the flag of the United States or to the United States flag's right.

The flag of the United States of America, when it is displayed with another flag against a wall from crossed staffs, should be on the right, the flag's own right, and its staff should be in front of the staff of the other flag.

The flag of the United States of America should be at the center and at the highest point of the group when a number of flags of states or localities or pennants of societies are grouped and displayed from staffs.

When the flags of two or more nations are displayed, they are to be flown from separate staffs of the same height. The flags are to be of approximately equal size. International usage forbids the display of the flag of one nation above that of another nation in time of peace.

When displayed either horizontally or vertically against a wall, the union should be uppermost and to the flag's own right, that is, to the observer's left. When displayed in a window, the flag should be displayed in the same way, with the union or blue field to the left of the observer in the street.

When used on a speaker's platform, the flag if displayed flat, should be displayed above and behind the speaker. When displayed from a staff in a church or public auditorium, the flag of the United States of America should hold the position of superior prominence, in advance of the audience, and in the position of honor at the clergyman's or speaker's right as he faces the audience. Any other flag so displayed should be placed on the left of the clergyman or speaker or to the right of the audience.

The flag, when flown at half-staff, should be hoisted to the peak for an instant and then lowered to the half-staff position. On Memorial Day the flag should be displayed at half-staff until noon only, then raised to the top of the staff. By order of the President, the flag should be flown at half-staff upon the death of principal figures of the United States government and the governor of a state, territory or possession, as a mark of respect to their memory. In the event of the death of other officials or foreign dignitaries, the flag is to be displayed at half-staff according to presidential instructions or orders, or in accordance with recognized customs or practices not inconsistent with law.

In the event of the death of a present or former official of the government of any state, territory or possession of the United States, the governor of the state, territory or possession may proclaim that the national flag shall be flown at half-staff.

- The flag should be hoisted briskly and lowered ceremoniously.
- The flag should be displayed in or near every polling place on election days.
- The flag should be displayed during school days in or near every schoolhouse.
- The flag, when it is such that it is no longer a fitting emblem for display, should be destroyed in a dignified way, preferably by burning.

The Pledge of Allegiance

I pledge allegiance to the Flag of the United States of America, and to the Republic for which it stands, one Nation under God, indivisible, with liberty and justice for all.

CHAPTER 10

PERSONNEL

Cape Rock Park, overlooking the Mississippi River at Cape Girardeau
Photo Courtesy of Missouri State Archives

Missouri Personnel

Missouri law (11.030, RSMo) requires the *Official Manual* contain certain personnel information. This information, provided by the Office of Administration and published as received after review by each state agency, appears in the same order here as the agency narrative listings appear in the earlier chapters. All listings are as of July 1, 2015.

Chapter 2: Executive Branch

Office of Governor
State Capitol, Jefferson City 65101

Nixon, Jeremiah W, governor, $133,821
Ansley, Channing, comm dir & policy adv, $101,000
Ardini, Edward R, counsel to the gov, $126,755
Bayer, Tiffany J, chief of staff to the first lady, $55,558
Blunt, Aaron, dir of opps, $50,000
Brauner, Sharon C, asst to legislative affairs, $52,000
Bundy, Seth D, dpty press sec & policy adv, $90,000
Harris, Robert J, dir of policy, $121,705
Barton, Taylor, admin asst/recept, $37,370
Hoelscher, Kimberly R, exec sec, $60,000
Holste, Scott A, press sec & policy advis, $81,305
Luebbering, Elizabeth, housekeeper, $24,200
Lyskowski, Peter A, deputy chief of staff, $111,605
Miller, William L, policy advisor, $100,000
Murray, Judy M, exec asst, $71,186
Nelson, Trey A, deputy dir of scheduling, $38,000
Nietzel, Michael, sr policy advisor, $76,129
Pieper, Christopher R, chief of staff, $126,755
Spillars, Andrea K, sr legal & policy advisor, $111,624
Thompson, Kelsey E, dir of scheduling, $70,000
Zamkus, Jason M, dir of legislative affairs, $111,605

Office of Lieutenant Governor
224 State Capitol, Jefferson City 65101

Kinder, Peter D, lt gov, $86,484
Bain, Matthew, staff asst, $34,000
Dawson, Laurie S, dir of administration, $62,317
Eastlick, Jay R, dir of comm, $71,205
Forrester, Reid K, chief of staff, $71,205
Jones, Willis A, dir constituent svcs & sr advoc, $41,285
Pondrom, Joseph R, dir of policy leg affairs, $36,000

Office of Secretary of State
PO Box 1767, Jefferson City 65102

Kander, Jason D, sec of state, $107,746
Adams, Andrew, dpty counsel, $52,002
Adeyeri, Temitope, comp info tech II, $48,156
Ahmedbani, Mariam S, auditor/acct II, $44,808
Ali, Mohamed, comp info tech II, $39,396
Allen, Julie A, dir of elections and info tech, $91,044
Allsbury, Phyllis A, exec sec, $53,040
Andrews, Archie, tech II, $30,384
Apperson, Kimberly, central servs technician, $30,000
Barge, Patricia G, research analyst I, $31,512
Barrett, Larry W, research analyst, $33,744
Barry, Jonathan, dir of business outreach, $54,504

Bauman, Lauren A, pers ofcr, $38,076
Baxley, Dixie I, compliance exam, $37,548
Bennett, Sandra D, accounting analyst II, $43,488
Benoist, Michael, dir of external opps, $42,924
Bilal, Deborah W, dir ref servs, $53,208
Blauvelt, Terry V, stat research analyst, $41,172
Blume, Jennifer S, tech II, $26,232
Bowen, Rebekah L, archivist, $37,548
Branch, Donald K, clerk I, $24,612
Branch, Dorothy E, tech III, $28,536
Branch, Jamie K, tech III, $29,004
Branstetter, Larry R, clerk I, $25,404
Brester, Kenna M, sup IV, $40,380
Brewer, Benjamin A, tech III, $28,104
Brock, Sharon E, archivist, $37,548
Brondel, Karen A, tech IV, $34,944
Brown, Sally, tech II, $28,908
Buchheit, Mark T, elections spec, $37,404
Burnett, Robyn K, archivist, $37,548
Burton, Nicholas, compliance exam, $37,548
Buschman, Joel A, tech II, $26,232
Butler, Matthew, digital collections coord, $41,940
Butler, Stacy J, tech II, $29,412
Caldera, Jose S, sr dpty counsel, $64,002
Carlson, Rebecca L, archivist, $40,380
Carter, Jase C, dir of bus serv/sr advisor, $75,264
Cebulak, Troy P, investigator II, $36,864
Christensen, Devon L, comp info tech spec I, $61,092
Clark, Casey, chief of staff, $90,900
Clevenger, Jack, comp info tech III, $45,156
Coker, Mary K, archivist, $38,928
Collings, Carolyn K, archivist, $40,380
Cook, Carolyn D, administrative aide III, $32,628
Cosby, Patrick J, accounting analyst II, $39,624
Crockett, Jamie, comm/publications asst, $30,984
Croteau, Shelly J, asst state archivist, $57,744
Crowley, Susan L, administrative aide III, $29,916
Crump, Dorinda A, investigator IV, $42,000
Degraffenreid, Mary E, tech III, $30,984
Dennis, Andrea M, tech II, $28,452
Denny, Keith, clerk I, $23,880
Desu, Venkata Suresh, dep dir of it/it opps, $77,868
Dickrader, Rhea, clerk I, $24,612
Dodd, Lance E, comp info tech spec I, $62,550
Dougan, John R, state archivist, $85,344
Douglas-Llyr, Michael L, graphic arts spec II, $30,984
Dudenhoeffer, Alisha L, administrative aide I, $27,084
Dudenhoeffer, Jane M, sup IV, $40,380
Durham, Brenda J, tech III, $29,976
Evans, Deborah J, dir-field opps, $47,340
Everman, Michael W, supervising archivist, $41,172
Evers, Bryan S, tech III, $29,976
Evers, Timothy J, sr ofc spt asst (keybrd), $28,908
Farris, Naoma R, archivist, $37,548
Ferguson, Dana L, central servs technician, $34,944
Fichter, Michael K, part-time other-research analyst I, $11.00/hr
Fischer, Amy S, tech III, $30,420
Fleming, Stephanie, dep dir of comm, $40,404
Fox, Lisa, sr conservator, $45,156
Frank, Evelyn D, spec, $38,928
Glankler, William L, archivist, $37,548
Graziano, Deann M, tech III, $30,420
Green, Jacqueline, tech III, $29,496
Grisham, Jennifer K, elections spec, $37,404
Hagerty, Shawn P, investigator IV, $42,000
Hahn, Kelsey, comp info tech III, $51,516
Haines, Ronald A, comp info tech spec I, $65,946
Hale, John D, dir of investor edu, $46,002
Han, You-Jin, sr dpty counsel, $57,000
Hanus, Ryan, electronic recs archivist, $38,928
Hartnett, Andrew M, commissioner of securities, $96,204
Hays, Kacey, licensing asst, $29,976
Heather, Sheila, sup IV, $40,380
Heet, Valerie D, dir of fiscal & facilities, $85,344
Heier, Devin, investigator I, $34,344
Hempe, Sandy L, conservator, $40,380
Henley, Jennifer, sr compliance exam, $43,440
Hentges, Lucille M, tech II, $27,084
Herron, Janice L, tech III, $28,536
Hiles, Waylene W, dir of admin rules/human rsrcs, $85,344
Hise, Kenneth L, sr ofc spt asst (keybrd), $29,904
Holloway, Arline M, tech II, $27,504
Hopkins, Richard G, sr ofc spt asst (keybrd), $29,412

Hosmer, Mary S, part-time other, $34.00/hr
Hotfelder, Aaron, special counsel, $60,600
Howard, Rebecca, tech III, $29,976
Hubbard, Michael A, sr ofc spt asst (keybrd), $28,452
Hughes, Lori M, asst dir fiscal & facilities, $75,948
Iriskic, Senada, tech III, $26,808
Irwin, Sarah B, librarian II, $38,928
James, Leslie A, archivist, $37,548
Johnson, Jamica, dir of examinations, $71,208
Jones, Sandra D, tech II, $27,084
Kaiser, Heather L, pers ofcr II, $45,756
Kammeier, Lynda E, investigator III, $39,396
Kemp, Marc, clerk I, $23,880
Kempf, Brandon C, reader advisor, $27,948
Kilbourn, Vonne, assoc editor, $32,052
Koetting, Amanda L, securities spec, $31,812
Korasick, John E, asst dir for local records, $56,520
Kraus, Erin, conservator, $37,548
Kromer, Laura A, tech II, $27,084
Lahr, Judith L, investigations mgr, $48,984
Lammers, Brandon L, tech I, $26,652
Lansford, Jill A, tech II, $27,948
Leimkuehler, Thomas B, librarian II, $38,928
Lennon, Brianna L, dep dir of eletions/sen dep counsel, $64,002
Lewis, Myra, dir-field opps, $46,980
Littrell, William P, compliance exam, $36,204
Long, Scott A, prog spec, $29,976
Lueckenotte, Lesley S, dir of corps/proj mgr, $63,996
Luker, Emily, historical educator, $37,548
Lusk, Megan E, sup I, $29,904
Maclin, Tonda S, tech III, $27,228
Mahaney, Stacy D, comp info tech mgr I, $66,750
Manolov, Roumen, dpty chief counsel, $49,500
Marlow, Christopher G, spec, $33,744
Martin, Jennifer, securities enforce counsel, $48,888
Martin, Ross, tech III, $26,808
Mathews, Carol W, reader advisor, $32,472
Mathews, Paul, reader advisor, $30,924
McCormick, Tyler B, securities enforce counsel, $48,888
McIntosh, Mary Kay V, archivist, $41,172
McKay, Amanda, editor, $36,888
McKinney, Diane F, conservator, $37,548
McNay, Karen S, recept II, $34,944
Meister, Bruce S, imaging servs mgr, $41,940
Melton, Sandra K, central servs sup, $39,780
Mentzer, Barbara, ofc spt asst (keybrd), $25,824
Miller, Christina M, sr reference archivist, $41,940
Miller, Ryan, comp info tech II, $41,172
Minze, Charles E, resource center sup, $36,204
Mitchell, Mary A, research analyst I, $31,512
Mitchell, Steven E, archivist, $37,548
Moorman, Amy, archivist, $38,928
Moots, Ann M, librarian II, $38,928
Morales, Tammy E, tech III, $30,984
Moran, Jaime M, tech III, $27,660
Morgan, Patrick T, dir of reg/chief counsel, $65,652
Moseley, Kimberly K, administrative aide III, $29,976
Musselman, Debra R, dir lib dev, $61,332
Myers, Linda S, archivist, $41,940
Nash, Joshua R, compliance exam, $36,204
Nield, Thomas C, electronic resource archivist, $43,488
O'Donnell, Bonnie, administative aide II, $28,452
Oduyeru, Olufunmilola, policy/comm asst, $29,976
Olson, Gregory A, curator of exhibits/spec prjct, $49,128
Pascoe, Kay C, accounting spec II, $19.19/hr
Peters, Christina L, elections coord, $38,736
Peters, Kimberly D, comp info tech II, $38,232
Hellman, Lisa J, youth services librarian/consult, $38,928
Pettit, Candice, clerk I, $23,880
Phillips, John R, dir of enforce, $85,344
Posz, Marsha, reader advisor, $27,948
Powers, Jennifer J, administrative aide III, $29,976
Prenger, Jeremy, tech II, $26,652
Presley, Marsha, securities ofc mgr, $40,404
Raetz, Kelly S, tech III, $29,976
Reading, Barbara A, state librarian, $85,344
Reed, Ruby M, tech II, $26,652
Reeder, Daniel, research analyst I, $11.00/hr
Reinkemeyer, Christine L, sup IV, $37,548
Riegel, Donna, dir-wolfner lib, $54,864
Rieke, Luke O, comp info tech sup I, $50,508
Rimel, Abbey J, dep dir for public services, $46,068
Roach, Samantha S, tech III, $27,228

Rogers, Brian E, princ asst for boards & comms, $38,928
Rouse, Frances, tech II, $27,948
Rowden, Sherry L, accounting spec II, $42,708
Ryan, Virginia V, reader advisor, $30,384
Schmitz, Melissa, tech II, $26,232
Schollmeyer, Diane M, comp info tech spec I, $54,288
Schreiber, Sharon B, elections spec, $44,808
Schreiman, Cheryl, tech I, $26,652
Scott, John B, deputy chief of staff, $85,344
Sengsourya, Bangone, tech III, $29,496
Sinha, Kirti, comp info tech spec I, $60,000
Sites, Brenda R, prog mgr, $53,208
Smith, Amanda L, tech II, $27,504
Smith, Nina D, tech II, $28,452
Snead, David E, archivist, $37,548
Spann, Martha, asst editor, $30,984
Stansfield, Mary, research analyst I, $31,512
Stark, Diann L, reader advisor, $27,948
Starks, Brandie, paralegal, $31,812
Stauffer, Justin D, part-time other-research analyst I, $11.84/hr
Steele, Anne H, mcvr elections spec II, $44,808
Stegeman, Julie A, deputy dir of publications, $42,924
Straub, Patricia D, administrative aide III, $33,132
Stroup, Deborah K, spec, $40,380
Struemph, Jason D, comp info tech spec I, $61,104
Swinford, Laura, comm dir, $70,002
Tomblinson, Barbara A, dir of constituent services, $41,928
Treat, Curtis W, managing editor, $43,488
Troup, Nathan E, asst dir for recs mgmt, $55,416
Trowbridge, Adam D, mcvr elections spec I, $37,404
Tunmire, Brandy, electronic recs archivist, $38,928
Turpin, Courtney, tech II, $27,084
Veltrop, Ronald L, clerk I, $23,880
Walker, Buford, special asst, $41,940
Warden, Cynthia A, tech II, $27,948
Watley, Michele, dir-field opps, $48,000
Weaver, Justin, comp info tech III, $47,520
Webb, Beverly M, tech III, $32,052
Werdehausen, Brooke A, tech II, $26,232
Werdehausen, Lisa, tech III, $29,976
White, Jacqueline D, composing equip operator II, $32,628
White, Stacy M, tech II, $27,948
Willard, Lois J, tech II, $13,332
Williams, Amy, tech II, $27,504
Wingo, Carl W, lib consult, $49,128
Winkelman, Tammy S, clerk I, $24,264
Winters, Verhonda D, sup II, $34,356
Woehlk, Erika, research analyst I, $31,512
Wood, Barbara J, gen counsel/exec dep sos, $99,960
Woodling, Drew, clerk I, $24,264
Wright, Megan, tech II, $26,232
Wyrick, Janet R, tech IV, $32,052
Young, Shaquanna, grant ofcr, $44,304
Zerr, Elizabeth, dir legislative & gov affairs, $55,002
Ziegelbein, Denise L, research analyst I, $32,052
Zweifel, Deanna R, acct I, $32,628

Office of State Auditor

121 State Capitol, Jefferson City 65101

Galloway, Nicole R, state auditor, $107,746
Alexander, Morgan M, staff auditor II, $38,736
Allen, Joshua L, sr auditor III, $51,923
Allison, Pamela D, audit mgr, $70,420
Anderson, Jennifer R, sr auditor I, $45,382
Applegate, James M, sr auditor I, $45,698
Arwe, Hussein A, staff auditor I, $37,222
Atout, Waleed K, sr auditor I, $42,655
Barton, Steven J, staff auditor II, $38,722
Becker, Shelbi M, intern, $18,000
Beeler, Susan J, audit mgr, $72,233
Bledsoe, Roberta P, sr auditor II, $46,666
Borde-Koufie, Albert P, staff auditor III, $43,633
Brown, Cynthia L, fiscal & administrative asst, $40,343
Bryant, Lori A, sr auditor I, $55,808
Cooper, Brenda J, administrative asst, $31,411
Cramer, Jay M, info tech sr analyst I, $49,067
Crosson, Katelyn L, staff auditor II, $38,722
Davis, Kelly M, audit mgr, $70,378
Dierksen, Erin N, staff auditor I, $37,222
Disney, Tina M, sr auditor II, $49,469
Doerhoff, Joan M, special advisor, $65,408

Dollens, Arthur W C, sr auditor I, $48,090
Druzenko, Oleksandr N, staff auditor III, $46,027
Eaves, Jeannette M, audit mgr, $72,624
Erfurth, Kenneth P, sr auditor I, $44,560
Erwin, Terri A, sr auditor II, $52,724
Freeman, Marjorie A, staff auditor II, $42,358
Fugitt, Ted C, sr auditor III, $56,054
Gardner, Cody J, intern, $18,000
Garrison, Gayle A, sr auditor III, $62,292
Gibler, Myrna L, audit mgr, $80,323
Gordon, Randall S, asst dir of audits, $85,143
Gorley, Rebecca L, public info ofcr, $43,500
Halwes, Jon E, dir of audits, $90,345
Hammann, Brian D, sr auditor II, $50,002
Hampson, Kim A, fiscal & administrative asst, $40,343
Harper, Paul M, gen counsel, $83,750
Henley, Dane T, custdn, $13.45/hr
Henley, Gina M, sr auditor I, $44,560
Henley, Mark T, equip-facilities supervisr, $38,070
Hoffman, Sheri A, exec asst, $37,930
Hohenstreet, Sheila K, staff auditor II, $38,722
Huddleston, Denise M, sr auditor I, $46,282
Jackson, Devin R, staff auditor II, $38,736
James, Connie J, sr auditor I, $46,571
Johnson, Mark T, staff attny, $60,600
Jung, Frank A, legal counsel, $89,385
Kauffman, Wayne T, sr auditor II, $48,425
Lara, Ruben, staff auditor II, $38,722
Lesmes, Sherrye-Lin, staff auditor II, $38,736
Lewis, Sara L, sr auditor I, $46,290
Lieser, John D, audit mgr, $67,825
Locke, Amanda S, sr auditor II, $55,154
Lockwood, Dennis L, audit mgr, $70,379
Luetkemeyer, John A, deputy state auditor, $99,500
McArthur, Robert L, sr auditor III, $59,394
McClain, Christopher A, staff auditor II, $38,722
McComas, Corey R, sr auditor III, $51,923
McDaniels, Marlon T, staff auditor II, $44,167
McDowell, Nancy A, staff auditor II, $38,736
McFadden, Angela M, sr auditor II, $44,506
McNish, Natalie B, sr auditor II, $50,178
Melton, Lori A, audit mgr, $70,378
Moore, Darrell L, chief litigation counsel, $89,385
Moorefield, Michael A, chief of staff, $92,000
Moulden, Julie A, sr auditor III, $53,517
Murdock, Rex A, sr auditor II, $48,137
Murray, Lavonda K, staff auditor I, $39,022
Neier, Kayla E, administrative asst, $28,880
Newgaard, Carol S, fiscal & administrative supvsr, $64,190
Nguyen, Anh D, staff auditor I, $37,222
O'Donnell, Hunter S, staff auditor I, $39,022
Olson, David T, sr auditor I, $44,791
Owens, Travis J, audit mgr, $70,379
Porting, Douglas J, dir of audits, $90,345
Prenger, Alex R, sr auditor I, $48,145
Pruitt, Regina M, dir of audits, $90,345
Pullins, Patrick M, sr auditor II, $49,991
Pummill, Michelle L, staff auditor I, $37,222
Re', Steven J, sr auditor III, $52,030
Renick, Cindy S, info technology mgr, $75,528
Reuter, Renee A, info tech sr analyst II, $61,121
Roberts, Jeffrey J, info systms sr auditor III, $65,254
Rogers, Seth J, staff auditor II, $40,540
Ruether, Mark G, asst dir of audits, $85,143
Rusatsi, Tessa A, sr auditor I, $46,290
Schafer, Nicholas A, staff auditor III, $42,354
Schlup, Lisa J, staff auditor II, $38,722
Schulenberg, Matthew M, sr auditor II, $48,360
Schuler, Todd M, audit mgr, $70,558
Seevers, Marian E, staff auditor II, $44,158
Shope, Joshua K, sr auditor I, $46,290
Showers, Robert E, audit mgr, $72,233
Sieg, Samantha R, staff auditor I, $37,222
Smith, Jason R, info tech sr analyst I, $43,531
Spicer, Shannon K, staff auditor III, $42,337
Spraggs, Kimberly R, asst dir of audits, $80,500
Stiles, Heather R, sr auditor III, $56,673
Stuck, Richard G, sr auditor II, $46,756
Summers, Terese J, staff auditor III, $48,390
Terlizzi, Gena M, dir of comm, $80,000
Thelen, Jeffrey W, info sys audit mgr, $77,346
Thompson, Rachelle L, sr auditor I, $42,655
Thomson, Joyce L, sr auditor II, $50,236

Vetter, Christopher B, audit mgr, $70,378
Vogt, Robyn L, audit mgr, $70,378
Walsh, Sara R, staff auditor II, $40,540
Wansing, Dana R, staff auditor III, $44,342
Warren, Emily J, intern, $18,000
Webb, Rebecca A, local government sup, $64,523
Whitis, Deborah S, audit mgr, $70,379
Williams, Keisha N, staff auditor III, $40,536
Wilson, Jill M, staff auditor III, $42,354
Withers, Ashtin N, staff auditor I, $37,222
Wright, Keriann E, audit mgr, $70,379

Office of State Treasurer

PO Box 210, Jefferson City 65102

Zweifel, Charles C, state treasurer, $107,746
Berkbuegler, Matthew M, research spec II, $29,976
Boone, Monica M, gen servs sup, $34,356
Bridges, Sonya C, processing clerk II, $26,652
Canale, Lisa F, processing clerk I, $24,264
Carranza, JoAnn, intern, $9.50/hr
Creech, Kelly J, securities spec, $34,944
Ferrell, Ryan M, info technologist III, $42,708
Girouard, Spencer, deputy dir of comm, $41,940
Grinston, Andre' S, business dev mgr, $46,068
Hackmann, Nicole A, dir of bank & invests, $100,812
Harper, Scott A, dir of unclaimed property & gen srvs, $82,788
Harrison, Lance A, treasury coord II, $36,888
Helmick, Jessica N, securities spec, $31,512
Hopkins, Lisa A, cash mgr I, $42,708
Howard, Gerri L, asst dir of bank, $68,160
Iler, Sarah M, treasury analyst II, $42,708
Keilholz, Dawna J, sr gen servs assoc, $28,908
Koeppen, Samantha F, linked deposit coord, $32,628
Lewis, Meghan M, dir of comm, $53,208
Luck, Roderick E, processing clerk I, $23,880
Massman, Lana J, asst dir of unclaimed property, $52,092
Masterson, David A, processing clerk I, $24,264
Morgan, Patrick T, general counsel, $74,304
Neidert, Maribeth, exec asst II, $41,940
Ocheskey, Rachelle L, invest analyst, $49,128
Oligschlaeger, Elizabeth D, processing clerk III, $29,976
Olmstead, Kyle A, leg liason & special projects coord, $41,940
Orscheln, Rebecca S, invest coord I, $36,888
Palmer, Thomas S, research spec, $27,228
Pearson, Marsha L, recept, $24,264
Peterson, Angela R, gen servs assoc, $23,880
Pettit, Tammy S, processing clerk II, $27,948
Pruitt, Bryce W, invest coord I, $33,744
Sanders, Jade, processing clerk I, $23,880
Schertzer, Debra M, exec asst II, $53,208
Schwartze, Lucas J, processing clerk II, $26,652
Spraggs, James B, gen servs assoc, $24,264
Swoboda, Sarah J, deputy state treasurer, $100,812
Tatum, Amanda M, treasury analyst I, $38,928
Tennison, Nancy E, administrative servs coord, $44,304
Thompson, Jennifer D, processing clerk II, $27,948
Toebben, Kimberly D, cash mgr II, $44,304
Uthe, Sarah M, processing clerk I, $23,880
Wagner, Judith A, processing clerk II, $26,652
Wetch, Vanessa M, info technologist IV, $55,416

Office of Attorney General

PO Box 899, Jefferson City 65102

Koster, Christopher A, attny gen, $116,437
Abner, Mary K, administrative sec, $41,713
Addadi, Jennifer O, asst attny gen, $54,540
Ahart, Carrie A, investigator I, $39,138
Ahrens, Maggie M, asst attny gen, $44,440
Akers, Siobhan K, asst attny gen, $54,540
Aquino, Nathan J, asst attny gen, $44,440
Asbridge, Ryan S, asst attny gen, $54,540
Ashlock, Lauri L, paralegal, $33,987
Atkinson, Samuel K, asst attny gen, $44,440
Backes, Nicholas J, consumer serv oper, $28,835
Bagby, Karen K, exec sec, $60,600
Baker, Tamula S, paralegal, $33,987
Ballard, Donald C, asst attny gen, $60,600
Balmer, James D, investigator I, $44,289

Bard, Jennifer E, asst attny gen, $60,600
Barker, Julie A, legal sec, $30,896
Barnes, Gregory L, asst attny gen, $58,866
Barresi, Lynn M, research analyst, $39,137
Barrett, Shelby L, legal sec, $30,896
Bartholomew, Robert J, asst attny gen, $54,540
Bealer, Rosalie K, administrative sec, $41,713
Bean, Caroline M, asst attny gen, $61,105
Bear, Brian T, asst attny gen, $51,005
Benke, Peter T, legal sec, $30,896
Beydler, Nick S, asst attny gen, $44,440
Bilyeu, Jason T, investigator I, $44,289
Bindbeutel, Joseph P, asst attny gen, div dir, $116,150
Bishop, Carla J, administrative sec, $41,713
Blackwell, Andrew W, asst attny gen, $49,490
Blackwell, Katherine L, consumer advocate, $29,866
Blackwell, Kristin M, legal sec, $30,896
Blackwell, Mary J, legal sec, $32,441
Blackwell, Timothy A, asst attny gen, $65,000
Blaine, Mary K, victim's advocate, $43,959
Bock, Nichole M, asst attny gen, $49,490
Boessen, Arlene R, fiscal ofcr, $65,145
Bokermann, Tracey E, asst attny gen, $27,270
Bommel, Lesha D, consumer advocate, $31,381
Boresi, Susan D, asst attny gen, div dir, $110,965
Branson, Eric A, info syss spec, $47,000
Brendel, Patrick J, info syss spec, $70,000
Brenner, Kelly A, investigator I, $39,138
Brenner, Terry A, legal sec, $30,896
Brethauer, Caroline A, legal sec, $30,896
Brown, Ross A, asst attny gen, $49,490
Bruce, Theodore A, asst attny gen, $45.55/hr
Bryant, Leann M, legal sec, $30,896
Buchheim, Evan, asst attny gen, $68,704
Burke, Laura K, asst attny gen, $54,540
Burkemper, T B, asst attny gen IV, $111,100
Burks, Skyler E, asst attny gen, $49,490
Burrows, Amanda M, investigator I, $39,137
Buxton, Malcolm, consumer serv oper, $30,390
Byrne, Michael J, asst attny gen, $65,650
Callahan, Elizabeth, asst attny gen, $76,255
Campbell, Megen J, asst attny gen, $49,490
Campbell, Rodney J Jr, asst attny gen, $49,490
Carlson, Robert E, asst attny gen, $65,000
Cherba, Michael R, asst attny gen, $54,540
Chirnside, Diane F, asst attny gen, $71,205
Churchill, Patricia J, asst attny gen, div dir, $97,465
Clark, Mary B, asst attny gen, $57,540
Clevenger, Susan B, investigator I, $44,289
Clinton, Thomas, info syss spec, supervisor, $59,085
Colburn, Susan F, asst attny gen, $54,633
Cole, Candace R, asst attny gen, $54,540
Colling, Jacob R, asst attny gen, $44,440
Collins, Darren W, clerk msngr, $31,411
Colon, Margarita E, investigator I, $43,430
Connelly, Anna E, asst attny gen, $44,440
Cook, Justine R, asst attny gen, $56,055
Coulter, Caroline M, asst attny gen, $57,176
Cowan, Don, asst attny gen, $54,540
Cox, Phillip B, asst attny gen, $70,700
Crank, Don W, asst attny gen, $54,540
Crow, Noralie T, fiscal ofcr, $38,380
Crowe, Austin D, asst attny gen, $49,490
Crowell, George B, asst attny gen, $72,720
Cunningham, Daniel A, asst attny gen, $54,540
Curtis, Woodie J, asst attny gen, $54,633
Dalton, Robert Q, investigator I, $39,137
Dandurand, Joseph P, deputy attny gen, $126,755
Danner, Audrey L, asst attny gen, $44,440
Daugherty, Maria W, asst attny gen, $49,490
Dees, Diana L, legal sec, $30,896
Dobecki, Sarah J, asst attny gen, $70,000
Dodge, Emily A, asst attny gen, $54,540
Doerhoff, Stephen C, asst attny gen, $52,000
Dolin, Katharine A, asst attny gen, $44,440
Drescher, David C, asst attny gen, $44,440
Duggan, Timothy P, asst attny gen, $75,407
Duncan, Elaine, legal sec, $30,896
Durkin, Thomas M, public education director, $52,015
Eierman, Anthony M, investigator I, $39,138
Ellis, Vanessa H, asst attny gen, $76,255
Elsbury, Laura E, asst attny gen, $69,185
Emanuel, James P, asst attny gen, $44,440

Farnsworth, James B, chief of staff, $116,150
Fee, Catherine V, asst attny gen, $77,858
Fey, Donna J, recept, $29,866
Fichter, Dora A, asst attny gen, $54,540
Flaster, Rachel S, asst attny gen, $49,490
Follett, Daniel W, asst attny gen, $60,381
Follmer, Nicole K, asst attny gen, $44,440
Folta, Thais A, asst attny gen, $65,000
Ford, Regina L, legal sec, $30,896
Fortenberry, Donna A, legal sec, $30,896
Fournier, Kimberley R, asst attny gen, $80,800
Fowler, Barbara A, legal sec, $30,896
Fox, Scott E, asst attny gen, $54,540
Frazier, Kristin M, asst attny gen, $54,540
Frizzell, Susan L, legal sec, $30,896
Frost, Lindsey, data entry clerk, $27,805
Frownfelter, Edwin R, asst attny gen, $64,385
Gabel, Denise N, asst attny gen, $68,500
Gardner, Gary L, asst attny gen, $38.05/hr
Gelber, Brandy R, investigator I, $39,137
Germinder, Julianne O, asst attny gen, $70,700
Getz, M J, asst attny gen, $30,499
Glass, Susan K, asst attny gen, $84,113
Glick, Margaret A, legal sec, $30,896
Gobble, Erica D, legal sec, $33,472
Godron, Michelle, recept, $28,836
Golightly, Andrew, info syss mgr, $85,850
Gonder, Nanci C, press sec, $78,275
Goodnight, Catherine D, asst attny gen, $58,075
Goodwin, Gregory M, asst attny gen, $44,440
Gordon, Meghan L, investigator I, $39,138
Gore, Shauna N, investigator I, $33,987
Grantham, John W, asst attny gen, $60,600
Grayson, Jennifer C, investigator I, $33,987
Greene, Gerald E, investigator I, $44,289
Griffith, Carol L, consumer advocate, $29,866
Gross, Elad J, asst attny gen, $44,440
Gummels, Joan F, general counsel, $116,150
Hahn, Sharie L, asst attny gen, $54,540
Hansen, David J, asst attny gen, $96,213
Harrel, Joshua D, asst attny gen, $60,600
Harris, Cara, asst attny gen, div dir, $97,465
Hawke, Stephen D, asst attny gen, $71,205
Hayden, Steve, director of investigations, $48,985
Haywood, Amy C, asst attny gen, $66,155
Heislen, Tricia A, web developer, $65,145
Henderson, Brandi N, legal sec, $30,896
Hensley, Jonathan M, asst attny gen, $54,540
Herman, Brian R, asst attny gen, $55,045
Hipkind, Yvette G, asst attny gen, $27,270
Hirschvogel, Michelle L, legal sec, $30,896
Hirth, John A, deputy general counsel, $98,475
Hisle, William J, investigator I, $39,137
Holdman, Sandra K, legal sec, $31,985
Holland, Kyra C, administrative asst, $31,411
Holliger, Ronald R, asst attny gen, $55.00/hr
Holtmeyer, Amanda G, administrative secretary, $40,905
Hooper, Andrew C, asst attny gen, $44,440
Hooper, Rebecca K, victim's advocate, $40,905
Horn, Joellen, asst attny gen, $71,205
Horton, Deborah A, accounting analyst , $48,985
Houser, Rachael K, asst attny gen, $57,000
Howie, Frances A, legal sec, $33,330
Huddleston, Heather R, legal sec, $30,896
Hudson, Ellen J, asst attny gen, $68,500
Hunt, Elaine C, administrative sec, $41,713
Hyder, Ii, chief investigator, $54,076
Hylton, Daryl R, asst attny gen, $73,225
Isaacson, Robert J, asst attny gen, $82,820
Jacobs, Craig H, asst attny gen, $56,560
Johnson, Charles W, mailroom sup, $31,411
Johnson, Sarah E, investigator I, $39,137
Johnson, Stephanie Y, consumer serv oper, $28,836
Keller, Lauren A, constituent services coord, $40,400
Kelly, Tiffany L, paralegal, $37,000
Kemp, Sheila R, Administrative secretary, $39,895
Kempf, Shannon T, asst attny gen, $62,317
Kimberly, Jennie J, paralegal, $33,987
Kincade, Mathew, asst attny gen, $44,440
Knaebel, Frances A, fiscal clerk, $35,666
Knight, Stuart, software engineer, $56,560
Knox, Sydney M, consumer serv oper, $28,835
Koetting, Melissa N, legal sec, $30,896

Kohler, Kathi S, administrative sec, $41,713
Kolb, Shirley J, data entry clerk, $11.85/hr
Komoroski, Nicholas J, asst attny gen, $61,105
Kopp, John J, asst attny gen, $84,335
Kramer, Karen L, asst attny gen, $68,704
Krispin, Eileen R, asst attny gen, $54,540
Kroll, Kerry A, hr manager, $65,145
Laird, Brandon D, asst attny gen, $49,490
Lamb, Jason H, asst attny gen, div dir, $106,555
Land, Shelly L, consumer investigations,dir, $73,326
Landwehr, Margaret, asst attny gen, $65,145
Laudano, Matthew J, asst attny gen, $60,600
Lawrence, Casey D, sunshine law coord, $35,855
Layton, James R, solicitor general, $126,755
Lehmen, Lindsay, paralegal, $33,986
Lemke, Linda S, asst attny gen, $24.00/hr
Lesicko, Christine K, asst attny gen, $44,440
Lewis, Caleb M, asst attny gen, $70,000
Lewis, Jeanine M, legal sec, $30,896
Leyshock, Douglas G, asst attny gen, $82,820
Light, Felicia M, pers clerk, $36,047
Little, Donald R, investigator I, $41,404
Long, Mary A, asst attny gen, $54,540
Lowe, Eric W, asst attny gen, $49,490
Lowry, Cynthia R, exec sec, $56,055
Lucas, Todd C, asst attny gen, $44,440
Luebbert, Nicholas A, info syss spec, $40,905
Lynch, John J, asst attny gen, $60,884
Mackelprang, Shaun J, asst attny gen, div dir, $97,465
Maddox, Kelly L, consumer advocate, $31,381
Manlove-Braxton, Linda K, asst attny gen, $58,431
Markley-Rutt, Carrie A, paralegal, $41,713
Marshall, Sherry L, victim's advocate, $40,905
Mattern, Suzanne L, software engineer, $65,145
McCain, David L, asst attny gen, $49,490
McCarrick, Brook D, asst attny gen, $60,600
McDowell, Saundra J, asst attny gen, $49,490
McElvein, Denise, asst attny gen, $80,295
McGaughey, Kimberly D, paralegal, $41,713
McKee, Jessica M, asst attny gen, $54,540
McManus, John K, asst attny gen, div dir, $97,465
McPherson, Daniel N, asst attny gen, $57,166
Mealy, William C, info syss spec, $52,015
Messonnier, Terrence M, asst attny gen, $71,205
Mettlen, Justin D, asst attny gen, $54,540
Meyer, Karen L, admin secretary, $41,713
Meyer, Rhonda S, dpty chief of staff, $98,475
Miller, Benjamin J, asst attny gen, $69,134
Millsap, Janice L, legal secretary, $36,360
Moore, Mary H, asst attny gen, $55,584
Morgan, Jeremiah J, asst attny gen, $96,213
Morris, Mary D, asst attny gen, $63,630
Morris, Michael D, asst attny gen, $54,540
Morris, Travis A, investigator I, $39,137
Mueller, Jillian M, asst attny gen, $44,440
Munoz, Crystal L, investigator I, $39,137
Nayyar, Faraz, asst attny gen, $49,490
Neeley, Caleb A, legal sec, $30,896
Nelson, Brent M, asst attny gen, $64,176
Nelson, Kevin A, asst attny gen, $54,540
Neuner, Colette, asst attny gen, $54,540
Niekamp, Carla A, investigator I, $39,138
Noland, R D, asst attny gen, $90,900
Nygard, Casey E, asst attny gen, $49,490
Ochoa, Melinda J, investigator I, $43,430
Osborne, Kareitha A, asst attny gen, $54,540
Ottenson, Emily B, asst attny gen, $44,440
Otto, Amy L, legal sec, $30,896
Pattengill, Natosha T, legal sec, $30,896
Pax, Amanda R, legal sec, $30,896
Payne, Leisa J, legal sec, $30,896
Peacock, Mary L, admin secretary, $41,713
Pearson, Stephanie, paralegal, $41,410
Perry, Greg, asst attny gen, div dir, $97,465
Phillips, Thomas M, asst attny gen, $54,540
Platz, Monty C, asst attny gen, $75,750
Poelker, Kyle A, asst attny gen, $44,440
Poole, Joel A, asst attny gen, div dir, $116,150
Powers, Ryan W, clerk msngr, $28,921
Presson, Robert L, asst attny gen, $40.00/hr
Rackers, Danielle E, consumer advocate, $29,866
Rackers, Tracy L, legal sec, $30,896
Ramos, Inan, legal sec, $30,896

Ramshead, Carla H, legal sec, $30,896
Randolph, John P, investigator I, $43,430
Ranfranz, Corey E, asst attny gen, $49,490
Rawlins, Stephanie A, legal sec, $30,896
Redmond, Kristina M, legal sec, $30,896
Reed, Susan, consumer advocate, $29,866
Reeves, Rochelle L, asst attny gen, $98,475
Reid, Camille M, paralegal, $33,987
Relys, Herbert A, asst attny gen, $58,075
Richardson, Lauren E, investigator I, $39,138
Rivero, Miguel G, investigator I, $39,137
Roark, Christine L, administrative sec, $33,411
Roark, Lacey E, legal sec, $33,472
Rodenbaugh, Donna J, registration specialist, $29,866
Roderick, Jared L, investigator I, $44,289
Ross, Stacey J, legal sec, $34,000
Roth, Lori A, legal sec, $31,833
Rowley, Adam S, asst attny gen, $44,440
Ryan, Kaela A, admin secretary, $40,400
Sandberg, Adam T, asst attny gen, $49,490
Sankar, Dion F, asst attny gen, $54,540
Sansone, Conrad, asst attny gen, $44,440
Scheulen, Beverly S, exec sec, $60,600
Schlotzhauer, Joseph R, asst attny gen, $49,490
Schneider, Anne E, asst attny gen, $73,326
Schoene, Charles A, paralegal, $33,987
Schube, Curtis M, asst attny gen, $49,490
Schuetze, Cheryl A, asst attny gen, $86,355
Sennott, Ashley L, consumer serv oper, $27,805
Sergent, Scott T, asst attny gen, $44,945
Shaffer, Tess A, paralegal, $33,986
Shansey, William M, asst attny gen, $54,540
Shine, Maureen T, asst attny gen, $54,540
Shiverdecker, Sharon J, legal sec, $30,896
Sholtz, Philip, asst attny gen, $61,105
Smith, Alicia A, legal sec, $30,896
Smith, Erin C, asst attny gen, $44,440
Smith, Matthew B, auditor, $48,985
Smith, Ronald Q, asst attny gen, $58,075
Snoke-Adams, Debra L, asst attny gen, $61,610
Spillane, Michael J, asst attny gen, $65,650
Stariwat, April, registered nurse, $52,015
Starnes, Richard, asst attny gen, $54,540
Stevens, Rebecca A, legal sec, $30,896
Stoppy, Lynn M, asst attny gen, $65,000
Strobel, Beth A, paralegal, $33,986
Sullivan, Rebecca L, paralegal, $33,987
Tarwater, Maureen E, recept, $29,866
Taulbee, Nicolas J, asst attny gen, $54,540
Taylor, Daryl R, asst attny gen, $49,490
Taylor, Shantell J, exec sec, $55,550
Teetzen, Samantha S, asst attny gen, $44,440
Thieme, Rhonda K, legal sec, $30,896
Thomsen, Patricia A, legal sec, $30,896
Thudium, Jacinda A, asst attny gen, $62,317
Tillman, Robert C, asst attny gen, $44,440
Toepke, Barbara L, asst attny gen, $27,270
Tolle, Julie L, asst attny gen, $75,750
Trachtenberg, Joanna L, asst attny gen, div dir, $97,465
Troesser, Matthew J, investigator I, $39,138
Trundle, Kendra L, legal sec, $30,896
Tucker, Dana W, asst attny gen, $96,213
Turner, Jaime D, legal sec, $30,896
Turner, Regina J, legal sec, $30,896
Urschler, Maria J, administrative sec, $36,562
Usher, Elliott J, asst attny gen, $44,440
Valentine, Kara L, asst attny gen, $71,205
Vanderpool, William S, asst attny gen, $86,355
Velasquez, Lindsey C, investigator I, $39,138
Vetter, Colleen J, asst attny gen, $75,750
Wales, Emily A, asst attny gen, $44,440
Walsh, Kathrine S, asst attny gen, $70,195
Ward, Jessica L, asst attny gen, $54,540
Watson, Stephanie L, asst attny gen, $68,175
Weider-Hatfield, Deborah J, asst attny gen, $54,540
Weisel, Brian P, asst attny gen, $54,540
Werdehausen, Megan K, legal sec, $30,896
Westen, Jacob T, asst attny gen, $44,440
Westhoff, Martha H, systems administrator, $56,560
Whipple, Peggy A, asst attny gen, $96,960
White, Linda J, legal sec, $30,896
Whitmer, Allison, legal sec, $30,896
Wilfong, Keyla S, asst attny gen, $54,540

Wille, Joshua A, asst attny gen, $54,540
Williams, Teresa, legal sec, $30,896
Willyard, Kelly J, asst attny gen, $44,440
Wilson, Gwen A, legal sec, $30,896
Winslow, Leslye, asst attny gen, $54,540
Wippermann, Maryann L, legal sec, $20.02/hr
Woodard, Winderlyn Y, recept, $33,472
Yates, Deborah, asst attny gen, $70,000
Yeager, B Joyce, asst attny gen, $73,326
Zerbonia, Renee E, asst attny gen, $44,440
Zoellner, Kevin M, asst attny gen, $96,213

Chapter 4: Legislative Branch

Missouri Senate

State Capitol, Jefferson City 65101

Richard, Ronald F, senate floor leader, $37,415
Allison, James, security specialist, $25.96/hr
Anderson, Nedra S, billroom clerk, $15.39/hr
Aubuchon, Kyle R, senators' staff, $47,000
Baker, Jessica R, staff attorney II, $49,490
Baker, Patrick A, senators' staff, $50,500
Barbarick, Michele A, research staff secretary, $40,081
Bashore, Brad A, public information specialist, $37,087
Bauer, Catherine A, senators' staff, $25.86/hr
Bauer, James A, carpenter II, $39,814
Beck, Marilyn E, senators' staff, $10,348
Bernskoetter, Janell L, joint committee tech analyst, $40,905
Berry, Ronald D, senators' staff, $58,833
Binkley, Robin, computer info technologist I, $35,351
Birk, Michela S, staff attorney II, $47,559
Bochat, Julie A, assistant secretary of senate, $58,952
Branson, Joan E, senators' staff, $22.66/hr
Brauner, Christine E, senators' staff, $47,235
Britton, Abby, resolution writer, $42,944
Broeker, Doris A, senators' staff, $51,912
Brown, Danny W, senator, $35,915
Brown, Jared D, senators' staff, $51,500
Burke, Ashley R, senators' staff, $37,500
Burton, Jon D, dir of operations/investigator, $84,500
Buschjost, Jacqueline M, senators' staff, $41,000
Bushman, Linda M, senators' staff, $26.51/hr
Butler, Andrea R, senators' staff, $32,000
Butler, Robin A, administrative/office support, $53,466
Byrd, Bryan C, network/commun specialist, $38,178
Cain, Beverly R, assistant secretary of senate, $25.25/hr
Carter, Alvin, assistant doorkeeper, $10,078
Carver, William C, maintenance supervisor II, $42,420
Chappelle-Nadal, Maria N, senator, $35,915
Christian, Amanda J, administrative assistant, $50,500
Clark, Pauline A, research staff secretary, $52,584
Creach, Michelle L, public information specialist, $34,400
Crider, Kayla J, research analyst II, $49,490
Crouse, Adriane D, secretary of senate, $90,500
Culp, Kathy L, senators' staff, $62,405
Cunningham, Michael J, senator, $35,915
Curls, Shalonn K, senator, $35,915
Dailey, Lisa, senators' staff, $40,408
Dampf, Drew A, senators' staff, $35,000
Davis, Paul, senators' staff, $40,000
Delano, Gwendolyn S, senators' staff, $16,082
Dempsey, Thomas, senate president pro tem, $38,415
Dixon, Robert A, senator, $35,915
Drewel, Martin R, assistant doorkeeper, $10,078
Dunnavant, James W IV, printing services tech IV, $20.19/hr
Eakin, Richard W, senators' staff, $6,180
Emery, Edgar G, senator, $35,915
Emily, Dean E, public information specialist, $39,402
Ertle, James O, director of research, $92,500
Falter, Christy L, accounting specialist, $45,000
Fiorini, David A, senators' staff, $3,600
Foley, Trevor S, assistant director-appropriations, $73,500
Foster, Bill I, senators' staff, $61,000
Foster, Joshua M, senators' staff, $44,440
Fulson, Sheron A, senators' staff, $58,927
Gauck, Carl R, chaplain, $6,124
Geisbuhler, Heidi L, majority caucus staff, $60,600
Germinder, Richard J, senators' staff, $60,000

Granich, Rose M, senators' staff, $40,829
Green, Stephen B, senators' staff, $62,620
Gresham, Adam, senators' staff, $69,636
Groce, Jason I, senators' staff, $50,500
Grothoff, Randy J, printing services tech IV, $42,110
Gwaltney, Kevin D, joint committee director, $65,650
Haskins, Sarah E, research analyst II, $47,470
Haslag, Kathleen A, senators' staff, $48,480
Hatcher, Charles L, minority caucus staff, $78,124
Hegeman, Daniel J, senator, $35,915
Hepburn-Darris, Lucille, enrolling & engrossing clerk, $41,842
Herschel, Anne B, senators' staff, $62,069
Hieger, Lauren F, majority caucus staff, $67,500
Hoelscher, Marga J, administrator, $93,000
Hoerschgen, Steven J, mailroom supervisor, $37,315
Holsman, Jason R, senator, $35,915
Hoppe, Thomas J, senators' staff, $50.52/hr
Huddleston, Robyn S, senators' staff, $26.60/hr
Hutschreider, Angela, public information specialist, $33,997
Hutton, Daniel L, senators' staff, $46,500
Hutton, Ryan S, computer info tech spec I, $44,500
Isenberg, Wilma J, senators' staff, $34.02/hr
Jacquin, Karen M, senators' staff, $54,386
Jenkins, Jackie A, research staff secretary, $34,058
Jennings, Eric D, senators' staff, $67,200
Jobes, Jordan T, senators' staff, $78,376
Jones, Gail L, assistant doorkeeper, $10,078
Jones, Mickey J, assistant doorkeeper, $10,078
Joyce, Tracey K, senators' staff, $36,360
Kadlec, Cindy S, joint committee director, $85,922
Keaveny, Joseph P, senate minority floor leader, $37,415
Kehoe, Mike L, senator, $35,915
Kesel, Jared R, computer info tech spec II, $40,909
Kleinsorge, Daniel J, senators' staff, $48,985
Kliethermes, Michelle G, budget staff secretary, $44,969
Koenigsfeld, Adam C, director of appropriations, $90,500
Koestner, Diane G, senators' staff, $42,420
Kolkmeyer, Heidi M, senators' staff, $55,567
Kraus, William G, senator, $35,915
Larue, William R, assistant doorkeeper, $10,078
Lawrence, Blake M, senators' staff, $45,450
Leake, Larry B, carpenter II, $18.42/hr
Lembke, James W, senators' staff, $58,000
Levota, Paul V, senator, $35,915
Lewis, Emily S, senators' staff, $37,532
Libla, Douglas E, senator, $35,915
Linhardt, Bonnie L, senators' staff, $30,000
Loethen, Carolyn C, senators' staff, $50,014
Logan, Elaine, enrolling & engrossing clerk, $37,876
Logsdon, James M, computer info technologist II, $49,433
Luehrman, Nancy E, senators' staff, $40,905
Luetkemeyer, Marylyn S, senators' staff, $43,479
Mackie, Keith R, senators' staff, $16,968
Marcel, Violet, senators' staff, $60,600
Martin, Kristina C, composing equipt operator II, $34,340
Maskery Luecke, Meghan E, staff attorney II, $55,197
Matthews-Smith, Shannon, computer info tech spec II, $49,741
McGhee, Robert L, resolution writer, $36,907
McMillen, Connie J, composing equipt operator III, $37,481
Michelson, Matthew R, senators' staff, $55,191
Miller, Deborah S, enrolling & engrossing clerk, $43,380
Monroe, Zachary, senators' staff, $57,500
Montgomery, Christa A, senators' staff, $25,250
Morse, Stacy E, senators' staff, $70,152
Mundell, Morgan M, chief financial officer/dir of CIS, $87,000
Munzlinger, Brian L, senator, $35,915
Murphy, Lorna, administrative/office support, $45,719
Mustoe, Barbara L, senators' staff, $64,236
Nasheed, Jamilah, senator, $35,915
Neustadt, Jennae M, senators' staff, $55,531
Newton, Carol R, enrolling & engrossing supv, $55,526
Niedergerke, Amy B, computer info tech spec III, $73,225
O'Bryan, Shelly, administrative/office support, $43,500
Olson, Andrew R, majority caucus staff, $69,500
Onder, Bob, senator, $35,915
Panik, Matthew J, senators' staff, $62,620
Parris, Pattie, senators' staff, $37.67/hr
Parson, Michael L, senator, $35,915
Patten, Roman W, assistant doorkeeper, $10,078
Pearce, David B, senator, $35,915
Pringer, Betty R, senators' staff, $23.23/hr
Proctor, Joan C, senators' staff, $34,340
Quick, Jill A, senators' staff, $38,380

Rackers, James O, assistant doorkeeper, $10,078
Rackers, Rosalie M, senators' staff, $26.50/hr
Rankin, James R, mailroom tech II, $34,035
Riddle, Jeanie K, senator, $35,915
Roach, Karen L, senators' staff, $33,835
Romine, Gary A, senator, $35,915
Rosen, Candace C, senators' staff, $10.00/hr
Rottmann, Anne G, library administrator, $49,701
Roundtree, Galisa L, billroom supervisor, $36,494
Rowden, Wilma, senators' staff, $40,404
Ruff, Michael R, joint committee director, $68,000
Saffa, Samuel J, senators' staff, $30,000
Sanchez, Leonardo, computer info tech spec II, $49,448
Sater, David D, senator, $35,915
Schaaf, Robert O, senator, $35,915
Schaefer, Kurt U, senator, $35,915
Schappe, Christopher M, minority caucus gen counsel, $96,354
Schatz, David A, senator, $35,915
Schellman, Gilbert H, assistant doorkeeper, $10,078
Schisler, Josh, senators' staff, $40,408
Schmitt, Eric S, senator, $35,915
Schmitz, Nicholas J, computer info tech spec II, $51,863
Schneider, Jan L, reading clerk, $8,712
Schnieders, Diana, research staff secretary, $23.44/hr
Schnieders, Dustin A, senators' staff, $64,236
Schulte, Donna M, administrative/office support, $41,842
Schupp, Jill, senator, $35,915
Scott, Jacob R, senators' staff, $35,000
Scott, Todd, majority caucus general counsel, $96,354
Sifton, Richard P, senator, $35,915
Silvey, Ryan A, senator, $35,915
Smith, Bill J, sergeant at arms, $14,977
Smith, Shantel A, public information specialist, $32,724
Spainhower, Theckla E, senators' staff, $12,000
Stone, Robin R, senators' staff, $29.29/hr
Sutherland, Christopher D, senators' staff, $60,000
Svagera, Scott A, research analyst II, $47,470
Swann, Hannah M, budget research analyst II, $46,460
Sweazea, Harrison E, photographer, $46,925
Sweets, Zachari D, senators' staff, $30,000
Tackett, Tamera G, computer info technologist II, $24.01/hr
Thalhuber, Donald W, minority caucus staff, $78,124
Thomas, Donna S, joint committee secretary, $41,084
Thomas, Janson M, senators' staff, $62,405
Thomas, Patricia N, senators' staff, $53,995
Thrash, Amy J, administrative/office support, $21.04/hr
Tuttle, Alex N, budget research analyst III, $57,736
Twehus, Tabitha N, computer info tech spec I, $31,500
Wade, Kimberly G, computer info technologist I, $39,479
Wallingford, Albert W, senator, $35,915
Walsh, Regina M, senator, $35,915
Walton, Garlanda J, senators' staff, $70,559
Wasson, John Jay M, senator, $35,915
Wheeler, Jordan T, budget research analyst II, $46,460
Wieland, Paul J, senator, $35,915
Wilde, Barbara L, legislative research clerk, $31,648
Willard, Aaron M, senators' staff, $75,000
Williams, Lillian A, senators' staff, $43,935
Williams, Margaret L, accounting specialist, $45,982
Williams, Yancy B, senators' staff, $78,376
Wilson, Mary C, asst director CIS, $74,740
Wingrath, Travis L, printing services tech II, $35,000
Winthorst, Cindy L, human resources specialist, $51,005
Wright, Billy P, senators' staff, $17.00/hr
Wright, Samuel F, senators' staff, $12.00/hr
Wyrick, Billy G, assistant doorkeeper, $10,078

Missouri House of Representatives

State Capitol, Jefferson City 65101

Richardson, Robert Todd, state rep-speaker, $38,415
Adams, Joseph L, state rep, $35,915
Alberts, Russell A, maint worker II, $38,232
Alferman, Justin T, state rep, $35,915
Allen, Susan K, state rep, $35,915
Alpers, Jeanette R, sr public spec, $37,548
Althoff, Carol J, dir, house admin, $86,484
Anders, Ira G, state rep, $35,915
Anderson, Douglas A, drafting servs attny II, $50,040
Anderson, Sonya A, state rep, $35,915
Andrews, Allen, state rep, $35,915
Arthur, Lauren, state rep, $35,915

Austin, Kevin L, state rep, $35,915
Ayer, Samantha, public spec II, $34,356
Babb, Kolton, legislator asst, $27,084
Backer, Brittany, legislator asst, $27,084
Backes, Dustin, legislative info coord, $34,944
Baepler, Connie J, legislator asst, $16.45/hr
Bahr, Kurt M, state rep, $35,915
Baker, Julia L, drafting servs attny II, $51,096
Balkenbush, Shirley, legislator asst, $20.53/hr
Barnes, Jason O, state rep, $35,915
Barninger, John W, legislator asst, $27,084
Barton, Morgan, legislator asst, $27,084
Basye, Charles R, state rep, $35,915
Bauer, Rachel M, exec I - leadership, $55,416
Bax, Greta, administrative asst, $58,908
Beard, Nathan G, state rep, $35,915
Beasley, Shana E, legislator asst, $27,084
Beckwith, Richard J, dir of info syst, $86,484
Bench, Louie, legislator asst, $27,084
Bernskoetter, Michael, state rep, $35,915
Berry, Thomas J, state rep, $35,915
Bias, Stephanie K, legislator asst, $27,084
Black, Linda R, state rep, $35,915
Boeth, Stephanie M, legislator asst, $27,084
Bogg, Rosemary, legislator asst, $14.87/hr
Bommel, Timmy B, public info spec II, $47,892
Bondon, Jack, state rep, $35,915
Bondurant, Christine M, exec I - cmmte, $44,304
Bondurant, Lisa G, exec I - leadership, $54,288
Bowles, Joseph J, legislator asst, $27,084
Bowman, Pam S, legislator asst, $28,908
Boyer, Kristin M, public info spec II, $18,444
Brandt, Linda D, legislator asst, $38,232
Brattin, Richard R Jr, state rep, $35,915
Brent, Michelle D, legislator asst, $27,084
Brown, Cloria C, state rep, $35,915
Brown, Wanda L, state rep, $35,915
Bruemmer, Alyssa R, legislator asst, $27,084
Bruemmer, William M, comp info tech III, $45,156
Bruns, Joseph, legislator asst, $27,084
Bruns, Marybeth, exec I - leadership, $50,040
Bryant, Danyale R, legislator asst, $27,084
Bryant, Dylan, legislator asst, $27,084
Bryar, Daniel J, exec I - leadership, $46,932
Buckler, Zachariah G, legislator asst, $27,084
Buhr, Lisa, legislator asst , $27,084
Burcham, Carrie A, legislator asst, $28,452
Burlison, Eric W, state rep, $35,915
Burns, Carl R, state rep, $35,915
Burns, Casey E, legislator asst, $27,084
Bush, Joyce M, legislator asst , $27,084
Butler, Michael P, state rep, $35,915
Byrd, Bryan C, net communication spec, $25,452
Cardwell, Lawanda J, legislator asst , $27,084
Carpenter, Jonathan D, state rep, $35,915
Carter, Donna G, legislator asst, $31,920
Caudle, Dorothy A, legislator asst, $13.22/hr
Chipman, Master J, state rep, $35,915
Choinka, Matthew J, legislator asst, $27,084
Cierpiot, Charles M, state rep, $35,915
Clarkson, Rita Z, legislator asst, $34,848
Clearwater, Ryan M, legislator asst, $27,084
Clifford, Mary C, legislator asst, $23.15/hr
Coats, Cheri M, legislator asst, $17.74/hr
Coller, Helen M, legislator asst, $34,224
Coller, Stephen C, legislator asst, $33,036
Colona, Michael J, state rep, $35,915
Conway, Kathie A, state rep, $35,915
Conway, Patrick R, state rep, $35,915
Cookson, Stephen C, state rep, $35,915
Corlew, Kevin R, state rep, $35,915
Cornejo, Robert W, state rep, $35,915
Cottom, Mary, legislator asst, $27,504
Crawford, Christopher, legislator asst, $27,084
Crawford, Sandra K, state rep, $35,915
Crews, Brian, legislator asst, $10.00/hr
Cronin, Kyle, legislator asst, $27,084
Cross, Gary L, state rep, $35,915
Crumbliss, D A, chief clerk, $88,368
Curchin, Alexander B, chief of staff, speaker's ofc, $86,484
Curtis, Courtney A, state rep, $35,915
Curtman, Paul R, state rep, $35,915
Darnall, John D, legislator asst, $27,084

David, Linda K, legislator asst, $28,908
Davis, Charles E, state rep, $35,915
Dean, Nina J, legislator asst, $27,084
Degenhardt, Marilyn S, legislator asst, $22.56/hr
Deneve, Rebecca D, publications sup, $71,100
Denkler, Clarissa, legislator asst, $37,548
Diemler, Cherie L, legislator asst, $27,084
Dinkins, Brett A, legislative info coord, $34,944
Dinkins, Christina L, legislator asst, $27,084
Dogan, Shamed, state rep, $35,915
Dohrman, Dean A, state rep, $35,915
Dominique, Robert D, sr legislative analyst, $61,332
Doss, Fredrick L, legislator asst, $27,084
Dugger, Tony R, state rep, $35,915
Dunn, Chris, administrative asst, $69,612
Dunn, Randy D, state rep, $35,915
Edgington, Anne E, drafting servs attny II, $63,996
Eggleston, John D, state rep, $35,915
Ellington, Brandon, state rep, $35,915
Engelby, Joy L, comp info spec II, $63,996
Engleman, Kelly E, legislator asst, $27,084
Engler, Joseph, exec I - cmmte, $39,624
Engler, Kevin P, state rep, $35,915
English, Keith A, state rep, $35,915
Entlicher, Jacklyn S, state rep, $35,915
Etter, Lisa M, exec I - leadership, $45,156
Evans, David W, legislator asst , $27,084
Farnam, Christopher A, district emp, $10.00/hr
Fields, Denia L, legislator asst , $27,084
Filardo, Kristin J, district emp, $10.00/hr
Findley, Joseph, district emp, $10.00/hr
Fischer, Marilee, district emp, $10.00/hr
Fisher, Vanessa L, legislator asst, $39,624
Fitzgerald, Glenn E, budget analyst IV, $68,160
Fitzpatrick, Scott M, state rep, $35,915
Fitzwater, Paul D, state rep, $35,915
Fitzwater, Travis L, state rep, $35,915
Flanigan, Thomas C, state rep, $35,915
Forck, Jamie R, comp info tech I, $36,204
Forck, Timothy E, comp info tech I, $37,548
Ford, Adam S, comp info technology spec I, $54,288
Foster, Gabrielle, legislator asst, $27,084
Foster, Holly B, legislator asst, $36,888
Fox, Trevor J, dir of comm, $71,100
Fraker, Lyndall D, state rep, $35,915
Franklin, Diane M, state rep, $35,915
Frederick, Keith J, state rep, $35,915
Fuller, James C, district emp, $10.00/hr
Gannon, Elaine F, state rep, $35,915
Gardner, Kimberly M, state rep, $35,915
Garoutte, Sarah A, legislative analyst II, $55,416
Gassmann, Karen, legislator asst, $27,084
Geary, Jacqueline A, legislator asst, $31,920
Gentzsch, Donna J, legislator asst, $34,848
Gesch, Deanna K, exec I - cmmte, $46,932
Glahn, Jason C, sr legislative analyst, $63,996
Gosen, Donald D Jr, state rep, $35,915
Gray, Maura N, legislator asst, $27,084
Gray, Rochelle W, state rep, $35,915
Green, Alan, state rep, $35,915
Green, Donna K, comp info tech III, $45,156
Griggs, Ronda S, legislator asst, $21.29/hr
Grounds, Diana G, public info spec II, $36,204
Haahr, Elijah, state rep, $35,915
Haefner, Marsha E, state rep, $35,915
Hager, Leann M, exec I - leadership, $54,288
Haid, June E, coord post office/bill room, $39,624
Hall, Kristal J, human resource analyst I, $35,568
Hansen, James E, state rep, $35,915
Harris, Ben S, state rep, $35,915
Haslag, Donna L, legislator asst, $37,548
Haynes, John N, legislator asst, $27,084
Helms, Stephen P, legislator asst, $27,084
Henderson, Meghan J, legislative analyst I, $51,096
Hicks, Ronald L, state rep, $35,915
Higdon, Galen W Jr, state rep, $35,915
Higgins, Christy A, exec I - staff, $32,628
Hildebrand, Charles B, doorkeeper, $9,650
Hill, Gary D, doorkeeper, $9,650
Hill, Justin, state rep, $35,915
Hinson, David A, state rep, $35,915
Hoey, Katherine E, drafting servs attny I, $46,932
Hollis, Beth R, legislator asst, $27,084

Hoskins, Denny, state rep-leadershp, $37,415
Hough, Lincoln P, state rep, $35,915
Houghton, Jay D, state rep, $35,915
Hubbard, Penny V, state rep, $35,915
Hubrecht, Tila L, state rep, $35,915
Huebert, Deborah, legislator asst, $27,084
Hueste, Jennifer R, comp info technology spec I, $53,208
Hummel, Jacob W, state rep-leadership, $37,415
Hurst, Lisa R, legislator asst, $36,204
Hurst, Thomas L, state rep, $35,915
Iken, Mitchell R, legislator asst, $27,084
Jackson, James, chaplain, $3,500
Jaco, Helen, asst dir appropriations, $69,612
Jamison, Joyce A, legislator asst, $27,084
Johnson, Delus K, state rep, $35,915
Johnson, Katie, admin asst staff, $38,232
Jones, Caleb M, state rep, $35,915
Justus, Jeffery D, state rep, $35,915
Kaliher, Gary, sound board oper, $9,530
Keeney, Shelley K, state rep, $35,915
Kelley, John M, state rep, $35,915
Kelly, Stevie, legislator asst, $27,084
Kelsey, Vern, reading clerk, $9,650
Kempf, Sherri L, legislator asst, $27,084
Kempker, Judith E, human resource analyst III, $58,908
Kendrick, Kip, state rep, $35,915
Kent, Jessica, legislator asst, $27,084
Kerns, Linda, legislator asst, $27,084
Kidd, William E, state rep, $35,915
King, Stewart N, state rep, $35,915
Kirkton, Jeanne M, state rep, $35,915
Kliethermes, Tammy J, sr bill room clerk, $30,420
Knollmeyer, Donald E, doorkeeper, $10,110
Koenig, Andrew P, state rep, $35,915
Kolkmeyer, Glen R, state rep, $35,915
Korman, Bartholomew J, state rep, $35,915
Korte, Leslie, legislative analyst II, $55,416
Kratky, Michele R, state rep, $35,915
Kuhn, Liane L, legislator asst, $38,928
Kurwicki, Robert A, chaplain, $3,500
Lafaver, Jeremy J, state rep, $35,915
Lair, Michael F, state rep, $35,915
Land, Janet, legislator asst, $27,084
Lant, William H, state rep, $35,915
Lauer, Jeanie, state rep, $35,915
Lavanchy, John F, legislator asst, $27,084
Lavender, Deb, state rep, $35,915
Leara, Michael A, state rep, $35,915
LePage, Antony, public spec I, $30,420
Lichtenegger, Donna S, state rep, $35,915
Licklider, Kathryn, legislator asst, $32,472
Limbach, Megan J, human resource analyst II, $26,093
Lindley, Chase W, legislator asst, $27,084
Lindsay, Lola D, legislator asst, $28,452
Long, Leticia, acct II, $41,172
Lorenz, Jonathan T, public info spec II, $37,548
Love, Warren D, state rep, $35,915
Luebbert, Carla J, legislator asst, $32,472
Lueckenhoff Vogel, Anne F, legislator asst, $31,416
Lynch, Steven M, state rep, $35,915
Maasen, Cheryl A, legislator asst, $28,452
Machon, Karen L, legislator asst, $38,928
Marshall, Nickolas A, state rep, $35,915
Martin, Jacinda, legislator asst, $33,036
Massman, Ron D, billroom clerk, $13.43/hr
Mathews, Roger K, state rep, $35,915
Maxey, Clinton J, legislative info coord, $34,944
May, Karla R, state rep, $35,915
Mayfield, Tad, legislative spec I - proc, $43,488
McCaherty, John C, state rep, $35,915
McCann Beatty, E G, state rep, $35,915
McCreery, Tracy L, state rep, $35,915
McDaniel, Andrew, state rep, $35,915
McDonald, Thomas J, state rep, $35,915
McGaugh, Joseph D, state rep, $35,915
McKnelly, Heather C, legislator asst, $27,084
McLemore, Claude, comp info tech III, $44,304
McManus, Kevin J, state rep, $35,915
McNeil, Margo G, state rep, $35,915
McNitt, Julie J, sr legislative analyst, $66,720
Medlin, Paula, legislator asst, $16,250
Mehmert, Jennifer J, comp info tech I, $36,204
Mehrhoff, Wanda, legislator asst, $27,084

Meller, Elaine C, legislator asst, $27,084
Meredith, Susan C, state rep, $35,915
Mertens, Barbara A, admin asst research, $22.56/hr
Messenger, Jeffery L, state rep, $35,915
Miller, Celeste R, legislator asst, $27,084
Miller, Dana L, dir procedures-asst chief clerk, $72,768
Miller, Julia Y, comp info tech III, $47,892
Miller, Rockne C, state rep, $35,915
Mims, Bonnaye V, state rep, $35,915
Mirts, Linda D, public spec II, $33,744
Mitten, Gina C, state rep, $35,915
Montecillo, Genise D, state rep, $35,915
Moon, Chris M, state rep, $35,915
Moreland, Christopher G, public info spec I, $30,420
Morff, Julie M, budget analyst III, $50,040
Morgan, Judith A, state rep, $35,915
Morris, Lynn A, state rep, $35,915
Mullally, Debra L, legislator asst, $32,472
Muntzel, David E, state rep, $35,915
Murray, Stuart, legislator asst, $27,084
Myers, David E, legislator asst, $27,084
Nally, Betty, legislator asst, $27,084
Naught, Kristina, drafting servs sup, $68,160
Neely, James W, state rep, $35,915
Newman, Stacey G, state rep, $35,915
Nichols, Mary F, state rep, $35,915
Nilges, Robin J, maint worker II, $33,744
Nittler, Stephen R, legislator asst, $27,084
Norr, Charlie, state rep, $35,915
Oberdahlhoff, Virginia S, district employee, $10.00/hr
O'Laughlin, Emily, legislator asst, $27,084
Ordway, Jaime, exec I - leadership, $38,232
Ortmeyer, Christopher R, comp info technology spec I, $51,096
Ott, Jill S, legislator asst, $34,848
Ott, Melaine A, legislator asst, $38,928
Otto, William B, state rep, $35,915
Overton, Lynn W, legislator asst , $27,084
Pace, Sharon L, state rep, $35,915
Painter, Diane L, drafting servs attny II, $62,664
Parkinson, Mark A, state rep, $35,915
Pearson, Scott E, legislator asst, $27,084
Percival, Latonya S, district employee, $10.00/hr
Perry, Jarad M, legislator asst, $27,084
Peters, Joshua, state rep, $35,915
Petrie, Jessica L, legislator asst, $27,084
Pfautsch, Donna S, state rep, $35,915
Pfister, Greggory S, legislator asst, $27,084
Phillips, Donald E, state rep, $35,915
Pierson, Tommie L, state rep, $35,915
Pietzman, James R, state rep, $35,915
Pike, Patricia, state rep, $35,915
Pleus, Patricia G, admin asst research, $45,156
Pogue, Jeffrey L, state rep, $35,915
Porter, Lisa J, legislator asst, $33,636
Powers, Marc P, administrative asst, $56,520
Price, Michael N, dir of appropriations, $79,296
Puyear, Charles, legislator asst, $27,084
Pyles, Michael S, legislator asst, $27,084
Rackers, Agnes R, district employee, $10.00/hr
Rackers, Anthony B, doorkeeper, $9,650
Rademan, Terri L, procurement ofcr I, $46,068
Redmon, Craig, state rep, $35,915
Rehagen, Karen A, legislator asst, $15.88/hr
Rehder, Holly R, state rep, $35,915
Reiboldt, William I, state rep, $35,915
Remole, Timothy G, state rep, $35,915
Rhoads, Robert S, state rep, $35,915
Rhodes, Deanna M, legislator asst, $27,084
Rhodes, Dennis L, legislator asst, $27,084
Richardson, Regina L, legislator asst, $27,084
Ritter, Janet M, legislator asst, $19.05/hr
Rizzo, John J, state rep, $35,915
Roark, James R, comp info technology spec I, $56,520
Roberts, Joseph D, budget analyst IV, $65,364
Robinett, Ralph W, sergeant-at-arms, $11,285
Robinson, Dylan, legislator asst, $27,084
Roden, Shane, state rep, $35,915
Rodieck, Tammy S, admin asst research, $39,624
Roeber, Rebecca, state rep, $35,915
Rogers, Kelley G, legislator asst, $27,084
Rohrbach, Beth, legislator asst, $28,908
Romalia, Kristin M, drafting servs attny II, $61,332
Rone, Donald, state rep, $35,915

Ross, Kenneth C, legislative dir, $71,100
Ross, Matthew W, comp info technology spec I, $53,208
Ross, Robert W, state rep, $35,915
Rowden, Caleb F, state rep, $35,915
Rowland, Lyle E, state rep, $35,915
Runions, Joseph E, state rep, $35,915
Ruth, Rebecca L, state rep, $35,915
Rutledge, Marietta E, legislator asst, $29,412
Sandbothe, Greg L, operations spec, $46,068
Savage, Paula A, legislator asst, $33,636
Schaben, Sarah L, public spec II, $37,548
Schaff, Megan, district employee, $10.00/hr
Schanzmeyer, Sandra K, legislator asst, $34,848
Scheulen, Donna J, legislator asst, $23.15/hr
Schmidt, Brian J, maint worker I, $28,908
Schnelting, Adam N, legislator asst, $27,084
Schwedler, Stacey R, legislator asst, $27,084
Seaton, Marilyn J, sr legislative spec-procedures, $25.57/hr
Shaul, Daniel Y, state rep, $35,915
Shull, Noel J, state rep, $35,915
Shumake, Lindell F, state rep, $35,915
Simmons, Chiquita, legislator asst, $27,084
Simpson, Rita Y, legislator asst, $27,084
Skinner, Scott A, comp info spec II, $63,996
Smith, Aaron M, public spec III, $37,548
Smith, Christina G, legislator asst, $27,084
Smith, Clement J, state rep, $35,915
Solon, Sheila Y, state rep, $35,915
Sommer, Chrissy, state rep, $35,915
Speak, Adam, legislator asst, $27,084
Spencer, Bryan, state rep, $35,915
St. Clair, Shelly A, legislator asst, $30,924
Stockman, Kathryn F, legislator asst, $15.88/hr
Strader, Dennis L, doorkeeper, $9,650
Strobel, Karla J, sr legislative analyst, $66,720
Strutton, Ethan D, comp info tech III, $43,488
Surface, Terry A, doorkeeper, $9,650
Suthoff, Nancy, legislator asst, $27,084
Sutton, Wesley, legislator asst, $27,084
Swan, Kathryn F, state rep, $35,915
Talken, Margaret M, legislator asst, $35,472
Taylor, Jered M, state rep, $35,915
Thessen, Angelia M, legislator asst, $28,908
Thiel, Maggie L, legislative analyst I, $49,128
Thoenen, Donna J, legislator asst, $30,924
Thompson, Matthew W, legislator asst, $27,084
Treppler, Rachel J, legislator asst, $27,084
Tucker, William B, dir of research, $86,484
Vescovo, Robert E, state rep, $35,915
Vest, Markus D, district employee, $10.00/hr
Volkart, Amy C, legislator asst, $27,084
Vought, Edward R, legislator asst, $27,084
Walker, Beth A, legislator asst, $34,848
Walker, Nathan B, state rep, $35,915
Webb, Marc T, asst dir research, $71,208
Webber, Stephen D, state rep, $35,915
Wehmeir, Patricia A, human resource analyst II, $50,040
Welch, David H, legislative counsel, $57,744
Werner, Brad A, dir of operations, $86,484
White, Emily, legislative spec II-proc, $48,156
White, Jefferson T, security guard - garage, $25,404
White, Kathalene L, sr legislative spec-procedures, $58,908
White, William E, state rep, $35,915
Wiemann, John D, state rep, $35,915
Wilhelm, Daniel, legislator asst, $27,084
Wilkinson, Romona, administrative asst, $54,288
Williams, Cullen J, legislator asst, $27,084
Williams, Jody K, legislator asst, $14.14/hr
Williams, Sharon K, legislator asst, $27,084
Willis, David E, chief of staff, speaker's ofc, $81,036
Wilson, Kenneth W, state rep, $35,915
Witte, Terry L, chief of staff, minority floor leader, $81,036
Wittenberger, Judy L, district employee, $10.00/hr
Wolfe, Myra R, legislator asst, $32,472
Wolters, Keri L, legislator asst, $30,384
Wood, Charles D, state rep, $35,915
Woolstenhulme, Marla G, public info spec II, $34,944
Wrenn, Andrew C, legislative analyst I, $47,892
Wright, Tracey, legislator asst, $27,084
Young, Carrie L, procurement ofcr I, $46,068
Zerr, Anne F, state rep, $35,915

Joint Legislative Committees

State Capitol, Jefferson City 65101

Hembree, Russell L, dir/revisor, $94,210
Basnett, Michael D, comp progmer-stat, $60,600
Donaldson, Emily M, administrative sec III, $44,999
Hagedorn, George W, comp info spec II, $38.47/hr
Kirkpatrick, James A, staff attny III, $61,889
Lueckenhoff, Sandra K, asst dir/chief bill drafter, $81,023
Mumpower, Lois A, lgl secretary, $46,397
Neuner, Charlotte M, editor II, $30.00/hr
Paschal, Cathy A, index sup, $36,010
Swisher, Greg A, business operations mgr/asst editor, $34,356
Veit, Donna A, comp info tech II, $55,068

Chapter 5: Judicial Branch

Supreme Court

PO Box 150 Jefferson City 65102

Breckenridge, Patricia A, supreme court judge (chief), $178,089
Aubuchon, Betsy, commission counsel, $84,540
Baehr, Jordan C, law clerk, $51,096
Barlow, Melanie M, judicial executive assistant, $53,208
Bay, Peter W, law clerk, $48,156
Bennett, Kristin, judicial executive assistant, $38,647
Blanton, Kathleen, judicial executive assistant, $53,208
Boessen, Mark P, maintenance worker I, $34,944
Bonine, Melvin D, maintenance worker I, $15.00/hr
Brade, Robin L, secretary III, $25,164
Breen, Thomas L, deputy marshal, $24.00/hr
Case, Julie D, deputy clerk bar enrollment, $14.79/hr
Conley, Lori C, librarian assistant, $27,084
Conley, Lori C, clerk typist I, $13.00/hr
Connell, Ryan L, maintenance worker I, $35,568
Cundiff, Curtis W, maintenance worker I, $36,204
Dickey, Donald W, chief deputy clerk, $74,304
Douglas, Roy L, deputy marshal, $25.00/hr
Draper, George W, supreme court judge, $170,292
Dunsford, Kelly D, law clerk, $56,151
Fischer, Zel M, supreme court judge, $170,292
Fishback, Tommy L, data processing officer, $63,996
Fletchall, Kathy K, administrative assistant, $43,488
Forck, Dennis L, maintenance supervisor, $38,928
Fredrick, Rebecca, judicial executive assistant, $53,208
Gallen, Kate, law clerk, $51,096
Geiser, Angel L, deputy clerk bar enrollment, $40,380
Hartman, Margie A, deputy clerk II, $71,100
Hennessey-Burch, Margaret, administrative assistant, $46,068
Heseman, Dwight E, deputy marshal, $24.00/hr
Hoelscher, Kari L, clerk typist II, $37,548
Holt, Jo G, secretary III, $44,304
Jansen, Carol D, law clerk, $48,156
Johnson, Amanda N, law clerk, $48,156
Jones, Allison, law clerk, $51,096
Kempker, Bryan J, maintenance worker I, $34,356
Knaebel, Lori S, deputy clerk II, $40,380
Koelling, Amanda K, clerk typist I, $8.00/hr
Korsmeyer, Dawn, fiscal officer I, $43,488
Lachenicht, Anthony J, deputy marshal, $25.00/hr
Lauer, Raymond B, deputy marshal, $25.00/hr
Leathers, Rebecca I, interpretive resource spec, $34,356
Lewis, Jacob A, law clerk, $48,156
Lucas, Elizabeth A, law clerk, $51,096
Luebbering, Greg J, general services supervisor, $54,288
Milinkov, Terri, administrative secretary, $53,208
Miller, Gail C, librarian, $46,068
Pasha, Mohsen, law clerk, $48,156
Peterson, Eric S, law clerk, $78,594
Phillips, Caleb P, law clerk, $51,096
Quinn, Mary J, clerk typist I, $10.10/hr
Ramirez, Misty A, law clerk, $56,151
Rehagen, Theresa M, deputy clerk bar enrollment, $41,933
Richardson, Delores J, judicial executive assistant, $53,208
Riggert, Beth S, communications counsel, $81,036
Ruehl, Arthur E, deputy marshal, $25.00/hr
Ruether, Cynthia L, judicial executive assistant, $53,208
Ruether, Cynthia L, clerk typist I, $13.00/hr

Russell, Mary R, supreme court judge, $170,292
Schanzmeyer, Rita C, director bar enrollment, $61,332
Smith, Carl, deputy marshal, $33,744
Smith, Crystal L, deputy marshal, $33,744
Stallion, Kristen, research assistant, $8.04/hr
Stearley, Harold E, counsel, $88,058
Stegeman, Mary L, fiscal officer I, $24.32/hr
Stieffermann, Robert P, marshal, $54,288
Stith, Laura D, supreme court judge, $170,292
Teitelman, Richard B, supreme court judge, $170,292
Thompson, Bill L, clerk of the supreme court, $131,843
Tiberghien, Kayle D, deputy clerk II, $37,548
Turley, Cynthia L, director court en banc, $84,540
Vinson, Christina S, deputy clerk II, $41,940
Vittetoe-moore, Falena L, judicial executive assistant, $53,208
Vittetoe-moore, Falena L, clerk typist I, $9.00/hr
Walter, Robert G, deputy marshal, $24.00/hr
Williams, Brian, research assistant, $8.04/hr
Wilson, Paul C, supreme court judge, $170,292

Office of State Courts Administrator

2112 Industrial Dr., Jefferson City 65101

Lloyd, Kathy S, administrator, $121,737
Abbott, Kimberly J, court services supervisor II, $58,908
Adams, Christopher K, education supervisor II, $58,908
Adamson, Patricia A, administrative specialist I, $30,984
Albert, Jonathan C, education mgmt analyst II, $41,940
Alexander, Jana L, ed principle mgmt analyst I, $47,892
Allen, Amanda B, court services mgmt analyst I, $39,624
Baker, Barbara M, sr computer support tech, $36,888
Baker, Meredith A, education supervisor I, $52,092
Barnett, Christina G, court services mgmt analyst II, $41,940
Battle, Kinica C, court services mgmt analyst II, $41,940
Belk, Coy D, computer support tech, $32,052
Bemboom, Nancy K, court services mgmt analyst I, $39,624
Bentivegna, Pierrette, ct svcs prin mgmt analyst I, $52,092
Benton, Travis L, application supv, $58,908
Berhorst, Nicole L, education mgmt analyst II, $43,488
Bestgen, Cory D, programmer supv, $66,720
Bias, Lisa J, transcription technician, $34,356
Bisges, Angela, facilities mgmt analyst I, $36,204
Boeckmann, Vanessa R, system administrator, $51,096
Boehlen, Nicholas E, court services mgmt analyst I, $40,380
Boessen, Carrie A, court services mgmt analyst II, $41,940
Brandes, Matthew R, server admin mgr, $75,948
Branson, Amy M, court services mgmt analyst I, $40,380
Braun, Emily M, sr computer support tech, $53,208
Brawn, Steven K, sr computer support tech, $35,568
Breeding, Lonnie W, accountant III, $50,040
Brendel, Larry J, app and supt dev mgr, $75,948
Brooks, Donald P, division director, $96,447
Bruce, Theresa, sr computer support engineer, $52,092
Bruchsaler, Robert W, pre-trial/prob svc supv I, $50,040
Buckley, Paul S, human resources manager, $72,768
Burnham, Teri L, sr customer support tech, $37,548
Buschjost, Douglas G, grants & projects mgr, $69,612
Butler, Lisa A, accountant II, $46,068
Buzard, Arbizene L, sr customer support tech, $54,288
Byland, Mary E, education mgmt analyst II, $42,708
Cassil, Courtney S, court services mgmt analyst II, $41,940
Caton, Shelley D, court services mgmt analyst I, $40,380
Cavender, Kendall J, customer support tech, $30,420
Chipley, Jennifer, customer support tech supv, $49,128
Cochran, Robert M, data systems supv, $69,612
Coffman, Denine A, court services mgmt analyst I, $40,380
Coles- Jones, Tina M, court services program manager, $71,100
Connell, Rebecca M, management analyst I, $36,888
Conner, Benjamin D, customer support tech, $30,420
Connery, Nicholas A, court services mgmt analyst I, $38,928
Cooper, Katlyn J, customer support tech, $30,420
Cox, Leslie M, court services mgmt analyst I, $40,380
Coy, Joseph L, ct svcs prin mgmt analyst I, $49,128
Cramer, Kelly, associate legal counsel, $53,208
Crawford, John T, programmer, $40,380
Cremer, Joseph L, desktop & device support mgr, $74,304
Davis, Janette M, temporary help, $14.41/hr
Davis, Vonda D, administrative specialist I, $30,984
Denney, Martha J, ct svcs prin mgmt analyst I, $47,892
Dial, Trenton A, court services mgmt analyst II, $41,940
Dillon, Tina M, education mgmt analyst II, $41,940
Doden, Lisa R, court services mgmt analyst II, $41,940

Doman, Katherine L, court services mgmt analyst II, $41,940
Dowden, D B, fiscal & general services mgr, $69,612
Doyle, Edward J, programmer, $41,940
Dunbar, Linda S, education supervisor I, $52,092
Evers, Derek W, computer support engineer, $34,944
Fischer, Christopher D, info security supervisor, $58,908
Fowler, Nathan P, audio visual support tech, $30,984
Friedewald, Janet L, hr principle mgmt analyst I, $46,068
Fringer, Michelle L, court services mgmt analyst II, $41,940
Garriott, Sherri L, sr database administrator, $53,208
Gathright, Kevin M, programmer, $45,156
Gaynor, Donna M, research management analyst II, $46,068
Gelber, Kevin P, court services mgmt analyst I, $39,624
Gerling, Kimberly A, sr programmer, $52,092
Gibson, Robin E, integrated services mgr, $71,208
Gilbert, Vanessia G, court services mgmt analyst II, $41,940
Graham, Debbie K, ct svcs prin mgmt analyst I, $47,892
Gray, Shelley M, ct svcs prin mgmt analyst I, $47,892
Green, Jennifer L, customer support tech, $30,420
Grove, Douglas W, programmer supv, $66,720
Gump, Carol L, sr database administrator, $56,520
Hagan, Martha J, court services mgmt analyst II, $41,940
Hagner, Jennifer L, sr software engineer, $52,092
Hall, Beth A, accountant III, $50,040
Hancock, Michael F, budget program manager, $72,768
Haslag, Joshua P, computer support engineer, $42,708
Hasler, George T, inventory specialist, $44,304
Hedrick, Carolyn D, sr programmer, $51,096
Hedrick, Kathleen A, ct svcs prin mgmt analyst I, $47,892
Hemmel, Marilue E, court services mgmt analyst II, $41,940
Hendricks, Curtis, education mgmt analyst II, $49,128
Henson, Sabrina S, info technology support tech, $33,180
Herman, Susan L, administrative specialist I, $32,628
Hilkerbaumer, Tristen K, temporary help, $12.00/hr
Hill, J S, sr system administrator, $55,416
Hoener, Amanda L, application supervisor, $54,288
Holzschuh, Joseph J, sr programmer, $52,092
Hopkins, Jacob R, research management analyst I, $41,172
Houts, Laura, administrative specialist II, $38,928
Huff, Jeffrey C, research supervisor I, $55,416
Huff, Samuel L, sr computer support tech, $34,356
Irminger, Tiffanie, publications mgmt analyst II, $41,940
Janku, Anne M, research program manager, $74,304
Jansen, Judy K, court services mgmt analyst II, $41,940
Jobe, Lyle L, network supervisor, $61,332
Johnson, Jeremy W, projects prin mgmt analyst I, $55,416
Johnson, Kristin M, research prin mgmt analyst I, $47,892
Kadow, Stacy L, computer support tech supv, $54,288
Kampeter, Melissa R, grants supervisor II, $58,908
Ketcherside, Adora M, sr system administrator, $55,416
Kliethermes, David J, app and support dev mgr, $75,948
Knipp, Christy M, accountant III, $50,040
Knipp, Clayton L, court services supervisor I, $51,096
Knollmeyer, Lori A, transcription supervisor II, $57,744
Knoth, Martha C, administrative specialist I, $30,984
Kopfer, Anita I, transcription technician, $36,204
Kraft, Jennifer D, computer support tech supv, $50,040
Kraus, Earl D, deputy state court adm and division dir, $96,447
Kunze, Aimee N, accountant I, $40,380
Lairmore, Melissa A, court services mgmt analyst I, $40,380
Langlotz, Laurie A, administrative specialist I, $34,944
Leeper, Sharon A, accountant III, $51,096
Lehman, Michael L, administrative support I, $33,180
Lemler, Michael A, accountant III, $51,096
Leskiw, Beth A, principal programmer, $57,744
Lesko, Valerie A, budget principle mgmt analyst I, $51,096
Loethen, Teresa A, transcription technician, $30,420
Luebbert, Ryan A, network administrator, $52,092
Maassen, Sandra L, fiscal management analyst II, $44,304
Maiura, Christopher M, server administration supv, $61,332
McCubbin, Dorothy L, sr database administrator, $24.57/hr
McElfresh, Ricky A, research supervisor II, $58,908
Mengwasser, Derek, software engineer, $41,172
Mengwasser, Justin J, software engineer, $45,156
Meyer, Tammy S, court services supervisor I, $51,096
Middleton, Dana, administrative specialist II, $43,488
Miller, Michael A, sr computer support engineer, $53,208
Miller, Pamela R, sr application support tech, $46,932
Minter, Samuel A, senior web developer, $45,156
Mitan, Andrew J, fiscal supervisor I, $56,520
Moffat, Mike, application support tech, $46,932
Monteer, Sherie L, sr software engineer, $51,096
Moore, Jeffrey J, sr programmer, $46,932

Morrisey, Richard, court services program manager, $71,100
Morrison, Gwendolyn G, accountant II, $44,304
Mote, Karen J, facilities mgmt analyst I, $36,204
Muenks, Kenny L, system administrator, $51,096
Norris, Terri A, publications unit supervisor I, $52,092
Northweather, Sean, database specialist, $45,156
Oligschlaeger, Glenda, sr software engineer, $52,092
Osmanovic, Fahrudin, research management analyst I, $40,380
Owens, Shannon J, projects prin mgmt analyst II, $58,908
Parsons-Jackson, Stephanie R, admin specialist I, $30,984
Paschal, Sherri A, division director, $96,447
Payne, Eric E, court services supervisor I, $51,096
Payne, Stefanie A, education mgmt analyst II, $41,940
Pearce, Mary C, administrative specialist I, $30,984
Peters, Michelle, fiscal management analyst I, $40,380
Pillai, Anupama S, sr programmer, $51,096
Plassmeyer, John P, temporary help, $12.00/hr
Plunkett, Angela M, court services supervisor II, $58,908
Rackers, Sue A, accounting specialist I, $38,232
Rafferty, Kristal, court services mgmt analyst II, $41,940
Ramsdell, Marla J, education mgmt analyst II, $45,156
Reeder, Daniel, customer support tech, $29,976
Renick, Patrick S, programmer, $45,156
Rex, Tammy L, court services supervisor I, $52,092
Reynolds, Kimberly A, hr mgmt analyst I, $39,624
Reynolds, Mary C, court services mgmt analyst II, $41,940
Richards, Deborah K, administrative specialist I, $30,984
Ricks, Lynette G, ct svcs prin mgmt analyst I, $46,068
Roark, David F, programmer supervisor, $61,332
Rodeman, Elizabeth A, contracts mgmt analyst I, $40,380
Rodieck, Karl J, court services supervisor II, $58,908
Rottmann, Russell W, contracts prin mgmt analyst I, $46,068
Russell, Rebecca S, court services program manager, $71,100
Salmons, Ian L, sr system administrator, $55,416
Sarver, William J, system administrator, $51,096
Schaffer, Dana K, human resources supervisor I, $52,092
Schnieders, Denise M, administrative specialist II, $23,238
Schroeder, Jill L, administrative specialist III, $45,156
Schulte, Shirley M, temporary help, $22.79/hr
Schwaller, Jessica L, court services mgmt analyst I, $38,928
Senter, Christina F, research management analyst II, $45,156
Shields, Susan E, accounting supervisor I, $53,208
Shiflett, Shelley P, court services supervisor II, $58,908
Simones, Anthony D, education program manager, $69,612
Smith, James W, computer support engineer, $37,548
Smith, Tara L, fiscal management analyst I, $40,380
Stalter, Aaron R, court services mgmt analyst I, $40,380
Stark, Sheila A, sr programmer, $53,208
Steinbeck, Rebecca L, programmer supervisor, $63,996
Stieferman, Christine A, customer support tech, $41,172
Stokes, Christina M, accounting specialist I, $33,180
Strope, Paul A, server administration supervisor, $61,332
Summers, William, programmer, $43,488
Suthoff, Samantha L, court services mgmt analyst II, $41,940
Sweeney, Danielle L, court services mgmt analyst I, $39,624
Tappel, Lori A, publications mgmt analyst I, $38,928
Taylor, Stephanie R, court services mgmt analyst I, $38,928
Toalson, Owen S, sr programmer, $52,092
Tuinstra, Brett, network administrator, $52,092
Upschulte, Julie R, court services mgmt analyst I, $40,380
Utermoehlen, Wanda E, administrative specialist II, $38,928
Vaidya, Kirtida, research management analyst I, $40,380
Vance, David D, sr computer support engineer, $52,092
Vaughan, Shelly L, sr quality assurance specialist, $46,932
Voss, Denise L, projects prin mgmt analyst II, $58,908
Wachter, Jenni K, administrative specialist I, $30,984
Wallace-Bay, Christine, education mgmt analyst II, $41,940
Waller, Kathy L, administrative specialist I, $30,984
Wibberg, Tina L, application supv, $58,908
Wilcox, Lisa L, research management analyst II, $24,564
Wiler, Gala S, accounting supervisor I, $56,520
Williams, Sarah L, administrative specialist I, $30,984
Wilson, Natalie, info security specialist, $45,156
Wing, Bradley W, research prin mgmt analyst I, $50,040
Wittrock, Bernice R, sr computer support engineer, $52,092
Wojtasik, Christine R, administrative specialist I, $30,984
Wunderlich, Tracy, sr system administrator, $55,416
Young, Kylie J, court services program manager, $71,100
Zacharias, Catherine N, legal counsel, $77,556

Court of Appeals—Eastern District

815 Olive St., St. Louis 63101

Van Amburg, Lisa, appellate judge, $155,709
Ahrens, Clifford H, appellate judge, $155,709
Anderson, Lisa B, law clerks, $52,092
Bader, Douglas R, court administrator - ap, $94,416
Berland, Rachel P, law clerks, $50,040
Borisch, Cynthia, judicial administrative asst, $39,624
Chamberlain, Alvin K, marshal, $40,380
Clayton, Robert M, appellate judge, $155,709
Cohen, Patricia L, appellate judge, $155,709
Conklin, Paul M, law clerks, $48,156
Dalton, Chad M, computer info tech spec, $53,208
Derousse, Candice E, deputy clerk, $36,204
Dowd, James M, appellate judge, $155,709
Dowd, Robert G, appellate judge, $155,709
Dyson, Erma D, deputy clerk, $36,204
Ellis, Roxane, judicial administrative asst, $39,624
Endres, Brenda K, judicial administrative asst, $39,624
Eswine, Jessica D, law clerks, $52,092
Everett, Tuesday R, judicial administrative asst, $39,624
Fuqua, Willa, law clerks, $50,040
Gaertner, Gary M, appellate judge, $155,709
Gonzalez, Judith E, judicial administrative asst, $39,624
Grieshaber, Dina M, judicial administrative asst, $39,624
Griffin, Laguerra R, judicial administrative asst, $39,624
Hannel, Joy, librarian III, $63,996
Heibel, Sandra, deputy clerk, $36,204
Hess, Philip M, appellate judge, $155,709
Hixson, Susan K, fiscal officer II, $49,128
Hoff, Mary K, appellate judge, $155,709
Hoffman, Matthew C, law clerks, $48,156
Jacquot, Maureen S, settlement secretary, $28,963
Johnson, Jennifer S, law clerks, $52,092
Jung, Hyo Jin J, law clerks, $48,156
Krings, Jennifer M, law clerks, $52,092
Lappas, Catherine, law clerks, $52,092
Machian, Jennifer M, law clerks, $50,040
Mackowiak, Lea M, law clerks, $52,092
Matteo, Laura E, law clerks, $50,040
Mooney, Lawrence E, appellate judge, $155,709
Morris, Joseph M, law clerks, $50,040
Motley, Kathy D, administrative assistant, $39,624
Motley-Cole, Delphine, deputy clerk, $36,204
Neal, Mary S, judicial administrative asst, $39,624
Odenwald, Kurt S, appellate judge, $155,709
Oslica, Amy E, law clerks, $48,156
Phillips, Megan E, law clerks, $52,092
Poole, Rebecca E, judicial administrative asst, $39,624
Prince, Tamatha S, judicial administrative asst, $40,380
Quigless, Angela T, appellate judge, $155,709
Rasnic, Tabitha A, data processing coord, $38,928
Richter, Roy L, appellate judge, $155,709
Rickman, Angela C, judicial administrative asst, $39,624
Roy, Laura E, clerk, $74,304
Ruehl, Arthur E, deputy clerk, $18,444
Schneider, Karen E, law clerks, $52,092
Sengheiser, Jason M, law clerks, $52,092
Skinner-Neuhaus, Deborah G, chief deputy clerk II, $46,932
Stevens, Julie A, law clerks, $52,092
Sullivan, Sherri B, appellate judge, $155,709
Taylor, Karen S, judicial administrative ast, $39,624
Taylor, Laura Y, law clerks, $52,092
Taylor, Sally M, deputy clerk, $36,204
Tooks, Lucius J, deputy clerk, $33,744
Tucker, Emily M, law clerks, $52,092
Van Dorn, Karen A, judicial administrative asst, $39,624
Wesselschmidt, Benjamin R, law clerks, $48,156
Westermann, Amy S, law clerks, $52,092
Williams, Shannon M, law clerks, $52,092
Wortman, Alice M, law clerks, $52,092

Court of Appeals—Southern District

300 Hammons Pkwy., Springfield 65806

Sheffield, Mary W, appellate judge, $155,709
Bailey, Amy L, librarian I, $42,708
Barber, Rose A, law clerks, $52,092
Bates, Jeffrey W, appellate judge, $155,709
Browne, Mary E, law clerks, $52,092

Budd, Sandra L, clerk, $88,368
Bunch, Douglas C, law clerks, $52,092
Burrell, Donald E, appellate judge, $155,709
Byrne, Jennifer L, law clerks, $48,156
Carmichael, James R, research attorney, $58,908
Francis, William W, appellate judge, $155,709
Goins, Debra S, judicial administrative asst, $39,624
Lessmeier, Jason J, law clerks, $52,092
Lynch, Gary W, appellate judge, $155,709
Mense, Lindy J, judicial administrative asst, $39,624
Newton, Susan E, fiscal officer II, $49,128
Pace, Laura B, judicial administrative asst, $39,624
Phillips, Janet A, judicial administrative asst, $39,624
Platter, Connie A, chief deputy clerk I, $43,488
Rahmeyer, Nancy S, appellate judge, $155,709
Rasmussen, Jamie P, law clerks, $52,092
Risberg, Michael, law clerks, $48,156
Sanders, Joel D, computer info tech spec, $54,288
Scott, Daniel E, appellate judge, $155,709
Shearer, Leana K, judicial administrative asst, $39,624
Shier, Blake M, law clerks, $48,156
Street, Craig A, staff counsel, $72,768
Travis, Jayme K, judicial administrative asst, $39,624
Vales, Laura A, law clerks, $52,092
Wilson, Kerry D, judicial administrative asst, $39,624
Woods, Mikel H, marshal, $22,529
Wygle, Traci A, deputy clerk, $36,204

Court of Appeals—Western District

1300 Oak St., Kansas City 64106

Ahuja, Alok, appellate judge, $155,709
Ball, Rockey A, deputy marshal II, $38,928
Becker, Susan L, law clerks, $46,932
Beckert, Tammy R, judicial administrative asst, $39,624
Boeding, Kimberly K, law clerks, $52,092
Bossert, Trevor S, law clerks, $46,068
Calvert, Monja M, judicial administrative asst, $39,624
Carpenter, Jawonia D, judicial administrative asst, $39,624
Casey, Susan M, law clerks, $51,096
Danner, Terri A, deputy clerk, $36,204
Daugherty, Nicholas R, law clerks, $46,068
Dewitt, Lydia E, law clerks, $46,068
Draper, Nicholas E, law clerks, $46,932
Ellis, Joseph M, appellate judge, $155,709
Estrada-lopez, Janine L, librarian II, $56,520
Fay, Whitney L, law clerks, $46,068
Gabbert, Anthony R, appellate judge, $155,709
Griffin, Marita A, law clerks, $46,068
Griffith, Rebecca L, judicial administrative asst, $29,718
Hardwick, Lisa W, appellate judge, $155,709
Harris, Alison K, law clerks, $48,156
Hasty, Brenda J, marshal, $41,940
Heenan, Paula J, judicial administrative asst, $39,624
Hooper, Heath A, law clerks, $48,156
Howard, Victor C, appellate judge, $155,709
Kellerman, Catherine D, deputy clerk, $36,204
Kennedy, David C, law clerks, $52,092
King, Susan L, law clerks, $52,092
Lohman, Christina S, law clerks, $51,096
Lord, Sherry L, deputy clerk, $36,204
Lord, Terence G, clerk, $88,368
Martin, Cynthia L, appellate judge, $155,709
Martin, Gene R, senior judge, $38.66/hr
Menke, Marie J, computer info tech spec, $54,288
Mitchell, Karen K, appellate judge, $155,709
Mitchell, Steven A, building manager, $55,416
Moran, John L, senior judge, $38.66/hr
Myers, Kathleen V, fiscal officer II, $49,128
Newton, Thomas H, appellate judge, $155,709
Pfeiffer, Mark D, appellate judge, $155,709
Price, Kendra Y, deputy clerk, $36,204
Ray, Katherine E, law clerks, $50,040
Seely, Nicole L, deputy clerk, $36,204
Sevier, Carol C, law clerks, $51,096
Skelton, Sara J, law clerks, $46,068
Sonnenberg, Susan C, staff counsel, $72,768
St John, Kathleen M, deputy clerk, $36,204
Stanford, Donna L, law clerks, $51,096
Washington, Charlotte, judicial administrative asst, $39,624
Welsh, James E, appellate judge, $155,709
Whitt, Kelsey D, law clerks, $51,096

Witt, Gary D, appellate judge, $155,709
Woods, Jayne T, law clerks, $52,092
Wurzer, Katherine E, law clerks, $46,932

Missouri Circuit Courts

Abbott, Brian P, juvenile officer IV, $46,932
Abbott, Lisa K, juvenile officer II, $37,548
Abbott, Marsha A, circuit clerk, $55,639
Abernathy, Christie T, court clerk II, $25,032
Abernathy, Renee T, court clerk III, $27,660
Acey, Angela M, court clerk II, $25,404
Adams, Amanda M, temporary help, $10.00/hr
Adams, Christina L, detention juvenile officer II, $36,888
Adams, Morgan C, court clerk II, $25,404
Adams, Peggy J, court clerk IV, $29,976
Adams, Rhonda S, court clerk III, $31,512
Adams, Suzanne C, court clerk IV, $32,628
Addison, Tressa M, court clerk II, $25,404
Adkins, Daren L, associate circuit judge, $135,059
Adkins, Mary B, court clerk II, $25,404
Agles, Jacqueline A, court clerk II, $25,404
Ahnert, Paula M, court clerk III, $27,660
Ahrens, Mark J, court clerk II, $25,404
Aiken, Carol, probate commissioner, $133,716
Akers, Kathy E, temporary rep, $15.00/hr
Akers, Laverne, unit manager II, $53,208
Akins, Stephanie L, court clerk II, $25,404
Albertson, Melissa N, detention aide II, $27,660
Aldridge, Lora L, court clerk II, $27,660
Alexander, Patricia, temporary rep, $14.70/hr
Alexander, Shane T, circuit judge, $146,804
Allee, Sherry L, court clerk III, $29,976
Allen, Catina C, court clerk II, $25,404
Allen, Donna L, court clerk IV, $18,772
Allen, Geoffrey E, family court commissioner, $133,716
Allen, Harvey S, associate circuit judge, $135,059
Allen, Julie L, unit manager I, $41,172
Allen, Julisa D, court clerk II, $25,404
Allen, Lorree A, court clerk III, $27,660
Allen, Melissa A, court reporter, $57,178
Allen, Nicholas L, court clerk III, $27,228
Allen, Russell C, juvenile officer IV, $44,304
Alley, Thomas R, associate circuit judge, $135,059
Allison, Kathleen S, juv/family court support wkr, $36,888
Allred, Amanda D, temporary help, $10.00/hr
Allred, Danielle E, court clerk II, $25,404
Allsberry, Gregory K, associate circuit judge, $135,059
Alonzo, Dawn C, court clerk III, $28,536
Alonzo, Ellen K, court clerk III, $31,512
Althide, Angela K, court clerk II, $25,404
Andel, Karen A, court reporter, $57,178
Anderson, Deborah F, court clerk II, $25,404
Anderson, Denise L, court clerk III, $27,660
Anderson, Elizabeth C, court clerk II, $25,404
Anderson, Julie A, juvenile officer I, $33,180
Anderson, Kimberly A, court program specialist II, $32,052
Anderson, Linda, court clerk III, $32,628
Anderson, Mary B, court clerk II, $25,032
Anderson, Rachelle D, court clerk II, $25,404
Anderson, Sharon K, court clerk V, $33,744
Anderson, Thelma Y, court program assistant IV, $43,488
Anderson, Vicky S, detention juvenile officer I, $33,180
Angle, Katelynn M, temporary help, $7.65/hr
Angles, Louis, associate circuit judge, $135,059
Angst, Kathleen S, court clerk III, $27,660
Ankrom, Rachelle R, court reporter, $57,178
Anthony, Nicole E, court clerk II, $25,404
Anthony, Shari L, court clerk II, $25,404
Archer, Donna L, court clerk II, $25,824
Armbruster, Amy S, court clerk II, $25,404
Arnold, Debora S, court clerk III, $32,628
Arterbery, Pearline, court clerk II, $27,504
Asel, Kaye F, court reporter, $57,178
Asel, Mary J, circuit judge, $146,804
Ash, David H, associate circuit judge, $135,059
Ashbaugh, Matthew T, temporary help, $11.67/hr
Ashley, Diedra K, juvenile officer III, $41,172
Ashley, Sandra L, court clerk II, $12,702
Askren, Jennie G, court clerk II, $25,404
Atchley, Michele L, juvenile officer II, $36,888
Atkins, Cheryl M, court clerk III, $27,660
Atkins, Dawn E, court clerk II, $25,404

Atkinson, Lizabeth M, court clerk II, $12,516
Atoe, Falepeau L, juvenile officer II, $37,548
Attebery, Amanda L, court clerk III, $27,660
Attwood, Dana J, court clerk II, $12,702
Atwell, Heidi H, juvenile officer II, $36,888
Aubuchon, Mary H, temporary help, $10.00/hr
Aurand, Ashley N, court clerk II, $25,032
Austin, Jan M, court clerk II, $25,404
Austin, Ruth A, court clerk III, $27,228
Aversman, Deana M, circuit clerk, $63,529
Aviles, Maria, court clerk II, $25,032
Ayers, Cynthia K, temporary rep, $25.00/hr
Aylward, Ellen L, secretary to presiding judge, $40,380
Aylward, Jane F, court clerk III, $37,548
Babb, Jeanne M, court clerk III, $36,204
Bachman, Linda L, court clerk III, $27,660
Bachtel, Chandra L, court clerk II, $12,702
Bacon, Douglas P, associate circuit judge, $135,059
Bail, Keith M, associate circuit judge, $135,059
Bailey, Gwendolyn Y, court clerk II, $25,824
Bailey, Karen D, court clerk IV, $29,976
Bailey, Roberta E, juvenile officer II, $36,204
Baird, Stacey L, court clerk III, $27,228
Baird-Schloemer, Brandi, associate circuit judge, $135,059
Bajric, Emina, court clerk II, $25,032
Baker, Alice M, court reporter, $57,178
Baker, Angela M, court clerk III, $28,104
Baker, Elizabeth A, court program specialist II, $32,052
Baker, Madisson L, temporary help, $10.00/hr
Baker, Michael L, detention aide I, $25,404
Baker, Sarah B, court clerk II, $25,404
Balinski, Denise M, secretary I, $25,404
Balk, Joyce A, temporary rep, $25.04/hr
Ball, Beverly S, court clerk III, $27,660
Ballay, Kimberly, court reporter, $57,178
Ballew, Tammy F, court reporter, $57,178
Ballinas, Madison L, court clerk II, $25,824
Banas, John P, circuit judge, $146,804
Bane, Tanya M, detention aide I, $12,698
Bankhead, Chanda R, juvenile officer IV, $44,304
Banning, Denise R, court clerk III, $27,660
Bannister, Kent T, detention juvenile officer I, $33,180
Banta, Natassi J, court clerk II, $17,522
Barber, Lisa R, detention aide II, $27,660
Barbosa, Deborah I, court clerk III, $27,660
Barhorst, Thomas, juvenile officer III, $41,172
Barker, Samuel R, associate circuit judge, $135,059
Barnard, Mary E, legal counsel, $54,288
Barnes, Jessica E, court clerk II, $25,404
Barnes, Perry T, juvenile officer III, $41,172
Barnes, Stacy M, court clerk II, $25,404
Barnett, Kaitlyn E, temporary help, $10.00/hr
Barnett, Sean M, detention aide I, $25,404
Barnett, Terri R, court clerk III, $27,660
Barnett-Stillings, Barbara D, circuit clerk, $70,437
Barnhart, Amy C, court clerk II, $25,404
Barnhart, Heather J, court clerk II, $25,032
Barnhart, Melissa A, court clerk II, $25,404
Barnhill, Emily E, court clerk II, $25,404
Barnhill, Rodney D, juvenile officer II, $45,156
Barr, Thomas R, circuit clerk, $70,437
Barry, Janette, court reporter, $57,178
Bartley, Donna A, court clerk II, $25,404
Barton, Elliott M, detention aide I, $15,238
Barton, Judith A, court clerk II, $27,504
Barton, Mary K, court clerk II, $30,384
Barton, Paula J, temporary rep, $15.00/hr
Bartram, Michelle, court clerk III, $29,496
Basham, Daimon L, detention aide II, $27,660
Baskins, Lori J, associate circuit judge, $135,059
Bass, Daphne, court clerk III, $27,660
Bastura, Jessica L, court clerk II, $25,032
Bateman, James J, legal counsel, $54,288
Bates, Jennifer E, court clerk III, $27,660
Battle, Gary, court clerk II, $27,504
Battle, Geraldine, court clerk II, $26,652
Battles, Mallory A, court clerk III, $27,660
Bauer, Diann K, court clerk II, $25,404
Baugus, Myrna L, court clerk III, $23,126
Baum, Jennae M, court clerk IV, $30,420
Baxter, Andrea L, temporary help, $10.00/hr
Baxter, Shirley M, temporary help, $10.00/hr
Bayes, Melody J, court clerk III, $33,744

Bays, Sarah E, court clerk II, $29,412
Baysinger, Sheryl V, court clerk II, $25,404
Beach, Douglas R, circuit judge, $146,804
Beal, Barbara A, court clerk V, $36,204
Beam, Dawna D, juvenile officer II, $36,888
Beard, R P, associate circuit judge, $135,059
Beard, Timothy C, court clerk V, $33,744
Beasley, Anita M, court clerk IV, $36,204
Beasley, Rachelle K, circuit clerk, $55,639
Beattie, Mary E, circuit clerk, $70,437
Beattle, Sherri L, court clerk II, $27,504
Becerra, Ann M, juvenile officer II, $36,888
Bechtel, Mary E, court clerk III, $27,660
Beck, Anita K, court clerk II, $25,404
Beck, Grant N, temporary help, $10.00/hr
Beck, James D, associate circuit judge, $135,059
Becker, David M, court clerk III, $27,660
Becker, Julie L, court reporter, $57,178
Becker, Linda M, court reporter, $57,178
Becker, Lisa M, court clerk II, $25,404
Becker, Zachary P, temporary help, $17.78/hr
Becker-Markovich, Christie M, treatment court adminstr II, $46,932
Beckner, Kelly E, court clerk II, $25,404
Beckwith, Pamela L, court clerk II, $25,404
Bedford, Marzita D, court clerk II, $25,404
Beetem, Jon E, circuit judge, $146,804
Begemann, Brenna L, court clerk II, $25,032
Begemann, Diane M, court clerk II, $32,472
Beger, John D, circuit judge, $146,804
Begley, Susan R, secretary to presiding judge, $33,180
Bektic, Jasna, court clerk II, $25,404
Belcher, Tina C, detention aide I, $28,452
Bell, Marylue, juvenile officer I, $33,180
Bell, Rickell A, court clerk II, $25,032
Bellamy, James T, associate circuit judge, $135,059
Bell-Thompson, Kristina L, court clerk II, $25,032
Belton, Carla A, court clerk III, $27,660
Beltz, Pamela G, court program specialist II, $32,052
Bendel, Paula J, court clerk IV, $32,052
Bennett, Brian C, juvenile officer II, $38,928
Bennett, Laurie A, court reporter, $57,178
Bennett, Nicole J, court clerk II, $12,516
Bennett, Rhonda D, court clerk II, $25,404
Bennett, Ricole S, court clerk II, $25,404
Berding, Heather M, court clerk IV, $30,420
Berding, Stacy M, court clerk II, $25,404
Bergen, Jessica J, court clerk II, $25,404
Berkel, Bonnie J, court clerk IV, $33,744
Bernstein, Scott L, associate circuit judge, $135,059
Berry, Janette R, court clerk II, $25,404
Berry, Nancy S, unit manager I, $41,172
Bertagnolli, Barbara J, court clerk II, $25,824
Besmer, Anne M, court clerk III, $37,548
Betsch, Barbara A, court clerk II, $12,702
Bevers, Jody K, court clerk III, $29,004
Bextermueller, Annie A, temporary help, $10.00/hr
Bice, Allyson R, court clerk II, $25,404
Bickel, James R, circuit judge, $146,804
Biddlecome, Morgan M, temporary help, $10.00/hr
Biederman, Christine A, court clerk III, $37,548
Bierman, Renee L, court reporter, $57,178
Biester, Charleen C, secretary to presiding judge, $33,180
Bigger, Sue K, court clerk II, $25,824
Billings, Shawn W, treatment court adminstr II, $46,932
Billington, Beth A, treatment court adminstr II, $46,932
Billington, Terry J, detention aide I, $12,698
Billington, Yvette M, court clerk II, $25,824
Bingham, Teresa L, associate circuit judge, $135,059
Binnie, Vickie L, court clerk II, $25,824
Bird, Kaitlin L, juvenile officer I, $24,885
Bird, Kayla L, temporary help, $10.00/hr
Bishop-Jones, Kimberly L, court clerk II, $23,816
Blake, Colleen C, court clerk III, $33,180
Blakemore, Christina R, circuit clerk, $70,437
Blakey, Jonathan R, court clerk II, $25,404
Blakey, Kristie J, detention juvenile officer IV, $44,304
Blakley, Mary D, court clerk II, $25,032
Blankenship, Alan M, associate circuit judge, $135,059
Blanks, Patrice L, court clerk II, $25,404
Blazer, Karen S, court clerk II, $25,032
Bleckman, Lori A, court clerk II, $25,404
Blincoe, T J, court clerk III, $32,052
Blissett, Theodore C, detention aide I, $25,404

Block, James M, court clerk IV, $30,420
Blockmon, Elaunda S, court clerk III, $27,660
Blood, Michelle L, court clerk II, $25,032
Bloodworth, John, associate circuit judge, $135,059
Bloomingdale, Tessa A, court clerk II, $25,404
Bock, Elizabeth A, associate circuit judge, $135,059
Bock, Ronald W, computer info tech supv II, $56,520
Bockman, Denise G, court clerk II, $19,989
Boeckmann, June, court clerk III, $27,660
Boerema, Amanda R, juvenile officer II, $36,888
Bogel, Diane M, court clerk III, $33,180
Bohannon, Maria A, court clerk IV, $30,420
Bohl, Holly A, court reporter, $57,178
Boles, Mickey A, juvenile officer II, $36,204
Boley, Amber L, court clerk II, $25,404
Bollinger, Linda L, secretary I, $25,404
Bollinger, Patricia L, court clerk II, $25,404
Bomgardner, Nicole R, temporary help, $10.00/hr
Bone, Kristina K, court clerk IV, $30,420
Bone, Michael W, court clerk IV, $30,420
Bone-Owen, Mary J, court reporter, $57,178
Bonnard, Connie A, court clerk II, $25,404
Book, Vicki L, circuit clerk, $55,639
Booker, Ella M, court clerk II, $30,924
Booker, Michaela L, court clerk II, $25,404
Booker, Natalie P, court clerk IV, $34,356
Booker, Teresa J, secretary II, $29,004
Boone, Kanesha J, court clerk II, $25,404
Booth, Heather L, court clerk II, $25,404
Borbonus, John N, associate circuit judge, $135,059
Borgmann, Scarlett M, court clerk II, $25,404
Boring, Rebekah J, food service worker II, $25,404
Boschert, M Diana K, court clerk II, $25,404
Boston, Dorothy H, court clerk III, $31,512
Boston, Melissa K, court clerk II, $25,404
Boston, Tiffany A, court clerk II, $25,824
Bottcher, Greta I, court clerk II, $28,908
Bouma, Sharon J, court clerk II, $25,404
Bova, Julie R, court clerk II, $25,404
Bowen, Heather E, juvenile officer I, $33,180
Bowers, Allen R, detention aide I, $25,404
Bowers, Pamela S, court clerk III, $28,104
Bowers-hutson, Melissa G, court clerk II, $25,404
Bowman, Candedia G, juvenile officer II, $36,888
Bowman, Cynthia, circuit clerk, $55,639
Boyce, Melissa D, court clerk II, $25,404
Boyd, Marla M, court clerk IV, $36,888
Boyer, Janet C, court clerk III, $32,052
Boyer, Jerry C, juvenile officer I, $33,180
Boyer, Kate L, court clerk II, $25,404
Boyer, Pamela J, court clerk III, $29,496
Boyer, Patricia J, circuit clerk, $55,639
Boyer, Rebecca K, court clerk III, $30,420
Boyer, Sarah N, temporary help, $10.00/hr
Braby, Dana, court reporter, $57,178
Braccini, Toni L, court clerk II, $29,904
Bracke, Brittany M, detention aide II, $16,596
Bracken, Frances L, secretary I, $25,032
Braddy, Carissa N, court clerk III, $27,660
Braden, Jill, juvenile officer IV, $43,488
Bradfield, Brittany, court clerk II, $25,404
Bradford, David P, court clerk II, $25,404
Bradley, Margo C, court clerk II, $25,404
Bradley, Michael W, associate circuit judge, $135,059
Brancato, Rozann, court reporter, $57,178
Brandes, Teresa L, court clerk IV, $30,420
Brandt, Ashlee D, court clerk II, $24,134
Brannon, Tammy S, court clerk III, $32,628
Branson, Rhonda J, detention aide I, $25,404
Braselman, Telisha R, court clerk II, $25,404
Braswell, Rita F, detention aide I, $25,032
Braylock, Catina S, court clerk IV, $34,356
Brecht, Sandra L, court clerk V, $40,380
Breckenridge, Brad A, court clerk II, $25,404
Breeden, Ralph K, juvenile officer III, $41,940
Brehe-krueger, Ada M, associate circuit judge, $135,059
Breite, Scott L, unit manager III, $56,520
Brelsford, Tammy L, court clerk II, $25,404
Brenner, Carol S, temporary rep, $15.00/hr
Breshears, Karlin M, court clerk III, $27,660
Bresnahan, Richard C, circuit judge, $146,804
Brewer, Craig D, associate circuit judge, $135,059
Brewer, Ella L, court clerk II, $27,084

Brewer, Tera R, court clerk IV, $29,976
Bridges, Lamond S, computer info tech II, $39,624
Bright, Belinda C, court clerk II, $25,404
Brinkley, Sherry A, circuit clerk, $55,639
Briscoe, Denise N, court clerk II, $23,816
Britt, Phillip M, drug court commissioner, $133,716
Brock, Mindy E, temporary help, $10.00/hr
Brockmeyer, Shirley, court clerk II, $12,698
Broeker, Roxann L, court reporter, $57,178
Broniec, Kelly C, associate circuit judge, $135,059
Brooks, Beverly A, court clerk II, $26,232
Brooks, Dana K, juvenile officer II, $38,928
Brooks, Kara E, temporary help, $10.00/hr
Brooks, Lana M, unit manager II, $53,208
Brothers, Beverly S, court clerk III, $31,512
Brown, Amanda J, court clerk II, $25,404
Brown, Betty J, court clerk II, $15,878
Brown, Cassie A, court clerk II, $25,824
Brown, Cody J, court clerk II, $25,404
Brown, Dennis L, detention aide I, $25,404
Brown, Evelyn M, court clerk II, $26,232
Brown, Jason R, associate circuit judge, $135,059
Brown, Kara M, court clerk II, $25,404
Brown, Karen D, court clerk III, $34,944
Brown, Kimberly J, associate circuit judge, $135,059
Brown, Nancy L, court clerk II, $25,404
Brown, Regina G, secretary II, $24,203
Brown, Sandy N, detention juvenile officer II, $36,204
Brown, Tammy L, court clerk V, $37,548
Brown, Tammy S, court clerk II, $25,404
Brown, Teresa, court clerk III, $31,512
Brown, Valerie G, court clerk II, $25,404
Brown, Wanda S, circuit clerk, $55,639
Brown Dugan, Claudia M, temporary help, $10.00/hr
Browning, Bradley C, food service worker II, $27,504
Bruch, Phyllis H, court clerk II, $25,824
Brucks, Rhiannon, juvenile officer II, $36,204
Bryan, Dani G, court clerk III, $32,052
Bryan, Kimberly K, court clerk IV, $30,420
Bryant, Deborah K, detention aide II, $28,104
Bryant, Paula P, associate circuit judge, $135,059
Buck, Kelley D, detention aide I, $25,032
Buckley, Raymond F, court clerk III, $27,660
Bucksath, Garrett L, circuit clerk, $70,437
Buechter, Genise L, circuit clerk, $55,639
Buechter, Irene H, court clerk II, $31,416
Bueno, Maria E, court clerk II, $25,404
Buie, Gail M, court clerk II, $25,404
Bull, Nancy L, court reporter, $57,178
Bullock, Jessica L, court clerk II, $25,404
Burbanks, Debra A, court clerk III, $32,052
Burch, Kayla M, court clerk II, $25,404
Burke, Laura A, temporary help, $10.00/hr
Burke, Mary J, juvenile officer II, $47,892
Burke, Nikki L, court clerk III, $27,660
Burke, Theresa C, associate circuit judge, $135,059
Burks, Tamatha A, court clerk II, $25,404
Burlison, Rex M, circuit judge, $146,804
Burlison-Huss, Erin S, associate circuit judge, $135,059
Burnell, Christopher A, court clerk II, $25,404
Burnett, Lisa A, court clerk II, $25,404
Burnett, Michele R, court clerk II, $25,404
Burnett, Susan M, circuit judge, $146,804
Burnham, Amanda M, court clerk IV, $32,052
Burnham, Lana J, court clerk III, $32,628
Burow, Scott F, juvenile officer III, $49,128
Burrow, Vicky D, court clerk III, $29,976
Burt, Herlinda R, court reporter, $57,178
Burton, Brittney M, secretary I, $25,404
Burton, Kathleen K, court clerk III, $32,052
Burton, Melissa S, secretary to presiding judge, $34,356
Burton, Michael D, circuit judge, $146,804
Burton, Michele E, court clerk II, $25,032
Buschmann, Mark A, circuit clerk, $55,639
Bush, Cynthia N, temporary help, $10.00/hr
Bush, Julian L, circuit judge, $146,804
Bushur, Jeffrey L, associate circuit judge, $135,059
Bussell, Kerry S, court clerk II, $25,404
Butcher, Janet M, temporary rep, $15.00/hr
Butler, Jessica R, court clerk II, $25,404
Butler, Stephine L, food service worker I, $12,340
Byers, Melissa D, court clerk II, $25,404
Byers, Natosha L, court clerk III, $27,228

Byler, Vera, court clerk III, $28,536
Byrd, Kim A, secretary II, $28,536
Byrn, David M, circuit judge, $146,804
Byron, Laura F, court clerk III, $28,104
Bywaters, Linda M, court clerk III, $27,660
Caddick, Jeremy A, juvenile officer II, $36,888
Cagle, Mary E, court clerk III, $27,660
Cahill, Kevin F, court clerk V, $34,356
Caine, Tracey L, court clerk III, $29,496
Caldwell, Trenna G, court clerk IV, $34,356
Callahan, Vickie L, temporary help, $12.21/hr
Callahan, Vickie L, court clerk II, $12,702
Calton, Amanda B, court clerk II, $25,404
Calvert, Mark D, associate circuit judge, $135,059
Calvin, Regina L, court clerk III, $27,228
Cammarata, Dodi L, court clerk III, $27,660
Campbell, Charrisa A, court clerk II, $25,404
Campbell, James L, court reporter, $57,178
Campbell, Latrease C, court clerk III, $28,104
Campbell, Monica T, court clerk II, $25,824
Campbell, Nikki K, juvenile officer II, $36,888
Campbell, Patrick W, circuit judge, $146,804
Campbell, Sandra P, court clerk III, $27,660
Campbell, Shavon G, court clerk II, $25,404
Campbell, Tammy K, court clerk II, $25,404
Campbell, Thomas B, juvenile officer III, $41,172
Campbell, Waymon L, juvenile officer II, $38,928
Campieri, Rosa M, court clerk II, $25,824
Candler, Kristi L, court clerk III, $27,660
Cannan, Paula R, court clerk III, $30,049
Cantrell, Andrea C, court clerk II, $25,404
Caples, Priscilla C, court clerk II, $25,032
Carden, Cheryl L, court clerk III, $33,180
Cardona, Troy A, circuit judge, $146,804
Cardwell, Ronda M, court clerk II, $25,404
Cargill, Margie, secretary II, $27,660
Carlson, Dwight W, court reporter, $57,178
Carlson, Michelle L, court clerk III, $28,908
Carlton, Stephen P, associate circuit judge, $135,059
Carmack, Erin, juvenile officer II, $36,204
Carpenter, Dorothea C, circuit judge, $146,804
Carpenter, Vicky L, court clerk V, $34,356
Carr, Timothy R, juvenile officer II, $38,232
Carrier, James R, associate circuit judge, $135,059
Carroll, Courtney B, court clerk III, $27,228
Carroll, Mary R, court clerk II, $28,908
Carron, Jennifer R, court clerk II, $25,404
Carrow, Terri, court clerk III, $27,660
Carter, Carolyn R, court clerk IV, $29,976
Carter, Cathy S, unit manager II, $46,932
Carter, Dylan T, juvenile officer II, $38,928
Carter, Robert C, circuit judge, $146,804
Carter, William W, associate circuit judge, $135,059
Carver, Dena E, juvenile officer II, $38,928
Cary, Karla L, court reporter, $57,178
Casaert, Susan K, court clerk III, $27,660
Casem, Karin J, court clerk II, $25,404
Casey, David L, detention aide II, $27,660
Casey, Theresa, secretary II, $14,522
Cash, Eddie, court clerk II, $25,404
Cashel, Chelsey A, court clerk II, $25,032
Castillo, Shannon R, court clerk II, $25,032
Cates, Mary C, court clerk II, $25,032
Catts, Kandi S, court program specialist II, $34,944
Caudle, Brad R, court clerk II, $25,404
Causey, Tonya, juvenile officer II, $38,928
Cecil, Michelle D, court clerk II, $28,908
Chadwell, Joe, circuit clerk, $55,639
Chamberlain, David P, associate circuit judge, $135,059
Chambers, Michelle L, juvenile officer II, $36,888
Chandler, Arrisa J, court clerk II, $25,404
Chandler, Kim L, court clerk II, $25,032
Chandler, Nicole C, court clerk II, $12,698
Chaney, Carrol H, temporary help, $10.00/hr
Chaney, Tara L, court clerk III, $27,660
Chanocua, Ana K, court clerk II, $25,404
Chapman, Michelle A, circuit clerk, $60,765
Chapman, Thomas N, circuit judge, $146,804
Charlton, Grace A, court clerk IV, $30,420
Chastain, Debra S, court clerk III, $24,336
Chasteen, Rhonda L, temporary rep, $15.00/hr
Chatman, Natalie J, juvenile officer II, $36,888
Cherry, Joan E, court clerk III, $33,744

Chervenak, Annette K, court clerk II, $25,404
Chestnut, Annie M, computer operator, $33,744
Childers, Lisa M, secretary II, $27,660
Childers, Sonja S, court clerk V, $34,356
Childress, Cindy L, secretary to presiding judge, $33,180
Childress, Rebecca L, court reporter, $57,178
Childs, Amanda L, court clerk II, $25,032
Chiodini, Louis A, court clerk II, $25,404
Choate, Debra L, court clerk II, $25,404
Chrisman, Carolyn S, family court commissioner, $133,716
Chrisman, Stacey L, court clerk II, $25,404
Christakis, Panagiota M, court clerk III, $27,660
Christensen, Sheryl A, temporary help, $10.00/hr
Christisen, Kelsey L, detention aide II, $27,660
Christmas, Tena M, circuit clerk, $55,639
Church, Sheri M, court clerk II, $25,404
Churchman, Shanieka M, temporary help, $10.00/hr
Claiborne, Lynn (Shellie) M, temporary help, $15.53/hr
Clariday, Becky R, juvenile officer II, $36,888
Clark, Adam W, detention aide II, $27,660
Clark, Beth L, court clerk II, $26,232
Clark, Christy A, detention aide I, $19,053
Clark, Craig, juvenile officer II, $36,204
Clark, Esther K, court clerk II, $28,908
Clark, Jill B, court clerk II, $25,404
Clark, Kasandra M, court clerk II, $25,404
Clark, Patricia K, court clerk IV, $35,568
Clark, Teresa A, court clerk IV, $30,420
Clark, Thomas C, associate circuit judge, $135,059
Clarke, Anne-Marie, family court commissioner, $133,716
Clary, Connie M, court clerk V, $38,232
Clay, Maysa L, temporary help, $10.00/hr
Clement, Tammy Y, court clerk II, $25,404
Clements, Chelsea L, temporary help, $9.50/hr
Clements, Elizabeth A, court clerk II, $25,404
Clifford, Patrick, associate circuit judge, $135,059
Cline-Pursell, Rose M, juvenile officer III, $41,172
Clinton, Kimberly A, court clerk III, $27,660
Close, Shirley K, temporary help, $10.00/hr
Clubbs, Talmage E, juvenile officer II, $36,888
Clyne, Catherine M, court clerk III, $34,356
Coberley, Shawna L, court clerk II, $25,404
Cody, Kathleen M, court clerk II, $25,824
Coffman, Brenda K, court clerk IV, $30,420
Cohen, Robert S, circuit judge, $146,804
Coker, Linda C, court clerk II, $28,908
Colbert, Annathesia N, court clerk II, $25,404
Cole, Martha K, court clerk III, $30,420
Coleman, Jeffrey T, associate circuit judge, $135,059
Coleman, Kathy E, court clerk II, $25,404
Coleman, Tamara R, temporary help, $11.67/hr
Coleman, Tammy R, court clerk III, $31,512
Coleman, Tracy A, court clerk III, $27,660
Coleman-King, Breanna G, court clerk III, $27,660
Collett, Carrie L, court clerk II, $25,032
Collins, Brenda L, detention aide II, $27,660
Collins, Cheryl G, court clerk II, $19,053
Collins, Elysia A, court clerk II, $25,404
Collins, Patrick A, court clerk III, $32,052
Collins, Sherrie T, temporary help, $10.43/hr
Collins, William B, circuit judge, $146,804
Collyott, Jeremy D, juvenile officer II, $36,888
Colon, Patricia A, juvenile officer IV, $46,932
Combs, Alice, court clerk II, $25,032
Comer, Kimberly S, court clerk II, $25,404
Comte, Shelly E, court clerk II, $25,404
Conard, Derek E, juvenile officer V, $60,120
Conklin, James D, circuit judge, $146,804
Connaghan, Patrick J, probate commissioner, $145,343
Conner, Jerry L, juvenile officer IV, $52,092
Conner, Margaret A, circuit judge, $55,639
Conners, Carolyn J, circuit clerk, $62,547
Connor, Lakeisha S, court clerk III, $27,660
Constable, Cortney L, juvenile officer II, $36,888
Cook, Andrew S, juvenile officer IV, $51,096
Cook, Heather A, court clerk II, $19,053
Cook, Kimberly R, juvenile officer I, $32,628
Cook, Marjorie J, court clerk II, $25,404
Cook, Rana A, court clerk IV, $30,420
Cook, Saydie A, court clerk II, $25,404
Cook, Stephanie L, court clerk III, $32,052
Cooksey, Jill K, court clerk III, $32,628
Cooksey, Sarah K, temporary help, $10.00/hr

Cooksey, William E, temporary help, $10.00/hr
Cooley, Tammie, court clerk II, $25,404
Coon, Kimberly A, deputy probate commissioner, $133,716
Cooper, Janie, temporary help, $10.00/hr
Cooper, Karrie L, secretary III, $29,496
Cooper, Natalie D, juvenile officer I, $33,180
Coover, Janet S, court program specialist I, $32,628
Copeland, Fred W, circuit judge, $146,804
Copeland, Vicki L, court clerk II, $25,404
Cordonnier, Michael J, circuit judge, $146,804
Cordova, Jennifer D, court clerk III, $27,660
Cornelius, Verla J, court clerk II, $19,688
Correa, Cynthia B, court clerk II, $25,404
Correia, Katie S, court clerk II, $25,404
Cothern, Amanda K, court clerk II, $25,404
Cothern, Katie C, temporary help, $8.50/hr
Cotton, Sheritha B, court clerk III, $28,104
Coulter, Margaret A, court clerk III, $37,548
Counce, Kaelon D, court clerk II, $25,404
Coureton, Delissa D, detention aide I, $12,516
Cowens, Monica Y, court clerk II, $26,652
Cowherd, Kyle B, court clerk II, $25,404
Cowin, Randy L, circuit clerk, $55,639
Cox, Diane A, court clerk II, $25,404
Cox, Erica L, juvenile officer IV, $44,304
Cox, Johnnie E, associate circuit judge, $135,059
Cox, Robin L, court reporter, $57,178
Cox, Thalia J, temporary help, $10.00/hr
Coy, Zack C, detention aide I, $25,404
Cozort, Presley E, court clerk II, $25,032
Craig, Kristi M, court clerk II, $25,404
Craig, Shirley A, secretary I, $25,404
Crane, Charlotte A, court clerk III, $27,660
Crane, Gail L, unit manager II, $60,120
Crane, Kevin M, circuit judge, $146,804
Crane, Shana L, court reporter, $57,178
Crane, Sue M, associate circuit judge, $135,059
Crawford, Sharon D, circuit clerk, $63,529
Crawford, Susan L, court clerk III, $34,944
Creed, Mary E, court reporter, $57,178
Creed-craghead, Penny J, circuit clerk, $55,639
Creekmore, Vickie J, court clerk II, $26,232
Creswell, Kimberly S, court clerk III, $27,660
Crews, Taylor M, temporary help, $10.00/hr
Crisp, Donna S, court clerk II, $23,816
Crites, Lisa L, secretary II, $28,536
Crockett, Marian J, court clerk III, $28,104
Crockom, Tyron L, detention aide II, $27,228
Crooks, Janet F, court clerk III, $27,660
Crosby, Kimberly M, court clerk II, $25,404
Crouse, Tammy J, circuit clerk, $55,639
Crowder, Cheryl A, unit manager II, $46,932
Crowder, Jaime L, detention aide II, $27,660
Crowder, Jill J, court reporter, $57,178
Crump, Sondra K, court clerk II, $25,404
Cruz, Tamala R, court reporter, $57,178
Culler, Geraldine A, court reporter, $57,178
Culler, Rebecca L, juvenile officer IV, $52,092
Cummings, Tracey R, court clerk III, $27,660
Cummins, Stephanie L, court clerk II, $25,404
Cundiff, Terry R, associate circuit judge, $135,059
Cunning, April R, court clerk III, $27,660
Cunningham, Amy J, court clerk II, $25,404
Cunningham, Jon A, circuit judge, $146,804
Cunnyngham, Jenny D, court clerk II, $25,404
Currie, William K, associate circuit judge, $135,059
Curtis, Julene R, court clerk II, $25,032
Curtman, Sheila M, court clerk III, $27,660
Cusick, Teresa A, court clerk IV, $35,568
Dabney, Larhonda Y, court clerk III, $27,660
Daffron, Ginger L, court clerk II, $25,404
Daffron, Stephanie M, court clerk III, $27,228
Dale, Mary M, court clerk II, $28,908
Dally, David C, circuit judge, $146,804
Dalton, Wesley C, circuit judge, $146,804
Dampier, Pamela L, juvenile officer II, $38,928
Damron, Cheryl L, court clerk II, $25,404
Daniel, Deirdre K, secretary to presiding judge, $33,180
Daniels, Chester E, court reporter, $57,178
Daniels, Deborah, associate circuit judge, $135,059
Daniels, Sheila E, court clerk II, $25,404
Danner, Ashton R, court clerk II, $25,032
Danner, Linda D, court clerk II, $25,404

Danuser, Julie L, court clerk II, $25,032
Darby, Shelby L, court reporter, $57,178
Darko, Karen, court clerk III, $28,536
Darr, Andrea L, court clerk II, $25,032
Darrough, Marian, court clerk II, $25,404
Darter, Kelly J, juvenile officer II, $36,888
Dattilo, Linda M, court reporter, $57,178
Daum, Kayla D, court clerk II, $25,404
Davenport, Susan L, court clerk II, $25,404
David, Carol E, court clerk V, $36,888
Davidson, Charles A, court program specialist II, $32,052
Davidson, Dawnel P, circuit clerk, $70,437
Davila, Patsy, court clerk II, $25,404
Davis, Jayne A, court clerk III, $34,356
Davis, Katheryn I, court clerk II, $25,824
Davis, Kathryn E, circuit judge, $146,804
Davis, Lynda, court clerk II, $25,404
Davis, Michael D, juvenile officer V, $55,416
Davis, Michelle L, juv/family court support wkr, $36,888
Davis, Peggy D, drug court commissioner, $133,716
Davis, Susan A, court clerk II, $26,232
Davis, Tayler A, court clerk II, $25,404
Davis, Titus, temporary help, $10.00/hr
Davis, Victoria, court clerk II, $25,404
Day, Andrew R, detention aide II, $27,660
Day, Denise R, court clerk III, $27,660
Day, Kayla R, court clerk II, $25,404
Day, Roylynna L, court clerk II, $25,404
Deak, Lisa A, court clerk II, $27,504
Debitetto, Cynthia A, court clerk V, $34,356
Debrot, Susan M, court clerk II, $25,404
Decker, Carisia, court clerk II, $25,404
Decker, Linda S, circuit clerk, $55,639
Decker, Mary D, court clerk III, $34,356
Decker, Patricia M, court clerk IV, $32,052
Dedmon, Regina L, court clerk II, $25,404
Deepe, Roger A, juvenile officer II, $36,888
Dees, Doloris, court clerk II, $25,404
Degonia, Isaiah L, detention aide I, $25,404
Degoosh, Toni K, court clerk II, $25,404
Deichmann, Mary H, court clerk III, $27,660
Del Muro, Justine E, circuit judge, $146,804
Del Percio, Julie M, court reporter, $57,178
Deline, Jaime N, court clerk II, $25,404
Delly, Aszelea, court clerk II, $25,404
Demarce, Karl A, associate circuit judge, $135,059
Dempsey, Melissa K, juvenile officer II, $43,488
Denniston, Katherine J, court clerk II, $26,232
Denny, Betty L, court clerk III, $27,660
Depriest, Tommy W, circuit judge, $146,804
Dering, Kendra S, temporary help, $12.00/hr
Deshay, Chyrell A, court clerk II, $25,404
Detchemendy, John A, court clerk II, $26,232
Determan, Sue E, court clerk II, $27,948
Devoto, Kathryn O, court reporter, $57,178
Devries, Sondra D, court reporter, $57,178
Dial, Gary, circuit judge, $146,804
Dickens, Pauletta L, court reporter, $57,178
Dickkut, Diana K, court clerk II, $17,190
Dickman, Mary C, court clerk III, $27,660
Diehl, Joy E, court clerk III, $28,536
Diehl, Madison R, temporary help, $10.00/hr
Dierker, Carol A, court clerk III, $31,512
Dierker, Robert H, circuit judge, $146,804
Dillard, Shelby E, court clerk II, $25,404
Dillon, Linda L, court clerk III, $30,984
Disney, Melisa D, court clerk II, $25,404
Ditzfeld, Alison M, court clerk II, $22,229
Dixon, Bryan T, juvenile officer II, $36,888
Dixon, Cynthia D, secretary to presiding judge, $37,548
Dixon, Ronnie M, juvenile officer III, $41,940
Dobbs, Gloria J, court clerk I, $22,872
Dobosz, Kathryn J, court clerk II, $25,404
Dobson, Cassidy A, court clerk II, $25,404
Dockery, Adam J, court clerk II, $25,824
Dodd, Monica A, court clerk IV, $29,976
Dodson, Angela M, juvenile officer I, $16,314
Dodson, Wanda S, associate circuit judge, $135,059
Dolan, Colleen, circuit judge, $146,804
Dolan, David A, circuit judge, $146,804
Doll, Dianne M, court clerk IV, $30,420
Doll, Patricia L, court clerk IV, $36,888
Donahue, Patricia M, court clerk II, $25,404

Donnelly, Margaret T, family court commissioner, $133,716
Donovan, Joyce M, court clerk II, $25,824
Dooley, Kayla K, detention aide I, $25,404
Dotson, Candice K, court clerk II, $25,032
Doublin, Jessica A, court clerk II, $12,516
Dougherty, Jacqueline R, court clerk III, $31,512
Dougherty, Paula M, temporary rep, $13.30/hr
Dougherty, Shannon R, associate circuit judge, $135,059
Douglas, Beth L, court clerk III, $29,004
Dowd, David, circuit judge, $146,804
Dowd, Melissa, juvenile officer III, $41,172
Dowd, Sandra L, circuit clerk, $70,437
Dowler, Krystina S, juvenile officer II, $36,204
Downey, Megan D, juvenile officer IV, $43,488
Doyle, Dustin W, juvenile officer IV, $44,304
Doyle, Shannon K, juvenile officer III, $40,380
Drace, Charles D, court clerk I, $22,536
Draper, Judy P, associate circuit judge, $135,059
Dreher, Shirley A, unit manager I, $44,304
Dreier, Jannelle L, detention aide I, $25,404
Druger, Linda D, secretary I, $25,404
Dubose, Victoria A, court clerk II, $25,404
Dubuque, Cecil J, juvenile officer II, $36,888
Duda, Steven, court clerk II, $25,404
Due, Sherry A, court clerk IV, $30,984
Dueker, Joseph S, associate circuit judge, $135,059
Dulaban, Marilyn L, court reporter, $57,178
Duncan, Malissa, court clerk III, $29,004
Duncan, Mishele T, court clerk V, $34,356
Dunkle, Patricia K, court clerk IV, $33,180
Dunn, Jennifer A, court reporter, $57,178
Dunn, Zachary T, detention juvenile officer I, $33,180
Dunnigan, Carla K, court clerk II, $25,404
Dunsford, Daniel T, court clerk II, $25,404
Dustman, Sandy E, court clerk II, $27,660
Duston, Charlene R, court clerk III, $27,660
Dutton, Billie L, court clerk III, $31,512
Duzenberry, Christina L, court reporter, $57,178
Dwane, Kerri L, temporary help, $10.00/hr
Dwight, Jamie D, juvenile officer II, $36,888
Dye, Karen A, court clerk II, $26,652
Dye, Katherine C, juvenile officer II, $36,888
Dyn, Allison M, temporary help, $10.00/hr
Eads, Amber M, court clerk III, $27,660
Eads, Jessica N, juvenile officer II, $36,204
Eads, Michelle S, court clerk III, $27,228
Eales, Sally J, juvenile officer II, $27,666
Earhart, Paula J, court clerk V, $38,928
Earls, Shanna M, court clerk II, $25,404
Easley, Leisa V, food service worker II, $25,404
East, Denise M, court clerk III, $27,660
Easter, Michelle D, court clerk II, $29,412
Easter, Patricia E, court program specialist I, $30,420
Eastling, Madeline, court clerk II, $25,824
Ebeling, Darla L, court clerk II, $25,404
Eberhard, Beverly L, court clerk II, $25,404
Eberting, Mary E, court clerk II, $26,232
Ebrecht, Annetta A, court clerk II, $25,404
Eck, Jenna L, juvenile officer II, $36,204
Eckert-Conaway, Gail M, court reporter, $57,178
Eckhoff, Adrian M, juvenile officer V, $48,156
Eckold, Dennis C, associate circuit judge, $135,059
Eckstein, Mary K, food service worker I, $11,575
Edelen, Patricia A, secretary III, $29,496
Edgar, Deborah M, court clerk V, $41,172
Edgar, Ronald J, detention aide I, $27,660
Edge, Renee L, court clerk V, $34,356
Edmundson, Jane A, court clerk III, $29,496
Edwards, Bethany J, court clerk II, $25,404
Edwards, Jerry D, court clerk V, $36,204
Edwards, Jimmie, circuit judge, $146,804
Edwards, Larry M, juvenile officer II, $36,888
Edwards, Mellissa L, court clerk II, $25,404
Egan, Sydney O, court clerk II, $25,404
Eggering, Brenda S, circuit clerk, $55,639
Ehler, Ann, court clerk IV, $33,744
Eighmy, Eric D, associate circuit judge, $135,059
Eisterhold, Charlene J, circuit clerk, $55,639
Eivins, Carol S, circuit clerk, $55,639
Elkins, Stephanie A, circuit clerk, $63,529
Elkins, Viola K, court program specialist II, $32,052
Ellenburg, Caleb D, temporary help, $10.00/hr
Elliott, Elizabeth F, court clerk II, $25,404

Elliott, Richard B, circuit judge, $146,804
Elliott, Shirley J, court clerk III, $27,660
Elliott, Sierra S, secretary I, $25,404
Ellis, Deborah A, juvenile officer II, $36,888
Ellison, April M, court clerk III, $27,660
Ellison, Kim L, court clerk II, $25,032
Elrod, Jennifer L, detention aide I, $12,698
Elsea, Stephanie A, detention aide I, $25,404
Emerick, Deborah S, court clerk III, $27,660
Emme, Kristina A, temporary help, $10.00/hr
Emory, Bonnie J, secretary to presiding judge, $34,944
Enax, Tina S, temporary help, $9.00/hr
Endicott, Gerall L, court clerk V, $34,356
Englaender, Andrew R, court clerk II, $25,032
England, Carol A, associate circuit judge, $135,059
England, Macalah H, temporary help, $10.00/hr
Enneking, Dasha L, court clerk II, $25,404
Ensminger, Janice M, court reporter, $57,178
Ensor, Melissa J, temporary help, $10.00/hr
Enyeart, Mary S, circuit clerk, $55,639
Epperson, Kari A, court clerk II, $25,032
Epperson, Rosanne L, court clerk II, $29,904
Epping, Mary K, family court administrator, $86,040
Eppy, Tara E, juvenile officer III, $41,172
Erbe, Lynn M, court reporter, $57,178
Erler, Amy K, court clerk III, $28,104
Erwin, Ronda A, court clerk IV, $36,888
Eslinger, Cory A, detention aide I, $25,404
Essner, John R, associate circuit judge, $135,059
Esteban-Dominguez, Angela M, court clerk II, $25,404
Estell, Sydney R, court clerk II, $25,032
Estes, Stephanie A, court clerk II, $28,908
Estraca, Stefanie A, court clerk I, $18,310
Evans, Anthony A, juvenile officer II, $36,888
Evans, David P, circuit judge, $146,804
Evans, Lucus C, juvenile officer I, $33,180
Evans, Marcy L, court clerk II, $28,908
Fahnestock, Joel P, circuit judge, $146,804
Failla, Linda S, temporary help, $10.00/hr
Fambrough, Jessica L, court clerk IV, $30,420
Fambrough, Mindy L, court clerk II, $25,404
Faris, Steven L, juvenile officer II, $36,888
Farmer, Iric D, detention juvenile officer I, $33,180
Farmer, Patrick W, detention aide I, $25,404
Faron, Natalie T, temporary help, $10.00/hr
Farragut-Hemphill, Sandra, circuit judge, $146,804
Farris, Kathryn E, court clerk II, $25,404
Faulconer, Jamie L, juvenile officer I, $33,180
Faulkner, Catherine D, court clerk III, $29,976
Faulkner, Susan R, court clerk III, $27,660
Fauser, Victoria M, court reporter, $57,178
Favazza, Anne M, court clerk III, $27,660
Favell, Sandra E, court clerk II, $26,232
Fechtelkotter, Jodi M, court clerk II, $25,404
Fellers, Teresa A, court clerk I, $13,752
Felty, Sandra A, temporary rep, $15.00/hr
Fennell, Glenn E, detention aide I, $25,404
Fergison, Ladonna L, court clerk II, $25,404
Ferguson, Melinda S, court clerk II, $25,032
Ferrari, Kerri A, juvenile officer III, $41,172
Ferrario, Eva J, court clerk III, $27,228
Ferris, Pamela L, court clerk II, $12,702
Ferris, Samuel P, court clerk II, $20,026
Fielder, Beth A, court clerk II, $25,404
Fields, Sheri A, court clerk II, $25,032
Fiene, Carla E, secretary to presiding judge, $36,204
Fincham, Thomas C, circuit judge, $146,804
Finders, Catherine M, court clerk V, $34,356
Findley, Jana L, circuit clerk, $55,639
Findley, Toi L, court clerk V, $38,232
Finley, Debra K, juvenile officer III, $41,172
Firestine, Angela S, court clerk II, $25,032
Fish, Terri J, court clerk II, $27,084
Fisher, Marsha F, court clerk II, $25,824
Fisher, Nancy L, circuit clerk, $55,639
Fitzgerald, Kimberly S, secretary to presiding judge, $34,356
Fitzpatrick, Shirley J, court clerk III, $27,228
Flaspohler, Charles J, circuit clerk, $55,639
Fleeman, Jennifer L, court clerk III, $27,660
Fletcher, Anna M, court clerk II, $25,032
Flook, Linda L, court clerk II, $29,904
Flores, Marcos A, juvenile officer II, $36,888
Flores, Norma L, court clerk II, $25,404

Fluker, Avis N, court clerk III, $33,744
Foley, Kathy J, court reporter, $57,178
Foots, Darlene A, court reporter, $57,178
Fordyce, Machaela M, court clerk II, $25,404
Foreman, Patricia L, temporary rep, $10.00/hr
Forster Krysl, Kelly C, court reporter, $57,178
Forsyth, Kathleen A, circuit judge, $146,804
Fortune, Georgina L, court clerk IV, $34,356
Foster, David L, juvenile officer II, $36,888
Foster, Karen M, court clerk II, $25,404
Foster, Kimberly A, court clerk II, $23,499
Foudree, Anne M, court clerk II, $25,404
Foulke, Robert J, associate circuit judge, $135,059
Fowler, Susan L, court clerk III, $30,420
Fox, Janeen C, court clerk II, $27,504
Fox, Nancy A, court reporter, $57,178
Francis, Amberlynn D, food service worker I, $11,754
Francis, Tamela L, temporary help, $10.00/hr
Francis, Traci D, marshal, $50,456
Frank, Samuel D, associate circuit judge, $135,059
Franklin, Carla R, court clerk II, $25,404
Franklin, Johnathan P, detention aide II, $27,660
Frasier, Carla M, court clerk III, $32,052
Frawley, Thomas J, circuit judge, $146,804
Frazier, Clarence J, detention aide I, $12,698
Frazier, Debbie L, court clerk II, $25,404
Freddie, Victoria L, court clerk II, $27,504
Frede, Karen L, court clerk III, $28,536
Freeman, Betty R, court clerk II, $25,404
French, Jackie M, court clerk II, $20,026
French, Tamara S, court clerk III, $27,660
Frick, Carolyn M, temporary rep, $15.00/hr
Fridley, Julie A, secretary to presiding judge, $33,180
Frieze, Sheila, court clerk II, $25,824
Fry, David J, drug court commissioner, $133,716
Fuchs, Kathleen L, court clerk II, $25,404
Fulton, Robin E, associate circuit judge, $135,059
Funk, Regina A, secretary II, $27,660
Furtak, Rebecca L, court clerk III, $27,660
Gaines, Candice C, court clerk III, $27,660
Gaines, Rick A, juvenile officer V, $51,096
Gaines-McPherson, Evelyn S, court clerk II, $25,404
Galate-Swartzbaugh, Judy M, court clerk IV, $30,420
Gall, Kathy R, secretary to presiding judge, $37,548
Gallagher, Holly A, temporary help, $10.00/hr
Gallagher, Yvonne N, court reporter, $57,178
Gallegos, Danette P, temporary help, $10.00/hr
Gamblin, Christina J, juvenile officer II, $36,888
Gann-Huseynov, Melissa, juvenile officer I, $33,180
Gans, Penny E, temporary help, $10.00/hr
Gantner, Sherry L, court reporter, $57,178
Garavaglia, Patricia M, court clerk III, $27,660
Garcia, Christy L, court clerk III, $27,660
Gardner, Michael E, circuit judge, $146,804
Gardner, Sara L, court clerk III, $30,579
Gardner, Timothy D, juvenile officer III, $41,940
Gargus, Paula S, circuit clerk, $55,639
Garner, Jessica D, court clerk II, $25,032
Garrett, Cynthia, court clerk III, $34,356
Garrett, Karen L, court clerk III, $27,660
Garrett, Kenneth R, circuit judge, $146,804
Garrett, Priscilla J, court clerk II, $25,404
Garrett, Rhonda J, court clerk II, $31,416
Garrison, Barbara J, court clerk II, $25,404
Garrison, Darren T, circuit clerk, $55,639
Garvey, John F, circuit judge, $146,804
Gasperoni, Maureen A, court clerk III, $27,660
Gaston, Douglas D, associate circuit judge, $135,059
Gatewood, April, court clerk III, $27,660
Gatewood, Latoya L, court clerk II, $25,404
Gavin, Nancy G, court clerk III, $28,104
Gay, Dimitri N, treatment court adminstr II, $46,932
Gebhardt, Mason R, associate circuit judge, $135,059
Geisendorfer, Jan E, circuit judge, $146,804
Gentry, Linda K, court program specialist I, $28,536
George, Robert E, associate circuit judge, $135,059
Gerhardt, Jennifer E, court clerk II, $25,404
Gerstenschlager, Sheila M, detention aide I, $25,404
Gettings, Earnestene P, court clerk II, $27,084
Ghisalberti, Kimberly R, court clerk II, $25,404
Giberson, Deborah M, juvenile officer IV, $45,156
Gibson, Marilyn M, treatment court adminstr II, $46,932
Gibson, Rashelle L, court clerk II, $25,404

Gildehaus, Kimberly J, court clerk II, $25,032
Gillespie, Kimberly A, court clerk II, $25,404
Gilligan, James, assistant accounting manager, $38,232
Gillis, Gregory B, associate circuit judge, $135,059
Gilmore, Chandra N, temporary help, $10.00/hr
Gilmore, Teresa L, court clerk II, $25,404
Girdley, Joseph A, court clerk II, $25,032
Givens, Tina M, court reporter, $57,178
Glasco, Kathryn J, temporary rep, $15.00/hr
Glaspie, Roberta J, detention aide I, $25,404
Gleason, Valerie A, court clerk II, $25,032
Glidewell, Carol L, temporary help, $10.00/hr
Godsy, Mary M, circuit clerk, $55,639
Goehring, Kimberly M, secretary II, $27,228
Goff, Joseph L, associate circuit judge, $135,059
Goings, Misty A, temporary juvenile officer III, $41,172
Golden, Peggy J, court clerk II, $32,472
Goldman, Steven H, circuit judge, $146,804
Gonzalez, Nancy L, court clerk II, $25,824
Goodall, Terri L, juvenile officer IV, $44,304
Goodman, Erica L, court clerk II, $25,824
Goodman, Jack A, circuit judge, $146,804
Goodrich, Melinda S, court clerk II, $22,229
Goodson, Adele E, court clerk III, $28,536
Gore, Sheila R, court clerk II, $25,404
Gorman, Grant C, associate circuit judge, $135,059
Goss, Linda M, court clerk II, $24,134
Graber-Knowles, Michelle L, court clerk II, $12,702
Grady, Gina M, unit manager I, $41,172
Graham, Aaron T, temporary help, $10.00/hr
Grass, Diana L, circuit clerk, $55,639
Grate, Jack R, circuit judge, $146,804
Graves, Christy, court clerk III, $27,660
Graves, Joseph, juvenile officer II, $36,888
Gravitz, Elizabeth M, court reporter, $57,178
Gray, Barbara J, court clerk II, $14,706
Gray, Dana L, court clerk III, $33,180
Gray, Joyce A, court clerk IV, $30,984
Gray, Tamira A, court clerk II, $20,026
Green, Daniel R, circuit judge, $146,804
Green, Felicia A, temporary help, $10.00/hr
Green, Heather R, detention aide I, $25,404
Greenfield, Stephanie L, court clerk V, $33,744
Greenwell, Carl M, associate circuit judge, $135,059
Greer, Madalyn C, court clerk II, $25,404
Gregor, Diane, temporary help, $10.00/hr
Gregory, Mary L, court clerk II, $29,904
Gresham, Dana M, detention aide II, $27,660
Greunke, Pamela R, circuit clerk, $55,639
Griffin, Debbie D, detention juvenile officer II, $36,204
Griffin, Deborah K, court clerk II, $25,032
Griffin, Yolanda D, court clerk II, $26,652
Griffith, Jennifer, court clerk III, $27,660
Griffith, Teresa G, court clerk II, $25,404
Griffy, Stacie L, detention aide II, $27,228
Grillo, Maria K, unit manager I, $42,708
Grobe, Doris F, court clerk II, $25,404
Groceman, Denise M, court clerk III, $29,004
Groff, Becky L, court clerk II, $27,504
Groner, Judith O, circuit clerk, $70,437
Groves, Haley M, court clerk II, $25,032
Gruber, Amy L, court clerk III, $27,228
Gruenwald, Kevin R, juvenile officer II, $36,888
Gschaar, Mary M, temporary help, $10.00/hr
Gudde, Denise M, court clerk II, $25,404
Guerrero, Luis R, detention aide I, $15,013
Guffey, Annette D, court clerk II, $25,404
Gum, Ashley R, court clerk II, $25,404
Gumm, Melinda A, circuit clerk, $55,639
Gunnels, Tonya M, court clerk II, $25,404
Gust, Jo A, court clerk IV, $41,940
Guzenski, Shannon S, secretary I, $25,404
Haase, Alexis N, temporary help, $10.00/hr
Hackett, James A, associate circuit judge, $135,059
Haddock, Brenda L, court clerk IV, $39,624
Hagan, Nikole J, temporary help, $10.00/hr
Hagar, Koni I, juvenile/family court aide, $27,660
Haglund-Miller, Maura E, court clerk II, $25,404
Hahn, Hailey N, temporary help, $9.00/hr
Hahne, Heather D, court clerk II, $25,032
Halbert, Katie L, temporary help, $12.03/hr
Halbert, Katie L, court clerk II, $12,516
Hale, Christine M, court reporter, $57,178

Hale, Dawn R, juvenile officer III, $41,172
Hale, Kimberly A, unit manager I, $41,172
Hale, Patrice M, court clerk II, $25,824
Haley, Teresa L, court clerk II, $29,904
Hall, Jeffery L, juvenile officer V, $49,128
Hall, Jennifer L, juvenile officer III, $41,172
Hall, Kathy J, secretary to presiding judge, $33,744
Hall, Lorie K, circuit clerk, $55,639
Hall, Michelle L, court reporter, $57,178
Hall, Waleeta, court clerk III, $32,628
Halley, Twila L, circuit clerk, $55,639
Hall-Reese, Angelina, court clerk III, $31,512
Hamilton, Chantaye K, temporary help, $10.00/hr
Hamilton, Laurietta M, court clerk II, $25,032
Hamilton, Nora M, temporary help, $7.65/hr
Hamilton, Toni M, secretary to presiding judge, $33,180
Hamlett, Linda R, associate circuit judge, $135,059
Hamlyn, James G, computer info tech trainee, $33,744
Hamm, Mary L, court clerk II, $28,452
Hammett, Victoria A, court reporter, $57,178
Hammontree, Rai J, court clerk II, $25,404
Hamner, Matthew P, associate circuit judge, $135,059
Hampel, Nathan A, detention aide I, $25,404
Hampton, Angelia M, court clerk III, $27,660
Hampton, Clara M, court clerk III, $29,004
Hampton, Judi D, detention juvenile officer IV, $44,304
Hampton, Sherri D, juvenile officer II, $36,888
Hamzabegovic, Adela, court clerk III, $27,660
Hancock, Kathleen J, temporary help, $10.00/hr
Hanes, Tamara A, court clerk III, $32,628
Hanley, Jill M, legal counsel, $54,288
Hann, Glenda L, court clerk II, $25,404
Hannaford, Lisa A, court clerk III, $31,920
Hannah, Melissa A, court reporter, $57,178
Hansbrough, W A, associate circuit judge, $135,059
Hansel, Susan M, court clerk II, $12,516
Harden, Madison D, temporary help, $10.00/hr
Hargadine, Rhonda L, juvenile officer I, $32,628
Hargrave, Sara E, court clerk III, $28,104
Harlan, Karen R, circuit clerk, $55,639
Harles, Cynthia K, secretary I, $23,816
Harless, Pamela L, court clerk III, $32,052
Harlin, Sandra A, court clerk III, $30,984
Harman, Larry D, circuit judge, $146,804
Harper, Angella C, juvenile officer II, $36,888
Harper, Peter D, juvenile officer II, $36,204
Harper, Sharon R, court clerk III, $27,660
Harrell, Athalia M, court clerk II, $25,032
Harrell, Kevin D, circuit judge, $146,804
Harrelson, Jerri L, circuit clerk, $55,639
Harrington, Judy, court clerk II, $27,948
Harrington, Kathy S, temporary help, $10.00/hr
Harris, Anissa D, juvenile officer II, $36,888
Harris, Kima K, court clerk III, $27,660
Harris, Sarah N, court clerk II, $25,032
Harris-Landers, Shannon, court clerk IV, $33,744
Harris-McNeal, Yvonne R, court clerk II, $25,404
Harrison, Brett, court reporter, $57,178
Harrison, Brittany M, court clerk II, $25,404
Harrison, Charles L, juvenile officer II, $36,888
Harrison, Dawn M, computer info tech II, $45,156
Harrison, Debra E, court clerk II, $26,232
Harrison, Toni L, court clerk V, $34,356
Hartman, Valerie G, unit manager II, $48,156
Hartman, Vera L, court clerk II, $25,404
Hartmann, Karen, court clerk II, $28,908
Hartzell, Joyce A, temporary help, $9.00/hr
Harvey, Arlando M, court clerk III, $27,660
Harvey, Hugh C, associate circuit judge, $135,059
Hatcher-Darden, Cheryl, court clerk II, $25,404
Hatfield, Kimberly A, court clerk II, $12,516
Hatfield, Kimberly A, temporary help, $12.03/hr
Hathcock, Kim, circuit clerk, $55,639
Hauser, Meghan D, court clerk II, $25,404
Hawkins, Myrtis L, court clerk II, $27,084
Hawkins, Stacy N, court clerk III, $27,660
Hawley, Luke A, temporary help, $10.00/hr
Hayden, Kenneth M, circuit judge, $146,804
Haydu, Justin, juvenile officer III, $40,380
Hayes, Brittany K, temporary help, $10.00/hr
Hayes, Donna B, court clerk II, $22,428
Hayes, Jacque I, court clerk II, $25,404
Hayes, Kristina R, court clerk II, $25,404

Hayes, Scott A, circuit judge, $146,804
Haynes, Amanda, court clerk II, $25,404
Haynes, Melanie E, court clerk II, $25,032
Hays, Angela N, secretary I, $25,404
Head, Randall L, associate circuit judge, $135,059
Headrick, Michael V, associate circuit judge, $135,059
Heagney, Philip D, circuit judge, $146,804
Heaney, Kenneth R, court clerk II, $26,232
Heese, Stasia A, court clerk II, $25,404
Hefner, Paula D, court reporter, $57,178
Heggie, Robert M, associate circuit judge, $135,059
Heimerman, Michelle J, juvenile officer II, $36,888
Heins, Cindy A, secretary to presiding judge, $33,744
Heitert, Christina, court clerk III, $27,660
Heitman, Anna R, court clerk II, $25,404
Helbing, Y L, temporary rep, $15.00/hr
Helms, Andy C, juvenile officer IV, $45,156
Helms, Deatte L, court clerk III, $30,984
Helsel, Krista K, court clerk II, $12,912
Helwig, Justin L, court clerk II, $25,032
Hembree, Kelly C, court clerk II, $25,404
Hemken, Jeannie M, court reporter, $57,178
Hency, Christy M, circuit clerk, $55,639
Henderson, Brenda J, court clerk II, $25,824
Henderson, Joyce M, court clerk IV, $30,420
Henderson, Lisa L, associate circuit judge, $135,059
Hendricks, Carolyn A, treatment court adminstr II, $46,932
Hendrickson, Michael O, circuit judge, $146,804
Hendrix, Paula J, court clerk II, $15,242
Hendrix, Paula J, temporary help, $12.21/hr
Hennon, Lisa M, court reporter, $57,178
Henry, Alisha J, detention aide I, $25,404
Henry, Brenda L, court clerk II, $26,232
Henry, Debra D, secretary I, $25,404
Henry, Donald M, associate circuit judge, $135,059
Henry, Larry D, treatment court adminstr II, $46,932
Henry, Sherrie A, secretary to presiding judge, $32,628
Hensley, Joseph L, associate circuit judge, $135,059
Heppe, Cheryl D, secretary II, $27,660
Herget, Amy M, court clerk II, $25,404
Herleth, Karen J, detention aide I, $25,404
Herman, Rhonda L, court clerk II, $28,452
Hermann, Tenia L, court clerk II, $16,513
Herrera, Amanda L, detention aide I, $25,404
Herring, Jillian D, juvenile officer II, $36,888
Herring, Lisa L, food service worker II, $25,032
Herrington, Janet L, court clerk II, $25,404
Herrold, Brittany M, court clerk II, $25,404
Herron, Corey K, associate circuit judge, $135,059
Hertel, Pamela L, temporary help, $10.00/hr
Hess, Kevin B, juvenile officer V, $48,156
Hess, Stephanie M, detention aide I, $25,404
Hessler, Deana L, accounting manager, $56,520
Hettenbach, Bryan L, circuit judge, $146,804
Hetzler, Shirley A, court clerk III, $34,944
Heumader, David M, court administrator, $52,092
Hewing, Melissa M, court clerk II, $25,404
Hickle, William E, circuit judge, $146,804
Hickman, Lori A, court clerk III, $27,660
Hickman, Sharon R, court clerk II, $25,404
Hicks, Janice C, temporary rep, $20.00/hr
Hicks, Janice D, court clerk II, $18,230
Hicks, Mary E, court clerk II, $25,404
Hicks, Tammi D, court clerk II, $25,404
Hicks, Timothy A, detention aide II, $27,660
Higby, Jeannette M, secretary II, $27,228
Higgins, Janice M, court clerk II, $25,824
Higgins, Jenna L, court reporter, $57,178
Higgins, Melanie B, court clerk II, $22,229
Higgins, Michele A, circuit clerk, $55,639
Higgins, Stacy L, court clerk II, $25,404
Higinbotham, Robert E, court clerk III, $27,228
Hill, Cara V, court clerk II, $25,824
Hill, Larry A, court program specialist II, $40,380
Hill, Michael P, detention juvenile officer I, $33,180
Hill, Shonda M, juvenile officer IV, $44,304
Hines, Allicia Y, court clerk II, $25,404
Hines, Karen L, court clerk II, $14,607
Hines, McKayla A, temporary help, $10.00/hr
Hinkle, Jeremy G, secretary to presiding judge, $33,744
Hinz, Bradley B, juvenile officer IV, $43,488
Hodges, Alexander R, court clerk II, $25,032
Hodges, Joanne L, court clerk II, $25,404

Hogan, Elizabeth B, circuit judge, $146,804
Hogan, Eugenie M, court clerk III, $27,660
Holcomb, Jerry L, family court commissioner, $133,716
Holcomb, Melissa K, circuit clerk, $74,653
Holden, Calvin R, circuit judge, $146,804
Holiman, Marsha V, circuit clerk, $55,639
Holland, Debra K, temporary rep, $15.00/hr
Hollaway, Kathryn A, court clerk II, $25,032
Holley, Peggy D, court clerk II, $25,404
Holliday, Brenda, court clerk III, $27,660
Holliday, Lori A, court clerk III, $27,660
Hollingsworth, Adele M, court clerk III, $27,660
Hollingsworth, Pierre D, temporary help, $8.00/hr
Holman, Mechelle D, court clerk III, $29,004
Holmes, Vanessa L, court clerk III, $27,660
Holt, Debra A, court clerk II, $14,454
Holt, Marlaina D, court clerk II, $25,404
Holt, Matthew D, treatment court adminstr II, $46,932
Holzum, Lisa M, court clerk II, $25,404
Hon, Diane R, court clerk II, $25,404
Hood, Dale W, associate circuit judge, $135,059
Hood, Georgenia B, secretary II, $29,496
Hoover, Tom W, juvenile officer IV, $57,744
Hopkins, Arlinda D, court clerk III, $27,660
Hopkins, Debra A, associate circuit judge, $135,059
Hopkins, Nicole R, court clerk II, $25,032
Hoppenthaler, Jennifer D, court clerk II, $25,404
Hopper, Karen S, court clerk II, $25,404
Hopwood, Lisa D, court clerk II, $25,404
Horine, Janet A, court clerk III, $31,512
Horman, Scott T, associate circuit judge, $135,059
Horne, Julie A, detention aide I, $20,659
Horton, Bettie M, temporary help, $7.65/hr
Horton, Brandi R, juvenile officer II, $36,888
Hoskins, Clarissa K, court clerk III, $27,660
Hoskins, Stephanie K, juvenile officer II, $41,172
Hosmer, Douglas A, associate circuit judge, $135,059
Hoss, Sharon, court clerk II, $25,404
House, Katie M, juvenile officer II, $36,888
House, Ted C, circuit judge, $146,804
Housewright, Ashley M, court clerk II, $25,404
Housewright, Beverly K, court reporter, $57,178
Houston, Alison C, juvenile officer II, $36,888
Houston, Christina M, court clerk II, $25,404
Hoven, David L, associate circuit judge, $135,059
Hovey, Juliet M, court reporter, $57,178
Hovis, Vicky S, detention juvenile officer I, $34,356
Howard, Pamela K, circuit clerk, $55,639
Howe, Jamie L, court clerk II, $25,404
Howell, Shelly R, court clerk II, $25,824
Hoysradt, Susan H, court clerk III, $27,660
Hubbard, Karen J, circuit clerk, $55,639
Hubbert, Mary E, court clerk II, $15,960
Hudson, Elizabeth A, secretary III, $29,496
Hudson, Kathy L, court clerk II, $25,404
Hudson, Mary A, secretary to presiding judge, $33,180
Hudson, Steven D, associate circuit judge, $135,059
Huff, David B, detention aide I, $12,702
Huff, Janet L, secretary I, $25,404
Huff, Karen A, court clerk III, $30,420
Huffaker, Julia L, court clerk II, $12,516
Huffman, Brittney L, secretary I, $15,242
Huffman, Brittney L, temporary help, $12.21/hr
Huffman, Jeanne Y, treatment court adminstr II, $46,932
Huffman, Mary A, court clerk II, $20,635
Hughes, Jennifer N, secretary I, $25,032
Hughes, Lawonda A, temporary help, $10.00/hr
Hughes, Patricia R, court clerk IV, $30,420
Hulsey, Bailey R, temporary help, $10.00/hr
Hummel, Lori K, court clerk II, $25,404
Humphrey, Jill C, court clerk II, $25,824
Humphrey, Julie D, court clerk II, $22,596
Hunt, Julia A, court reporter, $57,178
Hunt, Melinda S, court reporter, $57,178
Hunter, Carolyn J, court clerk II, $25,404
Hunter, Denise M, court clerk II, $27,660
Hunter, Elizabeth L, food service worker I, $19,368
Huntley, Brenda A, court clerk IV, $29,976
Hurd, Susan D, court clerk III, $34,356
Hurst, Jerry V, temporary help, $10.00/hr
Hutchings, Vicki H, court reporter, $57,178
Hutchison, Carrie L, court clerk III, $27,228
Hutchison, Jera E, court clerk II, $25,404

Hutchison, Nick S, juvenile officer II, $36,888
Hyde, Troy K, associate circuit judge, $135,059
Imhof, Daniel W, associate circuit judge, $135,059
Ingram, Ebony A, court clerk III, $27,660
Ingram, Gregory G, court clerk III, $29,496
Injenari, Kathy J, secretary to presiding judge, $36,888
Inman, Kelsea T, court clerk II, $25,404
Inman, Timothy W, associate circuit judge, $135,059
Iott, Brenda E, food service worker II, $25,404
Irons, Beverly E, court clerk II, $15,019
Irvin, Sheila C, court reporter, $57,178
Irving, Jarrell J, court clerk II, $25,032
Isbell, Tonya J, court clerk II, $25,404
Isom, Cynthia D, court clerk III, $30,984
Ivey, Carla R, court clerk III, $27,660
Jackson, Catherine O, court clerk IV, $30,420
Jackson, John J, associate circuit judge, $135,059
Jackson, Larry, court clerk II, $30,384
Jackson, Linda L, temporary rep, $12.00/hr
Jackson, Randall R, circuit judge, $146,804
Jackson, Sally J, court clerk III, $30,420
Jackson, Steven B, associate circuit judge, $135,059
Jaco, Angela R, juvenile officer II, $36,888
Jacquin, Maryann, court clerk III, $27,660
Jaeger, Glyda M, detention aide I, $26,232
Jaggard, Maureen A, court clerk III, $33,180
James, Holly J, court clerk II, $25,404
James, Sandra, court clerk III, $27,660
James, Sharon R, temporary rep, $13.02/hr
James, Teresa A, court clerk III, $28,104
Jameson, Anita J, temporary rep, $15.00/hr
Jameson, Gina G, circuit clerk, $55,639
Jamieson, Matthew R, court clerk III, $27,660
Jamison, Carman G, court clerk IV, $30,420
Jamison, Michael T, circuit judge, $146,804
Janish, Christina L, court clerk II, $25,404
Jansen, Joellen M, court clerk II, $21,339
Jasper, Lindsey D, court clerk II, $12,516
Jefferson, Roy A, juvenile officer II, $36,204
Jenkins, Caleb L, detention aide I, $13,614
Jenkins, Jaysa J, temporary help, $9.00/hr
Jenkins, Melba H, court clerk II, $25,032
Jennings, Kimmber D, juvenile officer I, $32,628
Jennings, Tammy F, court clerk II, $33,036
Jenry, Charlotte K, court clerk II, $30,384
Jensen, Dixie T, court clerk III, $27,228
Jerome, Kerri A, court clerk II, $26,232
Jett, Rebecca L, court clerk II, $25,032
Johnson, Amanda M, court clerk III, $27,660
Johnson, Brenda K, juvenile officer II, $36,888
Johnson, Carol S, court clerk II, $13,651
Johnson, Charles R, detention aide I, $25,404
Johnson, Crystal A, court clerk II, $25,824
Johnson, Doris M, court clerk II, $25,404
Johnson, Erin L, court clerk II, $25,032
Johnson, James R, juvenile officer IV, $45,156
Johnson, Janet K, court clerk III, $29,004
Johnson, Jennifer R, court reporter, $57,178
Johnson, Joni G, secretary I, $24,895
Johnson, Karen L, court clerk II, $25,404
Johnson, Kimberly K, court clerk V, $36,888
Johnson, Laura J, circuit judge, $146,804
Johnson, Lucretia A, temporary help, $10.00/hr
Johnson, Marleen K, secretary II, $27,660
Johnson, McKinley, court clerk II, $25,824
Johnson, Rita E, court clerk III, $28,536
Johnson, Shakir, unit manager II, $46,932
Johnson, Shannon, juvenile officer I, $33,180
Johnson, Sheila D, court clerk II, $25,404
Johnson, Shirley M, detention aide I, $25,404
Johnson, Survunah D, court clerk II, $30,384
Johnson, Tamika M, court clerk II, $25,404
Johnson, Tawanda, court clerk III, $29,004
Johnson, Tezetta G, court clerk II, $25,404
Johnson, Thomas, detention aide I, $25,404
Johnson, Trudy L, court clerk II, $25,404
Johnson-Massey, Kyerra M, court clerk II, $25,032
Johnston, Dena K, court clerk II, $25,404
Johnston, Kim M, court clerk II, $25,404
Jones, Alice L, temporary rep, $14.87/hr
Jones, Carrie D, court clerk III, $27,660
Jones, Charitie M, secretary to presiding judge, $33,180
Jones, Danielle S, court clerk III, $27,660

Jones, David C, circuit judge, $146,804
Jones, Denise N, court clerk III, $27,660
Jones, Diane K, court clerk II, $25,404
Jones, Elricka L, court clerk III, $27,660
Jones, Erika D, juvenile officer II, $36,888
Jones, Jackie, court clerk III, $27,660
Jones, Joaquinta, court clerk IV, $30,420
Jones, Lori A, court clerk II, $25,824
Jones, Margaret R, court clerk III, $27,228
Jones, Maria-Christine E, court clerk IV, $29,976
Jones, Mary J, detention aide II, $27,660
Jones, Natasha L, court clerk II, $25,404
Jones, Susan L, secretary II, $29,496
Jones, Timothy K, juvenile officer II, $36,888
Journey, James K, circuit judge, $146,804
Joyce, Patricia S, circuit judge, $146,804
Judah, Weldon C, circuit judge, $146,804
Juhl, Jessica J, juvenile officer II, $36,888
Julien, Andrea J, court clerk IV, $30,420
Julius, Casey L, juvenile officer II, $36,888
Jump, Shryl L, court clerk III, $27,660
Justice, Annisa B, court reporter, $57,178
Justus, Amy J, juvenile officer II, $36,888
Kahre, Steven W, circuit clerk, $55,639
Kaid-Allen, Andrea L, court clerk II, $25,404
Kaltenbronn, Erin M, court clerk II, $25,404
Kaltenbronn, Jon A, associate circuit judge, $135,059
Kamp, Gary A, associate circuit judge, $135,059
Kanatzar, James F, circuit judge, $146,804
Kanoy, Jason A, associate circuit judge, $135,059
Kardon, Antoinette, court clerk IV, $34,356
Karmel, Amber L, juvenile officer II, $36,888
Karr, Christopher E, juvenile officer II, $36,888
Keadle, Elizabeth A, court clerk II, $25,824
Keal, Jeffrey C, associate circuit judge, $135,059
Keathley, Jodi M, juvenile officer II, $41,172
Keener, Michael W, detention aide II, $27,660
Keeper, Lisa A, court clerk III, $29,496
Keim, Judy L, circuit clerk, $55,639
Keith, Joy O, court clerk II, $25,404
Kelley, Bryan E, court clerk II, $25,404
Kelley, Colleen P, court clerk II, $25,824
Kellogg, Daniel F, circuit judge, $146,804
Kelso, Michelle A, court clerk III, $27,660
Kendall, Linda N, court clerk III, $27,660
Kendrick, Whitney N, court clerk II, $25,404
Kennedy, Andreanna T, court clerk II, $25,404
Kennedy, Angela R, court clerk II, $25,404
Kennedy, Malinda K, court clerk II, $25,404
Kerr, Elizabeth K, court clerk II, $25,824
Kerr, Kristine A, circuit judge, $146,804
Kersha, Jonathan A, juvenile officer II, $36,888
Ketchum, Jennifer C, court clerk II, $25,404
Kettinger, Mary J, court clerk III, $30,420
Kiebach, Kristina M, court clerk III, $27,660
Kigar, James L, juvenile officer IV, $43,488
Kight, Caroline E, court clerk II, $25,404
Killebrew, Annie F, juvenile officer IV, $38,928
Kimbrell, Katie E, temporary help, $9.50/hr
Kimbrell, Sheryl A, court clerk II, $25,404
Kincaid, Darla D, court clerk II, $25,404
Kincy, Rose M, court clerk II, $26,652
Kinderknecht, Roger, court clerk III, $34,356
Kindhart, Christy, court clerk II, $27,948
King, Pamela S, court clerk II, $25,404
King, Virginia, temporary rep, $15.00/hr
Kingsolver, Ann M, court clerk II, $25,404
Kingston, Julie E, court clerk III, $35,568
Kinsley, Mary E, court clerk II, $25,404
Kinstler, Carmella M, court clerk III, $27,228
Kirn, Jeanna M, court clerk II, $25,404
Kiser, Alonna L, juvenile officer II, $38,928
Kiser, Jon A, drug court commissioner, $133,716
Kissee, Joni A, court clerk IV, $34,944
Kite, Linda S, court clerk II, $26,232
Kittelson, Tanya A, juvenile officer II, $36,888
Kleffner, Kathleen L, court clerk II, $25,404
Klein, Jamie M, court clerk III, $27,660
Kleinheider, Tammy L, court clerk II, $25,404
Klenke, Ruth A, unit manager I, $41,172
Klingler, Michael T, court clerk II, $25,404
Klouzek, Laura L, court clerk II, $25,404
Kniepman, Patricia A, court clerk II, $25,824

Knipmeyer, Kathryn D, court clerk II, $25,404
Knoeber, Breanna K, court clerk II, $25,404
Knox, Alicia L, court clerk II, $25,404
Knox, Rosa L, court clerk III, $32,052
Ko, Serena Y, court clerk III, $30,420
Koch, Pamela K, court reporter, $57,178
Koelzer, Juanita M, court clerk II, $25,032
Koeppen, Aaron G, associate circuit judge, $135,059
Koetting, Lauri E, detention aide I, $25,404
Koetting, Matthew J, legal counsel, $54,288
Koffman, Robert L, circuit judge, $146,804
Kohler, Colleen E, court clerk III, $28,536
Kohls, Kimberle D, temporary help, $10.00/hr
Kolkmeyer, Deann, court clerk III, $27,228
Kolling, Lilliann L, secretary I, $27,084
Komer, Jill D, court clerk II, $25,404
Komer, Susan L, court clerk II, $25,404
Koogler, Diane E, court clerk II, $25,404
Kopff, Christine M, court clerk II, $31,920
Kossmann, Aleaha M, court clerk II, $25,404
Kraft, Deborah L, court clerk II, $25,404
Krauser, Karen L, associate circuit judge, $135,059
Krautmann, Gary J, legal counsel, $56,520
Kreamalmyer, Lisa A, court reporter, $57,178
Kreuter, Anna M, court clerk III, $27,660
Krewson, Michael D, court clerk II, $26,652
Kriesmann, Joan M, court clerk III, $27,660
Krohn, Matthew M, associate circuit judge, $135,059
Krohne, Rebecca I, court clerk II, $25,404
Kroll, Kelci N, temporary help, $10.00/hr
Kroon, Deborah A, temporary help, $10.00/hr
Krueger, Patricia A, circuit clerk, $63,529
Krug, Jeanne T, court clerk V, $34,356
Kruger, Kymberlee S, court clerk II, $25,404
Kruse, Russell J, associate circuit judge, $135,059
Kudla, Barbara L, court clerk II, $18,095
Kuhns, Cami K, court clerk II, $25,404
Kunza Mennemeyer, Christina C, circuit judge, $146,804
Kunze, Jacqueline A, court clerk II, $12,702
Kyser, Janet, court clerk II, $25,404
Labeaume, Michelle A, unit manager II, $46,932
Labrot, Toni R, food service worker I, $11,754
Labunski, Carla, temporary help, $10.00/hr
Lafeber, Patricia M, court clerk II, $25,404
Laffoon, Terri A, court clerk II, $25,404
Lager, Irene L, temporary rep, $12.21/hr
Lager, Kent R, juvenile officer III, $41,172
Lajoie, Kristina N, court clerk III, $27,660
Lakin, Cynthia, court reporter, $57,178
Lakins, Robbie A, court clerk III, $29,004
Lamke, Isidore I, circuit judge, $146,804
Lampe, Barbara S, court clerk II, $25,404
Lancaster, Nancy D, court clerk II, $27,084
Land, Jordan C, juvenile officer V, $48,156
Landis, Justin L, juvenile officer I, $32,628
Landolt, Jeanne E, court clerk II, $23,780
Landon, Deborah J, court clerk II, $12,702
Lane, Leslie A, court clerk III, $27,660
Lane, Melissa J, court reporter, $57,178
Lane, Patricia J, secretary II, $27,660
Lane, Tim M, juvenile officer II, $38,928
Lang, Joyce E, court clerk II, $27,504
Lange-Kerns, Kirsten W, juvenile officer III, $40,380
Langkopf, Susan L, court clerk II, $12,702
Langley, Cody A, detention aide I, $25,404
Langsdale, Ashley M, juvenile officer I, $32,628
Lankford, Jill A, court clerk IV, $31,512
Lanning, Laura M, court clerk III, $27,660
Larkins, Beth A, court clerk III, $27,660
Larose, Yvonne D, temporary help, $9.00/hr
Larsen, Heidi A, court clerk II, $25,824
Lattin, Amber N, court clerk II, $25,032
Lauer, Gaylene, court clerk V, $44,304
Laughman, Cari C, court clerk II, $13,326
Lauhoff, Janet S, court clerk II, $12,516
Laurentius, Rhonda, court reporter, $57,178
Lawrence, Melissa K, court clerk II, $25,404
Lawrence, Sonya J, court clerk II, $25,404
Lawrence, Tina M, court clerk II, $25,404
Lawson, Holly M, court clerk II, $25,404
Lawson, Kelby M, temporary help, $9.00/hr
Lawson, Nadine L, court clerk II, $26,232
Lawson, Rhonda L, court clerk II, $25,404

Lawson, Terri L, secretary II, $27,660
Lawson, Tiffany A, court clerk III, $27,660
Leat, Elena, temporary help, $10.43/hr
Lebow, Mechelee, court clerk III, $27,660
Lebs, Dana S, court clerk III, $27,660
Ledbetter, Rhonda L, court program specialist IV, $46,932
Lee, Cynthia J, court clerk II, $25,404
Lee, Deborah L, court program specialist III, $35,568
Lee, Dixie C, secretary II, $27,660
Legrand, Christopher S, court clerk II, $25,404
Leigh, Sandra A, secretary II, $29,496
Lemke, Jessica D, juvenile/family court aide, $27,660
Lemmons, Stephanie N, treatment court adminstr II, $46,068
Lemuz, Ana I, court clerk III, $27,660
Lenoir, Melissa A, court clerk II, $25,404
Lenz, Susan M, court clerk II, $25,404
Lenzner, Sandy J, court clerk II, $25,032
Leonardt, Karen A, court clerk II, $25,824
LePage, John R, associate circuit judge, $135,059
Leslie, Elizabeth A, detention aide I, $12,511
Lett, Stacey J, associate circuit judge, $135,059
Letterman, Dusti M, court clerk II, $25,404
Leutert, Shayna D, temporary help, $10.00/hr
Leutert, Sheila L, court clerk V, $36,204
Lewis, Benjamin F, circuit judge, $146,804
Lewis, Mandy L, court clerk II, $25,404
Lewis, Sonya D, court clerk II, $25,404
Lewis, Tanya R, court clerk IV, $33,744
Ligons, Michael J, associate circuit judge, $135,059
Linberger, Elizabeth A, temporary help, $10.00/hr
Lind, Sondra J, temporary help, $10.00/hr
Lineberry, Charles S, computer info tech I, $35,568
Lingenfelter, Katrina, court clerk III, $27,228
Link, Lelia J, court clerk II, $25,404
Linn, Karie A, court clerk IV, $30,420
Lipke, Scott A, associate circuit judge, $135,059
Little, Mary M, unit manager I, $41,172
Litty, Jessica M, juvenile officer II, $36,888
Liu, Mengjiao, temporary help, $10.00/hr
Livia, Chrysanthi A, court clerk II, $20,958
Livingston, Molly L, circuit clerk, $55,639
Lloyd, Adrienne C, juvenile officer IV, $44,304
Lloyd, Richard L, detention aide I, $25,404
Lockhart, Jazmin A, court clerk II, $25,032
Locklin, Halee C, court clerk II, $25,404
Logan, Linda D, court clerk II, $25,404
Logsden, Tammy, court clerk II, $25,404
Lomax, Brenda S, court clerk II, $30,384
Long, Bobbi M, court clerk II, $25,032
Long, Colin P, associate circuit judge, $135,059
Long, Evelyn, court clerk II, $25,032
Long, Lyman J, court clerk II, $25,404
Long, Mary M, court reporter, $57,178
Long, Susan E, family court commissioner, $133,716
Longstreet, Debbie A, court clerk III, $27,660
Longworth, Jill R, court reporter, $57,178
Loper, Margie A, court clerk II, $25,404
Lopez, Dori A, court clerk II, $25,404
Lopez, Patricia R, court program specialist III, $42,708
Lorton, Lisa G, secretary I, $22,229
Lorusso, Barbara J, court clerk II, $25,404
Lorusso, Thomas S, court clerk V, $34,356
Loughrige, Valerie L, court clerk II, $25,404
Love, Maureen N, detention aide I, $25,404
Love, Richard B, juvenile officer I, $33,180
Lovekamp, Kelly L, associate circuit judge, $135,059
Lovett, Vanika, court clerk III, $27,660
Lowe, Crystal D, court clerk IV, $30,420
Lowery, Sarah E, court clerk II, $25,404
Lowry, Amanda B, court clerk II, $25,404
Lucas, Tiffeny N, court clerk III, $27,660
Lucht, Susan M, court reporter, $57,178
Lucy, Pamela S, secretary II, $29,004
Luebbering, Angela M, court clerk II, $22,596
Lukachick, John P, family court commissioner, $133,716
Luna, Larry G, associate circuit judge, $135,059
Lunceford, Brandi J, temporary help, $10.00/hr
Lund, Danielle J, court clerk II, $24,134
Luss, Aneca L, unit manager I, $41,172
Lute, Ashley M, court clerk III, $27,660
Lutz, Terry Y, court reporter, $57,178
Lutz, Tonya J, treatment court adminstr II, $46,932
Lynch, Angela R, court clerk II, $24,210

Lynch, Donna L, court clerk III, $32,052
Lyng, Terri N, juvenile officer II, $38,928
Lynn, Karen M, court reporter, $57,178
Lyon, Phyllis L, court clerk II, $25,032
Machelett, Rebecca L, court clerk IV, $30,420
MacPherson, Cynthia A, associate circuit judge, $135,059
Madigan, Mark J, juvenile officer II, $39,624
Madison, Melissa A, juvenile officer II, $37,548
Madson, Patricia L, court clerk II, $25,404
Magee, Kimberla L, court clerk II, $25,404
Mager, Mary K, court clerk II, $31,416
Maghe, Ana R, court clerk IV, $30,420
Maier, Brandy S, court clerk II, $25,404
Maier, Casaundra C, court clerk II, $25,404
Majka, Heather M, court clerk II, $25,404
Majors, Lory A, court clerk IV, $32,628
Manansala, Antonio M, associate circuit judge, $135,059
Maners, Kelly M, circuit clerk, $55,639
Manners, Patricia A, court reporter, $57,178
Manning, Jessica A, court clerk II, $25,404
Manning, Teresa D, court clerk II, $25,404
Manno, Christine M, court clerk II, $25,404
Manring, Edward M, associate circuit judge, $135,059
Mansfield, Sarah M, court clerk II, $25,404
Mansur, Cheryl A, circuit clerk, $55,639
Mantlo, Amanda K, detention aide I, $12,698
Manuel, Scott R, probate commissioner, $145,343
Manuel, Willie D, court clerk III, $27,660
Marcano, Mytrice, court clerk V, $34,356
Marcell, Sherry L, court clerk II, $25,032
March, Roma L, circuit clerk, $55,639
Marciano, Theresa M, court clerk II, $25,404
Marlett, Melissa L, court clerk V, $36,888
Marquardt, Jeffrey B, family court commissioner, $133,716
Marquart, Keith B, associate circuit judge, $135,059
Marquez, Guadalupe G, court clerk III, $27,660
Marquis, Teresa L, court clerk V, $34,356
Marshall, Robert L, maintenance worker, $29,976
Marshall, Sarah M, court reporter, $57,178
Marshall, Sherry, court reporter, $57,178
Martensen, Marlys A, court clerk II, $25,032
Martin, Ashley M, court clerk II, $25,032
Martin, Jessica M, court clerk II, $20,958
Martin, Karen F, court clerk II, $27,948
Martin, Kevin B, juvenile officer III, $41,172
Martin, Tamara L, court clerk IV, $30,984
Martinez, Kelly D, court clerk III, $27,660
Martinez, Sandra, circuit judge, $146,804
Martz, Rita J, juvenile officer IV, $44,304
Mason, David C, circuit judge, $146,804
Mason, Kimberly, court clerk II, $25,404
Mason, Mary G, court clerk II, $25,824
Mason, Susan D, court clerk II, $25,404
Mason-White, Tracey A, associate circuit judge, $135,059
Massey, Clinton W, juvenile officer III, $42,708
Mathews, Adrian K, detention aide I, $12,511
Mathews, Haley R, temporary help, $10.00/hr
Matlock, Sheronda S, court clerk III, $30,984
Matteson, Karen A, court clerk IV, $30,984
Matthews, Elaine R, court reporter, $57,178
Matthews, Joe B, temporary help, $10.00/hr
Mattlage, Ona S, court clerk II, $25,404
Matzen, Sassie M, temporary help, $10.00/hr
Maupin, Amy L, secretary II, $27,660
Maupin, Janet B, circuit clerk, $55,639
May, Deloris M, detention aide II, $27,660
May, Karen M, food service worker I, $11,752
May, Lily G, court clerk II, $25,404
May, Victoria S, court clerk II, $25,404
Mayer, Janis E, assistant accounting manager, $39,624
Mayer, Robert, circuit judge, $146,804
Mayes, Lathella J, court clerk II, $25,404
Mayes, Penny L, court clerk II, $25,404
Mayes, Rochelle M, court clerk III, $27,660
Mayfield, April F, secretary to presiding judge, $34,356
Mayfield, Cindy L, court clerk II, $12,702
Mayfield, Dana S, court clerk III, $30,984
Mayfield, Ruby J, court clerk II, $28,452
Mayfield, Veronica, secretary to presiding judge, $37,548
Mays, Sharika R, court clerk II, $25,824
Mays, Yvonne A, court clerk II, $26,652
Mayweather, Cheryl D, court clerk IV, $29,976
McBride, Sherry L, court clerk III, $32,628

McCadney, Phyllis A, court clerk III, $27,228
McCann, Jessica E, court clerk IV, $30,420
McCarty, Melissa D, court clerk II, $25,404
McCarver, Shawn R, associate circuit judge, $135,059
McClaran, Esther M, court clerk III, $27,660
McClure, Tanya M, court clerk II, $25,032
McCluskey, Ruth A, juvenile officer V, $47,892
McCollum, Chaise R, temporary help, $10.00/hr
McCollum, Tricia, court clerk III, $29,976
McCorkill, Myra A, court clerk II, $22,596
McCormick, Julie A, court clerk III, $31,512
McCoy, Libbi L, court clerk II, $30,384
McCrea, Dena J, secretary I, $25,404
McDaniel, Jennifer M, court clerk II, $25,404
McDaniel, Laveta S, court clerk IV, $36,888
McDermott, David, juvenile officer IV, $43,488
McDonald, Amy L, court clerk II, $19,053
McDonald, Karen J, court clerk IV, $34,944
McDonald, Mary J, temporary rep, $15.00/hr
McElwee, Jo E, circuit clerk, $70,437
McEnroe, Kimberley L, court clerk II, $25,404
McEntire, Misty N, court clerk III, $27,660
McFarlane, William A, temporary help, $17.78/hr
McGee, Lisa G, temporary help, $10.00/hr
McGee, Mary J, circuit clerk, $55,639
McGhee, Wendi J, court program specialist I, $32,052
McGinnis, Patrice, court clerk II, $25,404
McGowen, Dorinda E, court clerk III, $28,104
McGraugh, Christopher E, circuit judge, $146,804
McGuire, Cathy S, secretary II, $28,536
McIntosh, Patricia A, court clerk II, $25,404
McKalip, Alisha, court clerk IV, $29,976
McKee, Barbara A, court clerk III, $35,568
McKee, Mary V, family court commissioner, $133,716
McKeen, Connie J, court reporter, $57,178
McKenna, Karen D, court clerk III, $27,660
McKenzie, Charles H, circuit judge, $146,804
McKenzie, Dorothy G, circuit clerk, $55,639
McKinley, Latonya N, secretary to presiding judge, $33,180
McKinney, Lillian C, detention aide I, $12,516
McKinney, Lillian C, temporary help, $12.03/hr
McKinnon, Bruce T, juvenile officer IV, $46,932
McLane, Krystal M, court clerk III, $27,228
McLaughlin, Ellen M, secretary I, $25,032
McLeod, Sandra A, court reporter, $57,178
McMahan, Christie D, detention aide II, $27,660
McMillian, Carla J, temporary rep, $15.00/hr
McMullen, Michelle A, court clerk III, $27,660
McMullin, Jeffrey R, unit manager I, $41,172
McMullin, Kimberly A, secretary III, $32,052
McNair, Kimberly R, court clerk II, $22,229
McNairy, James A, detention juvenile officer I, $32,628
McNally, Lori A, court clerk III, $27,660
McNary, Paige M, court clerk II, $25,404
McNicholas, Daniel C, accounting specialist, $44,304
McPherson, Lisa R, court clerk III, $27,228
McPherson, Zaro, court clerk IV, $25,404
McShane, Maura B, circuit judge, $146,804
McTeer, Dawn, court reporter, $57,178
Meador, Sarah E, court clerk II, $25,404
Meadows-Jordan, Jessica N, court clerk II, $25,404
Means, Kelly A, detention aide I, $25,032
Mechler, Rachel A, court clerk II, $25,404
Meder, Kimberly S, court reporter, $57,178
Medley, Mary S, court clerk II, $25,404
Medley, Susan I, court clerk II, $12,702
Medlin, Kelly M, court clerk II, $25,404
Mehrhoff, Kimberly, secretary I, $12,516
Meinen, Matthew A, juvenile officer I, $33,180
Melkus, Jennifer A, court clerk III, $27,660
Melton, Matthew C, drug court commissioner, $133,716
Menconi, Robert E, juvenile officer II, $36,888
Menkhus, Tamara, unit manager II, $46,068
Meola, Lisa M, court clerk II, $25,404
Mercer, Yvonne, court clerk II, $25,404
Merling, Alex J, detention aide I, $15,013
Merrell, Shayla, court clerk II, $27,504
Merrigan, Molly M, family court commissioner, $133,716
Merseal, Kelly M, court clerk III, $27,660
Meseke, Mindie J, court reporter, $57,178
Messer, Peggy L, court clerk III, $29,496
Messina, Cynthia, court reporter, $57,178
Meyer, Linda M, juvenile officer VI, $60,120

Meyer, Shara L, court clerk II, $25,404
Meyers, Catherine L, court clerk II, $25,404
Meyers, Tonya S, court clerk II, $25,404
Michael, Kimberly A, court clerk II, $25,404
Midkiff, Sandra C, circuit judge, $146,804
Mike, Donah L, court clerk II, $25,404
Mikeska, Jennifer L, circuit clerk, $55,639
Mikulcza, Joann, court clerk II, $25,824
Miles, Barbara J, temporary rep, $15.00/hr
Miles, Toya S, court clerk III, $27,228
Miller, Angelina M, court clerk V, $34,944
Miller, Barbara A, court clerk III, $36,888
Miller, Bill D, circuit clerk, $70,437
Miller, Carrie M, circuit clerk, $55,639
Miller, David H, circuit judge, $146,804
Miller, Donna J, court clerk II, $27,504
Miller, Jerri L, court clerk III, $25,931
Miller, Joel A, associate circuit judge, $135,059
Miller, Michelle Y, court clerk III, $31,512
Miller, Patricia L, secretary I, $20,323
Miller, Pennie C, court clerk II, $28,908
Miller, Regan L, court clerk II, $25,404
Miller, Rosanna M, court clerk II, $25,404
Miller, Sandra L, secretary I, $25,824
Miller, Sara J, family court commissioner, $133,716
Miller, Timothy S, associate circuit judge, $135,059
Miller, Tina R, court reporter, $57,178
Miller-Beal, Jill A, detention aide I, $25,404
Mills, Garla, juvenile officer V, $49,128
Milne-Cathcart, Charla M, court reporter, $57,178
Minear, Cindy L, court clerk III, $29,976
Miner, Barbara J, court clerk III, $31,512
Mings, Heather J, court clerk II, $25,032
Minish, Susan N, court clerk II, $25,404
Missey, Darrell E, circuit judge, $146,804
Mitchell, Jill A, court clerk II, $25,032
Mitchell, Kelly D, juvenile officer I, $16,314
Mitchell, Stephen R, associate circuit judge, $135,059
Mitchell, Sylvia L, court clerk II, $25,404
Mittelhauser, Jeff A, associate circuit judge, $135,059
Mobley, David C, associate circuit judge, $135,059
Moeckli, D A, court clerk II, $14,393
Mohling, Kimberli K, court reporter, $57,178
Moll, Teresa, secretary I, $25,404
Mommens, Kathy A, secretary I, $25,404
Monaco, Rose Ann, court clerk II, $25,404
Monahan, Diane M, family court commissioner, $133,716
Moning, Lauren A, temporary help, $10.00/hr
Monken, James M, court clerk II, $25,404
Monnig, Cindy A, court clerk II, $25,404
Monroe, Carol A, secretary to presiding judge, $34,356
Monroe, Christina K, court clerk II, $25,404
Monroe, Tyrine O, court clerk II, $25,404
Montgomery, Caitlin E, detention aide II, $27,660
Montgomery, Judith K, court clerk II, $27,084
Montgomery, Norma J, court clerk II, $25,404
Moody, Susan M, court reporter, $57,178
Moon, Lori L, circuit clerk, $55,639
Moon, Susanne E, court reporter, $57,178
Moore, Cherri, court clerk II, $25,404
Moore, Eileen, court clerk V, $34,356
Moore, George S, circuit judge, $146,804
Moore, Jason D, juvenile officer II, $36,888
Moore, Lea A, court reporter, $57,178
Moore, Lee D, detention aide II, $27,660
Moore, Linda L, detention juvenile officer I, $33,180
Moore, Mary L, food service worker II, $25,404
Moore, Molly E, court clerk II, $25,404
Moore, Pamela H, court clerk II, $25,404
Moore, Sherry B, juvenile officer II, $36,888
Moppin, Judy A, court clerk III, $29,496
Morago, Brandon K, court clerk II, $25,404
Morales, Teresa L, court clerk II, $25,404
Morgan, Mary L, court clerk II, $25,404
Morgan, Stephanie L, court reporter, $57,178
Morgan, Valerie J, court clerk II, $25,032
Moriarty, Joan L, circuit judge, $146,804
Moroni, Gina R, temporary help, $10.00/hr
Morreale, Maria A, secretary II, $28,536
Morris, Allison F, court clerk II, $25,032
Morris, Christina, court clerk II, $25,404
Morris, Nicole K, court clerk II, $25,032
Morris, Teresa A, court clerk II, $25,404

Morrison, Bailey M, temporary help, $10.00/hr
Morrison, Carly O, temporary help, $10.00/hr
Morrow, Kameelah S, court clerk II, $25,824
Morse, Megan C, court clerk V, $34,356
Mosley, Marcia A, circuit clerk, $55,639
Mothersbaugh, Lori D, court reporter, $57,178
Mountjoy, Thomas E, circuit judge, $146,804
Mouton, David B, circuit judge, $146,804
Moyich, Kelly R, legal counsel, $54,288
Mueller, Jaclyn E, computer info tech II, $39,624
Mueller, Julie A, detention aide I, $18,774
Mueller, Mary B, legal counsel, $54,288
Muenks, Mary E, court clerk II, $12,702
Mulally, Susan J, secretary to presiding judge, $33,180
Mullen, Michael K, circuit judge, $146,804
Muller, Karen A, detention juvenile officer I, $32,628
Mungle, Vickie L, court clerk II, $18,230
Munton, David R, associate circuit judge, $135,059
Munzlinger, Valerie J, circuit clerk, $62,547
Murphy, Kristal R, court reporter, $57,178
Murphy, Stephanie K, court clerk III, $27,660
Murray, Dawn J, secretary I, $25,404
Murrell, Shannon M, court clerk III, $27,660
Musser, Jessica J, court reporter, $57,178
Myers, Meagan L, court clerk II, $25,404
Nabe, Karen L, temporary rep, $15.00/hr
Naile, Stacey A, court clerk III, $27,660
Nakashima-Moran, Kimberly A, court clerk V, $38,928
Nappi, Nancy L, court clerk II, $25,404
Nauman, David C, detention aide II, $27,660
Neal, Linda A, court clerk II, $26,232
Neal, Susan G, court clerk II, $20,323
Neese, Kevin M, juvenile officer I, $32,628
Neff, Crystal D, court clerk II, $25,824
Neill, Margaret M, circuit judge, $146,804
Neill, Mark H, circuit judge, $146,804
Nelson, Kevin R, court clerk II, $25,032
Nelson, Michelle R, court clerk II, $27,084
Newham, Deborah A, secretary to presiding judge, $33,180
Newman, Beverly A, juvenile officer V, $57,744
Newton, Ashley M, court clerk II, $25,404
Newton, Linda M, court clerk III, $30,420
Nicholas, John A, associate circuit judge, $135,059
Nichols, Debra J, court program specialist I, $30,420
Nichols, James V, associate circuit judge, $135,059
Nichols, Kara A, secretary II, $27,660
Nichols, Linda C, court reporter, $57,178
Nickols, Donald T, detention aide I, $25,404
Niemann, Scott C, court clerk III, $27,660
Nilges, Deanna, court clerk III, $27,660
Nilson, Patricia A, secretary to presiding judge, $33,180
Nimmo, Brooke, juvenile officer II, $36,888
Nixon, Dawn M, court clerk IV, $30,420
Nixon, Devon M, court clerk II, $25,404
Noble, Michael W, associate circuit judge, $135,059
Nolan, Thomas D, court clerk IV, $30,420
Nordsieck, Norma S, court clerk III, $27,660
Norman, Brooke D, court clerk II, $25,032
Norris, Jill A, treatment court adminstr II, $46,932
Norton, Daniel F, juvenile officer III, $48,156
Nowell, Cynthia L, court clerk III, $27,660
Nunn, Alma L, temporary help, $10.00/hr
Oaks, Seth C, juvenile officer II, $36,888
O'Brien, Jeffrey M, juvenile officer III, $44,304
O'Bryant, Mercedes L, court clerk II, $25,032
O'Dell, Amanda J, court clerk II, $25,404
O'Dell, Karen F, court clerk IV, $30,420
Odom, Lei A, court reporter, $57,178
O'Donnell, Barbara S, court clerk II, $25,404
O'Donnell, Kathleen M, court clerk II, $25,032
O'Dowd, Molly A, temporary help, $9.00/hr
Officer, Heather L, court clerk V, $34,356
Ogburn, Laura J, temporary help, $10.00/hr
Ogden, Judy R, court program specialist II, $32,052
Ohlms, Philip J, associate circuit judge, $135,059
Ohmer, Steven R, circuit judge, $146,804
O'Keefe, Rose F, court clerk II, $26,232
O'Leary, Patti, court clerk III, $31,512
Olinger, Rhonda K, court clerk II, $24,719
Oliver, Sharon J, detention aide II, $27,660
Oliver, Tonia L, court clerk II, $25,404
Ollar, Alisha A, court clerk II, $25,404
Olsen, Daniel W, associate circuit judge, $135,059

Ordnung, Michael J, associate circuit judge, $135,059
Orebaugh, Kimberly J, court clerk II, $25,404
O'Riley, Pam, court clerk II, $23,987
Orr, Amanda L, juvenile officer II, $36,204
Orr, Jared E, court clerk II, $25,824
Orr, Lavette M, temporary help, $10.00/hr
Orton, Janice E, court clerk II, $25,404
Osborne-Baston, Maxine B, temporary help, $10.00/hr
Ostmann, Tammy S, court clerk II, $25,404
Oswalt, Sandra S, court clerk V, $34,356
Othic, Scot T, associate circuit judge, $135,059
Ott, Mary E, associate circuit judge, $135,059
Ottinger, Lisa A, court clerk II, $25,824
Otto, Jalilah, associate circuit judge, $135,059
Overman, Darreld W, court clerk III, $27,660
Overstreet, Nancy S, court clerk II, $25,404
Owen, Claude C, juvenile officer II, $36,204
Owen, Hobart F, juvenile officer III, $41,940
Owens, Linda K, court clerk III, $27,660
Owens, Rachel L, court clerk II, $25,404
Owens, Rita S, court clerk IV, $33,744
Oxenhandler, Gary M, circuit judge, $146,804
Oyler-Hook, Kim J, court clerk III, $28,104
Ozbun, Laura L, court clerk II, $25,404
Pace, Sherrie J, court clerk II, $25,404
Page, Lisa, circuit judge, $146,804
Painter, Ernest M, juvenile officer IV, $52,092
Palmer, D E, temporary rep, $15.00/hr
Palmer, Wendy L, court clerk II, $25,824
Palmer, Willard D, detention aide II, $27,228
Paris, N D, court reporter, $57,178
Pariseau, Marla L, court clerk V, $33,744
Park, Brenda D, court clerk IV, $30,420
Parker, Kelly W, circuit judge, $146,804
Parker, Ronald L, court reporter, $57,178
Parks, Jackie J, court clerk II, $25,404
Parmentier, Karen L, court clerk V, $38,232
Parr, Pamela L, court clerk II, $23,780
Parrett, Renee R, court reporter, $57,178
Parris, Ashley D, court clerk II, $25,404
Parrott, Linda J, court clerk II, $25,824
Parsons, Janet S, circuit clerk, $55,639
Pastorfield, Timothy J, court clerk II, $25,032
Paszkiewicz, Gregory A, court clerk V, $41,940
Pate, Lena R, court clerk II, $25,404
Patt, Rose A, court clerk II, $20,026
Patterson, Andrea L, court reporter, $57,178
Patterson, Katherine J, temporary help, $10.00/hr
Patterson, Lisa M, court clerk II, $25,404
Patterson, Viki C, court clerk II, $25,404
Patterson-Hardaway, Sharlene D, court clerk III, $27,660
Pattison, Nadine M, court clerk II, $23,816
Paulus, Becky A, circuit clerk, $55,639
Payne, Dona J, court clerk II, $25,824
Payne, Sharon B, court clerk IV, $33,180
Pazera, Ann M, court clerk II, $25,404
Peace, Jack N, circuit judge, $146,804
Pearcy, Wendy G, court clerk II, $25,404
Pearson, Merrie E, court clerk IV, $34,944
Pearson, Sidney T, circuit judge, $146,804
Peasel, Michael D, court reporter, $57,178
Peat, Sally M, court reporter, $57,178
Peavler, Michelle A, juvenile officer II, $36,888
Peck, Jill K, circuit clerk, $55,639
Peebles, Barbara T, associate circuit judge, $135,059
Peel, Gregg A, detention aide I, $25,404
Peery, Rhonda J, secretary to presiding judge, $33,180
Peirce, Karen R, court clerk III, $27,228
Pelikan, Daniel G, circuit judge, $146,804
Pelton, Sherri R, court clerk III, $33,744
Pemberton, Kaci L, secretary I, $25,404
Penn, Roberta J, temporary help, $10.00/hr
Pennington, Sharon K, court clerk II, $25,404
Pennington, Stephanie D, temporary help, $10.00/hr
Peoples, Earline V, court clerk II, $25,404
Percival, Rhonda, secretary to presiding judge, $33,180
Perigo, Timothy W, circuit judge, $146,804
Perkins, Dena R, court clerk IV, $30,984
Perkins, Jennifer A, secretary III, $29,496
Permuter, Lawrence J, associate circuit judge, $135,059
Perney, Megan V, court clerk II, $25,404
Perrine, Lydia A, court clerk III, $28,536
Perry, Chelsea L, court clerk II, $25,404

Persons, Laura A, court clerk II, $25,404
Perumalla, Samuel R, court clerk II, $30,924
Peters, Camryn L, detention aide I, $15,019
Peterson, Cheryl A, court clerk III, $31,512
Peterson, Martina, family court commissioner, $133,716
Pettit, Sheena D, juvenile officer II, $36,888
Pettyjohn, Serena E, court clerk II, $25,404
Petzall, Constance D, court reporter, $57,178
Pfister, Chad N, associate circuit judge, $135,059
Phelan, Jeanne, court reporter, $57,178
Phillips, Jennifer, circuit judge, $146,804
Phillips, Margaret, temporary help, $10.00/hr
Phillips, Melissa K, juvenile officer IV, $47,892
Phillips, Samantha J, court clerk II, $12,698
Phillips, Tiffany, circuit clerk, $55,639
Pickett, Marsha C, secretary to presiding judge, $33,180
Piedimonte, Karen K, court clerk II, $25,404
Pigg, Brenda S, court clerk IV, $32,052
Pigg, Sylvia U, court clerk II, $25,404
Piles, Brenda J, court reporter, $57,178
Pilkington, Cameron M, temporary help, $10.00/hr
Pilley, Mark B, associate circuit judge, $135,059
Pingleton, Leslie J, court clerk II, $25,404
Pinkley, Tammy L, temporary help, $10.00/hr
Pinkston, James A, drug court commissioner, $133,716
Pippin, Virgil V, maintenance worker, $28,536
Pitts, Leslie D, detention aide I, $28,104
Pitts, Reanna M, juvenile officer II, $36,204
Plescher, Lena C, court clerk II, $25,404
Plunkett, Linda L, court clerk IV, $35,568
Podleski, Gayle L, circuit judge, $146,804
Poe, Carrie A, circuit clerk, $55,639
Poe, Jennifer A, court clerk II, $25,404
Poindexter, Yvette M, secretary II, $27,660
Pokorny, Debra M, temporary help, $10.00/hr
Pollihan, Patty G, unit manager I, $41,172
Porter, Christy L, court clerk II, $25,404
Porter, John C, associate circuit judge, $135,059
Postell, Blanche E, court clerk III, $27,660
Postlewait, Timothy A, court clerk II, $25,404
Potter, Brittany N, court clerk III, $27,228
Potter, Holly D, court clerk II, $25,404
Potter, Marissa A, court clerk III, $27,660
Potter, Susan L, circuit clerk, $55,639
Potter, Wendy E, secretary II, $33,180
Powell, Celeste A, court clerk II, $25,404
Powell, Dawn L, court clerk V, $34,356
Powell, Deborah F, juvenile officer III, $43,488
Powell, Kevin D, juvenile officer II, $36,888
Powell, Linda S, detention aide II, $27,660
Powell, Mark A, associate circuit judge, $135,059
Powell, Pamela M, court program specialist II, $32,052
Powell, Wesley B, circuit judge, $146,804
Poynter, Stacy N, court clerk II, $25,404
Prebil, Thomas J, circuit judge, $146,804
Prewitt, Philip E, associate circuit judge, $135,059
Preyer, Herbert M, associate circuit judge, $135,059
Price, Deborah J, court clerk III, $33,744
Price, Kendra R, court clerk III, $29,004
Price, Lois A, juvenile officer II, $38,928
Price, Nicole L, court clerk II, $25,404
Priest, Carman R, secretary to presiding judge, $33,180
Princivalli, Michael, treatment court adminstr II, $46,932
Pringer, Ellen M, court clerk II, $25,404
Pritchett, Michael M, circuit judge, $146,804
Pritt-Bothwell, Sharleen K, juvenile officer IV, $51,096
Proctor, Georgia L, unit manager I, $52,092
Prokes, Roger M, circuit judge, $146,804
Prost, Donna L, court clerk II, $22,596
Prothero, Jill E, court clerk II, $25,824
Provow, Eileen R, circuit clerk, $55,639
Pruett, Heidi E, court clerk III, $27,660
Pruitt, Melinda A, detention aide I, $13,968
Pulley, Courtney, juvenile officer II, $41,172
Puppel-Smith, Sue E, court clerk II, $25,404
Purvis, Staci A, court clerk III, $27,660
Pyle, G T, associate circuit judge, $135,059
Pyle, Peggy L, court clerk II, $25,404
Pyle, Shannon E, court clerk III, $27,660
Qualls, Debra A, court clerk II, $25,404
Qualls, Judy L, court clerk V, $34,356
Quitno, Neal R, associate circuit judge, $135,059
Rabbitt, Jean M, court clerk II, $25,032

Rabbitt, Lauren C, court clerk II, $25,404
Rackley, Mandy E, court clerk II, $25,404
Ramey, Stephanie L, court clerk II, $25,404
Ramirez, Melanie B, court clerk II, $25,404
Ramsay, Carol J, court clerk II, $12,702
Ramsey, Wilma, court clerk II, $29,412
Randall, Moria, court clerk II, $27,084
Randazzo, Kathleen A, secretary to presiding judge, $36,888
Randazzo, Kevin J, juvenile officer II, $36,888
Randle, Evelyn L, detention aide I, $25,404
Randolph, Stephanie, court clerk III, $27,660
Rapp, Mariah L, secretary to presiding judge, $33,180
Raske, Keith, court clerk III, $27,660
Rasnic, Kristin L, court clerk II, $25,404
Rathburn, Dennis M, detention aide II, $27,660
Ratzlaff, Dakotah B, temporary help, $10.00/hr
Ratzlaff, Delana, court clerk II, $27,660
Rawlings, Indre, court clerk II, $25,404
Raybon, Vinson, court clerk V, $33,744
Rayford, Carmela M, court clerk II, $25,404
Raymond, Anthony S, juvenile officer II, $36,888
Raymond, Vicky J, court clerk III, $27,660
Rea, Darlene, juvenile officer II, $37,548
Rea, Phyllis B, court reporter, $57,178
Reason, Carolyn D, court clerk II, $25,404
Reason, Justin R, temporary help, $10.00/hr
Reaves, Jacqueline A, court clerk II, $31,920
Redington, Thomas P, associate circuit judge, $135,059
Redmon, Robin S, juvenile officer II, $38,928
Reece, Donna F, court clerk II, $27,504
Reed, Tracy M, court clerk II, $25,032
Reeder, Cindy F, court clerk V, $37,548
Reel, Elisia M, court clerk II, $25,404
Reese, Jessica L, court clerk II, $25,404
Reese, Leandra C, court clerk II, $25,404
Reeves, Glenna K, legal counsel, $54,288
Reifsteck, Connie P, court clerk III, $27,660
Reinhard, Eric D, legal counsel, $54,288
Rellihan, Jerry J, associate circuit judge, $135,059
Renken, Amy D, court clerk II, $25,404
Renna, Joyce A, temporary rep, $15.00/hr
Reno, Gloria J, circuit judge, $146,804
Rensing, Kristie A, court clerk IV, $30,984
Replogle, Vickie D, court clerk II, $25,404
Retell, Reba L, court clerk II, $26,652
Reuschel, Cara L, juvenile officer II, $36,888
Reuter, Michael E, circuit clerk, $70,437
Revelle, Elizabeth A, detention aide II, $27,660
Reynolds, Jennifer L, court clerk II, $25,404
Reynolds, Lisa J, court clerk III, $27,660
Rhine, Tammy L, detention aide I, $25,032
Rhodes, Deborah S, temporary rep, $15.00/hr
Rhodes, Kim R, temporary help, $10.00/hr
Rhodes, Paula M, court clerk IV, $30,420
Rhodes, Randall G, juvenile officer V, $60,120
Rhone, Robbin D, court clerk II, $25,404
Rhone, Taylor J, court clerk II, $25,032
Rhymes, Minnie B, court clerk II, $25,824
Ribaudo, Ellen H, associate circuit judge, $135,059
Ricci, Tina L, court clerk III, $27,660
Rice, Lorraine T, juvenile officer II, $36,888
Rich, Diana L, circuit clerk, $55,639
Richard, Tracey L, court clerk III, $27,660
Richards, Alisha R, court clerk II, $22,529
Richards, Margie J, court clerk II, $25,404
Richards, Wm S, associate circuit judge, $135,059
Richardson, Monica C, court clerk II, $25,032
Richardson, Peggy D, associate circuit judge, $135,059
Richey, Charity, juvenile officer II, $36,888
Richley, Penny K, court clerk II, $25,032
Richmond, Kristin E, court clerk II, $25,404
Richmond, Michelle A, court clerk IV, $29,976
Richmond, Sharon R, circuit clerk, $55,639
Rickel, Cheryl A, court reporter, $57,178
Rickermann, Deborah K, court clerk II, $25,404
Ricks, Cindy G, court reporter, $57,178
Riddle, Christi J, court clerk IV, $34,356
Riddle, Donisha T, unit manager I, $41,172
Ridge, Janna L, court clerk II, $25,404
Riedesel, Misty D, temporary help, $10.00/hr
Riegel, Deborah J, court clerk II, $29,412
Riehl, Patricia A, associate circuit judge, $135,059
Riekeberg, Christopher R, court reporter, $57,178

Riekeberg, Toni K, court reporter, $57,178
Riffel, Lori E, court clerk II, $27,084
Rigby, Twila K, associate circuit judge, $135,059
Riggens, Antonio J, detention aide I, $25,032
Riggs-Spurlin, Dulcey A, court clerk II, $25,032
Rigney, Karen L, court clerk III, $34,944
Riley, Christina D, court clerk III, $30,420
Riley, John J, circuit judge, $146,804
Riley, John S, court administrator, $49,128
Riley, Theresa M, court clerk II, $25,404
Ringwald, Tina M, temporary help, $10.00/hr
Rippeto, Keely R, court clerk II, $25,404
Ritz, Cassie M, court clerk IV, $32,052
Robb, Becky L, court clerk V, $35,568
Robb, Patrick K, circuit judge, $146,804
Roberts, Brandy D, court clerk II, $25,404
Roberts, Judith A, temporary rep, $15.00/hr
Roberts, Kathryn M, court clerk III, $31,512
Roberts, Melinda J, court clerk I, $21,127
Roberts, Nancy R, court clerk II, $25,404
Roberts, Rickey R, associate circuit judge, $135,059
Roberts, Sherrill P, family court commissioner, $133,716
Roberts, Stacy L, juvenile officer V, $49,128
Roberts, Thomas P, court clerk V, $34,356
Robertson, Mary D, court clerk II, $12,702
Robey, Debra S, court clerk II, $25,404
Robinson, Nicole L, court clerk II, $22,229
Robinson, Roxanne C, court clerk II, $26,652
Robinson, Valerie, court clerk III, $27,660
Rocchio, David, court clerk V, $34,356
Roddy, Donald L, maintenance worker, $32,628
Rodecap, Janette K, associate circuit judge, $135,059
Roden, Brittany D, court clerk II, $25,404
Rodgers, Joni S, court clerk II, $26,652
Rodgers, Victoria L, court clerk II, $29,412
Rodriguez, Luis E, court clerk III, $27,660
Rodriquez, Kimberly J, detention aide I, $12,511
Rofkahr, Jessica K, court clerk II, $25,032
Rogado, Gracia S, court clerk II, $27,084
Rogers, Joyce E, detention aide II, $29,496
Rogers, Nancy A, temporary rep, $15.00/hr
Rogers, Teresa Y, court clerk IV, $38,232
Rogers, William J, juvenile officer II, $36,888
Rohrs, Elizabeth V, associate circuit judge, $135,059
Roldan, Marco A, circuit judge, $146,804
Rolf, Dennis A, circuit judge, $146,804
Rolufs, Edward M, court clerk III, $29,976
Roman, Rosa E, court clerk II, $15,878
Romans, Rosemary, circuit clerk, $55,639
Romine, Linelle J, juvenile officer I, $33,180
Rose, Jennifer L, temporary help, $10.00/hr
Rose, Kelly A, associate circuit judge, $135,059
Rose, Michael B, detention aide I, $20,026
Rosen, Sherrill L, family court commissioner, $133,716
Rosencrans, Lenna S, court clerk III, $28,536
Ross, Amanda J, court clerk II, $13,768
Ross, Andrew J, juvenile officer II, $36,888
Ross, Cynthia G, court clerk II, $29,904
Ross, Holly R, temporary help, $10.00/hr
Ross, Terry L, court clerk II, $13,749
Ross, Terry L, temporary help, $13.22/hr
Rothstein, D R, court clerk II, $25,404
Round, Bryan E, circuit judge, $146,804
Rowan, Kathleen E, court clerk II, $25,032
Rowden, Kerry G, associate circuit judge, $135,059
Rowe, Nicole D, court clerk II, $12,516
Rowe, Nicole D, temporary help, $12.03/hr
Rowland, Denise L, court clerk III, $27,660
Royalty, Katherine D, court clerk II, $26,652
Ruby, Robert T, court clerk IV, $37,548
Rucker, Aimee M, court clerk II, $25,404
Ruddick, Jeremy A, juvenile officer I, $33,180
Ruediger, Wanda F, court clerk II, $26,232
Ruff, Carol A, temporary help, $10.00/hr
Ruffcorn, Dalene M, court clerk V, $34,356
Rukavina, Kelly R, court clerk II, $25,404
Rumley, James M, associate circuit judge, $135,059
Rumley, Julie E, court clerk III, $27,660
Runkles, Amanda K, computer info tech supv I, $48,156
Rupp, Cynthia S, juvenile officer V, $33,180
Rupp, John D, drug court commissioner, $133,716
Rush, Gary E, court clerk II, $26,232
Rush, Pamela L, court clerk V, $38,928

Russell, Lori A, court clerk II, $12,702
Russell, Whitney R, court clerk II, $25,824
Rutter, Edith R, associate circuit judge, $135,059
Ryan, Holly A, secretary to presiding judge, $37,548
Ryerson, Elizabeth A, court clerk III, $30,984
Sadler, Susan M, circuit clerk, $63,529
Sago, Dawn R, court clerk II, $25,404
Salkil, Christina L, court clerk II, $25,032
Salyer, Casey K, juvenile officer II, $36,888
Sandefer, Tina M, court clerk IV, $30,420
Sander, Connie N, court clerk II, $25,404
Sander, Mishell R, court clerk III, $27,660
Sanders, Rosalind L, court clerk III, $27,660
Sandstrom, Gayla S, court clerk III, $27,228
Sandusky, Clifton L, detention aide I, $18,774
Sanford, Jessica, court reporter, $57,178
Sansegraw, Kimberly R, court clerk IV, $30,984
Sansom, Shane B, detention aide I, $25,404
Sapp, Angela J, court clerk III, $27,660
Sapp, Tonya L, detention aide I, $25,404
Saputo, Josephine A, court clerk III, $27,660
Sarratt, Danielle N, court clerk II, $25,404
Satterfield, Joe Z, associate circuit judge, $135,059
Sauer, Sheila R, treatment court adminstr II, $46,932
Saulsbury, Audrey E, court clerk II, $25,824
Saunders, Sherry L, court clerk II, $25,404
Saupe, Sara B, court clerk II, $25,404
Sawyer, Carissa R, court clerk II, $14,286
Sawyer, Kathryn I, court reporter, $57,178
Saxton, Lisa A, court clerk III, $31,512
Scaturro, Michele S, court clerk V, $43,488
Scavuzzo, Lydia M, court clerk II, $25,404
Schaeffer, Mary, juvenile officer II, $36,888
Schaffer, Amy J, court clerk II, $25,032
Schantz, Kimberly A, circuit clerk, $55,639
Schardan, Melissa A, court reporter, $57,178
Schatz, Doris D, court clerk V, $38,928
Schaumann, Dennis, circuit judge, $146,804
Schehr, Kevin P, associate circuit judge, $135,059
Scheibe, Richard L, associate circuit judge, $135,059
Schenck, Rebecca S, court clerk III, $27,660
Scherer, Melissa A, court clerk V, $34,356
Schiano, Tiffany M, temporary help, $10.00/hr
Schieber, Robert M, circuit judge, $146,804
Schierenbeck, Sharon, court clerk II, $25,824
Schimweg, Sheryl A, court clerk III, $30,420
Schlichting, Elaina D, court clerk II, $25,404
Schlueter, Julie K, secretary II, $27,660
Schmelz, Brenda L, court reporter, $57,178
Schmelzel, Jennifer S, temporary help, $10.00/hr
Schmidt, Beatrice C, detention aide I, $25,404
Schmidt, Donna C, court clerk III, $28,104
Schmidt, Lesley B, court clerk II, $12,516
Schmidt, Robyn R, circuit clerk, $55,639
Schneider, Cheri A, court clerk II, $27,948
Schneider, Denise M, court clerk III, $34,356
Schneider, Leslie A, associate circuit judge, $135,059
Schneider, Nancy L, circuit judge, $146,804
Schnell, Ann E, secretary II, $35,568
Schoenrock, Jennifer R, court clerk II, $25,404
Scholl, Brandy J, court clerk II, $25,824
Schollmeyer, Robert D, associate circuit judge, $135,059
Schoof, Melissa M, court clerk II, $15,019
Schoonover, Jestina S, court clerk II, $26,232
Schrader, Jason A, court clerk II, $25,824
Schremp, Donna E, court clerk III, $32,628
Schremp, Mary P, court clerk II, $30,924
Schridde, Belinda S, court clerk II, $25,404
Schroeder, Deborah J, court clerk IV, $35,568
Schroeder, Diana K, court clerk II, $25,824
Schroeder, Mary P, associate circuit judge, $135,059
Schuh, Amanda M, court clerk III, $30,420
Schuller, Randy P, associate circuit judge, $135,059
Schulte, Billye J, court reporter, $57,178
Schulte, Donald J, marshal, $59,534
Schultz, Cheryl L, circuit clerk, $55,639
Schultz, Shanda R, court clerk II, $25,404
Schulze, Elizabeth A, court reporter, $57,178
Schulze, Sara R, temporary help, $10.00/hr
Schupmann, Denise A, court clerk II, $25,404
Schutte, Pattie B, court clerk III, $29,032
Schwarzen, Michelle R, court clerk II, $25,404
Scobee, Deborah J, circuit clerk, $55,639

Scolaro, Nicholas S, detention juvenile officer I, $33,180
Scott, Angela M, juvenile officer I, $33,180
Scott, Ashley D, court clerk III, $27,660
Scott, Faye, temporary help, $10.43/hr
Scott, Gail D, court clerk II, $25,404
Scott, Gloria D, secretary II, $27,660
Scott, Michelle L, temporary help, $10.00/hr
Scott, Rebecca C, court clerk II, $25,032
Scott, Talia L, court clerk II, $25,032
Scrivner, Christy K, court clerk II, $25,404
Scruggs, Jay E, detention juvenile officer IV, $44,304
Seaman, Jason L, court clerk V, $33,744
Searcy, Lisa H, court clerk IV, $30,420
Sears, Chanda D, detention aide I, $25,404
Sears, Sheila K, court clerk V, $34,356
Sebastian, Aimee L, court clerk II, $25,404
Sedberry, Victoria L, unit manager II, $47,892
Seek, Sharie L, secretary III, $32,052
Seibel, Debra M, court clerk III, $32,052
Seiber, Lea A, court clerk V, $33,744
Seifert, Westley D, juvenile officer III, $41,172
Seiling, Sherry, court clerk V, $34,356
Seiller, Lorene H, court clerk III, $33,744
Selby, Kevin L, associate circuit judge, $135,059
Sellers, Lori A, court clerk II, $25,404
Selvey, Jaunita, court clerk III, $29,004
Selz, Shelly A, court clerk V, $38,232
Seneker, Harriet N, court clerk III, $32,628
Sexton, Laura M, juvenile officer III, $49,128
Seyler, Debra R, temporary help, $10.00/hr
Seymore, Julie R, treatment court adminstr II, $46,932
Shafer, Abe (Quint), associate circuit judge, $135,059
Sharp, Daniel E, juvenile officer IV, $45,156
Sharp, Jamey R, court clerk III, $29,496
Shaw, Beatrice, temporary rep, $15.00/hr
Shaw, Beverly A, temporary help, $10.00/hr
Shaw, Kara J, court clerk II, $25,032
Shaw, Vicki L, court clerk III, $32,628
Shegog, Karen S, unit manager II, $46,932
Shelby, Bridgett L, court clerk II, $25,404
Shelby, Kathy J, court clerk III, $27,660
Shellenbarger, Laurie, court clerk II, $25,404
Shelley, Stephni S, detention aide I, $25,404
Shephard, Talisha S, court clerk II, $25,404
Shepherd, Rachel L, circuit judge, $146,804
Sherry, Thea A, circuit judge, $146,804
Sherwood, Stacee L, court clerk II, $25,404
Shields, Diana L, juvenile officer II, $36,888
Shields, Molly M, court clerk II, $22,864
Shipley, Mitzi D, circuit clerk, $55,639
Shisler, Susan L, temporary help, $11.00/hr
Shively, Charrity E, court clerk II, $12,516
Shively, Rosalie A, circuit clerk, $55,639
Shivers, Angela D, court clerk III, $30,984
Shock, John H, associate circuit judge, $135,059
Short, Suzanne, court clerk II, $28,908
Shoults, Ronda D, court clerk II, $25,032
Shrader, Jacob N, detention juvenile officer I, $32,628
Shrauger, Brandy D, juvenile officer II, $36,204
Shrum, Linda L, court clerk II, $22,229
Shuck, Rose V, court clerk III, $34,944
Shy, Douglas R, computer info tech supv I, $49,128
Siavii, Rezetta K, court clerk III, $27,660
Siddiq, Amina, court clerk II, $25,404
Siebert, Theresa D, court clerk IV, $34,356
Siegel, Michele, court clerk II, $25,404
Siercks, Mary E, court clerk II, $25,404
Sifferman, Scott S, associate circuit judge, $135,059
Siler, David W, detention aide II, $27,660
Sillavan, Brooke S, court clerk III, $27,660
Sillyman, Darrell E, temporary help, $7.65/hr
Sillyman, Deana L, court clerk II, $28,452
Simmons, Joleene V, juvenile officer IV, $51,096
Simpson, Carol J, secretary I, $28,908
Simpson, Robert A, court clerk IV, $30,420
Simpson, Sheila M, court clerk II, $25,032
Sinclair, Grace C, circuit clerk, $63,529
Sisemore, Linda D, court clerk II, $25,824
Siwak, Ellen L, circuit judge, $146,804
Skaggs, Heather E, court clerk II, $25,404
Skaggs, Vickie L, court clerk II, $25,404
Skain, Mary C, court clerk II, $25,032
Skinner, Laura, secretary I, $25,404

Skinner, Mary K, detention aide II, $13,614
Skinner, Rebecca C, court clerk II, $20,323
Slater, Carrie L, juvenile officer II, $36,204
Slaughter, Diana H, court clerk III, $27,228
Slaughter, Susan A, secretary I, $25,404
Slesinski, Gregory, court clerk II, $25,404
Small, Brenda E, secretary I, $25,404
Small, Shelley R, court clerk II, $25,404
Smalley, Cheryl D, court clerk II, $25,404
Smith, Alice F, court clerk II, $13,142
Smith, Angela, court clerk III, $27,660
Smith, Ashlyn P, temporary help, $9.00/hr
Smith, Bobbie L, court clerk II, $25,404
Smith, Brandon L, juvenile officer II, $36,888
Smith, Cecilia S, circuit clerk, $55,639
Smith, Courtney N, court clerk II, $25,032
Smith, Crystal G, court clerk II, $25,032
Smith, Cynthia D, court clerk II, $25,404
Smith, Dennis N, associate circuit judge, $135,059
Smith, Donna K, court clerk II, $29,412
Smith, Erin M, court clerk II, $25,404
Smith, Hollie A, juvenile officer II, $38,928
Smith, Jeanne K, court clerk II, $25,824
Smith, Jennifer A, court clerk II, $26,232
Smith, Jerry S, court clerk II, $25,404
Smith, Jill M, court clerk III, $27,660
Smith, Joel Jay D, juvenile officer II, $38,928
Smith, Kelly, treatment court adminstr II, $46,932
Smith, Laura C, court clerk II, $25,404
Smith, Makayla C, temporary help, $10.00/hr
Smith, Mariana C, court clerk III, $27,660
Smith, Marla C, court clerk III, $29,004
Smith, Mary A, temporary help, $10.00/hr
Smith, Nina E, court clerk III, $33,744
Smith, Rebecca L, court clerk II, $28,452
Smithson, Ashley D, court clerk III, $27,660
Smoot, Deborah K, court clerk II, $30,384
Smoot, Erwin, court clerk IV, $30,420
Snelson, Julianne, computer operator, $27,660
Snider, Jennifer S, court clerk III, $29,976
Snider, Tameria L, court clerk II, $27,504
Snodgrass, Michael S, juvenile officer II, $36,888
Snow, Faye A, unit manager II, $51,096
Sobaski, Rachelle M, court reporter, $57,178
Sodergren, Thomas L, associate circuit judge, $135,059
Sokolowski, Earlene, temporary rep, $15.00/hr
Solomon, Connie D, court reporter, $57,178
Sondag, Sandra S, court reporter, $57,178
Sorensen, Marsha A, court clerk II, $25,404
Souders, Amanda R, court clerk II, $25,404
South, Cristina M, court clerk III, $27,228
Southard, Charolette J, temporary rep, $12.21/hr
Southern, Megan L, court clerk II, $25,404
Spalding, Christine R, juvenile officer II, $38,928
Sparks, Jacqueline L, court clerk III, $29,976
Spaunhorst, Donna K, court clerk II, $25,404
Spear, J B, associate circuit judge, $135,059
Speck, Debra S, computer info tech spec I, $48,156
Speis, Patricia A, court clerk V, $34,356
Spencer, Melissa A, court clerk II, $25,032
Spencer, Rebecca L, associate circuit judge, $135,059
Spencer, Shamika L, court clerk II, $25,404
Speth, Julia E, court clerk III, $28,104
Spielman, John C, associate circuit judge, $135,059
Spielman, Julie C, treatment court adminstr II, $46,932
Spitzer, Lari J, temporary help, $10.00/hr
Spiva, Brittany N, temporary help, $10.00/hr
Spiva, Charlotte D, detention aide II, $27,228
Spradling, Charmaine S, court reporter, $57,178
Sprague, Ann K, court reporter, $57,178
Spurgeon, Hope A, court clerk II, $27,084
Spurgeon, Mary C, temporary rep, $15.00/hr
Spurgeon, Stacie A, court clerk II, $25,404
Spurling, Jeremy J, juvenile officer II, $36,888
Squires, Jacquelin J, court clerk II, $25,404
Staashelm, Susan R, court clerk II, $25,032
Stacey, Brenda, associate circuit judge, $135,059
Stafford, Cynthia L, detention aide I, $25,404
Stafford, Willa D, court clerk II, $25,824
Stahl, Britney L, temporary help, $9.00/hr
Stallo, Eric W, circuit clerk, $55,639
Standridge, Richard T, associate circuit judge, $135,059
Stanfill, Kelly T, court clerk IV, $32,628

Stanturf, Rebecca J, circuit clerk, $55,639
Stark, Ashley R, juvenile officer I, $33,180
Stark, Pamela R, juvenile officer II, $36,888
Starkey, Billy J, detention aide II, $27,660
Stasiak, Brenda E, court clerk III, $37,548
Stearns, Martha J, court clerk II, $26,232
Steele, Heidi J, juvenile officer II, $40,380
Steele, Linda R, court clerk II, $27,948
Steele, Russell E, circuit judge, $146,804
Steen, Delola M, court clerk II, $19,053
Steen, Susan L, court reporter, $57,178
Steimel, Norman C, associate circuit judge, $135,059
Steinhoff, Janet A, court clerk III, $36,888
Steinkamp, Kenneth S, accounting manager, $62,664
Steinle McLain, Tammy J, court clerk II, $20,323
Stelzer, Michael F, circuit judge, $146,804
Stemmler, Christina L, temporary help, $10.00/hr
Stemmons, Tarran J, court clerk II, $25,404
Stephens, Debra S, court clerk II, $27,660
Stephens, Mark A, associate circuit judge, $135,059
Sterling, Don P, detention aide II, $27,660
Stevens, Carolyn, court clerk III, $30,984
Stevens, Deborah L, court clerk III, $28,536
Stevens, Marita S, court clerk III, $28,045
Stevens, Susan O, court reporter, $57,178
Stevenson, Liebe A, court reporter, $57,178
Stevenson, T M, court clerk II, $25,404
Stewart, Amanda S, court clerk II, $25,404
Stewart, Andrew T, detention aide I, $19,053
Stewart, Felicia J, court clerk III, $27,660
Stewart, Janet, court clerk IV, $30,984
Stewart, Kimberly G, court clerk III, $33,744
Stewart, Nathan B, circuit judge, $146,804
Stewart, Nicole G, court clerk IV, $30,420
Stillwell, Christi L, detention juvenile officer I, $32,628
Stinnett, Hillary L, detention aide II, $27,660
Stites, Natalia L, court clerk II, $25,404
Stockstill, Ashley A, court clerk III, $25,404
Stockton, Terra D, court clerk II, $25,404
Stoddard, Mary A, court clerk II, $27,948
Stokes, Debbie, court clerk III, $31,512
Stoll, Mark T, circuit judge, $146,804
Stolte, Florence E, court clerk II, $25,404
Stone, Tracy L, juvenile officer II, $38,928
Stoops, Katherine L, detention aide I, $15,013
Stoops, Paula M, secretary I, $25,404
Stovall-reid, Calea, associate circuit judge, $135,059
Street, Annette K, court clerk II, $25,032
Stremel, Gregory, associate circuit judge, $135,059
Strickland, Tianta A, court clerk III, $27,228
Strong, Charlotte A, court clerk III, $27,660
Strong, Rebecca E, circuit clerk, $55,639
Strope, Micayla R, court clerk II, $25,404
Strothmann, Wayne P, associate circuit judge, $135,059
Stuart, Beverley J, court clerk V, $34,356
Stump, Kristie L, court clerk III, $12,702
Sturdevant, Angela B, court clerk II, $25,404
Sturgell, Amanda S, temporary rep, $13.30/hr
Stutzman, Mary T, temporary help, $9.00/hr
Styles, Mark A, deputy probate commissioner, $133,716
Sullivan, Crystal T, court clerk II, $25,404
Sullivan, James E, circuit judge, $146,804
Summerlin, Penny L, court clerk III, $29,976
Summers, Tracy M, secretary I, $25,404
Suter-crayne, Cynthia A, associate circuit judge, $135,059
Sutton, Allyson N, temporary help, $10.00/hr
Sutton, Janet L, circuit judge, $146,804
Sutton, Sheree U, court clerk II, $25,404
Sutton, Sidney E, temporary help, $10.00/hr
Swaim, Kristie J, associate circuit judge, $135,059
Swann, Elizabeth W, associate circuit judge, $135,059
Swanson, Barbara J, temporary help, $10.00/hr
Sweeney, Edward W, circuit judge, $146,804
Sweet, Pamela A, court clerk II, $27,504
Swindle, Thomas D, associate circuit judge, $135,059
Swindler, Joshua T, detention aide I, $25,404
Swindler, Penny S, court clerk III, $24,202
Swindler, Randy T, maintenance worker, $28,536
Swiney, Becky J, circuit clerk, $55,639
Swing, Karen F, court clerk II, $25,404
Swope, Lauren R, detention aide II, $27,228
Swords, Brooke E, court clerk II, $25,404
Syms, Carolyn A, temporary rep, $12.21/hr

Tagai, Lori S, court clerk II, $23,467
Tallent, Monica D, court clerk II, $25,824
Tallman, Sandra A, court clerk II, $19,688
Tamerius, Yvonne, court clerk II, $25,404
Tann, Christina E, court clerk IV, $30,420
Tanner, Lisa A, court clerk II, $25,404
Tate, Christine K, court clerk III, $30,984
Tate, Sarah E, court clerk II, $25,404
Tatroe, Lana M, court clerk II, $27,084
Tatters, Susan K, secretary to presiding judge, $37,548
Taylor, Angela L, court clerk IV, $30,984
Taylor, Cindy J, court reporter, $57,178
Taylor, Diana M, court reporter, $57,178
Taylor, Jennifer R, court clerk III, $27,228
Taylor, Josh M, court clerk II, $25,404
Taylor, Patricia M, court clerk V, $35,568
Taylor, Shelia A, temporary help, $10.43/hr
Taylor, Vicky L, court clerk II, $12,516
Taylor, Vicky L, temporary help, $12.03/hr
Taylor-Whiteside, Valarie J, court clerk IV, $33,744
Teel, Lisa A, court clerk II, $25,087
Teer, Nancy G, unit manager II, $47,892
Teeter, Katherine A, temporary help, $10.00/hr
Teeter, Sophia K, temporary help, $10.00/hr
Terpening, Joy D, court clerk II, $25,404
Terry, Julie E, court clerk II, $25,404
Terry, Travis G, court clerk II, $25,404
Tharp, Connie F, court clerk III, $28,104
Thier, Martha K, secretary to presiding judge, $33,180
Thogmartin, Tammy L, court clerk IV, $32,052
Thomas, Adam E, detention juvenile officer IV, $43,488
Thomas, Ashley B, court clerk III, $27,660
Thomas, Deana F, court clerk II, $25,404
Thomas, Debra R, juvenile officer II, $36,888
Thomas, Jacqueline F, court clerk II, $31,416
Thomas, Jennifer D, juvenile officer II, $38,928
Thomas, Kyla L, temporary help, $10.00/hr
Thomas, Patricia R, court clerk II, $25,404
Thomas, Robin G, court clerk II, $25,404
Thomasson, Patrick L, court clerk IV, $38,232
Thompson, Amanda L, court clerk II, $25,032
Thompson, Beth J, court clerk II, $25,404
Thompson, Cathy A, secretary II, $28,536
Thompson, Cheryl L, court clerk II, $25,404
Thompson, Darren L, court clerk II, $25,404
Thompson, Diane L, secretary II, $26,752
Thompson, Gail J, court clerk III, $33,180
Thompson, Karen S, court clerk IV, $32,052
Thompson, Kenneth F, associate circuit judge, $135,059
Thompson, Linda J, court clerk II, $25,824
Thompson, Marcus A, detention aide II, $27,660
Thompson, Susan A, court clerk II, $25,824
Thompson, Tracy E, court clerk II, $25,404
Thompson, Virginia K, court clerk III, $25,175
Thomsen, Scott E, associate circuit judge, $135,059
Thomson, William D, associate circuit judge, $135,059
Thornhill, Matthew E, associate circuit judge, $135,059
Thurman, Amber D, juvenile officer II, $36,204
Tichenor, Tabitha L, court clerk III, $27,660
Tiggs, Neashalle, temporary help, $10.00/hr
Tiner, Cassaundra A, court clerk II, $25,404
Tinker-Saoirse, Tammy J, detention aide I, $12,698
Tinnin, Kimberley J, secretary to presiding judge, $32,628
Tinsley, Scott B, family court commissioner, $133,716
Tippin, Keener A, detention aide I, $25,404
Tipton, Carol J, juvenile officer II, $36,888
Tisdale, Alexis C, court clerk II, $25,404
Tisius, Nicole D, court clerk IV, $32,052
Tittsworth, Cheryl A, court clerk III, $32,628
Tobben, David B, associate circuit judge, $135,059
Todd, Denise R, secretary to presiding judge, $34,356
Todd, Velina L, court clerk II, $25,032
Tootle, Nancy A, court clerk II, $25,824
Torrence, John M, circuit judge, $146,804
Trachsel, Karla A, court clerk III, $27,660
Tracy, Sherry J, temporary rep, $15.00/hr
Treece, Twila D, court clerk IV, $36,888
Trickett-Harris, Constance L, court clerk II, $31,920
Triplett, Beth A, court clerk II, $25,032
Triplett, Linda A, detention aide I, $25,404
Trokey, Jenny J, court clerk II, $21,903
Troup, Joy B, secretary II, $28,536
Trout, Robert L, associate circuit judge, $135,059

Trout, Sandra L, court clerk II, $25,404
Trupiano, Carol A, court clerk II, $25,404
Trusty, Stacy N, temporary help, $10.00/hr
Tschannen, Terry A, circuit judge, $146,804
Tucker, Frederick P, circuit judge, $146,804
Tucker, Gerald V, court clerk III, $27,660
Tucker, Joshua C, temporary help, $10.00/hr
Tucker, Margaret, juvenile officer II, $36,888
Tuley, Rebecca S, court clerk III, $28,536
Tunnell, David T, associate circuit judge, $135,059
Turley, Melissa D, court clerk III, $27,660
Turner, Bradley A, juvenile officer III, $41,940
Turner, Carol B, court clerk III, $32,628
Turner, Kristin L, court clerk II, $25,404
Turner, Maria L, court clerk II, $18,413
Turner, Phillip E, detention juvenile officer I, $33,180
Turner, Sarah J, court clerk II, $12,702
Turner, Tasha D, court clerk II, $28,452
Turner, Tonya L, court clerk I, $22,536
Twyman, Amy J, court reporter, $57,178
Tyler, Judy, unit manager I, $41,172
Tyne, Rena S, court reporter, $57,178
Tyre, Wanda M, circuit clerk, $55,639
Uhlenbrock, Paige T, court clerk II, $25,404
Uhlich, Rebecca G, court clerk II, $20,323
Ulen, Sara L, juvenile officer II, $36,888
Underwood, Ashley N, court clerk III, $27,660
Underwood, Joshua D, associate circuit judge, $135,059
Underwood, Kathy D, temporary rep, $15.00/hr
Unnewehr, Brenda M, court clerk II, $25,404
Unverferth, Therese M, court clerk IV, $36,204
Urban, Kim R, court clerk III, $27,660
Ursery, Anna M, court clerk II, $33,036
Ussery, Angela K, juvenile officer II, $36,204
Vaira, Kevin, detention aide I, $25,404
Valbracht, James P, associate circuit judge, $135,059
Vallely, Stephanie L, court clerk II, $29,496
Valli, Jacqueline A, court clerk III, $27,660
Van Amburg, James W, circuit judge, $146,804
Van Doren, Tina M, court clerk II, $29,904
Vandeloecht, Andrea R, associate circuit judge, $135,059
Vander Veen, Kristine A, court clerk V, $34,356
Vanderhoof, Sheryl L, court clerk II, $25,404
Vandeven, Brenda J, circuit clerk, $55,639
Vandevender, Michelle, court clerk II, $25,404
Vandike, Cynthia A, secretary to presiding judge, $39,624
Vanlanker, Judy L, court clerk II, $25,404
Vanmatre, Traci L, court clerk IV, $30,420
Vannoy, Robin R, circuit judge, $146,804
Vanwyk, Shirley A, court clerk II, $25,404
Vaughn, Iva G, court clerk II, $25,824
Veach, Taylor J, detention aide I, $25,032
Veenstra, Lynette B, associate circuit judge, $135,059
Velazquez, Maribel, court clerk II, $25,404
Vernon, Jamie R, court clerk II, $25,404
Vernon, Jennifer L, court program specialist I, $28,104
Verrone, Erin N, court clerk III, $27,660
Vesser, Melissa S, juvenile officer I, $32,628
Vestal, Stephanie D, court clerk IV, $29,976
Vetter, Lisa A, secretary to presiding judge, $37,548
Villa, Melissa A, court clerk II, $25,404
Vince, Ellen L, court reporter, $57,178
Vincent, David L, circuit judge, $146,804
Vineyard, Ashleigh E, court clerk II, $25,404
Viox, Cody L, court clerk III, $27,228
Vitt, Gretchen L, court clerk III, $30,984
Vize, Karen M, court clerk III, $27,660
Vize, Mark R, court clerk IV, $30,420
Voelker, Reta F, court clerk II, $29,412
Volmert, Peggy, temporary rep, $13.00/hr
Vorhees, Frank G, juvenile officer I, $33,180
Vorhies, Marilyn K, court clerk III, $32,052
Vujnich, Timothy N, legal counsel, $56,520
Wade, Julie E, court clerk II, $25,824
Wagner, Diane E, court clerk II, $25,404
Wagner, Dorothy L, court clerk II, $25,404
Wagner, Mandi R, court clerk II, $27,228
Wagner, Raymond M, circuit judge, $146,804
Walden, Candace S, court clerk III, $31,512
Walden, Kevin L, associate circuit judge, $135,059
Walden, Tammy L, juvenile officer VI, $63,996
Walk, Robin K, court program specialist I, $33,744
Walker, Ashlee R, court clerk II, $25,032

Walker, David R, court clerk III, $27,660
Walker, Deborah S, court clerk III, $29,004
Walker, Emilee R, court clerk II, $25,032
Walker, Kristen A, juvenile officer I, $33,180
Walker, Michele L, court clerk II, $25,032
Walker, Roxane, court clerk II, $26,232
Walker, Ryan E, juvenile officer II, $36,888
Walker, Stephanie R, court clerk II, $25,404
Wallace, Barbara W, circuit judge, $146,804
Wallace, Karen I, court clerk II, $22,229
Wallace, Kelly L, court clerk II, $25,404
Waller, Daniel R, juvenile officer II, $36,888
Waller, Marjorie M, court clerk II, $25,824
Walls, Deborah S, court clerk V, $37,548
Walsh, Joseph L, circuit judge, $146,804
Walters, Douglas M, court clerk II, $25,404
Walters, Julie M, court clerk II, $25,404
Walters-Seamon, Jamie L, secretary I, $23,816
Walther, Jana M, court clerk II, $25,404
Walton, Dianna L, court clerk III, $34,356
Wansing, Michelle L, court clerk II, $19,368
Ward, Connie S, court clerk III, $29,004
Ward, Erin R, temporary help, $10.00/hr
Ward, Jamie L, court clerk II, $25,404
Ward, Katherine E, temporary help, $10.00/hr
Ward, Kelly M, court clerk II, $25,404
Ward, Robert A, deputy probate commissioner, $133,716
Ward, Sherre N, court clerk II, $25,824
Wardlow, Shannan N, temporary help, $10.00/hr
Ware, Jaisha R, detention aide I, $25,404
Warner, Amy L, juvenile officer II, $36,888
Warner, Janet L, juvenile officer, $47,624
Warner, John D, circuit judge, $146,804
Warren, Melissa S, secretary to presiding judge, $33,744
Warren, Phillip R, juvenile officer III, $40,380
Washburn, Jenifer S, secretary II, $27,228
Washington, Allicia, court clerk V, $36,204
Waterman, Judy A, temporary rep, $14.61/hr
Waterworth, Gwendolyn F, court program specialist II, $32,052
Watkins, Anita, circuit clerk, $55,639
Watkins, Bundini C, juvenile officer II, $36,888
Watkins, Nancy M, associate circuit judge, $135,059
Watral, Janet M, court clerk II, $25,824
Watson, Corissa T, court clerk III, $27,660
Watson, Geneva P, temporary help, $10.00/hr
Watson, Jennifer L, court program specialist II, $32,052
Watson, Mary M, court clerk II, $14,226
Watson, Pamela J, court clerk II, $25,824
Watts, Mary J, court clerk III, $28,104
Waugh, Gari A, court clerk II, $25,032
Weatherholt, Heather L, temporary help, $10.00/hr
Weatherspoon, Melanie N, court clerk II, $25,404
Weaver, Brittany N, temporary help, $10.00/hr
Weaver, Julie M, secretary I, $25,404
Webb, Barbara, court clerk II, $26,232
Webb, Dawn A, court clerk IV, $30,420
Webb, Stanley R, juvenile officer II, $36,888
Webb-Cline, Kayla S, court clerk II, $18,774
Weber, Janice L, juvenile officer III, $41,172
Webery, Erin K, court clerk II, $25,404
Weeks, Cynthia A, circuit clerk, $55,639
Weeks, Ryan L, temporary help, $10.00/hr
Wehmeier, Debbie L, court clerk IV, $35,568
Wehmeir, Stephanie L, juvenile officer II, $36,204
Weible, Vicki J, circuit clerk, $70,437
Weidman, Michele L, temporary help, $9.00/hr
Weinhold, Madison A, temporary help, $10.00/hr
Weir, Mary F, associate circuit judge, $135,059
Weis, Robert C, probate commissioner, $145,343
Weiskopf, Judy A, court clerk II, $25,824
Weiss, Christopher M, temporary help, $9.50/hr
Weiss, Katie D, court clerk II, $25,404
Weissmueller, Nancy J, court clerk V, $34,356
Weisz, Linda L, secretary I, $25,824
Welch, Nina M, court clerk III, $30,984
Weller, O W, marshal, $46,539
Wells, Carrie K, court clerk II, $25,404
Wells, Kellie L, juvenile officer II, $40,380
Werkowitch, Angela E, unit manager I, $53,208
Wertenberger, Prentha L, court clerk II, $25,404
Wesley, Angela M, temporary help, $10.00/hr
Wesley, Joy D, secretary I, $26,652
Wessell, Elizabeth S, court clerk V, $39,624

West, Beth S, court clerk V, $33,744
West, Carolyn F, court clerk II, $25,404
West, Sandra M, associate circuit judge, $135,059
Wester, Catherine M, court clerk II, $25,824
Westhoff, Fred L, associate circuit judge, $135,059
Weston, Camille, court clerk II, $25,404
Wexler Horn, Wendy L, circuit judge, $146,804
Wheeler, Cindy L, court clerk III, $27,660
Wheeler, Heather D, circuit clerk, $55,639
Wheeler, Polly A, court clerk II, $22,344
Whitaker, Kimberly A, secretary to presiding judge, $33,180
Whitby, Rufie, court clerk III, $28,536
White, Courtney S, temporary help, $10.00/hr
White, Franchesca N, temporary help, $10.00/hr
White, Geri M, court clerk II, $25,404
White, Laura L, court clerk II, $25,404
White, Ronald D, associate circuit judge, $135,059
White, Sammye G, circuit clerk, $55,639
White, Tracy M, court clerk II, $25,404
White, Victoria A, court clerk II, $19,053
Whitehead, Gayle L, court clerk III, $27,228
Whiteside, Courtney L, court clerk III, $27,660
Whitledge, Katina B, court clerk II, $25,404
Whitsell, Julie M, circuit clerk, $55,639
Whittington, Carolyn C, circuit judge, $146,804
Wholf, Anna, court clerk IV, $29,976
Whorlow, Karri M, court reporter, $57,178
Whorton, Rhonda I, temporary help, $11.00/hr
Wibbenmeyer, Patti K, circuit clerk, $74,653
Wiebe, Stacie M, court clerk II, $25,404
Wieman, Meagan D, court clerk II, $25,404
Wiese, Terry W, family court commissioner, $133,716
Wikowsky, Deborah S, court clerk II, $25,404
Wilburn, Michele L, court clerk II, $25,404
Wilcoxson, Frankie L, court clerk II, $25,404
Wilcoxson, Melody R, secretary to presiding judge, $33,744
Wiles, Truman L, associate circuit judge, $135,059
Wilkerson, Jeremy D, court clerk II, $25,404
Wilkerson, Joann, court clerk II, $25,824
Wilkins, Kenneth M, court clerk V, $33,744
Wilkins, Robert G, circuit judge, $146,804
Wille, Danny L, court clerk II, $28,452
Williams, Beryl L, secretary to presiding judge, $33,180
Williams, Billy R, juvenile officer I, $32,628
Williams, Carrie A, court clerk II, $29,412
Williams, Danielle J, court clerk II, $25,032
Williams, Glenna D, court clerk II, $26,652
Williams, Jessica E, court clerk II, $25,032
Williams, Johnny C, circuit clerk, $55,639
Williams, Kelly R, court clerk II, $25,404
Williams, Laura J, court clerk II, $15,242
Williams, Lesley G, temporary help, $10.00/hr
Williams, Madeliene L, court clerk II, $25,824
Williams, Mary J, court clerk II, $29,904
Williams, Melanie K, court reporter, $57,178
Williams, Melany D, circuit clerk, $55,639
Williams, Mildred S, court clerk III, $28,536
Williams, Rita A, court clerk III, $31,512
Williams, Rosemary, court clerk III, $27,660
Williams, Ryan K, juvenile officer III, $41,172
Williams, Stacy D, court clerk II, $25,404
Williams, Stanley D, associate circuit judge, $135,059
Williams, Swanetta R, unit manager I, $40,380
Williams, Tamika R, court clerk II, $25,404
Williams, Tony W, associate circuit judge, $135,059
Willis, Charmaine A, court clerk II, $25,032
Willis, Lucinda A, court clerk V, $34,356
Willis, Shelley R, court clerk II, $28,045
Wills-Christensen, Brenda, court reporter, $57,178
Wilmes, Sandra A, court clerk III, $32,628
Wilmot, Barbara E, court clerk II, $25,404
Wilroy, Monty J, detention aide II, $27,660
Wilson, Elaine M, circuit clerk, $55,639
Wilson, James L, detention aide I, $25,404
Wilson, Keenan R, temporary help, $10.00/hr
Wilson, Keyanna M, court clerk III, $27,660
Wilson, Linda M, court reporter, $57,178
Wilson, Michael P, associate circuit judge, $135,059
Wilson, Tammy, secretary I, $22,229
Wilson, Teresa R, court clerk II, $25,404
Wilson, Timothy J, circuit judge, $146,804
Winchester, William H, associate circuit judge, $135,059
Winckel, Pamela D, court clerk II, $30,924

Winfield, Shirley A, court clerk II, $25,404
Winfrey, Larry W, associate circuit judge, $135,059
Winger, Cathlene L, legal counsel, $54,288
Wise, Ladawn D, court clerk II, $25,824
Wise, Ora J, temporary help, $10.00/hr
Wiswall, Gina M, court clerk II, $15,960
Wolf, Angela M, court clerk II, $25,404
Wolf, Darlene M, court clerk III, $30,984
Wolo, Christina I, detention aide II, $27,228
Wood, Gael D, circuit judge, $146,804
Wood, Laurie L, treatment court adminstr II, $46,932
Wood, Pamela A, court clerk III, $27,660
Woodiest, Rochelle M, drug court commissioner, $133,716
Woodrum, Charlotte, temporary rep, $14.63/hr
Woods, Julie A, court clerk IV, $32,052
Woods, Rita M, court clerk III, $31,512
Wooldridge, Becki L, temporary help, $7.75/hr
Wright, Brenda L, circuit clerk, $55,639
Wright, Carmelita, detention aide II, $27,660
Wright, Christopher A, detention aide I, $12,698
Wright, Matthew C, juvenile officer II, $36,204
Wright, Michael S, associate circuit judge, $135,059
Wucher, Sally J, temporary help, $15.00/hr
Wyatt, Alaina N, court clerk II, $25,404
Wyatt, Kelsey E, court clerk II, $25,404
Wycoff, Patricia A, court clerk II, $25,404
Wylie, Glenda K, court reporter, $57,178
Wyman, Beth M, circuit clerk, $70,437
Yaeger, William S, temporary help, $10.00/hr
Yancey, Paula F, circuit clerk, $55,639
Yates, Christina L, court reporter, $57,178
Yeckel, Calvin, court clerk III, $27,660
Yergin, Mareike K, juvenile officer I, $33,180
Yonko, Sarah D, court clerk II, $25,404
York, Kimberly A, circuit clerk, $70,437
Young, Karmen M, detention aide I, $12,511
Young, Mark L, computer info tech III, $44,304
Young, Michael B, court clerk III, $30,984
Young, Michele L, detention aide I, $12,511
Young, Steven N, court clerk II, $25,032
Youngs, James D, circuit judge, $146,804
Yount, Cynthia L, court clerk III, $28,045
Yount, Laura A, court clerk III, $30,420
Yust, Alicia S, court clerk II, $25,404
Yust, Marty J, juvenile officer IV, $46,932
Zajdel, Michael H, court reporter, $57,178
Zakibe, Joyce I, court clerk III, $27,660
Zelle, Marsha M, court clerk III, $27,660
Zera, Mark J, unit manager I, $41,172
Zerr, Richard K, circuit judge, $146,804
Ziebarth, Denice M, court clerk II, $25,404

Commission on Retirement, Removal and Discipline of Judges

2190 Mason Rd., Ste. 201, St. Louis 63131

Huck, Jincey, administrative secretary, $22,578
Pettibone, Margaret R, administrative secretary, $22,578
Smith, James M, commission counsel, $145,343
Wise, Richard G, investigator, $21.51/hr

State Public Defender Commission

321 E Capitol Ave., Jefferson City 65101

Barrett, Michael K, dir, $145,343
Abeln, Rebecca M, asst pub defender, $62,664
Alladina, Natasha, asst pub defender, $46,068
Allen, Arthur E, asst pub defender, $63,996
Allen, Kathleen, sec, $29,496
Allen, Linda J, investigator, $37,548
Allen-Kemp, Crystal D, sec, $29,496
Altman, Amanda L, asst pub defender, $62,664
Anderson, Leslie J, asst pub defender, $46,068
Anderson, Michael W, asst pub defender, $38,928
Anderson, Nathaniel D, asst pub defender, $62,664
Annel, Jamie L, sec, $14,052
Anthony, Donna K, dist defender, $72,768
Aplin, Sarah J, asst pub defender, $51,096
Archer, Christine E, asst pub defender, $38,928

Archey, Jane E, mitigation spec, $40,380
Arens, Matthew J, asst pub defender, $46,068
Armfield, Zachary H, asst pub defender, $46,068
Ashley, Denise A, sec, $34,944
Assareh, Alexandria S, asst pub defender, $46,068
Aswad, Yazen, comp info spec, $36,204
Atkinson, Nathan M, asst pub defender, $46,068
Austermann, Patrick R, asst pub defender, $46,068
Bachman, Joshua C, asst pub defender, $46,068
Bagby, Everetta S, sec, $23,160
Bailey, Jonathan D, asst pub defender, $46,068
Bailey, Thomas J, asst pub defender, $51,096
Banks, Charles J, asst pub defender, $62,664
Bargeon, Travis C, asst pub defender, $46,068
Barron, Neil M, asst pub defender, $46,068
Bates, Nicholas A, asst pub defender, $38,928
Beesley, Megan A, asst pub defender, $51,096
Belfield, Tammy D, investigator, $37,548
Bell, Matthew J, asst pub defender, $38,928
Belts, Christopher P, asst pub defender, $51,096
Berrigan, Patrick J, asst pub defender, $62,664
Berry, Milan C, asst pub defender, $51,096
Bissenden, Elizabeth J, sec, $25,824
Blair, Ladonna M, investigator, $37,548
Blair, Norris G, investigator, $37,548
Blau, Ellen A, div dir, $97,236
Bledsoe, Sharlia E, sec, $22,536
Blue, Monette L, sec, $28,104
Boone Conley, Ella K, dist defender, $71,100
Booth, Dawn P, sec, $25,032
Booth, Jennifer L, asst pub defender, $62,664
Borgmeyer, David B, asst pub defender, $46,068
Bradley, Erin C, asst pub defender, $38,928
Braschler, Dusti L, investigator, $29,976
Brashears, Cynthia D, prog technician, $37,548
Brayer, Patrick C, asst pub defender, $69,612
Bremner, Paige N, asst pub defender, $51,096
Brewer, Maurice E, asst pub defender, $38,928
Brotherton, Ida F, sec, $28,104
Brown, Ara N, asst pub defender, $68,160
Brown, Jonathan J, investigator, $29,976
Brown, Kathleen H, asst pub defender, $66,720
Brown, Tracy, asst pub defender, $63,996
Bryant, David L, asst pub defender, $62,664
Buckmaster, Kevin D, investigator, $37,548
Buffaloe, Samuel E, asst pub defender, $46,068
Bullard, Stephanie J, asst pub defender, $51,096
Burnham, Emily D, mitigation spec, $37,548
Bushong, Linde L, sec, $30,984
Bustamante, Christine M, sec, $28,104
Byers, Timothy R, investigator, $37,548
Byrnes, Sylvia K, asst pub defender, $68,160
Cadigan, Kathleen M, sec, $26,232
Caldwell, Sandy S, sec, $31,512
Caldwell, Virginia H, sec, $25,824
Campbell, Beverly A, sec, $28,104
Canady, Shariece L, asst pub defender, $46,068
Cannon, Homer S, investigator, $37,548
Cantoni, Jordan M, asst pub defender, $46,068
Cardarella, Anthony C, dist defender, $72,768
Carlson, Tamara D, asst pub defender, $51,096
Carson, Arryn A, asst pub defender, $38,928
Carter, Pete E, asst pub defender, $68,160
Carter, Sharon R, sec, $29,496
Cartwright, Adam W, asst pub defender, $38,928
Carver, Justin T, dist defender, $71,100
Cassity, Heather L, sec, $28,104
Catlett, Donald L, dist defender, $72,768
Chapman-Kramer, William K, asst pub defender, $46,068
Chase, Kevin F, asst pub defender, $51,096
Chastain, Charlton C, asst pub defender, $62,664
Chigurupati, Srikant B, asst pub defender, $62,664
Christensen, Sara H, asst pub defender, $38,928
Clack, Paula, sec, $25,824
Clay, Amy M, asst pub defender, $62,664
Clifton, Rakefet L, investigator, $30,984
Clinton, Theresa S, investigator, $30,984
Colby, Juliane L, mitigation spec, $36,204
Collie, Crystal N, sec, $28,104
Collier, Joseph O, asst pub defender, $62,664
Commean, Amy L, asst pub defender, $62,664
Comstock, Karie E, dist defender, $71,100
Conley, Sandra M, sec, $30,384

Cook, Robert C, asst pub defender, $46,068
Corrado, Danielle K, prog mgr, $42,708
Coulter, Daniel, asst pub defender, $46,068
Counts, Robert, investigator, $37,548
Coyle, Tyler P, asst pub defender, $46,068
Crady, Lynnette N, sec, $29,412
Crane, Tara R, dist defender, $71,100
Crawford, Cynthia R, sec, $28,104
Creech, Angela S, sec, $23,160
Crick, Kirby A, asst pub defender, $38,928
Crocco, Thomas E, dist defender, $71,100
Crowell, Matthew D, asst pub defender, $71,100
Crowley, Bryce C, asst pub defender, $46,068
Davidson, Andrea J, asst pub defender, $46,068
Davidson, Anthony T, asst pub defender, $46,068
Davidson, Michelle K, dist defender, $71,100
Davis, Amy K, asst pub defender, $51,096
Davis, Christopher L, dist defender, $71,100
Davis, Deanna M, sec, $25,032
Davolt, Paul A, asst pub defender, $46,068
De Loyola, Damien S, asst pub defender, $46,068
Defilippo, Laura J, sec, $23,160
Degeorge, Susan A, asst pub defender, $62,664
Delleville, Bryan M, asst pub defender, $62,664
Demoss, Philip F, asst pub defender, $62,664
Denzel, Kent, asst pub defender, $63,996
Derryberry, Heidi R, investigator, $37,548
Deyoung, Judith L, sec, $11,580
Diemler, Janet S, investigator, $38,232
Dillard, Tisha K, paralegal, $30,984
Divine, Lorrie J, sec, $25,824
Dixon, Dawn D, sec, $25,824
Donnelly, Brice J, asst pub defender, $62,664
Donnelly, Kaitlynn M, asst pub defender, $38,928
Donohue, Joseph M, sec, $26,232
Donovan, Heather E, asst pub defender, $62,664
Douglas, Erin K, asst pub defender, $38,928
Douglas, Gabriel M, investigator, $37,548
Dowdy, Sherry M, investigator, $30,984
Dryden, Cynthia A, asst pub defender, $63,996
Duchscherer, Paul R, asst pub defender, $62,664
Duckering, Kellie L, asst pub defender, $51,096
Dudley, Angela R, asst pub defender, $46,068
Dujakovich, Heather M, sec, $26,232
Duncan, Jane C, prog mgr, $83,076
Dunn, Jane E, asst pub defender, $63,996
Dunnett, Robbe A, investigator, $40,380
Dutton, Jennifer L, sec, $26,232
Dyer, Roger W, asst pub defender, $46,068
Dysart, Trudy S, temp employee, $13.74/hr
Eddings, Betty L, sec, $31,512
Egan, James C, asst pub defender, $62,664
Eichler, Cinda, asst pub defender, $63,996
Eliason, Erika R, asst pub defender, $51,096
Elliston, Rebecca L, asst pub defender, $62,664
Elmer, Joel R, div dir, $120,192
Emmons, Jason M, asst pub defender, $46,068
Engelman, Caroline M, asst pub defender, $38,928
Estes, Jeffrey M, asst pub defender, $65,364
Eston, Christina N, investigator, $30,984
Euler, Richard A, asst pub defender, $62,664
Evans, Mark, asst pub defender, $63,996
Faerber, Amanda P, asst pub defender, $51,096
Feldman-Gary, Gara, asst pub defender, $46,068
Fenstermacher, Eric P, asst pub defender, $46,068
Fisk, Meagan L, sec, $23,160
Fleming, Robert L, asst pub defender, $65,364
Florez, Rita E, asst pub defender, $46,068
Flottman, Ellen H, dist defender, $71,208
Fogelberg, Julia C, asst pub defender, $46,068
Forneris, Timothy J, asst pub defender, $62,664
Fountain, Ronald, sec, $28,536
Foust, Reba E, sec, $25,824
Fox, Erica N, asst pub defender, $46,068
Fox, Mary D, dist defender, $84,540
Franklin-McMurry, Nike R, sec, $26,652
Friend, Robin R, sec, $26,232
Fry, Angela W, asst pub defender, $51,096
Fry, Tina M, sec, $22,536
Frye, Laura E, sec, $26,232
Garrison, Wendy E, asst pub defender, $51,096
Gass, Matthew T, asst pub defender, $38,928
Gau, Kevin B, asst pub defender, $62,664

Glenn, Sandra J, sec, $25,824
Goldberg, Robyn D, asst pub defender, $46,068
Gonzalez, Susana, sec, $25,824
Goodwin, Courtney G, dist defender, $71,100
Gordon, Sara E, asst pub defender, $51,096
Gotviagehya, Renee, asst pub defender, $62,664
Gray, James P, asst pub defender, $51,096
Gregg, Tiffany D, asst pub defender, $51,096
Griego, Kristen R, sec, $28,104
Griffith, Holly, asst pub defender, $62,664
Grimes, Quinn L, asst pub defender, $65,364
Grogan, Paddy L, sec, $25,824
Grothoff, Mark, asst pub defender, $62,664
Guemmer, Elizabeth A, paralegal, $37,548
Guinn, Edward L, dist defender, $71,100
Gunther, David M, investigator, $37,548
Hackathorn, Rodney, dist defender, $71,100
Hall, Gina L, prog mgr, $62,628
Hall, Leah R, investigator, $29,976
Hanson, Bethany R, asst pub defender, $46,068
Harding, Kenton D, asst pub defender, $38,928
Harness, Courtney M, asst pub defender, $62,664
Harnick, Daniel M, asst pub defender, $38,928
Harris, Chelsea L, asst pub defender, $46,068
Harris, Edna, sec, $25,824
Harris, Stephen J, dist defender, $77,556
Harvey, Maleaner R, asst pub defender, $62,664
Hatcher, John D, asst pub defender, $46,068
Hathaway, Jessica M, asst pub defender, $62,664
Hatley, Christopher S, asst pub defender, $68,160
Hawkins, Lareta C, sec, $26,232
Hayes, James R, asst pub defender, $46,068
Hayes, Kathryn E, asst pub defender, $46,068
Hays, Jeffrey A, comp info spec, $57,744
Hazama-Salerno, Yuko, sec, $25,404
Hazel, Leslie N, asst pub defender, $46,068
Heineman, Kenneth R, asst pub defender, $51,096
Hendershott, Lee M, asst pub defender, $46,068
Henry, Teresa A, sec, $28,104
Hentges, Andrew V, temp employee, $10.00/hr
Hernandez, Jennifer L, temp employee, $10.00/hr
Hesemann, Timothy D, asst pub defender, $38,928
Hicks, Barbara A, sec, $28,104
Hinkebein, Karl W, asst pub defender, $62,664
Hinkl, Michelle L, asst pub defender, $46,068
Hirth, Charles E, asst pub defender, $51,096
Hogan, Susan L, dist defender, $79,296
Holden, Donna L, dist defender, $62,664
Holder, Kathy L, sec, $28,104
Holzknecht, Beth, investigator, $40,380
Honse, Timothy E, asst pub defender, $38,928
Hoopes, Jodi L, sec, $28,104
Hoover, Jonathan S, asst pub defender, $62,664
Horneyer, Brian L, asst pub defender, $51,096
Hoskins, Charles D, asst pub defender, $68,160
Houck, Timothy J, asst pub defender, $51,096
Howsman, Jenni L, asst pub defender, $38,928
Hubbard, Latia R, asst pub defender, $46,068
Huckeby, Matthew W, asst pub defender, $51,096
Hudson, Lorrie A, investigator, $37,548
Huett, Elizabeth D, sec, $30,984
Hull, Natalie T, asst pub defender, $46,068
Hunt, Cynthia M, sec, $29,976
Hunt, Darla J, sec, $31,512
Hunt, Peggy J, sec, $25,824
Hunter, Donna M, sec, $28,104
Hustead, Michael A, asst pub defender, $46,068
Jackson, Christina D, sec, $25,824
Jackson, Gerald M, asst pub defender, $38,928
Jackson, Michelle D, sec, $28,104
Jackson, Steven B, investigator, $37,548
Jacobs, Michael, asst pub defender, $46,068
Jacquinot, Thomas, dist defender, $71,100
James, Jeanne M, investigator, $30,984
Jenkins, Harry M, asst pub defender, $51,096
Jesionowski, Leia E, sec, $25,824
Jimenez-mejia, Jacqueline V, asst pub defender, $46,068
Johnson, Amy E, sec, $28,104
Johnson, Anna W, asst pub defender, $46,068
Johnson, Danisha, sec, $25,032
Johnson, Janthony L, comp info spec, $60,120
Johnson, Laura L, asst pub defender, $46,068
Johnson, Sarah K, asst pub defender, $62,664

Johnson, Travis G, investigator, $29,976
Johnston, Charity R, investigator, $30,984
Johnston, Craig A, asst pub defender, $69,612
Johnston, Margaret M, asst pub defender, $62,664
Jones, Christina J, sec, $26,232
Jones, Katrina A, asst pub defender, $62,664
Jones, Leinati D, sec, $26,232
Jones, Teah B, investigator, $37,548
Kagay, Anthony M, asst pub defender, $46,068
Kaiser, Bret C, asst pub defender, $51,096
Kell, Shawn M, investigator, $37,548
Kelley, Lisa, sec, $28,104
Kellogg, Steven E, asst pub defender, $46,068
Kelly, Linda M, sec, $25,824
Kemp, Kimberly T, sec, $25,824
Kennedy, Colter, asst pub defender, $38,928
Kenyon, David J, asst pub defender, $65,364
Kerry, Beth A, asst pub defender, $69,612
King, Richard T, asst pub defender, $38,928
Kirsch, Thomas J, asst pub defender, $38,928
Klingbeil, Karen M, asst pub defender, $62,664
Knapp, Patrick W, investigator, $39,624
Koch, Rosalynn V, asst pub defender, $32,682
Koehler, Brent H, paralegal, $29,976
Kollmeyer, Kimberly R, asst pub defender, $46,068
Kraft, Karen E, div dir, $103,296
Krehmeyer, Joanne M, prog technician, $41,172
Krehmeyer, John R, asst pub defender, $65,364
Kroeger, Richard L, asst pub defender, $68,160
Kuehl, Sandra K, sec, $28,104
Kutz, Patrick R, asst pub defender, $46,068
Ladesh, Katherine E, asst pub defender, $71,208
Lambert, Roberta R, sec, $25,032
Lammert, Anna M, asst pub defender, $46,068
Lampley, Janise N, asst pub defender, $46,068
Lance, Horton J, asst pub defender, $69,612
Lance, Rebecca A, sec, $29,496
Lawrence, Samuel D, asst pub defender, $46,068
Lear, Kathleen L, prog mgr, $87,012
Leasure, Roy, investigator, $37,548
Lee, Kathleen S, prog technician, $37,548
Leftwich, Valerie S, asst pub defender, $62,664
Leggette, Tricia L, sec, $26,232
Lenyo, Mitchell E, asst pub defender, $38,928
Leuty, Tiffany M, asst pub defender, $62,664
Lewis, George R, sec, $25,824
Lewis, Knesha D, sec, $25,824
Lewis, Steven E, asst pub defender, $62,664
Lindewirth, Tiffany R, investigator, $30,984
Liszewski, Theodore E, asst pub defender, $62,664
Livingston, Neal C, investigator, $37,548
Llewellyn, Annette S, asst pub defender, $62,664
Locascio, Alec J, asst pub defender, $38,928
Locke, Kevin R, dist defender, $71,100
Lorenz, Kevin J, asst pub defender, $51,096
Lovelace, Gregory, mitigation spec, $40,380
Lowe, Amy E, asst pub defender, $51,096
Lowe, Craig E, asst pub defender, $46,068
Lowe, Lisa R, investigator, $37,548
Lowes, Susan J, sec, $30,420
Lucy, Daniel S, asst pub defender, $38,928
Lueken, Lori A, sec, $25,404
Lundt, Robert W, asst pub defender, $66,720
Lynxwiler, Steven F, dist defender, $71,100
Maguire, Kathleen D, asst pub defender, $38,928
Mahaffey, Matthew J, asst pub defender, $51,096
Mahon, Michael P, asst pub defender, $62,664
Mallonee, Aaron M, asst pub defender, $46,068
Malone, Cynthia J, mitigation spec, $40,380
Malugen, Ginia A, sec, $25,032
Maples, Larry, asst pub defender, $77,556
Marbough, Joy C, investigator, $37,548
Markin, Shawn R, asst pub defender, $62,664
Marsh, William T, asst pub defender, $62,664
Marshall, Thomas E, asst pub defender, $62,664
Martin, Jeffrey M, dist defender, $71,208
Martin, Laura G, asst pub defender, $71,100
Martin, Ryan A, asst pub defender, $68,160
Martin, Shara A, asst pub defender, $65,364
Martinez-Reyes, Jesus A, asst pub defender, $38,928
Matheson, Janeal, asst pub defender, $62,664
Mattox-Graham, Kimberly L, investigator, $30,984
McCallon, Deena L, sec, $23,160

McCarthy, Susan A, asst pub defender, $62,664
McCrady, Danielle L, investigator, $29,976
McDonnell, Nina M, sec, $25,404
McFarland, Debra L, paralegal, $18,774
McGee, Lisa D, sec, $33,744
McGinnis, Patricia A, asst pub defender, $62,664
McGowan, Andrew C, investigator, $30,984
McGuire, Jill M, sec, $28,104
McMahon, Shiante, asst pub defender, $38,928
McMurtrey, Terri M, investigator, $37,548
McRell, Katherine M, asst pub defender, $46,068
Mead, Andrew B, asst pub defender, $46,068
Meeker, Brett S, asst pub defender, $62,664
Megee, Jennifer R, sec, $26,232
Megerman, Alice K, asst pub defender, $62,664
Megerman, Joseph, asst pub defender, $68,160
Mermelstein, John G, div dir, $97,236
Merryman, Matthew T, asst pub defender, $46,068
Mettler, Morris W, asst pub defender, $62,664
Miller, Kelly L, dist defender, $71,100
Miller, Marshall A, asst pub defender, $62,664
Miller, Matthew R, asst pub defender, $46,068
Miller, Serena D, investigator, $28,161
Miller, Tami K, mitigation spec, $42,708
Milligan, Erin E, asst pub defender, $51,096
Miner, Amanda D, sec, $23,160
Mitchell, Chelsea R, asst pub defender, $51,096
Mitchell, Jana K, sec, $23,160
Mitchell, Max E, dist defender, $71,100
Moench, Anna C, asst pub defender, $46,068
Moore, Mary L, sec, $29,976
Moreland, Charles D, asst pub defender, $71,208
Morrison, John M, asst pub defender, $62,664
Moser, Gregory E, asst pub defender, $46,068
Mueller, Matthew G, asst pub defender, $46,068
Mullen, John, comp info spec, $63,996
Munday, Leon, div dir, $96,732
Musgrave, Pamela C, dist defender, $71,100
Napier, Norman C, asst pub defender, $51,096
Neighbors, Ruth E, dist defender, $84,540
Nilson, Jeffrey R, asst pub defender, $51,096
Noble, Cathy L, asst pub defender, $62,664
Nolan, Patrick M, asst pub defender, $38,928
Odorizzi, Diane M, sec, $25,404
O'hara, Deanna I, temp employee, $15.26/hr
Oliver, Alaina G, paralegal, $37,548
Olson, Kristina S, dist defender, $71,100
Oppelt, Charles G, asst pub defender, $62,664
Overbey, Tricia D, sec, $28,104
Pak, Bill, asst pub defender, $38,928
Parks, Heidi L, investigator, $30,984
Pasley, Devon S, asst pub defender, $51,096
Patterson, Stacy L, asst pub defender, $62,664
Payne, Kimberly A, paralegal, $37,548
Payne, Steven M, asst pub defender, $38,928
Payne, Yolanda, sec, $30,384
Pennant, Kyle K, sec, $12,912
Percival, Rosemary E, asst pub defender, $63,996
Perry, Dwayne F, dist defender, $71,208
Peter, Joshuah W, asst pub defender, $62,664
Peterson, Thomas D, asst pub defender, $38,928
Petesch, Margaret A, sec, $23,160
Phoenix, Lindsey N, asst pub defender, $51,096
Piatt, Christopher N, asst pub defender, $46,068
Picker, Chad T, asst pub defender, $62,664
Pike, Christopher V, comp info spec, $60,120
Pilkington, Jeremy L, asst pub defender, $51,096
Plank, Marsha, sec, $42,708
Polak, Colleen M, asst pub defender, $51,096
Ponce, Lindsay A, asst pub defender, $46,068
Ponder, Virginia J, comp info spec, $22,578
Porter, Jill S, asst pub defender, $62,664
Preddy, Lisa, dist defender, $71,208
Prenger, Myrna A, investigator, $38,232
Prenger, Susan A, sec, $12,912
Price, Tamara J, prog technician, $30,984
Pruneau, Tammy A, sec, $28,104
Puhlman, Julie C, asst pub defender, $46,068
Puhr, Stephanie N, asst pub defender, $51,096
Pyles, Kimberly M, investigator, $37,548
Queener, Emmett D, asst pub defender, $65,364
Radke, Daniel L, asst pub defender, $46,068
Randall, Sean P, asst pub defender, $46,068

Ranz, Stephen P, asst pub defender, $46,068
Rasnic, Melinda D, sec, $25,824
Regenbogen, Julie E, asst pub defender, $38,928
Reinagel, Scott T, asst pub defender, $51,096
Reiter, Warren A, asst pub defender, $62,664
Reuscher, Deborah L, investigator, $37,548
Reynolds, Stephen P, asst pub defender, $72,768
Rhodes, Leslie A, sec, $25,824
Rich, Daren C, asst pub defender, $38,928
Richardson, Jennifer A, asst pub defender, $62,664
Rinne, Susan R, dist defender, $71,100
Ripplinger, Timothy J, mitigation spec, $40,380
Robinson, Gwenda R, dist defender, $71,100
Robinson, Linda L, sec, $26,232
Roe, Derek M, asst pub defender, $62,664
Rolfingsmeier, Cort A, investigator, $30,984
Roper, Dane, asst pub defender, $62,664
Roper, Sarah E, sec, $28,104
Ross, Jessica L, asst pub defender, $46,068
Rowan, David E, asst pub defender, $62,664
Rowley, Aaron J, asst pub defender, $46,068
Ruess, Geralyn R, asst pub defender, $63,996
Rundquist, Jennifer L, asst pub defender, $38,928
Russell, Ruth K, asst pub defender, $51,096
Rynard, James A, asst pub defender, $46,068
Salazar, Evelyn A, asst pub defender, $38,928
Sams, Charles A, investigator, $30,984
Sartorius, Andrew J, asst pub defender, $38,928
Satchell, Elizabeth A, asst pub defender, $46,068
Savala, Mercede D, asst pub defender, $51,096
Sawyer, Christina L, asst pub defender, $62,664
Scanlon, Philip G, asst pub defender, $38,928
Scheets, Sarah L, sec, $30,984
Schneider, Deidre, sec, $25,824
Schofield, William R, asst pub defender, $38,928
Schulze, Todd A, dist defender, $71,100
Schumaker, Tay R, asst pub defender, $46,068
Schuman, Aaron R, asst pub defender, $38,928
Semet, Molly B, sec, $26,232
Serot, Sara S, asst pub defender, $63,996
Shah, Ankoor D, asst pub defender, $46,068
Shannon, Tyra B, sec, $28,104
Shellenbergar, Jeffrey M, asst pub defender, $62,664
Shepherd, Kayla M, sec, $25,824
Skornia, Christina S, sec, $28,104
Slone, Jennifer L, asst pub defender, $68,160
Smith, Angela K, sec, $25,824
Smith, Austin J, asst pub defender, $46,068
Smith, Brian D, asst pub defender, $62,664
Smith, Connie C, sec, $28,104
Smith, David B, asst pub defender, $62,664
Smith, Douglas J, asst pub defender, $38,928
Smith, Joshua M, asst pub defender, $68,160
Smith, Lesley D, asst pub defender, $38,928
Smith, Mary J, asst pub defender, $62,664
Solomon, Garrett M, asst pub defender, $62,664
Sommerich, Sherry L, sec, $26,652
Sowash, Theresa A, sec, $28,104
Spencer, Mona K, asst pub defender, $65,364
Springer, Deborah A, sec, $25,824
Staffey, Wendi R, sec, $25,824
Stanfield, Michael A, asst pub defender, $62,664
Stanley, Kayja E, asst pub defender, $51,096
Steele, Jemia R, asst pub defender, $51,096
Steele, Robert E, asst pub defender, $63,996
Stefan, Sheryl L, prog technician, $30,984
Stephens, Thomas J, dist defender, $71,208
Stephenson, Caitlin L, asst pub defender, $51,096
Stockstill, Stacey L, investigator, $39,624
Stokely, Walter J, asst pub defender, $46,068
Strange, Sharyn L, sec, $28,104
Stroup, Lisa M, asst pub defender, $66,720
Summers, Suzanne R, sec, $28,104
Swartwood, Liesl C, sec, $25,824
Swartz, Brandon A, asst pub defender, $46,068
Swerline, Stephen C, sec, $29,976
Swift, Melinda K, div dir, $97,236
Swift, William J, asst pub defender, $68,160
Swopes, Allison J, sec, $25,032
Tatro, Angela G, asst pub defender, $46,068
Taylor, Casey A, asst pub defender, $51,096
Tharp, Stacie L, investigator, $37,548
Thies, Robert M, investigator, $40,380

Thoman, Katy M, asst pub defender, $51,096
Thomas, Mintha M, sec, $26,232
Thompson, Amy, asst pub defender, $62,664
Thompson, Edward S, asst pub defender, $62,664
Thompson, Jenean L, asst pub defender, $62,664
Thompson, Rollin G, temp employee, $10.00/hr
Thompson, Wendy E, investigator, $39,624
Tolbert, Kyle A, asst pub defender, $46,068
Tomberlin, John M, asst pub defender, $46,068
Tomlin, John M, asst pub defender, $62,664
Troeger, Melinda A, asst pub defender, $62,664
Tucka, Mary P, dist defender, $71,100
Turlington, Sharon, asst pub defender, $71,100
Turner, Victoria A, sec, $23,160
Ugarte, Rene B, asst pub defender, $38,928
Ukman, Brian M, asst pub defender, $38,928
Ulman, Marissa R, asst pub defender, $46,068
Urick, Barbara A, asst pub defender, $46,068
Van Auken, Peter N, asst pub defender, $38,928
Vanholt, Susan J, sec, $25,824
Vannoy, Deborah L, sec, $25,404
Vigil, Matt W, asst pub defender, $46,068
Vitale, Sarah E, asst pub defender, $71,100
Vodnansky, Heather L, asst pub defender, $62,664
Wagner, Jeffery L, investigator, $37,548
Walker, Tamara S, investigator, $39,624
Wall, Judson D, asst pub defender, $46,068
Wallace, Darren, dist defender, $71,100
Wallace, Lisa M, sec, $25,824
Wallis, David R, asst pub defender, $71,100
Wallis, Marilin S, sec, $28,104
Wallut, Jerald S, asst pub defender, $38,928
Waltz, Matthew R, asst pub defender, $62,664
Ward, David H, asst pub defender, $46,068
Warr, Clement D, asst pub defender, $38,928
Warren, Susan R, asst pub defender, $71,100
Watson, Karla U, sec, $30,420
Weatherman, Matthew T, asst pub defender, $46,068
Webb, Kevin W, sec, $28,104
Webber, Sue K, asst pub defender, $62,664
Welborn, Lauren K, dist defender, $71,100
Welch, Nina L, investigator, $29,976
Welk, Gretchen R, investigator, $30,984
Wenell, Kelly D, asst pub defender, $46,068
White, Ryan M, asst pub defender, $38,928
White, Theresa R, asst pub defender, $46,068
Whitener, Joseph G, asst pub defender, $46,068
Wiegert, David E, asst pub defender, $46,068
Wilcox, Lori J, sec, $26,232
Wilhite, Pamela, paralegal, $37,548
Wilkinson, Sandra M, sec, $25,404
Williams, Carla A, sec, $25,824
Williams, Kayla L, asst pub defender, $38,928
Williams, Wayne R, dist defender, $71,208
Willibey, Jean M, asst pub defender, $62,664
Willingham, Mary S, prog mgr, $80,136
Willis, Christina A, sec, $25,824
Willis, James M, asst pub defender, $38,928
Wilson, James L, asst pub defender, $62,664
Winegarner, Curtis L, asst pub defender, $62,664
Winka Nordmann, Rebecca M, asst pub defender, $51,096
Wobig, Grant W, asst pub defender, $46,068
Wolpink, Jeannette L, asst pub defender, $62,664
Wolpink, Mark A, investigator, $30,984
Wood, Deidre F, asst pub defender, $51,096
Woodard, Jeffery R, investigator, $30,984
Woolley, Brian W, asst pub defender, $51,096
Wright, Eric N, comp info spec, $29,976
Wurst, Erika F, asst pub defender, $38,928
Yankoviz, Frank T, asst pub defender, $65,364
Young, Carol A, sec, $28,104
Younker, Michael S, asst pub defender, $46,068
Zacek Smith, Amy L, investigator, $29,976
Zieba, Carol S, prog mgr, $42,708
Zimmerman, John E, asst pub defender, $38,928
Zipfel, Stephanie G, asst pub defender, $46,068
Zleit, Andrew E, asst pub defender, $62,664
Zuzul, Joseph G, dist defender, $72,768

Chapter 6: Executive Departments

Office of Administration

PO Box 809 Jefferson City 65102

Nelson, Douglas E, state dept dir, $125,712
Aardsma, Walter, info technologist IV, $52,092
Abaffe, Anthony J, maint worker II, $29,004
Abbett, Sonya M, risk mgmt tech II, $30,984
Abbott, Dwayne C, info technologist IV, $49,128
Abbott, Ryan D, misc tech, $12.50/hr
Abbott, Tanner L, laborer, $10.75/hr
Abernathy, Robert W, printing/mail technician II, $27,084
Acree, Peter N, info technologist IV, $47,892
Adams, Michael S, info technology spec I, $51,096
Adams, Teresa A, info technologist III, $40,380
Addison, Amber M, info technology supv, $68,160
Aggeler, Carolyn A, info technology spec II, $68,160
Ahart, Brian, info technology spec II, $60,120
Ahmed, Diab M, info technologist IV, $48,156
Ahrens, Carla, ofc of administration mgr 2, $69,611
Akin, Vickie A, fiscal & administrative mgr b1, $55,045
Alexander, Dana A, info technology spec I, $53,208
Alexander, Daniel W, data processing mgr, $73,225
Allen, Gayle C, acct II, $41,940
Allen, Heather, examination monitor, $7.72/hr
Allen, Linda, examination monitor, $7.72/hr
Allen, Melinda B, pers analyst III, $45,156
Allen-Brown, Ashley E, public info spec I, $34,944
Allute, John, info technologist IV, $43,488
Amsden, William E, maint worker II, $29,976
Anderson, Angela M, info technologist IV, $45,156
Anderson, Christina A, info technologist III, $42,708
Anderson, Cory L, info technology spec I, $53,208
Anderson, Matthew, laborer, $10.75/hr
Anderson, Tammy L, exec II, $36,204
Anderson, William J, info technology spec I, $54,288
Andres, Jessica L, buyer I, $29,976
Andris, James, info technology spec II, $65,364
Angerer, Christopher W, info technology supv, $68,160
Antonio, Roxana N, hr mgr b1, $63,347
Aponte-Sanchez, John, info technologist I, $31,512
Arlen, Brenda L, info technology spec I, $48,156
Arms, Bobby J, maint worker II, $29,496
Arnel, Darrell K, skilled tradesman, $21.84/hr
Arnel, Jeffrey T, info technology spec I, $50,040
Arnett, Beverly, examination monitor, $7.72/hr
Arnold, Steven G, painter, $32,628
Arthur, Kenneth J, info technology spec I, $47,892
Ashby, Patricia E, acct I, $33,744
Ashley, Patrick, info technology spec I, $56,520
Atchison, Bernard J, comp info technology mgr I, $71,100
Augustine, Dana M, info technology spec I, $51,096
Augustine, Greg A, info technology spec II, $60,120
Ausley, Patrick D, printing/mail technician I, $23,880
Austin, Sherry L, account clerk II, $25,824
Auxier, Tammy, sr ofc spt asst (clerical), $25,824
Bacion, Raymond A, info technology spec II, $61,332
Backes, Michael E, info technology spec I, $63,996
Backes, Nicolle L, buyer II, $37,548
Bacon, Lisa L, acct II, $38,232
Bacon, Patricia A, fiscal & administrative mgr b2, $62,660
Bader, Leo W, maint worker II, $29,004
Bailey, Kristie L, info technologist II, $36,204
Bailey, Kristin D, info technologist II, $36,204
Bailey, Mark G, info technology spec I, $57,744
Baird, Eric, refrgrtn mech I, $32,628
Baker, Donald D, maint worker II, $29,004
Baker, Tom P, info technologist IV, $56,520
Balch, Deborah D, risk mgmt spec I, $43,488
Balke, Judith, ofc spt asst (keybrd), $26,652
Balken, Bruce K, info technologist III, $42,708
Ballesteros Lopez, Eladio, info technologist III, $40,380
Banuelos, Juan H, info technology spec II, $55,416
Barber, James, info technologist III, $41,172
Barbosa, Justin, info technologist III, $40,380
Barbour, Bryan, info technologist II, $36,204
Barnes, Frank R, info technology spec I, $58,908
Barnes, Sue, info technology spec I, $60,120
Barnett, Roger L, facilities opps mgr b1, $52,091
Barrett, James S, info technology oper II, $28,104

Barron, Kenneth A, info technologist II, $36,888
Baskette, Sandra K, pers analyst II, $37,548
Bass, Richard K, printing/mail technician III, $31,512
Bass, Zachary N, info technology spec I, $47,892
Bates, William D, info technology spec I, $56,520
Batson, Erin G, maint worker II, $31,512
Bax, Adam R, info technologist IV, $45,156
Bax, Rocky D, info technologist IV, $51,096
Bax, Scott B, info technology spec I, $55,416
Bax, Vicki L, info technology spec II, $62,664
Beakley, John, special asst prof, $67,670
Beard, David C, comp info tech spec III, $77,556
Beasley, Sheila D, exec II, $49,128
Beauchamp, Casey D, info technologist I, $30,984
Beck, Melissa M, info technology spec I, $54,288
Beck, Steve G, human rel ofcr I, $46,068
Becker, Clifford D, refrgrtn mech I, $30,984
Becker, David J, info technology spec I, $54,288
Becker, Scott C, groundskeeper II, $26,652
Beckmann, Brian D, info technology spec I, $56,520
Beddo, Dylan L, info technologist II, $42,708
Beers, Trenton D, info technologist IV, $45,156
Bell, Amy M, info technology spec I, $51,096
Bell, Brenda S, pers analyst III, $51,096
Beller, Ronald D, info technology spec I, $47,892
Beller, William, info technologist II, $36,888
Bellers, Stephen, info technologist I, $34,944
Belling, Jennifer J, examination monitor, $7.72/hr
Belveal, Edwin E, info technologist IV, $47,892
Beneke, Michael, info technologist III, $38,928
Bennett, Jesse, info technologist IV, $46,068
Bentch, Beverly J, court reporter II, $49,128
Bentley, Kevin L, crpntr, $29,976
Benton, John R, painter, $30,984
Benton, Sharon K, examination monitor, $7.72/hr
Berendzen, Bradley, maint spv I, $36,888
Berendzen, Michael L, misc prof, $50.74/hr
Berhorst, Abby M, info technologist IV, $45,156
Berhorst, Denise A, info technologist IV, $57,744
Berhorst, Hope A, info technology spec II, $60,120
Berhorst, John F, info technology spec I, $53,208
Berhorst, Leslie M, info technologist IV, $43,488
Berhorst, Melanie R, info technology spec II, $65,364
Berkbigler, Molly C, buyer I, $29,976
Berner, Thomas, electrcn, $32,052
Bernskoetter, James R, info technologist IV, $47,892
Berri, Brett W, special asst prof, $75,750
Berry, John M, examination monitor, $7.72/hr
Berry, Timothy B, info technologist II, $36,204
Bess, Larissa, sr ofc spt asst (keybrd), $25,032
Bess, Matthew D, fiscal & administrative mgr b2, $58,903
Bestgen, Brent, info technologist IV, $45,156
Bethmann, Rebecca A, acct II, $37,548
Beul, Lucas W, info technology spec II, $61,332
Bhattarai, Kriti, data processor tech, $14.87/hr
Bickel, Lesley, designated principal asst div, $40,400
Billingsley, Demekie, maint worker II, $30,420
Binggeli, Barbara A, info technology spec I, $53,208
Bingham, Terry W, info technologist IV, $45,156
Binkley, Vicki L, info technology spec I, $55,416
Bisges, Kyle S, info technology spec II, $61,332
Bisges, Nathan, info technology spec I, $55,416
Bisges, Ronald J, misc prof, $32.58/hr
Bittle, Joseph W, info technologist IV, $45,156
Blackburn, Marlene, contract spec II (ofc of adm), $47,892
Blackerby, Amanda, info technologist I, $36,204
Blackwood, Joseph A, maint worker II, $30,420
Blackwood, Kevin A, maint spv I, $38,928
Blackwood, Lee, maint worker II, $29,004
Blair, Russell W, info technologist III, $46,932
Block, Cody, tech asst III, $30,984
Block, Larry J, design/develop/survey mgr b3, $77,265
Blomberg, Sheila M, info technology spec II, $69,612
Blume, Joshua A, refrgrtn mech II, $37,548
Blumhorst, Dwight T, facilities opps mgr b1, $59,520
Bochat, Nancy L, info technology supv, $66,720
Bock, Michael J, info technology spec I, $68,160
Bockelman, Stacy M, graphic arts spec III, $38,928
Bocklage, Terry J, info technologist IV, $46,068
Boeckman, Scott J, info technologist II, $42,708
Boeger, Karen S, div dir, $96,746
Boehm, Nellie R, info technology spec I, $49,128
Boessen, Kimberly K, risk mgmt tech II, $30,984

Boessen, Roseanne L, info technology spec II, $71,100
Boland, Aaron S, info technologist II, $36,204
Bolden, Thomas A, info technology spec II, $62,664
Bomar, Alexander M, laborer, $10.75/hr
Bomar, Jason L, electrcn, $33,744
Bond, Patricia, info technology spec I, $52,092
Bond, Shayna R, risk mgmt spec II, $37,534
Bondurant, Douglas J, plumber, $31,512
Boney-Phillips, Frances F, info technology spec I, $53,208
Bonine, Mary A, printing/mail technician I, $23,880
Bonnie, Stephanie, info technologist IV, $45,156
Bonnot, Justin C, stationary engr, $34,944
Bonnot, Keith E, const insp, $46,068
Bonnot, Larry R, misc prof, $21.89/hr
Booker, Jannette F, info technologist IV, $47,892
Boone, Lorenzo L, bldg mgr II, $45,156
Borchelt, Laurie L, buyer IV, $62,664
Borgmeyer, Elizabeth A, info technologist IV, $47,892
Bosky, Mark W, info technologist II, $34,944
Boss, Robert, printing/mail technician III, $33,744
Bossaller, Herbert A, skilled tradesman, $21.84/hr
Bossom, Terry N, maint spv I, $40,380
Botkin, Timothy D, maint worker II, $29,004
Bottorff, Mika J, maint worker II, $29,976
Boyd, Jennifer M, info technologist IV, $48,156
Boyles, Tiffany S, info technologist IV, $43,488
Bracken, Michael J, info technology supv, $71,208
Bradley, Larry C, info technology supv, $71,208
Branch, Travis W, info technologist III, $40,380
Brand, Janice S, data processor tech, $27.52/hr
Brand, Larry D, facilities opps mgr b1, $63,986
Brand, Mary K, domestic serv worker, $11.41/hr
Brandt, Roger L, labor spv, $26,652
Branson, James V, info technology spec II, $77,556
Branson, Rodney F, data processor tech, $30.12/hr
Branson, Shannon L, buyer I, $29,976
Branstetter, Laura M, special asst prof, $81,305
Bratten, Cheryl, info technology spec I, $54,288
Braun, Daniel L, maint spv I, $43,488
Braun, Lee Ann M, fiscal & administrative mgr b2, $56,427
Bray, Kimberlyn R, accounting spec I, $36,204
Brazzell, Timmie L, facilities opps mgr b3, $63,000
Bremer, Jamie L, refrgrtn mech II, $34,944
Brengle, Michael K, painter, $37,548
Brennan, Albert B, info technologist IV, $45,156
Brenneke, Andrew J, laborer, $10.75/hr
Brenneke, Victoria M, acct I, $33,744
Brewer, Marvin L, crpntr, $29,976
Brickey, Jon M, info technologist IV, $45,156
Bridgewater, Eric T, maint worker II, $29,004
Briedwell, Deborah K, geographic info sys spec, $49,128
Bright, Randy, info technologist III, $46,068
Brinkley, Rebecca J, contract spec II (ofc of adm), $61,332
Briscoe, Joseph R, special investigator, $33.78/hr
Brock, James E, info technology sr spec, $71,100
Brockman, James D, info technology spec I, $56,520
Brooks, Stephanie, info technology supv, $74,304
Brothers, David M, info technology spec I, $63,996
Brown, Catherine F, div dir, $96,746
Brown, Donald R, info technologist I, $32,052
Brown, Jack, info technologist IV, $45,156
Brown, Nathan R, info technologist I, $31,512
Brown, Robert C, data processor tech, $27.84/hr
Brown, Tina M, const insp, $47,892
Brownawell, Susan, info technology spec I, $48,156
Browner, Claudia, exec I, $38,232
Bruemmer, Amy L, info technology spec I, $52,092
Brumley, Charlotte D, info technology spec I, $61,332
Brunk, Stephen E, info technology spec I, $49,128
Bruns, John E, printing/mail technician I, $27,948
Brunson, Kelly J, admin ofc spt asst, $32,628
Bryan, Stephanie D, info technology spec I, $56,520
Brzuchalski, Charles W, design/develop/survey mgr b3, $87,365
Buechler, Michael J, admin ofc spt asst, $36,888
Buffington, Kelli R, info technologist IV, $43,488
Buhr, Adam G, laborer, $10.75/hr
Bunselmeyer, Jennifer M, graphics spv, $40,380
Burchett, Billy, maint worker II, $31,512
Burec, Michael S, info technologist IV, $43,488
Burgess, Brad W, maint spv I, $32,628
Burgess, Carol A, principal asst board/commisson, $34,340
Burgess, Quentin, info technologist II, $36,204
Burgess, Roy E, buyer III, $43,488

Burkhart, Jeffrey L, info technologist IV, $43,488
Burns, Christopher T, info technologist IV, $45,156
Burns, Ryan L, special asst prof, $71,205
Burt, Gloria J, info technology spec I, $52,092
Busch, Wendell W, maint worker II, $29,976
Buschjost, James, storekeeper II, $28,104
Buschjost, Marian J, hr mgr b3, $69,690
Buschmeyer, Heath W, maint worker II, $29,004
Butzer, Douglas J, maint spv I, $37,548
Byers, Betsy R, dir of business servs, $71,205
Byrd, Deborah D, info technology spec I, $53,208
Byrd, George W, printing/mail technician III, $30,984
Byrd, Shirley K, info technologist III, $43,488
Caimi, John R, data processor tech, $27.17/hr
Cain, Kevin J, info technology spec I, $49,128
Calvin, Jennifer L, pers analyst IV, $53,208
Cameron, Barbara K, ofc spt asst (keybrd), $27,504
Cammarata, Steven R, crpntr, $37,548
Camp, Kelli D, info technology supv, $74,304
Campbell, Brian D, info technology spec I, $51,096
Campbell, Darryl L, maint worker II, $32,628
Campbell, Destiny, info technologist IV, $46,068
Campbell, Eve E, sr ofc spt asst (keybrd), $31,920
Campbell, James C, maint worker II, $29,004
Campbell, Joshua, info technologist IV, $29,976
Campbell, Mark B, info technologist IV, $46,068
Campbell, Rafael, info technologist IV, $46,068
Campbell, Roy P, info technology spec I, $63,996
Campbell, Yvonne W, maint worker II, $30,984
Cannon, Chris B, info technology spec I, $53,208
Cannon, Kristina M, budget & plng sr analyst, $52,092
Carel, Douglas D, info technologist IV, $46,068
Carey, John, geographic info sys analyst, $40,380
Carey, Tanner J, info technologist II, $36,888
Carl, Paul A, info technology spec I, $51,096
Carlton, Allana G, laborer I, $21,264
Carnaghi, Joann, examination monitor, $7.72/hr
Carranza, Gretchen, info technologist IV, $46,932
Carrender, Corey A, info technology spec I, $49,128
Carroll, Bryan K, info technologist I, $33,744
Carroll, John L, laborer II, $23,160
Carroll, Michael E, stationary engr, $33,744
Carroll, Robert C, crpntr, $34,356
Cartee, Dewayne G, info technologist IV, $47,892
Carter, Janet R, min purchasing asst, $27,660
Carter, Steven A, info technologist IV, $43,488
Caruthers, Brandi L, fiscal & administrative mgr b1, $50,076
Carwile, Justin D, info technologist IV, $50,040
Case, Carla M, info technologist IV, $38,928
Case, Janet C, info technology spec II, $58,908
Case, Levi S, maint worker II, $29,004
Case, Paul E, park maint wkr II, $26,652
Cassmeyer, Dale G, design/develop/survey mgr b2, $66,960
Cassmeyer, Jeffrey J, comp info tech spec III, $79,296
Cassmeyer, Kevin R, info technology spec II, $65,364
Cavender, Lisa A, facilities opps mgr b3, $87,365
Cavender, Tim A, info technologist IV, $45,156
Chandler, Tonya, admin ofc spt asst, $32,052
Chaney, Audrey, examination monitor, $7.72/hr
Chaney, John, examination monitor, $7.72/hr
Charbonneau, Todd A, maint worker II, $29,004
Charter, William E, info technologist II, $34,944
Chemweno, Caroline, info technologist IV, $45,156
Chiarletto, Joseph T, maint worker II, $29,004
Chinn, Kathy S, exec I, $41,940
Chinn, Paul B, design/develop/survey mgr b3, $77,265
Chojnacki, Joann B, info technology spec II, $71,100
Christian, Dennis A, maint worker II, $29,004
Christianson, David D, info technology spec I, $57,744
Chronister, Dale, examination monitor, $7.72/hr
Ciesluk, Scott A, info technologist III, $41,172
Cisco, Anastasia V, info technologist IV, $23,946
Cisco, Scott J, info technology spec I, $49,128
Clark, Cecil T, stationary engr, $35,568
Clark, Jody L, info technologist IV, $45,156
Clark-chapman, Dianna L, risk mgmt spec I, $43,488
Clayborn, Jared W, info technologist I, $30,984
Claypool, Jeffrey L, printing/mail technician III, $32,052
Clayton, Andrew C, info technologist III, $38,928
Cleveland, Rashad D, info technologist II, $36,888
Climer, James, hvac inst ctrls tech, $35,568
Clingman, Norman L, printing/mail technician III, $35,568
Closser, Colleen, examination monitor, $7.72/hr

Closser, James, examination monitor, $7.72/hr
Clover, Mary L, info technology spec I, $52,092
Coffelt, Linda K, sr ofc spt asst (clerical), $28,452
Cohen, Joseph B, info technology spec II, $71,100
Colbert-Botchway, Nicole J, commission mbr, $103,960
Cole, Marcus C, info technologist I, $30,984
Cole, Mark A, painter, $29,976
Coley, Matt, electrcn, $31,512
Collier, Jacqueline, info technology spec I, $53,208
Collier, Michelle P, admin ofc spt asst, $29,976
Collins, Earl E, maint worker II, $29,004
Collins, Timmy L, phys plant sup II, $38,928
Comer, Tristan R, misc tech, $12.50/hr
Connell, Victor, supply mgr II, $35,568
Conner, Bud, info technologist I, $31,512
Conover, Kirby A, laborer, $10.75/hr
Cook, Brian L, maint spv I, $34,944
Cook, Clyde K, info technology spec II, $68,160
Cook, Dustin N, info technologist II, $37,548
Cook, Jared A, misc tech, $12.50/hr
Cook, Julie A, info technology spec II, $60,120
Cook, Linda J, sr ofc spt asst (keybrd), $29,412
Coon, Thad, motor veh mech, $29,004
Coons, Dennis R, info technologist III, $40,380
Cooper, Katie B, exec I, $34,944
Cooper, Larry M, info technology spec I, $55,416
Copeland, Kelly S, exec I, $38,232
Cordry, Lisa R, admin ofc spt asst, $30,984
Cornett, Tonna K, info technology spec I, $54,288
Coroleuski, Linda C, examination monitor, $7.71/hr
Counsil, Charles A, maint worker II, $29,004
Coursey, Lance M, info technologist I, $30,984
Cox, Billy D, info technology spec II, $61,332
Cox, Francis L, info technology spec II, $69,612
Cox, Perry W, hvac inst ctrls tech, $30,984
Cox, Terry J, acct III, $42,708
Crabill, Robert N, info technology spec I, $49,128
Crader, Matt E, info technologist II, $47,892
Craig, Angela N, info technology spec I, $50,040
Craigg, David L, construction insp, $50,040
Craighead, Russell L, procurement ofcr II, $50,040
Cramer, Kristina M, buyer II, $37,548
Crawford, Charles E, crpntr, $34,944
Crawford, Joyce, fiscal & administrative mgr b1, $57,725
Crawford, Richard D, phys plant sup II, $41,940
Cretzmeyer, Trevor W, laborer, $10.75/hr
Crisp, Phillip L, maint worker II, $29,004
Crocker, Cory, info technologist I, $29,976
Crook, Andrew W, info technology spec II, $65,364
Crossland, Ricky L, maint worker II, $29,004
Crossnoe, Deborah S, fiscal & administrative mgr b2, $68,049
Crowley, Michelle L, info technology spec I, $53,208
Crump, Rebecca E, acct I, $33,744
Cundiff, Michael W, info technologist IV, $49,128
Cunningham, Donnie L, maint worker II, $29,004
Cunningham, Mitchell A, info technologist IV, $44,304
Cunningham, Paula A, public info coor, $49,128
Curren, Robert K, info technology supv, $71,208
Curry, Jeffrey M, info technology spec I, $53,208
Curry, Ronnie D, geographic info sys analyst, $41,940
Curtis, Evelyn, info technologist IV, $47,892
Cusumano, Steven R, data processor prof, $65,408
Dahler, Daniel, info technologist I, $31,512
Dallmeyer, Rudolph J, crpntr, $34,944
Dalton, Kevin, phys plant sup II, $43,488
Dame, Jeremy N, info technologist I, $31,512
Dampf, Tara, fiscal & administrative mgr b2, $68,049
Dandamudi, Sreenivasa R, commission mbr, $103,960
Daniels, Carl W, maint spv I, $46,932
Dann, Karl, electrcn, $33,744
Daugherty, Wendell K, info technologist IV, $49,128
Davault, Eric W, info technology spec II, $62,664
David, Charles R, maint worker II, $29,004
Davis, Courtney B, investigator, $22,058
Davis, Douglas K, info technology spec I, $54,288
Davis, Gary L, electrcn, $33,744
Davis, Larry M, maint worker II, $29,004
Davis, Lyle W, custodial worker I, $20,664
Davis, Max W, info technologist II, $36,204
Davis, Von B, info technologist I, $30,984
Dawson, Stacia L,-buyer IV, $53,208
De Leon, Thomas W, info technology spec I, $49,128
Deal, Timothy P, phys plant sup II, $41,940

Debrodie, Christopher, info technologist III, $41,172
Debroeck, Christopher A, printing/mail cust svc rep, $39,624
Decker, Ross R, data processor tech, $10.00/hr
Decker, William A, info technology spec I, $50,040
Deeken, Mary B, comp info tech supv I, $57,744
Deheer, Michael A, stationary engr, $34,356
Delaney, Charles D, capital imprvmts spec I, $44,304
Denkers, Erik A, info technology spec I, $58,908
Denkers, Teragram M, admin ofc spt asst, $33,180
Denney, Michael D, info technology spec II, $63,996
Dennison, Barry J, facilities opps mgr b2, $57,740
Dennison, Linda F, info technology spec I, $53,208
Dent, James B, info technology spec II, $65,364
Denton, Jerri L, pers analyst III, $55,416
Deville, Christina M, info technologist I, $32,052
Deville, Mark S, stationary engr, $33,744
Devore, Christopher G, facilities opps mgr b3, $70,700
Devore, Vandee V, fiscal & administrative mgr b3, $84,845
Dickens, Darrell E, maint worker II, $29,004
Dickerson, Adam, info technologist II, $36,888
Dickey, Aaron M, printing/mail technician II, $26,652
Dickneite, Gerard J, info technology spec II, $57,744
Dickson, William, info technology spec I, $52,092
Dicus, Lora A, info technology supv, $77,556
Didriksen, Robert A, planner I, $49,128
Diebold, Scott, info technology spec I, $49,128
Diestelkamp, Maretta S, info technologist IV, $49,128
Digennaro, William P, info technologist IV, $45,156
Dillard, Michael J, account clerk II, $25,824
Dillon, Elizabeth A, research analyst II, $36,204
Dilse, Stephanie, info technology oper II, $29,496
Distler, Christopher J, info technology spec I, $49,128
Distler, Cierra E, info technologist III, $40,380
Distler, Donald E, data processor tech, $28.90/hr
Distler, Joyce A, info technology spec I, $56,520
Distler, Laura B, info technology supv, $68,160
Distler, Rodney G, info technology spec II, $58,908
Dixon, Brent L, buyer IV, $62,664
Dixon, Cynthia A, ofc of administration mgr 3, $77,568
Dixon, James L, laborer, $10.75/hr
Dixon, Michael L, info technologist II, $36,204
Dodson, Teresa M, info technology spec I, $53,208
Doerhoff, Douglas F, maint worker II, $32,628
Doerhoff, Jennifer D, info technology spec II, $68,160
Doerrler, Tamara L, laborer II, $23,160
Dolson, Sharon A, info technology spec II, $58,908
Donley, Nathaniel J, info technologist IV, $45,156
Dooling, Jerry A, phys plant sup III, $57,744
Dooling, William M, crpntr, $29,976
Dorney, Michael R, crpntr, $33,744
Doskocil, Louis J, maint worker II, $31,512
Doss, Willis B, info technology spec II, $61,332
Doty, Diana, info technologist IV, $47,892
Douglas, Calvin, maint worker II, $29,004
Dover, Kenneth, comp info tech spec III, $65,364
Dowell, Ryan C, maint worker II, $29,004
Dowling, Douglas E, maint worker II, $29,496
Downing, John, info technologist III, $38,928
Drennen, Jill A, info technology spec I, $56,520
Drinkard, Daniel L, printing/mail technician IV, $36,888
Duckworth, Robert L, printing/mail technician IV, $33,744
Dudenhoeffer, Christina L, info technology spec I, $60,120
Dudenhoeffer, Deborah K, info technologist III, $43,488
Dudenhoeffer, Jena L, info technology spec I, $50,040
Dudenhoeffer, Valinda P, info technologist IV, $46,932
Dudzik, Matthew F, info technology sr spec, $75,948
Duemmel, Brenda M, info technology supv, $69,612
Duenow, William, info technology spec II, $62,664
Duewell, Colin E, geographic info sys spec, $49,128
Duff, Jacqueline S, info technology supv, $75,948
Dulle, Hal J, misc prof, $29.37/hr
Duncan, Barbara J, sr ofc spt asst (keybrd), $29,412
Duncan, Brian K, housekeeper II, $35,568
Duncan, Dennis J, info technologist III, $46,068
Duncan, Ronnie W, plumber, $29,976
Dunn, Logan, info technologist I, $30,984
Dunnaway, Gary, info technologist III, $40,380
Duppong, Carla J, exec I, $37,548
Durbin, Dylan M, info technologist I, $31,512
Durden, Joni R, examination monitor, $7.72/hr
Duren, Justin R, crpntr, $34,944
Durrill, J E, info technology spec I, $47,892
Dziadosz, David A, misc tech, $21.84/hr

Earl, Angela, info technology spec I, $50,040
Earl, Mallory A, groundskeeper I, $23,880
Eaton, Cory J, info technologist III, $41,172
Edgar, Benjamin A, info technologist II, $42,708
Edmonson, William T, misc tech, $25.49/hr
Edwards, Brian D, info technologist III, $42,708
Egbuchiri, Innocent U, info technologist IV, $46,932
Eggen, Gary L, fiscal & administrative mgr b2, $69,604
Eggen, Judy E, fiscal & administrative mgr b3, $88,819
Eghbali, Nathan, info technologist III, $40,380
Eidson, Cody M, info technologist III, $39,624
Eisterhold, Laura, info technology spec I, $47,892
Elliott, Glenda K, reporting spec, $29,969
Emerson, Cierra, info technologist III, $40,380
Emily, George N, info technology spec I, $54,288
Engelbrecht, Kevin D, info technology spec I, $57,744
Engler, Daniel R, printing/mail technician I, $23,880
Enlow, Karen L, budget & plng sr analyst, $65,364
Estes, Jessica M, examination monitor, $7.72/hr
Evans, Christina, accounting spec II, $40,380
Evans, Dawn R, disability prog spec, $40,380
Evans, Kerry J, info technology spec I, $50,040
Evers, Duane A, info technology spec II, $57,744
Evers, Lindsey A, info technologist IV, $45,156
Ewing, David, info technology spec I, $49,128
Ewing, Robert L, laborer, $10.75/hr
Ezell, Joe H, boiler oper, $28,104
Faerber, Susan R, data processor tech, $28.06/hr
Faherty, Charles A, info technologist IV, $45,156
Falter, Jeffrey F, comp info technology mgr I, $71,208
Farley, Jessica A, sr ofc spt asst (clerical), $32,472
Farnen, Jean M, info technologist IV, $49,128
Farrell, Libbie D, fiscal & administrative mgr b2, $65,636
Farrenburg, Robert W, maint worker II, $30,420
Farris, Kelley L, info technology spec I, $53,208
Farris, Wade P, maint worker II, $29,004
Fast, Thomas, hr mgr b1, $56,964
Feeler, Preston D, info technologist III, $38,928
Feller, Steven W, painter, $36,204
Feltrop, Lisa L, admin ofc spt asst, $35,568
Fender, David A, info technology spec I, $51,096
Ferguson, Jeffrey C, info technology spec II, $71,208
Ferkel, Timothy J, info technologist IV, $43,488
Ferrell, Charles M, skilled tradesman, $21.59/hr
Ferrier, John, info technology supv, $68,160
Fester, Rita A, info technology supv, $62,664
Fetes, Eric M, info technology oper I, $26,652
Finnell, Mark, info technology spec II, $71,100
Fischer, Robbie L, stationary engr, $33,744
Fish, Christopher, info technologist II, $34,944
Fisher, Anthony J, maint worker II, $29,004
Fisher, Brandon L, info technologist II, $30,984
Fisher, Michael W, phys plant sup II, $38,928
Fitzpatrick, Doris M, comp info tech supv I, $53,208
Fletchall, Brianna J, examination monitor, $7.72/hr
Fletchall, Karen R, examination monitor, $7.72/hr
Fletchall, Sheena, examination monitor, $7.72/hr
Fletcher, Allen D, boiler oper, $28,104
Fletcher, Heath W, info technologist III, $38,928
Foley, Samuel, info technologist II, $37,548
Forbis, Allan J, hr mgr b3, $73,225
Forck, Curtis, fiscal & administrative mgr b1, $51,991
Fortson, Rodney L, accounting spec III, $53,208
Foster, Colleen M, info technology spec I, $50,040
Foster, Stephon L, laborer, $10.75/hr
Foster, Stewart C, maint worker II, $29,004
Fouts, Bonita L, info technology spec I, $58,908
Fowler, Shirley M, info technologist III, $46,068
Frank, Amy L, admin ofc spt asst, $31,512
Frank, Dale W, printing/mail technician III, $33,744
Frank, Deborah, data processor clerical, $16.80/hr
Frank, Mary E, info technology spec I, $51,096
Frank, Valiente K, pers clerk, $28,104
Frank, William J, info technology spec I, $52,092
Franzen Stephens, Eileen V, info technologist IV, $50,040
Freand, Troby L, sr ofc spt asst (keybrd), $27,084
Freeman, Christina M, fiscal & administrative mgr b2, $68,000
Frommel, Theresa S, info technologist IV, $63,996
Fry, Harold L, stationary engr, $38,928
Fudge, Eric D, examination monitor, $7.72/hr
Fudge, Jodi, examination monitor, $7.72/hr
Fuller, James W, printing/mail technician I, $23,880
Furlong, Cheryl L, info technology oper II, $32,052

Furman, Billy G, painter, $36,888
Gabelsberger, Kevin J, info technology spec II, $68,160
Gabelsberger, Michelle L, info technology spec II, $62,664
Gaffney, Mary, info technology spec I, $50,040
Gaines, Philip L, maint worker II, $29,004
Gal, Michele L, info technologist III, $39,624
Gann, Faith A, examination monitor, $7.72/hr
Garrad, Hannah K, examination monitor, $7.72/hr
Garrett, Gregory D, info technology oper I, $26,652
Gasper, Timothy P, maint worker II, $29,004
Gass, Joshua, info technologist III, $41,172
Gatson, Michael, info technologist IV, $51,096
Geeding, Brenda K, examination monitor, $7.72/hr
Geeding, Tommy, examination monitor, $7.72/hr
Geers, Jonathan R, info technology spec I, $52,092
Gentges, Barbara L, info technology spec I, $54,288
Gentges, Meghan, info technologist III, $38,928
George, Andrew D, info technology spec II, $71,208
Gerling, Richard W, data processing mgr, $75,000
Gerloff, Debbie L, info technology oper I, $27,084
Gerstner, Christine M, fiscal & administrative mgr b2, $75,245
Gerstner, Michelle M, special asst prof, $40,400
Getty, Ronald W, business analyst II, $62,317
Giboney, Tony R, info technology spec II, $61,332
Gibson, Brenda, ofc of administration mgr 1, $56,516
Gieseker, Alexis M, geographic info sys spec, $50,040
Gilbert, Katie A, risk mgmt tech II, $30,984
Giles, Craig A, info technology spec I, $51,096
Gillespie, Frederick, laborer II, $28,452
Gillespie, Thomas C, info technology spec I, $55,416
Gilliam, Susan M, info technologist IV, $43,488
Gilliland, Helen M, examination monitor, $7.72/hr
Gilmore, Loretta M, training tech III, $46,068
Girouard, Paul M, design/develop/survey mgr b1, $46,068
Glasgow, Lisa A, info technology spec II, $68,160
Glawson, Susan L, info technology spec I, $52,092
Goeller, Amanda M, risk mgmt tech II, $30,984
Goeller, Jerome A, painter, $29,976
Goff, Brooke S, info technologist I, $30,984
Gonterman, Jordan M, info technologist I, $31,512
Goodrick, Jodell K, acct II, $37,548
Gordon, Kenton L, maint spv I, $34,944
Gourley, Robert J, data processing mgr, $60,095
Govreau, Teresa, examination monitor, $7.72/hr
Gramblin, Steven D, info technology sr spec, $77,556
Grannemann, Mark A, facilities opps mgr b1, $56,798
Grant, William L, info technology spec I, $62,664
Graves, Cindy, admin ofc spt asst, $31,512
Green, Paul L, maint worker II, $30,984
Green, Rick W, painter, $37,548
Green, Rodney G, maint spv I, $35,568
Grellner, Jennifer M, info technology spec I, $55,416
Gresham, Theodore K, info technologist IV, $45,156
Griddine, Eugene V, storekeeper I, $29,412
Griffaw, Steve, info technology spec I, $53,208
Griffith, Joshua A, info technology spec I, $47,892
Grindle, Simone C, sr ofc spt asst (keybrd), $29,412
Groner, Pamela L, risk mgmt spec II, $54,288
Groner, Terence B, misc tech, $16.00/hr
Grothoff, Gary L, printing/mail technician I, $23,880
Grothoff, Judy A, reporting spec, $27,084
Groven, William E, maint spv I, $32,628
Groves, Larry L, printing/mail technician I, $24,612
Gruber, Brenda S, admin ofc spt asst, $31,512
Guagliata, Stephen E, storekeeper I, $25,824
Guffey, Monica E, info technologist II, $31,512
Hackney, James R, info technologist II, $36,204
Hadley, Traci, acct I, $32,052
Hager, Suzanne E, paralegal, $36,047
Haines, Krystal M, acct I, $29,976
Hake, Harry D, info technology spec I, $50,040
Hale, Keith D, info technology spec I, $52,092
Hale, Vicki L, exec I, $41,940
Haley, Carl L, const insp, $42,708
Haller, Alissa M, info technologist II, $36,888
Hallford, Michelle A, exec I, $41,940
Hamilton, Monica L, info technology spec II, $61,332
Hammack, Kelly D, design/develop/survey mgr b2, $56,448
Hampton, Johnny T, info technologist III, $38,928
Hance, Landon E, labor spv, $35,472
Hanks, Gary, misc tech, $9.60/hr
Hannaford, David M, administrative analyst III, $43,488
Hansen, Craig A, printing/mail technician III, $34,356

Harbison, Bradley L, info technologist IV, $45,156
Harbison, Jo A, info technology spec II, $63,996
Harden, Andy J, maint spv I, $32,628
Hardesty, Brian S, phys plant sup I, $39,624
Hargus, Diana L, info technology spec I, $49,128
Harley, Luther J, park maint wkr II, $30,924
Harmon, Tracye R, info technology spec I, $51,096
Harrell, Harvey, maint spv II, $44,304
Harrell, Paul, info technologist III, $46,068
Harrington, Robert A, examination monitor, $7.72/hr
Harrington, Robert J, info technologist IV, $46,068
Harrington, Victoria J, examination monitor, $7.72/hr
Harris, Greg, plumber, $36,888
Harris, Lois A, info technologist IV, $45,156
Harris, Shane R, tractor trailer driver, $30,420
Harrison, Thomas M, info technologist III, $41,172
Hart, Aaron J, hr mgr b2, $71,999
Hartman, Kenneth L, info technology spec II, $62,664
Hartman, Paul, info technologist III, $42,708
Hartmann, Joe F, info technology spec II, $63,996
Hartmann, Rose M, info technologist IV, $46,932
Harvey, Carol A, storekeeper I, $29,904
Harvey, Jesse T, laborer, $10.75/hr
Harvey, Robert, laborer I, $21,264
Harwood, Ronni, sr ofc spt asst (clerical), $28,452
Hasenbeck, Patrick A, info technology spec I, $54,288
Haslag, Brenda, ofc of administration mgr 1, $23.31/hr
Haslag, Karen R, data processor tech, $36.51/hr
Haslag, Ronald J, info technology spec I, $55,416
Hassler, Cynthia A, info technology spec II, $69,612
Hassler, Katharine J, info technologist I, $31,512
Hastings, Dane, refrgrtn mech II, $34,944
Hatch, Betty J, sr ofc spt asst (keybrd), $27,948
Hathaway Giles, Heather D, info technology spec I, $50,040
Haupt, Logan, info technologist III, $41,172
Hayes, Cindy L, info technologist II, $42,708
Hayes, Isaac, info technologist IV, $58,908
Hayes, Ryan N, info technology spec II, $61,332
Hayes, Sharon D, sr ofc spt asst (keybrd), $29,412
Haymaker, Scott A, plumber, $29,976
Haynes, Ray C, locksmith, $35,568
Hazlett, Joseph I, laborer II, $23,160
Healy, Timothy T, maint worker II, $29,004
Hearod, Kathy, info technologist IV, $45,156
Heberle, Nicholas P, special asst prof, $61,109
Heckman, Holly J, info technology spec I, $50,040
Heidemann, Brian K, maint worker II, $29,004
Heidlage, Kyle, info technologist IV, $46,068
Heimericks, Scott A, maint worker II, $32,052
Hein, Judith R, info technologist IV, $51,096
Heinrich, Tyler J, data processor tech, $17.17/hr
Heislen, Cory M, info technology supv, $61,332
Heislen, Ryan, info technology spec I, $49,128
Heislen, Stacey L, asst dir, $76,255
Heller, Michael B, info technology spec II, $61,332
Helmers, Lukas, info technologist I, $30,984
Helton, Sandra L, info technologist IV, $52,092
Helton, Tricia R, info technologist II, $47,892
Hemmelgarn, Robert D, info technologist II, $34,944
Henderson, Carla J, comp info tech supv I, $47,892
Henderson, Jennifer D, info technologist II, $36,204
Henderson, Mabel, sr ofc spt asst (clerical), $29,412
Hendrix, Korrine J, examination monitor, $7.72/hr
Henley, Dianne D, info technologist III, $41,940
Henrickson, Drew M, design/develop/survey mgr b3, $77,265
Henry, James L, info technologist IV, $45,156
Henry, Robert N, maint worker II, $29,004
Hensley, Janet L, info technologist IV, $47,892
Henson, Kenneth G, info technology spec I, $55,416
Herigon, Alexander D, comp info tech II, $35,568
Herigon, Mitchell V, printing/mail technician IV, $33,744
Herigon, Shawn T, info technologist II, $36,888
Heritage, Kristi L, info technology spec I, $53,208
Herman, Karen L, sr ofc spt asst (keybrd), $30,924
Herrick, Donald L, electrcn, $37,548
Herron, Randy L, maint worker I, $31,416
Hesser, Matthew B, state demographer, $71,208
Heuser, Kenneth W, maint worker II, $29,496
Heuvelman, Michael, laborer II, $23,160
Hickman, Mark D, plumber, $29,976
Hickman, Tammy L, housekeeper II, $34,944
Hicks, Phillip S, info technologist IV, $46,068
Hicock, William A, acct I, $37,548

Higgins, Hance, info technologist II, $36,888
Highfill, Kevin L, fiscal & administrative mgr b3, $73,035
Highland, Melanie J, budget & plng sr anal, $57,744
Hildenbrand, John, acct I, $33,744
Hilke, David L, info technologist IV, $54,288
Hill, James D, info technology oper II, $29,496
Hill, Kathryn J, sr ofc spt asst (keybrd), $27,084
Hill, Mark W, design/develop/survey mgr b3, $87,365
Hill, Sabrina N, sr ofc spt asst (clerical), $25,032
Hillen, Britni, accounting spec I, $36,204
Hillman, Bridget L, info technology spec I, $54,288
Hillman, Kent L, data processor prof, $84,335
Himmerick, Sheila R, acct I, $30,984
Hobart, Matthew J, maint worker II, $29,004
Hodde, Marvin L, info technology spec I, $56,520
Hodge, Gina L, comp info technology mgr I, $71,208
Hodge, Paul, storekeeper I, $25,032
Hodge, Rebecca J, pers clerk, $27,228
Hodges, Aaron M, info technologist II, $38,232
Hodges, Renee L, acct I, $34,944
Hoelscher, Karen, info technology spec I, $52,092
Hoelscher, Theresa, info technology spec I, $54,288
Hoepfinger, Clyde, maint worker II, $30,420
Hoerschgen, Ryan, info technology spec II, $60,120
Hogue, Deamon L, comp info tech supv I, $57,744
Holland, Craig A, printing/mail technician III, $29,976
Holliday, Marsha L, acct I, $30,984
Hollis, Craig W, dir of info tech, $65,000
Holman, Mark W, refrgrtn mech II, $36,204
Holmes, Arlan, fiscal & administrative mgr b2, $72,215
Holtmeyer, Jerome M, clerk, $28.90/hr
Holton, Ricardo, maint worker II, $34,356
Holton, Sammie D, stationary engr, $40,380
Holzem, Kenneth W, data processor tech, $28.90/hr
Holzer, David L, locksmith, $32,628
Honan, Robert W, principal asst board/commisson, $55,946
Hooks, Robert S, laborer II, $23,508
Hopson, Michael J, maint worker II, $29,004
Horn, Stephanie A, exec I, $34,944
Horn, Travis, info technologist IV, $45,156
Hosenfelt, James L, maint spv I, $32,628
Hoskins, Jacob S, info technologist I, $30,984
Hoskins, Nicole L, info technologist I, $31,512
Hoskins, Travis G, info technology spec I, $55,416
Houston, Johnn, info technologist I, $30,984
Houts, Meggan C, info technologist IV, $43,488
Howard, Karen M, pers analyst III, $54,048
Howard, Michael J, info technology spec II, $62,664
Howell, Bob L, designated principal asst div, $51,005
Howren, Kerry, info technology spec II, $58,908
Hubble, Felicia, fiscal & administrative mgr b2, $60,797
Huber, Michael R, info technology spec I, $48,156
Huddleston, B S, info technology spec II, $65,364
Hughes, Angela R, exec I, $36,888
Hughes, Barbara L, data processor tech, $28.90/hr
Hughes, Christopher A, stationary engr, $34,944
Hughes, Jessica, info technologist IV, $43,488
Hughes, Michael T, info technology spec I, $54,288
Hughes, Tony A, maint worker II, $29,004
Hughes Luebbering, Melissa G, sr field investigator, $42,708
Hughey, Shelley L, administrative asst, $32,053
Huhmann, Russell A, info technology spec I, $61,332
Huhn, Brittany K, info technology oper I, $26,652
Hulett, Robert K, electrcn, $32,628
Hulsey, Dustin, maint worker II, $29,004
Hulsey, Krysten G, acct I, $34,944
Hultberg, Kevin L, maint spv I, $41,172
Hume, Travis, planner II, $41,172
Hummer, Patrick A, maint spv I, $33,180
Hunter, Donna L, acct I, $33,744
Hunter, Melissa D, info technologist II, $36,888
Hurlburt, Debra K, storekeeper I, $29,904
Hursman, Matthew E, phys plant sup III, $47,892
Hutcheson, Dakota, info technologist II, $35,568
Hutinger, James M, info technology spec I, $49,128
Hutinger, William E, printing/mail technician I, $23,880
Hutton, Deborah J, info technologist IV, $58,908
Hutton, Randall D, info technology supv, $68,160
Hyde, Sandra M, designated principal asst div, $45,159
Iliff, James E, info technologist II, $36,888
Imhoff, Grayson T, risk mgmt tech II, $38,928
Indelicato, Joseph M, info technologist IV, $56,520
Inhof, Joseph, maint worker II, $29,004

Inturi, Mallikharjuna R, info technology spec II, $71,208
Ipock, Steven J, maint worker II, $29,004
Irving, Milton D, maint worker II, $32,052
Irwin, Richard E, info technologist IV, $53,208
Isenberg, Samuel J, info technology spec II, $55,416
Iven, Michelle L, info technologist IV, $54,288
Ivy, Shawn F, info technology spec II, $65,364
Jackson, Cory P, info technologist I, $30,984
Jackson, Delbert L, maint worker II, $34,356
Jaco, Brian L, maint worker II, $29,004
Jacobs, John E, phys plant sup II, $41,940
Jacobs, Paula C, exec I, $41,940
Jacobsen, Erik R, info technologist III, $40,380
Jahnke, Mark S, info technology spec II, $63,996
Jakubielski, Joseph L, const insp, $47,892
James, Terry L, info technology spec I, $54,288
Jeffress, Stephen D, info technology supv, $61,332
Jeffries, Nicholas S, info technologist I, $31,512
Jennewein, Christopher, info technologist II, $35,568
Jimenez, Jason P, printing/mail cust svc rep, $36,888
Jimenez, John A, info technology spec I, $55,416
John, Magnus, info technology spec I, $49,128
Johns, Ronald A, info technologist I, $34,944
Johnson, Bryan S, info technologist IV, $49,128
Johnson, Carolyn, examination monitor, $7.72/hr
Johnson, Kenneth E, maint worker II, $29,004
Johnson, Kevin, maint worker II, $32,628
Johnson, Kimberly A, pers analyst II, $49,128
Johnson, Lisa A, data processor tech, $30.00/hr
Johnson, Melissa S, paralegal, $36,889
Johnson, Michelle D, info technologist II, $39,624
Johnson, Parker Q, data processor tech, $10.00/hr
Johnson, Randy S, info technology supv, $58,908
Johnson-Townsend, Angela, risk mgmt tech I, $28,536
Johnston, Nancy R, div dir, $96,746
Joiner, Patti L, info technology spec I, $47,892
Jones, David M, info technology spec I, $54,288
Jones, Debra A, housekeeper II, $33,744
Jones, Janene A, risk mgmt tech II, $30,984
Jones, Karen F, info technology oper I, $27,084
Jones, Keith W, info technology supv, $71,208
Jones, Sherry J, examination monitor, $7.72/hr
Julson, David, info technologist IV, $53,208
Juneau, Michael, info technologist I, $31,512
Kaiser, Emily, info technologist II, $34,944
Kaiser, Mark S, div dir, $96,746
Kalia, Anil, comp info tech spec III, $72,768
Kallenbach, Janet F, fiscal & administrative mgr b1, $59,085
Kalugin, Vasily V, info technology spec I, $51,096
Kamara, Edith A, mgmt analysis spec II, $45,156
Karaff, Debra L, info technologist IV, $48,156
Kauffman, Lisa M, pers clerk, $28,104
Keeling, Darlene T, acct II, $37,548
Keeney, Kenneth W, plumber, $29,976
Keep, Pamela J, info technology supv, $63,996
Keeran, Angela M, admin ofc spt asst, $31,512
Keilholz, Celeste R, info technology sr spec, $72,768
Keilholz, Marilyn K, admin ofc spt asst, $31,512
Keisker, David L, comp info tech supv II, $57,744
Kelly, Connie S, info technologist IV, $46,068
Kelly, David J, maint worker II, $29,004
Kelly, Elizabeth A, geographic info sys analyst, $40,380
Kelly, Gavan B, laborer II, $23,160
Kemna, Leslie, buyer III, $43,488
Kemna, Luann, info technologist IV, $43,488
Kemna, Sharon A, misc prof, $29.91/hr
Kemp, Diana S, info technologist III, $32,298
Kempf, Sherry K, dsgnr III, $48,001
Kempker, Carolyn, info technology spec II, $61,332
Kempker, Joseph G, printing/mail technician III, $36,888
Kempker, Marvin, maint worker II, $29,004
Kendle, Julie, info technology spec I, $51,096
Kennedy, Brenda K, admin ofc spt asst, $30,420
Kennedy, Steve, maint worker II, $29,004
Kennett, Karl L, info technology spec I, $49,128
Kern, Nick A, maint spv I, $34,944
Kerr, Dorothy B, printing/mail technician II, $31,416
Kerr, Michael D, maint worker II, $34,356
Kessler, Benjamin, data processor tech, $10.00/hr
Ketterman, Francis N, info technology spec I, $51,096
Key, Kerry D, maint worker II, $29,976
Kilfoil, Steven J, info technologist IV, $45,156
Kimlinger, Jonathan T, info technologist II, $36,888

King, Donald L, designated principal asst div, $79,285
Kingston, David W, maint worker II, $29,004
Kinney, Wesley E, maint worker II, $29,004
Kirkweg, Aaron M, info technologist I, $31,512
Kirkweg, Rhonda M, pers analyst III, $45,156
Kirsch, Paul E, info technologist IV, $46,068
Kirschman, Kevin D, info technologist III, $46,068
Kirschner, Richard M, stationary engr, $34,944
Kiso, Barbara A, info technology spec II, $63,996
Kiso, Jason M, info technology spec I, $47,892
Kistler, Chad T, maint worker II, $29,004
Klahr, James H, exec dir, $86,355
Klatt, Nicole R, training tech III, $46,068
Kleffner, Julie A, buyer IV, $62,664
Kleffner, Larry, misc tech, $9.84/hr
Kleindienst, John H, info technologist IV, $45,156
Klenklen, Patricia C, pers analyst IV, $57,744
Kliethermes, George A, info technologist IV, $56,520
Kliethermes, Gregory A, printing/mail technician II, $32,472
Kliethermes, Lauren, info technologist IV, $44,304
Kliethermes, Richard C, data processing mgr, $78,000
Kliethermes, Twyla E, mgmt analysis spec II, $49,128
Klusmeier, Jeffrey E, legal counsel, $67,620
Kneibert, Christopher, info technologist IV, $50,040
Knight, Dustin, info technologist II, $36,888
Knipfel, Jared S, laborer II, $23,160
Knipp, Lucas J, info technology spec I, $50,040
Koelling, Bobbie S, info technology spec I, $53,208
Koelling, Deborah L, examination monitor, $7.72/hr
Kolb, Craig T, info technology oper II, $37,548
Kolks, Jason W, buyer II, $37,548
Kraft, Emily J, special asst prof, $51,000
Krakue, Ekow D, info technologist III, $39,624
Kraus, David, info technology spec II, $60,120
Kraus, Stephen M, info technologist I, $31,512
Krause, Guy R, hr mgr b3, $89,895
Kroell, Vincent R, stationary engr, $33,744
Kromschroeder, Donald W, plumber, $29,976
Kroner, Steven M, facilities opps mgr b2, $63,986
Kuebler, Joshua, info technologist IV, $43,488
Kuljak, Vladimir, info technologist IV, $46,068
Kumar, Geetha, info technologist III, $41,172
Kumwenda, Alex M, info technology spec I, $49,128
Kuntz, Raymond C, info technology spec I, $55,416
Kuntze, Thomas, info technology oper IV, $46,932
Kusick, Monica G, info technology spec I, $47,892
Labedz, Charles J, info technologist I, $30,984
Labonte, Janette R, info technology spec II, $63,996
Lackman, David, admin ofc spt asst, $33,180
Lagore, Khristopher M, maint worker II, $29,004
Lammert, Richard, info technologist IV, $45,156
Lane, Andrew, info technologist IV, $43,488
Lankford, Calvin, maint worker I, $26,652
Lapp, Ronald E, electrcn, $29,976
Larkins, Scott W, info technologist IV, $58,908
Laroe, John W, boiler oper, $29,976
Larue, Julie K, laborer II, $25,032
Lauberth, Cassie M, info technologist IV, $43,488
Lauer, George M, info technologist IV, $49,128
Laughlin, Bonnie J, info technologist IV, $46,068
Laughlin, Christine A, info technology spec II, $63,996
Laughlin, Peter R, stationary engr, $34,944
Laut, Marcus L, painter, $29,976
Lawson, Merry L, risk mgmt tech II, $31,512
Layson, Tina M, info technology spec I, $50,040
Leeper, Brandon G, refrgrtn mech I, $30,984
Lehman, Joseph, printing/mail technician III, $29,004
Lehmen, Patrick J, acct II, $37,548
Lehmen, Seth, data processor tech, $10.00/hr
Leimkuehler, Yona, info technology spec II, $55,416
Lemport, Timothy S, refrgrtn mech II, $37,548
Leonard, William, heavy equip mech, $32,628
Lepper, Craig R, telecommun analyst IV, $49,128
Lester-wyss, Gail A, info technology spec II, $61,332
Levin, Thomas E, info technology spec II, $57,744
Levy, Kelly A, staff training & dev coor, $48,156
Lewis, David Z, info technologist I, $31,512
Lewis, Eddie J, housekeeper I, $29,004
Lewis, Elbert, info technology spec I, $50,040
Lewis, Jennifer L, research analyst IV, $55,416
Lewis, Kenneth A, maint worker II, $29,004
Lewis, Mickey L, maint worker II, $31,512
Li, Qing, info technologist IV, $45,156

Libbert, Darlene R, data processor tech, $24.06/hr
Libbert, Michael A, info technologist II, $36,888
Libbert, Sara A, data processing mgr, $74,752
Lidge, Charles E, maint worker II, $30,420
Limbach, Mary L, sr ofc spt asst (keybrd), $29,412
Limback, Terry D, maint worker II, $29,004
Lindell, Carl L, maint worker I, $26,652
Lindsay, Jaden A, laborer, $10.75/hr
Linhardt, Paul, buyer II, $37,548
Linsenbardt, Thomas L, info technologist IV, $47,892
Lister, Jamie, info technology spec I, $47,892
Littich, Ronald L, facilities opps mgr b2, $68,639
Loar, Wade G, info technologist III, $38,928
Lock, Randall, info technology spec II, $65,364
Lockhart, William A, info technologist II, $34,944
Loesch, Delores K, data processor tech, $28.90/hr
Loethen, Darlene M, info technology supv, $68,160
Loethen, Nancy J, acct II, $46,932
Loftis, Rex H, maint spv I, $32,628
Logan, Kristy J, info technologist IV, $45,156
Logston, Edythe H, info technology spec II, $58,908
Lohmann, Elizabeth A, reporting spec, $27,496
Long, Amos, info technologist III, $38,928
Long, Curtis S, info technologist II, $36,888
Long, Gary L, maint spv I, $37,548
Long, Mark E, legal counsel, $84,335
Love, Leesa A, acct I, $33,744
Lovel, Jason D, info technologist IV, $49,128
Lowe, David A, info technologist I, $31,512
Lowry, Carla S, info technologist IV, $48,156
Lowry, Scot D, info technologist IV, $54,288
Luaders, Della L, sr field investigator, $49,128
Luadzers, Brenda E, spt asst, $24,612
Lucas, James M, info technology spec II, $71,100
Ludy, Lyndsay R, sr ofc spt asst (keybrd), $25,032
Luebbering, Johann B, info technology spec I, $51,096
Luebbering, Lauri G, data processing mgr, $78,275
Luebbering, Linda S, div dir, $103,525
Luebbert, Daniel W, maint spv II, $41,940
Luebbert, Delana L, exec I, $30,984
Luebbert, Paul D, info technologist IV, $47,892
Luebbert-Howser, Megan L, buyer III, $43,488
Luecke, Brad R, design/develop/survey mgr b2, $71,205
Lueckenotte, Kurtis L, refrgrtn mech II, $33,744
Lunsford, William R, laborer, $10.75/hr
Lupo, Karen S, admin ofc spt asst, $36,888
Lutz, Deborah, risk mgmt spec I, $48,156
Lutz, Thomas E, maint spv I, $42,708
Lynch, Kenneth S, info technologist IV, $46,932
Maddox, William D, maint worker II, $29,004
Magee, Brian D, phys plant sup III, $57,744
Maher, Zachary A, info technology oper II, $28,104
Mahurin, Bobby L, maint worker II, $29,004
Major, Terry T, maint worker II, $29,004
Malhotra, Vipan, info technology sr spec, $75,948
Malone, Christina A, info technology spec I, $50,040
Maloy, James A, info technology spec II, $65,364
Malzner, Laura K, st cnslt on child welfare, $51,096
Manczuk, Mikel, data processor tech, $26.63/hr
Maness, Eric T, info technology spec II, $63,996
Manion, Amber, sr ofc spt asst (keybrd), $26,652
Mankin, Michael, stationary engr, $34,944
Manning, Guy L, maint spv I, $37,548
Mantle, Colleen K, custodial work spv, $25,404
Mantle, Mark A, info technology spec II, $58,908
Marcus, Michael S, comp info tech spec III, $74,304
Markway, Daniel J, crpntr, $38,928
Markway, Eric T, electrcn, $33,744
Markway, Robert, info technology supv, $63,996
Marrant, Steve D, maint worker II, $30,420
Marshall, Brent D, info technologist IV, $46,068
Martin, Alan R, stationary engr, $37,548
Martin, Annette R, admin ofc spt asst, $32,628
Martin, Clifford, info technology spec II, $68,160
Martin, Gina M, pers analyst II, $44,304
Martin, Jose L, printing/mail technician I, $27,084
Martin, Kevin D, comp info tech supv II, $63,996
Martin, Matthew, info technology spec I, $50,040
Martin, Robin M, pers clerk, $30,984
Martin, Stephen L, info technology spec I, $55,416
Maschmeyer, Louis C, maint worker II, $29,004
Maseles, Richard M, legal counsel, $58,196
Maslen, Jimmie J, motor veh mech, $32,628

Mason, Luke P, info technologist II, $36,888
Mason, Tina L, pers analyst II, $36,204
Massman, Andrew A, maint worker II, $32,628
Massman, Bradley J, printing/mail technician II, $28,452
Massman, Michael F, phys plant sup III, $49,128
Massman, Samuel, maint worker II, $29,004
Massman, William J, crpntr spv, $38,232
Masters, Larry R, stationary engr, $34,944
Matheis, Karen A, info technology spec II, $60,120
Mathenia, Randall W, info technologist IV, $58,908
Mathis, Melissa A, state leasing coor, $57,744
Mattison, Dennis E, maint spv I, $32,628
Maupin, Christopher, pers analyst III, $46,932
Maxwell, Rodney K, info technology spec II, $71,208
May, Michael W, phys plant sup II, $42,708
Mayfield, Elijah, data processor tech, $10.10/hr
Mayfield, Todd C, info technology spec I, $53,208
Maylee, Dale D, phys plant sup II, $46,068
Mazza, Matthew J, storekeeper I, $26,652
McBride, Linda K, info technologist III, $41,940
McBurney, Samuel D, info technologist IV, $43,488
McCann, Karen J, exec I, $41,940
McCann, Mark W, info technology spec I, $57,744
McCarty, Megan, risk mgmt spec I, $40,380
McCarty, Micah J, printing/mail technician II, $25,824
McCarty, Michelle L, risk mgmt tech III, $34,944
McCarty, Theodore M, info technologist IV, $43,488
McCauley, Shawn P, fiscal & administrative mgr b1, $47,878
McClatchery, Angie M, info technologist IV, $45,156
McConkey, Larry G, maint worker II, $32,052
McCoy, Michael D, info technologist IV, $51,096
McCray, Michael J, risk mgmt spec I, $46,932
McDaniel, Allen T, maint spv I, $32,628
McDermit, Elizabeth A, account clerk II, $25,824
McDonald, Carla A, info technologist IV, $50,040
McDougal, Sara A, info technology spec I, $57,744
McFarland, Mark W, refrgrtn mech II, $37,548
McFarland, Rick D, comp info technology mgr I, $81,036
McGartland, Patricia A, ofc spt asst (keybrd), $23,508
McGhee, Sylvia M, exec I, $37,548
McGlasson, Dale, info technologist IV, $43,488
McGonigal, Christopher G, info technologist I, $30,984
McGowen, Thomas E, maint spv I, $32,628
McIntosh, Audrey, commission mbr, $103,960
McKenna, William J, facilities opps mgr b1, $55,152
McLucas, Phillip N, info technologist IV, $45,156
McQuary, Pamela R, exec I, $47,892
McTavish, Marissa, info technologist IV, $47,892
Mealy, Sandra R, info technologist I, $51,096
Means, Nicholas J, park maint wkr I, $23,880
Meili, James P, info technology spec I, $54,288
Meine, Steven E, info technology spec I, $55,416
Mendoza, Rony V, info technology spec I, $71,208
Mengwasser, Kevin, info technology spec II, $71,100
Merchant, James D, maint spv I, $38,232
Merchant, Larry W, plumber, $34,944
Merrell, Durk B, info technology spec II, $71,208
Mertens, Laura A, ofc of administration mgr 2, $58,869
Meyer, Leann M, pers analyst II, $44,304
Meyer, Robert E, info technology spec I, $61,332
Meyer, Stephen W, info technology spec II, $71,208
Meyer, Tiffanie, procurement ofcr I, $46,068
Michel, Megan J, info technologist IV, $23,946
Michel, Tammy L, buyer II, $43,488
Migogo, Felix, info technology spec I, $50,040
Mihalevich, Matthew C, info technologist IV, $56,520
Milam, James L, construction insp, $47,892
Miller, Alan F, account clerk II, $27,084
Miller, April J, pers clerk, $28,104
Miller, Clinton W, maint worker II, $29,004
Miller, Cori N, info technologist II, $36,204
Miller, David L, maint worker II, $29,976
Miller, Diana L, info technology spec II, $60,120
Miller, George L, painter, $29,976
Miller, James E, maint worker II, $36,888
Miller, Jennifer L, info technologist III, $40,380
Miller, Kathy L, pers analyst III, $46,932
Mills, Marianne E, planner IV, $59,640
Mincks, Robert D, info technology supv, $71,208
Miner, Jeff T, info technologist IV, $49,128
Minkin, Erik, info technology spec II, $62,664
Minks, Mark A, maint worker II, $29,004
Miriello, Umberto, info technologist IV, $46,932

Mistler, Trisha A, graphic arts spec II, $28,536
Mitchell, Alexander D, info technologist III, $41,940
Mitchell, Harold, maint worker II, $29,004
Mitchem, Mandy L, admin ofc spt asst, $34,944
Moeller, Jennifer L, info technology spec I, $52,092
Moe-Omoigui, Cherece D, info technology spec II, $63,996
Moore, Christopher H, info technology spec I, $54,288
Moore, Richard E, info technology spec I, $60,120
Mora, Blanca, pers analyst II, $39,624
Moran, John L, special investigator, $37.49/hr
Moran, Michael, info technology spec II, $62,664
Morfeld, Melanie K, pers clerk, $29,496
Morgan, Claud A, maint worker II, $30,420
Morris, Angela C, procurement ofcr II, $50,040
Morris, David G, maint worker II, $29,004
Morris, James R, printing/mail technician IV, $37,548
Morris, Jordan E, accounting spec I, $35,568
Morris, Kevin A, stationary engr, $33,744
Morris, Lendia, printing/mail technician II, $27,948
Morris, Vernon, facilities opps mgr b2, $59,611
Morrow, Bradley J, info technology spec I, $52,092
Morrow, Garrick D, info technologist II, $38,232
Morts, Tyler G, maint spv I, $35,568
Moses, Rebecca M, misc prof, $18.42/hr
Mosha, Richard F, info technologist IV, $46,068
Mowatt, Kimarley N, info technologist III, $41,172
Moyer, William P, data processing mgr, $65,145
Mueller, Cathy J, pers analyst I, $40,380
Mueller, Heather M, info technology spec I, $50,040
Muenks, Angeline J, pers analyst III, $45,156
Muenks, Eric V, comp info tech supv II, $62,664
Muenks, Steve, info technology spec I, $58,908
Mueth, Laura F, disability prog rep, $34,944
Murdick, Jessica L, risk mgmt tech II, $32,052
Murdock, James B, stationary engr, $33,744
Murphy, Brianna G, special asst ofc & clerical, $33,330
Murphy, Michael W, info technologist IV, $46,068
Murray, Carla J, info technology spec II, $60,120
Murray, Kevin, ofc of administration mgr 1, $51,021
Mustoe, Daniel B, ofc of administration mgr 1, $51,025
Mutert, Joyce E, data processor tech, $28.90/hr
Muzy, Joseph E, info technologist II, $36,888
Myers, Joseph A, hvac inst ctrls tech, $36,888
Nadreau, Lee W, info technology spec I, $51,096
Naik, Rashmi Y, info technology spec II, $66,720
Nations, Dennis B, stationary engr, $35,568
Neal, Jody D, maint spv I, $32,628
Neal, Stacy, div dir, $96,746
Neel, Tristin R, examination monitor, $7.72/hr
Neely, Nathan R, info technology spec II, $68,160
Neff, Paula S, painter, $29,976
Neiman, Angela L, info technology spec I, $51,096
Nelson, Charles T, laborer I, $21,264
Nenninger, Sheri M, exec I, $38,232
Neuhart, Wallace, info technology spec II, $65,364
Neuner, Matthew G, info technology spec I, $47,892
Neuner, Michael B, clerk, $8.83/hr
Nevels, Derek W, maint worker II, $29,004
Newland, Christopher, info technology spec I, $51,096
Newman, Donald R, stationary engr, $33,744
Newman, Douglas, comp info tech spec III, $68,160
Newton, Jarrod R, info technologist II, $42,708
Nichols, Raymond L, info technology spec I, $55,416
Nichols, Susan K, misc prof, $24.75/hr
Niedergerke, Carey L, maint worker II, $29,004
Nilges, Randy R, maint worker II, $29,496
Nix, Steven, info technology oper II, $36,204
Nold, Mary F, sr ofc spt asst (keybrd), $31,416
Nott, Raleigh M, park maint wkr III, $34,944
Novak, Gerry D, info technologist IV, $50,040
Nzoiwu, Festus M, info technologist III, $41,172
O'Bannon, Lon W, info technologist IV, $47,892
O'Connell, Timothy P, info technologist IV, $50,040
Odneal, Lori A, printing/mail technician III, $29,496
Odom, James L, ofc of administration mgr 1, $54,274
Offutt, Devon J, info technologist I, $29,976
Ogbevoen, Nicholas O, info technologist IV, $45,156
Ogden, Jeffrey, info technology spec II, $65,364
Ogega, Nyankuru O, info technologist II, $36,888
Oligschlaeger, Jennifer L, info technology spec II, $58,908
Oligschlaeger, Jocelyn Y, accounting spec II, $40,380
Oligschlaeger, Michelle A, info technologist IV, $47,892
Oliver, Austin R, info technologist I, $31,512

Olson, Robert B, info technology spec II, $62,664
Onsongo, Edwin N, info technologist IV, $43,488
Opehem, Hope J, info technologist IV, $50,040
Opie, Jessica L, fiscal & administrative mgr b3, $84,845
Oppy, Erin R, info technologist IV, $45,156
Orman, Lori A, info technologist IV, $45,156
O'Rourke, Daniel C, fiscal & administrative mgr b2, $65,977
Ortmeyer, Laura L, fiscal & administrative mgr b2, $69,604
Orton, Bret, info technologist III, $44,304
Oser, Connie L, storekeeper II, $33,744
Ostrom, David B, maint spv I, $32,628
Oswald, Geoffrey S, info technologist II, $41,940
O'toole, James P, designated principal asst div, $62,317
Ousley, Brandon M, info technology spec I, $52,092
Overbey, Beverley L, comp info tech supv I, $56,520
Owen, James M, legal counsel, $71,000
Owens, Jerry J, reporting spec, $35,568
Owens, Stephen E, info technology sr spec, $71,208
Ownbey, Jamie F, printing/mail technician IV, $37,548
Pace, Dylann J, laborer, $10.75/hr
Pahl, Eric N, data processing mgr, $76,255
Palazzolo, Elizabeth, fiscal & administrative mgr b2, $69,604
Palmer, Kenneth, info technologist II, $37,548
Pappenfort, Cary R, info technology spec I, $60,120
Parkes, Dustin J, info technologist I, $31,512
Parks, Rhiannon M, info technologist I, $30,984
Parks, Richard R, state leasing coor, $57,744
Parris, Greg, info technology spec I, $51,096
Parry, Dustin D, account clerk II, $25,824
Patridge, Jeffrey D, geographic info sys analyst, $44,304
Patterson, Douglas W, supply mgr I, $32,628
Paudel, Dipendra, accounting spec I, $34,944
Pauley, Lynda, exec I, $31,512
Paulsmeyer, Kristen E, legal counsel, $69,135
Payne, Jeremiah D, maint worker II, $29,004
Pearson, Bryan R, maint worker II, $29,004
Pearson, Walter, designated principal asst dept, $98,766
Pecher, Leanne, facilities opps mgr b1, $57,740
Peery, Donnie, info technologist IV, $43,488
Pendleton, Leighann, acct I, $30,984
Penserum, Jason A, custodial worker II, $21,864
Percy, Nathan R, designated principal asst div, $45,159
Perkins, Stanley W, ofc of administration mgr 1, $55,550
Perrey, Janet L, data processor tech, $26.72/hr
Perrin, Spencer D, plumber, $29,976
Peters, David, data processor tech, $10.00/hr
Peters, Donald W, design/develop/survey mgr b1, $58,899
Peters, Kenneth J, info technology supv, $60,120
Peters, Matthew D, state leasing coor, $57,744
Peters, Paula M, comp info technology mgr I, $77,556
Pettit, Earl, buyer IV, $53,208
Pettit, James W, info technology spec I, $56,520
Phanichkul, Patrick L, info technologist III, $42,708
Phelps, Barbara L, acct I, $30,984
Phillips, Angela, designated principal asst div, $84,351
Phillips, Douglas R, info technologist IV, $46,932
Phillips, Nathan L, info technology spec II, $57,744
Phillips, Sarah, info technologist III, $41,172
Phillips, Stephanie C, info technologist I, $31,512
Pierce, John B, info technology spec II, $62,664
Pilkington, Matthew, info technologist III, $40,380
Pillai, Girish S, comp info tech spec III, $72,768
Pinet, Jon A, maint worker II, $29,004
Pinkston, Susan L, info technologist IV, $45,156
Pippen, John W, info technology spec I, $52,092
Pippins, Derek A, info technologist IV, $43,488
Pitt, Edward, plumber, $36,888
Plassmeyer, Kimberly, acct I, $30,984
Pleus, Kevin J, printing/mail technician I, $23,880
Plybon, Dawn, pers analyst I, $37,548
Pointer, Paul E, maint spv I, $37,548
Pointer, William T, stationary engr, $37,548
Polendo, Andrea L, account clerk II, $25,824
Pool, Gary, info technology spec II, $62,664
Pope, Jeremy, info technology oper II, $28,104
Porter, Alex, info technologist II, $36,888
Porter, Micah J, info technology spec I, $47,892
Potts, Patricia J, info technologist IV, $55,416
Potts, Patrick L, info technologist I, $40,380
Potts, Ray G, comp info technology mgr I, $66,720
Potts, Tamara S, acct I, $30,984
Prater, Christine M, acct II, $39,624
Prater, Jessica K, fiscal & administrative mgr b1, $53,207

Prater, Tamira K, info technology supv, $61,332
Prenger, C D, info technology spec II, $71,100
Prenger, Diane J, info technology spec II, $60,120
Prenger, Glen E, account clerk II, $26,652
Prenger, Matthew R, info technologist III, $41,172
Prevallet, Clayton M, maint worker II, $29,004
Prewett, Jessica L, exec I, $34,944
Prila, Herald, info technologist IV, $45,156
Pringer, Jeana F, budget & plng analyst II, $46,932
Proctor, Tammy S, info technology spec I, $50,040
Propst, Donald H, state leasing coor, $60,120
Provance, Christopher L, info technologist IV, $46,932
Pruitt, Jack L, laborer I, $26,652
Pruitt, Roger D, maint spv I, $43,488
Puckett, Steven M, refrgrtn mech II, $35,568
Pyatt, Jesse, data processor tech, $10.00/hr
Quick, Byron G, electrcn, $29,976
Qutami, Connie S, accounting spec III, $51,096
Qutami, Michael M, design/develop/survey mgr b3, $77,265
Raburn, Amy L, info technology spec II, $65,364
Rackers, Carol S, pers analyst I, $32,052
Rackers, Cynthia L, info technology spec I, $51,096
Rackers, Nathan J, info technology spec II, $63,996
Rackers, Susan, risk mgmt tech II, $30,420
Rademan, Debra S, misc tech, $24.48/hr
Ragar, D L, info technology sr spec, $72,768
Ragland, Daniel J, info technology spec I, $52,092
Rahim, Mustafa R, geographic info sys spec, $47,892
Ralston, Sarah, acct II, $38,232
Ramelb, Tami L, info technology spec II, $72,768
Randle, Darren T, maint worker II, $29,004
Raps, Billy R, sheet metal worker, $30,984
Rasmussen, Austin T, data processor tech, $10.00/hr
Rasmussen, Dwayne A, fiscal & administrative mgr b2, $67,726
Ratchford, Lynn, info technology spec II, $71,208
Ratzel, Ali P, info technologist I, $31,512
Rauba, Lisa D, comp info tech supv II, $57,744
Rawlings, David, data processor tech, $10.00/hr
Ray, Michael E, maint worker II, $29,004
Readenour, Monica D, info technology spec II, $68,160
Redel, Kathleen K, info technology spec I, $54,288
Reed, Philip S, data processing mgr, $81,297
Reeves, Hollis R, maint worker II, $29,004
Rehagen, Mary L, comp info tech supv I, $49,128
Rehagen, Robert J, electrcn, $33,744
Rehagen, Travis F, info technologist IV, $46,932
Rehkop, Phillip E, info technology spec I, $54,288
Reichert, Christopher M, phys plant sup III, $52,092
Reinkemeyer, Benjamin M, info technology spec II, $71,100
Reinstein, Bert, info technology spec I, $56,520
Rench, Vanessa J, info technologist IV, $46,932
Renno, Eddie L, maint spv I, $32,628
Retherford, Elizabeth S, geographic info sys analyst, $41,940
Reynolds, Deborah A, misc tech, $16.16/hr
Rhea, Kimberly L, acct I, $30,984
Rhoads, Kenneth O, info technology spec II, $61,332
Rhoads, Stephanie, account clerk II, $26,652
Rhodes, Damon J, info technology supv, $69,612
Rhodes, Mark A, stationary engr, $38,928
Richardson, Helen C, examination monitor, $7.72/hr
Richardson, Jason M, info technologist III, $38,928
Richardson, Troy, examination monitor, $7.72/hr
Richart, Jerry C, painter, $36,204
Richey, George D, crpntr, $34,944
Richey Winkelman, Donna L, info technology spec II, $71,208
Ridenhour, Paul W, phys plant sup II, $46,068
Riegel, Patricia I, info technologist II, $41,940
Riegel, Patricia L, info technology spec I, $49,128
Rieman, Kyle, budget & plng analyst II, $46,932
Riley, Aaron R, info technologist I, $31,512
Ritter, Timothy A, printing/mail cust svc rep, $41,940
Rivera, Ralph A, info technology spec I, $63,996
Roach, Mitzi J, info technology spec I, $56,520
Roark, Janice A, info technology spec II, $62,664
Robb, Barry L, facilities opps mgr b1, $63,986
Roberson, Amanda R, admin ofc spt asst, $34,944
Roberts, Anthony L, fiscal & administrative mgr b3, $74,544
Robertson, Jay M, info technology spec I, $50,040
Robinette, Emily C, info technologist I, $30,984
Robinson, Shelly L, info technology spec II, $65,364
Robyn, Timothy P, designated principal asst dept, $111,605
Rockelman, Christian, dsgnr I, $36,204
Rockers, Clayton W, laborer, $10.75/hr

Rodgers, Jerry L, maint worker II, $30,984
Roehl, Terrence, pers analyst III, $48,156
Rogers, David E, info technologist IV, $45,156
Rogers, Dustin A, info technologist III, $42,708
Rogge, Mitchell D, facilities opps mgr b1, $55,152
Roling, Michael T, special asst prof, $90,395
Rollins, Jake, comp info tech spec III, $68,160
Rose, Beverly, account clerk II, $27,084
Rose, John K, maint worker II, $34,356
Rosslan, Kelcee L, data processor tech, $10.00/hr
Rothove, Kathy G, data processor tech, $25.58/hr
Rothove, Mary K, info technology spec I, $36,888
Roundcount, Jerome B, maint spv I, $32,628
Rouse, Steven H, info technologist IV, $46,068
Rowland, Jeremy M, electronics tech, $30,984
Rowland, Theresa L, pers clerk, $28,104
Royer, Kevin L, maint worker II, $29,004
Rozelle, Janine, info technologist II, $35,568
Rucker, Billy, storekeeper II, $28,104
Rucker, Louis G, facilities opps mgr b2, $63,985
Ruessler, Patrick M, acct I, $30,984
Ruether, Gary P, storekeeper II, $25,032
Ruppel, Barbara, geographic info sys spec, $47,892
Ruppel, John H, refrgrtn mech I, $34,356
Ruppel, Justin M, maint worker II, $29,004
Rush, Gayle A, info technologist I, $32,052
Rush, Marty J, info technologist IV, $46,068
Rush, Melody S, info technologist IV, $45,156
Russell, Zachary, design/develop/survey mgr b1, $52,091
Russler, Jacqueline A, designated principal asst div, $36,990
Ryan, Jason L, info technologist IV, $45,156
Sackett, Melissa, buyer I, $29,976
Saltink, Robert W, info technologist IV, $45,156
Samson, Roger W, data processor tech, $30.76/hr
Samuel, Ronald, crpntr, $35,568
Sandbothe, Christopher D, printing/mail technician III, $29,496
Sands, Frank, maint worker II, $29,496
Sanning, Evan J, info technologist IV, $51,096
Sanning, Joe L, design/develop/survey mgr b2, $60,261
Santa Cruze, James J, info technologist IV, $45,156
Sappington, John W, data processor tech, $31.43/hr
Sarver, William J, info technologist IV, $49,128
Satterlee, Jacqueline, buyer II, $37,548
Savala, Nicolas W, laborer, $10.75/hr
Savka, Gary C, maint worker II, $30,420
Schaefer, Kirsten R, research analyst IV, $48,156
Schaefer, Michael D, printing/mail technician IV, $38,232
Schaefer, Roger, laborer, $20.14/hr
Schaefer, Sandra M, acct II, $37,548
Schaefer, Viola M, misc tech, $26.26/hr
Schaffer, Barbara J, sr ofc spt asst (keybrd), $26,652
Schaffer, Derrick J, info technologist II, $38,928
Schaffer, Nancy K, info technology supv, $55,416
Schanuth, Tyler W, data processor tech, $10.00/hr
Schelich, Paul W, info technologist IV, $47,892
Scheperle, Matthew A, info technologist III, $41,172
Schepers, Christopher M, info technology spec I, $50,040
Schepers, Eric, info technology oper II, $28,104
Scheppers, Andrew T, info technologist II, $36,888
Scherer-Morris, Diane M, info technologist IV, $46,068
Scheulen, Steven C, info technology spec I, $52,092
Schlereth, Steven E, maint spv I, $32,628
Schloss, Jeffrey, geographic info sys coordinatr, $68,160
Schloss, Teresa M, geographic info sys spec, $49,128
Schmid, Dennis R, fiscal & administrative mgr b2, $65,980
Schmidt, Jared C, info technologist III, $41,940
Schmidt, Justin W, laborer II, $27,084
Schmidt, Thomas L, facilities opps mgr b3, $72,755
Schmidt, Timothy D, design/develop/survey mgr b2, $71,205
Schmolzi, Kevin P, info technologist IV, $43,488
Schmolzi, Kristina R, sr ofc spt asst (keybrd), $28,452
Schmutzler, Darryl P, printing/mail technician IV, $34,356
Schmutzler, Kathy J, info technology spec I, $53,208
Schneider, Jared A, maint worker II, $29,004
Schneider, Paula J, info technologist IV, $45,156
Schnieders, Tracy L, acct I, $33,180
Schobey, Betty A, comp info tech supv II, $58,908
Schoelch, Wesley C, power plant mech, $30,984
Schollmeyer, Eric W, maint worker II, $29,004
Schollmeyer, Holly M, info technology spec I, $50,040
Schrader, Karen M, examination monitor, $7.72/hr
Schraer, Karen, sr ofc spt asst (keybrd), $28,452
Schreiber, Kirk M, principal asst board/commisson, $74,311

Schrimpf, Thomas A, info technologist IV, $45,156
Schroder, Leo E, maint worker II, $32,628
Schroeder, David, info technology sr spec, $81,036
Schubert, Aaron L, info technology spec II, $71,208
Schubert, Amanda M, mgmt analysis spec I, $41,940
Schuemann, Jason D, maint worker II, $29,004
Schuett, Breanna C, info technologist II, $36,204
Schuldt, Justin A, refrgrtn mech II, $38,232
Schulte, Catherine B, fiscal & administrative mgr b1, $60,600
Schulte, Garret J, motor veh mech, $29,976
Schulte, Joyce, info technologist IV, $45,156
Schulte, Kevin J, crpntr, $30,420
Schulte, Melvin W, misc tech, $16.91/hr
Schulte, Scott E, info technology spec II, $71,208
Schulte, Teri L, buyer III, $43,488
Schulte, Valerie M, acct I, $34,944
Schultz, Kelly D, prog mgr, $70,927
Schwartz, Dennis J, storekeeper I, $25,824
Schwartze, Derek, reporting spec, $11.00/hr
Schwartze, Lindsay F, info technologist III, $41,172
Schweiss, Michael J, info technology supv, $66,720
Scott, Charlene L, info technologist IV, $36,125
Scott, Dennis L, storekeeper II, $28,104
Scott, Keron K, info technologist II, $35,568
Scrivner, Brandon, storekeeper II, $27,228
Seaboldt, Grover W, labor spv, $26,652
Seals, Ollie P, sr ofc spt asst (keybrd), $26,232
Seeley, Philip, info technologist IV, $43,488
Seeney, Wanda L, ofc of administration mgr 2, $71,205
Self, Jr, maint worker II, $31,512
Senter, Frank K, info technology spec II, $62,664
Shaefer, Aaron E, info technology spec I, $49,128
Shalbot, Cheryl, info technologist II, $34,944
Shanklin, David L, info technologist IV, $51,096
Shans, Vivian, examination monitor, $7.72/hr
Shavers, Rebecca L, risk mgmt spec I, $41,940
Sheley, Jeffery D, maint worker II, $29,004
Shelton, Michael C, phys plant sup II, $44,304
Shepherd, Kristy A, info technology spec I, $34,944
Sheppard, Howard V, info technology spec I, $47,892
Sheputis, Kenneth P, maint worker II, $34,944
Sheridan, Teresa L, sr ofc spt asst (keybrd), $27,084
Sherrill, John D, phys plant sup II, $45,156
Shikles, Krista D, info technology spec II, $60,120
Shimmens, Barbara, misc prof, $36.42/hr
Shockley, Joseph W, info technology supv, $65,364
Sholes, Thomas L, info technology supv, $62,664
Short, Kendra L, info technologist II, $36,204
Shouse, Guy K, stationary engr, $33,744
Shrum, Ronald J, maint spv I, $32,628
Shuey, Richard A, info technology spec I, $56,520
Shultz, Randy A, info technologist II, $34,944
Shultz, Thomas E, info technology spec I, $53,208
Sidahmed Ahmed, Mula Ihfid, info technologist II, $36,888
Siebeneck, Chelsea, accounting spec I, $36,204
Siebeneck, Joshua A, refrgrtn mech II, $33,744
Siebeneck, Perry L, groundskeeper II, $23,880
Siegler, Steven R, designated principal asst div, $92,572
Siemons, Jason, info technologist IV, $45,156
Siemons, Lucinda K, accounting spec II, $40,380
Sieve, Steven, laborer II, $24,264
Sifford, Shawn, info technologist IV, $45,156
Sikes, Athena M, acct I, $34,944
Silvey, Louis D, maint worker II, $29,004
Simms, Robert F, data processing mgr, $76,255
Simpson, Corigan P, info technologist II, $36,204
Sims, Brandon P, info technologist I, $30,984
Sinden, Leslie A, laborer I, $21,264
Singer, Bruce A, info technology spec I, $56,520
Sipakati, Patro M, info technology spec I, $50,040
Sissom, John W, info technology spec I, $49,128
Siverly, Brenton, fiscal & administrative mgr b3, $71,205
Skaggs, Daniel E, maint worker II, $29,004
Skelton, Betty A, info technologist IV, $45,156
Skidmore, Brenda K, info technologist IV, $53,208
Skiles, Gary W, laborer, $10.75/hr
Slusher, Renee T, dpty state dept dir, $115,064
Small, Christopher S, maint worker II, $29,004
Smalley, Brett W, laborer II, $23,160
Smith, Cathy J, printing/mail technician I, $23,880
Smith, Chaun L, laborer, $10.75/hr
Smith, Glenn C, design engr I, $52,092
Smith, Greg, printing/mail technician II, $25,824

Smith, Jeffery D, plumber, $34,356
Smith, Nancy D, info technologist IV, $45,156
Smith, Robert A, maint spv I, $32,628
Smith, Sara R, info technologist IV, $46,932
Smith, Sherrece R, designated principal asst dept, $52,985
Smith, William T, maint spv I, $32,628
Snellen, Brian D, info technology spec II, $55,416
Snider, Billy J, stationary engr, $33,744
Snyder, Jordan T, info technologist I, $31,512
Snyder, Zheng, accounting spec I, $36,204
Sokolowski, Kimberly A, info technology spec I, $50,040
Solomon, Cathy L, info technology sr spec, $74,304
Sommerer, Ginger, court reporter II, $35,927
Sommerer, Joseph, data processor tech, $10.00/hr
Sommerer, Marvin L, supply mgr II, $38,232
Sommerer, Tammy I, info technology spec I, $51,096
Sooter, John H, laborer II, $28,908
Sorensen, David E, info technologist II, $34,944
Sosnowski, Paula, exec I, $40,380
Sparks, Daniel S, info technology spec I, $53,208
Spears, Alan D, info technology spec II, $71,208
Speidel, Kimberly A, acct III, $57,744
Spencer, William L, phys plant sup III, $46,068
Spillars, John L, info technology spec I, $49,128
Sprague, Reynetta D, info technologist IV, $45,156
Spray, Amy R, facilities opps mgr b1, $59,611
Sprenger, Dewayne L, info technologist IV, $57,744
Stafford, Cynthia S, fiscal & administrative mgr b3, $77,557
Stains, Dianne K, info technologist IV, $45,156
Staley, Velda M, designated principal asst div, $39,529
Stalter, Courtney R, fiscal & administrative mgr b2, $55,000
Stapleton, Angela G, pers analyst I, $32,628
Stapleton, Timothy, info technologist II, $34,944
Stapp, David L, maint worker II, $29,004
Stark, Jerry A, maint worker II, $29,004
Statler, David P, info technology spec II, $71,100
Steele, Thelma E, info technologist IV, $43,488
Steenburgen, Bonnie J, fiscal & administrative mgr b1, $57,744
Steffens, Jonathan, info technology supv, $61,332
Stegeman, Judy V, data processor tech, $28.90/hr
Stegeman, Kevin, info technologist III, $41,172
Steinbeck, Greg S, info technologist III, $38,928
Steinman, Anthony W, info technologist IV, $45,156
Stemmler, Bernard J, maint worker II, $29,004
Stephenson, John J, info technology supv, $63,996
Stevens, Chris J, phys plant sup II, $45,156
Stevens, Eveleen, info technologist III, $41,940
Stevens, Kenneth B, refrgrtn mech II, $38,232
Stevenson, Daniel J, info technology spec I, $54,288
Stieferman, Vincent A, refrgrtn mech I, $38,232
Stiefermann, Diane M, info technologist IV, $47,892
Stiers, Bryan A, maint worker II, $29,496
Still, Ronald, info technologist III, $43,488
Stobbart, John T, buyer III, $50,040
Stock, Terry L, maint worker II, $29,004
Stokes, Bradley, info technologist IV, $45,156
Stokes, Curtis R, staff attny, $60,257
Stokes, James R, info technology spec I, $51,096
Stokes, Ruth A, ofc of administration mgr 1, $63,985
Stone, Angela M, info technologist IV, $46,932
Stone, Thomas, construction insp supv, $52,092
Storm, George M, info technology spec I, $50,040
Storms, Thompson A, info technologist III, $40,380
Stout, Michael A, info technology supv, $71,100
Stovall, Janet R, info technologist IV, $46,932
Stover, Terry L, info technology spec I, $60,120
Strange, Chalaine E, comp info tech supv I, $52,092
Strein, Tammie S, info technology supv, $61,332
Stringer, Justin, risk mgmt spec II, $43,488
Strong-goeke, Lori L, fiscal & administrative mgr b3, $88,819
Strope, Dawn M, info technologist IV, $46,068
Strope, Stacy, info technology spec I, $54,288
Strube, Glynne D, info technologist IV, $43,488
Struempf, Elizabeth A, info technologist IV, $45,156
Struemph, Dustin M, tech asst IV, $37,548
Struemph, Linda M, state leasing coor, $57,744
Struemph, Lynn A, budget & plng sr anal, $57,744
Stuecken, Victoria, info technologist III, $39,624
Sullens, John L, info technology spec I, $51,096
Sullwold, Michael R, refrgrtn mech II, $34,944
Summerlott, Tommy F, maint worker II, $29,004
Summers, David J, maint worker II, $29,004
Sundermeyer, Michael S, design/dev/survey mgr b2, $71,205

Suresh, Anuncia M, info technology spec II, $71,208
Surface, Scott, printing/mail technician II, $26,652
Sutherland, Danny L, maint worker II, $15,496
Sutter, Glenda J, info technologist IV, $51,096
Swanigan, Carolyn J, asst prog mgr, $54,591
Swartz, Mark, info technology spec II, $66,720
Sweeten, Nicolle A, info technologist II, $36,888
Sweetwood, Matthew G, budget & plng sr analyst, $60,120
Sykes, Dennis W, info technologist IV, $45,156
Tackett, Steven M, info technologist IV, $48,156
Taggart, Dale A, info technologist IV, $46,932
Talley, Bradford W, plumber, $29,976
Tallman, Stephanie L, info technologist IV, $45,156
Tambke, Bernadine, acct I, $30,984
Tappel, Trevor P, maint worker II, $29,004
Taylor, Elishia S, info technologist IV, $46,932
Taylor, John W, printing/mail technician II, $25,824
Taylor, Kelly A, info technology spec II, $57,744
Taylor, Shelby L, admin ofc spt asst, $31,512
Teasley, Laura R, info technology spec II, $65,364
Temmen, Donna M, sr ofc spt asst (keybrd), $30,924
Templeton, Tammy W, info technologist III, $42,708
Tessereau, Steven J, refrgrtn mech I, $30,984
Theis, Melissa K, pers analyst III, $46,932
Thoenen, Wayne A, info technologist IV, $45,156
Thomas, Fonda M, info technology spec II, $61,332
Thomas, Gay B, info technologist IV, $45,156
Thomas, Ronald E, comp info tech spec III, $81,036
Thompson, Andrew J, info technologist I, $29,976
Thompson, Christine K, budget & plng sr analyst, $57,744
Thompson, Gary L, info technology spec II, $61,332
Thompson, Jonathan L, phys plant sup III, $52,092
Thompson, Mark R, supply mgr I, $34,944
Thompson, Michael G, info technologist IV, $49,128
Thompson, Shannon, phys plant sup III, $49,128
Thornton, Barry D, info technologist IV, $49,128
Thornton, Carmela E, fiscal & administrative mgr b3, $77,557
Thurman, Erik, info technologist III, $38,928
Tiethoff, Tracey A, info technology spec II, $62,664
Tindle, Steven A, info technology spec I, $50,040
Todd, Douglas C, electrcn, $31,512
Todd, Dwight L, info technologist IV, $47,892
Toebben, Amanda N, sr ofc spt asst (keybrd), $25,824
Tordoff, Wade G, printing/mail cust svc rep, $33,180
Toth, Rowland, info technologist IV, $45,156
Townsend, Keith J, info technology spec I, $49,128
Townsend, Timothy, supply mgr I, $31,512
Trabue, Bryan C, info technology spec I, $56,520
Trachsel, Marilyn, misc tech, $30.54/hr
Tracy, Daniel A, info technologist I, $33,180
Treece, Alan B, info technology spec II, $74,304
Tribout, Scott E, electrcn, $29,976
Tripp, Robert D, info technologist IV, $45,156
Troesser, Melissa, exec I, $34,944
Troup, David L, info technologist IV, $47,892
Trusley, Charlene K, printing/mail technician III, $29,004
Trussell, Diana L, info technologist IV, $60,120
Tull, Annette C, pers analyst III, $45,156
Tupper, Ray D, maint worker II, $29,004
Turner, Benjamin J, info technologist III, $40,380
Turner, Gentry J, electrcn, $29,976
Turpin, Payton D, park maint wkr II, $26,652
Tuttle, Cynthia, acct I, $34,944
Twehus, Jason M, info technologist III, $39,624
Twehus, Tanya L, sr ofc spt asst (keybrd), $26,652
Twehus, Terry M, info technology spec I, $51,096
Tyler, Michael, maint spv I, $32,628
Tyner, Cheryl L, info technology spec II, $66,720
Ulstad, Tony L, info technologist IV, $45,156
Umphrey, David T, maint worker II, $30,420
Underwood, Todd, refrgrtn mech I, $30,984
Usyk, Larysa M, info technology spec I, $51,096
Utrecht, John A, misc tech, $9.50/hr
Van Nostrand, Belinda J, data processor tech, $30.77/hr
Van Nostrand, Jean P, info technology supv, $71,100
Vance, Marcia A, storekeeper I, $25,824
Vandeloecht, Heather, acct II, $37,548
Vanderfeltz, Glenda S, ofc of administration mgr 1, $56,510
Vanderfeltz, Sara L, special asst ofc & clerical, $47,975
Vanhooser, Barbara J, account clerk II, $25,824
Vanloo, Judy, examination monitor, $7.72/hr
Vaughan, Jincy, info technology spec II, $65,364
Vaughn, Andrew C, info technologist I, $31,512

Veit, David, info technology sr spec, $68,160
Veit, Dennis R, data processor tech, $34.58/hr
Veit, Nikki J, info technology spec II, $74,304
Veit, Ronald C, maint worker II, $29,976
Veit, Theresa A, info technology supv, $63,996
Vennavalli, Leelavathi, info technologist IV, $45,156
Verhoff, Anthony, acct II, $37,548
Vermillion, David, maint spv I, $32,628
Vernon, Miranda, acct I, $30,984
Verslues, Donna S, pers analyst II, $40,380
Verslues, Gina, accounting spec III, $47,892
Verslues, Peter J, design/develop/survey mgr b1, $65,145
Vessell, Rodney J, ofc of administration mgr 3, $71,205
Vestal, Michael G, maint worker II, $29,004
Viebrock, Cherie L, info technology spec I, $56,520
Vinyard, Ranada S, legal counsel, $60,975
Vogel, Michael G, data processor tech, $28.90/hr
Volkart, Danny W, printing/mail technician I, $23,880
Volkart, Jason L, data processing mgr, $84,335
Vollmer, Greg J, electrcn, $36,888
Volmert, Janna E, risk mgmt tech I, $27,228
Von Der Bruegge, Michael A, info technology spec I, $55,416
Vuppala, Mahendar, info technology sr spec, $72,768
Wade, Theresa, printing/mail technician II, $25,824
Wagner, Donald L, phys plant sup II, $43,488
Wagner, Michelle L, info technologist IV, $45,156
Wagner, Randall O, info technology spec II, $65,364
Wagoner, Donald R, maint spv I, $35,568
Walker, Bryan, info technology oper II, $28,104
Walker, Daniel A, electronics tech, $30,984
Walker, Dwayne T, info technology spec II, $62,664
Walker, Kyle L, refrgrtn mech I, $30,984
Walker, Leroy R, refrgrtn mech I, $30,984
Walker, Thomas J, laborer, $10.75/hr
Wall, Tammy, acct II, $39,624
Wallace, Jerry L, stationary engr, $33,744
Wallenmeyer, Crystal G, info technology spec I, $50,040
Walls, Sylvester, comp info tech spec III, $66,720
Walther, Sandra K, design/develop/survey mgr b2, $71,205
Wankum, Jacqueline M, info technology spec I, $60,120
Warner, Cherry G, pers clerk, $30,420
Warren, Dennis, info technology spec II, $57,744
Washburn, Patricia M, info technology sr spec, $71,208
Waters, Cody, design/develop/survey mgr b2, $67,791
Watkins, Vicki L, pers analyst II, $37,548
Watson, Aaron, info technologist IV, $56,520
Watson, Eric S, printing/mail technician I, $23,880
Watson, Katherine A, investigator, $40,400
Watts, Sherry L, reporting spec, $33,181
Weaver, Bryan, info technology spec I, $55,416
Weber, Aaron J, printing/mail technician I, $23,880
Weber, Delilah, sr ofc spt asst (keybrd), $27,948
Weber, Lawrence, principal asst board/commisson, $87,365
Weible, Samuel G, painter, $35,568
Weible, Sarah C, info technologist III, $40,380
Weider, James W, comp info tech supv II, $68,160
Welch, Suzanna F, printing/mail technician II, $25,824
Welschmeyer, Timothy, info technologist I, $36,204
Wendler, Jennifer C, examination monitor, $7.72/hr
Wessing, Crystal D, fiscal & administrative mgr b3, $75,245
West, Bryan S, printing/mail technician II, $30,924
West, Kelly, info technology spec I, $55,416
West, Tracey J, pers analyst I, $30,984
West, Tyler S, info technology oper I, $26,652
Westbrook, Claybon, info technology spec I, $49,128
Whisler, Angela M, acct I, $30,984
White, Bret G, plumber, $32,052
White, Melissa E, info technologist IV, $46,068
White-Frieling, Stacy, fiscal & administrative mgr b1, $47,904
Whitfield, Carla M, info technology spec I, $52,092
Whitson, Alicia M, exec I, $41,172
Whitworth, Jason, info technologist III, $38,928
Wibberg, Robert J, phys plant sup III, $50,040
Wieberg, Amy, dsgnr III, $52,092
Wieberg, Janice L, sr ofc spt asst (keybrd), $29,412
Wilbers, Daniel J, exec I, $33,744
Wilbers, Elizabeth J, info technology spec I, $53,208
Wilde, Adam J, info technologist IV, $49,128
Wilde, Anthony S, info technology spec II, $62,664
Wilde, Kyle T, buyer II, $37,548
Wiles, Robert C, sr ofc spt asst (keybrd), $28,452
Wilfred, Neefa, info technologist III, $40,380
Wilfred, Sunil C, info technology spec II, $71,208

Wilkerson, Chris E, data processing mgr, $92,572
Wilkerson, Joan C, info technology spec I, $62,664
Wilkins, Arthur T, info technology spec I, $49,128
Williams, Arnold D, geographic info sys spec, $50,040
Williams, Charles H, info technology sr spec, $81,036
Williams, Connie S, info technologist IV, $45,156
Williams, Don, info technologist IV, $45,156
Williams, Edward V, maint worker II, $29,004
Williams, Kathy E, info technologist IV, $45,156
Williams, Marshall L, maint worker I, $26,652
Williams, Terry, info technologist IV, $45,156
Williams-Rooney, Eric T, laborer, $10.75/hr
Willig, Rickey L, facilities opps mgr b1, $57,726
Willmeno, Angela L, sr ofc spt asst (keybrd), $25,824
Wilmes, Norbert E, maint spv I, $39,624
Wilson, Christopher D, info technology spec I, $55,416
Wilson, Florence E, info technology spec I, $54,288
Wilson, Gregory, comp info tech supv II, $68,160
Wilson, John L, maint worker II, $29,004
Wilson, Michael A, maint spv I, $32,628
Wilson, Steven G, info technologist IV, $45,156
Wilson, Thomas H, info technology spec I, $54,288
Wilson, Timothy G, park maint wkr II, $26,652
Wingate, Jase J, garage spv, $33,744
Wingrath, Bernard, misc tech, $9.84/hr
Winn, Karen A, commissmbr, $103,960
Wisner, Jana M, info technologist IV, $45,156
Wisnewski, Lindsey D, budget & plng analyst II, $46,932
Wittkop, Richard W, info technology oper I, $26,652
Wixon, William M, maint spv I, $44,304
Woehr, Denise M, info technology supv, $60,120
Woerner, Darcy A, info technologist III, $40,380
Woerner, Scott S, info technologist III, $42,708
Wolf, Steven, info technology spec I, $54,288
Wolfe, Leslie F, design/develop/survey mgr b1, $49,123
Wolfe, Megan V, info technologist I, $31,512
Wolken, Troy A, maint worker II, $32,628
Womack, Barbara A, info technologist IV, $45,156
Woodling, Kathy A, info technologist IV, $50,040
Woods, Levi, exec I, $38,232
Woods, Lori D, examination monitor, $7.72/hr
Wooton, James F, info technology spec I, $52,092
Wright, Corey A, laborer II, $23,160
Wright, Paul G, data processor prof, $82,985
Wright, Renee A, info technology spec I, $49,128
Wright, Willie J, maint spv II, $41,940
Wyatt, Johnny B, hvac inst ctrls tech, $33,744
Wyss, George, info technologist II, $36,204
Xu, Michelle, info technologist I, $30,984
Yang, Jufang, info technologist III, $38,928
Yocum, Robert W, info technology spec I, $50,040
Young, Jan, custodial worker I, $21,264
Youngblood, Derrick A, info technology spec I, $49,128
Yount, Daniel C, refrgrtn mech II, $40,380
Zahner, Starr, info technology spec II, $57,744
Zaring, Roger G, locksmith, $34,944
Zayumba, Sarah K, pers analyst II, $37,548
Zdybel, Peter J, maint spv I, $37,548
Zeller, Don R, design/develop/survey mgr b3, $77,265
Zeller, Scott A, design/develop/survey mgr b2, $60,261
Zemke, Douglas E, info technology spec I, $51,096
Ziegler, Elizabeth L, gen counsel, $76,255
Zimmerman, Jennifer L, info technology spec I, $49,128
Zweifel, Andrew J, info technologist III, $41,172
Zweifel, Gregory W, refrgrtn mech II, $38,232

Department of Agriculture

1616 Missouri Blvd., PO Box 630, Jefferson City 65102

Fordyce, Richard L, state dept dir, $121,705
Abney, Donald W, seasonal fair worker, $7.65/hr
Adkins, Linda J, admin ofc spt asst, $32,628
Albert, John D, agric mgr b2, $56,507
Alsager, Sarah M, designated principal asst dept, $65,650
Anderson, Emily K, correctional worker, $22.45/hr
Anderson, Emily S, env public hlth spec IV, $40,380
Anderson, James, principal asst board/commisson, $75,000
Archuleta, Ilana M, mkting spec II, $41,940
Arnold, Carol A, acct I, $36,204
Arway, Michael R, pesticide use investigator, $36,204
Asbury, Tristan O, mkting spec II, $41,940
Ash, Skyla E, grain insp V, $52,092

Bailey, Paul, agric mgr b2, $56,507
Baker, Joseph A DVM, veterinarian I, $65,364
Baker, Latiffany L, ofc worker misc, $10.00/hr
Baker, Timothy D, correctional worker, $22.85/hr
Baldon, Leah B, grain regulatory auditor II, $38,928
Bales, Raymond H, correctional worker, $21.73/hr
Ball, Aleesha M, ofc worker misc, $10.00/hr
Bargielski, Daniel J, env pub hlth spec III, $40,380
Barr, Yvonne V, pesticide use investigator, $36,204
Bashor, Evart C, grain insp I, $28,452
Baslee, Daniel, correctional worker, $24.05/hr
Bassham, Larry T, env public hlth spec IV, $47,892
Baugh, Aaron P, feed & seed insp II, $36,204
Beach, Harvey J, grain regulatory auditor III, $47,892
Beasley, Jason R, tech asst III, $32,052
Becker, Susan A, agric mgr b1, $54,220
Beedle, Dawn D, agric mgr b2, $60,000
Beerman, Steven R, env public hlth spec IV, $47,892
Beery, Cheryl D, grain regulatory auditor II, $42,708
Bell, Johnny J, chemist III, $43,488
Bennett, Olivia W, animal hlth ofcr, $36,204
Bennett, Susan S, planner II, $43,488
Benz, William A, designated principal asst dept, $65,650
Berendzen, Buffy R, designated principal asst div, $40,384
Berendzen, Sue, exec I, $40,380
Berwanger, Eric, grain regulatory auditor III, $47,892
Billingsley, Gary R, grain inspection worker, $10.10/hr
Bishop, Tammie L, admin ofc spt asst, $32,628
Boatwright, John R, sr pub hlth lab scintst, $41,940
Boggs, Kim A, seasonal fair worker, $15.39/hr
Bohnert, Catherine A, mkting spec II, $41,940
Bouse, Nancy L, admin ofc spt asst, $36,204
Branson, Floyd, correctional worker, $22.85/hr
Breyer, Merrel M, emergency mgmnt spec, $46,932
Bristow, Jay L, grain insp I, $28,452
Brocke, Tina C, pesticide use investigator, $36,204
Brown, Dennis, maint spv I, $36,888
Brownfield, Wanda F, correctional worker, $24.05/hr
Brundick, Emily M, designated principal asst dept, $41,935
Brunnert, John M, agric mgr b2, $56,512
Buckland, Amber L, special asst prof, $36,566
Burnside, Brandon D, grain insp III, $34,356
Bush, Ronnie D, correctional worker, $21.39/hr
Bushan, Lawrence W, plant industries worker, $12.00/hr
Buttry, William A, grain inspection worker, $10.10/hr
Byrd, David W, correctional worker, $22.45/hr
Caldwell, Jimmy L, grain inspection worker, $10.10/hr
Capps, Andrew C, correctional worker, $25.32/hr
Carbone-Scott, Amy S, seasonal fair worker, $9.00/hr
Carroll, Mikiata L, pesticide use investigator, $36,204
Casagrande, Steven P, fuel device safety insp, $34,356
Cave, James R, seasonal fair worker, $8.32/hr
Chafin, Zachary A, fuel device safety insp, $32,628
Chamberlin, Ryan K, grain insp I, $26,652
Chappell, Joseph J, grain inspection worker, $10.10/hr
Chatman, Darryl M, dpty state dept dir, $106,050
Chevalier, Melissa M, grain inspection worker, $10.10/hr
Christiansen, Ryan D, grain insp I, $27,504
Clements, Alan N, fiscal & administrative mgr b3, $75,750
Collop, Tonya M DVM, veterinarian I, $65,364
Conner, Walter L, plant protect spec, $38,928
Cook, Andrew M, weights & measures insp I, $32,628
Cook, Kevin R, sr public hlth lab scientist, $41,940
Cook, Rachel E DVM, veterinarian I, $65,364
Cook, Rick, fuel device safety insp, $35,568
Cook, Stanley E, agric mgr b2, $56,507
Cooper, Joann M, exec I, $32,052
Cooper, Matthew G, seasonal fair worker, $7.65/hr
Corbin, Brit E, correctional worker, $23.23/hr
Cornejo, Staci M, sr ofc spt asst (keybrd), $27,504
Corpening, Daniel L, correctional worker, $21.39/hr
Council, Diane N, sr ofc spt asst (keybrd), $28,908
Covey, Jackie L, grain inspection worker, $17.73/hr
Cox, Gerald W, grain inspection worker, $10.10/hr
Danback, Ronald L, plant industries worker, $12.00/hr
Davis, Robert R, grain inspection worker, $10.10/hr
De La Rocha, Xavier O, chemist I, $32,628
Deal, Kimberly K, sr ofc spt asst (keybrd), $28,908
Debauch, Marin K DVM, veterinarian I, $65,364
Delhotal, Steven D, correctional worker, $21.39/hr
Dent, Randy S, weights & measures insp I, $32,628
Dieckhoff, Darin T, sr pub hlth lab scintst, $41,940

Disselhorst, Ken E, feed & seed insp II, $36,204
Disselhorst, Steven, agric mkt reporter, $37,548
Dodd, Michael L, weights & measures insp I, $32,628
Donovan, Maria R, ofc worker misc, $10.00/hr
Dowden, Rebecca J, env pub hlth spec III, $40,380
Driskill, Cassie M, anml hlth ofcr, $36,204
Duncan, Derek A, grain insp III, $32,628
Dunn, John P, designated principal asst div, $72,720
Eddy, Danae E, grain insp II, $29,976
Edmonds, Eric S, grain insp II, $29,004
Edwards, Kristofor A, correctional worker, $21.39/hr
Edwards, Winston D, ofc worker misc, $10.00/hr
Ehlenbeck, Susan M, plant protect spec, $41,172
Eichholz, Sandra S, seasonal fair worker, $8.00/hr
Eilermann, Chris, weights & measures insp I, $32,628
Elliott, James E, tech asst IV, $36,888
Emanuel, Shanta L, sr ofc spt asst (keybrd), $28,908
Embree, Vickie C, ofc spt asst (keybrd), $24,264
Endsley, Edward, correctional worker, $22.85/hr
Eveler, Glenda R, ofc spt asst (keybrd), $26,652
Evers, Breylee A, chemist I, $34,944
Ewers, Callie S, env pub hlth spec III, $46,068
Faenger, Jeffrey S, land surv I, $48,156
Falls, Donald L, env pub hlth spec V, $51,096
Falter, Nathan L, env pub hlth spec III, $40,380
Fann, Judy L, grain inspection worker, $10.10/hr
Fellows, James A, correctional worker, $23.65/hr
Ferguson, James, fuel device safety insp, $36,204
Ferrell, Wanda J, sr ofc spt asst (keybrd), $28,908
Ficken, William J, maint worker II, $34,356
Fields, Bonnie L, correctional worker, $22.45/hr
Finn, Denise L, sr ofc spt asst (keybrd), $28,908
Fisher, Pauline J, ofc worker misc, $13.17/hr
Fitzgerald, William R, grain inspection worker, $10.10/hr
Fizer, Glen W, painter, $29,976
Fizer, Joseph D, grain inspection worker, $10.10/hr
Fleig, James J, plant industries prg coor, $45,156
Forck, Jacqueline S, assoc public hlth lab scientist, $32,628
Forgey, Larry W DVM, veterinary pathologist, $72,768
Forsythe, Amy D, admin ofc spt asst, $32,628
Frederick, Anastacia N, sr ofc spt asst (keybrd), $28,908
Freeman, Alan, mkting spec III, $46,068
Freeman, Samantha J, pub info spec II, $41,940
Garmon, Adrian A, grain insp II, $32,052
Garrett, Gary A, grain inspection worker, $10.10/hr
Gaynor, John, fuel device safety insp, $32,628
Gibbs, Linda L, seasonal fair worker, $8.50/hr
Gibson, Roger D, grain inspection worker, $12.02/hr
Giese, Laurie D, correctional worker, $22.06/hr
Giese, Steven, correctional worker, $23.23/hr
Gilgour, Chase S, special asst prof, $35,000
Gill, Thomas M, env public hlth spec III, $43,488
Gilson, Debora M, correctional worker, $21.73/hr
Goodwin, Marquette D, grain inspection worker, $10.10/hr
Goran, Brittny L, public info spec I, $30,984
Gottschalk, Penny R, exec I, $35,568
Grabau, Jennifer L, fiscal & administrative mgr b1, $46,925
Graves, Alicia M, animal hlth ofcr, $36,204
Gretlein, Richard D, prop asst, $16.96/hr
Grundler, Judy A, div dir, $85,561
Guymon, Kayden K, ofc worker misc, $10.00/hr
Haden, John K DVM, veterinary epidemiologist, $72,768
Hake, Austin M, pesticide use investigator, $36,204
Hall, Stacy A, sr ofc spt asst (keybrd), $28,908
Hamlett, Philip K, fuel device safety insp, $32,628
Hampton, India L, sr ofc spt asst (keybrd), $28,908
Hancock, Tony D, agric mgr b2, $56,507
Hanger, Jerry D, seasonal fair worker, $7.65/hr
Hankins, Sharon F, exec I, $33,744
Hanson, Kevin J, lab mgr b1, $54,282
Hardin, William T, seasonal fair worker, $15.00/hr
Harlin, Brandon C, grain insp I, $27,504
Hart, Devin, feed & seed insp II, $41,940
Harter, Michael D, feed & seed insp II, $40,380
Hartman, Marsha A, plant industries worker, $12.12/hr
Haslag, Rochelle L, designated principal asst div, $37,924
Hawcroft, Bart A, agric mgr b1, $53,203
Hawkins, Terry L, grain inspection worker, $10.10/hr
Haworth, Meridee K, feed & seed insp II, $36,204
Hayes, Ronald, div dir, $85,561
Hays, Teresa L, env public hlth spec III, $40,380
Heffel, Bradley H, grain inspection worker, $14.44/hr
Heimbaugh, Ron L, design/develop/survey mgr b2, $58,899

Heimericks, Andrew C, assoc public hlth lab scientist, $32,628
Heimericks, Rachel E, admin ofc spt asst, $36,204
Henderson, Jane, seasonal fair worker, $7.73/hr
Henderson, Kenneth D, agric mgr b2, $56,507
Henderson, Lydia J, seasonal fair worker, $8.08/hr
Henderson, Tami J, seasonal fair worker, $8.58/hr
Hensley, Brent L, weights & measures insp I, $32,628
Herron, Bryan W, seasonal fair worker, $15.39/hr
Hibdon, Colin W, correctional worker, $22.45/hr
Hickam-Fountain, Linda S, div dir, $86,355
Higgins, Nevelyn G, seed analyst II, $33,180
Hill, Danny E, agric mkt reporter, $26,208
Hoellering, Paul D, correctional worker, $21.73/hr
Holland, Kayla M, seasonal fair worker, $7.65/hr
Holman, Judith A, seasonal fair worker, $7.65/hr
Holtsclaw, Emily J, designated principal asst div, $37,960
Holtzclaw, Christa C, mkting spec II, $41,940
Hoormann, Elizabeth A, seasonal fair worker, $7.65/hr
Hopkins, Jacob W, grain insp I, $28,452
Hopper, Charles P, mkting spec III, $50,040
Horn, Denise K, pers analyst II, $41,940
Hoskins, David, seed analyst III, $38,232
Huffman, John, agric mkt reporter, $37,548
Hughes, Bradley W, env pub hlth spec III, $46,932
Hughes, John R, laborer II, $23,160
Hughes, Thomas E, metrology spec, $38,232
Inglish, Shawn N, agricultural loan ofcr, $41,172
Jackson, Shannon C, seasonal fair worker, $15.39/hr
James, Jeremy D, grain inspection worker, $10.10/hr
James, Tyler C, land surv I, $48,156
Jameson, Samuel W, veterinarian I, $65,364
Jamison, Jennifer J, fuel device safety insp, $32,628
Jenkins, Jeffrey S DVM, veterinarian I, $65,364
Johnson, David A, plant protect spec, $44,304
Johnson, Taylor, ofc worker misc, $10.00/hr
Jolliff, Kevin A, ofc worker misc, $15.00/hr
Jones, Lindsey J, mkting spec III, $51,096
Jones, Lori J, correctional worker, $21.39/hr
Jordan, Fred L, correctional worker, $21.39/hr
Jordan, John S, env public hlth spec V, $49,128
Jubell, Scott W, correctional worker, $22.85/hr
Judy, Dan T, pesticide use investigator, $36,204
Kallenbach, Steven J, env pub hlth spec III, $40,380
Kasak, Barbara H, seasonal fair worker, $8.25/hr
Kasak, Karl E, seasonal fair worker, $15.00/hr
Keele, Ryan E, maint worker II, $29,004
Kelley, Michael R, grain inspection worker, $10.10/hr
King, Olivia R, seasonal fair worker, $7.65/hr
Kleiboeker, Donald A, agric mkt reporter, $17,472
Kleindienst, Angela F, acct II, $38,928
Klenklen, John C, div dir, $81,305
Kliethermes, Dana M, acct II, $41,940
Kliethermes, Jean, agric mgr b2, $56,507
Knipp, Rosalee M, ofc worker misc, $10.00/hr
Koechner, Kathleen A, lab technician, $20.91/hr
Koestner, Mary L, lab mgr b2, $54,800
Kramer, Richard L, agric mkt reporter, $33,744
Land, Thomas E, grain inspection worker, $10.10/hr
Landes, William I, correctional worker, $24.05/hr
Lane, Kelly, admin ofc spt asst, $32,628
Langton, Sean D, correctional worker, $22.85/hr
Lather, Ronald L, land surv I, $48,156
Lauber, Thomas L, grain insp II, $30,984
Leake, Kevin R, grain inspection worker, $10.10/hr
Leake, Nicholas A, chemist III, $40,380
Ledoux, Douglas G, plant industries prg coor, $46,932
Leffert, William H, correctional worker, $22.45/hr
Leonard, James M, grain insp IV, $43,488
Lewis, Joyce A, exec I, $38,928
Li, Yuhong, plant protect spec, $38,928
Libhart, Marcheta A, correctional worker, $22.85/hr
Liter, Paul A, weights & measures insp I, $32,628
Locke, Wesley E, chemist III, $40,380
Loera, Linda S, grain inspection worker, $10.10/hr
Loesing, Matthew R, grain inspection worker, $11.10/hr
Long, Jason E, weights & measures insp I, $32,628
Luecke, Amy K, exec II, $36,204
Lueckenotte, Sydney M, sr ofc spt asst (keybrd), $28,908
Lunsford, Chris A, grain insp V, $52,092
Lybyer, Stephen J, weights & measures insp I, $32,628
Lynch, Terry M, grain inspection worker, $10.10/hr
Lyons, Tony L, plant industries worker, $10.00/hr
Ma, Hank K, misc prof, $52,179

Marburger, Matthew D, grain inspection worker, $10.10/hr
Martin, Mary A, animal hlth ofcr, $36,204
Martin, Nathaniel G, fuel device safety insp, $34,944
Mastin, Chretta A, env pub hlth spec V, $49,128
Mausbach, Doreen E, feed & seed insp II, $36,204
May, Melissa G, plant industries prg coor, $45,156
McBride, Brittney G, seasonal fair worker, $7.65/hr
McCloud, Tracie L, grain inspection worker, $10.10/hr
McCorkendale, David B, anml hlth ofcr, $36,204
McGowin, Joshua, plant industries worker, $10.00/hr
McIntosh, Jane L, planner IV, $63,996
McKay, James B, env pub hlth spec III, $40,380
McKinney, Norman F, grain inspection worker, $10.10/hr
McKnight, Nicole L, env public hlth spec III, $40,380
McMullin, Amanda R, sr ofc spt asst (keybrd), $28,908
McNeal, Russell A, correctional worker, $25.78/hr
Melson, John W, pub hlth lab scientist, $37,548
Melton, Mary E, lab mgr b2, $56,507
Mendenhall, Erin L, animal hlth ofcr, $36,204
Mergen, Kari L, public inf & mktg coor state fair, $45,156
Merrick, Melba, ofc spt asst (clerical), $22,536
Meyer, David H, principal asst board/commisson, $75,000
Meyer, Gloria J, env public hlth spec III, $40,380
Miller, Mark L, agric mgr b1, $53,025
Miller, Melissa A, mkting spec II, $41,940
Mills, Hillary D, ofc worker misc, $13.13/hr
Miner, Christy G, land survey spec I, $32,628
Mohr, Christine E, anml hlth ofcr, $36,204
Moody, Christa L, special asst prof, $45,450
Moon, Courtney L, seasonal fair worker, $9.09/hr
Moore, Glenn, seasonal fair worker, $7.65/hr
Moore, Jason L, bldg mgr I, $46,932
Moore, Joshua B, animal hlth ofcr, $36,204
Moore, Lisa L, weights & measures insp I, $32,628
Moreland, Terry L, fuel device safety insp, $34,356
Morgan, Bradley E, chemist III, $40,380
Moritz, Steven R, correctional worker, $26.72/hr
Morris, Steven F, plumber, $34,944
Muenks, Quintin P, lab mgr b2, $49,110
Muhammad, Paul C, fuel device safety insp, $32,628
Mulwee, James A, lab technician, $20.49/hr
Murphy, Mark J, agric mgr b2, $47,878
Murray, Deborah L, seasonal fair worker, $7.65/hr
Musick, Timothy A, fuel device safety insp, $35,568
Muths, Michelle L, seasonal fair worker, $7.65/hr
Nachreiner, Mark E, pesticide use investigator, $37,548
Nagel, Dennis, agric mkt reporter, $17,472
Ndessokia, Jaquline M, hr mgr b1, $56,507
Neff, Douglas A, fuel device safety insp, $34,944
Neill, Roger A, env public hlth spec III, $40,380
Newsom, Darrel A, grain insp I, $28,452
Newson, Jaleesa P, grain inspection worker, $10.10/hr
Newton, Robert A, correctional worker, $21.39/hr
Nichols, James L, grain inspection worker, $10.10/hr
Nilges, Anthony H, fuel device safety insp, $34,356
Noring, Dennis, chemist IV, $49,128
Norris, Richard E, fuel device safety insp, $32,628
Oldham, Justin R, correctional worker, $21.39/hr
Olsen, Kurt T, mkting spec III, $41,674
Onstott, Gregory, agric mgr b2, $71,205
Orr, Martha, weights & measures insp I, $32,628
Otto, Kayla L, mkting spec II, $41,940
Otto, Paige N, ofc worker misc, $10.10/hr
Owen, Herschel, weights & measures insp I, $32,628
Ozburn, Steven C, electrcn, $34,944
Pace, Kenneth D, correctional worker, $23.65/hr
Parker, Roger M, agric mkt reporter, $38,928
Parks, Todd, grain inspection worker, $10.66/hr
Parrish, Tony M, correctional worker, $21.73/hr
Parrott, Daniel K, grain inspection worker, $10.10/hr
Pate, Jimmy W, correctional worker, $26.72/hr
Pauls, Kenneth L, correctional worker, $22.45/hr
Payne, Barbara G, correctional worker, $21.39/hr
Payne, Carol J, land survey spec II, $46,068
Payne, Erica D, grain insp III, $36,204
Peeks, Chandler D, grain inspection worker, $10.10/hr
Perryman, Anthony H, animal hlth ofcr, $36,204
Perso, Robin K, fiscal & administrative mgr b2, $75,750
Phillips, Jacob R, plant industries worker, $10.00/hr
Phillips, Robert H, plant protect spec, $38,928
Phillips, Robert T, admin ofc spt asst, $33,744
Phipps, Sarah J, plant industries prg coor, $45,156
Pirtle, Jerry L, plant industries worker, $10.00/hr

Pittenger, William R, anml hlth prog coor, $45,156
Pleus, Whitney L, sr ofc spt asst (keybrd), $28,908
Plochberger, Jason L, chemist III, $42,708
Pohlmann, Kayla A, env public hlth spec III, $40,380
Pool, Darla K, env public hlth spec III, $40,380
Praswater, Ronald D, animal hlth ofcr, $37,548
Pratte, Darrell D, design/develop/survey mgr b3, $69,376
Preston, Misti D, designated principal asst dept, $91,405
Provance, April N, seasonal fair worker, $7.65/hr
Quinones, Brandian L, grain inspection worker, $10.10/hr
Rackers, Cleta L, chemist III, $43,488
Raef, Glenn A, weights & measures insp I, $32,628
Ramey, Mark C, correctional worker, $27.57/hr
Ransdell, Jeffrey M, crpntr, $29,976
Raymond, Leroy, weights & measures insp II, $40,380
Reddick, Lisa D, weights & measures insp I, $32,628
Reid, Tanner D, ofc worker misc, $10.00/hr
Reynolds, Jackie, grain inspection worker, $17.73/hr
Reynolds, Timothy L, correctional worker, $24.45/hr
Richardson, Adam D, fuel device safety insp, $32,628
Richter, Jeffrey S, grain insp V, $52,092
Riley, Bob J, fuel device safety insp, $35,568
Riley, Douglas R, grain insp III, $33,180
Riordan-Lolli, Judi, animal hlth ofcr, $36,204
Robertson, Duane, agric mkt reporter, $17,472
Rogers, Robyn K, sr ofc spt asst (keybrd), $28,908
Rogers, Timothy E, weights & measures insp I, $32,628
Rold, Matthew C, agric mgr b2, $56,507
Root, Jeffrey L, weights & measures insp I, $32,628
Roslawski, Michael S, weights & measures insp I, $32,628
Rowe, Tommy C, grain inspection worker, $10.10/hr
Rybolt, David A DVM, veterinarian I, $65,364
Salzman, Thomas B, correctional worker, $22.45/hr
Sandgren, Jay, grain inspection worker, $10.10/hr
Scantlin, Susan D, grain inspection worker, $10.10/hr
Schaefer, Laura N, lab technician, $12.87/hr
Schilb, Hubert L, grain inspection worker, $10.10/hr
Schlueter, Richard P, grain regulatory auditor II, $42,708
Schmidt, Jean A, veterinarian II, $71,208
Schnakenberg, Randall K, seasonal fair worker, $8.32/hr
Schofield, Bradley J, anml hlth ofcr, $36,204
Schofield, Joseph A, weights & measures insp I, $32,628
Scholl, Scott D, correctional worker, $21.39/hr
Schwartze, Jodie L, chemist II, $36,204
Scott, Kirk D, correctional worker, $24.45/hr
Seifner, Thomas J, seasonal fair worker, $11.00/hr
Sexton, Helen E, sr pub hlth lab scintst, $41,940
Shaw, Robert E, seasonal fair worker, $8.32/hr
Shehorn, Kenneth A, correctional worker, $21.39/hr
Shewmaker, Michael S, correctional worker, $24.79/hr
Shirky, Monica G, groundskeeper II, $26,652
Siegel, Regina K, seasonal fair worker, $7.65/hr
Silmon, Daniel, grain inspection worker, $10.10/hr
Simpson, William D, fuel device safety insp, $32,628
Sims, Charles J, insp, $14.74/hr
Sims, Vanessa, correctional worker, $21.39/hr
Sindle, Kyle B, grain regulatory auditor I, $36,204
Slade, Darryl R, plant industries prg coor, $50,040
Smith, Alan B, grain regulatory auditor I, $36,204
Smith, Catherine R, plant protect spec, $38,928
Smith, James E, security guard, $26,232
Smith, Justin C, grain inspection worker, $10.10/hr
Smith, Vanessa A, seasonal fair worker, $10.00/hr
Snapp, Jaret K, laborer II, $23,160
Snider, Brandon W, fuel device safety insp, $32,628
Sponsler, P K, weights & measures insp I, $32,628
Stackhouse, Gwendolyn E, grain insp I, $28,452
Stafford, Mark, correctional worker, $22.85/hr
Stafford, Patricia K, correctional worker, $21.39/hr
Stamp, Adam K, fuel device safety insp, $38,232
Starke, Heidi L, plant industries worker, $12.00/hr
Starr, Zachariah W, plant protect spec, $38,928
Stayton, Loretta L, correctional worker, $22.85/hr
Steed, Jeffery W, grain inspection worker, $10.10/hr
Steele, Roy M, correctional worker, $22.85/hr
Stegeman, Dustin L DVM, veterinarian II, $68,160
Steinman, Amy L, acct II, $38,928
Stevenson, G'darius, grain inspection worker, $10.10/hr
Steward, Brian J, grain regulatory auditor II, $42,708
Stiens, Gregory L, weights & measures insp I, $32,628
Stokes, Linda K, exec I, $36,204
Stone, Dusty L, grain insp I, $29,412
Strenfel, Barbara A, env public hlth spec III, $40,380

Stropp, Joseph F, env public hlth spec III, $49,128
Struemph, Kenneth C, div dir, $81,305
Sumner, Harold, weights & measures insp I, $32,628
Swartz, Dennis J, grain inspection worker, $10.10/hr
Talbott, Zachary R, grain regulatory auditor I, $36,204
Telford, Cecily M, plant industries worker, $10.00/hr
Terrell, Levi J, grain insp I, $28,452
Thomas, James W, grain inspection worker, $10.10/hr
Thompson, Chad P, correctional worker, $21.39/hr
Thompson, Julia W, plant protect spec, $18,774
Tizon, Amanda K, plant protect spec, $38,928
Trapp, Joseph F, grain insp III, $40,380
Travis, Jacob J, fuel device safety insp, $32,628
Treese, Harold A, veterinarian II, $71,208
Trimble, Justin L, correctional worker, $21.39/hr
Troup, Mark H, plant industries prg coor, $50,040
Tyler-Carter, Caroline M, agric mkt reporter, $30,984
Upschulte, Kevin B, lab mgr b2, $56,507
Verslues, Brenda L, mkting spec II, $41,940
Voland, Steven L, correctional worker, $22.45/hr
Volkart, Lori E, admin ofc spt asst, $32,628
Vollmer, Edna, admin ofc spt asst, $32,628
Wake, Guy R, correctional worker, $21.39/hr
Walker, Joe E, acct II, $46,932
Wall, Curtis P, fuel device safety spec, $41,172
Wall, Dawn M, investigator II, $46,932
Walters, Jacquline K, land survey spec I, $32,628
Wamsley, Collin S, agric mgr b2, $56,507
Wansing, Kayla R, env public hlth spec III, $40,380
Ward, Terri B, seasonal fair worker, $8.00/hr
Warren, Debby S, seasonal fair worker, $10.10/hr
Warrick, Michael E, legal counsel, $91,405
Webb, Kali N, seasonal fair worker, $7.75/hr
Webb, Michael W, correctional worker, $21.73/hr
Weber, Jennifer L, animal hlth ofcr, $36,204
Weible, Robert W, fuel device safety insp, $34,356
Weil, Harold G, grain inspection worker, $10.10/hr
Welch, Michael R, pesticide use investigator, $40,380
Wempe, Reagan A, mkting spec II, $41,940
Whitaker, Clinton G, fuel device safety spec, $38,928
White, Danny D, correctional worker, $24.45/hr
White, Joseph E, correctional worker, $21.39/hr
Wilde, Karen S, designated principal asst div, $44,723
Wilde, Lisa A, designated principal asst div, $41,661
Wilkerson, James E, correctional worker, $23.65/hr
Wilkerson, Willis D, correctional worker, $21.39/hr
Williams, Jimmy L, agric mgr b2, $60,745
Wilson, Bruce L, tech asst IV, $42,708
Wilson, Hannah E, seasonal fair worker, $8.00/hr
Wilson, Kevin O, grain inspection worker, $14.28/hr
Wilson, Loyd N, designated principal asst dept, $91,405
Winkelman, Joleen L, sr ofc spt asst (keybrd), $28,908
Wiseman, Gene, principal asst board/commisson, $67,355
Witt, Shelly D, admin ofc spt asst, $32,628
Witten, Michael A, ofc worker misc, $10.00/hr
Wolfe, Carole A, sr ofc spt asst (keybrd), $28,908
Wolfe, Mark R, principal asst board/commisson, $91,405
Wolpers, Margaret M, seasonal fair worker, $8.00/hr
Wood, Karen M, acct II, $40,380
Woody, Denise L, correctional worker, $21.39/hr
Woody, Randall S, correctional worker, $22.85/hr
Woolery, Robert H, correctional worker, $25.32/hr
Worden, William T, correctional worker, $21.39/hr
Worsley, William B, correctional worker, $21.39/hr
Wright, Bruce G, seasonal fair worker, $7.65/hr
Wulff, James E, maint worker II, $29,004
Wyatt, Jo A, grain regulatory auditor II, $38,928
Wyckoff, Eric R, designated principal asst div, $45,450
Wyman, Ricky L, plant industries worker, $10.00/hr
Wyss, Sandra, exec II, $39,624
Young, Marla M, planner II, $46,932
Zurmiller, Thomas E, correctional worker, $22.85/hr

Department of Conservation

2901 W. Truman Blvd., Jefferson City 65109

Ziehmer, Robert L, dir, $140,004
Abbott, Eric E, conservation agent, $50,280
Abdon, Michael W, conservation agent, $46,488
Abel, Steffanie L, resource science asst, $31,488
Abner, Johsua K, resource technician, $9.86/hr
Ackerson, Johnathan R, fisheries mgmt biologist, $44,712

Ackley, Kenneth B, wildlife biologist, $41,352
Ackley, Rachel K, resource technician, $9.86/hr
Acosta Saldana, Juan D, resource asst, $8.58/hr
Adams, Chris T, resource technician, $39,768
Adams, Clarence M, resource asst, $24,024
Adams, Donald B, construction & maint supt, $51,264
Adams, Michael D, resource asst, $24,480
Adams, Ralph E, lead facilities mgmt tech, $39,768
Adams, Tim E, resource technician, $42,996
Adamson, Kathy A, public serv asst, $7.82/hr
Adkins, Casey L, intern, $11.90/hr
Aery, Jessica R, wildlife biologist, $12.47/hr
Akin, Danny L, conservation agent, $45,588
Albright, Garret E, info tech field spt supv, $68,784
Alleger, Max R, wildlife ecologist, $58,800
Allen, Lisa G, state forester/forestry div chief, $98,748
Allen, Michael J, resource asst, $26,460
Allison, Regina A, administrative staff asst, $8.98/hr
Allman, Jasper L, fisheries mgmt biologist, $58,296
Allmon, William H, equip shop technician, $39,768
Althoff, Lance E, contract sup, $47,412
Amass, Barbara S, public serv asst, $26,976
Amerman, Samuel D, resource technician, $33,372
Amerman, Yvette, resource forester, $44,712
Ames, Catlin W, resource staff scientist, $37,500
Anderson, Bryan C, resource technician, $38,232
Anderson, Charles W, resource science supv, $62,352
Anderson, Lisa M, hr data analyst, $41,352
Anderson, Lucas M, private land conservationist, $37,500
Anderson, Michael E, fisheries mgmt biologist, $51,264
Anderson, Michelle R, fisheries biologist, $12.47/hr
Andrews, Franklin E, resource technician, $34,044
Angus, Matthew P, intern, $11.90/hr
Archer, Vernon L, ofc mgr, $35,388
Armstrong, Karen P, conservation educ consult, $44,712
Arnall, William F, resource asst, $28,044
Arnett, Kenneth W, public serv asst, $8.00/hr
Arnold, Adam L, conservation agent, $40,548
Arnold, Don M, construction & maint supt, $55,440
Arnold, Jeffrey A, fleet servs spec, $53,304
Arnold, Leah G, resource technician, $9.86/hr
Arnold, Rae E, resource asst, $8.58/hr
Asahl, Derick J, resource technician, $10.57/hr
Asher, Allison M, resource asst, $8.58/hr
Asher, Jeffery B, maint sup, $47,412
Asher, Marcus N, private land conservationist, $39,000
Aslakson, James D, mechal engr, $68,784
Asmus, Leigh A, administrative staff asst, $8.58/hr
Aspen, Joshua N, conservation asst, $7.82/hr
Atkinson, Stephen D, proj engr, $74,400
Auffet, Shirley Y, administrative staff asst, $30,288
Ausbury, Austin D, resource aide, $7.82/hr
Austin, Andrew G, fisheries rgnal supv, $64,848
Austin, Jerome B, conservation agent, $61,140
Bachmann, Levi T, resource asst, $8.58/hr
Badgley, Kevin E, interpretive center mgr, $42,996
Baebler, Elisa N, fisheries biologist, $12.47/hr
Bagley, Marc J, conservation agent, $42,996
Bailey, Bruce T, resource technician, $32,748
Bailey, Cody D, resource forester asst, $10.83/hr
Bailey, Dalton L, resource asst, $8.58/hr
Bailey, Wesley P, facility maint tech, $16.69/hr
Bakameyer, Jeffrey S, resource forester, $40,548
Baker, Deborah K, ofc sup, $39,768
Baker, Ethan R, resource asst, $8.58/hr
Baker, James M, fisheries biologist, $12.47/hr
Baker, James S, equip shop technician, $44,712
Baker, Logan G, resource asst, $8.58/hr
Baker, Randy D, resource asst, $27,516
Baldridge, David R, conservation agent, $40,548
Baldwin, Donna S, ofc mgr, $38,232
Bale, Adam M, resource forester, $37,500
Ballard, Jared A, resource asst, $24,480
Ballard, Russell J, excess prop technician, $9.42/hr
Bancroft, Jacob I, resource asst, $24,024
Bandelier, Dorothy M, public serv asst, $9.86/hr
Banks, Onis W, resource aide, $7.82/hr
Banner, Kimberly A, naturalist, $36,792
Barber, Jay M, conservation educ consult, $59,952
Barker, Theodore W, public serv asst, $8.00/hr
Barnes, Andrea F, administrative staff asst, $28,596
Barnes, Andrew J, conservation agent, $40,548
Barnes, Kent R, resource asst, $31,488

Barnes, Perry T, lead crpntr, $13.71/hr
Barnes, Wesley G, maint sup, $42,996
Barns, Don L, maint sup, $49,296
Barr, Gregory P, lead crpntr, $51,264
Barrioz, Seth A, private land conservationist, $39,000
Barry, Peggy A, ofc sup, $32,100
Bartlett, Brian K, conservation agent, $54,360
Bartley, Donald P, resource asst, $9.42/hr
Bartnicki, Lia Raquel O, naturalist, $12.17/hr
Barton, James A, private land conservationist, $44,712
Barton, William D, conservation agent, $40,548
Basham, Danny S, heavy equip oper, $38,232
Bassett, Kent E, fire prog asst supv, $42,168
Bataille, Karen J, resource science supv, $62,352
Bateman, Denise M, administrative asst, $41,352
Bates, Daryl R, resource technician, $30,876
Bates, Kathy M, administrative staff asst, $8.78/hr
Bath, Terry L, resource technician, $33,372
Batkiewicz, Stephen F, resource asst, $8.58/hr
Batson, Stanley W, lead crpntr, $40,548
Batten, Jasmine K, wildlife hlth spec, $38,232
Battles, John D, resource asst, $8.58/hr
Battson Warren, Jennifer J, wildlife div chief, $85,368
Bauer, John E, range ofcr, $29,148
Bauer, Katie L, resource asst, $8.58/hr
Baumberger, Erick C, asst natural history biologist, $10.83/hr
Baumer, Michele D, public involvement coord, $54,360
Baumer, Samuel H, lead maint technician, $9.86/hr
Baumhoer, Nichole J, administrative asst, $41,352
Bax, Kimberly D, ofc mgr, $37,500
Bax, Melinda S, accounting technician, $28,596
Bay, James E, heavy equip oper, $32,748
Bayless, Michael A, fisheries mgmt biologist, $48,336
Bealmer, Brian W, resource technician, $34,716
Beasley, Trincy A, intern, $11.90/hr
Beck, Nanci E, pub serv asst, $7.82/hr
Beckett, Jerry W, maint sup, $36,084
Bedford, Melissa A, education outreach coord, $39,000
Beggs, Hunter S, conservation agent, $7.82/hr
Behle, Patricia A, public serv asst, $8.58/hr
Belfiore, Vincent A, resource science asst, $10.83/hr
Bellipanni, Dorothy A, resource asst, $8.78/hr
Benchabane, Ahmed, resource asst, $26,460
Bender, Catlin M, resource aide, $7.82/hr
Benedict-wiseman, Geri L, training & dev coord, $57,660
Benton, Kendall C, info tech field spt spec, $47,412
Beres, Audrey L, policy coord, $47,412
Bergfield, Matthew O, conservation agent, $42,996
Bergthold, Brandy S, resource science asst, $10.83/hr
Beringer, Jeffrey J, resource scientist, $64,848
Berry, Lyndsea R, resource aide, $7.82/hr
Berti, Jeffrey A, conservation agent, $52,284
Beshears, Jordon S, wildlife biologist, $33,372
Bess, Robert N, financial servs analyst, $43,848
Bethel, Judith A, ofc sup, $36,084
Beul, Michael W, aircraft mech, $58,800
Beuterbaugh, Caleb M, resource asst, $25,452
Bill, Michael D, forestry dist sup, $47,412
Bilyeu, David A, facility maint tech, $29,148
Binsbacher, Ruddyard R, conservation agent, $42,996
Binsbacher, Ryan N, conservation agent, $40,548
Biram, Noella C, forest nursery mgr, $42,168
Bisges, Gary F, contract sup, $57,660
Bishop, Ric L, protect dist supv, $48,336
Bixler, Timothy M, it gis sup, $53,304
Blackmon, Joan L, administrative staff asst, $29,724
Blanchard, Paul E, fisheries prog coord, $58,800
Blanks, Michael G, crpntr, $32,100
Blatz, Richard J, forestry field progs supv, $69,612
Bledsoe, Joanna K, protect dist supv, $61,140
Block, Elizabeth E, deisgner/editor, $42,168
Blocker, Kayla A, resource asst, $8.58/hr
Bloskovich, Brian J, fac maint tech, $26,460
Blunk, Christopher G, wildlife mgmt biologist, $42,168
Boaz, Joan T, private land svs regional supv, $57,660
Bock, Craig S, contract sup, $41,352
Bock, Frances D, info technology coord, $74,292
Bockman, Skyler T, education center mgr, $42,168
Bokern, Brian P, wildlife biologist, $36,792
Bolden, James E, conservation agent, $40,548
Boman, Adam D, fisheries mgmt biologist, $40,548
Bommarito, Nicholas J, resource asst, $22,680
Bond, Lucas C, news services coord, $40,548

Bonnot, Rhonda J, engring design tech, $45,588
Bono, Dominick V, lead maint technician, $9.86/hr
Borges, Leon E, wildlife biologist, $42,168
Borisenko, Kevin C, private land servs chief, $72,948
Borowiak, James L, resource asst, $30,876
Boshears, Ricky V, heavy equip oper, $45,588
Boss, Rachel N, wildlife mgmt asst, $10.83/hr
Botard, Shane A, resource forester, $37,500
Bothwell, Christopher L, pub serv asst, $7.82/hr
Bowyer, Matthew W, wildlife regional supv, $47,412
Box, Aaron M, resource asst, $8.58/hr
Boyd, Brian K, conservation agent, $63,588
Boyd, Christopher B, conservation agent, $39,768
Boyer, Phillip D, resource technician, $25,452
Boze, Jeromy C, resource technician, $34,368
Bracken, Adam S, conservation agent, $42,996
Bradford, Alan D, conservation agent, $54,360
Braithwait, James M, wildlife damage biologist, $56,544
Branch, Leother, conservation agent, $57,660
Brandes, Allen M, fisheries regional prog spv, $45,588
Brandsgaard, Adam A, conservation educ consult, $44,712
Brandsma, Justin P, resource technician, $29,724
Branson, Andrew F, fisheries progs spec, $50,280
Branson, Glenda E, safety coord, $71,532
Brauch, Dalton H, resource asst, $8.58/hr
Braunecker, Jason M, protect dist supv, $45,588
Brauner, Brittnie L, environmental rev coord, $29,724
Brawley, Brandon R, resource asst, $26,976
Bray, Diana L, public serv asst, $24,024
Bredesen, Richard E, wildlife mgmt biologist, $44,712
Breuer, Jeffrey V, conservation agent, $45,588
Brewer, Lora J, resource technician, $9.86/hr
Bridgeman, Donald E, equip shop technician, $42,996
Bridges, Cameron B, resource asst, $23,580
Bridges, Kearby G, conservation agent, $40,548
Briggler, Jeffrey T, resource scientist, $50,280
Briggler, Malissa L, resource scientist, $45,588
Brillhart, Michael L, resource asst, $28,596
Brinkley, Phillip D, naturalist, $36,084
Brisco, Stuart J, resource technician, $9.86/hr
Brixey, Michael E, heavy equip oper, $30,876
Broaddus, Dustin W, resource asst, $8.58/hr
Brocaille, Michael L, resource aide, $7.82/hr
Brolaski, Samantha M, resource asst, $7.82/hr
Brondel, Dylan A, special projs asst, $9.86/hr
Brooks, Betty L, resource aide, $8.19/hr
Brooks, Michael E, outdoor educ cntr supv, $49,296
Brooks, Timothy W, private land conservationist, $57,660
Brostoski, Jordanya I, naturalist, $33,372
Brown, Doyle F, federal aid coord, $64,848
Brown, Edward K, private land svs regional supv, $71,532
Brown, Jeffrey S, conservation agent, $57,660
Brown, Kelby J, resource aide, $7.82/hr
Brown, Mary C, public serv asst, $9.42/hr
Brown, Scott M, conservation agent, $42,996
Brown, Timothy D, resource asst, $24,024
Brown, Tyler S, conservation agent, $40,548
Brunke, Kevin D, wildlife mgmt biologist, $40,548
Bruns, David J, conservation educ consult, $47,412
Bryan, Patricia D, ofc mgr, $35,388
Bryan, Robert P, resource asst, $34,044
Bryant, Darlene E, wildlife mgmt biologist, $57,660
Bryant, Matthew S, conservation agent, $39,000
Bryant, Scott, info technology spec, $42,168
Buback, Steven M, natural history reg biologist, $41,352
Buck, Lydia M, administrative staff asst, $8.58/hr
Buckley, Gregory L, lead crpntr, $43,848
Buckner, Ben J, resource asst, $25,956
Buechler, Amy C, pub involvement coord, $54,360
Bueltmann, Andrew T, fisheries biologist, $12.47/hr
Buescher, Brian A, wildlife biologist, $12.47/hr
Bullock, Andrew L, conservation agent, $54,360
Bullock, Caleb C, resource asst, $8.58/hr
Bullock, Wyatt L, resource asst, $8.58/hr
Bumgardaner, Corbin S, conservation agent, $61,140
Burdick, Andrew P, asst htchry mgr, $36,084
Burgdorf, William E, resource asst, $25,452
Burger, Scott B, protect dist supv, $64,848
Burk, Jeremy W, lead crpntr, $38,232
Burke, Alicia D, wildlife mgmt asst, $11.62/hr
Burke, Ronald L, fisheries spec, $42,168
Burns, Alton P, wildlife biologist, $34,044
Burns, Billy J, resource technician, $37,500

Burns, Debra A, wildlife regional supv, $52,284
Burns, Donald W, info tech field spt spec, $64,848
Burns, Robert N, resource asst, $8.78/hr
Burrell, Nicholas C, wildlife biologist, $36,084
Burton, Michael R, protect dist supv, $71,532
Bush, Shane C, fisheries mgmt biologist, $40,548
Busse, Sherry L, resource aide, $8.38/hr
Bussell, Dylan R, resource aide, $7.82/hr
Butler, Dorothy J, progmer/db mgr, $57,660
Buxman, Stan L, resource asst, $8.78/hr
Byrd, Bryan W, wildlife biologist, $36,084
Byrd, Christin M, private land conservationist, $37,500
Caby, Michael D, wildlife biologist, $36,084
Cadden, Luann M, naturalist, $12.47/hr
Cady, Briggs J, info technology spec, $50,280
Caffey, Julie A, public serv asst, $34,716
Callow, Clayton J, resource technician, $9.86/hr
Calvert, Eric T, resource asst, $24,984
Calvert, Gary L, wildlife mgmt biologist, $53,304
Calvert, Martin R, resource forester, $49,296
Calvert, Paul D, fisheries field opers chief, $68,784
Camden, James J, resource asst, $23,112
Campa, Francisco L, conservation agent, $58,800
Campbell, Christine M, conservation agent, $54,360
Campbell, Craig R, equip shop technician, $36,084
Campbell, Jennifer K, policy coord, $54,360
Campbell, Mary P, facility maint tech, $28,044
Campbell, Robert H, resource asst, $8.58/hr
Canaday, Brian D, fisheries div chief, $82,080
Cannon, Shelli A, administrative staff asst, $28,596
Cantoni, David L, resource technician, $10.11/hr
Cantrell, Jeffrey N, conservation educ consult, $47,412
Capps, Jeremy L, resource technician, $29,148
Capps, Steven R, resource asst, $24,024
Capps, William C, outdoor skills spec, $57,660
Careaga, Jacob D, design & devel div chief, $85,368
Carlisle, David S, conservation agent, $46,488
Carmack, Andrew S, private land conservationist, $40,548
Carr, Glenda J, lead maint technician, $9.86/hr
Carr, Willie A, conservation agent, $42,996
Case, Dennis L, equip mech II, $10.11/hr
Case, Kyle A, resource technician, $29,148
Case, Ryan L, resource aide, $8.00/hr
Cassell, Gregory W, resource forester, $51,264
Cato, Brendan S, resource aide, $7.82/hr
Cato, William L, resource asst, $23,112
Cavanaugh, Daniel D, resource technician, $32,748
Cavender, Kathleen F, nature center mgr, $55,440
Chapin, William A, info tech field spt spec, $57,660
Chapman, Ben D, resource asst, $24,024
Chasteen, Bonnie L, editor, $54,360
Chenoweth, Joshua D, resource asst, $8.58/hr
Chesher, Christopher L, conservation agent, $48,336
Chew, Kevin, resource asst, $24,480
Chilton, Bryant C, resource technician, $40,548
Chorice, Linda F, nature center mgr, $61,140
Christal, Kameron L, resource aide, $7.82/hr
Christensen, Michael J, conservation agent, $58,800
Cieslewicz, Paul G, fisheries mgmt biologist, $54,360
Civiello, James A, htchry syss mgr, $70,140
Clark, Darrell G, resource asst, $34,044
Clark, George D, forest nursery sup, $67,452
Clark-Barry, Janine A, public serv asst, $7.82/hr
Classey, Dawn M, resource technician, $9.86/hr
Clay, Jerry D, resource technician, $32,748
Cleary, Sean D, wildlife mgmt biologist, $44,712
Clennin, Russell N, facility maint tech, $26,976
Clever, Donald R, conservation agent, $39,000
Clift, Gordon M, resource asst, $27,516
Cloyd, Christopher A, digital comm mgr, $62,352
Coates, Daniel P, warehouse servs technician, $34,044
Cobden, Jason S, info tech field spt spec, $44,712
Cockerham, Jeffrey L, outreach & edu chief, $68,784
Cofer, Robert L, resource technician, $28,596
Colatskie, Shelly N, wildlife biologist, $12.47/hr
Colborn, Ryan C, resource asst, $9.20/hr
Cole, Derek L, conservation agent, $57,660
Cole, Kimberly K, conservation educ consult, $37,500
Colehour, Jacob D, htchry mgr, $45,588
Coleman, Andrea N, resource asst, $8.58/hr
Coleman, Kendall L, private land conservationist, $42,168
Colley, Dalton R, administrative staff asst, $24,480
Collier, Cecil, pump repair sup, $45,588

Collier, Gregory W, outdoor skills spec, $45,588
Collins, Michael J, conservation agent trainee, $36,084
Collins, Shaun A, resource asst, $8.58/hr
Combes, Matthew D, resource scientist, $49,296
Comer, Sierra F, resource science asst, $10.83/hr
Conaway, Lesly K, aquaculture biologist, $48,336
Conner, Charles C, cmnty forester, $48,336
Conway, Chris L, administrative staff asst, $36,792
Conway, Stephen D, lead crpntr, $40,548
Cook, Deanna L, fin servs mgr, $54,360
Cook, Richard J, fisheries rgnal prog spv, $53,304
Cook, Terry J, resource technician, $38,232
Cooke, Dennis E, outdoor skills spec, $47,412
Cooper, G R, resource asst, $8.98/hr
Cooper, Gary L, lead equip oper, $50,280
Cooper, Kathy L, private land conservationist, $15.82/hr
Cooper, Lorinda L, administrative staff asst, $30,288
Cooper, Ricky E, resource asst, $26,976
Cooper, Stephanie L, resource aide, $7.82/hr
Cooper, Steven B, wildlife mgmt biologist, $50,280
Copeland, Forrest D, resource aide, $7.82/hr
Copple, Lauren A, public serv asst, $9.64/hr
Cordell, Keith L, wildlife biologist, $36,792
Corlew, Lindsey R, resource asst, $24,480
Corley, Scott G, protect dist supv, $51,264
Cornforth, Lawrence A, hatchery mgr, $50,280
Corrigan, John M, resource aide, $7.82/hr
Corson, Angela M, fisheries prog coord, $52,800
Corwin, Michael J, resource technician, $9.86/hr
Cosbey, Elizabeth S, pub serv asst, $8.00/hr
Cotton, Jane E, resource technician, $40,548
Courtois, Roger D, lead maint technician, $10.33/hr
Cowell, Andrew M, resource asst, $25,956
Cox, Christa D, conservation agent, $39,000
Cox, Christopher C, conservation agent, $50,280
Cox, Cortney L, resource aide, $7.82/hr
Cox, Elijah R, resource asst, $8.58/hr
Cox, Shelly R, naturalist, $12.47/hr
Coy, Aimee M, private land conservationist, $40,548
Coy, Isaac W, resource asst, $8.58/hr
Coy, Nathan J, wildlife biologist, $34,044
Crabtree, Keith R, resource technician, $38,232
Crabtree, Malanna K, resource aide, $7.82/hr
Craft, Margaret M, digital media producer, $59,952
Craig, Fred, construction & maint supt, $70,140
Craig, Jerry L, resource asst, $30,876
Crain, Scott A, asst hatchery mgr, $43,848
Crane, Melanie L, asst fin servs chief, $61,140
Crase, Wendy N, administrative staff asst, $25,452
Cravens, Chester G, protect rgnal supv, $78,912
Crawford, Bryon D, resource technician, $32,748
Crawford, Gary D, gen servs supv, $71,532
Crawford, Robert D, maint sup, $41,352
Creamer, David J, crpntr, $28,596
Creasy, Shane R, resource technician, $29,148
Creech, Clay J, conservation agent, $54,360
Creed, Mark J, conservation agent, $42,996
Crewse, Robert L, resource asst, $26,460
Crider, Albert S, wildlife technician, $10.57/hr
Crider, Raymond G, resource technician, $9.86/hr
Crisler, Craig A, wildlife mgmt biologist, $53,304
Crites, Jason W, fisheries mgmt biologist, $40,548
Crites, Jeffrey G, conservation agent, $45,588
Crocker, Sarah M, accounting technician, $29,148
Crouse, Jarrett C, resource asst, $24,480
Crowe, Richard D, private land conservationist, $37,500
Cumberledge, Catherine S, info tech field spt spec, $58,800
Cunningham, Darrel E, resource technician, $38,232
Cunningham, Shawn P, distrib center mgr, $50,280
Curry, Matthew D, private land conservationist, $45,588
Cussimanio, Josh A, wildlife biologist, $39,768
Dake, Brad O, contract sup, $14.38/hr
Dalbey, Michelle M, aquaculture spec, $32,100
Dames, Howard R, fisheries mgmt biologist, $51,264
Damron, Daryl R, wildlife damage biologist, $44,712
Danaher, Carlin F, resource technician, $9.86/hr
Daniel, Chris A, wildlife mgmt biologist, $43,848
Daniels, Martha J, exhbs coord, $70,140
Daniels, Richard A, protect dist supv, $64,848
Darnall, Christine A, aquatic animal hlth spec, $45,588
Darnell, Michael T, lead equip oper, $39,768
Darrow, David, wildlife mgmt biologist, $49,296
Dattilo, John C, resource science asst, $10.83/hr

Davis, Benjamin J, resource asst, $24,024
Davis, Candice D, media spec, $42,996
Davis, Joseph W, info technology spec, $67,452
Davis, Lisa K, protect technician, $29,724
Davis, Sarah H, resource technician, $9.86/hr
Davis, Stacey D, discovery center mgr, $55,440
Davis, Tyler I, resource asst, $8.58/hr
Day, Trevor A, resource asst, $8.58/hr
Debold, Joseph L, urban wildlife biologist, $42,168
Debow, Keith C, resource asst, $34,716
Decoske, Christine C, conservation agent, $54,360
Decoske, Jamey J, resource science asst, $42,996
Dejong, Catherine S, forestry rgnal supv, $72,948
Delaney, Kerrie L, administrative staff asst, $23,580
Dellamano, Jan A, private land conservationist, $48,336
Demand, Jefferey A, wildlife mgmt biologist, $44,712
Dennis, Eric L, fisheries mgmt biologist, $42,168
Dent, Billy J, resource asst, $34,716
Dentner, Holly J, forestry field progs supv, $53,304
Derryberry, Harold D, resource aide, $8.00/hr
Desanty-combes, Jackie A, asst natural history bio, $10.83/hr
Desanty-combes, Jackie A, resource technician, $9.86/hr
Devaul, William G, resource asst, $8.58/hr
Devine, Kimberly S, ofc mgr, $37,500
Dickey, Jason M, protect dist supv, $54,360
Dickson, Stephen M, land surv, $58,800
Diefendorf, Larry F, resource asst, $8.58/hr
Diekmann, Benjamin D, intern, $11.90/hr
Diekmann, Terri L, ofc mgr, $35,388
Diel, Steven M, resource aide, $8.19/hr
Dierking, Jeffrey W, private land conservationist, $41,352
Dinsdale, Travis C, area biologist, $50,280
Dirnberger, Ryan R, wildlife mgmt biologist, $37,500
Distefano, Robert J, resource scientist, $64,848
Distefano, Will M, resource asst, $8.58/hr
Dixon, James C, wildlife damage biologist, $44,712
Dixon, Kevin S, conservation agent, $57,660
Dobbins, Michelle D, hr spec, $50,280
Dockins, Dee A, outdoor skills spec, $42,168
Doerhoff, Adam J, conservation agent, $40,548
Doerhoff, Roberta R, resource forester asst, $30,288
Doering, Branden T, resource aide, $7.82/hr
Doherty, Kyle P, resource asst, $8.58/hr
Doman, Kenneth R, protect field chief, $64,848
Doolen, Rodney D, wetland servs biologist, $44,712
Doran, Christopher W, conservation agent, $40,548
Dorge, Sandra M, ofc sup, $36,084
Douglas, Leia M, administrative staff asst, $25,956
Douglas, Lucas J, resource asst, $8.58/hr
Dow, Stephen M, administrative staff asst, $8.58/hr
Doyle, David P, resource forester asst, $28,596
Dozier, Ricky L, resource technician, $34,044
Draper, Thomas A, dpty dir-resource mgmt, $115,620
Drecktrah, Bruce M, fisheries field opers chief, $61,140
Drenon, Russell K, policy coord, $18.70/hr
Driscoll, Katharine M, resource aide, $7.82/hr
Drummond, Frank D, wildlife biologist, $48,336
Drummond, Kimberly J, administrative staff asst, $8.58/hr
Drury, Danny L, heavy equip oper, $35,388
Dry, Douglas G, info tech field spt spec, $51,264
Dubbs, Matthew A, lead maint technician, $9.86/hr
Duckworth, Russell B, protect dist supv, $54,360
Duckworth, Shawn C, wetland servs biologist, $45,588
Duemmel, Corey J, purchasing & fleet analyst, $50,280
Duffin, Donnamarie H, asst natural history biologist, $10.83/hr
Duffin, Donnamarie H, asst gis spec, $12.47/hr
Dufur, Brett R, editor, $49,296
Duncan, James L, equip shop technician, $39,000
Dunda, Kyle C, conservation agent trainee, $36,084
Dunham, Lisa L, ofc mgr, $35,388
Dunn, Nelson J, it spt technician, $36,084
Dyer, Jimmy L, resource asst, $28,044
Dyer, Timothy W, resource asst, $24,480
Ebbesmeyer, James M, private land conservationist, $44,712
Eberwein, Sue L, hr spec, $16.20/hr
Eckhardt, Perry W, cmnty conserv planner, $48,336
Eden, Leah R, naturalist, $39,000
Edgar, William W, resource asst, $8.98/hr
Edwards, Eric K, edu outreach coord, $40,548
Edwards, Jeremy H, conservation agent trainee, $36,084
Edwards, Scott W, resource asst, $8.98/hr
Edwards, Tiffany A, resource asst, $8.78/hr
Eikermann, Jason B, conservation agent, $42,996

Elder, Elizabeth L, public serv asst, $7.82/hr
Elkins, Elizabeth A, administrative staff asst, $8.58/hr
Elledge, Matthew S, resource asst, $25,956
Elliott, Anthony G, resource scientist, $50,280
Elliott, Jerry D, protect dist supv, $54,360
Elliott, Steven E, outdoor educ cntr supv, $42,996
Elliott, Utah G, equip shop technician, $39,768
Ellis, Dale W, it spt technician, $46,488
Elsea, Cole L, resource asst, $8.78/hr
Ely, Christopher D, conservation agent, $42,996
Emery, Justin D, conservation agent, $40,548
Emmerich, Beth A, resource scientist, $45,588
Engel, Matthew A, fisheries mgmt biologist, $42,168
Engelke, Chad A, resource asst, $24,024
English, Kelly, accounting technician, $32,100
Enright, Thomas A, wildlife biologist, $32,100
Entrop, Kara D, public serv asst, $8.58/hr
Ernst, Sarah H, wildlife mgmt asst, $10.83/hr
Ernst, Sean P, conservation agent, $42,996
Esely, Jeffrey D, private land conservationist, $44,712
Eulinger, Kevin G, conservation agent, $40,548
Evans, Randall J, asst natural history biologist, $11.09/hr
Evers, Lindsey N, financial servs analyst, $36,084
Evert, Joseph M, resource asst, $8.58/hr
Ewigman, Robert J, construction & maint supt, $52,284
Ewing, Chance E, resource technician, $25,956
Expose, Sonja D, administrative staff asst, $33,372
Faiman, John S, resource science asst, $39,000
Faith, Samuel K, conservation educ consult, $44,712
Fakes, Jennifer L, outreach & educ reg supv, $51,264
Falconer, Rick A, resource technician, $36,792
Fantz, Debra K, resource scientist, $55,440
Fantz, John R, fisheries staff biologist, $54,360
Farmer, Madison P, resource asst, $8.58/hr
Farnsworth, Judith M, resource asst, $9.20/hr
Farr, Robert R, conservation agent, $59,952
Farrington, Susan J, natural history reg biologist, $41,352
Farwell, Brad M, asst htchry mgr, $36,084
Farwell, Derek R, conservation agent, $52,284
Faunce, Kaycee E, resource aide, $7.82/hr
Feeler, Heather D, comm mgr, $55,440
Fees, Douglas W, info tech servs chief, $93,732
Feighert, Donald N, resource technician, $9.86/hr
Feistel, Andrew W, conservation agent trainee, $36,084
Ferguson, David E, equip shop sup II, $58,800
Fessler, Justin A, proj engr, $63,588
Fey, Cheryl A, protect progs supv, $74,400
Fiaoni, Michael G, resource forester, $51,264
Fike, Terri D, resource asst, $9.20/hr
Finn, Margaret D, resource aide, $8.00/hr
Fischer, Kent A, maint sup, $43,848
Fischer, Sherry L, stream servs prog supv, $57,660
Fischer, Christopher D, resource technician, $10.33/hr
Fisher, Jackie A, contract sup, $50,280
Fisher, Timothy G, lead equip oper, $38,232
Flaspohler, Michael G, wildlife mgmt biologist, $50,280
Fleischhauer, Michael D, resource forester, $40,548
Fleming, Julie A, progmer/db mgr, $53,304
Fletcher, Rebecca L, resource forester, $44,712
Flinn, Emily B, resource scientist, $45,588
Flora, Anthony R, lead equip oper, $49,296
Flores, Diane R, it business analyst, $71,532
Flores, Kenda S, aquatic habitat spec, $53,304
Flowers, Brian D, outdoor skills spec, $46,488
Focht, Justin D, resource asst, $29,148
Foerster, Donald E, private land conservationist, $15.82/hr
Fogle, Justin W, conservation agent, $42,996
Ford, Zachary L, resource scientist, $45,588
Fore, Daniel A, resource asst, $24,024
Foreman, Malissa D, resource asst, $8.58/hr
Forster, James A, equip shop technician, $39,768
Fortenberry, Leslie A, dsgnr, $48,336
Foster, Alex C, wildlife biologist asst, $29,724
Foster, Clark E, resource technician, $30,288
Foster, Jennifer L, public serv asst, $7.82/hr
Foster, Jodean, protect technician, $30,288
Foster, Thomas C, resource technician, $28,044
Fountain, Daryl G, lead equip oper, $49,296
Fowler, Carl A, resource asst, $8.58/hr
Franks, Matthew L, conservation agent, $40,548
Frazier, Curtis J, intern, $11.90/hr
Frazier, Jennifer S, gen counsel, $85,368
Frazier, Larry D, lead crpntr, $36,792

Frazier, Roger L, priority habitat coord, $50,280
Frederick, Shelby M, resource asst, $8.98/hr
Freeman, Nathaniel C, maint mech, $9.42/hr
Freeman, Philip C, wildlife mgmt biologist, $46,488
Freese, John M, resource aide, $7.82/hr
Frey, Dolores M, accounting technician, $11.62/hr
Fritz, Gregory E, protect rgnal supv, $68,784
Fronterhouse, Quenten A, conservation agent, $42,996
Frye, Matthew B, warehouse servs technician, $25,956
Fuller, Craig J, fisheries mgmt biologist, $51,264
Gailey, Justin W, wildlife mgmt biologist, $42,996
Gaines, Audrey L, intern, $11.90/hr
Gale, James M, equip shop technician, $33,372
Gall, Lloyd D, resource asst, $36,792
Gant, Isaac B, gis spec, $15.08/hr
Gao, Xiaoming, biometrician, $63,588
Gardner, Bradley D, resource asst, $24,024
Gardner, Michael, resource aide, $8.00/hr
Gardner, Randy A, conservation agent, $39,000
Garner, Cynthia D, cmnty forester, $50,280
Garner, Darrick L, resource science asst, $32,100
Garner, Shawn O, resource asst, $8.58/hr
Garrett, Molly J, resource technician, $9.86/hr
Garrison, Heather A, fisheries mgmt biologist, $36,084
Gartner, Justine T, forest mgmt chief, $80,484
Garver, Robert L, outdoor skills spec, $40,548
Garvey, Joseph M, forestry regional supv, $74,400
Gaskins, Michael D, private land conservationist, $40,548
Gauck, Inge, public serv asst, $8.00/hr
Gehin, Amanda R, crpntr, $10.83/hr
Geiger, Alex L, resource asst, $24,024
Gelly, Grant A, conservation agent, $42,996
Gemming, Craig S, fisheries mgmt biologist, $57,660
Gentry, Caleb W, resource aide, $8.00/hr
George, Angela C, resource forester, $40,548
George, John R, wildlife regional supv, $55,440
Gerken, Jack R, resource asst, $9.42/hr
Gerling, Donald M, resource asst, $28,596
Gettys, Geanna, ofc mgr, $32,748
Gibbs, Jessica M, wildlife biologist, $12.47/hr
Gibson, Gregory J, fac maint tech, $28,596
Gieck, Brenda L, accounting asst, $8.78/hr
Gilbert, Brian C, wildlife mgmt biologist, $40,548
Gilby, Travis A, resource asst, $25,956
Gilmore, Len E, resource asst, $9.64/hr
Girdner, Michael R, resource asst, $8.98/hr
Girondo, Jennifer A, fisheries mgmt biologist, $40,548
Girondo, Nicholas M, fisheries mgmt biologist, $40,992
Gladbach, Tim J, heavy equip oper, $45,588
Gleckler, Annie R, resource asst, $8.58/hr
Glen, Andrew R, resource technician, $9.86/hr
Glenn, Stuart R, resource forester, $46,488
Glover, Micah F, resource asst, $24,480
Goetz, Anthony T, equip shop technician, $34,716
Goggins, Lynn, accounting technician, $29,724
Gognat, Gary L, resource forester, $44,712
Goin, Jeffrey H, resource technician, $34,044
Golden, Rick L, resource asst, $37,500
Good, Chris S, resource technician, $42,996
Goodrich, Kristen E, resource forester, $45,228
Goreham, Travis M, conservation agent, $40,548
Gorrell, Gary L, resource asst, $34,044
Gould, Grant P, lead maint technician, $9.86/hr
Govero, Steven M, range ofcr, $28,044
Grace, Timothy B, fisheries regional supv, $74,400
Gragg, Bryan N, forestry regional supv, $51,264
Graham, George W, media spec, $43,848
Grass, Brandon L, resource technician, $29,148
Gray, Chad T, resource asst, $24,024
Gray, Laurie E, fisheries technician, $9.42/hr
Green, Cynthia B, conservation educ consult, $63,588
Green, Heather S, accounting asst, $27,516
Green, Tyler B, conservation agent, $39,000
Gregg, Cory D, resource forester, $40,548
Gregg, Richard L, resource asst, $28,596
Gregory, Deborah A, public serv asst, $7.82/hr
Gregory, Trent W, crpntr, $31,488
Gregory, Tyler M, resource asst, $22,680
Grellner, Michael J, distrib center asst, $36,792
Griddine, Mark E, resource technician, $36,792
Griggs, Richard C, duplicating equip oper II, $33,372
Griggs, Robin R, ast natural history biologist, $10.83/hr
Grimes, Mitchell S, resource aide, $8.00/hr

Grishow, David A, lead crpntr, $37,500
Grishow, Richard L, const & maint supt, $66,144
Gross, Jacob A, equip shop technician, $34,716
Grote, Christopher M, conservation agent, $40,548
Gruber, Shawn M, outreach & educ reg supv, $51,264
Grueber, Mark E, cmnty forester, $53,304
Grumm, Robin, asst nature center mgr, $45,588
Grusenmeyer, Evan D, wildlife biologist, $12.47/hr
Haas, Randall D, private land conservationist, $59,952
Habina, Brenda K, resource aide, $8.19/hr
Hadley, Bradley M, conservation agent, $45,588
Haefke, Christopher S, web developer, $45,588
Hager, Brent T, resource asst, $8.58/hr
Hager, Brent T, fisheries technician, $9.42/hr
Hager, Joshua L, wildlife mgmt biologist, $39,000
Hagerman, Ramona L, printing prod spec, $42,168
Hake, Audrey G, resource aide, $8.00/hr
Hale, Earnest C, hatchery mgr, $45,588
Halford, Megan S, ofc mgr, $35,388
Hall, Kasey T, lead crpntr, $13.71/hr
Hall, Nicholas T, resource aide, $7.82/hr
Halley, Bart E, resource asst, $28,596
Ham, Brian F, protect dist supv, $56,544
Ham, Tyler D, resource science asst, $10.83/hr
Hambelton, Ronnie W, resource asst, $30,288
Hamilton, Thomas J, info technology spec, $63,588
Hanks, Laura L, it spt technician, $47,412
Hanks, Wesley A, resource asst, $24,024
Hanley, Joann L, hr compliance coord, $47,412
Hanna, Lynndon R, maint sup, $43,848
Happekotte, Eric M, resource asst, $28,596
Harding, Mark A, heavy equip oper, $35,388
Harding, Tyler K, conservation agent, $37,500
Harlan, Bryant J, resource asst, $8.78/hr
Harlan, James B, resource technician, $37,500
Harmon, Brian K, lead equip oper, $40,548
Harms, David S, conservation agent, $45,588
Harre, Dean C, protect field chief, $66,144
Harris, Carol L, administrative staff asst, $11.09/hr
Harris, Dustin B, resource asst, $23,580
Harris, Jeffrey W, conservation agent, $46,488
Harris, Susan L, conservation educ consult, $13.71/hr
Harrison, Scott H, range ofcr, $29,724
Hart, Larry T, it business analyst, $70,140
Hart, Roger D, resource technician, $32,748
Hartley, Aaron J, lead crpntr, $42,996
Hartman, Laura B, resource technician, $9.86/hr
Hartshorn, Tyson A, conservation agent, $40,548
Hartwig, Daniel A, forestry regional supv, $51,264
Hasenbeck, David A, elk prog mgr, $57,660
Haslag, Austin M, info tech analyst, $13.71/hr
Haslag, Kenny D, info technology spec, $71,532
Haslag, Shannon L, accounting technician, $31,488
Haslag, Whitney M, intern, $11.90/hr
Haslerig, Janet M, resource scientist, $67,452
Havens, Benjamin A, asst hatchery mgr, $38,232
Hawkins, Danny D, lead crpntr, $13.71/hr
Haydon, Randall L, resource technician, $37,500
Hayes, Rocky D, cmnty forester, $59,952
Head, Terry G, resource technician, $29,148
Headland, Ronda K, cmnty conserv planner, $42,168
Hedges, Robert K, wildlife mgmt biologist, $46,488
Hedgpeth, Kevin L, wildlife mgmt biologist, $53,304
Heerlein, Yvonne M, ofc mgr, $39,000
Hees, Patsy D, heavy equip oper, $32,748
Heidy, Vicki L, resource science supv, $67,452
Heimericks, Kevin J, lead maint technician, $9.86/hr
Heimos, Lisa R, resource asst, $8.58/hr
Heislen, Dale L, entprs technology archtct, $62,352
Heisler, Kurt G, conservation agent, $57,660
Heisler, Nicolas K, resource aide, $7.82/hr
Heitman, Theodore R, resource asst, $24,480
Hempel, Mark T, fisheries biologist, $12.47/hr
Hempen, Kevin A, resource technician, $32,100
Hendershott, Arron J, outreach & educ reg supv, $57,660
Henderson, Dawn E, resource science fld sta supv, $52,284
Hendrickson, Ray C, resource technician, $36,792
Henry, Bruce M, natural history reg biologist, $39,000
Henry, John W, wildlife mgmt asst, $10.83/hr
Henry, Mark A, conservation agent, $42,996
Henry, Robert L, wildlife biologist, $39,000
Henry, Travis C, resource technician, $33,372
Hensley, Roger L, resource asst, $8.58/hr

Hentschke, Kurt W, htchry mgr, $45,588
Heppermann, Lia C, private land conservationist, $43,848
Herigon, Heather C, hr recruitment technician, $37,500
Herndon, Matthew V, resource asst, $8.58/hr
Hertel, Bryant W, outdoor educ cntr supv, $39,768
Herzog, David P, resource science fld sta supv, $68,784
Hetherington, Kathryn E, ofc sup, $30,876
Heuring, Eric L, conservation agent, $42,996
Hibler, Christine L, resource asst, $8.58/hr
Hicks, David J, info technology spec, $43,848
Higgins, Chelsea N, resource aide, $8.00/hr
Higgins, Tamra J, resource asst, $24,024
Highfill, Taylor M, resource asst, $8.58/hr
Hilgedick, Kristie S, news servs coord, $44,712
Hill, Evan B, intern, $13.71/hr
Hill, Jane E, public serv asst, $7.82/hr
Hill, Justin A, resource asst, $29,148
Hill, Matthew A, wildlife mgmt biologist, $42,996
Hillen, Debra L, data entry oper II, $8.58/hr
Hilliard, Robyn S, realty technician, $38,988
Hime, Sydney K, vol & interprtv prgm crd, $56,544
Hindman, Jake W, outreach & educ dist supv, $42,168
Hinkle, John D, maint sup, $43,848
Hinnah, Russell R, forestry dist sup, $50,280
Hirschman, Susan R, accounting technician, $11.62/hr
Hitchings, Matthew L, conservation agent, $40,548
Hobson, Paul M, resource asst, $9.20/hr
Hodges, Brandon J, resource asst, $25,956
Hodges, Nathaniel R, conservation agent, $40,548
Hodson, Nacomi M, resource aide, $7.82/hr
Hoehn, Christopher S, resource aide, $7.82/hr
Hoel, Stephen M, private land conservationist, $44,712
Hoelscher, Douglas M, chief aircraft pilot, $68,784
Hoerner, Sharon R, asst gis analyst, $14.04/hr
Hofstetter, Johna J, resource asst, $25,956
Hogsett, Jacob C, research asst, $9.42/hr
Holcomb, Samantha L, resource asst, $8.58/hr
Holden, Tisha M, excess prop technician, $29,724
Holder, Logan L, resource asst, $8.58/hr
Hollabaugh, Scott J, resource asst, $24,024
Holland, Michele D, conservation agent, $57,660
Holloway, Patricia J, conservation educ consult, $46,488
Holsapple, Aaron L, resource forester, $42,996
Holt, Lesly M, private land conservationist, $43,848
Holt, Robert C, lead equip oper, $51,264
Holt, Todd C, it infrastructure supv, $76,296
Holtsclaw, Thaddeus W, resource asst, $28,596
Hommertzheim, John G, resource asst, $8.78/hr
Hood, Mary M, resource aide, $8.78/hr
Hoover, David E, wildlife mgmt biologist, $50,280
Hoover, John W, heavy equip oper, $39,768
Hoover, Sammy D, resource asst, $25,956
Hopwood, Seth E, resource asst, $8.58/hr
Horack, Edward P, resource aide, $7.82/hr
Horton, Richard A, fisheries mgmt biologist, $47,016
Houf, Paul T, conservation agent, $45,588
Houf, Ryan J, wildlife mgmt biologist, $42,996
Houston, Brian K, fac maint tech, $28,596
Hovis, Edward L, resource technician, $42,168
Howard, Lee E, resource technician, $33,372
Howard, Wayne E, resource aide, $8.00/hr
Hrabik, Robert A, fisheries progs spec, $71,532
Hubbard, Katherine, clerk typist, $8.00/hr
Hubbard, Kathie J, ofc mgr, $40,548
Hubbard, Michael W, resource science div chief, $85,368
Hudson, Karen M, mkting spec, $45,588
Huebner, Jerod M, wildlife biologist, $34,044
Huff, Brody M, resource asst, $8.58/hr
Huff, Elaine K, accounting technician, $9.42/hr
Hufferd, James M, resource technician, $42,168
Huffman, Thomas R, resource science asst, $32,100
Hughes, Andrew H, resource asst, $24,024
Hughes, Jacob E, resource asst, $25,452
Hughes, Lee G, public land coord, $53,304
Hull, Paula A, resource asst, $8.58/hr
Hullinger, Michael A, resource forester, $33,372
Humble, Andrew J, private land conservationist, $40,548
Hunsaker, Denise A, conservation agent, $57,660
Hunt, Kimberly K, ofc sup, $34,044
Hunter, Daryl W, resource asst, $26,976
Hunter, John N, excess prop technician, $9.64/hr
Huntley, Jessie L, resource asst, $29,148
Hurayt, Melissa M, naturalist, $12.76/hr

Hurayt, Melissa M, pub serv asst, $7.82/hr
Hurley, Everett H, lead crpntr, $39,768
Hurley, Mason L, resource asst, $23,580
Hurt, James M, crpntr, $33,372
Hutton, Dennis L, resource asst, $8.78/hr
Hutton, Walter L, conservation agent, $57,660
Hyland, Theresa R, resource asst, $8.58/hr
Idel, Doris E, administrative staff asst, $11.50/hr
Ingram, John D, conservation agent, $45,588
Ireland, Robert D, engring design tech, $37,500
Isabelle, Jason L, resource scientist, $45,588
Jackson, Bridget L, conservation educ consult, $44,712
Jaco, Tony J, private land svs rgnal supv, $64,848
Jacobs, Leslie A, administrative staff asst, $25,452
Jacobs, Robert B, wildlife ecologist, $59,952
Jacobsen, Steven L, asst discovery center mgr, $47,412
Jacobson, Jason J, resource forester, $44,712
Jacomb, Joshua E, gis technician, $40,548
Jacquin, Sherry K, accounting technician, $10.11/hr
James, Elise M, public serv asst, $7.82/hr
James, Tim J, wildlife mgmt biologist, $49,296
Jansky, Kyle J, resource technician, $9.86/hr
Janzow, Marcus C, private land conservationist, $15.82/hr
Jasumback, Christopher M, resource technician, $26,976
Jeffries, Aaron P, asst to dir-gov rel, $90,660
Jeffries, Chelsea R, fisheries technician, $9.42/hr
Jellison, Jared D, resource asst, $26,460
Jenkins, Richard R, it info mgmt mgr, $75,876
Jennings, Jeffrey B, lead crpntr, $41,352
Jennings, Jeffrey L, resource asst, $8.58/hr
Jennings, Tara E, accounting technician, $31,488
Jensen, Jason E, private land servs chief, $72,948
Jerek, Joseph S, news servs coord, $53,304
Jewell, Jarrad S, conservation agent, $40,548
Jewett, Samuel L, resource technician, $30,288
Jingst, Thomas S, resource technician, $39,000
Joerger, Danielle R, asst natural history biologist, $10.83/hr
Johanson, Mark D, resource forester, $42,648
Johns, Caleb E, resource asst, $23,112
Johnson, Curtis L, conservation asst, $7.82/hr
Johnson, Lue V, administrative staff asst, $33,372
Johnson, Mary K, info tech analyst, $40,548
Johnson, Paul J, resource forester, $40,548
Johnson, Shannon S, resource technician, $9.86/hr
Johnston, Danelia L, forestry administrative tech, $33,372
Johnston, Darlene H, resource aide, $9.64/hr
Johnston, Kolt J, wildlife technician, $10.33/hr
Jonaitis, David V, resource asst, $9.20/hr
Jones, Adam W, wildlife mgmt biologist, $40,548
Jones, Colby J, naturalist, $11.90/hr
Jones, Colby J, resource asst, $8.58/hr
Jones, Gregory W, permit servs sup, $71,532
Jones, Landry E, private land conservationist, $40,548
Jones, Marsha S, conservation agent, $57,660
Jones, Matthew E, resource forester, $57,660
Jones, Matthew R, resource asst, $8.58/hr
Jones, Michael L, protect dist supv, $48,336
Jones, Micheal J, wildlife rgnal supv, $63,588
Jones, Russell C, resource asst, $24,024
Jones, Ryan S, wildlife mgmt biologist, $41,352
Jordan, Keith J, resource asst, $8.78/hr
Jordan, Zebulon Z, conservation agent, $40,548
Jourdon, Glenda M, data entry oper II, $8.78/hr
Joyce, Byron M, resource technician, $37,500
Juhala, Amy J, administrative staff asst, $26,460
Juhlin, Steven E, conservation educ consult, $47,412
Karr, Amanda J, administrative staff asst, $25,956
Katt, Stephanie N, resource asst, $8.58/hr
Kavan, Timothy G, private land conservationist, $41,352
Keeley, Michael T, resource forester, $44,712
Keene, Kent A, resource asst, $8.58/hr
Keeran, Randy L, private land conservationist, $36,084
Keller, Barbara J, resource scientist, $44,712
Keller, Dennis D, lead equip oper, $49,296
Kelly, Jared M, resource aide, $7.82/hr
Kelly, Katherine M, wildlife biologist, $12.76/hr
Kelly, Ryan P, wildlife biologist, $39,000
Kelsay, Christina L, resource science asst, $29,724
Kelso, Brice D, resource forester, $39,000
Kemp, Philip L, administrative staff asst, $30,288
Kemper, Stacy L, administrative staff asst, $30,876
Kemple, Randall L, contract sup, $14.73/hr
Kendrick, Sarah A, wildlife progs supv, $47,412

Kennedy, Christopher J, fisheries regional supv, $51,264
Kernodle, Barton E, resource asst, $30,876
Ketterman, Lane M, resource asst, $8.58/hr
Kienzler, Peter C, resource technician, $9.86/hr
Kiger, Jeremy C, conservation agent, $42,996
Kile, Troy M, resource asst, $8.58/hr
Killian, Darren W, conservation agent, $45,588
King, Bryson E, hr analyst, $38,232
King, Kevin R, resource aide, $8.19/hr
King, Norma S, public serv asst, $8.58/hr
King, Steven W, resource asst, $25,452
Kinserlow, Clarissia M, resource technician, $29,724
Kinsey, Truman P, conservation asst, $7.82/hr
Kipp, George M, forestry progs spec, $45,588
Kippenberger, Jeanne M, lead maint technician, $9.86/hr
Kiral, Alan G, heavy equip oper, $31,488
Kirby, Samuel J, entprs info archtct, $75,876
Kirchner, Dawn R, ofc mgr, $32,748
Kistner, Stephen C, conservation agent, $39,000
Kleeman, Cesare C, resource asst, $29,148
Kleeman, Louis H, resource asst, $10.83/hr
Kleeschulte, Morgann L, resource technician, $9.86/hr
Klein, Michael L, gis spec, $51,264
Kliegel, Matthew T, heavy equip oper, $36,792
Kliethermes, Justin R, resource asst, $24,024
Knauer, Regina A, outreach & edu chief, $66,144
Knipp, Brian J, maint sup, $38,232
Knorr, Janelle L, resource aide, $7.82/hr
Knowles, Bryan H, resource asst, $8.78/hr
Knudsen, John B, private land svs regional supv, $51,264
Knuth, David S, fisheries mgmt biologist, $40,548
Koehler, Jamie S, asst nature center mgr, $42,168
Koelling, Blake E, resource asst, $8.58/hr
Koenig, Ann C, cmnty forester, $50,280
Koenig, Charlotte F, administrative staff asst, $8.78/hr
Koger, Jason S, resource asst, $26,460
Kokel, Haley N, public serv asst, $7.82/hr
Koppelman, Jeffrey B, resource scientist, $64,848
Korthas, Kent, wildlife mgmt spec, $59,952
Kottemann, Katherine A, administrative staff asst, $26,460
Kramer, Randy J, resource asst, $7.82/hr
Krause, Kevin L, resource technician, $30,876
Kraxberger, Joe D, lead maint technician, $11.62/hr
Krumm, Jeffrey D, electrical engr, $77,376
Kuder, Douglas E, resource asst, $8.58/hr
Kuehn, Ezekiel A, resource aide, $7.82/hr
Kuester, Cassey J, it proj mgr, $47,412
Kuhn, Linda R, asst natural history biologist, $10.83/hr
Kuhn, Nicholas T, forestry field progs supv, $51,264
Kulowiec, Thomas G, resource science adm coord, $72,948
Kunce, Bradley L, resource asst, $26,976
Kusgen, Dennis L, heavy equip oper, $39,000
Lackman, Kathryn A, fisheries staff biologist, $40,548
Lacombe, Lisa M, nature center mgr, $51,264
Lacrosse, Guy M, info technology spec, $48,336
Lairmore, Kyle M, hunter ed/shooting range coord, $48,336
Lake, Timothy C, lead equip oper, $49,296
Lalk, Sara R, resource asst, $8.58/hr
Lamb, Alan S, conservation agent, $40,548
Lamb, Claudine A, outreach & educ reg supv, $55,440
Lambert, John B, resource aide, $8.00/hr
Lambeth, Gregory A, conservation asst, $7.82/hr
Lamzik, Kenneth S, resource asst, $8.58/hr
Lanahan, Kevin M, web developer, $58,800
Lancaster, Charles M, protect dist supv, $67,452
Landstad, Christopher P, asst htchry mgr, $36,084
Landwer, Brett H, resource staff scientist, $40,548
Lane, Alex Q, resource asst, $8.58/hr
Lane, Trent, protect dist supv, $61,140
Langston, Jason W, conservation agent, $42,996
Lanham, Annabelle, administrative staff asst, $30,288
Lanigan, Pamela A, fisheries rgnal supv, $57,660
Lanning, Seth W, research asst, $9.86/hr
Lanning, Seth W, fisheries biologist, $12.47/hr
Laposha, Nicholas A, protect rgnal supv, $72,948
Larivee, Lisa K, special projects asst, $9.86/hr
Larivee, Todd C, it infrastructure & opertn mgr, $77,376
Larsen, Michael L, resource asst, $8.58/hr
Larson, Renee M, resource asst, $34,044
Lashley, Jeremiah D, mail servs asst, $21,444
Latz, Marcus W, resource aide, $7.82/hr
Laval, Steven A, resource forester, $54,960
Lawler, Joseph M, resource technician, $28,596

Lawrence, Billy A, resource asst, $9.42/hr
Lawrence, Robert K, forest entomologist, $56,544
Layman, Wyatt J, naturalist, $33,372
Layne, Jason T, wildlife biologist, $12.47/hr
Leahy, Michael J, natural areas coord, $51,264
Leary, Alan, wildlife mgmt coord, $64,848
Leary, Kathryn D, asst gis analyst, $11.35/hr
Leeker, Thomas W, conservation agent, $45,588
Leeman, Elizabeth A, resource technician, $9.86/hr
Leftwich, Jeffrey L, design & dev chief, $90,492
Legg, Tony L, outdoor educ cntr supv, $55,440
Leiber, Wes E, heavy equip oper, $32,100
Leisenring, Allison S, resource asst, $24,024
Lemaster, Nicholas C, resource technician, $29,148
Leonard, William R, resource asst, $8.58/hr
Leppin, Leslie A, administrative staff asst, $11.35/hr
Leppin, Leslie A, clerk typist, $11.35/hr
Letterman, Danton D, protect dist supv, $51,264
Lewis, Cheryl A, resource technician, $39,000
Lewis, David L, contract sup, $79,644
Lichtenberg, Brady M, resource asst, $8.58/hr
Light, Clayton J, wildlife biologist, $33,372
Light, Savannah M, accounting technician, $9.42/hr
Liles, Hugh D, administrative staff asst, $8.98/hr
Lindeman, Larry R, outdoor skills spec, $44,712
Linder, Tracey L, public serv asst, $7.82/hr
Linebaugh, Nicholas J, resource asst, $26,460
Lininger, Jacob C, resource asst, $8.58/hr
Linnenbrink, Donna C, ofc mgr, $38,232
Lipe, Jared D, resource aide, $7.82/hr
Little, David R, resource asst, $24,984
Little, James M, resource asst, $25,956
Liverar, Michael A, maint sup, $41,352
Lloyd, George D, equip shop technician, $45,588
Lobb, M Delbert, resource scientist, $62,352
Lock, Kendric A, resource asst, $8.58/hr
Lockard, Haley N, wildlife mgmt asst, $10.83/hr
Lockard, Kevin W, conservation agent, $39,000
Loethen, Margaret D, administrative staff asst, $26,460
Lofstrom, Chris M, equip shop technician, $39,000
Logan, Linda K, proj engr, $67,452
Lohraff, Kevin M, edu prog/curriculum supv, $56,544
Lombardo, Alicia M, public serv asst, $7.82/hr
Loncarich, Frank L, wildlife mgmt biologist, $42,168
Long, Darren P, resource asst, $23,112
Long, Eric A, conservation agent, $42,996
Long, Jonah D, public serv asst, $8.00/hr
Long, Jonah D, resource asst, $8.58/hr
Longhofer, Michael G, resource asst, $28,596
Lonning, Kermit A, equip shop technician, $43,848
Looten, Fay R, accounting technician, $35,388
Lorenz, Kyle L, wildlife biologist, $32,748
Lorraine, John D, resource technician, $9.86/hr
Love, Daniel L, protect dist supv, $67,452
Love, Julie M, accounting technician, $31,488
Lucas, Lisa M, it proj mgr, $53,304
Luebbering, Justin B, crpntr, $30,288
Luecke, Danielle A, accounting technician, $31,488
Lueckenhoff, Ryan W, private land conservationist, $37,500
Lueckenhoff, William F, policy spec, $20.09/hr
Lueckenotte, Debra L, administrative staff asst, $33,372
Luna, Benjamin P, resource asst, $8.58/hr
Lutes, Carol R, administrative staff asst, $8.58/hr
Lutes, Carol R, resource technician, $9.86/hr
Lyddon, Brandon D, conservation agent, $40,548
Lyons, Robert A, conservation agent, $42,996
Mabee, William R, resource staff scientist, $42,168
Mabry, Preston L, wildlife biologist, $36,792
Mace, Sherry D, resource aide, $8.00/hr
Madsen, Megan G, crpntr, $11.09/hr
Madsen, Trana N, naturalist, $36,792
Magoc, Matthew S, conservation educ consult, $38,232
Mahan, Christopher G, resource asst, $31,488
Mahan, Danny R, lead maint technician, $9.86/hr
Mahan, Gary R, fac maint tech, $36,792
Main, Sara F, resource forester, $53,304
Mallady, Conrad L, outdoor skills spec, $56,544
Malmborg, Marlene J, intern, $11.90/hr
Manglik, Deepti V, it proj sup, $75,876
Manning, Claudia K, public serv asst, $8.00/hr
Manuel, Mark C, resource aide, $8.38/hr
Manuel, Mark C, resource asst, $8.58/hr
Maples, Rhonda L, exec asst, $54,996

Markley, Matthew G, protect dist supv, $51,264
Marks, Martin M, wildlife biologist, $39,000
Marler, Jonathan S, resource asst, $8.78/hr
Marley, Philip H, gis spec, $42,996
Marshall, John T, wildlife biologist, $39,000
Martin, Christie M, accounting technician, $38,232
Martin, Joseph C, it business dev mgr, $72,948
Martinez, David J, fac maint tech, $29,148
Martinez, Rudy G, asst nature center mgr, $43,848
Mason, Shaun E, resource asst, $9.20/hr
Mason, Torrance D, fisheries mgmt biologist, $44,712
Mason, Tyler G, conservation agent, $37,500
Massey, Mark E, lead crpntr, $40,548
Matheney, Matthew P, fisheries staff biologist, $54,360
Mathis, Fred L, resource aide, $7.82/hr
Matney, Rebecca A, naturalist, $36,792
Mattucks, Robert H, fisheries mgmt biologist, $57,660
Maupin, Michael A, conservation agent, $40,548
Maupins, Robert J, fac maint tech, $35,388
May, Leora M, accounting technician, $11.62/hr
May, Melisa F, exhbs dsgnr, $37,500
Mayers, David A, resource asst, $8.58/hr
Mazzulla, Mary P, ofc mgr, $32,100
McAllister, David A, dpty counsel, $83,712
McAteer, Sarah M, fisheries biologist, $12.47/hr
McBride, Georgia M, resource aide, $8.78/hr
McBride, James L, resource asst, $8.98/hr
McCann, Christian L, resource aide, $7.82/hr
McCann, Lewis A, special asst to dir, $40.00/hr
McCann, Tyler L, resource asst, $24,480
McClain, Jacob C, resource asst, $8.58/hr
McClamroch, Lucas K, conservation agent, $39,000
McCleary, Dustin C, resource asst, $25,452
McClellan, Ricky P, resource technician, $38,232
McCloud, Bradley D, land surv, $58,800
McClure, Michael K, wetland servs biologist, $47,412
McConnell, Matthew D, resource technician, $30,876
McCorkell, David M, conservation agent, $37,500
McCracken, Rhys A, resource asst, $8.58/hr
McCracken, Rhys A, resource technician, $9.86/hr
McCray, Joseph E, resource asst, $9.42/hr
McDaniel, Adam J, resource staff scientist, $38,232
McDaniel, Tim S, conservation agent, $54,360
McDonald, Jill L, administrative staff asst, $29,148
McDougald, Scott A, resource asst, $8.58/hr
McDougald, Scott A, resource aide, $7.82/hr
McElfresh, Wendy K, resource asst, $27,516
McGallagher, Lawrance G, resource science asst, $30,288
McGhee, Nathan E, resource aide, $7.82/hr
McGowan, Travis A, resource asst, $8.58/hr
McGrane, Mary C, asst nature center mgr, $43,848
McGregor, Christopher T, lead equip oper, $39,768
McKeage, Brian L, fisheries spec, $42,168
McKee, Brad D, private land svs regional supv, $51,264
McKee, Jeremy J, resource asst, $8.58/hr
McKee, Michael J, resource scientist, $54,360
McKim, Alan D, heavy equip oper, $36,084
McKinney, Stephanie A, conservation educ consult, $40,548
McLain, Mark A, wildlife mgmt biologist, $40,548
McLain, Travis R, protect progs spec, $57,660
McLeland, Christopher A, private land svcs biologist, $45,588
McMillan, Eric W, maint sup, $41,352
McMullen, Chelsea J, resource technician, $9.86/hr
McMullen, Joseph A, big river spec, $45,588
McMurray, Stephen E, resource scientist, $54,360
McNeely, Mark A, conservation agent, $37,500
McNeil, Edis C, crpntr, $34,716
McNutt, Tori L, resource asst, $8.58/hr
McQuillen, Monte R, wildlife mgmt biologist, $50,280
McSpadden, Kara A, private land conservationist, $37,500
McWilliams, Scott N, wildlife damage biologist, $61,140
Meade, Richard, fisheries training coord, $57,660
Mechlin, Nathan M, private land conservationist, $43,848
Medlock, Chad T, resource asst, $26,460
Medlock, Sarah J, resource forester, $40,548
Meese, Todd M, wildlife damage biologist, $45,588
Meier, Amy K, fisheries staff biologist, $42,168
Meier, Eileen D, administrative staff asst, $8.98/hr
Meister, Thomas R, wildlife damage biologist, $45,588
Meneau, Kevin J, fisheries mgmt biologist, $57,660
Mengel, Doreen C, resource scientist, $64,848
Mernick, Michael B, crpntr, $31,488
Mertz, Ashley M, wildlife mgmt asst, $10.83/hr

Mertz, Ashley M, resource science asst, $10.83/hr
Messbarger, Lonnie A, resource forester, $49,296
Metcalf, Edward L, private land conservationist, $44,712
Meyer, Bret O, lead crpntr, $13.71/hr
Meyer, Dean N, lead crpntr, $35,388
Michaletz, Paul H, resource scientist, $64,848
Middleton, Elizabeth L, resource scientist, $45,588
Midkiff, Shari A, resource aide, $7.82/hr
Midyett, Jason C, conservation agent, $42,996
Mieser, Adam C, resource asst, $29,724
Mifflin, Sheldon L, resource technician, $29,148
Miles, Robert C, resource aide, $7.82/hr
Miller, Angela L, resource asst, $29,148
Miller, Gary R, conservation agent, $52,284
Miller, Jeffrey W, resource asst, $25,956
Miller, John D, interpretive center mgr, $53,304
Miller, John D, resource technician, $42,996
Miller, Kirby G, resource technician, $41,352
Miller, Mark R, outdoor skills spec, $44,712
Miller, Marlyn L, fisheries progs supv, $72,948
Miller, Melissa A, resource technician, $9.86/hr
Miller, Mitchell L, wildlife rgnal supv, $71,532
Miller, Rebecca, asst nature center mgr, $41,352
Miller, Stuart F, policy coord, $59,952
Miller, Timothy J, outdoor skills spec, $41,352
Milligan, Jarad D, conservation agent, $40,548
Mills, William T, resource forester, $48,336
Mitchell, Margaret R, asst gis spec, $15.08/hr
Mitchell, Michael J, htchry mgr, $50,280
Moffitt, Andrew C, resource aide, $7.82/hr
Mohrman, Janet L, resource asst, $31,488
Mondragon, Salvador J, fisheries mgmt biologist, $40,548
Monroe, Kyle S, resource forester, $40,548
Montgomery, Derek M, resource asst, $8.58/hr
Moore, Kathryn R, conservation educ consult, $44,712
Moore, Lance M, conservation agent, $40,548
Moore, Matthew E, heavy equip oper, $36,084
Moore, Shelly L, resource technician, $38,232
Moore, Travis L, fisheries mgmt biologist, $45,588
Moreno, Thresia M, special permits technician, $27,516
Morfeld, Angela K, editor, $45,588
Morfeld, Nathan J, resource asst, $26,460
Morgan, Amy M, accounting asst, $24,024
Morgan, Scott A, resource asst, $39,768
Mormann, Kyle J, survey spec, $42,168
Morris, Dale R, resource asst, $25,452
Morris, Gary L, resource asst, $8.78/hr
Morris, Loryssa L, resource asst, $8.58/hr
Morris, Michael J, forestry field progs supv, $61,140
Morris, Richard B, resource aide, $9.86/hr
Morris, William Z, resource asst, $8.58/hr
Morris, William Z, fisheries technician, $9.42/hr
Morrow, Christopher M, protect regional supv, $68,784
Morton, Steven K, intern, $11.90/hr
Morton, William D, resource science asst, $10.83/hr
Mosley, Luke H, resource asst, $8.58/hr
Mothershead, Andrew R, conservation agent, $40,548
Moulder, Jodi E, private land conservationist, $47,040
Muckler, Frank W, resource asst, $25,956
Mueller, Margaret S, chief fin ofcr, $96,048
Mueller, Russell W, sr cartographer, $25.00/hr
Muenks, Kevin G, vidgrapher, $47,412
Muenks, Nathan D, habitat mgmt coord, $50,280
Muich, Stephen E, resource science asst, $11.09/hr
Mullock, Alexander L, resource asst, $24,024
Murphy, John C, private land conservationist, $44,712
Murphy, Ryan J, resource forester asst, $11.09/hr
Murray, Jeannine M, resource asst, $29,724
Murray, Norman L, species & habitat chief, $70,140
Murray, Sean P, resource asst, $8.58/hr
Musick, Matthew S, resource asst, $8.58/hr
Napoli, James A, resource asst, $8.78/hr
Naramore, Tyler R, equip serv technician, $24,024
Neal, Diane R, naturalist, $13.38/hr
Neal, Matthew W, resource asst, $8.58/hr
Neece, Kaleb W, conservation agent trainee, $36,084
Needham, Phil S, conservation agent, $54,360
Nelson, Frank A, resource scientist, $45,588
Nelson, Justin C, wildlife biologist, $12.47/hr
Nelson, Mark A, forestry rgnal supv, $64,848
Neubauer, Thomas D, hr div chief, $88,788
Neuenschwander, William E, resource technician, $33,372
Newbold, Christopher D, natural history reg biologist, $46,488

Nichols, Christopher P, resource technician, $30,288
Niebruegge, David J, private land conservationist, $50,280
Niederjohn, Michaela J, resource aide, $8.19/hr
Niemeyer, Eric W, private land conservationist, $39,000
Niswonger, Darby J, resource staff scientist, $40,548
Noble, Peter J, resource forester, $36,084
Noel, Krista M, natural history reg biologist, $41,352
Nofsinger, Charles T, protect dist supv, $48,336
Noll, Steven R, wildlife mgmt biologist, $44,712
Norris, Julie A, private land conservationist, $39,000
Norris, Michael W, const & maint supt, $53,304
Novinger, Douglas C, resource science supv, $57,660
Nowak, Karl R, heavy equip oper, $34,716
Oeldrich, Vicki D, legal sec, $45,588
Ofodile, Dianna L, resource asst, $9.20/hr
O'Hearn, Rebecca A, resource scientist, $45,588
Ohrenberg, Kimberly S, conservation agent, $42,996
O'Keefe, Donald R, resource asst, $23,580
Oligschlaeger, Dorothy A, accounting asst, $10.11/hr
Oliver, Scott P, crpntr, $37,500
Oliver, Tucker L, resource asst, $8.58/hr
Olson, Elizabeth K, resource scientist, $43,848
Olson, Matthew G, resource scientist, $43,848
Ong, Moses K, conservation educ consult, $38,232
O'Quinn, Clayton W, resource asst, $26,976
Orchard, Steve A, resource forester, $47,412
Ormsby, Matthew A, naturalist, $12.47/hr
Ostendorf, David E, resource staff scientist, $43,848
Ostheller, Dean E, maint asst, $8.58/hr
Oswald, Hayden K, asst gis spec, $12.47/hr
Otte, Cheryl L, administrative staff asst, $26,460
Otterstein, Kurt W, range ofcr, $44,712
Otto, Denise C, fisheries mgmt biologist, $40,548
Otto, William L, resource asst, $8.58/hr
Owens, David E, resource asst, $24,984
Owens, June A, resource aide, $7.82/hr
Owens, Stephen K, resource asst, $26,976
Ozias, Paulette, public serv asst, $8.98/hr
Packard, Aimee E, administrative staff asst, $23,580
Paes, Steven C, resource forester, $56,544
Palmer, James R, conservation agent, $57,660
Paothong, Noppadol, photographer, $39,000
Parker, Robyn L, naturalist, $12.47/hr
Parnell, Todd B, fisheries spec, $32,748
Parrett, Gwendolyn K, conservation educ consult, $45,588
Parrish, Joshua S, resource technician, $25,452
Parsons, Dale O, proj engr, $67,452
Patterson, Daniel J, resource technician, $32,100
Patton, Michael R, resource asst, $29,724
Patton, Shauna C, accounting asst, $24,480
Payne, James M, heavy equip oper, $34,044
Payne, Sandy J, contract technician, $47,412
Payton, Amanda C, naturalist, $12.76/hr
Peacher, Thomas E, outreach & educ dist supv, $48,336
Peacock, William S, fac maint tech, $30,876
Pearson, Ashley N, accounting asst, $22,680
Pearson, Kamaria L, fisheries technician, $9.42/hr
Peck, Ronald D, info technology spec, $69,132
Peine, John G, heavy equip oper, $31,488
Pelton, John M, resource forester, $57,660
Pemberton, Caleb J, maint asst, $7.82/hr
Pendergrass, Taliaa D, special progs coord, $13.71/hr
Pennington, Adam A, resource technician, $9.86/hr
Pennington, Shawn A, conservation agent, $45,588
Peper, Sarah J, fisheries mgmt biologist, $42,168
Perry, April L, fisheries biologist, $33,372
Perry, Michael V, asst htchry mgr, $39,000
Perry, Scott A, maint sup, $41,352
Persinger, Jason W, resource scientist, $46,488
Peter, John L, resource technician, $39,000
Peter, John M, resource asst, $8.58/hr
Petersen, Michael D, private land conservationist, $55,440
Peterson, Leon D, resource technician, $35,388
Petras, Megan A, resource forester, $37,500
Pettijohn, Sheila L, resource aide, $7.82/hr
Petty, Jeffrey J, lead equip oper, $49,296
Petzoldt, Duane L, resource asst, $30,876
Phelps, Quinton E, resource scientist, $45,588
Philips, Phil W, outreach & educ proj coord, $70,140
Phillips, Jacob M, resource asst, $8.58/hr
Phillips, Nicola M, ofc mgr, $35,388
Phillips, Richard L, lead crpntr, $36,084
Phillips, Travis H, resource aide, $7.82/hr

Philpott, Logan M, resource technician, $9.86/hr
Piccoli, Dylan S, resource asst, $8.58/hr
Pierce, Angela D, naturalist, $36,084
Pierson, James L, private land conservationist, $44,712
Pierson, Tammy Y, conservation agent, $46,488
Pilz, Matthew J, resource forester, $37,500
Pinkowski, John A, private land conservationist, $46,488
Piper, John W, lead maint technician, $9.86/hr
Pitchford, Gregory D, fisheries mgmt biologist, $57,156
Pitts, Phillip R, fisheries mgmt biologist, $54,360
Pitzer, Sarah E, naturalist, $12.47/hr
Pleimling, Justin K, resource asst, $23,112
Plunkett, Michael J, conservation agent, $59,952
Pobst, Brad S, private land conservationist, $54,360
Pogue, Brandon T, resource asst, $24,480
Polk, Jacob B, resource aide, $7.82/hr
Polka, S J, public serv asst, $8.98/hr
Polley, Kenneth D, protect dist supv, $48,336
Polley, Kevin A, conservation agent, $42,996
Pollreisz, Allan J, it desktop sup, $66,144
Pondrom, Aaron J, protect dist supv, $51,264
Ponting, Connie L, ofc sup, $38,232
Poore, Kenneth E, arch, $70,140
Porath, Joel W, wildlife mgmt chief, $66,144
Porter, Coda M, resource aide, $7.82/hr
Porter, Marci L, dsgnr, $42,168
Porting, Pam S, accounting technician, $33,372
Post, Aaron J, conservation agent, $40,548
Post, Margaret A, comm asst, $26,460
Posten, David A, const & maint supt, $65,532
Potter, Lisa M, private land progs supv, $51,264
Powell, John C, resource asst, $8.58/hr
Powell, Kevin W, conservation agent, $37,500
Powelson, Donald J, private land conservationist, $44,712
Powers, Laura K, resource asst, $8.78/hr
Prater, Darren P, resource asst, $8.58/hr
Prater, Donald M, info tech field spt spec, $50,280
Pratt, Anthony J, fisheries rgnal supv, $61,140
Pratt, John D, conservation agent, $62,352
Pratt, Timothy C, conservation agent, $42,996
Prenger, Clinton M, resource asst, $23,580
Prenger, Mattheuw R, proj engr, $61,140
Prenger, Tracey L, resource asst, $24,480
Prentice, Alexander L, fisheries info syss mgr, $40,548
Preston, Thomas L, crpntr, $36,792
Price, James M, resource technician, $34,716
Prichard, Leroy O, equip shop technician, $39,768
Pride, Justin D, resource technician, $29,148
Priesendorf, Thomas A, fisheries mgmt biologist, $54,360
Priester, Dominique, ofc mgr, $33,372
Prost, Donald K, purchasing & fleet supv, $59,952
Pryor, Benny L, protect dist supv, $66,144
Pryor, Caleb J, conservation agent trainee, $36,084
Puetz, C Jordan, resource aide, $7.82/hr
Pulley, Jeremy W, private land conservationist, $37,500
Pulliam, Robert D, fisheries mgmt biologist, $54,360
Pund, Jonathan C, info technology spec, $42,168
Pursell, Dyanna L, gis spec, $43,848
Pursley, Benjamin C, conservation agent, $42,996
Putman, Bryon L, naturalist, $16.98/hr
Putnam, Craig A, resource asst, $25,956
Pyburn, Justin J, conservation agent trainee, $36,084
Quade, Jack C, cadd sys mgr, $61,140
Rackers, Carol B, accounting technician, $12.17/hr
Rackers, Susan R, compensation/benefits mgr, $63,588
Rademan, Amanda J, hr spec, $43,848
Rademan, Janet H, accounting technician, $18.20/hr
Radford, Michael S, area biologist, $45,588
Raedeke, Andrew H, resource scientist, $55,440
Raeker, August C, forestry dist sup, $52,284
Rahm, Donald C, fisheries technician, $9.42/hr
Rahm, Eric J, fisheries staff biologist, $41,352
Raithel, Mark S, wildlife artist, $49,296
Randecker, Michelle R, naturalist, $12.17/hr
Randle, William J, heavy equip oper, $39,768
Randolph, Clayton W, lead exhbs crpntr, $42,168
Raney, James W, resource aide, $8.19/hr
Rankin, Benjamin J, contract sup, $40,548
Rath, Ricky D, private land conservationist, $40,548
Rauch, Luke C, resource asst, $8.58/hr
Ray, Karen L, resource aide, $8.98/hr
Reckamp, Dustin J, crpntr, $32,748
Recktenwald, Nathan M, fisheries spec, $32,100

Reed, Charles A, naturalist, $42,168
Reed, Mark E, conservation agent, $58,800
Reed, Michael S, fisheries mgmt biologist, $51,264
Reel, Timothy J, resource technician, $38,232
Reese, Patrice J, conservation agent, $39,000
Reeves, Dalton W, resource asst, $8.58/hr
Rehmer, Connie S, administrative staff asst, $8.58/hr
Reimund, Mark C, maint technician, $8.98/hr
Reinagel, Susan K, administrative staff asst, $9.20/hr
Reinkemeyer, Curtis J, gis spec, $15.08/hr
Reinkemeyer, Kelly A, hr benefits analyst, $36,084
Reitz, Ronald A, survey coord, $49,296
Remmert, Paul A, permit servs spec, $55,440
Renick, Brian C, pump repair spec, $36,084
Renkemeyer, Ashley D, accounting asst, $23,580
Renken, Rochelle B, resource science field chf, $71,532
Rennison, George B, equip shop technician, $36,084
Reno, Kyle D, private land svs regional supv, $63,588
Reynolds, Gerald G, resource asst, $8.78/hr
Reynolds, Glenn R, resource asst, $26,976
Rezac, Kelly M, wildlife diversity coord, $48,336
Rhea, John W, heavy equip oper, $38,232
Rhoades, Samantha N, conservation agent trainee, $36,084
Rhodes, Andrew D, outdoor skills spec, $37,500
Rice, Christopher J, fisheries biologist, $12.47/hr
Rice, Scott D, protect dist supv, $51,264
Rice, Shane J, resource forester, $44,712
Richardson, John D, resource technician, $32,748
Richter, Gabriel P, info technology spec, $49,296
Richter, Lisa R, naturalist, $36,084
Rieken, Larry T, wildlife rgnal supv, $64,848
Rigby, Patrick E, info tech field spt spec, $56,544
Riggert, Christopher M, vol water qual cord, $45,588
Rimer, Rhonda L, natural history reg biologist, $49,296
Ringler, Keith M, resource asst, $8.58/hr
Ripperger, Tim D, deputy dir-admin/commun, $115,620
Rising, Billy C, resource asst, $24,480
Riter, Lexis M, conservation agent, $37,500
Rittel, Deanna J, fisheries technician, $9.42/hr
Rizzo, Larry J, natural history reg biologist, $49,296
Roam, Mason R, resource technician, $30,876
Roberts, Herbert M, resource technician, $42,168
Roberts, Mark A, info technology coord, $50,280
Roberts, William C, wildlife mgmt asst, $10.83/hr
Robertson, Becky M, conservation agent, $40,548
Robertson, Carl G, lead crpntr, $14.04/hr
Robertson, Harold, lead maint technician, $9.86/hr
Robertson, Samantha M, administrative staff asst, $34,716
Robinson, Kevin C, crpntr, $36,084
Robinson, Ronald, maint sup, $36,084
Rockelman, Luann J, administrative staff asst, $8.58/hr
Rockelman, Patti A, accounting technician, $38,232
Rodriguez, Rebecca A, naturalist, $34,716
Roe, Patricia J, info technology spec, $59,952
Rogers, Austin L, lead crpntr, $13.71/hr
Roller, Joshua R, conservation agent, $40,548
Rollins, Johnnie L, equip shop technician, $48,336
Rome, Lloyd J, resource technician, $34,044
Romesburg, Carl B, mkting asst, $10.83/hr
Roney, Christopher S, aircraft pilot, $55,440
Rose, Warren D, outreach & educ reg supv, $55,440
Ross, Preston L, lead crpntr, $13.71/hr
Ross, Zachary E, resource asst, $8.58/hr
Rousselot, Edward W, maint asst, $32,100
Routh, Billie R, resource asst, $8.58/hr
Rowden, John E, fac maint tech, $30,288
Rowold, David, forestry dist sup, $58,800
Roy, Breilly N, resource asst, $8.58/hr
Roy, James S, private land conservationist, $42,996
Roy, Randall L, wildlife mgmt biologist, $43,848
Ruff, Alex J, resource technician, $26,976
Rugelio, Jose L, resource technician, $9.86/hr
Ruman, Laura C, environ compliance speci, $54,360
Ruoff, Tyler R, resource science asst, $28,044
Ruse, Janet A, proj coord, $13.71/hr
Ruskamp, Christine N, intern, $11.90/hr
Russell, Bradley A, asst htchry mgr, $39,000
Russell, Timothy L, wildlife rgnal supv, $62,352
Rutledge, Betty J, it spt technician, $40,548
Ryan, Douglas A, resource technician, $39,000
Ryan, Warren S, fisheries rgnal supv, $52,284
Sachs, Alan D, resource asst, $8.58/hr
Sackett, Craig E, lead crpntr, $42,168

Samson, Anthony A, distrib ctr admin, $36,084
Sanders, Zachary L, resource asst, $8.58/hr
Sangster, Wendy H, cmnty forester, $45,588
Sarantakis, Scott M, outdoor skills spec, $42,996
Sartwell, Joel F, syss analyst, $59,952
Savaiano, Kathleen A, interpretive progs supv, $14.38/hr
Schaefer, Richard C, fac maint tech, $26,460
Schafer, Stanley G, lead equip oper, $50,280
Schenewerk, Harold F, resource asst, $9.42/hr
Scheperle, William H, proj engr, $67,452
Schepis, Daniel J, conservation agent, $39,000
Schertler, Tanner J, resource technician, $9.86/hr
Scheuler, Laura L, outreach & educ technician, $35,388
Schiwitz, Beverly A, public serv asst, $8.00/hr
Schmidt, Roger L, forest mgmt technician, $10.57/hr
Schmidt, Roger L, lead equip oper, $12.17/hr
Schmidt, Ryan R, resource asst, $7.82/hr
Schmiedeskamp, Connie D, naturalist, $14.04/hr
Schmitz, James P, resource asst, $8.58/hr
Schnake, Ashley D, urban wildlife biologist, $37,500
Schneidler, Kyle D, resource asst, $24,984
Schrader, Lynn H, fisheries rgnal supv, $66,144
Schreck, Patricia A, public serv asst, $12,978
Schremp, Bradley A, crpntr, $30,288
Schriener, William M, resource aide, $7.82/hr
Schroer, Michael D, wildlife mgmt chief, $73,488
Schroeter, Anita M, resource technician, $9.86/hr
Schubert, Jennifer L, accounting technician, $26,460
Schuenemeyer, Susan G, hris coord, $71,532
Schuette, Timothy J, lead equip oper, $40,548
Schuhmann, Andrea N, natural history reg biologist, $39,000
Schulte, Clyde F, resource aide, $8.19/hr
Schulte, Michael G, resource technician, $34,716
Schulte, Nicholas W, resource asst, $8.58/hr
Schwalbert, Michael G, lead maint technician, $9.86/hr
Schwartze, David P, resource asst, $8.58/hr
Schweiss, Brian E, forestry administrative mgr, $62,352
Schweissguth, Lafe W, resource asst, $24,984
Schwendemann, Marley J, resource asst, $8.58/hr
Scott, Colleen S, interpretive center mgr, $43,848
Scott, Craig L, resource aide, $7.82/hr
Scott, Jeffrey L, conservation agent, $48,336
Scott, Mary E, fisheries mgmt biologist, $45,588
Scott, William C, resource asst, $8.58/hr
Scroggins, Craig D, gis spec, $51,264
Sechler, Stan B, private land svs rgnal supv, $51,264
Seek, Matthew N, editor, $50,280
Seidel, Lorri L, employment mgr, $75,876
Seiler, Ted P, private land conservationist, $44,712
Sell, Lillian R, resource forester, $44,712
Sellars, Raymond E, resource asst, $25,956
Sentman, Rachelle L, resource aide, $7.82/hr
Sercl, Jason E, sign technician, $30,876
Settle, Benjamin D, resource asst, $8.58/hr
Settle, Rachel A, intern, $13.71/hr
Severe, Jason R, resource forester, $44,712
Sevits, Christopher L, resource technician, $30,288
Shadwick, Joshua L, conservation agent, $39,000
Shank, Erin D, urban wildlife biologist, $44,712
Shanks, Lorrie J, accounting technician, $25,452
Shanks, Weylin M, lead crpntr, $13.71/hr
Sharon, Julie K, resource technician, $31,488
Sharp, Warren W, resource asst, $24,984
Shave, Susan M, administrative staff asst, $28,596
Shaw, Thomas J, resource asst, $8.78/hr
Sheffler, Allison R, resource aide, $7.82/hr
Shelby, Cody M, heavy equip oper, $28,596
Shelby, Jeffrey J, resource asst, $8.58/hr
Shellenberg, Heather, ofc sup, $27,516
Shelton, Brian E, conservation agent, $40,548
Shenk, Robert B, resource aide, $9.64/hr
Sherrill, Bradley S, resource aide, $7.82/hr
Shieh, David Y, resource technician, $28,596
Shifflett, Russell L, protect dist supv, $64,848
Shipman, Stephanie A, administrative staff asst, $23,112
Shomaker, Miranda S, public serv asst, $7.82/hr
Shores, Daniel K, conservation agent, $40,548
Short, Timothy A, resource technician, $34,716
Shortt, Nick D, resource asst, $8.58/hr
Shumate, Terry W, resource asst, $24,024
Shurvington, George E, private land svs rgnal supv, $53,304
Sickler, Stephanie M, administrative staff asst, $8.58/hr
Siech, Kathleen A, resource asst, $8.58/hr

Sieren, Chris J, resource technician, $36,084
Sigman, Scott W, mkting asst, $10.33/hr
Sikes, Kenneth D, resource technician, $39,000
Simmons, Casey W, conservation agent, $42,996
Sims, Alan D, progs coord, $30.00/hr
Singer, Sheila A, hr safety tech, $36,084
Sinha, Debashree, resource technician, $9.86/hr
Sisson, Charles T, resource technician, $42,168
Sizemore, Jake R, resource asst, $8.58/hr
Skaggs, Carrie L, sign shop sup, $40,548
Skalicky, Francis J, media spec, $47,412
Skinner, Jon P, cmnty forester, $50,280
Skinner, Monty L, resource asst, $28,596
Slagle, Zachary W, resource asst, $25,956
Sleeper, Wesley G, resource technician, $9.86/hr
Smith, Brooke A, resource asst, $8.58/hr
Smith, Chad N, wildlife mgmt biologist, $40,548
Smith, Gerald W, protect dist supv, $51,264
Smith, Janet K, administrative staff asst, $36,084
Smith, Joseph D, resource technician, $39,000
Smith, Kevin W, resource asst, $8.58/hr
Smith, Laroy R, resource technician, $38,232
Smith, Matthew D, conservation agent, $42,996
Smith, Merle K, resource technician, $41,352
Smith, Michael D, const & maint supt, $51,264
Smith, Michael S, fisheries administrative mgr, $71,532
Smith, Patty J, administrative staff asst, $29,148
Smith, Ricky L, resource asst, $8.58/hr
Smith, Rodney S, conservation agent, $48,336
Smith, Sophia I, resource asst, $8.58/hr
Smith, Stephanie A, resource asst, $29,724
Smith, Steven J, resource asst, $36,792
Sneed, Philip M, resource forester, $46,488
Snell, Gary W, lead maint technician, $9.86/hr
Snelson, Gregory J, contract sup, $50,280
Snyder, Cody J, forest mgmt technician, $10.33/hr
Snyder, Jason, it spt technician, $42,168
Sobotka, Molly J, resource staff scientist, $39,000
Sones, Brittney M, ofc mgr, $36,792
Soucy, Jeremy J, conservation educ consult, $41,352
Southers, Doug S, resource asst, $8.58/hr
Sowerwine, Joshua J, lead maint technician, $9.86/hr
Spencer, John P, resource asst, $8.58/hr
Sperry, Mark L, resource asst, $34,044
Spicci, Anna-Sophia E, lead maint technician, $9.86/hr
Spicci, Anthony A, gis sup, $71,532
Springer, Austin M, resource asst, $8.58/hr
Spurgeon, Matthew J, conservation agent, $42,996
Spurgeon, Paul S, hatchery mgr, $50,280
Stamper, Ashton K, conservation agent trainee, $36,084
Starke, Douglas J, grounds sup, $43,848
Starks, Trevor A, resource science asst, $28,596
Stearns, Phillip A, resource aide, $7.82/hr
Steding, Larry W, resource technician, $34,716
Steeby, Sandra L, facility maint tech, $32,100
Steele, Diana J, public serv asst, $26,976
Steele, Jay R, resource technician, $39,000
Steelman, Jason D, lead equip oper, $38,232
Steelman, Norman C, conservation agent, $42,996
Steen, Christopher L, resource aide, $8.98/hr
Stephens, Blake R, fisheries mgmt biologist, $37,500
Stephens, George A, resource asst, $31,488
Stephens, Robert L, lead crpntr, $13.71/hr
Stephens, Scott J, conservation agent, $45,588
Stephenson, Danielle M, resource forester asst, $28,596
Sterling, Edward M, resource aide, $7.82/hr
Sternburg, Janet E, policy coord, $61,140
Stevens, Ryan H, resource asst, $24,480
Stevenson, Aaron P, resource scientist, $45,588
Stewart, Samuel A, naturalist, $11.90/hr
Stieferman, Mary E, hr spec, $16.20/hr
Stiek, Jenna D, resource asst, $24,984
Stirts, Richard E, resource technician, $41,352
Stockton, Francesca M, conservation asst, $7.82/hr
Stogsdill, Preston L, wildlife biologist, $13.71/hr
Stogsdill, Ray D, resource aide, $8.19/hr
Stolle, Samantha J, naturalist, $12.17/hr
Stoltzfus, Matthew D, resource technician, $29,148
Stoner, Alex I, resource asst, $8.58/hr
Stoner, Gregory A, fisheries mgmt biologist, $56,544
Stonitsch, Elizabeth A, resource technician, $9.86/hr
Stonner, David W, photographer, $37,500
Storts, Nathan S, asst htchry mgr, $33,372

Strader, Steven A, conservation agent, $42,996
Straka, Kelly A, state wildlife veterinarian, $66,144
Straka, Thomas G, conservation agent, $37,500
Stratman, Leann C, arch, $18.70/hr
Stratton, Benjamin J, conservation agent, $40,548
Straub, Joan H, outreach & edu div chief, $71,268
Street, Robin L, administrative staff asst, $33,372
Stricklin, Ronnie L, resource aide, $7.82/hr
Strodtman, Samantha J, intern, $11.90/hr
Strother, Mitchell L, proj engr, $78,912
Strother, Thomas M, protect rgnal supv, $72,948
Strozewski, Jacob R, conservation agent, $42,996
Struchtemeyer, Marilyn S, administrative staff asst, $8.58/hr
Struckhoff, Alicia N, resource scientist, $43,848
Struemph, Careen L, accounting technician, $12.47/hr
Struemph, Jerry L, equip shop technician, $36,084
Stucker, Vern D, private land conservationist, $36,084
Sudkamp, Scott D, private land conservationist, $52,284
Sulkowski, Robert J, conservation agent, $46,488
Sullivan, Kevin P, resource science field station supv, $74,400
Sullivan, Theresa L, public serv asst, $8.58/hr
Sumner, Luke A, aircraft pilot, $55,440
Sumners, Jason A, resource scientist, $45,588
Swainston, Eric B, conservation agent, $42,996
Swan, Lenora M, administrative staff asst, $28,596
Swarthout, Jeffrey D, resource asst, $29,148
Swee, Wesley E, htchry mgr, $45,588
Swem, Susan A, conservation agent, $57,660
Swindle, Zachary P, lead crpntr, $13.71/hr
Switzer, Mark T, resource asst, $34,044
Swopes, Ricky D, resource asst, $9.42/hr
Sykes, Jason T, area biologist, $45,588
Syrigos, Jan L, special progs coord, $14.04/hr
Tallent, Danny T, conservation agent, $42,996
Tallman, Troy N, resource asst, $8.58/hr
Tapp, Jessica L, wildlife biologist, $34,716
Tappmeyer, Andrew R, wildlife mgmt biologist, $47,412
Tappmeyer, Brandon S, resource asst, $8.58/hr
Taylor, Stetson A, resource asst, $8.58/hr
Terrell, Randy G, htchry mgr, $59,952
Terrill, Nichole L, pubations mgr, $47,412
Theis, Chris P, lead crpntr, $41,352
Thiele, Kathleen L, public serv asst, $7.82/hr
Thierfelder, Andrea J, ofc sup, $29,148
Thomas, Billy E, resource asst, $34,044
Thomas, Dejuan L, ofc mgr, $37,500
Thomas, Howard D, design & dev chief, $88,788
Thomas, Luke C, resource aide, $7.82/hr
Thompson, Austin G, resource asst, $8.58/hr
Thompson, Debra L, empl rel mgr, $72,948
Thompson, Donald T, forestry rgnal supv, $59,952
Thompson, Patrick G, equip shop technician, $38,232
Thompson, Rita E, administrative staff asst, $11.50/hr
Thompson, Thomas R, resource scientist, $45,588
Thorne, David H, policy sup, $70,140
Thornhill, Darren R, fisheries mgmt biologist, $42,168
Thornton, Bethany D, resource asst, $8.58/hr
Thurber, Stephanie L, dsgnr, $36,084
Thurman, Levi C, resource asst, $8.58/hr
Thurston, Ronnie L, const & maint supt, $51,264
Tiberghien, Dylan J, resource aide, $8.00/hr
Tiberghien, Keith M, resource aide, $8.00/hr
Tieman, Chad A, resource aide, $7.82/hr
Tiller, Donald P, conservation agent, $57,660
Tillman, Michael A, facility maint tech, $30,288
Tipton, Matthew A, resource asst, $25,452
Todd, Brian L, fisheries rgnal supv, $71,532
Tomlin-McCrary, Martha L, resources analyst, $56,544
Toombs, Bobby L, resource asst, $28,596
Toombs, Gene A, resource technician, $39,768
Tousignant, Joe N, area biologist, $57,660
Trantham, Jeffrey T, resource asst, $8.58/hr
Trautman, Cara J, resource asst, $9.20/hr
Travnichek, Vincent H, resource science center chief, $71,532
Treasure, Sarah K, administrative staff asst, $8.58/hr
Treasure, Sarah K, resource asst, $8.58/hr
Treiman, Thomas B, resource scientist, $56,544
Trice, Patricia A, accounting asst, $8.58/hr
Trinkle, Gregory H, contract spec, $56,544
Tripp, Sara J, resource scientist, $43,848
Troxel Dewitt, Susan M, forestry regional supv, $63,588
Truesdell, Linda J, administrative staff asst, $29,148
Tucker, Lindell, resource asst, $31,488

Tucker, Matthew J, resource asst, $26,976
Tucker, Rodney L, forestry rgnal supv, $50,280
Tuckus, Jesse M, resource asst, $8.58/hr
Tuma, George E, wildlife technician, $10.33/hr
Turnbough, Gregory A, resource asst, $25,452
Turner, Andrew W, resource scientist, $45,588
Turner, Dustin B, resource asst, $28,596
Turner, Richard A, conservation educ consult, $44,712
Turner, Sara C, nature center mgr, $51,264
Tuter, Joseph M, engring design tech, $36,792
Tuttle, Erin M, naturalist, $32,100
Tuttle, Johnny G, forest mgmt chief, $66,144
Tvedt, Kara J, fisheries mgmt biologist, $45,588
Twenter, Brett E, resource asst, $8.78
Twyman, Dennis L, protect dist supv, $64,848
Tyson, Wayne T, resource asst, $8.78/hr
Underwood, Ali J, resource asst, $24,984
Underwood, Dennis D, resource technician, $32,100
Urban, Joseph P, resource technician, $10.57/hr
Utrecht, Mary R, administrative staff asst, $28,596
Valenti, Warren F, private land conservationist, $16.20/hr
Valentine, James J, resource technician, $32,100
Valentine, Kristina M, resource asst, $28,044
Vallance, Jonathan S, resource technician, $27,516
Van Ausdoll, Joseph D, resource science asst, $10.83/hr
Van Patten, Mark N, fisheries staff biologist, $49,296
Van Rhein, Stephen L, cmnty conserv planner, $46,488
Vance, David C, resource forester, $40,548
Vandelicht, Rachel L, info technology spec, $40,548
Vandeloecht, Brent K, agric liaison, $50,280
Vanderhoef, Daniel B, conservation agent, $40,548
Vanhorn, Jason A, resource aide, $7.82/hr
Vanmatre, Gary D, conservation agent, $58,800
Vaughan, Clarence, duplicating equipoper II, $36,792
Vaughn, Jason D, conservation agent, $42,996
Vaughn, Rodney S, resource asst, $29,148
Veatch, Paul W, conservation agent, $59,952
Vessels, Patti A, resource asst, $27,516
Villarreal, Rachel E, administrative staff asst, $8.98/hr
Villeme, Forrest H, resource aide, $7.82/hr
Villmer, Steven W, resource asst, $30,876
Villwock, Jason L, resource forester, $39,000
Vining, Ivan W, biometrician, $61,140
Vogel, John A, wildlife rgnal supv, $51,264
Vogel, William J, proj coord, $13.71/hr
Vogt, Guy R, resource asst, $26,460
Volmert, Angie D, resource asst, $34,044
Volmert, Eric H, lead crpntr, $40,548
Volmert, Jason L, heavy equip oper, $34,044
Voney, Scott J, fisheries mgmt biologist, $44,712
Voss, Cynthia K, asst fin servs chief, $74,400
Voss, Gary M, survey spec, $57,660
Voss, Ryan M, maint asst, $7.82/hr
Voyles, Cynthia M, sign technician, $32,100
Wadel, Kelly L, resource asst, $8.98/hr
Wagoner, Patricia A, proj coord, $13.71/hr
Waldrop, Brian J, mkting asst, $10.57/hr
Wales, Christina L, clerk typist, $8.00/hr
Walker, Laura M, resource aide, $8.00/hr
Walker, Nicole L, wildlife biologist, $36,084
Wall, Paul D, equip shop sup II, $53,304
Wallace, Ronald E, lead crpntr, $49,296
Walls, Jennifer I, resource technician, $9.86/hr
Wankum, Donna M, ofc sup, $39,000
Ward, Joshua G, private land conservationist, $36,084
Ward, Pamela D, resource asst, $34,044
Ward, Thomas W, resource aide, $7.82/hr
Warnke, Derek A, conservation agent, $40,548
Warren, Justin H, resource forester, $33,372
Wash, Trina M, pub serv asst, $23,580
Watson, Lee A, editor/dsgnr, $15.44/hr
Watts, Greg A, resource asst, $25,452
Weaver, Alicia, administrative mgr, $75,876
Webster, Benjamin C, forestry field progs supv, $51,264
Wehmeyer, Lisa, internal auditor, $68,784
Wehmhoff, Luke A, resource asst, $8.58/hr
Weidenbenner, Bryan A, resource technician, $25,956
Weidinger, Joe F, realty spec, $61,140
Welch, Wendel G, heavy equip oper, $32,748
Wells, Christopher J, resource technician, $27,516
Wells, Jerry D, lead maint technician, $9.86/hr
Wells, Roger L, crpntr, $40,548
Welsh, Kevin W, resource technician, $32,100

Wessel, Chris A, crpntr, $31,488
Wesselschmidt, Raenhard O, wildlife mgmt biologist, $40,548
West, John L, resource staff scientist, $37,500
West, Kayla M, resource asst, $8.98/hr
West, Kenneth D, protect rgnal supv, $72,948
West, William D, conservation agent, $40,548
Westcott, Ryan A, resource asst, $24,984
Westin, Stephen C, forestry field progs supv, $67,452
Whalen, James P, edu spec, $45,588
Wheaton, Nichole J, naturalist, $12.47/hr
Whelan, Thomas L, htchry mgr, $52,284
Whisler, Samuel M, maint technician, $8.98/hr
Whitaker, Stasia D, resource technician, $27,516
White, Clifford P, art dept sup, $46,488
White, James R, equip shop technician, $47,412
White, Stephanie C, hr spec, $49,296
White, William T, private land svcs div chief, $87,060
Whitehead, Tim D, resource technician, $39,000
Whiteman, Kasey W, resource science field statation supv, $48,336
Whitener, David M, forest mgmt technician, $45,588
Whitsell, Paul M, resource forester, $40,548
Whittaker, Stanley D, excess prop technician, $29,724
Wieberg, Christopher M, administrative mgr, $62,352
Wiechman, Jerry D, fisheries mgmt biologist, $49,296
Wilcoxon, Mark W, conservation agent, $52,284
Wilder, Christina M, intern, $11.90/hr
Wilgers, Kyle D, resource asst, $8.58/hr
Wilkinson, Amy L, interpretive center mgr, $40,548
Wilkinson, Jerid M, conservation agent, $42,996
Willard, Jacob D, resource forester, $40,548
Willbur, Timothy T, resource asst, $8.58/hr
Williams, Scott C, fisheries mgmt biologist, $44,712
Williamson, Christopher J, fisheries mgmt biologist, $42,168
Williamson, Craig W, private land conservationist, $40,548
Wilsdorf, Amy A, public serv asst, $10,908
Wilson, Allen J, it spt technician, $34,716
Wilson, Bonnie M, resource aide, $8.58/hr
Wilson, Cliff, resource science asst, $32,100
Wilson, Hannah-ruth J, public serv asst, $7.82/hr
Wilson, Jenna M, administrative staff asst, $8.58/hr
Wilson, Lana K, administrative staff asst, $36,792
Wilson, Peter M, lead maint technician, $11.09/hr
Winchester, David A, resource asst, $25,956
Winders, Kyle R, resource scientist, $46,488
Wiseman, Matthew S, purchasing serv analyst, $42,996
Wissehr, Sharon K, administrative staff asst, $8.78/hr
Witt, Spenser L, resource technician, $9.86/hr
Wofford, Jerry A, equip shop sup I, $54,360
Wolf, Alexander J, resource staff scientist, $39,000
Wolf, Kathleen D, fisheries technician, $9.42/hr
Wolfe, Robert J, equip shop technician, $36,084
Wolken, Matthew J, protect rgnal supv, $74,400
Wolken, Roger E, protect rgnal supv, $74,400
Wollard, Bryan K, conservation agent, $58,800
Wolters, Jordan T, intern, $11.90/hr
Wood, Darrin L, conservation agent, $40,548
Wood, Devin L, private land conservationist, $37,500
Wood, Mark E, maint mech, $10.11/hr
Wood, Ronald D, resource asst, $8.98/hr
Wood, Ryan W, conservation agent, $37,500
Woodland, Nathan N, outdoor educ cntr supv, $40,548
Woodring, Michael R, resource asst, $8.58/hr
Woods, David A, fisheries mgmt biologist, $40,548
Woods, Kipp O, digital media producer, $62,352
Woodward, Lonnie N, aircraft mech, $21.08/hr
Woolf, David A, maint asst, $7.82/hr
Worley, James M, edu spec, $36,792
Worth, Austin M, resource asst, $8.58/hr
Wright, Amy L, policy spec, $15.82/hr
Wright, Chase H, conservation agent, $37,500
Wright, John D, conservation agent, $42,996
Wright, Rachel D, asst natural history biologist, $11.90/hr
Wright, Simeon, forest pathologist, $48,336
Wright, Todd W, conservation agent, $46,488
Yamnitz, Larry D, protect div chief, $101,352
Yasger, Patricia A, fisheries mgmt biologist, $54,360
Yates, Toby W, resource aide, $7.82/hr
Yeager, Douglas J, conservation agent, $56,544
Yegge, Tamie M, nature center mgr, $58,800
Young, Neal B, wetland servs biologist, $43,848
Young, Patrick J, resource asst, $26,460
Zachary, Tyler J, info tech field spt spec, $44,712
Zaczek, Nicholas E, resource forester, $36,792

Zarlenga, Daniel H, media spec, $47,412
Zerwig, Cherie L, administrative staff asst, $26,976
Ziebarth, Donald E, equip shop technician, $39,768
Zielke, Kevin H, conservation agent, $46,488
Zimmer, Katie N, progs coord, $15.44/hr
Zimmerman, Shaun T, it spt technician, $46,488
Zimmerschied, Meghan M, aquaculture spec, $36,084
Zurowski, Kellie R, range ofcr, $26,460

Department of Corrections

PO Box 236, Jefferson City 65102

Lombardi, George A, state dept dir, $121,705
Aaron, Brian K, corrections ofcr I, $29,661
Aaron, Sherry A, corrections ofcr I, $31,668
Abarca, Elvia, prob & parole ofcr II, $36,204
Abarca, Linda S, cook III, $28,104
Abbott, Gary W, corrections ofcr II, $31,668
Abbott, George D, maint spv I, $32,628
Abbott, Gregory L, corrections ofcr I, $29,652
Abbott, Lisa G, corrections recs ofcr I, $28,104
Abbott, Michael, storekeeper I, $25,824
Abell, Christopher W, corrections ofcr I, $29,652
Abeln, Dennis L, corrections ofcr I, $29,652
Abioye, Mary A, corrections ofcr I, $29,652
Abmeyer, Christine M, prob & parole ofcr II, $36,204
Abram, Scott A, prob & parole ofcr II, $36,204
Abrams, Eugene W, chaplain, $34,932
Achter, David G, garage spv, $32,628
Achterberg, Sydney A, sr ofc spt asst (keybrd), $26,652
Acklin, Michael L, corrections ofcr I, $29,652
Acklin, Tami C, prob & parole ofcr II, $39,624
Ackman, Joeseph M, corrections ofcr I, $29,652
Acord, Jackie R, corrections ofcr I, $29,652
Acres, Kris L, corrections ofcr I, $29,652
Adair, Deanna M, corrections ofcr I, $29,652
Adair, John J, corrections ofcr I, $28,692
Adair, Linda A, acad tchr III, $41,172
Adair, Richard J, investigator III, $38,928
Adamek, Gary L, maint spv I, $32,628
Adams, Barry L, corrections ofcr II, $35,724
Adams, Benjamin, prob & parole asst I, $28,536
Adams, Brian L, corrections ofcr I, $29,652
Adams, Carla B, prob & parole ofcr II, $39,624
Adams, Daniel W, corrections ofcr III, $33,744
Adams, Danny E, functional unit mgr corr, $38,928
Adams, Donna M, ofc spt asst (keybrd), $23,160
Adams, Jacob M, corrections ofcr I, $29,652
Adams, Joshua C, corrections ofcr I, $29,652
Adams, Kathryn L, admin ofc spt asst, $28,104
Adams, Kody D, corrections ofcr I, $29,652
Adams, Lili T, corrections recs ofcr III, $36,204
Adams, Lisa K, prob & parole ofcr II, $36,204
Adams, Loretta D, corrections ofcr I, $29,652
Adams, Mandy M, prob & parole ofcr II, $36,204
Adams, Matthew B, recrtn ofcr I, $32,052
Adams, Matthew J, corrections ofcr I, $29,652
Adams, Melinda K, prob & parole unit spv, $44,304
Adams, Melissa A, prob & parole ofcr II, $36,204
Adams, Miriam D, prob & parole ofcr I, $36,888
Adams, Nathan S, corrections ofcr I, $28,692
Adams, Rebecca K, ofc spt asst (keybrd), $22,536
Adams, Reginald D, prob & parole ofcr II, $36,204
Adams, Robert B, corrections ofcr I, $29,652
Adams, Scott E, prob & parole ofcr II, $36,204
Adams, Stephanie D, prob & parole ofcr II, $36,204
Adams, Teresa V, corrections case mgr II, $36,888
Adams, Wendy J, ofc spt asst (keybrd), $23,160
Adams, Zachary, prob & parole ofcr II, $36,204
Adamson, Joyce D, corrections case mgr II, $34,944
Addie, James A, corrections ofcr I, $31,678
Adey, Randy E, corrections ofcr I, $29,652
Adkerson, Connie L, prob & parole unit spv, $45,156
Adkerson, Travis A, corrections ofcr I, $29,652
Adkins, James D, recrtn ofcr I, $33,744
Adkins, James W, corrections mgr b1, $51,096
Adkison, Brett R, phys plant sup III, $46,068
Adkison, David A, maint spv I, $32,628
Adzah, Emma S, corrections ofcr I, $28,692
Agenstein, Rita S, admin ofc spt asst, $32,052
Agers, Robert W, boiler oper, $28,104
Aggers, Christopher L, corrections ofcr I, $29,652

Aholt, Gregory J, storekeeper I, $26,232
Ahrens, Joann L, prob & parole ofcr II, $38,232
Ahrens, Joshua W, corrections ofcr I, $29,652
Aiello, Tiffany B, subs abuse cnslr I, $29,976
Aitkens, Lauretta K, corrections spv II, $46,068
Akee, Kaleb L, voc enter spv I, $28,104
Akers, Cody L, corrections ofcr I, $29,652
Akers, Herbert E, corrections ofcr II, $32,220
Akers, Kimberly R, cook III, $28,104
Akers, Wendle L, subs abuse cnslr III, $38,232
Akins, James F, corrections ofcr I, $29,652
Akins, Stephen D, corrections ofcr I, $29,652
Alagna, Susan, prob & parole ofcr II, $38,232
Albach, Adam L, corrections case mgr II, $34,944
Alberts, Maghan R, prob & parole ofcr II, $36,204
Alberts, Richard C, maint spv II, $38,928
Albertson, Daryl L, prob & parole ofcr II, $40,380
Albertson, Thomas A, corrections ofcr I, $29,652
Albin, Justin L, corrections ofcr I, $29,652
Albin, Lee E, maint spv I, $33,180
Albright, Jesse J, corrections ofcr I, $29,652
Albring, Paul A, corrections ofcr I, $28,692
Alderman, Cari A, exec I, $30,984
Alderman, Robert A, corrections ofcr III, $36,888
Alderman, Tracy R, corrections ofcr I, $31,140
Alderson, Melanie J, storekeeper I, $25,824
Alexander, Danny K, stationary engr, $33,744
Alexander, Michael E, corrections ofcr III, $37,056
Alexander, Michael R, prod spec I corr, $40,380
Alexander, Spencer T, corrections ofcr I, $29,652
Alexander, Susan L, cook III, $29,976
Alfaro, Daniel E, corrections ofcr I, $29,652
Alford, Kenneth W, corrections ofcr I, $29,652
Alford, Kiska M, ofc spt asst (keybrd), $23,160
Alicie, James E, corrections ofcr I, $29,652
Allard, Jenna, prob & parole ofcr I, $29,976
Allard, Scott T, prob & parole ofcr II, $40,380
Allee, Amanda F, acad tchr III, $37,548
Allen, Ann R, prob & parole asst I, $32,628
Allen, Ashley R, ofc spt asst (keybrd), $23,880
Allen, Austin J, corrections ofcr I, $28,692
Allen, Brian, corrections case mgr II, $40,380
Allen, Carl E, corrections ofcr I, $33,348
Allen, Cody D, corrections ofcr I, $29,652
Allen, Darrell W, corrections ofcr I, $29,652
Allen, Debera L, corrections ofcr I, $29,652
Allen, Denise L, corrections ofcr I, $29,652
Allen, Dennis M, corrections mgr b1, $45,661
Allen, Eric, prob & parole ofcr II, $34,944
Allen, Gary D, corrections ofcr I, $29,652
Allen, Homer R, inst activity coor, $33,744
Allen, Jared M, corrections ofcr I, $29,652
Allen, Jason L, corrections ofcr I, $29,652
Allen, Jason R, corrections ofcr I, $29,652
Allen, Jeff D, corrections ofcr I, $29,652
Allen, Jennifer, special para prof, $38,928
Allen, Jodi M, sr ofc spt asst (keybrd), $25,824
Allen, Kenneth D, corrections ofcr I, $28,692
Allen, Kimberly K, prob & parole ofcr I, $32,052
Allen, Larry W, food serv mgr II, $36,888
Allen, Lee D, cook III, $28,104
Allen, Lee T, corrections ofcr I, $29,652
Allen, Lindsay A, corrections ofcr I, $29,652
Allen, Marc H, corrections ofcr I, $29,652
Allen, Mathew D, corrections ofcr I, $29,652
Allen, Patricia L, storekeeper I, $25,824
Allen, Richard W, stationary engr, $33,744
Allen, Shirley M, corrections ofcr I, $29,652
Allen, Skyler J, corrections ofcr I, $29,652
Allen, Steven A, recrtn ofcr I, $31,512
Allen-Leonard, Tonia M, ofc spt asst (keybrd), $23,160
Alley, Brenda L, functional unit mgr corr, $38,928
Allgaier, Timothy, voc enter spv II, $34,944
Allgier, Justin N, corrections ofcr I, $29,652
Allgier, Richard C, boiler oper, $28,104
Allhands, Hannah C, prob & parole ofcr II, $36,204
Allison, Amy C, prob & parole ofcr II, $36,888
Allison, Brenda, ofc spt asst (keybrd), $23,160
Allison, Eric, tractor trailer driver, $30,984
Allison, Julia A, corrections ofcr I, $31,140
Allison, Ricky L, corrections ofcr I, $29,652
Allison, Roxanne E, subs abuse cnslr II, $34,944
Allnutt, Ritchie L, corrections ofcr I, $30,132

Austin, Scott D, corrections ofcr I, $29,652
Autrey, Eve, corrections ofcr I, $29,652
Avant, Danielle M, corrections ofcr I, $29,652
Avery, Cole R, corrections ofcr I, $29,652
Avery, Douglas J, prob & parole asst I, $29,496
Avery, John C, prob & parole ofcr II, $36,204
Avery, Trenae M, corrections ofcr I, $29,652
Awai, Mendi W, corrections ofcr I, $29,652
Axtell, Valerie E, ofc spt asst (keybrd), $26,652
Axton, Kent D, electronics tech, $31,512
Aycock, Neil, prob & parole unit spv, $41,940
Ayers, Aaron J, corrections ofcr I, $29,652
Ayers, Bradley D, corrections mgr b1, $50,045
Ayers, Brenda E, corrections ofcr I, $29,652
Ayers, Chester A, corrections ofcr I, $28,692
Ayers, Greg S, corrections ofcr I, $28,692
Ayers, James A, phys plant sup I, $37,548
Ayres, Becky D, prob & parole ofcr II, $34,944
Ayres, Cody J, corrections ofcr I, $29,652
Babayco, Heath A, corrections ofcr I, $29,652
Babbitt, Jacob W, corrections ofcr I, $29,652
Bachtel, Betty S, storekeeper I, $27,084
Backes, Christofer B, corrections ofcr I, $29,652
Backman, James C, corrections ofcr I, $28,692
Backues, Anita E, account clerk II, $25,824
Backues, Kanon C, corrections ofcr I, $29,652
Bacon, Paul E, corrections mgr b1, $47,391
Bade, Timothy W, corrections ofcr I, $28,692
Bader, Bryan S, corrections ofcr I, $29,652
Bagby, Claude W, corrections ofcr I, $29,652
Bagley, Kaleb A, corrections ofcr I, $28,692
Bagwill, Leslianne, acad tchr III, $37,548
Baheyadeen, Majeeda H, ofc spt asst (keybrd), $23,160
Bahlman, Britany N, corrections ofcr I, $29,652
Bailey, Arnold E, corrections ofcr I, $29,652
Bailey, Chelsea N, prob & parole ofcr II, $36,204
Bailey, Cheri A, corrections ofcr II, $31,668
Bailey, Cortney S, corrections ofcr I, $29,652
Bailey, Debra S, prob & parole ofcr II, $38,232
Bailey, Ellen J, cook III, $28,104
Bailey, Gale E, registered nurse mgr b2, $70,983
Bailey, Jeffery J, corrections ofcr I, $29,652
Bailey, John T, corrections ofcr I, $29,652
Bailey, Mahlon D, corrections ofcr I, $29,652
Bailey, Natasha N, corrections ofcr I, $29,652
Bailey, Nathan L, corrections ofcr II, $31,668
Bailey, Richard L, corrections ofcr I, $31,140
Bailey, Robert L, special educ tchr III, $45,156
Bailey, Ronald F, corrections ofcr II, $35,724
Bailey, William F, corrections ofcr II, $33,348
Bair, Mark E, investigator I, $30,984
Baker, Anthony J, corrections ofcr I, $29,652
Baker, Charles E, corrections ofcr III, $33,744
Baker, Charles T, parole hearing analyst, $56,520
Baker, Christina L, sr ofc spt asst (clerical), $25,824
Baker, Cynthia D, corrections ofcr I, $29,652
Baker, Dalene L, sr ofc spt asst (keybrd), $27,504
Baker, David W, corrections ofcr I, $29,652
Baker, Donald E, corrections ofcr I, $28,692
Baker, Douglas W, corrections case mgr II, $38,928
Baker, Gary W, prob & parole ofcr II, $38,232
Baker, Jeffrey D, corrections ofcr I, $30,132
Baker, Jon E, corrections ofcr I, $29,652
Baker, Kathleen A, corrections ofcr I, $29,652
Baker, Kelly R, corrections ofcr I, $29,652
Baker, Kenneth A, corrections ofcr I, $29,652
Baker, Mark R, recrtn ofcr III, $41,172
Baker, Mary E, corrections ofcr I, $28,692
Baker, Michael, corrections ofcr I, $29,652
Baker, Novalea F, corrections case mgr II, $37,548
Baker, Robert E, corrections ofcr I, $29,652
Baker, Robert L, corrections ofcr III, $33,744
Baker, Rusty S, corrections ofcr I, $29,652
Baker, Stanley R, corrections ofcr I, $31,140
Baker, Teri L, prob & parole unit spv, $48,156
Baker, Theresa J, voc edu spv, $41,172
Baker, Timothy D, corrections ofcr II, $31,668
Bald, Anthony, prob & parole ofcr II, $39,624
Baldeh, Momodou, prob & parole asst I, $28,536
Baldwin, Christopher L Jr, corrections ofcr I, $29,652
Baldwin, Dennis R, prob & parole ofcr II, $40,380
Baldwin, Michael L, corrections ofcr I, $29,652
Baldwin, Miles A, corrections ofcr I, $29,652

Balentine, Bruce, corrections ofcr I, $31,668
Bales, Ashley B, corrections case mgr II, $34,944
Bales, Joyce E, corrections ofcr I, $31,140
Bales, Lyle, corrections case mgr II, $39,624
Bales, Mark D, corrections ofcr I, $29,652
Bales, Raymond H, corrections ofcr I, $30,132
Balfour, Bonnie L, corrections ofcr II, $31,668
Ball, April D, sr ofc spt asst (clerical), $25,824
Ball, David A, stationary engr, $33,744
Ball, George J, corrections ofcr I, $28,692
Ball, Jeffrey L, special asst paraprof, $31,800
Ball, Susan J, corrections case mgr II, $34,944
Ballance, Joseph J, corrections ofcr I, $28,692
Ballard, Glenda M, cook II, $24,264
Ballard, Jason, prob & parole ofcr I, $30,984
Ballew, Michael, corrections ofcr I, $28,692
Balliett, Stephen M, corrections ofcr I, $28,692
Ballinger, Joshua A, corrections ofcr I, $29,652
Ballinger, Terrena M, corrections mgr b2, $52,091
Bambrough, Darbe L, ofc spt asst (keybrd), $23,160
Bamburg, Robert O, corrections ofcr I, $28,692
Banks, Bria J, ofc spt asst (keybrd), $22,536
Banks, Kimberly S, ofc spt asst (keybrd), $12,912
Banks, Libby L, prob & parole ofcr II, $36,204
Banks, Renee A, prob & parole ofcr II, $36,204
Bannan, Carmelia F, corrections ofcr I, $29,652
Bannan, Gary L, corrections ofcr I, $29,652
Banning, Cecil S, corrections ofcr I, $33,348
Banta, Vicky M, prob & parole asst I, $29,496
Baquet, Zachary L, corrections ofcr I, $28,692
Barbagiovanni, Joseph W, corrections training ofcr, $38,928
Barber, Victoria M, corrections ofcr I, $28,692
Barber-Neal, Rebecca J, corrections case mgr I, $30,984
Barbour, Benjamin, prob & parole ofcr II, $36,204
Barbre, Thomas C, corrections ofcr II, $37,056
Barck, Jody C, corrections ofcr I, $29,652
Bardoner, Jesse W, prob & parole ofcr II, $34,944
Bargfrede, John L, corrections ofcr I, $28,692
Barker, David A, corrections ofcr II, $31,668
Barker, Derek, corrections case mgr II, $34,944
Barker, Guymon G, electronics tech, $29,976
Barker, John F, corrections ofcr I, $33,348
Barker, Kevin A, corrections ofcr I, $32,220
Barker, Laura J, sr ofc spt asst (keybrd), $27,504
Barker, Michael A, prob & parole ofcr II, $36,204
Barker, Robert C, prob & parole asst II, $34,944
Barker, Robert E, corrections ofcr I, $29,652
Barkho, Shawn L, edu asst II, $28,584
Barksdale, Michele L, ofc spt asst (keybrd), $23,160
Barlow, Brian K, corrections ofcr II, $31,668
Barlow, Marjorie A, ofc spt asst (keybrd), $23,160
Barlow, Regina A, cook II, $26,232
Barnaba, Laurie J, recrtn ofcr II, $32,628
Barnard, Marshall R, corrections ofcr II, $31,668
Barnes, Adrian M, functional unit mgr corr, $39,624
Barnes, Andrew J, corrections ofcr I, $29,652
Barnes, Chad B, corrections ofcr I, $29,652
Barnes, Charles T, corrections ofcr II, $31,668
Barnes, Christie J, corrections ofcr II, $31,668
Barnes, David L, corrections ofcr I, $29,652
Barnes, Emily G, prob & parole ofcr II, $36,204
Barnes, Jennifer L, corrections ofcr I, $28,692
Barnes, Kimberly A, prob & parole ofcr II, $40,380
Barnes, Kristin D, corrections ofcr I, $29,652
Barnes, Lisa, functional unit mgr corr, $38,928
Barnes, Pamela J, cook II, $24,264
Barnes, Robert L, corrections ofcr I, $29,652
Barnes, Terry S, sr ofc spt asst (clerical), $29,412
Barnett, Benjimin K, corrections ofcr I, $29,652
Barnett, Cheryl A, subs abuse cnslr II, $34,944
Barnett, David F, corrections mgr b2, $51,220
Barnett, Jessica N, corrections mgr b1, $45,333
Barnett, Wyatt M, corrections ofcr I, $29,652
Barnhart, Richard A, corrections ofcr I, $29,652
Barnhart, Tommy G, chaplain, $34,932
Barnhill, Lloyd D, cook II, $24,264
Baron, Lauren E, sr ofc spt asst (keybrd), $25,824
Barr, James M, prob & parole ofcr II, $38,232
Barraclough, Matthew A, corrections ofcr I, $29,652
Barrett, Deborah A, corrections case mgr II, $34,944
Barrett, Frances E, voc tchr III, $37,548
Barrett, John W, corrections ofcr II, $33,900
Barrios, Ana D, prob & parole asst I, $29,496

Barron, Sheila Y, storekeeper I, $26,652
Barroso, Eric J, acad tchr III, $38,232
Barry, Lee M, prob & parole asst I, $29,496
Barry, Robert G, prob & parole asst I, $29,496
Bartels, Timothy D, corrections ofcr I, $29,652
Bartholomew, Bruce E, phys plant sup I, $36,204
Bartlett, Deanna J, ofc spt asst (keybrd), $25,404
Bartlett, Jamon M, corrections ofcr I, $29,652
Bartlett, John, prob & parole ofcr II, $36,204
Bartlett, Laurin A, prob & parole ofcr II, $36,204
Bartlett, Lavern, corrections ofcr I, $29,652
Bartlett, Mark A, corrections case mgr II, $34,944
Bartley, Troy E, dietitian III, $50,040
Bartolo, Darlene A, storekeeper I, $25,824
Barton, Adam D, corrections ofcr I, $29,652
Barton, Ashton K, recrtn ofcr I, $30,420
Barton, Brady L, inst activity coor, $31,512
Barton, Casey S, corrections ofcr I, $28,692
Barton, Christopher B, corrections ofcr I, $31,668
Barton, Christopher L, corrections ofcr I, $29,652
Barton, Cynthia A, prob & parole ofcr II, $38,232
Barton, Donald R, corrections case mgr II, $34,944
Barton, Jacquiline N, ofc spt asst (clerical), $22,536
Barton, Lynette R, admin ofc spt asst, $28,104
Barton, Micheal P, corrections ofcr I, $29,652
Barton, Nicolle L, prob & parole unit spv, $41,940
Barton, Teresa, corrections ofcr I, $29,652
Bartz, Lonny J, functional unit mgr corr, $41,940
Bartz, Sandra J, corrections case mgr II, $39,624
Barwick, Kimberly D, corrections ofcr I, $29,652
Basham, Clayborn L, corrections ofcr I, $28,692
Basham, Michele L, corrections ofcr III, $34,356
Bashford, Timothy E, maint worker II, $30,984
Bashor, Alex E, corrections ofcr I, $28,692
Bashor, Amos M, corrections ofcr I, $28,692
Basinger, Christine E, cook II, $24,264
Basinger, Jordan L, corrections case mgr I, $31,512
Baskett, Melissa S, recrtn ofcr II, $32,628
Baskette, Steven C, storekeeper II, $28,104
Baslee, Daniel, corrections ofcr I, $33,348
Baslee, Ricky L, corrections ofcr I, $29,652
Basler, Kimberly A, storekeeper I, $25,824
Bass, Jeannette R, prob & parole ofcr II, $36,204
Bass, Jody E, recrtn ofcr I, $29,976
Bate, Allen A, corrections ofcr I, $29,652
Bateman, Loren L, corrections ofcr II, $30,576
Bates, Carol J, lab mgr b1, $42,845
Bates, Ronald G, corrections case mgr II, $38,232
Bates, Sabrina N, corrections ofcr I, $29,652
Bates, Terry L, storekeeper I, $27,084
Batson, George M, corrections ofcr I, $29,652
Batson, John M, electronics tech, $30,984
Batson, Tyson L, corrections ofcr I, $29,652
Battles, Gwendolyn E, corrections ofcr II, $31,668
Battreal, Donnie M, corrections ofcr I, $28,692
Batts, Jason A, corrections ofcr I, $28,692
Bauer, William C, corrections ofcr I, $29,652
Baugher, Margaret R, cook II, $24,264
Baumann, Michelle, corrections ofcr II, $31,668
Baumann, Steven P, corrections ofcr III, $35,568
Baumbach, William R, corrections ofcr I, $29,652
Baumgartner, David A, corrections ofcr I, $28,692
Baumhoer, Shane M, admin ofc spt asst, $28,104
Bax, Justin D, maint spv II, $38,232
Bax, Shawn H, subs abuse cnslr II, $33,744
Baxley, Scott C, prob & parole ofcr II, $40,380
Baxley, Thomas A, corrections case mgr II, $39,624
Baxter, Dennis R, corrections ofcr I, $28,692
Baxter, James E, stationary engr, $33,744
Baxter, Sherri L, corrections ofcr I, $29,652
Baxter, Steven L, corrections ofcr I, $29,652
Bayless, Timothy B, corrections ofcr II, $31,668
Baysinger, Karen, admin ofc spt asst, $30,984
Baysinger, Randy L, corrections ofcr I, $29,652
Beach, Mackenzie L, corrections ofcr I, $28,692
Beach, Melvin L, stationary engr, $34,356
Beach, Thomas M, corrections ofcr I, $28,692
Beale, James, prob & parole asst I, $28,536
Bealer, Kelsey P, cook II, $24,264
Bealmear, Vicki, corrections mgr b1, $51,144
Bealmer, Nathan M, corrections ofcr I, $29,652
Beane, Roger, prob & parole ofcr I, $29,976
Bearce, Justin P, prob & parole ofcr II, $36,204

Beard, Douglas R, inst activity coor, $33,180
Bearden, Cherese A, ofc spt asst (clerical), $22,536
Bearden, Cora Y, corrections ofcr I, $29,652
Bearden, Edward K, corrections ofcr I, $29,652
Bearden, James W, prob & parole ofcr II, $34,944
Bearden, Joel E, prob & parole ofcr II, $39,624
Bearden, Roy L, prob & parole ofcr II, $36,204
Beasley, Deseri, prob & parole ofcr I, $29,976
Beasley, Michael R, corrections ofcr I, $28,692
Beasley, Michelle E, corrections ofcr I, $28,692
Beasley, William S, voc enter spv II, $34,356
Beason, Carl L, corrections spv I, $37,548
Beattie, Jaymi S, corrections ofcr I, $29,652
Beatty, Joann L, ofc spt asst (keybrd), $25,824
Beaty, Trevor L, corrections ofcr III, $32,628
Beauchamp, Chantal S, prob & parole ofcr II, $36,204
Beauchamp, Donald L, corrections ofcr I, $34,512
Beauchamp, Jill R, prob & parole ofcr II, $36,204
Beauchamp, Kelsey M, corrections ofcr I, $28,692
Beauchamp, Victoria M, corrections ofcr I, $29,652
Beaver, Aaron T, corrections ofcr I, $29,661
Beaver, Timothy J, corrections ofcr I, $29,652
Beavers, Adeesha, prob & parole asst I, $28,536
Becerra, Julie A, prob & parole ofcr II, $39,624
Beck, Brenda A, prob & parole ofcr II, $38,232
Beck, Brian S, corrections ofcr I, $29,652
Beck, Cody P, corrections ofcr I, $29,652
Beck, Corry J, corrections ofcr I, $29,652
Beck, Joshua R, corrections ofcr I, $29,652
Beck, Julia J, corrections ofcr I, $29,652
Beck, Lisa A, planner III, $45,156
Beck, Lisa A, budget analyst III, $53,208
Beck, Robin L, prob & parole ofcr II, $36,204
Beck, Tonia S, cook III, $29,004
Beck, Trisha L, corrections ofcr I, $29,652
Beck-clithero, Jeanine M, sr ofc spt asst (keybrd), $25,032
Beckemeyer, Mark J, corrections ofcr I, $33,348
Becker, Carole D, corrections case mgr I, $30,420
Becker, Russell R, recrtn ofcr I, $31,512
Beckett, Jarred C, corrections ofcr I, $28,692
Beckett, Robert G, corrections ofcr I, $29,652
Beckham, Paul A, corrections ofcr I, $29,652
Bedrosian, Pamela, prob & parole ofcr II, $36,204
Bedrosian-Vandermark, Carol M, corrections ofcr I, $28,692
Bee, Richard G, corrections ofcr III, $35,568
Beecham, Debra A, admin ofc spt asst, $30,420
Beel, Randall S, corrections ofcr II, $31,668
Beelek, Demetrice J, corrections ofcr I, $29,652
Beer, Daniel D, corrections ofcr I, $29,652
Beers, Dora L, corrections ofcr II, $31,668
Beers, Linda S, ofc spt asst (keybrd), $23,880
Beers, Opal E, corrections ofcr I, $31,140
Beers, Terry M, power plant mech, $30,984
Beers, Tony W, corrections ofcr I, $29,652
Beers, Wade R, special asst technician, $46,925
Beesler, William B, corrections ofcr I, $29,652
Beeson, Amy M, corrections ofcr III, $33,744
Beeson, Steven W, account clerk II, $25,824
Beggs, Regina L, functional unit mgr corr, $38,928
Begley, Aaron P, corrections ofcr I, $29,652
Beiser, Philip G, cook III, $28,104
Beister, Heather D, ofc spt asst (keybrd), $23,160
Belcher, Jami L, prob & parole asst I, $29,496
Belfield, Heather D, corrections case mgr II, $34,944
Belfield, Timothy E, corrections ofcr I, $30,576
Bell, Brian F, corrections ofcr I, $29,652
Bell, Candice L, corrections ofcr I, $29,652
Bell, Cordell A, corrections ofcr I, $31,140
Bell, Damien D, corrections ofcr I, $29,652
Bell, Dawn L, corrections ofcr I, $31,140
Bell, Dianna M, corrections ofcr I, $29,652
Bell, Jason J, prob & parole ofcr II, $37,548
Bell, Jesse D, corrections ofcr I, $29,652
Bell, Lois M, sr ofc spt asst (keybrd), $26,232
Bell, Michele L, corrections ofcr I, $29,652
Bell, Robert D, corrections ofcr I, $31,140
Bell, Steven D, prob & parole unit spv, $45,156
Bell, Thomas W, cook III, $27,228
Bell, Tully L, corrections ofcr I, $29,316
Bellamy, Danielle C, prob & parole ofcr II, $36,204
Belleville, Thomas J, prob & parole ofcr II, $36,204
Bellew, Jacob T, special educ tchr I, $30,984
Belstle, Mary V, admin ofc spt asst, $29,976

Belt, Randy E, corrections case mgr I, $30,420
Belt, Richard S, maint worker II, $29,004
Bemboom, Russell L, corrections case mgr II, $34,944
Bembry, Ramona, prob & parole asst II, $30,420
Benavidez, Richard J, corrections ofcr I, $28,692
Bench, Eric J, corrections ofcr II, $31,668
Bench, Julie A, acad tchr III, $37,548
Bench, Kelly L, corrections ofcr II, $31,668
Bench, Robin L, prob & parole ofcr II, $36,204
Bendure, Zachary P, corrections ofcr I, $29,652
Benedict, Timothy M, corrections ofcr I, $29,652
Benford, Kimberly D, corrections ofcr I, $29,652
Benitez, Caleb M, corrections ofcr I, $28,692
Benjamin, Logan S, corrections ofcr I, $29,652
Benker, Lorena F, corrections ofcr I, $28,692
Benn, Danny L, serv mgr I, $33,744
Bennett, Bon, ofc spt asst (keybrd), $23,160
Bennett, Ciara M, corrections ofcr I, $28,692
Bennett, Cody A, corrections ofcr I, $28,692
Bennett, Corey L, corrections ofcr I, $29,652
Bennett, Dennis K, corrections ofcr I, $29,652
Bennett, Donna A, corrections ofcr I, $29,652
Bennett, Harold G, corrections ofcr I, $29,652
Bennett, Isaac, corrections ofcr I, $29,652
Bennett, Katherine A, prob & parole ofcr II, $39,624
Bennett, Kelisha L, corrections ofcr I, $29,652
Bennett, Kimberly R, corrections ofcr II, $31,668
Bennett, Lyndsay J, prob & parole ofcr II, $36,204
Bennett, Mark G, corrections ofcr I, $29,652
Bennett, Rita J, special educ tchr III, $40,380
Bennett, Roger L, corrections ofcr I, $33,900
Bennett, Ron, cook II, $24,264
Bennett, Shawn E, corrections ofcr I, $29,652
Benskin, Carol J, pers clerk, $28,104
Benson, Anthony L, corrections ofcr I, $29,652
Benson, Brian J, corrections ofcr I, $29,652
Benson, Jacquin, prob & parole ofcr II, $40,380
Benson, Nathan A, corrections ofcr I, $29,652
Benson, Norman P, stationary engr, $33,744
Benson, Stephen K, corrections ofcr II, $31,668
Bentley, Lori L, ofc spt asst (keybrd), $25,824
Bentley, Patricia L, corrections ofcr I, $29,652
Bentley, Shreve, investigator II, $36,204
Bentley-Monnig, Barbara A, prob & parole ofcr II, $36,888
Benton, Christain A, corrections case mgr II, $34,944
Benton, Sean R, corrections ofcr I, $29,652
Benton, Thomas M, corrections ofcr I, $29,652
Benton, Timothy W, maint spv I, $32,628
Bentsen, Travis J, corrections ofcr II, $31,668
Bentz, Jonmichael S, corrections ofcr II, $31,668
Bentz, Keith E, corrections ofcr III, $33,744
Berends, Traci A, corrections ofcr I, $29,652
Berendzen, David A, heavy equip mech, $35,568
Berendzen, Kelley D, sr ofc spt asst (keybrd), $25,824
Berens, Thomas C, pers clerk, $28,104
Berg, Brian T, corrections ofcr I, $28,692
Berggren, Kimberly J, prob & parole ofcr II, $36,204
Bergman, Melissa K, corrections mgr b1, $53,208
Bergren, Brandon L, corrections ofcr I, $29,652
Berhorst, Gerald R, corrections ofcr I, $34,512
Berkbigler, Scott E, corrections mgr b1, $48,808
Bernand, Susan E, corrections ofcr I, $31,140
Bernskoetter, Hollie R, voc tchr III, $37,548
Berrey, Bryan C, corrections ofcr I, $29,652
Berry, Charles S, cook II, $24,264
Berry, Chris M, functional unit mgr corr, $42,708
Berry, David Q, corrections ofcr I, $29,652
Berry, Deanna L, corrections ofcr II, $30,576
Berry, Heather J, corrections ofcr I, $29,652
Berry, James L, corrections mgr b1, $53,206
Berry, Kimberly, prob & parole ofcr II, $39,624
Berry, LeAnn M, serv mgr II, $38,928
Berry, Linda D, ofc spt asst (keybrd), $23,160
Berry, Rosemary B, ofc spt asst (keybrd), $23,160
Berry, Terry L, corrections ofcr II, $33,348
Bertel, Zachary R, corrections ofcr I, $28,692
Bertelsmeyer, Timothy W, corrections ofcr I, $29,652
Berten, D Wayne, exec II, $39,624
Bertrand, David E, prob & parole ofcr II, $41,940
Beshears, Susan A, prob & parole ofcr II, $36,888
Besher, Steven D, corrections ofcr I, $29,652
Bess, Chad E, corrections ofcr I, $29,652
Bess, Elizabeth A, inst activity coor, $31,512

Bess, Joshua, human rel ofcr II, $41,940
Best, Christopher A, corrections ofcr I, $29,652
Best, John, maint spv I, $31,512
Bestgen, Edwin A, corrections mgr b1, $49,108
Bestgen, Reta, ofc spt asst (keybrd), $26,232
Bestgen, Shawn K, recrtn ofcr I, $29,976
Bettes, Daniel C, corrections ofcr I, $29,652
Bettis, James A, corrections ofcr I, $31,140
Betts, Betsie R, functional unit mgr corr, $38,928
Betts, Dionna M, prob & parole ofcr II, $39,624
Betts, Lynette, prob & parole ofcr II, $40,380
Betz, Brenda L, corrections ofcr I, $29,652
Betz, Pamela S, corrections ofcr I, $31,140
Beucke, Denise R, ofc spt asst (keybrd), $22,536
Beverage, Kyle-Christophe S, corrections ofcr I, $28,692
Beverage, Michael L, corrections ofcr I, $29,652
Bezner, James J, corrections ofcr III, $39,624
Biach, Eric D, corrections ofcr I, $29,652
Bibby, John D, corrections ofcr I, $29,652
Biberdorf, Theresa M, prob & parole unit spv, $43,488
Bidding, Kathleen M, functional unit mgr corr, $45,156
Bieker, Laura A, corrections ofcr I, $29,652
Bieri, Neva K, ofc spt asst (keybrd), $23,160
Biggs, James W, corrections ofcr I, $29,652
Bilderback, Mark A, corrections ofcr I, $31,140
Bilinski, Edward D, prob & parole unit spv, $46,932
Billings, Donna K, corrections ofcr I, $29,652
Billingsley, Samuel, corrections spv II, $43,488
Bimm, Carl S, prob & parole ofcr II, $36,204
Bingaman, Brian, corrections ofcr III, $32,628
Bingham, Jerry, functional unit mgr corr, $40,380
Bingham, Tamra J, corrections ofcr I, $29,652
Bingham, Tawanna T, corrections ofcr I, $28,692
Binion, Vivian L, ofc spt asst (keybrd), $23,160
Bird, Joshua A, maint spv I, $33,180
Bird, Martha L, ofc spt asst (keybrd), $23,880
Bird, Pammy S, corrections ofcr I, $29,652
Bird, Paul A, corrections ofcr I, $29,652
Birdsong, Connie M, prob & parole asst I, $29,496
Birmingham, Laura L, prob & parole ofcr II, $40,380
Birmingham, Pamela S, cook II, $24,264
Bisel, Darrel L, corrections ofcr III, $35,568
Bisel, Janita, functional unit mgr corr, $38,928
Bishop, Joseph N, prob & parole asst II, $31,512
Bishop, Steven L, corrections ofcr I, $29,652
Bishop, Tracy L, prob & parole ofcr II, $36,204
Bishop, William A, corrections ofcr I, $29,652
Bisker, Scotty G, corrections ofcr I, $30,132
Bivens, Patricia A, cook II, $24,264
Bix, Melva J, corrections ofcr I, $29,652
Bixenman, Julie R, voc tchr II, $34,944
Black, Deborah E, corrections ofcr III, $34,356
Black, Debra L, admin ofc spt asst, $28,104
Black, Dylan C, corrections ofcr I, $28,692
Black, Edward C, corrections ofcr II, $31,668
Black, Karen, admin ofc spt asst, $28,104
Black, Kevin M, recrtn ofcr II, $32,628
Black, Lora L, ofc spt asst (clerical), $22,536
Black, Michael G, stationary engr, $32,628
Black, Rhonda R, corrections classif asst, $30,984
Black, Rodney K, corrections training ofcr, $40,380
Black, Ryan, corrections ofcr I, $28,692
Black, William M, corrections ofcr I, $29,652
Blackard, James A, corrections ofcr I, $29,652
Blackburn, Gilbert L, garage spv, $36,204
Blackburn, Shari L, corrections ofcr I, $29,652
Blackman, Lillie M, prob & parole ofcr II, $36,204
Blackman, Lloyd A, corrections ofcr I, $29,652
Blackmon, Romelle P, corrections case mgr II, $34,944
Blacksher, Donita M, ofc spt asst (keybrd), $23,160
Blackwell, Benjamin L, prob & parole asst I, $29,496
Blair, David E, storekeeper I, $25,824
Blair, Kristi M, ofc spt asst (keybrd), $23,160
Blair, Paul D, functional unit mgr corr, $41,940
Blair, Tammy K, acad tchr III, $41,172
Blair, Tony D, maint spv I, $35,568
Blake, Crystal D, prob & parole ofcr II, $36,204
Blake, Josephine K, corrections ofcr I, $29,652
Blake, Kevin D, corrections ofcr I, $29,652
Blakely, Carol L, prob & parole ofcr II, $36,888
Blakely, Cynthia K, corrections case mgr III, $39,624
Blakely, Hunter R, corrections mgr b1, $49,735
Blakemore, Kayrene, ofc spt asst (keybrd), $25,032

Blakemore, Paul E, factory mgr II, $38,928
Blakley, Michael M, prob & parole asst I, $30,984
Blalock, James B, cook II, $24,264
Blanco, Jason D, prob & parole ofcr II, $36,204
Bland, Makeitra, ofc spt asst (keybrd), $23,160
Bland, Richard S, prob & parole ofcr II, $39,624
Bland, Roger D, corrections ofcr II, $35,100
Blank, Troy L, corrections ofcr III, $34,356
Blanke, Verla E, acad tchr III, $38,232
Blankenship, Anthony D, corrections ofcr I, $29,652
Blankenship, Gaithel A, corrections ofcr I, $29,652
Blankenship, Joshua P, corrections ofcr I, $28,692
Blankenship, Nakisha L, prob & parole ofcr I, $29,976
Blankenship, Rhonda M, prob & parole ofcr II, $36,204
Blankenship, Rosalyn R, corrections ofcr I, $29,652
Blankenship, William, corrections ofcr I, $28,692
Blank-parmeley, Shanna K, prob & parole ofcr II, $36,204
Blanton, Troy D, corrections ofcr I, $29,652
Blasingain, Travis C, corrections ofcr I, $28,692
Blaylock, Jody B, corrections ofcr I, $29,652
Bleau, Ronald J, storekeeper II, $28,104
Bleazard, Andre M, maint spv I, $32,628
Bleazard, Paula L, ofc spt asst (keybrd), $23,160
Bledsoe, Nancy S, corrections mgr b1, $49,757
Blegen, Michael A, prob & parole asst II, $38,232
Bleigh, Gregory L, corrections ofcr I, $29,652
Bliesath, Jessica M, prob & parole ofcr II, $36,204
Bliss, Robert B, corrections ofcr III, $33,744
Blissett, Adrain M, corrections ofcr II, $31,668
Blissett-smith, Linda C, corrections ofcr I, $29,652
Blizzard, Kevin R, corrections ofcr I, $29,652
Bloate, Debora A, prob & parole asst I, $29,496
Block, David J, phys plant sup I, $38,232
Blocker, Craig A, functional unit mgr corr, $45,156
Blocker, Diana R, prob & parole ofcr II, $36,204
Blodgett, Randall I, corrections ofcr I, $31,140
Bloomer, Wanda J, corrections ofcr I, $29,652
Blount, Christopher J, prob & parole asst I, $29,496
Blount, Jeffery L, corrections ofcr I, $29,652
Blount, Marjorie D, corrections ofcr I, $28,692
Bluhm, Jerry D, corrections ofcr I, $29,652
Blum, Monty G, corrections ofcr I, $34,512
Blumenthal, Scott E, ofc spt asst (keybrd), $23,160
Blumhorst, Melanie, ofc spt asst (keybrd), $23,160
Blunt, David T, corrections ofcr I, $29,652
Blunt, Dennis H, corrections ofcr I, $29,652
Blunt, Tenika D, corrections ofcr I, $29,652
Blunt, Tyler J, corrections ofcr I, $29,652
Blythe, Morgan C, corrections ofcr I, $29,652
Boardman, Kevin T, corrections ofcr I, $29,652
Boatright, Henry W, corrections spv I, $38,928
Boatright, Kim, prob & parole ofcr II, $38,928
Boatright, Sarah M, prob & parole ofcr II, $34,944
Boatwright, Brett L, prob & parole ofcr II, $36,204
Bobzien-Wade, Donna J, cook II, $24,264
Bochantin, Matthew, prob & parole ofcr II, $36,204
Bock, Sarah L, corrections ofcr I, $28,692
Bockstruck, Tony A, corrections ofcr I, $29,652
Bode, Donald L, corrections ofcr I, $29,661
Bodimer, Larry E, corrections ofcr I, $29,652
Body, Betty J, food serv mgr II, $39,624
Body, Steven T, corrections ofcr I, $33,348
Boeckman, Dennis R, phys plant sup I, $38,928
Boeckman, Stefan W, corrections ofcr I, $29,652
Boehm, Amanda A, corrections ofcr I, $29,652
Boehmer, Curt L, corrections ofcr I, $29,652
Boesing, Bryan T, corrections ofcr III, $33,744
Boettcher, Tina M, corrections ofcr I, $30,276
Bogart, Andrew J, corrections ofcr I, $29,652
Bogeart, David R, corrections ofcr I, $29,652
Boggs, Daniel R, corrections ofcr II, $30,576
Boggs, Delmer R, corrections ofcr I, $29,652
Boggs, Mitchell R, corrections ofcr I, $31,140
Boggs, Teresa A, corrections ofcr I, $29,652
Boggs, Timothy D, maint spv I, $32,628
Bogue, Jeffrey E, prob & parole ofcr II, $36,204
Boguslaw, David L, corrections ofcr I, $29,652
Bohacik, Keith, ofc spt asst (keybrd), $23,160
Bohannon, April A, corrections ofcr I, $29,652
Bohling, John H, corrections ofcr I, $33,900
Bohlke, Nancy R, corrections ofcr I, $29,652
Bohnert, Angela C, prob & parole ofcr II, $36,204
Bohnert, George E, corrections ofcr I, $29,652

Bohning, Mary A, account clerk II, $25,824
Bohon, Celia M, cook II, $24,264
Bohonsky, Michelle L, corrections ofcr I, $29,652
Bohrn, Scott D, corrections ofcr I, $33,348
Bol, Adelia L, corrections ofcr I, $29,652
Boland, Robert J, corrections ofcr I, $28,692
Bolden, Amanda L, ofc spt asst (keybrd), $23,160
Bolden, Linda C, sr ofc spt asst (keybrd), $27,504
Boles, Troy E, corrections ofcr I, $29,652
Boley, Janet L, voc enter spv II, $33,744
Bolin, Korrie L, prob & parole ofcr II, $38,232
Bolin, Robert S, corrections ofcr I, $29,652
Bolinger, Louisa S, corrections mgr b2, $52,741
Bolling, Joseph G, corrections ofcr I, $28,692
Bollinger, Charles D, corrections ofcr I, $33,900
Bollinger, Gale E, corrections classif asst, $35,568
Bollinger, Kenneth W, corrections ofcr II, $33,900
Bolte, Jeffrey, corrections ofcr II, $31,668
Bolton, Dolores L, cook III, $29,496
Bommarito, Anthony V, corrections ofcr I, $29,652
Bonacker, Nancy A, corrections mgr b1, $51,678
Bond, Michael D, corrections ofcr I, $29,652
Bond, Thomas K, prob & parole asst II, $36,888
Bond, Twila T, corrections ofcr I, $29,652
Bonds, Diane, prob & parole ofcr II, $36,204
Bone, Daniel L, corrections ofcr I, $29,652
Bone, Kelly, prob & parole ofcr I, $37,548
Bone, Tommy R, corrections ofcr I, $29,652
Bonilla, Denise H, prob & parole ofcr II, $36,204
Bonner, Carolyn N, prob & parole ofcr II, $36,888
Bonnett, David, corrections ofcr I, $29,652
Bontz, Crystal D, cook II, $24,264
Bontz, Margie S, prob & parole unit spv, $48,156
Booher, Anthony K, prob & parole ofcr II, $41,172
Book, V J, account clerk II, $25,824
Booker, Donnie R, corrections ofcr I, $28,692
Booker, Jason E, corrections ofcr II, $31,668
Booker, Sondra J, admin ofc spt asst, $29,004
Boone, Jennifer S, ofc spt asst (keybrd), $23,160
Booth, Anita J, corrections recs ofcr III, $36,204
Boothe, Shirley A, corrections ofcr I, $29,652
Boots, Christopher J, corrections ofcr I, $29,652
Bordelon-Pearson, Robert J, corrections ofcr I, $29,652
Borden-Wheat, Kayla X, corrections ofcr I, $29,652
Boren, Bruce A, corrections ofcr I, $29,652
Boresi, Jay D, legal counsel, $45,450
Borghardt, Gary L, corrections ofcr I, $29,652
Borgmeyer, Jennifer R, sr ofc spt asst (keybrd), $25,824
Bork, Roger K, corrections ofcr I, $31,140
Bornhop, Blake S, corrections ofcr II, $30,576
Borron, Max L, stationary engr, $35,568
Borrowman, Bonnie R, corrections ofcr I, $29,652
Borrowman, Kenneth O, corrections ofcr I, $29,652
Borrowman, Ronnie L, corrections ofcr I, $29,652
Borske, Evelyn I, corrections case mgr II, $36,204
Borton, Leah D, corrections mgr b1, $48,775
Borts, Cynthia L, ofc spt asst (keybrd), $23,160
Boss, Melissa A, prob & parole ofcr II, $36,204
Bostwick-kenkel, Debra L, ofc spt asst (keybrd), $23,880
Boswell, David K, prob & parole ofcr II, $36,204
Bosworth, Jo E, corrections ofcr I, $30,132
Bothe, Michael L, corrections ofcr I, $28,692
Bothwell, John R, corrections ofcr I, $29,652
Botts, Angela R, corrections ofcr I, $28,692
Botts, Christopher R, recrtn ofcr II, $32,628
Botts, Julie A, ofc spt asst (keybrd), $23,160
Boucher, Christopher J, corrections ofcr I, $29,652
Bouge, Marla A, corrections ofcr I, $30,132
Boulger, Beverly J, ofc spt asst (keybrd), $23,160
Boulware, Dean L, maint spv I, $32,628
Bouman, Mary C, corrections mgr b1, $51,856
Bounds, Kasi M, corrections ofcr I, $28,692
Bourn, Kristen, prob & parole ofcr I, $29,976
Bourne, Caleb J, corrections ofcr I, $29,652
Bourrage, Valerie, ofc spt asst (keybrd), $23,160
Bowe, John M, corrections ofcr I, $29,652
Bowen, Aaron M, corrections ofcr I, $28,692
Bowen, Cheryl L, prob & parole ofcr II, $36,204
Bowen, Laura L, ofc spt asst (keybrd), $23,160
Bowen, Lori M, corrections case mgr II, $34,944
Bowen, Megan E, corrections ofcr I, $28,692
Bowen, Tate A, corrections ofcr I, $29,652
Bower, Philip M, corrections ofcr II, $31,668

Bowers, Casey L, corrections ofcr I, $28,692
Bowers, Kimberly N, corrections ofcr II, $31,668
Bowers, Linda J, corrections ofcr I, $31,140
Bowers, Michael K, maint spv II, $37,548
Bowersox, Michael S, corrections mgr b3, $77,557
Bowersox, Rodney S, corrections ofcr II, $34,512
Bowes, Jeremy D, maint worker II, $29,496
Bowlin, Rocky S, corrections ofcr I, $29,652
Bowling, Donald C, correctional worker, $13.96/hr
Bowman, Daniel R, corrections ofcr I, $29,652
Bowyer, Tamara S, corrections recs ofcr III, $36,204
Bowyer, William S, corrections mgr b1, $47,881
Box, Nathan F, corrections ofcr I, $29,652
Boyce, David R, corrections ofcr I, $31,140
Boyd, Angelica D, inst activity coor, $32,628
Boyd, Ashley M, ofc spt asst (keybrd), $23,160
Boyd, Derris D, prob & parole ofcr II, $39,624
Boyd, Farrah L, corrections ofcr I, $29,652
Boyd, Jocelyn R, corrections ofcr I, $29,652
Boyd, Linda M, account clerk II, $28,908
Boyd, Michael L, corrections case mgr I, $31,512
Boyd, Patricia G, corrections ofcr I, $30,132
Boyd, Rebecca S, corrections ofcr I, $30,132
Boyd, Vickie, prob & parole ofcr II, $36,204
Boyer, Brian J, corrections case mgr II, $34,944
Boyer, Cheryl Y, corrections ofcr I, $29,652
Boyer, Colbey J, corrections ofcr I, $29,652
Boyer, David P, subs abuse cnslr II, $34,944
Boyer, Jacqueline K, corrections mgr b1, $41,605
Boyer, John, corrections ofcr I, $29,652
Boyer, Kathleen A, acad tchr III, $37,548
Boyer, Kathleen M, food serv mgr II, $33,744
Boyer, Stacy G, sr ofc spt asst (keybrd), $25,824
Boyer, Tara J, prob & parole unit spv, $43,488
Boyet, Jaron D, corrections ofcr I, $29,652
Boyet, Tina A, corrections ofcr I, $29,652
Boylan, Sandra E, corrections ofcr I, $29,652
Boyle, Dylan T, corrections ofcr I, $29,652
Boyle, Joshua S, corrections ofcr I, $29,652
Boyles, Alana C, corrections mgr b3, $62,081
Boyles, Ellen Y, corrections ofcr I, $29,652
Boze, Patrick W, corrections ofcr II, $31,668
Brack, Thomas C, subs abuse cnslr II, $34,944
Bracken, Carol D, labor spv, $29,412
Bradford, Kerri K, corrections ofcr I, $29,652
Bradford, Lillian C, corrections ofcr II, $33,348
Bradhurst, Nelson W, maint worker II, $30,420
Bradley, Brianna C, subs abuse cnslr I, $30,984
Bradley, Carolyn K, corrections ofcr I, $31,140
Bradley, James E, corrections ofcr I, $29,652
Bradley, Jason C, corrections ofcr I, $29,652
Bradley, Jeffry L, corrections ofcr II, $35,724
Bradley, Nicki S, cook II, $23,508
Bradley, Steven D, corrections ofcr III, $33,744
Bradshaw, Eric V, corrections ofcr I, $29,652
Bradshaw, Eunice M, ofc spt asst (keybrd), $24,264
Bradshaw, Johnnie L, corrections ofcr I, $29,652
Brady, Daniel T, corrections ofcr I, $29,652
Brady, Huston, prob & parole ofcr II, $34,944
Brady, Lonnie G, corrections ofcr I, $29,652
Brady, Thomas M, corrections ofcr I, $29,652
Brady, Thomas P, corrections ofcr I, $31,140
Brakefield, Sherry L, acad tchr III, $36,204
Bramblett, Devin D, prob & parole ofcr II, $36,204
Brammer, Larry E, corrections ofcr I, $32,784
Brammer, Timothy A, maint spv II, $36,888
Branch, Karen A, pers clerk, $28,104
Branch, Tara J, corrections ofcr I, $29,652
Brand, Douglas R, corrections ofcr I, $29,652
Brandl, Linda A, ofc spt asst (steno), $27,084
Brandon, David L, corrections ofcr I, $29,652
Brandt, Andrew C, prob & parole ofcr II, $36,888
Brandt, Joel A, cook III, $27,228
Brandt, Rebecca C, account clerk II, $25,824
Brannum, Carl, corrections ofcr II, $31,668
Brannum, Lola A, corrections ofcr I, $29,652
Brannum, Marvin L, corrections classif asst, $33,744
Bransford, Juanita, ofc spt asst (keybrd), $23,160
Branson, Alexis L, ofc spt asst (keybrd), $23,160
Branson, Curt A, prob & parole ofcr II, $36,204
Branson, Denice, sr ofc spt asst (keybrd), $28,452
Branson, Floyd, corrections ofcr I, $31,668
Branson, Timothy C, voc enter spv II, $32,628

Branstetter, Amanda G, ofc spt asst (keybrd), $23,160
Branstetter, James A, cook II, $24,264
Branstetter, Julia A, inst activity coor, $32,052
Branstetter, Kelly A, prob & parole ofcr II, $40,380
Brashear, Timothy J, corrections ofcr I, $28,692
Brashers, Carla C, corrections ofcr II, $31,668
Brashers, James D, corrections ofcr II, $31,668
Braswell, Sterling, corrections case mgr II, $36,888
Braswell, Warren H, corrections ofcr I, $31,140
Bratton, Isreal A, corrections ofcr I, $31,140
Bratton, Katherine S, prob & parole ofcr II, $36,204
Brauner, Patrick C, corrections ofcr I, $29,652
Bravo, William E, corrections ofcr II, $35,100
Brawley, Anna L, corrections ofcr II, $31,668
Brawley, Carl E, corrections ofcr II, $31,668
Brawley, Marvin R, corrections ofcr II, $31,668
Brawley, Travis S, corrections ofcr I, $29,652
Brayton, Joseph M, maint spv I, $32,628
Breakfield, George M, corrections ofcr I, $29,652
Breckenridge, John M, corrections ofcr I, $29,652
Breeden, Cathy A, corrections ofcr II, $33,348
Breeden, Danny R, corrections ofcr I, $29,652
Breeding, Jesse A, corrections ofcr II, $30,576
Breedon, Stacey D, prob & parole ofcr II, $38,232
Breeze, Terry D, corrections ofcr I, $31,668
Brendel, Sarah A, pers clerk, $30,420
Brenizer, Nancy M, corrections ofcr II, $31,668
Brenneke, Chad M, corrections ofcr I, $29,652
Brenneke, Jeffrey A, maint spv II, $35,568
Breshears, Cynthia J, storekeeper I, $25,824
Bresnahan, Kimberly A, special asst prof, $41,923
Bresnahan, William H, corrections case mgr II, $34,944
Brewer, Christopher E, corrections spv II, $43,488
Brewer, Hugh D, acad tchr III, $37,548
Brewer, Janet L, ofc spt asst (keybrd), $23,160
Brewer, Joshua T, corrections ofcr I, $29,652
Brewer, Lynda K, ofc spt asst (keybrd), $24,264
Brewer, Thomas L, electronics tech, $30,984
Brewer, Truman E, corrections ofcr I, $30,276
Bricker, Tracy Y, voc enter spv II, $29,976
Bricker, William R, tractor trailer driver, $30,984
Bridgeman, Barbara J, sr ofc spt asst (keybrd), $27,084
Bridges, Gale L, prob & parole ofcr II, $36,204
Bridges, Jonathan R, corrections ofcr I, $29,652
Bridwell, Misty L, corrections ofcr I, $29,652
Briesacher, Matthew B, legal counsel, $76,255
Brigance, Thomas W, corrections ofcr I, $31,140
Briggs, Hannah J, subs abuse cnslr II, $33,744
Briggs-Ray, Joaquin M, corrections ofcr I, $31,140
Brightwell, Jeremy W, corrections ofcr I, $29,652
Brill, Anthony M, corrections ofcr II, $31,668
Brimer, Jared M, corrections ofcr I, $29,652
Brink, Kristi L, ofc spt asst (keybrd), $22,536
Brinkley, Larry W, corrections ofcr III, $33,744
Brinkley, Shawn M, corrections ofcr I, $29,652
Brinkley, Shelby K, corrections ofcr I, $29,652
Brinkley, Timothy J, corrections ofcr I, $29,652
Brinkman, Treasa M, subs abuse cnslr II, $33,744
Brinton, Anthony M, corrections ofcr I, $29,652
Briones, Bryan S, corrections ofcr I, $30,276
Brister, Haskell B, prob & parole ofcr I, $31,512
Bristol, Christina M, ofc spt asst (keybrd), $23,160
Bristow, V L, prob & parole ofcr II, $40,380
Britt, Cammy L, prob & parole ofcr I, $39,624
Britton, Gary S, corrections ofcr I, $29,652
Brix, Garry E, special asst prof, $41,414
Brizendine, Thomas M, corrections ofcr III, $36,204
Broaden, Julie M, prob & parole ofcr II, $36,204
Broadway, Barbara, cook III, $28,104
Broadway, Jason D, corrections ofcr I, $29,652
Broadway, Kristina L, corrections case mgr II, $34,944
Brock, Justin R, corrections ofcr I, $28,692
Brockman, Brandice, corrections ofcr I, $29,652
Brockmeyer, Kim, ofc spt asst (keybrd), $23,160
Brody, Julia M, corrections ofcr I, $29,652
Brody, Phyllis J, ofc spt asst (keybrd), $23,160
Brody, Robert L, corrections ofcr II, $31,668
Broleman, Theresa A, prob & parole unit spv, $46,068
Bromley, Miranda J, cook II, $24,264
Bromley, Thomas L, corrections ofcr I, $29,652
Bromwich, Allen K, corrections ofcr I, $29,652
Bronakowski, Jill M, acad tchr III, $37,548
Bronakowski, John J, corrections ofcr II, $30,576

Brondel, Brian J, corrections ofcr I, $29,652
Brondel, Cora L, corrections ofcr I, $29,652
Brondel, Jay J, recrtn ofcr II, $37,548
Brooke, Benjamin D, functional unit mgr corr, $38,928
Brooks, Doris V, librarian II, $34,356
Brooks, Jennifer K, prob & parole ofcr II, $36,204
Brooks, Jeremy K, corrections training ofcr, $38,928
Brooks, Londa, ofc spt asst (keybrd), $23,160
Brooks, Michael A, corrections ofcr I, $29,652
Brooks, Ryan A, corrections ofcr I, $29,652
Brooks, Ryan P, corrections ofcr I, $29,652
Brooks, Samantha, prob & parole ofcr II, $34,944
Brooks, Terek, prob & parole asst II, $30,420
Brothers, Robert W, corrections training ofcr, $39,624
Brothers, Shari L, exec II, $34,944
Brouk, Steven D, corrections ofcr I, $29,652
Broussard, Amy D, prob & parole ofcr II, $36,204
Browers, Baretta E, corrections ofcr I, $29,652
Browers, Jimmy D, corrections ofcr I, $30,132
Browers, Joshua, corrections ofcr I, $29,652
Browers, Mark S, corrections ofcr III, $38,928
Browers, Monique R, admin ofc spt asst, $28,104
Brown, Alaina N, corrections ofcr I, $29,652
Brown, Anthony L, prob & parole ofcr I, $30,984
Brown, Ashlee N, corrections recs ofcr I, $28,104
Brown, Ashley N, corrections ofcr I, $29,652
Brown, Beverly J, prob & parole ofcr II, $37,548
Brown, Brandon D, corrections ofcr I, $29,652
Brown, Carole L, special educ tchr III, $38,928
Brown, Cedric K, corrections ofcr I, $28,692
Brown, Channa N, prob & parole ofcr II, $38,232
Brown, Charles A, corrections ofcr II, $35,724
Brown, Charles T, corrections ofcr I, $29,652
Brown, Christopher A, corrections mgr b1, $48,149
Brown, Dakota W, corrections ofcr I, $29,652
Brown, Daniel J, corrections ofcr II, $35,724
Brown, Danielle N, corrections ofcr I, $28,692
Brown, David G, fire & safety spec, $30,984
Brown, David L, corrections ofcr I, $29,652
Brown, Denise Y, corrections ofcr I, $31,140
Brown, Donald L, corrections ofcr I, $28,692
Brown, Donna R, corrections ofcr II, $33,348
Brown, Dwight J, corrections case mgr II, $40,380
Brown, Gary A, stationary engr, $37,548
Brown, Greg A, phys plant sup III, $47,892
Brown, Heather M, prob & parole asst I, $28,536
Brown, Helena, prob & parole ofcr I, $29,976
Brown, James E, prob & parole unit spv, $43,488
Brown, James M, corrections ofcr I, $29,652
Brown, Janet C, cook II, $24,264
Brown, Janet M, corrections ofcr I, $28,692
Brown, Jeffrey T, boiler oper, $28,104
Brown, Jennifra M, corrections ofcr I, $29,652
Brown, Jeremiah W, corrections ofcr I, $29,652
Brown, Jesse D, corrections ofcr I, $29,652
Brown, Jim C, corrections ofcr I, $28,692
Brown, Jim E, corrections ofcr III, $35,568
Brown, Joseph E, corrections case mgr I, $29,976
Brown, Joy V, prob & parole asst I, $30,984
Brown, Kasha-Marie A, corrections ofcr I, $29,652
Brown, Katherine E, corrections ofcr I, $29,652
Brown, Keandria C, prob & parole ofcr II, $36,204
Brown, Kristina R, ofc spt asst (steno), $26,232
Brown, Larry R, corrections ofcr I, $30,276
Brown, Laura Denise A, cook II, $23,508
Brown, Lindsay D, corrections ofcr I, $29,652
Brown, Lori E, prob & parole ofcr II, $39,624
Brown, Lori L, corrections case mgr II, $36,888
Brown, Mark, corrections ofcr I, $29,652
Brown, Mary A, prob & parole ofcr II, $36,204
Brown, Mechelle L, prob & parole ofcr II, $36,204
Brown, Michael L, supply mgr II, $41,940
Brown, Michael L, corrections ofcr I, $29,652
Brown, Michael R, corrections ofcr II, $31,668
Brown, Michael W, corrections ofcr I, $34,512
Brown, Randy O, stationary engr, $33,744
Brown, Rhonda L, ofc spt asst (keybrd), $24,264
Brown, Richard D, corrections ofcr I, $29,652
Brown, Samuel E, corrections ofcr I, $30,132
Brown, Seddrix, corrections ofcr I, $28,692
Brown, Steven D, corrections ofcr I, $29,652
Brown, Steven K, corrections ofcr I, $31,668
Brown, Ted R, maint spv I, $36,888

Brown, Terrell, corrections ofcr I, $29,652
Brown, Timothy J, corrections ofcr I, $29,652
Brown, Timothy L, corrections ofcr II, $31,668
Brown, Timothy T, corrections ofcr I, $29,652
Brown, Tracy L, prob & parole ofcr II, $39,624
Brown, Travis L, corrections ofcr III, $33,744
Brown, Zachary T, corrections case mgr II, $34,944
Brownfield, Tammy D, ofc spt asst (keybrd), $24,264
Brownfield, Wanda F, corrections ofcr II, $33,348
Brownfield, Wayne A, corrections ofcr I, $29,652
Browning, Allen R, prob & parole asst I, $29,496
Browning, Christopher, corrections case mgr II, $36,204
Browning, Jesse A, corrections ofcr I, $28,692
Browning, Laurel A, ofc spt asst (keybrd), $23,160
Browning, Mark E, corrections case mgr II, $35,568
Brownlee, Christopher B, corrections spv I, $38,232
Brownlee, Kelley E, corrections ofcr I, $31,140
Brownlow, Ryan F, corrections mgr b1, $40,876
Brownsberger, Mary B, ofc spt asst (keybrd), $23,160
Broyles, Hugh R, prob & parole ofcr II, $39,624
Bruce, Alice, prob & parole ofcr II, $34,944
Bruce, Brandi L, ofc spt asst (keybrd), $23,160
Bruce, Denise H, corrections mgr b1, $49,104
Bruce, Kelly, corrections ofcr I, $29,652
Brugger, Christina, prob & parole ofcr II, $39,624
Brune, Michael R, corrections ofcr I, $29,652
Brunkhorst, Darren K, corrections ofcr II, $30,576
Brunner, Michael E, prob & parole ofcr II, $36,204
Brunner, Michael S, storekeeper II, $28,104
Bruns, Kevin S, maint spv II, $34,944
Bryan, Andrew P, corrections ofcr I, $29,652
Bryan, Claude M, maint spv I, $32,628
Bryan, Daniel W, functional unit mgr corr, $38,928
Bryan, Isaac B, corrections ofcr I, $29,652
Bryan, Kevin, prob & parole asst I, $29,496
Bryan, Lori N, prob & parole ofcr II, $36,204
Bryan, Timothy A, corrections ofcr I, $28,692
Bryant, Andrew J, corrections ofcr I, $28,692
Bryant, Cody R, corrections ofcr III, $33,744
Bryant, Jacqulyn E, corrections ofcr II, $30,576
Bryant, Kenny A, phys plant sup II, $38,928
Bryant, Treecia L, prob & parole unit spv, $41,940
Bryson, Christine I, corrections ofcr I, $29,652
Buchanan, Colleena M, corrections ofcr I, $29,652
Buchanan, Neva J, corrections spv I, $37,548
Bucher, Daniel R, corrections ofcr I, $28,692
Bucher, Sharon, corrections spv I, $42,708
Buchholz, Karen A, ofc spt asst (keybrd), $25,032
Buck, John P, corrections mgr b1, $46,931
Buck, Monroe, cook II, $26,232
Buck, Ronald L, corrections ofcr I, $29,652
Buckallew, Kenneth J, corrections ofcr I, $28,692
Buckingham, Ronnie D, corrections ofcr I, $29,652
Buckley, Amee E, corrections ofcr I, $28,692
Buckley, Donald E, corrections spv I, $42,708
Buckman, Daryn S, corrections ofcr I, $29,652
Buckman, Tyler B, prob & parole ofcr II, $36,204
Buck-Morgan, Wilma, ofc spt asst (keybrd), $11,580
Buckner, Dustin L, locksmith, $32,628
Buckner, Dwight E, corrections ofcr II, $31,668
Buckner, Ladonna M, corrections mgr b1, $42,852
Buckner, Thomas E, corrections ofcr I, $29,652
Bucksath, Jennifer M, prob & parole ofcr II, $39,624
Buechter, Dale J, factory mgr II, $38,928
Buechter, John L, cook II, $24,264
Buechter, Joseph A, factory mgr I, $34,944
Buechter, Luke J, stationary engr, $38,232
Buechter, Stephen E, voc enter dist supv, $36,888
Buehrlen, Von W, corrections ofcr I, $29,652
Bueker, William J, corrections ofcr I, $29,652
Buell, John, corrections ofcr II, $30,576
Buerck, Charles P, corrections mgr b1, $45,162
Buerky, Matthew R, recrtn ofcr I, $30,420
Buffington, Jordan L, corrections ofcr I, $29,652
Bufford, Gregory S, corrections ofcr I, $29,652
Buford, Charles D, corrections case mgr II, $40,380
Buhler, Susan G, corrections ofcr I, $29,652
Buholt, Terry W, subs abuse cnslr II, $34,944
Buhs, Steven R, corrections case mgr II, $34,944
Buie, Chris D, functional unit mgr corr, $42,708
Bull, Michael C, corrections ofcr I, $29,652
Bullard, Christian N, corrections ofcr I, $29,652
Bulson, Amanda R, corrections ofcr I, $29,652

Bumgardner, Shelbie L, corrections ofcr I, $29,652
Bunch, David L, prob & parole ofcr II, $36,204
Bunch, Kimberly G, corrections ofcr I, $31,140
Bunch, Ricky L, corrections ofcr I, $29,652
Bundy, Donald E, corrections ofcr I, $29,652
Bunfill, Ryan D, corrections ofcr I, $29,652
Bunker, Haley N, prob & parole ofcr I, $30,984
Bunnell, Michael S, corrections ofcr I, $28,692
Bunton, Donald M, corrections spv I, $42,708
Bunton, E R, corrections ofcr I, $29,652
Bunton, Melanie H, subs abuse cnslr II, $34,944
Buol, Meagan E, prob & parole ofcr II, $38,232
Burch, Charles E, storekeeper II, $28,104
Burch, Christopher M, prob & parole ofcr II, $36,204
Burch, Eric L, functional unit mgr corr, $44,304
Burch, Gregory, prob & parole ofcr I, $30,984
Burch, Lisa M, sr ofc spt asst (keybrd), $25,824
Burch, Mickey L, corrections ofcr I, $29,652
Burch, Shawn C, corrections ofcr I, $29,652
Burcham, Dustin M, corrections ofcr I, $28,692
Burcham, Rebecca, prob & parole ofcr II, $36,204
Burchard, Scott D, prob & parole ofcr II, $36,204
Burchett, Christopher M, corrections ofcr I, $29,652
Burchett, Stephanie A, prob & parole ofcr II, $37,548
Burd, Bradley K, corrections case mgr II, $36,204
Burgener, Sherry L, corrections ofcr I, $29,652
Burger, Bradley W, prob & parole unit spv, $45,156
Burger, Brenda K, prob & parole ofcr II, $41,940
Burgess, Adam C, corrections ofcr I, $28,692
Burgess, David L, corrections ofcr I, $31,140
Burgess, James D, corrections ofcr I, $30,132
Burgess, Karen, prob & parole ofcr II, $36,204
Burgess, Tony D, corrections ofcr I, $29,652
Burgett, Rhonda L, prob & parole ofcr II, $39,624
Burgett, Steven M, corrections ofcr I, $29,652
Burk, Lori J, corrections mgr b1, $47,876
Burkard, Ryan T, corrections ofcr I, $29,652
Burkdoll, Amanda K, corrections case mgr I, $29,976
Burkdoll, Johnny L, corrections spv I, $45,156
Burke, Brett J, corrections training ofcr, $41,172
Burke, Bruce M, factory mgr I, $38,928
Burke, Kelley J, prob & parole ofcr III, $43,488
Burke, Rose M, corrections ofcr I, $31,140
Burkemper, Jill K, prob & parole unit spv, $41,940
Burkemper, Todd M, corrections ofcr I, $29,652
Burkert, Anna M, corrections ofcr I, $31,668
Burkeybile, Robin J, corrections ofcr I, $29,652
Burlage, Michael L, corrections ofcr I, $29,652
Burlage, Robert F, corrections spv I, $44,304
Burleigh, Steven M, corrections ofcr I, $29,652
Burleson, Melissa J, ofc spt asst (keybrd), $23,160
Burleson, William M, corrections ofcr II, $31,668
Burlison, Andrew J, corrections ofcr I, $29,652
Burnett, Cynthia, sr ofc spt asst (keybrd), $25,032
Burnett, James D, corrections ofcr I, $31,140
Burnett, Lauren A, corrections ofcr I, $28,692
Burnett, Michael J, corrections ofcr I, $31,140
Burnett, Nancy E, ofc spt asst (keybrd), $24,264
Burnett, Odessa, ofc spt asst (keybrd), $23,160
Burnett, Pamela S, prob & parole ofcr II, $39,624
Burnett, Randy C, corrections mgr b1, $48,781
Burnett, Tara, prob & parole ofcr I, $29,976
Burnette, Barbara A, prob & parole ofcr II, $41,940
Burns, Christopher L, corrections ofcr I, $30,576
Burns, Cynthia A, corrections ofcr I, $28,692
Burns, Donna K, cook II, $24,264
Burns, Donna M, corrections spv I, $40,380
Burns, Ellen L, cook III, $28,104
Burns, Michael L, locksmith, $29,976
Burns, Rachel N, corrections ofcr I, $29,652
Burns, Ryan E, corrections ofcr I, $31,140
Burns, Shannan, prob & parole asst II, $31,512
Burns, Tina R, corrections ofcr II, $31,668
Burris, Jonathan T, corrections ofcr I, $29,652
Burris, Roger G, prob & parole asst I, $29,496
Burris, Timothy, corrections mgr b2, $53,034
Burroughs, Betsy M, prob & parole ofcr II, $36,888
Burrow, Brandon, corrections ofcr I, $28,692
Burt, Keith A, corrections ofcr I, $31,140
Burtnett, Karen D, corrections ofcr II, $35,724
Burton, Arthur W, corrections ofcr I, $29,652
Burton, Carol A, corrections ofcr I, $31,140
Burton, James C, prob & parole ofcr II, $36,888

Burton, Phillip W, corrections ofcr I, $29,652
Burton, Rejeana F, sr ofc spt asst (clerical), $27,948
Burton, Roger E, prob & parole asst II, $32,052
Burton, Trevor H, corrections ofcr I, $28,692
Buschman, Angela M, corrections ofcr I, $29,652
Buschman, Paul A, corrections ofcr I, $29,652
Bush, Brittany, ofc spt asst (keybrd), $22,536
Bush, Margaret L, sr ofc spt asst (keybrd), $26,652
Bush, Ronnie D, corrections ofcr I, $29,652
Bushery, Emily K, corrections ofcr I, $29,652
Bushnell, Glenda, ofc spt asst (keybrd), $23,160
Busken, Michelle R, prob & parole ofcr II, $36,204
Buss, Andrew G, corrections ofcr I, $30,132
Buss, Marilyn S, functional unit mgr corr, $44,304
Bussio, Darold L, corrections ofcr I, $29,652
Buster, Vicki S, corrections recs ofcr I, $28,104
Buswell, Tracy J, ofc spt asst (keybrd), $23,880
Butcher, Doug L, corrections ofcr I, $29,652
Butcher, Elizabeth M, prob & parole ofcr II, $40,380
Butler, Donald L, corrections ofcr I, $29,652
Butler, Jadonna A, subs abuse cnslr II, $38,928
Butler, Joshua, corrections ofcr I, $29,652
Butler, Kristi L, prob & parole ofcr II, $36,204
Butler, Richard A, corrections ofcr I, $29,652
Butler, Shandra A, corrections ofcr I, $29,652
Butler, Tom D, corrections ofcr I, $29,652
Butler, Willie L, corrections ofcr I, $29,652
Butterworth, Alan R, functional unit mgr corr, $38,928
Buttz, Rodney E, prob & parole asst I, $29,496
Buxton, Christina L, correctional worker, $26,400
Buzbee, Danielle, prob & parole ofcr II, $36,888
Buzzard, James H, corrections ofcr I, $31,140
Byassee, Michael O, cook II, $24,264
Bybee, Ronnie W, corrections ofcr I, $31,140
Bycraft, Tylor J, corrections ofcr I, $28,692
Bye, Robert E, storekeeper I, $25,824
Bye, William L, storekeeper II, $28,104
Byerley, Lucas J, corrections ofcr I, $28,692
Byers, Jennifer M, prob & parole ofcr II, $39,624
Byington, Earl K, corrections ofcr I, $29,652
Byington, Sheri, corrections ofcr III, $34,356
Byland, Phyllis, misc prof, $19.41/hr
Byler, Bryan W, prob & parole ofcr I, $36,204
Bynum, Gail M, prob & parole unit spv, $44,304
Bynum, Kathleen J, corrections case mgr II, $36,888
Byram, Kenneth R, corrections spv I, $36,888
Byram, Lana S, recrtn ofcr I, $31,512
Byrd, Amy J, corrections ofcr I, $29,652
Byrd, David W, corrections ofcr I, $31,140
Byrd, Mary J, ofc spt asst (keybrd), $23,160
Caban, Michelle L, ofc spt asst (keybrd), $23,160
Caby, Ginger K, storekeeper II, $28,104
Caddell, David L, corrections ofcr I, $31,140
Cade, Carmela L, corrections ofcr I, $30,132
Cade, Mitchell L, corrections ofcr I, $28,692
Cage, Janet L, prob & parole ofcr II, $41,940
Cage, Jennifer G, prob & parole ofcr II, $36,204
Cagle, Kirby A, prob & parole ofcr II, $36,204
Cahalin, Michael C, corrections ofcr III, $36,204
Cahill, Kimberly D, cook II, $23,508
Cain, Amanda G, corrections ofcr I, $28,692
Cain, Andrew C, corrections ofcr II, $31,668
Cain, Dennis J, special asst official & admstr, $46,460
Cain, Douglas R, corrections ofcr II, $31,668
Cain, Eric S, maint worker II, $29,004
Cain, James D, maint spv I, $32,628
Cain, Jerry A, corrections ofcr I, $29,652
Cain, John E, prob & parole asst I, $29,496
Cain, Mable L, special asst ofc & clerical, $22,520
Cain, Nicholas D, corrections ofcr I, $28,692
Cain, Ricky L, corrections ofcr I, $29,652
Cain, Roxanne T, corrections ofcr I, $31,140
Cain, Spencer D, maint spv I, $32,628
Cain, Tina M, corrections ofcr I, $29,652
Cain, Tommy D, corrections ofcr III, $35,568
Calaway, Margaret S, corrections ofcr I, $33,348
Caldwell, Anthony R, corrections ofcr I, $29,652
Caldwell, Bradley R, corrections ofcr I, $28,692
Caldwell, Misty R, corrections ofcr I, $29,652
Calhoun, Patricia A, corrections ofcr I, $29,652
Calhoun, Wendall L, functional unit mgr corr, $41,172
Call, Janice A, exec II, $40,380
Call, Lance E, cook III, $30,984

Callahan, Erin D, prob & parole ofcr II, $36,204
Callahan, James J, corrections ofcr I, $29,652
Callen, Robert L, corrections ofcr I, $29,652
Calonne, Kevin, corrections ofcr I, $29,652
Calvert, Brenda L, corrections spv I, $40,380
Calvert, Everett L, corrections training ofcr, $40,380
Calvert, Nicholas A, cook II, $24,264
Calvin, Adam L, recrtn ofcr I, $30,420
Calvin, Bryce A, corrections ofcr I, $29,652
Calvird, Deborah A, storekeeper I, $25,824
Camarador, Willie L, exec II, $36,204
Camden, Bryan T, corrections ofcr I, $29,652
Camden, Randy L, corrections ofcr III, $44,304
Camden, Raymond M, corrections ofcr I, $29,652
Camden, Sandra L, admin ofc spt asst, $28,104
Cameron, Michael A, corrections ofcr I, $29,652
Cameron, Timothy D, prob & parole ofcr II, $38,232
Camp, Amanda R, prob & parole ofcr II, $36,204
Camp, Devin L, corrections ofcr I, $28,692
Campanelli, Charles A, maint spv II, $34,944
Campbell, Alexander R, corrections ofcr I, $29,652
Campbell, Catherine L, sr ofc spt asst (keybrd), $27,504
Campbell, Charles A, corrections ofcr I, $33,348
Campbell, Charles L, corrections ofcr I, $29,652
Campbell, Charles M, corrections ofcr I, $29,652
Campbell, David H, corrections ofcr I, $28,692
Campbell, Dustan Y, prob & parole ofcr II, $36,204
Campbell, Frank T, corrections ofcr II, $33,348
Campbell, Gloria L, corrections ofcr I, $29,652
Campbell, James F, correctional worker, $26,400
Campbell, James R, prob & parole ofcr II, $38,232
Campbell, John L, corrections ofcr II, $30,576
Campbell, Joseph E, cook III, $28,104
Campbell, Joshua, cook II, $23,508
Campbell, Linda K, prob & parole ofcr II, $36,204
Campbell, Mary A, corrections ofcr I, $29,652
Campbell, Richard L, fire & safety spec, $34,944
Campbell, Sonia L, corrections case mgr II, $34,944
Campbell, Whitney, prob & parole ofcr I, $29,976
Cane, Dakota L, prob & parole asst I, $29,496
Cannady, August J, corrections ofcr I, $28,692
Cannon, Bryan K, prob & parole asst I, $29,496
Cannon, Connie L, corrections ofcr I, $29,652
Cannon, Jeremy A, corrections ofcr I, $29,652
Cantoni, David J, corrections ofcr I, $29,652
Cantrell, Bobby J, corrections ofcr I, $29,652
Cantrell, Bradley J, corrections ofcr I, $29,652
Cantrell, Edward B, corrections ofcr I, $29,652
Cantrell, Jeremy H, prob & parole ofcr II, $37,548
Cantrell, Kendra S, investigator I, $32,628
Cantrell, Lesley L, maint spv I, $32,628
Cantrell, Peggy S, corrections ofcr I, $29,652
Cantrell, Sherry D, ofc spt asst (keybrd), $23,160
Cantua, Mark E, maint spv I, $32,628
Capestro, Jeffrey J, corrections ofcr I, $29,652
Caples, Robert, corrections ofcr I, $33,348
Capps, Aaron W, prob & parole ofcr II, $38,232
Capps, Andrew C, corrections ofcr I, $35,100
Capps, Ronda N, prob & parole ofcr II, $36,204
Carder, Timothy R, corrections ofcr III, $33,744
Carey, Michael J, corrections ofcr I, $29,652
Carey, Zach M, corrections ofcr I, $28,692
Carignan, Dennis M, cook III, $30,984
Carlin, Matthew A, budget analyst II, $37,548
Carlisle, Lisa, account clerk II, $26,232
Carlson, Anthony, prob & parole ofcr I, $29,976
Carlton, Richard D, corrections ofcr I, $29,652
Carman, Linda L, prob & parole ofcr II, $39,624
Carmichael, Bruce W, corrections case mgr I, $30,984
Carmine, Jeffery M, corrections ofcr I, $28,692
Carmon, Penny E, acad tchr III, $37,548
Carnahan, Keyla K, ofc spt asst (keybrd), $23,160
Carnal, Myron L, prob & parole unit spv, $43,488
Carothers, Ernest E, corrections ofcr II, $31,668
Carothers, Sonny, voc enter spv I, $30,420
Carpenter, Cheryl A, corrections case mgr II, $38,928
Carpenter, Christy L, prob & parole unit spv, $45,156
Carpenter, Joey A, corrections ofcr I, $29,652
Carpenter, Jordan T, corrections ofcr I, $29,652
Carpenter, Michael L, prob & parole ofcr II, $39,624
Carpenter, Ronald W, prob & parole asst I, $29,496
Carper, Anthony F, corrections ofcr I, $29,652

Carr, Christopher M, corrections ofcr I, $28,692
Carr, David E, corrections ofcr I, $31,140
Carr, Jason H, driver, $14.86/hr
Carr, Jason T, prob & parole ofcr II, $34,944
Carr, Jeromy G, corrections spv I, $38,232
Carr, Patricia A, ofc spt asst (keybrd), $23,160
Carr, Sandra L, ofc spt asst (steno), $27,084
Carr, Sara J, corrections case mgr II, $34,944
Carrel, Helen I, exec II, $36,204
Carrier, Heather N, corrections ofcr I, $29,652
Carriker, Erin H, corrections ofcr I, $29,652
Carriker, Kathleen, prob & parole unit spv, $46,068
Carrillo, Pedro, corrections ofcr I, $29,652
Carroll, Alex C, corrections ofcr I, $29,652
Carroll, Derrick L, prob & parole ofcr II, $36,204
Carroll, Joseph N, corrections ofcr I, $29,652
Carroll, Kimberly G, prob & parole ofcr II, $36,204
Carroll, Robert A, corrections ofcr I, $29,652
Carsey, Leslie D, investigator II, $37,548
Carson, Cody L, corrections ofcr I, $28,692
Carson, Shelly L, training tech II, $44,304
Carter, Arnold R, sr ofc spt asst (keybrd), $27,504
Carter, Cody D, corrections ofcr I, $28,692
Carter, Don, cook III, $27,228
Carter, Jay L, corrections ofcr I, $29,652
Carter, Karen F, corrections case mgr II, $34,944
Carter, Marc E, prob & parole unit spv, $43,488
Carter, Mary L, corrections ofcr I, $29,652
Carter, Patrick J, corrections ofcr I, $29,652
Carter, Randy E, voc enter spv II, $30,984
Carter, Rhonda C, prob & parole ofcr II, $36,204
Carter, Shanyon K, prob & parole unit spv, $41,940
Carter, Shelley, prob & parole ofcr II, $36,204
Carter-Schackmann, Christopher A, corrections ofcr I, $30,276
Cartrette, Sandra G, corrections ofcr I, $29,652
Caruthers, Bethany I, corrections ofcr I, $29,652
Caruthers, James C, corrections ofcr I, $29,652
Carver, Michael J, corrections ofcr I, $29,652
Carver, Scott L, cook II, $24,264
Cary, David J, corrections ofcr I, $29,652
Cary, Tyrone, corrections ofcr I, $31,140
Case, Darrell D, corrections ofcr II, $32,220
Case, Evan B, corrections ofcr I, $28,692
Case, Evan B, maint spv I, $33,744
Case, Jacob A, corrections ofcr I, $28,692
Case, Travis D, storekeeper II, $29,496
Caselman, Heather S, corrections ofcr I, $29,652
Caselman, Susan E, corrections classif asst, $31,512
Caselman, Timothy C, corrections ofcr I, $29,652
Casey, Elizabeth L, sr ofc spt asst (keybrd), $25,824
Casey, Kelly D, prob & parole ofcr II, $36,204
Casey, Marie E, acad tchr III, $41,172
Cash, Martha G, storekeeper II, $29,496
Cashatt, James C, prob & parole ofcr II, $36,204
Casidy, William M, corrections ofcr II, $31,668
Casper, Randy L, corrections ofcr I, $31,140
Cassady, Barbara A, serv mgr II, $38,928
Cassady, Joseph L, corrections mgr b3, $66,438
Cassidy, Brad D, prob & parole asst I, $29,496
Cassidy, Brian, boiler oper, $28,104
Cassity, Carolyn J, corrections case mgr II, $34,944
Casteel, Kenneth R, cook III, $28,104
Castelli, Christine, prob & parole ofcr II, $38,232
Castillo, Teddi L, ofc spt asst (keybrd), $24,612
Castle, Bonnie K, cook II, $24,264
Caswell, Rickie R, corrections ofcr I, $31,678
Cates, Anthony L, corrections ofcr I, $28,692
Cathey, Gregory S, corrections ofcr I, $29,652
Caudle, Brad A, corrections ofcr I, $29,652
Caudle, Nancy J, corrections ofcr I, $33,900
Causey, Alberta K, ofc spt asst (keybrd), $23,160
Cavanaugh, Carol L, corrections ofcr I, $29,652
Cavanaugh, Mathew S, corrections ofcr I, $28,692
Cavender, Leila R, cook III, $28,104
Cavins, Justin J, corrections ofcr I, $29,652
Cayer, Donna Y, corrections mgr b2, $54,014
Cecil, David F, corrections ofcr I, $29,661
Cecil, Loretta S, corrections ofcr I, $29,652
Cecil, Rick J, corrections ofcr I, $29,652
Cecil, Steven A, corrections ofcr I, $29,652
Cephus, Joshua A, corrections ofcr I, $29,652
Cerny-Cordes, Tamara L, inst activity coor, $34,944
Chaffin, Heather, prob & parole ofcr II, $36,204

Chaidez, Danice M, exec II, $36,204
Chamberlain, Juanita, subs abuse cnslr III, $41,940
Chambers, Cathie M, corrections ofcr I, $29,652
Chambers, Jessica L, prob & parole ofcr II, $36,204
Chambers, Kellee M, prob & parole unit spv, $41,940
Chance, Jennifer J, corrections recs ofcr II, $30,984
Chandler, Ada S, ofc spt asst (clerical), $22,536
Chandler, Beverly, prob & parole ofcr II, $34,944
Chandler, Brian K, storekeeper II, $31,512
Chandler, David R, factory mgr I, $34,944
Chandler, Jill D, storekeeper II, $28,104
Chandler, Joshua E, corrections ofcr II, $31,668
Chandler, Norvella L, prob & parole ofcr II, $41,940
Chaplin, Mark A, corrections ofcr III, $35,568
Chapman, Amy E, ofc spt asst (keybrd), $23,160
Chapman, Becky S, prob & parole ofcr II, $36,204
Chapman, Cheryl M, cook III, $28,104
Chapman, Christopher A, maint worker II, $29,496
Chapman, Heather H, corrections mgr b1, $40,380
Chapman, John W, prob & parole ofcr II, $36,888
Chapman, Kenneth, special asst technician, $43,935
Chapman, Kenneth D, phys plant sup I, $36,204
Chapman, Marvin H, corrections ofcr III, $33,900
Chapman, Russ L, corrections ofcr I, $29,652
Chapman, Schaffer D, corrections ofcr I, $30,276
Chapman, William T, planner III, $45,156
Chapman-Mitchell, Julie A, prob & parole ofcr II, $36,204
Chappell, Howard E, maint spv I, $33,180
Charboneau, Anthony J, voc enter spv I, $27,228
Charleston, Ida A, corrections ofcr I, $29,652
Charlton, Anthony D, corrections ofcr I, $29,652
Charlton, Carmen, prob & parole ofcr II, $36,204
Charlton, John W, recrtn ofcr II, $33,744
Charlton, Matthew G, recrtn ofcr I, $30,984
Chase, Amy L, corrections ofcr I, $29,652
Chase, Brian W, corrections ofcr I, $31,140
Chase, Christopher R, corrections ofcr II, $31,668
Chastain, Kenneth W, corrections ofcr I, $29,652
Chastain, Kevin W, tractor trailer driver, $29,976
Chastain, Mishea L, corrections ofcr I, $28,692
Chatfield, Brooke M, corrections ofcr I, $28,692
Chatman, Jeffrey A, corrections ofcr I, $31,140
Chatman, Melinda M, corrections ofcr I, $28,692
Chatman, Tina C, corrections ofcr I, $28,692
Chatwell, Dawana E, subs abuse cnslr II, $34,944
Chauvin, Cozette A, corrections ofcr I, $29,652
Cheadle, Lashella R, corrections ofcr I, $28,692
Cheatham, Laura E, ofc spt asst (keybrd), $23,160
Chen, Tung W, corrections ofcr I, $29,652
Cheney, Clifton M, corrections ofcr I, $29,652
Cheney, Gina M, corrections ofcr I, $29,652
Chenoweth, Brooke N, corrections ofcr I, $29,652
Chenoweth, Terrie A, corrections ofcr I, $31,140
Cherico, Donald D, corrections ofcr I, $31,140
Cherry, Kim A, admin ofc spt asst, $28,104
Chester, Kyle C, corrections ofcr I, $29,652
Childers, Joshua D, corrections ofcr I, $28,692
Childers, Natashia L, account clerk II, $25,032
Childrey, Philip L, corrections ofcr I, $29,652
Childrey, Travis, corrections ofcr I, $29,652
Childs, Joseph A, electronics tech, $30,984
Chillers, Kimerly E, corrections case mgr II, $34,944
Chipman, Kyle, prob & parole ofcr I, $29,976
Chisenhall, Robert, prob & parole ofcr II, $36,204
Chishko, Cynthia A, corrections ofcr I, $29,652
Chism, Eldonna M, corrections ofcr I, $29,652
Chmielewski, Simone C, cook III, $28,104
Cholak, Thomas J, corrections ofcr I, $29,652
Chor, Amy L, corrections case mgr II, $36,888
Christensen, Ronald J, corrections spv I, $38,928
Christensen, Steven L, corrections training ofcr, $39,624
Christian, Anthony B, corrections case mgr II, $34,944
Christian, Daniel R, corrections ofcr I, $29,652
Christian, Howard L, special educ tchr III, $42,708
Christian, James A, corrections ofcr II, $33,348
Christian, Stacy L, corrections ofcr I, $29,652
Christianer, Mark L, prob & parole ofcr II, $36,204
Christians, Johannes, corrections ofcr I, $28,692
Christopher, Ashton M, corrections classif asst, $30,420
Christopher, Brent N, corrections ofcr I, $29,652
Christopher, David T, tractor trailer driver, $30,984
Christopher, Nancy R, ofc spt asst (keybrd), $23,160
Christos, Charles J, labor spv, $26,652

Christus, Julie A, corrections mgr b1, $52,402
Christy, Geoffrey E, corrections ofcr I, $29,652
Christy, Mitchel A, corrections ofcr I, $28,692
Chronister, Craig R, prob & parole ofcr II, $40,380
Chronister, Timothy W, corrections ofcr II, $32,784
Chumley, Christopher E, locksmith, $30,420
Church, Ammenda M, corrections ofcr I, $28,692
Church, Sylvia H, corrections ofcr I, $31,140
Church, Tammy L, corrections ofcr I, $29,652
Chute, Alexander S, corrections ofcr I, $30,276
Cisco, Lewis J, corrections ofcr I, $29,652
Clack, Shane, corrections ofcr I, $29,652
Clampitt, Cheryl A, prob & parole ofcr II, $19,116
Clare, James W, corrections ofcr I, $29,652
Clariday, Jessica R, corrections case mgr I, $30,984
Clark, Angela K, corrections ofcr I, $28,692
Clark, April M, corrections ofcr I, $29,652
Clark, Brad K, corrections ofcr III, $33,744
Clark, Bradley, prob & parole ofcr II, $34,944
Clark, Brenda E, ofc spt asst (keybrd), $25,824
Clark, Christopher L, corrections ofcr I, $29,652
Clark, Diane J, prob & parole ofcr I, $31,512
Clark, Donald R, corrections ofcr I, $33,348
Clark, Donna M, acad tchr III, $38,232
Clark, Edwin B, corrections ofcr I, $28,692
Clark, Effie A, ofc spt asst (keybrd), $26,232
Clark, Jonathan P, corrections spv I, $38,928
Clark, Julie D, prob & parole ofcr II, $36,888
Clark, Karen S, corrections recs ofcr I, $28,104
Clark, Kyle A, prob & parole ofcr II, $36,204
Clark, Lacey D, ofc spt asst (keybrd), $22,536
Clark, Laura S, investigator II, $37,548
Clark, Lisa K, corrections spv I, $41,172
Clark, Lisa S, special educ tchr III, $38,928
Clark, Michael A, prob & parole ofcr II, $39,624
Clark, Omer L, corrections mgr b2, $51,466
Clark, Scott L, prob & parole asst I, $29,496
Clark, Sheila A, ofc spt asst (keybrd), $23,160
Clark, Stephan V, corrections ofcr I, $29,652
Clark, Teresa L, prob & parole ofcr II, $36,204
Clark, Vivien, prob & parole ofcr II, $36,204
Clarke, Anita, registered nurse–clinic opers, $68,532
Clarke, Dereck M, corrections spv I, $38,232
Clarke, Sonia L, storekeeper II, $28,104
Clary, Christopher M, corrections ofcr I, $28,692
Clausen, Alexander D, corrections ofcr I, $29,652
Clausen, Tommy R, corrections ofcr II, $30,576
Clay, Gary J, corrections ofcr I, $29,652
Clay, Steven J, corrections ofcr I, $29,652
Claycomb, Scott A, garage spv, $34,356
Claypool, Tyeson N, corrections ofcr I, $29,652
Clayton, John M, corrections ofcr I, $29,652
Clayton, Nathan A, corrections ofcr I, $29,652
Cleek, Paul R, stationary engr, $35,568
Cleeton, Larry J, corrections ofcr I, $30,132
Clemens, Jeffrey S, voc tchr III, $37,548
Clemens, Mary C, ofc spt asst (keybrd), $11,580
Clement, Misty S, corrections ofcr I, $28,692
Clemons, Melissa, prob & parole asst I, $29,496
Clendenny, Sandra K, corrections ofcr I, $29,652
Clennin, Tracy, storekeeper II, $31,512
Clevenger, Penney A, sr ofc spt asst (clerical), $25,824
Clevenger, Victor A, corrections ofcr III, $33,744
Clifford, Abagail M, ofc spt asst (keybrd), $23,160
Clifford, Douglas A, corrections ofcr I, $29,652
Clifford, Kathryn J, ofc spt asst (keybrd), $23,160
Clifton, Audrey A, corrections ofcr I, $29,652
Cline, Anita D, ofc spt asst (keybrd), $23,160
Cline, David M, storekeeper I, $25,824
Cline, Keith A, corrections ofcr II, $35,100
Cline, Valarie A, corrections ofcr I, $28,692
Cline, William J, corrections ofcr I, $29,652
Clinkenbeard, Randall L, corrections ofcr I, $31,668
Clinkenbeard, Tammy J, corrections case mgr II, $36,204
Clinton, Audrey J, corrections spv I, $37,548
Clinton, Jason D, corrections ofcr I, $29,652
Clodfelter, Ryan L, prob & parole ofcr II, $36,204
Cloninger, Charles L, corrections ofcr I, $29,652
Clouse, Carla Y, cook II, $23,508
Clover, Robert L, corrections ofcr I, $29,652
Clubbs, Laura E, ofc spt asst (keybrd), $23,160
Clubbs, Shannon R, corrections ofcr II, $31,668
Clyburn, Jennifer E, prob & parole ofcr II, $38,232

Clymer, Michael T, corrections ofcr I, $31,668
Coates, Rose C, cook III, $27,228
Coatney, Wesley, investigator II, $38,928
Coats, Gary D, corrections ofcr I, $32,784
Coats, Leisha A, corrections ofcr I, $28,692
Cobaugh, Jane E, corrections ofcr I, $29,652
Cobb, Amanda L, corrections ofcr I, $29,652
Cobb, Andrea M, corrections ofcr I, $29,652
Cobb, Clayton J, corrections ofcr I, $29,652
Cobb, Kellie, prob & parole ofcr II, $19,812
Cobb, Michael W, corrections ofcr I, $29,652
Cobb, Tina L, prob & parole ofcr II, $36,204
Coble, Nicholas R, prob & parole unit spv, $44,304
Coburn, Kayla, ofc spt asst (keybrd), $22,536
Coburn, Theodore O, prob & parole ofcr II, $36,204
Cochenour, Floyd E, corrections ofcr I, $29,652
Cochran, Joyce C, ofc spt asst (clerical), $22,536
Cochran, Ralph M, acad tchr III, $37,548
Cockrum, Lester G, corrections ofcr II, $31,668
Coday, Aubrey M, corrections ofcr I, $29,652
Coday, Tresa D, inst activity coor, $36,204
Coello, Robert J, corrections ofcr I, $29,652
Cofer, Heather D, corrections mgr b1, $41,975
Cofer, Thomas H, corrections ofcr I, $31,668
Coffee, Joseph M, corrections ofcr I, $28,692
Coffelt, Aaron A, corrections ofcr I, $29,652
Coffelt, Ashley L, corrections ofcr I, $29,652
Coffelt, Jimmy D, corrections ofcr I, $31,140
Coffelt, Joe D, facilities opps mgr b1, $52,092
Coffer, Andrew, corrections ofcr I, $29,652
Coffman, Amanda L, corrections mgr b1, $48,781
Coffman, Britney R, corrections ofcr I, $29,652
Coffman, James H, corrections ofcr I, $30,132
Coffman, Melanie M, cook II, $24,264
Coffman, Ryan D, phys plant sup III, $47,892
Coffman, Willie, corrections spv I, $37,548
Coker, Jacob V, corrections ofcr I, $29,652
Colbert, Dillon O, corrections ofcr I, $29,316
Colbert, Melinda K, storekeeper I, $25,824
Colbert, Patsy R, corrections ofcr I, $31,140
Colbert, Scott J, prob & parole ofcr II, $41,940
Colborn, Gaye A, corrections mgr b2, $49,909
Colborn, Jonathan L, corrections ofcr III, $38,232
Colby, Sherry R, acct I, $30,984
Cole, Alonzo A, corrections ofcr I, $28,692
Cole, Dale F, garage spv, $32,628
Cole, James K, corrections ofcr I, $28,692
Cole, James R, corrections ofcr I, $29,652
Cole, Karen S, prob & parole unit spv, $42,708
Cole, Kiara, prob & parole asst I, $29,496
Cole, Mark Q, corrections ofcr I, $29,652
Cole, Robert L, maint spv I, $32,628
Cole, Ronald L, boiler oper, $28,536
Cole, Samuel H, corrections ofcr I, $30,276
Cole, Terance L, laundry mgr, $37,548
Coleman, Amy L, ofc spt asst (keybrd), $23,160
Coleman, Angela M, corrections ofcr I, $29,652
Coleman, Bettie M, corrections ofcr I, $29,652
Coleman, Connie F, ofc spt asst (keybrd), $23,160
Coleman, Danetta, prob & parole ofcr II, $36,204
Coleman, Dennis J, corrections ofcr I, $29,652
Coleman, Eric D, corrections ofcr I, $29,652
Coleman, Jason H, subs abuse cnslr III, $39,624
Coleman, Joshua E, corrections ofcr I, $28,692
Coleman, Leonard W, corrections ofcr I, $29,652
Coleman, Linda S, factory mgr I, $34,944
Coleman, Mark E, corrections ofcr I, $28,692
Coleman, Nancy I, acad tchr III, $39,624
Coleman, Paul B, maint spv I, $32,628
Coleman, Paul R, corrections training ofcr, $42,708
Coleman, Penny K, prob & parole ofcr II, $40,380
Coler, Gabriella, corrections ofcr I, $29,652
Coley, Donald B, maint spv I, $36,888
Collard, Ronald E, corrections ofcr I, $29,652
Collett, Stefanie D, corrections ofcr I, $29,652
Colley, Billy W, corrections ofcr I, $29,652
Colliatie, Spencer G, storekeeper II, $28,104
Collier, Cynthia R, corrections mgr b1, $48,371
Collier, James R, corrections ofcr I, $29,652
Colligan, John P, corrections mgr b1, $54,282
Collins, Barry A, stationary engr, $33,744
Collins, Caleb M, corrections ofcr I, $29,652
Collins, Cari D, div dir, $86,363

Collins, Christian, corrections ofcr I, $28,692
Collins, Cody L, corrections ofcr I, $29,652
Collins, Cory A, corrections ofcr I, $28,692
Collins, Donald J, cook II, $23,508
Collins, Frances L, corrections ofcr I, $29,652
Collins, Frankie L, corrections ofcr I, $29,652
Collins, Isaac L, corrections mgr b3, $59,910
Collins, Keeton W, corrections ofcr I, $28,692
Collins, Logan Z, corrections ofcr I, $29,652
Collins, Lonnie D, corrections ofcr I, $29,652
Collins, Michael K, corrections ofcr I, $29,652
Collins, Rodney T, corrections mgr b1, $50,730
Collins, Ronnie C, corrections ofcr I, $29,652
Collins, Sara L, cook II, $24,264
Collins, William S, corrections ofcr I, $29,652
Colter, Angela L, prob & parole unit spv, $43,488
Colter, Neena, corrections ofcr I, $31,140
Colter, Scott A, corrections spv II, $46,932
Colvin, Donald C, corrections ofcr I, $33,348
Colvin, Kristi, ofc spt asst (keybrd), $23,160
Colyer, Devin C, corrections ofcr I, $28,692
Colyer, Jeremy L, corrections ofcr I, $29,652
Combs, Angela K, account clerk II, $25,824
Combs, Angie J, prob & parole ofcr II, $36,204
Combs, Justin A, labor spv, $26,652
Combs, Robyn R, librarian II, $34,356
Conard, Kevin M, corrections ofcr II, $31,668
Conaway, Clark E, corrections ofcr I, $28,692
Condict, Mark E, corrections ofcr I, $29,652
Condron, Jeremy L, maint spv I, $32,628
Cone, Terry S, prob & parole ofcr II, $36,204
Conger, Tonya D, corrections ofcr I, $29,652
Conklin, Harold L, corrections ofcr I, $29,652
Conklin, Meredith, prob & parole ofcr II, $34,944
Conley, Christopher M, maint spv I, $32,628
Conley, Jacob A, corrections ofcr I, $28,692
Conley, Jacob A, recrtn ofcr I, $30,420
Conley, Kim R, prob & parole asst I, $33,180
Conley, Meeka J, prob & parole ofcr III, $39,624
Conn, Richard D, corrections ofcr II, $33,900
Connell, Deanne M, corrections ofcr I, $29,652
Connell, Gary A, stationary engr, $36,204
Connell, Kenneth A, voc tchr III, $41,172
Connell, Lenuta, corrections ofcr I, $29,652
Connell, Marshall D, corrections ofcr I, $29,652
Connell, Timothy A, stationary engr, $33,744
Connelly, Timothy J, corrections case mgr II, $40,380
Conner, Amy R, prob & parole ofcr II, $36,204
Conner, Ashly H, corrections ofcr I, $29,652
Conner, Darren, electronics tech, $30,984
Conner, Kenneth R, corrections ofcr I, $29,652
Conner, Kimberly J, corrections ofcr I, $29,652
Conner, Nathan B, corrections ofcr I, $29,652
Conover, Brant A, corrections ofcr I, $29,652
Conrad, Charles T, corrections ofcr I, $29,652
Conrad, Marshall D, corrections ofcr I, $29,652
Conrad, Tony M, recrtn ofcr II, $37,548
Constable-Keesaman, Peggy L, cook III, $28,104
Constant, Freddie S, corrections ofcr I, $29,652
Conway, Daniel J, corrections ofcr I, $29,652
Conway, Sandy L, corrections case mgr II, $33,744
Cook, Brenda S, special asst technician, $40,374
Cook, Carol E, acad tchr III, $37,548
Cook, Craig L, corrections ofcr I, $29,652
Cook, Darin R, corrections ofcr I, $28,692
Cook, Darrell E, corrections ofcr I, $29,652
Cook, Darren G, corrections ofcr I, $33,348
Cook, David E, cook III, $27,228
Cook, Heather N, ofc spt asst (keybrd), $23,160
Cook, Jennifer P, librarian II, $33,744
Cook, Kimberly M, corrections ofcr I, $29,652
Cook, Kyleigh T, corrections ofcr I, $28,692
Cook, Laura J, corrections mgr b1, $47,944
Cook, Matthew G, corrections ofcr I, $31,140
Cook, Melyne N, corrections ofcr I, $29,652
Cook, Norman G, corrections ofcr I, $33,900
Cook, Reuben A, corrections ofcr I, $29,652
Cook, Ricky D, corrections ofcr I, $29,652
Cook, Roxanne M, prob & parole ofcr II, $36,888
Cook, Wayne E, corrections ofcr I, $29,652
Cooke, Camilla J, prob & parole ofcr II, $36,204
Cooke, Chad A, corrections ofcr II, $32,220
Cooke, Christine M, corrections ofcr I, $29,652

Cook-Hannon, Effie L, prob & parole asst I, $29,496
Cookson, Michael D, voc tchr III, $37,548
Cooley, Christopher R, acad tchr III, $39,624
Cooley, Jeff A, maint spv I, $32,628
Coomes, Greg A, recrtn ofcr I, $31,512
Coon, Douglas F, subs abuse unit spv, $41,940
Coonce, Deborah A, cook III, $27,228
Coons, Brandon M, corrections ofcr I, $29,652
Coontz, Waylon L, corrections ofcr I, $28,692
Cooper, Adam B, corrections ofcr I, $28,692
Cooper, Charles T, corrections ofcr I, $29,652
Cooper, Christopher T, maint spv I, $31,512
Cooper, Cierra, ofc spt asst (keybrd), $23,160
Cooper, Connie J, ofc spt asst (keybrd), $23,160
Cooper, Donald L, corrections ofcr I, $31,140
Cooper, Douglas C, prob & parole ofcr II, $39,624
Cooper, Dustin J, maint spv I, $32,628
Cooper, Faith A, corrections ofcr I, $29,652
Cooper, Jerry L, corrections ofcr I, $29,652
Cooper, Larry R, prob & parole ofcr II, $36,204
Cooper, Patrick R, corrections ofcr I, $29,652
Cooper, Robert F, ofc spt asst (clerical), $21,864
Cooper, Scott C, corrections ofcr II, $31,668
Coots, Robert W, corrections classif asst, $32,052
Cope, Amy L, prob & parole ofcr II, $36,204
Cope, Maria C, corrections ofcr I, $29,652
Cope, Ronald L, prob & parole ofcr II, $38,232
Cope, Thomas E, corrections ofcr I, $29,652
Copeland, Albert A, corrections ofcr I, $29,652
Copeland, Deidre C, prob & parole ofcr II, $38,232
Copeland, John D, subs abuse cnslr II, $34,944
Copeland, Ryun E, corrections ofcr I, $28,692
Coplin, Nathaniel D, corrections ofcr I, $29,652
Coplin, Robert A, stationary engr, $33,744
Coppedge, Bryan K, corrections ofcr I, $29,652
Corbin, Brit E, corrections ofcr I, $32,220
Corbin, Mandy A, corrections ofcr I, $29,652
Corbin, Nelson T, maint spv I, $32,628
Corchado, Marcus A, corrections ofcr I, $29,652
Corcimiglia, Lanny C, prob & parole unit spv, $44,304
Cordell, Johnny E, corrections ofcr I, $29,652
Cordes, Ginger A, sr ofc spt asst (keybrd), $27,504
Cordes, Robert B, corrections ofcr I, $29,652
Cordes, Robert E, corrections ofcr I, $31,668
Cordio, Toni G, ofc spt asst (keybrd), $27,084
Cordray, Larry E, stationary engr, $33,744
Corey, Carmen N, prob & parole ofcr II, $36,204
Corinthos, Miranda, account clerk II, $25,824
Corkell, Angela F, corrections ofcr I, $28,692
Corkell, Daniel A, corrections ofcr I, $29,652
Corkell, Joshua E, corrections ofcr I, $29,652
Corkell, Sharon A, cook II, $24,264
Corley, Margo T, ofc spt asst (keybrd), $23,160
Cornelison, Jerry W, corrections ofcr I, $30,132
Cornelison, Nancy K, corrections ofcr I, $29,652
Cornelius, Carolyn J, corrections case mgr II, $38,928
Cornelius, James L, corrections ofcr I, $29,652
Cornelius, Ruthoni M, corrections ofcr I, $29,652
Cornelius, Sasha N, corrections ofcr I, $28,692
Cornelius, Travis, prob & parole ofcr II, $36,204
Cornett, Susan M, sr ofc spt asst (keybrd), $28,452
Coronado, Daniel A, accounting spec I, $37,548
Corpening, Daniel L, corrections ofcr I, $29,652
Corser, Richard G, corrections spv I, $42,708
Corum, David L, corrections spv I, $42,708
Corvaia, Johnathan M, corrections ofcr II, $31,668
Cory, Lauren M, prob & parole ofcr II, $36,204
Cossey, Carey L, ofc spt asst (keybrd), $22,536
Cossey, Clifton J, corrections case mgr II, $35,568
Costa, Cathy J, corrections ofcr I, $29,652
Cotten, Jonathan R, corrections ofcr I, $31,668
Cotten, Truly A, corrections ofcr I, $29,652
Cottingham, Terri R, corrections ofcr I, $28,692
Cottrell, Crystal D, prob & parole ofcr II, $39,624
Cottrell, Marlene K, corrections ofcr II, $31,668
Couch, David P, corrections ofcr I, $29,652
Couch, Jason O, corrections ofcr I, $29,652
Couch, Paul B, corrections ofcr I, $30,132
Couch, Paula F, exec II, $36,888
Coughlin, Kevin R, corrections ofcr I, $29,652
Coulter, Daniel R, corrections ofcr III, $37,548
Courson, Caitlin M, prob & parole ofcr II, $36,204
Courtney, Sharon L, corrections case mgr II, $38,928

Courtois, Megan L, prob & parole ofcr II, $36,204
Courtway, Tracy A, voc enter spv II, $29,976
Courville, Alan W, corrections ofcr I, $29,652
Cousin, E F, corrections ofcr I, $29,652
Cowan, Jerico B, corrections ofcr I, $28,692
Cowan, Julie A, corrections case mgr II, $36,204
Cowden, Chris S, corrections ofcr I, $31,140
Cowie, James C, corrections ofcr I, $29,652
Cowley, Lisa A, corrections ofcr I, $29,652
Cowley, Ronald D, corrections ofcr I, $29,652
Cox, Aaron P, corrections ofcr II, $30,576
Cox, Brenda J, cook II, $23,508
Cox, Dale W, corrections ofcr I, $32,784
Cox, Dana L, prob & parole ofcr II, $34,944
Cox, Debra Y, account clerk II, $25,032
Cox, Dennis D, corrections ofcr I, $29,652
Cox, Dennis E, guidance cnslr II, $37,548
Cox, Janice K, cook II, $24,264
Cox, Jeanette L, storekeeper I, $29,412
Cox, John E, corrections ofcr II, $31,668
Cox, Kimberly K, ofc spt asst (keybrd), $23,160
Cox, Michael G, subs abuse cnslr II, $34,944
Cox, Nicholas J, prob & parole ofcr II, $36,204
Cox, Ricky D, corrections ofcr II, $31,668
Cox, Ronald L, corrections ofcr I, $33,900
Cox, Sara E, corrections ofcr I, $29,652
Cox, Skye E, corrections ofcr II, $31,668
Cox, Steven W, corrections ofcr I, $29,652
Cox, Tyler R, corrections ofcr I, $28,692
Coy, Brandy, prob & parole ofcr I, $29,976
Coyle, Krista, prob & parole ofcr II, $36,204
Crabtree, Justin R, corrections ofcr I, $28,692
Craddock, Michael V, corrections ofcr I, $33,348
Craddock, Nicole C, corrections ofcr I, $29,652
Crader, Daniel A, cook II, $24,264
Crader, Joshua C, corrections ofcr II, $31,668
Crafton, Jeremy D, corrections ofcr I, $29,652
Crago, Erick J, corrections ofcr I, $29,652
Craig, Christina, corrections ofcr I, $29,652
Craig, Daniel A, corrections ofcr I, $28,692
Craig, Danielle S, ofc spt asst (keybrd), $23,160
Craig, John P, storekeeper II, $29,004
Craig, Kurt L, corrections ofcr I, $31,140
Craig, Lacy A, prob & parole ofcr II, $39,624
Craig, Ryan M, corrections ofcr I, $29,652
Craig, Thomas L, corrections ofcr I, $29,652
Craig, Timothy A, corrections ofcr I, $29,652
Crandall, Phillip L, corrections spv I, $38,928
Crandell, Robert C, corrections ofcr I, $29,652
Crane, Craig M, corrections ofcr III, $32,628
Crane, James M, prob & parole ofcr I, $29,976
Craner, Diana E, prob & parole asst I, $29,496
Craney, Diana, sr ofc spt asst (keybrd), $25,824
Crary, Scott L, corrections ofcr I, $29,652
Crawford, Antoinette C, sr ofc spt asst (keybrd), $25,824
Crawford, Barton D, corrections ofcr I, $29,652
Crawford, Bob D, corrections ofcr I, $33,348
Crawford, Daniel E, corrections ofcr I, $29,652
Crawford, Davey S, corrections ofcr I, $33,348
Crawford, James A, corrections ofcr I, $28,692
Crawford, Jason P, corrections ofcr I, $35,724
Crawford, Joyce I, special asst ofc & clerical, $26,260
Crawford, Kaci L, corrections ofcr I, $30,132
Crawford, Mark R, corrections ofcr I, $30,276
Crawford, Reuben, corrections ofcr I, $28,692
Crawford, Ricky W, corrections ofcr I, $29,652
Crawford, Tessa M, administrative analyst II, $34,944
Crawford, Tina M, ofc spt asst (keybrd), $23,160
Creason, Catherine L, corrections case mgr I, $29,976
Creed, Lynnette, corrections mgr b1, $48,338
Creek, Melissia A, corrections case mgr II, $33,744
Creg, Dena L, corrections ofcr I, $29,652
Cregar, Carolyn D, corrections recs ofcr I, $28,104
Cremer, Charlotte M, subs abuse cnslr II, $34,944
Cress, Alex D, prob & parole ofcr II, $36,204
Cress, Aric K, prob & parole ofcr II, $36,204
Creswell, Justin W, corrections ofcr I, $29,652
Crews, Leann, corrections case mgr II, $34,944
Crews, Ryan M, corrections mgr b3, $66,438
Crews, Steven T, corrections mgr b1, $40,874
Crews, Travis L, corrections ofcr I, $29,652
Crick, Catherine L, corrections ofcr I, $29,652
Crippen, Andrew M, corrections ofcr I, $29,652

Crisler, Janiece K, admin ofc spt asst, $27,228
Crisman, James M, corrections ofcr I, $29,652
Crisman, Kasey D, corrections ofcr I, $29,652
Crisp, Barbara A, ofc spt asst (keybrd), $23,160
Crites, Allen M, prob & parole ofcr I, $31,512
Crites, Amber C, prob & parole ofcr II, $36,204
Crites, Debra S, account clerk II, $25,824
Crocker, Dennis J, corrections ofcr I, $34,512
Crocker, Elizabeth S, corrections case mgr II, $37,548
Crocker, Richard H, corrections ofcr I, $29,652
Crocker, Tracy L, prob & parole ofcr II, $36,204
Crockett, Kay G, special asst technician, $51,510
Cromer, Jacob E, corrections ofcr I, $28,692
Cromer, Norman W, corrections ofcr I, $29,652
Cronin, Haley, prob & parole ofcr II, $34,944
Cronin, Justin B, electronics tech, $31,512
Cronin, Sarah J, prob & parole ofcr II, $34,944
Cronk, Lisa L, corrections case mgr I, $29,976
Crook, David A, prob & parole ofcr II, $36,204
Cross, Anita A, corrections ofcr I, $29,652
Cross, Brad A, recrtn ofcr I, $29,976
Cross, Brent A, corrections ofcr I, $29,652
Cross, Cheryl D, acad tchr III, $37,548
Cross, Deana M, corrections ofcr I, $29,652
Cross, John F, prob & parole unit spv, $45,156
Crossgrove, Jeffrey L, corrections ofcr I, $29,652
Crosthwait, David, tractor trailer driver, $30,984
Crothers, Antonio, prob & parole asst I, $28,536
Crouch, Eugene D, corrections ofcr I, $29,652
Crouch, Karen L, corrections ofcr I, $31,140
Crouch, Kimberly J, corrections mgr b1, $49,738
Crow, Ashton N, acct I, $30,984
Crow, Audra L, ofc spt asst (keybrd), $23,160
Crow, Dorothy, storekeeper I, $26,232
Crow, Richard N, corrections ofcr I, $29,652
Crowder, Russell J, locksmith, $32,052
Crowley, Brittany L, corrections ofcr I, $28,692
Crowley, Robert J, maint worker II, $29,004
Crowley, Robert W, corrections ofcr I, $28,692
Crowley, Sherri R, ofc spt asst (keybrd), $23,160
Crubaugh, Jamey, prob & parole ofcr I, $29,976
Crull, Lynn, corrections ofcr I, $29,652
Crum, Ronald W, corrections ofcr II, $32,220
Crum, Tina M, corrections ofcr I, $29,652
Crump, James D, corrections mgr b2, $47,599
Crump, Jay W, corrections ofcr II, $33,348
Crump-Tuttle, Taryen R, prob & parole ofcr II, $36,204
Cruz, Colby J, corrections ofcr I, $28,692
Cruz, Ricky M, boiler oper, $27,228
Cruz Balestier, Stacy L, corrections ofcr I, $28,692
Culbertson, Donald E, prob & parole ofcr II, $36,204
Culbertson, Gerard T, cook III, $28,104
Culbreath, James L, corrections case mgr II, $34,944
Cullen, Michael A, corrections ofcr I, $28,692
Cullen, Sandra, ofc spt asst (keybrd), $23,160
Cullom, Monica L, storekeeper I, $27,084
Culton, Pamela K, sr ofc spt asst (keybrd), $27,948
Culver, David S, cook II, $24,264
Culwell, Joyce M, storekeeper II, $29,496
Cummings, Carol J, investigator III, $38,928
Cummings, Jacob D, corrections ofcr I, $29,652
Cummings, Victoria D, storekeeper I, $25,824
Cummins, Douglas, corrections ofcr I, $29,652
Cummins, James A, corrections ofcr I, $29,652
Cummins, Justin D, corrections ofcr I, $29,652
Cummins, Marianne, subs abuse cnslr III, $37,548
Cummins, Nancy L, corrections ofcr II, $31,668
Cundiff, Tyler V, prob & parole ofcr I, $29,976
Cunningham, Ashley N, ofc spt asst (keybrd), $23,160
Cunningham, Frank R, maint spv I, $32,628
Cunningham, Glen A, tractor trailer driver, $33,744
Cunningham, Jesse E, corrections ofcr I, $28,692
Cunningham, Lindsey N, corrections ofcr I, $29,652
Cunningham, Melinda, prob & parole ofcr II, $36,204
Cunningham, Wesley R, acad tchr III, $37,548
Cupp, Aaron M, corrections ofcr I, $29,652
Curlile, Kyra E, ofc spt asst (keybrd), $22,536
Curnutt, Katrina J, ofc spt asst (keybrd), $23,160
Curran, Pamela L, prob & parole ofcr II, $39,624
Currence, Richard D, corrections ofcr I, $29,652
Currington, Bobby L, corrections ofcr I, $33,348
Curry, Megan D, corrections ofcr I, $30,276
Curry, Phillip L, storekeeper II, $28,104

Curtin, Todd E, cook II, $24,264
Curtis, Andrew T, corrections ofcr I, $29,652
Curtis, Brandon K, corrections ofcr I, $29,652
Curtis, Kevin S, maint spv I, $33,744
Curtis, Laura, prob & parole ofcr II, $41,172
Curtis, Nevin R, corrections ofcr I, $29,652
Curtis, Ralph J, cook II, $23,508
Curtis, Randy, corrections ofcr I, $29,652
Curtis, Rubeno G, prob & parole asst I, $29,496
Cutt, David W, corrections ofcr III, $35,568
Cutt, Kristin L, corrections case mgr II, $36,204
Czarnecki, Brian M, corrections ofcr I, $29,652
Dade, Toneta, prob & parole ofcr II, $36,204
Daffron, Billie D, maint spv I, $32,628
Daffron, Darlene D, corrections ofcr I, $31,668
D'agostino, Christine S, prob & parole ofcr II, $40,380
Dahlem, Eric D, corrections ofcr I, $29,652
Daiber, Sandra M, prob & parole ofcr II, $38,232
Dailey, Tammy L, prob & parole ofcr II, $38,232
Daise, Diane J, ofc spt asst (keybrd), $24,612
Dalechek, Deanna L, prob & parole ofcr II, $18,102
Dalgetty, Ronald A, corrections ofcr I, $29,652
Dallas, Toni C, ofc spt asst (keybrd), $23,508
Dallmier, Aaron M, corrections ofcr I, $29,652
Dally, Maree, prob & parole ofcr II, $36,204
Dalton, Mark D, corrections ofcr I, $34,512
Dalton, Michael W, corrections ofcr I, $29,652
Dalton, Michelle S, subs abuse cnslr II, $34,944
Dalton, Patricia M, corrections ofcr I, $33,348
Dalton, Robin L, ofc spt asst (keybrd), $23,160
Dalton, Thomas J, corrections ofcr I, $31,140
Dame, Amelia M, corrections ofcr I, $29,652
Dameron, Ashley N, prob & parole ofcr I, $30,984
Damewood, Frank L, corrections ofcr I, $29,652
Dampier, Brian T, corrections ofcr I, $29,652
Dane, Jason K, garage spv, $32,628
Danels, George A, corrections ofcr I, $29,661
Daniel, Brenda, food serv mgr I, $32,052
Daniel, Kenneth, corrections ofcr I, $30,132
Daniels, Avera L, research analyst III, $40,380
Daniels, Carrie M, corrections ofcr I, $28,692
Daniels, Dacia R, ofc spt asst (keybrd), $23,160
Daniels, Jack, prob & parole ofcr II, $36,204
Daniels, Jack A, maint worker II, $29,004
Daniels, Michelle L, prob & parole ofcr II, $36,204
Daniels, Samantha R, corrections ofcr I, $29,652
Daniels-Grigg, Corrina J, acad tchr III, $37,548
Danner, Ryan W, corrections ofcr II, $31,668
Danuser, Clay A, prob & parole ofcr II, $38,232
Dare, Melisa E, prob & parole ofcr II, $38,232
Darling, James W, corrections ofcr I, $29,652
Darling, Mary L, storekeeper I, $25,824
Darnell, Candy J, cook II, $24,264
Daro, Jason R, corrections ofcr I, $29,652
Dashner, Wendy L, functional unit mgr corr, $38,928
Daugherty, Janice G, prob & parole ofcr II, $38,232
Daugherty, John W, stationary engr, $37,548
Daugherty, Richard L, recrtn ofcr I, $31,512
Daugherty, Sherri L, prob & parole ofcr II, $39,624
Daugherty, Tracy L, acad tchr III, $37,548
Daugherty, William R, corrections ofcr I, $29,652
Daum, Delmar E, locksmith, $29,976
Dauster, Dylan D, corrections ofcr I, $29,652
Davenport, Austin L, corrections ofcr I, $29,652
Davenport, Dillon E, corrections ofcr I, $29,652
Davenport, William C, corrections ofcr I, $29,652
David, Lauren, prob & parole asst I, $28,536
Davidson, Derek A, corrections ofcr I, $29,652
Davidson, Derek A, prob & parole ofcr II, $38,232
Davidson, Glenn A, corrections ofcr II, $35,724
Davidson, Nathaniel R, corrections ofcr I, $29,652
Davidson, Randy J, recrtn ofcr III, $38,928
Davidson, Rhonda R, corrections ofcr I, $29,652
Davidson, Shane C, corrections ofcr I, $29,652
Davis, Adam W, corrections ofcr I, $29,652
Davis, Andrew R, corrections ofcr I, $29,652
Davis, Brian L, corrections case mgr I, $30,984
Davis, Charles W, corrections ofcr III, $33,744
Davis, Christopher A, corrections ofcr I, $29,652
Davis, Cody R, corrections ofcr I, $29,652
Davis, Dale K, corrections ofcr I, $28,692
Davis, Daniel B, corrections ofcr I, $29,652
Davis, Darin L, corrections ofcr I, $29,652

Davis, Darrell D, corrections ofcr I, $28,692
Davis, Darrell W, prob & parole asst II, $31,512
Davis, David A, corrections ofcr I, $29,652
Davis, Debra J, corrections ofcr I, $29,652
Davis, Dennis L, corrections ofcr I, $28,692
Davis, Dianne R, prob & parole asst I, $30,984
Davis, Diona L, corrections ofcr I, $31,140
Davis, Dominique M, corrections ofcr I, $28,692
Davis, Dorothy L, corrections ofcr I, $31,140
Davis, Eric L, corrections ofcr I, $28,692
Davis, Fannie L, corrections mgr b1, $51,965
Davis, Gary L, corrections ofcr I, $29,652
Davis, Grace M, ofc spt asst (clerical), $22,536
Davis, Gregory S, corrections ofcr I, $29,652
Davis, Jarrett W, corrections ofcr I, $29,652
Davis, Jason A, corrections ofcr II, $31,668
Davis, Jason A, corrections ofcr I, $29,652
Davis, Jefferson D, corrections ofcr II, $31,668
Davis, Kathleen D, ofc spt asst (keybrd), $23,160
Davis, Katrina A, corrections ofcr I, $29,652
Davis, Keith M, prob & parole ofcr II, $41,940
Davis, Kelly M, prob & parole ofcr II, $36,204
Davis, Kristine A, prob & parole unit spv, $44,304
Davis, Ladonna N, corrections ofcr III, $33,744
Davis, Leon Q, recrtn ofcr II, $32,628
Davis, Lesa G, prob & parole ofcr II, $36,204
Davis, Margaret K, corrections ofcr I, $29,652
Davis, Marian A, corrections ofcr II, $32,784
Davis, Marshal L, corrections ofcr I, $28,692
Davis, Matthew T, corrections ofcr I, $29,652
Davis, Michael D, corrections ofcr I, $29,652
Davis, Michael E, laundry mgr, $34,944
Davis, Michael L, parole hearing analyst, $49,128
Davis, Michael R, corrections ofcr I, $31,140
Davis, Mildred A, cook II, $24,264
Davis, Mitchell D, human rel ofcr II, $41,940
Davis, Myra J, corrections ofcr I, $31,140
Davis, Nancy E, prob & parole ofcr II, $37,548
Davis, Natasha D, corrections ofcr I, $28,692
Davis, Pamela J, ofc spt asst (keybrd), $23,880
Davis, Paula J, ofc spt asst (keybrd), $23,160
Davis, Rodney D, corrections ofcr I, $29,652
Davis, Sandra K, prob & parole ofcr II, $36,888
Davis, Scott M, corrections ofcr I, $28,692
Davis, Spencer D, corrections ofcr I, $29,652
Davis, Steven G, prob & parole ofcr II, $40,380
Davis, Steven R, corrections ofcr I, $29,652
Davis, Tayte E, corrections ofcr I, $29,652
Davis, Timothy, prob & parole ofcr II, $36,204
Davis, Tina R, ofc spt asst (keybrd), $22,536
Davis, Tracey D, corrections case mgr II, $34,944
Davis, Tracey R, account clerk II, $25,824
Davis, Wesley R, corrections ofcr I, $31,140
Davis, William H, prob & parole asst I, $29,496
Davis, Zachariah I, corrections ofcr I, $29,652
Davitz, Katie M, admin ofc spt asst, $28,104
Dawes, Billy, corrections ofcr I, $29,652
Dawson, Corey L, corrections ofcr I, $28,692
Dawson, Derek R, corrections case mgr II, $34,944
Dawson, Ernest M, corrections ofcr I, $29,652
Dawson, Stacia, sr ofc spt asst (keybrd), $25,824
Day, Clarence R, maint spv II, $34,944
Day, Daralyn A, prob & parole ofcr II, $36,204
Day, Diane K, ofc spt asst (clerical), $22,536
Day, James A, corrections ofcr II, $31,668
Day, Jared W, corrections ofcr I, $29,652
Day, Paula A, cook II, $24,264
Day, Samantha R, ofc spt asst (keybrd), $22,536
Day, Shelley L, prob & parole ofcr II, $39,624
Day, Timothy L, corrections ofcr I, $28,692
Day, Travis A, corrections ofcr I, $29,652
Dayton, Michael D, corrections ofcr I, $29,652
de la Cruz, Matthew B, corrections ofcr I, $29,652
Deacon, Charles M, corrections ofcr I, $29,652
Dean, Derek T, corrections ofcr I, $28,692
Dean, Donald E, prob & parole asst II, $33,180
Dean, Donald J, corrections ofcr I, $29,652
Dean, Misty D, corrections ofcr I, $29,652
Deao, Kristen, prob & parole ofcr I, $30,984
Deardeuff, Jerline E, misc prof, $18.37/hr
Deardeuff, Kelly L, corrections ofcr I, $29,652
Deardorff, Kevin J, corrections ofcr II, $33,900
Dearing, John A, prob & parole ofcr II, $36,204

Deason, Paul D, corrections case mgr II, $34,944
Deaton, Stacy R, prob & parole ofcr II, $36,204
Deblois, Robert E, maint spv I, $34,356
Debord, Joshua A, corrections ofcr I, $29,652
Debord, Terry, sr ofc spt asst (keybrd), $25,824
Debrecht, Debra M, special educ tchr III, $38,928
Decker, Jeffrey L, maint spv I, $32,628
Decker, John P, prob & parole ofcr II, $36,204
Decker, Nathaniel J, correctional worker, $26,400
Decker, Stephen R, corrections ofcr I, $29,652
Decker, Terri Jo C, prob & parole ofcr II, $36,204
Declue, Gail A, corrections ofcr I, $29,652
Declue, Melinda E, prob & parole ofcr II, $36,204
Declue, Michael R, maint spv I, $31,512
Declue, Tanya D, corrections ofcr I, $29,652
Declue, Tracie L, corrections mgr b1, $46,177
Declue, Walter J, corrections ofcr II, $31,668
Deen, Derek A, prob & parole ofcr II, $36,204
Dees, Terry L, investigator I, $31,512
Deets, Matthew A, corrections ofcr I, $32,784
Deets, Matthew A, corrections ofcr I, $28,692
Degonia, Lynn E, corrections ofcr I, $29,652
Degregorio, Michael J, corrections ofcr I, $28,692
Deguire, Pamela J, ofc spt asst (keybrd), $23,160
Deien, Darren, prob & parole ofcr II, $39,624
Deiter, Chris C, corrections ofcr III, $36,888
Delashmit, Sandra F, corrections ofcr I, $28,692
Delhotal, Steven D, corrections ofcr I, $29,652
Delong, Jonathan D, corrections ofcr I, $29,652
Delozier, Jennifer E, corrections ofcr II, $30,576
Delpercio, Michael J, corrections ofcr I, $29,652
Demaris, Glenn E, corrections ofcr I, $29,652
Dement, Anthony G, corrections ofcr I, $29,652
Dement, Benjamin E, corrections ofcr II, $31,668
Demerchant, Nicole C, prob & parole ofcr II, $36,204
Demkowicz, Jennifer L, corrections ofcr I, $29,652
Demkowicz, Michael J, corrections ofcr II, $33,348
Demoss, Anna M, correctional worker, $26,400
Demott, Michael A, maint worker II, $29,004
Dempsey, Chad D, corrections ofcr I, $31,140
Dempsey, Daniel C, corrections ofcr I, $29,652
Dempsey, Lisa C, prob & parole unit spv, $43,488
Dempsey, Melinda A, corrections ofcr I, $31,140
Denham, Dwayne A, corrections ofcr I, $29,652
Denham, Dwight E, corrections ofcr I, $29,652
Denison, David G, corrections ofcr I, $29,652
Denler, Ronald D, prob & parole asst I, $29,496
Denney, Cheryl J, corrections ofcr I, $29,652
Dennis, Christopher S, corrections ofcr II, $31,668
Dennis, Jessica M, prob & parole ofcr II, $36,204
Dennis, Joanna D, ofc spt asst (keybrd), $23,160
Dennis, Ryan A, corrections ofcr I, $29,652
Dennis, Stanley G, voc enter spv II, $29,976
Dennis, William H, corrections ofcr III, $33,744
Denny, Anna M, ofc spt asst (keybrd), $24,612
Denton, Bradley A, prob & parole ofcr II, $40,380
Denton, Justin L, corrections ofcr II, $31,668
Denton, Molly J, admin ofc spt asst, $27,228
Denton, Steven M, corrections ofcr I, $31,140
Depue, Betty J, corrections ofcr I, $29,652
Depuy, William R, corrections ofcr I, $29,652
Derboven, Deborah E, food serv mgr II, $34,944
Derboven, Melvin K, corrections ofcr I, $29,652
Derboven, Susan A, ofc spt asst (steno), $26,652
Derboven, Tara D, corrections case mgr II, $34,944
Derosa, Mary A, cook II, $24,264
Derousse, Amy J, ofc spt asst (keybrd), $23,880
Derousse, Christina D, cook II, $24,264
Derrick, John L, corrections ofcr I, $29,652
Derrickson, Rose M, functional unit mgr corr, $43,488
Derrington, Sharon M, corrections mgr b2, $56,200
Derryberry, Vicki L, ofc spt asst (keybrd), $23,160
Derstine, Stephen R, corrections ofcr I, $29,652
Deshon, Brian J, corrections ofcr III, $33,744
Despain, Harry G, corrections ofcr I, $29,652
Despain, Lloyd A, corrections case mgr II, $38,928
Despain, Teresa M, corrections case mgr II, $36,204
Detienne, Gary L, corrections ofcr II, $31,668
Dettmer, Brenda J, ofc spt asst (clerical), $22,536
Dettmer, Richard A, corrections ofcr I, $29,652
Deville, Joseph M, corrections ofcr III, $38,232
Devine, Patricia D, subs abuse cnslr II, $34,944
Devos, Andrew L, special educ tchr III, $42,708

Deweese, Marlene B, corrections ofcr II, $33,348
Deweese, Wesley W, corrections spv I, $42,708
Dewey, Denise S, corrections classif asst, $32,628
Dewey, Duane A, storekeeper I, $25,032
Dews, Melissa D, corrections recs ofcr I, $28,104
Dexheimer, John L, corrections ofcr I, $29,652
Diamond, Angela M, prob & parole ofcr II, $36,204
Diaz, Ali M, investigator II, $30,420
Diaz, Taleta K, ofc spt asst (keybrd), $23,880
Dickerson, George E, prob & parole ofcr II, $41,940
Dickerson, James D, recrtn ofcr I, $31,512
Dickerson, John E, corrections ofcr I, $29,652
Dickerson, Joyce J, corrections case mgr II, $34,944
Dickerson, Sandra K, corrections case mgr II, $34,944
Dickey, Bobby L, corrections ofcr I, $29,652
Dickey, Derek W, corrections ofcr II, $31,668
Dickey, Lauren K, ofc spt asst (keybrd), $23,160
Dickey, Sonya L, corrections ofcr I, $28,692
Dickey, Terry L, corrections ofcr I, $29,652
Dickinson, Gary W, maint spv I, $32,628
Dickson, Bridgette M, prob & parole unit spv, $45,156
Dickson, Gregory D, prob & parole ofcr I, $18,774
Dickson, Sheila A, corrections mgr b1, $45,661
Dicus, Daniel, corrections ofcr II, $36,360
Dicus, Scott A, corrections ofcr II, $31,668
Didlo, Dustin L, prob & parole ofcr II, $36,204
Dieckman, Robert R, corrections ofcr I, $29,652
Diedrich, Leslie K, ofc spt asst (keybrd), $23,880
Diekemper, Sherry, prob & parole ofcr II, $40,380
Diener, Courtney B, corrections case mgr I, $29,976
Diener, David E, corrections ofcr I, $28,692
Dierks, Robert S, corrections classif asst, $30,420
Dietiker, Terry M, corrections ofcr I, $30,132
Dietz, Meschelle K, account clerk II, $25,824
Dilks, Stephen A, acad tchr III, $36,204
Dill, Lona M, cook II, $24,264
Dillard, Tracy L, ofc spt asst (keybrd), $23,160
Dillman, Elizabeth A, corrections ofcr I, $29,652
Dillon, Kathy L, prob & parole ofcr II, $36,204
Dillon, Tereasa L, food serv mgr II, $35,568
Dills, Kelly L, corrections mgr b2, $57,727
Dilport, Henry F, corrections ofcr I, $29,652
Dilse, James M, corrections spv I, $40,380
Dimmitt, Troy E, corrections ofcr I, $29,652
Din-Gabisi, Bouraan, corrections ofcr I, $29,652
Dinolfo, Janis R, ofc spt asst (keybrd), $23,160
Dinsmore, Nita F, ofc spt asst (steno), $27,084
Dinwiddie, Dale D, corrections case mgr II, $36,888
Dinwiddie, Paula K, corrections case mgr II, $36,204
Dinwiddie, Sheila L, ofc spt asst (keybrd), $22,536
Diotte, David S, voc enter sales mgr, $38,928
Dittman, Almalee S, corrections case mgr II, $36,888
Dittman, Paul H, corrections ofcr I, $31,140
Dittmeier, Melinda G, functional unit mgr corr, $48,156
Divine, Craig, prob & parole ofcr I, $30,984
Dixon, Angie, prob & parole ofcr II, $39,624
Dixon, Brian A, corrections ofcr II, $31,668
Dixon, Desirae D, correctional worker, $26,400
Dixon, Jeffrey A, corrections ofcr I, $29,652
Dixon, Jeremy D, prob & parole ofcr II, $36,204
Dixon, Tammy K, corrections ofcr I, $29,652
Dixon, Tracy S, corrections ofcr I, $29,652
Dixon, William F, prob & parole ofcr II, $36,204
Dixson, Richard L, prob & parole asst II, $34,944
Dlugos, Matthew, prob & parole asst I, $29,496
Dobbins, Angela L, corrections ofcr I, $29,652
Dobbins, Mike T, prob & parole ofcr II, $36,204
Dobbins, Shaundi S, corrections ofcr I, $29,652
Dodd, Nicolette A, storekeeper II, $28,536
Dodd, Sherrie A, prob & parole ofcr II, $36,204
Dodd, Thomas M, corrections ofcr I, $29,652
Dodd-Henderson, Angela R, prob & parole asst II, $34,356
Dodson, Anthony J, corrections ofcr I, $29,652
Dodson, Ruth A, corrections recs ofcr I, $28,104
Doerhoff, Dewayne C, storekeeper II, $29,004
Doiel, Kevin L, corrections ofcr III, $33,744
Dolan, Christopher R, corrections ofcr I, $29,652
Dolan, Gary P, corrections ofcr I, $29,652
Dolan, Ryan P, prob & parole ofcr II, $36,204
Dollar, James P, storekeeper II, $29,004
Dollens, Dustin D, corrections ofcr I, $29,652
Dolson, John E, corrections ofcr I, $28,692
Domenico, Norman, corrections ofcr I, $29,652

Domiano, Robert J, prob & parole ofcr II, $34,944
Dominguez, John F, corrections ofcr I, $29,652
Domkoski, Melanie L, prob & parole ofcr II, $18,102
Donaldson, Justin D, prob & parole ofcr I, $32,628
Dondle, Stanley L, prob & parole ofcr II, $38,232
Donley, Bryan R, corrections ofcr I, $29,652
Donnelli, John R, investigator I, $31,512
Donner, Jeffrey, voc enter spv II, $29,976
Donohue, Nicole D, prob & parole ofcr I, $30,984
Donze, Carl S, corrections ofcr I, $29,652
Dooley, Connie J, corrections recs ofcr III, $36,204
Dooley, David M, maint worker II, $33,180
Dooley, David M, corrections ofcr I, $28,692
Dooley, Jennifer A, corrections case mgr I, $32,628
Doran, Daniel J, correctional worker, $26,400
Dority, James D, corrections ofcr I, $29,652
Dormire, David R, div dir, $91,163
Dorner, Matthew A, corrections ofcr I, $30,276
Dorney, Patrick J, corrections ofcr I, $29,652
Dorney, Valerie J, admin ofc spt asst, $28,104
Dorrell, Aimee L, corrections case mgr II, $34,944
Dorrell, Virgil, corrections ofcr I, $29,652
Dorsey, Barry L, prob & parole ofcr II, $38,232
Dorsey, Charles S, corrections ofcr I, $29,652
Dorsey, Christopher A, corrections ofcr I, $29,652
Dorton, Christie L, special asst paraprof, $47,767
Dosiak, Jennifer V, corrections ofcr II, $31,668
Doss, Brandon N, corrections ofcr I, $28,692
Doss, Brian C, corrections ofcr I, $30,132
Doss, David F, corrections ofcr I, $29,652
Doss, Erma J, corrections ofcr I, $29,652
Doss, Nicholas B, corrections ofcr I, $29,652
Doss, Sabrina D, corrections case mgr II, $35,568
Doss, Thomas G, corrections ofcr I, $29,652
Dotson, Cynthia G, cook II, $24,264
Dotson, Kevin, corrections ofcr I, $29,652
Dotson, Michael W, prob & parole ofcr II, $36,888
Doty, Angella M, ofc spt asst (keybrd), $23,160
Dotzman, Bartholomew, maint spv I, $33,180
Doughty, Christopher L, prob & parole ofcr II, $36,204
Doughty, Michael J, corrections ofcr III, $35,568
Douglas, Jennifer E, corrections ofcr I, $29,652
Douglas, Kevin C, prob & parole ofcr I, $30,984
Douglas, Kylie D, corrections ofcr I, $29,652
Douglas, Laura L, corrections ofcr I, $29,652
Douglas, Michael S, corrections ofcr I, $29,652
Douglass, Amanda E, prob & parole ofcr II, $36,204
Douglass, Judy E, prob & parole ofcr II, $38,232
Doutre, Michael T, corrections ofcr I, $29,652
Dow, Quinten, ofc spt asst (keybrd), $23,160
Dowd, Colleen M, special asst official & admstr, $62,317
Dowd, James M, corrections ofcr I, $29,652
Dowell, Gary W, prob & parole ofcr II, $36,204
Downard, Chad A, corrections ofcr I, $29,652
Downing, Franklin B, maint worker II, $29,004
Downing, Heather M, fiscal & administrative mgr b1, $51,684
Downs, Elmita J, cook II, $24,264
Downs, Gary E, corrections training ofcr, $41,172
Downs, Matthew W, corrections ofcr I, $29,652
Doyle, Laura S, ofc spt asst (keybrd), $23,160
Draffen, Christopher, prob & parole ofcr II, $36,204
Draffen, Kenny J, recrtn ofcr II, $33,744
Draffen, Mary B, cook II, $24,264
Draffen, Melissa A, sr ofc spt asst (keybrd), $25,824
Draffen, Vanessa J, corrections case mgr II, $40,380
Drage, Marilyn J, corrections ofcr I, $29,652
Drake, Alan W, corrections ofcr II, $33,348
Drake, Joseph P, functional unit mgr corr, $38,928
Drake, Kathy M, ofc spt asst (keybrd), $23,160
Drake, Kelsey R, corrections ofcr I, $29,652
Drake, Teri D, cook III, $28,104
Drane, Douglas D, fire & safety spec, $33,180
Draper, Andrea R, cook II, $24,264
Draper, Curtis A, maint spv I, $32,628
Dravenstott, Larry D, corrections ofcr II, $30,576
Drechsel, Nicholas J, investigator I, $29,976
Dredge, Scott D, corrections ofcr III, $32,628
Dredge, Valerie L, ofc spt asst (keybrd), $23,880
Drennen, Alvin F, food serv mgr II, $41,172
Drew, Brad D, corrections ofcr I, $29,652
Drew, Kenneth S, corrections ofcr I, $29,652
Dreyer, Patrick, corrections training ofcr, $41,172
Dreyer, Stephen J, corrections ofcr I, $29,652

Drinjak, Adela, prob & parole ofcr I, $29,976
Droney, Dawn M, corrections ofcr I, $29,652
Drope, Cotie, corrections ofcr I, $29,652
Drought, Michael A, corrections ofcr I, $30,132
Drummond, Jared M, prob & parole unit spv, $41,940
Drummond, Jessica, prob & parole ofcr II, $34,944
Drummond, Loraine R, ofc spt asst (keybrd), $23,160
Dryden, Catherine L, ofc spt asst (keybrd), $22,536
Dryden, Terry L, maint spv I, $34,356
Duba, Anita L, corrections ofcr I, $29,652
Dubach, Karen R, ofc spt asst (keybrd), $23,160
Dubbert, Leo J, storekeeper II, $28,104
Dubois, Ronni K, prob & parole ofcr II, $40,380
Dubose, Stanley E, prob & parole asst I, $29,496
Dubose, Vicky, prob & parole ofcr II, $41,940
Ducich, Douglas D, corrections case mgr II, $34,944
Duckett, Matthew G, prob & parole ofcr II, $36,204
Duckett, Todd L, corrections ofcr I, $28,692
Duckworth, David W, corrections ofcr II, $31,668
Duckworth, Ernest E, corrections ofcr I, $28,692
Duckworth, Howard J, corrections ofcr II, $31,668
Dudenhoeffer, Alicia M, admin ofc spt asst, $29,004
Duff, Deanna, prob & parole unit spv, $41,940
Duff, Diana L, prob & parole unit spv, $41,940
Dufrain, Joey P, prob & parole ofcr I, $37,548
Dugger, Cameron T, corrections ofcr I, $29,652
Dugger, Gregory L, corrections ofcr I, $30,132
Duing, Stanley H, corrections ofcr I, $29,652
Dulaney, Steven W, phys plant sup I, $36,204
Dulworth, Tarah L, corrections ofcr I, $29,652
Duly, Robert B, voc enter spv II, $30,984
Dunagan, Melvin W, prob & parole ofcr II, $39,624
Dunagan, Timothy A, electronics tech, $30,984
Dunavant, Donna J, subs abuse cnslr II, $34,944
Dunaway, David W, maint spv I, $31,512
Dunbar, Billy D, corrections mgr b1, $45,333
Duncan, Braden S, corrections ofcr I, $28,692
Duncan, Cassie J, prob & parole ofcr II, $38,232
Duncan, Christel A, corrections ofcr I, $29,652
Duncan, Dalton J, corrections ofcr I, $29,652
Duncan, Doyle, corrections ofcr I, $29,652
Duncan, James L, corrections ofcr I, $29,652
Duncan, Johnna, prob & parole ofcr II, $34,944
Duncan, Michael D, corrections ofcr I, $29,652
Duncan, Sandy D, voc enter spv II, $36,888
Duncan, Shane M, corrections ofcr I, $28,692
Duncan, Terry G, corrections ofcr I, $29,652
Duncan, Timothy K, maint spv I, $32,628
Dungan, Karen A, corrections mgr b1, $52,999
Dunlap, Brandy A, corrections case mgr II, $34,944
Dunlap, John C, corrections ofcr I, $32,784
Dunlap, Patrick D, functional unit mgr corr, $41,940
Dunlap, Patrick J, corrections ofcr I, $33,348
Dunlap, William C, corrections spv I, $41,172
Dunman, Ellen M, prob & parole ofcr II, $38,232
Dunn, Bruce L, corrections case mgr II, $36,204
Dunn, Garry H, corrections ofcr I, $29,652
Dunn, Gregory R, corrections spv II, $47,892
Dunn, Robert B, recrtn ofcr I, $32,052
Dunn, Sharon A, prob & parole unit spv, $49,128
Dunn, Thomas A, corrections mgr b2, $51,491
Dunn, William C, corrections ofcr I, $29,652
Dunn, Winfield S, factory mgr II, $38,928
Dunn, Zachary E, corrections ofcr I, $29,316
Dunnigan, Ronald J, corrections ofcr I, $29,652
Dunnington, Russell L, corrections ofcr I, $31,140
Dunwoody, Randy G, corrections ofcr I, $30,132
Dunwoody, Sean S, corrections ofcr I, $30,132
Dunwoody, Wilma J, pers clerk, $28,104
Duplin, Shawn J, edu sup, $41,940
Dupree, Keith E, storekeeper II, $29,976
Durbin, John E, corrections ofcr I, $29,652
Durbin, Michael W, prob & parole ofcr II, $36,888
Durbin, Yvonne C, corrections ofcr I, $32,784
Durden, Lashonda E, corrections ofcr I, $29,652
Durdle, Nicholaus L, prob & parole asst I, $29,496
Durfee, Todd M, corrections ofcr I, $28,692
Durham, Brian K, corrections ofcr I, $29,652
Durham, Delilah J, cook II, $24,264
Durham, Elizabeth, prob & parole ofcr II, $36,204
Durham, James W, corrections ofcr I, $29,652
Durham, Virgil M, corrections ofcr III, $39,624
Durrow, George W, corrections ofcr II, $31,668

Dusheke, Gary L, cook II, $24,264
Dusheke, Wesley, corrections ofcr I, $28,692
Dutcher, Christopher M, maint spv I, $32,628
Dwiggins, Samuel K, corrections ofcr I, $29,652
Dwyer, Linda A, account clerk II, $25,824
Dwyer, Stephanie A, subs abuse cnslr II, $34,944
Dydell, Karen L, corrections ofcr I, $32,784
Dye, Earl A, investigator II, $37,548
Dye, Terry P, corrections ofcr I, $29,652
Dyer, Amy E, corrections ofcr I, $29,652
Dysart, Robin L, corrections ofcr I, $29,652
Dysart, Tamara A, exec II, $39,624
Dysinger, Hollie A, corrections ofcr II, $31,668
Dzindolet, Justin A, corrections ofcr I, $28,692
Eadie, Rebecca L, corrections case mgr I, $29,976
Eads, Charity S, corrections ofcr I, $29,652
Eads, Donald D, corrections ofcr I, $29,652
Eads, Reba R, pers clerk, $28,104
Eady, Tarena T, corrections ofcr I, $29,652
Eagle, Andrew T, corrections ofcr I, $28,692
Eales, Charla K, corrections mgr b1, $49,738
Earl, Jeffrey K, designated principal asst dept, $60,000
Earls, Alan R, dpty div dir, $77,467
Earls, Alexander W, corrections case mgr I, $31,512
Earls, Bryan K, corrections ofcr III, $38,232
Earnest, Lonni R, corrections ofcr II, $31,668
Earnheart, Christopher M, corrections ofcr I, $29,652
Easler, Robert P, factory mgr I, $34,944
Eason, Beverly J, area sub abuse trtmnt coor, $45,156
Eason, Joshua D, corrections ofcr I, $29,652
Eason, Nicole R, corrections ofcr II, $31,668
Eason, Pamela S, corrections ofcr I, $29,652
East, Amy E, ofc spt asst (keybrd), $23,160
Easterwood, Andrea B, prob & parole ofcr II, $36,204
Eastland, Chester A, corrections ofcr I, $33,348
Eastman, Cody J, corrections ofcr I, $28,692
Eastwood, Terri A, pers clerk, $28,104
Eatherton, Dana S, ofc spt asst (keybrd), $23,160
Eaton, Erika M, corrections ofcr I, $29,652
Eaton, Randall G, phys plant sup III, $46,932
Eaton, Theodore T, corrections case mgr II, $36,204
Eaves, Sheila M, corrections ofcr I, $29,652
Eberhart, Caleb M, corrections ofcr I, $29,652
Eberle, Sandra K, corrections recs ofcr I, $28,104
Ebersold, Kathy, ofc spt asst (keybrd), $24,264
Ebersole, Jodie L, prob & parole ofcr II, $36,204
Ebert, James A, corrections ofcr II, $31,668
Ebert, Robert G, investigator I, $32,628
Ebert, Stephanie E, registered nurse - clin opers, $52,608
Ebong, Kini S, corrections ofcr I, $29,652
Echols, Alicia J, corrections ofcr I, $29,652
Eck, Amy R, prob & parole ofcr II, $36,204
Eckert, Randy D, corrections ofcr I, $28,692
Eckert, Stephanie J, corrections ofcr III, $32,628
Eckert, Tiffany M, corrections ofcr I, $29,652
Eckhoff, Adam R, corrections ofcr I, $29,652
Eckhoff, Ashley E, inst activity coor, $31,512
Eckhoff, David I, corrections ofcr I, $29,652
Eckhoff, Deena M, corrections ofcr I, $30,132
Eckhoff, Kevin E, corrections ofcr III, $36,888
Eckles, Haddie M, corrections ofcr I, $28,692
Eckrich, Matthew R, prob & parole ofcr II, $36,888
Eddleman, Caleb J, corrections ofcr I, $29,652
Eddy, Joseph P, special asst official & admstr, $76,861
Eddy, Tony L, maint spv I, $32,628
Edgar, Billy G, maint spv I, $32,628
Edgar, Cynthia M, corrections ofcr I, $30,132
Edgar, H Lynn, maint worker II, $29,004
Edgar, Robert L, corrections ofcr I, $30,132
Edging, Ronnie J, corrections ofcr I, $28,692
Edgmond, Patsy S, ofc spt asst (keybrd), $23,160
Edmond, Troy D, prob & parole asst I, $34,356
Edmonds, Lindell R, corrections case mgr III, $45,156
Edmondson, Patrick B, corrections ofcr I, $28,692
Edwards, Brandon L, prob & parole asst I, $29,496
Edwards, Casey L, corrections ofcr I, $29,652
Edwards, Deborah, prob & parole ofcr II, $36,204
Edwards, James C, facilities opps mgr b3, $72,507
Edwards, Jeannette M, sr ofc spt asst (keybrd), $27,084
Edwards, Jessie D, corrections ofcr I, $29,652
Edwards, Katherine S, corrections mgr b1, $49,735
Edwards, Kristofor A, corrections ofcr I, $29,652
Edwards, Loretta, prob & parole asst I, $29,496

Edwards, Michael G, prob & parole ofcr II, $36,204
Edwards, Natalie J, prob & parole ofcr II, $36,204
Edwards, Richard S, recrtn ofcr I, $30,984
Edwards, Rodney P, corrections ofcr I, $29,652
Edwards, Tommie L, phys plant sup II, $40,380
Edwards, Whitney M, corrections case mgr II, $34,944
Efnor, Alyson C, corrections ofcr II, $31,668
Efnor, Judy A, corrections ofcr I, $29,652
Efnor, Justin M, corrections ofcr I, $29,652
Eggers, Cheryl K, corrections ofcr I, $33,348
Egharevba, Friday O, corrections case mgr III, $37,548
Ehlers, Rebecca L, corrections mgr b2, $55,861
Ehovuon, Anthony, prob & parole ofcr II, $36,204
Eichholz, Lisa M, corrections ofcr I, $29,652
Eickelman, Richard E, maint spv I, $32,628
Eiman, Richard D, corrections ofcr I, $31,140
Ekeanyanwu, Charles, voc enter rep, $33,744
Ekstam, Teena M, corrections recs ofcr I, $28,104
Elam, Caleb, corrections ofcr I, $28,692
Elbert, Jordan B, prob & parole ofcr II, $36,204
Elbert, Sheila R, cook II, $24,264
Elbert, Susan E, ofc spt asst (keybrd), $23,160
Eldredge, Tristan R, corrections ofcr I, $29,652
Eldridge, Pamela D, special educ tchr III, $37,548
Eldridge, Roy J, corrections ofcr I, $29,652
Elger, Robert E, cook II, $24,264
Elgert, Gina J, corrections case mgr II, $34,944
Eliott, Darrell O, corrections ofcr I, $29,652
Elkins, Brandon A, corrections ofcr I, $29,652
Elkthunder, Jim, corrections ofcr I, $29,652
Ellerbeck, Gayle E, corrections ofcr I, $29,652
Ellermann, Cheryle A, prob & parole ofcr II, $40,380
Ellington, Mary L, corrections ofcr I, $29,652
Elliott, Amie L, prob & parole ofcr II, $36,204
Elliott, Benjamin V, corrections ofcr I, $28,692
Elliott, Elizabeth D, prob & parole ofcr II, $36,204
Elliott, Janet A, corrections ofcr I, $29,652
Elliott, Jody T, corrections ofcr I, $29,652
Elliott, Pamela L, investigator I, $30,984
Elliott, Pearl E, corrections ofcr I, $29,652
Elliott, Randall L, corrections ofcr III, $39,624
Elliott, Richard L, corrections ofcr I, $29,652
Elliott, Rick R, prob & parole asst I, $29,496
Elliott, Seth T, corrections ofcr II, $31,668
Elliott, Timothy W, corrections ofcr I, $29,652
Ellis, Charles L, corrections ofcr I, $29,652
Ellis, Dana M, prob & parole asst I, $29,496
Ellis, Daniel A, fire & safety spec, $31,512
Ellis, Darla K, ofc spt asst (keybrd), $23,160
Ellis, Donna J, acad tchr III, $37,548
Ellis, James E, corrections ofcr I, $29,652
Ellis, Jodi L, prob & parole ofcr II, $36,204
Ellis, Mark S, corrections ofcr II, $33,900
Ellis, Melissa R, storekeeper II, $28,104
Ellis, Robert E, corrections ofcr II, $33,348
Ellis, Roger D, corrections spv I, $38,232
Ellis, Ronald L, corrections ofcr III, $35,568
Ellis, Sierra R, corrections ofcr I, $29,652
Ellis, Stephanie L, corrections ofcr I, $29,652
Ellison, Melinda K, prob & parole ofcr II, $36,204
Ellzey, Charles M, corrections ofcr I, $33,348
Ellzey, David O, corrections ofcr II, $34,524
Elrod, Patricia C, cook III, $29,976
Elsberry, Kelsey, ofc spt asst (keybrd), $23,160
Elseman, Stacy M, admin ofc spt asst, $28,104
Emanuel, Marc D, corrections ofcr I, $33,348
Emberry, David W, corrections ofcr I, $31,140
Embree, Susan R, prob & parole ofcr II, $38,232
Embrey, Jason S, corrections ofcr I, $29,652
Embrey, Scott A, corrections ofcr I, $29,652
Embry, Erin E, acad tchr I, $29,976
Emerson, Rod B, corrections ofcr II, $31,668
Emerson, Sheryl E, ofc spt asst (keybrd), $23,160
Emert, Barbara, cook II, $24,264
Emery, Joshua A, corrections ofcr II, $33,348
Emmerich, Christopher A, corrections ofcr I, $28,692
Emmerich, Robert A, corrections ofcr II, $31,668
Emmons, Billy J, corrections ofcr I, $29,652
Emmons, Cynthia N, corrections ofcr II, $31,668
Emmons, Joel D, corrections ofcr I, $30,276
Emrick, Fred L, corrections ofcr I, $29,652
Enderle, Joseph B, corrections ofcr I, $29,652
Endsley, Edward, corrections ofcr I, $31,668

Engberg, Terry C, corrections ofcr I, $29,652
Engberg, Tina M, corrections ofcr I, $29,652
Engel, Danny W, corrections ofcr II, $28,692
Engelbrecht, Sara D, account clerk II, $26,652
Engelking, Sonya K, prob & parole ofcr II, $39,624
Engelman, Amanda P, corrections ofcr I, $29,652
Engelmann, Stephen E, corrections ofcr I, $29,652
England, Jason W, corrections ofcr II, $33,348
England, Laura R, corrections ofcr I, $29,652
Englehart, Rebecca A, corrections ofcr I, $28,692
Englert, Edward M, corrections ofcr I, $29,652
Eniade, Elias O, corrections case mgr II, $34,944
Enloe, Christopher W, corrections ofcr I, $29,652
Ensign, Jill E, ofc spt asst (keybrd), $23,880
Entrikin, Debra S, ofc spt asst (keybrd), $23,160
Epperson, Jessica E, corrections ofcr I, $29,652
Epperson, Lori A, corrections case mgr II, $35,568
Epping, Susan E, subs abuse cnslr II, $34,944
Epps, Jeremy G, corrections ofcr I, $29,652
Erickson, James, corrections ofcr I, $29,652
Erisman, Kayla, prob & parole ofcr II, $34,944
Erke, Carla S, corrections ofcr I, $31,140
Erke, Gail L, subs abuse cnslr III, $37,548
Erker, Bert D, prob & parole ofcr II, $38,232
Ernst, Matthew G, parole hearing analyst, $55,416
Ervin, Carlie H, subs abuse cnslr II, $33,744
Ervin, Charles M, recrtn ofcr I, $30,420
Ervin, Jessica D, cook II, $23,508
Eskridge, Stephen J, power plant mech, $30,984
Eslahi, Tom S, corrections ofcr I, $29,652
Esqueda, Tosha M, corrections ofcr I, $28,692
Essary, John M, chaplain, $39,529
Essary, Zelda K, ofc spt asst (keybrd), $23,160
Estes, Aaron S, storekeeper I, $25,824
Estes, Courtney D, corrections ofcr I, $28,692
Estes, Gary A, corrections ofcr I, $29,652
Estes, Lora E, prob & parole ofcr II, $36,204
Estes, Mandy L, corrections ofcr I, $29,652
Estes, Ryan D, corrections ofcr I, $29,652
Estes, Vivian L, ofc spt asst (keybrd), $23,160
Estes, William D, corrections ofcr II, $30,576
Estill, Jerri A, prob & parole ofcr II, $34,944
Etzler, Shammara J, corrections ofcr I, $29,652
Eudy, Gary, corrections ofcr I, $34,512
Eustace, Matthew W, corrections ofcr I, $29,652
Evans, Aaron G, corrections ofcr II, $31,668
Evans, Anita B, prob & parole asst I, $29,496
Evans, Ann J, corrections ofcr I, $29,652
Evans, David T, corrections ofcr I, $29,652
Evans, Diane K, corrections ofcr I, $29,652
Evans, Harvey L, corrections ofcr I, $29,652
Evans, Ian P, prob & parole unit spv, $41,940
Evans, James M, corrections ofcr I, $28,692
Evans, Jessica P, corrections ofcr I, $28,692
Evans, Johnny C, corrections ofcr I, $32,784
Evans, Kimberly M, special asst official & admstr, $53,025
Evans, Latonja L, prob & parole asst II, $33,180
Evans, Megan M, ofc spt asst (keybrd), $22,536
Evans, Michelle J, prob & parole asst II, $31,512
Evans, Nicole L, ofc spt asst (keybrd), $23,160
Evans, Thomas E, maint spv I, $32,628
Evans, Tracy J, prob & parole ofcr II, $39,624
Eveler, Keith A, fire & safety spec, $30,984
Everall, John S, corrections ofcr I, $29,652
Everhart, Sandra L, cook III, $28,104
Everhart, Terry M, corrections ofcr I, $29,652
Evers, Bethany A, sr ofc spt asst (keybrd), $25,824
Eversole, Christine V, corrections ofcr I, $29,652
Ewin, Daniel B, corrections ofcr II, $30,576
Ewing, Calena, corrections ofcr I, $29,652
Exendine, Nicholas T, corrections ofcr I, $28,692
Ezell, Cheryl L, ofc spt asst (keybrd), $23,160
Ezersky, David I, corrections ofcr II, $31,668
Ezzell, Colton L, corrections ofcr I, $29,316
Fagan, Kevin L, corrections ofcr I, $29,652
Fahland, Laurie A, corrections ofcr I, $29,652
Fahland, Stanley E, corrections ofcr I, $29,652
Fahning, Timothy J, prob & parole ofcr II, $36,204
Fahrlander, Gregory A, prob & parole ofcr II, $39,624
Fain, Patrick G, ofc spt asst (keybrd), $23,160
Fain, Thomas A, corrections ofcr I, $31,668
Fair, William E, corrections ofcr II, $31,668
Fairchild, Perry L, acad tchr III, $37,548

Fairclough, Pamela K, ofc spt asst (keybrd), $23,160
Falcon, Amanda A, corrections case mgr II, $34,944
Falkenrath, Doris E, designated principal asst div, $42,000
Falkenrath, Jeffrey D, corrections spv I, $38,928
Falls, Thomas J, maint worker II, $29,496
Fane, Terrell D, corrections ofcr I, $29,652
Fangman, Roger L, corrections ofcr I, $29,652
Fann, Maude H, corrections ofcr I, $29,652
Fannon, James H, prob & parole unit spv, $42,708
Fanter, Lora O, ofc spt asst (keybrd), $23,160
Farley, Justin B, corrections ofcr I, $29,652
Farley, Karen S, corrections case mgr II, $40,380
Farley, Terry M, corrections ofcr I, $30,132
Farley-Getty, Debbie A, prob & parole ofcr II, $40,380
Farmer, Christopher N, voc edu spv, $41,940
Farmer, Joan G, ofc spt asst (keybrd), $23,160
Farmer, Yulaunda S, corrections ofcr I, $29,661
Farnsworth, Gerald D, corrections ofcr I, $29,652
Farr, Jenny, prob & parole asst I, $29,160
Farr, William R, tractor trailer driver, $30,984
Farr, William W, corrections ofcr I, $29,652
Farr, Zachary T, corrections ofcr I, $29,652
Farrah, Jason D, corrections ofcr I, $29,661
Farrah, Randy M, corrections ofcr I, $28,692
Farrar, Lindsay, prob & parole ofcr II, $36,204
Farrell, Clayton D, corrections ofcr I, $29,652
Farrell, Dennis L, stationary engr, $33,744
Farrell, Ryan, prob & parole ofcr I, $30,984
Farrell, Thomas D, corrections ofcr II, $31,668
Farris, Bobby J, corrections ofcr I, $29,652
Farris, Corey L, corrections ofcr I, $28,692
Farris, Greg L, corrections ofcr I, $28,692
Farris, Richard D, storekeeper II, $29,976
Farrow, Sandra L, prob & parole ofcr II, $41,940
Fasching, Stacey M, corrections ofcr II, $33,348
Fassnacht, Leo J, corrections ofcr II, $30,576
Fast, Cameron T, corrections case mgr II, $36,204
Fattig, Gerald W, corrections ofcr I, $29,652
Fauke, Casey A, corrections ofcr I, $29,652
Faul, Stephanie G, storekeeper I, $25,824
Faulk, June L, ofc spt asst (steno), $25,032
Faulkner, Deborah, prob & parole asst I, $29,496
Faulkner, Donald, maint spv I, $32,628
Faulkner, Gena E, cook II, $24,264
Faulkner, Jason A, corrections ofcr I, $29,652
Faulkner, Roger L, corrections ofcr II, $31,668
Fay, Peggy J, storekeeper II, $28,104
Fearn, Kimberly E, sr ofc spt asst (keybrd), $25,824
Feely, William M, corrections ofcr II, $31,668
Fehling, Sheryl K, ofc spt asst (clerical), $22,536
Fehrenbach, James W, prob & parole unit spv, $41,940
Fehrenbach, William J, prob & parole unit spv, $41,940
Feigenspan, Donna K, storekeeper I, $25,824
Feiste, Tim W, corrections ofcr I, $29,652
Feith, Cherie L, corrections ofcr II, $33,348
Feith, Kenneth W, corrections ofcr III, $35,568
Feldman, Dorinda K, corrections ofcr I, $29,652
Feldmann, Kathryn L, corrections ofcr II, $31,668
Felgar, Mary J, recrtn ofcr III, $41,940
Felix, Andre, corrections ofcr I, $28,692
Feller, Jack D, corrections ofcr II, $35,724
Fellows, James A, corrections ofcr I, $32,784
Fels, Michael J, prob & parole ofcr II, $39,624
Feltner, Christopher G, corrections ofcr I, $29,652
Feltner, William J, corrections ofcr I, $29,652
Felton, Marla K, functional unit mgr corr, $39,624
Fenner, James E, stationary engr, $36,888
Fenton, Craig E, corrections ofcr II, $31,668
Fenton, Thomas C, corrections ofcr I, $28,692
Fenwick, Gary A, corrections ofcr I, $28,692
Fergerson, Nancy, sr ofc spt asst (keybrd), $25,824
Ferguson, Adam K, corrections ofcr I, $29,652
Ferguson, Craig E, maint worker II, $29,004
Ferguson, Karen D, prob & parole ofcr II, $41,172
Ferguson, Kimberly J, fire & safety spec, $31,512
Ferguson, Robert L, corrections ofcr I, $31,678
Ferguson, Ryan A, prob & parole ofcr I, $29,976
Ferguson, Samantha A, corrections ofcr I, $29,652
Ferry, Mary R, corrections ofcr I, $28,692
Fessler, Vicki L, corrections mgr b1, $47,913
Fester, Glen E, corrections ofcr I, $29,652
Fetterhoff, Dennis L, stationary engr, $33,744
Fewins, Clay L, corrections ofcr I, $29,652

Fick, Karen A, corrections recs ofcr III, $39,624
Fick, Paula J, admin ofc spt asst, $29,496
Fidler, Dwayne J, corrections ofcr II, $31,668
Fiedler, Melinda L, cook II, $24,264
Fielder, Larry E, fire & safety spec, $30,984
Fielder, Tonya D, corrections ofcr I, $31,140
Fields, Bonnie L, corrections ofcr I, $31,140
Fields, Darrel L, corrections ofcr I, $29,652
Fields, Katherine L, prob & parole ofcr III, $39,624
Fields, Marsha A, prob & parole ofcr II, $41,172
Fields, Patrick L, corrections ofcr I, $29,652
Fields, Richard, maint spv I, $34,356
Fields, Russell R, prob & parole ofcr I, $29,976
Fields, Susan L, corrections case mgr II, $34,944
Fife, Gay L, corrections recs ofcr III, $36,204
Figge, Margaret L, corrections ofcr I, $29,652
Figueroa, David E, corrections ofcr II, $31,668
Fike, Bret L, maint spv II, $36,204
Filbert, Tabetha L, prob & parole ofcr II, $38,232
Files, Charles R, subs abuse cnslr III, $39,624
Finch, Duane K, stationary engr, $33,744
Finden, Craig, prob & parole ofcr II, $36,204
Findley, Betty J, ofc spt asst (keybrd), $23,160
Findley, Brian W, corrections ofcr I, $30,276
Findley, Michelle L, prob & parole asst I, $29,496
Finley, Amanda L, corrections ofcr I, $29,652
Finley, Barbara M, ofc spt asst (keybrd), $23,160
Finley, Charles, corrections ofcr II, $31,668
Finley, Cory D, prob & parole asst I, $31,512
Finley, David R, garage spv, $32,628
Finley, Tara L, corrections ofcr II, $31,668
Finley, William J, corrections ofcr I, $29,652
Finney, Billy F, corrections ofcr I, $31,140
Finney, Jean L, corrections ofcr III, $33,744
Finton, John A, corrections ofcr I, $29,652
Fiorino, Jennifer K, ofc spt asst (keybrd), $23,160
Fipps, Jason A, corrections ofcr I, $29,652
Firebaugh, Lonnie, corrections ofcr I, $29,652
Firebaugh, Randy L, electronics tech, $30,984
Firkins, Wesley E, corrections ofcr I, $28,692
Firkus, Matthew T, corrections ofcr I, $29,652
Firkus, Thomas S, boiler oper, $27,660
Firnbach, Joseph W, corrections ofcr I, $29,652
Fisch, Francis R, corrections ofcr I, $29,652
Fisch, Lori A, corrections ofcr I, $29,652
Fischer, Clarissa K, prob & parole asst I, $29,496
Fischer, Devin R, supply mgr I, $31,512
Fischer, Jackie, graphic arts spec III, $36,204
Fischer, Julie A, ofc spt asst (keybrd), $23,160
Fischer, Mary D, account clerk II, $27,948
Fischer, Nancy M, cook III, $28,104
Fischer, Richard E, boiler oper, $28,104
Fish, Sherry K, corrections ofcr I, $29,652
Fisher, Alan L, corrections ofcr II, $37,056
Fisher, Angela D, accounting spec I, $34,944
Fisher, Brian K, corrections ofcr II, $31,668
Fisher, Gerald E, labor spv, $26,652
Fisher, Joseph C, maint spv I, $32,628
Fisher, Leroy F, corrections ofcr I, $29,652
Fisher, Rickey L, voc enter rep, $33,744
Fisk, Johnny R, corrections ofcr II, $33,348
Fitch, Gregory B, corrections ofcr I, $29,652
Fithen, George E, acad tchr III, $37,548
Fitzgerald, Daniel R, acad tchr III, $37,548
Fitzgerald, Esther M, prob & parole ofcr II, $39,624
Fitzgerald, Patrick, corrections case mgr II, $36,204
Fitzpatrick, Barbara H, ofc spt asst (keybrd), $23,160
Fitzpatrick, Dirk A, prob & parole asst I, $29,496
Fitzpatrick, Kelly L, prob & parole ofcr II, $39,624
Fitzwater, Sylvia K, ofc spt asst (keybrd), $25,032
Fjell, Ryan A, corrections ofcr II, $31,668
Flaherty, Brianne, prob & parole ofcr I, $30,984
Flaherty, Peter M, corrections ofcr I, $29,652
Fleetwood, Christopher S, corrections ofcr I, $29,652
Fleetwood, Melissa R, corrections ofcr I, $29,652
Fleetwood, Travis L, prob & parole ofcr II, $36,204
Fleharty, Jennifer, prob & parole ofcr II, $38,232
Fleharty, Todd D, prob & parole unit spv, $43,488
Fleischer, Brandon S, corrections ofcr I, $29,652
Fleischman, William G, prob & parole ofcr II, $38,232
Fleming, Ki A, corrections ofcr I, $28,692
Fleming, Ralph C, corrections ofcr I, $29,652
Flennoy, Jasimane D, corrections ofcr I, $29,652

Flentge, John D, corrections ofcr I, $34,512
Fleser, Michael, prob & parole ofcr I, $29,976
Fletchall, David D, corrections ofcr I, $29,652
Fletcher, Dakota, corrections case mgr II, $33,744
Fletcher, Heather L, prob & parole ofcr II, $36,204
Fletcher, John E, corrections ofcr I, $29,652
Fletcher, Joshua T, corrections ofcr I, $29,652
Fletcher, Paula D, corrections case mgr II, $36,204
Fletcher, Richard K, corrections ofcr I, $28,692
Fletcher, Steven E, recrtn ofcr II, $33,180
Flieg, Scott R, corrections ofcr I, $28,692
Fliegel, Laura E, med technologist trne, $28,104
Flies, Don W, corrections ofcr II, $33,348
Flint, Deborah K, cook III, $27,228
Flint, Elizabeth, subs abuse cnslr II, $34,944
Flint, James M, corrections ofcr I, $28,692
Flock, Catherine L, cook III, $28,104
Florea, Ashly L, corrections ofcr II, $30,576
Florea, Tammy S, storekeeper I, $25,824
Flores, Eduardo, prob & parole ofcr II, $36,204
Flowers, Elisha D, corrections ofcr I, $29,652
Flowers, Josh M, corrections ofcr I, $29,652
Flowers, Russell L, corrections ofcr II, $33,348
Fluellen, Diana L, prob & parole ofcr II, $41,172
Fluharty, Wesley A, corrections ofcr I, $28,692
Flynn, Eric, refrgrtn mech II, $33,744
Flynn, Lance, corrections ofcr I, $28,692
Flynn, Rhonda J, ofc spt asst (keybrd), $23,160
Fohey, Robert W, corrections mgr b1, $47,876
Foley, Brian D, corrections ofcr II, $30,576
Foley, Grace L, corrections ofcr II, $31,668
Foley, Susan J, prob & parole ofcr II, $40,380
Foley, William C, corrections ofcr I, $29,652
Foli, Jeffery C, corrections ofcr I, $28,692
Folker, Terrence, prod spec I corr, $42,708
Foly, Komla M, corrections ofcr I, $28,692
Forbes, Andrea S, prob & parole ofcr II, $36,204
Forbes, Norman M, corrections case mgr II, $34,944
Forbis, Joshua W, corrections ofcr I, $28,692
Forck, Christopher W, facilities opps mgr b2, $66,196
Ford, Don E, hvac inst ctrls tech, $30,984
Ford, James M, corrections ofcr II, $31,668
Ford, Kristen D, admin ofc spt asst, $28,104
Ford, Patrick R, corrections ofcr I, $31,668
Ford-Henry, Fontella, investigator III, $40,380
Foree, Alice M, storekeeper I, $26,652
Foreman, Daniel N, prob & parole ofcr I, $30,420
Forman, Glenn C, corrections ofcr II, $31,668
Forrest, Brandon J, corrections ofcr I, $28,692
Forster, David J, corrections ofcr I, $30,132
Forsyth, Catherine, prob & parole ofcr II, $36,204
Fort, Johnny W, corrections ofcr I, $29,652
Fortier, Nicholas R, corrections ofcr I, $29,652
Fortner, Debra L, corrections ofcr I, $31,140
Fortner, Donald G, corrections ofcr I, $31,668
Fortner, Donna J, ofc spt asst (keybrd), $23,160
Fortune, Kenneth J, corrections ofcr I, $29,652
Fostek, Nicholas J, corrections ofcr I, $29,652
Foster, Brian W, corrections ofcr I, $29,652
Foster, Charles A, corrections ofcr I, $29,652
Foster, Darlene A, storekeeper I, $28,452
Foster, David R, thrpst, $36.21/hr
Foster, Dustin C, corrections ofcr I, $29,652
Foster, Jacquelyn M, ofc spt asst (keybrd), $23,160
Foster, James R, corrections ofcr I, $29,652
Foster, Jenneca M, special asst ofc & clerical, $38,002
Foster, John G, prob & parole ofcr III, $42,708
Foster, Kimberlie H, prob & parole ofcr II, $36,204
Foster, Marie A, corrections ofcr I, $29,652
Foster, Mercedes D, corrections ofcr I, $28,692
Foster, Michael K, corrections ofcr I, $29,652
Foster, Sarah E, corrections ofcr I, $29,652
Foster, Scott A, corrections spv I, $42,708
Foster, Sidney B, corrections ofcr I, $29,652
Foster, Todd L, maint spv I, $32,628
Foster, Walter, corrections spv I, $38,928
Foulke, Nancy J, prob & parole ofcr II, $39,624
Fountain, Billy J, acad tchr III, $37,548
Foushee, Justin L, corrections ofcr I, $29,652
Fouts, Bryan D, corrections ofcr I, $29,652
Fowler, David M, corrections ofcr I, $31,140
Fowler, Dorothy J, ofc spt asst (keybrd), $23,160
Fowler, Glenn E, corrections ofcr I, $29,652

Fowler, Seneva S, account clerk II, $25,824
Fowler-Wieberg, Crystal L, corrections ofcr I, $29,652
Fox, Barbara J, corrections ofcr I, $28,692
Fox, James D, corrections ofcr I, $29,652
Fox, Jeni M, factory mgr II, $38,928
Fox, Melissa A, prob & parole ofcr II, $38,232
Fox, Scott A, corrections case mgr I, $40,380
Fraley, Dennis R, corrections ofcr I, $29,652
France, Brenda K, corrections classif asst, $32,052
Francis, Charla A, corrections ofcr I, $29,652
Francis, Crystal L, ofc spt asst (keybrd), $23,508
Francis, Daniel R, corrections ofcr III, $33,744
Francis, Dwight D, fire & safety spec, $31,512
Francis, Henry D, corrections ofcr I, $33,348
Francis, John A, corrections ofcr I, $29,652
Francis, John W, corrections ofcr I, $29,652
Francis, Judith A, corrections ofcr I, $29,652
Francis, Lori A, ofc spt asst (clerical), $24,612
Francis, Nicholas R, corrections ofcr I, $29,652
Francis, Nicole L, corrections case mgr I, $29,976
Francis, Rickey H, phys plant sup I, $36,204
Francis, Steven T, recrtn ofcr I, $29,976
Francis, Todd D, corrections mgr b2, $49,937
Francke, Christopher, prob & parole ofcr II, $36,204
Francois, Shanan L, cook II, $23,508
Frank, Floyd G, maint spv II, $38,232
Frank, Jamie L, corrections case mgr I, $31,512
Franke, David R, corrections ofcr II, $33,348
Franken, Justin W, corrections ofcr III, $32,628
Franken, Lorena M, corrections ofcr I, $29,652
Franklin, Douglas L, electronics tech, $31,512
Franklin, Kenneth L, prob & parole asst I, $29,976
Franklin, Leslie L, admin ofc spt asst, $31,512
Franklin, Linda M, corrections ofcr I, $31,140
Franklin, Regina D, prob & parole ofcr II, $36,204
Franklin, Richard A, edu asst II, $24,804
Franklin, Robert L, prob & parole asst II, $30,420
Frans, Brandon, corrections ofcr I, $28,692
Fredrich, Travis D, corrections ofcr I, $29,652
Fredrick, Diana M, procurement ofcr II, $49,128
Fredrick, Patrick J, corrections ofcr I, $29,652
Freeland, Joseph, maint worker II, $29,004
Freelin, Jeannie M, corrections ofcr I, $29,652
Freels, Jennifer L, corrections ofcr III, $32,220
Freeman, Agnas C, corrections ofcr I, $29,652
Freeman, Barbara A, sr ofc spt asst (keybrd), $25,824
Freeman, Charles M, corrections training ofcr, $38,928
Freeman, Donna M, cook III, $30,984
Freeman, Gary, corrections classif asst, $32,628
Freeman, John C, cook III, $32,052
Freeman, Orville C, corrections ofcr I, $32,784
Freeman, Richard C, corrections ofcr I, $29,652
Freeman, Tammy L, prob & parole ofcr II, $36,204
Freeman, Timothy A, corrections case mgr II, $36,204
Freie, Tiffany C, prob & parole ofcr II, $36,204
Freiheit, Paul W, corrections ofcr I, $29,652
French, Derek S, corrections ofcr II, $30,576
French, Jerry L, corrections ofcr I, $28,692
French, Missy M, prob & parole ofcr II, $36,204
Frerk, Todd P, corrections ofcr I, $33,348
Frese, Joseph R, corrections ofcr I, $29,652
Freund, Alex L, corrections ofcr I, $29,652
Frey, Lori M, functional unit mgr corr, $40,380
Friedrich, Dwight D, corrections ofcr I, $29,652
Friend, Derrel P, corrections ofcr I, $29,652
Friend, Patricia L, sr ofc spt asst (keybrd), $25,824
Friend, Timmy R, recrtn ofcr II, $36,204
Friesen, Leland O, corrections ofcr II, $31,668
Friesen, Walter A, corrections ofcr III, $35,568
Friesz, Charles G, corrections ofcr I, $29,652
Friesz, George M, phys plant sup I, $36,204
Friesz, Keith M, recrtn ofcr I, $30,984
Friesz, Laura J, investigator I, $35,568
Frimpong-Derkyi, Theophilus, corrections ofcr II, $30,576
Frisbie, Melanie A, prob & parole ofcr II, $36,204
Frisbie, Michael E, electronics tech, $30,984
Frisbie, Robertia L, corrections case mgr II, $40,380
Fritz, Jeremy W, corrections ofcr I, $28,692
Fritz, Richard H, corrections ofcr II, $31,668
Fritz, Robert C, corrections ofcr I, $29,652
Fritzinger, Andrew W, corrections ofcr II, $31,668
Fritzinger, Mary, corrections ofcr II, $34,512
Frock, Robert D, corrections ofcr I, $29,652

Fronick, Mark E, corrections ofcr II, $31,668
Frost, Grant D, corrections ofcr II, $31,668
Frost, Leroy G, corrections ofcr I, $29,652
Frump, Michael A, corrections ofcr I, $29,652
Fry, Jeffrey E, corrections ofcr I, $29,652
Fry, Tina L, admin ofc spt asst, $32,628
Fryman, Ronda, ofc spt asst (keybrd), $23,160
Fuchs, Robyn M, prob & parole ofcr II, $40,380
Fugate, Kevin L, corrections ofcr I, $29,652
Fuhr, Larry D, maint spv I, $36,888
Fuller, Donald F, corrections ofcr I, $31,668
Fuller, Garry L, corrections ofcr I, $33,900
Fuller, Heather E, ofc spt asst (keybrd), $23,160
Fuller, Joshua C, corrections ofcr I, $29,652
Fuller, Nathaniel, corrections ofcr I, $29,652
Fulmer, Jennifer A, prob & parole ofcr II, $38,232
Fulop, Nicolas J, corrections ofcr I, $30,132
Fulton, Catherine, ofc spt asst (keybrd), $22,536
Fults, Rex M, prob & parole asst I, $29,496
Funk, Nichole M, prob & parole ofcr II, $36,204
Funk, William T, corrections ofcr II, $33,348
Funston, Cheryl A, corrections ofcr I, $29,652
Furgason, Richard C, corrections ofcr II, $31,668
Furlong, Connie S, cook II, $24,264
Fuwell, Allen L, corrections ofcr II, $31,668
Fuwell, Gary W, corrections case mgr II, $34,944
Gabel, Keith A, corrections ofcr I, $29,652
Gabel, Paul D, corrections ofcr I, $29,652
Gabing, Joel, corrections ofcr I, $29,652
Gaertner, Gary E, corrections ofcr I, $30,132
Gage, Christopher J, ofc spt asst (keybrd), $23,160
Gage, Frederick F, corrections ofcr I, $29,652
Gainer, Gene H, corrections ofcr I, $29,652
Gaines, Charles L, corrections ofcr I, $29,652
Gaines, David A II, corrections ofcr I, $29,652
Gaines, Leda D, cook II, $24,264
Gaines, Mary A, prob & parole ofcr II, $36,204
Gaines, Richard A, corrections spv I, $44,304
Gaither, Carrie, ofc spt asst (keybrd), $23,160
Gaither, Mark L, corrections ofcr I, $31,140
Galbreath, Andrea R, corrections ofcr II, $33,900
Galbreath, Charles E, corrections ofcr I, $29,652
Galbreath, Deetrilynn, account clerk II, $25,032
Galbreath, Kimberly S, recrtn ofcr II, $34,944
Galbreath, Marshall E, food serv mgr II, $37,548
Gall, Rocky A, corrections ofcr I, $29,652
Gallaher, Michael, maint spv II, $36,888
Gallego, Tina M, corrections ofcr I, $29,652
Galloway, Donald, corrections ofcr I, $30,132
Gamble, Andrew W, corrections ofcr III, $38,232
Gamble, Kevin, corrections ofcr I, $28,692
Gammon, Jason A, corrections ofcr I, $29,652
Gammons, Roger D, recrtn ofcr I, $34,356
Gann, Douglas L, corrections ofcr I, $29,652
Gann, Jennifer, sr ofc spt asst (keybrd), $25,032
Gann, Michael D, corrections mgr b2, $55,589
Gann, Nancy J, ofc spt asst (keybrd), $22,536
Gannon, Franklin D, corrections ofcr I, $29,652
Gansner, Timothy M, corrections ofcr I, $28,692
Gant, Laura D, maint worker II, $29,004
Gant, Terry E, stationary engr, $37,548
Garcia, Patricia, ofc spt asst (keybrd), $23,880
Gardner, Chad W, corrections ofcr I, $28,692
Gardner, Clay S, prob & parole ofcr II, $40,380
Gardner, Elizabeth K, corrections ofcr I, $28,692
Gardner, Merritt T, corrections ofcr I, $29,652
Gardner, Roxane M, ofc spt asst (keybrd), $23,160
Garner, Carolyn S, prob & parole ofcr II, $36,204
Garner, Jason D, corrections ofcr I, $29,652
Garner, Justin B, corrections ofcr I, $29,652
Garner, Tara B, prob & parole ofcr II, $36,204
Garner, Theresa K, corrections ofcr I, $31,140
Garnett, Jerry D, corrections spv II, $45,156
Garnett, Jolene J, corrections ofcr I, $30,132
Garoutte, Valerie M, prob & parole ofcr II, $36,204
Garrett, Hunter D, corrections ofcr I, $29,652
Garrett, John M, corrections ofcr I, $29,652
Garrett, Megan N, corrections ofcr I, $29,652
Garrett, Paul D, corrections case mgr II, $38,928
Garrigus, Holly N, corrections ofcr I, $29,652
Garrigus, Steven A, corrections ofcr I, $31,140
Garrison, Ashley M, corrections ofcr I, $28,692
Garrison, Julie D, admin ofc spt asst, $27,228

Garsee, Rickey D, prob & parole ofcr II, $36,204
Gartman, John M, corrections ofcr I, $29,652
Garton, Mary R, corrections ofcr I, $29,652
Garvis, Carolyn A, corrections ofcr I, $29,652
Garwood, Cassie D, prob & parole unit spv, $41,940
Garza, Danila M, corrections ofcr I, $28,692
Gash, Tracy J, corrections ofcr I, $29,652
Gaskin, Christina A, prob & parole ofcr II, $36,204
Gastineau, Noreen G, cook I, $22,872
Gaston, Debra K, account clerk II, $25,824
Gates, Sue E, voc tchr III, $37,548
Gatewood, Heather R, corrections ofcr I, $29,652
Gatewood, Robert R, corrections ofcr I, $29,652
Gatlin, Carl F, acad tchr III, $37,548
Gatson, Brent M, corrections ofcr III, $33,744
Gatton, Karen L, corrections case mgr II, $34,944
Gatton, Rose L, corrections ofcr II, $33,900
Gaudet, Jessica G, ofc spt asst (keybrd), $22,536
Gaughan, William E, prob & parole ofcr II, $34,944
Gault, Amanda N, corrections ofcr I, $28,692
Gaunt, Cheree R, prob & parole ofcr II, $36,204
Gaunt, Janette S, cook II, $24,264
Gavin, Jill S, sr ofc spt asst (keybrd), $25,824
Gaydos, Allen, corrections ofcr I, $31,668
Gaye, Victor B, prob & parole asst I, $29,976
Geary, Timothy M, corrections ofcr I, $29,652
Geasley, John M, corrections ofcr I, $28,692
Gebhard, Michael P, corrections ofcr I, $29,652
Gee, Willie W, corrections ofcr I, $32,292
Geer, Joseph M, corrections ofcr I, $29,652
Geesing, Ryan M, corrections ofcr I, $29,652
Gehlert, Kenneth J, corrections ofcr I, $29,652
Geiger, Michael R, corrections ofcr I, $29,652
Geiser, Teddy L, corrections ofcr I, $29,652
Geiser, William, corrections ofcr I, $29,652
Geldner, John E, corrections ofcr II, $30,576
Gelski, Kyle D, functional unit mgr corr, $37,548
Gentry, Dalton L, corrections ofcr II, $31,668
Gentry, Jimmie L, corrections case mgr II, $38,232
Gentry, Meredith, prob & parole ofcr II, $36,204
Gentry, Patrick W, corrections case mgr II, $34,944
George, Brian T, parole hearing analyst, $49,128
George, Candas J, cook III, $27,228
George, Eric, prob & parole ofcr II, $34,944
George, Rita A, corrections ofcr I, $28,692
Gerard, Michael S, corrections ofcr I, $29,652
Gerard, Waylon M, corrections ofcr I, $28,692
Gerard, Wayne, corrections ofcr I, $32,784
Gerdes, Marvin G, subs abuse cnslr III, $37,548
Gerding, Nelda J, corrections recs ofcr III, $36,204
Gerke, John D, functional unit mgr corr, $38,928
Gerke, Steven M, corrections ofcr I, $28,692
Gerlt, Willa J, corrections ofcr I, $29,652
German, Kelli J, corrections ofcr I, $29,652
German, Michael A, corrections ofcr I, $29,652
Gerrish, Richard A, corrections case mgr II, $40,380
Gerrish, Sherry K, corrections case mgr II, $34,944
Gerstenberger, Phillip R, prob & parole ofcr II, $40,380
Gertz, Amy R, functional unit mgr corr, $41,940
Gette, Jason E, corrections ofcr I, $29,652
Gette, Joseph I, corrections ofcr I, $29,652
Gettinger, Steven P, corrections ofcr I, $29,652
Giallongo, Giovanni S, corrections ofcr I, $29,652
Gibbs, Jenny B, ofc spt asst (keybrd), $23,160
Gibbs, Johnny S, corrections spv II, $48,156
Gibson, April E, special asst paraprof, $41,425
Gibson, Beth L, corrections classif asst, $29,976
Gibson, Brennan S, investigator III, $38,928
Gibson, Harold L, maint spv I, $35,568
Gibson, Jeffrey M, corrections ofcr I, $28,692
Gibson, Joseph P, corrections ofcr I, $30,276
Gibson, Kevin C, maint worker II, $29,004
Gibson, William G, tractor trailer driver, $30,984
Gidney, Jack A, corrections ofcr I, $33,348
Gier, Karla D, admin ofc spt asst, $32,628
Giese, Laurie D, corrections ofcr I, $30,576
Giese, Steven, corrections ofcr I, $32,220
Gifford, Clyde L, corrections ofcr I, $29,652
Gifford, Ronald G, maint spv I, $33,180
Gifford, Steven D, corrections spv I, $40,380
Gilbert, Frank M, corrections ofcr I, $29,652
Gilbert, Thelma J, prob & parole ofcr II, $39,624
Gilchrist, Kirk R, corrections ofcr I, $29,652

Gildehaus, Julie M, corrections ofcr II, $31,668
Gildersleeve, Christina N, prob & parole unit spv, $44,304
Gile, Joseph D, corrections ofcr I, $29,652
Giles, Russell A, corrections ofcr I, $29,652
Gilgour, David W, corrections ofcr I, $28,692
Gilgour, James L, corrections ofcr I, $29,652
Gilgour, Judy L, corrections ofcr I, $33,900
Gillam, Donna L, food serv mgr II, $35,568
Gillam, Joseph C, corrections ofcr I, $29,652
Gillam, Joseph L, corrections ofcr I, $34,512
Gillespie, Jason B, corrections ofcr I, $29,652
Gillespie, Stacy D, sr ofc spt asst (keybrd), $26,232
Gilliam, Tia J, account clerk II, $28,908
Gilliam, Winford R, corrections ofcr II, $31,668
Gillilan, Robert J, corrections ofcr II, $32,220
Gilmer, Jennifer M, corrections ofcr I, $29,652
Gilmore, Affton C, prob & parole ofcr I, $30,420
Gilmore, Albert R, tractor trailer driver, $34,356
Gilmore, Carina L, corrections ofcr I, $28,692
Gilmour, William R, acad tchr III, $37,548
Gilpin, Teresa A, ofc spt asst (keybrd), $23,160
Gilson, Debora M, corrections ofcr I, $30,132
Gilyard, Belinda, ofc spt asst (keybrd), $22,536
Gingerich, Cynthia L, prob & parole unit spv, $45,156
Gipson, Amanda S, admin ofc spt asst, $28,104
Girardier, Bridgette M, corrections ofcr I, $29,652
Gisselbeck, Erin M, prob & parole ofcr II, $36,888
Gittemeier, Frank, corrections spv I, $40,380
Gittemeier, Lynn F, corrections ofcr III, $35,568
Gittemeier, Matt J, corrections ofcr II, $33,900
Gittemeier, Tammi G, corrections case mgr II, $34,944
Givens, Jacob A, corrections ofcr I, $30,276
Givens, Steven W, corrections ofcr I, $28,692
Gladbach, Shelly R, admin ofc spt asst, $28,104
Glaser, Rhonda L, corrections ofcr II, $33,348
Glasgow, Jackie G, corrections spv I, $41,172
Glasgow-Cobb, Karla L, corrections mgr b1, $49,104
Glass, James A, corrections ofcr II, $35,100
Glawson, Alan D, storekeeper I, $25,824
Glendening, Theresa M, area sub abuse trtmnt coor, $45,156
Glenn, Helga N, storekeeper II, $28,104
Glenn, Steven A, entprss mgr b1, $44,493
Gloe, Linda L, prob & parole asst I, $28,536
Gloe, Susanne R, corrections ofcr II, $31,668
Glore, Candida M, sr ofc spt asst (keybrd), $29,412
Glore, Larry J, recrtn ofcr III, $40,380
Glore, Lonnie G, stationary engr, $33,744
Glover, Jessica, prob & parole ofcr I, $29,976
Glover, Jessica M, acad tchr III, $36,204
Glover, Kelly J, corrections ofcr I, $29,652
Glydewell, Charles N, corrections ofcr I, $29,652
Glydewell, Diana R, corrections ofcr I, $29,652
Goad, Douglas D, corrections ofcr II, $37,056
Goad, Kenneth D, corrections ofcr I, $29,652
Gober, James T, corrections spv II, $46,068
Gober, Michael R, voc enter spv II, $29,976
Goble, Monica K, corrections ofcr I, $29,652
Godat, Lydia S, ofc spt asst (keybrd), $23,160
Godert, Chantay R, corrections mgr b2, $49,909
Godfirnon, Penny S, corrections ofcr I, $31,140
Godley, Tracey D, corrections ofcr I, $29,652
Godsey, Terri L, prob & parole ofcr II, $36,204
Goebel, Timothy J, corrections spv II, $46,068
Goedeke, Kimberly R, admin ofc spt asst, $28,104
Goedken, Lori, corrections training ofcr, $42,708
Goedken, Matthew J, subs abuse cnslr III, $37,548
Goen, Marcia S, ofc spt asst (keybrd), $25,824
Goeppner, K Renee, prob & parole unit spv, $43,488
Goetsch, Beverly A, cook II, $24,264
Goetz, Rebecca A, prob & parole ofcr II, $19,116
Goff, Gregory B, maint spv I, $33,180
Goff, Jennifer A, ofc spt asst (keybrd), $23,160
Goff, Kendall R, acad tchr III, $37,548
Goff, Kyler A, corrections ofcr I, $29,652
Goforth, Devon M, corrections ofcr I, $28,692
Goforth, Mark, corrections ofcr I, $29,652
Goheen, Candy L, sr ofc spt asst (keybrd), $25,824
Gold, Hans, prob & parole ofcr I, $29,976
Golden, Crystal S, corrections ofcr I, $29,652
Golden, Daniel W, corrections ofcr I, $28,692
Golden, Jeremiah, prob & parole ofcr I, $29,976
Golden, Mishelle D, sr ofc spt asst (keybrd), $25,824
Golden, Rhonda, prob & parole ofcr II, $39,624

Golden, Sherman K, corrections ofcr I, $29,652
Goldman, Ruby M, prob & parole asst I, $30,984
Goldsmith, Robert S, corrections ofcr I, $29,652
Goldsmith, Roy D, corrections ofcr I, $29,652
Golian, Justin M, corrections ofcr II, $31,668
Golian, Michael P, corrections ofcr III, $33,744
Gollon, Jason H, prob & parole ofcr II, $36,204
Goltra, Sandra M, ofc spt asst (clerical), $22,536
Gomez, Natalie L, prob & parole unit spv, $46,068
Gonzalez, Isaiah T, prob & parole ofcr I, $30,984
Gonzalez, Michael, corrections ofcr I, $33,348
Gooch, Patricia M, corrections ofcr I, $28,692
Good, Dale L, corrections mgr b1, $55,143
Good, Keith A, prob & parole asst II, $31,512
Good, Timothy W, corrections ofcr I, $29,652
Good, Tosha M, subs abuse cnslr III, $37,548
Goodin, Heather M, prob & parole ofcr I, $36,204
Gooding, Dale L, corrections ofcr I, $30,132
Goodman, Gail S, corrections ofcr I, $29,652
Goodrich, Diann, corrections ofcr I, $29,652
Goodrich, Krista S, ofc spt asst (keybrd), $23,160
Goodroad, Dana M, subs abuse cnslr II, $34,944
Goodson, Brenda K, corrections ofcr I, $29,652
Goodson, Cody D, corrections ofcr I, $29,652
Goodson, Martina L, sr ofc spt asst (keybrd), $25,824
Goodson, Terry D, corrections ofcr I, $30,132
Goodwin, Elizabeth A, corrections ofcr I, $29,652
Goodwin, Gregory T, corrections ofcr I, $29,652
Goodwin, Jamie C, prob & parole ofcr II, $36,204
Goodwin, Kimberly, prob & parole ofcr II, $36,204
Goolie, Lora A, corrections ofcr I, $28,692
Goon, Michelle L, corrections ofcr I, $29,652
Gordley, Illyssa, prob & parole ofcr II, $34,944
Gordon, Delora L, corrections case mgr II, $34,944
Gordon, Ellis E, corrections ofcr I, $31,140
Gordon, George F, corrections ofcr III, $33,744
Gordon, Richard A, corrections ofcr I, $29,652
Gorham, Jay P, functional unit mgr corr, $38,928
Gorham, Jimmie R, corrections ofcr I, $29,652
Gorman, James, prob & parole ofcr II, $36,888
Gorman, Joseph, prob & parole ofcr I, $30,420
Gosche, Crystal G, prob & parole ofcr II, $36,204
Gose, Maria C, ofc spt asst (keybrd), $23,160
Goss, Jason W, corrections ofcr I, $29,652
Gottman, Jordan, prob & parole ofcr II, $34,944
Gould, Lawrence W, corrections ofcr I, $28,692
Govero, Audrey D, storekeeper I, $25,824
Govreau, Jerry L, laundry mgr, $34,944
Grable, Kristal L, corrections ofcr I, $28,692
Grace, Shunn Q, corrections ofcr I, $29,652
Graczyk, William G, corrections ofcr I, $29,652
Grady, Kiatah J, prob & parole ofcr II, $36,204
Graeff, Faith H, corrections case mgr II, $34,944
Graen, Thomas N, cook II, $24,264
Graen, Thomas N, storekeeper I, $26,232
Graf, Lisa M, ofc spt asst (keybrd), $23,160
Graf, Shelly L, corrections training ofcr, $42,708
Gragg, Thomas E, corrections ofcr I, $29,652
Graham, Andrew L, corrections ofcr I, $28,692
Graham, Deanna D, corrections ofcr I, $29,652
Graham, Donald G, maint spv I, $32,628
Graham, Edward E, corrections ofcr I, $31,140
Graham, Kenneth W, factory mgr II, $40,380
Graham, Larry C, corrections ofcr III, $37,548
Graham, Lisa A, procurement ofcr I, $37,548
Graham, Nicholas R, corrections ofcr I, $29,652
Graham, Norman M, corrections ofcr III, $33,744
Graham, Robert K, corrections ofcr I, $29,652
Graham, Russell D, corrections ofcr I, $33,348
Graham, Sherri L, ofc spt asst (keybrd), $25,404
Gramlich, Douglas H, corrections case mgr II, $38,928
Gramlich, Joseph C, functional unit mgr corr, $40,380
Grange, James D, corrections ofcr I, $29,652
Granger, Gina D, prob & parole unit spv, $43,488
Granger, Katherine, prob & parole ofcr II, $36,204
Granneman, William D, corrections ofcr II, $33,348
Grant, Bryant T, corrections ofcr I, $28,692
Grant, Cary E, corrections spv I, $38,928
Grant, Christopher, prob & parole ofcr II, $34,944
Grant, Sharon E, voc edu spv, $40,380
Gratto, Thomas J, investigator II, $37,548
Graul, Jeremy G, corrections ofcr I, $29,652
Graver, David W, corrections ofcr II, $31,668

Graver, Joyce L, corrections case mgr II, $34,944
Graver, Robin L, ofc spt asst (keybrd), $23,160
Graves, Katherine A, corrections ofcr I, $29,652
Graves, Patricia L, corrections ofcr I, $29,652
Gravett, Carl, corrections ofcr I, $29,652
Gray, Aaron D, corrections ofcr I, $29,652
Gray, Antonio M, prob & parole asst I, $29,496
Gray, Brian L, garage spv, $32,628
Gray, Christopher M, maint spv I, $31,512
Gray, Deantwan C, corrections ofcr I, $29,652
Gray, Elaine K, account clerk II, $25,824
Gray, Gary W, corrections ofcr III, $35,568
Gray, Janie C, corrections ofcr I, $31,668
Gray, Kara N, ofc spt asst (keybrd), $22,536
Gray, Michael D, corrections case mgr II, $39,624
Gray, Orval D, boiler oper, $28,104
Gray, Phyllis R, corrections ofcr II, $31,668
Gray, Rosie L, corrections ofcr I, $28,692
Gray, Sammie J, corrections ofcr I, $29,652
Gray, Shelley L, corrections ofcr III, $35,568
Gray, Stephen W, prob & parole asst I, $30,984
Gray, Toya A, prob & parole ofcr I, $29,976
Grayson, David J, corrections ofcr I, $33,348
Grayson, Kelli J, corrections ofcr I, $29,652
Graze, Bridget, ofc spt asst (keybrd), $22,536
Graziano, Brett M, recrtn ofcr I, $29,976
Grebner, Steven D, maint spv I, $32,628
Green, Carol, ofc spt asst (keybrd), $23,160
Green, Carrie A, prob & parole ofcr II, $36,204
Green, Charlene K, inst activity coor, $31,512
Green, Donald E, corrections ofcr I, $29,652
Green, Joyce A, accounting spec II, $40,380
Green, Joyce E, prob & parole ofcr II, $38,232
Green, Melissa L, ofc spt asst (keybrd), $23,160
Green, Michael R, prob & parole ofcr II, $38,232
Green, Randall J, corrections ofcr I, $29,652
Green, Randy A, corrections ofcr I, $31,668
Green, Roger L, corrections ofcr I, $29,652
Green, Ronald L, voc tchr III, $41,940
Green, Russell L, corrections ofcr II, $31,668
Green, Shari K, prob & parole ofcr II, $39,624
Green, Teresa L, prob & parole ofcr II, $36,888
Green, Thomas E, corrections ofcr I, $29,652
Green, Tracy E, corrections ofcr I, $29,652
Green, William B, corrections ofcr II, $35,724
Green, Willis B, corrections ofcr I, $28,692
Greene, Angela, prob & parole ofcr II, $34,944
Greene, Jennifer A, corrections ofcr III, $33,744
Greene, Keyshane C, corrections ofcr I, $29,652
Greene, Monica L, prob & parole asst I, $29,496
Greene, Terrese R, prob & parole asst II, $33,180
Greene, Todd D, corrections ofcr I, $28,692
Greenfield, Schelby B, corrections ofcr I, $29,652
Greenlee, Dustin A, corrections ofcr I, $29,652
Greenwood, Charles E, corrections ofcr I, $29,652
Greenwood, Garry L, corrections ofcr II, $31,668
Greer, Krishonya R, corrections case mgr I, $29,976
Greer, Steven J, prob & parole ofcr II, $36,204
Gregg, Esther M, corrections ofcr I, $33,900
Gregg, Roxanne J, corrections ofcr I, $29,652
Gregorc, Anthony C, corrections ofcr I, $29,652
Gregory, Curtis W, corrections ofcr I, $29,652
Gregory, Melanie, prob & parole asst I, $29,496
Gregory, Robert H, corrections ofcr I, $29,652
Greiner, Stephanie M, training tech II, $40,380
Gremmel, Brian J, prob & parole ofcr II, $37,548
Gremminger, Broc A, corrections ofcr II, $31,668
Gremminger, Christopher L, corrections training ofcr, $38,928
Gremminger, Tammy L, prob & parole ofcr II, $39,624
Gresham, Kraig A, corrections training ofcr, $41,940
Gresham, Tonya L, storekeeper II, $25,824
Grider, Carel J, corrections ofcr III, $35,568
Grider, Joseph C, corrections ofcr I, $29,652
Grier, Brian, corrections ofcr I, $29,652
Grierson, Jennifer L, prob & parole ofcr II, $36,204
Grieshaber, Christopher J, corrections ofcr I, $29,652
Grieshammer, Joshua D, corrections ofcr I, $28,692
Griffin, Donna S, corrections ofcr I, $31,140
Griffin, James R, corrections ofcr I, $29,652
Griffin, Melody H, registered nurse - clin opers, $68,532
Griffin, Michael J, corrections ofcr I, $29,652
Griffin, Robert A, corrections case mgr II, $38,232
Griffin, Stephanie M, prob & parole asst I, $29,496

Griffin, Wanda E, corrections ofcr I, $31,140
Griffith, Cindy A, corrections mgr b3, $62,081
Griffith, David W, recrtn ofcr II, $34,356
Griffith, James D, storekeeper I, $25,824
Griffith, Steven D, corrections ofcr I, $28,692
Griffith, Steven G, corrections ofcr I, $33,348
Griffiths, James S, corrections ofcr I, $29,652
Grigery, James D, corrections ofcr I, $29,652
Grigg, Mark A, corrections ofcr I, $29,652
Grigg, Sharon K, corrections ofcr I, $29,652
Griggs, Charles R, corrections ofcr I, $29,652
Griggs, Donald J, prob & parole ofcr II, $36,204
Griggs, Richard S, corrections mgr b1, $45,340
Grillo, Crystal A, corrections ofcr I, $28,692
Grimes, Jeremiah R, prob & parole ofcr II, $40,380
Grimes, Joseph P, corrections ofcr I, $30,132
Grimes, Kristopher G, corrections ofcr I, $29,652
Grimes, Warren E, corrections ofcr I, $30,132
Grimm, Beverly S, corrections ofcr III, $34,356
Grimm, Christa I, corrections ofcr I, $29,652
Grimsley, Jeff W, maint spv I, $35,568
Grinder, Tina K, prob & parole ofcr II, $36,204
Grindstaff, Jodi R, storekeeper II, $30,420
Grindstaff, Shelia A, cook II, $24,264
Grinstead, Pamela K, cook III, $28,104
Grivas, John M, corrections ofcr I, $28,692
Groce, Stacey L, ofc spt asst (clerical), $22,536
Groce, Virginia L, ofc spt asst (keybrd), $22,536
Groes, Rebecca L, prob & parole ofcr II, $36,888
Groff, Lori A, ofc spt asst (keybrd), $11,580
Grohmann, Eric E, corrections ofcr I, $29,652
Groll, Jeremiah R, corrections ofcr I, $29,652
Groll, Kyle T, corrections case mgr II, $35,568
Groom, Staci, prob & parole ofcr II, $39,624
Gross, Anna M, cook II, $24,264
Gross, Cynthia L, prob & parole asst I, $34,356
Gross, Deborah J, prob & parole asst I, $29,496
Gross, Dennis C, storekeeper I, $25,824
Gross, Elizabeth A, prob & parole ofcr II, $36,204
Gross, Fred E, corrections ofcr I, $29,652
Gross, Glenn F, corrections case mgr II, $40,380
Grossman, Tamara S, prob & parole ofcr II, $37,548
Grote, Brenda S, cook II, $26,232
Grote, Jimi M, recrtn ofcr I, $29,976
Grote, Robert H, corrections ofcr I, $29,652
Groven, Tammy L, ofc spt asst (keybrd), $23,160
Grovenor, Trey C, corrections ofcr I, $29,652
Grover, Daniel, recrtn ofcr III, $38,232
Grover, Jacob M, corrections ofcr I, $29,316
Groves, Mary J, prob & parole ofcr II, $41,940
Groves, William J, corrections ofcr I, $29,661
Groza, Marcus W, corrections ofcr II, $33,900
Grubbs, Jerry D, stationary engr, $33,744
Grubbs, Jonna, functional unit mgr corr, $43,488
Gruber, Connie L, sr ofc spt asst (keybrd), $27,504
Gruber, Robert W, entprss mgr b2, $51,831
Gschwender, Elmer A, recrtn ofcr III, $37,548
Gudgell, Deborah J, ofc spt asst (keybrd), $23,160
Guenther Redington, Amie G, prob & parole ofcr II, $36,204
Guerrero, Kymberly L, corrections ofcr I, $32,784
Guhlke, Jay C, corrections ofcr I, $29,652
Guile, Bruce E, chaplain, $34,932
Guinn, Faron C, corrections ofcr I, $29,652
Guinn, Randy D, corrections ofcr I, $29,652
Guise, Aimee J, corrections ofcr I, $29,652
Gulick, Laura M, prob & parole ofcr II, $36,204
Gulledge, Julie K, ofc spt asst (keybrd), $23,160
Gullett, Thomas A, corrections ofcr I, $29,652
Gulley, Michael T, corrections ofcr I, $29,652
Gully, Joseph L, storekeeper II, $28,536
Gully, Joseph M, corrections ofcr I, $31,140
Gumm, Becky L, ofc spt asst (keybrd), $23,160
Gunn, Rebecca C, corrections ofcr I, $29,652
Gunnett, Robert L, corrections ofcr I, $29,652
Gunter, James L, corrections ofcr I, $29,652
Gunter, Troy A, corrections ofcr I, $29,652
Gutches, Steven L, corrections ofcr I, $29,652
Guy, Janet M, storekeeper I, $25,032
Guyer, Charles N, corrections ofcr I, $29,652
Haarlammert, Stephen, corrections ofcr I, $29,652
Haarmann, Joyce A, corrections ofcr I, $29,652
Haase, Cheryl G, corrections ofcr I, $29,652
Hacker, Gary D, corrections ofcr I, $29,652

Hackett, Cristi D, corrections ofcr I, $29,652
Hackett, John E, storekeeper I, $29,904
Hackmann, Arin N, sr ofc spt asst (keybrd), $25,824
Hadaller, Scott A, prob & parole ofcr II, $38,232
Hadley, Gregory M, exec II, $36,204
Hadley-Maycroft, Heather M, prob & parole ofcr II, $36,204
Haefner, Ladonna R, cook II, $24,264
Hagar, Christine, storekeeper I, $29,904
Hagen, Meaghan, prob & parole ofcr II, $34,944
Hagenhoff, Sandra L, corrections ofcr I, $30,132
Hager, Deborah R, prob & parole unit spv, $46,932
Hagerty, James V, corrections spv I, $38,232
Hagerty, John R, corrections case mgr II, $34,944
Hagerty, Lara A, storekeeper I, $25,824
Haggard, Connie L, admin ofc spt asst, $28,104
Haggard, Olivia R, ofc spt asst (keybrd), $23,160
Hagins, John G, recrtn ofcr I, $31,512
Hagnas, Tashana M, corrections ofcr I, $28,692
Hagood, David K, corrections ofcr I, $29,652
Hahn, Blake E, investigator I, $31,512
Hahn, Daniel L, corrections ofcr I, $29,652
Hahn, Daniel P, corrections ofcr I, $29,652
Hahn, Mary J, corrections ofcr I, $29,652
Hahn, Nicholas L, corrections ofcr I, $29,652
Hahn, Patricia L, prob & parole ofcr II, $40,380
Hahn, Timothy J, corrections ofcr I, $29,652
Haile, Amy E, prob & parole ofcr II, $36,204
Hainen, Charles, maint spv I, $32,628
Haintel, Daniel M, corrections ofcr II, $31,668
Halbach, Corina M, corrections ofcr I, $29,652
Halbert, Ryan P, prob & parole ofcr II, $36,204
Halbrook, Vicki, cook II, $24,264
Hale, Dale E, corrections training ofcr, $38,928
Hale, Donald L, corrections ofcr II, $31,668
Hale, Janet E, corrections ofcr I, $29,652
Hale, Larry E, corrections ofcr I, $29,652
Hale, Laveta F, corrections ofcr I, $31,140
Hales, Jacqueline, prob & parole ofcr II, $36,204
Haley, Michael D, corrections ofcr I, $29,652
Halik, Raym J, corrections ofcr I, $29,652
Hall, Amy, prob & parole ofcr I, $29,976
Hall, Bonnie E, supply mgr I, $33,744
Hall, Bradley J, corrections ofcr I, $31,668
Hall, Brian D, corrections ofcr I, $29,652
Hall, Carrie M, corrections ofcr I, $29,652
Hall, Chad A, corrections ofcr I, $29,652
Hall, Chelsey N, corrections ofcr I, $29,652
Hall, David E, prob & parole ofcr II, $36,888
Hall, Douglas C, corrections ofcr I, $29,652
Hall, Eugene, corrections ofcr I, $29,652
Hall, James A, electronics tech, $31,512
Hall, Jennifer A, ofc spt asst (keybrd), $26,652
Hall, Jerry, corrections case mgr II, $36,888
Hall, Joshua J, recrtn ofcr I, $31,512
Hall, Joshua M, corrections ofcr I, $29,652
Hall, Kathryn L, prob & parole ofcr II, $18,102
Hall, Kenneth P, corrections ofcr I, $28,692
Hall, Lawrence S, corrections ofcr I, $33,348
Hall, Matthew P, corrections ofcr I, $29,652
Hall, Robbie G, corrections ofcr I, $33,900
Hall, Ryan G, corrections ofcr I, $28,692
Hall, Shelly J, corrections case mgr II, $34,944
Hall, Terry A, prob & parole ofcr II, $36,204
Hall, Van, corrections ofcr I, $31,140
Hall, Vanessa R, corrections ofcr I, $29,652
Hallam, Amber R, corrections ofcr I, $28,692
Haller, Loren L, corrections ofcr I, $29,652
Halley, Colby M, corrections ofcr I, $33,348
Hallquist, Jay A, corrections ofcr I, $31,140
Hallsted, Ryan C, corrections ofcr I, $28,692
Halter, Faith A, ofc spt asst (clerical), $22,536
Halton, Stacey L, corrections ofcr I, $29,652
Halton, Travis J, corrections ofcr I, $29,652
Ham, Christopher J, corrections ofcr II, $30,576
Ham, Dora E, subs abuse cnslr II, $37,548
Hamacher, Matthew P, corrections ofcr I, $29,652
Hamburg, Bonnie G, prob & parole ofcr II, $36,204
Hamby, Ronald W, corrections ofcr II, $31,668
Hamelton, Charlann L, cook II, $24,264
Hamilton, Barbara J, corrections ofcr I, $31,140
Hamilton, Charlene E, corrections ofcr I, $31,140
Hamilton, David A, corrections ofcr II, $32,220
Hamilton, Gary L, corrections ofcr II, $32,220

Hamilton, Jeffry W, corrections ofcr I, $29,652
Hamilton, Joan K, instructor, $25.26/hr
Hamilton, John P, corrections ofcr I, $28,692
Hamilton, Lonnie W, prob & parole ofcr III, $41,172
Hamilton, Myong H, corrections ofcr I, $29,652
Hamilton, Steven W, maint spv I, $32,628
Hamilton-Kresl, Jennifer G, corrections ofcr I, $29,652
Hamlin, Clarence C, corrections case mgr I, $34,944
Hamlin, Delila L, sr ofc spt asst (keybrd), $27,504
Hamm, Jenifer R, prob & parole ofcr II, $36,204
Hammer, Aaron M, corrections ofcr I, $29,652
Hammers, Edwin H, cook II, $24,264
Hammock, Dana A, ofc spt asst (keybrd), $23,160
Hammond, Julie D, sr ofc spt asst (keybrd), $26,232
Hammond, Samuel L, procurement ofcr II, $45,156
Hammonds, John C, corrections ofcr I, $28,692
Hammons, Paul A, corrections ofcr I, $31,140
Hammontree, Justin M, corrections ofcr I, $28,692
Hampton, Amy M, corrections ofcr I, $31,140
Hampton, Bonnie K, sr ofc spt asst (clerical), $25,032
Hampton, Brian J, corrections ofcr I, $29,652
Hampton, Maleena B, corrections ofcr I, $30,984
Hamsher, Mary L, ofc spt asst (keybrd), $23,160
Hanafusa, Michael K, corrections ofcr II, $33,900
Hanafusa, Traci N, prob & parole asst I, $28,536
Hancock, Gregory B, corrections ofcr III, $33,744
Hand, Harold, corrections spv I, $41,172
Hand, Robert D, corrections ofcr I, $29,652
Hanebrink, Bruce A, corrections case mgr II, $33,744
Hanes, Adam R, corrections ofcr I, $29,652
Hanes, Carl O, corrections ofcr III, $38,928
Hanewinkel, James C, corrections ofcr I, $29,652
Haney, Sharon E, cook II, $24,264
Hankins, Cory L, corrections ofcr I, $28,692
Hankins, Dale V, prob & parole unit spv, $45,156
Hankins, Justin P, prob & parole asst II, $31,512
Hankins, Mary, ofc spt asst (keybrd), $23,160
Hankins, Matthew, corrections ofcr I, $28,692
Hankins, Pamela J, prob & parole ofcr III, $38,928
Hankins, Tonya, corrections ofcr I, $29,652
Hanks, Leland G, corrections ofcr I, $29,652
Hanline, Michael R, corrections classif asst, $33,180
Hanlon, Janice K, cook III, $28,104
Hannaford, Jane E, acad tchr III, $37,548
Hannan, John F, corrections ofcr I, $29,652
Hannel, Augustus E, corrections ofcr III, $38,232
Hanning, Raymond D, corrections ofcr I, $29,652
Hansen, Casey J, ofc spt asst (keybrd), $23,160
Hansen, Jeremy S, corrections ofcr III, $34,944
Hansen, Lynn E, prob & parole ofcr II, $36,888
Hansen, Melissa K, ofc spt asst (clerical), $22,872
Hanson, Rita E, cook III, $29,004
Hanson, Teresa A, corrections case mgr II, $34,944
Hanway, Katina D, corrections ofcr I, $29,652
Happel, Marlin C, corrections ofcr I, $30,132
Harbaugh, Jonathan, prob & parole ofcr I, $29,976
Harbin, Janie A, cook II, $24,264
Hardee, Sean S, corrections ofcr II, $30,576
Hardin, Chico V, corrections ofcr I, $29,652
Hardin, Rebecca M, ofc spt asst (keybrd), $23,160
Hardin, Roy A, corrections ofcr I, $29,652
Hardy, Adrienne D, registered nurse - clin opers, $68,532
Hardy, Maria J, prob & parole ofcr II, $38,232
Hardy, Narrie L, ofc spt asst (keybrd), $23,880
Hare, Melanie J, prob & parole ofcr II, $40,380
Hargrave, Christopher R, corrections ofcr II, $33,900
Hargrave, Sandra K, acad tchr III, $37,548
Harkins, Joshua R, corrections ofcr I, $29,652
Harkins, Michele J, acad tchr II, $34,944
Harkins, Rodney M, corrections ofcr II, $31,668
Harlan, Justin L, corrections ofcr I, $29,652
Harlow, Douglas P, prob & parole ofcr II, $36,204
Harmon, Andrew K, cook II, $23,508
Harms, Cara S, corrections ofcr II, $38,232
Harms, Cora L, prob & parole ofcr II, $40,380
Harms, James D, maint spv I, $31,512
Harms, Kelly G, corrections ofcr I, $29,652
Harness, Steven E, corrections ofcr II, $31,668
Harper, Coleen M, cook III, $28,104
Harper, Jeffrey D, corrections ofcr III, $33,744
Harper, Mary A, prob & parole ofcr II, $36,204
Harper, Robert S, corrections ofcr I, $29,652
Harper, Travis D, corrections ofcr I, $29,652

Harrell, Gaytha J, cook II, $24,264
Harrell, Marshinna K, prob & parole ofcr II, $36,204
Harrington, Todd E, corrections ofcr I, $29,652
Harris, Adrian L, corrections ofcr I, $28,692
Harris, Anthony J, corrections ofcr I, $29,652
Harris, Billy D, corrections mgr b3, $66,438
Harris, Bryan K, corrections ofcr I, $28,692
Harris, Catherine S, sr ofc spt asst (keybrd), $25,824
Harris, Charles E, corrections ofcr II, $31,668
Harris, Charles R, corrections ofcr I, $34,512
Harris, Darryl, prob & parole ofcr II, $36,204
Harris, Diana Y, area sub abuse trtmnt coor, $47,892
Harris, Elizabeth J, ofc spt asst (clerical), $22,536
Harris, Eugene W, corrections ofcr I, $34,512
Harris, Hope L, prob & parole asst II, $31,512
Harris, James R, corrections ofcr I, $31,668
Harris, Jeffery W, corrections ofcr I, $29,652
Harris, Joshua A, account clerk II, $25,824
Harris, Karolean R, prob & parole ofcr II, $36,204
Harris, Kenneth J, labor spv, $26,652
Harris, Kristina J, corrections ofcr I, $31,140
Harris, Laramie Q, corrections ofcr I, $30,276
Harris, Linda F, corrections ofcr II, $31,668
Harris, Lora, ofc spt asst (keybrd), $22,536
Harris, Lynn A, prob & parole ofcr II, $36,204
Harris, Randall L, storekeeper II, $31,512
Harris, Robert W, corrections ofcr I, $29,652
Harris, Sandra D, prob & parole asst I, $29,496
Harris, Steven G, corrections ofcr I, $29,652
Harris, Tammy M, corrections ofcr I, $29,652
Harris, Winona M, cook II, $24,264
Harrison, Allen R, corrections ofcr I, $30,132
Harrison, Autumn N, prob & parole ofcr II, $36,204
Harrison, Bradford A, corrections ofcr I, $29,652
Harrison, Carl L, corrections ofcr I, $29,652
Harrison, Debra L, ofc spt asst (keybrd), $23,160
Harrison, Gerald E, corrections ofcr I, $33,348
Harrison, Gregory K, stationary engr, $33,744
Harrison, Jason W, labor spv, $26,652
Harrison, Lindsey R, corrections ofcr I, $28,692
Harrison, Melissa L, prob & parole ofcr II, $34,944
Harrison, Richard A, corrections ofcr II, $30,576
Harrison, Robert L, corrections ofcr I, $29,652
Harrison, Roy A, corrections ofcr II, $33,348
Harrison, Thomas A, voc enter spv II, $29,976
Harrison, Tim W, corrections ofcr I, $30,132
Harrison, Trevor P, prob & parole ofcr II, $36,204
Harrison, William D, corrections ofcr I, $29,652
Harris-Whalen, Julie A, storekeeper II, $28,104
Harrower, James A, corrections spv I, $39,624
Hart, Carl, corrections ofcr I, $29,652
Hart, Dena S, prob & parole ofcr II, $40,380
Hart, Dwayne L, corrections ofcr I, $29,652
Hart, Rusty J, ofc spt asst (keybrd), $22,536
Hartel, Virgil N, prob & parole ofcr II, $36,204
Harter, Dennis E, corrections ofcr I, $29,652
Hartman, Kimberly S, corrections recs ofcr III, $36,204
Hartman, Linda S, corrections ofcr I, $29,652
Hartness, Timothy M, corrections classif asst, $31,512
Hartrup, Randy W, corrections case mgr II, $36,888
Hartwig, Bradley E, corrections ofcr I, $29,652
Hartwig, Richard W, corrections ofcr I, $29,652
Hartzell, Gena K, corrections ofcr I, $28,692
Harvey, Ariel L, corrections ofcr I, $28,692
Harvey, Heidee N, corrections ofcr I, $29,652
Harvey, Rick D, corrections ofcr II, $32,220
Harwood, Bethene F, storekeeper II, $28,536
Harwood, Connie J, corrections ofcr I, $31,140
Hasker, Jonathan C, corrections ofcr II, $31,668
Haskins, Hope E, correctional worker, $26,400
Haslag, Emily R, storekeeper I, $25,824
Haslag, Larry W, prod spec I corr, $44,304
Haslag, Yvonne J, corrections ofcr II, $31,668
Haslip, Travis L, locksmith, $29,976
Hasselman, Justin M, corrections ofcr I, $29,652
Hastings, Aaron, prob & parole ofcr II, $37,548
Hastings, Aaron M, corrections ofcr I, $29,652
Haston, Ronald G, corrections ofcr I, $29,652
Hasty, Travis J, corrections ofcr I, $29,652
Hatch, Brandon L, corrections ofcr I, $28,692
Hatcher, Matthew D, corrections ofcr I, $29,652
Hatcher, Renita K, corrections ofcr I, $29,652
Hatfield, Christopher M, prob & parole asst I, $29,496

Hathaway, Reginald S, corrections ofcr III, $34,356
Hathcock, Samuel C, corrections ofcr I, $29,652
Hatton, Casey R, maint spv II, $34,944
Haug, Geoffrey A, corrections ofcr II, $31,668
Hawanchak, David A, corrections ofcr I, $29,652
Hawk, Gwendolyn K, account clerk II, $25,824
Hawk, Joseph P, corrections ofcr I, $28,692
Hawkins, Danel R, corrections ofcr II, $31,678
Hawkins, Eric W, corrections ofcr I, $29,652
Hawkins, Georgianna, prob & parole asst I, $30,984
Hawkins, Heather J, ofc spt asst (keybrd), $23,160
Hawkins, Jacqueline R, cook III, $28,536
Hawkins, James A, corrections ofcr II, $31,668
Hawkins, Jason R, cook II, $24,264
Hawkins, Judith A, corrections ofcr II, $36,360
Hawkins, Julia E, corrections ofcr I, $33,900
Hawkins, Linda D, sr ofc spt asst (keybrd), $27,504
Hawkins, Michael W, corrections ofcr I, $29,652
Hawkins, Sandra A, ofc spt asst (keybrd), $12,132
Hawn, Rendy L, corrections ofcr I, $30,132
Haws, Jamie L, corrections ofcr I, $29,652
Haws, Terra N, corrections ofcr II, $31,668
Hawthorn, Jeffrey L, corrections ofcr II, $31,668
Hayden, Christopher, corrections ofcr I, $28,692
Hayden, Jerry W, corrections ofcr I, $29,652
Hayden, Rachel M, corrections ofcr II, $31,668
Hayes, Alex W, corrections ofcr I, $31,140
Hayes, Brennan E, corrections ofcr I, $29,652
Hayes, Edna M, corrections ofcr I, $29,652
Hayes, George E, corrections mgr b2, $47,600
Hayes, Ginger L, storekeeper II, $29,496
Hayes, John E, corrections ofcr II, $34,512
Hayes, Meckenzie M, prob & parole ofcr I, $29,976
Hayes, Ronnie D, corrections ofcr II, $31,668
Hayes-Sterbenz, Barbie, prob & parole ofcr II, $39,624
Hayhurst, Candice L, prob & parole ofcr II, $36,888
Haymart, Cynthia L, corrections ofcr I, $29,652
Haynes, Cora J, special official & admstr, $52,419
Haynes, Heather A, corrections ofcr I, $29,652
Haynes, Jeffrey W, corrections ofcr II, $30,576
Haynes, Jerry J, corrections ofcr I, $29,652
Haynes, Lindsay N, acad tchr III, $37,548
Haynes, Marvin L, functional unit mgr corr, $41,940
Haynie, Elda J, corrections ofcr I, $29,652
Haynie, Kim E, cook III, $28,104
Hays, Amanda E, prob & parole ofcr I, $29,976
Hays, Brett E, corrections ofcr II, $30,576
Hays, Charles A, corrections ofcr II, $31,668
Hays, Dustin W, corrections ofcr I, $29,652
Hays, Joan M, special asst paraprof, $20.00/hr
Hays, Kim M, corrections case mgr II, $38,232
Hays, Ricky L, corrections case mgr II, $34,944
Hays, Roy W, supply mgr I, $34,356
Hays, Susan R, corrections ofcr I, $29,652
Hays, Timothy S, corrections case mgr II, $37,548
Hays, Trina R, corrections case mgr II, $34,944
Hayward, Brenda L, corrections ofcr I, $29,652
Hazel, Melinda R, corrections ofcr I, $29,652
Hazel, Ricky L, corrections ofcr I, $29,652
Head, George C, prob & parole ofcr II, $38,232
Heady, Chad D, laundry mgr, $34,944
Heard, Rose M, prob & parole ofcr II, $36,204
Hearn, Anita M, ofc spt asst (clerical), $23,508
Hearn, Jessica, corrections ofcr I, $29,652
Hearn, Michelle L, voc tchr II, $34,944
Heath, Ash S, corrections ofcr I, $29,652
Heath, William R, corrections ofcr II, $31,668
Heavens, Beverly J, ofc spt asst (steno), $27,084
Hebblethwaite, Doug A, corrections ofcr I, $31,140
Hebert, Christopher R, corrections ofcr II, $30,576
Heckenbach, Michael L, maint spv II, $31,512
Hecker, Brian D, corrections ofcr I, $28,692
Hedgcoth, Brandy L, cook II, $24,264
Hedrick, Jason A, corrections ofcr I, $29,652
Hedrick, Machelle M, storekeeper I, $26,232
Hedrick, Timothy J, corrections ofcr II, $30,576
Hedrick, Tyler S, corrections ofcr I, $29,652
Heet, David P, capital imprvmts spec I, $45,156
Heether, James E, corrections ofcr I, $29,652
Heffelfinger, Virginia A, prob & parole ofcr II, $38,232
Heffner, Don M, corrections ofcr I, $31,668
Heffner, Jeremy M, corrections case mgr I, $31,512
Hefley, Kayle A, corrections ofcr I, $29,652

Hegerfeld, Ken N, corrections ofcr I, $29,652
Hehner, Scott A, corrections ofcr I, $29,652
Heidle, Richard A, corrections ofcr I, $30,132
Heightman, Gary J, recrtn ofcr I, $29,976
Heightman, Linda K, corrections ofcr III, $33,744
Heikal, Amr A, corrections ofcr II, $31,668
Heil, Benjamin K, laundry mgr, $34,944
Heimericks, Geneva A, sr ofc spt asst (keybrd), $25,824
Heimericks, Kathryn B, ofc spt asst (keybrd), $22,536
Heinrich, Andrea M, corrections ofcr I, $29,652
Heinrich, Jamie F, prob & parole unit spv, $41,940
Heinrich, John W, corrections ofcr I, $29,652
Heinrich, John W, corrections ofcr II, $31,668
Heins, Deborah R, cook II, $24,264
Heisse, Dustin J, corrections ofcr I, $28,692
Heitman, Joseph F, corrections ofcr I, $31,140
Heitzer, Benjamin R, corrections ofcr I, $29,652
Heldenbrand, Chris W, maint spv I, $32,628
Heldenbrand, Russell L, corrections ofcr I, $29,652
Heldenbrand, Steven K, storekeeper I, $28,908
Helfrich, Daniel, maint worker II, $28,104
Helkey, C R, corrections case mgr I, $36,888
Heller, Jessida, prob & parole ofcr II, $36,204
Hellman, Lynn E, prob & parole ofcr II, $39,624
Helm, Benjamin W, corrections ofcr I, $29,652
Helm, Paula D, ofc spt asst (keybrd), $23,160
Helm, Richard W, corrections ofcr I, $29,652
Helm, Susan S, food serv mgr II, $40,380
Helm, Valerie J, corrections ofcr II, $32,220
Helmig, Christina R, prob & parole ofcr II, $36,204
Helms, Allen E, corrections ofcr I, $29,652
Helms, Amanda K, corrections ofcr I, $28,692
Helms, Charles R, corrections classif asst, $30,984
Helms, Crystal R, corrections ofcr I, $29,652
Helms, Devin L, corrections ofcr I, $29,652
Helms, Maureen M, corrections ofcr I, $31,140
Helms, Ronald E, corrections ofcr I, $29,652
Helms, Steven L, phys plant sup III, $46,932
Helms, Terri L, storekeeper II, $29,004
Helms, Thomas C, corrections ofcr I, $29,652
Helms, Wendy L, ofc spt asst (keybrd), $23,160
Helton, Jon E, corrections ofcr I, $29,652
Helton, Kevin M, corrections ofcr I, $34,512
Helton, Krista I, corrections mgr b2, $52,278
Helton, Lisa A, corrections ofcr II, $31,668
Helton-Siebuhr, Kim, prob & parole spv, $43,488
Hemingway, James R, corrections ofcr I, $28,692
Hemkens, Michael P, corrections ofcr I, $29,652
Henderson, Carol A, corrections ofcr II, $31,668
Henderson, David W, corrections ofcr I, $31,140
Henderson, Jenna A, prob & parole ofcr I, $31,512
Henderson, Jennifer M, corrections case mgr II, $34,944
Henderson, John R, stationary engr, $32,628
Henderson, Richard L, corrections ofcr I, $29,652
Henderson, Robert S, corrections case mgr II, $37,548
Henderson, Sandra L, corrections ofcr I, $29,652
Hendren, Derek L, corrections spv I, $41,940
Hendren, Timothy L, corrections ofcr I, $28,692
Hendricks, Curtis M, prob & parole ofcr II, $40,380
Hendricks, Deanna E, prob & parole ofcr II, $36,204
Hendrickson, Scott A, storekeeper II, $28,104
Hendrix, Andrew C, corrections ofcr II, $31,668
Hendrix, Tamara L, corrections ofcr II, $30,576
Henggeler, Carrie L, functional unit mgr corr, $37,548
Henke, John F, corrections ofcr I, $29,652
Henke, Roger D, corrections ofcr III, $34,356
Henley, Bobby L, acct II, $43,488
Henley, Polly J, ofc spt asst (keybrd), $24,612
Henley, Sara K, prob & parole ofcr II, $40,380
Henley, Trinette R, prob & parole ofcr II, $39,624
Hennigh, Joseph D, corrections ofcr I, $29,652
Henning, Garry L, corrections ofcr I, $29,652
Henningfeld, Devin M, corrections ofcr II, $31,668
Hennings, Justin A, corrections ofcr II, $31,668
Hennings, Melissa J, prob & parole ofcr II, $36,204
Henry, Cheryl L, corrections ofcr I, $29,652
Henry, Michael, correctional worker, $26,400
Henry, Michael D, prob & parole asst II, $31,512
Henry, Steven D, corrections ofcr I, $28,692
Henslee, Eric S, corrections ofcr I, $29,652
Henslee, Jeffrey, prob & parole asst I, $29,976
Hensley, Alan P, corrections ofcr I, $31,140
Hensley, Benjamyn M, cook II, $24,264

Hensley, Christopher J, corrections ofcr I, $29,652
Hensley, Kathleen M, corrections ofcr I, $28,692
Henson, Beverly A, ofc spt asst (keybrd), $26,232
Henson, Brett T, corrections ofcr I, $28,692
Henson, Carol S, corrections ofcr I, $29,652
Henson, Christine E, corrections ofcr II, $31,668
Henson, Donald C, prob & parole ofcr II, $36,204
Henson, Elizabeth A, ofc spt asst (keybrd), $23,160
Henson, John M, corrections ofcr I, $29,652
Henson, Justin D, corrections ofcr I, $28,692
Henson, Laura J, exec II, $36,204
Henson, Rodney S, corrections spv I, $38,232
Henson, Rone F, maint spv I, $32,628
Henson, Thomas A, bldg const wkr II, $30,984
Hentges, Megan K, sr ofc spt asst (keybrd), $25,032
Henton, Charles E, corrections ofcr I, $30,132
Henton, Patrisha L, laundry spv, $30,420
Herbert, Richard L, corrections ofcr I, $33,348
Hercules, Bartley S, prob & parole ofcr II, $39,624
Heriford, Sandra L, corrections ofcr I, $29,652
Herigon, Kathern S, sr ofc spt asst (keybrd), $27,084
Herlein, Eric K, corrections ofcr I, $29,652
Herlofson, Erik J, corrections case mgr II, $34,944
Herman, Bonnie A, functional unit mgr corr, $38,928
Herman, Jennifer L, ofc spt asst (keybrd), $23,160
Herman, Kimberly D, prob & parole ofcr II, $36,888
Hermann, Anna, ofc spt asst (keybrd), $11,268
Hernandez, David M, corrections ofcr I, $29,652
Hernandez, Paul I, corrections ofcr I, $29,652
Herndon, Brandon C, corrections ofcr II, $30,576
Herndon, Christy L, ofc spt asst (keybrd), $23,160
Herndon, Pamela S, corrections ofcr I, $29,652
Herndon, Tiffaney L, corrections ofcr I, $29,652
Herndon, William J, corrections ofcr II, $31,668
Herrell, Cody W, corrections ofcr I, $28,692
Herrera, Dianna, corrections ofcr I, $29,652
Herrin, Daniel E, corrections ofcr I, $29,652
Herring, Della J, corrections ofcr I, $33,900
Herring, Kimberly M, corrections mgr b1, $40,380
Herrington, Michelle L, corrections ofcr I, $28,692
Herrington, Regina A, ofc spt asst (keybrd), $23,160
Herron, Alivia N, corrections ofcr I, $28,692
Herzberg, Kathy L, corrections ofcr I, $30,132
Herzog, Eric M, corrections ofcr I, $29,652
Heselton, Robert M, corrections ofcr I, $29,652
Hess, Donnie W, corrections ofcr I, $29,652
Hess, Jason R, corrections ofcr II, $31,668
Hess, Jordan P, corrections ofcr I, $28,692
Hess, Nathan H, corrections ofcr II, $31,668
Hesse, Debra L, prob & parole asst I, $29,496
Hesse, Vicky E, storekeeper I, $25,824
Hesse, Walter C, maint spv I, $32,628
Hessell, Jennifer C, prob & parole ofcr II, $36,204
Hester, James R, storekeeper I, $25,824
Heussner, Cherie L, cook III, $27,228
Heusted, Karen S, sr ofc spt asst (keybrd), $25,824
Hewett, Holly A, prob & parole ofcr II, $36,204
Hewitt, Jason S, cook II, $24,264
Hewitt, Jonathon, corrections ofcr I, $29,652
Hibbitts, Marty R, corrections ofcr I, $29,652
Hibbs, Betty L, maint worker II, $33,180
Hibdon, Colin W, corrections ofcr I, $31,140
Hibdon, Tammy J, corrections ofcr I, $29,652
Hibler, Matthew A, storekeeper II, $28,536
Hickey, Brandy L, corrections ofcr I, $29,652
Hickman, Joshua P, corrections ofcr I, $28,692
Hickman, Randal G, corrections ofcr I, $29,652
Hicks, Garret R, prob & parole ofcr II, $36,888
Hicks, Jimmie D, corrections ofcr III, $33,744
Hicks, Joey W, recrtn ofcr I, $29,976
Hicks, Lyndle A, corrections ofcr I, $29,652
Hicks, William D, corrections ofcr I, $32,784
Higashi, Roy T, corrections ofcr II, $31,668
Higgenbotham, Angela M, corrections ofcr I, $29,652
Higgins, Tammy J, ofc spt asst (keybrd), $25,032
Highfill, Coreen A, corrections ofcr I, $29,652
Highfill, David A, corrections ofcr I, $29,652
Hightower, Angela G, ofc spt asst (keybrd), $23,160
Hightower, Jerome D, corrections ofcr II, $30,576
Higley, April S, corrections ofcr I, $28,692
Hilbert, Levi J, prob & parole asst I, $29,496
Hildebrand, Vicki A, corrections ofcr II, $31,668
Hilden, William E, cook III, $29,976

Hildreth, Sheri A, sr ofc spt asst (keybrd), $27,084
Hill, E Duane, storekeeper II, $28,536
Hill, Edwin D, corrections ofcr I, $29,652
Hill, James Kevin, prob & parole ofcr II, $39,624
Hill, Jennifer L, corrections ofcr I, $28,692
Hill, Neil B, prob & parole ofcr II, $39,624
Hill, Robert E, corrections case mgr II, $34,944
Hill, Sha-Shona S, prob & parole ofcr II, $36,204
Hill, Shery A, ofc spt asst (keybrd), $23,880
Hill, Theresa L, corrections case mgr II, $34,944
Hill, Tiffany N, corrections ofcr I, $29,652
Hill, Tyrone C, corrections ofcr I, $29,652
Hillebrand, Mark B, corrections ofcr I, $29,652
Hillerman, Kenneth L, recrtn ofcr III, $41,940
Hillis, Kimberly A, ofc spt asst (keybrd), $23,160
Hillis, Ryan J, corrections ofcr II, $31,668
Hilpert, John W, corrections mgr b1, $40,876
Hilton, Roger B, corrections ofcr I, $29,652
Hilton, Weston, corrections ofcr I, $29,652
Himebrook, Mark A, laundry mgr, $37,548
Hineman, John D, maint spv I, $31,512
Hines, Blaire P, prob & parole ofcr II, $36,204
Hines, Derek R, corrections spv II, $49,128
Hines, James R, labor spv, $26,652
Hinkle, Deanna N, prob & parole ofcr II, $39,624
Hinkle, Lowell D, corrections ofcr I, $29,652
Hinkle, Melanie M, corrections case mgr II, $34,944
Hinkle, Richard I, power plant mech, $30,984
Hinkle, Sheldon R, corrections ofcr I, $29,652
Hinnard, Joanna L, corrections ofcr I, $28,692
Hinnen, Diana J, sr ofc spt asst (keybrd), $28,452
Hinson, David E, corrections ofcr I, $29,652
Hinton, Emily J, corrections ofcr I, $28,692
Hinton, Gary L, recrtn ofcr II, $33,180
Hinz, Nicole M, ofc spt asst (keybrd), $26,232
Hirsch, Anastacia M, corrections ofcr I, $29,652
Hirschman, Shane T, prob & parole ofcr III, $38,928
Hirst, Aimee L, corrections case mgr II, $34,944
Hitchcock, Sallie A, prob & parole unit spv, $41,940
Hite, Tammy L, prob & parole ofcr II, $36,888
Hitt, Nathan, corrections ofcr I, $28,692
Hittle, Daniel L, corrections ofcr I, $29,652
Hixon, Toni C, ofc spt asst (keybrd), $23,160
Hoaglund, Mark A, corrections ofcr II, $35,724
Hobbs, Cheryl R, corrections classif asst, $29,976
Hobbs, Joel C, corrections ofcr I, $29,652
Hobbs, Scott E, corrections ofcr I, $30,132
Hobeck, Valerie E, prob & parole ofcr II, $36,204
Hockemeyer, Toby A, cook II, $23,508
Hocker, Elizabeth D, subs abuse cnslr II, $34,944
Hodge, Carrie R, prob & parole ofcr II, $36,204
Hodge, Denise L, prob & parole ofcr II, $38,232
Hodges, Armand R, corrections ofcr I, $29,652
Hodges, Brian K, corrections ofcr I, $30,132
Hodges, Lloyd W, corrections ofcr II, $36,360
Hodges, Pamela L, procurement ofcr I, $37,548
Hodges, Patrick S, prob & parole ofcr II, $47,892
Hoecker, Kelly B, corrections ofcr I, $29,652
Hoecker, Shawn P, prob & parole asst I, $29,496
Hoeft, Judy K, cook II, $24,264
Hoellering, Paul D, corrections ofcr I, $30,132
Hoelscher, Gary W, fire & safety coor, $38,928
Hoepf, Steven H, recrtn ofcr I, $29,496
Hoer, Carl M, maint worker II, $30,420
Hoff, John R, corrections spv I, $42,708
Hoff, Tamara Y, corrections ofcr I, $29,652
Hoffelmeyer, Paul H, recrtn ofcr I, $30,984
Hoffman, Jerry G, corrections mgr b1, $52,730
Hoffman, Michael T, prob & parole asst II, $36,888
Hoffman, Philip D, corrections ofcr I, $28,692
Hoffman, Randy R, corrections ofcr III, $33,744
Hoffman, Regina G, corrections ofcr II, $33,348
Hoffmaster, James A, corrections classif asst, $35,568
Hoffmeister, Joseph P, corrections mgr b2, $55,123
Hoffmeister, Michelle L, psychologist II, $63,996
Hofstetter, Wayne K, storekeeper II, $32,052
Hogan, Cynthia D, ofc spt asst (keybrd), $11,580
Hogan, Jared R, prob & parole ofcr II, $36,204
Hogan, Jennifer C, prob & parole ofcr II, $38,232
Hogan, Timothy J, prob & parole ofcr II, $36,204
Hogard, Dewayne T, corrections ofcr II, $36,360
Hoggatt, Roy E, prob & parole ofcr II, $36,204
Hogue, James V, chaplain, $34,356

Holcomb, Carl F, corrections ofcr I, $33,348
Holcomb, Charles O, locksmith, $29,976
Holcomb, Karron R, ofc spt asst (keybrd), $26,232
Holcomb, Rise R, storekeeper I, $27,084
Holden, Nicole R, prob & parole ofcr II, $38,232
Holder, Christine S, ofc spt asst (keybrd), $23,160
Holder, Michael D, corrections ofcr I, $29,652
Holder, Michael E, corrections ofcr I, $29,652
Holdman, Brian J, corrections ofcr I, $28,692
Holdman, Rodney B, fire & safety spec, $31,512
Holdren, Christine L, prob & parole ofcr II, $36,204
Holford, William L, laundry mgr, $34,944
Holifield, John, stationary engr, $33,744
Holland, Carolyn M, cook II, $24,264
Holland, Darren C, recrtn ofcr II, $36,204
Holland, Karl B, maint spv I, $32,628
Holland, Rodney D, corrections ofcr I, $29,652
Holland, Tina M, inst activity coor, $31,512
Hollander, Stefanie J, corrections ofcr I, $29,652
Hollen, James B, maint worker II, $29,004
Hollinger, Jerrel D, corrections ofcr II, $31,668
Hollingsworth, Chad A, phys plant sup I, $38,928
Hollingsworth, Chelsea F, corrections ofcr I, $28,692
Hollinsworth, Terry L, labor spv, $25,824
Hollis, Jacklynn D, corrections ofcr I, $28,692
Hollis, Linda K, prob & parole ofcr II, $36,204
Hollon, John E, corrections ofcr I, $29,652
Holloway, Freddie, prob & parole asst I, $29,496
Holloway, Kimberly D, corrections ofcr I, $29,652
Holman, Donna L, ofc spt asst (keybrd), $24,264
Holman, Pamela L, corrections ofcr I, $29,652
Holmes, Arthur W, corrections training ofcr, $39,624
Holmes, Bryant L, corrections mgr b1, $47,414
Holmes, Johnny J, prob & parole asst I, $29,496
Holmes, Keith L, corrections ofcr II, $30,576
Holmes, Lisa M, corrections case mgr I, $29,976
Holmes, Patrick S, corrections ofcr II, $35,100
Holmes, Raymond D, corrections ofcr I, $29,652
Holmes, Sonia M, ofc spt asst (keybrd), $22,536
Holohan, Beverly J, ofc spt asst (keybrd), $24,264
Holstein, William J, corrections ofcr I, $29,652
Holsten, Timothy B, corrections case mgr II, $34,944
Holt, Emily J, corrections ofcr I, $28,692
Holt, George H, corrections ofcr I, $29,652
Holt, Jani J, investigator I, $30,984
Holt, Justin H, corrections ofcr I, $29,652
Holt, Melissa D, corrections ofcr I, $29,652
Holt, Nathan W, prob & parole asst I, $29,496
Holt, Rebecca G, librarian II, $36,888
Holt, Steven D, prob & parole asst I, $29,496
Holterman, Danielle, admin ofc spt asst, $28,104
Holtzclaw, Daniel E, corrections ofcr I, $29,652
Holtzhouser, Larry J, stationary engr, $33,744
Holyfield, Pamela L, prob & parole ofcr II, $40,380
Homan, Barry J, corrections ofcr I, $29,652
Homan, Charley D, corrections ofcr I, $29,652
Homes, William W, corrections ofcr I, $30,276
Honerkamp, Jason S, storekeeper I, $25,824
Honerkamp, Karen, storekeeper II, $28,104
Honerkamp, Ronald E, corrections ofcr I, $29,652
Honeycutt, Kerry E, corrections ofcr I, $29,652
Honse, Susan J, ofc spt asst (keybrd), $23,160
Hood, Dawn M, corrections ofcr I, $29,652
Hood, Laddie K, corrections ofcr II, $31,668
Hood, Lita S, admin ofc spt asst, $30,984
Hood, Robert V, refrgrtn mech II, $33,744
Hood, Robin E, corrections ofcr I, $29,652
Hood, Sandra K, prob & parole ofcr II, $40,380
Hooker, John W, corrections ofcr III, $33,744
Hooker, Lisa M, corrections ofcr I, $29,652
Hooks, Terry, prob & parole asst I, $29,496
Hooper, Jackie W, maint spv I, $32,628
Hoose, Ashleigh E, sr ofc spt asst (keybrd), $25,824
Hoosemans, Catharina M, ofc spt asst (keybrd), $22,536
Hooss, Bryan D, corrections ofcr I, $29,652
Hootselle, Thomas W, corrections ofcr I, $29,652
Hoover, Paul D, corrections ofcr I, $29,652
Hoover, Randall D, corrections ofcr I, $29,652
Hoover, Sara L, prob & parole ofcr II, $36,204
Hoover, Stacy D, corrections ofcr II, $31,668
Hoover, William J, corrections ofcr I, $29,652
Hope, David L, corrections ofcr I, $29,652
Hopke, David L, corrections ofcr I, $31,140

Hopke, Vicki L, ofc spt asst (keybrd), $23,160
Hopkins, Daniel R, corrections training ofcr, $38,928
Hopkins, David L, maint worker II, $29,004
Hopkins, Marvin L, corrections ofcr I, $29,652
Hopkins, Roy D, serv mgr II, $41,940
Hopkins, Sheila L, corrections ofcr I, $28,692
Hoppe, Greg A, recrtn ofcr II, $37,548
Hoppe, Stephony J, acad tchr III, $41,940
Hopper, Christopher M, prob & parole ofcr II, $39,624
Hopper, Matthew R, corrections ofcr I, $29,652
Hopping, Robert C, corrections ofcr III, $33,744
Hopson, Tanesha Y, prob & parole ofcr II, $36,204
Horn, Christopher, corrections ofcr II, $31,668
Horn, Jason L, corrections ofcr III, $33,744
Horn, Michael W, corrections ofcr I, $29,652
Horn, Tommie E, corrections case mgr II, $34,944
Horne, Donald C, chaplain, $34,932
Horton, Charles, corrections case mgr II, $37,548
Horton, Larry J, corrections ofcr I, $30,132
Horton, Laura A, cook II, $24,264
Horton, Matthew W, corrections ofcr I, $28,692
Horvath, Michael A, corrections ofcr I, $29,652
Hosfeld, Karla A, prob & parole ofcr II, $36,204
Hoskins, Blake R, corrections ofcr I, $29,652
Hoskins, Bryan A, corrections ofcr I, $30,132
Hoskins, Dustin M, prob & parole ofcr II, $34,944
Houchins, Mark R, food serv mgr II, $34,944
Houchins, Steven G, labor spv, $25,824
Hough, Trindle D, prob & parole ofcr II, $36,204
Houk, Russell D, corrections ofcr I, $28,692
Hounihan, Anthony T, corrections ofcr I, $29,652
Houpt, Anthony W, tractor trailer driver, $30,984
Houpt, Tammy A, corrections ofcr I, $29,652
House, Curtis L, cook II, $24,612
House, Cynthia A, investigator II, $37,548
House, Debra K, corrections ofcr I, $29,652
House, Donald W, corrections ofcr I, $29,652
House, Margaret E, sr ofc spt asst (keybrd), $25,824
House, Sharon A, ofc spt asst (keybrd), $23,160
House, Steven, food serv mgr I, $29,976
Householder, Jeffry S, corrections ofcr II, $30,576
Houser, Tabitha S, prob & parole ofcr I, $29,976
Houser, William F, prob & parole ofcr II, $36,888
Houston, Ernest B, driver, $14.19/hr
Houston, Steven J, tractor trailer driver, $30,984
Houtz, David L, corrections ofcr I, $29,652
Hovde, Christopher A, corrections ofcr I, $28,692
Hoven, Christopher, prob & parole ofcr II, $36,204
Hovis, Chad J, corrections ofcr II, $33,348
Hovis, Kenneth D, corrections case mgr III, $37,548
Howard, Amanda J, corrections ofcr I, $29,652
Howard, Darla J, corrections ofcr I, $29,652
Howard, David F, functional unit mgr corr, $42,708
Howard, Dequincy D, investigator I, $29,976
Howard, Jacqueline M, corrections ofcr I, $29,652
Howard, Jamie S, corrections ofcr I, $29,652
Howard, Jeffrey, serv mgr I, $34,944
Howard, Marcene Y, ofc spt asst (keybrd), $22,536
Howard, Matthew B, corrections ofcr II, $30,576
Howard, Michael B, corrections ofcr I, $29,652
Howard, Ricky B, phys plant sup I, $38,928
Howard, Robin S, exec II, $36,204
Howard, Shona M, sr ofc spt asst (keybrd), $27,084
Howard, Warren P, voc enter spv II, $31,512
Howe, Carl L, corrections ofcr I, $29,652
Howe, Darrell R, corrections spv I, $42,708
Howe, David E, corrections ofcr II, $31,668
Howe, Debra A, corrections ofcr I, $29,652
Howe, Edward P, corrections ofcr I, $29,652
Howe, Shawn B, corrections ofcr I, $28,692
Howe, Sherry D, corrections ofcr I, $29,652
Howell, Steven D, factory mgr II, $40,380
Howell, Travis R, corrections ofcr I, $28,692
Howery, Kelly M, corrections mgr b1, $43,221
Howland, Kayla R, correctional worker, $26,400
Howland, Rodney E, correctional worker, $26,400
Howser, James W, prob & parole ofcr II, $36,204
Hoxworth, Rick C, corrections ofcr I, $29,652
Hoy, Richelle D, prob & parole ofcr II, $20,190
Hoylman, Robert A, corrections ofcr I, $29,652
Hoyt, Terence M, maint worker I, $26,652
Hrabak, Jessica F, prob & parole ofcr II, $36,204
Hubbard, Daryl G, storekeeper II, $28,536

Hubbard, James J, corrections ofcr I, $28,692
Hubbard, Jeffery A, corrections ofcr II, $31,668
Hubbard, Jonathan J, corrections ofcr I, $29,652
Hubbard, Marilyn L, corrections ofcr I, $29,652
Hubbard-Stewart, Kimberly E, prob & parole unit spv, $44,304
Hubbart, Michael J, corrections ofcr I, $29,652
Huber, James M, prob & parole ofcr II, $38,232
Huber, Thomas W, corrections spv I, $41,172
Huckelberry, Emma L, ofc spt asst (keybrd), $26,652
Huckstep, David A, corrections ofcr I, $29,652
Huckstep, Tina B, corrections ofcr I, $30,132
Huddleston, Calvaletta C, corrections ofcr I, $29,652
Huddleston, Dustin D, maint spv I, $33,744
Huddleston, Edward J, corrections ofcr I, $29,652
Huddleston, Mindy L, prob & parole ofcr III, $39,624
Huddleston, Ottis W, corrections ofcr I, $29,652
Hudelson, Robert G, corrections ofcr I, $29,652
Hudgens, Joseph K, corrections ofcr I, $29,652
Hudlemeyer, Dennis, corrections ofcr I, $29,652
Hudson, Donna M, admin ofc spt asst, $29,976
Hudson, Harold W, prob & parole asst I, $32,628
Hudson, Ii, corrections ofcr II, $31,668
Hudson, Jacob A, corrections ofcr I, $29,652
Hudson, Lisa M, corrections ofcr I, $29,652
Hudson, Mariesha M, corrections ofcr I, $28,692
Hudson, Samantha R, ofc spt asst (keybrd), $23,160
Hudson, Sarah E, ofc spt asst (keybrd), $23,880
Hudson, Scott W, corrections ofcr I, $29,652
Hudson, Tom A, corrections ofcr I, $29,652
Hudspeth, Jay S, corrections ofcr I, $29,652
Huett, Joseph M, corrections ofcr I, $29,652
Huff, Gary W, corrections case mgr II, $34,944
Huff, Jaimie L, storekeeper I, $25,824
Huff, Jason M, corrections ofcr I, $29,652
Huff, Lawrence E, corrections ofcr I, $29,652
Huff, Margaret A, corrections ofcr I, $29,652
Huff, Oliver T, corrections ofcr II, $31,668
Huff, Ronda M, storekeeper I, $25,824
Huff, Shawn D, corrections ofcr II, $33,348
Huff, Tamara, corrections ofcr I, $29,652
Huffman, Carla J, storekeeper I, $26,232
Huffman, Jason K, corrections ofcr I, $28,692
Huffman, Jeremy J, corrections ofcr II, $31,668
Huffman, Richard M, recrtn ofcr I, $29,976
Huffman, Tracy J, corrections ofcr I, $29,652
Hufford, Steven C, prob & parole ofcr II, $39,624
Huggins, Gary W, corrections ofcr I, $29,652
Huggins, Rebecca J, corrections ofcr I, $28,692
Hughes, Allen L, corrections training ofcr, $38,928
Hughes, Billie B, factory mgr II, $38,928
Hughes, Dana R, functional unit mgr corr, $38,928
Hughes, Jane D, corrections ofcr I, $29,652
Hughes, Jonathan G, cook I, $22,200
Hughes, Juanita A, prob & parole ofcr II, $41,172
Hughes, Kelly M, voc tchr II, $34,944
Hughes, Linda A, ofc spt asst (keybrd), $23,160
Hughes, Matayla M, prob & parole ofcr I, $29,976
Hughes, Michael L, corrections ofcr III, $32,628
Hughes, Ophelia M, prob & parole ofcr II, $39,624
Hughes, Randell S, mgmt analysis spec II, $41,940
Hughes, Robert V, corrections ofcr I, $29,652
Hughes, Ruth M, ofc spt asst (keybrd), $25,824
Hughes, Stacy M, admin ofc spt asst, $28,104
Hughlette, Shawna L, prob & parole ofcr II, $36,204
Huhn, Kylie R, corrections ofcr I, $29,652
Huhn, Lori A, account clerk II, $28,908
Huitt, Joshua G, corrections ofcr I, $29,652
Huitt, Kimberly A, corrections ofcr I, $29,652
Hulet, Jonell L, corrections ofcr I, $29,652
Hulett, Randy W, corrections ofcr II, $31,668
Hulett, Zachary L, corrections ofcr I, $29,652
Hull, Crystal L, voc tchr III, $37,548
Hull, James R, corrections ofcr I, $29,652
Hullinger, Howard G, corrections ofcr I, $31,668
Huls, Dana M, corrections ofcr I, $28,692
Hulse, Lee D, corrections ofcr I, $28,692
Hulsey, Roseanne K, ofc spt asst (keybrd), $26,232
Hume, Brenda K, ofc spt asst (keybrd), $23,160
Humfeld, Simon W, corrections ofcr III, $39,624
Hummel, Jeannie, corrections case mgr II, $34,944
Humphrey, Gracie L, functional unit mgr corr, $41,933
Humphreys, John R, guidance cnslr II, $37,548
Humphreys, Summer S, acad tchr III, $37,548

Hundley, Betty L, pers clerk, $31,512
Hundley, Dennis, maint spv I, $35,568
Hunger, Heather L, ofc spt asst (keybrd), $22,536
Hunger, Sally M, ofc spt asst (keybrd), $23,160
Hunnell, Kenneth D, corrections case mgr II, $35,568
Hunsaker, Cameron E, corrections case mgr II, $38,928
Hunt, Daniel R, corrections ofcr I, $29,652
Hunt, Heather, corrections ofcr I, $29,652
Hunt, Janice K, ofc spt asst (keybrd), $23,160
Hunt, Larry W, corrections ofcr I, $29,652
Hunt, Nancy A, ofc spt asst (keybrd), $23,160
Hunt, Steven L, corrections ofcr I, $29,652
Hunt, Velma A, corrections ofcr I, $29,652
Hunter, Dustin T, corrections ofcr I, $29,652
Hunter, Dwain W, corrections spv I, $39,624
Hunter, John W, corrections ofcr I, $29,652
Hunter, Laura A, prob & parole ofcr III, $38,928
Hunter, Lorieann M, corrections ofcr III, $35,568
Hunter, Mandy L, prob & parole ofcr II, $19,116
Hunter, Maranda L, corrections ofcr I, $29,652
Hunter, Martin R, labor spv, $26,652
Hunter, Matthew L, corrections ofcr I, $28,692
Hunter, Patricia A, prob & parole ofcr II, $40,380
Huntsman, Katlin M, cook II, $24,264
Hurlburt, Melody A, inst activity coor, $31,512
Hurlburt, Timothy N, corrections ofcr I, $29,652
Hurley, Diane D, corrections case mgr II, $34,944
Hurley, Helen J, corrections mgr b2, $54,807
Hurley, James A, corrections mgr b3, $66,438
Hurley, Kurtis A, corrections ofcr I, $29,652
Hurley, Wayne D, corrections ofcr I, $34,512
Hurst, Eric R, corrections ofcr I, $29,652
Hurst, Jerami D, prob & parole ofcr III, $40,380
Hurst, Jimmy R, corrections ofcr I, $29,652
Hurt, Brandy D, corrections ofcr I, $29,652
Hurt, Daniel A, corrections ofcr I, $29,652
Hurt, Daniel O, prob & parole ofcr II, $40,380
Hurt, Henry P, cook II, $24,264
Huskey, Adam, corrections ofcr II, $31,668
Huskey, Brandy, ofc spt asst (keybrd), $23,160
Huss, Larry A, voc tchr II, $34,944
Hutchason, Shaun W, corrections ofcr I, $29,652
Hutchcraft, Valerie, corrections case mgr II, $34,944
Hutcherson, Keeley N, corrections ofcr I, $29,652
Hutcheson, Sandria L, librarian II, $33,744
Hutcheson, Victoria L, ofc spt asst (clerical), $22,536
Hutcheson, Yolanda L, corrections recs ofcr III, $36,204
Hutchings, Deborah E, cook II, $24,264
Hutchison, Sherry D, corrections ofcr I, $29,652
Hutsell, Rickey D, corrections ofcr I, $29,652
Hutson, Aaron D, maint spv I, $34,356
Hutson, Donald J, prob & parole asst I, $29,496
Hutson, John R, fire & safety coor, $38,928
Hutson, Larry J, electronics tech, $30,984
Hutson, Mark D, corrections ofcr III, $35,568
Hutson, Nicholas J, corrections ofcr I, $29,652
Hutter, Kathrine M, corrections ofcr I, $29,652
Hutton, Joshua, corrections case mgr I, $31,512
Hutton, Michael T, corrections ofcr III, $33,744
Huxol, Sheryl L, prob & parole ofcr II, $40,380
Hyatt, Myrna L, storekeeper I, $25,824
Hyde, Clinton J, corrections ofcr I, $29,652
Hyden, Timothy R, corrections ofcr I, $28,692
Hygrade, Cynthia A, prob & parole unit spv, $41,940
Hying, Keith R, corrections ofcr I, $29,652
Hymer, A S, prob & parole ofcr II, $39,624
Hyte, Darron L, corrections case mgr II, $34,944
Ibrahim, Yahaya O, prob & parole asst I, $29,496
Iburg, Dianne B, corrections ofcr I, $31,140
Iburg, Stacey L, corrections case mgr II, $38,928
Ida, Justin D, corrections ofcr I, $29,652
Ike, Andrea O, corrections ofcr I, $29,652
Iler, Bruce W, cook III, $28,104
Ilgenfritz, Robert J, corrections ofcr I, $29,652
Imler, Henry L, voc enter rep, $33,744
Immekus, Charles D, corrections ofcr II, $31,668
Immel, James J, corrections ofcr II, $33,348
Immel, Kimberly D, corrections ofcr I, $29,652
Ince, Terry L, corrections ofcr II, $33,900
Ingram, Brandon L, corrections ofcr I, $29,652
Ingram, Harold L, corrections ofcr I, $29,652
Ingram, James E, corrections ofcr I, $31,140
Ingram, Jennifer L, corrections ofcr I, $29,652

Ingrassia, James P, corrections ofcr I, $29,652
Inlow, Eric W, corrections ofcr I, $29,652
Inlow, Kimberly K, corrections case mgr II, $38,232
Inman, Cindy A, sr ofc spt asst (keybrd), $25,824
Inman, Kendrick L, prob & parole asst I, $29,496
Inman, Philip G, storekeeper I, $26,232
Inman, Robert P, corrections ofcr II, $35,100
Inman, Tiffany M, corrections ofcr I, $29,652
Innes, Dakota J, corrections ofcr I, $29,652
Innes, Edward L, corrections ofcr I, $29,652
Ipock, Ronald L, corrections ofcr II, $31,668
Irby, Kimberly A, corrections ofcr I, $29,652
Ireland, Betty S, corrections ofcr I, $29,652
Ireland, Daniel W, corrections ofcr I, $29,652
Ireland, Edgar D, corrections ofcr I, $29,652
Ireland, Marcie, corrections case mgr II, $37,548
Ireland, Ricky L, corrections ofcr I, $29,652
Irions, Michael D, prob & parole ofcr II, $36,204
Irvin, Debra L, corrections ofcr I, $28,692
Irvin, Robert W, maint spv I, $33,744
Irwin, Dixie J, voc enter spv II, $29,976
Isenberg, Kyle J, prob & parole ofcr II, $34,944
Isgrig, Andrew W, corrections ofcr I, $29,652
Isgrig, David, corrections ofcr I, $28,104
Ishmael, Brenda K, laundry mgr, $34,944
Ishmael, Christopher L, maint spv I, $32,628
Iske, Richard F, chaplain, $17,159
Issleib, Todd W, corrections case mgr II, $34,944
Iven, Linda S, admin ofc spt asst, $30,984
Ives, Donald R, corrections ofcr I, $33,348
Ives, Teresa J, corrections ofcr I, $32,784
Ivey, Drew W, corrections ofcr I, $29,652
Ivie, Heather L, prob & parole ofcr II, $36,204
Ivy, Kimberly A, prob & parole asst I, $31,512
Ivy, Michael K, corrections ofcr II, $31,668
Jacho, Lawanda, prob & parole asst I, $29,496
Jack, Billy, prob & parole asst I, $29,496
Jackman, Matthew B, corrections ofcr I, $29,652
Jackson, Adam B, corrections ofcr I, $29,652
Jackson, Anita S, ofc spt asst (keybrd), $23,160
Jackson, Barbara A, corrections ofcr I, $31,140
Jackson, Catherine M, corrections ofcr II, $31,668
Jackson, Cheri N, corrections ofcr I, $28,692
Jackson, Clara S, human rel ofcr I, $38,928
Jackson, Coel M, corrections ofcr I, $28,692
Jackson, Cornell, prob & parole asst I, $29,496
Jackson, Daniel J, corrections ofcr II, $31,668
Jackson, Daniel L, corrections ofcr I, $29,652
Jackson, Dawn, sr ofc spt asst (keybrd), $25,824
Jackson, Deborah K, prob & parole ofcr II, $40,380
Jackson, George W, corrections ofcr I, $28,692
Jackson, Haywood L, corrections ofcr I, $28,692
Jackson, Jerry L, corrections case mgr II, $39,624
Jackson, Krystle L, prob & parole ofcr II, $34,944
Jackson, Latashia, cook II, $23,508
Jackson, Louis A, corrections ofcr I, $29,652
Jackson, Mark L, corrections ofcr I, $31,140
Jackson, Mona H, corrections ofcr I, $33,348
Jackson, Rebekah B, prob & parole unit spv, $46,932
Jackson, Regina M, corrections case mgr II, $34,944
Jackson, Richard T, corrections ofcr I, $31,140
Jackson, Scott A, corrections ofcr I, $29,652
Jackson, Stan A, corrections mgr b1, $50,714
Jackson, Tamara D, ofc spt asst (keybrd), $23,160
Jackson, Tequilla, corrections ofcr I, $29,652
Jaco, Jeremy W, corrections ofcr I, $29,652
Jacobi, Gary W, corrections ofcr II, $31,668
Jacobs, Christopher A, corrections ofcr I, $29,652
Jacobs, Connie M, cook II, $24,264
Jacobs, Eric D, corrections case mgr II, $34,944
Jacobsen, Carl E, corrections case mgr II, $33,744
Jacobson, Rachel R, ofc spt asst (keybrd), $23,160
Jacques, Roger L, prob & parole ofcr II, $39,624
Jacquin, Mathew J, corrections ofcr I, $29,652
Jaeger, Edward L, maint worker II, $29,496
Jager, Bill W, corrections ofcr II, $31,668
Jaggie, Jon C, corrections ofcr I, $29,652
Jaggie, Sherry D, storekeeper I, $25,824
Jahraus, Donald A, corrections ofcr I, $29,652
Jakob, Bill A, corrections ofcr I, $28,692
Jakoubek, Jason S, corrections ofcr II, $31,668
James, Anthony D, corrections case mgr II, $41,172
James, Derrick L, corrections ofcr I, $29,652

James, James P, laundry mgr, $34,944
James, Jeri L, registered nurse - clin opers, $68,532
James, Jesse L, prob & parole asst I, $29,496
James, Marshall E, acad tchr III, $41,940
James, Paula A, storekeeper II, $28,536
James, Randall N, corrections ofcr II, $33,900
Jamison, Thomas I, corrections ofcr I, $30,276
Jane, Rhadonna, corrections ofcr I, $29,652
Janecek, James D, corrections ofcr I, $29,652
Jansen, Stanley C, corrections ofcr II, $30,576
Janssen, Kim, ofc spt asst (keybrd), $23,160
Jaques, Keven L, prob & parole asst II, $31,512
Jaramillo, Raeanne M, special educ tchr III, $38,928
Jarrett, Aaron P, prob & parole unit spv, $43,488
Jarrett, Darrell G, maint spv I, $32,628
Jarrett, Joseph G, voc enter spv II, $29,976
Jarrett, Lindell E, tractor trailer driver, $32,052
Jarvis, Jeffrey S, corrections ofcr I, $29,652
Jarvis, Jerome A, maint spv I, $32,628
Jarvis, Scott M, corrections ofcr I, $29,652
Jarvis, Shane W, corrections ofcr I, $29,652
Jarvis, Tina M, ofc spt asst (keybrd), $25,032
Jasmon, Kelby R, corrections ofcr I, $29,652
Jaycox, Kimberly A, corrections ofcr I, $31,140
Jaycox, Randy D, corrections ofcr I, $31,668
Jefferson, Tony A, corrections ofcr I, $29,652
Jeffries, Douglas R, corrections ofcr III, $33,744
Jeffries, Pamela A, ofc spt asst (steno), $26,232
Jeffries, Ronald E, corrections ofcr I, $33,348
Jeffris, Wesley D, corrections ofcr I, $34,512
Jemes, Joshua P, corrections ofcr I, $29,652
Jenkins, Acle D, corrections ofcr I, $31,140
Jenkins, Amy M, ofc spt asst (keybrd), $23,160
Jenkins, Brian K, corrections ofcr II, $31,668
Jenkins, Cody A, corrections ofcr I, $29,652
Jenkins, Donald W, corrections ofcr I, $29,652
Jenkins, Evalina D, corrections ofcr I, $29,652
Jenkins, Jaime J, prob & parole ofcr II, $36,204
Jenkins, Jerry L, corrections ofcr III, $32,628
Jenkins, Justin C, corrections ofcr I, $29,652
Jenkins, Justin M, corrections ofcr I, $29,652
Jenkins, Lea M, corrections ofcr I, $28,692
Jenkins, Regina, corrections ofcr I, $29,652
Jenkins, Robert J, prob & parole ofcr II, $40,380
Jenkins, Shawn C, corrections ofcr I, $29,652
Jenkins, Tony S, corrections ofcr I, $29,652
Jenkins, Zachery E, corrections ofcr II, $31,668
Jenness, Elvin F, corrections ofcr I, $34,512
Jennings, Adam R, corrections ofcr I, $28,692
Jennings, Brenda L, librarian II, $35,568
Jennings, Darrell W, corrections ofcr I, $29,652
Jennings, Jaramiah R, corrections ofcr I, $29,661
Jennings, Joseph W, corrections ofcr I, $29,652
Jennings, Karen L, corrections ofcr I, $29,652
Jennings, Kathleen S, corrections ofcr I, $29,652
Jennings, Marcia K, corrections case mgr II, $34,944
Jennings, Mark J, corrections ofcr I, $28,692
Jennings, Michael R, corrections ofcr I, $29,652
Jennings, Mindy G, corrections ofcr I, $31,140
Jennings, Raymond L, corrections ofcr I, $29,652
Jennings, Richard, functional unit mgr corr, $38,928
Jennings, Stacy D, sr ofc spt asst (clerical), $25,824
Jensen, Matthew C, electronics tech, $31,512
Jensen, Thomas E, corrections spv I, $42,708
Jensen, Vickie L, ofc spt asst (keybrd), $23,160
Jepsen, Jamie M, prob & parole ofcr II, $36,204
Jerozal, Raymond J, corrections case mgr II, $38,232
Jessmer, Matthew L, corrections ofcr I, $29,652
Jestes, Brent K, corrections ofcr III, $35,568
Jeter, Kathryn A, prob & parole ofcr II, $36,204
Jett, Debra S, acad tchr III, $37,548
Jewell, Laura, ofc spt asst (keybrd), $23,880
Jewell, Michael J, maint worker II, $29,004
Jimmerson, Sandra M, corrections mgr b1, $47,036
Jimminson, Sylvia I, prob & parole ofcr II, $39,624
Jisa, Joseph V, corrections ofcr I, $29,652
Job, Jessica J, cook II, $23,508
Job, Melissa D, storekeeper II, $28,104
Job, Shelby, stationary engr, $33,744
Jobe, Jason L, locksmith, $29,976
Jobe, Stephen G, corrections ofcr I, $29,652
Jochem, Kelly L, cook III, $28,104
John, Prince, corrections ofcr I, $28,692

Johnke, Aaron S, corrections ofcr I, $29,652
Johnmeyer, Renee B, ofc spt asst (keybrd), $23,160
Johns, Lisa, sr ofc spt asst (keybrd), $25,824
Johnson, Adam, cook III, $31,512
Johnson, Alexsa P, corrections ofcr I, $29,652
Johnson, Andre J, corrections ofcr I, $29,652
Johnson, Arnold M, corrections ofcr I, $29,652
Johnson, Beth, prob & parole unit spv, $41,940
Johnson, Bobby D, corrections ofcr II, $31,668
Johnson, Branden K, corrections ofcr III, $33,744
Johnson, Brandon A, corrections ofcr I, $29,652
Johnson, Carmen C, corrections case mgr II, $34,944
Johnson, Chase L, corrections ofcr I, $28,692
Johnson, Christina L, prob & parole ofcr II, $20,190
Johnson, Christopher R, corrections ofcr I, $29,652
Johnson, David C, corrections ofcr I, $29,652
Johnson, David E, corrections ofcr I, $29,652
Johnson, Dean, corrections ofcr I, $29,652
Johnson, Derrick A, corrections ofcr I, $29,652
Johnson, Dorine P, corrections ofcr I, $29,652
Johnson, Edward G, corrections ofcr I, $34,512
Johnson, Elise D, prob & parole asst I, $29,496
Johnson, Florene H, corrections ofcr I, $29,652
Johnson, Gene R, corrections ofcr I, $29,652
Johnson, Glendale M, corrections training ofcr, $41,940
Johnson, Jacob T, corrections case mgr II, $35,568
Johnson, James A, corrections ofcr I, $29,652
Johnson, James E, prob & parole asst I, $32,052
Johnson, James R, corrections ofcr II, $31,668
Johnson, Jeffrey E, corrections case mgr II, $38,232
Johnson, Jeffrey S, corrections ofcr II, $33,348
Johnson, Jeremiah J, corrections ofcr II, $31,668
Johnson, Jessica M, corrections ofcr I, $29,652
Johnson, Jewell T, corrections ofcr I, $29,652
Johnson, John A, corrections ofcr I, $32,784
Johnson, Joseph P, corrections ofcr I, $28,692
Johnson, Josephine L, prob & parole ofcr II, $40,380
Johnson, Kelly C, ofc spt asst (keybrd), $23,160
Johnson, Kim A, prob & parole ofcr II, $36,888
Johnson, Kimberly L, corrections ofcr I, $28,692
Johnson, Kirk E, corrections spv I, $41,172
Johnson, Lawrence, acad tchr II, $33,744
Johnson, Levi B, corrections ofcr I, $29,652
Johnson, Linda F, ofc spt asst (keybrd), $23,160
Johnson, Lisa M, sr ofc spt asst (keybrd), $25,824
Johnson, Matthew B, corrections ofcr I, $29,652
Johnson, Mavis R, corrections ofcr II, $31,668
Johnson, Michael C, corrections ofcr I, $29,652
Johnson, Michael D, corrections ofcr I, $29,652
Johnson, Nicki U, prob & parole asst I, $29,496
Johnson, Oliver S, corrections ofcr I, $29,652
Johnson, Oscar, corrections ofcr III, $34,356
Johnson, Paula L, corrections ofcr II, $35,100
Johnson, Robert D, prob & parole asst II, $32,052
Johnson, Ronnie, corrections ofcr I, $29,652
Johnson, Shawn V, prob & parole ofcr II, $36,204
Johnson, Sheila D, corrections ofcr I, $29,652
Johnson, Shirl B, librarian II, $33,744
Johnson, Shirley F, corrections ofcr I, $29,652
Johnson, Steven A, chaplain, $34,356
Johnson, Tamara, prob & parole ofcr II, $36,204
Johnson, Thaddeus, corrections ofcr I, $32,784
Johnson, Tina M, corrections ofcr I, $29,652
Johnson, Troy A, corrections case mgr II, $34,944
Johnson, Wendell P, corrections ofcr II, $37,056
Johnson, William D, maint worker II, $29,004
Johnson, Willie J, prob & parole ofcr II, $36,888
Johnston, Amber L, corrections case mgr III, $38,928
Johnston, Christopher N, corrections ofcr I, $29,652
Johnston, Diana L, ofc spt asst (keybrd), $23,160
Johnston, Patricia A, acad tchr III, $37,548
Johnston, Rebecca E, exec II, $36,204
Johnston, Shirley A, prob & parole ofcr II, $36,204
Jomp, John W, corrections ofcr I, $28,692
Jones, Adam J, corrections ofcr I, $28,692
Jones, Antoine, prob & parole asst I, $28,536
Jones, Athen B, corrections ofcr II, $31,668
Jones, Barry B, inst activity coor, $32,052
Jones, Brandon W, corrections ofcr I, $29,652
Jones, Carl J, corrections ofcr I, $29,652
Jones, Carl J, chaplain, $34,356
Jones, Catherine Y, sr ofc spt asst (keybrd), $25,824
Jones, Charles E, corrections ofcr I, $33,348

Jones, Cheryl, prob & parole ofcr I, $14,988
Jones, Connie S, prob & parole asst I, $29,496
Jones, Damon P, prob & parole ofcr II, $36,204
Jones, Darryl W, corrections ofcr I, $29,652
Jones, David L, corrections ofcr I, $33,348
Jones, Donald E, corrections ofcr III, $33,744
Jones, Donald G, corrections ofcr I, $29,652
Jones, Dusty L, corrections spv II, $43,488
Jones, Edwin D, corrections spv I, $38,928
Jones, Elisabeth L, prob & parole ofcr II, $36,204
Jones, Eric S, factory mgr I, $34,944
Jones, Ethan T, corrections ofcr I, $29,652
Jones, Frankie L, corrections ofcr I, $29,652
Jones, Gregory L, corrections ofcr I, $29,652
Jones, James D, corrections ofcr I, $29,652
Jones, Jamie E, corrections ofcr I, $28,692
Jones, Jeffrey D, corrections ofcr I, $29,652
Jones, Jeffrey T, corrections case mgr II, $33,744
Jones, Jimmie S, corrections ofcr I, $29,652
Jones, Joe A, maint spv II, $33,744
Jones, Johnathon T, corrections ofcr I, $28,692
Jones, Joseph S, prob & parole ofcr II, $36,204
Jones, Josephine E, prob & parole ofcr II, $41,940
Jones, Karen M, corrections ofcr I, $29,652
Jones, Karin E, prob & parole ofcr II, $36,204
Jones, Kathryn H, acad tchr III, $38,232
Jones, Kenneth C, corrections ofcr I, $29,652
Jones, Kenneth C, board mbr, $84,431
Jones, Kenneth R, corrections ofcr II, $35,100
Jones, Kenneth W, prob & parole ofcr II, $39,624
Jones, Kimberly A, corrections ofcr I, $33,348
Jones, Larry J, corrections ofcr I, $29,652
Jones, Lisa, special educ tchr III, $42,708
Jones, Lorene J, corrections case mgr II, $34,944
Jones, Lori J, corrections ofcr I, $29,652
Jones, Matt E, corrections ofcr I, $29,652
Jones, Matthew B, functional unit mgr corr, $41,940
Jones, Megan, prob & parole ofcr II, $36,204
Jones, Michael P, corrections spv I, $41,172
Jones, Michael T, corrections ofcr I, $28,692
Jones, Nancy J, corrections ofcr I, $32,784
Jones, Pamela J, admin ofc spt asst, $28,104
Jones, Patricia K, prob & parole asst I, $29,496
Jones, Philip, corrections ofcr I, $29,652
Jones, Ralph D, corrections ofcr I, $29,652
Jones, Rebecca S, sr ofc spt asst (clerical), $25,824
Jones, Renee M, ofc spt asst (keybrd), $23,160
Jones, Robert A, corrections ofcr I, $31,140
Jones, Robert J, corrections ofcr I, $29,652
Jones, Roger J, corrections ofcr I, $29,652
Jones, Ronal D, corrections ofcr II, $32,292
Jones, Sarah E, corrections ofcr I, $28,692
Jones, Sarah K, cook II, $23,508
Jones, Sheila M, ofc spt asst (keybrd), $23,160
Jones, Tammy L, prob & parole ofcr II, $36,204
Jones, Tammy M, corrections ofcr I, $30,132
Jones, Thea P, corrections ofcr I, $29,652
Jones, Timmy A, corrections ofcr I, $29,652
Jones, Trina L, cook II, $23,508
Jones, Walker R, prob & parole ofcr I, $29,976
Jones, Walter E, prob & parole ofcr II, $40,380
Jones, Walter L, corrections ofcr II, $31,668
Jones, William E, corrections mgr b2, $49,908
Jones, William L, corrections ofcr III, $34,356
Joplin, Hanna L, corrections ofcr I, $29,652
Joplin, Shelly A, admin ofc spt asst, $28,104
Jordan, Elizabeth K, corrections ofcr I, $29,652
Jordan, Fred L, corrections ofcr I, $29,652
Jordan, Shanica A, prob & parole asst I, $29,496
Jordan, Thomas J, cook II, $24,264
Jorgensen, Robert H, corrections ofcr I, $31,140
Jorgenson, Matthew W, prob & parole ofcr II, $36,204
Joseph, Dawn A, corrections ofcr II, $33,348
Joseph, John J, maint worker II, $28,104
Josephson, Cheryl A, corrections ofcr I, $29,652
Joslyn, Donna L, prob & parole ofcr II, $38,232
Jovanovic, Margaret C, prob & parole ofcr II, $41,940
Joy, Judy B, ofc spt asst (keybrd), $23,160
Joyce, Steven W, corrections ofcr II, $30,576
Juan, Oliver R, corrections ofcr I, $29,652
Jubell, Scott W, corrections ofcr I, $31,668
Judd, Daniel W, corrections ofcr I, $29,652
Juhl, Rebecca L, corrections ofcr I, $29,652

Julian, Steve R, investigator I, $35,568
Jump, Kathie H, prob & parole ofcr II, $36,204
Jundy, Frederick E, corrections ofcr I, $29,652
Jung, Denise E, sr ofc spt asst (keybrd), $25,824
Justus, Daniel L, corrections ofcr II, $31,668
Kaden, Janice M, librarian II, $33,744
Kaelin, Denna R, corrections ofcr I, $29,652
Kaempfe, Jason S, corrections ofcr I, $28,692
Kaiser, Jeffrey L, corrections ofcr I, $29,652
Kaiser, Joshua S, corrections ofcr I, $28,692
Kalamon, Mykola, corrections ofcr I, $33,348
Kalnas, Charles R, stationary engr, $33,744
Kamer, Arnett E, corrections ofcr I, $29,652
Kamp, Jennifer L, corrections recs ofcr III, $36,204
Kampeter, Heather M, admin ofc spt asst, $28,104
Kampeter, Jennifer L, ofc spt asst (keybrd), $23,160
Kane, Amanda M, ofc spt asst (keybrd), $23,160
Kane, Brenda J, prob & parole ofcr II, $38,232
Kane, Cynthia A, prob & parole ofcr II, $36,204
Kapelski, Donald L, corrections ofcr I, $29,652
Karaff, Michael L, maint spv I, $32,628
Karnes, Ashley A, corrections ofcr I, $29,652
Karr, Andrew J, corrections ofcr I, $29,652
Kasak, Kathleen M, corrections mgr b2, $58,424
Kaslin, Cori R, prob & parole ofcr I, $30,984
Kastning, Joshua J, corrections ofcr I, $29,652
Kastning, Steven E, corrections ofcr I, $29,652
Kater, Melanie G, corrections case mgr II, $34,944
Kattelman, Susan R, corrections ofcr II, $31,668
Kavanaugh, David C, garage spv, $32,628
Kavanaugh, Sherria K, ofc spt asst (clerical), $25,032
Kaylor, Larry D, corrections case mgr II, $36,204
Kearns, Brandon S, corrections ofcr I, $29,652
Kearns, Deborah A, ofc spt asst (keybrd), $22,536
Kearns, Gina G, corrections ofcr II, $31,668
Kearns, Kristopher S, corrections ofcr II, $31,668
Keck, Aaron R, power plant mech, $32,628
Keckley, Ronald E, corrections ofcr I, $29,652
Kedge, Leroy J, corrections ofcr I, $29,652
Keedy, Patricia A, corrections ofcr I, $28,692
Keegan, Greg R, acad tchr III, $39,624
Keehler, Lori A, admin ofc spt asst, $28,104
Keely, Lisa J, ofc spt asst (keybrd), $23,160
Keely, Rockiesha, prob & parole ofcr II, $36,204
Keely, Stanley H, functional unit mgr corr, $45,156
Keen, Nona C, cook II, $23,508
Keener, Susan R, prob & parole unit spv, $43,488
Keeney, Charlene E, sr ofc spt asst (keybrd), $25,824
Keenoy, Justin L, prob & parole ofcr I, $29,976
Keeran, Dennis L, voc enter spv II, $34,944
Keeran, Layton E, tractor trailer driver, $29,976
Keeran, Robert W, corrections ofcr II, $31,668
Keesaman, Jacqueline N, corrections ofcr II, $31,668
Keeth, Tamra L, prob & parole ofcr II, $41,940
Keeting, Lisabeth L, prob & parole ofcr II, $36,204
Keith, Brian A, corrections ofcr II, $31,668
Keith, David M, corrections ofcr II, $31,668
Keith, Sally, factory mgr II, $38,928
Keithley, Larry W, storekeeper I, $25,824
Kellams, Lynn M, prob & parole ofcr II, $39,624
Kellar, Nickolas R, corrections ofcr I, $28,692
Keller, Dana L, corrections mgr b2, $60,216
Keller, Ethan J, corrections ofcr I, $29,652
Keller, Michael D, corrections ofcr I, $28,692
Keller, Richard W, corrections ofcr I, $29,652
Keller, Rodney K, prob & parole ofcr II, $36,204
Keller, Stephanie L, corrections ofcr I, $29,652
Keller, Tamara L, corrections ofcr I, $29,316
Kellerhals, Robert R, prob & parole asst I, $29,496
Kellerman, Kim E, prob & parole ofcr II, $36,204
Kelley, Amanda S, ofc spt asst (keybrd), $23,160
Kelley, Brian M, recrtn ofcr I, $31,512
Kelley, Coy C, corrections ofcr I, $29,652
Kelley, Harold W, corrections ofcr I, $29,652
Kelley, Isabella, corrections ofcr I, $29,652
Kelley, Jacqueline R, prob & parole ofcr II, $39,624
Kelley, James O, corrections ofcr I, $29,652
Kelley, Larry, corrections ofcr I, $29,652
Kelley, Leslie M, prob & parole ofcr II, $36,204
Kelley, Raechel S, corrections ofcr I, $31,140
Kelley, Steffi, corrections ofcr I, $29,652
Kelley, Steve, corrections ofcr II, $33,900
Kelley, Thomas A, corrections ofcr I, $29,652

Kelly, Ashley N, corrections case mgr I, $29,976
Kelly, Colby A, corrections ofcr I, $28,692
Kelly, Donald L, corrections ofcr I, $29,652
Kelly, Kevin W, corrections ofcr I, $31,140
Kelly, Lisa C, prob & parole ofcr II, $38,232
Kelly, Maclean M, corrections ofcr I, $28,692
Kelly, Paula S, prob & parole ofcr II, $38,232
Kelly, Peyton N, corrections ofcr I, $28,692
Kelly, Sean M, corrections ofcr I, $29,652
Kelly, Shannon D, prob & parole asst I, $29,496
Kelso, Michael, corrections ofcr I, $31,140
Kelts, Deana C, corrections ofcr I, $29,652
Kemp, Brandon R, corrections ofcr I, $29,652
Kemp, Cynthia E, acad tchr III, $37,548
Kempa, Nelson R, corrections ofcr I, $29,652
Kempa, Ronald, corrections ofcr I, $30,132
Kemper, Dana L, supply mgr I, $36,204
Kemper, Sheila L, corrections ofcr I, $29,652
Kempf, Kenneth D, corrections ofcr I, $29,652
Kempf, Roylene E, ofc spt asst (keybrd), $23,160
Kempker, Dwayne V, dpty div dir, $78,216
Kempker, Julie, special asst official & admstr, $82,315
Kempker, Kyle W, corrections ofcr II, $30,576
Kempker, Linda L, corrections ofcr I, $31,668
Kempker, Mark A, voc enter spv II, $29,004
Kempker, Tammy S, corrections recs ofcr I, $29,496
Kemry, Tyler W, cook II, $23,508
Kenna, Toni L, prob & parole ofcr II, $41,172
Kennedy, Bobbie S, corrections spv I, $38,928
Kennedy, James E, tractor trailer driver, $30,984
Kennedy, Jeremy, corrections ofcr I, $29,652
Kennedy, Krystle L, corrections ofcr I, $29,652
Kennedy, Tommi J, ofc spt asst (keybrd), $23,160
Kennison, Denise A, storekeeper I, $25,824
Kennison, Fred M, corrections ofcr I, $34,512
Kennon, Brandy, prob & parole ofcr II, $34,944
Kennon, Darlene L, corrections ofcr I, $29,652
Kennon, James, factory mgr II, $41,940
Kennon, Jason P, corrections ofcr I, $29,652
Kennon, Jimmy L, corrections ofcr I, $29,652
Kennon, Nancy A, acad tchr III, $38,232
Kennon, Tessa N, corrections ofcr I, $29,652
Kensinger, Casey R, corrections ofcr I, $29,652
Kent, Finesa, prob & parole asst I, $29,496
Kent, Joshua G, corrections ofcr I, $28,692
Kent, Theresa L, prob & parole asst I, $29,496
Kentner, Alex L, corrections ofcr I, $29,652
Kepler, James P, corrections ofcr I, $29,652
Kern, Belinda A, storekeeper I, $25,824
Kern, Sandra E, prob & parole asst I, $29,496
Kernan, Laura L, account clerk II, $27,084
Kerns, Alanna C, corrections ofcr II, $30,576
Kerns, Katie M, corrections ofcr I, $29,652
Kersey, Vanessa, ofc spt asst (keybrd), $23,160
Kerwin, Shannon B, sr ofc spt asst (keybrd), $27,504
Kesselring, Sarah E, account clerk II, $25,824
Kessler, James, prob & parole ofcr II, $38,232
Ketcherside, Abby M, corrections ofcr I, $28,692
Ketchum, Nathan C, corrections ofcr I, $29,652
Key, Gregory C, prob & parole ofcr II, $36,888
Key, Henry W, storekeeper I, $25,824
Key, Tammy L, corrections ofcr I, $29,652
Kibbe, Benjamin F, corrections ofcr II, $35,100
Kidd, Jefferson E, corrections ofcr I, $29,652
Kidd, Richard P, corrections ofcr I, $29,652
Kidd-Mitchell, Juanita E, prob & parole ofcr II, $41,172
Kidwell, William D, locksmith, $34,356
Kiefer, Cristina N, ofc spt asst (keybrd), $23,160
Kiefer, David R, corrections ofcr I, $29,652
Kiefer, Jesse, maint worker II, $28,104
Kiefer, Joshua A, maint spv I, $32,628
Kieffer, Keith E, functional unit mgr corr, $38,928
Kieffer, Rhonda K, corrections case mgr II, $36,204
Kiel, Stacey R, admin ofc spt asst, $28,104
Kiker, Kimberly A, corrections ofcr I, $29,652
Kilgore, Ashley A, ofc spt asst (keybrd), $23,160
Kilgore, Mary, corrections ofcr I, $29,652
Killian, Evan D, corrections ofcr I, $28,692
Killian, Robert F, corrections case mgr II, $34,944
Killion, John E, storekeeper I, $27,504
Kimbell, Jason A, corrections ofcr I, $29,652
Kimberlin, Jennifer J, prob & parole ofcr II, $39,624
Kimbro, James A, subs abuse cnslr II, $34,944

Kimbrough, Chante, prob & parole ofcr I, $34,944
Kimbrough, Elizabeth A, corrections recs ofcr I, $28,104
Kimbrough, Michael D, functional unit mgr corr, $41,172
Kimmich, Patricia A, prob & parole ofcr II, $41,940
Kimsey, Matthew R, parole hearing analyst, $49,128
Kimsey, Shannon L, corrections mgr b1, $48,839
Kincade, Deborah R, special asst paraprof, $20.78/hr
Kincaid, James M, corrections ofcr II, $31,668
Kinder, Kelly A, account clerk II, $25,824
Kinder, Shanna J, ofc spt asst (keybrd), $23,160
Kinder, Trista M, corrections case mgr I, $30,984
Kindle, Amanda L, ofc spt asst (keybrd), $23,160
Kindle, Lyndon P, corrections ofcr II, $31,668
Kinealy, Daniel M, corrections ofcr I, $29,652
King, Brad S, corrections ofcr I, $29,652
King, Brandon T, corrections ofcr I, $29,652
King, Dana, prob & parole ofcr II, $36,204
King, Danetta S, cook III, $28,104
King, David, recrtn ofcr III, $40,380
King, Denver, corrections ofcr I, $34,512
King, Denver J, recrtn ofcr I, $30,984
King, Donna, corrections mgr b2, $52,753
King, Emmett J, corrections ofcr I, $29,652
King, Ernest F, garage spv, $32,628
King, George R, corrections spv I, $41,940
King, Heather A, corrections ofcr I, $29,652
King, Heather S, prob & parole asst I, $29,496
King, Isadore, prob & parole asst I, $29,496
King, James R, corrections training ofcr, $38,928
King, Joel H, locksmith, $29,976
King, Joshua J, corrections ofcr I, $29,652
King, Justin E, fire & safety spec, $30,420
King, Kielly M, ofc spt asst (keybrd), $23,160
King, Kimberly E, corrections ofcr I, $28,692
King, Mable A, corrections ofcr I, $29,652
King, Matthew E, corrections ofcr I, $29,652
King, Matthew P, corrections ofcr I, $29,652
King, Nicholas R, corrections ofcr I, $29,652
King, Robin L, corrections ofcr I, $29,652
King, Rolland B, corrections ofcr I, $29,652
King, Rosie D, corrections ofcr I, $29,652
King, Tasha M, corrections ofcr I, $29,652
King, Teresa M, prob & parole unit spv, $46,068
Kingcade, Terry, corrections ofcr I, $29,652
Kingsley, Denise E, prob & parole unit spv, $41,940
Kinman, Geraldine L, food serv mgr I, $31,512
Kintner, Scott A, corrections case mgr II, $39,624
Kirby, Abby, prob & parole asst I, $29,496
Kirby, Christie L, corrections ofcr I, $31,140
Kirby, Christopher L, corrections ofcr I, $29,652
Kirby, Christopher P, prob & parole ofcr II, $36,204
Kirby, Dennis W, corrections ofcr III, $36,888
Kirby, Durwood M, prob & parole ofcr II, $39,624
Kirchner, Balinda S, ofc spt asst (keybrd), $23,160
Kirchoff, Lisa M, corrections ofcr I, $29,652
Kirchoff, Roland S, corrections ofcr I, $29,652
Kirk, Ashley N, corrections ofcr I, $29,652
Kirk, Robert N, corrections ofcr I, $29,661
Kirk, Ronald L, corrections ofcr I, $29,652
Kirk, Tammie L, inst activity coor, $32,052
Kirkhart, Andrea N, cook II, $24,264
Kirkhart, Anthony W, corrections ofcr II, $31,668
Kirkhart, Johnathan M, corrections ofcr I, $29,652
Kirkley, Hugh W, cook II, $24,264
Kirkman, David A, maint spv I, $32,628
Kirkman, Michael C, corrections ofcr I, $29,652
Kirkman, Tammy J, corrections ofcr I, $30,132
Kirkpatrick, Kyle M, corrections ofcr I, $29,652
Kirks, Timothy H, corrections ofcr I, $29,652
Kirksey, Tracy J, corrections ofcr I, $29,652
Kirn, Peter S, corrections ofcr I, $29,652
Kirtley, Alice L, corrections ofcr I, $31,668
Kisch, Michael J, maint worker II, $28,104
Kissick, Beverly S, exec II, $36,204
Kissick, Ellen K, corrections ofcr I, $31,140
Kissick, Jerry L, stationary engr, $33,744
Kissick, Kelly L, prob & parole ofcr II, $38,232
Kissinger, Norman, corrections training ofcr, $41,940
Kitchell, Howard L, corrections ofcr I, $29,652
Kitchell, Jeremiah J, corrections ofcr I, $29,652
Kitchell, William E, corrections ofcr I, $29,652
Kitchen, Benjamen P, corrections ofcr I, $29,652
Kitchens, Amy L, registered nurse - clin opers, $52,608

Kitchin, Clinton E, maint worker II, $29,004
Kittelson, Shane C, corrections ofcr I, $29,652
Kizeart, Stecia D, corrections ofcr I, $28,692
Kizer, Jerome D, corrections ofcr I, $29,652
Klamert, John E, prob & parole ofcr II, $36,204
Kleier, Stacy J, corrections mgr b2, $49,909
Klein, Brenda M, ofc spt asst (keybrd), $26,232
Klein, Kenton H, tractor trailer driver, $31,512
Klein, Kerry M, functional unit mgr corr, $41,940
Kleinsorge, Paul H, corrections ofcr I, $29,652
Klempke, Lawrence M, corrections ofcr I, $28,692
Klever, Jerry D, corrections case mgr II, $39,624
Klick, Anita M, admin ofc spt asst, $28,104
Kliethermes, Amy S, cook II, $24,264
Kliethermes, Carol J, admin ofc spt asst, $28,104
Kliethermes, Daniel J, corrections ofcr I, $34,512
Kliethermes, Gerald P, voc enter rep, $33,744
Kliethermes, Michael W, cook III, $28,104
Kliewer, Doug M, recrtn ofcr III, $37,548
Kline, John M, corrections ofcr I, $29,652
Kline, Keith A, corrections ofcr I, $29,652
Kline, Richard L, corrections ofcr I, $31,140
Klingel, Ginger R, prob & parole ofcr II, $36,204
Klingeman, Shirley A, corrections ofcr I, $30,132
Klipfel, Paula A, ofc spt asst (keybrd), $23,880
Klockenkemper, Terry J, corrections ofcr I, $28,692
Kloeppel, Teresa A, corrections ofcr I, $29,652
Klueppel, Jennifer M, prob & parole ofcr II, $40,380
Klumper, Matthew R, functional unit mgr corr, $38,928
Klumper, Steven R, corrections ofcr I, $29,652
Knapp, Cheryl L, storekeeper I, $25,824
Knapp, Marvin D, corrections ofcr I, $29,652
Knapp, Michael J, maint spv I, $32,628
Knarr, Marc D, corrections spv I, $37,548
Knatcal, Audra R, sr ofc spt asst (keybrd), $25,824
Kneib, Tara K, corrections ofcr I, $28,692
Knickerbocker, Kevin L, corrections mgr b1, $50,235
Kniess, Rose M, corrections ofcr I, $29,652
Knight, Benjamin P, corrections ofcr I, $28,692
Knight, Joyce J, corrections ofcr I, $29,652
Knight, Robert H, corrections ofcr II, $31,668
Knipp, Gabriel R, maint worker II, $29,004
Knipp, Sheri, admin ofc spt asst, $30,420
Knipp, Stanley W, corrections ofcr II, $31,668
Knorr, Brenda L, cook III, $29,004
Knoske, William A, corrections ofcr I, $29,652
Knott, Christina L, ofc spt asst (keybrd), $26,232
Knott, Donnie E, corrections spv I, $42,708
Knowles, Tyler R, corrections ofcr I, $29,652
Knox, Brenda J, ofc spt asst (keybrd), $26,652
Kobert, Cassie L, corrections ofcr I, $29,652
Kobielush, Calvin L, corrections ofcr I, $29,652
Koch, Daniel A, prob & parole asst I, $29,496
Koch, Thomas D, corrections ofcr I, $29,652
Koderick, Frank J, corrections ofcr I, $29,652
Koderick, Joshua C, corrections ofcr I, $28,692
Koechner-Talley, Amy M, prob & parole ofcr II, $36,204
Koelling, Scott A, corrections ofcr I, $29,652
Koenig, Elizabeth C, prob & parole ofcr II, $36,204
Koenig, Nicholas P, corrections ofcr I, $29,652
Koenig, Peter L, corrections ofcr I, $33,348
Koenigsfeld, Julie A, librarian II, $36,204
Koerner, David J, corrections ofcr I, $29,652
Koessel, Paul C, prob & parole ofcr II, $40,380
Koestner, Adam R, corrections case mgr II, $34,944
Koffman, Teresa A, corrections ofcr III, $38,232
Koger, Jon W, corrections ofcr I, $30,132
Kohler, Craig A, corrections ofcr II, $31,668
Kohn, James F, voc enter spv II, $29,004
Kohnz, Julie M, prob & parole ofcr II, $36,204
Kolb, Carol J, cook I, $24,264
Kolb, David T, prob & parole ofcr II, $36,204
Koller, Larry J, tractor trailer driver, $30,984
Kolling, Martin W, corrections ofcr I, $28,692
Komer, Shawnda K, corrections ofcr I, $29,652
Koncor, Rhonda L, ofc spt asst (keybrd), $23,160
Konik, Mark S, prob & parole asst I, $29,976
Konopka, Cassondra M, corrections ofcr II, $31,668
Koon, Walter, corrections ofcr II, $31,668
Koonse, Nancy K, corrections case mgr II, $36,888
Koontz, Candy L, corrections ofcr I, $29,652
Kopczenski, Nicholas A, corrections ofcr I, $29,652
Kornbrust, Diamond A, corrections ofcr I, $28,692

Kornbrust, Shawn, corrections ofcr I, $29,652
Korneman, Sherie L, corrections mgr b2, $50,853
Korte, Edmund G, storekeeper I, $27,084
Korte, Howard J, corrections ofcr I, $31,140
Kosanke, Karen S, ofc spt asst (keybrd), $23,160
Kosanke, Patrick J, corrections ofcr III, $36,204
Kosfeld, Martin R, corrections ofcr III, $37,548
Kosfeld, Samona J, human rel ofcr I, $38,928
Kost, Wendy L, ofc spt asst (keybrd), $23,160
Kottwitz, Greg D, corrections ofcr I, $29,652
Kovachik, Albert H, corrections ofcr I, $29,652
Krachey, Daniel R, inst activity coor, $33,744
Kraft, Hayley L, corrections case mgr II, $34,944
Krajewski, Amanda A, corrections ofcr I, $29,652
Kramer, Jeremy W, corrections ofcr I, $28,692
Kramer, Joshua A, corrections ofcr I, $29,652
Kramer, Shane P, maint worker II, $29,004
Krampe, Jerome D, corrections spv I, $41,940
Krantz, Justin R, corrections case mgr II, $34,944
Krasnicki, Charles, prob & parole ofcr II, $36,204
Krattli, Priscilla, corrections ofcr I, $31,140
Kraus, Terrie S, ofc spt asst (keybrd), $23,160
Krause, Mark J, corrections ofcr I, $29,652
Krawiecki, Matthew J, corrections ofcr II, $30,576
Krawl, Paula L, corrections ofcr II, $31,668
Krawl, Robert A, corrections ofcr II, $31,668
Kreilick, John K, voc enter rep, $33,744
Kreisler, Robby, corrections ofcr I, $29,652
Kreisler, Sharae L, corrections ofcr I, $29,652
Kremer, Sandra K, account clerk II, $25,824
Kreutzer, Gregory A, corrections ofcr I, $29,652
Krieg, Curt G, maint worker II, $29,004
Krieg, Holly A, admin ofc spt asst, $33,180
Krieg, Kevin R, prob & parole ofcr II, $36,204
Krieger, Adam, prob & parole ofcr II, $30,984
Krieger, Kelly, labor spv, $26,652
Krigbaum, Brandon L, corrections ofcr I, $29,652
Krisher, Renae L, prob & parole ofcr II, $38,232
Kroenung, Eugene P, corrections ofcr I, $29,652
Kroll, Nelda R, corrections ofcr I, $29,652
Kroner, Amanda K, corrections case mgr II, $34,944
Kroush, Beverly F, corrections ofcr I, $31,140
Krug, Charles E, corrections ofcr I, $34,512
Kruger, Sarah D, acad tchr III, $37,548
Krull, Terri, corrections ofcr I, $29,652
Kruse, Kyle O, corrections ofcr I, $29,652
Kruse-McKeown, Melissa A, prob & parole unit spv, $42,708
Krydynski, Thomas J, prob & parole ofcr II, $40,380
Krzyzanowski, Randi M, prob & parole ofcr II, $34,944
Kuck, Lee A, corrections ofcr III, $35,568
Kuck, Scott E, corrections ofcr I, $31,140
Kucsik, Richard J, prob & parole ofcr II, $36,204
Kuda, Connie S, factory mgr I, $36,888
Kuda, Pamela A, ofc spt asst (clerical), $22,872
Kuder, Russell P, corrections ofcr I, $29,652
Kueck, Lisa G, corrections ofcr I, $29,652
Kueckelhan, Patricia, edu sup, $44,304
Kuehn, Dena M, ofc spt asst (clerical), $22,536
Kugler, Mark S, corrections ofcr I, $31,140
Kugler, Steven P, prob & parole ofcr II, $40,380
Kuhler, Rhonda J, exec II, $36,888
Kukovich, Shannon L, ofc spt asst (keybrd), $25,032
Kukulka, Ron S, corrections case mgr II, $36,888
Kulhanek, Kenneth P, corrections ofcr I, $29,652
Kumberg, James H, functional unit mgr corr, $43,488
Kundert, Brian T, corrections ofcr I, $28,692
Kunkel, Kristopher C, corrections ofcr I, $29,652
Kuntz, Cynthia M, ofc spt asst (keybrd), $24,612
Kuntz, Danial D, corrections ofcr I, $29,652
Kunzler, Carl L, maint spv I, $33,180
Kupihea, Tasha C, prob & parole asst I, $29,496
Kurgas, Angela G, corrections ofcr I, $29,652
Kurth, Brook J, corrections case mgr II, $34,944
Kurtz, Jerry D, corrections ofcr I, $29,652
Kurtz, Kathleen A, ofc spt asst (keybrd), $23,160
Kush, Brian P, corrections ofcr I, $28,692
Kutscher, Michelle A, sr ofc spt asst (keybrd), $25,032
Kuttenkuler, Christina, admin ofc spt asst, $28,104
Kuttenkuler, David J, corrections ofcr I, $29,652
Kuttenkuler, Richard, prob & parole unit spv, $43,488
Kyle, Elbert G, corrections ofcr III, $38,232
Kyle, Todd A, corrections ofcr I, $29,652
Labang, Oscar, prob & parole asst I, $29,496

Labon, Leslie L, corrections case mgr II, $34,944
Labrash, Christopher E, voc tchr II, $33,744
Lachance, Denise L, cook II, $24,264
Lack, Michelle, prob & parole asst I, $29,496
Lackey, Eileen M, ofc spt asst (clerical), $22,536
Lacy, Rick S, corrections ofcr I, $29,652
Lafavor, Jimmy L, corrections ofcr I, $31,140
Lafferty, James A, corrections ofcr II, $31,668
Lafleur, Jennifer I, prob & parole asst I, $29,496
Lafontaine, Brian D, corrections ofcr I, $29,652
Lafountain, Ray R, storekeeper II, $28,104
Lahmeyer, Brad L, corrections ofcr I, $31,140
Laird, Jacquline D, admin ofc spt asst, $30,984
Laird, John J, corrections ofcr I, $29,652
Laird, Joshua T, corrections ofcr I, $29,652
Lairmore, Jeannie M, account clerk II, $25,824
Lairmore, Stacy D, corrections case mgr II, $33,744
Lake, Amanda L, functional unit mgr corr, $37,548
Lake, Deana S, corrections ofcr I, $31,140
Lake, Ryan E, corrections ofcr I, $29,652
Lakey, Lori M, corrections mgr b2, $49,909
Lamarche, John W, corrections ofcr I, $29,652
Lamarche, Patricia K, cook II, $24,264
Lamasney, Stephen D, cook II, $23,508
Lamb, Jordan A, corrections ofcr I, $29,652
Lamb, Richard C, stationary engr, $33,744
Lambe, Ricky D, corrections ofcr II, $31,668
Lamberson, Blake A, corrections ofcr I, $29,652
Lambert, Christopher D, storekeeper II, $28,104
Lambert, Marc A, corrections ofcr I, $29,652
Lambert, Tammy R, corrections ofcr III, $35,568
Lamm, Pamela R, cook II, $24,264
Lammers, Deborah L, prob & parole ofcr II, $36,204
Lammers, Douglas D, corrections ofcr I, $29,652
Lammers, Mary Kay, prob & parole ofcr II, $39,624
Lammers, Steven J, corrections ofcr I, $29,652
Lamp, Jeffrey A, voc tchr II, $34,944
Lampe, Debbie I, ofc spt asst (keybrd), $23,160
Lamphier, Allen L, corrections ofcr I, $28,692
Lamphier, Monica L, prob & parole unit spv, $46,068
Lamunion, Rebecca K, ofc spt asst (keybrd), $23,160
Lancaster, Melissa J, inst activity coor, $29,004
Lancaster, Timothy. R, investigator I, $37,548
Lance, James D, storekeeper II, $27,228
Land, David B, corrections ofcr I, $29,652
Landers, Nathan C, corrections ofcr I, $29,652
Landers, Tammy L, corrections classif asst, $31,512
Landes, William I, corrections ofcr II, $33,348
Landreth, Jeremy A, cook II, $23,508
Landrum, Libby A, registered nurse mgr b1, $66,786
Landry, James L, corrections ofcr I, $28,692
Lands, Marie E, prob & parole ofcr II, $40,380
Landwehr, Robert L, corrections ofcr II, $33,348
Lane, Daniel D, acad tchr III, $37,548
Lane, Edward L, maint worker II, $29,004
Lane, Michael W, corrections ofcr I, $29,652
Lane, Patricia S, laundry mgr, $34,944
Lane, Richard A, maint spv I, $32,628
Laney, Douglas L, corrections ofcr I, $29,652
Lanfersieck, Katie L, ofc spt asst (keybrd), $23,160
Lang, Cody A, labor spv, $26,652
Lang, Mark, maint spv I, $34,356
Lang, Nora E, ofc spt asst (keybrd), $23,160
Lange, Daniel J, prob & parole asst I, $29,496
Lange, Jerry B, corrections ofcr II, $33,900
Langgin, Christopher H, corrections ofcr I, $29,316
Langley, Emma D, cook II, $24,264
Langley, Ian R, corrections ofcr I, $28,692
Langley, Lori G, corrections mgr b1, $42,368
Langston, Marie, corrections ofcr I, $32,784
Langton, Sean D, corrections ofcr I, $31,668
Lankford, Billy M, corrections ofcr I, $29,652
Lankford-Wilcox, Michelle R, prob & parole ofcr III, $41,172
Lansche, Tammy M, corrections case mgr II, $34,944
Laplant, Brock W, corrections case mgr II, $35,568
Lara, Adriana R, ofc spt asst (keybrd), $23,160
Larabee, Carmen A, corrections ofcr I, $29,652
Laramore, Donna, prob & parole ofcr II, $37,548
Laramore, Nichole V, corrections ofcr I, $29,652
Lark, James D, corrections ofcr I, $29,652
Lark, Teresa C, recrtn ofcr II, $33,744
Larkins, Jeanne S, prob & parole ofcr II, $39,624
Larm, Charles W, corrections ofcr I, $29,652

Larry, Melissa, prob & parole ofcr II, $36,204
Larson, Erik S, corrections ofcr I, $29,652
Larson, Thorne K, corrections ofcr I, $29,652
Larue, Alan L, corrections ofcr I, $29,652
Larue, Dalton J, corrections ofcr I, $29,652
Lasher, Sandy L, ofc spt asst (keybrd), $24,612
Lashley, Gabriel W, electronics tech, $30,984
Lassley, Dennis R, corrections ofcr I, $29,652
Laster, Angela D, prob & parole ofcr II, $39,624
Laswell, Norita I, corrections ofcr I, $34,512
Latchford, Bruce L, stationary engr, $33,744
Laub, Luke A, corrections ofcr I, $29,652
Laughlin, Barbara L, storekeeper I, $25,824
Laughlin, Jason R, bldg const spv, $33,744
Lauhoff, Barry A, stationary engr, $33,744
Laurent, Julie A, prob & parole ofcr II, $36,204
Laux, Daniel J, food serv mgr I, $32,052
Lavender, Tina M, cook II, $24,264
Lavigne, Michael L, corrections ofcr I, $29,652
Law, Levi D, corrections ofcr I, $29,652
Law, Linda, corrections spv I, $41,172
Law, Sandra P, corrections ofcr I, $29,652
Lawless, Melissa, prob & parole ofcr II, $36,204
Lawrence, Billie, prob & parole ofcr II, $36,204
Lawrence, Caitlin N, corrections ofcr I, $28,692
Lawrence, Charles K, prob & parole asst I, $29,496
Lawrence, Jacob M, corrections ofcr I, $28,692
Lawrence, Jonathan J, corrections ofcr I, $29,652
Lawrence, Lee E, corrections ofcr I, $29,652
Lawrence, Lori A, storekeeper II, $27,504
Lawrence, Mark E, corrections ofcr I, $29,652
Lawrence, Patrick A, corrections ofcr I, $29,652
Lawrence, Randall C, corrections ofcr I, $29,652
Lawrence, Rhonda R, corrections classif asst, $33,180
Lawrence, Rodney A, corrections ofcr I, $29,652
Lawrence, Sandra G, corrections ofcr I, $29,652
Lawrence, Scott A, corrections mgr b3, $66,438
Lawrence, Tana R, corrections ofcr I, $28,692
Lawson, Aaron L, corrections ofcr I, $30,132
Lawson, Chad E, corrections ofcr I, $29,652
Lawson, Charles H, corrections ofcr I, $29,652
Lawson, Charles L, corrections ofcr I, $29,652
Lawson, Cody C, cook II, $23,508
Lawson, Darren L, phys plant sup I, $36,204
Lawson, Dolores L, acad tchr III, $36,204
Lawson, James H, prob & parole ofcr II, $36,204
Lawson, Kenneth D, corrections mgr b2, $57,379
Lawson, Michael D, corrections ofcr III, $39,624
Lawson, Patricia, corrections ofcr I, $29,652
Lawson, Roger H, corrections ofcr I, $29,652
Lawson, Shawn A, cook II, $24,264
Lawson, Teri N, corrections mgr b1, $42,403
Lawson, Walter E, corrections ofcr I, $29,652
Lawzano, Michael, special asst prof, $53,016
Laxton, Benjamin, corrections ofcr I, $29,652
Layden, Michael J, corrections case mgr II, $38,928
Layfield, Ronald D, corrections ofcr I, $29,652
Laymon, Kelly V, corrections ofcr I, $29,652
Laytham, Mike G, corrections ofcr I, $29,652
Layton, Dustin D, corrections ofcr I, $29,652
Layton, Jill S, prob & parole ofcr II, $36,204
Layton, John-Riley A, corrections ofcr I, $29,652
Layton, Linda L, ofc spt asst (keybrd), $23,160
Lea, Casey J, corrections ofcr I, $29,652
Lea, Jeremiah J, corrections ofcr III, $35,568
Lea, Jessica L, corrections ofcr I, $29,652
Lea, Sherri L, prob & parole ofcr II, $40,380
Leach, Billy D, corrections ofcr II, $31,668
Leach, Stephen L, corrections ofcr II, $31,668
Leach, Timmy R, corrections case mgr II, $40,380
Leak, Andy J, corrections ofcr I, $29,652
Leak, Gregory C, corrections ofcr I, $29,652
Leak, Tracy A, corrections ofcr I, $29,652
Leake, Floyd D, corrections ofcr I, $32,220
Learue, Patricia L, pers clerk, $28,104
Leathers, Rosina R, corrections ofcr I, $29,652
Lebcowitz, Gary T, corrections ofcr I, $29,652
Lechman, Dara M, corrections ofcr I, $29,652
Leclair, Christopher J, corrections ofcr I, $28,692
Ledbetter, Jeffrey S, corrections ofcr I, $29,652
Ledford, Josh A, corrections ofcr I, $29,652
Ledl, Diana S, prob & parole ofcr II, $36,204
Lee, Catherine M, prob & parole ofcr II, $39,624

Lee, Christopher E, corrections ofcr I, $28,692
Lee, Craig A, storekeeper I, $25,824
Lee, Devin J, corrections ofcr I, $29,652
Lee, Dylan A, corrections ofcr I, $29,652
Lee, Dylan S, corrections ofcr I, $33,348
Lee, James D, cook III, $28,104
Lee, Jami J, corrections ofcr I, $29,652
Lee, Jason M, corrections ofcr II, $31,668
Lee, Jennifer S, pers clerk, $28,104
Lee, Jerry W, corrections ofcr I, $29,652
Lee, Kathi M, prob & parole ofcr II, $36,888
Lee, Mark L, prob & parole ofcr II, $39,624
Lee, Matthew E, corrections ofcr I, $29,652
Lee, Miranda D, corrections ofcr I, $29,652
Lee, Shannon T, special asst technician, $44,432
Lee, Shari L, sr ofc spt asst (clerical), $25,824
Lee, Shari M, prob & parole ofcr II, $40,380
Lee, Valerie D, prob & parole ofcr II, $40,380
Leeder, Kenneth W, corrections case mgr II, $35,568
Leeper, Douglas, prob & parole ofcr II, $36,204
Leer, Judy K, sr ofc spt asst (keybrd), $28,908
Leffert, William H, corrections ofcr I, $31,140
Leffler, Ricky M, corrections ofcr I, $29,652
Lefkowitz, Valerie A, prob & parole unit spv, $41,940
Lefmann, Dennis S, recrtn ofcr I, $31,512
Leftridge, Benjamin A, recrtn ofcr I, $31,512
Leggans, Hazel L, subs abuse cnslr III, $37,548
Leggans, James R, corrections ofcr I, $29,652
Leggins, Danielle J, corrections ofcr I, $28,692
Leggins, Jonathon D, corrections ofcr I, $29,652
Legrand, Aaron J, corrections classif asst, $32,628
Legreid, Kevin, med technologist III, $38,928
Lehmen, John H, cook II, $24,264
Lehmen, Theresa M, prob & parole ofcr II, $39,624
Leith, Sarah R, voc tchr I, $30,984
Leitz, Richard W, corrections ofcr I, $34,512
Leivan, Chad A, corrections ofcr II, $31,668
Lejeune, Jeannie C, prob & parole unit spv, $44,304
Lemberger, Sara R, prob & parole unit spv, $43,488
Lenger, Lenard D, fiscal & administrative mgr b3, $72,508
Lenhardt, Kathleen L, corrections ofcr I, $29,652
Leninsky, Michael S, corrections ofcr I, $29,652
Lenney, Brandon D, corrections ofcr I, $28,692
Lent, Michael A, stationary engr, $33,744
Lentz, Leslie L, corrections ofcr III, $35,568
Lentz, Rebecca J, prob & parole ofcr II, $39,624
Leonard, Aaron J, corrections ofcr I, $29,652
Leonard, Christopher M, corrections ofcr I, $30,132
Leonard, David B, corrections ofcr I, $31,764
Leonard, Dorris M, prob & parole ofcr II, $38,232
Leonard, James F, acad tchr III, $37,548
Leonard, Mark E, corrections ofcr II, $31,668
Leonard, Phillip A, corrections ofcr II, $31,668
Leonard, Toni D, corrections ofcr I, $28,692
Leroy, Maureen, acad tchr III, $37,548
Leroy, Ronnie F, corrections ofcr I, $29,652
Lescalleet, Stacie L, corrections case mgr I, $31,512
Leslie, Daniel S, corrections ofcr I, $29,652
Leslie, Franklin G, corrections ofcr I, $29,652
Leslie, Glen R, corrections ofcr I, $29,652
Leslie, Gregory C, corrections ofcr III, $33,744
Lessard, Mario J, corrections ofcr II, $33,900
Lester, John L, corrections ofcr I, $29,652
Lester, Raymond D, corrections ofcr I, $31,668
Lester, Todd S, corrections ofcr I, $29,652
Leu, Margaret M, corrections case mgr II, $34,944
Leuthauser, Darrin L, corrections ofcr I, $29,652
Levell, Shane A, corrections ofcr I, $29,652
Lewallen, Gary L, maint spv I, $34,356
Lewellen, Curtis K, acad tchr III, $37,548
Lewis, Arin K, corrections ofcr I, $29,652
Lewis, Ashley M, corrections ofcr I, $29,652
Lewis, Carl D, corrections training ofcr, $38,928
Lewis, Cody L, corrections ofcr I, $29,652
Lewis, Elizabeth D, corrections ofcr I, $28,692
Lewis, Harold E, corrections ofcr I, $29,652
Lewis, Heather J, corrections case mgr I, $29,976
Lewis, Jacqueline, corrections ofcr I, $31,140
Lewis, James D, serv mgr I, $34,944
Lewis, James E, corrections ofcr I, $29,652
Lewis, Jason W, corrections mgr b2, $61,033
Lewis, John A, corrections case mgr II, $40,380
Lewis, Jonathan W, corrections ofcr I, $29,652

Lewis, Justin D, prob & parole ofcr I, $30,984
Lewis, Kelly L, prob & parole ofcr II, $39,624
Lewis, Kendra L, ofc spt asst (keybrd), $23,160
Lewis, Lesia A, special educ tchr III, $38,928
Lewis, Mark A, stationary engr, $33,744
Lewis, Paul G, corrections ofcr I, $29,652
Lewis, Ray W, maint spv I, $32,628
Lewis, Roger L, corrections ofcr I, $29,652
Lewis, Samantha E, corrections ofcr I, $29,652
Lewis, Scott D, corrections ofcr I, $33,900
Lewis, Stephen M, corrections ofcr I, $29,652
Lewis, Teresa L, admin ofc spt asst, $30,984
Lewis, Terry D, corrections ofcr I, $31,668
Leyerle, David R, prob & parole ofcr II, $36,888
Liakos, Jeremy K, corrections mgr b1, $46,178
Libbert, Kent V, maint worker II, $29,004
Libbert, Shelly M, voc enter spv I, $30,420
Libbert, Taylor J, corrections ofcr I, $28,692
Libby, Michael, corrections ofcr I, $34,512
Libel, Charles W, maint spv I, $32,628
Libhart, Marcheta A, corrections ofcr I, $31,668
Libla, Justin R, corrections ofcr I, $29,652
Lietch, Michele R, ofc spt asst (keybrd), $25,824
Lietzke, Ferd C, corrections ofcr I, $31,140
Lietzke, Karla M, corrections ofcr I, $31,140
Liggett, Jim L, corrections ofcr I, $29,652
Light, Bradley L, corrections ofcr I, $29,652
Light, Joni L, corrections case mgr II, $34,944
Light, Layton, prob & parole ofcr II, $36,204
Lightfoot, Cody B, corrections ofcr I, $29,652
Lightfoot, Wendy M, corrections ofcr I, $29,652
Ligons, Larry E, prob & parole asst II, $32,628
Lilge, Karis L, corrections ofcr I, $30,276
Lillard, Nancy B, sr ofc spt asst (keybrd), $27,084
Lilley, Bradley S, corrections ofcr I, $29,652
Lilley, Ii, corrections ofcr I, $29,652
Lima, Robert E, corrections classif asst, $31,512
Limanen, Whitney L, prob & parole ofcr II, $34,944
Lin, Raymond, prob & parole ofcr II, $36,204
Lincoln, Richard B, corrections ofcr II, $31,668
Lincoln, William D, corrections ofcr I, $29,652
Lind, Bryce A, corrections ofcr I, $28,692
Lind, Gary D, prob & parole unit spv, $42,708
Lindquist, Albert C, voc enter mktng coor, $43,488
Lindsay, Christine M, prob & parole ofcr II, $36,204
Lindsay, Leanne M, corrections ofcr II, $31,668
Lindsey, Betty J, corrections case mgr II, $34,944
Lindsey, Donald J, corrections ofcr I, $28,692
Lindsey, Jeremiah A, corrections ofcr I, $29,652
Lindsey, Kevin A, corrections ofcr I, $29,652
Lineberry, Cheryl J, corrections ofcr II, $31,668
Lingua, James M, recrtn ofcr I, $31,512
Linhardt, Shannon M, corrections ofcr I, $29,652
Link, April D, corrections ofcr II, $31,668
Link, Edward L, corrections ofcr I, $29,652
Link, Gloria L, corrections case mgr II, $34,944
Link, Randy D, functional unit mgr corr, $41,940
Linley, Juanita O, corrections ofcr I, $29,652
Linne, Amy K, prob & parole ofcr II, $36,204
Linney, Sheila K, corrections case mgr I, $29,976
Lint, Bonita L, corrections ofcr I, $29,652
Lipe, Nathan A, corrections ofcr I, $29,652
Lipp, Dawn D, corrections ofcr I, $29,652
Lipp, Gary W, corrections case mgr II, $34,944
Lisenbee, Jason A, corrections ofcr I, $28,692
Litherland, Jonathan P, corrections ofcr I, $29,652
Little, Beverly, prob & parole ofcr II, $36,888
Little, Donald L, corrections ofcr I, $29,652
Little, John L, corrections ofcr I, $28,692
Little, Russell L, prob & parole unit spv, $45,156
Littleton, Kari L, prob & parole ofcr II, $36,204
Littleton, Michael D, corrections ofcr I, $29,652
Litton, Hope E, corrections case mgr II, $34,944
Litwiller, Joseph C, exec II, $38,928
Litzelman, Gerry S, corrections ofcr I, $28,692
Livesay, Earl D, corrections ofcr II, $30,576
Livingston, Bailey D, corrections ofcr I, $28,692
Lizama, Fritz R, corrections ofcr I, $30,132
Lloyd, Michelle M, ofc spt asst (keybrd), $23,160
Lober, Elizabeth E, storekeeper I, $25,824
Loch, Kayla, prob & parole ofcr I, $30,984
Lock, Brian J, corrections ofcr III, $33,744
Lockard, Jeffrey L, tractor trailer driver, $32,052

Locke, Anna M, sr ofc spt asst (keybrd), $25,824
Lockett-Hamilton, Shari C, prob & parole ofcr II, $36,204
Lockhart, Lukendra L, corrections ofcr I, $29,652
Lockhart, Richard L, corrections ofcr I, $29,652
Lockwood, Jerry R, corrections ofcr I, $31,140
Lockwood, Keith A, prob & parole asst I, $29,496
Lockwood, Kristina S, prob & parole unit spv, $44,304
Loeffelman, Jendra, acad tchr III, $37,548
Loehner, Kenneth C, recrtn ofcr I, $34,944
Loehr, Sarah D, corrections ofcr I, $29,652
Loftin, Dovie L, corrections ofcr I, $29,652
Lohmeyer, Gary A, corrections ofcr II, $31,668
Lohmeyer, Robert G, corrections ofcr I, $29,652
Lohsandt, Scott F, corrections ofcr I, $29,652
Loker, Julie A, laundry mgr, $34,944
Loker, Paul E, maint spv I, $32,628
Lollar, Calvin W, recrtn ofcr I, $29,004
Lollar, Richard W, corrections ofcr I, $29,652
Lombard, Joy D, prob & parole ofcr II, $36,204
Lomedico, Julie L, prob & parole ofcr II, $36,204
Lomosi, Tiffany L, prob & parole unit spv, $41,940
London, Joyartisha, prob & parole ofcr II, $36,204
Loner, Ronald W, corrections ofcr I, $29,652
Long, Cathy S, ofc spt asst (keybrd), $25,032
Long, Christina D, prob & parole ofcr I, $32,628
Long, Darlene A, ofc spt asst (keybrd), $23,160
Long, Devona G, prob & parole asst I, $29,496
Long, Dianne P, corrections ofcr I, $29,652
Long, Gilbert J, accounting spec I, $36,204
Long, James C, prob & parole unit spv, $41,940
Long, Joshua, corrections ofcr I, $29,652
Long, Joshua D, prob & parole ofcr II, $36,204
Long, Karen S, prob & parole ofcr II, $41,940
Long, Maggie L, corrections ofcr I, $28,692
Long, Mary A, prob & parole ofcr II, $36,204
Long, Matthew J, prob & parole ofcr II, $36,888
Long, Matthew T, corrections case mgr II, $33,744
Long, Parks A, stationary engr, $33,744
Long, Ronald L, corrections ofcr III, $35,568
Long, Sandy K, ofc spt asst (keybrd), $23,880
Long, Scott R, corrections ofcr II, $31,668
Long, Susan A, ofc spt asst (keybrd), $23,160
Long, Terry L, recrtn ofcr I, $31,512
Long, Velma M, pers ofcr I, $40,380
Long, William L, maint spv I, $32,628
Lonis, Jesse L, corrections ofcr I, $29,652
Lonis, Larry, corrections ofcr II, $35,724
Looten, Paul R, corrections ofcr I, $29,652
Loper, Le R, prob & parole asst I, $31,512
Lopez, Derek R, corrections ofcr I, $29,652
Lopez, John C, corrections ofcr I, $29,652
Lopez, Rogelio, corrections ofcr I, $29,652
Lopez, Shirley A, prob & parole ofcr II, $36,204
Lorance, Michael T, corrections ofcr I, $29,652
Lorenz, Ronald D, cook II, $25,404
Lott, Bradley K, corrections ofcr I, $28,692
Loucks, James C, corrections ofcr I, $29,652
Loucks, Samantha F, corrections ofcr I, $29,652
Loudon, Thomas C, prob & parole ofcr II, $38,232
Louiselle, David M, corrections ofcr I, $29,652
Love, Dana C, storekeeper I, $28,452
Love, Jevon, cook II, $24,264
Love, Joan A, prob & parole ofcr II, $36,204
Love, Roy, corrections ofcr I, $29,652
Loveall, Julie K, sr ofc spt asst (keybrd), $25,824
Lovingier, Crystal K, corrections ofcr III, $33,180
Lowe, James M, corrections ofcr I, $29,652
Lowe, Katie N, cook II, $24,264
Lowe, Thomas C, corrections ofcr I, $29,652
Lower, John A, corrections spv II, $43,488
Lowery, Alvin L, corrections case mgr II, $33,744
Lowman, Kwanshae R, prob & parole asst I, $29,496
Lowrance, Maria N, corrections case mgr II, $33,744
Loyche, Janine M, laundry mgr, $34,944
Lucas, Bradley, voc enter spv II, $30,420
Lucas, Connie S, cook II, $24,264
Lucas, Kenneth G, corrections ofcr I, $29,652
Lucas, Stanley G, corrections case mgr II, $38,232
Lucas, Teresa A, librarian II, $34,356
Lucas, Wanda J, voc edu spv, $46,932
Lucas, Wendie L, corrections ofcr I, $29,652
Lucia, Catherine F, fiscal & administrative mgr b1, $48,809
Luck, John D, prob & parole ofcr II, $36,204

Luck, Lyndi L, corrections ofcr I, $29,652
Luckett, Nicole M, ofc spt asst (keybrd), $23,160
Luebbers, Amy J, exec II, $36,204
Luebbers, Debra M, food serv mgr II, $34,944
Luebbert, Ronald F, corrections spv I, $41,940
Luetjen, Chad E, inst activity coor, $31,512
Luetjen, James L, edu sup, $41,940
Luetkemeyer, Jennifer L, ofc spt asst (keybrd), $23,160
Lujan, Penni A, corrections ofcr I, $29,652
Luke, Erica N, prob & parole ofcr II, $36,204
Luke, William L, prob & parole ofcr II, $39,624
Luna, Manuel L, corrections ofcr I, $29,652
Lund, Gary M, corrections ofcr I, $29,652
Lundy, Donnie L, corrections ofcr I, $29,652
Lundy, Ronnie D, corrections ofcr II, $31,668
Lundy, Tonya R, corrections ofcr I, $28,692
Lunsford, Lindell D, corrections ofcr I, $28,692
Lunsford, Lisa L, corrections ofcr I, $29,652
Lunsford, Mary J, corrections ofcr I, $31,140
Lunsford, Rodney G, serv mgr II, $38,928
Luntsford, Danny G, corrections ofcr I, $31,668
Luntsford, James E, corrections ofcr I, $29,652
Luntsford, Robert W, corrections ofcr I, $29,652
Luntsford, Tammy D, corrections case mgr II, $37,548
Luntsford, Tommie L, corrections ofcr I, $31,140
Luster, Dale W, corrections ofcr II, $31,668
Lutes, Melinda K, prob & parole ofcr II, $39,624
Lutz, Brandi T, prob & parole ofcr II, $39,624
Lutz, Edward L, corrections case mgr II, $35,568
Luvin, Derrick J, corrections ofcr II, $31,668
Lybarger, Dustin W, corrections ofcr I, $29,652
Lybarger, Joshua A, corrections ofcr I, $29,652
Lybarger, Natalie B, corrections ofcr I, $29,316
Lynch, Eric C, voc tchr III, $38,928
Lynch, Kathy A, prob & parole asst I, $29,496
Lynch, Marion M, corrections ofcr I, $29,652
Lynch, Randall L, acad tchr III, $37,548
Lynde, Kimberly A, corrections ofcr I, $28,692
Lynn, Frank J, corrections ofcr I, $29,652
Lynn, Robert H, corrections ofcr I, $33,900
Lynn, Timothy M, corrections ofcr I, $29,652
Lynn, Warren, corrections ofcr I, $29,652
Lyon, David R, electronics tech, $30,984
Lyons, Naomi R, special educ ofcr I, $29,976
Lysinger, Tyler, prob & parole ofcr I, $29,976
Maberry, Cassie, prob & parole ofcr II, $36,204
Maberry, Chad, prob & parole ofcr I, $29,976
Maberry, Edward L, corrections ofcr I, $29,652
Maberry, Robin E, corrections ofcr I, $29,652
Mabery, James F, boiler oper, $28,104
Mabry, Michelle L, prob & parole ofcr II, $34,944
Macclugage, Sana K, corrections ofcr I, $28,692
Machiran, Daniel J, prob & parole ofcr II, $40,380
Mackesty, Joshua A, corrections ofcr I, $28,692
Macklin, David E, corrections ofcr I, $29,652
Maclin, David N, cook III, $28,104
Macmurchy, Grace, prob & parole ofcr II, $36,204
Macomber, Deborah I, storekeeper I, $25,824
Macomber, Henry M, garage spv, $32,628
Madden, Corey E, corrections ofcr I, $29,316
Madden, Jesse S, corrections ofcr I, $29,652
Maddox, Elisa M, corrections ofcr I, $29,652
Madison, Tamara L, corrections ofcr I, $33,348
Madison, Thomas J Jr, fire & safety spec, $30,984
Maez, Danielle, prob & parole ofcr II, $36,204
Magee, Darrel E, corrections ofcr I, $29,652
Magers, John T, corrections ofcr I, $31,140
Maggard, Amanda N, ofc spt asst (keybrd), $23,160
Maggard, Ronald L, corrections ofcr I, $29,652
Magill, Marvin L, prob & parole ofcr II, $36,204
Magnus, Steve E, prob & parole ofcr II, $38,232
Magnuson, Kirk A, corrections ofcr I, $29,316
Maguire, Deborah L, prob & parole ofcr II, $36,204
Maguire, Robert T, corrections ofcr I, $29,652
Mahan, Dennis R, prob & parole ofcr II, $36,204
Mahaney, James P II, cook II, $24,264
Maharas, Devona A, admin ofc spt asst, $32,052
Mahoney, Emily, ofc spt asst (keybrd), $11,580
Mahurin, Robbie L, corrections training ofcr, $41,172
Maiden, Brian O, corrections ofcr I, $29,652
Maiden, Deena, ofc spt asst (keybrd), $24,264
Maier, Megan A, prob & parole ofcr II, $36,204
Main, Jamie, prob & parole ofcr I, $29,976

Main, Joy A, ofc spt asst (keybrd), $23,160
Maithya, Daniel M, prob & parole ofcr II, $38,232
Major, Darla K, pers clerk, $28,104
Majors, Ty R, corrections ofcr I, $29,652
Malady, Paul R, corrections ofcr II, $30,576
Malear, Kevin R, corrections ofcr I, $31,668
Malita, Craig S, prob & parole ofcr II, $39,624
Mallen, Keith A, corrections ofcr I, $32,784
Mallen, Kevin E, acad tchr III, $37,548
Mallett, Wesley N, corrections ofcr I, $29,652
Mallory, Patricia S, corrections ofcr I, $29,652
Mallow, David P, factory mgr I, $37,548
Malloy, Tiffanie M, corrections ofcr I, $28,692
Malone, Justin J, corrections ofcr I, $28,692
Malott, Trinity L, corrections ofcr I, $29,652
Malugen, Jeremy W, corrections ofcr I, $29,652
Malugen, Lucy L, ofc spt asst (keybrd), $23,160
Manche, Tyson D, corrections ofcr I, $29,652
Mandeville, Sharon G, corrections ofcr I, $29,652
Mandino, Nicole M, corrections ofcr I, $29,652
Manes, Linda J, cook III, $28,104
Maness, Kelly D, prob & parole ofcr II, $38,232
Manire, Nancy L, prob & parole ofcr II, $36,888
Manis, Jeffrey W, corrections ofcr I, $29,652
Manker, Clarence D, storekeeper II, $28,104
Manley, Cody M, corrections ofcr I, $29,652
Manley, Michael D, prob & parole ofcr II, $38,232
Mann, Bonnie S, corrections ofcr I, $30,132
Mann, Sara E, corrections ofcr I, $29,652
Mann, Tim M, recrtn ofcr II, $36,204
Manning, Sharon M, corrections ofcr III, $32,628
Manno, Brendan M, corrections ofcr I, $28,692
Manno, Michael J, maint spv I, $32,628
Manseau, Steven A, cook II, $26,232
Mansell, Paul R, corrections ofcr I, $29,652
Manson, William C, labor spv I, $26,652
Mapa, Eric T, prob & parole asst I, $29,496
Maple, Cheryl L, corrections ofcr I, $28,692
Marcink, William H, chaplain, $34,356
Marcum, Deena L, sr ofc spt asst (keybrd), $26,652
Mares, Nathaniel F, corrections ofcr I, $29,652
Marhanka, Joddie, corrections ofcr I, $28,692
Mark, Austin F, corrections ofcr I, $29,652
Marker, Timothy P, corrections ofcr I, $29,652
Markham, Christopher A, maint spv I, $32,628
Markley, Glenn E, corrections ofcr II, $33,348
Marks, Christopher, librarian II, $33,744
Marks, Chrystal E, corrections ofcr I, $29,652
Markway, Jeananne, designated principal asst div, $48,600
Marlay, Steven D, recrtn ofcr III, $41,940
Marler, Dustin L, corrections ofcr I, $29,652
Marler, Lana S, ofc spt asst (keybrd), $23,160
Marler, Shae M, corrections ofcr I, $29,652
Marlow, Gwenn L, librarian II, $33,744
Marmet, David W, corrections ofcr I, $29,652
Marriott, Carrie L, corrections ofcr I, $28,692
Marriott, James A, corrections ofcr II, $33,900
Marriott, Steven D, corrections case mgr II, $34,944
Marsch, Danielle M, ofc spt asst (keybrd), $22,536
Marsh, Shelby D, corrections ofcr I, $28,692
Marshall, Dennis K, corrections case mgr II, $34,944
Marshall, Heather K, corrections case mgr I, $29,976
Marshall, Karen L, prob & parole unit spv, $43,488
Marshall, Kenya L, corrections ofcr I, $28,692
Marshall, Kevin L, garage spv I, $32,628
Marshall, Michael D, maint spv I, $32,628
Marshall, Michelle D, corrections ofcr I, $29,652
Marshall, William J, prob & parole unit spv, $41,940
Martel, Douglas S, stationary engr, $36,204
Marten, Steven D, corrections ofcr I, $29,652
Martensen, Valerie F, corrections ofcr I, $29,976
Martin, Allison N, corrections ofcr I, $28,692
Martin, Billie J, storekeeper I, $25,824
Martin, Brian E, corrections ofcr I, $29,652
Martin, Bryan A, corrections ofcr II, $31,668
Martin, Chad E, tractor trailer driver, $30,420
Martin, Chelsea L, corrections ofcr I, $29,652
Martin, Christopher W, corrections ofcr I, $29,652
Martin, Clarissa M, investigator I, $29,976
Martin, Corrinn E, corrections ofcr I, $29,652
Martin, Darren C, corrections ofcr I, $28,692
Martin, David L, corrections ofcr I, $29,652
Martin, David R, corrections ofcr I, $30,132

Martin, David V, corrections ofcr I, $29,652
Martin, Denise K, ofc spt asst (keybrd), $23,160
Martin, Dennis A, corrections ofcr I, $29,652
Martin, Douglas D, corrections ofcr II, $31,668
Martin, Gary W, corrections ofcr II, $31,668
Martin, Huston J, prob & parole unit spv, $41,940
Martin, Jack L, subs abuse cnslr II, $34,944
Martin, Jacob D, corrections ofcr II, $31,668
Martin, Jersan, prob & parole ofcr I, $29,976
Martin, Joe L, corrections ofcr I, $29,652
Martin, Joseph A, corrections ofcr I, $29,652
Martin, Karen M, sr ofc spt asst (keybrd), $27,948
Martin, Kimberlee L, corrections ofcr I, $29,652
Martin, Kody W, corrections ofcr I, $29,652
Martin, Larissi Y, corrections ofcr I, $28,692
Martin, Mark E, stationary engr, $33,744
Martin, Martha M, cook II, $24,264
Martin, McKenzie L, ofc spt asst (keybrd), $23,160
Martin, Patrick M, corrections training ofcr, $41,940
Martin, Raina A, functional unit mgr corr, $38,928
Martin, Rebecca B, account clerk II, $27,084
Martin, Richard, tractor trailer driver, $29,976
Martin, Richard D, corrections case mgr II, $34,944
Martin, Robin, prob & parole asst I, $29,496
Martin, Samantha J, ofc spt asst (keybrd), $23,880
Martin, Stanley S, recrtn ofcr III, $41,940
Martin, Steven W, factory mgr II, $38,928
Martin, Terrie L, prob & parole ofcr II, $38,232
Martin, Theresa A, cook II, $24,264
Martineau, Douglas R, corrections ofcr III, $35,568
Martinez, Daniel A, corrections mgr b1, $44,037
Martinez, Joseph D, corrections ofcr I, $29,652
Martinez, Richard, corrections ofcr II, $31,668
Martinez, Richard M, corrections ofcr III, $35,568
Martinez, Tamiko N, prob & parole ofcr II, $36,204
Martino, Paul D, corrections ofcr I, $29,652
Marton, Mary L, corrections ofcr II, $33,348
Masegian, Charles, corrections ofcr I, $29,652
Masegian, Kenneth, electronics tech, $31,512
Masek, Jayne L, fiscal & administrative mgr b2, $54,377
Mason, Angela L, corrections ofcr I, $29,652
Mason, Crystal, ofc spt asst (keybrd), $22,536
Mason, David A, corrections ofcr I, $28,692
Mason, David R, prob & parole ofcr II, $37,548
Mason, Jatealia M, corrections ofcr I, $28,692
Mason, Jeffery A, corrections ofcr I, $29,652
Mason, Jeremy L, corrections ofcr I, $29,652
Mason, Kenneth G, corrections ofcr I, $29,652
Mason, Matthew D, chaplain, $34,356
Mason, Pearl M, cook II, $24,264
Mason, Rebecca R, storekeeper I, $25,824
Mason, Shelby S, corrections ofcr I, $29,652
Massenburg-Thomas, Doloress L, prob & parole ofcr II, $41,940
Massey, Laurel, prob & parole ofcr I, $29,976
Massey, Melissa D, ofc spt asst (keybrd), $23,160
Massey, Stacey L, prob & parole ofcr II, $38,232
Massey, Steven D, corrections ofcr I, $30,132
Massey, Thomas J, corrections ofcr I, $29,652
Massey, Tyler J, corrections ofcr I, $29,652
Massman, Melissa A, designated principal asst dept, $50,419
Masson, Johnathan J, corrections ofcr I, $29,652
Masson, William D, maint spv I, $33,180
Masten, Jesse B, corrections ofcr I, $33,900
Masters, Billy T, corrections ofcr I, $29,652
Masterson, Beverly A, prob & parole ofcr II, $36,204
Masuch, Daniel R, corrections ofcr I, $28,692
Matheney-Jewell, Rae D, storekeeper I, $25,824
Mathes, Angela D, prob & parole ofcr II, $36,204
Mathes, Kevin, corrections ofcr II, $32,220
Mathews, Brandon L, corrections ofcr I, $29,652
Mathias, Ronald S, prob & parole ofcr II, $38,928
Mathis, Justin A, corrections ofcr I, $29,652
Mathis, Yolanda N, account clerk II, $25,824
Mathison, Archie L, voc enter rep, $33,744
Matich, Jolene R, corrections ofcr I, $29,652
Matlock, Paul B, electronics tech, $30,984
Matlock, Rachel K, corrections ofcr I, $29,652
Matney, Robin A, account clerk II, $27,504
Matos, Jeffrey A, corrections ofcr I, $28,692
Matt, Alyson K, prob & parole ofcr I, $39,624
Mattern, Taylor M, ofc spt asst (keybrd), $23,160
Matteson, Sean P, corrections ofcr I, $29,652
Matthews, Charles W, corrections ofcr I, $29,652

Matthews, Debra A, corrections ofcr I, $29,652
Matthews, John W, corrections ofcr I, $29,652
Matthews, Marketa N, prob & parole ofcr I, $30,984
Matthews, Sarah A, ofc spt asst (clerical), $22,536
Mattingly, Chadwick M, corrections ofcr I, $29,652
Mattingly, Kolin, prob & parole ofcr II, $36,204
Mattison, Crystal A, prob & parole unit spv, $40,380
Mattison, Daniel S, prob & parole ofcr I, $30,420
Mattox, Christopher G, corrections case mgr II, $41,940
Mattox, Jami L, corrections ofcr I, $29,652
Mattox, Ryan C, corrections ofcr II, $31,668
Matzenbacher, Vanessa D, corrections ofcr I, $29,652
Mauderly, Wade F, corrections ofcr I, $31,140
Maulsby, Tracy J, investigator I, $33,744
Maune, Mark A, corrections ofcr I, $33,348
Maupin, Kathryn R, corrections ofcr I, $29,652
Maurer, Lindell T, storekeeper I, $26,652
Mausser, Cory R, corrections ofcr I, $29,652
Maxey, Jesse L, corrections ofcr I, $29,652
Maxvill, Michael K, corrections ofcr III, $33,744
Maxwell, Michael W, corrections ofcr I, $29,652
Maxwell, Nonley L, corrections ofcr I, $29,652
May, Bill W, corrections ofcr I, $30,132
May, Jesse N, corrections ofcr II, $31,668
May, Kathy L, corrections ofcr I, $32,784
May, Natalie R, storekeeper I, $25,824
May, Robert W, corrections ofcr II, $30,576
May, Susan K, entprss mgr b1, $49,255
May, Tabbatha D, corrections ofcr I, $28,692
Mayberry, Brandon S, corrections ofcr I, $29,652
Mayberry, Daniel S, corrections ofcr I, $29,652
Mayberry, Dennis L, corrections spv I, $42,708
Mayberry, Jennifer A, prob & parole unit spv, $43,488
Mayer, Elizabeth A, exec I, $32,628
Mayes, Michele L, corrections ofcr I, $29,652
Mayes, Thomas E, corrections ofcr I, $29,652
Mayfield, Eulisa R, prob & parole unit spv, $41,940
Mayfield, Latorria E, corrections ofcr I, $29,652
Mayfield, Linda F, corrections ofcr I, $29,652
Mays, Jeremy T, corrections ofcr III, $33,744
Mays, Linda M, ofc spt asst (keybrd), $24,264
Mayson, Alexander D, corrections ofcr I, $29,652
Maziarka, Kasey S, corrections case mgr I, $29,976
Mazur, Christopher B, corrections ofcr I, $29,652
Mbuya, Elicia E, prob & parole ofcr II, $36,204
McAdams, Abby M, prob & parole ofcr II, $40,380
McAdams, James E, storekeeper I, $25,824
McAfee, Lance E, corrections case mgr II, $35,568
McAfee, Michelle L, prob & parole ofcr II, $36,204
McAlister, Travis Q, prob & parole ofcr II, $38,232
McAllister, Amber D, cook II, $24,264
McAllister, Benjamin M, corrections ofcr I, $30,276
McArdle, John R, corrections ofcr I, $29,652
McBee, Kenneth C, corrections mgr b2, $49,909
McBee, Mark A, corrections ofcr I, $29,652
McBee, Rocky N, corrections ofcr I, $30,132
McBride, Brian K, corrections ofcr I, $29,652
McBride, Cynthia A, prob & parole ofcr II, $41,940
McBride, Ginger R, acad tchr III, $37,548
McBride, Jeffery J, prob & parole ofcr II, $36,204
McBride, Kristen L, sr ofc spt asst (keybrd), $25,824
McBride, Kyle R, corrections ofcr I, $29,652
McBride, Paul K, corrections case mgr II, $34,944
McBride, Victoria L, investigator II, $37,548
McCabe, Steven, corrections ofcr I, $29,652
McCaffrey, Matthew A, prob & parole ofcr II, $36,204
McCain, Harvey R, corrections ofcr I, $29,661
McCall, Drew M, corrections ofcr I, $28,692
McCall, Randy A, maint spv I, $32,628
McCallan, Tony L, corrections ofcr III, $32,628
McCallister, Michelle L, prob & parole ofcr II, $36,204
McCallum, David D, corrections ofcr I, $28,692
McCampbell, Andrew R, corrections ofcr I, $28,692
McCann, Ashley A, cook I, $22,872
McCann, Christopher C, corrections ofcr I, $29,652
McCann, Matt G, recrtn ofcr I, $29,976
McCarey, Daniel J, corrections ofcr I, $31,668
McCart, Jonnette L, librarian II, $39,624
McCarter, Caroline A, prob & parole ofcr II, $18,102
McCarthy, Angela D, corrections ofcr I, $29,652
McCarthy, Christina M, corrections mgr b1, $46,177
McCarthy, James E, corrections ofcr I, $29,652
McCarthy, Joseph M, corrections ofcr I, $29,652

McCarthy, Nancy J, special asst official & admstr, $69,610
McCarthy, Troy S, investigator II, $40,380
McCarty, Daniel R, corrections case mgr II, $34,944
McCarty, Dylan J, corrections ofcr I, $29,652
McCarty, Jonathan I, garage spv, $32,628
McCarty, Shad P, corrections ofcr I, $29,652
McCarty, Shannon W, phys plant sup III, $46,068
McCarver, Monna A, corrections spv I, $41,172
McCauley, Matthew L, corrections ofcr I, $29,652
McCauley, Shelly A, corrections ofcr I, $29,652
McCauley, Troy L, food serv mgr II, $34,944
McClain, Dawnelle L, corrections ofcr I, $31,140
McClaine, Buddy A, corrections ofcr I, $29,652
McClard, Kimberly D, sr ofc spt asst (keybrd), $26,652
McCleary, Dolly M, corrections ofcr I, $30,132
McCleery, James L, functional unit mgr corr, $46,068
McClellan, Gerald W, corrections ofcr I, $28,692
McClellan-Fox, Lacie J, investigator I, $30,984
McCloud, Mike E, corrections ofcr I, $29,652
McCloy, Jonathan I, corrections ofcr I, $29,652
McClung, Michael W, corrections ofcr I, $29,652
McClure, David J, corrections ofcr I, $29,652
McClure, Jessie J, corrections ofcr I, $34,512
McClure, Kellie A, corrections ofcr I, $29,652
McClure, Peggy L, special asst official & admstr, $70,700
McClurg, Donald L, stationary engr, $33,744
McCollum, Justin D, corrections ofcr I, $29,652
McCollum, Michelle L, corrections ofcr I, $29,652
McComb, W C, corrections ofcr I, $29,652
McConnell, Arthur J, corrections ofcr I, $28,692
McConnell, Christopher D, corrections ofcr I, $29,652
McConnell, Erin J, corrections ofcr I, $29,652
McConnell, James O, corrections ofcr I, $29,652
McConnell, John S, prob & parole unit spv, $44,304
McConnell, Lori A, ofc spt asst (steno), $27,084
McConnell, Michael D, corrections ofcr I, $31,140
McConnell, Michael J, corrections ofcr I, $29,652
McConnell, Yolanda R, prob & parole ofcr II, $36,204
McCord, Gary E, corrections training ofcr, $38,928
McCormack, Madison N, corrections ofcr I, $29,652
McCormick, Robert E, corrections ofcr I, $29,652
McCormick, Timothy C, electronics tech, $32,052
McCormick, William H, recrtn ofcr I, $31,512
McCory, Carl, corrections ofcr II, $37,056
McCourtney, Gregory, maint spv II, $34,944
McCourtney, Tracy M, corrections ofcr I, $29,652
McCoy, Dennis J, corrections ofcr I, $33,348
McCoy, Jerad S, corrections ofcr I, $28,692
McCoy, Kyle T, corrections ofcr I, $29,652
McCoy, Nicholas A, corrections ofcr I, $29,652
McCoy, Walter R, corrections ofcr I, $31,140
McCracken, Eric V, motor veh mech, $29,976
McCrady, Patricia, sr ofc spt asst (keybrd), $26,232
McCrary, Brooke R, corrections classif asst, $32,052
McCreary, Adam S, corrections classif asst, $30,420
McCrimmons, William D, prob & parole ofcr II, $36,204
McCrorey, Kevin D, corrections ofcr I, $29,652
McCulley, Leah M, ofc spt asst (keybrd), $23,160
McCulley, Valarie A, storekeeper I, $25,824
McCulloch, Troy J, recrtn ofcr I, $29,976
McCullough, Darrell F, corrections ofcr I, $28,692
McCumber, Angela M, corrections ofcr I, $28,692
McCumber, Joe E, corrections ofcr I, $29,652
McCune, Rodney R, corrections ofcr I, $29,652
McCurdy, Bonnie J, voc enter spv II, $31,512
McCurdy, Lloyd W, stationary engr, $33,744
McCush, Doyle E, corrections ofcr I, $29,652
McCutchen, Tyla R, prob & parole ofcr II, $36,204
McDaniel, Bart A, corrections ofcr I, $29,652
McDaniel, Carla K, corrections ofcr I, $29,652
McDaniel, Erica D, corrections ofcr I, $29,652
McDaniel, Jeffery L, corrections ofcr II, $31,668
McDaniel, Joanna L, corrections ofcr I, $28,692
McDaniel, Robert W, inst activity coor, $30,420
McDaniels, Jim B, corrections case mgr II, $39,624
McDaniels, Joy Y, storekeeper I, $28,104
McDonald, Alden F, maint spv I, $37,548
McDonald, Diana E, corrections ofcr II, $31,668
McDonald, Julia L, corrections case mgr II, $37,548
McDonald, Kevin, subs abuse cnslr II, $34,944
McDonald, Larry W, corrections classif asst, $29,976
McDonald, Orville L, corrections ofcr I, $29,652
McDonald, Sean E, prob & parole ofcr II, $36,888

McDonald, Thomas W, prob & parole ofcr II, $36,204
McDonnal, Jamie L, corrections ofcr I, $31,668
McDonnell, Christopher R, phys plant sup III, $47,892
McDowell, Johnna M, corrections spv I, $37,548
McDowell, Mary B, corrections ofcr I, $29,652
McDowell, Matthew D, account clerk II, $25,824
McDowell, Robert M, corrections ofcr I, $33,348
McElroy, Jesse J, prob & parole ofcr II, $36,204
McElroy, Marilyn G, account clerk II, $27,084
McElroy, Patric C, corrections ofcr I, $28,692
McElwee, Joshua, corrections ofcr I, $29,652
McEntire, Ronald D, corrections ofcr I, $33,348
McEuen, Cynthia M, sr ofc spt asst (keybrd), $25,824
McFall, Jesse D, corrections ofcr II, $31,668
McFall, John W, corrections ofcr I, $29,652
McFann, Jerry S, corrections ofcr I, $28,692
McFarland, Jeffrey J, maint spv I, $32,628
McFarland, Timothy J, corrections case mgr II, $34,944
McFarland, William, prob & parole ofcr I, $30,420
McFerrin, Derek, prob & parole ofcr II, $36,204
McFerron, Samuel P, corrections spv I, $38,232
McGary, David L, corrections ofcr I, $29,652
McGaughey, Margaret A, account clerk II, $29,412
McGee, Gary D, investigator I, $37,548
McGee, Larry L, corrections ofcr I, $29,652
McGee, Michael L, corrections ofcr III, $38,232
McGee, Stephen R, corrections ofcr I, $29,652
McGhee, Amanda J, prob & parole asst I, $29,496
McGhee, Cynthia D, prob & parole ofcr II, $39,624
McGhee, Jerry D, recrtn ofcr I, $31,512
McGill, Jill L, ofc spt asst (keybrd), $23,160
McGill, Michael S, investigator I, $30,420
McGinley, Kevin E, functional unit mgr corr, $41,940
McGinley, Mary E, prob & parole ofcr II, $36,204
McGinnis, Christine L, prob & parole ofcr II, $39,624
McGinnis, Julie A, prob & parole ofcr II, $41,172
McGinnis, Tildon J, corrections ofcr I, $29,652
McGlothlin, Jessica M, corrections ofcr I, $29,652
McGowan, Amie M, corrections case mgr I, $30,984
McGowan, Evelyn D, inst activity coor, $35,568
McGowan, Shelby J, corrections ofcr I, $29,652
McGowan, Wayne A, corrections ofcr I, $29,652
McGowin, Sheldon F, corrections ofcr I, $29,652
McGuire, Alexis M, ofc spt asst (keybrd), $23,160
McGuire, Corey T, corrections ofcr I, $29,652
McGuire, Diana M, laundry mgr, $34,944
McGuire, Justin M, prob & parole asst II, $30,420
McGuire, Kathleen V, prob & parole ofcr II, $39,624
McGuire, Lee C, ofc spt asst (keybrd), $23,160
McGuire, Michael L, corrections ofcr I, $29,652
McHatton, Sandra L, edu asst II, $24,804
McIntire, James C, corrections ofcr II, $31,668
McIntire, Michele R, prob & parole ofcr II, $36,204
McIntosh, Craig E, corrections ofcr I, $29,652
McKay, Brian C, prob & parole ofcr II, $38,232
McKay, Kevin C, corrections ofcr III, $33,744
McKee, Christina L, prob & parole ofcr II, $36,204
McKee, James E, corrections ofcr I, $29,652
McKee, James P, corrections ofcr I, $29,652
McKee, James S, corrections ofcr I, $29,652
McKee, Jerry R, corrections ofcr I, $29,652
McKee, Kara I, account clerk II, $25,824
McKee, Laura S, storekeeper I, $25,824
McKee, Lora L, corrections ofcr II, $31,668
McKee, Robert E, acad tchr III, $37,548
McKee, Travis A, corrections ofcr I, $29,652
McKenna, Matthew T, corrections ofcr I, $29,652
McKenzie, Brian H, corrections ofcr I, $29,652
McKenzie, Jason D, food serv mgr II, $34,944
McKenzie, Saralyn J, corrections spv I, $41,172
McKernan, Phillip C, prob & parole ofcr II, $40,380
McKiddy, Steven D, corrections ofcr I, $29,652
McKiddy, Vicki L, corrections ofcr I, $29,652
McKinney, Allen L, corrections ofcr I, $29,652
McKinney, Charlotte S, corrections ofcr III, $35,568
McKinney, Dennis L, corrections ofcr I, $33,348
McKinney, Edward L, corrections ofcr I, $31,140
McKinney, Joshua, corrections ofcr I, $28,692
McKinney, Joshua D, recrtn ofcr I, $29,652
McKinney, Molly E, ofc spt asst (keybrd), $23,160
McKinney, Steffan A, corrections ofcr I, $28,692
McKinney, Thomas P, corrections ofcr I, $30,276
McKinnies, Katrena, ofc spt asst (keybrd), $23,160

McKinnon, Mary J, corrections ofcr I, $29,652
McKinzie, Kelly S, functional unit mgr corr, $40,380
McKlintic, Kimberly J, corrections mgr b1, $50,045
McLain, Keith L, corrections ofcr I, $29,652
McLaughlin, Terrie L, ofc spt asst (keybrd), $24,264
McLellan, Edward J, corrections ofcr I, $29,652
McLeroy, Geary K, corrections ofcr III, $33,744
McMahan, Kathryn L, corrections ofcr I, $28,692
McMahan, Kathy R, corrections ofcr I, $29,652
McMahan, Pamela, ofc spt asst (keybrd), $23,160
McMahan, Robert F, maint spv I, $32,628
McMahan, Robert T, corrections ofcr II, $31,668
McMahon, Casey R, corrections ofcr II, $31,668
McMahon, Lloyd J, corrections spv I, $36,204
McMasters, Terry L, corrections ofcr II, $31,668
McMenamy, Jennifer, ofc spt asst (keybrd), $11,580
McMenemy, Randi L, prob & parole unit spv, $43,488
McMillen, Cheryl, prob & parole ofcr II, $36,888
McMillen, Elizabeth M, corrections ofcr I, $29,652
McMillen, Richard G, locksmith, $29,976
McMiller, Tonya D, prob & parole unit spv, $41,940
McMorris, Andrew, prob & parole asst I, $28,536
McMullen, Patrick B, corrections ofcr I, $29,652
McMullin, Heather L, ofc spt asst (keybrd), $23,160
McMunn, Garrett L, corrections ofcr I, $28,692
McMurray, Charles G, corrections ofcr I, $29,652
McNeal, Russell A, corrections ofcr II, $35,724
McNease, John C, prob & parole asst I, $29,496
McNeely, Terry L, corrections ofcr I, $33,348
McNeil, Stephanie R, prob & parole ofcr II, $36,204
McNew, Carol A, acad tchr III, $37,548
McNew, Danny J, corrections ofcr I, $29,652
McNulty, Brittany N, corrections ofcr I, $29,652
McNutt, Josh L, corrections training ofcr, $41,940
McPherson, Kelly A, prob & parole unit spv, $42,708
McPhillips, Keli, prob & parole ofcr II, $36,204
McQueen, Shane K, corrections ofcr I, $29,652
McQuinn, Cili A, corrections ofcr I, $28,692
McRoy, Ronald D, prob & parole ofcr II, $41,940
McSorley, Molly R, prob & parole ofcr II, $36,204
McSpadden, Branden C, corrections ofcr I, $29,652
McSpadden, Dean A, corrections ofcr I, $29,652
McSwain, C S, prob & parole ofcr II, $40,380
McSwain, Ellis, board chair, $88,750
McVey, Jimmie W, prob & parole asst II, $35,568
McWhorter, Rob D, phys plant sup I, $36,204
Mead, Letha V, corrections ofcr I, $31,140
Mead, Mary L, prob & parole ofcr II, $39,624
Meade, Gene P, corrections ofcr I, $31,140
Meade, Patricia E, prob & parole ofcr II, $39,624
Meador, Bobbie, prob & parole ofcr II, $36,204
Meador, Bryan W, corrections ofcr II, $31,668
Meador, Dennis W, corrections ofcr I, $29,652
Meadors, Bruce F, corrections ofcr I, $28,692
Meadows, James A, prob & parole ofcr II, $36,204
Meadows, John P, maint spv I, $31,512
Mealy, David R, stationary engr, $33,744
Mecca, Daniel L, corrections ofcr I, $29,652
Mecey, Henry C, voc enter spv II, $29,976
Mecey, Troy W, stationary engr, $33,744
Medina, Emilio, prob & parole asst I, $28,536
Medina, Michael B, corrections ofcr I, $29,652
Medley, Jasmine, prob & parole ofcr II, $34,944
Medley, Terry D, corrections ofcr I, $28,692
Medlin, Joshua L, corrections ofcr I, $29,652
Medlock, Tracey L, ofc spt asst (keybrd), $23,160
Medrow, Steven A, training tech III, $46,068
Medsker, Kimberly A, acad tchr III, $37,548
Meehan, Peggy, prob & parole ofcr II, $38,232
Meek, Janet S, corrections ofcr I, $28,692
Meek, Mary K, ofc spt asst (keybrd), $23,160
Meek, Michael L, voc tchr II, $34,944
Meek, Steven L, locksmith, $33,180
Meers, Barbara J, corrections recs ofcr I, $28,104
Mefford, Sheila V, prob & parole ofcr II, $36,204
Megas-Loucks, Mindy M, corrections ofcr I, $29,652
Meier, Christopher W, corrections ofcr I, $29,652
Meiller, Rachael L, corrections ofcr I, $29,652
Meisel, Marcus, corrections ofcr I, $29,652
Melion, Michael J, subs abuse cnslr III, $37,548
Mell, Paul H, subs abuse cnslr I, $30,984
Melte, Dana A, pers clerk, $31,512
Melte, Thomas A, corrections ofcr III, $34,356

Melton, Richard A, corrections ofcr I, $29,652
Melzer, John, corrections classif asst, $31,512
Memhardt, Mark R, corrections ofcr I, $29,652
Menaugh, Barin L, maint spv I, $32,628
Mendell, Barry D, corrections ofcr I, $29,652
Mendenhall, Melody M, corrections ofcr I, $30,132
Mendenhall, Michael, prob & parole asst I, $29,496
Mendenhall, Michael J, corrections ofcr II, $32,220
Mendenhall, Robert D, corrections ofcr I, $31,140
Meng, Allen L, corrections ofcr I, $28,692
Meng, Makayla A, corrections ofcr I, $28,692
Menke, Joshua E, corrections ofcr I, $28,692
Mensah, Eric W, corrections ofcr I, $29,652
Menteer, Richard K, corrections spv I, $36,204
Menz, Jennifer L, prob & parole ofcr I, $36,888
Mercer, Cynthianne G, prob & parole ofcr II, $36,204
Mercer, John T, corrections ofcr II, $30,576
Merideth, Brandi A, functional unit mgr corr, $38,928
Merrick, Melissa M, corrections ofcr I, $29,652
Merriett, Dustin W, corrections ofcr I, $29,652
Merriett, Sarah M, prob & parole ofcr II, $36,204
Merrill, Heather A, prob & parole ofcr I, $36,888
Merrill, Leon N, corrections ofcr II, $35,100
Merrill, Matthew R, prob & parole unit spv, $41,940
Merriman, Sie L, corrections ofcr I, $29,652
Merritt, George L, corrections ofcr I, $29,652
Merritt, Stephen J, cook III, $28,104
Merritt, Walter V, prob & parole asst I, $29,496
Mertens, Jennifer B, prob & parole ofcr II, $39,624
Merz, Kathleen M, prob & parole ofcr II, $36,204
Meservey, Mari, corrections ofcr I, $29,652
Mesger, Christopher A, corrections ofcr I, $29,652
Mesmer, Angela M, corrections mgr b3, $66,438
Messer, Shawn L, asst prog mgr, $14.71/hr
Messick, Brian, corrections ofcr I, $28,692
Messner, Diana S, corrections ofcr I, $29,652
Metcalf, Dixie E, corrections ofcr I, $29,652
Metcalf, Mark E, corrections ofcr I, $29,652
Metcalfe, Mavick D, corrections ofcr I, $29,652
Metivier, James, corrections ofcr I, $29,652
Meyer, Aaron D, corrections ofcr I, $28,692
Meyer, Anthony L, prob & parole ofcr II, $36,888
Meyer, Ashley M, account clerk II, $25,824
Meyer, Carl L, corrections ofcr I, $29,652
Meyer, Carol J, sr ofc spt asst (keybrd), $25,824
Meyer, David L, corrections mgr b1, $46,178
Meyer, David W, corrections ofcr I, $31,140
Meyer, Emerson S, corrections ofcr I, $29,652
Meyer, Jason H, corrections ofcr I, $29,652
Meyer, Karen A, prob & parole ofcr II, $19,116
Meyer, Margaret L, corrections ofcr I, $29,652
Meyer, Martin D, corrections ofcr II, $34,512
Meyer, Marty L, prob & parole ofcr II, $34,944
Meyer, Melanie, ofc spt asst (keybrd), $22,536
Meyer, Paul R, corrections ofcr I, $29,652
Meyer, William R, corrections ofcr I, $29,652
Meyers, David E, corrections ofcr I, $30,132
Meyers, Jeffrey C, corrections ofcr II, $30,576
Meyers, John S, corrections ofcr I, $29,652
Meyers, Sarah L, corrections ofcr I, $29,652
Meyers, Sharron I, corrections ofcr I, $29,652
Meyers, Terry L, prob & parole ofcr II, $40,380
Meyners, Nathanael A, corrections ofcr I, $29,652
Meza, Santiago R, corrections ofcr I, $29,652
Mezo, Christina D, corrections ofcr II, $30,576
Miceli, Gregory, prob & parole ofcr II, $36,204
Michael, David J, labor spv, $26,652
Michaud, Michael T, corrections ofcr II, $31,668
Michels, Rebecca, prob & parole ofcr II, $36,204
Michenfelder, Stephanie M, corrections ofcr II, $31,668
Mick, Daniel J, corrections ofcr I, $29,652
Mickens, Carleton C, maint spv I, $32,628
Mickler, Steven L, corrections ofcr I, $31,140
Middaugh, Natasha K, prob & parole ofcr II, $36,204
Middaugh, Traca J, storekeeper II, $28,104
Middendorf, Jon P, corrections ofcr I, $28,692
Middleton, Stanley R, corrections ofcr II, $33,348
Midgyett, Amy R, corrections ofcr I, $29,652
Midgyett, Tyrone G, corrections ofcr I, $29,652
Mika, Melissa M, prob & parole ofcr II, $36,204
Milam, William A, corrections ofcr I, $29,652
Milam, William A, functional unit mgr corr, $37,548
Milburn, Bruce E, corrections ofcr I, $29,652

Milburn, Howard D, corrections case mgr II, $36,204
Miles, Ethan J, corrections ofcr I, $28,692
Militzer, Richard T, corrections ofcr I, $28,692
Miller, Amanda J, corrections ofcr I, $29,652
Miller, Amy L, sr ofc spt asst (keybrd), $25,824
Miller, Amy M, corrections ofcr II, $31,668
Miller, Angela M, sr ofc spt asst (keybrd), $25,824
Miller, Brandon L, corrections ofcr I, $28,692
Miller, Brian, corrections ofcr I, $31,668
Miller, Brian R, corrections ofcr I, $28,692
Miller, Calvin C, stationary engr, $33,744
Miller, Carl B, corrections case mgr II, $36,888
Miller, Cassey L, inst activity coor, $31,512
Miller, Christopher A, corrections ofcr I, $29,652
Miller, Christopher L, corrections ofcr I, $29,652
Miller, Claudine C, corrections ofcr II, $33,348
Miller, Cortney N, corrections ofcr I, $29,652
Miller, David A, corrections ofcr II, $31,668
Miller, David W, corrections ofcr I, $29,652
Miller, Deborah J, corrections mgr b1, $48,783
Miller, Donald R, corrections ofcr I, $29,652
Miller, Easton L, corrections ofcr I, $28,692
Miller, Elizabeth A, ofc spt asst (keybrd), $23,160
Miller, Franklin G, voc enter spv I, $28,104
Miller, Jack S, corrections ofcr II, $33,348
Miller, Jacob J, correctional worker, $26,400
Miller, James O, corrections ofcr I, $29,652
Miller, Janet R, ofc spt asst (clerical), $21,864
Miller, Jemima J, cook III, $28,104
Miller, Jennifer L, corrections ofcr I, $28,692
Miller, Jolene E, prob & parole ofcr II, $36,888
Miller, Jonathan D, corrections ofcr I, $29,652
Miller, Jonathan M, prob & parole asst II, $32,052
Miller, Joseph L, corrections ofcr I, $29,652
Miller, Julie, ofc spt asst (keybrd), $23,160
Miller, Justin M, corrections ofcr I, $29,652
Miller, Kerby R, recrtn ofcr I, $31,512
Miller, Leland K, phys plant sup III, $47,892
Miller, Leon C, chaplain, $34,356
Miller, Lisa R, prob & parole ofcr II, $36,204
Miller, Lloyd L, prob & parole ofcr II, $40,380
Miller, Lyle G, storekeeper II, $32,052
Miller, Lynda M, corrections ofcr I, $29,652
Miller, Mark L, corrections ofcr I, $31,140
Miller, Mark M, recrtn ofcr II, $32,628
Miller, Marlene, sr ofc spt asst (keybrd), $25,824
Miller, Melba J, librarian II, $33,744
Miller, Meryl F, corrections ofcr II, $31,668
Miller, Michael J, corrections case mgr II, $38,232
Miller, Myeshia E, corrections ofcr I, $28,692
Miller, Nicholas A, investigator III, $38,928
Miller, Nicole D, corrections ofcr I, $28,692
Miller, Priscilla A, prob & parole ofcr II, $40,380
Miller, Richard E, corrections ofcr I, $30,132
Miller, Robert E, corrections ofcr I, $29,652
Miller, Robert W, electronics tech, $30,984
Miller, Roger P, corrections ofcr I, $29,652
Miller, Roxann L, cook III, $28,104
Miller, Rue A, prob & parole ofcr II, $39,624
Miller, Ryan D, corrections ofcr I, $29,652
Miller, Ryan M, corrections ofcr I, $28,692
Miller, Sara C, prob & parole ofcr II, $40,380
Miller, Sara K, corrections ofcr I, $29,652
Miller, Sarah, prob & parole asst I, $28,536
Miller, Scott C, corrections ofcr I, $29,652
Miller, Tamara D, corrections ofcr I, $28,692
Miller, Trieste R, prob & parole asst I, $29,496
Miller, William L, corrections ofcr I, $29,652
Millett, Esarae, maint worker II, $29,004
Millikin, Brandon K, prob & parole asst I, $29,496
Million, Tanner R, corrections ofcr I, $28,692
Mills, Chelsea D, corrections ofcr I, $29,652
Mills, Darrin L, corrections ofcr I, $29,652
Mills, Eric A, corrections ofcr I, $28,692
Mills, Ethan M, corrections ofcr I, $28,692
Mills, John C, corrections ofcr I, $29,652
Mills, Joseph H, corrections ofcr I, $29,652
Mills, Kimberly J, prob & parole ofcr II, $39,624
Mills, Mark R, corrections ofcr I, $29,652
Mills, Robert E, corrections ofcr I, $29,652
Milne, Janet L, corrections ofcr I, $31,140
Milner, Norman B, corrections ofcr I, $29,652
Milton, Frank L, corrections ofcr III, $36,204

Minchue, Samuel, corrections spv I, $36,204
Minich, Jerry L, corrections ofcr I, $29,652
Minor, Dean M, corrections mgr b3, $66,438
Minor, Dillon D, corrections ofcr I, $28,692
Minor, Michael E, corrections ofcr I, $31,140
Minor, William E, corrections ofcr I, $31,140
Minson, Mary A, cook II, $24,264
Mintidis, Kimberly A, prob & parole ofcr II, $36,204
Mirgain, Alicia A, prob & parole ofcr II, $36,204
Miro, Matthew J, corrections ofcr I, $28,692
Misbauer, Timothy M, corrections ofcr I, $28,692
Mishler, Krystal D, corrections ofcr I, $29,652
Missey, Diane L, voc enter spv II, $29,976
Mistler, Denver R, maint spv I, $32,628
Mitchell, Charles V, corrections ofcr II, $31,668
Mitchell, Eric L, prob & parole ofcr II, $36,204
Mitchell, James W, corrections ofcr II, $31,668
Mitchell, Megan E, prob & parole ofcr II, $36,204
Mitchell, Ronald K, corrections case mgr III, $37,548
Mitchell, Timothy L, corrections ofcr I, $29,652
Mitchell, Valerie D, corrections ofcr I, $29,652
Mitchell, Yavonna G, admin ofc spt asst, $28,104
Mitchem, Robert C, corrections ofcr I, $29,652
Mitchener, Derek L, ofc spt asst (keybrd), $23,160
Mittag, David A, voc tchr II, $34,944
Moad, Aaron D, corrections ofcr I, $29,652
Moak, Randall L, corrections ofcr I, $29,652
Mobley, Karen A, cook II, $26,232
Mobley, Kimberly J, corrections training ofcr, $39,624
Mobley, Randall F, functional unit mgr corr, $43,488
Mobley, Reshonda R, inst activity coor, $31,512
Mobley, Robert D, corrections ofcr I, $29,652
Mobley, Ronald L, training tech II, $44,304
Moden, Jennifer, prob & parole ofcr II, $36,204
Moe, Lindsay A, prob & parole ofcr II, $36,204
Moeckel, Kathryn A, prob & parole ofcr II, $36,204
Moeller, Adrienne, acad tchr III, $37,548
Moffet, Michael R, corrections ofcr I, $28,692
Moise, Roy W, corrections ofcr I, $31,140
Mokwah, Joseph A, corrections ofcr I, $29,652
Moles, Joshua L, corrections ofcr II, $30,576
Moles, Lee E, corrections ofcr I, $31,138
Monarch, Gregory S, corrections ofcr I, $29,652
Moncrief, Chance W, corrections ofcr I, $28,692
Moncrief, Larry D, corrections ofcr I, $31,140
Money, Jonathan T, corrections ofcr II, $31,668
Monnig, Bert C, voc enter spv II, $29,976
Monroe, Diane L, corrections ofcr I, $29,652
Monroe, Wardell, cook III, $29,976
Montague, Dylan S, corrections ofcr I, $29,652
Montavy, Danyail A, corrections ofcr I, $29,652
Montavy, Douglas W, corrections ofcr II, $32,784
Monteer, Tracy C, acad tchr III, $37,548
Montemayor, Jesse P, corrections ofcr I, $31,140
Montemayor, Latisha L, corrections classif asst, $33,744
Montgomery, David E, corrections ofcr II, $31,668
Montgomery, Diane M, corrections case mgr II, $36,204
Montgomery, Douglas W, functional unit mgr corr, $41,940
Montgomery, Jennifer A, prob & parole ofcr II, $36,204
Montgomery, Lora B, corrections case mgr II, $38,928
Montgomery, Marion M, corrections ofcr III, $38,928
Montgomery, Mark B, functional unit mgr corr, $38,928
Montgomery, Martin H, voc edu spv, $41,940
Montgomery, Sharron K, cook III, $28,104
Montgomery, Teresa A, corrections ofcr I, $29,652
Moody, Catherine J, corrections ofcr I, $31,140
Moody, Charles E, phys plant sup II, $42,708
Moody-Edmond, Vashon L, sr ofc spt asst (keybrd), $29,412
Moody-Mahone, Valarie N, prob & parole ofcr II, $36,204
Moon, Billy J, corrections ofcr I, $29,652
Mooney, Steven A, corrections training ofcr, $37,548
Moore, Adela V, corrections ofcr I, $29,652
Moore, Amanda M, prob & parole ofcr II, $36,204
Moore, Amanda N, prob & parole ofcr II, $36,204
Moore, Ammy M, corrections ofcr I, $29,652
Moore, Anna M, ofc spt asst (keybrd), $11,580
Moore, Billie J, corrections ofcr I, $29,652
Moore, Brandi L, corrections case mgr II, $34,944
Moore, Brenda D, prob & parole ofcr II, $36,204
Moore, Brian A, corrections ofcr I, $29,652
Moore, Chandra D, ofc spt asst (keybrd), $23,160
Moore, Charles R, electronics tech, $32,052
Moore, Christina M, corrections ofcr I, $29,652

Moore, Clinton W, corrections ofcr I, $31,140
Moore, Curtis M, corrections ofcr I, $30,132
Moore, David C, corrections ofcr I, $28,692
Moore, Debra J, med technologist II, $34,944
Moore, Debra S, corrections case mgr II, $36,204
Moore, Douglas R, recrtn ofcr II, $33,180
Moore, Dustin A, electronics tech, $30,984
Moore, Elizabeth A, ofc spt asst (keybrd), $23,160
Moore, Erika L, prob & parole ofcr II, $36,204
Moore, Glendon P, corrections ofcr II, $30,576
Moore, Heather N, prob & parole ofcr II, $36,204
Moore, Henrietta, corrections ofcr I, $29,661
Moore, Jared D, corrections ofcr I, $30,276
Moore, Jennifer S, prob & parole ofcr II, $36,888
Moore, Joey D, prob & parole ofcr II, $38,232
Moore, Kalipulako N, corrections ofcr I, $29,652
Moore, Kathy L, corrections case mgr II, $38,928
Moore, Kimi J, prob & parole ofcr II, $40,380
Moore, Lindell L, corrections ofcr I, $33,348
Moore, Loraine K, corrections ofcr I, $31,668
Moore, Mark D, corrections ofcr III, $35,568
Moore, Marquita, prob & parole ofcr I, $36,204
Moore, Michael W, corrections ofcr I, $29,652
Moore, Paul T, corrections ofcr I, $29,652
Moore, Richard A, corrections ofcr I, $29,652
Moore, Roger L, corrections ofcr II, $31,668
Moore, Samantha K, corrections ofcr I, $28,692
Moore, Sarah E, ofc spt asst (clerical), $22,536
Moore, Shelley R, special asst prof, $63,986
Moore, Skyler L, corrections ofcr I, $29,652
Moore, Stephanie N, prob & parole ofcr I, $30,984
Moore, Terri L, storekeeper I, $25,824
Moore, Tina M, corrections ofcr I, $31,140
Moore, Todd A, corrections case mgr II, $34,944
Moore, Virginia F, prob & parole ofcr II, $41,172
Moots, William L, corrections ofcr I, $29,652
Morales, Oscar D, corrections ofcr I, $28,692
Morales, Raphael, prob & parole ofcr I, $30,984
Moran, Lisa M, cook II, $24,264
Morard, Donald J, corrections ofcr I, $29,652
Moravec, Timothy J, corrections ofcr I, $29,652
Morelan, Jeremy R, corrections ofcr I, $29,652
Moreland, Julia M, corrections ofcr I, $29,652
Moreland, Shawn M, corrections ofcr I, $29,652
Morgan, Charles A, corrections ofcr I, $29,652
Morgan, Connie F, ofc spt asst (keybrd), $24,264
Morgan, Connie F, admin ofc spt asst, $28,536
Morgan, Darin L, corrections mgr b2, $52,091
Morgan, Georgianne M, acad tchr III, $37,548
Morgan, James A, corrections ofcr I, $29,652
Morgan, Jesse A, corrections spv I, $37,548
Morgan, Kristin N, prob & parole ofcr II, $36,204
Morgan, Roslyn M, prob & parole ofcr II, $36,204
Morgan, Roy B, corrections ofcr I, $29,652
Morgan, Stacey L, corrections ofcr I, $31,140
Morgan, Troy B, corrections ofcr I, $29,652
Morgan, Tye D, corrections ofcr I, $29,652
Morgan, William, functional unit mgr corr, $40,380
Morgan, Wilma M, sr ofc spt asst (clerical), $27,504
Morgans, Barbara K, prob & parole ofcr II, $36,204
Moritz, Lacey L, corrections ofcr I, $29,652
Moritz, Steven R, corrections ofcr II, $37,056
Morlang, Shari R, corrections mgr b1, $50,041
Morris, Andrew A, prob & parole ofcr II, $36,204
Morris, Brent D, corrections mgr b2, $61,852
Morris, Brian S, corrections ofcr I, $29,652
Morris, Charles E, corrections ofcr II, $31,668
Morris, David F, corrections ofcr I, $31,140
Morris, Donna, corrections ofcr I, $29,652
Morris, Eddie P, corrections ofcr I, $29,652
Morris, John A, corrections ofcr II, $31,668
Morris, Julie A, cook II, $24,264
Morris, Justin M, corrections ofcr I, $29,652
Morris, Keith A, corrections ofcr I, $29,652
Morris, Leslie E, corrections ofcr I, $29,652
Morris, Michael J, corrections ofcr I, $29,652
Morris, Nicholas W, maint worker I, $26,652
Morris, Pamela S, prob & parole ofcr II, $36,204
Morris, Richard L, corrections ofcr I, $29,652
Morris, Rickie D, corrections ofcr I, $29,652
Morris, Robert L, corrections ofcr I, $29,652
Morris, Robert P, corrections ofcr I, $30,132
Morris, Sarah D, ofc spt asst (keybrd), $23,160

Morris, Sharita, prob & parole asst I, $29,496
Morris, Teresa J, sr ofc spt asst (clerical), $25,824
Morris, William F, corrections ofcr I, $29,652
Morrison, Caleb A, corrections ofcr I, $28,692
Morrison, Christopher L, prob & parole ofcr II, $41,940
Morrison, Megan N, corrections case mgr II, $34,944
Morrison, Michael, prob & parole ofcr II, $34,944
Morrison, Michelle J, acad tchr III, $37,548
Morrison, Sarah C, prob & parole asst I, $29,496
Morriss, Jane D, corrections ofcr I, $31,140
Morriss, Kelly R, corrections mgr b2, $56,218
Morriss, Mandie M, facilities opps mgr b1, $60,000
Morrow, Janice M, special educ tchr III, $41,172
Morrow, John W, corrections ofcr I, $29,652
Morrow, Scott M, corrections ofcr I, $28,692
Morse, Alan B, corrections ofcr I, $32,784
Morse, Richard S, corrections ofcr III, $34,356
Morton, Catina T, corrections ofcr I, $29,652
Morton, James E, corrections ofcr I, $29,652
Morton, Kirsten D, sr ofc spt asst (keybrd), $25,824
Morton, Vaughn R, corrections ofcr I, $29,652
Morts, Ryan, prob & parole ofcr I, $36,888
Moser, Annette, prob & parole ofcr II, $36,204
Moser, Jackie L, corrections ofcr I, $29,652
Moses, Daniel, corrections ofcr I, $29,652
Moses, Daniel J, corrections ofcr I, $29,652
Mosier, Elijah L, corrections ofcr II, $30,576
Mosley, John R, prob & parole unit spv, $41,940
Moss, Brandon M, corrections ofcr I, $29,652
Moss, Chad A, maint worker II, $29,004
Moss, David J, human rel ofcr I, $38,928
Moss, David T, corrections ofcr I, $29,652
Moss, Gary W, corrections ofcr I, $30,132
Moss, Justin B, corrections ofcr I, $28,692
Moss, Linda I, laundry mgr, $34,944
Moss, Lisa L, corrections ofcr I, $31,140
Moss, Loretta E, corrections case mgr II, $38,928
Moss, Ryan D, corrections ofcr II, $31,668
Mosser, Gregg A, corrections ofcr I, $29,652
Motel, John E, corrections spv I, $42,708
Motley, Deandre J, corrections ofcr I, $28,692
Motley, Dustin W, corrections ofcr I, $29,652
Moudy, Ann E, corrections ofcr I, $29,652
Moulder, Michelle L, sr ofc spt asst (keybrd), $25,824
Mouser, Justin K, corrections ofcr I, $29,652
Mowen, Christina M, corrections ofcr I, $30,276
Mowen, Keith E, corrections ofcr I, $29,652
Mowrey, Nolan M, corrections ofcr I, $28,692
Mowry, John D, corrections ofcr I, $29,652
Moxley, Jay J, corrections ofcr I, $29,652
Moyer, Haylie A, corrections ofcr I, $29,652
Moyer, Joshua J, prob & parole ofcr II, $36,204
Moyers, Ryan S, corrections ofcr I, $29,652
Moynahan, Mark T, corrections ofcr I, $29,652
Mozee, Aaron M, corrections ofcr II, $31,668
Mudd, Helen D, corrections case mgr II, $36,204
Muehlman, Steven D, electronics tech, $30,984
Mueller, John A, prob & parole asst II, $31,512
Mueller, Joshua A, cook II, $24,264
Mueller, Katherine A, prob & parole ofcr II, $40,380
Mueller, Keith A, corrections ofcr II, $35,100
Mueller, Laura A, prob & parole ofcr II, $36,204
Mueller, Margaret P, cook III, $28,104
Mueller, Nicole L, corrections ofcr I, $29,652
Mueller, Ryan D, subs abuse cnslr II, $34,944
Mueller, Steven D, parole hearing analyst, $54,288
Mueller, Terry E, corrections ofcr I, $29,652
Muenks, Rhonda M, prob & parole ofcr II, $40,380
Muessig, John J, stationary engr, $33,744
Muessig, Stacy K, ofc spt asst (keybrd), $22,536
Muff, Shane J, corrections ofcr II, $35,100
Muff, Tracy M, corrections ofcr I, $29,652
Muhammad, Antonio, prob & parole ofcr II, $36,204
Muir, Nicholas E, corrections ofcr I, $29,652
Mulford, Daniel W, corrections ofcr I, $29,652
Mull, Sidney A, corrections ofcr II, $33,348
Mullen, Christopher M, corrections ofcr I, $29,652
Mullen, Randy D, corrections ofcr I, $31,140
Mullen, Richard J, corrections case mgr II, $34,944
Mullican, Timothy P, corrections ofcr I, $29,652
Mullinax, Karen D, supply mgr II, $34,944
Mullinax, Russell D, corrections case mgr II, $38,232
Mullins, Keith, prob & parole ofcr II, $38,232

Mullins, Randy E, recrtn ofcr I, $32,052
Mullock, Michael D, corrections case mgr II, $33,744
Mundell, Jessica D, corrections case mgr I, $29,976
Mundwiller, Erica T, prob & parole ofcr II, $36,204
Mundwiller, Joseph M, corrections case mgr II, $34,944
Munger, David E, corrections ofcr I, $29,652
Munson, Brandine M, prob & parole ofcr II, $40,380
Munson, Terry L, stationary engr, $33,744
Munson, William C, corrections ofcr I, $29,652
Munsterman, Kelsie J, corrections ofcr I, $29,652
Muntz, Daniel W, corrections ofcr I, $29,652
Muntz, Frank A, corrections ofcr I, $29,652
Murdock, Gary W, prob & parole asst I, $29,496
Murdock, Jason D, corrections ofcr I, $31,140
Murdock, Patrick P, corrections ofcr I, $30,132
Murdock, Tim L, corrections ofcr I, $31,140
Murphy, Ashleigh, prob & parole ofcr I, $29,976
Murphy, Austin T, stationary engr, $34,944
Murphy, Brent A, corrections ofcr I, $29,652
Murphy, Charles E, corrections ofcr I, $29,652
Murphy, Darrell W, stationary engr, $33,744
Murphy, Diana L, cook II, $24,264
Murphy, Dylan L, corrections ofcr I, $29,652
Murphy, Eric A, corrections ofcr I, $28,692
Murphy, Gregory H, chaplain, $34,356
Murphy, Heather L, prob & parole ofcr II, $36,204
Murphy, Johnna L, corrections ofcr I, $32,784
Murphy, Linette D, storekeeper I, $27,504
Murphy, Lisa B, prob & parole ofcr II, $38,232
Murphy, Mary A, ofc spt asst (keybrd), $23,508
Murphy, Merideth E, ofc spt asst (keybrd), $23,508
Murphy, Robert D, corrections ofcr I, $29,652
Murphy, Tara D, corrections recs ofcr II, $30,984
Murphy, Zachary C, corrections ofcr I, $28,692
Murray, Brittany M, cook II, $23,508
Murray, Johann P, recrtn ofcr I, $30,420
Murray, Justin A, corrections ofcr I, $29,652
Murray, Rebecca L, prob & parole ofcr II, $36,204
Murray, Ricky A, corrections ofcr I, $34,512
Murray, Robert, functional unit mgr corr, $41,940
Murray, Timothy J, correctional worker, $26,400
Murrell, Lori D, prob & parole ofcr II, $38,232
Murry, Robert L, corrections ofcr II, $31,668
Musgrave, Tracey A, prob & parole unit spv, $40,380
Musick, Dennis K, prob & parole ofcr II, $41,940
Musser, David L, corrections ofcr I, $29,652
Mustain, Gloria S, corrections ofcr I, $29,652
Mustain, Todd E, corrections ofcr I, $29,652
Mutota, Walt, corrections training ofcr, $38,928
Myer, Marjorie O, corrections ofcr I, $29,652
Myers, Ashley M, corrections ofcr I, $29,652
Myers, Brian K, corrections spv I, $41,172
Myers, Jo Ann, corrections ofcr I, $29,652
Myers, John E, corrections ofcr I, $29,652
Myers, Kenya J, corrections ofcr I, $29,652
Myers, Linda D, corrections ofcr I, $31,140
Myers, Marga R, functional unit mgr corr, $41,172
Myers, Miccola S, ofc spt asst (keybrd), $25,824
Myers, Michael J, prob & parole ofcr II, $36,204
Myers, Michelle A, exec I, $30,984
Myers, Tammy R, ofc spt asst (keybrd), $22,536
Myers, Teri L, exec II, $36,204
Myler, Sharon J, prob & parole ofcr III, $39,624
Myler, Tresa L, ofc spt asst (keybrd), $25,824
Myracle, Edie A, storekeeper I, $25,824
Myrick, Jennifer, corrections training ofcr, $38,928
Myscofski, Joseph E, labor spv, $27,948
Nabors, Leslie J, ofc spt asst (keybrd), $23,160
Naeger, Jeremy M, corrections ofcr I, $29,652
Naes, Carla D, prob & parole ofcr II, $41,940
Nagel, Chloe A, corrections ofcr I, $28,692
Nail, Bruce A, corrections ofcr I, $29,652
Nally, Jonell L, account clerk II, $25,824
Namassy, Adel K, corrections ofcr I, $28,692
Nangosyah, Ivan, corrections ofcr I, $29,652
Nanney, Gene M, corrections ofcr I, $28,692
Napier, Evan M, corrections ofcr I, $29,652
Narancich, Daniel A, corrections ofcr I, $28,692
Nash, Amanda L, ofc spt asst (keybrd), $23,160
Nash, Frances E, sr ofc spt asst (keybrd), $25,824
Nash, John B, corrections ofcr I, $29,652
Nash, Nicole D, corrections ofcr II, $31,668
Nash, Randy S, corrections ofcr I, $29,652

Nash, Vernetta S, prob & parole ofcr II, $36,204
Nations, Laura L, ofc spt asst (keybrd), $23,160
Naughton, Eric J, corrections ofcr I, $28,692
Naylor, Ken E, corrections ofcr II, $33,348
Nazu, Mimi R, functional unit mgr corr, $37,548
Neal, Linda J, corrections ofcr I, $29,652
Neal, Paul R, corrections ofcr I, $29,652
Nease, Larry R, cook III, $28,104
Nease, Michael R, corrections ofcr I, $28,692
Neece, Tamara R, prob & parole asst I, $29,496
Neel, Charles M, corrections training ofcr, $38,928
Neel, David A, corrections ofcr I, $29,652
Neel, Kim, prob & parole ofcr II, $36,204
Neel, Laura M, storekeeper II, $30,984
Neel, Renee L, corrections ofcr II, $31,668
Neely, Amy K, prob & parole ofcr II, $36,204
Neff, Daniel J, power plant mech, $30,420
Neff, Diane M, corrections ofcr I, $29,652
Nefferdorf, Matthew L, corrections ofcr I, $28,692
Negus, Vincent J, corrections classif asst, $31,512
Neher, Kristie D, corrections ofcr I, $29,652
Neighbor, Ronald P, subs abuse cnslr III, $36,204
Neill, Deanna L, prob & parole ofcr II, $40,380
Neiman, Ronald C, special asst technician, $40,716
Neitzel, Christopher S, corrections ofcr I, $29,652
Nelson, Ashley, prob & parole ofcr II, $36,204
Nelson, Beth A, recrtn ofcr I, $31,512
Nelson, Celace A, prob & parole ofcr II, $37,548
Nelson, Christopher A, corrections ofcr I, $29,652
Nelson, Dallas L, corrections ofcr I, $28,692
Nelson, Daniel C, maint spv I, $32,628
Nelson, David E, training tech III, $45,156
Nelson, David M, corrections ofcr I, $29,652
Nelson, Frederick J, corrections ofcr II, $33,348
Nelson, James R, corrections ofcr III, $37,548
Nelson, Jason P, corrections ofcr I, $29,316
Nelson, Kelli R, prob & parole ofcr II, $39,624
Nelson, Kerry J, corrections mgr b1, $51,096
Nelson, Lisa M, corrections ofcr I, $29,652
Nelson, Roger G, corrections ofcr I, $29,652
Nelson, Ronald D, corrections ofcr I, $33,348
Neman, Malek K, corrections ofcr I, $28,692
Nesbit, Derek A, corrections ofcr I, $29,652
Nesler, Courtney R, ofc spt asst (keybrd), $23,160
Ness, Brandon, corrections ofcr I, $28,692
Ness, Chad T, corrections ofcr I, $28,692
Ness, Chuck T, corrections ofcr II, $31,668
Nethington, Jeremy L, corrections ofcr I, $28,692
Nettles, Lindsay K, corrections ofcr I, $28,692
Nettles, Rosetta, corrections ofcr I, $29,652
Neubauer, Laura L, corrections ofcr I, $29,652
Neudorff, Dylan S, corrections ofcr I, $28,692
Neumann, James R, corrections ofcr I, $29,652
Nevels, Robert W, corrections ofcr I, $29,652
Newbern, Antonio, prob & parole ofcr II, $34,944
Newbold, Dominic F, corrections ofcr I, $28,692
Newell, Joshua J, corrections ofcr I, $29,652
Newkirk, Jennifer K, prob & parole ofcr II, $38,232
Newman, Daniel A, acad tchr III, $39,624
Newman, Doris M, corrections ofcr I, $29,652
Newman, Kevin R, maint worker II, $31,512
Newman, Matthew D, corrections ofcr I, $29,652
Newman, Stephanie A, corrections ofcr I, $29,652
Newsom, Jonathan N, corrections ofcr I, $28,692
Newton, Robert A, corrections ofcr I, $29,652
Ney, Christine C, pers clerk, $29,004
Nibarger, Steven L, corrections ofcr I, $29,652
Nicholls, Peter, corrections ofcr I, $29,652
Nichols, Beverley A, maint spv II, $34,944
Nichols, Colin E, prob & parole asst I, $33,180
Nichols, Danielle M, corrections ofcr I, $28,692
Nichols, Gary E, corrections case mgr II, $38,232
Nichols, Gerald L, corrections ofcr I, $29,652
Nichols, Jackie L, account clerk II, $27,084
Nichols, Jerry A, corrections ofcr I, $31,140
Nichols, Joseph E, corrections ofcr I, $28,692
Nichols, Pagena M, special asst prof, $59,590
Nichols, Rebecca M, ofc spt asst (clerical), $22,536
Nichols, Tina M, prob & parole ofcr II, $36,204
Nicholson, James A, investigator II, $37,548
Nickell, John A, prob & parole ofcr III, $37,548
Nickell, Larry J, corrections ofcr I, $31,140
Nickell, Stephanie L, prob & parole ofcr II, $36,204

Nickelson, Angela J, acad tchr III, $39,624
Nickelson, Douglas W, investigator I, $31,512
Nickelson, Marah J, corrections ofcr I, $29,652
Nickelson, Mindi A, prob & parole ofcr II, $36,204
Nickelson, Randy A, corrections ofcr I, $29,652
Niederkorn, Lisa C, subs abuse cnslr II, $34,944
Niehaus, Martin K, recrtn ofcr I, $30,420
Nieland, David J, prob & parole ofcr II, $36,204
Nielsen, Leland R, corrections ofcr II, $32,292
Nielsen, Wanda F, cook II, $24,264
Niemet, Desiree M, corrections case mgr II, $34,944
Nieves, Yeriel, prob & parole asst I, $29,496
Niffen, Lori A, corrections ofcr I, $29,652
Niffen, Stacy K, ofc spt asst (keybrd), $23,880
Niggemeier, Melissa M, prob & parole ofcr II, $39,624
Nilges, Mary L, ofc spt asst (keybrd), $23,880
Ninedorf, Daniel J, corrections ofcr I, $29,652
Ninness, Michael A, prob & parole ofcr II, $36,204
Nipper, Billy, corrections training ofcr, $39,624
Nipper, Bruce S, voc enter spv II, $29,976
Nivens, Patsy J, corrections ofcr I, $29,652
Nivens, Roger A, corrections ofcr I, $29,652
Nivert, Mark N, corrections ofcr I, $29,652
Njong, Princewill, prob & parole asst I, $29,496
Nkwocha, George C, corrections ofcr I, $29,652
Nkwocha, Onyewuchi I, corrections ofcr I, $29,652
Nobert, John C, corrections ofcr I, $29,652
Noble, Amanda G, ofc spt asst (keybrd), $23,160
Noble, Vivian J, corrections recs ofcr I, $28,104
Nobles, Roberto J, cook II, $23,508
Nocks, Ricky D, corrections ofcr I, $29,652
Noe, Mark D, maint spv I, $36,204
Noel, Brian K, corrections ofcr I, $29,652
Noel, Cynthia G, prob & parole ofcr II, $36,204
Noeller, Kelly J, corrections ofcr I, $29,652
Noeth, Gail D, corrections ofcr I, $29,652
Noisworthy, Stephanie, corrections ofcr I, $28,692
Nokes, David, prob & parole ofcr II, $36,204
Nokes, Nicole, sr ofc spt asst (keybrd), $25,824
Nokes, William G, corrections ofcr I, $31,140
Nolan, Deanna R, account clerk II, $28,908
Nolan, Troy D, corrections ofcr I, $29,652
Noland, Shawn P, corrections ofcr I, $29,652
Nold, Mark B, corrections training ofcr, $43,488
Nold, Robert J, corrections ofcr I, $29,652
Nolden, Herbert J, corrections ofcr I, $29,652
Nolin, Martha V, designated principal asst div, $71,668
Nolting, Patricia M, ofc spt asst (keybrd), $23,160
Nordbye, Tom F, corrections ofcr I, $29,652
Norman, Darlene Y, ofc spt asst (keybrd), $23,160
Norman, Jeffrey R, corrections mgr b3, $71,205
Norman, Michael J, corrections ofcr I, $28,692
Norris, Bobby W, corrections ofcr I, $29,652
Norris, Derek D, prob & parole ofcr II, $36,204
Norris, Heidi M, corrections ofcr I, $29,652
Norris, James B, corrections ofcr I, $29,652
Norris, Keli N, corrections ofcr I, $29,652
Norris, Kelly G, electronics tech, $33,744
Norris, Robin D, nutrition/dietary svcs mgr b2, $60,125
Norris, Sharon K, corrections ofcr I, $30,132
North, Christopher S, corrections ofcr II, $31,668
Northern, Rachelle L, corrections ofcr I, $29,652
Norton, Brandon M, corrections case mgr I, $32,628
Norton, Linda C, prob & parole ofcr I, $29,976
Norvell, George A, corrections ofcr I, $31,140
Novack, Diane R, prob & parole ofcr II, $36,204
Novak, Laura A, storekeeper I, $25,824
Novak, Lee A, corrections ofcr I, $28,692
Novak, Melissa K, corrections ofcr I, $29,652
Novich, Tyler J, corrections ofcr I, $28,692
Nowack, Jacob O, corrections ofcr I, $29,652
Noyes, Crystal G, corrections ofcr I, $29,652
Nuccio, Rebecca N, prob & parole ofcr II, $36,204
Nuckols, James R, corrections ofcr II, $35,724
Nuernberger, Paul A, acct I, $30,984
Null, David A, corrections ofcr I, $29,652
Null, Erik C, corrections ofcr I, $29,652
Null, Heather E, ofc spt asst (keybrd), $23,160
Null, Kris L, prob & parole ofcr II, $36,204
Nungesser, Amanda N, corrections ofcr I, $29,652
Nunn, Daniel J, prob & parole ofcr II, $36,204
Nunn, Elisha A, corrections ofcr I, $29,652
Nunn, Ramona A, ofc spt asst (keybrd), $23,160

Nunn, Thomas L, corrections ofcr I, $29,652
Nutter, Jacob L, storekeeper II, $28,104
Nye, Maelma, ofc spt asst (keybrd), $23,160
Oaker, Jeffery J, maint spv I, $33,180
Oakley, Brian C, corrections ofcr II, $30,576
Oaks, John C, corrections ofcr I, $29,652
O'banion, Gail O, ofc spt asst (keybrd), $23,160
Oberbeck, Jerry L, recrtn ofcr I, $35,568
Oberhaus, Emmie M, corrections ofcr I, $29,661
Oberhaus, Gina M, prob & parole ofcr II, $36,204
Oberhaus, Jeremy J, corrections ofcr I, $29,652
Obermark, Craig S, corrections ofcr I, $29,652
Obermark, Jason T, prob & parole ofcr II, $36,204
Obermark, Lonnie R, corrections ofcr I, $29,652
Obermier, Robert, corrections ofcr I, $31,668
Obi, Noel M, corrections case mgr II, $34,944
Obrien, Edward J, corrections ofcr I, $29,652
O'callaghan, Chad M, prob & parole ofcr II, $36,204
O'callaghan, Pamela S, subs abuse cnslr II, $34,944
O'cheltree, Andrew L, corrections ofcr I, $29,652
Ochoa, Isabel E, corrections ofcr II, $31,668
Ochs, Catherine C, ofc spt asst (keybrd), $23,160
Ochs, Jesscelia K, corrections ofcr II, $31,668
Ochs, Randall L, corrections ofcr III, $34,356
Ochse, Steven J, corrections ofcr II, $35,724
Ockenfels, David, prob & parole ofcr II, $39,624
O'connell, Brian S, corrections mgr b3, $59,940
O'connell, Emmett E, corrections ofcr II, $31,668
O'connor, Alice E, prob & parole unit spv, $43,488
O'connor, Andrew D, corrections ofcr I, $29,652
O'connor, Michael X, recrtn ofcr I, $29,976
O'connor, Thomas C, recrtn ofcr I, $31,512
Odell, Stephen G, corrections ofcr I, $28,692
O'dell, Brenda L, account clerk II, $26,232
O'dell, Hallie R, corrections ofcr I, $31,140
Odom, David L, corrections ofcr I, $29,652
Odom, Preston W, corrections ofcr I, $29,652
Odom, Rodney W, maint spv II, $35,568
Oellerich, Robert M, corrections ofcr I, $29,652
Oesterling, Ronald D, corrections ofcr I, $29,652
Oetting, Clifford L, correctional worker, $15.94/hr
Oetting, Peter N, corrections ofcr I, $34,512
Offield, Shelley L, prob & parole ofcr I, $30,984
Ogle, David W, corrections ofcr I, $29,652
Ognenovski, Boshko, corrections ofcr I, $28,692
Ohanaja, Festus I, corrections ofcr I, $28,692
O'hara, Philip M, correctional worker, $26,400
Ohlberg, John H, storekeeper I, $25,824
O'kelley, Scott S, special asst official & admstr, $66,660
Okoiron, Peter E, corrections ofcr I, $31,140
Okoiron, Victoria, prob & parole ofcr II, $39,624
Olalde, Nicolas D, corrections ofcr I, $29,652
Oldfield, David J, research mgr b2, $60,848
Oldham, Del L, voc tchr III, $38,232
Oldham, Justin R, corrections ofcr I, $29,652
Oldham, Sherry L, cook III, $28,104
Oldridge, Darren E, corrections ofcr I, $29,652
Oldridge, Robin A, corrections ofcr I, $28,692
Olenhouse, Marsha L, ofc spt asst (keybrd), $23,160
Oleson, Jennifer, prob & parole ofcr I, $29,976
Oligschlaeger, Kenneth J, tractor trailer driver, $32,628
Olinger, John A, corrections ofcr I, $29,652
Oliver, Adam J, corrections ofcr I, $29,652
Oliver, Gerald L, prob & parole ofcr II, $38,232
Oliver, Ira B, stationary engr, $33,744
Oliver, Laura J, corrections ofcr I, $29,652
Oliver, Melinda S, prob & parole unit spv, $44,304
Oliver, Roger D, corrections ofcr I, $33,348
Oliver, William L, corrections ofcr I, $29,652
Oller, Suzanne L, prob & parole ofcr II, $36,204
Olmem, Matthew E, corrections ofcr I, $29,652
Olmstead, Timothy R, corrections ofcr II, $31,668
Olsen, Jerry P, corrections ofcr I, $29,652
Olson, Janel A, corrections ofcr I, $29,652
Olson, Robert M, corrections ofcr I, $31,140
Olson, Silas N, corrections ofcr I, $29,652
Omerovic, Amra, prob & parole ofcr II, $29,976
O'neal, Amber, ofc spt asst (keybrd), $23,160
O'neal, Eric T, corrections ofcr I, $29,652
O'neal, Kyleigh A, corrections ofcr I, $28,692
O'neal, Michael R, prob & parole ofcr II, $36,204
Onwuemegbulem, Ray, prob & parole ofcr II, $36,204
Opare, Michael, corrections ofcr I, $29,652

Oppeau, Kurt R, prob & parole ofcr II, $36,204
Oppermann, Amy N, subs abuse cnslr II, $34,944
Orbin, Sonny L, corrections ofcr II, $31,668
Orcutt, Bobby D, corrections ofcr I, $29,652
Orcutt, Jesse R, corrections ofcr I, $29,652
O'riley, Donald E, corrections ofcr I, $31,140
Oroke, Kimberly C, special asst technician, $45,955
O'rourke, Caleb P, corrections ofcr I, $29,652
O'rourke, Maureen, prob & parole ofcr II, $36,204
Orr, James G, corrections ofcr I, $29,652
Ortega, Kellye R, functional unit mgr corr, $37,548
Ortega, Samantha L, ofc spt asst (keybrd), $23,160
Orton, Deryl, corrections ofcr I, $33,900
Osborn, Earl R, prob & parole ofcr II, $36,204
Osborne, Christopher C, prob & parole ofcr II, $36,204
Osborne, James L, corrections ofcr I, $28,692
Oser, Walter D, corrections ofcr I, $29,652
Osgood, Patrick L, maint worker II, $29,004
Osia, Sonia J, prob & parole ofcr II, $36,204
Osiecki, Donna L, prob & parole ofcr II, $41,940
Osman, Cindy D, ofc spt asst (keybrd), $27,504
Osmon, Joshua G, corrections ofcr I, $29,652
Osmon, Terry R, corrections ofcr I, $29,652
Ostermann, Jeffry W, corrections ofcr I, $33,900
Ostrander, Christina M, ofc spt asst (keybrd), $23,160
Otto, Dale N, voc enter rep, $33,744
Ottomeyer, Phoebe E, prob & parole ofcr II, $41,940
Ouren, Matthew H, prob & parole ofcr II, $36,204
Ourth, Marni, acad tchr III, $37,548
Ousley, James E, corrections ofcr I, $29,652
Ousley, Mary K, cook II, $24,264
Overkamp, Matthew C, corrections ofcr II, $32,220
Overstreet, David L, fire & safety spec, $34,944
Overstreet, Jared R, corrections ofcr II, $31,668
Overstreet, Michael W, corrections ofcr I, $29,652
Overton, Keith Z, corrections ofcr I, $29,652
Owen, Carrie L, corrections mgr b1, $47,888
Owen, David J, designated principal asst dept, $53,033
Owen, Doug, inst activity coor, $34,356
Owen, E Jolene, acad tchr III, $41,172
Owen, Eric J, corrections ofcr I, $29,652
Owen, Mary L, prob & parole asst I, $29,496
Owen, Sara M, corrections ofcr I, $28,692
Owens, Charles E, corrections ofcr I, $28,692
Owens, Eric J, corrections ofcr I, $31,668
Owens, George E, corrections ofcr I, $29,652
Owens, Glenda, ofc spt asst (keybrd), $22,536
Owens, Jordon L, corrections ofcr I, $28,692
Owens, Kimberly S, account clerk II, $25,824
Owens, Marilyn K, ofc spt asst (clerical), $22,536
Owens, Randall E, investigator II, $37,548
Owens, Rodney D, corrections ofcr I, $29,652
Owens, Shawn A, corrections ofcr I, $29,652
Ownby, Kevin J, corrections training ofcr, $38,928
Owotutu, Janice K, corrections ofcr I, $29,652
Owusu, Frank, corrections ofcr I, $28,692
Oxendine, Tracey L, corrections training ofcr, $42,708
Oxford, John M, corrections case mgr II, $38,928
Oxley, Amber R, corrections ofcr I, $29,652
Oyer, Douglas E, prob & parole ofcr II, $36,204
Ozanich, Levi M, corrections ofcr III, $32,628
Ozenberger, Georgette, corrections ofcr I, $29,652
Pace, Kenneth D, corrections ofcr I, $32,784
Pace, Todd J, corrections ofcr I, $28,692
Pacheco, Michael J, corrections ofcr I, $29,652
Paden, Denise D, functional unit mgr corr, $39,624
Padget, Trevor J, corrections ofcr I, $29,652
Padgett, Jean M, pers analyst II, $37,548
Padgett, Sarah N, prob & parole ofcr II, $36,204
Page, Cara B, inst activity coor, $31,512
Page, Dawn, admin ofc spt asst, $33,180
Page, Joseph W, corrections ofcr I, $30,276
Page, Justin L, corrections mgr b1, $46,178
Page, Lisa D, laundry mgr, $34,944
Page, Terry L, corrections mgr b2, $53,058
Pagett, Nancy J, corrections ofcr III, $33,744
Paige, Todd A, corrections ofcr I, $29,652
Painter, Rickie D, corrections spv I, $40,380
Paker, Richard P, labor spv, $26,652
Palmer, Jessie U, corrections ofcr I, $29,652
Palmer, Mark, corrections ofcr I, $29,652
Palmer, Shelly L, corrections ofcr I, $29,652
Palmer, Teri L, corrections ofcr I, $31,140

Palmeri, Linda F, cook II, $23,508
Palmier, Ronald L, corrections ofcr I, $29,652
Pankau, Steven M, corrections case mgr II, $34,944
Pantaleo, Bryan E, correctional worker, $26,400
Pantaleo, Luke C, corrections ofcr I, $28,692
Pantaleo, Matthew J, corrections ofcr I, $29,652
Paolino, David J, corrections ofcr I, $31,140
Papen, Joshua W, corrections ofcr I, $29,652
Paris, Kenneth V, corrections ofcr I, $30,139
Parker, Anthony J, corrections ofcr I, $29,652
Parker, Astra L, corrections ofcr I, $29,652
Parker, Devin S, corrections ofcr II, $31,668
Parker, Donald V, maint spv I, $32,628
Parker, Joshua W, voc enter spv II, $29,976
Parker, Kelly R, prob & parole ofcr II, $39,624
Parker, Randell L, corrections ofcr I, $31,668
Parker, Timothy R, corrections ofcr I, $28,692
Parker, Wesley G, boiler oper, $27,228
Parker, William E, maint spv I, $31,512
Parker, Yu-Li Y, ofc spt asst (keybrd), $23,160
Parkey, Jeffrey W, corrections ofcr I, $31,140
Parkhurst, Amy A, corrections case mgr I, $36,204
Parkhurst, Mark, corrections mgr b1, $46,233
Parkman, Timmy L, maint spv I, $32,628
Parks, Jason P, corrections ofcr II, $31,668
Parks, Patricia J, ofc spt asst (keybrd), $22,536
Parks, Tina R, prob & parole ofcr II, $39,624
Parnas, Deborah A, prob & parole ofcr II, $39,624
Parnell, Samantha J, corrections ofcr I, $28,692
Parr, Niki J, corrections ofcr I, $29,652
Parrish, Christopher N, corrections ofcr I, $29,652
Parrish, Sandra K, cook III, $30,984
Parrish, Tony M, corrections ofcr I, $30,132
Parrott, Charles, corrections ofcr I, $29,652
Parrott, James B, corrections ofcr I, $28,692
Parshall, Darrin S, corrections ofcr I, $31,668
Parshall, Kelly J, admin ofc spt asst, $32,628
Parson, John N, corrections ofcr I, $29,652
Parsons, Christopher R, corrections ofcr I, $29,652
Parsons, Cristi W, corrections ofcr I, $29,652
Parsons, David E, corrections ofcr I, $33,348
Parsons, John L, corrections ofcr II, $31,668
Parsons, Johnathon J, librarian II, $33,744
Parsons, Randal A, locksmith, $31,512
Partridge, Audrey E, subs abuse cnslr II, $34,944
Pasch, Eldon L, corrections ofcr I, $29,652
Pash, Ronda J, corrections mgr b3, $66,438
Pashia, Christy, corrections case mgr I, $31,512
Pashia, Shane A, corrections ofcr I, $29,652
Pashik, Samantha J, corrections case mgr I, $30,984
Paskins, Tiona, prob & parole asst II, $30,420
Pasley, Amy N, ofc spt asst (keybrd), $23,160
Pasley, Cherry L, librarian II, $34,356
Pasley, Quinten J, corrections ofcr II, $31,668
Pass, Scott A, corrections ofcr I, $29,652
Passig, Erick S, corrections ofcr I, $29,652
Pate, Brandon M, cook II, $24,264
Pate, Jimmy W, corrections ofcr II, $37,056
Pate, Joshua A, corrections ofcr I, $28,692
Patrick, Gregory, corrections ofcr I, $31,140
Patrick, Melinda R, ofc spt asst (keybrd), $23,160
Patrick, Ryan J, corrections ofcr I, $29,652
Patrick, Sherri L, acad tchr III, $36,204
Patterson, Brian T, corrections ofcr I, $29,652
Patterson, Bryan L, prob & parole ofcr II, $38,232
Patterson, Courtney, prob & parole ofcr II, $36,204
Patterson, Curtis E, corrections ofcr I, $29,652
Patterson, Darrell D, corrections ofcr I, $30,132
Patterson, Gina L, admin ofc spt asst, $28,104
Patterson, Juli E, corrections ofcr II, $31,668
Patterson, Kelle D, corrections ofcr I, $29,652
Patterson, Lashaunta M, prob & parole ofcr II, $37,548
Patterson, Mike G, prob & parole asst I, $29,496
Patterson, Rebecca E, corrections case mgr I, $29,976
Patterson, Robert L, maint worker II, $28,104
Patterson, Robert W, corrections ofcr I, $29,652
Patton, Brian D, corrections ofcr III, $33,744
Patton, Jeffrey W, corrections ofcr I, $30,576
Patton, John A, maint spv I, $32,628
Patton, Steven M, corrections ofcr I, $29,652
Paul, Kenneth R, corrections ofcr II, $37,056
Paul, Tiffany T, prob & parole ofcr II, $36,204
Pauley, Daniel J, storekeeper II, $28,104

Pauley, James A, corrections ofcr I, $29,652
Pauls, Kenneth L, corrections ofcr I, $31,140
Pauls, Richard D, corrections ofcr I, $29,652
Pawling, Shanin L, corrections ofcr I, $28,692
Paxton, Gregory A, storekeeper I, $25,824
Paxton, James H, prob & parole asst II, $31,512
Paxton, Kathy A, corrections ofcr I, $29,652
Payne, Barbara G, corrections ofcr I, $29,652
Payne, Brady A, corrections ofcr I, $28,692
Payne, Courtney A, corrections ofcr I, $28,692
Payne, Deborah K, corrections ofcr I, $29,652
Payne, Derek L, corrections ofcr II, $31,668
Payne, James A, corrections ofcr I, $29,652
Payne, James R, corrections ofcr I, $35,724
Payne, Jean R, prob & parole ofcr II, $36,204
Payne, Jennifer R, ofc spt asst (keybrd), $23,160
Payne, Kristina L, corrections case mgr II, $34,944
Payne, Michael B, corrections mgr b2, $57,970
Payne, Michelle L, corrections mgr b1, $43,497
Payne, Paula S, corrections ofcr I, $29,652
Payne, Robert M, cook II, $23,508
Payne, Romie R, corrections ofcr I, $31,668
Payne, Stanley D, corrections mgr b2, $47,556
Payne, Terry L, corrections ofcr III, $33,744
Payne, Tracy V, corrections ofcr I, $33,348
Payton, Shannon L, corrections ofcr I, $29,661
Peak, Dawn N, cook II, $24,264
Pearl, Kathy L, cook II, $23,508
Pearon, Robert D, corrections ofcr I, $29,652
Pearson, Alice D, ofc spt asst (keybrd), $23,160
Pearson, Angelique K, corrections ofcr II, $31,668
Pearson, Cherise R, prob & parole ofcr II, $40,380
Pearson, Kevin J, corrections ofcr I, $29,652
Pearson, Lonnie D, corrections ofcr I, $29,652
Pearson, Robert S, corrections ofcr I, $31,668
Pearson, Tamra R, prob & parole ofcr II, $36,204
Pearson, Thomas W, functional unit mgr corr, $43,488
Pease, Ricky R, corrections ofcr I, $29,652
Peavler, Gordon D, corrections case mgr II, $36,888
Peeler, Richard E, corrections ofcr I, $31,140
Peeper, Charles E, corrections ofcr I, $29,652
Peery, Michele C, ofc spt asst (keybrd), $24,612
Peery, Shawn, storekeeper I, $26,232
Peifer, Samuel T, maint worker II, $29,004
Peiter, Rebecca N, sr ofc spt asst (clerical), $25,824
Pelletier, Anthony D, investigator I, $31,512
Penberthy, Rita F, corrections ofcr I, $30,576
Pence, April D, corrections case mgr II, $36,204
Pendergraft, Jonathon A, corrections ofcr I, $29,652
Pendleton, Ronald O, corrections ofcr III, $33,744
Pendley, Thomas J, corrections ofcr I, $29,652
Penfield, Judy K, cook II, $24,264
Penland, Michael D, corrections spv I, $37,548
Penland, Teri A, corrections ofcr I, $31,140
Pennington, Jack N, recrtn ofcr II, $35,568
Penrod, David J, corrections spv I, $38,928
Peppers, Jason P, cook II, $24,264
Peppers, Kristen D, prob & parole unit spv, $46,068
Peppers, Martin L, corrections ofcr I, $29,652
Perdue, Michelle J, prob & parole ofcr II, $34,944
Perez, Pamela L, corrections ofcr I, $29,652
Perkins, April N, ofc spt asst (keybrd), $22,536
Perkins, Cynthia L, special educ tchr III, $37,548
Perkins, David E, power plant mech, $30,984
Perkins, Donald L, phys plant sup I, $34,944
Perkins, Dwayne R, corrections ofcr I, $29,652
Perkins, Randall, prob & parole unit spv, $41,940
Perrin, Thomas C, corrections ofcr I, $28,692
Perry, Alana N, corrections case mgr II, $34,944
Perry, Amber M, ofc spt asst (keybrd), $22,536
Perry, B E, sr ofc spt asst (keybrd), $27,948
Perry, Delores A, ofc spt asst (keybrd), $23,160
Perry, Eric L, corrections ofcr II, $31,668
Perry, George L, corrections ofcr I, $31,140
Perry, James L, corrections ofcr I, $33,348
Perry, Jill A, prob & parole unit spv, $45,156
Perry, Joyce L, ofc spt asst (keybrd), $27,084
Perry, Steven L, maint worker II, $29,004
Persch, Dale O, investigator I, $40,380
Pershing, David L, corrections mgr b1, $42,403
Peskar, James E, acad tchr III, $38,232
Peterman, Angela A, corrections ofcr I, $29,652
Peters, Christopher W, corrections ofcr I, $29,652

Peters, Dana K, fiscal & administrative mgr b2, $47,556
Peters, Donna J, corrections ofcr III, $33,744
Peters, Dustin H, corrections ofcr II, $31,668
Peters, Gary L, corrections ofcr I, $29,652
Peters, Kimberly D, corrections ofcr I, $29,652
Peters, Michelle L, corrections mgr b1, $46,926
Peters, Patrick V, corrections ofcr I, $29,652
Peters, Richard R, corrections ofcr I, $31,678
Petersen, Mike L, prob & parole ofcr II, $39,624
Peterson, Davianne R, corrections ofcr I, $29,652
Peterson, Hope, prob & parole ofcr II, $36,204
Peterson, Jerald A, corrections ofcr III, $33,744
Peterson, Ryne J, corrections ofcr I, $29,652
Petifurd, Anita, labor spv, $26,652
Petifurd, Danny B, laundry mgr, $33,744
Petri, Jacqueline K, corrections case mgr II, $37,548
Petri, John A, maint spv I, $36,204
Petroff, Lisabeth D, cook III, $28,104
Petruczenko, Gregory K, prob & parole unit spv, $41,940
Petsche, Brad J, corrections ofcr I, $29,652
Pettigrew, Mandy, corrections classif asst, $30,984
Pettigrew, Shawn M, corrections case mgr II, $34,356
Pettijohn, Jeffrey A, subs abuse cnslr II, $37,548
Pettis, Bryan W, corrections ofcr I, $29,652
Pettit, Jamie N, prob & parole ofcr II, $34,944
Pettit, Jennifer L, ofc spt asst (keybrd), $23,160
Pettitt, Blane, corrections ofcr I, $28,692
Pettus, Brian K, corrections ofcr III, $38,928
Pettus, Bruce J, corrections ofcr I, $29,652
Pettus, Clint B, corrections ofcr I, $29,652
Pettus, Rachel J, corrections ofcr I, $29,652
Petty, Matthew D, corrections classif asst, $31,512
Petty, William H, corrections ofcr II, $31,668
Peura, Robert W, corrections mgr b1, $51,684
Pfeifer, Carrie L, investigator I, $33,180
Pfeifer, Michael A, recrtn ofcr II, $31,512
Pfeiffer, David R, corrections ofcr II, $31,668
Pfeiffer, Robin R, corrections ofcr I, $29,652
Pfeiffer, Tilena M, corrections ofcr I, $29,652
Pfenenger, Richard J, maint worker II, $29,004
Pfuehler, Phillip A, stationary engr, $33,744
Phares, Blake J, corrections ofcr I, $28,692
Phegley, Gary W, fire & safety spec, $33,180
Phegley, Richard B, corrections ofcr I, $29,652
Phelps, Derin S, corrections ofcr I, $29,652
Phelps, Nicholas G, voc enter spv I, $28,104
Phelps, Relby R, corrections ofcr I, $32,784
Phiffer, Angela E, prob & parole ofcr II, $34,944
Phillippe, Maryann, corrections case mgr II, $38,232
Phillips, Alex D, storekeeper II, $28,104
Phillips, Clayton, prob & parole ofcr II, $36,204
Phillips, Dale E, functional unit mgr corr, $43,488
Phillips, Donald L, corrections ofcr I, $29,652
Phillips, Gail L, corrections case mgr II, $34,944
Phillips, George T, corrections ofcr I, $29,652
Phillips, James C, corrections ofcr I, $29,652
Phillips, Justin D, prob & parole ofcr II, $36,204
Phillips, Kaylee A, prob & parole asst I, $29,496
Phillips, Kevin R, corrections ofcr I, $28,692
Phillips, Lanny J, corrections ofcr I, $29,652
Phillips, Marion B, ofc spt asst (keybrd), $26,652
Phillips, Nadine N, corrections ofcr I, $28,692
Phillips, Ronald A, corrections ofcr I, $29,652
Phillips, Scott D, hr mgr b1, $46,234
Philpot, Amy J, prob & parole ofcr II, $39,624
Phipps, Christopher S, corrections ofcr I, $30,132
Phipps, Cory L, investigator II, $37,548
Piazza, Harry J, voc enter spv II, $29,976
Pich, Jack R, corrections ofcr I, $33,348
Pickens, Michelle R, prob & parole ofcr I, $30,420
Pickens, Travis A, corrections ofcr I, $29,652
Pickett, Jeremy A, corrections ofcr II, $30,576
Pickett, Keith E, corrections ofcr I, $29,652
Pickett, Melanie E, ofc spt asst (keybrd), $22,536
Pickett, Richard J, labor spv, $29,412
Pickett, Sherry L, corrections case mgr I, $31,512
Pickett, Timothy B, corrections ofcr III, $34,356
Picraux, Julie D, sr ofc spt asst (keybrd), $25,824
Pidcock, Vanessa R, cook III, $28,104
Pierce, Candice P, ofc spt asst (keybrd), $23,160
Pierce, Jeffery L, corrections ofcr I, $29,652
Pierce, Jennifer N, subs abuse cnslr II, $33,744
Pierce, Jerry W, corrections ofcr I, $28,692

Pierce, Matthew R, special asst official & admstr, $44,444
Pierce, Michael E, corrections ofcr I, $33,348
Pierce, Patricia, prob & parole ofcr II, $36,888
Pierce, Sherry L, ofc spt asst (steno), $24,612
Pierceall, John L, corrections ofcr I, $29,652
Pierick, John, corrections ofcr I, $32,784
Piers, Taryn L, prob & parole ofcr II, $36,204
Pierson, Rebecca J, functional unit mgr corr, $40,380
Pierson, Stacy L, ofc spt asst (keybrd), $22,536
Pietoso-taylor, Nicole M, prob & parole ofcr II, $36,204
Pigmon, Shelia D, subs abuse cnslr II, $34,944
Pike, Andre L, prob & parole unit spv, $42,708
Pike, Shannon J, ofc spt asst (keybrd), $23,160
Pilcher, Colton J, corrections ofcr I, $29,652
Pilcher, Onie L, ofc spt asst (keybrd), $11,580
Pilkington, Barry S, corrections ofcr I, $28,692
Pilkington, Daniel M, corrections ofcr I, $29,652
Pilkington, Jacob R, storekeeper II, $29,496
Pilny, Richard E, corrections ofcr II, $31,668
Pindell, David L, corrections ofcr I, $34,512
Pineau, Emily, ofc spt asst (keybrd), $22,536
Pinkava, Michael J, corrections ofcr I, $29,652
Pinkham, Jaramie R, corrections ofcr I, $28,692
Pinkham, Krista L, corrections ofcr I, $28,692
Pinkley, James L, corrections case mgr II, $34,944
Pinkley, Michael D, corrections ofcr I, $29,652
Pinkley, Roger C, phys plant sup III, $49,128
Pinkstaff, Cynthia A, ofc spt asst (keybrd), $23,160
Piper, Kevin L, corrections ofcr I, $29,652
Piper, Mark L, corrections ofcr I, $29,652
Pipkin, Robert L, corrections ofcr I, $31,140
Pippins, Neila P, ofc spt asst (keybrd), $23,160
Pirtle, Andrea, ofc spt asst (keybrd), $23,160
Pirtle, Rodney L, supply mgr I, $32,628
Pirtle, Stuart G, storekeeper I, $28,908
Pirtle, Terry L, recrtn ofcr II, $37,548
Pitford, Todd A, corrections ofcr I, $29,652
Pitman, James A, prob & parole ofcr II, $40,380
Pittman, Craig A, corrections ofcr I, $29,652
Pittman, Dawn M, prob & parole asst I, $29,496
Pittman, Tommy G, corrections ofcr II, $31,668
Pitts, Glen A, corrections ofcr I, $29,652
Pitzer, Skyler F, corrections ofcr I, $29,652
Piva, Michael, prob & parole ofcr II, $36,204
Piveral, Donald R, corrections ofcr I, $28,692
Planalp, Eric S, corrections ofcr I, $29,652
Planalp, Jennifer J, ofc spt asst (keybrd), $23,160
Plate, Lisa A, corrections case mgr II, $34,944
Platt, Brian K, corrections ofcr I, $34,512
Platt, David W, stationary engr, $35,568
Platt, Marilyn L, cook II, $24,264
Platte, Brian E, corrections ofcr I, $29,652
Plickebaum, Robyn L, prob & parole ofcr II, $36,888
Pliska, Derek V, corrections ofcr II, $31,668
Plowman, Steve E, maint spv II, $36,204
Plowman, Travis W, corrections spv I, $38,232
Plummer, George R, corrections ofcr I, $31,140
Plunkett, Dana L, ofc spt asst (keybrd), $23,160
Plunkett, Kristin D, prob & parole ofcr II, $41,940
Plymell, Carole J, sr ofc spt asst (keybrd), $27,084
Plymell, Kenton D, corrections ofcr I, $29,652
Podadera, Riza M, ofc spt asst (keybrd), $23,160
Poe, Debra F, corrections ofcr I, $30,132
Poe, Pamela S, fire & safety spec, $30,984
Poe, Shawn R, maint spv I, $31,512
Poeppe, Duane J, corrections ofcr I, $34,512
Poeppe, Sherry L, corrections ofcr I, $29,652
Pogue, Brent E, functional unit mgr corr, $41,172
Pogue, Deborah J, corrections ofcr I, $29,652
Pogue, Lisa D, corrections mgr b2, $49,909
Pogue, Mary, corrections ofcr I, $29,652
Pogue, Tonya J, corrections ofcr I, $29,652
Pointer, Andrew P, corrections ofcr I, $29,652
Polachek, Chris, phys plant sup III, $46,068
Poland, Judy L, storekeeper I, $25,824
Polette, Michael, corrections ofcr I, $28,692
Polhamus, Victoria K, corrections ofcr I, $28,692
Politte, Dwight D, hr mgr b2, $52,000
Politte, Mary J, storekeeper II, $28,104
Politte, Paul M, maint spv I, $32,628
Polk, Michael W, prob & parole unit spv, $46,932
Polk, Robert W, voc enter spv II, $29,976
Pollack, Adam J, corrections ofcr I, $29,652

Pollard, Johnnie D, corrections ofcr II, $30,576
Pollard, Roger D, corrections case mgr II, $38,232
Polley, Byron L, corrections ofcr I, $28,692
Polley, Dakota L, corrections ofcr I, $29,652
Pollion, Vonzetta L, corrections ofcr I, $29,652
Polmateer, Lyle W, corrections ofcr I, $29,652
Polsky, Bruce D, recrtn ofcr I, $30,420
Polston, Clinton J, corrections ofcr II, $31,668
Pona, Keith T, corrections ofcr III, $32,628
Pona, Theresa H, corrections ofcr I, $29,652
Pool, Sylvia J, ofc spt asst (keybrd), $22,536
Poor, Dale C, corrections ofcr I, $29,652
Pope, Kelly R, acad tchr III, $37,548
Pope, Kitty L, sr ofc spt asst (keybrd), $25,032
Pope, Leslie, prob & parole asst I, $29,496
Pope, Michael C, corrections ofcr I, $31,140
Pope, Robert D, garage spv, $32,628
Pope, Sherry L, corrections ofcr I, $29,652
Poppa, Terry D, corrections ofcr I, $29,652
Popplewell, Deborah L, account clerk II, $25,032
Porembski, Vanessa M, prob & parole ofcr II, $40,380
Poretti, David J, corrections ofcr I, $29,652
Portell, Kristan E, ofc spt asst (keybrd), $23,160
Porter, Beatrice L, corrections ofcr I, $29,652
Porter, Gabriel B, corrections ofcr II, $31,668
Porter, James T, electronics tech, $30,984
Porter, Lori A, ofc spt asst (keybrd), $23,160
Porter, Robert, prob & parole ofcr II, $40,380
Porter, Stacy A, prob & parole ofcr II, $41,172
Porterfield, James K, corrections ofcr I, $32,220
Portiner, Eric S, corrections ofcr II, $30,576
Portiner, Tess R, corrections ofcr I, $29,652
Posch, Mark G, corrections ofcr I, $29,652
Poschel, Jessica S, account clerk II, $25,824
Post, Judy E, corrections ofcr I, $30,276
Posten, Susan A, inst activity coor, $29,976
Postlewait, Randell D, corrections ofcr I, $29,652
Poston, Elizabeth M, prob & parole ofcr I, $33,744
Poteet, Ryan M, corrections ofcr II, $31,668
Potter, Charles E, factory mgr II, $38,928
Potts, Sandra C, corrections mgr b1, $42,368
Potts, Terry A, corrections ofcr I, $29,652
Poulin, Brandelin A, corrections ofcr I, $29,652
Poulson, Veronica L, corrections ofcr I, $28,692
Powe, Tonia M, storekeeper I, $26,232
Powell, Amanda M, ofc spt asst (keybrd), $23,160
Powell, Andrew P, corrections ofcr I, $28,692
Powell, Carla R, prob & parole ofcr II, $39,624
Powell, Christopher B, corrections classif asst, $33,744
Powell, Heather D, prob & parole ofcr II, $39,624
Powell, James C, corrections mgr b1, $48,149
Powell, Jason E, corrections ofcr I, $28,692
Powell, Kevin R, prob & parole asst I, $29,496
Powell, Maria A, corrections ofcr I, $29,652
Powell, Martha L, corrections ofcr I, $29,652
Powell, Raydell, prob & parole asst I, $29,496
Powell, Richard L, prob & parole unit spv, $42,708
Powell, Tom F, prob & parole ofcr II, $36,204
Powell, Walter E, corrections ofcr I, $29,652
Powelson, Kimberly S, corrections ofcr II, $33,348
Power, Randy L, corrections ofcr I, $29,652
Powers, Amanda J, admin ofc spt asst, $28,104
Powers, Kenneth J, corrections ofcr I, $29,652
Powers, Mark D, corrections ofcr I, $29,652
Powers, Ruth E, corrections ofcr I, $31,140
Powless, Stacia N, corrections ofcr I, $29,652
Poynter, Grant S, corrections ofcr I, $29,652
Poyser, Michael D, maint spv I, $32,628
Pracchia, Steven C, corrections ofcr I, $29,652
Praiswater, Earlene E, registered nurse mgr b1, $65,092
Pratcher, Harvey L, prob & parole asst I, $29,004
Prater, Curt, voc enter spv II, $33,744
Prather, Charlene L, corrections ofcr I, $29,652
Pratt, Chestine, corrections case mgr II, $36,204
Pratt, Deborah J, corrections case mgr II, $34,944
Pratt, Jamie A, corrections ofcr I, $28,692
Pratte, Amy L, prob & parole ofcr II, $36,204
Pratte, Michael K, prob & parole ofcr II, $36,204
Pratte, Michelle D, corrections case mgr II, $34,944
Predmore, Gregory K, corrections ofcr I, $29,652
Prentzler, James P, investigator I, $33,744
Prentzler, Tina M, corrections mgr b1, $50,800
Presberry, Brian S, recrtn ofcr I, $29,976

Presberry, Kammi S, cook II, $24,264
President, Mary E, prob & parole asst I, $29,496
Presswood, Justin D, prob & parole ofcr II, $36,204
Preston, Bryan W, corrections ofcr II, $30,576
Preston, Christina, prob & parole asst I, $29,496
Preston, Lawrence E, maint spv II, $36,888
Preston, Rusty N, corrections ofcr III, $35,568
Preston, Taylor L, corrections case mgr I, $30,420
Preston, Thomas J, prob & parole ofcr II, $36,204
Prewitt, Elizabeth K, corrections ofcr I, $29,652
Prewitt, Jessica R, ofc spt asst (keybrd), $23,160
Prewitt, Stephanie N, corrections ofcr I, $29,652
Pribble, Corey, corrections ofcr I, $29,652
Price, Angela K, prob & parole ofcr II, $38,232
Price, Brandon H, corrections ofcr II, $31,668
Price, Carollyree, prob & parole ofcr II, $36,204
Price, Chad A, corrections ofcr I, $29,652
Price, Gregory R, corrections ofcr I, $29,652
Price, Janelle S, sr ofc spt asst (keybrd), $25,824
Price, Jennifer A, corrections case mgr II, $34,944
Price, Jennifer C, ofc spt asst (keybrd), $23,160
Price, Kimberly R, corrections ofcr I, $29,652
Price, Michael W, acad tchr I, $29,004
Price, Paul A, electronics tech, $29,976
Price, Roberta C, corrections ofcr I, $29,652
Price, Sonya L, corrections ofcr I, $29,652
Price, Susan A, corrections case mgr II, $34,944
Price, Tamara M, corrections ofcr I, $29,652
Price, Tracy J, corrections ofcr III, $33,744
Price, Vicki R, sr ofc spt asst (keybrd), $26,652
Prichard, Rebecca S, ofc spt asst (keybrd), $23,160
Pride, Sarah, prob & parole ofcr I, $30,984
Pride, Stefan A, corrections ofcr I, $29,652
Priebe, Melinda L, prob & parole ofcr II, $41,940
Prier, John S, corrections ofcr II, $33,348
Prier, Katherine J, ofc spt asst (keybrd), $23,160
Prier, Mary L, corrections ofcr I, $29,652
Priest, Luann N, corrections recs ofcr III, $36,204
Primo, Justin D, corrections ofcr I, $29,652
Prindle, Rhonda K, corrections ofcr I, $33,348
Prino, Jessica N, ofc spt asst (keybrd), $23,160
Prino, Melody A, ofc spt asst (keybrd), $23,160
Pritchett, Jason R, corrections ofcr I, $29,652
Pritchett, Renee F, corrections ofcr I, $29,652
Privett, Jessie L, corrections ofcr I, $31,668
Privett, Lisa K, storekeeper II, $28,104
Probst, Christopher A, cook II, $24,264
Proctor, Arthur J, corrections ofcr II, $33,348
Proctor, Timothy J, corrections ofcr I, $29,652
Proffer, Christopher, functional unit mgr corr, $37,548
Proffer, Trevor L, corrections ofcr I, $29,652
Propst, Darryl E, corrections ofcr I, $29,652
Province, Kevin E, stationary engr, $33,744
Province, Norman W, special educ tchr III, $38,928
Provow, Paul L, storekeeper II, $32,628
Prudden, Cynthia M, dpty div dir, $77,467
Prudden, Douglas J, corrections mgr b3, $66,438
Prude-Rose, Jessica T, prob & parole ofcr II, $36,204
Pruett, Karen R, corrections ofcr I, $29,652
Pruett, Stanley W, corrections case mgr II, $38,928
Pruitt, Karen E, sr ofc spt asst (keybrd), $26,232
Pruitt, Myrtle L, corrections ofcr II, $31,668
Pruitt, Samuel, prob & parole asst I, $29,496
Prussman, Janet M, cook III, $32,052
Puckett, Henry M, electronics tech, $30,984
Puckett, Mark D, corrections ofcr I, $29,652
Puckett, Phillip L, stationary engr, $33,744
Puckett, Sandra K, ofc spt asst (keybrd), $23,160
Puckett, Timothy C, tractor trailer driver, $32,628
Pueppke, Kirk E, corrections spv I, $40,380
Puff, Linda M, corrections ofcr I, $29,652
Puffenberger, Francis D, corrections ofcr I, $29,652
Pugh, Amanda, corrections ofcr I, $29,652
Pullen, Diana L, acad tchr III, $37,548
Pullen, Jamie L, corrections ofcr I, $29,652
Pullen, Jarrod C, recrtn ofcr I, $31,512
Pullen, Paul M, maint worker II, $28,104
Pullett, Allen M, corrections ofcr I, $28,692
Pulley, Daniel L, maint worker II, $29,004
Pulley, James L, corrections ofcr I, $29,652
Pulley, Theresa D, ofc spt asst (keybrd), $26,652
Pulliam, Jason, corrections case mgr I, $37,548
Pulliam, Richard L, corrections ofcr II, $33,348

Pultz, Matthew, functional unit mgr corr, $37,548
Pumel, Glen D, corrections ofcr I, $28,692
Purdy, Kenneth L, corrections ofcr I, $29,652
Purnell, Kayla E, corrections ofcr I, $29,652
Pursel, Robert D, corrections ofcr II, $31,668
Purvis, Paul W, acad tchr III, $37,548
Puterbaugh, Stephen R, boiler oper, $28,104
Putnam, Michael A, corrections ofcr I, $29,652
Pyatt, John C, corrections ofcr I, $29,652
Pyatt, Patti J, acad tchr III, $37,548
Pyle, Duke C, corrections ofcr I, $29,652
Pyle, Phyllis A, corrections ofcr I, $28,692
Pyles, George E, corrections ofcr I, $29,652
Quainoo, Isaac, corrections ofcr I, $28,692
Qualls, Derek, labor spv, $26,652
Quattrocchi, Frank T, corrections ofcr II, $31,668
Quick, Deborah, sr ofc spt asst (keybrd), $25,824
Quick, Tony M, corrections ofcr I, $29,652
Quigley, James D, corrections ofcr I, $31,668
Quillin, Tyson A, corrections ofcr I, $29,652
Quimby, Cary L, corrections ofcr I, $29,652
Quinlan, Esther C, cook II, $24,264
Quinlan, Jack F, corrections ofcr I, $29,652
Quinn, John M, inst activity coor, $31,512
Quint, Scott D, corrections ofcr I, $29,652
Quiring, Bryce T, corrections ofcr I, $28,692
Rabe, Miles L, corrections ofcr I, $29,652
Rabey, Timothy, prob & parole asst I, $28,536
Rackers, Crystal, typist, $12.12/hr
Rackers, Dana M, ofc spt asst (keybrd), $22,536
Rackers, Lisa J, account clerk II, $25,032
Rackers, Sharon, acad tchr III, $37,548
Rackers, Thomas O, maint spv I, $34,356
Rackley, Janis C, corrections ofcr I, $29,652
Rackovan, Joseph S, corrections ofcr I, $29,652
Raddatz, Rebecca C, corrections ofcr I, $29,652
Radford, Rose, corrections ofcr I, $29,652
Radford, Timothy A, corrections ofcr I, $29,652
Radmer, Ronnie C, corrections ofcr I, $29,652
Radmer, Savannah V, corrections ofcr I, $29,652
Rafi, Arif B, acad tchr III, $39,624
Ragain, Michael D, corrections case mgr II, $36,204
Ragan, Julianna, corrections ofcr I, $29,652
Ragan, Julie A, ofc spt asst (keybrd), $25,824
Ragan, Kimberly D, storekeeper I, $25,824
Ragan, Troy D, phys plant sup II, $42,708
Ragland, Randy, corrections ofcr I, $29,652
Ragsdale, Paul R, corrections ofcr I, $29,652
Ragsdale, Sharon E, storekeeper I, $25,404
Railey, Randall J, corrections ofcr I, $28,692
Raines, Aaron R, corrections ofcr I, $29,652
Rainey, Rickie D, corrections case mgr II, $36,888
Rains, Beth A, ofc spt asst (keybrd), $23,160
Rains, Regina A, corrections case mgr II, $34,944
Rainwater, Douglas W, corrections ofcr II, $32,220
Rainwater, Hollis A, serv mgr I, $35,568
Rajput, Atif K, corrections case mgr II, $34,944
Rake, Margaret A, ofc spt asst (keybrd), $23,160
Rakes, Heather N, corrections ofcr I, $29,652
Rakes, Robert E, corrections ofcr I, $29,652
Raletz, John A, prob & parole ofcr II, $36,204
Rameriz, Misty L, corrections case mgr II, $35,568
Ramey, Eileen M, corrections mgr b2, $51,466
Ramey, Mark C, corrections ofcr I, $29,652
Ramey, Mark C, corrections ofcr III, $38,232
Ramey, Parrish L, corrections spv I, $41,172
Ramic, Jasmin, corrections ofcr I, $29,652
Ramirez, Alan J, corrections ofcr I, $29,652
Ramirez, Jose' M, corrections ofcr I, $29,652
Ramirez, Paula M, corrections mgr b1, $54,000
Ramsey, Christopher E, corrections ofcr I, $29,652
Ramsey, Patrick W, corrections ofcr II, $31,668
Ramsey, Rachael L, prob & parole ofcr II, $36,204
Ramsey, Rachel J, acad tchr III, $37,548
Ramsey, Robert M, corrections ofcr I, $29,652
Ramsey, Roy J, corrections ofcr I, $29,652
Ramsey, Shelby J, ofc spt asst (keybrd), $22,536
Ramsey, Theresa A, corrections ofcr I, $29,652
Rand, Deborah S, cook II, $24,264
Randall, Brad A, corrections ofcr I, $29,652
Randall, Willie J, corrections ofcr I, $29,652
Randazzo, Adam M, corrections ofcr II, $31,668
Randle, Laronda L, cook II, $24,264

Randolph, Kristy L, prob & parole ofcr II, $36,204
Rangel, Darcie J, corrections ofcr I, $29,652
Rannebarger, Jason L, prob & parole ofcr II, $36,204
Ransom, Anthony D, corrections ofcr I, $29,652
Raper, Rejeana R, corrections ofcr I, $28,692
Raps, Hope R, sr ofc spt asst (keybrd), $29,412
Rardon, Chrystal R, human rel ofcr II, $41,940
Rardon, Derek K, corrections case mgr II, $34,944
Rascher, Nathan W, corrections ofcr II, $31,668
Rash, Sundeep, corrections ofcr I, $29,652
Rasnic, Jonathan, prob & parole ofcr I, $29,976
Raspberry, Jennifer M, corrections case mgr II, $36,204
Ratlif, Trinis M, prob & parole ofcr II, $37,548
Ratliff, Erica S, ofc spt asst (keybrd), $23,160
Ratliff, Kenneth W, corrections ofcr I, $33,348
Ratliff, Rusty W, corrections case mgr II, $36,888
Ratterree, Dustin L, corrections ofcr I, $28,692
Ratterree, Terry L, corrections ofcr I, $29,652
Raufer, Mark H, stationary engr, $33,744
Rawlins, Carol M, prob & parole ofcr II, $38,232
Rawls, David, corrections ofcr I, $29,652
Rawson, Bryan D, corrections ofcr I, $28,692
Rawson, Rozanne L, subs abuse cnslr II, $33,744
Ray, Catherine, ofc spt asst (keybrd), $23,160
Ray, Deborah K, corrections ofcr III, $38,928
Ray, Jason D, labor spv, $26,652
Ray, Kevin S, corrections ofcr II, $35,100
Ray, Michelle L, corrections ofcr I, $29,652
Ray, Ralph F, corrections spv I, $41,172
Ray, Randi F, storekeeper I, $25,824
Ray, Randy W, phys plant sup III, $48,156
Ray, Sabrina A, corrections classif asst, $31,512
Ray, Scott L, corrections ofcr II, $33,348
Ray, Thomas P, corrections ofcr I, $29,652
Rayfield, Amber N, corrections ofcr I, $29,652
Rayford, Leslie, prob & parole asst II, $33,744
Rayl, Angela M, ofc spt asst (keybrd), $24,612
Raymond, Donna L, corrections case mgr III, $38,232
Raymond, Matthew R, recrtn ofcr III, $37,548
Rea, Brian, prob & parole ofcr II, $34,944
Reade, Andrew K, corrections ofcr I, $29,652
Reading, Mike, labor spv, $26,652
Reagan, Lauren, ofc spt asst (keybrd), $22,536
Ream, Chad I, corrections ofcr II, $31,668
Reardon, Linda C, functional unit mgr corr, $44,304
Reaves, Brent C, prob & parole ofcr II, $36,204
Reavis, Charles A, corrections ofcr I, $29,652
Rebman, Michelle, special asst prof, $40,653
Rech, William C, corrections ofcr I, $29,652
Reckner, Donald W, corrections spv I, $41,172
Rector, Randy G, corrections ofcr III, $37,548
Redburn, Michael J, corrections ofcr I, $29,652
Redburn, Patsy L, corrections ofcr I, $29,652
Redd, Demegee, corrections ofcr I, $29,652
Redd, Sandie C, corrections ofcr I, $29,661
Redden, James A, corrections ofcr II, $31,668
Redden, Larry K, maint spv I, $31,512
Reddick, Sonya K, corrections ofcr I, $29,652
Redding, Jerome, prob & parole ofcr II, $36,204
Reddy, Steven E, maint spv I, $33,180
Redington, Daniel W, corrections mgr b2, $53,742
Redington, Micheal E, phys plant sup III, $46,068
Redmon, Dustin A, corrections ofcr I, $28,692
Redmon, Gary D, corrections case mgr I, $30,420
Redmon, Michael J, corrections ofcr I, $31,668
Redmond, Frances E, prob & parole asst I, $29,496
Redmond, Lauretta J, special educ tchr II, $36,204
Redmond, Lawana R, corrections ofcr I, $29,652
Redmond, Robert E, maint worker II, $31,512
Reece, Kyle A, corrections ofcr I, $29,652
Reed, Abigail M, cook III, $27,228
Reed, Amber L, ofc spt asst (keybrd), $23,160
Reed, Andrew T, corrections ofcr I, $29,652
Reed, Betty L, corrections ofcr I, $31,140
Reed, Charles A, corrections ofcr II, $31,668
Reed, Charles D, stationary engr, $33,744
Reed, Cole A, corrections ofcr I, $29,652
Reed, Daniel J, corrections ofcr I, $28,692
Reed, Debra K, corrections ofcr III, $36,204
Reed, Edward P, corrections ofcr I, $29,652
Reed, Harold E, corrections ofcr II, $31,668
Reed, James D, boiler oper, $28,104
Reed, James O, corrections spv I, $42,708

Reed, Jamie L, prob & parole unit spv, $41,940
Reed, Jean M, corrections ofcr I, $31,140
Reed, Jessica M, corrections ofcr I, $29,652
Reed, Jimmy C, corrections ofcr I, $31,140
Reed, John A, corrections ofcr I, $29,652
Reed, Johnny M, maint worker I, $25,824
Reed, Jonathan M, corrections ofcr I, $29,652
Reed, Keith K, storekeeper I, $27,084
Reed, Kevin L, corrections ofcr I, $29,652
Reed, Latrieze E, prob & parole ofcr II, $36,204
Reed, Margaret D, voc enter spv II, $29,976
Reed, Matthew D, corrections ofcr I, $29,652
Reed, Paula K, corrections mgr b1, $43,681
Reed, Stacey N, corrections ofcr I, $28,692
Reed, Steven K, corrections ofcr I, $29,652
Reed, Steven R, corrections ofcr I, $29,652
Reed, Timothy N, prob & parole ofcr II, $39,624
Reed-hancock, Julie K, prob & parole unit spv, $42,708
Reedy, Chester, corrections ofcr I, $29,652
Reel, Brenda L, ofc spt asst (keybrd), $23,160
Rees, Jennie L, special asst technician, $45,155
Reese, Charles M, corrections ofcr I, $29,652
Reese, Christopher A, corrections ofcr I, $29,652
Reese, Diane E, corrections recs ofcr I, $30,984
Reeter, Justin C, corrections ofcr I, $29,652
Reeter, Mary A, special asst paraprof, $22.97/hr
Reeves, Cynthia G, acad tchr III, $36,204
Reeves, Eileen K, admin ofc spt asst, $33,180
Reeves, John H, storekeeper II, $31,512
Reeves, Shauna R, corrections ofcr I, $28,692
Reeves, Tammy L, prob & parole ofcr II, $36,204
Regan, Joseph C, corrections ofcr I, $33,348
Reger, Anita M, corrctions case mgr II, $34,944
Reger, Jeremiah J, corrections ofcr I, $29,652
Reger, Thomas W, corrections ofcr II, $33,900
Rehagen, Carl A, corrections ofcr I, $29,652
Rehagen, Frank A, maint spv I, $35,568
Rehkop, Carl D, corrections ofcr II, $31,668
Rehkop, Jessica R, corrections ofcr II, $31,668
Rehkop, Kathryn D, ofc spt asst (keybrd), $23,160
Reichard, Susan L, corrections ofcr I, $29,652
Reichelt, Barbara A, ofc spt asst (keybrd), $27,084
Reidlinger, Eric E, corrections ofcr II, $31,668
Reidt, Keith R, prob & parole ofcr II, $40,380
Reighard, Jacqueline N, prob & parole asst I, $29,496
Reighley, Nyla J, corrections ofcr I, $29,652
Reiner, Karen L, corrections ofcr I, $29,652
Reinig, Brenda D, prob & parole ofcr II, $36,204
Reinkemeyer, Joan M, special asst official & admstr, $70,500
Reital, Richard E, storekeeper I, $26,232
Reital, Roger H, corrections spv I, $40,380
Reiter, Danny L, corrections ofcr II, $33,900
Reiter, Kenneth L, corrections ofcr II, $36,360
Reith, Kurt D, corrections ofcr II, $32,220
Rekart, Allison S, prob & parole unit spv, $42,708
Remer, David M, corrections ofcr I, $29,652
Reminger, Steven M, maint worker II, $29,004
Rench, Bruce A, corrections ofcr I, $29,652
Rencher, Raleigh J, maint spv I, $32,628
Rendall, Mechelle H, prob & parole ofcr II, $36,204
Renfro, Michael W, corrections ofcr I, $29,652
Renk, Brett A, corrections ofcr I, $29,652
Renn, Rance A, recrtn ofcr III, $41,940
Renneke, David F, corrections ofcr I, $29,652
Renner, Robby C, corrections ofcr I, $29,652
Rentfro, Bradley W, corrections ofcr I, $29,652
Resendiz, Jesus, prob & parole ofcr II, $36,888
Resonno, Walter L, corrections ofcr I, $29,652
Resor, Julie A, corrections ofcr I, $28,692
Ressel, Daphne L, prob & parole unit spv, $45,156
Restemayer, Pamela J, corrections case mgr II, $34,944
Revels, Martin E, prob & parole ofcr II, $39,624
Revolorio, Jennifer V, corrections ofcr I, $29,652
Rex, Kevin R, corrections ofcr I, $29,652
Rex, Penny L, cook III, $28,104
Rexroat, Joseph M, corrections ofcr I, $29,652
Reynolds, Craig A, corrections ofcr I, $28,692
Reynolds, Denise A, corrections mgr b1, $64,135
Reynolds, Jessica, prob & parole ofcr II, $36,204
Reynolds, Timothy L, corrections ofcr II, $33,900
Rhew, Paul D, factory mgr I, $34,944
Rhives, Deandra, ofc spt asst (keybrd), $23,160
Rhoades, Chelsey R, account clerk II, $25,824

Rhoades, Heather R, corrections ofcr I, $29,652
Rhoades, Janet S, corrections recs ofcr I, $28,104
Rhoades, Mindy T, corrections ofcr I, $29,652
Rhoades, Richard D, corrections ofcr I, $29,652
Rhoades, Tammy J, corrections ofcr I, $29,652
Rhoades, William E, corrections ofcr II, $31,668
Rhodes, Allen C, corrections ofcr I, $29,652
Rhodes, Alysha L, corrections ofcr I, $29,652
Rhodes, Benjamin E, corrections ofcr I, $29,652
Rhodes, David A, corrections ofcr I, $29,652
Rhodes, Gregory W, functional unit mgr corr, $38,928
Rhodes, James M, investigator I, $34,356
Rhodes, Jeffrey D, corrections ofcr I, $29,652
Rhorer, Christopher L, recrtn ofcr I, $30,984
Rhorer, Lorraine M, corrections ofcr I, $29,652
Rice, Katina L, admin ofc spt asst, $28,536
Rice, Michele M, corrections ofcr I, $29,652
Rice, Sharon W, ofc spt asst (keybrd), $23,160
Rich, Terrie L, corrections ofcr III, $33,744
Richards, Andrew D, corrections ofcr I, $29,652
Richards, Benjamin W, food serv mgr II, $39,624
Richards, Billie J, corrections ofcr I, $29,652
Richards, Bradley J, corrections ofcr II, $31,668
Richards, Cynthia D, ofc spt asst (keybrd), $23,508
Richards, Early J, corrections spv I, $38,928
Richards, Freddie J, corrections ofcr I, $29,652
Richards, Hannah L, corrections ofcr I, $29,652
Richards, James L, corrections ofcr I, $32,784
Richards, Jill R, corrections ofcr II, $31,668
Richards, Tony N, maint spv I, $32,628
Richards, Tracy E, corrections ofcr I, $28,692
Richardson, Fredrick W, corrections ofcr I, $28,692
Richardson, Jermiah B, corrections ofcr I, $29,652
Richardson, Justin S, corrections ofcr I, $28,692
Richardson, Kurt D, electronics tech, $31,512
Richardson, Loyd N, corrections ofcr I, $29,652
Richardson, Melvina F, cook II, $24,264
Richardson, Patrick E, corrections ofcr I, $28,692
Richardson, Stephen B, prob & parole ofcr II, $40,380
Richardson, Steven L, corrections ofcr I, $29,652
Richardson, Sylvia J, inst activity coor, $31,512
Richardson, Tammy L, corrections ofcr II, $31,668
Richardson, Timothy E, corrections ofcr I, $29,652
Richardson, Tyler D, corrections ofcr I, $31,140
Richardson, Wesley A, corrections ofcr I, $29,652
Richars, Michael F, corrections ofcr I, $28,692
Richey, Cheryl R, corrections case mgr II, $36,204
Richey, Julianne M, ofc spt asst (keybrd), $23,160
Richey, Lisa L, corrections ofcr I, $31,140
Richey, Loraine G, corrections case mgr II, $39,624
Richie, Rhonda A, ofc spt asst (keybrd), $23,160
Richman, Justine, prob & parole ofcr II, $36,204
Richmond, Shaneal T, corrections ofcr I, $29,652
Richmond-Rohn, Cathy, prob & parole ofcr II, $18,444
Richter, Scott R, corrections ofcr I, $28,692
Richtman, Kyla C, librarian II, $33,744
Rick, Donna M, corrections ofcr I, $29,652
Rick, Patricia A, corrections ofcr I, $30,576
Rick, Steven P, corrections ofcr I, $33,348
Rickard, David A, corrections ofcr I, $28,692
Rickard, Terry W, maint spv I, $32,628
Ricker, James H, corrections ofcr I, $33,348
Rickman, Dillon, corrections ofcr I, $29,652
Rickmon, Renwick L, corrections ofcr I, $29,652
Ricotta, Alan V, corrections ofcr I, $29,652
Rictor, Lawrence D, corrections ofcr I, $29,652
Riddell, Roy J, corrections training ofcr, $38,928
Riddle, David L, corrections ofcr I, $29,652
Ridenbark, Kimberly A, corrections ofcr I, $29,652
Ridgel, Charles, corrections ofcr I, $31,668
Ridgeway, Donald A, corrections case mgr II, $34,944
Ridgeway-Lopez, Ronda J, corrections case mgr II, $34,944
Riedel, Gunter D, corrections ofcr II, $31,668
Riedel, Jayme L, corrections ofcr I, $29,652
Riedesel, Dustin K, corrections ofcr I, $28,692
Riegel, Paul L, corrections ofcr I, $29,652
Rieger, Arlen W, maint spv I, $32,628
Rieke, Dorothy M, sr ofc spt asst (keybrd), $28,908
Ries, Seth A, corrections ofcr I, $28,692
Rigdon, Victoria J, corrections ofcr I, $29,652
Rigg, Nongrak, recrtn ofcr I, $31,512
Riggins, Susan G, cook II, $24,264
Riggs, Dennis D, corrections ofcr I, $29,652

Riggs, Jo A, prob & parole ofcr II, $36,204
Riggs, Jordan J, prob & parole ofcr II, $36,204
Riggs, Shawnna, ofc spt asst (keybrd), $23,160
Righetti, Kirk R, corrections ofcr I, $29,652
Riley, Carmen L, corrections ofcr I, $29,652
Riley, Christopher M, corrections ofcr I, $28,692
Riley, Cicely T, prob & parole unit spv, $41,940
Riley, Deborah L, prob & parole ofcr II, $18,102
Riley, Jeffery, prob & parole ofcr II, $36,204
Riley, Kent M, corrections ofcr I, $28,692
Riley, Marge A, registered nurse mgr b1, $58,657
Riley, Michael D, corrections ofcr I, $29,652
Riley, Travis K, voc enter spv II, $29,976
Rimel, John W, corrections ofcr I, $29,652
Rimmer, Jacqueline A, corrections ofcr I, $29,652
Rimson, Leslie A, sr ofc spt asst (keybrd), $25,824
Rinati, Brandon M, corrections ofcr I, $28,692
Rinehart, Linda V, storekeeper I, $26,232
Rinehart, Zachary W, prob & parole asst I, $29,496
Ring, Guy P, corrections ofcr I, $31,668
Ring, Valerie S, librarian II, $33,744
Rios, Federico H, corrections ofcr I, $28,692
Rios, Javier C, corrections ofcr I, $29,652
Rios, Sharon K, corrections mgr b1, $48,783
Rippinger, Phillip A, corrections ofcr II, $33,900
Risher, Fredrick P, corrections ofcr III, $32,628
Risner, Adam E, prob & parole ofcr II, $34,944
Ritchie, Brian M, storekeeper II, $28,104
Ritter, Daniel J, corrections ofcr I, $29,652
Ritter, Keshia D, prob & parole ofcr II, $36,204
Ritter, Laura A, cook III, $27,228
Ritter, William J, corrections ofcr I, $29,652
Ritzmann, August J, corrections ofcr I, $29,652
Rivera, Jose J, corrections ofcr II, $31,668
Rivera, Matthew D, corrections ofcr I, $32,784
Rivers, Christian L, corrections ofcr I, $29,652
Rivers, James M, acad tchr III, $37,548
Rives, Wallisa, prob & parole asst I, $32,628
Roach, Derick M, corrections ofcr II, $32,220
Roach, Dewayne P, corrections mgr b1, $46,178
Roach, Earl A, corrections ofcr I, $29,652
Roach, Jeremy W, corrections ofcr I, $29,652
Roach, Rhonda L, ofc spt asst (keybrd), $23,160
Roam, George W, corrections ofcr I, $29,652
Roan, Penny J, ofc spt asst (keybrd), $26,232
Roark, Dedra A, prob & parole ofcr I, $36,204
Roark, Melissa S, prob & parole ofcr II, $37,548
Robb, Randall L, subs abuse unit spv, $41,940
Robben, Michael E, corrections ofcr I, $29,652
Robbins, Brandon D, corrections ofcr I, $28,692
Robbins, Dennis D, corrections ofcr I, $29,652
Roberds, Regina, ofc spt asst (keybrd), $23,160
Roberson, Karen E, prob & parole asst I, $29,496
Roberts, Charles D, prob & parole ofcr II, $36,204
Roberts, Frank L, corrections ofcr I, $28,692
Roberts, Gary H, corrections ofcr I, $30,132
Roberts, Glenna M, ofc spt asst (keybrd), $22,536
Roberts, Jeffrey L, corrections ofcr II, $31,668
Roberts, John M, corrections ofcr I, $28,692
Roberts, John W, corrections ofcr I, $29,652
Roberts, Lisa M, ofc spt asst (keybrd), $23,160
Roberts, Monica A, corrections ofcr I, $29,652
Roberts, Montana O, cook III, $23,508
Roberts, Paul D, corrections mgr b1, $44,037
Roberts, Rhonda L, prob & parole asst I, $29,496
Roberts, Ronnie L, corrections ofcr I, $29,652
Roberts, Shawn F, corrections ofcr II, $31,668
Roberts, Shelley L, maint worker II, $31,512
Roberts, Stephanie S, prob & parole ofcr II, $38,232
Roberts, Tracy A, corrections ofcr I, $29,652
Roberts, William R, corrections ofcr I, $29,652
Robertson, Brian L, corrections ofcr I, $29,652
Robertson, Christopher D, corrections ofcr I, $29,652
Robertson, Cole D, corrections ofcr I, $29,652
Robertson, Erin M, ofc spt asst (keybrd), $23,160
Robertson, Harold, recrtn ofcr III, $41,940
Robertson, Jeremy A, corrections spv I, $37,548
Robertson, Kevin S, subs abuse cnslr II, $34,944
Robertson, Michael R, corrections ofcr I, $29,652
Robertson, Savanna K, corrections ofcr I, $29,652
Robertson, Tammari D, corrections recs ofcr I, $28,104
Robertson-riley, Tena G, corrections mgr b1, $47,876
Robin, Gerald A, corrections ofcr I, $29,652

Robinett, Ashley, corrections case mgr I; $33,744
Robins, Michael, acad tchr III, $41,172
Robinson, Arney L Jr, storekeeper I, $25,032
Robinson, Brian K, prob & parole ofcr II, $40,380
Robinson, Brian L, corrections ofcr I, $29,652
Robinson, Chad, corrections ofcr I, $29,652
Robinson, Daniel K, corrections ofcr I, $29,652
Robinson, Davita K, cook II, $24,264
Robinson, Dimple K, cook III, $28,104
Robinson, Fred, storekeeper II, $30,984
Robinson, Heidi L, prob & parole ofcr II, $36,204
Robinson, James L, corrections ofcr I, $29,652
Robinson, Jerry G, corrections ofcr I, $29,652
Robinson, Kathryn R, corrections ofcr I, $29,652
Robinson, Latoya D, corrections ofcr I, $29,652
Robinson, Linnell T, prob & parole ofcr II, $38,232
Robinson, Lora L, account clerk II, $25,824
Robinson, Millie E, special asst technician, $45,450
Robinson, Monik, storekeeper II, $28,104
Robinson, Nani R, corrections ofcr I, $29,652
Robinson, Richard, corrections ofcr I, $29,652
Robinson, Robby J, corrections ofcr I, $30,132
Robinson, Shaunrelle T, corrections ofcr I, $29,652
Robinson, Sueane, prob & parole ofcr II, $36,204
Robinson, Thelma H, corrections ofcr I, $32,784
Robinson, Therese R, ofc spt asst (keybrd), $23,160
Robison, Jeremy, corrections ofcr I, $28,692
Robke, Thomas, corrections ofcr I, $29,652
Robson, Jeff W, prob & parole ofcr II, $38,232
Roche, Kellee K, corrections ofcr I, $29,652
Rockenfield, Deloris J, sr ofc spt asst (keybrd), $25,824
Rodebaugh, Jason G, corrections case mgr I, $33,744
Rodenberg, Kaley M, ofc spt asst (keybrd), $23,160
Roderick, Amy L, designated principal asst dept, $67,468
Roderick, Kathy D, account clerk II, $25,824
Roderick, Kevin W, cook II, $24,264
Rodey, Joseph G, corrections ofcr I, $28,692
Rodgers, Melissa R, prob & parole ofcr II, $36,204
Rodgers, Ricky L, corrections ofcr I, $29,652
Rodrick, Maria A, inst activity coor, $32,628
Rodrick, Richard L, corrections ofcr I, $31,140
Rodriguez, Alberto R, corrections ofcr I, $31,140
Rodriguez, Daniel C, corrections training ofcr, $38,928
Rodriguez, David, prob & parole asst I, $30,120
Rodriguez, Miguel A, prob & parole ofcr II, $36,204
Roesch, Rhonda R, corrections ofcr I, $29,652
Roesner, James R, corrections case mgr II, $38,232
Roever, Ashley, prob & parole ofcr I, $29,976
Rogan, Cavin A, corrections ofcr I, $29,652
Rogers, Barbara L, cook II, $24,264
Rogers, Bobby J, corrections case mgr II, $34,944
Rogers, Carla S, corrections ofcr I, $31,140
Rogers, Donnie V, acad tchr III, $37,548
Rogers, Gary R, corrections ofcr III, $33,744
Rogers, Jeffrey S, corrections case mgr I, $34,944
Rogers, John G, recrtn ofcr III, $40,380
Rogers, Kelli N, prob & parole unit spv, $41,940
Rogers, Marilyn M, corrections ofcr III, $38,232
Rogers, Nathanial J, corrections ofcr I, $28,692
Rogers, Nya R, prob & parole unit spv, $41,940
Rogers, Pamela M, principal asst board/commisson, $47,767
Rogers, Sara R, sr ofc spt asst (clerical), $26,232
Rogers, Trish A, cook III, $28,104
Rogers-denham, Kyle J, corrections ofcr I, $30,132
Rohrbach, Melisa D, accounting spec II, $40,380
Roland, David W, corrections ofcr I, $29,652
Roland, Teresa, prob & parole ofcr II, $36,204
Roller, Keith, corrections ofcr I, $31,140
Rollins, Melvin D, cook II, $24,264
Rollins, Nynva N, corrections ofcr II, $31,668
Rollins, Tracy L, corrections ofcr I, $29,652
Rollins, William R, voc enter spv II, $31,512
Romey, Cynthia A, special educ tchr III, $40,380
Romig, Jimmy L, corrections ofcr I, $29,652
Romine, Brett R, prob & parole ofcr I, $31,512
Roney, Jessika P, corrections ofcr I, $29,652
Roney, John E, stationary engr, $33,744
Roney, Sarah E, corrections ofcr I, $29,652
Ronning, Thor D, corrections ofcr I, $29,652
Roodman, Renee, sr ofc spt asst (keybrd), $27,504
Roof, Lacey L, prob & parole ofcr II, $36,204
Rook, Brandon W, corrections ofcr I, $28,692
Rooks, Farrell T, corrections ofcr I, $29,652

Roos, Noal C, corrections case mgr I, $30,984
Roper, Ronald G, corrections ofcr I, $29,652
Rorah, John L, acad tchr III, $39,624
Rose, David W, corrections ofcr I, $28,692
Rose, Tammy L, corrections ofcr I, $28,692
Rose, Tina M, prob & parole ofcr II, $36,204
Rosemann, Jennifer L, ofc spt asst (keybrd), $23,508
Rosenauer, Courtney M, corrections ofcr I, $29,652
Rosenbohm, Elizabeth A, subs abuse cnslr II, $34,944
Rosenbum, Donny R, corrections ofcr I, $29,652
Rosenbum, Sherry L, corrections ofcr II, $31,668
Rosenfield, Robert L, dietitian III, $50,040
Rosinski, David A, corrections ofcr III, $32,628
Ross, Brenda K, admin ofc spt asst, $31,512
Ross, Cody B, corrections spv I, $41,172
Ross, Darren K, corrections ofcr I, $29,652
Ross, Edward A, corrections ofcr II, $33,348
Ross, Erica E, prob & parole ofcr II, $34,944
Ross, Gary L, corrections case mgr II, $34,944
Ross, James L, electronics tech, $31,512
Ross, Kimberly S, corrections case mgr I, $36,888
Ross, Vickie L, prob & parole ofcr II, $38,232
Rost, David E, dpty state dept dir, $99,194
Rost, Vincent E, prob & parole ofcr II, $34,944
Roth, Joy M, corrections ofcr I, $29,652
Roth, Kevin A, corrections classif asst, $33,180
Roth, Mary J, ofc spt asst (keybrd), $23,508
Roth, Oscar R, corrections ofcr III, $38,928
Rothenay, David A, corrections ofcr I, $30,132
Rothlisberger, Kevin W, corrections ofcr I, $32,784
Rothove, Hannah M, ofc spt asst (keybrd), $23,160
Rotter, Michael J, corrections ofcr II, $31,668
Roubik, Martin W, prob & parole ofcr II, $36,204
Rousan, Kevin L, corrections ofcr I, $29,652
Rousan, Patricia F, corrections ofcr III, $33,744
Routh, Bradley R, corrections ofcr I, $29,652
Routh, Joshua D, corrections ofcr I, $28,692
Rowden, Stephanie A, acad tchr II, $29,976
Rowe, Brian M, corrections ofcr I, $29,652
Rowland, Ammiel N, pers clerk, $28,104
Rowland, James E, corrections spv I, $41,172
Rowland, James R, corrections ofcr I, $30,276
Rowland, Tina L, prob & parole ofcr II, $39,624
Rowland, William J, corrections ofcr I, $29,652
Rowles, Charlene R, ofc spt asst (steno), $27,084
Rowlett, Jerry M, corrections ofcr I, $29,652
Rowley, Allen D, prob & parole ofcr II, $41,940
Rowley, Penny M, corrections ofcr I, $30,132
Rowlison, Gwenna J, ofc spt asst (keybrd), $23,160
Royle, Jason B, corrections ofcr II, $31,668
Royster, William J, corrections ofcr I, $29,652
Rozier, Timothy R, corrections ofcr I, $29,652
Ruark, Larry D, corrections ofcr I, $31,140
Rubenstein, Stephanie M, prob & parole ofcr II, $38,928
Rubino, Monica J, corrections ofcr I, $29,652
Rubio, Corey J, corrections ofcr I, $28,692
Ruble, Dan E, corrections ofcr I, $31,140
Ruble, Hazel E, prob & parole ofcr II, $39,624
Ruble, Justin G, prob & parole ofcr II, $36,204
Ruble, Kenneth M, corrections ofcr I, $29,652
Ruble, Yvonne G, ofc spt asst (keybrd), $23,160
Ruby, Cynthia S, corrections ofcr I, $29,652
Ruby, Lesa A, corrections ofcr I, $29,652
Ruch, Richard L, corrections mgr b1, $47,881
Rucker, Andy, corrections ofcr I, $31,140
Rucker, Martin T, board mbr, $84,431
Rudd, Shelly R, corrections ofcr I, $29,652
Rudder, Charles T, prob & parole ofcr II, $36,204
Rueschhoff, John C, acad tchr III, $36,204
Ruessing, Deborah S, cook II, $24,264
Ruffing, David J, stationary engr, $33,744
Ruffino, Nathaniel J, corrections ofcr I, $29,652
Rugado, Austin J, corrections ofcr I, $28,692
Ruiz, Robert, fire & safety spec, $37,548
Rulo, Christopher F, corrections ofcr I, $28,692
Rulo, Mickey L, corrections ofcr I, $29,652
Ruminer, Jody S, factory mgr I, $34,944
Runde, James A, laundry mgr, $35,568
Runde, Logan, prob & parole ofcr II, $36,204
Runnels, Dawn A, prob & parole ofcr II, $36,204
Runyan, James G, boiler oper, $28,104
Runyon, Deanna M, sr ofc spt asst (keybrd), $26,652
Runyon, Joey E, investigator II, $37,548

Ruoff, Cody G, prob & parole ofcr II, $36,204
Ruppel, Bradley P, corrections ofcr I, $29,652
Ruppel, Christopher W, corrections ofcr I, $29,652
Ruppel, Dwan, exec I, $33,180
Ruppel, Edward L, corrections case mgr II, $38,232
Ruppel, Sheilah L, ofc spt asst (keybrd), $25,824
Rus, Cheri L, prob & parole ofcr II, $38,232
Ruselowski, Candance D, cook II, $24,264
Rush, Betty L, corrections ofcr I, $29,652
Rush, Jeffrey L, corrections ofcr I, $29,652
Rush, Shalita, ofc spt asst (keybrd), $23,160
Russell, Angela S, prob & parole ofcr II, $34,944
Russell, Beverly A, cook III, $28,104
Russell, Brit J, prob & parole ofcr II, $36,204
Russell, Darrell W, food serv mgr II, $33,744
Russell, Denny E, maint spv I, $32,628
Russell, James E, corrections ofcr I, $29,652
Russell, James L, corrections ofcr III, $38,928
Russell, Kristi L, storekeeper I, $25,824
Russell, Lilah, prob & parole ofcr II, $36,204
Russell, Lloyd J, corrections ofcr I, $29,652
Russell, Margaret L, corrections ofcr II, $34,512
Russell, Robert S, corrections ofcr I, $29,652
Russell, Terry J, corrections ofcr I, $29,652
Russell, Tye A, cook II, $23,508
Rustemeyer, Andrew C, corrections ofcr I, $33,348
Ruth, Kristine N, prob & parole unit spv, $41,940
Ruth, Mitchell C, stationary engr, $33,744
Rutherford, Rachel D, corrections ofcr I, $28,692
Rutherford, Shirley B, pers clerk, $29,004
Rutling, Sencerity, prob & parole ofcr I, $30,984
Ruzicka, Donald T, board mbr, $84,431
Ryan, Lisa K, corrections ofcr I, $29,652
Ryberg, Heather F, ofc spt asst (keybrd), $23,160
Rybolt, Tammy L, ofc spt asst (keybrd), $23,160
Rydberg, Rylan J, special educ tchr III, $38,928
Ryder, Philip J, corrections ofcr I, $28,692
Ryno, Jerry W, corrections ofcr I, $31,140
Ryno, Mary B, voc tchr II, $34,944
Saale, Michael J, corrections ofcr II, $31,668
Sacca, Pamela J, subs abuse cnslr II, $36,204
Sachse, Adam C, corrections ofcr I, $28,692
Sachse, Jennifer M, corrections mgr b3, $66,438
Sackrey, Brad J, corrections ofcr I, $29,652
Sadler, Keith A, corrections ofcr I, $29,652
Saffold, Roberta M, prob & parole ofcr II, $38,232
Sagastume, Alex A, corrections ofcr I, $28,692
Sailor, Terri L, sr ofc spt asst (keybrd), $25,824
Saine, Todd A, corrections ofcr I, $29,652
Saint, Joseph S, corrections case mgr II, $38,928
Salamone, Anne E, prob & parole ofcr II, $36,204
Salazar, Kayla M, corrections ofcr I, $28,692
Salem, Hesham R, cook III, $28,104
Saliger, Steven D, corrections ofcr I, $29,652
Salisbury, Thomas J, corrections ofcr I, $29,652
Salmons, James R, corrections ofcr I, $29,652
Salsberry, Karl D, corrections ofcr I, $29,652
Salzman, Kacee C, corrections ofcr I, $29,652
Salzman, Robert J, labor spv, $29,412
Salzman, Thomas B, corrections ofcr I, $31,140
Samm, Mark L, corrections case mgr II, $40,380
Samm, Renee J, corrections case mgr III, $40,380
Samm, Todd S, corrections ofcr I, $30,132
Sample, Michael E, corrections ofcr I, $29,652
Sample, Tiffany D, corrections case mgr II, $34,944
Samples, April L, corrections case mgr I, $29,976
Sampsel, Kenneth R, corrections ofcr I, $29,652
Sampson, Joseph T, corrections mgr b2, $49,924
Sams, Ronald C, corrections ofcr I, $29,652
Samson, Meritt E, ofc spt asst (keybrd), $25,404
Samson, Steve R, exec II, $38,232
Samuels, Shirey L, corrections ofcr I, $29,652
Sancegraw, Francis B, corrections ofcr I, $29,652
Sancegraw, Regina M, corrections ofcr I, $29,652
Sand, Rich L, prob & parole ofcr II, $36,888
Sandau, Seth, corrections ofcr I, $28,692
Sandeberg, Michael W, corrections ofcr I, $28,692
Sanders, Aaron N, corrections ofcr I, $29,652
Sanders, Abijah B, prob & parole asst II, $30,420
Sanders, Amy J, prob & parole unit spv, $44,304
Sanders, Christine, corrections case mgr III, $40,380
Sanders, Dustin J, corrections ofcr I, $29,652
Sanders, Kathryn M, ofc spt asst (keybrd), $22,536

Sanders, Margaret M, prob & parole ofcr II, $18,102
Sanders, Paul S, corrections ofcr I, $29,652
Sanders, Vickie L, corrections ofcr I, $29,652
Sandoval, Dennis M, corrections ofcr I, $31,140
Sands, Jennifer L, prob & parole ofcr II, $36,204
Sandy, Darrell D, recrtn ofcr III, $39,624
Sanges, Michelle R, prob & parole ofcr II, $36,204
Sanner, Steven R, storekeeper I, $28,908
Sanning, Laura L, exec II, $34,944
Sansegraw, Zachary A, corrections ofcr I, $29,652
Sanson, David L, corrections ofcr I, $31,140
Sansoucie, Daniel P, maint spv II, $34,944
Sansoucie, David J, corrections ofcr I, $29,652
Sansoucie, Deborah, cook III, $28,104
Sansoucie, Michael E, corrections ofcr I, $28,692
Sansoucie, Ronald L, corrections ofcr I, $29,652
Sansoucie, Shane P, corrections ofcr I, $29,652
Sansoucie, Sharon M, ofc spt asst (keybrd), $26,652
Santhuff, Karen M, prob & parole unit spv, $47,892
Sapp, Brandon M, corrections ofcr I, $29,652
Sapp, David E, corrections ofcr I, $29,652
Sapp, Melissa, prob & parole ofcr II, $34,944
Sapp, Scott D, storekeeper I, $26,232
Sapp, Theresa A, admin ofc spt asst, $28,104
Sappington, James L, corrections ofcr I, $29,652
Sappington, Roberta D, corrections ofcr I, $29,652
Sarchett, Christopher M, prob & parole unit spv, $41,940
Sargent, Adam, corrections ofcr I, $29,652
Satterfield, Jared D, maint worker II, $29,004
Satterfield, Joseph L, corrections case mgr II, $34,944
Satterfield, Melissa A, ofc spt asst (keybrd), $23,160
Satterthwaite, Thomas E, corrections ofcr I, $29,652
Sauberan, Olivia N, corrections ofcr I, $28,692
Saucedo, Alex, corrections ofcr I, $29,652
Sauerbrei, Beverly J, corrections ofcr I, $28,692
Saunders, Connie F, corrections ofcr I, $29,652
Saunders, Jessica D, corrections ofcr I, $28,692
Saunders, Keith A, corrections ofcr I, $30,132
Saunders, Mike R, corrections ofcr III, $33,744
Saunders, Quinten C, corrections ofcr I, $30,276
Savage, David E, corrections spv I, $40,380
Savage, Ellen M, corrections ofcr I, $31,668
Savage, Robert J, corrections case mgr II, $38,928
Saville, Cathy J, corrections ofcr I, $29,652
Savner, Emily Y, cook III, $28,104
Sawyer, Curtland S, corrections ofcr I, $29,652
Sawyer, Nathan T, corrections ofcr I, $29,652
Saxton, Amy T, account clerk II, $25,032
Sayer, Alison L, prob & parole ofcr II, $40,380
Sazonov, Dennis Y, corrections ofcr I, $29,652
Scallion, Kimberly A, corrections case mgr II, $34,944
Scaringello, Michael D, corrections ofcr I, $29,652
Schaefer, Matthew R, corrections ofcr I, $28,692
Schaeffer, Shawn J, cook II, $24,264
Schafer, Eric T, investigator II, $37,548
Schafer, Linda K, storekeeper I, $26,652
Schanzmeyer, Cynthia A, corrections ofcr I, $29,652
Schanzmeyer, Janice V, pers clerk, $33,180
Schanzmeyer, Joseph G, maint spv II, $34,944
Scharbrough, Emily S, prob & parole ofcr III, $38,928
Scharbrough, Fredrick, prob & parole ofcr II, $36,888
Scharff, Evelyn J, corrections ofcr I, $29,652
Schartz, Catherine H, prob & parole ofcr II, $39,624
Schauperl, Mady, voc enter spv II, $33,744
Scheel, Justin L, corrections ofcr II, $30,576
Scheets, Vonda D, special educ tchr III, $37,548
Scheiffele, Linda A, corrections ofcr I, $29,652
Scheldberg, Amy B, subs abuse cnslr II, $34,944
Schenewerk, Charles P, maint spv I, $32,628
Scherder, Gary W, maint worker II, $29,004
Scherder, Jeffrey J, corrections ofcr I, $31,140
Scherder, Kevin F, recrtn ofcr I, $31,512
Scherder, Mary K, ofc spt asst (keybrd), $23,160
Scherer, Cheryl L, corrections mgr b1, $47,033
Scherrer, Natasha M, ofc spt asst (keybrd), $23,160
Scheulen, Leroy W, acct II, $37,548
Scheulen, Melissa A, special asst paraprof, $47,767
Scheulen, William L, corrections ofcr I, $29,652
Schien, David K, corrections ofcr I, $29,652
Schilli, Cynthia A, cook II, $24,264
Schilling, Gina K, corrections ofcr I, $29,652
Schilling, Shirley, acad tchr III, $41,172
Schimming, Clarita J, corrections ofcr I, $29,652

Schimming, Maggie L, corrections ofcr I, $28,692
Schlattman, Lucille A, corrections ofcr I, $29,652
Schlosser, Joseph S, corrections mgr b1, $49,846
Schlottach, Ronald D, corrections ofcr I, $29,652
Schlude, Joseph J, prob & parole ofcr II, $36,204
Schmelz, Herbert L, corrections ofcr I, $29,652
Schmidt, Corey A, corrections ofcr I, $29,652
Schmidt, Jeff, prob & parole ofcr II, $34,944
Schmidt, Louise D, ofc spt asst (steno), $27,084
Schmidt, Stacey L, corrections ofcr I, $29,652
Schmidt, Stacie L, cook II, $25,404
Schmidt, Todd A, corrections ofcr I, $29,652
Schmiedeskamp, Kurt W, voc enter spv II, $31,512
Schmieg, Amber E, ofc spt asst (keybrd), $23,160
Schmieg, Jason J, corrections ofcr I, $29,652
Schmitt, John A, maint spv I, $32,628
Schmitz, Chrystal D, corrections mgr b1, $45,330
Schmitz, Kristy D, ofc spt asst (keybrd), $25,824
Schmitz, Ryan P, cook II, $24,264
Schmutz, Brian C, functional unit mgr corr, $38,928
Schmutz, Randy A, recrtn ofcr II, $37,548
Schmutz, William D, corrections mgr b2, $59,790
Schneedle, John T, corrections ofcr I, $29,652
Schneider, Andrew D, corrections ofcr I, $29,652
Schneider, Joel D, corrections ofcr I, $28,692
Schnepf, Barbara L, prob & parole ofcr II, $40,380
Schnick, William H, corrections ofcr I, $29,652
Schnieders, Kevin M, corrections ofcr I, $29,652
Schoenherr, Jennifer S, prob & parole ofcr II, $36,888
Schoenhofer, Shane M, corrections ofcr I, $29,652
Schoening, Jeffery, corrs id ofcr, $31,512
Schofield, Paul E, corrections ofcr I, $29,652
Schofield, Wayne S, corrections ofcr I, $28,692
Scholl, Denise M, sr ofc spt asst (clerical), $25,824
Scholl, Scott D, corrections ofcr I, $29,652
Schoneboom, Lisa G, corrections case mgr II, $36,888
Schoppe, Derrick P, cook III, $28,104
Schouten, Douglas E, corrections ofcr II, $31,668
Schrader, Adam M, corrections ofcr I, $29,652
Schrader, Steven L, corrections ofcr I, $29,652
Schraft, Donald E, corrections ofcr I, $31,140
Schreck, Adam W, corrections ofcr I, $28,692
Schreck, Dale W, corrections ofcr I, $31,668
Schreck, Susan F, account clerk II, $25,032
Schriefer, Barry L, corrections ofcr I, $29,652
Schrimpf, Gabriel S, corrections ofcr I, $29,652
Schroeder, Derek W, corrections ofcr I, $29,652
Schroeder, Kenneth C, corrections ofcr I, $29,652
Schroeder, Nathan C, prob & parole ofcr II, $36,204
Schroer, James C, corrections ofcr I, $29,652
Schrum, Christopher M, corrections ofcr I, $29,652
Schrum, Kevin S, corrections ofcr I, $29,652
Schubert, Erin, prob & parole ofcr II, $34,944
Schul, Teresa L, prob & parole ofcr II, $36,204
Schulke, Emil W, corrections ofcr I, $29,652
Schulte, Daemian M, storekeeper I, $25,824
Schulte, Jennifer A, admin ofc spt asst, $28,104
Schulte, Judy L, corrections ofcr I, $31,668
Schulte, Marvin L, storekeeper II, $32,052
Schulte, Samantha E, admin ofc spt asst, $28,104
Schultz, Jordon W, corrections ofcr I, $28,692
Schultz, Lora Mae, prob & parole ofcr II, $36,204
Schultz, Ralph A, corrections case mgr II, $34,944
Schultz, Thomas W, corrections case mgr II, $34,944
Schulze, Lisa H, corrections mgr b2, $55,856
Schulze, Ruth A, ofc spt asst (keybrd), $24,612
Schumann, Kenya G, sr ofc spt asst (keybrd), $25,032
Schurman, Marcelle R, ofc spt asst (keybrd), $25,824
Schussler, Daryl W, corrections ofcr I, $28,692
Schuster, Randy S, corrections ofcr I, $29,652
Schutte, Michael D, stationary engr, $33,744
Schwaninger, Linda K, ofc spt asst (keybrd), $23,160
Schwartz, Margaret E, ofc spt asst (keybrd), $23,160
Schwartz, Pamela S, ofc spt asst (keybrd), $23,160
Schwartze, Tina M, sr ofc spt asst (keybrd), $25,824
Schwede, Joan M, exec II, $36,888
Schweder, Carol J, cook II, $24,264
Schweder, Courtney W, corrections spv II, $46,068
Schweder, Tammy L, admin ofc spt asst, $29,976
Schwent, Brian P, cook III, $28,104
Schwent, Todd J, corrections mgr b1, $47,913
Scoon, Gregor A, corrections case mgr II, $34,944
Scott, Ashton, prob & parole ofcr I, $29,976

Scott, Cheryl A, prob & parole ofcr II, $39,624
Scott, Darryl W, corrections ofcr I, $28,692
Scott, David L, corrections classif asst, $31,512
Scott, David M, corrections ofcr I, $29,652
Scott, Doris A, cook II, $27,084
Scott, James R, corrections ofcr I, $29,652
Scott, Jason A, corrections ofcr II, $30,576
Scott, Jimmie D, corrections ofcr I, $30,132
Scott, John E, special asst official & admstr, $71,205
Scott, Julie J, sr ofc spt asst (keybrd), $25,824
Scott, Karen F, cook II, $24,264
Scott, Karen M, corrections ofcr I, $29,652
Scott, Kirk D, corrections ofcr II, $33,900
Scott, Kristi L, ofc spt asst (keybrd), $23,160
Scott, Kyle J, corrections ofcr I, $29,652
Scott, Larry C, corrections case mgr II, $38,232
Scott, Michael W, maint spv I, $32,628
Scott, Tyrel C, corrections mgr b1, $50,790
Scott, William J, corrections ofcr I, $29,652
Scranton, Penny L, corrections ofcr I, $29,652
Scrivner, Donald J, stationary engr, $33,744
Scroggins, Wayne E, corrections ofcr II, $31,668
Scruggs, David W, prob & parole unit spv, $43,488
Scruggs, Laura J, storekeeper II, $28,104
Scurlock, Rebecca L, prob & parole ofcr II, $39,624
Seabaugh, Timothy E, corrections case mgr II, $34,944
Seals, Teresa M, corrections ofcr I, $33,900
Seamon, David W, corrections ofcr I, $33,348
Searcy, Marla K, corrections ofcr I, $31,140
Searles, Richard, cook II, $24,264
Sears, David S, corrections ofcr II, $30,576
Sears, Gary W, maint spv I, $32,628
Sears, Michelle L, prob & parole asst I, $30,984
Sears, Ronald G, corrections ofcr III, $37,548
Seaton, Melanie B, ofc spt asst (clerical), $25,404
Seaton, Michael D, prob & parole ofcr II, $36,204
Seaton, Michelle C, prob & parole ofcr II, $36,204
Sederstrom, Carrie A, corrections case mgr I, $30,984
Sedgwick, Anne K, ofc spt asst (keybrd), $24,264
See, Darin L, voc enter spv II, $30,420
See, David L, corrections ofcr II, $30,576
See, Jason W, corrections ofcr I, $29,652
Seehusen, Steven H, investigator I, $31,512
Seeley, Adam V, corrections ofcr I, $28,692
Seeley, Jeffrey, corrections ofcr III, $38,928
Seeley, Jennifer L, functional unit mgr corr, $38,928
Seever, Cynthia L, corrections ofcr II, $31,668
Seginak, John P, corrections ofcr II, $30,576
Seiger, Melody S, corrections ofcr I, $29,652
Seiller, Wayne J, electronics tech, $31,512
Seipel, Thomas L, corrections mgr b1, $46,935
Seise, Stephanie A, corrections ofcr I, $29,652
Sekoni, Oluropo B, corrections ofcr I, $29,652
Self, Kenney R, corrections ofcr I, $29,652
Selig, Justin, prob & parole ofcr I, $34,944
Sellers, Gary M, corrections spv I, $37,548
Sells, Rickey W, corrections ofcr I, $29,652
Semar, Leslie W, functional unit mgr corr, $43,488
Senor, Erin R, corrections case mgr II, $34,944
Sentman, Brandon S, corrections ofcr I, $29,652
Sentman, Jason L, corrections ofcr I, $29,652
Sepulveda, Carlos W, corrections ofcr I, $29,652
Serviss, Daniel A, corrections ofcr I, $29,652
Settles, Crystal D, corrections ofcr I, $29,652
Settles, Daniel J, corrections ofcr III, $33,744
Severson, Pamela S, cook II, $24,264
Sexton, Jeremy T, corrections ofcr II, $31,668
Sexton, Judy, prob & parole ofcr I, $29,976
Seyler, Melvin L, maint spv I, $32,628
Seymour, Micaela R, ofc spt asst (keybrd), $22,536
Seymour, Robert A, corrections ofcr I, $29,652
Seymour, Ryan M, corrections ofcr I, $29,652
Shackelford, Angela B, corrections ofcr I, $31,140
Shade, Shaun A, corrections ofcr I, $29,652
Shadrick, Donald L, corrections ofcr I, $28,692
Shaeffer, Jason M, corrections ofcr I, $29,652
Shafer, James D, locksmith, $29,976
Shafer, Jerry T, corrections spv I, $39,624
Shafer, Linda K, ofc spt asst (keybrd), $23,160
Shafer, Nancy E, cook III, $28,104
Shaffer, Shelley D, corrections case mgr I, $29,976
Shamily, Gwendolyn D, prob & parole ofcr II, $36,204
Shands, James A, corrections ofcr I, $29,652

Shanefelter, Thomas V, food serv mgr II, $35,568
Shankle, Jennifer L, prob & parole unit spv, $46,068
Shanks, Michael R, corrections ofcr I, $29,652
Shannon, Carol D, prob & parole ofcr II, $41,940
Shannon, Darla A, ofc spt asst (steno), $26,652
Shannon, Marquitte K, corrections case mgr II, $34,944
Sharp, Adron D, corrections ofcr I, $29,652
Sharp, Artisha V, corrections ofcr I, $28,692
Sharp, Bryan K, prob & parole asst I, $30,984
Sharp, Dustin R, corrections ofcr I, $29,652
Sharp, Elonda L, corrections ofcr III, $33,744
Sharp, Gary R, cook III, $28,104
Sharp, James A, factory mgr I, $36,888
Sharp, Stephanie A, prob & parole ofcr II, $38,232
Sharp, Stephanie J, ofc spt asst (keybrd), $11,580
Sharp, Stephanie N, corrections ofcr II, $30,576
Sharp, Tyler, corrections ofcr I, $29,652
Sharp, Vernon E, corrections ofcr I, $34,512
Sharp, Wanda J, corrections ofcr I, $33,900
Sharpes, Richard A, corrections ofcr II, $31,668
Shaver, Jennifer M, corrections ofcr I, $28,692
Shavnore, Brandon E, corrections ofcr I, $29,652
Shavnore, Stephen L, corrections ofcr I, $29,652
Shavnore, Stephen W, supply mgr I, $37,548
Shaw, Christopher E, corrections ofcr III, $33,744
Shaw, Dennis, prob & parole asst II, $36,888
Shaw, Jeremy L, prob & parole asst II, $31,512
Shaw, Mark V, corrections ofcr I, $29,652
Shaw, Terry L, maint spv II, $36,888
Shawgo, Sharon A, ofc spt asst (keybrd), $24,612
Shawver, Sheri L, prob & parole ofcr II, $36,204
Shea, John K, corrections ofcr I, $28,692
Shearin, Bernice D, cook II, $28,104
Shears, Gloria J, ofc spt asst (keybrd), $23,160
Sheehan, Tony L, corrections ofcr I, $30,576
Sheets, Jessica, prob & parole ofcr II, $36,204
Sheets, Sara M, ofc spt asst (keybrd), $23,508
Sheffield, Chasity M, admin ofc spt asst, $28,104
Sheffield, David A, corrections classif asst, $30,420
Shehorn, Kenneth A, corrections ofcr I, $29,652
Sheible, Melinda, ofc spt asst (keybrd), $22,536
Shelby, Jamie J, ofc spt asst (keybrd), $23,160
Shell, Clayton A, corrections ofcr I, $28,692
Shelmadine, Randy A, corrections ofcr I, $29,652
Shelton, Charles G, corrections case mgr II, $36,888
Shelton, Chris C, corrections ofcr I, $29,652
Shelton, Christy D, acad tchr III, $37,548
Shelton, Jason R, tractor trailer driver, $30,984
Shelton, Shanna N, corrections ofcr I, $29,652
Shelton, Tamara E, prob & parole ofcr II, $38,232
Shepard, Eric, recrtn ofcr I, $31,512
Sheperd, Stephanie A, corrections case mgr III, $37,548
Shepherd, Angela M, cook II, $23,508
Shepherd, Cynthia L, admin ofc spt asst, $28,104
Shepherd, Dennis W, factory mgr II, $38,928
Shepherd, Michael D, recrtn ofcr I, $31,512
Shepherd, Paige L, corrections ofcr I, $29,652
Shepherd, Terry R, corrections ofcr I, $31,140
Shepherd, Tina M, ofc spt asst (keybrd), $23,160
Sherer, Dena L, corrections ofcr I, $31,140
Sherer, Rebecca D, corrections ofcr III, $36,204
Sherman, Brett A, corrections ofcr I, $28,692
Sherman, Canessa A, prob & parole asst II, $31,512
Sherman, Edward P, factory mgr I, $34,944
Sherman, Mitchell T, corrections ofcr I, $29,652
Sherman, Richard, maint spv II, $38,928
Sherman, Robbert, functional unit mgr corr, $45,156
Sherrill, Charles D, maint spv I, $32,628
Sherrod, Lelonda, prob & parole unit spv, $42,708
Sherwood, Donald P, corrections ofcr I, $29,652
Sherwood, Traycie, prob & parole ofcr II, $36,888
Sherzad, Sardar A, med technologist II, $34,944
Shewell, Kristi D, ofc spt asst (keybrd), $23,160
Shewmaker, Brian G, maint worker II, $29,004
Shewmaker, Michael S, corrections spv I, $36,204
Shiflett, Daniel E, corrections ofcr I, $29,652
Shiflett, Jay A, corrections ofcr I, $31,140
Shilling, William A, prob & parole asst I, $29,496
Shine, Tiffany J, corrections ofcr I, $28,692
Shinkle, Amanda, prob & parole ofcr II, $36,204
Shipley, Deanna M, corrections ofcr I, $29,652
Shipley, John R, corrections ofcr II, $33,348
Shipley, Martha J, corrections ofcr I, $30,132

Shipley, Sharon A, storekeeper II, $28,104
Shipley, Zachary A, corrections ofcr I, $28,692
Shipman, John A, corrections spv II, $51,096
Shipman, Samuel L, corrections ofcr I, $31,668
Shirk, Nathaniel W, corrections ofcr I, $28,692
Shirrell, Jerry K, prob & parole ofcr II, $40,380
Shirrell, Teresa K, corrections mgr b2, $47,559
Shively, Charles J, corrections ofcr I, $29,652
Shively, Daniel R, corrections spv I, $39,624
Shively, Shelly L, corrections ofcr I, $32,784
Shobe, Victor, corrections ofcr I, $29,652
Shockey, Zachary W, corrections ofcr I, $29,652
Shockley, Bruce E, corrections training ofcr, $41,940
Shockley, James L, corrections case mgr II, $38,232
Shockley, Matthew R, corrections ofcr I, $29,652
Shoemaker, Robert E, corrections ofcr I, $29,652
Shoemate, Steven L, corrections ofcr I, $29,652
Shoemyer, William J, garage spv, $34,356
Shook, Joseph M, corrections ofcr I, $29,652
Shores, Deborah K, cook II, $24,264
Short, Brenda S, corrections mgr b2, $52,741
Short, Matthew E, corrections case mgr II, $33,744
Shoults, Andrew L, corrections ofcr I, $29,652
Shoults, Brandon M, corrections ofcr I, $29,652
Shoults, Mary A, corrections classif asst, $31,512
Showers, Beth A, prob & parole ofcr II, $36,204
Shrewsbury, John C, labor spv, $26,652
Shrewsbury, Megan K, corrections case mgr I, $29,976
Shrewsbury, Todd A, prob & parole ofcr II, $39,624
Shriner, Gary A, tractor trailer driver, $30,984
Shryock, Barbara A, inst activity coor, $29,976
Shryock, Michael W, corrections ofcr I, $29,652
Shuck, Dewella A, corrections ofcr I, $29,652
Shull, William R, corrections ofcr I, $29,652
Shutt, Sandra L, corrections ofcr I, $34,512
Shy, Damon, prob & parole ofcr I, $29,976
Sibley, Jamie E, ofc spt asst (clerical), $22,536
Siciliani, Joseph R, corrections ofcr I, $29,652
Siebeneck, Timothy W, acad tchr III, $37,548
Siefkas, Michael S, corrections ofcr I, $29,652
Siegel, Michelle A, prob & parole ofcr II, $40,380
Siegler, Bryan K, corrections ofcr I, $29,652
Siela, Brian M, corrections ofcr I, $29,652
Sievers, Connie M, prob & parole ofcr II, $41,940
Sifford, William E, prob & parole unit spv, $43,488
Sigman, Barry L, corrections ofcr III, $34,356
Sigman, Trevor D, corrections ofcr I, $29,652
Sikes, Corey K, corrections ofcr I, $29,652
Sikoutris, Dena, special asst prof, $62,317
Siliven, Karen D, corrections ofcr I, $29,652
Siliven, Michael D, corrections ofcr I, $29,652
Silkett, Lionors A, prob & parole ofcr II, $37,548
Silkwood, Cathryn P, ofc spt asst (keybrd), $23,160
Silver, Jericks E, corrections ofcr II, $31,668
Silver, Terry E, corrections ofcr II, $33,348
Silvey, Judith A, corrections ofcr I, $29,652
Silvey, Steve D, stationary engr, $33,744
Simar, Anne M, corrections ofcr I, $33,348
Simar, David J, corrections ofcr I, $29,652
Simmerly, Diana L, functional unit mgr corr, $38,928
Simmers, Paula R, corrections ofcr I, $29,652
Simmons, Alice M, sr ofc spt asst (clerical), $25,824
Simmons, Amanda J, cook II, $24,264
Simmons, Anthony B, supply mgr I, $32,628
Simmons, Billy J, voc enter spv II, $29,976
Simmons, Brandi D, corrections ofcr I, $29,652
Simmons, Brice W, corrections case mgr I, $30,984
Simmons, Charles M, corrections ofcr I, $29,652
Simmons, Justin, corrections ofcr I, $29,652
Simmons, Kimberly D, corrections case mgr II, $34,944
Simmons, Latrese R, prob & parole ofcr II, $38,232
Simmons, Steven W, corrections spv II, $47,892
Simmons, Tonya E, corrections ofcr I, $29,652
Simmons, Willie J, corrections ofcr I, $28,692
Simpson, David L, corrections ofcr I, $29,652
Simpson, David S, corrections ofcr I, $29,652
Simpson, Gayle L, corrections ofcr I, $29,652
Simpson, John A, corrections ofcr I, $31,140
Simpson, Justin L, corrections case mgr I, $30,420
Simpson, Kenneth L, recrtn ofcr III, $43,488
Simpson, Myla J, ofc spt asst (keybrd), $24,612
Simpson, Shona D, inst activity coor, $31,512
Simpson, Sonja L, industries sup, $27,228

Simpson, Tryxie M, ofc spt asst (clerical), $21,864
Sims, Grace A, ofc spt asst (keybrd), $23,160
Sims, Jennifer L, subs abuse cnslr II, $33,744
Sims, Kristina K, corrections ofcr I, $29,652
Sims, Loral N, recrtn ofcr I, $29,976
Sims, Seth E, corrections ofcr I, $29,652
Sims, Vanessa, corrections ofcr I, $29,652
Since, Billie J, corrections ofcr I, $29,652
Since, Roger L, special educ tchr III, $38,928
Since, Ryan J, corrections spv I, $37,548
Sinden, Charles D, corrections ofcr I, $28,692
Singleton, Audrey N, prob & parole ofcr II, $36,204
Singleton, John D, corrections ofcr I, $29,652
Singleton, Mathew, corrections ofcr I, $28,692
Singleton, Terkesha C, prob & parole ofcr II, $36,204
Sipi, Sondra H, corrections ofcr I, $29,652
Sirmons, Marty, corrections mgr b2, $49,937
Sirois, Nancy J, cook II, $24,264
Sisk, Corey, corrections ofcr I, $31,668
Sisson, Donald R, storekeeper, $15.05/hr
Sitzes, Michael E, maint spv II, $33,744
Sitzes, Shawntay L, prob & parole ofcr II, $36,204
Skaggs, Christopher O, corrections case mgr II, $34,944
Skaggs, Douglas L, recrtn ofcr I, $34,964
Skaggs, Lance E, corrections ofcr I, $29,652
Skaggs, Mark L, corrections ofcr II, $32,220
Skaggs, Nicholas D, corrections ofcr I, $29,652
Skaggs, Richard, recrtn ofcr III, $37,548
Skaggs, Robert M, power plant mech, $30,984
Skaggs, Tiffany J, ofc spt asst (keybrd), $22,536
Skeen, Melvin J, chaplain, $34,356
Skeene, Stephanie M, corrections ofcr I, $29,652
Skelton, Patricia M, ofc spt asst (keybrd), $23,880
Skiles, Andrew J, corrections ofcr I, $28,692
Skiles, Bryan, investigator I, $33,180
Skiles, Chad E, maint spv I, $35,568
Skiles, Christopher L, corrections ofcr I, $28,692
Skiles, Marvin F, labor spv, $26,652
Skiles, Shirley J, corrections ofcr I, $29,652
Skinner, Wendy H, prob & parole ofcr II, $38,232
Skipper, Robbie W, labor spv, $26,652
Skjeveland, Beth E, prob & parole ofcr II, $39,624
Skornia, Jane, prob & parole ofcr II, $36,204
Skouby, Robert D, corrections ofcr I, $33,900
Slack, Jeffrey L, corrections ofcr I, $33,348
Slack, Karen M, subs abuse cnslr II, $33,744
Slankard, Karen K, corrections ofcr I, $29,652
Slape, James L, corrections ofcr I, $28,692
Slape, Lawrence R, corrections ofcr III, $31,668
Slater, Nina J, corrections ofcr I, $29,652
Slates, Lisa D, ofc spt asst (keybrd), $23,160
Sliger, Jeremy, corrections ofcr I, $29,652
Slinkard, Dewayne T, storekeeper II, $28,536
Sloan, Chanta, ofc spt asst (keybrd), $23,160
Sloan, Danny S, corrections case mgr II, $36,888
Sloan, Glenda L, corrections ofcr I, $29,652
Sloan, Ira M, maint spv I, $32,628
Sloan, Jere S, corrections ofcr III, $35,568
Sloan, Tonya L, storekeeper I, $25,824
Sloan, Tyler, prob & parole ofcr II, $36,204
Sloat, Codey W, corrections ofcr I, $28,692
Slote, Michael D, corrections ofcr I, $31,140
Slote, Ray W, corrections ofcr I, $29,652
Slovensky, Cyrus W, corrections ofcr I, $28,692
Slugantz, Kristie M, corrections training ofcr, $46,068
Sluis, Peter S, corrections ofcr I, $29,652
Smail, Phillip E, corrections ofcr III, $33,744
Smallen, Lonnie K, corrections case mgr II, $34,944
Smallen, Matthew B, corrections ofcr I, $29,652
Smalley, Janice R, ofc spt asst (keybrd), $23,160
Smallwood, Michael L, corrections ofcr I, $29,652
Smallwood, Ronald D, prob & parole ofcr II, $36,204
Smetzer, Nicholas S, corrections ofcr I, $29,652
Smit, Wade A, corrections ofcr II, $31,668
Smith, Aaron J, corrections ofcr I, $29,652
Smith, Albert L, corrections ofcr I, $29,652
Smith, Alicia M, prob & parole ofcr II, $39,624
Smith, Andrea K, ofc spt asst (keybrd), $23,160
Smith, Andrew L, corrections ofcr I, $28,692
Smith, Barry W, corrections ofcr III, $38,232
Smith, Blaine R, functional unit mgr corr, $37,548
Smith, Bradley D, voc tchr I, $29,976
Smith, Bradley J, corrections ofcr I, $28,692

Smith, Bradley L, corrections ofcr III, $33,744
Smith, Branden C, corrections ofcr II, $30,576
Smith, Brandon M, corrections ofcr I, $29,652
Smith, Buck E, corrections ofcr III, $34,356
Smith, Carl M, corrections ofcr I, $34,512
Smith, Chad A, corrections ofcr I, $28,692
Smith, Chad D, corrections mgr b1, $47,876
Smith, Chantelle M, prob & parole unit spv, $41,940
Smith, Charlene E, ofc spt asst (keybrd), $22,536
Smith, Charles J, corrections ofcr II, $35,724
Smith, Christina L, corrections ofcr I, $29,652
Smith, Christopher E, corrections ofcr I, $29,652
Smith, Christopher L, corrections ofcr I, $29,652
Smith, Chrystala J, corrections ofcr I, $30,276
Smith, Cindy D, special asst prof, $39,624
Smith, Clifford A, corrections ofcr I, $29,652
Smith, Cody D, maint worker II, $29,004
Smith, Cory L, corrections ofcr I, $29,652
Smith, Courtney L, prob & parole ofcr II, $36,204
Smith, Dana L, prob & parole ofcr II, $38,232
Smith, Daniel B, corrections ofcr I, $29,652
Smith, Daniel E, factory mgr II, $41,172
Smith, Daniel J, corrections ofcr I, $29,652
Smith, Danielle, prob & parole asst I, $29,496
Smith, Darlene A, corrections mgr b2, $58,897
Smith, David A, corrections ofcr I, $29,652
Smith, Debra A, ofc spt asst (keybrd), $23,160
Smith, Debra L, ofc spt asst (keybrd), $23,880
Smith, Dennis J, corrections ofcr II, $31,668
Smith, Douglas M, corrections ofcr III, $38,928
Smith, Dustin L, corrections ofcr I, $29,652
Smith, Edward J, corrections ofcr I, $29,652
Smith, Elizabeth A, corrections ofcr I, $29,652
Smith, Elizabeth A, corrections training ofcr, $38,928
Smith, Erikka, prob & parole ofcr II, $36,204
Smith, Gary R, corrections ofcr I, $29,652
Smith, Gregory J, corrections ofcr II, $30,576
Smith, Hannah A, prob & parole ofcr II, $34,944
Smith, Jacob T, corrections ofcr I, $29,652
Smith, Jadyn P, corrections ofcr I, $29,652
Smith, James D, corrections ofcr I, $29,652
Smith, James E, recrtn ofcr I, $31,512
Smith, James E, corrections ofcr II, $31,668
Smith, Jason B, corrections ofcr I, $28,692
Smith, Jeffrey J, corrections ofcr I, $29,652
Smith, Jennifer A, corrections training ofcr, $38,232
Smith, Jennifer L, cook II, $23,508
Smith, Jeremy D, corrections ofcr I, $29,652
Smith, John C, corrections mgr b1, $42,368
Smith, John E, corrections ofcr I, $29,652
Smith, Jonathan N, corrections ofcr I, $29,652
Smith, Joseph K, corrections ofcr I, $29,652
Smith, Joseph L, corrections ofcr I, $28,692
Smith, Julie A, corrections case mgr II, $34,944
Smith, Karen A, corrections ofcr I, $29,652
Smith, Kenneth R, cook II, $24,264
Smith, Kevin, prob & parole ofcr II, $20,586
Smith, Kevin W, corrections case mgr II, $34,944
Smith, Kimberly S, ofc spt asst (keybrd), $23,160
Smith, Kristopher M, corrections ofcr I, $29,652
Smith, Kyle A, corrections ofcr I, $28,692
Smith, Leigh S, prob & parole ofcr II, $34,944
Smith, Leland T, corrections mgr b1, $53,196
Smith, Lesi G, corrections case mgr II, $34,944
Smith, Linda Y, corrections ofcr I, $29,652
Smith, Lindy R, ofc spt asst (keybrd), $23,160
Smith, Lisa A, corrections recs ofcr I, $28,104
Smith, Lisa G, cook II, $24,264
Smith, Lori E, ofc spt asst (keybrd), $22,536
Smith, Lori L, prob & parole ofcr II, $36,204
Smith, Marcia, research analyst II, $36,204
Smith, Marie C, cook III, $28,104
Smith, Mark A, prob & parole ofcr II, $36,888
Smith, Michelle N, prob & parole ofcr II, $36,204
Smith, Mona, prob & parole ofcr II, $41,172
Smith, Nathan E, corrections ofcr I, $29,652
Smith, Neona D, ofc spt asst (steno), $25,824
Smith, Pari M, prob & parole unit spv, $41,940
Smith, Paula D, prob & parole asst I, $31,512
Smith, Rebecca L, corrections ofcr I, $29,652
Smith, Richard J, corrections ofcr I, $28,692
Smith, Robbin D, cook II, $24,264
Smith, Robert L, maint worker II, $29,004

Smith, Robert L, corrections ofcr I, $29,652
Smith, Roberta L, ofc spt asst (keybrd), $23,160
Smith, Rodney E, fire & safety spec, $30,984
Smith, Roger W, corrections ofcr I, $29,652
Smith, Ronald E, corrections ofcr I, $29,652
Smith, Ronald W, corrections ofcr I, $29,652
Smith, Ronda K, sr ofc spt asst (keybrd), $25,824
Smith, Roy L, corrections ofcr I, $29,652
Smith, Russell L, corrections ofcr II, $31,668
Smith, Sarah B, parole hearing analyst, $50,040
Smith, Sharon A, prob & parole ofcr II, $39,624
Smith, Sheila M, corrections case mgr II, $36,204
Smith, Shereda S, corrections mgr b1, $47,393
Smith, Staci S, functional unit mgr corr, $38,928
Smith, Stephen M, prob & parole ofcr II, $36,204
Smith, Steven K, prob & parole unit spv, $41,940
Smith, Ted B, tractor trailer driver, $30,984
Smith, Teresa L, supply mgr I, $33,744
Smith, Timothy A, subs abuse cnslr II, $34,944
Smith, Tina D, corrections ofcr I, $30,132
Smith, Tyler G, corrections ofcr I, $29,652
Smith, Victoria J, ofc spt asst (keybrd), $25,824
Smith, Zachary D, corrections ofcr I, $28,692
Smithey, Dominga, ofc spt asst (keybrd), $22,536
Smith-Webster, Kenisha L, prob & parole ofcr II, $36,204
Smody, Sonya E, corrections ofcr I, $28,692
Smothers, Kelly L, prob & parole ofcr II, $36,204
Smyser, David W, corrections ofcr I, $31,140
Smyser, Treva J, corrections ofcr I, $29,652
Smyth, Colin N, corrections mgr b1, $46,926
Smyth, Kelley D, prob & parole unit spv, $44,304
Snapp, Leah M, corrections ofcr I, $29,652
Snapp, Pattie G, prob & parole ofcr II, $38,232
Snavely, Joshua P, cook II, $23,508
Sneed, Robert W, corrections ofcr II, $31,668
Sneed, Teresa A, corrections ofcr I, $29,652
Snellen, Darren J, investigator I, $31,512
Snelling, Josef D, corrections ofcr I, $29,652
Snider, Anthony D, corrs id ofcr, $31,512
Snider, Chase S, corrections ofcr I, $28,692
Snider, Floyd D, corrections ofcr I, $29,652
Snider, Jo Ann, prob & parole ofcr II, $39,624
Snider, Theresa L, corrections ofcr I, $29,652
Snoderly, Michael D, corrections ofcr I, $31,140
Snodgrass, Norman A, corrections ofcr II, $31,668
Snow, Cari S, ofc spt asst (keybrd), $23,160
Snow, Michael J, corrections ofcr I, $29,652
Snow, Rachel A, corrections ofcr I, $29,652
Snow, Robert E, corrections ofcr I, $29,652
Snow, Samantha E, subs abuse cnslr I, $29,976
Snow, Terry W, corrections ofcr I, $30,132
Snyder, Bernie, corrections ofcr I, $29,652
Snyder, John M, factory mgr II, $38,928
Snyder, Kelsey J, corrections ofcr I, $29,652
Snyder, Timothy M, corrections ofcr I, $29,652
Snyder, William D, corrections ofcr I, $29,652
Soden, Michael A, corrections ofcr I, $31,140
Sodomka, Dean C, voc tchr III, $37,548
Soldan, Lisa, ofc spt asst (clerical), $22,536
Sollars, Stephanie, prob & parole ofcr II, $36,204
Solomon, Marla D, prob & parole ofcr II, $36,888
Somers, Michael W, corrections ofcr II, $30,576
Somerville, Kevin W, corrections ofcr I, $29,652
Somerville, Peggy M, corrections ofcr I, $29,652
Sommerfeld, Jack W, corrections ofcr I, $29,652
Soncrant, David L, corrections ofcr I, $29,652
Sorenson, Ronald L, corrections ofcr I, $29,652
Soto, Eric A, corrections ofcr I, $28,692
Souders, Connie J, corrections ofcr II, $32,220
South, Carl M, tractor trailer driver, $33,744
Southard, Eric L, corrections ofcr I, $29,652
Southers, Bonieta J, corrections ofcr I, $29,652
Sovanski, Dawn A, edu sup, $45,156
Sowards, Jr, recrtn ofcr II, $33,744
Sowards, Sheila J, corrections ofcr I, $31,668
Sowers, Kevin S, prob & parole ofcr II, $36,204
Spackler, Chelsea A, training tech II, $41,172
Spackler, Richard H, corrections mgr b3, $62,081
Spainhour-George, Christina M, storekeeper I, $28,908
Spalding, Cary S, corrections ofcr I, $29,652
Spalding, Jane A, functional unit mgr corr, $41,172
Sparks, Eugene E, corrections ofcr I, $29,652
Sparks, Janet V, corrections ofcr II, $31,668

Sparks, Jason S, corrections ofcr I, $28,692
Sparks, Valorie J, corrections mgr b1, $46,519
Sparrow, Nicole M, prob & parole ofcr II, $36,204
Speagle, Roxane M, functional unit mgr corr, $38,928
Spear, Shana M, account clerk II, $25,824
Spears, Melissa M, corrections ofcr I, $28,692
Spears, Steven W, phys plant sup I, $41,172
Spease, Cody M, corrections ofcr I, $29,652
Speck, Gary L, voc tchr III, $37,548
Speckhals, Christine A, corrections mgr b1, $48,809
Speed, Chara M, investigator I, $31,512
Speed, Patricia A, corrections ofcr I, $33,348
Spegal, Daniel M, phys plant sup III, $46,068
Spegal, Sherry L, corrections ofcr I, $29,652
Speidel, Jennifer L, corrections ofcr I, $29,652
Spence, Jared L, prob & parole ofcr II, $38,232
Spence, Joseph S, prob & parole ofcr II, $36,204
Spencer, Carrie E, ofc spt asst (keybrd), $23,160
Spencer, Darcey M, librarian I, $29,004
Spencer, Darla K, corrections recs ofcr III, $36,204
Spencer, David K, corrections ofcr I, $29,652
Spencer, Mary A, maint worker II, $28,104
Spencer, Matthew L, corrections ofcr II, $31,668
Spencer, Tracy L, ofc spt asst (keybrd), $23,880
Sperry, Alison G, ofc spt asst (keybrd), $23,160
Sperry, Christopher W, corrections ofcr I, $29,652
Spicer, Elton L, corrections ofcr I, $29,652
Spicer, Theresa M, corrections ofcr I, $28,692
Spickard, Thomas C, corrections ofcr I, $29,652
Spies, Virginia L, prob & parole ofcr II, $40,380
Spillars, Debbie J, corrections ofcr I, $31,140
Spiniolas, Gerald C, corrections spv I, $37,548
Spinka, Christine M, research analyst IV, $45,156
Spire, Jennifer L, corrections ofcr I, $29,652
Spire, Ryan A, corrections ofcr I, $29,652
Spitzer, Kevin E, corrections ofcr I, $29,652
Spitzmiller, Stephen A, corrections ofcr I, $29,652
Spivey, John P, corrections ofcr I, $29,652
Splain, Crystal L, ofc spt asst (keybrd), $23,160
Spoo, Harry A, corrections ofcr II, $31,668
Spooner, Chelsi L, ofc spt asst (keybrd), $23,160
Spooner, Ronda, ofc spt asst (keybrd), $23,160
Spor, Lisa L, corrections ofcr I, $29,652
Spradley, Courtney A, ofc spt asst (clerical), $22,536
Spradlin, Daniel B, corrections ofcr I, $28,692
Spradling, Jonathan M, corrections ofcr I, $29,652
Sprague, Donald R, maint spv I, $31,512
Sprague, Jesse W, corrections ofcr I, $29,652
Spree, Jean E, ofc spt asst (keybrd), $23,160
Spriggs, Emily, prob & parole ofcr I, $29,976
Spring, Daniel D, prob & parole ofcr II, $39,624
Springborn, Kayla J, corrections ofcr I, $29,652
Springborn, Sean D, corrections ofcr I, $29,652
Springer, Thomas E, stationary engr, $35,568
Sprofera, Anthony C, corrections ofcr I, $29,652
Sprofera, Elnora L, ofc spt asst (keybrd), $26,232
Sprous, Larry E, corrections ofcr I, $29,652
Sprouse, Mark S, corrections ofcr I, $28,692
Spurgeon, Sherri C, corrections ofcr II, $31,668
Spurgin, Amy L, subs abuse cnslr I, $29,976
Spurgin, Christopher J, maint spv II, $34,944
Spurr, Stephen P, corrections ofcr I, $29,652
St. John, Mark A, corrections case mgr II, $39,624
Staab, Carissa M, prob & parole ofcr II, $36,204
Staats, Danielle R, prob & parole ofcr II, $36,204
Stacy, Brad L, corrections ofcr I, $33,348
Stadt, Claire R, corrections case mgr II, $34,944
Stafford, Charles W, maint spv I, $34,356
Stafford, Mark, corrections ofcr I, $31,668
Stafford, Patricia K, corrections ofcr I, $29,652
Stafford, Robert L, corrections ofcr I, $29,652
Stafford, Ronald K, corrections ofcr I, $29,652
Stafford, Troy E, corrections ofcr I, $29,652
Staggs, Susan L, prob & parole ofcr II, $36,204
Stagner, Matthew W, corrections ofcr I, $29,652
Stahl, Dustin M, corrections ofcr I, $29,652
Stahlhuth, Rebekah, ofc spt asst (keybrd), $23,160
Staley, Carla J, corrections mgr b1, $50,759
Stallbories, Ronald V, corrections ofcr I, $28,692
Stallings, Regina, ofc spt asst (keybrd), $23,160
Stallman, Donald W, maint worker II, $31,512
Stallsworth, Devin L, corrections ofcr I, $28,692
Stalter, Mark A, recrtn ofcr II, $36,204

Stamper, Ashley E, corrections ofcr I, $28,692
Stamper, James W, corrections ofcr I, $29,652
Standiford, Christina A, corrections ofcr I, $29,652
Standiford, Dylan M, corrections ofcr I, $28,692
Stange, William R, corrections mgr b2, $54,833
Stanifer, Bradley R, fire & safety spec, $30,984
Stanley, Brian L, corrections ofcr I, $29,652
Stanley, Christina L, prob & parole ofcr II, $36,204
Stanley, Dawn, prob & parole ofcr II, $38,928
Stanley, Kevin O, corrections ofcr I, $29,652
Stanley, Michael R, corrections ofcr I, $29,652
Stansbury, Steve R, factory mgr II, $38,928
Stanton, Clay M, corrections spv I, $38,232
Stark, Brenda J, sr ofc spt asst (keybrd), $29,412
Stark, Cary M, corrections ofcr I, $29,652
Stark, Christopher W, corrections ofcr II, $35,724
Stark, Cody W, corrections ofcr I, $29,652
Stark, Della, account clerk II, $25,824
Stark, Jamie M, corrections classif asst, $31,512
Stark, Shea E, corrections ofcr I, $29,652
Stark, Wilma G, corrections ofcr I, $29,652
Starke, Julia J, ofc spt asst (keybrd), $23,160
Starkey, Aaron T, prob & parole asst I, $29,496
Starkey, Jodi R, prob & parole ofcr II, $36,204
Starling, Linda F, corrections case mgr II, $34,944
Starner, Andrew P, prob & parole ofcr II, $39,624
Stathem, Patricia L, corrections case mgr II, $34,944
Staton, Shelley C, inst activity coor, $33,180
Stayton, Loretta L, corrections ofcr I, $31,668
Stearley, Christopher M, corrections ofcr I, $29,652
Stearns, Annette, sr ofc spt asst (keybrd), $25,824
Steel, Jason A, corrections ofcr I, $29,652
Steele, Judy A, ofc spt asst (keybrd), $23,160
Steele, Lamontria L, sr ofc spt asst (keybrd), $27,948
Steele, Roy M, corrections ofcr I, $31,668
Steele, Troy L, corrections mgr b3, $71,205
Steen, Carrie R, research analyst III, $40,380
Steffen, Kristie A, corrections ofcr I, $29,652
Stegall, Gregory S, corrections ofcr I, $29,652
Stegall, Norman D, corrections case mgr III, $43,488
Stegall, Steven K, recrtn ofcr I, $30,984
Steger, Charles J, corrections ofcr I, $29,652
Steger, Robert W, corrections ofcr I, $28,692
Stein, Jana L, corrections ofcr I, $29,652
Stein, Loretta L, corrections ofcr I, $29,661
Stein, Stephanie S, prob & parole ofcr II, $41,172
Steinbeck, Lisa M, prob & parole ofcr II, $40,380
Steinmetz, Joseph P, maint worker II, $29,004
Steitz, Mark A, prob & parole ofcr II, $36,204
Stell, Tamara L, corrections case mgr II, $36,204
Stemmler, Brenda J, acad tchr III, $37,548
Stengel, Leroy C, corrections ofcr I, $29,652
Stenhoff, Dennis L, corrections ofcr I, $29,652
Stepanek, Richard H, corrections mgr b2, $47,568
Stephan, Marilyn K, ofc spt asst (keybrd), $23,160
Stephan, Ronald W, corrections ofcr I, $29,652
Stephens, Bruce C, functional unit mgr corr, $43,488
Stephens, Jennifer M, corrections ofcr I, $29,652
Stephens, Mark C, corrections training ofcr, $45,156
Stephens, Monika R, ofc spt asst (keybrd), $23,160
Stephens, Scott C, power plant mech, $30,984
Stephens, Zachary S, corrections ofcr I, $29,652
Stephenson, Kimberly E, ofc spt asst (keybrd), $23,880
Stephenson, Lynette R, corrections ofcr I, $30,132
Stephenson, Robert D, voc enter spv II, $33,744
Stepleton, Bethany B, acad tchr III, $37,548
Stepp, James C, corrections ofcr I, $29,652
Sterling, Heather A, corrections ofcr I, $29,652
Sternberg, Paul E, supply mgr I, $32,628
Sterzinger, Trevor L, corrections ofcr I, $29,652
Stetina, Amy L, special educ tchr I, $29,976
Stetina, Christopher J, corrections ofcr I, $30,132
Steuber, Cynthia L, corrections mgr b2, $55,957
Stevener, Robert G, locksmith, $30,984
Stevens, Christy L, inst activity coor, $31,512
Stevens, Crystal D, corrections ofcr I, $28,692
Stevens, Denny A, corrections ofcr II, $31,668
Stevens, Holly J, corrections ofcr II, $30,576
Stevens, James B, corrections ofcr I, $29,652
Stevens, Stuart A, corrections ofcr I, $29,652
Stevens, Vicki L, sr ofc spt asst (keybrd), $25,824
Stevenson, Charles E, prob & parole ofcr II, $36,204
Stevenson, David L, prob & parole ofcr II, $36,204

Stevenson, Robert T, corrections ofcr I, $29,652
Stever, Alice, special asst technician, $43,935
Steward, Crystal N, corrections ofcr I, $30,576
Steward, Rhonda F, pers clerk, $29,496
Steward, Scotty D, storekeeper II, $28,536
Stewart, Brenda D, corrections ofcr I, $29,652
Stewart, Donald. N, corrections ofcr II, $31,668
Stewart, Floyd D, corrections ofcr I, $29,652
Stewart, Gary L, corrections ofcr I, $31,140
Stewart, Jacob R, corrections ofcr I, $29,652
Stewart, Kathleen E, corrections case mgr II, $34,944
Stewart, Keith M, corrections ofcr I, $29,652
Stewart, Mary B, corrections mgr b1, $49,735
Stewart, Melissa D, prob & parole unit spv, $41,940
Stickney, Charles D, corrections ofcr I, $31,140
Stidham, Timothy W, corrections ofcr I, $29,652
Stieferman, Dennis A, maint spv I, $37,548
Stieferman, Judith E, ofc spt asst (keybrd), $23,160
Stiens, Diana J, ofc spt asst (keybrd), $23,160
Stiens, Mark A, prob & parole ofcr II, $41,172
Stiers, Mattie C, corrections ofcr II, $33,348
Stierwalt, Kurt A, prob & parole ofcr II, $39,624
Stigall, Jeffrey D, cook II, $24,264
Stigall, Rhonda G, storekeeper II, $27,084
Still, Curtis D, corrections ofcr III, $36,204
Still, Jessica R, corrections case mgr II, $34,944
Still, Jimmie L, maint worker II, $29,004
Still, Joyce A, prob & parole ofcr II, $43,488
Still, Kristi M, ofc spt asst (keybrd), $23,160
Stillwell, Christina M, corrections ofcr I, $29,652
Stimpson, Harold E, corrections ofcr I, $31,140
Stimpson, Jason S, maint spv II, $34,944
Stinnett, Alicia A, cook II, $23,508
Stinnett, Deborah L, corrections ofcr I, $29,661
Stinnett, Gayla J, storekeeper I, $25,824
Stith, Amanda B, pers clerk, $28,104
Stith, Bernis D, corrections ofcr I, $32,784
Stith, Christopher M, corrections ofcr I, $33,900
Stith, Donald D, corrections ofcr III, $33,744
Stith, John T, corrections ofcr I, $29,652
Stith, Leslie D, corrections ofcr III, $33,744
Stith, Tammy L, supply mgr I, $33,744
Stithem, Douglas C, corrections ofcr I, $29,652
Stock, Louis S, corrections ofcr I, $29,652
Stock, Tracy E, corrections ofcr I, $28,692
Stockdale, Cassie R, corrections ofcr II, $31,668
Stockhausen, Robert M, corrections ofcr I, $29,652
Stockton, Frederick J, corrections ofcr III, $35,568
Stockton, Grant E, inst activity coor, $29,976
Stockton, Larry, prob & parole ofcr I, $30,984
Stockwell, Edward L, corrections ofcr I, $31,668
Stoecklein, Andrew J, acct I, $31,512
Stoehr, Mark D, corrections training ofcr, $41,172
Stokes, Sarah R, investigator I, $29,976
Stoll, Gary J, fiscal & administrative mgr b2, $56,210
Stoll, Stephen G, locksmith, $33,744
Stoll, Susan A, corrections ofcr I, $29,652
Stollings, Karen L, functional unit mgr corr, $39,624
Stoltz, Stephen A, prob & parole ofcr II, $34,944
Stone, Arnold J, phys plant sup I, $40,380
Stone, Brian D, fire & safety spec, $31,512
Stone, Dennis J, corrections ofcr I, $29,652
Stone, Jennifer M, corrections ofcr I, $29,652
Stone, Kaley J, corrections case mgr II, $33,744
Stone, Melinda B, subs abuse cnslr II, $34,944
Stone, Nina, prob & parole ofcr II, $36,204
Stone, William J, corrections ofcr I, $29,652
Stoneburner, James B, factory mgr II, $38,928
Stonecipher, Diana L, corrections recs ofcr III, $36,888
Stone-Eudy, Gwendolyn A, ofc spt asst (keybrd), $11,580
Stoner, Cody J, corrections ofcr I, $28,692
Stonfer, Amy D, prob & parole ofcr II, $36,204
Storoz, Leo I, maint spv II, $36,888
Stotler, Stacy L, ofc spt asst (keybrd), $23,160
Stotts, Thomas D, maint spv I, $36,888
Stout, David J, corrections ofcr I, $29,652
Stout, Johnathon R, corrections ofcr I, $30,276
Stout, Kendall B, prob & parole ofcr II, $36,204
Stout, Thimothy W, corrections ofcr II, $31,668
Stout, Thomas W, food serv mgr II, $34,944
Stover, Kenneth A, corrections training ofcr, $38,928
Stover, Matthew E, corrections ofcr I, $29,652
Stowell, Merle, corrections ofcr II, $37,056

Strahm, Elden, corrections ofcr II, $33,348
Strait, John R, corrections ofcr I, $29,652
Strait, Michael W, corrections ofcr II, $34,512
Stralka, John M, corrections case mgr II, $34,944
Strange, Bryan K, corrections ofcr II, $31,668
Strange, Courtney M, corrections ofcr I, $28,692
Strange, Dennis W, corrections ofcr I, $29,652
Strange, Dustin A, corrections ofcr I, $29,652
Strange, Melvin R, corrections ofcr II, $33,348
Strange, William L, corrections ofcr I, $29,652
Strathman, Letitia A, ofc spt asst (keybrd), $23,160
Strating, Kerry D, cook III, $28,104
Stratton, Helen, corrections ofcr I, $30,132
Straube, Barbara J, exec II, $36,492
Straube, Christopher W, maint spv I, $32,628
Strauch, Matthew M, corrections ofcr I, $29,652
Strauss, Margaret K, corrections ofcr I, $29,652
Strauss, Peter C, corrections ofcr I, $29,652
Strebeck, Beau J, corrections ofcr I, $28,692
Streck, Milton W, corrections ofcr I, $29,652
Streeter, Katheryn S, sr ofc spt asst (keybrd), $25,824
Strehlow, Samantha, prob & parole ofcr I, $29,976
Stretch, Jeff N, corrections ofcr I, $29,652
Stricker, Brian T, corrections ofcr I, $29,652
Strickland, Alisha D, ofc spt asst (keybrd), $23,160
Strickland, Robert A, corrections ofcr I, $29,652
Strickland, Sarah E, ofc spt asst (keybrd), $22,536
Strid, Myles B, corrections ofcr III, $33,744
Strobel, Michael E, stationary engr, $33,744
Strong, Chelsie, prob & parole asst I, $29,496
Strong, Darrell J, corrections ofcr I, $31,668
Strong, Dwight E, corrections ofcr I, $31,140
Strong, Jeffrey A, corrections ofcr I, $29,652
Strong, Michael P, facilities opps mgr b1, $54,288
Strope, Corey D, corrections ofcr I, $28,692
Strough, Brian S, acad tchr III, $45,156
Stroup, Adam M, corrections ofcr I, $29,652
Stroup, Jeffery L, painter, $36,204
Stroup, William G, corrections ofcr I, $29,652
Strube, Jeffrey W, corrections ofcr I, $29,652
Struemph, Daniel E, voc enter analyst, $46,932
Struttmann, Kevin G, storekeeper I, $27,948
Strzyzewski, Andrew J, corrections ofcr I, $28,692
Stuart, Curtis F, prob & parole ofcr II, $36,204
Stuchell, Karen A, librarian II, $33,744
Studley, Peggy S, ofc spt asst (keybrd), $23,508
Stuedle, Ruth E, pers clerk, $28,536
Stufflebean, Andy L, functional unit mgr corr, $37,548
Stufflebean, Kristina M, corrections ofcr I, $29,652
Stump, Melissa, prob & parole asst I, $29,496
Sturdefant, Rick L, garage spv, $32,628
Sturdevant, Ralph E, investigator II, $37,548
Sturgeon, Tina L, corrections ofcr I, $31,668
Sturm, Brent A, corrections ofcr I, $29,652
Sturm, Matthew R, div dir, $86,363
Sturm, Michael R, corrections ofcr I, $29,652
Sturm, Vevia L, special asst prof, $49,955
Stutsman, Cassie L, corrections ofcr I, $29,652
Stutsman, Joshua A, corrections ofcr I, $29,652
Suddarth, Michael W, corrections training ofcr, $41,940
Sugden, Karen M, corrections ofcr I, $29,652
Sullens, Charles, corrections ofcr II, $31,668
Sullins, Cindy L, corrections ofcr I, $29,652
Sullins, Gary W, corrections ofcr I, $28,692
Sullivan, Brenda J, recrtn ofcr III, $39,624
Sullivan, Carrie A, corrections ofcr I, $29,652
Sullivan, Cherrie L, ofc spt asst (keybrd), $23,880
Sullivan, Jason D, corrections ofcr I, $29,652
Sullivan, Joshua, corrections ofcr I, $29,652
Sullivan, Kimberly M, ofc spt asst (steno), $24,612
Sullivan, Margaret R, corrections ofcr I, $31,140
Sullivan, Paula L, corrections ofcr I, $29,652
Sullivan, Tim W, corrections ofcr I, $29,652
Sulser, Susanne R, corrections ofcr I, $29,652
Summers, Jerry R, corrections ofcr I, $29,652
Sumner, Shirley A, corrections case mgr II, $34,944
Sumpter, Elizabeth S, corrections case mgr II, $38,232
Sumpter, Nathan B, corrections ofcr I, $29,652
Sumy, R G, prob & parole ofcr II, $36,204
Sunderland, Joe A, maint spv I, $33,180
Sunderman, Dennis W, corrections ofcr I, $29,652
Sunderman, Dianna S, subs abuse cnslr II, $34,944
Sunfield, Jamie L, voc tchr II, $33,744

Suntken, Cynthia M, ofc spt asst (keybrd), $23,160
Supple, Lori J, prob & parole asst I, $30,984
Surface, Charles A, maint spv II, $35,568
Surface, Heidi M, prob & parole asst I, $29,496
Surface, Tami L, corrections case mgr II, $38,232
Sutherland, Teresa L, corrections ofcr I, $30,132
Suthoff, Lucille A, account clerk II, $25,824
Sutton, Benjamin L, corrections ofcr I, $29,652
Sutton, Concepcion A, ofc spt asst (keybrd), $24,264
Sutton, Conrad H, functional unit mgr corr, $38,928
Sutton, David D, corrections ofcr I, $29,652
Sutton, John L, electronics tech, $30,984
Sutton, Matthew L, corrections ofcr II, $30,576
Sutton, Tina L, functional unit mgr corr, $38,928
Swain, Kelly D, corrections ofcr I, $29,652
Swainston, Francis A, prob & parole ofcr II, $36,204
Swaller, Timothy J, garage spv, $31,512
Swan, Douglas A, corrections ofcr I, $31,140
Swan, Gloria A, corrections ofcr I, $33,348
Swan, Jeremy L, corrections ofcr I, $29,652
Swan, Joshua E, corrections case mgr I, $30,984
Swank, Destiny D, corrections ofcr I, $29,652
Swank, Justin D, corrections ofcr III, $33,744
Swanson, Dennis D, corrections ofcr I, $29,652
Swanson, Valencia N, ofc spt asst (keybrd), $23,160
Swarens, Melissa L, ofc spt asst (keybrd), $23,160
Swartz, Javan L, corrections ofcr I, $29,652
Swartz, Mindy M, corrections case mgr II, $34,944
Swearengin, Scott, corrections ofcr II, $36,360
Sweazey, Raymond L, corrections ofcr I, $29,652
Swederske, Jessica L, prob & parole ofcr II, $36,204
Sweem, Samantha D, corrections ofcr I, $29,652
Sweet, Donald, corrections ofcr I, $29,652
Sweeten, Steve P, maint spv I, $32,628
Swift, Micki, prob & parole ofcr I, $29,976
Swinford, Brett W, corrections ofcr I, $29,652
Swinford-kimes, Deborah C, prob & parole ofcr II, $36,204
Swingle, Amy J, ofc spt asst (keybrd), $23,160
Swink, Desiree L, corrections ofcr I, $29,652
Swint, Valencia F, cook II, $23,508
Swisher, John C, chaplain, $34,932
Swopes, Donald G, corrections spv I, $41,940
Swymeler, David K, prob & parole ofcr II, $36,204
Sybert, Bobby R, corrections ofcr I, $29,652
Sybert, Terry L, corrections ofcr I, $29,652
Sydenstricker, Katherine L, cook III, $28,104
Sydney, Deana R, corrections ofcr I, $29,652
Sykes, Martin E, chaplain, $34,932
Sykes, Natisha A, corrections ofcr I, $29,652
Symons, Michael E, corrections ofcr I, $28,692
Sympson, Johnny B, corrections ofcr I, $30,132
Sympson, Valerie A, corrections spv I, $36,204
Tabor, Evelyn, cook II, $24,264
Tackett, Franklin D, corrections ofcr I, $29,652
Taft, Robyn, prob & parole ofcr II, $36,204
Tagai, Edward B, prob & parole unit spv, $43,488
Talbot, Brian W, corrections ofcr I, $29,652
Taliaferro, Norma A, prob & parole ofcr II, $40,380
Tallent, Jeffrey, corrections ofcr I, $29,652
Tallent, Leaetta A, corrections ofcr I, $29,652
Talley, Jeffery R, prob & parole ofcr II, $36,204
Tallman, Amy M, corrections ofcr I, $29,652
Tallman, Craig S, prob & parole unit spv, $46,932
Tam, Jerome, corrections ofcr I, $29,652
Tambke, Mary, sr ofc spt asst (keybrd), $25,824
Tandarich, Stephanie M, corrections spv I, $37,548
Tandy, Cecelia A, corrections ofcr I, $29,652
Tangen, Susan S, corrections ofcr I, $29,652
Tank, Brian R, corrections ofcr I, $29,652
Tanner, Glenn A, corrections ofcr I, $31,668
Tanner, Robert J, corrections ofcr I, $28,692
Tanner, Victoria A, ofc spt asst (keybrd), $27,084
Tapley, Michael O, corrections classif asst, $31,512
Tarleton, Amber N, ofc spt asst (keybrd), $22,536
Tarrants, Lacie S, corrections ofcr I, $29,652
Tarrants, Rhonda T, corrections ofcr II, $31,668
Taschner, Carol F, prob & parole unit spv, $41,940
Tate, Shelby L, ofc spt asst (clerical), $22,536
Tate, Vincent R, corrections ofcr I, $29,652
Tate, Warren A, corrections ofcr I, $29,652
Tate, Zachary C, corrections ofcr I, $29,652
Tatman, Jimmie L, maint spv I, $32,628
Tatro, Daniel R, corrections ofcr I, $30,132

Taul, Jeff R, corrections ofcr I, $29,652
Tausend, David C, corrections ofcr I, $31,668
Tausend, Victoria L, corrections ofcr I, $29,652
Taylor, Anthony B, recrtn ofcr II, $34,356
Taylor, Brianna N, corrections ofcr I, $29,652
Taylor, Christopher L, corrections ofcr I, $29,652
Taylor, Damon J, labor spv, $26,652
Taylor, Daniel J, corrections ofcr I, $29,652
Taylor, Daryl R, corrections ofcr I, $29,652
Taylor, Dawn M, edu asst II, $24,804
Taylor, Deborah F, corrections ofcr II, $33,348
Taylor, Donna J, corrections ofcr I, $29,652
Taylor, Edna M, prob & parole ofcr II, $41,940
Taylor, Heather M, acad tchr III, $37,548
Taylor, Holly M, corrections ofcr I, $29,652
Taylor, James, corrections ofcr II, $30,576
Taylor, Jaramaine R, prob & parole ofcr II, $36,204
Taylor, Jill A, prob & parole ofcr II, $36,204
Taylor, John C, corrections ofcr I, $29,652
Taylor, Kathryn R, ofc spt asst (keybrd), $26,232
Taylor, Lisa J, ofc spt asst (keybrd), $23,880
Taylor, Lyle M, corrections ofcr I, $29,652
Taylor, Marc E, corrections recs ofcr I, $28,104
Taylor, Mary A, corrections case mgr III, $37,548
Taylor, Melody J, admin ofc spt asst, $28,104
Taylor, Nicholas S, corrections ofcr II, $31,668
Taylor, Nichole L, corrections ofcr I, $29,652
Taylor, Nicole E, prob & parole ofcr II, $36,204
Taylor, Reginald, prob & parole ofcr II, $40,380
Taylor, Sheldon W, corrections ofcr I, $29,652
Taylor, Shelly, prob & parole ofcr I, $29,976
Taylor, Shelly D, corrections ofcr I, $29,652
Taylor, Shirley A, prob & parole asst I, $29,496
Taylor, Stanley D, corrections ofcr I, $29,652
Taylor, Stephanie D, prob & parole ofcr II, $36,204
Taylor, Stephen F, corrections ofcr II, $33,348
Taylor, Steven G, corrections ofcr I, $31,140
Taylor, Tamara L, corrections ofcr I, $29,652
Taylor, Thomas L, cook III, $27,228
Taylor, Timothy L, corrections ofcr I, $29,652
Taylor, Tony, corrections ofcr I, $29,652
Taylor, Ty N, corrections ofcr I, $29,652
Taylor, Veronica A, sr ofc spt asst (keybrd), $25,824
Taylor-tallent, Lindsey M, corrections ofcr I, $29,652
Teague, Mary E, corrections ofcr I, $30,132
Teal, Karen D, storekeeper II, $28,104
Teater, Joshua, prob & parole asst I, $29,496
Tebbe, Ronald J, corrections ofcr I, $29,652
Tebbenkamp, Corey P, subs abuse cnslr I, $30,984
Tedder, Gregory L, corrections ofcr I, $31,140
Tedder, Nathan A, corrections ofcr I, $29,652
Teegarden, Ruth A, acad tchr III, $39,624
Teems, Brian J, corrections mgr b1, $48,149
Teitsort, Alexzander D, prob & parole ofcr I, $30,420
Teller, Eli V, corrections ofcr I, $29,652
Tellman, Dana J, prob & parole ofcr II, $36,888
Tellman, John M, locksmith, $29,976
Tellman, Michael D, corrections ofcr I, $31,668
Templeman, Lavanna, corrections ofcr I, $29,652
Templeton, Alexander W, corrections ofcr I, $29,652
Tennison, Lorrie A, prob & parole ofcr II, $40,380
Tennyson, Christopher A, corrections ofcr I, $29,652
Ter Maat, Susan, prob & parole ofcr II, $36,204
Terrell, Larry E, prob & parole unit spv, $41,940
Terrell, Lorrie G, corrections ofcr I, $32,784
Terrell, Robin L, corrections spv I, $36,888
Terrell, Sonya D, corrections ofcr I, $31,140
Terrell, Terry W, corrections ofcr I, $34,512
Terrill, Nathaniel, prob & parole asst I, $29,496
Terry, Brad S, corrections ofcr III, $38,928
Terry, Caleb, corrections ofcr I, $29,652
Terry, David K, corrections ofcr III, $34,356
Terry, Jeffery W, corrections ofcr I, $29,652
Terry, Jennifer N, corrections ofcr I, $31,668
Terry, Jimmy L, corrections ofcr I, $29,652
Terry, Merrilyn L, prob & parole ofcr II, $39,624
Terry, Rita K, corrections case mgr II, $36,888
Terry, Roger D, corrections mgr b2, $54,097
Terry, Stephen R, corrections spv I, $42,708
Terry, Tamara A, investigator I, $30,984
Terry, Tammy K, corrections ofcr I, $31,140
Terry, Travis W, corrections mgr b1, $46,203
Teson, Rebecca A, corrections ofcr II, $31,668

Testerman, Andrew E, prob & parole ofcr II, $36,204
Thacker, Janie S, account clerk II, $27,504
Thacker, Jarrod R, cook II, $24,264
Thatcher, Steven M, corrections ofcr I, $28,692
Thayer, Jamie, prob & parole ofcr II, $36,204
Thebeau, Charity N, cook III, $28,104
Thebeau, Robert, corrections ofcr I, $29,652
Theerman, Deborah L, acad tchr III, $41,940
Thele, Jacob W, corrections ofcr I, $29,652
Thessen, William E, corrections ofcr I, $29,652
Thiara, Amanda, ofc spt asst (keybrd), $23,160
Thibault, Keith L, corrections ofcr I, $29,652
Thibault, Mark E, corrections ofcr I, $28,692
Thiel, Amy D, prob & parole ofcr II, $36,204
Thieme, Ashley A, prob & parole unit spv, $43,488
Thieme, James W, corrections ofcr I, $29,652
Thieme, William R, corrections ofcr I, $29,652
Thierfelder, Kevin P, corrections ofcr I, $29,652
Thimmesch, Deborah, corrections case mgr II, $34,944
Thiongane, Khadijatou, corrections ofcr I, $29,652
Thogmartin, Bret A, corrections ofcr II, $31,668
Thomalla, Mary A, corrections ofcr I, $31,140
Thomas, Abra S, corrections ofcr I, $29,652
Thomas, Allen D, corrections ofcr II, $31,668
Thomas, Austin J, account clerk II, $25,032
Thomas, Brian M, corrections ofcr III, $33,744
Thomas, Cheryl K, cook II, $24,264
Thomas, Christopher R, investigator III, $40,380
Thomas, Coty M, corrections ofcr I, $29,652
Thomas, Debbie, corrections ofcr I, $29,652
Thomas, James P, corrections ofcr II, $30,576
Thomas, Jeremy M, corrections ofcr I, $28,692
Thomas, Julie A, corrections ofcr I, $29,652
Thomas, Julie J, functional unit mgr corr, $38,928
Thomas, Justin D, corrections ofcr II, $31,668
Thomas, Justin L, research analyst II, $36,204
Thomas, Keesila R, corrections ofcr I, $28,692
Thomas, Kenneth D, corrections ofcr I, $29,652
Thomas, Lakesha, prob & parole ofcr II, $36,204
Thomas, Lionell, prob & parole ofcr II, $34,944
Thomas, Margie A, corrections ofcr I, $29,652
Thomas, Martin J, corrections ofcr I, $29,652
Thomas, Merlin, corrections case mgr II, $40,380
Thomas, Michael T, corrections ofcr I, $29,652
Thomas, Paul W, recrtn ofcr I, $31,512
Thomas, Richard D, corrections ofcr I, $29,652
Thomas, Robin R, corrections case mgr II, $34,944
Thomas, Rodney E, prob & parole ofcr II, $38,232
Thomas, Ronald, corrections ofcr I, $29,652
Thomas, Stephanie M, corrections mgr b2, $60,216
Thomas, Steven P, storekeeper II, $28,104
Thomas, Tamonia C, corrections ofcr I, $28,692
Thomas, Vivian J, corrections ofcr I, $29,652
Thomas, William A, prob & parole unit spv, $44,304
Thomas, William E, corrections ofcr I, $29,652
Thomas-Jett, Vicki E, corrections ofcr I, $29,652
Thomason, David O, corrections ofcr I, $29,652
Thompson, Billy G, tractor trailer driver, $32,052
Thompson, Brian S, corrections ofcr I, $32,784
Thompson, Cade A, corrections spv I, $40,380
Thompson, Chad E, corrections ofcr I, $29,652
Thompson, Chad P, corrections ofcr I, $29,652
Thompson, Jarrett H, tractor trailer driver, $30,984
Thompson, Jeffrey A, corrections ofcr I, $33,348
Thompson, Jessica L, prob & parole ofcr II, $36,204
Thompson, Kenneth W, corrections ofcr I, $29,652
Thompson, Kevin L, corrections ofcr III, $33,744
Thompson, Kimberly J, corrections ofcr II, $31,668
Thompson, Lawrence E, corrections ofcr I, $29,652
Thompson, Lori C, prob & parole ofcr II, $36,204
Thompson, Martin L, ofc spt asst (clerical), $22,536
Thompson, Michael G, corrections ofcr I, $29,652
Thompson, Michelle R, functional unit mgr corr, $38,928
Thompson, Nelson P, corrections ofcr III, $37,548
Thompson, Roger G, maint worker II, $28,104
Thompson, Shawn W, corrections training ofcr, $41,940
Thompson, Sheila D, ofc spt asst (keybrd), $26,232
Thompson, Stephen L, corrections ofcr II, $31,668
Thompson, Todd N, recrtn ofcr I, $31,512
Thompson, Vanessa Y, ofc spt asst (keybrd), $23,508
Thomsen, Stephanie, prob & parole asst I, $28,536
Thomure, Sebastian L, corrections ofcr I, $29,652
Thornburg, Keith B, subs abuse cnslr II, $34,944

Thornburg, Teresa G, corrections mgr b2, $56,510
Thorne, Mary R, corrections ofcr I, $29,652
Thorne, Susan E, ofc spt asst (keybrd), $23,160
Thorne, Tavis J, prob & parole ofcr II, $36,204
Thorne, Timothy R, prob & parole ofcr II, $41,940
Thornton, Charles E, corrections ofcr I, $29,652
Thornton, Perry D, corrections ofcr I, $29,652
Thornton, Ricky W, corrections ofcr I, $29,652
Thornton, Roberta, prob & parole ofcr II, $38,232
Thrasher, Jessica A, corrections ofcr I, $29,652
Threadgill, Stacey A, subs abuse cnslr III, $37,548
Throckmorton, Johnathan W, corrections ofcr II, $31,668
Throckmorton, Todd N, cook II, $23,508
Thurman, Joshua E, corrections ofcr I, $29,652
Thurman, Larry H, recrtn ofcr II, $32,628
Thurston, Benny H, corrections ofcr I, $29,652
Tiefenauer, Kevin D, maint spv I, $32,628
Tiemann, Paul B, corrections ofcr I, $30,132
Tiffany, Michelle L, corrections ofcr I, $29,652
Tillett, Justin, corrections ofcr I, $29,652
Tilley, Shannon K, prob & parole ofcr II, $38,928
Tilson, Jennifer E, corrections ofcr I, $29,652
Timbers, Jacob, prob & parole asst I, $28,536
Timmons, Janese M, ofc spt asst (keybrd), $25,824
Tinker, Chad A, corrections ofcr I, $28,692
Tinker, Dennis E, corrections ofcr I, $29,652
Tinnin, Kaitlin M, corrections ofcr I, $28,692
Tinoco, James, prob & parole asst I, $29,496
Tinsley, Rita, prob & parole ofcr II, $36,204
Tintinger, Jonathan H, prob & parole unit spv, $43,488
Tipp, Jeremiah G, corrections ofcr I, $29,652
Tippen, Dustin A, corrections ofcr I, $29,652
Tippie, Amy R, prob & parole ofcr II, $36,204
Tipton, Darrin D, corrections mgr b1, $49,831
Tipton, Gregory J, corrections ofcr I, $29,652
Tipton, Thomas E, voc tchr III, $37,548
Tittle, J E, prob & parole ofcr II, $36,204
Tobin, Anthony K, stationary engr, $33,744
Todaro, Nickolas T, corrections ofcr I, $29,652
Todd, Christopher W, prob & parole ofcr II, $36,204
Todd, Eric N, corrections ofcr I, $29,652
Todd, Matthew R, corrections case mgr I, $31,512
Todd, Robert J, corrections ofcr II, $31,668
Todd, Thomas T, corrections case mgr II, $37,548
Toebben, Dennis D, tractor trailer driver, $34,944
Tolbert, Juanita, cook II, $24,264
Toler, Roy W, corrections ofcr I, $31,140
Tolle, Dale W, corrections ofcr III, $36,204
Tollenaar, Mary K, prob & parole ofcr II, $39,624
Tolliver, David J, chaplain, $34,356
Tomlin, Dawne, prob & parole ofcr II, $37,548
Tomson, Jeffrey A, voc enter spv II, $31,512
Toney, Terrie D, storekeeper I, $26,232
Toot, Christopher E, corrections ofcr I, $29,652
Toot, Tammy S, corrections case mgr II, $38,928
Topash, David S, corrections spv I, $41,172
Torkelson, Rana A, ofc spt asst (keybrd), $23,160
Torres, Melvin, corrections ofcr I, $28,692
Touchette, Lucas W, corrections ofcr II, $31,668
Townsend, Daniel, recrtn ofcr I, $33,744
Townsend, Heather K, functional unit mgr corr, $39,624
Townsend, Marcia D, prob & parole ofcr II, $38,232
Tracer, Bonita L, prob & parole ofcr II, $41,940
Tracy, Charles D, chaplain, $34,356
Trammell, Robert W, storekeeper I, $25,824
Tranbarger, Iola R, corrections ofcr I, $29,652
Trapp, Larry E, phys plant sup II, $38,928
Trask, Alexandria N, corrections ofcr I, $28,692
Traver, Kimberly, prob & parole ofcr II, $36,204
Travis, David C, corrections ofcr II, $31,668
Travis, Rhonda F, ofc spt asst (keybrd), $23,160
Travis, Rufus K, maint spv I, $34,356
Travis-Johnson, Lisa, prob & parole ofcr II, $39,624
Traylor, April L, prob & parole ofcr II, $39,624
Traynor, Earl E, corrections ofcr I, $29,652
Traynor, Edward E, boiler oper, $28,104
Traynor, Katinell F, ofc spt asst (keybrd), $23,160
Traynor, Terry W, maint spv I, $32,628
Treadwell, Mitchell R, recrtn ofcr II, $32,628
Trebing, Daniel J, corrections ofcr I, $29,652
Treece, Brenda G, ofc spt asst (keybrd), $23,160
Treece, Ryan D, storekeeper I, $26,232
Trehal, Russell E, corrections ofcr I, $30,132

Trent, Belinda M, cook III, $27,228
Trevino, Samuel S, corrections ofcr I, $29,652
Trezise, Cynthia M, corrections case mgr II, $34,944
Tribbitt, Tina A, prob & parole ofcr II, $36,204
Trimble, Justin L, corrections ofcr I, $29,652
Triplett, Aaron M, corrections ofcr I, $29,652
Triplett, Garry F, corrections ofcr I, $29,652
Triplett, Jennifer M, corrections ofcr I, $30,276
Triplett, Kyle C, corrections ofcr I, $28,692
Tripp, Brian P, prob & parole ofcr II, $39,624
Tripp, Michael D, corrections ofcr I, $29,652
Troesser, Dedie R, special asst ofc & clerical, $35,350
Troncoso, Michael E, corrections case mgr II, $36,204
Trotter, Christopher D, corrections ofcr I, $29,652
Trotter, Marla L, corrections ofcr I, $31,668
Trout, Richard A, corrections classif asst, $30,420
Trowbridge, Erin S, recrtn ofcr I, $29,976
Trowbridge, Janet K, corrections ofcr I, $29,652
Trower, Daniel B, voc tchr II, $34,944
Troxel, Kimberly S, corrections ofcr I, $28,692
Troxel, Matthew L, corrections ofcr I, $29,652
Trueblood, Benjamin T, corrections ofcr I, $29,652
Truelove, Timothy P, corrections spv II, $46,068
Truitt, Jeremy Z, prob & parole unit spv, $41,940
Truman, Eric S, corrections ofcr I, $31,668
Truman, Karen S, corrections ofcr I, $29,652
Trussell, Craig A, acad tchr III, $38,232
Trustee, Darrel D, corrections ofcr I, $32,784
Trustee, Pamela R, cook II, $24,264
Trusty, Mark M, functional unit mgr corr, $39,624
Tubbs, Tyler A, corrections ofcr I, $28,692
Tucker, Brian S, corrections ofcr I, $29,652
Tucker, Charles E, corrections ofcr I, $29,652
Tucker, Randall E, investigator I, $29,976
Tucker, Shane E, corrections ofcr I, $29,652
Tucker, Whitney E, corrections case mgr II, $34,944
Tuggle, Katherine L, corrections ofcr I, $33,348
Tune, Arron W, corrections ofcr I, $29,652
Tunget, Cody N, corrections ofcr I, $29,652
Tunks, Mark A, labor spv, $26,652
Turbak, Robert A, corrections ofcr I, $29,652
Turley, Joe G, corrections ofcr I, $31,668
Turley, Kenneth W, maint worker II, $33,744
Turlington, Brad F, corrections ofcr I, $31,140
Turner, Candy L, prob & parole ofcr II, $36,888
Turner, Carman A, corrections ofcr I, $31,140
Turner, Charles R, functional unit mgr corr, $41,940
Turner, George W, investigator II, $37,548
Turner, Gregory, corrections ofcr I, $31,140
Turner, Jason L, corrections ofcr I, $29,652
Turner, Jason M, corrections ofcr I, $28,692
Turner, Jeffrey A, corrections ofcr I, $29,652
Turner, Jeffrey A, corrections spv I, $38,928
Turner, Justin T, corrections ofcr II, $31,668
Turner, Kenneth P, corrections ofcr I, $29,652
Turner, Larry D, corrections ofcr I, $31,140
Turner, Lisa M, corrections case mgr II, $36,204
Turner, Melissa K, pers clerk, $30,984
Turner, Paul A, voc tchr II, $34,944
Turner, Paulette F, prob & parole ofcr II, $36,888
Turner, Pearl M, ofc spt asst (keybrd), $23,508
Turner, Raquel A, corrections ofcr I, $28,692
Turner, Robert S, corrections ofcr I, $29,652
Turner, Sharon L, corrections case mgr II, $38,928
Turner, Tammye E, corrections ofcr I, $30,132
Turner, Taylar L, corrections ofcr I, $29,652
Turner, Timothy A, corrections ofcr I, $29,652
Turner, Zachary W, corrections ofcr I, $28,692
Turpin, Travis W, cook II, $24,264
Turpin, Wayne R, corrections ofcr I, $29,652
Tutor, Janet L, corrections case mgr III, $39,624
Tutt, Kathy M, corrections training ofcr, $41,172
Tuttle, James D, corrections ofcr I, $29,652
Tuttle, James M, maint worker II, $29,004
Tuttle, Kathleen A, ofc spt asst (keybrd), $25,824
Tuttle, Kimberly A, prob & parole ofcr II, $40,380
Tuttle, Paul G, prob & parole asst I, $29,496
Tuttle, Robert J, maint worker II, $29,004
Tuttleton, Randy W, prob & parole asst I, $29,496
Twenter, Melinda J, corrections ofcr I, $28,692
Twenter, Shannon D, functional unit mgr corr, $42,708
Twilla, Mary J, corrections ofcr I, $29,652
Twitchell, James T, corrections ofcr I, $29,652

Twyman, Shawn C, corrections mgr b1, $46,178
Twyman, Teri L, corrections case mgr II, $34,944
Tye, James A, corrections ofcr I, $29,652
Tyler, Bridget A, storekeeper I, $25,824
Tyler, Robert K, corrections ofcr I, $29,652
Tyler, Terry M, acad tchr III, $36,204
Typaldos, Dathan L, corrections ofcr I, $28,692
Tyre, Calvin N, maint worker I, $27,084
Tyrone, Barbara A, storekeeper I, $25,824
Uding, Lynn R, subs abuse cnslr III, $41,172
Uebinger, Jeffrey K, prob & parole ofcr II, $37,548
Uebinger, Verlena L, corrections ofcr II, $34,512
Ukoh, Lawrence C, prob & parole asst I, $30,984
Ulrich, Rebecca J, prob & parole ofcr II, $36,204
Umfleet, Dawn M, sr ofc spt asst (keybrd), $25,824
Umfleet, Dennis R, prob & parole asst I, $29,496
Umfleet, Nathan A, corrections ofcr I, $28,692
Umfleet, Timothy M, fire & safety spec, $29,976
Umfress, Cody J, corrections ofcr I, $29,652
Umstattd-schmutz, Angela R, functional unit mgr corr, $38,928
Underhill, Sharon S, exec II, $36,204
Underwood, Darcy L, corrections ofcr I, $28,692
Underwood, Kimberly S, ofc spt asst (keybrd), $23,160
Underwood, Michael J, corrections ofcr I, $33,348
Underwood, Misty G, prob & parole unit spv, $42,708
Unger, Lisa R, corrections ofcr I, $29,652
Upchurch, Jeannette M, corrections ofcr I, $29,652
Urhahn, Melvin L, sr ofc spt asst (keybrd), $25,824
Usher, Lisa M, cook II, $24,264
Usher, Marc C, corrections ofcr II, $31,668
Ussery, Jason D, corrections ofcr I, $29,652
Utterback, Nicole M, prob & parole ofcr II, $36,204
Vails, Jason, corrections ofcr II, $31,668
Valentine, Cassandra S, corrections ofcr I, $29,652
Valentine, Ronald S, corrections ofcr I, $29,652
Valire, Stephanie M, sr ofc spt asst (keybrd), $30,384
Vallier, William R, corrections spv II, $46,068
Van Buskirk, Daniel J, recrtn ofcr I, $33,180
Van Fleet, Teresa A, corrections ofcr I, $29,652
Vanbelkum, Brian D, corrections ofcr I, $29,652
Vanbibber, Richard L, stationary engr, $37,548
Vance, Deborah L, special asst paraprof, $53,291
Vance, Michael A, corrections ofcr I, $29,652
Vance, Peggy B, prob & parole ofcr II, $34,944
Vandenhoek, Timothy R, corrections ofcr I, $29,652
Vandergriff, David M, corrections spv II, $46,068
Vandergriff, Kenneth D, corrections ofcr I, $29,652
Vandergriff, Kenneth S, corrections ofcr I, $29,652
Vandergriff, Rickie E, corrections ofcr I, $29,652
Vandergriff, Todd A, corrections spv I, $37,548
Vandermark, Ronald, corrections ofcr I, $28,692
Vanderpool, Clinton G, garage spv, $32,628
Vanderpool, Wayne E, corrections ofcr II, $31,668
Vandevender, James R, acad tchr III, $42,708
Vandorin-laire, Anita S, prob & parole ofcr II, $42,708
Vang, Kou, corrections ofcr I, $29,652
Vang, Lonnie, corrections ofcr I, $29,652
Vangennip, Olga, prob & parole asst II, $31,512
Vangundy, Vincent A, prob & parole ofcr II, $36,204
Vanhooser, Brenda K, corrections ofcr I, $29,652
Vanisko, Marsha L, pers clerk, $32,628
Vanlandingham, Ralph D, corrections ofcr I, $29,652
Vanlandingham, Rickie G, corrections ofcr I, $30,139
Vanloo, Brock H, special asst prof, $45,333
Vanloo, Lisa G, prob & parole ofcr II, $36,204
Vanmeter, Darin, prob & parole ofcr II, $41,172
Vannaman, Preston S, corrections ofcr I, $28,692
Vannoy, James, prob & parole ofcr II, $39,624
Vantilburg, Jacqueline S, corrections ofcr III, $39,624
Varner, Gregory H, corrections ofcr I, $29,652
Varner, Jamie W, storekeeper I, $26,232
Vaugh, Christopher, prob & parole asst II, $31,512
Vaughan, Scott M, stationary engr, $33,744
Vaughn, Darren K, prob & parole ofcr II, $39,624
Vaughn, Debra S, ofc spt asst (keybrd), $23,160
Vaughn, Derek, prob & parole ofcr II, $36,204
Vaughn, Jeanne L, prob & parole ofcr II, $36,204
Vaughn, Samantha S, prob & parole unit spv, $41,940
Vaughn, Shawn S, prob & parole ofcr II, $36,204
Vaught-massey, Tamie K, electronics tech, $30,984
Vawter, Jason L, corrections ofcr I, $28,692
Vedane-finn, Julia E, acad tchr III, $37,548
Veit, Norbert C, maint spv I, $32,628

Veit, Scott J, bldg const wkr II, $30,984
Veltrop, Leon V, supply mgr I, $33,180
Venable, Norma R, voc tchr III, $38,232
Venable, Philip C, storekeeper II, $30,420
Venn, Charles W, corrections ofcr I, $29,652
Verdugo, Christopher M, corrections ofcr II, $30,576
Vernon, Eric C, investigator II, $37,548
Vessar, Christina M, corrections ofcr I, $28,692
Vessar, Dorothy J, corrections ofcr I, $29,652
Vester, Lacee L, corrections ofcr I, $29,652
Vetere, Christopher S, corrections ofcr I, $28,692
Vetere, Mathew C, corrections ofcr I, $29,652
Veulemans, Tracey A, storekeeper II, $30,420
Vich, Lynne R, corrections ofcr I, $29,652
Vick, Andrea R, sr ofc spt asst (keybrd), $25,032
Vilcinskas, Sheryll A, prob & parole ofcr II, $36,204
Villasenor, Frank, prob & parole ofcr II, $36,204
Villmer, Thomas W, corrections mgr b3, $71,205
Vincent, Bradley W, phys plant sup I, $35,568
Vincent, Colin M, corrections ofcr I, $29,652
Vincent, Dale, corrections ofcr I, $29,652
Vincent, Jacob J, corrections ofcr I, $29,652
Vinluan, Rogelio J, electronics tech, $30,984
Vinson, Jason L, recrtn ofcr II, $32,628
Vinson, Joshua L, corrections ofcr I, $29,652
Vinson, Michael J, corrections ofcr III, $34,356
Vinyard, Abby J, account clerk II, $25,824
Vivian, Kalvin L, maint worker II, $30,420
Voelkel, Joshua E, corrections ofcr I, $29,652
Vogel, Gary D, maint worker II, $29,004
Vogel, Michelle L, corrections ofcr I, $29,652
Vogelgesang, Shannon M, corrections case mgr II, $34,944
Vogelsang, Victor W, corrections ofcr I, $29,652
Voland, Steven L, corrections ofcr I, $31,140
Volkart, Kenneth D, corrections ofcr II, $30,576
Vollmer, Karla Y, corrections ofcr I, $29,652
Volner, Leland A, corrections ofcr I, $29,661
Volz, Alicia R, prob & parole asst II, $33,744
Von Opitz, Donald, corrections ofcr I, $30,276
Vorhees, Scott M, corrections case mgr III, $41,172
Voss, Debra S, corrections ofcr I, $29,652
Voss, James L, corrections ofcr III, $34,356
Voss, Robert J, corrections ofcr I, $29,652
Voyles, Terry J, corrections ofcr I, $29,652
Vrba, Donald W, prob & parole ofcr II, $36,204
Wade, Charles A, maint spv I, $33,180
Wade, Corey N, corrections ofcr I, $29,652
Wade, Dexter E, corrections ofcr I, $31,140
Wade, Jon F, corrections ofcr I, $28,692
Wade, Jonna M, corrections case mgr II, $33,744
Wade, Mark S, corrections case mgr II, $36,888
Wade, Michelle R, functional unit mgr corr, $38,928
Wade, Steven F, corrections ofcr I, $31,140
Wade, Troy D, functional unit mgr corr, $38,928
Wade, William R, corrections ofcr I, $29,652
Wadley, Jerry D, corrections ofcr I, $29,652
Wadley, Terry E, corrections ofcr II, $31,668
Wagaman, Barry L, corrections ofcr I, $31,668
Wagaman, Jared W, corrections ofcr I, $29,652
Wagers, Beth A, admin ofc spt asst, $28,104
Wagers, Cheri E, ofc spt asst (keybrd), $23,160
Wagers, Gabriel A, corrections training ofcr, $38,928
Wagers, Richard L, corrections ofcr I, $33,348
Wagganer, Danny E, corrections ofcr I, $29,652
Wagganer, Darrell G, investigator II, $37,548
Wagner, Dana C, acad tchr III, $36,204
Wagner, Douglas S, prob & parole ofcr II, $36,204
Wahlers, Brenda, food serv mgr II, $35,568
Wainscott, Jose' M, corrections ofcr I, $33,348
Waite, Kylah S, prob & parole ofcr II, $36,204
Waite, Richard I, corrections ofcr I, $29,652
Waites, James D, corrections ofcr I, $29,652
Wake, Guy R, corrections ofcr I, $29,652
Wakeman, James P, phys plant sup I, $40,380
Walberg, Charlcie L, corrections ofcr I, $29,652
Walberg, Steven M, corrections ofcr II, $33,348
Walcott, Donald L, corrections ofcr I, $29,652
Walden, Cy J, corrections ofcr I, $28,692
Walden, Susan M, corrections ofcr I, $30,276
Waldrep, Marlin K, corrections ofcr I, $29,652
Waldrup, Thomas W, corrections spv I, $37,548
Walker, Alexandre G, corrections ofcr I, $29,652
Walker, Barbara L, corrections ofcr I, $29,652

Walker, Billy R, corrections ofcr I, $28,692
Walker, Bronie V, prob & parole asst I, $30,984
Walker, Chase C, corrections ofcr I, $28,692
Walker, Craig A, corrections ofcr I, $29,652
Walker, Darla S, cook II, $24,264
Walker, David L, prob & parole asst I, $29,496
Walker, Deborah L, corrections ofcr I, $29,652
Walker, Debra S, acad tchr III, $37,548
Walker, Jabari D, corrections ofcr I, $29,652
Walker, James A, corrections ofcr I, $29,652
Walker, James T, corrections ofcr I, $29,652
Walker, Jared L, corrections ofcr I, $28,692
Walker, Keely, prob & parole ofcr I, $29,976
Walker, Leroy, stationary engr, $33,744
Walker, Melissa R, corrections ofcr I, $28,692
Walker, Michael P, chaplain, $34,356
Walker, Nancy S, corrections ofcr I, $29,652
Walker, Paul R, stationary engr, $37,548
Walker, Rhonda, sr ofc spt asst (keybrd), $27,504
Walker, Robyn G, sr ofc spt asst (keybrd), $25,032
Walker, Ronnie D, corrections ofcr I, $29,652
Walker, Shawn D, corrections ofcr I, $29,652
Walker, Sheryle A, ofc spt asst (keybrd), $23,160
Walker, Wyatt W, corrections ofcr I, $28,692
Wall, Roberta L, prob & parole ofcr II, $38,232
Wallace, David L, corrections ofcr I, $29,652
Wallace, David L, corrections ofcr I, $29,652
Wallace, Ian N, corrections mgr b3, $66,438
Wallace, Kevin S, corrections ofcr I, $29,652
Wallace, Kristopher J, corrections ofcr I, $28,692
Wallace, Lashonda R, correctional worker, $26,400
Wallace, Ralph L, corrections training ofcr, $38,928
Wallace, Timothy A, corrections case mgr II, $34,944
Wallace, Troy E, corrections ofcr I, $29,652
Wallace, Zella M, registered nurse - clin opers, $52,608
Wallen, Eric L, corrections ofcr I, $29,652
Wallen, James A, corrections spv I, $41,172
Wallen, Kyle A, corrections ofcr I, $29,652
Wallen, Linda D, ofc spt asst (keybrd), $23,160
Waller, Matthew K, corrections ofcr II, $31,668
Waller, Samuel A, electronics tech, $29,976
Waller, Wesley I, corrections ofcr I, $29,652
Wallingford, David M, corrections case mgr II, $38,232
Walls, Jerry A, corrections ofcr I, $28,692
Walls, Lawrence, corrections ofcr I, $28,692
Walls, Mark D, corrections ofcr I, $29,652
Walls, William, corrections ofcr I, $29,652
Walmer, Timothy J, corrections ofcr I, $28,692
Walsh, Brock A, corrections ofcr I, $29,652
Walsh, Jesse M, corrections ofcr I, $29,652
Walsh, Robert A, corrections ofcr I, $29,652
Walsh, Sherry L, cook II, $24,264
Waltemeyer, Lorraine K, corrections ofcr I, $33,900
Walters, Beverly A, storekeeper II, $28,104
Walters, Jarrett L, corrections ofcr I, $28,692
Walters, Kevin L, prob & parole asst I, $29,496
Walters, Ryan K, corrections ofcr I, $28,692
Walters, Scott K, corrections ofcr I, $29,652
Walton, Charles E, corrections ofcr I, $29,652
Walton, Jane L, licensed prof cnslr II, $47,892
Walton, Jeffrey S, prob & parole ofcr II, $36,204
Walton, Julianne, cook II, $24,264
Walton, Shaun S, prob & parole asst I, $29,496
Walton, Shertia K, corrections ofcr I, $28,692
Walton, Thomas D, corrections ofcr II, $34,512
Waltz, Joshua J, corrections ofcr I, $29,652
Wampler, Herbert D, maint spv I, $32,628
Wampler, Michael S, corrections ofcr I, $29,652
Wampler, Travis J, corrections ofcr I, $29,652
Wampler, Wayne M, corrections ofcr I, $29,652
Wankel, Susan M, corrections ofcr I, $30,132
Wankum, Janet L, ofc spt asst (keybrd), $23,160
Wankum, Michael E, corrections ofcr I, $29,652
Wann, Myers C, corrections ofcr I, $29,652
Wansing, Cynthia S, corrections mgr b2, $47,556
Ward, Carol L, prob & parole unit spv, $43,488
Ward, Charity N, corrections ofcr I, $29,652
Ward, Dennis M, stationary engr, $35,568
Ward, Erin L, corrections ofcr I, $28,692
Ward, Jennifer M, corrections case mgr I, $32,052
Ward, Justin M, corrections ofcr I, $28,692
Ward, Micheal T, corrections ofcr I, $29,652
Ward, Phillip R, corrections ofcr I, $29,652

Ward, Tenna A, corrections classif asst, $31,512
Ward, Willie B, corrections ofcr II, $31,668
Warden, Aaron K, corrections ofcr I, $29,652
Warden, Alicia C, corrections ofcr I, $28,692
Warden, Robert N, corrections ofcr I, $29,652
Ware, Eric B, recrtn ofcr I, $29,976
Warford, Tyler R, corrections ofcr I, $29,652
Warner, Robert, functional unit mgr corr, $43,488
Warner, Robert, prob & parole asst I, $29,496
Warning, Jeremy I, corrections case mgr II, $34,944
Warnke, Dietrick P, corrections ofcr I, $29,652
Warren, Adrienne A, corrections ofcr I, $29,652
Warren, Derrick L, prob & parole asst II, $33,744
Warren, Mark T, corrections ofcr I, $29,652
Warren, Todd W, corrections mgr b1, $42,864
Washburn, Jacob S, corrections ofcr I, $29,652
Washington, Batina C, prob & parole unit spv, $42,708
Washington, Devona, prob & parole ofcr II, $37,548
Washington, Fugenia V, ofc spt asst (keybrd), $23,160
Wasielewski, Donald, prob & parole ofcr II, $36,204
Wassell, Matthew M, corrections ofcr I, $29,652
Wasson, Amy E, corrections ofcr III, $35,568
Wasson, Thomas P, corrections ofcr I, $29,652
Waterbury, Lauren F, corrections ofcr I, $29,652
Waterhouse, Philip C, corrections ofcr I, $29,652
Waters, Jackie A, corrections ofcr I, $29,652
Waters, Teresa D, ofc spt asst (keybrd), $24,612
Waters, Wayne A, corrections ofcr I, $33,348
Watie, Barbara J, ofc spt asst (keybrd), $24,264
Watkins, Bryan L, corrections ofcr I, $29,652
Watkins, Clinton R, subs abuse cnslr III, $37,548
Watkins, Dan, corrections ofcr I, $28,692
Watkins, David R, corrections ofcr I, $29,652
Watkins, Joshua D, corrections ofcr I, $29,652
Watkins, Judy L, cook III, $28,104
Watkins, Michael D, cook II, $24,264
Watkins, Samuel G, corrections ofcr I, $28,692
Watkins, Tcheanina J, prob & parole ofcr II, $36,204
Watkins, Tiah M, corrections ofcr I, $29,652
Watson, Brittany L, corrections ofcr I, $29,652
Watson, Eboney, prob & parole ofcr II, $34,944
Watson, Garry S, corrections ofcr I, $31,140
Watson, Gary L, corrections ofcr I, $29,652
Watson, James R, corrections case mgr II, $33,744
Watson, Keith A, corrections case mgr II, $34,944
Watson, Luann C, corrections case mgr II, $36,204
Watson, Mack E, corrections ofcr I, $29,652
Watson, Richard A, corrections case mgr II, $36,204
Watson, Robert D, maint spv I, $31,512
Watson, Robert W, prob & parole ofcr II, $36,204
Watson, Robin L, prob & parole ofcr II, $40,380
Watson, Thomas E, corrections ofcr I, $31,140
Watson-hunnell, Teresa A, prob & parole ofcr II, $40,380
Wattenbarger, Aaron D, corrections ofcr I, $29,652
Wattree, Michelle M, prob & parole asst I, $29,496
Watts, Michael D, storekeeper II, $29,004
Watts, Paul R, prob & parole ofcr II, $38,232
Watts, Randall L, corrections ofcr II, $33,348
Watts, Thomas C, corrections ofcr I, $29,652
Waugh, Linda D, investigator I, $30,984
Waugh, Patrick T, prob & parole ofcr I, $31,512
Way, Carole J, corrections case mgr II, $34,944
Waymon, Matthew D, corrections ofcr I, $29,652
Weakley, Callie M, corrections ofcr I, $29,652
Weatherby, Abraham M, corrections ofcr I, $29,652
Weatherby, Henry R, corrections ofcr I, $31,140
Weatherford, Patricia A, speech-language pathologist, $41,940
Weatherford-williams, kimberly L, prob & parole ofcr II, $38,232
Weathers, Ronald J, corrections ofcr I, $29,652
Weaver, Charles M, corrections ofcr I, $29,652
Weaver, Denise M, exec II, $38,232
Weaver, Michael L, corrections ofcr III, $33,744
Weaver, Miranda, prob & parole asst I, $29,496
Weavers, John B, corrections ofcr I, $34,512
Weavers, Tamara R, corrections classif asst, $33,180
Webb, Andrew W, corrections case mgr II, $34,944
Webb, David A, corrections ofcr I, $29,652
Webb, David E, investigator I, $30,984
Webb, Gay L, prob & parole ofcr II, $40,380
Webb, Jerry D, corrections ofcr I, $29,652
Webb, Kyle D, corrections ofcr II, $31,668
Webb, Lonnie D, corrections ofcr I, $31,668

Webb, Michael D, corrections ofcr II, $37,056
Webb, Michael W, corrections ofcr I, $30,132
Webb, Michelle S, corrections ofcr I, $29,652
Webb, Richard A, corrections ofcr I, $33,348
Webb, Terry A, functional unit mgr corr, $42,708
Webb, Terry L, corrections ofcr I, $29,652
Webb, Theresa L, cook II, $24,264
Webber, Cybelle M, corrections mgr b2, $51,806
Weber, Dennis J, corrections ofcr I, $29,652
Weber, John P, corrections ofcr I, $32,220
Weber, Kevin L, corrections ofcr I, $35,100
Weber, Michael J, functional unit mgr corr, $37,548
Weber, Ryan C, corrections ofcr I, $29,652
Weber, Scott J, functional unit mgr corr, $40,380
Weber, Susan K, sr ofc spt asst (keybrd), $25,824
Weber, Timothy D, corrections ofcr II, $31,668
Webster, Carol, ofc spt asst (keybrd), $23,160
Webster, Essence, sr ofc spt asst (keybrd), $26,232
Weed, Ashley A, subs abuse cnslr II, $33,744
Weed, Jessica R, ofc spt asst (keybrd), $23,160
Weed, Jody H, corrections ofcr II, $31,668
Weeks, James R, corrections ofcr I, $29,652
Weese, Kari L, corrections ofcr I, $28,692
Wehmeyer, Casey J, corrections case mgr I, $30,984
Wehmeyer, Teresa A, administrative analyst III, $40,380
Weide, Christopher, corrections ofcr I, $29,652
Weidenbenner, Cletus R, prob & parole unit spv, $45,156
Weidenbenner, Edward K, corrections ofcr I, $29,652
Weiland-thomas, Kasey D, corrections ofcr I, $29,652
Weiner, Helen M, ofc spt asst (keybrd), $11,940
Weinert, Nathan S, legal counsel, $45,450
Weir, Joel M, cook II, $23,508
Weis, Linda L, sr ofc spt asst (keybrd), $25,824
Weisenborn, Mary L, sr ofc spt asst (keybrd), $25,824
Weiss, Lori J, prob & parole asst I, $30,984
Weiss, Stanley G, corrections ofcr I, $29,652
Weiss, Zachery A, maint worker II, $29,004
Weitlich, Ronald D, corrections ofcr I, $31,668
Welch, Andrew T, corrections ofcr I, $28,692
Welch, Craig A, corrections ofcr II, $32,220
Welch, Gary A, corrections classif asst, $29,976
Welch, Grace A, corrections case mgr II, $36,204
Welch, James C, maint spv I, $32,628
Welch, James K, maint worker II, $29,496
Welch, Kevin J, corrections ofcr I, $31,140
Welch, Michael R, corrections ofcr I, $28,692
Welch, Robert L, corrections ofcr I, $29,661
Weldon, Jennifer L, ofc spt asst (keybrd), $23,160
Welker, Denise L, prob & parole ofcr II, $38,232
Welling, Lorri R, corrections ofcr III, $33,744
Wells, Brian M, corrections ofcr I, $29,652
Wells, Cynthia I, acad tchr III, $37,548
Wells, Danielle M, corrections ofcr I, $28,692
Wells, Dusty L, corrections ofcr I, $29,652
Wells, Gary L, corrections ofcr I, $31,668
Wells, Gloria J, ofc spt asst (keybrd), $23,508
Wells, Jamie L, prob & parole ofcr II, $36,204
Wells, Jimmie L, board mbr, $84,431
Wells, Kenneth J, corrections ofcr III, $33,744
Wells, Lyndsey R, prob & parole ofcr II, $36,204
Wells, Michael D, corrections ofcr I, $29,652
Wells, Robert M, corrections case mgr I, $36,204
Wells, Sara E, corrections ofcr I, $29,652
Wells, Sharon A, pers clerk, $30,420
Wells, Thomas H, corrections ofcr I, $33,900
Wells, Victoria A, corrections ofcr I, $29,652
Wells, Wesley, prob & parole ofcr II, $37,548
Welschmeyer, Barbara R, sr ofc spt asst (clerical), $25,824
Welschmeyer, Matthew A, corrections ofcr I, $29,652
Welschmeyer, Michael S, corrections ofcr I, $29,652
Welsh, Eugene W, corrections ofcr I, $29,652
Wendt, Benjamin S, corrections ofcr I, $28,692
Wendt, Michael G, corrections ofcr II, $31,668
Wentworth, Marilyn K, ofc spt asst (keybrd), $24,612
Wenzl, Angela R, corrections ofcr I, $29,652
Werder, Robin G, parole hearing analyst, $53,208
Werner, Kristen L, prob & parole ofcr II, $36,204
Werning, Stephanie L, prob & parole unit spv, $41,940
Wernsman, Brooke, prob & parole ofcr II, $36,204
Wesbecher, Rae D, corrections ofcr I, $29,652
Wescott, Sean K, corrections ofcr III, $33,744
Wesely, Mary A, prob & parole ofcr II, $36,204
Wesley, George R, food serv mgr I, $32,628

Wessing, John K, prob & parole ofcr II, $37,548
Wessling, Denise M, prob & parole ofcr II, $36,204
West, Ashley, corrections ofcr I, $29,652
West, Chad E, corrections ofcr I, $29,652
West, David P, corrections ofcr I, $29,652
West, Gregory D, corrections case mgr II, $38,928
West, Jacqueline R, ofc spt asst (keybrd), $24,264
West, James J, corrections ofcr I, $31,140
West, Jeremiah L, corrections ofcr I, $29,652
West, Pamela L, corrections ofcr II, $31,668
West, Tab R, corrections ofcr III, $32,628
West, Travis W, corrections ofcr I, $29,652
Westbrook, Charlotte, prob & parole ofcr II, $38,232
Westermier, Mark W, storekeeper II, $30,420
Westfall, Jared M, corrections ofcr I, $29,652
Westling, Kim K, ofc spt asst (keybrd), $23,160
Weston, Angelia L, corrections training ofcr, $39,624
Weston, Damian A, corrections ofcr I, $29,652
Weston, Davonna M, sr ofc spt asst (keybrd), $30,924
Weston, James B, prob & parole ofcr II, $40,380
Wetherell, Joseph C, heavy equip mech, $33,744
Wethington, Shawn A, corrections spv I, $38,232
Wettengel, Robyn L, corrections ofcr I, $29,652
Wetton, James W, corrections ofcr I, $29,652
Wetzel, Jonathan D, prob & parole ofcr II, $40,380
Weybright, David D, recrtn ofcr I, $29,976
Weybright, David P, corrections ofcr I, $30,132
Whalen, Joseph P, corrections ofcr I, $29,652
Whaley, Kevin T, corrections case mgr III, $41,940
Wheat, Russell A, corrections ofcr I, $29,652
Wheatley, Charles D, corrections mgr b1, $42,366
Wheeler, Craig L, factory mgr I, $33,744
Wheeler, Dan L, corrections ofcr I, $29,652
Wheeler, Haley R, prob & parole ofcr II, $36,204
Wheeler, Joseph W, prob & parole ofcr II, $36,204
Wheeler, Kevin M, corrections ofcr I, $29,652
Wheeler, Lisa M, thrpst, $36.21/hr
Wheeler, Nancy L, cook II, $24,264
Wheeler, William F, corrections ofcr I, $29,652
Wheelis, Justin M, corrections ofcr I, $28,692
Whelchel, Jonathan W, prob & parole ofcr I, $29,976
Whelen, Scott P, corrections ofcr I, $29,652
Whisler, Iii, corrections ofcr I, $29,652
Whitaker, Bonnie G, corrections ofcr I, $33,348
Whitaker, Corey H, corrections ofcr I, $29,652
Whitaker, James R, prob & parole ofcr II, $36,204
Whitaker, Jeff L, corrections ofcr I, $29,652
Whitaker, Marion C, corrections ofcr I, $29,652
Whitaker, Mark D, voc enter spv II, $31,512
White, Anthony J, prob & parole ofcr II, $36,204
White, Barry W, corrections ofcr I, $32,784
White, Billy, prob & parole asst I, $28,536
White, Bobbi J, corrections ofcr I, $30,276
White, Brandon L, corrections ofcr II, $30,576
White, Catherine, prob & parole unit spv, $45,156
White, Chelsea D, corrections ofcr I, $28,692
White, Christopher H, corrections ofcr I, $29,652
White, Crystal N, corrections ofcr I, $29,652
White, Dale W, corrections ofcr I, $31,140
White, Danny D, corrections ofcr I, $33,900
White, David B, prob & parole ofcr II, $36,204
White, Debra J, sr ofc spt asst (clerical), $28,452
White, Felicia, prob & parole ofcr II, $36,204
White, Gordon C, med technologist II, $34,944
White, Jason N, corrections ofcr I, $29,652
White, Joann M, registered nurse - clin opers, $63,084
White, John J, corrections ofcr I, $29,652
White, John K, prob & parole asst II, $30,420
White, John L, corrections ofcr I, $29,652
White, Jon A, corrections ofcr I, $29,652
White, Joseph E, corrections ofcr I, $29,652
White, Melissa, corrections case mgr II, $36,204
White, Michael C, corrections case mgr III, $41,940
White, Richard, corrections case mgr III, $38,928
White, Robert J, corrections ofcr I, $29,652
White, Ronald R, corrections ofcr I, $30,132
White, Selita C, prob & parole ofcr II, $40,380
White, Steven M, prob & parole ofcr II, $36,204
White, Tamera L, corrections mgr b2, $54,784
White, Terry L, corrections spv II, $44,304
White, Tina M, subs abuse cnslr II, $34,944
White, Tina M, storekeeper I, $27,084
White, Vicky S, special asst technician, $35,738

White, Wendy R, corrections ofcr I, $29,652
Whited, James B, corrections ofcr I, $29,652
Whited, James B, corrections ofcr I, $33,348
Whited, Sara E, prob & parole ofcr II, $36,204
Whitehead, Charles D, corrections ofcr I, $29,652
Whitehead, Michelle L, corrections ofcr I, $28,692
Whitehead, Zackary S, investigator I, $31,512
Whitfield, Mersharn L, recrtn ofcr I, $31,512
Whitford, Anthony C, corrections ofcr I, $29,652
Whitley, Lois M, prob & parole ofcr II, $38,232
Whitley, Patsy E, corrections ofcr I, $31,140
Whitmer, Reba F, functional unit mgr corr, $42,708
Whitmore, Audrey E, supply mgr I, $34,944
Whitnell, Cheryl L, corrections ofcr I, $29,652
Whitney, Tylone D, corrections ofcr I, $29,652
Whitsell, Gregory P, prob & parole ofcr II, $36,204
Whitson, Elizabeth A, corrections ofcr I, $29,652
Whitt, David R, prob & parole ofcr II, $41,172
Whitt, Pamela S, ofc spt asst (keybrd), $26,652
Whitt, Rodney J, maint spv I, $34,356
Whitt, Sue A, corrections ofcr I, $29,652
Whittington, Colleen D, prob & parole ofcr II, $36,888
Whittle, Curtis R, corrections ofcr II, $31,668
Whittle, Eric S, functional unit mgr corr, $42,708
Whittle, Matthew D, corrections ofcr III, $35,568
Wicker, Douglas L, corrections ofcr I, $29,652
Wicker, James Z, prob & parole ofcr II, $36,204
Wickes, Eric E, corrections ofcr I, $28,692
Wickey, Patricia L, prob & parole ofcr II, $36,204
Wickey, Scott C, prob & parole ofcr II, $39,624
Wickins, Brian W, prob & parole ofcr II, $36,204
Wickles, Terri D, sr ofc spt asst (clerical), $25,824
Wickliffe, Allen E, corrections ofcr III, $36,204
Wickstrom, Emily K, prob & parole ofcr I, $29,976
Wideman, Amy T, prob & parole ofcr II, $34,944
Wideman, Nikki L, prob & parole ofcr II, $38,232
Widener, Charise M, corrections ofcr I, $29,652
Widener, Robert, special asst technician, $48,016
Wiederholt, Karen D, corrections case mgr I, $29,976
Wiederholt, Rhonda S, prob & parole ofcr II, $39,624
Wiedmaier, Deborah E, corrections ofcr I, $30,576
Wiegel, Mark S, corrections ofcr I, $29,652
Wiegers, Robert A, corrections case mgr II, $35,568
Wiemholt, Benjamin T, corrections classif asst, $31,512
Wienecke, Steve L, prob & parole asst I, $30,984
Wiens, Loyal K, corrections ofcr I, $29,652
Wiesner, Alexander M, corrections ofcr I, $29,652
Wiesner, Rick A, corrections ofcr II, $31,668
Wiest, Patrick W, corrections ofcr I, $29,652
Wigal, Laurette P, corrections ofcr I, $28,692
Wigfall, Donna R, functional unit mgr corr, $38,928
Wigger, Sandra J, prob & parole ofcr II, $38,232
Wiggington, Adam F, cook I, $22,200
Wiggins, Clifton K, corrections ofcr I, $29,652
Wilbanks, Tara A, ofc spt asst (keybrd), $23,160
Wilbers, Michael C, corrections ofcr I, $30,132
Wilburn, Elizabeth B, corrections ofcr II, $31,668
Wilder, Lyndelle M, corrections case mgr II, $34,944
Wildhaber, Todd M, corrections ofcr II, $31,668
Wildhagen, Robert C, corrections ofcr I, $29,652
Wiles, Brian K, prob & parole ofcr II, $39,624
Wiles, Pamela L, corrections case mgr II, $40,380
Wiles, Ronald E, entprss mgr b1, $42,920
Wiley, Daniel D, corrections ofcr II, $33,348
Wiley, Harold W, corrections ofcr I, $29,652
Wilfong, Paul J, corrections ofcr I, $28,692
Wilfong, Russell S, corrections ofcr III, $38,232
Wilfong, Terry W, corrections ofcr II, $31,668
Wilford, Magdalene, corrections ofcr I, $29,652
Wilhite, James T, maint worker II, $29,496
Wilhite, Randall A, corrections ofcr I, $29,652
Wilhite, Raymond L, corrections ofcr I, $29,652
Wilhite, Travis W, corrections spv I, $37,548
Wilhoit, Jason M, prob & parole ofcr II, $36,204
Wilkerson, Barry W, corrections ofcr I, $29,652
Wilkerson, David H, corrections ofcr I, $29,661
Wilkerson, Dawn N, prob & parole unit spv, $44,304
Wilkerson, James E, corrections ofcr I, $32,784
Wilkerson, Timothy A, corrections case mgr II, $38,928
Wilkerson, Willis D, corrections ofcr I, $29,652
Wilkes, Dale W, corrections training ofcr, $39,624
Wilkins, Stephanie R, corrections case mgr I, $31,512
Wilkinson, Brenda L, prob & parole ofcr II, $37,548

Wilkinson, Chris A, maint spv I, $32,628
Wilkinson, Karey E, corrections ofcr I, $29,652
Wilkinson, Mark W, chaplain, $32,638
Wilkinson, Sara, prob & parole ofcr II, $34,944
Will, Gregory C, corrections ofcr I, $28,692
Will, Paul, maint worker II, $29,976
Wille, Mark S, food serv mgr I, $32,052
Willett, Jasmine S, ofc spt asst (keybrd), $22,536
Willette, Calvin J, corrections ofcr I, $29,652
Willette, Megan K, corrections ofcr I, $29,652
Williams, Aaron M, corrections ofcr I, $29,652
Williams, Alexander C, corrections ofcr I, $28,692
Williams, Allison M, prob & parole asst I, $29,496
Williams, Annette C, corrections ofcr I, $29,652
Williams, Bill R, corrections ofcr I, $29,652
Williams, Bobby W, corrections ofcr I, $31,140
Williams, Brad L, corrections ofcr I, $29,652
Williams, Bradley J, cook II, $24,264
Williams, Briana N, cook III, $27,228
Williams, Bryan R, corrections ofcr I, $31,140
Williams, Carmen L, prob & parole ofcr II, $38,232
Williams, Charles B, corrections ofcr I, $28,692
Williams, Dakota L, corrections ofcr I, $28,692
Williams, Daniel J, corrections ofcr I, $29,652
Williams, Darrel R, corrections ofcr I, $29,652
Williams, Darron W, corrections ofcr I, $29,652
Williams, Debra A, cook II, $24,264
Williams, Debra F, food serv mgr II, $34,944
Williams, Debra K, corrections spv I, $42,708
Williams, Deloise, special asst official & admstr, $70,000
Williams, Edward O, corrections ofcr I, $29,652
Williams, Ellen A, corrections ofcr I, $30,139
Williams, Erica R, corrections mgr b1, $44,032
Williams, Falonda, prob & parole asst I, $28,536
Williams, Freddie, prob & parole asst I, $31,044
Williams, Ginger A, ofc spt asst (keybrd), $25,032
Williams, Jacqueline M, corrections ofcr I, $29,652
Williams, James, corrections ofcr I, $28,692
Williams, James L, corrections ofcr I, $29,652
Williams, Jamie L, corrections ofcr II, $30,576
Williams, Jana L, corrections ofcr I, $29,652
Williams, Jarrell L, corrections ofcr I, $29,652
Williams, Jason J, corrections ofcr I, $29,652
Williams, Jennifer L, corrections ofcr I, $28,692
Williams, Jennifer S, corrections ofcr I, $29,652
Williams, Joe C, stationary engr, $33,744
Williams, John R, corrections ofcr II, $31,668
Williams, Johnnie A, corrections ofcr I, $29,652
Williams, Joseph C, corrections ofcr I, $29,652
Williams, Kaliah R, cook II, $24,264
Williams, Kasey S, corrections ofcr I, $29,652
Williams, Katherine S, ofc spt asst (keybrd), $12,912
Williams, Katie H, prob & parole ofcr II, $36,204
Williams, Keith, corrections training ofcr, $41,172
Williams, Kevin M, recrtn ofcr I, $33,744
Williams, Kimberly, prob & parole ofcr II, $38,232
Williams, Larry, corrections case mgr II, $36,888
Williams, Leroy S, food serv mgr II, $38,928
Williams, Linda L, corrections case mgr II, $37,548
Williams, Lisa D, sr ofc spt asst (keybrd), $25,032
Williams, Mary L, prob & parole ofcr II, $38,232
Williams, Merl E, corrections ofcr I, $31,668
Williams, Michael A, corrections ofcr I, $29,652
Williams, Michael H, corrections ofcr I, $29,652
Williams, Nicole Y, prob & parole ofcr II, $39,624
Williams, Patrick D, corrections ofcr I, $28,692
Williams, Raeshaun, prob & parole ofcr II, $34,944
Williams, Richard G, chief counsel, $80,804
Williams, Rickey A, corrections ofcr I, $29,652
Williams, Rodney D, corrections ofcr I, $31,668
Williams, Rodney G, acad tchr III, $43,488
Williams, Roger L, corrections ofcr I, $29,652
Williams, Rusty G, voc enter spv II, $30,984
Williams, Ruth E, corrections ofcr I, $29,652
Williams, Ryan L, corrections ofcr I, $30,132
Williams, Ryan L, corrections ofcr I, $28,692
Williams, Samantha L, corrections ofcr I, $29,652
Williams, Samuel D, corrections ofcr I, $28,692
Williams, Sandra L, admin ofc spt asst, $28,104
Williams, Sharon R, acad tchr III, $37,548
Williams, Shawne C, corrections ofcr I, $29,652
Williams, Sherry, corrections classif asst, $33,744
Williams, Shirley L, ofc spt asst (keybrd), $23,508

Williams, Skyler B, corrections ofcr I, $29,652
Williams, Susan D, sr ofc spt asst (keybrd), $25,824
Williams, Timothy L, corrections ofcr I, $31,668
Williams, Toya S, cook II, $23,508
Williams, Walter, corrections ofcr I, $29,652
Williams, Wayne H, corrections ofcr III, $39,624
Williams-glover, Nancy, prob & parole ofcr II, $38,232
Williamson, April L, corrections ofcr II, $30,576
Williamson, Bryant M, correctional worker, $26,400
Williamson, David P, corrections ofcr I, $29,652
Williamson, Heather A, ofc spt asst (clerical), $22,536
Williamson, Jason R, corrections ofcr I, $29,652
Williamson, Katrina, ofc spt asst (keybrd), $23,160
Williamson, William H, corrections ofcr I, $29,652
Williford, Devin L, corrections ofcr I, $29,652
Williford, Michelle L, corrections ofcr I, $29,652
Williford, Star S, corrections ofcr I, $28,692
Williford, Timothy E, corrections ofcr I, $29,652
Willingham, Sheri L, ofc spt asst (keybrd), $25,032
Willis, Candace R, corrections training ofcr, $41,940
Willis, Cathy L, special educ tchr III, $38,928
Willis, Don R, subs abuse cnslr II, $34,944
Willis, Jack C, corrections ofcr I, $29,652
Willis, Jennifer R, ofc spt asst (keybrd), $22,536
Willis, Linda S, corrections ofcr I, $29,652
Willis, Renee L, corrections recs ofcr I, $28,536
Willmeno, Jay A, maint spv II, $34,944
Willoughby, Robert E, corrections ofcr I, $29,652
Wills, James M, corrections ofcr I, $29,652
Wilmes, Diana E, corrections ofcr I, $31,668
Wilmsmeyer, Chris W, corrections ofcr I, $31,668
Wilmsmeyer, Christopher L, corrections ofcr I, $29,652
Wilmurth, Calvin E, corrections ofcr I, $29,661
Wilson, A S, corrections ofcr I, $29,652
Wilson, Alicia N, ofc spt asst (clerical), $22,536
Wilson, Amanda K, corrections ofcr II, $31,668
Wilson, Angela K, ofc spt asst (keybrd), $22,536
Wilson, Angela S, sr ofc spt asst (keybrd), $25,824
Wilson, Artricia M, prob & parole asst I, $29,496
Wilson, Carol D, corrections ofcr I, $29,652
Wilson, Charity E, prob & parole ofcr II, $36,204
Wilson, Charles R, corrections ofcr II, $31,668
Wilson, Crystal R, prob & parole ofcr II, $36,204
Wilson, Dallas E, corrections ofcr I, $29,652
Wilson, Dana L, prob & parole unit spv, $41,940
Wilson, Debra K, corrections case mgr II, $36,204
Wilson, Dennis W, corrections ofcr II, $31,668
Wilson, Dysart E, maint spv I, $32,628
Wilson, Gary D, phys plant sup III, $46,068
Wilson, Gina M, cook II, $27,084
Wilson, Gregory A, prob & parole unit spv, $41,940
Wilson, Ian P, corrections ofcr I, $31,140
Wilson, James E, corrections ofcr II, $33,348
Wilson, James L, corrections ofcr I, $29,652
Wilson, James M, corrections ofcr I, $33,900
Wilson, Jennie L, corrections ofcr I, $30,139
Wilson, Jenny M, prob & parole ofcr II, $36,888
Wilson, Joshua J, corrections ofcr I, $29,652
Wilson, Judy K, cook III, $27,228
Wilson, Kara J, acad tchr II, $33,744
Wilson, Keith L, corrections ofcr I, $29,652
Wilson, Kevin G, corrections ofcr I, $29,652
Wilson, Krista, prob & parole ofcr II, $36,204
Wilson, Mark F, corrections ofcr I, $29,652
Wilson, Melissa M, corrections case mgr II, $34,944
Wilson, Monica E, corrections ofcr I, $30,132
Wilson, Paul E, special asst official & admstr, $46,965
Wilson, Phillip R, corrections ofcr I, $29,652
Wilson, Robert L, corrections ofcr II, $31,668
Wilson, Robin R, ofc spt asst (keybrd), $23,160
Wilson, Shannon M, admin ofc spt asst, $28,104
Wilson, Shemika F, prob & parole ofcr II, $36,204
Wilson, Starr N, corrections ofcr I, $29,652
Wilson, Stephanie A, corrections case mgr II, $37,548
Wilson, Susan M, storekeeper II, $30,420
Wilson, Terry T, maint spv I, $33,180
Wilson, Tommy R, corrections ofcr I, $28,692
Wilson, Tracy A, ofc spt asst (keybrd), $23,160
Wilson, Veronica K, corrections ofcr I, $29,652
Wilson, Waylon L, corrections case mgr II, $36,204
Wilson, Willa R, corrections ofcr I, $29,652
Wilson, William B, corrections case mgr II, $38,232
Wilson, Zachery T, corrections ofcr I, $28,692

Wilt, Ted T, electronics tech, $30,984
Wimmer, Brittany A, sr ofc spt asst (keybrd), $25,824
Winch, Tina L, ofc spt asst (keybrd), $23,160
Winder, Randy S, maint worker II, $31,512
Winders, Warren F, corrections case mgr II, $34,944
Windle, Chris S, corrections ofcr I, $29,652
Windmiller, Anthony, corrections ofcr II, $31,668
Winfield, Barbara J, corrections case mgr II, $37,548
Winfield, Gary J, corrections ofcr I, $31,140
Wingate, Ricky L, corrections ofcr I, $29,652
Wingate, Sherry L, cook II, $23,508
Winget, Heather D, corrections ofcr I, $29,652
Winholtz, Alice, account clerk II, $25,824
Winingear, Carol A, prob & parole ofcr II, $40,380
Winkler, Catherine A, acad tchr III, $37,548
Winkler, Paul R, corrections ofcr II, $31,668
Winkowski, Richard A, maint worker II, $29,004
Winn, James B, corrections ofcr I, $29,652
Winn, Sammie L, corrections ofcr I, $29,652
Winningham, Cherylon G, corrections mgr b1, $52,331
Winschel, Craig A, corrections ofcr I, $31,140
Winter, James W, corrections ofcr I, $29,652
Winter, Mindi M, corrections ofcr I, $29,652
Winter, Shelly D, prob & parole ofcr II, $37,548
Winter, Travis D, corrections ofcr II, $32,220
Winterbower, Joseph T, corrections ofcr I, $30,132
Winterbower, Mark J, corrections case mgr II, $34,944
Winterwolf, Connor D, corrections ofcr I, $28,692
Wiorek, Jason J, corrections ofcr I, $29,652
Wirtel, William J, prob & parole ofcr II, $36,204
Wirths, Lorri D, prob & parole ofcr II, $36,204
Wirtz, Lori A, prob & parole ofcr II, $36,204
Wirtz, Ronald V, corrections spv I, $37,548
Wirtz, Stephani R, corrections ofcr I, $29,652
Wisdom, Kelleeta N, corrections ofcr I, $29,652
Wisdom, Stephen A, corrections ofcr I, $30,132
Wisdom, Warren A, recrtn ofcr I, $31,512
Wise, Donald I, maint worker II, $29,004
Wise, Marisa A, corrections ofcr I, $28,692
Wiseman, Christopher A, prob & parole ofcr II, $36,204
Wiseman, Dennis B, corrections ofcr I, $33,348
Wiseman, James A, hr mgr b2, $66,489
Wiseman, James J, prob & parole asst I, $29,496
Wiseman, Leesa, corrections mgr b1, $48,809
Wissel, Darlene A, prob & parole asst I, $29,496
Witherbee, Cassandra, ofc spt asst (keybrd), $23,160
Witt, Douglas J, corrections ofcr I, $29,652
Witt, Justin M, corrections ofcr I, $29,652
Witt, Randy N, corrections ofcr I, $28,692
Witthaus, Anita M, special asst paraprof, $47,767
Wixom, Jeffrey K, corrections ofcr II, $31,668
Woeger, Kathy A, ofc spt asst (keybrd), $23,160
Woemmel, Jeffrey S, corrections ofcr I, $29,652
Wofford, Neil E, functional unit mgr corr, $40,380
Wofford, Rachelle, prob & parole ofcr III, $38,928
Wohlgemuth, Larry D, corrections ofcr I, $34,512
Wohlwend, Leo V, corrections ofcr II, $31,668
Wojtowicz, Sherri D, prob & parole ofcr II, $36,204
Wolf, April D, corrections ofcr I, $29,652
Wolf, Judith A, prob & parole ofcr II, $39,624
Wolf, Teal R, corrections ofcr I, $29,652
Wolf, Vincent J, corrections ofcr I, $29,652
Wolfe, Diane E, accounting spec II, $40,380
Wolfe, James R, prob & parole ofcr II, $37,548
Wolfe, Jay B, prob & parole ofcr II, $36,204
Wolfe, Laura A, special asst prof, $45,834
Wolfe, Stacia M, sr ofc spt asst (keybrd), $25,032
Wolfe, Terry K, corrections ofcr I, $29,652
Wolfenbarger, S R, corrections ofcr I, $31,140
Wolfrum, Janet L, special asst prof, $46,897
Wolfskill, Delores J, cook II, $24,264
Wolken, Kimberly A, admin ofc spt asst, $28,104
Wolz, Brian W, corrections ofcr I, $29,652
Womack, Lisha B, corrections training ofcr, $40,380
Womack, Trudy G, recrtn ofcr I, $31,512
Wombles, Daniel A, corrections ofcr III, $33,744
Wombles, Renee D, corrections spv I, $38,232
Wonders, Charles E, corrections ofcr I, $29,652
Wood, Abbey K, storekeeper II, $28,104
Wood, Cynthia S, corrections classif asst, $30,420
Wood, Danny T, corrections ofcr I, $31,140
Wood, Karen L, storekeeper I, $26,652
Wood, Kimberly D, corrections ofcr I, $29,652

Wood, Lisa A, ofc spt asst (keybrd), $26,232
Wood, Martha F, corrections case mgr II, $38,232
Wood, Matthew S, cook II, $23,508
Wood, Melissa B, prob & parole unit spv, $41,940
Wood, Michael A, corrections ofcr I, $28,692
Wood, Michael E, corrections ofcr I, $28,692
Wood, Raymond C, corrections ofcr I, $29,652
Wood, Richard D, corrections ofcr I, $28,692
Wood, Robert L, corrections ofcr I, $33,348
Wood, Shannon, corrections ofcr I, $29,652
Wood, Stacy Y, corrections spv I, $38,232
Wood, Susan D, fiscal & administrative mgr b2, $56,210
Wood, Theresa A, corrections ofcr I, $29,652
Wood, Timothy P, functional unit mgr corr, $42,708
Wood, Tonya A, voc enter spv II, $29,976
Wood, Tonya S, corrections ofcr I, $29,652
Woodall, Randall E, corrections ofcr I, $29,652
Woodard, Alexander L, corrections ofcr I, $28,692
Woodard, Tommie V, corrections ofcr II, $33,348
Woodcock, Alan J, corrections ofcr I, $29,652
Woodhurst, Jason A, corrections ofcr III, $35,568
Woodhurst, Katie A, corrections ofcr I, $29,652
Woodley, Amanda Y, corrections case mgr II, $34,944
Woodring, Kimberly R, corrections ofcr I, $29,652
Woodrow, Susan K, corrections ofcr I, $29,652
Woodruff, Alison, prob & parole unit spv, $41,940
Woodruff, Candise L, subs abuse cnslr II, $36,204
Woodruff, Daniel P, corrections ofcr II, $31,668
Woodruff, Dolores M, corrections ofcr I, $29,652
Woodruff, Matthew P, corrections ofcr I, $29,652
Woodruff, Michelle L, corrections ofcr I, $28,692
Woodruff, Paul A, corrections ofcr II, $35,100
Woods, Adam R, corrections ofcr I, $28,692
Woods, Heidi J, functional unit mgr corr, $37,548
Woods, James D, corrections ofcr I, $29,652
Woods, Lowell C, voc enter spv II, $33,180
Woods, Lynne B, ofc spt asst (keybrd), $24,264
Woods, Michelle R, corrections ofcr I, $29,652
Woods, Monica L, prob & parole ofcr II, $36,204
Woods, Paul G, corrections ofcr I, $29,652
Woods, Randy L, maint spv I, $32,628
Woods, Robert, corrections ofcr I, $32,784
Woods, Robert M, maint spv I, $32,628
Woods, Sara, ofc spt asst (keybrd), $23,160
Woods, Trula L, admin ofc spt asst, $28,104
Woodson, Jerry V, corrections ofcr I, $30,132
Woodson, Marvin E, corrections ofcr I, $29,652
Woodson, Myron R, correctional worker, $26,400
Woodward, George, corrections ofcr I, $28,692
Woodward, Gregory K, corrections ofcr I, $31,668
Woodworth, Vera H, admin ofc spt asst, $28,536
Woody, Denise L, corrections ofcr I, $29,652
Woody, James W, corrections ofcr I, $29,652
Woody, Randall S, corrections ofcr I, $31,668
Woody, William D, corrections ofcr I, $29,652
Wooldridge, Christine C, ofc spt asst (keybrd), $23,160
Wooldridge, Craig L, corrections ofcr III, $33,744
Woolery, Robert H, corrections ofcr II, $35,100
Woolfolk, Dennis, corrections ofcr II, $31,678
Wooten, Darren L, corrections ofcr I, $30,276
Word, Donnie L, corrections ofcr I, $29,652
Worden, William T, corrections ofcr I, $29,652
Workes, Charles E, corrections ofcr I, $28,692
Workman, Darla A, corrections ofcr II, $30,576
Workman, Thomas J, corrections ofcr I, $29,652
Worley, Pamela J, corrections case mgr II, $36,888
Wormington, Christopher E, corrections ofcr I, $29,652
Wormington, Sarah M, corrections ofcr I, $29,652
Wormsley, Kelly D, corrections ofcr I, $29,652
Worrell, Charles B, corrections ofcr I, $32,784
Worrell, Lisa M, prob & parole ofcr II, $36,204
Worsham, Douglas A, pastoral cnslr, $50,438
Worsley, William B, corrections ofcr I, $29,652
Worthen, Ronald G, corrections ofcr I, $28,692
Wren, Ashley D, corrections ofcr I, $28,692
Wright, Amelia, ofc spt asst (keybrd), $25,824
Wright, Anthony J, prod spec I corr, $40,380
Wright, Barbara A, ofc spt asst (keybrd), $25,824
Wright, Bradley A, corrections ofcr I, $33,348
Wright, Cynthia K, corrections ofcr I, $29,652
Wright, Dorothy J, librarian II, $33,744
Wright, Douglas K, corrections ofcr I, $31,140
Wright, Freedom R, corrections ofcr I, $29,652

Wright, J B, prob & parole asst I, $29,496
Wright, Jack E, corrections ofcr II, $31,668
Wright, Jack L, corrections ofcr I, $29,652
Wright, Jeffrey A, prob & parole ofcr II, $39,624
Wright, Johnny W, corrections ofcr I, $29,661
Wright, Joy K, corrections ofcr I, $31,140
Wright, Keith, prob & parole asst II, $35,568
Wright, Mark E, corrections case mgr II, $37,548
Wright, Paul L, corrections ofcr I, $29,652
Wright, Randal J, corrections ofcr I, $29,652
Wright, Rebecca S, corrections ofcr I, $31,140
Wright, Richard A, corrections ofcr I, $29,652
Wright, Richelle A, pers clerk, $27,228
Wright, Ronald E, corrections ofcr I, $31,668
Wright, Teresa G, admin ofc spt asst, $28,104
Wright, Toni R, acad tchr III, $37,548
Wright, William E, corrections ofcr I, $29,652
Wrinkles, Alan G, corrections ofcr I, $29,652
Wrinkles, Billy R, maint spv I, $32,628
Wrinkles, Karen L, corrections ofcr I, $31,140
Wrisinger, Tyler M, corrections ofcr I, $29,652
Wulfers, Connie A, prob & parole ofcr II, $41,172
Wulff, Allison, prob & parole asst I, $29,496
Wunderlich, Jenny L, corrections case mgr I, $31,512
Wyatt, Charles R, corrections ofcr I, $29,652
Wyatt, Jessieca R, corrections ofcr I, $28,692
Wyatt, Justin W, corrections ofcr III, $33,744
Wyatt, Kelsey M, corrections ofcr I, $28,692
Wyatt, Micah U, corrections ofcr I, $29,652
Wyatt, Vernon R, cook II, $24,264
Wyble, Jamie L, prob & parole ofcr II, $36,204
Wyhs, Susan M, prob & parole ofcr II, $38,232
Wykert, April S, cook II, $24,264
Wykert, Wilem O, corrections ofcr I, $29,652
Wykes, Greg D, phys plant sup II, $38,928
Wyman, Misty D, corrections ofcr II, $31,668
Wynn, David P, prob & parole ofcr II, $37,548
Wynne, Terry M, corrections ofcr I, $33,348
Wyrick, Bevin E, investigator II, $38,928
Wyrick, Cheryl L, sr ofc spt asst (keybrd), $25,032
Wyrick, Joshua P, corrections training ofcr, $38,928
Wyrick, Mark W, corrections ofcr I, $31,668
Yaeger, William A, cook II, $24,264
Yager, Christopher A, cook II, $23,508
Yahnig, Edward L, corrections mgr b1, $55,119
Yamry-reeves, Mona C, corrections ofcr I, $30,132
Yancey, Dwight S, corrections ofcr I, $29,652
Yancey, Kevin H, corrections ofcr I, $29,652
Yancey, Steven A, corrections ofcr I, $29,652
Yancy, Andrea M, ofc spt asst (keybrd), $25,032
Yarbrough, Dale E, corrections ofcr I, $28,692
Yarmy, Kimberly C, corrections ofcr I, $29,652
Yarnell, Jacob A, prob & parole asst I, $29,496
Yates, Justin P, corrections ofcr II, $31,668
Yates, Paul M, voc tchr III, $37,548
Yates, Stephanie R, prob & parole ofcr II, $38,232
Yates, Wallace A, corrections ofcr I, $29,652
Yavrouian, Steve, prob & parole asst I, $31,512
Ybarra, Kelsey C, prob & parole ofcr II, $36,204
Yelton, Brian G, functional unit mgr corr, $38,928
Yoder, Julie R, corrections ofcr I, $29,652
Yokem, Judy L, corrections ofcr I, $30,132
Yonkers, Jason P, corrections ofcr I, $29,652
York, Aaron R, corrections ofcr II, $31,668
York, Amanda L, corrections case mgr I, $31,512
York, Calvin F, corrections ofcr I, $31,140
York, Christy L, corrections ofcr I, $29,652
York, Michael S, corrections ofcr I, $29,652
York, Milton L, corrections ofcr I, $29,652
York, Richard W, corrections ofcr I, $29,661
Yotter, Lynda K, acad tchr III, $37,548
Young, Annette, acad tchr III, $41,172
Young, Beatrice S, corrections ofcr I, $29,652
Young, Billy E, corrections ofcr I, $29,661
Young, Billy J, cook II, $24,264
Young, Bretton R, corrections ofcr I, $31,140
Young, Brian L, corrections ofcr II, $31,668
Young, Cheryl L, sr ofc spt asst (keybrd), $25,824
Young, Cynthia A, corrections recs ofcr III, $36,204
Young, David G, corrections ofcr I, $29,652
Young, David S, corrections ofcr I, $31,140
Young, Deborah A, corrections ofcr I, $29,652
Young, Delores I, ofc spt asst (steno), $25,824
Young, Denese L, librarian II, $33,744
Young, Everett A, prob & parole asst I, $29,496
Young, Heather L, corrections ofcr I, $31,140
Young, Jeffrey A, corrections ofcr I, $29,652
Young, Jeffrey E, corrections case mgr II, $36,888
Young, John D, corrections mgr b3, $59,904
Young, Joshua I, corrections ofcr I, $29,652
Young, Keith W, storekeeper II, $28,104
Young, Kimberley S, corrections ofcr I, $29,652
Young, Paul W, corrections ofcr I, $29,652
Young, Rachel A, sr ofc spt asst (keybrd), $25,824
Young, Robyn L, corrections ofcr I, $30,132
Young, Rodney E, corrections ofcr I, $29,652
Young, Stanley L, labor spv, $29,412
Young, Thomas W, corrections ofcr I, $29,652
Young, Wanda S, corrections case mgr II, $34,944
Young-griffin, Latonia N, corrections case mgr II, $34,944
Youngs, Krystal F, prob & parole ofcr II, $36,204
Youngs, Patricia W, ofc spt asst (keybrd), $23,160
Youngs, Tonya L, investigator II, $37,548
Yount, Alan M, corrections ofcr I, $29,652
Yount, Charles, corrections ofcr I, $33,348
Yount, Kelvin E, stationary engr, $32,628
Yount, Trina K, prob & parole ofcr II, $36,204
Youtsey, Brian, recrtn ofcr I, $29,976
Yuill, Kimberly A, ofc spt asst (keybrd), $23,160
Yuille, Naomi F, corrections ofcr I, $29,652
Zabel, Lisa F, corrections ofcr I, $31,140
Zahn, Jason T, corrections ofcr III, $33,744
Zahner, Garrie J, corrections ofcr I, $30,132
Zaiger, Amanda R, prob & parole ofcr I, $31,512
Zaiss, Jennifer L, prob & parole ofcr II, $39,624
Zamkus, Jennifer M, special asst official & admstr, $72,508
Zander, Daniel, prob & parole ofcr II, $36,204
Zarcone, Deborah G, prob & parole ofcr II, $38,232
Zartler, Jeanna M, corrections case mgr I, $30,420
Zartler, Loring R, corrections ofcr II, $31,668
Zeger, Francis H, corrections ofcr I, $29,652
Zeigel, Jeremy L, corrections ofcr III, $36,204
Zeigel, Monica L, subs abuse unit spv, $42,708
Zeigler, Carl L, corrections ofcr I, $29,652
Zeih, Ashley R, corrections ofcr I, $28,692
Zeit, Michelle R, prob & parole ofcr II, $39,624
Zeornes, Randy A, corrections ofcr I, $29,652
Zerbster, Eveline C, corrections ofcr II, $32,220
Zettler, Joseph O, maint worker II, $29,004
Zeugin, Thomas F, corrections ofcr I, $29,652
Ziebarth, Bruce C, corrections ofcr I, $29,652
Ziegler, Shawn M, prob & parole ofcr II, $40,380
Zimmer, Mary A, corrections ofcr I, $29,652
Zimmerman, Dylan J, corrections ofcr I, $28,692
Zimmerman, Robert W, maint spv I, $34,356
Zimmerman, Shayna M, prob & parole ofcr II, $36,204
Zimmerman, Steven, corrections ofcr I, $33,348
Zimmerman, Tracy A, corrections ofcr I, $29,316
Zink, Rosalie, corrections ofcr I, $30,132
Ziolkowski, Donald C, corrections ofcr I, $29,652
Zolman, Kenneth, storekeeper I, $25,824
Zona, Lori J, exec II, $36,204
Zook, Tracy D, subs abuse unit spv, $44,304
Zubeck, Kurt J, corrections ofcr I, $29,652
Zuccarini, David W, corrections ofcr I, $29,652
Zuccarini, Joshua W, corrections ofcr I, $29,652
Zuidervaart, Robert W, corrections ofcr I, $29,652
Zumbehl, Casey M, ofc spt asst (keybrd), $23,160
Zurmiller, Thomas E, corrections ofcr I, $31,668
Zuroweste, Lori B, designated principal asst div, $55,303
Zwick, Courtney E, sr ofc spt asst (keybrd), $25,824

Department of Economic Development

PO Box 1157, Jefferson City 65102

Downing, John M, state dept dir, $121,200
Able, Nancy M, fiscal & administrative mgr b1, $51,098
Acklin, Darron, workforce dev spec I, $33,180
Adams, Deborah L, workforce dev spec I, $32,052
Adams, Jeanna, workforce dev spec I, $32,052
Adams, Melissa A, admin ofc spt asst, $29,976
Addo, William E, pub utl acct II, $41,172
Admire, Lori L, workforce dev spec I, $32,052
Akins, Kenneth W, acct II, $43,488

Alaniz, Frank C, workforce dev supv III, $48,156
Alber, Nicole, hsng prgm auditor & insp, $49,128
Albertson, Tracie L, workforce dev spec IV, $43,488
Aldridge, Janice L, workforce dev spec I, $36,888
Allen, Cathy, workforce dev spec II, $36,888
Allen, Dustin A, housing dev ofcr II, $40,380
Allison, Dustin J, div dir, $91,405
Althoff, Lisa, principal asst board/commisson, $57,338
Ames, Belinda J, workforce dev supv I, $32,628
Amos, Marya, research analyst III, $45,156
Ancell, Brenda B, workforce dev spec IV, $43,488
Anderson, Andy, workforce dev spec I, $32,052
Anderson, Bongkotch, economic dev incentive spc III, $46,932
Anderson, Melissa S, sr ofc spt asst (steno), $29,904
Anderson, Michele L, workforce dev spec I, $32,052
Anderson, Regina Y, workforce dev spec IV, $45,156
Anderson, Ronda R, research mgr b1, $56,400
Anderson, William, special asst prof, $91,910
Angel, Jamie P, mkting spec II, $38,928
Antal, Alexander J, legal counsel, $54,000
Anton, Sally R, tourist center spv, $30,984
Appelbaum, Christine A, workforce dev spec I, $32,052
Archer, Aaron, utl engring spec II, $51,096
Archer, Jason V, mkting spec III, $51,096
Arens, Heather D, administrative asst, $41,013
Armstead, Debora, workforce dev spec I, $32,052
Arnold, Donna K, manuf hsng insp supv, $43,488
Arnold, Laurie, admin ofc spt asst, $28,104
Arthur, Richard, workforce dev spec I, $29,976
Awosanmi, Jacob, workforce dev spec I, $32,052
Baker, Cheri L, loan servicing ofcr, $53,208
Baker, Christina, dpty counsel, $68,498
Baker, Denise, housing dev ofcr II, $36,888
Ballew, Theresa L, workforce dev spec I, $32,052
Bangert, Gary R, utl mgmt analyst III, $58,908
Barbour, Pamela, workforce dev spec I, $32,052
Barlow, Robert E, workforce dev spec I, $29,004
Barnes, Bryan, cmnty & economic dev mgrb1, $52,500
Barnes, Matthew L, utl regulatory auditor IV, $54,288
Barnhill, Connie S, admin ofc spt asst, $36,888
Barr, Cecilia D, consumer servs spec I, $36,204
Bashore, Cody G, workforce dev spec IV, $43,488
Bauer, Mark A, misc prof, $33.99/hr
Baugh, Deborah L, cmnty & economic dev mgrb1, $52,500
Baugher, Roger B, misc tech, $27.39/hr
Baughman, Kimberly J, economic dev incentive spc III, $48,156
Bax, Alan J, utl engring spec III, $56,520
Bax, Melanie K, sr ofc spt asst (keybrd), $25,824
Beard, Heather L, workforce dev spec I, $30,984
Beas, Terry G, workforce dev spec I, $32,052
Beck, Daniel I, utl regulatory eng spv, $68,160
Becker, Joyce S, exec II, $46,932
Beer, Tina B, dpty div dir, $91,405
Bellomy, William J, workforce dev spec I, $29,004
Benko, Michele, mkting spec I, $31,512
Benson, Marcel Y, workforce dev spec I, $32,052
Benson, Victoria, special asst prof, $30,984
Benz, Linda K, workforce dev spec I, $38,232
Bequette, Donald W, workforce dev spec I, $32,052
Berg, Erik A, housing prog loan admstr, $57,744
Berlin, Robert S, dpty counsel, $66,720
Bernsen, Deborah A, utl mgmt analyst III, $58,908
Bernskoetter, Greg G, exec I, $41,940
Bevelle, Nathan, workforce dev spec IV, $43,488
Bieniek, Geoffrey T, workforce dev spec I, $29,976
Bisges, Matthew J, info technologist III, $41,172
Bishop, Percy, arch III, $61,332
Black, Terrie A, workforce dev spec I, $32,052
Blair, Alice J, housing dev ofcr I, $38,928
Block, Leann, misc prof, $14.52/hr
Boateng, Kofi A, utl regulatory auditor IV, $57,744
Bocklage, Michelle A, rate & tariff exam III, $45,156
Boettcher, Mark, housing dev appraiser, $61,332
Boggs, Michael, tourist center spv, $30,984
Bolin, Kimberly K, utl regulatory auditor V, $63,996
Bolinger, Barbara E, sr ofc spt asst (keybrd), $23,923
Bonnot, Tina M, workforce dev spec IV, $46,932
Boone, Robert, legislative coord, $58,908
Borgmeyer, John, dpty counsel, $70,902
Boustead, Korin J, rate & tariff exam II, $40,380
Brackney, Beverly A, housing dev ofcr II, $41,940
Bramlett, Kamala J, tourist center spv, $31,512
Branson, Lisa A, account clerk II, $27,948

Brenner, Steven, exec I, $34,944
Brewer, Deborah S, workforce dev spec I, $32,628
Brewster, Paula, accounting spec III, $58,908
Brightwell, Suzanne D, housing dev ofcr I, $36,888
Brinker, Donald M, fiscal & administrative mgr b2, $71,205
Brown, Aaron, housing dev ofcr I, $36,204
Brown, Diana J, workforce dev spec I, $38,232
Brown, Jerry M, workforce dev spec I, $32,052
Brown, Lamont D, workforce dev spec IV, $44,304
Brown, Marsha A, workforce dev spec I, $38,928
Brown, Sherrie, pers ofcr I, $45,156
Brown, Tracey L, fiscal & administrative mgr b3, $75,750
Brown Bowers, Patti J, sr ofc spt asst (keybrd), $27,084
Brueggeman, Barbara B, pub info spec II, $34,944
Brueggemann, Shelley E, div dir, $90,000
Buchanan, Brian J, utl opps tech spec I, $37,548
Buchanan, John A, planner III, $60,120
Buckman, Jerene A, sr ofc spt asst (keybrd), $31,920
Buechler, Jennifer L, workforce dev spec IV, $43,488
Bugalski, Michael R, mkting spec I, $34,356
Burch, Shawn, workforce dev spec I, $32,052
Burke, Angela J, sr counsel, $76,255
Burton, Kim S, regulatory law judge, $60,120
Busch, Darnell, info technologist IV, $54,288
Busch, James A, utl regulatory mngr, band3, $74,304
Buschjost, Martha J, misc prof, $18.50/hr
Bushmann, Michael, regulatory law judge, $64,219
Butler, Sheryl L, hsng prgm auditor & insp, $53,208
Butts, Steven, workforce dev spec I, $32,052
Cabe, Brianne, acct II, $42,708
Calderon, Guadalupe, housing dev ofcr I, $40,380
Campbell, Marian B, legal counsel, $91,405
Cannon, George M, workforce dev spec I, $29,976
Canuteson, Gregory B, dpty div dir, $116,655
Cardwell, Lynda J, clerk, $13.90/hr
Carle, Erin M, utl regulatory auditor II, $41,940
Carroll, Cynthia J, energy spec III, $49,128
Carroll, Donny J, cmnty & economic dev mgrb1, $55,550
Carrow, Pamela L, workforce dev spec I, $32,052
Carter, Julie A, fiscal & administrative mgr b2, $61,234
Carter, Lauren N, economic dev incentive spec I, $30,984
Carter, Renae, info technologist III, $44,304
Cassels, Mary K, pers clerk, $33,180
Cassidy, John P, utl regulatory auditor V, $65,364
Cecil, Walter C, regulatory econ III, $55,416
Chapman, Phyllis L, workforce dev spec I, $32,052
Cheshire, Jennifer, workforce dev supv I, $33,744
Childs, Aaron D, economic dev incentive spec II, $38,928
Chittum, James M, workforce dev spec IV, $43,488
Choe, Kwang Y, regulatory econ II, $45,156
Christine, Tom, workforce dev spec I, $32,052
Chughtai, Shams U, cmnty & economic dev mgrb1, $48,150
Churchill, Mary M, admin ofc spt asst, $32,052
Clark, Randall E, research analyst III, $51,096
Clark, Wendy N, housing prog loan admstr, $58,908
Clavin-Clubine, Melody K, sr housing dev ofcr, $45,156
Clevenger, David L, workforce dev spec I, $29,976
Collier, Sheila A, hsng prgm auditor & insp, $47,892
Collop, Cathy J, cmnty & economic dev mgrb1, $55,550
Comstock, Suzanne A, consumer servs spec I, $36,204
Connolly, Karen L, workforce dev spec I, $36,204
Corbett, Leander, workforce dev spec I, $32,052
Coronel, Paola, mkting spec I, $31,512
Cottrell, Randy L, cmnty & economic dev mgrb2, $58,879
Couch, Myron E, misc tech, $25.04/hr
Coventry, Carol L, workforce dev spec I, $32,052
Cox, Kimberly S, utl policy analyst II, $55,416
Cox, Linda, tourist asst, $23,880
Cracraft, Kara H, pers analyst II, $39,624
Craig, Carol, housing dev ofcr II, $44,304
Craig, Pamela S, consumer servs spec II, $36,204
Crihfield, Terry W, workforce dev spec I, $37,548
Crowe, Anne M, utl regulatory auditor IV, $56,520
Cruikshank, Lorinda, mgmt analysis spec I, $37,548
Cull, Mary K, workforce dev spec I, $32,052
Dale, Colleen M, sr counsel, $74,304
David, Kim A, workforce dev spec I, $32,052
Davidson, Bryant C, economic dev incentive spec II, $38,928
Davidson, Janette K, utl policy analyst I, $46,068
Davis, Helen B, acct III, $46,068
Davis, Kristie L, cmnty & economic dev mgrb1, $55,000
Davis, Rachel R, sr housing dev ofcr, $45,156
Davis Vandegriffe, Donna M, workforce dev spec IV, $45,156

Day, Bridgett M, hsng prgm auditor & insp, $49,128
Days, Rita H, principal asst board/commisson, $70,000
Delaney, Sharon S, admin ofc spt asst, $33,744
Dempsey, Stephen M, workforce dev spec IV, $43,488
Denham, Kenneth, housing dev ofcr I, $35,568
Derks, Denise J, economic dev incentive spc III, $46,932
Dietrich, Natelle R, designated principal asst div, $83,430
Dishong, Patrick A, workforce dev spec I, $32,052
Distler, Laura D, sr ofc spt asst (keybrd), $29,904
Dixson, Anita P, workforce dev spec IV, $43,488
Doerhoff, Ronald F, ofc servs asst, $32,628
Donovan, Michael P, div dir, $81,600
Dottheim, Steven R, dpty counsel, $78,446
Douglas, Tasha, sr hsng prgm auditor & inspctr, $56,520
Drace, Jason H, acct II, $40,380
Drake, Jeffrey R, research mgr b1, $56,400
Driver, John R, hsng prgm auditor & insp, $52,092
Drummond, Carran A, workforce dev spec I, $32,052
Duckett, Tecora, research analyst III, $40,380
Dunham, Courtney L, consumer servs coord, $43,488
Dupre, Joan L, workforce dev spec I, $32,052
Durr, Caleb, workforce dev spec I, $32,052
Eaves, Dana E, utl regulatory auditor IV, $54,288
Ebbinghaus, Pamela D, tourist center spv, $30,984
Edwards, Justin S, consumer servs coord, $41,940
Ehrhard Reid, Sarah, economic dev incentive spec I, $31,512
Eichelberger, Pamela S, misc prof, $20.69/hr
Eiken, Michelle A, administrative asst, $41,013
Eimer, Elise, designated principal asst div, $30,979
Elrod, Lisa A, cmnty & economic dev mgrb3, $75,750
Elwood, Thomas E, environ spec II, $37,548
Enloe Hargus, Kimberley S, research analyst III, $47,892
Ensrud, Michael J, rate & tariff exam II, $40,380
Epperson, Connie E, workforce dev supv I, $33,744
Eubanks, Claire M, utl regulatory engr I, $55,416
Evans, Rebecca, workforce dev spec I, $32,052
Ewing, Lawanda H, workforce dev spec I, $36,204
Ewing, Tammi R, housing dev ofcr II, $46,068
Fangmann, Mandy, human rel ofcr I, $45,156
Featherstone, Cary G, utl regulatory auditor V, $68,160
Fee, Gabrielle, economic dev incentive spc III, $43,488
Fender, Kelly R, workforce dev supv II, $34,944
Ferguson, Lisa M, utl regulatory auditor IV, $55,416
Feuerborn, Geneva, sr ofc spt asst (keybrd), $32,472
Fife, Brenda K, info technology spec I, $56,520
Finnell, Kay, misc prof, $20.53/hr
Fischer, Carol S, workforce dev supv I, $40,380
Fischer, Janis E, utl policy analyst II, $69,612
Fitzgerald, Linda K, mkting spec I, $32,628
Fitzpatrick, Daniel L, utl engring spec II, $52,092
Fletcher, Eldon, workforce dev spec I, $32,052
Fletcher, Patricia, workforce dev spec I, $31,512
Fletcher, Rebecca J, workforce dev spec IV, $41,940
Flood, Cynthia E, fiscal & administrative mgr b2, $69,728
Flowers, James C, research mgr b2, $58,879
Floyd, Evelyn, workforce dev spec I, $29,976
Floyd, Tamara A, workforce dev spec IV, $47,892
Fortson, Bradley J, designated principal asst div, $46,200
Fortson, Michae'l D, acct I, $33,180
Foster, Clinton, utl engring spec II, $51,096
Foster, Keith D, utl regulatory auditor IV, $54,288
Foutes, Stephen A, cmnty & economic dev mgrb1, $42,513
Fox, Maudie J, workforce dev spec I, $32,052
Francis, Donald R, workforce dev spec I, $37,548
Franklin, Darryl L, workforce dev spec I, $36,204
Fred, Carol G, utl regulatory mngr, band1, $60,120
Freeman, Anne M, economic dev incentive spec II, $38,928
Freeman, David A, manuf hsng insp II, $36,888
Freshour, Rhonda K, workforce dev spec I, $38,928
Friedman, Jules M, hsng prgm auditor & insp, $49,128
Funk, Kristin M, workforce dev spec IV, $43,488
Gage, Katherine M, workforce dev spec I, $29,976
Gage, Nico S, special asst prof, $49,000
Gainous, Robert W, workforce dev spec I, $29,004
Galeano, Manuel H, misc tech, $16.00/hr
Gallivan, Kathy, workforce dev spec I, $29,004
Garber, Landon D, economic dev incentive spc III, $43,488
Garber, Robert, energy spec II, $36,204
Gardner, Christine M, economic dev incentive spc III, $47,892
Gassner, Joe L, environ mgr b2, $55,411
Gateley, Curtis B, utl policy analyst II, $55,416
Gavura, Michael A, special asst prof, $75,750
Gettys, Jeff, special asst prof, $67,000

Ghomsi, Noumvi G, utl engring spec II, $52,092
Gibby, Carol S, workforce dev spec I, $29,976
Gilliland, Nancy J, workforce dev spec I, $32,628
Givens, Gina A, workforce dev spec I, $34,356
Glasgow, Scott J, utl mgmt analyst III, $44,304
Glover, Barbara L, designated principal asst div, $73,000
Gourley, Sarah A, workforce dev spec I, $38,232
Gray, Harry L, workforce dev spec I, $32,052
Gray, Keisha L, admin ofc spt asst, $30,984
Greble, Gail A, mkting spec III, $43,488
Green, Audrie D, workforce dev spec I, $32,052
Green, Jacqueline, workforce dev spec I, $34,944
Green, Jermaine D, utl regulatory auditor III, $47,892
Green, Monica A, sr ofc spt asst (keybrd), $25,032
Green, Thomas S, designated principal asst div, $68,680
Greenbaum, Denise, info technology supv, $65,364
Greenslit, Edward L, workforce dev spec IV, $43,488
Gregory, Sheryl L, pers analyst II, $41,172
Griffin, Shana E, utl regulatory auditor III, $47,892
Gross, Randy S, utl regulatory engr I, $55,416
Hafner, Richard, workforce dev spec IV, $43,488
Hagan, Isaac K, research analyst I, $29,976
Hahn, Joyce M, workforce dev spec IV, $43,488
Haigh, Nicole L, research analyst I, $30,984
Hake, Dawn L, designated principal asst div, $41,013
Hale, Julia V, arts council prgm spec II, $41,940
Hall, Daniel Y, commissmbr, $106,625
Hall, Dennis G, pub info coor, $38,928
Hamby, Steven C, workforce dev spec IV, $43,488
Hanak, Scott A, cmnty & economic dev mgrb3, $68,583
Hanauer, John, info technology mgr, $71,100
Hanneken, Lisa K, utl regulatory auditor V, $65,364
Happy, Kimberly, administrative analyst III, $46,932
Happy, Layne M, misc prof, $8.12/hr
Hardy, Donna M, workforce dev spec I, $32,052
Hardy, Joyce, housing dev ofcr I, $41,940
Harmon, Paula M, housing prog loan admstr, $57,744
Harper, Kimberly R, economic dev incentive spec I, $35,568
Harps, Chiqueta M, hsng prgm auditor & insp, $41,940
Harris, Maurice S, planner II, $41,940
Harris, V W, utl regulatory auditor III, $49,128
Harrison, Paul R, utl regulatory auditor IV, $54,288
Hassani, Rachel G, prog consult, $76,259
Havener, Gregory B, economic dev incentive spec II, $38,928
Hawes, Carrie M, accounting analyst I, $46,932
Hawkins, John D, workforce dev spec II, $32,628
Hayton, Ryan L, info technology spec I, $56,520
Hearn, Rodney M, workforce dev spec I, $29,976
Heidbreder, Angela, sr ofc spt asst (keybrd), $30,384
Heifner, Tammy S, tourist asst, $23,880
Heimericks, Michael R, planner III, $55,416
Heinrich, Kevin D, workforce dev spec I, $38,928
Heintz, Jennifer L, chief counsel, $78,487
Hemenway, Sarah Y, div dir, $104,838
Henderson, Brenda S, tourist asst, $23,880
Henderson, Wess A, div dir, $90,000
Hensley, John F, mkting spec III, $45,156
Hiatte, Darrell L, misc prof, $30.77/hr
Higgins, Ronald C, sr housing dev ofcr, $46,932
Hildebrand, Tiffany R, designated principal asst div, $34,000
Hill, Billy R, tourist asst, $24,264
Hinrichs, Krista S, mkting spec III, $47,892
Hirniak, Justin, workforce dev spec I, $32,052
Hirst, Stacey D, fiscal & administrative mgr b2, $75,000
Hobbs, Elizabeth M, sr ofc spt asst (keybrd), $28,452
Hoehn, Kim R, admin ofc spt asst, $28,104
Hoffman, John P, info technologist IV, $53,208
Hollis Setser, Deborah D, workforce dev spec I, $32,052
Holmes, Laura L, tourist asst, $26,232
Holtmeyer, Rita A, misc prof, $24.24/hr
Holtschneider, Lucas C, designated principal asst div, $65,000
Homan, Lisa R, workforce dev spec I, $32,052
Hope, Ashleigh D, workforce dev supv II, $41,940
Hopkins, Amanda, acct II, $43,488
Hopper, Adrian, workforce dev spec I, $32,052
Hopper, Margaret, mkting spec I, $31,512
Horman, Darla J, planner III, $45,156
Horstman, Brenda S, cmnty & economic dev mgrb2, $75,000
Horton, Licia S, workforce dev supv I, $32,628
Hoskins, Laura L, hr mgr b1, $56,520
Hoss, Denise D, hsng prgm auditor & insp, $49,128
Houtman, Wayne W, workforce dev spec I, $29,976
Howard, Lyric S, misc tech, $10.00/hr

Huber, Tammy L, utl policy analyst II, $55,416
Huck, Linda L, workforce dev spec I, $38,928
Huelsing, Dave, workforce dev spec I, $32,052
Huff, Eric S, workforce dev spec I, $29,976
Huffman, Jason M, utl regulatory auditor II, $41,172
Huggins, April L, housing dev ofcr II, $34,356
Hughes, Mark D, prog consult, $76,259
Huhmann, Myra J, workforce dev spec IV, $43,488
Huhn, Elizabeth A, consumer servs spec II, $36,204
Hummel, Martin L, utl engring spec III, $58,908
Hunziker, William C, hsng prgm auditor & insp, $49,128
Hurt, Erica A, administrative asst, $41,013
Hutchins, Karen, workforce dev spec I, $32,052
Hyman, Martin R, planner II, $42,708
Hyneman, Charles R, utl regulatory auditor V, $66,720
Ice, Alissa R, housing prog loan admstr, $57,744
Imhoff, Thomas M, rate & tariff examination spv, $66,720
Ishida, Keiko C, arts council prgm spec II, $41,940
Jackson, Denise L, workforce dev supv II, $36,204
Jackson, Grey D, hsng prgm auditor & insp, $47,892
Jackson, Jonathan C, research analyst I, $30,984
Jackson, Shirley M, workforce dev spec I, $32,628
Jefferson, Nathaniel P, cmnty & economic dev mgrb2, $65,016
Jeffries, Kathy E, mgmt analysis spec I, $45,156
Jenkins, Andrea, acct I, $36,204
Jenkins, Lesa A, utl regulatory engr II, $65,364
Jensen, Gary, workforce dev spec IV, $41,940
Jeter-Boldt, Katherine, legal counsel, $67,584
Jimenez, Janet R, mkting spec I, $30,420
Johannes, Emily A, acct II, $36,204
Johannpeter, Kay A, designated principal asst div, $41,620
Johnson, Charles, workforce dev supv I, $33,744
Johnson, Jerron M, economic dev incentive spc III, $41,940
Johnson, Julian R, acct III, $53,208
Johnson, Lisa K, cmnty & economic dev mgrb2, $58,879
Johnson, Lincoln Sr, workforce dev supv II, $36,204
Johnson, Tracy, principal asst board/commisson, $42,523
Jones, Dorothy E, workforce dev spec IV, $41,172
Jones, Kennard L, regulatory law judge, $64,219
Jones-Kaufman, Ashley A, economic dev incentive spec I, $31,512
Jordan, Daniel, regulatory law judge, $64,219
Justice, Karen K, housing dev ofcr II, $40,380
Kabler, Anna M, sr ofc spt asst (keybrd), $29,904
Kaemmerer, Daniel W, legal counsel, $43,305
Kalthoff, James P, designated principal asst div, $91,405
Keckler, David, workforce dev spec IV, $41,940
Keevil, Jeffrey A, sr counsel, $57,744
Kehner, Annette, exec II, $46,068
Keilholz, Julie A, fiscal & administrative mgr b1, $57,744
Kelley, Michael, mkting spec III, $50,040
Kelly, Kevin T, pub info admstr, $57,744
Kempker, Lynne, budget analyst III, $57,744
Kenney, Robert S, commisschair, $106,625
Kenney, William P, commissmbr, $106,625
Ketchum, Steven L, workforce dev spec I, $32,052
Kiesling, Mark B, utl mgmt analyst II, $39,624
Kilker, Elizabeth, workforce dev spec I, $32,052
Kilker, Michael A, energy spec III, $40,380
Kimes, Reida M, tourist center spv, $32,052
King, Beverly F, tourist center spv, $32,052
Kingsbury, Jennifer L, economic dev incentive spc III, $43,488
Kinnett, Janet R, workforce dev supv I, $41,940
Klevorn, Jim G, housing prog loan admstr, $49,128
Kliethermes, Robin M, regulatory econ II, $45,156
Kliethermes, Sarah L, regulatory econ III, $57,744
Kline, Jill I, special asst prof, $41,172
Kocher, Martin, mkting spec I, $31,512
Koenigsfeld, Christine R, paralegal, $42,708
Kohly, Sherri L, utl policy analyst I, $47,892
Korenberg, Kevin M, research analyst I, $30,984
Kornelis, Susan M, acct I, $41,940
Kottwitz, John D, utl engring spec III, $60,120
Kraus, Steven A, misc prof, $31.15/hr
Kremer, Lisa A, utl regulatory mngr, band2, $66,720
Kronholm, Connie M, workforce dev spec IV, $43,488
Kunst, Jason P, utl regulatory auditor II, $39,624
Kyei, Zurett, research analyst I, $30,984
Lake, Jeanne L, workforce dev spec I, $37,548
Lake, Terry E, workforce dev spec I, $33,180
Landolt, Constance M, acct III, $46,932
Lange, Shawn E, utl engring spec III, $55,416
Lappin, Marilyn V, special asst prof, $97,455
Laramore, Laura K, workforce dev spec I, $32,052

Lawhon, Donna L, sr housing dev ofcr, $50,040
Lawrence, Mindy P, workforce dev spec I, $36,204
Lawson, Carla D, workforce dev spec I, $33,744
Lay, Thomas W, workforce dev supv II, $36,204
Lee, Darryl, workforce dev spec I, $29,004
Lee, Debra, workforce dev spec IV, $41,940
Lee-Robinson, Benita, acct II, $43,488
Leidy, Kelly L, workforce dev spec I, $33,180
Lennon, William D, div dir, $78,000
Leonard, Ted, misc prof, $15.00/hr
Leonberger, Robert R, utl regulatory eng spv, $74,304
Leonberger, Tracy F, consumer servs spec II, $37,548
Lester, Laura S, planner III, $45,156
Levesque, Andrea, manuf hsng insp II, $36,204
Levin, Benjamin N, misc prof, $14.41/hr
Lewis, Rachel M, prog consult, $80,868
Li, Yan, mkting spec III, $51,096
Lindeman, Linda I, workforce dev spec I, $32,052
Ling, Lynnea S, consumer servs spec II, $36,204
Linhardt, Darla K, workforce dev spec I, $32,052
Linville, Linda K, acct I, $36,204
Lock, Philip S, misc prof, $23.15/hr
Lohraff, Jane E, planner III, $45,156
Long, Jason M, info technologist IV, $46,932
Lopez, Carol R, housing dev ofcr I, $37,548
Lucas, Deborah, workforce dev spec I, $32,628
Luebbert, Jessica D, admin ofc spt asst, $33,744
Lyon, Belinda, workforce dev spec I, $34,944
Lyons, Karen K, utl regulatory auditor IV, $55,416
Mack, Jonathan D, cmnty & economic dev mgrb1, $50,924
Macrobie, Barbara A, pub info coor, $38,928
Magee, Douglas C, workforce dev spec I, $36,888
Maglich, Terrance M, mkting spec III, $61,332
Mahan, Kyle B, workforce dev supv I, $33,744
Mahaney, Jay, arch II, $61,332
Majors, Keith A, utl regulatory auditor IV, $55,416
Malone, Anne E, workforce dev spec IV, $41,940
Maloney, Cheryl R, workforce dev spec I, $32,052
Maloney, Erin L, utl regulatory engr I, $55,416
Mankin, D S, designated principal asst div, $40,291
Manning, Kristy J, designated principal asst div, $95,950
Manning, Tiffany, workforce dev spec IV, $41,940
Mannon, Alexander W, workforce dev spec I, $33,180
Mantle, Donna M, workforce dev spec IV, $46,068
Mantle, Lena M, misc prof, $35.72/hr
Marevangepo, Zephania, utl regulatory auditor III, $47,892
Marke, Geoffrey Q, designated principal asst div, $58,580
Marshall, Lisa J, workforce dev spec I, $32,052
Marshall, Lula O, workforce dev spec I, $30,984
Martin, Ryan W, utl regulatory engr I, $53,208
Massman, Chad, economic dev incentive spec I, $30,984
Masters, Daniel, workforce dev spec I, $32,628
Matranga, Audrey, workforce dev spec I, $32,052
Matthews, Michelle, workforce dev spec I, $29,004
Maupins, Candace, sr hsng prgm auditor & inspctr, $57,744
May, Brian H, special asst prof, $111,605
May, Cori S, accounting spec II, $41,172
May, Tim B, mkting spec II, $40,380
Mayfield, Cydney, sr counsel, $57,744
McAllister, Melody L, acct III, $47,892
McBride, Annie T, workforce dev spec I, $31,512
McCrady, Cheryl A, workforce dev spec I, $38,928
McCullough, C S, pub info coor, $38,928
McDonald, Kristy D, workforce dev spec I, $32,052
McKinney, Dee A, cmnty & economic dev mgrb2, $55,406
McKinnie, Adam C, ch utl econ, $62,664
McKnight, Linda A, workforce dev spec I, $34,356
McMellen, Amanda C, utl regulatory auditor V, $63,996
McNelis, Kathleen A, utl engring spec III, $55,416
McVicker, Todd M, environ spec III, $45,156
Mealy, Marcia, economic dev incentive spc III, $45,156
Meisenheimer, Barbara A, planner IV, $63,996
Merciel, James A, utl regulatory eng spv, $72,768
Mers, Nicole J, legal counsel, $46,068
Metz, August W, cmnty & economic dev mgrb3, $75,750
Meyer, Barbara J, energy engr II, $49,128
Middleton, Deborah J, pers clerk, $33,180
Middleton, Sandra D, fiscal & administrative mgr b2, $69,072
Mieir, Glen O, planner III, $47,892
Miles, Derick A, utl regulatory engr II, $61,332
Miller, Jan R, special asst prof, $46,932
Miller, Jennifer, housing prog loan admstr, $54,288
Miller, Joseph E, workforce dev spec I, $32,052

Mills, Lewis R, div dir, $101,000
Minish, Debra K, workforce dev spec IV, $46,068
Minor, Dylan M, workforce dev spec IV, $43,488
Mirabella, Glenn P, workforce dev spec I, $33,180
Mizer, Lisa J, workforce dev spec I, $32,052
Mock, Robert W, fiscal & administrative mgr b2, $62,115
Modlin, Emily, workforce dev supv II, $36,204
Molina, Joel A, utl regulatory auditor II, $39,624
Mondello, Kellie, fiscal & administrative mgr b2, $68,140
Monehan, Michael D, workforce dev spec I, $33,180
Moore, Amy E, prog consult, $76,259
Moore, Andrew, workforce dev spec I, $32,052
Moore, Jacqueline S, pub utl acct I, $34,944
Moore, Rosemary, housing dev ofcr I, $33,744
Moore, Sheila L, acct III, $42,708
Moore, Valerie L, cmnty & economic dev mgrb1, $55,550
Mormann, Brittney L, cmnty dev rep I, $34,356
Morris-sapp, Cynthia K, pub info spec II, $41,172
Morton, Craig A, workforce dev spec I, $32,628
Mueth, Marcella, legal counsel, $46,068
Mullins, Gretchen O, workforce dev spec I, $33,180
Murphy, Alyssa, pub info spec II, $36,888
Murray, Byron M, regulatory econ II, $45,156
Murray, David F, utl regulatory mngr, band2, $68,160
Murrell, Terry L, workforce dev spec I, $36,888
Myers, Jamie, misc prof, $14.41/hr
Myers, Leslie J, admin ofc spt asst, $33,180
Nagel, Marsha A, exec I, $34,944
Nance, Alisa, workforce dev spec I, $32,052
Nara, Zatuilla D, economic dev incentive spc III, $49,128
Neuner, Evan P, utl opers tech spec II, $41,940
Nguyen, Joann, legal counsel, $67,584
Niblack, William C, research mgr b2, $73,008
Nichols, Lori, workforce dev supv I, $33,744
Nickolaus, Nathan M, chief counsel, $106,555
Nussbaum, Sarah A, designated principal asst dept, $60,000
Oberreither, Mary A, admin ofc spt asst, $31,512
Ochoa, Gregg A, pub info coor, $46,068
Oerly, Marcy, energy spec IV, $50,040
Oetting, Beth A, hr mgr b1, $61,332
Oligschlaeger, Mark L, utl regulatory mngr, band3, $72,768
Onunkwor, Daniel, research analyst II, $41,940
Opitz, Timothy J, sr counsel, $57,744
Otto, Tracy J, designated principal asst div, $41,940
Overbey, Dawn E, designated principal asst dept, $46,068
Painter, Deborah L, workforce dev spec I, $40,380
Papen, Michael A, cmnty & economic dev mgrb2, $75,000
Pardalos, Ann G, cmnty & economic dev mgrb2, $70,008
Parish, Dana R, utl policy analyst I, $45,156
Parker, Tracy L, exec II, $38,232
Parkhurst, David, tourist asst, $23,880
Parks, Linda L, workforce dev supv III, $43,488
Parsons, Sarah, fiscal & administrative mgr b2, $71,205
Patterson, Samuel L, workforce dev spec I, $29,976
Pauley, Mark, economic dev incentive spc III, $50,040
Payne, Whitney A, legal counsel, $46,068
Pennington, Scottie, hr mgr b2, $71,205
Perry, Dianna I, workforce dev spec I, $32,052
Perry-jones, Antoinette, hsng prgm auditor & insp, $49,128
Person, Dorothy A, sr hsng prgm auditor & insptr, $53,208
Peterson, Julie, cmnty & economic dev mgrb1, $52,015
Pfliegier, Joselyn, housing dev ofcr II, $41,940
Phillips, Jeri, mkting spec I, $31,512
Phillips, Linda C, admin ofc spt asst, $28,104
Pinthuprapa, Chatchai, energy engr II, $50,040
Pitchford, Leslie K, workforce dev spec IV, $41,940
Pool, Nichelle P, workforce dev spec I, $32,052
Poole-king, Contessa J, pub info coor, $46,068
Pope, Judy A, admin ofc spt asst, $35,568
Popp, Andy W, environ mgr b2, $54,900
Poston, Charles T, utl regulatory engr I, $55,416
Poston, Marc D, dpty counsel, $71,023
Potts, Douglas, mkting spec III, $45,156
Potts, Rachel D, hr mgr b2, $75,000
Prenger, Deborah J, admin ofc spt asst, $37,548
Pridgin, Ronald D, regulatory law judge, $70,902
Pritchett, Cassie, research analyst II, $36,204
Pruitt, Michelle I, economic dev incentive spec I, $30,420
Quagraine, Frank A, designated principal asst div, $91,405
Rademan, Mark G, info technologist IV, $50,040
Rainbolt, Eric J, workforce dev spec I, $33,180
Rains, Wendy S, mkting spec I, $34,356
Ransdall, Billy L, designated principal asst div, $81,305

Rawlins, Karen A, workforce dev spec I, $32,052
Reeves, Sherry J, acct II, $46,068
Reinhart, Sandra L, admin ofc spt asst, $33,180
Reznicek, Steven D, cmnty & economic dev mgrb2, $58,879
Rice, Donald M, arts council prgm spec II, $41,172
Rice, Lorenzo, fiscal & administrative mgr b2, $71,205
Richter, Brooke M, utl regulatory auditor II, $39,624
Riechers, Charles M, hsng prgm auditor & insp, $49,128
Riley, Terry G, workforce dev spec I, $32,628
Riordan, James, acct II, $39,624
Ritchie, Joel E, misc tech, $16.00/hr
Roberts, Julie A, workforce dev spec I, $33,180
Robertson, Kimberly J, sr housing dev ofcr, $41,940
Robertson, Ted, ch pub utl acct, $71,208
Robinett, John A, utl engring spec III, $55,416
Robinson, Lester W, workforce dev supv II, $36,888
Robinson, Peggy A, economic dev incentive spc III, $45,156
Robnett, James Jr, economic dev incentive spc III, $56,520
Rogers, John A, utl regulatory mngr, band2, $68,160
Rogers, Megan R, workforce dev spec IV, $43,488
Roling, Alicia J, workforce dev spec IV, $47,892
Rollins, Jesse, energy engr I, $41,940
Ronan, Taylor, designated principal asst dept, $30,300
Rooffener, Michelle, workforce dev spec I, $32,052
Roos, David C, regulatory econ III, $55,416
Ross, Wanda S, workforce dev spec I, $32,052
Roth, Keriann N, pub utl acct II, $41,172
Rowell, Nasonya A, workforce dev spec I, $32,052
Rubin, Marsha A, hsng prgm auditor & insp, $49,128
Ruble, Robert L, cmnty & economic dev mgrb2, $58,897
Rupp, Scott T, commissmbr, $106,625
Russo, James M, rate & tariff examination spv, $62,664
Sabella, Jonathan R, misc prof, $14.41/hr
Salsman, Kari A, utl policy analyst I, $45,156
Sanders, Charles A, telecommun tech II, $39,624
Sanders, Lindsay N, acct I, $36,204
Sanders, Pamela A, housing dev ofcr II, $40,380
Sanders, Virginia R, admin ofc spt asst, $33,744
Sapp, Christine A, admin ofc spt asst, $28,104
Sarver, Ashley R, utl regulatory auditor II, $41,172
Sauter, Arthur P, tourist asst, $23,880
Schaben, Kristen M, economic dev incentive spec I, $30,420
Schad, Lauren J, designated principal asst div, $43,056
Schafer, Lance, pub utl fin anal, $49,128
Schallenberg, Robert E, designated principal asst div, $83,430
Scheible, Jerry, utl regulatory mngr III, $60,120
Schenewerk, Sharon, workforce dev spec IV, $43,488
Scheperle, Michael S, mgr economic analysis, $66,720
Scherr, Kevin J, energy spec IV, $49,128
Schlueter, Courtney, arts council prgm spec I, $34,944
Schmidt, Curtis D, info technology spec I, $56,520
Schmidt, Jennifer, housing prog loan admstr, $60,120
Schnittger, Marcia S, sr ofc spt asst (clerical), $33,036
Scholz, David, workforce dev supv I, $33,744
Scurlock, Eugene, acct II, $43,488
Seidner, Kendelle R, administrative asst, $41,013
Sharpe, Sarah B, utl regulatory auditor III, $46,932
Shea, Lynne, cmnty & economic dev mgrb2, $70,008
Shemwell, Lera L, dpty counsel, $66,720
Shipp, Joe N, workforce dev spec I, $30,984
Shofler, Kathryn S, workforce dev spec I, $32,052
Sieg, Susan, planner III, $48,156
Sigler, Leticia, fiscal & administrative mgr b1, $55,000
Simmons, Beverly S, workforce dev spec I, $32,052
Simms, Lori K, cmnty & economic dev mgrb2, $65,923
Simms, Wanda, account clerk II, $26,652
Simons, Christine, workforce dev spec I, $36,204
Sims, Darlene L, sr hsng prgm auditor & insptr, $62,664
Singler, Judith A, workforce dev spec I, $38,232
Sloan, Scott, workforce dev spec I, $32,052
Smith, Alan, workforce dev spec I, $32,052
Smith, Daniel D, info technologist IV, $54,288
Smith, Danielle L, cmnty & economic dev mgrb2, $60,257
Smith, Dave L, tourist center spv, $30,984
Smith, Donald E, workforce dev spec IV, $43,488
Smith, Julie E, housing dev ofcr II, $41,940
Smith, Justin F, utl regulatory mngr, band2, $53,208
Smith, Lana M, workforce dev spec I, $32,628
Smith, Lynn, workforce dev spec IV, $43,488
Smith, Marietta, sr housing dev ofcr, $41,940
Smith, Patricia A, utl mgmt analyst III, $46,068
Smith, Sabrina L, paralegal, $46,727
Sneed, Ashley L, tourist asst, $23,880

Snell, Christine, paralegal, $45,264
Soma, James, workforce dev spec I, $33,180
Sommerer, David M, utl regulatory mngr, band2, $71,100
Sowder, Stephen, training tech III, $45,156
Sparkman, Evelyn, acct II, $43,488
Spell, Alan E, designated principal asst div, $73,008
Sporcic, Andrea, pub info spec II, $41,172
Sprague, Shelly, workforce dev spec I, $29,004
Spratt, David A, utl opers tech spec II, $42,708
Spurgeon, Michael D, tourist center spv, $30,984
Stahlman, Michael L, regulatory econ III, $55,416
Stamper, Don, principal asst board/commisson, $60,000
Steck, Deborah L, sr ofc spt asst (steno), $29,904
Steck, Mary, misc prof, $25.49/hr
Steffan, Deborah L, fiscal & administrative mgr b1, $49,803
Stepp, Denise, workforce dev spec I, $33,744
Stetzler, Kip A, div dir, $121,705
Stevens, Ashley, consumer servs spec I, $32,052
Stevens, Debbie, sr ofc spt asst (clerical), $29,904
Stevens, William A, workforce dev spec IV, $41,940
Stine, Philip D, workforce dev spec I, $38,928
Stockman, Lisa A, acct II, $37,548
Stokely, Kristin R, legal counsel, $53,000
Stokes, Melanie, workforce dev spec I, $32,052
Stoll, Stephen M, commissmbr, $106,625
Struckhoff, Mark D, utl engring spec II, $52,092
Studstill, Jerry, workforce dev spec I, $32,052
Stueber, John S, accounting analyst III, $53,208
Sublett, Amy J, div dir, $94,510
Sullivan, Michael B, info technology spec II, $65,364
Sullivan, Terence L, info technologist IV, $57,744
Summerford, Amy M, economic dev incentive spec I, $30,984
Sundermeyer, Susan L, designated principal asst div, $38,223
Susan, Amy, designated principal asst dept, $76,255
Swartz, Robert T, workforce dev spec I, $40,380
Taylor, Jennifer C, workforce dev supv I, $34,944
Taylor, Trudi M, sr ofc spt asst (keybrd), $33,036
Tejan, Sharon D, mgmt analysis spec II, $41,940
Templemire, Janice E, sr ofc spt asst (keybrd), $29,904
Terrill, Glenda D, planner III, $53,208
Thomas, Accashia M, pub info spec I, $29,976
Thomas, Patricia A, admin ofc spt asst, $48,156
Thomas, Susan R, admin ofc spt asst, $30,984
Thompson, Deborah M, printing/mail technician II, $34,224
Thompson, Kevin A, managing counsel, $90,000
Tippin, Keener A, pub info coor, $41,940
Tisdale, Sherri S, workforce dev spec I, $32,052
Tompkins, Goldie L, prog consult, $80,868
Torufa, Edward S, labor econ, $56,520
Tripp, Mary S, workforce dev spec I, $32,052
Tucker, Ruth, mkting spec I, $31,512
Tune, Cheryl L, designated principal asst div, $60,000
Turk, Sara, fiscal & administrative mgr b2, $70,843
Turner, James A, workforce dev spec I, $32,052
Turner, Mary P, research analyst III, $42,708
Turner, Sally A, workforce dev spec I, $36,888
Turner, Tara L, workforce dev spec I, $32,052
Tyler, Brenda, housing dev ofcr I, $33,744
Van Eschen, John B, utl regulatory mngr, band3, $74,304
Van Slyck, Harold E, economic dev incentive spc III, $43,488
Van Wart, Deana M, workforce dev spec I, $34,944
Vander Meulen, Gretchen, workforce dev spec I, $35,568
Vander Veen, Mary K, account clerk II, $25,824
Vanleer Weig, Denise F, workforce dev spec I, $32,052
Vaught, Dianna L, designated principal asst div, $40,291
Velasco, Ricardo D, workforce dev spec I, $29,976
Vernier, Robert J, workforce dev supv I, $32,628
Vernon, Cynthia J, workforce dev spec I, $29,976
Verslues, Rebecca S, mkting spec III, $47,892
Verslues, Robert L, exec II, $37,548
Vollenweider, Brian, pub info admstr, $61,332
Von Seckendorff, Helene L, workforce dev spec I, $32,628
Voss, Cherlyn D, div dir, $90,000
Walker, Jr, workforce dev spec I, $32,628
Walker, Mallory, housing dev ofcr I, $34,944
Walker, Sarnia, workforce dev spec I, $29,004
Wallace, Annette, mkting spec III, $43,488
Wallace, Wanda S, workforce dev supv I, $33,744
Walls, Angela, anthony E, workforce dev spec I, $32,052
Walsh, Nikki, housing dev ofcr I, $33,744
Warren, Henry E, regulatory econ II, $57,744
Warren, Sarah A, economic dev incentive spc III, $45,156
Watson, Shytria, workforce dev supv I, $33,744

Watson, Weylin, legal counsel, $91,405
Watts, Amanda V, economic dev incentive spec II, $38,928
Weed, Danielle M, accounting spec I, $36,204
Weiler, Laura C, acct II, $40,380
Weingart, Steven J, workforce dev spec I, $29,976
Weiss, Llona, designated principal asst div, $86,169
Wells, Brian, utl regulatory auditor I, $38,928
Wells, Jennie R, paralegal, $40,291
Wheeler, Jessica E, auditor I, $33,744
White, Joan M, exec I, $41,940
White, Kenneth T, cmnty & economic dev mgrb1, $57,533
White, Lynette L, workforce dev supv II, $40,380
White, Sheldon L, info technologist IV, $54,288
Whitehead, Thomas E, workforce dev supv I, $33,744
Wiebe, Leslie R, admin ofc spt asst, $33,180
Wiederholt, Rebecca, mkting spec I, $31,512
Wilbers, Brenda R, environ mgr b3, $73,225
Wilbers, Christy L, acct II, $37,548
Wilfong, Tracy E, training tech II, $40,380
Will, Christopher G, research analyst II, $37,548
Williams, Gregory A, utl engring spec III, $56,520
Williams, Jill E, arts council prgm spec II, $40,380
Williams, Judy V, workforce dev spec I, $32,628
Williams, Mindy J, research analyst III, $45,156
Williams, Nathan C, dpty counsel, $66,720
Williams, Samantha L, workforce dev spec I, $29,004
Williams, Sheila P, workforce dev spec IV, $43,488
Williams, William H, legal counsel, $46,068
Wilson, Billie L, pers ofcr I, $45,156
Wilson, Debra, workforce dev spec I, $32,628
Winters, Michelle, workforce dev spec I, $32,052
Woltkamp, Melissa R, cmnty & economic dev mgrb2, $61,610
Won, Seoung Joun, regulatory econ III, $55,416
Woodruff, Morris L, regulatory law judge, $78,487
Woodworth, Wayne L, workforce dev supv I, $33,744
Woolery, Gayla D, workforce dev supv I, $32,628
Word, Megan M, cmnty & economic dev mgrb3, $72,720
Worley, Melody K, economic dev incentive spc III, $46,932
Wright, Charity Y, housing dev ofcr II, $34,356
Wright, Cheryl L, designated principal asst div, $40,291
Wright, Marcus, misc prof, $12.24/hr
Wright, Wanda L, workforce dev spec I, $40,380
Xu, Ming, energy engr III, $55,416
Yarbrough, Karen R, workforce dev spec I, $32,052
Yarnell, John B, pub info spec I, $30,984
York, John M, workforce dev spec I, $29,976
Young, Matthew, utl regulatory auditor III, $46,932

Department of Elementary and Secondary Education

205 Jefferson St., PO Box 408, Jefferson City 65101

Vandeven, Margaret M, commissioner, $187,776
Aaron, Bonnie L, asst supt, $57,336
Aaron, Cara L, dd cnslr, $38,040
Abbey, Holly, dd cnslr II, $43,008
Abernathy, Judith A, tchr aide, $11.36/hr
Ables, Marilyn S, short term sub tchr, $14.03/hr
Abotobik, Alice M, short term sub tchr, $14.33/hr
Abotobik, Alice M, tchr aide, $11.36/hr
Acton, Kayla M, residential advisor I, $20,856
Adam, Sharon T, dd case ctrl analyst, $25,296
Adam, Suzanne E, sec, $15,936
Adams, Christie J, tchr aide, $18,528
Adams, Donna M, student life dir, $42,960
Adams, Jenifer L, short term sub tchr, $14.03/hr
Adams, Pat O, short term sub tchr, $14.03/hr
Adams, Robert W, residential advisor I, $12.09/hr
Adamson, Jennifer N, bus attendant, $10.05/hr
Adamson, Jennifer N, tchr aide, $11.36/hr
Adamson, Jennifer N, short term sub tchr, $14.03/hr
Adamson, Lacy M, tchr aide, $11.36/hr
Adamson, Lacy M, custodial worker I, $10.05/hr
Adkins, Stacy L, tchr, $28,704
Ajuzie, Elizabeth C, nutrition prog spec, $38,880
Alber, Juliana D, tchr, $27,792
Albers, Anthony T, tchr, $31,944
Aldridge, Lisa A, short term sub tchr, $22.10/hr
Aldridge, Lisa A, tchr aide, $11.36/hr
Alejo, Lyla M, tchr aide, $11.36/hr
Alexander, Catherine, vr cnslr III, $47,712

Alexander, Maureen T, rgnal mgr, $66,648
Alexander, Rene M, registered nurse, bsn, $42,120
Alexander, Sarah F, tchr aide, $11.36/hr
Ali, Yvonne, sup, $45,480
Allan, Gavin S, dir, $51,864
Allan, Karen E, dir, $51,360
Allee, Tammy D, exec asst, $35,952
Allegrini, Beth A, vr cnslr II, $43,008
Allen, Amy C, tchr aide, $18,600
Allen, Anita L, billing spec, $25,272
Allen, Deborah A, short term sub tchr, $14.03/hr
Allen, Diana L, custodial worker II, $27,984
Allen, Ethan R, tchr aide, $11.36/hr
Allen, Haley V, tchr aide, $19,632
Allen, Marsha L, short term sub tchr, $14.33/hr
Allen, Marsha L, tchr aide, $11.36/hr
Allen, Marsha L, long term sub tchr, $20.90/hr
Allen, Richard L, hearing ofcr, $53,472
Allen, Tracy L, home school coord, ms, $44,424
Allen, Wanda K, legal asst, $34,608
Allison, Charlene S, tchr aide, $21,144
Althiser, Mary C, hr analyst, $43,008
Althoff, John C, dd cnslr I, $39,960
Amour, Marion P, sec, $10.73/hr
Ancipink, Jacquelyn, dd cnslr II, $43,008
Anderson, Crystal L, interpreter, $36,528
Anderson, Giana M, asst dist supv, $51,864
Anderson, Kenneth E, asst dir, $47,712
Anderson, Megan S, tchr aide, $11.36/hr
Anderson, Summer, tchr aide, $14,904
Anderson, Susan F, registered nurse, bsn, $22.65/hr
Andes, Grover S, bldg admin, $46,896
Andrews, Priscilla, residential advisor I, $26,736
Angerer, Kaylie L, billing spec, $24,768
Annis, Meredith L, tchr aide, $11.36/hr
Arbuckle, Stacey L, tchr aide, $13,584
Ardrey, Brenne L, vr cnslr III, $47,712
Arellin, John C, dist sup, $55,728
Arl, Lisa M, tchr aide, $14,832
Arl, Lisa M, short term sub tchr, $2.03/hr
Arl, Lisa M, long term sub tchr, $8.90/hr
Arland, Daniel, vr cnslr IV, $50,568
Arnette, Sara L, vr cnslr II, $43,008
Arnold, Janet L, short term sub tchr, $14.33/hr
Arnold, Janet L, tchr aide, $11.36/hr
Arnold, Janet L, bus attendant, $10.05/hr
Arnold, Janet L, tchr In charge, $17.27/hr
Arnold, Julie Y, tchr aide, $17,808
Arnold, Nancy F, tchr, $44,784
Arthur, Joshua L, tchr aide, $11.36/hr
Atkins, Courtney R, registered nurse, bsn, $33,480
Atterberry, Patty L, nurse lpn, $13.94/hr
Aubuchon, Gail M, sup, $55,344
Aubuchon, Kristen A, residential advisor I, $20,448
Audrain, Kathleen F, administrative asst, $29,328
Aust, Crystal J, nurse lpn, $23,640
Austin, Tiffany J, dd cnslr I, $39,960
Avant, Eric L, administrative asst, $27,480
Avicola, Karla, vr cnslr I, $39,960
Babb, Amber L, tchr aide, $11.36/hr
Babcock, Deanna, dd cnslr II, $43,008
Bachwirtz, Charles E, vr cnslr II, $43,008
Backes, Carol S, tchr aide, $11.36/hr
Backes, Cathy J, dd cnslr, $38,040
Bacon, Tonia R, sec, $25,296
Bader, Eric W, tchr, $31,584
Badji, Yaya, sup, $41,952
Bailey, Jill S, tchr, $39,144
Bailey, Jill S, homebound tchr, $24.23/hr
Bailey, Tisha J, asst dist supv, $51,864
Baker, Anita L, asst dir, $53,616
Baker, Ann M, vr cnslr III, $47,712
Baker, David D, sup, $52,128
Baker, James F, short term sub tchr, $14.03/hr
Baker, Joseph M, sup, $37,968
Baker, Mildred M, tchr aide, $14,208
Baker, Mildred M, short term sub tchr, $2.53/hr
Baker, Nancy J, tchr, $46,488
Baker, Nancy J, homebound tchr, $24.23
Baker, Nancy J, residential advisor III, $30,720
Baker, Rachel E, short term sub tchr, $14.03/hr
Balabas, Bradley S, dd cnslr II, $43,008
Barbee, Donald E, custodial worker II, $25,536

Barber, Jamie E, tchr, $30,288
Barber, Jamie E, homebound tchr, $24.23/hr
Barber, Lesa C, vr cnslr II, $43,008
Barbour, Robin E, exec asst, $41,688
Barchers, Kristi J, tchr, $28,704
Barchers, Kristi J, homebound tchr, $24.23/hr
Bardwell, Melissa D, sup, $39,144
Barjenbruch, Jesse L, tchr aide, $14,832
Barnard, Marilyn J, short term sub tchr, $14.03/hr
Barnard, Marilyn J, long term sub tchr, $20.90/hr
Barner-gordon, Lashawn R, tchr aide, $13,584
Barnes, Dawn Y, sec, $22,320
Barnes, Faith A, tchr aide, $11.36/hr
Barnes, Faith A, short term sub tchr, $14.03/hr
Barnes, Gary, custodial worker II, $24,168
Barnett, Joycie R, tchr aide, $15,120
Barney, Geoffrey Q, supt, $77,136
Barr, Stephen L, asst commissioner, $96,432
Bartimus, Jennifer L, tchr aide, $11.36/hr
Bartimus, Jennifer L, short term sub tchr, $14.03/hr
Barton, Brenda S, custodial worker I, $10.05/hr
Barton, Brenda S, tchr aide, $11.36/hr
Bartram, Penni L, administrative asst, $29,040
Bashore, Chrissy A, sup, $38,880
Bastean, Thomas W, asst supt, $27.20/hr
Bates, Chantel L, dd cnslr II, $43,008
Bates, Kathryn S, bldg admin, $37,200
Bates, Kathryn S, homebound tchr, $24.23/hr
Bates, Shaun C, dir, $50,232
Bath, Stepheny J, phys edu tchr, $40,728
Battle, Ali J, billing spec, $24,504
Batts, Kathleen J, tchr aide, $11.36/hr
Baucom, Laura A, tchr, $30,960
Baucom, Laura A, homebound tchr, $24.23/hr
Baugher, Darlene R, dir, $67,128
Bauman, Kim R, tchr aide, $14,208
Baumgartner, Danielle A, tchr aide, $11.36/hr
Bax, Elizabeth S, dd case ctrl analyst, $28,056
Bax, Kristen N, dd cnslr III, $47,712
Bax, Monica M, dd cnslr III, $47,712
Baxter, Lorna L, short term sub tchr, $14.03/hr
Baxter, Lorna L, tchr aide, $11.36/hr
Baxter, Lorna L, sec, $10.73/hr
Bayless, Brenda H, registered nurse, bsn, $42,120
Bean, Caressa B, tchr aide, $11.36/hr
Beasley, Saundra J, tchr aide, $14,832
Beattie, Jeannette L, cook II, $15,024
Beatty, Noel L, supply mgr, $36,936
Becherer, Nicholas P, dd cnslr, $21.87/hr
Beck, Andrea K, state & fed compliance ofcr, $72,792
Beck, Claire F, dist sup, $55,728
Beck, Hermetta S, administrative asst, $34,200
Beck, Robin D, tchr aide, $14,208
Becker, Candice D, procurement spec, $31,656
Beckham, Elise D, sec, $20,352
Beeman, Lisa C, tchr aide, $14,136
Begay, Ralphfred D, dd cnslr, $38,040
Behl, Larhonda J, tchr aide, $11.36/hr
Behl, Larhonda J, registered nurse, $21.66/hr
Behle, Tanya A, billing spec, $25,272
Bell, Stephanie F, homebound tchr, $24.23/hr
Bell, Stephanie F, tchr, $28,704
Belt, Peggy L, interpreter, $42,432
Belt, Sharon K, hearing ofcr, $56,208
Belton, Eileen, sup, $44,328
Benitz, Melanie A, vr cnslr II, $43,008
Bennett, Angela R, dd cnslr II, $43,008
Benton, Chokaio P, home school coord, ms, $43,560
Berensen, Kerry L, long term sub tchr, $20.90/hr
Berensen, Kerry L, short term sub tchr, $14.09/hr
Bergman, Lorie A, administrative asst, $30,432
Bergmann, Karen A, dd cnslr, $21.87/hr
Berhorst, Gretchen M, sup, $49,200
Berlin-bates, Kara M, vr cnslr, $38,040
Bernardino, Arminda L, registered nurse, $21.66/hr
Bernskoetter, Mark J, asst field opps mgr, $67,872
Berry, Amanda M, tchr aide, $11.36/hr
Berry, Amanda M, bus attendant, $10.05/hr
Bertram, Julie A, dd cnslr, $38,040
Bertucci, Crystal S, accounting spec, $37,344
Bess, Catherine A, tchr aide, $14,208
Bess, Catherine A, short term sub tchr, $2.53/hr
Beussink, Rebecca J, dd cnslr, $38,040

Bibbs, Christopher R, vr cnslr III, $47,712
Biles, Stephen J, tchr aide, $11.36/hr
Biles, Stephen J, short term sub tchr, $14.33/hr
Billings, Constance, bldg admin, $55,152
Bishoff, Lynn A, dd case ctrl analyst, $28,056
Bitterman, Latisha D, tchr aide, $11.36/hr
Bittle, Kandy J, tchr aide, $11.36/hr
Black, Rebecca A, short term sub tchr, $14.33/hr
Black, Rebecca A, tchr aide, $11.36/hr
Blackwell, Lucille R, tchr, $35,928
Blair, Brandi N, tchr, $29,184
Blair, Brandi N, homebound tchr, $24.23/hr
Blakley, Dwayne D, custodial worker II, $24,144
Blakley, Leo J, sup, $19.79/hr
Blankley, Sheila M, tchr, $42,360
Blankley, Sheila M, homebound tchr, $24.23/hr
Blattel, Amy R, hearing ofcr, $53,472
Bledsoe, Bradley L, dir, $60,408
Bledsoe, Michelle D, billing spec, $25,272
Bloch, Jessica L, vr cnslr I, $39,960
Blue, Vickie E, tchr aide, $15,624
Blue, Vickie E, short term sub tchr, $1.39/hr
Boan, Betty J, tchr aide, $14,832
Board, Melba A, bldg admin, $47,904
Bobbett, Lois A, dist mgr, $59,856
Boeckmann, Julie A, comm technician, $38,544
Boeger, Geraldine A, dd cnslr III, $47,712
Boehmer, Donald J, tchr aide, $11.36/hr
Boehmer, Donald J, short term sub tchr, $14.03/hr
Boessen, Lora J, sup, $39,648
Boldt, Shane W, custodial worker II, $21,168
Boles, Janet V, administrative asst, $26,952
Bolin, Kathy J, dd ce spec, $26,184
Bommarito, Natalie A, vr cnslr II, $43,008
Bonderer, Mary D, tchr aide, $13,608
Bone, Herbert L, tchr aide, $11.36/hr
Bonk, Marianne R, tchr aide, $11.36/hr
Bonner, Susan D, sup, $51,672
Bonsall, Barbara, hr analyst, $36,624
Bonsall, Gary L, short term sub tchr, $14.03/hr
Bonsall, Gary L, long term sub tchr, $20.90/hr
Boone, Jane M, hearing ofcr, $59,856
Boone, Regina L, billing spec, $25,272
Booth, Janice R, tchr aide, $15,792
Boren, Linda S, tchr aide, $11.36/hr
Borgel, Emily J, vr cnslr IV, $50,568
Borgmeyer, Mary L, registered nurse, $21.66/hr
Bosman, Anthony D, residential advisor I, $23,184
Boston, Virginia A, sec, $10.84/hr
Boudreau, Jennifer E, dd cnslr, $38,040
Bowen, Amy L, vr cnslr IV, $50,568
Bowles, Nancy L, communication spec, $42,840
Bowlin, Sheila M, cook II, $15,024
Bowman, Mary C, short term sub tchr, $14.03/hr
Bowman, Mary C, tchr aide, $11.36/hr
Bowmar, Joyce R, tchr aide, $15,624
Bown, Marlene K, tchr aide, $14,520
Boyd, Pamela A, asst dir, $53,616
Boyer, Brenda E, tchr aide, $14,832
Boykins-Walls, Marleta R, tchr aide, $14,208
Boykins-Walls, Marleta R, short term sub tchr, $2.53/hr
Brackett, Laurie G, vr cnslr I, $39,960
Bradfield, Elizabeth R, tchr aide, $11.36/hr
Bradfield, Elizabeth R, short term sub tchr, $22.10/hr
Bradford, Candice M, dd case ctrl analyst, $26,952
Bradley, Jonathan D, residential advisor I, $20,856
Bradley-Sias, Cynthia, residential advisor I, $21,264
Bradshaw, Donna J, qual assurance spec, $51,864
Brady, Marjorie A, vr cnslr II, $43,008
Brady, Terry J, tchr aide, $11.36/hr
Brake, Deborah K, tchr aide, $11.36/hr
Brake, Deborah K, cook I, $9.45/hr
Brandl, Erika D, sup, $41,160
Brandt, Juell M, tchr, $32,136
Bransfield, Somer E, tchr aide, $11.36/hr
Branson, Vickie A, dd cnslr I, $39,960
Branstetter, Judy L, billing spec, $25,272
Braswell, Betty J, administrative asst, $28,224
Braxton, Charles E, residential advisor III, $26,424
Bray, Kelly A, dd cnslr, $38,040
Brejcha, Kay K, bldg admin, $47,856
Breshears, Joan B, nurse lpn, $13.94/hr
Brewner, Kimberly L, tchr aide, $15,624

Briscoe, Deloris A, tchr aide, $14,376
Brock, Lori G, tchr aide, $11.36/hr
Brockmeier, Richard H, sup, $18.36/hr
Brogoto, Victoria A, tchr aide, $11.36/hr
Brooks, Lana S, dir, $53,160
Brooks, Rebecca L, tchr aide, $11.36/hr
Brooks, Stephanie A, dir, $51,864
Broom, John H, coord, $72,072
Brower, Christina A, dd cnslr II, $43,008
Brown, Betty J, short term sub tchr, $14.33/hr
Brown, Betty J, tchr aide, $11.36/hr
Brown, Betty J, homebound tchr, $24.23/hr
Brown, Jessica S, tchr aide, $11.36/hr
Brown, Jessica S, short term sub tchr, $14.33/hr
Brown, Jessica S, cook I, $9.45/hr
Brown, Kathy L, tchr aide, $14,832
Brown, Kiersten M, vr cnslr I, $39,960
Brown, Kimberly D, tchr aide, $15,696
Brown, Magen R, vr cnslr I, $39,960
Brown, Rebecca L, tchr aide, $11.36/hr
Brown, Troy L, custodial worker II, $26,544
Brown, Walter L, sup of instruction, $55,344
Browner, Lina M, exec asst, $38,544
Brownewell, Tracy D, tchr aide, $14,832
Brownewell, Tracy D, short term sub tchr, $2.03/hr
Brownlee, Chanee M, tchr aide, $11.36/hr
Brozovich, Rebecca S, home school coord, ms, $40,824
Bruce, Connie L, tchr In charge, $40,656
Bruner, Jacqueline A, sup, $23.95/hr
Bruning, Kristi A, qual assurance spec, $52,896
Bryan, Elaine M, dir, $55,320
Bryan, Miranda J, billing spec, $25,272
Bryant, Angela M, billing spec, $25,272
Bryant, Bruce A, asst dir, $56,448
Bryant, Marsha, coord, $61,464
Bu, Valerie S, asst dist supv, $51,864
Bubulka, Virginia S, tchr aide, $15,432
Buhr, Lisa B, dd cnslr II, $43,008
Bunton, Arlene S, tchr aide, $11.36/hr
Burch, Janelle M, instructional spec, $42,552
Burgess, Vernetta M, tchr aide - bus atnd, $20,064
Burke, Patricia M, tchr, $29,280
Burkhart, Robin A, dir, $52,200
Burkhead, Karen C, hr analyst, $35,976
Burks, Lisa M, accounting spec, $28,008
Burlison, Susan L, short term sub tchr, $14.03/hr
Burnaman, Debbie L, tchr, $34,392
Burney, Karen J, bus attendant, $11,136
Burney, Karen J, tchr aide, $11.36/hr
Burns, Jennifer A, home school coord, ms, $42,720
Burns, Kenneth L, custodial worker I, $10,896
Burns, Lauren A, tchr aide, $11.36/hr
Burns, Tina T, vr cnslr IV, $50,568
Burton, Loraine, bus attendant, $10.05/hr
Burton, Loraine, short term sub tchr, $14.33/hr
Burton, Loraine, tchr aide, $11.36/hr
Burton, Talea R, tchr aide, $11.36/hr
Busdieker, Leon C, dir, $50,544
Bush, Fritz E, dd cnslr I, $39,960
Buss, Stacy L, instructional spec, $34,272
Butcher, Deborah L, sup, $41,160
Butler, Lorraine A, vr business spec I, $39,960
Butler, Yvonne R, tchr aide, $11.36/hr
Butler, Yvonne R, cook I, $9.45/hr
Cable, Heather J, tchr aide, $14,064
Cachero, Robin L, registered nurse, $39,672
Caddell, Jessica R, sup, $38,352
Cafolla, Sharon K, vr cnslr III, $47,712
Cairer, Travis L, phys edu tchr, $29,160
Caldwell, Kristen M, dd cnslr II, $43,008
Calhoun, Linda S, sec, $10.73/hr
Calhoun, Susan H, tchr aide, $15,096
Callan, James E, custodial worker I, $10.05/hr
Callan, James E, tchr aide, $11.36/hr
Calton, Kimberly R, tchr aide, $14,544
Calvert, Paul D, dd cnslr II, $43,008
Calvin, Edward L, residential advisor III, $26,016
Calvin, Timothy I, tchr aide, $11.36/hr
Camden, Sandra L, tchr aide, $15,888
Camp, Sarah C, dir, $50,832
Campbell, Sarah E, tchr aide, $11.36/hr
Campbell, Sarah E, short term sub tchr, $14.33/hr
Cann, Charlene A, registered nurse, $40,392

Cardetti, Dorothy G, long term sub tchr, $8.90/hr
Cardetti, Dorothy G, tchr aide, $14,832
Cardetti, Dorothy G, short term sub tchr, $2.03/hr
Carel, Lisa A, short term sub tchr, $14.03/hr
Carlisle-moresi, Diana M, dd cnslr III, $47,712
Carlson, Tracy A, custodial worker II, $29,280
Carlstrom, Todd A, dd cnslr I, $39,960
Carlyle, Tamara J, tchr aide-bus driver, $20,400
Carney, Vickie P, tchr aide - bus atnd, $19,176
Carr, Mary I, tchr aide, $11.36/hr
Carrera, Jennifer J, tchr aide, $14,208
Carrington, Joan I, activities dir, $44,352
Carrington, Roy L, residential advisor I, $12.09/hr
Carroll, Amanda M, residential advisor I, $12.09/hr
Carroll, Julie A, administrative asst, $29,928
Carroll, Karen M, residential advisor I, $21,264
Carson, Catherine R, dir, $24,288
Carson, Larachel, residential advisor I, $25,992
Carter, Amber, tchr aide, $20,064
Carter, Jessica M, tchr aide, $13,320
Carter, Mary A, vr cnslr II, $43,008
Carter, Oscar E, dir, $49,056
Carter, Rebecca J, short term sub tchr, $14.33/hr
Carter, Rebecca J, long term sub tchr, $20.90/hr
Carter, Stephen, vr cnslr II, $43,008
Carwile, Abigail S, dd cnslr III, $47,712
Casey, Sandra A, tchr aide, $14,208
Cash, Amanda J, data spec, $34,608
Cash, Donna J, sup, $41,160
Cashmer, Wanda D, tchr aide, $11.36/hr
Cashmer, Wanda D, bus driver, $10.36/hr
Castillo-lara, Angela D, administrative asst, $26,952
Castleman, Amber M, asst dir, $47,712
Castrop, Cassandra, procurement spec, $33,552
Catt, Donna L, dir, $49,056
Celeslie, Mary J, sec, $27,984
Chambers, J'aysha K, dd cnslr I, $39,960
Chandler, Gregory D, dd cnslr II, $43,008
Chandler, Pamela D, dd spec, $21.87/hr
Chaney, Mark S, tchr aide, $11.36/hr
Chaplin, Kimberly R, asst dist supv, $51,864
Chaplin, Patricia S, dd cnslr II, $47,712
Chappelow, Marsha A, charter schools field dir, $39,672
Charlton, Denise I, registered nurse, $40,392
Cheek, Eric P, phys edu tchr, $33,840
Chen, Shaojun, mobl and orient inst, $36,432
Chesnut, Joy L, short term sub tchr, $14.03/hr
Childers, Janet L, dist sup, $55,728
Chin, Sarah-cortney R, tchr aide, $11.36/hr
Christian, Virgil R, tchr aide, $13,320
Christiansen, Catherine V, short term sub tchr, $14.03/hr
Christiansen, Judith, tchr, $33,456
Christiansen, Judith, homebound tchr, $24.23/hr
Christiansen, Veronica M, short term sub tchr, $22.10/hr
Christopher, Joyce M, vr cnslr IV, $50,568
Cieslewicz, Carlene, registered nurse, bsn, $42,120
Clancy-may, Maureen E, sup of instruction, $55,344
Clardy, Sarah L, rgnal mgr, $66,648
Clark, Debra L, tchr aide, $14,208
Clark, Michelle J, asst dist supv, $51,864
Clary, Ashley B, tchr aide, $11.36/hr
Clary, Ashley B, bus attendant, $10.05/hr
Clause, Chris B, dir, $57,000
Clay, Danna S, administrative asst, $26,952
Cleaveland, Sara L, vr cnslr II, $43,008
Clements, Margaret S, sec, $12.81/hr
Clevenger, Carol L, tchr aide, $14,352
Clifford, Joseph K, custodial worker II, $24,168
Cline, Tammy J, tchr aide, $11.36/hr
Clink, Debra A, sch transp/fin consult, $47,640
Clinton, Teresa M, short term sub tchr, $14.03/hr
Clinton, Teresa M, tchr aide, $11.36/hr
Clinton, Teresa M, bus attendant, $10.05/hr
Cloninger, Larry H, short term sub tchr, $14.33/hr
Cloninger, Larry H, tchr aide, $11.36/hr
Clubb, Verna J, tchr aide, $18,168
Cluckey, Coleman P, cook II, $17,184
Clutter, Olivia C, short term sub tchr, $14.33/hr
Clutter, Olivia C, tchr aide, $11.36/hr
Clymer, Scott A, residential advisor I, $20,448
Cobb, Timothy L, tchr, $32,520
Cochran, Catherine A, dd cnslr III, $47,712
Cochran, Matthew C, dd cnslr, $38,040

Cockrum, Leslie A, vr cnslr III, $47,712
Cockrum, Shawn H, dir, $53,280
Coffman, Christopher A, sup, $38,352
Coffman, Robin E, chief of staff, $96,432
Coffman, Stephen D, rgnal field technician, $50,016
Coldiron, Codie N, tchr aide, $14,520
Cole, Adrian B, tchr aide, $19,632
Cole, Brian A, custodial worker II, $24,168
Cole, Julie A, tchr aide, $11.36/hr
Cole, Kathleen L, tchr, $30,096
Cole, Kathleen L, homebound tchr, $24.23/hr
Cole, Melinda M, custodial worker II, $24,168
Collaso, Barbara J, vr cnslr III, $47,712
Collins, Arki L, tchr aide, $15,624
Collins, Johnny D, short term sub tchr, $14.03/hr
Collins, Johnny D, tchr aide, $11.36/hr
Collins, Johnny D, bus driver, $0.19/hr
Collins, Johnny D, bus attendant, $10,632
Collins, Karen M, tchr, $29,160
Collins, Kathy L, asst dir, $53,616
Collins, Kelly L, dd cnslr, $38,040
Collins, Lashonda C, administrative asst, $26,952
Collins, Linda, vr cnslr III, $47,712
Collins, Nicholas P, tchr aide, $11.36/hr
Collins, Nicholas P, bus attendant, $10.05/hr
Collins, Nicholas P, short term sub tchr, $14.33/hr
Collins, Shanda M, tchr, $28,152
Colopy, Robert E, residential advisor I, $22,488
Conklin, Deanna L, custodial worker I, $10.05/hr
Conklin, Deanna L, tchr aide, $11.36/hr
Conklin, Deanna L, cook I, $9.45/hr
Conn, Teresa G, short term sub tchr, $14.03/hr
Conn, Teresa G, tchr aide, $11.36/hr
Conrad, Kimberly L, dist sup, $57,000
Cook, Bobbie A, sec, $23,736
Cook, Kelly R, asst dir, $53,616
Cook, Michael J, vr spec, $26.24/hr
Cook, Rea L, short term sub tchr, $14.33/hr
Cook, Rea L, long term sub tchr, $20.90/hr
Cook, Rea L, tchr aide, $11.36/hr
Cook, Rhonda J, short term sub tchr, $22.10/hr
Cooke, Abigail R, dd cnslr III, $47,712
Coon, John C, tchr aide, $11.36/hr
Coon, John C, short term sub tchr, $14.33/hr
Cooper, Mary M, short term sub tchr, $14.33/hr
Cooper, Mary M, tchr aide, $11.36/hr
Cooper, Tracy L, tchr, $32,520
Cooper-brown, Mary A, tchr aide, $14,856
Cooperrider, Lois P, sec, $10.73/hr
Corcoran, Christina L, dd cnslr II, $43,008
Corey, Mary K, dir, $51,864
Cottam, Brittany E, tchr aide, $11.36/hr
Cottam, Brittany E, short term sub tchr, $14.03/hr
Cotten, Klarissa J, tchr aide, $11.36/hr
Counsil, Charles A, residential advisor I, $20,856
Counsil, Patricia A, sec, $24,720
Cousins, Kelly A, cook II, $17,520
Couzens, Marilena, tchr aide, $11.36/hr
Cowell, Julia A, dir, $51,864
Cox, Ted D, hearing ofcr, $28.64/hr
Coy, Mara L, tchr aide, $14,520
Coy, Mara L, homebound tchr, $24.23/hr
Coy, Mara L, short term sub tchr, $2.28/hr
Coy, Mara L, long term sub tchr, $9.15/hr
Crabtree, Staci R, tchr aide, $14,520
Craft, Sarah E, tchr aide, $14,856
Craighead, Johnnie L, custodial worker I, $27,000
Craigmiles, Rian A, tchr, $28,152
Craigmiles, Rian A, homebound tchr, $24.23/hr
Crawford, Kevin P, tchr aide, $14,208
Crawford, Loretta A, tchr aide, $17,256
Cremer, Emily R, hr school spec, $42,264
Cremer, Jill M, dir, $57,000
Crihfield, Rhoda M, tchr, $36,864
Crihfield, Rhoda M, homebound tchr, $24.23/hr
Crismas, Michelle T, dd cnslr III, $47,712
Crismon, Tammy E, qual assurance spec, $51,864
Crocker, Deanna J, tchr aide, $14,352
Crockett, Wanda M, residential advisor I, $12.09/hr
Crosby, Heather L, dir, $51,864
Crosby, Teresa L, tchr aide, $18,312
Cross, Angela M, tchr aide, $14,208
Cross, Catherine L, sec, $21,024

Crow, Sherri M, tchr aide, $14,376
Crowder, Patricia L, residential advisor I, $21,264
Crumbie, Brenda M, short term sub tchr, $2.28/hr
Crumbie, Brenda M, tchr aide, $14,520
Crust, Lisa K, dd cnslr II, $43,008
Cruzen, Christine A, dd cnslr III, $47,712
Cryts, Kathryn A, tchr aide, $11.36/hr
Culliton, Thomas, short term sub tchr, $14.03/hr
Cunningham, Lynne M, tchr, $35,928
Cunningham, Nickie A, tchr aide, $14,208
Curran, Patricia L, dir, $40,464
Curry, Aleada D, tchr aide, $15,336
Curry, Aleada D, short term sub tchr, $1.62/hr
Curtman, Lore'e A, accounting spec, $35,664
Dacila, Georgeta, billing spec, $27,336
Dacila, Ioan, dd cnslr IV, $50,568
Daily, Christopher M, asst supt, $56,256
Dalpiaz-Brown, Abigail R, tchr aide, $14,832
Dannenmueller, Michael R, residential advisor I, $12.09/hr
Dannenmueller, Sheila H, hearing ofcr, $53,472
Danuser, Ronald D, dormitory dir, $32,112
Darby, Jennifer L, administrative asst, $26,952
Darnell, Olivia M, tchr aide, $11.36/hr
Dauber, Elizabeth A, vr cnslr II, $43,008
Dautenhahn, Toni L, home school coord, $40,824
Davidson, Christine, tchr aide, $24,432
Davie, Suzette L, tchr aide, $17,352
Davie, Suzette L, long term sub tchr, $6.86/hr
Davie, Suzette L, homebound tchr, $24.23/hr
Davis, Adam R, residential advisor I, $21,264
Davis, Amarie, billing spec, $25,272
Davis, Dara M, dd cnslr I, $39,960
Davis, Donna F, tchr, $46,560
Davis, Donna F, homebound tchr, $24.23/hr
Davis, Janiece D, billing spec, $24,504
Davis, June M, short term sub tchr, $14.03/hr
Davis, Marie A, sup, $37,968
Davis, Mary K, short term sub tchr, $14.33/hr
Davis, Mary K, tchr aide, $11.36/hr
Davis, Rochelle F, dd cnslr IV, $50,568
Davis, Samuel J, residential advisor I, $12.09/hr
Day, Kevin S, phys edu tchr, $32,496
Day, Linda K, tchr aide, $13,584
Dean, Karen D, vr cnslr II, $43,008
Debrodie, Trisha A, asst dormitory dir, $26,856
Dee, Dylan J, dd cnslr, $38,040
Dekeyser, Glenda E, sec, $25,608
Delgado, Michele L, dd cnslr II, $43,008
Deluce, Heather M, vr cnslr I, $39,960
Denney, Dale E, custodial worker II, $25,536
Dennis, Erin E, administrative asst, $26,952
Derboven, Archie E, supt, $77,664
Derickson, Gay L, tchr aide, $14,064
Desmond, Dana S, prog spec, $37,608
Deterding, Angela J, dd cnslr I, $39,960
Deubler-White, Jane A, vr cnslr I, $39,960
Deuster, Brian K, rgnal mgr, $66,648
Devers, Danielle M, tchr aide, $11.36/hr
Devers, Danielle M, bus attendant, $10.05/hr
Dial, Carlean, tchr aide - bus atnd, $23,976
Dial, Darren D, custodial worker II, $24,168
Dibert, Chasity L, dd cnslr I, $39,960
Dibooglu, Ali, dd cnslr II, $43,008
Dickey, Kelli E, exec asst to the comm of educ, $47,760
Diebold, Kathleen M, tchr, $29,472
Diederich, Marie D, tchr aide, $17,304
Diehl, Wendy S, tchr aide, $15,624
Dierking, Michael J, sup, $39,648
Dietzel, Rachel S, procurement mgr, $44,112
Dietzschold, Keith A, sup, $41,160
Dignan, Arthur G, short term sub tchr, $14.03/hr
Dignan, Joyce B, short term sub tchr, $14.03/hr
Dingus, Mary H, school librarian, $42,672
Dinsmore, Pamala D, tchr aide, $11.36/hr
Dinwiddie, Lauren A, billing spec, $25,272
Dinwiddie, Shelia S, sec, $13,728
Distler, Jill R, administrative asst, $16.79/hr
Dittlinger, Diane L, dd cnslr, $21.87/hr
Dixon-Wallack, Samala, vr cnslr II, $43,008
Dixson, Angela D, residential advisor II, $21,648
Dobbins, Heather L, tchr aide, $11.36/hr
Dobbins, Heather L, short term sub tchr, $14.03/hr
Dobson, Mary L, vr driver, $9.23/hr

Dobson, Raymond J, vr driver, $9.23/hr
Dodds, Alisa K, vr cnslr IV, $30,360
Doerhoff, Dana L, dir, $50,232
Doke, Anna M, dd ce spec, $26,160
Dollins, Davy J, administrative asst, $26,160
Donaldson, Carol, tchr aide, $18,120
Donaldson, Carolyn J, tchr aide, $15,408
Donaldson, Rosalie M, tchr aide, $18,552
Donze, Kristin, vr cnslr II, $43,008
Dooling, Linda L, dir, $51,864
Dorsey, Casey J, administrative asst, $26,952
Dorson, Roger D, coord, $80,688
Doster, Tonya R, asst dist supv, $51,864
Dotter, Allison L, tchr, $29,640
Dowling, Mary B, tchr aide, $14,856
Downing, Debora L, sup, $41,160
Downs, Latoya S, long term sub tchr, $20.90/hr
Downs, Latoya S, short term sub tchr, $14.33/hr
Downs, Latoya S, tchr aide, $11.36/hr
Downs, Latoya S, sec, $10.73/hr
Downs, Latoya S, short term sub tchr, $14.33/hr
Downs, Latoya S, tchr aide, $11.36/hr
Downs, Latoya S, bus attendant, $10.05/hr
Doyel, Shaughnessy, tchr, $35,664
Doza, Cheryl R, dir, $49,056
Draisey, Shannon L, sec, $17,808
Drake, Raymond E, dist sup, $57,000
Drew, Bradley H, residential advisor I, $22,488
Drew, Tosha A, tchr aide, $21,144
Drinkall, Edith A, billing spec, $25,272
Dubbert, Alane R, asst dist supv, $51,864
Dudenhoeffer, Andrew S, food distrib spec, $39,648
Dudley-Antoine, Montia S, tchr aide, $11.36/hr
Duede, Alan L, phys edu tchr, $33,480
Duggins, Meghan M, tchr, $28,152
Duley, Nicole L, tchr aide, $11.36/hr
Dunavant, James D, storekeeper II, $29,544
Duncan, Charles L, residential advisor I, $12.09/hr
Duncan, Janet L, asst dir, $47,712
Duncan, Starla D, administrative asst, $31,440
Dunlap, Jennifer S, asst dist supv, $51,864
Dunn, Douglas W, residential advisor I, $12.09/hr
Dunn, Heather J, tchr, $28,704
Dunn, Maureen E, dir, $51,864
Dutton, Linda G, tchr aide, $13,584
Dzurick, Christopher P, sup, $38,352
Dzurick, John J, residential advisor I, $21,264
Eads, Jennifer L, custodial worker II, $23,688
Eakens, Melissa D, dd case ctrl analyst, $30,312
Eary, Joy D, tchr aide, $14,520
Eastin, Aubren D, tchr aide, $11.36/hr
Eastin, Aubren D, short term sub tchr, $14.03/hr
Eckert, Toby K, rgnal mgr, $66,648
Edmonds, Melissa A, administrative asst, $26,952
Edmonds, Paula G, short term sub tchr, $1.39/hr
Edmonds, Paula G, tchr aide, $15,624
Edwards, Earlene T, tchr aide, $11.36/hr
Edwards, Gayle A, tchr aide, $15,144
Edwards, Gayle A, long term sub tchr, $8.65/hr
Edwards, Gayle A, short term sub tchr, $1.78/hr
Edwards, Keri R, vr cnslr III, $47,712
Edwards, Patricia L, tchr aide, $14,832
Edwards, Shawna L, tchr aide, $11.36/hr
Effinger, John W, asst dir, $55,656
Egbert, Sharon K, sup, $44,976
Egley, Allison J, intake cnslr, $38,040
Ehresman, Paul, short term sub tchr, $14.03/hr
Eidson, Susan E, dd cnslr, $21.87/hr
Eifert, Tammy S, short term sub tchr, $22.10/hr
Eighmy, Julie K, tchr aide, $15,120
Elbasani, Barry, sup, $47,712
Ellingsworth, Cathy M, prog spec, $33,744
Elliott, Elizabeth A, residential advisor I, $21,264
Elliott, Robin A, residential advisor I, $12.09/hr
Ellis, Jeremy J, dir, $49,560
Ellison, Willie L, residential advisor I, $20,856
Elmonis, Nadia, tchr aide, $14,208
Elmonis, Renide, tchr aide, $11.36/hr
Elsner, Danielle R, short term sub tchr, $14.33/hr
Elsner, Danielle R, tchr aide, $11.36/hr
Elsner, Danielle R, bus attendant, $10.05/hr
Emerick, Vanae S, asst dist supv, $51,864
Emery, Stacey R, tchr aide, $14,520

Emmendorfer, Leigh A, vr cnslr II, $43,008
Emory, Jennifer L, asst dist supv, $51,864
Endsley, Tacey L, cook II, $17,184
Engelage, Shanna L, tchr aide, $14,832
Engelmeier, Renae, tchr aide, $11.36/hr
Engelmeier, Renae, short term sub tchr, $14.03/hr
Erkenbrack, Ellen K, dd cnslr II, $44,520
Erlandsen, Jill R, vr cnslr II, $43,008
Ernst, Carrie E, tchr aide, $14,208
Ernst, Carrie E, short term sub tchr, $2.53/hr
Ernst, Carrie E, long term sub tchr, $9.40/hr
Ernst, Debbie J, short term sub tchr, $14.33/hr
Ernst, Debbie J, tchr aide, $11.36/hr
Ernst, Debbie J, bus attendant, $10.05/hr
Eschbach, Virginia R, sec, $28,416
Espiricueta, Tabatha, tchr aide, $14,832
Esposito-perfetto, Laura K, tchr aide, $11.36/hr
Essner, Clara M, sec, $21,600
Essner, Matthew E, dir, $50,232
Eubanks, Cassandra J, dd cnslr I, $39,960
Evanoski, Brian S, vr cnslr III, $47,712
Evans, Debra L, tchr aide, $11.36/hr
Evans, Debra L, short term sub tchr, $14.33/hr
Evans, Lisa A, sup, $41,160
Even, Ashley N, sec, $9.23/hr
Even, Martha K, gen servs spec, $33,216
Evers, Candace, dd cnslr, $38,040
Ewers, Tameria Y, communication asst, $35,376
Exler, Deena A, qual assurance spec, $51,864
Exline, Charles M, dir, $67,272
Faaborg, Mary J, cook II, $13,176
Fair, Rae L, tchr aide, $13,032
Fairchild, Susan R, tchr, $30,408
Falk, Suzanne M, asst dist supv, $51,864
Falker, Christy L, tchr, $36,744
Falker, Christy L, homebound tchr, $24.23/hr
Falter, Cara B, dd cnslr II, $43,008
Falter, Sharon A, hearing ofcr, $53,472
Fambro, Tonya D, dir, $57,000
Fannon, Deborah J, asst dist supv, $51,864
Farrell, Cleve R, residential advisor I, $20,448
Farris, Elizabeth H, sec, $12.81/hr
Faughn, Tammie M, tchr aide, $11.36/hr
Faughn, Tammie M, short term sub tchr, $14.33/hr
Fayne, Gloria D, cook II, $11,760
Feger, Joseph C, residential advisor I, $21,720
Fennewald, Loretta C, prog spec, $33,384
Ferguson, Cynthia M, registered nurse, $21.66/hr
Ferguson, Cynthia M, registered nurse, $21.66/hr
Ferrand, Brandi N, long term sub tchr, $20.90/hr
Ferrand, Brandi N, short term sub tchr, $14.03/hr
Ferrand, Brandi N, tchr aide, $11.36/hr
Fick, Cami E, administrative asst, $26,424
Fick, Linda B, dir, $65,328
Figgins, William E, dd cnslr II, $43,008
Filley, Jamie B, sec, $20,352
Finke, Janet L, long term sub tchr, $25.08/hr
Fiocco, Judith M, speech thrpst, $35,688
Fischer, Judy C, tchr aide, $11.36/hr
Fischer, Judy C, short term sub tchr, $14.03/hr
Fisher, Bradley M, dd cnslr II, $43,008
Fisher, Georgetta, sec, $25,296
Fisher, Rebecca K, tchr aide, $11.36/hr
Fisher, Rebecca K, short term sub tchr, $14.33/hr
Fitzpatrick, Rory K, dd cnslr II, $43,008
Fitzpatrick, Susan A, short term sub tchr, $14.03/hr
Fitzsimmons, Kimberly D, billing spec, $25,272
Fitzwater, Brandi R, tchr aide, $11.36/hr
Fitzwater, Rebecca L, tchr aide, $11.36/hr
Flaugher, Kelly L, coord, $71,208
Fleischmann, Cheryl J, dd ce spec, $29,256
Fleming, Diana M, tchr aide, $13,032
Fleming, Sandra J, tchr aide, $16,608
Florence, Patricia A, tchr aide, $11.36/hr
Flowers, Rebekah K, instructional spec, $36,312
Floyd, Angel D, tchr aide, $11.36/hr
Floyd, Angel D, short term sub tchr, $14.03/hr
Floyd, Angel D, bus attendant, $10.05/hr
Floyd, Angel D, bus driver, $10.36/hr
Flynn, Rebecca A, sec, $22,584
Folscroft, Cynthia D, tchr, $27,792
Foltz-schlegel, Kristen A, dd cnslr I, $39,960
Fonville, Michelle R, tchr aide, $11.36/hr

Fonville, Michelle R, short term sub tchr, $22.10/hr
Foote, Jacqueline D, administrative asst, $26,952
Ford, Rebecca L, billing spec, $24,504
Ford, Tonnette, residential advisor I, $24,864
Fort, Michelle L, long term sub tchr, $20.90/hr
Fort, Michelle L, tchr aide, $11.36/hr
Fort, Michelle L, homebound tchr, $24.23/hr
Fort, Michelle L, short term sub tchr, $14.33/hr
Foster, Brent E, communication spec, $42,840
Foster, Nancy K, residential advisor I, $26,376
Foster, Teresa G, dd cnslr II, $43,008
Foulks, Angie, tchr aide, $11.36/hr
Foulks, Angie, bus driver, $10.36/hr
Foulks, Angie, bus attendant, $10.05/hr
Francis, Kelly R, tchr aide, $14,208
Francis, Kelly R, short term sub tchr, $2.53/hr
Francis, Kelly R, long term sub tchr, $9.40/hr
Francis, Kelly R, homebound tchr, $24.23/hr
Francis, Kirsten M, tchr aide, $11.36/hr
Frank, Carol A, administrative asst, $28,224
Frank, Jennifer L, asst dir, $43,704
Frankhouser, Alma J, tchr aide, $14,376
Franklin, Amy E, dd cnslr II, $43,008
Franklin, Lonnie L, residential advisor I, $12.09/hr
Franklin, Melia K, dir, $49,560
Franzi, Fulvio I, dir, $56,472
Frazier, Patrick D, custodial worker/tchr aide, $19,560
Frazier, Patrick D, short term sub tchr, $2.16/hr
Freeman, Andrea K, short term sub tchr, $14.33/hr
Freeman, Andrea K, tchr aide, $11.36/hr
Freeman, Andrea K, sec, $10.73/hr
Freeman, Andrea K, homebound tchr, $24.23/hr
Freeman, Andrea K, bus attendant, $10.05/hr
Freeman, Angela F, dd cnslr III, $47,712
Freeman, Christy K, tchr aide, $11.36/hr
Freeman, Christy K, short term sub tchr, $14.33/hr
Freeman, Denise R, tchr aide, $14,520
Freeman, Jackie L, tchr aide, $14,520
Freeman, Jamie S, tchr aide, $11.36/hr
Freeman, Jamie S, short term sub tchr, $22.10/hr
Freeman, Jamie S, long term sub tchr, $20.90/hr
Freeman, Jason S, tchr, $27,792
Freeman, Krista L, tchr aide - bus atnd, $18,792
Freeman, Lois A, bldg admin, $40,944
Freiling, Mary V, tchr, $36,456
Frese, Nicholas J, dd cnslr, $38,040
Friedmeyer, Carolyn L, tchr aide, $14,832
Frink-hedglin, J D, sup, $46,656
Frisbee, Byron D, bus driver, $10,968
Fritts, Suzanne K, tchr aide, $14,520
Fritts, Suzanne K, short term sub tchr, $2.28/hr
Fry, Danielle P, asst dir, $53,616
Fry, Samantha R, tchr aide, $11.36/hr
Frye, Roger, residential advisor I, $23,184
Fuchs, Curt R, coord, $66,240
Fuhrmann, Margaret M, tchr aide, $11.36/hr
Fuller, Dee Ann M, dist sup, $55,728
Futrell, Pavla, tchr aide, $14,376
Gahagan, Barbara P, administrative asst, $27,168
Gaines, Richard S, residential advisor I, $21,720
Gaines, Timothy E, coord, $71,208
Galbreath, Charles H, short term sub tchr, $14.03/hr
Galbreath, Charles H, long term sub tchr, $20.90/hr
Galbreath, Deshawna J, tchr aide, $20,064
Gallup, Melissa, vr cnslr III, $47,712
Gammill-jones, Mary L, tchr aide, $14,064
Gann, Mary K, tchr aide, $15,624
Gannon, Angela A, tchr, $33,696
Garbiso, Carla J, tchr aide, $11.36/hr
Garcia, Leslie J, rgnal mgr, $66,648
Gardner, Beverly A, vr cnslr IV, $50,568
Gardner, Elizabeth V, billing spec, $29,256
Gardner, John G, tchr, $27,792
Gardner, Melody S, dd cnslr I, $39,960
Garner, Judith A, short term sub tchr, $14.03/hr
Garner, Judith A, tchr aide, $11.36/hr
Garretson, Lynn J, tchr aide, $11.36/hr
Garretson, Lynn J, short term sub tchr, $14.33/hr
Garrett, Ernest E, supt, $77,136
Garthe, Pamela G, dd cnslr II, $43,008
Gartland, Sadye S, vr spec, $26.24/hr
Garton, Martha L, long term sub tchr, $6.90/hr
Garton, Martha L, tchr aide, $17,304

Garton, Martha L, short term sub tchr, $0.03/hr
Gassner, Melissa M, tchr aide, $11.36/hr
Gatewood, Louis E, dist sup, $55,728
Gathing, Ernestine M, tchr aide, $18,648
Gawatz, Monica M, tchr, $36,432
Gawatz, Monica M, homebound tchr, $24.23/hr
Gee, Kimberly L, asst dir, $53,616
Gehrs-Gurley, Lisa M, tchr aide, $11.36/hr
Gely, Rafael, hearing ofcr, $28.64/hr
Gerber, David L, asst dir, $43,704
Gergs, Angela M, qual assurance spec, $51,864
Gerken, Janice J, bldg admin, $43,416
Germeroth, Debra L, tchr aide, $13,032
Gertz, Rachel D, tchr aide, $11.36/hr
Gibson, Judy A, tchr aide, $15,624
Gibson, Lana K, tchr aide, $11.36/hr
Gier, Dan A, rgnal field technician, $43,704
Gilb, Marita M, asst dist supv, $51,864
Gillam, Leonard W, dir, $57,000
Gillaspie, Trina L, sec, $22,656
Gilleland, Kent L, residential advisor I, $12.09/hr
Gilleland, Naomi J, residential advisor I, $21,264
Gillman, Susan M, tchr aide, $11.36/hr
Gilman, Pamela D, tchr aide, $21,384
Gilmore, Beverly J, tchr aide, $14,520
Gilmore, Lora K, tchr aide, $13,320
Gilpin, Barbara J, asst dir, $47,712
Gilpin, Charles L, vr cnslr II, $43,008
Gipson, Kevin D, custodial worker II, $29,712
Giseburt, Kaitlin L, tchr aide, $14,208
Giseburt, Kaitlin L, short term sub tchr, $2.53/hr
Givans, Eric E, cook II, $17,784
Glore, Alecia M, tchr aide, $14,856
Goans, Judith E, prog analyst, $31,656
Godat, Claudia E, tchr aide, $11.36/hr
Godley, Karan J, tchr aide, $27,552
Goins, Darnay M, custodial worker II, $29,592
Golden, Margret A, long term sub tchr, $20.90/hr
Golden, Margret A, short term sub tchr, $14.33/hr
Golden, Margret A, tchr aide, $11.36/hr
Gonzales, Lindsey J, residential advisor I, $20,856
Gonzalez, Marty S, phys edu tchr, $28,704
Goodin, Pamela J, administrative asst, $29,328
Gordon, Ruby C, bus driver, $11,424
Gordon, Ruby C, tchr aide, $11.36/hr
Gorsage, Kevin P, nutrition prog spec, $38,352
Gorse, Anna M, tchr, $28,992
Gove-Ortmeyer, Stacie A, dd cnslr, $38,040
Grace, Michelle L, tchr aide, $11.36/hr
Graham, Erica M, tchr aide, $11.36/hr
Graham, Robert G, custodial worker I, $10.05/hr
Granger, Jamie L, long term sub tchr, $22.10/hr
Granger, Jamie L, short term sub tchr, $14.03/hr
Granger, Jamie L, tchr aide, $11.36/hr
Granger, Jamie L, long term sub tchr, $20.90/hr
Granger, Jamie L, short term sub tchr, $22.10/hr
Grant-Engle, Leigh A, asst commissioner, $96,432
Graudin, Julia, short term sub tchr, $14.03/hr
Gravier, Timothy W, dir, $57,000
Gray, Deborah R, tchr aide, $13,320
Gray, Richard R, residential advisor I, $12.09/hr
Gray, Sharon L, short term sub tchr, $14.03/hr
Graziano, Michelle D, administrative asst, $26,952
Greeley, Nancy D, sup of instruction, $54,792
Green, Barbara A, vr cnslr II, $43,008
Green, Jordan R, tchr aide, $11.36/hr
Green, Linda T, residential advisor I, $12.09/hr
Green, Rhonda S, administrative asst, $26,424
Greenberg, Shani R, asst dist supv, $51,864
Greene, Matthew R, tchr aide, $11.36/hr
Greer, Anthony H, tchr aide, $11.36/hr
Gregg, Diane J, tchr, $47,016
Gregg, Matthew P, vr cnslr I, $39,960
Gregoire, Ashley J, short term sub tchr, $14.03/hr
Gregoire, Ashley J, tchr aide, $11.36/hr
Gregory, Crystal E, tchr aide, $14,856
Greife, Mary B, short term sub tchr, $14.03/hr
Greife, Mary B, tchr aide, $11.36/hr
Grieshaber, Regina D, rgnal mgr, $66,648
Griffin, Barbara L, tchr, $36,768
Griffith, Julia M, vr cnslr I, $39,960
Griggs, Danielle N, tchr aide, $11.36/hr
Griggs, Danielle N, bus attendant, $10.05/hr

Griggs, Richard M, sup, $41,160
Gritten, Kimberly A, tchr aide, $11.36/hr
Gritten, Kimberly A, short term sub tchr, $14.33/hr
Grooms, Denise L, short term sub tchr, $14.03/hr
Grooms, Denise L, tchr aide, $11.36/hr
Groskurth, F A, tchr, $34,752
Gross, Ashley N, tchr aide, $11.36/hr
Gross, Nicky L, tchr aide, $14,520
Grosse, Donna L, tchr aide, $18,144
Gruenewald, Diane K, vr cnslr II, $43,008
Grzesiak-Burzynska, Weronika I, dd cnslr I, $39,960
Guffey, Judy, sec, $10.73/hr
Guffey, Judy, tchr aide, $11.36/hr
Guilliams, Melissa H, dd cnslr IV, $50,568
Guined, Audrea N, tchr aide, $11.36/hr
Guined, Audrea N, sec, $10.73/hr
Guinn, Amy Sue E, residential advisor I, $12.09/hr
Gundy, Deborah A, phys edu tchr, $36,408
Gunnels, Cassandra L, tchr aide, $15,624
Guth, Diana L, tchr, $32,256
Gutic, Adnan, tchr, $28,152
Haag, Patricia A, registered nurse, $33,048
Hack, Katherine N, dd ce spec, $26,184
Hackmann, Amanda N, accounting analyst, $32,040
Hagenhoff, Margaret, administrative asst, $29,928
Hagenhoff, Sara M, asst dir, $47,712
Hager, Ellen G, registered nurse, $40,392
Hagston, Jean M, tchr aide, $11.36/hr
Hairston, Gale L, dir, $54,816
Halderman, Amy L, administrative asst, $27,480
Hall, Lea M, custodial worker I, $22,128
Hall, Myra K, dd cnslr II, $43,008
Hall, Sandra, cook II, $20,352
Hallum, Sarah C, dd cnslr II, $43,008
Halter, Patty A, qual assurance spec, $52,896
Haltom, Hans P, vr cnslr I, $39,960
Hamilton, Brittany K, dd cnslr II, $43,008
Hamilton, Jennifer K, dd cnslr I, $39,960
Hamilton, Julie A, tchr aide, $11.36/hr
Hamilton, La Mart, custodial worker II, $24,144
Hamlett, Mindy E, tchr, $34,224
Hamlin-Eaves, Angela D, long term sub tchr, $8.90/hr
Hamlin-Eaves, Angela D, short term sub tchr, $2.03/hr
Hamlin-Eaves, Angela D, tchr aide, $14,832
Hamman, Lauren M, registered nurse, bsn, $33,840
Hammergren, Rania C, tchr aide, $14,208
Hampton, Rebecca A, tchr aide, $14,520
Hancock, Chelsey J, tchr aide, $11.36/hr
Hancock, Chelsey J, short term sub tchr, $22.10/hr
Hanesack, Holly A, billing spec, $24,768
Hanna, Mary B, tchr, $33,264
Hanner, Sarah E, dd cnslr II, $43,008
Hanselman, Ginger R, dd cnslr III, $47,712
Harden, Dennis D, coord, $66,240
Harder, Kelly R, tchr aide, $14,520
Hardimon, Jermaine D, tchr aide, $13,032
Hardin, Kali P, tchr aide, $11.36/hr
Hardin, Kali P, sec, $10.73/hr
Hardman, Virginia L, bldg admin, $35,688
Harley, Crystal N, tchr aide, $14,208
Harms, Neil W, dir, $57,000
Harper, Jessica K, tchr aide, $14,832
Harper, Jessica K, short term sub tchr, $2.03/hr
Harper, Jessica K, long term sub tchr, $8.90/hr
Harper, John G, dir, $57,000
Harper, Kelsey A, sec, $9.23/hr
Harper-Jackson, Gwen, dist sup, $55,728
Harrell, Marcia M, tchr aide, $13,608
Harrington, Trisha C, vr cnslr I, $39,960
Harris, Cynthia K, residential advisor I, $12.09/hr
Harris, Cynthia K, short term sub tchr, $14.03/hr
Harris, Deanna L, home school coord, $40,104
Harris, Eunice D, hearing ofcr, $28.64/hr
Harris, Karen L, short term sub tchr, $14.03/hr
Harris, Karen L, tchr aide, $11.36/hr
Harris, Karen L, registered nurse, $21.66/hr
Harris, Tyler J, custodial worker II, $22,944
Harris, Valerie B, administrative asst, $28,896
Harris, Yvette L, tchr aide, $11.36/hr
Harris, Yvette L, short term sub tchr, $14.03/hr
Harris Watkins, Mary, instructional spec, $42,336
Harris Watkins, Mary, bldg admin, $3.47/hr
Harrison, Joyce D, tchr aide, $16,632

Harrison, Laura M, administrative asst, $16.50/hr
Harrison, Michelle L, laundry worker, $16,896
Hart, Alfred A, short term sub tchr, $14.03/hr
Hart, Alfred A, long term sub tchr, $22.10/hr
Hartenbower, Forrest W, short term sub tchr, $14.03/hr
Hartenbower, Forrest W, tchr aide, $11.36/hr
Harter, Jessica F, tchr aide, $11.36/hr
Hartgroves, Donna C, long term sub tchr, $20.90/hr
Hartgroves, Donna C, bus attendant, $10.05/hr
Hartgroves, Donna C, tchr aide, $11.36/hr
Hartgroves, Donna C, short term sub tchr, $22.10/hr
Hartman, Kenneth L, residential advisor III, $28,992
Hartman, Kristine L, dd cnslr II, $43,008
Hase-rish, Ryvana D, tchr aide, $11.36/hr
Hastings, Amy L, vr cnslr II, $43,008
Hastings, Heather D, tchr aide-bus driver, $18,912
Hasty, Renee M, administrative asst, $29,328
Hatfield, James R, data spec, $28,320
Hatterman, Lyn A, tchr aide-bus driver, $23,520
Havlik, Linda, tchr, $48,336
Hawkins, Kourtney A, sec, $23,064
Hawkins, Mary L, tchr, $36,768
Hawkins, Regina K, custodial worker I, $16,128
Hayes, Amy M, tchr aide, $14,832
Hayes, Beverly, tchr aide, $26,184
Hayes, Teraveya T, dd cnslr, $38,040
Haymes, Grace G, short term sub tchr, $14.33/hr
Haymes, Grace G, tchr aide, $11.36/hr
Haymes, Grace G, cook II, $10.05/hr
Haymes, Grace G, sec, $10.73/hr
Haymes, Krista A, bldg admin, $42,528
Hays, Billy A, tchr aide, $11.36/hr
Hays, Jessica A, dd cnslr III, $47,712
Hays, Jessica N, dd cnslr II, $43,008
Hazelwood, Virginia, cook II, $15,840
He, Ning S, vr cnslr III, $47,712
Hearn, Sandra M, billing spec, $25,272
Hecht, Kara N, homebound tchr, $24.23/hr
Hecht, Kara N, phys edu tchr, $28,704
Heckemeyer, Samantha K, vr cnslr II, $43,008
Heckman, April L, accounting spec, $31,656
Hedderman, Betty J, tchr aide, $11.36/hr
Hedges, Teresa D, tchr aide, $15,624
Hegadorn, Luke T, food serv mgr, $35,208
Hegerfeld, Emilie D, tchr aide, $11.36/hr
Heilmann, Peggy A, phys edu tchr, $34,176
Heislen, Cynthia L, dir, $51,864
Heislen, Kyle J, sup, $42,192
Hellmann, Jennifer R, tchr aide, $11.36/hr
Helming, Terri L, dd cnslr III, $47,712
Helms, Lisa D, sec/tchr aide, $23,592
Helwig, Glenda S, asst commissioner, $96,432
Hemme, Donna S, administrative asst, $29,256
Henderson, Ashley N, tchr aide, $11.36/hr
Henderson, Kerri J, tchr, $39,144
Henderson, Kerri J, homebound tchr, $24.23/hr
Hendricks, Tabitha M, dd cnslr, $38,040
Hendrickson, Deanna J, dd cnslr II, $43,008
Hendrix, Lisa J, dd cnslr II, $43,008
Henning, Laura M, tchr aide, $11.36/hr
Henning, Laura M, bus attendant, $10.05/hr
Henning, Laura M, short term sub tchr, $14.33/hr
Henningsen, Blaine A, career pathways mgr, $54,792
Henrickson, Michele L, dd case ctrl analyst, $31,728
Henry, Heather M, tchr aide, $11.36/hr
Henry, Heather M, short term sub tchr, $14.33/hr
Henry, Susan E, dd cnslr III, $47,712
Henry, Virginia L, dir, $51,864
Hernandez, Natasha J, nurse lpn, $13.94/hr
Herndon, Tabitha L, administrative asst, $31,248
Herring, Jessica L, dir, $49,056
Herrmann, Charles A, dd cnslr, $21.87/hr
Herron, Jennifer M, tchr aide, $13,320
Herx, Diane A, administrative asst, $26,424
Hess, Emily M, tchr aide, $11.36/hr
Hibbs, Jason E, tchr aide, $14,520
Hibler, Chaneyll A, billing spec, $24,768
Hickey, Darla A, administrative asst, $29,328
Hickman, April J, sec, $22,320
Hickson, Ronald L, residential advisor I, $21,264
Higgins, Danielle S, tchr aide, $11.36/hr
Higgins, James T, dist sup, $55,728

Higgins, Robert D, sup, $38,880
Hilderbrand, Linda G, vr cnslr III, $47,712
Hill, Cozett, administrative asst, $30,576
Hill, Jaimie L, tchr aide, $13,608
Hill, Marti L, administrative asst, $31,656
Hill, Misty C, tchr aide, $14,856
Hill, Tammy L, tchr, $29,280
Hill-grant, Brenda D, sec, $12.81/hr
Hill-mayes, Angela E, home school coord, ms, $43,560
Hirner, Paula S, sec, $21,360
Hirsch, Sheila J, sup, $49,200
Hirst, Barbara E, vr cnslr IV, $50,568
Hitch, Christina M, billing spec, $24,504
Hoard, Larry R, dir, $23.34/hr
Hockaday, Debbie L, billing spec, $26,184
Hodge, Demetra D, tchr aide, $11.36/hr
Hodges, Angela B, tchr, $27,792
Hodges, Holly N, tchr, $28,152
Hodges, Susan E, sup, $41,160
Hoelzer, Barbara D, dir, $57,000
Hoffman, Staci S, asst dist supv, $51,864
Hoffmesiter, Alex P, tchr aide, $11.36/hr
Hogan, Edwin J, dir, $49,056
Holaday, Barbara A, short term sub tchr, $14.33/hr
Holaday, Barbara A, tchr aide, $11.36/hr
Holguin, Julie A, tchr aide, $14,520
Holland, Darren C, night watch, $9.16/hr
Holland, Mary E, bus driver, $11,232
Holland, Mary E, tchr aide, $11.36/hr
Holland, Mary E, short term sub tchr, $14.03/hr
Hollingsworth, Dale L, accounting analyst, $32,040
Hollingsworth, M A, tchr aide, $11.36/hr
Hollis, Cynthia L, coord, $61,416
Holloway, Ashley L, sec, $19,896
Holloway, Debra M, tchr aide, $17,880
Holloway, Debra M, long term sub tchr, $6.43/hr
Holloway, Mary A, cook I, $16,728
Holloway, Tonya C, tchr aide, $14,832
Holman, Dale W, home school coord, $40,104
Holman, Misty D, nurse lpn, $13.94/hr
Holmes, Carol A, prof rel ofcr, $51,864
Holmes, Kathryn L, dd cnslr I, $39,960
Holzbauer, Jennifer D, vr cnslr II, $43,008
Hombs, Robin E, tchr aide, $11.36/hr
Hombs, Robin E, sec, $10.73/hr
Hoogveld, Jennifer L, tchr aide, $14,208
Hoover, Louann P, short term sub tchr, $14.03/hr
Hoover, Louann P, long term sub tchr, $20.90/hr
Hoover, Louann P, bldg admin, $24.75/hr
Horn, Dawn M, dd cnslr II, $43,008
Horrell, Dawn M, dd cnslr II, $43,008
Horrell, Timothy L, dd cnslr II, $43,008
Horton, Danielle R, tchr aide, $14,520
Hose, John H, sup, $25.14/hr
Hosier, Joanna J, nutrition contract spec, $41,184
Hough, Linda C, billing spec, $25,272
House, Misty R, tchr aide, $11.36/hr
House, Misty R, short term sub tchr, $14.33/hr
House, Reta K, bldg admin, $45,528
Houtz, Catherine E, bus attendant, $10,632
Houtz, Catherine E, tchr aide, $11.36/hr
Houtz, Catherine E, bus driver, $0.19/hr
Howard, Bryan N, dir, $57,000
Howard-owens, Carla, tchr aide, $24,432
Howe, Cynthia J, tchr aide, $16,608
Howe, Terry L, tchr aide, $14,520
Howrey, Christina L, vr cnslr III, $33,408
Hoxworth, Veronica M, administrative asst, $29,664
Hubbard, Cathy J, sup, $23.13/hr
Hubbard, Erin E, dd cnslr, $38,040
Hudgens, Sandra L, dormitory dir, $33,936
Hudson, Bonnie M, tchr, $38,328
Hudson, Christina J, data spec, $32,832
Hudson, Erniesha D, tchr aide, $11.36/hr
Hudson-brooks, Victoria, tchr, $27,792
Huff, Christy R, dd cnslr III, $47,712
Huffman, Barbara A, dd cnslr III, $47,712
Huffman, Lisa M, tchr aide, $11.36/hr
Hug, Stormey R, custodial worker I, $7.65/hr
Huggins, Melinda M, dist mgr, $59,856
Huggins, Patricia A, tchr aide, $11.36/hr
Huggins, Tamara A, dd cnslr I, $39,960
Hughes, Barbara K, dd case ctrl analyst, $26,952

Hughes, Crystal, tchr, $31,848
Hughes, Joyce A, tchr aide, $11.36/hr
Hughey, Joy M, billing spec, $25,272
Hughey, Sandra J, vr cnslr II, $34,440
Hummel, Robert P, sup, $19.79/hr
Humphrey, Allison M, residential advisor I, $20,448
Humphrey, Bernadette, vision educ tchr aide, $21,264
Humphries, Margaret, homebound tchr, $24.23/hr
Humphries, Margaret, tchr, $37,704
Hunt, Deston M, accounting spec, $27,504
Hunt, Jessica R, tchr aide, $14,520
Hunt, Kristy D, custodial worker II, $24,168
Hunter, April A, tchr aide, $14,832
Hunter, Melissa A, hearing ofcr, $53,472
Huskey, Dusty J, custodial worker II, $25,200
Hutchison, Kimberly, tchr aide, $14,520
Hutchison, Mary C, tchr aide, $11.36/hr
Huyck, Esther J, administrative asst, $31,248
Iles, Margee A, tchr, $35,592
Inglish, Leanna C, tchr aide, $11.36/hr
Inman, Angela L, vr cnslr II, $43,008
Inman, Deanna L, dd cnslr II, $39,960
Ipock, Michelle L, dd cnslr, $38,040
Isaac, Daniel D, tchr aide, $21,000
Isaac, Shawna M, cook I, $19,992
Isaacs, Amanda S, tchr aide, $11.36/hr
Isaacs, Amanda S, bus attendant, $10.05/hr
Isaacs, Elena F, tchr aide - bus atnd, $20,280
Islam, Rezwan, physician, $18,576
Jackson, Kenneth R, sup of instruction, $55,344
Jackson, Laura L, tchr aide, $15,672
Jackson, Linda K, tchr aide, $18,072
Jackson, Mary E, dd cnslr II, $43,008
Jackson, Nadine K, short term sub tchr, $2.04/hr
Jackson, Nadine K, tchr aide, $13,584
Jackson, Tameika D, administrative asst, $26,952
Jackson, Timothy L, vr business spec, $38,040
Jackson, Tina A, tchr aide - bus atnd, $20,136
Jacobson, Tia M, dd cnslr II, $43,008
Jahne, Annette D, tchr aide, $13,320
Jameson, Debra D, asst dir, $41,904
Janes, Jill J, sup of instruction, $54,792
Janes, Kelly M, tchr, $32,592
Janes, Kelly M, homebound tchr, $24.23/hr
Jarrell, Debra S, tchr aide - bus atnd, $19,992
Jarrett, Joan M, asst dir, $42,336
Jarvis-Scott, Roxane Y, dd cnslr II, $43,008
Jeffers, Melissa S, tchr aide, $14,832
Jeffries, Cindy L, tchr aide, $18,336
Jeffs, Lisa R, tchr aide, $11.36/hr
Jeffs, Lisa R, tchr In charge, $24.53/hr
Jeffs, Lisa R, short term sub tchr, $14.33/hr
Jenkins, Cheryl, dd cnslr, $38,040
Jenkins, Henry A, tchr aide, $16,632
Jennings, Kathon D, storekeeper II, $22,944
Jennings, Laurie A, tchr aide, $14,232
Jensen, Jesse M, qual assurance spec, $51,864
Jerles, Sara C, residential advisor I, $20,448
Jesse, Rosemary A, billing spec, $25,272
Jessup, Ellen G, phys edu tchr, $34,416
Johns, James D, vr cnslr II, $43,008
Johns, Terry A, sup, $20.14/hr
Johns, Virginia, school librarian, $32,520
Johnson, Barbara L, tchr, $35,136
Johnson, Cherity D, bldg admin, $41,496
Johnson, Cynthia L, vr driver, $9.23/hr
Johnson, Kelly M, dd cnslr III, $47,712
Johnson, Laurie L, billing spec, $25,272
Johnson, Matthew A, tchr, $30,984
Johnson, Melinda C, short term sub tchr, $14.03/hr
Johnson, Melinda C, registered nurse, $21.66/hr
Johnson, Melinda C, tchr aide, $11.36/hr
Johnson, Melinda C, bus attendant, $10.05/hr
Johnson, Melinda C, homebound tchr, $24.23/hr
Johnson, Melissa S, cook I, $16,728
Johnson, Michelle L, dd cnslr II, $43,008
Johnson, Sheila R, tchr aide, $11.36/hr
Johnson, Ted A, tchr aide, $13,560
Johnson, Teresa, residential advisor I, $21,264
Johnson-Sumowski, L, nursing asst, $21,576
Johnston, Deborah J, long term sub tchr, $20.90/hr
Johnston, Deborah J, short term sub tchr, $22.10/hr
Johnston, Deborah J, tchr aide, $11.36/hr

Johnston, Debra A, dd cnslr III, $47,712
Johnston, Kristina K, vr cnslr II, $43,008
Johnston, Therese L, administrative asst, $27,168
Jones, Alvin Z, dd cnslr I, $39,960
Jones, Bridget A, tchr, $28,032
Jones, Bridget A, homebound tchr, $24.23/hr
Jones, Cara A, dd cnslr I, $39,960
Jones, Cecelia, custodial work sup, $29,712
Jones, Diana A, cook II, $18,504
Jones, Greg M, phys edu tchr, $28,152
Jones, Harriet, dd case ctrl analyst, $28,056
Jones, Leslie R, tchr aide, $14,208
Jones, Leslie R, short term sub tchr, $2.53/hr
Jones, Mari, prog spec, $30,312
Jones, Marshelle L, residential advisor I, $12.09/hr
Jones, Pandora D, tchr aide, $15,624
Jones, Sarah B, dd cnslr II, $43,008
Jones, Steve, storekeeper II, $17,208
Jones, Tammy J, tchr, $34,752
Jones, Wendell L, residential advisor I, $12.09/hr
Jones, Yulanda S, vr cnslr I, $39,960
Joplin, Brenda L, tchr aide, $11.36/hr
Jordan, Jane E, dir, $30.00/hr
Jordan, Jennifer A, dir, $51,864
Judd, Melissa D, tchr aide, $11.36/hr
Judd, Melissa D, bus attendant, $10.05/hr
Julian, Terry M, tchr aide, $18,096
Julius, Kathy J, administrative asst, $33,000
Juneau, Raymond W, dd cnslr II, $43,008
Kachris, Peter T, sup of instruction, $44,280
Kaemmerer, Kimberly M, rgnal mgr, $66,648
Kaiser, Mary L, sec, $17,808
Kaiser, Patricia C, dir, $51,864
Kaiser, Tammy S, tchr aide, $15,624
Kambouris, Sara J, tchr aide, $11.36/hr
Kambouris, Sara J, bus attendant, $10.05/hr
Karnes, Mary R, short term sub tchr, $14.03/hr
Karnes, Mary R, long term sub tchr, $20.90/hr
Kassing, Debbie S, dd cnslr, $21.87/hr
Katnik, Paul J, asst commissioner, $96,432
Katt-Haycraft, Beverly M, tchr aide, $11.36/hr
Kaufman, Michele R, dd cnslr, $38,040
Kay, Dawn M, residential advisor I, $21,264
Kaylor, Marilyn J, short term sub tchr, $2.03/hr
Kaylor, Marilyn J, tchr aide, $14,832
Keating, Nancy K, asst dir, $47,712
Keays, Deborah A, tchr aide, $18,600
Keber, Katie L, tchr aide, $11.36/hr
Keber, Katie L, short term sub tchr, $14.03/hr
Kedzierski, Urszula, bldg admin, $42,408
Keegan, Linda K, tchr aide, $11.36/hr
Keesling, Hope M, tchr, $29,064
Keesling, Hope M, homebound tchr, $24.23/hr
Keim, Billie J, legal asst, $32,856
Keller, Richard, short term sub tchr, $14.03/hr
Keller, Richard, long term sub tchr, $20.90/hr
Keller, Virginia L, data spec, $29,712
Kelley, Rudolph V, tchr aide, $15,624
Kelly, Kathy M, human resource mgr, $57,000
Kelly, Kimberly M, tchr aide, $11.36/hr
Kelly, Shelly M, tchr aide, $14,832
Kelly, Shelly M, short term sub tchr, $2.03/hr
Kemna, Natalie R, dd cnslr II, $43,008
Kemp, Sandra K, tchr aide, $18,072
Kemp, Sandra K, long term sub tchr, $6.28/hr
Kempf, Margaret M, tchr aide, $11.36/hr
Kempker, Kelly L, sup, $41,160
Kempker, Nathan L, hearing ofcr, $53,472
Kemple, Kimberly R, dd cnslr, $38,040
Kendall, Michael D, asst dir, $47,712
Kenkel, Jennifer S, dd cnslr IV, $50,568
Kenny, Caroline A, tchr, $35,136
Kerns, D-Ann, tchr aide, $11.36/hr
Kerns, Kenneth G, sup, $41,160
Kessell, Donna S, tchr aide, $15,624
Kessell, Donna S, short term sub tchr, $1.39/hr
Kessell, Donna S, homebound tchr, $24.23/hr
Kestermont, Dolores M, tchr aide, $13,872
Kettwig, Joseph H, tchr aide-bus driver, $19,320
Kettwig, Joseph H, short term sub tchr, $2.31/hr
Kettwig, Joseph H, long term sub tchr, $9.18/hr
Kiel, Bethany M, dd cnslr II, $43,008
Kiesling, Shelley R, hr analyst, $43,008

Kilson, Deanna, administrative asst, $29,400
Kincaid, Jennifer E, vr cnslr II, $43,008
King, Erica D, vr cnslr I, $39,960
King, Sara A, tchr, $33,360
King, Teresa W, dist sup, $55,728
Kingsbury, Alison E, residential advisor I, $21,264
Kinney, Angela C, cook II, $20,400
Kinney, Stephanie A, tchr, $35,736
Kirchner, April, billing spec, $25,272
Kirchner, Stephanie L, short term sub tchr, $14.33/hr
Kirchner, Stephanie L, tchr aide, $11.36/hr
Kiser, Millissa R, tchr aide, $14,520
Kiser, Millissa R, short term sub tchr, $2.28/hr
Kiso, Andrea E, registered nurse, $32,400
Kleine, Yvonne M, tchr aide, $11.36/hr
Klenke, Karen M, dist sup, $55,728
Kliethermes, Sandra, sup, $38,880
Klima, Katherine C, billing spec, $25,272
Knapp, Doris E, tchr aide, $14,832
Knapp, Evelyn V, dd cnslr III, $47,712
Knapp, Paula S, tchr aide, $11.36/hr
Knapp, Paula S, short term sub tchr, $22.10/hr
Knight, Paul D, instructional spec, $33,792
Knipp, Juanita B, nurse lpn, $13.94/hr
Knisely, Kelvin L, phys edu tchr, $30,456
Knittel, Elaine K, tchr aide, $16,824
Knowles, Linda L, short term sub tchr, $22.10/hr
Knowles, Linda L, tchr aide, $11.36/hr
Knowles, Linda L, long term sub tchr, $20.90/hr
Knowles, Linda L, homebound tchr, $24.23/hr
Knowlton, Catherine, vr cnslr IV, $50,568
Kobzej, Janice E, vr cnslr IV, $50,568
Kocian, Catherine C, vr cnslr I, $39,960
Koehler, Lisa R, tchr aide, $14,352
Koenig, Sherry A, registered nurse, $33,048
Koetting, Angela M, accounting spec, $30,456
Komrska, Arbrey M, tchr aide, $14,208
Komrska, Arbrey M, long term sub tchr, $9.40/hr
Komrska, Arbrey M, short term sub tchr, $2.53/hr
Kopp, Todd M, tchr aide, $11.36/hr
Kopriva, Kathleen, vr cnslr III, $47,712
Kosmatka, Cheryl L, sup, $39,648
Kotlin, Amy K, homebound tchr, $24.23/hr
Kotlin, Amy K, tchr, $33,216
Kovach, Ashley M, tchr aide, $11.36/hr
Kraus, Jonathan M, residential advisor I, $21,264
Krauth, Stacy L, tchr aide, $15,624
Krawitz, Lori L, tchr aide, $13,584
Kreiensieck, Jennifer L, dd cnslr, $38,040
Kreutz, Jean, residential advisor I, $12.09/hr
Kreutz, Jean, cook I, $9.45/hr
Kujath, Julie A, dd cnslr II, $43,008
Kumsher, Kelsey N, tchr aide, $11.36/hr
Kunselman, Carol A, short term sub tchr, $14.33/hr
Kunselman, Carol A, tchr aide, $11.36/hr
Kunselman, Carol A, bus attendant, $10.05/hr
Kuster, Sydnee R, residential advisor I, $20,856
Kyle, Heather A, registered nurse, $21.66/hr
Lafollette, J C, dd cnslr II, $43,008
Lalk, Alisha N, tchr aide, $11.36/hr
Lamar, Rebecca A, dist sup, $55,728
Lamons, Brian J, sup, $41,928
Lampe, Logan M, tchr, $27,792
Lancaster, Amy, administrative asst, $12.58/hr
Landers, Cheri R, hr analyst, $21.39/hr
Landgraf, Luke T, dd cnslr II, $43,008
Landon, Deborah F, administrative asst, $28,896
Lane, Ashley N, vr cnslr I, $39,960
Lane, Lori A, comp info tech, $47,832
Lang, Sandra M, nutrition prog spec, $41,184
Langhorst, Steven W, charter schools field dir, $49,560
Lankford, Ronald L, dpty commissioner, $125,352
Largent, Rebecca J, asst dir, $55,728
Larose, Gaye D, tchr aide, $14,352
Larue, Melissa D, tchr aide, $11.36/hr
Larue, Melissa D, bus attendant, $10.05/hr
Lascuola, Gina M, tchr, $34,032
Lasswell, Glenda, custodial worker II, $14,856
Latz, Alecia A, dds admin, $72,072
Launius, Elaine L, tchr aide, $11.36/hr
Lawson, Rebecca A, sec, $23,856
Lawson, Rose M, cook II, $21,000
Lawson, Tina K, dir, $51,864

Lawson, Tracey L, comp info tech, $36,936
Layman, Melissa, vr cnslr III, $47,712
Le, Phung T, billing spec, $29,256
Lear, Kathleen M, long term sub tchr, $7.81/hr
Lear, Kathleen M, tchr aide, $16,176
Lear, Kathleen M, short term sub tchr, $0.94/hr
Lee, Amy S, administrative asst, $29,328
Lee, Brenda S, tchr aide, $11.36/hr
Lee, Jerrell R, residential advisor I, $20,856
Lee, Robert J, custodial worker I/bus driver, $16,896
Lee, Robert J, tchr aide, $11.36/hr
Leeka, Lindsay R, phys edu tchr, $30,240
Legrand, Leanne R, tchr aide, $16,776
Lehmen, Tammy M, school finance consult, $45,384
Lemon, Connie L, tchr aide, $11.36/hr
Lemons, Sarah E, dd cnslr II, $43,008
Lenard, Chyrisse, tchr aide, $14,832
Lentz, Montroe L, tchr aide, $17,856
Lenzy, Joyce L, billing spec, $25,272
Lepage, Barbara J, exec asst, $38,544
Lepage, Erin A, dd cnslr, $38,040
Lepage, Sharon L, chief budget ofcr, $72,792
Leroux, Allen L, residential advisor I, $21,264
Levin, Sherry L, sup, $38,352
Lewis, Janice F, sec, $12.81/hr
Lewis, Jessica A, residential advisor I, $21,648
Lewis, Kimberly S, tchr aide, $11.36/hr
Lewis, Markeith T, residential advisor I, $20,856
Lewis, Oneita K, tchr ln charge, $32,880
Lewis, Paula K, nurse lpn, $24,912
Lewis, Rickey J, sup, $20,592
Lewis, Robert J, tchr aide, $11.36/hr
Lewis, Sara E, home school coord, $40,104
Lewis, Taylor M, tchr aide, $11.36/hr
Libbert, Amy L, dist mgr, $59,856
Libbert, Randy J, dir, $63,408
Licklider, Elizabeth A, billing spec, $24,936
Lincoln, Saundra S, administrative asst, $27,984
Lindsay, Diane E, tchr aide, $14,376
Lindsey, Vernie D, tchr aide, $11.36/hr
Linke, Kristina, short term sub tchr, $14.03/hr
Linkon, Andrew W, asst dir, $47,712
Linneman, Debra L, sup, $40,944
Liontas, Lindsey B, tchr aide, $14,520
Lipscomb, Miranda R, vr cnslr II, $43,008
Lister, Laurie A, mcdhh ofc spt specialis, $30,312
Littleton, Adele C, tchr aide, $14,520
Lloyd, Noelle N, dd cnslr II, $43,008
Lobmire, Daniel J, short term sub tchr, $14.03/hr
Lock, Dennis C, dd cnslr I, $39,960
Lockett, Larry W, residential advisor I, $12.09/hr
Lockwood, Lisa R, tchr aide, $11.36/hr
Lockwood, Lisa R, cook I, $9.45/hr
Lococo, Joshua I, tchr aide, $19,632
Lococo, Sherryl L, tchr, $29,928
Loeb, Elisa A, billing spec, $25,272
Logston, Kimberly D, home school coord, $40,104
Lohman, Janella B, tchr aide, $14,832
Lohmann, Thomas, tchr, $33,336
Lombas, Alexis K, tchr aide, $11.36/hr
Long, Rose A, short term sub tchr, $2.03/hr
Long, Rose A, tchr aide, $14,832
Longley, Rick D, coord, $71,208
Longley, Teri L, exec asst, $34,752
Long-McClelland, Bridgette L, tchr aide, $14,832
Lonjers, Juanita M, tchr aide, $15,672
Lor, Bao, dd cnslr, $38,040
Lorenz, Anna M, vr cnslr II, $43,008
Losh, Kelly R, homebound tchr, $24.23/hr
Losh, Kelly R, tchr, $28,152
Lossman, Delayne C, billing spec, $25,272
Lossman, Paul H, asst dist supv, $51,864
Louis, Monese, tchr aide, $11.36/hr
Louis, Monese, short term sub tchr, $22.10/hr
Louis, Monese, long term sub tchr, $20.90/hr
Loveland, Sharon C, qual assurance spec, $52,896
Lowe, Denise M, residential advisor I, $25,992
Loyd, C J, asst commissioner, $96,432
Luallin, Abby M, tchr aide, $11.36/hr
Lucas, Justin M, vr cnslr I, $39,960
Lucy, Tammy R, tchr aide, $14,520
Ludvigsen, Christopher A, cmnty spt liaison, $37,032
Luebbering, Kimberly R, sup, $37,968

Luebbert, Carla J, comp info tech, $36,936
Luebbert, Jessica B, nurse lpn, $13.94/hr
Luebbert, Kristy J, data spec, $36,696
Lueckenotte, Mary J, sec, $27,912
Luedloff, Regina L, data spec, $31,032
Luetkemeyer, Alan R, dd cnslr, $38,040
Luetkemeyer, Beverly K, asst dir, $43,704
Luffman, Adriana K, tchr aide, $11.36/hr
Luna, Angela D, registered nurse, bsn, $33,840
Maas, Robert J, tchr aide, $14,208
Mackey, Rachel, sec, $22,176
Maddox, Edward D, residential advisor I, $12.09/hr
Madsen, Kathleen T, qual assurance spec, $53,472
Mahala, Lori D, vr cnslr II, $43,008
Mahurin, Christina M, tchr, $28,704
Major, April M, administrative asst, $26,952
Mallory, Candace F, tchr aide, $11.36/hr
Mallory, Candace F, short term sub tchr, $14.33/hr
Mallory, Candace F, sec, $10.73/hr
Mallory, Candace F, bus attendant, $10.05/hr
Mallory, Candace F, bldg admin, $18.03/hr
Mallory, Candace F, long term sub tchr, $20.90/hr
Mallory, Candace F, homebound tchr, $24.23/hr
Mallory, Trina R, tchr aide, $13,584
Maness, Jodeen J, sup, $37,968
Manetzke, Rebecca, dd cnslr II, $43,008
Mann, Lori R, tchr, $35,688
Manthey, Shandy S, tchr aide, $11.36/hr
Manthey, Shandy S, short term sub tchr, $14.33/hr
Mantooth, Scott A, field opps mgr, $69,168
Maples, Lacey N, administrative asst, $26,952
Marcano, Abigail A, tchr aide, $11.36/hr
Marcano, Abigail A, cook I, $9.45/hr
Marcano, Michelle M, long term sub tchr, $20.90/hr
Marcano, Michelle M, homebound tchr, $24.23/hr
Marcano, Michelle M, tchr in charge, $24.31/hr
Marcano, Michelle M, short term sub tchr, $14.03/hr
Marcano, Michelle M, tchr aide, $11.36/hr
Markley, Ellvan D, hearing ofcr, $53,472
Markley, Jane E, tchr aide, $11.36/hr
Markley, Jane E, short term sub tchr, $14.03/hr
Marler, Rachael L, dd cnslr II, $43,008
Marquart, Bonnie L, tchr aide, $14,208
Marsch, Ronald L, sup, $19.79/hr
Marshall, Tamara L, dist sup, $55,728
Marshall, Treavor L, tchr aide, $14,208
Marshall, Treavor L, long term sub tchr, $9.40/hr
Marsicovetere, Samantha N, sup, $39,648
Martin, Andy S, dir, $52,776
Martin, Dakotah R, tchr aide, $11.36/hr
Martin, Donna L, sec, $23,736
Martin, Jim W, short term sub tchr, $14.33/hr
Martin, Jonathan B, residential advisor I, $12.09/hr
Martin, Lori A, residential advisor I, $12.09/hr
Martinek, Rebecca L, tchr aide, $14,520
Martinek, Rebecca L, short term sub tchr, $2.28/hr
Martinez, Anna, dd cnslr, $38,040
Mascheck, Jennie S, coord, $61,464
Masek, Lisa M, asst dist supv, $51,864
Mason, Andrea L, tchr aide, $14,208
Mason, Denise M, vr cnslr III, $47,712
Mason, Laretta M, sec, $10.73/hr
Mason, Laretta M, tchr aide, $11.36/hr
Mason, Sarah E, tchr aide, $14,520
Mason-Donovan, April, vr cnslr II, $43,008
Massey, Jennifer A, hearing ofcr, $53,472
Massey, Rebecca A, vr cnslr III, $47,712
Massie, Linda M, tchr aide, $17,352
Massman, Sara A, sup, $41,160
Mathews, Christine L, dd cnslr III, $47,712
Mathis, Patricia A, sec, $24,288
Matson, Janet L, cook II, $17,520
Matthews, Mechelle L, dd cnslr II, $43,008
Mawby, Frank R, custodial worker II, $24,168
Mayes, Breanna N, tchr aide, $14,520
Mayes, Linda T, vr cnslr III, $47,712
Mayginnes, Abby L, tchr, $28,704
Mayginnes, Abby L, homebound tchr, $24.23/hr
Mayhall, Connie K, coordinating speech thrpst, $36,888
Maynard, Lisa G, dd cnslr, $38,040
Maynard, Rebecca L, dist sup, $55,728
McAfee, Deborah A, tchr aide, $13,872
McCamy-Henderson, Elizabeth J, tchr, $32,064

McCamy-Henderson, Elizabeth J, homebound tchr, $24.23/hr
McCann, Amy E, vr cnslr II, $43,008
McCarron, Pamela A, vr cnslr IV, $50,568
McClay, Robin M, sup, $37,968
McClintock, Marada, vr cnslr II, $43,008
McCrary, Rose M, tchr aide, $14,832
McCrary, Rose M, short term sub tchr, $2.03/hr
McCrary, Rose M, long term sub tchr, $8.90/hr
McCrary, Rose M, homebound tchr, $24.23/hr
McCray, Athena M, administrative asst, $26,160
McCray, Melanie N, tchr aide, $20,424
McCrory, Heather R, tchr aide, $11.36/hr
McCrory, Heather R, short term sub tchr, $22.10/hr
McCrory, Heather R, custodial worker I, $10.05/hr
McCush, Roger S, phys edu tchr, $28,704
McDavis, Artricia L, cook II, $16,752
McDonald, Carol E, tchr aide, $11.36/hr
McDonald, Cynde A, administrative asst, $27,480
McDowell, Lura J, registered nurse, $40,392
McDowell, Rebecca J, tchr, $38,328
McElhaney, Sharon K, tchr aide, $14,832
McElwain, Gina L, bus driver, $10.36/hr
McElwee, Lynn, tchr, $34,248
McFarland, Mary E, tchr, $34,392
McFarland, Mary E, homebound tchr, $24.23
McFarlin, Toby L, tchr aide, $14,832
McGhee, Tiauni J, tchr aide, $11.36/hr
McGill, Chelsea H, tchr aide, $11.36/hr
McGinnis, Patricia J, tchr aide, $14,328
McGowin, Jim E, dd cnslr II, $43,008
McGuirk, Avella O, tchr aide, $11.36/hr
McKinzie, Betty L, asst dir, $43,704
McKissack, Robert L, tchr aide, $15,696
McLaughlin, Sherri E, vr cnslr II, $26.24
McLelland, Janet E, sup, $49,200
McLemore, Carla D, tchr aide, $11.36/hr
McManis, Lisa M, bus driver, $11,472
McManis, Lisa M, tchr aide, $11.36/hr
McMullen, Georgia A, tchr aide, $14,376
McNair, Gela, billing spec, $25,272
McNece, Vernon R, tchr, $29,280
McNeill, Louella Y, dist sup, $55,176
McPhearson, Frank, residential advisor I, $12.09/hr
McQuerter, Doris D, vr cnslr I, $39,960
McSorley, Tamra E, administrative asst, $29,328
Meadows, Sondra H, short term sub tchr, $14.03/hr
Meadows, Sondra H, long term sub tchr, $20.90/hr
Mealman, Catherine K, custodial worker II, $29,592
Mehrle, Blayne A, tchr aide, $14,520
Meisenheimer, Lisa J, vr cnslr II, $43,008
Mengwasser, Claire S, speech thrpst, $29,520
Merrick, Joshua K, dist mgr, $59,856
Merrill, Joyce D, billing spec, $24,504
Merrill, Susan K, tchr aide, $18,072
Mertens, Julie A, administrative asst, $26,160
Messex, Franklin E, custodial worker II, $11.03/hr
Messick, Juanita R, tchr aide, $14,208
Metz, Ivory C, dd cnslr III, $47,712
Meyer, David R, dd cnslr II, $43,008
Meyer, Kathy A, tchr, $34,680
Meyer, Teresa A, tchr aide, $15,408
Michael, Janet L, tchr aide, $11.36/hr
Michel, Anita D, rgnal mgr, $66,648
Midgyett, Gwenlyn J, billing spec, $25,272
Milam, Emily D, tchr aide, $14,208
Milgrim, Nancy A, dist sup, $55,728
Miller, Annette E, sup, $48,360
Miller, Brenda F, cook II, $18,504
Miller, Carol, short term sub tchr, $14.33/hr
Miller, Carol, tchr aide, $11.36/hr
Miller, Cristy G, tchr aide, $11.36/hr
Miller, Cynthia F, dd ce spec, $26,160
Miller, Gary R, custodial worker II, $23,688
Miller, Heather C, tchr aide, $11.36/hr
Miller, Heather C, bus attendant, $10.05/hr
Miller, Heather C, bus driver, $10.36/hr
Miller, Irell J, short term sub tchr, $14.33/hr
Miller, Janis C, dist sup, $55,728
Miller, Karen L, billing spec, $12,672
Miller, Kelly D, dd cnslr I, $39,960
Miller, Kevin M, qual assurance spec, $50,520
Miller, Kim W, hearing ofcr, $53,472
Miller, Kimberly A, sup, $37,968

Miller, Nicole L, dd cnslr, $38,040
Miller, Regina D, administrative asst, $29,400
Miller, Robert A, vr cnslr IV, $50,568
Miller, Shanda L, residential advisor I, $12.09/hr
Miller, Shantelle L, tchr aide, $11.36/hr
Miller, Susan K, home school coord, $40,104
Miller, Terry D, dd cnslr II, $43,008
Mills, Robin E, sec, $22,656
Minor, Miye F, billing spec, $25,272
Misenhelter, Lana K, tchr aide, $18,336
Mitcham, Mary E, tchr aide, $11.36/hr
Mitchell, Barbara J, tchr, $31,152
Mitchell, Lydia M, dist sup, $55,728
Mitchell, Rebekah K, residential advisor I, $24,864
Mitchell, Steven P, residential advisor I, $26,040
Moad, Deborah J, sec, $12.81/hr
Mobley, Robert D, asst dist supv, $51,864
Moen, Tim S, bus driver, $11,232
Mohamed, Umalhassan B, tchr aide, $11.36/hr
Molitor, Wendy T, vr cnslr, $38,040
Mollerus, Nichole S, tchr aide, $11.36/hr
Monahan, Stephanie, administrative asst, $26,952
Moncrief, Joann, dist sup, $57,000
Monroe, Karen E, administrative asst, $33,504
Montez, Debbie M, residential advisor II, $23,904
Montgomery, Barbara, short term sub tchr, $22.10/hr
Montgomery, Barbara, tchr aide, $11.36/hr
Montgomery, Barbara, long term sub tchr, $20.90/hr
Montgomery, Ruth R, tchr aide, $11.36/hr
Montgomery, Sandra G, sec, $27,168
Moon, Joyce A, tchr aide, $15,120
Mooney, Kimberly A, tchr aide, $14,208
Mooney, Kimberly A, short term sub tchr, $2.53/hr
Mooney, Kimberly A, long term sub tchr, $9.40/hr
Moore, Almeda E, cook II, $13,416
Moore, Beverly A, dd cnslr IV, $50,568
Moore, Donna L, tchr aide - bus atnd, $22,368
Moore, Lamonica L, short term sub tchr, $22.10/hr
Moore, Lamonica L, tchr aide, $11.36/hr
Moore, Melissa A, tchr, $37,968
Mora, Bradley J, bldg admin, $42,672
Morales, Jennifer S, tchr In charge, $34,536
Moreland, Jennifer G, sup, $41,160
Morelock, Susan K, tchr aide, $16,608
Morgan, Shauna A, home school coord, $41,832
Morgan, Teresa C, long term sub tchr, $20.90/hr
Morgan, Teresa C, tchr In charge, $24.31/hr
Morris, Cary R, qual assurance spec, $51,864
Morris, Desiree D, school sup, $36,648
Morris, Lisa M, administrative asst, $27,480
Morris, Robert L, tchr In charge, $47,712
Morrison, Marcy D, dir, $51,864
Morrow, Belinda G, sec, $24,096
Morrow, Kristen A, coord, $71,208
Moses, Joanne K, dist mgr, $59,856
Moss, Brenda F, tchr aide - bus atnd, $19,176
Moyers, Jessica P, tchr aide, $14,520
Moyers, Jessica P, short term sub tchr, $2.28/hr
Moyers, Lori L, dd cnslr II, $43,008
Moyers, Tony R, asst dist supv, $51,864
Mueller, Mary A, tchr aide, $11.36/hr
Mueller, Mary A, short term sub tchr, $14.03/hr
Mueller, Michele R, sup, $37,968
Mueller-sparrow, Jennifer A, vr cnslr IV, $30,360
Muenks, Michael J, coord, $66,240
Muessig, Tiffani J, asst dir, $41,904
Mulvaney, Frances A, short term sub tchr, $14.33/hr
Mulvaney, Frances A, tchr aide, $11.36/hr
Mulvaney, Frances A, sec, $10.73/hr
Murphy, Heather L, dd cnslr II, $43,008
Murphy, Misty R, tchr, $30,192
Myers, Meagan R, tchr aide, $11.36/hr
Myers, Shannon R, tchr aide, $16,656
Nalagan, Bryant E, dd cnslr II, $43,008
Narup, Martha R, tchr aide, $15,624
Narup, Martha R, short term sub tchr, $1.39/hr
Narup, Martha R, long term sub tchr, $8.26/hr
Nash, Carolyn S, tchr aide, $15,696
Navy, Lynn, school sup, $48,792
Neal, William J, residential advisor I, $21,264
Neale, William C, asst commissioner, $96,432
Neeley, Wyvonnia M, dd cnslr, $38,040
Neeley-kienzle, Anita M, cook I, $9.45/hr

Neeley-kienzle, Anita M, tchr aide, $11.36/hr
Nehring, Becky K, asst dist supv, $51,864
Nelson, Bonnie M, tchr aide, $18,048
Nelson, Donald E, tchr aide, $11.36/hr
Nelson, Yalonna M, tchr aide, $14,520
Neu, Terri L, administrative asst, $26,952
Neumann, Sarah M, tchr In charge, $36,216
Neumeyer, Teresa L, tchr, $36,432
Newman, Gloria A, cook II, $21,528
Newman, Marlo J, sec, $23,808
Nichols, Mary H, tchr aide, $11.36/hr
Nichols, Mary H, bus attendant, $10.05/hr
Nichols, Tom O, sup of instruction, $32.00/hr
Nicholson, Cathleen M, vr cnslr, $13.60/hr
Nickell, Angela D, dir, $51,864
Niekamp, Lori L, dir, $49,056
Niswonger, Paula R, prof rel ofcr, $51,864
Noel, Audra L, dd cnslr III, $47,712
Northway, Heather J, exec asst, $34,752
Norton, Rosa L, tchr aide, $11.36/hr
Nutting, Teresa M, home school coord, ms, $43,560
Oakes, Jean J, registered nurse, $21.66/hr
Oakes, Jean J, tchr aide, $11.36/hr
Oakes, Jean J, short term sub tchr, $14.33/hr
Oakes, Jean J, long term sub tchr, $20.90/hr
O'brien, Connie M, sup, $41,160
Odean, Brenda C, registered nurse, $33,048
Odegard, Eva D, short term sub tchr, $14.03/hr
Oestreich, Joe B, night watch, $20,184
Oestricker, Desiree D, tchr, $29,280
Oetman, Lauretta G, registered nurse, $21.66/hr
O'hara, Amanda L, tchr aide-bus driver, $18,624
Okeke, Peter C, dd cnslr, $38,040
Olaoye, Bolanle T, vr cnslr II, $43,008
Oligschlaeger, Kim R, asst dir, $47,712
Oligschlaeger, Sheila A, asst dist supv, $51,864
Oliver, Diane E, short term sub tchr, $14.33/hr
Oliver, Diane E, tchr aide, $11.36/hr
Olson, Debra K, tchr, $29,640
Olvera, Nicki J, registered nurse, $40,392
O'neal, Megan D, dd cnslr, $38,040
Orr, Janice W, dd cnslr I, $39,960
Osoro, Linet N, dd cnslr II, $43,008
Ostendorf, Kimberly S, short term sub tchr, $2.03/hr
Ostendorf, Kimberly S, long term sub tchr, $8.90/hr
Ostendorf, Kimberly S, tchr aide, $14,832
Ostertag, Jill A, tchr aide, $11.36/hr
Otekunrin, Helen A, administrative asst, $26,160
Ottermann, Diane L, tchr aide, $14,352
Ottersbach, Margaret A, vr cnslr III, $47,712
Otterson, Carolyn S, dd spec, $21.87/hr
Ottman, Shelia R, instructional spec, $39,072
Oxford, Lucinda, tchr, $29,424
Pace, Mary H, tchr, $34,392
Pace, Mary H, homebound tchr, $24.23/hr
Palmer, Barbara K, bus attendant, $10.05/hr
Palmer, Barbara K, short term sub tchr, $14.33/hr
Palmer, Barbara K, tchr aide, $11.36/hr
Palmer, Charlynda G, administrative asst, $31,248
Palmer, Corree D, tchr aide, $13,032
Palmer, Rebecca L, short term sub tchr, $14.03/hr
Palmer, Veronica O, tchr aide, $11.36/hr
Palmer, Veronica O, short term sub tchr, $14.33/hr
Parente, Jackson S, tchr aide, $11.36/hr
Parker, Christy A, dd cnslr III, $47,712
Parker, Jennifer, residential advisor I, $20,232
Parker, Judy K, sec, $22,584
Parks, Tracy Y, vr cnslr II, $43,008
Patterson, Paula S, bldg admin, $45,528
Payne, Mary M, tchr aide, $14,208
Payne, Rebecca S, sup, $36,480
Payne, Sherrie L, billing spec, $29,256
Peabody, Robert J, dd cnslr, $38,040
Peake, Emmanuel A, tchr aide, $11.36/hr
Pearson, Barbara J, tchr aide, $14,832
Peck, Pamela L, tchr aide, $11.36/hr
Peck, Pamela L, short term sub tchr, $14.33/hr
Peck, Pamela L, homebound tchr, $24.23/hr
Peeple, William J, custodial worker II, $24,144
Pegues, Ariel J, tchr aide, $11.36/hr
Peitzmeier, Atina M, tchr aide, $14,520
Peneston, Dee A, school sup, $51,480
Peneston, Robert E, dormitory dir, $34,752

Penninger, Christy L, speech thrpst, $36,432
Pepper, Catherine L, tchr aide, $13,344
Peralta, Traci J, tchr aide, $14,832
Perkins, Bess L, instructional spec, $33,792
Perkins, Dianne M, vr cnslr II, $43,008
Perkins, Elizabeth D, vr cnslr IV, $50,568
Perkins, Michelle D, hearing ofcr, $53,472
Perrigo, Daniel L, bus driver, $13.50/hr
Perstrope, Gina K, tchr aide, $11.36/hr
Perstrope, Gina K, cook I, $9.45/hr
Peters, Rebecca R, administrative asst, $26,160
Peterson, Kimberly J, residential advisor I, $21,264
Peterson, Lisa M, vr cnslr III, $47,712
Peterson, Matt W, dd cnslr II, $43,008
Pettit, Debra L, registered nurse, $40,392
Pfaff, Brian J, short term sub tchr, $22.10/hr
Pfleger, Donald F, dd cnslr IV, $50,568
Phegley, Kristan D, tchr aide, $14,856
Phillips, Heather I, tchr aide, $11.36/hr
Phillips, Heather I, bus attendant, $10.05/hr
Phillips, Ruth E, tchr aide, $11.36/hr
Pickett, Patricia R, administrative asst, $27,480
Piel, Andrea L, guidance cnslr, $29,280
Piel, Megan E, vr cnslr II, $43,008
Pike, Deborah S, tchr aide, $13,320
Pike, Tina R, bldg admin, $40,656
Pille, Marie R, tchr, $31,224
Pille, Marie R, homebound tchr, $24.23/hr
Pinet, Allison P, tchr aide, $11.36/hr
Pittman, Betty S, residential advisor I, $21,264
Pittmon, Stacy L, residential advisor I, $21,720
Pivirotto, Doreen M, short term sub tchr, $14.33/hr
Pixley, Brooke A, tchr, $28,152
Planty, Dakeeta A, tchr aide, $14,832
Platt, Heather M, dd cnslr II, $43,008
Plein, Catherine A, dd cnslr II, $43,008
Pleus, Tanya S, planner, $42,720
Pointer, Robin, residential advisor I, $22,440
Pollard, Debbie L, tchr aide, $11.36/hr
Pollard, Debbie L, tchr aide, $11.36/hr
Pollard, Debbie L, bus attendant, $10.05/hr
Ponder, Beverly J, administrative asst, $27,480
Porter, Gary W, tchr, $32,808
Porter, Kayla S, tchr aide, $14,208
Porter, Kayla S, short term sub tchr, $2.53/hr
Potter, Sarah L, comm coord, $72,792
Powell, Katie I, tchr, $30,240
Powell, Katie I, homebound tchr, $24.23/hr
Powell, Krystall D, sup, $31,920
Powell, Mieka M, asst dist supv, $51,864
Pratt, Mary B, sec, $22,656
Pratt, Vickie J, registered nurse, $21.66/hr
Preis, Stacey J, dpty commissioner, $125,352
Prenger, Cecilia C, short term sub tchr, $14.03/hr
Presberry, Richard L, vr spec, $26.24/hr
Prewett, Bertie I, tchr aide, $11.36/hr
Price, Bonnie S, tchr aide - bus atnd, $18,504
Price, Bonnie S, short term sub tchr, $2.80/hr
Price, Clara A, tchr aide, $11.36/hr
Price, Clara A, short term sub tchr, $14.33/hr
Price, Earnestine, short term sub tchr, $14.33/hr
Price, Earnestine, tchr aide, $11.36/hr
Price, Jared R, dd cnslr II, $43,008
Price, Loretta M, prof rel ofcr, $51,864
Price, Sandra A, custodial worker II, $23,184
Price, Sandra A, tchr aide, $0.33/hr
Pride, Mariah M, tchr aide, $11.36/hr
Proctor, Beth E, billing spec, $29,520
Proehl-Burnett, Patrice A, hearing ofcr, $53,472
Prueitt, Dianna J, tchr aide, $11.36/hr
Pruitt-Smith, Vanessa B, custodial worker II, $24,168
Pugh, Carrie, qual assurance spec, $52,896
Pulliam, Toni E, sec, $24,288
Purcell, Melinda S, sec, $23,808
Purnell, Edith G, administrative asst, $26,952
Purvis, Victoria V, sec, $15,120
Purvis, Victoria V, short term sub tchr, $1.80/hr
Quade, Linda K, sec, $12.81/hr
Quetsch, Cynthia A, coord, $72,864
Quick, Stephanie L, residential advisor I, $22,488
Quinn-Davis, Willie J, dd cnslr II, $43,008
Rackers, Bethany R, sec, $9.23/hr
Rackers, Courtney C, administrative asst, $27,504

Rackers, Myra L, asst field opps mgr, $67,872
Rader, Patsy J, short term sub tchr, $14.33/hr
Rader, Patsy J, bus attendant, $10.05/hr
Rader, Patsy J, tchr aide, $11.36/hr
Raines, Rhonda K, tchr aide, $11.36/hr
Raines, Rhonda K, cook I, $9.45/hr
Ralston, Joanne S, coord, $59,088
Randall, Cameron L, tchr aide, $11.36/hr
Rangel, Jacquelyn S, billing spec, $24,504
Rantz, Christina L, administrative asst, $29,328
Rathert, Regina L, vr cnslr III, $47,712
Ray, Jeremy J, vr cnslr II, $43,008
Raymer, Virgie E, short term sub tchr, $14.03/hr
Raymer, Virgie E, tchr aide, $11.36/hr
Reagan, Victoria M, tchr aide, $14,832
Ream, Shari J, tchr, $32,520
Reaves, Traci L, tchr, $29,208
Reaves, Traci L, homebound tchr, $24.23/hr
Rector, Craig D, coord, $66,240
Redden, Glenn, tchr aide, $11.36/hr
Redding, Julia A, dd cnslr II, $43,008
Redeker, Karen, tchr aide, $14,208
Redfering, Ruth E, tchr, $35,328
Reed, Barbara J, tchr aide, $15,624
Reed, James D, sup, $41,160
Reed, Kimberly D, dd cnslr II, $43,008
Reed, Rachel D, tchr aide, $11.36/hr
Reed, Rachel D, bus attendant, $10.05/hr
Reed, Rosemary J, comp info tech, $39,408
Reed, Sherry L, sec, $15,288
Reese, Jay W, sup of instruction, $56,472
Reese, Judith A, custodial worker I, $12,864
Rehagen, Jill A, accounting analyst, $41,184
Rehagen, Kacey, short term sub tchr, $14.03/hr
Rehagen, Kacey, long term sub tchr, $20.90/hr
Rehagen, Mark S, sup, $38,352
Rehak, Janice M, coord, $61,416
Renfro, Tammy L, bus driver, $10.36/hr
Ressel, Kyla J, asst dist supv, $51,864
Reyes, Janet M, prof rel ofcr, $51,864
Reynolds, Angela M, dd cnslr II, $43,008
Reynolds, Mary M, tchr aide, $11.36/hr
Rhamy, Natalie B, tchr aide-bus driver, $18,912
Rhoads-Ashley, Jeannie C, vr cnslr, $38,040
Rhodes, Stephanie D, dd cnslr I, $39,960
Ricci, Sandra M, tchr aide, $11.36/hr
Rice, Bridgette M, tchr aide, $11.36/hr
Rice, Laura L, custodial work sup, $36,816
Rice, Mary A, residential advisor I, $22,440
Richards, Jonathan D, vr cnslr II, $43,008
Richmond, Gloria J, custodial worker II, $23,184
Rickabaugh, Cory L, residential advisor I, $12.09/hr
Ricker, Timothy A, sup of instruction, $56,472
Riddle, Joletta K, tchr aide, $11.36/hr
Ridings, Priscilla K, tchr aide, $15,384
Riggs, Debra K, billing spec, $25,272
Rikard, Rebecca J, administrative asst, $26,952
Riley, April J, dd cnslr II, $43,008
Riley, Regina A, tchr, $31,704
Riley, Stephanie A, hearing ofcr, $53,472
Riley, William B, custodial worker I, $10.05/hr
Rimer, Mary L, dir, $49,056
Riner-Mooney, Angela G, dir, $51,864
Riney, Marsha R, bldg admin, $50,280
Riney, Rashelle L, tchr aide, $14,208
Riney, Rashelle L, short term sub tchr, $2.53/hr
Ring, Kelli R, tchr aide, $18,072
Ripley, Debora E, tchr ln charge, $44,832
Ripley, Jeffrey M, field opps mgr, $69,168
Ritter, Brenda A, tchr aide, $11.36/hr
Ritter, Brenda A, sec, $10.73/hr
Ritz, Kelley A, dd cnslr II, $43,008
Rivera, Luis A, long term sub tchr, $20.90/hr
Rizzo, Julie K, tchr, $40,080
Roach, Denise A, exec asst, $41,688
Roach, Douglas J, asst dir, $49,488
Roark, Shai E, registered nurse, $32,400
Robbins, Thomas F, coord, $61,416
Roberson, Brenda J, tchr aide, $11.36/hr
Roberson, Brenda J, short term sub tchr, $14.03/hr
Roberson, Laura D, cook II, $20,736
Roberts, C D, hearing ofcr, $28.64/hr
Roberts, Linda D, tchr aide, $11.36/hr

Robertson, Erica L, dd cnslr II, $43,008
Robertson, Pamela K, comp info tech, $42,024
Robinson, Christine, vr cnslr IV, $50,568
Robinson, Michelle L, tchr aide, $11.36/hr
Robinson, Nancy D, tchr aide, $18,576
Robinson, Peggy L, bldg admin, $52,896
Robinson, Priscilla A, tchr, $36,744
Robinson, Terraine G, tchr, $29,592
Robinson, Tracy R, dd ce spec, $26,568
Robinson-kidd, Anissa D, tchr aide, $14,520
Roetto, Jill M, vr cnslr II, $43,008
Roetto Verburgt, Mary E, dd cnslr III, $47,712
Rogers, Jo E, tchr aide, $11.36/hr
Rogers, Michael D, custodial worker II, $29,280
Rogers, Shaunta E, tchr, $29,880
Rogers, Steven R, sup, $41,160
Rohde, Nancy M, registered nurse, $34,848
Rois-delpha, Molly E, vr cnslr III, $47,712
Rojas, April M, tchr aide, $11.36/hr
Rojas, April M, sec, $10.73/hr
Rolloos, Megan E, dd cnslr II, $43,008
Romans, Ashley D, tchr aide, $11.36/hr
Romans, Ashley D, short term sub tchr, $14.03/hr
Romans, Ashley D, registered nurse, $21.66/hr
Romine, Heather M, vr cnslr II, $43,008
Rooff, Kristine M, administrative asst, $33,504
Rosa-chiodini, Linda, short term sub tchr, $14.03/hr
Rose, Annette E, tchr aide, $11.36/hr
Rose, Anthony, custodial worker I, $10.05/hr
Rose, Anthony, tchr aide, $11.36/hr
Rose, Anthony, cook I, $9.45/hr
Rosenkoetter, R D, dir, $54,072
Rosenstengle, Jacquelyn A, vr cnslr I, $39,960
Ross, Angela R, dd cnslr II, $43,008
Ross, Linda M, registered nurse, bsn, $50,856
Ross, Margie M, tchr aide, $11.36/hr
Ross, Mary R, vr cnslr II, $43,008
Ross, Patricia I, tchr aide, $24,456
Rosser, Kathy S, tchr aide, $11.36/hr
Rowland, Christopher A, billing spec, $24,768
Rowland, Paula L, tchr aide, $13,320
Roycraft, Donna C, sec, $14,184
Rudolph, Amber M, dd cnslr I, $39,960
Ruettgers, Marsha R, sup, $41,160
Runzo, William D, food serv mgr, $32,064
Rush, Brenda H, procurement spec, $39,744
Rush, Constance J, gen counsel, $51,864
Rush, T K, procurement spec, $33,552
Russell, Angela D, tchr, $28,968
Russell, Brian D, residential advisor I, $12.09/hr
Russell, Celeste M, tchr aide, $13,320
Rust, Catherine M, sup, $20,592
Rutledge, Catherine L, tchr aide, $13,320
Rutledge, Kevan K, asst dir, $53,616
Rutledge, Sarah K, asst dist supv, $51,864
Ryan, John P, vr cnslr, $21.87/hr
Ryce, Cynthia A, short term sub tchr, $22.10/hr
Rynning, Roberta L, administrative asst, $26,424
Saltzman, Mary K, long term sub tchr, $25.08/hr
Samelak, Joseph A, nutrition prog spec, $38,880
Samit, Daniel M, vr cnslr II, $43,008
Sampson, Thomas, vr cnslr IV, $50,568
Samson-pestka, Becky J, tchr aide, $11.36/hr
Samson-pestka, Becky J, short term sub tchr, $14.03/hr
Samuelson, Eve M, dd cnslr, $38,040
Sandbothe, Pamela M, dir, $57,000
Sanders, Gary L, asst dir, $47,712
Sanders, Sherry A, tchr aide, $14,064
Sanderson, Deborah A, tchr, $45,720
Sanderson, Deborah A, homebound tchr, $24.23/hr
Sanfilippo Solindas, Terry D, sup, $38,472
Santoriello, Cherise M, tchr, $28,152
Satterfield, Treva M, tchr, $36,432
Satterfield, Treva M, homebound tchr, $24.23/hr
Sauer, Joann, dd cnslr II, $43,008
Saunders, Honey N, tchr aide, $11.36/hr
Sawyer, Sharon D, sec, $15,936
Schank, Carla L, tchr aide, $13,320
Schatz, Chad C, dir, $55,320
Scheele, Amy J, tchr aide, $11.36/hr
Scheele, Amy J, custodial worker I, $10.05/hr
Scheffing, Dianne E, homebound tchr, $24.23/hr
Scheffing, Dianne E, tchr, $34,392

Schell, Anna M, tchr aide, $20,712
Schellman, Steven R, asst dir, $42,336
Schepers, Donna L, hr analyst, $43,008
Scherer, Samalynn D, dd cnslr, $38,040
Scherer, Tonia M, tchr, $28,152
Schiffner, Michael D, dir, $63,408
Schilling, Deborah L, dd cnslr III, $47,712
Schindler, Angela R, dd cnslr II, $43,008
Schlag, Amy R, dd cnslr III, $47,712
Schlimpert, Thomas L, asst dir, $43,704
Schlottman, Tina M, tchr, $33,360
Schlottman, Tina M, homebound tchr, $24.23/hr
Schlotz, Lauren E, tchr aide, $11.36/hr
Schmid, Anna C, tchr aide, $11.36/hr
Schmidt, Jesse G, residential advisor I, $20,856
Schmitt, Marianne, sec, $12.81/hr
Schmutzler, Patricia L, phys edu tchr, $36,744
Schneider, Linda S, long term sub tchr, $20.90/hr
Schneider, Linda S, short term sub tchr, $14.03/hr
Schneider, Valerie J, dd case ctrl analyst, $30,312
Schnieders, Allison M, tchr aide, $11.36/hr
Schnurbusch, Arlene, dd case ctrl analyst, $33,888
Schofield, Christine, administrative asst, $28,896
Schreier, Diana L, tchr aide, $16,632
Schremp, Stephanie M, tchr, $28,152
Schroeder, Pamela R, asst dir, $47,712
Schulte, Norbert H, coord, $71,208
Schulte, Rebekah G, billing spec, $12,672
Schultz, Danielle L, dd cnslr IV, $50,568
Schumacher, Pamela J, homebound tchr, $24.23/hr
Schumacher, Pamela J, long term sub tchr, $8.67/hr
Schumacher, Pamela J, tchr aide, $15,120
Schumacher, Pamela J, short term sub tchr, $1.80/hr
Schutzenhofer, Darla, tchr aide, $17,880
Schwarzer, Ashley R, tchr aide, $11.36/hr
Schweer, Stacy A, billing spec, $25,272
Schweizer, Brooke A, tchr aide, $11.36/hr
Scott, James K, tchr aide, $11.36/hr
Scott, Kristyn M, tchr aide, $11.36/hr
Scott, Laura A, sup, $22.48/hr
Scott, Shari L, tchr, $36,816
Scott, Shari L, homebound tchr, $24.23/hr
Scott, Thea F, dir, $51,864
Scroggs, Bradley J, dir, $56,472
Sears, Amanda G, tchr aide, $11.36/hr
Secrest, Tammy S, tchr aide, $14,856
Sederburg, Jennifer M, dd cnslr II, $43,008
Seek, Rachel E, tchr aide, $11.36/hr
Segall, Robyn M, sup, $41,160
Seiberlich, Debra L, tchr, $35,520
Seiberlich, Debra L, homebound tchr, $24.23/hr
Seiler, Carol A, dd cnslr II, $43,008
Selinger, Ronald D, dd cnslr II, $43,008
Sellinger, Kelly L, homebound tchr, $24.23/hr
Sellinger, Kelly L, phys edu tchr, $28,152
Semkin, Todd R, administrative asst, $33,504
Sexton, Shawn C, tchr aide, $11.36/hr
Shanahan, Michele L, vr cnslr I, $39,960
Shanks, Karen M, administrative asst, $30,432
Shannon, Theresa D, custodial worker I, $13,968
Shannon, Theresa D, tchr aide, $11.36/hr
Sharpe, Donna S, sup, $38,352
Shaul, Samantha L, vr cnslr I, $39,960
Shaw, Barbara J, nutrition prog spec, $38,880
Shaw, Rebecca A, short term sub tchr, $14.03/hr
Shaw, Rebecca A, tchr aide, $11.36/hr
Shaw, Rebecca A, long term sub tchr, $20.90/hr
Shaw, Robert E, vr cnslr II, $43,008
Sherwood, Kendra L, tchr aide, $14,832
Sherwood, Kendra L, short term sub tchr, $2.03/hr
Sherwood, Kendra L, long term sub tchr, $8.90/hr
Shifflet, Scott A, hearing ofcr, $53,472
Shipman, Aubrey T, sup, $41,160
Shively, Bernadette C, asst dist supv, $51,864
Shively, Beverly A, tchr aide, $15,624
Shively, Beverly A, short term sub tchr, $1.39/hr
Shively, Beverly A, long term sub tchr, $8.26/hr
Short, Debby J, sec, $19,776
Short, Savannah B, short term sub tchr, $14.03/hr
Short, Savannah B, tchr aide, $11.36/hr
Shrum, Heather N, bus attendant, $10.05/hr
Shrum, Heather N, short term sub tchr, $14.03/hr
Shrum, Heather N, tchr aide, $11.36/hr

Shrum, Heather N, long term sub tchr, $20.90/hr
Shrum, Heather N, tchr In charge, $24.53/hr
Shultz, Debra L, tchr, $37,920
Sidney, Jonathan T, custodial worker I, $7.65/hr
Siebeneck, Diane M, hr analyst, $36,624
Siebert, Harold W, dir, $25.00/hr
Siebert, Kathy L, administrative asst, $27,480
Siehr, Cathy M, vr cnslr II, $43,008
Siekerman, Amy J, vr cnslr II, $43,008
Sievert, Sean W, cook I, $16,392
Siler, Harold D, residential advisor I, $12.09/hr
Sillas-Rodriguez, Kathy L, tchr aide, $11.36/hr
Silvey, Monica L, administrative asst, $29,256
Simmons, Brenda K, dir, $57,000
Simmons, Stephanie A, tchr aide, $13,032
Simon, Sheila M, administrative asst, $14.52/hr
Sims, Amanda K, tchr, $28,704
Sims, Sandy M, tchr aide, $14,832
Sims, Shannon N, tchr, $28,152
Sims, Shannon N, homebound tchr, $24.23/hr
Sisco, Kathy A, dd ce spec, $31,992
Sissom, Sherry A, dd ce spec, $29,256
Sisson, Jr, custodial worker I, $10.05/hr
Sitton, Michelle R, tchr, $29,472
Sitton, Michelle R, homebound tchr, $24.23/hr
Skaggs, Doris L, tchr aide, $11.36/hr
Skaggs, Doris L, short term sub tchr, $14.33/hr
Skinner, Kerri E, tchr aide, $11.36/hr
Slawson, Starla A, tchr aide, $11.36/hr
Sloat, Timothy A, residential advisor I, $12.09/hr
Smith, Alissa C, tchr aide, $11.36/hr
Smith, Audrey, residential advisor II, $27,984
Smith, Autumn R, vr cnslr I, $39,960
Smith, Betty J, tchr aide, $11.36/hr
Smith, Betty J, custodial worker I, $10.05/hr
Smith, Bettye J, residential advisor I, $24,120
Smith, Carley F, tchr, $34,176
Smith, Carley F, homebound tchr, $24.23/hr
Smith, Carol A, vr cnslr III, $28,632
Smith, Cynthia G, vr spec, $26.24/hr
Smith, Dean E, bldg admin, $41,328
Smith, Elizabeth, vr cnslr III, $47,712
Smith, Janet M, administrative asst, $39,624
Smith, Jeather L, dist sup, $55,728
Smith, Joanne F, comp info tech, $32.90/hr
Smith, Kelly S, dd cnslr II, $43,008
Smith, Laura A, tchr, $32,760
Smith, Leah I, dd cnslr I, $21.87/hr
Smith, Mattie L, tchr aide, $11.36/hr
Smith, Mellissa D, administrative asst, $30,816
Smith, Rick L, dd cnslr III, $48,336
Smith, Robyn L, vr cnslr III, $47,712
Smith, Sabrina R, tchr aide, $16,776
Smith, Sabrina R, short term sub tchr, $0.46/hr
Smith, Sabrina R, long term sub tchr, $7.33/hr
Smith, Sabrina R, homebound tchr, $24.23/hr
Smith, Shirley E, tchr aide, $11.36/hr
Smith, Tracy E, tchr aide, $14,832
Smith, Zol-licia J, short term sub tchr, $14.33/hr
Smith, Zol-licia J, tchr aide, $11.36/hr
Smoot, Jonathan D, residential advisor I, $21,264
Sneller, Larry E, custodial worker I, $16,176
Snook, Donna J, tchr aide, $14,328
Snow, Donna K, tchr aide, $14,832
Snow, Laura J, sec, $22,560
Snyder, Annette M, long term sub tchr, $8.25/hr
Snyder, Annette M, tchr aide, $14,328
Snyder, Annette M, short term sub tchr, $1.38/hr
Snyder, Kristin M, vr cnslr I, $39,960
Snyder, Rhonda K, tchr aide, $14,208
Snyder-Miller, T L, prof rel ofcr, $51,864
Soars, Lewis M, tchr aide, $14,208
Sohn, Carole S, administrative asst, $29,328
Sokol, Kathleen H, short term sub tchr, $14.03/hr
Sommerville, Russell, short term sub tchr, $14.33/hr
Sommerville, Russell, tchr aide, $11.36/hr
Sommerville, Russell, long term sub tchr, $20.90/hr
Sone, Lisa A, asst dir, $53,616
Soto, Alison R, audiologist, $24.50/hr
Sotonwa, Opeoluwa S, dir, $63,864
South, Kimberly D, tchr aide, $11.36/hr
Sowder, Carol A, short term sub tchr, $14.03/hr
Spalty, Thomas J, dir, $51,864

Spears, Geri S, dd cnslr III, $47,712
Spencer, Marcia E, sec, $15,288
Spiess, Nicole M, tchr, $30,192
Spilker, Renay S, phys edu tchr, $36,432
Sprague, Cathy L, tchr aide, $16,608
Srigley, Elizabeth L, tchr aide, $11.36/hr
Srigley, Elizabeth L, short term sub tchr, $22.10/hr
Srigley, Elizabeth L, long term sub tchr, $20.90/hr
Stains, Johnny R, sup, $41,160
Stains, Tammy J, sup, $38,352
Stamper, Adriane R, long term sub tchr, $8.90/hr
Stamper, Adriane R, tchr aide, $14,832
Stamper, Adriane R, short term sub tchr, $2.03/hr
Stamper, Letha M, tchr, $31,224
Standfield, Chelsea A, tchr aide, $11.36/hr
Stanley, Leslie E, vr cnslr IV, $50,568
Stansberry, Tony L, sup of instruction, $56,472
Stark, Barbara A, cook II, $21,720
Starke, Starla A, vr cnslr II, $45,360
Starks, Farrah, residential advisor I, $14,064
Starlin-Horner, Ann H, dir, $24,792
Starnes, Pamela K, tchr aide, $17,352
Starr, Stephen P, vr cnslr III, $47,712
Steele, Gloria J, tchr aide, $15,624
Stegeman, Caitlin N, dd cnslr, $38,040
Stegeman, Russell J, billing spec, $24,768
Stephens, Danny H, vr spec, $26.24/hr
Stephens, Donna M, tchr aide, $18,072
Stephens, Josie K, tchr aide, $15,624
Stephens, Josie K, long term sub tchr, $8.26/hr
Stephens, Lindi D, tchr, $28,608
Stephenson, Nora I, tchr aide, $17,352
Stephenson, Roger W, vr cnslr II, $43,008
Stevens, Delpha R, tchr aide, $14,208
Steward, Sharon D, vr cnslr III, $48,336
Steward, Shirley L, tchr aide, $18,072
Stewart, Brenda J, accounting spec, $33,552
Stewart, Gailene L, dir, $24,792
Stewart, Helen N, dir, $50,832
Stewart, Julie M, short term sub tchr, $22.10/hr
Stewart, Julie M, tchr aide, $11.36/hr
Stichler, Michele L, administrative asst, $27,480
Stieber, Michael P, asst dormitory dir, $27,816
Stites, John R, tchr aide, $11.36/hr
Stock, Cheryl A, sup, $37,968
Stock, Joan A, tchr aide, $11.36/hr
Stock, Joan A, short term sub tchr, $14.33/hr
Stock, Joan A, long term sub tchr, $20.90/hr
Stoecker, Jennifer, dd cnslr II, $43,008
Stoll, Deborah K, sec, $10.73/hr
Stoll, Deborah K, tchr aide, $11.36/hr
Stone, Christopher, residential advisor II, $21,648
Stone, Reva M, administrative asst, $28,224
Stoneking, Brittney C, tchr aide, $11.36/hr
Stowers, Vicki L, tchr aide, $11.36/hr
Strand, Jocelyn M, coord, $66,240
Strange, Jennifer L, tchr, $36,144
Stranimier, Lorretta S, sec, $22,656
Stratman, Nancy L, tchr, $36,168
Strein, Marla K, tchr aide, $11.36/hr
Strickland, Sharon L, short term sub tchr, $14.03/hr
Strickland, Sharon L, tchr aide, $11.36/hr
Strothmann, Nancy M, vr cnslr II, $43,008
Strothmann, Patrick K, dd cnslr, $38,040
Struemph, Lindsey M, qual assurance spec, $51,864
Stuart, Lynne A, dd spec, $21.87/hr
Stuart, Roxanne K, tchr aide, $11.36/hr
Stuart, Roxanne K, custodial worker I, $10.05/hr
Student, Angela E, tchr aide, $11.36/hr
Studer, Jamie E, asst dormitory dir, $26,568
Stumbaugh, Michele L, tchr aide, $14,208
Stumbaugh, Michele L, short term sub tchr, $2.53/hr
Stump, Pamela S, registered nurse, $33,048
Sturgeon, Colt T, tchr aide, $11.36/hr
Sublett, La'Kesha R, tchr aide, $11.36/hr
Suerig, Heather D, tchr, $31,440
Suerig, Heather D, homebound tchr, $24.23/hr
Sullinger, Mona D, dd cnslr II, $43,008
Sullins, Andrea D, tchr aide, $14,520
Summers, Kristy R, data spec, $20,040
Sumowski-Bradley, Kayla D, residential advisor I, $20,856
Suppes, Colleen C, tchr aide, $14,520
Surface, Karen L, sec, $27,168

Sutherland, Anna Marie L, tchr aide, $14,520
Sutter, Lisa K, tchr, $34,632
Sutton, Douglas K, dir, $52,776
Sutton, Patty A, billing spec, $25,272
Swaim, Maureen M, custodial worker II, $24,168
Swain, Amy E, asst dist supv, $51,864
Swain, Kevin L, tchr, $28,152
Swank, Cinthia M, tchr aide, $14,208
Swank, Cinthia M, short term sub tchr, $2.04/hr
Swann, Robert, custodial worker I, $22,080
Swyhart, Roxanne K, tchr aide, $13,032
Sybert, Pamela J, registered nurse, $41,448
Tackett, Larissa J, tchr aide, $13,032
Tadsen, Jeffrey D, vr driver, $12.81/hr
Taggart, Samantha J, nutrition prog spec, $38,880
Talley, Della L, short term sub tchr, $14.33/hr
Talley, Della L, custodial worker I, $10.05/hr
Talley, Della L, tchr aide, $11.36/hr
Tanner, Angela J, tchr aide, $13,608
Tanner, Bryan M, nutrition prog spec, $38,352
Tanner, Margery A, dir, $51,864
Tate, Deanna M, administrative asst, $26,424
Taylor, Charlotte Y, residential advisor I, $12.09/hr
Taylor, Cleophus, custodial worker I, $20,904
Taylor, Linda K, sec, $12.81/hr
Taylor, Mihui S, long term sub tchr, $8.26/hr
Taylor, Mihui S, tchr aide, $15,624
Taylor, Mihui S, short term sub tchr, $1.39/hr
Taylor, Rebecca M, sup, $39,648
Taylor, Stacy R, sup, $48,408
Taylor, Tara D, instructional spec, $33,792
Tenholder, Carol J, qual assurance spec, $51,864
Tennessen-cusumano, Beatrix, tchr, $31,896
Terrill, Alysha I, dd cnslr, $38,040
Terry, Hattie T, tchr, $28,704
Terry, Hattie T, homebound tchr, $24.23/hr
Thele, Crystal A, asst dist supv, $51,864
Thieme, Charolette R, administrative asst, $26,952
Thomas, Brenda K, short term sub tchr, $14.03/hr
Thomas, Kayla N, tchr aide, $11.36/hr
Thomas, Kayla N, bus attendant, $10.05/hr
Thomas, Kayla N, custodial worker I, $10.05/hr
Thomas, Lindsay B, administrative asst, $28,224
Thomas, Lisa R, tchr aide, $11.36/hr
Thomas, Lisa R, short term sub tchr, $22.10/hr
Thomas, Nancy O, asst dir, $47,712
Thomas, Nancy S, dd cnslr IV, $50,568
Thomas, Pamela S, coord, $66,240
Thomas, Robin M, vr cnslr II, $43,008
Thomas, Vanassa D, dd cnslr II, $43,008
Thomason, Jim L, tchr aide, $11.36/hr
Thomlinson, Mark A, tchr aide, $11.36/hr
Thompson, Casey R, vr cnslr I, $39,960
Thompson, Cheryl A, sup, $18,984
Thompson, Susan K, administrative asst, $26,952
Thorbergson, Allison K, home school coord, ms, $44,112
Thorne, Tammy L, tchr aide, $11.36/hr
Thornton, Brooke D, billing spec, $25,272
Thornton, Virginia J, tchr aide, $13,320
Thornton, William R, gen counsel, $96,432
Threlkeld, Sara E, tchr aide, $11.36/hr
Threlkeld, Sara E, short term sub tchr, $14.33/hr
Throop, Elizabeth N, tchr aide, $11.36/hr
Thuli, Cari A, billing spec, $24,768
Tice, Heather M, vr cnslr I, $39,960
Tiggemann, Kyle J, dd cnslr, $38,040
Tilley, Angela N, tchr aide, $11.36/hr
Tilley, Angela N, short term sub tchr, $14.33/hr
Tinker, Alexandra A, tchr aide, $11.36/hr
Tinker, Alexandra A, short term sub tchr, $14.33/hr
Tobias, Thomas J, dir, $48,552
Tochtrop, Laurie, dd cnslr, $38,040
Tolliver, Juria, residential advisor I, $20,232
Toole-bowles, Sheryl L, vr cnslr II, $43,008
Torrence, Rosemarie, sec, $12.81/hr
Townsend, Teresa L, tchr aide, $17,880
Tracy, Bryan W, qual assurance spec, $51,864
Tracy, Patty M, tchr aide, $14,856
Trandahl, Cassandra J, tchr aide, $11.36/hr
Triplett, Pearlene B, sec, $12.81/hr
Trovillion, Melinda, administrative asst, $27,984
Tucker, Daniel L, phys edu tchr, $27,792
Turley, Bethany A, tchr aide, $13,320

Turner, Amanda L, short term sub tchr, $14.03/hr
Turner, Debra L, dd cnslr IV, $50,568
Turner, Greg L, qual assurance spec, $51,864
Turner, Madonna S, tchr aide, $14,856
Turner, Marian, tchr aide, $22,608
Turner, Mario J, residential advisor I, $12.09/hr
Turner, Mary J, tchr aide, $14,520
Turner, Suanne, tchr, $37,920
Turner, Teri A, tchr aide, $14,208
Turpin, Leslie B, sup, $38,880
Uhrhan, Michael R, dd cnslr, $38,040
Underwood, Kimberly J, dd cnslr II, $43,008
Underwood, Steven E, dd cnslr III, $47,712
Unger, Clarinda F, vr spec, $26.24/hr
Utt, Michele R, dir, $51,864
Valadez, Amanda S, tchr aide, $14,208
Van Oostrom, Claudia K, qual assurance spec, $55,416
Van Pelt, Megan B, dd cnslr II, $43,008
Van Winkle, Laura G, tchr aide, $11.36/hr
Van Winkle, Laura G, bus attendant, $10.05/hr
Vandeloecht, Fawn M, nurse lpn, $23,640
Vanderkuur-earl, Kristina K, tchr aide, $11.36/hr
Vanderslice, Kathy J, tchr aide, $13,320
Vandeven, Sheryl A, tchr aide, $14,856
Vandyke, Felicia D, vr cnslr II, $43,008
Vanvolkinburg, Dorothy F, tchr aide, $11.36/hr
Vanvolkinburg, Dorothy F, cook II, $10.05/hr
Vanvolkinburg, Jr, tchr aide, $14,520
Vanvolkinburg, Jr, short term sub tchr, $14.03/hr
Vanvolkinburg, Jr, tchr aide, $11.36/hr
Vanvolkinburg, Jr, custodial worker I, $10.05/hr
Vanzant, Brandy S, tchr aide, $11.36/hr
Vaugh, Kelly M, registered nurse, $21.66/hr
Vernon-peoples, Deborah L, long term sub tchr, $9.52/hr
Vernon-peoples, Deborah L, tchr aide, $14,064
Vernon-peoples, Deborah L, short term sub tchr, $2.65/hr
Vickers, Bradley V, asst dormitory dir, $26,568
Vickers, Bradley V, residential advisor I, $12.09/hr
Vickers, Norlian V, interpreter, $37,176
Vickers, Norma L, sup, $27.20/hr
Viehmann, Christie L, vr cnslr III, $42,960
Vilkanskas, Lydia A, tchr, $28,032
Villmer, M T, sup, $45,312
Villmer, Rich A, asst dir, $52,200
Vincent, Gerene E, hearing ofcr, $53,472
Vincent, Kristen N, dd cnslr, $38,040
Vitellaro, Gina M, short term sub tchr, $2.40/hr
Vitellaro, Gina M, tchr aide, $14,520
Volkerding, John W, dd cnslr I, $39,960
Vos, Joyce M, tchr aide, $11.36/hr
Waddell, Joyce C, asst supt, $58,824
Wade, Davine J, nursing asst, $10.29/hr
Wade, Toni N, accounting audit analyst, $46,944
Wadley, Sandra L, sup, $49,200
Wagner, Glenda A, dd case ctrl analyst, $30,360
Wagoner, Esther S, tchr aide, $15,696
Wahby, Robbyn G, csc exec dir, $145,008
Waldon, Carol A, tchr, $28,152
Walker, Cynthia P, accounting spec, $29,256
Wallace, Karen S, tchr aide, $17,832
Wallack, Blaise P, dd cnslr, $38,040
Wallen, Laura A, dist sup, $55,728
Wallis, Terrilee S, tchr aide, $15,408
Wallis, Terrilee S, short term sub tchr, $0.43/hr
Wann, Brenda K, tchr aide, $15,648
Ward, Patricia A, billing spec, $24,768
Warden, Tammy, tchr, $29,280
Warfield, Victoria J, cook I, $16,392
Warman, Twyla, tchr aide, $14,520
Warn, Cocoa A, tchr aide, $14,520
Warn, Cocoa A, short term sub tchr, $2.28/hr
Warn, Cocoa A, homebound tchr, $24.23/hr
Warren, Douglas A, short term sub tchr, $14.03/hr
Warren, Douglas A, bus driver, $10.36/hr
Warren, Douglas A, bus attendant, $10.05/hr
Warren, Douglas A, tchr aide, $11.36/hr
Warren, Douglas A, homebound tchr, $24.23/hr
Warren, Robinne L, short term sub tchr, $14.03/hr
Washburn, Victor R, dd cnslr II, $43,008
Washington, Bobby G, long term sub tchr, $20.90/hr
Washington, Bobby G, short term sub tchr, $14.03/hr
Washington, Kristina Y, residential advisor I, $12.09/hr
Wasman, Cynthia L, custodial worker I, $10.05/hr

Wasman, Cynthia L, tchr aide, $11.36/hr
Wasman, Cynthia L, sec, $10.73/hr
Watkins, Kristen M, tchr aide, $11.36/hr
Watson, Alena C, residential advisor I, $20,856
Watson, Cynthia A, administrative asst, $31,608
Watts, Shirley A, sec, $25,608
Wayne, Susan T, dd cnslr III, $48,576
Weamer-Lee, Julia E, tchr, $29,592
Webster, Aubrey A, tchr aide, $11.36/hr
Webster, Aubrey A, short term sub tchr, $14.33/hr
Webster, Rebecca S, tchr aide, $11.36/hr
Wegman, Jacob J, vr spec, $26.24/hr
Weiss, Carrie A, tchr, $28,704
Weitkamp, Sandra S, vr cnslr IV, $50,568
Welch, David K, dir, $60,240
Wells, Amy E, tchr aide, $19,632
Wells, Jennifer K, tchr, $29,472
Wells, Karen L, bldg admin, $51,936
Wells, Nancy M, tchr aide, $14,832
Wells, Randall G, asst dir, $50,496
Wensmann, Tamara, cook II, $11,808
West, Angela L, tchr, $29,280
West, Cody D, dd cnslr III, $47,712
West, Kevin L, vr cnslr IV, $50,568
West, Rebecca A, dd cnslr II, $43,008
Westbrooks, Sara J, dd cnslr I, $39,960
Westergaard, Gayla R, sup, $47,640
Wheeler, Laura J, administrative asst, $29,328
Whitaker, Patricia, long term sub tchr, $20.90/hr
Whitaker, Patricia, short term sub tchr, $14.03/hr
Whitaker, Patricia, tchr aide, $11.36/hr
White, Angela D, billing spec, $25,272
White, Clarissa L, dist sup, $55,728
White, Keith J, dd cnslr, $38,040
Whitlock, Brenda E, sup, $47,016
Wibberg, Kathleen A, tchr aide, $11.36/hr
Wideman, Janell E, administrative asst, $28,224
Wieberg, Jackie E, exec asst, $34,752
Wiegand, Amber L, sup, $37,968
Wiggins, Shereeta I, dd cnslr, $38,040
Wiggs, Lorraine E, sec, $21,000
Wilbers, Staci L, tchr aide, $11.36/hr
Wilcox, Lachana S, residential advisor I, $20,856
Wiley, Carla D, tchr aide - bus atnd, $19,200
Wiley, Carla D, long term sub tchr, $9.25/hr
Wiley, Carla D, short term sub tchr, $2.38/hr
Wiley, Cassandra L, dd cnslr II, $43,008
Wilfong, Allison M, administrative asst, $26,952
Wilhoit, Sandra A, dd cnslr II, $43,008
Wilken, Ronald L, sup of instruction, $56,472
Wilkowski, Tracy R, tchr aide, $14,208
Willenbrock, Michelle M, vr cnslr II, $43,008
Williams, Barbara A, registered nurse, $32,400
Williams, Christine, accounting spec, $15.02/hr
Williams, Dennis K, asst dist supv, $51,864
Williams, Janice, tchr aide-bus driver, $19,296
Williams, Joann L, tchr aide, $14,520
Williams, Levi J, tchr aide, $20,016
Williams, Pamela J, coord, $66,240
Williams, Ronald K, vr business spec, $38,040
Williams, Shelly R, residential advisor I, $21,264
Williams, Terri D, homebound tchr, $24.23/hr
Williams, Terri D, short term sub tchr, $14.03/hr
Williams, Urail S, dd cnslr, $38,040
Williams, Virginia L, sup, $40,296
Williamson, Stephanie R, dd cnslr, $38,040
Willis, Tanya J, sup, $37,968
Willson, Maria A, dd cnslr II, $43,008
Willtrout, Barbara A, sec, $19,824
Wilsie, Kenneth, short term sub tchr, $14.03/hr
Wilsie, Kenneth, tchr aide, $11.36/hr
Wilsie, Kenneth, tchr In charge, $24.31/hr
Wilson, Artimio J, vr cnslr II, $43,008
Wilson, Candice, billing spec, $25,056
Wilson, Christopher, vr cnslr IV, $50,568
Wilson, Jonah R, residential advisor I, $12.09/hr
Wilson, Karen L, rgnal mgr, $66,648
Wilson, Kelly J, tchr aide - bus atnd, $19,176
Wilson, Stephanie D, dd cnslr II, $43,008
Wilson, Thomas B, vr cnslr III, $47,712
Wilson, Tomago C, dd cnslr II, $43,008
Wimer, Dale D, sup, $47,640
Wimer, Margaret A, prog analyst, $31,656

Wineland, Kimberly D, sr hr analyst, $45,504
Winfield, Evelyn M, cook I, $9.45/hr
Winfield, Evelyn M, tchr aide, $11.36/hr
Winkelman, Michael A, tchr, $30,984
Winters, Joshua B, nutrition prog spec, $41,184
Wiseman, Linda F, tchr aide, $11.36/hr
Witcher, Angela A, tchr aide, $11.36/hr
Witcher, Angela A, short term sub tchr, $14.33/hr
Withers, Cassandra J, asst dir, $47,712
Wittek, Janet S, phys edu tchr, $49,344
Wittmann, Timothy J, dir, $25.50/hr
Wolf, Kimberly J, accounting spec, $30,432
Wolfe, Daniel A, residential advisor I, $21,264
Wolfe, Donna M, sec, $27,480
Wolfe, Paul A, tchr, $28,704
Wolford, Cathee A, dist sup, $55,728
Wood, Landon D, dir, $48,552
Wood, Mary C, dir, $27.75/hr
Wood, Melisa A, tchr aide, $11.36/hr
Wood, Nancy L, sup, $44,760
Woodard, Ruby M, tchr aide, $11.36/hr
Woodard, Ruby M, custodial worker I, $10.05/hr
Woodard, Ruby M, cook I, $9.45/hr
Woods, Leslie R, asst dir, $43,248
Woods, Michelle L, coord, $66,240
Woods, Stephanie M, vr cnslr II, $43,008
Woolard, Sheila M, tchr, $32,496
Woolard, Sheila M, homebound tchr, $24.23/hr
Wooton, Karen A, coord, $66,240
Workman, Carol A, administrative asst, $29,928
Worthington, Keven W, asst dist supv, $51,864
Wren, Kenneth R, tchr aide, $14,208
Wren, Kenneth R, short term sub tchr, $2.53/hr
Wright, Jessica M, bldg admin, $34,464
Wright, Marva E, vr cnslr III, $47,712
Wright, Yvonne R, dir, $57,000
Wutke, Michael A, sup of instruction, $55,344
Wynne, Jennifer L, vr cnslr II, $43,008
Yates, Douglas O, tchr, $28,152
Yates, Douglas O, homebound tchr, $24.23/hr
Yates, Mary E, tchr aide, $14,880
Yinger, Jenny, asst dist supv, $51,864
Yoesel, Margaret R, dir, $49,056
Young, Claire S, tchr aide, $11.36/hr
Young, Jason, coord, $73,248
Young, Jayne, vr cnslr II, $43,008
Young, Judy C, short term sub tchr, $14.03/hr
Young, Judy C, tchr aide, $11.36/hr
Young, Judy C, long term sub tchr, $20.90/hr
Young, Kimberly S, tchr aide - bus atnd, $19,176
Young, Yvonne M, hearing ofcr, $59,856
Younger-Loesing, Melissa A, tchr aide, $14,208
Younger-Loesing, Melissa A, short term sub tchr, $2.53/hr
Younger-Loesing, Melissa A, long term sub tchr, $9.40/hr
Yount, Jennifer C, dd cnslr II, $43,008
Zeller, Kayla M, prof rel ofcr, $51,864
Ziehmer, Carleen R, dd cnslr IV, $50,568
Zirfas, Robert J, dist sup, $55,728

Department of Health and Senior Services

PO Box 570, Jefferson City 65102

Vasterling, Carolyn G, state dept dir, $121,709
Abbott, Jane, hlth prog rep II, $44,304
Adams, Frank L, fac surv II, $46,068
Adey, Richard L, ofc spt asst (keybrd), $26,232
Adrian, Diana L, admin ofc spt asst, $28,536
Adrian, Hellen I, registered nurse mgr b1, $59,046
Ahlemeyer, Caron R, child care fac spec III, $41,940
Alberti, Cassia M, adlt prot & cmty wkr II, $33,744
Alexander, Joyce E, hlth prog rep III, $42,708
Alfred, Stephanie L, adlt prot & cmty wkr II, $33,744
Allen, Katrina D, adlt prot & cmty wkr II, $33,744
Allen, Lori A, fac adv nurse II, $46,956
Allen, Rachel H, hlth prog rep I, $30,984
Alsberge, Karla A, sr ofc spt asst (keybrd), $25,824
Althouse-Hill, Nancy L, hlth prog rep III, $44,304
Ambati, Praveena, sr epidemiology spec, $50,040
Ambrosius, Celeste A, fac adv nurse II, $46,956
Ament, Cynthia J, fac surv II, $41,940

Anderson, Becky L, acct II, $38,232
Anderson, Jana, adlt prot & cmty wkr II, $33,744
Anderson, Joan T, hlth & sr svcs mgr 2, $65,902
Anderson, Katrina M, fac adv nurse II, $45,204
Anderson, Shane L, proj spec, $25.00/hr
Angell, Bryan D, research analyst III, $46,932
Arends, Anne N, proj spec, $14.00/hr
Arnel, Bria L, fac surv II, $40,380
Arnett, Calah M, adlt prot & cmty supv, $40,380
Arni, Rita F, nutrition spec, $50,040
Arnold, Charles, hlth facilities cnslt, $56,520
Arnold, Christine A, hlth & sr svcs mgr 1, $55,410
Arnold, Tabitha A, sr ofc spt asst (keybrd), $25,824
Ash, Shelly D, budget analyst III, $54,288
Ashlock, Debbie L, child care fac spec II, $39,624
Asi, Lori L, adlt prot & cmty wkr II, $34,356
Atkinson, Bobbi L, sr ofc spt asst (keybrd), $25,824
Atkinson, David P, hlth prog rep I, $30,984
Atkinson, Gina M, exec I, $36,204
Avery-williams, Sara K, admin ofc spt asst, $28,536
Avis, Karen J, pub hlth nurse, $47,904
Ayers, Sharon K, sr counsel, $73,175
Ayres, Nicole K, sr pub hlth lab scintst, $41,940
Backer, Ann E, hlth prog rep III, $40,380
Backers, Gregory A, investigator III, $40,380
Bacon, Steven W, planner III, $51,096
Baer, Donna J, adlt prot & cmty wkr II, $33,744
Bailey, Dawn M, admin ofc spt asst, $28,104
Bailey, Frederick D, hlth facilities nrsng cnslt, $55,320
Bailey, Michele L, nutritionist III, $43,488
Baker, Anna M, admin ofc spt asst, $29,976
Baker, Douglas B, sr epidemiology spec, $49,128
Baker, James F, fac insp, $41,172
Baker, Jamie R, hlth prog rep III, $44,304
Baker, Judy L, fac adv nurse II, $46,956
Baker, Melissa D, fac surv II, $40,380
Baker, Molly D, proj spec, $18.53/hr
Baker, Patricia L, adlt prot & cmty supv, $46,068
Baldwin, Chris A, adlt prot & cmty wkr II, $33,744
Ball, Dana D, fac adv nurse II, $48,780
Ball, Linda G, pub hlth consult nurse, $60,036
Ballard, Donna S, proj spec, $14.00/hr
Ballard, Harry A, environ spec III, $46,932
Ballew, Marie R, hlth prog rep III, $41,940
Banks-smith, Jamieka C, adlt prot & cmty wkr II, $34,944
Barber, Lynn D, adlt prot & cmty wkr II, $34,356
Barding, Nanette M, sr ofc spt asst (keybrd), $27,948
Barnard, Leslie M, proj spec, $15.00/hr
Barnes, Anne M, adlt prot & cmty wkr II, $33,744
Barnes, Patricia L, sr ofc spt asst (keybrd), $25,824
Barnes, Stephanie M, child care fac spec II, $38,232
Barnes, Tracy J, adlt prot & cmty wkr II, $33,744
Barr, Susan, nutritionist II, $45,156
Barron, Amy N, adlt prot & cmty supv, $40,380
Bartlett, Heather M, adlt prot & cmty wkr II, $33,744
Bartlett, Linton H, planner III, $50,040
Barton, Frances M, aging prog spec II, $44,304
Barton, Jana L, child care fac spec II, $42,708
Barton, Kurry S, hlth prog rep III, $41,172
Bassford, Karen, hlth prog aide, $27.00/hr
Bastean, Lisa M, fac surv II, $49,128
Bateman, Jessica J, adlt prot & cmty wkr II, $33,744
Bates, Theresa A, sr ofc spt asst (keybrd), $26,652
Bathon, Kathy D, fac adv nurse II, $46,956
Battles, Cathy D, adlt prot & cmty wkr II, $33,744
Bauer, Jessica L, lab mgr b2, $57,735
Bauman, Timothy G, fac surv II, $41,940
Bax, Jessica, hlth & sr svcs mgr 2, $64,200
Bax, Kimberly A, acct II, $38,928
Bayless, Alicia C, long-term care spec, $36,204
Baylor, Sharon M, proj spec, $28.00/hr
Baysinger, Cherri L, hlth & sr svcs mgr 3, $71,493
Baysinger, Lori K, sr ofc spt asst (keybrd), $28,452
Beaird, Leigh A, adlt prot & cmty wkr II, $33,744
Beatty, Virginia A, planner III, $54,288
Beck, Cynthia S, sr ofc spt asst (keybrd), $27,084
Beckett, Janice K, adlt prot & cmty wkr II, $33,744
Beddo, Monica L, assoc pub hlth lab scientst, $31,512
Bedell, Patricia A, dpty div dir, $84,858
Beeson, Danette L, hlth prog rep III, $50,040
Behrens, Shelly A, fac adv nurse II, $53,124
Bell, Jessica C, admin ofc spt asst, $29,496
Bell, Laura L, adlt prot & cmty wkr II, $36,888

Bell, Laurie A, adlt prot & cmty wkr II, $33,744
Bell, Myesha D, proj spec, $14.00/hr
Bellamy, Jeffrey, proj spec, $27.00/hr
Bellinger, Linda F, aging prog spec II, $46,068
Bellinger, Linda F, proj spec, $15.00/hr
Bemboom, Dena M, adlt prot & cmty wkr II, $33,744
Bembrick, Mary A, adlt prot & cmty wkr II, $38,232
Benford, Gloria J, sr ofc spt asst (keybrd), $26,652
Bening, Tammy E, proj spec, $14.00/hr
Bennett, Natasha N, hlth prog rep I, $29,976
Bennett, Ronnie G, fac surv II, $47,892
Bennett, Sherrita V, adlt prot & cmty wkr II, $33,744
Bennett-davis, Rita L, hlth facilities nrsng cnslt, $53,124
Benton, Betty J, adlt prot & cmty wkr II, $33,744
Berger, Kevin T, investigator II, $37,548
Berger, Mellisa K, adlt prot & cmty wkr II, $33,744
Berndt, Sarah E, adlt prot & cmty wkr I, $30,984
Berry, Jeanine Y, adlt prot & cmty wkr II, $32,628
Berwanger, Anita R, proj spec, $30.00/hr
Betts, Karen L, ofc spt asst (keybrd), $21,665
Beussink, Amy L, adlt prot & cmty supv, $40,380
Bexten, Joyce M, designated principal asst div, $42,711
Beyer, Nancy F, env pub hlth spec IV, $48,156
Bierschwal, Carol J, sr ofc spt asst (keybrd), $26,652
Bietsch, Charlotte R, adlt prot & cmty wkr II, $33,744
Bilyeu, Heather M, assoc pub hlth lab scientst, $31,512
Bilyeu, Kathleen A, long-term care spec, $36,204
Bisges, Deborah L, pub hlth sr nurse, $50,052
Bishop, Brian A, exec I, $30,984
Bixler, Teresa L, adlt prot & cmty wkr II, $33,744
Bixler, Thomas L, env pub hlth spec IV, $43,488
Black, Terry C, hlth & sr svcs mgr 2, $60,000
Blair, Cindy L, exec II, $37,548
Blanke, Yavanna L, pers clerk, $28,536
Blankenship, Robert D, adlt prot & cmty wkr II, $33,744
Blau, Elizabeth A, planner III, $48,156
Blessing, Debra L, adlt prot & cmty supv, $43,488
Blevins, Mary E, account clerk II, $25,824
Blocker, Karen K, sr ofc spt asst (keybrd), $25,824
Bloemke, Janet K, proj spec, $25.00/hr
Blum, Cassie L, fac surv III, $53,208
Bock, Keith J, sr pub hlth lab scintst, $41,940
Bock, Ruth M, proj spec, $10.40/hr
Bode Oliver, Elaine C, proj spec, $25.00/hr
Boeckman, Julie M, prog coord dmh dohss, $49,128
Boeckman, Lindsay M, admin ofc spt asst, $28,536
Boeckmann, Molly J, fiscal & administrative mgr b2, $74,312
Boeger, Michael R, hlth & sr svcs mgr 2, $64,802
Boessen, Matthew D, special asst prof, $34,942
Bohannan, Candy M, aging prog spec II, $45,156
Bolden, Aaron D, adlt prot & cmty wkr II, $33,744
Bomarito, Crystal A, adlt prot & cmty wkr II, $33,744
Bonchonsky, Deborah J, hlth prog rep II, $34,944
Bonilla, Denise C, hlth prog rep II, $34,944
Bonnett, Michael L, info spt coor, $33,180
Bontempo, Carol A, research analyst III, $44,304
Boos, Cecelia R, sr ofc spt asst (keybrd), $25,824
Borders, Jolene K, pub hlth consult nurse, $63,768
Borgmann, Myra, fac surv II, $41,940
Bos, John E, hlth & sr svcs mgr 1, $63,996
Bosh, Karin A, research analyst IV, $54,288
Boston, Robert T, hlth prog rep III, $42,708
Bowers, Michael S, sr ofc spt asst (keybrd), $25,824
Bowman, Stephen C, fac surv II, $41,940
Boyd, Lindsay M, pub hlth lab scientist, $37,548
Boyd, Thomas M, ofc spt asst (clerical), $22,536
Boyer, Carey M, hlth & sr svcs mgr 2, $54,257
Bradbury, Shannon M, proj spec, $18.53/hr
Bradley, Kirk E, fac surv II, $41,940
Bradley, Kristi R, adlt prot & cmty wkr II, $36,204
Bradshaw, Amy M, pub hlth sr nurse, $56,448
Brake, Kimberly B, adlt prot & cmty wkr II, $33,744
Braloski, John M, supply mgr I, $32,628
Brand, Jennifer L, adlt prot & cmty wkr II, $33,744
Brandenburg-simonin, Lisa G, acct I, $30,984
Brands, Andrea L, adlt prot & cmty wkr II, $33,744
Branson, Amanda S, admin ofc spt asst, $28,536
Branson, Kathy G, special asst ofc & clerical, $48,157
Branson, Lisa G, hlth prog rep II, $41,940
Brantley, William R, environ scientist, $56,520
Braun, Carol R, epidemiology spec, $50,040
Braun, Jennifer L, training tech II, $40,380
Braun, Jordan G, adlt prot & cmty wkr II, $33,744

Bray, Brenda S, acct II, $37,548
Brendel, Barbara A, hlth prog rep III, $49,128
Brendel, Justa J, acct II, $41,940
Brenneke, Lori A, hlth & sr svcs mgr 2, $63,049
Brewer, Michael C, hlth & sr svcs mgr 2, $64,200
Brewer, Randi J, adlt prot & cmty wkr II, $33,744
Brickey, Leigh A, pub hlth sr nurse, $49,788
Bridge, Melinda, adlt prot & cmty wkr II, $33,744
Bridges, Angela K, adlt prot & cmty wkr II, $36,888
Bright, Andrea N, hlth prog rep III, $40,380
Brill, Johna K, fac adv nurse II, $46,956
Brison, Danica L, adlt prot & cmty wkr II, $33,744
Brizendine, Todd W, adlt prot & cmty wkr II, $36,888
Brockman, Stephanie A, fac surv II, $41,940
Brondel, Jordyn R, adlt prot & cmty wkr I, $30,984
Brooke, Jolie R, adlt prot & cmty wkr II, $33,744
Brown, Adam C, adlt prot & cmty wkr II, $33,744
Brown, Carrie S, sr ofc spt asst (keybrd), $25,824
Brown, Cynthia L, sr ofc spt asst (keybrd), $25,824
Brown, Lisa A, special asst prof, $84,858
Brown, Meghan R, fac adv nurse II, $48,780
Brown, Melissa A, fiscal & administrative mgr b1, $55,704
Brown, Reba A, sr ofc spt asst (keybrd), $28,908
Brown, Reba S, adlt prot & cmty wkr II, $33,744
Brown-Watson, Carol A, sr ofc spt asst (keybrd), $26,232
Bruemmer, Wendy M, aging prog spec II, $40,380
Bruning, Janice L, child care fac spec II, $42,708
Bryan, Stacey M, fac adv nurse III, $51,072
Bryant, Anna R, adlt prot & cmty wkr II, $33,744
Bryant, Jean W, hlth & sr svcs mgr 1, $57,512
Buchanan, Lori M, pub info coor, $42,708
Buckland, Margaret M, pub hlth consult nurse, $62,508
Buckley, Julie, pub hlth lab scientist, $37,548
Buckley, Michael J, adlt prot & cmty wkr II, $33,744
Buechler, Jeffrey A, hlth prog rep III, $39,624
Burch, Sarah J, hlth prog rep I, $31,512
Burchardt, Alexandra A, adlt prot & cmty wkr II, $33,744
Burgess, Angela M, exec II, $36,204
Burk, Keri D, nutrition spec, $50,040
Burris, Denise M, fac surv II, $41,940
Burrow, Jessy N, pub hlth nurse, $47,904
Bursnall, Felicia A, sr ofc spt asst (keybrd), $25,824
Buschjost, Brenda S, hlth prog rep II, $39,624
Butler, Cindy L, sr epidemiology spec, $52,092
Butler, Valerie A, hlth prog rep II, $44,304
Butner, Bethany C, adlt prot & cmty wkr II, $33,744
Buxton, Jerry M, planner III, $50,040
Byram, J D, info spt coor, $31,512
Byrd, Amy J, adlt prot & cmty wkr II, $35,568
Byrd, David J, lab mgr b1, $54,578
Byrd, Yvonne J, adlt prot & cmty wkr II, $33,744
Cable, Lora, hlth prog rep II, $34,944
Cade, Linda M, fiscal & administrative mgr b1, $63,989
Cadman, Aaron S, environ spec III, $45,156
Cain, Mackenzie M, epidemiology spec, $38,928
Cale-Cohoon, Elizabeth F, adlt prot & cmty wkr II, $33,744
Call, Shyanne N, sr ofc spt asst (keybrd), $25,824
Calvin, Danielle L, sr ofc spt asst (keybrd), $25,824
Cameron, Lani L, adlt prot & cmty supv, $42,708
Campbell, Jessica A, env pub hlth spec III, $44,304
Campbell, Kenneth W, adlt prot & cmty supv, $44,304
Campbell, Kimberly D, long-term care spec, $34,944
Campbell, Pamela F, admin ofc spt asst, $28,536
Campbell, Rick A, environ spec III, $44,304
Canning, Mary L, hlth & sr svcs mgr 2, $65,360
Carey, Evelyn S, info spt coor, $29,004
Carlton, Rachael L, long-term care spec, $34,944
Carrell, Gregory P, adlt prot & cmty wkr II, $33,180
Carrender, Robyn R, hlth prog rep III, $41,940
Carrier, Tammy F, hlth prog rep II, $27,659
Carron, Heather R, pub hlth nurse, $47,904
Carter, Jan L, child care fac spec III, $46,068
Carter, John D, adlt prot & cmty wkr II, $38,232
Carter, Julie A, child care fac spec II, $40,380
Carter, Michael G, hlth educator III, $55,416
Carter, Miranda L, pub hlth lab scientist, $37,548
Carter, Robyn S, adlt prot & cmty wkr II, $38,232
Carver, Cynthia J, hlth prog rep II, $36,888
Case, Elizabeth P, hlth facilities cnslt, $53,208
Cassidy, Betty A, mgmt analysis spec II, $50,040
Casteel, September L, adlt prot & cmty wkr II, $33,744
Castrodale, Michael D, adlt prot & cmty wkr II, $33,744
Cates, Paula M, env pub hlth spec IV, $49,128

Cavender, Brett A, legal counsel, $45,764
Cawa, Christi K, adlt prot & cmty wkr II, $33,744
Chadbourne, Ayla M, adlt prot & cmty wkr II, $33,744
Chaidez, Tina M, ofc spt asst (keybrd), $23,160
Chambers, Gabriel A, adlt prot & cmty wkr II, $33,744
Chambers, Lowynta R, admin ofc spt asst, $27,228
Chamley, Kristina L, adlt prot & cmty wkr II, $34,944
Chandler, Stephanie R, child care fac spec III, $38,928
Chase, Patricia L, fac adv nurse II, $46,956
Chavez-Hauser, Lina, epidemiology spec, $40,380
Chavosky, Stephanie M, adlt prot & cmty wkr II, $32,628
Chitima-Matsiga, Rebecca T, research analyst III, $41,172
Chou, Joyce, hlth prog rep II, $34,944
Chrisco, Marla L, child care fac spec II, $36,204
Chrismer, Sandra L, fac adv nurse III, $54,156
Christian, James M, pub hlth lab scientist, $37,548
Christian, Kelley L, admin ofc spt asst, $29,496
Christiansen, Jill E, adlt prot & cmty wkr II, $36,888
Christopher, Maureen K, adlt prot & cmty wkr II, $34,944
Churchill, Neelie M, hlth & sr svcs mgr 1, $53,160
Cisewski, Joseph D, adlt prot & cmty wkr II, $33,744
Clark, Angela M, child care fac spec III, $41,940
Cleeton, Tracy D, hlth facilities cnslt, $56,520
Clemons, Linda V, adlt prot & cmty wkr II, $34,944
Clevenger, Elizabeth A, adlt prot & cmty wkr II, $33,744
Clinton, Dennis A, proj spec, $25.00/hr
Closson, Karen K, mgmt analysis spec II, $43,488
Clow, Carrie E, adlt prot & cmty supv, $40,380
Clutter, Linda S, hlth prog rep III, $45,156
Coats, Ella R, adlt prot & cmty wkr II, $33,744
Cobb, Roxanne L, fac surv II, $43,488
Cockrum, Jamie L, adlt prot & cmty wkr II, $33,744
Coday, Maureen A, adlt prot & cmty wkr II, $38,232
Coffey, Whitney B, research analyst III, $40,380
Coffman, Diane E, hlth prog rep III, $42,708
Cole, Jamia L, account clerk II, $25,824
Cole, Lynn G, hlth & sr svcs mgr 1, $57,735
Cole, Marjorie, pub hlth consult nurse, $62,508
Coleman, Donna M, adlt prot & cmty wkr II, $36,204
Coleman, Elizabeth S, adlt prot & cmty wkr II, $35,568
Coleman, Roberta L, pers clerk, $28,536
Collier, Mary G, hlth & sr svcs mgr 2, $66,722
Collinge, Rachelle, registered nurse mgr b1, $66,628
Collins, Marc D, adlt prot & cmty wkr II, $36,888
Conaway, Jessica D, adlt prot & cmty wkr II, $33,744
Conaway, Phyllis L, sr ofc spt asst (keybrd), $25,824
Cone, Touree, hlth prog rep III, $39,624
Conger, Deborah L, spec hlth care needs reg coord, $58,908
Connell, Jessica, storekeeper II, $34,356
Connell, Karen W, hlth prog rep III, $46,932
Connell, Susan A, hlth prog rep III, $38,928
Conner, Gina M, fac surv II, $41,940
Conner, Kriston D, adlt prot & cmty wkr II, $33,744
Conner, Latavia W, adlt prot & cmty wkr II, $33,744
Connor, Rebecca E, adlt prot & cmty wkr II, $35,568
Cook, Melinda J, fac surv II, $43,488
Cook, Susanna A, ofc spt asst (keybrd), $22,536
Coonce, Sharon L, adlt prot & cmty supv, $43,488
Coopwood, Martin S, fac surv II, $41,940
Coots, Lisa A, registered nurse mgr b2, $74,189
Copeland, Shari S, child care fac spec II, $40,380
Cornelius, Kathryn M, adlt prot & cmty wkr II, $33,744
Corum, Erin M, hlth prog rep I, $31,512
Costillo, Katie E, adlt prot & cmty wkr II, $33,744
Cotterman, James B, adlt prot & cmty wkr II, $34,944
Courter, Jennifer J, fac adv nurse II, $48,780
Covington, Casey R, adlt prot & cmty supv, $41,172
Cowsette, Synetta F, adlt prot & cmty wkr II, $33,744
Cox, Elaine S, child care fac spec II, $41,940
Cox, Lana L, sr ofc spt asst (keybrd), $26,232
Cox, Patty A, adlt prot & cmty wkr II, $33,744
Cox, Verena L, adlt prot & cmty supv, $40,380
Crabtree, Chaz A, child care fac spec II, $36,204
Crafton, Kimberly L, hlth prog rep II, $17,472
Craig, Caron A, admin ofc spt asst, $29,496
Craig, Kathy A, hlth educator III, $46,068
Cramer, Steve W, hlth & sr svcs mgr 3, $71,493
Crandall, Lisa J, hlth & sr svcs mgr 2, $66,038
Crawford, Dora L, admin ofc spt asst, $28,104
Crawford, Jennifer M, adlt prot & cmty wkr II, $33,744
Creach, Julie G, designated principal asst div, $80,155
Cripps, Melinda K, adlt prot & cmty wkr II, $37,548
Crockett, Katherine L, emergency med svcs insp I, $36,204

Cross, Hollee R, hlth facilities nrsng cnslt, $53,124
Cross, Karen C, fac adv nurse II, $53,124
Crowe, Tina L, hlth prog rep II, $34,944
Culbertson, Janice D, fac surv II, $44,304
Cullifer, Angela L, adlt prot & cmty wkr II, $34,944
Cummins, Jason S, env pub hlth spec IV, $45,156
Cummins, Todd G, hlth facilities cnslt, $54,288
Curlile, Patricia J, sr ofc spt asst (keybrd), $26,232
Curry, Kayla A, adlt prot & cmty wkr II, $33,744
Curry, Meredith A, pers ofcr I, $43,488
Czuba, Denise, hlth facilities cnslt, $48,156
Da Silva, Candace A, proj spec, $15.00/hr
Dabbs, Tammy L, sr ofc spt asst (keybrd), $25,824
D'alessandro, Renee, research analyst III, $41,940
Daly, Richard P, proj spec, $25.00/hr
Dambach, Karl T, hlth & sr svcs mgr 1, $51,538
Daniel, Adria K, adlt prot & cmty wkr II, $33,744
Daniels, Donald B, storekeeper I, $26,232
Daro, Heather M, accounting spec II, $38,928
Darr, Paula J, pub hlth consult nurse, $61,248
Davenport, Deandre M, adlt prot & cmty wkr II, $33,744
Davenport, Heather J, env pub hlth spec III, $41,172
David, Angela M, fac adv nurse II, $53,124
Davidson, Brenna, administrative analyst II, $34,944
Davis, Cheryl Y, adlt prot & cmty wkr II, $33,744
Davis, Erica L, ofc spt asst (keybrd), $22,536
Davis, Kathleen I, hlth & sr svcs mgr 1, $55,410
Davis, Kathy D, adlt prot & cmty wkr II, $33,744
Davis, Lorraine, long-term care spec, $39,624
Davis, Marcia D, hlth prog rep II, $34,944
Davis, Mark A, hlth & sr svcs mgr 2, $64,534
Davis, Sarah D, adlt prot & cmty wkr II, $33,744
Dawson, Donald D, pub hlth nurse, $47,904
Day, Carol L, sr ofc spt asst (keybrd), $25,824
Deal, Betsy D, sr ofc spt asst (keybrd), $26,652
Dear, Sandra L, sr ofc spt asst (keybrd), $25,824
Dearixon, Betsy E, sr ofc spt asst (keybrd), $25,824
Debroeck, Angela K, hlth prog rep II, $45,156
Degreef, Marjorie L, hlth facilities nrsng cnslt, $53,124
Dekoster, Jeannine A, fac surv II, $46,068
Delaporte, Christine A, adlt prot & cmty wkr II, $38,232
Delgman-yawberry, Bridgette A, nutritionist III, $45,156
Delmain, Rhonda S, child care fac spec II, $36,204
Demier, Tom C, adlt prot & cmty wkr II, $33,744
Demsko, Susan M, sr ofc spt asst (keybrd), $25,824
Denight, Emily A, hlth educator II, $36,204
Despain, Alisha D, adlt prot & cmty wkr II, $33,744
Dettman, Ellen J, env pub hlth spec V, $57,744
Dewert, Fern F, hlth facilities nrsng cnslt, $62,508
Dicarlo, Deborah K, adlt prot & cmty wkr II, $37,548
Dickens, Deana L, child care fac spec II, $37,548
Dicks, V J, pub hlth consult nurse, $63,768
Dickson, Dana L, fac adv nurse II, $46,956
Dieleman, Patsey L, fac adv nurse II, $53,124
Dietle, Eden G, sr epidemiology spec, $46,068
Dill, Tracy, hlth prog rep II, $38,928
Dinkela, Patricia F, ofc spt asst (keybrd), $23,880
Dinolfo, Kay, designated principal asst div, $64,200
Dixon, Jamie L, fac surv III, $47,892
Dixon, Tanya D, fiscal & administrative mgr b1, $55,410
Dodds, Susan E, fac surv II, $42,708
Dodge, Nola D, adlt prot & cmty wkr II, $33,744
Doman, Cynthia L, adlt prot & cmty supv, $41,172
Donahue, Colleen A, acct II, $37,548
Donoho, Ellen G, child care fac spec II, $38,928
Dormire, Rhonda F, facilities opps mgr b1, $52,024
Doty, Neysa L, adlt prot & cmty wkr II, $33,744
Dougan, Gayle M, sr ofc spt asst (keybrd), $25,824
Douglas, Jessica N, adlt prot & cmty wkr II, $33,744
Douglas, Linda, adlt prot & cmty wkr II, $37,548
Douglas, Susan M, child care fac spec II, $38,928
Douglas, Tonya, proj spec, $14.00/hr
Douglas, Tracy L, fac insp, $33,744
Dowdy, Douglas E, adlt prot & cmty wkr II, $33,744
Downing, Nancy A, long-term care spec, $40,380
Doyen, Tamara L, adlt prot & cmty wkr II, $33,744
Dresel, David W, fac adv nurse II, $46,956
Drew, Linda K, fac adv nurse II, $53,124
Driver, Theresa B, sr ofc spt asst (keybrd), $27,948
Drury, Russell L, lab mgr b2, $57,735
Duckett, Loren L, proj spec, $14.41/hr
Dudenhoeffer, Nancy, acct II, $43,488
Duewell, Rhonda L, epidemiology spec, $47,892

Duggan, Marie K, hlth prog rep II, $34,944
Dukes, Latoya S, adlt prot & cmty wkr II, $33,744
Dunger, Samantha N, adlt prot & cmty wkr II, $33,180
Dunlap, Terrance L, proj spec, $15.00/hr
Dunlap, Terrance L, fac surv III, $46,068
Dunn, Mary J, admin ofc spt asst, $32,628
Dunn, Sarah C, child care fac spec II, $36,888
Dunnegan, Melisa, fac adv nurse II, $53,124
Durham, Lisa J, ofc spt asst (keybrd), $23,160
Durst, Karen S, fac adv nurse II, $45,204
Duvall, Angela D, fac adv nurse III, $53,124
Dyson, Beverly A, child care fac spec III, $41,940
Easley, Angela E, child care fac spec II, $36,204
East, David C, design engr I, $61,332
Eastman, Lisa L, planner III, $56,520
Edgar-avery, Kimbra D, adlt prot & cmty wkr II, $38,232
Edwards, Diane L, admin ofc spt asst, $33,180
Edwards, Kristen L, designated principal asst div, $80,155
Edwards, Michelle, sr ofc spt asst (keybrd), $25,824
Edwards, Sandra J, fac adv nurse II, $45,204
Edwards, Travis J, adlt prot & cmty wkr II, $33,744
Eftink, Karen K, pub hlth nurse, $50,052
Egan, Melissa K, pub hlth sr nurse, $53,124
Ehrenreich, Mary K, fac surv II, $41,940
Eichemier, Nancy E, fac adv nurse II, $46,956
Eiken, Darla S, lab mgr b1, $56,445
Eiler, Ashley L, pub hlth lab scientist, $37,548
Eisterhold, Megan L, pub hlth lab scientist, $37,548
Elbert, Rochelle J, fac surv II, $47,892
Elders, Wesley L, adlt prot & cmty wkr II, $33,744
Eldridge, Brenda F, sr ofc spt asst (keybrd), $25,824
Eller, Mary F, nursing consult, $31.20/hr
Ellis, Candice J, adlt prot & cmty wkr II, $33,744
Ellis, Shirley A, child care fac spec II, $41,940
Ellison, Margaret D, sr ofc spt asst (keybrd), $25,824
Ellis-young, Joan L, adlt prot & cmty wkr II, $33,744
Ellsworth, Terry S, emergency med svcs insp II, $44,304
Elwood, Christina, epidemiology spec, $43,488
Engler, Kathleen, aging prog spec II, $40,380
Ermeling, Nancy J, fac adv nurse II, $53,124
Ervin, Tisa E, adlt prot & cmty wkr II, $36,204
Eslahi, Terry, epidemiology spec, $46,932
Evans, Alison M, child care fac spec II, $36,204
Evans, Elizabeth E, environ spec II, $36,204
Evans, Jannis K, hlth prog rep III, $43,488
Evans, Sandra D, adlt prot & cmty wkr II, $33,744
Everhart, Rose A, sr ofc spt asst (keybrd), $25,824
Evers, Laura E, acct II, $41,172
Ewing, Hillary A, fac adv nurse II, $53,124
Ewing, Tanya R, fac adv nurse II, $46,956
Fabro, Laura K, sr epidemiology spec, $45,156
Falls, Linda M, adlt prot & cmty wkr II, $33,744
Farmer, Diana, acct III, $50,040
Farmer, Elizabeth R, proj spec, $25.00/hr
Farnsworth, Nicole M, hlth prog rep I, $30,984
Farthing, Michelle T, fac surv II, $45,156
Fazekas, Tunde, procurement ofcr I, $37,548
Featherston, Joshua, pub hlth lab scientist, $37,548
Feigly, Carla A, fac adv nurse II, $46,956
Feisel, Keith E, training tech II, $40,380
Feltrop, Joann C, hlth prog rep III, $43,488
Fennelly, Rebecca L, fac adv nurse III, $58,752
Fennewald, Sharon K, admin ofc spt asst, $32,628
Fensterman, Emilee F, fac adv nurse I, $48,780
Ferguson, Shanna, fac surv III, $48,156
Ferlazzo, Damon A, planner III, $53,208
Ferlet, Kerrie L, adlt prot & cmty wkr II, $38,232
Ferro, Constance M, child care fac spec II, $36,888
Ferry, Shelly A, sr ofc spt asst (keybrd), $26,232
Feuers, Dorothy I, typist, $10.96/hr
Fields, Michael J, hlth facilities nrsng cnslt, $55,320
Fischer, Bret S, dpty state dept dir, $110,000
Fisher, Pamela, sr ofc spt asst (keybrd), $25,824
Fisher, Susan M, account clerk I, $22,536
Fisher, Tracy A, sr ofc spt asst (keybrd), $27,948
Fitzpatrick, Cory A, adlt prot & cmty wkr II, $33,744
Fletcher, Trudie L, exec I, $36,888
Flieg, Angela A, adlt prot & cmty wkr II, $33,744
Flippo, Sandra K, adlt prot & cmty supv, $40,380
Flores, Brian T, sr pub hlth lab scintst, $42,708
Flow, Penny K, proj spec, $14.00/hr
Fluekiger, Kristin N, adlt prot & cmty wkr II, $33,744
Folks, Eric C, env pub hlth spec V, $49,128

Forbis, Amy L, hlth & sr svcs mgr 2, $64,763
Forck, Amiee J, hlth prog rep II, $38,928
Forck, Josetta M, ofc spt asst (keybrd), $23,160
Formon, Genevieve B, sr ofc spt asst (keybrd), $25,824
Forrest, Mitzi J, admin ofc spt asst, $32,628
Forsythe, Aaron E, mgmt analysis spec II, $46,932
Fort, Simone M, fac surv II, $43,488
Foster, Diana L, acct II, $41,172
Foster, Eron P, training tech II, $41,940
Foster, Michelle A, adlt prot & cmty wkr II, $33,744
Foster, Perry A, storekeeper II, $28,536
Foster, Rachel, admin ofc spt asst, $28,536
Fox, Matthew J, pub hlth lab scientist, $36,204
Fox, Tera L, adlt prot & cmty wkr II, $33,744
Francis, Larissa E, adlt prot & cmty wkr II, $33,744
Francken, Leah E, adlt prot & cmty wkr II, $38,232
Frank, Stacie L, fac adv nurse II, $46,956
Franklin, Janice D, adlt prot & cmty wkr II, $39,624
Franklin, Patrick B, epidemiology spec, $46,932
Frazier, Caitlin E, fac insp, $36,204
Frazier, Shawna L, fac adv nurse II, $53,124
Free, Alanta S, long-term care spec, $36,204
Freiburger, Andrew P, env pub hlth spec IV, $44,304
Frevert, Marsha, exec I, $31,512
Friedberg, Yelena M, sr epidemiology spec, $55,416
Fritch, Angela M, hlth prog rep II, $34,944
Fruchtnicht, Chloe, adlt prot & cmty wkr II, $33,744
Fuller, Phyllis E, hlth & sr svcs mgr 1, $55,410
Gaddy, Peggy D, prog coord dmh dohss, $56,520
Gailey, David L, hlth facilities cnslt, $55,416
Gailey, James A, sr ofc spt asst (keybrd), $25,032
Gallatin, April A, ofc spt asst (clerical), $22,536
Galloway, Catherine S, fac adv nurse III, $54,156
Gamm, Nicole E, hlth facilities nrsng cnslt, $53,124
Gansmann, John G, accounting analyst III, $54,288
Garber, Bobbi J, dpty div dir, $84,858
Garcia, Nancy L, pub hlth nurse, $47,904
Gardner, Sandra G, pub hlth nurse, $50,052
Gardner, Troy M, adlt prot & cmty wkr II, $34,944
Garikapaty, Venkata P, pub hlth epidemiologist, $74,304
Garner, Jason D, adlt prot & cmty supv, $41,172
Garner, Stacey D, hlth & sr svcs mgr 2, $55,706
Garoutte, Jonathan D, hlth & sr svcs mgr 2, $66,028
Garr, Natisha J, fac adv nurse II, $46,956
Garrison, James D, fac surv II, $47,892
Garrison, Trisha A, hlth prog rep II, $34,944
Gash, Glenda, hlth prog rep III, $38,928
Gates, Sandra L, hlth & sr svcs mgr 1, $57,744
Gathright, William R, proj spec, $26.00/hr
Gaughan, James E, environ engr IV, $62,664
Gaw, Erica L, admin ofc spt asst, $27,660
Gaw, Susan, sr ofc spt asst (keybrd), $25,824
Gegg, Stacey R, adlt prot & cmty wkr II, $33,744
Gentner, Kortney K, accounting spec II, $41,172
Gestring, Theresa J, fac adv nurse II, $60,036
Gibson, Lisa, exec II, $38,928
Gibson, Roger W, sr epidemiology spec, $57,744
Gilbert, Lisa, sr ofc spt asst (keybrd), $25,032
Gillmore, Lori A, admin ofc spt asst, $28,536
Gilmore, Lynn M, sr auditor, $45,156
Gladbach, Stephen E, lab mgr b2, $61,343
Glastetter, Dayneen Y, child care fac spec II, $37,548
Glenn, John M, adlt prot & cmty wkr II, $33,744
Goans, Renee E, hlth prog rep II, $36,204
Godsey, Renee A, fiscal & administrative mgr b3, $80,156
Goetz, Darice R, admin ofc spt asst, $28,536
Goetz, Kathryn M, sr ofc spt asst (keybrd), $25,824
Goldammer, Deborah, proj spec, $25.00/hr
Goldrick, Tamara L, long-term care spec, $39,624
Good, Pamela E, admin ofc spt asst, $34,356
Gorman, Kimberly D, fac adv nurse II, $55,320
Goslin, Teresa H, hlth prog rep III, $46,068
Graham, Cheryl L, adlt prot & cmty wkr II, $33,744
Graham, Jessica L, child care fac spec II, $36,204
Graham, Shalonda R, fiscal & administrative mgr b1, $59,889
Grahlman, Mary F, fac adv nurse II, $46,956
Grannemann, Nanci M, procurement ofcr I, $37,548
Grant, Elizabeth S, adlt prot & cmty supv, $40,380
Gray, Laura, fac surv II, $41,940
Gray, Michelle L, adlt prot & cmty supv, $41,172
Green, Leashie A, adlt prot & cmty wkr II, $33,744
Green, Nancy J, nutritionist III, $47,892
Gregory, Kathleen, admin ofc spt asst, $28,104

Gregory, Natalie R, pub hlth sr nurse, $48,780
Grellner, Sharon A, pers clerk, $36,888
Greninger, Jessica L, adlt prot & cmty wkr II, $33,744
Grim, Autumn M, prog coord dmh dohss, $54,288
Grimes, George E, fac adv nurse II, $53,124
Grindstaff, Richard L, hlth & sr svcs mgr 2, $56,514
Grote, Beverly A, accounting spec II, $44,304
Grover-Slattery, Carmen M, hlth & sr svcs mgr 1, $54,288
Guein, Doris J, child care fac spec III, $43,488
Guerrant, Susan M, info spt coor, $29,004
Gwanfogbe, Philomina N, epidemiology spec, $51,096
Haberberger, Bryan A, environ spec I, $29,976
Hackmann, Douglas W, hlth prog rep II, $41,940
Hader, Peggy N, admin ofc spt asst, $28,536
Hadley, Traci A, pub hlth consult nurse, $62,508
Hagenhoff, Amy, pub hlth lab scientist, $37,548
Hagner, Dinah, hlth facilities cnslt, $54,288
Hagood, Laura L, hlth prog rep III, $41,172
Hahn, Rachael S, prog coord dmh dohss, $50,040
Hahs-Ross, Rhonda, fac surv II, $44,304
Haile, Christen E, proj spec, $25.00/hr
Haley, Carrie L, hr mgr b2, $65,865
Hall, Christina L, sr ofc spt asst (keybrd), $28,452
Hall, Dixie L, adlt prot & cmty wkr II, $33,744
Hall, Melissa L, adlt prot & cmty wkr II, $38,232
Hall, Rhonda J, pub hlth nurse, $47,904
Hall, Virginia C, info spt coor, $31,512
Haller, Shirley A, account clerk II, $26,232
Hamilton, Gail, proj spec, $14.00/hr
Hamlet, Lila S, hlth facilities nrsng cnslt, $55,320
Hamlet, Sharon S, adlt prot & cmty supv, $43,488
Hamm, Robert H, med cnslt, $122,280
Hammann, Megan L, hlth prog rep II, $34,944
Hammes, Toni R, pub hlth nurse, $50,052
Hammond, Warshieta M, child care fac spec II, $36,204
Hampton, Amy C, coor of childrens progs, $41,940
Hampton, Cindy J, sr ofc spt asst (keybrd), $25,824
Hand, Karie A, adlt prot & cmty wkr II, $33,744
Haner, Kelly L, adlt prot & cmty wkr II, $33,744
Hansen, Deborah D, proj spec, $30.00/hr
Harbert, Karen D, epidemiology spec, $40,380
Harbison, Catherine B, pub hlth consult nurse, $57,612
Harbison, Pamela L, adlt prot & cmty wkr II, $33,744
Hardgrove, Shawn, account clerk II, $25,824
Hardin, Angela K, fac adv nurse II, $48,780
Hardy, Rachel L, sr pub hlth lab scintst, $41,940
Hargis, Robert C, planner III, $50,040
Hargus, Rebecca L, hlth prog rep III, $38,928
Harp, Deborah A, adlt prot & cmty wkr II, $33,744
Harper, Emma J, fac surv II, $48,156
Harris, Elizabeth A, hlth & sr svcs mgr 2, $61,338
Harris, Kathy L, child care fac spec II, $41,940
Harris, Rebecca S, accounting spec III, $49,128
Harris Franklin, Lori J, sr epidemiology spec, $48,156
Harrison, Jennifer M, planner II, $41,172
Hartgraves, Celesta S, div dir, $89,676
Hartley, Mary J, adlt prot & cmty wkr II, $33,744
Hartman, Michelle D, environ spec II, $46,068
Harvey, Benjamin R, special asst prof, $66,046
Harvey, Sheena D, ofc spt asst (keybrd), $23,160
Harvey, Susan W, hlth prog rep III, $43,488
Harvey, Tanya K, coor of childrens progs, $44,304
Haslag, Alexis R, pub hlth lab scientist, $37,548
Hastings, Peggy P, child care fac spec II, $40,380
Haug, Abigayle L, proj spec, $10.00/hr
Haulman, Angela C, adlt prot & cmty wkr II, $34,944
Hausman, Mendy J, adlt prot & cmty wkr II, $33,744
Havens, Randell, spec hlth care needs reg coord, $54,288
Hawk, Steven C, env pub hlth spec IV, $46,068
Hawkins, Arlene D, long-term care spec, $34,944
Hayden, Andrew C, investigator II, $37,548
Hays, Warren A, planner II, $38,928
He, Rong, research analyst III, $40,380
Heard, Shanna L, sr ofc spt asst (keybrd), $25,824
Heathman, Amber D, accounting spec II, $40,380
Heaton, Darwin D, adlt prot & cmty wkr II, $33,744
Heckman, Jill S, adlt prot & cmty wkr II, $33,744
Hedges, Patrick B, adlt prot & cmty wkr II, $33,744
Hedrick, Eddie R, proj spec, $30.00/hr
Heidbreder, Carla M, fac insp, $32,628
Heinkel, Jennifer L, ofc spt asst (keybrd), $23,160
Heisinger, Shena M, proj spec, $14.85/hr
Helems, Dana F, sr ofc spt asst (keybrd), $25,824

Helmers, John H, adlt prot & cmty wkr II, $39,624
Helton, Sharon A, fiscal & administrative mgr b1, $62,026
Hendee, Audrey M, proj spec, $27.00/hr
Henderson, Bridgett A, mgmt analysis spec II, $46,932
Henderson, Erik N, adlt prot & cmty wkr II, $32,628
Henderson, Gloria, sr ofc spt asst (keybrd), $26,652
Henderson, Michael C, hlth & sr svcs mgr 1, $58,394
Henderson, Peggy L, hlth prog rep III, $43,488
Hendricks, Carol J, fac adv nurse II, $52,032
Henke, Keith G, hlth & sr svcs mgr 1, $61,327
Henschel, Kathleen M, epidemiology spec, $40,380
Henson, Katherine A, fac adv nurse II, $46,956
Henson, Linda J, hlth facilities nrsng cnslt, $55,320
Henson, Sonya M, epidemiology spec, $46,068
Henson, Tracy A, sr ofc spt asst (keybrd), $25,824
Hentges, Sandra, hlth & sr svcs mgr 2, $66,038
Herigon, Julie A, training tech II, $41,172
Herigon, Kelly L, accounting spec I, $36,204
Herring, Barbara, ofc spt asst (keybrd), $23,160
Hessling, Susan A, dietitian IV, $45,156
Heuett, Vickie L, hlth facilities nrsng cnslt, $53,124
Hiatte, Linda K, account clerk II, $25,824
Hibi, Robin L, hlth & sr svcs mgr 2, $55,706
Hickox, Mary L, adlt prot & cmty wkr II, $33,744
Highfill, Craig D, prog coord dmh dohss, $53,208
Hilbert, Holly A, fac adv nurse II, $53,124
Hildebrand, Terry D, aging prog spec II, $49,128
Hilker, Teresa A, hlth & sr svcs mgr 2, $54,257
Hill, Joan M, adlt prot & cmty supv, $46,068
Hill, Karen A, adlt prot & cmty wkr II, $33,744
Hilton, Matthew J, adlt prot & cmty wkr II, $33,744
Hines, Laurie J, special asst prof, $83,830
Hinkle, C J, sr epidemiology spec, $55,416
Hobart, Ryan D, special asst prof, $62,119
Hoerr, Matthew H, adlt prot & cmty wkr II, $34,356
Hoerschgen, Bethany M, sr ofc spt asst (keybrd), $25,032
Hoffman, Ann M, proj spec, $27.00/hr
Hoffman, Crystal D, adlt prot & cmty wkr II, $33,744
Hoffman, Nancy L, proj spec, $34.40/hr
Hoffmann, Marilyn K, ofc spt asst (keybrd), $23,880
Hogrefe, Wanda J, info spt coor, $32,052
Hollandsworth, Jason S, hlth facilities nrsng cnslt, $60,036
Hollandsworth, Jenny M, hlth & sr svcs mgr 1, $51,538
Hollis, Emily E, sr ofc spt asst (keybrd), $29,904
Holman, Daphne E, admin ofc spt asst, $28,536
Holshouser, Brandy J, adlt prot & cmty wkr II, $33,744
Holtkamp, Charlotte M, sr ofc spt asst (keybrd), $26,652
Holtmeyer, Rosetta M, typist, $12.00/hr
Hooker, Joyce L, exec II, $38,232
Hooper, Brittney N, hlth prog rep III, $23,951
Hoover, Kayci J, sr ofc spt asst (keybrd), $25,824
Hope, Melissa K, planner III, $50,040
Hopkins, Alma M, nutrition spec, $52,092
Hopkins, Patrick V, lab mgr b2, $61,343
Hopkins, Tyler L, adlt prot & cmty wkr I, $30,984
Horn, Christie E, adlt prot & cmty wkr II, $33,744
Horvath, Eugenia K, admin ofc spt asst, $28,536
Hoskins, Mary M, proj spec, $25.00/hr
Houchins, Karla J, principal asst board/commisson, $55,411
House - Henry, Douglas W, proj spec, $14.00/hr
Housh, Heather D, adlt prot & cmty wkr II, $33,744
Howard, Heather R, adlt prot & cmty wkr II, $36,888
Howard, Jacqueline S, hlth facilities nrsng cnslt, $53,124
Howren, Dolan W, fac surv II, $44,304
Howser, Shellie M, admin ofc spt asst, $28,104
Hubner, Deloris F, hlth prog rep II, $36,204
Hudanick, Lana K, pub hlth consult nurse, $53,124
Huddleston, Peggy A, admin ofc spt asst, $32,052
Hudson, Donna R, pub hlth sr nurse, $57,612
Hueste, Eric A, hlth & sr svcs mgr 2, $66,038
Huffman, Carol A, adlt prot & cmty wkr II, $33,744
Hughes, Caroyln D, adlt prot & cmty wkr II, $33,744
Hulett, Jill L, hlth prog rep II, $36,888
Hunter, Andrew D, research mgr b2, $63,482
Hunter, Anita M, adlt prot & cmty wkr II, $33,744
Hunter, Charity J, hlth & sr svcs mgr 1, $53,200
Hurla, Paul G, fac surv III, $47,892
Husong, Judith J, ofc spt asst (keybrd), $24,264
Hutchison, Heather L, admin ofc spt asst, $28,536
Ice, Shauna M, pub hlth nurse, $47,904
Indelicato, Jennifer L, adlt prot & cmty supv, $41,172
Inman, Brian D, admin ofc spt asst, $28,536
Inman, Robert F, hlth prog rep III, $47,892

Ives, Tasha R, sr ofc spt asst (keybrd), $25,824
Ivory-dixon, Tina, adlt prot & cmty wkr II, $32,628
Ivy, Lisa A, chld care prgm spec, $44,304
Jackson, Carla L, fac surv II, $45,156
Jackson, Elmer D, investigator III, $40,380
Jackson, Jeanette L, adlt prot & cmty wkr II, $33,744
Jackson, Lynette A, admin ofc spt asst, $29,496
Jackson, Staci L, fac surv II, $46,068
Jackson, Tiffany N, fac surv II, $41,940
Jackson, Tim L, hlth & sr svcs mgr 2, $55,706
Jaco, Brenda L, hlth prog rep II, $35,568
Jacobs, Holly J, adlt prot & cmty wkr II, $33,744
Jacobs, Kelly A, sr ofc spt asst (keybrd), $25,824
Jacobsen, Michelle M, hr mgr b1, $50,080
Jahanpour, Ehsan, proj spec, $28.50/hr
James, Charlene, proj spec, $14.00/hr
James, Christine, admin ofc spt asst, $32,628
Jameson, Charles W, ofc spt asst (clerical), $22,536
Jameson, Sarah B, ofc spt asst (keybrd), $22,536
Jameson, Veronica A, adlt prot & cmty wkr II, $33,744
Jamison, Janice I, exec II, $36,888
Jansen, Beverly M, hlth prog rep II, $40,380
Jarrell, Alan M, pub hlth lab scientist, $37,548
Jarvis, Vicky L, sr ofc spt asst (keybrd), $29,412
Jefferies, Ingrid, adlt prot & cmty wkr II, $34,944
Jenkerson, Mark A, env pub hlth spec IV, $48,156
Jenkins, Alicia D, chld care prgm spec, $53,208
Jenkins, Ashley E, pub hlth consult nurse, $55,320
Jenkins, Karen D, hlth facilities nrsng cnslt, $53,124
Jennings, Carla D, registered nurse mgr b2, $63,996
Jerome, Brandi L, fac adv nurse II, $48,780
Jevarajah, David S, adlt prot & cmty wkr II, $33,744
Jobe, Cynthia J, hlth & sr svcs mgr 2, $64,200
Jobe, Leslie E, hlth & sr svcs mgr 2, $64,802
Johnson, Cynthia, fac surv II, $41,940
Johnson, Doyle J, adlt prot & cmty supv, $40,380
Johnson, Dustin S, env pub hlth spec V, $48,156
Johnson, Eric D, adlt prot & cmty supv, $40,380
Johnson, Johnathan, ofc spt asst (clerical), $22,872
Johnson, Juaniata R, sr ofc spt asst (keybrd), $28,452
Johnson, Juanita Y, ofc spt asst (keybrd), $23,160
Johnson, Kate M, adlt prot & cmty wkr II, $33,744
Johnson, Mary A, sr ofc spt asst (keybrd), $25,824
Johnson, Mary S, fac surv II, $41,940
Johnson, Percy S, env pub hlth spec IV, $46,932
Johnson, Shondra, hlth & sr svcs mgr 2, $60,101
Johnson, Toyka L, info spt coor, $31,512
Johnson, Tracy M, proj spec, $14.00/hr
Joiner, Samantha L, hlth facilities nrsng cnslt, $51,072
Jones, Abby J, adlt prot & cmty wkr II, $34,944
Jones, Angela D, env pub hlth spec IV, $41,940
Jones, Ashley M, sr ofc spt asst (keybrd), $25,404
Jones, Georgia B, fac adv nurse III, $53,124
Jones, Mary N, fac surv II, $41,940
Jones, Rita V, ofc spt asst (clerical), $22,536
Jones, Sandra K, hlth prog rep II, $40,380
Jones, Tracy L, adlt prot & cmty wkr II, $35,568
Jones-major, Carolyn I, adlt prot & cmty wkr II, $36,888
Jordan, Alice M, hlth facilities nrsng cnslt, $55,320
Jorgensen, Cory R, environ scientist, $54,288
Josupait, Christi D, adlt prot & cmty wkr II, $33,744
Jung, Marineda J, proj spec, $20.00/hr
Jungmeyer, Andra E, coor of childrens progs, $41,940
Jury, Richard J, proj spec, $24.55/hr
Kamara, Haroun O, fiscal & administrative mgr b1, $61,244
Kamper, Clarence R, epidemiology spec, $47,892
Kanagawa, Jennifer M, pub hlth nurse, $47,904
Karr, Eunice D, child care fac spec II, $38,928
Karstetter, Mary D, fac adv nurse III, $58,752
Kayani, Noaman, research analyst IV, $51,096
Keen, Barbara K, nutrition spec, $50,040
Keen, Heather N, fac adv nurse II, $46,956
Keeran, Billie J, admin ofc spt asst, $28,104
Keim, Nancy J, nutritionist III, $46,068
Keith, Deborah D, admin ofc spt asst, $28,536
Keller, Erica M, adlt prot & cmty supv, $40,380
Keller, Keith R, proj spec, $14.00/hr
Keller, Mary B, adlt prot & cmty wkr II, $33,744
Keller, Matthew R, research analyst III, $40,380
Keller, Michael B, fac insp, $32,628
Keller-crites, Elizabeth, fac adv nurse II, $45,204
Kelley, June D, sr ofc spt asst (keybrd), $26,232
Kelly, David H, research analyst I, $31,512

Kelly, Erin C, pub hlth sr nurse, $47,904
Kelly, Glenda L, proj spec, $30.00/hr
Kelly, Kimberly D, adlt prot & cmty supv, $40,380
Kelsey, Amy L, hlth & sr svcs mgr 1, $53,534
Kelton, Carolyn, sr ofc spt asst (keybrd), $28,908
Kemezys, Monica, child care fac spec II, $42,708
Kempker, Stacy L, designated principal asst div, $42,711
Kempker, Valerie C, adlt prot & cmty wkr II, $32,628
Kennedy, Courtney J, adlt prot & cmty wkr II, $33,744
Kennedy, Sally J, fac adv nurse II, $48,780
Kennon, Catherine D, hlth prog rep III, $41,940
Keran, Carrie A, proj spec, $14.00/hr
Kerber, James V, adlt prot & cmty wkr II, $33,744
Kern, Deborah A, adlt prot & cmty wkr II, $33,744
Kerns, Debbie S, admin ofc spt asst, $28,104
Kerns, Julie L, sr ofc spt asst (keybrd), $27,084
Kerr, Danielle G, fac adv nurse II, $46,956
Kiesling, Jami L, pub hlth consult nurse, $56,448
Kilfoil, Barbara J, acct II, $42,708
Kindell, Diana, adlt prot & cmty wkr II, $33,744
Kinder, Paula K, adlt prot & cmty wkr II, $34,356
King, Brenda L, hlth prog rep I, $32,052
King, Rick L, fac surv II, $41,940
Kingsbury, Melissa M, fac insp, $32,628
Kinkead, Arlinda K, hlth facilities nrsng cnslt, $53,124
Kinney, Connie C, ofc spt asst (keybrd), $23,160
Kinsaul, Donna, adlt prot & cmty wkr II, $33,744
Kirbey, Harold C, div dir, $94,878
Kitchell, Dorothy D, sr ofc spt asst (keybrd), $25,824
Klapp, D S, hlth facilities nrsng cnslt, $53,124
Kleffner-Wansing, Melissa L, hlth & sr svcs mgr 1, $59,946
Klemm, David J, fac surv II, $41,940
Kliethermes, Debby A, sr ofc spt asst (keybrd), $12,917
Kliethermes, Karen A, hlth prog rep III, $48,156
Kliethermes, Laura A, planner III, $57,744
Kline, Kally J, sr ofc spt asst (keybrd), $25,824
Klug, Tracy L, lab mgr b1, $52,092
Knaust, Sarah M, hlth prog rep II, $34,944
Kneeskern, Susan K, hlth facilities nrsng cnslt, $63,768
Knipp, Lindsey N, sr ofc spt asst (keybrd), $25,824
Knott, Elizabeth A, proj spec, $14.00/hr
Koch, Denise E, child care fac spec II, $36,204
Koch, Mary R, hlth & sr svcs mgr 1, $50,198
Koebel, William M, hlth & sr svcs mgr 3, $77,180
Koechner, Tammy S, fac insp, $31,512
Koetters, Alexandria J, ofc spt asst (keybrd), $22,536
Koffarnus, Nathan A, epidemiology spec, $40,380
Kolb, Carla J, ofc spt asst (keybrd), $25,824
Kolb, Kevin L, facilities opps mgr b2, $74,312
Kolb, Richard E, sr auditor, $48,156
Korsmeyer, Cheryl A, proj spec, $18.00/hr
Kosmatka, Ronald S, budget analyst II, $37,548
Kothe, Cynthia A, spec hlth care needs reg coord, $54,288
Kothe, Marcia E, fac insp, $32,628
Kowieski, Rose A, hlth prog rep III, $45,156
Kramel, Tracy A, special asst ofc & clerical, $43,050
Krattli, Joyce A, sr ofc spt asst (keybrd), $25,824
Kreiling, Sheila A, fac adv nurse II, $46,956
Kreitzer, Penny J, child care fac spec II, $36,204
Kreter, Chester A, fac surv II, $40,380
Kreutz, Amber M, admin ofc spt asst, $28,536
Kroeger, Samuel S, typist, $10.83/hr
Krogstad, Linda D, hlth prog rep II, $42,708
Kroll, Sharlet E, hlth prog rep III, $44,304
Kuchem, Stephanie M, sr ofc spt asst (keybrd), $26,232
Kummerfeld, Kris L, planner II, $48,156
Kurrelmeyer, Stacy L, account clerk II, $25,824
Kuster, Rachelle L, env pub hlth spec V, $53,208
Lacey, Troy V, fac surv II, $41,940
Lackey, Ainsley S, env pub hlth spec IV, $43,488
Laddusaw, Dalonda P, adlt prot & cmty wkr II, $33,744
Lamb, Jennifer F, fac adv nurse II, $46,956
Laneave, Melissa R, admin ofc spt asst, $34,944
Lang, Marie L, adlt prot & cmty supv, $42,708
Langston, John W, hlth & sr svcs mgr 2, $64,802
Lara, Joyce A, hlth prog rep III, $44,304
Larsen, Hether M, adlt prot & cmty supv, $41,172
Lasater, Danielle M, proj spec, $28.00/hr
Lasley, Morgan M, accounting spec I, $36,204
Lauderback, Travis C, adlt prot & cmty wkr II, $34,944
Laughlin, Melinda A, hlth & sr svcs mgr 3, $71,493
Lawrence, Micheal A, long-term care spec, $37,548
Lee, Michelle, hlth facilities nrsng cnslt, $61,248

Lee, Michelle L, adlt prot & cmty wkr II, $33,744
Lehnhoff, Roger C, maint spv I, $32,628
Lemen, Patricia A, adlt prot & cmty wkr II, $33,744
Lenberg, Stacey N, adlt prot & cmty wkr II, $33,744
Lene, Tammy J, fac adv nurse II, $48,780
Leonard, Emily L, fiscal & administrative mgr b1, $62,662
Lepold, Kristie L, fac insp, $32,628
Leseberg, Lisa D, clin soc work spv, $52,092
Lewis, Cassandra E, adlt prot & cmty supv, $41,172
Lewis, Laura B, hlth prog rep II, $34,944
Lewis, Sandra, human rel ofcr III, $52,092
Li, Jiaqing, research analyst III, $51,096
Libby, Kathy D, fac adv nurse II, $46,956
Lile, Aaron A, proj spec, $25.00/hr
Liley, M S, proj spec, $20.00/hr
Lilly, Nathan R, env pub hlth spec V, $56,520
Limbach, Bridgette A, hlth prog rep I, $30,984
Lindberg, Dale W, env pub hlth spec IV, $48,156
Linneman, Dean A, dpty div dir, $84,858
Linton-Redel, Deborah R, fac adv nurse II, $53,124
List, Mary L, hlth prog rep III, $41,172
Litchfield, David B, research analyst III, $44,304
Liu, Qian, research analyst III, $41,940
Llanos, Patricia, hlth prog rep III, $40,380
Locke, Lorena W, hlth educator III, $45,156
Lococo, Bonnie S, adlt prot & cmty wkr II, $33,744
Loehr, Gregory E, fac adv nurse II, $46,956
Loethen, Loretta J, mgmt analysis spec II, $48,156
Loethen, Nicole L, chief counsel, $89,688
Logan, Kylene A, sr ofc spt asst (keybrd), $25,824
Lomax, Angela J, adlt prot & cmty wkr II, $33,744
Long, Anna L, hlth educator III, $40,380
Long, Bryon, proj spec, $25.00/hr
Long, Katie A, nutritionist III, $42,708
Longanecker, Michael H, fiscal & admin mgr b2, $72,760
Longley-olson, Patricia A, sr pub hlth lab scintst, $41,940
Lopes, Annette, admin ofc spt asst, $29,496
Lovelace, Wendy J, hlth prog rep I, $31,512
Lowrie, Donya L, registered nurse mgr b2, $69,058
Lubia, Eileen M, sr ofc spt asst (keybrd), $25,824
Lucas, Jo A, proj spec, $14.00/hr
Luebbering, Joyce E, hlth & sr svcs mgr 1, $55,498
Luebbering, Kathy M, hlth prog rep II, $39,624
Luebbering, Kristi A, fac adv nurse II, $54,156
Luebbering, Leon J, lab mgr b1, $54,578
Luebbering, Lindsay J, adlt prot & cmty wkr II, $33,744
Luebbering, Tami R, sr ofc spt asst (keybrd), $13,978
Lueckenotte, Jean M, admin ofc spt asst, $28,536
Lueckenotte, Terri A, fac adv nurse III, $53,124
Lurten, Kevin D, adlt prot & cmty wkr II, $32,628
Lusher, Cera M, hlth prog rep I, $33,180
Lute, Christopher D, maint worker II, $29,976
Lutmer, Brian M, lab mgr b1, $52,092
Lydon, Frank, epidemiology spec, $46,932
Lynch, Lori L, admin ofc spt asst, $28,536
Lyon, Matthew G, proj spec, $25.00/hr
Maasen, Tammy L, designated principal asst div, $42,711
Macgregor, David J, fac surv II, $46,932
Madonna, Michael, sr ofc spt asst (keybrd), $28,908
Madore, Melanie B, hlth & sr svcs mgr 2, $62,655
Mahaney, Marcia, fiscal & administrative mgr b2, $72,760
Mahfood, Nadia J, info spt coor, $30,984
Mahon, Bryan C, admin ofc spt asst, $28,536
Maine, Karen J, hlth facilities nrsng cnslt, $58,752
Maley, Brenda K, prog coord dmh dohss, $55,416
Maley, Randall, env pub hlth spec IV, $51,096
Malone, Deborah D, hlth prog rep II, $37,548
Maloney, Pamela J, fac adv nurse II, $46,956
Malzner-Underwood, Cara L, pers ofcr I, $46,932
Marberry, Erin L, nutritionist III, $42,708
Marks, Ronda R, admin ofc spt asst, $29,976
Marr, Linda J, sr ofc spt asst (keybrd), $28,908
Marriott, Cathy L, fac surv II, $40,380
Marsch, Ryan M, training tech II, $43,488
Marsh, Erifilie C, fac adv nurse II, $48,780
Marshall, Mary E, sr ofc spt asst (keybrd), $25,824
Marshall, Tracy E, child care fac spec III, $41,940
Martin, Gregrey A, investigator III, $43,488
Martin, John C, fac adv nurse II, $49,788
Martin, Laurie A, adlt prot & cmty wkr II, $34,944
Martin, Norma D, admin ofc spt asst, $28,536
Martin, Peter N, proj spec, $25.00/hr
Martin, Rebecca R, fac surv II, $46,068

Martin, Sandra K, adlt prot & cmty wkr II, $36,888
Martorelli, Meagan V, fac surv II, $43,488
Martz, Nola B, pub hlth consult nurse, $65,148
Marx, Harvey L, proj spec, $30.00/hr
Mason, Emanuel A, adlt prot & cmty wkr II, $36,888
Massey, Nicole D, hlth & sr svcs mgr 1, $57,631
Massman, Michael J, lab mgr b3, $70,997
Matheney, Shanna R, fac adv nurse II, $48,780
Matheny, Brian S, ofc spt asst (keybrd), $23,160
Mathieson, Samantha A, epidemiology spec, $40,380
Matlick, Wendi M, child care fac spec II, $36,204
Maupin, Peggy L, hlth prog rep II, $38,232
May, Steven A, environ spec III, $46,932
Mayberry, Stephanie L, adlt prot & cmty wkr II, $33,180
Maynard, Morgan L, adlt prot & cmty wkr II, $33,744
Maynard-brown, Debra C, fac surv II, $40,380
Mazurek, Kathryn R, aging prog spec II, $40,380
McAbee, Trina R, sr ofc spt asst (keybrd), $28,452
McAboy-young, Morgan A, pub info coor, $41,940
McBride, David G, sr epidemiology spec, $52,092
McBride-mooty, Molly J, proj spec, $27.00/hr
McCain, Wanda J, adlt prot & cmty wkr II, $33,744
McCart, Karen S, adlt prot & cmty wkr II, $33,744
McCarter, Deanna K, hlth facilities nrsng cnslt, $53,124
McCartney, Danielle S, adlt prot & cmty supv, $39,624
McClanahan, Ashley L, adlt prot & cmty wkr II, $33,744
McClaskey, Sandra L, sr ofc spt asst (keybrd), $25,824
McClurg-hitt, Deborah J, nutritionist III, $46,932
McComb, Tonya S, admin ofc spt asst, $28,104
McConkey, Barbara D, fac adv nurse III, $51,072
McCorcle, Karyn M, adlt prot & cmty wkr II, $33,744
McCormack, Camille Z, adlt prot & cmty wkr II, $33,744
McCoy, Jacqueline M, admin ofc spt asst, $32,628
McCrary, Karen A, adlt prot & cmty wkr II, $32,628
McDonald, Jarrett J, fac insp, $36,204
McElroy-otis, Michele R, hlth & sr svcs mgr 2, $60,729
McElwaine, Samuel A, hlth prog rep II, $40,380
McGee, Marlon J, adlt prot & cmty wkr II, $33,744
McGlocklin, James A, adlt prot & cmty wkr II, $33,744
McGrath, Molly K, adlt prot & cmty wkr II, $33,744
McGrath, Wayne D, env pub hlth spec IV, $43,488
McKee, Angela J, research analyst III, $40,380
McKee, Sally L, principal asst board/commisson, $49,959
McKeever, Richard D, hlth prog rep III, $41,940
McKinney, Andrew L, environ spec III, $50,040
McKinney, Tara G, hlth prog rep III, $39,624
McKinnis, Cheryl A, adlt prot & cmty wkr II, $33,744
McMasters, Tammy J, pub hlth nurse, $50,052
McNeely, Lois D, adlt prot & cmty wkr II, $35,568
McNeely, Shelly L, adlt prot & cmty wkr II, $33,744
McQuitty, Maranda S, fac insp, $32,628
Mead, Rhonda J, fac adv nurse II, $46,956
Mebruer, Brandon D, environ spec III, $40,380
Mebruer, Deborah K, special asst ofc & clerical, $56,760
Medrano, Brianna, pub hlth lab scientist, $37,548
Meers, Jeffrey L, accounting spec III, $54,288
Mehmert, Ashley R, sr pub hlth lab scintst, $41,940
Meller, Jessica A, sr pub hlth lab scintst, $41,940
Meller, Lavonda G, fac surv II, $43,488
Menges, Mary T, hlth & sr svcs mgr 3, $74,312
Mercer, Melanie G, sr ofc spt asst (keybrd), $25,824
Mertens, April D, sr ofc spt asst (keybrd), $25,824
Mertzlufft, Kathy A, nutrition spec, $55,416
Metzger, Robert W, proj spec, $24.96/hr
Meyer, Lori D, adlt prot & cmty wkr II, $33,744
Meyer, Thomas S, fac insp, $31,512
Meyers, Debra L, ofc spt asst (keybrd), $22,536
Meystedt, Rachel, legal counsel, $44,935
Michnal, Dawn M, hlth prog rep III, $44,304
Mickels, Rebecca A, research analyst IV, $49,128
Miller, Belvy L, admin ofc spt asst, $32,052
Miller, Daniel M, adlt prot & cmty wkr II, $33,744
Miller, Gabrielle L, adlt prot & cmty wkr II, $33,744
Miller, Janet L, adlt prot & cmty wkr II, $34,944
Miller, Stephanie E, fac adv nurse III, $57,612
Mills, Robin S, fac adv nurse II, $46,956
Mills-McCullough, Courtnee R, adlt prot & cmty wkr II, $33,744
Miner, Margie M, pub hlth nurse, $50,052
Minter, Nancy A, coor of childrens progs, $51,096
Mitchell, Rebecca, sr ofc spt asst (keybrd), $25,824
Mitchem, Amy L, hlth prog rep II, $34,944
Mobley, Evan L, research analyst II, $36,204
Mock, Barbara A, fac insp, $34,944

Moeller, Sarah M, account clerk I, $22,536
Monnig, Jessica L, accounting spec II, $46,932
Montecino, December J, hlth prog rep I, $31,512
Montgomery, Carrie D, sr ofc spt asst (keybrd), $26,652
Mooney, Regena S, adlt prot & cmty wkr II, $38,232
Moore, Alice M, sr ofc spt asst (keybrd), $25,824
Moore, Betty J, proj spec, $14.00/hr
Moore, Jodie L, long-term care spec, $34,944
Moore-lewis, Joanne P, admin ofc spt asst, $28,536
Morelock, Susan J, fac adv nurse III, $58,752
Moreno, Amanda C, adlt prot & cmty wkr II, $33,744
Morgan, Daria, admin ofc spt asst, $28,536
Morgan, Kevin T, adlt prot & cmty supv, $40,380
Morris, Jean A, fac adv nurse II, $45,204
Morris, Judith K, hlth facilities nrsng cnslt, $53,124
Morris, Natalie S, sr ofc spt asst (keybrd), $25,824
Morris, Pamela D, adlt prot & cmty wkr II, $33,744
Morrison, Charlotte A, admin ofc spt asst, $31,512
Morts, Laura C, fac adv nurse III, $51,072
Mosier, Susan L, fac adv nurse II, $45,204
Mosley, Mary J, research analyst III, $50,040
Moss, Kimberly A, accounting spec I, $36,204
Moss, Tammie E, adlt prot & cmty wkr II, $37,548
Moylan, Rickey G, fac surv II, $47,892
Mu' Min, Charmane M, adlt prot & cmty wkr II, $34,944
Mueckl, Kimberly M, fac insp, $36,204
Mullen, Heather J, fac surv II, $41,940
Murdock, Michael L, proj spec, $25.00/hr
Murphy, Leslie R, hlth prog rep III, $41,172
Murray, Patricia D, sr ofc spt asst (keybrd), $25,032
Murrow, Denise L, adlt prot & cmty wkr II, $33,744
Muza, Glenda J, admin ofc spt asst, $29,496
Myhre, Thelma J, environ spec II, $38,928
Myler, Margaret A, adlt prot & cmty wkr II, $37,548
Nagle, Maura K, adlt prot & cmty wkr II, $33,744
Nall, Dana E, fac adv nurse II, $46,956
Nance, Keven S, adlt prot & cmty wkr II, $33,744
Naught, Laura E, lab mgr b2, $61,343
Needy, Tiffany A, accounting spec I, $34,944
Neely, Terri B, fac adv nurse II, $48,780
Nelluri, Supriya, research analyst IV, $49,128
Nelson, Dawn M, accounting spec III, $60,120
Nelson, Patricia L, sr ofc spt asst (keybrd), $28,908
Nelson-mumin, Sadiah N, proj spec, $14.00/hr
Netter, Monica J, sr ofc spt asst (keybrd), $25,824
Newman, Angelia D, adlt prot & cmty wkr II, $33,744
Newton, Latasha A, child care fac spec II, $36,204
Nguyen, Minh, fac surv II, $41,940
Nichols, Catherine R, hlth prog rep II, $34,944
Nichols, Joy L, child care fac spec II, $39,624
Nickels, Paula M, adlt prot & cmty wkr II, $33,744
Nickelson, Paula F, prog coord dmh dohss, $60,120
Nickerson, Jodi L, fac surv II, $43,488
Nicoll, Rachel T, fac adv nurse II, $53,124
Niekamp, Tracy J, hlth & sr svcs mgr 2, $62,664
Nkweti, Celestine, adlt prot & cmty wkr II, $32,628
Nobe, Michelle L, adlt prot & cmty wkr II, $30,984
Noble, Devona, adlt prot & cmty supv, $41,172
Noeltner, Jill, fac adv nurse II, $53,124
Nolan, Angela L, adlt prot & cmty wkr II, $33,744
Nolte, Amy C, child care fac spec II, $36,204
Norrell, Thomas G, adlt prot & cmty wkr II, $33,744
Novinger, Mary E, pub hlth consult nurse, $53,124
Nugent, Teri A, hlth prog rep II, $34,944
Nugent, William I, hlth & sr svcs mgr 2, $64,802
Obermeier, Mary R, fac surv II, $41,940
O'brien, Douglas P, investigation mgr b1, $55,410
O'brien, Raelene A, fac surv III, $53,208
Ochsner, Debra, admin ofc spt asst, $27,228
Oden, Jackie S, hlth prog rep I, $30,420
Odom, Sharon G, environ sup, $49,128
Oeser, David L, sr epidemiology spec, $49,128
Oesterly, Angela J, coor of childrens progs, $44,304
Oligschlaeger, Timothy A, acct I, $31,512
Olivas, Tiffany L, fac insp, $32,628
Oliver, Christina J, sr ofc spt asst (keybrd), $29,904
Oliver, Gary L, adlt prot & cmty wkr II, $39,624
Olson, Marianne R, adlt prot & cmty wkr II, $33,744
O'neal, Peggy J, sr ofc spt asst (keybrd), $25,032
O'neill, Erica N, adlt prot & cmty wkr II, $33,744
Opie, Stephanie K, acct I, $31,512
Osman, Patricia A, hlth & sr svcs mgr 2, $60,003
Oster, Jeffery M, fac adv nurse II, $55,320

Ostermeier, Diane K, pub hlth nurse, $52,032
Ott, Ammanda M, fac adv nurse III, $51,072
Ott, Patricia E, fac adv nurse II, $45,204
Otto, Ashlie J, pub hlth sr nurse, $51,072
Otto, Holly M, coor of childrens progs, $44,304
Otto, Karen R, hlth prog rep III, $39,624
Owens, Janet S, pers analyst II, $44,304
Ownbey, Martaun L, proj spec, $14.00/hr
Pagan, Jeanine A, pub hlth sr nurse, $48,780
Palermo, Kenneth J, hlth & sr svcs mgr 2, $66,028
Palm, Joseph S, special asst prof, $67,472
Pape, Sarah, admin ofc spt asst, $28,104
Pappas, Charisse A, pub info coor, $50,040
Pappas, Cheryl G, nursing consult, $27.14/hr
Pardoe, Lisa A, exec I, $30,984
Parish, La Shun N, adlt prot & cmty wkr II, $32,628
Parker, Dawn L, hlth prog rep III, $47,892
Parker, Rachel M, sr ofc spt asst (keybrd), $25,824
Parker, Tiffany L, adlt prot & cmty wkr II, $33,744
Paro, Carolyn L, hlth prog rep II, $44,304
Parsley, James R, child care fac spec II, $39,624
Parsons, Constance M, hlth facilities cnslt, $52,092
Parsons, Kathryn E, fac surv III, $47,892
Pashi, Arthur K, research analyst IV, $49,128
Patino, Evelyn J, admin ofc spt asst, $28,536
Patrickus, Mary M, admin ofc spt asst, $31,512
Patterson, Anita, sr ofc spt asst (keybrd), $25,824
Patterson, Irene Z, adlt prot & cmty wkr II, $36,888
Patterson, Robert W, research analyst IV, $50,040
Patterson, Scott B, research analyst IV, $47,892
Patterson, Shay E, fac surv III, $47,892
Patton, Margaret L, sr ofc spt asst (keybrd), $25,824
Paulsen, Lisa L, sr ofc spt asst (keybrd), $28,908
Payne, Lisa G, admin ofc spt asst, $28,104
Peel, Mary M, adlt prot & cmty wkr II, $39,624
Pennell, Jennifer A, fac adv nurse II, $48,780
Perkins, Adam J, sr pub hlth lab scintst, $41,940
Perkins, Katherine S, adlt prot & cmty wkr II, $36,888
Perkins, Patricia L, admin ofc spt asst, $28,104
Perkins-Dumas, Carla D, adlt prot & cmty wkr II, $33,744
Persley, Ernestine, nutritionist III, $41,172
Peters, Tracy L, fac adv nurse I, $42,792
Petershagen, Paula M, sr ofc spt asst (keybrd), $25,824
Peterson, Lesha C, hlth prog rep III, $38,928
Petet, Gwendolyn L, pers analyst II, $37,548
Pethan, Michael W, spec hlth care needs coord, $50,040
Petty, Vicki D, child care fac spec II, $44,304
Pfenenger, Jackie O, facilities opps mgr b1, $46,979
Pfitzner, Sarah K, adlt prot & cmty wkr II, $33,744
Phelan, Lawrence P, sr epidemiology spec, $55,416
Phelps, Christopher W, emergency med svcs insp I, $36,204
Phelps, Jeanine, hlth prog rep II, $34,944
Phelps, Jessica D, adlt prot & cmty wkr II, $33,744
Pherigo, Mary E, hlth prog rep III, $42,708
Philbert, Patricia A, typist, $12.00/hr
Phillips, Dawn R, admin ofc spt asst, $36,888
Phillips, Doug P, research analyst III, $40,380
Phillips, Lola B, hlth & sr svcs mgr 1, $57,609
Phillips, Tim F, child care fac spec II, $42,708
Phillips, Virginia A, env pub hlth spec IV, $46,932
Pierce, Amy K, lab mgr b1, $54,286
Pierce, Loretta, pub hlth nurse, $50,052
Pierson, Kassie L, sr ofc spt asst (keybrd), $25,032
Pieters, Rudolph S, fac surv II, $43,488
Pikes, Willa M, adlt prot & cmty wkr II, $33,744
Pinard, Heidi A, adlt prot & cmty wkr II, $33,744
Pinkston, Nerissa D, fac adv nurse II, $45,204
Pinney, Donna S, adlt prot & cmty wkr II, $33,744
Pittman, Rhonda, admin ofc spt asst, $31,512
Pitts, Sarah L, sr ofc spt asst (keybrd), $25,824
Plaster, Samuel F, hlth & sr svcs mgr 2, $56,511
Platter, Cynthia L, proj spec, $15.00/hr
Poettgen, Ralph R, procurement ofcr I, $46,068
Pogue, Tommi K, account clerk II, $25,824
Ponder, Laura G, planner II, $46,932
Ponder, Michael, fac surv III, $53,208
Porting, M S, special asst prof, $80,155
Poskin, Brooke A, child care fac spec II, $36,888
Potter, Kelvin W, adlt prot & cmty wkr II, $36,204
Potter, Mallory A, env pub hlth spec IV, $43,488
Powell, Betty, typist, $13.25/hr
Powell, Linda L, hlth prog rep III, $42,708
Pratt, Pamela D, sr epidemiology spec, $52,092

Pratte, Megan C, ofc spt asst (keybrd), $22,536
Premnath, Sri V, sr ofc spt asst (keybrd), $25,824
Prenger, Diana S, fac surv II, $46,932
Prenger, Viola M, admin ofc spt asst, $28,536
Price, Marjorie E, adlt prot & cmty wkr II, $33,744
Pritchard, Thomas L, hlth facilities cnslt, $52,092
Pruitt, James L, prog coord dmh dohss, $57,744
Pryor, Louella, sr ofc spt asst (keybrd), $25,032
Puckett, Barbara J, adlt prot & cmty wkr II, $33,744
Puckett, Barbara L, adlt prot & cmty wkr II, $38,232
Puckett, Donna C, prog coord dmh dohss, $60,120
Pue, Howard L, hlth & sr svcs mgr 2, $74,312
Pulley, Tiffany A, adlt prot & cmty wkr II, $32,628
Purcell, Dawn R, fac adv nurse II, $53,124
Putman, Antonette M, pub hlth nurse, $47,904
Pyle, Deborah L, long-term care spec, $36,204
Quick, Bonnie S, nursing consult, $26.00/hr
Quinn, Karla M, nutritionist III, $43,488
Quinn, Kristine C, adlt prot & cmty supv, $41,940
Raburn-Miller, Julie I, prog coord dmh dohss, $57,744
Race, Dianna M, adlt prot & cmty wkr II, $33,744
Rackers, Brenda K, legal counsel, $51,350
Rackers, Cindy R, hlth & sr svcs mgr 3, $73,113
Rackers, Diane C, proj spec, $14.85/hr
Rackers, Joyce A, registered nurse mgr b1, $65,359
Rademan, Kim C, sr ofc spt asst (keybrd), $25,824
Raithel, Sharon C, hlth facilities nrsng cnslt, $60,036
Ramsey, Steven A, designated principal asst dept, $63,630
Ramza-Gay, Maria J, adlt prot & cmty wkr II, $33,744
Randolph, Susan L, account clerk II, $25,824
Reasoner, Vicky L, hlth facilities nrsng cnslt, $61,248
Record, Richard A, adlt prot & cmty wkr II, $33,744
Redcay, Ryan L, adlt prot & cmty supv, $40,380
Redding, Susan M, proj spec, $27.50/hr
Redmon, Denise M, nutrition spec, $50,040
Reed, David T, adlt prot & cmty wkr II, $34,944
Reed, John P, adlt prot & cmty wkr II, $33,744
Reed, Sheila M, planner III, $50,040
Reese, Cindy A, prog coord dmh dohss, $55,416
Reese-Okosi, Tracy D, nutritionist III, $43,488
Reeter, Christal A, adlt prot & cmty wkr II, $33,744
Rehard, Amy L, hlth & sr svcs mgr 2, $56,514
Reid, Christopher R, research analyst I, $32,628
Reinhardt, Kimberly A, hlth prog rep III, $44,304
Reinkemeyer, Amy K, admin ofc spt asst, $34,944
Reisenbichler, Deborah K, proj spec, $14.00/hr
Reitz, Hollis A, hlth facilities nrsng cnslt, $62,508
Renfro, Cynnamon M, adlt prot & cmty supv, $40,380
Renner, Matthew R, med technologist II, $34,944
Rettig, Wendy R, adlt prot & cmty wkr II, $33,744
Rettle, Deborah A, sr ofc spt asst (keybrd), $28,908
Rex, Beverly A, hlth facilities nrsng cnslt, $65,148
Rexing, Julie A, adlt prot & cmty wkr II, $33,744
Rexroad, Cynthia C, fac surv III, $50,040
Reynolds, Angela A, adlt prot & cmty wkr II, $33,744
Reynolds, John R, account clerk II, $25,824
Reynolds, Kim Saskia M, long-term care spec, $34,944
Reynolds, Melissa J, environ spec III, $44,304
Reynolds, Patricia D, adlt prot & cmty wkr II, $38,232
Rhodes, Aleesha, hlth prog rep II, $34,944
Rhodes, Heather N, sr ofc spt asst (keybrd), $25,824
Rice, Michelle R, pub hlth sr nurse, $49,788
Richardson, Drucilla A, adlt prot & cmty wkr II, $34,944
Richardson, Dustin R, adlt prot & cmty wkr II, $33,744
Richardson, Laura C, sr ofc spt asst (keybrd), $25,824
Rickard, Rebecca L, proj spec, $14.00/hr
Ricks, Bonnie S, sr pub hlth lab scintst, $42,708
Rider, Larry D, adlt prot & cmty wkr II, $34,944
Riehn, Lori L, fiscal & administrative mgr b2, $61,343
Riley, Alyssa M, child care fac spec II, $36,204
Risse, Alice A, admin ofc spt asst, $32,052
Roadruck, Nicoshia R, acct I, $30,984
Roark, Tracy J, hlth prog rep II, $34,944
Roberts, Lynn L, fac surv III, $49,128
Robertson, Kathleen R, legal counsel, $49,444
Robinson, Ayla K, ofc spt asst (keybrd), $23,160
Robinson, Dori M, pub hlth nurse, $47,904
Robinson, Kathy G, hlth prog rep II, $38,928
Robinson, Tara D, hlth prog rep III, $41,940
Robison, Jason E, adlt prot & cmty wkr II, $33,744
Rockers, Mark A, storekeeper I, $25,824
Rodemeyer, Michelle A, fiscal & administrative mgr b2, $66,679
Rodgers, Cynthia A, adlt prot & cmty wkr II, $38,232

Roe, Jamie M, adlt prot & cmty wkr II, $33,744
Rogers, Sharmini V, hlth & sr svcs mgr 2, $68,736
Rohman, Nancy J, sr ofc spt asst (keybrd), $25,824
Roling, Michael R, hlth facilities cnslt, $47,892
Rommel, Deborah L, hlth prog rep III, $41,172
Rorrer, Regina D, fac adv nurse II, $46,956
Rosack, Randi L, epidemiology spec, $40,380
Ross, Karen E, adlt prot & cmty supv, $46,068
Ross, Megan E, adlt prot & cmty supv, $41,940
Ross, Patricia I, fac surv II, $42,708
Rowland, Katie L, admin ofc spt asst, $28,536
Roy, Laura A, adlt prot & cmty wkr II, $33,744
Rozier, Shomari A, aging prog spec II, $47,892
Rueter, Barbara L, training tech III, $47,892
Rumans, Leslie A, hlth prog rep II, $34,944
Rush, Latisha S, long-term care spec, $36,204
Rushing, Kathy, adlt prot & cmty supv, $41,940
Russell, Billie J, child care fac spec II, $36,204
Russell, Leona K, long-term care spec, $38,928
Russell, Lynn M, adlt prot & cmty wkr II, $33,744
Russler, Teresa L, designated principal asst div, $42,711
Rustemeyer, Mindy S, sr pub hlth lab scintst, $41,940
Rustemeyer, Nicholas J, environ spec II, $36,204
Ryun, Katelyn M, adlt prot & cmty wkr I, $30,984
Sabogal De Guerrero, Eliasa J, fac surv II, $41,940
Sadler, Wanda R, mgmt analysis spec II, $45,156
Sahagun, Jennie L, adlt prot & cmty wkr II, $33,744
Salifu, Abdul W, research analyst III, $38,928
Salik, Anjail S, hlth & sr svcs mgr 1, $51,538
Salmon, Angela M, adlt prot & cmty wkr II, $33,744
Salter, Joseph T, adlt prot & cmty supv, $40,380
Salyer, Krista A, sr ofc spt asst (keybrd), $27,948
Salzwedel, Beverly A, sr ofc spt asst (keybrd), $28,452
Samson, Barbara J, env pub hlth spec IV, $41,940
Sanders, Euliana, adlt prot & cmty wkr II, $33,744
Sanders, James M, adlt prot & cmty wkr II, $33,744
Sanders, Kathy, adlt prot & cmty wkr II, $33,744
Sanders, Melinda D, hlth & sr svcs mgr 3, $78,840
Sanders, Theresa A, adlt prot & cmty wkr II, $33,744
Sapp, Kathryn, hlth & sr svcs mgr 2, $64,200
Sardis, Karen A, adlt prot & cmty wkr II, $33,744
Sartain, Terena L, sr ofc spt asst (keybrd), $25,824
Sassi, Barbara J, environ spec III, $46,932
Sauriol, Stacy G, sr ofc spt asst (keybrd), $25,824
Sayers, Amanda D, exec I, $30,984
Sayles, Kathy G, sr ofc spt asst (keybrd), $25,824
Saylor, Jan R, adlt prot & cmty wkr II, $33,744
Schaben, Andrea M, adlt prot & cmty wkr II, $33,744
Schaben, Angela D, sr auditor, $43,488
Schaefer, Kellie D, fac adv nurse II, $46,956
Schafer, Brandy A, pub hlth lab scientist, $37,548
Schafer, Brian E, proj spec, $25.00/hr
Schaffer, Alan J, lab mgr b2, $57,735
Schanbacher, Janice K, admin ofc spt asst, $28,104
Schaperclaus, Dawn M, account clerk II, $25,824
Scherer, Nancy A, hlth & sr svcs mgr 1, $57,759
Scheulen, Diann C, proj spec, $25.00/hr
Schillers, Randy W, lab mgr b2, $57,735
Schilligo, Linda, proj spec, $19.04/hr
Schlater, Sybil R, mgmt analysis spec II, $44,304
Schlemmer, Julie N, long-term care spec, $35,568
Schlesselman, Deana L, adlt prot & cmty supv, $41,172
Schmidt, Valerie N, hlth prog rep II, $39,624
Schmitz, Dennis D, sr pub hlth lab scintst, $47,892
Schmutzler, Ross A, assoc pub hlth lab scintst, $31,512
Schneider, Kaye L, adlt prot & cmty wkr II, $38,232
Schneider, Todd A, environ spec III, $43,488
Schnieders, Craig G, fiscal & administrative mgr b1, $55,411
Schnieders, Melanie A, sr ofc spt asst (keybrd), $25,824
Schondelmeyer, Rio S, assoc pub hlth lab scientst, $32,628
Schootman, Mario, proj spec, $50.00/hr
Schott, Philip A, pub hlth lab scientist, $37,548
Schramm, Wayne F, proj spec, $26.00/hr
Schremp, Krista E, fac surv II, $44,304
Schroer, Kristi A, proj spec, $14.85/hr
Schrum, Tonya R, adlt prot & cmty supv, $39,624
Schubert, Kimberly S, hlth prog rep II, $17,472
Schuchardt, Sheri L, adlt prot & cmty wkr II, $33,744
Schultz, Kristina L, hlth prog rep III, $44,304
Schultz, Michael G, proj spec, $25.00/hr
Schuman, Leslie A, sr ofc spt asst (keybrd), $25,032
Schwandtner, Waunita J, hlth & sr svcs mgr 2, $64,200
Schwartz, Kristi L, research analyst III, $41,172

Schwartze, Kayla J, ofc spt asst (keybrd), $23,160
Schweer, Gina M, fac adv nurse II, $60,036
Schweitzer, Cheryl A, admin ofc spt asst, $28,536
Scott, Jennifer, fac surv II, $41,940
Scott, Lakeasha Y, adlt prot & cmty wkr II, $33,744
Scott, Nancy L, exec I, $30,984
Seaman, Reantha K, pub hlth nurse, $50,052
Seamon, Jayne J, fac surv III, $51,096
Seaver, Melissa, hlth prog rep III, $41,940
Sebastian, Leslie A, hlth prog rep I, $31,512
Seboldt, Bryon J, fac surv II, $41,940
Secrest, Barbara J, fac insp, $32,628
Seehusen, Jason R, hlth prog rep I, $30,984
Sehr, Veronica K, adlt prot & cmty wkr I, $29,976
Seifert, Leslie P, hlth prog rep III, $42,708
Selkie, Elena M, adlt prot & cmty wkr II, $33,744
Semkiw, Elizabeth S, environ spec III, $46,932
Sergent, Sarah M, hlth & sr svcs mgr 2, $65,298
Serra, Jeanne M, div dir, $89,676
Servey, Amber D, aging prog spec II, $40,380
Seyfert, Valarie A, pub hlth sr nurse, $60,036
Shannon, Patrick R, lab mgr b2, $61,343
Sharr, Sarah M, sr pub hlth lab scintst, $41,940
Shell, Ray M, research mgr b1, $51,062
Shellenberger, Melissa A, pub hlth nurse, $47,904
Shelton, Donna J, sr ofc spt asst (keybrd), $25,824
Shelton, Kellie G, adlt prot & cmty wkr II, $33,744
Sheridan, Helen A, adlt prot & cmty wkr II, $32,628
Sherman, Christina L, adlt prot & cmty supv, $40,380
Shields, Linda L, pub hlth nurse, $52,032
Short, Brenda D, sr ofc spt asst (keybrd), $27,504
Shortal, Amanda J, exec II, $36,204
Shoultz, Angela R, fac surv II, $41,940
Siebert, Deborah A, hlth prog rep II, $35,568
Siegel, Karen L, adlt prot & cmty supv, $41,172
Siler, Kristi D, adlt prot & cmty supv, $40,380
Silman, Karen, long-term care spec, $39,624
Silva, Christine L, environ sup, $54,288
Silvey, Lindsey, adlt prot & cmty wkr II, $33,744
Simmons, Patricia L, hlth & sr svcs mgr 1, $58,168
Simms-homan, Sherri G, pub hlth epidemiologist, $74,304
Simpson, Mandy K, adlt prot & cmty wkr II, $33,744
Sims, Brenda L, fac adv nurse II, $46,956
Sims, Brenda S, ofc spt asst (keybrd), $23,160
Sims, Ronda C, hlth & sr svcs mgr 1, $51,538
Sindle, Amber M, adlt prot & cmty wkr II, $33,744
Singer, Stacey L, accounting spec III, $41,172
Sinn, Shannon M, assoc pub hlth lab scientst, $32,628
Sipakati, Rose N, nutritionist III, $44,304
Sire, Thomas M, adlt prot & cmty wkr II, $32,628
Sisson, Amy E, sr ofc spt asst (keybrd), $25,824
Skaggs, Teresa A, hlth prog rep II, $34,944
Skipper, Thomas C, fac surv II, $41,940
Sloan, Jacqueline K, admin ofc spt asst, $32,628
Sluyter, Kathy A, fac adv nurse III, $53,124
Small, Chiquita Y, hlth prog rep II, $34,944
Smith, Amber N, pub hlth lab scientist, $37,548
Smith, Christine E, prog coord dmh docs, $54,288
Smith, Christine M, admin ofc spt asst, $29,496
Smith, Debi R, sr ofc spt asst (keybrd), $25,032
Smith, Dona L, sr ofc spt asst (keybrd), $25,824
Smith, Glenna A, adlt prot & cmty wkr II, $37,548
Smith, Hollie, hlth prog rep II, $36,888
Smith, Laura L, fac adv nurse III, $53,124
Smith, Lori A, sr ofc spt asst (keybrd), $25,824
Smith, Martha J, pub hlth consult nurse, $62,508
Smith, Matthew C, adlt prot & cmty wkr II, $33,744
Smith, Melissa J, child care fac spec III, $43,488
Smith, Miss Toni S, adlt prot & cmty wkr II, $34,944
Smith, Monica N, hlth prog rep II, $36,204
Smith, Nancy, child care fac spec II, $36,204
Smith, Rhonda H, pub hlth nurse, $50,052
Smith, Shawn N, adlt prot & cmty wkr II, $33,744
Smith, Teresa L, admin ofc spt asst, $31,512
Smith, Traci R, adlt prot & cmty wkr II, $33,744
Sneller, Patricia A, hlth prog rep III, $39,624
Snodgrass, Penny S, child care fac spec I, $30,984
Snook, Barbara A, pub hlth nurse, $52,032
Snyder, Pamela A, sr ofc spt asst (keybrd), $25,824
Snyder, Susan M, adlt prot & cmty wkr II, $34,944
Solomon, Jill R, child care fac spec II, $34,944
Solomon, Wendy P, adlt prot & cmty wkr II, $32,628
Sommerhauser, Lisa E, fac adv nurse II, $53,124

Spaulding, Stephanie R, sr ofc spt asst (keybrd), $25,824
Spaw, Barbara G, pub hlth sr nurse, $56,448
Spears, Austin, adlt prot & cmty wkr II, $33,744
Speed, Dylan E, storekeeper I, $25,824
Spencer, Helen S, adlt prot & cmty supv, $41,172
Spencer, Stacey M, sr ofc spt asst (keybrd), $27,084
Spencer, Teresa D, fac adv nurse III, $51,072
Spencer, William J, long-term care spec, $39,624
Spencer, William L, adlt prot & cmty wkr II, $33,744
Spohn, Mary L, fac adv nurse II, $53,124
Srikanta, Hemalatha, aging prog spec II, $42,708
Stafford, Jason C, adlt prot & cmty wkr II, $33,744
Stafford, Teresa A, sr ofc spt asst (keybrd), $25,824
Staley, Wanda R, adlt prot & cmty supv, $40,380
Stancil, Michael G, planner III, $49,128
Stansbury, Angel D, sr ofc spt asst (keybrd), $25,032
Starns, Sandra K, sr ofc spt asst (keybrd), $25,824
Starr, Mary, hlth & sr svcs mgr 1, $53,449
Starr, Mary E, proj spec, $25.78/hr
Stayton, Lauren L, fac adv nurse III, $60,036
Steeby, Ashley E, pub hlth lab scientist, $37,548
Steele, Tamara D, adlt prot & cmty wkr II, $33,744
Stegall, Kimberlyn S, adlt prot & cmty wkr II, $34,356
Stephenson, Zana A, hlth prog rep III, $39,624
Stevens, Deborah L, fac adv nurse II, $46,956
Steward, Toni K, fac adv nurse III, $52,032
Stewart, Chris A, adlt prot & cmty wkr II, $36,888
Stewart, Nancy L, adlt prot & cmty wkr II, $33,744
Stieferman, Beth A, pub hlth consult nurse, $57,612
Stieferman, Kathleen A, exec II, $36,204
Stiles, Jana M, long-term care spec, $36,204
Stith, Sandra, long-term care spec, $42,708
Stock, Terri L, adlt prot & cmty wkr II, $34,944
Stockman, Sally K, admin ofc spt asst, $28,536
Stokes, Sharon K, sr ofc spt asst (keybrd), $27,084
Stone, Rebekah L, hlth facilities nrsng cnslt, $53,124
Stout, Annette A, accounting spec II, $40,380
Stoverink, Jessica D, adlt prot & cmty wkr II, $33,744
Strange, Linda L, proj spec, $14.00/hr
Stratman, Terry, storekeeper II, $28,536
Strauss, Tonya L, fac adv nurse II, $46,956
Strickland, Vicki A, nutrition spec, $55,416
Strifler, Vivian E, hlth facilities nrsng cnslt, $62,508
Strope, Dana S, lab mgr b2, $61,343
Strubinger, Edwyn T, adlt prot & cmty wkr II, $33,744
Stuart, Victoria A, sr ofc spt asst (keybrd), $25,032
Studebaker, Glenn W, prog coord dmh dohss, $49,128
Sturma, Connalee, procurement ofcr I, $40,380
Sturtz, Wanda D, hlth prog rep II, $37,548
Stutman, Jeremiah L, adlt prot & cmty wkr II, $33,744
Sullentrup, Gwendolyn J, adlt prot & cmty wkr II, $33,744
Sullivan, Catherine R, hlth & sr svcs mgr 2, $66,038
Sullivan, Craig A, env pub hlth spec IV, $43,488
Sullivan, Monica M, adlt prot & cmty wkr II, $36,888
Summers, Rita P, proj spec, $25.00/hr
Summers, Verla J, hlth prog rep III, $43,488
Sutherland, Elizabeth J, hlth facilities nrsng cnslt, $60,036
Sutterer, Cheryl L, adlt prot & cmty wkr II, $38,232
Sutterer, Karen S, hlth facilities cnslt, $47,892
Swan, Dana E, adlt prot & cmty wkr II, $33,744
Swartwood, Maurita J, sr ofc spt asst (keybrd), $28,908
Sweaney, April D, pub hlth nurse, $47,904
Sweet, Vicki S, adlt prot & cmty wkr II, $33,744
Sweezer, Melinda A, investigator III, $40,380
Swoger, Tina M, adlt prot & cmty supv, $40,380
Taber, Crystal D, adlt prot & cmty wkr I, $30,984
Tagami, Takako, nutrition spec, $50,040
Talbert, Selma L, adlt prot & cmty wkr II, $33,744
Talbot, Candice S, hlth & sr svcs mgr 2, $56,516
Talken, Sharon A, sr ofc spt asst (keybrd), $27,084
Talley, Crystal G, epidemiology spec, $40,380
Tappel, Larraine P, administrative analyst II, $41,172
Taube, Jennifer M, hlth & sr svcs mgr 1, $44,297
Taylor, Johnny J, accounting spec II, $40,380
Taylor, Jonea L, proj spec, $14.00/hr
Taylor, Judy C, admin ofc spt asst, $28,536
Taylor, Wanda I, child care fac spec II, $40,380
Temmen, Lee, hlth & sr svcs mgr 1, $54,039
Terrill, Melissa D, adlt prot & cmty wkr II, $33,744
Tesreau, Kerri A, dpty div dir, $84,858
Theroff, Angela M, fac surv III, $47,892
Thoenen, Betty A, account clerk II, $25,824
Thomas, Angela D, adlt prot & cmty wkr II, $33,180

Thomas, Blake C, fac surv III, $54,288
Thomas, Karen S, adlt prot & cmty wkr II, $36,204
Thomas, Kathie J, registered nurse mgr b1, $65,359
Thomas, Larry J, vid spec, $42,708
Thomas, Shawnta D, adlt prot & cmty wkr II, $33,744
Thomas, Susan E, hlth & sr svcs mgr 1, $62,660
Thomas-Randall, Detra Y, ofc servs asst, $38,232
Thompson, Barbara L, adlt prot & cmty wkr II, $36,888
Thompson, Carla K, fac adv nurse III, $53,124
Thompson, Diane E, admin ofc spt asst, $30,984
Thompson, Elizabeth E, info spt coor, $32,628
Thompson, Elizabeth J, hlth & sr svcs mgr 1, $54,286
Thompson, Frances L, sr pub hlth lab scintst, $41,940
Thompson, Laura R, hlth prog rep II, $34,944
Thompson, Rebecca A, hlth prog rep II, $34,944
Thornhill, Judith A, fac adv nurse II, $46,956
Thorp, Christine E, adlt prot & cmty wkr II, $33,744
Thurmond, Marqus J, adlt prot & cmty supv, $40,380
Thurston, Lourdes A, accounting spec III, $46,068
Tidwell, Debra J, nutritionist III, $44,304
Tighe, Patricia, research analyst III, $41,940
Tillison, Deanna S, acct III, $47,892
Tillison, Lisa A, adlt prot & cmty wkr II, $33,744
Tilly, Alice M, sr ofc spt asst (keybrd), $25,824
Timmons, Deborah L, adlt prot & cmty wkr II, $38,232
Todd, Brenda A, fac adv nurse II, $45,204
Todd, Edith E, env pub hlth spec IV, $44,304
Toebben, Clayton M, sr ofc spt asst (keybrd), $26,232
Toebben, Tanya M, hlth prog rep II, $34,944
Tomson, Heather R, adlt prot & cmty wkr II, $33,744
Tonarely, Susan A, aging prog spec I, $36,204
Tordoff, Yvonne C, account clerk II, $25,824
Townsend, Martha A, fac insp, $32,628
Troxel, Dana L, nutritionist III, $44,304
Truesdale, Michelle E, child care fac spec II, $36,204
Trussell, Michelle R, child care fac spec II, $39,624
Tucker, Raymond P, ofc spt asst (clerical), $24,264
Tumbleson, Teresa C, adlt prot & cmty supv, $45,156
Turabelidze, George, med cnslt, $124,656
Turner, Alyce G, hlth educator II, $43,488
Turney, Janelle, adlt prot & cmty wkr II, $34,356
Tuschhoff, Ronda C, child care fac spec II, $40,380
Tuttle, Ruth E, fac surv III, $47,892
Tuua, Roy P, lab mgr b2, $57,735
Tuua, Tiffany A, hlth prog rep III, $39,624
Tyler, Jeneva J, adlt prot & cmty wkr II, $34,944
Tyler, Justin D, adlt prot & cmty wkr II, $33,744
Tyler, Kamilah R, adlt prot & cmty wkr II, $33,744
Tyler, Margaret R, proj spec, $23.12/hr
Ulstad, Melinda M, aging prog spec II, $41,940
Umana, Uyama A, adlt prot & cmty wkr II, $33,744
Utter, Teresa A, hlth prog rep III, $40,380
Van Horn, Ann N, fac adv nurse II, $53,124
Van Loo, Tara J, aging prog spec II, $40,380
Van Tuinen, Mark, proj spec, $26.00/hr
Vandyne, Mary B, special asst prof, $71,436
Vandyne, Melissa L, planner III, $53,208
Vaughan, Denise H, adlt prot & cmty wkr II, $33,744
Veasman, Dianne R, pub hlth lab scientist, $32,931
Veit, Shirley A, sr ofc spt asst (keybrd), $27,084
Veltrop, Lisa M, hlth prog rep II, $34,944
Venerable, Cassandra, adlt prot & cmty wkr II, $33,744
Veo, Parrie V, hlth facilities nrsng cnslt, $53,124
Vermette, Lacey D, sr pub hlth lab scintst, $40,380
Verslues, Amy M, pub hlth lab scientist, $37,548
Verslues, Angela N, fac adv nurse II, $46,956
Vest, Steven E, fac surv II, $43,488
Viele, Constance S, adlt prot & cmty wkr II, $33,744
Vieth, Patricia L, pub hlth sr nurse, $47,904
Vietmeier, Cynthia M, adlt prot & cmty wkr II, $33,744
Villalobos, Darlene R, adlt prot & cmty wkr II, $33,744
Vincent, Christi L, hlth prog rep III, $40,380
Volner, Cheri J, account clerk II, $29,412
Voss, Brittany D, accounting spec II, $38,928
Voss, Karla L, hlth educator III, $40,380
Wade, Cynthia L, adlt prot & cmty wkr II, $33,744
Wade, Randall L, fac adv nurse II, $46,956
Wagner, Elana D, fac surv II, $43,488
Walkenhorst, Terry L, hlth & sr svcs mgr 2, $62,664
Walker, Janett R, procurement ofcr I, $37,548
Wallace, Shalinda E, child care fac spec II, $36,204
Walley, Nancy K, fac adv nurse II, $46,956
Walton, Randy J, prog coord dmh dohss, $56,520

Walusiku-Todd, Mulima, fiscal & admin mgr b1, $58,872
Wambuguh, Dennis, environ sup, $56,520
Wambuguh, Loise N, research analyst III, $41,940
Wankum, Cherie C, fac adv nurse II, $46,956
Ward, Craig B, research mgr b2, $66,731
Ward, D'Anne L, nutritionist III, $42,708
Ward, Janet, hlth prog rep I, $30,984
Ward, Marie E, adlt prot & cmty wkr II, $38,232
Warren, Victoria L, prog coord dmh dohss, $58,908
Washington, Stephanie L, hlth prog rep III, $39,624
Waters, Mary K, fac adv nurse II, $48,780
Watkins, Gordon S, epidemiology spec, $44,304
Watkins, Patricia M, legal counsel, $58,584
Watson, Dean A, special asst prof, $56,758
Watson, Debra A, fac adv nurse II, $53,124
Watson, Robert W, fac surv II, $46,068
Waweru, Luke M, adlt prot & cmty wkr II, $33,744
Weaver, Randy G, adlt prot & cmty supv, $46,068
Weaver, Rebecca R, adlt prot & cmty wkr II, $33,744
Webb, Grace A, sr ofc spt asst (keybrd), $28,908
Webb, Judith A, hlth prog rep II, $35,568
Weddle, Carol, adlt prot & cmty supv, $41,172
Wehmeyer, Kimberly S, hlth prog rep II, $34,944
Wehrle, Mary S, proj spec, $35.00/hr
Welch, Kelly A, sr ofc spt asst (keybrd), $25,824
Wells, Jennafer M, adlt prot & cmty wkr II, $33,744
Wells, Samantha A, account clerk II, $25,032
Wells, Stephanie D, adlt prot & cmty wkr II, $35,568
Welschmeyer, Paige A, pub hlth lab scientist, $37,548
Welty, Barbara R, hlth prog rep II, $37,548
Wendel, Angela C, adlt prot & cmty wkr II, $33,744
Wenzel, Jeffrey A, sr epidemiology spec, $46,068
Werdehausen, Breanna E, hlth prog rep I, $31,512
Werner, Barbara J, adlt prot & cmty wkr II, $39,624
Werth-Morgan, Helga, adlt prot & cmty supv, $46,068
West, Daniel B, fac surv II, $46,068
West, Jamie L, adlt prot & cmty supv, $40,380
West, Janice L, fac insp, $32,628
West, Julie A, adlt prot & cmty wkr II, $33,744
Whipple, Noah R, info spt coor, $29,004
White, Janie M, fac adv nurse II, $46,956
White, Leah R, child care fac spec III, $41,940
White, Susan B, hlth & sr svcs mgr 2, $65,298
Whitmar, William W, lab mgr b3, $80,155
Whitson, Leslie A, sr epidemiology spec, $46,068
Whitson, Nedra K, fac surv III, $56,520
Whittenberg, Summer N, adlt prot & cmty wkr II, $33,744
Whittington, Ellen M, sr ofc spt asst (keybrd), $26,232
Wiebe, Debra J, long-term care spec, $37,548
Wieberg, Alicia M, hlth prog rep I, $30,420
Wieberg, Sandra A, proj spec, $14.10/hr
Wiebers, Katelyn A, adlt prot & cmty wkr II, $33,744
Wiggs, Imogene, hlth prog rep III, $41,940
Wilbers, Barbara A, hlth prog rep I, $39,624
Wilbers, Patricia A, accounting spec III, $55,416
Wilde, Janice T, prog coord dmh dohss, $53,208
Wilde, Megan C, registered nurse, $44,904
Wildhaber, Jonathan H, typist, $10.83/hr
Wiley, Scott M, fac surv III, $46,068
Wilfong, Christy G, sr ofc spt asst (keybrd), $27,948
Wilkerson, Linda L, hlth prog rep II, $43,488
Wille, Jane E, sr ofc spt asst (keybrd), $25,824
Williams, Amanda E, sr ofc spt asst (keybrd), $25,032
Williams, Brandi N, adlt prot & cmty wkr II, $33,744
Williams, Bruce, adlt prot & cmty wkr II, $33,744
Williams, Carrie A, child care fac spec II, $36,204
Williams, Debra L, long-term care spec, $37,548
Williams, Gwenda D, adlt prot & cmty wkr II, $33,744
Williams, Jeanne N, ofc spt asst (keybrd), $22,536
Williams, Jeffery W, adlt prot & cmty wkr II, $36,888
Williams, Jessica A, fac adv nurse II, $45,204
Williams, Joel D, pub hlth lab scintst, $41,940
Williams, Michelle A, adlt prot & cmty wkr II, $33,744
Williams, Pamela F, sr ofc spt asst (keybrd), $26,652
Williams, Penny L, prog coord dmh dohss, $55,416
Williams, Sheri A, pub hlth sr nurse, $60,036
Williams-Fry, Lacey M, adlt prot & cmty wkr II, $33,744
Williamson, Margie J, adlt prot & cmty wkr II, $33,744
Williamson, Mary A, sr ofc spt asst (keybrd), $25,824

Williamson, Michelle D, hlth & sr svcs mgr 3, $77,180
Willis, Rosie C, account clerk II, $27,948
Wilson, Brandy L, adlt prot & cmty wkr II, $34,944
Wilson, Brenda J, adlt prot & cmty wkr II, $35,568
Wilson, Janet S, hlth & sr svcs mgr 2, $63,716
Wilson, Jeremy A, pub hlth lab scientist, $38,928
Wilson, Katherine S, adlt prot & cmty supv, $45,156
Wilson, Marcia D, prog coord dmh dohss, $55,416
Wilson, Melessa A, hlth prog rep I, $33,744
Wilson, Michelle D, adlt prot & cmty wkr II, $36,204
Wilson, Stephanie M, fac insp, $32,628
Wimbley, Ryan P, adlt prot & cmty wkr II, $33,744
Winchester, Sheila C, fac surv III, $46,932
Winder, Diana R, admin ofc spt asst, $29,976
Winemiller, Teresa A, child care fac spec II, $40,380
Winford, Cindy L, sr ofc spt asst (keybrd), $25,824
Winkler, Ann L, env pub hlth spec V, $50,040
Winslow, Aaron L, env pub hlth spec V, $56,520
Winters, Diane, adlt prot & cmty supv, $40,380
Withrow, Holly L, research analyst II, $44,304
Witte, Jacquelyn S, fac adv nurse II, $46,956
Woemmel, Patricia K, acct I, $30,984
Wolfe, Kathryn J, fac surv III, $52,092
Wolfe, Ladonna G, hlth facilities cnslt, $54,288
Wolff, Kathleen A, fac insp, $42,708
Wong, Lana I, hlth prog rep I, $33,180
Wood, Catherine A, hlth prog rep II, $34,944
Wood, Kimberly R, legal counsel, $41,935
Wood, Nicole D, hlth & sr svcs mgr 1, $51,538
Wood, Roselyn M, admin ofc spt asst, $37,548
Wood, Stacey J, hlth prog rep III, $40,380
Wood, Venice P, prog coord dmh dohss, $57,744
Woods, Destini M, sr ofc spt asst (keybrd), $25,824
Woodsmall, Paula A, proj spec, $14.41/hr
Woodward, Terri L, hlth & sr svcs mgr 2, $64,196
Worthington, Karen, adlt prot & cmty wkr II, $38,928
Wortmann, Teresa A, pub hlth sr nurse, $50,052
Wrather, Kimberly A, fac adv nurse II, $46,956
Wright, Mark S, nutritionist III, $47,892
Wright, Randall G, investigator II, $38,232
Wu, Fei, sr epidemiology spec, $52,092
Yates, Karen F, sr epidemiology spec, $47,892
Yeager, Amanda B, env pub hlth spec V, $48,156
Yeager, Kathryn L, adlt prot & cmty wkr II, $35,568
Yeager, Pamela M, hlth facilities nrsng cnslt, $55,320
Young, Sarah R, nutritionist III, $43,488
Young, Treaka N, aging prog spec II, $41,940
Yun, Shumei, pub hlth epidemiologist, $74,304
Zacek Smith, Daniel P, adlt prot & cmty wkr II, $33,744
Zehaie, Mehari, exec I, $36,204
Zeigenbein, Jill E, child care fac spec II, $37,548
Zeilman, Michelle A, hlth & sr svcs mgr 2, $65,298
Zoellner, Jeffrey, fiscal & administrative mgr b2, $74,163
Zungura, Daniel, adlt prot & cmty wkr II, $33,744

Department of Higher Education

3515 Amazonas, Jefferson City 65109

Russell, David R, commissioner, $172,205
Anderson, Erik J, Research associate III, $41,172
Barner, Devon M, office support assistant, $24,612
Beck, Cheryl L, coordinator II, $38,928
Bestgen, Connie L, program spec, $36,888
Blecha, Carol A, research associate IV, $48,156
Branch, Kerry R, senior associate, $52,092
Burnette, Debra J, assistant commissioner, $71,100
Buschjost, Vicky L, admin asst, $41,165
Cardwell, Leanne, assistant commissioner, $79,285
Clemons, Jennifer L, executive assistant, $40,905
Coleman, Elizabeth A, assistant commissioner, $62,664
Day, Daniel N, senior associate, $52,092
Duren, Jessica E, public information specialist II, $38,928
Erbschloe, Patricia D, program specialist, $33,180
Falter, Kathleen F, office support assistant, $30,385
Gilliland, Norma J, coordinator II, $37,548
Hall, Samantha, research associate I, $36,888
Haller, Amy, program specialist, $34,944

Hamburg-Butterfield, Dory J, research associate II, $37,548
Hendrix, Lesley E, public information coord, $41,940
Howe, Kim L, client service rep II, $41,940
Kaiser, Sheila, compliance reviewer II, $41,172
Karle, Ashley N, coordinator I, $37,548
Kintzel, Jeremy J, assistant commissioner, $65,364
Kixmiller, Dana L, program specialist, $33,180
Knee, Jeremy D, general counsel, $77,000
Landrum, Marilyn G, student assistant associate, $41,172
Maxwell, Nora, senior associate, $52,092
McLeod, Alyssa M, program specialist, $33,180
Meyer, Julie B, director, $66,720
Monhollon, Rusty L, assistant commissioner, $79,285
Plemons, Jennifer E, research associate II, $37,548
Potter, Kathryn S, coordinator I, $38,928
Powell, Robert E, senior associate, $52,092
Pritchett, Angelette L, research associate III, $43,488
Randall, Susan M, accounting specialist II, $40,068
Reed, Kelli, account clerk II, $43,488
Reed, Keyna R, student assistant associate, $29,412
Robertson, Marla B, senior associate, $57,744
Schedler, Sarah M, program specialist, $34,356
Schwartz, Jessica L, executive I, $32,052
Sees, Dawn D, public info specialist II, $41,172
Schockley, Ida M, snr office support asst, $27,948
Slote, Kimberly D, policy analyst, $43,488
Tews, Diann V, office support assistant, $24,612
Thomas, Penny J, program specialist, $33,180
Vail, Jaron D, research associate I, $34,356
Valentine, Elizabeth, senior associate, $52,092
Vedenhaupt, Laura, L, senior associate, $50,040
Wade, Leroy, B, deputy commissioner, $92,908
Werner, Amy, M, research associate I, $35,568
Westerwald, Greta, L, program specialist, $29,976
Wilson, Lisa, M, public info coordinator, $41,940
Winter, Leslie, A, admin asst, $30,420
Wolken, Paula, J, budget analyst III, $53,208

University of Missouri

Columbia 65211

Wolfe, Timothy Michael, president, $459,000
Aarns, Christian D, police officer, $17.50/hr
Aaron, William W III, grounds keeper, $12.70/hr
Aaron, William Walter Jr, mech, small engine, $17.68/hr
Aaron, Deena Kathleen, office support assistant IV, $15.25/hr
Aasen, Caitlin Marina, office support assistant II, $12.00/hr
Abadir, Danna Kay, coor, reimbursement, $44,426
Abadir, Erin Rochelle, research/lab technician sr, $15.00/hr
Abagiu, Catalin Ion, instructor, adjunct, $27,000
Abayan, Nilvie O, sterile processing tech, $17.08/hr
Abbett, Dylan Michael, emrg med techn, $11.61/hr
Abbett, Julie Ann, resp therapist reg, $30.00/hr
Abbott, Monte L Jr, prof, ast adjunct, $9,000
Abbott, Brooklyn Jean, clerk, diet, $9.95/hr
Abbott, Carmen Casanova, prof, clincl, $67,254
Abbott, Carmen Casanova, physical therapist, $39.20/hr
Abbott, Cristopher Matthew, temporary technical, $16.00/hr
Abbott, Daniel R, lecturer, $42,779
Abbott, Elizabeth Ames, business support specialist sr, $17.48/hr
Abbott, Ellen Elizabeth, business support specialist II, $21.40/hr
Abbott, Gary Bernard, prof, ast, $46,900
Abbott, Gary L, research engineering tech II, $25.88/hr
Abbott, Gregory William, event assistant I, $7.55/hr
Abbott, Jeanne Martha, prof, asoc profl practice, $66,642
Abbott, Joyce E, executive assistant, $19.00/hr
Abbott, Kati Marie, academic advisor, $36,000
Abbott, Linda, coor, care, $69,906
Abdallah, Mouin S, resident physician-7th yr, $63,475
Abdel Karim, Abdul Rahman Riyad, res physician-4th yr, $54,425
Abdel-Khalik, Jasmine C, prof, asoc, $100,000
Abdelhadi, Adam Tawfik, mental health tech, $13.72/hr
Abdeljalil, Asem, adjunct, $15,000
Abdelrazeq, Abdallah, resident physician-1st yr, $49,025
Abdimalik, Muhidin Idris Bana, tutor, $9.00/hr
Abdirahman, Ahmed Osman, temporary clerical, $10.50/hr
Abdou Ali, Mohamed Ali Mahmoud, fellow, post doctoral, $37,200

Abdul Hafidh, Jamal, prof, ast adjunct, $19,200
Abel, Jane Fowlkes, pharmacist III, $60.00/hr
Abell, Kristen L, strat comm associate II, $46,125
Abella, Romualdo L, dental equip spclst, $24.13/hr
Abeln, Timothy R, prof, ast teach, $38,000
Abels, Arnold Vernon, dir II student support svcs, $92,808
Aberbach, Ian M, professor, $103,159
Abercrombie, Karen C, custodian, $12.94/hr
Abernathy, James L Jr, communications coord sr, $23.85/hr
Abernathy, Lloyd R, instructor, adjunct, $3,885
Abernathy, Nadine C, business support specialist II, $23.94/hr
Abernathy, Steven P, research/lab technician sr, $18.85/hr
Abioye, Alechia Danielle, instructor, adjunct, $4,200
Ablabutyan, Lilit, resident physician-3rd yr, $52,470
Abner, Marita, prof, ast teach, $29,421
Abraham, Ashley, resident physician-3rd yr, $52,470
Abraham, Meredith Frances, clerk, diet, $9.50/hr
Abrams, Douglas E, prof, asoc, $150,188
Abreu, Eduardo Limongi Marques, prof, ast, $82,000
Abron, Laura Elizabeth, business ops associate sr, $46,512
Absheer, Michael S, research lab supervisor, $43,276
Abt, Byron Joseph, temporary technical, $10.00/hr
Abts, Patricia Joan, office support assistant III, $11.30/hr
Abu ghanimeh, Mouhanna, resident physician-1st yr, $49,025
Abu Omar, Mohannad Naheid I, resident physician-3rd yr, $52,470
Abuamr, Khalil Mohammad, resident physician-5th yr, $56,120
Abutu, Victor Ogwu, med coding spclst-certified, $18.23/hr
Acamovic, Milica, grader, $4,800
Acar, Levent, prof, asoc, $86,010
Accurso, Anthony J, press IV, $22.21/hr
Achtenberg, David, professor, $125,000
Achterberg, Steven C, research specialist sr, $55,115
Achuff, Elizabeth Colleen, program/project supprt coor I, $9,600
Ackerman, Justin A, asoc media producer, $12.37/hr
Ackerman, Sharon Ann, central regstry-data spclst, $19.40/hr
Ackert, Jayne Marie, supv nursing acute care, $37.63/hr
Acock, Linda, care team assoc-clinical, $13.33/hr
Acsay, Peter, prof, asoc teach, $57,170
Acsenvild, Alex, programmer analyst-entry, $52,530
Acton, Amanda Leigh, med office assistant, $12.57/hr
Acton, Angela Renae, business tech analyst-expert, $54,234
Acton, Becky Jean, business support specialist sr, $20.29/hr
Acton, Elise Ann, temporary clerical, $8.00/hr
Acton, Eric C, operations support tech sr, $18.73/hr
Acton, James D, prof, asoc clincl dept, $196,090
Acton, Jason Ray, bldg cntrl sys tech II, $22.49/hr
Acton, John E, mech trades spclst lead, $22.49/hr
Acton, Patricia L, mgr II business admin, $65,166
Acton, Richard Dale, event assistant I, $7.85/hr
Acton, Ronald B, bts carpenter, $21.71/hr
Acuff, Michael, prof, asoc clincl dept, $150,409
Adair, Zakiya Renicia, prof, ast, $64,303
Adam, Amy Elizabeth, academic advisor, $41,254
Adam, Balkozar S, prof, asoc clincl dept, $181,564
Adam, Cheryl L, office support assistant IV, $16.34/hr
Adams, John D Jr, fellow, post doc clncl-yr3, $60,415
Adams Remson, Patrice M, dental assistant II, $15.02/hr
Adams Sr, Stephen L Sr, mts/hvac, $24.13/hr
Adams-Kloepfer, Mercedes Christine, care team assoc-clinical, $11.10/hr
Adams-Salter, Tina Marie, sys privacy offcr, $155,250
Adams-Tisdale, Kaye Denise, student support spec sr, $17.53/hr
Adams, Cassandra Denise, strat comm associate I, $43,000
Adams, Catherine Comely, dir II advancement, $69,274
Adams, Christina Fern, fin and acctg manager, $47,880
Adams, Curt D, mts/hvac, $21.05/hr
Adams, Frieda F, office support assistant III, $15.98/hr
Adams, Guy B, prgm director, $45,008
Adams, Ida C, event assistant I, $7.50/hr
Adams, Jason Christopher, instructor, adjunct, $3,000
Adams, Johanna R, prof, ast extns, $69,800
Adams, John E, prof, curator teach, $92,555
Adams, John V, retail sales manager, $54,108
Adams, Jonathan F, internet administrator-expert, $22.73/hr
Adams, Kimberly H, patient svc rep, $12.76/hr
Adams, Lucinda Jane, mgr research activities, $49,600
Adams, Mark T, custodian, $11.00/hr
Adams, Mary Anna, office support assistant IV, $15.00/hr
Adams, Mary Jo, ast dir advancement, $53,186

Adams, Michael, program/project supprt coor I, $40,000
Adams, Patricia Leigh, office support assistant IV, $14.24/hr
Adams, Penny Lou, mgr, medical educ, $56,917
Adams, Ryan Archer, stage services assistant sr, $16.00/hr
Adams, Ryan D, bts carpenter, $21.71/hr
Adams, Sharon, dental hygienist, $34.34/hr
Adams, Shayna Ann, office support assistant III, $11.67/hr
Adams, Stephanie Jo, service rep III, $14.08/hr
Adams, Steven Lee, strat comm associate II, $50,980
Adams, Tamekquia Lapree, event assistant I, $7.50/hr
Adams, Tammy Lynn, lecturer, $35,000
Adams, Teresa Ann, business support specialist II, $19.76/hr
Addison, Christopher Jacob Ray, food svc wrkr I, $9.60/hr
Adegoke, Jimmy Omoniyi, prof, asoc, $72,281
Adejo, Kelechi Ihunanya, food svc wrkr I, $9.60/hr
Adekpedjou, Akim Mouhamadou, prof, asoc, $34,781
Adelman, Mason Alexander, emrg med techn, $11.61/hr
Adelstein, Edward H, prof, asoc, $124,380
Adeola, Oluwaseun Gbolabo, resident physician-2nd yr, $52,007
Aderton, Andrea Hope, instructor, clincl, $49,939
Adicks, John Calvin II, office support assistant IV, $15.27/hr
Adjekughele, Ajemina, care team assoc-clinical, $12.15/hr
Adkins, Barbara A, resrch ast, $45,000
Adkins, DeeAnna K, strat comm associate sr, $67,926
Adkins, Denice C, prof, asoc, $76,802
Adkins, Eric C, research specialist I, $33,229
Adkins, Grant, support systems admin-entry, $51,000
Adkins, James Ryan, student support specialist I, $13.75/hr
Adkins, Marsha, coor, service, $22.11/hr
Adkins, Rita E, asoc dir program/project ops, $59,057
Adkisson, Cary D, nurse, staff II, $20.54/hr
Adkisson, Wendy Leaann, nurse, licensed prac, $16.29/hr
Adl Tabatabaei, Negar, mentor, $8.00/hr
Adler, Kalie Elizabeth, resident physician-3rd yr, $52,470
Affalter, Jonathan David, mgr student support svcs, $40,000
Agai, Milly Kavoki, office support assistant IV, $15.68/hr
Agali, Priscilla Obianuju, instructor, clincl, $15,375
Agarwal, Ajay, prof, ast clincl dept, $250,000
Agarwal, Kirti, fellow, post doc clncl yr1, $60,415
Agca, Cansu, resrch scientist/academic, $45,000
Agca, Yuksel, prof, asoc, $120,265
Agee, Kenneth, food svc wrkr I, $11.29/hr
Aggarwal, Ajay, prof, ast clincl dept, $260,113
Aggarwal, Arpit, resident physician-5th yr, $58,083
Aggarwal, Kul B, prof, clinical dept, $40,695
Agha, Mohammad Tariq, prof, ast clincl dept, $150,000
Aghedo, Naomi Mae, nurse, licensed prac sr, $20.90/hr
Agnew, Candace A, exec ast to the gen offcr, $81,000
Agnew, Katharine Marie, student service coor II, $39,600
Agnew, Rhonda Lynn, office support assistant IV, $13.61/hr
Agrawal, Harsh, fellow, post doc clncl-yr2, $58,083
Aguilar Monteagudo, Miguel, mentor, $8.00/hr
Aguilar Ramos, Gerardo, prof, ast adjunct, $45,600
Aguilar-Parks, Anita Manuelita, office support asst IV, $15.20/hr
Aguilar, Francisco Xavier, prof, asoc, $99,879
Aguilar, Leslie Michelle, grader, $52
Ahad, Roomana, resident physician-2nd yr, $50,810
Ahlersmeyer, Alice F, nurse, staff II, $34.18/hr
Ahmad, Diana L, professor, $73,378
Ahmad, Khaldoun Ibrahim, instructor, adjunct, $27,000
Ahmad, Salman, prof, ast, $319,770
Ahmad, Zafar, physician ast, $93,811
Ahmed, Arif, prof, asoc, $82,425
Ahmed, Fadha, health physicist, $51,493
Ahmed, Khulood T, instructor, clincl, $102,000
Ahmed, Muhammad Farooq, fellow, post doctoral, $21.05/hr
Ahmed, Zaheer, resident physician-2nd yr, $50,810
Ahner, Allen Steven Jos, sftware supprt analyst-speclst, $42,301
Ahner, Carin Elizabeth, fellow, resrch, $45,432
Aholt-Gayler, Mandy L, service rep III, $12.24/hr
Aholt, Dana J, resrch ast, $55,000
Aholt, Justine Camille, nurse, staff II, $24.28/hr
Aholt, Michael, mgr csm operations, $60,618
Ahrens, Cheryl Sue, fin and acctg manager, $49,640
Ahrens, Kent J, programmer analyst-entry, $46,135
Ahrens, Mallory Elizabeth, serv line spclst, $67,810
Ahrens, Maria B, office support assistant IV, $19.00/hr
Ahsan, Humera, prof, asoc clincl dept, $250,000
Ailor, Melissa Anne, physical therapist, $73,088

Ailor, Susan Kay, prof, asoc clincl, $12,000
Ainley, Dennis James, model, $15.00/hr
Ainsworth, Elizabeth Grace, office support asst IV, $14.00/hr
Ainsworth, Jovita T, nurse, staff II rnwp, $34.18/hr
Airuehia, Patricia Amuche, pharmacist II, $106,746
Aistrope, Daniel Scott, prof, ast clincl, $96,000
Aites, Richard William, police officer, $17.50/hr
Aitken, Timothy R, powr plnt maint spclst III mec, $25.85/hr
Aitkens, Dayne Edward, grounds keeper, $12.12/hr
Aitkens, Dylan Gene, animal caretaker, $10.78/hr
Aitkens, Karen A, office support assistant III, $14.34/hr
Aitkens, Keith W, mts/machinist lead, $22.11/hr
Aitkens, Susan Joyce, business support specialist sr, $24.43/hr
Ajans, Lena S, temporary professional, $13.50/hr
Ajemba, Ogugua G, resident physician-3rd yr, $52,470
Ajmi, Ayyoub, librarian I, $62,500
Akers, Dennis Patrick, media producer sr, $34,400
Akers, Jaynee Marie, custodian, $10.00/hr
Akers, Jeffrey Wayne, retail sales associate, $13.43/hr
Akers, Jill Elizabeth, coor protocol svcs, $20.35/hr
Akers, Kathleen McKenzie, programmer analyst-expert, $56,488
Akers, Michael Lynn, genl stores attd, $14.85/hr
Akers, Sheila Rose, business support specialist II, $21.37/hr
Akers, Susan Raeann, custodian, $12.94/hr
Akerson, Alan W, prof, ast teach, $42,225
Akerson, Dorothy S, prof, teach, $77,713
Akhmadullin, Iskander V, prof, asoc, $52,254
Akin, Elvan, prof, asoc, $69,777
Akinduro, Christianah Bose, program/proj supprt coor I, $42,000
Akinmoladun, Femi-Jide Anthony, custodian, $10.00/hr
Akins, Daniel S, library info specialist, $12.98/hr
Akiwumi, William Adebayo, dir II research ops / plng, $114,153
Akkaladevi, Narahari, fellow, post doctoral, $46,000
Aksoy, Bayram S, prof, ast teach, $80,000
Al Bahhash, Ghassan Najm Abdullah, research eng tech I, $18.01/hr
Al Dahhan, Muthanna Hikmat, professor, $170,482
Al Hassan, Qasim Ahmed, resident physician-2nd yr, $50,810
Al Qadri, Syeda Laila, resident physician-2nd yr, $51,134
Al-Albani, Laura George Vangelos, instructor, adjunct, $30,900
Al-Khalisi, Nabil, resident physician-1st yr, $49,025
Al-Khashti, Noelle K, healthcare admin fellow, $50,000
Al-Suyyagh, Raed Farestouma, fellow, post doc clncl-yr3, $60,415
Alafaireet, Patricia Elaine, prof, ast teach, $92,596
Alagha, Lana Zakaria, prof, ast, $76,915
Alajo, Ayodeji Babatunde, prof, ast, $79,235
Alamdari, Habibollah Shahriar, res physician-3rd yr, $53,763
Alaniz, Terry, office support assistant IV, $17.37/hr
Alba-Marshall, Candace Alicia, office support asst III, $12.24/hr
Albadarin, Sakher Mohamed, resident physician-4th yr, $54,425
Albers, Gail M, program/project supprt coor I, $53,317
Albers, Timothy L, dir I, student support svcs, $73,555
Albert, Patrice, research specialist sr, $58,095
Albert, Philip Arthur, mts/hvac, $24.13/hr
Albert, Selena D, office support assistant IV, $14.87/hr
Alberts, Annette Marie, temporary professional, $18.57/hr
Alberty, Jermine Dornell, sr dir program/project ops, $81,600
Albl, Jeri, business support specialist II, $19.01/hr
Albrecht, Kristen Leigh, student support specialist sr, $17.31/hr
Albrecht, Mariden Carmona, office support asst III, $11.90/hr
Albrecht, Marlene N, office support assistant IV, $16.27/hr
Albright, Amber Dawn, rec/athletic assistant sr, $10.25/hr
Albright, David Luther, prof, ast, $72,930
Albright, Joseph Elmer, mts/pipefitter, $21.05/hr
Albright, Joyce Gay, prof, ast teach, $91,908
Albu, Cristina, prof, ast, $55,605
Alcabasa, Rodeth Quines, patient svc rep, $13.21/hr
Alcantara, Alma, accountant I, $17.43/hr
Alcazar-Estela, Asier, prof, asoc, $64,212
Alcorn, Shirley Jean, central sterile assistant, $10.68/hr
Alden, Michael F, athletic director, $317,193
Alden, Seth Leigh, healthcare admin fellow, $50,000
Alderson, Lisa G, office support assistant IV, $13.22/hr
Aldrich-Watson, Deborah, prof, asoc, $59,335
Aldrich, Eric Michael, on-air talent television, $38,000
Aldrich, Jonathan Andrew, mts/electrician mrc, $18.74/hr
Aldrich, Mary Katherine, mgr env health and safety, $83,000
Aldridge, Ann Crystal, nurse, staff now II, $28.00/hr
Aldridge, Danny, security officer sr, $16.60/hr
Aldridge, Dorothy D, nurse clinician, $52,153

Aldridge, Kristina J, prof, asoc, $95,101
Aldridge, Robyn Renee, surgical technl certified, $16.92/hr
Aldridge, Tanya Renee, revenue cycle trainer, $47,942
Aleman, Peter P, mech trades spclst (mts), $22.42/hr
Alemi, Farzad, adjunct, $15,000
Aleto, Thomas Joseph Jr, prof, ast clincl dept, $260,097
Alewel, Austin Allen, communications assistant sr, $15.39/hr
Alex, Linda, fellow, post doctoral, $42,000
Alexander, Amanda B, veterinarian, residnt, $26,315
Alexander, Amanda Caroline, prof, ast teach, $60,000
Alexander, Anne Michele, prof, asoc teach, $80,800
Alexander, Christy L, patient svc rep, $12.76/hr
Alexander, Danette K, media production director II, $40,000
Alexander, David D, mental health tech, $13.16/hr
Alexander, Gene Owen, care team assoc-suppt, $10.64/hr
Alexander, Gregory Lynn, prof, asoc, $99,004
Alexander, Jared P, ast athletic director, $45,031
Alexander, Jennafer Marie Leone, instructor, adjunct, $18,000
Alexander, Jennifer Aiko Nosaka, mgr student support svcs, $30,000
Alexander, Jennifer Lynn, dir III business admin, $112,532
Alexander, Julie Sara, resident physician-1st yr, $50,219
Alexander, Marsha A, extns professional, $74,373
Alexander, Nancy Ann, library info specialist sr, $19.71/hr
Alexander, Sam, custodian, $12.90/hr
Alexander, Stephen, professor, $115,270
Alexenko, Andrei Petrovitch, prof, ast resrch, $49,089
Alford, Dulce Gonzalez, technology resource manager, $51,500
Alfred, Chantae Hardin, family fincl edu spclst, $47,922
Algeo, Erin Maureen, resident physician-2nd yr, $50,810
Algren, Mark Stephen, prgm director, $102,000
Ali Akbarpour, Hadi, fellow, post doctoral, $34,000
Ali, Fatima Hadi, resident physician-3rd yr, $52,470
Ali, M Ishrat N, prof, ast, $151,000
Ali, Omaima, resident physician-7th yr, $63,475
Ali, Saima, specialist, $10.00/hr
Alioto, Armine, nurse clinician, $67,518
Allada, Venkata, vice provost, $178,032
Allai, Mariah Victoria, cat scan technl (ct), $21.79/hr
Allam, Mohamed Yosef, food svc wrkr I, $9.60/hr
Allbee, Roger H Jr, media producer II, $14.95/hr
Alleman, Stephen P, librarian III, $61,603
Allemang, Mary Christine, nurse, staff II, $21.37/hr
Allen, Adria L, finance systems specialist sr, $70,212
Allen, Angela Selena, office support assistant IV, $14.24/hr
Allen, Anne Foster, library info specialist sr, $15.32/hr
Allen, Anne Mary, strat comm associate I, $39,500
Allen, Brandon Derrick, driver emerg road svc, $13.42/hr
Allen, Bryant Lamar, stage services assistant sr, $16.00/hr
Allen, Carla McCaghren, prof, asoc clincl, $62,050
Allen, Charles W, mgr research technical svcs, $93,869
Allen, Charlotte Nicole, nurse, staff I, $19.00/hr
Allen, Chasidy Ladine, office support assistant I, $9.05/hr
Allen, Deanna Evelyn, nurse, staff II, $22.24/hr
Allen, Debra E, program/project supprt coor I, $57,741
Allen, Donna J, med office assistant, $13.60/hr
Allen, Dorthea E, telecomm opr-h, $10.37/hr
Allen, Gary Keith, vice president, $240,698
Allen, Holly Ann, student support specialist sr, $16.87/hr
Allen, Isaac Curtis, program/project supprt coor I, $34,680
Allen, Jane Karen, human resources specialist sr, $57,200
Allen, Jennifer Ashley, business support specialist sr, $20.81/hr
Allen, Jessica Denise, student support specialist sr, $17.03/hr
Allen, Kelli Danielle, adjunct, $21,000
Allen, Kelsey Diane, strat comm associate I, $35,088
Allen, Kelsey Rachelle, resp therapist reg, $28.00/hr
Allen, Kimberly A, programmer analyst-princpl, $72,806
Allen, Kimberly Ruth, prof, asoc teach, $99,591
Allen, Lorna Hon, office support assistant III, $13.77/hr
Allen, Mark D, program/project supprt coor sr, $72,100
Allen, Mary Ellen, nurse, staff II, $34.18/hr
Allen, Mary Renee, patient svc rep, $14.76/hr
Allen, Marzell, distribution techn-mtls mgmt, $15.26/hr
Allen, Mitchell John, research/lab technician, $11.00/hr
Allen, Nanette Marie, patient svc rep, $14.88/hr
Allen, Rachael Chloe, prof, ast teach, $52,500
Allen, Raye L, research lab supervisor, $45,900
Allen, Robert W, mech trades spclst (mts), $24.45/hr
Allen, Robin L, custodian, $10.19/hr
Allen, Ryan Douglas, student service coor II, $40,000

Allen, Stephanie Marie, instructor, clincl, $67,524
Allen, Tara Jeffrey, prof, teach, $80,000
Allen, Wesley Lloyd, resident physician-4th yr, $55,804
Allen, William D, instructor, adjunct, $16,000
Allen, William H, prof, ast teach, $60,504
Allenbrand, Jackie Jo, seasonal farm ast, $10.51/hr
Allers, Jewel R, academic advisor, $44,318
Alleyne, Janel A, mgr student support svcs, $33,666
Allinder, Maridel, strat comm consultant sr, $63,000
Allinson, Kayla Paulette, clinical nursing supvsr, $50,198
Allison, Cathy S, project manager-princpl, $67,220
Allison, Jeanne Marie, prof, ast teach, $47,802
Allison, Jennifer Karen, engineer sr, $76,385
Allison, Kathleen S, temporary professional, $11.00/hr
Allison, Kenneth Harold, research maint tech sr, $26.90/hr
Allison, Michael, prof, asoc teach, $56,763
Allison, Rholinda Dianne, clncl imprvmnt spclst, $25.57/hr
Allison, Tommie Jo, office support assistant IV, $15.50/hr
Allison, Wendy Sue, strat comm associate II, $43,630
Allman, Richard W Jr, prof, asoc, $60,883
Allmon, Amanda Lou Ann, prof, asoc clincl dept, $148,063
Allmon, Kelly Ann, nurse, staff II, $20.54/hr
Allred, Olga, office support assistant III, $12.50/hr
Allsworth, Jenifer, prof, asoc resrch, $82,000
Allyn, William Nicholas, instructor, adjunct, $15,000
Alm, John C, resident physician-4th yr, $55,804
Almaliky, Kathim Hassab, food svc wrkr III, $13.21/hr
Almashhrawi, Ashraf Abdelhalim, fellow, post doc clncl-yr3, $60,415
Almasri, Mahmoud Faud, prof, asoc, $99,960
Almeer, Zainab S, resident physician-2nd yr, $50,810
Almeida, Ray, event assistant I, $16.66/hr
Almenoff, Maxwell, resident physician-1st yr, $49,025
Alnazer, Sarah Constance, office support assistant II, $11.00/hr
Alnijoumi, Mohammed Mustafa, fellow, post doc clncl-yr3, $60,415
Alobaidan, Tina Jean, business support specialist II, $19.83/hr
Alonso, Ruben, lecturer, $9,000
Alpert, Martin Alvin, professor, $270,608
Alqalyoobi, Shehabaldin, resident physician-2nd yr, $50,810
Alshami, Hamza, resident physician-5th yr, $56,120
Alsharit, Ahmed Mohammed, bus tech analyst-speclst, $39,998
Alston, LaTonya Annette, nurse, licensed prac, $18.17/hr
Altena, Robert James, mts/pipefitter, $22.50/hr
Altheide, Richard W, network engineer-master, $93,317
Althof, Wolfgang, professor, $140,517
Althoff, James Frances, media producer sr, $17.83/hr
Altman, Maria Ann, strat comm consultant, $48,201
Altman, Sally Jean, strat comm consultant, $45,320
Altnether, Scott T, cook, $13.21/hr
Altomare, Robert H, prof, ast adjunct, $125.00/hr
Alton II, William Eugene, hospital security officer, $14.31/hr
Aluri, Lata Madhavi, fellow, post doc clncl-yr2, $58,083
Alvarez, Frances V, pat acct rep, $16.12/hr
Alvarez, Renee C, mgr II business admin, $71,750
Alviso, Debbie Susan, business support specialist sr, $24.80/hr
Aly, Abdelrahman Abdallah A, res physician-3rd yr, $52,470
Alzoubi, Rana Khazar Talla, resident physician-5th yr, $56,120
Amari, Eileen M, prof, ast clincl, $71,000
Amatya, Jennifer Rose, student support specialist sr, $17.67/hr
Ambrus, Howard Lee, food svc wrkr I, $9.60/hr
Amelon, George Crighton, research specialist I, $34,979
Ames, Clint Anton, instructor, adjunct, $45,000
Ames, Kelsey Lee, phlebotomist, $11.95/hr
Amick, Michael D, maintenance supervisor, $54,100
Amigo, Maria Julia, instructor, adjunct, $14,400
Amin, Maaya B, child dev assistant, $8.12/hr
Amor, Lahcen, trades helper, $12.55/hr
Amorim, Juliana, research/lab technician sr, $15.39/hr
Amoroso, Mark Alexander, office support assistant II, $10.24/hr
Amos Landgraf, James Michael, prof, ast, $93,745
Amos, Britney Lynn, med coding spclst-certified, $18.96/hr
Ampong, Dan Tiloy, business support specialist sr, $21.64/hr
Amponsah, David Kofi, instructor, visiting, $56,228
Amrhein, Ann Marie, accountant sr, $47,625
Amyot, Cynthia C, professor, $136,282
Anbari, Allison Brandt, nurse, resrch, $38,613
Ancel, Judith, program/project supprt coor II, $56,845
Ancell, Joseph M, farm wrkr II, $14.27/hr
Andemariam, Ephrem Mehret-AB, prog/proj sup coor I, $41,212
Anders, Gary Dale, event assistant I, $9.00/hr

Andersen, Elizabeth Gerber, instructor, adjunct, $1,700
Andersen, Mary, research specialist sr, $39,600
Anderson-Gross, Chadwyck Alan, food svc wrkr II, $10.10/hr
Anderson, Aaron Travis, office support assistant II, $14.63/hr
Anderson, Alex I, academic advisor, $35,001
Anderson, Amanda Jane, psychotherapist, $51,000
Anderson, Amy Marlene, program/project supprt coor I, $30,593
Anderson, Andrew Felix, temporary professional, $20.00/hr
Anderson, Angela Renee, nurse, licensed prac, $20.06/hr
Anderson, Barry S, professor, $69,116
Anderson, Blake Alexander, tutor, $8.50/hr
Anderson, Bradd L, state spclst, asoc, $63,046
Anderson, Carolyn Kay, healthcare programs spec, $15.10/hr
Anderson, Cayla J, retail sales associate sr, $18.49/hr
Anderson, Crissy Lynn, sterile processing tech, $15.00/hr
Anderson, David Paul, db programmer analyst-expert, $62,316
Anderson, Deborah Mae, prof, asoc, $109,077
Anderson, Debra K, office support assistant IV, $16.02/hr
Anderson, Debra Kay, sr ast dir studnt supprt svcs, $54,381
Anderson, Elaine R, 4-h spclst, $44,700
Anderson, Emily Elizabeth, office support assistant III, $11.53/hr
Anderson, Eric L, system administrator-princpl, $76,214
Anderson, Eric W, business svcs consultant sr, $62,383
Anderson, Erin Abbott, editor II, $100.00/hr
Anderson, Gary Lee, event assistant I, $7.55/hr
Anderson, Glen Michael, prof, ast, $50,989
Anderson, Janae, office support assistant II, $10.25/hr
Anderson, Jeffery Cooper, resrch scientist/academic sr, $45,999
Anderson, Jessica C, stock clerk, $12.94/hr
Anderson, Jessica L, csm associate I, $14.96/hr
Anderson, Jo Ann, educational prgm coor sr, $56,500
Anderson, Jordan Elizabeth, pharmacist, $119,543
Anderson, K Kim, head coach, $300,000
Anderson, Karen Elaine, nurse, staff now plus, $30.00/hr
Anderson, Kassandra Ellen, environmental health tech II, $15.17/hr
Anderson, Katherine Marie, librarian III, $72,500
Anderson, Kenneth C, professor, $65,556
Anderson, Kerin Kay, academic advisor sr, $42,499
Anderson, Kevin L, busi spclst, agri, $51,990
Anderson, Kim Marie, prof, asoc, $69,500
Anderson, Kristina Marie, resident physician-3rd yr, $53,763
Anderson, Laura L, academic advisor sr, $40,800
Anderson, Lauren Elizabeth, lab assistant, $10.00/hr
Anderson, Leslie P, grader, $1,200
Anderson, Mark Alan, instructor, $52
Anderson, Marquetta, office support assistant IV, $16.99/hr
Anderson, Mary E, library specialist, $48,793
Anderson, Michael A, telecom engineer-master, $82,118
Anderson, Nathan C, mgr event services, $52,500
Anderson, Neil L, professor, $108,824
Anderson, Paul B, mgr fl csm operations, $46,467
Anderson, Sarah Christine, med lab techn, $15.87/hr
Anderson, Sarah Kathleen, fin / acctg consultant lead, $81,000
Anderson, Sharlette Dawn, prof, ast clincl, $67,140
Anderson, Shelley W, patient svc rep, $14.55/hr
Anderson, Stephanie Ann Heffernan, mgr advancement, $47,959
Anderson, Stephen H, professor, $126,796
Anderson, Tanya Lynn, office support assistant IV, $14.76/hr
Anderson, Terri L, coor, care, $64,398
Anderson, Tiffany Chane'l, prof, ast adjunct, $10,672
Anderson, Tiffany N, sr asoc dir business admin, $77,732
Anderson, Troy D, mechanical maint IV, $20.23/hr
Anderson, Valerie Reeves, histologic technl, $23.13/hr
Anderson, Vera, business ops associate II, $47,377
Anderson, Victor, mts/hvac, $20.45/hr
Anderson, Wayne Perry, emeritus, $15,000
Anderson, William David, instructor, adjunct, $9,000
Anderson, William G, dir I, broadcast operations, $66,077
Anderson, Winona K, educational pgm coor III, $55,613
Andert, Jennifer Anne, resp therapist reg, $26.47/hr
Andes, Thomas D, instructor, adjunct, $2,700
Andolino, Debra Elizabeth, ast mgr hospitality services, $39,600
Andre, Marilyn Jones, instructor, adjunct, $4,955
Andre, Paul Alan, educational pgm coor II, $16.54/hr
Andreasen, Shawn Lynn, nurse, staff II, $30.77/hr
Andreasen, Stacey J, office support assistant IV, $15.89/hr
Andres, Cheryl Y, nurse, staff II, $30.27/hr
Andrews, Jack H, research specialist I, $15.00/hr
Andrews, Justin K, mechl plant spclst, $19.64/hr

Andrews, Leigh Ann, nurse, licensed prac, $21.19/hr
Andrews, Linda Kathryn, office support assistant III, $13.09/hr
Andrews, Tammy K, nurse, clincl charge-lpn, $22.52/hr
Andrews, Thomas Wesley, fellow, $21,000
Androff, Emily Suzanne, instructor, clincl, $77,000
Angel, Elizabeth, custodian, $12.94/hr
Angell, Lisa M, hris specialist-entry, $53,500
Angell, Natasha J, director it, $109,725
Angle, Brittany Marie, research specialist I, $38,000
Anglo, Lisa M, care team assoc-clinical, $14.88/hr
Angolia, Christine A, librarian II, $52,287
Anjum, Bushra, prof, ast teach, $70,000
Anliker, Christina M, nurse, staff II, $30.36/hr
Anliker, Darwin E, police lieutenant, $69,310
Anliker, Megan Nicole, occl therapy ast cert, $16.35/hr
Anselmo, Martalea Grubb, instructor, clincl, $73,708
Anstine, Kris L, library info specialist, $12.98/hr
Anthoney, Stephen Michael, network engineer-speclst, $49,233
Anthony, Christopher Steven, research/lab tech sr, $16.65/hr
Anthony, Daniel R, athletic trainer, $15,000
Anthony, Janet V, instructor, adjunct, $12,552
Anthony, Kathleen K, office support assistant IV, $17.34/hr
Anthony, Sarah Elizabeth, academic advisor, $39,000
Anthony, Scott T, teaching ast, $31.80/hr
Antimi, Christina Helen, safety comm operator, $17.23/hr
Anton, Katie Jo, student support specialist sr, $17.25/hr
Anye, Emeline Sungla, resp therapist reg, $18.97/hr
Anyokwu, Okah Justin, instructor, clincl, $35,000
Anzaldo, Demetrio, prof, asoc teach, $43,268
Aouad, Nassib Samir, prof, ast, $76,701
Apel, David E, mts/sheet metal, $22.49/hr
Appel, Heidi M, resrch scientist/academic sr, $72,098
Appelman, Howard R, prof, asoc adjunct, $22,050
Apperson, Bradly Michael, event assistant I, $8.50/hr
Applebaum, Marla Nancy, prog/project supprt coor II, $64,739
Appleton, Pollyana C, network engineer-speclst, $49,768
Applewhite, Robert Lee, custodian, $12.94/hr
Appling, Paul A, steam plant opr II, $24.15/hr
Appold, Martin Stephan, prof, asoc, $68,175
Appuhn-Hodges, Katharine Ellen, comm coord sr, $18.79/hr
Apt, Janessa Lynn, retail sales associate sr, $18.63/hr
Aquino, Anita Sue, office support assistant IV, $15.43/hr
Araiza, Christian Nicholas Storm, surgical technl certified, $16.83/hr
Araiza, Christopher A, supv food svc I,-h, $35,860
Araiza, Kenneth Dakota, cook, $12.64/hr
Aramjoo, Ashley, fellow, post doctoral, $30,000
Arand, Roseanna Marie Christal, audiologist, $59,280
Arbore Granner, Laura Michele, media producer II, $18.25/hr
Arbuckle, Nathanael Lee, academic advisor, $39,000
Arce, Moises, professor, $101,832
Archambault, Nicholas Samuel, veterinarian, residnt, $26,315
Archambault, Paul Michael, bts painter, $20.23/hr
Archer, Patricia E, compositor, $19.13/hr
Arden, Adrienne Judith, library info specialist, $14.27/hr
Ardhanari, Sivakumar, fellow, post doc clncl yr1, $50.00/hr
Ardhanari, Sivakumar, fellow, post doc clncl-yr3, $60,415
Ardini, Sheri J, nurse, staff II, $34.18/hr
Aregbe, Farouk Olufunmilayo, student service coor II, $43,646
Arellano, Crystal Jean, student support specialist II, $17.51/hr
Arend, Richard James, professor, $185,500
Arends, Brigett Kay, event assistant I, $8.50/hr
Arens, Christy Lee Ann, nurse, staff, $22.37/hr
Arft, Elaine Renee, nurse, staff II, $22.79/hr
Arico, Adam James, instructor, adjunct, $10,500
Ariew, Andre I, prof, asoc, $86,771
Arif, Murtaza, prof, ast clincl dept, $208,080
Arment, Christian D, resrch anlyst, $47,296
Armentrout, Jerry R, police sergeant, $27.33/hr
Armentrout, Lindsey Anne, communications asst sr, $16.25/hr
Armentrout, Tammy L, office support assistant sr, $18.25/hr
Armer, Jane M, professor, $122,653
Armer, Nathan Charles, research specialist I, $15.00/hr
Armistead, Joan Elyse, office support aide II, $8.08/hr
Armstrong, Elizabeth Gemma, lecturer, $44,126
Armstrong, Lisa Lynn, patient svc rep, $13.15/hr
Armstrong, Robert Paul, construction manager I, $46,284
Arndorfer, Paul Wayne, dir strength and conditioning, $52,400
Arndt, Jamie L, professor, $115,986
Arndt, Justin James, research specialist I, $31,722

Arneal, Renee Jean, nurse, staff per diem, $35.00/hr
Arnet, Benjamin Paul, media producer sr, $43,600
Arnet, Nicole Ashley, office support assistant IV, $16.78/hr
Arnett, Krista L, research specialist I, $40,706
Arnold-Cook, Jerri Lynne, sr dir program/project ops, $66,400
Arnold, Alan Dale, db administrator-expert, $69,624
Arnold, Anthony Burton, ast dir business admin, $53,657
Arnold, Anya Elaine, instructor, adjunct, $26,850
Arnold, Brenda Mae, extension asoc, $32,000
Arnold, Cheri, nurse, staff now III, $30.00/hr
Arnold, Jennifer M, business support specialist II, $19.54/hr
Arnold, Judith Dione, resrch ast, $41,200
Arnold, Kimberly M, business support specialist II, $17.65/hr
Arnold, Krysta J, physician ast, $109,700
Arnold, Laura W, prof, ast adjunct, $12,000
Arnold, Lory J, student service coor II, $46,161
Arnold, Matthew T, office support assistant III, $14.31/hr
Arnold, Noelle Witherspoon, prof, asoc, $70,199
Arnold, Pamela Kay, police officer, $16.54/hr
Arnold, Ryan Tristan, ast mgr hospitality services, $63,672
Arnold, Willis Ryder, strat comm consultant, $39,800
Arns, Megan Elizabeth, prof, ast teach, $37,800
Aro, Michael R, prof, ast clincl dept, $250,000
Aronson, Elizabeth Marian, nursing ast sr, $13.00/hr
Aronson, Rochelle, office support assistant III, $13.12/hr
Aronstam, Robert Steven, professor, $156,194
Aroor, Annayya R, prof, ast resrch, $56,838
Arora, Rajinder, professor, $158,126
Arora, Simran-Jyot, resident physician-2nd yr, $52,610
Arp, Elizabeth Ashley, program/project supprt coor I, $34,400
Arp, Robert, instructor, adjunct, $18,000
Arredondo, Alice Lee, dean, ast, $90,000
Arredondo, Margaret Alice, user support analyst-spec, $19.00/hr
Arredondo, Monica, office support assistant IV, $15.00/hr
Arri, Matthew Drake, student service coor II, $53,150
Arribas, Jason Robert, resident physician-2nd yr, $50,810
Arroyo, Pablo A, extns professional, ast, $46,826
Arsenault, Andre, resident physician-2nd yr, $50,810
Arshadi, Nasser, vice provost, $199,551
Arteaga-Cox, Irma Angela, prof, ast, $76,361
Arthur, Cheyenne Adele, temporary crafts service, $13.00/hr
Arthur, Connie B, student service coor I, $40,000
Arthur, Dakota Sue, temporary crafts service, $13.00/hr
Arthur, Gerald Lee, prof, ast resrch, $75,013
Arthur, Randall Lee, lecturer, $45,000
Arthur, Russell James, maint svc attd, $17.60/hr
Artioli, Jennifer L, athletic trainer, $48,260
Artist, Erma, office support assistant IV, $20.01/hr
Artman, Deborah N, instructor, adjunct, $17,100
Arunachalam, Vairam, professor, $291,818
Arya, Bindu, prof, asoc, $118,023
Arya, Monika, fellow, post doc clncl-yr3, $60,415
Asadi, Ebrahim, fellow, post doctoral, $55,000
Asano, Ashley Emiko Piilani, specialist, $10.00/hr
Asarch, Allison Beth, intern, $26,265
Asay, Kayla Leann, resident physician-3rd yr, $52,899
Asbee, Joanne Siri, nurse clinician, $67,727
Asbell, Henry C, media production director I, $46,598
Asbill, Steven John Jr, pharmacy resident, $38,500
Asbury, Beth M, dir construction and planning, $119,912
Asbury, Cathy Ann, csm associate II, $20.47/hr
Asbury, Danny Lee, mobile mammogr van driver/psr, $14.95/hr
Asbury, Wanda Sue, custodian, $12.94/hr
Asbury, Wayne F, animal caretaker-equine/food, $11.85/hr
Asche, Sarah Margaret, resp therapist reg, $20.55/hr
Asencio, Angelica, temporary crafts service, $9.10/hr
Asfaw, Amha, instructor, resrch, $4,226
Ash, Ken R, sr dir program/project ops, $91,326
Ashbaugh, Catherine Messina, nurse spclst, clincl, $97,469
Ashbaugh, Margaret Ann, animal techn, $13.89/hr
Ashbaugh, Mark S, professor, $153,050
Ashcraft, Nikki L, prof, ast teach, $59,276
Asher, Ellen Mary, office support assistant III, $14.42/hr
Asher, Imani, resident physician-2nd yr, $50,810
Asher, Irving Mark, prof, ast clincl dept, $166,145
Asher, Lori A, temporary professional, $11.30/hr
Asher, Phillip Joseph, business support specialist II, $16.81/hr
Asher, Susan R, education nurse, $73,117
Ashford, Nancy Jane, academic advisor, $54,931

Ashley, Deidra Elyse, strat comm associate I, $50,000
Ashley, Kevin, support systems admin-princpl, $65,557
Ashley, Lee Ann, office support assistant IV, $15.01/hr
Ashraf, Imran, fellow, post doc clncl-yr2, $58,083
Ashraf, Muhammad Javed, adjunct, $15,000
Ashurst, Cherry Sherie, dental assistant II, $15.37/hr
Ashworth, William B Jr, prof, asoc, $67,630
Askew, Devon Marcus, tutor, $14.08/hr
Askew, Jessica Ann, patient svc rep, $11.30/hr
Asle Zaeem, Mohsen, prof, ast, $88,663
Asmar, Nakhle, professor, $101,300
Asokan, Vibha Rajagopalan, veterinarian, residnt, $26,000
Asombang, Akwi Wasi, prof, ast clincl dept, $204,000
Assioun, Zehdi, electronics technician II, $14.72/hr
Aston, Barbara Kay, instructor, clincl, $14,974
Aston, Julie Frances, office support assistant II, $15.37/hr
Aswad, Saadiya, business support specialist sr, $28.08/hr
Atallah, Najdat A, physician, $242,420
Atasoy, Ulus, prof, asoc, $183,302
Atencio-Spears, Jennifer Marie, executive assistant, $23.64/hr
Athans, Gaitha Christine, teaching ast, $13.00/hr
Atherly, Damon Allen, office support assistant IV, $16.32/hr
Atherton, Kevin James, programmer analyst-speclst, $59,874
Athey, Kimberly Kay, care team assoc-clinical, $13.33/hr
Athey, Michael Ryan, med techl reg, $23.23/hr
Atiles, Julia, prof, asoc, $78,000
Atkins, Robert E Jr, farm wrkr III, $15.72/hr
Atkins, Amanda Grace, program/project supprt coor I, $29,000
Atkins, Amy E, office support assistant II, $10.95/hr
Atkins, Andrea Marie, nurse clinician, $58,000
Atkins, Carisa A, nurse, staff now III, $30.00/hr
Atkins, Lori N, clerk, diet, $11.46/hr
Atkinson, Curtiss J, mts/pipefitter, $22.50/hr
Atkinson, David Thomas, telecom tech-speclst, $15.13/hr
Atkinson, Terry W, mts/pipefitter, $22.50/hr
Atkinson, Trish Marie, surgical technl certified, $17.09/hr
Atkisson, David W, cooling tower techn lead, $21.07/hr
Atkisson, Eva Marie, neurodiagnostic tech (reg), $23.26/hr
Atkisson, Justin Cruse, pharmacy techn II, $13.26/hr
Atkisson, Steven Douglas, mech, bldg maint, $18.12/hr
Attebery, Autumn Lorene, custodian, $10.00/hr
Attebery, Jeffrey R, fin and acctg manager sr, $88,821
Atwell, Anne P, executive assistant, $17.12/hr
Atwell, Samuel Dale, agronomy spclst, $53,155
Atwell, Theodore Clyde, security officer, $11.90/hr
Atwood, Amy Elizabeth, nurse, staff prn, $26.00/hr
Atwood, Jerry L, prof, curators, $172,349
Atwood, Justin Henry, fellow, post doc clncl yr1, $55,804
Aubuchon, Gregory Paul, instructor, adjunct, $12,000
Aubuchon, Mira, prof, ast clincl dept, $166,480
Auer, Michael Robert, asoc dir program/project ops, $53,344
Aufdenberg, Donna Irene, extns professional, asoc, $53,247
Augustine, Rachel Elaine, strat comm associate II, $40,400
Augustyn, James Patrick, operations support tech II, $11.30/hr
Auinbauh, Melanie Katherine, physical therapist, $35.00/hr
Aura, Saku Petteri, prof, asoc, $105,844
Ausmus, Andrew Michael, physician, $50.00/hr
Ausmus, Ashley Marie, pharmacy resident, $42,000
Ausmus, Julie Ann, event assistant I, $11.00/hr
Aust, John M, coor athletic operations sr, $45,829
Austin-Bythell, Suzanne Holly, prof, ast adjunct, $9,000
Austin, April Louise, instructor, adjunct, $12,500
Austin, Elizabeth Ann, instructor, adjunct, $4,800
Austin, Katherine L, prof, ast clincl dept, $193,000
Austin, Kathryn M, health records techn II, $14.39/hr
Austin, Kimberly A, certif pharmacy techn, $14.09/hr
Austin, Lorrie L, internet administrator-entry, $18.54/hr
Austin, Mary A, sr asoc athletic director, $150,000
Austin, Roberta L, temporary professional, $12.00/hr
Austin, Ron Anthony, adjunct, $10,500
Austin, Sarah Kate, tutor, $10.00/hr
Austin, Sharon Marie, occl therapist, $55,080
Austin, Susan Lisa, nurse clinician, $57,958
Autenrieth, Debra K, office support assistant IV, $17.98/hr
Autenrieth, Melissa Lynn, coor, service, $16.71/hr
Auwarter, Douglas Dale, instructor, adjunct, $27,600
Avenell, Christa Ann, nurse anesthetist, $147,900
Avery, Patricia L, instructor, adjunct, $1,601
Avila-Becerra, Blanca Estela, custodian, $10.94/hr

Avila, Hailey Ann, resident physician-1st yr, $49,025
Avila, Jeremy S, resident physician-2nd yr, $52,610
Aviles Quinones, Alicia, prof, ast teach, $41,208
Awoniyi, Ruth Oluwaseun, adjunct, $17,100
Awuah-Offei, Kwame, prof, asoc, $96,496
Axley, Rosemary E, office support assistant III, $14.32/hr
Aycock, Mary Beth, librarian III, $50,175
Ayers, Alison Ruth, student service coor I, $41,000
Ayers, Autumn Leigh, student service coor II, $45,000
Ayers, Timothy, maint svc attd, $18.41/hr
Ayers, Van Harrison, extns professional, $60,478
Aylesworth, Cheryl Jo, instructor, adjunct, $6,276
Ayllon, Miguel Elias, student service coor II, $48,000
Aylward, Ann Louise, internet administrator-speclst, $21.70/hr
Aylward, Carol A, adjunct, $15,000
Ayoub, Amir Z, business ops associate sr, $46,512
Ayres, Christina, nurse, or/recovery-ch, $20.95/hr
Azhar, Javeria, resident, clincl, $31,104
Aziz, Fahad, fellow, post doc clncl yr1, $55,804
Azizan-Gardner, Noor S, ast deputy chanclr-diversity, $121,870
Azizi, Orchideh, scientist lead, $86,520
Azmeh, Ashley Renee, strat comm associate II, $45,015
Babbar, Shilpa, resident physician-6th yr, $58,200
Babcock, David W, program/project supprt coor I, $57,957
Babel, Christine Elise, project manager-expert, $64,114
Babel, Kent Michael, network engineer-expert, $62,581
Baber, Susan J, event assistant sr, $16.50/hr
Babilon, Stacie Ann, asoc dir program/project ops, $49,500
Babiuch, Ryan N, programmer analyst-speclst, $51,765
Babski, Christopher A, designer, commercial sign, $20.52/hr
Baccam, Chiengkham, lab assistant, $11.25/hr
Bach, Emily Ann, asoc dir student support svcs, $62,950
Bach, Vicki Lyn Foley, executive assistant, $22.73/hr
Bachman, Bonnie J, professor, $121,762
Bachman, Janet Marie, office support assistant III, $18.50/hr
Bachman, Ryan, resident physician-1st yr, $49,025
Bachmann, Bethany Nicole, nutrition spclst, $40,602
Bachrach, Bert E, prof, asoc clincl dept, $235,257
Back, Jessica Ruth, social worker-non acute care, $34,977
Backe, Susan A, revenue recovery spclst, $49,996
Backes, Karen M, nurse, staff II, $35.23/hr
Backues, Andrew A, system support analyst-expert, $24.99/hr
Backues, Julia Carlene, office support assistant IV, $14.65/hr
Backus, Bob C, prof, asoc, $108,690
Backus, James Gregory, instructor, adjunct, $5,994
Backus, Kathleen Q, veterinary technician sr, $17.23/hr
Bacon, Kathryn Julia, system support analyst-speclst, $22.68/hr
Bacon, Raymond R, user support analyst-princpl, $48,904
Bade, Karl M, custodian, $11.41/hr
Bade, Martha Virginia, supv nursing acute care, $36.13/hr
Baden, James Henry, student support specialist sr, $21.57/hr
Bader, Kenneth, research specialist I, $36,208
Bader, Sheryl L, pat acct rep, $14.92/hr
Bader, Valerie Gwen, instructor, clincl, $49,163
Bader, Valerie Gwen, nurse, staff II, $40.00/hr
Badiane, Mamadou, prof, asoc, $58,804
Badoer, Dominique Carlo, prof, ast, $180,000
Badr, Mostafa Z, professor, $103,433
Badresingh, Kimberly Annalise, physical therapist, $35.00/hr
Baehman, Beau Jonathon, temporary technical, $25.00/hr
Baehman, Stephanie Diane, strat comm associate II, $60,000
Baek, Juheon, lab assistant, $8.00/hr
Baepler, Mark A, mgr research activities, $52,278
Baer, Bonita G, clincl documnt spclst, $60,402
Baer, Regina Kay, office support assistant II, $14.81/hr
Baerwald, Charles H, security analyst-entry, $47,000
Baez Medero, Yiliam, custodian, $13.36/hr
Baez, Fausto Rangel, custodian, bldg maint, $12.64/hr
Bagby-Stone, Stephanie D, prof, asoc clincl dept, $46,500
Bagby, Elizabeth Lucille Chandler, clinical nursing supv, $51,750
Baggett, Adam Martin, internet administrator-expert, $24.04
Baggett, Michelle Patrice, library info specialist sr, $14.95/hr
Baggett, Sarah Dawn, mgr student support svcs, $44,605
Bagnall, Lindsay L, temporary clerical, $10.00/hr
Baguio, Ramses Canete, nurse anesthetist, $95.00/hr
Bagwill, Joseph Edward, bldg cntrl sys techn I, $20.31/hr
Bahador, Farshad, physician, $25.00/hr
Bahadori, Shannon Marie Schreck, nurse, staff II, $29.14/hr
Bahar, Patricia Ann, custodian, $13.36/hr

Bahar, Sonya, professor, $80,062
Bahena Garcia, Miguel Angel, instructor, ast, $6,804
Bahl, Deepti, resident physician-1st yr, $50,219
Bahm, Katie Lyn, prof, ast adjunct, $8,004
Bahner, Nancy L, mgr III business admin, $66,650
Bahr, Michael W, prof, asoc, $78,762
Bahr, Tamara Dee, office support assistant IV, $16.00/hr
Bai, Baojun, prof, asoc, $128,197
Bai, Qian, temporary technical, $8.25/hr
Baier, Michelle Marie, nurse, staff II, $20.54/hr
Bailes, Allison, student recruitment spclst, $20.21/hr
Bailey Burch, Brendolyn, resrch asoc, $71,231
Bailey, Angela Michelle, on-air talent television, $44,841
Bailey, Chastidy Anne, research specialist I, $35,977
Bailey, Courtney Oehler, resident physician-3rd yr, $52,470
Bailey, Deborah Ann, program/project supprt coor II, $39,600
Bailey, Douglas B, nurse, licensed prac, $21.69/hr
Bailey, Kevin S, director it, $120,011
Bailey, Kimberly Jo, office support assistant IV, $17.58/hr
Bailey, Kira Marie, fellow, post doctoral, $53,333
Bailey, Kristen, office support assistant III, $11.50/hr
Bailey, Matthew A, electronics technician I, $11.92/hr
Bailey, Rachel Michelle, instructor, clincl, $24,000
Bailey, Robert Gary, dean, ast, $126,488
Bailey, Sandra L, serv line spclst, $95,000
Bailey, Sarah Pulliam, dir I, strat communications, $90,000
Bailey, Sonya Merwin, temporary clerical, $15.50/hr
Bailey, Steven, lecturer sr, $18,600
Bailey, Tara Lynn, office support assistant II, $10.34/hr
Bailey, Wayne C, prof, asoc, $83,755
Bailey, Zachary D, resident physician-3rd yr, $52,470
Bain, Andrew, mental health tech, $12.20/hr
Bain, Wesly Ryan, emergency services rep, $11.61/hr
Baines, Christopher Philip, prof, ast, $111,110
Baird, Jason, prof, asoc, $90,351
Baird, Jessica Anne, research/lab technician, $10.51/hr
Baird, Michele Gail, coor, care, $65,447
Baise, Kenneth W, distribution techn-mtls mgmt, $15.48/hr
Bajwa, Ata Ur Rahim, resident physician-3rd yr, $52,470
Baker, Donald Southwood III, bus tech analyst-speclst, $60,650
Baker-Alley, Thara Sabri, programmer analyst-speclst, $55,381
Baker, Abby Marie, nurse practitioner, $78,000
Baker, Alyson Elizabeth, media production director I, $42,000
Baker, Alyssa, office support assistant IV, $14.50/hr
Baker, Amanda Dale, med office assistant, $14.41/hr
Baker, Amy Elizabeth, asoc dir finl svcs-mrc, $82,613
Baker, Brittany Haley, patient svc rep, $11.40/hr
Baker, Cara E, nurse, licensed prac, $18.00/hr
Baker, Casey D, strat comm consultant sr, $62,264
Baker, Charles, distribution techn-mtls mgmt, $15.26/hr
Baker, Christopher Lee, mover, $12.90/hr
Baker, Clarinda L, nurse clinician, $72,675
Baker, Courtney Renay, patient svc rep, $12.76/hr
Baker, Crystal D, child dev assistant, $11.81/hr
Baker, Daniel Paul, dir II advancement, $92,474
Baker, David E, dean, ast, $133,793
Baker, Dolores Anne, nurse, staff, $29.79/hr
Baker, Donald Warren, instructor, adjunct, $21,000
Baker, Elizabeth A, professor, $67,704
Baker, Erin Janene Angst, instructor, lab, $38,480
Baker, Gail Marie, patient svc rep, $13.73/hr
Baker, Gary, instructor, adjunct, $3,000
Baker, Gary Allen, prof, ast, $101,784
Baker, Gary W, event assistant I, $7.55/hr
Baker, Gaye A, coor, reimbursement, $54,551
Baker, Janet L, patient svc rep, $13.17/hr
Baker, Jason R, resident physician-1st yr, $49,025
Baker, Jenifer Lee, data cntr support tech-expert, $22.40/hr
Baker, Jennifer Elizabeth, nurse, staff II, $20.54/hr
Baker, Jennifer Laura, nurse, licensed prac, $18.37/hr
Baker, Jerry, community dev spclst, $57,595
Baker, Jessica Ann, human resources specialist sr, $48,045
Baker, Jessica Lynn, business support specialist II, $15.62/hr
Baker, Jodi Marie, educational pgm coor III, $25,417
Baker, Kenneth E, custodian, $10.69/hr
Baker, Kenneth Scott, prof, asoc, $68,604
Baker, Linda, office support aide II, $11.06/hr
Baker, Lisa Lynn, academic advisor, $34,400
Baker, Lora Ann, food svc wrkr I, $9.98/hr

Baker, Makayla Nicole, high school student, $8.50/hr
Baker, Matthew C, resident physician-5th yr, $56,120
Baker, Molly Danielle, instructor, adjunct, $14,400
Baker, Monica Elaine, office support assistant IV, $14.93/hr
Baker, Nancy, instructor, adjunct, $7,059
Baker, Nancy A, business ops associate sr, $46,740
Baker, Patrick L, emrg med techn paramedic, $19.71/hr
Baker, Phillip, maint tech III, prev, $18.45/hr
Baker, Rebecca Ann, nurse, or/recovery-ch, $30.04
Baker, Rhonda Pauline, office support assistant IV, $13.09/hr
Baker, Richard, distribution techn-mtls mgmt, $15.26/hr
Baker, Robert F, fellow, post doctoral, $51,597
Baker, Robert Michael, programmer analyst-princpl, $80,237
Baker, Ronald, custodian, $12.94/hr
Baker, Sheila N, prof, ast, $90,875
Baker, Sonya M, dental assistant I, $12.25/hr
Baker, Stafford Harold, dir II research ops and plng, $152,930
Baker, Stephanie L, care team assoc-suppt, $13.61/hr
Baker, Sylvia Nicole, academic advisor, $39,145
Baker, Timothy P, extns professional, $60,820
Baker, Vickie L, office support assistant IV, $13.18/hr
Baker, Vicky Lynn, instructor, adjunct, $8,400
Baker, Wendy Louise, cook, $12.20/hr
Bakert, Vidia Devi, nurse, staff now II, $28.00/hr
Bal, Bhajanjit, professor, $260,033
Bal, Simran Kaur, temporary clerical, $8.00/hr
Balakrishnan, Bimal, prof, assoc, $85,703
Balakrishnan, S N, prof, curators, $135,325
Balaraman, Velmurugan, fellow, post doctoral, $40,000
Balcerzak, Phyllis, resrch ast, $29,667
Balch, Tina Marie, office support assistant III, $12.50/hr
Baldini, Deborah Kristine S, dean, asoc, $106,083
Baldridge, Robert A, office support assistant IV, $14.50/hr
Baldridge, Shanna S, nurse, staff II, $30.80/hr
Baldus, Kimberly, prof, teach, $46,751
Baldwin, Barbara L, office support assistant IV, $14.49/hr
Baldwin, Hazel R, custodian, $13.36/hr
Baldwin, Kurt S, prof, asoc, $67,420
Baldwin, Marques Robert, ast coach, $34,340
Baldwin, Melissa H, compliance specialist I, $17.23/hr
Baldwin, Michael Robert, prof, ast, $99,960
Baldwin, Patricia Lynn, mgr III business admin, $53,000
Baldwin, Taylor Shannon, temporary crafts service, $8.00/hr
Baldwin, Traci Lynn, business spclst, $46,500
Balestreri, Teresa A, dir I, student support svcs, $78,429
Ball, Alexia Jane, phys therapy ast, $18.96/hr
Ball, Angela Dawn, child life spclst, $21.56/hr
Ball, Anna Leigh, professor, $116,688
Ball, Brianna Nicole, patient svc rep, $11.70/hr
Ball, Debra Jo, office support assistant IV, $20.32/hr
Ball, Elizabeth Quarles, academic advisor sr, $44,880
Ball, John David, prof, ast clincl, $93,000
Ball, Stephen Daniel, prof, asoc, $96,985
Balla, Sudarshan, prof, ast clincl dept, $210,000
Balla, Sudarshan, fellow, post doc clncl-yr2, $50.00/hr
Ballah, Danielle Elizabeth, office support assistant IV, $14.69/hr
Ballantyne, John Charles, resident physician-1st yr, $50,219
Ballard, Amber Rose, care team assoc-clinical, $11.10/hr
Ballard, Deborah, office support assistant IV, $18.22/hr
Ballard, Erica Embry, resident physician-2nd yr, $52,007
Ballard, Stevi Ranae, operations support tech I, $10.94/hr
Ballegeer, Joseph, resrch ast, $8,640
Ballenger, Kevin, hospital security officer, $10.64/hr
Ballenger, Roland L, event assistant I, $7.50/hr
Ballenger, Sandra Kay, physical therapist, $82,764
Ballew, Karen I, environmental health tech sr, $19.42/hr
Ballew, Natasha Lynne, nurse, staff II, $25.64/hr
Ballew, Rebecca L, office support assistant II, $14.75/hr
Ballinger, Marc R, garage attendant, $13.19/hr
Ballmann, Jacob Alan, emrg med techn paramedic, $15.31/hr
Ballou, Janice R, nurse advisor, telephone, $27.58/hr
Ballou, Matthew Glenn, prof, asoc teach, $51,720
Balogh, Maria Teresa, prof, asoc teach, $41,977
Balsam, Nina Penny, asoc dir program/project ops, $56,223
Balser, Christina J, student service coor sr, $72,775
Balser, Deborah B, prof, asoc, $104,727
Balser, Nicholas P, academic advisor, $36,720
Balthazor, Troy Philip, communications assistant sr, $16.68/hr
Balvin, Carolyn Sue, food svc wrkr III, $13.21/hr

Bamber, James W, med techl reg, $26.29/hr
Bame, Karen J, prof, asoc, $96,025
Bammes, Nathan O, resident physician-3rd yr, $52,470
Banaszynski, Jacqueline M, professor, $160,065
Bandari, Rajendra Prasad, fellow, post doctoral, $40,014
Banderas, Julie Wright, professor, $148,637
Bandla, Nitya, resident physician-3rd yr, $53,763
Bandyopadhyay, Susanta, prof, ast clincl dept, $150,000
Bane, Margaret Share, instructor, adjunct, $7,500
Bangert, Linda, lecturer, $27,000
Bangs, John Kendrick, instructor, adjunct, $14,667
Banholzer, Peter M, business svcs consultant, $50,750
Bani Yaghoub, Majid, prof, ast, $64,213
Banister, Randy Lee, bts carpenter, $22.43/hr
Bank, Barbara Millier, nurse, staff II rnwp, $33.84/hr
Bank, David Bernard, resp therapy techn/icu cert, $25.70/hr
Banken, Amy Elizabeth, office support assistant IV, $13.92/hr
Banken, Mary Jo, dir I, strat communications, $104,993
Bankhead, Douglas Clair, prof, ast clincl dept, $200,000
Banks, Adelle M, editor sr, $74,473
Banks, Calvin Lee, custodian, $12.50/hr
Banks, Mark Allen, nurse, staff, $34.70/hr
Banks, Michael Jacob, student recruitment spclst, $14.96/hr
Banks, William D, professor, $91,424
Banning, Adam D, system administrator-expert, $58,240
Bannister, Barbara Lynne, office support assistant III, $13.75/hr
Bansah, Kenneth Joseph, fellow, teaching, $48,000
Banta, Nicole Marie, revenue cycle trainer, $47,671
Bao, Lei, food svc wrkr III, $12.20/hr
Bao, Suping, instructor, clincl, $86,000
Bar Nadav, Hadara R, prof, asoc, $57,431
Barabtarlo, Alla P, librarian III, $61,218
Barabtarlo, Gene, professor, $96,320
Baragiola, Martin John, media producer sr, $40,935
Barajas Munoz, Ignacio Alejandro, resrch asoc, $45,015
Barajas Munoz, Marcie Renee, sr ast dir studnt supprt svcs, $53,448
Barbaro, Erin Elizabeth, geo info system specialist sr, $46,973
Barbaro, Michael C, programmer analyst-spclst, $60,886
Barbee, Ernest James, event assistant I, $15.00/hr
Barber, Anna Camille, security officer, $11.25/hr
Barber, Carolyn Elizabeth, prof, asoc, $64,538
Barber, Cheri Ann, prof, ast clincl, $80,000
Barber, Cynthia Lea, hospital lab tech, $15.05/hr
Barber, Gary Edward, instructor, adjunct, $7,500
Barber, Jeffrey Ray, housing&envirn design spclst, $59,201
Barber, Joshua Andrew, resident physician-1st yr, $50,219
Barber, Lance Anthony, db programmer analyst-spclst, $48,398
Barber, Laura L, office support assistant III, $14.70/hr
Barber, Shelby Lynn, mental health tech, $11.00/hr
Barbero, David John, research project analyst, $41,000
Barbero, Joy E, event assistant I, $15.50/hr
Barbieri, Veronica Rose, cat scan technl (ct), $23.07/hr
Barbina, Anastasiya A, neurodiagnostic tech (reg), $25.00/hr
Barbis, Anthony M, prof, asoc teach, $57,570
Barchak, Joseph Patrick, social worker, $49,491
Barchak, Michele Jean, nurse, staff II, $32.44/hr
Barchenski, Julia Ann, asoc dir program/project ops, $27,500
Bardhan, Sougata, fellow, post doctoral, $39,731
Bardol, Nicholas J, chemist II, $60,000
Bardwell, Deborah K, med techl reg, $30.36/hr
Bare, Jessica B, resident physician-4th yr, $54,425
Barfknecht, Lisa C, clinical nursing supvsr, $69,360
Bargar, John W, custodian, $10.94/hr
Bargen, Walter L, office support assistant III, $11.30/hr
Barger, Melanie W, mgr external relations, $48,564
Barger, Rita S, prof, asoc, $71,009
Barik, Subhasis, fellow, post doctoral, $36,750
Barile, Mary Margaret, administrative consultant II, $30.00/hr
Barker, Robert Eugene Jr, mts/insulator, $21.05/hr
Barker, Alex W, director, $149,903
Barker, Anne K, librarian III, $61,861
Barker, Bruce F, prof, adjunct, $10.00/hr
Barker, Jordan P, resident physician-2nd yr, $50,810
Barker, Kendra, instructional designer-spclst, $48,494
Barker, Kristin Hansen, asoc dir program/project ops, $49,000
Barker, Susan E, nurse, staff II, $30.87/hr
Barklage, Adam Kent, student recruitment spclst, $19.39/hr
Barkley, Mary Lou, office support assistant I, $8.99/hr
Barkley, Terry Alan, maint svc attd, $16.12/hr

Barks, Phyllis Elaine, lecturer, $100.00/hr
Barksdale, Debra David, instructor, adjunct, $10,800
Barkwell, Gregory Joe, bts mason/tuckptr, $20.23/hr
Barmann, Eric Michael, business ops associate II, $46,350
Barna, Mark R, editor II, $42,032
Barnard, Natalie Rae, nurse, staff II, $29.94/hr
Barner, Rhonda, temporary professional, $12.00/hr
Barner, Terry Lee, media producer sr, $40,800
Barnes, Amanda K, office support assistant III, $12.00/hr
Barnes, Barry M, agriculture foreman, $16.54/hr
Barnes, Blake William, resident physician-3rd yr, $53,763
Barnes, Charles, investigator, resrch, $81,312
Barnes, Cody J, resident physician-2nd yr, $52,007
Barnes, Courtney Leigh, prof, ast clncl dept, $168,096
Barnes, Dianne Julia, pat acct rep, $14.56/hr
Barnes, Donald, rec/athletic sports prof, $71,788
Barnes, Donald Scott, support systems admin-speclst, $46,512
Barnes, Donna L, business support specialist II, $20.19/hr
Barnes, Edward B, strat comm consultant sr, $55,105
Barnes, Everett Wayne, librarian II, $53,271
Barnes, James W, resident physician-3rd yr, $52,470
Barnes, Jeffrey F, supv hosptlty & pat suprt svcs, $46,565
Barnes, Jennifer Dawn, student support specialist sr, $18.96/hr
Barnes, Kristin Leigh, nurse, clncl charge-rn, $29.26/hr
Barnes, Kylie Nicole, prof, ast clncl, $96,000
Barnes, Laura Marie, child developmentalist, $55,724
Barnes, Margaret A, office support assistant III, $14.14/hr
Barnes, Michael Heath, prof, asoc teach, $48,845
Barnes, Michelle Lory, office support assistant III, $13.50/hr
Barnes, Nicholas H, high school student, $7.50/hr
Barnes, Stephen L, professor, $535,191
Barnes, Stephen Michael, student support specialist II, $15.25/hr
Barnes, Susan Jane, library info specialist sr, $14.95/hr
Barnes, Terry Lynn, ast provost, $24,240
Barnett, Amber Nicole Niles, temporary technical, $15.00/hr
Barnett, Carter Wyatt, food svc wrkr I, $9.60/hr
Barnett, Christopher J, resrch asoc, $80,201
Barnett, Christopher W, user support analyst-expert, $20.62/hr
Barnett, Jessica Lynn, office support assistant IV, $14.30/hr
Barnett, Ryan Lucas, research specialist sr, $42,000
Barnett, Sarah Swain, counselor, genetic, $60,114
Barnett, Yan Zhou, resrch asoc, $82,255
Barnette, Mary B, clerk, unit, $14.78/hr
Barnette, Stephanie L, clerk, operating room supply, $12.22/hr
Barnhart, Bradley Ivan, instructor, adjunct, $1,601
Barnhart, Mary Jo, office support assistant IV, $16.31/hr
Barnhart, Rachael Mae, event assistant I, $7.55/hr
Barnhart, Robert, custodian, $12.94/hr
Barnhill, Kelly Marie, office support assistant IV, $13.52/hr
Barnidge, Joan M, media producer sr, $46,720
Barnstone, Aliki Dora, professor, $97,401
Barnthouse, Kimberly Gail, office support assistant IV, $14.19/hr
Barondes, Royce De Rohan, prof, asoc, $129,724
Barquero-Molina, Miriam, director, $69,710
Barr, Darin Jay, instructor, adjunct, $10,560
Barr, Kristi Lee, office support associate, $20.35/hr
Barr, Stacy Lynn, research specialist I, $39,497
Barraza, Blanca, custodian, $12.94/hr
Barrera Macedo, Felicitas, custodian, $12.94/hr
Barrera, Caroline Rae, nurse, staff, $30.24/hr
Barrera, Juan, nurse, procedures, $30.77/hr
Barrera, Paula, custodian, $10.94/hr
Barreto, Kathryn Anne, event assistant I, $7.50/hr
Barrett, Amy C, emrg med techn, $12.90/hr
Barrett, Bruce Allen, professor, $83,689
Barrett, Marla Lynn, fin and acctg manager, $61,429
Barrett, Patricia Ruth, busi spclst, agri, $46,500
Barrett, Paula, strat comm associate II, $46,683
Barrett, Robert W, sr mgr csm operations, $64,467
Barrett, Steve W, instructor, adjunct, $12,000
Barrier, Breton Foster, prof, asoc, $179,591
Barrois, Lyndon Joseph Jr, adjunct, $9,000
Barron, Christopher M, event assistant I, $10.50/hr
Barron, Gary, mts/insulator, $22.50/hr
Barron, Jason P, ast coach, $24,000
Barron, Martha Lynne, reimbursement spclst, $22.97/hr
Barron, Paul Michael, prof, ast teach, $53,251
Barron, Rebecca Lea, telecomm opr-h, $9.90/hr
Barrow, Catherine Lynn, occl therapist, $73,174

Barrow, Lloyd H, professor, $64,592
Barrow, Marianne Downey, instructor, adjunct, $1,601
Barry, Timothy Michael, prof, ast adjunct, $125.00/hr
Barry, William B, instructor, adjunct, $2,585
Barsky, Lili Lohi, resident physician-1st yr, $50,219
Bartelli, Nicholas L, fellow, post doctoral, $42,000
Bartels, Amy McBride, educational pgm associate I, $14.35/hr
Bartels, Ashley N, resident physician-3rd yr, $53,763
Bartels, Brett, resident physician-1st yr, $49,025
Bartels, Justine Marie, office support assistant IV, $13.24/hr
Barth, Amy Elizabeth, prof, ast, $76,300
Barth, Cathi Dawn, office support assistant III, $11.90/hr
Barthel, Brandon Daniel, physician, resident chief, $64,425
Bartholome, Rachael Marie, office support asst IV, $13.37/hr
Bartholow, Bruce D, professor, $115,000
Bartkoski, Katherine Michelle, 4-h youth dev educr, $28,901
Bartkoski, Scott Jacob, resident physician-2nd yr, $52,007
Bartlett, David V G, media production director I, $65,000
Bartlett, Denise Michelle, nurse, staff II rnwp, $26.55/hr
Bartlett, Leah Anne, teaching ast, $13.00/hr
Bartlett, Lyria Dickason, instructor, $42,000
Bartlett, Nicholas I, research/lab technician sr, $13.37/hr
Bartley, Natalie Del, serv line spclst, $69,117
Bartley, Sharon Diane, mgr III business admin, $74,623
Barton-Burke, Margaret, prof, asoc, $131,849
Barton, Ariel E, fellow, post doctoral, $48,000
Barton, Christina Marie, office support assistant III, $11.56/hr
Barton, Cynthia Lynn, office support assistant IV, $13.20/hr
Barton, Elizabeth Ann, resident physician-2nd yr, $52,007
Barton, Elizabeth Anne, care team assoc-clinical, $12.08/hr
Barton, Elizabeth Anne, student service coor II, $42,394
Barton, Gary Edward, custodian, $10.94/hr
Barton, Gayla Jean, nurse clinician, $67,518
Barton, James Ernest, temporary technical, $27.50/hr
Barton, Jessica Anne, med office assistant, $13.33/hr
Barton, John Cyril, prof, asoc, $58,577
Barton, John D, fin and acctg specialist, $15.19/hr
Barton, Johnathan Jackson, food svc wrkr I, $9.60/hr
Barton, Kelli Nicole, resrch asoc, $39,000
Barton, Lawrence, emeritus, $5,000
Barton, Stephanie Arlene, bus support specialist I, $16.62/hr
Bartoni, Karen Marie, business support specialist II, $18.82/hr
Barua, Dipak, prof, ast, $80,000
Barua, Sutapa, prof, ast, $80,000
Bascom, Daryle E, mgr II csm operations, $73,000
Bashkin, James K, professor, $98,100
Bashyal, Shristy, student support specialist II, $15.04
Basi, Christian, ast dir strat communications, $86,173
Basile, Carole Gaynes, dean, $190,999
Basinger, Diane, med office assistant, $13.46/hr
Basinger, Glenda Fay, care team assoc-clinical, $13.33/hr
Basinger, Teresa Elkin, pat acct rep, $16.50/hr
Basker, Emek Meira, prof, asoc, $91,278
Baskett, Carol K, temporary clerical, $10.50/hr
Baskett, Jennifer Kay, nurse, staff now I, $26.00/hr
Baskett, Joe Donavan, electronics technician sr, $24.67/hr
Baskett, Lois Lanelle, executive assistant, $23.28/hr
Baskett, Randall A, hospital security officer, $13.62/hr
Basler, Beth D, talent assessment spclst, $45,540
Basler, Janna D, asoc dir student support svcs, $67,813
Basnett, Christopher Ryan, food svc wrkr I, $9.98/hr
Basnett, Daniel D, csm operations supervisor, $36,742
Basnett, Jaime Denise, nurse practitioner, $82,207
Bass, April Renee, student service coor sr, $47,461
Bass, Ellamae, office support assistant IV, $13.17/hr
Bass, Kristin Ronnetta, student support specialist sr, $16.87/hr
Bassa, Reginald L, dir II student support svcs, $79,221
Bassett, Cynthia L, office support assistant IV, $16.31/hr
Bassett, Cynthia Wyatt, librarian II, $46,575
Bassett, Eric, managing engineer, $86,636
Bassett, Kenneth N, mts/pipefitter, $22.50/hr
Bassett, Michael Ray, maintenance supervisor, $51,976
Bassham, Jennifer Nicole, serv line spclst, $66,827
Bassi, Carl Joseph, prof, asoc, $113,542
Bast, Sandra R, lecturer, $5,393
Basu, Amit Kumar, student support specialist I, $12.99/hr
Batal, Joelle Maureen, tutor, $10.25/hr
Batal, Joseph James, pharmacist III, $118,798
Batarick, John Paul, operations support tech II, $11.30/hr

Bate, Bate, prof, ast, $78,550
Bate, Michael John, system administrator-speclst, $46,589
Bateman, Susan Yvonne, academic advisor, $34,937
Bates Slone, Jamie Morgan, instructor, adjunct, $7,500
Bates, Camryn Lynne, care team assoc-suppt, $10.85/hr
Bates, Carla Pauline, prof, ast teach, $60,000
Bates, Elizabeth A, system support analyst-princpl, $63,648
Bates, Jessica Alexandra, enrollment advisor sr, $16.80/hr
Bates, Marc William, bts locksmith, $22.78/hr
Bates, Mark Sterling, electronics technician sr, $26.67/hr
Bates, Martez Demond, temporary clerical, $10.82/hr
Bates, Shyloh Faith, care team assoc-clinical, $12.08/hr
Bateson, Paul Eric, specialist, $70,299
Batsch, Dianna Theresa, business ops associate II, $57,051
Batson, Karly Michelle, veterinary technician, $13.58/hr
Batson, Linda K, clinical educator, $74,346
Batson, Wendy Kristine, library info specialist sr, $14.99/hr
Batten, Tracy Michele, psychotherapist, $51,000
Battershell, Steven Grey, dairy worker, $14.27/hr
Batterson, Jack A, library info specialist, $13.06/hr
Battles, Catherine M, program/project supprt coor I, $53,318
Batye, Michael Travis, care team assoc-suppt, $13.12/hr
Bauche, Kathryn Lynn, student service coor II, $43,884
Bauer, Amber Lynn, office support assistant III, $12.69/hr
Bauer, Casey Marie, office support assistant IV, $14.87/hr
Bauer, Eike, prof, asoc, $68,224
Bauer, John S, med techl reg, $31.10/hr
Bauer, Laura Branit, specialist, $30,000
Bauer, Lisa M, prof, ast teach, $59,152
Bauer, Matthew David, office support assistant I, $8.89/hr
Bauer, Robert L, prof, asoc, $68,275
Bauer, Sheila M, nurse, staff now plus, $30.00/hr
Baugh, Shannon T, asoc coach, $60,000
Baugh, Tiffany Patterson, resident physician-2nd yr, $52,007
Baugh, Wesley Clay, programmer analyst-speclst, $48,960
Baughan, Kirk A, dir II advancement, $90,000
Baumann, Casie, fin and acctg analyst sr, $46,821
Baumann, James Frank, professor, $168,199
Baumann, Robert A, sr ast dir studnt supprt svcs, $63,466
Baumgartner, Alana Rachel, nurse, staff II, $25.00/hr
Baumgartner, Becky Anne, office support assistant II, $10.34/hr
Baumgartner, Cody Michael, seasonal farm ast, $8.93/hr
Baumgartner, Michael James, bts carpenter, $21.71/hr
Baur, Stuart W, prof, asoc, $77,275
Bausano, Brian J, prof, ast clincl dept, $290,000
Bautista, Javier F, custodian, $12.94/hr
Bavel, Ari Lloyd, instructor, adjunct, $16,800
Bawl, Ashley Nicole, admiss liaison-mrc (rn), $51,858
Bax, Chelsea Lynn, mental health tech trainee, $9.27/hr
Bax, Dawn M, business support specialist II, $16.67/hr
Bax, John Michael, director it, $90,877
Bax, Joshua T, instructor, adjunct, $13,500
Bax, Kristin Nicole, cat scan technl (ct), $21.36/hr
Bax, Lisa M, instructional developr-expert, $21.63/hr
Baxendale, James Gilbert, asoc dir program/proj ops, $90,000
Baxley, Scott Christopher, event assistant I, $7.55/hr
Baxter, Alison Taylor, care team assoc-clinical, $12.08/hr
Baxter, Bonita Enette, dir I, business admin, $76,899
Baxter, Ethan Bryant, hospital lab tech, $12.22/hr
Baxter, Jana L, custodian, $10.94/hr
Baxter, Michael Joseph, db programmer analyst-speclst, $52,500
Baxter, Stephanie Lynn, care team assoc-clinical, $13.53/hr
Baybrook, Heidi Jean, nurse, staff I, $19.00/hr
Baybrook, Nicholas Alsendair Waite, nurse, staff II rnwp, $20.54/hr
Baye, Alicia Louise, nurse, licensed prac, $20.67/hr
Bayer, Mary Margaret, teaching ast, $13.00/hr
Bayless, Jennifer L, ast dir student support svcs, $55,631
Bayless, Jerry R, prof, asoc, $114,311
Bayless, Peter Neil Deubner, instructor, adjunct, $15,000
Baysinger, Ashley Nicole, nurse, staff II, $20.95/hr
Bazat, Jaime Lynn, human resources assistant, $16.50/hr
Bazat, JoEllen, business svcs consultant sr, $42.57/hr
Baze, Brandy Michelle, student recruitment spclst sr, $20.92/hr
Bea, Anthony Lee, food svc wrkr II, $11.83/hr
Beachler, Connie Jo, student service coor II, $52,086
Beahan, Gary W, event assistant I, $7.55/hr
Beal, Elizabeth Christine, business support spec sr, $22.18/hr
Beal, Katie Elizabeth, resident physician-2nd yr, $52,007
Beale, Geoffrey D, prof, asoc clincl, $250.00/hr

Beall, Mark A, manager it, $76,000
Beam, Hilary Michelle, office support assistant IV, $15.00/hr
Beaman-Kogan, Joshua Paul, psychologist, $55,000
Beaman, Darlene F, business support specialist II, $15.98/hr
Beaman, James M, research maintenance tech sr, $21.11/hr
Beaman, Laney E, strat comm associate II, $42,845
Beamer, Brook Erin, radiologic techl, $18.59/hr
Beamer, Kimberly Nicole, office support assistant IV, $14.46/hr
Beamer, Lesa J, prof, asoc, $89,784
Bean, Evette De'Jon, mental health professional, $46,500
Bean, Kaylin Takata, resrch ast, $16,255
Beard, Cory C, prof, asoc, $87,035
Beard, Mark N, prof, ast clincl dept, $142,800
Beard, Mark N, physician, $100.00/hr
Beard, Shawn Marie, office support assistant III, $13.98/hr
Bearden, Audrey Jan, resident physician-3rd yr, $52,470
Bearelly, Dilip, prof, ast clincl dept, $200,000
Beary, Jacqueline, business support specialist II, $17.63/hr
Beary, Mark O, research lab manager, $76,125
Beasley, Larry D Jr, steam plant opr II, $24.15/hr
Beasley, Baylee Eulalia, lab assistant, $8.08/hr
Beasley, Deborah Blaine, fin and acctg analyst sr, $40,986
Beasley, Elizabeth McCoy, bus support specialist II, $18.91/hr
Beasley, Nicole Michelle, event assistant I, $15.50/hr
Beasley, Patricia Faye, patient svc rep, $11.29/hr
Beasley, Sandra Jean, office support assistant IV, $15.82/hr
Beaston, Margaret M, nurse, staff II, $34.05/hr
Beaton, Whitney Nikole, education nurse, $62,200
Beattie, Sally, nurse, advanced practice, $66,233
Beatty, Alicia Marie, professor, $75,000
Beatty, Jennifer Ann, student service coor sr, $48,561
Beatty, Tami L, academic advisor, $41,453
Beaty, Mollee McCray, nurse, staff II, $21.26/hr
Beaty, Sandra K, strat comm associate II, $53,992
Beauchamp, Joseph W, nurse, licensed prac, $20.88/hr
Beaudoin, Alysia Ann, business support specialist II, $19.84/hr
Beaumont, Benjamin Francis, physician ast, $102,613
Beaumonte, John, driver, $12.72/hr
Beaumonte, Nicole Renee, executive assistant sr, $57,475
Becchi, Michela, prof, ast, $97,608
Becevic, Mirna, asoc dir program/project ops, $62,791
Bechtel, Sandra Marie, prof, ast, $120,235
Bechtold, Matthew L, prof, asoc clincl dept, $217,688
Bechtoldt, Marcel G, manager it, $81,417
Beck, Niels Christian Jr, emeritus, $49,095
Beck, Barbara J, educational pgm associate I, $13.72/hr
Beck, Brittany K, temporary clerical, $10.00/hr
Beck, Carmen Lynn, instructional designer-speclst, $55,182
Beck, Corrina Moria, academic advisor, $36,977
Beck, David A, prof, asoc clincl dept, $166,262
Beck, Emily Christine, emrg med techn, $12.14/hr
Beck, Mary M, prof, clincl, $128,251
Beck, Robert T, specialist, $60,309
Becker, Billy Ray, research/lab technician, $12.50/hr
Becker, Bryan R, professor, $97,549
Becker, Crystal H, police officer, $19.10/hr
Becker, Jacob Joseph, resident physician-4th yr, $55,804
Becker, Jessie Amanda, office support assistant IV, $13.26/hr
Becker, Lynn K, office supervisor, $44,160
Becker, Matthew C, programmer analyst-speclst, $53,506
Becker, Paul Abram, system support analyst-speclst, $19.85/hr
Becker, Russell G, patient svc rep, $12.09/hr
Beckering, Susan Marie, instructor, clincl, $87,000
Beckerman, Marvin Marshall, resrch ast, $4,539
Beckett, Adam Harty, prof, ast adjunct, $150,360
Beckett, Daniel Wesson, grader, $3,000
Beckett, Judy D, lecturer, $30,947
Beckfield, Felicity Jo, health physicist, $70,040
Beckham, Trevor H, resident physician-2nd yr, $50,810
Becklenberg, Susan D, dir II finance, $138,137
Beckley, Diana R, instructor, clincl, $15,440
Beckman, Brian C, food svc wrkr I, $9.60/hr
Beckmann, Cynthia C, resrch asoc, $54,862
Beckmann, Joseph Albert, prof, ast clincl dept, $147,900
Beckmann, Leissa S, nurse, procedures, $28.50/hr
Beckmann, Lindsey Beth, student support specialist sr, $24.94/hr
Beckmann, Patrick, athletic trainer, $57,235
Beckmann, Robert W, mgr III business admin, $88,500
Beckwith, Lynn L, prof, teach, $105,799

Becwar, Megan Hanna, child dev assistant, $11.90/hr
Beddoe, Nicole Dawn, physical therapist, $71,971
Bedell, Robert Allen, student service coor I, $34,400
Bedford, Carolyn K, nurse, staff II, $34.18/hr
Bedford, Tammy L, office support assistant IV, $14.15/hr
Bedy, Andrew Imre, emrg med techn paramedic, $15.61/hr
Bedy, Starr-Mar'ee Concelia, pharmacist, $117,341
Beeler, William, resident physician-1st yr, $49,025
Beene, Kenneth, enrollment advisor sr, $19.62/hr
Beerntsen, Brenda T, professor, $125,245
Beeson, Dennis Allen, prof, ast adjunct, $9,450
Beeson, Marilyn S, social worker, $69,056
Beeson, Stella Marie, patient svc rep, $13.61/hr
Beetner, Daryl G, professor, $145,000
Beffa, Lindsey Brooke Martin, resident physician-4th yr, $58,804
Beffa, Lucas Randall Anton, resident physician-4th yr, $55,804
Begemann, Brian D, powr plnt opr II, $28.70/hr
Begemann, Dawn Kimberly, service rep IV, $16.13/hr
Begemann, Jim Mark, powr plnt opr lead, $31.58/hr
Begley, Laura A, program/project supprt coor I, $51,163
Begley, Mary Theresa, security officer, $10.87/hr
Begonia, Mark Gregory, resrch asoc, $37,002
Behle, Michael Joseph, prof, asoc teach, $49,765
Behlmann, Bradley Alan, mts/electrician, $20.31/hr
Behm, Angela Marie, temporary crafts service, $7.50/hr
Behrick, Connie Gay, office support assistant IV, $16.96/hr
Behringer, Erik J, prof, ast resrch, $57,810
Behrle, Andrew C, fellow, post doctoral, $35,508
Behrle, Natalie Marie Iacopelli, res physician-2nd yr, $52,007
Behrouzi-Jareh, Parvin, nurse practitioner, $92,061
Beisser, Nicholas Paul, custodian, $10.69/hr
Bel, Susan Elizabeth, nurse, staff II, $21.80/hr
Belaustegui, Luis V, lecturer, $38,760
Belaustegui, Maria Ivonne, instructor, adjunct, $28,800
Belben, Erin, teaching ast, $6,720
Belcher, David C, prof, ast teach, $70,000
Belcher, Katherine A, office support assistant IV, $16.56/hr
Belcher, Suzanne Renee, nurse, staff II rnwp, $20.95/hr
Belden, Jeffery L, prof, clinical dept, $176,442
Beldor, Sandra Maria, supv nursing acute care, $33.10/hr
Belew, Kathryn M, nurse spclst, clincl, $87,886
Belezos, Desiree N, academic advisor, $35,088
Belford, Linda J, manuscript specialist sr, $41,943
Belgrave, Melita J, prof, ast, $48,960
Bell-Christian, Amber Deniece, office support asst III, $12.00/hr
Bell-Hale, Lindsey Mae, office support assistant III, $14.50/hr
Bell, Angela D, grader, $100.00/hr
Bell, Bill Stetson, temporary crafts service, $9.00/hr
Bell, Brenda K, office support assistant I, $9.51/hr
Bell, Brittany Bickford, lab assistant, $8.08/hr
Bell, Brooke Renee, advancement associate II, $22.36/hr
Bell, Charles E, prof, ast teach, $46,100
Bell, Clare V, prof, asoc, $62,222
Bell, Debora Jeneen, professor, $79,542
Bell, Evan R, student service coor I, $38,760
Bell, Heather Leigh, operations support tech sr, $22.00/hr
Bell, Jacquelyn Sue, prof, asoc profl practice, $70,399
Bell, Jasmine Marie, custodian, $10.00/hr
Bell, Jennifer, instructor, adjunct, $975
Bell, Jennifer Carey, rec/athletic assistant sr, $10.25/hr
Bell, Lauren Nicole, lab assistant, $8.75/hr
Bell, Linda, tutor, $22.70/hr
Bell, Marcia L, office support assistant IV, $19.87/hr
Bell, Natalie, radiologic techl, $20.51/hr
Bell, Rhodes P, veterinarian, residnt, $26,315
Bell, Robert Dale, instructor, clincl, $154,512
Bell, Savannah Nicole, event assistant I, $8.40/hr
Bell, Teresa G, educational pgm associate I, $14.84/hr
Bell, Tiffany Marie, teaching ast, $31.80/hr
Bell, Valerie J, instructor, adjunct, $3,600
Bellew, Kathleen Ann, security analyst-speclst, $61,000
Bellis, Kelly McKenna, clerk, diet, $10.42/hr
Bellome, John, prof, asoc adjunct, $92,570
Bellovich, Tena J, lecturer, $38,304
Belmore, Dawn Lanae, athletic trainer, $44,303
Belmore, James M, custodian, $10.94/hr
Belmore, Keith M, prof, ast teach, $76,105
Belsare, Aniruddha Vasudeo, fellow, post doctoral, $38,000
Beltey, Portia, food svc wrkr I, $9.60/hr

Belton, Henry Lee, custodian, $13.23/hr
Belveal, Michael, network engineer-princpl, $68,000
Bemis, Lori Ann, office support assistant IV, $22.69/hr
Bempah, Doreen O, care team assoc-suppt, $13.12/hr
Bemrose, Kimberly Michelle, temporary clerical, $9.49/hr
Benard, Julie Ann, resident physician-3rd yr, $56,263
Benben, Richard, head coach, $60,600
Bence, Victoria Lyn, patient svc rep, $11.51/hr
Bender, Shawn B, prof, ast, $95,500
Bender, Shilo Alena, research/lab technician, $15.00/hr
Bendorf, Ricky D, nurse anesthetist, $95.00/hr
Bene, Stephen A, facilities supervisor, $57,697
Benedicktus, Dana M, advancement officer sr, $61,935
Benedict, Ashley Renae, care team assoc-clinical, $13.33/hr
Benedict, Christianne Janine, temporary crafts service, $10.00/hr
Benedict, Heather Rose, agronomy spclst, $45,961
Benedict, Nancy G, executive assistant, $19.25/hr
Beneke, Andrea Faith, coor, service, $16.45/hr
Benenati, Debbie J, student support specialist sr, $23.52/hr
Benesova, Veronica, scholar, visiting, $14,400
Benevides, James M, prof, asoc teach, $77,951
Bengtson, Stephanie A, program/project supprt coor sr, $55,401
Benigno, Jaclyn Jennifer, resrch asoc, $47,045
Benjamin, Antonio L, temporary professional, $16.54/hr
Benjamin, Keith, professor, $74,636
Benjamin, Kishia Dalaine, operations support tech II, $11.53/hr
Benjamin, Leaha C, office support assistant III, $13.46/hr
Benn, Wendy Renae, ultrasonographer, $25.51/hr
Benna, Andrea Elizabeth, compliance manager, $48,000
Benne, Christopher Michael, nurse, staff II, $23.56/hr
Benne, Joshua Anthony, research specialist I, $31,411
Benner, Dennis George, mech plant speclst, mrc, $18.09/hr
Benner, Kalea E, prof, ast teach, $53,122
Benner, Mary Elizabeth, intern, $25,500
Benner, Nicholas S, strat comm associate I, $42,740
Bennett-Brush, Nicholas Spenser, pharmacy tech, $10.64/hr
Bennett, Bethany J, mgr, medical educ, $58,300
Bennett, Denise Jo, csm specialist sr, $18.87/hr
Bennett, Edward S, professor, $124,601
Bennett, James C, business support specialist sr, $24.16/hr
Bennett, Jeffrey Scott, prof, asoc, $64,209
Bennett, Jerry Richard, mech trades spclst (mts), $22.42/hr
Bennett, John, mgr business devlpmnt-mrc, $77,609
Bennett, John Falls, prof, asoc teach, $75,736
Bennett, Justin M, instructor, adjunct, $3,400
Bennett, Kimberly K, prof, asoc, $66,169
Bennett, Lara Zwarun, prof, asoc, $63,700
Bennett, Linda, prof, asoc, $116,894
Bennett, Lorna Gayle, office support assistant III, $11.73/hr
Bennett, Nancy A, office support assistant IV, $17.20/hr
Bennett, Nelia Herico, nurse, or/recovery-ch, $34.32/hr
Bennett, Susan Elizabeth, prof, ast clincl, $52,275
Bennett, Wendy Annette, custodian, $12.94/hr
Benney, Erin Michelle, nurse, staff I, $19.00/hr
Benney, Gregory Scott, program/project supprt coor I, $34,400
Benoit, Lauren Beth Dante, development officer, $47,333
Benskin, Terri Lynn, coor audit & quality monitor, $58,065
Benson, Connie Louise, office support assistant IV, $18.01/hr
Benson, Craig A, mgr student support svcs, $59,178
Benson, Errol, asoc dir human resources, $95,444
Benson, Heather Renee, architectural associate, $38,872
Benson, Jacquelyn J, prof, ast, $76,000
Benson, Kathryn Anne, executive assistant, $18.80/hr
Benson, Kelly Lyn, academic advisor, $41,389
Benson, Kyla Marie, physician ast, $82,000
Benson, Roy, bldg cntrl sys techn iv lead, $25.37/hr
Bent, Elizabeth Oliver-Savio, business ops associate sr, $52,544
Bent, Emily Susan, library info specialist sr, $17.74/hr
Bent, Michael James, office support assistant IV, $14.48/hr
Bentch, Carmen Jean, nurse, staff II, $22.24/hr
Bentch, Felicia Lea, patient svc rep, $11.50/hr
Benter, Stephanie R, business support specialist II, $15.45/hr
Bentlage, Marci Jo, office support assistant III, $12.72/hr
Bentley, Clyde, prof, asoc, $76,866
Bentley, Reginald Lee, stores clerk, $13.74/hr
Benton, Parker Nash, event assistant I, $8.50/hr
Benton, Rita A, patient svc rep, $13.01/hr
Benwell, Amy Lynn, office support assistant IV, $19.09/hr
Benz, Barbara Jean, office support assistant III, $12.58/hr

Benz, Doris Ann, student support specialist I, $12.98/hr
Bequette, Amanda Renee Whitworth, prof, ast resrch, $48,233
Berardini, Nicholas Ryan, instructor, adjunct, $18,000
Berck, Charles Wayne, event assistant I, $7.55/hr
Berendzen, Gerri Lee, prof, ast visiting, $65,000
Berent, Linda Marie, prof, asoc clincl dept, $138,936
Berey, Lewis, instructor, adjunct, $12,000
Berg, Christina, office support assistant IV, $15.50/hr
Berg, Deanna Ruth, sterile processing coord, $17.68/hr
Berg, John Norman, emeritus, $26,530
Berg, Nova Eileen, nurse, licensed prac, $20.37/hr
Bergendahl, Francis Neil, mts/pipefitter, $21.05/hr
Berger, Joyce Ann, office support assistant IV, $18.64/hr
Berger, Kelly Marie, mental health tech, $11.85/hr
Berger, Mark, prof, adjunct, $53,333
Berger, Terence M, media producer II, $17.00/hr
Bergerson, Andrew S, professor, $73,081
Bergesch, Rebecca Lynn, nurse, licensed prac, $18.46/hr
Bergeson, Lisa M, nurse, staff II, $26.89/hr
Bergfield, Rebecca Ann, environmental health prof sr, $47,000
Bergin Jr, Patrick Michael Taylor, lecturer, $9,000
Bergin, Christi A, prof, asoc resrch, $62,500
Bergin, David, prof, asoc, $76,491
Bergin, Melissa Grace, high school student, $7.50/hr
Bergman, Becky, mgr II student support svcs, $53,427
Bergman, Greg A, event assistant I, $9.50/hr
Bergman, Katherine F H, event assistant I, $7.75/hr
Bergman, Roger L, grader, $52
Bergoudian, Rita L S, instructor, adjunct, $4,267
Bergstrom, Dean E, research specialist II, $51,266
Berhorst, Bridget Maureen, occl therapist, $35.00/hr
Berhorst, Melissa Renee, radiologic techl, $23.46/hr
Beringer, Patricia A, audiologist, $33.00/hr
Berka, Charles Melvin, lab assistant, $11.73/hr
Berkbigler, Jeffrey A, library information assistant, $12.44/hr
Berkel, Laverne A, prof, asoc, $79,596
Berkelman, Robert Jeffrey, student support spec sr, $16.80/hr
Berkey, Jess, fin and acctg consultant, $60,000
Berkley Patton, Jannette, prof, asoc, $68,648
Berkley, Annette, mammography technl, $30.36/hr
Berkley, Clint A, telecom it analyst-princpl, $54,771
Berkowitz, Marvin W, professor, $156,925
Berlemann, James D, emrg med techn paramedic, $14.98/hr
Berlin, Aaron R, sr manager it, $92,716
Berlin, Sarah E, media production ast, $40,115
Berlyn, Mark A, dir iv advancement, $119,819
Bernal II, Anthony John, student support specialist sr, $17.25/hr
Bernard, Jessica Marie, instructor, adjunct, $9,000
Bernards, Matthew T, ast, $91,455
Bernath, Maureen Dominique, student service coor II, $42,630
Berndt, Harold D, dir I, finance, $91,169
Bernfeld, Jeremy, editor II, $45,000
Bernhard, Christa Lynne, veterinarian, residnt, $26,000
Bernhardt, Deborah J, instructor, ast, $33,486
Bernhardt, John Raymond, med techl reg, $28.58/hr
Bernhardt, Mark, professor, $75,000
Bernier Gosselin, Veronique, veterinarian, residnt, $26,000
Bernskoetter, Nicole Elizabeth, research specialist I, $32,640
Bernstein, Moira Michelle Jablon, oper support tech I, $20.00/hr
Bernt, Beth Ann, practice manager, $78,000
Bernt, John Paul, nurse, staff II, $34.18/hr
Berry, Alisha R, student support specialist sr, $16.87/hr
Berry, Anita June, office support assistant III, $12.62/hr
Berry, Barbara, instructor, clincl, $15,375
Berry, Clinton L, librarian III, $47,574
Berry, Daniel G, emrg med techn paramedic, $15.37/hr
Berry, David Robert, nurse, staff II, $28.80/hr
Berry, Emanuele Mikala, program/project supprt coor I, $34,400
Berry, Jamie A, sr dir program/project ops, $87,101
Berry, Jennifer Kay, reimbursement ast-cert, $18.76/hr
Berry, Mara G, office support assistant III, $11.50/hr
Berry, Meridith J, extns professional, asoc, $61,025
Berry, Michael P, athletic trainer, $49,147
Berry, Nicholas Forrest, event assistant I, $7.50/hr
Berry, Robert Taylor, prof, asoc adjunct, $20,475
Berry, Tracey Gillian, strat comm consultant sr, $60,047
Bertram, Barry, instructor, adjunct, $22,500
Bertram, Rosalyn M, prof, asoc, $68,009
Besenyi, Gina Marie, research/lab technician, $15.00/hr

Beshears, Jacqueline Lea, nurse practitioner, $78,030
Besleme, Harry James, food svc wrkr I, $11.29/hr
Bess, Melissa M, nutrition spclst, $49,973
Best, Brad A, prof, ast/profl pract, $66,261
Best, Gail Maureen, office support assistant II, $10.40/hr
Best, Rebecca Hope, prof, ast, $56,100
Bestgen, Brenda, office support assistant IV, $18.15/hr
Bethea, Walter Kenneth Jr, student service coor I, $42,345
Bethel, Kelly J, business support specialist II, $19.50/hr
Bethel, Samuel Reed, mental health professional, $36,285
Bethell, Lance M, instructor, $52
Bethman, Brenda Lee, dir II student support svcs, $72,595
Bethune, Christine Elizabeth, office support asst IV, $15.66/hr
Bettencourt, B Ann, professor, $120,749
Betts, Aaron B, patient svc rep, $13.55/hr
Betts, Philip Patrice, strat comm consultant, $21.96/hr
Betz, Bridgette Anne, dir II student support svcs, $74,601
Betz, Christian Kelly, event assistant I, $7.70/hr
Betz, Deborah Lynn, student support specialist sr, $22.13/hr
Beucke, Nathan Lewis, prof, asoc clincl dept, $136,866
Beutenmiller, Brett Gregory, nurse, staff II, $20.54/hr
Beutenmiller, Melissa Ann, care team assoc-clinical, $11.10/hr
Bevard, Kevin G, reactor operator, $26.42/hr
Bever, Tadd C, polysomnograph techn reg, $20.97/hr
Beversdorf, David Q, prof, asoc, $182,334
Bewley, Jeffrey Lee, advancement officer sr, $62,131
Beyer, Gene C, sr ast dir studnt supprt svcs, $60,405
Beyer, Madeline Carroll, communications assistant sr, $16.25/hr
Bhandari, Ramji Kumar, prof, ast resrch, $65,400
Bharadwaj, Pratiksubramany, event assistant I, $8.50/hr
Bhardwaj, Bhaskar, resident physician-1st yr, $49,025
Bhardwaj, Mohit, prof, ast clincl dept, $150,000
Bhargava, Rhea, resident physician-2nd yr, $50,810
Bhartee, Harsh, resident physician-1st yr, $50,219
Bhaskar, Michelle Mary, specialist, $10.00/hr
Bhat, Hari Krishen, prof, asoc, $106,882
Bhat, Nimee Kotha, resrch ast, $29,502
Bhatia, Sanjiv K, prof, asoc, $93,813
Bhatnagar, Udit Bhaskar, resident physician-2nd yr, $50,810
Bheemisetty, Shyamala Deepti, resident physician-4th yr, $55,804
Bhullar, Pushpajit, librarian III, $63,950
Bi, Lian Xiang, prof, asoc resrch, $8,000
Bianco, Julie Ann, nurse, licensed prac, $20.07/hr
Bibbs, Deidra Lashawn, office support assistant I, $9.05/hr
Bibby, John E, event assistant I, $7.50/hr
Bichianu, Daniela Cristina, prof, ast adjunct, $125.00/hr
Bichu, Prasad Balkrishna, prof, ast clincl dept, $145,503
Bickel, Barry R, db programmer analyst-speclst, $54,621
Bickel, Gavin Wesley, radiologic techl, $18.96/hr
Bickel, Judith A, pat admiss advisor, $30.36/hr
Bickerton, Andrea Dawn H, resident physician-1st yr, $50,219
Bickford, Edmund Cooney, event assistant I, $9.45/hr
Bickhaus, Jennifer Ann, resident physician-4th yr, $55,804
Biedenstein, Becky L, grounds keeper, $12.18/hr
Biegen, Sharon, dir II student support svcs, $88,836
Bielicke, Delite, admiss liaison-mrc, $56,016
Bien, Joseph Julius, professor, $88,783
Bier, Gregory L, prof, asoc teach, $106,641
Bier, Melinda C, academic dir, $130,370
Bieri, Alan E, physical therapist, $35.00/hr
Bieri, Joni Renee, reimbursement ast, $15.87/hr
Bierman, Barbara June, grader, $52
Biesemeyer, Janis, coor, service, $17.10/hr
Bietsch, Deborah, office support assistant IV, $14.87/hr
Biever, Jessica Jo, fellow, post doctoral, $36,000
Biggs, Andrew Knox, research specialist I, $43,502
Biggs, Joedd Harrison, resident physician-1st yr, $50,219
Biggs, Meghan Elizabeth, research specialist I, $31,200
Bigham, Richard Hunt, dean, ast, $92,520
Bihlmaier, Jennifer Kristin, resident physician-3rd yr, $52,470
Bihlmaier, Matthew Douglas, resident physician-4th yr, $54,425
Bihmidine, Saadia, fellow, post doctoral, $44,100
Bihomora, Stanislas Rutsinga, custodian, $12.94/hr
Bilderback, Bobbie Lea, office support assistant IV, $16.93/hr
Bildner, Amy Marie, ultrasonographer, $24.10/hr
Bildner, Carl, pat admiss advisor, $31.20/hr
Bildner, Carl, clincl documnt spclst, $69,515
Bildner, Judith I, nurse manager, $107,415
Bill, Tammy, office support assistant I, $11.71/hr

Billings, Laura Lisa, nurse spclst, clincl, $78,250
Billings, Steve P, prof, ast adjunct, $125.00/hr
Billings, Veci Lynn, reimbursement ast sr, $18.93/hr
Billington, Joshua D, resident physician-2nd yr, $52,007
Billstein, Catherine A, business support analyst sr, $26.72/hr
Bilyeu, Brad Patrick, system administrator-speclst, $47,314
Bilyeu, Neal, prof, ast adjunct, $38,000
Bin Abdulhak, Aref Abdulrahman, res physician-3rd yr, $52,470
Binalsheikh, Ibrahim Makki, prof, ast clincl dept, $185,000
Binder, Lindi Bell, physician ast, $78,500
Binfield, Julian, prof, ast resrch, $99,959
Bingaman, Jerry Wayne, custodian mrc, $10.50/hr
Bingaman, Susan, research specialist sr, $41,218
Bingham, Colby S, resident physician-2nd yr, $52,007
Bingham, Gregory R, police officer, $18.56/hr
Bink, Cinnamon Ann, nurse, licensed prac, $17.85/hr
Binkley, Jana Marie, clerk, unit, $11.00/hr
Bintzer, Jeanne Ann, media producer, $41,454
Biondo Bell, Deanna Lynn, veterinary technician sr, $18.56/hr
Birch, O Tyrone, food svc wrkr I, $10.53/hr
Birchler, Donald Eugene, custodian, $12.69/hr
Birchler, James A, prof, curators, $237,097
Birchler, Wanda G, office support assistant III, $11.30/hr
Bird, Scott Gawain, ast athletic director, $77,250
Bird, Susan Kristen, resrch ast, $37,080
Birdsong, Jaimie Lynn, coor, service, $17.32/hr
Birdsong, Jamie E, custodian, $10.69/hr
Birdsong, Mary Etta, custodian, $13.23/hr
Birisci, Esma, statistician, $21.97/hr
Birk, Heather Lynn, strat comm manager, $52,250
Birk, Michael David, user support analyst-expert, $20.86/hr
Birkenbach, David Charles, temporary clerical, $10.50/hr
Birkholz, Robin M, office support assistant sr, $18.22/hr
Birkner, Betty A, office support assistant IV, $15.35/hr
Birkner, Rebecca Rose, office support assistant IV, $13.06/hr
Birman, Victor, professor, $147,728
Birmingham, Keith A, business support specialist II, $24.09/hr
Birt, Jeffrey T, engineer I, $56,184
Birt, Julie Amanda, teaching ast, $20,850
Birtley, Nancy Michele, instructor, adjunct, $8,412
Birzer, Megan Christine, resrch ast, $40,000
Bischoff, Christian M, fellow, post doctoral, $44,000
Bisges, Heather Ann, nurse clinician, $60,000
Bisges, Kevin H, construction manager II, $67,854
Bish, Mandy Danielle, research specialist sr, $55,000
Bish, Ryan L, library info specialist sr, $14.95/hr
Bish, Samuel E, business svcs consultant sr, $78,280
Bishop, Michael W Jr, nurse, staff II rnwp, $20.54/hr
Bishop Perera, Helene, nurse, licensed prac, $17.91/hr
Bishop, Alicia Reine, nurse, staff now III, $30.00/hr
Bishop, Barbara A, prof, ast teach, $32,564
Bishop, Bradley W, healthcare admin fellow, $50,000
Bishop, Brian Travis, ast coach, $34,000
Bishop, Danielle E, security officer, $11.71/hr
Bishop, Donna Michelle, hris specialist-expert, $65,975
Bishop, Kendra Renee, nursing ast, $12.08/hr
Bishop, Molly J, temporary professional, $11.30/hr
Bishop, Nancy I, research/lab technician sr, $14.99/hr
Bishop, Shane Barton, athletic trainer, $48,260
Bishop, Teresa Antha, educational pgm coor II, $39,034
Bismark, Veronika, grader, $100.00/hr
Bissen, Michael S, support systems admin-speclst, $45,600
Bissram, Jeremy, intern, $26,265
Bittle, Carol Ann, health records techn II, $14.09/hr
Bittle, Charles Richard, bts carpenter, $21.71/hr
Bittle, Duane, delivery attd, libry lead, $14.98/hr
Bittle, Laurie E, telecom inst analyst-expert, $22.36/hr
Bittner, Mary Katharine, nurse, licensed prac, $15.06/hr
Bivens, Michael W, stage services assistant sr, $16.00/hr
Bivens, Nathan J, ast dir research, $77,613
Bixby, Alicia, instructor, $44,734
Bixby, James A, mgr csm operations, $25.96/hr
Bixby, Mary Katherine, student service coor sr, $72,228
Bixler-Funk, Anne-Marie, instructor, adjunct, $25,050
Bjes, Edward S, resrch ast, $38,215
Bjornstrom, Eileen E Spitznas, prof, ast, $69,269
Black, Andrew, prof, teach, $47,739
Black, Angela Lynn Curl, prof, ast, $61,845
Black, Anthony F, instructor, adjunct, $18,000

Black, Brandee S, resident physician-5th yr, $58,083
Black, Cheryl D, professor, $67,261
Black, David James, forensic investigator, $21.36/hr
Black, Debra, office support assistant IV, $19.19/hr
Black, Elizabeth Ann, research specialist sr, $51,761
Black, Frederick C, distribution techn-mtls mgmt, $14.25/hr
Black, Grant C, academic dir, $96,801
Black, Heather Nicole, pharmacy tech, $12.51/hr
Black, Jamette M, human resources specialist sr, $60,241
Black, Jaryn Shea, nurse, staff II, $20.54/hr
Black, Lahne Jean, student support specialist sr, $17.14/hr
Black, Mary Dell, resrch asoc, $26,500
Black, Nathan Douglas, custodian, $10.94/hr
Black, Rebecca Anne, nurse, staff I, $19.00/hr
Black, Samuel Travis, business support analyst II, $17.64/hr
Black, Sharon A, executive assistant, $18.60/hr
Black, William Kurt, prof, asoc, $60,900
Blackburn, Botswana Toney, prof, ast teach, $71,781
Blackburn, Ronnie, sftware supprt analyst-speclst, $39,600
Blackburn, Steven K, resp therapist reg, $28.60/hr
Blacklock, Judy Lee, telecomm opr-h, $13.12/hr
Blackman, Abigail Shniter, resident physician-2nd yr, $50,810
Blackman, Kimberly Kay, program/project supprt coor II, $60,000
Blackmon, Betty L, prof, asoc, $64,853
Blackmore, Lisa A, lecturer, $12,108
Blackmore, Mark Powell, lecturer, $4,404
Blackshear, Nicholas Brake, care team assoc-clinical, $12.08/hr
Blackstone, Jennifer Em, programmer analyst-speclst, $45,600
Blackwell, Joshua P, support systems admin-expert, $54,758
Blackwell, Justin R, user support analyst-expert, $21.16/hr
Blackwell, Kenneth Dale, mech trades spclst (mts), $24.45/hr
Blackwell, Phyllis Elaine, office support assistant sr, $15.56/hr
Blackwell, Traci Ann, business support specialist II, $20.63/hr
Blackwell, Valerie Gayle, program/project supprt coor sr, $19,975
Blackwood, Matthew Joseph, system administrator-entry, $43,259
Blades, Amy Lynn, strat comm consultant, $44,849
Blagg, Rene M, med coding spclst-certified, $20.75/hr
Blaine, Edward H, professor, $126,158
Blair-Bruce, Pamela, instructor, adjunct, $7,059
Blair, Andrew C, lecturer, $30,000
Blair, Carolyn Elizabeth, instructor, adjunct, $4,200
Blair, David Nelson, custodian, $12.94/hr
Blair, Ellen Louise, business support specialist sr, $23.29/hr
Blair, Jeanette Grace, accountant I, $16.60/hr
Blair, Jennifer Ann, resident physician-3rd yr, $52,470
Blair, Jennifer Annette, research lab supervisor, $45,000
Blair, Jennifer L, business support specialist II, $19.66/hr
Blair, Johnette E, office support assistant IV, $14.32/hr
Blair, Richard F, bts locksmith, $21.71/hr
Blair, Steven R, mechanical plant speclst, mrc, $18.09/hr
Blaisdell, Deborah Sue, office support assistant IV, $19.45/hr
Blaisdell, Garion Matthew, temporary technical, $7.50/hr
Blaise, Gerry, account executive, $6,000
Blaise, Janet Lucille, nurse, staff II, $34.18/hr
Blaise, Kristina Michelle, surgical technl certified, $15.87/hr
Blake, Celeste Renee, pharmacy tech, $10.85/hr
Blake, Joni M, administrative consultant, $103,947
Blake, Kevin Ray, lecturer, $45,000
Blake, Sarah Frances, resident physician-1st yr, $49,025
Blakemore, Amanda L, office support assistant III, $11.80/hr
Blakemore, Casey Lee, instructor, adjunct, $6,300
Blakemore, Danielle L, nurse, staff now plus, $30.00/hr
Blakemore, Lisa Marie, nurse, staff now III, $30.00/hr
Blakley, Norman D, optometric techn, $12.42/hr
Blanc, Teresa Williams, instructor, clincl, $9,000
Blancarte, Deborah Anna, instructor, adjunct, $12,600
Blancett, John Michael, instructor, adjunct, $6,000
Blanche, Adrienne, media producer II, $17.41/hr
Bland, Angela Marie, custodian, $10.69/hr
Bland, Lisa Ann, business support specialist II, $17.51/hr
Bland, Thomas Alan, mts/refrigeration mech, $22.50/hr
Blandon, Erick, prof, asoc, $59,478
Blank, Anne Sophie, prof, asoc teach, $44,108
Blank, Penny Lea, executive assistant, $25.37/hr
Blankenship, Amanda Lee, nurse manager, $77,753
Blankenship, Shannon Dale, mts/electrician, $21.05/hr
Blankson, Richard Kuntu, office support assistant II, $100.00/hr
Blanton, Gerald, ast dir student support svcs, $59,160
Blanton, Robert John, resp therapist reg, $20.98/hr

Blanton, Sarah H, support systems admin-princpl, $70,373
Blanton, Virginia Yvette, professor, $92,463
Blazis, Debra J, nurse, staff now III, $30.00/hr
Blea, Tyrone, office support aide II, $9.92/hr
Blease, Lauren Ashley, nurse, staff I, $19.00/hr
Blecha, Kelley Jon, mgr surgical svcs-h, $124,200
Blecha, Kyle M, program/project supprt coor I, $25.00/hr
Bledsoe, Steven R Jr, user support analyst-expert, $20.47/hr
Bledsoe, Wayne Mitchell, media production director I, $23,793
Bleha, Saleh Ali, instructor, adjunct, $54,000
Bleich, Mary Louise, office support assistant IV, $12.98/hr
Bleiler, Jennifer Dawn, librarian III, $45,602
Bleisch, Amy D, research/lab technician, $15.00/hr
Bleneau, Virginie Annie, grader, $100.00/hr
Blevins, Gary D, custodian mrc, $11.02/hr
Blevins, Michelle M, executive assistant sr, $56,382
Blickhan, Danielle Elizabeth, care team assoc-clinical, $12.32/hr
Bliss, Robert McKinley, dean, $145,450
Blissett, Dorothy J, educational pgm associate I, $13.45/hr
Blitz, Bryan, head coach, $132,000
Bloch, Peter H, professor, $153,726
Blocher, Erin Elizabeth, instructor, $57,913
Blocker, Rebecca Sue, housing&envirn design spclst, $62,081
Blockus, Linda, dir program/project operations, $67,891
Blodgett, Clayton F, resrch asoc, $53,048
Blodgett, Elaine L, office support assistant III, $11.30/hr
Blodgett, John G, programmer analyst-princpl, $38,577
Blodgett, Kelsey Elizabeth, veterinary technician sr, $14.95/hr
Blodgett, Monika, office support assistant IV, $14.80/hr
Blodgett, Stacey Michelle, extension asoc, $50,880
Bloemker, Katherine Hoffman, prof, asoc teach, $73,974
Blomenkamp, Kyle J, technical trainer-expert, $47,248
Blomenkamp, Mandy Ann, nurse, staff II, $22.24/hr
Blomquist, Gregory E, prof, asoc, $57,609
Blood, Adelina J, tutor, $13.39/hr
Bloom, Tina Lee, prof, asoc, $73,013
Bloss, Jennifer Rebecca, academic advisor, $40,076
Bloss, Jeremy S, student support specialist II, $20.08/hr
Blount, Jessica Michelle, resident physician-4th yr, $54,425
Blow, Constance A, instructor, clincl, $64,036
Blower, Erin Elizabeth, library info specialist, $12.98/hr
Blueitt, Bennie Shawdale, custodian, $10.39/hr
Bluel, Reagan J, extns professional, ast, $46,000
Bluestone, Kenneth I, physician, $135.00/hr
Blumberg, Eric M, instructor, adjunct, $9,000
Blumer, Jeffrey S, business support specialist II, $19.49/hr
Blumer, Tammy Jean, certif pharmacy techn, $17.37/hr
Blumhagen, Teresa L, nurse, staff, $30.24/hr
Blundell, Robert Eugene Jr, prof, asoc clincl, $115,024
Blust, Dennis Michael, social worker, $38,229
Blust, Heather N, office support assistant IV, $14.00/hr
Boatman, Nancy C, program/project supprt coor sr, $54,867
Bobb, Logan Christopher, office support assistant III, $12.00/hr
Bobitan, Luciana Maria, instructor, $13,404
Bobka, Andrew Lawrence, emrg med techn, $11.61/hr
Bobo, Lucius James III, custodian, $13.23/hr
Bobowski, Michael Richard, temporary clerical, $8.50/hr
Bobryk, Christopher W, fellow, post doctoral, $44,000
Bobzien Wade, Donna J, care team assoc-suppt, $21.74/hr
Bock Apperson, Jennifer Nicole, nurse, staff II, $20.54/hr
Bock, Anagha Sawant, research specialist I, $37,790
Bock, Margaret Mason, lecturer, $100.00/hr
Bocke, Dana D, teaching ast, $10.00/hr
Bocklage, Todd G, ast mgr respiratory care, $84,760
Bocklage, Tracy Kay, nurse manager, $84,000
Bockting, Benjamin M, office support assistant II, $10.24/hr
Bodapati, Surya Narayan, prof, adjunct, $56,700
Bode, Robert Perry, professor, $123,627
Bodle, Jamie Nicole, ophthalmic ast cert, $14.15/hr
Body, Melanie Jessica, fellow, post doctoral, $34,000
Boeckmann, Andrew Z, engineer, resrch, $79,560
Boeckmann, Kathleen Zak, editor ast, $73,729
Boedeker, Terri Lea, reimbursement ast-cert, $18.41/hr
Boehlow, Rachel E, mgr student support svcs, $49,538
Boehm, Clinton J, csm associate II, $16.64/hr
Boehm, Lawrence F, strat comm associate II, $51,252
Boehm, Randall Gene, mgr security-h, $82,214
Boeke, Paul Steven, resident physician-4th yr, $55,804
Boelsen, Regina G, patient svc rep, $16.55/hr

Boerman, Erika Mary, fellow, post doctoral, $44,340
Boessen, Adam Michael, prof, ast, $65,000
Boessen, Christian R, prof, asoc teach, $78,005
Boessen, Norma Denise, academic advisor sr, $43,268
Bogan, Barbara, reimbursement spclst, $23.51/hr
Bogart, Raymon L, police lieutenant, $47,377
Bogdanov, Anna Mari, pharmacy tech, $10.64/hr
Bogener, James Winston, adjunct, $15,000
Bogener, Jennifer L, nursing ast sr, $13.00/hr
Boggs, Eugenia Inez, coor, service, $19.14/hr
Boggs, H Ronald, construction manager II, $73,313
Boggs, Jerry W, bts carpenter, $21.71/hr
Boggs, Kathleen R, instructor, adjunct, $43,000
Boggs, Rebecca, educational pgm coor III, $50,000
Bogle, Angela, adjunct, $15,000
Bogler, David John, prof, ast adjunct, $9,000
Bogue, Michael G, mts/welding, $21.05/hr
Bohan, Ruth L, professor, $77,208
Bohanek, Jennifer Geraldine, prof, ast resrch, $17,394
Bohannan, Eric W, research specialist sr, $63,127
Bohaty, Brenda S, professor, $203,017
Bohlmeyer, Rebecca Faye, db programmer analyst-expert, $61,854
Bohm, Jacqueline Leigh, business support specialist II, $20.28/hr
Bohm, Tiffany C, care team assoc-clinical, $12.32/hr
Bohn, Joan Rene, sterile processing tech, $18.86/hr
Bohn, Marybeth A S, executive assistant, $22.64/hr
Bohner, Martin Juergen, prof, curators, $100,000
Bohnert, Amy N, mgr II business admin, $53,596
Bohon, Tiffany M, prof, ast clincl dept, $141,400
Bohorquez, Laura G, child dev teacher sr, $25,272
Boies, Genevieve N, food svc wrkr II, $11.83/hr
Boisseau, Michelle, professor, $88,553
Boit, Elizeba Jepotib, nurse, staff II, $21.37/hr
Bok, Sangho, fellow, post doctoral, $65,000
Bokemper, Meghen, resident physician-1st yr, $49,025
Bolabola Taboada, Marie Ann, instructor, clincl, $15,375
Boland, Denise Ann, office support assistant IV, $20.26/hr
Boland, Kathleen J, prof, asoc clincl, $90,225
Boland, Sharon Kay, reimbursement ast-cert, $19.11/hr
Boland, Sherri Kay, office support assistant IV, $18.77/hr
Bolden, Brenda E, office support assistant IV, $13.75/hr
Boldt, Jessica Lynn, museum paraprofessional II, $15.10/hr
Bolen, Angela Celesta, student support specialist sr, $27,773
Bolerjack, Kaela G, resp therapist reg, $21.18/hr
Boles, Catherine Diann, prof, ast, $65,344
Boles, Cynthia Lynn, office support assistant IV, $14.70/hr
Boles, Katrina Kouba, media producer sr, $37,653
Boles, Michael K, media producer sr, $39,577
Boles, Nadine, educational pgm associate I, $13.05/hr
Boles, Rhonda L, research specialist sr, $25.78/hr
Boley, Adam J, network engineer-expert, $63,000
Boley, Cynthia, teaching ast, $13.00/hr
Boliaux, Matthew Gordon, tutor, $10.75/hr
Boling, Brad, student support specialist sr, $16.74/hr
Boling, Geneva Lynn, sr asst dir studnt supprt svcs, $56,854
Boling, Melody A, resrch asoc, $46,350
Bolinger, Autum Laine, nurse, staff II, $22.24/hr
Bollig, Craig A, resident physician-1st yr, $50,219
Bollin, John J III, resrch asoc, $61,538
Bollinger, David Wayne, research specialist I, $36,720
Bollinger, Holly Lynn, strat comm associate II, $48,231
Bollinger, Michelle Elizabeth, student service coor II, $53,500
Bolls, Paul David, prof, asoc, $90,507
Bollu, Pradeepchakrava, fellow, post doc clncl-yr3, $60,415
Bolman, Lee G, professor, $224,400
Bolon, Cynthia Pearl, lecturer, $45,930
Bolshakova, Natalia, prof, ast adjunct, $31,733
Bolte, Cheryl Ann, veterinary technician, $15.76/hr
Bolte, Kenneth A, busi spclst, agri, $62,172
Bolton, Julie Ann, care coordinator, $64,375
Bolton, Natalie Anne, prof, ast, $61,675
Bolton, Tiffany Leeann, instructor, $63,630
Bolzenius, Jacob, temporary clerical, $16.92/hr
Bomar, Marilee Green, nurse spclst, clincl, $87,209
Bommel, Tommy Gene, mech, bldg maint, $19.64/hr
Bompadre, Silvia G, prof, ast, $76,500
Bonaparte, Marla Dennise, food svc wrkr III, $13.21/hr
Bonaparte, Voronica Inez, business support spec II, $20.21/hr
Bond, Nancy Celeste, library info specialist sr, $15.32/hr

Bond, Nancy Suzanne, supply chain systems prin muhc, $63,984
Bond, Van Burian, bts mason/tuckptr, $20.23/hr
Bondy, Kathleen Noland, extns professional, $61,038
Bone, Terry Lynn, lecturer, $45,935
Bonebrake, Beatrice Anne, office support assistant IV, $13.20/hr
Bonello, Joseph P, office support assistant IV, $16.44/hr
Bonen, Michael Garth, nurse, staff prn, $26.00/hr
Bonen, Tiffany Dawn, nurse, staff II, $23.89/hr
Boness, Matthew Thomas, office support assistant III, $11.30/hr
Bonewald, Lynda F, prof, curators, $214,150
Bongartz, Charlotte Marie, csm professional sr, $57,888
Bongartz, Michael, dir I, university police, $86,098
Bongiorno, Angelo Giuseppe, ast athletic trainer, $34,400
Bonner, Donna R, office support assistant IV, $19.02/hr
Bonnett, Anne Louise, nurse clinician, $72,675
Bonnot, Julie Alane, nurse, staff II, $29.44/hr
Bonnot, Thomas W, research specialist I, $40,472
Bono, Mary Louise, office support assistant IV, $16.31/hr
Bonsall, Aaron, prof, ast, $73,440
Bonsignore, Diego, teaching ast, $4,608
Bontrager, Megan Michelle, office support assistant II, $10.55/hr
Bonuchi, Jimmy Louis, mts/electrician, $22.49/hr
Bonzer, William E, reactor manager, $65,196
Book, Neil L, emeritus, $6,000
Book, William, instructor, adjunct, $9,000
Booker, Brent Eldon, agriculture associate sr, $19.08/hr
Booker, Joshua Michael, seasonal farm ast, $8.93/hr
Bookout, Mark E, director it, $94,976
Books, Heather E, hris specialist-expert, $58,000
Bookter, Edwin Faust Jr, sterile processing tech, $17.95/hr
Boomer, Joanne Patricia, manager it, $85,833
Boon, Robert Eric, instructor, $29,750
Boone, Elizabeth Katherine, instructor, adjunct, $4,800
Boone, Elton R, instructional developr-princpl, $25.73/hr
Boone, Faith A, ast athletic trainer, $34,916
Boone, John Paul, temporary technical, $8.25/hr
Boone, Lashonda R, research consultant II, $67,641
Boone, Luke, resident physician-1st yr, $49,025
Boonseng, Thitinun, student support specialist sr, $22.11/hr
Boos, Nancy L, pharmacy tech, $13.61/hr
Booska, Danielle Nicole, nurse, staff II, $21.37/hr
Booth, Frank W, professor, $185,275
Booton, Brian H, program/project supprt coor I, $49,710
Booze, Rosie, custodial supervisor, $35,270
Boozer, Thomas Mark, prgm director, $90,000
Bopp, Anthony L, mts/pipefitter, $22.50/hr
Bopp, Kenneth D, prof, ast clincl, $62,487
Bopp, Michael Corin, mts/electrician, $21.05/hr
Bordelon, Camille Elise, athletic trainer, $45,000
Bordenkircher, Shelley Anne, mammography technl, $28.91/hr
Border, Marilyn J, custodian, $11.00/hr
Bordere, Tashel C, prof, ast, $76,000
Borders, James David, retail sales manager, $47,610
Borduin, Charles M, professor, $122,584
Bordy, Harold Phillip, instructor, adjunct, $15,000
Borelli, Gail S, editor II, $47,000
Boren, Suzanne Austin, prof, asoc, $119,900
Boren, Thomas L, sr dir program/project ops, $97,919
Borengasser, Tracy Lynn, office supervisor, $34,500
Borenstein, Marc A, prof, clinical dept, $410,962
Borgelt, Steven C, prof, asoc, $95,182
Borgers, Karen R, executive assistant, $22.48/hr
Borges Domingues, Livia Cristina Miranda, hlr spec I, $17.00/hr
Borgmann, Elizabeth Anne, research specialist I, $42,000
Borgmeyer, Ashley Elizabeth, nurse, staff II, $23.34/hr
Borgmeyer, Susan K, program/project supprt coor I, $51,250
Borja, Jonathan, prof, ast teach, $35,510
Born, Christopher Andrew, instructor, adjunct, $9,000
Bornhauser, Allison Rae, recruiter, hlth care, $58,068
Bornhop, Jason Wayne, sr ast dir studnt supprt svcs, $53,972
Bornschein, Robert J, athletic attd, $12.02/hr
Borsheski, Betsy Lynn Barnett, physician, $200.00/hr
Borusky, Jessica, instructor, adjunct, $7,500
Borwick, James B, internet administrator-entry, $20.00/hr
Boschert, Jana Lynn, dir I, advancement, $68,850
Boshard, Barbara Josephine, coor, qlty assess/improv, $68,606
Boss, Amanda Marie, business support specialist II, $17.16/hr
Boss, Jessica Nichole, nurse, staff II, $21.26/hr
Bossaller, Clifford T, system administrator-expert, $70,358

Bossaller, Jenny Simpson, prof, ast, $62,926
Bossaller, Stephanie Doyle, manager it, $77,676
Bosslet, Janet Marie, temporary clerical, $11.09/hr
Bostick, Brian P, fellow, post doc clncl-yr2, $58,083
Bostick, Jane E, prof, asoc clincl, $64,658
Boston, Leah Rachelle, nurse, staff II, $22.56/hr
Boston, Nicholas A, resident physician-4th yr, $55,804
Boswell, Cathy Lynn, custodian mrc, $9.42/hr
Botero, Blanca Cecilia, pharmacist II, $115,884
Bott, Jana Dawn, manager it, $88,716
Bottoms, Christopher A, programmer analyst-expert, $68,979
Botts, Ashton J, admin consultant I, $20.00/hr
Botts, Dayla Lashawn, office support assistant IV, $17.02/hr
Botts, Michelle Marie, educational pgm assistant, $9.65/hr
Botts, Shelley Scott, student support specialist I, $14.00/hr
Botts, Steven D, powr plnt matrl handling opr, $21.05/hr
Bouchard, Christopher D, sr dir program/project ops, $97,000
Boucher, Alexandra Nicole, patient svc rep, $12.09/hr
Boudreau, Karissa Dawn, nurse, licensed prac, $15.06/hr
Boughan, Breanne Amanda, lab assistant, $10.00/hr
Boulanger, Matthew T, research specialist sr, $40,252
Boulware, Travis Leon, coor athletic operations, $36,150
Bounds, Dinah Lynn, office support assistant IV, $14.71/hr
Bouras, Mohamed, asoc dir program/project ops, $62,526
Bourbia, Amine, resident physician-1st yr, $49,025
Bourisaw, Diana M, prof, ast adjunct, $16,008
Bourne, Carol, prof, ast adjunct, $10,500
Bourne, Godfrey R, prof, asoc, $61,883
Bourne, Steve, prof, ast clincl, $85,000
Bouscaren, Durrie Watson, strat comm consultant, $39,600
Bouse, Chuck D Jr, managing architect, $84,900
Bouse, Michael Richard, custodian, $10.69/hr
Bouse, Stephanie Renee, student support specialist sr, $17.48/hr
Bouska, Kristen Leah, fellow, post doctoral, $45,000
Bousquet, Lorie A, executive assistant, $19.17/hr
Boutros, Nashaat, professor, $35,000
Boutwell, Curtiss W, pharmacist II, $124,045
Bouyain, Samuel Eric Andre, prof, asoc, $100,188
Bovier, Michael Francis, prof, ast teach, $62,500
Bowden, Christopher Sean, db administrator-princpl, $73,393
Bowden, Deborah Kay, office support assistant I, $12.14/hr
Bowden, Jennifer Lynn, telecomm opr-h, $11.28/hr
Bowders, John J Jr, professor, $148,465
Bowdoin, Elizabeth Marie, clinical nursing supvsr, $61,940
Bowe Thompson, Carole, resrch asoc, $56,000
Bowe, Jeanne M, staff nurse, $24.35/hr
Bowen, Aaron Michael, hospital security officer, $10.64/hr
Bowen, Jessica Carol, student support specialist sr, $19.49/hr
Bowen, Kelly A, business support specialist II, $15.40/hr
Bowen, Marisa Lynn, resrch asoc, $26,500
Bowen, Misty Dawn, resident physician-2nd yr, $50,810
Bowens, Lynn Marie, lecturer, $9,910
Bower, Melinda J, patient svc rep, $13.62/hr
Bowerman, Loretta L, care team assoc-clinical, $13.89/hr
Bowers, Bart S, nurse, staff II, $22.24/hr
Bowers, Gregory Glenn, prof, asoc profl practice, $61,784
Bowers, Jessica L, fellow, post doctoral, $30,000
Bowes, Allyson Dayle, program/project supprt coor I, $47,589
Bowie, Daniel Christopher, office support assistant I, $9.05/hr
Bowie, Rita L, dir II human resources, $102,996
Bowler, Jennifer Nicole, nurse, staff II rnwp, $23.72/hr
Bowles, Douglas, resrch asoc, $70,000
Bowles, Douglas K, professor, $166,640
Bowling, Alan C, office support assistant IV, $15.10/hr
Bowling, Carrie E, instructor, clincl, $92,000
Bowling, Thomas Joseph, executive assistant, $16.95/hr
Bowman, Frank O III, professor, $194,228
Bowman, Christopher P, custodian, $12.94/hr
Bowman, Jesse W, research specialist I, $39,010
Bowman, Katherine G, prof, ast teach, $51,418
Bowman, Kyle Scott, emrg med techn paramedic, $14.65/hr
Bowman, Robert Dwight, instructor, adjunct, $9,600
Bowman, Robin Josephine, prof, ast teach, $66,586
Bowman, Shirl Anne, cook mrc, $11.33/hr
Bowman, Steven E, dental equip spclst, $22.39/hr
Bowman, Tiffany S, student service coor II, $52,234
Bowne, Joni B, supv nursing acute care, $23.90/hr
Bowne, Tamara K, nurse, staff, $29.31/hr
Boyce, Christopher, dir I, student support svcs, $82,513

Boyce, Christopher John, sftware supprt analyst-expert, $46,398
Boyce, Diane Ray, patient svc rep, $12.76/hr
Boyce, Kenneth A, prof, ast, $60,696
Boyce, Richards Merrell, tutor, $10.00/hr
Boyd, Leonard Jay Jr, seasonal farm ast, $10.51/hr
Boyd-Kennedy, Victoria Anne, academic advisor, $44,892
Boyd-Lee, LaToshia, program/project supprt coor I, $50,900
Boyd-Mills, Becky Sue, educational pgm associate I, $14.27/hr
Boyd, Ashleigh Ohmes, speech/lang pathologist, $47,792
Boyd, Catherine Nichole, office support assistant I, $11.00/hr
Boyd, Edward Ray, data cntr support tech-entry, $16.96/hr
Boyd, Irene Denise, phlebotomist, $13.87/hr
Boyd, Jamillah, strat comm associate II, $46,236
Boyd, Kara N, lecturer sr, $18,000
Boyd, Karen O, fin and acctg manager, $77,498
Boyd, Leanne Elaine, office support assistant III, $12.65/hr
Boyd, Rebecca Lynn, office support assistant IV, $15.37/hr
Boyd, Robert Greenville, floor care techn lead, $14.62/hr
Boyd, Trenton, librarian IV, $78,444
Boyer, Chrisann L, telecom tech-princpl, $20.27/hr
Boyer, Heidi Aleta, office support assistant IV, $18.85/hr
Boyer, John, prof, adjunct, $50,000
Boyer, John A, internet administrator-expert, $25.15/hr
Boyer, Joshua Bruce, event assistant I, $10.20/hr
Boyer, Matt, research/lab technician sr, $15.00/hr
Boyer, Megan A, academic advisor, $43,125
Boyer, Nathan P, prof, asoc, $57,792
Boyer, Patricia G, prof, asoc, $64,702
Boyer, Sheila F, office support assistant IV, $16.41/hr
Boyes, Andrea Laurel, custodian, $10.00/hr
Boyes, Timothy S, nurse, licensed prac sr, $20.37/hr
Boyles, Laurie R, nurse, or/recovery-ch, $31.48/hr
Boyles, Rebecca Anne, nurse, staff II, $31.47/hr
Bozarth, Andrew L, resident physician-4th yr, $54,425
Bozarth, Eric J, fin and acctg specialist, $18.93/hr
Bozarth, Margaret Rose, resident physician-3rd yr, $54,270
Boze, Joe N, engineering technician II, $19.37/hr
Bozek, Weiwen Wang, fin and acctg analyst sr, $40,788
Bozynski, Chantelle Carole, instructor, clincl, $86,472
Bozzette, Maryann, prof, asoc, $86,063
Bozzolo, Arianna, prof, ast resrch, $77,500
Brackeen, Winona M, nurse, staff II, $22.24/hr
Bracken Carroll, Alice, lecturer, $9,000
Bracken, Lauri L, office support assistant III, $11.41/hr
Bradbury, John F Jr, mgr research activities, $49,748
Braddix, D'Andre Cortez, sr dir studnt supprt svcs, $91,740
Braddock, Stephen Charles, office support asst IV, $13.59/hr
Bradfield, Katherine Anne, office support assistant III, $12.56/hr
Bradford, Blythe Maria, child dev asoc teacher, $15.42/hr
Bradford, Connie Lea, fin and acctg specialist, $19.85/hr
Bradford, Deborah Jean, custodian, $12.94/hr
Bradford, Deshayda Rayshell Anee, care team assoc-clinical,
  $12.08/hr
Bradford, Victor Alonso, student support specialist II, $16.51/hr
Bradley, Aric Connor, human resources assistant, $13.39/hr
Bradley, Cara Anne, dental assistant II, $19.65/hr
Bradley, Crystal Antoinette, temporary crafts service, $9.10/hr
Bradley, Deborah J, office support assistant IV, $14.00/hr
Bradley, Donald K, insulation svcs wrkr II, $20.07/hr
Bradley, James O, maintenance supervisor, $55,093
Bradley, Jonathan R, fellow, post doctoral, $77,250
Bradley, Karen, nurse, staff, $30.00/hr
Bradley, Kendall Dale, communications assistant sr, $19.24/hr
Bradley, Kevin W, prof, asoc, $107,583
Bradley, Kristina Marie, academic advisor, $36,000
Bradley, Linda K, resrch asoc, $42,448
Bradley, Memoree Lynn, executive assistant sr, $65,520
Bradley, Michelle, nurse, staff II, $22.96/hr
Bradley, Ronda Zinser, instructor, clincl, $6,240
Bradley, Scott W, sftware supprt analyst-speclst, $40,392
Bradley, Teresa Lynn, office support assistant III, $11.30/hr
Bradley, Vanessa Renee, intern, $25,500
Bradshaw-Straub, Laura, business support specialist II, $17.06/hr
Bradshaw, Audrie Louis, office support assistant I, $9.79/hr
Bradshaw, Christopher C, grader, $100.00/hr
Bradshaw, Cynthia A, business ops associate I, $38,300
Bradshaw, Frankie E, bts painter, $21.71/hr
Bradshaw, Gary F, custodian, $11.00/hr
Bradshaw, Kaylyn, high school student, $10.20/hr

Bradshaw, Laqueta Shanta, custodian, $12.94/hr
Bradshaw, Rodney M, bts carpenter, $20.23/hr
Brady, Amber Megann, director it, $92,966
Brady, Elaine D, med techl reg, $28.62/hr
Brady, James, head coach, $50,647
Brady, Joan, teaching ast, $22,800
Brady, Kathy Jo, ultrasonographer, $33.37/hr
Brady, Kevin E, fin and acctg manager, $61,820
Brady, Neal Laurence, clerk, operating room supply, $13.63/hr
Brady, Scott, mgr III business admin, $80,000
Braff, Lea C, office support assistant I, $10.00/hr
Brafford, Emery W, mgr engineering-mrc, $70,319
Bragg, Jack Dwayne, prof, asoc clincl, $126,825
Braiuca, Stacy Lynette, instructor, adjunct, $15,000
Brake, Jennifer Lynn, advancement officer, $45,600
Bramel, Linda G, executive assistant, $28.17/hr
Brammer, Karen Lucille, office support assistant IV, $15.66/hr
Branch, Autumn Charity, safety monitor, $9.27/hr
Branch, Breann, office support assistant IV, $16.00/hr
Branch, Yolanda Yvette, executive assistant, $18.87/hr
Brand, Kevin, sftware supprt analyst-speclst, $43,962
Brandes, Gary Wayne, prof, asoc teach, $60,730
Brandkamp, Joanne Frances, bus support specialist sr, $21.69/hr
Brandmeyer, Andrew Michael, adjunct, $9,000
Brandon, Leah J, resident physician-3rd yr, $54,270
Brandon, Tyler, dental assistant II, $15.00/hr
Brandow, Jason Dale, csm operations coordinator, $26.30/hr
Brandt, Donna K, research specialist I, $15.00/hr
Brandt, Evan Randolph, lecturer, $9,000
Brandt, John R, system administrator-expert, $79,070
Brandt, Julie L, administrative consultant II, $83,640
Brandt, Kimberly R, instructor, clincl, $145,000
Brandt, Kimberly R, resident physician-1st yr, $50.00/hr
Brandt, Lea Cheyney, prof, asoc clincl, $92,845
Brandt, Nathan R, horticulture spclst, $46,871
Brandt, Nicole Elaine, nursing ast, $12.08/hr
Brandt, Rebecca Lynn, ast registrar, $75,376
Brandt, Ted E, dir clinic ops, $114,240
Branson, Amanda Jane, educational pgm associate I, $12.91/hr
Branson, Angela Susann, student service coor II, $41,500
Branson, Bonnie S, professor, $89,511
Branson, Keith Richard, prof, ast teach, $118,170
Branson, Lillie D, nurse, staff II, $28.47/hr
Branson, Samantha Louise, adjunct, $15,300
Branson, Walter J, vice chancellor, $204,800
Branson, William A, bts painter, $21.71/hr
Branstetter, Karen B, 4-h spclst, $50,690
Brase, Todd D, ast mgr hospitality services, $42,231
Brasington, Dianna Lynn, office support assistant IV, $14.87/hr
Brassfield, Peggy Lorraine, patient svc rep, $13.73/hr
Bratt, Alaina M Oestreich, nurse clinician, $45,012
Bratt, Hanah Marlee, child dev assistant, $8.16/hr
Brauch, Michael Kristian, event assistant I, $9.00/hr
Braudis, Kara M, prof, ast clincl dept, $250,000
Braun, Joseph A Jr, lecturer, $100.00/hr
Braun, Caleb David, reactor operator sr, $28.99/hr
Braun, Carole Lynne, office support assistant IV, $13.00/hr
Braun, David Meyer, prof, asoc, $105,705
Bravo, Rosalba, custodian, $12.94/hr
Braxton, Darryl D, office support assistant IV, $15.46/hr
Braxton, Michael LaMar, custodian, $12.18/hr
Bray, Kimberly Sue, professor, $93,292
Braylock, Kenneth, mail carrier, $14.24/hr
Brazeal, James B, dir III business admin, $103,500
Breaugh, James, professor, $183,631
Brechbuhler, Alex Fremont Daniel, lab assistant, $10.75/hr
Breckinridge, Alberta, administrative consultant, $83,503
Bredehoeft, Cole Tyler, hospital lab tech, $12.22/hr
Bredemeier, Brenda Jo, prof, asoc, $77,304
Breedlove, Boyd Henry, police officer, $18.44/hr
Breedlove, Linda Sue, instructor, ast, $19.47/hr
Breedlove, Michael, bts carpenter, $21.71/hr
Breedlove, Ruth Remley, office support assistant IV, $16.35/hr
Breems, Luke Gordon, instructor, adjunct, $4,200
Breen, Barbara L, dir I, business admin, $100,829
Brehmer, Monie Lashon, educational pgm assistant, $9.24/hr
Breithaupt, Dean Philip, bldg cntrl sys techn IV, $24.15/hr
Breitweiser, Susanna Michelle, nurse, staff II, $20.54/hr
Brekhus, Rachel L, librarian II, $48,779

Brekhus, Wayne H, prof, asoc, $82,369
Brekke, Diana M, cat scan technl (ct), $23.56/hr
Brekke, Lindsay Marie, mgr II business admin, $48,760
Brekke, Mark Joshua, radiologic techl, $18.41/hr
Brekke, Mark W, radiologic techl, $26.47/hr
Bremer, Jennifer Lynn, physician assistant, $81,000
Bremer, Kathy, tutor, $12.00/hr
Brendler, Beth Monica, prof, ast, $68,347
Breneman, Rhonda Carter, nurse, licensed prac sr, $20.58/hr
Brennaman, Lisa M, prof, ast clincl dept, $175,000
Brennan, Donald E, system administrator-speclst, $49,179
Brennan, Margaret Kindler, patient svc rep, $11.28/hr
Brenner, Casey Lauren, nurse, staff I, $19.67/hr
Brenner, John M, editor sr, $57,200
Brenner, Torin A, nurse, staff II, $22.32/hr
Brent, Edward Everett Jr, professor, $95,115
Breshears, Derrick, user support analyst-entry, $16.01/hr
Breshears, Lauren Wood, nurse, staff now III, $30.00/hr
Breske, Shannon Marie Barney, student service coor sr, $62,210
Bresnahan, Claire Elyse, temporary crafts service, $7.50/hr
Bresnahan, Michelle Elaine, dir I, env health / safety, $85,000
Bressie, Mary Elizabeth, office support assistant III, $11.70/hr
Bretz, Rachel L, couns hlth/welfare/wellness sr, $30.00/hr
Bretz, Sandra Joan, system support analyst-speclst, $27.23/hr
Breuer, David I, sr mgr csm operations, $73,316
Brewer, Anna, pat acct rep, $15.42/hr
Brewer, Carla W, pat acct rep, $15.99/hr
Brewer, Connie Sue, business support specialist II, $20.53/hr
Brewer, Marcia J, office support assistant IV, $17.66/hr
Brewer, Todd F, lecturer, $58,667
Brewer, Tricia Ann, nurse, staff II, $25.00/hr
Breyfogle, Russel P Jr, event assistant I, $8.18/hr
Breyfogle, Matthew, event assistant I, $10.00/hr
Breytspraak, Linda M, olson professorship, $12,963
Brian, Mitchell L, prof, asoc teach, $43,800
Brice, James Shawn, resrch ast sr, $51,000
Brichoux, David Wayne, instructor, adjunct, $21,000
Bricker, Petra Rae, student service coor I, $36,714
Brickler, Emily Walker, mgr III business admin, $53,600
Bridewell, Lanee Charlotte, student service coor II, $39,600
Bridgeman, Jay Thomas, prof, ast clincl dept, $260,000
Bridges, Jeff A, prof, ast teach, $83,481
Bridges, Jessie L, business support specialist II, $23.51/hr
Bridges, Larry Dale, program/project supprt coor II, $32.00/hr
Bridges, Sandra Denise, custodian, $11.41/hr
Bridgford, Shelley Hagan, resident physician-2nd yr, $50,810
Bridwell, Shelby Leigh, clerk, diet, $9.50/hr
Briedwell, Teresa A, prof, asoc teach, $92,391
Briesacher, Sandra Lee, research specialist I, $28,226
Brietzke, Stephen August, prof, clinical dept, $250,000
Briggs, Donald G, hospital security officer, $13.24/hr
Briggs, Elizabeth Christian, sales & service rep, $9.46/hr
Briggs, Joette Arlene, pat acct rep, $16.88/hr
Briggs, Kelley Marie, resp therapist reg, $20.55/hr
Briggs, Leah Ann Miller, business support specialist sr, $22.81/hr
Briggs, Lesli Theresa, serv line spclst, $81,859
Brigham, Dale Edward, prof, asoc teach, $48,959
Bright, Jessica Erin, ultrasonographer, $30.25/hr
Brightwell, Daniel L, radiologic techl, $28.92/hr
Brightwell, Jerry D, office support assistant IV, $16.06/hr
Brilley, Jennifer Lee, couns hlth/welfare/wellness sr, $30.00/hr
Brillhart, Mary Louise Bowen, patient svc rep, $14.88/hr
Brillhart, Matthew J, asoc dir program/project ops, $55,480
Brimer, Janelle Marie, office support assistant III, $14.33/hr
Brimmer, Gary W, med techl reg, $30.36/hr
Brimmo, Olubusola Abiye, research/lab technician sr, $19.23/hr
Brinegar, Holly Anne, business tech analyst-expert, $54,234
Brines, Terri R, strat comm consultant, $49,165
Brinkerhoff, Mark Russell, telecomm opr-h, $11.11/hr
Brinkhoff, Julie Anna, asoc dir program/project ops, $64,361
Brinkman, Barbara L, prof, asoc adjunct, $13,500
Brinkman, Brian, resident physician-1st yr, $49,025
Brinkman, Carolyn Kay, office support assistant IV, $13.88/hr
Brinkmann, Darryl Lee, instructor, adjunct, $12,000
Brinkmann, Rieanne Elizabeth, office support asst IV, $14.49/hr
Brinson, Carol, reimbursement ast, $16.87/hr
Brintnall, Piper Harlan, event assistant I, $10.00/hr
Brintnall, Thomas C, csm operations supervisor, $49,500
Brion, Elise Rechtin, patient svc rep, $11.63/hr

Briscoe, Dana A, patient svc rep, $14.88/hr
Briseno, Katherine A, student support specialist sr, $16.87/hr
Bristow, Douglas A, prof, asoc, $83,079
Britt Rankin, Jo, dean, asoc, $131,395
Britt, Douglas W, system support analyst-expert, $23.22/hr
Britt, Lisa G, prof, ast teach, $72,410
Britt, Mihaela Iuliana, student service coor sr, $52,702
Brittin, Michelle L, nurse, staff II, $26.94/hr
Britton, Alzina, nurse, staff II rnwp, $32.78/hr
Britton, Jordan Douglas, anesthesia techn, $12.77/hr
Britton, Joshua M, nurse anesthetist, $145,760
Brixey, Elizabeth K, prof, asoc profl practice, $64,655
Brizendine Esq, Lyle Wayne, sr dir advancement, $103,327
Broadus, Tamala Roshall, care team assoc-suppt, $14.88/hr
Brocato, Emily Rose, research specialist I, $32,250
Brocco, Correy Patrick, nurse, staff II, $20.54/hr
Brock, Carol Ann, nurse, licensed prac, $20.37/hr
Brock, Caroline C, prof, ast teach, $66,000
Brock, Devara D, student support specialist I, $19.71/hr
Brock, Natalie Annette Deford, ast coach, $34,400
Brocker, Brian L, system administrator-expert, $67,038
Brockhouse, John Glenn, distrib techn-mtls mgmt, $15.26/hr
Brockland, John J, resident physician-1st yr, $50,219
Brockman, John D, prof, ast resrch, $74,826
Brockman, Lisa, nurse, licensed prac, $22.16/hr
Brockmann, Lorraine B, prof, asoc, $73,677
Brockmann, William G, prof, asoc clincl, $88,743
Broderick, Brianna Kylie, head coach, $32,320
Brodersen, Timothy John, security officer, $12.31/hr
Brodkorb II, Gary Wade, social worker sr, $53,000
Brodsky, Nash J, tutor, $10.00/hr
Brodwin, Mark, prof, ast, $64,260
Brody, Deborah Ann, nurse, licensed prac sr, $19.78/hr
Broerman, Victor Michael, temporary technical, $10.00/hr
Brogan, David Micah, prof, ast, $50,000
Brokaw, Dawn Marie, office support assistant I, $11.33/hr
Bromert, Karen Higgs, research specialist I, $37,142
Brommelsiek, Margaret, instructor, $117,096
Brondel, Richard, mts/sheet metal, $22.50/hr
Bronsman, Karen Elaine, dental assistant II, $12.98/hr
Brooker, Kathryn S, instructor, adjunct, $2,933
Brookins, Oscar, event assistant I, $7.55/hr
Brookman, James S III, retail sales associate sr, $33,495
Brooks-Neely, Catherine Judith Marie, temp prof, $12.00/hr
Brooks, Audrey Lynn, resident physician-3rd yr, $52,470
Brooks, Barret K, educational pgm coor I, $34,441
Brooks, Bonnie M, patient svc rep, $13.29/hr
Brooks, Brian Shedd, prof, adjunct, $20,000
Brooks, Christi Leianne, nurse, staff II, $22.44/hr
Brooks, Constance Moore, prof, ast clincl, $84,600
Brooks, Danny R, pat acct rep, $15.53/hr
Brooks, Dayna Rose, executive assistant, $17.09/hr
Brooks, Dierk L, temporary crafts service, $9.50/hr
Brooks, Erin Marie, prof, ast clincl, $70,553
Brooks, George H, business support specialist I, $15.40/hr
Brooks, Hayley Stevie Jean, custodian, $10.39/hr
Brooks, Jeremy C, stage services assistant sr, $16.00/hr
Brooks, Joey Carnell, security officer, $11.00/hr
Brooks, John Thomas, mechanical plant speclst, mrc, $18.09/hr
Brooks, Jon D, orthopedic techn, $16.19/hr
Brooks, Karen Kathryn, human resources specialist sr, $54,000
Brooks, Kenneth Ellis, police officer, $17.56/hr
Brooks, Kenneth W, asoc dir research, $119,151
Brooks, Kim Marie, mgr II business admin, $53,384
Brooks, Michelle A, csm operations coordinator, $21.25/hr
Brooks, Phillip Duane, building/mechanical maint I, $16.50/hr
Brooks, Phillips R, prof, asoc, $83,964
Brooks, Scott N, prof, asoc, $98,172
Brooks, Tanjela R, sr mgr business admin, $61,812
Brooks, Vicki L, security officer, $12.49/hr
Brooks, Whitney Nicole, finl counselor(eligibility), $16.08/hr
Brooks, William P, event assistant I, $8.00/hr
Brookshier, Scott Alen, health physics technician I, $18.50/hr
Broombaugh, Jeffrey L, communications coordinator, $15.00/hr
Brosch, Tracy Lynn, resrch ast, $1,333
Brost, Amy Kristina, office support assistant IV, $15.53/hr
Brotherton, Gussie Dean III, resident physician-1st yr, $50,219
Brotto, Leticia Souza, resrch asoc, $48,175
Brotto, Marco Aurelio, professor, $138,375

Broughton, Alisa Ann, resp therapist reg, $22.27/hr
Brow, Richard K, prof, curators, $148,363
Brower, Danny C, custodian, $11.41/hr
Brown Emmons, Morgan Lee, temporary clerical, $7.50/hr
Brown II, Ernest E, retail sales assistant sr, $11.70/hr
Brown, McLawrence Vodman III, custodial supervisor, $34,572
Brown, Steven Lamont Jr, cook, $11.24/hr
Brown, Willie A Jr, custodian, $12.94/hr
Brown-Hood, Deana Lynn, office support assistant IV, $16.78/hr
Brown, Adam J, resident physician-1st yr, $50,219
Brown, Adelaide B, librarian II, $46,400
Brown, Andre K, histologic technl, $24.67/hr
Brown, Andrea J, business support specialist II, $18.12/hr
Brown, Arminta L, business ops associate sr, $46,512
Brown, Ayanna Ronique, office support assistant III, $11.30/hr
Brown, Beth Ann, office support assistant IV, $16.25/hr
Brown, Beverly Kay, coor, service, $18.31/hr
Brown, Brandon Daniel, resident physician-5th yr, $58,083
Brown, Carl Marquis, user support analyst-entry, $13.00/hr
Brown, Carol K, library info specialist sr, $16.25/hr
Brown, Carolyn Ilene, instructor, adjunct, $12,552
Brown, Charles Augustus, food svc wrkr I, $9.60/hr
Brown, Charles E, business ops associate I, $58,083
Brown, Charles R, professor, $121,236
Brown, Cheryl Ann, med techl reg, $30.36/hr
Brown, Cheryl Lynn, nurse, staff II, $32.99/hr
Brown, Chrisanthia, dean, $156,721
Brown, Christina L, business support specialist sr, $29.60/hr
Brown, Christopher William, floor care techn, $11.96/hr
Brown, Claude David, event assistant I, $7.55/hr
Brown, Courtney Elise, extension asoc, $30,750
Brown, Courtney Lee, fellow, post doctoral, $39,000
Brown, Cynthia A, office support assistant III, $13.50/hr
Brown, Cynthia Kelly, dental assistant II, $16.37/hr
Brown, David Gerard, grounds lead, $15.92/hr
Brown, David J, forensic investigator, $24.49/hr
Brown, Dennis G, bindery opr I, $14.85/hr
Brown, Diane Marie, business ops associate sr, $45,828
Brown, Douglas Paul, custodian, $12.94/hr
Brown, Douglas Scott, prof, ast resrch, $127,612
Brown, Emma Barnard, temporary professional, $9.00/hr
Brown, Eric S, prof, asoc, $70,943
Brown, Ernest Kyle, custodian, $10.00/hr
Brown, Felice, food svc wrkr I, $9.60/hr
Brown, Gerald A, nurse anesthetist, $147,900
Brown, Helana Kylek, event assistant I, $7.50/hr
Brown, Henry Choate, engineer, resrch, $76,500
Brown, Jacqueline Mary, mgr pat accts-h, $100,880
Brown, James Michael, environmental health prof sr, $50,007
Brown, Jared J, farm wrkr III, $16.47/hr
Brown, Jason Wayne, communications coordinator, $16.03/hr
Brown, Jeffery D, dir II csm operations, $132,600
Brown, Jenee Bernadette, custodian, $11.41/hr
Brown, Jerry Lemone, event assistant I, $7.50/hr
Brown, Jessica N, educational pgm associate I, $13.32/hr
Brown, Jordan, teaching ast, $4,000
Brown, Joshua Page, mgr student support svcs, $30,805
Brown, Juanita, custodian, $12.94/hr
Brown, Julie A, nurse, staff II, $34.18/hr
Brown, Justin Chase, asoc dir student support svcs, $74,263
Brown, Justin V, mech, bldg maint, $18.12/hr
Brown, Katelyn Jane, nurse, staff II, $20.95/hr
Brown, Kathleen S, prof, asoc, $84,575
Brown, Kevin Bryon, pat acct rep, $14.84/hr
Brown, Kevin P, prof, ast, $57,873
Brown, Khatrina Denise, tutor, $13.13/hr
Brown, Laura Elizabeth, prof, ast adjunct, $125.00/hr
Brown, Linda A, med records transcript, $16.30/hr
Brown, Linda Sue, nurse, staff II, $32.78/hr
Brown, Lisa K, nurse, staff II, $27.00/hr
Brown, Lorita M, office support assistant IV, $13.76/hr
Brown, Luke E, resident physician-2nd yr, $50,810
Brown, Margaret Saunders, physician ast, $35.93/hr
Brown, Marie A, clerk, unit, $15.15/hr
Brown, Marilyn Louise, office support assistant IV, $20.66/hr
Brown, Mark Stacy, custodian, $13.96/hr
Brown, Marla Kay, nurse, licensed prac, $19.74/hr
Brown, Marquis C, fin and acctg analyst sr, $50,182
Brown, Mary Ann, mgr III business admin, $89,100

Brown, Mary E, office support assistant IV, $18.33/hr
Brown, Mary K, resp care clinical coor, $31.54/hr
Brown, Mary Kathleen, sr dir program/project ops, $71,577
Brown, Mary Luella, sr manager it, $103,758
Brown, Marybeth, prof, adjunct, $35,804
Brown, Matthew John Micheal, manager it, $63,000
Brown, Maury P, office support assistant II, $14.28/hr
Brown, Megan Lyn, resident physician-2nd yr, $50,810
Brown, Michael, nurse, staff II, $27.42/hr
Brown, Michael C, driver, route, $15.20/hr
Brown, Michael David, mts/electrician, $21.05/hr
Brown, Michael Steven, prof, ast clincl dept, $200,000
Brown, Monty Eugene, bts carpenter, $21.71/hr
Brown, Nathan Alan, custodian, $12.94/hr
Brown, Nathaniel Harrison, strat comm associate II, $47,940
Brown, Nicholas Gregory, user support analyst-spec, $16.89/hr
Brown, Pamela Jane Bonner, prof, ast, $80,560
Brown, Patrick L, instructor, adjunct, $9,600
Brown, Peter D, network engineer-expert, $71,813
Brown, Pia L, office support assistant IV, $15.01/hr
Brown, Rachel Margaret Ann, dean, asoc, $213,902
Brown, Raeshara Diana, communications coord sr, $21.64/hr
Brown, Randy Lee, construction manager II, $63,050
Brown, Rhonda S, asst dir prof rev coding, $82,774
Brown, Richard E, bts plasterer, $20.23/hr
Brown, Rita Bess, instructor, adjunct, $600
Brown, Robert Thomas, custodian, $10.69/hr
Brown, Roger Wayne, anesthesia techn, $15.45/hr
Brown, Sandra Lee, office support assistant III, $12.91/hr
Brown, Sarah Kathryn, event assistant I, $8.00/hr
Brown, Sarah Tobermann, instructor, adjunct, $4,035
Brown, Sean R, ast mgr hospitality services, $42,514
Brown, Shelby Rae, head athletic trainer, $50,500
Brown, Shelley, custodian, $12.94/hr
Brown, Tammey, lab techn, persl svc-clin lab, $14.28/hr
Brown, Tara J, office support assistant IV, $14.12/hr
Brown, Timothy D, ultrasonographer, $34.94/hr
Brown, Vicky Laux, business support specialist II, $20.80/hr
Brown, Wayne M, prof, asoc, $127,000
Brown, Wesley Carl, temporary crafts service, $9.10/hr
Brown, Wilfred A, media producer I, $14.55/hr
Browne II, Albert W, program/project supprt coor sr, $63,960
Browne, Albert Harvey, food svc wrkr I, $9.60/hr
Browne, Christopher John, agriculture associate sr, $24.50/hr
Brownell, Susan E, professor, $39,186
Brownfield, Angela, prof, ast clincl, $96,000
Brownfield, Jessica Lee, interior designer sr, $56,175
Browning, Jimmy Douglas Jr, research specialist II, $51,673
Browning, Robert Jr, chiller techn III, $25.15/hr
Browning, Caitlyn Noel, office support assistant I, $9.05/hr
Browning, Jody Lee, business support specialist II, $18.75/hr
Browning, John E, electrician, powr plant sr, $27.26/hr
Browning, Lee J, prof, ast adjunct, $9,461
Browning, Tammy Marie, supervisor II, $61,914
Brownsworth, Christopher Aaron, res physician-4th yr, $58,304
Brox, Denene, business support specialist II, $18.03/hr
Broz, Karen L, coor of emr education, $73,092
Broz, Robert R, prof, ast extns, $86,926
Bruce, Jared M, prof, asoc, $68,075
Bruce, Melissa Lynette, patient svc rep, $12.76/hr
Bruce, Steven Edward, prof, asoc, $83,407
Bruce, Tia Chantal, nurse, staff II, $24.26/hr
Brucks, Glenna K, nurse, staff II, $33.11/hr
Brucks, Kimberly Ann, practice manager, $85,890
Brueggenjohann, Jean M, professor, $95,505
Bruemmer, Stacy E, office support assistant III, $11.79/hr
Bruening, Jeanine Elise, ast dir student support svcs, $55,339
Bruening, Michael W, prof, asoc, $63,307
Bruer, Amy E, academic advisor, $35,539
Brugmann, Monica M, nurse, staff now III, $30.00/hr
Brulez, Morgan, teaching ast, $15,200
Brumagin, Matthew W, bts carpenter, $21.71/hr
Brumbaugh, Diane Nicole, certif pharmacy techn, $16.87/hr
Brumbaugh, Wendeline S, family fincl edu spclst, $52,232
Brumble, Shana Breann, licensed practical nurse, $15.00/hr
Brumett, Loren D, mgr csm operations, $41,650
Brumett, Wendy L, custodian, $11.41/hr
Brumfield, Irma Louise, nurse advisor, telephone, $32.37/hr
Brummet, Sam Earl, food svc wrkr I, $9.60/hr

Brune, David Edward, professor, $105,077
Brune, Mary, teaching ast, $22,400
Bruner, Mary B, neurodiagnostic tech (non-reg), $19.76/hr
Brunette, Charles A, compliance manager, $45,000
Brunholtz, Lynne, office support assistant IV, $16.30/hr
Brunig, Brian James, prof, ast adjunct, $14,491
Bruning, Maryjane L, central sterile supervisor, $65,226
Brunnworth, Nolan Carter, asoc dir advancement, $79,000
Bruno, Christopher James, system administrator-expert, $76,440
Bruno, Don, system support analyst-speclst, $20.00/hr
Bruno, Mary Angeline Lyon, strat comm associate II, $44,000
Bruns-Clarke, Teresa Mae, nurse, staff II, $23.98/hr
Bruns, Candace Marie, pat acct rep, $14.31/hr
Bruns, Jean Griessel, internet administrator-expert, $27.65/hr
Bruns, Kayle Dawne, instructor, clincl, $15,375
Bruns, Meagan Elizabeth, hlth prgm ast, $12.50/hr
Bruns, Sheila Renee, educational pgm associate I, $18.08/hr
Brush, Larry J, mech, small engine, $19.39/hr
Bruza, Robert M, carpenter, $21.87/hr
Bruzzese, Leonard J, prof, asoc profl practice, $116,116
Bruzzini, Daniel Blaise, prof, ast adjunct, $125.00/hr
Bryan, Donald G Jr, manager it, $79,097
Bryan, Benjamin David, temporary crafts service, $9.50/hr
Bryan, Cynthia Anne, temporary crafts service, $9.50/hr
Bryan, Eric Shane, prof, asoc, $59,069
Bryan, Jeffrey N, prof, asoc, $151,358
Bryan, Josiah Asher, instructor, $60,000
Bryan, Lori Michelle, ultrasonographer, $32.87/hr
Bryan, Margaret Elena, instructor, $44,044
Bryan, Neil, resident physician-1st yr, $49,025
Bryan, Olivia Dana, coor, reimbursement, $46,575
Bryan, Rachel D, temporary crafts service, $9.50/hr
Bryan, Susie, office support assistant IV, $14.25/hr
Bryan, Victoria Jean, office support associate, $28.17/hr
Bryan, William Dean, interventional technl (ir), $21.36/hr
Bryant, Aftan Shea, dietitian, clincl, $45,981
Bryant, Cheryl Denise, office support assistant III, $14.39/hr
Bryant, Christian Phillip, on-air talent television, $17.00/hr
Bryant, Fay J, office support assistant II, $10.51/hr
Bryant, Melissa, office support assistant IV, $16.98/hr
Bryant, Micheal A, nurse, staff stat, $25.73/hr
Bryant, Patrick J, prof, clincl, $121,000
Bryant, Robert Scott, building/mechanical maint I, $17.95/hr
Bryant, Taylor Louise, 4-h spclst, $42,500
Bryda, Elizabeth A, professor, $139,842
Bryson, Jeffrey Robert, powr plnt maint spclst III wld, $25.85/hr
Bryson, Jody Marie, internet administrator-speclst, $19.26/hr
Bubach, Susan K, retail sales associate sr, $15.47/hr
Bubacz, Bruce Stephen, prof, curator teach, $171,714
Buchanan, Carla Denise, custodian, $12.94/hr
Buchanan, Crystal Alexis, office support assistant IV, $17.00/hr
Buchanan, Curtis, resident physician-1st yr, $49,025
Buchanan, Kelli Anne, business support specialist II, $16.83/hr
Bucher, Andrew M, custodian, $10.69/hr
Bucher, Christopher Lamar, system sup analyst-entry, $18.02/hr
Buchheit, Adam Richard, asoc media producer, $11.53/hr
Buchheit, Kevin Charles, police officer, $17.50/hr
Buchheit, Maura Kay, retail sales assistant sr, $11.50/hr
Buchheit, Sarah Renee, nurse, staff II, $22.89/hr
Buchheit, Yvonne, supv resp care, $73,463
Buchholz, Nancy Ann, physical therapist, $84,760
Buchmiller, Micki N, surgical technl certified, $17.18/hr
Buck, Alicia Darcelle, mental health professional, $35,088
Buck, Brian W, prof, ast clincl dept, $250,000
Buck, Dawne Lyn Stelle, staff nurse, $27.05/hr
Buck, Laura C, library info specialist sr, $14.95/hr
Buckallew, Kelsey Ann, nurse, staff II, $24.48/hr
Buckaloo, George Warren Jr, admin consultant, $50.00/hr
Buckholtz, Kenneth R, prof, adjunct, $22,050
Buckingham, Andrew Eric, sftware supprt analyst-entry, $34,400
Buckingham, Krystine Nykole, nurse, licensed prac, $15.06/hr
Buckler, Nicole Lynn Krejci, office support asst III, $13.78/hr
Buckley, Matthew E, student service coor II, $41,105
Buckman, Eric M, powr plnt cntrl sys techn, $23.75/hr
Buckman, Meng-Ping, nurse, staff II, $27.30/hr
Buckner, John W IV, resident physician-3rd yr, $52,470
Buckner, Kaylon Leann, enrollment advisor sr, $16.98/hr
Buckner, Velma Ann, office support assistant IV, $15.90/hr
Bucko, Luray C, dietitian, clincl, $62,197

Buckridge, Tiffany Rae, surgical technl certified, $16.84/hr
Buday, Sarah K, psychologist, $55,000
Budd, John M, professor, $100,955
Buddemeyer, Sherry Denise, nurse, staff II wkend II, $28.61/hr
Budds, Michael J, prof, curators, $71,602
Budesheim, Phyllis Rae, program/project supprt coor I, $38,438
Budiselich, Mallory Nicole, radiologic techl, $18.59/hr
Budny, Elizabeth M, nurse, staff II, $20.54/hr
Budreau, Jennifer Elizabeth, psychologist, $40.00/hr
Buechter, Michel L, nurse, staff I, $19.00/hr
Buehler, Jonathon Sanford, physical therapist, $60,480
Bueltmann, Jilian Rae, instructor, adjunct, $9,318
Bueneman, Puspa Leela, office support assistant III, $14.92/hr
Bueno, Andrea Melissa, academic advisor sr, $46,170
Bueno, Jillian Christine, library information assistant, $11.30/hr
Buffaloe, Lucas Robert, prof, ast clincl dept, $137,700
Buffaloe, Robert Neal, prof, ast clincl dept, $161,262
Buford, Anneke Amelia, nurse, staff, $22.66/hr
Buford, Kenya R, academic advisor, $43,512
Buford, Mareeka Shray, custodian, $10.39/hr
Buford, Zachary Marcum, food svc wrkr I, $9.60/hr
Bugg, Leon Hayes, teaching ast, $36.40/hr
Buhr, Laurie Beth, radiologic techl, $21.67/hr
Buie, Amelia Jean, instructor, adjunct, $7,059
Bukoski, Alex D, prof, ast, $120,416
Bulla, Andrew James, research/lab technician, $10.24/hr
Bullard, Jimmie DeAnn, educational prgm coor sr, $57,000
Bullard, John David, bts plasterer, $20.23/hr
Bullerdieck, Michelle Ann, pharmacist II, $118,368
Bullett, Erin Shelton, psychologist, $71,500
Bullion, John Lewis, professor, $102,739
Bullock, John Robert, engineering technician I, $16.70/hr
Bullock, Paula Castle, lab quality assurance spclst, $76,746
Bullock, Richard L, emeritus, $15,000
Bulmann, Jennifer Kane, prof, ast adjunct, $16,645
Bunce, Larry W II, dir institutional research, $90,126
Bunch, Angelia Christine, office support assistant III, $14.55/hr
Bunch, Collin Michael, specialist, $56,459
Bunch, James L, lecturer, $34,200
Bunch, Matthew Raymond, operations support tech sr, $15.44/hr
Bunde, Rachel Whitney, nurse, staff II, $20.84/hr
Bundrick, Jeffrey David, physical therapist, $58,753
Bunger, Chase L, compliance manager, $58,425
Bunn, Katharine S, counsel, $142,561
Bunnell, Dale Leon, driver, $12.80/hr
Bunton, Peggy Jean, office support assistant III, $16.15/hr
Bunton, Timothy W, bts mason/tuckptr, $20.23/hr
Bunyak, Filiz, prof, ast resrch, $41,000
Bunyard, Mary Ann, office support assistant III, $14.56/hr
Buran, Sarah A, nurse, staff II, $23.04
Burbank, Malena Ann, pat acct rep, $15.09/hr
Burch, Joni L, mgr student support svcs, $42,000
Burch, Kevin D, occl therapy ast cert, $22.82/hr
Burch, Mary M, temporary professional, $11.30/hr
Burch, Milbre Elizabeth, commercial talent, $20.00/hr
Burch, Patricia J, business tech analyst-expert, $55,444
Burden, Ashley Smallwood, strat comm consultant sr, $58,219
Burden, Michael J, program/project supprt coor sr, $52,000
Burdick, Bruce A, resrch asoc, $72,728
Burg, Jillian Ruth, office support assistant III, $12.23/hr
Burgan, Lynn Ann, mgr II business admin, $68,670
Burge, Christine R, dental assistant II, $17.27/hr
Burger, Lisa Renee, research specialist II, $55,099
Burger, Melissa Anne, resident physician-3rd yr, $53,763
Burger, Robert C, prof, asoc clincl dept, $161,262
Burgeson, Harold M Jr, med techl reg, $29.83/hr
Burgess, Andre Ralph, clerk, operating room supply, $13.72/hr
Burgess, Karin Denise, office support assistant IV, $13.30/hr
Burgess, Laura Lynn, food svc wrkr I, $11.29/hr
Burgess, Leslie A, executive assistant, $17.31/hr
Burgess, Olivia Anne, grader, $100.00/hr
Burgess, Pamela L, business support specialist II, $22.58/hr
Burgess, Taran Elyse, nurse, staff I, $19.00/hr
Burgess, Veronica Marie, media producer II, $18.10/hr
Burgett, Lamyia Sharmae, nurse, licensed prac, $14.76/hr
Burgett, Tammy Elaine, custodian, $10.94/hr
Burgoyne, Suzanne, prof, curators, $87,137
Burk, Eric Leon, maint svc attd, $16.24/hr
Burk, Kent, adjunct, $15,000

Burke Aguero, Hannia Lorena, interpreter, medical, $25.00/hr
Burke-Aguero, Donald Harrison, professor, $142,677
Burke, Daltyn Kole, radiologic techl, $19.62/hr
Burke, Diane Louise Mutti, prof, asoc, $63,214
Burke, Dorinda Dawn, forensic investigator, $26.93/hr
Burke, Jennifer Barbara, nurse, staff II rnwp, $23.16/hr
Burke, Kenneth Andrew, av instal service tech-speclst, $14.96/hr
Burke, Lana M, office support assistant III, $12.81/hr
Burke, Mary Christine, office support assistant III, $11.50/hr
Burke, Roger Lee, mts/pipefitter, $21.05/hr
Burkeen, Bruce Allen, research engineering tech I, $25.26/hr
Burken, Joel G, professor, $182,427
Burkett, Charlotte Ann, office support assistant IV, $15.53/hr
Burkett, Elisa Ann, ast dir clinic opns-shc, $72,348
Burkett, Glenna, business support specialist sr, $23.68/hr
Burkett, Kathleen Maureen, compliance specialist I, $16.00/hr
Burkeybile, Alyson Anne, physician ast, $96,652
Burkhardt, Aaron R, resident physician-1st yr, $50,219
Burkhardt, Elizabeth Lake, advancement officer, $45,600
Burkhardt, Victoria Ann, nurse clinician, $57,483
Burkhart, Mary Beth, emrg med techn paramedic, $17.72/hr
Burkholder, Mark Alan, professor, $150,438
Burks, Cathy D, pat acct rep, $14.95/hr
Burks, Dilauna G, office support assistant IV, $14.92/hr
Burks, Melody Michelle, serv line spclst, $67,808
Burks, Patrick Carroll, bts mason/tuckptr, $20.23/hr
Burks, Stacy Lynn, office supervisor, $38,475
Burks, Steve M, mgr cardiopulm svcs-mrc, $95,128
Burky, Robyn Carol, program/project supprt coor II, $41,184
Burle, Lindsay K, research/lab technician, $12.00/hr
Burleson, Dustin Shane, prof, ast adjunct, $125.00/hr
Burnam, Larry Randall, mts/refrigeration mech, $22.49/hr
Burnam, Megan A, nurse, staff II rnwp, $22.89/hr
Burnett, Barbara Lynne, business support specialist II, $23.45/hr
Burnett, Brian Douglas, vice president, $300,000
Burnett, Brooke E, research specialist I, $45,320
Burnett, Claudine, event assistant I, $7.50/hr
Burnett, Kimberly Ann, office support assistant IV, $17.91/hr
Burnett, Laura June, assoc dir clinic operations-up, $101,803
Burnett, Michael, bts mason/tuckptr, $21.71/hr
Burney Miller, Katherine L, business support spec II, $23.42/hr
Burney, Rusty Joe, ast athletic director, $70,040
Burnham, Connie J, specialist, $62,073
Burnham, Sharon Lynn, office support assistant IV, $14.68/hr
Burns-Wallace, Deangela Jenise, admin consultant II, $101,800
Burns, Amy L, nurse, licensed prac, $15.36/hr
Burns, Anthony Tyrone, custodian, $12.18/hr
Burns, Carl F, ast vice chancellor, $100,000
Burns, Dexter W, supv resp care, $82,648
Burns, Dolores L, pharmacy tech, $14.88/hr
Burns, Gary E, maint wrkr, prev, $16.95/hr
Burns, Kathleen A, academic dir, $71,031
Burns, Kelsey Elizabeth, office support assistant II, $10.24/hr
Burns, Linda Mary, instructor, adjunct, $9,000
Burns, Mary Ann, sr dir program/project ops, $68,000
Burns, Mary Y, office support assistant II, $11.84/hr
Burns, Matthew Kevin, dean, asoc, $165,000
Burns, Nancy Beatrice, educational pgm associate I, $13.45/hr
Burns, Thomas G, librarian II, $46,920
Burns, Wesley Marcus, ast coach, $80,000
Burr II, Mark Owen, utility dist wrkr II, $18.55/hr
Burridge, Kimberly Nanette, retail sales assistant sr, $11.70/hr
Burris, Connie M, human resources specialist I, $17.57/hr
Burris, Deborah J, dir III business admin, $125,000
Burris, Edwin E, prof, asoc teach, $64,900
Burris, Jennifer Lynn, nurse, or/recovery-ch, $26.34/hr
Burris, Joseph E, prof, asoc clincl dept, $194,304
Burris, Russell, patient svc rep, $14.73/hr
Burris, Sharon Kay, office support assistant IV, $16.33/hr
Burry, Jessica Marie, event assistant I, $9.00/hr
Burry, Steven Earl, electrician, high voltage, $27.26/hr
Bursik, Robert J Jr, professor, $101,450
Burton, Brandon D, police officer, $17.57/hr
Burton, Cameron Lynn, office support assistant III, $13.39/hr
Burton, Cherie Dione, office support assistant IV, $16.50/hr
Burton, David L, extns professional, asoc, $57,497
Burton, Erin Nicole, veterinarian, residnt, $30,467
Burton, Geoffrey Lynn, advancement associate I, $33,512
Burton, Gera C, director, $107,434

Burton, John Michael, maint svc attd, $18.41/hr
Burton, Judith K, program/project supprt coor I, $19.23/hr
Burton, Justin Michael, custodian, $12.72/hr
Burton, Laura Grace, nurse, staff I, $19.00/hr
Burton, Lauren V, reimbursement ast-cert, $20.08/hr
Burton, Mark C, db programmer analyst-princpl, $83,254
Burton, Mark J, supv radiology, $37.44/hr
Burton, Michael Thomas, ast coach, $34,340
Burton, Sharnice Dawn, custodian, $13.23/hr
Burwell, Christopher James, ast dir advancement, $88,813
Burwell, Melissa Dawn, nurse, staff II, $20.54/hr
Busby, Amy Kathleen, tutor, $13.53/hr
Busch, Jamey Andrew, maint wrkr, prev, $16.88/hr
Busch, Kathryn Ann, student service coor II, $50,165
Busch, Nikolaus S, strat comm associate I, $39,600
Busch, Tammie Marie, library info specialist sr, $15.75/hr
Busch, Tanika Lea, administrative consultant, $80,037
Busch, Theresa Kay, office support assistant IV, $14.00/hr
Busch, William M, instructor, adjunct, $8,640
Buschman, Michael D, maintenance supervisor, $56,578
Buse-Oberto, Alexander Henley, food svc wrkr I, $9.98/hr
Bush Rowe, Shelley Pauline, sr dir program/proj ops, $88,707
Bush, Gregg Aaron, nurse, staff II, $21.26/hr
Bush, Holly J, business support specialist II, $20.14/hr
Bush, Lyle A, mts/pipefitter, $21.05/hr
Bush, Richard B, pharmacist III, $126,501
Bush, Sarah L, prof, asoc teach, $49,616
Bush, Tamara Anne, nurse, staff, $22.06/hr
Bushnell, Matthew A, custodian, $11.44/hr
Bushur, Donna Marie, instructor, adjunct, $15,000
Bushur, John Fidelis, mentor, $15.00/hr
Busick, Chris D, mechl plant spclst, $19.64/hr
Busken, Sharon D, nurse, licensed prac, $20.68/hr
Bussard, Kimberly S, executive assistant, $16.87/hr
Bussman, Marlene Ruth, nurse, staff now III, $30.00/hr
Buszek, Keith Richard, professor, $103,801
Butcher, Brandon M, instructor, adjunct, $24,000
Butcher, Clayton J, instructor, clincl, $150,000
Butcher, Marion Mark, research/lab technician sr, $16.00/hr
Butcher, Nick T, instructor, adjunct, $24,000
Butikofer, Scott, resident physician-2nd yr, $50,810
Butkievich, Karen Nicole, med office assistant, $12.75/hr
Butkievich, Laura E, pharmacy clincl coor, system, $133,344
Butkus, Alvin Adam, instructor, adjunct, $7,500
Butler, Diedre S, office support assistant III, $11.92/hr
Butler, Ge Maya Vaneese, temporary crafts service, $12.00/hr
Butler, James M, ast coach, $36,000
Butler, Johanne, house manager h, $84,090
Butler, Kelly John, performace improvement prof, $68,598
Butler, Lauren Blair, student recruitment spclst sr, $17.00/hr
Butler, Mellissia D, educational pgm associate I, $13.45/hr
Butler, Michael K, mgr II business admin, $64,473
Butler, Miriam D, prof, ast teach, $66,957
Butler, Nellie J, house mgr h prn, $35.00/hr
Butler, Nicholas K, asoc dir program/project ops, $68,979
Butler, Ralph A, executive director, $227,941
Butler, Rhonda Elaine, office support assistant IV, $18.22/hr
Butler, Rochelle B, student support specialist I, $16.78/hr
Butler, Sandra Louise, nurse, staff II, $34.18/hr
Butler, Vanessa Jean, patient svc rep, $13.58/hr
Butner, Bonita Key, prof, asoc, $36,823
Butt, Jane E Loudermilk, office support assistant IV, $15.71/hr
Button, Debra Hull, proj mgr, appeals, $87,913
Butts, Tim W, fin and acctg analyst sr, $56,375
Buxton, Chris Lee, office support assistant I, $9.05/hr
Buxton, Heather Leanne, nurse, staff I, $19.00/hr
Buzzanga, Terra Lynn, prof, ast adjunct, $17,100
Buzzard, Sharon Kay, prof, ast teach, $30,345
Buzzola, Rino A, fellow, post doc clncl-yr2, $58,083
Byars, Katherine S, student support specialist I, $15.30/hr
Byars, Michael, media producer II, $19.22/hr
Byerly-Duke, Eli Lewis, seasonal farm ast, $8.93/hr
Byerly, Kyna Anne, counselor, genetic, $51,725
Byers, William L Jr, director it, $120,933
Byers, Dana C, office support assistant IV, $17.28/hr
Byers, Patrick L, extns professional, asoc, $67,028
Byers, Rhonda Faye, human resources manager sr, $69,710
Byishimo, Rubin Nkunda Bantu, hospital lab tech, $13.04
Byland, James Franklin, sr prgm mgr studnt supprt svcs, $52,400

Byland, Tamara Cloutier, dir II student support svcs, $87,230
Byler, Brandy Lynn, business support specialist II, $20.25/hr
Byler, Marshall J, support systems admin-speclst, $48,560
Bylinowski, Catherine Ann, temporary professional, $17.17/hr
Bylo, Kay Denise, temporary professional, $14.95/hr
Bynum, Mary B, mental health tech, $13.46/hr
Bynum, Patricia A, bts painter, $21.71/hr
Byrd, Aaron Darcy, custodian, $13.23/hr
Byrd, Alan K, sr dir studnt supprt svcs, $102,004
Byrd, Richard Eugene, facilities supervisor, $42,924
Byrne, Andreina Patrice, grader, $4,800
Byrne, Emily D, office support assistant III, $15.97/hr
Byrnes, Brandy Jo, radiologic techl, $21.60/hr
Bythell, Benjamin James, prof, ast, $68,250
Bzowyckyj, Andrew Stefan, prof, ast clincl, $96,000
Caba Fernandez, Marilyn, food svc wrkr I, $10.53/hr
Cabarcas, Michelle, instructor, adjunct, $9,600
Cable, Carol E, electronics technician II, $17.31/hr
Cable, John W, lecturer, $15,000
Cable, Richard, bts carpenter, $21.71/hr
Cabrera Azpiroz, Mirel Lucia, scholar, visiting, $7,071
Cabrera Rodriguez, Belkis, custodian, $13.36/hr
Cabrera, Brenda K, office support assistant III, $13.74/hr
Caccamo, Nancy Jane, office support assistant III, $11.30/hr
Cacek, Debra D, pharmacist II, $67.20/hr
Caddell, Bridget Nicole, executive assistant, $19.00/hr
Caddell, Robert D, chef apprentice, $9.69/hr
Caddell, Scott D, research specialist I, $35,421
Cade, Elliott Matson, research/lab technician, $10.24/hr
Cadwell, Alexandra Teandra Shavee, nurse, lic prac, $15.89/hr
Caeiro, Martha, prof, teach, $46,842
Caffrey, Connie J, med techl reg, $29.05/hr
Cagle, Christopher Aaron, mgr student support svcs, $32,401
Cagle, Lisa Lynette, instructor, adjunct, $10,500
Cahalan, Terry James, farm wrkr I, $10.78/hr
Cahill, John T Jr, locksmith, $21.42/hr
Cahill, Nathanial Elsworth, busi spclst, agri, $39,500
Cahill, Thomas James, anesthesia techn, $14.65/hr
Cai, Haiyan, prof, asoc, $105,111
Cai, Zhen, fellow, post doctoral, $41,370
Cain, Brian J, librarian I, $43,260
Cain, Courtney J, occl therapist, $52,634
Cain, Kerry L, office support assistant IV, $15.84/hr
Cain, Kevin Michael, custodian, $11.41/hr
Cain, MacKenzie M, patient svc rep, $12.55/hr
Cairns, Scott, professor, $105,084
Cairns, Whitney Carlisle, lecturer, $15,300
Cairns, Zachary A, prof, ast, $56,930
Calaluce, Margaret Elizabeth, nurse, staff II rnwp, $34.18/hr
Calcutt, Michael J, prof, asoc, $109,617
Calder, Bradford D, nurse, staff II, $30.50/hr
Calder, Deborah J, chargemaster spclst, $65,097
Calderon, Nichole Christine, central sterile assistant, $10.51/hr
Caldwell, Ashley Elaine, fin and acctg consultant, $50,760
Caldwell, Benjamin Tolly, research/lab technician, $15.00/hr
Caldwell, Clifford Michael, operations support tech I, $10.94/hr
Caldwell, Heather L, instructor, adjunct, $1,200
Caldwell, J Douglas, strat comm consultant, $49,439
Caldwell, Robert Demetris, nurse, licensed prac, $16.53/hr
Caldwell, Teresa Jane, nurse, staff II, $35.15/hr
Calhoon, Barbara A, med coding spclst-certified, $22.80/hr
Calhoon, Larry L, support systems admin-expert, $75,000
Calhoun, Sarah Lynne, prof, ast clincl dept, $142,380
Calkins, Carl F, sr dir research and inst prgms, $217,132
Callahan, Adam Christian, mgr student support svcs, $34,239
Callahan, Margaret Susan, pharmacist II, $119,945
Callahan, Richard J, prof, asoc, $101,708
Callahan, Zachary D, research specialist I, $31,500
Callais, Cheston, research engineering tech I, $20.00/hr
Callan, Peter O, dir talent acquisition & mgmt, $143,082
Callaway, Cathy L, museum professional I, $30,845
Callaway, Vicki Marie, director it, $82,621
Callen, Becky S, office support assistant IV, $13.12/hr
Callender, Alexis A, prof, ast teach, $48,033
Callier, Jayne M, programmer analyst-expert, $64,390
Calliotte, Whitney Nicole, student support spec sr, $16.87/hr
Callison, Marc Max, storage admin-expert, $68,375
Callister, Paul Douglas, professor, $156,000
Calloway, Iris Muzette, dir II advancement, $71,365

Calloway, Stephen Michael, pharmacist III, $121,121
Calvert, Christopher James, high school student, $7.90/hr
Calvert, Deborah K, nurse, staff II, $27.14/hr
Calvert, Krista, instructor, adjunct, $7,200
Calvert, Tammy, custodian, $12.94/hr
Calvert, Wilma J, prof, ast, $80,252
Calvin-Weeks, Danna Marie, instructor, clincl, $23,040
Calvin, Barbara Lynn, office support assistant IV, $16.21/hr
Calvin, Belinda B, pat acct rep, $14.84/hr
Calvin, James Halvorsen, prof, asoc, $58,245
Calvin, Latrina M, office support assistant IV, $17.07/hr
Calvin, Rebecca Ann, strat comm associate II, $52,947
Calvin, Rebekah Lynn, mgr III business admin, $71,065
Calvin, Steven Eugene, farm wrkr II, $13.59/hr
Calyam, Anjaneyaprasad Prabhakar, prof, ast, $106,820
Camden, Jean Mary, resrch ast, $80,201
Camden, Ryan Eugene, pharmacist II, $123,882
Cameron, Joseph Alfred III, pharmacist III, $128,835
Cameron, Aunya, resident physician-1st yr, $50,825
Cameron, Donald H, resp therapist reg, $26.47/hr
Cameron, Evan R, physician, $250.00/hr
Cameron, Glen T, professor, $155,919
Cameron, Jason Bernard Keezell, system admin-expert, $55,025
Cameron, Roger W, prof, ast clincl dept, $125,000
Cameron, Susan C, media production director I, $61,500
Cameron, Velynda Jo, 4-h spclst, $47,830
Camille, Mary Smith, coor, surg supply, $56,618
Cammack, Sarah Elizabeth, nurse, staff II, $26.60/hr
Camp, Amy Elizabeth, coor phy suprt, $56,818
Camp, Casey William, supv radiology, $39.95/hr
Camp, Charlene Esther, office support assistant IV, $14.00/hr
Camp, Courtney, ultrasonographer, $30.60/hr
Camp, Milene D, patient svc rep, $14.77/hr
Camp, Patricia Ann, human resources assistant, $15.88/hr
Camp, Simone R, ast mgr pathology, $81,600
Camp, Terrance Jordan, genl stores attd, $14.14/hr
Campbell, Michael Carl II, prof, ast, $70,000
Campbell, Brett L Jr, educational pgm associate I, $13.58/hr
Campbell, Anita Sethi, instructor, adjunct, $30.00/hr
Campbell, Austin R, pharmacist II, $128,835
Campbell, Carla Anne, lecturer, $36,000
Campbell, Daniel Ralph, hospital security officer, $11.29/hr
Campbell, Danielle Rose Simone, office support asst IV, $15.00/hr
Campbell, Darla Lea, busi spclst, agri, $49,700
Campbell, David D, insulation svcs wrkr III lead, $21.55/hr
Campbell, Deborah M, coor, care, $72,675
Campbell, Donald, bldg cntrl sys techn iv lead, $25.37/hr
Campbell, Doreen C, custodian, $12.94/hr
Campbell, Gina N, office support assistant IV, $14.50/hr
Campbell, Glenda L, nurse, staff II, $29.86/hr
Campbell, Jabez Duane, temporary technical, $10.00/hr
Campbell, James Davis, professor, $102,945
Campbell, James F, professor, $137,376
Campbell, James M, mgr csm operations, $55,045
Campbell, Julia Ann, prof, ast teach, $61,800
Campbell, Katie Lynn, executive assistant, $18.99/hr
Campbell, Lori A, office support assistant III, $11.58/hr
Campbell, Michelle Kaye, patient svc rep, $13.02/hr
Campbell, Rhonda Michelle, nurse, licensed prac, $19.49/hr
Campbell, Rowenda Carlos, nurse, licensed prac, $16.83/hr
Campbell, Scheryl K, human resources specialist I, $20.72/hr
Campbell, Scott D, environmental health prof II, $50,351
Campbell, Teresa Jeanne, fin and acctg analyst, $19.47/hr
Campbell, Terrie Rae, office support assistant IV, $16.13/hr
Campione-Barr, Nicole Marie, prof, asoc, $71,313
Campione, Sharon Anne, research specialist I, $15.00/hr
Campoli, Jeanne Marie, clerk, unit, $14.26/hr
Canada, Kelli Elizabeth, prof, ast, $71,500
Canady, Lakeisha, dental assistant II, $13.24/hr
Canady, Shilo, child dev assistant, $8.08/hr
Canavan, Alice, business support specialist II, $23.74/hr
Cancila, Jack Michael, lecturer, $10,500
Cancilla, Devon A, vice provost, $150,000
Candela, Amber Grace, prof, ast, $60,000
Candice, Christopher G, child dev aide, $8.90/hr
Candrl, Julie M, fin and acctg analyst sr, $54,710
Canfield, Chad B, care team assoc-clinical, $12.32/hr
Canfield, Richard E, custodian, $10.39/hr
Canfield, Shannon Marie, asoc dir program/project ops, $52,020

Canhasi, Ilir, supv food svc I,-h, $35,855
Canis, Randy Lawrence, prof, adjunct, $26,775
Canlas, Benjamin T, sr manager it, $94,999
Cannaday Adams, Carrie, nurse, licensed prac, $19.23/hr
Cannon, John F, prof, asoc, $89,474
Cannon, Tracey LaRhein, instructor, adjunct, $6,354
Canole, Edith, custodian, $10.00/hr
Canole, Jeff, building/mechanical maint I, $17.95/hr
Canole, Mark David, mail carrier, $14.85/hr
Canole, Roberta L, bindery opr I, $14.85/hr
Canote, Melody D, animal caretaker-equine/food, $12.72/hr
Canoy, Margaret B Minihan, reimbursement ast-cert, $20.19/hr
Canton, Shanae Denise, office support assistant IV, $15.68/hr
Cantrell-Walker, Jennifer Jean, instructor, adjunct, $15,000
Cantrell, Amanda Nicole, cook, $12.64/hr
Cantrell, Emily Anne, research specialist I, $37,698
Cantu, Edward III, prof, asoc, $91,750
Cantu, Norma Elia, professor, $113,300
Cantwell, Christopher D, prof, ast, $56,000
Cao, Hongyuan, prof, ast, $87,000
Cao, Tam Bang, temporary technical, $8.50/hr
Cao, Yangrong, fellow, post doctoral, $41,200
Cao, Zongxuan, resident physician-1st yr, $50,219
Capinpin, Cindy Sue, custodian, $11.41/hr
Capinpin, Tony A, custodian, $10.69/hr
Capito, Marie Dabbs, pharmacist II, $60.00/hr
Capito, Nicholas Michael, resident physician-5th yr, $58,083
Caples, Gary Dean Jr, surgical technl certified, $17.09/hr
Caples, Dawn Elizabeth Kay, surgical technl certified, $17.43/hr
Caplinger, Gregory Weldon, nurse, staff II, $22.56/hr
Caplinger, Leighton Ariane, nurse, staff II, $21.68/hr
Caplow, Julie A, prof, asoc, $72,134
Capuano, Kayla Nicole, care team assoc-clinical, $12.08/hr
Carani, Stephanie Rebecca, dir II advancement, $83,000
Caratti, Adela, food svc wrkr I, $11.29/hr
Caraway, Barbara Jean, anesthesia techn, $17.10/hr
Caraway, Ron N, security analyst-entry, $41,937
Caraza-de-Holland, Xanath, lecturer, $32,232
Carbone, Kristin, prof, asoc, $79,500
Carbonell, Roberto, police officer, $17.50/hr
Cardenas Haro, Jose Antonio, prof, ast teach, $65,000
Cardenas, Lauren Graciela, adjunct, $18,000
Cardenas, Tabatha Leann, supv housekeeping, $29,893
Carder, Rachel Marie, office support assistant III, $11.50/hr
Cardwell, Barry Lee, coor, service, $17.10/hr
Cardwell, Laura Denise, instructor, adjunct, $7,200
Careaga, Andrew P, dir II strat communications, $99,671
Carey, Jeanie, educational pgm coor III, $50,000
Cargile, Donna J, nurse, licensed prac sr, $19.39/hr
Carl, Jacqueline Rebekah, instructor, $52
Carl, Jane M, professor, $83,479
Carlisle, Gretchen K, fellow, post doctoral, $10,110
Carlisle, Terry E, physician ast, $128,320
Carlo Contreras, Gustavo, professor, $135,905
Carlo, Teresa Anna, nurse, licensed prac, $17.71/hr
Carlos, Joseph L, custodian, $12.69/hr
Carlos, Justin Dean, grounds keeper, $11.76/hr
Carlos, Rodney J, mts/pipefitter, $21.05/hr
Carlsen Krause, Monica Maria, post doctoral asoc, $40,000
Carlson, Brad Michael, prof, ast, $56,855
Carlson, Gwendolyn Diane, bus support specialist II, $22.00/hr
Carlson, Kimberly Jean, resrch asoc, $55,934
Carlton, Joshua Andrew, resident physician-1st yr, $50,219
Carlyon, Joshua Caleb, research activities supervisor, $34,744
Carmack, Carli Marie, executive assistant, $16.54/hr
Carmack, Terry Lee, research/lab technician sr, $18.07/hr
Carmack, Tina M, office support assistant IV, $17.74/hr
Carmichael, Angela Marie, bus support specialist sr, $26.83/hr
Carmichael, Tammy Merlean, office support asst IV, $17.58/hr
Carmody, John H, scientific photographer, $17.20/hr
Carmona, Estrella, educational pgm associate I, $12.25/hr
Carnahan, Dava Marie, instructor, clincl, $79,000
Carnahan, Lacey Brooke, mgr student support svcs, $31,305
Carner, Dorothy J, librarian IV, $83,863
Carner, Inge Patricia, educational pgm associate I, $13.76/hr
Carnes, Bridgette Nicole, instructor, adjunct, $15,300
Carnes, Christopher Ryan, cook, $13.21/hr
Carnes, Zachary T, radiologic techl, $18.59/hr
Carney, John P III, ast coach, $77,250

Carney, Eugene Davis, media producer sr, $16.54/hr
Carney, Jacqueline Louise, tutor, $10.00/hr
Carney, Megan Strawsine, couns hlth/welfare/wellness, $40,000
Carney, Michael T, prof, asoc adjunct, $12,000
Carney, Rita M, nurse, staff II, $34.18/hr
Caron, Normand Robert, prof, ast clincl dept, $65,093
Carothers, Donna M, ast dir advancement, $59,679
Carothers, Marsha G, librarian I, $38,399
Carothers, Sheila K, med coding spclst-certified, $20.83/hr
Carpenter, Angie M, patient svc rep, $14.88/hr
Carpenter, Brent D, extns professional, asoc, $60,053
Carpenter, Brittany G, specialist, $10.00/hr
Carpenter, Corinne Meloni, executive assistant, $17.45/hr
Carpenter, LaQuanda, instructor, adjunct, $8,325
Carpenter, William Russell, resident physician-3rd yr, $53,763
Carpentier-Anderson, Melissa Catherine, veterinarian, res, $26,000
Carpintero, Barbie Iyula, histologic technl, $21.78/hr
Carr, Amanda Marie, student support specialist sr, $16.87/hr
Carr, Brandi Rae, office support assistant II, $11.04
Carr, Chaka Sharrinet, office support assistant III, $13.00/hr
Carr, David Boice, driver, $12.80/hr
Carr, Deborah L, director, $120,919
Carr, Gregory Stephen, lecturer, $18,000
Carr, Laura Elizabeth, nurse, staff I, $19.00/hr
Carr, Lauren Leigh, prof, ast adjunct, $125.00/hr
Carr, Lucinda Jackson, educational pgm associate I, $13.66/hr
Carr, Patricia Ann, phlebotomist, $10.64/hr
Carraher, Melanie McGregor, bus support specialist II, $20.18/hr
Carraher, Michael R, research specialist sr, $50,500
Carranza, Miguel Antonio, professor, $132,090
Carrell, Janice M A, program/project supprt coor I, $50,019
Carrell, Tamara Janelle, instructor, adjunct, $7,200
Carreras, Kylie Frances, care team assoc-clinical, $12.55/hr
Carriker, Gordon L, extns professional, asoc, $52,656
Carrington, Clayton Tyler, event assistant I, $8.50/hr
Carrington, Leland K, food svc attd I,-mrc, $10.20/hr
Carroll, Bobbi Jo, custodian, bldg maint, $12.64/hr
Carroll, Cameron Eugene, event assistant I, $8.50/hr
Carroll, Douglas R, prgm director, $138,314
Carroll, Janet L, business tech analyst-princpl, $58,423
Carroll, Jason Robert, reactor operator, $26.42/hr
Carroll, John Davis, instructor, adjunct, $12,000
Carroll, Joseph C, professor, $100,400
Carroll, Kellie R, resp therapist reg, $20.42/hr
Carroll, Kimberly Gail, event assistant I, $7.55/hr
Carroll, Mark M, prof, asoc, $61,811
Carroll, Mary Katherine, care team assoc-clinical, $11.10/hr
Carroll, Vincent Anthony, mgr student support svcs, $30,805
Carroz, Jodi Laverne, nurse, staff II, $20.54/hr
Carroz, Laura Lyng, academic advisor, $43,786
Carson Jones, Jessica, prof, ast adjunct, $14,400
Carson, Bryan L, custodian, $13.23/hr
Carson, Catherine Roberta, grader, $52
Carson, Ronald S, prof, asoc adjunct, $18,000
Carson, Tamara Bella, office support assistant IV, $16.33/hr
Carstens, Stephanie J, resident physician-4th yr, $55,804
Carstens, Vicki M, prof, asoc, $100.00/hr
Cartee, Dominique Marie, nurse, or/recovery-ch, $20.54/hr
Cartee, Eugena Lee, food svc wrkr I, $9.60/hr
Cartee, Jacob Tyler, food svc wrkr I, $9.60/hr
Carter Dochler, Jennifer Lynne, instructor, adjunct, $9,000
Carter Fischer, Wendy Jo, sr ast dir studnt supprt svcs, $58,087
Carter-Simmons, Bertha Yvonne, instructor, clincl, $90,000
Carter, Anita F, mgr II business admin, $63,390
Carter, Barbara Sue, nurse, staff II, $31.70/hr
Carter, Brian Andrew, pat acct rep, $13.98/hr
Carter, Brooke Nicole, nurse, licensed prac, $14.76/hr
Carter, Charles K, care team assoc-suppt, $13.58/hr
Carter, Clara Louise, office support assistant III, $16.48/hr
Carter, Dawn, food svc wrkr II, $11.83/hr
Carter, Diana L, program/project supprt coor I, $41,600
Carter, Eric J, student service coor sr, $52,485
Carter, Helga E, office support assistant II, $10.56/hr
Carter, Karen A, nurse, staff II rnwp, $20.54/hr
Carter, Karla A, executive assistant, $25.10/hr
Carter, Kate L, nurse, staff II rnwp, $20.54/hr
Carter, Kelly Ann, lecturer, $25,005
Carter, Lance Crawford, prof, ast teach, $81,039
Carter, Lyanna Renee, office support assistant II, $14.79/hr

Carter, Maria Jenet, media production director I, $45,000
Carter, Maridella Elizabeth, instructor, adjunct, $7,500
Carter, Marilyn L, custodian, $13.36/hr
Carter, Martha Linda, asoc vice chancellor, $115,566
Carter, Marty M, business ops associate sr, $66,300
Carter, Michael Wayne, prof, ast teach, $80,600
Carter, Mildred Louise, business support specialist II, $18.71/hr
Carter, Pat A, mts/hvac, $21.05/hr
Carter, Robyn Delea, radiologic techl, $20.12/hr
Carter, Tara Eileen, nurse, staff prn, $26.00/hr
Carter, Taylor, child dev assistant, $8.08/hr
Carter, Tracy A, nurse, licensed prac sr, $20.37/hr
Cartier, Catherine Ann, instructor, adjunct, $9,000
Cartwright, Charles E, construction manager I, $48,450
Cartwright, Eric David, executive chef, $66,070
Caruso, Anthony Nicholaus, prof, asoc, $130,000
Caruthers, Loyce E, prof, asoc, $67,556
Carver, Colleen Merie, museum paraprofessional II, $17.51/hr
Carver, Mary Heather, professor, $100,242
Cary, Ann H, dean, $210,000
Cary, Becky Jo, executive assistant, $19.37/hr
Cary, Paul L, coor tox/drug monitor svc, $82,002
Cary, Shannon N, strat comm associate I, $43,711
Cary, Suzanne M, prof, ast clincl, $59,051
Casad, Bettina J, prof, ast, $71,200
Casady, Brandon Ryan, care team assoc-clinical, $12.80/hr
Casady, Jacob Michael, hospital security officer, $11.07/hr
Casares, Amanda Christene, surgical techn certified, $16.84/hr
Casati-Zajicek, Jennifer, research specialist sr, $59,745
Casazza, Peter, prof, curators, $179,065
Case-Halferty, Anne Elizabeth, mgr advancement, $46,000
Caselman, Deborah Sue, finance systems specialist III, $78,054
Casey, Erin Elizabeth Ryan, office support assistant IV, $14.75/hr
Casey, William R, temporary clerical, $9.10/hr
Cash, Daniel Richard, community dev acct rep, $52,000
Cason, Myra O, anesthesia techn, $16.46/hr
Cason, Robin Kay, custodian, $10.94/hr
Casperson, Cassandra Lee, academic advisor, $35,894
Cass, Brittany K, advancement officer, $45,600
Cass, Dylan Lee, accountant I, $15.70/hr
Cass, Sherry A, executive assistant, $21.08/hr
Cassels, John W Jr, prof, asoc clincl dept, $141,400
Cassil, Michele Leigh, nurse, staff II, $25.91/hr
Cassmeyer, Diane Catherine, business support spec II, $20.15/hr
Cassone, Deandra Tillman, prof, asoc adjunct, $18,000
Castaner, Leilani Jeanette, veterinary technician sr, $19.96/hr
Castano, Carlos Henry, prof, asoc, $86,539
Casteel, David B, mts/electrician, $21.05/hr
Casteel, Stan, professor, $133,574
Castello, Anthony W, police officer, $16.54/hr
Castille, Bryan Steven, instructor, adjunct, $18,000
Castleman, Heather Wynn, patient svc rep, $11.00/hr
Castor, Gary Wayne, instructor, adjunct, $8,000
Castro Guerrero, Norma Angelica, resrch scientist/acad, $25,200
Castro, Antonio Jamie, prof, ast, $77,297
Castrop, Joseph Bruno, project manager-expert, $70,700
Castulik, Kathy, couns hlth/welfare/wellness, $46,415
Caszatt, Michelle, nurse, staff II, $34.18/hr
Catalano, Brock Michael, research/lab technician, $10.24/hr
Catalano, Theresa Diane, supv, lab, $61,371
Cataldo, Barbara, reimbursement ast-cert, $18.59/hr
Cater, Seth R, security analyst-speclst, $52,000
Cates, Christopher Wayne, resident physician-1st yr, $50,219
Cates, Judy, business support specialist II, $18.22/hr
Cates, Megan K, resident physician-2nd yr, $52,007
Cates, Michelle, physician, $200.00/hr
Cates, Paula Kay, educational pgm associate I, $13.45/hr
Cathey, Andrea M, dir II advancement, $64,292
Catley, Delwyn, professor, $89,359
Catlin, Angie Marie, nurse, staff II, $21.75/hr
Cato, Sarah, tutor, $25.25/hr
Catron, Brian L, engineer, resrch, $45,000
Catron, Courtney Marie, radiologic techl, $18.96/hr
Cattanach, John R, dir event operations, $111,104
Caubet, William L Jr, physicist, $163,951
Caudle, Sonya Nadine, nurse, staff II, $32.65/hr
Cauthon, Jordan Kristine, program/project supprt coor I, $19,041
Cavanaugh, Anna Pearl, phlebotomist, $14.88/hr
Cavanaugh, Crystal Lynn, nurse, staff II, $20.54/hr

Cavender, Colin K, custodian, bldg maint, $11.76/hr
Cavender, Deborah L, custodian lead, $11.98/hr
Cavigioli, Rita C, professor, $66,495
Cavins, David Matthew, programmer analyst-speclst, $40,636
Cawlfield, Jeffrey D, vice provost, $167,635
Cays, Donna, prof, asoc teach, $40,617
Cecil, Gregory A, dir III advancement, $73,294
Cecil, Michelle A, prof, curator teach, $160,333
Cedeck, Karen A, human resources assistant, $18.30/hr
Cen, Yigang, scholar, visiting, $18,000
Cepel, Christian M, programmer analyst-speclst, $46,000
Cerneka, Erin Suzanne Ramsay, nurse practitioner, $91,127
Cerney, Lisa Marie, accountant II, $18.72/hr
Cernusca, Mihaela Mariana, resrch asoc, $2,000
Cerutti, Jessica Ellen, lecturer sr, $10,500
Cesario, Robert James, prof, ast teach, $62,957
Cessac, Susan M, fin and acctg consultant lead, $76,138
Cetinkaya, Egemen Kemal, prof, ast, $79,790
Cha, Ho Seop, prof, ast adjunct, $18,900
Chabot, Kara Nicole, emergency services rep, $10.75/hr
Chaddad, Fabio, prof, asoc, $96,041
Chadha, Rohit, prof, ast, $86,700
Chaffin, Carla Ann, strat comm consultant, $47,337
Chagnon, Napoleon Alphonseau, prof, resrch, $130,000
Chairman, Dennis Baskaran, prof, ast clincl dept, $257,040
Chakraborty, Sounak, prof, asoc, $83,440
Chakraborty, Uday Kumar, professor, $96,744
Chalfant, Cozetta, resp therapy techn/icu cert, $26.11/hr
Chaligoj, Erica Dawn, nurse, staff II, $21.59/hr
Challacombe, Rosana, student service coor II, $40,000
Chamberlain, Don Louis, audiologist, $57,000
Chamberlain, Roger Wade, prof, ast adjunct, $8,004
Chamberlain, Ronda Marcemia, custodian, $10.39/hr
Chamberlin, Glen A, managing engineer, $80,856
Chambers, Brenda Williams, pat acct rep, $15.42/hr
Chambers, Carol Lorene, med techl reg, $28.19/hr
Chambers, Christopher Daniel, dir prog/project oper, $81,411
Chambers, Krista, executive assistant, $20.86/hr
Chambers, Melissa Ann, business support specialist II, $15.40/hr
Chambers, Yvette Gerre, educational pgm coor I, $33,330
Champ, Sandee Anne, office support assistant II, $10.67/hr
Champlin, David M, strat comm associate II, $39,600
Chan, Albert K, prof, ast clincl dept, $164,475
Chan, Chin Ting, instructor, adjunct, $10,800
Chan, Hoi Yuen, student service coor I, $37,048
Chan, Lisa Kim, intern, $24,014
Chan, Paul Chun Ho, prof, asoc, $93,917
Chan, Sokphon Julia, care team assoc-clinical, $12.08/hr
Chance, Callie, nurse, staff II, $21.37/hr
Chance, Deborah L, prof, ast resrch, $51,000
Chance, Louanne, nurse, resrch, $30.54/hr
Chancellor, Beth Claudette, chief info security officer, $161,924
Chandlee, Jessica Dawn, nurse, licensed prac, $16.14/hr
Chandlee, Kayla Renee, certif pharmacy techn, $13.56/hr
Chandler, Saronda Thomas Jr, dental assistant I, $12.06/hr
Chandler, Courtney Rae, patient svc rep, $10.64/hr
Chandler, Donna Gail, bts painter, $20.23/hr
Chandler, Jeffrey M, custodian, $10.94/hr
Chandler, Jessica Brianne, ast athletic director, $60,903
Chandler, Patricia C, office support assistant IV, $16.14/hr
Chandler, Patricia Dawn, temporary crafts service, $9.10/hr
Chandran, Arul Velavan, fellow, post doc clncl-yr2, $58,083
Chandrasekhar, Anand, professor, $93,687
Chandrasekhar, H R, professor, $106,966
Chandrasekhar, Meera, prof, curator teach, $134,908
Chandrashekhara, K, prof, curators, $169,976
Chang, Cheng Hsiung Alec, prof, asoc, $83,521
Chang, Chia-Wai David, prof, asoc clincl dept, $253,777
Chang, Elizabeth Hope, prof, asoc, $67,162
Chang, Jonathan L, research specialist I, $14.95/hr
Chang, Qin, resident physician-4th yr, $54,425
Chang, Qing, programmer analyst-speclst, $47,277
Chang, Qing, prof, ast adjunct, $18,000
Chansley, Jackie Ray, office support assistant IV, $17.12/hr
Chapins, Jessica Lynn, office support assistant II, $10.56/hr
Chaplin, Linda M, dental hygienist, $33.82/hr
Chapman, Alan D, prof, ast, $81,675
Chapman, Becky S, event assistant I, $7.55/hr
Chapman, Cherie J, dir program/project operations, $91,767

Chapman, Cinda Rebecca, instructor, adjunct, $21,000
Chapman, Connie Sue, pat acct rep, $15.40/hr
Chapman, Haley Mariah, research/lab technician, $11.00/hr
Chapman, Jeffrey, dir II advancement, $90,000
Chapman, Jennifer J, physician ast, $88,293
Chapman, John Patrick, temporary clerical, $8.75/hr
Chapman, Karen Sue, human resources manager, $47,800
Chapman, Lauren Danielle, nursing ast, $12.08/hr
Chapman, Patricia S, office support assistant IV, $14.29/hr
Chapman, Paula Gayle, clinical educator, $67,215
Chapman, Sean Kevin, bldg cntrl sys techn III, $23.33/hr
Chapman, Sheila Jeanne, dietitian, clincl, $53,820
Chapman, Sherri Marie, radiologic techl, $24.51/hr
Chapman, Steve W, network engineer-expert, $64,731
Chapman, Troy L, bldg cntrl sys tech II, $22.49/hr
Chappelear, Andrea Lee, internet admin-expert, $24.25/hr
Charatonik, Wlodzimierz Jan, professor, $80,228
Charboneau, Heather N, staff dev spclst, $47,500
Charles, Nicholas Tyler, office support assistant I, $9.05/hr
Charlton, Douglas D, reactor engineer, $74,370
Charlton, Jennifer, clinical lab manager I, $51,000
Charrier, Richard J, geo info system specialist, $48,340
Charrier, Taresa Delayne, nurse, staff II, $27.43/hr
Chartkov, Jolene Noel, nurse clinician, $52,153
Chase, Jo-Ana Dolojan, prof, ast, $66,482
Chase, Leslie, nurse anesthetist, $147,900
Chase, Phyllis Ann, prgm director, $106,600
Chastain, Claud B, professor, $137,784
Chasteen, Janessa Cae, lecturer, $26,513
Chatterjee, Deb, prof, asoc, $81,782
Chattin, Lisa Diane, reimbursement ast-cert, $18.41/hr
Chaudhary, Juhi, research specialist I, $38,850
Chaudhry, Ghulam M, professor, $135,482
Chaudhry, Irfan, resident physician-1st yr, $49,025
Chauvin, Stephanie Kay, educational pgm coor I, $33,000
Chavers, Devin Vershawn, student recruitment spclst, $14.96/hr
Chavez, Concepcion Z, custodian, $13.23/hr
Chavez, Paulette, safety communications operator, $13.16/hr
Che, Ann K, supervisor it, $45,594
Cheadle, Carl Edward, research specialist sr, $40,800
Cheak Zamora, Nancy Christine, prof, ast, $79,143
Cheatom, Tameka Roshae, office support assistant III, $11.47/hr
Cheatom, Teresa Mae, hospital lab tech, $15.40/hr
Cheatum, Ackren Jarnell, care team assoc-suppt, $13.25/hr
Cheavens, John Caleb, coor protocol svcs, $19.61/hr
Cheavens, Stacy Turpin, cert med illustrator, $24.10/hr
Cheek, Amber J, compliance manager, $47,000
Cheek, Franklin V, dairy worker, $14.27/hr
Cheesman, Marjorie Ruth, nurse, licensed prac, $15.35/hr
Cheesman, Nathan Elisha, mgr student support svcs, $34,564
Cheffen, Sheila Renee, human resources assistant, $14.90/hr
Chegwidden, Anne E, business support specialist II, $21.65/hr
Chela, Harleen Kaur, resident physician-2nd yr, $52,007
Chelladurai, Cary Alicia Lyon, mgr II student support svcs, $55,350
Chellappan, Sriram, prof, asoc, $100,000
Chen, Adam Albert, lab assistant, $9.00/hr
Chen, Chung-Lung, professor, $134,453
Chen, Daqing Ann, finance systems specialist sr, $84,500
Chen, Dongqing, research/lab technician, $17.17/hr
Chen, Elton Chengyi, resident physician-4th yr, $54,425
Chen, Genda, professor, $200,000
Chen, Hsiu-Hung, prof, ast resrch, $46,000
Chen, Jen-Hao, prof, ast, $72,000
Chen, Jianping, research specialist I, $32,400
Chen, Jinn Kuen, professor, $125,302
Chen, Julie Zongwei, db programmer analyst-princpl, $73,463
Chen, Katherina Ying Ru, research/lab technician sr, $13.24/hr
Chen, Ke, office support assistant III, $11.80/hr
Chen, Mingjie, resrch scientist/academic sr, $39,534
Chen, Nina Yuh Hsien, extns professional, $61,417
Chen, Shanshan, nutrition spclst, $38,500
Chen, Shi Jie, professor, $130,400
Chen, Weihong, research/lab technician, $12.63/hr
Chen, Xiaobo, prof, ast, $66,390
Chen, Xuemei, fellow, post doctoral, $52,700
Chen, Yi, professor, $110,482
Chen, Yuan, academic advisor, $37,555
Chen, Zhen, professor, $160,719
Chen, Zhenrui, scholar, visiting, $25.00/hr

Chen, ZhiQiang, prof, ast, $75,030
Chen, Zihong, research specialist I, $31,100
Chenault, Jacqueline Ann, office support assistant III, $14.27/hr
Cheney, Amy Renee, patient svc rep, $13.97/hr
Cheney, Robert C, resident physician-1st yr, $50,219
Cheng, An-Lin, prof, asoc, $88,888
Cheng, Fei, scholar, visiting, $18.46/hr
Cheng, Jianlin, prof, asoc, $119,386
Cheng, Kun, prof, asoc, $138,000
Cheng, Maggie Xiaoyan, prof, asoc, $45,695
Cheng, Ya-Wen, educational pgm coor III, $54,000
Chernookaya, Nadezhda, coor, perf imprv pat safty-acs, $53,820
Cherrington, Mindy L, nurse practitioner, $85,084
Cherry, Cheryl L, office support assistant IV, $17.51/hr
Chertoff, Keyna, resrch ast sr, $53,321
Cheslik, Julie, dean, asoc, $143,109
Chester, Aaron James, stage services assistant sr, $16.00/hr
Chester, Amy R, ast registrar, $48,812
Chester, Bryan G, strat comm manager, $65,975
Chettiar, Ram, resident physician-3rd yr, $52,470
Chew, Jesslyn Tenhouse, strat comm associate I, $44,137
Chew, Lindell Phillip, instructor, $14,000
Chi, Cletus Fonchingong, resp therapist reg, $24.00/hr
Chi, Junzhe, temporary technical, $11.18/hr
Chi, Ming Bruce, resident physician-2nd yr, $50,810
Chick, Queteria A, certif pharmacy techn, $13.82/hr
Chickey, Carol A, office support assistant IV, $14.20/hr
Chickos, James, professor, $83,498
Chicone, Carmen Charles, professor, $125,295
Chiesi, Matthew D, instructor, adjunct, $18,648
Chievous, Tami Lynn, ast athletic director, $105,000
Chikhladze, George, prof, ast teach, $57,311
Childers, Sharleen K, clncl imprvmnt spclst, $58,063
Childs, Amy, office support assistant IV, $18.50/hr
Childs, Angela Jean, paralegal, $42,500
Childs, Deborah Wildman, educational prgm coor sr, $58,174
Childs, Thomas E, research specialist sr, $54,365
Childs, Yasmin R, patient svc rep, $12.34/hr
Chiles, Linda Sue, media producer I, $16.08/hr
Chiles, Todd H, prof, asoc, $122,774
Chindris, Calin Ioan, prof, ast, $85,194
Chinea, Zachary, police officer, $17.30/hr
Ching, Wai Yim, professor, $126,466
Chinn, Stephanie T, library info specialist, $13.45/hr
Chinnakotla, Bhavana, resident physician-2nd yr, $52,007
Chinni, Connie Rafalko, waiter/waitress, $8.51/hr
Chipman, James Wayne, ast vice chancellor, $159,500
Chipman, Stephanie Dawn, mgr II student support svcs, $49,750
Chirillo, Jennifer Ann, business support specialist II, $15.25/hr
Chirillo, Joseph A, system administrator-entry, $46,865
Chisholm, Julia Marie, mgr outpatient pharmacy, $142,520
Chism, Jay S, sr dir program/project ops, $94,030
Chism, Jennifer Lynne, academic advisor, $37,500
Chism, Patti Jeanine, dir II advancement, $70,157
Chism, Sean Jeremy, student service coor II, $46,500
Chism, Thresa D, office support assistant IV, $14.93/hr
Chittum, Joshua Goss, office support assistant IV, $13.33/hr
Chiu, Eric Shao Yuan, internet administrator-entry, $15.45/hr
Chiu, Yu Hsien, prof, asoc teach, $63,070
Chiuchiarelli, Sera Roberta, resrch asoc, $53,550
Chmura, Victor Henry, custodian, $10.00/hr
Cho, Seonghee, prof, asoc, $82,114
Cho, Soo Yeon, research project analyst, $57,000
Cho, Sung Hwan, fellow, post doctoral, $38,760
Cho, Uee Wan, prof, asoc, $82,923
Cho, Yong Jin, scholar, visiting, $12,000
Cho, Yonghee Kristina, resident physician-3rd yr, $52,470
Chockalingam, Anand, prof, asoc clincl dept, $137,659
Choi, Baek-Young, prof, asoc, $82,977
Choi, Emily Nicole, patient svc rep, $11.92/hr
Choi, Minsu, prof, asoc, $83,940
Choi, Myong Hee, office support assistant I, $10.00/hr
Chole, Dana Marie, physical therapist, $35.00/hr
Choma, Rachel Lee, temporary clerical, $8.00/hr
Choma, Theodore John, professor, $269,322
Chopra, Pooja, resident physician-1st yr, $49,025
Chorlins, Jason Adam, grader, $100.00/hr
Chott, Mary L, office support assistant IV, $16.35/hr
Chott, Steve L, system support analyst-entry, $17.51/hr

Chou, Fenfen, sr dir program/project ops, $106,080
Choudhary, Asif Saeed, resident physician-2nd yr, $52,007
Choudhry, Hadia A, resident physician-2nd yr, $52,007
Choudhry, Kiran Siddique, prof, ast, $115,900
Choudhury, Amitava, prof, ast, $67,170
Chowdhury, Masud Hasan, prof, asoc, $102,465
Chrisman, Frances Dawn, office support assistant sr, $18.37/hr
Chrisman, Katharine Danelle, nurse, licensed prac, $16.56/hr
Chrisman, Lori Ellen, food svc wrkr II, $10.10/hr
Christ, Shawn Edward, prof, asoc, $77,650
Christensen Murray, Pia E, strat comm associate I, $48,691
Christensen, Cortnee Lee, office support assistant IV, $16.53/hr
Christensen, Erin Frances, student service coor II, $39,600
Christensen, Gordon, professor, $127,903
Christensen, Kirk Le, prof, ast teach, $68,516
Christian, Nakisha Anelda, fin and acctg analyst sr, $46,200
Christian, Natasha Kenyata, nurse, clincl charge-lpn, $21.37/hr
Christian, Sheila Abby, operations support tech sr, $14.16/hr
Christiansen, Rachel J, program/project supprt coor II, $40,968
Christiansen, Tanya, professor, $103,560
Christiansen, Teri Ellen, prof, asoc teach, $75,558
Christianson, Scott, prof, ast teach, $78,594
Christie, Robert Walter Jr, med techl reg, $30.36/hr
Christie, Connilee J, asoc dir program/project ops, $54,228
Christopher, Jimmy Dale Jr, mgr csm operations, $61,000
Christopher, Caitlin Jewell, food svc wrkr II, $10.10/hr
Christopher, Kourtney Lea, research specialist I, $43,260
Christopher, Patrick, resident physician-1st yr, $49,025
Christopher, Un Chong, instructor, adjunct, $40,320
Christus, Pete E III, security officer, $13.89/hr
Christy, Cynthia Ann, program/project supprt coor II, $40,590
Chronister, Mary E, nurse, staff II rnwp, $31.67/hr
Chronwall, Bibie M, prof, asoc adjunct, $19,392
Chrucky, SerhII, lecturer, $9,000
Chu, Asa Sebastian, resident physician-1st yr, $50,219
Chu, Cindy Yue-Xin, research specialist I, $46,263
Chu, Jingxi, research consultant sr, $70,454
Chu, Shirley, veterinarian, residnt, $26,000
Chu, Xiangping, prof, asoc, $93,000
Chua, Winnie L, specialist, $10.00/hr
Chubiz, Lon Michael, prof, ast, $69,000
Chughtai, Mahmooda Ashraf, mental health tech, $14.24/hr
Chui, Charles, founders professor, $20,011
Chuick, Allison Beth Seplak, academic advisor, $40,800
Chun, Sanghun, scholar, visiting, $26,904
Chung, Jae-Won, temporary technical, $15.00/hr
Chung, Je Kook, program/project supprt coor I, $42,000
Chung, Kyung H, resident physician-6th yr, $58,200
Chung, Younghee, temporary clerical, $11.30/hr
Chuquilin Arista, Miguel, prof, ast clincl dept, $154,671
Church, Ann E, nurse, staff II, $33.70/hr
Church, Ashley Diane, nurse, staff I, $19.37/hr
Church, Dane Jack, resident physician-2nd yr, $50,810
Church, Daniel J, nurse, staff II, $20.85/hr
Church, Karla Turney, executive assistant sr, $57,450
Church, Kimberly Swanson, prof, ast, $145,550
Churchill, Andrew Michael, system sup analyst-expert, $25.47/hr
Churchman, Monte Rae, business tech analyst-expert, $65,633
Chval, Kathryn B, dean, asoc, $146,250
Chyan, Meei Fenq, med coding spclst-certified, $20.75/hr
Cicak, Amanda Jane, research specialist I, $31,969
Cil, Akin, adjunct, $15,000
Cindrich, Brenda Lynn, office support assistant IV, $23.06/hr
Ciolli, Alicia Jeanne, grounds keeper II, $14.39/hr
Cirstea Apostol, Mihaela Carmen, prof, ast resrch, $80,800
Cisar, Renee Elizabeth, tutor, $10.00/hr
Cisco, Jonathan Randall, educational prgm coor sr, $47,040
Cissell, Christopher Scott, head coach, $55,550
Claas, Jared Anthony, food svc wrkr I, $9.60/hr
Clack, Jennifer Lynn, nurse, staff II rnwp, $22.22/hr
Claiborn, Charles David, instructor, adjunct, $12,000
Clair, Elissa Batshaw, instructor, adjunct, $7,059
Clampitt, Hannah Marie Sultzman, bus ops assoc sr, $50,242
Clapp, Lauren Kay, nurse, staff II, $20.95/hr
Clapper, Rachel E, resident physician-3rd yr, $53,763
Clark Gibson, Denise Michelle, pat acct rep, $14.57/hr
Clark II, Randall B, resident physician-2nd yr, $52,007
Clark, Ara Elizabeth, ast dir strat communications, $52,400
Clark, Barbara A, nurse, staff II, $27.16/hr

Clark, Carol A, mgr purchasing-h, $86,786
Clark, Cary Lee, resrch ast, $50,400
Clark, Charles T, bts carpenter lead, $24.74/hr
Clark, Christina Annette, retail sales assistant sr, $14.28/hr
Clark, Clayton Charles, serv line spclst, $65,517
Clark, Cristin Cay, dir II advancement, $63,240
Clark, Dennis D, mts/hvac, $24.13/hr
Clark, Douglas A, student service coor sr, $53,664
Clark, Emily Denise, fin and acctg specialist, $16.50/hr
Clark, Frances Ann, food svc wrkr II, $10.49/hr
Clark, Gary F, prof, asoc resrch, $112,199
Clark, Gary L, security officer, $10.66/hr
Clark, Howard Anthony, event assistant I, $10.00/hr
Clark, Jamaro D, custodian lead, $13.96/hr
Clark, Jana L, business support specialist II, $17.24/hr
Clark, Jennifer M, reactor specialist, $57,282
Clark, Jennifer Nicole, nurse anesthetist, $147,900
Clark, Jeremy, insulation svcs wrkr II, $20.07/hr
Clark, John M, prof, asoc, $134,916
Clark, Judith Dryden, teaching ast, $13.00/hr
Clark, Kerry Maureen, resrch asoc, $58,994
Clark, Kristen Joannie, office support assistant III, $12.50/hr
Clark, Kristen Nicole, office support assistant IV, $12.98/hr
Clark, Lesley Sue, office support assistant IV, $15.01/hr
Clark, Linda Faye, instructor, adjunct, $15,000
Clark, Lori Michelle Kramer, asoc dir program/proj ops, $77,497
Clark, Mark D, custodian, $12.94/hr
Clark, Mark F, powr plnt opr II, $28.70/hr
Clark, Mary Beth, strat comm associate II, $46,000
Clark, Mary J, research consultant II, $28.56/hr
Clark, Matthew Gill, resident physician-4th yr, $58,804
Clark, Mavis Anita, prof, ast adjunct, $16,008
Clark, Megan Elizabeth, resident physician-3rd yr, $53,763
Clark, Megan Renee, anesthesia techn, $16.70/hr
Clark, Megan Ruth, lab assistant, $14.00/hr
Clark, Melody Lynn, custodian, $12.94/hr
Clark, Michael Patrick, food svc wrkr I, $9.98/hr
Clark, Patrick C, prof, ast adjunct, $21,300
Clark, Rhiannon M, nurse, staff now III, $30.00/hr
Clark, Robert D, lecturer, $75,000
Clark, Shanchez Rashid, high school student, $7.50/hr
Clark, Stephanie Dawn, grader, $52
Clark, Stephen L, professor, $123,530
Clark, Stephen Paul, custodian, $10.39/hr
Clark, Susan W, supv pat accts-up, $53,183
Clark, Tami Jo, mgr training-revenue cycle, $71,894
Clark, Thomas C, research specialist sr, $50,191
Clark, Tina Renee, office support assistant III, $17.68/hr
Clark, Toby Brewer, surgical technl certified, $15.87/hr
Clark, Vickie L, event assistant I, $10.00/hr
Clarke Ekong, Sheilah F, prof, asoc, $104,561
Clarke, Andrew D, prof, asoc, $71,967
Clarke, Felisha Monicque, coor, service, $17.10/hr
Clarke, Lane L, professor, $168,795
Clarke, Robert Bede, professor, $77,522
Clarkson, Bonnie Sue, system support analyst-expert, $28.46/hr
Clarkston, Joshua Jacob, custodian, $10.94/hr
Clary, Kevin W, prof, ast clincl dept, $187,782
Clary, Megan Leigh, prof, ast clincl dept, $82,820
Clary, Terressa Linette, educational pgm associate I, $14.53/hr
Clatfelter, Matthew Eric, boiler maint opr, $20.45/hr
Clatterbuck, Brant Michael, resident physician-1st yr, $50,219
Clatterbuck, Mallory Rose, serv line spclst, $67,810
Clatterbuck, Thomas, csm associate III, $29.36/hr
Claunch, Hillary Lauren, instructor, $41,616
Clausen, Ashley Nicole, patient svc rep, $11.07/hr
Clawson, Anna Mae, business support specialist II, $19.74/hr
Clawson, Gregory Lawrence, coor hlthcare compliance, $64,367
Clawson, Stacee Wise, nurse clinician, $65,374
Claxton Rogers, Kathleen Y, student support spec I, $17.31/hr
Claxton, Marianne, patient svc rep, $13.73/hr
Clay, Aaron Ray, custodian, $10.00/hr
Clay, Antonio Charles, mail carrier, $14.24/hr
Clay, Daniel Leland, dean, $212,851
Clay, Robin Blake, student recruitment spclst sr, $17.31/hr
Clay, Sarah E, veterinarian, residnt, $26,315
Claybaugh, Craig C, prof, ast, $102,840
Clayborn, Becky L, coor, service, $20.27/hr
Clayborn, Miton S, lecturer sr, $9,000

Claybrook, Shelly Ann, office support assistant IV, $13.00/hr
Claycamp, Kevin L, mts/hvac, $21.05/hr
Claypole, Kandace Lea, office support assistant IV, $15.00/hr
Claypool, Annmarie A, nurse, staff, $27.81/hr
Claypool, James B, engineer I, $44,052
Clayton, Amanda Michelle, instructor, $60,602
Clayton, Heather Elaine, nurse, staff II, $20.54/hr
Clayton, Leigh A, program/project supprt coor I, $43,475
Clayton, Malika Ann, nurse, licensed prac, $18.70/hr
Clayton, Mitzi R, asoc athletic director, $109,000
Clayton, Patricia J, network engineer-princpl, $73,580
Clayton, Rhonda Sue, executive assistant, $20.91/hr
Clayton, Stephen P, library info specialist, $12.98/hr
Cleaves, Barbara A, educational pgm associate I, $13.45/hr
Cleeton, Matthew, nurse, staff II, $34.18/hr
Clem, Douglas Wayne, prof, asoc clincl, $72,591
Clem, Travis O, neurodiagnostic tech (reg), $21.93/hr
Clemens, Patrick M, ast mgr hospitality services, $54,200
Clemente, Jennifer Leigh, office support assistant III, $14.28/hr
Clements, Brandi Rifner, business ops associate sr, $54,375
Clements, Koby L, asoc dir program/project ops, $77,500
Clementz, Anna Louise, nurse, staff II, $26.00/hr
Clemons, Georgia, nurse, staff II, $34.18/hr
Clemons, Latonyia Nicole, office support assistant IV, $13.52/hr
Clemsen, Alex T, ast coach, $75,000
Cleveland, Ashley Darlene, food svc wrkr I, $9.60/hr
Cleveland, David Raymond, food svc wrkr I, (g), $11.89/hr
Cleveland, Mary Helen, accountant sr, $47,353
Clevenger, Ann Marie, event assistant I, $7.55/hr
Clevenger, Peggy Jean, hospital lab tech, $15.18/hr
Clevenger, Zachary James, event assistant I, $7.55/hr
Cliburn, Paula J, teaching ast, $13.00/hr
Cliburn, Tamara Lynn, nurse, staff II rnwp, $26.94/hr
Click, Melissa Anne, prof, ast, $57,798
Clickner, Aimee Elizabeth, nurse, staff II, $23.35/hr
Clifford, Jacob Paul, security officer, $12.02/hr
Clifford, Karen Marie, strat comm associate II, $42,439
Clifton, Brian Marshall, av instal service tech-entry, $13.50/hr
Clingher, Adrian, prof, asoc, $76,547
Clinton, Robert Lowry, instructor, adjunct, $9,000
Clippard, Nina Marie, coor, care, $59,146
Clithero Crane, Loretta Ann, support systems admin-expert, $57,644
Clithero, Lauren Ashley, research specialist I, $40,500
Clooten, Michael Gene, student support specialist I, $12.99/hr
Clough, Amanda Jane, business tech analyst-expert, $63,429
Clouser, Roseanne E, pat acct rep, $15.37/hr
Clow, Jeannine I, office support assistant II, $11.07/hr
Clubb, Michael W, research specialist sr, $44,560
Coalier, Paula F, prof, ast teach, $38,159
Coates, Joan Ripley, professor, $159,768
Coats, Dale L, laborer II, $14.47/hr
Coats, Delores Marie, nurse, staff II rnwp, $34.18/hr
Coats, Diana Rose Roberts, fellow, post doctoral, $36,045
Coats, Karen Renee, food svc wrkr III, $13.21/hr
Coats, Kellie Ann, dir II advancement, $66,416
Coats, Linda N, business support specialist II, $20.85/hr
Coats, Micheal Robert, nurse, staff now plus, $30.00/hr
Coats, Sally, business support specialist II, $25.47/hr
Cobb Orr, Rachael Elizabeth, dean, ast, $75,000
Cobb, Charles Madison, prof, adjunct, $125.00/hr
Cobb, Kimberly Dee, health records techn II, $12.97/hr
Cobb, Melissa Gia, athletic attd, $13.04
Cobb, Melissa Sue, research specialist I, $37,740
Cobb, Michael W, construction manager II, $74,940
Coberly, Beverly Ann, asoc vice provost, $163,410
Coberly, Emily Alicia, instructor, clincl, $12,000
Coberly, Jared S, resident physician-3rd yr, $55,013
Coburn, Katherine Marie, temporary clerical, $15.50/hr
Coburn, Meghan Rheanne, nurse, staff II, $20.54/hr
Cochran, Autumn Marie, temporary crafts service, $7.65/hr
Cochran, Barbara Marie, office support assistant III, $12.48/hr
Cochran, Barbara Stubbs, prof, profl practice, $129,952
Cochran, Dallas, mts/pipefitter, $22.50/hr
Cochran, Debra J, pat acct rep, $14.95/hr
Cochran, Dorothy J, instructor, adjunct, $15,300
Cochran, GeJuan, executive assistant, $19.17/hr
Cochran, Jamison Michael, electronics technician III, $16.50/hr
Cochran, Judith A, professor, $113,118
Cochran, Kelly A, prof, ast clincl, $96,500

Cochran, Lisa Ellen, nurse clinician, $50,000
Cochran, Pamela Marie, custodian, $12.94/hr
Cochran, Paula Marie, office support assistant II, $18.52/hr
Cochran, Sarah E, hospital lab tech, $12.22/hr
Cochran, Steve A, network engineer-princpl, $82,725
Cochran, Steven Kelly, hyprbric chmbr spclst/anest as, $28.05/hr
Cocjin, Eileen Lao, prof, asoc clincl, $94,408
Cockrell, Linda S, serv line spclst, $84,000
Cockrum, Angie Dawn, operations support tech sr, $14.76/hr
Cocroft, Reginald B, professor, $93,921
Coder, Elaine Anne, prof, ast adjunct, $9,000
Codilla, Sharon Ann, dental assistant sr, $19.73/hr
Cody, Megan Nicole, nurse, staff II, $23.30/hr
Cody, Zinda G, office support assistant IV, $15.63/hr
Coe, Benjamin L, nurse, staff II rnwp, $21.57/hr
Coffel, Traci Nichole, office support assistant sr, $16.50/hr
Coffelt, Jo A, nurse, or/recovery-ch, $33.44/hr
Coffin, Floyd Larry, ast athletic director, $63,474
Coffin, Gregg P, asoc dir csm operations, $114,515
Coffin, Ryan Alexander, business support specialist II, $14.95/hr
Coffman, Deborah R, nurse, staff II, $28.72/hr
Coffman, Jewel H, instructor, extns, $70,990
Coffman, Stoney E, farm wrkr III, $15.05/hr
Coggeshall, Mark V, prof, ast resrch, $71,049
Coggins, Megan Nicole, nurse, or/recovery-ch, $21.37/hr
Cogswell, Elizabeth A, dir III advancement, $101,907
Cogswell, James Alan, dir libraries mu, $161,568
Cohagen, Kara Elaine, educational pgm coor I, $34,441
Cohen, Ann M, instructor, adjunct, $24,909
Cohen, Blake E, resident physician-4th yr, $54,425
Cohen, Daniel Jay, prof, ast teach, $39,585
Cohen, David E, prof, asoc clincl, $106,930
Cohen, Deborah, prof, asoc, $61,920
Cohen, Gerald Leonard, professor, $90,654
Cohen, Michael Edward Sackheim, mgr student sup svcs, $40,000
Cohen, Roxanna E, nurse clinician, $63,465
Cohen, Samuel Schlesinger, prof, asoc, $66,894
Cohen, Signe M, prof, asoc, $61,206
Cohn, Leah Ann, professor, $144,090
Cohn, Susan V, mgr student support svcs, $33,231
Coil, Connie L, pat acct rep, $14.92/hr
Coil, Justin Lee, media production associate, $8.89/hr
Coker, Adeniyi A, professor, $132,113
Coker, Angela, prof, asoc, $64,711
Colaner, Colleen Michele Warner, prof, ast, $58,714
Colanese, Justin Patrick, resident physician-4th yr, $54,425
Colbert, Dory Ann, communications coordinator, $21.26/hr
Colbert, Lindsey Michelle, physical therapist, $60,425
Colbert, Sharon LeAnn, curriculum / assessment coor, $67,644
Colbert, Shirley Engle, instructor, ast, $19.47/hr
Colbert, Stephen, prof, ast clincl dept, $138,531
Coldiron, Jennifer Leigh, student service coor II, $46,575
Coldiron, Marti Jo, surgical technl certified, $16.19/hr
Cole Manney, Ronalda Venie, prof, ast clincl, $69,742
Cole, Amy, asoc registrar, $60,062
Cole, Anthony Wayne, maintenance supervisor, $58,635
Cole, Cathy L, mgr medical records-mrc, $63,240
Cole, Eldon Willard, extns professional, $83,718
Cole, Hayley J, prof, ast visiting, $39,886
Cole, Jennifer L, nurse, staff II rnwp, $20.54/hr
Cole, Keith, utility dist wrkr IV, $23.75/hr
Cole, R Julia, instructor, adjunct, $7,500
Cole, Richard A, bts plasterer, $21.71/hr
Cole, Theodore M, prof, asoc teach, $89,000
Cole, Vinson, professor, $102,485
Coleman Dade, Tiffany Lynn, nurse, licensed prac, $16.05/hr
Coleman, Anna E, business support specialist sr, $23.37/hr
Coleman, Anthony Lee, custodian, $13.36/hr
Coleman, Beverly Ann, instructor, adjunct, $7,200
Coleman, Brianna Telise, care team assoc-suppt, $10.64/hr
Coleman, Charles R, mts/pipefitter, $22.50/hr
Coleman, Daniel P, construction manager II, $64,494
Coleman, Diane Lynette, student support specialist I, $15.14/hr
Coleman, Donna M, office support assistant III, $13.60/hr
Coleman, Ernest O, laborer II, $14.47/hr
Coleman, Hanna Christine, food svc wrkr II, $10.49/hr
Coleman, Jacqueline, resrch asoc, $12,000
Coleman, Jacquelyn Renee, educational pgm assoc I, $14.07/hr
Coleman, Janet Carter, med office assistant, $13.53/hr

Coleman, Janine Fay, orthopedic techn-trainee, $13.02/hr
Coleman, Krista Danielle, patient svc rep, $11.07/hr
Coleman, Laura J, office support assistant III, $13.70/hr
Coleman, Nancy Lynn, 4-h spclst, $52,775
Coleman, Patricia Ann, custodian, $11.41/hr
Coleman, Paul M, managing engineer, $102,752
Coleman, Shianna Irene, office support assistant III, $14.49/hr
Coleman, Stephanie, food svc wrkr II, $11.83/hr
Coletti, Maryann Rose, instructor, clincl, $69,000
Coley, Marcy L, business support specialist II, $20.70/hr
Collard, Michael, resident physician-1st yr, $49,025
Collet, Denise Lorraine, reimbursement ast, $17.49/hr
Colletta, Angela Marie, research specialist I, $31,700
Collevechio, Alyssa C, intern, $14,400
Colley, Ashley Elizabeth, high school student, $7.50/hr
Colley, Bobby, business support specialist sr, $21.37/hr
Colley, Deborah R, pat acct rep, $16.63/hr
Colley, Frances M, academic advisor, $36,511
Colley, Stacy Joann, office support assistant IV, $16.59/hr
Collier, Brian J, nurse, staff now III, $30.00/hr
Collier, Carrie Michelle, student service coor sr, $54,366
Collier, Kimberly Ann, research specialist I, $40,856
Collier, Robin L, office support assistant IV, $18.85/hr
Collier, Robyn Ann, office support assistant III, $11.42/hr
Collier, Thomas A, mgr info svcs-mrc, $76,486
Colligan, Judy Minako, educational pgm associate I, $14.53/hr
Collins, Adela, instructor, adjunct, $28,800
Collins, Brittnea V, healthcare admin fellow, $50,000
Collins, Cynthia Lynn, neurodiagnostic tech (reg), $25.00/hr
Collins, Dawnelle Renae, program/project supprt coor I, $35,700
Collins, Diane M, library info specialist, $13.26/hr
Collins, Emiliana Sebastian, care team assoc-clinical, $12.08/hr
Collins, Jillian Kay, student support specialist sr, $16.54/hr
Collins, Jonathan M, prof, ast clincl dept, $257,040
Collins, Joseph Linn, user support analyst-expert, $19.61/hr
Collins, Julie Ann, sr dir program/project ops, $89,175
Collins, Kawajalyn E, attd, personal, $9.90/hr
Collins, Kent S, prof, asoc profl practice, $91,502
Collins, Kimberly Joann, instructor, adjunct, $9,600
Collins, Kris A, bts painter, $21.23/hr
Collins, Marcia Yvette, patient svc rep, $14.08/hr
Collins, Melissa Jill, fellow, post doctoral, $42,979
Collins, Michael, director, $182,618
Collins, Michael Gerard, office support assistant I, $9.79/hr
Collins, Monica Watkins, advancement associate, $46,000
Collins, Quentin A, food svc wrkr I, $9.60/hr
Collins, Robert Lee, instructor, adjunct, $10,500
Collins, Robert W, instructor, adjunct, $22,200
Collins, Sarah Dawn, nurse, licensed prac, $17.36/hr
Collison, Connie Annette, physical therapist, $74,784
Collum, Emily Ann, surgical technl trainee, $14.09/hr
Collum, Lisa Renea, event assistant I, $7.50/hr
Collum, Mark Waymon, event assistant I, $7.50/hr
Colman, Ryan Hughes, advancement associate II, $18.93/hr
Colman, Tamara L, mgr II business admin, $50,003
Colt, David Eaton, prof, asoc teach, $95,000
Colter, Dustin LeAllen, event assistant I, $8.50/hr
Colvin, Ania L, office support assistant III, $11.50/hr
Colvin, April A, police lieutenant, $65,125
Colvin, Carolyn Marie, instructor, adjunct, $3,200
Colvin, Megan M, veterinary technician, $14.91/hr
Colwell, Carol Greiner, nurse, staff, $31.84/hr
Colwell, John C, internet administrator-speclst, $20.15/hr
Colwill, Jack M, emeritus, $72,550
Combs, Angela YeVette, office support assistant IV, $14.74/hr
Combs, Tammy Monique, instructor, adjunct, $18,660
Comer, Bryan E, geo info system specialist sr, $60,907
Comer, Carolyn, event assistant I, $7.55/hr
Comes, Johanna Claire Frankel, nurse practitioner, $35.74/hr
Comfort, William Joseph, care team assoc-suppt, $12.14/hr
Comley, Victoria S, custodian, $12.69/hr
Commons, Andrea Louise, mgr research activities, $51,500
Compain-Romero, Ana M, dir program/project oper, $57,970
Comparato, Bridget Greer, patient svc rep, $10.64/hr
Comparato, Corey V, nursing ast sr, $13.00/hr
Comparato, Melissa Faye, office support assistant IV, $14.00/hr
Compton, Heather Campbell, office support asst III, $11.30/hr
Comstock, Meghan Marie, accountant I, $15.55/hr
Conant, Gavin C, prof, asoc, $91,799

Conant, Marjorie Mae, instructor, clincl, $167,000
Conatser, Jolena Kay, sterile processing tech, $18.26/hr
Conatser, Richard Allen, event assistant I, $7.55/hr
Conaway, Susan N, phlebotomist, $13.39/hr
Conaway, Veronica Marie, resident physician-1st yr, $50,219
Concannon, Chaeleigh Barrett, physical therapist, $59,928
Concannon, Marie C, librarian III, $60,234
Concannon, Stephen McKinley, student service coor II, $49,425
Conde, Gina Michelle, educational pgm associate I, $14.20/hr
Conde, Kimberly Brooke, intern, $26,265
Condray, Elizabeth S, educational pgm coor III, $52,412
Cone, Michelle A, dir program/project operations, $63,152
Conklin, Carli N, prof, asoc, $102,839
Conklin, Joyce S, business support specialist sr, $18.02/hr
Conklin, Randall S, mts/pipefitter, $22.50/hr
Conklin, Sandra Kay, instructor, clincl, $107,161
Conley, Mary Shannon, office support assistant IV, $15.00/hr
Conley, Tammie Michelle, instructor, clincl, $49,713
Conn, Vicki S, dean, asoc, $196,258
Connaghan-Gross, Kathleen Teresa, bus support spec II, $15.40/hr
Connell-Dent, Debra Jane, prof, ast teach, $61,801
Connell, Angela Christine, instructor, adjunct, $21,450
Connell, Joetta, office support assistant IV, $16.87/hr
Connell, Jordyn Mackenzie, patient svc rep, $10.85/hr
Connell, Margaret Catherine, nurse, staff prn, $26.00/hr
Connelly, Frances, professor, $83,506
Connelly, Jamie Michelle, human resources mgr sr, $60,770
Connely IV, Charles Conner, prof, asoc teach, $60,000
Conner, Alyssa L, custodian, $10.94/hr
Conner, Jennifer Renee, coord, distribution-matls dist, $17.16/hr
Conner, Medea M, custodian, $12.94/hr
Conners, Angel I, bindery opr I, $14.85/hr
Conners, Laura Annette, office support assistant IV, $15.75/hr
Connett, Frank Davis III, geo info system specialist, $52,063
Connett, Deborah Finfgeld, professor, $72,712
Connette, Grant M, fellow, post doctoral, $42,000
Connolly, Shawn, supv, lab, $58,166
Connor, Donald Lee, strat comm associate II, $44,294
Connor, Lois Marie, temporary clerical, $10.50/hr
Connor, Malnaisia Louishua, event assistant I, $7.50/hr
Connor, Melissa A, business support specialist II, $16.73/hr
Connor, Wanda Lea, nurse, staff II, $27.54/hr
Connors, Kristen Marie, nurse, staff II, $21.80/hr
Connot, Donna Sue, business support specialist II, $18.30/hr
Connot, Stacie L, patient svc rep, $13.10/hr
Conrad, Jodi Renee, patient svc rep, $11.92/hr
Conrad, Kristina Marie, business ops associate sr, $57,205
Conrad, Shannon Lee, care team assoc-clinical, $14.17/hr
Conrad, Tammy S, academic advisor, $43,858
Constant-Eskew, Jena Ann, educational pgm assoc I, $13.51/hr
Constantinescu, Gheorghe M, prof, adjunct, $38,683
Constantinescu, Ileana A, prof, asoc teach, $74,000
Constantino, Joselito Austria, dir I, advancement, $63,000
Conti, Genevieve Nicole, strat comm associate I, $37,806
Convery, Laura, communications coordinator sr, $18.03/hr
Conway, Patrick C, police officer, $22.01/hr
Conway, Robert R, prof, adjunct, $65,280
Conyers, Jessica Diane, business support specialist sr, $18.65/hr
Cook, Aaron Curt, student recruitment spclst, $22.07/hr
Cook, Alissa Diane, nurse, staff prn, $26.00/hr
Cook, Amy Stewart, office support assistant IV, $13.76/hr
Cook, Angelia Jill, office support assistant IV, $15.42/hr
Cook, Barbara J, office support assistant IV, $15.97/hr
Cook, Billy Arthur, supv bldg trades-h, $55,058
Cook, Brenda Jean, business support specialist sr, $23.87/hr
Cook, Cathy Lee, library info spclst II, $20.28/hr
Cook, Christopher R, project manager-princpl, $74,288
Cook, Cindy Rose, mgr environmental svcs, $108,299
Cook, Crystel Reeves, prof, ast resrch, $51,834
Cook, Darrell Wayne, bts carpenter, $21.71/hr
Cook, David M, db programmer analyst-expert, $30.52/hr
Cook, Dawn Kay, asoc dir program/project ops, $51,983
Cook, Deetta, lecturer, $61,800
Cook, Gabriel A, prgm mgr II studnt supprt svcs, $45,900
Cook, Gregory Allen, reimbursement ast-cert, $18.59/hr
Cook, James L, professor, $200,738
Cook, Jeremy Alexander, db programmer analyst-princpl, $63,073
Cook, John Alexander, office support associate, $16.54/hr
Cook, Joseph C, internet administrator-expert, $19.75/hr

Cook, Juanita L, custodian, $11.41/hr
Cook, Justin W, physician ast, $93,917
Cook, Justin W, physician ast, $80.00/hr
Cook, Kathy, nurse, staff II, $34.18/hr
Cook, Kelley M, nurse, licensed prac, $16.53/hr
Cook, Kristi Lynne, business support specialist II, $16.07/hr
Cook, Kristy Ann, business ops associate I, $35,174
Cook, Lauren P, resident physician-4th yr, $55,804
Cook, Lisa Kay, supv radiology, $36.30/hr
Cook, Mary Angela, educational pgm associate I, $12.55/hr
Cook, Megan Louise, nurse, staff II, $20.54/hr
Cook, Melody Rachel, communications assistant, $10.30/hr
Cook, Michael L, professor, $236,891
Cook, Nancy Dill, accountant I, $19.90/hr
Cook, Norman Timothy, surgical technl trainee, $18.00/hr
Cook, Pamela Sue, business support specialist sr, $19.12/hr
Cook, Phyllis Jean, instructor, adjunct, $4,800
Cook, Richard M, professor, $71,410
Cook, Roger F, professor, $86,138
Cook, Rose Marie, custodian, $12.94/hr
Cook, Sheri L, food svc wrkr II, $10.10/hr
Cook, Sylvia Jenkins, founders professor, $25,617
Cook, Timothy Isaac, food svc wrkr II, $10.49/hr
Cook, Tony D, instructor, clincl, $86,251
Cook, Travis Shane, bts painter, $19.59/hr
Cook, William M, research engineering tech I, $23.31/hr
Cooke, Alexandra Rose, pharmacy tech, $11.07/hr
Cooke, Roberta L, student support specialist I, $16.93/hr
Cool, Dona Sue, instructor, ast, $19.47/hr
Cooley, Cassidy S, office support assistant IV, $17.24/hr
Cooley, Jason Warren, prof, ast, $68,984
Cooley, Serena V, hospital lab tech, $13.24/hr
Coonrod, Curtis C, vice provost, $203,320
Coonrod, Morgan Taylor, temporary clerical, $11.00/hr
Coons, Patricia I, nurse, staff II rnwp, $22.24/hr
Cooper, Brian L, pacs technologist, $29.22/hr
Cooper, Carl E, csm associate I, $18.04/hr
Cooper, Cathy A, instructor, lab, $46,000
Cooper, Cathy Ann, student service coor II, $45,033
Cooper, Cody Lee, food svc wrkr I, $9.60/hr
Cooper, Delores Ann, office support assistant III, $14.08/hr
Cooper, Jane M, nurse, advanced practice, $86,052
Cooper, Jeff G, police sergeant, $19.86/hr
Cooper, Jessica Leigh, lab techn, persl svc-clin lab, $13.91/hr
Cooper, Jill K, research specialist sr, $50,368
Cooper, Judith K, strat comm associate II, $39,600
Cooper, Krystin Jennifer, executive assistant, $18.13/hr
Cooper, M Lynne, prof, curators, $148,601
Cooper, Maegan Krystel, grader, $52
Cooper, Megan Danielle, office support assistant IV, $17.51/hr
Cooper, Monika Nikole, pat acct rep, $14.34/hr
Cooper, Pamela Jeanne, office support assistant IV, $18.77/hr
Cooper, Pamela Sue, research specialist sr, $60,000
Cooper, Perry M, asoc media producer, $15.54/hr
Cooper, Shelley Janelle, instructor, adjunct, $14,700
Cooper, Shontreal, resident physician-1st yr, $49,025
Cooper, Steven C, grader, $52
Cooper, Thomas Jefferson, prof, ast clincl, $26,000
Cooper, Thomas V, dir payer strat & hlth sys con, $181,043
Cooperstock, Linda R, research specialist I, $20.00/hr
Cooperstock, Michael Steven, emeritus, $107,521
Cope, Brianna Lee, supv pat admiss, $41,592
Cope, David Eli, field superintendent, $78,000
Cope, Glen H, provost, $250,000
Cope, Jonna S, cook mrc, $11.33/hr
Cope, Leveta Dale, hospital lab tech, $17.10/hr
Cope, Reed, resident physician-1st yr, $49,025
Copeland, Alison, state spclst, asoc, $68,295
Copeland, Candy R, clerk, unit, $14.29/hr
Copeland, Christy M, dir program/project operations, $76,300
Copeland, Ereka Lynn, reimbursement ast-cert, $18.59/hr
Copeland, Matthew Evan, resrch ast, $12.00/hr
Copeland, Nicole Rose Polney, care team assoc-clinical, $11.32/hr
Copeland, Serena Elizabeth, custodian, $10.94/hr
Copeland, Stephen Jay, mech, bldg maint, $18.12/hr
Copher, Renee Lynn, instructor, adjunct, $27,000
Copling, Kenneth L, mts/refrig mech-r, $21.91/hr
Coppersmith, Sarah A, prof, ast adjunct, $16,008
Coram, Jeana Rae, surgical technl certified, $16.75/hr

Corbett, Mark A, reactor operator sr, $31.83/hr
Corbin, Jackie Dale, seasonal farm ast, $9.75/hr
Corbin, Trista Rene, emrg med techn, $13.35/hr
Corcoran, Blake Cooper, resident physician-3rd yr, $53,763
Corcoran, Julie Michelle, project manager-speclst, $54,648
Cordes, Lisa Gay, asoc dir program/project ops, $62,000
Cordes, Vonda Kay, office support assistant IV, $17.72/hr
Cordones Cook, Juanamaria, professor, $84,280
Cordova, Ralph Adon Jr, prof, ast, $62,711
Cordova, Terri L, rehab therapy aide, $12.94/hr
Cordsmeyer, Angela J, business support specialist II, $15.00/hr
Corley, Heather Ann, prof, ast adjunct, $27,000
Corn, Robert Steven, resident physician-3rd yr, $52,470
Corneillier, Brittony Page, student recruitment spclst, $14.96/hr
Cornelison, Brittany Hope, care team assoc-clinical, $11.10/hr
Cornelison, Dawn D, prof, asoc, $79,264
Cornelison, Meredith Louise, supv, food svc II-h, $36,950
Cornelison, Robin A, patient svc rep, $15.10/hr
Cornelison, Sharon M, teaching ast, $13.00/hr
Cornelius-Green, Jennifer Nicole, research lab supv, $61,897
Cornell, Barbara E, nurse, or/recovery-ch, $34.59/hr
Cornell, David W, dean, asoc, $250,008
Cornell, Kasey Catherine, resident physician-3rd yr, $65,763
Cornell, Raina D, business support specialist II, $18.22/hr
Cornford, Ernest A, dir II finance, $120,000
Cornish, Barbara Jean, academic advisor, $32,302
Cornish, Peter Verle, prof, ast, $90,225
Corns, Melissa Lorene, temporary clerical, $9.50/hr
Corns, Steven M, prof, asoc, $88,342
Cornwall, Adrienne Camille, strat comm associate I, $52,000
Cornwell, Dustin, sr dir research and inst prgms, $140,000
Corona, Hille Charmaine, resident physician-3rd yr, $53,763
Corpuz, Sara Melissa, instructor, clincl, $15,375
Corridori, Frank Salvatore, prof, ast/profl pract, $66,422
Corrigan, Jeff D, research specialist sr, $38,665
Corson, Barbara L, executive assistant, $25.50/hr
Corson, Paul William, certif pharmacy techn, $17.63/hr
Cortalezzi, Francisco Jose, resrch scientist/academic, $55,550
Cortes Di Lena, Yovanna, fellow, post doctoral, $60,000
Cortes, Antonio Ceballos, custodian, $12.94/hr
Cortez, Brennen Kade, event assistant I, $8.50/hr
Corwin, Kaitlin Nicole, emrg med techn, $12.68/hr
Corwin, Sherry L, mgr acctg/budget-h, $99,916
Cosby, Daniel P, environmental health tech II, $17.82/hr
Cosby, Robin B, animal techn, lab, $15.90/hr
Cosgrove, Michael A, resrch ast, $17.50/hr
Cosmopoulos, Michael, professor, $135,625
Cossairt, Diana J, mammography technl, $24.29/hr
Cossey, George Anne M, office support assistant III, $12.50/hr
Cossey, Kevin, security officer, $11.10/hr
Costanza, Lauren Patricia, clerk, unit, $12.00/hr
Costello, Christine, prof, ast resrch, $75,750
Costello, Michael Joseph, prof, ast teach, $48,715
Costigan, Kelly Rae, pat care techn, $11.61/hr
Costoplos, Lauren Ashley, office support assistant IV, $15.42/hr
Cotner, Cynthia S, librarian III, $61,062
Cott, Ronald K, prof, ast clincl, $206,727
Cotter, Zachariah Davis, event assistant I, $10.00/hr
Cotterill, Anne Lucile, prof, asoc, $61,714
Cotton, Anne Elizabeth, nurse, staff II, $34.18/hr
Cotton, Erika, office support assistant III, $13.07/hr
Cotton, Kimberly Ann, db programmer analyst-speclst, $64,309
Cottone, R Rocco, professor, $106,091
Cottrell, Angela M, dir II student support svcs, $71,604
Cottrell, John L, instructor, clincl, $76,143
Cottrell, Mitchell, research engineering tech II, $29.01/hr
Couch, Jessica Lynn, care team assoc-clinical, $11.10/hr
Coughenour, Jeffrey P, prof, ast clincl dept, $326,165
Coulson, Kim Jr, nurse, staff per diem, $35.00/hr
Coulter, Jennifer Leigh, nurse, staff I, $19.00/hr
Coulter, Matthew Sean, office support associate, $18.75/hr
Coulter, Maureen Elizabeth, enrollment advisor sr, $16.54/hr
Coulthard, Jennifer Joan, animal techn, $15.12/hr
Counsil, Joseph A, engineer, ast resrch, $58,423
Countryman, Marcia Marie, lecturer, $48,000
Couper, John Lee, temporary technical, $9.00/hr
Coupland, Alison Leigh, instructor, adjunct, $15,000
Cousins, David Shane, nurse, staff now plus, $30.00/hr
Couts, Alvin Louis Jr, animal techn, $15.12/hr

Coutts, Linda D, instructor, adjunct, $3,300
Couzens, Elizabeth Kay, office support assistant IV, $15.62/hr
Coveney, Raymond M Jr, prof, adjunct, $3,756
Cover, Cindy Lou, human resources mgr-enterprise, $80,451
Covert, Orrie T III, asoc vice chancellor, $203,863
Covert, David D, care team assoc-suppt, $14.50/hr
Covert, David J, prof, ast visiting, $55,000
Covington, Betty J, executive assistant, $27.20/hr
Covington, Carl D, cook, $12.95/hr
Covington, John Michael, surgical technl certified, $19.00/hr
Cowan, Anita C, executive assistant, $17.92/hr
Cowan, Christine, instructor, adjunct, $27,000
Cowan, Derrick Todd, event assistant I, $8.50/hr
Cowan, Michael E, central sterile assistant, $10.73/hr
Cowan, Mitchell Alan, research/lab technician sr, $15.93/hr
Cowan, Nelson, prof, curators, $187,616
Cowan, Ricky A, temporary crafts service, $14.50/hr
Cowans, Laron S, wait service supervisor, $14.95/hr
Cowden, John W, prof, clncl, $72,000
Cowell, Kimberly Sue, lecturer, $9,000
Cowgill, Libby Windred, prof, ast, $58,960
Cox, Andrea Renee, mental health professional, $36,000
Cox, Anissa T, temporary clerical, $10.50/hr
Cox, Anna Christine, lab assistant, $10.20/hr
Cox, Anne, manuscript specialist, $34,750
Cox, Bruce T, business ops associate sr, $47,540
Cox, Christina Lynn, med coding spclst-certified, $23.13/hr
Cox, Gary D, archivist II, $47,111
Cox, George Michael, temporary professional, $15.00/hr
Cox, Jason M, fellow, post doc clncl yr1, $60,415
Cox, Jason N, research specialist sr, $41,356
Cox, Jeremy A, accountant sr, $57,750
Cox, Karen Rose, mgr, quality improvement, $109,375
Cox, Kyron Damar, temporary crafts service, $9.50/hr
Cox, Laura J, event assistant I, $7.58/hr
Cox, Lisa Kay, office support associate, $20.30/hr
Cox, Mariah, child dev assistant, $8.08/hr
Cox, Melissa, office support assistant IV, $15.27/hr
Cox, Peggy Ann, care team assoc-clinical, $14.19/hr
Cox, Ralph J, event assistant I, $7.58/hr
Cox, Shannon Kaye, office support assistant IV, $14.44/hr
Cox, Willie H, ast coach, $107,200
Coy, Connie L, video comm admin-princpl, $76,586
Coy, Matthew Kurtis, lecturer, $15,000
Coyle, Mindy Dawn, ast coach, $38,100
Cozad, David Brian Jr, research/lab technician sr, $12.98/hr
Cozad, Kristin Danielle, reactor engineer, $48,252
Cozad, Tonya Rena, office support assistant IV, $16.98/hr
Cozart, Jatata Monique, office support assistant III, $11.30/hr
Crabb, Richard Paul, professor, $103,674
Crabtree, Bridget F, reimbursement ast-cert, $20.89/hr
Crabtree, Joshua Daniel, research maintenance tech, $16.82/hr
Crabtree, Pamela J, office support assistant IV, $16.40/hr
Craddock, Anthony Farris, user support analyst-entry, $14.00/hr
Crader, Gary D, resrch anlyst sr, $49,499
Crader, Lisa Sue, executive assistant, $20.92/hr
Craft, Jean S, lecturer, $43,147
Crafton, Janet Marie, educational pgm coor III, $52,412
Craghead, Kathy Sue, grader, $52
Craghead, Richard Gene, temporary clerical, $10.85/hr
Craig, Brittany Morgan, nurse, staff II rnwp, $20.54/hr
Craig, Cynthia Louise, office support assistant IV, $18.36/hr
Craig, James Richard, prof, asoc teach, $102,500
Craig, Julia Christine, student support specialist sr, $16.87/hr
Craig, Justin D, communications coordinator, $15.40/hr
Craig, Kevin W, prof, ast clncl dept, $161,058
Craig, Lora, temporary crafts service, $9.19/hr
Craig, Rachel Marie, temporary technical, $10.00/hr
Craig, Stacy Kaylyn, office support assistant III, $12.37/hr
Craighead, Ferrie Lee, business support specialist II, $17.17/hr
Craighead, Kathryn Irene, office support assistant IV, $13.43/hr
Cram, Debra Mardell, office support assistant III, $17.14/hr
Cram, Megan Leigh, serv line spclst, $67,810
Cramer, Ronda Raye, office support assistant IV, $16.80/hr
Cramer, Tara Lynn, program/project supprt coor I, $37,048
Crandall-Witte, Nancy Renee, library info specialist, $15.93/hr
Crandall, Elizabeth M, child dev teacher sr, $25,000
Crane, Danny J, mech/opr II, heavy equip, $22.12/hr
Crane, Jennine Marie, resrch scientist/academic, $36,589

Crane, Linda Sue, executive assistant, $22.86/hr
Crane, Megan Elizabeth, nurse, licensed prac, $18.70/hr
Crane, Stacy B, research specialist sr, $36,875
Cranford, Daniel Lee, research activities supervisor, $42,200
Cranmer, Christina D, adminr, grad med educ prgms, $55,416
Craven, Jennifer Lee, coor, service, $15.68/hr
Cravens, Eric Maurice Jr, food svc wrkr I, $9.60/hr
Cravens, David D, prof, asoc clncl dept, $158,661
Cravens, Nicole Jonine, educational pgm associate I, $13.66/hr
Craver, Andrew Larkin, program/project supprt coor I, $43,260
Craver, Mary D, coor, wellness-mrc, $36,612
Crawford, Christina L, educational pgm coor II, $38,914
Crawford, Craig Geoffrey, electronics technician sr, $17.83/hr
Crawford, Cynthia E, sr dir program/project ops, $103,076
Crawford, David Allen, research maintenance tech, $20.65/hr
Crawford, Emily R, prof, ast, $68,227
Crawford, Glenn David, engineering technician II, $22.62/hr
Crawford, James J W, extns professional, asoc, $58,066
Crawford, Jeffrey H, dir finance-enterprise, $173,400
Crawford, Jonathan Clay, lab assistant, $9.00/hr
Crawford, Karen D, office support assistant sr, $22.36/hr
Crawford, Mason Joseph, nurse, staff II, $21.37/hr
Crawford, Melinda C, office supervisor, $46,028
Crawford, Patrick John, strat comm associate I, $42,000
Crawford, Penny Leola, asoc dir program/project ops, $48,647
Crawford, Quinn Adam, temporary technical, $9.00/hr
Crawford, Rusty L, sr mgr business admin, $89,971
Crawford, Shelly Irene, office supervisor, $45,885
Crawford, Taylor Renee, food svc wrkr I, $9.60/hr
Crawford, Tonya Ann, manuscript specialist sr, $42,456
Crawford, Willie M, ast dir env health and safety, $94,685
Creach, Cary S, asoc dir program/project ops, $51,055
Creagh, Sharon L, office supervisor, $41,383
Creamer, Thomas Lloyd Jr, nurse, staff II, $24.60/hr
Creamer, Angela A, supv radiology, $30.57/hr
Creamer, John Hunter, accountant sr, $43,260
Creamer, Julie B, business support specialist II, $15.19/hr
Crean, Allan R, academic dir, $107,994
Creason, Connie Adena, supv outpatient svcs, $46,122
Creason, Dustin Wiliam, grounds keeper, $12.12/hr
Creason, Jennifer Lynne, custodian, $12.94/hr
Creason, Marybeth E, student service coor I, $38,146
Crecelius, Cory R, physical therapist, $63,135
Crecelius, Jessica Elizabeth, nurse, staff II, $22.51/hr
Creech, Michael R, support systems admin-expert, $58,942
Creed-Baker, Brenda Gaye, cardiovasc tech invasive, $22.88/hr
Creed, Cory Alexander, horticulture spclst, $38,500
Creed, M Jane, pharmacy tech, $14.88/hr
Creedon, Sarah A, health records techn I, $11.31/hr
Creel, Alana Nicole, nurse, staff II, $21.90/hr
Creger, Mary Virginia, instructor, adjunct, $9,600
Creighton, Erica Kay, research specialist I, $35,168
Cremeens, Karyn Lynn, student service coor II, $47,421
Crenshaw, Benjamin Hardy, prof, ast clncl dept, $142,500
Crescenzo, Connor Daniel, event assistant I, $10.00/hr
Crespino, Curtis J, vice chancellor, $184,748
Crespy, David A, professor, $67,847
Cress, David L, lecturer, $15,000
Cresswell, Christina Jane, office support assistant IV, $13.73/hr
Crews, Amy Elizabeth, office support assistant IV, $14.01/hr
Crews, Elizabeth Nicole, nurse, staff I, $19.00/hr
Crews, Sandra M, prof, asoc teach, $94,963
Crim, Julia Ruth, prof, clinical dept, $260,000
Cripps, Bryce V, pharmacist II, $118,798
Crisel, Melissa Ann, resrch asoc, $61,488
Crisp, Christi J, educational pgm associate I, $14.40/hr
Crist, Brett D, prof, asoc, $260,294
Crist, Frank H, prof, ast adjunct, $125.00/hr
Crist, Jamie Daniel, resident physician-1st yr, $49,025
Criswell, Ali F, nurse, staff II, $27.46/hr
Crites, Alisha Dawn Baker, nurse, staff II, $24.09/hr
Crites, Brenda Kaye, telecom it analyst-expert, $22.14/hr
Crites, Darryl M, data cntr support tech-princpl, $21.43/hr
Crocker, Amanda K, surgical technl certified, $22.88/hr
Crocker, Brandon F, orthotist, $24.37/hr
Crocker, Gabrial Lynn, instructor, adjunct, $9,000
Crockett, Philip, nurse, staff II, $28.98/hr
Croft, Barbetta, sftware supprt analyst-spclst, $47,858
Croft, David Eugene, lecturer, $15,000

Croft, Jeffrey G, maint svc attd, $18.41/hr
Croft, Kayla Eloise, child dev assistant, $8.20/hr
Crombie, Kathryn Frances, research/lab technician, $13.75/hr
Crone Willis, Kelly R, manager it, $84,465
Cronin, Andrew Dorsey, research/lab technician, $10.24/hr
Cronin, Jacob, resrch anlyst, $45,460
Cronin, Sigrid, resrch aide, $20.00/hr
Cronk, Nikole J, prof, ast teach, $75,013
Crook, Deborah Kay, serv line spclst, $84,924
Crook, Leo Gerald, maintenance supervisor, $60,605
Crook, Megan, strat comm associate II, $46,500
Crook, Wayne, agronomy spclst, $50,863
Crooks, Brooke Bratten, nurse, staff II, $26.00/hr
Crooks, Scott Douglas, couns hlth/welfare/wellness sr, $30.00/hr
Crooks, Troy D, bts painter, $18.85/hr
Cropp IV, Frederick William, dean, asoc, $115,066
Cropp, Jeadawn Elizabeth, office support assistant III, $13.75/hr
Crosbie, Alfred Linden, prof, curators, $130,011
Crosby, Daniel Irving, research specialist I, $28.00/hr
Crosby, Frank Blair, csm associate I, $18.39/hr
Crosby, Marci Jennings, instructor, $55,818
Cross Sr, Darrell Wayne, custodian, $12.94/hr
Cross-Davis, Diarra Tene, mental health professional, $43,100
Cross, Darrell, food svc wrkr I, $9.60/hr
Cross, David T, prof, asoc teach, $91,760
Cross, Jason Andrew, office support assistant IV, $15.50/hr
Cross, Jessica Nicole, surgical technl certified, $15.87/hr
Cross, Kathleen Tara, child dev teacher sr, $29,943
Cross, Megan Nicole, student service coor sr, $45,600
Cross, Neal C, telecom it analyst-speclst, $19.42/hr
Cross, Vonda Kaye, ophthalmic imager, $22.35/hr
Crossfield, Sherrie Lynn, office support assistant III, $12.35/hr
Crossland, Jill Marie, dietitian, clincl, $46,882
Crosson, Mary, sftware supprt analyst-princpl, $52,400
Crothers, Renee, custodial supervisor, $41,400
Crouch, Dennis D, prof, asoc, $121,445
Crouch, Diane Lynn, custodial supervisor, $40,259
Crouch, Jennifer V, resident physician-2nd yr, $52,007
Crow, Emery Lee, custodian, $12.94/hr
Crow, Emily LeeAnn, event assistant I, $8.00/hr
Crow, Joseph A, resrch asoc, $38,000
Crow, Mariesa L, professor, $197,399
Crowder, Verna Jean, central sterile assistant, $12.35/hr
Crowe, Emily Marie, nutrition spclst, $40,000
Crowe, Laura Elizabeth, child dev teacher sr, $26,441
Crowe, Robin L, nurse, licensed prac, $18.46/hr
Crowell, Christopher Robert, supt systems admin-expert, $60,600
Crowell, Kelly Y, student support specialist sr, $17.93/hr
Crowley, Charles Christopher, mech, bldg maint, $19.64/hr
Crowley, Jennifer E, business support specialist II, $17.50/hr
Crowley, Julie A, nurse, staff II, $30.77/hr
Crowley, Kevin J, custodian, $11.41/hr
Crowley, Lisa A, temporary professional, $13.00/hr
Crowley, Michelle Lynn, surgical technl certified, $16.84/hr
Crowley, Nicholas Joseph, resident physician-1st yr, $50,219
Croy, Dwayne E, resp therapist reg, $26.89/hr
Croy, Lori A, media production director sr, $77,651
Crozier II, James H, grader, $100.00/hr
Crozier, Ruth E, dir program/project operations, $68,160
Cruise, Dusty Joseph, sr dir program/project ops, $136,500
Cruise, Mary J, hlth prgm ast, $15.76/hr
Crull, Kimber R, communications coordinator sr, $16.83/hr
Crull, Reed Kolby, ast mgr hospitality services, $40,788
Crum, Mark J, mechl plant spclst, $19.64/hr
Crum, Shermica L, care team assoc-suppt, $13.37/hr
Crum, Vida, pat acct rep, $17.01/hr
Crumbliss, Angela Leigh, mgr II business admin, $59,160
Crumley, Carolyn Elizabeth, instructor, adjunct, $36,000
Crump, Martha Lou, business support specialist II, $16.51/hr
Crump, Ramona Collins, pat acct rep, $15.81/hr
Crump, Sara Lyn, instructor, adjunct, $7,200
Crump, Spencer N, bts painter, $20.23/hr
Crumpecker, Christina Colleen, adjunct, $15,000
Crumpton, Constance A, occl therapist, $72,675
Crumpton, Roger Eugene, event assistant I, $15.00/hr
Crupe, Stefanie A, office support assistant IV, $14.83/hr
Cruse, Ashley Nicole, nurse, staff II rnwp, $22.24/hr
Cruse, Lori Lynn, patient svc rep, $12.13/hr
Crutcher, Stephanie Ann, care team assoc-clinical, $14.06/hr

Crutchfield, Angela Dawn, nurse, licensed prac, $18.81/hr
Crutsinger, Bob Glen, dir I, finance, $112,349
Cruzan, Devon Nicole, mental health tech trainee, $9.27/hr
Csabafi, Tamas Z, resrch asoc, $44,000
Csapo Sweet, Rita, prof, asoc, $53,540
Cubias Argueta, Nancy Johana, hospital lab tech, $13.44/hr
Cuchta, Brittany M, lecturer, $30,948
Cuddy, Rhonda, reimbursement spclst, $23.01/hr
Cudney, Elizabeth Anne Fargher, prof, asoc, $95,270
Cuenca, Alexander, lecturer, $100.00/hr
Cuesta, Luis Francisco, prof, ast teach, $41,000
Cui, Jiankun, prof, ast resrch, $81,151
Cui, Yaya, research specialist I, $44,331
Cui, Yi, fellow, post doctoral, $35,000
Culbertson, Amy E, human resources assistant, $15.56/hr
Culbertson, Michael, bldg cntrl sys techn III, $23.33/hr
Cullen, Christopher L, csm operations supervisor, $53,328
Cullen, Cory Reece, high school student, $9.50/hr
Cullen, Rachel Mary, event assistant I, $8.50/hr
Culley, Rebecca Lee, nurse, staff II rnwp, $22.24/hr
Cullimore, Miriam E, coor children's miracle netwrk, $39,200
Cullina, Adam, manager it, $62,046
Cullina, Sheryl Nicole, human resources manager sr, $58,500
Cullom, Frances Pauline, mental health tech, $13.69/hr
Cullom, Kimberly R, educational pgm associate I, $13.00/hr
Culp, Daniel Michael, student service coor II, $22.51/hr
Culp, Judith Anne, temporary professional, $35,175
Culp, Robert A, psychologist, $65,979
Culp, Sarah Marie, commercial talent, $20.00/hr
Culpepper, Tammy, educational pgm associate I, $13.45/hr
Culver, Mark E, resrch asoc, $54,980
Cumbie, Billy G, emeritus, $8,000
Cummings SR, Larry J, nurse, staff II, $30.25/hr
Cummings, Brett Alan, patient svc rep, $14.88/hr
Cummings, James M, prof, clinical dept, $259,996
Cummings, Jerry D, operations support tech sr, $19.71/hr
Cummings, Karen Lynn, prof, asoc, $57,253
Cummings, Kevin James, prof, ast, $87,281
Cummins, Christopher Marshal, office support ast II, $10.56/hr
Cummins, Daniel Mathias, support systems admin-entry, $40,000
Cummins, Jacqueline Yvette, strat comm manager, $63,859
Cummins, John Steven, resident physician-1st yr, $50,219
Cummins, Karen A, temporary professional, $11.30/hr
Cummins, Michael Richard, mts/refrigeration mech, $21.05/hr
Cunningham, Beverly Joann, accountant sr, $50,641
Cunningham, Billie M, prof, teach, $122,520
Cunningham, Brook Elaine, nurse, licensed prac, $16.20/hr
Cunningham, James Noel, mgr csm operations, $45,500
Cunningham, Julie A, office support assistant III, $14.57/hr
Cunningham, Kristan L, office support assistant IV, $18.23/hr
Cunningham, Laura Beth, resp therapist reg, $20.12/hr
Cunningham, Mary Louise, nurse spclst, clincl, $92,373
Cunningham, Michael, student service coor I, $53,428
Cunningham, Michelle, asoc dir program/project ops, $62,400
Cunningham, Ruth Ann, patient svc rep, $12.76/hr
Cunningham, Sandra Lynn, retail sales assistant, $9.99/hr
Cunningham, Simone Avier, student service coor II, $39,600
Cunningham, Theodore C, livestock spclst, $48,373
Cuno, Hillary Ann, nurse, staff prn, $26.00/hr
Cupp, Kristopher Joel, research/lab technician, $10.24/hr
Cupp, Kyle Joseph, patient svc rep, $12.81/hr
Curd, Judith Darlene, patient svc rep, $12.36/hr
Curl, Joseph Kent, food svc wrkr I, $9.60/hr
Curnutte, Cynthia, interior designer, $58,473
Curnutte, Todd Alan, bts painter, $21.71/hr
Curran, Alicia Lynn, research specialist I, $29,838
Currans, Cynthia Marie, resrch ast, $12,792
Current, Neeley A, office support associate, $19.26/hr
Currey, John R Jr, teaching ast, $32.50/hr
Currey, David E, sr ast dir studnt supprt svcs, $82,160
Currie, Cheryl L, nurse, staff II, $34.18/hr
Curry, Mark J Jr, enrollment advisor, $16.87/hr
Curry, Adam Paul, mts/electrician, $21.05/hr
Curry, Alphia Minnette, business support specialist II, $17.99/hr
Curry, Daren Richard, dir program/project operations, $56,341
Curry, Jan, office support assistant III, $14.70/hr
Curry, Jessica Whitney, resident physician-4th yr, $54,425
Curry, Lora, office support assistant IV, $16.50/hr
Curry, Lydia Ellen, office support assistant III, $13.60/hr

Curry, Marc Patrick, extns professional, asoc, $53,000
Curry, Monica Joleen, office support assistant IV, $16.19/hr
Curry, Randy D, professor, $164,552
Curry, Russell D, mts/insulator, $21.05/hr
Curry, Susan Kay, nurse, staff II, $34.18/hr
Curry, Timothy Michael, system administrator-expert, $63,858
Curry, Tonia Lynn, nurse, staff per diem, $35.00/hr
Curs, Bradley R, prof, asoc, $85,743
Curtis-Wingfield, Gayla Danne, student support spec sr, $20.00/hr
Curtis, Ashley Danielle, nurse, staff II, $20.84/hr
Curtis, Brian H, mech, custdl equip, $16.24/hr
Curtis, Darrick Tyler, student recruitment spclst, $16.35/hr
Curtis, Deontae M, mental health tech, $12.65/hr
Curtis, Elaine Carole, nurse, licensed prac, $18.43/hr
Curtis, Lori, prof, ast teach, $44,415
Curtis, Mildred Barbara, nurse, staff now I, $26.00/hr
Curtis, Scott Alan, librarian III, $54,652
Curtis, Shaquille Mar Shawn, care team assoc-suppt, $12.14/hr
Curtright, Thomas C, nurse, staff I, $19.00/hr
Cushman, Brittany Nicole, nurse, staff I, $19.00/hr
Cusick, Cynthia Anne, mgr III business admin, $73,986
Cusick, Eric Lee, library information assistant, $11.30/hr
Custard, Claudia Joana, care team assoc-clinical, $12.32/hr
Custard, Wendy Lynn, nurse, licensed prac, $18.46/hr
Cusumano, Dominic Vincent, office support asst IV, $13.00/hr
Cutburth, Aimey Lynn, safety comm operator, $13.67/hr
Cutitaru, Mihail Tudor, prof, ast teach, $70,000
Cutkosky, Steven Dale, prof, curators, $161,590
Cutler, Cathy S, prof, resrch, $107,133
Cutts, James H, project manager-princpl, $73,418
Cutts, Trina R, courier, $14.95/hr
Czebrinski, Edward C, test engineer-speclst, $46,974
D'Agostino, Katherine Mary, grant writer, $21.58/hr
D'Agrosa, Amy, instructor, adjunct, $18,000
D'Amour, Peter Jeremy, ast coach, $68,000
D'Souza, Valerian T, prof, asoc, $62,353
Da Silva, Claudio, custodian, $13.23/hr
Dabson, Brian, prof, resrch, $155,621
Dacey, Catherine E, nurse, staff II, $22.01/hr
Dache-Gerbino, Amalia Z, prof, ast, $68,500
Dachroeden, Arthur Eric, nurse, staff II, $23.34/hr
Dade, Alice Katharine, prof, ast, $58,860
Daehne, Alexander, instructor, adjunct, $16,200
Dagenais, Lydia F, mgr II student support svcs, $65,000
Daghlas, Asaad Fawzi, db programmer analyst-princpl, $80,862
Dagli, Cihan H, professor, $165,624
Dagostino, Maria Theresa, office support assistant IV, $13.24/hr
DaGue, Beverly Blum, scientist lead, $68,740
Dahlberg, Juliann, office support assistant IV, $16.00/hr
Dahling, Amanda Kate, editor II, $40,500
Dahlke, Donald Kirk, coord, distribution-matls dist, $18.43/hr
Dahlke, Lezlie R, nurse, or/recovery-ch, $34.18/hr
Dahlmann, Diane, dir II student support svcs, $127,089
Dahlstrom, Chelsea K, business ops associate sr, $45,600
Dahman, Angela Elizabeth, strat comm associate II, $58,995
Dahms, Cindy L, patient svc rep, $14.88/hr
Dahms, Wesley Guy, emrg med techn paramedic, $15.50/hr
Dai, Aihua, research specialist sr, $42,411
Daifallah, Thaer Ali, adjunct, $15,000
Dailey, Fred Duane, emeritus, $22,000
Dailey, Jennifer Lynn, csm project manager, $72,760
Daily, Melody A R, prof, clincl, $131,406
Daily, Sally K, office support assistant IV, $12.98/hr
Daiprai, Linda Marie, service rep IV, $16.13/hr
Dakich, Joy L, lecturer, $52,601
Dakshinesh, Parameshwaraiah Sugganahally, fellow, post doc
   clncl-yr3, $60,415
Dalabih, Abdallah Riad, prof, ast clincl dept, $194,250
Dalabih, Abdallah Riad, physician, $100.00/hr
Dalabih, Sevilay, resident physician-1st yr, $50,219
Dalay, Stephen M, lecturer, $21,500
Dalba, Natalie Dworshak, nurse, staff I, rnwp, $19.00/hr
Dalby, Theresa E, educational pgm associate I, $13.72/hr
Dale, Heather Nicole, nursing ast, $12.32/hr
Dale, Hollis M, hyperbaric med techn, $26.47/hr
Dale, Sandra K, mgr student support svcs, $48,361
Dale, Shari L, resp therapist reg, $27.36/hr
Dale, Virginia C, executive assistant sr, $49,018
Daley, Sean David, nurse, staff II rnwp, $20.54/hr

Dall, Lawrence H, adjunct, $15,000
Dallas, Mark Robert, resrch ast, $40,800
Dallas, Sarah L, professor, $119,613
Dalton, Benjamin Paul, resident physician-6th yr, $58,200
Dalton, Bernadette Mary, office support assistant IV, $16.77/hr
Dalton, John Hiram, prof, asoc, $60,696
Dalton, Mona Salama, nurse, or/recovery-ch, $30.18/hr
Dalton, Norman Sylvester, grounds supervisor, $49,452
Dalton, Richard Overton, mgr II student support svcs, $63,216
Daltoso, Christina Marie, office support assistant III, $12.75/hr
Daly, Kevin James, clerk, unit, $13.37/hr
Daly, Martin, prof, resrch, $40,000
Daly, Peggy Jean, office support assistant III, $13.00/hr
Dameron, Stacy Ann, patient svc rep, $14.88/hr
Dameron, Taryn Amber, 4-h youth devlmnt educr, $36,500
Dames, Christopher, dean, $138,587
Damon, Della, fin and acctg manager, $68,806
Damon, Rachel Loretta, care team assoc-clinical, $13.07/hr
Dampier, Christine, custodian, $12.94/hr
Damron, Jeanne Margaret, nurse, staff I, $19.00/hr
Damyen, Taylor Leigh, health physics technician I, $19.00/hr
Dang, Jason, instructor, adjunct, $7,200
Daniel, Christopher James, librarian I, $44,423
Daniel, Gertraud, child dev assistant, $10.79/hr
Daniel, Jeremy J, research specialist I, $36,750
Daniel, Klista Ilene, distribution techn-mtls mgmt, $14.04/hr
Daniel, Lesley B, educational pgm assistant, $10.86/hr
Daniel, Mary Lee Neyland, office support assistant IV, $16.41/hr
Daniel, Nancy M, strat comm associate II, $55,656
Daniel, Richard E, student support specialist II, $18.51/hr
Daniels, Wayne Jr, media producer I, $13.18/hr
Daniels, Clinton Ross, resp therapist reg, $19.54/hr
Daniels, Courtney, human resources assistant, $14.00/hr
Daniels, Dana Beteet, program/project supprt coor II, $63,162
Daniels, Devonte M, event assistant I, $7.50/hr
Daniels, Kimberly K, psychologist, $78,506
Daniels, Malesa Gaye, mgr II business admin, $51,394
Daniels, Mark Allen, prof, ast, $100,858
Daniels, Melissa R, retail sales ast manager, $18.00/hr
Daniels, Steven G, garage attendant, $13.89/hr
Daniels, Taylor Morgan, dental assistant II, $12.98/hr
Danielsen, Brooke Currin, bus support specialist II, $17.46/hr
Daniggelis, Christopher Stephen, prof, ast, $55,079
Danila, Cristina Ileana, prof, ast clincl dept, $210,000
Danker, Rebecca J, certif pharmacy techn, $17.10/hr
Dannecker, Erin A, prof, asoc, $108,617
Danner, Chelsea Hoover, nurse, staff prn, $26.00/hr
Dantzler, Heather Ann, research specialist I, $31,722
Dappas, Corinne Marcia, telecomm opr-h, $10.10/hr
Darandari, Hamza, dir II csm operations, $116,000
Dare, Donna D, office support assistant II, $12.86/hr
Darknell, Mitchell William, human resources asst, $12.99/hr
Darko, Samuel O, custodian, $13.23/hr
Darkow, Margaret Kay, occl therapist, $51,345
Darling, Ashley M, asoc dir program/project ops, $63,085
Darling, Lisa A, instructor, adjunct, $62.50/hr
Daro, Melissa G, office support assistant III, $12.41/hr
Daro, Tara L, reimbursement ast-cert, $18.59/hr
Darolia, Rajeev, prof, ast, $84,840
Darr, Clint Eugene, educational pgm coor I, $35,148
Darr, Jennifer Leah, radiologic techl, $18.23/hr
Darr, Katie Ann, finl counselor(eligibility), $17.24/hr
Darrah, Carly Ann, office support assistant IV, $14.00/hr
Darter, Tommy G, mts/electrician mrc, $18.74/hr
Das, Sajal K, professor, $211,088
Dasho, Isabeau Valerie, library info specialist, $12.98/hr
Datsov, Petar Datskov, temporary professional, $25.00/hr
Datsova, Mitsa Borisova, custodian, $12.94/hr
Datwyler, Marjorie Lyn, asoc dir program/project ops, $52,275
Datz, Craig A, administrative consultant sr, $100.00/hr
Daud, AbdulRahman, custdl suply delvry attd, $13.45/hr
Daugherty, Amber D, mgr II student support svcs, $45,600
Daugherty, Bradley K, physical therapist, $77,940
Daugherty, Claude Anthony, mts/pipefitter, $22.49/hr
Daugherty, Erin Lynn, child life spclst, $18.23/hr
Daugherty, Kimberly L, operations support tech sr, $18.99/hr
Daugherty, Linda J, asoc dir program/project ops, $61,329
Daugherty, Mary Ann, physical therapist, $56,733
Daugherty, Nathan A, program/project supprt coor I, $35,880

Daughton, William Joseph, prof, adjunct, $18,000
Dauksch, Janice Kay, user support analyst-entry, $11.41/hr
Daumas, Taneska Rae, business support specialist II, $16.64/hr
Daume, Debbie S, office support assistant IV, $14.50/hr
Dauve, Jan L, prof, teach, $33,939
Davenport, Deanna Kathline, nurse practitioner, $61,425
Davenport, Felia Katherine, prof, asoc, $51,202
Davenport, Heather L, nurse, licensed prac, $19.84/hr
Davenport, Lavonna Raschelle, food svc wrkr II, $10.49/hr
Davenport, Leeann Renee, business ops associate II, $46,446
Davenport, Loni Elise, resrch ast, $45,900
Davenport, Tamara L, office support assistant IV, $13.94/hr
David, Ana, office support associate, $16.76/hr
David, Craig A, dir sponsored programs, $130,000
David, Jeanne S, communications coordinator sr, $19.93/hr
David, John Dewood, prof, asoc, $128,500
Davidson, Amy Katherine, nurse, licensed prac, $16.45/hr
Davidson, Gethorio, temporary crafts service, $8.89/hr
Davidson, Jami Le, research/lab technician sr, $17.89/hr
Davidson, Linda J, instructor, adjunct, $16,650
Davidson, Martina Ann, nurse, staff II, $29.85/hr
Davidson, Sandra Ann, prof, curator teach, $100,116
Davidson, Tamara J, student service coor I, $36,754
Davidson, Tyrone Hugh, mgr II student support svcs, $50,998
Davies, Caroline Pickens, prof, asoc, $72,464
Davies, Laura Kristine, clerk, unit, $14.88/hr
Davis, Joseph L Jr, bts painter, $20.23/hr
Davis, Robert Lane Jr, program/project supprt coor II, $46,199
Davis, Alicia Finnus, custodian, $12.94/hr
Davis, Amanda Lea, extension asoc, $33,750
Davis, Ashley D, office support assistant IV, $13.30/hr
Davis, Beth Ann, nurse, licensed prac, $21.07/hr
Davis, Chad E, resident physician-2nd yr, $50,810
Davis, Chelsea McCray, rec/athletic specialist sr, $25.00/hr
Davis, Christina Susanne, dir program/proj operations, $79,516
Davis, Cody Alan, health records techn II, $12.37/hr
Davis, Curt H, professor, $186,333
Davis, Cynthia Denise, surgical technl certified, $18.87/hr
Davis, Dale L, educational pgm assistant, $10.74/hr
Davis, Daniel John, research specialist I, $44,625
Davis, Danyelle A, office support assistant II, $11.59/hr
Davis, David Karl, field superintendent, $73,008
Davis, Dawn M, business support specialist sr, $24.77/hr
Davis, Dawn Renee, office support assistant III, $12.79/hr
Davis, Debra D, 4-h spclst, $46,451
Davis, Diane Marie, office support assistant IV, $15.00/hr
Davis, Donna M, prof, asoc, $68,207
Davis, Eric S, db administrator-entry, $54,060
Davis, Everett E, bts locksmith, $20.23/hr
Davis, Floyd W, custodian, $12.94/hr
Davis, Geetha Kancherla Rao, prof, ast clincl dept, $142,800
Davis, George E, professor, $234,269
Davis, Glon Louise, patient svc rep, $11.50/hr
Davis, Heather Jane, lab assistant, $10.00/hr
Davis, Heiddi Lynn, dir II csm operations, $125,100
Davis, Jan Ellen, resrch asoc, $39,750
Davis, Janice F, nurse, staff II, $33.11/hr
Davis, Janis M, care coordinator, $65,545
Davis, Jennifer Michelle, student support specialist II, $18.63/hr
Davis, Jernia A, event assistant I, $8.00/hr
Davis, Jerry E, educational pgm assistant, $11.81/hr
Davis, Jerry Lee, custodian, bldg maint, $12.64/hr
Davis, Joanna Louise, student service coor II, $46,463
Davis, Jodee, prof, asoc, $63,268
Davis, John Mark, maint tech III, prev, $18.45/hr
Davis, June M, office support assistant II, $11.51/hr
Davis, Justin Wade, prof, asoc adjunct, $41,715
Davis, Kaitlin Elizabeth, office support assistant IV, $12.98/hr
Davis, Karen L, business support specialist II, $16.04/hr
Davis, Karen Louise, instructor, adjunct, $125.00/hr
Davis, Karen Sue, business support specialist II, $19.75/hr
Davis, Karli Ann, strat comm associate II, $50,000
Davis, Kelly J, office support assistant III, $12.18/hr
Davis, Kenneth R, sr ast dir csm operations, $105,085
Davis, Kimberli Morgan, fellow, $49,000
Davis, Kimberly Renee, instructor, adjunct, $27,000
Davis, Kirk Gavin, coor, care, $66,292
Davis, Kory A, system administrator-expert, $61,200
Davis, Larissa Renae, patient svc rep, $11.23/hr

Davis, Larry J, dean, $167,510
Davis, Lashira, custodian, $10.39/hr
Davis, Leesa Marie, office support assistant III, $13.20/hr
Davis, Liane Marie, resp therapist reg, $26.85/hr
Davis, Linda Gail, fin and acctg manager sr, $90,909
Davis, Linda Maria, snack bar attd, $11.91/hr
Davis, Lindsay W, professor, $70,184
Davis, Lonnie S, mail carrier, $14.85/hr
Davis, Lori Lynn, psychology techn, $15.36/hr
Davis, Matthew Donald, prof, asoc, $64,420
Davis, Matthew T, research/lab technician sr, $14.71/hr
Davis, Melissa D, instructor, adjunct, $10,796
Davis, Melissa S, nurse, licensed prac, $18.83/hr
Davis, Melvin, sr dir program/project ops, $102,050
Davis, Michael C, prof, asoc, $83,808
Davis, Michael John, professor, $213,037
Davis, Michael Larry, temporary crafts service, $11.24/hr
Davis, Michael Lee, event assistant I, $7.55/hr
Davis, Michael Patrick, extns professional, ast, $48,784
Davis, Michele Monique, office support assistant IV, $15.70/hr
Davis, Monica Reba, office support assistant III, $12.74/hr
Davis, N Kay, dir pat revenue cycle, $175,592
Davis, Natashua R, administrative consultant II, $83,232
Davis, Neville, physician, $100.00/hr
Davis, Patricia A, office support assistant IV, $14.95/hr
Davis, Patricia Ann, temporary professional, $23.00/hr
Davis, Peter N, emeritus, $24,000
Davis, Pierre W, instructor, adjunct, $27,000
Davis, Rachel Kristen, patient svc rep, $10.64/hr
Davis, Ralph C, bts painter-mrc, $16.36/hr
Davis, Randal L, sr ast dir csm operations, $67,534
Davis, Rebecca Miller, prof, ast teach, $47,500
Davis, Roy A, event assistant I, $7.55/hr
Davis, Ruby J, custodial supervisor, $48,360
Davis, Ryan M, prof, ast clincl dept, $250,000
Davis, Sara D, editor sr, $55,000
Davis, Shawn Thomas, strat comm associate I, $35,432
Davis, Stefani R, coor head injury svc, $38,628
Davis, Steven Dean, professor, $98,682
Davis, Steven L, mts/insulator, $22.50/hr
Davis, Teresa L, executive assistant sr, $51,180
Davis, Teresa Nicole, food svc wrkr I, $9.60/hr
Davis, Terry J, maint tech II, prev, $14.89/hr
Davis, Theresa, anesthesia techn, $16.14/hr
Davis, Tina R, ast mgr pat accts, $72,675
Davis, Tonya Jo, nurse, staff II rnwp, $21.75/hr
Davis, Tracy Lynn, custodian, $10.69/hr
Davis, Trinity Marie, instructor, adjunct, $12,395
Davis, Vanha Lynn, care team assoc-clinical, $14.17/hr
Davis, Wanda Sue, custodian, $11.41/hr
Davis, Winifred Ann, dental assistant I, $13.17/hr
Davison, Chad A, bts carpenter, $21.71/hr
Davolt, Victoria Renaye White, mental hlth prof, $46,675
Dawes, Richard, prof, asoc, $92,352
Dawn, Kenneth, instructor, adjunct, $7,500
Dawood, Hala A W, db programmer analyst-princpl, $83,759
Daws, Koni Janine, academic advisor sr, $51,508
Dawson, Carolyn Kay, office support assistant IV, $17.36/hr
Dawson, Cindy L, nurse, staff II rnwp, $30.60/hr
Dawson, Cody Dawn, patient svc rep, $10.64/hr
Dawson, Delema Suzanne, media production assoc, $8.89/hr
Dawson, Joyce Beatrice, custodian, $12.94/hr
Dawson, Kristin Michelle, office support assistant III, $11.85/hr
Dawson, Maurice Eugene, prof, ast, $120,000
Dawson, Nancy Lee, histologic technl, $26.47/hr
Dawson, Peter A, resident physician-4th yr, $55,804
Dawson, Rhonda R, office support assistant IV, $13.81/hr
Dawson, William P, instructor, ast, $15,000
Dawson, Yolanda Celeste, nurse, licensed prac, $17.19/hr
Day, Arden Dorothy, resrch ast, $36,383
Day, Brennen Michael, temporary technical, $11.00/hr
Day, David Michael, csm associate III, $29.20/hr
Day, Delbert E, emeritus, $12,000
Day, Don Ray, extension ast, $37,407
Day, Jo Ann, academic advisor, $37,181
Day, Larry J, bts carpenter, $21.71/hr
Day, Margaret Ann, prof, ast clincl dept, $142,800
Day, Melinda Renae, office support assistant IV, $14.70/hr
Day, Nancy, prof, asoc, $120,580

Day, Patricia Lynn Klinger, nurse, staff II, $21.26/hr
Day, Tamara Marie, performace improvement prof, $66,279
Day, Victoria D, human resources specialist sr, $45,241
Dayton, Susan Denise, mgr II hospitality services, $71,818
De Araujo, Zandra U, prof, ast, $69,106
De Armas, Rosamaria, executive assistant, $21.01/hr
de Graffenreid, Ellen Forderhase, vice chancellor, $220,000
De La Cruz Serverino, Manuel E, athletic attd, $13.04/hr
De La Cruz Severino, Benito Manuel, food svc wrkr I, $9.98/hr
De La Cruz, Jacqueline, food svc wrkr III, $12.20/hr
De La Cruz, Sonlly Y, food svc wrkr III, $13.21/hr
De La Torre, Nidya, prof, ast clincl, $90,387
De La Torre, Roger Anibal, prof, asoc, $563,318
De Leon Franklin, Onekia Renee, office support asst III, $15.93/hr
De Melo, Karen Michelle, med techl reg, $23.79/hr
De Rosier, Christopher J, communications assistant sr, $13.24/hr
De Silva Udawatta, Mihiri Nilanthi, health rec tech II, $12.50/hr
De Stadler, Marie Jean, speech/lang pathologist, $35.00/hr
De, Debraj, fellow, post doctoral, $50,000
Deakyne, Carol A, professor, $87,747
Deal, Janelle D, surgical technl certified, $23.01/hr
Dean Baar, Susan L, dean, $210,120
Dean, Grace Elizabeth, psychologist, $40.00/hr
Dean, Jennifer Marie, pat acct rep, $13.46/hr
Dean, Joan F, prof, curators, $95,139
Dean, Kenneth D, provost, deputy, $242,178
Dearlove, Sandra Tucker-Levins, grant writer, $21.02/hr
DeArmond, Janel Rae, temporary technical, $20.00/hr
Deaton, Brady James, executive director, $200,000
Deaver, Karla J, extns professional, asoc, $67,372
Deaver, Margaret L, nurse clinician, $72,675
Deaver, Shawn Allan, business support specialist II, $16.65/hr
DeBartolomeo, Melissa Noel, programmer analyst-spec, $36,750
DeBates, Paula Arlene, instructional designer-speclst, $49,920
DeBenedetti, Kathryn A, lecturer, $35,000
DeBlauw, Cindy K, extension asoc, $51,105
Debnath, Deepayan, fellow, post doctoral, $54,936
DeBoef, Amannda Gail Maphies, office support asst IV, $15.50/hr
Debroy, Saptarshi, fellow, post doctoral, $51,000
Dechter, Christopher J, audiovisual designer-speclst, $26.93/hr
Decker, Gentry Thomas, research specialist I, $31,100
Decker, Jared Egan, prof, ast, $73,000
Decker, Jayme, resident physician-1st yr, $49,025
Decker, Karen, office support assistant IV, $15.15/hr
Decker, Mark E, system support analyst-speclst, $24.61/hr
Deckert, Eileen Louise, nurse, staff prn, $26.00/hr
Deckert, William Joseph, nurse anesthetist, $147,900
DeClue, Amy Elizabeth, prof, asoc, $123,565
DeClue, Lindsey Hayden, nurse, licensed prac, $15.59/hr
Declue, Rochelle, ast dir student support svcs, $73,203
DeClue, Stacie Elizabeth, veterinary technician, $15.50/hr
Decourley, Rebecca Michelle, temp professional, $13.00/hr
Dedmon, Allyssa Denise, office support assistant III, $11.96/hr
Dedrick, Nicole Suzanne, reimbursement ast, $17.46/hr
Deeds, Dexter Damian, patient svc rep, $11.01/hr
Deehr, Dale F, supv, lab, $77,940
Deeken, Debra J, dir ambulatory pat care svcs, $117,300
Deere, Ashley Raye, nurse clinician, $61,343
Deering, Annette E, 4-h spclst, $44,144
Deering, Julie B, operations support tech II, $16.06/hr
Deering, Shawn W, extns professional, asoc, $51,784
Dees-Burnett, Keichanda Inger, dir I, student support svcs, $60,600
Dees, Sylvia K, office support assistant III, $12.00/hr
Defelice, Kimi, reimbursement ast-cert, $18.23/hr
DeFord Petefish, Teresa Lynn, program/proj supprt coor I, $35,857
DeFrangesco, Larisa, office support assistant IV, $12.98/hr
Defreese, Carol J, instructor, adjunct, $27,000
DeFroy, Mary Agnes, sr manager it, $89,124
DeGonia, John N, instructor, adjunct, $62.50/hr
Degraff, Clifford R, supv radiology, $28.56/hr
DeGraffenreid, Keri Nicole, ast coach, $34,230
DeGraffenreid, Todd Courtney, head coach, $40,400
DeGroodt, Tina Marie, coor, reimbursement, $63,149
Dehaemers, Jennifer, asoc vice chancellor, $124,800
Dehart, Carmen Ann, dir II business admin, $99,000
Dehaven, Gregory W, hospital security officer, $14.88/hr
Dehaybi, Sarah Lauren, resident physician-2nd yr, $50,810
Deidrick, Kathleen Keely McCann, instructor, adjunct, $24,000
Deines, Donna New, prof, asoc, $102,000

DeJaynes, Shelly, business support specialist sr, $22.84/hr
DeJong, James, instructor, $114,673
DeKinder, Julie Lynn Ott, prof, asoc clincl, $99,777
Dekker, Steve Elliot, instructor, adjunct, $17,520
Del Porto-Dahms, Alda Magda, nurse anesthetist, $143,720
Del Priore, Angela, resident physician-1st yr, $50,219
Dela Cruz, Genevieve, certif pharmacy techn, $17.10/hr
Delach Leonard, Mary J, strat comm consultant, $58,231
Delaney, Margaret Elizabeth, nurse, staff II, $34.62/hr
DeLanois, Jack J, mts/plumber, $19.21/hr
Delap, Melissa, education nurse, $77,204
Delashmutt, Stephanie Lynn, nurse, staff II, $21.37/hr
Delaunay, Anne, olson professorship, $21,109
Delaware, Richard, prof, asoc teach, $52,783
Delbert, Dianne, office support assistant IV, $18.36/hr
Deleon, Kara Beth Bowen, fellow, post doctoral, $47,840
Delgado, Galo Fernando, instructor, adjunct, $14,400
Delima, Teresa A, nurse, staff II, $34.18/hr
DeLisle, James R, prof, asoc, $160,000
Della Rocca, Gregory John, prof, asoc, $260,294
Dellamano, Natalie Paige, patient svc rep, $11.00/hr
Deloach-Packnett, Gwendolyn, ast vice chancellor, $100,214
DeLong, Paula Sue, compliance manager sr, $55,179
Delong, Tony Ray, program/project supprt coor I, $47,536
DeLouche, Tracie L, care team assoc-clinical, $14.17/hr
Delp, Jennifer Renae, nurse, staff now plus, $30.00/hr
Delston, Jill B, prof, ast teach, $42,900
Demarco, Vincent G, prof, asoc resrch, $79,574
DeMars, Kyle Jordan, prof, ast, $79,765
Demchenko, Alexei, prof, curators, $85,203
Demelo, Ryan, resident physician-5th yr, $61,683
Dement, Megan Michelle, nurse, staff I, $19.37/hr
Demian, Susan H, office support assistant IV, $20.81/hr
Demien, Coradina Sue, nurse, licensed prac, $19.23/hr
Deming, Philip E, dir I, student support svcs, $93,360
Demiroz, Erdem, instructor, adjunct, $7,200
Demkowicz, Michelle Lynn, event assistant I, $12.00/hr
Dempsey, Heather Nicole, accountant sr, $47,470
Dempsher, John Paul, research specialist I, $32,000
Demse, Elizabeth Sara, nurse, staff I, $19.37/hr
Denbigh, John Louis Jr, farm manager, $49,363
Denbigh, Beverly K, office support assistant III, $16.96/hr
Denbow, Victoria Clair, care team assoc-clinical, $11.10/hr
Deneke, Janet Leslie, temporary professional, $11.30/hr
Deng, Baolin, professor, $186,198
Deng, Wen, prof, ast, $81,000
Deng, Yang, ast coach, $60,000
Denham, Debra, business support specialist II, $21.01/hr
Denise, Daniel W, system support analyst-expert, $29.08/hr
Denker, Laura Anne, student service coor sr, $51,071
Denkler, Sarah R G, extns professional, asoc, $54,965
Denneny, James C III, prof, clinical dept, $227,250
Denney, Isaac Abraham, patient svc rep, $11.28/hr
Denney, Vivien Therese Mier, med techl reg, $23.75/hr
Denninghoff, Joanna M, nurse, staff I, $19.00/hr
Dennis, Amy Michelle, nurse, staff per diem, $35.00/hr
Dennis, Barbara Lynn, office support assistant IV, $15.46/hr
Dennis, Brandon E, central sterile assistant, $10.43/hr
Dennis, Brenda J, executive assistant, $23.41/hr
Dennis, Donald L, ast dir csm operations, $77,363
Dennis, Eric L, custodian, $13.36/hr
Dennis, Heather Dee, nurse, staff, $30.24/hr
Dennis, Nancy D, patient svc rep, $12.14/hr
Dennis, Shannon Elizabeth, bus support specialist II, $21.40/hr
Dennis, Wanda Rochelle, custodian, $13.36/hr
Dennis, William Ray, prof, ast clincl dept, $304,000
Dennison, Stephanie Lynne, patient svc rep, $11.01/hr
Dennison, Vicki Sumiyo, program/proj supprt coor II, $88,293
Denny, Dorothy R, asoc dir program/project ops, $50,763
Denny, Krystle Dawn, food svc wrkr I, $9.60/hr
Denson, Stuart Benjamin, user support analyst-speclst, $17.50/hr
Dent, Eunice Marie, custodian, $13.23/hr
Denton, Kayla Beth, pat acct rep, $13.61/hr
Denton, Mary F, supv pat admiss, $45,891
Denton, Miriam Leigh, nurse, staff, $21.36/hr
Denzel, Laura Ann, coordinator, loa, $16.65/hr
Denzel, Michael K, support systems admin-princpl, $61,812
Deo, Shekhar Hari, resrch scientist/academic, $40,706
DeOrnellas, Walter L, sterile processing tech, $17.79/hr

DePriest, Amy Nicole, student support specialist sr, $16.54/hr
DePriest, Kristan M, mri technologist, $27.10/hr.10/hr
Depriest, Melanie Elaine, bus support specialist II, $15.81/hr
Depriest, Robert Lynn, system support analyst-expert, $22.96/hr
Depue, Jade Rachael, temporary professional, $13.00/hr
Depue, Susan Marie, prof, ast resrch, $64,708
Derakhshani, Reza, prof, asoc, $87,241
Derboven, Sonja M, business svcs consultant sr, $82,000
Derda, Grace Chaudet, student service coor sr, $52,508
Dereberry, Melissa Ann Green, lecturer, $27,500
Deremer, James J, support systems admin-speclst, $47,861
Derham, Billie Jo, prof, ast adjunct, $45,000
Derix, Christopher James, psychologist, $40.00/hr
Derix, Heather Renee, psychologist, $58,350
Dermitzel, Daniel, instructor, adjunct, $18,000
Derrell, Anna Theresa, program/project supprt coor I, $45,600
Derrick, Chase D, resident physician-4th yr, $55,804
Derrick, Karen E, mgr clinical nutrition, $70,663
Derryberry, Dannie Sue, temporary professional, $14.00/hr
Des Marteau, Genevieve Rose, media producer II, $14.95/hr
Desai-Ramirez, Bijal Manoj, sr dir program/project ops, $80,800
Desai, Kalpesh, professor, $200,000
Desai, Neal A, resident physician-4th yr, $54,425
Desai, Neil Kishor, fellow, post doc clncl yr1, $55,804
Desai, Rini, resident physician-1st yr, $49,025
Desantis, Sadie R, prof, ast teach, $50,000
Desch, Gretchen E, radiologic techI, $27.92/hr
Deshmukh, Rupesh, fellow, post doctoral, $43,050
Deshmukh, Sanaa Khan, fellow, post doc clncl-yr2, $58,083
Desimio, Maria L, business ops associate II, $47,148
DeSmith, Marsha Renee, student support specialist II, $15.25/hr
Desnoo, Laura Denise, infection control profl, $31.86/hr
Desnoyer, Brad M, prof, asoc teach, $80,800
Desota, Joseph Preston, instructor, adjunct, $24,000
Desouches, Stephane Louis, resident physician-3rd yr, $52,470
DeSouza, Guilherme Nelson Fernandes, prof, asoc, $94,397
DeSouza, Luiza Queiroz, instructor, $45,450
Despins, Laurel A, prof, ast, $61,734
Dessem, Ralph L, professor, $200,788
Dessenberger, Jennifer Elda, nurse, staff II rnwp, $21.37/hr
Dessenberger, William J, phlebotomist, $15.62/hr
Deters, Robin David, db programmer analyst-princpl, $75,403
Dethman, John P, librarian II, $49,702
Detlor, Dylan Rudi, certif pharmacy techn, $12.75/hr
Deuel, Derrick Duane, bldg cntrl sys techn I, $20.31/hr
Deuser, Cecelia M, specialist, $15.23/hr
Deutsch, Jonathan Paul, temporary crafts service, $7.50/hr
Deutscher, Susan L, professor, $90,982
Devaney, Cheryl L, instructor, adjunct, $10,500
Devaney, Michael Joseph, emeritus, $24,000
Devasahayam, Joe Vasanth M, fellow, post doc clncl yr1, $55,804
DeVault, Annette Nina, nurse, staff II, $21.35/hr
DeVault, Julie Ann, nurse, licensed prac, $18.83/hr
Devault, Tracie Marie, lecturer, $40,000
Devereaux, Qwan, food svc wrkr II, $10.10/hr
Devilbiss, Alexander Scott, db programmer analyst-entry, $42,000
Devlin, Colleen Elizabeth, dir I, strat communications, $93,024
Devlin, Karisha V, busi spclst, agri, $48,706
Devlin, Steven Leon, dean, ast, $117,160
DeVore, Jessie L, research/lab technician sr, $17.40/hr
Dewar, Jennifer L, strat comm associate I, $35,432
DeWeese, June LaFollette, tutor, $10.00/hr
Dewit, Deborah A, nurse, licensed prac, $18.46/hr
DeWitt, Petra, prof, ast, $55,000
Dews, Amy Catherine, office support assistant II, $11.90/hr
Dews, Diane, business support specialist sr, $27.88/hr
Dexter, Janet L, office support assistant IV, $15.90/hr
Dey, Janiene Marie, service rep III, $13.03/hr
Dhaliwal, Sonia, psychologist, $68,486
Dhanapal, Arun Prabhu, fellow, post doctoral, $38,000
Dharani, Lokeswarappa R, prof, curators, $177,038
Dhillon, Gurminder Singh, resident physician-3rd yr, $52,470
Dhoot, Jashdeep, resident physician-7th yr, $63,475
Dhoot, Sonia Brar, resident physician-4th yr, $54,425
Dhuper, Sonal, prof, ast clincl dept, $153,000
Diamant, Richard L, sftware supprt analyst-princpl, $55,736
Diamond, David D, director, $95,084
Diamond, Elizabeth Ellen, office support assistant III, $12.00/hr
Diamond, Michael A, professor, $186,095

Diamond, Rand J, prof, teach, $147,159
Diamond, Sandra I, program/project supprt coor I, $25.75/hr
Dias, Jerry Ray, prof, curators, $102,885
Diaw, Angela Marie, teaching ast, $31.80/hr
Diaz Guerrero, Raquel Joselyn, res physician-5th yr, $58,083
Diaz, Armando, media producer I, $14.30/hr
Diaz, Graciela Cecilia, instructor, adjunct, $32,400
Diaz, Raymond Jo, custodian, $11.00/hr
Dibb, Susan Ford, student service coor II, $30,146
Dibble, Cameron Shawn, teaching ast, $36.40/hr
Diblasi, Lea Anne, nurse clinician, $66,300
Dibooglu, Selahattin, professor, $95,097
Dick, Thomas A, temporary professional, $11.30/hr
Dickerson, Lawrence Elmer III, extension asoc, $26,753
Dickerson, John Michael, phlebotomist, $11.07/hr
Dickerson, Marlana Love, business support spec sr, $21.92/hr
Dickerson, Nathan Thomas, couns hlth/welfare/wellness sr, $30.00/hr
Dickerson, Rhiannon Leigh, lecturer, $30,000
Dickerson, Susan M, project manager-princpl, $77,454
Dickey, Cheryl A, office support assistant IV, $15.36/hr
Dickey, David E, lecturer, $8,010
Dickey, Frances, prof, asoc, $73,235
Dickey, Karen Lucille, executive assistant, $17.57/hr
Dickey, Marlene A, office support assistant III, $14.52/hr
Dickinson, Andrew A, press IV, $22.21/hr
Dickinson, Deborah D, business support specialist II, $19.41/hr
Dickinson, Leslie Dawn, prof, ast teach, $51,500
Dickinson, Matthew George, system admin-expert, $69,666
Dickmann, Dane A, stage services assistant sr, $16.00/hr
Dickson, Christine N, student service coor II, $51,519
Dickson, Deborah Ruth, patient svc rep, $12.13/hr
Dickson, Jason Ross, student support specialist II, $15.58/hr
Dickson, Jessica Ann, asoc athletic director, $65,650
Dickson, Rachel Darrylyn, office support assistant III, $11.53/hr
DiDonato, Kristen Lee, prof, ast clincl, $96,000
Die, Rony, student service coor II, $41,715
Diecker, Judith Ann, office support assistant sr, $15.00/hr
Dieckmann, Rebecca E, executive assistant sr, $66,672
Diehl, Becky Sue, student service coor II, $45,993
Diehl, Jonathan Eugene, event assistant I, $8.50/hr
Diehl, Kathleen Marie, instructor, adjunct, $1,706
Diehl, Leslie C, utility dist wrkr III, $20.77/hr
Diehls, Brenda Jewell, reimbursement ast, $16.03/hr
Diekhuis, Stacy Helen, custodian, $10.39/hr
Diekmann, Marilyn M, fin and acctg analyst sr, $67,400
Diem, Sarah L, prof, ast, $76,039
Diener, Jeremy W, dir III advancement, $85,260
Diener, Jill Suzanne, student service coor sr, $50,004
Dieringer, Lara Christine, office support assistant IV, $15.00/hr
Dierker, Philip Dennis, csm associate I, $17.67/hr
Dierkes, Daron, library info specialist, $16.50/hr
Dierking, Adam Michael, temporary crafts service, $9.28/hr
Dierks, Travis A, prof, ast adjunct, $18,900
Diesh, Colin Michael, resrch anlyst, $52,320
Dietrich, Bryce Jensen, prof, ast visiting, $40,000
Dietrich, Maria Magdalena, prof, ast, $77,520
Dietrich, Simone Susanne, prof, ast, $63,246
Dietterle, Luke Herbers, tutor, $10.50/hr
Dietz, Kathryn M, nurse, staff per diem, $35.00/hr
Dietzel, Gary, high school student, $7.50/hr
Digby, Jonathan S, temporary professional, $11.30/hr
Diggs, Benard, dir student/univ center, $73,726
DiGiovanni, Peter Mark, instructor, adjunct, $16,875
Dikhaminjia, Nana, visiting asst research prof, $30,000
Diliberto, Michael Anthony, media producer sr, $40,000
Dilks, Deborah E, mgr student support svcs, $50,922
Dilks, Stephen, professor, $78,664
Dill, Amanda Marie, nurse, licensed prac, $15.67/hr
Dill, Larry Nelson, specialist, $64,530
Dillamon, Laura Elizabeth, nurse, staff II rnwp, $30.28/hr
Dillard, Allison B, office support assistant III, $14.00/hr
Dillard, Debra Ann, service rep IV, $16.13/hr
Dillard, Shericka Antoinette, office support asst IV, $13.50/hr
Dilley, Teresa V, instructor, adjunct, $4,200
Dillinger, Wendy Marie, head coach, $45,225
Dillon, Bonnie G, nurse, staff II, $34.18/hr
Dillon, Dana Louise, dental assistant sr, $20.27/hr
Dillon, Darrell W, electrician, undrgrnd dist I, $21.05/hr

Dillon, Tina Marie, office support assistant II, $10.36/hr
Dillon, Wade Gordon, police officer, $17.05/hr
Dilse, Diane Elaine, pat acct rep, $16.32/hr
Dilse, Don S, supv bldg trades-h, $55,058
Dilse, Micah Warner, system support analyst-entry, $19.37/hr
Diltz, Darlisa Jeanette, business spclst, $50,000
Dimaggio, Sherry Diane, business support spec sr, $24.53/hr
Dimond, Paul Vernon, nurse anesthetist, $147,900
Dinakarpandian, Deendayal, prof, asoc, $83,738
Dinehart, Karlee Rose, fin and acctg consultant, $60,900
Ding, Cody Shuai, professor, $93,581
Ding, Huan, program/project supprt coor I, $43,899
Ding, QingQing, resident physician-4th yr, $55,804
Ding, Shinghua, prof, asoc, $97,421
Dingley, Brenda L, librarian II, $97,755
Dingo, Rebecca A, prof, asoc, $72,161
Dinino, Megan, coor, service, $15.15/hr
Dinsdale, Blake J, media producer sr, $55,869
Dinsmore, Michael T, operations support tech sr, $17.32/hr
Dinwiddie, Karol M, business support specialist II, $21.21/hr
DiPietro, Stephanie Maura, prof, ast, $70,000
DiRaimo, Andrea Gail, fin and acctg manager, $59,257
DiRie, Christine Marie, prof, ast teach, $63,540
Dirks, Bradley R, prof, ast teach, $90,000
Dirksmeyer, Stephanie A, pat acct rep, $17.10/hr
Dismang, Megetta Marcene, care team assoc-clinical, $13.77/hr
Disney, Stephani Leeann, clinical technician II, $15.16/hr
Disselhorst, Rick B, research activities supervisor, $47,729
Disser, Marilyn S, executive assistant, $17.00/hr
Ditch, Jonas A, sftware supprt analyst-speclst, $41,000
Dittmeier, William J, prof, ast adjunct, $10,200
Dittmer, Joel P, prof, ast, $53,469
Ditzfeld, Jennifer L, temporary professional, $11.30/hr
Divine, Peggy Jean, business support specialist II, $17.17/hr
Dixey, Jennifer, instructional tech-speclst, $50,000
Dixon-Hall, Janice Lorraine, program/proj supprt coor I, $47,000
Dixon, Amber Dawn, nurse, licensed prac, $18.37/hr
Dixon, Bradley Scott, student service coor II, $42,500
Dixon, Cindy Lee, physician ast, $100.00/hr
Dixon, Darlene, office support assistant IV, $16.90/hr
Dixon, Jamie L, nurse, staff II, $22.24/hr
Dixon, Lonny W, director, $172,343
Dixon, Marijo, system administrator-expert, $56,100
Dixon, Tahji Rashaad, care team assoc-clinical, $11.00/hr
Dixon, Tiphani Yvonne, office support assistant III, $15.00/hr
Dixon, Travis W, program/project supprt coor II, $39,600
Dixson, Debra J, nurse, staff II, $32.09/hr
Dixson, Jonathan, research specialist I, $37,648
Dizdarevic, Denis, couns hlth/welfare/wellness sr, $50,000
Djunaidi, Harjanto, business ops associate sr, $50,000
Dluhos-Sebesto, Casey, resident physician-4th yr, $65,000
Do Amaral, Fernanda Plucani, fellow, post doctoral, $38,000
Dobbins, Jeffrey Edward, custodian, $10.39/hr
Dobbins, Kristine Joyce, curator, $49,094
Dobbs, Linda Sue, prof, ast adjunct, $125.00/hr
Dobbs, Sherry Kaye, instructor, adjunct, $6,400
Dobek, Amy V, office support assistant V, $13.72/hr
Dobens, Elizabeth A, resrch ast, $12,000
Dobens, Leonard, prof, asoc, $88,194
Dobey, Ronald J, mgr health physics, $100,221
Dobey, Tarilyn Starzinger, clincl documnt spclst, $65,909
Dobies, Pamela Anne, prof, ast teach, $81,221
Dobson, Catherine Marie, human resources spec II, $24.55/hr
Dobson, Ramona Kay, instructor, adjunct, $9,093
Dockweiler, Christine Marie, student service coor II, $46,000
Doctor, Abbas Abdulla, specialist, $10.00/hr
Dodam, Ginny G, research/lab technician sr, $13.00/hr
Dodam, John R, professor, $168,586
Dodd, Daniel Lee, library info specialist, $12.98/hr
Dodd, Matthew Wright, hospital security officer, $11.06/hr
Dodds, Bradley Vernon, network engineer-expert, $58,726
Dodson, Catherine Sue, event assistant I, $7.75/hr
Dodson, Jaime Elizabeth, clinical educator, $57,000
Dodson, Marsha Rene, business ops associate I, $40,992
Dodson, Monique Ann, business support specialist II, $16.31/hr
Doebelin, Adrienne Renee, radiologic techl, $21.48/hr
Doebelin, Stephanie Dawn, sr asoc dir bus admin, $105,060
Doerhoff, Faye Elizabeth, physician, $200.00/hr
Doering, Deborah, business support specialist sr, $18.83/hr

Doerr, Aaron, asoc media producer, $12.18/hr
Doerr, Daniel Justin, student service coor sr, $46,056
Doescher, Kaitlyn Ware, nurse, staff I, $19.00/hr
Doffoney, Crystal Chanae, educational pgm assoc I, $12.85/hr
Dogan, Fatih, professor, $126,225
Doherty, Elaine Eggleston, prof, asoc, $80,000
Dohm, Christopher Clark, technical writer-princpl, $66,951
Dohm, Kimberly Jean, supv, clinical-rehab svcs, $82,317
Dohrmann, Mary L, prof, clinical dept, $181,649
Dokken, Dee Ann, nurse, staff, $30.24/hr
Dolan, Andrew B, event assistant I, $7.55/hr
Dolan, Kathleen A, sr dir program/project ops, $104,000
Dolan, Kathryn C, prof, ast, $56,450
Dolan, Levi Joseph, event assistant I, $9.00/hr
Dolan, Patricia A, asoc dir program/project ops, $24,960
Dolbashian, Edward, prof, asoc, $60,640
Dolezal, Darry L, prof, asoc, $52,224
Doljanac, Robert Frank, resrch asoc, $28,325
Doll, Amy Jo, resident physician-3rd yr, $52,470
Doll, Donald C, prof, clinical dept, $337,620
Doll, Jennifer L, controller-h, $205,000
Dollar, Diane, instructor, adjunct, $6,300
Dollard, Patrick, bindery opr, $19.13/hr
Dollens, Emily Anne, lab techn, persl svc-clin lab, $12.22/hr
Dollens, Jacqueline Rene, hris specialist-entry, $40,395
Dollens, Melanie Ann, nurse, staff I, $19.00/hr
Dollens, Michelle, nurse, procedures, $29.25/hr
Dollerschell, John T, resident physician-1st yr, $49,025
Domagtoy, Janet Ruth, office support assistant V, $17.13/hr
Domanowski, Michael Edmund, supv, food svc II-h, $47,303
Domeier, Timothy L, prof, ast, $85,000
Domenick, Korey Michael, intern, $12.48/hr
Domingo, Ma Francesca Del Rosario, hr spec II, $40,800
Domingo, Maria Paula Del Rosario, care team assoc-clinical, $13.33/hr
Domingues da Silva, Daniel Barros, prof, ast, $57,134
Dominguez Rosa, Cesar, custodian, $12.90/hr
Dominguez, Shayelle Courtney, temporary clerical, $14.68/hr
Dominick, Clint Cameron, rec/athletic specialist sr, $39,600
Dominique, Katharine Courtney, asoc media prod, $11.30/hr
Domke, Barbara E, program/project supprt coor I, $45,000
Domon, Tiffany Leeann, patient svc rep, $10.85/hr
Donahoe, Timothy J, electronics technician I, $13.70/hr
Donahue II, John T, user support analyst-expert, $19.66/hr
Donaldson, Joe F III, educational pgm manager, $49,440
Donaldson, Brooke Ellen, nurse, licensed prac, $16.04/hr
Donaldson, Jessica Lynn, rehab therapy aide, $11.88/hr
Donato, Phillip Richard Jr, asoc dir program/proj ops, $69,509
Donegan, Brett T, resident physician-4th yr, $54,425
Doner, Alyssa S, veterinary technician sr, $16.30/hr
Dong, Nianbo, prof, ast, $85,600
Dong, Shengzhang, fellow, post doctoral, $40,800
Dong, Xiaoqing, prof, ast resrch, $38,000
Dong, Yanming, fellow, post doctoral, $38,760
Dong, Yuan, resrch asoc, $36,000
Donley, Alex J, strat comm associate II, $44,733
Donley, Lyle D, polysomnograph techn reg, $30.05/hr
Donnell Hilgedick, Kristen Marie, prof, ast, $82,050
Donnell, Thomas, business tech analyst-expert, $50,000
Donnelly, David Patrick, dean, $425,000
Donnelly, Kevin Shane, veterinarian, residnt, $49,776
Donnelly, Lindsay Lee, veterinarian, residnt, $26,315
Donnelly, Stephanie Katherine, temporary clerical, $12.00/hr
Donoho, Paula Gerber, library info specialist, $12.98/hr
Donohoe, Charles, adjunct, $15,000
Donovan, Edlyn F, supv gift shop, $18.56/hr
Donovan, John D, event assistant I, $9.50/hr
Donovan, Judith M, med techl reg, $30.36/hr
Donovan, Kathleen, coor, resrch partcpnt advocacy, $59,905
Donovan, Martha S, office support assistant III, $17.74/hr
Donovan, Michael T, dir sports operations, $45,000
Donze, Joni S, office support assistant II, $10.24/hr
Dooley, Amyjo Anne, mgr student support svcs, $52,155
Dooley, Brian D, ast coach, $64,000
Dooley, Dawn Angel, office support assistant III, $13.25/hr
Dooley, Judy Lynn, business support specialist II, $19.97/hr
Dooley, Terry W, custodian, $13.36/hr
Dooley, Troy Lee, courier, $15.77/hr
Doolittle, Derek W, asoc athletic director, $54,400

Dop, Dani Jo, office support assistant III, $12.69/hr
Dopp, Alex Richard, grader, $100.00/hr
Dopplick, Suzin Marie, coor protocol svcs, $17.00/hr
Doran, Mary E, librarian III, $54,675
Doran, Sean Patrick, resident physician-1st yr, $49,025
Dorani, Sahar Sarah, intern, $23,000
Dorflinger, Connie A, executive assistant sr, $55,539
Dority, Alicia D, educational pgm coor III, $54,035
Dority, Sandra Kay, linen attd, $12.96/hr
Dorman, Pamela R, business support specialist II, $22.32/hr
Dorn, Julie Ann, dir II advancement, $67,295
Dorner, Lisa Marie, prof, ast, $72,534
Dorsey, Jennifer Lee, instructor, adjunct, $9,000
Dorsey, Michaelle E, library info specialist sr, $15.13/hr
Dorth, David G, csm professional II, $65,168
Dorward, Darla J, reimbursement ast-cert, $18.87/hr
Doshier, Laura Jane, resident physician-4th yr, $55,804
Doskey, Paul Matthew, prof, ast clincl dept, $200,000
Doss, Carrie Ann, nurse, advanced practice, $82,335
Doss, Chelsea Cheyenne, custodian, $10.00/hr
Doss, Crystal Rae, prof, ast teach, $50,000
Doss, Crystal Shannon, custodian, $10.39/hr
Doss, Heather Elaine, resident physician-4th yr, $58,265
Doss, Kourtney Leigh, nurse, staff I, $19.00/hr
Doss, Marc Duane, sr dir program/project ops, $89,258
Dostoglou, Stamatis, professor, $98,717
Dothage, Andrea Bickford, dietitian, clincl, $59,685
Dothage, Bertha Lynn, custodian, $12.94/hr
Dothage, Kenneth R, custodian, $10.39/hr
Dothage, Mary Kathryn, extns professional, $84,193
Dotson, Carl, construction manager II, $68,557
Dotson, Shelley Marie, mgr event management, $58,773
Doty, Amanda Lou, radiologic techl, $21.53/hr
Doty, Jennifer, clinical program coordinator, $82,499
Doty, Jeri Lee, chief planning ofcr, $240,000
Doty, Micah Renee, educational pgm associate I, $12.25/hr
Doty, Randa Elise, busi spclst, agri, $41,267
Doty, Timothy Thomas Warren, security analyst-expert, $53,476
Dotzel, Qiang Sun, prof, asoc teach, $51,475
Dotzel, Ronald M, prof, asoc, $64,418
Dou, Gary J, student support specialist sr, $23.88/hr
Dougherty, Barbara J, prof, resrch, $128,467
Dougherty, Clinton B, business spclst, $43,512
Dougherty, Debbie S, professor, $84,600
Dougherty, Thomas Warren, professor, $185,895
Doughty, Joy Kim, nurse, staff II rnwp, $34.50/hr
Douglas, Clayton Irving, research lab supervisor, $48,946
Douglas, Debra G, central regstry-data coor sr, $23.70/hr
Douglas, Diana Lynn, research specialist I, $39,520
Douglas, Paul E, grounds keeper, $11.76/hr
Douglas, Rodney D, custodian, $13.36/hr
Douglas, Ryan Nathaniel, fellow, post doctoral, $40,518
Douglas, Tanner Anton, stage services assistant sr, $16.00/hr
Douglas, Tyron Michael O'Shea, prof, ast, $72,620
Dourlain-Kerley, Tracey Marie, nurse, staff II, $20.14/hr
Dourty, Brian R, assoc director it, $111,140
Dourty, Jill Suzanne, communications coordinator, $25.00/hr
Doutt, Gerald Lee, instructor, adjunct, $30,000
Dove, Amy Catherine, business support specialist II, $16.16/hr
Dow, Jay K, professor, $81,682
Dowd, Colleen M, event assistant I, $7.67/hr
Dowd, Karla Ann, dir I, finance, $94,000
Dowdell, Jaimi L, administrative consultant, $78,867
Dowden-White, Priscilla Anne, prof, asoc, $54,983
Dowe, Kenneth X, custodian, $12.18/hr
Dowell, Carol Jeanine, finl counselor(eligibility), $15.69/hr
Dowell, Elizabeth A, custodian, $13.36/hr
Dowell, Jason L, office support associate, $18.84/hr
Dowell, Lonnie R, agriculture foreman, $21.74/hr
Dowis, Ryan Robert, instructor, adjunct, $7,500
Dowlatshahi, Shahdad, professor, $144,668
Dowler, Melissa Dawn, clinical mgr, $90,689
Dowlut-McElroy, Tazim, resident physician-5th yr, $75,000
Downer, Natalie Lorraine, fellow, post doctoral, $35,721
Downes, Connor Charles, student service coor II, $39,624
Downey, Barbara S, prof, asoc teach, $91,551
DowneyEber, Cheryl Lynn, mgr student support svcs, $41,000
Downing, Daniel Leon, extension asoc, $55,481
Downing, Lillie I, office support assistant IV, $15.54/hr

Downing, Robert, resident physician-1st yr, $49,025
Downing, Stuart McKinley, temporary crafts service, $7.50/hr
Downs Espinoza, Stacy Lynn, strat comm associate II, $53,523
Downs, Andrew, high school student, $9.86/hr
Downs, Craig, prof, ast clincl dept, $201,433
Downs, Harry W, professor, $118,295
Downs, John Eric, radiologic techl, $24.15/hr
Downs, Julie Ann, instructor, adjunct, $9,000
Downs, Robert Carl, professor, $132,100
Doyle-Wright, Aaric Marquise, intern, $8.50/hr
Doyle, Afton Nicole, care team assoc-clinical, $11.10/hr
Doyle, James Francis, instructor, adjunct, $14,400
Doyle, Lauren Michelle, care team assoc-suppt, $10.64/hr
Doyle, Meredith Paige, ast coach, $45,000
Doyle, Suzanne A, instructor, adjunct, $10,800
Doyon, Melinda Sue, user interfce designer-speclst, $46,500
Drage, Joshua John, event assistant I, $8.50/hr
Dragich, Martha, professor, $145,371
Drainer, Margaret Dianne, administrative consultant II, $50,000
Draisey, Tyler Colby, event assistant I, $10.00/hr
Drake, Angela Kim, instructor, $40,400
Drake, Jalina Elise, office support assistant III, $13.22/hr
Drake, Joan Morgan, medical base supervisor, $72,993
Drake, Kathleen Elizabeth, student service coor II, $39,600
Drake, Krystal L, prof, ast clincl, $81,200
Drake, Perry Dean, academic dir, $104,037
Draker, Andrew L, sr manager it, $77,532
Drallmeier, James A, prof, curator teach, $164,274
Drane, Edward, csm professional sr, $70,263
Draper, Jack A, prof, asoc, $57,139
Draper, Nancy J, office supervisor, $41,552
Draper, Robert A, emrg med techn paramedic, $19.65/hr
Drbal, Larry Frank, instructor, adjunct, $22,500
Drees, Betty Marie, professor, $310,000
Drennan, Anthony E, user support analyst-speclst, $15.64/hr
Drennan, Kaci Mulvaney, student service coor II, $40,788
Drennan, Rachel M, physical therapist, $56,472
Dresbach, Russell I, research lab supervisor, $53,688
Dresner, Thomas J, safety communications operator, $13.48/hr
Dressel, Kimberly Jo, coor, service, $16.81/hr
Drew Gounev, Andrea, prof, asoc teach, $59,644
Drew, Rozlyn Dee, nurse, or/recovery-ch, $27.05/hr
Drewel, Janice Sue, academic advisor, $38,533
Drewel, Scott Arthur, temporary technical, $10.50/hr
Drewniak, James L, prof, curators, $176,895
Drewry, Katherine Laura, asoc dir program/project ops, $52,000
Dreyfus, Lawrence A, vice chancellor, $201,623
Driemeier, Donald H, emeritus, $3,000
Driever, Steven L, professor, $93,946
Drinkard, Keri Rose, nurse, staff II, $24.63/hr
Driscoll, Denise Duke, instructor, adjunct, $6,276
Driskel Hawxby, Lisa, prgm director, $49,920
Driskill, Karla Kaye, business support specialist II, $17.84/hr
Driskill, Nathan Richard, instructor, adjunct, $10,452
Driver, Laura Elizabeth, prof, ast clincl, $85,000
Driver, Patrick, specialist, $10.00/hr
Drobnis, Erma Z, prof, ast/profl pract, $79,590
Droke, Wilma Lee, program/project supprt coor I, $30,588
Drowne, Kathleen M, prof, asoc, $84,203
Drtina, Amy Smith, commercial talent, $20.00/hr
Drtina, Jon A, prof, asoc teach, $57,869
Druce, Robert L, prof, resrch, $113,400
Drum, David K, project manager-princpl, $88,199
Drury, A Cooper, professor, $108,665
Drury, Julie Lynne, student service coor sr, $46,640
Dryer, Kaitlyn Ruth, educational pgm coor III, $48,000
Drymalski, Amanda Suzanne, pharmacist II, $60.00/hr
Drymalski, Mark W, prof, ast clincl dept, $163,710
Dsouza Prabhu, Newton Santosh, prof, asoc, $83,769
DSouza, Irene Jane, lecturer, $28,431
Du, Wei, support systems admin-expert, $62,088
Du, Xiaoping, professor, $103,991
Dua, Rohit, prof, ast teach, $69,302
Duan, Dongsheng, professor, $198,135
Duan, Kaixuan, fellow, post doctoral, $36,225
Duan, Lian, prof, ast, $80,388
Duan, Ye, prof, asoc, $116,494
Dubin, Jonathan R, adjunct, $15,000
Dubois, Kay Roberta, lecturer, $21,210

DuBois, Melissa Faye, educational pgm associate I, $14.51/hr
Dubois, Robert D, professor, $96,328
Dubose, Nadie Antranette, ast dir student support svcs, $52,920
Duchaine, Chandler Marie, tutor, $9.00/hr
Ducharme, Kristen M, resp therapist reg, $22.84/hr
Duchmann, Kristin Lorena, nurse, staff II, $23.79/hr
Duck, Scott A, maintenance supervisor, $57,288
Duckworth, Jessica Lynne, research/lab technician sr, $12.98/hr
Duckworth, Justin C, nurse, staff II, $22.56/hr
Duckworth, Linda M, medical coding spclst, $19.83/hr
Duckworth, Rylee S, nurse, staff prn, $26.00/hr
Duckworth, Suzanne, nurse, staff II, $28.82/hr
Dude, Kim, asoc dir student support svcs, $79,133
Dudek, Edward Frank, nurse, staff II rnwp, $32.74/hr
Dudenhoeffer, Christopher James, research specialist I, $41,858
Dudenhoeffer, Patricia G, security analyst-expert, $69,208
Duderija, Jasmina, nurse, staff II, $20.95/hr
Dudgeon, Wesley Kennon, custodian, $10.39/hr
Dudley, Beth A, prof, ast teach, $77,197
Dudley, Brenda K, mgr II business admin, $66,632
Dudley, Robert Martin, event assistant I, $7.50/hr
Dudziak, Douglas Andrew, custodian, $12.94/hr
Duever, Valerie R, business ops associate I, $35,346
Duewell, Mark E, geo info system specialist sr, $64,574
Duewell, Timothy J, system administrator-speclst, $52,020
Duff, DeAnna Nichelle, patient svc rep, $14.16/hr
Duff, Sara Elizabeth, stage services assistant sr, $16.00/hr
Duffey, Suellynn Kay, prof, asoc, $69,496
Duffy, Kathleen Landie, student service coor II, $40,788
Duffy, Margaret E, professor, $116,500
Duffy, Mary Pat, resrch asoc, $20,600
Duffy, Meg Shanon, office support assistant IV, $13.92/hr
Duffy, Robert, dir II advancement, $80,730
Dufresne, Jean Marie-Wigton, lecturer, $32,480
Dugan, Mary C, prof, ast resrch, $73,693
Dugan, Thomas G, account manager, $79,599
Dugger, Ellen L, teaching ast, $13.00/hr
Duhadway, Meghan R, instructor, clncl, $90,000
Duitsman, Pamela Kay, nutrition spclst, $58,961
Duke, James Charles Jr, instructor, adjunct, $8,946
Duke, Aaron C, internet administrator-speclst, $18.27/hr
Duke, Linda Sue, instructor, adjunct, $5,400
Duke, Rachelle Marie, executive assistant, $21.92/hr
Dulle, Michael, event assistant I, $10.00/hr
Dullovi, Emrush, custodian, $13.23/hr
Dullovi, Hasim, custodian, $13.23/hr
Dumas, Andrew Glynn, temporary technical, $15.00/hr
Dumlao, Perseveranda L, nurse, or/recovery-ch, $30.33/hr
Dumond, Lynda A, educational pgm associate I, $14.29/hr
DuMont, JoAnne, instructor, adjunct, $12,552
Dunavant, Jill Kathryn, nurse, staff II, $34.18/hr
Dunaway, Amy Marie, program/project supprt coor I, $46,079
Dunbar Sr, James, custodian, $12.72/hr
Dunbar, Andrea Marie, office support assistant IV, $19.85/hr
Dunbar, Burton, professor, $103,351
Dunbar, Carrie Lee, office support assistant IV, $13.37/hr
Duncan, Adam C, instructor, extns, $49,655
Duncan, Carrie E, prof, ast, $62,226
Duncan, Charles James, facilities supervisor, $51,438
Duncan, Diana Rovena, temporary technical, $8.10/hr
Duncan, Khesha R, program/project supprt coor I, $40,630
Duncan, Kristin Lee, resident physician-2nd yr, $50,810
Duncan, Lori Michelle, business support specialist II, $15.19/hr
Duncan, Mary Virginia, lecturer, $41,209
Duncan, Rochelle L, business ops associate II, $52,527
Duncan, Scott George, audiovisual designer-speclst, $26.93/hr
Duncan, Tina Lynn, custodian, $10.94/hr
Duncan, Tracy G, business tech analyst-expert, $57,568
Duncan, Vernon M, mts/pipefitter, $21.05/hr
Dundulis, Jason A, resident physician-6th yr, $58,200
Dungan, Financy Leo, nurse, staff now III, $30.00/hr
Dunham, Mary Smith, instructor, adjunct, $18,000
Dunham, Theresa J, nurse, staff II rnwp, $34.18/hr
Dunivan, Deborah Elaine, instructor, clncl, $30,750
Dunkle, Ronald E, csm professional II, $65,664
Dunkley, Daive Anthony, prof, ast, $61,425
Dunlap Lehtila, Aimee Sue, prof, ast, $70,500
Dunlap, Phillip Andrew, lecturer, $9,000
Dunlap, Shara M, prof, asoc clncl, $93,761

Dunn, James E Jr, food svc wrkr IV, $14.77/hr
Dunn, Kenneth R Jr, db programmer analyst-princpl, $81,588
Dunn, Roger Leo Jr, bts carpenter, $20.23/hr
Dunn Norman, Shari, prof, asoc, $107,576
Dunn-Morton, Julie Anita, manuscript specialist sr, $61,106
Dunn, Andrew Joseph, patient svc rep, $11.28/hr
Dunn, Catherine M, physician, $135.00/hr
Dunn, David John, extension asoc, $53,025
Dunn, Edward J, csm professional II, $40,586
Dunn, Holly Ann, coor, care, $62,630
Dunn, Jerry, prof, asoc clncl, $74,736
Dunn, Kathy Ann, pat acct rep, $14.95/hr
Dunn, Lora L, nurse, licensed prac, $15.51/hr
Dunn, Marilee, speech/lang pathologist, $35.00/hr
Dunn, Michael Wayne, dir I, broadcast operations, $105,379
Dunn, Peggy Jo, instructor, adjunct, $3,000
Dunn, Sara D, office support associate, $18.79/hr
Dunnaway, Shawna R, occl therapy clncl spclst, $65,863
Dunne, Mary Christine, nurse, staff II, $22.24/hr
Dunning, Charles, rec/athletic assistant sr, $10.25/hr
Dunning, Jan Kittredge, patient svc rep, $13.55/hr
Dunnuck, Hope Diane, office support assistant IV, $15.90/hr
Dunscombe, Linda H, nurse, staff II, $25.71/hr
Dunseith, Theodore D, emrg med techn paramedic, $18.90/hr
Dunsmore, Margaret Ellen, med techl reg, $21.00/hr
Dunwoody, Kathryn Jane, recreation spclst, therapu, $38,076
Duong, Jane, resident physician-1st yr, $50,825
DuPree, Sandra Marie, enrollment advisor sr, $16.54/hr
Dupuis, Terrence E, media production director I, $66,122
Dupureur, Cynthia M, professor, $75,241
Durairaj, Anita, fellow, post doctoral, $46,350
Duran Severino, Kelvin Santiago, food svc wrkr I, $10.53/hr
Duran, Carrie Lynne, pharmacist, $95,587
Duran, Christine Lea Nichols, office support asst IV, $13.89/hr
Duran, Joel A, food svc wrkr I, $9.60/hr
Durante, Kelly Joy Peyton, resrch asoc, $66,011
Durante, William, professor, $161,479
Durbak, Amanda Rita, fellow, post doctoral, $42,993
Durbin, Brooke Michelle, programmer analyst-expert, $55,200
Durbin, Robin Marie, office support assistant I, $12.73/hr
Durbin, Susan D, event assistant I, $21.18/hr
Durden, Jamesia, resident physician-1st yr, $50,825
Durden, Terkrisha Neomia, temporary technical, $10.85/hr
Durdina, Lukas, scholar, visiting, $11.31/hr
Durdle, Erika Leigh, pat care techn, $11.00/hr
Durdle, Leigh Ann, director it, $114,334
Durham, Harris E Jr, veterinary technician sr, $22.14/hr
Durham, Amanda Michelle, nurse, staff I, $19.00/hr
Durham, John Samuel, pharmacist, $112,937
Durham, Rhonda L, project manager-expert, $61,810
Durham, Robert S, mts/electrician lead, $26.61/hr
Durham, Roxann J, instructor, adjunct, $24,677
Durham, Sarah Marie, pharmacist, $110,943
Durham, Zachary Louis, research specialist I, $14.96/hr
Durig, James R, prof, curators, $158,314
Durk, Alaina R, nurse clinician, $62,498
Durlam, Kim Ellen, construction manager II, $70,313
Durnin, Dina Marie Basta, instructor, adjunct, $4,706
Duron, Kelly Marie, adjunct, $9,000
Durrwachter, Weston Thomas, tutor, $9.00/hr
Dusenberg, Christopher Sean, temporary technical, $20.00/hr
Dusevich, Vladimir M, resrch ast, $68,069
Dussel, Phyllis K, business support specialist sr, $25.60/hr
Dutcher, Catherine A, instructor, adjunct, $14,118
Dutcher, Marcia Veronica, resrch ast sr, $36,400
Dutt, Somosree, db administrator-speclst, $53,000
Duval, Gordon W Jr, resident physician-1st yr, $50,219
Duvaleus, Ashley Marie, nurse, staff prn, $26.00/hr
Duvall, Amalie Ann, business support specialist II, $19.89/hr
Dvorak, Aiman A, fellow, teaching, $28,000
Dvorani, Shpend, custodian, $12.72/hr
Dwiggins, Caleb R, programmer analyst-speclst, $48,960
Dwiggins, Kathryne J, lecturer, $41,200
Dwight, Mary Phyl, prof, ast clncl, $48,289
Dwilewicz, Roman, professor, $42,132
Dwyer, Cynthia Dianne, instructor, adjunct, $4,200
Dwyer, Jaclyn J, academic advisor, $35,000
Dwyer, John Patrick, instructor, $12,000
Dwyer, Timothy Alan, business tech analyst-speclst, $50,553

Dye-Fetrow, Alissa Rose, human resources consultnt sr, $66,814
Dye, Dustin K, enrollment advisor sr, $16.54/hr
Dye, Jan Susan, system administrator-expert, $69,707
Dye, Joseph Sonny, custodian, bldg maint, $11.76/hr
Dyer Chenoweth, Diane Lynn, prof, ast clincl, $85,000
Dyer, Arthur H, chaplain, $55,058
Dyer, Carla Alexander, prof, asoc clincl dept, $190,852
Dyer, Darla Dawn, business support specialist II, $17.16/hr
Dyer, Jacqueline Goodwin, tutor, $25.25/hr
Dyer, John, prof, ast teach, $55,246
Dyer, Jonathan Alden, prof, asoc clincl dept, $193,357
Dyer, Justin B, prof, asoc, $91,978
Dyer, Linda Kay, office support assistant II, $11.66/hr
Dyer, Susan Renee, nurse, licensed prac, $20.68/hr
Dykas, Felicity A, librarian IV, $68,634
Dyke II, Peter C, prof, ast clincl dept, $234,291
Dykes, James, dental technician sr, $19.81/hr
Dykes, Shelly Ann, central sterile assistant, $10.51/hr
Dykhouse, Vance J, prof, ast adjunct, $125.00/hr
Dyle, Rufus, fin and acctg analyst sr, $50,925
Dysart, Christopher, nurse anesthetist, $95.00/hr
Dysart, Janice Louise, librarian III, $58,269
Dysvick, Ronald, instructor, adjunct, $72,000
Dziadek, Olivia L, resident physician-3rd yr, $52,470
Dzunu, Edem Samuel Kwame, instructor, adjunct, $18,000
Eaden, Shaun Mikiel, db programmer analyst-specist, $45,920
Eades, Megan Mia, nurse, staff II, $20.95/hr
Eads, Max Alan, head coach, $67,680
Eads, Stephanie Nicole, nurse, staff II, $21.60/hr
Eady, Cornelius Robert, professor, $135,067
Eagan, Emilie Michel, safety monitor, $9.27/hr
Eagen, Hannah Marie, radiologic techl, $20.12/hr
Eagen, Mary K, nurse, staff II, $33.59/hr
Eager, Loubna Bekkali, grader, $15.00/hr
Eagle, Doris Faye, executive assistant, $18.71/hr
Eaker, Alyssa Marie, care team assoc-clinical, $12.08/hr
Eakins, Roger Lee, temporary professional, $29.52/hr
Earhart, Melanie L, interior designer, $49,716
Earickson, Renee Lynn, nurse, staff II, $23.76/hr
Earl, Dedra S, business support specialist sr, $26.35/hr
Earl, Joshua Joseph, resident physician-1st yr, $50,219
Earl, Sara K, office support assistant IV, $14.00/hr
Earla, Ravinder, resrch asoc, $46,836
Earle, James A, head coach, $7,212
Earleywine, Ehren Larry, head coach, $178,000
Earleywine, Larry Bruce, event assistant I, $20.00/hr
Earll, Sarah Annette, lecturer sr, $18,000
Early, Christine Marie, nurse, staff II, $34.18/hr
Early, David James Judson, bts painter, $21.23/hr
Early, Tina M, office support assistant II, $12.26/hr
Early, Zac James, instructional designer-expert, $58,000
Earlywine, Daniel Thomas, research specialist I, $39,500
Earnest, Brad Kent, head therapist cert, $83,538
Earnest, Kimberly Michelle, prgm mgr I, studnt supprt svcs, $55,418
Earnest, Kristen Michelle, nurse, staff II, $24.37/hr
Earney II, Billy C, programmer analyst-specist, $61,868
Earney, Kim Gibson, business support specialist II, $20.80/hr
Easley, Thomas N Jr, bts carpenter, $20.23/hr
Easley, Amy June, nurse, staff II rnwp, $21.69/hr
Easley, Barbara A, instructor, adjunct, $6,276
Easley, Samuel T, police officer, $19.95/hr
Easley, Terry Lynn, project manager-entry, $39,603
East, Kristopher S, office support assistant II, $12.13/hr
Easter, Matthew Adam, instructor, adjunct, $12,339
Easterling, Justin L, ast coach, $41,000
Eastin, L Clint, ast mgr hospitality services, $43,141
Eastling-Stewart, Zakia Nyila, mgr student support svcs, $28,500
Eastman-Mueller, Heather Paige, hlth educator, $52,616
Eastman, Amanda Zoe, radiologic techl, $18.59/hr
Eastman, Kristin Lambert, tutor, $15.00/hr
Easton, Robert W Jr, mech trades spclst (mts), $22.42/hr
Easton, Aaron W, chemist I, $39,317
Easton, Tina Marie, instructor, adjunct, $7,059
Eatherton, Nathan S, assoc director it, $103,588
Eatinger-Sprague, Jennifer Margaret, nurse, staff II rnwp, $20.14/hr
Eaton, James Howard Jr, powr plnt maint spclst II, $23.75/hr
Eaton, Lucretia Ann, business support specialist II, $17.17/hr
Eaton, Michael E, pharmacist II, $119,962
Eaton, Miriam D, patient svc rep, $14.88/hr

Eaton, Peter James, prof, asoc, $84,501
Eaton, Stephanie Ann, asoc dir business admin, $55,184
Eaves, Breezie Renee, service rep III, $10.64/hr
Ebarb, Kristopher Jason, fellow, post doctoral, $40,000
Ebben, Jane M, veterinary technician sr, $22.37/hr
Ebeling, Joseph James, pharmacy tech, $10.85/hr
Eber, Carl T, resp therapy techn/icu cert, $21.23/hr
Eberhart, Dorthy J, office support assistant III, $16.27/hr
Eberhart, James Louis, event assistant I, $7.50/hr
Ebers, Kevin M, instructor, adjunct, $8,760
Ebersol, Kimberly L, nurse practitioner, $84,052
Ebersold, Erika Angelise, patient svc rep, $11.01/hr
Ebersole, Gary L, professor, $96,592
Ebert, Jared Edwin, resident physician-1st yr, $50,219
Eberwein, Mary, office support assistant IV, $14.39/hr
Ebest, Sally Barr, professor, $68,767
Eby, Tim John, dir I, strat communications, $140,000
Echelmeyer, David W, physical therapist, $55,965
Echols, Angel Deon, tutor, $13.00/hr
Eck II, John Joseph, prof, ast teach, $47,920
Eckelkamp, Elizabeth, dean, asoc, $90,412
Eckerle, Jason Eugene, grounds keeper II, $15.09/hr
Eckert, Andreas, prof, ast, $96,800
Eckert, Anne Marie, office support assistant IV, $13.73/hr
Eckert, Anthony D, system administrator-expert, $80,003
Eckert, Rophel, rec/athletic specialist sr, $25.00/hr
Eckes, Hannah Darlene, enrollment advisor sr, $16.54/hr
Eckhardt, William G, prof, teach, $87,250
Eckstrom, Kevin R, dir I, strat communications, $96,275
Economon, Kristen Marie, prof, ast teach, $62,500
Edara, Praveen Kumar, prof, asoc, $101,861
Eddings, Denise, office support assistant IV, $17.79/hr
Eddings, Timothy C, security officer, $10.71/hr
Eddleman, Amanda Dawn, nurse, staff I, $19.00/hr
Eddy, Holly Lynn, activity aide, $13.61/hr
Eddy, Janet Marie, mental health tech, $12.90/hr
Edelen, Ashley Nicole, nurse, staff II, $20.54/hr
Eden, David W, pharmacist III, $124,983
Edgar, Amanda Faith, temporary technical, $8.57/hr
Edgar, Camilla S, cook mrc, $10.76/hr
Edgar, John E, technology resource coor, $60,454
Edgar, Judy Ann, office support assistant III, $12.25/hr
Edgerton, Samantha, office support assistant III, $11.98/hr
Edholm, Christina Lee, office support asst IV, $14.11/hr.11/hr
Edidin, Dan S, professor, $104,991
Edie, Michelle Dawn, hospital lab tech, $15.73/hr
Edison, Karen, prof, clinical dept, $405,475
Edmonds, Robert James, resident physician-2nd yr, $50,810
Edmondson, Cynthia D, office support assistant IV, $17.06/hr
Edmunds, Mackinsey Lee, care team assoc-clinical, $12.55/hr
Edmundson, Rebecca Ann, program/project supprt coor sr, $59,774
Edris, Jerry Ronald, instructor, adjunct, $9,000
Edwards-Ellsworth, Pat, instructor, adjunct, $1,200
Edwards, Amber D, program/project supprt coor I, $33,436
Edwards, Anthony T, instructor, adjunct, $28,500
Edwards, April A, office support assistant III, $15.71/hr
Edwards, Ashley Rhiannon, resp therapist reg, $22.65/hr
Edwards, Charles F, prof, ast clincl dept, $200,000
Edwards, Colby Frank, farm wrkr II, $13.59/hr
Edwards, Gary Christophe, cook, $12.20/hr
Edwards, Jill, academic advisor, $42,066
Edwards, Josie Michele, office supervisor, $45,175
Edwards, Katherine Francis, prof, ast clincl dept, $131,811
Edwards, Kathleen A, coor quality improvement, $51,750
Edwards, Kelly, editor II, $40,986
Edwards, Kimberly Jean, student service coor I, $40,933
Edwards, Linda Kay, executive assistant, $19.31/hr
Edwards, Mark Charles, prof, ast adjunct, $125.00/hr
Edwards, Mary Katherine, media production director II, $56,389
Edwards, Matthew Janes, prof, ast, $51,000
Edwards, Michael A, program/project supprt coor I, $43,628
Edwards, Paula S, nurse manager, $96,173
Edwards, Rachel Alice, resrch ast, $32,320
Edwards, Rebecca Sue, supv, clinical-rehab svcs, $72,450
Edwards, Robert Russell, prof, clincl, $95,790
Edwards, Tanner Archie, recruiter, hlth care, $51,131
Edwards, Tracie L, instructor, adjunct, $31,500
Edwards, Vicki Kay, business support specialist II, $23.93/hr
Edwards, Wesley Robert, mechl plant spclst, $18.82/hr

Efker, Tandi E, nurse, staff I, $19.00/hr
Egan, Kimberly Diane, nurse, staff now plus, $30.00/hr
Egbert Nichols, Michele Ann, coor, reimbursement, $47,826
Egbert, Teresa Elizabeth, office supervisor, $43,216
Ege, Edward Joseph, pharmacist III, $124,935
Ege, Joseph Wilber, seasonal farm ast, $8.93/hr
Ege, Patrick Joseph, pharmacy tech, $11.65/hr
Egekeze, Nkemakolam Chukuma, resrch ast, $30,000
Egen, Tina Evon, research specialist sr, $40,400
Eggeman, Paul K, mgr research activities, $55,511
Eggering, Tom W, mechl plant spclst, $19.64/hr
Eggers, John P, resident physician-4th yr, $54,425
Eggerstedt, Amanda Nicole, nurse, staff I, rnwp, $19.00/hr
Eggert, Lori Suzanne, prof, asoc, $81,600
Eggleston, Patricia M, office support assistant III, $15.52/hr
Eggleston, Timothy Michael, student recruitment spclst, $21.17/hr
Egley, Brittany Ann, nurse, staff II, $22.00/hr
Ehlers, Leta Jean, pharmacist III, $120,000
Ehlert, Karen Kealoha, office support assistant sr, $22.17/hr
Ehlert, Mark, prof, asoc resrch, $86,769
Ehmke, Melissa Lynn, prof, ast teach, $77,611
Ehrhard, Peter John, communications coordinator sr, $16.87/hr
Ehrhardt, Mary Erica, event assistant I, $15.00/hr
Ehteshami Rad, Arash, resident physician-2nd yr, $52,007
Eiberger, Rachel Marie, office support assistant III, $17.85/hr
Eich, Florian Gregor, fellow, post doctoral, $42,000
Eichelberger, Bernard Hoke, bts carpenter, $21.71/hr
Eichelberger, Debra, mgr clinical trials, $75,655
Eichelberger, Marvin Morris, sterile processing tech, $18.31/hr
Eichen, Peggy A, research specialist sr, $39,600
Eichenberger, Amy Leann, nurse, staff II rnwp, $25.23/hr
Eichhorn, Victoria Lynne, office supervisor, $54,576
Eick, J David, prof, adjunct, $7,340
Eickenhorst, Danielle Rhea, lecturer, $12,000
Eickhoff, Natalie, event assistant I, $7.50/hr
Eickhorst, Nina C, office support assistant IV, $14.25/hr
Eide, Benjamin Edward, waiter/waitress, $10.19/hr
Eidson II, David L, sftware supprt analyst-expert, $53,040
Eidson, Darren Scott, event assistant I, $8.50/hr
Eigel, Alice Ann, nurse, staff II, $32.83/hr
Eigsti, Jennifer L, ast dir business admin, $65,300
Eiken, Beth T, office support associate, $22.14/hr
Eiken, Douglas Kent, instructor, adjunct, $13,200
Eiler, Catherine Sue, prof, ast adjunct, $8,004
Eimers, Lisa Cole, dir II advancement, $73,182
Eimers, Mardy T, v provost, $140,977
Einsiedel, Julie A, reimbursement ast-cert, $18.93/hr
Einsiedel, Maurissa Nichol, emergency services rep, $13.25/hr
Eiring, Katherine Ardythe, mental health tech trainee, $9.27/hr
Eisele, Robert J, surgical technl trainee, $14.29/hr
Eisenbarth, Timothy P, communications assistant sr, $14.57/hr
Eisenberg, Lawrence A, ast vice chancellor, $125,000
Eisentrager, Peter E, asoc dir business admin, $66,981
Eisentrager, Shana Kathleen, business support spclst II, $20.43/hr
Eisleben, Lauren Elizabeth, instructor, adjunct, $27,000
Eissinger, Sandra Paige, media producer I, $13.76/hr
Eklund, Lana Ruth, media producer I, $15.00/hr
Ekstam, Fred, prof, ast teach, $41,212
El Boher, Arie, dir I, research ops and plng, $102,526
El Gizawy, Ahmed S, professor, $101,267
El Kady, Rasha Mahmoud Ibrahim, res physician-3rd yr, $53,763
El-Halawany, Hani N, resident physician-3rd yr, $52,470
El-Midany, Ayman Abdel-Hamid, prof, asoc teach, $85,000
Elam, Angela C, prof, ast teach, $39,141
Elam, Karissa Marie, patient svc rep, $12.75/hr
Elder, Anthony W, system administrator-spclst, $46,284
Elder, Brandon Aaron, resident physician-1st yr, $49,025
Elder, James E, food svc wrkr III, $11.24/hr
Elder, Keshia Sims, prof, asoc clincl, $99,849
Elder, Melanie J, patient svc rep, $11.79/hr
Elderbrook, Molly Jeanne, research/lab technician, $10.24/hr
Elderbrook, Paula K, pat acct rep, $15.41/hr
Eldridge, Jerri Rae, library info specialist sr, $14.95/hr
Eldridge, Keith A, programmer analyst-expert, $65,925
Elfrink, Cory J, program/project supprt coor I, $40,000
ElGawady, Mohamed Abdelmonem, prof, asoc, $87,646
Elgin, Richard L, prof, ast adjunct, $18,587
Elgin, Shannon C, temporary clerical, $15.00/hr
Elias, Martille Rene, prof, asoc adjunct, $9,519

Elias, Rebecca Sue, office supervisor, $36,496
Elkady, Essam Nazar, physician, $212,023
Elkhananany, Ahmed Muhammad Ezaj, res physician-2nd yr, $50,810
Elking, Chalyn, office support assistant IV, $14.25/hr
Elkins, Diana Sue, lab techn, persl svc-clin lab, $15.60/hr
Ell, Matthew R, reactor operator sr, $29.36/hr
Ell, Paul R, program/project supprt coor II, $40,000
Ell, Wendy Shay, occl therapist, $35.00/hr
Ellebracht, Ann K, coor graphic svcs, $51,225
Ellebracht, Mary E, nurse, licensed prac, $19.37/hr
Ellebracht, Rita A, db programmer analyst-princpl, $76,090
Ellebracht, Tammy Raye, executive assistant, $22.02/hr
Elledge, Dean A, prof, asoc adjunct, $10.00/hr
Elledge, Sally A, prof, ast clincl, $64,000
Eller, Kristen Marie, nurse, staff II, $22.22/hr
Ellerbusch, Lisabeth, office support assistant III, $16.60/hr
Ellerman, Michael J Sr, mech, small engine, $19.90/hr
Ellerman, Michael John, temporary clerical, $10.00/hr
Ellersieck, Mark Robert, prof, resrch, $48,037
Elli, Andrew J, emrg med techn paramedic, $16.28/hr
Ellifrit, Paul B, bts carpenter, $21.71/hr
Ellinger, Jill R, instructor, adjunct, $10,800
Ellinghausen, Laurie Marie, prof, asoc, $60,333
Ellingsworth, Chase Richard, resident physician-1st yr, $50,219
Ellington, Erin Elizabeth, prof, ast clincl, $73,288
Ellington, Vanessa Jo, cook, $13.21/hr
Elliot, Lyn E, prof, asoc, $58,140
Elliott-Engel, Jeremy J, 4-h spclst, $46,460
Elliott-Vowiell, LaRae Gena, office support asst IV, $18.12/hr
Elliott, Alexandra Alida, fellow, post doctoral, $37,100
Elliott, Brandie Ann, executive assistant sr, $51,250
Elliott, Carol Ann, nurse, staff II, $25.24/hr
Elliott, Cheryl Ann, office support assistant IV, $18.03/hr
Elliott, Christopher Thomas, med techl reg, $22.23/hr
Elliott, David L, grader, $100.00/hr
Elliott, Denise Catherine, office support assistant IV, $14.85/hr
Elliott, Diane E, central sterile assistant, $17.21/hr
Elliott, Grant P, prof, ast, $68,347
Elliott, Jacquelyn D, specialist, $86,700
Elliott, Jason, dir II advancement, $80,000
Elliott, Jason Christopher, emrg med techn paramedic, $16.15/hr
Elliott, Kayla Breann, radiologic techl, $18.23/hr
Elliott, Lee Farrar, research specialist sr, $56,707
Elliott, Linda M, patient svc rep, $13.96/hr
Elliott, Lisa Michelle, support systems admin-expert, $56,106
Elliott, Marie Elizabeth, animal techn, ast lab, $13.89/hr
Elliott, Marsha Frese, head coach, $114,635
Elliott, Melissa J, health records techn I, $11.72/hr
Elliott, Michael Lee, system administrator-spclst, $54,000
Elliott, Michael T, prof, asoc, $171,536
Elliott, Nancy L, office support assistant II, $14.97/hr
Elliott, Richard James, maint svc attd, $17.54/hr
Elliott, Steven Jeffrey, sr manager it, $91,505
Elliott, Susan G, librarian I, $41,511
Elliott, Tammy Carol, care team assoc-clinical, $14.17/hr
Elliott, Tyra Wade, csm associate sr, $30.28/hr
Elliott, Yvonne, lecturer, $15,000
Ellis-Claypool, Janis Kathleen, prof, ast teach, $66,667
Ellis, Charles E, extns professional, asoc, $54,736
Ellis, Jason Scott, prof, ast resrch, $42,000
Ellis, Jeffrey B, support systems admin-spclst, $46,850
Ellis, Krissy Anne, coor athletic operations, $46,000
Ellis, Loquita Kay, office support assistant IV, $13.24/hr
Ellis, Mark W, executive assistant, $18.49/hr
Ellis, Mary Louise, cook, $12.95/hr
Ellis, Sarah Lynn, human resources specialist III, $40,788
Ellison, Brian Douglas, media producer II, $14.95/hr
Ellison, Gordon O, research engineering tech I, $18.18/hr
Ellsmore, Kimberly N, med techl reg, $27.44/hr
Ellsworth, Harold S Jr, resident physician-2nd yr, $50,810
Ellsworth, Kevin Scott, bts mason/tuckptr, $22.14/hr
Elman, Julie Passanante, prof, ast, $65,290
Elmestad, Alex Conrad, prof, ast adjunct, $9,000
Elmore, A Curt, professor, $100,000
Elmore, Andrew L, advancement officer, $50,023
Elmore, Andrew S, fin and acctg analyst sr, $55,345
Elmore, Cecilia Ann, dir I, student support svcs, $67,200
Elmore, Dennis C, mgr env health and safety, $85,000
Elmore, Patrick Harrison, student recruitment spclst, $20.29/hr

Elrod, Cassandra Carlene, prof, asoc, $117,780
Elsberry, David Lynn, nurse, staff II, $34.18/hr
Elsberry, Kristin Renee, nurse, staff II, $20.84/hr
Elsherbiny, Hisham, resident physician-1st yr, $49,025
Elsik, Christine G, prof, asoc, $137,800
Elson, Billy J, security officer, $13.68/hr
Elswick, Beth L, prof, ast teach, $38,207
Elswick, James T, mgr II student support svcs, $59,160
Elwood, Lisa K, business support specialist II, $15.25/hr
Ely, Katie A, ast coach, $52,000
Emanuel, Gregory R Jr, research lab manager, $65,346
Emanuel, Larita Michelle, business support spclst sr, $24.10/hr
Embree, Alexandra Withrow, student service coor I, $42,757
Embree, Amanda Lee, hospital lab tech, $12.46/hr
Embree, Angela Nacole, nurse advisor, telephone, $28.61/hr
Embree, Mary F, research specialist sr, $47,555
Embrey, Danny L, instructor, adjunct, $11,000
Embry, Kelli K, csm operations supervisor, $48,451
Emerich, David William, professor, $119,961
Emerich, Nila Jane, office support assistant III, $16.72/hr
Emerson, Abigail Kilpatric, prof, ast clincl dept, $165,463
Emerson, Andy Kinney, office support associate, $21.92/hr
Emerson, Eric Lynn, custodian, $12.90/hr
Emerson, Hugh Sprague, environmental health prof sr, $47,346
Emerson, Jane Anne, prof, asoc clincl dept, $194,037
Emerson, Virginia Michelle, office support assistant III, $12.01/hr
Emery, Debra Walker, sr dir program/project ops, $70,000
Emery, Janice Diane, 4-h spclst, $41,000
Emmanouilidis, Panagiotis, prof, ast clincl, $93,000
Emring, Angela R, mgr I, business admin, $54,956
Emter, Craig Allen, prof, ast, $95,139
Enciso, Angel Jaime Sison, resident physician-2nd yr, $52,007
Endaya, Yolanda Paranal, instructor, clincl, $23,040
Enderle, Logan, event assistant I, $8.50/hr
Endersby, James W, prof, asoc, $79,558
Endicott, Renee D, instructor, clincl, $72,000
Endres, Tammy, reimbursement ast-cert, $20.01/hr
Endsley, Eric Allen, driver, $13.19/hr
Endsley, Jennifer Joshalynne, care team assoc-suppt, $12.14/hr
Endsley, Kayla Lin, nurse, licensed prac, $16.69/hr
Eng, Li-Li, prof, asoc, $136,388
Engel, Elizabeth E, manuscript specialist sr, $39,600
Engel, Thomas G, prof, asoc, $100,030
Engelhardt, Christopher R, fellow, post doctoral, $37,740
Engelman, Peter C, adjunct, $15,000
Engelstein, Stefani, prof, asoc, $59,964
England-Biggs, Laura Elizabeth, lecturer, $100.00/hr
England, Danny J, research specialist sr, $54,090
England, Donald R, ast mgr plant engrg-h, $83,028
England, Jackie Earl, support systems admin-spcclst, $50,906
England, Kelli Ann, office support assistant IV, $13.82/hr
England, Kenneth D, support systems admin-expert, $58,393
Englander, Janice Lynn, pharmacist II, $128,444
Engle, Ellen A, office support assistant III, $15.13/hr
Engle, Judith Renee, human resources specialist I, $17.98/hr
Engle, Steven Craig, instructor, adjunct, $27,000
Englehart, Andrea Lynn, nurse, licensed prac, $15.96/hr
Englert, Terry Lynn, patient svc rep, $14.88/hr
English, Carla Renae, custodian, $12.94/hr
English, D Nicole, instructor, adjunct, $19,200
English, David M, professor, $185,218
English, James T, professor, $123,243
English, James Terrell, anesthesia techn, $14.50/hr
English, Karen Farrar, dir I, advancement, $63,354
English, Kimberly Kay, patient svc rep, $15.09/hr
English, Noel A, compliance manager, $46,594
English, Ronald Wayne, event assistant I, $7.55/hr
Engram, Mary Wescoat, human dev spclst, $42,823
Enke, David L, professor, $159,626
Enlow, Michell Ranae, programmer analyst-expert, $59,726
Ennis, Betty Kay, educational prgm coor sr, $57,887
Ennis, Jerry D, agriculture associate II, $15.39/hr
Enoch, Jerol B, student service coor II, $40,333
Enochs, Amanda J, office support assistant II, $14.15/hr
Enochs, Britney Meryl, child dev teacher sr, $25,000
Enright, Jennifer Jolene, telecomm opr-h, $11.01/hr
Enright, Linda Mae, office support assistant IV, $14.14/hr
Enriquez, Jonathan R, adjunct, $15,000
Enriquez, Maithe, prof, asoc, $78,763

Ensign, Susan K, educational pgm coor I, $34,845
Enyard, Harold D, custodian, $12.94/hr
Enyard, Tiffany Dawn, clerk, unit, $11.50/hr
Enyart, Tyrone E, office support assistant IV, $13.72/hr
Enyeart, Carter, professor, $107,371
Enzor, Terrie Robin, pat acct rep, $15.01/hr
Eoff, Heather N, educational pgm associate I, $12.81/hr
Eplee, Matthew C, csm operations supervisor, $54,000
Epperly, Kerri M, nurse, staff II, $34.18/hr
Epperson, Alyssa Ann, psychology techn, $14.54/hr
Epperson, Patricia Kay, nurse, staff prn, $26.00/hr
Epperson, Regan R, nurse, staff II rnwp, $27.95/hr
Epping, Shane Christopher, strat comm associate II, $43,697
Epstein, Joel, prof, asoc resrch, $92,840
Erandio, Jexter Mallare, event assistant I, $7.55/hr
Erb, Laura Jane, prof, asoc resrch, $105,844
Erbschloe, Shirley A, nurse, staff, $28.59/hr
Ercal, Fikret, professor, $123,904
Ercal, Nuran, professor, $149,061
Erdel, Shara Ann, instructor, adjunct, $5,647
Erdelez, Sanda, professor, $94,767
Eren, Metin I, fellow, post doctoral, $40,000
Erhardt, Benjamin F, resident physician-3rd yr, $53,763
Eric, Sibomana, high school student, $9.41/hr
Erickson, Chad Anthony, event assistant I, $8.50/hr
Erickson, Dee Anne Speiser, supv outpatient svcs, $54,633
Erickson, Francilda Ann, lecturer, $18,150
Erickson, Jeffrey P, business support specialist II, $19.37/hr
Erickson, Kelvin Todd, professor, $134,405
Erickson, Rita K, maint svc attd, $17.78/hr
Erickson, Sonja Lucille, resrch anlyst, $43,696
Erickson, Toni L, instructor, adjunct, $125.00/hr
Ericsson, Aaron C, prof, ast resrch, $80,080
Ernst, John P, asoc dir research, $113,124
Ersoy, Ilker, fellow, post doctoral, $40,000
Ertl, Tenise Michelle, licensed practical nurse, $15.06/hr
Ervie, Katherine Gale, prof, ast teach, $145,000
Ervin, Crystal Renee, pat acct rep, $14.95/hr
Ervin, Donna Sue, office support assistant I, $9.89/hr
Ervin, Keona K, prof, ast, $57,134
Ervin, Spencer Allen, food svc wrkr I, $9.98/hr
Erwin, Richard W Jr, fin and acctg manager sr, $87,071
Erwin, Ruth Ann, mgr II business admin, $56,970
Erwin, Zachary L, livestock spclst, $43,275
Erzen, Laura Janell, enrollment advisor, $14.95/hr
Esbensen, Finn Aage, professor, $141,194
Eschenbrenner, Barry, farm manager, $45,000
Eschenroeder, Jackman Christian, lab assistant, $10.25/hr
Escott, Amy Dribin, asoc dir program/project ops, $51,010
Escott, Stephanie L, hris specialist-specialist, $47,196
Esebua, Magda, prof, asoc clincl dept, $200,568
Eshete, Solomon Getahun, custodian, $13.36/hr
Eskew, Linda Joanne, human resources specialist sr, $54,631
Eskridge, Bernard R, prof, asoc clincl dept, $142,644
Espanol, Eloy, office support assistant sr, $17.85/hr
Espenschied, Ricky D, facilities attd, $13.89/hr
Esping, Amy Larissa, custodian, $10.69/hr
Esping, David R, director it, $81,400
Essen, Crystal L, office support assistant III, $12.79/hr
Esser, Anna Marie, temporary technical, $9.80/hr
Esser, Gregory Jason, bts carpenter, $21.71/hr
Essig, Benjaman W, police officer, $19.27/hr
Essing, Anne Kathleen, instructor, adjunct, $13,500
Estes, Brian Kent, sterile processing tech, $16.67/hr
Estes, Kristina S, event assistant sr, $21.91/hr
Estes, Leandre Darrell, food svc wrkr I, $9.60/hr
Estes, Michelle I, custodian, $12.94/hr
Estes, Rhonda Jean, mental health tech, $13.00/hr
Estes, Sarah Elizabeth, educational pgm associate I, $13.30/hr
Estes, Shane Demarco, cook, $12.64/hr
Estienne, Robert Mark, intern, $18,000
Estill, Beverly A, med lab techn, $22.39/hr
Eston, Christopher W, emrg med techn, $11.99/hr
Etingov, Igor, fellow, post doctoral, $42,000
Ettling, Jeffery Alan, prof, ast adjunct, $6,000
Eubanks, Alien Odon, food svc wrkr III, $13.21/hr
Eubanks, Cassandra Gwen, temporary technical, $16.00/hr
Eubanks, Gail Lynn, instructor, adjunct, $14,000
Eubanks, Janisha Rashea, patient svc rep, $12.31/hr

Eubanks, Karen K, library information assistant, $12.72/hr
Eugster, Pamela J, csm project manager, $73,607
Eultgen, Amy Kristine, student support specialist II, $15.40/hr
Eultgen, Theresa Kathryn, prog/project supprt coor I, $37,761
Evans Blumer, Melissa, research/lab technician sr, $19.08/hr
Evans, Brian, bts roofer, $21.71/hr
Evans, Brock Steven Fortner, research specialist I, $35,000
Evans, Caleb Thomas, db administrator-expert, $74,220
Evans, Debora L, service rep III, $13.12/hr
Evans, Deborah J, dental ast certd, $14.83/hr
Evans, Diana Marie, pat acct rep, $14.31/hr
Evans, Eric S, dir program/project operations, $77,250
Evans, Gary Lee, radiologic techl, $23.26/hr
Evans, Ian Willey, research/lab technician, $10.24/hr
Evans, Jason Frederick, program/project supprt coor sr, $60,000
Evans, Jennifer Pearline, office support assistant IV, $14.57/hr
Evans, Judson R, mts/machinist, $21.05/hr
Evans, Mary Grace, model, $15.00/hr
Evans, Nickolas C, student service coor II, $49,158
Evans, Rebecca Ellen, office support assistant IV, $17.60/hr
Evans, Sarah Elizabeth, licensed practical nurse, $15.06/hr
Evans, Sean Michael, event assistant I, $8.50/hr
Evans, Sherry L, patient svc rep, $13.55/hr
Evans, Stephen Mark, ast mgr hospitality services, $41,580
Evans, Timothy, prof, asoc, $113,414
Evans, Travis, specialist, $25.00/hr
Evans, Virginia Dee, program/project supprt coor II, $50,136
Evans, Wendelin J, instructor, adjunct, $9,600
Evelev, John O, prof, asoc, $65,813
Eveloff, Vivian L, academic dir, $113,180
Even, Christine Elaine, psychologist, $71,231
Even, Susan E, dir stu hlth cntr, $171,440
Even, Victoria Anne, patient svc rep, $11.07/hr
Even, Yael, professor, $72,611
Evenski, Andrea J, prof, ast clincl dept, $250,000
Everest, Arvind Andrew, network engineer-expert, $56,000
Everett, Case Calvin, resident physician-2nd yr, $50,810
Everett, Christina Angelina, prog/project supprt coor I, $36,050
Everett, Kevin Dale, prof, asoc, $116,415
Everett, Nicole Luanne, office support assistant IV, $16.08/hr
Everett, Thomas A, prof, ast resrch, $65,000
Everett, William A, professor, $79,920
Everhart, Jesse Edward, clerk, diet, $9.50/hr
Evers, Brett Frederick, trades helper, $10.78/hr
Evers, Cathy L, custodian, $12.94/hr
Evers, Jeffrey J, mgr II csm operations, $66,077
Evers, Thomas Frederick, bts carpet installer, $21.71/hr
Eversman, Walter, emeritus, $40,246
Eversmeyer, Lindsay, temporary professional, $22.23/hr
Everson, Kristin M, temporary professional, $25.00/hr
Ewens, Shirley A, temporary crafts service, $12.69/hr
Ewigman, Sara Ann, temporary clerical, $10.85/hr
Ewing, David Eric, resident physician-2nd yr, $52,007
Ewing, Derek D, system support analyst-speclst, $21.75/hr
Ewing, Katie L, temporary professional, $11.30/hr
Ewing, Mitchel Sage, food svc wrkr I, $9.60/hr
Exner, Judy Lynn, safety communications operator, $15.46/hr
Eyberg, Caitlin Ann, instructor, adjunct, $5,400
Eye, Mark A, temporary professional, $45,000
Eyler, Richard T, programmer analyst-princpl, $68,725
Eyssell, Thomas H, professor, $200,629
Ezashi, Toshihiko, prof, asoc resrch, $72,127
Ezell, Charity Catherine, resp therapy techn cert, $21.12/hr
Ezell, John D, professor, $85,574
Ezoulin, Miezan, post doctoral asoc, $36,414
Ezzell, Scott Andrew, academic advisor, $37,179
Faaborg, Janice E, academic advisor, $33,098
Faaborg, John Raynor, professor, $128,005
Faber, Jackie Dee, nurse clinician, $67,518
Faber, John C, network engineer-expert, $58,000
Faber, Shari L, nurse, staff I, $19.00/hr
Facklam, Carol S, student support specialist sr, $21.18/hr
Faddis, Kent W, strat comm associate sr, $60,600
Fadel, Erika Simone, student service coor II, $55,162
Fadel, Paul Joseph, prof, asoc, $148,835
Fadler, Cheryl A, tutor, $10.00/hr
Fadler, Kayci Lee, temporary technical, $10.50/hr
Fagan, Mary Kathleen, prof, ast, $77,562
Fagerlin, Melanie Corine, lab assistant, $10.00/hr

Fahrendorf, Whitney Rae, veterinary technician sr, $15.25/hr
Fahrenholtz, William G, prof, curators, $138,013
Fahrmeier, Lorin Elaine, program/project supprt coor I, $36,647
Fails, Cynthia Lenecia, student service coor sr, $47,430
Fainter, Jennifer Marie, office support assistant IV, $15.15/hr
Fair, Russell Lee, project manager-princpl, $83,000
Fairbanks, Stephen A, instructor, adjunct, $9,000
Fairchild, Mary, instructor, clincl, $15,375
Fairfax, Charles A, programmer analyst-expert, $64,836
Fairley, Connie K, service rep IV, $18.43/hr
Fairley, Joy Pedego, program/project supprt coor I, $52,275
Fairley, Mark S, video comm admin-expert, $69,829
Faisal, Mir Fahad, resident physician-3rd yr, $52,470
Fajen, Aaron, network engineer-entry, $50,000
Fakiri, Maryam Shabaz, tutor, $9.00/hr
Falchi, Laura D, distribution techn-mtls mgmt, $14.74/hr
Falco, Michael Anthony Jr, asoc media producer, $11.53/hr
Falcon, Kathleen Marie, office support assistant IV, $16.85/hr
Fales, Roger C, prof, asoc, $87,336
Fales, William Harold, professor, $120,957
Falk, Patricia Jean, office support assistant IV, $20.74/hr
Fallert, Adam C, db programmer analyst-speclst, $47,914
Falles, Tyrone Lamont, floor care techn, $14.25/hr
Fallon, Rebecca M, academic advisor, $37,000
Falls, Dominique J, clerk, diet, $12.96/hr
Famuliner, Ryan M, prof, ast/profl pract, $53,000
Fan, Jun, prof, asoc, $119,486
Fancher, Richard M, environmental health prof II, $43,578
Fandek, Neal William, strat comm associate II, $46,543
Fang, Zhiwei David, resrch asoc, $53,576
Fann, Michael R, nurse anesthetist, $95.00/hr
Fann, Stephanie Lee, custodian, $11.41/hr
Fannin, David P, db programmer analyst-princpl, $72,605
Fantroy-Ross, Sherry Susan, business support spclst II, $15.52/hr
Fantroy, Jennifer Drake, dir program/project operations, $55,999
Farberman, Susann M, prof, teach, $95,245
Fares, Hala Nabil, office support assistant I, $12.14/hr
Farfan, William Jeffrey, teaching ast, $13.00/hr
Farid, Reza S, prof, asoc clincl dept, $190,603
Farid, Talha Ahmad, resident physician-3rd yr, $52,470
Farina, Anne Shim Jee, instructor, adjunct, $10,500
Faris, Bushra Ali, interpreter, medical, $25.00/hr
Farmer, Ashley Lynne, nurse, staff I, $19.00/hr
Farmer, Gregory, instructor, adjunct, $18,000
Farmer, Janet E, dean, asoc, $179,214
Farmer, John William, resrch scientist/academic sr, $99,329
Farmer, Matthew Cullen, prof, ast, $56,560
Farnejad, Farshad, adjunct, $15,000
Farnsworth, Erica Louise, teaching ast, $11,664
Farr, Emily Catherine, nurse, staff II, $21.69/hr
Farra, Hassan, prof, ast clincl dept, $210,000
Farrah, Shirley J, dean, ast, $101,261
Farrar, Ashley Nicole, nurse, staff II, $22.24/hr
Farrar, Matthew Wayne, police officer, $17.08/hr
Farrar, Patricia Lynn, veterinarian, $99,144
Farrell, Monica L, academic advisor, $48,608
Farrell, Sherry A, library specialist, $51,669
Farrens, Justin Paul, emrg med techn paramedic, $14.99/hr
Farris-Folkerts, Pamela Deanne, teaching ast, $13.00/hr
Farris, Donna J, csm specialist sr, $19.32/hr
Farris, Kerry D, scientist, $63,985
Farris, Steven Todd, sterile processing tech, $17.53/hr
Fasciotti, Mary T, mgr II business admin, $63,156
Fasina, Olufemi Olusogo, fellow, post doctoral, $34,000
Fasken, Brenda, office support assistant III, $13.81/hr
Fasken, Kevin Lee, environmental health prof sr, $48,222
Fast, Katie Marie, resident physician-1st yr, $50,219
Faubion, Kelly Lee, care team assoc-clinical, $14.88/hr
Faucett, Bruce, bts painter, $21.28/hr
Faucett, Danielle Marie, office support assistant IV, $14.70/hr
Faucett, Rhonda Jean, office support assistant III, $13.92/hr
Faulk, Danae Michelle, grader, $100.00/hr
Faup, Kelley A, business support specialist sr, $24.08/hr
Fauske, Julianne Elizabeth, resident physician-2nd yr, $52,007
Fausz, J Frederick, prof, asoc, $83,558
Favaregh, Emily Ladan, resrch ast, $48,451
Favignano, Rodney Jr, sftware supprt analyst-speclst, $40,194
Fay, James D, prof, asoc, $58,940
Fay, Rebecca Ann, educational pgm assistant, $12.25/hr

Fay, William Philip, professor, $301,951
Fay, William Robert, hospital security officer, $13.05/hr
Fayad, Melissa H, library info specialist, $14.24/hr
Fearing, Nicole Marie, prof, ast adjunct, $23,868
Fearn, Sara Rachel, resident physician-3rd yr, $52,470
Feazel, Mark A, stage services assistant sr, $16.00/hr
Fech, Jonathan Alan, coor protocol svcs, $14.09/hr
Fedde, Arianna Michelle, food svc wrkr II, $10.10/hr
Federa, Austin Moran, media producer sr, $35,088
Feeley, Diane J, educational prgm coor sr, $59,320
Feener, Raymond S, prof, asoc, $65,487
Fegley, Andrew J, resp therapist reg, $20.55/hr
Fegley, Ruth Erin, nurse, staff II, $24.01/hr
Fehrenbach, Patrick T, media producer I, $16.29/hr
Feibish, Natalie Ann, instructional developr-expert, $23.08/hr
Feilner, Ronald D, mgr csm operations, $62,517
Feintuch, Yossi, lecturer, $13,333
Feistman, Richard E, instructor, adjunct, $10,000
Feldkamp, Ruth E, library information assistant, $11.30/hr
Feldman, Bernard Joseph, dean, asoc, $121,115
Feldman, Marvin Fredrick, prof, ast clincl, $74,108
Feldmann, Heather N, business support specialist sr, $22.23/hr
Feldt, Margaret Marian, event assistant I, $8.00/hr
Felkner, Penny Sue, db administrator-expert, $73,686
Fellabaum, Jennifer Melissa, prof, ast teach, $71,340
Feller, Tracy Ann, mgr external relations, $72,441
Felling, Kyle B, media producer sr, $37,708
Felock, Matthew Joseph, user support analyst-entry, $15.22/hr
Felps, Stacy A, instructor, adjunct, $3,300
Fels, Rebecca Janice, media producer sr, $34,400
Felt, Joyce Ellen, office support assistant III, $14.35/hr
Felten, Elizabeth A, care coordinator, $68,289
Felten, Martha Mae, reimbursement ast-cert, $18.41/hr
Felten, Susan, nurse practitioner, $84,907
Feltner, Buddy J, mechl plant spclst, $19.64/hr
Feltner, Lucinda, coor business-up, $19.71/hr
Felton, Courtney Lea, nurse, licensed prac, $18.00/hr
Felton, Diane M, temporary clerical, $10.50/hr
Felts, Kathryn Schmidtke, asoc dir research activities, $80,341
Feltz, Jean L, occ therapist-adult day connec, $29,802
Femrite, Stephanie Viola, extns professional, ast, $43,462
Fender, Christopher M, dir III business admin, $139,444
Fendler, Timothy James, resident physician-5th yr, $56,120
Feng, Linda, resrch asoc, $48,101
Feng, Qi, research/lab technician sr, $16.29/hr
Feng, Sherry Xumin, research specialist I, $42,114
Feng, Zaichun Frank, professor, $107,169
Fenical, Robin L, care team assoc-suppt, $13.12/hr
Fenley, Brenda Joyce, sftware supprt analyst-speclst, $46,244
Fenley, William David, powr plnt maint spclst II, $23.75/hr
Fennel, Barbara M, ultrasonographer, $35.54/hr
Fennell, Hilda Martinez, instructor, ast, $19,035
Fennell, John W, prof, asoc profl practice, $80,400
Fenner, Bruce Allen, custodian, $10.94/hr
Fenner, Bryant W, floor care techn, $11.96/hr
Fenner, Marie, custodian, $12.94/hr
Fennewald, Andrew J, pharmacy intern second year, $13.50/hr
Fennewald, Annie Lynn, business ops associate sr, $61,065
Fennewald, Kristen Anna, temporary crafts service, $7.50/hr
Fennewald, Tara Catherine, nurse, staff II, $20.95/hr
Fenske, Margret Kristine, theatre ast, $39,000
Fenster, Howard A, health records techn II, $13.37/hr
Fent, Lee A, db programmer analyst-expert, $30.00/hr
Fenton, Connie L, nurse clinician, $70,502
Fenton, Jason A, office support assistant III, $13.26/hr
Fenwick, Tyler Jae, head coach, $74,600
Ferdowsi, Mehdi, prof, asoc, $114,869
Ferguson, Ameia Lkay, med techl reg, $20.94/hr
Ferguson, Brian Steven, fellow, post doctoral, $42,000
Ferguson, Cydney Jae, student recruitment spclst, $14.96/hr
Ferguson, Cynthia D, executive assistant, $18.96/hr
Ferguson, Eric Lee, program/project supprt coor I, $52,273
Ferguson, Ian, dean, $230,000
Ferguson, Jeffrey R, prof, ast resrch, $72,104
Ferguson, Jeremy S, support systems admin-expert, $55,965
Ferguson, Jill Suzanne, compliance manager sr, $66,000
Ferguson, Justin T, csm specialist sr, $17.17/hr
Ferguson, Kendra Renee, care team assoc-clinical, $11.10/hr
Ferguson, Kenneth D, prof, asoc, $96,500

Ferguson, Lesli Suzanne, nurse, staff prn, $26.00/hr
Ferguson, Lori A, emrg med techn, $14.56/hr
Ferguson, Mae Alice, office support assistant II, $10.45/hr
Ferguson, Nathan Flynn, temporary crafts service, $9.10/hr
Ferguson, Rebecca Ann, resident physician-6th yr, $58,200
Ferguson, Rita Marie, office support assistant IV, $20.97/hr
Ferguson, Starsha Dawn, office support assistant IV, $13.62/hr
Fernandez, Alfonso, lecturer, $9,000
Fernandez, John Vincent, strat comm associate I, $14,400
Fernandez, Kimberly Michele, nurse, staff now III, $30.00/hr
Fernandez, Kristen Lynn Heins, prof, ast clincl dept, $185,000
Fernando, Lakdas N, resrch anlyst, $49,920
Fernlund, Kevin, professor, $67,621
Ferrari, Francesca, asoc dir program/project ops, $47,284
Ferree, Nancy S B, program/project supprt coor I, $31,752
Ferreira-Nichols, Stephanie Claudia, research/lab tech, $12.50/hr
Ferrel, Thomas R, resrch asoc, $48,185
Ferrell, Jane Dauten, administrative consultant, $47,615
Ferrell, Sarah D, nurse, staff II, $20.95/hr
Ferris, Stephen P, professor, $301,096
Fessler, Jamie Theresa, physical therapist, $35.00/hr
Fete, Mary Donna, instructor, clincl, $43,701
Fete, Timothy Joseph, prof, clinical dept, $337,365
Fetsch, Jessica Lynn, nurse, staff I, rnwp, $19.00/hr
Fetters, Mark S, office support assistant III, $15.82/hr
Feutz, Cynthia E, nurse spclst, clincl, $96,720
Fewell, John L, telecom tech-princpl, $23.37/hr
Feys, Dimitri, prof, ast, $80,601
Fiala, Kyle C, prof, ast/profl pract, $194,577
Fichter, Lucille Mary, sr manager it, $102,001
Fick, Rachel Anne, lecturer, $18,120
Fick, Susan T, patient svc rep, $13.55/hr
Fickel, Nicole A, student support specialist sr, $19.24/hr
Ficklen, William G, library info specialist, $20.07/hr
Fidalgo, Maria Marta, prof, asoc, $103,040
Fidler, Roger F, administrative consultant II, $92,011
Fieldman, Hali, prof, asoc, $54,177
Fields II, Burt Lee, library information assistant, $11.30/hr
Fields, David L, mts/refrigeration mech, $21.05/hr
Fields, Denise Marie, program/project supprt coor sr, $82,400
Fields, Linda, office support assistant IV, $16.08/hr
Fields, Linda Sun, physician ast, $100.00/hr
Fields, Travis Duane, prof, ast, $75,000
Fierro, Erica Alicia, program/project supprt coor II, $40,000
Figard, Rachel Joann, nurse, licensed prac, $17.11/hr
Figge, Lindsay Brooke, patient svc rep, $11.07/hr
Figueroa, Tomasina, custodian, $13.36/hr
Figures, Constance Veronica, food svc wrkr II, $11.83/hr
Fikru, Mahelet, prof, ast, $81,432
Filcoff, Eric Craig, media producer sr, $42,716
Filer, Deborah J, social worker, $58,548
Filion, Diane L, dean, asoc, $130,330
Filkins, Brittany Nicole, office support assistant sr, $16.35/hr
Filkins, Emily Lauren, office support assistant I, $8.90/hr
Fillingim, Debra K, instructor, adjunct, $21,600
Finch, Jonathan Andrew, lecturer, $40,509
Fincher, Camellia Faye, office support assistant III, $12.86/hr
Fincher, Joshua Cameron, patient svc rep, $10.64/hr
Fincher, Larry Dean, orthopedic techn, $15.86/hr
Findeis, Jill L, director, $197,728
Finders, Kristin Marie, social worker, $51,409
Fines, Barbara Glesner, dean, asoc, $161,300
Fink, Adrienne Brynn, student service coor sr, $48,348
Fink, Kathleen Theresa, sr dir program/project ops, $82,215
Fink, Lieschen Ann, prof, ast adjunct, $16,008
Fink, Michael K, fellow, resrch, $43,680
Finke, Alan Wayne, nurse, staff II, $33.76/hr
Finke, Darin Andrew, prof, ast teach, $44,572
Finke, Deborah L, prof, asoc, $98,630
Finkel, Claire Elizabeth, resident physician-1st yr, $50,219
Finlay, Diana L, educational pgm associate I, $13.58/hr
Finley, Amanda Leah, lecturer, $75,372
Finley, Catlyn El, surgical technl certified, $16.19/hr
Finley, Kenneth W, administrative consultant II, $86,305
Finlinson, Tyson R, resident physician-2nd yr, $50,810
Finn, Allison Nichole, social worker, $46,221
Finn, Lavernia D, nurse, staff II, $27.00/hr
Finn, Martin J, retail sales manager, $70,000
Finnegan, Megan C, office support assistant IV, $15.11/hr

Finney, Dawn M, temporary professional, $11.30/hr
Finnigan, Ruth Leah, nurse, staff II, $20.54/hr
Firestone, Pola Rae, program/project supprt coor sr, $52,000
Firman, Jeffre D, professor, $98,612
First, Jennifer Marie, program/project supprt coor I, $47,025
Firwana, Belal, resident physician-3rd yr, $53,763
Fischer Messmer, Jane Ann, prof, ast adjunct, $34,200
Fischer, Amanda Jo, resident physician-1st yr, $49,025
Fischer, Carol Ann, supv nursing acute care, $38.67/hr
Fischer, Connie Irene, office support assistant IV, $15.30/hr
Fischer, James D, instructor, residnt, $65,548
Fischer, Jeffrey D, human resources specialist I, $19.95/hr
Fischer, Kohri Nicole, clerk, unit, $10.64/hr
Fischer, Marsha Blakemore, counsel, $142,561
Fischer, Mary McIlrath, program/project supprt coor I, $38,000
Fischer, Monika, prof, asoc teach, $54,408
Fischetti, William M, mgr research activities, $54,180
Fish, Alan L, police sergeant, $21.47/hr
Fish, Anne, prof, asoc, $89,537
Fish, Emily Luanne, reimbursement ast sr, $22.47/hr
Fish, James L, instructor, adjunct, $10,800
Fish, Kristin Gail, pharmacist II, $116,232
Fish, Laura Rosemary, safety communications oper, $13.73/hr
Fish, Michael Nathaniel, prof, ast clincl dept, $200,000
Fish, Natalie Mary, event assistant I, $8.50/hr
Fish, Rebecca A, resident physician-2nd yr, $52,007
Fish, William Brian, event assistant I, $7.55/hr
Fishback, Nathan John, support systems admin-expert, $52,400
Fisher-McLean, Kandace Lenae, housing & envirn design spclst, $42,997
Fisher, Alexandra Julia, intern, $15.00/hr
Fisher, Chelsea Rae, resident physician-4th yr, $54,425
Fisher, Collin Lee, waiter/waitress, $9.50/hr
Fisher, Delores Ann, library info specialist sr, $17.32/hr
Fisher, Frances Jennelle, office support assistant III, $16.75/hr
Fisher, Jason Eric, temporary technical, $12.00/hr
Fisher, Jeanne L, temporary technical, $25.00/hr
Fisher, Kelsy Loren, prof, ast clincl, $64,297
Fisher, Kesha Renee, care team assoc-clinical, $11.10/hr
Fisher, Laverne Kay, supv outpatient svcs, $49,298
Fisher, Lori Ann, nurse, staff II rnwp, $24.62/hr
Fisher, Nola M, hospital security officer, $13.15/hr
Fisher, Patricia Ann, 4-h spclst, $60,613
Fisher, Patricia Marie, executive assistant, $21.70/hr
Fisher, Robert B, prof, ast clincl dept, $200,000
Fisk, James L, student support specialist sr, $16.54/hr
Fisk, Norma J, tutor, $12.00/hr
Fister, Daniel R, temporary crafts service, $9.50/hr
Fitch, Dale Kent, prof, ast, $69,497
Fitch, Mark W, prof, asoc, $91,002
Fitch, Stephanie L, prof, asoc teach, $58,911
Fitts, Lauren Nicole, rehab therapy aide, $10.75/hr
Fitzgerald, Barry Kent, db administrator-speclst, $66,963
Fitzgerald, Cole A, resident physician-3rd yr, $52,470
Fitzgerald, Daniel W, prgm director, ast, $48,930
Fitzgerald, Gail, professor, $109,650
Fitzgerald, James L, farm wrkr III lead, $17.29/hr
Fitzlaff, Ernest D, mechanical plant speclst, mrc, $18.09/hr
Fitzpatrick, Ann B, research/lab technician sr, $15.95/hr
Fitzpatrick, Carol M, human resources manager sr, $67,113
Fitzpatrick, Steven Neal, mts/sheet metal, $22.49/hr
Fitzsimmons, Abigail Katherine, med lab techn, $15.87/hr
Fitzsimmons, Anne B, prof, asoc clincl dept, $152,159
Fitzsimmons, Natalie Marie, sr reimbursement analyst, $80,730
Fix, Michael, prof, teach, $45,491
Fjone, Heather Louise, mental health professional, $38,595
Flachsbart, Barry B, professor, $105,253
Flack, Adam B, resident physician-3rd yr, $52,470
Flack, Eric Phillip, instructor, adjunct, $7,760
Flagg, Michael Afton, asoc dir research, $109,182
Flaherty, Victoria Lucinda, resp therapist reg, $30.00/hr
Flaigle, Connie Jo, programmer analyst-expert, $63,110
Flaker, Greg C, professor, $278,929
Flakne, Larry Louis, asoc dir program/project ops, $50,625
Flamm, Kayla Mary, temporary professional, $9.00/hr
Flanagan, John R, prof, ast teach, $42,557
Flanagan, Kyle Michael, office support assistant III, $16.48/hr
Flanagan, Lori, athletic director, $108,231
Flanagan, Shawn K, instructor, ast, $33,486

Flanagin, Phillip Randall, supv resp care, $84,760
Flanary, Wayne Edwin, extns professional, $72,611
Flanders, Hillary, instructor, adjunct, $6,276
Flanegin, Suzanne M, dir iv advancement, $110,635
Flanigan, Phyllis Ann, extns professional, asoc, $73,862
Flanner, Julie Ann, nurse, staff II, $20.54/hr
Flannigan, Jessica Lynn, office support assistant III, $12.00/hr
Flaspohler, Carrie Lee, nurse, staff II rnwp, $21.17/hr
Flatt, Curtis R, managing engineer, $98,576
Flatt, Jenny L, 4-h spclst, $50,812
Flatt, Tisha Rena, supv hosptlty & pat suprt svcs, $53,645
Flatt, Wendy Renee, livestock spclst, $43,591
Flattem, Deborah D, clerk, unit, $13.62/hr
Flaugher, Kathy Elaine, executive assistant, $18.00/hr
Fleagle, Brian Joseph, media producer I, $12.99/hr
Fleagle, Jessica M, prof, ast clincl dept, $178,847
Fleak, Kenneth Paul, prof, ast teach, $42,032
Fleck, Alissa R, business tech analyst-speclst, $45,207
Fleck, Patti J, sr asoc dir studnt supprt svcs, $80,000
Fleeger, John W, lecturer, $16,000
Fleeks, Lavera A, office support assistant III, $11.30/hr
Fleeman, Rodney Thomas, instructor, adjunct, $7,200
Fleenor, Ernest C, bts painter, $18.00/hr
Fleenor, Jeffrey H, csm project manager, $72,775
Fleenor, Traci R, advancement officer, $46,968
Fleer, Cynthia Kay, nurse, staff per diem, $35.00/hr
Fleharty, Rosemary A, program/project supprt coor I, $62,428
Fleisher, Carol Watson, program/project supprt coor sr, $60,719
Fleming, Willie Jr, custodian, $13.23/hr
Fleming, Adela L, mgr II student support svcs, $60,000
Fleming, Callie J, student service coor sr, $47,880
Fleming, David Avery, professor, $405,756
Fleming, Dorothy Glen, student support specialist sr, $17.40/hr
Fleming, Gail Hagler, lecturer, $45,456
Fleming, James Daniel, prof, ast adjunct, $125.00/hr
Fleming, Jennifer Lynn, temporary professional, $13.00/hr
Fleming, Jordan Bernard, tutor, $10.00/hr
Fleming, Matthew Craig, student service coor II, $39,624
Fleming, Paula Marilynn, business support spclst II, $19.01/hr
Flerlage, Allen E, programmer analyst-expert, $56,224
Flesch, Brian Scott, pat care ast-ophthalm, $12.96/hr
Flesner, Marcia, instructor, clincl, $65,720
Fletcher, Angela M, human dev spclst, $53,308
Fletcher, Dwayne E, mts/refrig mech-r, $20.10/hr
Fletcher, Kevin J, strat comm associate II, $40,788
Fletcher, Michelle Lynn, fin and acctg analyst sr, $49,524
Flink, James Duncan, prof, ast/profl pract, $65,000
Flink, Jamie Bono, prof, ast/profl pract, $62,347
Flinn, Allison Marie, intern, $25,500
Flinn, Mark V, professor, $106,050
Flinn, Regina D, patient svc rep, $14.88/hr
Flood-Lorber, Nicole Almora, nurse, staff II, $22.44/hr
Flood, Christine Ann, couns hlth/welfare/wellness sr, $30.00/hr
Flood, David Louis, prof, ast clincl dept, $260,113
Flood, Kelli Lynn, reimbursement spclst, $21.51/hr
Flood, Nicole Marie, program/project supprt coor I, $35,000
Florance, Megan C, business support specialist II, $17.50/hr
Florence, Ludia Belle, patient svc rep, $14.88/hr
Florence, Tuesday Rochelle, student support spclst sr, $18.79/hr
Flores Noyola, Juan Esteban, system sup analyst-spclst, $23.08/hr
Flores, Benjamin Warren, db administrator-speclst, $55,890
Flores, David Chandler, business support specialist II, $19.71/hr
Flores, Lisa Y, professor, $104,583
Flores, Mary Lucille, business support specialist sr, $25.30/hr
Flores, Ricardo A, professor, $69,165
Flori, Ralph E Jr, prof, asoc, $143,278
Flotron, Gary L, lecturer sr, $18,600
Flournoy, Nancy, prof, curators, $185,003
Flowers, Barbara Jean, instructor, adjunct, $11,400
Flowers, JoAnne Brannon, sr mgr business admin, $79,228
Flowers, Kara Michelle, prof, ast clincl, $46,874
Flowers, Linda S, pat admiss advisor, $30.24/hr
Flowers, Peggy Ann, nurse, licensed prac, $21.37/hr
Flowers, Portia Patrice Elizabeth, fellow, post doctoral, $40,000
Flowers, Thomas Elliott, mental health tech, $13.69/hr
Floyd, Angela Diane, advancement associate I, $18.00/hr
Floyd, Christina Marie, coor, profl practice & stds, $74,549
Floyd, Margaret E, office support assistant III, $15.53/hr
Floyd, Randall C, prof, asoc clincl dept, $229,451

Fluesmeier, Katherine D, office support assistant IV, $16.87/hr
Flynn Peters, Kristin Joan, prof, ast clincl, $50,997
Flynn, Holly Erin, business tech analyst-speclst, $47,905
Flynn, Samantha Ann, nurse, staff I, $19.00/hr
Flynn, William E, pat acct rep, $14.86/hr
Focella, Elizabeth S, fellow, post doctoral, $39,264
Fock, Jakob Alexander, temporary crafts service, $8.00/hr
Foecking, Mark F, research specialist I, $34,424
Fogarty, Brian J, prof, asoc, $112,692
Fogel, Catherine Abigail, office support assistant III, $13.50/hr
Fogel, Steven Tedd, physician, $135.00/hr
Fogelbach, Gary M, human resources analyst lead, $40,102
Fogle, Derrick Glenn, technology resource manager, $63,240
Fogle, Jeremy L, clerk, stores sr, $14.85/hr
Fogle, Sonya Michelle, service rep IV, $17.55/hr
Fogue, Jared Richard, media producer II, $17.55/hr
Folescu, Marina Radiana, prof, ast, $62,068
Foley, Richard F Jr, prof, asoc, $51,323
Foley, Anne-Marie, director, $94,415
Foley, Cynthia J, student support specialist II, $15.82/hr
Foley, David S, concierge-hospitality svcs, $18.46/hr
Foley, Henry C, executive vice president, $367,500
Foley, Karin Elizabeth, asoc dir research, $107,100
Foley, Kimberly A, office support assistant IV, $15.00/hr
Foley, Laura Michelle, instructional developr-expert, $21.77/hr
Foley, Mark A, business support specialist II, $16.37/hr
Folk, William, professor, $220,825
Folkerts, Amy A, office support assistant III, $14.27/hr
Folkerts, Ella F, teaching ast, $13.00/hr
Follett, Travis G, custodian, $10.39/hr
Follmer, Beth C, program/project supprt coor II, $50,058
Folsom, Chainy Jerome, resrch ast, $9,000
Foltz, James A, custodian, $10.39/hr
Folzenlogen, Darcy D, emeritus, $11,700
Fondren, Kevin Reed, custodian, $11.44/hr
Fonseca, Elizabeth Anne, prof, ast teach, $40,400
Font-Montgomery, Esperanza Enid, prof, asoc clincl dept, $148,000
Fontenot, Justin Lee, ast mgr hospitality services, $41,235
Foo, Albert Siong Wai, manager it, $88,034
Foote, Christopher Andrew, research specialist sr, $49,000
Foote, Karen M, fin and acctg specialist, $19.21/hr
Forbes, Sheryl A, care team assoc-clinical, $13.80/hr
Forbes, William T, instructor, adjunct, $7,200
Forbis, Brenda L, business support specialist I, $18.61/hr
Forbis, Casey E, program/project supprt coor II, $62,250
Forbis, Diana L, office support assistant IV, $16.36/hr
Forbis, Emily Suzanne, nurse, licensed prac, $15.79/hr
Forbis, James K, maintenance supervisor, $57,053
Forbis, Lisa Michelle, patient svc rep, $13.77/hr
Forbis, Tara Nicole, nurse, clincl charge-rn, $27.45/hr
Forbis, Terry L, seasonal farm ast, $8.93/hr
Force, Jenny M, ast mgr respiratory care, $69,227
Force, John Dale, hospital security officer, $12.44/hr
Forciniti, Daniel, professor, $109,290
Ford, Anitha Delphine, custodian, $10.00/hr
Ford, Cornell, ast coach, $300,500
Ford, Holly Beth, prof, ast clincl dept, $133,488
Ford, Jake, human resources specialist III, $41,004
Ford, Jenny W, office support assistant I, $10.49/hr
Ford, Jessica Lee, resp therapist reg, $19.73/hr
Ford, Jill Halbrook, dir I, student support svcs, $88,550
Ford, Kate Linn G, temporary clerical, $12.50/hr
Ford, Leslie A, maint tech II, prev, $16.50/hr
Ford, Lindy Sue, nurse practitioner, $87,085
Ford, Peggy A, chief comp, rsk mgmt & reg aff, $214,245
Ford, Sarah Ann, social worker, $21.36/hr
Ford, Stephanie Marie, nurse, staff II, $20.95/hr
Ford, Wayne Keith, mts/electrician, $22.50/hr
Ford, Zaneta Denise, office support assistant III, $12.57/hr
Foreman, Mary Carolyn, ast mgr hospitality services, $40,788
Foreman, Paul Michael, asoc dir program/project ops, $68,159
Foreman, Stanley Rafe, prof, asoc teach, $153,000
Foreman, Timothy Daniel, temporary clerical, $8.00/hr
Forester, Kenneth G, mts/refrig mech-r, $20.87/hr
Forgy, Nancy Jane, nurse, staff II rnwp, $22.89/hr
Forman-Brunell, Miriam, professor, $85,568
Forrest, Larry G, bts painter, $21.71/hr
Forrest, Rhonda K, student support specialist sr, $31.01/hr
Forrest, Stewart L, cook, $13.21/hr

Forrester, April L, lab assistant, $10.50/hr
Forrester, Delmer J, equip opr/mech II, agri, $17.78/hr
Forrester, Judy Est, instructor, $19,317
Forsee, Brenda Marie, nurse, licensed prac, $21.07/hr
Forsha, Angelique Louise, program/proj supprt coor I, $42,014
Forstater, Mathew, professor, $85,902
Forsyth, Jennifer Jean, resident physician-4th yr, $54,425
Fortman, John T, db programmer analyst-speclst, $57,570
Fortner, Amelia S, library info specialist sr, $15.32/hr
Forward, Ann Hayden, cook, $12.20/hr
Forward, Jim W, athletic attd, $14.47/hr
Fossett, Theresa L, asoc dir program/project ops, $48,934
Foster Jr, Jack B, distribution techn-mtls mgmt, $14.84/hr
Foster-Neal, Racheal Marie, office support asst IV, $13.50/hr
Foster, Angela A, nurse, licensed prac, $15.67/hr
Foster, Anserd Julius, agronomy spclst, $46,872
Foster, Antoine Chaveuz, temporary crafts service, $7.50/hr
Foster, Brian, emeritus, $47,250
Foster, Brian P, instructl technl, $51,999
Foster, Deborah E, business support specialist II, $19.88/hr
Foster, Gregory Mark, instructor, ast, $15,000
Foster, James R, pat acct rep, $14.26/hr
Foster, Jason Eric, enrollment advisor sr, $16.54/hr
Foster, Jennifer Rae, strat comm consultant, $45,293
Foster, JoAnn, custodian, $10.94/hr
Foster, Julie A, business tech analyst-expert, $63,318
Foster, Kathleen Ann, sr ast dir studnt supprt svcs, $53,186
Foster, Mary Ann, event assistant I, $7.55/hr
Foster, Matthew, resident physician-1st yr, $49,025
Foster, Michele Lynn, professor, $163,200
Foster, Priscilla D, veterinary technician sr, $19.83/hr
Foster, Raymond T, prof, asoc, $189,507
Foster, Sally Seagull, theatre ast, $20.00/hr
Foster, Susan E, business svcs consultant sr, $87,727
Fougere, John, dir strat comm-enterprise, $128,754
Foulkes, Matthew Walton, prof, asoc, $62,864
Foulkes, Teresa Diane, asoc dir program/project ops, $57,693
Foundas, Anne Leigh, professor, $75,000
Fountain, John A Jr, health records techn II, $17.00/hr
Fountain, Alana Ranae, pat acct rep, $14.86/hr
Foursha, Leslie A, care team assoc-clinical, $12.75/hr
Foust, Catherine A, reimbursement ast-cert, $18.59/hr
Foust, Jonathan Scott, custodian, $11.00/hr
Foutch, Gary, prof, adjunct, $54,000
Fowler Smith, Charla Jenea, physical therapist, $37.25/hr
Fowler, Bruce Allen, specialist, $45,030
Fowler, Dana Renee, lecturer, $9,000
Fowler, Justin Michael, research/lab technician, $10.24/hr
Fowler, Kaneshia K, reimbursement ast-cert, $19.86/hr
Fowler, Mary K, director it, $101,566
Fowler, Nancy Marie, strat comm consultant, $43,575
Fowler, Patricia J, temporary professional, $12.00/hr
Fowler, Rebecca Thurmond, manager it, $85,833
Fowler, Stephanie L, system support analyst-speclst, $19.75/hr
Fowler, Thomas Randall, horticulture spclst, $60,524
Fox, Andrew Mark, prof, ast, $58,137
Fox, Beverly Y, instructor, $49,392
Fox, David Gary, asoc dir business admin, $53,448
Fox, Derek Bradford, prof, asoc, $139,640
Fox, Diana Marie, certif pharmacy techn, $13.50/hr
Fox, Jamal James, prof, ast adjunct, $21,060
Fox, Jessica Rose, office support assistant II, $13.77/hr
Fox, Jill Anette, strat comm associate II, $48,433
Fox, Linda, library info specialist sr, $17.68/hr
Fox, Linda J, library info specialist sr, $15.32/hr
Fox, Lori Ann, academic advisor, $41,096
Fox, Neil Ian, prof, asoc, $66,890
Fox, Roy F, professor, $92,881
Fox, Susan Kay, instructor, adjunct, $19,820
Fox, Tina R, strat comm associate II, $47,000
Fox, Travis R, psychologist, $72,105
Fox, Victoria Lynn, business support specialist II, $22.18/hr
Foyto, Leslie P, asoc dir research, $132,032
Frahm, Katherine Christine, office support assistant IV, $13.23/hr
Frahm, Randy James, nurse, staff II, $34.18/hr
Fraizer, Katherine Suzanne Neville, office support asst III, $12.25/hr
France, Galynn Renee, human resources manager sr, $66,950
France, John L, media producer I, $13.18/hr
Francis, Amber Marie, internet administrator-entry, $19.49/hr

Francis, Dale William, messenger, $9.55/hr
Francis, Grace Lucille, asoc dir program/project ops, $69,500
Francis, Harriet, business svcs consultant sr, $82,735
Francis, Jean E, instructor, $57,775
Francis, Jere R, prof, curators, $297,077
Francis, John R, media production director II, $50,600
Francis, Lorie Lynne, lecturer, $41,826
Francis, Rebecca Anne, central regstry-data coor, $23.74/hr
Francisco, Benjamin David, prof, asoc teach, $117,790
Francisco, Benjamin Isaac, fin and acctg specialist, $19.73/hr
Francisco, Jacquelyn, fellow, post doctoral, $35,000
Francisco, Lei Wang, fin and acctg analyst sr, $42,383
Franck, Susan Faye, instructor, $45,450
Francois, Julie K, nurse, staff, $33.80/hr
Frandsen, Gary Michael, prof, ast teach, $63,788
Frandsen, Sherl F, hospital security officer, $13.29/hr
Frangos, Jennifer Elaine, prof, asoc, $56,621
Frank, Amelia E, resident physician-2nd yr, $52,007
Frank, Beth Ellen, db programmer analyst-expert, $60,000
Frank, Harold J, managing engineer, $88,427
Frank, Jerritt J, prof, ast, $97,200
Frank, Logan Anthony, resident physician-5th yr, $58,083
Frank, Meghan M, nurse, staff now III, $30.00/hr
Frank, Monica Marie, business ops associate sr, $54,026
Frank, Ronald L, prof, asoc, $72,599
Frank, Stephanie B, prof, ast, $62,000
Franke, Cynthia D, supv nursing acute care, $38.88/hr
Franke, James Michael, resp therapist reg, $28.58/hr
Franken, Ashley Rose, physical therapist, $56,472
Franklin, Andrew Lawrence, resident physician-3rd yr, $53,763
Franklin, Carl Benjamin, resrch asoc, $25,000
Franklin, Craig, professor, $154,273
Franklin, Jeffrey Lynn, media producer II, $15.17/hr
Franklin, JoAnn, instructor, clincl, $92,000
Franklin, Kerry A, custodian, $12.94/hr
Franklin, Laura Beth, business support specialist II, $20.04/hr
Franklin, Ryan Lee, asoc media producer, $12.37/hr
Franks, Eric Marshall, program/project supprt coor II, $65,876
Franta, Jeffrey T, temporary professional, $19.54/hr
Franta, Linda K, office support assistant III, $15.65/hr
Frantz, Mary K, teaching ast, $13.00/hr
Frantz, Mary M, human resources specialist I, $19.89/hr
Franz, Alexander W E, prof, ast, $97,675
Franz, Charles, prof, asoc, $91,497
Franz, Lori, professor, $194,236
Franzel, Aaron Stephen, prof, ast clincl, $92,128
Franzel, G A, prof, adjunct, $22,241
Franzel, Sean B, prof, asoc, $62,151
Frappier, Brian Lee, prof, asoc clincl, $119,320
Frappier, Doreen C, hospital lab tech, $13.73/hr
Fraser, Jacob S, research specialist I, $40,000
Frasher, Judith Lynn, social worker asoc, $40,316
Fratila, Alexandra Maria, high school student, $7.50/hr
Fraundorf, Philip, prof, asoc, $71,742
Fraunfelder, Frederick Web, professor, $517,120
Frazer, Kevin G, prof, ast clincl dept, $137,700
Frazer, Nicholas Christiano, patient svc rep, $11.07/hr
Frazier, Cindy J, fin and acctg manager sr, $87,041
Frazier, Gloria S, office support assistant IV, $14.85/hr
Frazier, Harry, powr plnt opr lead, $31.58/hr
Frazier, Keenya Sierra, patient svc rep, $10.64/hr
Frazier, Kelli Ann, nurse, staff II, $21.37/hr
Frazier, Shellaine R, prof, ast clincl dept, $183,056
Freborg, Myles Ryan, grader, $52
Frede, Elaina Crews, strat comm associate II, $48,956
Frederick-Hudson, Katherine Harrington, fellow, post doctoral,
    $21,000
Frederick, Benjamin Keith, resident physician-3rd yr, $53,763
Frederick, Dawn, nurse clinician, $72,675
Frederick, Jessica Leigh, nurse clinician, $61,747
Frederick, Lawrence William, chief info officer-campus, $175,000
Fredericksen, Michael C, security officer, $11.48/hr
Frederiksen, Tayler M, nurse, staff I, $19.00/hr
Frederking, Clarissa Leigh, veterinary technician sr, $15.60/hr
Fredrickson, Lance R, nurse anesthetist, $147,900
Freeburne, Alex B, programmer analyst-speclst, $23.87/hr
Freelin, Tammy Lee W, instructor, clincl, $39,632
Freelon, Deidrea Lachelle, custodian, $10.39/hr
Freelon, Teresa Lynn, temporary crafts service, $9.50/hr

Freeman, David R Jr, instructor, $24,000
Freeman, Angela K, med office assistant, $13.06/hr
Freeman, Brian, resident physician-1st yr, $49,025
Freeman, Cheryl Sue, patient svc rep, $12.81/hr
Freeman, Clinton S, supervisor it, $53,004
Freeman, David Fors, prof, ast, $53,508
Freeman, Derrick, student service coor II, $54,951
Freeman, Diana L, neurodiagnostic tech (reg), $22.44/hr
Freeman, Elizabeth Ann, dietitian, clincl, $55,794
Freeman, Erica Loren, office support assistant I, $8.89/hr
Freeman, James L, nurse, staff II, $28.25/hr
Freeman, James P, bts painter-mrc, $16.36/hr
Freeman, Katie Lynn, resident physician-3rd yr, $53,763
Freeman, Melissa Diane, compliance specialist I, $18.54/hr
Freeman, Melody D, mgr I, business admin, $60,000
Freeman, Seth C, resident physician-3rd yr, $56,763
Freeman, Stanley Dean, mgr II csm operations, $71,651
Freeman, Susan Marie, business support specialist II, $16.75/hr
Freemyer, Angela June, business support specialist sr, $21.00/hr
Frees, Scott P, messenger, $12.96/hr
Freese, Megan Elizabeth, strat comm associate I, $34,500
Freese, Rebekah Ann, instructor, clincl, $49,939
Freese, Ross Arden, system support analyst-speclst, $23.18/hr
Freese, Terry L, bldg cntrl sys techn III, $24.49/hr
Freese, Victoria Nicole, asoc dir advancement, $75,000
Freese, William C, sr manager it, $101,279
Freesemann, Lisa Ann, user support analyst-speclst, $16.92/hr
Freet, Danny Jack, police officer, $19.99/hr
Freeze, David Alan, nurse, staff II, $22.00/hr
Freeze, Leah Kathryn, advancement officer, $46,512
Freiberg, Tristan Munro, fellow, post doctoral, $48,000
Freiburghaus, Mary Katherine, nurse practitioner, $80,157
Freie, Lori Ann, business support specialist II, $18.15/hr
Freivogel, Margaret Wolf, sr dir program/project ops, $77,625
French, Anne Shields, office support assistant II, $11.36/hr
French, Brandi Rose, prof, ast clincl dept, $155,150
French, Dan Wright, professor, $265,219
French, Marvin Lee Everett, food svc wrkr I, $9.60/hr
French, Tom N, mgr csm operations, $50,600
Frese, Robert Curran, lecturer sr, $10,500
Fresenburg, Brad Steven, prof, ast extns, $72,867
Freuler, Sela Kate, psychology techn, $13.20/hr
Freund, Stefan R, prof, asoc, $66,357
Frevert, Amanda Lee, student support specialist II, $17.11/hr
Frevert, Max Wesley, mgr hosptly & env svcs, $56,111
Frey, Brian Patrick, police officer, $19.76/hr
Frey, Jay M, prepress sr, $21.95/hr
Frey, Linnea H, instructor, clincl, $43,701
Frey, Scott Harold, professor, $187,006
Freyermuth, Robert W, prof, curator teach, $165,396
Freyermuth, Sharyn K, prof, asoc teach, $85,000
Frick, Kenneth Joseph, prof, ast clincl, $103,000
Fridley, Carol Ann, business support specialist II, $20.00/hr
Fridley, Cullen Michael, athletic trainer, $42,280
Fried, Elliott Asher, resident physician-2nd yr, $50,810
Fried, Gabriel W, prof, ast teach, $36,000
Fried, Kristen J, resident physician-3rd yr, $52,470
Frieda, Dustin Bennett, prof, ast adjunct, $6,800
Friedell, Mark Lowry, professor, $75,000
Frieden, Richard Arthur, csm associate I, $16.91/hr
Friedlander, Richard J, founders professor, $24,967
Friedlein, Sasha Marie, animal caretaker, $12.55/hr
Friedli, Amber Jo, nurse, licensed prac, $19.92/hr
Friedline, Gerianne, prof, ast teach, $38,381
Friedman, Chelsie Marie, sr ast dir studnt supprt svcs, $53,448
Friedman, Gene E, prof, asoc, $56,221
Friedman, Marianne S, business support specialist II, $18.99/hr
Friedman, Negina Battzion, office support assistant III, $11.50/hr
Friedman, Sara Tsharna, office support assistant IV, $13.00/hr
Friedman, Simon H, professor, $115,185
Friedman, Steven C, editor sr, $62,504
Friedrich, Andrea Dawn, nurse, licensed prac sr, $18.12/hr
Friedrich, Deborah, business support specialist II, $21.60/hr
Friedrich, Donald W, cook, $13.21/hr
Friedrich, James M, distribution techn-mtls mgmt, $15.06/hr
Friedrich, Judith R, librarian II, $52,689
Friedrich, Michael Lee, mts/pipefitter, $21.05/hr
Friedrich, Richard, bts carpenter lead, $21.24/hr
Friedrichsen, Patricia J, prof, asoc, $72,388

Friel, Cathryn L, instructional designer-expert, $64,818
Friel, Jeffrey Alan, business tech analyst-expert, $54,063
Friend, Alyson K, advancement associate II, $18.42/hr
Friend, Beata Jo, reactor engineer, $51,784
Friend, Jennifer Ingrid, dean, ast, $95,000
Friend, Russell Franklin, telecom tech-expert, $15.44/hr
Friend, Timothy Eugene, grader, $3,600
Frierson, Carla Celeste, office support assistant III, $17.55/hr
Friese, James Owen, system support analyst-speclst, $25.86/hr
Friesen, Lynn Roosa, prof, ast clincl, $82,620
Friess, Susan Elaine, office support assistant IV, $18.70/hr
Friesz, Melody, office support assistant IV, $18.76/hr
Friesz, Stephen M, maint tech III, prev, $17.63/hr
Frimpong, Samuel Jr, temporary technical, $10.00/hr
Frimpong, Samuel, professor, $166,618
Frink, Karen L, nurse, clincl charge-lpn, $21.71/hr
Frisbee, Patricia A, dir I, student support svcs, $69,938
Frisbee, Rebecca M, strat comm manager, $76,984
Frisbee, Tobias J, retail sales associate, $17.89/hr
Frisby, Craig L, prof, asoc, $74,095
Frisby, Cynthia M, prof, asoc, $82,710
Frisch, Michael, prof, asoc, $74,216
Friskey, Sarah Ann, research lab supervisor, $52,092
Fritsche, Kevin L, professor, $101,002
Fritschi, Felix Beat, prof, asoc, $112,200
Fritschie, Kristen Jo, coor children's miracle netwrk, $47,861
Fritts, Mary Lou A, chief info officer-campus, $167,879
Fritz Hoerchler, Tarren Denise, prof, ast adjunct, $16,008
Fritz, Dana R, prof, asoc clincl dept, $70,000
Fritz, Douglas T, health records techn II, $13.50/hr
Froehlich, Markus Gerd, fellow, post doctoral, $49,008
Froese, Ethan A, support systems admin-princpl, $65,671
Froese, Michelle M, sr advance dir studnt supprt svcs, $63,613
Frogge, Elizabeth Marie, prof, ast/profl pract, $58,802
Frost, Allen R, mgr csm operations, $52,500
Frost, Kristen Duda, nurse, staff II, $21.68/hr
Frost, Salisa Roselie, mental health tech, $13.50/hr
Frost, Tyson Mark, nurse, staff I, $19.00/hr
Fruits, John Leland, reactor manager, $115,347
Fry, Alice Lauralyn, business support specialist sr, $22.31/hr
Fry, Daniel David, specialist, $25.00/hr
Fry, Geoffrey David, instructor, adjunct, $1,726
Fry, Nicholas B, librarian II, $53,572
Fry, Pamela Rae, fellow, post doctoral, $35,000
Fry, Shannon, ast coach, $40.37/hr
Frye, Laura Marie, instructor, clincl, $55,500
Frye, Martin Joseph, research/lab technician, $11.00/hr
Frye, Nyonia Jones, human resources assistant, $17.20/hr
Fryer, Larry A, custodian, $11.41/hr
Frymire, John M, prof, asoc, $60,197
Fu, Man Shun, rsrch asoc, $39,996
Fu, Mingui, prof, ast, $85,000
Fu, Qingbo, prof, asoc, $126,885
Fu, Tian, accountant I, $19.82/hr
Fuchs, Adam Gerard, event assistant I, $7.55/hr
Fudge, Kathleen N, office supervisor, $51,325
Fudge, Tod Michael, sr mgr csm operations, $59,022
Fuegner, Nancy E, lecturer, $77,051
Fuehrer, Aaron, specialist, $10.00/hr
Fuemmeler, Brenda K, business support specialist II, $16.50/hr
Fuemmeler, Chris D, db programmer analyst-expert, $66,889
Fuemmeler, Daniel F, dir I, business admin, $94,900
Fuemmeler, Marta L, coor protocol svcs, $17.79/hr
Fuemmeler, Mary N, nurse, licensed prac, $18.49/hr
Fuemmeler, Melinda Rae, office support assistant IV, $17.34/hr
Fuemmeler, Niki Ann, business support specialist II, $16.65/hr
Fuemmeler, Stacy Jill, mental health tech, $12.45/hr
Fuemmeler, Tracy Lynn, exec ast to gen offcr, $72,680
Fugate, Carley Ann, business support specialist II, $18.54/hr
Fugate, Rachel Elizabeth, office support assistant I, $9.25/hr
Fuger PhD, Kathryn L, resrch asoc, $92,274
Fuhlage, Luisa Gimenez, instructional designer-speclst, $52
Fuhrman, Thomas W, housing&envirn design spclst, $54,662
FujII, Nicholas J, specialist, $10.00/hr
Fukawa, Nobuyuki, prof, ast, $102,545
Fulcher, Christopher, prof, ast resrch, $85,584
Fulcher, Yan G, fellow, post doctoral, $39,556
Fulford, Robert Walter, ast coach, $160,000
Fulhage, Jane M, event assistant I, $7.70/hr

Fulk, David Mark, advancement officer sr, $75,000
Fulkerson, Erin Elizabeth, fellow, post doctoral, $35,000
Fuller, Becky Sue, office support assistant III, $12.25/hr
Fuller, Donald Joe, programmer analyst-speclst, $45,613
Fuller, Jeana, nurse, licensed prac, $19.42/hr
Fuller, Marsha E, library info specialist, $13.81/hr
Fuller, Pamela L, nurse, staff, $31.20/hr
Fuller, Timothy Floyd, asoc coach, $325,000
Fuller, Tina Marie, custodian, $11.41/hr
Fullerton, Megan Katherine, temporary professional, $11.30/hr
Fullum, C Michael, specialist, $10.00/hr
Fulps, Linda Young, executive assistant, $21.63/hr
Fulton, Alexandria Mary, research/lab technician, $10.24/hr
Fultz, Jennifer Lee, office support assistant IV, $15.81/hr
Fultz, Jordan E, db programmer analyst-speclst, $48,738
Fung, Hung Gay, professor, $228,354
Funk, Crystal Anne, care team assoc-clinical, $14.86/hr
Funke, Ervalene Fay, sr reimbursement analyst, $59,303
Funke, Joy Davis, office support assistant IV, $13.53/hr
Funkenbusch, Karen Brents, resrch ast, $58,944
Fuqua, Melissa S, supv pat accts-up, $52,400
Furby, Sharon Ann, prof, asoc clincl, $93,761
Furgason, Dea Lu, case manager, $64,158
Furgason, Kathern Lee, prof, ast adjunct, $12,000
Furkin, Casey Marie, certif pharmacy techn, $17.10/hr
Furlong, Clarence Wayne, custodian, $12.94/hr
Furlong, Jacklyn Lucille, custodian, $10.39/hr
Furlong, Mark D, press IV, $22.21/hr
Furlong, Robert M, custodian, $12.94/hr
Furlong, Stacey J, telecomm opr sr-h, $13.24/hr
Furlow, Teri A, academic advisor sr, $46,105
Furnish, Ben A, ast editor, $18.84/hr
Furrer, Jason Lawrence, prof, ast teach, $58,834
Furst, Scott C, environmental health tech sr, $17.64/hr
Furstenau, Nina, prgm director, $55,000
Furtwengler, Dale Charles, lecturer, $10,800
Fusinatto, Jenna Rae, academic advisor, $37,500
Gaar, James R, editor II, $54,589
Gabel, Candance E Dixon, prof, asoc extns, $88,344
Gabel, Carolyn Sue, custodian lead, $11.98/hr
Gabel, Joan Therese Alexander, dean, $367,126
Gable, Sara E, prof, asoc, $73,023
Gabriel-Schaper, Kim, temporary clerical, $10.00/hr
Gace, Janice Lou, nurse, clincl charge-lpn, $23.01/hr
Gachpaz, Babak, resident physician-3rd yr, $52,470
Gaddis, Monica, prof, ast adjunct, $61,000
Gaddy, Amber J, program/project supprt coor II, $63,240
Gaddy, Melissa Ann, office support assistant III, $13.02/hr
Gadel, Alice M, student support specialist I, $13.03/hr
Gadi, Rajyalakshmi, adjunct, $15,000
Gadsden, Christopher T, lecturer, $24,000
Gadson, Shalone Monecia, office support assistant IV, $13.86/hr
Gadson, Sharon Ann, office support assistant III, $12.11/hr
Gaffey, Karen, food svc wrkr II, $11.83/hr
Gaffney, Amy Denise, program/project supprt coor I, $42,935
Gafke, Roger A, emeritus, $90,898
Gage, Colin C, business svcs consultant sr, $80,550
Gagnon, Dennis R, dir I, strat communications, $105,080
Gagnon, Terri Loibl, editor II, $42,848
Gahl, John Michel, professor, $152,892
Gahl, Martha Trauth, high school student, $10.00/hr
Gai, Andrew John, instructor, adjunct, $24,456
Gaidi, Sekou S, event assistant I, $8.00/hr
Gaines, Carol L, patient svc rep, $14.28/hr
Gaines, Julia R, prof, asoc, $100,000
Gaines, Karen Lee, instructor, adjunct, $9,000
Gaines, Sarah R, dietitian, clincl, $22.00/hr
Gainor, Barry J, emeritus, $118,828
Gajda, Laura Anne, exec dir advancement-hsc, $146,985
Gakali, Jimmy Ngobo, custodian, $12.94/hr
Galambos, Colleen M, professor, $114,863
Galatta, Aboma, support systems admin-speclst, $57,296
Gale, Leslie L, student service coor II, $44,500
Galeassi, Mark Allen II, programmer analyst-expert, $66,950
Galecki, Grzegorz, prof, asoc, $95,042
Galen, Candace, professor, $114,625
Galen, Jeff A, instructor, adjunct, $11,250
Galen, Melody R, editor II, $49,701
Galenas, Isabel Paulette, nurse, staff II, $21.37/hr

Galenas, Rimas G, prof, ast teach, $34,680
Galindo, Narbeli, instructor, $60,000
Gall, Audra L, human resources specialist III, $48,720
Gallagher, Patrick Edward, telecomm opr-h, $11.32/hr
Gallagher, Ryan D, custodian, $12.94/hr
Gallagher, Ryan Patrick, temporary clerical, $8.00/hr
Gallardo, Mark, asoc dir business admin, $57,620
Gallazzi, Fabio, prof, ast resrch, $71,616
Gallemore, Cassie Nichole, nurse, staff I, $19.00/hr
Galler, Tracy Michelle, office support assistant IV, $14.56/hr
Gallihugh, Stanley M Jr, office support assistant IV, $14.12/hr
Gallimore, Rangira Bea, prof, asoc, $66,091
Gallimore, Salama Mieretta, bus svcs consultant sr, $68,000
Gallion, Michael Eugene, nurse anesthetist, $95.00/hr
Gallop, Amy A, pat care techn, $11.75/hr
Galloway, Kristi Erin, strat comm associate I, $37,875
Galloway, Rockford Dale, supv, food svc II-h, $47,861
Galloway, Tabitha Lynn Ireland, res physician-5th yr, $58,083
Galloway, Tina Marie, office support assistant IV, $13.11/hr
Gallup, Amanda Marie, food svc wrkr II, $10.49/hr
Gallup, Bridget A, business support specialist sr, $22.31/hr
Gallup, Cara D, program/project supprt coor I, $38,800
Gallup, Fonda M, anesthesia techn, $16.22/hr
Gallup, Kourtney Michelle, temporary crafts service, $7.75/hr
Gallup, Lianna Marie, nurse, staff II, $29.33/hr
Gallup, Renetta J, dir II human resources, $110,148
Galmore, Kimberly Ann, adjunct, $15,300
Galovan, Adam Michael, grader, $100.00/hr
Galovski, Tara Ellen, prof, asoc, $79,235
Galvin, Victoria, office support assistant IV, $19.03/hr
Galyen, Krista Dawn, instructional designer-expert, $54,000
Gambaro, Stephen Colin, strat comm associate I, $34,400
Gamble, Sean James, resident physician-3rd yr, $52,470
Gamblin, Sarah Marie, office support assistant II, $10.69/hr
Gamboa, Amanda Brooke, nurse, staff now III, $30.00/hr
Gamboa, Jose Leonardo Bugayong, nurse, staff II rnwp, $21.57/hr
Gamez de Levy, Patricia, resident physician-3rd yr, $53,763
Ganahl, Dennis J, prof, ast visiting, $61,500
Ganaway, Chad Orie, food svc wrkr II, $11.07/hr
Gandara, Madeline E, patient svc rep, $12.76/hr
Gandolfi, Barbara, prof, ast resrch, $81,600
Gandy, Stefanie Renee, library info specialist, $12.98/hr
Gangloff, Karen Ashley, fellow, post doctoral, $72,600
Gangloff, Mark D, ast coach, $50,000
Gangopadhyay, Keshab, prof, resrch, $87,347
Gangopadhyay, Shubhra, professor, $187,684
Ganjam, Irene K, supv, lab, $57,601
Ganley, Brian C, prof, ast teach, $66,045
Gann, James R, business svcs consultant sr, $88,400
Gannan, Franklin D, network engineer-expert, $62,412
Gannan, Laurie M, business support specialist II, $17.92/hr
Ganong, Lawrence H, professor, $133,624
Gansmann, Amy Renee, nurse, licensed prac, $21.19/hr
Ganss, Paul Edward, clinical lab manager II, $73,916
Gant, Austin Dylan, user support analyst-entry, $19.25/hr
Gant, Cortaiga Anteggina, research/lab technician sr, $14.50/hr
Gant, Kelly Ray, environmental health prof II, $47,162
Ganti, Latha, physician, $250.00/hr
Gantzer, Clark J, professor, $70,598
Ganz, David R, emeritus, $30,564
Gao, Jie, prof, ast, $80,523
Gao, Stephen Shangxing, professor, $109,447
Gao, Yong, prof, asoc, $127,710
Gaona, Emma Jean, mental health tech, $14.88/hr
Garavalia, Linda S, dean, asoc, $150,000
Garb, Candace Todd, program/project supprt coor I, $47,277
Garcelon, Marc, prof, asoc, $73,260
Garcia Dominguez, Juan Diego, csm project manager, $85,000
Garcia Rubio, Joni Lynn, strat comm associate II, $42,840
Garcia Touza, Mariana, prof, ast clincl dept, $143,263
Garcia, Barbara J, custodian, $11.41/hr
Garcia, Cynthia S, program/project supprt coor I, $35,002
Garcia, Debra S, office supervisor, $43,000
Garcia, Donna Marie, temporary professional, $20.00/hr
Garcia, Gail C, pat care phy suprt, $60,565
Garcia, Kelly Miller, office support assistant II, $10.24/hr
Garcia, Kristin Michelle, instructor, adjunct, $125.00/hr
Garcia, Michael Leonard, prof, asoc, $75,323
Garcia, Natalie Brooke, custodian, $12.94/hr

Garcia, Nicholas Avel, media producer II, $15.17/hr
Garcia, Sarah A, temporary professional, $13.00/hr
Garcia, Sydney Lynn, food svc wrkr I, $9.60/hr
Garcia, Tamara J, optician, $40,030
Garcia, Virginia Brooke, research specialist sr, $20.00/hr
Garcia, Zacheriah James, mental health tech, $11.73/hr
Garcille, Erika Lynn, business ops associate I, $42,400
Gard, Amber Rose, media production associate, $8.89/hr
Gard, Lisa Michelle, physician, $200.00/hr
Gardi, Lisa Marie, instructor, adjunct, $4,200
Gardiner, Edith N, coor, care, $67,544
Gardner, Frank B III, prof, ast adjunct, $300.00/hr
Gardner-Andrews, Anna, tutor, $25.00/hr
Gardner, Allison Michelle, instructor, clincl, $6,667
Gardner, Beverly Ann, instructor, visiting, $64,921
Gardner, Cheryl Michelle, nurse practitioner, $78,134
Gardner, Christine Lynn, nurse anesthetist, $147,900
Gardner, Debra Lynn, patient svc rep, $14.88/hr
Gardner, James R, professor, $50,000
Gardner, Matthew R, system support analyst-expert, $28.68/hr
Gardner, Meghan Kate, temporary clerical, $16.00/hr
Gardner, Michael Jay, prof, ast clincl dept, $148,881
Gardner, Ruth L, student support specialist I, $15.76/hr
Gardner, Sally Lyn, nurse, staff II, $34.04/hr
Gardner, Shannon Lee, surgical technl certified, $15.87/hr
Garey, Katherine M, asoc dir student support svcs, $61,812
Garfias, Cesar L, radiologic techl, $18.59/hr
Garfias, Pamela A, business support specialist II, $22.32/hr
Garg, Megha, prof, ast clincl dept, $250,000
Gargus, Almyra Louise, office support assistant III, $12.73/hr
Gargus, Jan, office support assistant II, $11.28/hr
Gargus, Jessica Elaine, couns hlth/welfare/wellness, $42,000
Garhart, Christine A, prof, ast teach, $70,433
Garikapaty, Venkata, prof, ast adjunct, $27,000
Garipalli, Archana, resident physician-3rd yr, $53,763
Garland, Noah M, research specialist sr, $50,416
Garlock, Shelby Lynne, nurse, staff II, $20.54/hr
Garman, Carol J, resrch asoc, $15,600
Garmon, Patricia Anne, business support specialist II, $18.07/hr
Garms, Michael Eugene, police officer, $16.54/hr
Garneau, Chelsea Lynn, prof, ast, $70,000
Garner, Emily Anne, student support specialist II, $17.15/hr
Garner, Erin Michelle, temporary professional, $11.30/hr
Garner, George A, system support analyst-expert, $22.09/hr
Garner, Nicole Lynn, business support specialist II, $17.85/hr
Garner, Paula C, accountant sr, $63,123
Garnett, Jeremy Owen, animal caretaker, $12.12/hr
Garnett, Lori A, cardiovasc techn invasive, $23.92/hr
Garnov, Alexander Yuryevich, chemist II, $64,023
Garr, Pamela J, business support specialist II, $19.76/hr
Garr, Shauntel Rayette, patient svc rep, $13.67/hr
Garrard, Leigh A, instructor, adjunct, $62.50/hr
Garrett, David Claybourne IV, resident physician-4th yr, $54,425
Garrett, Arwood Jr, program/project supprt coor sr, $55,291
Garrett, Deborah C, mgr II business admin, $59,433
Garrett, Elizabeth Ann, prof, clinical dept, $182,070
Garrett, Harold, emeritus, $85,000
Garrett, Jason Thomas, recruiter, hlth care, $63,631
Garrett, Jennifer Lee, instructor, adjunct, $13,214
Garrett, Jennifer Rae, food svc wrkr I, $9.60/hr
Garrett, Jeremy Ray, instructor, adjunct, $9,000
Garrett, Jerry D, athletic attd, $14.47/hr
Garrett, Jonah Walker, resident physician-4th yr, $54,425
Garrett, Krista Leigh, intern, $26,265
Garrett, Lawrence W, bts equip opr, $21.71/hr
Garrett, Mary Lou, security officer, $10.24/hr
Garrett, Matthew C, dir program/project operations, $56,502
Garrett, Miranda Jean, hospital lab tech, $12.46/hr
Garrett, Scott Lee, grounds keeper, $12.12/hr
Garrett, Susan, resrch asoc, $50,000
Garrett, Will Anderson, research/lab technician, $12.80/hr
Garrett, Zachary Ryan, electronics technician I, $11.92/hr
Garris, David R, prof, asoc teach, $71,615
Garrison, Annemarie L, nurse, staff II, $20.95/hr
Garrison, Carol Jeanne, grader, $52
Garrison, Douglas W, ast mgr pat admissions, $63,174
Garrison, Julie Renee, pat acct rep, $14.95/hr
Garrison, Kathy Ann, office support assistant IV, $15.12/hr
Garrison, Lanette Marie, occl therapist, $71,053

Garrison, Larry, professor, $139,714
Garrison, Leanna Catherine, business support spclst II, $18.42/hr
Garrison, Linda K, business support specialist II, $17.03/hr
Garrison, Robert Strickler, network engineer-expert, $60,222
Garro, Mona, research/lab technician sr, $18.37/hr
Garry, Vanessa Bean, prof, ast, $60,000
Garson, Scott Arnold, prof, ast teach, $34,680
Garth, Linda C, program/project supprt coor II, $64,653
Gartner, Carrie Nell, dir communications & pub rel, $110,000
Garton, Bryan L, dean, asoc, $199,863
Garton, Susan Lynn, instructor, ast, $35,100
Garvey, Jacqueline Sue, histologic technl, $25.00/hr
Garvin, Michael Roy, human resources specialist III, $59,303
Garzia, Ralph P, prof, asoc, $129,789
Garzon, Dawn L, prof, teach, $98,252
Gash, Patricia L, csm operations supervisor, $50,688
Gassmann, Walter, professor, $120,298
Gastecki, Michelle Lynn, research specialist I, $16.00/hr
Gastineau, Elizabeth Ann, office support assistant III, $13.00/hr
Gastler, Amanda Leigh, communications coord sr, $16.87/hr
Gatapia, Dramises I, mts/hvac lead, $26.61/hr
Gateley, Crystal Aileen, prof, asoc teach, $76,996
Gater, Teena Eileen, nurse advisor, telephone, $29.25/hr
Gates, Callie Elizabeth Holmes, office support asst IV, $14.33/hr
Gates, Kent S, professor, $128,963
Gates, Stephanie Jeanette, dir clinic ops, $134,550
Gatewood, Simona D, sterile processing tech, $18.86/hr
Gathercole, Kathy A, stores clerk, $12.98/hr
Gatica, Maria Resurreccion L, med lab techn, $23.34/hr
Gatson, Linda Marie, office support assistant III, $23.15/hr
Gatzke, Carolin Gotnimi, pharmacist III, $128,835
Gaubatz, Douglas Frederick, prof, ast adjunct, $9,000
Gaughan, Keith M, db programmer analyst-princpl, $60,743
Gaughan, Sharon Kay, library information assistant, $11.30/hr
Gaughran, Jacob E, fire inspector III, $21.05/hr
Gault, Sandra L, dir II student support svcs, $75,741
Gaunt, Matthew Moore, dir II advancement, $79,931
Gavett, Christine Elizabeth, prof, ast clincl, $71,946
Gavett, Neil Bruce, model, $10.50/hr
Gavin, Lauren Elizabeth, care team assoc-clinical, $12.80/hr
Gavin, Ryan Robert, strat comm associate I, $35,290
Gavin, Stephanie Lynn, instructor, adjunct, $9,000
Gawin, Jennifer R, instructor, adjunct, $6,300
Gawlik, Justin Arthur, athletic trainer, $15,000
Gawron, Mary Lynnette, office support assistant IV, $15.86/hr
Gay, Cassandra L, office support assistant III, $12.59/hr
Gay, John W, dean, asoc, $150,000
Gayer, Patricia, business support specialist II, $18.17/hr
Gayou, Audrey M, museum paraprofessional II, $15.76/hr
Gayou, Douglas, prof, ast teach, $46,513
Gazda, Jeanette M, business support specialist II, $15.53/hr
Ge, Bin, statistician, $59,433
Ge, Mao Chen, prof, asoc, $100,500
Geary, David C, prof, curators, $199,600
Gebhardt, Christopher Lawrence, supv, food svc II-h, $40,428
Gebhardt, Melinda Kay, patient svc rep, $14.88/hr
Gee, Mara Jean, business support specialist II, $24.16/hr
Gee, Ryan Lynn, resrch ast sr, $49,000
Geehan, Douglas M, adjunct, $15,000
Geerlings, Karla L, library info specialist sr, $15.03/hr
Geery, Wayne L, network engineer-speclst, $53,560
Gehrig, Dustin L, patient svc rep, $12.92/hr
Gehrig, Kathy L, patient svc rep, $15.33/hr
Gehrke, Suzanne Victoria Arnold, prof, ast resrch, $75,000
Geiger, David Stuart, mgr respiratory care, $112,154
Geiger, Lisa K, patient svc rep, $14.06/hr
Geisert, Rodney Dean, professor, $171,307
Geisert, Susan K, academic advisor, $36,826
Geisler, Angelee Michelle, nurse, staff prn, $26.00/hr
Geisler, Carol S, business support specialist II, $17.37/hr
Geisler, Gregory Gerard, prof, asoc, $134,665
Geiss, Mary Bridget, lecturer, $36,240
Geissert, Lori Ann, patient svc rep, $13.74/hr
Geist, Linda Ann, strat comm associate I, $40,400
Geitz, Samantha Michele, temporary technical, $20.00/hr
Gelder, Jennifer Breneman, nurse, staff II rnwp, $25.74/hr
Geldner, Michael Shane, mts/electrician, $21.05/hr
Geller, Noah F, prof, adjunct, $5,760
Gelles, Gregory, professor, $140,148

Gellman, David, system administrator-speclst, $54,872
Gellman, Suzanne Zemelman, family fincl edu spclst, $56,983
Gely, Rafael, professor, $222,991
Gemignani, Cynthia, office support assistant IV, $17.36/hr
Geno, Kendal L, resident physician-2nd yr, $52,007
Genochio, Jerry J, dir repertory theatre, $123,552
Genovese, Nicholas John, fellow, post doctoral, $37,000
Gensamer, Connie L, system support analyst-entry, $17.70/hr
Gensamer, Joseph Arthur, user support analyst-spec, $17.69/hr
Gentges, Ryan William, waiter/waitress, $13.22/hr
Gentis, Jennifer Michelle, med office assistant, $11.07/hr
Gentry, Bettina Anne, veterinarian, $21,959
Gentry, Brenda J, phlebotomist, $13.20/hr
Gentry, Lindsey Raye, program/project supprt coor I, $40,198
Gentry, Roxanne Marie, nurse, staff II, $34.68/hr
Gentry, Shelby, dental assistant II, $12.98/hr
Gentry, Todd, csm associate III, $27.92/hr
Gentzler, Evan W, event assistant I, $12.50/hr
Gentzsch, Judy Lynne, office support assistant III, $16.14/hr
Genualdi, Joseph Fred, professor, $83,230
George, Ameera Domonique, phlebotomist, $11.88/hr
George, Angela M, office support assistant IV, $15.58/hr
George, Britney Taylor, office support assistant IV, $13.96/hr
George, Christina Beth, office support assistant IV, $13.05/hr
George, Christina Rose, user support analyst-entry, $14.95/hr
George, Darwin Floyd, event assistant I, $9.50/hr
George, Dionne Natalie, student service coor II, $43,990
George, Gary G, utility dist wrkr III, $20.77/hr
George, Kevin Randall, manuscript specialist, $34,500
George, Thomas F, chancellor, $319,802
Georges, Anthony, dir II student support svcs, $95,559
Georges, George T, fellow, post doc clncl yr1, $55,804
Geotz, Judy Marie, office support assistant III, $14.49/hr
Gephardt, Timothy, managing engineer, $74,037
Gerald II, Rex E, scientist lead, $91,860
Gerardy, Nancy Lynn, instructor, adjunct, $16,800
Gerau, John Edward, supv engineering, $54,676
Gerau, Sue Carol, nurse, licensed prac, $19.59/hr
Gerber, Michael David, nurse, staff II rnwp, $23.12/hr
Gerbes, Jessica Dawn, nurse, staff per diem, $35.00/hr
Gerdes, Becky S, hlth prgm ast, $16.72/hr
Gerdes, Bryan C, resrch ast, $41,200
Gerding, Billy R, electronics technician sr, $25.94/hr
Gerding, Laura Ann, strat comm associate II, $54,310
Gerding, Zachary J, electronics technician II, $15.26/hr
Geren, Karen Maree, business ops associate sr, $70,000
Gerhardt, Howard Carl Jr, prof, curators, $155,201
Gerhardt, Jared David, prof, ast adjunct, $125.00/hr
Gerhardt, Klaus O, scientist lead, $29.13/hr
Gerhart, Deborah Louise, prof, ast teach, $65,975
Gerhart, Sandra L, office support assistant IV, $17.83/hr
Gerhart, Tammy Diann, retail sales manager, $51,500
Gerke, Daneal Blanche, educational pgm associate I, $13.30/hr
Gerke, Janice L, educational pgm associate I, $13.53/hr
Gerke, Susan A, instructor, adjunct, $1,600
Gerkovich, Mary M, prof, asoc, $86,500
Gerlach, Corin N, insulation svcs wrkr I, $17.78/hr
Gerlach, Donald, csm professional sr, $77,500
Gerlach, Heather Dawn, supv pat accts-up, $52,400
Gerlach, Stephanie, office support assistant IV, $15.64/hr
Gerling, Hannah Laura, nurse, staff II, $20.95/hr
Gerling, Vernon Lee, police officer, $20.04/hr
Gerlt, Scott A, resrch asoc, $74,017
Germain, Dustin P, business support specialist II, $19.55/hr
German, Abby Christine, veterinary technician, $15.50/hr
German, Debi L, nurse, staff II, $34.18/hr
Germann, Marla E, technology resource coor, $70,852
Germeroth, Cynthia Bryant, db administrator-princpl, $74,491
Germeroth, Paul H, telecom engineer-speclst, $49,911
Gernander, Emily Ivy, nurse, staff prn, $26.00/hr
Gerrein, Sheryl Lee, business support specialist II, $17.65/hr
Gerry, Matthew Elbridge, media producer II, $16.44/hr
Gerstein, Emily D, prof, ast, $65,000
Gerstlauer, Janmari H, educational pgm associate I, $14.44/hr
Gerteis, Louis Saxton, professor, $111,520
Gerth, Daniel J, dean, asoc, $82,000
Gertler, Erica Lynn Nuttall, temporary technical, $8.00/hr
Gertsch, Leslie Sour, prof, asoc, $78,023
Gervino, Christopher J, on-air talent television, $53,591

Gestring, Johnathan Scott, ast mgr hospitality services, $40,788
Gesztesy, Friedrich, professor, $156,641
Gett, Michael Gregory, rec/athletic specialist, $14.43/hr
Getz, Keith, powr plnt opr lead, $31.58/hr
Getz, Stephen P, nurse, staff prn, $26.00/hr
Getzendaner, Gail A, dir nursing designee, $89,735
Gewecke, Kenton Donald, on-air talent television, $28,000
Gewinner, Kim M, enrollment advisor sr, $17.22/hr
Geyer, Brooke D, prof, ast clincl dept, $144,813
Geyer, Elizabeth O, instructor, lab, $47,000
Geyer, Francis A, child dev asoc teacher, $11.30/hr
Ghan, Cheri R, student recruitment spclst sr, $23.16/hr
Ghan, Christopher Brent, temporary professional, $8.00/hr
Ghanem, Yazan, resident physician-1st yr, $49,025
Gharahbeigi, Sara, fellow, post doctoral, $48,000
Ghasr, Mohammad Tayeb, prof, ast resrch, $74,220
Ghatehorde, Namratta Kaur, resident physician-2nd yr, $52,007
Ghazali, Amira Hamed A A, resident physician-5th yr, $56,120
Ghazanfarpour, Nayereh, research/lab technician sr, $14.00/hr
Gherardini, Mary Catherine, teaching ast, $13.00/hr
Ghio, Katie Anne, child dev teacher sr, $29,362
Gholson, Ginger K, resp care clinical coor, $28.10/hr
Gholson, Talia J, human resources specialist III, $23.61/hr
Ghosh, Atreyo, lab assistant, $10.00/hr
Ghosh, Jaya, fellow, $50,219
Ghosh, Rajgourab, fellow, post doctoral, $31,000
Ghosh, Tushar K, professor, $101,954
Giacomelli, Kristy Kay, ast registrar, $48,000
Gianino, Kevin G, prof, ast adjunct, $2,250
Gianladis, Eugene James, psychologist, $54,200
Gianladis, John James, speech/lang pathologist, $72,675
Gibb, Erika L, professor, $76,982
Gibbons, Amanda Lea, nurse, staff II rnwp, $22.12/hr
Gibbons, Carolyn L, fin and acctg manager, $80,871
Gibbons, Julie Ann, custodian, $10.00/hr
Gibbons, Vicki, sr ast dir studnt supprt svcs, $65,693
Gibbs, Gregory L, business tech analyst-expert, $69,163
Gibbs, James Jr R, maint svc attd, $16.24/hr
Gibbs, Mary Vanette, infection control profl, $69,639
Gibbs, Vanessa W, cook, $15.03/hr
Gibler, Michelle M, instructor, clincl, $87,616
Gibler, Rhonda K, vice chancellor, $234,000
Giboney, Robert W, house manager h, $78,227
Gibson, Melvin Lee Jr, event assistant I, $7.55/hr
Gibson, Abigail Maryce, nurse, staff I, $19.00/hr
Gibson, Carla Roussin, strat comm associate I, $43,458
Gibson, David B, dir I, strat communications, $94,860
Gibson, David D, supv ambulance svcs, $21.61/hr
Gibson, Ginger R, serv line spclst, $68,793
Gibson, Heather Lindsey, research specialist I, $31,969
Gibson, Kyle, prof, asoc teach, $124,817
Gibson, Mara B, prgm director, $54,535
Gibson, Maya C, prof, ast, $57,950
Gibson, Rhonda K, med coding spclst-certified, $22.32/hr
Gibson, Russell Wade, reactor operator sr, $31.30/hr
Gibson, Tammy Michelle, nurse anesthetist, $147,902
Gibson, Tanya Marie, prof, ast, $95,325
Gibson, Twyla Gail, prof, ast, $71,563
Gibson, Warren, office support assistant III, $14.95/hr
Gielow, Kelsie Renee, care team assoc-clinical, $11.32/hr
Gielow, Kurt Hanson, research/lab technician, $10.24/hr
Gieras, Angela Lee, dir repertory theatre, $140,000
Gierse, Jo M, strat comm consultant, $56,811
Giesel, Janett G, pat acct rep, $15.78/hr
Giesel, Stephen Frederick, instructional designer-expert, $59,590
Giesing, Nicole Marie, nurse, staff II, $20.95/hr
Giesler, Julie Sue, business support specialist II, $22.32/hr
Giessman, Jacob Adam, instructor, adjunct, $8,400
Giessmann, Rebecca Kay, anesthesia techn, $16.14/hr.14/hr
Giessmann, Sarah Louise, nurse, staff II rnwp, $21.37/hr
Gifford, Christopher Michael, resident physician-2nd yr, $50,810
Gifford, Kim A, stage services assistant lead, $18.45/hr
Gilbert, Danielle Wiggins, specialist, $10.00/hr
Gilbert, Janet M, surgical technl certified, $18.00/hr
Gilbert, Nicholas D, operations support tech sr, $16.13/hr
Gilbert, Paul E, emrg med techn paramedic, $15.29/hr
Gilbert, Steven A, custodian mrc, $10.50/hr
Gilbertsen, Lisa Anne, resrch ast, $2,667
Gilbertson, Peggy K, student service coor sr, $36,503

Gilbertson, Samuel Charles, custodian, $10.94/hr
Gilbreth, David Greg, resp therapist reg, $23.97/hr
Gilbreth, Timothy M, research/lab technician sr, $17.66/hr
Giles, Justin R, user support analyst-expert, $20.37/hr
Giles, Lydia Cathleen, executive assistant, $21.78/hr
Gilford, Tyrone Anthony, custodian, $12.50/hr
Gilgour, Katelyn Elizabeth, patient svc rep, $10.85/hr
Gilkison, Natalie Grace, executive assistant, $18.00/hr
Gill, Dorothy Elizabeth, nurse, staff II, $21.27/hr
Gill, Janet L, fin and acctg manager, $49,165
Gill, Jonathan Jabez, care team assoc-clinical, $11.10/hr
Gill, Megan Leis, strat comm consultant sr, $68,848
Gill, Olivia S, office support assistant IV, $14.92/hr
Gill, Rita, care team assoc-clinical, $13.33/hr
Gill, Shareen, care team assoc-clinical, $11.10/hr
Gilland, Ashley Rose, office support assistant III, $13.00/hr
Gillard, Rebecca Lynn, clerk, unit, $11.07/hr
Gillenwater, Kristin Stonebraker, adjunct, $15,000
Gilles, Carol, prof, asoc, $72,313
Gilles, Jere Lee, prof, asoc, $81,172
Gillespie, Daniel L, hospital security officer, $13.57/hr
Gillespie, Erin N, nurse, staff II, $29.34/hr
Gillespie, Tammy, educational prgm coor sr, $56,931
Gillespie, Torian Darshon, temporary crafts service, $14.00/hr
Gillette, Maris Boyd, professor, $120,000
Gillette, Mary Patrice, executive assistant, $22.34/hr
Gilliam, Stephanie Nicole, veterinary technician sr, $17.67/hr
Gillies, Argyle Douglas Stewart, professor, $114,606
Gilligan, Christopher James, custodian, $11.44/hr
Gilligan, Joseph Justin, custodian, $12.50/hr
Gilliland, Shanna Michelle, business tech analyst-spclst, $59,784
Gillin, Douglas P, sr asoc athletic director, $219,000
Gillingham, John Rowley III, founders professor, $37,395
Gillis, William L III, managing engineer, $87,500
Gillis, Kevin D, professor, $135,155
Gillis, Paul, high school student, $10.00/hr
Gillispie, John Patton, executive director, $183,731
Gillman, Max Kenneth, professor, $213,300
Gilman, Randall L, pharmacy tech, $10.64/hr
Gilmore, Amy C, program/project supprt coor I, $43,500
Gilmore, Courtney M, office support assistant III, $16.35/hr
Gilmore, Kevin D, sr manager it, $86,000
Gilmore, Wilbur Dean, fleet vehicle attd, $14.27/hr
Gilness, Siiri Marie, office support assistant IV, $13.15/hr
Gilpin, Abby Gayle, business support specialist II, $17.85/hr
Gilpin, Alison Kay, nurse, staff now III, $30.00/hr
Gilpin, Gwen Renee, office support assistant III, $12.59/hr
Gilpin, Jodi L, network engineer-expert, $62,338
Gilpin, Lisa J, linen attd, $12.96/hr
Gilzow, Joshua F, business tech analyst-spclst, $62,118
Gilzow, Paul F, programmer analyst-expert, $69,530
Ginger Horne, Selisa Ann, custodian, $10.39/hr
Gingerich, Levi J, bts carpenter, $21.71/hr
Gingrich, Kari Michelle, instructor, adjunct, $40,000
Ginn, Cynthia, program/project supprt coor I, $48,551
Ginnings, Tiffany Lea, office support assistant IV, $13.24/hr
Ginsburg, Mark A, operations support tech I, $10.24/hr
Ginter-Novinger, Sarah Ann, temporary clerical, $13.65/hr
Giordano, J Christopher, system administrator-expert, $68,434
Gipson, Jonathan Leigh, custodian, $10.39/hr
Gipson, Nellie, telecomm opr-h, $11.64/hr
Gipson, Scott Allan, library info specialist sr, $15.32/hr
Gipson, Teresa Lynn, library info specialist sr, $17.46/hr
Girard, Tiffney Gayle, emrg med techn, $13.16/hr
Girivaru, Ravindra Venkata, prof, asoc, $75,207
Gish, Melissa Jean, clerk, unit, $14.09/hr
Gish, Orral S, research engineering tech I, $27.66/hr
Gisi, Greta Marie, educational pgm coor I, $33,330
Gitan, Raad Shebib, research specialist sr, $52,804
Gitonga, DeNae Leanna, community dev spclst, $41,000
Gittemeier, Thomas S, sr manager it, $88,486
Giuliano, Elizabeth A, prof, asoc, $126,988
Giuliano, Molly, media producer sr, $42,000
Givan, Scott A, asoc director, $100,815
Givens, James Arthur Jr, db programmer analyst-princpl, $76,171
Givens, Gwen Lynn, food svc wrkr I, $9.60/hr
Givens, Jason Matthew, custodian, $13.36/hr
Gizer, Ian R, prof, ast, $74,970
Glaab, David Lee, mover, $14.27/hr

Glaab, Linda Susan, linen attd, $11.16/hr
Gladbach, Pamela K, educational pgm associate I, $13.45/hr
Glahn, Anastasia, veterinary technician sr, $15.67/hr
Glascock, Callie Kathryn, dir II business admin, $95,190
Glascock, Jacqueline Jean, fellow, post doctoral, $35,000
Glascock, Michael Dean, resrch scientist/academic sr, $111,293
Glascock, Nicholas Barrett, nurse clinician, $60,000
Glaser, Rainer Ernst, professor, $75,524
Glasgow, Arlandis Sharod, office support assistant III, $12.28/hr
Glasgow, Leora, rehab therapy aide, $17.82/hr
Glash, James R, head coach, $61,670
Glasker, Sharon, communications coordinator sr, $17.67/hr
Glaskey, David Aamon, seasonal farm ast, $10.51/hr
Glaskey, Marsha Kay, ultrasonographer, $25.56/hr
Glass, Alisa D, reimbursement ast-cert, $18.59/hr
Glass, Bret Amittae, csm operations coordinator, $20.20/hr
Glass, Kay Lynn, radiation ther therapist, $34.94/hr
Glass, Sarah Beth, speech/lang pathologist, $49,920
Glass, Timothy E, professor, $88,185
Glassberg, Andrew Durst, temporary professional, $15.00/hr
Glassmaker, Kelsey Lynn, nurse, staff II, $20.54/hr
Glassman, Joel Norman, academic dir, $135,368
Glaubitz, Jeanna Marie, instructor, adjunct, $4,800
Gleason, Catherine Honore, prof, ast teach, $37,124
Gleason, Deborah Ann, human resources specialist I, $15.06/hr
Gleason, Julia E, business support specialist II, $18.85/hr
Gleason, Nancy L, emeritus, $65,000
Gleba, Richard J Jr, strat comm consultant sr, $89,100
Glendening, Matthew Ryan, prof, ast, $173,400
Glenn, Brandon Nicole, coor business-up, $19.02/hr
Glenn, John R, architect II, $59,884
Glenn, Mary Maxine Gill, nurse, staff, $24.97/hr
Glick, Elisa Fern, prof, asoc, $71,256
Glidewell, Bob, grant writer sr, $40,048
Glidewell, Kimberly Rochelle, mental health tech, $11.50/hr
GlinskII, Olga V, prof, ast resrch, $44,342
GlinskII, Vladislav, prof, asoc, $45,081
Glise, Anthony Leroy, prof, ast adjunct, $35,700
Glissmann, Christine Nicole, office support asst III, $13.08/hr
Glosson, Lori Lee, certif pharmacy techn, $12.71/hr
Glover, Drew W, resident physician-4th yr, $54,425
Glover, Max A, agronomy spclst, $45,148
Glushko, Anna Yurievna, tutor, $9.00/hr
Glynn, Earl F, db programmer analyst-princpl, $76,000
Go, Steven, adjunct, $15,000
Goad, Jonathan Giles, media producer I, $12.99/hr
Goans, Matthew Brant, fin and acctg analyst sr, $50,600
Gochenour, Julie B, business tech analyst-expert, $71,796
Goddard, Kara Brooke, pharmacist, $117,341
Godec, Jesse Adam, medical base supervisor, $64,584
Godefroid, Kathleen Mae, mental health tech, $11.50/hr
Godsey, Deanna Lee, mgr managed care contracting, $150,075
Godsy, Gary M, technology resource coor, $66,230
Godsy, Lauren Elizabeth, food svc wrkr II, $10.10/hr
Godwin, Blake M, temporary technical, $20.00/hr
Godwin, Deborah Hohlt, dir II advancement, $98,850
Godwin, Linda Maxine, professor, $99,224
Goe, Gregory, network engineer-speclst, $67,131
Goedert, Martha Hoffman, prof, ast adjunct, $12,000
Goedrich, Sammy Harvey, hand therapist cert, $59,640
Goeller, Emily Griffard, resident physician-4th yr, $55,804
Goerke, Marilyn Joyce, instructor, adjunct, $7,386
Goerndt, Angela Marie, research/lab technician sr, $15.33/hr
Goerndt, Michael E, fellow, post doctoral, $45,895
Goers, Bryan K, student service coor II, $41,531
Goettemoeller, Dareth Ann, teaching ast, $55.00/hr
Goff, Carol L, office support assistant III, $12.00/hr
Goff, Jessie Marie, nurse, staff I, rnwp, $19.00/hr
Goff, Veronica Lynn, nurse, staff II, $21.37/hr
Goggins, Sean Patrick, prof, ast, $90,470
Gogol, Edward P, prof, asoc, $83,846
Gohar, Ashraf Anwar Samy, adjunct, $15,000
Goins, Rickey A, patient svc rep, $14.75/hr
Goins, Yhanika, student support specialist sr, $17.59/hr
Gokel, George William Jr, prof, distinguished, $188,213
Gold, Gloria Jean, food svc attd II-mrc, $10.71/hr
Gold, Kathleen Helen, student service coor sr, $46,512
Gold, Michael, prof, resrch, $120,614
Golda, Nicholas J, prof, ast clincl dept, $321,860

Goldberg, Marsha S, product support rep-expert, $53,544
Goldberg, Mathew R, prof, ast teach, $41,415
Golden, Frances E, specialist, $45,224
Golden, Jason Andrew, architect sr, $66,889
Golden, John H, social worker-non acute care, $52,836
Golden, Max Hunter, office support assistant I, $9.05/hr
Goldenberg, Zeena Finer, instructor, adjunct, $7,539
Goldenhersh, Elizabeth D, recreation spclst, therapu, $38,076
Goldman, Artice L, custodian, $12.94/hr
Goldman, Linda A, instructor, adjunct, $1,601
Goldman, Marcus DeJuan, custodian, $10.00/hr
Goldman, Tony Darnell, custodian, $10.39/hr
Goldschmidt, Benjamin Samuel, research specialist I, $23,712
Goldschmidt, Lisa Ann, instructor, adjunct, $9,600
Goldschmidt, Michael, prof, ast teach, $63,647
Goldschmidt, Steven Richard, instructor, $58,000
Goldstein Hode, Marlo Billie, fellow, post doctoral, $35,000
Goldstein, Christina Lynn, prof, ast, $260,000
Goldstein, David Evan, emeritus, $5,576
Goldstein, Laurie J, human resources specialist III, $41,420
Goldwasser, Cary Merle, strat comm manager, $56,917
Golian, Daniel L, floor care techn lead, $13.34/hr
Golian, Lanette S, cook, $13.21/hr
Goller, Donna M, nurse, staff per diem, $35.00/hr
Golomb, Miriam W, prof, asoc, $70,000
Gomero, Estela, custodian, $12.94/hr
Gomez, Francisco Gustavo, prof, asoc, $70,084
Gomez, Kenia L, instructor, adjunct, $8,325
Gomez, Maria, custodian, $13.36/hr
Gomez, Ruby Griselda, educational pgm associate I, $14.51/hr
Gompper, Matthew E, professor, $113,303
Gong, Xiaofen, med techl reg, $22.44/hr
Gonsher, Phillip, instructor, $60,000
Gonzales, Jacob Luis, office support assistant IV, $12.98/hr
Gonzalez, Abelardo, custodian, $13.36/hr
Gonzalez, Ben Dody, lecturer sr, $9,000
Gonzalez, Christian Eunice, resident physician-1st yr, $50,219
Gonzalez, David S, dir II advancement, $89,500
Gonzalez, Eleazar Ubaldo, resrch asoc, $44,558
Gonzalez, Irene, custodian, $13.36/hr
Gonzalez, Jaime, sterile processing tech, $18.31/hr
Gonzalez, Lorenzo Fernando, instructor, adjunct, $7,500
Gonzalez, Nancys, custodian, $13.36/hr
Gonzalez, Pamela Sue, compliance anlyst, $61,500
Gonzalez, Rosa Julia, pat acct rep, $14.86/hr
Gonzalez, Solange Andrea, instructor, adjunct, $21,600
Gooch, Dennis Ray Jr, custodian, $10.00/hr
Gooch, Jeremy, bts carpenter, $20.23/hr
Good, Robert Andrew, prof, ast adjunct, $8,004
Good, Talyn, instructor, adjunct, $18,648
Goodenow, Andrew J, asoc chief information officer, $130,000
Goodin, Audrey J, revenue recovery spclst, $28.48/hr
Gooding, Rylee Elaine, food svc wrkr II, $10.10/hr
Goodman II, Walter R, pat care techn, $12.65/hr
Goodman, Christopher M, nurse, staff II, $21.80/hr
Goodman, Dennis S, sr dir studnt supprt svcs, $157,900
Goodman, James A, asoc provost, $2,400
Goodman, Judith C, prof, asoc, $119,188
Goodman, Peter J, supv hosptlty & pat suprt svcs, $53,205
Goodman, Renae Darlene, educational pgm coor I, $34,441
Goodnick, Carol Elizabeth, nurse clinician, $72,675
Goodrich, Jeannine Gehrs, specialist, $66,971
Goodridge, Connie H, executive assistant, $25.75/hr
Goodridge, Nye Joel, strat comm manager, $46,114
Goodridge, Zachary Kurtis, police officer, $16.54/hr
Goodrum, Sherry Ann, reimbursement ast, $16.16/hr
Goodson, Repps B, telecom tech-princpl, $20.71/hr
Goodwin, Audrey Beth, office support assistant IV, $13.78/hr
Goodwin, Diane A, executive assistant, $21.57/hr
Goodwin, Gerald B, ast dir csm operations, $63,241
Goodwin, Joan L, db programmer analyst-princpl, $70,929
Goodwin, Martha R, instructor, clincl, $31,854
Goodyear, Michelle Lea, educational pgm associate I, $12.85/hr
Goolsby, Tiffany Nicole, educational pgm coor I, $34,441
Goosen, Brittany N, ast coach, $34,400
Gopalakrishna, Ganesh, prof, ast clincl dept, $177,900
Gopalakrishna, Srinath, professor, $172,484
Gopalaratnam, Ananthalakshmi, bus support spec sr, $19.23/hr
Gopalaratnam, Vellore S, professor, $122,530

Goran, Jason Lee, business tech analyst-expert, $69,894
Goran, Lisa Gail, instructor, adjunct, $9,900
Gordon, Gayle Anne, instructor, adjunct, $12,000
Gordon, Jalonn Earl, police officer, $18.33/hr
Gordon, Jean, instructor, clincl, $15,000
Gordon, Kathryn Ruth, pharmacy intern fifth year, $16.50/hr
Gordon, Malcolm Eugene, resrch ast, $29,920
Gordon, Marilyn Kathryn, tutor, $7.50/hr
Gordon, Matthew J, prof, asoc, $76,770
Gordon, Michelle Lynn, patient svc rep, $12.21/hr
Gordon, Rachel L, asoc dir program/project ops, $49,055
Gordon, Robert Lyle, asoc dir program/project ops, $61,200
Gordon, Tony Don, custodian, $11.44/hr
Gordy Panhorst, Karen Lynn, educational pgm coor III, $56,265
Gore, Lisa Ellen, nurse anesthetist, $147,900
Gore, Megan A, resrch ast, $40.00/hr
Gore, Nancy Jean, nurse, staff, $31.20/hr
Goree-Hamilton, Latoya Monique, prog/proj supprt coor sr, $66,625
Gorges, Jeffrey Graham, system administrator-princpl, $91,962
Gorham, Jennie L, physician, $247,931
Gorham, Lucas Michael, student support specialist II, $16.82/hr
Gorman-McAdams, Barbara Jan, office support asst IV, $16.99/hr
Gorman, Alison Kay, student support specialist II, $19.69/hr
Gorman, Kristi Ann, pat acct rep, $14.03/hr
Gormley, Sheri Annette, ast dean strategy & planning, $97,773
Gorrell, Jordan R, ophthalmic ast cert, $13.60/hr
Gorsage, Daniel Michael, resident physician-3rd yr, $53,763
Gorsegner, Whitney D, tutor, $10.00/hr
Gorski, Jeffrey P, professor, $114,255
Gorski, Jerome L, professor, $178,618
Gosavi, Abhijit, prof, asoc, $79,850
Gosche, Mary Louise, extns professional, asoc, $69,035
Goshorn, Mitchell S, office support assistant I, $10.24/hr
Goss, Morgan Nicole, nurse practitioner, $100.00/hr
Gosselin, Amy Michelle, nurse, licensed prac, $16.29/hr
Gossen, Ronald Howard, sr asoc vice chancellor, $170,158
Goswami, Lalit Nath, prof, ast resrch, $86,591
Goswami, Rashmi, temporary professional, $11.30/hr
Gotfredson, Jillian Evans, temporary clerical, $15.50/hr
Gotham, Heather J, prof, asoc resrch, $78,797
Gott, Sarah Margaret, program/project supprt coor I, $56,160
Gottman, Eric E, prof, asoc clincl, $105,956
Gotto, George Swift IV, prgm director, $67,883
Gough, James Patrick, agriculture associate II, $13.72/hr
Gould, Iva Jo, instructor, $9,910
Gould, Joanna L, resident physician-2nd yr, $50,810
Gounev, Todor K, prof, asoc teach, $55,516
Gouwens, Donald A, prof, asoc clincl, $76,583
Gov-Ari, Eliav, prof, ast clincl dept, $252,046
Gov-Ari, Hanna Klara, prof, ast clincl dept, $135,660
Gov-Ari, Hanna Klara, physician, $100.00/hr
Govindarajan, Raghav, prof, ast clincl dept, $130,000
Gowdy, Kathryn Laker, high school student, $8.75/hr
Gowdy, Mary Ann, prof, ast teach, $87,816
Gower, Joseph Raymond, custodian, $12.72/hr
Gowin, Elijah, professor, $81,151
Goyal, Mala, resident physician-4th yr, $54,425
Goyal, Munish Kumar, prof, ast clincl dept, $154,671
Goyal, Neha, fellow, post doc clncl yr1, $55,804
Goyne, Jennifer Lynn, programmer analyst-speclst, $58,566
Goyne, Keith William, prof, asoc, $86,262
Grabau, Andrew S, dir III advancement, $90,954
Grabau, Ashli Armstrong, student service coor II, $40,000
Grace, Win, office support assistant IV, $20.16/hr
Gracey, Thomas Burke, grounds keeper II, $16.07/hr
Gracia, Daniel, radiologic techl, $18.59/hr
Grady, Francis W, professor, $124,557
Graessle, Lisa Marie, nurse, advanced practice, $78,307
Graf, Paul G Jr, office support assistant IV, $14.60/hr
Graf, Devin Elizabeth, instructor, clincl, $52,015
Grafakos, Loukas, professor, $153,153
Graff, Teresa Naomi, supv, clinical-rehab svcs, $80,342
Gragg, Larry Dale, prof, curator teach, $137,942
Graham, April, sr dir program/project ops, $60,600
Graham, Barbara Luck, prof, asoc, $64,199
Graham, Charles Hauser, asoc dir program/project ops, $49,440
Graham, Deanna Sue, educational pgm associate I, $13.55/hr
Graham, Diana Lynn, mgr hskpg/laundry-mrc, $44,945
Graham, Eric Robert, health physics technician II, $22.75/hr

Graham, James P, account executive, $31,517
Graham, Kendra K, extns professional, asoc, $54,140
Graham, Louis K, resident physician-3rd yr, $53,763
Graham, Maqual R, professor, $117,500
Graham, Sheila Shelp, prof, ast adjunct, $28,500
Graham, Steven W, asoc vice president, $203,174
Grailer, Joseph George III, instructor, adjunct, $18,000
Gramlich, Lisa, nurse, staff II rnwp, $32.12/hr
Granade, Samuel A II, prof, asoc, $62,829
Grandestaff, Lauren R, business ops associate I, $39,011
Grane-Johnson, Patricia, interpreter, medical, $25.00/hr
Graney, Kelcy Laraine, nurse, staff I, $19.37/hr
Granger, Charles Ralph, professor, $135,265
Granger, Debra A, custodian, $13.23/hr
Granger, Kurt William, bts carpenter-mrc, $16.36/hr
Granger, Ryan Matthew, certif pharmacy techn, $14.70/hr
Granger, Shannon Patrick, sftware supprt analyst-entry, $40,000
Granneman, Jim, event assistant I, $7.75/hr
Granneman, Marcia Ann, nurse, clincl charge-lpn, $22.31/hr
Grant, Amber Lacrystal, office support assistant III, $13.72/hr
Grant, David A, engineer II, $58,050
Grant, Deana G, research/lab technician, $14.42/hr
Grant, Erin Ann, program/project supprt coor I, $35,886
Grant, India Lamae, event assistant I, $7.50/hr
Grant, Jason Greer, nurse anesthetist, $95.00/hr
Grant, Jennifer Leigh, care team assoc-clinical, $11.10/hr
Grant, Joshua Shwayne, custodian, $10.94/hr
Grant, Judy Kathleen, nurse, staff II rnwp, $34.18/hr
Grant, Julia Marjorie, grader, $52
Grant, Kiana Raeann, child dev assistant, $11.14/hr
Grant, Mary Rose, prof, asoc adjunct, $1,725
Grant, Nakish D, physician, $135.00/hr
Grant, Sheila Ann, professor, $129,641
Grant, Steven Leslie, prof, asoc, $103,530
Grant, Trisha, mgr II hospitality services, $56,930
Grantham, Katie A, prof, asoc, $84,500
Grantham, Kristopher E, teaching ast, $55.00/hr
Gras, Elizabeth M, patient svc rep, $14.81/hr
Grasman, Kellie Sue, lecturer, $64,142
Grass, Marlene Rae, veterinary technician sr, $15.00/hr
Gratton, Danielle Ann, ast coach, $37,875
Gratton, Matthew C, adjunct, $15,000
Gratton, Sean, adjunct, $15,000
Graue, Julie, educational pgm associate I, $13.72/hr
Graumann, Cayle C, programmer analyst-princpl, $73,538
Graves, Beverly Dark, prof, ast adjunct, $93,000
Graves, D'Andre Keion, event assistant I, $7.50/hr
Graves, Gina G, executive assistant, $16.95/hr
Graves, Jennie M, office support assistant IV, $14.94/hr
Graves, Meghan Elizabeth, pharmacy tech, $10.85/hr
Graves, Rebecca S, librarian IV, $60,400
Graves, Sarah Marie, care team assoc-suppt, $14.88/hr
Graves, Steven Lynn, db programmer analyst-expert, $71,210
Gravitt, William Fletcher Jr, temporary clerical, $10.94/hr
Gray, Aaron D, prof, ast clincl dept, $147,113
Gray, Amanda Elizabeth, mgr student support svcs, $32,191
Gray, Antionette C, nurse, licensed prac, $17.00/hr
Gray, Barry K, supv sterile processing, $40,576
Gray, Betty Jean, office support assistant I, $9.79/hr
Gray, Cheryl L, support systems admin-speclst, $46,284
Gray, Emily Kahn, resident physician-1st yr, $49,025
Gray, Gwendolyn, librarian III, $58,980
Gray, Hannah Marie, veterinary technician, $13.72/hr
Gray, Kevin, resident physician-1st yr, $49,025
Gray, Krista Erin, student service coor II, $47,000
Gray, Margaret L, program/project supprt coor I, $54,133
Gray, Paula K, program/project supprt coor I, $35,396
Gray, Stefanie Zimmerman, advancement associate II, $20.68/hr
Gray, Traci Nikol, program/project supprt coor II, $46,868
Gray, Tracy Lea, communications coordinator, $16.63/hr
Grayer, Carla J, pat acct rep, $16.21/hr
Grayer, Marsha L, office support assistant III, $17.40/hr
Grayson, Rhonda M, office support assistant IV, $14.82/hr
Greathouse, Scott Alan, system support analyst-expert, $25.26/hr
Greber, Jamie Corryn, prof, ast/profl pract, $60,000
Green Conaway, Darcy, adjunct, $15,000
Green Sappington, Harriett, sr ast dir csm operations, $99,839
Green, Ashley Mae, care team assoc-clinical, $12.50/hr
Green, Bernard, food svc wrkr I, $9.60/hr

Green, Bernard JonTerre, event assistant I, $7.50/hr
Green, Cameron, event assistant I, $8.50/hr
Green, Chante Michelle, office support assistant IV, $14.35/hr
Green, Cindy Jane, nurse, staff II, $24.61/hr
Green, Daniel A, office support assistant IV, $14.50/hr
Green, Daniel Keith, prof, ast teach, $34,000
Green, Deborah Kay, office support assistant IV, $15.53/hr
Green, Deborah Lee, teaching ast, $28.00/hr
Green, Donna Marie, custodian, $12.94/hr
Green, Edna Caroline, business support specialist II, $19.10/hr
Green, Fanda R, educational pgm associate I, $13.45/hr
Green, Gerald E, care team assoc-suppt, $13.31/hr
Green, James Robert, prof, asoc clincl, $115,166
Green, Jennifer Lynn, fin and acctg manager, $61,828
Green, John W, office supervisor, $51,925
Green, Jonathan Andrew, prof, asoc, $82,315
Green, Kevin M, network engineer-speclst, $62,435
Green, Kimberley A, psychologist, $74,593
Green, Linda Sue, business ops associate sr, $47,940
Green, Margaret Bright, hospital lab tech, $12.46/hr
Green, Martha A, custodian, $13.23/hr
Green, Megan N, dir I, student support svcs, $60,600
Green, Robert Ronald, administrative consultant, $48,000
Green, Sherri L, nurse, staff II rnwp, $34.47/hr
Green, Stephanie Venee, office support assistant IV, $14.50/hr
Green, Tammy, library info specialist sr, $14.95/hr
Green, Tamra A, nurse, staff II, $30.00/hr
Green, Thomas D, mgr III business admin, $77,400
Green, Wandra Brooks, ast dir strat communications, $56,838
Greene, Clinton A, prof, asoc, $74,735
Greene, Debra Lou, office support assistant IV, $18.43/hr
Greene, Russell Clayton, instructor, adjunct, $21,000
Greening, Daniel W, prof, asoc, $106,383
Greening, Dorothy Lou, office support assistant IV, $19.03/hr
Greening, Janelle Marie, compliance manager sr, $63,423
Greening, Nancy N, patient svc rep, $14.32/hr
Greenlaw, Kimberly Ann, business support spclst sr, $21.74/hr
Greenlaw, Russell R, bts carpenter, $21.71/hr
Greenlee, Brittany Irene, child dev teacher sr, $26,747
Greenlief, C Michael, prof, asoc, $77,055
Greenslet, Dawn Rae, nurse, staff II rnwp, $20.14/hr
Greenup, Richard Lee, programmer analyst-speclst, $53,452
Greenup, Tammy J, business ops associate sr, $52,875
Greenup, Tracy, dir II finance, $103,218
Greenway, Jaymie Dawn, media producer I, $14.25/hr
Greenwell, Hairong Liu, db programmer analyst-princpl, $71,535
Greenwell, Mallory Lu, office support assistant IV, $14.31/hr
Greenwell, Peter, system administrator-expert, $69,329
Greenwell, Ronetta Marie, patient svc rep, $11.07/hr
Greenwood, B K, prof, asoc, $69,642
Greenwood, Bunnia Jane, nurse, staff II, $32.09/hr
Greenwood, Cynthia Ann, office support assistant IV, $16.10/hr
Greenwood, Wanda M, clincl documnt spclst, $68,395
Greer, Edward Shelton, grounds keeper, $12.12/hr
Greer, Jane, prof, asoc, $69,355
Greer, Julia Ann, clerk, unit, $13.94/hr
Greer, Scott L, educational pgm associate I, $13.15/hr
Greer, Tiffany, instructor, clincl, $23,040
Greever Rice, Tracy Kay, resrch asoc, $66,273
Gregg, Anne E, nurse, staff now III, $30.00/hr
Gregg, Bonnie E, human resources manager sr, $60,182
Gregg, Kristi Dawn, db programmer analyst-expert, $66,926
Gregg, Vilas R, anesthesia techn, $16.46/hr
Gregory, Clarence Jr, sr dir program/project ops, $71,658
Gregory, Gretchen Anne, instructor, clincl, $52,153
Gregory, Gretchen Anne, nurse, staff prn, $45.00/hr
Gregory, Kelly B, strat comm consultant, $57,410
Gregory, Michael R, powr plnt opr II, $28.70/hr
Gregory, Michelle L, research/lab technician, $14.00/hr
Gregory, Nathaniel, event assistant I, $7.50/hr
Gregory, Rabia Anne-Geha, prof, asoc, $67,640
Gregory, Sheila R, custodian, $10.69/hr
Greim, Robert Douglas, compliance manager, $60,782
Greimann, Beth Marie, instructor, ast, $18.00/hr
Greiner, Michael Dale, rec/athletic specialist sr, $25.00/hr
Grelle, Andrea Marie, educational pgm associate I, $13.28/hr
Grellner, Karrisa Ann, resident physician-4th yr, $55,804
Gremp, Diane L, technology resource coor, $46,481
Gresham, Marshanna Kay, executive assistant, $22.54/hr

Gresham, Michelle Marie, business support spec II, $15.11/hr
Gresham, Steven D, grounds keeper, $12.70/hr
Grethen, Tyler James, temporary clerical, $7.50/hr
Grevers, Andrew Joseph, ast coach, $53,560
Grewe-Nelson, Emily Kathryn, res physician-1st yr, $49,025
Grgurich, Tara Macseene, nurse anesthetist, $95.00/hr
Grice, Bonita R, office support assistant IV, $17.83/hr
Grider, Chris, instructor, clincl, $49,147
Grieco, Viviana Leticia, prof, asoc, $62,682
Griesedieck, David J, prof, teach, $54,829
Griesemer, Julia A, nurse, staff II rnwp, $27.00/hr
Grieshaber, Vickie Lynn, serv line spclst, $83,491
Griffen, Jacklyn M, nurse, staff II, $34.23/hr
Griffen, Jerry R, nurse, staff II, $34.25/hr
Griffin, Andrew L, dir II student support svcs, $71,253
Griffin, Brandon Dominique, care team assoc-clinical, $12.08/hr
Griffin, Dora J, accountant I, $18.05/hr
Griffin, Jaime M, pat acct rep, $13.76/hr
Griffin, Kimberly Dawn, temporary technical, $10.00/hr
Griffin, Marshall Courtney, strat comm consultant, $44,163
Griffin, Melissa Brook, nurse, staff II, $22.24/hr
Griffin, Michael G, prof, asoc, $101,994
Griffin, Nathan Allen, food svc wrkr I, $9.98/hr
Griffin, Ryan Merrell, mgr student support svcs, $46,000
Griffin, Skye B, system administrator-speclst, $49,350
Griffin, Stephenia, mgr III business admin, $93,005
Griffin, William Howard, instructor, adjunct, $27,000
Griffith, Connie L, educational pgm associate I, $13.87/hr
Griffith, Drew Benton, temporary clerical, $9.00/hr
Griffith, Felicia M, care team assoc-clinical, $13.60/hr
Griffith, Grace Erin, nurse, staff I, $19.00/hr
Griffith, Ieshia Nicole, business support specialist II, $20.61/hr
Griffith, Jean, office support associate, $18.83/hr
Griffith, Laura Ann, nurse, staff per diem, $35.00/hr
Griffith, Sharon D, office support assistant IV, $15.20/hr
Griffith, Stanford A, communications assistant sr, $14.00/hr
Griffith, Stephen Patrick, prof, ast clincl dept, $206,250
Griffith, Susan B, nurse, staff prn, $26.00/hr
Grigaitis, Elise Suzanne, staff nurse, $20.81/hr
Grigg, Jennifer Jean, nurse spclst, clincl, $85,653
Griggs, Judith A, surgical technl certified, $24.01/hr
Griggs, Marilyn Louise, event assistant I, $7.55/hr
Griggs, Melissa Dawne, prof, ast resrch, $65,850
Griggs, Patrick Martin, nuclear med techni, $24.58/hr
Grigsby, Gary Scott, prof, asoc profl practice, $62,024
Grigsby, Kendra Kay, med office assistant, $10.85/hr
Grigsby, Mary, professor, $99,138
Grigsby, Sheila Renee, prof, ast teach, $63,747
Grill, J B, prof, asoc, $58,191
Grillo, Michael Anthony, fellow, post doctoral, $40,000
Grillo, Stephanie Louise, resrch scientist/academic, $42,024
Grim, Ericka L, student support specialist sr, $16.54/hr
Grimaldi, Gabriel J, instructor, adjunct, $9,000
Grimes, Amanda Rhenee, prof, ast teach, $57,913
Grimes, Marrisa D, temporary professional, $11.30/hr
Grimes, Terrie Lynn, mgr patient admissions-h, $94,806
Grimm-Howell, Elizabeth Marie, lecturer sr, $18,600
Grimm, Kenneth K, mts/refrig mech-r, $21.91/hr
Grimme, Beverly Ann, patient svc rep, $12.53/hr
Grimshaw, Connie, executive assistant, $23.11/hr
Grimshaw, John Randall, revenue cycle trainer, $43,457
Grimsley, Ruth Ellen, office support assistant IV, $17.68/hr
Grimsley, Sterling Lloyd, electronics technician II, $16.01/hr
Grinch, Alexander G, ast coach, $260,000
Grinch, Andrew G, asoc athletic director, $94,937
Grinch, Carin Nicole Huffman, dir II advancement, $73,182
Grindstaff, Melissa Jane, office support assistant IV, $15.00/hr
Grindstaff, Regina Rae Randolph, prof, ast teach, $59,304
Griner, Catherine J, resrch ast, $667
Grisham, Clayton Matthew, instructor, adjunct, $2,250
Grisham, Heather Faith, surgical technl certified, $17.45/hr
Grisham, Martha Ellen, business support specialist II, $22.01/hr
Grissom, Elizabeth A, business support specialist II, $19.20/hr
Grissum, Kimberly R, patient svc rep, $14.56/hr
Griswold, Jeffrey S, csm operations supervisor, $40,290
Grizzle, Kelly Dawn, coor, care, $68,465
Grobman, Megan Elizabeth, veterinarian, residnt, $26,000
Grodzinsky, Anna, resident physician-5th yr, $56,120
Groene, Robert W II, prof, asoc, $61,817

Groh, Ashley Marie, prof, ast, $72,765
Groman, Kimberly Sue Reese, educational pgm coor I, $34,845
Groner-Skopec, Jana L, extension asoc, $48,720
Gronkiewicz, Kristina Marie, veterinarian, residnt, $26,000
Grooms, L Doug, head coach, $46,040
Gros, Jean Germain, professor, $70,955
Grose, Sarah Jessie Lee, office support assistant II, $10.25/hr
Groshong, Susan Ruth, human resources specialist III, $60,601
Groshong, Ted Donald, emeritus, $88,773
Grospitch, Robert E, sr dir studnt supprt svcs, $98,283
Gross, Fonda J, mgr II csm operations, $59,017
Gross, Joetta, business support specialist II, $22.02/hr
Gross, Kelly D, nurse, or/recovery-ch, $22.56/hr
Gross, Kevin James, stock clerk, $12.94/hr
Gross, Kiki L, custodian, $13.96/hr
Gross, Linda Sue, office support assistant IV, $16.60/hr
Gross, Melissa A, pat acct rep, $16.19/hr
Gross, Richard Vernon, event assistant I, $9.25/hr
Gross, Sylvia M, media production director II, $45,600
Gross, Tammie R, business support specialist sr, $23.11/hr
Grosz, Nathaniel N, mts/pipefitter lead, $23.62/hr
Grotewiel, Lindsay Nicole, program/proj supprt coor II, $72,121
Grotewiel, Morgan Marie, instructor, adjunct, $6,300
Grotha, Michael W, mts/plumber, $21.91/hr
Grove, Christina Joi, instructor, adjunct, $4,200
Grove, Joshua Tyler, research/lab technician sr, $14.00/hr
Grover-Bisker, Edna May, dir I, student support svcs, $72,800
Groves, Christopher R, police sergeant, $28.12/hr
Groves, James L, prof, asoc, $80,616
Groves, Nicole Lynn, office support assistant IV, $14.50/hr
Grow, David E, prof, asoc, $71,963
Grubaugh, Sarah Lynn, business support specialist II, $19.18/hr
Grubbs II, Garry Smith, prof, ast, $71,050
Grube, Sean Allan, dir II student support svcs, $78,000
Grueber, Sarah D, infection control profl, $74,587
Gruen, Ingolf Uwe, prof, asoc, $82,935
Gruen, Karen D, business support analyst II, $25.33/hr
Gruender, Kayla Leann, custodian, $12.94/hr
Gruenewald, Don Allen, event assistant I, $7.75/hr
Gruenewald, Jean Borgelt, bus support specialist II, $20.30/hr
Gruenewald, Kate D, student service coor II, $41,184
Gruer, Adrianna Michelle, high school student, $7.50/hr
Grullon, Carolina, custodian, $10.94/hr
Grumich, Timothy P, retail sales assistant sr, $18.79/hr
Gruner, Barbara A, prof, asoc clincl dept, $169,544
Grupe, Dixie Johnson, instructor, adjunct, $3,360
Grupe, Gregory A, instructor, adjunct, $6,400
Grus, Terrence M, dir I, student support svcs, $94,057
Gruzdev, Vitaly, prof, ast resrch, $42,166
Gu, Chao, prof, asoc, $115,961
Gu, Li-Qun, prof, asoc, $118,889
Gu, Zezong, prof, asoc, $98,501
Guardiola, Ivan, prof, asoc, $80,800
Gubbels, Rebecca L, business spclst, $68,004
Gubbins, Erin M, nurse practitioner, $77,520
Gubbins, Paul, dean, asoc, $150,000
Gubera, Christopher C, instructor, residnt, $52,595
Gubrium, Jaber Fandy, professor, $212,984
Gubrud, Ross E, psychologist, $53,250
Gudino De Herrera, Alejand, extension asoc, $41,616
Guenther, Emily Anne, mental health tech, $11.00/hr
Guenther, Karl J, research specialist sr, $50,290
Guerrant, Jacob Wesley, med techl reg, $21.36/hr
Guerrero, Herminia F, animal techn, ast lab, $12.72/hr
Guese, Megan Nicole, sterile processing tech, $16.50/hr
Guess, Cynthia Kay, student service coor I, $44,477
Guess, Trent M, prof, asoc, $121,200
Guest, Kody J, office support assistant IV, $15.03/hr
Guest, Marlin J, support systems admin-expert, $53,186
Guetterman, Linda Marie, academic advisor sr, $48,384
Guevara, Kevin Aquino, teaching ast, $9,000
Guevara, Milagros A, nurse, staff II, $33.60/hr
Guffey, Brandon J, mgr III business admin, $69,800
Guffey, Judy Loraine, care team assoc-suppt, $12.80/hr
Guggenberger, Joe David, prof, ast, $80,000
Guggenmos, Justin L, director it, $85,680
Guha, Subharup, prof, asoc, $81,051
Guha, Suchismita, professor, $88,301
Gui, Peichun, resrch asoc, $50,653

Guidetti, Richard Samuel, resident physician-2nd yr, $50,810
Guier, Karla Ann, nurse, staff II rnwp, $22.55/hr
Guignon, Amy Michelle, instructor, adjunct, $7,059
Guile, Robin L, nurse, staff II, $30.26/hr
Guilford Davis, Tammy, library info specialist sr, $15.10/hr
Guilford, Deborah J, patient svc rep, $13.74/hr
Guilford, Sara Lea, supv, operating room nursing, $36.74/hr
Guilford, Tamera Elyse, nurse, staff II, $20.95/hr
Guilfoyle, Thomas J, professor, $156,777
Guillemette, Ashley Lynn, extension asoc, $38,625
Guillemette, Michael Adrien, prof, ast, $86,700
Guilliams, Donald Joseph, instructor, residnt, $67,486
Guinan, Patrick E, prof, asoc extns, $76,570
Guinn, Neil William, sftware supprt analyst-entry, $45,612
Guinnip, Pinky Sue, food svc wrkr II, $10.70/hr
Gulick, Sharon Ann, state spclst, asoc, $73,028
Gullapalli, Yochita, resident physician-3rd yr, $53,763
Gummersheimer, Sandra Beth, academic advisor, $46,987
Gunasekera, Jagath Chandana, fellow, post doctoral, $40,000
Gund, Kathleen Mary, accountant sr, $53,500
Gundel, Jamie Austin, temporary crafts service, $13.00/hr
Gunier, Elizabeth Ann, nurse clinician, $59,516
Gunier, Rick L, mech, bldg maint, $18.12/hr
Gunn, Gregory Floyd, ast reactor manager, $76,500
Gunn, James Alan, custodian, $11.41/hr
Gunn, Kate, advancement officer, $50,023
Gunn, Victoria, prof, ast clincl dept, $231,657
Gunter, Joshua Lee, event assistant I, $9.00/hr
Gunter, Mallie Allison, educational pgm associate I, $13.45/hr
Guntur, Vamsi P, prof, asoc clincl dept, $267,580
Guo, Baorong, prof, asoc, $66,300
Guo, Binhui, research/lab technician sr, $18.00/hr
Guo, Huatao, prof, ast, $91,800
Guo, Juyuan, research specialist sr, $44,455
Guo, Shun Hua, resident physician-4th yr, $55,804
Guo, Xiaoli, fellow, post doctoral, $40,698
Guo, Ya, resrch scientist/academic sr, $55,000
Gupta, Bhanu Prakash, resident physician-6th yr, $58,200
Gupta, Bina, prof, curators, $138,385
Gupta, RajIV, lecturer, $20,400
Gupta, Sagar, fellow, post doctoral, $43,200
Gupta, Shikha, psychologist, $71,500
Gupta, Sumit Kumar, prof, ast clincl dept, $260,000
Gupta, Suneel, fellow, post doctoral, $30,000
Gupta, Vikas, prof, ast clincl dept, $165,000
Gurd, Sean Alexander, prof, asoc, $72,576
Gurney, Ursula Kim, asoc athletic director, $94,896
Gurskis, Frank Clary, security officer, $10.45/hr
Gurwit, Margery R, resrch ast, $19,890
Gusie, Courtney Nicole, patient svc rep, $11.28/hr
Gustafson, Amber D, nurse, staff I, $19.00/hr
Gustafson, Emily Louise, prof, ast teach, $60,000
Gustafson, Nicholas A, research/lab technician, $13.50/hr
Gustofson, Wendy Jane, dir I, strat communications, $100,495
Gutenko, Gregory, prof, asoc, $62,959
Guth, Brandon Lee, police officer, $17.19/hr
Gutheil, William G, prof, asoc, $87,820
Guthrie, Ellen K, executive assistant sr, $56,992
Guthrie, James M, chemist II, $58,767
Guthrie, Jane Frances, nurse, staff, $31.87/hr
Guthrie, Joyce Merlene, veterinary technician, $13.70/hr
Guthrie, Krista Mae, service rep III, $14.28/hr
Guthrie, Melanie J, prof, ast teach, $125,974
Gutierrez Aguilar, Manuel, fellow, post doctoral, $38,495
Gutierrez, Brenda, care team assoc-clinical, $11.10/hr
Gutierrez, Sara Christine, nurse, staff I, rnwp, $19.00/hr
Gutmann, Lee William, driver emerg road svc, $15.15/hr
Gutschow, Susan E, resident physician-5th yr, $56,120
Gutta, Aditya, resident physician-2nd yr, $50,810
Gutweiler, John L, lecturer, $39,448
Guy, Reginald Jermaine, care team assoc-clinical, $12.80/hr
Guy, Tracie Jae, intern, $25,500
Guyette, Richard, prof, resrch, $75,674
Guyton-Gladden, Linda Ann, office support asst IV, $17.58/hr
Guyton, Thomas W, maint wrkr, prev, $16.95/hr
Guzman, Joanna, office support assistant I, $9.88/hr
Guzman, John Samuel, custodian, $10.94/hr
Guzman, Marla K, phlebotomist, $10.64/hr
Guzy, Michael William, instructor, adjunct, $9,000

Gwaltney, Sarah J, care team assoc-clinical, $12.55/hr
Gwinner, Autumn Lea, food svc wrkr II, $11.07/hr
Gyllenborg, Richard M, head coach, $43,515
Gysbers, Katherine Elise, prof, ast clincl, $14,300
Gysbers, Norman C, prof, curators, $146,346
Ha-Brookshire, Jung Eun, prof, asoc, $85,201
Ha, Oh Ryeong, instructor, adjunct, $18,000
Ha, Theodore T, instructor, adjunct, $9,000
Haaf, Joan, police officer, $18.68/hr
Haaf, Monica Elizabeth, educational pgm associate I, $13.45/hr
Haak, Kristoph, resident physician-1st yr, $49,025
Haar, Barbara Imler, instructor, adjunct, $22,500
Haarmann, Kathryn J, seasonal farm ast, $8.93/hr
Haarmann, Michael P, farm wrkr III, $16.47/hr
Haas, Megan B, nurse, staff per diem, $35.00/hr
Haas, Ronald E, research engineering tech I, $20.26/hr
Habibi, Javad, prof, ast resrch, $59,686
Habibi, Shagayeg, nurse, staff II, $22.24/hr
Habteab, Biniyam S, food svc wrkr I, $9.60/hr
Hackert Kiralfy, Janet M, extns professional, asoc, $60,105
Hackett, Gail, provost, $261,694
Hackleman, Jay Martin, prof, asoc teach, $92,000
Hackleman, Kelly Ker, prof, asoc adjunct, $27,900
Hackley, Steven A, prof, asoc, $72,952
Hackley, Suzanne May, office support assistant IV, $14.65/hr
Hackman, Anne Marie, coor nrsg outcomes prof devl, $80,292
Hackman, Sarah Denise, resident physician-3rd yr, $55,013
Hackmann, Debra K, reimbursement ast, $19.31/hr
Hackmann, Karen Cavender, nurse spclst, clincl, $89,482
Hackmeister, Mary Elizabeth, office support asst IV, $16.15/hr
Hackney, Oesuk, nurse, staff II rnwp, $26.21/hr
Hacquard, Laura, student service coor sr, $62,625
Haddix, Charles J, library specialist, $55,102
Haddock, Michelle Diane, office support assistant III, $12.00/hr
Haddox, Meghan Nicole, patient svc rep, $11.28/hr
Haden, Hana LeAnn, ast coach, $23,660
Haden, Tyler Drew, resident physician-2nd yr, $52,007
Hader, KayMaree, office support assistant IV, $14.28/hr
Hadfield, Juliann, program/project supprt coor I, $35,568
Hadsell, Susan Marie, nurse, licensed prac, $16.29/hr
Haeussler, Tanya M, strat comm consultant sr, $65,000
Haeussler, Ted, environmental health prof sr, $46,999
Haffer, Randy L, system administrator-expert, $62,152
Haffey, Ronald Lee, dir II business admin, $54,190
Hafford, Jeromy Christian, phlebotomist, $12.37/hr
Hagan, Ann K, business support specialist II, $17.68/hr
Hagan, Catherine Elizabeth, prof, ast, $99,554
Hagan, June M, nurse, lpn now plus sr, $20.00/hr
Hagans-Reynolds, Gail Janene, bus support spclst II, $18.84/hr
Hagarty, Mary Brenn, nurse, staff I, $19.67/hr
Hagedorn, Ariel Nicole, hospital lab tech, $12.71/hr
Hagedorn, Shannon L, nurse, staff prn, $26.00/hr
Hagelin, Jerold L, strat comm associate I, $26.27/hr
Hagemeyer, David A, system administrator-expert, $74,440
Hagen, Brad, steam plant opr II, $24.15/hr
Hagen, Darren E, prof, ast resrch, $68,670
Hagen, Donald Edward, professor, $101,168
Hagen, Gretchen, prof, resrch, $69,280
Hagen, Michael P, supv, food svc II-h, $38,516
Hagenow, Jennifer Jean, radiologic techl, $18.23/hr
Hager, Nora Lynn, instructor, $51,204
Hagewood, Lindsey Dawn, med lab techn, $17.09/hr
Haggard, Trent, dir I, research ops and plng, $116,000
Haggiagi, Jehad, resident physician-6th yr, $58,200
Haggins, Ile, prof, ast teach, $45,000
Hagglund, Kristofer, dean, $202,000
Hagglund, Lindsey N, academic advisor, $39,330
Haghighi, Emily H, program/project supprt coor II, $50,000
Hagler, Joyce Ann, certif pharmacy techn, $14.31/hr
Hagni, Diane M, office support associate, $16.97/hr
Hagni, Victoria, temporary professional, $16.00/hr
Hague, Robert Daniel, psychology techn sr, $15.90/hr
Hahm, Bumsuk, prof, asoc, $115,505
Hahn Cover, Kristin, prof, asoc clincl dept, $270,890
Hahn, Allen W, emeritus, $19,913
Hahn, Elizabeth, resident physician-1st yr, $49,025
Hahn, Eric Von, grader, $52
Hahn, Morgan Rae, audiology coordinator, $71,008
Haider, Ali, sftware supprt analyst-princpl, $57,153

Haight, Matthew Duane, veterinary technician sr, $18.76/hr
Haile, Melissa J, office support assistant IV, $15.31/hr
Hainen, Mary Ann, library info specialist sr, $14.95/hr
Hainsworth, Dean P, professor, $264,271
Hairston, Casey A, athletic trainer, $51,350
Hairston, Thomas W, asoc dir program/project ops, $54,806
Haithcoat, Lindlie Jean, geo info system tech, $15.76/hr
Haithcoat, Louisa Mae, temporary technical, $11.00/hr
Haithcoat, Timothy L, dir program/project operations, $79,558
Haj Mahmoud, Khaldoun, resident physician-3rd yr, $53,763
Hake, Angela Marie, business ops associate sr, $50,004
Hakim, Chady H, fellow, post doctoral, $42,294
Halai, Umme Aiman, resident physician-3rd yr, $53,763
Halbert, Alicia M, coor, service, $16.39/hr
Haldiman, Lindsey Jo, resident physician-4th yr, $54,425
Hale, Amanda Sue, serv line spclst, $67,810
Hale, Barbara N, professor, $95,132
Hale, Kathy Marie, ast registrar, $48,000
Hale, Kendell L, head coach, $65,000
Hale, Shannon A, office support assistant IV, $16.28/hr
Hale, Wendy S, nurse, staff II rnwp, $33.11/hr
Halenda, Stephen P, prof, asoc, $98,952
Haley, Glenn L, lecturer, $20,475
Haley, John Arlend, farm wrkr III, $15.05/hr
Haley, Michelle Renee, office support assistant III, $13.79/hr
Halford, Jana Marie, ultrasonographer, $30.13/hr
Halka, Jeremy Robert, research/lab technician, $11.00/hr
Hall Jones, Lori Beth, office support assistant IV, $13.33/hr
Hall, Alexander James, high school student, $7.50/hr
Hall, Alice E, prof, asoc, $71,300
Hall, Angela Elaine, research/lab technician, $14.28/hr
Hall, Cheryl L, prof, asoc teach, $45,346
Hall, Deborah A, student support specialist I, $15.48/hr
Hall, Denise Nicole, radiologic techl, $21.10/hr
Hall, Dorian Curtis, program/project supprt coor I, $35,315
Hall, Eric Jonathan, prof, asoc, $66,005
Hall, Gabriel M, head coach, $40,400
Hall, Jason Ferrell, communications coordinator, $17.16/hr
Hall, Jennifer L, med lab techn, $22.88/hr
Hall, Jim D, telecom tech-princpl, $22.19/hr
Hall, John R, prof, ast clincl dept, $136,000
Hall, Judy K, social worker-non acute care, $56,160
Hall, Kevin Michael, instructor, adjunct, $4,200
Hall, Kim Elizabeth, extns professional, ast, $48,503
Hall, Kim Reanetta, custodian, $12.69/hr
Hall, Kimberly Nelson, tutor, $10.00/hr
Hall, Leslie W, prof, clinical dept, $412,216
Hall, Lorrie Lynn, office support assistant III, $11.79/hr
Hall, Mary A, nurse, licensed prac sr, $20.37/hr
Hall, Matthew Bret, pharmacist, $105,875
Hall, Melba Rose, nurse, advanced practice, $63,131
Hall, Michelle Marie, strat comm associate II, $44,444
Hall, Pamela Jane, business support specialist II, $26.16/hr
Hall, Patricia A, office support assistant IV, $19.46/hr
Hall, Richard H, professor, $102,685
Hall, Robert Dickinson, asoc v chancl research, $217,237
Hall, Robert Michael, customer service supervisor, $58,002
Hall, Sarah Patricia, care team assoc-clinical, $14.00/hr
Hall, Shirley Ann, patient svc rep, $13.57/hr
Hall, Shirley I, office support assistant III, $13.48/hr
Hall, Sonja Denise, custodian, $13.36/hr
Hall, Steve W, lecturer, $30,000
Hall, Susan Gillahan, prof, ast adjunct, $125.00/hr
Hall, Teresa Ann, library info specialist sr, $17.49/hr
Hall, Tony Andrew, ast vice president, $181,309
Hall, Troy S, grader, $100.00/hr
Haller, John Michael, prof, ast teach, $112,200
Halleran, William T, agronomy spclst, $50,000
Halley, Joni L, educational pgm associate I, $12.70/hr
Halley, Mary Margaret, instructor, adjunct, $17,892
Halliburton, Laura Jill, nurse, staff II, $29.54/hr
Halliburton, Susan D, supv pat accts-up, $45,244
Halliburton, Taylor Lashell, temporary clerical, $8.00/hr
Hallman, Jennifer Cornett, social worker-non acute care, $40,227
Halmen, Ceki, prof, ast, $71,750
Halpin, Jared Scott, resident physician-5th yr, $56,120
Halpin, Rachel Elizabeth, veterinarian, residnt, $26,315
Halsall, Viannella, resrch asoc, $48,500
Halsey, Julia Struble, instructor, clincl, $100,000

Halsted, Kristen Lynne, occl therapist, $81,024
Halstenson, Nancy Ann, prof, asoc profl practice, $103,977
Halter, Brett, head coach, $104,000
Halterman, Heather Ann, educational pgm assoc I, $14.07/hr
Halterman, Troy W, head coach, $10,260
Ham, Lindsey Michelle, care team assoc-clinical, $11.10/hr
Hamadto, Fikreta, business support specialist sr, $19.99/hr
Hambelton, Renee D, educational pgm associate I, $14.25/hr
Hambelton, Stacy Lionel, busi spclst, agri, $57,717
Hambright, Lori J, care team assoc-clinical, $12.80/hr
Hamed, Omama Mubarak Ahmed, care team assoc-clinical, $12.32/hr
Hamel, Sarah Katherine, grader, $8.00/hr
Hames, Kasey A, fellow, post doctoral, $36,500
Hamilton-Mueller, Laurie Lavonne, mgr busi/fiscal opns, $72,675
Hamilton, Amber J, nurse, staff now plus, $30.00/hr
Hamilton, Anna Lynn, business support specialist sr, $17.48/hr
Hamilton, Dale G, certif pharmacy techn, $12.46/hr
Hamilton, Deborah, nurse clinician, $63,858
Hamilton, Denice D, advancement officer sr, $59,061
Hamilton, James Donald, pat acct rep, $13.52/hr
Hamilton, Jennifer Lynn, executive assistant, $16.96/hr
Hamilton, Kelli, office support assistant IV, $14.98/hr
Hamilton, Lauri Knowles, nurse, hlth educ, $20.82/hr
Hamilton, Margaret Louise, prof, as adjunct, $51,300
Hamilton, Robin K, executive assistant sr, $48,960
Hamilton, Rosemary Michelle, lab tech, persl svc-clin lab, $13.04/hr
Hamilton, Scott D, prof, ast adjunct, $125.00/hr
Hamilton, Scott Lee, system administrator-princpl, $74,910
Hamilton, Stacey A, instructor, $52,958
Hamilton, Susan Lynette, business support spec sr, $20.37/hr
Hamilton, Tausha Nicole, food svc wrkr II, $10.49/hr
Hamilton, Yvetta Mae, office support assistant IV, $16.05/hr
Hamlyn, Krystal R, patient svc rep, $11.07/hr
Hamm, Chuck W, ophthalmic imager, $26.47/hr
Hamm, Lisa Marie, executive assistant, $19.60/hr
Hammad, Hazem Tawfiq-Fayez, prof, ast clincl dept, $208,080
Hammann, Kenneth R, dean, asoc, $122,519
Hammer, Barbara L, dir I, student support svcs, $87,972
Hammer, Mary A, supv med records, $46,968
Hammer, Richard David, prof, asoc clincl dept, $280,500
Hammer, Steven D, office support assistant IV, $13.23/hr
Hammock, Lenora Anne Lindsey, prof, ast/profl pract, $65,496
Hammond, Caitlin Anne, physical therapist, $64,791
Hammond, David Joseph, coord, distrib-matls dist, $18.09/hr
Hammond, Karen Marie, nurse, staff II, $24.24/hr
Hammond, Karl Daniel, prof, ast, $90,000
Hammond, Kelsey W, student service coor II, $44,494
Hammond, Myko S, instructor, adjunct, $4,200
Hammond, Nonetta, office support assistant IV, $13.16/hr
Hammonds, Herschel Frederick, custodian, $12.94/hr
Hammonds, Wanda Denise, custodian, $12.94/hr
Hammons, Angela Christine, manager it, $63,212
Hammons, Jerry L, business ops associate sr, $70,161
Hammoud, Ghassan M, prof, asoc clincl dept, $225,424
Hamner, Joe Van III, supv ambulance svcs, $20.96/hr
Hamper, Bruce Cameron, prof, ast teach, $45,800
Hampton, Chad E, finance systems specialist I, $59,537
Hampton, Conner Mack, coor athletic operations, $34,400
Hampton, Jeffrey Keith, instructor, clincl, $92,000
Hampton, Jeremy P, prof, ast clincl, $96,000
Hampton, Joseph Clifton, pharmacy tech, $10.85/hr
Hampton, Melissa Virginia, nurse, staff II rnwp, $22.45/hr
Hampton, Natalie Jean Botsch, strat comm associate I, $38,633
Hampton, Sara Deanne, mgr II business admin, $59,440
Hampton, Shachunda L, educational pgm associate I, $14.25/hr
Han, James Edward, programmer analyst-expert, $90,411
Han, Xu, prof, asoc, $51,579
Han, Yijie, prof, asoc, $95,425
Hanberry, Brice Bond, resrch asoc, $50,000
Hanberry, Phillip Ashley, geo info system tech, $16.60/hr
Hancock, John C III, compliance specialist II, $46,938
Hancock, Denis C Jr, system administrator-expert, $70,372
Hancock, Liam Aaron, temporary technical, $9.75/hr
Hancock, Tamara Suzanne, fellow, resrch, $30,000
Hand, Tammy Sue, clerk, unit, $14.09/hr
Handel, Peter Herwig, emeritus, $49,699
Hander, Trisha, prof, ast resrch, $103,603
Handley, Debora Jean, instructor, adjunct, $6,400

Hanenberger, Kelley Lynn, nurse, staff II, $21.68/hr
Hanes, Jennifer Lea, human resources manager sr, $57,500
Haney, Anita R, office support assistant IV, $17.59/hr
Haney, Megan Marie, fellow, resrch, $42,000
Haney, Pamela Marie, strat comm associate II, $45,396
Hanford, Charles, business ops associate II, $51,101
Hanford, Jennifer Lynn, nurse, staff II, $26.85/hr
Hanft, Laurin Michelle, resrch scientist/academic, $53,856
Hanke, Justin J, resident physician-4th yr, $54,425
Hanke, Ralph C, prof, ast, $105,325
Hankel-Shepherd, Paula R, resrch ast, $29,245
Hankemeier, Rita D, med coding spclst-certified, $23.13/hr
Hankins, Brooke Lynn, clerk, diet, $9.84/hr
Hankins, Miriam A, research lab supervisor, $49,378
Hankins, Susan Diane, executive assistant, $20.19/hr
Hankinson, Chad A, prof, asoc teach, $39,853
Hankle, Ramone Lamar, safety monitor, $9.27/hr
Hanko, Shelly Marlene, prof, asoc teach, $94,692
Hanks, Patrick Dean, emrg med techn paramedic, $14.75/hr
Hanley, Linda Lea, clncl imprvmnt spclst, $54,101
Hanlin, Robert Leroy, instructor, $41,400
Hanlon, Brian R, bts painter, $21.71/hr
Hanna, David A, support systems admin-expert, $52,400
Hanna, Francis M, prof, adjunct, $120,000
Hanna, Todd Lewis, strat comm consultant, $51,043
Hanna, William A, prof, asoc adjunct, $18,900
Hanneken, Daniel Joseph, instructor, adjunct, $18,000
Hanner, Martha J, system support analyst-specist, $20.47/hr
Hannink, Mark, professor, $133,214
Hannoun, Maureen Ann, dir sponsored programs, $104,000
Hanrahan, Stephen G, lecturer, $3,600
Hansbrough, Andrew Rory, library info specialist sr, $15.32/hr
Hansen, Bonnie J, business ops associate II, $49,063
Hansen, Brittany Ann, hlth prgm ast, $12.50/hr
Hansen, Christopher Paul, research specialist sr, $44,679
Hansen, Cynthia Lou, nurse, staff II, $29.89/hr
Hansen, Elizabeth A, office support associate, $23.76/hr
Hansen, Jason Robert, specialist, $10.00/hr
Hansen, Kelli Bruce, librarian I, $42,024
Hansen, Kevin R, business support specialist sr, $22.30/hr
Hansen, Lonnie Paul, research specialist I, $35,000
Hansen, Matthew Leo, db programmer analyst-princpl, $67,618
Hansen, Raechelle L, specialist, $10.00/hr
Hansen, Ryan Paul, nursing ast sr, $13.26/hr
Hansen, Sarah Ann, fellow, resrch, $49,128
Hansen, Suzon Lorriane, reimbursement ast, $16.50/hr
Hansford Bowles, Suzanne Lynn, grant writer lead, $42.87/hr
Hanson, Brenda M, instructor, clincl, $47,923
Hanson, Carrie Lin, prof, ast, $74,000
Hanson, Casey Bruce, program/project supprt coor I, $37,000
Hanson, Edwin William, teaching ast, $13.00/hr
Hanson, Jessica R, office support assistant II, $12.79/hr
Hanson, Peter George, waiter/waitress, $8.00/hr
Hanson, Russell Scott, chemist sr, $57,283
Hanson, Stephanie, product support rep-specist, $40,883
Hanson, Steven E, med techl reg, $24.04/hr
Hanson, Thomas Matthew, veterinarian, residnt, $26,315
Hanson, Willard L, prof, ast resrch, $51,000
Hanssen, Elizabeth Elaine, library info specialist, $13.30/hr
Hanuscin, Deborah L, prof, asoc, $85,536
Happe, Kimberly Renee, business support specialist II, $14.95/hr
Happel, Lisa Gail, custodian, $10.69/hr
Haque, Irfan Ul, office support assistant IV, $13.43/hr
Harbach, Barbara Carol, prof, curator teach, $82,201
Harbke, Kelly Lynne, nurse, staff II rnwp, $21.58/hr
Harbour, Kenneth D, quick copy cntr opr, $14.27/hr
Harcharras, Asma, prof, asoc, $70,942
Hardaway, Melissa Nicole, radiologic techl, $21.83/hr
Harden, Karen Marie, student support specialist sr, $17.01/hr
Harder, Dana B, field superintendent, $78,000
Hardesty, Ashley Marie, nurse, staff II, $23.67/hr
Hardesty, Becky, support systems admin-expert, $64,271
Hardesty, Lauren Breen, academic advisor, $35,000
Hardin, Andrea Nicole, nurse, staff now III, $30.00/hr
Hardin, Candias Deshaun, custodian, $10.00/hr
Hardin, Christopher D, professor, $209,008
Hardin, Corey M, nurse, staff II, $22.00/hr
Hardin, Karen Lea, surgical techn certified, $23.64/hr
Hardin, Lisa G, patient svc rep, $14.88/hr

Hardin, Tina Marie, clinical nursing supvsr, $64,107
Harding, Billie Yvonne, custodian, $12.94/hr
Harding, John Fredric, db programmer analyst-expert, $56,100
Harding, Victoria Elizabeth, project manager-expert, $67,983
Hardinger Braun, Karen Louise, prof, clincl, $110,500
Hardouin, Scott A, resident physician-3rd yr, $52,470
Hardt, Elizabeth Ann, executive assistant, $23.18/hr
Hardwick, John E, ast dir csm operations, $68,461
Hardy, Beth Ann, nurse, staff II, $27.70/hr
Hardy, Jessica L, recruiter, hlth care, $64,819
Hardy, Leah Nichole, nurse, staff II, $22.24/hr
Hardy, Lorilie Ann, performace improvement prof, $64,949
Hardy, Marilyn, office support assistant IV, $15.44/hr
Hardy, Michael, geo info system specialist, $46,492
Hare, Brian, prof, asoc teach, $51,705
Harger, Jason Tyler, prof, ast adjunct, $8,004
Hargett, Dean A, manuscript specialist, $37,605
Hargis, Christy Ruth, pat admiss advisor, $25.75/hr
Hargis, Christy Ruth, coor, care, $32.00/hr
Hargis, Christy Ruth, case mgr, workers comp, $72,675
Hargis, David C, media producer sr, $45,012
Hargis, Michael Edward, floor care techn lead, $14.25/hr
Hargrove, Marilyn Sanford, prof, asoc adjunct, $26,607
Haring, William Edward, nurse, staff II, $22.24/hr
Harkey, Jeff H, prof, ast clincl dept, $150,000
Harkins, Doreen Renae, office support assistant IV, $18.28/hr
Harkness, Rhonda M, custodian, $13.23/hr
Harlan, Denise R, clinical nursing supvsr, $75,458
Harlan, James Dale, research specialist I, $16,304
Harlan, Kelly Fay, office support assistant IV, $14.20/hr
Harlan, Lana Marie, pharmacist III, $128,835
Harlan, Lisa Faye, nurse, licensed prac, $16.53/hr
Harlow, Charles Russell, event assistant I, $9.00/hr
Harlow, James M, electronics technician III, $20.47/hr
Harmata, Michael, professor, $136,159
Harmelink, Heidi Elizabeth, dir II advancement, $68,135
Harmon, Catherine Nicole, service rep III, $13.02/hr
Harmon, Cindy Sue, administrative consultant II, $78,423
Harmon, Corinne Mary, prof, ast teach, $45,000
Harmon, Darla A, asoc dir advancement, $79,000
Harmon, Gere Jo, business tech analyst-expert, $66,503
Harmon, Janie Ausburn, dir III advancement, $120,095
Harmon, Lawrence J, system administrator-expert, $57,306
Harmon, Lisa, nurse, staff II rnwp, $34.18/hr
Harmon, Mark William, maintenance, residnt, $26,000
Harmon, Richard, bldg cntrl sys tech II, $22.49/hr
Harms, Aaron A, student service coor sr, $48,312
Harms, Debra S, business support specialist sr, $23.76/hr
Harms, Karen Annette, business support specialist II, $19.15/hr
Harms, Kristi Ann, business ops associate II, $43,525
Harn, Lein, professor, $105,560
Harper-Judd, Jill Alexandra, prof, ast teach, $61,200
Harper, Anthony David, mental health professional, $46,509
Harper, Casandra E, prof, asoc, $77,039
Harper, Cindy L, executive assistant sr, $52,943
Harper, Dana Sue, program/project supprt coor I, $29,120
Harper, Dyan, prof, teach, $31,500
Harper, Emily Rebecca, social worker, $44,429
Harper, Janine Ann, nurse anesthetist, $165,000
Harper, Jeffrey G, architect sr, $69,712
Harper, Jessica Darcel, supv, acute care nursing rnwp, $26.53/hr
Harper, Joni Rae Ross, agronomy spclst, $43,506
Harper, Kellen M, grounds keeper, $12.12/hr
Harper, Kimberly D, manuscript specialist, $35,605
Harper, Patrick, resident physician-1st yr, $49,025
Harper, Rachel P, student service coor sr, $56,354
Harper, Sylvia L, business ops associate sr, $45,600
Harper, Travis W, agronomy spclst, $43,509
Harper, Vanessa Louise, office support assistant IV, $15.00/hr
Harpham, Linda S, nurse, staff II, $29.30/hr
Harre, Edward J, instructor, adjunct, $900
Harrel, Shawn A, media producer II, $14.95/hr
Harrell, Amanda Marie, resident physician-2nd yr, $50,810
Harrell, Ann M, prof, asoc, $57,105
Harrell, Jennifer R, office support assistant IV, $13.70/hr
Harrell, Linda Sue, business support specialist I, $18.82/hr
Harrell, Michael D, manager it, $79,160
Harrington, Amanda B, resident physician-4th yr, $55,804
Harrington, Amber Diane, nurse, licensed prac, $17.61/hr

Harrington, Marcia D, compliance specialist I, $20.16/hr
Harrington, Patricia A, service rep III, $15.37/hr
Harris Lyttle, Deanna Patrice, resident physician-4th yr, $55,009
Harris, Alexander Donald, prof, asoc clincl, $98,569
Harris, Barbara Jean, temporary professional, $15.00/hr
Harris, Bradford H, db programmer analyst-speclst, $56,700
Harris, Carrie Jane, animal techn, lab, $15.90/hr
Harris, Catharine Jean, prof, asoc clincl dept, $180,173
Harris, Cecilia Marie, child dev teacher sr, $24,500
Harris, Chrishonda Lachelle, custodian, $10.39/hr
Harris, Christie M, central sterile assistant, $10.48/hr
Harris, David Allen, event assistant I, $7.55/hr
Harris, David Edwin, supv engineering, $53,340
Harris, Deanna, instructor, clincl, $22,800
Harris, E Barbara, teaching ast, $10.00/hr
Harris, Elizabeth Marie, teaching ast, $13.00/hr
Harris, Gina Linda, nurse, advanced practice, $81,671
Harris, Harold Hart, founders professor, $21,905
Harris, Harry, student service coor II, $47,102
Harris, Jackie L, research specialist I, $19.50/hr
Harris, Jamie L, care team assoc-clinical, $12.50/hr
Harris, Jennifer Lynn, operations support tech II, $13.11/hr
Harris, Jon Paul N, temporary technical, $30.00/hr
Harris, Jose, food svc wrkr III, $13.21/hr
Harris, Joyce L, educational pgm associate I, $13.89/hr
Harris, Justin M, system support analyst-expert, $24.33/hr
Harris, Karen D, coor pat fam & emp engagement, $97,469
Harris, Katherine Lockwood, prof, ast, $63,628
Harris, Kathryne Louise, reimbursement ast, $17.58/hr
Harris, Lesley Joy, emrg med techn, $13.16/hr
Harris, Lindsey Nicole, patient svc rep, $12.35/hr
Harris, MaKesha LaChe', instructor, adjunct, $4,200
Harris, Mark E, engineering technician II, $18.90/hr
Harris, Mary E, office support assistant III, $12.17/hr
Harris, Maude M, nutrition spclst, $54,066
Harris, Michael C, security analyst-princpl, $71,997
Harris, Michael E, safety communications operator, $14.01/hr
Harris, Natalie M, resp care clinical coor, $27.09/hr
Harris, Nathan H, resident physician-3rd yr, $52,470
Harris, Nicole Rush, prgm mgr I, studnt supprt svcs, $54,751
Harris, Norma J, office support assistant IV, $16.72/hr
Harris, Paige L, pharmacist III, $128,835
Harris, Robin Christine, prof, ast teach, $71,000
Harris, Sandra Dawn, custodian, $11.41/hr
Harris, Shanika Nicole, program/project supprt coor II, $40,000
Harris, Tamara Dawn, nurse clinician, $66,679
Harris, Tanya S, office support assistant IV, $15.83/hr
Harris, Tavon L, event assistant I, $7.55/hr
Harris, Trevor N, media producer sr, $34,400
Harris, Wesley R, professor, $83,884
Harrison, A Wilson III, resident physician-2nd yr, $50,810
Harrison, Alaina Pauline, nursing ast, $12.08/hr
Harrison, Amanda Joy Staley, museum paraprofessional II, $15.00/hr
Harrison, Christopher Dean, food svc wrkr I, $9.60/hr
Harrison, Gigi Suzanne, office support assistant IV, $16.00/hr
Harrison, Holly Rachele, care team assoc-clinical, $12.32/hr
Harrison, John Anthony, user support analyst-speclst, $16.50/hr
Harrison, Jonathan Scott, prof, clinical dept, $345,000
Harrison, Mary M, nurse, staff II, $33.43/hr
Harrison, Patricia Jean, programmer analyst-expert, $60,244
Harrison, Ronald, trades helper-ssd, $12.55/hr
Harrison, Sheri-Marie Laura, prof, ast, $61,073
Harrison, Stephanie R, human resources assistant, $15.69/hr
Harrison, Susan Marie, pat acct rep, $15.42/hr
Harrison, William L, prof, asoc, $111,387
Harrold, Adam Lee, resident physician-2nd yr, $52,007
Harrold, Joanna Marie, nurse, staff now III, $30.00/hr
Harrold, Stephanie Ann, food svc wrkr I, $9.60/hr
Harry, Bruce E, prof, asoc, $165,600
Harryman, Sandra J, serv line spclst, $87,512
Harstad, Ronald M, professor, $182,256
Hart, Deirdre M, resident physician-4th yr, $54,425
Hart, Elsa Marie, business support specialist II, $16.83/hr
Hart, Eric S, prof, asoc clincl, $92,411
Hart, Jane Ann, nurse, procedures, $33.76/hr
Hart, Jennifer Lynn, prof, asoc, $97,158
Hart, Lauren E, teaching ast, $27.00/hr
Hart, Marcia L, fellow, resrch, $45,432
Hart, Mark D, mts/electrician, $21.05/hr

Hart, Megan Leanore, prof, ast, $75,000
Hart, Rebekah Kumanovo, executive assistant, $18.39/hr
Hartenberger, Aurelia Winifred, prof, asoc adjunct, $27,000
Harter, Andrew H, user support analyst-entry, $15.09/hr
Harter, Donald R, csm associate sr, $33.28/hr
Harter, Jessica Ann, patient svc rep, $12.36/hr
Harting, Martha Lynn, lecturer sr, $18,000
Hartleip, Jill E, instructor, ast, $13,608
Hartley-Martz, Fay A, business support specialist II, $18.28/hr
Hartley, Dannah Jo, student service coor II, $39,600
Hartley, Donna Kaye, pat admiss advisor, $30.71/hr
Hartley, Joshua Ray, system support analyst-princpl, $61,445
Hartley, Kathryn Ann, pharmacy intern second year, $13.50/hr
Hartline, Roy S, dir II advancement, $78,008
Hartman, Bridget A, resident physician-1st yr, $50,219
Hartman, Emily Brooke, office support assistant III, $12.96/hr
Hartman, Jessica Leann, tutor, $10.00/hr
Hartman, Lori A, business tech analyst-princpl, $81,797
Hartman, Mary Francis Marn, comm coord sr, $17.25/hr
Hartman, Todd W, support systems admin-speclst, $47,671
Hartmann, Tad Aaron, program/project supprt coor I, $50,000
Hartnagel, Susan Lynn, student support specialist sr, $17.44/hr
Hartsfield, Noah Rakestraw, office support asst III, $13.86/hr
Hartwick, Jennifer Ramsey, student service coor II, $42,661
Hartz, Analise Lyn, reimbursement ast-cert, $18.59/hr
Hartz, Megan Elizabeth, sr manager it, $84,960
Hartze Pithua, Maranda Ann, certif pharmacy techn, $14.73/hr
Harvey, Edward J III, lecturer, $15,000
Harvey, William P Jr, mail carrier, $14.85/hr
Harvey, Alexandria Correll, nurse, staff I, $19.00/hr
Harvey, Deborah M, ast dir registration svcs-up, $84,397
Harvey, James Michail-Richard, media production assoc, $8.89/hr
Harvey, Kayla, child dev teacher sr, $25,000
Harvey, LaShonda Beatrice, office support asst IV, $14.89/hr
Harvey, Loyola E, executive assistant, $24.19/hr
Harvey, Matthew Charles, food svc wrkr II, $10.49/hr
Harvey, Merle Edward, custodian, $12.94/hr
Harvey, Patrick J, custodian, $12.94/hr
Harvey, Robyn Chanelle, care team assoc-clinical, $11.32/hr
Hasan, Kristen M, ast mgr hospitality services, $42,186
Hasan, Rim, resident physician-3rd yr, $53,763
Hasan, Syed Eqbal, instructor, adjunct, $20,000
Hasan, Syed Z, mgr II hospitality services, $56,576
Hasegawa, Lee T, academic advisor, $35,088
Hasekamp, Jodi A, office support associate, $16.54/hr
Haselhorst, Ross, technology resource director, $95,506
Hasenkamp, Rebecca Lee, event assistant I, $10.00/hr
Hashman, Jennifer Elaine, student support spclst sr, $17.51/hr
Haskamp, Deborah Lucille, office support assistant IV, $14.95/hr
Haskamp, Mary Adah, human resources specialist II, $50,743
Haskins, Sandra S, lecturer, $100.00/hr
Haskins, Sarah Elizabeth, temporary clerical, $8.00/hr
Haslag, Barbara Louise, patient svc rep, $13.02/hr
Haslag, Joseph H, professor, $176,994
Hasner, Kevin L, business support specialist II, $17.58/hr
Hasner, Velvet Irene, strat comm associate II, $48,227
Hasselriis, Barbara Jeanne, dir III advancement, $86,170
Hassenflug, Jeffrey A, resident physician-2nd yr, $50,810
Hasser, Eileen Mary, professor, $158,760
Hassett, Daniel E, asoc director, $90,450
Hassinger, Megan J, care team assoc-clinical, $13.06/hr
Hassler, Danelle Breann, office support assistant III, $11.44/hr
Hassler, Thomasina Frenchie, prof, ast adjunct, $16,008
Hatch, Nancy Elizabeth, mgr advancement, $45,840
Hatcher, E Ann, office supervisor, $56,000
Hatcher, Gregory, chiller techn III, $25.15/hr
Hatcher, Lachelle Denee, nurse, staff now III, $30.00/hr
Hatcher, Patrice L, office support assistant IV, $14.22/hr
Hatfield-Callen, Jenny Arlene, resrch asoc, $49,718
Hatfield, Amanda J, coor, reimbursement, $50,362
Hathaway, Lisa Ledell, instructor, $30,392
Hathaway, Samantha C, resident physician-3rd yr, $53,763
Hathman, Kelli Michelle, human resources specialist sr, $46,370
Hathman, Theresa Lynn, custodian, $12.94/hr
Hatley, Clarissa Ann, temporary clerical, $10.10/hr
Hattman, Melissa, administrative consultant, $91,790
Hatton, Ante Frances, clerk, diet, $12.96/hr
Hatton, Anthony De'Arthur, event assistant I, $7.50/hr
Hatton, Helen E, nurse, staff, $29.74/hr

Hatton, Jennifer M, strat comm associate II, $47,766
Hauck, Gayla D, office support assistant IV, $14.21/hr
Hauck, Henry A, business ops associate II, $50,005
Hauck, Virginia Mae, custodian, $11.41/hr
Hauf, Susan, instructor, adjunct, $14,667
Haug, Stephen B, mgr I, business admin, $41,004
Haulenbeek, Derrick Ray, business ops associate sr, $45,600
Haun, Leigh Anne, advancement officer, $46,968
Haupt, Nancy Lynne, instructor, adjunct, $1,109
Haury, Emily M, adjunct, $15,000
Hausam, Susan Faye, business support specialist II, $18.72/hr
Hauschild, Mark Walter, prof, ast visiting, $65,000
Hauser, Megan M, office support assistant IV, $14.21/hr
Hausheer, Monelle S, mgr II hospitality services, $60,112
Hausman, Timothy A, dir iv advancement, $107,100
Haverkamp, Benjamin Thomas, resident physician-4th yr, $54,425
Havner, James Allen, csm supervisor, $56,148
Hawk, Phyllis W, office support associate, $22.53/hr
Hawk, William A, prof, asoc, $57,932
Hawke, Nancie D, counsel, $150,426
Hawkins, Claude Millard Jr, grounds keeper, $12.23/hr
Hawkins, Addie Faye, instructor, adjunct, $18,750
Hawkins, Alyssia, business svcs consultant sr, $63,954
Hawkins, Blake Aaron, food svc wrkr I, $9.60/hr
Hawkins, Darren Charles, research/lab technician sr, $16.32/hr
Hawkins, Diana L, office support assistant IV, $13.18/hr
Hawkins, Gary W, electronic sys techn III, $22.01/hr
Hawkins, Jacqueline Ann, office support assistant IV, $18.00/hr
Hawkins, Kathlene, academic advisor, $45,050
Hawkins, Martha F, instructor, adjunct, $3,067
Hawkins, Sara Lynn Ann, sterile processing tech, $18.31/hr
Hawley, Erin Morrow, prof, asoc, $102,839
Hawley, Jana M, professor, $149,815
Hawley, Joshua D, prof, asoc, $102,839
Hawley, Kristin M, prof, asoc, $73,769
Hawthorne, Marion Fred, professor, $298,572
Hay, Amy Lynn, student support specialist II, $15.32/hr
Hay, Marilyn Louise, educational pgm coor III, $56,244
Hayat, Muhammad Badar, fellow, teaching, $48,000
Hayday, Megan, high school student, $7.50/hr
Hayden, Melvin Ray, prof, resrch, $21,112
Hayden, Rose M, executive assistant, $25.42/hr
Haydon, Cynthia Ann, grant writer sr, $50,300
Hayes-Hewitt, Gwendolyn Ezella, child dev assistant, $11.85/hr
Hayes, Alisa Kristine, prof, ast clincl dept, $275,000
Hayes, Angela Denise, retail sales assistant, $10.00/hr
Hayes, Ashley D, business support specialist sr, $20.09/hr
Hayes, Brett E, mgr, therapy, $157,435
Hayes, Carla Denise, custodian, $12.94/hr
Hayes, Charles M, prof, ast resrch, $68,795
Hayes, Gregory Dean, dir I, student support svcs, $67,626
Hayes, Karen Diana, educational pgm coor I, $23,733
Hayes, Karla Jo, nurse, staff I, rnwp, $19.00/hr
Hayes, Kathryn Korrell, prof, ast adjunct, $68,850
Hayes, Kay Lynn, office support assistant sr, $16.92/hr
Hayes, Kelly D, custodian lead, $16.43/hr
Hayes, Kristina Marie, hospital security officer, $12.11/hr
Hayes, Laura Ann, office support assistant IV, $16.41/hr
Hayes, Melissa D, office support assistant III, $13.56/hr
Hayes, Michael Joseph, resrch scientist/academic, $68,647
Hayes, Michelle A, nurse, staff II, $29.12/hr
Hayes, Mike, office support assistant IV, $13.26/hr
Hayes, Mina Noelle, nurse, staff per diem, $35.00/hr
Hayes, Nancy Jo, coor, reimbursement, $61,098
Hayes, Paula, food svc wrkr IV, $14.77/hr
Hayes, Rana C, custodian, $12.94/hr
Hayes, Rita A, office support assistant IV, $15.26/hr
Hayes, Shawnda R, police officer, $17.56/hr
Hayes, Timothy J, fellow, post doc clncl-yr3, $60,415
Hayes, Tommy L, mts/electrician-r, $20.87/hr
Hayes, Toni, executive assistant, $18.56/hr
Hayes, Veronica J, academic advisor sr, $48,878
Hayes, Vicki Jo, custodian, $11.41/hr
Hayes, Wesley Adam, event assistant I, $7.50/hr
Haymon, Beverly, custodian, $13.23/hr
Haynes, Cheryl Lynn, telecomm opr-h, $12.96/hr
Haynes, Courtney Alexis, waiter/waitress, $8.47/hr
Haynes, Dana Brown, asoc dir program/project ops, $36,565
Haynes, Dennis J, construction manager II, $64,556

Haynes, Gary L, mts/machinist, $21.05/hr
Haynes, John M, sr director, $128,021
Haynes, Kathy J, dir III business admin, $137,700
Haynes, Tonya Maria, prof, asoc adjunct, $31,500
Haynes, William L, professor, $127,316
Hays, Amber Lynn, nurse, staff II, $26.70/hr
Hays, Fred H, prof, asoc, $175,964
Hays, Lauren A, student recruitment spclst, $15.83/hr
Hays, Malcolm E, instructional developr-expert, $23.90/hr
Hays, Pamela M, patient svc rep, $15.43/hr
Hays, Whitney R, student service coor sr, $47,940
Hayward, Kevin, asoc athletic director, $81,600
Hayward, Robert S, prof, asoc, $71,160
Haywood, Kathleen Marie, dean, asoc, $133,194
Haywood, Scot Bradford, police sergeant, $20.04/hr
Hazan, Sara Melissa, educational pgm associate I, $13.41/hr
Hazelbauer, Gerald L, professor, $280,144
Hazell, Rachael, grader, $3,600
Hazelrigg, Conner W, research/lab technician, $13.00/hr
Hazelwood, Susan E, lecturer, $25.00/hr
Hdeib, Ecaterina Mariana, prof, asoc clincl, $68,191
Hdeib, Moses M, prof, clincl, $97,709
He, Gaofei, post doctoral asoc, $37,000
He, Hong S, professor, $83,321
He, Jinghao, scientist lead, $86,100
He, Wenjie, prof, asoc, $79,605
He, Xiaoming, prof, ast, $65,100
He, Zhihai, professor, $116,580
He, Zhuoqiong, professor, $101,684
Head, Jeweletta Lynn, nurse, staff II, $34.30/hr
Head, Michael D, resp therapy techn cert, $21.77/hr
Headd, Chrystal Glennice, office support assistant IV, $14.00/hr
Headd, Heather Renee, nurse, licensed prac, $18.01/hr
Headrick, Linda Ann, professor, $297,729
Headrick, Nancy Jo, lecturer, $100.00/hr
Headrick, Virginia J, business tech analyst-princpl, $56,901
Heagy, Christina Lynne, office support assistant IV, $13.24/hr
Healey, Erica A, intern, $24,014
Healy-Mendez, Judith Marie, business support spclst II, $20.52/hr
Heaps, Jodi Michelle, prof, ast resrch, $71,396
Heard, James Edward Jr, sterile processing tech, $17.53/hr
Heard, Amanda Lynn, nurse, licensed prac, $16.78/hr
Heard, Jennifer Jean, event assistant I, $7.50/hr
Heard, Michelle Renee, office support assistant IV, $16.05/hr
Hearne, Joanna Megan, prof, asoc, $66,323
Hearne, Leonard B, prof, ast teach, $58,566
Hearst, Kevin D, instructor, adjunct, $75.00/hr
Hearst, Linda Marie, business svcs consultant, $53,710
Heater, Brandy A, ophthalmic ast cert, $12.75/hr
Heath, Christine M, business support analyst sr, $27.97/hr
Heath, Erin Christine, nurse, staff I, $19.37/hr
Heath, Jamey L, mts/electrician, $20.64/hr
Heath, Myra L, custodian, $12.94/hr
Heath, Tanya Suzanne, instructor, adjunct, $30,000
Heathcock, Geoffrey H, instructor, adjunct, $12,300
Heaviland, Paula E, dir I, business admin, $127,170
Heavin, Geoffrey Lee, emrg med techn paramedic, $17.51/hr
Heberer, Paige Rachelle, pharmacy tech, $10.64/hr
Heberle, Heather Noel, dietitian, clincl, $52,000
Heberlein, Kendyl Jane, nurse, staff I, $19.00/hr
Hebert, Karen R, prof, ast, $84,256
Hecht, Corina Bethany, business tech analyst-spclst, $49,980
Hecht, Martin Lynn, mgr III business admin, $77,347
Heck, Cynthia Lynn, office support assistant III, $15.00/hr
Heck, Michelle Lynn, mgr II student support svcs, $63,533
Heckathorn, Jeffery Wayne, db programmer analyst-expert, $64,656
Heckel, Mary Ellen, mgr II student support svcs, $61,399
Heckemeyer, James F, construction manager II, $87,359
Heckenkamp, Joseph E, system administrator-princpl, $75,770
Hecker, Melinda Michelle Zion, prof, ast clincl dept, $128,520
Heckler, Bridget Elaine, waiter/waitress, $7.71/hr
Heckman, Chad, electrician, high voltage, $27.26/hr
Heckman, Cherine Daree, student service coor sr, $47,940
Heckman, Jennifer Marie, nurse, staff per diem, $35.00/hr
Heckmaster, Dustin Lonnie, police officer, $19.10/hr
Hedberg, Riley Curtis, emrg med techn, $11.70/hr
Heddinghaus, Carol M, dir III business admin, $100,791
Hedges, Kimberly Ann, academic advisor, $36,867
Hediger, Marla, student support specialist II, $20.37/hr

Hedlund, Aaron Douglas, prof, ast, $102,060
Hedrick, Benjamin J, teaching ast, $13.00/hr
Hedrick, David, director, $105,160
Hedrick, Jill A, serv line spclst, $87,290
Hedrick, Lynne Marie, clinical educator, $63,038
Hedrick, Ryan Anthony, grounds keeper II, $13.09/hr
Hedrick, Taleka T, temporary crafts service, $9.50/hr
Heendaliya, Lasanthi, instructor, adjunct, $18,000
Heesch, Cheryl M, professor, $150,595
Heese-Peck, Antje, prof, ast, $90,489
Heeter, Elizabeth Ann, serv line spclst, $67,810
Heether, Shaun Caleb, histologic techn tr, $12.22/hr
Heffernan, Amber Leigh, accountant sr, $43,347
Heffernan, Jane Elizabeth, educational pgm assoc I, $14.14/hr
Heffner, Carol Jo, executive assistant, $19.81/hr
Hefley, Jenna Marie, academic advisor, $35,895
Heflin, Colleen M, prof, asoc, $118,662
Hegeman, Mary Crawford, assoc director it, $107,906
Hegger, Joseph D, prof, ast teach, $82,200
Hegger, Susan Carey, asoc dir program/project ops, $63,342
Heggie, Glen David, prof, clincl, $116,463
Hegle, Jeremy W, sr dir program/project ops, $73,500
Hegstad, Geri Lee, office supervisor, $49,234
Hegstrom, Jessica L, nurse, staff per diem, $35.00/hr
Heibel, Dottie, office support assistant III, $13.64/hr
Heibel, Lyndsie Nicole, temporary crafts service, $8.96/hr
Heiberg, Mike D, athletic attd, $14.72/hr
Heidari, Amanda Jo, orthopedic techn, $14.22/hr
Heidari, Angela Faye, office support assistant IV, $14.53/hr
Heidari, Manijeh B, resrch asoc, $56,244
Heidebrecht, Sherry Coe, admiss liaison-mrc (rn), $63,149
Heidlage, Judith Anne, nurse, staff II, $34.65/hr
Heidolph, Erich Philip, operations support tech sr, $13.49/hr
Heidt, Jonathan W, prof, ast clincl dept, $247,000
Heikes, Brandon Wayne, veterinarian, residnt, $26,000
Heim, Kristin Nicole, instructor, ast, $31,938
Heim, Lloyd L, custodian, $10.19/hr
Heiman, Suzette T, prof, profl practice, $99,720
Heimericks, Kenda Sue, office support assistant IV, $16.74/hr
Heimericks, Pamela Jean, educational pgm assoc I, $13.88/hr
Heimsoth, Susan, clinical mgr, $92,127
Heine, Anne Gray, instructor, clincl, $48,665
Heine, Anne Gray, nurse, staff II, $40.00/hr
Heinrich, Markus Steven, seasonal farm ast, $9.26/hr
Heinrich, Natalie Elizabeth, food svc wrkr I, $9.60/hr
Heinrich, Steven Ray, research maintenance tech sr, $24.62/hr
Heins, Carla J, fin and acctg manager, $78,741
Heins, Lynn Caroline, busi spclst, agri, $41,717
Heinz, John Steven, lab assistant, $9.00/hr
Heinz, Robert D, research specialist I, $47,400
Heinz, Ryan J, strat comm manager, $51,000
Heischmidt, Brett Andrew, tutor, $10.25/hr
Heisel, Alan D, prof, asoc, $89,528
Heisel, Leighanne, prof, asoc teach, $50,987
Heiser, James William, resrch asoc, $52,920
Heisner, Brandy Raye, phlebotomist, $11.57/hr
Heiss, Andrea Brandenburg, prof, ast/profl pract, $61,091
Heissler, Kelly M, program/project supprt coor I, $37,882
Heisterberg, Arlie Christopher, radiation ther therapist, $31.00/hr
Heithaus, Peter A, asoc vice chancellor, $129,000
Heithold, Bonni Nicole Welch, physician, $100.00/hr
Heitmann, Thomas W, engineer sr, $66,179
Heitmeyer, Jana C, ast athletic director, $64,260
Heivilin, James E, data cntr support tech-speclst, $19.25/hr
Held II, John Dennis, dir iv advancement, $94,089
Held, Anthony James, emrg med techn paramedic, $15.51/hr
Held, Philip, fellow, post doctoral, $36,000
Helfer, Adam D, professor, $84,159
Helfers, Diane Marie, prof, asoc, $98,053
Hellensmith, Donnell Nicole, nurse, licensed prac sr, $17.07/hr
Heller, Randall Lane III, resident physician-4th yr, $54,425
Heller, Burton Lee Jr, managing engineer, $78,591
Heller, Aaron Neal, resident physician-1st yr, $49,025
Heller, Margaret Jarrell, nurse, staff II rnwp, $34.18/hr
Heller, Patricia White, resident physician-2nd yr, $52,007
Hellwege, Darren Michael, media producer sr, $40,985
Helm, Michael Nolan, fire protec/equip tech I, $12.12/hr
Helm, Nicoya, tutor, $25.00/hr
Helm, Scott T, prof, asoc teach, $77,177

Helm, Sherri K, executive assistant, $26.49/hr
Helming, Dyann L, nurse, advanced practice, $77,000
Helming, Susan Amanda, research specialist II, $37,830
Helmka, Roger Matthew, food svc wrkr I, $9.60/hr
Helms, Esta, surgical technl certified, $17.34/hr
Helms, Kristy Nicole, ultrasonographer, $28.74/hr
Helms, Michelle Kay, accountant sr, $50,562
Helphingstine, Cynthia J, prgm director, $104,040
Helton, Keith L Jr, mts/electrician mrc, $18.74/hr
Helton, James A, custodian, $10.94/hr
Hemen, Teresa Ann, nurse, licensed prac sr, $22.16/hr
Hemenway, Charles K, med techl reg, $28.31/hr
Hemeyer, Tylisha Michelle, office support asst IV, $15.47/hr
Hemmann, Christine S, nurse advisor, telephone, $29.98/hr
Hemmann, Gregory, event assistant I, $8.50/hr
Hemmer, Toni L, office support assistant IV, $18.70/hr
Hemmersmeier, Kimberly Ann, temporary clerical, $9.00/hr
Hemmings, Roland Andre Jr, facilities supervisor, $39,600
Hemmings, Shelby Dawn, teaching ast, $7,600
Hempen, Maryann J, office support assistant III, $16.98/hr
Hemphill, John M, health physicist, $70,501
Hemphill, Mary Eve, strat comm associate II, $43,008
Henderson, Ronald L Jr, ast athletic director, $55,500
Henderson, Tony Maurice Sr, custodian, $12.50/hr
Henderson, Baylee Ann, nurse, staff I, $19.37/hr
Henderson, Beth A, prof, ast adjunct, $28,204
Henderson, Callie Suzanne, nurse, staff I, $19.00/hr
Henderson, Connor Grae, food svc wrkr I, $9.60/hr
Henderson, Eugene, food svc wrkr I, $9.60/hr
Henderson, Jamie L, nurse, staff II, $33.11/hr
Henderson, Jane Gay, educational pgm associate I, $12.55/hr
Henderson, Jeffrey S, user support analyst-entry, $14.00/hr
Henderson, Jennifer Nicole, guest house attd, $9.27/hr
Henderson, Kay Keiko, office support assistant IV, $14.90/hr
Henderson, Lamar, internet administrator-entry, $18.04/hr
Henderson, Laura Elizabeth, prof, ast clincl dept, $180,000
Henderson, Linda L, nurse, licensed prac now, $17.00/hr
Henderson, Robert Lee, nurse, staff II rnwp, $20.95/hr
Henderson, Rodney Orlando, custodian, $12.94/hr
Henderson, Sarah Lynn, business support specialist II, $19.28/hr
Henderson, Scott A, instructor, $52
Henderson, Scott T, ast dir stu hlth, $159,261
Henderson, Tanya Genea, office support assistant IV, $17.83/hr
Henderson, Whitney Lee, occl therapist, $57,260
Hendrell, Jonathan H, environmental health tech II, $15.44/hr
Hendren, Andrew Curtis, floor care techn lead, $14.25/hr
Hendren, Beth Ann, pat acct rep, $13.83/hr
Hendren, Jacqueline Sue, reimbursement ast-cert, $18.59/hr
Hendren, Jessie Love, care team assoc-clinical, $11.10/hr
Hendren, Nora J, business support specialist II, $19.78/hr
Hendren, Steven Wayne, food svc wrkr II, $10.10/hr
Hendricks, Charolette A, coor, care, $67,359
Hendricks, Lena Hallmon, office support assistant III, $13.34/hr
Hendrickson, Wendell J, maint equip opr, $19.23/hr
Hendrickson, Mary K, prof, ast, $83,060
Hendrickson, Ruth Suzanne, prof, asoc teach, $38,950
Hendrix, Patricia L, radiologic techl, $26.47/hr
Henegar, Jeffrey R, dir II research ops and plng, $127,500
Heng, Xiao, prof, ast, $80,000
Henggeler, Joseph Aloys, temporary technical, $8.50/hr
Henggeler, Joseph Charles, prof, asoc extns, $93,299
Henggeler, Mary H, temporary professional, $11.30/hr
Heniff, Jeffrey Paul, research engineering tech I, $17.50/hr
Henik, Kacey, event assistant I, $10.00/hr
Henk, Debra L, 4-h spclst, $43,015
Henke, Brent A, nurse, staff II, $23.85/hr
Henke, Daniel Joseph, library info specialist, $13.86/hr
Henke, Diane Marie, office support assistant II, $13.80/hr
Henke, Jennifer Marie, cat scan technl (ct), $24.29/hr
Henke, Kristi B, nurse, staff I, $22.19/hr
Henke, Michael Joseph, asoc media producer, $11.53/hr
Henke, Robin M, office support assistant IV, $16.47/hr
Henley, Courtney Brianne, office support assistant IV, $12.98/hr
Henley, Eric M, bts roofer, $21.71/hr
Henley, L C, custodian lead, $14.03/hr
Henley, Marshall, event assistant I, $7.55/hr
Henneberry, Roger Bradford, mechl plant spclst, $19.64/hr
Hennen, Douglas V, resp therapist reg, $22.93/hr
Henness, Steven A, extns professional, asoc, $55,870

Hennessey, Linda A, med techl reg, $29.00/hr
Hennessy, Kevin Raymond, instructor, adjunct, $3,375
Hennessy, Maryrose, office support assistant IV, $15.66/hr
Hennings, Justin M, research/lab technician, $12.25/hr
Hennkens, Heather Marie, prof, ast resrch, $72,415
Henrickson, Celeste N, grader, $100.00/hr
Henry-Smetana, Erik Eugene, dir II human resources, $108,000
Henry, Albertina B, educational pgm associate I, $12.55/hr
Henry, Ashley Elizabeth, educational pgm associate I, $12.49/hr
Henry, Bill D, facilities attd, $13.19/hr
Henry, Caitlyn Erin, pat care techn, $11.75/hr
Henry, Carolyn J, professor, $201,967
Henry, Coty Demond, custodian, $12.50/hr
Henry, Holly Renae, instructional designer-expert, $52,000
Henry, James E, prof, asoc, $84,066
Henry, Janna A, reimbursement ast, $16.35/hr
Henry, Jonathan M, educational pgm coor III, $42,787
Henry, Mary Pat, professor, $93,254
Henry, Matthew Aaron, prof, ast teach, $49,099
Henry, Maureen, office support assistant III, $12.95/hr
Henry, Michael P, instructor, adjunct, $19,200
Henry, Vinita, prof, clincl, $118,648
Hensel, Brian K, instructor, $91,800
Henshaw, Marilyn Lea, house mgr h prn, $35.00/hr
Henslee, Amber M, prof, ast, $67,850
Hensley-Ward, Rebecca, instructor, adjunct, $9,000
Henson, Bob Londes, professor, $68,623
Henson, Charles Dewayne, prof, teach, $124,800
Henson, Charmaine, office support assistant IV, $17.61/hr
Henson, Joshua Aaron, ast coach, $550,000
Hentges, Jaimie Nicole, reimbursement ast-cert, $19.68/hr
Henze, Hannah Lynn, research/lab technician sr, $16.00/hr
Henzel, Laura Lynn, nurse, staff II, $34.18/hr
Henzl, Michael T, professor, $102,663
Heppner, Mary Jean, professor, $103,451
Heppner, Puncky Paul, prof, curators, $146,957
Hequembourg, John Lester, construction manager II, $62,220
Herald, William K, bts mason/tuckptr lead, $23.25/hr
Herbert, Stephen T, library info specialist sr, $18.85/hr
Herberts, Richard C, system administrator-entry, $45,686
Herbold, Carl Albert Jr, ast reactor manager, $86,537
Herbst, Diane M, office support assistant IV, $15.37/hr
Herd, Sasha Joel, nurse, staff II, $26.67/hr
Herde, Mary Josephine, instructor, ast, $24.40/hr
Herdzina, Denise L, accountant sr, $48,794
Herdzina, John K, student support specialist II, $17.68/hr
Herico, Nayda Buena, retail sales assistant, $9.22/hr
Heriford, Cheryl Sue, certif pharmacy techn, $17.10/hr
Herigon, Diane M, student support specialist II, $17.92/hr
Herin, Brent E, nurse, staff II, $25.35/hr
Heringman, Noah I, professor, $79,406
Heritage, James Francis, athletic attd, $13.82/hr
Herling, Sarah E, csm professional I, $37,960
Herman, Jason Michael, communications coordinator, $19.47/hr
Herman, John M, emrg med techn paramedic, $14.77/hr
Herman, Keith C, professor, $116,317
Herman, Rachel Jenean, pat care techn, $12.25/hr
Hermann, Trina A, surgical technl non cert, $20.09/hr
Hermsen, Joan M, prof, asoc, $102,354
Hern, Augustus III, event assistant I, $7.55/hr
Hern, Wm Jonathan James, library info specialist, $13.30/hr
Hernandez Lopez, Gabriela, nurse, staff II, $21.26/hr
Hernandez, Erica K, prof, asoc teach, $49,783
Hernandez, Jacquelyne A, care team assoc-clinical, $14.29/hr
Hernandez, Katherine L, office support assistant IV, $16.28/hr
Hernandez, Maya Dionne, student service coor sr, $50,413
Hernandez, Michelle Marie, dental assistant II, $15.81/hr
Hernandez, Sarah A, office support assistant IV, $16.92/hr
Hernandez, Stephanie Marie, prog/proj supprt coor I, $38,000
Hernandez, Tammy Annette, research/lab technician sr, $13.00/hr
Hernandez, Veronica, educational pgm associate I, $12.43/hr
Hernandez, Veronica Yolanda, custodian, $12.94/hr
Herndon, Betty Larue, prof, asoc resrch, $47,827
Herndon, Rayla Ny'Cole, instructor, adjunct, $4,200
Herndon, Sierra Nicole, high school student, $9.00/hr
Herr, Cameron Cody Lynn, resident physician-3rd yr, $53,763
Herren, Andrew Jay, patient svc rep, $10.64/hr
Herrick, Joseph Robert, mental health tech, $14.88/hr
Herrin, Daniel John, athletic trainer, $15,000

Herrin, Jeremy Alexandre, waiter/waitress, $9.19/hr
Herring, Matthew Alan, ast athletic director, $90,000
Herring, Matthew David, extns professional, asoc, $67,583
Herring, Vanessa Marie, advancement officer sr, $62,500
Herrman, Alia Rochelle, asoc dir strat communications, $66,500
Herron, Gloria Maria, office support assistant IV, $14.40/hr
Herron, Gregory Allen, business tech analyst-expert, $61,891
Herron, John Paul, prof, asoc, $78,319
Herron, Kristin Kathryn Lindner, temp professional, $13.00/hr
Herron, Misti Ann, office support assistant III, $12.50/hr
Herron, Stara Michelle, library info specialist, $12.98/hr
Herron, Theresa Lynn, custodian lead, $11.98/hr
Hersey, Darren A, custdl suply delvry attd, $13.97/hr
Hert, Bill, custodian, $12.94/hr
Hertel, Laura Jane, student service coor sr, $52,151
Hervey, Elizabeth I, grader, $52
Herwig, Robert Vaughan, prof, ast adjunct, $125.00/hr
Herx, Dylan Lane, instructional designer-expert, $52,780
Herzog, David L, prof, asoc profl practice, $70,959
Herzog, Emily Dawn, music therapist, $29,294
Herzog, Melissa J, prof, ast resrch, $69,314
Hess, Robert Lee II, counsel, $144,668
Hess, Amy E, media producer II, $18.34/hr
Hess, Dana L, nurse, staff II rnwp, $30.49/hr
Hess, Jamie Renee, pat acct rep, $13.69/hr
Hess, Lucie A, social worker, $25.00/hr
Hess, Michael R, db programmer analyst-princpl, $74,856
Hess, Mitchell R, mgr II business admin, $72,840
Hess, Natalie M, pat acct rep, $14.78/hr
Hess, Shauna Denise, nurse, advanced practice, $77,152
Hesse, Constance Ann, event assistant I, $7.75/hr
Hessenkemper, Terry L, nurse, staff II, $34.18/hr
Hessler, Greg C, mech trades spclst (mts), $24.45/hr
Hester, Robert Lorenzo Jr, food svc wrkr I, $9.60/hr
Hester, Helen A, credentialing spclst, $18.36/hr
Heston, Dawn M, prof, ast teach, $40,496
Hether, Tamara J, supv clncl neurophys lab, $35.57/hr
Hettich, Douglas J, student recruitment spclst, $16.93/hr
Heuer Sr, Brian Dale, distribution techn-mtls mgmt, $15.06/hr
Heuer, Alexander Steven Henry, media producer sr, $45,518
Heuer, Angelina Marie, nurse, staff I, $19.00/hr
Heuer, Brooke Anne, patient svc rep, $10.85/hr
Heuer, Debbie Joann, patient svc rep, $15.14/hr
Heuer, Marie Nicole, mgr II business admin, $55,435
Heuer, Sabrina Leann, teaching ast, $55.00/hr
Heuer, Tammy Dawn, nurse, staff II, $31.33/hr
Heun, Dennis E, surgical technl certified, $23.01/hr
Heutinck, Melinda Ann, nurse practitioner, $34.33/hr
Hewett, John, director, $12,737
Hewitt, Whitney Nicole Deforest, specialist, $10.00/hr
Heydn, Beth L, certif pharmacy techn, $17.14/hr
Heyen, Kevin D, dir iv advancement, $110,511
Heyer, Tara Marie, nurse, staff II rnwp, $24.05/hr
Heying, Parker, child dev assistant, $8.08/hr
Hiatt, Karen A, service rep IV, $16.30/hr
Hiatt, Roger L, instructor, adjunct, $32,400
Hiatt, Stephen V, resident physician-4th yr, $54,425
Hibbard, Anna, high school student, $8.50/hr
Hibbard, Mariah Alexis, student support specialist II, $15.57/hr
Hibbs, Lori Ann, executive assistant, $24.56/hr
Hibbs, Sally A, reimbursement ast-cert, $19.76/hr
Hibdon, Rodger Lloyd, mts/hvac, $21.05/hr
Hickam, George Harold, temporary clerical, $9.76/hr
Hickem, Debra Ann, anesthesia techn, $16.22/hr
Hickem, Lorenzo D, mail carrier, $14.85/hr
Hickem, Sharice Nicole, office support assistant III, $14.07/hr
Hickem, Vanessa, telecomm opr-h, $11.66/hr
Hickerson, Leo J, telecom tech-princpl, $30.64/hr
Hickey, Debbie L, compliance manager sr, $47,230
Hickey, Keith, physicist, $79.56/hr
Hickey, Sandra Kay, nurse, staff II, $33.93/hr
Hickman, Chase R, human resources analyst sr, $59,168
Hickman, Christopher, mts/electrician, $25.35/hr
Hickman, Clark Joseph, dean, asoc, $114,848
Hickman, Jennifer Diane, physical therapist, $35.00/hr
Hickman, Joshua V, care team assoc-clinical, $13.60/hr
Hickman, Megan Marie, talent assessment spclst, $48,043
Hickman, Sondra Jean, certif pharmacy techn, $15.15/hr
Hickman, Tammy L, nurse, clncl charge-lpn, $23.01/hr

Hickman, Timothy L, sr asoc athletic director, $165,000
Hickman, Timothy Patrick, prof, asoc teach, $117,267
Hicks, Carrie L, office support assistant III, $14.62/hr
Hicks, Dawn Renee, educational pgm associate I, $14.00/hr
Hicks, Debbie L, driver, $13.89/hr
Hicks, Lanis Lucille, professor, $167,076
Hicks, Matthew Scott, mts/refrig mech-r, $20.10/hr
Hicks, Melissa Jean, nurse, staff II, $24.35/hr
Hicks, Michael Dewayne, media production director II, $68,951
Hicks, Pamela Kay, patient svc rep, $12.61/hr
Hicks, Ramona Lynn Sparks, media producer II, $16.65/hr
Hicks, Richard Berkley, instructor, adjunct, $30.00/hr
Hicks, Rita Sue, nurse, clncl charge-rn, $33.88/hr
Hicks, Sarah Jane, hr informatics spclst, $53,698
Hicks, Shannon Robinnett, event assistant sr, $16.21/hr
Hidalgo Johnson, Lorena J, lecturer, $32,130
Hidden, Natalia ACH, nurse, staff II, $21.68/hr
Hieken, Sherry M, administrative consultant, $71,400
Hiers, Hannah, teaching ast, $15,200
Hiett, DeeAnna Lynn, prof, asoc, $55,605
Higbee, Alexia Ann, psychology techn, $19.01/hr
Higbee, Dena K, sr dir program/project ops, $108,000
Higdon, Patricia, prof, asoc teach, $54,560
Higginbotham, Holly, prof, ast/profl pract, $62,000
Higginbotham, Roger D, exec dir support svcs, $193,735
Higgins, Frank Herbert Jr, instructor, adjunct, $12,000
Higgins, Alex Howard, seasonal farm ast, $10.51/hr
Higgins, Barry J, research technical svcs supv, $31.91/hr
Higgins, Bryan Lee, health physicist, $50,000
Higgins, Darcy Oram, research/lab technician, $10.50/hr
Higgins, Darla Jane, business ops associate sr, $64,539
Higgins, Donna Lynne, lecturer sr, $27,000
Higgins, Jennifer Lynn, cardiovasc techn invasive, $26.72/hr
Higgins, Lisa L, program/project supprt coor II, $42,845
Higgins, Nicole D, lecturer, $30,399
Higgins, Rebecca Carolyn, advancement officer, $50,000
Higgins, Robin Marie, radiologic techl, $19.24/hr
High, Christopher C, food svc wrkr I, $9.60/hr
Highbarger, Tommy R, office support assistant II, $10.44/hr
Highman, Lindsay Marie, nurse, staff II, $20.95/hr
Higley, Glenn G, specialist, $41,300
Hilboldt, Evangeline, child dev assistant, $8.08/hr
Hilburn, Patrick Michael, dir I, business admin, $84,092
Hilden, Patrick T, mts/refrigeration mech, $22.49/hr
Hilderbrand, Tonya Marie, office support assistant IV, $16.05/hr
Hildreth, Joyce, custodian, $12.94/hr
Hildreth, Micah Louis, academic advisor, $37,000
Hile, Matthew G, prof, asoc resrch, $109,359
Hileman, Christina Mitef, resrch asoc, $66,713
Hileman, David Leon, 4-h spclst, $57,857
Hiler, Kathryn Elizabeth, media producer sr, $36,000
Hiles, Mary Alene, histologic techn, $20.21/hr
Hiles, Rachel Kathleen, resrch ast, $35,521
Hiles, Sara Shipley, prof, ast/profl pract, $57,222
Hiles, Thomas Scott, vice chancellor, $277,956
Hilgedick, Steven Austin, prof, ast resrch, $65,650
Hilger, Debra Jean, office support assistant III, $15.08/hr
Hilgers, Michael Gene, professor, $103,331
Hill II, Kelvin Bernard, custodian, $12.90/hr
Hill-Turney, Lisa Marie, instructor, adjunct, $9,600
Hill, Anita R, custodian mrc, $10.50/hr
Hill, Brian K, grounds keeper II, $16.07/hr
Hill, Christop Lee, custodian, $11.44/hr
Hill, Clayton Travis, student service coor II, $41,011
Hill, Dennis L, nurse, staff II, $31.26/hr
Hill, Donald, food svc wrkr III, $11.24/hr
Hill, James Curtis, fellow, post doctoral, $36,691
Hill, Jana Marie Wilson, prof, ast clncl dept, $128,520
Hill, Jonathan Lynn, prof, ast clncl dept, $200,000
Hill, Joshua Greenstein, instructor, ast, $33,000
Hill, Kathy M, med techl reg, $30.25/hr
Hill, Kristy Michele, strat comm associate sr, $63,000
Hill, Larry Ross, bts carpenter, $19.59/hr
Hill, Larry W, mts/welding, $21.05/hr
Hill, Lyssa Alexandra, event assistant I, $8.50/hr
Hill, Mary Susan, nurse, staff II, $28.98/hr
Hill, Melissa Gaye, business tech analyst-princpl, $66,298
Hill, Michael Andrew, professor, $209,091
Hill, Michael Brooks, nurse, staff II, $28.45/hr

Hill, Michelle L, mgr II business admin, $73,057
Hill, Michelle Ramona, business ops associate II, $44,918
Hill, Nancy Kay, business svcs consultant, $49,763
Hill, Patrick Elwood, event assistant I, $10.00/hr
Hill, Regina Marie, nurse, staff II, $21.37/hr
Hill, Richard K, teaching ast, $31.80/hr
Hill, Robert A, ast coach, $357,500
Hill, Robert Paul, strat comm associate I, $57,900
Hill, Robert T, prof, ast clincl dept, $200,000
Hill, Robin Dianne, student service coor II, $43,000
Hill, Saed Deryck, instructor, adjunct, $5,004
Hill, Sarah A, educational pgm associate III, $20.61/hr
Hill, Sharon Marie, surgical technl certified, $21.54/hr
Hill, Susanna Jane, educational prgm coor sr, $57,630
Hill, Teneka Marie, office support assistant IV, $16.50/hr
Hill, Terry D, db administrator-expert, $85,428
Hill, Timothy David, academic advisor, $36,856
Hillebrand, Miranda Lynne, nurse, licensed prac, $15.35/hr
Hillemann, Linda K, instructor, clincl, $49,939
Hillen, Christopher Robert, network engineer-entry, $40,000
Hillerman, Wanda Lee, nurse, staff II, $34.43/hr
Hilliard, Lara Kirsten, instructor, adjunct, $14,400
Hillman, Alicia A, docent, $10,000
Hillman, Emily Anne, adjunct, $15,000
Hillman, Laura Smith, emeritus, $55,692
Hillman, Richard E, emeritus, $108,000
Hills, Angela Marie, certif pharmacy techn, $15.89/hr
Hillstrom, Victoria J, human resources manager sr, $69,500
Hillyer, Laurel A, custodian, $12.94/hr
Hilmas, Gregory E, prof, curators, $155,123
Hilton, Brieanne Michelle, student recruitment spec sr, $17.00/hr
Hilton, Shelley A, grant writer lead, $61,618
Himmelberg, Dale Joseph, bts locksmith, $21.71/hr
Himmelberg, Glen R, emeritus, $108,762
Himmelberg, Melanie, executive assistant, $16.54/hr
Hina, Audra M, hospital lab tech, $12.65/hr
Hinck, Shawn Michael, police officer, $17.56/hr
Hindeleh, Elias C, library info specialist, $20.82/hr
Hinderliter, Iris Ariel, student service coor II, $50,752
Hinderliter, Jon M, ast dir strat communications, $64,269
Hinds, Alisha Marie, resident physician-3rd yr, $53,763
Hinds, Matthew Allen, custodian, $11.00/hr
Hinds, Stuart L, librarian II, $62,473
Hinds, Tamara S, care team assoc-suppt, $14.88/hr
Hindsley, Thomas M, adjunct, $15,000
Hine, Angelynn G, med records transcript, $16.67/hr
Hinecker, William Rex Leroy, custodian, $11.44/hr
Hinerman, Monica Lynn, nurse, staff I, rnwp, $19.37/hr
Hines, Carol E, resp therapist reg, $19.34/hr
Hines, Christine C, educational pgm associate I, $14.39/hr
Hines, G Dennis, mts/pipefitter, $22.50/hr
Hines, Jonathan, dir II advancement, $69,993
Hines, Mary Ann, office support assistant IV, $14.83/hr
Hines, Melissa Daun, coor, service, $15.16/hr
Hines, Samantha Anne, resp therapist reg, $19.54/hr
Hines, Sheri L, account executive, $26,600
Hines, Stacy Machelle, radiologic techl, $18.87/hr
Hinkebein, Brian Patrick, nurse anesthetist, $95.00/hr
Hinkebein, Lyndsay Dayle, nurse, licensed prac, $15.06/hr
Hinkel, Lora Renee, instructor, clincl, $12,132
Hinkelman, Kirk Lee, office support assistant III, $13.22/hr
Hinkle, Larry G, animal techn II, $16.17/hr
Hinkle, Teresa K, med techl reg, $28.59/hr
Hinnant, Amanda L, prof, asoc, $74,966
Hinrichs, Elizabeth Leann, accountant I, $17.36/hr
Hinrichs, Gregory P, accountant sr, $49,008
Hinsen, Jason Bradley, research specialist I, $41,520
Hinshaw, Becky L, office support assistant III, $13.13/hr
Hinshaw, Heidi M, nurse practitioner, $89,844
Hinten, Patty A, clerk, diet, $12.62/hr
Hinton, Elaine L, staff dev spclst, $58,316
Hinton, Michael J, hospital security officer, $13.29/hr
Hinton, Pamela S, prof, asoc, $76,080
Hintz, Carol Ann, vice chancellor, $149,968
Hinz, Lori A, patient svc rep, $12.76/hr
Hinz, Mary Adele, coor, service, $15.22/hr
Hinz, Paige Nichole, nurse, licensed prac, $15.06/hr
Hinze, Mary L, temporary clerical, $13.50/hr
Hippenmeyer, Paul J, business svcs consultant sr, $86,822

Hirner, Cara Marie, supv nursing acute care, $32.27/hr
Hirner, Leo J, instructor, adjunct, $5,460
Hirni, Kirstin Claire, resident physician-3rd yr, $54,270
Hironaka, Mieko, specialist, $25.50/hr
Hirsch, Craig Wiley, resident physician-1st yr, $49,025
Hirsch, Gerald Lee, asoc dir research activities, $78,300
Hirsch, Paul D, educational pgm coor III, $43,192
Hirschinger, Laura Elizabeth, performace improvement prof, $73,686
Hirschman, Kyle D, resident physician-5th yr, $58,083
Hirshberg, Martha J, prof, ast teach, $65,101
Hirt, Diana S, extension asoc, $31,212
Hirte, Angela, teaching ast, $31.80/hr
Hirtz, Paul D, prgm mgr II studnt supprt svcs, $55,000
Hischier, Amy Jean, ophthalmic med technl cert, $20.00/hr
Hiskey, Lisa Marie, resident physician-2nd yr, $52,007
Hitchcock, Aaron Tyler, office support assistant IV, $14.14/hr
Hitchcock, Charlotte, business support specialist sr, $27.59/hr
Hitt, Susan M, nurse clinician, $60,980
Hitzhusen, Gerald Lee, prof, asoc, $66,173
Hladky, Dan T, prof, ast teach, $142,800
Ho, Andrea, resident physician-1st yr, $49,025
Ho, Andrew G, teaching ast, $11.00/hr
Ho, Dominic King Choi, professor, $162,979
Ho, Shanyu, research/lab technician sr, $15.16/hr
Ho, Thi Le, research specialist I, $34,684
Hoagland, Carl, prof, teach, $143,024
Hoagland, Joshua Jess, neurodiagnostic tech (reg), $20.50/hr
Hoang, Mary Sawlai, resident physician-3rd yr, $52,470
Hoard, Adrienne Walker, professor, $92,500
Hoard, Anna Louise, model, $17.00/hr
Hoard, Mary Katharine, research specialist sr, $51,150
Hobart, Brennan L, media producer sr, $42,774
Hobbs, Erin Christine, asoc dir program/project ops, $65,000
Hobbs, Gilda J, coor, service, $16.75/hr
Hobbs, John C, ag & rurl devlpmnt spclst, $51,730
Hobbs, Joseph John, professor, $110,159
Hobbs, Lydia Darlene, certif pharmacy techn, $17.10/hr
Hoberek, Andrew P, prof, asoc, $72,201
Hobson, Angela Donetta, resrch ast, $20,800
Hockaday, Heather Marie, nurse, staff II rnwp, $22.24/hr
Hockaday, Stephanie Dawn, custodian, $10.00/hr
Hockenbury, Jon L, retail sales ast manager, $18.08/hr
Hockenbury, Sandra L, instructional developr-speclst, $19.34/hr
Hockman, Kristen Michelle, prof, ast teach, $72,521
Hodel, Maria Kathleen Pope, asoc dir program/project ops, $69,600
Hodge, Denise Michele, patient svc rep, $13.21/hr
Hodge, Douglas W, rec/athletic specialist sr, $25.00/hr
Hodge, Genola B, cytotechnologist reg, $34.94/hr
Hodge, Harlan Bryant, instructor, adjunct, $10,500
Hodge, Jessica P, prof, ast, $61,914
Hodge, Kaitlyn Rose, custodian, $10.69/hr
Hodge, Lloyd C, radiologic techl, $29.54/hr
Hodge, Mary, mail carrier sr, $14.04/hr
Hodge, Seth Lucas, custodian, $11.00/hr
Hodges, Kellie Leona, qa/control technician, $21.63/hr
Hodges, Kristin Diane, office support assistant IV, $19.77/hr
Hodges, Rebecca McLain, prof, ast adjunct, $9,600
Hodges, Tamar Elise, nurse, staff now III, $30.00/hr
Hodges, Traci Lynn, lecturer, $78,821
Hodgson, Kathryn Ellen, prof, ast teach, $64,744
Hodill, Rebekah Lynn, office support assistant IV, $14.48/hr
Hodler, Stacey Lynn, business support specialist II, $18.50/hr
Hodnett, Daryl M, sr dir program/project ops, $82,404
Hodson, Mary Frances, program/project supprt coor sr, $45,600
Hoefelman, M Ann, ultrasonographer, $37.00/hr
Hoeft, Jason M, sftware supprt analyst-speclst, $40,194
Hoehn, Andrea Theresa, occl therapist, $35.00/hr
Hoehne, Jessica Dawn, serv line spclst, $67,810
Hoehne, John Albert, educational pgm manager, $50.00/hr
Hoeing, Michelle Christine, dietitian, clincl, $43,555
Hoek, Donna Suzanne, office support assistant III, $12.00/hr
Hoelscher, Beverly Fermill, office support assistant IV, $16.76/hr
Hoelscher, Jeffrey D, coor media rels-medicine, $51,393
Hoemann, Paul R, dir II csm operations, $136,209
Hoeme, Kaylene, educational pgm associate I, $13.73/hr
Hoernschemeyer, Daniel Gerard, prof, ast clincl dept, $260,037
Hoerr, Thomas R, resrch ast, $6,000
Hoerstkamp, Mark, architectural associate, $46,268

Hofen, Richard J, farm manager, $61,817
Hofer, Laura F, db programmer analyst-expert, $71,922
Hofer, Nathan Charles, prof, ast, $67,807
Hofer, Violet Jean, ast vice chancellor, $97,800
Hoff, Amy Elizabeth, nurse, staff II, $28.84/hr
Hoff, Justina Lynne, nurse, staff II, $28.14/hr
Hofferber, Scott Shane, executive director, $305,510
Hoffman, Ann M, instructor, adjunct, $125.00/hr
Hoffman, Benjamin Daniel, tutor, $10.00/hr
Hoffman, Charles Edward, dean, $227,700
Hoffman, Christopher, prof, asoc adjunct, $10,500
Hoffman, David Paul, livestock spclst, $53,397
Hoffman, Heather Joy, business support specialist II, $19.46/hr
Hoffman, Jeffrey M, bldg cntl sys techn I, $20.64/hr
Hoffman, Jerry D, sr ast dir studnt supprt svcs, $67,409
Hoffman, Kimberly G, dean, asoc, $180,000
Hoffman, Kurt William, prof, ast adjunct, $125.00/hr
Hoffman, Linda C, nurse, staff II, $34.18/hr
Hoffman, Linda Sue, prof, asoc teach, $47,793
Hoffman, Mark, prof, asoc, $240,000
Hoffman, Morgan Jade, rehab therapy aide, $10.64/hr
Hoffman, Sunny Jo, research specialist sr, $52,197
Hoffman, Tamra Jan, instructor, clincl, $53,300
Hoffman, Timothy, professor, $8,271
Hoffman, Wanda Pearl, office support assistant IV, $13.80/hr
Hoffmann, Dustin R, support systems admin-entry, $39,600
Hoffmann, Kyle Joseph, system support analyst-expert, $22.36/hr
Hoffmeister, Alex Paul, event assistant I, $7.55/hr
Hoffsette, Leon M, research consultant sr, $89,058
Hofherr, Peter William, prgm director, $14,040
Hofmann-Graf, Mala Anne, nurse, staff now I, $26.00/hr
Hofmann, Ashlee Kathleen, nurse, staff I, $19.37/hr
Hofmann, Hunter V, prof, asoc clincl dept, $288,130
Hofmann, Steven, prof, curators, $200,000
Hogan, Cody Patrick, accountant sr, $43,500
Hogan, Janine M, office support assistant IV, $14.42/hr
Hogan, John Patrick, prof, asoc, $80,800
Hogan, Katherine Elise, 4-h yth devlmnt educr, $33,500
Hogan, Kerri Marie, event assistant sr, $15.75/hr
Hogan, Rosemary Grace, prof, asoc clincl, $97,750
Hogan, Shahn A, programmer analyst-expert, $62,164
Hogan, Suzanne M, media producer II, $14.95/hr
Hogan, Timothy, coor, qlty assess/improv, $92,158
Hogan, William Russell, emrg med techn paramedic, $17.79/hr
Hogenkamp, Brenda, administrative consultant, $69,200
Hogg, Anna D, child developmentalist, $49,173
Hogg, Kevin Daniel, dir II business admin, $97,000
Hogg, Rebecca Lynn, resident physician-2nd yr, $52,007
Hogue, Ryan Stuart, emrg med techn, $12.25/hr
Hohmeier, Sylvia, veterinary technician, $15.76/hr
Hoien, Barbara Elaine, recruiter, hlth care, $55,890
Holan, Scott Harold, prof, asoc, $99,480
Holbrook, Kesi Erin, fin and acctg analyst sr, $64,077
Holden, Ashley Krisanne, nurse, staff II, $20.95/hr
Holden, Hilary Anne, enrollment advisor sr, $16.54/hr
Holder, Andrew, professor, $91,835
Holder, Brandon Lee, temporary crafts service, $10.00/hr
Holder, Sheila Kay, business support specialist sr, $19.37/hr
Holder, Tyson R, student service coor II, $40,218
Holdmeier, Shirley A, academic advisor, $39,236
Holdo, Ricardo Martin, prof, ast, $82,035
Holladay, Bonna Rae, resrch ast, $40,449
Holladay, John N, academic advisor, $40,036
Holland, Alicia Denee, mri technologist, $28.00/hr
Holland, Ashley C, safety communications operator, $14.01/hr
Holland, Charles A, business spclst, $49,239
Holland, D Jane, office support assistant IV, $14.89/hr
Holland, Deborah Crosley, instructional developr-spec, $14.95/hr
Holland, James R, radiologic techl, $19.26/hr
Holland, Jennifer, program/project supprt coor I, $56,000
Holland, Kara Susanne, adjunct, $9,000
Holland, Kelli Ann, human resources manager sr, $60,900
Holland, Lene J, professor, $99,329
Holland, Lindsay Ellen, student recruitment spclst, $16.84/hr
Holland, Michael A, resident physician-2nd yr, $51,134
Holland, Michael E, archivist IV, $86,978
Holland, Paige Janae, nursing ast, $11.11/hr
Holland, Stephen P, specialist, $37,911
Holle, Julie Michelle, veterinary technician sr, $22.28/hr

Holle, Shawna Lynn, office support assistant II, $10.50/hr
Holley, Margaret M, instructor, adjunct, $19,425
Holliday, Casey Monahan, prof, ast, $88,509
Holliday, Gregory A, dir hr prgrms/proj-enterprise, $119,033
Holliday, Pamela Ann, mgr surgical svcs-h, $116,900
Holliday, Zachary M, resident physician-3rd yr, $65,763
Hollinger, Cassandra N, counselor, genetic, $57,222
Hollinger, Leigh, business support specialist II, $18.09/hr
Hollinger, Robert E, business ops associate sr, $62,730
Hollingshead, Jennifer Anne, mgr, marketing, $112,154
Hollingsworth-Smith, Kristel Dawn, police officer, $17.50/hr
Hollingsworth, Heather Sue, temporary professional, $15.00/hr
Hollingsworth, Meili Jo, office support assistant II, $12.50/hr
Hollingsworth, Susan B, dir I, student support svcs, $94,812
Hollins, Etta Ruth, professor, $194,255
Hollins, Octavia, office support assistant II, $11.17/hr
Hollis, Jennifer M, strat comm associate I, $37,513
Hollister, Vannessa Brandy, custodian, $10.69/hr
Hollman, Edward J, temporary technical, $20.00/hr
Holloway, Amanda L, asoc dir program/project ops, $51,983
Holloway, Gregory Maurice, av instal service tech-spec, $16.17/hr
Hollrah, Sean D, cat scan technl (ct), $30.36/hr
Holly, David Ward, csm associate III, $25.07/hr
Holly, Jason Scott L, prof, ast clincl dept, $153,000
Holly, Rita Virginia, business support specialist sr, $26.37/hr
Holm, Jason Scott, user support analyst-speclst, $16.30/hr
Holm, Lisa Jo, nurse, staff, $28.48/hr
Holm, Michael Kevin, boiler maint opr, $24.13/hr
Holman, Christopher Michael, professor, $106,700
Holman, J Martin, prof, ast teach, $48,699
Holman, Jeremy Pearl, farm wrkr II, $14.27/hr
Holman, Lauren Nichole, media producer II, $14.95/hr
Holmes, Robert Ray Jr, prof, adjunct, $28,800
Holmes, Byron, insulation svcs wrkr II, $20.07/hr
Holmes, Cady Jean, human resources specialist II, $35,640
Holmes, Derrick, facilities supervisor, $46,894
Holmes, Donald J, sr manager it, $72,682
Holmes, Eileen Marie, human resources assistant, $16.58/hr
Holmes, Keeta Martin, prgm director, ast, $72,136
Holmes, Lyndal Gray, prof, asoc adjunct, $284.00/hr
Holmes, Nila Jean, temporary professional, $11.30/hr
Holmes, Richard G, research specialist I, $34,122
Holmes, Sarah Elizabeth, activity aide, $14.00/hr
Holmes, Stanley J, program/project supprt coor I, $34,658
Holmes, Stephen Michael, prof, asoc, $76,650
Holsinger, Alexander, professor, $78,098
Holsinger, Kristi, professor, $77,893
Holsinger, Linda Mariko, executive assistant sr, $106,015
Holsinger, Robin D, resp therapy techn/icu cert, $24.05/hr
Holt, Amon Eugene III, specialist, $10.00/hr
Holt, Angela M, care team assoc-clinical, $14.72/hr
Holt, Ashley Lynn, pat acct rep, $14.98/hr
Holt, James Leon, mts/pipefitter, $25.35/hr
Holt, Jason A, head coach, $45,740
Holt, Jeffrey A, med office assistant, $13.60/hr
Holt, Jessica Marie, nurse, staff II, $23.34/hr
Holt, Lorie Anne, prof, asoc, $77,046
Holt, Richard F, resident physician-4th yr, $55,804
Holt, Scott Christopher, sterile processing tech, $18.31/hr
Holt, Steven Calvin, temporary professional, $50.00/hr
Holte, Misha Anne, physician ast, $86,000
Holtgrave, Darcy Elizabeth, ast editor, $18.18/hr
Holtkamp, Kelly L, program/project supprt coor I, $48,048
Holtkamp, Robin C, office support assistant IV, $14.72/hr
Holtmeyer, Kimberli N, mgr III business admin, $64,152
Holton, Abby M, neurodiagnostic tech (reg), $24.00/hr
Holtzclaw, Brennan J, commercial talent, $20.00/hr
Holub Taylor, Leticia Ann, instructor, adjunct, $16,650
Holwerda, Ross A, resident physician-3rd yr, $52,470
Holznecht, Mackenzie, rec/athletic specialist sr, $39,600
Holzum, Hannah Renee, dietitian, clincl, $48,685
Homan, Bryce Mark, mts/electrician, $21.05/hr
Homan, Kelly O, prof, asoc, $86,059
Homer, Shelli Elizabeth, instructor, $33,821
Honan, John M, temporary professional, $21.07/hr
Honas, Kenneth G, temporary technical, $13.91/hr
Honeyman, Joshua A, resident physician-3rd yr, $52,470
Hong, Zhongkui, resrch scientist/academic, $50,459
Honig, Sheila, lecturer, $32,294

Honigberg, Saul M, prof, asoc, $86,377
Honnold, Adrianne L, lecturer, $18,360
Honse, Elizabeth Failynn, student support specialist I, $14.44/hr
Honse, Rebecca Jo, sterile processing tech, $14.09/hr
Honse, Victoria Anne, clerk, operating room supply, $14.09/hr
Hood, Daffany J, business support specialist sr, $21.99/hr
Hood, David James, custodian, $11.41/hr
Hood, Diana Klemme, emp rel spec hlthcr, $84,760
Hood, Edwin Thomas, prof, adjunct, $64,750
Hood, Jennifer Lynn, resp therapist reg, $24.34/hr
Hood, Margaret Ann, waiter/waitress, $9.00/hr
Hook, Benjamin Austin, instructor, adjunct, $10,500
Hook, Gregory Alan, operations support tech sr, $14.90/hr
Hooker, Sabrina LuAnn, media production associate, $9.00/hr
Hooks, Jessica LeDean, nurse, staff II, $24.45/hr
Hooper, Sarah E, fellow, resrch, $43,680
Hoormann, Jackie A, rev cycle perf, qlty & tr mgr, $80,593
Hoormann, Richard G, agronomy spclst, $53,132
Hoover, Adam L, patient svc rep, $13.02/hr
Hoover, Emily A, student support specialist sr, $17.03/hr
Hoover, John N, librarian IV, $94,889
Hoover, Nancy A, student service coor II, $52,433
Hopewell, Bridget Leann, resident physician-4th yr, $55,804
Hopgood, Vicki L, program/project supprt coor sr, $55.00/hr
Hopkins, Adrian Maurice, mech, auto cntrl, $21.62/hr
Hopkins, Daniel Jacob, dir sports operations, $95,613
Hopkins, Daniel Price, professor, $76,082
Hopkins, Keith Allen, custodian lead, $13.96/hr
Hopkins, Keron E, business ops associate sr, $45,600
Hopkins, Lori Brooke, patient svc rep, $15.24/hr
Hopkins, Mary J, office support assistant IV, $13.19/hr
Hopkins, Melanie Sue, csm associate I, $14.96/hr
Hopkins, Michael A, programmer analyst-entry, $39,600
Hopkins, Olivia May, nurse, staff now III, $30.00/hr
Hopkins, Raphael Nicolle, business support spec II, $16.98/hr
Hopkins, Taisiya Mikhailovna, office support asst IV, $16.00/hr
Hopkins, Tamara V, prof, ast clincl, $187.50/hr
Hopkins, Travis A, custodian, $12.94/hr
Hopp, Bethany Ann, office support assistant IV, $13.75/hr
Hoppe, Mary A, program/project supprt coor I, $40,170
Hopper, Billie J, med coding spclst-certified, $23.94/hr
Hopper, Ryan Phillip, care team assoc-clinical, $12.32/hr
Hopper, Stacy Ray, custodian, $12.94/hr
Hoppock, Patty A, nurse, staff II, $22.67/hr
Hopson, Cheryl Ann, supv pat accts-up, $50,903
Hopson, Neil B, mts/pipefitter, $22.49/hr
Hor, Yew San, prof, ast, $75,515
Horine, Andrew D, resident physician-3rd yr, $53,763
Horisk, Claire S, prof, asoc, $63,310
Horman, Deborah L, nurse, licensed prac, $21.42/hr
Horn, Alex Burdett, student support specialist II, $15.37/hr
Horn, Katelyn Marie, research/lab technician, $10.24/hr
Horn, Nathan E, db administrator-expert, $69,000
Horn, William F, asoc dir research inst prgms, $125,034
Horne, Malaika B, dir III business admin, $120,621
Horner, Jennifer Leann, research specialist I, $41,202
Horner, Joe L, extension asoc, $75,941
Horner, Margaret M, instructor, clincl, $13,500
Horner, William Thomas, prof, teach, $54,393
Hornick, John A, dir nursing svcs um, $143,645
Hornsby, Jeffrey Scott, professor, $329,555
Horsford, Emily Kathleen, retail sales associate sr, $31,722
Horsley, James L, cook, $13.21/hr
Horsmon, Caitlin Marie, prof, asoc, $58,670
Horstman, Haley Ann, prof, ast, $60,600
Horstmeier, Robin Leann, prof, asoc adjunct, $18,000
Horton, Christa Jo, business ops associate I, $39,385
Horton, Rose Marie, sr dir program/project ops, $90,660
Horton, Tiffany J, office support assistant IV, $14.05/hr
Horvatich, Christopher Travis, peoplesoft admin-spclst, $73,000
Horvit, Beverly Jane, prof, ast/profl pract, $59,160
Horvit, Mark Harris, prof, asoc profl practice, $113,499
Horwitz, Bruce, prof, ast clincl, $39,397
Horwitz, Mara H, resident physician-2nd yr, $52,610
Hoscher, Joan M, teaching ast, $14.28/hr
Hosder, Serhat, prof, asoc, $86,662
Hosey, Craig A, coor info systems, $64,484
Hosey, Jessica Anne, program/project supprt coor II, $60,099

Hoskins, Anna Catherine, social worker, $25.00/hr
Hoskins, David G, telecom tech-expert, $16.06/hr
Hoskins, Gerald S, cat scan technl (ct), $30.91/hr
Hoskins, Heidi M, care team assoc-suppt, $13.37/hr
Hoskins, Holly D, pat acct rep, $14.84/hr
Hoskins, Phillip J, deputy general counsel, $210,120
Hosokawa, Michael Charles, professor, $131,722
Hoss, John D, custodian, $11.41/hr
Hoss, William Henry, mts/refrig mech-r, $20.87/hr
Hossain, Akm Mosharraf, prof, ast clincl dept, $255,000
Hossain, Md Shakhawat, resrch scientist/academic, $45,008
Hosseini, Virginia Lee, patient svc rep, $14.88/hr
Hosto-Marti, Barbara Jean, instructor, adjunct, $12,000
Hotard, Michelle Catherine, nurse, staff II, $19.00/hr
Hotchkiss, Mark, account manager, $24,000
Hotop, Philip Anton, operations support tech I, $10.24/hr
Hou, Chen, prof, ast, $66,250
Houchins, Mallory Ann, educational pgm coor I, $32,825
Houck, Meghann Victoria, resident physician-4th yr, $55,804
Houg, Lynn R, bts carpenter, $21.71/hr
Houg, Rita E, mgr II csm operations, $67,030
Hough, Brandon D, assoc director it, $109,242
Houghton, Howard Louis, prof, asoc clincl dept, $210,958
Houk, Selena, food svc wrkr II, $10.10/hr
Hourchi, Daniel Abbas, mental health tech, $13.66/hr
Hournou, Ivonne Beatriz, instructor, adjunct, $9,000
House, James E Jr, sterile processing tech, $18.31/hr
House, Aimee Rene, social worker, $44,426
House, Alicia Marie, nurse, licensed prac, $19.59/hr
House, Heath H, electronic sys techn III, $22.01/hr
House, Jason R, mech, bldg maint, $19.64/hr
House, Misty Michelle, office support associate, $17.43/hr
House, Sandra Jo, office support assistant IV, $15.57/hr
Houseman, Richard M, prof, asoc, $78,688
Housley, Sonja Lou, care team assoc-clinical, $12.97/hr
Housman, Gillian Kathleen, resident physician-2nd yr, $50,810
Houston, Dana Denise, security officer sr, $13.56/hr
Houston, Eugenia Marie, educational pgm associate I, $13.65/hr
Houston, Gregory C, prof, ast clincl, $106,982
Houston, John Brian, prof, ast, $83,000
Houston, Judith A, patient svc rep, $13.44/hr
Houston, Kathryn S, dir I, advancement, $63,350
Houston, Kimberlie A, business support specialist II, $18.86/hr
Houston, Monica Ellen, office support assistant IV, $13.92/hr
Houston, Tammy R, office support assistant III, $15.61/hr
Houts, Todd A, dir II env health and safety, $128,438
Houttuin, Melissa A, nurse, staff II, $21.37/hr
Houx, Lucy Virginia, instructor, $52
Howald, Linda Sue, pharmacist II, $128,835
Howard, Amelia Rose, academic advisor sr, $42,000
Howard, Bryce T, media producer I, $13.25/hr
Howard, Deborah Ann, tutor, $10.00/hr
Howard, Debra Ann, practice manager, $66,279
Howard, Derek Arthur, high school student, $8.00/hr
Howard, Genevieve Andrea, strat comm associate II, $49,555
Howard, James Thomas, strat comm consultant, $68,500
Howard, Jeremy Bryant, retail sales assistant sr, $11.73/hr
Howard, Logan Blain, office support assistant III, $12.48/hr
Howard, Melissa, resident physician-1st yr, $49,025
Howard, Michael Joseph, prof, ast teach, $45,750
Howard, Michael Montez, custodian, $10.39/hr
Howard, Rhonda Jennifer, supv, lab, $58,166
Howard, Rita Loree, office support assistant IV, $17.82/hr
Howard, Robert G, surgical technl certified, $21.24/hr
Howard, Sherry Ann, office support assistant IV, $14.14/hr
Howard, Tammi Marie, patient svc rep, $13.19/hr
Howard, Teresa L, executive assistant, $28.11/hr
Howdeshell, Donald Marcus, system administrator-spclst, $54,230
Howe, Donald R, hospital security officer, $12.68/hr
Howe, John S, professor, $236,944
Howe, Michael, research engineering tech I, $26.07/hr
Howe, Theron Dikeman, temporary professional, $10.00/hr
Howe, Timothy E, prof, ast, $54,924
Howell, Whitcomb Steve III, nurse, staff I, $19.00/hr
Howell, Bradley M, emrg med techn paramedic, $14.20/hr
Howell, Dana S, speech/lang pathologist, $27,865
Howell, Jaqueline I, educational pgm associate I, $12.85/hr
Howell, Karen H, office support assistant IV, $15.00/hr
Howell, Renette Reshelle, office support assistant IV, $14.05/hr

Howenstine, Debra A, prof, asoc clincl dept, $153,301
Howerton, Tracey Lynn, manuscript specialist sr, $40,000
Howes, William Seth, prof, ast, $58,590
Howland, Jane L, prof, teach, $64,622
Howland, Rachel Margaret, pharm intern third year, $15.00/hr
Howren, Arthur Ronald, programmer analyst-expert, $47,619
Howsare, Robert Roy, instructor, adjunct, $15,000
Howse, Christopher J, resident physician-3rd yr, $53,763
Howze, Carolyn K, finance systems specialist II, $47,895
Hoxworth, William D, emrg med techn, $14.88/hr
Hoyos Escobar, Daniela, high school student, $8.00/hr
Hoyos, Jessica Ivette, temporary crafts service, $8.00/hr
Hoyos, Mary Elizabeth, resrch scientist/academic, $37,520
Hoyt-Vail, Martina Louise, student support spclst II, $18.02/hr
Hoyt, Christopher R, professor, $118,600
Hoyt, Daniel Seth, prof, ast clincl dept, $56,100
Hrach, Chatchaya T, student service coor II, $39,600
Hritsco, Jennifer Dawn, reimbursement consultant, $59,511
Hruban, Gina M, office support assistant IV, $15.75/hr
Hsieh, Fu Hung, professor, $163,935
Hsieh, Hsin-Yeh, resrch scientist/academic, $43,243
Hsueh, Kuei-Hsiang, prof, asoc, $70,013
Hu, Jiu, custodian, $12.94/hr
Hu, Parker John, resident physician-5th yr, $61,683
Hu, Qiong, fellow, post doctoral, $43,680
Hu, Shenghui, research specialist I, $46,932
Hu, Zhiqiang, prof, asoc, $111,591
Huaco, Yoni, custodian, $12.94/hr
Huang, Bo, tutor, $13.13/hr
Huang, Chi Ming, prof, asoc, $72,936
Huang, Donghua, research specialist I, $40,578
Huang, Francis Howard Lim, prof, ast, $73,365
Huang, Guoliang, prof, asoc, $105,000
Huang, Haigen, fellow, post doctoral, $40,000
Huang, Jian, fellow, post doctoral, $48,175
Huang, Johnny Guo-Xun, office support assistant III, $11.30/hr
Huang, Junying, scholar, visiting, $18.75/hr
Huang, Rosa H, professor, $87,046
Huang, Sheng-You, system administrator-speclst, $58,080
Huang, Shengping, fellow, post doctoral, $37,669
huang, Susan, event assistant I, $8.50/hr
Huang, Wei, engineer I, $40,000
Huang, Xian, prof, ast, $79,500
Huang, Yue-Wern, professor, $85,784
Hubbard, Brett M, temporary professional, $19.54/hr
Hubbard, Calvin L, coor, securty opns & tech sup, $23.01/hr
Hubbard, Elizabeth, office support assistant IV, $18.32/hr
Hubbard, Loretta J, patient svc rep, $14.07/hr
Hubbard, Mary Karen Riechers, instructor, adjunct, $18,636
Hubbard, Nancy L, supv, operating room nursing, $31.91/hr
Hubbard, Rachel Lorraine, nurse, staff II, $22.22/hr
Hubbard, Theresa Lynne, physical therapist, $35.00/hr
Hubbard, Victoria C, research specialist I, $49,700
Hubbart, Jason A, prof, asoc, $87,789
Huber, Ann L, executive assistant, $19.64/hr
Huber, Patrick J, professor, $71,547
Huberman, Jennifer M, prof, asoc, $62,317
Hubert, Brenda Carol, nurse, staff II, $26.44/hr
Hubert, Lucy Carr, office support assistant III, $15.32/hr
Hubert, Teri Rae, resp therapist reg, $21.47/hr
Huble, Kayley Rose, office support assistant II, $10.55/hr
Hubler, Graham Kelder Jr, administrative consultant II, $91,052
Huck, Randall Albert, coor, safety, $66,586
Huck, Stacey Marie, office support assistant III, $14.35/hr
Huckabay, Cassandra Lee, nurse, staff II, $21.26/hr
Huckabey, Marsha L, business support specialist II, $22.37/hr
Huckla, Virginia L Feldpausch, instructor, ast, $13,608
Huddleston, Megan Marie, clinical nursing supvsr, $65,748
Huddleston, Megan Marie, nurse, staff prn, $26.00/hr
Hudgens, Connie J, human resources manager, $55,893
Hudgins, Vicki Louise, student support specialist II, $20.83/hr
Hudlow, Lucinda A, office support assistant IV, $17.46/hr
Hudnut, Mary Jo, db programmer analyst-princpl, $67,966
Hudnut, Patricia Susan, office support assistant IV, $16.46/hr
Hudson II, Robert Allen, reactor operator sr, $36.09/hr
Hudson Weems, Clenora, professor, $84,082
Hudson, Bonnie Joy, account executive, $6,000
Hudson, Christine Marie, bus support specialist II, $19.43/hr
Hudson, Doranne Meny, prof, asoc teach, $92,281

Hudson, Eskil C, environmental health tech II, $15.25/hr
Hudson, Fraser Berkley, prof, asoc, $73,613
Hudson, LeGreta, prof, ast teach, $55,000
Hudson, Nicholas Michael, nurse, licensed prac, $14.76/hr
Hudson, Paula A, db programmer analyst-expert, $65,017
Hudson, Rebekah Marie, physician ast, $100.00/hr
Hudson, Repps Bedford, instructor, adjunct, $5,250
Hudson, Rhonda G, nurse, licensed prac sr, $20.18/hr
Hudson, Samuel Levi, media producer II, $17.50/hr
Hudson, Stanton T, asoc dir healthcare programs, $88,301
Hudson, Terry G, occl therapist, $70,502
Hudson, Tracy L, business support analyst sr, $26.23/hr
Hudson, Troy, bldg cntrl sys techn iv lead, $25.37/hr
Hudspeth, Paula Rae, teaching ast, $13.00/hr
Huebner, Beth M, prof, asoc, $90,500
Huebner, Jacqueline D, research/lab technician II, $13.90/hr
Huebner, John W, specialist, $10.00/hr
Huebner, Wayne, professor, $172,158
Huebner, Zachary Tate, temporary crafts service, $17.50/hr
Huelsbergen, Anselm Martin, archivist III, $52,302
Huelsbergen, Deborah L, prof, curators, $79,936
Hueske, Christine A, compliance specialist I, $18.23/hr
Huether, Linda G, executive assistant, $23.40/hr
Huey, Loretta J, educational pgm associate I, $13.45/hr
Huff, Harold Eugene, research specialist sr, $31.15/hr
Huff, Nicole Ann, nurse, licensed prac, $16.29/hr
Huffington, Deborah Sue, nurse, staff II, $34.53/hr
Huffington, Gabrial Edgar, instructor, adjunct, $7,500
Huffman, Abram Patrick, resp therapist reg, $30.00/hr
Huffman, Amber Mae, social worker, $50,151
Huffman, Angie L, enrollment advisor sr, $17.10/hr
Huffman, Chelsey Lynn, nurse clinician, $52,153
Huffman, David, db administrator-expert, $74,164
Huffman, Gale Delmar, bts carpenter, $19.59/hr
Huffman, Nichole Tennille, temporary technical, $20.84/hr
Huffman, Sarah Rose, research specialist I, $38,545
Huffmon, Jennifer L, program/project supprt coor I, $54,536
Hufford, Jonathan, resident physician-1st yr, $49,025
Hufker, Barbara Jean, library info specialist sr, $21.84/hr
Huggins, Karen Renee, business support specialist II, $18.22/hr
Hughes II, Joseph Clinton, lecturer, $35,781
Hughes, Andrea Leigh, instructor, adjunct, $7,059
Hughes, Ann E, nurse, staff II, $30.21/hr
Hughes, Anne Maureen, mgr III business admin, $77,035
Hughes, Bruce R, cooling tower techn, $20.07/hr
Hughes, Carey Marie, grader, $52
Hughes, Clarissa Evette, temporary clerical, $8.58/hr
Hughes, Dana N, instructor, clincl, $14,400
Hughes, Delbert D, sterile processing tech, $18.31/hr
Hughes, Ellen Camille, certif pharmacy techn, $17.10/hr
Hughes, Erin Leigh, intern, $14,400
Hughes, Fred Darrell, driver, $12.80/hr
Hughes, Heather Anne, event assistant I, $7.55/hr
Hughes, Jeffrey Phillip, tutor, $9.00/hr
Hughes, Joshua Dennett, internet admin-expert, $25.20/hr
Hughes, Kari Dee, fin and acctg analyst sr, $52,876
Hughes, Krista Lynn, prof, qlty assess/improv, $71,770
Hughes, Laura Diane, temporary technical, $25.00/hr
Hughes, Margaret Ellen, food svc wrkr IV, $13.30/hr
Hughes, Mary, nurse, or/recovery-ch, $33.43/hr
Hughes, Michael Evan, prof, ast, $70,000
Hughes, Rhonda Sue, business support specialist sr, $20.15/hr
Hughes, Stanley J, mts/pipefitter, $22.50/hr
Hughes, Stephanie, electronics technician I, $12.55/hr
Hughes, Tiffany, mgr III business admin, $58,741
Hughes, Tracey Michelle, librarian II, $47,976
Hughey, Douglas A, support systems admin-expert, $54,228
Hughey, Tyler Lynn, mts/electrician, $20.31/hr
Huhman, Andrew Craig, care team assoc-clinical, $11.10/hr
Huhman, Carol J, office support assistant IV, $12.98/hr
Hui, Oi Chi, library info specialist sr, $14.95/hr
Huilman, Kevin M, db programmer analyst-expert, $54,500
Huisman, Daniel Linn, physical therapist, $72,028
Huisman, Sarah Esther, prof, ast adjunct, $50
Huke, Michael A, instructor, clincl, $9,000
Hulbert, Anna E, resident physician-2nd yr, $52,007
Hulbert, Molly Anne, resrch ast, $31,000
Hulen, Kenneth D, temporary crafts service, $14.50/hr
Hulen, Nadeen Marie, office support assistant IV, $15.66/hr

Hulen, Taylor Nicole, temporary clerical, $8.35/hr
Hulett, Joycelin Louise, instructor, adjunct, $9,600
Hulett, Tabitha A, pat acct rep, $14.52/hr
Hull, Angela Marie, prof, ast teach, $62,000
Hull, Caitlin N, accountant sr, $47,940
Hull, Christopher R, student service coor II, $41,011
Hull, Ed, mts/electrician, $21.05/hr
Hull, Greta Thompson, instructor, clincl, $56,270
Hull, Kimberly L, mgr III business admin, $72,583
Hull, Rose Marie, resp therapist reg, $20.52/hr
Hull, Sherri L, educational pgm associate I, $13.89/hr
Hulsey, Thomas Aaron, research/lab technician, $10.24/hr
Hultine Massengale, Sarah Ann, community dev spclst, $45,679
Hults, Lawrence R, theatre ast, $15.00/hr
Humble, Taylor Marguerite, temporary crafts service, $7.65/hr
Hume, Deborah Louise, prof, asoc teach, $75,748
Hume, Gary Lee, grant writer, $22.30/hr
Humfeld, Sarah Conditt, fellow, post doctoral, $51,008
Hummel, Amanda Marie, service rep IV, $16.13/hr
Hummel, Angela Renae, office support assistant IV, $15.12/hr
Hummel, Christy J, student recruitment spclst, $16.48/hr
Hummer, Haley RaeAnn, office support assistant III, $12.00/hr
Hummert, Matthew David, stage services assistant, $14.00/hr
Humpf, Max Julian, mental health tech, $11.44/hr
Humphrey, James R Jr, extns professional, asoc, $51,690
Humphrey, Brenda Gwen, educational pgm assistant, $10.40/hr
Humphrey, Julia C, program/project supprt coor I, $30,815
Humphrey, Kimberly A, administrative consultant II, $85,971
Humphrey, Nolan W, mts/electrician-r, $20.87/hr
Humphrey, Phillip, av instal service tech-entry, $14.00/hr
Humphrey, Tera G, student service coor I, $35,100
Humphries, William Edward III, prof, ast visiting, $255,000
Hund, Jonathan David, care team assoc-clinical, $12.08/hr
Hundle, James R, administrative consultant II, $100,378
Huneke, Diane Lynne, nurse, resrch, $47,380
Huneycutt, Lois L, prof, asoc, $65,628
Hunsburger, Dale R, educational pgm associate I, $12.68/hr
Hunsley, Richard Walter, resp therapist reg, $26.47/hr
Hunt-Carter, Erin Elizabeth, grader, $100.00/hr
Hunt, Christina Bree, tutor, $25.00/hr
Hunt, Diane Lynn, business support specialist sr, $16.66/hr
Hunt, Emily Elizabeth, nurse, staff II, $24.89/hr
Hunt, Heather K, prof, ast, $86,969
Hunt, Herbert O, event assistant I, $11.40/hr
Hunt, Jamie Joellen, prof, ast teach, $58,425
Hunt, Jared Tyler, custodian, $10.39/hr
Hunt, Linda A, event assistant II, $13.83/hr
Hunt, Marcia Diane, nurse, staff II, $34.18/hr
Hunt, Sharen Kay, 4-h spclst, $69,946
Hunt, Stephanie Gentry, serv line spclst, $80,268
Hunt, Tony L, ast dir env health and safety, $62,504
Hunter, James Douglas Jr, dir program/project operations, $84,357
Hunter, Brenda K, business support specialist sr, $20.40/hr
Hunter, Charles S, boiler maint opr, $24.13/hr
Hunter, Daphne Denita, accountant I, $18.07/hr
Hunter, Diane K, librarian III, $72,408
Hunter, Dominic E, event assistant I, $7.55/hr
Hunter, Jennifer Lynn, prof, asoc, $81,195
Hunter, Joan R, resrch asoc, $55,328
Hunter, Latoya L, temporary crafts service, $9.50/hr
Hunter, Mark Ira, prof, ast clincl dept, $183,960
Hunter, MaryMargaret Katharine, event assistant I, $8.00/hr
Hunter, Nichelle, mgr III business admin, $53,668
Hunter, Shelby Lyn, nurse, staff I, $19.00/hr
Huntley, John W, prof, ast, $64,640
Hunton, Katrina Joy, veterinary technician, $14.27/hr
Hunts, Chelsey Ann, research/lab technician, $10.24/hr
Huntsperger, Jason D, research lab supervisor, $43,332
Huppert, Patrick W, security access spclst, $22.53/hr
Hura, Paul, docent, $5,000
Hurcomb, Laura G, instructor, adjunct, $15,000
Hurley, Andrew, professor, $95,747
Hurley, Tobi L, accountant II, $20.95/hr
Hurson, Alireza, professor, $183,102
Hurst-Bayless, Connie Marie, instructor, adjunct, $6,276
Hurst, Debra A, mri technologist, $35.80/hr
Hurst, Gayle Ann, program/project supprt coor I, $39,206
Hurst, Heather Danielle, event assistant sr, $16.48/hr
Hurst, Nathan Gregory, strat comm associate II, $44,533

Hurst, Robin D, prof, asoc teach, $64,427
Hurt, Douglas Allan, prof, ast teach, $53,930
Hurt, Jennifer Lenae, nurse, staff II, $22.93/hr
Hurt, Meghan L, resident physician-4th yr, $54,425
Hurwicz, Margo Lea, prof, asoc, $73,610
Husain, Syed Arshad, emeritus, $70,218
Husbye, Nicholas E, prof, ast, $60,684
Huscher, Krista M, veterinary technician, $14.63/hr
Huseva, Katsiaryna Serheeuna, fellow, post doc clncl yr1, $27,000
Huskey, Debby Sue, office support assistant IV, $19.39/hr
Huskey, Linda G, nurse, staff II, $20.54/hr
Huskey, Ramona June, courier, $12.40/hr
Hussain, Muhanad, mental health tech, $11.44/hr
Hussey, Kelsey Simpson, dir I, business admin, $104,245
Hustead, Andrew D, temporary crafts service, $10.00/hr
Husted, Kristofor Hoagnelson, media producer sr, $37,400
Huston, Dale W, custodian, $13.23/hr
Huston, Kristin Nicole, lecturer, $30,000
Hutcheson, Estrella Lynn, certif pharmacy techn, $14.52/hr
Hutcheson, Kyle David, veterinarian, residnt, $26,000
Hutcheson, Ryan S, prof, ast teach, $36,000
Hutchins, Julie Lyn, instructor, adjunct, $4,400
Hutchins, Sarah Elizabeth, communications asst sr, $18.76/hr
Hutchinson, Corrie Ann, librarian II, $66,000
Hutchinson, Karen D, child dev teacher sr, $27,945
Hutchinson, Lisa Ann, sftware supprt analyst-entry, $39,634
Hutchinson, Lisa Ann, patient svc rep, $12.76/hr
Hutchinson, Rashaun Lamar, media production assoc, $9.00/hr
Hutchinson, Roderick A, advancement associate II, $17.04/hr
Hutchison, Alisa G, instructor, clincl, $78,413
Hutchison, Bobby G, custodian, $11.41/hr
Hutchison, Brian Lewis, prof, ast, $64,016
Hutchison, Gregory K, grounds keeper, $13.21/hr
Hutsler, Shannon M, student service coor II, $40,000
Hutson, Mary Darlene, nurse, staff II, $31.17/hr
Hutton, Christy Ann Clark, psychologist, $76,071
Hutton, Kyle Glenn, office support assistant III, $13.00/hr
Hutton, Stacy, instructor, adjunct, $8,325
Huxley, Virginia H, professor, $197,828
Huxtable, Brian R, system administrator-entry, $56,810
Huynh, Danny L, resident physician-4th yr, $55,804
Hwang PhD, Soo Duck, scientist lead, $66,810
Hwang, Peter Y, prof, ast clincl dept, $156,060
Hwang, Sarah Kathryn, prof, ast clincl dept, $156,060
Hwang, Tzyh Chang, professor, $171,912
Hyatt-Wade, Sharyn Jane, instructor, adjunct, $9,910
Hyatt, Zoe R, strat comm associate sr, $45,828
Hyde, Cynthia Renee, ophthalmic ast cert, $16.70/hr
Hyder, Salman M, professor, $156,087
Hyder, Zeshan, prof, ast teach, $80,000
Hyken, Tina A, administrative consultant, $95,532
Hyland, Nancy, nurse, staff II, $34.18/hr
Hyler, Billy, care team assoc-suppt, $13.37/hr
Hyler, Bonita Marcia, instrument techn II lead, $16.69/hr
Hyler, William Melvin, bts painter, $21.71/hr
Hynes, Steven Edward, mgr env health and safety, $82,000
Hysa, Burhan, custodian, $12.18/hr
Hysong, Christopher Robert, grader, $52
Iadevito, Deborah Ann, specialist, $3,147
Ianke, Donna M, clinical educator, $78,374
Ianke, Leesa, business support specialist II, $21.65/hr
Ibdah, Jamal A, professor, $490,248
Ibendahl, Erica Lynne, resident physician-3rd yr, $53,763
Ibrahim, Abdullahi Ali, prof, visiting, $14,667
Ibrahim, Gulsen I, med techl reg, $26.41/hr
Ibrahim, Ibsa Mussa, custodian, $10.00/hr
Ibrahim, Mervat A, instructor, adjunct, $17,700
Ibraimi, Arian, office support assistant IV, $14.91/hr
Ice, Jennifer Lee, office support assistant III, $12.15/hr
Icenogle, Coney Elizabeth, custodian, $10.39/hr
Ichim, Ana Maria, prof, ast, $78,960
Ickler, Donald W, fin and acctg manager sr, $96,390
Ickler, Donald W, occl therapist, $35.00/hr
Ide, Bridget Nicole, nurse, staff II, $21.15/hr
Idle, Linda Slinkard, mgr revenue management, $102,342
Idle, Ruby A, office support assistant IV, $18.21/hr
Igel, Kyle Donald, advancement officer, $45,600
Igwe, Orisa J, prof, asoc, $86,412
Ihler, Mary Ann, executive assistant, $20.77/hr

Ihler, Olin Lee, grounds keeper, $12.70/hr
Ill, Kelsey Lee, nurse, staff I, $19.37/hr
Illingworth, Catherine Chott, office support asst III, $11.86/hr
Ilsley, Karen Sue, mammography technl, $30.62/hr
Imhoff, Gary Mark, dir II research ops and plng, $148,824
Imhoff, Karla L, user support analyst-speclst, $18.50/hr
Imhoff, Melinda G, office support assistant IV, $15.77/hr
Imig, Kathleen Cory Harrell, resrch ast, $27,216
Immel, Heath Eric, sr asoc dir business admin, $98,003
Immken, Erin Kathleen, couns hlth/welfare/wellness sr, $31,000
Imparato, Amy Christina, office support assistant III, $11.53/hr
Imperiale, Louis, professor, $77,516
Imperiale, Sam J, event assistant I, $11.17/hr
Imsland, Brice Eugene John, temporary technical, $12.00/hr
Infranca, Cynthia L, office support assistant IV, $18.50/hr
Ingalls, Cannon E, emrg med techn paramedic, $17.56/hr
Ingalls, Kevin L, prof, ast clincl dept, $250,000
Ingalls, Korrin P, nurse, staff II, $27.04/hr
Inge, Tamara K, business support specialist II, $18.74/hr
Ingebritson, Daphne L, nurse, staff II, $34.18/hr
Ingebritson, Robynn Marie, nurse, staff I, $19.00/hr
Ingebritson, Samantha Marie, nurse, staff I, $19.37/hr
Ingersoll, Amanda P, nurse, staff I, $19.37/hr
Ingersoll, Elizabeth Ellen, nurse, staff II, $21.80/hr
Ingersoll, Weber P, psychologist, $43,920
Ingraham, Holly E, instructor, adjunct, $12,000
Ingram, Ellis Andrew, dean, asoc, $109,609
Ingram, Melissa Ann, program/project supprt coor sr, $60,936
Ingram, Robert G, project manager-princpl, $69,718
Inman, Kathy L, office support assistant IV, $14.08/hr
Inn, Kimhon, phlebotomist, $14.88/hr
Innes, Kimberle Bourn, nurse, staff II, $34.77/hr
Innes, Mary Theresa, nurse, staff II, $34.18/hr
Inniss, Enos C, prof, ast teach, $85,644
Insall, Eugene M Jr, prof, asoc, $63,625
Inskeep, Matthew L, rec/athletic specialist sr, $44,500
Inskip, Nathaniel W, research engineering tech I, $19.12/hr
Ion, Mariana, accountant sr, $44,887
Iqbal, Ahmad, resident physician-6th yr, $58,200
Ireland, Christine G, research/lab technician, $13.11/hr
Ireton, Sean M, prof, asoc, $65,327
Irish, Chantal Nicole, temporary professional, $13.00/hr
Irish, John Michael, resident physician-2nd yr, $52,007
Irish, Melanie Lynn, office support assistant IV, $14.21/hr
Irons, Chrystal Dawn, business spclst, $46,716
Irons, Jean Marie Elizabeth, instructor, adjunct, $10,000
Irons, Larry Roland, prof, asoc teach, $46,000
Irovic, David T, db administrator-princpl, $83,938
Irsheidat, Nadia Ahmad, student support specialist I, $13.79/hr
Irsik, Cynthia Lea, office support assistant IV, $15.87/hr
Irvin, Michael, maint svc attd, $16.92/hr
Irwin, Daniel Paul, event assistant I, $8.00/hr
Irwin, Erica Leigh, mental health professional, $38,150
Irwin, Gregory Neal, grader, $52
Irwin, Patricia A, office support assistant I, $11.26/hr
Irwin, Stephanie E, resident physician-2nd yr, $52,007
Irwin, Thomas Glenn, prof, ast teach, $40,985
Isaac-Savage, Evelyn Paulette, asoc provost, $123,500
Isaac, Kakkattukuzhy M, professor, $95,922
Isaac, Letensie T, nurse, staff II rnwp, $34.51/hr
Isaac, Michael J, resident physician-4th yr, $54,425
Isaac, Tseggai, prof, asoc, $59,599
Isaacs, Kelley Sue, nurse, staff II, $26.06/hr
Isabelle, Abby Elizabeth, research specialist I, $30,823
Isbell-Robertson, Rachel Lynn, media producer I, $14.39/hr
Isbell, Galen Craig, bts carpenter, $22.43/hr
Isbell, Rae Ann, nurse, staff I, $23.04/hr
Isenberg, Macey Nicole, pharmacy tech, $11.07/hr
Isenberg, Pamela Ellen, nurse, staff II, $34.18/hr
Isgrig, Bobby Jo, temporary clerical, $9.00/hr
Isgrig, Dwayne E, system support analyst-entry, $16.92/hr
Ishmael, Madeline Corey, mental health tech trainee, $9.27/hr
Islam, Naz E, professor, $112,921
Ispa, Jean Mona, professor, $120,930
Isselhard, Annette, instructor, adjunct, $6,276
Ithman, Muaid Hilmi, prof, ast clincl dept, $185,858
Ituarte, Darcy Marie Dubinsky, physician ast, $90,500
Ituarte, Felipe, resident physician-1st yr, $50,219
Iveson, Candace Jacob, instructor, clincl, $49,939

Ivey, Jan R, research specialist I, $45,537
Ivey, Patrick Alton, dir strength and conditioning, $260,000
Ivey, Starla Lynn, prof, ast teach, $61,200
Ivicsics, Antoinette, cook, $13.21/hr
Ivliyeva, Irina, prof, asoc, $69,858
Ivy, Sharon M, patient svc rep, $14.70/hr
Ivy, Steven F, 4-h spclst, $46,500
Iwasaki, Laura Rei, prof, asoc, $180,354
Iyob, Ruth, professor, $72,872
Izard, Tiffany Anne, program/project supprt coor I, $39,149
Jack, Otonye Haniel, user support analyst-speclst, $19.20/hr
Jackman, Ashlee Rae, care team assoc-clinical, $12.32/hr
Jackman, Michelle Louise, coor, care, $67,213
Jackman, Reno Eugene, custodian, $12.94/hr
Jackman, Ricky Howard, food svc wrkr II, $12.45/hr
Jackson, Catia Andrea III, av instal service tech-entry, $12.98/hr
Jackson, Robert L Jr, emrg med techn paramedic, $17.89/hr
Jackson-Thompson, Jeannette, prof, asoc resrch, $103,364
Jackson, Alfaye, office support assistant III, $11.75/hr
Jackson, Antoinette Micaela Balino, enrollment advisor sr, $17.12/hr
Jackson, Ashante Kaleilani, office support assistant IV, $16.37/hr
Jackson, Brett Thomas, teaching ast, $27.00/hr
Jackson, Brian Adam, police officer, $17.30/hr
Jackson, Brian Anthony, temporary technical, $20.00/hr
Jackson, Carolyn Nutt, office support assistant IV, $14.05/hr
Jackson, Chara K, sterile processing tech, $19.71/hr
Jackson, Clara L, student support specialist I, $18.09/hr
Jackson, Dana Latrice, instructor, adjunct, $6,300
Jackson, Daniel E, research specialist I, $44,100
Jackson, Daniel Lee, instructor, clincl, $30,000
Jackson, Darius Thomas, student service coor I, $41,000
Jackson, Darryl D, temporary clerical, $10.25/hr
Jackson, David A, prof, ast adjunct, $125.00/hr
Jackson, Deanne Marie, registrar, $83,292
Jackson, Donna Marie, student support specialist sr, $17.52/hr
Jackson, Florastine Marie, custodian, $12.94/hr
Jackson, James M, mech trades spclst (mts), $23.61/hr
Jackson, Jesse Lee, custodian, $12.50/hr
Jackson, Joseph A, programmer analyst-entry, $49,945
Jackson, Kalie, office support assistant III, $13.74/hr
Jackson, Katie Jo RIndahl, asoc dir advancement, $61,812
Jackson, Kelly Nicole, office support assistant IV, $13.61/hr
Jackson, Kelsey H, office support assistant I, $9.32/hr
Jackson, Kennetha K, hris specialist-specialist, $65,018
Jackson, Kerrick Diondre, ast coach, $85,000
Jackson, Kristina Alene, office support assistant IV, $16.06/hr
Jackson, Kristine Helen, med techl reg, $23.93/hr
Jackson, LaQuita Apasha, human resources assistant, $15.36/hr
Jackson, Lathoria Deniece, custodian, $12.94/hr
Jackson, Laura Courtright, resrch ast sr, $53,778
Jackson, Lauren R, business support specialist sr, $23.35/hr
Jackson, Lindsey Morgan Rae, mental health tech, $12.45/hr
Jackson, Louise Verdell, office support assistant I, $9.31/hr
Jackson, Lucy Erin, office support assistant IV, $15.13/hr
Jackson, Michael J, custodian, $12.18/hr
Jackson, Needra L, librarian III, $68,106
Jackson, Norma J, program/project supprt coor sr, $73,440
Jackson, Ric T, pharmacist II, $60.00/hr
Jackson, Richard Eugene, seasonal farm ast, $8.93/hr
Jackson, Rollin F, prof, ast teach, $57,570
Jackson, Russell E, nurse, staff II, $28.46/hr
Jackson, Ryan Henry, rec/athletic specialist sr, $39,600
Jackson, Scott A, bts carpenter, $21.71/hr
Jackson, Shannon M, prof, asoc, $62,456
Jackson, Shawn Cameron, temporary crafts service, $12.00/hr
Jackson, Shawnna Dianne, instructor, adjunct, $28,800
Jackson, Sonia M, educational pgm associate I, $14.27/hr
Jackson, Syreeta Contrell, nurse, clincl charge-lpn, $20.89/hr
Jackson, Tara Lynn, office support assistant IV, $14.72/hr
Jackson, Tekela RayShon, office support assistant IV, $13.99/hr
Jackson, Terri R, custodian, $12.94/hr
Jackson, Theresa L, clincl documnt spclst, $56,181
Jackson, Tiffany Chavon, instructor, adjunct, $10,500
Jackson, Travis Eugene, event assistant I, $7.50/hr
Jackson, Tremar Yvonne Caroline, food svc wrkr I, $9.60/hr
Jackson, Walter D, mts/hvac, $24.13/hr
Jackson, William Charles, office support assistant I, $9.31/hr
Jacob, Arthur A, prof, ast clincl, $79,959
Jacob, Dany, resident physician-3rd yr, $52,470

Jacob, Gretchen K, educational pgm assistant, $10.64/hr
Jacobi, Jessica Rene Zumbehl, sup systems admin-spec, $46,284
Jacobi, Teresa D, emrg med techn paramedic, $19.01/hr
Jacobo, Felix Joaquin, custodian, $10.00/hr
Jacobs, David L, laborer II, $14.35/hr
Jacobs, Joyce Ann, office support assistant IV, $13.41/hr
Jacobs, Judy Ann, office support assistant IV, $13.37/hr
Jacobs, Kayla Nicole, business support specialist sr, $19.54/hr
Jacobs, Lauren Clare, nurse, staff II, $20.54/hr
Jacobs, Melinda L, veterinary technician sr, $15.76/hr
Jacobs, Robert T, electronics technician II, $17.10/hr
Jacobs, Roy Scott, strat comm associate I, $33,910
Jacobson, Brad Martin, office support assistant III, $15.15/hr
Jacobson, Jacqueline Rae, human resources spec I, $19.14/hr
Jacobson, Janice Kay, business support specialist sr, $24.05/hr
Jacobson, Victoria Ann, dir III business admin, $101,048
Jacobus, Laurie Ann, instructor, adjunct, $19,200
Jacoby, Sharon L, instructor, adjunct, $9,910
Jacoby, William A, prof, asoc, $92,365
Jacome Sosa, Maria Miriam, fellow, post doctoral, $43,680
Jacques, Chantal Hermina, prof, ast adjunct, $13,831
Jacquin, Kenneth R, office support assistant sr, $16.83/hr
Jacquinot, Elizabeth Cristina, instructor, adjunct, $15,000
Jaddoo, Julie Patrina, research project analyst, $50,000
Jadwin, Wade A, business ops associate sr, $50,765
Jaeger, Darrell, manager it, $77,807
Jaeger, Lauren Anne, temporary crafts service, $7.50/hr
Jaeger, Tracy Ann, office support assistant III, $14.21/hr
Jaegers, Dena M, nurse, staff II, $32.65/hr
Jagdagdorj, Bolor Erdene, high school student, $7.50/hr
Jago, Arthur G, professor, $145,790
Jahan, Sultana, prof, asoc clincl dept, $173,200
Jahnsen, Megan Brianne, business support spclst sr, $22.36/hr
Jain, Kanupriya, resident physician-3rd yr, $53,763
Jain, Kaushik Kumar, resident physician-4th yr, $54,425
Jain, Nishant Rajkumar, sftware supprt analyst-princpl, $58,541
Jakubovska, Marika, grader, $15.00/hr
Jakubovskis, Aldis, specialist, $60,669
Jakubowicz, Richard Anthony, police officer, $17.50/hr
Jalalzai, Farida, prof, asoc, $86,453
Jalisatgi, Satish Subray, prof, ast resrch, $158,075
Jalisatgi, Shubhaga Satish, executive assistant, $16.87/hr
James Kracke, Marilyn R, prof, asoc, $73,510
James, Alexandra Frances, resident physician-2nd yr, $52,007
James, Allen W, electrician, pwr plant sr lead, $28.63/hr
James, Allison Rene, care team assoc-clinical, $11.10/hr
James, Annalise C, resident physician-3rd yr, $52,470
James, Caroline C, library info specialist, $12.98/hr
James, Christopher B, manager it, $59,513
James, Christopher R, resident physician-1st yr, $50,219
James, Harvey S, prof, asoc, $100,508
James, Hongying Li, programmer analyst-princpl, $71,723
James, Kellie N, nurse practitioner, $87,720
James, Lindsey J, ast coach, $58,000
James, Michael Jay, custodian, $11.00/hr
James, Mona Lea, nurse, staff II rnwp, $20.54/hr
James, Rebecca Gale, pat acct rep, $15.68/hr
James, Rhonda Jean, executive assistant, $24.43/hr
James, Tiffany A, student support specialist II, $16.13/hr
James, Toni K, nurse, staff II wkend II, $34.18/hr
Jameson, Carol, nurse, staff II, $31.65/hr
Jameson, Haley Hoss, instructor, adjunct, $32,400
Jameson, Helen G, med techI reg, $29.81/hr
Jameson, Sally McAlpine, mgr II business admin, $59,055
Jamieson, Bobbi Jo, nurse, staff II, $23.89/hr
Jamieson, Saralee, human dev spclst, $48,524
Jamieson, Tim, head coach, $208,080
Jamison, Billy P Jr, business support specialist II, $21.20/hr
Jamison, Connie L, dental hygienist, $34.15/hr
Jamison, Rachael Fern, student support specialist II, $15.00/hr
Jamtgaard, Keith A, resrch asoc, $65,991
Janasz, Shelly Marie, dir I, student support svcs, $90,137
Jandegian, Caitlin Marie, research/lab technician sr, $17.00/hr
Jandeska, Adam Martin, ast mgr health physics, $85,002
Janes, Emily Anne, nurse, staff II, $20.14/hr
Janes, Jennifer Nicole, nurse, staff now III, $30.00/hr
Jang, Su Ahn, prof, asoc, $64,250
Jang, Wooseung, professor, $106,274
Jani, Piyushkumar Jayantilal, resident physician-2nd yr, $50,810

Janikow, Cezary, prof, asoc, $97,125
Jankowski, Helen, coor nursing informatics, $92,772
Janney, Teresa L, nurse, staff II, $35.04/hr
Janovy, Cynthia Anne, media production director I, $50,000
Janssen, Janice L, fin and acctg manager sr, $84,445
Janzen, Mark L, prof, ast clincl dept, $191,174
Jaramillo, Carmen Anita, dental hygienist, $34.51/hr
Jarboe, Mark Ellis, instructor, adjunct, $6,400
Jarboe, Seth Markland, operations support tech II, $13.21/hr
Jardine, Jeremy, media producer II, $15.25/hr
Jarka, Edward, prof, ast clincl, $95,578
Jarman, Mona Lee, dental assistant II, $13.97/hr
Jarnegan, Joseph Thomas, project manager-speclst, $60,180
Jarosik, Jerry Joseph, construction manager II, $77,625
Jarosik, Lisa, temporary professional, $15.00/hr
Jarrett, Kim Louise, student support specialist sr, $16.54/hr
Jarrett, Lindsey G, instructor, adjunct, $9,000
Jarrett, Sonia B, office support assistant III, $15.02/hr
Jarvie Eggart, Michelle Edith, lecturer, $15,000
Jarvis, Mark A, business tech analyst-expert, $69,781
Jasenowski, Claudia Lorraine, academic advisor, $37,750
Jasinski, Margaret Eva, hlth educator, $46,488
Jasper, Anthony Arondall, floor care techn, $13.57/hr
Jasper, Cynthia Louise, custodian, $10.69/hr
Jauregui, Sylvia L, mgr student support svcs, $40,641
Jay, Charla Lynne, nurse, resrch, $48,352
Jayarao, Elisha Marie, physician ast, $89,319
Jayarao, Mayur, resident physician-4th yr, $55,804
Jean, Yanching Jerry, prof, adjunct, $6,000
Jeanetta, Eliana Felgueiras, student support spclst I, $15.64/hr
Jeanetta, Stephen C, prof, asoc extns, $80,933
Jeans, Pamela S, health records techn I, $12.17/hr
Jeff-Agboola, Yemisi Adefunke, scholar, visiting, $14,400
Jefferis, Shelia Ann, patient svc rep, $12.30/hr
Jefferson, Cynthia Maria, nurse, licensed prac, $20.60/hr
Jefferson, Jeffrey Laron, event assistant I, $7.85/hr
Jefferson, Raquel Lynn, retail sales manager, $40,973
Jefferson, Sandra Kaye, custodian, $10.94/hr
Jefferson, Urmeka Taylor, prof, ast, $71,761
Jeffrey, Angela Kelly, instructional designer-speclst, $53,300
Jeffrey, Linda D, nurse, staff II, $33.43/hr
Jeffrey, Sophia Blenerhasset, dir II research ops / plng, $80,106
Jeffries, Andrea Dawn, care team assoc-suppt, $10.64/hr
Jeffries, Gail Ann, coor, care, $64,398
Jeffries, Jody Dean, dir student/univ center, $79,995
Jeffries, Joel Travis, prof, asoc clincl dept, $214,022
Jeffries, Keith Allen, csm professional sr, $65,805
Jeffries, Mark R, student support specialist sr, $16.54/hr
Jeffries, Ruth Ann, business support specialist II, $18.79/hr
Jeffries, Sandra K, nurse, staff II, $27.00/hr
Jellison, Judith A, dir I, student support svcs, $72,851
Jen, Philip Hung Sun, prof, adjunct, $21,000
Jendoubi, Rougaya, nurse, staff II, $21.37/hr
Jenkins, Aaron Garth, db programmer analyst-princpl, $71,020
Jenkins, Adam Cole, programmer analyst-entry, $44,762
Jenkins, Angela Dawn, construction manager I, $59,160
Jenkins, Anna Florine, office support assistant III, $11.53/hr
Jenkins, Audra Elizabeth, office support assistant IV, $14.99/hr
Jenkins, Bradley Clark, temporary technical, $30.00/hr
Jenkins, Brandie Denise, instructor, adjunct, $4,200
Jenkins, Bridgette, student service coor II, $70,881
Jenkins, Carla Gene, nurse, licensed prac, $20.88/hr
Jenkins, Carol E, prof, ast teach, $37,000
Jenkins, Chantell E, resp therapist reg, $30.00/hr
Jenkins, Dwayne Edmund, custodian, $13.23/hr
Jenkins, Jeffrey Lloyd, maint svc attd-mrc, $13.36/hr
Jenkins, Jessica Christina, office support assistant IV, $14.03/hr
Jenkins, Joel W, instructor, adjunct, $15,000
Jenkins, Mary Gwen, mgr public relations, $97,469
Jenkins, Maureen Erin, internet administrator-entry, $16.65/hr
Jenkins, Olivia Leigh, resp therapist reg, $19.83/hr
Jenkins, Rachael Marie, nurse, clincl charge-rn, $26.45/hr
Jenkins, Stancia Jolene, ast vice chancellor, $97,800
Jenkins, Susan Diane, nurse anesthetist, $147,900
Jenkins, Toya Antoinette, office support assistant IV, $14.75/hr
Jenkins, Wade A, hospital security officer, $11.97/hr
Jenks, Christopher Scott, resident physician-4th yr, $54,425
Jenks, Steven Mark, grounds supervisor, $53,909
Jenner, Mark Wallace, extns professional, asoc, $54,500

Jenner, Michael Mollet, prof, profl practice, $127,731
Jennewein, August Harvey, strat comm associate II, $47,251
Jennings, Cynthia Lynn, business support specialist sr, $20.09/hr
Jennings, Debbie R, med techl reg, $29.44/hr
Jennings, Deborah C, office support assistant IV, $16.15/hr
Jennings, Diane, sftware supprt analyst-princpl, $55,237
Jennings, Eddie J, maint svc attd, $17.78/hr
Jennings, Eric D, distribution techn-mtls mgmt, $15.26/hr
Jennings, Erica Danielle, patient svc rep, $11.40/hr
Jennings, Jeff W, instructional tech-speclst, $48,549
Jennings, Jeremy, resident physician-1st yr, $50,825
Jennings, Krista Hediger, human resources manager sr, $52,400
Jennings, Lacey Dawn, care team assoc-clinical, $13.07/hr
Jennings, Martha Ott, office support assistant IV, $21.84/hr
Jennings, Mary C, extension asoc, $31,212
Jennings, Michael L, db programmer analyst-princpl, $70,408
Jennings, Raynea T, animal caretaker, $11.76/hr
Jennings, Roy L, maint svc attd, $17.78/hr
Jennings, Terri L, business support specialist II, $16.17/hr
Jennings, Vicki A, nurse, staff, $30.24/hr
Jensby, Joshua Allen, temporary clerical, $9.75/hr
Jensen, Glenn A Jr, supv engineering, $46,336
Jensen, Andrew D, instructor, $32,170
Jensen, Cheryl Ann, research/lab technician sr, $19.52/hr
Jensen, Julie Elizabeth, instructor, adjunct, $6,300
Jensen, Kurtis Charles, asoc dir program/project ops, $56,000
Jensen, Lisa A, ast editor, $17.00/hr
Jensen, Ronald V, instructor, clincl, $44,065
Jenson, Ronda Jean, resrch asoc, $91,620
Jentschura, Ulrich David, prof, asoc, $76,733
Jeon, Kyung Seong, resrch asoc, $65,966
Jepson, Steven Baker, prof, ast teach, $39,690
Jerman, Linda, custodian, $10.00/hr
Jernigan, Adriane Eric, food svc wrkr I, $9.60/hr
Jerome Beckmann, Carla, student service coor sr, $47,424
Jesse, Heather L, nurse, staff II rnwp, $26.16/hr
Jesse, Robert Michael, powr plnt opr II, $28.70/hr
Jesse, Roger C, optician, $42,755
Jessie, Katie Marie, office support assistant III, $14.16/hr
Jester, Amelia Suzanne, mental health tech, $11.00/hr
Jestis, Benny Stewart, mts/pipefitter, $22.50/hr
Jeter, Chelsea Marie, lab assistant, $9.50/hr
Jeter, John Mark, db programmer analyst-speclst, $50,063
Jeter, Kelsey Maureen, extns professional, $43,000
Jett, Leslie Glenn, prof, ast teach, $65,378
Jett, Robert Andrew, pharmacist, $121,282
Jett, Roger Dennis, dir I, human resources, $24,011
Jett, Shelly Yvonne, nurse, staff II, $21.80/hr
Jett, Stacey A, nurse clinician, $68,340
Jewell, Gavin Michael, media producer I, $13.61/hr
Jeyapaul, Elbert, fellow, post doctoral, $19.26/hr
Ji, Juan, research specialist sr, $46,680
Ji, Li, teaching ast, $13.00/hr
Ji, Tieming, prof, ast, $83,373
Ji, Wei, professor, $90,473
Ji, Yan, resrch asoc, $41,135
Jia, Guanghong, prof, ast resrch, $56,100
Jia, Shuhui, lab assistant, $9.00/hr
Jiang, Lin, prof, ast, $138,691
Jiang, Qian, resrch asoc, $36,771
Jiang, Qingtang, professor, $84,809
Jiang, Shan, fellow, post doctoral, $48,001
Jiang, Shaokai, research specialist sr, $63,604
Jiang, Wei, prof, asoc, $96,096
JiJi, Renee Denise, prof, asoc, $71,423
Jimenez, Biancka D, supervisor it, $46,904
Jimenez, Columba, nurse, licensed prac, $18.51/hr
Jin, Daozhong, prof, ast resrch, $40,000
Jin, Minshan, research/lab technician sr, $13.77/hr
Jin, Wei, fellow, post doctoral, $35,520
Jindal, Ankur, fellow, post doc clncl yr1, $55,804
Jindal, Nidhi, prof, ast clincl dept, $135,000
Jivan, Ashik J, resident physician-4th yr, $54,425
Jobe, Cynthia A, grant writer sr, $56,100
Jobe, Helen Wheeler, executive assistant, $22.89/hr
Johannesen, Eric, prof, ast clincl dept, $142,800
Johannesen, Jamison D, user support analyst-entry, $15.56/hr
Johanning, Allen D, human resources mgr-enterprise, $67,500
Johanning, Amanda Johnson, hospital lab tech, $14.66/hr

Johanning, Christopher William, hospital lab tech, $12.90/hr
Johanning, Donna J, dir II finance, $96,600
Johanning, Gina K, instructor, adjunct, $6,607
Johanning, Janet Diane, nurse, staff II, $34.18/hr
Johanning, Rebecca Elizabeth, qa/control technician, $21.25/hr
Johanningmeier, Daniel S, resp therapist reg, $28.45/hr
Johanningmeier, Patricia I, nurse, or/recovery-ch, $34.18/hr
Johansen, Andrew E, resident physician-2nd yr, $50,810
John, Anush Abraham, resident physician-6th yr, $58,200
John, Susan Zacharias, physician, stu hlth, $140,766
Johnmeyer, Ashley Elaine, patient svc rep, $11.28/hr
Johnoff, Michael J, finl counselor(eligibility), $17.37/hr
Johns, Bill Edward, mts/electrician, $25.35/hr
Johns, Ricky R, maintenance supervisor, $50,228
Johns, Robert D, water chemical spclst, $23.33/hr
Johnsen, Donald A, custodian, $11.41/hr
Johnson, Julius H Jr, prof, asoc, $123,815
Johnson, Robert Paul Jr, mech, bldg maint, $19.64/hr
Johnson Moxley, Melanie K, lecturer, $45,000
Johnson-Arnold, Camille Yvette, bus support spec sr, $21.12/hr
Johnson, Aaron T, food svc wrkr I, $9.60/hr
Johnson, Alexandria Lashae, custodian, $10.00/hr
Johnson, Alexia Jean, instructor, adjunct, $18,000
Johnson, Alfred J, system support analyst-speclst, $19.75/hr
Johnson, Andrea Lucille, supv resp care, $67,792
Johnson, Arbie W, mail processor II, $15.26/hr
Johnson, Arionna E, high school student, $7.50/hr
Johnson, Bonnie Jean, pat acct rep, $13.46/hr
Johnson, Bonnie Lynn, temporary clerical, $9.00/hr
Johnson, Bradley Alan, strat comm associate I, $34,400
Johnson, Briana Lynne, instructional designer-speclst, $52,268
Johnson, Bryan W, system support analyst-speclst, $19.56/hr
Johnson, Carmen Leanne, office support assistant IV, $16.92/hr
Johnson, Catrin Maureen, office support assistant IV, $14.75/hr
Johnson, Chi Lan, business support specialist sr, $25.04/hr
Johnson, Christopher A, patient svc rep, $11.28/hr
Johnson, Cierra, resident physician-1st yr, $49,025
Johnson, Connie J, student support specialist I, $13.79/hr
Johnson, Cory Eugene, med techl reg, $26.55/hr
Johnson, Crystal L, office support assistant IV, $18.11/hr
Johnson, Danita, student support specialist II, $19.17/hr
Johnson, Darcy Deane, nurse, staff II, $26.98/hr
Johnson, David Charles, chiller techn, $23.04/hr
Johnson, David M, custodian, bldg maint lead, $13.27/hr
Johnson, Dawn, child dev assistant, $8.08/hr
Johnson, Debbie S, strat comm associate I, $42,866
Johnson, Dennis Tallyn, office support assistant IV, $14.50/hr
Johnson, Diana, registrar, $70,902
Johnson, Dorothy T, coor, service, $19.06/hr
Johnson, Douglas D, clncl imprvmnt spclst, $58,063
Johnson, E Diane, librarian IV, $72,910
Johnson, Eboni Shakell, office support assistant IV, $12.98/hr
Johnson, Elena K, nurse, licensed prac, $20.18/hr
Johnson, Elizabeth A, student service coor II, $47,000
Johnson, Elizabeth Anne, library info specialist sr, $15.32/hr
Johnson, Emily Anne, resrch anlyst sr, $57,228
Johnson, Eric Darren, physician ast, $75.00/hr
Johnson, Eric'el Nelshon, tutor, $15.00/hr
Johnson, Fred B, custodian, $12.94/hr
Johnson, Gaile Tanyea, human resources specialist sr, $48,564
Johnson, Galen D, emrg med techn paramedic, $16.17/hr
Johnson, Garry A, prof, ast clincl dept, $200,000
Johnson, Gary Steven, prof, asoc, $114,448
Johnson, Gary Thomas, csm associate I, $18.98/hr
Johnson, Gayle Christy, professor, $134,948
Johnson, Gina Maria, business tech analyst-expert, $57,848
Johnson, Grecia A, office support assistant III, $12.33/hr
Johnson, Gregory K, prof, clincl, $96,578
Johnson, Harold Albert, prof, ast adjunct, $160,000
Johnson, Heather, resrch ast, $20,000
Johnson, Ivan D, food svc wrkr IV, $14.77/hr
Johnson, Jacob M, patient svc rep, $12.55/hr
Johnson, Jasmine Cyriess, nurse, staff II, $20.54/hr
Johnson, Jason David, system support analyst-expert, $24.96/hr
Johnson, Jeffrey D, prof, ast, $74,005
Johnson, Jeffrey Scott, prof, ast, $130,000
Johnson, Jenika L, nurse, staff now III, $30.00/hr
Johnson, Jennifer Christine, intern, $23,000
Johnson, Jennifer Lynn, office support assistant IV, $13.62/hr

Johnson, Jeremy D, system administrator-speclst, $47,822
Johnson, Jerri Kay, nurse, staff II, $22.56/hr
Johnson, Jessica Marie, specialist, $10.00/hr
Johnson, Jessica Rachel, nurse, staff now III, $30.00/hr
Johnson, Jill L, prof, ast adjunct, $8,004
Johnson, Jocelyn Nicole, sterile processing tech, $17.53/hr
Johnson, John H, mts/hvac, $24.13/hr
Johnson, Joseph A, nurse, staff II, $35.21/hr
Johnson, Joseph W, prof, asoc, $58,961
Johnson, Kandice K, prof, clincl, $131,616
Johnson, Karen Jo, docent, $5,000
Johnson, Kari M, teaching ast, $36.40/hr
Johnson, Kathryn Marie, office support assistant IV, $16.68/hr
Johnson, Kelly L, fin and acctg analyst sr, $43,470
Johnson, Kevin L, construction manager II, $67,782
Johnson, Kimberly Delaine, executive assistant sr, $61,200
Johnson, Krystal Nicole, lab assistant, $9.75/hr
Johnson, Larry, custodian, $13.36/hr
Johnson, LaShan Marchelle, dental assistant II, $12.98/hr
Johnson, Lashanda Renee, food svc wrkr II, $11.83/hr
Johnson, Laurie Nicole, business support analyst II, $22.91/hr
Johnson, Leeann Overstreet, mgr trauma prgm-hospt, $97,469
Johnson, Lena Michelle, office support assistant IV, $18.30/hr
Johnson, Letitia Ann, patient svc rep, $14.88/hr
Johnson, Letitia K, community dev spclst, $51,224
Johnson, Lilly, reimbursement ast, $18.18/hr
Johnson, Linda S, mgr infection control, $97,881
Johnson, Lori Ann, dir I, business admin, $112,200
Johnson, Lori Jean, coor quality improvement-oce, $76,965
Johnson, Marc C, prof, asoc, $116,975
Johnson, Marjorie C, business support specialist II, $20.91/hr
Johnson, Mark, maint svc attd, $18.41/hr
Johnson, Mark A, student service coor II, $40,926
Johnson, Mark L, db programmer analyst-expert, $54,464
Johnson, Mark L, chair, dept, $175,539
Johnson, Marsha L, surgery, first ast, $24.87/hr
Johnson, Mary Elizabeth, cook, $12.20/hr
Johnson, Matthew F, strat comm associate I, $51,500
Johnson, Matthew Garrett, programmer analyst-entry, $25.00/hr
Johnson, May L, custodian, $13.36/hr
Johnson, Michael Dennis, dir II advancement, $85,000
Johnson, Miyosha Michelle, educational pgm assoc I, $13.58/hr
Johnson, NaChelle Nicole, custodian, $12.94/hr
Johnson, Nanci W, asoc dir program/project ops, $63,710
Johnson, Nancy L, educational pgm coor III, $56,729
Johnson, Nicole Patrice, office support assistant IV, $13.73/hr
Johnson, Nina M, librarian III, $51,780
Johnson, Philip J, professor, $133,981
Johnson, Quinn Lamar, prof, ast clincl dept, $420,240
Johnson, Quintanella Bennet, student service coor II, $43,000
Johnson, Rachel J, tutor, $12.00/hr
Johnson, Rania Shawntre, central sterile assistant, $10.73/hr
Johnson, Rebecca A, professor, $110,819
Johnson, Rebecca Lynn, nurse anesthetist, $147,900
Johnson, Richard A, professor, $188,984
Johnson, Richard Arden, resident physician-6th yr, $58,200
Johnson, Robert N, professor, $109,089
Johnson, Ryan J, instructor, adjunct, $100
Johnson, Ryan P, office support assistant IV, $13.39/hr
Johnson, Sarah, resident physician-1st yr, $49,025
Johnson, Sarah Ashley, research specialist II, $34,500
Johnson, Sarah Elizabeth, office support assistant III, $11.40/hr
Johnson, Sharon D, professor, $80,700
Johnson, Sharon L, fin and acctg manager sr, $81,436
Johnson, Sheila Marie, office support assistant IV, $16.08/hr
Johnson, Shelby Leanne, custodian, $10.39/hr
Johnson, Tamra Gene, surgical technl trainee, $15.25/hr
Johnson, Taylore Rose, office support assistant III, $12.00/hr
Johnson, Terrance A, anesthesia techn, $15.30/hr
Johnson, Thomas G, professor, $156,903
Johnson, Tim S, animal techn, ast lab, $12.72/hr
Johnson, Tina Marie, reimbursement ast-cert, $18.59/hr
Johnson, Travis D, media producer II, $16.46/hr
Johnson, Turner James, office support assistant III, $12.24/hr
Johnson, Tyler L, student recruitment spclst, $15.19/hr
Johnson, Victoria L, prof, asoc, $76,357
Johnson, Vivian I, office support assistant IV, $14.36/hr
Johnson, Yolanda Joyce, executive assistant, $19.74/hr

Johnson, Zane Matthew, emrg med techn, $13.16/hr
Johnston, Joseph Andrew Jr, professor, $106,788
Johnston, Amy E, executive assistant, $17.04/hr
Johnston, David K, director it, $90,553
Johnston, Joseph Daniel, ast coach, $50,610
Johnston, Laura C, prof, ast/profl pract, $56,550
Johnston, Melisa Anne, nurse practitioner, $57,732
Johnston, Nicole Ruth, archivist III, $35,197
Johnston, Rhonda Kay, program/project supprt coor sr, $48,076
Johnston, Sara Elizabeth, resident physician-1st yr, $50,219
Johnston, Thomas, professor, $108,363
Johnston, Vickie L, nurse, licensed prac, $19.11/hr
Johnstone, George, professor, $146,890
Joiner, Gary Lamont, custodian, $12.18/hr
Jolley, Laura Robinson, manuscript specialist sr, $40,565
Jones Sr, Kemani Lee, programmer analyst-speclst, $45,600
Jones-Jackson, Kimberly Ann, bus support spclst sr, $22.94/hr
Jones, Alahandra Angelita Charit, tutor, $10.25/hr
Jones, Alexander Benjamin, resident physician-1st yr, $50,219
Jones, Alicia A, nurse, licensed prac, $20.37/hr
Jones, Allan William, emeritus, $34,680
Jones, Alva Susan, business ops associate sr, $49,782
Jones, Andrea Shawn, resrch asoc, $57,493
Jones, Angela Kay, communications coordinator, $15.00/hr
Jones, Antoinne Marquis, student support specialist I, $19.71/hr
Jones, Ashanti Camela, nurse, licensed prac, $17.00/hr
Jones, Ashley Kaye, nurse clinician, $62,956
Jones, Barbara Bowers, librarian IV, $65,400
Jones, Brent Allen, strat comm consultant, $46,275
Jones, Brett Michael, med techl reg, $20.94/hr
Jones, Brian, ast coach, $291,500
Jones, Brock P, mgr II business admin, $57,171
Jones, Carol Jean, nurse, staff II, $28.07/hr
Jones, Carolyn Ann, specialist, $61,213
Jones, Carolyn D, business support specialist II, $19.90/hr
Jones, Carrie E, nurse, staff II, $20.95/hr
Jones, Cason H, academic advisor, $44,803
Jones, Catherine Messick, prof, clinical dept, $200,000
Jones, Cecil A, mts/hvac, $21.05/hr
Jones, Charles A, ast coach, $6,432
Jones, Charles Phillips, fellow, $21,000
Jones, Cheryl Lynn, office support assistant IV, $13.70/hr
Jones, Cory Terrell, police sergeant, $20.04/hr
Jones, Cynthia, lecturer, $48,801
Jones, Debra Linn, office support assistant III, $16.65/hr
Jones, Debra S, business support specialist II, $22.12/hr
Jones, Deon, custodian, $12.94/hr
Jones, Diana Christine, business ops associate sr, $46,512
Jones, Dianne Elizabeth, office support assistant III, $11.88/hr
Jones, Dillon Tyler, temporary crafts service, $7.65/hr
Jones, Edward, maint tech III, prev, $18.45/hr
Jones, Elizabeth A, nurse clinician, $61,477
Jones, Emily Sue, pharmacy tech, $11.00/hr
Jones, Endsley Terrence, founders professor, $38,458
Jones, Erin Noelle, supv nursing acute care, $29.03/hr
Jones, Felicia Ann, surgical technl certified, $15.87/hr
Jones, Franklin Alanzo, floor maint wkr, $13.84/hr
Jones, Garrett James, system support analyst-expert, $20.74/hr
Jones, Gillian Leray, resident physician-3rd yr, $52,470
Jones, Grace C, patient svc rep, $13.74/hr
Jones, Harold Alan, library info specialist sr, $15.44/hr
Jones, Hazel Marie, office support assistant III, $11.53/hr
Jones, Heather Marie, serv line spclst, $67,810
Jones, Jack G, research technical svcs supv, $20.99/hr
Jones, James Christopher, mri technologist, $38.22/hr
Jones, James Jesse, office support assistant IV, $13.50/hr
Jones, Jamie Sue, neurodiagnostic tech (reg), $20.40/hr
Jones, Jason Matthew, nurse, staff now III, $30.00/hr
Jones, Jay J, prof, asoc clincl, $110,373
Jones, Jeana Marie, nurse, staff now plus, $30.00/hr
Jones, Jennifer Grace, resp therapist reg, $21.50/hr
Jones, John Richard, prof, curators, $169,671
Jones, Johnny B, custodian, $10.94/hr
Jones, Jordan Kelley, prof, ast adjunct, $7,200
Jones, Jordan Whitney, office support assistant IV, $17.51/hr
Jones, Joseph P, human resources specialist II, $37,000
Jones, Julie Elizabeth, nurse, staff per diem, $35.00/hr
Jones, Kathryn Jo Baker, fellow, post doctoral, $42,442
Jones, Kathryn Lynn, service rep III, $13.74/hr

Jones, Katie Ann, student support specialist I, $15.15/hr
Jones, Keesha Lenise, human resources specialist III, $45,455
Jones, Larry Dale, instructor, adjunct, $12,000
Jones, Leland S, security officer, $11.79/hr
Jones, Lena D, custodian, $13.36/hr
Jones, Linda Jo, care team assoc-clinical, $15.05/hr
Jones, Linda K, nurse, licensed prac, $17.31/hr
Jones, Lindsey Lee, human resources manager sr, $62,100
Jones, Lisa, business support specialist II, $18.73/hr
Jones, Lisa Raquel, contract spclst-managed care, $50,524
Jones, Lynette Dawn, nurse, licensed prac, $15.67/hr
Jones, Marianne Clare, mgr III business admin, $72,513
Jones, Mark E, custodian, $10.69/hr
Jones, Marlene B, instructor, adjunct, $15,000
Jones, Marvia, resrch asoc, $45,000
Jones, Misty Rae, nurse manager, $77,563
Jones, Moneen Marie, prof, ast resrch, $74,500
Jones, Nancy Jane, event assistant I, $7.70/hr
Jones, Nathan Allan, prof, asoc adjunct, $12,000
Jones, Nikki V, clerk, unit, $12.11/hr
Jones, Patricia Ann, csm operations coordinator, $19.44/hr
Jones, Patricia Elaine, office support assistant III, $18.08/hr
Jones, Peter D, hospital security officer, $11.50/hr
Jones, Rachel Tanner, mental health tech trainee, $9.27/hr
Jones, Reed, custodian, $10.39/hr
Jones, Richard Allen, maint svc attd, $17.78/hr
Jones, Richard L, event assistant I, $7.57/hr
Jones, Richard Sterling, temporary crafts service, $9.50/hr
Jones, Ricky, mts/pipefitter, $21.05/hr
Jones, Ronald Edward, dir I, broadcast operations, $70,000
Jones, Ronald W, bts painter, $21.71/hr
Jones, Sara Tylor, nurse, staff II, $21.35/hr
Jones, Scott E, boiler maint opr, $24.13/hr
Jones, Sherry D, custodian mrc, $10.50/hr
Jones, Skip Williams, media producer II, $16.00/hr
Jones, Stacy L, safety communications operator, $14.46/hr
Jones, Stacy L, sr mgr business admin, $62,762
Jones, Tammy Dee, business support analyst II, $23.24/hr
Jones, Tammy Lynn, program/project supprt coor I, $26,520
Jones, Tracy Christyne, office support assistant IV, $15.19/hr
Jones, Trenton A, asoc coach, $42,420
Jones, Wilbert James, custodian, $12.94/hr
Jones, Willie Matthew, business support analyst I, $19.58/hr
Jones, Youlanda Yvonne, office support assistant III, $16.39/hr
Jones, Zachary Lee, telecomm opr-h, $10.74/hr
Joo, Jee Young, prof, ast, $72,900
Joo, Jhi Young, prof, ast, $81,000
Joos, Steven D, fin and acctg manager sr, $76,981
Joplin, Corinne Annette, child life spclst, $41,030
Joplin, John D, rec/athletic assistant, $10.00/hr
Jordan, Carter M, clerk, unit, $11.00/hr
Jordan, James Ralph, program/project supprt coor II, $44,341
Jordan, Jenny Redix, mgr II student support svcs, $57,000
Jordan, Jessica L, fin and acctg manager, $62,400
Jordan, Jill E, media producer II, $14.95/hr
Jordan, Karen Lynnette, food svc wrkr IV, $14.77/hr
Jordan, Kevin C, operations support tech sr, $20.00/hr
Jordan, Kevin Dion, food svc wrkr IV, $14.77/hr
Jordan, Margaret Renee, home hlth aide, $11.32/hr
Jordan, Monette Lindeice, office support assistant IV, $13.75/hr
Jordan, Sara Elizabeth, care team assoc-suppt, $10.85/hr
Jordan, Yolanda D, phlebotomist, $14.88/hr
Jorgensen, Erik L, support systems admin-princpl, $66,780
Jorgensen, Erin Rachael McNeill, strat comm assoc II, $42,000
Jorgensen, Jason Donald, office support assistant IV, $13.00/hr
Jorgensen, Jeffrey Brian, prof, ast clincl dept, $244,014
Jorgensen, Michael Edward, lecturer, $45,900
Jorgensen, Stephen Robert, dean, $185,674
Jorgenson, Courtney Don, hlth prgm ast, $12.50/hr
Jorgenson, Katherine Clare, instructor, adjunct, $6,300
Jose, Philip Marshall, mts/electrician, $21.05/hr
Jose, Shibu, professor, $159,938
Joseph, Nilufer E, dir II finance, $101,892
Joshi, Christopher L, fellow, post doc clncl yr1, $60,415
Joshi, Kailash, professor, $118,100
Joshi, Trupti Subhash, prof, ast resrch, $84,000
Jost, Amanda Boehm, pharmacy resident, $38,500
Jost, Glenona B, patient svc rep, $14.32/hr
Jost, Melissa M, nurse manager, $80,057

Josten, Jane M, nurse, licensed prac sr, $20.77/hr
Joswara, Andry Solihin, fin and acctg consultant, $68,291
Jouret, James Jacob, nurse, staff I, $19.00/hr
Journey, Linda Joyce, business support specialist II, $17.49/hr
Joy, Morgan N, programmer analyst-expert, $57,790
Joy, Tyler R, telecom tech-princpl, $21.19/hr
Ju, Min, prof, ast, $107,590
Juarez, Larry Anthony, dental lab supervisor, $69,713
Juba, Thomas R, research specialist sr, $44,462
Judy March, Jan, research/lab technician sr, $16.78/hr
Judy, Megan Elizabeth, on-air talent television, $42,657
Juengermann, Ann M, dir I, business admin, $129,080
Juengermann, Cecilia A, fin and acctg manager, $71,495
Juengermann, Lee, reactor specialist, $59,077
Juergens, Ashley Marie, care team assoc-clinical, $12.08/hr
Juergens, Elaine Beatrice, patient svc rep, $13.33/hr
Juergens, Victoria Jo, hospital security officer, $10.64/hr
Julo, Anthony T, office support assistant IV, $14.42/hr
Jun, Bokkwan, prof, ast, $170,000
Junek, Andrea N, system support analyst-entry, $17.26/hr
Jung, Catherine Pitts, resident physician-4th yr, $54,425
Jung, Jae Chul, prof, asoc, $108,871
Juniel, Cedric Durell, event assistant I, $7.50/hr
Jurczyk, Michael, prof, asoc, $99,194
Jurgesmeyer, Kristin Michelle, nurse advisor, telephone, $27.31/hr
Jurisson, Silvia S, professor, $125,601
Jurkevich, Alexander, mgr research activities, $63,672
Jurkevich, Olga, fin and acctg specialist, $15.50/hr
Jurkouich, Heather Rose, waiter/waitress, $7.50/hr
Justice, John D, instructor, adjunct, $18,000
Justice, Marjorie Ann, instructor, adjunct, $9,000
Juzkiw, Irene Ann, instructor, $79,857
Kabel, Allison M, prof, ast, $79,143
Kabir, Asad Waseem, resident physician-6th yr, $58,200
Kabler, Ashley Erin, lab assistant, $9.50/hr
Kabugi, Caroline Njeri, mental health tech, $11.85/hr
Kaburia, Dereck Gitau, mental health tech, $13.74/hr
Kabytaev, Kuanysh Zeinullovich, fellow, post doctoral, $45,000
Kadam, Suhas Baliram, fellow, post doctoral, $39,000
Kaeberle, Jean Marie, instructor, clincl, $15,375
Kagay, Kathy L, grader, $52
Kahl, Laura J, office support assistant IV, $16.50/hr
Kahler, Bobby, mail carrier, $15.77/hr
Kahng, SungWoo, prof, asoc, $115,000
Kail, Jeffrey E, prof, adjunct, $19,440
Kaimann, Stephanie Lauren, fin and acctg manager, $54,683
Kain, Meri Amanda, instructor, adjunct, $12,487
Kaiser, Andrea, account executive, $6,000
Kaiser, Helmut, prof, resrch, $92,502
Kaiser, Sandra L, office support assistant III, $12.00/hr
Kaitheri Kandoth, Pramod, resrch asoc, $45,689
Kaja, Simon, prof, ast resrch, $75,705
Kakie, Kingsley, support systems admin-speclst, $59,518
Kalahurka, William P, prof, ast teach, $45,000
Kalaitzandonakes, Nicholas, professor, $153,663
Kalb, Heather Marie, office support assistant III, $13.39/hr
Kale, Aaron C, temporary clerical, $9.00/hr
Kale, Anupama M, resident physician-5th yr, $58,083
Kale, Gautam Kishore, fellow, post doc clncl-yr2, $58,083
Kalinkos, Bill, prof, ast visiting, $37,800
Kalinowski, Michael Kevin, animal techn, ast lab, $13.19/hr
Kalista, Lyndsay Gayle, nurse, staff II, $20.54/hr
Kallenbach, Nena C, executive assistant, $21.75/hr
Kallenbach, Robert L, professor, $150,431
Kaller, Zachary A, tutor, $15.00/hr
Kalogeris, Theodore John, prof, ast resrch, $72,338
Kaloudis, Naomi R, lecturer, $45,000
Kamau, David K, event assistant I, $8.50/hr
Kamau, Virginia E, custodian, $10.73/hr
Kamler, Bill J, nurse, staff II, $34.18/hr
Kamler, Kathryn Ann, med coding spclst-certified, $23.94/hr
Kammer, Jenna Frances, instructional designer-expert, $58,134
Kammerich, Carolyn K, custodian, $10.94/hr
Kammerich, Julie Selck, instructor, $21,447
Kammerich, Mark Alan, instructor, adjunct, $9,000
Kammler, Kate J, horticulture spclst, $42,783
Kamp, Timothy Joseph, security sgt-h, $14.58/hr
Kampelman, Janine Agnes, instructor, clincl, $88,000
Kamran Disfani, Amy Lynn, patient svc rep, $12.37/hr

Kanaley, Jill A, professor, $117,215
Kanatzar, Iris Ellen, business support specialist II, $25.00/hr
Kander, Diana Kagan, prof, ast teach, $116,667
Kandlik, Jennifer Michelle, coor emergency svcs ed, $63,551
Kane, Addie Marie, resp therapist reg, $20.12/hr
Kane, Kevin Yurll, prof, clinical dept, $173,910
Kane, Thomas C, program/project supprt coor I, $36,000
Kang, Henry Hyungwoo, prof, asoc, $92,287
Kang, Jeehoon, lab assistant, $8.00/hr
Kang, Min Soo, prof, asoc, $65,429
Kang, Terry S, resident physician-4th yr, $54,425
Kannan, Raghuraman, prof, asoc, $125,000
Kanne, Christine Marie, physical therapist, $35.00/hr
Kanne, Stephen Michael, director, $197,613
Kannuswamy, Rohini, resident physician-2nd yr, $52,007
Kanter, Steven, dean, $500,000
Kantor, Jeff Lawrence, prof, ast clncl dept, $176,501
Kapellusch, Andrew C, temporary crafts service, $10.15/hr
Kapila, Shubhender, professor, $125,737
Kapka, Kenneth D, user support analyst-speclst, $17.49/hr
Kaplan, Chad W, resident physician-4th yr, $54,425
Kaplan, David M, prof, ast, $106,700
Kaplan, Deborah, nurse clinician, $66,536
Kaplan, Lorie F, director, $86,700
Kaplan, Martin Russell, office support assistant IV, $20.24/hr
Kaplan, Michael B, couns hlth/welfare/wellness, $29.64/hr
Kapoor, Ragini, prof, ast adjunct, $67,250
Kapp, Julie M, prof, asoc, $115,000
Kapros, Tamas, prof, asoc teach, $66,010
Kapuria, Devika, resident physician-2nd yr, $50,810
Karan, Dejan, system administrator-speclst, $46,284
Karanja, Damaris Mumbi, extns professional, asoc, $50,375
Karanja, Elizabeth Njeri, tutor, $9.00/hr
Karasseva, Natalia G, resrch scientist/academic sr, $68,378
Karcher, Catherine A, custodian, $10.39/hr
Kardakos, Petros Dimitrios, distribution techn-mtls mgmt, $14.84/hr
Kardell, Christine Ann, lecturer, $8,400
Kardon, Mike J, distribution techn-mtls mgmt, $14.55/hr
Karhoff, Lana Marie, nurse, staff II, $33.71/hr
Karian, Stephen Edwin, prof, asoc, $75,609
Karicho, Peter Karuga, mental health tech, $13.27/hr
Karig, Maureen F, lecturer, $12,000
Kariuki, Michael Muchiri, nurse, staff now III, $30.00/hr
Karl, Eric Norman, supv electric-h, $53,886
Karlin, Joshua Gerard, resident physician-1st yr, $50,219
Karmakar, Srabani, fellow, post doctoral, $38,000
Karmann, Courtney Jean, office support assistant IV, $13.50/hr
Karnes, Matthew D, nurse, staff per diem, $35.00/hr
Karney, Lewis Eugene, utility dist wrkr IV, $23.75/hr
Karpinski, Gary, lecturer sr, $9,000
Karr, Matthew Levon, pharmacy tech, $11.00/hr
Karslake, James E, business support specialist II, $20.54/hr
Karthas, Ilyana, prof, ast, $55,315
Karthikeyan, Kamalesh Rajah, resident physician-2nd yr, $52,007
Karuga, Teresiah Wambui, mental health tech, $12.81/hr
Karwaa, Moid, prof, ast clncl, $87,000
Karwoski, Debra Jean, office support assistant II, $15.15/hr
Karwoski, Roger Wayne, media production director I, $32,796
Kase, Teresa Mae, cancer registrar, $17.83/hr
Kashubeck West, Susan, professor, $84,386
Kasica, Paula J, lecturer, $4,590
Kasmann, Janice Ann, physical therapist, $72,028
Kasper, Donna Marie, human resources assistant, $15.57/hr
Kasper, Martin J, mgr env health and safety, $71,181
Kasper, Rhonda R, educational pgm associate I, $14.09/hr
Kasper, Susan J, program/project supprt coor I, $47,092
Kass, Gary Alan, editor II, $48,000
Kassel, Andrew S, system administrator-princpl, $63,984
Kassel, Candace Reba, supv, lab, $59,943
Kassel, Erica J, educational prgm coor sr, $50,723
Kassel, Lynn E, prof, ast clncl, $96,000
Kasten, Michael C, prgm director, $83,000
Kaster, Alyona Renae, food svc wrkr I, $9.60/hr
Kaster, Wesley Brian, reactor operator sr, $29.60/hr
Kater, Marcus A, resident physician-5th yr, $56,120
Katoch, Bandhana, business ops associate sr, $67,524
Katski, Gregory Matthew, strat comm associate II, $45,000
Katta, Natraj, prof, ast clncl dept, $183,600
Katti, Kattesh, professor, $217,695

Katti, Kavita Kattesh, scientist lead, $62,510
Katunar, Cecil C Jr, grounds keeper II, $14.26/hr
Katz, Allan Jack, prof, distinguished, $150,000
Katz, Daniel Thedore, event assistant I, $20.00/hr
Katz, Elijah, resident physician-1st yr, $49,025
Katz, Jacqueline Maria, nurse, licensed prac, $21.07/hr
Katz, Jerald Owen, professor, $113,289
Katz, Martin L, professor, $136,402
Kauffman, Sheri Joyce, police officer, $18.68/hr
Kaufman, James D, asoc dir program/project ops, $69,051
Kaufman, Kevin L, maintenance supervisor, $59,134
Kaufman, Linda Lou, executive assistant, $18.02/hr
Kaufman, Robyn E, nurse, staff II, $33.41/hr
Kaufmann, Gina Brooke, media production director I, $43,000
Kaume, Lydia Karimi, extns professional, ast, $52,535
Kaup, Ann M, mgr I, business admin, $67,400
Kaur, Amardeep, prof, ast teach, $67,000
Kaussen, Valerie M, prof, asoc, $66,441
Kavanagh, Kristin E, resident physician-4th yr, $55,804
Kavanaugh, Anna, instructor, adjunct, $6,300
Kay, Bruce C, office support assistant IV, $14.00/hr
Kay, Gary Roger, custodian, $12.94/hr
Kay, William, instructor, adjunct, $13,500
Kaylen, Michael S, prof, asoc, $66,355
Kaylen, Myoung Lee, prof, asoc teach, $69,785
Kazem, Bahaa Ibraheem, scholar, visiting, $30,000
Kazic, Toni, prof, asoc, $106,775
Ke, Bin, business support specialist sr, $22.80/hr
Kean, John N Jr, mgr external relations, $49,123
Kean, Stacy Lynn, instructor, ast, $31,200
Kearney, Karina, office support assistant IV, $14.50/hr
Kearney, Matthew L, sr ast dir studnt supprt svcs, $56,511
Kearns, Michael Joseph, bldg cntrl sys techn III, $23.28/hr
Keating, Margaret, instructor, adjunct, $22,500
Keaton, Danielle Tadra, prof, ast adjunct, $25,650
Keefer, Matthew W, professor, $79,499
Keegan, Kathleen Marie, telecomm opr-h, $9.27/hr
Keegan, Kevin G, professor, $146,972
Keel, Hannah Elizabeth, event assistant I, $11.00/hr
Keel, Robert O, prof, teach, $63,582
Keeler, Matthew Robert, assoc director it, $75,961
Keeler, Meghan C, instructor, adjunct, $16,800
Keely, Jennifer Loraine, prof, ast clncl, $55,686
Keely, John L, asoc dir student support svcs, $72,637
Keene, Bradly Allen, cook, $12.20/hr
Keene, Charles W, prof, ast teach, $78,001
Keener, Elizabeth A, pharmacist II, $68.50/hr
Keenoy, Jessica Jory, prgm director, ast, $21,226
Keers, Christa Jane DeMarke, media producer II, $17.23/hr
Keesal, Marlene Ann, instructor, adjunct, $7,386
Keeter, David Patrick, media producer sr, $46,692
Keeton, David Kenneth, nurse anesthetist, $95.00/hr
Keeton, Debbie, library info specialist sr, $19.50/hr
Keeton, William Robert, instructor, $72,000
Keffer, Dustin Wayne, resident physician-3rd yr, $52,470
Keffer, Marilyn Y, med coding spclst-certified, $20.83/hr
Kehner, Kenneth William, lecturer, $18,240
Keicher, Emma Sofia, child developmentalist, $47,741
Keightley, John A, prof, asoc resrch, $86,367
Keilholz, Caitlin C, pharmacy tech, $13.16/hr
Keiser, Lael R, prof, asoc, $100,129
Keisler, Duane H, professor, $100,335
Keith, Benjamin R, med techl reg, $25.58/hr
Keith, Kyler Lee, student recruitment spclst sr, $19.00/hr
Keith, Scott F, grounds supervisor, $53,002
Keith, Trisha D, office support assistant IV, $16.23/hr
Keithahn, Stephen Timothy, prof, ast clncl dept, $189,145
Keithly, Melina Tatyana, resident physician-2nd yr, $50,810
Keleher, Lauren Louise, research specialist I, $31,100
Kell, Mendy E, business ops associate sr, $47,222
Kell, Shannon P, mts/electrician-r, $20.87/hr
Kellar, Chieko, lecturer, $27,063
Kellar, Vivian L, nurse, staff II rnwp, $31.54/hr
Kellenberger, Allison K, nurse, staff II, $31.13/hr
Kellenberger, Joseph A, nurse, licensed prac sr, $20.77/hr
Keller, William J Jr, supv radiology, $36.69/hr
Keller-Tracy, Rebecca Lynn, resident physician-1st yr, $50,219
Keller, Barbara J, fellow, post doctoral, $48,286
Keller, Edwin Roy, instructor, ast, $18.72/hr

Keller, James M, professor, $187,684
Keller, Karen, prof, ast adjunct, $16,728
Keller, Kelly Kathleen, office support assistant II, $13.00/hr
Keller, Kimberly Jean Miller, resrch asoc, $63,513
Keller, Kirk L, enterprise architect, $81,600
Keller, Mason C, instructor, adjunct, $12,000
Keller, Shayla Beth, nurse, staff II, $20.54/hr
Keller, Steven W, prof, asoc, $76,332
Keller, Whitney J, executive assistant, $19.70/hr
Kellerhaus, Midge E, executive assistant, $24.08/hr
Kelley, Orville Edward Jr, business ops associate sr, $65,032
Kelley, Cheryl A, professor, $69,650
Kelley, Dennis Francis, prof, ast, $59,587
Kelley, Elizabeth Spencer, prof, ast, $76,500
Kelley, Henry A, animal techn, ast lab, $13.89/hr
Kelley, Jeanne Marie, business support specialist II, $15.10/hr
Kelley, Joseph Allen, care team assoc-clinical, $13.74/hr
Kelley, Justin M, media producer II, $17.50/hr
Kelley, Kate Stockton, grader, $100.00/hr
Kelley, Katlin Marie, office support assistant IV, $13.09/hr
Kelley, Patricia Ann, office support assistant IV, $14.35/hr
Kelley, Rachel Elaine, safety communications oper, $13.40/hr
Kelley, Ronald B, ast vice chancellor, $131,306
Kelley, Stephen Scot, system support analyst-entry, $18.31/hr
Kelley, Tanya, instructor, adjunct, $28,800
Kellner, Lauren Pinder, nurse, staff II, $20.54/hr
Kellogg, Leonard Frank, programmer analyst-expert, $55,808
Kellogg, Theresa Ann, business svcs consultant sr, $84,456
Kelly, Calvin F Jr, supv housekeeping, $34,866
Kelly, Mark Anthony Sr, driver, $13.89/hr
Kelly, Charles Allen, mech, bldg maint, $19.64/hr
Kelly, Christopher S, dir III advancement, $81,782
Kelly, Cindi Rae, mgr II business admin, $58,580
Kelly, Colleen L, asoc dir program/project ops, $57,785
Kelly, Dana J, mail processor II lead, $16.79/hr
Kelly, Dana Lou, office support assistant III, $12.74/hr
Kelly, David Joseph, grounds keeper II, $13.09/hr
Kelly, Deasha Nicole, food svc wrkr I, $9.60/hr
Kelly, Debra Ann, horticulture spclst, $49,500
Kelly, Dedrae Marcella, office support assistant I, $9.05/hr
Kelly, Eric Lawrence, distribution techn-mtls mgmt, $15.26/hr
Kelly, Gregory D, supervisor it, $60,000
Kelly, James Eugene, care team assoc-suppt, $13.12/hr
Kelly, Janet Taylor, executive assistant, $16.71/hr
Kelly, June Charlene, business support specialist II, $16.00/hr
Kelly, Karen S, business support analyst sr, $28.73/hr
Kelly, Martha M, prof, ast, $61,295
Kelly, Michael Joseph, professor, $91,682
Kelly, Michael William, instructor, $43,672
Kelly, Michelle M, tutor, $15.00/hr
Kelly, Myra J, office support assistant IV, $15.94/hr
Kelly, Patricia Jane, dean, asoc, $120,345
Kelly, Robert A, busi spclst, agri, $50,767
Kelm, Lyddia B, nurse, staff II, $29.75/hr
Kelsay, Michael P, lecturer, $35,700
Kelsay, Wendi Rechelle, nurse, staff / in house agency, $40.00/hr
Kelsey, Hailee Jade, radiologic techl, $18.59/hr
Kelso, Angel Whisper, custodian, $10.00/hr
Kelso, Angela Berneice, nurse, licensed prac sr rnwp, $15.06/hr
Kelton, Stephanie Ann, prof, asoc, $89,499
Kelty, Blanca Gonzalez, instructor, ast, $13,608
Kelty, Javier Alexander, instructor, ast, $25,381
Kemble, Cara Marie, nurse, staff II, $22.00/hr
Kemboi-Melly, Edna, nurse anesthetist, $145,760
Kemna, Abby Marie, nurse, staff II, $20.54/hr
Kemp, Oscar P Jr, police lieutenant, $47,085
Kemp, David J, instructor, $57,041
Kemp, Gregory, mech, bldg maint, $19.64/hr
Kemp, Maureen J, office support assistant IV, $16.13/hr
Kemp, Michelle Stephens, mgr II student support svcs, $61,260
Kemp, Shane Michael, food svc wrkr II, $10.10/hr
Kemp, Tamera L, patient svc rep, $14.51/hr
Kemper, Brittany N, educational pgm associate I, $11.80/hr
Kemper, David Lee-Andrew, resp therapist reg, $20.22/hr
Kemper, Jackielyn Dawn, supv, acute care nursing rnwp, $25.36/hr
Kemper, Jonathan W, system administrator-entry, $42,630
Kempf, Bobby Joe, maintenance supervisor, $53,654
Kempf, Jerold J, bts carpenter, $21.71/hr
Kempf, Lana Dianne, patient svc rep, $11.23/hr

Kempf, Patrick W, fin and acctg consultant sr, $58,625
Kempf, Zachary Joseph, care team assoc-clinical, $13.33/hr
Kempker, Jennifer Marie, educational pgm assistant, $10.19/hr
Kempker, Richard Herman, bts roofer, $21.71/hr
Kempker, Samantha Marie, temporary crafts service, $10.00/hr
Kempker, Stacey Marie, pat admiss advisor, $28.58/hr
Ken, Jonathan, resident physician-1st yr, $50,219
Kendhari, Jusleen, instructor, clincl, $191,250
Kendig, Susan M, prof, teach, $95,283
Kendrick, Bethany Michele, office support assistant II, $13.00/hr
Kendrick, Raymond, electronics technician III, $15.51/hr
Kendrick, Sarah Ann Wolken, research/lab tech sr, $15.00/hr
Kendrick, Theresa Michelle, prog/proj supprt coor sr, $56,229
Keneipp, Cynthia A, care coordinator, $65,586
Kenley-Morris, Corina Kay, nurse, staff II, $27.16/hr
Kennedy, Anne Marie, patient svc rep, $12.76/hr
Kennedy, Devin Scott, resident physician-1st yr, $50,219
Kennedy, Donald Eugene, head coach, $40,000
Kennedy, George, prof, adjunct, $28,267
Kennedy, Helen E, nurse, licensed prac, $17.11/hr
Kennedy, Jason E, support systems admin-expert, $54,999
Kennedy, Kathleen M, patient svc rep, $14.12/hr
Kennedy, Kelsey Sue, event assistant I, $8.50/hr
Kennedy, Madeline Grace, office support assistant III, $11.50/hr
Kennedy, Molli Kaye, clerk, operating room supply, $12.22/hr
Kennedy, Robin Clark, curator, $25.31/hr
Kennedy, Secley R, office support assistant IV, $14.79/hr
Kennedy, William L, physicist, $170,174
Kennett, Kurt, support systems admin-expert, $53,448
Kennett, Michele R, ast vice chancellor, $133,404
Kenney, Carl William, instructor, adjunct, $9,000
Kenney, Michael P, maintenance supervisor, $57,592
Kenny, Ann Louise, research specialist sr, $42,000
Kensinger, Kraig William, extension asoc, $35,233
Kensinger, Sherry L, nurse, lpn now plus sr, $20.00/hr
Kent, Robert E II, food svc wrkr III, $13.21/hr
Kent, Karelia Grace, patient svc rep, $10.64/hr
Kenty, Jorang, business support specialist II, $15.90/hr
Kenyon, Nathan T, resident physician-3rd yr, $53,763
Kenyon, Sarah Lynn, agronomy spclst, $43,072
Kenzior, Alexander L, resrch scientist/academic, $48,847
Keown, Christine A, nurse advisor, telephone, $29.97/hr
Kerl, Marie E, prof, teach, $130,217
Kerley, Emily Elizabeth, office support assistant IV, $13.50/hr
Kerley, Monty S, professor, $137,762
Kerley, Shelley A, sr dir advancement, $97,800
Kern, Andrew E, prof, ast teach, $95,000
Kerner, Daniel B, human resources manager sr, $66,950
Kerns, John Gerald, professor, $80,915
Kerns, Kalvin K, asoc dir business admin, $63,917
Kerns, Resa J, librarian II, $62,206
Kerr-Totten, Morgan Lynn, nurse, licensed prac, $14.76/hr
Kerr, Audrey Grace, nurse, staff II rnwp, $23.12/hr
Kerr, Bouchra I, clinical technician sr, $21.60/hr
Kerr, Cynthia Diane, nurse, staff, $21.58/hr
Kerr, Kathleen Patricia, academic advisor, $42,487
Kerr, Mary Ellen, nurse, staff II rnwp, $32.75/hr
Kerr, Stepfon O, custodian, $12.18/hr
Kerridge, Bonnie Daria, prof, ast adjunct, $36,101
Kertz, Maria Louise, care team assoc-clinical, $11.10/hr
Kerwin, Razmus Y, instructional developr-speclst, $17.25/hr
Kerwin, William J, prof, asoc, $73,067
Kerwood, Roxanna L, program/project supprt coor sr, $55,843
Kesinger, Kelly Ann, student support specialist II, $18.70/hr
Kesler, Dylan Charles, prof, ast, $66,767
Kesler, Ellen Marie, research specialist sr, $56,042
Kespohl, Gregory G, account executive, $56,797
Kessel, James White, prof, clinical dept, $279,314
Kessinger, Chad R, mts/hvac, $18.74/hr
Kessler, David C, network engineer-expert, $55,000
Kessler, Karen E, human resources specialist II, $57,496
Kessler, Stanton Scott, instructor, adjunct, $7,200
Kester, Cassandra Chance, student support spec sr, $17.94/hr
Kesterson, Jacob P, prof, ast clincl dept, $214,200
Kesterson, Julia Marie, prof, ast adjunct, $90,354
Ketcherside, Tori Christine, telecomm opr-h, $9.64/hr
Ketharnath, Dhivya, instructor, adjunct, $16,500
Ketring, Alan R, asoc director, $129,314
Kettenbach, Gerard Francis, instructor, $32,821

Kettenbrink, Anne Elizabeth, strat comm associate II, $53,500
Ketter, Traci Lynn, instructor, adjunct, $22,000
Ketterlin, Brianne M, nurse, staff II, $23.23/hr
Ketterman, Christina Michele, nurse, staff prn, $26.00/hr
Kettinger, Jane Marie, office support assistant I, $10.57/hr
Kettle, Jacob Kinley, pharmacist, $124,851
Keuss, Theresa Lynn, ast registrar, $47,899
Kevern, John T, prof, asoc, $79,378
Kewley, Leslie M, lab techn, persl svc-clin lab, $15.25/hr
Key, Beth Ann, audiometric techn, $14.84/hr
Key, Elisabeth Elaine, dean, ast, $94,915
Key, Kelly Marie, serv line spclst, $68,793
Key, Kevin B, custodian, $12.94/hr
Key, Linda Jean, rehab therapy aide, $14.88/hr
Keys, Morgan Ann, veterinary technician sr, $16.16/hr
Khairallah, Joelle, academic advisor, $39,848
Khakh, Gurpreet Singh, resident physician-1st yr, $50,219
Khaleel, Fuad I, business ops associate sr, $47,472
Khaleel, Nabila I, prof, ast clincl dept, $138,380
Khaleel, Rakiya, diet techn, $15.42/hr
Khalsa, Kartapurkh Singh, instructor, adjunct, $4,200
Khan, Asif Bashir, food svc wrkr III, $11.24/hr
Khan, Aslam Ali, fellow, post doctoral, $49,159
Khan, Erum Z, resident physician-5th yr, $58,083
Khan, Faeza Fahmee, resident physician-2nd yr, $52,007
Khan, Fahad, resident physician-2nd yr, $50,810
Khan, Hassan Mansoor, fellow, post doc clncl yr1, $55,804
Khan, Marydell E, nurse, licensed prac, $20.18/hr
Khan, Mather Ali, fellow, post doctoral, $36,771
Khan, Ricardo Mohamed, prof, visiting, $50,750
Khan, Salman Ali, resident physician-1st yr, $49,025
Khan, Soly Remo, nurse, staff II, $34.18/hr
Khan, Uzma Zubair, prof, asoc clincl dept, $153,768
Khanal, Navadeep, librarian I, $46,000
Khangura, Darshan Singh, resident physician-2nd yr, $52,007
Khanna, Ramesh, professor, $255,197
Khanna, Sanjeev K, professor, $132,176
Khare, Sharad, prof, asoc, $30,735
Khare, Tripti, temporary technical, $30.00/hr
Khatri, Naresh, prof, asoc, $105,000
Khayat, Kamal, professor, $232,135
Khelouz, Nacer, prof, asoc, $51,818
Khengar, Payal N, high school student, $10.00/hr
Khengar, Vibhaveri, med lab techn, $23.01/hr
Khilkevich, Victor, prof, ast, $80,000
Khir, Nadir, physician, $75.00/hr
Khodakhast, Beheshteh, prof, ast clincl, $88,434
Khoobchandani, Menka, fellow, post doctoral, $35,000
Khosla, Nidhi, prof, ast, $75,205
Khreis, Rula Iyad, resident physician-2nd yr, $52,007
Khurana, Inder K, professor, $250,014
Kibbee, Nicole, adjunct, $15,000
Kickbusch, Scott W, library info specialist sr, $17.66/hr
Kidane, Mehret G, custodian, $12.94/hr
Kidd, Ambrose Raiford III, prof, ast teach, $43,250
Kidd, Doretta S, asoc dir student support svcs, $62,216
Kidd, Joseph Benton, asoc curator, $43,529
Kidder, Stephanie Lynn, fellow, post doctoral, $44,340
Kidwell, Carolyn J, office support assistant IV, $17.85/hr
Kidwell, Greg K, nurse, staff II, $34.18/hr
Kiehl, William C, fin and acctg manager sr, $102,154
Kiehn, Julaine R, dir II csm operations, $144,945
Kiehne, Melissa Anne, child dev assistant, $8.16/hr
Kiesendahl, John K, prof, ast adjunct, $200.00/hr
Kiesling, Jerry Wayne, dir program/project operations, $62,130
Kiger, Sam A, professor, $167,549
Kilbourn, Daniel Lee, maint tech III, prev, $18.45/hr
Kilbourn, Sheryl, office support assistant IV, $15.02/hr
Kilburn, Terry L, bts painter, $21.71/hr
Kile, Bernie James, mts/pipefitter, $21.05/hr
Kile, Tina Lynn, nurse, staff II rnwp, $23.12/hr
Kilgore, Connie Larue, health records techn I, $10.74/hr
Kilgore, Daniel J, police lieutenant, $46,976
Kilgore, Katherine W, pharmacist II, $117,822
Kilgore, Lindsay Maye, office support assistant IV, $15.67/hr
Kilgore, Nicole Elizabeth, fin and acctg analyst sr, $47,491
Kilgus, Stephen Patrick, prof, ast, $73,000
Killday, Mary Carolyn, social worker, $55,751

Killingsworth, Ronald Lynn, instructor, adjunct, $62.50/hr
Killip, John W, prof, adjunct, $125.00/hr
Killoren, Jack Judge, high school student, $8.00/hr
Killoren, Sarah E, prof, ast, $69,500
Killpack, Scott Collin, agronomy spclst, $65,628
Kilpatrick, Colin J, dir iv advancement, $132,391
Kilway, Kathleen, prof, curator teach, $109,490
Kim, Baek Hyun, fellow, post doctoral, $39,000
Kim, Benny, prof, asoc, $77,085
Kim, Byungmin, prof, adjunct, $21,000
Kim, Chang-Soo, professor, $93,120
Kim, Cheehyung, prof, ast, $65,000
Kim, Dae Young, prof, asoc clincl dept, $120,181
Kim, Dae-Young, prof, asoc, $83,195
Kim, Hyunho, scholar, visiting, $14,688
Kim, Jae Woo, prof, ast resrch, $59,083
Kim, James E, resident physician-3rd yr, $54,270
Kim, Jarim, prof, ast, $58,500
Kim, Jung Hyup, prof, ast, $85,714
Kim, JuRyoung, fellow, post doctoral, $38,000
Kim, Kyonghee, prof, ast, $184,871
Kim, Min Soon, prof, ast, $99,878
Kim, Mirae, prof, ast, $74,000
Kim, Sang Hee, fellow, post doctoral, $39,634
Kim, Sang Soon, sr dir program/project ops, $83,679
Kim, Sangchul, post doctoral asoc, $39,727
Kim, So Mi, fellow, post doctoral, $48,000
Kim, Sola, resident physician-1st yr, $49,025
Kim, Sophia Younjoo, programmer analyst-expert, $54,790
Kim, Sujeong, programmer analyst-entry, $40,966
Kim, Sujin, post doctoral asoc, $16,800
Kim, Suk Jin, scholar, visiting, $25.00/hr
Kim, Sungyop, prof, asoc, $65,571
Kim, Won-Seok, research specialist sr, $42,000
Kim, YoonHa, fellow, post doctoral, $39,000
Kimaru, John Ndungo, mental health tech, $13.66/hr
Kimball, David C, professor, $76,572
Kimball, Jonathan William, prof, asoc, $104,590
Kimber, Tusha D, student service coor II, $53,222
Kimberlin, Robin Michelle, social worker sr, $37,569
Kimberling Jr, David John, coor, care, $61,387
Kimberling, Jessica Ann, care team assoc-clinical, $14.17/hr
Kimble, Susan J, prof, asoc clincl, $88,061
Kimbrel, Cindi J, nurse, licensed prac, $19.03/hr
Kimbrell, Matthew H, lecturer, $41,200
Kimbrough, Tamy Maria, coor, service, $14.76/hr
Kimmel, Cameo Elizabeth, nurse, staff I, $19.37/hr
Kimura, Andrea Lynn, hlth educator, $48,328
Kincade, Larry F, telecom tech-expert, $21.64/hr
Kincade, Patricia Ann, instructor, clincl, $57,396
Kincaid, Derik Tyler, temporary crafts service, $20.00/hr
Kincaid, Margaret Mercedes, prof, ast teach, $55,000
Kincaid, Sara Jane, strat comm associate II, $53,000
Kinder, Beth Joann, nurse, licensed prac sr, $19.84/hr
Kinder, Cory Michael, human resources specialist II, $39,996
Kinder, Jeffrey W, operations support tech II, $16.13/hr
Kinder, Kimberly S, prof, ast teach, $52,486
Kinder, Laura Ann, instructor, adjunct, $9,600
Kindle, Carl, db programmer analyst-princpl, $70,249
Kindle, Lara, academic advisor, $34,400
Kindley, James, instructor, adjunct, $22,500
Kindlund, Konny Michael II, grounds keeper II, $13.73/hr
Kinds, William K, programmer analyst-spclst, $46,284
King, Dana M III, prof, ast clincl, $107,369
King, D Randall Jr, prof, asoc adjunct, $9,519
King-Stephens, Deborah Kathryn, prof, ast adjunct, $8,004
King, Amy Christine, office support assistant IV, $13.75/hr
King, Andrew Kenneth, technical trainer-spclst, $52,531
King, Betty J, pat admiss advisor, $31.59/hr
King, Bradley, instructor, adjunct, $14,118
King, Carroll J, prof, asoc clincl dept, $257,555
King, Chad L, grader, $4,800
King, Charles Brandon, business ops associate I, $45,000
King, Daniel M, head coach, $43,002
King, Donna K, temporary crafts service, $12.66/hr
King, Eileen M, social worker, $62,704
King, Elizabeth Griep, prof, ast, $79,000
King, Gavin M, prof, asoc, $95,912
King, Gregory W, prof, asoc, $81,735

King, James David, hospital security officer, $13.20/hr
King, Karen Emily Lunn, prof, ast teach, $41,712
King, Karen Lee, program/project supprt coor I, $55,815
King, Kathryn, pharmacist III, $128,835
King, Kristin Delaney, resident physician-2nd yr, $52,007
King, Lacy C, business support specialist II, $20.02/hr
King, Laura A, prof, curators, $124,928
King, Leesa Lynn, nurse, staff II rnwp, $34.18/hr
King, Makini Lateefah, instructor, adjunct, $8,325
King, Philip W, security officer, $15.00/hr
King, Richard K, custodian, $11.41/hr
King, Ryan Matthew, student service coor II, $61,800
King, Sharon A, business support specialist II, $20.47/hr
King, Skyler, grader, $6,400
King, Suzanne M, business support specialist sr, $23.15/hr
King, Wendy C, student recruitment spclst, $14.96/hr
King, Wilma, director, $183,523
Kingsbury, Joseph S, police officer, $19.15/hr
Kingsbury, Justine Charity, office support assistant IV, $14.35/hr
Kingsley, Clint Daniel, prof, asoc clincl dept, $300,000
Kingsley, Laurie Ellen, prof, asoc teach, $66,557
Kingsley, Rebecca Lea, office support assistant IV, $13.18/hr
Kingston, Amanda Maride, resident physician-2nd yr, $52,007
Kinkade, Scott Edward, prof, asoc clincl dept, $164,383
Kinne, Whitney Elizabeth, mgr student support svcs, $46,000
Kinnear, Jason A, asoc dir program/project ops, $62,476
Kinnee, Aaron M, tutor, $15.00/hr
Kinney, Joseph P, forensic techn, $18.00/hr
Kinnison, Dana Kay, prof, asoc teach, $65,076
Kinred, David Christopher, office support assistant II, $10.24/hr
Kinser, Lisa Rhea, care team assoc-clinical, $12.32/hr
Kintner, Christine Louise, office support assistant sr, $17.43/hr
Kinworthy, James L, hospital security officer, $14.88/hr
Kinworthy, Julie Anne, coor, service, $16.30/hr
Kinworthy, Leslie Ellen, coor, service, $14.50/hr
Kinzel, Edward C, prof, ast, $80,201
Kirby, Jason Michael, pharmacy tech, $10.64/hr
Kirby, Jessica Marie, office support assistant I, $9.05/hr
Kirby, Karen A, resrch scientist/academic, $48,022
Kirby, Vicki G, library info specialist sr, $15.32/hr
Kirch-Holliday, Jean Marie, bus support specialist II, $21.11/hr
Kirchner, Jeanette M, office support assistant IV, $15.05/hr
Kirk, Harriet Louese, house manager h, $84,760
Kirk, Mark D, professor, $93,750
Kirk, Shannon Dale, academic advisor, $37,005
Kirkham, Deborah Lucille, office support assistant IV, $16.76/hr
Kirkpatrick, James Raymond, resident physician-2nd yr, $50,810
Kirkpatrick, John Carter, fire protec/equip tech III, $19.91/hr
Kirkpatrick, Kathy J, office support assistant III, $15.67/hr
Kirkpatrick, Kevin P, prof, asoc teach, $52,646
Kirkpatrick, Lauren Elizabeth, resident physician-3rd yr, $56,263
Kirkpatrick, Michael Joseph, custodian, $11.00/hr
Kirkpatrick, Windy D, business support specialist II, $16.67/hr
Kirkwood, Karen Elizabeth, director it, $94,862
Kirleis, Kristina L, pat acct rep, $14.58/hr
Kirouac-Fram, Jaclyn Heather, dir II advancement, $72,709
Kirrane, Kayla R, nurse, staff now III, $30.00/hr
Kirtley, Jacob Abbet, nurse, staff II, $20.95/hr
Kirubakaran, Silvas Jebakumar Prince, fellow, post doctoral, $43,800
Kiser, Brenna Lorraine, instructor, adjunct, $18,000
Kishi, Erin Noriko, veterinarian, residnt, $26,000
Kisra, Sood S Aman, resident physician-3rd yr, $52,470
Kissane, Betty L, office support assistant IV, $17.51/hr
Kist, Dylan James, pharmacy intern first year, $12.00/hr
Kisthardt, Mary Kay, professor, $128,100
Kitase, Yukiko, resrch scientist/academic sr, $56,000
Kitch, Evelyn Kay, pat admiss advisor, $33.06/hr
Kitchel, Tracy J, prof, asoc, $109,333
Kitchen, Charles R, event assistant I, $8.50/hr
Kitchen, Jacqueline Rhea, resident physician-4th yr, $56,225
Kite, Cora Ann, nurse, staff, $30.24/hr
Kite, Kody L, pacs technologist, $28.77/hr
Kite, Randy Eugene, patient svc rep, $14.28/hr
Kite, Terry Wayne, instructor, adjunct, $7,059
Kitson, Megan Deshay, program/project supprt coor I, $37,402
Kittaka, Mizuho, fellow, post doctoral, $38,000
Kittle, Clayton Dale, cardiovasc techn invasive, $30.36/hr
Kittle, Dian Braun, nurse, resrch, $67,811
Kittle, Penny Renee, educational pgm assistant, $10.40/hr

Kittrell, Joan Jacqualine, patient svc rep, $13.17/hr
Kiundi, Emma Ngina, certified med asst trainee, $12.22/hr
Kiviniemi-Moore, Jordan, intern, $25,500
Klaassen, Joann G, prof, asoc clincl, $61,026
Klamm, Loretta Ann Sanderson, instructor, adjunct, $22,000
Klaric, Matthew N, prof, ast resrch, $104,101
Klatt, Janice L, nurse, licensed prac, $17.65/hr
Klausner, Carla, olson professorship, $34,740
Klay, John Joseph, physical therapist, $72,315
Klearman, Kimberly Janette, mgr csm operations, $46,892
Kleen, Penny Lynn, prof, ast teach, $69,576
Kleeschulte, Cheryl S, pat acct rep, $15.90/hr
Kleffner, Kristen C, student service coor II, $45,540
Klein Trull, Meg A, prof, asoc clincl, $62,694
Klein, Brandi A, prof, ast, $61,996
Klein, Carla Trowbridge, office support assistant II, $10.25/hr
Klein, Cerry M, professor, $163,301
Klein, Erin Louise, program/project supprt coor I, $50,000
Klein, Lesa Mueller, prof, ast adjunct, $46,200
Klein, Michael S, prof, ast adjunct, $125.00/hr
Klein, Michelle Lee, office support assistant IV, $14.77/hr
Klein, Peter G, professor, $117,588
Klein, Sandra K, prof, ast adjunct, $36,640
Klein, William, prof, teach, $49,035
Kleiner, Dan L, nuclear med technl, $35.60/hr
Kleiner, Karen T, medical dosimetrist, $49.96/hr
Kleinsorge, Andrea Marie, event assistant I, $7.50/hr
Kleinsorge, David L, research specialist I, $37,792
Klekamp, Sarah Elizabeth, academic advisor, $39,145
Klem, Anna Mary, educational pgm assistant, $9.15/hr
Klem, Michelle D, 4-h spclst, $53,122
Klem, Rachel Ann, human resources assistant, $14.00/hr
Klemme, Brenda Kay, office support assistant IV, $15.50/hr
Klemme, Jeffrey P, bts carpenter, $21.71/hr
Klemmer, Lauren E, academic advisor, $52,264
Klenklen, Michelle, supv radiology, $40.75/hr
Kleopfer, Natalie Rose, advancement officer, $55,000
Klevorn, Tegan Lynnel, student service coor II, $42,723
Kleypas, Jackie Sue, instructor, clincl, $59,106
Kliethermes, Benita Esther, cancer registrar sr, $19.51/hr
Kliethermes, Matthew D, prof, asoc clincl, $67,835
Kliethermes, Paul T, business support specialist II, $16.36/hr
Klimczak, Aimee, prof, ast teach, $49,307
Kline, David D II, prof, asoc, $112,651
Kline, Janet Lee, sr dir program/project ops, $96,670
Kline, Katie Maureen, lecturer, $39,128
Klinefelter, James Whitney, emrg med techn, $13.10/hr
Kling, Nathaniel, research/lab technician sr, $15.33/hr
Klinger, David A, professor, $93,096
Klinger, Joan M, pharmacist, $104,819
Klinginsmith, Barbara A, office support assistant II, $11.04/hr
Klippel, Herman E, grounds keeper lead, $15.84/hr
Kloeppel, Garrick Joseph, food svc wrkr I, $9.60/hr
Kloeppel, Terence L, event assistant I, $7.55/hr
Kloeppel, Veronica Pilar, nurse, staff II, $21.26/hr
Klooster, Anya Dodgson, nursing ast, $12.08/hr
Klosterman, M Jean, executive assistant sr, $66,150
Klote, Allen E, facilities attd, $13.89/hr
Klote, Christopher M, anesthesia techn, $14.65/hr
Klote, Michael Anthony, instructor, adjunct, $21,000
Klott, Hillary Anne, nurse, staff II, $21.57/hr
Klotz, Daryl P, office support assistant IV, $16.11/hr
Klovstad, James David, intern, $25,500
Kludtke, Erica L, nurse, staff II, $22.67/hr
Kluever, Craig Allan, professor, $107,991
Klug, Charlene Denice, instrument techn II, $15.90/hr
Klund, Barbara D, business support specialist II, $19.78/hr
Klusmeier, Susan Marie, academic advisor, $51,750
Kluthe, Deborah E, physician ast, $98,408
Knackstedt, Keely Dawn, student support specialist II, $15.40/hr
Knadler, Jill Kristine, business support specialist II, $15.63/hr
Knapp, Benjamin O, prof, ast, $71,000
Knapp, Christina J, interior designer, $47,861
Knapp, James A, supervisor it, $50,000
Knapp, Jessica Lynne, veterinarian, residnt, $26,315
Knapp, Joshua Brandon, research/lab technician sr, $16.00/hr
Knapp, Megan Elizabeth, academic advisor, $38,213
Knapp, Patricia J, office support assistant IV, $17.12/hr
Knapp, Victoria L, editor sr, $56,517

Knaus, Abbey J, db programmer analyst-expert, $56,227
Knausenberger, Walter Ingolf H, dir II research ops and plng, $155,500
Knedlik, Lana M, counsel, $144,668
Knell, Maureen E, prof, asoc clincl, $103,000
Knell, Paul Frederick, instructor, adjunct, $2,800
Knerr, Delbert Ray, research specialist sr, $55,917
Knerr, Marilee Kae, event assistant II, $10.75/hr
Knewtson, Carly Jo, instructor, adjunct, $125.00/hr
Knierim, Tammy L, office support assistant IV, $14.48/hr
Knight, Emily Allison, academic coor, $2,400
Knight, Katherine Ruth, compliance specialist I, $17.61/hr
Knight, Korbin Nathaniel, care team assoc-suppt, $12.32/hr
Knight, Mary H, educational pgm associate I, $13.15/hr
Knipfel, Renee Marie, social worker, $56,286
Knipp, Brenda Marie, educational pgm associate I, $12.25/hr
Knipp, Lauren Leigh, hospital security officer, $10.64/hr
Knipp, Trevor Ryan, custodian, $10.00/hr
Knipping, Nancy, prof, asoc, $70,045
Knoche, Marvin L, office support assistant IV, $16.40/hr
Knoedelseder, Beth Anne, instructor, adjunct, $14,118
Knoernschild, Amy R, nurse, staff II, $27.00/hr
Knoesel, Benjamin James, high school student, $7.50/hr
Knoesel, James R, rec/athletic sports prof, $62,034
Knoesel, John Francis, high school student, $8.25/hr
Knoll, Sarah, program/project supprt coor I, $50,000
Knoll, Yasuyo M, library information assistant, $11.72/hr
Knollmeyer, Edward J, dir III business admin, $131,590
Knoop, Andrew, prof, asoc clincl, $71,729
Knoop, Marie Ann, office support assistant IV, $16.71/hr
Knopf-Amelung, Sarah, resrch asoc, $47,000
Knopf, Melissa Ann, nurse, staff I, $19.50/hr
Knopick, David A, prof, ast adjunct, $15,000
Knopp, Jerome, prof, asoc, $94,591
Knorr, Stephen C, vice president, $223,604
Knoten, Thomas P, instructor, adjunct, $13,333
Knotts, Paige Kathryn, communications assistant sr, $14.30/hr
Knox, Candy J, nurse, or/recovery-ch, $34.62/hr
Knox, Eric W, nurse, or/recovery-ch, $34.18/hr
Knox, James, steam plant opr II, $24.15/hr
Knudsen, Kathaleen Marie, phlebotomist, $10.85/hr
Knudson, Dennis K, mental health tech, $13.69/hr
Knudson, Sarah Elizabeth, nurse, staff II, $22.79/hr
Koan, Bridget Hurney, strat comm associate II, $47,000
Kobashigawa, Estela Haverstick, research specialist I, $22,075
Koblitz, Courtland W Jr, instructor, adjunct, $2,933
Koboldt, Timothy J, prof, ast clincl dept, $237,000
Koburov, George T, prof, ast clincl dept, $345,000
Koc, Ali Bulent, prof, ast, $68,638
Koc, Nazire Pinar, prof, ast teach, $47,735
Koch, Colleen Susan, administrative consultant II, $135.00/hr
Koch, Dietrich M, teaching ast, $27.00/hr
Koch, Julie Christine, student support specialist sr, $17.02/hr
Koch, Katherine Allryse, health records techn I, $9.83/hr
Koch, Matthew Joseph, stage services assistant lead, $18.12/hr
Koch, Natalie L, business support specialist II, $19.24/hr
Kochin, Frank S, dir III business admin, $109,000
Kochtanek, Thomas R, prof, asoc, $77,263
Kodali, Lavanya, prof, ast clincl dept, $178,500
Kodali, Murali Krishna, fellow, post doc clncl-yr3, $60,415
Koditschek, Theodore, professor, $72,100
Kodros, Gus J III, media producer I, $13.70/hr
Koedel, Cory R, prof, asoc, $130,000
Koehly, Ellie Diane, fellow, $50,219
Koehn, Adria Lee, office support assistant IV, $15.66/hr
Koehn, Eric C, media producer sr, $40,527
Koehn, Kristin L, prof, asoc clincl dept, $151,395
Koehn, Kristin L, physician, $100.00/hr
Koehner, Patrice A, office support assistant IV, $19.42/hr
Koeller, Kevin James, prof, ast resrch, $51,500
Koelzer, Peter J, custodian, $13.36/hr
Koen, Mary Ann, prof, ast adjunct, $56,250
Koenen, Joseph William, extns professional, $68,979
Koenig, Dianna S, educational pgm assistant, $11.87/hr
Koenig, Kelly Nicole, resident physician-2nd yr, $52,007
Koenig, Sheila D, reimbursement ast sr, $18.53/hr
Koenig, Sheryl Faye, grant writer lead, $62,424
Koenig, Susan E, dir academic compliance, $114,109
Koenigsdorf, Brian R, system support analyst-princpl, $61,764

Koerber, Kelly Marie, nurse, staff per diem, $35.00/hr
Koerber, Scott M, fellow, post doc clncl yr1, $55,804
Koerner, Patrick B, student service coor sr, $45,600
Koerper, Richard Arthur, instructor, adjunct, $1,251
Koertel, Michael A, academic advisor, $38,150
Koester, Tess Jean, pat acct rep, $14.92/hr
Koesterer, Emily, dental assistant II, $12.98/hr
Koestner, Christine Marie, nurse, staff now III, $30.00/hr
Koestner, Cynthia R, advancement associate II, $23.25/hr
Kofahl, Robert Jasen, care team assoc-suppt, $12.76/hr
Koffarnus, Nathan A, supv, food svc II-h, $39,467
Koger, Katrina, nurse, staff II, $34.18/hr
Kohl, Sara Nichole, radiologic techl, $18.59/hr
Kohler, Edward A, sterile processing tech, $18.41/hr
Kohler, James N, network engineer-speclst, $51,982
Kohler, Peter A, environmental health tech sr, $17.85/hr
Kohlhart, Julie Dawn, psychologist, $55,000
Kohli, Ritesh, fellow, post doc clncl yr1, $55,804
Kohlscheen, Patricia A, office support assistant IV, $15.95/hr
Kohnen, Patti J, office support assistant IV, $16.25/hr
Kohnle, Kendall, resrch ast, $15,600
Kohnle, Sarah Leslie, instructor, adjunct, $9,000
Kohout, Regina P, temporary clerical, $13.50/hr
Kohut, Michael Robert, prof, ast adjunct, $27,000
Koivunen, Debra G, prof, asoc, $208,409
Koldobskiy, Aleksandr, professor, $129,692
Kolgushev, Roman, db programmer analyst-entry, $19.04/hr
Kolker, Allison N, resident physician-3rd yr, $53,763
Kolker, Lila R, business support specialist II, $17.78/hr
Kolkmeier, Andrea, lecturer, $35,000
Kollenberg, Joan L, nurse, staff II rnwp, $33.83/hr
Koller, James P, prof, asoc clincl dept, $172,640
Koller, Sara Jean, hospital lab tech, $12.71/hr
Kome, Gregory A, emrg med techn paramedic, $17.84/hr
Komes, Kevin Donserm, prof, asoc clincl dept, $181,900
Konakondla, Sanjay, resident physician-3rd yr, $53,763
Konie, Jared A, resident physician-5th yr, $58,083
Konig, Peter, emeritus, $70,710
Konkle, Maureen A, prof, asoc, $65,236
Konstanzer, James A, food svc attd II-mrc, $10.71/hr
Konstanzer, Jennifer R, care team assoc-clinical, $13.60/hr
Konur, Dincer, prof, ast, $74,766
Konzal, John C, manuscript specialist, $36,351
Koo, Jeong-Kyu, prof, ast, $81,000
Koob, Kelley Renee, lecturer, $26,526
Koob, Perry B, db administrator-expert, $58,528
Koonce, Patricia C, prof, ast clincl, $5,000
Koopman, Peter J, prof, asoc clincl dept, $158,457
Koopman, Richelle Diane, prof, asoc, $156,060
Kopeikin, Sergei M, professor, $74,880
Kopeikin, Zoia, tutor, $10.25/hr
Kopetz, Patricia Bowersox, prof, teach, $131,271
Kopfle, Sue Ann, chief hr officer-umhcs, $275,441
Kopolow, Jeffrey, instructor, $52
Kopp, Kristin Leigh, prof, asoc, $67,594
Koppel, Paul, prof, ast adjunct, $12,000
Koppinger, Laura Michelle, social worker, $44,426
Koppisetti, Rama Krishna, research specialist I, $31,100
Kopriva, Noel Renee, librarian II, $46,000
Korando, Donna Kay, asoc dir program/project ops, $63,342
Korasick, Candace Anne, instructor, ast, $15,000
Korbeck, Glenn Robert, reactor operator, $26.42/hr
Korku, Velma P, care team assoc-clinical, $14.00/hr
Korn, Katrina, fellow, post doctoral, $40,000
Kornrumpf, Kyle Brett, reactor operator, $26.42/hr
Korpella, Helyn D, speech/lang pathologist, $67,765
Korschgen, Ann J, v prov enrollment mgmt, $168,231
Korsmeyer, Nikki Kay, ultrasonographer, $30.00/hr
Kort, Allison, prof, visiting, $40,000
Korte, Scott W, mgr research technical svcs, $88,668
Korthuis, Ronald J Jr, professor, $257,919
Korucuoglu, Ozlem, fellow, post doctoral, $42,000
Kos, Ryan Adam, temporary technical, $8.50/hr
Kosbar, Kurt Louis, prof, asoc, $115,272
Koscielski, Stephanie Dawn, sr dir program/project ops, $61,509
Koshoeva, Kairy, instructor, $40.00/hr
Koske, Timothy Thomas, sr ast dir studnt supprt svcs, $88,338
Koskela, Mark J, powr plnt opr lead, $31.58/hr
Kosnik, Lea-Rachel Defne, prof, asoc, $92,060

Kostal, Joshua Douglas, food svc wrkr I, $9.60/hr
Kostal, Larae, human resources specialist sr, $54,230
Kostas, Haley Janene, instructor, adjunct, $5,700
Kostina, Ekatherina Vladilenovana, office supt asst IV, $14.85/hr
Kostjerevac, Raza, mental health tech, $14.67/hr
Kosztin, Dorina C, prof, teach, $67,439
Kosztin, Ioan, professor, $86,269
Kottemann, Karl William, administrative consultant, $66,332
Kouba, Melissa Miller, prof, ast clincl dept, $163,719
Koucherik, Elena, instructor, $45,450
Koulen, Peter, professor, $308,000
Koval, Nick S, nurse anesthetist, $95.00/hr
Kovalenko, Mikhail Leonidovich, system support analyst-spec, $22.06/hr
Kovaleski, Scott D, professor, $122,689
Kovarik, Mary Cathleen, prof, asoc teach, $94,492
Kovatch, Jennifer Ann, resident physician-1st yr, $50,219
Kowalewski, Shirley A, research/lab technician sr, $19.80/hr
Kowert, Marilyn Helene, accountant sr, $49,428
Koylu, Umit O, professor, $103,844
Koza, Jakub Adam, fellow, post doctoral, $40,500
Koziol, Catherine, prof, ast adjunct, $35,400
Kracke, George R, prof, asoc, $74,226
Kraemer, Julie A, student service coor II, $40,600
Kraft, Damon, grader, $100.00/hr
Kraft, J Brooks, police officer, $18.90/hr
Kraft, Jeffrey Darren, event assistant I, $22.40/hr
Kraft, Katelyn Marie, instructor, adjunct, $17,333
Krajicek, Jennifer D, stage services assistant lead, $21.17/hr
Kralina, Linda M, instructor, adjunct, $2,000
Kramel, Sherri L, patient svc rep, $10.85/hr
Kramer, Jeffrey Alan, bldg cntrl sys techn IV, $24.15/hr
Kramer, Joanne, prof, asoc teach, $111,294
Kramer, Johanna Ingrid, prof, asoc, $63,984
Kramer, Joseph P, spectrometrist, $53,580
Kramer, Justin Michael, communications coord sr, $23.08/hr
Kramer, Kimberly Jo, coor, service, $18.35/hr
Kramer, Marvin L, prof, clincl, $96,826
Kramer, Paula Jane, nurse, staff I, $19.00/hr
Kramme, Ken, instructor, adjunct, $8,000
Krampe, Melissa Anne, nurse, staff II, $20.54/hr
Krantz, Steven R, prof, asoc, $23,308
Kraske, Kathryn McMaster, strat comm associate sr, $58,100
Kraske, Steven Douglas, prof, asoc teach, $79,000
Krasne, Darcy A, prof, ast visiting, $42,000
Kratzer, Brian W, prof, ast/profl pract, $72,474
Kratzer, Deborah Lynn, pat care ast-ophthalm, $11.67/hr
Kraus, Gail Lynn, mgr research activities, $45,600
Kraus, James Duane, ast mgr hospitality services, $41,485
Kraus, Meghan Marie, counselor, genetic, $56,610
Kraus, Michael Patrick, csm professional I, $46,622
Kraus, Robert Peter, sftware supprt analyst-expert, $22.32/hr
Krause II, William John, professor, $117,960
Krause, Anette Marie, surgical technl certified, $17.52/hr
Krause, Carolyn Kathleen, office support assistant sr, $22.51/hr
Krause, Kathy M, professor, $74,856
Krause, Matthew Philip, instructor, clincl, $10,710
Kraxberger, Lynda S, dean, asoc, $89,775
Kray, Jared Eugene, resident physician-6th yr, $60,415
Kreimid, Mosbah M, physician, $255,042
Kreisler, Donna Joyce, environmental health prof I, $41,395
Kreklow, Susan, dir sports operations, $37,408
Kreklow, Wayne, head coach, $155,000
Kremer, Gary R, dir st hist society, $145,000
Kremer, Howard L, adjunct, $15,000
Kremer, Kevin Michael, resident physician-1st yr, $50,219
Kremer, Linda M, med office assistant, $13.80/hr
Krenz, Maike, prof, ast, $89,100
Kreps, Patricia C, prof, ast adjunct, $21,944
Kresta, Laura Elizabeth, resident physician-3rd yr, $52,470
Kretzschmar, Michelle Denice, nurse, staff, $24.85/hr
Kribben, David R, mgr payroll/cntrl proc-h, $84,760
Kribben, Sarah, paramed aesthetician, $15.24/hr
Kribbs, Barbara J, office support assistant IV, $16.11/hr
Kridel, Donald J, prof, asoc, $88,018
Krieckhaus, Jonathan T, prof, asoc, $75,200
Krimmer, Kalissa Marie, temporary technical, $8.50/hr
Krishnamurthy, K, vice provost, $195,921
Kroeckel, John O, reactor operator, $26.42/hr

Krohn, Michael James Jr, instructor, adjunct, $35.00/hr
Kroll, Melody M, strat comm associate I, $49,516
Kroll, Michele M, 4-h spclst, $55,164
Kroll, Stanley R, db administrator-princpl, $86,175
Krom, Laurie Jean, prgm director, $87,360
Kroner, Crystal Lynn, educational prgm coor sr, $46,500
Kroner, Michelle M, student service coor II, $40,392
Kronk, Kristel Cherisse, speech/lang pathologist, $57,273
Krost, Nancy S, library info specialist sr, $15.81/hr
Krouse, Renee Michelle, office support assistant IV, $15.61/hr
Krstic, Megan Ashley, student recruitment spclst sr, $17.98/hr
Krtek, Kurtis W, physical therapist, $95.00/hr
Krueger, Amanda Lea, nurse, staff - in house agency, $40.00/hr
Krueger, James M, vice chancellor, $199,000
Krueger, Lavern E, instructor, adjunct, $26,265
Krueger, Whitney Lauren, social worker, $45,080
Kruessel, Marcia Rae, event assistant I, $7.50/hr
Krug, Giulianne, prof, asoc clincl, $85,021
Krug, Jeffrey, prof, ast teach, $83,528
Kruger, Caroline Denise, reimbursement ast-cert, $20.57/hr
Kruger, Michael B, dean, asoc, $129,799
Krulewich, Susanne Jean, academic advisor, $36,360
Krull, Ryan W, student support specialist I, $13.00/hr
Krumeich, Andrew W, system administrator-speclst, $49,500
Krumm, Beth, dir II advancement, $83,768
Krumme, John William, resident physician-1st yr, $49,025
Krumsiek, Rebecca Charity, sterile processing tech, $16.50/hr
Kruse Smith, Sandra L, instructor, $78,409
Kruse, Cecilia Marvlene, food svc wrkr I, $9.60/hr
Kruse, Curtis G, mech, small engine, $19.39/hr
Kruse, Lisa, business support specialist sr, $23.97/hr
Kruse, Melissa Ann, reactor specialist, $72,000
Kruse, MIchael Scott, instructor, $18,000
Kruse, Robin L, prof, asoc resrch, $100,008
Kruser, Keaton Dean, theatre ast, $10.00/hr
Krvavac, Armin, resident physician-3rd yr, $53,763
Kryah, Rachel Elizabeth, asoc dir program/project ops, $53,716
Krysa, Mitchel Stephen, instructor, adjunct, $15,000
Ku, Tabitha, resident physician-1st yr, $50,219
Kubas, Stephanie Nicole, coor, marketing, $52,000
Kubas, Thomas Anthony, research/lab technician, $13.77/hr
Kuby, Candace Ross, prof, ast, $76,447
Kucher, Anastasiia, extension asoc, $25.54/hr
Kucherovsky, Evelyn, business support specialist II, $18.37/hr
Kuchuk, Maryna Victorovna, research/lab tech sr, $17.56/hr
Kuchy, Maureen T, temporary clerical, $9.00/hr
Kudav, Siddharth, resident physician-4th yr, $55,804
Kueffer, Peter James, chemist II, $51,500
Kuehl, Peggy G, prof, asoc clincl, $100,000
Kuehner, Summer Nicole, nurse, licensed prac, $14.76/hr
Kuehnle, Jennifer F, program/project supprt coor sr, $57,587
Kuensting, Andrea Theresa, nurse, staff II, $26.67/hr
Kuensting, Laura L, prof, ast teach, $63,048
Kueny, Stacey Lynn, speech/lang pathologist, $57,272
Kuhail, MohammadAmin, prof, ast teach, $58,300
Kuhl, Chauncey G, mts/electrician, $24.13/hr
Kuhl, Erin Kathleen, nurse, staff II, $24.49/hr
Kuhlman, Dana Kay, business support specialist sr, $22.26/hr
Kuhlman, John Melville, library information assistant, $13.17/hr
Kuhn, Brian Thomas, business tech analyst-entry, $40,897
Kuhn, Erik Schreen, stage services assistant sr, $16.00/hr
Kuhnert, Mark Edward, prof, asoc teach, $83,101
Kuhrts, Elise N, nurse, staff II, $23.67/hr
Kuhrts, Eric N, hospital security officer, $12.43/hr
Kuipers, David R, prof, asoc, $145,258
Kujath, Roger Alan, custodian, $13.23/hr
Kujawa, Kathleen, rec/athletic specialist sr, $25.00/hr
Kuklenko, Nina Kosmin, central sterile assistant, $10.51/hr
Kulczycki, Judith Mary, instructor, adjunct, $7,059
Kuligowski, Craig, ast coach, $302,500
Kulikov, Sergey, resident physician-1st yr, $49,025
Kulkarni, Atul Anil, prof, ast, $124,845
Kulkarni, Gaurav Ashok, resident physician-5th yr, $58,083
Kullman, Zane Alexander, event assistant I, $9.06/hr
Kulow, Benjamin Jeffrey, resident physician-2nd yr, $50,810
Kulp, Valerie Jo, office support assistant IV, $14.43/hr
Kumanomido, Mariko Christine, lecturer, $16,800
Kumar, Anil, professor, $170,780
Kumar, Arun, prof, ast clincl dept, $209,508

Kumar, Gaurav, prof, ast clincl dept, $250,000
Kumar, Kalayarasi S, chemist I, $37,445
Kumar, Lala, extns professional, asoc, $54,182
Kumar, Nishant, prof, ast teach, $70,585
Kumar, Pragati, prof, ast clincl dept, $200,000
Kumar, Senthil Annamalai, prof, ast clincl dept, $182,590
Kumar, Senthil R, prof, ast resrch, $55,724
Kumar, Sonali Mukherjee, student support spec sr, $17.15/hr
Kumar, Vandana, prof, asoc, $99,597
Kumar, Vijay, prof, curators, $113,492
Kumar, Yolanda Izenner, tutor, $10.00/hr
Kumari, Harshita, resrch asoc, $38,314
Kumia, John K, office support assistant IV, $17.58/hr
Kummerfeld, Emily Lynn, temporary clerical, $10.50/hr
Kummerfeld, Robin, care team assoc-clinical, $14.90/hr
Kump, Jan Marie, pat acct rep, $15.25/hr
Kunkel, Malea Jan, supv radiology, $28.95/hr
Kunkel, Nancy J, student service coor II, $42,800
Kunkle, Karen, business tech analyst-expert, $50,750
Kuntz, Deborah Lynn, hospital lab tech, $17.10/hr
Kunz, Carol Isola, nurse, staff stat, $31.17/hr
Kunz, Joann Marie, instructor, clincl, $80,000
Kunza, Josephine Ann, office support assistant IV, $16.93/hr
Kuo, Carolyn Olson, mgr interior design, $71,600
Kurakula, Deepthi Christina, fellow, post doc clncl-yr2, $58,083
Kurdestany, Jamshid Moradi, fellow, post doctoral, $39,000
Kureshi, Faraz, resident physician-6th yr, $58,200
Kurlowski, Drew A, prof, ast visiting, $40,000
Kuroki, Keiichi, prof, asoc, $121,857
Kurrelmeyer, Michelle Renee, resp therapist reg, $25.00/hr
Kurter, Cihan, prof, ast, $70,000
Kurtz, Michael John, temporary crafts service, $16.50/hr
Kurtz, Patrick A, business support specialist II, $15.50/hr
Kurukulasuriya, Lilamani Rg, prof, asoc clincl dept, $156,575
Kurup, Vishal, assoc director it, $83,475
Kuruvilla, Mili, prof, ast, $81,600
Kurzejeski, Eric Walter, prgm director, $15,000
Kurzweil, Kaily Cecelia, pharmacy tech, $10.64/hr
Kuschel, Douglas M, db programmer analyst-expert, $68,823
Kusgen, Diana Rose, nurse, licensed prac, $21.13/hr
Kusgen, Samantha Leigh, radiologic techl, $20.07/hr
Kuster, Carrie Ann, nurse, staff II, $25.23/hr
Kutikkad, Geetha Vettathmangot, test engineer-expert, $52,400
Kutikkad, Kiratadas, ast reactor manager, $88,865
Kutty, Asha, instructor, $42,000
Kuuskoski, Jonathan, prof, ast teach, $43,104
Kuzvard, Tomas, head coach, $39,996
Kvapil, Audrey Lynn, business support specialist sr, $21.42/hr
Kwamin, Brittany Oluwabunmi, care team assoc-suppt, $12.14/hr
Kwan, Wing-Yin, resident physician-2nd yr, $50,810
Kwasinski, David R, resident physician-2nd yr, $52,007
Kwasniewski, Misha T, prof, ast resrch, $80,000
Kwon, Jae Wan, prof, asoc, $106,723
Kyd, Michael E, arborist, $16.62/hr
Kyd, Michael T, bldg cntrl sys techn IV, $24.15/hr
Kyle, William C Jr, professor, $153,243
Kyle, Sheryl Renee, nurse, staff II rnwp, $29.46/hr
Kyles, Robin Denise, instructor, adjunct, $4,200
Kyles, Shanta Latrice, academic advisor, $35,326
Kyupelyan, Levon, research specialist I, $19.23/hr
Kyvig, James W, operations support tech sr, $15.20/hr
La Brier, Amanda Marie, business ops associate sr, $48,428
Laakman, Anna L, research specialist sr, $61,058
Laas, Michele Gay, chief flight nurse, $77,520
Labadie, Meredith Margaret, instructor, adjunct, $7,059
Labarbera, Anthony C, coord, distribution-matls dist, $18.34/hr
Labedz, Kara Kreikemeier, mental health professional, $39,114
Labelle, John W, mts/electrician, $21.05/hr
LaBoube, Roger Allen, prof, adjunct, $36,840
LaCapra, Veronique C, strat comm consultant, $45,018
Lacarrubba, Alison M, prof, ast teach, $84,190
Lacey, Carrie Elizabeth, coor, reimbursement, $53,875
Lacey, Gary S, bldg cntrl sys tech II, $22.49/hr
Lacey, Tamara Gae, pat acct rep, $13.72/hr
Lach, Barbara Teresa, executive assistant, $21.50/hr
LaChance, Amanda G, educational pgm assistant, $10.77/hr
Lachhman, Reynald Ulysses, nurse, licensed prac, $15.36/hr
Lacity, Mary C, professor, $151,741
Lackamp, Mary Geralyn, strat comm associate II, $46,350

Lackey, William J, prof, ast teach, $43,230
Lackland, Connie Marie, nurse, staff II, $29.45/hr
Lacy, Linda, program/project supprt coor I, $37,500
Lacy, Matthew Trey, temporary clerical, $7.50/hr
Lacy, Sarah A, prof, ast, $55,000
Ladd, Megan Elizabeth, asoc dir program/project ops, $49,692
Lade, Amy, supv, acute care nursing rnwp, $32.30/hr
Ladehoff, Paul H, director, $71,445
Ladyman, Kenneth P, research specialist I, $47,000
Lafalce, Maria D, instructor, adjunct, $7,200
LaFevers, William D, prof, ast clincl, $70,000
Laffey, James M, professor, $129,755
LaFon, Janet Carol, extns professional, $68,615
Lafrenz, David E, research specialist I, $18,915
Lafrenz, Kimberly Marie, office support assistant IV, $17.85/hr
Lagares, David A, nurse, staff II rnwp, $22.44/hr
Lage, Kraig Jason, prof, ast clincl dept, $250,000
Lago, Jane H, ast dir student support svcs, $30.00/hr
Lai, Wing Cheung, research specialist I, $47,983
Lai, Yi, prof, ast resrch, $61,681
Lair, Angela Rose, business tech analyst-speclst, $57,064
Lair, Linda Marie, prof, ast clincl, $57,821
Lair, Trenton L, chiller techn III, $25.15/hr
Laird, Karen E, grader, $100.00/hr
Laity, John, prof, asoc, $88,087
Lajubutu, Oyebanjo Ayorinde, dir institutional research, $125,000
Lake, Dorothea F, emerg svcs educator, $53,820
Lake, Leanne M, business support specialist II, $18.47/hr
Lake, Stacey Marie, nurse, staff II, $22.78/hr
Lakin, Kate Elizabeth, strat comm associate I, $40,143
Lakshmanan, Manika, instructor, adjunct, $10,500
Lalli Hills, Daniel Ryan, resident physician-3rd yr, $52,470
Lam, Jinming, network engineer-entry, $40,600
Lam, Thomas Fung, research specialist sr, $62,500
Lamar, Andrew Leroy, dir II finance, $98,100
Lamartina, Joyce Ann, office support assistant IV, $20.56/hr
LaMaster, Phyllis Rene, office support assistant IV, $13.24/hr
Lamb, Heather S, prof, ast/profl pract, $64,200
Lamb, James David, office support assistant IV, $17.88/hr
Lamb, Jonathan Patrick, media production director I, $47,000
Lamb, Richard L, resp therapy techn cert, $21.70/hr
Lamb, Terri Christine, nurse, staff II, $34.18/hr
Lambdin, Aaron Spencer, emrg med techn, $11.50/hr
Lamberson, William R, professor, $125,324
Lambert, Garrett D, resident physician-1st yr, $50,219
Lambert, Jermon Rafael, floor care techn, $11.96/hr
Lambert, Kimberly Ann, student service coor II, $75,000
Lambert, Lyndia Mariette, custodian, $10.00/hr
Lambert, Megan Elise, teaching ast, $13.00/hr
Lambert, Michael H, mgr cardiology svcs, $123,402
Lambert, Michelle Desiree, research specialist I, $33,000
Lambert, Thomas Andrew, professor, $173,260
Lambert, Troy Dean, nurse, staff prn, $26.00/hr
Lambrecht, Daniel, resident physician-1st yr, $50,825
Lambrechts, Robert, instructor, adjunct, $22,500
Lambson, Steven W, librarian III, $56,717
Lamere, Kathy L, business support specialist sr, $26.52/hr
Lamers, Nellie, family fincl edu spclst, $51,274
Lami, Carol Sue, med coding spclst-certified, $23.94/hr
Lamm, Lisa A, nurse, staff, $28.57/hr
Lamme, Kaylie Elizabeth, executive assistant, $16.54/hr
Lammers, Erin Michelle, pharmacist, $119,543
Lammers, James, teaching ast, $31.80/hr
Lammers, Jerratt, athletic attd lead, $15.20/hr
Lammers, Katherine Marie, physical therapist, $67,273
Lammers, Lori A, office support assistant IV, $18.65/hr
Lammers, Mary A, house manager h, $84,291
Lammers, Mary Kathryn, nurse, licensed prac, $18.46/hr
Lammers, Robby D, office support assistant IV, $15.17/hr
Lammers, Seth T, manager it, $60,000
Lammers, Sharon Lynne, office support assistant IV, $17.22/hr
Lamond, Colleen, asoc athletic director, $92,000
Lamont, Leigh Ann, nurse, staff II, $32.12/hr
LaMoure, Kara Anne, prof, ast, $48,195
Lampe, Lori L, nurse, staff, $30.24/hr
Lampe, Melinda Diane, med techl reg, $23.11/hr
Lampe, Sara Nell, asoc dir program/project ops, $27,500
Lamphear, Laura Marie, instructor, clincl, $35,250
Lamphear, Sarah Jean, teaching ast, $13.00/hr

Lampitt, Kathleen Row, prof, asoc clincl, $53,342
Lancaster, William L Jr, stage services assistant lead, $17.92/hr
Lancaster, Eric Lee, instructor, ast, $22,215
Lancaster, Lori L, med techl reg, $29.58/hr
Lancaster, Michelle Lynn, veterinary technician sr, $18.39/hr
Lancaster, Pamela Sue, patient svc rep, $14.88/hr
Lance, Brandy Rene, nurse, staff II, $25.09/hr
Lancey, Robert W, prof, asoc clincl dept, $218,475
Land, Norman Earl Jr, professor, $84,898
Land, Jillian Lee, event assistant I, $12.00/hr
Land, Sonya Ellen, instructor, adjunct, $200
Land, Tonya Rachelle, office support assistant IV, $13.19/hr
Lande, John M, professor, $143,990
Lander, Linda Jenelle, nurse, staff II, $29.97/hr
Landers-Ochsner, Michelle Renae, office supt asst IV, $13.59/hr
Landers, Benjamin R, research specialist I, $45,003
Landers, Robert G, professor, $114,993
Landes, Judy A, instructor, adjunct, $4,200
Landess, Babs M, office support assistant IV, $13.33/hr
Landgraf, Thomas Joseph, prof, asoc clincl, $102,641
Landhuis, Louis Wayne, phys therapy ast, $24.90/hr
Landhuis, Pauline Marie, prof, ast, $68,705
Landis, Amber Elizabeth, hospital lab tech, $15.30/hr
Landor, Antoinette Marie, prof, ast, $76,000
Landreth, Michael R, bts painter, $21.71/hr
Landreth, Sara Ann, nurse, staff II, $23.33/hr
Landrum, Alice L, physician, $135,001/hr
Landrum, Donald Gene, building security spclst, $23.75/hr
Landrum, E M, bts carpenter, $21.71/hr
Landrum, Lisa Gail, office support assistant IV, $23.15/hr
Landry, Linda Calvert, nurse clinician, $72,555
Landwier, Michael James, safety comm oper, $13.48/hr
Lane, Alexander Timothy, central sterile assistant, $13.08/hr
Lane, Amber Cheyane, custodian, $10.69/hr
Lane, Carolyn, med records transcript, $16.19/hr
Lane, David B, certif pharmacy techn, $15.95/hr
Lane, Emily K, lecturer, $47,547
Lane, Jill Alene, educational pgm associate I, $14.61/hr
Lane, Kari Rae, prof, ast, $68,508
Lane, Lisa Ann, patient svc rep, $12.77/hr
Lane, Marcia K, human resources specialist I, $16.40/hr
Lane, Mary E, office support assistant II, $12.41/hr
Lane, Patrick S, instructor, adjunct, $3,200
Lane, Ralph Hill, instructor, adjunct, $7,800
Lane, Sherry Sadler, prof, ast adjunct, $8,004
Lane, Tara Jo, office support assistant IV, $15.11/hr
Lane, William A, supv housekeeping, $38,805
Laney, Tamieka Lashay, patient svc rep, $12.10/hr
Lang, Beth Ann, instructor, adjunct, $7,059
Lang, Elizabeth Christine, office support assistant I, $9.27/hr
Lang, James D, grounds keeper II, $16.07/hr
Lang, Krystal Proctor, ast dir student support svcs, $46,284
Langbart, Jamie L, office support assistant III, $17.04/hr
Langbart, Jared Ray, care team assoc-clinical, $13.06/hr
Langdon, Susan Helen, professor, $91,369
Lange-Osborn, Margaret Jean, prof, ast resrch, $60,500
Lange, Thomas W, mail carrier, $14.24/hr
Langen, Timothy C, prof, asoc, $74,990
Langeneckert, Babette C, cancer registrar sr, $22.31/hr
Langeneckert, Mark G, prof, ast teach, $54,155
Langeslag, Sandra Juliette Elisabeth, prof, ast, $70,000
Langford, Barry Robert, instructor, adjunct, $13,333
Langford, Elena Mila, care team assoc-clinical, $12.08/hr
Langford, Howard Dale, temporary technical, $30.30/hr
Langford, Lauren E, nurse, staff II, $21.68/hr
Langley, April C E, prof, asoc, $71,518
Langley, Candice Deanne, interventional technl (ir), $23.68/hr
Langlotz, Paul W, emrg med techn paramedic, $20.01/hr
Langlotz, Sheila Kaye, nurse manager, $90,780
Langrehr, Kimberly June, prof, ast, $61,200
Langston, Benjamin Robert, lecturer, $45,000
Langston, Wayne W, mechanical plant speclst, mrc, $18.09/hr
Langworthy, Mark Alan, dir III advancement, $94,319
Lanham, Caroline U B, dir I, advancement, $59,423
Lanier, John Brian, library info specialist, $13.65/hr
Lanigar, Sean E, prof, ast clincl dept, $168,000
Lankachandra, Kamani M, adjunct, $15,000
Lankachandra, Manesha, resident physician-3rd yr, $52,470
Lankerd, Adam D, nurse, licensed prac, $15.36/hr

Lankford, Deanna M, fellow, post doctoral, $37,139
Lankford, Edwin Louis, professor, $118,635
Lanman, Lorraine A, student support specialist I, $18.28/hr
Lannin, Amy Alison, director, $80,462
Lannin, John, prof, asoc, $135,738
Lansford, Blair E, nurse, staff II, $23.67/hr
Lantiainen, Satu Maarit, research specialist I, $32,033
Lantzer, Ryan F, system administrator-expert, $58,000
Lapadatescu, Martian Cezar, care team assoc-clinical, $12.32/hr
Lara, Nuria, resrch asoc, $43,911
Larbie, Andrews Kojo, mentor, $8.00/hr
Larew, Melissa C, supv matls mgmt+b, $47,116
Larimore, Erin Louise, livestock spclst, $38,917
Lark, Kylie B, office support assistant IV, $14.48/hr
Lark, Michael Anne, office support assistant II, $13.60/hr
Larkin, Lyndell Dean, community dev spclst, $51,546
Larkin, Randee R, office support assistant IV, $14.80/hr
Larm, Shanna Lee, office support assistant II, $13.00/hr
LaRocca, John David, dir II event services, $109,094
Larocca, Patricia L, nurse, staff II, $22.66/hr
Larocque-Smerdon, Laura L, med lab techn, $17.51/hr
Larocque, William J, med lab techn, $18.48/hr
LaRosa, Thomas John, instructor, adjunct, $4,035
Larrick, Lee A, programmer analyst-expert, $59,898
Larsen, Annelsbeth Trouten, bus support specialist II, $15.74/hr
Larsen, David R, professor, $73,776
Larsen, Hae-Jung, library info specialist, $12.98/hr
Larsen, Soren C, prof, asoc, $74,826
Larson, Diane Louise, nurse clinician, $72,675
Larson, Hendra Berry, event assistant I, $7.75/hr
Larson, Jossalyn Gale, library info specialist sr, $15.49/hr
Larson, Lorence W, event assistant I, $10.00/hr
Larson, Michael James, rec/athletic specialist sr, $40,000
Lary, Sherri D, office support assistant IV, $16.26/hr
Lashley, Amber Dawn, child life spclst, $43,513
Lashley, Angela G, network engineer-princpl, $68,360
Lashley, Sally Rae, nurse, or/recovery-ch, $27.39/hr
Lasker, Zammone L, office supervisor, $36,200
Lasley, Adam Thomas, landscape gardener, $14.66/hr
Lasley, Raymond Dean, research/lab technician, $11.40/hr
Lasley, Susan Lynn, mgr II business admin, $66,945
Lasley, Tyler R, research/lab technician, $14.20/hr
Lass, Daniel Lyle, theatre ast, $10.00/hr
Lass, Joseph Martin, stage services assistant lead, $16.56/hr
Lasseter, Dean B, prof, ast clincl dept, $150,000
Lasseter, Hana D, temporary crafts service, $7.50/hr
Lassiter, Lee R, mri technologist, $35.10/hr
Lasta, Lynhart Blanche, nurse clinician, $65,843
Lastra Gonzalez, Guido, prof, ast, $147,113
Laswell, Robert W, mts/pipefitter, $22.50/hr
Lathan, Jasmine Delynn, care team assoc-clinical, $12.08/hr
Latore, Theresa Marie, instructor, adjunct, $7,059
Lattimer, Jimmy Christian, prof, asoc, $125,579
Latushkin, Yuri, professor, $134,838
Latz, Jeanie Kay, instructor, adjunct, $42,000
Lau-Sieckman, Alisa Marie, nurse clinician, $35,109
Lau, Cheri Lee, patient svc rep, $14.92/hr
Lau, Rebecca Lynn, nurse clinician, $52,000
Laubert, Derick Patrick, construction manager I, $60,000
Lauchstaedt, Elizabeth Anne, student service coor sr, $57,111
Laudel, Karis Ann, clinical casework ast, $15.87/hr
Lauer Vornholt, Julie Ann, student support spec II, $18.93/hr
Laufer, Cynthia A, resrch ast, $51,150
Laughlin, Christine Lynn, dir I, university police, $92,200
Laughlin, James P, boiler maint opr, $24.13/hr
Laughlin, Maurice Harold, professor, $213,065
Laughlin, Peggy A, supv outpatient svcs, $51,298
Laughlin, Tammy Lynn, event assistant I, $7.50/hr
Laupp, Deborah June, mgr II hospitality services, $73,707
Laur, Bryce T, operations support tech II, $14.00/hr
Laurent, R Scott, prgm mgr I, studnt supprt svcs, $52,622
Laurenti, Melissa Rose, business ops associate II, $52,521
Lauriello, John, professor, $374,556
Lauriello, Naomi F, prof, ast clincl dept, $203,611
Lauritsen, Janet Lynn, professor, $120,010
Lauterbach, Joshua Alexander, lab assistant, $10.00/hr
Laux, Sharon Catherine, educational pgm manager, $74,307
Lauzier, Stephan Eugene, dir research facilities, $116,559
Lavaute, Alicia Beth, office support assistant IV, $16.20/hr

Lavelle, Ellen, prof, asoc resrch, $81,566
Lavendusky, Karen Louise, business ops associate II, $52,369
Lavigne, Eleanor T, advancement officer sr, $60,000
Lavin, Roberta Proffitt, prof, teach, $140,000
Law, Ryan H, instructor, $68,621
Lawhorn, Evelyn Champale, care team assoc-clinical, $12.32/hr
Lawhorn, Zachary Ryan, media producer sr, $39,000
Lawler, Larry L, architectural associate, $46,942
Lawless, Andrea Leigh, office support assistant IV, $15.00/hr
Lawless, Elaine, prof, curator teach, $113,292
Lawman, Eric E, research specialist I, $46,177
Lawman, Janice M, nurse, licensed prac sr rnwp, $18.57/hr
Lawrence, Alverda G, office support assistant IV, $14.66/hr
Lawrence, Ashley J, ultrasonographer, $27.80/hr
Lawrence, Brooke Ashley, office support assistant II, $11.59/hr
Lawrence, Edward C, professor, $163,559
Lawrence, Leanna Beth, prof, ast clincl, $65,000
Lawrence, Linda Sue, student support specialist sr, $23.01/hr
Lawrence, Lynne Dupont, educational pgm coor III, $59,160
Lawrence, Megan Marie, nurse, staff I, $19.00/hr
Lawrence, Shasta Brewer, office support assistant III, $11.30/hr
Lawson, Andrea L, office support assistant IV, $13.16/hr
Lawson, David Carter, ast mgr hospitality services, $42,384
Lawson, Deborah Ann, prof, asoc adjunct, $18,900
Lawson, Donna Lorraine, custodian, $12.94/hr
Lawson, Jamica Shanae, custodian, $10.00/hr
Lawson, Jennifer Nannette, nurse, staff II, $31.93/hr
Lawson, Jon, ast mgr hospitality services, $49,711
Lawson, Laura S, business ops associate I, $42,965
Lawson, Lee Ann, pharmacist II, $128,835
Lawson, Lynn C, patient svc rep, $13.83/hr
Lawson, Lynna J, specialist, $47,478
Lawson, Martin W, nurse, staff per diem, $35.00/hr
Lawson, Melissa, prof, asoc clincl dept, $139,558
Lawson, Michael William, certif pharmacy techn, $13.08/hr
Lawson, Misty Leigh, certif pharmacy techn, $12.46/hr
Lawton, Brian, lecturer sr, $30,000
Lawton, Caroline Barbara, instructor, adjunct, $3,360
Lawzano, Ryan Michael, police officer, $17.69/hr
Lay, Carol J, office support assistant II, $10.94/hr
Lay, David Edward, lecturer, $39,789
Lay, Marsha Lee, resrch asoc, $56,000
Layfield, Lester James, professor, $435,450
Layman, John F, fin and acctg analyst sr, $42,230
Layman, Timothy Joe, police sergeant, $25.18/hr
Layton, Aaron Jimail, instructor, adjunct, $4,200
Layton, Sandra F, office support assistant II, $12.03/hr
Lazarus, David M, library info spclst II, $15.32/hr
Lazzaro-Weis, Carol M, professor, $110,279
Le Tourneau, Justin John, db programmer analyst-spclst, $46,740
Le, Khang Duc, resident physician-3rd yr, $52,470
Le, My Chi Han, resident physician-6th yr, $60,415
Le, Phuong Thanh Thi, pharmacy intern third year, $15.00/hr
Le, Vy Khoi, professor, $83,858
Lea, Bih-Ru, prof, asoc, $115,547
Lea, Ronnie D, geo info system specialist, $43,528
Leach, Kristen A, fellow, post doctoral, $47,011
Leach, Stacey B, prof, ast teach, $118,320
Leach, Tab R, bldg cntrl sys techn IV, $24.15/hr
Leachman, Robert Earl, prgm director, $56,939
Leacock, Krystle A, resident physician-3rd yr, $52,470
Leaders, Dustin Anthony, phlebotomist, $10.85/hr
Leahy II, Joseph M, strat comm consultant, $46,575
Leake, Patricia Faye, office support assistant IV, $13.00/hr
Leal, Manuel Salvador, prof, asoc, $86,940
Leamon, Gerri A, boiler maint opr, $24.13/hr
Leap, Braden T, grader, $100.00/hr
Leary, Emily Vanessa, prof, ast resrch, $95,000
Leasure, Harold Stephen, operations support tech II, $17.75/hr
Leasure, Jacqueline Diane, practice manager, $75,996
Leatherman, Teresa L, business support specialist II, $21.63/hr
Leathers, Rebecca Lynn, office support assistant IV, $13.95/hr
Leaton, Larry G, mts/electrician, $21.05/hr
Leaton, Patricia, custodian, $12.94/hr
Leavitt, Patience Nicole, custodian mrc, $9.95/hr
LeBeau, Christopher, librarian IV, $78,577
Lebel, Danielle Leigh, radiologic techl, $21.32/hr
Lebens, Mary Domenica, nurse, staff per diem, $35.00/hr

LeBrell, Carrie Ann, couns hlth/welfare/wellness sr, $30.00/hr
Lecci, Stephanie Ashley, strat comm consultant, $43,500
Lederer, Jason Alan, police officer, $17.93/hr
Ledford, Donald R, support systems admin-expert, $54,496
Ledford, Julie A, educational pgm associate I, $13.45/hr
Ledoux, David R, professor, $101,534
Lee, Mark W Jr, prof, ast, $104,175
Lee, Alice Irene, office support assistant II, $13.98/hr
Lee, Alta May, security officer, $11.25/hr
Lee, Brenda L, central regstry-data coor sr, $23.58/hr
Lee, Britlyn, nurse, staff II, $20.95/hr
Lee, Bryan David, user support analyst-entry, $13.00/hr
Lee, Catherine Elizabeth, rec/athletic specialist, $13.37/hr
Lee, Charles E, surgical technl certified, $23.01/hr
Lee, Chi H, professor, $102,613
Lee, Christopher B, prof, ast teach, $63,262
Lee, Courtney Ellen, office support assistant IV, $15.00/hr
Lee, David E, custodian, $12.94/hr
Lee, David R, prof, asoc, $100,919
Lee, Debra J, library info specialist, $13.30/hr
Lee, Geongsik, temporary clerical, $13.45/hr
Lee, Hye Young, research specialist I, $40,847
Lee, Hyoung Koo, prof, asoc, $119,474
Lee, Ilhyung, professor, $135,264
Lee, Jae Cheul, physician, stu hlth, $145,311
Lee, James Chak Man, prof, asoc, $98,863
Lee, Jason B, system administrator-expert, $71,100
Lee, Jeffrey, ast mgr hospitality services, $42,077
Lee, Jejung, prof, asoc, $75,000
Lee, Jennifer Michelle, office support assistant IV, $14.30/hr
Lee, Johnishca Dazjuan, nurse, staff II rnwp, $22.26/hr
Lee, Kaitlyn McKenzie, care team assoc-clinical, $11.10/hr
Lee, Kang Jae, prof, ast teach, $65,000
Lee, Kay Sohee, dental hygienist, $28.56/hr
Lee, Kelsey, resident physician-1st yr, $49,025
Lee, Krishna Corrin, ast coach, $42,050
Lee, Kristin Cliburn, prof, ast clincl, $54,542
Lee, Mark A, specialist, $65,975
Lee, Megan Renee, research specialist I, $15,550
Lee, Pamela J, patient svc rep, $13.23/hr
Lee, Phillip Steven, pharmacist II, $128,835
Lee, Rae L, specialist, $53,297
Lee, Rayman Kwok Yeung, cook, $12.95/hr
Lee, Rebekah May, compliance manager sr, $56,925
Lee, Rhonda L, pat acct rep, $18.24/hr
Lee, Scott, prof, asoc, $59,137
Lee, Seokhyung, scholar, visiting, $16,800
Lee, Seonah, prof, ast, $72,900
Lee, Suhwon, prof, asoc teach, $59,852
Lee, SungKyoung, prof, ast, $66,300
Lee, Taekgi, scholar, visiting, $16,800
Lee, Tracy L, med distrib & supply assoc, $13.76/hr
Lee, Trenda L, coor, reimbursement, $62,642
Lee, William R, research/lab technician, $13.46/hr
Lee, Wing Mann, prof, ast clincl, $82,000
Lee, Woojin, visiting asst research prof, $41,267
Lee, Yeonkyung, temporary professional, $12.00/hr
Lee, Ying Ying, scientist, $30.00/hr
Lee, Yugyung, prof, asoc, $92,185
Leeman, Lauren Cathleen, manuscript specialist, $36,115
Leemis, Eric B, surg materials mgr, $70,799
Leeth, David Anthony, care team assoc-suppt, $12.14/hr
Leewright, Troy S, pathology asst, $99,624
Leezy, Charles F, system support analyst-expert, $23.42/hr
Lefever, Daniel David, ast coach, $70,500
LeFevre, Michael L, professor, $249,791
Leftwich, Valerie S, prof, asoc adjunct, $6,000
Legarsky, Justin J, prof, asoc, $88,037
Legg, Jeffrey Lane, contract spclst-managed care, $59,555
Lehenbauer, Dorothy Paulette, health records techn I, $11.11/hr
Lehenbauer, Kara Jo Heidbreder, office support asst IV, $14.00/hr
Lehman, Mark Alan, support systems admin-spclst, $55,325
Lehman, Merideth, care coor, journeys prgm-ch, $60,244
Lehmann, Rochelle Leigh, office support assistant I, $8.90/hr
Lehnen, Gerada Sue, business support specialist II, $20.93/hr
Lehocky, Daniel Leroy, instructor, adjunct, $31,500
Lehr-Lehnardt, Rana R, lecturer, $56,000
Leible, Jessica Ann, home hlth aide, $11.32/hr
Leibold, Kimberly, academic advisor, $35,500

Leibsle, Fred M, prof, asoc, $69,413
Leidy, Heather J, prof, ast, $99,331
Leifeld, Martin, vice chancellor, $216,500
Leigh, Morgan Brittany, research/lab technician, $11.73/hr
Leigh, Nathan D, resrch asoc, $59,627
Leighton, Caprice Leonette, sftware supprt analyst-speclst, $45,272
Leighton, Lori Ann, instructor, adjunct, $39,900
Leija, Leila Alexandria, animal caretaker, $10.78/hr
Leimkuehler, Ashley Nicole, office support asst IV, $14.00/hr
Leimkuehler, Cherie, instructor, adjunct, $14,400
Leimkuehler, Donald Glenn, care team assoc-clinical, $14.88/hr
Leinert, Shannon Marie, instructor, adjunct, $12,000
Leishman, Lisa Louise, resident physician-3rd yr, $53,763
Leisman, Jo Ann, coor, care, $72,675
Leiss, Eric E, support systems admin-expert, $65,601
Leiss, Frankie, office support assistant IV, $15.48/hr
Leiss, Hattie M, executive assistant, $19.81/hr
Leiter, Debra L, prof, ast, $55,000
Leith, Philip Gerard, system administrator-princpl, $70,166
Lekakh, Simon Naumovich, prof, resrch, $82,698
Leland, Andrew Simon, office support assistant II, $10.00/hr
Lemay, Alysha Christine, office support assistant I, $10.00/hr
Lemberger, John C, house manager h, $70,461
Lembke, Erica Suzanne, prof, asoc, $83,235
Lemme, Veronica Lynne, student recruitment spclst, $19.42/hr
Lemmitt, Kalisha Dawn, office support assistant IV, $13.17/hr
Lemon, William John, system administrator-expert, $78,764
Lemus Alarcon, Mauro Enrique, db admin-master, $109,523
Lenart, Urska, academic advisor, $36,720
Lenger, Bonita Sue, executive assistant, $52,179
Lenger, Dale Martin, agriculture supervisor, $28.99/hr
Lenon-Davis, Caitlin Arwen, office support asst IV, $15.20/hr
Lenon, Hannah E, office support assistant IV, $14.61/hr
Lenox, Mark H, lecturer, $15,000
Lenser, Jodette Clarice, academic advisor, $38,512
Lentz, Kathy Jolene, prof, ast clincl, $48,960
Lentz, Larry Wayne, tab techn III lead, $22.11/hr
Lenz, Dean, electronics technician III, $21.15/hr
Lenzenhuber, Sarah Beth, human resources spec I, $15.55/hr
Lenzini, Ronda R, business support specialist sr, $20.41/hr
Leon, Thomas James, ast athletic director, $66,950
Leonard, Donna Marie, state spclst, asoc, $83,562
Leonard, Gloria, dir III business admin, $120,000
Leonard, Gregory A, business support analyst sr, $27.58/hr
Leonard, Karen, prof, ast adjunct, $28,500
Leonard, Lynn Marie, instructor, adjunct, $8,325
Leonard, Sheila M, custodian, $12.94/hr
Leonard, Travis L, coord, distribution-matls dist, $17.95/hr
Leonardelli, Michael John, extension asoc, $40,178
Leone, Nicolas A, dir II broadcast operations, $103,500
Leone, Nicole, temporary professional, $30.00/hr
Leong, Lampo, professor, $74,858
Leonhard, Barbara H, instructor, $57,775
Leopold, Jennifer Lynn, prof, asoc, $95,678
Leopold, Lisa Ann, finl counselor(eligibility), $16.29/hr
Leppien, Parker K, media producer I, $12.98/hr
Lerch, Martha J, research/lab technician sr, $15.42/hr
Lerche, Anne Marie, mgr human res-mrc, $72,675
Lerner, David Jacob, resident physician-5th yr, $56,120
Lero, Tyler Francis, med techI reg, $22.55/hr
Leroux, Christopher L, emrg med techn paramedic, $15.61/hr
Leroux, Mark Anthony, head coach, $110,000
Leroy, Matthew John, resident physician-1st yr, $50,219
Les, Zelly, health physics technician I, $18.07/hr
Lesan, Bret L, engineer II, $64,890
Lesh, Ralph Floyd, research/lab technician II, $17.37/hr
Leshner, Glenn M, professor, $97,674
Leslie, Cecilia J, prgm mgr II studnt supprt svcs, $67,158
Leslie, Dawn Frances, office support assistant IV, $16.31/hr
Leslie, Lawrence H, custodian, $13.23/hr
Leslie, Michelle Erin, fellow, post doctoral, $36,720
Leslie, Philip A, temporary professional, $20.00/hr
Leslie, Scott N, building/mechanical maint I, $16.50/hr
Lesniak, Melissa Marie, couns hlth/welfare/wellness sr, $30.00/hr
Lessiack, Dawn R, temporary professional, $15.00/hr
Lessley, Pamela K, project manager-expert, $69,428
Lessor, Rachel E, instructor, clincl, $20,500
Lester, Ashlie Marie, prof, ast teach, $57,000
Lester, Cassandra June, mental health tech, $14.24/hr

Lester, Cheri Lynn, office support assistant IV, $16.36/hr
Lester, Deedward A, food svc wrkr I, $9.60/hr
Lester, Deirdre Maria, accountant I, $17.34/hr
Lester, Rebecca Sue, nurse, staff II, $22.56/hr
Letchworth, Shelia Marie, educational pgm assoc I, $13.45/hr
Letourneau, Stephanie Mechelle, office support asst III, $14.37/hr
Letsky, Philippa Margaret, instructor, ast, $19,035
Leu, Ming C, professor, $222,597
Leuci, Mary Simon, dean, ast, $102,520
Leuenberger, Brenda K, business ops associate sr, $52,000
Leung, Javier Alberto, educational pgm coor III, $60,750
Leung, Kit Sang, prof, ast resrch, $73,678
Leutschaft, Susan Kay, office support assistant III, $11.67/hr
Leutzinger, Rachelle A, scientific photographer, $21.20/hr
Leutzinger, William P, dir II env health and safety, $95,625
Leveke, Karin Renee, educational prgm coor sr, $56,500
Leventhal, Jacob J, founders professor, $45,099
Leventis, Nicholas, prof, curators, $104,499
Leveque, Michael R, psychologist, $40.00/hr
Lever, John R, prof, asoc, $109,615
Lever, Susan Z, prof, asoc, $77,821
Lever, Teresa Elaine, prof, ast, $86,700
Leverett, Charles Enoch, programmer analyst-speclst, $47,424
Leverett, Laura Ann, nurse, staff II, $21.58/hr
Leverette, Jonee Michelle, office support assistant IV, $13.49/hr
Levin, Brian M, head coach, $46,146
Levin, James H, ast director, $89,825
Levin, Kristen Woodstuff, instructor, adjunct, $7,059
Levin, Russella Nell, lecturer, $18,000
Levine, Alan, instructor, $31,500
Levine, Marlene Hauser, prof, ast teach, $42,000
Levins, Matthew S, business support specialist II, $16.39/hr
Levinstein, Adee, diet techn, $11.00/hr
Levit, Nancy, prof, curators, $159,650
Levsen, Emily Marie, nurse, staff II, $20.54/hr
Levsen, Janis L, technical writer-expert, $49,267
Levsen, Matthew A, dir fin mgmt svcs & assoc cfo, $176,051
Levsen, Tyler J, compliance specialist I, $15.00/hr
Levy, Gayle Annette, prof, asoc, $64,369
Levy, Mary Jean, business support specialist II, $19.16/hr
Lewis Harris, Jacquelyn A, prof, asoc, $60,166
Lewis, Cornell Edward Jr, business ops associate II, $42,840
Lewis, Robert Eric Jr, food svc wrkr I, $9.60/hr
Lewis-Jones, Ann Marie, student recruitment spclst sr, $16.54/hr
Lewis, Alexandria Monique, social worker, $44,862
Lewis, Amanda Lynn, nurse, licensed prac, $18.24/hr
Lewis, Amber Lynn, physical therapist, $56,472
Lewis, Ashley Elizabeth, instructor, adjunct, $4,200
Lewis, Blake Carlton, db administrator-expert, $72,833
Lewis, Brent J, retail sales manager, $62,399
Lewis, Christie Lynne, asoc dir program/project ops, $50,000
Lewis, Cloyd Lee, hospital security officer, $14.23/hr
Lewis, Crystal Gene, resrch asoc, $41,800
Lewis, David J, dir I, student support svcs, $65,975
Lewis, Dionne M, dir I, advancement, $61,673
Lewis, Donald Van, network engineer-princpl, $87,923
Lewis, Faith Annette, nurse, staff II rnwp, $21.26/hr
Lewis, Hershe Renee, nurse, licensed prac, $15.28/hr
Lewis, Jane Ann, med distrib & supply assoc, $13.76/hr
Lewis, Jodie L, human resources assistant, $20.89/hr
Lewis, Johnny Michael, educational pgm coor III, $6,500
Lewis, Judy Ann, instructor, adjunct, $12,000
Lewis, Julie Marie, nurse clinician, $51,882
Lewis, Justina Ruth, mgr student support svcs, $45,000
Lewis, Kay C, 4-h youth devlmnt educr, $34,128
Lewis, Keith E, office support assistant III, $11.95/hr
Lewis, Kenny Ray, bts equip opr, $20.23/hr
Lewis, Laura Ann, nurse, staff prn, $26.00/hr
Lewis, Mattie L, office support assistant III, $16.25/hr
Lewis, Miachel, bts carpenter, $21.71/hr
Lewis, Michael Robert, professor, $43,148
Lewis, Michelle Nicole, serv line spclst, $67,810
Lewis, Myron Evan, food svc wrkr I, $11.29/hr
Lewis, Nadine A, nurse, licensed prac sr, $20.77/hr
Lewis, Nathan C, stage services assistant sr, $16.00/hr
Lewis, Nicolle M, student service coor II, $41,200
Lewis, Patricia A, care team assoc-clinical, $13.33/hr
Lewis, Paul David, instructor, adjunct, $4,200
Lewis, Randall S, research engineering tech II, $20.76/hr

Lewis, Robert C, custodian, $10.69/hr
Lewis, Robert G, bts mason/tuckptr, $21.71/hr
Lewis, Sara Marie, mgr student support svcs, $44,003
Lewis, Scott Alan, tutor, $9.00/hr
Lewis, Stacey Ann, office support assistant III, $15.14/hr
Lewis, Stephanie Anne, student service coor I, $34,750
Lewis, Tameka Lavonne, care team assoc-clinical, $13.46/hr
Lewis, Timothy J, professor, $156,519
Lewis, Trudy Lynne, professor, $100,828
Lewis, Whitney Sue, strat comm associate II, $52,520
Lewyn, Michael, prof, ast visiting, $60,000
Leykamp, Rose M, business support specialist II, $18.01/hr
Li, Aigen, professor, $102,812
Li, Chunyan, resrch asoc, $53,265
Li, Feng, resrch scientist/academic, $39,557
Li, Haitao, prof, asoc, $118,038
Li, Hanbing, resrch scientist/academic, $44,562
Li, Hao, prof, asoc, $111,987
Li, Lin, fellow, post doctoral, $35,000
Li, Ling, programmer analyst-expert, $52,998
Li, Liping, fellow, post doctoral, $40,000
Li, Maoyin, prof, ast resrch, $48,812
Li, Min, prof, ast resrch, $71,776
Li, Mingshan, resrch scientist/academic, $57,762
Li, Rong, research specialist sr, $24,000
Li, Shixin, db programmer analyst-speclst, $50,597
Li, Xianghuan, db programmer analyst-speclst, $45,600
Li, Xianping, prof, ast, $62,000
Li, Xuechang, programmer analyst-expert, $66,164
Li, Yan, prof, ast teach, $38,000
Li, Yanguang, professor, $84,222
Li, Yijun, ultrasonographer, $28.00/hr
Li, Yong, resrch asoc, $30,000
Li, Yuek Yin M, office support assistant IV, $14.85/hr
Li, Zhaofeng, scholar, visiting, $27,600
Li, Zhaohui, research specialist I, $31,722
Li, Zhixuan, db programmer analyst-princpl, $69,211
Liang, Huichun, lecturer, $26,533
Liang, Shaobo, scholar, visiting, $36,000
Liang, Xinhua, prof, ast, $84,589
Liang, Yan, fellow, post doctoral, $40,816
Liang, Yayun, prof, asoc resrch, $62,190
Liao, Yu-Hsin, prof, ast teach, $59,287
Liao, Yuguo, prof, ast, $64,000
Liapis, Athanasios I, professor, $146,105
Libbus, Nicholas, cook, $13.21/hr
Libre, Nicolas Ali, scholar, visiting, $36,000
Liccione, Jamarra Lashawn, serv line spclst, $76,382
Lichtenauer, Anna Marie, research specialist sr, $39,600
Lichty, Elizabeth L, sftware supprt analyst-expert, $51,209
Licklider, Catherine Rochelle, office support asst IV, $16.92/hr
Licklider, David Robert, police officer, $19.83/hr
Licklider, Marilyn S, office support assistant IV, $13.13/hr
Licklider, Mary M, instructor, adjunct, $6,000
Lidge, Kenneth, prof, ast teach, $44,528
Lidgus, Jonathan A, dir II student support svcs, $71,078
Liesen, James G, prof, ast clincl dept, $163,026
Liesen, James G, physician, $100.00/hr
Lietzan, Erika Fisher, prof, asoc, $118,500
Lige, Tamica Lynn, office support assistant IV, $15.97/hr
Liggatt, Keanon, system administrator-entry, $48,000
Light, Carrie L, operations support tech II, $14.28/hr
Light, Dennis J, laborer II, $14.35/hr
Light, Katherine Marie, med lab techn, $16.35/hr
Light, Kenneth L, lecturer, $27,000
Light, Lisa Marie, nurse, staff II, $32.78/hr
Light, Sherri L, office support assistant IV, $15.54/hr
Lightbody, Geri L, occl therapy ast cert, $21.51/hr
Lightfoot, Jeffrey S, custodian, $12.94/hr
Lightfoot, Rhonda Stone, temporary professional, $12.00/hr
Like, Toya Z, prof, asoc, $65,661
Likhitsup, Alisa, resident physician-4th yr, $54,425
Likholetov, Vladislav A, prof, ast resrch, $74,591
Likholetova, Natalia Vladimirovna, teaching ast, $20.00/hr
Likins, Floyd Leo, instructor, resrch, $55,430
Lilienkamp, Jonathan Andrew, system administrator-spclst, $50,162
Lilienkamp, Paul L, research/lab technician sr, $16.25/hr
Liljequist, Erin M, resrch ast, $41,820
Lillebo, Troy, ast vice chancellor, $106,543

Lilley, Stephanie Lynne, nurse, staff II rnwp, $22.11/hr
Lillie, Cheryl Lee, lecturer, $41,212
Lillig, Shawn Phillip, resident physician-3rd yr, $52,470
Lilly, Angela Ann, research specialist sr, $59,050
Lilly, Angela Y, dean, ast, $91,800
Lilly, Christine Elizabeth, resident physician-1st yr, $49,025
Lilly, Megan Rena, dental assistant II, $13.76/hr
Lilyquist, Michael Bradley, resident physician-5th yr, $56,120
Lim, Hyun Jin, instructor, adjunct, $12,000
Lim, Mona Man Nor, med techl reg, $30.36/hr
Lim, Robert W, prof, asoc, $83,039
Lim, Seung Lark, prof, ast, $67,320
Lim, Teng Teeh, prof, asoc extns, $86,906
Limbach, Tammy R, office support assistant IV, $16.52/hr
Limback, Mindy Marie, asoc dir strat communications, $73,500
Limmer, Matthew A, fellow, post doctoral, $53,200
Limpic, Kelly Daun, human resources specialist sr, $48,410
Lin, Chien Fu, prof, ast adjunct, $27,000
Lin, Chung Ho, prof, ast resrch, $69,655
Lin, Dan, prof, ast, $88,082
Lin, Hongy, prof, adjunct, $20,475
Lin, Jian, prof, ast, $85,000
Lin, Jingyi, research/lab technician sr, $12.98/hr
Lin, Li, fellow, post doctoral, $44,560
Lin, Mengshi, prof, asoc, $88,913
Lin, Sz Chyuan, system administrator-speclst, $52,803
Lin, Yuyi, prof, asoc, $79,336
Lincoln, Candy Suzanne, resident physician-2nd yr, $52,007
Lincoln, Jaime L, enrollment advisor, $15.37/hr
Lincoln, Judith Ann, data cntr support tech-entry, $17.06/hr
Lind, Joshua Arron, compliance specialist II, $45,330
Lindahl, David L Jr, librarian IV, $110,000
Lindahl, Cheryl A, nurse, staff II, $33.11/hr
Lindaman, Susan F, instructor, adjunct, $39,000
Lindberg, Thomas R, network engineer-expert, $58,337
Lindbloom, Erik J, prof, asoc, $166,464
Lindeman, Barbara A, sr ast dir studnt supprt svcs, $79,812
Lindeman, Sara Ann, student service coor I, $41,500
Linden, Shelley S, office support assistant III, $13.60/hr
Lindenbaum, Sharon B, vice chancellor, $205,920
Linder, Andrea Dannielle, nurse, licensed prac, $15.94/hr
Linder, Douglas Owen, professor, $143,600
Linder, Sarah E, office support aide II, $9.52/hr
Lindholm, Lyla Jo, prof, ast clincl, $71,328
Lindner, Garth Ashley, fellow, post doctoral, $45,000
Lindner, Hillary Renee, temporary crafts service, $9.50/hr
Lindquist, Jonathan, research engineering tech I, $23.31/hr
Lindquist, Matthew Boyd, resident physician-2nd yr, $52,610
Lindquist, Patricia Darlene, bus support analyst sr, $23.98/hr
Lindsay, Doris J, nurse, staff II, $34.18/hr
Lindsay, Kirby L, building/mechanical maint I, $17.19/hr
Lindsay, Stefanie Ann, resrch ast, $30,000
Lindsey, Cameron C, professor, $123,000
Lindsey, Candace Carlette, event assistant I, $7.50/hr
Lindsey, Catherine Renee, library info specialist, $13.65/hr
Lindsey, Dee Ann, nurse, staff II, $34.71/hr
Lindsey, Juliana L, executive assistant, $20.50/hr
Lindsey, Laura Jo, strat comm associate sr, $63,630
Lindsey, Levita A, care team assoc-clinical, $14.17/hr
Lindsey, Michael John, custodian lead, $13.96/hr
Lindsey, Pamela, clinical nursing supvsr, $73,257
Lindsey, Stacey D, nurse, staff II, $31.94/hr
Linebaugh, Jeanette A, mgr outpatient clinic-ef, $95,313
Lineberry, David C, asoc dir program/project ops, $50,715
Linenfelser, Ian James, recreation spclst, therapu, $36,500
Lingard, Christopher N, specialist, $10.00/hr
Lingle, Deborah Carol, business support specialist II, $22.78/hr
Linhardt, Richard D, research activities supervisor, $37,273
Linhares, Shannon Marie, human resources spclst sr, $57,120
Linit, Marc Jeffrey, dean, asoc, $243,983
Link, Gary L, ast athletic director, $50,429
Link, Thomas Jeremiah, electronics technician II, $14.50/hr
Linn, Jacob K, ast athletic director, $57,094
Linneman, Damon Ross, reactor engineer, $49,859
Linneman, Larry W, asoc registrar, $82,007
Linneman, Natalie Rene, nurse, staff I, $19.37/hr
Linneman, Paul Kevin, nurse clinician, $84,992
Linneman, Taylor Jay, supv housekeeping, $35,706
Linsin, James R W, psychologist, $69,354

Linthacum, Michael J, nurse, licensed prac sr, $20.37/hr
Lintner, Debora Renee, educational prgm coor sr, $57,000
Linton, Carrie Lea, phlebotomist, $10.85/hr
Lintzenich, Ryan Scott, anesthesia techn, $15.37/hr
Linville, Malcolm Eugene Jr, instructor, adjunct, $8,325
Linville, Dana A, fin and acctg manager sr, $71,703
Linville, Ina Metzger, prgm director, $114,940
Linville, Michael Lynn, mgr research technical svcs, $98,083
Linwood, Kisha Marie, nurse, staff now III, $30.00/hr
Liou, FueWen Frank, professor, $149,625
Lippard, Suzanne C, library info specialist sr, $14.95/hr
Lippincott Dunn, Chelsea Lynette, educational pgm assoc I, $13.62/hr
Lippmann, Rachel D, strat comm consultant, $40,955
Lippold, Michael A, hospital security officer, $10.85/hr
Lipscomb, Delores Joanne, nurse, licensed prac, $20.67/hr
Lipscomb, Patricia Anne, pat acct rep, $14.26/hr
Liptak, Jeffrey, csm associate sr, $33.75/hr
Lipton, Emma E, prof, asoc, $66,005
Lischwe, Shannon Patricia, office support assistant III, $12.84/hr
Liscum, Emmanual III, ast vice provost, $143,111
Lising, Michael J, instructor, adjunct, $6,943
Liss, Beth Kaplan, child dev assistant, $13.52/hr
Lister, Brittany Nicole, genl stores attd, $14.14/hr
Liston, Martha, teaching ast, $11,400
Litofsky, Scott, professor, $287,900
Litt, Jeffrey Scott, prof, ast clincl dept, $380,000
Littell, Tracey Anne, coor protocol svcs, $16.22/hr
Little, Joseph D, bts locksmith, $21.71/hr
Little, Linda Mann, office support assistant IV, $14.86/hr
Little, Nancy L, pharmaceutical purchsn ast, $13.71/hr
Little, Randie Raderman, prof, resrch, $122,298
Little, Raymond D, program/project supprt coor I, $20.39/hr
Little, Tyeece E, business ops associate sr, $60,911
Littlepage, Farrah Sue, lecturer, $39,462
Littleton, Donald N, mts/electrician, $25.35/hr
Littleton, Paula Sue, mgr reim fed/state payers, $98,070
Litton, Paul J, professor, $127,560
Littrell, Rachel Lynn, fellow, post doc clncl yr1, $50.00/hr
Littrell, Rachel Lynn, fellow, post doc clncl-yr3, $60,415
Litwiller, Lauren Elizabeth, occl therapist, $53,167
Litzsinger, Lee Anne, library information assistant, $11.47/hr
Liu, Chaohui, program/project supprt coor II, $34,787
Liu, Chihsien, system administrator-expert, $77,226
Liu, Cuilan, research/lab technician, $14.82/hr
Liu, Don, prof, clinical dept, $268,195
Liu, Fang, business support specialist II, $16.23/hr
Liu, Gwo-Yuh, research specialist I, $40,902
Liu, Hongzeng, resrch asoc, $46,125
Liu, Hua, fellow, post doctoral, $39,140
Liu, Jinghua, resrch asoc, $39,385
Liu, Juan, instructor, $15,000
Liu, Kelly Hong, professor, $115,021
Liu, Kun, research specialist II, $16.54/hr
Liu, Lewis, construction manager II, $77,063
Liu, Mian, prof, curators, $116,350
Liu, Shan-Lu, prof, asoc, $116,699
Liu, Shanliang, physician, $237,991
Liu, Weijie, fellow, post doctoral, $40,706
Liu, Xiao-Ming, resrch asoc, $55,640
Liu, Xiaoqing Frank, professor, $114,478
Liu, Xin, resrch scientist/academic, $60,000
Liu, Xin, prof, ast, $78,397
Liu, Yajun, fellow, post doctoral, $38,500
Liu, Yi, resrch asoc, $38,950
Liu, Yidong, research specialist sr, $30,306
Liu, Yifei, prof, asoc, $98,000
Liu, Ying, programmer analyst-speclst, $47,499
Liu, Ying, resrch ast, $35,977
Liu, Ying, prof, ast clincl, $81,549
Liu, Ying-Hsiu, instructional designer-speclst, $57,610
Liu, Zhengbin, fellow, post doctoral, $45,000
Livengood-Clouse, Matthew Alan, instructional designer-princpl, $78,000
Livingston, Jennifer L, adjunct, $15,000
Livingston, Kimberly A, research specialist I, $40,839
Livingston, Kristi, program/project supprt coor II, $65,266
Livingston, Melissa Perry, academic advisor, $35,350
Llanos, Samuel, academic coor, $2,400
Llewellyn-Neff, Peggy Ann, event assistant I, $7.75/hr

Lloyd, David R, instructor, adjunct, $9,300
Lloyd, Ian Michael, food svc wrkr I, $9.60/hr
Lloyd, Jamie C, system administrator-speclst, $48,691
Lloyd, Jessica Ann, athletic trainer, $39,600
Lloyd, Melody J, office support assistant IV, $13.30/hr
Lloyd, Tim Steven, strat comm consultant, $47,424
Lo, Chieh Cheng, fellow, post doctoral, $24,000
Lo, Clarence Y, prof, asoc, $79,002
Lobati, Frederick Ntum, prof, ast clincl dept, $183,600
Lobati, Winifred Muyang, pharmacist II, $60.00/hr
Loberiza, Verona Ester Aza, care team assoc-clinical, $12.08/hr
Lobo, Prem, sr asoc dir business admin, $96,276
Locher, Bonnie Elizabeth, pat care techn, $11.61/hr
Lock, Lori Karen, care team assoc-clinical, $13.33/hr
Lock, Marie Helen, nurse, licensed prac sr, $22.16/hr
Lock, Sydney Alex, nurse, staff II, $21.37/hr
Lock, Thomas R, research specialist sr, $59,596
Lock, Timothy S, bts roofer, $21.71/hr
Locke, Jean R, clerk, unit, $14.88/hr
Locke, Kenneth, lecturer, $18,600
Locke, Levi Justin, strat comm associate II, $40,194
Lockett, Anissa B, strat comm associate sr, $49,889
Lockett, Heather Lynn, nurse, or/recovery-ch, $22.67/hr
Lockett, Michelle Y, custodian, $13.23/hr
Lockette, Warren, professor, $300,000
Lockhart, James O, temporary crafts service, $10.00/hr
Lockhart, Linda Susan, strat comm consultant, $52,019
Lockwood, Jason, sr manager it, $101,120
Lockwood, Katie E, project manager-princpl, $75,168
Lockwood, Kristy, instructor, adjunct, $6,300
Lockwood, Melinda Anne, executive assistant, $20.66/hr
Lockwood, Tammy Kim, patient svc rep, $14.22/hr
Lococo, Brandon Anthony, hospital security officer, $10.64/hr
Lodes, Lisa Diane, custodian, $13.23/hr
Lodge, Marjorie, student support specialist I, $12.98/hr
Lodwick, Terry Ann, event assistant I, $7.55/hr
Loeb, Joseph, resident physician-1st yr, $49,025
Loeb, Nanette P, nurse, staff II, $33.49/hr
Loehr, John Erik, prof, asoc, $148,537
Loerzel, Wendy Nicole, business support specialist II, $16.60/hr
Loesing, Cathie Shook, educational pgm coor III, $55,914
Loethen, Denise Dawn, business tech analyst-expert, $70,168
Loew, Thomas W, prof, clinical dept, $232,833
Loew, Thomas W, physician, $100.00/hr
Lofgreen, Kaj Burdge, office support assistant III, $13.77/hr
Lofgreen, Martha Ann, prof, ast clincl, $64,268
Loftin, Adam Christopher, office support assistant IV, $14.28/hr
Loftin, Brenda J, instructor, adjunct, $9,000
Loftin, Julie Baker, student support specialist II, $15.59/hr
Loftin, Richard Bowen, chancellor, $450,000
Logan-Lewis, Tania Cherea, clinical casework ast, $37,524
Logan, Anna Laurose, sales & service rep, $12.96/hr
Logan, Emily Nicole, academic advisor, $34,855
Logan, James Robert, event assistant I, $7.55/hr
Logan, Kenneth W, physicist, $167,459
Logan, Laqueisha, office support assistant III, $14.50/hr
Loggains, Britney Michelle, office support assistant I, $11.15/hr
Loggins, Louis William, temporary clerical, $8.00/hr
Loginova, Oksana, prof, asoc, $94,088
Logsdon, Lynnette Marie, clinical nursing supvsr, $73,597
Logsdon, Richard Raymond, temporary clerical, $9.00/hr
Logue, Jeannene Nicole, office support assistant IV, $17.93/hr
Logue, Richard Thomas, physician, $250.00/hr
Lohe, Katherine A, coor athletic operations, $43,900
Lohe, Mikala Rae, temporary crafts service, $8.50/hr
Lohman, Christopher Ray, strat comm consultant, $48,461
Lohmann, Mary Ellen, communications coordinator, $19.09/hr
Lohmeyer, Steve W, mts/sheet metal, $22.50/hr
Loman, Brett T, research specialist I, $31,100
Loman, Samantha Michele Donelson, care team assoc-clinical, $13.06/hr
Lomax, Tewania, academic advisor sr, $43,216
Lombardo-Muff, Maria Antoinette, nurse, licensed prac sr, $19.58/hr
Lombardo, Stephen J, professor, $102,194
Londre, Felicia, professor, $120,419
Londre, Venne R, instructor, adjunct, $14,400
Lonergan, Owen S, resident physician-2nd yr, $50,810
Long-Middleton, Matthew, media production director I, $39,600
Long-Pease, Jessica Marie, dir I, student support svcs, $63,500

Long, Adrianne, office support aide II, $10.00/hr
Long, Alexander Ross, research specialist I, $46,350
Long, Christopher Alan, event assistant I, $10.00/hr
Long, Desiree, instructor, adjunct, $15,000
Long, Elizabeth F, clerk, unit, $12.00/hr
Long, Erica Lea, academic advisor sr, $47,754
Long, Gary John, professor, $86,171
Long, James E, system administrator-princpl, $74,302
Long, Justin Matthew, custodian, $10.94/hr
Long, Kenneth Wayne, mts/pipefitter, $22.50/hr
Long, Kimm Christine, nurse, staff II rnwp, $28.08/hr
Long, Leyanna Kaye, business support specialist II, $15.29/hr
Long, Natalie Abert, resident physician-3rd yr, $56,763
Long, Suzanna K, prof, asoc, $107,004
Long, Tahna Brook, prof, ast teach, $34,680
Long, Teresa J, human resources manager sr, $62,542
Long, Theresa Marie, fellow, $21,000
Long, Tina Ann, custodian, $11.41/hr
Long, Tina Marie, resp therapist reg, $19.37/hr
Longaker, Jessica G, library info specialist sr, $16.11/hr
Longmore, Ryan Bradley, resident physician-6th yr, $58,200
Longsworth, Mary Lynn Elizabeth, office support asst I, $10.91/hr
Loos, Brad Stewart, ast coach, $160,000
Lopes, Marco Aurelio Ferreira, veterinarian, residnt, $26,315
Lopez, Curtis V, administrative consultant, $88,500
Lopez, Daniel Avin, emrg med techn paramedic, $15.44/hr
Lopez, Juan Ernesto, custodian, $12.94/hr
Lopez, Juana, educational pgm associate I, $15.58/hr
Lopez, Kristi Takeko, fellow, post doc clncl-yr3, $60,415
Lopez, Liliana, educational pgm associate I, $13.04/hr
Lopez, Maria F, staff nurse, $26.29/hr
Lopez, Micaela Francesca, hlth prgm ast, $12.50/hr
Lopez, Myra Beatriz Brittamart, strat comm associate II, $47,256
Lopez, Samantha Lene Sheets, office support assistant I, $9.50/hr
Lopez, Vanesa Crystal, phlebotomist, $11.49/hr
Lopinot, Justin R, lecturer, $9,060
Lore, Savannah Nicole, grader, $4,800
Lorenson, Tami N, student support specialist II, $18.07/hr
Lorenz-Anderson, Penny L, human resources spclst III, $51,283
Lorenz, Emily Patricia, strat comm associate I, $29,664
Lorenz, Linda Lee, student service coor II, $54,000
Lorenz, Nancy Frances Fox, resrch ast, $34,374
Lorenz, Todd E, extns professional, asoc, $61,665
Lorenzen, Carol L, professor, $92,036
Lorenzo, Delfino, resident physician-1st yr, $49,025
Lorenzo, Rachel, child dev assistant, $8.08/hr
Loring, David C, event assistant I, $8.74/hr
Lorio, Julio C, tutor, $10.00/hr
Lorraine, Lacey Dawn, office support assistant III, $12.23/hr
Lorson, Christian Lawrence, professor, $172,598
Lorson, Monique Ann, prof, asoc resrch, $61,015
Lortz, Carolee, coor, service, $14.97/hr
Lory, John A, prof, asoc extns, $97,554
Loseman, Robert Arthur Jr, mgr, sfty, telecomm & emer pre, $81,600
Loshbaugh, Alan J, media producer sr, $43,271
Loskutov, Anatoly, resident physician-1st yr, $49,025
Lotven, Jeremiah, business ops associate sr, $46,626
Loucks, Billy Joe, peoplesoft admin-princpl, $85,000
Loucks, Tonya Renee, fin and acctg analyst sr, $58,917
Lough, Tiffany Dawn, physical therapist, $35.00/hr
Loughman, Amy Dawn, dir I, advancement, $61,812
Loughrey, Thomas James, prof, asoc, $49,340
Loughridge, Shelly D, fin and acctg specialist, $15.19/hr
Louie, Alison C, prof, ast clncl, $98,525
Love, Carolyn White, occl therapist, $40,102
Love, Emily Elizabeth, program/project supprt coor II, $42,000
Love, Jacob C, media production associate, $9.00/hr
Love, Jennifer Bolinger, couns hlth/welfare/wellness sr, $30.00/hr
Love, John A, tab techn III, $21.05/hr
Lovelace, Daryl W, office support assistant III, $12.00/hr
Lovelace, Mark E, retail sales assistant sr, $16.55/hr
Lovelace, Victoria Leigh, nurse, staff prn, $26.00/hr
Lovell, Carla Jean, pat acct rep, $15.57/hr
Lovell, Jeff A, mgr II business admin, $59,371
Lovenduski, Tristan Noel, instructor, adjunct, $9,000
Lovercamp, Erica L, business support specialist sr, $20.75/hr
Lovewell, Andrew Heath, hipaa/hitech privacy spclst, $51,882
Lovitt, Brian T, resident physician-2nd yr, $50,810
Lovitt, John R, administrative consultant, $87,652

Lovstad, Jessica Nina, intern, $25,500
Low, Tanya E, grader, $52
Lowe IV, Albert J, instructor, adjunct, $15,000
Lowe, Jasmine V, patient svc rep, $11.63/hr
Lowe, Jason Eric, grounds keeper, $11.76/hr
Lowe, Jonathan Paul, student service coor II, $40,000
Lowe, Margaret Mary, media coordinator, $60,000
Lowen, Deanne Lynn, ultrasonographer, $30.71/hr
Lowenkamp, Christopher T, instructor, adjunct, $10,500
Lower, Sammy Dean, 4-h spclst, $46,965
Lowery, Paul Sr, floor maint wkr, $12.54/hr
Lowery, Lea Ann, prof, asoc clincl, $64,002
Lowery, Roy J, research specialist sr, $39,600
Lowes, Jennifer Lynn, nurse, staff II, $29.86/hr
Lowhorn, Mitchell Alan, bts carpenter, $21.71/hr
Lowrey, Julie K, office support assistant IV, $17.07/hr
Lowrey, Susan Marie, custodian, $12.94/hr
Lowry, Deborah Jane, nurse, licensed prac sr, $20.37/hr
Lowry, Karen Eileen, academic advisor, $37,213
Lowry, Krista Lea, nurse, clincl charge-rn, $34.68/hr
Lowry, Nancy, education nurse, $80,185
Loy, James, telecom tech-princpl, $23.37/hr
Loyacono, Laura Louise, prgm director, $103,000
Loyalka, Sudarshan Kumar, professor, $207,590
Loyd Minear, Karen Lee, 4-h spclst, $57,952
Loyd, Jennifer, office support assistant III, $12.82/hr
Loyd, Laci Nicole, care team assoc-clinical, $12.08/hr
Loyd, Samuel E, environmental health tech II, $15.40/hr
Loyd, Sherry J, executive assistant, $25.88/hr
Loyd, Vanessa, prof, ast teach, $66,483
Lozano, Justin D, student service coor II, $41,642
Luabeya, Ntshila Vicky, student support specialist sr, $16.78/hr
Luan, Zhijian, programmer analyst-entry, $45,806
Lubahn, Dennis Bryant, professor, $134,030
Lubischer, Kara K, community dev spclst, $50,315
Lucaci, Patrick, resident physician-4th yr, $54,425
Lucas, Carrie Ann, nurse practitioner, $82,144
Lucas, David B, security officer, $11.71/hr
Lucas, David E, nurse anesthetist, $147,900
Lucas, Elizabeth Katherine, manager it, $63,036
Lucas, Erica Ladawn, nurse, licensed prac, $17.91/hr
Lucas, Faith, fin and acctg manager, $64,020
Lucas, Gina Marie, office support assistant IV, $13.00/hr
Lucas, Karen G, resrch asoc, $62,200
Lucas, Mark L, dir II student support svcs, $115,034
Lucas, Rachel Francene, office support assistant IV, $13.25/hr
Lucas, ReNia Chrishay, office support assistant IV, $12.98/hr
Lucas, Wayne L, olson professorship, $6,453
Lucchese, Scott A, prof, ast clncl, $13,000
Lucchesi, Kathryn Renee, strat comm associate I, $35,432
Luce-Durfee, Georgia Rae, office support assistant III, $11.50/hr
Luchene, Leslie J, psychologist, $67,074
Lucht, Jill R, asoc dir program/project ops, $59,303
Luckenotte, Patricia Rose, office support assistant IV, $18.67/hr
Luckey, Evon, office support assistant IV, $15.02/hr
Lucy, Matthew C, professor, $143,630
Lucz, John Joseph, mech, auto cntrl, $21.62/hr
Ludden-Schlatter, Alicia Kathryn, res physician-2nd yr, $52,007
Ludeman, Christine Marie, business support spclst II, $17.56/hr
Ludeman, James G, building/mechanical maint I, $17.95/hr
Ludlam, Julianne Gray, prof, ast teach, $44,364
Ludlow, Douglas K, professor, $113,389
Ludwig, Bruce, construction manager II, $60,109
Ludwig, Debra L, student support specialist sr, $21.15/hr
Ludwig, Justin Ryan, police officer, $19.15/hr
Ludwig, Kyle P, pharmacist II, $128,835
Ludwig, Shannon L, pharmacist II, $100,527
Ludwig, Sydney Erin, social worker, $45,302
Luebbering, Aric Ashley, reactor operator sr, $30.26/hr
Luebbering, Brooke Nicole, nurse, staff II, $20.54/hr
Luebbert, Stephen H, emrg med techn, $11.73/hr
Luechtefeld, Donna S, office support assistant IV, $14.05/hr
Lueck, Ronald G, event assistant I, $7.62/hr
Lueckenhoff, Ryan W, research specialist sr, $39,600
Lueckenotte, Annette Marie, instructor, clncl, $77,000
Lueckenotte, Diana Kay, office support assistant IV, $17.00/hr
Lueckert, Kendra Leigh, strat comm associate II, $42,000
Lueders, Aaron Charles, strat comm consultant, $57,846
Luetkemeyer, Craig Alan, resident physician-3rd yr, $53,763

Luetkemeyer, Jamie Brianne, resident physician-3rd yr, $56,763
Luke, Christine Rose, resident physician-2nd yr, $50,810
Luker, James Matthew, business support specialist II, $15.70/hr
Lukomski, Jennifer S, advancement associate II, $20.36/hr
Luks, Christi Patton, prof, asoc teach, $88,000
Lumley, Robin Theresa, clerk, unit, $14.40/hr
Lumpkin, David Craig, research/lab technician, $10.24/hr
Lunceford, Joni Marie, nuclear med technl, $30.60/hr
Lunceford, Julie Nan, mngd care reimbursmt spclst, $63,149
Lunceford, Kevin R, supv nuclear medicine, $38.83/hr
Lund, Angela Dawn, nurse manager, $92,269
Lundberg, Alicen Dawne, office support assistant IV, $17.32/hr
Lundgren, Jennifer D, prof, asoc, $77,449
Lundstrom, Marc D, educational pgm manager, $90,573
Lundy, Jordan R, event assistant I, $13.50/hr
Lundy, Kacey E, veterinary technician sr, $16.08/hr
Lung, Heidi Kristina, adjunct, $9,000
Luntsford, Rita, reimbursement ast sr, $19.66/hr
Luo, Mao, fellow, post doctoral, $33,000
Luo, Rensheng, prof, asoc resrch, $65,130
Luo, Yuyan, prof, asoc, $72,268
Lupo, Anthony R, professor, $46,506
Luppino, Anthony J, professor, $132,900
Lusby, Crystal Lee, patient svc rep, $13.06/hr
Lusher, Steven Michael, research specialist sr, $64,686
Lusk, Susan Gail, food svc attd II-mrc, $9.62/hr
Luster-Smith, Marsha Faye, instructor, clincl, $86,000
Luster, Shatomi Nicole, family fincl edu spclst, $48,983
Luterman, Joan R, social worker, $25.00/hr
Luther, Jessica Marie, office support assistant IV, $18.67/hr
Luther, Jill Kristine, prof, ast teach, $112,000
Luther, John W, system support analyst-expert, $25.55/hr
Luther, Megan Marie, administrative consultant, $65,053
Lutz, Lacey Francis, care team assoc-clinical, $14.17/hr
Lutz, Patricia Ann, hlth prgm spclst, $17.08/hr
Lutzen, Karl F, information security officer, $76,620
Lybeck-Brown, Jennette C, asoc dir student support svcs, $95,226
Lyddon, Penny Louise, csm specialist sr, $18.87/hr
Lyddon, Terri Diane, research lab supervisor, $44,363
Lydon, John D Jr, scientist lead, $84,161
Lykins, Ronald J, prgm mgr I, studnt supprt svcs, $54,200
Lyle, Alexis Rae, nurse, staff II, $20.54/hr
Lyle, Heidi Marie, executive assistant, $21.89/hr
Lyle, Scott Allen, lecturer, $12,000
Lyles-Maqsood, Jennifer M, academic advisor, $36,906
Lyles, Carjay N, ast coach, $74,600
Lyles, Rosalind, tutor, $25.25/hr
Lyman, Barbara M, certif pharmacy techn, $18.49/hr
Lyman, Carissa Jean, human resources specialist III, $42,227
Lyman, Richard Lee, professor, $102,809
Lynch, Claudia Rene, business support specialist II, $21.50/hr
Lynch, Emily Claire, instructor, $15,000
Lynch, Gretchen M, student support specialist II, $22.61/hr
Lynch, Ivy E, temporary professional, $11.30/hr
Lynch, Jennifer Ann, police sergeant, $21.12/hr
Lynch, Jennifer Ashley, patient svc rep, $11.51/hr
Lynch, Mary Cullen, office support assistant III, $12.69/hr
Lynch, Robert Francis, fellow, post doctoral, $40,000
Lynch, Scott, chiller techn III, $25.15/hr
Lynch, Timothy Edward, prof, asoc, $92,250
Lynd, Ashley Rebecca, lecturer, $35,000
Lyne, Mona Marie, prof, asoc, $78,895
Lynem, Wendy Sue, custodian, $12.94/hr
Lynn, Becky Kaufman, prof, ast clincl dept, $182,016
Lynn, Joetta J, office support assistant IV, $16.45/hr
Lynn, Jolene J, prof, ast clincl, $83,532
Lyon IV, James F, prof, ast teach, $47,470
Lyon, Jessica Pearl, office support assistant sr, $14.95/hr
Lyon, M Boden, technology resource coor, $57,009
Lyon, Sally Beth, lecturer, $100.00/hr
Lyons, William Jackson Jr, patient svc rep, $10.64/hr
Lyons-Burney, Heather, prof, ast clincl, $98,000
Lyons, Amanda Michelle, instructor, adjunct, $14,400
Lyons, Leslie A, professor, $188,600
Lyons, Terry Dale, custodian, $10.39/hr
Lyttle, Kayson Andrew, research project analyst, $57,000
Ma, Hongbin, professor, $159,907
Ma, Li, fellow, $55,804
Ma, Lixin, prof, asoc, $96,505

Ma, Shen Ying, prof, ast, $250,000
Ma, Yinfa, prof, curator teach, $126,868
Maag, Jennifer Melynne McAfee, prof, ast clincl, $43,987
Maas, Jenny Lynn, nurse, or/recovery-ch, $23.35/hr
Maasen, Rebecca Ellen, speech/lang pathologist, $58,500
Maass, Amy A, ast mgr hospitality services, $43,973
Maassen, Marvin J, research engineering tech I, $26.10/hr
Mabary, Judith A, prof, asoc, $57,348
Mabe, Shawna Alise, nurse clinician, $57,926
Mabery, Christy N, surgical technl certified, $17.78/hr
Mabery, Kathleen J, nurse, staff II rnwp, $22.24/hr
Mabrey, Kimberly Allison Traxler, geo info system tech, $15.54/hr
Mabry, Laura Elizabeth, office support assistant III, $14.02/hr
Mabury, Amber Lynne, nurse, staff, $20.95/hr
Macan, Therese Hoff, professor, $88,455
Mace, Amy Kathleen, office support assistant III, $12.98/hr
Mace, Milissa A, custodian, $11.41/hr
Mace, Tammy Renae, office support assistant III, $14.50/hr
Mace, Zachary Gerard, nurse, staff I, rnwp, $19.00/hr
Mach, Georgia Ruth Black, prof, ast adjunct, $17,133
Machella, Kenneth Titus, mental health tech, $14.28/hr
Mack, Carolyn A, prof, ast teach, $31,416
Mack, Elisa J, custodian, $13.23/hr
Mack, Shamela Rene, pat acct rep, $15.42/hr
Mackay, Janet, business support specialist II, $18.76/hr
Mackender, Gregory Von, prof, ast teach, $46,400
MacKenzie, Jennifer J, prof, teach, $44,060
Mackey, Katelin Michelle, nurse, staff II rnwp, $20.54/hr
Mackey, Vanessa L, resrch ast, $38,684
Mackinney, Mikael Judson, resident physician-3rd yr, $52,470
Mackley, Nathan M, fin and acctg specialist, $17.46/hr
Mackley, Richard Todd, asoc dir fin and acctg, $86,520
Macklin, Nan Lynne, educational pgm associate I, $12.55/hr
Maclachlan, Lawrence D, librarian IV, $83,700
MacLeod, Kenneth G, professor, $80,660
MacMorran Maboneza, Jennifer A, couns hlth/welfare/wellness sr, $30.00/hr
MacNeill, Simon R, professor, $140,341
Macomber, Kathryn Evelyn, community dev spclst, $49,958
MacPherson, Casey Jo Magee, ast coach, $46,350
Macsithigh, Gearoid P, prof, asoc, $73,847
Maczynski, David D, sftware supprt analyst-expert, $46,284
Maddela, Surender, prof, ast resrch, $102,284
Madden, Nicholas A, resident physician-4th yr, $56,225
Maddex, Kaitlyn Nicole, nurse, staff I, $19.00/hr
Maddi, Charles V III, strat comm consultant, $21.51/hr
Maddox, Alva, resp therapist reg, $26.47/hr
Maddox, Marcy Lynn, rev cycle spclst, $62,109
Maddux, Scott D, prof, ast teach, $63,561
Maddy, Aaron C, operations support tech II, $14.18/hr
Maddy, Allen L, mgr csm operations, $52,686
Mader, Curt H, instructor, adjunct, $6,000
Madewell, Jane M, office support assistant III, $12.62/hr
Madison-Cannon, Sabrina Lynnette, prof, asoc, $80,098
Madison, Ahmed, sterile processing tech, $18.31/hr
Madison, Daniel C, resrch asoc, $61,414
Madison, Don H, prof, curators, $139,056
Madore, Lawrence Roy, emrg med techn, $13.57/hr
Madria, Ninu, research/lab technician sr, $14.00/hr
Madria, Sanjay Kumar, professor, $142,000
Madsen, Richard, prof, adjunct, $19,533
Maedgen, Shelly Lynn, student support specialist sr, $17.19/hr
Maerz, Norbert H, prof, asoc, $98,739
Maestas, Violet Anne, nurse, staff II, $27.16/hr
Magana-Zavala, Yesenia, custodian, $13.36/hr
Magana, Cinthia Ivette, custodian, $12.90/hr
Magana, Samuel, custdl suply delvry attd, $13.97/hr
Magee, Joseph David III, resrch scientist/academic, $75,168
Magee, Sheri L, nurse, staff now II, $30.00/hr
Magers, Diane Marie, business support specialist II, $17.78/hr
Maggard, Bryan S, sr asoc athletic director, $175,000
Maggard, Leilani, executive assistant, $21.71/hr
Maggard, Lindsey Ann, couns hlth/welfare/wellness sr, $30.00/hr
Magill, Justin L, environmental health tech II, $15.55/hr
Maglio, Nicholas S, temporary clerical, $11.50/hr
Magnier Demaisonneuve, Alexandre, prgm director, $73,513
Magnino, Bennett Clark, internet administrator-spclst, $20.51/hr
Magnuson, Nancy M, prof, clincl, $128,659
Magrone, Francis A Jr, manager it, $74,500

Magrone, Lyndsey M, manager it, $56,996
Maguffee, Paul Ray, counsel, $178,602
Maguffee, Sarah Ross, prof, asoc adjunct, $12,000
Maguire, Dianne S, instructor, $52
Magundho, Nellie Mildred, mental health tech, $12.70/hr
Mahala, Daniel, prof, asoc, $64,178
Mahan, Joseph Bradley, event assistant I, $9.25/hr
Mahan, Wanda N, event assistant I, $9.46/hr
Mahari, Patricia A, office support assistant III, $12.65/hr
Mahdi, Amin Omar, fellow, post doc clncl-yr2, $58,083
Maher, Cecilee Brooke, communications assistant sr, $15.05/hr
Maher, Jessica Ann, social worker, $23.03/hr
Maher, Lindell M, ast dir csm operations, $76,244
Maher, Marissa Elizabeth Neff, bus support spclst II, $17.94/hr
Maher, Mary Carol, prof, asoc teach, $77,864
Maher, Timothy M, prof, teach, $86,942
Mahler, Emily M, student service coor II, $47,895
Mahlin, Amy Christeen, nurse, staff II, $22.00/hr
Mahlin, Laurisa Cathlyn, strat comm associate II, $43,630
Mahmood, Hina, student recruitment spclst, $17.58/hr
Mahnken, Sherry L, librarian II, $42,964
Mahoney, James F Jr, instructor, adjunct, $18,000
Mahoney, Patrick B, mech/opr II, heavy equip, $22.12/hr
Mahurin, Melissa Ann, research specialist I, $37,231
Mai, Liuqing, prof, ast visiting, $72,838
Maichel, Joel Robert, tutor, $15.00/hr
Maier, Gayla D, education nurse, $75,361
Mains, Christopher Dean, custodian, $10.39/hr
Mairs, Katey Chandra, mgr III business admin, $52,400
Maitz, Charles A, prof, ast teach, $110,000
Majchrzak, Sandra S, educational pgm coor III, $56,766
Majee, Wilson, prof, ast, $74,542
Majerus, Timothy Christopher, instructor, $10,796
Major, Alma Claire, db programmer analyst-expert, $58,392
Major, Marci Lynn, prof, ast, $58,000
Major, Sarah J, enrollment advisor sr, $16.87/hr
Majors, James Raymond, event assistant I, $7.50/hr
Majors, Myles Preston, temporary professional, $9.50/hr
Majumder, Moumita, fellow, post doctoral, $40,000
Majzoub, Eric H, prof, asoc, $88,984
Makarov, Konstantin A, professor, $97,286
Makarova, Marina Alexandrovna, instructor, adjunct, $32,170
Makler, Vyacheslav Isaakovich, res physician-1st yr, $50,219
Malan, Denise N, programmer analyst-expert, $61,800
Maland, Brett M, business svcs consultant sr, $79,796
Malaney, Karla B, nurse spclst, clincl, $95,472
Malcolm, Kelly Ann, patient svc rep, $11.07/hr
Malcom, Megan Renee, academic advisor, $35,088
Maldeney, Jill Elizabeth, academic advisor sr, $47,322
Maldonado, Belinda Marie, custodian, $10.69/hr
Maledy, Grant McHenry, high school student, $10.00/hr
Maledy, Scott H, media production director II, $49,308
Malfatti, Gabrielle, director, $83,830
Malherek, Jill Suzanne, student support specialist I, $12.99/hr
Malhotra, Kunal, prof, ast clincl dept, $151,000
Malik, Janelle Pascuzzi, programmer analyst-speclst, $48,519
Malik, Mohammad Zubair, fellow, post doc clncl yr1, $55,804
Malinee, Kirsten, program/project supprt coor II, $60,544
Malinski, Cheri L, nurse, staff II rnwp, $30.96/hr
Malinski, Garrett, event assistant I, $8.50/hr
Malinski, Nathaniel, event assistant I, $8.50/hr
Malinski, Scott M, security officer, $12.71/hr
Malkin, Dena Ann, nurse, staff I, $19.00/hr
Mallams, Deanna Kay, instructor, adjunct, $4,200
Mallams, Robert D, prof, ast adjunct, $8,004
Mallare, Alfredo Garcia, custodian, $11.29/hr
Mallen, Scott M, media producer II, $17.19/hr
Mallett, Erin Marie, pharmacy intern third year, $15.00/hr
Mallick, Connie Maurine, nurse, licensed prac sr, $20.49/hr
Mallioux, Susan Lynn, library info specialist sr, $21.43/hr
Mallory, Daniel A, livestock spclst, $42,266
Mallory, Jason D, lecturer, $23,250
Mallory, John O, cook, $13.21/hr
Malloy, David Caroll, bts carpenter, $21.71/hr
Malloy, Thomas Charles, research/lab technician, $10.71/hr
Malloy, Thomas M, research/lab technician sr, $14.83/hr
Malm-Buatsi, Elizabeth Ashiokor, prof, ast, $425,000
Malm, Sheri Elaine, office support assistant IV, $16.83/hr
Malm, Thomas A, garage attendant, $13.89/hr

Malmstrom, Steven D, prof, ast adjunct, $125.00/hr
Malon, Robert Anthony, security officer, $13.61/hr
Malone, Alexis M, lab assistant, $8.08/hr
Malone, Bernard Robert, instructor, adjunct, $14,400
Malone, Ed A, prof, asoc, $70,958
Malone, Mary Susan Maupin, student support spclst sr, $20.19/hr
Malone, Phayon Gay, patient svc rep, $14.88/hr
Malone, Shana Renee, office support assistant III, $11.30/hr
Malone, William Eugene, custodian, $10.69/hr
Malone, Williard F, custodian, $13.23/hr
Maloule, Ossama, resident physician-4th yr, $54,425
Maltby, Deborah B, prof, asoc teach, $42,820
Maltsberger, Beverly Ann, extns professional, $86,418
Malugani, Izelda, grader, $52
Malwitz, Kari A, resident physician-3rd yr, $53,763
Malyn, Justin D, information security officer, $88,228
Manary, Susan Denise, nurse, staff II, $32.31/hr
Mandel, Jane Lynn, business tech analyst-expert, $58,970
Mandel, Keith E, chief clinical integration, $350,000
Mandy, David M, professor, $150,501
Manes, Kevin K, stage services assistant lead, $18.00/hr
Maness, Chad W, pharmacist II, $110,582
Manfra, Louis Paul II, prof, ast, $75,213
Manfra, Kelly Moon, nurse, staff prn, $26.00/hr
Mangano, Christopher Lee, supv support services moi, $48,457
Mangano, Emily L, business support specialist sr, $23.47/hr
Mangunta, Lakshmi, mental health tech, $14.24/hr
Manguvo, Angellar, sr prgm mgr studnt supprt svcs, $54,200
Manhas, Gurdeep Singh, resident physician-2nd yr, $52,007
Manie, Brett A, media producer II, $19.00/hr
Manier, AnneMarie Frieda, med techl reg, $21.67/hr
Manies, Shawne Marie, prof, ast teach, $63,540
Manion II, Marion William, nurse anesthetist, $147,900
Manion, Lee B, prof, ast, $63,514
Maniriques, Rafaela Maestrello, scholar, visiting, $15,600
Mankey, Erin Lynn, educational pgm assistant, $10.25/hr
Mankey, Jacalyn Margaret, office support assistant IV, $20.82/hr
Mankin, Matthew Christopher, lecturer, $29,813
Mankin, Mclpomeni, sr mgr advancement, $55,000
Manley, Robert Neal III, library info specialist, $14.50/hr
Manley, Beth, office supervisor, $42,024
Manley, Jessica, office support assistant IV, $15.20/hr
Manley, Susan Ellen, nurse, staff per diem, $35.00/hr
Manlove, Addie Lee, dental assistant I, $15.11/hr
Mann, Adam Michael, tutor, $10.00/hr
Mann, Amber Michelle, research specialist I, $36,082
Mann, Angela Lynn, food svc wrkr I, $9.60/hr
Mann, Ashley Ann, resident physician-4th yr, $54,425
Mann, Bryce Phillip, care team assoc-suppt, $12.64/hr
Mann, Carmen L, office supervisor, $54,254
Mann, Christina, mgr interior design, $67,172
Mann, Fred Anthony, professor, $124,892
Mann, James B, prof, ast teach, $63,036
Mann, Jason J, mechl plant spclst, $19.64/hr
Mann, Michael, custodian, $10.00/hr
Mann, Monica Renee, coor, service, $16.10/hr
Mannebach, Brent D, ast mgr hospitality services, $41,988
Mannebach, Kimberly Dawn, dietitian, clincl, $52,292
Mannigel, Becky J, program/project supprt coor I, $35,310
Manning, Chesly E, security sgt-h, $17.82/hr
Manning, Edwina Jean, cook mrc, $11.11/hr
Manning, Leisha R, office support assistant IV, $18.96/hr
Mannino, Tony, prof, asoc adjunct, $21,000
Mano, Haim, prof, asoc, $141,233
Manring, Noah, professor, $166,585
Manring, Reuben Denver, cook, $11.24/hr
Manrique Acevedo, Camila Margarita, prof, ast, $147,113
Mansell, Kate Bowra, temporary professional, $16.54/hr
Mansell, Susan L, house mgr h prn, $35.00/hr
Manson, Leonard H III, asoc dir program/project ops, $75,341
Manthravadi, Sashidhar, resident physician-1st yr, $49,025
Mantle, Jennifer M, office support assistant IV, $15.94/hr
Mantle, Margery Paige, care team assoc-clinical, $11.10/hr
Mantrala, Murali Krishna, professor, $285,693
Mantych, Elizabeth A, prof, ast teach, $78,621
Manuel, Ann Shenethia, asoc vice chancellor, $131,700
Manuel, Jamie Renee, temporary technical, $11.00/hr
Manuel, Theresa Ann, office support assistant III, $14.00/hr
Manzella, Abigail Genee Hughes, prof, ast visiting, $36,000

Manzo, Angelo A, prof, asoc, $55,122
Manzo, Erica France, prof, ast adjunct, $18,000
Mao, Chunfeng, resrch scientist/academic, $57,955
Mao, Jiude, resrch scientist/academic, $47,053
Mao, Limin, prof, resrch, $110,000
Mao, Yijin, fellow, post doctoral, $36,000
Mapes, Kathrine Elizabeth, reimbursement spclst, $20.06/hr
Mapes, Renee L, psychologist, $32.96/hr
Maphies, Duane Alan, farm wrkr I, $11.76/hr
Maples, Amber Rene, nurse, staff II, $20.54/hr
Mapp, Maya Telesford, prgm mgr I, studnt supprt svcs, $40,392
Maqbool, Maaz Sohail, resident physician-3rd yr, $53,763
Maras, Melissa Ann, prof, ast, $61,241
Marasigan, Joanne Abby, resident physician-1st yr, $49,025
Marberry Van Asselt, Gwendolyn Eugenia, instructor, adjunct, $37,500
March, Betty L, executive assistant, $21.44/hr
March, Chamelle Jan, nurse, advanced practice, $78,995
March, Jeffrey S, veterinary technician, $15.00/hr
March, John Zachary, director, $133,800
March, Rebecca L, nurse, staff now I, $26.00/hr
March, Sarah Marie, program/project supprt coor I, $37,434
March, Teri Michelle, nurse, licensed prac, $20.49/hr
March, Tina Lynn, custodian, $10.00/hr
March, Torie Michelle, care team assoc-clinical, $12.32/hr
Marchal, Noah Joseph, research specialist sr, $53,500
Marchand, Charles L, rec/athletic assistant, $10.00/hr
Marchbanks, Eli E, business support specialist II, $18.41/hr
Marchbanks, Suzette L, business support specialist II, $16.39/hr
Marchi, Leticia Monteiro, scholar, visiting, $15,600
Marciarille, Ann Marie, prof, asoc, $92,000
Marcks, Carter Bryson, temporary clerical, $7.50/hr
Marcos Llinas, Monica, prof, asoc teach, $43,724
Marcum, Michael Anthony, teaching ast, $13.00/hr
Marcus, Al J, administrative consultant, $80,000
Mardikes, Anastasios M, professor, $111,624
Mares, Kenneth R, resrch ast, $59,944
Mareschal, Teresa Lynn, human dev spclst, $52,155
Mareske, Richard D, prgm mgr I, studnt supprt svcs, $43,939
Mareth, Leslie Rebecca, instructor, $52
Margeson, Dyana Lyn, support systems admin-entry, $39,600
Margolies, Daniel Seth, media coordinator, $61,000
Marian, Stacy Ann, office support assistant III, $12.50/hr
Maric, Nevena, prof, ast, $68,007
Maricic, Kimberly A, prof, asoc adjunct, $15,000
Mariea, Sherry Ann, grader, $100.00/hr
Mariles, Rosalinda E, lecturer, $34,067
Marin Carlson, Amy Rose, instructor, adjunct, $31,050
Marin Ruiz, Sandra Delina, specialist, $55,000
Marinova, Detelina Christova, prof, asoc, $156,548
Marinova, Irena Ivanova, hris specialist-expert, $66,873
Maris, Ryan Lee, retail sales associate sr, $15.39/hr
Marken, Patricia A, dean, asoc, $157,500
Market, Breanna Joyce, clerk, diet, $11.47/hr
Market, Patrick S, professor, $97,355
Markie, Peter Joseph, prof, curator teach, $131,061
Markley, John G, prof, ast adjunct, $75,000
Markley, Kathleen Louise, nurse clinician, $30.29/hr
Markley, Rebecca Lee, executive assistant sr, $58,000
Markoe, Lauren E, editor II, $30,600
Markou, Stella I, prof, asoc, $55,096
Marks, Cheri L, program/project supprt coor I, $48,433
Marks, Linda R, prof, asoc clincl, $91,807
Marks, Raymond D, prof, asoc, $61,791
Markward, Martha J, instructor, adjunct, $18,000
Marler, Harold A Jr, facilities supervisor, $66,744
Marley, Keri M, tutor, $10.00/hr
Marley, Robert J, provost, $240,000
Marlin Horst, Kristen Elizabeth, finance systems spec I, $48,000
Marling, Garet Joe, instructional designer-speclst, $54,392
Marlo Daugherty, Tracy, community dev spclst, $46,965
Marlo, Alyssa Marie, office support assistant III, $13.62/hr
Marlo, Jacinta B, hospital lab tech, $14.42/hr
Marlo, Michael Robert, prof, ast, $65,856
Marlo, Todd L, veterinarian, residnt, $26,000
Marlow, Darcy Lynn, care team assoc-clinical, $12.96/hr
Marlow, Jeffrey V, surgical technl certified, $24.28/hr
Marney, Amanda Sue, extension asoc, $48,960
Marquez-Alvarez, Connie A, office support asst IV, $15.12/hr

Marquez, Stacy Jo, med office assistant, $14.55/hr
Marquez, Stephanie Nicole Coleen, lecturer, $32,130
Marquier, Janice D, nurse, licensed prac sr, $20.37/hr
Marquis, Robert J, professor, $91,030
Marr, Joel W, insulation svcs wrkr II, $20.07/hr
Marr, Matthew, resident physician-1st yr, $49,025
Marr, Shaylee Richele, ast coach, $42,450
Marra, Rose M, professor, $100,901
Marren, Karey Frances, nurse, staff II, $26.81/hr
Marrero, T R, professor, $102,448
Marriott, Kenneth E, csm associate sr, $32.06/hr
Marriott, Kevin Lee, mental health tech, $14.79/hr
Marroquin, Rafael, resident physician-4th yr, $55,804
Marroquin, Rafael, perfusionist, $122,767
Marrs, Mary Elizabeth, prof, asoc teach, $177,036
Marschall, Joseph M J Jr, research specialist sr, $45,147
Marschall, Emily Christine, instructor, adjunct, $10,500
Marsden, Michelle Louise, office support assistant IV, $16.77/hr
Marse, William A, dir I, student support svcs, $96,373
Marsh, Henry H Jr, mgr csm operations, $53,425
Marsh, Don W, media producer sr, $23.71/hr
Marsh, Larry A, student service coor II, $30,146
Marsh, Melinda A, office support assistant IV, $16.87/hr
Marshall, Alan Lee, system administrator-princpl, $89,754
Marshall, Barbara J, office support assistant IV, $17.72/hr
Marshall, Catherine A, nurse, staff, $22.60/hr
Marshall, Christine E, academic advisor, $43,725
Marshall, Herbert Lincoln, prof, visiting, $72,000
Marshall, Jennifer Bechard, nurse, staff II, $21.69/hr
Marshall, Jody M, lecturer, $100.00/hr
Marshall, John Bryson, professor, $167,627
Marshall, Julie Marie, prof, ast clincl dept, $185,000
Marshall, Karen K, library info specialist sr, $14.95/hr
Marshall, Kirsten Straub, nurse, staff II, $23.12/hr
Marshall, Lavelle J, mts/electrician, $21.05/hr
Marshall, Ronald D, csm operations coordinator, $18.57/hr
Marso, Garrett, event assistant I, $8.50/hr
Marston, Carrie Chronister, nurse, staff I, $19.00/hr
Marston, Christine Renee, bus support specialist II, $21.57/hr
Marszalek, Christine Susan, instructor, adjunct, $16,650
Marszalek, Deborah Kay, instructor, adjunct, $12,600
Marszalek, Jacob M, prof, asoc, $64,675
Marte, Ricardo, prof, ast teach, $45,788
Marteen, Clara A, custodian, $12.94/hr
Marteen, Delline Louise, patient svc rep, $12.94/hr
Martel, Paulette Janice, nurse clinician, $71,468
Martellaro, John August, 4-h youth devlmnt educr, $32,240
Martellaro, John P, asoc dir strat communications, $86,700
Martens, Amy Michelle, mammography technl, $30.97/hr
Martens, Brad Joseph, practice manager, $96,773
Martens, Brad M, academic advisor, $43,350
Martens, Matthew P, professor, $169,004
Martensen, Stephanie W, couns hlth/welfare/wellness, $43,000
Martie-Moss, Roberta Jacklyn, food svc wrkr III, $13.21/hr
Martin II, Sterling B, head coach, $45,170
Martin, William Arthur III, operations support tech II, $15.49/hr
Martin Kratzer, Renee Ann, instructor, adjunct, $12,000
Martin-Anderson, Sarah Marie, prof, ast, $88,000
Martin, Aaron James, farm wrkr I, $10.78/hr
Martin, Adam Lee, research specialist sr, $43,583
Martin, Alison Tharp, mgr II student support svcs, $58,515
Martin, Amber Laine, executive assistant, $16.54/hr
Martin, Amy Elizabeth, office support assistant III, $11.30/hr
Martin, Andrea L, resident physician-1st yr, $50,219
Martin, Angela Camille, central regstry-data coor sr, $23.47/hr
Martin, April D, nurse, staff II, $34.18/hr
Martin, Barbara J, mri technologist, $38.62/hr
Martin, Belinda Elaine, instructor, clincl, $14,000
Martin, Brittany Michelle, food svc wrkr I, $9.60/hr
Martin, Carla, office support assistant IV, $14.30/hr
Martin, Carol Ann, student service coor sr, $55,640
Martin, Carolyn Nichole, instructor, clincl, $72,000
Martin, Cheryle L, 4-h youth devlmnt educr, $34,128
Martin, Clancy William, professor, $94,854
Martin, Connie S, nurse, licensed prac, $17.92/hr
Martin, Craig Joseph, prof, ast adjunct, $18,000
Martin, Dana Elizabeth, prof, ast teach, $73,315
Martin, Danae Michele, patient svc rep, $11.50/hr
Martin, Darren W, press III, $20.77/hr

Martin, David William, editor II, $46,000
Martin, Deirdre Lynn, educational pgm assistant, $10.50/hr
Martin, Dustin Lee, care team assoc-suppt, $13.12/hr
Martin, Elaine A, business support analyst sr, $21.42/hr
Martin, Eric D, care team assoc-clinical, $14.88/hr
Martin, Frances C, human resources specialist I, $18.55/hr
Martin, Gregg Dale, prof, asoc teach, $72,442
Martin, Gregory Cortez, student service coor II, $51,252
Martin, Holly Ann, supv pat accts-up, $52,391
Martin, Jason Matthews, prof, ast, $52,000
Martin, Jerry D, nurse anesthetist, $165,000
Martin, Jessica Lauren, reimbursement spclst, $21.07/hr
Martin, Karen R, dental assistant II, $16.09/hr
Martin, Kari Lyn, prof, ast clincl dept, $185,000
Martin, Kathryn Anne, pharmacy tech, $10.64/hr
Martin, Kelley Kammeyer, library specialist, $33,825
Martin, Kimberly Danielle, retail sales associate sr, $15.00/hr
Martin, Kyle Christine, coor, reimbursement, $51,750
Martin, Logan H, steam plant opr II, $24.15/hr
Martin, Lori M, user support analyst-specist, $18.90/hr
Martin, Marcia K, office support assistant III, $14.36/hr
Martin, Marian Winifred, instructor, adjunct, $6,667
Martin, Mark E, prof, asoc, $100,660
Martin, Mary Jane, nurse, licensed prac sr now, $20.00/hr
Martin, Matthew B, research specialist sr, $52,871
Martin, Megan L, human resources specialist III, $54,034
Martin, Melanie Lynn, care team assoc-suppt, $13.37/hr
Martin, Michael S, press II, $17.78/hr
Martin, Nina Skye, temporary technical, $8.50/hr
Martin, Orrena L, custodian, $12.94/hr
Martin, Paul R, csm associate III, $24.78/hr
Martin, Rankin F, research/lab technician sr, $19.05/hr
Martin, Rebecca Elizabeth, reimbursement ast-cert, $18.41/hr
Martin, Rebecca Lynn, nurse, clincl charge-rn, $34.18/hr
Martin, Robert Earl, technical trainer-expert, $55,571
Martin, Robyn Marie, instructor, $55,000
Martin, Ruth Ann Marie, research/lab technician, $12.98/hr
Martin, Sandra Jean, office support assistant III, $13.04/hr
Martin, Shannon Lea, office support assistant III, $11.61/hr
Martin, Shawn T, research/lab technician, $11.75/hr
Martin, Shelli Lynn, reimbursement consultant, $60,000
Martin, Sherry L, care team assoc-clinical, $14.88/hr
Martin, Stephen D, programmer analyst-entry, $49,424
Martin, Susan L, coor, qlty assess/improv, $58,000
Martin, Tammy Jeanette, office support assistant IV, $17.12/hr
Martin, Tammy Lynn, care coordinator, $64,260
Martin, Tenille Rose, office support assistant IV, $16.67/hr
Martin, Thomas A, prof, clincl, $117,523
Martin, Tonia Nicole, clinical nursing supvsr, $70,663
Martin, Virginia Lea, office support assistant III, $12.63/hr
Martin, William D, mgr III business admin, $80,439
Martin, William Henry, delivery attd, libry, $11.76/hr
Martin, William M, nuclear med technl, $35.29/hr
Martinez Esteban, Noelia, instructor, ast, $38,071
Martinez-Castilla, Domingo A, resrch asoc, $58,008
Martinez-Lemus, Luis Arturo, prof, asoc, $99,637
Martinez, Anthony Michael, temporary crafts service, $7.50/hr
Martinez, Danielle Elizabeth, executive assistant, $19.23/hr
Martinez, Gerardo Raul, resrch ast, $45,000
Martinez, Heather Lael, nurse, staff prn, $26.00/hr
Martinez, Karla, executive assistant, $18.50/hr
Martinez, Leanndra Nicole, instructor, adjunct, $4,200
Martinez, Matthew Casey, resident physician-4th yr, $55,804
Martinez, Norma Camarena, custodian, $12.94/hr
Martinez, Orlando, custodian, $13.96/hr
Martinez, Rebecca Gilda, prof, ast, $61,840
Martinez, Sebastian, temporary crafts service, $7.50/hr
Martinez, Viviana Maribel, dental assistant II, $13.17/hr
Martinez, Wendi Marie, patient svc rep, $12.76/hr
Martinich, Joseph S, founders professor, $28,364
Martino, John Michael, resident physician-3rd yr, $53,763
Martino, Tracy McWhorter, physician ast, $92,700
Marty, Carmen Renee, strat comm consultant, $53,344
Martz, Nola Beth, instructor, adjunct, $12,000
Marulanda, Angela M, high school student, $8.00/hr
Marulanda, Jaime Mauricio, veterinary technician sr, $15.84/hr
Maruniak, Joel, prof, asoc, $79,023
Marushak, Sheila Kay, sr dir program/project ops, $80,000
Marvin, Charles W, prof, ast teach, $34,700

Marx, Celeste S, asoc dir advancement, $62,930
Marx, Deanna G, student service coor sr, $62,424
Marx, Kenna Elise, pharmacy intern third year, $15.00/hr
Maschmann, Matthew R, prof, ast, $86,700
Maseles, Judy Siebert, librarian IV, $75,883
Mash, Debra A, fin and acctg analyst sr, $47,947
Mashhoon, Bahram, professor, $96,348
Masih, Susan T, health physicist, $70,707
Maslar, Cheryl Lynn, temporary crafts service, $9.50/hr
Maslar, David A, prof, ast visiting, $110,000
Mason, April Nicole, student support specialist sr, $18.50/hr
Mason, Debra L, prof, profl practice, $128,494
Mason, Gina Marie, program/project supprt coor I, $46,690
Mason, Howard L, resrch asoc, $84,642
Mason, Kathleen J, nurse, staff II, $34.18/hr
Mason, Larry K, food svc wrkr IV, $12.19/hr
Mason, Minda Corinne, dir II advancement, $83,640
Mason, Vivian Joyce, extns professional, asoc, $60,891
Masseau, Isabelle, prof, ast teach, $110,849
Massey, Adam Chase, resident physician-2nd yr, $52,007
Massey, David G, research specialist I, $39,629
Massey, Jane Ellen, patient svc rep, $12.93/hr
Massey, Judith Lee, coor reg affs qual imprv safty, $73,351
Massey, Merriam Maria, student support specialist I, $15.50/hr
Massey, Raymond E, prof, extns, $105,196
Massey, Vera Lee, extns professional, $85,571
Massie, Matt D, research specialist ast, $51,718
Massman, Steve J, system administrator-princpl, $66,728
Massman, Valerie Jo, nurse, staff, $28.65/hr
Masson, Jill P, executive assistant sr, $56,650
Mast, Audrey M, lecturer, $9,000
Mastain-Hausman, Raigan Elizabeth, patient svc rep, $11.28/hr
Masten, John T, user support analyst-specist, $16.24/hr
Masters, Brandon J, ast coach, $38,760
Masters, Glenda L, data cntr support tech-expert, $20.95/hr
Masters, Joan P, student service coor sr, $53,043
Masters, Leslie R, food svc wrkr II, $11.83/hr
Masters, Lindsay Meredith, nurse, staff prn, $26.00/hr
Masud, Jahangir, fellow, post doctoral, $29,289
Matchefts, Samantha Mae, sr ast dir studnt supprt svcs, $72,831
Materer, Timothy John, emeritus, $15,000
Mathai, Cherian Joseph, resrch scientist/academic, $70,000
Matheny, Lila Kay, patient svc rep, $13.74/hr
Matheny, Pamela M, mgr II business admin, $63,364
Mathes, Stacey L, animal techn, ast lab, $13.89/hr
Mathes, Zachary A, research specialist I, $40,002
Mathew, Nithin, fellow, post doctoral, $49,003
Mathews, Cynthia Sue, med techl reg, $25.93/hr
Mathews, Eric Wade, grounds keeper, $12.23/hr
Mathews, Jason Stephen, office support assistant I, $9.05/hr
Mathews, Melisa Jo, coor, service, $16.03/hr
Mathews, Michelle C, prof, ast teach, $65,000
Mathews, Patricia Christine, office support asst IV, $15.43/hr
Mathews, R Blake, admiss liaison-mrc (rn), $60,777
Mathis, Kaitlin Marie, nurse, staff II rnwp, $21.37/hr
Mathis, Sarah K, office support assistant III, $11.53/hr
Mathis, Susan M, prof, ast adjunct, $31,500
Mathis, Taylor Caine, emrg med techn, $11.84/hr
Matisziw, Timothy C, prof, asoc, $83,963
Matlock, Edie M, reimbursement consultant, $50,007
Matlock, Joni Lynn, office support assistant III, $11.48/hr
Matlock, Tammie Lee, office support assistant III, $11.30/hr
Matney, Devin Lee, high school student, $7.65/hr
Matney, Staci Leree, business support specialist sr, $21.15/hr
Matney, Troy A, office support assistant III, $11.81/hr
Matney, Virginia L, event assistant I, $7.55/hr
Matott, Michael P, fellow, post doctoral, $40,444
Matson, Larry D Jr, mech trades spclst (mts), $24.45/hr
Matson, Sharon L, office support associate, $18.92/hr
Matsui, Fumihiro, fellow, post doctoral, $40,000
Matter, Molly Catherine, nurse, staff prn, $26.00/hr
Mattes, Armin, scholar, visiting, $53,333
Matteson-Kome, Michelle Leigh, nurse, advanced pract, $75,937
Matteson, Jeremy W, system administrator-expert, $58,219
Matthew, Sandra Kay, executive assistant, $65,500
Matthews, Bertt M, dir comp serv-umhc, $116,733
Matthews, Charles C, resrch scientist/academic, $48,490
Matthews, Clinton F, prgm director, ast, $60,000
Matthews, Heather L, physician ast, $93,811

Matthews, Joy Wylie, prof, asoc clincl, $105,694
Matthews, Julie K, research specialist II, $35,088
Matthews, Kimberly Malinda, nurse practitioner, $82,969
Mattingly, Joseph R Jr, prof, ast teach, $68,563
Mattingly, Jennifer Leigh, research specialist I, $32,640
Mattson, Laurie Joann, care team assoc-clinical, $12.32/hr
Mattson, Randy A, supv pharmacy, $128,835
Matturro Morgan, Mary Ann, mgr III business admin, $74,308
Matulewski Phipps, Teresa, system support analyst-expert, $22.60/hr
Matz, Scott Thomas, resident physician-5th yr, $58,083
Mauck, Nathan A, prof, ast, $151,983
Mauldin, Elaine G, prof, asoc, $195,014
Mauler, Daniela Alice, instructor, clincl, $102,000
Maulik, Dev, professor, $75,750
Maupin, Cathy A, dir I, business admin, $87,192
Maupin, Misty Dawn, nurse, licensed prac, $16.86/hr
Maurel, Delphine, fellow, post doctoral, $39,270
Maurer, Alexandra Helene, office support assistant II, $11.03/hr
Maurer, Brian David, prof, ast teach, $35,350
Maurer, Kathleen Ann, office support assistant IV, $13.91/hr
Maurer, Sha'Day Lachell, food svc wrkr II, $10.10/hr
Mauzey, Kyle, office support assistant III, $14.85/hr
Mavrakis, Nora Regeb Halim, teaching ast, $13.00/hr
Mawhinney, Thomas Patrick, professor, $143,059
Mawson, Ashley Nicole, nurse, staff II, $21.67/hr
Maxey, Robert Wayne, health physics technician II, $20.65/hr
Maxville, Hannah Marie, certified med asst, $12.83/hr
Maxwell, Heather J, animal techn, $14.33/hr
Maxwell, Jordan Nicole, research specialist I, $33,660
Maxwell, M Kirt, coor, reg affrs, qlty & infrmt, $75,555
Maxwell, Mary Frances, office support assistant IV, $17.84/hr
Maxwell, Monty Lee, temporary crafts service, $8.50/hr
Maxwell, Nancy J, office support assistant III, $13.50/hr
Maxwell, Peter E, business svcs consultant, $49,820
May, Charles Andrew, dir II student support svcs, $106,929
May, Frank, investigator, resrch, $22.00/hr
May, Jennifer Pratt, administrative consultant II, $91,800
May, Lisa Ann, food svc wrkr II, $11.07/hr
May, Lisa Nicole, educational pgm associate I, $13.37/hr
May, Regina A, exec ast to gen offcr, $87,817
Maybell, Timothy Wayne, police sergeant, $19.66/hr
Mayberry, Holly A, hospital lab tech, $13.10/hr
Mayberry, Melissa Ann, neurodiagnostic tech (non-reg), $27.00/hr
Mayen Green, Denise Lia, mobile mammograph techl, $21.36/hr
Mayer, Joy Mathis, prof, asoc profl practice, $66,993
Mayer, Melissa A, office support assistant IV, $12.98/hr
Mayer, Nancy Denise, prof, asoc teach, $40,401
Mayer, Warren E, internet administrator-princpl, $27.42/hr
Mayes, Kari Jo, office support assistant IV, $14.77/hr
Mayes, Latisha Terrase, executive assistant, $20.03/hr
Mayfield, Cori Ann, library info specialist, $12.98/hr
Mayfield, Jessica Lynne, spvsr, rev mgmt, $62,345
Mayfield, Julie Lynn, operations support tech sr, $13.21/hr
Mayfield, Wayne Andrew, resrch asoc, $65,545
Mayhan, Bryan D, resrch asoc, $63,377
Mayhan, Maggie E, research specialist sr, $39,600
Mayhan, William Francis, instructor, adjunct, $27,000
Mayhew, Beth Suzanne, office support assistant IV, $19.37/hr
Maynard, Deanna Kay Stokes, educational prgm coor sr, $56,500
Mayo II, Robert J, administrative consultant, $66,720
Mayo, Jean, office support assistant III, $17.75/hr
Mayotte, Jonathan M, db programmer analyst-expert, $66,595
Mays, Joyce, custodian, $13.23/hr
Mays, Tatiana LaShae, care team assoc-clinical, $11.10/hr
Mayuiers, Doris, advancement associate II, $22.15/hr
Mazdra, Michael Joseph, programmer analyst-entry, $49,407
Maze, Susan Nabb, programmer analyst-expert, $59,484
Mazuch Bassham, Laura Nicole, comm coord, $18.85/hr
Mazurek, Micah Osborne, prof, ast, $93,409
Mazuru, Dana, prof, ast clincl dept, $250,000
Mazza, Joseph Michael, prof, ast visiting, $45,710
McConnell, Cyrus Michael, research specialist I, $31,100
McDonald, Thomas Patrick, research/lab technician, $12.00/hr
McEntire, Jacob Anthony, tutor, $13.39/hr
McAfee, Steven Ray, resident physician-1st yr, $50,219
McAlister, Shannon Michelle, instructor, adjunct, $15,000
McAlister, William H, prof, asoc, $105,345
McAllister, Mary Beth, resp therapist reg, $19.24/hr
McAllister, Richard David, video comm admin-expert, $68,527

McAllister, Wesley A, steam plant opr II, $24.15/hr
McAllum, Lynetta Patrice, student support specialist I, $12.98/hr
McAlpin, Nanell Joni, instructor, adjunct, $12,600
McAmis, Ronald W, prof, ast clincl, $90,000
McAroy, Jennifer Lynn, prof, ast adjunct, $125.00/hr
McArthur, Carole P, professor, $117,684
McBee-Black, Kerri Beth Maurine, instructor, $40,066
McBride Jackson, R Maxine, office support asst IV, $13.77/hr
McBride, Charlese Yvonne, educational pgm assoc I, $14.37/hr
McBride, Deborah C, lecturer, $133,930
McBride, Gail Roberta, home hlth aide, $13.33/hr
McBride, Janet Ford, instructor, adjunct, $350
McBride, Luke Benjamin, resident physician-4th yr, $55,804
McCabe, Denise Michelle Suzanne, patient svc rep, $13.64/hr
McCabe, Martha Brook, student service coor II, $60,000
McCaffrey, Kimberly A, prof, asoc teach, $38,964
McCain, Courtney Allison, office support assistant IV, $17.66/hr
McCain, Diane, chaplain, $32,312
McCain, George Edward, archivist II, $52,000
McCall, Adam John, teaching ast, $55.00/hr
McCall, John Daryl, environmental health prof II, $42,128
McCall, Shannon, reactor operator sr, $32.19/hr
McCall, Zachary Allen, prof, ast, $57,346
McCallen, Tiffany Anne, strat comm associate II, $55,080
McCallie, Jay S, animal techn, $13.89/hr
McCallister, Ricci L, nurse, staff II, $23.23/hr
McCally, Ryan Edward, veterinarian, residnt, $26,315
McCanless, Rachel Lynn, nurse, staff II, $23.24/hr
McCann, Cynthia Ellen, student support specialist II, $17.49/hr
McCann, Laura M J, prof, asoc, $94,762
McCann, Leslie A, med coding spclst-certified, $23.13/hr
McCarrison, Kevin L, office support assistant IV, $18.35/hr
McCarrison, Pamela, office support assistant II, $10.25/hr
McCarroll, Daniel J, prgm director, $77,250
McCarter, Ashley Nicole, temporary professional, $13.00/hr
McCarter, David J, farm wrkr I, $10.78/hr
McCarter, Justen Lee, educational pgm assistant, $10.00/hr
McCarter, Stella Kate, snack bar attd, $11.15/hr
McCarther, Shirley M, prof, asoc, $64,511
McCarthy, Darla Lorraine, prof, asoc teach, $84,000
McCarthy, Denis Michael, professor, $79,402
McCarthy, Elizabeth Ann, teaching ast, $25,020
McCarthy, Judith C, pat acct rep, $15.56/hr
McCarthy, Peter R, library information assistant, $14.83/hr
McCarthy, Renee Ann, pharmacist, $122,902
McCarthy, Robert J, lecturer sr, $27,900
McCarthy, Travis Roger, biological safety prof lead, $89,923
McCarty, Justine Erin, student support specialist sr, $16.87/hr
McCarty, Stephanie Dawn, nurse, staff II rnwp, $22.97/hr
McCarty, Timothy James, account executive, $25,976
McCathren, Rebecca, prof, asoc, $69,628
McCauley, Brent Riley, advancement officer, $47,045
McCauley, Joseph Edward, head coach, $40,400
McCauley, Megan Jelley, academic advisor, $36,643
McCaulley, Graham E, extension assoc, $45,000
McCaulley, Sheila Martin, med techl reg, $25.65/hr
McClain II, William E, agronomy spclst, $50,204
McClain-McKinney, Morgan Brennay, mgr research tech svcs, $71,837
McClain, Ashley Desire, nurse, staff II, $20.14/hr
McClain, Gregory Dewayne, prof, ast, $129,204
McClain, Karen L, nurse, staff II, $21.80/hr
McClain, Paul Edward, care team assoc-suppt, $13.37/hr
McClain, Shana Deshay, temporary crafts service, $9.50/hr
McClanahan, Audrey Michelle, office support asst II, $13.50/hr
McClanahan, Sabrina Aurelia, office support asst III, $14.60/hr
McClanahan, Scott Clinton, instructor, adjunct, $21,600
McClaren, Irina Aleksandrovna, office support asst IV, $14.00/hr
McClaskey, Diane, prof, ast clincl, $98,000
McClaskey, Laura L, executive assistant, $21.58/hr
McCleland, Tara Elaine, athletic trainer, $45,805
McClellan, Andrew D, professor, $113,088
McClellan, Chrissa Lea, prof, ast clincl dept, $150,000
McClellan, Jennifer, nurse, staff II, $29.92/hr
McClellan, Shannon Gail, office support assistant IV, $13.47/hr
McClendon, Jennifer Keeley Buxton, student recruitment spclst, $22.51/hr
McClernon, Mark Francis, prof, asoc, $131,610
McCloud, Shane J, nurse, staff II rnwp, $20.95/hr

McClure, Bruce A, professor, $124,569
McClure, Erica, office support assistant III, $17.07/hr
McClure, Hannah Susan, office support assistant IV, $13.51/hr
McClure, Linda S, med techl reg, $29.14/hr
McClure, Robert Charles, event assistant I, $7.55/hr
McCluskey, Frank N, system administrator-expert, $63,493
McClusky, John, specialist, $21,624
McCoig, Myra M, coor risk/liability-h, $82,161
McCollegan, Kelly Jo, nurse anesthetist, $147,900
McCollom-Hull, Kimberly Marie, office support asst sr, $16.30/hr
McCollum, Mary Anne, strat comm associate II, $64,608
McCollum, Meghan Nicole, clerk, diet, $11.11/hr
McCollum, Teresa L, resp therapy techn/icu cert, $23.01/hr
McComb, Ardith A, media producer II, $18.40/hr
McCombs, Amy S, prof, profl practice, $129,953
McConnell, Diane Dolores, histologic technl, $22.00/hr
McConnell, Mary E, program/project supprt coor I, $52,275
McCord, Deborah Jo, service rep IV, $16.13/hr
McCord, William T, project manager-princpl, $108,669
McCorkill, Andrew M, livestock spclst, $41,035
McCormack, Lacey Leanne, phlebotomist, $13.67/hr
McCormack, Ruth Schaefer, social worker, $25.00/hr
McCormack, Susan R, business support specialist II, $15.04/hr
McCormick, Amanda Elizabeth, educational pgm assoc I, $14.27/hr
McCormick, Chad Meyer, resident physician-2nd yr, $52,007
McCormick, Evelyn F, program/project supprt coor I, $32,048
McCormick, Gary Paul, prof, ast teach, $66,008
McCormick, Judith K, prof, asoc teach, $86,851
McCormick, Katheryn Ann, application spclst, $45,946
McCormick, Martha Louise, dir planning & bus devlmnt, $162,945
McCormick, Tamara Filip, speech/lang pathologist, $35.00/hr
McCowan, Jerry D, mts/sheet metal, $22.50/hr
McCowan, Karla Kay, business support specialist II, $17.51/hr
McCowan, Roger, mts/electrician, $22.49/hr
McCoy, Glenda L, ops prgm coord revenue cycle, $72,675
McCoy, Kyle John, emrg med techn paramedic, $14.88/hr
McCoy, Lauren Elizabeth, instructor, adjunct, $12,000
McCoy, Marina R, fellow, resrch, $47,244
McCoy, Matthew S, specialist, $10.00/hr
McCoy, Paulina Morgan, instructor, adjunct, $2,400
McCoy, Tom E, grounds keeper II, $15.15/hr
McCracken, Charles B, reactor engineer, $76,489
McCracken, James M, electronics technician III, $21.66/hr
McCracken, Janet Lee, business support specialist II, $19.47/hr
McCrate, Denis M, agriculture associate II, $18.35/hr
McCreary, Rod P Jr, event assistant I, $8.50/hr
McCroskey, Amanda A, social worker, $25.00/hr
McCubbin, Rachael Marie, coor, service, $17.10/hr
McCubbin, Todd A, asoc vice chancellor, $180,803
McCubbin, Tracy L, storage admin-princpl, $80,493
McCubbins, Jeffrey C, maint svc attd, $17.78/hr
McCudden, Sara Suzanne, program/project supprt coor II, $55,075
McCuistion, Curtis Josh, food svc wrkr II, $10.10/hr
McCulloch, Corey L, db administrator-expert, $66,000
McCulloch, Timothy Lee, med techl reg, $28.91/hr
McCullough, Ladonna A, office support assistant IV, $17.51/hr
McCullough, Michael Wayne, prof, ast teach, $58,140
McCullough, Rona Marie, executive assistant, $21.74/hr
McCullough, S Scott, csm associate II, $22.17/hr
McCune, Elizabeth Ellen, sr mgr external relations, $67,830
McCune, Lornaida M, prof, ast teach, $36,778
McCunniff, Michael D, prof, asoc, $125,460
McCurdy, Kristen, office support assistant II, $10.24/hr
McCush, Mary M, business support specialist II, $23.89/hr
McCutcheon, Robert B, strat comm associate II, $48,480
McDaniel, Christopher Scott, strat comm consultant, $40,658
McDaniel, Clinton Leroy, mental health tech, $12.65/hr
McDaniel, Elizabeth Lynne, care team assoc-clinical, $12.32/hr
McDaniel, Everett Koichi, human resources manager, $55,395
McDaniel, Jason Allen, rec/athletic specialist sr, $25.00/hr
McDaniel, Kelsey Nichole, office support assistant IV, $13.70/hr
McDaniel, Linda Sue, reimbursement ast, $18.85/hr
McDaniel, Roxanne W, dean, asoc, $141,772
McDaniel, Wayne Charles, admin consultant sr, $116,953
McDaniels, Lisa, mgr II hospitality service, $61,673
McDaniels, Robert M, sr prgm mgr studnt supprt svcs, $71,786
McDannald, Katie Lynn Karl, social worker, $43,555
McDavid, Eric L, db programmer analyst-expert, $53,448
McDavid, Shelly Rae, library information assistant, $11.30/hr

McDermit, April Dawn, nurse, licensed prac, $15.06/hr
McDermott, Courtney M, prof, ast teach, $41,711
McDonald, Daniel Keith II, office support assistant III, $11.30/hr
McDonald, David Paul Jr, maint svc attd, $18.41/hr
McDonald, Daniel K Sr, custodian, $12.50/hr
McDonald, Andrew, specialist, $10.00/hr
McDonald, Angela Sue, asoc dir program/project ops, $49,113
McDonald, Annette H, nurse spclst, clincl, $84,407
McDonald, Billie Sue, patient svc rep, $12.76/hr
McDonald, Bryce Matthew, support systems admin-spclst, $50,000
McDonald, Charles Thomas, media producer II, $15.17/hr
McDonald, Cynthia Eick, academic advisor, $35,088
McDonald, Gabriel Paul, bts carpenter, $18.85/hr
McDonald, Kerry Ann, supv nursing acute care, $37.67/hr
McDonald, Kerry S, professor, $138,390
McDonald, Marjorie V, office support assistant II, $13.26/hr
McDonald, Michael Kelly, prof, asoc, $71,197
McDonald, Paula Faye, temporary clerical, $10.50/hr
McDonald, Steven J, academic advisor, $37,312
McDonald, Theresa Marie, social worker, $25.00/hr
McDonald, Vicki Lynne, reimbursement ast sr, $20.62/hr
McDonnell, Dwight E, athletic trainer, $51,491
McDougal, Kathy Helen, asoc dir program/project ops, $51,973
McDougle, Roger, instructor, adjunct, $16,317
McDow, Christy Lea, office support assistant IV, $15.81/hr
McDowd, Joan M, professor, $110,430
McDowell, Flora Lee, med office assistant, $13.60/hr
McDowell, Kirsten, central regstry-data coor, $20.00/hr
McDowell, Landon Patrick, research lab supervisor, $44,370
McDowell, Michelle A, research specialist I, $33,619
McDuffie, Clinton Eugene, instructor, adjunct, $7,500
McElderry, Jonathan Alan, program/project supprt coor I, $41,600
McElroy, Brittany Pieper, on-air talent television, $50,000
McElroy, Jan J, instructor, adjunct, $23,184
McElroy, Jane A, prof, asoc, $107,684
McElroy, Richard Colin, event assistant I, $18.00/hr
McEndarfer, Melinda, advancement officer sr, $63,945
McEniry, Kelly P, library info specialist sr, $15.32/hr
McEntire, Leslie Ann, prof, ast adjunct, $24,012
McEvoy, Kathryn, resident physician-3rd yr, $52,470
McEwan, Abigail Catherine, instructor, clincl, $152,000
McEwan, Thomas W, resident physician-6th yr, $60,415
McEwen, Leslie Ann, coor, service, $15.22/hr
McEwen, Thomas Wayne, police sergeant, $24.69/hr
McFadden, Thomas B, director, $194,425
McFarland, Jacob Andrew, prof, ast, $85,000
McFarland, Julian Lee, office support assistant I, $9.05/hr
McFarland, Katherine Ross, nurse, staff II, $22.24/hr
McFarland, Michael Hiatt, ast coach, $40,000
McFarland, Victor Robert, prof, ast, $59,000
McFarling, Paula L, educational prgm coor sr, $46,966
McField, Shameika Shontae, head coach, $63,000
McGaha, Erin Mitzel, pat acct rep, $15.14/hr
McGannon, Rhonda, nurse, procedures, $34.18/hr
McGarr, Jennifer L, human resources specialist III, $56,400
McGarvey, Ronald Glenn Jr, prof, ast, $96,350
McGaugh, Melaney Anne, nurse, staff per diem, $35.00/hr
McGaughey, Glenda, mgr II business admin, $52,302
McGavock, Daniel James, emrg med techn, $14.88/hr
McGavock, Nicholas Adam, emrg med tech paramedic, $15.78/hr
McGee, Robert Eugene, security officer, $11.48/hr
McGee, Aaron Leslie, user support analyst-spclst, $16.27/hr
McGee, Andre, ast coach, $75,000
McGee, Eve J, resrch asoc, $60,000
McGee, Janet A, custodian, $12.94/hr
McGee, Sharon Kay, office support assistant IV, $12.98/hr
McGennis, Faydre Lane, technology resource coor, $46,512
McGeorge, Jamie W, pat acct rep, $14.84/hr
McGeorge, Jenna Lynn, accountant I, $15.85/hr
McGhee, Kara E, grader, $100.00/hr
McGhee, Meghan G, nurse, staff II, $21.37/hr
McGill, Tiffany M, custodian, $12.90/hr
McGillivary, Jennifer Lee, lecturer, $9,300
McGillivray, Ian Patrick, media producer II, $17.31/hr
McGinity, Margaret Ann, office support assistant IV, $14.99/hr
McGinn, Scott B, athletic trainer, $39,600
McGinnie, Carol Louise, office support assistant IV, $18.35/hr
McGinnis Millsap, Rachael Marie, extension asoc, $34,599
McGinnis, Jill S, db programmer analyst-princpl, $80,026

McGinnis, Jon D, professor, $91,500
McGinnis, Julie Hutchinson, prof, ast clincl, $73,121
McGinnis, Lynn E, office support assistant IV, $18.48/hr
McGinnis, Sandra Kay, pat acct rep, $14.69/hr
McGinty, Bryan K, animal caretaker-equine/food, $12.26/hr
McGinty, Eric Robert, nurse, staff II rnwp, $23.37/hr
McGinty, Kara Beth, office support assistant IV, $16.31/hr
McGinty, Trinette Renee, reimbursement ast-cert, $18.59/hr
McGowan, Cheryl Louise, nurse practitioner, $92,000
McGowan, Kelly Gail, extension asoc, $29,800
McGowan, Micheal D, dir I, business admin, $144,100
McGowan, Violeta, dental assistant II, $13.39/hr
McGowin, James H Jr, mts/electrician, $21.05/hr
McGowin, Susan L, office support assistant III, $15.20/hr
McGrath, Brandi Kay, business support specialist II, $17.87/hr
McGrath, Matthew S, professor, $101,807
McGrath, Pamela, office support assistant IV, $13.50/hr
McGrosso, John, prof, asoc, $66,997
McGruder, Ann Celeste, exec ast to the gen officr, $115,077
McGruder, Rebecca Mary, nurse, staff II, $27.70/hr
McGuff, Megan Elizabeth, nurse, staff I, $19.00/hr
McGuffey, Chelsea Nicholle, nurse, staff II, $20.14/hr
McGuffey, Logan William, resident physician-1st yr, $50,219
McGuffin, Tara Renee, enrollment advisor sr, $17.50/hr
McGuire Craig, Lacrissa Jean, nurse, staff II, $22.50/hr
McGuire, Dana E, educational pgm associate I, $14.67/hr
McGuire, Marcella Lynn, instructional designer-expert, $56,177
McGuire, Richard T, psychologist, $78,030
McGuire, Sean Michael, surgical technl certified, $15.87/hr
McHatton, Patricia, dean, asoc, $120,000
McHenry, Gwendolyn Delores, reimbursement spclst, $24.26/hr
McHenry, Milton Arthur, event assistant I, $7.50/hr
McHenry, Renee E, temporary clerical, $22.83/hr
McHugh, Sandra C, nurse, or/recovery-ch, $34.26/hr
McIlvaney, Nancy L, manuscript specialist, $35,605
McIntire, Michelle Allen, teaching ast, $8,000
McIntosh, Bill R, sr manager it, $96,239
McIntosh, Daniel H, prof, asoc, $71,389
McIntosh, Jill Erica, dir II advancement, $69,934
McIntosh, Mark Alan, professor, $241,909
McIntosh, Renae Lynn, instructor, $42,230
McIntosh, Renae Lynn, nurse, staff II, $35.00/hr
McIntosh, Timothy S, human resources manager sr, $62,068
McIntyre, Anita A, nurse, staff II, $33.25/hr
McKane, Edward B, environmental health prof sr, $52,045
McKarns, Susan Carol, prof, ast, $104,847
McKay, Cheryl A, strat comm manager, $63,179
McKay, Diane P, student support specialist sr, $20.00/hr
McKay, Terry D, bindery opr II, $17.78/hr
McKean, Melissa D, resident physician-3rd yr, $52,470
McKean, Michael L, prof, asoc, $112,314
McKee, Forest R Jr, supv, food svc II-h, $43,661
McKee, Adryan Marc, prof, ast teach, $34,680
McKee, Jennifer Mariah, floor care techn, $12.15/hr
McKee, Lindsey L, instructor, adjunct, $40,320
McKee, Rachel Leah, medical coding spclst, $19.71/hr
McKee, Sarah Elizabeth, student support specialist sr, $17.31/hr
McKee, Teresa Elizabeth, agriculture assistant II, $16.43/hr
McKelvey, William A Jr, program/project supprt coor I, $49,955
McKelvie, Thomas Scott, prof, asoc teach, $39,865
McKelvy, Terrence Malcolm, mts/hvac, $24.13/hr
McKendry, Anne Leslie, prof, asoc, $84,670
McKenna, Ryan F, resident physician-3rd yr, $53,763
McKenney, Charlotte Ann, coor, care, $64,822
McKenney, William Thomas, professor, $74,235
McKenzie, Wayland N Jr, prof, asoc clincl, $5,000
McKenzie, Amber Jean, pat acct rep, $13.10/hr
McKenzie, Amy Noelle, asoc dir human resources, $78,795
McKenzie, Cassandra, specialist, $10.00/hr
McKenzie, Charlene K, office support assistant IV, $17.07/hr
McKenzie, John D, electrician, high voltage, $27.26/hr
McKenzie, Marjorie L, retail sales assistant, $12.15/hr
McKenzie, Susan, office support assistant II, $14.18/hr
McKeon, Patrick J, mgr event services, $58,976
McKerlie, Elizabeth Anne, instructor, adjunct, $6,300
McKibben, James Charles, asoc dir research, $56.97/hr
McKiddy, Clayton E, instructor, clincl, $82,000
McKie, Anna Lee, nurse, staff I, $19.37/hr
McKinley, Cynthia Denise, nurse anesthetist, $147,912

McKinney, Beverly K, nurse, staff now I, $26.00/hr
McKinney, Kathleen Margaret, event assistant I, $9.31/hr
McKinney, Mitchell S, professor, $94,225
McKinney, Patrick Joseph, db programmer analyst-expert, $53,827
McKinney, Vincent Mardell, temporary professional, $15.00/hr
McKinnon, Pamela S, pat acct rep, $15.26/hr
McKinstry, Megan Louise, prof, ast teach, $30,399
McKinzie, Edward D, system administrator-princpl, $79,559
McKinzie, Misty Marie, mgr III business admin, $67,291
McKinzie, Ramonna Anne, ast adminr pat accts-up, $84,595
McKnight, Jennifer M, prof, asoc, $65,800
McLain, Ellen H, dir III advancement, $103,000
McLane, Tayler Rae, research/lab technician sr, $13.26/hr
McLaughlin, Tim W, dir II advancement, $61,800
McLaurin, Christopher T, prof, adjunct, $25,200
McLay, Barbara, prof, asoc clincl, $75,058
McLay, Breanne N W, nurse, staff I, $19.00/hr
McLeland, Rebecca Diane, human resources spec I, $16.23/hr
McLeod, Alyssa M, office support assistant III, $12.89/hr
McLeod, Hyosun, student support specialist I, $14.32/hr
McLure, Jason David, editor sr, $54,000
McMahan, Ryan Michael, custodian, $10.00/hr
McMahill, Anna Beth, account executive, $6,000
McMahon, Aaron Gabriel, nurse, licensed prac, $16.04/hr
McMahon, Judith, coor, reimbursement, $63,149
McManus, James D, surgical technl certified, $16.35/hr
McManus, John C, professor, $74,793
McMichael, Luci Mauricio, prof, asoc teach, $44,327
McMichael, Susan Rose, nurse, staff II rnwp, $26.89/hr
McMichael, Tiffany Marie, office support assistant sr, $17.55/hr
McMickle, Laura L, business support specialist II, $18.53/hr
McMillan, Dana M, instructor, field, $19,333
McMillan, Kendell, pharmacist III, $128,835
McMillen, Amy Louise, student support specialist II, $17.34/hr
McMillen, Clinton Thomas, media producer sr, $42,925
McMillen, Edward M, bts carpenter, $21.71/hr
McMillen, Jennifer Emilie, television producer, $31,899
McMillen, Travis W, media producer II, $20.37/hr
McMillian, Joshua James, head coach, $41,209
McMillian, Melanie Ann, user support analyst-speclst, $17.25/hr
McMillin, Bruce M, professor, $145,312
McMillin, Colin M, grader, $100.00/hr
McMillin, Ian Alexander, food svc wrkr III, $12.20/hr
McMillion, Clark A, prof, teach, $44,100
McNally, Jennifer, temporary professional, $11.30/hr
McNamara, James Barry III, tutor, $15.00/hr
McNamara, Vicki Renee, prof, ast adjunct, $16,008
McNamee, Brian J, dir II finance, $88,797
McNamee, Ian Joseph, programmer analyst-entry, $41,200
McNamee, Matthew, counsel, $124,085
McNamee, Turi Ann, prof, asoc clincl dept, $297,330
McNary, Robert Leon, extns professional, asoc, $57,191
McNay, Jennifer L, advancement officer, $52,560
McNeeley, Jeffrey Quintin, customer service supervisor, $48,816
McNeely, John H Jr, serv line spclst, $79,000
McNeely, Tammy L, emergency services rep, $14.88/hr
McNeil, Hilary Dawn, instructor, field, $46,818
McNeil, Patrick E, prof, ast, $50,900
McNeill, Brian J, instructor, adjunct, $9,000
McNeley, Kimberly Ann, asoc vice provost, $124,200
McNew, Karla G, clinical nursing supvsr, $74,876
McNickle, Susan F, educational pgm associate I, $13.30/hr
McNiel, Tammy Lynn, program/project supprt coor I, $53,881
McNolty, Leslie Ann, instructor, adjunct, $18,000
McNulty, Idalia Marisol, educational pgm associate I, $13.45/hr
McNutt, Justin M, network engineer-princpl, $79,333
McPeak, Katherine Elizabeth, office support asst IV, $16.15/hr
McPhail, Brenda M, asoc vice chancellor, $136,706
McPhail, Thomas L, professor, $144,283
McPheeters, Dawn Michelle, instructor, clincl, $23,040
McPherson, Joshua Paul, field superintendent, $73,000
McQuary, Linda Jean, mgr I, business admin, $65,395
McQuay, Christine Ione, nurse, staff II, $22.32/hr
McQueen, Cydney, prof, asoc clincl, $101,000
McQueen, Penny Dawn, student support specialist II, $17.51/hr
McQueen, Rebecca Kay, supv engineering, $55,058
McQuegge, William Gene Jr, coor, service, $16.49/hr
McQuitty, Mark C, accountant I, $16.28/hr
McQuitty, Ronald L, maint tech III, prev, $18.45/hr

McQuitty, Shayana T, temporary clerical, $9.50/hr
McReynolds, David S, csm professional sr, $66,175
McReynolds, Gary D, prof, ast clincl, $103,254
McReynolds, Michelle J, office support assistant IV, $18.90/hr
McRoberts, Jon Tyler, fellow, post doctoral, $50,000
McSherry, Allison Renee, nurse, staff I, $19.00/hr
McSherry, Brenda K, nurse practitioner, $93,444
McSherry, David T, nurse, staff I, rnwp, $19.00/hr
McSpadden, David Craig, supv, clinical-rehab svcs, $74,970
McSteen, Paula Catherine Mary, prof, asoc, $105,807
McSwain, Eric Nathan, manager it, $76,500
McTye, Willie Linda, custodian, $13.96/hr
McVeigh, Thomas F, resrch asoc, $98,473
McVey, Janette Dianne, prof, ast clincl dept, $200,000
McWhorter, Lucy M, patient svc rep, $14.88/hr
McWilliams, Ashley Beth, patient svc rep, $12.33/hr
McWilliams, Emma Lee, emergency services rep, $11.07/hr
McWilliams, Lorie A, med office assistant, $14.00/hr
Meacham, Crystal Dianne, resident physician-4th yr, $54,425
Mead, Molly, manager it, $73,704
Mead, Samuel T, office support assistant III, $11.57/hr
Mead, Tatum Nicole, prof, ast clincl, $95,000
Meade, Kristen J, dir III business admin, $106,500
Meador, Timothy T, resp therapist reg, $31.66/hr
Meadows, Barton T, prof, ast adjunct, $10,500
Meadows, Ellen E, academic advisor, $34,916
Meadows, John F, floor maint wkr, $13.84/hr
Meadows, Richard L, prof, teach, $131,453
Meadows, Susan Elaine, librarian IV, $57,956
Meagher, Michael E, prof, asoc, $60,507
Mealancon, Doretha A, pharmacy tech, $11.90/hr
Means, John Cecil, resrch asoc, $36,000
Means, Martha Raye, nurse, staff II, $20.95/hr
Mears, Cassidy Alan, ast coach, $34,400
Mease, Kristina Marie, student support specialist II, $14.95/hr
Mebane, Carla Deanne, dir program/project operations, $65,000
Mecham, Kathi Sue, horticulture spclst, $46,500
Meckfessel, Michele D, prof, ast, $145,000
Medeiros, Denis Michael, vice provost, $184,500
Medellin, Josephine, executive assistant, $21.23/hr
Medhi, Deepankar, prof, curators, $127,613
Medina, Jennifer Lynne, prof, ast, $39,546
Medina, Silvia, custodian, $12.94/hr
Medley, Beth Anne Dinslage, sr prgm mgr studnt sup svcs, $53,448
Medley, John H, prof, ast clincl dept, $220,000
Medley, Kristen Leigh, nurse, staff II, $24.01/hr
Medlin, Jack K, mail carrier, $14.59/hr
Medling, Noah E, db programmer analyst-specist, $47,048
Medlock, Eve, sr prgm mgr studnt supprt svcs, $65,867
Medvedeva, Ioulia Y, prof, asoc, $79,411
Meeder, Michael, instructor, adjunct, $18,648
Meek, Amanda Marie, 4-h spclst, $41,000
Meek, Richard Shawn, agriculture associate II, $13.66/hr
Meek, Sabrina R, temporary clerical, $9.00/hr
Meeks, Kathy S, business ops associate II, $44,688
Meers, Brett A, research/lab technician sr, $19.76/hr
Meers, Grace M, research specialist sr, $45,007
Meffert, Bruce Albert, ast reactor manager, $96,901
Mefford, Connie, extns professional, asoc, $55,162
Mehmert, Michelle A, media producer II, $15.86/hr
Mehmood, Sabah, tutor, $10.00/hr
Mehr, David R, professor, $191,174
Mehra-Chaudhary, Ritcha, research specialist sr, $42,032
Mehrer, Cynthia Susan, mgr nursing svcs, $54,614
Mehrhoff, Nancy Lynn, reimbursement ast sr, $19.45/hr
Mehrhoff, Wayne Arthur, program/project supprt coor I, $21.86/hr
Mehrle, Donna Joann, extension asoc, $58,609
Mehta, Navina, resident physician-4th yr, $54,425
Mehta, Ravish, db programmer analyst-expert, $60,334
Mehta, Sanjay S, resident physician-4th yr, $55,804
Meier, Kay Elaine, nurse, licensed prac, $19.58/hr
Meier, Lesley Renee, extns professional, asoc, $43,848
Meiners, Wanda J, lab techn, persl svc-clin lab, $17.10/hr
Meinhardt, Clinton G, research specialist I, $46,020
Meinhardt, Katherine Kay, nurse, staff, $24.07/hr
Meininger, Gerald Alan, director, $258,182
Meisenbach, Rebecca J, prof, asoc, $64,827
Meisenheimer, Kathleen Elizabeth, pat acct rep, $14.31/hr
Meissen, Laura E, pat admiss advisor, $29.78/hr

Meissen, Roger W, program/project supprt coor I, $45,777
Meives, Danny F, nurse, staff II, $34.18/hr
Melchert, Russell B, dean, $217,485
Melegrito, Jeffrey P, ast mgr hospitality services, $54,503
Melegrito, Joan M, event assistant I, $9.41/hr
Meler, Christine Ann, office support assistant IV, $18.85/hr
Melgren, Spencer Edward, tutor, $10.00/hr
Meller, Daryl, mts/sheet metal, $22.50/hr
Meller, Tiffany Suzette, nurse, advanced practice, $81,224
Mellerup, Delvin C, engineering technician II, $21.56/hr
Melling, Steven P, lecturer, $30,900
Mellinger, Mark Andrew, event assistant I, $7.50/hr
Mello, Magda, mgr II hospitality services, $58,543
Melloway, Angela K, business support specialist II, $19.68/hr
Melloway, C Dale, system support analyst-expert, $27.33/hr
Melloway, Deborah L, operations support tech sr, $16.64/hr
Melly, Elias K C, nurse, staff I, rnwp, $19.37/hr
Melnyk, Andrew, professor, $98,267
Melnyk, Julie A, prof, ast teach, $36,000
Melton, Cenitoria Latreice, academic advisor, $34,400
Melton, Jennifer Jill, resp therapist reg, $21.53/hr
Melton, Katherine Hettwer, couns hlth/welfare/wellness, $39,600
Melton, Rebecca L, event assistant sr, $14.72/hr
Melville, Tina L, student service coor II, $41,750
Melvin, Deborah Diane, library info specialist, $12.98/hr
Melvin, Joseph Conor, resident physician-2nd yr, $52,007
Melvin, Kelley Lynn, lecturer, $32,130
Men, Hongsheng, prof, ast resrch, $71,400
Menand, Shannon Lee Fogg, prof, asoc, $63,738
Menand, Stephane, student service coor I, $37,578
Menard, Kimberly Ann, veterinarian, residnt, $26,000
Mendelsohn, Bill, sr dir program/project ops, $90,024
Mendenhall, Denice L, instructor, clincl, $52,103
Mendez Babcock, Erica Chong, prof, ast/profl pract, $50,980
Mendez, James Alexander III, office support asst II, $13.15/hr
Mendez, Carlos A, instructor, ast, $22,843
Mendez, Raquel Chong, temporary clerical, $9.70/hr
Mendoza-Cozatl, David Guillermo, prof, ast, $98,253
Mendoza, Cesar, prof, asoc, $92,213
Mendoza, Joanna Rosalie, prof, asoc, $63,058
Menees, Thomas, prof, asoc, $92,299
Menefee, Amy Elizabeth, business support spclst II, $18.96/hr
Menendez, Martha, administrative consultant, $86,959
Meng, Chunxia, fellow, post doctoral, $46,092
Meng, James H, programmer analyst-expert, $74,721
Mengwasser, Lindsey Jane, physical therapist, $62,334
Menifield, Charles E, professor, $109,502
Menning, Michael F Sr, csm operations supervisor, $50,387
Mense, David Hunter, ast coach, $71,000
Mense, Nancy Elkins, 4-h spclst, $70,567
Mentis, David M, teaching asoc, $59,277
Mercer, Anne, instructor, clincl, $4,500
Merchant, Cherry Ann, educational pgm associate I, $12.55/hr
Mercier, Katherine Augusta, museum paraprofessional I, $15.00/hr
Meredith, Melynda Ann, prof, ast clincl, $81,000
Merfeld-Langston, Audra Lynn, prof, asoc, $66,285
Meriac, John Patrick, prof, ast, $66,950
Merideth, Cindy Lou, resp therapist reg, $28.00/hr
Meriwether, Nichelle S, couns hlth/welfare/wellness sr, $30.00/hr
Merkle, Edgar C, prof, ast, $78,475
Merlenbach, Matthew Joseph, user support analyst-entry, $14.85/hr
Merrell, Rebecca S, library info specialist sr, $17.83/hr
Merrick, Danielle Abernethy, teaching ast, clincl, $65,750
Merrick, Lana Jo, program/project supprt coor I, $49,875
Merrick, Ramona Lea, care team assoc-clinical, $14.17/hr
Merrill, Brandon Patrick, resident physician-2nd yr, $52,007
Merrill, Catherine, clinical mgr, $92,400
Merrill, Dennis, prof, curator teach, $94,280
Merrill, Haley Marie, resident physician-5th yr, $56,120
Merrill, Megan L, student service coor sr, $52,485
Merriman, Donald G, mts/pipefitter, $22.50/hr
Merriman, Gary J, support systems admin-expert, $53,186
Merriman, Michelle Lynn, db programmer analyst-speclst, $46,288
Merriman, Philip K, support systems admin-entry, $40,498
Merritt, Chris A, nutrition spclst, $49,351
Merritt, Jamie Marie, educational pgm associate I, $13.45/hr
Merritt, Karen Susan, nurse, staff II, $29.82/hr
Merritt, Sherry Mitchel, home hlth aide, $13.33/hr
Merritt, Stephanie Marie, prof, asoc, $72,665

Mertens, Randall J, strat comm associate sr, $53,845
Mertensmeyer, Carol A, prof, asoc clincl, $67,426
Merz, Chris J, prof, ast adjunct, $23,625
Mesa, Rodolfo, security officer, $10.82/hr
Mescher, Kelly K, counsel, $130,304
Mesenbrink, Angel Renee, nurse, staff II, $31.77/hr
Mesfin, Fassil Brian, prof, ast, $249,900
Mesplay, Brenda K, business support specialist II, $19.34/hr
Messbarger, Joann L, grant writer sr, $50,000
Messbarger, Quinten Ceddell, bus svcs consultant sr, $89,026
Messer, Elizabeth E, nurse, staff stat, $24.27/hr
Messervy, Jason C, resident physician-1st yr, $50,219
Messina, Nancy Joan, librarian I, $40,000
Messner, Albert R, maint svc attd, $14.72/hr
Mestres, Jaime Lynn, academic advisor, $41,244
Metcalf-Wilson, Kristin, prof, ast teach, $18,535
Metcalf, Meredith, resident physician-1st yr, $49,025
Mette, Andrew Michael, sftware supprt analyst-expert, $50,863
Mette, Rebecca Ann Schwartz, grader, $100.00/hr
Mettes, Beth Ellyn, nurse, staff II, $23.12/hr
Mettu, Sangeeta, resident physician-4th yr, $55,804
Metz, Cynthia H, intern, $8,000
Metz, Melanie Suzanne, radiologic techl, $22.50/hr
Metzen, Jeremiah Adam, programmer analyst-speclst, $55,000
Metzgar, Karma June, sr dir program/project ops, $97,586
Metzger, Kenan Lewis, instructor, adjunct, $16,650
Meuser, Thomas Michael, prof, asoc, $78,260
Meuth, Alexander I, research specialist I, $33,899
Meyer, Allison Marie, prof, ast, $76,000
Meyer, Amanda Elizabeth, instructor, adjunct, $17,100
Meyer, Anne Marie, asoc dir student support svcs, $97,972
Meyer, Benjamin Abraham, mts/electrician, $20.31/hr
Meyer, Beverly E, food svc wrkr I, $11.29/hr
Meyer, Caitlin E, office support assistant III, $13.46/hr
Meyer, Chandra Lynette, educational pgm associate I, $12.85/hr
Meyer, Christine Elizabeth Allen, office support asst III, $13.50/hr
Meyer, David W, hospital security officer, $14.88/hr
Meyer, Dennis, csm associate III, $26.10/hr
Meyer, Donald George, prof, prof, ast, $71,400
Meyer, Emily Marie, executive assistant, $18.00/hr
Meyer, Ginger Rae, temporary crafts service, $25.00/hr
Meyer, James E, nutrition spclst, $57,291
Meyer, Janet Marie, finance systems manager, $81,923
Meyer, Jayson L, dir I, advancement, $63,721
Meyer, Jeffrey E, agriculture associate I, $13.69/hr
Meyer, Jennifer Marie, program/project coor II, $46,056
Meyer, Jill Zimmerman, business spclst, $72,100
Meyer, John L, library info specialist sr, $18.29/hr
Meyer, John Stephen, system administrator-expert, $61,221
Meyer, Mary L, business support specialist sr, $30.00/hr
Meyer, Mary Suzanne, physical therapist, $35.00/hr
Meyer, Patricia Rose, animal technician sr, $13.39/hr
Meyer, Rebecca Marie, pat acct rep, $16.65/hr
Meyer, Richard A, security sgt-h, $19.17/hr
Meyer, Shelley R, nurse, staff II, $22.96/hr
Meyer, Tammy J, custodian, $11.41/hr
Meyer, Tara Marie, office support assistant III, $15.52/hr
Meyer, Walter A, asoc dir research, $56.00/hr
Meyer, Wilbert E, instructor, clincl, $93,600
Meyerhardt, Gail Louise, patient svc rep, $13.74/hr
Meyers, Christina Rose, nurse, lpn now plus yr, $20.00/hr
Meyers, Courtney Ann, patient svc rep, $11.50/hr
Meyers, Debra M, student support specialist sr, $17.36/hr
Meyers, Gail A, nurse, staff II, $35.57/hr
Meyers, James, office support assistant IV, $16.00/hr
Meyers, Jody Lynn, office support assistant IV, $13.06/hr
Meyers, Maria E, sr dir research and inst prgms, $166,215
Meyers, Monica Lee, student support specialist I, $12.98/hr
Meyers, William H, professor, $165,522
Mezzanotte, Shannon Marie, office support asst IV, $13.59/hr
Micek, Benjamin T, mgr student support svcs, $39,171
Miceli, Paul, professor, $100,192
Michael, Amy K, lecturer, $38,000
Michael, Kelly Gaye, veterinary technician sr, $16.23/hr
Michael, Kristen Nicole, resident physician-3rd yr, $52,470
Michael, Valarie Ann, mental health tech, $11.85/hr
Michaels, Sarah Nicole, office support assistant II, $14.00/hr
Michaelson, Jill Elizabeth, nurse anesthetist, $147,900
Michaletz, Heather N, food svc wrkr I, $10.53/hr

Micheas, Athanasios, prof, asoc, $74,010
Micheas, Lada, user support analyst-princpl, $55,857
Michelson, Randal Cerf, resident physician-3rd yr, $52,470
Middelkoop, Pilar Mendoza, prof, asoc, $75,414
Middelkoop, Timothy, director it, $104,500
Middleton, Richard T IV, prof, asoc, $62,572
Middleton, Florence J, office support assistant III, $14.32/hr
Middleton, Jessica, instructor, adjunct, $27,200
Middleton, John R, professor, $141,849
Middleton, Julie N, extns professional, $117,107
Middleton, Kevin M, prof, asoc, $91,800
Middleton, Michael, deputy chancellor, $211,891
Middleton, Robert C, resrch ast, $4,800
Middleton, Scott D, media producer II, $15.93/hr
Midgyett, Terbo Stephen, event assistant I, $7.50/hr
Midha, Ashok, professor, $168,253
Midha, Christine Rose, lecturer, $15.00/hr
Midyett, Justin Paul, physical therapist, $73,088
Mielke, Megan Michelle, nurse, staff II, $21.69/hr
Miener, Lauren A, occl therapist, $51,714
Mierzwa, Patra Ann, research specialist I, $46,233
Mihail, Jeanne Denyse, professor, $104,214
Mihalevich, Connie Jean, mgr finl counslg, $85,865
Mihok, Deborah E, specialist, $20.00/hr
Mikayelyan, Arpine, research/lab technician, $12.75/hr
Mikesell, Dustin Lee, high school student, $8.00/hr
Mikhail, Samuel, resident physician-4th yr, $65,000
Mikkelsen, Mark, dir I, business admin, $100,000
Mikles, Ashley Marie, nurse, staff now III, $30.00/hr
Mikuleza, Brittany Rose, office support assistant III, $13.50/hr
Milam, Maurice Dale, user support analyst-speclst, $16.81/hr
Milam, Michael R, agronomy spclst, $53,262
Milanick, Mark, professor, $135,591
Milbach, Erica Renee, nurse anesthetist, $147,900
Milburn, Laurie Anne, prof, ast adjunct, $8,004
Mildenhall, Robert Priday, fellow, post doc clncl yr1, $55,804
Miles, Judith Helen, emeritus, $60,641
Miles, Randall J, prof, asoc, $86,117
Milescu, Lorin Silviu, prof, ast, $83,416
Milescu, Mirela, prof, ast, $80,050
Milford, Peggy Ann, educational pgm associate I, $12.49/hr
Milhollin, Ryan Keane, extension asoc, $57,442
Miliaresis, Ismini Alexandra, prof, ast visiting, $41,000
Millam, Clifford Wayne, care team assoc-clinical, $15.30/hr
Millard, Joy L, sr dir program/project ops, $109,100
Millen, Andrew James, care team assoc-clinical, $13.60/hr
Millen, Janet L, nurse, staff II, $30.78/hr
Millen, Kristen M, nurse, staff II, $22.32/hr
Miller, Dennis K Jr, prof, asoc, $70,045
Miller, Gerald Leo Jr, prof, ast, $77,931
Miller, Robert Lee Jr, security officer, $10.24/hr
Miller, Russell Edison Jr, bts carpenter, $21.71/hr
Miller, Stanley Leroy Jr, high school student, $10.70/hr
Miller Struttmann, Nicole Elizabeth, fellow, post doctoral, $40,000
Miller-Hoover, Millie T, business spclst, $56,624
Miller, Alexis Lee, high school student, $8.00/hr
Miller, Allison Elizabeth, executive assistant, $19.17/hr
Miller, April Lynn, nurse, staff II rnwp, $21.26/hr
Miller, Ashley Marie, chemist I, $41,586
Miller, Blair Rich, temporary crafts service, $7.50/hr
Miller, Brenda Deanna, instructor, clincl, $4,500
Miller, Carol Ann, tutor, $15.00/hr
Miller, Carrie Lynn, hospital lab tech, $14.88/hr
Miller, Christina Kathleen, resrch ast, $11,333
Miller, Christopher Stephen, resident physician-1st yr, $50,219
Miller, Cindy L, med records transcript, $15.37/hr
Miller, Cole Dowdy, temporary clerical, $8.00/hr
Miller, Colton Duane, psychologist, $77,394
Miller, Courtney Sue, resrch ast, $55,000
Miller, Don L, human dev spclst, $61,804
Miller, Donna Lee, office support assistant III, $14.98/hr
Miller, Douglas C, prof, clinical dept, $213,282
Miller, Douglas James, prof, asoc adjunct, $31,500
Miller, Elizabeth D, grant writer sr, $57,793
Miller, Emily Christine, interior design associate, $37,668
Miller, Emily I, prof, ast teach, $112,200
Miller, F Scott, prof, teach, $94,700
Miller, Gail, nurse, staff now III, $30.00/hr
Miller, George H, video comm admin-expert, $69,428

Miller, Gloria J, operations support tech sr, $13.35/hr
Miller, Grant Wyman, instructor, adjunct, $7,500
Miller, James Isaac, prof, asoc, $120,961
Miller, James Madison, professor, $75,863
Miller, Janel Evelyn, business tech analyst-entry, $43,860
Miller, Jason Dewayne, support systems admin-speclst, $50,000
Miller, Jason Wayne, dir, hris, $118,878
Miller, Jean, dean, $168,300
Miller, Jennifer Leah, pharmacist, $60.00/hr
Miller, Jennifer Nichole, nurse clinician, $71,015
Miller, Joel B, lecturer, $9,300
Miller, Judith Ann, dean, $205,602
Miller, Judy Kay, nurse, staff II, $28.69/hr
Miller, Kassia Amber, veterinary technician sr, $15.92/hr
Miller, Kathleen K, prgm director, $72,456
Miller, Kathleen M, office support assistant IV, $16.83/hr
Miller, Keith W, professor, $140,070
Miller, Kerby Alonzo, prof, curators, $102,122
Miller, Kevin L, custodian, $12.94/hr
Miller, Kurt Russell, high school student, $7.65/hr
Miller, Laura Ann, professor, $127,879
Miller, Lindsey Elizabeth, advancement coordinator, $44,000
Miller, Lionell, system administrator-speclst, $47,830
Miller, Livia Marie, clerk, diet, $9.50/hr
Miller, Lynda, telecom it analyst-princpl, $64,187
Miller, Magda Denes, resident physician-2nd yr, $52,007
Miller, Margaret Louise, food svc wrkr I, $11.29/hr
Miller, Marsha A, business support specialist II, $21.52/hr
Miller, Matthew Brian, instructional designer-princpl, $60,133
Miller, Matthew T, library info specialist sr, $14.95/hr
Miller, Megan Tambi, physical therapist, $62,334
Miller, Nicholas Jay, resident physician-1st yr, $49,025
Miller, Patricia D, agronomy spclst, $51,024
Miller, Renee Marie, nurse, staff II, $24.67/hr
Miller, Renita Suzette, office support assistant IV, $16.03/hr
Miller, Richard Everett, food svc wrkr I, $9.60/hr
Miller, Rosetta, nurse, staff now I, $26.00/hr
Miller, Sarah C, mail processor I, $13.74/hr
Miller, Stacey A, counselor, genetic, $71,710
Miller, Stephen W, hospital security officer, $13.21/hr
Miller, Steven, db administrator-entry, $50,171
Miller, Steven, maint svc attd, $18.41/hr
Miller, Susan R, nurse, staff II, $32.19/hr
Miller, Suzanne Kilcoyne, resident physician-3rd yr, $52,470
Miller, Talley M, health records techn II, $14.88/hr
Miller, Tammie J, nurse, staff, $26.72/hr
Miller, Thomas H, advancement associate II, $19.69/hr
Miller, Vicki Lynn, mgr III business admin, $74,567
Miller, Vickie J, anesthesia techn, $16.22/hr
Miller, Willard O, nurse, staff II, $34.18/hr
Miller, William H, resrch scientist/academic sr, $121,457
Miller, William Vencill, prof, clinical dept, $265,200
Miller, Wyatt Wayne, agronomy spclst, $42,229
Miller, Yvonne M D, dir iv advancement, $141,687
Milles, Jeffrey Lee, resident physician-2nd yr, $52,007
Millier, Romain Pierre, dir I, csm operations, $93,355
Milligan, Ashley Marie, nuclear med technl, $29.40/hr
Milligan, Debra Annette, patient svc rep, $13.75/hr
Milligan, Larry L, distribution techn-mtls mgmt, $15.26/hr
Million, Stephanie Katherine, resident physician-3rd yr, $52,470
Mills Gray, Susan L, state spclst, asoc, $83,526
Mills-Sandoval, Toby Mackenzie, soc worker-non acute care, $44,146
Mills, Brandon James, student recruitment spclst, $19.62/hr
Mills, Britney, surgical technl certified, $16.19/hr
Mills, Eric, ast mgr ambulance svcs, $54,304
Mills, Janice Achs, office support assistant III, $11.63/hr
Mills, Maude Elizabeth, patient svc rep, $13.06/hr
Mills, Mistie Renee Peil, prof, ast clincl dept, $170,708
Mills, Rilla Dean, dean, $218,991
Mills, Scott, office support assistant IV, $14.25/hr
Mills, Sharlyn Leanne, dental assistant II, $13.17/hr
Mills, Sherry L, office support assistant IV, $16.02/hr
Mills, Stacie Lee, office support assistant I, $9.32/hr
Millspaugh, Joshua J, professor, $164,506
Millstein, Mitchell Alan, prof, adjunct, $9,300
Milne, Diana R, human dev spclst, $57,396
Milner, Stephanie N, 4-h spclst, $41,019
Milstead, Toni J, business support specialist sr, $26.77/hr

Milyo, Jeffrey Dennis, professor, $161,088
Minczuk, Kathryn Elizabeth, research/lab technician, $10.32/hr
Miner, Thomas W, credentialing spclst, $18.13/hr
Mingucci, Monica M, prgm director, $80,323
Minnis, Tracy Jo, educational pgm associate I, $14.54/hr
Minor, Angela Nicole, recreation spclst, therapu, $37,524
Minor, Deborah Ann, teacher, special educ-mpc, $47,281
Minor, Elizabeth Faye, db programmer analyst-princpl, $81,529
Minor, Frankie D, sr dir studnt supprt svcs, $142,758
Minor, George Alan, telecom engineer-speclst, $52,500
Minor, Marian Adams, instructor, adjunct, $6,000
Minor, Susan Elaine, event assistant I, $8.40/hr
Minta, Michael David, prof, asoc, $77,051
Minturn, Hannah Rupp, prgm mgr I, studnt supprt svcs, $45,900
Minturn, Neil B, prof, asoc, $55,264
Mir, Fazia Ahmed, fellow, post doc clncl yr1, $55,804
Miranda, Maria Esther, custodian, $13.96/hr
Mirchandani, Dinesh A, prof, asoc, $129,700
Mirth, Christina Alyssa, couns hlth/welfare/wellness sr, $30.00/hr
Mirts, Leigh Ann, nurse, licensed prac, $17.00/hr
Mirtz, John L, business tech analyst-expert, $53,829
Misfeldt, Michael Lee, professor, $195,100
Mishra, Bhawani Prasad, resrch asoc, $49,470
Mishra, Jennifer, prof, asoc, $63,623
Mishra, Santosh Kumar, chemist II, $54,303
Mislan, Cristina, prof, ast, $64,500
Misner, Aaron Shane, pharmacy tech, $13.91/hr
Misra, Madhukar, prof, clinical dept, $220,000
Misra, Shamita, prof, asoc clincl dept, $153,255
Mitchel, Heidi S, compliance specialist I, $17.25/hr
Mitchell, Billy Joe Jr, mts/pipefitter, $24.13/hr
Mitchell, William J Jr, prof, asoc, $114,124
Mitchell, Aaron Blair, human resources specialist III, $43,325
Mitchell, Alexis Shantay, tutor, $10.00/hr
Mitchell, Amber Lynn, care team assoc-clinical, $12.08/hr
Mitchell, Andrea Blair, practice manager, $75,480
Mitchell, Angus Levi, bts carpenter, $21.71/hr
Mitchell, Anthony Deshaun, custodian, $10.94/hr
Mitchell, Ashley Elizabeth, student recruitment spclst sr, $20.59/hr
Mitchell, Barbara S, fellow, post doctoral, $65,000
Mitchell, Cheryl A, lab techn, persl svc-clin lab, $16.73/hr
Mitchell, Dawn Marie, food svc wrkr I, $11.29/hr
Mitchell, Debra Jo, mgr III business admin, $87,860
Mitchell, Denise Dianne, nurse, staff II, $28.25/hr
Mitchell, Donald Dean, event assistant I, $7.65/hr
Mitchell, Donald Stephen, instructor, $53,554
Mitchell, Eric Lamont, sterile processing tech, $17.53/hr
Mitchell, Garry Lee, custodian, $12.94/hr
Mitchell, Geri Lynne, media production director I, $50,960
Mitchell, Jacqueline Sue, office support assistant III, $15.30/hr
Mitchell, Jamie Sue, business tech analyst-speclst, $42,617
Mitchell, Jerome, custodian, $13.36/hr
Mitchell, John P, food svc wrkr I, $11.29/hr
Mitchell, Karen Kay, prof, ast/profl pract, $62,265
Mitchell, Katrina Lea, instructor, adjunct, $11,600
Mitchell, Kelly Ann, med coding spclst-certified, $20.08/hr
Mitchell, Kenneth, prof, asoc, $92,004
Mitchell, Laura Grace, nurse practitioner, $76,602
Mitchell, Linda E, professor, $103,449
Mitchell, Lisa A, nurse, licensed prac, $18.89/hr
Mitchell, Marion S, hospital security officer, $12.73/hr
Mitchell, Mary Ann, ast athletic director, $55,000
Mitchell, Maurice Lee, mts/pipefitter, $22.50/hr
Mitchell, Patrick Christopher, instructor, adjunct, $18,648
Mitchell, Rachel Magdalene, nurse, staff II rnwp, $21.68/hr
Mitchell, Randy Joe, office support assistant IV, $15.45/hr
Mitchell, Samuel E, biomed equip techn III, $27.37/hr
Mitchell, Sarah Nichole, grader, $100.00/hr
Mitchell, Simon D, prof, asoc, $123,560
Mitchell, Starlene Marie, care team assoc-suppt, $10.64/hr
Mitchell, Tanya Villalpando, prof, asoc, $77,994
Mitchell, Tracey Lee, mts/refrigeration mech lead, $22.11/hr
Mitchell, Wil E, sftware supprt analyst-expert, $50,750
Mitchell, William Alfred, executive director, $88,840
Mitchum, Melissa Goellner, prof, asoc, $122,480
Mite, Robby, tutor, $9.00/hr
Mitra, Ashim K, vice provost, $206,500
Mitra, Moonmoon, office support assistant IV, $17.65/hr
Mitra, Ranjana, resrch asoc, $44,277

Mitrea, Dorina Irena Rita, professor, $92,825
Mitrea, Marius, professor, $109,092
Mitsuyama, Yoshihiro, athletic trainer, $39,900
Mittal, Mayank Kumar, fellow, post doc clncl-yr2, $58,083
Mitten, Gloria Manette, perfusionist, $137,030
Miyamoto, Peter Marc, prof, asoc, $60,623
Mize, Brenda, nurse clinician, $72,920
Mize, Robert Blake, strat comm associate sr, $57,621
Mizutani, Yuima, educational pgm associate I, $12.98/hr
Mo, Cheng Lin, fellow, post doctoral, $38,000
Moats, Benjamin Charles, lecturer, $29,970
Moats, Michael Scott, prof, asoc, $104,900
Moattar, Aliraad, specialist, $10.00/hr
Mobberley, James C, prof, curators, $120,772
Moberly, Deborah Ann, prof, asoc adjunct, $19,038
Moberly, Kenneth Leland, police officer, $16.54/hr
Mobley, Angela D, user support analyst-expert, $21.03/hr
Mobley, Kimberly Lynne, patient svc rep, $12.76/hr
Modica, Natalie E, office support assistant III, $13.50/hr
Moe, Brittany Anne, office support assistant IV, $13.98/hr
Moehrle, Stephen R, professor, $188,086
Moeller, Brice Eugene, event assistant I, $10.00/hr
Moeller, Kimberly Nicole, librarian I, $42,000
Moeller, Linda Sue, mgr III business admin, $29.01/hr
Moeller, Stephanie Rae, payroll/cntrl proc spclst, $49,992
Moen, Daryl R, professor, $122,537
Moen, Heidi Erin, business support specialist sr, $17.60/hr
Moen, Michelle Lynn, nurse, staff II, $22.19/hr
Moentmann, Shellie, nurse, staff II, $29.55/hr
Moersch, Valerie Lorraine, office support assistant IV, $12.99/hr
Moes, Jim, instructor, adjunct, $9,000
Moesel, Douglas D, prof, asoc, $143,329
Moffitt, Amanda J, psychology techn, $14.25/hr
Moghadam, Behjat K H, professor, $98,742
Moghadam, Keivan N, support systems admin-speclst, $51,125
Mohammed, Waseemuddin Ansari, res physician-2nd yr, $50,810
Mohan, Mary Jo, business support specialist II, $19.16/hr
Mohan, Rajiv Ravindra, professor, $173,300
Mohesky, Catherine L, human resources specialist III, $48,691
Mohi, Christie Linn, med techl reg, $27.62/hr
Mohlman, Clayton, db programmer analyst-expert, $73,296
Mohrman, Mary Beth, founders professor, $26,000
Mohrmann, Gregory G, operations support tech II, $20.00/hr
Mohrmann, Rae J, operations support tech sr, $26.78/hr
Molinar Thorne, Emanuel E, tutor, $9.00/hr
Molitor, Katelynn Rose, office support assistant II, $9.50/hr
Molitoris, Cassie Ann, strat comm manager, $48,480
Moller, Chad, asoc athletic director, $78,000
Molloy, Whitney Suzanne, dir I, student support svcs, $64,236
Moloney, Timothy Hayes, instructor, $49,490
Molteni, Agostino, prof, adjunct, $22,407
Monahan, James L III, asoc dir program/project ops, $64,754
Monahan, Kelly Marie, resident physician-1st yr, $50,219
Mondy, Jessica Erin, hospital lab tech, $13.40/hr
Mondy, Kerrie Anne, stage services assistant sr, $16.00/hr
Monge Palacios, Manuel, fellow, post doctoral, $47,000
Mongillo, Diane F, executive assistant, $20.86/hr
Mongler, Clifford L, research engineering tech I, $17.40/hr
Mongler, Joshua B, resident physician-3rd yr, $53,763
Monibi, Farrah Ann, fellow, post doctoral, $30,600
Monk, Terri Gay, prof, clinical dept, $187,500
Monnier, Nicole M, prof, asoc teach, $52,360
Monnig, Candice Danielle, office support assistant IV, $15.44/hr
Monnig, Jason, bts carpenter, $21.71/hr
Monnig, Mindy Leanne, serv line spclst, $83,070
Monnig, Sandra M, program/project supprt coor II, $46,101
Monroe, Heidi Marie, instructor, clncl, $33,762
Monroe, Heidi Marie, nurse, staff II, $40.00/hr
Monroe, Holly Orr, prof, ast clncl, $68,160
Monroe, Jessica Marie, specialist, $10.00/hr
Monroe, Mark A, information security officer, $86,166
Monroe, Richard, student service coor II, $39,600
Monroe, Tori Nicole, care team assoc-clinical, $12.32/hr
Monsen, Toni Dee, business support specialist II, $21.83/hr
Monserrate, Lisa M, business support specialist II, $19.11/hr
Monson, Beth Ann, executive assistant, $16.79/hr
Monson, Michael J, prof, asoc, $85,929
Monson, Sandra J, prof, ast resrch, $171,875
Montano, Jacqueline Graham, temporary crafts service, $8.00/hr

Monteer, Amy Michelle, speech/lang pathologist, $35.00/hr
Monteer, Nancy S, sr asoc dir business admin, $85,168
Montes, Miguel, custodian, $12.94/hr
Montfrooij, Wouter Theodorus, prof, asoc, $70,753
Montgomery Smith, Stephen, professor, $102,739
Montgomery, Aaron M, system administrator-entry, $46,350
Montgomery, April Rachelle, nurse, staff I, $19.00/hr
Montgomery, Barbara Sue, program/pro supprt coor II, $65,516
Montgomery, Brooke Ashley, temporary technical, $8.50/hr
Montgomery, Christa Lynn, resrch scientist/academic, $42,000
Montgomery, Christina Elizabeth, hospital lab tech, $14.20/hr
Montgomery, Christine, grant writer sr, $52,000
Montgomery, Emily Michel, social worker, $46,249
Montgomery, Emma Elizabeth, office support asst IV, $13.50/hr
Montgomery, Frances Haemmerlie, chancellors prof, $27,843
Montgomery, John H, prof, ast clncl dept, $275,000
Montgomery, Lisa Marie, asoc dir business admin, $62,500
Montgomery, Mark A, instructor, adjunct, $6,000
Montgomery, Michael Lloyd, student support spec I, $13.93/hr
Montgomery, Rebecca Ila, care team assoc-clinical, $12.99/hr
Montgomery, Scott Brooks, instructor, adjunct, $3,000
Montgomery, Tammie Lea, event assistant I, $7.55/hr
Montie, Paula Jean, nurse, staff II, $22.24/hr
Montonye, Daniel R, fellow, resrch, $42,000
Montoya De Rivera, Maria Monserrat, educational pgm associate I, $13.45/hr
Montoya Pantoja, Rosa Maria, custodian, $13.36/hr
Montoya Salazar, Maria Elena, educational pgm assoc I, $15.64/hr
Montoya, Scott A, police officer, $17.08/hr
Montoya, Sunshine Dawn, safety comm operator, $14.00/hr
Monzingo, Chantell Nicole, pat acct rep, $14.92/hr
Moody, Mikki L, temporary professional, $15.00/hr
Moody, Susan C, academic advisor sr, $41,227
Mookkan, Muruganantham, fellow, post doctoral, $39,253
Moon, Gregory Allen, pat care techn, $11.99/hr
Mooney, Brian P, prof, ast resrch, $78,338
Mooney, Bryan F, security analyst-entry, $45,000
Mooney, Gayle L, office support assistant III, $13.00/hr
Mooneyham, Shanon Lynn, farm wrkr I, $12.12/hr
Moore II, Kenneth Lamont, event assistant I, $8.50/hr
Moore, Ralph C Sr, instructor, adjunct, $12,552
Moore-Porter, Valorie Nan, business support spclst II, $17.59/hr
Moore, Alex Michael, fellow, post doctoral, $30,000
Moore, Ali Michelle, animal technician sr, $23.00/hr
Moore, Alyssa Dawn, office support assistant IV, $15.30/hr
Moore, Ashley Elizabeth Hays, office supervisor, $55,000
Moore, Ben, prof, visiting, $75,000
Moore, Bobby D, nurse anesthetist, $147,900
Moore, Bridgette Elizabeth, lecturer sr, $9,000
Moore, Brittany, resident physician-1st yr, $49,025
Moore, Bruce A, csm professional II, $43,534
Moore, Cameron Todd, teaching ast, $8,424
Moore, Cameron Todd, phlebotomist, $10.64/hr
Moore, Cecil P, administrative consultant sr, $48,054
Moore, Dale, security officer, $14.09/hr
Moore, Danna Lynn, office support assistant IV, $16.00/hr
Moore, David F, advancement associate II, $24.12/hr
Moore, David Joshua, temporary clerical, $7.50/hr
Moore, David N, supv engineering, $56,055
Moore, Deaudrea L, custodian, $12.50/hr
Moore, Diana K, rehab therapy aide, $12.94/hr
Moore, Donna Sue, patient svc rep, $14.23/hr
Moore, Duane S, mech, bldg maint, $19.64/hr
Moore, Emily Ann, theatre ast, $10.00/hr
Moore, Emma, nurse, staff I, $19.00/hr
Moore, Gail Dian, telecom tech-expert, $20.11/hr
Moore, Gary T, prof, adjunct, $4,800
Moore, Harold L, resrch asoc, $50,657
Moore, Ivan Charles, manager it, $82,891
Moore, Jana E, program/project supprt coor sr, $56,360
Moore, Jennifer Marie, resident physician-2nd yr, $52,007
Moore, Jessica M, child dev aide, $9.65/hr
Moore, Joi L, prof, asoc, $95,240
Moore, Julia A, instructor, ast, $35,823
Moore, Juliet Marie, food svc wrkr II, $10.49/hr
Moore, Kate, educational pgm manager, $76,506
Moore, Kay Lynn, neurodiagnostic tech (non-reg), $19.68/hr
Moore, Kevin C, prof, asoc, $82,400
Moore, Kim D, resrch asoc, $15,600

Moore, Linda Sue, care team assoc-clinical, $14.92/hr
Moore, Lindsey Nicole, resident physician-4th yr, $55,804
Moore, Marsha C, executive assistant, $22.97/hr
Moore, Mary Clare, academic advisor, $43,100
Moore, Megan Elizabeth, prof, ast, $55,729
Moore, Phyllis A, dir program/project operations, $78,981
Moore, Rebecca Sue, reimbursement ast-cert, $18.59/hr
Moore, Robert L, boiler maint opr, $24.13/hr
Moore, Sandra L, office support assistant IV, $16.45/hr
Moore, Sarah Lee, student recruitment spclst, $17.16/hr
Moore, Sarah Louise, resrch asoc, $46,818
Moore, Sarah S, nurse, staff now I, $26.00/hr
Moore, Shane Edward, hospital lab tech, $12.46/hr
Moore, Shanelle E, patient svc rep, $11.28/hr
Moore, Shannon Baker, instructor, adjunct, $21,000
Moore, Stephanie Renee, pat acct rep, $15.14/hr
Moore, Steven J, distribution techn-mtls mgmt, $15.48/hr
Moore, Tanya L, office support assistant IV, $13.76/hr
Moore, Terrence, sftware supprt analyst-entry, $34,916
Moore, Terry D, supv skilled trades, $46,145
Moore, Tonya Erin, nurse, licensed prac, $18.19/hr
Moore, Traci A, teaching ast, $13.00/hr
Moore, Tracie L, 4-h spclst, $43,499
Moore, Vickie M, fin and acctg consultant, $52,368
Moorefield, Mackenzie Jane, human resources mgr sr, $60,000
Moorehead, Dawn Marie, mgr II business admin, $60,297
Moormeier, Jill A, adjunct, $15,000
Moosmann, Angelia S, nurse, or/recovery-ch, $33.77/hr
Moosmann, Thomas Ray, mts/pipefitter, $22.50/hr
Mora, Diane Marie, program/project supprt coor I, $50,000
Mora, Kendyll Rose, phlebotomist, $14.77/hr
Morales, Angel Ricardo, prof, ast teach, $60,075
Morales, Fidencio, custodian, $12.94/hr
Morales, Paula Maria, pat acct rep, $13.69/hr
Moran, Frances Ellen, office support assistant IV, $15.73/hr
Moran, Joseph C, media producer sr, $41,501
Moran, Robert, business support specialist II, $18.00/hr
Morash-Littell, Lynn Ann, instructor, adjunct, $19,200
Morawitz, Elizabeth Anne, prof, asoc, $64,149
Mordica, Dustin Ryan, user support analyst-speclst, $20.03/hr
Moreau, Leah R, office support assistant IV, $18.37/hr
Morehouse, Dale William, prof, asoc, $60,929
Morehouse, Douglas Dwight, temporary technical, $14.50/hr
Moreland, Jill Annette, instructor, $52,500
Moreland, Michael, resident physician-1st yr, $49,025
Morell, Casey Allan, temporary technical, $13.08/hr
Morello, Peter, prof, asoc, $63,192
Moreno, Gabriela Isabel, office support assistant I, $11.00/hr
Moreno, Jeannie Ann, educational pgm assistant, $11.65/hr
Morey, Michael E, programmer analyst-speclst, $21.92/hr
Morey, Sharon S, grant writer, $22.91/hr
Morff, Bree Mashell, med techl reg, $22.99/hr
Morgan Talley, Michele Lezlie, rec/athletic specialist, $3,531
Morgan, Brandie Renee, fellow, post doctoral, $32,320
Morgan, Cindy Lou, nurse, staff, $27.64/hr
Morgan, Fred Keith, custodian mrc, $10.50/hr
Morgan, Gerald J, construction manager II, $80,112
Morgan, Ilene H, prof, asoc, $73,227
Morgan, Jason C, mgr csm operations, $52,562
Morgan, John Mark, prof, asoc, $71,470
Morgan, Joseph A, resident physician-5th yr, $58,083
Morgan, Linda Jean, asoc dir program/project ops, $59,214
Morgan, Lindsey Hope, mental health tech, $11.85/hr
Morgan, Lori, mgr III business admin, $84,660
Morgan, Matthew D, office support associate, $21.65/hr
Morgan, Michelle Renee, office support assistant III, $14.03/hr
Morgan, Nancy L, librarian II, $55,000
Morgan, Nathan G, powr plnt cntrl sys techn sr, $27.26/hr
Morgan, Ralph Speer, professor, $137,313
Morgan, Raymund Michael, support systems admin-spclst, $46,284
Morgan, Rebecca Ann, educational pgm associate I, $13.64/hr
Morgan, Rex Alan, nurse, staff, $22.83/hr
Morgan, Roberta, program/project supprt coor sr, $56,657
Morgan, Ruth Ellen, nurse practitioner, $70,680
Morgan, Scott W, mts/electrician, $21.05/hr
Morgan, Stacy Aniece, psychologist, $40.00/hr
Morgan, Veronica S, lecturer, $34,721
Morgan, William D, bts carpenter, $21.71/hr
Morgensen, Cynthia Ann, business support spclst II, $23.10/hr

Morgensen, Phillip Lee, teaching ast, $13.00/hr
Mori, Anatole, prof, asoc, $59,431
Moriarty, Roberta Charlene, finl counselor(eligibility), $18.47/hr
Morice, Melissa Sue, nurse, staff II, $20.54/hr
Moritz, Ashton Ann, safety monitor, $9.27/hr
Mormile, Melanie R, professor, $85,106
Moroni, Joseph R, ast mgr hospitality services, $41,500
Moroni, Tawnya L, temporary crafts service, $9.50/hr
Morpurgo, Carlo, professor, $85,790
Morrey, Christopher Anthony, student service coor II, $41,006
Morrill, Renee J, office support assistant IV, $14.00/hr
Morris, Corey Dremond Sr, event assistant I, $7.50/hr
Morris, Adam M, db programmer analyst-princpl, $69,140
Morris, Andrew A J, event assistant I, $9.25/hr
Morris, Brandi Kay, office support assistant IV, $16.68/hr
Morris, Brian, asoc athletic director, $85,000
Morris, Darla M, nurse, staff II, $29.20/hr
Morris, Debbie Kay, event assistant I, $7.55/hr
Morris, E Matthew, fellow, post doctoral, $48,331
Morris, Ed F, instructor, adjunct, $11,680
Morris, Ellen Kathleen, student support specialist II, $15.39/hr
Morris, Frank W, mgr broadcast operations, $69,281
Morris, Hannah Louise, child dev assistant, $8.08/hr
Morris, Hayley Suzanne, patient svc rep, $11.28/hr
Morris, Heather, executive assistant sr, $46,740
Morris, Heather Lynn, student service coor II, $50,000
Morris, Hope Lynette, executive assistant, $17.63/hr
Morris, James Haden, pat care techn, $11.61/hr
Morris, Jennifer Ann, nurse, licensed prac, $16.62/hr
Morris, John Steven, resrch scientist/academic sr, $52,948
Morris, Judith A, office support assistant IV, $16.39/hr
Morris, Kathleen Ann, office support assistant IV, $17.26/hr
Morris, Laura Elizabeth, prof, ast clincl dept, $142,800
Morris, Lori Lynn, reimbursement ast, $16.00/hr
Morris, Mark R, mts/welding, $22.50/hr
Morris, Mary Michelle Jarrett, prof, asoc, $63,026
Morris, Megan Lynn, business support specialist II, $15.71/hr
Morris, Melanie Appel, reimbursement ast, $16.00/hr
Morris, Michelle Lee, coor, service, $17.10/hr
Morris, Rachel Jane, programmer analyst-speclst, $65,000
Morris, Rachel K, program/project supprt coor sr, $61,441
Morris, Rosemary A, technical writer-expert, $46,284
Morris, Sandra, media producer sr, $59,569
Morris, Sarah L, ast vice chancellor, $122,871
Morris, Shannon Thomas, media producer II, $17.97/hr
Morris, Sharon Lee, office support assistant III, $11.64/hr
Morris, Sherezad Jonathan, patient svc rep, $12.20/hr
Morris, Tamara, dir I, advancement, $62,000
Morris, Tammie K, food svc wrkr II, $11.83/hr
Morrison, Ariel Schroder, temporary technical, $10.00/hr
Morrison, Christopher Wallace, resident physician-3rd yr, $52,470
Morrison, Ginnie D, fellow, post doctoral, $41,500
Morrison, Glenn, professor, $92,834
Morrison, Jack, custodian, $12.94/hr
Morrison, Julie Rene, supv food svc I,-h, $36,382
Morrison, Kimberly L, business support specialist II, $18.95/hr
Morrison, Lisa M, 4-h spclst, $44,959
Morrison, Margaret Zonia, lecturer, $18,600
Morrison, Michael Gene, mech trades spclst (mts), $21.62/hr
Morrison, Michael James, storage admin-entry, $64,482
Morrison, Scott Dewayne, stage services asst lead, $18.12/hr
Morrissey, John Michael, asoc dir fin and acctg, $85,485
Morrissey, Jordan Elizabeth, office support asst III, $15.30/hr
Morrissey, William Joseph, physician, $250.00/hr
Morrow, Alyssa Anne, child dev teacher sr, $26,000
Morrow, Derek Stefen, temporary technical, $20.00/hr
Morrow, Eva, instructor, ast, $37,531
Morrow, Jason A, hospital lab tech, $13.16/hr
Morrow, Jesse J, bts carpenter, $20.23/hr
Morrow, Johanna Lynn, research specialist I, $41,140
Morrow, Sally Ann, media producer II, $18.00/hr
Morrow, Susan Kay, supv housekeeping, $34,898
Morrow, Willard, prof, asoc teach, $89,250
Morse, Jacqueline Ann, office support assistant II, $11.87/hr
Morse, Leona Ruth, library info specialist, $15.76/hr
Mortimer, Denise Christine, dir II research ops and plng, $56,550
Mortimer, Dylan J, instructor, adjunct, $7,500
Morton, D Patrick, dir research activities, $78,917
Morton, Duane E, model, $17.00/hr

Morton, Ellen E, dental assistant II, $17.10/hr
Morton, Jennifer A, academic advisor sr, $51,462
Morton, Kera Kay, nurse, staff II rnwp, $21.80/hr
Morton, Lea-Ann, ast vice chancellor, $115,000
Morton, Leo E, chancellor, $296,514
Morton, Rebecca Ann, mgr med records-h, $102,327
Morton, Scotta L, student service coor II, $60,000
Morton, Stephen Carlyle, lecturer, $16,830
Morton, Vickie Lynn, nurse, licensed prac, $20.58/hr
Mosa, Abu Saleh Mohammad, engineer II, $61,800
Mosbrucker, Christine Anne, 4-h spclst, $41,700
Mosbrucker, Stephanie Anne, educational pgm assoc I, $12.55/hr
Mosel, Alison Beth, athletic trainer, $53,410
Mosel, Paul W, mts/electrician, $20.31/hr
Moseley, Lorna, cook, $13.21/hr
Mosely, Jessica Renee, health records techn I, $9.99/hr
Moser, Ashley R, resident physician-6th yr, $58,200
Moser, Heike, office support assistant IV, $16.96/hr
Moser, Joyce Marie, coor info systems, $76,309
Moser, Lisa M, business support specialist II, $17.48/hr
Moser, Suzan Anne, temporary technical, $34.85/hr
Moses-Nunley PhD, Dianna N, psychologist, $40.00/hr
Moses, Christopher Austin, high school student, $7.90/hr
Moses, Dennis Alfred, bts glazier, $20.23/hr
Moses, Kristin Jeanine, nurse, staff II, $23.00/hr
Mosher, Sonya Marie, nurse, staff II, $24.43/hr
Moskowitz, Jacob Ezra, fellow, resrch, $42,000
Mosley Ayuk, Kendra, temporary professional, $19.00/hr
Mosley, Geoffrey D Jr, mgr inpatient rehab svcs, $91,080
Moss, Nels C III, nurse, staff II, $22.00/hr
Moss, Aaron D, programmer analyst-speclst, $53,614
Moss, Cynthia J, resp therapist reg, $21.74/hr
Moss, Kathryn Sue, prof, asoc clincl, $65,777
Moss, Linda Faye, reimbursement spclst, $19.20/hr
Moss, Lisa, nurse, staff II rnwp, $34.18/hr
Moss, Randy Hays, professor, $117,670
Moss, Takisha Rachele, office support assistant III, $11.53/hr
Mossine, Olga, nurse, staff II, $27.07/hr
Mossine, Paul Valerievich, instructor, adjunct, $27,000
Mossine, Valeri V, scientist lead, $69,818
Mossman, Karen Ann, tutor, $15.00/hr
Mota, Araceli, food svc wrkr IV, $14.77/hr
Motavalli, Gertrud Elisabeth, physical therapist, $35.00/hr
Motavalli, Peter P, professor, $92,969
Mote, Sarah Elizabeth, strat comm associate II, $51,000
Moten, Ronnie Steven, food svc wrkr I, $9.60/hr
Mott, Lori Jean, office support assistant IV, $14.35/hr
Mott, Rebecca Louise, office support assistant IV, $15.61/hr
Mott, Susan Lynn, office support assistant IV, $16.95/hr
Mottaz, Kelly Lynn, research specialist I, $40,697
Mottl, Rebecca L, office support assistant IV, $18.52/hr
Mottl, Robert O, lecturer, $3,060
Moua, Pangku, student service coor II, $41,918
Mouber, Bryan E, instructor, adjunct, $9,000
Moulaison, Heather L, prof, ast, $73,649
Moum, Amy J, temporary professional, $11.30/hr
Moum, Glenda Ellen, strat comm associate II, $46,128
Mounter, Sarah Ann, research specialist I, $46,500
Mountjoy, Larry, mts/machinist, $21.07/hr
Mountz, William T, grader, $100.00/hr
Mousadakos, Kasiani, occl therapist, $69,033
Movitz, Norman Randal, media production director I, $41,250
Mowrer, Constance J, program/project supprt coor I, $35,224
Moxley, Callie Lynn, serv line spclst, $67,810
Moxley, David E, instructor, clincl, $80,327
Moxley, Elle R, media production director I, $41,000
Moyer, Lorena Ann Lanford, ast mgr nutri/fs patient fs, $62,975
Moyer, Paul, safety communications operator, $14.21/hr
Moyes, William E, event assistant I, $7.50/hr
Mozingo, Allan Lee, custodian lead, $13.96/hr
Mozingo, Nathan, nurse, staff II rnwp, $22.89/hr
Mramor, Sandra M, med techl reg, $30.36/hr
Mreen, Fern B, business support specialist II, $19.24/hr
Mroz, Jordan Michael, research specialist I, $38,850
Mu, Hao, project manager-princpl, $101,429
Muchhala, Nathan C, prof, ast, $70,000
Muchow, Michael D, librarian III, $56,737
Muck, Patrick S, fin and acctg specialist, $19.73/hr
Muckerman, Dale, csm professional sr, $50,317

Muckerman, James G, stores clerk, $19.25/hr
Muckerman, Sean Michael, care team assoc-clinical, $12.80/hr
Mudd, Gidget M, educational pgm associate I, $14.19/hr
Muehlebach, Kurt L, prof, ast adjunct, $125.00/hr
Muehlrath, Kathryn, prof, ast adjunct, $16,008
Mueller, Alexander Heinrich, scholar, visiting, $12,000
Mueller, Elizabeth Ashley, nurse, staff I, $19.00/hr
Mueller, Gary Edward, prof, asoc, $97,318
Mueller, Georgia Leigh, resrch ast, $34,500
Mueller, Jessica Marie, program/project supprt coor I, $48,376
Mueller, Jonathan D, internet administrator-expert, $24.68/hr
Mueller, Kevin A, police sergeant, $20.34/hr
Mueller, Larry, research specialist II, $53,296
Mueller, Marie Therese, nurse practitioner, $85,686
Mueller, Mark Robert, resident physician-3rd yr, $56,763
Mueller, Melody Noel, office support assistant III, $11.47/hr
Mueller, Michelle Lee, office support assistant IV, $15.30/hr
Mueller, Ronald F, specialist, $69,237
Mueller, Tonya J, support systems admin-speclst, $60,159
Mueser, Peter, professor, $118,182
Mueth, Jill Symmonds, prof, ast adjunct, $8,004
Mueth, Marcella L, temporary crafts service, $9.60/hr
Mugel, Hannah Margaret, temporary professional, $12.00/hr
Mugisha, Okello, fellow, post doctoral, $39,264
Muhammad, Ludie Coretta, student service coor II, $43,988
Muhoza, Justin, food svc wrkr I, $9.60/hr
Muin, Michael J, strat comm associate II, $51,603
Mukherjee, Nivedita, student support specialist II, $19.18/hr
Mukherjee, Sumit, resident physician-5th yr, $56,120
Mukherji, Mridul, prof, asoc, $92,410
Mulcahey, Jamie Lee, data cntr support tech-entry, $15.00/hr
Mulcahy, Ellyn Rosemarie, instructor, adjunct, $9,600
Mulderig, John P, administrative consultant sr, $125,736
Muleski, Gregory E, instructor, $36,400
Mulholland, Pamela A, asoc vice chancellor, $217,350
Mullaguri, Naresh, resident physician-2nd yr, $52,007
Mullaly Quijas, Margaret P, librarian III, $94,430
Mullanix, Deborah Valene, office support assistant III, $11.30/hr
Mullanix, Janet Ann, lab techn, persl svc-clin lab, $14.06/hr
Mullen, Anthony Floyd Jr, food svc wrkr I, $9.60/hr
Mullen, Chad Edwin, cook, $12.20/hr
Mullen, Dennis Marvin, mgr II csm operations, $71,508
Mullen, Gentry Marion, media producer sr, $51,000
Mullen, Helen Braley, emeritus, $1,200
Mullen, Robert W G, dir II research ops and plng, $120,120
Mullen, Roberta, dir II business admin, $103,168
Muller, Alyssa Merrillyn, care team assoc-clinical, $12.08/hr
Muller, Majorie Terbugh, event assistant I, $22.40/hr
Muller, Virginia Lee, prof, asoc teach, $37,680
Mulligan, Heather Angelique, nurse, licensed prac, $20.02/hr
Mulligan, Zora Zoa, chief of staff, $165,000
Mullin, Kevin P, media producer II, $21.42/hr
Mullin, Mark E, athletic director, $115,000
Mullin, Patricia R, office support assistant IV, $13.33/hr
Mullins, April Elizabeth, nurse, staff II rnwp, $25.53/hr
Mullins, Christopher O'Brian, event assistant I, $7.50/hr
Mullins, Rachel Marie, med techl reg, $23.87/hr
Mulyala, Rajasekhar Reddy, prof, ast clincl dept, $180,000
Mumm, Tyler John, hospital lab tech, $12.46/hr
Mundey, Alan J, 4-h spclst, $46,721
Mundt, Cassandra J, strat comm associate II, $39,600
Mundy, Ray A, professor, $177,683
Munford, Donald Ray, patient svc rep, $13.55/hr
Munk, Patricia Ruth, care team assoc-clinical, $13.53/hr
Munoz, Alexis M, nurse, staff I, $19.00/hr
Munro, John S, prof, clincl, $150,000
Muns, Raleigh Clayton, librarian III, $65,803
Munteanu, Gregory Alexander, media production dir I, $40,194
Muratore, Mary Jo, professor, $105,312
Murdie, Amanda Marie, prof, asoc, $77,453
Murdock, Fred A Jr, research specialist sr, $57,884
Murdock, Amy Marie, nurse, or/recovery-ch, $26.31/hr
Murdock, Andrea Faye, nurse, staff II, $29.40/hr
Murdock, Linda Joan, resp care clinical coor, $29.59/hr
Murdock, Nancy L, professor, $94,292
Murdock, Tamera B, professor, $92,246
Muri, Regan Macal, nurse, staff II rnwp, $20.95/hr
Muri, Taylor Rene, care team assoc-clinical, $11.10/hr
Murillo, Maria Daveiva, instructor, ast, $24,746

Murillo, Sandra E, custodian, $12.94/hr
Murowchick, James, prof, asoc, $71,007
Murphy, Analise Noel, nurse, staff II, $23.12/hr
Murphy, Bridget E, educational pgm coor III, $40,036
Murphy, Carl W, bts painter, $20.23/hr
Murphy, Carole, founders professor, $20,193
Murphy, Christopher Edward, lecturer sr, $9,300
Murphy, Clifton N, prof, ast resrch, $26,902
Murphy, Courtney Leann, nurse, staff II, $21.26/hr
Murphy, David L, temporary crafts service, $10.00/hr
Murphy, Dennis James, temporary professional, $18.33/hr
Murphy, James H, ast vice chancellor, $119,000
Murphy, Jeffrie Blake, mts/pipefitter, $22.49/hr
Murphy, Jody Lea, nurse, staff II, $34.18/hr
Murphy, Kevin Robert, waiter/waitress, $10.19/hr
Murphy, Mackensie Christian, research specialist I, $38,850
Murphy, Michelle Lynn, student service coor sr, $46,968
Murphy, Phillip John, police officer, $17.93/hr
Murphy, Phyllis Kay, environmental health prof sr, $47,043
Murphy, Ronald Alan, db programmer analyst-princpl, $70,408
Murphy, Shaun Eric, 4-h spclst, $48,865
Murphy, Stephanie Lynn, research/lab technician sr, $14.04/hr
Murphy, Steven Francis, rec/athletic assistant, $8.00/hr
Murphy, Terry Eugene, custodian, $12.94/hr
Murphy, Theresa L, business support specialist sr, $20.13/hr
Murphy, Tina Kay, tutor, $10.00/hr
Murray-Jones, Cynthia Rene, office support asst IV, $13.37/hr
Murray, Brandon Marshall, custodian, $10.00/hr
Murray, Carri L, office support assistant IV, $13.72/hr
Murray, Cynthia A, hlth prgm spclst, $18.91/hr
Murray, David Lee, custodian, $12.90/hr
Murray, Emily Ann, temporary crafts service, $7.50/hr
Murray, Janet Y, professor, $197,638
Murray, Jerry Dewayne, custodian, $12.90/hr
Murray, John S, dir III business admin, $115,000
Murray, Johnna, lecturer, $51,765
Murray, Joshua M, strat comm associate I, $44,827
Murray, Kathy A, asoc dir student support svcs, $79,896
Murray, Lisa A, nurse, staff II, $31.58/hr
Murray, Michael D, prof, curator teach, $94,640
Murray, Ramona, office support assistant sr, $18.22/hr
Murray, Ryan J, student support specialist II, $20.92/hr
Murray, Sandra K, mgr I, business admin, $44,101
Murray, Susan L, professor, $106,757
Murrell, Eric Dean, clerk, stores, $15.20/hr
Murtha, Yvonne, prof, ast clincl dept, $175,000
Musaev, Omar R, resrch asoc, $16,800
Muscato, Andrea Lea, nurse, staff II, $20.54/hr
Muse, Carol Ann, nurse, staff I, $19.37/hr
Muse, Jeanne M, office support assistant IV, $18.86/hr
Musgrove, Robin Yvette, system support analyst-spclst, $22.53/hr
Mushaben, Joyce Marie, professor, $101,820
Mushrush, Willis C Jr, business spclst, $60,436
Musick, Shane T, mts/hvac, $24.13/hr
Musket, Paul J, sr asoc dir business admin, $86,114
Musket, Theresa A, research lab supervisor, $57,500
Muskett-Lyon, Virginia Lee, event assistant I, $7.50/hr
Musonda, Chiluba John, student service coor sr, $46,512
Mussatt, Susan, nurse clinician, $62,174
Musser, Dale Roy, prof, asoc teach, $117,068
Mussman, Denise Carpenter, prof, asoc teach, $46,668
Mustain, Charlotte Fay, library information assistant, $11.89/hr
Mustapha, Azlin, professor, $92,903
Mustapha, Sara Jeanette, nurse, staff now III, $30.00/hr
Musterman, Kathryn Irene, mgr, nrsing for aging in place, $55,713
Mutangadura, Tendai, research specialist I, $51,546
Mutava, Raymond Ngao, fellow, post doctoral, $43,050
Muter, Amal Qassim, food svc wrkr II, $10.10/hr
Mutrux, Ellen Rachel, sr dir program/project ops, $86,601
Muzaffar, Arshad R, prof, asoc, $231,900
Muzika, Rosemarie, professor, $114,210
Muzinich, Michael Curtis, resident physician-5th yr, $58,083
Myer, Julie Kay, student support specialist sr, $16.74/hr
Myers, Aleatha Anne, nurse, staff II, $35.07/hr
Myers, Anna L, rehab therapy aide, $13.12/hr
Myers, Anne Marie, prof, asoc, $65,186
Myers, Annunziata M, coor, service, $16.99/hr
Myers, Bridget Crowley Kevin, prof, ast teach, $66,667
Myers, Danny R, program/project supprt coor II, $58,308

Myers, David Brenton, prof, ast, $77,000
Myers, Elaine Elizabeth, office support assistant II, $11.00/hr
Myers, Elizabeth J, supv pat accts-up, $52,480
Myers, Felicita Anna, academic advisor, $38,545
Myers, Forest Everette, instructor, $72,000
Myers, Gary, dean, $257,550
Myers, Jessica Lynn, dietitian, clincl, $47,475
Myers, John J, professor, $138,737
Myers, John William, director it, $109,849
Myers, Kevin, csm associate sr, $30.99/hr
Myers, Laurie Ellen, lecturer, $15,000
Myers, Lindsy L, prof, ast teach, $42,820
Myers, Lucille Joan, lecturer, $41,485
Myers, Mary A, prof, asoc teach, $73,960
Myers, Mike Neal, research engineering tech I, $20.00/hr
Myers, Noah Turner, instructor, ast, $29,485
Myers, Prudence A, business tech analyst-expert, $54,234
Myers, Raymond I, prof, clincl, $64,957
Myers, Richard E, dairy worker, $14.27/hr
Myers, Richard Joseph, educational pgm coor II, $34,914
Myers, Robert Lee, prgm director, $133,048
Myers, Sheila R, media producer II, $15.06/hr
Myers, Susan M, child dev teacher sr, $27,780
Myers, Trenton M, resident physician-2nd yr, $50,810
Myler, Matthew T, event assistant I, $11.00/hr
Myles, Erin Nichole, care team assoc-clinical, $11.10/hr
Myrda, Tom J, stage services assistant lead, $19.47/hr
Myre, Debbie E, library info specialist, $13.10/hr
Myrick, Kory Dion, event assistant I, $10.50/hr
Mysliwiec, June Bernice, coor, service, $16.74/hr
Naaman, Harira Ladi, food svc wrkr II, $10.10/hr
Nabelek, Carol R, chemist II, $19.04/hr
Nabelek, Peter I, professor, $97,498
Nabhan, Tareq Issam, prof, ast adjunct, $30,600
Nabli, Henda, research specialist I, $37,708
Nacarato, Matthew Scott, event assistant I, $10.00/hr
Nace, Rebecca Rose, specialist, $70,596
Nadafy, Somaye, temporary clerical, $8.00/hr
Nadin, Andrew, prof, adjunct, $18,600
Nadler, Ann W, asoc dir business admin, $89,099
Naeger, Joyce A, business support specialist II, $18.84/hr
Naes, Margaret Mary, supervisor it, $48,000
Nagam, Nivedita, fellow, post doc clncl yr1, $55,804
Nagarkar, Sushama A, lecturer, $100.00/hr
Nagel, David Lee, powr plnt opr lead, $31.58/hr
Nagel, Mary C, health records techn I, $11.96/hr
Nagel, Susan Carol, prof, asoc, $93,488
Nagel, Terrie R, ast director, $71,605
Nagele, Ryan P, resident physician-2nd yr, $50,810
Nagy, Dusty Weaver, prof, asoc teach, $109,376
Nagy, Wayne R, student service coor II, $39,791
Nah, Fui Hoon, professor, $164,209
Naidzionak, Uladzislau, fellow, post doc clncl-yr3, $60,415
Nail, Michelle Anna, business support specialist II, $18.96/hr
Nail, Sandra Kay, supv, lab, $69,900
Nair, Satish S, professor, $166,029
Najera, Omar Fabian, resident physician-1st yr, $50,219
Naji, Darwish I, physician, resident chief, $64,425
Nall, Donna J, reimbursement ast-cert, $18.23/hr
Nam, Paul Ki Souk, prof, asoc, $62,674
Nance, Sally Ann, grader, $52
Nanda, Ashish, prof, ast clincl dept, $291,200
Nandimandalam, Bharath Kumar Reddy, resident physician-1st yr, $50,219
Nanney, John T, prof, ast clincl, $85,500
Nanney, Spencer Craig, mri technologist, $24.94/hr
Napier, Kari Jane, csm operations supervisor, $36,865
Nappier, Elanora Mary, lecturer sr, $27,000
Naqvi, Syed Hasan Raza, prof, ast clincl dept, $239,700
Narotzky, Sarah, resident physician-5th yr, $56,120
Narsingam, Saiprasad, resident physician-2nd yr, $50,810
Nash, Kindel Turner, prof, ast, $61,200
Nash, Nancy Carolyn, reimbursement ast sr, $20.05/hr
Nash, Tiffany Joyce, nurse, licensed prac, $17.44/hr
Nassir, Fatiha, prof, ast resrch, $72,100
Nath, Manashi, prof, ast, $68,647
Nathan, Christopher Michael, library information asst, $11.30/hr
Nathan, Manjula, prof, asoc extns, $92,798
Nation, Angela Denise, executive assistant, $22.92/hr

Nation, Jessica Marie, office support assistant IV, $14.83/hr
Nation, Theresa J, nurse, procedures, $34.18/hr
Nations, Amy Melissa, nurse, staff II, $20.54/hr
Nations, Elizabeth Anne Hines, high school student, $8.25/hr
Natwick, Sandra Lee, instructor, clincl, $90,000
Nauert, Paul John, lecturer, $22,500
Naufel, Brenna Renee, program/project supprt coor II, $70,000
Naufel, Zeyna Josephine, clerk, diet, $9.75/hr
Naughton, Bethany A, mgr inpatient rehab svcs, $96,703
Naughton, Blake Alan, director, $137,700
Naugle, Ryan, temporary crafts service, $9.50/hr
Naumann, Joseph A Jr, prof, asoc adjunct, $38,064
Naumann, Harley Dean, prof, ast, $78,500
Naumann, Michael Steven, system admin-expert, $61,959
Nauss, Robert M, professor, $207,760
Nava, Guadalupe L, custodian, $10.94/hr
Navarro, Richard Alan, prof, ast teach, $29,775
Navarro, Sean Matthew, business support specialist II, $18.00/hr
Navarro, Virginia L, prof, asoc, $91,942
Naveh-Benjamin, Esther, prof, ast teach, $59,152
Naveh-Benjamin, Moshe, professor, $129,515
Navin, Lynn M, sr dir program/project ops, $67,007
Nay Lor, Jesse A, security officer, $11.80/hr
Naylor, Brenda D, office support assistant I, $9.11/hr
Naylor, Jackson B, agriculture foreman, $24.73/hr
Naylor, John Porter, farm wrkr III, $15.72/hr
Naylor, Sharon Kay, office support assistant IV, $14.93/hr
Nayyar, Manav, prof, ast clincl dept, $180,000
Naz, Sabiha, prof, ast teach, $37,822
Nazario, Jason A, finl counselor(eligibility), $16.30/hr
Nazario, Karen Colby, executive assistant, $18.92/hr
Nazeer, Sarah A, resident physician-2nd yr, $50,810
Ndengue, Steve, fellow, post doctoral, $39,996
Ndiaye, Ndeye Marieme, nurse, staff now III, $30.00/hr
Ndungu, Sylvester Chege, mental health tech, $12.95/hr
Neal, Connie Ann, housing&envirn design spclst, $49,133
Neal, David R, distribution techn-mtls mgmt, $15.26/hr
Neal, Donna S, clinical nursing supvsr, $76,419
Neal, John F, asoc dir csm operations, $105,523
Neal, Leslie R, serv line spclst, $79,134
Neal, Paula J, asoc dir program/project ops, $68,978
Neal, Steven Phelps, prof, asoc, $92,617
Neal, Toni Michelle, nurse, staff II, $24.64/hr
Neckermann, Adrienne Rae, prog/proj supprt coor sr, $52,000
Nedblake, Cassandra L, manager it, $52,400
Nedblake, Dennis M, support systems admin-spcclst, $45,600
Neds, Timothy Evan, event assistant I, $9.50/hr
Needham, Martha Elaine, instructor, adjunct, $1,000
Needles, Becky Jo, nurse, staff per diem, $35.00/hr
Needles, Philip R, instructor, adjunct, $27,000
Neef, Kermon W Jr, building/mechanical maint I, $17.95/hr
Neel, Dustin R, adjunct, $15,000
Neel, Gwendolyn Kay, instructor, clincl, $145,000
Neel, James David, resident physician-7th yr, $61,960
Neelin, Patrick, media production director I, $45,000
Neely, Amber Brookes, mgr II business admin, $54,888
Neely, Jean E, nurse, staff, $23.00/hr
Neely, Laneshia Shanay, office support assistant II, $10.25/hr
Neely, Travis M, db programmer analyst-expert, $58,000
Neff, Angela Louise, nurse, staff, $30.24/hr
Neff, Jeffery Lynn, event assistant I, $7.50/hr
Neff, Kenneth E, event assistant I, $9.75/hr
Neff, Philip M, system support analyst-expert, $27.04/hr
Neff, Sherrie E, human resources specialist III, $22.01/hr
Neff, Suzanne E, office supervisor, $58,602
Negin, Saeedeh, fellow, post doctoral, $38,411
Neier, Leigh P, prof, ast teach, $60,920
Neighbors, Beckie Sue, nurse, staff II, $25.50/hr
Neiss, Jana Lynne, prof, ast teach, $84,497
Neitz, Mary Jo, professor, $108,297
Neitzert, Alyssa Renne, nurse, staff per diem, $35.00/hr
Nejedly, Kathleen Nicole, food svc wrkr II, $9.60/hr
Nell, Amanda E, student service coor sr, $55,997
Nelsen, Debra D, nurse, staff II, $34.18/hr
Nelson, John William Jr, prof, ast clincl, $81,000
Nelson, Christopher S, prof, ast clincl dept, $319,770
Nelson, Claudia L, human resources specialist I, $20.57/hr
Nelson, Eugene Joseph, grounds keeper lead, $15.84/hr
Nelson, Florence Leann, customer service supervisor, $20.00/hr

Nelson, Gregory A, hris specialist-expert, $66,573
Nelson, Gregory Stafford, sr mgr advancement, $69,156
Nelson, Janice, child dev assistant, $13.70/hr
Nelson, Jean, prof, teach, $80,898
Nelson, Jeanette Yvonne, coor, service, $17.10/hr
Nelson, Jennifer M, strat comm associate I, $35,088
Nelson, Jessica Marie, custodian, $12.94/hr
Nelson, John C, dairy worker, $14.27/hr
Nelson, Kecia Liane, social worker, $59,687
Nelson, Kelly A, prof, resrch, $107,151
Nelson, LaTamera Shanae, clerk, diet, $10.63/hr
Nelson, Leigh Anne, prof, asoc, $101,000
Nelson, Lilian Malab, custodian, $12.69/hr
Nelson, Lorine Sue, coor, service, $18.91/hr
Nelson, Marcia Marie, business support specialist II, $21.64/hr
Nelson, Mary Jo, office support assistant I, $9.31/hr
Nelson, Mary L, prof, adjunct, $10,890
Nelson, Matthew B, building/mechanical maint I, $16.50/hr
Nelson, Patricia Lavonne, office support assistant IV, $13.24/hr
Nelson, Rose Marie, care coordinator, $65,545
Nelson, Ryan W, stage services assistant lead, $17.53/hr
Nelson, Sherry F, human dev spclst, $51,476
Nelson, Steven Brian, bts paperhanger, $22.49/hr
Nelson, Tanys Christi Reed, manager it, $77,438
Nelson, Taylor Brooke, resident physician-1st yr, $50,219
Nelson, Teresa Ann, nurse, licensed prac sr, $21.81/hr
Nelson, Terry John Lynn, stage services assistant lead, $19.97/hr
Nelson, Terry Wayne, custodian, $11.00/hr
Nelson, Tiffany J, instructor, clincl, $79,000
Nelson, Timothy P, librarian I, $42,582
Nemec, John Edward III, director IT, $130,050
Nemmers, Charles J, prgm director, $95,990
Neogi, Parthasakha, professor, $99,990
Nepper, Jennet I, program/project supprt coor I, $42,000
Ner, Zarah Hernandez, prof, ast clincl dept, $150,840
Nesbitt, Joan Marie, vice chancellor, $195,500
Nesterova, Maria, patient svc rep, $11.28/hr
Netemeyer, Paula Marie, mgr II business admin, $64,260
Nettles-Strong, Alisa Carol, office support assistant IV, $15.07/hr
Nettles, Duane V, programmer analyst-expert, $68,766
Nettles, Martha Judith, instructor, adjunct, $24,000
Nettles, Tanya D, business support specialist sr, $28.17/hr
Netzer, Anthony J, instructor, clincl, $175,000
Neuerburg, Sharon M, office support assistant IV, $18.30/hr
Neujahr, Joyce Sharon, instructor, adjunct, $8,400
Neukomm, Martha Jane, instructor, adjunct, $6,900
Neulinger, Nathan R, system administrator-master, $72,565
Neuman, Dale A, prgm director, $12,000
Neuman, Jill Ann, asoc dir program/project ops, $60,097
Neuman, Stevanie Schneider, prof, ast, $195,000
Neumann, Joy Aileen, dental assistant II, $17.45/hr
Neumann, Kay Lynn, instructor, adjunct, $41,000
Neumeyer, Gayla Marie, asoc dir program/project ops, $77,500
Neuner, Gregory J, engineer lead, $88,075
Neuner, Katharyn Kay, nurse clinician, $60,489
Neunuebel, Brittany Lynn, academic advisor, $35,018
Neuschafer, Caverly D, office support assistant III, $12.81/hr
Nevalga, Jeimmie Deguzman, prof, ast/profl pract, $61,290
Nevatt, Jennifer Rebekah, educational pgm assoc I, $14.14/hr
Nevel, Rebekah Joy, resident physician-3rd yr, $56,263
Nevels, Carlous R, lead sr mail carrier, $16.69/hr
Nevels, Chassity Sharrel, office support assistant III, $12.00/hr
Nevels, Clifford Donell, stock clerk, $12.94/hr
Nevels, Marilyn Estes, office support assistant IV, $16.01/hr
Never, Brent Ryan, prof, ast, $85,409
Neverman, Eric Mitchell, resident physician-3rd yr, $53,763
Nevins, Louis Preston, business support specialist II, $18.54/hr
New, Laura Lee, instructor, $30,000
Newberry, Rosalie Grace, on-air talent television, $45,000
Newcomb, Henry E, research specialist I, $35,690
Newcomer, Helen M, distribution techn-mtls mgmt, $14.04/hr
Newcomer, Lauren Marie, enrollment advisor sr, $16.54/hr
Newcomer, Lori L, prof, asoc resrch, $76,103
Newcomer, Nara L, librarian III, $60,600
Newell Groshong, Kyle, business support specialist sr, $28.17/hr
Newell, Sharae Lyn, nurse, licensed prac, $15.35/hr
Newell, Traci Alane, office support assistant II, $13.67/hr
Newhouse, Nancy L, prof, ast adjunct, $125.00/hr
Newkirk, Deborah D, nurse, licensed prac sr, $19.41/hr

Newkirk, Joseph W, prof, asoc, $84,224
Newkirk, Melissa Kaye, resrch ast sr, $11,033
Newland, Dominique Terri, sup systems admin-spec, $52,000
Newlin, Joseph William, accountant I, $22.05/hr
Newman, Alan Richard, prof, resrch, $2,860
Newman, Amanda Elizabeth, care team assoc-clinical, $12.57/hr
Newman, Ashley Nicole, custodian, $10.69/hr
Newman, Cara L, psychologist, $40.00/hr
Newman, Carol Dell, prof, asoc, $116,150
Newman, Dorothy M, mental health tech, $12.63/hr
Newman, Jack S, mts/plumber, $20.10/hr
Newman, Jessica Michelle, child dev teacher sr, $26,312
Newsham, Judy H, instructor, adjunct, $12,552
Newsom, Carol Gean, pat acct rep, $15.29/hr
Newton Northup, Jessica Rose, research specialist sr, $48,985
Newton, Carol M, programmer analyst-entry, $48,005
Newton, Jerry Allan, event assistant I, $7.50/hr
Newton, Kalia, office support assistant IV, $13.10/hr
Newton, Kathleen J, professor, $103,010
Newton, Michael D, nurse, clincl charge-rn, $34.68/hr
Newton, Nathan J, prof, ast, $183,800
Newton, Rachel C, office support assistant II, $14.37/hr
Neylon, Karen M, program/project supprt coor I, $48,503
Ngassi, Felix, resrch asoc, $47,254
Ngo, Hilton Lim, prof, ast clincl dept, $192,308
Ngom, Martin Raobert, instructor, adjunct, $8,325
Nguyen, Barbara, resident physician-1st yr, $49,025
Nguyen, Caitlyn Ngoc, resident physician-2nd yr, $50,810
Nguyen, Eric Hoang, programmer analyst-speclst, $49,206
Nguyen, Henry Thien, professor, $229,180
Nguyen, Katy, instructor, clincl, $65,847
Nguyen, Kim Thoa Huynh, safety monitor, $9.27/hr
Nguyen, Linda Thi, educational pgm associate I, $13.28/hr
Nguyen, Nam Tuan, temporary professional, $12.00/hr
Nguyen, Quynh, med techl reg, $20.94/hr
Nguyen, Raymond, temporary technical, $25.26/hr
Nguyen, Son Thengoc, fellow, post doctoral, $48,000
Nguyen, Tho Kim, prof, ast clincl, $52,480
Nguyen, Thuan Ba, resident physician-5th yr, $58,083
Nguyen, Van Thi, prof, ast clincl dept, $141,882
Nguyen, Vu Hoai, instructor, adjunct, $15,000
Nguyen, Yen, mgr student support svcs, $56,606
Ngwenyama, Ruth A, research specialist sr, $49,869
Ngwoke, Grace I, custodian, $10.94/hr
Ni, Xiaoguang, professor, $140,476
Nice, Emily Grace, clerk, diet, $9.55/hr
Niceswanger, Brian, prof, ast adjunct, $7,500
Nicewarner, Daniel Scott, academic advisor sr, $42,500
Nichoalds, Demitra Marie, nurse, staff I, $19.00/hr
Nichols, Howard Vincent Jr, emrg med techn, $13.82/hr
Nichols, James Melvin Jr, custodian, $12.94/hr
Nichols, Alice, business support specialist II, $20.08/hr
Nichols, Andrea M, office supervisor, $40,091
Nichols, Anna Laura, event assistant I, $7.65/hr
Nichols, Cheryl Lynn, office support assistant IV, $14.43/hr
Nichols, Craig T, network engineer-expert, $60,960
Nichols, Dalesa N, telecomm opr-h, $10.41/hr
Nichols, David Christopher, grounds keeper, $12.55/hr
Nichols, Debra Joy, patient svc rep, $13.25/hr
Nichols, Debra Kay, office support assistant IV, $15.01/hr
Nichols, Dina Rae, office support assistant IV, $14.91/hr
Nichols, Francesca Lee, nurse, staff I, $19.00/hr
Nichols, Gina, resident physician-1st yr, $49,025
Nichols, Hannah Marie, office support assistant IV, $17.81/hr
Nichols, Heather N, office support assistant III, $14.77/hr
Nichols, Jarrod Cameron, research/lab technician, $13.50/hr
Nichols, Jerale Eugene, custodian, $10.94/hr
Nichols, Jerry Stephen, mts/pipefitter, $21.05/hr
Nichols, Jessica Wroath, coor audit & quality monitor, $45,540
Nichols, John Anthony, student recruitment spclst, $16.85/hr
Nichols, Joshua Carroll, internet administrator-expert, $25.50/hr
Nichols, Karen J, cook, $13.21/hr
Nichols, Kirby D, mail carrier sr, $15.90/hr
Nichols, Kristi Lea, business support specialist sr, $17.94/hr
Nichols, Kurt A, powr plnt matrl handling opr, $21.05/hr
Nichols, LaNita A, research specialist sr, $45,150
Nichols, Leona May, business support specialist II, $21.31/hr
Nichols, Lisa Kraner, office support assistant IV, $14.04/hr
Nichols, Maggie A, office support assistant IV, $13.39/hr

Nichols, Melinda Kay, business support specialist II, $21.93/hr
Nichols, Michael Anthony, nurse anesthetist, chief, $184,875
Nichols, Michael D, health physics technician II, $21.77/hr
Nichols, Michael R, project manager-expert, $67,803
Nichols, Michael R, prof, asoc, $67,320
Nichols, Raeona K, psychologist, $71,951
Nichols, Randy, print services supervisor, $54,101
Nichols, Robin K, office support assistant IV, $15.35/hr
Nichols, Robin Marie, custodian, $10.39/hr
Nichols, Ruth Lynn, nurse, staff, $30.48/hr
Nichols, Sarah Louise, surgical technl certified, $17.34/hr
Nichols, Shawna Lee, program/project supprt coor I, $44,083
Nichols, Stephanie Loriane, certif pharmacy techn, $17.28/hr
Nichols, Tommy Dale, mts/pipefitter, $22.49/hr
Nichols, Walter Kirt, professor, $554,064
Nicholson, Carrie Sue, program/project supprt coor II, $53,040
Nicholson, Donald Jay, extns professional, $84,366
Nicholson, Janet Sue, fin and acctg manager, $59,019
Nickel, Jeffrey Charles, prof, asoc, $180,022
Nickell, Franklin Delano, mgr research activities, $25,000
Nickell, Glenda, instructor, clincl, $59,945
Nickelson, Karen Johanna, research specialist I, $34,292
Nickens, Flynn Rodale Jr, floor care techn lead, $13.34/hr
Nickerson, Eric L, building/mechanical maint I, $17.19/hr
Nickerson, Rhobenya K, office support assistant III, $15.37/hr
Nicklas, Eric W, account executive, $63,237
Nickler, John M, 4-h spclst, $60,145
Nickolaus, Daniel W, health physics technician II, $24.98/hr
Nickolaus, David G, engineering technician sr, $25.94/hr
Nicks, Courtney A, research specialist I, $31,100
Nicolaescu, Jessica Marie, occl therapist, $52,225
Nieder, Brittany Nicole, 4-h youth devlmnt educr, $32,000
Niederberger, Margaret, lecturer, $35,757
Niedergerke, Sarah Rochelle, nurse, staff II, $21.68/hr
Niederhelm, Henry F, director it, $113,413
Niederhelm, Kathleen M, project manager-expert, $72,466
Niedt, Douglas Ashton Jr, prof, asoc, $54,795
Niehaus, Mary Rebecca, advancement associate II, $17.37/hr
Niekamp, Julia D, office support assistant IV, $16.08/hr
Niekamp, Thomas Anthony, asoc dir opns/devlmnt-h, $153,667
Nielsen, Marie Suzanne, nurse, licensed prac, $15.67/hr
Nielson, Mary A, pat acct rep, $14.84/hr
Nielson, Pamela K, nurse, staff, $19.21/hr
Nielson, Peter Blake, lab assistant, $11.50/hr
Nieman, Adriana Oerly, program/project supprt coor I, $38,143
Niemeier, Stephanie Lynn, nurse, staff II, $28.00/hr
Niemeyer, Christopher, librarian III, $53,987
Niemeyer, Michelle Shannon, executive assistant, $24.44/hr
Niemi, Tina M, professor, $83,281
Nienhaus, Angela Brianna, temporary clerical, $8.60/hr
Nieto, Kathryn Marguerite, nurse, licensed prac, $15.36/hr
Nietzel, Debra J, human resources specialist sr, $61,202
Nietzel, Kari Michelle, resrch asoc, $43,860
Nieuwenhuizen, Farah, grader, $52
Nieuwenhuizen, Timothy M, technology resource coor, $51,525
Nieves, Victor Alberto, hospital lab tech, $15.09/hr
Nigh, Margaret S, coor protocol svcs, $15.00/hr
Nigro, Kathleen Butterly, prof, asoc teach, $42,698
Nikodim, Betty Elaine, db administrator-speclst, $64,791
Nikolenko, Amanda B, nurse, staff I, $19.00/hr
Niles, Daniel D, system administrator-princpl, $74,718
Niles, Vironica Marie, patient svc rep, $13.61/hr
Nilges, Jeffrey L, designer, commercial sign, $20.52/hr
Nilon, Charles H, professor, $82,621
Nilsson, Johanna E, professor, $84,000
Nimley, Marcella Elaine, nurse, staff II, $34.23/hr
Nimsakont, Emily Elizabeth Dust, lecturer, $100.00/hr
Nisbett, J Keith, prof, asoc, $91,798
Nistala, Puja, prof, ast clincl dept, $250,000
Nistala, Ravi, prof, ast clincl dept, $151,000
Nistendirk, Amber N, serv line spclst, $65,517
Nistendirk, Sonya, executive assistant sr, $67,863
Nitcher, Deborah Ann, cardiovasc techn invasive, $25.83/hr
Nittler, Jessica Rae, prof, ast adjunct, $31,580
Niu, Xiaofan, research specialist I, $42,000
Nixon, Jennifer L, project manager-speclst, $59,134
Nixon, Marsha L, office support assistant III, $12.53/hr
Nixon, Sheila Taft, house manager h, $77,501
Nixon, Susan D, instructor, adjunct, $5,400

Niyogi, Dev K, prof, asoc, $71,251
Njuguna, Esther Wanjiku, mental health tech, $14.44/hr
Noack, Carla E, prof, ast, $54,149
Noble-Triplett, Deborah Suzanne, ast vice president, $126,130
Noble, David Wallace, distribution techn-mtls mgmt, $14.66/hr
Noble, Heather Lynn, psychologist, $57,448
Noble, James Stewart, professor, $120,545
Noble, Jerry D, event assistant I, $9.95/hr
Noble, Kim, media producer II, $17.47/hr
Noble, Scott Patrick, forensic techn, $20.64/hr
Noble, Summer D, research/lab technician, $11.00/hr
Noblin, Jeffrey L, office support assistant IV, $15.00/hr
Noel, Catherine Burke, ast dir managed care-up, $97,889
Noel, Connie M, office support assistant I, $9.05/hr
Noel, Jeffrey G, prof, ast resrch, $76,244
Noel, Tammy W, human resources assistant, $16.19/hr
Noffke, Carli A, academic advisor, $34,400
Nofong, Valentine, resident physician-3rd yr, $53,763
Noguera, Erika Cecilia, program/project supprt coor II, $53,500
Nohava, Samantha Jean, resident physician-2nd yr, $50,810
Nolan, Gwen L, instructor, clincl, $55,682
Nolan, Jennifer J, prof, ast teach, $40,000
Nolan, Jonathan David, distribution techn-mtls mgmt, $15.48/hr
Nolan, Mark Kenneth, nurse, staff II rnwp, $20.95/hr
Nolan, Michael F, emeritus, $52,151
Nolan, Telesa, business ops associate sr, $55,946
Noland, Jaleh M, office support assistant IV, $16.85/hr
Nolasco, Emanuel Ortega, user support analyst-entry, $15.86/hr
Nolasco, Nichole Marie, rev cycle spclst, $59,311
Nolen, Rose M, communications assistant sr, $15.61/hr
Nolin, Colette A, ast mgr clncl registr svcs, $86,957
Nolke, Cody D, certif pharmacy techn, $12.73/hr
Nolke, Korrin Nicole, care team assoc-clinical, $11.10/hr
Nolke, Melissa Marie, ast mgr hospitality services, $42,431
Noll, Birgit, prof, teach, $71,728
Nolte, Robert J, business support specialist I, $15.87/hr
Noltie, Douglas B, prof, asoc, $59,503
Nolting, Jeffrey Kyle, seasonal farm ast, $10.51/hr
Nolting, Rachael Michelle, office support assistant III, $13.30/hr
Noonan-Lowry, Deborah Kay, nurse, staff II, $26.27/hr
Noordsy, Lisa, resp therapy techn cert, $20.91/hr
Nordin, Nicole Rhea, lecturer, $33,612
Nordman, Robert William, prof, teach, $88,540
Nordstrom, Jennifer Anna, dietitian, clncl, $43,555
Norell, Shane Thomas, user support analyst-speclst, $17.73/hr
Norgard, Peter, resrch scientist/academic, $50,000
Norman, James R, custodian, $12.94/hr
Norman, Sarah Anne, mental health professional, $16.54/hr
Norregaard, Thorkild Vad, ast clincl dept, $218,484
Norris, Amanda Gloria, resrch ast, $11.89/hr
Norris, Andrew T, managing engineer, $42.64/hr
Norris, Cailin Ann, mental health tech, $11.00/hr
Norris, Deborah Lynn, patient svc rep, $12.44/hr
Norris, J Michael, engineering technician II, $30.11/hr
Norris, Kelly Andrea Felicia, research/lab tech sr, $15.00/hr
Norris, Laurie K, certif pharmacy techn, $17.10/hr
North, Jason Scott, nurse, staff II, $29.92/hr
North, Melanie Ann, radiologic techl, $24.07/hr
North, Wayne Allan, project manager-speclst, $51,408
Northcut, Kathryn Michele, prof, asoc, $69,785
Northcutt, Ariel Kristine, activity aide, $12.77/hr
Northern, Jason S, asoc dir advancement, $75,000
Northrup, Melinda, ultrasonographer, $34.94/hr
Norton, John Alan, dir research and inst prgms, $158,749
Norwood, Donnell Bussey, custodian, $10.00/hr
Nossaman, Larry D, grant writer lead, $57,018
Nourian, Zahra, fellow, post doctoral, $42,605
Novak, Kenneth J, professor, $94,497
Novinger, Tony Lee, cook, $12.20/hr
Nowack, Adam Jacob, radiation ther therapist, $25.81/hr
Nowlin, Bethany Elaine, food svc wrkr II, $10.10/hr
Nowlin, Daniel L, data cntr support tech-expert, $19.83/hr
Nowlin, Jessica Marie, care team assoc-clinical, $12.99/hr
Nowlin, Kimberly A, clerk, unit, $14.46/hr
Nowlin, Mary L, pat acct rep, $17.70/hr
Nowlin, Ollie L, reimbursement ast-cert, $18.84/hr
Nowlin, Rebecca Diane, care team assoc-clinical, $11.10/hr
Noyes, Barbara Ann, med records coder, $16.00/hr
Nuelle, Clayton W, fellow, post doc clncl-yr3, $60,415

Nuelle, Julia Ann Vetter, resident physician-4th yr, $55,804
Nugent, Alexis Brianne, strat comm associate II, $46,235
Nugent, Lara D, research specialist sr, $47,777
Nuhanovic, Muska, nurse, staff II, $22.24/hr
Null, Crystal B, office support assistant IV, $16.69/hr
Nunez, Dawn, clinical nursing supvsr, $74,000
Nunez, Rosa Isela, asoc dir student support svcs, $60,600
Nunn, Joshua Wingate, environmental health tech II, $15.46/hr
Nunnelly, Micheline, coor, marketing, $56,985
Nusbaum, Matthew Sean, clinical mgr, $91,049
Nutter, Michelle A, asoc dir program/project ops, $56,096
Nwaneri, Stephine Chinwendu, care team assoc-clinical, $12.44/hr
Nwankwo, Vincent Nwabufo, res physician-4th yr, $55,804
Nyberg, Ginny Marie, prof, ast clincl, $65,129
Nye, Michael P, lecturer, $62,397
Nygaard, Runar, prof, asoc, $114,826
Nyoni, Joakim Cashmir, dir II advancement, $88,000
O'Banner, Calvin James, waiter/waitress, $9.00/hr
O'Bannon, Daniel Patrick, research engineering tech I, $23.11/hr
O'Bannon, Gary Maurice, instructor, adjunct, $19,500
O'Brian, Andrea Jane, nurse, staff II, $20.54/hr
O'Brian, Taylor Gregory, surgical technl certified, $16.19/hr
O'Brien, Dennis, professor, $166,881
O'Brien, Diane Beckerle, prof, ast teach, $57,300
O'Brien, Gloria, executive assistant, $76,000
O'Brien, James J, professor, $80,642
O'Brien, Janet Jo, nurse, staff II, $20.54/hr
O'Brien, Michael John, dean, $250,036
O'Brien, Sean D, prof, asoc, $103,000
O'Bryan, Marlena Deann, nurse, staff II, $23.64/hr
O'Bryan, Michael Brendan, instructor, adjunct, $12,000
O'Bryan, Shannon Marie, student service coor II, $23,660
O'Connell, Christopher R, resident physician-3rd yr, $53,763
O'Connell, Elizabeth Ann, office support assistant IV, $13.63/hr
O'Connell, Rachel Anne, student service coor II, $46,823
O'Connell, Thomas Helton, mgr II business admin, $48,403
O'Connor, Aubrey Ann, resident physician-3rd yr, $52,470
O'Connor, Daniel Franklin, research/lab tech sr, $15.00/hr
O'Connor, Karen Visovsky, prof, ast resrch, $70,000
O'Connor, Kevin Andrew, prof, ast resrch, $102,999
O'Connor, Mary Agnes, chair, dept, $6,000
O'Connor, Michael J, prof, asoc, $88,532
O'Day, Maureen Helen, nurse, staff II, $23.82/hr
O'Dell, Michael L, professor, $75,000
O'Doherty, Michael S, prof, ast, $183,953
O'Donnell, Frederick Thomas, prof, ast clincl dept, $200,000
O'Donnell, Mallory Lynn, interior designer, $44,000
O'Hara, Linley Erin, nurse, staff I, $19.00/hr
O'Hara, Sullavan Patrick, mental health tech, $11.00/hr
O'Higgins, Briana M, strat comm associate II, $42,000
O'Kane, Devon Joseph, temporary technical, $10.00/hr
O'Malley, Brendan Joyce Chong, res physician-2nd yr, $50,810
O'Malley, Mary K, prof, clincl, $86,000
O'Malley, Ronald J, professor, $152,464
O'Mara, Kelly, office support assistant sr, $47,644
O'Neal, Glenda Jean, instructor, adjunct, $10,500
O'Neal, Gregory Lee, custodian, $13.36/hr
O'Neal, Rebecca Ann, executive assistant, $19.20/hr
O'Neal, Thomas John, prof, asoc, $68,417
O'Neal, Thomas W, dir III advancement, $102,000
O'Neil, Alysha Marie, dir III business admin, $101,851
O'Neil, Nicholas Cory, system administrator-entry, $44,370
O'Neil, Rochelle Lynn, intern, $24,014
O'Neill-Jones, Mary Catherine, tutor, $10.50/hr
O'Neill, James John, maint svc attd, $16.88/hr
O'Neill, JoAnna, office support assistant IV, $15.19/hr
O'Neill, Mary Shannon, instructor, clincl, $15,375
O'Reilly, Deborah Sanders, program/project supprt coor I, $40,560
O'Renick, Elam, manager it, $64,371
O'Riley, Samantha Ann, educational pgm associate I, $11.80/hr
O'Rourke, Daniel Eugene, high school student, $7.75/hr
O'Rourke, Kevin, adjunct, $15,000
O'Rourke, Nicole Marie, nurse, staff II, $21.37/hr
O'Shea, Janine Marie, lecturer, $35,000
O'Steen Jr, James Michael, ast dir student support svcs, $47,169
O'Sullivan, Catherine Margaret, dir I, advancement, $49,205
O'Sullivan, Laura Eileen, prof, clincl, $89,600
O'Toole, Peggy Anne, lecturer sr, $21,000
Oakes, Mary A, office support assistant IV, $16.78/hr

Oakes, Susan Benton, teaching ast, $7,500
Oakley, Diane E, nurse, staff II, $35.06/hr
Oakley, Nicholas James, research specialist I, $31,300
Oakson, James Stephen, prof, ast adjunct, $330.00/hr
Oatman, Katherine Jo, specialist, $10.00/hr
Oba, Junko, grader, $52
Oba, Yuji, prof, asoc clincl dept, $262,820
Obafemi-Ajayi, Olutayo Yenola, fellow, post doctoral, $19.23/hr
Obannon, Deborah Jean, professor, $97,517
Oberg Roberts, Kathryn Altajean, social worker, $53,836
Oberhaus, Deana Kay, coor, care, $32.00/hr
Oberhaus, Shawn Lynette, health physics technician I, $18.70/hr
Oberle, Hannah Elizabeth, occl therapist, $50,128
Obermark, Lauren E, prof, ast, $56,300
Obert, Brenda J, care team assoc-clinical, $14.17/hr
OBlennis, Gavin K, patient svc rep, $12.09/hr
Oboh Ikuenobe, Francisca, professor, $104,761
Obourn, Lula M, office support assistant IV, $12.98/hr
Obrecht, Daniel V, research specialist sr, $59,118
Obrennan, Gerald Keith, manager it, $74,326
Obrian, Lori Lee, office support assistant IV, $15.45/hr
Obrien, David J, professor, $104,600
Obrien, Dianna Borsi, instructor, adjunct, $9,000
OBrien, Jacquelyn D, teaching ast, $13.00/hr
Obrien, Stacey Jane, nurse, staff II, $26.41/hr
Ocampo, Cristian, custodian, $10.00/hr
Occena, Kathleen Martin, nurse, staff now III, $30.00/hr
Occena, Luis G, prof, asoc, $145,661
Ochester, Tracy Elizabeth, temporary professional, $100.00/hr
Oconnell, Robert M, professor, $112,416
Oconnor, Erin K, mgr research technical svcs, $87,818
OConnor, Margaret Ellen, office support assistant IV, $16.12/hr
Oconnor, Michael J, managing engineer, $90,824
Odell, Lawrence L, dental technician sr, $18.37/hr
Odell, Robert Lee, sterile processing tech, $18.31/hr
Oden, Courtney Lynne, psychology techn, $13.65/hr
Oden, Mary B, educational pgm assistant, $9.96/hr
Odom, Arthur Louis, professor, $83,350
Odum, Lauren Elizabeth, prof, ast clincl, $96,000
Odunayo, Theresa Avosuahi, prof, ast teach, $67,802
Oehl, Dustin Hunter, office support assistant IV, $13.20/hr
Oehler, Julie Christine, nurse, staff II, $19.00/hr
Oerly, Patty Marie, house manager h, $67,907
Oerly, Terry D, animal technician sr, $13.97/hr
Oerther, Daniel B, professor, $177,477
Oesterreich, Joshua Caleb, police officer, $17.47/hr
Oestreich, Gavin T, reactor operator, $26.42/hr
Oetting, Helen E, strat comm consultant sr, $66,449
Oetting, Jennifer Suzanne, human resources spclst II, $48,960
Oetting, Martin Christy, dir external relations, $104,956
Ofem, Brandon Rowan Ibiang, prof, ast, $115,000
Offutt, Cheryl Ann, prof, asoc teach, $78,496
Offutt, Cory L, resident physician-2nd yr, $50,810
Oforiwaa, Rosemond Akua, mental health tech, $12.14/hr
Ogan, John, model, $10.50/hr
Ogar, Megan Marie, advancement officer, $47,000
Ogawa, Kenneth M, physician, stu hlth, $143,205
Ogburn, Freda Jeanette, instructor, adjunct, $14,400
Ogden, Dwain Lee, lab assistant, $9.06/hr
Ogden, Jamie Alise, prof, ast clincl dept, $140,454
Ogden, Terri S, office support assistant IV, $14.82/hr
Ogilvie, Gerald W, prof, ast clincl, $81,000
Ogle, Sandra Suzette, nurse, staff II rnwp, $21.68/hr
Ogorman, Chad Warren, research specialist sr, $39,600
Ogungbade, Juliet Omosi, patient svc rep, $13.21/hr
Ogunleye, Ayodeji Idowu, resident physician-1st yr, $50,219
Oh, Seungly, fellow, post doctoral, $48,000
Oh, Sookhee, prof, asoc, $61,268
Ohiemu, Cyril Benelu, floor care techn, $12.39/hr
Ohmes, George A Jr, agronomy spclst, $62,638
Ohnesorge, Erin Shawn, practice manager, $78,846
Ohrenberger, Ayako, office support assistant III, $12.05/hr
Oilar, Molly Elizabeth, instructor, adjunct, $7,059
Okafor, Anthony Chukwujekwu, professor, $96,520
Okamura, Lawrence, prof, asoc, $69,390
Okamura, Linda Suzanne, db administrator-princpl, $81,083
Okanovich, Elena Markovna, instructor, adjunct, $7,059
Okeefe, Adrianne Darby, student support specialist sr, $17.63/hr
Okeefe, Matthew J, professor, $152,172

OKeefe, Samuel E, strat comm associate II, $39,600
Okiring, Patience Idewait, executive assistant, $17.20/hr
Okker, Patricia, professor, $186,723
Okonkwo, Christopher, prof, asoc, $65,195
Okruch, Kelsey Marie, physical therapist, $65,750
Oladiran, Olawale B, asoc dir research, $107,886
Olayiwola, Modinat Labake, nurse, staff I, $19.00/hr
Olberding, Brian L, support systems admin-expert, $55,162
Olbricht, Gayla Renee, prof, ast, $65,611
Old, Christy Leigh, student support specialist II, $17.21/hr
Old, Melissa L, fin and acctg analyst sr, $56,375
Old, Tammy Lynn, business support specialist II, $18.88/hr
Oldenburg, Andrew Dean, intern, $18,000
Oldham, John Timothy, physician, $250.00/hr
Oldham, Ryan Patrick, prof, ast adjunct, $39,000
Olds, Bryan L, custodian, $12.94/hr
Olds, Lisa L, office support assistant IV, $14.11/hr
Olds, Steven J, athletic attd, $14.72/hr
Olds, Tyson J, resident physician-2nd yr, $52,007
Oleski, Francesca Victoria, driver, $13.89/hr
Olin, Georgia Lynn, supv nursing acute care, $27.25/hr
Olisah, Lisa Ann, anesthesia techn, $16.22/hr
Olishile, Terry Ann, educational pgm associate I, $12.88/hr
Olivas, Wendy M, prof, asoc, $66,530
Olive, Jerry Wayne, instructor, adjunct, $8,067
Oliver, Harvey A III, resident physician-3rd yr, $53,763
Oliver, John W Jr, maint svc attd, $16.92/hr
Oliver, Angelina Marie, coor, service, $15.13/hr
Oliver, Beatrice Kim, finl counselor(eligibility), $15.56/hr
Oliver, Christina Lynne, office support assistant IV, $16.92/hr
Oliver, Connie Coleen, care team assoc-clinical, $13.33/hr
Oliver, Diane Lynette, office support assistant IV, $15.11/hr
Oliver, Gina M, prof, ast clincl, $61,212
Oliver, Kassie Rebbecca, nurse, staff now III, $30.00/hr
Oliver, Kassie Rebbecca, coor, trauma outrch edu, $39,520
Oliver, Lorenzo L, mental health tech, $12.33/hr
Oliver, Mary Jane, nurse, staff II, $25.30/hr
Oliver, McCall Madeline, nurse, staff I, $19.00/hr
Oliver, Meral, custodian, $13.23/hr
Oliver, Michael Ray, event assistant I, $8.50/hr
Oliver, Nancy Lynn, office support assistant III, $11.44/hr
Oliver, Richard Edward, prof, asoc adjunct, $129,467
Oliver, Sarah Miranda, prof, ast teach, $50,000
Oliver, Theda Renee, office support assistant III, $15.47/hr
Oliveri, Rigel Christine, prof, asoc, $144,924
Oliveros, Luz A, business support specialist I, $14.86/hr
Olmstead, Lindsay Anne, nurse, staff I, $19.00/hr
Olmsted, James Russell, mechanical plant spec, mrc, $18.09/hr
Olmsted, Julianne K, physical therapist, $76,020
Olree, Meghan Yvonne, stage services assistant sr, $16.00/hr
Olsan, Jonel Marie, resp therapist reg, $26.67/hr
Olsen, Anastasia Marie, intern, $25,500
Olsen, Erik Kristopher, prof, asoc, $76,936
Olson, David W, network engineer-master, $95,998
Olson, Evan A, resident physician-4th yr, $55,804
Olson, Judy Ann, student support specialist II, $21.26/hr
Olson, Kristy L, mammography technl, $30.36/hr
Olson, Michelle A, food svc wrkr III, $13.21/hr
Olson, Neil C, dean, $262,874
Olson, Robert H, professor, $108,470
Olson, Ronald E, emeritus, $8,400
Olver, Terry Dylan, fellow, post doctoral, $42,000
Omar, Fahad, fellow, post doc clncl-yr2, $58,083
Omar, Mussa Ali, athletic attd lead, $15.20/hr
Omer, Mohamed Abdelbary F, res physician-2nd yr, $50,810
Omeragic, Zerina, resp therapist reg, $21.36/hr
Omorodion, Alexander, instructor, adjunct, $12,300
Omoscharka, Evanthia, resident physician-4th yr, $54,425
Omran, Jad, fellow, post doc clncl yr1, $55,804
Oncken, Ehren G, academic advisor, $40,671
Oncken, Stephenie Marie, office support assistant IV, $15.18/hr
Onderbeke, Timothy G, animal techn, ast lab, $13.89/hr
ONeal, James Edward, linen attd, $11.16/hr
Oneal, James M, nurse, staff II, $28.59/hr
Oneal, Kevin W, case worker, rehab, $39,158
Oneil, Christopher S, nurse, staff II, $23.82/hr
ONeill, Armedia Lorrain, animal technician sr, $13.73/hr
ONeill, James Alan, csm professional II, $30,591
Oneill, Kathleen F, social worker, $61,230

Oneill, Susan E, prof, ast clincl, $57,000
Ong, Cesar Lee, prof, ast clincl dept, $250,000
Ong, Vu Xuan, lecturer, $35,368
Opat, Keith M, resident physician-2nd yr, $52,007
Opfer, David E, maint svc attd, $18.41/hr
Opfer, Dennis J, mech trades spclst (mts), $22.42/hr
Oppenheim, Stephen Barry, prof, ast clincl dept, $200,000
Oppenheimer, Carla L, instructor, adjunct, $10,500
Oppenlander, Jamison Arthur, care team assoc-clinical, $13.06/hr
Orbann, Carolyn Marie, prof, ast teach, $68,340
Ordway, David Andrew, media producer II, $15.55/hr
Orford, Jennifer Marie, student service coor sr, $63,247
Origel, Gabriela, custodian, $12.94/hr
Orns, Elizabeth Anne, social worker, $56,324
Ornstein, Hayley Renee, psychologist, $40.00/hr
Orr, Brandon Harrell, prof, ast teach, $57,787
Orr, Debbie, patient svc rep, $11.62/hr
Orr, Kathy Lynn, office support assistant III, $11.39/hr
Orscheln, Jennifer Marie, resp therapist reg, $27.09/hr
Orscheln, Lori Dianne, nurse, staff per diem, $35.00/hr
Orscheln, Michael S, strat comm manager, $62,727
Orsini, Jessica L, user support analyst-specist, $16.70/hr
Ortbals, Jeanne Michele, care coordinator, $63,036
Ortega, Jeanne M, research specialist sr, $65,730
Orth, Teresa Ann, resident physician-7th yr, $63,475
Ortiz, April Elaine, office support assistant III, $12.02/hr
Ortiz, Lorena, custodian, $13.36/hr
Ortiz, Luis Enrique, specialist, $67,150
Ortiz, Maria Rita, office support assistant III, $12.91/hr
Ortiz, Nancy, custodian, $13.36/hr
Ortmann, Kelsey Elizabeth, pat care techn, $11.61/hr
Orton, Dianne Joy, strat comm consultant sr, $22,040
Orton, Kayla Renee, nurse, licensed prac, $14.76/hr
Orton, Sarah Lynn, prof, asoc, $84,227
Osberg, Nicole Jamie, temporary clerical, $9.35/hr
Osborn, David C, mgr I, business admin, $49,515
Osborn, Matthew Warner, prof, ast, $54,209
Osborne, Joseph E III, custodian, $11.41/hr
Osborne, James Walter, prof, ast adjunct, $500.00/hr
Osborne, Leigh A, nurse, staff II, $30.66/hr
Osby, Kenneth L, mail carrier, $14.24/hr
Oser, Claire, ast editor, $20.64/hr
Oser, Sarah Marie, educational pgm associate I, $12.55/hr
Osgood, Alicia Lucille, nurse, licensed prac, $17.00/hr
Osgood, James Gale, prof, ast clincl dept, $304,016
Osibin, Willard Stafford III, fellow, $45,000
Osman, Bryce Edward, advancement associate II, $18.27/hr
Osman, Pamela J, dir program/project operations, $75,997
Osman, Sara Marie, media producer sr, $36,120
Osmundson, Kacey A, emrg med techn, $12.81/hr
Osoego, Elochukwu Anthony, nuclear med technl, $26.39/hr
Oster, Andrew Stewart, resident physician-2nd yr, $50,810
Ostercamp, Gary L, chaplain, $55,058
Ostergaard, Carolyn A, optician, $41,580
Osterlind, Steven J, statistician, $4,741
Ostrow, Jill, prof, asoc teach, $53,459
Ostrowski, Tim Daniel, fellow, post doctoral, $45,390
Osullivan, Abigail R, sr manager it, $86,637
Oswald, Clay A, bts carpenter, $20.23/hr
Oswald, Holly Z, office support assistant IV, $13.78/hr
Oswald, Lauren Brady, supervisor it, $49,038
Oswald, Nicholas S, system support analyst-specist, $18.11/hr
Oswald, Tricia Leeann, fin and acctg manager, $56,000
Oswell Holmes, Andrea L, educational pgm assoc I, $14.04/hr
Otabela Mewolo, Joseph Desire, prof, ast teach, $46,000
Otoole, Judy A, office support assistant II, $10.24/hr
Otrok, Christopher M, professor, $207,237
Ott, Deana Lynette, coor, service, $17.10/hr
Ott, Kathryn Lynne, instructor, clincl, $24,919
Ott, Samuel Joseph, media producer II, $14.95/hr
Otte, Paul M, nurse, staff II, $22.67/hr
Otten, Samuel J, prof, ast, $68,513
Ottenson, Jason Matthew, maint svc attd, $16.88/hr
Otterbacher, Nicholas C, dir sports operations, $69,000
Ottery, Susan E, nurse, clincl charge-rn, $33.54/hr
Otteson, Kayla Deanne, dietitian, clincl, $49,588
Otteson, Theodore, instructor, adjunct, $17,500
Ottis, Erica Jean, prof, ast clincl, $96,500
Otto, Adrienne Nichole, nurse, staff II, $22.24/hr

Otto, Donna C, emeritus, $56,685
Otto, Jacob P, communications coordinator sr, $17.12/hr
Otto, Julia, instructor, adjunct, $2,006
Otto, Thomas G, retail sales associate, $13.71/hr
Ou, Ruguang, research specialist sr, $43,002
Ouart, Michael D, vice provost, $218,042
Ours, Ron L Jr, custodian, $11.41/hr
Ours, Lisa Alexandra, office support assistant I, $8.99/hr
Ousley, Anthony, event assistant I, $9.00/hr
Ousley, Jeffrey S, csm associate I, $17.55/hr
Ouyang, Wen, specialist, $65,926
Overby, Leroy Marvin, professor, $113,232
Overly, Sheri F, food svc wrkr II (g), $12.45/hr
Overman, Pamela Rae, dean, asoc, $164,646
Overstreet, Christina Lee, med techl reg, $24.51/hr
Overstreet, Keith W, steam plant opr II, $24.15/hr
Overton, Cheryl L, care team assoc-clinical, $14.21/hr
Overton, Tina Rene, coor, reimbursement, $44,644
Owen, Anna Kristine, office supervisor, $42,840
Owen, Caleb Joshua, program/project supprt coor I, $40,000
Owen, Denise Kay, business tech analyst-specist, $42,082
Owen, Shirley Jane, reimbursement ast sr, $21.00/hr
Owens, Carly Marie, pharmacy intern second year, $13.50/hr
Owens, David, librarian III, $57,188
Owens, George Christopher, food svc wrkr I, $9.60/hr
Owens, Jennifer Lynn, prof, ast, $59,000
Owens, Judith Donna, animal techn, lab, $15.58/hr
Owens, Julia L, office support assistant III, $13.19/hr
Owens, Lois R, office support assistant IV, $14.07/hr
Owens, Marcia J, office support assistant III, $14.65/hr
Owens, Marshae Janiece, retail sales assistant, $10.00/hr
Owens, Reta Gay, custodian mrc, $9.42/hr
Owens, Ryan Daniel, strat comm associate I, $36,000
Owens, Stephen James, general counsel, $401,855
Owens, Teddy Alan, custodian, $10.39/hr
Owings, Valerie Ann, instructor, adjunct, $6,300
Ownby, P Darrell, emeritus, $6,000
Owsley, Dennis C, media producer II, $15.17/hr
Oxford, Faith A, mri technologist, $34.60/hr
Oyelola, Emmanuel, animal techn, ast lab, $13.89/hr
Oyelola, Rebecca A, care team assoc-suppt, $13.33/hr
Oyinloye, Gbolahan Damilola, res physician-3rd yr, $53,763
Oyler, Nathan Andrew, prof, asoc, $66,961
Ozaki, Jon H, specialist, $10.00/hr
Ozias, John Peter, academic advisor sr, $47,500
Pabst-Bostic, Valera Lynn, executive assistant, $18.40/hr
Pabst, A William, temporary professional, $32.66/hr
Pace, Colleen Therese, student service coor II, $40,020
Pace, Heather Anne, prof, asoc clincl, $98,000
Pace, Jeneva Jean, business support specialist II, $20.21/hr
Pace, Jennifer Kay, nurse, staff II, $23.54/hr
Pace, Pamela Janel, office support assistant IV, $14.12/hr
Pacheco, Dylan T, teaching ast, $13.00/hr
Pacini, Tracy Jeanne, instructor, adjunct, $22,950
Packard, James H, dir II csm operations, $104,600
Packard, Jenna Marie, nurse, staff II, $20.54/hr
Packard, Kerri S, prof, asoc profl practice, $64,673
Packard, Raymond Dean, prof, asoc profl practice, $64,533
Packer, Christina, nurse, staff I, $19.00/hr
Packnett, Barry, custodian lead, $14.03/hr
Padash-Barmchi, Mojgan, fellow, post doctoral, $29,000
Paddock, Kyle John, research specialist I, $31,722
Padgett, Michelle Marie, office support assistant IV, $18.45/hr
Padgett, Stephanie Ann, instructor, adjunct, $9,000
Padilla Parellada, Jaume, prof, ast, $76,300
Padilla, Debra L, mgr nutrition/diet-mrc, $49,758
Padilla, Derrick D, custodian mrc, $10.29/hr
Paes, Jennifer Katheleen, educational pgm associate I, $12.25/hr
Pagano, Matthew James, human resources assistant, $14.06/hr
Page, James W IV, ast dir advancement, $53,186
Page, Carey Fishburn, research/lab technician sr, $18.00/hr
Page, Heather Michelle, dir sports operations, $60,000
Page, Jonathan James, temporary clerical, $9.10/hr
Page, Matthew Philip, prof, ast clincl dept, $217,546
Page, Nicholas Patrick, event assistant I, $8.50/hr
Page, Suzie Mae, custodian, $10.39/hr
Page, Tyler J, student service coor sr, $51,497
Pagett, Lisa Renee, office support assistant III, $13.60/hr
Pai, P Frank, professor, $133,117

Paige, Lisa R, office support assistant IV, $16.37/hr
Paige, Robert L, professor, $81,460
Paik, Sung Wook, fellow, post doctoral, $50,000
Paine, Dorothy Elizabeth, dir II student support svcs, $75,000
Painter, Angie Annette, reimbursement spclst, $26.37/hr
Painter, Brian, building/mechanical maint I, $17.95/hr
Painter, Madalyn C, strat comm manager, $57,343
Painter, William R, mechl plant spclst, $19.64/hr
Pal, Dhananjay, prof, asoc resrch, $49,620
Palacios Rivera, Jamille, prof, ast teach, $75,000
Palade, Kimberly Diane, office support assistant IV, $15.69/hr
Palangpour, Elaine M, office support assistant IV, $17.57/hr
Palaniappan, Anand, temporary technical, $15.00/hr
Palaniappan, Kannappan, prof, asoc, $112,540
Palaniappan, Krishnan Kanna, temporary technical, $7.50/hr
Palaniappan, Sala Manian, office support assistant III, $12.00/hr
Palermo, Francisco, prof, ast, $68,500
Palipatana, Janpen, peoplesoft admin-spclst, $79,468
Palipatana, Panprai, db administrator-princpl, $80,285
Palisch, Nicholas Greg, asoc dir program/project ops, $48,336
Palizzi, Barry A, resident physician-3rd yr, $52,470
Paller, Karla K, nurse, staff II rnwp, $34.17/hr
Palm, Alysia Renee, custodian, $12.72/hr
Palma, Thiago Olmos, theatre ast, $8.00/hr
Palmer, Aaron D, farm wrkr I, $12.12/hr
Palmer, Barbara J, office support associate, $21.90/hr
Palmer, Caitlin Nelle, tutor, $10.25/hr
Palmer, Craig T, prof, asoc, $59,984
Palmer, Dain R, resrch asoc, $40,000
Palmer, Dana Gale, bts carpenter, $20.23/hr
Palmer, Debra Fern, social worker, $54,633
Palmer, Elliott Ross, temporary crafts service, $8.00/hr
Palmer, Kaitlin Lene, temporary technical, $9.00/hr
Palmer, Karen Lavern, office support assistant III, $12.42/hr
Palmer, Mark Henry, prof, asoc, $71,942
Palmer, Nancy R, nurse clinician, $47,032
Palmer, Patricia A, instructor, field, $40,775
Palmer, Susan Starke, sterile processing tech, $18.05/hr
Palmer, William Owings, instructor, adjunct, $2,468
Palmgren, Jayme Elizabeth, business support spclst II, $15.25/hr
Palmier, Mark Oliver, fellow, post doctoral, $45,000
Palmieri, William, student service coor II, $46,460
Palonsky, Stuart Barry, emeritus, $15,000
Paluri, Deepthi, resrch ast sr, $45,000
Pamulapati, Hema, resident physician-2nd yr, $50,810
Pan, Heng, prof, ast, $80,190
Pan, Jianli, prof, ast, $89,500
Pan, Xiufang, fellow, post doctoral, $44,558
Pancella, Thomas G, asoc dir program/project ops, $54,663
Panchanathan, Karthik, prof, ast, $61,206
Pandjiris, James, lecturer sr, $27,900
Pandompatam, Govind, resident physician-2nd yr, $50,810
Pandya, Vishwam Rajendrakumar, fellow, post doc clncl-yr2, $58,083
Paneck, James Edwin, temporary technical, $10.25/hr
Panethiere, Vicki Renee, office support assistant IV, $14.35/hr
Pang, Kejia, fellow, post doctoral, $39,000
Pang, Michael Man Ho, professor, $88,958
Pankau, Deborah Ann, temporary professional, $13.43/hr
Pankau, Debra Christine, instructor, $18,000
Pankey, Steven William, student service coor II, $47,000
Pannell, Diana Jordan, food svc wrkr II, $10.10/hr
Pantaleo, Ashley M, student support specialist sr, $17.03/hr
Pantaleo, Jarrod A, mgr II student support svcs, $60,000
Panther, Leah, instructor, adjunct, $6,300
Pantuso, Alison B, coor outreach prgms, $41,600
Papageorge, Diane Margo, instructor, adjunct, $6,276
Papasian, Christopher J, professor, $190,797
Pape, Glenda Lynn, patient svc rep, $14.30/hr
Pape, Kristen Tara, program/project supprt coor I, $43,318
Pappas, Julie Marie, waiter/waitress, $8.47/hr
Paquette, Michelle Marie, prof, ast resrch, $53,281
Paquin, George, mover, $14.27/hr
Paracha, Majid Bakhsh, temporary technical, $12.00/hr
Parcell, Joseph L, professor, $130,957
Parcell, Julia Hammes, program/project supprt coor I, $16.54/hr
Pardalos, John A, prof, asoc clncl dept, $239,736
Paredes, Kea Elizabeth, nurse, staff II, $22.89/hr
Paretsky, Nicholas G, custodian, $12.69/hr

Parham, Weston Carr, mgr II student support svcs, $58,000
Parikh, Tanvi, fellow, post doctoral, $40,000
Parish, Timothy Alan, supv, food svc II-h, $42,908
Parisi, Joseph, professor, $76,677
Parisse, Joshua, student recruitment spclst sr, $19.00/hr
Park, Benjamin Earl, fellow, post doctoral, $50,000
Park, Carolynn Rae, supv, lab, $74,603
Park, Chanwoo, prof, asoc, $110,000
Park, Eun Soo, prof, asoc, $85,505
Park, Jinkyu, fellow, post doctoral, $37,000
Park, Jonghyun, prof, ast, $80,000
Park, Joontaek, prof, ast, $83,338
Parker, Charles James Jr, business support specialist II, $17.34/hr
Parker, Marion E Jr, anesthesia techn, $14.43/hr
Parker-Oliver, Debra Rae, professor, $130,876
Parker, Aileen Mae, nurse, licensed prac, $21.07/hr
Parker, Catherine Dore, resident physician-1st yr, $50,219
Parker, Crista Leigh, instructor, adjunct, $10,200
Parker, Dannial J, custodian, $10.69/hr
Parker, David J, sr dir professional svcs, $239,429
Parker, Debbie Sue, instructor, ast, $41,843
Parker, Derek Shea, office support assistant IV, $15.48/hr
Parker, Jerry Calvin, dean, asoc, $225,505
Parker, Julie A, ast registrar, $51,052
Parker, Kathryn Marie, nurse, staff now III, $30.00/hr
Parker, Lee Ann, office support assistant III, $12.42/hr
Parker, Patricia G, professor, $149,180
Parker, Rafeal Lee, support systems admin-entry, $42,025
Parker, Rochelle M, prof, ast clncl dept, $202,878
Parker, Sandra Dee, office support assistant I, $9.32/hr
Parker, Sara Wing, instructor, clncl, $43,021
Parker, Sara Wing, resp therapist reg, $30.00/hr
Parker, Stephen L, arborist, $17.40/hr
Parker, Tammy Denise, nurse, staff II, $29.50/hr
Parker, Taybor William, research specialist I, $31,100
Parkins, George K, prof, ast clncl dept, $261,670
Parkinson, Deidre Leann, fin and acctg manager, $70,338
Parkinson, Tressa J, prof, clncl, $98,761
Parks, Cynthia L, dir I, business admin, $72,011
Parks, Elizabeth Jane, professor, $159,135
Parks, Gera Nae, temporary crafts service, $9.50/hr
Parks, Veronica Joan, pharmacy intern fifth year, $16.50/hr
Parmalee, Donald R, custodian, $13.36/hr
Parmer, Kenneth Jr, mgr csm operations, $60,059
Parra, Claire Anne, research/lab technician, $11.00/hr
Parris, Matthew Stephen, account manager, $89,198
Parris, Paul E, professor, $103,344
Parrish, Alan Ray, prof, asoc, $147,600
Parrish, Amy Anne, nurse, staff II, $21.59/hr
Parrish, William S, telecom tech-expert, $18.28/hr
Parrott, James L, prof, asoc clncl, $91,115
Parrow, Kenny Earl, food svc wrkr III, $13.21/hr
Parry, Mark E, professor, $297,429
Parry, Pamela Juliet, program/project supprt coor I, $28,000
Parshall, Jordan Elizabeth, student recruitment spclst sr, $16.84/hr
Parshall, Timothy H, asoc dir program/project ops, $75,025
Parsons, Eric S, prof, ast resrch, $65,644
Parsons, Gina Denise, office support assistant III, $13.00/hr
Parsons, Holly S, business support specialist II, $20.20/hr
Parsons, James Hamilton, nurse, staff II, $23.45/hr
Parsons, Jean L, prof, asoc, $89,049
Parsons, Lindsay N, resrch ast, $20.00/hr
Parsons, Roger W, construction manager I, $54,555
Parsons, Roy L, biological safety prof, $56,556
Parsons, Scott David, office support assistant IV, $15.30/hr
Parsons, Trish Elizabeth, temporary crafts service, $15.00/hr
Partee, Nigel Coleman, police officer, $17.50/hr
Partington, Mark E, office support assistant IV, $15.57/hr
Partise, Mark Joseph, office supervisor, $42,121
Partise, Nicholas Shane, storage admin-spclst, $54,611
Partridge, Paula Renee, office support assistant IV, $15.05/hr
Partyka, Edward K, physician, $125.00/hr
Parzych, Jennifer Lee, nurse, staff II rnwp, $22.78/hr
Pasala, Saikiran, operations support tech I, $12.50/hr
Pasch, Deborah Lynn, exec dir univ hosp chf nurs ex, $244,000
Paschang, Lisa G, asoc dir program/project ops, $67,957
Pasco, Rebecca Jeanne, instructor, adjunct, $3,300
Pasley, James Neville, instructor, adjunct, $10,286
Pasley, Jeffrey L, professor, $101,413

Pasley, Lois N, med techl reg, $30.64/hr
Pasqua-Wright, Jackson Lawerence, db programmer analyst-entry, $42,000
Pastor, Mary Rebecca, strat comm associate II, $51,707
Patchell, Andrew N, db programmer analyst-entry, $43,050
Pate, Christina Marie, instructional designer-entry, $18,712
Patel, Ami Akshaykumar, business ops associate II, $61,167
Patel, Amit J, adjunct, $15,000
Patel, Amit R, resident physician-1st yr, $50,219
Patel, Andrew Paul, resident physician-2nd yr, $52,007
Patel, Bhoomit Sumantbhai, med techl reg, $21.79/hr
Patel, Chirag Rasiklal, resident physician-2nd yr, $50,810
Patel, Harsha N, prof, ast clincl dept, $131,883
Patel, Kamlesh, sterile processing tech, $18.58/hr
Patel, Kinnari Vinodrai, temporary crafts service, $7.50/hr
Patel, Megha Bharatkumar, med techl reg, $22.44/hr
Patel, Nayan M, resident physician-3rd yr, $52,470
Patel, Nitu, med techl reg, $24.03/hr
Patel, Purav Prakash, resident physician-3rd yr, $53,763
Patel, Ravi J, resident physician-2nd yr, $50,810
Patel, Rupal C, hospital lab tech, $13.35/hr
Patel, Sajal, resident physician-1st yr, $50,219
Patel, Samrat, resident physician-3rd yr, $52,470
Patel, Sunil Ramesh, nurse, staff II rnwp, $20.14/hr
Paten, Christin Michelle, nurse, staff I, $19.00/hr
Pathak, Seemantini Madhukar, prof, ast, $120,000
Pathan, Safiullah Md, resrch scientist/academic sr, $59,150
Patharkar, Osric R, fellow, post doctoral, $43,000
Patibandla, Sruthi, resident physician-2nd yr, $50,810
Patil, Ashutosh, prof, ast, $140,000
Patil, Gunvant Baliram, fellow, post doctoral, $42,000
Patil, Harshal Rohidas, resident physician-7th yr, $63,475
Patil, Sonal Ashutosh, fellow, $60,000
Patillo, Amy Rachel, extns professional, ast, $53,586
Patlan, Justin Joseph, police officer, $19.57/hr
Patney, Vikram, fellow, post doc clncl yr1, $55,804
Patrick, Howard Eugene, event assistant I, $7.50/hr
Patrick, Jennifer Michele, social worker, $56,020
Patrick, Jeri K, surgical techl certified, $23.83/hr
Patrick, Sandra Michelle, nurse, licensed prac, $16.26/hr
Patrick, Shawn Cannon, grounds keeper, $11.76/hr
Patrick, Tammy Jo, nurse, staff II, $27.05/hr
Patrick, Terry Bruce, custodian, $10.94/hr
Patterson, Cheri L, asoc dir program/project ops, $25,325
Patterson, Chris, cooling tower techn, $20.07/hr
Patterson, Danny Paul, engineering technician II, $17.57/hr
Patterson, David J, professor, $158,639
Patterson, Debra Anne, custodian, $12.94/hr
Patterson, Heather McKenzie, prof, ast adjunct, $18,315
Patterson, Jacob Sly, certif pharmacy techn, $13.85/hr
Patterson, Julia Winzerling, office support assistant IV, $15.35/hr
Patterson, Kathy W, retail sales assistant sr, $11.70/hr
Patterson, Laura J, manager IT, $72,152
Patterson, Leslie Anne, strat comm manager, $48,882
Patterson, Lisa Marie, prof, ast adjunct, $18,000
Patterson, Mark Elliot, prof, ast, $91,500
Patterson, Miles L, founders professor, $38,020
Patterson, Shira K, retail sales assistant sr, $11.32/hr
Patterson, Terry L, support systems admin-princpl, $61,465
Patterson, Theresa Mae, event assistant I, $7.55/hr
Pattillo, Shelia, nurse, licensed prac, $21.25/hr
Patton, Adell Jr, founders professor, $26,090
Patton, Corinne, instructor, adjunct, $12,000
Patton, Evan A, pat acct rep, $15.00/hr
Patton, Leigh Walker, temporary clerical, $12.00/hr
Patton, Ruth Eileen, nurse, staff prn, $26.00/hr
Patton, Sean, internet administrator-expert, $26.43/hr
Patton, Trudis Ann, programmer analyst-expert, $75,146
Pattrin, Helen Marie, executive assistant, $19.17/hr
Patwardhan, Anjali, prof, ast clincl dept, $152,537
Paul, Dylan Brooke Houston, nurse, staff II, $20.54/hr
Paul, Lori L, prof, ast teach, $47,655
Paul, Robert Harris, academic dir, $170,004
Paul, Teresa Lynn, business support specialist sr, $19.76/hr
Pauley, Tony, mts/pipefitter, $22.50/hr
Paulk, Holli Leigh, prof, ast teach, $72,000
Paulsell, Mary Elizabeth, state spclst, asoc, $85,000
Paulson, Lindsay Ann, nurse, staff II rnwp, $22.12/hr
Pauly, Daniel Frank, professor, $50,000

Pauly, Rebecca Rainer, professor, $50,000
Pautz, Gail Ann, patient svc rep, $14.32/hr
Paver, Emily Katherine, social worker, $50,477
Pavich, Michael Ewald, office support assistant IV, $14.69/hr
Paxton, Charles W, sr mgr csm operations, $71,319
Payne, Andrew Joseph, resrch scientist/academic, $60,300
Payne, Craig Alan, prof, asoc extns, $101,889
Payne, Debra Ann, custodian, $10.94/hr
Payne, Glenda S, custodian, $12.94/hr
Payne, Kayla Renee, food svc wrkr I, $9.98/hr
Payne, Kelsey Rae, care team assoc-clinical, $12.08/hr
Payne, Leonard DeWayne, custodian, $10.39/hr
Payne, Lynda, professor, $101,600
Payne, Scotty B, bldg cntrl sys techn IV, $24.15/hr
Payne, Thomas L, v chancl&dean agri/food/natrl, $269,412
Paynter, Christopher Aaron, resident physician-3rd yr, $52,470
Peace, Andrew W, emrg med techn paramedic, $14.59/hr
Peace, Leanne J, dir program/project operations, $75,281
Peace, Nathan K, emrg med techn, $11.61/hr
Peach, Janis Kay, librarian III, $64,166
Peacher, Jerry Lee, professor, $96,441
Peacher, Joel F, lecturer, $39,324
Peacock, Mary Malissa, tutor, $15.00/hr
Pearce, Ibitola, professor, $100,412
Pearce, Jacqueline Winona, prof, ast teach, $105,211
Pearce, Rita Denise, instructor, adjunct, $9,000
Pearl, Lacy Ann, educational pgm associate I, $13.45/hr
Pearman, Chris J, environmental health prof sr, $51,992
Pearman, Renee Lynn, system support analyst-expert, $26.01/hr
Pearsall, Camella Elizabeth, dental hygienist, $25.00/hr
Pearse, John E Jr, office support assistant IV, $16.24/hr
Pearson, Douglas A, prof, ast clincl, $84,050
Pearson, Erin R, resident physician-1st yr, $50,219
Pearson, Katheryn Y, custodian, $11.44/hr
Pearson, Linda Rae, home hlth aide, $12.32/hr
Pearson, Spencer Winston, model, $10.50/hr
Peart, Eunice Kay, nurse, licensed prac, $17.86/hr
Peart, Marvin Maurice, nurse, staff I, $19.37/hr
Pease, Dennis Carl, research specialist lead, $54,075
Pease, Kailyn Brooke, nurse, staff II, $21.68/hr
Pease, Susan Gail, operations support tech II, $12.23/hr
Peavey, Judith A, speech/lang pathologist, $69,772
Pecina, Uzziel Hernandez, prof, ast clincl, $56,182
Peck, Barbara A, instructional developr-expert, $20.50/hr
Peck, Dawn, counselor, genetic, $72,673
Peck, Sarah Kay, supv, acute care nursing rnwp, $27.79/hr
Peck, Scott C, prof, asoc, $108,606
Peckham, Nicholas Hughes, instructor, adjunct, $12,000
Pecorak, Cee Jaye, pharmacist III, $60.00/hr
Peculis, Brenda A, prof, asoc, $90,184
Pederson, Alison Joy, cardiovasc techn invasive, $23.00/hr
Pederson, David M, bts mason/tuckptr, $22.14/hr
Pederson, Germaine C, nurse, staff now III, $30.00/hr
Peebles, Janett Lee, care team assoc-clinical, $14.17/hr
Peek, Danielle Rene, nurse, staff I, $19.00/hr
Peek, Shelby Lynn, nurse, staff II, $20.95/hr
Peel, Gary Richard, fin and acctg manager, $56,197
Peeler, Anita K, nurse, staff II, $29.95/hr
Peeno, Margaret Marie, instructor, adjunct, $6,276
Peery, Kelly J, strat comm manager, $49,400
Peet, Benjamin, instructor, adjunct, $18,000
Pegler, Eugene A Jr, mgr II student support svcs, $63,000
Peiser, Megan L, grader, $100.00/hr
Peiter, Kenneth Lee, custodian, $10.00/hr
Peiter, Laura Christine, student support specialist II, $15.50/hr
Pekkala, Elizabeth Sue, office support assistant IV, $14.48/hr
Peknik, Hilary Renee Wheat, dir II advancement, $76,875
Pelc, Jessica Kay, office support assistant IV, $14.41/hr
Pele, Nicole Andrea, instructor, adjunct, $101.70/hr
Pelfrey, Brenda Hines, mail processor II, $13.63/hr
Pelikan, Andrew Robert, resident physician-1st yr, $50,219
Pelikan, Joseph, environmental health tech II, $16.04/hr
Pelikan, Morgan Leigh, custodian, $10.69/hr
Pellegrin, Richard Scott, prof, ast teach, $47,000
Pellegrini, Ekin, prof, asoc, $118,604
Pellot, Brian D, dir I, strat communications, $86,000
Pelmore, Mark Edward, educational pgm associate I, $13.45/hr
Pemberton, Cynthia Lea, deputy provost, $164,440
Pemberton, Joshua J, grounds keeper, $12.12/hr

Pemberton, Megan Christine, office support asst III, $12.75/hr
Pemberton, Melissa L, student service coor sr, $52,485
Pena, Wendy Lynn Brasses, hris specialist-entry, $46,350
Pence-Johnson, Vickie Renee, physician ast, $99,835
Pence, Jamie Nicole, couns hlth/welfare/wellness sr, $30.00/hr
Pendergrass, Laura Kelly, media producer I, $13.83/hr
Pendleton, Chelsea Megan, nurse, staff now III, $30.00/hr
Pendleton, Micheal James, mts/pipefitter, $21.05/hr
Pendleton, Randall W, office support assistant IV, $15.90/hr
Penfield, Jonathan Foster, supv nursing acute care, $23.31/hr
Peng, Huiling, resrch asoc, $106,206
Peng, Ying, fellow, post doctoral, $40,000
Peng, Zhonghua, prof, curators, $109,682
Peniston, Eric Brian, model, $15.00/hr
Penn, Christina M, social worker, $49,996
Penn, David A, resp care clinical coor, $29.82/hr
Penn, Paul D, perioperative ast, $15.17/hr
Pennathur, Shiva Kumar, business ops associate sr, $65,895
Pennell, Hillary D, prof, ast visiting, $39,886
Pennella, Mario A, prof, ast teach, $63,262
Penning, Christa Catherine, office support assistant III, $14.28/hr
Pennington, Buddy D Jr, librarian II, $72,855
Pennington, Delilah, prof, ast clincl, $73,383
Pennington, Kara Kirchhoff, ast mgr hospitality services, $43,808
Pennington, Kathleen Ann, fellow, post doctoral, $42,622
Pennington, Mary A, educational pgm associate I, $13.45/hr
Peoples, Allison Dawn, nurse, staff II, $20.54/hr
Peoples, Channon D, ast dir student support svcs, $55,143
Peplinski, Roman, resident physician-1st yr, $49,025
Pepper, Mary Beth, executive assistant sr, $60,439
Peralta, Angel Rolando, fellow, post doc clncl-yr2, $58,083
Percival, Julie Paulyne, office support assistant IV, $13.30/hr
Percy, Nancy AnnLevy, office support assistant I, $11.77/hr
Pereira, Raynolde, prof, asoc, $200,274
Pereira, Susan Lynne, prof, asoc clincl dept, $161,217
Perera, Amanda Marie, patient svc rep, $10.75/hr
Pereverzev, Andrey Yuryevich, resrch asoc, $52,000
Perez Anzaldo, Guadalupe, prof, ast, $56,801
Perez Herrera, Misael Francisco, supv sup services moi, $52,119
Perez, Johnson Joseph III, academic advisor sr, $45,170
Perez, Amanda Marie, mentor, $8.00/hr
Perez, Angela Kim, activity aide, $13.88/hr
Perez, Jessica Marie, phlebotomist, $13.04/hr
Perez, Lacey Doreen, care team assoc-clinical, $10.85/hr
Perkins, Robert L Jr, custodian, $12.94/hr
Perkins, Beth Erin, hlth educator, $45,000
Perkins, Daryl Eugene, student recruitment spclst, $16.85/hr
Perkins, Debbie Jean, strat comm consultant, $50,282
Perkins, Deborah, office support assistant sr, $19.59/hr
Perkins, Deseri J, office support assistant IV, $16.88/hr
Perkins, Dorothea, user support analyst-expert, $18.17/hr
Perkins, Janice M, business support specialist II, $17.77/hr
Perkins, Jeffrey Scott, asoc dir program/project ops, $55,694
Perkins, Joann R, fin and acctg manager, $74,250
Perkins, M Paulina, student service coor sr, $52,108
Perkins, Michael James, athletic attd, $14.72/hr
Perkins, Michael Ray, pharmacist, $116,688
Perkins, Michael T, maint svc attd, $18.41/hr
Perkins, Ruthann, administrative consultant, $88,777
Perkins, Seth, office support assistant IV, $14.44/hr
Perkins, Shana Leigh, care team assoc-suppt, $12.14/hr
Perkins, Sonia A, ast mgr hskpg, $54,272
Perkins, Tressie Mae, dental assistant I, $14.64/hr
Perkins, Willy Ray, csm associate II, $18.24/hr
Perkinson, Lora Lynn, pharmacist III, $128,835
Perkowski, Michael H, sr prgm mgr studnt supprt svcs, $70,301
Perley, Sandra L, business ops associate sr, $66,737
Perna, Leslie, professor, $62,530
Perna, Mark J, prof, ast, $249,900
Pernicka, Henry J, prof, asoc, $102,205
Peroff, Nicholas Carl, professor, $109,742
Perrigo, Cyndia Kay, reimbursement ast-cert, $19.62/hr
Perrigo, Mark W, bts painter, $21.71/hr
Perrigo, Shelley, patient svc rep, $14.88/hr
Perrin, Mona Sue, reimbursement ast-cert, $18.59/hr
Perrin, Roy, resp therapy techn cert, $21.45/hr
Perry, Alan Leon II, cook, $12.39/hr
Perry, Earnest Lee Jr, prof, asoc, $112,200
Perry, Amanda C, 4-h spclst, $45,000

Perry, Ashley Elizabeth, supv nursing acute care, $26.75/hr
Perry, Briona Catherine, tutor, $9.00/hr
Perry, Clint Robert, seasonal farm ast, $9.75/hr
Perry, Donna Marie, office support assistant IV, $14.24/hr
Perry, Erin Elizabeth, coor ultrasound svcs, $65,525
Perry, Helen Mary, mgr II student support svcs, $53,324
Perry, Jamin William, fellow, post doctoral, $42,000
Perry, Justin James, food svc wrkr I, $9.60/hr
Perry, Kathleen, radiologic techl, $26.64/hr
Perry, Keith Allen, custodian, $10.69/hr
Perry, Kendra Elaine, program/project supprt coor II, $55,397
Perry, Kristi Kay, office support assistant IV, $15.98/hr
Perry, Lana J, event assistant I, $7.70/hr
Perry, Madeline Lindsey, high school student, $7.50/hr
Perry, Rex D, program/project supprt coor I, $38,125
Perry, Sarah Elizabeth, student service coor I, $34,400
Perry, Sherri L, nurse, licensed prac sr, $22.16/hr
Perry, Vanessa Denise, nurse, licensed prac, $18.89/hr
Perryman, Carol D, nurse, licensed prac sr now, $19.25/hr
Persak, Deborah A, teaching ast, $13.00/hr
Persechini, Anthony J, professor, $128,966
Persinger, Cathy Lynn, temporary clerical, $8.50/hr
Perso, Genevieve F, physical therapist, $66,481
Perti, Bhisham Kumar Jr, floor care techn, $11.02/hr
Perti, Kellie Renee, surgical technl certified, $18.59/hr
Pesala, Siva Prasad Reddy, resident physician-1st yr, $50,219
Pesek, Donna DeBres, office support assistant III, $11.73/hr
Pestle, Jody L, office support assistant IV, $18.15/hr
Pesto, Marilyn Marie, sr dir program/project ops, $68,124
Peter, Kaitlyn Jo, office support assistant IV, $15.00/hr
Peterman, Shahla, prof, teach, $66,424
Peters, Philip G Jr, professor, $166,246
Peters, Clark M, prof, ast, $70,324
Peters, Elizabeth Ann, prof, ast clincl dept, $222,836
Peters, Gary J, powr plnt maint spclst III mw, $25.85/hr
Peters, Jeffrey Craswell, research/lab technician sr, $18.59/hr
Peters, Kathleen L, business support specialist II, $16.25/hr
Peters, Lesley Ann, student service coor II, $34,572
Peters, Nickie James Jamel, reactor specialist, $71,417
Peters, Paula K, research/lab technician ast, $13.50/hr
Peters, Shannon L, surg techn, micrograph-mohs, $19.74/hr
Petersen, Alan W, mgr II hospitality services, $70,883
Petersen, Andrea N, nurse, staff II, $21.69/hr
Petersen, Emily M, architectural associate, $47,779
Petersen, Jodi L, neurodiagnostic tech (reg), $32.50/hr
Petersen, Laura Anne, office support assistant IV, $15.34/hr
Petersen, Michele A, pat admiss advisor, $34.52/hr
Petersen, Rod W, television producer, $34,000
Petersen, Susan Marie, temporary professional, $28.85/hr
Petersen, Sylvia Marie, seasonal farm ast, $9.26/hr
Peterson, Robert Benjamin III, dir I, broadcast operations, $94,913
Peterson, Anne Louise, instructor, adjunct, $4,200
Peterson, Barbara Payne, strat comm consultant sr, $86,165
Peterson, Beverly Jo, research project analyst, $41,600
Peterson, Blake Edward, resident physician-3rd yr, $53,763
Peterson, Catherine A, prof, asoc, $86,217
Peterson, Crystal Lynn, office support assistant IV, $15.76/hr
Peterson, Cynthia Buchta, nurse, staff II, $36.71/hr
Peterson, Dwight James, fellow, post doctoral, $38,500
Peterson, Eldon D, powr plnt maint spclst III wld, $25.85/hr
Peterson, Emily Elaine, temporary crafts service, $15.40/hr
Peterson, Jane Anthony, prof, asoc clincl, $82,907
Peterson, Jessica Dawn, social worker, $63,149
Peterson, Joshua Steven, bts carpenter, $19.59/hr
Peterson, Julie, nurse, staff now II, $28.00/hr
Peterson, Laura M, resident physician-2nd yr, $50,810
Peterson, Patti Ann, student support specialist I, $13.13/hr
Peterson, Rex, sr manager it, $88,255
Peterson, Ted L, system administrator-entry, $46,457
Peterson, Zoe D, prof, asoc, $80,000
Pethan, Courtney Lynn, food svc wrkr II, $11.83/hr
Petner, Christiane Ellen, mgr nursing-mpc, $74,651
Petre, Kenneth Eugene, radiologic techl, $23.26/hr
Petree, Marcus J, research specialist I, $31,700
Petree, Matthew, office support assistant III, $13.47/hr
Petrella, Nicholas E Jr, prof, ast adjunct, $21,600
Petri, Alexis, resrch asoc, $79,888
Petrie, Cynthia Spiliopoulou, prof, asoc, $93,634
Petrik, Bethany Michelle, prof, ast teach, $34,680

Petrik, Michael D, grader, $100.00/hr
Petrikovitsch, John F, instructional developr-expert, $26.84/hr
Petrillo, Lauren Kay, executive assistant, $17.81/hr
Petris, Carisa Kay, instructor, adjunct, $40,000
Petris, Michael J, prof, asoc, $102,537
Petrosinelli, Alexandra Diane, student service coor I, $41,000
Petroski, Gregory F, prof, ast resrch, $99,489
Petrovic, Kara Lynn, editor II, $51,000
Pettey, Dix Hayes, professor, $70,475
Pettig, Rachel Nicole, patient svc rep, $11.01/hr
Pettigrew, Jack Melvin, mts/electrician-ssd, $21.05/hr
Pettijohn, Robert L, bts carpenter, $22.43/hr
Pettis, Ethel Luciana L H, office support assistant IV, $16.15/hr
Petty, Charlotte Diane, lecturer sr, $9,000
Petty, Janice M, custodian, $13.23/hr
Petty, Jordan Danielle, instructor, adjunct, $7,059
Petty, Therese Ruhland, resrch asoc, $35,000
Petty, Tyrome, ast registrar, $55,287
Pew, Susan May, nurse, staff per diem, $35.00/hr
Peycke, Daniel Justin, teaching ast, $27.00/hr
Pezley, Gina Maria, nurse, staff II rnwp, $31.13/hr
Pezold, Matthew Anthony, prof, ast extns, $57,000
Pezza, Maria Andrea, temporary clerical, $15.00/hr
Pfaff, Christina Nicole, office support assistant IV, $14.35/hr
Pfaff, Elizabeth C, instructor, clincl, $36,000
Pfaff, Joyce M, business ops associate sr, $26,586
Pfannenstiel, Shaun Daniel, academic advisor, $36,000
Pfefer, Joleen M, sr manager it, $86,439
Pfeffer, Ana Victoria, custodian, $10.94/hr
Pfeifer, Alex K, business support specialist II, $17.94/hr
Pfeifer, Angela Marie, office support assistant IV, $13.75/hr
Pfeifer, Peter, professor, $166,101
Pfeiffer, Ferris Michael, prof, ast, $85,680
Pfeiffer, Kimberley Sue, nurse, staff II, $28.18/hr
Pfingsten, Christopher, system administrator-speclst, $56,704
Pfister, Michelle Roxanne, intern, $30,000
Pflieger, Jo Ann, office support assistant II, $11.05/hr
Pflughaupt, Sharon Anne, bus support specialist II, $17.64/hr
Pham, Anh Thi Ngoc, media producer sr, $36,000
Phan, Nghi U, system administrator-expert, $67,210
Phanichkul, Tamara E, office support assistant III, $16.63/hr
Phaup, J Glenn, research specialist I, $46,558
Phegley, Jennifer, professor, $86,486
Phelan, Robert John, mgr I, business admin, $40,880
Phelps, Akiela Breonia, nurse, licensed prac, $14.76/hr
Phelps, Amber Victoria, hlth prgm spclst, $19.42/hr
Phelps, C DeWayne, engineering technician II, $17.05/hr
Phelps, Cristy A, business support specialist II, $20.72/hr
Phelps, Deborah L, nurse, licensed prac, $16.53/hr
Phelps, Deloris Elizabeth, advancement associate sr, $50,665
Phelps, Julie Ann, instructional designer-speclst, $51,485
Phifer, Erik Stephen, food svc wrkr I, $9.60/hr
Philip, Benjamin Allen, fellow, post doctoral, $47,244
Phillippe, Donna Jo, clinical integration liaison, $82,800
Phillips, Harvey Jr, custodian lead, $14.03/hr
Phillips, Ann E, veterinary technician sr, $19.70/hr
Phillips, Camille Marie, media producer sr, $39,600
Phillips, Cecile Arden, office support assistant IV, $17.27/hr
Phillips, Charlotte L, prof, asoc, $95,848
Phillips, Christopher Wayne, bts carpenter-mrc, $16.36/hr
Phillips, Courtney Rae, nurse, staff II, $22.24/hr
Phillips, Darlene Vivian, care team assoc-clinical, $14.17/hr
Phillips, Deborah G, business support specialist II, $14.95/hr
Phillips, Denise Renee, temporary professional, $17.25/hr
Phillips, Eileen C, infection control profl, $69,372
Phillips, Gordon L, security sgt-h, $17.97/hr
Phillips, James H, radiologic techl, $28.70/hr
Phillips, Katherine L, food svc wrkr I, $11.29/hr
Phillips, Kathryn Eleanor, lab assistant, $8.50/hr
Phillips, Kathy J, student service coor sr, $48,410
Phillips, Keith E, boiler maint opr, $24.13/hr
Phillips, Kirsten Elaine, nurse anesthetist, $147,900
Phillips, Kodi Allen, cook, $12.64/hr
Phillips, Lorraine June, prof, asoc, $93,470
Phillips, Lynelle Mae, instructor, $60,628
Phillips, Margaret Bagwell, instructor, adjunct, $9,000
Phillips, Margaret L, teaching ast, $13.00/hr
Phillips, Margaret Rose, instructor, adjunct, $7,059
Phillips, Russell G, powr plnt maint spclst III mw, $25.85/hr

Phillips, Ruthanne, office support assistant IV, $13.78/hr
Phillips, Samuel Owen, care team assoc-clinical, $10.85/hr
Phillips, Shani R, nurse, licensed prac, $18.46/hr
Phillips, Shawn M, clinical mgr, $119,025
Phillips, Shelly M, ultrasonographer, $30.11/hr
Phillips, Teresa B, reimbursement spclst, $20.44/hr
Phillips, Thomas E, professor, $107,425
Phillips, Tommy L, maint wrkr, prev, $18.37/hr
Phillips, Walter Ray, prof, adjunct, $27,000
Phillips, William Barton, administrative consultant sr, $34,124
Phillips, Winfred George, prof, asoc teach, $92,945
Philpot, Nicholas James, athletic trainer, $25.00/hr
Philpot, Timothy A, prof, asoc, $89,020
Phinyophan, Piyarat, cook, $12.64/hr
Phipps, Anita Diane, instructor, adjunct, $13,000
Phipps, Jeanie Maupin, business support specialist II, $16.48/hr
Phipps, Steven, prof, ast visiting, $67,500
Phouk, Vannak, research/lab technician sr, $20.80/hr
Piasecki, Thomas M, professor, $76,471
Piatnitskaia, Galina N, prof, teach, $53,138
Picard, Michele L, custodian, $11.41/hr
Piccinini, Gualtiero, professor, $73,204
Piccirillo, Sarah, resrch ast, $42,822
Picco, Kelly J, nurse, staff now III, $30.00/hr
Piccolomini, Sara Elizabeth, research/lab technician, $10.32/hr
Picht, Randy N, executive director, $169,918
Pick, Roger, professor, $127,124
Pickard, Emmett B, sterile processing tech, $18.58/hr
Pickard, Joseph G, prof, asoc, $64,586
Pickens, Clayton Burke Jr, med lab techn, $15.87/hr
Pickens, Clayton B Sr, med techl reg, $22.44/hr
Pickens, Charlene K, med lab techn, $15.87/hr
Pickens, Martha Lynn, business support specialist II, $20.95/hr
Pickens, Matthieu J, av instal service tech-speclst, $14.96/hr
Pickens, Richard Matthew, librarian II, $40,408
Pickens, Tracy L, business support specialist II, $18.58/hr
Picker, Mary Ellen, prof, ast adjunct, $9,000
Pickerel, Lynn Ann, editor I, $25.00/hr
Pickerell, Roberta Audrey, service rep IV, $15.81/hr
Pickerill, Heath A, mgr research technical svcs, $79,386
Pickering, Lindsay Ann, student recruitment spclst, $16.60/hr
Pickett, Christine Theresa, strat comm consultant sr, $53,448
Pickett, Glenn E, tutor, $10.00/hr
Pickett, Ilayna H, tutor, $10.00/hr
Pickett, Janice L, office support assistant III, $13.59/hr
Pickett, Melissa Anne, nurse, advanced practice, $39.05/hr
Pickup, Julia Marie, instructor, adjunct, $10,500
Piech, Tara L, veterinarian, residnt, $29,000
Piel, Jessica M, nurse, staff II rnwp, $21.37/hr
Piepenbring, Nancy B, manuscript specialist, $34,750
Pieper, Kimberly Ann, recruiter, hlth care, $69,522
Pierard, Victor Allen, event assistant I, $7.55/hr
Pierce II, Robert A, prof, asoc extns, $60,736
Pierce, Ashley N, office support assistant IV, $14.16/hr
Pierce, Heather L, prof, ast clincl dept, $142,800
Pierce, Jeannette Ellen, librarian IV, $100,000
Pierce, Jeffrey A, grounds keeper, $13.21/hr
Pierce, Jennifer Irene, nurse, staff now plus, $30.00/hr
Pierce, Jerry Allen, nurse, staff now plus, $30.00/hr
Pierce, John Neal, pharmacist III, $125,375
Pierce, Laura Lee, temporary professional, $11.30/hr
Pierce, Lois H, academic dir, $112,800
Pierce, Michael Anthony, bldg cntrl sys tech II, $23.33/hr
Pierce, Rachel Anne, psychologist, $42,759
Pierce, Teresa Jean, custodian, $10.94/hr
Pierce, Vern L, prof, asoc extns, $88,181
Pierre, Karen A, mgr advancement, $51,392
Piesbergen, Frances Rapking, librarian III, $61,735
Pigg, Lloyd, safety communications operator, $14.01/hr
Pike, Sharon M, research specialist I, $15.45/hr
Pilcher, Steve Douglass, csm associate III, $25.90/hr
Pile, Allyson Margaret, radiologic techl, $18.59/hr
Pille, Joseph G Jr, construction manager sr, $87,120
Pillen, Timothy J, nurse anesthetist, $147,900
Pilley, Susan Woodson, lecturer, $29,063
Pilz, Jenifer Slade, technology resource associate, $15.25/hr
Pina, Zorina M, instructor, clincl, $1,324
Pinckney, Donald Rickey, temporary clerical, $12.47/hr
Pine, Darren W, grader, $100.00/hr

Pineda, Eynar G, temporary crafts service, $10.00/hr
Pineda, Nicole Sumayo, community suprt spclst, $36,050
Pingeton, Robin Renee, head coach, $208,080
Pinhero, Patrick Joseph, professor, $130,644
Pinkel, Gary, head coach, $350,000
Pinkerton, Denise R, social worker, $51,262
Pinkston, John R, resrch ast, $59,092
Pinnow, Rachel JaDean, prof, ast, $62,648
Pintel, David J, professor, $217,859
Pinto, Suyopa Chinchilla, custodian, $13.36/hr
Pintz, Joseph Edmund, prof, ast, $55,979
Piorkowski, James R, resident physician-5th yr, $58,083
Piorkowski, Jessica Mordarski, nurse, staff prn, $26.00/hr
Piper, Karen L, professor, $81,272
Pipes, Jeffery D, bts carpenter, $21.71/hr
Pippa, Aristotle Lawrence, tutor, $10.00/hr
Pippen, Todd, custodian, $10.00/hr
Pippin, Hanna Marie, office support assistant IV, $16.22/hr
Pippins, Willie Sam, event assistant I, $7.50/hr
Piranio, Michelle M, dir compliance effectiveness, $144,900
Pirch, Nikkole Kaylene, communications coord sr, $17.03/hr
Pires, Joseph C, prof, asoc, $104,498
Piringer, Nancy L, account executive, $66,680
Pirotte, Mary, student service coor II, $49,992
Pirtle, James Clifford, sr mgr broadcast operations, $60,000
Pirtle, Marsha, dir II student support svcs, $85,107
Piryani, Komal, resident physician-3rd yr, $52,470
Pitchford, Thomas Lee, mgr II business admin, $54,610
Pitford, Penny E, nurse, staff II rnwp, $20.95/hr
Pithua, Patrick, prof, ast, $101,064
Pitre, Jennifer Lee, med lab techn, $16.43/hr
Pittman, David L, prof, asoc adjunct, $21,600
Pittman, Demetria, food svc wrkr III, $13.21/hr
Pitts, Brian Drexel, temporary technical, $40.63/hr
Pitts, Shirley Ann, custodian, $10.94/hr
Pittser, Julie Renee, sr prgm mgr studnt supprt svcs, $55,850
Pivovarov, Peter, prof, ast, $77,571
Pizzo, Terra R, student recruitment spclst, $15.87/hr
Place, Jerry P, dean, asoc, $50,000
Place, Linna F, dir I, student support svcs, $63,806
Placke, Sara D, educational pgm associate I, $13.45/hr
Plagman, Rexene Lenore, independ living spclst, $12.78/hr
Plain, Cuba A, ast vice president, $148,661
Plain, Ronald L, professor, $129,455
Plamann, Lynda Schulte, dean, asoc, $122,369
Plamann, Michael D, professor, $100,355
Planitz, Jerome J Jr, mgr II csm operations, $66,333
Plank, Adrian Sloan, powr plnt matrl handling opr, $20.31/hr
Plaster, Nicole Ann, nurse, staff II, $19.00/hr
Platner, Erik Shane, office support assistant III, $14.20/hr
Platt, Melvin C, professor, $159,476
Platto, Christine L, student support specialist II, $16.85/hr
Platto, Edward C, custodian lead, $13.96/hr
Platto, Ronald J, media producer sr, $39,856
Platz, Trent A, prof, ast adjunct, $7,575
Pliska, Daniel M, executive chef, $110,610
Pliske, Martin J, distribution techn-mtls mgmt, $15.26/hr
Ploesser, Daniel William, event assistant I, $9.00/hr
Plovanich, Rebecca, radiologic techl, $26.47/hr
Plue, Raymond E, teaching ast, $13.00/hr
Plummer, Alvin Alexander, tutor, $15.00/hr
Plummer, Barbara Ann, business support specialist II, $20.10/hr
Plummer, Christopher Raymond, hospital sec officer, $11.07/hr
Plummer, Peggy L, business support specialist sr, $22.07/hr
Plummer, Sheila Yvonne, tutor, $15.00/hr
Pluym, Mark C, resident physician-4th yr, $54,425
Podgursky, Michael J, professor, $202,356
Poe, Alyssa Rose Ann, animal caretaker, $10.78/hr
Poe, April Dawn, animal caretaker, $10.78/hr
Poe, Brenda Marie, nurse, staff I, $19.00/hr
Poe, G Thomas, prof, asoc, $68,140
Poe, Jane A, executive assistant, $20.45/hr
Poe, Melissa Tapley, executive assistant sr, $54,755
Poe, Sonny Marie, mgr outpatient svc-mrc, $63,149
Poe, Tracy Lynn, custodian, $13.23/hr
Poehling, James C, ast vice chancellor, $38,316
Poehlmann, Carl John, resrch asoc, $117,087
Poelling, Cheryl R, office support assistant IV, $15.44/hr
Poettgen, Mary Mildred, event assistant I, $7.70/hr

Pogue, Adrian Elizabeth, nurse, staff I, $19.00/hr
Pogue, Beverly J, office support assistant IV, $13.18/hr
Pogue, Jerry Dean, maint svc attd, $17.60/hr
Pogue, Tayor James, temporary clerical, $8.60/hr
Pohlman, Deborah K, business tech analyst-spclst, $58,917
Poindexter, Monica Marie, instructor, ast, $31,110
Poirier, Carla Raye, prgm director, $26,556
Poirier, Deborah Ann, nurse, staff, $30.08/hr
Pojmann, Karen M, editor II, $45,335
Pokala, Naveen, prof, ast, $212,160
Pokala, Suhasini, instructor, clincl, $87,000
Polacco, Joseph Carmine, emeritus, $9,720
Poli, Sravan Kumar Reddy, tutor, $9.00/hr
Politte, Lenard L, prof, clincl, $16,444
Polkow Haight, Jennifer, veterinary technician lead, $22.70/hr
Pollard, Carol, research/lab technician sr, $16.98/hr
Pollard, Freedom Danielle, care team assoc-clinical, $12.75/hr
Pollard, Jawann A, student recruitment spclst, $22.18/hr
Pollard, Margo, executive assistant, $18.73/hr
Pollard, Sherry L, dir III business admin, $131,064
Pollion, LaToya A, patient svc rep, $11.90/hr
Pollitt, Daniel, instructor, adjunct, $8,325
Pollock, Amanda Gayle, radiologic techl, $20.42/hr
Pollock, Graham Robertson, resident physician-5th yr, $56,120
Pollock, Kelly Elizabeth, fellow, post doctoral, $19.23/hr
Pollock, Melisa Ann, office support assistant IV, $14.00/hr
Polo Parada, Luis, prof, asoc, $100,768
Polson, Beth Ann, nurse, clincl charge-rn, $32.40/hr
Polson, John L, system administrator-spclst, $49,500
Polston, David L, telecom tech-princpl, $21.60/hr
Pomerleau, Thomas J, athletic trainer, $40,050
Pommerenke, David, professor, $121,240
Ponce, Jasely K Torres, food svc wrkr III, $12.20/hr
Pond, Donna S, nurse, staff II, $29.23/hr
Ponder, Debra Jo, instructor, adjunct, $6,276
Ponder, Devin Anthony, patient svc rep, $11.07/hr
Ponferrada, Leonor Corazon, office support associate, $19.03/hr
Ponikvar, Michael John, specialist, $10.00/hr
Ponnapureddy, Rakesh, resident physician-1st yr, $49,025
Pons, Lisa Michelle, instructor, ast, $32,112
Pontz, John David, ast coach, $61,800
Poock, Scott Ervin, prof, asoc extns, $99,412
Pooker, Kristin M, office support assistant IV, $15.75/hr
Pool, Stephen Dewayne, instructor, adjunct, $12,300
Poole, Coledia Marie, program/project supprt coor I, $36,500
Poole, Janice M, nurse, staff, $29.52/hr
Poole, Mark W, emrg med techn, $13.24/hr
Poole, Melinda A, office support assistant IV, $16.30/hr
Poole, Melissa J, grant writer sr, $25.00/hr
Poole, Stephanie Y, system support analyst-spclst, $19.27/hr
Poor, Joel C, prof, asoc teach, $77,071
Pope, Christina Veloso, academic advisor sr, $41,108
Pope, Jodie Lynn, nurse, staff II, $28.39/hr
Pope, Mark L, professor, $109,200
Popejoy, Connie L, med records transcript, $18.45/hr
Popejoy, Lori L, prof, asoc, $96,638
Popescu, Mihaela Florentina, coor protocol svcs, $21.40/hr
Popescu, Mihail, prof, asoc, $114,400
Popkes-Johnson, Jennie Elizabeth, nurse, staff II, $31.10/hr
Popoola, Christine Renee, executive assistant sr, $49,964
Popoola, Oluwole, resident physician-1st yr, $50,219
Popovic, Zoran Slavko, prof, visiting, $50,000
Popp, Donald Wesley, custodian, $10.94/hr
Popp, Jennifer Ann, business ops associate sr, $53,544
Popper, Judith S, prof, clincl, $75,220
Porcel, Jorge, prof, asoc, $63,303
Portell, Grant August, temporary technical, $10.00/hr
Porter, Blake Wilson, resident physician-5th yr, $56,120
Porter, Brian J, electronics technician III, $16.95/hr
Porter, Brian P, office support assistant III, $17.57/hr
Porter, Elaine S, nurse, staff II, $32.96/hr
Porter, Jana Leann, asoc dir program/project ops, $60,000
Porter, Jennifer Elaine, program/project supprt coor I, $40,599
Porter, Lisa M, surgical technl certified, $23.26/hr
Porter, Mary I, business support specialist II, $21.94/hr
Porter, Michael L, ast coach, $140,000
Porter, Quilla N, custodian, $12.94/hr
Porter, Ralph J, asoc dir program/project ops, $77,500
Porter, Ruth A, office support assistant I, $11.93/hr

Porterfield, Amanda S, office support assistant IV, $15.58/hr
Porterfield, Michael David, instructional designer-expert, $55,617
Porterfield, Shirley Lynn, prof, asoc, $74,820
Porth, Mark Matthew, housing&envirn design spclst, $38,885
Porting Jackson, Elizabeth Renee, office support asst III, $15.90/hr
Portley, Erica Carmen, office support assistant IV, $14.66/hr
Portman, Julie Anne, lecturer, $100.00/hr
Portwood, Hannah Dale, office support assistant IV, $15.19/hr
Portwood, Lisa Ann, staff nurse, $21.98/hr
Poses, Jonathan W, asoc dir program/project ops, $61,509
Posey, Christia Ann, head coach, $56,100
Posey, John Randall, instructor, adjunct, $24,000
Posey, Robin A, office support assistant III, $11.76/hr
Poskin, Jane E, temporary clerical, $9.25/hr
Posses, Mary, prof, asoc, $65,881
Possin, Michael E, resident physician-3rd yr, $53,763
Postlethwaite, Bonnie Sue, dean, $123,600
Pothoff, Chad Edward, media production director II, $48,000
Potochnick, Stephanie Rodriguez, prof, ast, $78,683
Potrafka, Richard M, dir II student support svcs, $74,600
Potrafka, Susan R, sr ast dir studnt supprt svcs, $54,892
Pott, Rosemary, business ops associate II, $51,787
Pottebaum, Rebecca Ann, bus support specialist sr, $17.59/hr
Pottebaum, Stephen J, sr manager IT, $65,205
Potter, Dan S, media production director sr, $89,166
Potter, Erik R, strat comm associate I, $41,208
Potter, Joshua Michael, network engineer-expert, $71,527
Potter, Kelvin Wayne, med lab techn, $16.50/hr
Potter, Roy Allen, technology resource manager sr, $65,000
Potter, Stephen E, media producer sr, $45,364
Potter, Terry Eugene, seasonal farm ast, $10.51/hr
Potthoff, Jason Alan, ast coach, $41,000
Pottinger IV, Hardy J, programmer analyst-expert, $57,490
Pottinger, Anastasia Lee, teaching ast, $55.00/hr
Pottinger, Joan D, teaching ast, $13.00/hr
Pottorff, Mark G, ast dir student support svcs, $46,600
Potts, Sammie L Jr, research engineering tech I, $25.00/hr
Potts, Lisa M, business support specialist II, $17.31/hr
Potts, Shelley Ann, social worker, $53,503
Potts, Shelley Ann, mental health tech, $12.90/hr
Potts, Sonia Kay, business support specialist II, $23.37/hr
Potts, Tracey A, office support assistant IV, $14.00/hr
Potucek, Erica Brooke, mental health tech, $12.45/hr
Poulin, Rachelle Renee, coor, service, $17.15/hr
Poulopoulos, Nikolaos, prof, ast visiting, $45,000
Pounds, Krista Ann, office support assistant IV, $13.21/hr
Pounds, Madison, event assistant I, $8.50/hr
Pounds, Savannah Marie, event assistant I, $8.50/hr
Pournelle, Dana Michelle, 4-h spclst, $46,093
Pourney, Christy Ellen, advancement associate II, $18.60/hr
Pourney, Matthew K, prgm director, $55,106
Powell, Larson M Jr, professor, $69,236
Powell, Amber Lynn, care team assoc-clinical, $12.08/hr
Powell, Brittany Ann, care team assoc-clinical, $11.10/hr
Powell, Claudia Lane, manuscript specialist sr, $20.26/hr
Powell, Connie Renee, office support assistant IV, $19.68/hr
Powell, Duane Lee, nurse, staff II, $27.48/hr
Powell, Jodie Lynn, radiologic techl, $23.97/hr
Powell, Kyleene F, nurse, staff II, $20.54/hr
Powell, Laura, speech/lang pathologist, $58,000
Powell, Leslie McBride, business support specialist sr, $25.97/hr
Powell, Lisa Michelle, temporary clerical, $12.00/hr
Powell, Mary Ann, nurse, staff, $30.24/hr
Powell, Megan M, tqip coordinator, $17.18/hr
Powell, Melvin D, telecom tech-expert, $18.53/hr
Powell, Mike S, exec dir mo rehab cntr, $141,120
Powell, Rachael Nicole, nurse, staff II, $24.25/hr
Powell, Richard Stevan, custodian, $11.00/hr
Powell, Rosetta Marie, office support assistant IV, $14.11/hr
Powell, Roslyn, office support assistant IV, $14.28/hr
Powell, Scott J, library info specialist sr, $15.32/hr
Powell, Shaquille Tyshawn, patient svc rep, $10.85/hr
Powell, Toney, custodian, $11.44/hr
Powelson, Misty Ann, nurse, licensed prac, $18.24/hr
Power, Chelsey D, temporary crafts service, $7.50/hr
Power, Lisa K, student support specialist sr, $16.87/hr
Powers, Donald W Jr, powr plnt opr I, $25.85/hr
Powers Scott, Renee Lee, couns hlth/welfare/wellness, $59,594
Powers, Cary L, advancement officer, $52,464

Powers, Dale J, communications coordinator sr, $22.37/hr
Powers, Lisa Jo, instructor, adjunct, $9,900
Powers, Rachel A, intern, $23,000
Powers, Robyn Ellen, nurse, staff II, $27.00/hr
Prabhushankar, Roopashree, fellow, post doc clncl-yr2, $58,083
Prager, Bradley J, prof, asoc, $76,155
Prahlad, Anand, professor, $95,290
Prangcharoen, Narong, teaching ast, $31.80/hr
Prasad, Amit, prof, asoc, $74,688
Prasad, Srirupa, prof, ast, $58,848
Praschan, Stephanie Anne, academic advisor sr, $45,900
Prater, Joseph Chet, event assistant I, $7.50/hr
Prater, Lacey B, social worker, $50,568
Prather, Randall S, prof, curators, $212,495
Prativadi, Narasimhachar Govindarajan, physician, $250.00/hr
Prato, Anthony A, emeritus, $64,019
Pratt, Joseph B, custodian, $10.94/hr
Pratt, Nathan A, nurse, staff per diem, $35.00/hr
Pratt, Pamela Drew, instructor, adjunct, $8,571
Pratt, Wayne J, strat comm consultant, $53,000
Pratte, Brenda S, resrch asoc, $47,375
Pratte, Claire Elise, nurse, staff I, rnwp, $19.37/hr
Pratte, Evan, ast coach, $78,030
Pratte, Laura Marie, reimbursement ast-cert, $18.59/hr
Pratte, Paul Simon, director it, $107,376
Prayer, Joseph Jacob Jr, food svc wrkr I, $9.60/hr
Preckshot, Geoffrey W, library info specialist, $12.98/hr
Prelas, Mark Antonio, professor, $136,578
Prendergast, Polly Draper, sr dir program/project ops, $62,115
Prenger, Sharon Monica Knipp, physical therapist, $81,151
Prenger, Susan G, nurse, staff, $31.28/hr
Presberg, Charles D, prof, asoc, $80,077
Presley, Andrew James, network engineer-speclst, $46,534
Presser, Nan R, asoc dir healthcare programs, $79,007
Pressley, Linda Jo, physical therapist, $37.11/hr
Prestigiacomo, Carl Christopher, prof, asoc teach, $97,757
Preston, James Orval, dir III advancement, $86,631
Preston, Karson Lynn, nurse, staff II, $21.37/hr
Preston, Keri A, educational pgm associate I, $13.66/hr
Preston, Morgan Ann, care team assoc-clinical, $12.50/hr
Preston, Stephen James, pharmacist II, $60.00/hr
Prettejohn, Amy M, ast dir institutional research, $66,950
Pretz, Shari Lynn, business support specialist II, $15.25/hr
Preul, Jamy Lena, temporary professional, $21.64/hr
Preuss, Carla Christine, media producer sr, $35,088
Preuss, Timothy A, db programmer analyst-speclst, $46,398
Prevette, Danelle Elizabeth, nurse, staff I, $19.00/hr
Prevo, Judy, office support assistant IV, $15.89/hr
Prewett, Barb S, prgm mgr II studnt supprt svcs, $65,000
Prewett, Beverly Deanne, office support assistant IV, $18.84/hr
Prewett, Montana Danse, custodian, $11.41/hr
Prewett, Nicholas W, dir II student support svcs, $119,765
Prewett, Rachael B, temporary professional, $50.00/hr
Prewitt, Alissa Ann, surgical technl certified, $18.50/hr
Prewitt, Christopher Thomas, sup systems admin-expert, $52,400
Prewitt, Nicole Lynn, radiologic techl, $18.23/hr
Prewitt, Terry, system support analyst-expert, $22.76/hr
Prewitt, Wayne R, sr dir program/project ops, $97,493
Preyer, David Lee, supv sterile processing, $54,633
Preyer, Melvin, agriculture foreman, $24.88/hr
Price, Amy Michelle, nurse, staff II, $24.96/hr
Price, Brittani Lynn, advancement coordinator, $14,400
Price, Catherine J, nurse, staff, $33.23/hr
Price, Clayton E, prof, asoc teach, $67,955
Price, David A, agriculture associate II, $15.43/hr
Price, Diana J, pat acct rep, $15.98/hr
Price, Jeffrey, prof, asoc, $91,956
Price, Jin Yuan, prof, ast resrch, $38,215
Price, Michael D, custodian, $11.00/hr
Price, Nancy Ann, instructor, $57,775
Price, Sandra Elise, instructor, adjunct, $9,600
Price, Tina D, office support assistant IV, $14.77/hr
Price, Victor Owen, ast registrar, $68,738
Prichard, Stephanie, program/project supprt coor I, $50,000
Prichodko Ray, Victoria, resident, clncl, $31,104
Pridgeon, Carolyn S, custodian, $11.00/hr
Pridgeon, Sean Christopher, nurse, staff now III, $30.00/hr
Priebe, Cynthia Jane, custodian, $10.94/hr
Priebe, Thomas R, utility dist wrkr IV, $23.75/hr

Priesmeyer, Stephanie Cooper, head coach, $66,244
Priest, Colin J, research/lab technician, $10.24/hr
Priest, Dennis Frank, student support specialist sr, $17.94/hr
Primers Egans, Lindra, dental assistant I, $16.84/hr
Primich, Tracy Lynn, sr director, $104,530
Primos, Jeffrey Louis, dir I, business admin, $89,024
Prince, Allante Marcell, event assistant I, $7.50/hr
Prince, Arianna Marquis, care team assoc-clinical, $12.32/hr
Prince, Georgia Semone, office support assistant III, $12.39/hr
Prince, Monique R, office support assistant IV, $14.84/hr
Prince, Sarah Ann, nurse, staff II, $23.36/hr
Principi, Alessandro, fellow, post doctoral, $42,000
Princivalli, Melissa D, nurse, staff II, $22.24/hr
Prine, Lynn Ann, dental assistant II, $16.54/hr
Prine, Richard G, prof, ast clincl, $121,126
Pringle, Oran Allan, prof, curator teach, $105,418
Prior, Stephen Harry, fellow, post doctoral, $43,269
Pritchett, Kathy J, human resources assistant, $16.76/hr
Pritchett, Kristen Elizabeth, ast coach, $46,000
Pritchett, Michael S, prof, asoc, $61,973
Pritzl, Curtis J, fellow, post doctoral, $38,571
Probert, Ted Russel, extns professional, asoc, $68,143
Procopio, Sebastiano J, intern, $22,783
Procter, Adam M, fellow, post doctoral, $50,000
Procter, Brenda J, prof, asoc extns, $39,077
Procter, Donna S, academic advisor sr, $41,350
Proctor, Phyllis May, health records techn I, $13.09/hr
Proell, Benjamin Jon, adjunct, $9,000
Proffer, Richard Dale, business spclst, $54,929
Proffitt, Rachel Christina, instructor, $52
Proffitt, Sarah Ann, research/lab technician, $10.24/hr
Prost, Evan, prof, ast teach, $47,024
Prothero, Leslie A, office support assistant IV, $14.66/hr
Protzel, Edward Howard, instructor, adjunct, $9,000
Proud, Kelsey E, strat comm consultant, $47,213
Prouhet, Paula Marie, prof, ast teach, $63,540
Proulx, Christine M, prof, asoc, $73,328
Prouty, Mary Ann, office support assistant IV, $18.97/hr
Provencher, William Jay, ast mgr hospitality services, $50,500
Provolt, Chloe Lyn, mental health tech, $12.45/hr
Provorse, Christopher D, mgr III business admin, $64,416
Provost, Karen Lois, business support analyst II, $18.52/hr
Prue, Robert E, prof, ast, $60,993
Pruett, Colleen Evelyn, instructor, adjunct, $16,500
Pruett, Jennifer Renee, custodian, $12.94/hr
Pruett, Kenneth R, care team assoc-clinical, $15.17/hr
Pruett, Sharon G, nurse advisor, telephone, $30.36/hr
Pruett, Stacie Nicole, high school student, $7.50/hr
Pruitt, Howard D, cms operations supervisor, $54,565
Pruitt, Robert L, powr plnt maint spclst III mec, $25.85/hr
Pruitt, Stephen W, professor, $191,996
Pryor, Christina Nichole, instructor, adjunct, $8,400
Pryor, Jonathan Thomas, student service coor II, $40,392
Prysock, Monica, temporary professional, $11.30/hr
Pu, Hefu, prof, ast, $78,000
Puckett, Carrie Lynn, office support assistant IV, $15.87/hr
Puckett, Charles Linwood, professor, $358,184
Puckett, Samuel Van, csm project manager, $72,775
Pudenz, Carla J, business support specialist sr, $28.17/hr
Pue, Dianna, office support assistant III, $14.99/hr
Puetz, Joseph R, resident physician-1st yr, $50,219
Pugh, Laura Lynne, office support assistant III, $12.92/hr
Pugh, Pamela B, office support assistant IV, $19.36/hr
Puglis, Mary Ann, nurse, staff II, $34.72/hr
Pugsley, Delilah Lorraine, pharmacy tech, $10.85/hr
Pukthuanthong, Kuntara, prof, asoc, $290,563
Pulakat, Lakshmidevi, professor, $137,996
Puleo, Donna J, dir I, event services, $77,555
Pulley, Leticia Passi, nurse, staff prn, $26.00/hr
Pulliam, Cameron Bradley, media production assoc, $8.89/hr
Pummill, John Charles, student support specialist I, $12.98/hr
Pung, Lyda, resident physician-1st yr, $49,025
Puntenney, Bryce F, communications coordinator sr, $19.70/hr
Puntenney, Patrick Quin, editor II, $48,798
Purcell, Angie Marie, temporary clerical, $10.50/hr
Purchase Roberts, Amanda Michelle, studnt service coord II, $43,860
Purdome, Roberta Ann, nurse, staff, $27.55/hr
Puricelli, Michael D, resident physician-3rd yr, $53,763
Purk, John H, professor, $122,741

Purnell-Ford, Kayla Marie, care team assoc-suppt, $10.64/hr
Purnell, Andrea M, strat comm associate II, $45,909
Purnell, Charles, retail sales assistant, $10.15/hr
Pursell, Dyanna Lenore, geo info system tech, $17.65/hr
Purves, Cameron A, business support specialist II, $19.39/hr
Purves, Emily Adrienne Smith, serv line spclst, $67,810
Purvis-Dierks, Jenifer Lee, patient svc rep, $12.84/hr
Pushechnikov, Oleksiy, fellow, post doctoral, $57,689
Pushechnikova, Lina, research/lab technician sr, $15.81/hr
Pushechnikova, Yuliya, high school student, $7.50/hr
Putnam, Darcie L, instructor, adjunct, $9,093
Putnam, James W, csm associate II, $21.09/hr
Putnam, Jennifer Lynn, ast coach, $160,000
Putnam, Tina E, ast mgr acctg-h, $75,296
Puttaswamy, Sachidevi, fellow, post doctoral, $38,000
Putterman, Hana, resident physician-1st yr, $50,219
Puttur, Santhoshkumar, prof, ast resrch, $51,456
Puttur, Shuba, histologic technl, $20.94/hr
Pyle, Marsha Agnes, dean, $238,703
Pyron, Donna N, specialist, $26.00/hr
Qasem, Abdulraheem M.S, prof, ast clincl, $175,250
Qazi, Abdul Haseeb, resident physician-2nd yr, $50,810
Qi, Wenchuan, programmer analyst-entry, $44,000
Qin, Hua, prof, ast, $75,400
Qin, Ruwen, prof, ast, $77,587
Qin, Zhenbo, professor, $110,581
Qiu, Dan, fellow, post doctoral, $42,000
Qiu, Liming, fellow, post doctoral, $36,750
Qiu, Yunsheng, temporary technical, $8.50/hr
Qu, Zhe, resrch scientist/academic, $37,500
Quackenbush, Stephen Lee, prof, asoc, $65,770
Quade, James Carl, mts/electrician, $22.50/hr
Quade, Mary Ann, office support assistant IV, $15.12/hr
Quaintance, Jennifer Lynn, dir I, student support svcs, $82,000
Quearry, Jayson William, grader, $7,200
Queathem, Kelly Renee, care team assoc-clinical, $11.49/hr
Quezada, Jose Ydanis, custodian lead, $14.03/hr
Quick, Angela Denise, nurse, staff II, $31.47/hr
Quick, Daniel Thomas, office support assistant I, $9.05/hr
Quick, Deborah M, coor, marketing, $56,985
Quick, Hillary Anne, nurse, staff I, $19.00/hr
Quick, Jacob Adam, prof, ast, $313,500
Quick, Rebecca Ann, patient svc rep, $13.74/hr
Quick, Roy Evan Dalton, research/lab technician sr, $18.00/hr
Quigley, Maureen R, prof, asoc teach, $56,222
Quilty, Katherine Bishop, nurse, staff II, $22.32/hr
Quinata, Michael A, resrch mgr-medicine, $68,900
Quinlan, Brenda K, emp rel spec hlthcr, $70,104
Quinlan, Constance, office support assistant III, $16.21/hr
Quinlan, Denise E, office support assistant IV, $15.43/hr
Quinn, Colleen, resident physician-1st yr, $49,025
Quinn, James Thomas, extns professional, asoc, $58,362
Quinn, Kathleen J, dean, asoc, $139,500
Quinn, Michael P, system administrator-expert, $52,400
Quinn, Paula Kay, nurse, staff II, $23.54/hr
Quinn, Peggy Colleen, med techl reg, $30.36/hr
Quinn, Raymond, maintenance supervisor, $54,159
Quinn, Thomas P, professor, $120,968
Quinn, Tim Lee, research/lab technician sr, $17.50/hr
Quiriconi, Margo, instructor, adjunct, $13,500
Quirk, Kelly Kathleen, patient svc rep, $10.64/hr
Quiros, Monica Elisa, child dev teacher sr, $26,485
Qurashi, Farheen A, resident physician-4th yr, $54,425
Qureshi, Nilofer, professor, $125,782
R, Juan Lopez, custodian, $12.94/hr
Raab, Ann Margaret, instructor, adjunct, $7,200
Raack, William J Jr, asoc dir program/project ops, $63,342
Raaf, Deborah M, educational pgm associate I, $14.91/hr
Rabara, Viral Kantilal, fellow, post doc clncl yr1, $55,804
Rabbitt, Philip James, clerk, operating room supply, $13.46/hr
Race, Katelyn Marie, lab assistant, $10.00/hr
Rachow, Jennifer A, program/project supprt coor I, $40,511
Rackers, Bethany Ann, social worker, $52,239
Rackers, Logan John, temporary technical, $10.25/hr
Rackers, Mitchell T, security analyst-princpl, $68,785
Rackets, Reese Tyler Thomas, editor II, $40,400
Radchenko, Christopher Char, res physician-4th yr, $54,425
Radcliff, Jennifer Michelle, instructor, clincl, $30,750
Rademan, Maxwell Aaron, nurse, staff II, $22.00/hr

Radice, Anthony Robert, police officer, $16.79/hr
Radom, Virginia, instructor, clincl, $11,400
Radulescu, Alexandru Viorel, prof, ast, $59,153
Rae, Frank David, event assistant I, $8.35/hr
Rae, Jacquelyn Elaine, pat acct rep, $16.08/hr
Raedeke, Maurine Darling, prof, ast teach, $67,703
Rafferty, Holly, pharmacy tech, $10.85/hr
Raftopoulos, Demitrios Andrew, office support asst IV, $14.54/hr
Ragan, Diane M, veterinary technician sr, $16.98/hr
Ragan, Lauren S, child dev teacher sr, $26,747
Ragan, Roland D, house manager h, $84,760
Ragan, Sean Matthew, student recruitment spclst, $16.03/hr
Rages, Lorri Amber, teaching ast, $13.00/hr
Ragon, Katharine Elayne, resrch asoc, $39,977
Ragsdale, John W Jr, professor, $132,400
Ragsdale, Debra L, coor, reimbursement, $52,977
Ragsdell, Jennifer Ann, teaching ast, $55.00/hr
Rahaman, Lennard Ishmael, office support asst III, $13.92/hr
Rahaman, Mohamed N, professor, $105,933
Raheja, Aman, instructor, adjunct, $11,700
Rahman, Rubayat Naila, fellow, post doc clncl-yr2, $58,083
Rahman, Tahir, prof, ast clincl dept, $177,900
Rahmani, Esmaeel, research specialist I, $30,000
Rahn, Ruby M, office support assistant IV, $13.24/hr
Rahner, Matthew R, temporary technical, $8.00/hr
Railton, Barbara E, operations support tech II, $17.00/hr
Railton, Charles R, press III, $20.77/hr
Railton, David Joseph, accountant I, $16.63/hr
Raine, Elizabeth C, hlth educator, $41,662
Raines, Gary Alan Jr, business support specialist sr, $19.42/hr
Raines, Benjamin Todd, resident physician-1st yr, $50,219
Raines, Donna S, supv nursing acute care, $32.07/hr
Raines, Kim Mary, mgr III business admin, $64,416
Raines, Neus, resrch asoc, $46,600
Raines, Penelope Ann Phyllis, prog/proj supprt coor I, $51,625
Rainey, Antonio J, animal caretaker, $12.12/hr
Rainey, George, system administrator-expert, $55,820
Rainey, Hannah K, event assistant I, $7.50/hr
Rainey, Larry Darnell, event assistant I, $7.50/hr
Rainey, Trinity Ann, food svc wrkr II, $10.49/hr
Rainsberger, Paul K, director, $96,894
Rainwater, Gary P, mts/electrician, $21.05/hr
Raitt, Jill, prof, visiting, $18,000
Rajagopalan, Anuradha, prof, asoc clincl dept, $134,885
Rajan, Suraj, resident physician-2nd yr, $52,007
Raju, Murugesan, resrch asoc, $41,630
Ralph, Gregory Michael, research/lab technician sr, $12.99/hr
Ralph, Sarah Jane, program/project supprt coor II, $41,580
Ralston, Andrew C, hospital security officer, $14.81/hr
Ramachandran, Venkataraman, prof, asoc clincl dept, $212,295
Ramakrishna, Malavika, student support specialist I, $13.66/hr
Ramalingam, Anupama, resident physician-4th yr, $55,804
Ramamoorthy, Ezhiludai Nambi, fellow, post doc clncl yr1, $55,804
Raman, Srikar, fellow, post doctoral, $44,000
Ramirez, Alejandro, prof, ast clincl dept, $206,701
Ramirez, Ana Mirca, custodian, $10.94/hr
Ramirez, Cathi Ann, event assistant I, $9.00/hr
Ramirez, Elizabeth, program/project supprt coor I, $45,582
Ramirez, Rigoberto, resident physician-4th yr, $54,425
Rammaha, Osama I, custodial supervisor, $50,232
Ramphal, Ronald, support systems admin-speclst, $52,040
Ramsay, Christopher Wayne, sr asoc dir research, $91,350
Ramsay, Darlene S, ast vice chancellor, $104,000
Ramsey, Amanda Sue, med techl reg, $24.27/hr
Ramsey, John C, business support specialist sr, $24.89/hr
Ramsey, Lisa Ann, nurse, licensed prac sr, $16.62/hr
Ranabargar, Courtney Renee, reimbursement ast, $18.59/hr
Randall, Douglas D, emeritus, $64,544
Randall, Linda Lea, professor, $236,440
Randall, Paula M, nurse, staff II rnwp, $31.20/hr
Randle, Ernestine, custodian, $13.23/hr
Randle, Nanette Nicole, instructor, clincl, $80,000
Randolph, Dennis A, instructor, adjunct, $15,000
Randolph, Jena K, prof, ast resrch, $74,800
Randolph, Jennifer Leah, nurse, staff I, $19.00/hr
Randolph, Joshua Cole, radiologic techl, $18.87/hr
Randolph, LaShaundra R, student service coor II, $40,392
Randolph, Patrick David, student recruitment spclst, $15.25/hr
Raney, Suzanne King, communications coordinator, $19.25/hr

Rangarajan, Rajesh, resident physician-2nd yr, $50,810
Rani, Prityi, resident physician-4th yr, $55,804
Rankin II, Robert L, animal caretaker-equin/fd lead, $13.37/hr
Ranow, Ashley Nichole, nurse, staff now III, $30.00/hr
Ransdell, Brennan Myles, instructor, $41,769
Ransom, Curtis Joel, research specialist sr, $45,000
Rantz, Marilyn J, prof, curators, $180,006
Rao, Akhilesh, fellow, post doc clncl-yr2, $58,083
Rao, Prabhakar Aroor, professor, $92,067
Rao, Praveen Ramesh, prof, asoc, $82,100
Rao, Sirish C, resident physician-1st yr, $50,219
Raper, Shelby Marie, student recruitment spclst, $14.96/hr
Raper, Stephen A, prof, asoc, $116,405
Rapier, Dana S, academic advisor, $38,371
Rapko, Emily K, sr prgm mgr studnt supprt svcs, $57,854
Rapley, John W, professor, $149,712
Rapp, Angela M, office support assistant IV, $16.00/hr
Rapp, James Vincent, office support aide II, $8.50/hr
Rapp, Melissa Leigh, social worker, $54,628
Rapp, Ryan, ast vice president, $163,175
Rapsilber, Kenneth Matthew, academic advisor sr, $40,988
Rardin, Theresa A, tutor, $15.00/hr
Rasa Edwards, Beth Charlene, 4-h spclst, $49,279
Rasberry, Melissa Ann, reimbursement ast, $16.71/hr
Rash, Estella, child dev assistant, $12.83/hr
Rash, Jacqueline Marie, student support specialist I, $13.24/hr
Raskin, Gail Lemp, research specialist sr, $66,460
Rasmussen, Jacqueline Anne, business spclst, $64,131
Rasmussen, Lynn M, prof, ast clincl, $35,148
Rasoolvali, Zulfikar Ali, psychiatrist, $150.00/hr
Rassman, Shane A, resident physician-4th yr, $54,425
Raterman, Donna S, patient svc rep, $14.88/hr
Rath, Nigam, prof, resrch, $90,750
Rathbone McCuan, Eloise, professor, $89,185
Rathke, Donna J, business support specialist II, $21.86/hr
Rathmann, Carla M, office support assistant IV, $15.90/hr
Rathmann, Rodney L, prof, asoc adjunct, $9,519
Rathmann, Thomas D, grounds keeper-mrc, $11.11/hr
Rathz, Paula Maryann, child life spclst, $40,229
Ratliff, Deborah, executive assistant, $20.20/hr
Ratliff, Mark Harris, instructor, adjunct, $375
Ratneshwar, Srinivasan, professor, $212,065
Rattani, Ajita, resrch asoc, $44,000
Ratterman, Lisa M, safety communications operator, $14.01/hr
Rau, Adam D, fellow, $56,803
Rau, Matthew James, office support assistant III, $12.50/hr
Rau, Rene Collins, executive assistant, $19.86/hr
Rauch, Todd Allen, event assistant I, $7.55/hr
Raumschuh, Terry E, media producer sr, $48,176
Rautman, Marcus, professor, $83,858
Ravandoust, Yasaman, prof, asoc, $95,000
Ravenscraft, Patricia, reimbursement ast-cert, $21.35/hr
Ravert, April Anderson, research/lab technician sr, $18.73/hr
Ravert, Russell Douglas, prof, asoc, $76,938
Raw, Kathy E, med techl reg, $22.55/hr
Rawat, Gagneesh Gaurav, peoplesoft admin-princpl, $85,105
Rawlings, Arthur L, prof, ast clincl dept, $212,242
Rawlings, Catherine Ann, office support assistant IV, $14.49/hr
Rawlings, Sharon S, dietitian, clincl, $22.00/hr
Rawson, Vanessa Aharoyn, research/lab technician sr, $15.11/hr
Ray, Anthony L, data cntr support tech-princpl, $26.86/hr
Ray, Bimal Kumar, professor, $113,767
Ray, Chandra S, prof, resrch, $42,000
Ray, Denise Lynn, business support specialist II, $18.27/hr
Ray, Donald P, mts/hvac, $24.13/hr
Ray, Eva R, linen attd, $12.96/hr
Ray, Gerda W, prof, asoc, $53,070
Ray, Jill Ann, patient svc rep, $14.45/hr
Ray, Kimberly K, med lab techn, $21.70/hr
Ray, S Don, family fincl edu spclst, $48,288
Ray, Sandra Meeks, office support assistant IV, $17.08/hr
Ray, Sandy Leah, office support assistant III, $13.50/hr
Ray, Sheila Barrett, nurse anesthetist, $147,900
Ray, Terry A, custodian, $11.41/hr
Ray, Wendy Renee, educational pgm associate I, $13.21/hr
Raybon, Tyrone Jeffrey, stores clerk, $14.43/hr
Raychaudhuri, Ratul, resident physician-7th yr, $61,960
Rayford, Sharon Veronica, research/lab technician, $10.25/hr
Raymer, Justin Marshall, student service coor I, $37,550

Raymon, Neil A, prof, asoc, $61,004
Raymond, Melinda Kay, phlebotomist, $12.69/hr
Raysheldi, Samuel, tutor, $15.00/hr
Raza, Shahzad, fellow, post doc clncl-yr3, $60,415
Read, David T, professor, $96,064
Read, Deborah Elaine, staff dev spclst, $55,183
Read, Diane Michelle, student support specialist II, $16.19/hr
Read, Emily Meghan, pharmacy tech, $10.85/hr
Read, G Sullivan, professor, $107,774
Reagan, Ryan Scott, food svc wrkr I, $11.35/hr
Reagan, Tina Renee, student support specialist II, $15.11/hr
Real, Jordan Anne, ast mgr pat admissions, $55,058
Reams, Cheryl Lee, asoc dir program/project ops, $71,033
Reams, Kelly Ann, patient svc rep, $12.76/hr
Reams, Laura Beth, nurse, licensed prac, $15.06/hr
Reams, Mary L, mgr, medical educ, $61,036
Reams, Michelle Jude, instructor, $37,990
Reams, Pamela R, med tchnl reg, $25.89/hr
Reams, Robert C, resident physician-2nd yr, $52,007
Reape, Kevin Michael, internet administrator-entry, $16.83/hr
Reardon, Daniel Charles, prof, ast, $58,648
Reasoner, Lynda E, telecom it analyst-spcclst, $19.42/hr
Reasons, Brittany Leann, pat acct rep, $14.54/hr
Reavey, Daphne A, instructor, clincl, $62,663
Reaws, Gwendolyn S, educational pgm associate I, $13.72/hr
Reay, Craig, office support assistant II, $13.39/hr
Rebe, Kathryn L, system support analyst-spcclst, $28.37/hr
Rebeck, Patricia Sarah, instructor, adjunct, $8,325
Reber, Leo William, administrative consultant sr, $93,997
Reberry, Ann, business support specialist II, $20.72/hr
Reboli, Alan J, support systems admin-spcclst, $48,000
Reboli, Sarah Lenore, business ops associate II, $48,960
Rebstock, Michael Rex, fin and acctg specialist, $16.79/hr
Rechtien, Johnathan David, system support analyst-entry, $17.26/hr
Recker, Lane L, event assistant I, $7.55/hr
Reckley, Alice, prof, asoc, $64,425
Recko, Susan Lee, exec dir learning, $157,435
Recktenwald, Christine M, prof, ast teach, $63,344
Records, Holly Anne, temporary professional, $17.26/hr
Records, Kathryn Ann, professor, $141,750
Rector, Randy S, prof, ast, $26,867
Redd, Matthew Kenneth, resident physician-5th yr, $56,120
Redd, Richard L, floor care techn, $13.57/hr
Redden, Diana Michelle, enrollment advisor sr, $16.87/hr
Redden, James Andy, custodian, $11.41/hr
Redden, Jessica Renee, nurse advisor, telephone, $27.37/hr
Redden, Roger R, custodian, $11.00/hr
Redden, Timothy D, resp therapist reg, $26.12/hr
Reddick, Tracy, office support assistant IV, $16.49/hr
Reddick, Travis Wayne, system administrator-expert, $67,897
Redding, Chelsea Renee, research specialist I, $35,001
Redding, Deborah Lydia, instructor, adjunct, $6,800
Redding, Kenneth E, csm associate I, $19.97/hr
Reddy, Anvesh C, resident physician-4th yr, $54,425
Reddy, Chada Sudershan, prof, asoc, $103,856
Reddy, G Mallikarjun, resident physician-3rd yr, $53,763
Reddy, Jyotsna Batapati Krishna, fellow, post doc clncl yr 1, $55,804
Reddy, V Prakash, prof, asoc, $68,523
Redfield Jacobs, Laura M, office support assistant IV, $14.50/hr
Redford, Gloria Juliana, prof, ast clincl, $86,351
Redmon, Leiona Elizabeth, custodian, $10.39/hr
Redmon, Philip, programmer analyst-spcclst, $46,886
Redmon, Tawana Antionette, temporary clerical, $9.00/hr
Redmond, Breanna, child dev assistant, $8.08/hr
Redohl, Sarah Margaret, instructor, adjunct, $18,000
Redwine, Michael George, custodian, $10.69/hr
Reece, Jea Hyun, media producer sr, $38,000
Reed II, Earl Thomas, support systems admin-spcclst, $48,585
Reed, Aaron Wesley, prof, asoc teach, $59,841
Reed, Andrew, research/lab technician sr, $15.00/hr
Reed, Daniel Ryan, hospital security officer, $11.28/hr
Reed, David James, editor II, $6,480
Reed, Heather Renee, business ops associate sr, $57,835
Reed, Ingrid, prof, ast clincl, $107,033
Reed, JoAnn, nurse, staff II, $28.45/hr
Reed, Katherine Trimarco, prof, asoc profl practice, $60,795
Reed, Kenyon, office support assistant III, $13.87/hr
Reed, Lloyd Wayne, custodian, $12.94/hr
Reed, Melissa K, office support assistant IV, $14.94/hr

Reed, Nicole L, custodian, $10.94/hr
Reed, Patricia Lee, custodian, $12.94/hr
Reed, Paula Lucille, office support assistant III, $15.14/hr
Reed, Ricky A, support systems admin-expert, $72,480
Reed, Rita, prof, profl practice, $88,477
Reed, Robby Adam, supv sterile processing, $45,250
Reed, Robert Edward, prof, asoc resrch, $97,934
Reed, Shannon Kelly, prof, ast teach, $100,934
Reed, Sharon Ann, strat comm consultant sr, $77,836
Reed, Sharon E, resrch scientist/academic, $38,500
Reed, Spencer M, communications assistant sr, $17.25/hr
Reed, Terry Wayne, hospital security officer, $13.42/hr
Reed, William Calvan, floor care techn, $13.57/hr
Reeder, Angela Leigh, supv nursing acute care, $29.28/hr
Reeder, Anne Janel, program/project supprt coor I, $43,430
Reeder, David Allen, mts/electrician, $21.05/hr
Reeder, Joe S, supv bldg trades-h, $55,058
Reeder, Le Ann, child life spclst, $47,311
Reeder, Linda S, prof, asoc, $64,228
Reeder, Tammy L, nurse, staff, $27.85/hr
Reedy, Lindsay Marie, business support specialist II, $18.63/hr
Reedy, Mark J, user support analyst-expert, $21.09/hr
Rees, David L, prof, profl practice, $88,681
Rees, Jo Merle, nurse, staff II, $33.35/hr
Reese Sr, Emery Dennis, custodian, $10.69/hr
Reese, James W, strat comm associate II, $41,000
Reese, Leah Marie, nurse, licensed prac, $15.06/hr
Reese, Lori K, instructor, $45,095
Reese, Sylkia R, central sterile assistant, $10.25/hr
Reese, Tempeste N, executive assistant, $17.71/hr
Reeser, Cassie L, mgr advancement, $46,928
Reesman, Sarah K, sr asoc athletic director, $167,000
Reeter, Kara Lea, nurse, staff I, $19.00/hr
Reeter, Scott C, strat comm associate I, $40,422
Reever, Jennifer Ann, nurse, staff II rnwp, $22.59/hr
Reeves Viets, Joseph Loren, prof, clinical dept, $437,604
Reeves, Andrew M, assoc director it, $77,250
Reeves, Betsy Lewin, clinical educator, $72,272
Reeves, Darryl R, rehab therapy aide, $12.14/hr
Reeves, Donna Sue, nurse, staff II rnwp, $34.18/hr
Reeves, Hannah R, prof, ast adjunct, $31,854
Reeves, Jeffory A, business support specialist II, $18.22/hr
Reeves, Jennifer Ann, resident physician-2nd yr, $50,810
Reeves, Joe, custodian, $11.44/hr
Reeves, Kelly S, office support assistant IV, $18.19/hr
Reeves, Lois Marie, office support assistant II, $10.35/hr
Reeves, Randy A, prof, asoc profl practice, $68,026
Reeves, Samantha Gail, patient svc rep, $12.44/hr
Reeves, Shunda L, office support assistant IV, $13.33/hr
Reeves, Stacey Marie, resrch aide, $32,000
Reeves, Trista, linen attd, $9.27/hr
Regan, Blaine Lee, patient svc rep, $10.85/hr
Regan, Sarah Margaret, certif pharmacy techn, $12.65/hr
Regester, April Jayne, prof, ast, $63,599
Register, Melissa Joyce, nurse, staff per diem, $35.00/hr
Regunath, Hariharan, fellow, post doc clncl-yr2, $58,083
Reh, Su, high school student, $9.41/hr
Rehagen, Diana Maria, office support assistant III, $14.05/hr
Rehard, David Galen, teaching ast, $16,680
Rehmer, Steven Royal, grounds keeper II, $14.52/hr
Rehmert, Mona Ann, office support assistant IV, $14.66/hr
Reich, Emily Nicole, nurse, staff II, $25.00/hr
Reich, Jay H, adjunct, $15,000
Reich, Linda Marie, advancement associate I, $36,295
Reichel, Mary C, environmental health tech sr, $20.13/hr
Reichel, Susan Kay, supv pat admiss, $48,128
Reicks, Meghan E, resident physician-5th yr, $58,083
Reid Arndt, Stephanie A, dean, asoc, $136,800
Reid, Anita Jean, educational pgm associate I, $12.49/hr
Reid, Barbara J, office support assistant II, $11.04/hr
Reid, David H, assoc director it, $91,225
Reid, Joshua Stephen, event assistant I, $10.50/hr
Reid, Lisa Marie, nurse, staff II, $28.09/hr
Reid, Rita-Marie Cain, professor, $116,669
Reidmeyer, Mary R, prof, asoc teach, $79,498
Reidy, Jennifer Lynn, research specialist I, $44,152
Reifschneider, Brenda K, business ops associate sr, $46,056
Reighard, Amelia Marguerite, resrch ast, $38,400
Reilly, Daniel William, student service coor II, $51,933

Reilly, Thomas James, prof, asoc clincl, $93,720
Reinbott, David L, busi spclst, agri, $56,682
Reinbott, Molly Grace, care team assoc-clinical, $12.08/hr
Reinbott, Timothy M, field superintendent, $74,603
Reindel, Sara G, tutor, $12.75/hr
Reine, Benjamin S, resident physician-3rd yr, $52,470
Reineke, Charles E, editor sr, $55,393
Reinero, Carol Rose, prof, asoc, $134,180
Reinhart, Amber Marie, prof, asoc, $62,150
Reinhart, James Anthony, care team assoc-clinical, $12.57/hr
Reinke, Wendy M, prof, asoc, $91,663
Reinkemeyer, Ross, construction manager II, $63,359
Reinsel, Thomas E, prof, ast, $259,436
Reisenbichler, Marilyn B, director it, $93,597
Reising, Patricia Lynn, student support specialist II, $15.08/hr
Reiske, Matthew Lawrence, sr ast dir studnt supprt svcs, $82,278
Reisner, Craig Thomas, reactor operator sr, $19.40/hr
Reiss, Laura Langford Gordon, bus support spec II, $15.51/hr
Reiss, Philip E, system administrator-speclst, $48,267
Reissing, Rebecca Danielle, user interfce designer-expert, $49,395
Reisweber, Mia Starmer, lecturer, $45,000
Reith, Dennis Frederick, office support assistant III, $14.92/hr
Rekab, Kamel, professor, $108,689
Rele, Maureen, telecomm opr-h, $12.96/hr
Releford, Alfreda J, accountant I, $19.18/hr
Reliford-Miller, Bobbie J, office support assistant IV, $20.08/hr
Rellergert, Linda Sue, extns professional, $68,234
Remeika, Joseph G Jr, temporary technical, $11.91/hr
Remelius, Susan E, patient svc rep, $14.88/hr
Remier, Michael Charles, system administrator-expert, $72,171
Remlinger, Christina M, nurse, staff II, $29.40/hr
Remming, Lizabeth Ann, instructor, adjunct, $2,133
Remole, Brenda M, nurse, staff now III, $30.00/hr
Rempfer, Brooke Nicole, nurse, staff II rnwp, $21.37/hr
Rempfer, Melisa V, prof, asoc, $67,226
Rendo, Carla Christine, office support assistant IV, $14.69/hr
Reneker, Joseph Li, high school student, $7.50/hr
Reneker, Lixing W, prof, asoc, $97,085
Renfro, Kevin Charles, lab assistant, $9.00/hr
Renfrow, Catherine M, pat acct rep, $16.59/hr
Rengasamy Venugopalan, Shankar, prof, ast, $102,000
Renken, Deanna Naomia, surgical technl certified, $17.52/hr
Renna, Sarah Marie, research specialist sr, $60,000
Renner, Gregory J, emeritus, $119,200
Reno, Teresa Lynn, office support assistant III, $13.63/hr
Renoe, Susan Dixon, dir program/project operations, $45,900
Renschen, Patrick Charles, instructor, $34,939
Rensing, Kimi Lyn, instructor, adjunct, $27,000
Renson, Virginie Paule C, fellow, post doctoral, $43,500
Rentel, Jennifer Mary, business support specialist II, $21.59/hr
Renz, David O, professor, $147,706
Repuyan, Christina Shea, instructor, adjunct, $125.00/hr
Resch, Timothy Michael, dir II research ops and plng, $138,136
Resnik, Andrew G, prof, asoc clincl dept, $190,958
Restrepo, Ricardo J, research specialist I, $36,057
Rettke, Cindee K Smalley, resrch asoc, $32,402
Retzloff, David George, prof, asoc, $87,675
Reuben, Richard C, professor, $133,610
Reust, Carin E, prof, asoc clincl dept, $163,863
Revelle, Sara M, instructor, clincl, $21,335
Revels, Preshus S, tutor, $10.00/hr
Rex, Jacob Powell, seasonal farm ast, $9.75/hr
Rexroat, Richard Joseph, librarian III, $61,521
Rexroth, Linda Sue, nurse, staff II, $38.14/hr
Reyes Estrada, Maria G, custodian, $12.94/hr
Reyes, Jessie Jill, dir I, human resources, $93,898
Reyes, Marcos, prof, ast clincl dept, $167,076
Reyland, Emily James, office support assistant III, $14.25/hr
Reyland, Margaret Rose, student support specialist II, $18.69/hr
Reyna, Ivan Roberto, prof, asoc, $59,478
Reynard, Paul Raymond II, csm associate I, $16.86/hr
Reynolds Moehrle, Jennifer, prof, asoc, $150,929
Reynolds, Adam N, stage services assistant lead, $18.00/hr
Reynolds, Alexandra Way, mental health tech, $11.22/hr
Reynolds, Don F, prof, ast resrch, $95,509
Reynolds, Frances E, instructor, ast, $24.89/hr
Reynolds, Jade Lynn, food svc wrkr II, $11.60/hr
Reynolds, Jamel S, care team assoc-clinical, $11.10/hr
Reynolds, James A, surgical technl certified, $15.87/hr

Reynolds, Michelle C, resrch asoc, $70,192
Reynolds, Naomi, educational pgm associate I, $13.16/hr
Reynolds, Rebecca D, health records techn II, $13.07/hr
Reynolds, Tarah Marie, nurse, staff II, $20.54/hr
Reys, Barbara Bestgen, prof, curators, $146,739
Reys, Robert Edward, emeritus, $32,000
Rezaei, Fateme, prof, ast, $80,000
Reznicek, Samantha Alyse, nursing ast, $12.08/hr
Rhee, Noah, professor, $70,284
Rhine, Matthew D, resrch asoc, $52,570
Rhoad, Angela Renea, educational pgm associate I, $14.15/hr
Rhoades, Jamie, research/lab technician, $14.28/hr
Rhoades, Kathline V, patient svc rep, $14.96/hr
Rhoades, Teresa K, cook, $12.95/hr
Rhoads, Aaron Bruce, floor care techn lead, $14.25/hr
Rhoads, Mary K, executive assistant, $23.92/hr
Rhoads, Ty Allen, student support specialist I, $13.95/hr
Rhode, Ashley A, program/project supprt coor II, $47,041
Rhode, Luke Shane, reactor operator trainee II, $22.65/hr
Rhodenbaugh, Gregory Scott, head coach, $132,870
Rhodes, Calvin C, custodian, $13.23/hr
Rhodes, Ciera Ashton, research/lab technician, $10.24/hr
Rhodes, Jana Marie, coor, service, $14.09/hr
Rhodes, Jodelle B, veterinary technician sr, $17.14/hr
Rhodes, Karen C, program/project supprt coor I, $46,880
Rhodes, Rebecca C, research/lab technician, $10.24/hr
Rhodes, Sarabeth A, db programmer analyst-princpl, $76,181
Rhomberg, Mary Beth, prof, ast clincl, $72,201
Rial, Christina Virginia, student service coor II, $39,600
Ribble, Dale J, ast coach, $37,931
Ribiat, Ronald Louis, office support assistant IV, $14.28/hr
Ricci, Cassie Marie, physician, resident chief, $64,425
Rice, Cheryl E, reimbursement ast sr, $22.46/hr
Rice, Christopher D, prof, asoc, $101,441
Rice, Donald S, prof, ast/profl pract, $61,391
Rice, Gale Borkowski, speech/lang pathologist, $35.00/hr
Rice, Glenn P, programmer analyst-expert, $56,753
Rice, Melanie S, nurse, licensed prac, $17.28/hr
Rice, Rachel Eleanor, nurse, staff I, $19.00/hr
Rice, Timothy G, bts carpenter, $20.23/hr
Rich, George J, fin and acctg specialist, $17.26/hr
Rich, Justin Keith, academic advisor, $36,720
Rich, Kelly Jean, educational pgm associate I, $13.80/hr
Richard, Sharon Ernestine, nurse, staff, $29.08/hr
Richards, James E Jr, professor, $130,000
Richards, Anthony Lawrence, maint svc attd, $18.41/hr
Richards, Cynthia Alice, support systems admin-speclst, $51,062
Richards, Holly Ann, health records techn II, $13.56/hr
Richards, Jennifer M, nurse, staff II, $26.80/hr
Richards, Jo Beth, asoc dir program/project ops, $60,119
Richards, Jordan Spencer, telecom tech-expert, $18.51/hr
Richards, Katherine Nadine, nurse, staff II, $21.37/hr
Richards, Mary Jo, fin and acctg consultant, $57,500
Richards, Pamela R, office support assistant IV, $15.49/hr
Richards, Rhonda C, office support assistant IV, $16.22/hr
Richards, Thomas F, asoc vice president, $237,481
Richards, Von L, professor, $118,639
Richardson, Andrew, event assistant I, $8.50/hr
Richardson, Anglique Michelle, pat acct rep, $14.29/hr
Richardson, Catherine Marie, library information asst, $12.97/hr
Richardson, Chaves Shanqay, care team assoc-suppt, $12.69/hr
Richardson, David N, prof, asoc, $94,598
Richardson, Holli Mishelle, med techl reg, $30.36/hr
Richardson, James Alexander, mech, auto-mrc, $15.76/hr
Richardson, James D, db programmer analyst-expert, $52,400
Richardson, James R, geo info system tech, $14.39/hr
Richardson, Jared Thomas, event assistant I, $8.50/hr
Richardson, Jennifer Lynn, student recruitment spclst, $16.75/hr
Richardson, Jerry R, prof, asoc, $87,023
Richardson, Jesse Douglas, reactor operator, $26.42/hr
Richardson, Kareem Andre, head coach, $257,500
Richardson, Katherine R, business support spclst II, $22.00/hr
Richardson, Kevin Scott, police captain, $84,276
Richardson, Kyle Patrick, office support assistant III, $12.00/hr
Richardson, Kylene S, advancement officer, $50,000
Richardson, Lauren Kristyne, educational pgm assoc I, $13.45/hr
Richardson, Mark Douglas, reactor specialist, $74,257
Richardson, Melinda Ellen, mgr II business admin, $49,500
Richardson, Molly A, advancement associate II, $18.42/hr

Richardson, Tanisha Janeal, office support assistant II, $11.22/hr
Richardson, Thomas E, food svc wrkr I, $11.29/hr
Richardson, Traci Anne, care team assoc-suppt, $13.58/hr
Richardson, William E, operations support tech II, $16.27/hr
Richardson, Zackery D, system support analyst-spclst, $22.55/hr
Richerson, Condra J, nurse, licensed prac, $21.02/hr
Richeson, Christian Francis, instructor, adjunct, $10,500
Richey, Joseph F, instructor, adjunct, $1,778
Richey, Judy K, office support associate, $19.95/hr
Richins, Marsha L, professor, $178,698
Richison, Susan Ilene, office support assistant IV, $18.36/hr
Richmond, Heather Deann, manuscript specialist, $34,400
Richmond, Michelle Elizabeth, nurse, staff I, $19.00/hr
Richmond, Renee E, med techl reg, $26.53/hr
Richmond, Renita Michelle, library information asst, $11.30/hr
Richmond, Stacy Lynn, pat acct rep, $15.33/hr
Rickard, Diana Elizabeth, business support spclst II, $23.27/hr
Rickard, Joshua Aaron, security analyst-speclst, $55,000
Rickard, Sherry Ann, practice manager, $74,520
Ricker, Andrew Joseph, ast coach, $256,000
Ricker, Timothy J, fellow, post doctoral, $39,264
Ricklefs, Marcelene Ann, instructor, adjunct, $29,175
Ricklefs, Robert E, professor, $147,594
Riddell, Lynne E, office support assistant IV, $16.40/hr
Riddick, Kaliantha, student support specialist sr, $18.26/hr
Riddle, Raquel Cherice, service rep III, $12.47/hr
Riden, Rebecca Jo, instructor, adjunct, $15,000
Ridenhour, Bonnie Sue, custodian, $10.69/hr
Ridenhour, Sarah M, business support analyst II, $17.12/hr
Ridenhour, Suzanne Elizabeth, research specialist sr, $44,576
Ridge, Joy Marie, instructor, adjunct, $4,500
Ridgeway, Victoria Ann, mobile mammogr van driver/psr, $16.59/hr
Ridgley, Devin Michael, fellow, post doctoral, $43,000
Ridgway, Edward Eugene, network engineer-princpl, $70,820
Ridgway, Kenneth E, bts carpenter, $21.71/hr
Ridgway, Robyn A, prgm mgr II studnt supprt svcs, $64,498
Ridolfi, Janice Kristine, advancement officer, $46,600
Riebeling, Shari Lynn, social worker, $41,607
Riebschlager, Chris, prof, ast adjunct, $10,500
Riechmann, Allison Marie, pharmacist III, $128,835
Riedel, Edward Girard, asoc dir program/project ops, $51,587
Riedy, Jennifer M, student service coor II, $48,500
Riegerix, Michael J Jr, temporary technical, $8.00/hr
Riek, James V, on-air talent television, $58,500
Riek, Sara Garcia, interpreter, medical, $15.92/hr
Rielley, David F, student service coor sr, $52,555
Riemann, Christie Hodgen, prof, asoc, $59,347
Ries, Lawrence D, prof, asoc teach, $85,790
Riess, Jennifer M, office support assistant IV, $15.25/hr
Rife, Danita G, nurse practitioner, $98,141
Rife, Isabel Pinto, asoc dir program/project ops, $64,946
Rifenbark, Kelly L, mgr student support svcs, $29,004
Rigdon, Charles D, technology resource coor, $55,227
Riggins, David W, prof, curator teach, $112,905
Riggins, Matthew Q, emrg med techn, $11.75/hr
Riggins, Robin D, nurse practitioner, $93,811
Riggs, Ashley Charlotte, athletic trainer, $39,600
Riggs, Brenda D, academic advisor sr, $45,894
Riggs, Mary Lenore, care team assoc-suppt, $13.37/hr
Riggs, Robert Christensen, prof, ast teach, $55,000
Rikoon, James S, dean, asoc, $127,740
Riley-Tillman, Timothy Christopher, professor, $116,365
Riley, Ann Campion, librarian IV, $121,043
Riley, Heather Dawn, care team assoc-clinical, $12.08/hr
Riley, Helen Ann, office support assistant IV, $15.58/hr
Riley, Joey D, sr ast dir business admin, $64,650
Riley, John R, technical trainer-princpl, $56,483
Riley, Megan Johanna, nurse, clincl charge-rn, $31.62/hr
Riley, Melissa A, mgr II hospitality services, $55,952
Riley, Melissa Dawn, nurse, staff II, $26.00/hr
Riley, Melissa S, reimbursement ast-cert, $18.59/hr
Riley, Morgan Lynn, lab assistant, $11.00/hr
Riley, Nancy C, library specialist, $38,044
Riley, Renee Valerie, technical writer-expert, $51,685
Riley, Ronald R, prof, asoc clincl, $95,004
Riley, Shawn Patrick, user support analyst-entry, $14.71/hr
Rimmer Rouser, DaWuan L, custodian, $13.36/hr
Rinacke, Robert D, mts/hvac, $22.49/hr
Rinaldi, Caroline, prof, asoc teach, $84,000

Rinck, Johnathan Martin, office support assistant III, $12.82/hr
Rindt, Hansjorg, resrch asoc, $50,000
Rinehart, Jameson M, audiovisual designer-speclst, $26.93/hr
Rinehart, Kelsay Rebecca, business support spclst sr, $16.54/hr
Rinehart, Teresa Ann, nurse, licensed prac, $15.67/hr
Ringbauer, Sara Elizabeth, db programmer analyst-expert, $63,477
Ringdahl, Erika N, prof, clinical dept, $168,025
Ringo, Terry D, mech, auto cntrl, $22.42/hr
Rinker, Brandon L, pat acct rep, $14.29/hr
Rinkus, Samantha Marie, tutor, $10.00/hr
Rinne, Luke A, communications coordinator sr, $17.76/hr
Rinta-Evans, Catherine, office support assistant IV, $15.84/hr
Rios, Elizabeth Navarro, custodian, $12.94/hr
Rios, James Edward, police officer, $17.58/hr
Rioux-Forker, Dana, resident physician-2nd yr, $52,007
Ripley, Regina G, educational pgm associate I, $14.36/hr
Rippe II, William F, resident physician-4th yr, $55,804
Rippeto, Timothy Leroy, electrician, undrgrnd dist I, $21.05/hr
Rippey, John Hodsden, security officer, $12.75/hr
Rippey, Susan J, ultrasonographer, $31.85/hr
Risch, Sherri Margaret, temporary professional, $13.00/hr
Rish, Melissa D, mgr, managed care reimbursmnt, $98,088
Ritchie, Debra K, nurse practitioner, $93,444
Ritland, Bradley Douglas, resident physician-2nd yr, $50,810
Ritter, Angela M, nurse clinician, $68,349
Ritter, Kathy Ann, educational pgm manager, $21,673
Ritter, Sharon E, prof, ast adjunct, $34,200
Ritter, Steven Ray, custodian, $13.36/hr
Ritz, Matthew Gregory, custodian, $10.69/hr
Ritzo, Ashley Nichole, dietitian, clincl, $45,297
Rivas, Griselda, custodian, $13.36/hr
Rivera, Luis Antonio Jr, system administrator-princpl, $72,530
Rivera, Anitra Chyrell, human resources manager, $46,900
Rivera, Arnaldo Luis, prof, asoc, $245,000
Rivera, Jennifer Lynne, lecturer, $30,000
Rivera, Natalia, prof, ast teach, $46,690
Rivera, Rocio Melissa, prof, ast, $83,731
Rivers, Rocky Dean, maintenance supervisor, $52,044
Roach, Barbette Alberta, enrollment advisor sr, $16.87/hr
Roam, Alexis Brooke, instructor, clincl, $45,925
Roark, Abrea Ann, resident physician-4th yr, $54,425
Roark, Angel Rose, office support assistant II, $10.35/hr
Roark, Phillip L, mail carrier, $12.40/hr
Roark, Rebecca A, educational pgm associate I, $13.58/hr
Roark, Rhenda R, db programmer analyst-princpl, $63,030
Roark, Shannon Dee, office support assistant IV, $13.90/hr
Robak, Michael James, librarian III, $86,350
Robb, George Bertis III, system administrator-princpl, $75,770
Robb, Misty Dawn, pat acct rep, $15.13/hr
Robb, Stacy Jo, program/project supprt coor I, $35,224
Robb, Terrence Lyon, event assistant I, $11.00/hr
Robb, Terry L, project manager-princpl, $90,882
Robb, Vickie Lynn, asoc dir program/project ops, $55,654
Robbins, Annette Kline, office support assistant I, $9.05/hr
Robbins, Arnold J, director, $120,000
Robbins, Bridgett, clinical mgr, $105,610
Robbins, Gwen A, dir II advancement, $74,130
Robbins, Jeffery Edward, practice manager, $85,000
Robbins, Jeremy Joseph, resident physician-1st yr, $50,219
Robbins, Kate Lynn, research specialist I, $32,000
Robbins, Lance C, resident physician-2nd yr, $52,007
Robbins, Michael Cook, grader, $100.00/hr
Robbins, Philip Alexander, prof, asoc, $70,365
Robbins, Tamra K, business support specialist II, $22.94/hr
Roberson, Daniel S, custodian, $12.69/hr
Roberson, Elizabeth Marie, asoc editor, $18.49/hr
Robert, Christopher A, prof, asoc, $133,202
Roberts-Higgins, Brooke Alison, strat comm consultant, $53,036
Roberts, Allan D, bindery opr III, $20.77/hr
Roberts, Amanda Mechaele, pat care techn, $12.08/hr
Roberts, Ashlee K, ast dir student support svcs, $46,284
Roberts, Ashley Renae, patient svc rep, $12.24/hr
Roberts, Barrek Austin, programmer analyst-entry, $44,000
Roberts, Becky Jo, media producer sr, $35,000
Roberts, Carter J, health physics technician II, $22.44/hr
Roberts, Charlene M, physical therapist, $78,397
Roberts, Craig, professor, $93,484
Roberts, Cristine A, prof, ast, $65,867
Roberts, Cynthia A, nurse, or/recovery-ch, $34.26/hr

Roberts, Donnell, educational pgm associate I, $13.54/hr
Roberts, Emily Grace, nurse, staff now plus, $30.00/hr
Roberts, Grant Steven, radiologic techl, $18.59/hr
Roberts, Gretchen Diana, program/proj supprt coor I, $18.11/hr
Roberts, Jana L, nurse, or/recovery-ch, $29.99/hr
Roberts, Jennifer A, police officer, $19.27/hr
Roberts, Jonathan L, programmer analyst-expert, $70,562
Roberts, Justin L, strat comm manager, $49,275
Roberts, Katherine Dee, health records techn II, $13.14/hr
Roberts, Kenneth L, bts mason/tuckptr, $21.71/hr
Roberts, Kenneth T, system support analyst-spclst, $21.75/hr
Roberts, Larry J, program/project supprt coor I, $38,400
Roberts, Marcia, student support specialist sr, $16.87/hr
Roberts, Mary Jeanne, prof, ast adjunct, $7,575
Roberts, Melissa J, dean, asoc, $100,000
Roberts, Michael, pat care techn, $12.50/hr
Roberts, Michael B, powr plnt matrl handling opr, $21.05/hr
Roberts, Penelope A, office support assistant IV, $13.18/hr
Roberts, Robert Michael, prof, curators, $304,080
Roberts, Russell H, resrch ast sr, $53,000
Roberts, Severin, dir II advancement, $76,200
Roberts, Stephanie R, prof, asoc, $56,250
Roberts, Stephen, dean, $190,000
Roberts, Susan Marie, office support assistant III, $12.32/hr
Roberts, Tamara T, extns professional, asoc, $70,291
Roberts, Vicky L, reimbursement consultant, $54,425
Robertson, Angela, custodian, $12.94/hr
Robertson, Ashley Brooke, office support assistant IV, $14.44/hr
Robertson, Barbara A, office support associate, $23.29/hr
Robertson, Brian Kendall, instructor, $44,945
Robertson, David B, professor, $98,670
Robertson, Deborah, mgr occl hlth svcs-umhs, $93,811
Robertson, Denzel L, temporary crafts service, $9.50/hr
Robertson, Gail Lynn, event assistant I, $7.75/hr
Robertson, Jeffrey Dell, lecturer, $9,300
Robertson, John D, professor, $142,489
Robertson, Juanita, educational pgm associate I, $14.14/hr
Robertson, Michael W, prof, ast clincl dept, $255,000
Robertson, Patricia Colleen, office support asst IV, $19.98/hr
Robertson, Sarah Nicole, nurse, staff I, rnwp, $19.00/hr
Robertson, Sheila Marie, coor ped inj prev safty outrch, $18.09/hr
Robertson, Teresa A, certif pharmacy techn, $15.03/hr
Robertson, Terry Alan, lecturer, $40,800
Robertson, Timothy R, business tech analyst-spclst, $42,513
Robinett, Andrea Arlyne, nurse advisor, telephone, $26.51/hr
Robinett, Lori Lynn, paralegal, $52,400
Robinette, Elizabeth Marie, stage services assistant sr, $16.00/hr
Robinette, Sean D, programmer analyst-entry, $19.04/hr
Robins, Velda M, sr mgr csm operations, $53,920
Robinson IV, Elijah Davis, event assistant I, $8.50/hr
Robinson, Ronald Jr, stage services assistant sr, $16.00/hr
Robinson, Alexander, police officer, $17.30/hr
Robinson, Anita Renea, event assistant I, $7.55/hr
Robinson, Billie Lee, tutor, $14.08/hr
Robinson, Carol Ann, nurse, licensed prac, $19.78/hr
Robinson, Carrie Ann, business support specialist II, $16.48/hr
Robinson, Charles R, professor, $95,375
Robinson, Chauntae M, dental assistant II, $14.86/hr
Robinson, Courtney Denise, safety monitor, $9.27/hr
Robinson, Debra A G, vice chancellor, $179,786
Robinson, Diane, office support assistant IV, $13.24/hr
Robinson, Dianne Kay, office support assistant III, $11.30/hr
Robinson, Eric K, radiologic techl, $26.47/hr
Robinson, James Max, instructor, adjunct, $900
Robinson, Joanne Rochelle, food svc wrkr I, $9.60/hr
Robinson, Joshua M, cook, $12.20/hr
Robinson, Karen Margaret, librarian III, $64,394
Robinson, Kenneth Dale, care team assoc-clinical, $14.88/hr
Robinson, Kimberlee Suzanne, strat comm assoc II, $25.00/hr
Robinson, Linnell T, event assistant I, $12.00/hr
Robinson, Manda Page, supv nursing acute care, $33.33/hr
Robinson, Marva, office support assistant IV, $17.65/hr
Robinson, Matthew Timothy, prof, asoc clincl dept, $345,000
Robinson, Phillip, prof, asoc, $57,407
Robinson, Ricky Lynn, farm wrkr II, $13.59/hr
Robinson, Rivian D, office support assistant IV, $15.58/hr
Robinson, Samantha Lee, custodian, $10.39/hr
Robinson, Scott A, hospital security officer, $11.97/hr
Robinson, Shayla Marie, food svc wrkr I, $9.60/hr

Robinson, Starla J, nurse, staff II, $29.40/hr
Robinson, Stephanie Lynn, resp therapist reg, $18.96/hr
Robinson, Twyla Sue, office support assistant IV, $15.30/hr
Robison, Kent Andrew, instructor, adjunct, $6,276
Robison, Sue A, educational pgm associate I, $14.78/hr
Robison, Susan Faith, temporary professional, $14.00/hr
Robledo, Judith, custodian, $13.96/hr
Robles, Rodolfo, food svc wrkr I, $11.29/hr
Robnett, Sandra, library information assistant, $13.43/hr
Roby, Aisha Janiah, surgical technl certified, $20.12/hr
Roccia, Miriam I, sr dir studnt supprt svcs, $91,740
Rocco, Christopher M, grounds keeper II, $15.31/hr
Rocha Gomes, Nicoya Sha Von, office support asst IV, $15.53/hr
Roche, Kelley Renae, nurse, staff II, $22.24/hr
Rochester, J Martin, professor, $101,281
Rockers, Linda E, nurse, staff II, $34.18/hr
Rockford, Deborah, program/project supprt coor II, $43,442
Rodden, Debra Ann, emrg med techn paramedic, $18.99/hr
Rodeman, Barbara J, nurse spclst, clincl, $87,886
Roderick, Arlene, office support assistant IV, $18.35/hr
Roderick, Douglas Lee, teaching ast, $4,500
Rodes, Sharon G, media producer II, $19.05/hr
Rodewald, Brandon S, manager it, $73,068
Rodgers, Audrey Danielle, temporary technical, $10.95/hr
Rodgers, Elton Reid, emrg med techn paramedic, $19.71/hr
Rodgers, Jacqueline Marie, office support assistant IV, $18.00/hr
Rodgers, Kevin D, police lieutenant, $74,379
Rodgers, Marilyn L, dean, asoc, $95,247
Rodgers, Megan Eileen, nurse, staff I, $19.00/hr
Rodgers, Shelly Lanette, professor, $105,806
Rodier, Jason T, resident physician-2nd yr, $52,007
Rodman, Debbie Ann, fin and acctg manager sr, $73,555
Rodriguez Ramirez, Antonio Del Rosario, food svc wrkr I, $9.98/hr
Rodriguez-Pedroza, Sandy Kay, custodian, $10.00/hr
Rodriguez, Abraham H, resident physician-2nd yr, $52,007
Rodriguez, Elizabeth Ann, vice president, $261,331
Rodriguez, Julia, business ops associate sr, $50,254
Rodriguez, Lorraine Frances, advancement coordinator, $35,535
Rodriguez, Mary Michelle, office support assistant I, $9.05/hr
Rodriguez, Nicholas Brandon, office support assistant I, $9.05/hr
Rodriguez, Sandy, librarian II, $48,303
Rodriquez, Jason Leonard, prof, ast, $71,447
Roe-Quilici, Amy Elizabeth, mgr III business admin, $77,356
Roe, Cindy L, business support specialist sr, $24.97/hr
Roe, Pamela K, strat comm associate I, $52,188
Roe, Robert Paul, prof, asoc, $72,341
Roebuck, Lynette L, education nurse, $58,731
Roedel, Thomas O'Brien, technical trainer-entry, $35,690
Roehrs, Julie G, nurse, staff II rnwp, $20.54/hr
Roenfeldt, Connor Adam, human resources spclst I, $15.00/hr
Roeseler, Charles Aloys, police captain, $57,500
Roesslet, Bryan W, director it, $142,262
Roettgen, Carl F, csm associate II, $23.83/hr
Roettgen, Nathan Owen, system administrator-princpl, $75,600
Rogers Denham, Trudy Ann, prof, ast adjunct, $18,404
Rogers, Ashley Nicole, enrollment advisor sr, $16.83/hr
Rogers, Barbara Jean, resrch asoc, $26,500
Rogers, Braeden Mitchell, event assistant I, $9.00/hr
Rogers, Carol Tucker, nurse, staff per diem, $35.00/hr
Rogers, Christine L, office support assistant IV, $20.51/hr
Rogers, Clay Leslie, student service coor II, $40,000
Rogers, Doris M, coor conference, $51,217
Rogers, Emeline Rose Tucker, student support spclst I, $16.42/hr
Rogers, Evelyn S, editor sr, $51,990
Rogers, Gordon Craig, nurse, staff now II, $28.00/hr
Rogers, J David, prof, asoc, $113,936
Rogers, James L, maint svc attd, $18.41/hr
Rogers, Janet Ann, executive assistant, $17.83/hr
Rogers, John D, peoplesoft admin-expert, $80,368
Rogers, Jonice K, library info specialist sr, $15.32/hr
Rogers, Kayla Suann, nurse, licensed prac, $15.20/hr
Rogers, LaDora Marie, office support assistant IV, $17.89/hr
Rogers, Lawanda, mgr II hospitality services, $59,090
Rogers, Mark Joseph, media production director I, $47,300
Rogers, Nicole Diane, prof, ast adjunct, $45,600
Rogers, Rebecca L, professor, $80,026
Rogers, Tiara L, office support assistant III, $13.64/hr
Rogers, Treva May, nurse, staff II, $24.57/hr
Rogers, William H, prof, asoc, $87,998

Rohde, Geralf, media producer II, $15.17/hr
Rohlfing, Curt, technical writer-expert, $61,256
Rohloff II, Waldemar Mark, prof, ast teach, $47,450
Rohr, Stacy Lynn, executive assistant, $17.59/hr
Rohrbough, Alan J, instructor, ast, $31,098
Rohrer, Daniel K, user support analyst-entry, $16.39/hr
Rohrs, Sara Elizabeth, diet techn, $11.00/hr
Rohs, Jovanna M, resrch asoc, $63,000
Rojas Moreno, Christian Andres, prof, ast clincl dept, $153,000
Rojas, Cheryl L, supv, lab, $58,650
Rolan, Terry D, prof, ast adjunct, $13,000
Roland, Clarabelle, custodian, $12.94/hr
Roland, Jason W, dir II advancement, $65,150
Roland, William, prof, clinical dept, $14,745
Rold, Nancy Hunt, hlth prgm spclst sr, $54,021
Rold, Tammy Lynn, research specialist sr, $56,359
Roll, Marissa Lorraine, hlth prgm ast, $15.45/hr
Roller, Cindy Rene, med lab techn, $23.01/hr
Rollins, Jason L, strat comm manager, $58,411
Rollins, Kathryn Lauren, instructor, clincl, $25,000
Rollins, Kristina Elizabeth, lecturer, $9,910
Roloff, David B, dir I, advancement, $67,163
Roloff, Laura Yarbrough, strat comm associate II, $62,692
Rolufs, Jimmy Dale Jr, environmental health tech II, $15.22/hr
Rolufs, Angela Beechner, dir III business admin, $117,528
Roman, Alexandra, resident physician-1st yr, $49,025
Romana, Bhupinder Singh, resident physician-2nd yr, $52,007
Romanetto, Krista Dawn, supv med records, $43,296
Romano, Michael V, lecturer, $9,000
Rome, Stefanie Baker, dir program/project operations, $75,750
Romei, Ann Catherine, mgr student support svcs, $31,805
Romeiser, Kurt R, pharmacy techn II, $14.28/hr
Romero Perez, Rebecca Faye, nurse, staff now III, $30.00/hr
Romero, Anna Marie, prof, asoc profl practice, $66,377
Romero, Brianna Swann, lecturer, $39,462
Romesburg, Mary Kathryn, research specialist I, $39,373
Romig, Tiffany D, nurse, licensed prac, $15.67/hr
Romine, Matthew Scott, emrg med techn, $12.00/hr
Romkema, Lisa Rose, nurse anesthetist, $110,925
Ronan, Melissa Kay, student support specialist II, $16.88/hr
Ronchetto, Camille Lynn, emrg med techn, $13.70/hr
Ronci, Raymond C, prof, asoc teach, $40,873
Rondomanski, Amber, office support assistant IV, $13.50/hr
Ronen, David, professor, $119,075
Ronnebaum, Jill M, care team assoc-clinical, $13.80/hr
Rood, Kyle D, research specialist lead, $33.65/hr
Rood, Tammy Lynn, nurse practitioner, $72,312
Roodman, Allison A, psychologist, $53,038
Roof, Katie L, patient svc rep, $13.65/hr
Roohparvar-Brumfield, Jennifer Audrey, office sup asst IV, $14.92/hr
Roohparvar, Mohammed Ali, surgical technl certified, $23.02/hr
Roohparvar, Rhonda R, telecomm opr-h, $10.71/hr
Rook, Mary Elizabeth, instructor, adjunct, $19,820
Rooks, Brigitte Latrise, child dev assistant, $8.08/hr
Rooney, Jeanne Marie, fin and acctg manager, $73,000
Rooney, Stephen Craig, ast dir mental health-shc, $88,150
Root, Deanna Christine, pat acct rep, $14.78/hr
Root, Marsha Lynne, office support associate, $21.96/hr
Roper, Nancy Sue, physical therapist, $84,760
Roper, Paula Lajean, librarian III, $56,176
Roquette, Krista L, resident physician-4th yr, $54,425
Rorah, Rosalie M, business support specialist II, $20.53/hr
Rorvig, Paul Edward, dir sports operations, $60,000
Rosario, Mary Esther, lecturer, $30,300
Rosas, Antonio, driver emerg road svc, $15.63/hr
Roscher, Jennifer Lynn, mental health tech, $12.90/hr
Rose, Amanda J, professor, $99,587
Rose, Amy Nicole, nurse, clincl charge-lpn, $20.37/hr
Rose, Chad Allen, prof, ast, $66,990
Rose, Cynthia A, nurse, advanced practice, $78,290
Rose, David C, professor, $133,020
Rose, Erica Catherine, instructor, adjunct, $8,400
Rose, Margaret Anne, resrch ast, $10.00/hr
Rose, Mary Katherine, care team assoc-clinical, $12.08/hr
Rose, Nancy P, nurse, staff II, $24.20/hr
Rose, Sharree Nicole, executive assistant, $19.30/hr
Rose, Simon Edward John, temporary technical, $25.00/hr
Rose, Thomas Ray, executive assistant, $24.16/hr
Rose, Tina Faye, care team assoc-clinical, $14.17/hr

Rose, Valerie Anne, patient svc rep, $13.02/hr
Roseberry, Jarett E, intern, $24,014
Roselli, Laura Elizabeth, lecturer, $35,368
Roseman, Lisa C, office support assistant IV, $15.15/hr
Rosen, Eric Brent, dir repertory theatre, $200,594
Rosen, Gary D, bts painter, $21.71/hr
Rosen, Kathleen Routier, prof, clinical dept, $250,000
Rosen, Mitzi Gay, health records techn I, $11.84/hr
Rosenbaum, David Michael, dir II strat comm, $135,000
Rosenbaum, Jason A, strat comm consultant, $43,200
Rosenberg, Leah Alice, prof, ast visiting, $19,000
Rosenberger, Till, program/project supprt coor I, $31,450
Rosenblad, Brent Lyndon, prof, asoc, $99,408
Rosenburg, Troy W, custodian, $11.41/hr
Rosenfeld, Cheryl S, prof, asoc, $105,917
Rosenfeld, Julie Anne, prof, ast, $56,700
Rosenfeld, Richard Bruce, founders professor, $43,541
Rosenhauer, Eric B, sr asoc dir business admin, $156,220
Rosenkoetter, Alan Charles, lecturer, $1,530
Rosenkranz, Patrice B, instructor, adjunct, $2,844
Rosenthal, Patricia Anne, academic dir, $70,550
Ross, Candy S, reimbursement ast-cert, $18.59/hr
Ross, Chanua Kosa, instructor, adjunct, $7,869
Ross, Christopher Terence, bts painter, $19.59/hr
Ross, Emily, prof, asoc teach, $50,764
Ross, Guy Alan, bts carpenter, $18.12/hr
Ross, Jacqueline Marie, nurse, staff now III, $30.00/hr
Ross, James T, research technical svcs supv, $24.98/hr
Ross, Janet Nalubega, prof, ast teach, $48,000
Ross, Jeffery Scott, mgr III business admin, $72,000
Ross, Joshua Todd, mts/pipefitter, $20.31/hr
Ross, Kelly A, student recruitment spclst sr, $19.22/hr
Ross, Paul Robert, ast vice chancellor, $156,000
Ross, Robert, library info specialist, $17.72/hr
Ross, Robert Raymond, instructor, ast, $19.47/hr
Ross, Sara C, business ops associate II, $46,835
Ross, Shannon Marie, office support assistant II, $10.37/hr
Ross, Stephanie Andrea, professor, $76,106
Ross, William Tennyson, mgr student support svcs, $30,000
Rossano, Margaret H, student support specialist II, $16.27/hr
Rosse, Martha Jean, physical therapist, $66,732
Rosser, Jennifer L, resrch asoc, $50,160
Rosson, Amy Christine, business support specialist sr, $19.70/hr
Rosson, Peggy Starr, custodian, $12.94/hr
Rossy, John Christopher Jr, powr plnt opr, $21.09/hr
Rossy, Carrie Lee, office support assistant II, $11.09/hr
Rossy, Lynn Ann, psychologist, $84,016
Rosteet, Cherie Kathryn, event assistant I, $7.50/hr
Rostron, Allen Kent, professor, $115,000
Rota, Charles David, instructor, adjunct, $13,333
Rota, Christopher T, fellow, post doctoral, $60,000
Rotach, Carol Ann, asoc dir student support svcs, $60,600
Rotert, Gregory A, support systems admin-spclst, $46,100
Rotert, Joanne F, strat comm associate II, $44,372
Rotert, Mary Ann, ast dir student support svcs, $61,695
Roth, Emily Danae, resident physician-3rd yr, $52,470
Roth, Jamie Lynne, nurse, staff I, $19.00/hr
Roth, Laura Erna, business ops associate sr, $50,137
Roth, Luanne K, prof, ast teach, $40,000
Rother, Chase Lawrence, mgr student support svcs, $30,639
Rothermich, Joyce A, instructor, adjunct, $7,059
Rotter, Vera Leanne, compliance anlyst, $57,176
Rottinghaus, George Edwin, prof, clincl, $115,901
Rottinghaus, Jennifer Lynn, instructor, $50,000
Rottman, Joseph, prof, asoc, $152,238
Rouder, Jeffrey N, professor, $128,074
Rounds, James H, founders professor, $46,186
Roundtree, William V Jr, supv housekeeping, $36,572
Rouse Luebbert, Donna, reimbursement ast-cert, $19.31/hr
Rouse, Ronald McCollom, teaching ast, $13.00/hr
Rouyer, Jennifer Stallbaumer, instructor, adjunct, $15,000
Rovey, Joshua Lucas, prof, asoc, $108,343
Rowan, Carman Nicole, nurse, staff I, $19.00/hr
Rowan, Steven William, professor, $80,384
Rowden, Charitey Lee, nurse, staff II, $21.15/hr
Rowden, Olytha M, patient svc rep, $15.14/hr
Rowden, Troy L, custodian, $10.69/hr
Rowe, Adam Jerome, custodian, $10.94/hr
Rowe, Carmen Elaine, executive assistant, $21.11/hr

Rowe, Erin Danielle, office support assistant I, $9.75/hr
Rowe, Jennifer Lynn, prof, asoc profl practice, $72,837
Rowland, Diana L, account executive, $6,000
Rowland, Katrina Lynnette, hlth educator, $47,249
Rowland, Linda M, research specialist I, $40,965
Rowles, Brian ONeil, office support assistant III, $11.50/hr
Rowles, Jessica Marie, nurse, staff I, $19.00/hr
Rowles, Sheryl L, nurse, licensed prac, $19.48/hr
Rowlett, Lori A, mgr II business admin, $55,880
Rowlett, Matthew C, athletic trainer, $55,114
Rownaghi, Ali Asghar, prof, ast resrch, $80,000
Roy, Jennifer Marie, office support assistant III, $14.75/hr
Royal, Angela B, prof, ast clincl, $103,464
Royal, Floyd T, custodian lead, $11.98/hr
Royal, Lauren Shephard, adjunct, $15,200
Royer, Gene W, media producer II, $15.82/hr
Royse, Julianne, asoc dir program/project ops, $52,286
Royse, Lisa Anne, educational pgm coor III, $60,622
Royster, Thomas E, construction manager II, $74,500
Rubemeyer, Merry D, reimbursement ast sr, $18.78/hr
Rubenstein, Sara Garner, internet admin-expert, $23.53/hr
Rubin, Allison Dawn, instructor, adjunct, $4,706
Rubin, Leona Joyce, asoc vice chancellor, $180,000
Rubin, Zachary C, grader, $100.00/hr
Rubio-Reyes, Carlos Armando, res physician-1st yr, $50,219
Rubio, Ivan Pacheco, food svc wrkr I, $9.60/hr
Rubio, Jorge Derrick, pat acct rep, $13.44/hr
Ruch Graham, Evelyn K, program/proj supprt coor II, $57,425
Rucinski, Garrett Bryan, office support assistant III, $13.92/hr
Rucinski, Joseph Michael, police captain, $58,349
Rucinski, Kylee Jenae, coor, service, $13.79/hr
Rucker, Edwinna Lynn, care team assoc-suppt, $13.58/hr
Rucker, James, event assistant I, $7.55/hr
Rudakov, Fedor, prof, ast, $65,000
Rudel, Bettejane C, chemist I, $18.75/hr
Rudelson, Larisa, nurse, staff II, $29.19/hr
Rudigier, Jana Elizabeth, instructor, clincl, $45,867
Rudkin, Charles C, executive assistant, $17.12/hr
Rudkin, Nicole Lee, office support assistant IV, $14.28/hr
Rudkin, Regina, business support specialist sr, $21.39/hr
Rudloff, Crystal M, office support assistant IV, $16.65/hr
Rudolph, Christopher W, police sergeant, $20.04/hr
Rudolph, Kimberly Kay, office support assistant IV, $18.90/hr
Rudolph, Shelby Marielle, med techl reg, $20.94/hr
Rudy, Duane, prof, asoc, $61,623
Rudy, Paul, prof, curators, $76,552
Ruebel-Marshall, Mary Christine, instructor, adjunct, $7,500
Ruediger, Dylan Lane, event assistant I, $8.50/hr
Ruehter, Valerie Leeann, prof, asoc clincl, $106,000
Ruekberg, Carey Elizabeth, office support assistant IV, $15.39/hr
Ruff, Christopher Michael, security officer, $12.20/hr
Ruff, Jeri Lynn, social worker, $54,506
Ruffel, Audrianna Nicole, nurse, staff II, $21.37/hr
Ruffin, Candace E, student support specialist II, $15.61/hr
Ruffin, Clyde, professor, $117,229
Ruffus, Anthony Paul, instructor, adjunct, $10,500
Rugen, Lewis L, system administrator-princpl, $83,261
Ruggiero, Fiorillo M, lecturer, $48,322
Ruh, Brandi Lee, nurse, staff II rnwp, $22.24/hr
Ruhland, Michael R, lecturer sr, $36,000
Ruhr, Eric, food svc wrkr III, $13.21/hr
Ruiz, Hannayd, program/project supprt coor I, $50,000
Ruiz, Maria Paula, resident physician-2nd yr, $50,810
Rulis, Paul M, prof, ast, $61,200
Rumble, Derek B, bts plasterer, $20.23/hr
Rumpf, Rachel L, instructor, adjunct, $15,000
Runge, Catherine Paige, office support assistant III, $11.30/hr
Runnebaum, Linda Margaret, office support asst IV, $14.73/hr
Runnion, Paul N, prof, ast teach, $47,003
Runyan, Callie Renee, nursing ast, $12.08/hr
Runyan, Robert M, program/project supprt coor II, $61,260
Runyon, Mark C, office support assistant I, $9.05/hr
Runyon, Molly J, research specialist I, $32,000
Runyon, Susan Lynn, care coordinator, $67,626
Rupkey, Kristy Lynn, patient svc rep, $15.41/hr
Ruplinger, Jacqueline M, prof, asoc clincl dept, $144,585
Rupp, Laura E, dir I, event services, $65,000
Ruppar, Todd M, prof, ast, $77,553
Ruppert, Joan Hart, prof, ast teach, $81,090

Rush, Atonja Laciene, csm operations supervisor, $45,000
Rush, Jacqueline Marie, nurse, staff II, $26.00/hr
Rush, Jodi L, business support specialist II, $20.99/hr
Russell, Adam Jeffrey, tutor, $10.00/hr
Russell, Charles Todd, mts/sheet metal, $22.49/hr
Russell, Colin St. Aubyn, programmer analyst-speclst, $51,227
Russell, Cynthia Lorraine, professor, $110,700
Russell, Dennis M, integ farm syst spclst, $23.33/hr
Russell, Graham Cameron, media producer I, $13.25/hr
Russell, Heather Hendrix, media producer I, $13.77/hr
Russell, Jan Elizabeth, executive assistant, $23.57/hr
Russell, Jim D, event assistant I, $7.55/hr
Russell, Johari, av instal service tech-entry, $12.98/hr
Russell, John D, engineering technician II, $16.80/hr
Russell, Judy Marie, office support assistant IV, $14.77/hr
Russell, Leslie Ann, pharmacy intern second year, $13.50/hr
Russell, Mallory Elizabeth, office support assistant II, $12.00/hr
Russell, Mike Kent, grounds keeper lead, $15.84/hr
Russell, Nancy Lee, patient svc rep, $12.76/hr
Russell, Robert A, labor educ spclst, $54,116
Russell, Robert K, research/lab technician, $13.00/hr
Russell, Sherilyn Sue, business support specialist sr, $29.09/hr
Russell, Thomas, prof, ast clincl, $81,000
Russo, Michael Reynard, instructor, visiting, $40,000
Rust, Daniel Lee, prof, ast teach, $44,429
Rust, Dylan Stephens, resp therapist reg, $19.00/hr
Ruth, Ted E, dir II csm operations, $105,100
Ruth, Zachary, high school student, $7.50/hr
Ruthengael, Varyanna Chryzhtjanok, research spclst I, $33,899
Rutherford, Paul Mason Jr, instructor, adjunct, $8,325
Rutherford, Donald William, security officer, $13.99/hr
Rutherford, Doris Fay, office support assistant sr, $18.97/hr
Ruthmann, Nicholas Peter, resident physician-2nd yr, $52,007
Rutter-Chu, Christy Suzanne, instructor, clincl, $46,080
Rutter, Sara B, lecturer, $100.00/hr
Ruud, Jessica Anne, resp therapist reg, $18.23/hr
Ruzhitskaya, Lanika Yanovna, grader, $100.00/hr
Ruzich, Lawrence J, library info specialist, $13.30/hr
Ryals, Mitchell Andrew, office support assistant II, $10.24/hr
Ryan, Aaron Paul, police officer, $17.50/hr
Ryan, Gary Ray, research engineering tech I, $23.31/hr
Ryan, Jacqueline Renee, serv line spclst, $68,793
Ryan, Linda Alfs, instructor, adjunct, $34,200
Ryan, Mark Russ-Ell, director, $191,900
Rychlewski, Walter Joseph III, instructor, adjunct, $18,000
Rychnovsky, Alisha L, fin and acctg manager, $72,636
Rydberg-Cox, Jeffrey, professor, $97,954
Ryder, Katelyn Alexandra, program/project supprt coor I, $35,568
Ryle, Margaret Ann, office support assistant IV, $14.87/hr
Rymph, Catherine E, prof, asoc, $61,013
Rynearson, Penny Renee, nurse, licensed prac, $20.67/hr
Rynning, Lance Christopher, stores clerk, $12.98/hr
Rynning, Stacy Nicole, care team assoc-clinical, $13.06/hr
Rysavy, Robin M, teaching ast, $31.80/hr
Saab, Youssef, prof, asoc, $85,693
Saad, Cheryl Lynn, custodian, $12.69/hr
Saale, Lawrence A, engineer sr, $75,148
Saalfeld, Sarah Therese, research/lab technician sr, $18.00/hr
Saavedra, Venessa Maria, food svc wrkr I, $9.60/hr
Sabates, Nelson Raymond, prof, adjunct, $15,000
Sabharwal, Chaman L, professor, $101,950
Sabin, Derrek Joseph, temporary clerical, $10.20/hr
Sable-Smith, Bram Eric, office support assistant II, $10.00/hr
Sable, Marjorie R, professor, $162,843
Saboor, Wanda Jean, office support assistant IV, $14.08/hr
Sachdev, Sherri Lynn Weiss, business ops associate sr, $61,200
Sachdev, Shrikesh Chandrakant, resrch scientist/acad sr, $53,416
Sackett, Leah Marie, instructor, adjunct, $27,000
Saddler, Jeffrey L, ast reactor manager, $78,795
Sade, Randy J, research project analyst, $47,021
Sadler, Nicole Lynn, occl therapy ast cert, $23.01/hr
Sadler, Troy D, professor, $166,089
Sadowski, Christina Y, nurse, staff prn, $26.00/hr
Sadowski, Jatha Bounous, dir II human resources, $118,454
Sadowski, Kaitlyn T, human resources specialist I, $16.23/hr
Saeki, Elina, instructor, adjunct, $9,600
Saenz, Francisco Jose Boland, hospital lab tech, $12.46/hr
Saenz, Sara Kay, nurse, staff II, $20.95/hr
Saffran, Lisa Jeanne, director, $73,542

Safranski, Timothy J, prof, asoc, $93,213
Safranski, Trista Ann, prof, ast teach, $84,000
Safronov, Alexander Valentinovich, prof, ast resrch, $86,591
Sagastume, Samantha Carolyn Belinda, lecturer, $35,700
Sager, Janet L, educational pgm associate I, $12.68/hr
Sager, Renee Marie, custodian, $10.94/hr
Saghari, Amir-Hossein, resident physician-4th yr, $55,804
Saguiguit, Leo Contreras, prof, asoc, $61,744
Saharay, Rita, prof, visiting, $71,443
Saheli, Ali, programmer analyst-speclst, $53,337
Sahota, Pradeep K, professor, $351,551
Saidian, Lila, resident physician-5th yr, $58,083
Saifullah, Abu Sayeed Muhammad, prof, ast, $85,000
Saigh, Jessica Lynn, instructor, adjunct, $27,900
Sakharova, Julia, prof, ast, $59,440
Sala, Rhael R, business support specialist II, $15.25/hr
Salam, Muhammad Waqar Us, prof, ast clincl dept, $165,000
Salameh, Hassan A, resident physician-3rd yr, $52,470
Salamon, Jessica Lee, office support assistant III, $14.70/hr
Salamon, Steven, police captain, $57,500
Salas Martinez, Mabel Leonor, prof, ast clincl, $89,913
Salau, Muskinni Olanrewaju, instructor, clincl, $35,000
Salazar, Valerie Anne, program/project supprt coor I, $40,170
Sale, Elizabeth W, prof, asoc resrch, $92,881
Salem, Jason D, peoplesoft admin-princpl, $85,217
Salerno-Denninghoff, Lucille Dorothy, asoc dir prog/proj ops, $46,232
Salerno, Laura Marie, asoc dir student support svcs, $65,121
Saleska, Diane Debra, prof, asoc teach, $66,987
Salim, Hani A, prof, asoc, $105,935
Salinas, Erica H, prof, ast adjunct, $100,000
Salisbury, Adam C, resident physician-8th yr, $64,175
Sall, Candace Ann, asoc curator, $39,393
Sall, Joseph C, business support specialist II, $18.36/hr
Sallee, Timothy E, custodian, $12.94/hr
Salley, Paul Adam, media producer I, $13.25/hr
Sallinger, Elizabeth Janelle, instructor, adjunct, $32,400
Salmon, Linda K, office support assistant IV, $15.41/hr
Salmon, Megan A, service rep III, $11.50/hr
Salmons, Hayden Scott, temporary clerical, $7.50/hr
Salmons, Michael E, strat comm associate II, $42,000
Salmons, Veronica Lynn, student service coor II, $43,500
Salter, Cody J, user support analyst-speclst, $18.00/hr
Salter, Lisa Nicole, human resources specialist I, $17.00/hr
Salter, Mike V, mts/electrician-r, $20.10/hr
Salucci, Diane Lynne, instructor, adjunct, $9,000
Salvatore, Dominick, prof, ast clincl, $96,000
Salvo-Eaton, Jennifer Rose, librarian I, $45,955
Salyer, Perry David, user support analyst-speclst, $17.94/hr
Salzer, William L, prof, clinical dept, $205,583
Salzsieder, Leigh William, prof, ast, $148,909
Samaranayake, V A, prof, curator teach, $99,500
Samborski, Jeff J, business spclst, $54,000
Samp, Sheri L, business support specialist II, $17.50/hr
Sample, Jacquelyn Marie, instructor, clincl, $25,759
Samples, Robert, ast vice chancellor, $126,958
Sampson, Amber Marie, serv line spclst, $84,870
Sampson, Charles L, emeritus, $42,000
Sampson, Cheryl L, prof, asoc, $55,834
Sampson, Christopher S, prof, ast clincl dept, $275,000
Sampson, Elizabeth, program/project supprt coor II, $47,047
Samuel, Melissa S, research specialist sr, $40,392
Samuels, Austyn Lewis, intern, $19,311
Samuels, Larry Lee, finl counselor(eligibility), $14.95/hr
Samuelson, Cody Bruce, user support analyst-entry, $15.76/hr
Sanburn, Karen L, business support analyst II, $23.49/hr
Sanchegraw, Ricky D, db administrator-speclst, $61,058
Sanchez Canales, Yoel, care team assoc-suppt, $10.64/hr
Sanchez, Barbara L, nurse practitioner, $86,769
Sanchez, Carlos, custodian, $13.36/hr
Sanchez, Cristina, child dev assistant, $8.08/hr
Sanchez, Hessell, office support assistant I, $9.69/hr
Sanchez, Nathan Daniel, event assistant I, $8.50/hr
Sanchez, Olman L, prof, ast, $69,705
Sandberg, Danielle Erin, nurse, licensed prac, $19.22/hr
Sander, Aaron, event assistant I, $8.50/hr
Sander, Kristen Marie Wellemeyer, specialist, $10.00/hr
Sander, Todd P, research specialist sr, $43,350
Sanders, Frank Jr, custodian, $11.41/hr

Sanders, Harlow Stewart Jr, instructor, adjunct, $12,000
Sanders, Amy L, strat comm consultant sr, $54,872
Sanders, Brian Douglas, dir I, finance, $82,192
Sanders, Chris K, manager it, $70,219
Sanders, Colleen M, clincl documnt spclst, $78,312
Sanders, Dale B, sr asoc dir business admin, $91,872
Sanders, Dedra L, human resources assistant, $13.75/hr
Sanders, Gina M, academic advisor, $40,596
Sanders, Heather Nicole, lab assistant, $8.65/hr
Sanders, Jennifer E, mgr student support svcs, $32,714
Sanders, Judith, nurse clinician, $26,520
Sanders, Kristyn S, nurse, staff, $29.66/hr
Sanders, Larry Russell, manager it, $88,341
Sanders, Lee A, nurse, staff II, $23.42/hr
Sanders, Linda Beth, ast mgr hospitality services, $54,043
Sanders, Patricia K, office support assistant I, $12.50/hr
Sanders, Rebecca L, cardiovasc techn invasive, $22.89/hr
Sanders, Robert Lawrence, academic advisor, $43,275
Sanders, Sara Nicole, hospital lab tech, $13.20/hr
Sanders, Shelly Lynn, nurse, licensed prac, $18.83/hr
Sanders, Susan Ursula, librarian III, $54,719
Sanders, Suzanne D, temporary crafts service, $10.00/hr
Sanders, Terry Ray, resp therapist reg, $19.34/hr
Sanders, Wayne A, librarian III, $57,084
Sanderse, Nathan Michael, resident physician-2nd yr, $50,810
Sanderson, Alan, instructor, adjunct, $7,500
Sanderson, Christina Jean, audiology coordinator, $69,967
Sandford, David Matthew, event assistant I, $8.50/hr
Sandford, Nancy Ann, nurse practitioner, $78,134
Sandidge, CortneyJo Mychelle, sr ast dir studnt supprt svcs, $56,543
Sandifer, Thomas M, pharmacist II, $123,595
Sandlin, Gregory Daniel, food svc wrkr III, $13.21/hr
Sandone, Jacquelyn, prof, ast teach, $45,450
Sandoval, Maria Rivas, custodian, $12.94/hr
Sandreczki, Thomas C, professor, $103,454
Sandri, Kelly Jo, adjunct, $15,000
Sandritter, Tracy L, instructor, clincl, $1,050
Sandrock-Swearingen, Jill Marie, office sup asst III, $12.50/hr
Sandroff, Nancy Elizabeth, prof, ast adjunct, $8,004
Sands, Laura L, occl therapist, $63,428
Sands, Linda Beth, office support assistant IV, $16.23/hr
Sandvol, Eric A, professor, $87,775
Sandy, Shastri Stefan, prof, ast, $169,820
Sanford, Matthew R, asoc dir research, $105,836
Sangha, Harbaksh Singh, prof, ast clincl dept, $260,100
Sankar, Soundrapandian, instructor, adjunct, $16,500
Sankovich, Richard, lecturer, $31,296
Sanner-Stiehr, Ericka, instructor, clincl, $15,375
Sansberry II, Kevin Deron, human resources manager, $57,408
Santaularia, Luciana Theresa, nurse, staff II, $20.95/hr
Santee, Jennifer, prof, asoc clincl, $101,000
Santi, Tyler Lee, user support analyst-entry, $14.00/hr
Santiago, Vicente Raul, mental health tech, $11.85/hr
Santirojprapai, Anthony Dhirasilph, lecturer, $18,000
Santos, Vernice L, care team assoc-clinical, $10.85/hr
Sanyal, Soumya Deepta, fellow, post doctoral, $45,000
Sapp, Aaron V, physician, stu hlth, $141,143
Sapp, Ashley Lynae, nurse, staff II rnwp, $20.95/hr
Sapp, Betty M, office support assistant IV, $14.05/hr
Sapp, Eddie Lee, genl stores attd lead, $15.59/hr
Sapp, Janet E, executive assistant sr, $59,858
Sapp, Jani Lou, business support specialist II, $22.73/hr
Sapp, Jenna M, mgr II business admin, $55,950
Sapp, Jim, garage attendant, $13.19/hr
Sapp, Kristina L, fin and acctg consultant sr, $62,000
Sapp, Kristopher R, research engineering tech I, $23.31/hr
Sapp, Lesley Jeanne, student support specialist sr, $20.95/hr
Sapp, Mark Anthony, electronics technician sr, $24.61/hr
Sapp, Stanley Dean, bts carpenter, $20.23/hr
Sapp, Stephanie, office support assistant IV, $17.05/hr
Sappington, James Duane, system support analyst-princpl, $60,768
Sappington, John R, hospital security officer, $14.14/hr
Saputo, Wilhelmina L, educational pgm assistant, $10.06/hr
Sarafianos, Stefanos, prof, asoc, $147,704
Sarangapani, Jagannathan, professor, $181,265
Sardis, Forrest Harrell, animal caretaker-equine/food, $10.91/hr
Sargent, Thomas W Jr, building/mechanical maint I, $16.50/hr
Sargent, Angie Lynn, nurse, staff I, $19.00/hr
Sargent, Carol L, program/project supprt coor sr, $61,533

Sargent, Jalisa Latoya, temporary clerical, $8.35/hr
Sargentini, Michael J, facilities supervisor, $39,600
Sarma, Saurav Jyoti, fellow, post doctoral, $44,571
Sarmini, Muhammad Talal, resident physician-3rd yr, $53,763
Sarpong, Yaw Dwomoh, resident physician-5th yr, $58,083
Sarr, Lucy C, dental assistant I, $11.65/hr
Sartain, Debby Faye, reimbursement ast-cert, $18.59/hr
Sarva, Sivatej, prof, ast clncl dept, $252,000
Satheesh, Keerthana Menagara, prof, asoc, $125,000
Sathyamurthy, Anjana, fellow, post doc clncl yr1, $55,804
Satpathy, Sashi, prof, curators, $138,518
Sattenspiel, Lisa, professor, $65,597
Satterfield, Emmalou Theresa, prof, ast teach, $56,260
Satterfield, Jessica Rochelle, office support assistant II, $10.40/hr
Satterfield, William David, electronics technician III, $19.00/hr
Sauer, Gordon C III, prof, ast teach, $34,000
Sauer, Brian Robert, resident physician-4th yr, $54,425
Sauer, Michael F, db programmer analyst-speclst, $50,472
Saul, Ellen Wendy, professor, $159,916
Saulsbury, Tina Louise, teaching ast, $1,548
Saults, John Scott, prof, asoc resrch, $67,165
Saunders, Alison Lynette, grader, $52
Saunders, Lindsey Anne, business support specialist II, $18.03/hr
Sauro, Benjamin L, office support assistant IV, $15.33/hr
Sauter, Vicki L, professor, $130,579
Sautner, David J, lab attd, $10.51/hr
Sautter, Jason L, ast coach, $70,000
Savage, Kathleen Patrice, coor, care, $65,345
Savage, Patricia Ann Marie, family fincl edu spclst, $42,500
Saverson, Elaine Kay, custodian, $10.39/hr
Savesky, Janet Ann, dir nutrition/fd svcs, $100,000
Savich, Tim, csm associate II, $18.25/hr
Savio, Barbara F, business ops associate sr, $51,000
Savu, Anna Barbara, research specialist sr, $50,023
Savvidou, Paola, prof, ast, $56,255
Sawalich, William Adam, prof, ast adjunct, $6,000
Sawkin, Mark T, prof, ast clncl, $96,000
Sawyer, Aaron M, grader, $100.00/hr
Sawyer, Betty J, dietitian, clncl, $50,071
Saxena, Vikas, fellow, post doctoral, $43,000
Saxton, Christopher K, instructor, $52
Sayed, Ramy medhat, resident physician-1st yr, $50,825
Sayedahmed, Ahmed, prof, ast teach, $75,000
Sayers, Melanie Leanne, nurse, staff II, $24.61/hr
Sayers, Stephen P, prof, asoc, $108,617
Saylor, James A, emrg med techn paramedic, $19.71/hr
Sbabo, Sharon S, fin and acctg specialist, $15.19/hr
Scaboo, Andrew M, prof, ast resrch, $84,000
Scales, Karen McCallum, instructor, $43,357
Scallan, Joshua Paul, fellow, post doctoral, $44,340
Scantlin, Aaron Joseph, temporary technical, $14.00/hr
Scantlin, Betty Ann, telecom it analyst-entry, $16.79/hr
Scardina, Traci Marie, student support specialist sr, $25.08/hr
Scarlett, Linca A Jr, care team assoc-clinical, $12.32/hr
Scarlett, Amy Jo, neurodiagnostic tech (reg), $23.93/hr
Scates, Kimberly Michelle, instructor, adjunct, $9,000
Scavone, Gina R, office support assistant IV, $14.54/hr
Schaaf-Petty, Barbara Anne, strat comm associate II, $51,763
Schaak, Sarah M, nurse anesthetist, $147,900
Schaal, Bob A, exec dir mo orthopaedic instit, $176,530
Schaal, Katie Porter, physical therapist, $61,000
Schaal, Ryan Andrew, physical therapist, $60,516
Schacht, Megan M, psychologist, $40.00/hr
Schachtel, James, veterinarian, residnt, $26,000
Schachtman, Todd R, professor, $89,853
Schaefer, Christopher J, resident physician-3rd yr, $53,763
Schaefer, Danielle Renee Chastain, physical therapist, $35.00/hr
Schaefer, Jane Ellen, office support assistant IV, $33,252
Schaefer, Jeffrey A, stage services assistant sr, $16.00/hr
Schaefer, Joseph K, business tech analyst-speclst, $52,416
Schaefer, Julie Marie, instructor, adjunct, $7,200
Schaefer, Michael Wayne, lecturer, $30,600
Schaefer, Scott J, media producer II, $14.95/hr
Schaefer, Sean M, reactor operator sr, $31.31/hr
Schaefer, Susan Degginger, instructor, adjunct, $4,800
Schaefer, Tammie Janell, prof, ast, $148,625
Schaefer, Thomas Joseph, lecturer, $9,300
Schaeffer, Joshua W, instructor, clncl, $45,000
Schaeffer, Scott Bryan, prof, asoc adjunct, $9,519

Schaefferkoetter, Karen Nanette, account executive, $6,000
Schafer, Carmen Gail, user support analyst-expert, $21.44/hr
Schafer, Carolyn S, certif pharmacy techn, $15.50/hr
Schafer, Charlea Michelle, nurse, licensed prac, $16.97/hr
Schafer, Janis M, office support assistant IV, $15.77/hr
Schafer, Kerri J, intern, $35,000
Schaffer, Jennifer M, academic advisor, $40,986
Schaffner, Mike R, agriculture foreman, $22.48/hr
Schaffnit, Scott Edwin, instructor, adjunct, $9,000
Schalk, George T, forest worker, $10.53/hr
Schall, Janice Joan, prof, adjunct, $15,000
Schaller, Kara Marie, pharmacy resident, $38,500
Schams, Karen, polysomnograph techn reg, $31.64/hr
Schanot, Laurel Ann, business support specialist II, $17.50/hr
Scharf, Martha Elizabeth, instructor, clncl, $61,224
Scharf, Peter C, professor, $94,589
Scharfenberg, Buddy L, system administrator-entry, $40,194
Scharlott, Donald Gary, pharmacist III, $60.00/hr
Scharp, Daniel G, nurse, staff II, $22.10/hr
Schart, William Lawrence, event assistant I, $7.75/hr
Schartel, Valarie Gail, curriculum and assessment coor, $60,281
Schatten, Heide, professor, $90,808
Schatz, Enid Joy, prof, asoc, $108,537
Schauflinger, Martin, research specialist I, $49,700
Schauner, Stephanie Michelle, prof, asoc clncl, $100,000
Scheberle, Nancy Young, business support spclst II, $18.00/hr
Schedler, Rebecca R, library info specialist, $12.98/hr
Scheer, Amy Michelle, nurse, staff II, $23.12/hr
Scheer, Lisa K, professor, $175,068
Scheer, Melissa B, 4-h spclst, $45,499
Scheerer, Christopher R, stage services assistant sr, $16.91/hr
Scheese, Lisa Marie, student service coor sr, $46,500
Scheetz, Christopher, manager it, $73,440
Scheffer, Kelly Ann, lecturer, $9,000
Scheiderer, Ronald Dean, specialist, $42,396
Scheidt, Christopher W, ultrasonographer, $29.01/hr
Scheidt, Jill Kaytlyn, agronomy spclst, $42,334
Scheidt, Maureen E, retail sales manager, $41,580
Scheiner, Cynthia, support systems admin-expert, $69,354
Schell, Georgia Mae, telecomm opr-h, $11.56/hr
Schellman, Kelly Leann, nurse, staff II, $25.97/hr
Schelp, Ginger Lynn, performce improvement prof, $64,979
Schelp, William, research specialist sr, $55,217
Schempf Bernhardt, Sarah Ruth, lecturer, $9,000
Scheneman, Mary Ann, prof, ast clncl, $60,954
Schenewerk, Keith Stone, maintenance supervisor, $51,741
Schenker, David Joseph, prof, asoc, $94,827
Schepker, Angela Renee, nurse, staff II, $32.01/hr
Scherer, Laura Danielle, prof, ast, $76,189
Scherrer, Juanita M, care team assoc-clinical, $14.50/hr
Scheufler, Jason A, electronics technician I, $15.14/hr
Scheve, Kenneth, specialist, $64,840
Schibig, Monica Ann, prof, asoc clncl, $80,252
Schick, Carol Anne, prof, ast teach, $60,260
Schieber, Amanda Leann, physician ast, $93,636
Schiefer, Sandra Lynn, librarian II, $46,036
Schieltz, Kelly Michele, prof, ast teach, $60,000
Schiermeier, Heather Marie, nurse, staff II rnwp, $22.24/hr
Schiermeier, Morgan J, resident physician-3rd yr, $53,763
Schiessl, Christoph Eugen, prof, ast teach, $40,300
Schiffbauer, James D, prof, ast, $64,640
Schifman, Adam Gabriel, prof, ast clncl dept, $243,000
Schilb, Jill Elizabeth, physical therapist, $35.00/hr
Schilke, Lawrence E, managing engineer, $102,550
Schillinger, Mary Beth, social worker, $58,500
Schindler, Donald Neil, farm manager, $61,825
Schindler, Stephanie M, 4-h spclst, $41,792
Schiradelly, Kimberly Ann, custodian, $10.39/hr
Schiska, Amy Louise, office support assistant IV, $17.43/hr
Schisla, Gretchen, prof, asoc, $61,355
Schlager, Bruce C, nurse, staff now plus, $30.00/hr
Schlager, Paula J, business svcs consultant, $52,000
Schlarman, Jacqueline Babka, ast dir strat comm, $62,349
Schlegel, Joshua Paul, prof, ast, $75,500
Schleicher, Amie D, extns professional, asoc, $54,698
Schleicher, Janolyn Jean, office support assistant IV, $16.00/hr
Schlein, Candace Melissa, prof, ast, $57,741
Schlemper, Kristel Dawn, academic advisor, $39,290
Schler, Cayley Leann, patient svc rep, $13.51/hr

Schlesinger, Mark E, professor, $95,474
Schlichting, Frederick W, asoc coach, $47,854
Schlieder, Vern F, mechl plant spclst, $19.64/hr
Schliesman, Jeremy L, user support analyst-expert, $19.45/hr
Schlink, Amanda S, strat comm associate sr, $51,175
Schlink, Carla Susan, executive assistant sr, $58,667
Schloss, Jacob A, human resources assistant, $13.00/hr
Schlotzhauer, Cathy Lynn, infection control profl, $66,409
Schlotzhauer, Ciara DaLynn, patient svc rep, $11.07/hr
Schlotzhauer, Roderic D, research lab manager, $63,150
Schlotzhauer, Tailor Lorean, patient svc rep, $10.64/hr
Schlup, Brittany Lynn, program/project supprt coor I, $36,720
Schlup, Dasi H M, social worker, $63,398
Schmaltz, Chester Lee, statistician sr, $70,036
Schmaltz, Richard Allen, prof, asoc clncl dept, $40,469
Schmalz, Carrie A, business support specialist sr, $17.74/hr
Schmalz, Patricia Corder, resp therapist reg, $29.28/hr
Schmer, Carol Elizabeth, prof, ast clncl, $75,276
Schmick, Darell Douglas, librarian II, $45,424
Schmid, Kenneth R, teaching asoc, $65,484
Schmid, Sasha Ayn, head coach, $86,000
Schmidt Clay, Kelly Michele, prof, ast adjunct, $17,500
Schmidt, Christopher J, pharmacist II, $60.00/hr
Schmidt, Claire M, grader, $100.00/hr
Schmidt, David Charles, prof, asoc extns, $98,189
Schmidt, Francis John, professor, $107,468
Schmidt, Harland S, nurse, staff II, $33.81/hr
Schmidt, Jana Elizabeth, asoc dir program/project ops, $61,199
Schmidt, Jennifer Nora, office supervisor, $43,331
Schmidt, Karen A, media producer sr, $31,615
Schmidt, Lauren B, prof, ast, $54,850
Schmidt, Michael Stephen, lecturer, $24,000
Schmidt, Olaf, prof, ast teach, $39,754
Schmidt, Patricia D, health records techn II, $13.64/hr
Schmidt, Scott D, media producer sr, $45,000
Schmidt, Shane Michael, safety comm operator, $12.98/hr
Schmidt, Sheryl A, business ops associate II, $42,639
Schmidt, Timothy Michael, temporary crafts service, $7.50/hr
Schmidt, Vanessa Michele, resident physician-2nd yr, $52,007
Schmidtlein, Margaret Mary, instructor, clncl, $21,000
Schmitt, Frank Bernhardt, police sergeant, $20.04/hr
Schmitt, Matthew D, resident physician-4th yr, $56,225
Schmitt, Wendy Susanne, nurse, staff I, $19.00/hr
Schmitter, Kala Danae, radiologic techl, $23.75/hr
Schmitz, Eugene G, extns professional, asoc, $61,817
Schmitz, Jessica Joann, athletic trainer, $40,050
Schmitz, Lindsay N, librarian I, $41,754
Schmutz, Linda Ann, nurse, licensed prac, $21.78/hr
Schnabel, Jennifer Lyn, research lab supervisor, $53,500
Schnabel, Robert D, prof, asoc resrch, $91,241
Schnable, Amber M, instructor, adjunct, $15,300
Schnadt, Sara Louise, programmer analyst-expert, $61,200
Schnakenberg, C Tim, extns professional, asoc, $74,756
Schnase, Esther Washington, library info specialist sr, $15.70/hr
Schnatterly, Karen Ann, prof, asoc, $158,175
Schneeberger, Kenneth C, dean, ast, $13,862
Schneider, Amanda Rose, library info specialist sr, $17.00/hr
Schneider, Barbara S, prgm mgr II studnt supprt svcs, $90,000
Schneider, Chris, program/project supprt coor sr, $66,000
Schneider, Christine, resident physician-2nd yr, $52,007
Schneider, Christine Lynn, office support assistant II, $11.85/hr
Schneider, Gina M, ast coach, $47,000
Schneider, Jacqueline P, hlth prgm ast, $12.73/hr
Schneider, James J, temporary technical, $25.00/hr
Schneider, Jeffery L, csm associate III, $29.43/hr
Schneider, Mary B, student support specialist sr, $22.68/hr
Schneider, Rebecca Irene, research specialist ast, $46,941
Schneider, Samantha Leigh, research/lab technician, $14.54/hr
Schneider, Scott J, admin consultant I, $20.00/hr
Schneider, Tina Delaine, office support assistant IV, $14.00/hr
Schnell, Randall R II, custodian, $12.94/hr
Schnell, Thomas R II, founders professor, $25,302
Schnell, Janet L, nurse, staff II rnwp, $23.42/hr
Schnell, Jennifer Dianna, prof, ast teach, $50,000
Schnell, Letta Jean, custodian, $12.94/hr
Schnell, Randall R, bldg cntrl sys techn IV, $24.15/hr
Schneller, Jacqueline M, academic advisor, $36,575
Schneller, John T, prof, asoc profl practice, $61,120
Schnepp, Charles H, mts/pipefitter, $22.49/hr

Schnetzler, Bobby Dean, ast mgr plant engrg-h, $75,872
Schnetzler, Susan M, nurse, staff II, $30.79/hr
Schnieders, Christopher Paul, health physics tech II, $24.00/hr
Schnieders, Pamela Gail, supv resp care, $77,985
Schnitzer, Patricia G, prof, asoc, $81,143
Schnurman, Aaron M, user support analyst-expert, $18.45/hr
Schoebinger, Robert Eugene, distrib techn-mtls mgmt, $15.26/hr
Schoelz, James E, professor, $133,253
Schoemehl, Jessica Ann, human resources assistant, $14.06/hr
Schoengarth, Amanda Jane, nurse, staff II, $24.08/hr
Schoengarth, Shelby Columbus, ultrasonographer, $24.10/hr
Schoenike, JoAnn, fin and acctg analyst sr, $48,654
Schoenleber, Dana B, prof, asoc adjunct, $20,000
Schofield, Blake Andrew Ackerman, counsel, $118,500
Schofield, Jessica Hanson, nurse, staff II, $25.00/hr
Scholes, Roberta J, prof, teach, $70,908
Scholl, David A, student service coor I, $42,140
Scholten, Joshua H, enrollment advisor sr, $16.54/hr
Scholten, Melissa Lea, student service coor II, $40,392
Scholtz, George E, student recruitment spclst, $21.13/hr
Schomaker, Amy Marie, office support assistant IV, $15.18/hr
Schommer, Susan K, prof, ast clncl dept, $90,451
Schonberg, William P, professor, $219,513
Schondelmeyer, Terry, office support assistant IV, $18.70/hr
Schonemann II, James R, director it, $97,551
Schooler, Lois Marie, business support analyst sr, $23.26/hr
Schooler, Payton Scot, attd, personal, $9.90/hr
Schooler, Roy L, mts/hvac, $21.05/hr
Schooley, Kimberley, nurse, licensed prac, $14.76/hr
Schoonover, Carol Lynn, educational pgm assistant, $9.16/hr
Schoonover, Meredith Linn, med office assistant, $13.80/hr
Schoor, Rachel A, resrch ast, $33,500
Schopflin, Pamela A, office support assistant IV, $17.04/hr
Schoplin, Susan Murray, instructor, adjunct, $9,000
Schopp, Laura, professor, $135,252
Schopp, Luciana DiSanto, high school student, $8.25/hr
Schott, Christopher Ryan, lecturer, $41,950
Schouten, Charles Lynn, maintenance supervisor, $61,162
Schouten, Christopher Lorne, grounds keeper, $11.76/hr
Schouten, Jonathan Ray, police sergeant, $20.72/hr
Schouten, Lindsey Neal, office support assistant IV, $14.20/hr
Schouten, Seth Danial, seasonal farm ast, $9.75/hr
Schrader, Alicia, resident physician-4th yr, $54,425
Schrader, Cheryl Bunnett, chancellor, $304,500
Schrader, Lucy Jane, prof, ast extns, $56,159
Schramm, Christine, research/lab technician sr, $18.79/hr
Schramm, David G, prof, asoc, $90,986
Schramm, Jeffrey W, prof, asoc, $55,570
Schranck, Rebecca Christine, animal caretaker-equine/food, $10.91/hr
Schrand, Michael, media production director II, $55,824
Schreffler, Jon, farm manager, $47,773
Schreffler, Keri Nichole, seasonal farm ast, $9.75/hr
Schreiber, Cathy I, nurse, staff, $30.24/hr
Schreiber, Kathy L, ast dir research, $72,406
Schreiner, Steven M, prof, asoc, $57,950
Schremp, Terri Denise, nurse, staff II rnwp, $34.18/hr
Schreyer, Kurt A, prof, asoc, $61,500
Schrimpf, Cassidy Elizabeth, food svc wrkr I, $9.60/hr
Schrimpf, Jessica L, resp therapist reg, $30.00/hr
Schrimpf, Lindsey A, prof, ast clncl dept, $132,319
Schroeder, Amber June, dental assistant II, $13.30/hr
Schroeder, Elizabeth Ann, nurse, advanced practice, $85,695
Schroeder, Elliot Robert, user support analyst-speclst, $16.36/hr
Schroeder, Kae Dee, nurse, staff II, $27.41/hr
Schroeder, Kimberly N, resrch asoc, $37,550
Schroeder, Lucy Marie, stage services assistant sr, $16.00/hr
Schroeder, Peter Nathan, stage services assistant sr, $16.00/hr
Schroeder, Sandra M, grader, $52
Schroeder, Sara Michelle, nurse, staff II, $31.88/hr
Schroeder, Stefanie Anne, resident physician-3rd yr, $53,763
Schroepfer, Mary Siebert, nutrition spclst, $59,646
Schroll, Sarah Emily, teaching ast, $13.00/hr
Schrufer-Poland, Tabitha Lee, res physician-2nd yr, $50,810
Schubert, April Renee, nurse, staff II rnwp, $22.96/hr
Schubert, Sascha, prof, ast clncl, $205,000
Schubert, Shari L, business support specialist II, $19.19/hr
Schubring, Barbara B, business support specialist II, $15.31/hr
Schubring, Paul Bernard, business ops associate II, $42,033

Schuck, Oliver Winters, event assistant I, $8.00/hr
Schuermann, Susan M, library info specialist sr, $17.20/hr
Schuh, Jennifer Rose, nurse, staff I, $19.37/hr
Schuh, Robert P, resident physician-2nd yr, $52,007
Schul, Johannes, professor, $97,255
Schulte, Abigail M, executive assistant, $20.50/hr
Schulte, Erica Michelle, business support specialist sr, $23.06/hr
Schulte, Heather Marie, support systems admin-speclst, $45,600
Schulte, Jo Ann, office support assistant IV, $15.22/hr
Schulte, Kristi M, ast dir student support svcs, $57,730
Schulte, Lynn, research specialist II, $25.00/hr
Schulte, Martin W, supv, lab, $68,310
Schulte, Michael W, prof, asoc teach, $61,409
Schulte, Taylor Lynn, food svc wrkr I, $9.60/hr
Schultheis, Robert A, extns professional, asoc, $66,994
Schultz, Ashley Sue Porter, nurse, or/recovery-ch, $22.24/hr
Schultz, Courtney Lynne, research/lab technician, $15.00/hr
Schultz, Elizabeth Ann, business ops associate I, $37,840
Schultz, Eric D, instructor, adjunct, $6,000
Schultz, John Charles, director, $241,217
Schultz, Loren G, prof, asoc teach, $106,747
Schultz, Nancy L, dir III advancement, $77,580
Schultz, Tom E, asoc dir student support svcs, $61,812
Schultz, Tracy Lynn, sr ast dir studnt supprt svcs, $69,799
Schultzel, Mark, resident physician-5th yr, $56,120
Schulz, Benjamin J, programmer analyst-expert, $53,448
Schulz, David J, prof, asoc, $91,780
Schulz, John Hubert, research/lab technician sr, $15.00/hr
Schulz, Laura Clamon, prof, ast, $82,735
Schulz, Michael, prof, curators, $115,272
Schulze, Carmen K, prof, adjunct, $18,000
Schulze, Jennifer Marie, prof, ast adjunct, $17,100
Schumacher, Edward Joseph, instructor, $10,796
Schumacher, Jacqueline A, resrch anlyst, $44,569
Schumacher, Kristopher Ray, instructor, adjunct, $18,000
Schumacher, Leon George, professor, $104,628
Schumacher, Mary Kay, nurse advisor, telephone, $31.70/hr
Schumacher, Megan Dawn, strat comm associate I, $39,015
Schumacher, Michael W, mgr broadcast operations, $55,455
Schuman, Joan Barker, prof, ast teach, $65,200
Schuman, Thomas, prof, asoc, $80,928
Schumann, Sarah Kaylynn, educational pgm assoc I, $11.92/hr
Schumann, Tyler K, cook, $12.20/hr
Schupp, James R, mechl plant spclst, $18.82/hr
Schupp, Joni L, oper prgm coord-radiology, $92,219
Schupp, Ryan P, radiologic techl, $21.11/hr
Schupp, Shirley M, office support assistant IV, $15.99/hr
Schurk, Mary Kathleen, prof, ast teach, $77,471
Schurman, Susan L, office support assistant III, $14.04/hr
Schust, Danny Joseph, professor, $212,805
Schuster, Robert L Jr, db programmer analyst-expert, $59,201
Schuster, Amanda L, mgr, ticket sales, $41,000
Schuster, Andrea M, resident physician-1st yr, $50,219
Schuster, Andrew N, rec/athletic specialist, $13.24/hr
Schuster, Carisa Marise, office support assistant IV, $13.39/hr
Schuster, Paige M, nurse, staff II, $22.24/hr
Schutte, Jenny Beth, veterinarian, residnt, $26,000
Schutte, Michele Mary, nurse, staff, $34.60/hr
Schutter, Jennifer, extns professional, asoc, $52,509
Schutter, Penny Alisha, nurse, staff I, $19.00/hr
Schutz, William Joseph, mts/hvac, $24.13/hr
Schuyler, Justin Robert, prof, ast teach, $65,000
Schwab, David M, research specialist I, $49,700
Schwab, Dennis E, data cntr support tech-expert, $19.89/hr
Schwain, Kristin A, prof, asoc, $66,424
Schwandt, Robert Douglas, ast dir institutional safety, $87,002
Schwantes, Carlos A, professor, $146,519
Schwartz, Alison Kae, temporary crafts service, $9.50/hr
Schwartz, Jeffrey Rich, mts/electrician, $21.05/hr
Schwartz, Lindsay Margaret, resident physician-1st yr, $49,025
Schwartz, Lisa Renee, dir II advancement, $79,776
Schwartz, Mary Elizabeth, instructor, adjunct, $9,000
Schwartz, Paul N, dir I, business admin, $79,341
Schwartz, Richard B, professor, $170,094
Schwartz, Robert W, dean, $240,000
Schwartz, Tony Allen, library info specialist, $13.03/hr
Schwarz, Benyamin, professor, $97,112
Schweder, Michael S, operations support tech II, $12.96/hr
Schwedtmann, Cara Michelle, nurse, staff now I, $26.00/hr

Schwein, Anna Marie, student support specialist sr, $16.80/hr
Schweiss, Connie K, technology resource coor, $52,412
Schweitzberger, Kathleen A, librarian III, $68,577
Schwertz, Deborah K, office support assistant IV, $14.56/hr
Scoggins, Donna G, executive assistant, $18.44/hr
Scogin, Joseph M, instructor, adjunct, $9,600
Sconce, R Wesley, mgr supp svcs-moi, $84,760
Scordias, Margaret Ann, prof, ast adjunct, $750
Scotland, Eric, fellow, $45,000
Scott, David M Jr, nurse, staff II rnwp, $29.26/hr
Scott, Dennis James Jr, mgr student support svcs, $32,305
Scott, Paul R Jr, resrch ast, $1,200
Scott-Showalter, Polly, lecturer, $34,800
Scott, Alexander Winfield, fellow, $21,000
Scott, Angie Christine, reimbursement ast-cert, $18.59/hr
Scott, Benjamin Michael, mental health tech trainee, $9.27/hr
Scott, Christopher L, account executive, $24,000
Scott, Craig P, resp care clinical coor, $28.67/hr
Scott, Cynthia Carol, temporary crafts service, $25.00/hr
Scott, David M, education nurse, $69,499
Scott, Elpida Marie, lecturer, $43,791
Scott, Gena L, dir II advancement, $84,797
Scott, Grant J, prof, ast resrch, $141,115
Scott, James Craig, instructor, adjunct, $24,000
Scott, James K, director, $139,930
Scott, Jana L, asoc dir program/project ops, $57,811
Scott, Jared Wade, user support analyst-entry, $14.00/hr
Scott, Jessica Rene, grader, $100.00/hr
Scott, Joseph Brian, lecturer, $44,126
Scott, Joshua Lamarr, care team assoc-clinical, $11.10/hr
Scott, Karissa E, editor II, $39,996
Scott, Kelly Joy, nurse practitioner, $50,828
Scott, Lasar D, pharmacy tech, $11.69/hr
Scott, Lisa Danielle, nurse, staff I, $19.37/hr
Scott, Lisa Karen, prof, ast adjunct, $27,000
Scott, Marcy L, office support assistant IV, $16.79/hr
Scott, Matthew Douglas, research specialist sr, $54,631
Scott, Patricia A, resrch ast, $12.00/hr
Scott, Patricia Ann, prof, ast teach, $57,000
Scott, Patrick Joseph, operations support tech II, $11.30/hr
Scott, Paula Michelle, sterile processing tech, $19.13/hr
Scott, Rebecca R, prof, asoc, $72,256
Scott, Reggie A, office support assistant IV, $17.11/hr
Scott, Rexroy Anthony, db programmer analyst-expert, $65,545
Scott, Riotta M, technical trainer-princpl, $52,834
Scott, Sally Sue, nurse, staff II, $30.36/hr
Scott, Susan Donnell, mgr, patient sfty & risk mgmnt, $94,692
Scott, Tabitha Renee, supv pat accts-up, $52,718
Scoville, Caryn L, librarian III, $51,902
Scowden, Angela M, resp therapist reg, $22.20/hr
Scroggins, Erin Nicole, nurse, staff I, rnwp, $19.00/hr
Scroggins, Rebecca Jean, research specialist I, $32,033
Scroggs, Catherine Cox, vice chancellor, $185,436
Scrogin, Kalee Joe, mental health tech, $11.50/hr
Scruggs Hicks, Maya M, ast dir student support svcs, $46,284
Scruggs, Sherry Ann, pat acct rep, $14.33/hr
Scumpu, Ioan-Andrei, resident physician-1st yr, $50,219
Seabaugh, Janice Louise, prof, ast clincl, $75,000
Seabourne, Marcia Gay, office support assistant III, $14.43/hr
Seabrooks, Joseph Jr, instructor, adjunct, $8,325
Seagraves, Janice Ethel, executive assistant, $18.40/hr
Sealock, Glenn E Jr, grounds keeper, $13.21/hr
Search, John Derek, farm wrkr I, $12.12/hr
Sears, Carla F, med techl reg, $25.39/hr
Sears, Melissa Ann, laundry attd-mrc, $9.95/hr
Seaton, Jennifer, ultrasonographer, $34.94/hr
Seaton, Lauren Kathlene, office support assistant II, $11.00/hr
Seaton, Sharon Elaine, business support specialist II, $21.79/hr
Seay, Kathy R L, student support specialist II, $20.44/hr
Sebacher, Mary C, prof, ast clincl, $53,064
Sebastian, Jimmy, prof, ast, $69,993
Seckington, Theron L, stage services assistant lead, $19.00/hr
Secrease, Teresa L, nurse, licensed pract, $19.97/hr
Seda, Julie Sue, nurse practitioner, $84,365
Sederburg, Shelia S, office support assistant IV, $12.99/hr
Sedgwick, Genet Michelle, mri technologist, $26.86/hr
Sedgwick, Kathleen Alice, nurse, staff II rnwp, $32.11/hr
Sedighsarvestani, Sahra, prof, asoc, $87,700
Sedillo, Lorinda Lynne, nurse, staff per diem, $35.00/hr

Sedovic, Jennifer Christina, central regstry-data coor, $20.00/hr
See, Joni, nurse, staff, $30.35/hr
See, William Mitchel, prof, ast clincl dept, $235,000
Seebart, Scott J, instructor, adjunct, $15,000
Seeger, Cheryl M, lecturer, $10,008
Seeger, Karen Wyatt, office support assistant III, $16.31/hr
Seeger, Thomas Hilliard, electronics technician sr, $28.43/hr
Seelbinder, Wendy, resrch asoc, $53,907
Seely, Shane R, prof, ast, $57,050
Sees, Dawn, media producer sr, $25.11/hr
Seever, Richard L, mts/pipefitter, $21.05/hr
Sega, Liana Mihaela, prof, asoc, $60,689
Segal, Steven S, professor, $206,000
Segal, Uma A, professor, $83,400
Segert, Ines L, prof, ast teach, $59,152
Segert, Jan, prof, asoc, $85,236
Seghi, Connie Leigh, patient svc rep, $14.07/hr
Segura, Maria T, custodian, $13.36/hr
Sehgal, Ravi, health records techn I, $11.66/hr
Seiber, Pa'reesha Ma'kenzee, patient svc rep, $10.85/hr
Seibert, Eva Lou, executive assistant, $19.23/hr
Seidel, Teresa L, support systems admin-expert, $66,793
Seiler, Vickie Lynn, educational pgm associate I, $12.85/hr
Seithel, Michelle Lynn, physician ast, $105,000
Seitz, Christine O, prof, asoc teach, $54,500
Seitz, Paul Thomas, prof, ast adjunct, $50,333
Sekscinski, Jerry D, mech trades spclst (mts), $21.09/hr
Selby, Amanda B, serv line spclst, $68,793
Selby, Ashley R, coor value anlyst, $64,563
Self, Delbert Eugene Jr, emrg med techn, $14.24/hr
Self, Dana R, strat comm manager, $58,735
Self, Deborah S, office support assistant III, $16.14/hr
Self, Irven Jerold, mts/hvac, $24.13/hr
Self, Jennifer Melaina, instructor, adjunct, $4,002
Self, Sharon D, office support assistant III, $14.99/hr
Self, William Thomas, prof, ast, $166,188
Seligson, Theodore H, prof, adjunct, $30,000
Selkoe, Clifford Jr, nurse, staff II, $30.61/hr
Sell, Jennifer Dawn, office support assistant IV, $14.08/hr
Selle, Matthew Louis, nurse, staff II rnwp, $20.54/hr
Sells, Drew Jeffery, office support assistant IV, $13.37/hr
Sells, Lorelei K, business ops associate sr, $47,880
Selman, Brenda V S, sr dir studnt supprt svcs, $139,051
Selsor, Heather J, coor, care, $65,345
Selting, Bonita R, educational prgm coor sr, $66,073
Selting, Kimberly Anne, prof, asoc teach, $118,774
Selva, Regina M, prof, ast clincl, $42,344
Selva, Thomas J, prof, clinical dept, $310,338
Selves, Stewart Wayne, research specialist I, $42,450
Semarge, Renee Marie, prof, ast teach, $50,000
Semke, Rosemary Kathleen, nurse, staff I, $19.00/hr
Semler, Jessica Lynn, psychologist, $72,805
Semlitsch, Raymond, prof, curators, $139,810
Semmes, Clovis Eugene III, professor, $142,474
Semon, Julie A, prof, ast, $65,000
Senaviratne, G M M M A, fellow, post doctoral, $41,200
Senevey, Susan Jeannette, nurse, staff II, $21.69/hr
Sengupta, Shramik, prof, asoc, $89,819
Sennott, Lisa Ann, instructor, adjunct, $5,042
Senter, David A, prof, ast adjunct, $47,431
Seok, Ji Yeon, fellow, post doctoral, $41,000
Seper, Shannon Lianne, nurse, staff II, $20.54/hr
Seppo, Jonathan Luke, office support assistant III, $16.50/hr
Serati, David Anthony, tutor, $15.00/hr
Seris, Christopher C, mgr csm operations, $64,170
Seris, Jennifer Christine, strat comm associate II, $49,163
Serna, Pablo Andres, instructor, ast, $22,843
Serota, Susan B, instructor, adjunct, $9,360
Sertell, Jill Kathryn, office support assistant III, $12.13/hr
Servey, Jessica Dawne, nurse, licensed prac, $18.12/hr
Sessions, Jordan Rulon, resident physician-6th yr, $58,200
Sessions, Sharon Ann, care coordinator, $65,650
Sessler, Mary J, patient svc rep, $15.08/hr
Sethi, Anmol, high school student, $7.50/hr
Setser, Laci Renee, nurse, staff II rnwp, $20.95/hr
Settergren, Roberta N, executive assistant sr, $70,542
Settlemyer, Derek G, bts mason/tuckptr, $18.71/hr
Settles, Karla Denise, custodian, $13.36/hr

Setzer, David R, professor, $87,500
Sevem, Mark W, program/project supprt coor I, $34,916
Severino, Andri Medrano, stock clerk, $10.94/hr
Severson, Carol A, custodian mrc, $10.50/hr
Seville, Karlan M, strat comm consultant sr, $66,186
Sewell, Laurie Renee, physician assistant, $81,610
Sewell, Thomas Dan, professor, $118,533
Sewell, Travis Darren, mgr advancement, $46,600
Sexten, William Justin, prof, ast, $85,200
Sexton-Green, Datyn Mikel, high school student, $7.50/hr
Sexton, Lori A, prof, ast, $60,157
Sexton, Mary Jean, custodian, $12.94/hr
Sexton, Michael Todd, csm associate II, $19.43/hr
Sexton, Sarah Brie, office support assistant IV, $12.98/hr
Sexton, Ty Jacob, supv housekeeping, $33,000
Seyedmahmoud, Rasoul, fellow, post doctoral, $38,000
Seymour, Kyle Robert, system support analyst-spectst, $23.32/hr
Seymour, Rachel, resident physician-1st yr, $49,025
Shababi, Monir, prof, ast resrch, $47,000
Shabani, Elizabeth Kathleen, prog/proj supprt coor I, $37,742
Shabel, Joshua Forrest, temporary technical, $20.00/hr
Shackelford, Jeffrey David, sr dir program/project ops, $90,000
Shad, Yasar, prof, ast clincl dept, $180,000
Shadwell, Michael S, office support assistant II, $11.15/hr
Shafel, Kristin F, communications coordinator, $15.22/hr
Shafer, Chelsea Elise, clerk, diet, $9.90/hr
Shafer, Gentrie L, livestock spclst, $41,250
Shafer, Rebecca S, research specialist I, $41,895
Shafer, Rhonda M, 4-h spclst, $52,174
Shaffer Johnson, Cassandra Elizabeth, student service coor I, $36,714
Shaffer, Dixie L, custodian lead, $11.98/hr
Shaffer, Julie A, mgr laboratory-mrc, $71,650
Shaffer, Paul E, custodian, bldg maint, $12.13/hr
Shaffer, Stephanie Anne, research/lab technician, $15.00/hr
Shaffer, Travis L, prof, ast teach, $48,026
Shaffer, Victoria A, prof, ast, $80,765
Shafiq, Ali, resident physician-4th yr, $54,425
Shagdarova, Seseg, care team assoc-clinical, $12.08/hr
Shah, Ankit Bharatkumar, fellow, post doctoral, $39,264
Shah, Raj, resident physician-1st yr, $49,025
Shah, Syed A, resident physician-3rd yr, $53,763
Shahan, Morgan Ashley, nurse, staff per diem, $35.00/hr
Shahan, Victoria, mgr II student support svcs, $69,612
Shahdadi, Neima, office support assistant II, $12.98/hr
Shahmohammadi, Niloofar, couns hlth/welfare/wellness, $41,382
Shalenko, Lacey Ann, ast coach, $31,364
Shalenko, Mark Paul, mech, bldg maint, $20.29/hr
Shaller, David Allyn, emeritus, $23,625
Shamim, Shariq, resident physician-5th yr, $56,120
Shamkhalov, Eduard A, food svc wrkr II, $10.10/hr
Shamsi, Pourya, prof, ast, $79,790
Shanahan, Margaret Rose, care team assoc-suppt, $13.58/hr
Shang, Yi, professor, $127,610
Shankar, Ravi, prof, ast clincl dept, $191,250
Shanklin, John, system support analyst-expert, $25.97/hr
Shanks, Amanda Kay, nurse, or/recovery-ch, $24.36/hr
Shanks, Chelsea Marie, child dev asoc teacher, $11.75/hr
Shanks, Patti A, prof, ast adjunct, $37,658
Shannon Simms, Brenda, mgr student support svcs, $69,533
Shannon, Donald Kent, extns professional, $67,379
Shannon, Dorothy A, neonatal nurse practitioner, $85,904
Shannon, James Grover, professor, $174,498
Shannon, Joshua W, serv line spclst, $65,517
Shannon, Katie B, prof, asoc teach, $64,656
Shannon, Marcia Carlson, professor, $96,138
Shannon, Mark W, electronics technician I, $11.68/hr
Shannon, Michael Aaron, radiological technologist, $21.20/hr
Shannon, Sutro Wayne, livestock spclst, $58,561
Shapiro, Allan James, prof, ast adjunct, $120,000
Shapiro, Katrina Gatti, office support assistant IV, $13.00/hr
Sharif, Shan, resident physician-2nd yr, $52,007
Shariff, Adam Richmond, prof, ast adjunct, $8,004
Sharma, Ajay, prof, ast resrch, $45,900
Sharma, Akshit, resident physician-1st yr, $49,025
Sharma, Amit Kumar, resident physician-5th yr, $56,120
Sharma, Krishna, professor, $163,993
Sharma, Praneet Kumar, resident physician-8th yr, $64,175
Sharma, Rishi, fellow, post doctoral, $37,500

Sharma, Sandhya, speech/lang pathologist, $35.00/hr
Sharp, Adam, hospital security officer, $10.85/hr
Sharp, Brad A, mts/insulator, $21.05/hr
Sharp, Brian W, coor protocol svcs, $15.00/hr
Sharp, Claudia Melina, coor protocol svcs, $14.83/hr
Sharp, Denise G, office support assistant IV, $14.69/hr
Sharp, Garry L, temporary crafts service, $11.24/hr
Sharp, Gordon Craig, emeritus, $10,131
Sharp, Gregg Lloyd, instructor, clincl, $6,750
Sharp, Jason Lee, instructor, extns, $54,269
Sharp, Jered, emrg med techn, $11.61/hr
Sharp, Jodi A, security officer, $12.29/hr
Sharp, Judith A, prof, clincl, $65,200
Sharp, Kathy Leann, business support specialist II, $20.95/hr
Sharp, Latonya Rena Moore, surgical technl certified, $17.78/hr
Sharp, Paul R, professor, $104,369
Sharp, Rex L, head athletic trainer, $119,160
Sharp, Robert E, professor, $191,937
Sharp, Sarah Elizabeth, nurse, clincl charge-lpn, $18.58/hr
Sharp, Victoria Christine, emrg med techn, $11.75/hr
Sharp, Wesley Duane, powr plnt opr II, $28.70/hr
Sharpe, Deanna L, prof, asoc, $94,676
Sharpe, Mary Elizabeth, prof, ast teach, $62,500
Sharpe, Paul A, librarian II, $65,553
Sharpsteen, Donald J, prof, asoc, $63,108
Sharrock, Dee Ann, ultrasonographer, $29.16/hr
Shatto, James E, business ops associate sr, $55,272
Shatto, Nathan E, dir I, advancement, $79,801
Shaub, Audery Maria, business ops associate sr, $50,596
Shaver, Jason Thomas, lecturer, $42,021
Shavers, Cyrhonda Denise, prof, ast adjunct, $8,004
Shaw, Adam Franklin, resident physician-5th yr, $56,120
Shaw, Alicia Christine, nurse, staff prn, $26.00/hr
Shaw, Becky Ann, pat acct rep, $14.68/hr
Shaw, Catherine E, business support specialist II, $17.24/hr
Shaw, Christopher M, resident physician-6th yr, $58,200
Shaw, Christopher Patrick, system support analyst-expert, $25.06/hr
Shaw, Daniel Porter, professor, $141,049
Shaw, Ernest Cornelius, manager it, $70,667
Shaw, Helen A, librarian III, $47,526
Shaw, Hubert P, csm associate II, $20.00/hr
Shaw, Kara Mattes, office support assistant IV, $15.70/hr
Shaw, Katherine, temporary technical, $17.00/hr
Shaw, Kenneth William, prof, asoc, $183,601
Shaw, Kevin Christopher, mgr event services, $40,650
Shaw, Kimberlee Ann, instructor, adjunct, $1,800
Shaw, Loretta Hogans, executive assistant, $30.96/hr
Shaw, Mary L, research specialist I, $37,790
Shaw, Meredith Dawn, student service coor II, $48,960
Shaw, Nancy Ann, nurse, staff II, $36.81/hr
Shaw, Nathan Eugene, custodian, $10.73/hr
Shaw, Nichole Suzanne, nurse, licensed prac, $18.46/hr
Shaw, Rebecca Lynn, research specialist I, $43,026
Shaw, Richard Franklin, administrative consultant II, $77,838
Shaw, Roxie June Edwards, sup systems admin-expert, $55,917
Shaw, Roy L, video comm it tech-speclst, $16.13/hr
Shaw, Steven, specialist, $10.00/hr
Shay, Aaron Eugene, mts/refrigeration mech, $22.50/hr
Shay, Matthew W, mts/sheet metal, $21.05/hr
Shayatovich, Paul E, retail sales assistant sr, $12.80/hr
Shea, Julie Marie, business support specialist II, $19.47/hr
Sheaffer, Kelley D, nurse, staff II rnwp, $25.44/hr
Sheahan, Bridget Martin, psychologist, $40.00/hr
Shear, Jennifer Anne, communications coordinator, $17.52/hr
Sheard, Sandra G, custodian, $12.94/hr
Shearer, Cristina Marie, nurse, licensed prac, $16.04/hr
Shearer, Heidi J, student service coor sr, $48,410
Shearer, Mary Chantelle, interventional technl (ir), $22.11/hr
Shearrer, Cassidy Diane, media producer II, $16.30/hr
Shearrer, Cynthia D, librarian III, $65,095
Shearrer, Joe, organizational dvlpmt consult, $93,150
Sheble, Brian Anthony, instructor, adjunct, $6,000
Shedd, Stefanie Raquel, office support assistant IV, $14.53/hr
Sheeder, Megan Miranda, care team assoc-suppt, $10.85/hr
Sheehan, John Joseph, instructor, adjunct, $15,000
Sheehey, Haley Lynn, care team assoc-clinical, $11.10/hr
Sheerin, Matthew James, event assistant I, $7.55/hr
Sheets, Curtis D, mail carrier, $14.85/hr
Sheets, Lincoln Ralph, fellow, post doctoral, $50,000

Sheffel, Christina Frances, educational pgm coor III, $52,412
Sheffield, Bret J, instructor, adjunct, $15,000
Shekailo, Donald J Jr, occl therapist, $72,000
Shelby, Jonathan Hughes, advancement officer, $50,000
Shelby, Joyce Renee, business support analyst sr, $26.23/hr
Sheldon, Kennon M, professor, $101,383
Sheldon, Melanie S, prof, ast teach, $59,152
Sheley, Brooke Lee, nurse, staff I, $19.00/hr
Sheley, Dale W, animal techn, ast lab, $13.89/hr
Sheley, David C, powr plnt maint spclst II, $23.75/hr
Sheley, Marvin L, cook, $12.95/hr
Sheley, Rodney Eugene, office support assistant III, $13.00/hr
Shellabarger, Mary J, nurse spclst, clincl, $49,390
Shellenberger, John Marc, resident physician-2nd yr, $52,007
Sheller, Mary Frances, human resources specialist I, $23.37/hr
Shellhart, Laurie A, supv, operating room nursing, $31.11/hr
Shelly, Beverly J, ast mgr pat accts, $67,188
Shelton, Brian, custodian, $13.23/hr
Shelton, Charity F, coor therapy svcs-mrc, $76,864
Shelton, Danyele Renee, fellow, post doctoral, $35,000
Shelton, James David, prof, asoc adjunct, $19,038
Shelton, Joshua Brian, police officer, $17.50/hr
Shelton, Kamesha Anell, child dev assistant, $8.08/hr
Shelton, Kevin L, professor, $123,045
Shelton, Kourtney, child dev assistant, $8.08/hr
Shelton, Linda D, educational pgm associate I, $13.44/hr
Shelton, Linda L, nurse, staff prn, $26.00/hr
Shelton, Lynn Jean, office support assistant sr, $17.16/hr
Shelton, Michael Patrick, instructor, $10,796
Shelton, Patrick J, ast coach, $4,992
Shelton, Tammy Lynn, office support assistant IV, $15.00/hr
Shemon, Mary Kathleen Bassett, teaching ast, $27.50/hr
Shemon, Zachary Joseph, prof, ast, $55,000
Shen, Chin Tina, instructor, adjunct, $18,000
Shen, Huei-Wern, prof, ast, $59,201
Shen, Xiaojun, professor, $100,942
Sheng, Hong, prof, asoc, $118,627
Shenk, Mary Katherine, prof, asoc, $67,579
Shenker, Joel Isaac, prof, ast clincl dept, $165,600
Shenoi, Raveen B, resident physician-1st yr, $50,219
Shepard, Beth A, student support specialist II, $18.51/hr
Shepard, Richard Charles, specialist, $72,000
Shepard, Summer Augusta, nurse advisor, telephone, $27.91/hr
Shepherd-Miles, Robin L, patient svc rep, $14.88/hr
Shepherd, Christine Marie, nurse, staff II, $34.18/hr
Shepherd, Dana Jermaine, custodian, $10.94/hr
Shepherd, Seth David, powr plnt matrl handling opr, $20.31/hr
Sheppard, James W, prof, asoc, $64,644
Sheppard, Kathleen Lynn, prof, ast, $55,027
Sher, Kenneth, prof, curators, $209,561
Sher, Linda, media producer II, $17.17/hr
Sher, Philip Fei-Yu, mental health professional, $40,800
Sherbondy, Karen S, extension asoc, $46,137
Sheremeta, Alyena, patient svc rep, $11.07/hr
Sheridan, Jennifer L, coor, service, $17.10/hr
Sherman, Abigayle M, program/project supprt coor I, $17.04/hr
Sherman, Angela Christine, nurse, staff, $24.03/hr
Sherman, Cynthia Dee, house manager h, $74,353
Sherman, Helene, founders professor, $27,825
Sherman, Janice, prof, asoc teach, $62,000
Sherman, Jerry Allen, distribution techn-mtls mgmt, $15.06/hr
Sherman, Melissa Dawn, polysomnograph techn reg, $20.12/hr
Sherman, Michael Parker, prof, adjunct, $50,796
Sherman, Seth L, prof, ast, $260,000
Sherraden, Margaret S, founders professor, $28,080
Sherrill, Meredith K, veterinarian, residnt, $26,315
Sherwood, Jesse, prof, ast teach, $52,500
Shetler, Cheryl Ann, custodian, $10.39/hr
Shettlesworth, Janice M, sterile processing tech, $18.31/hr
Shettlesworth, Kimberly Marie, student support spclst II, $16.34/hr
Shettlesworth, Theresa Rose, credentialing spclst, $19.67/hr
Shi, Haiying, research specialist I, $46,562
Shi, Honglan, prof, asoc resrch, $82,400
Shi, Junxiang, prof, ast resrch, $42,000
Shi, Yiyu, prof, ast, $89,500
Shibles, Eleanor Sue, custodial supervisor, $48,360
Shibusawa, Yoshiaki, advancement officer, $12,000
Shields, Nancy A, prof, asoc, $72,011
Shields, Nicole Jo, nurse, staff II rnwp, $24.25/hr

Shields, Phyllis Jean Devine, distrib techn-mtls mgmt, $14.95/hr
Shields, Yakima Young, prof, ast teach, $88,366
Shiflett, Lora Ann, resrch asoc, $47,200
Shiflett, Pamela K, coor, service, $17.10/hr
Shiflett, William Jefferson, dir II advancement, $83,768
Shigaki, Cheryl Lynn, prof, asoc, $95,295
Shih, Han M, sr manager it, $85,749
Shih, Shu-Fen, security officer, $10.24/hr
Shilcrat, Stewart Joel, advancement officer, $50,000
Shimron, Yonat, strat comm consultant sr, $76,500
Shin, Dmitriy, prof, ast, $117,300
Shin, Geiguen, scholar, visiting, $6,000
Shin, Hye Young, prof, ast, $55,000
Shiner, Jeanne Dian, office support assistant IV, $15.15/hr
Shiner, Mark A, resp therapist reg, $27.36/hr
Shingleton, Randy Alan, dir II csm operations, $107,500
Shinkut, Esther Swatdunie, pharmacist II, $60.00/hr
Shinn, Tatyana N, library info specialist sr, $15.81/hr
Shiozaki, Teisha, resident physician-3rd yr, $52,470
Shipers, Dana Charlene, nurse, staff II, $26.60/hr
Shipley, Landon Christopher, ast coach, $24,255
Shipley, Thomas Nathan, media producer sr, $25.78/hr
Shipman, Amber Elizabeth, nurse, staff I, $19.00/hr
Shipman, Kimberly Beth, patient svc rep, $13.68/hr
Shipman, Ronnie Dale, research specialist I, $32,760
Shipova, Ekaterina, research specialist I, $37,874
Shire, Stephanie Sue, waiter/waitress, $8.44/hr
Shirley, Benaud St Aldeen, asoc coach, $41,000
Shirley, Taysia Josphine, patient svc rep, $11.07/hr
Shiu, Anthony S, prof, asoc, $58,216
Shiu, Patrick Ka Tai, prof, asoc, $91,480
Shivaprakash, Shivasankalp, technology resource coor, $55,125
Shiveley, Brenda M, custodian mrc, $10.50/hr
Shivers, Beatrice A, office support assistant IV, $19.94/hr
Shives, Janice K, bts painter, $20.23/hr
Shives, Linda M, office support assistant III, $14.00/hr
Shives, Timothy Edward, floor care techn, $12.15/hr
Shlyakhtina, Natalia Ivanovna, research specialist II, $50,142
Shobassy, Mazen N, resident physician-2nd yr, $50,810
Shocklee, Philip J, driver, $13.19/hr
Shoemake, Brian McMillan, veterinarian, residnt, $26,000
Shoemaker, Adam M, asoc dir program/project ops, $48,934
Shoemaker, Charles Edward, coord, distrib-matls dist, $17.46/hr
Shoemaker, Christopher Lee, business spclst, $50,572
Shoemaker, Doris J, program/project supprt coor II, $27,606
Shoemaker, Hea Kyung Jeong, business support spclst sr, $21.63/hr
Shoemaker, Kelly Marie, pharmacy tech, $10.64/hr
Shoemaker, Wayne Edgar, research tech svcs supv, $29.62/hr
Shoemaker, William Kylle, ast coach, $34,340
Sholtis, Gina Marie, ast vice chancellor, $135,000
Sholy, Carol S, business ops associate sr, $64,000
Sholy, Joumana Ibrahim, custodian, $13.23/hr
Shomper, Jeremy L, veterinarian, residnt, $26,000
Shonekan, Jamimah Olagbenle, educational pgm assoc I, $12.55/hr
Shonekan, Stephanie Uku, prof, asoc, $76,914
Shoot, Rebecca Lyn, nurse, staff II, $32.37/hr
Shore, Deborah Ann, nurse, staff II rnwp, $31.99/hr
Shorney, Lorrene J, health records techn II, $13.06/hr
Shorr, Margaret Ann, nurse, staff now III, $30.00/hr
Short, Christopher, student support specialist II, $14.95/hr
Short, Melinda Lou, nurse, staff prn, $26.00/hr
Short, Robert L, mts/pipefitter, $22.50/hr
Shortridge, James Riley, fellow, post doc clncl-yr2, $58,083
Shory, Lein N, strat comm associate sr, $50,268
Shotwell, William Matthew, sterile processing tech, $14.89/hr
Shoults, Derek Steven, user support analyst-speclst, $16.86/hr
Shouse-Carnoali, Mindy Jo, office support assistant III, $11.30/hr
Shover, Thomas J, certif pharmacy techn, $13.35/hr
Showalter, Stephen Duane, event assistant I, $7.50/hr
Showalter, William Eric, prof, asoc, $85,221
Showers, Debra K, instructor, adjunct, $9,600
Showers, Steven Brent, med techl reg, $24.86/hr
Showmaker, Jason Andrew, resident physician-5th yr, $58,083
Showmaker, Rebecca Lynn, student service coor sr, $43,600
Shows, Justin H, prof, ast teach, $60,000
Shoyinka, Adekemi, pharmacist II, $60.00/hr
Shoyinka, Sosunmolu Opeyemi, prof, ast adjunct, $13,048
Shrensker, Jennifer Loren, prof, ast teach, $45,905
Shrestha, Anuj, resident physician-4th yr, $54,425

Shrestha, Bijaya, prof, asoc teach, $69,614
Shrestha, Srijana, resident physician-4th yr, $55,804
Shroyer, Jonathan D, bts painter lead, $22.29/hr
Shrull, Richard, user support analyst-expert, $20.66/hr
Shryock, Merry M, speech/lang pathologist, $70,456
Shryock, Sydney Madison, patient svc rep, $10.85/hr
Shuaib, Abdulgader H, clinical technician II, $16.00/hr
Shue, Sandra Sue, patient svc rep, $11.92/hr
Shufeldt, Mary Ann, nurse, staff, $26.48/hr
Shukla, Shivendra D, professor, $175,354
Shuls, James Virgil, prof, ast, $60,000
Shults, Julie Lynn, user interfce designer-expert, $53,961
Shults, Michelle, advancement associate II, $18.50/hr
Shultz, Angela Marie, nurse, staff II, $20.54/hr
Shultz, Patti H, prof, ast adjunct, $34,010
Shultz, Rudane Edward, prof, adjunct, $25,000
Shumate, Amy Nicole, educational pgm coor III, $49,200
Shumway, Nora Kyle, resident physician-3rd yr, $53,763
Shurtz, Joseph C, resident physician-2nd yr, $52,007
Shy, Lindsay Zoellner, business support specialist II, $19.05/hr
Shymansky, James A, professor, $140,164
Shyu, Chi Ren, professor, $226,958
Siau, Keng Leng, professor, $177,525
Sibghat Tul Llah, resident physician-1st yr, $49,025
Sibigtroth, Christine M, veterinarian, residnt, $26,315
Sicht, Caroline Marie, office support assistant II, $10.34/hr
Siciliani, Jennifer L, prof, teach, $64,537
Sickels, Katelyn Nicole, emrg med techn, $12.32/hr
Sickler, Deborah Lee, office support assistant IV, $13.27/hr
Sida, Jessica Lea, lab assistant, $8.08/hr
Siddall, Martin L, sr dir broadcast operations, $187,422
Siddens, Adrienne Danea, veterinary technician, $15.76/hr
Siddens, Randall T, mgr III business admin, $80,000
Siddiki, MD Mahbube Khoda, instructor, adjunct, $33,000
Siddiqi, Nasir H, physician, $250.00/hr
Siddique, Sameer, fellow, post doc clncl-yr3, $60,415
Sidebottom, Neal A, nurse, staff II, $29.58/hr
Sides, Connie Johanna, nurse, advanced practice, $76,888
Sidhu, Manavjot, fellow, post doc clncl yr1, $50.00/hr
Sidhu, Manavjot, fellow, post doc clncl-yr3, $60,415
Sidio, Gandolf John George, programmer analyst-entry, $43,671
Sidwell, Jonathon R, research specialist sr, $48,381
Siebenaler, Ashley G, student service coor sr, $47,880
Sieberg, Lisa M, instructor, adjunct, $27,200
Siebert, Haley Katherine, temporary technical, $9.50/hr
Siebert, Ryan Bernarr, resident physician-4th yr, $55,804
Siegel, Alana D, temporary professional, $15.00/hr
Siegel, Jerrold, instructor, adjunct, $15,000
Siegel, Krista Marie, care team assoc-suppt, $13.01/hr
Siegel, Marcelle Arra, prof, asoc, $68,242
Siegel, Steven Frank, engineer II, $60,343
Siegenthaler, Kimberly Lake, sr dir program/project ops, $107,635
Siegler, Karen Marie, service rep III, $14.55/hr
Siegmund, Mandi Renae, nurse, staff I, $19.00/hr
Sielert, Deborah Ann, executive assistant, $23.56/hr
Sieli, Michael, sftware supprt analyst-expert, $46,968
Sieli, Paizlee Tenaj, research/lab technician, $12.75/hr
Sieli, Ralph G, library info specialist, $12.98/hr
Siem, Carol A, instructor, clncl, $67,126
Siemers, Laurel T, lecturer sr, $18,000
Sieveking, Jamie Jo, nurse advisor, telephone, $26.00/hr
Sieveking, Michael J, business svcs consultant, $47,701
Sieveking, Steven W, research/lab technician sr, $17.86/hr
Sievel, Janet E, academic advisor, $35,539
Sievert, Connie J, office support assistant IV, $17.22/hr
Sievert, Donald Edward, professor, $72,220
Sievert, Rebecca, instructor, clncl, $25,833
Siewert, Walter Michael, academic dir, $89,759
Sifers, Travis McCann, resident physician-3rd yr, $54,270
Sigdel, Krishna Prasad, resrch asoc, $46,113
Sigholtz, Shelley Evans, food svc wrkr I, $9.60/hr
Signorino, Russell D, instructor, adjunct, $24,000
Sikes, Nicole Carraher, office support assistant III, $14.25/hr
Silkman, Gregory L, sr ast dir csm operations, $84,595
Silkman, Julie Janel, executive assistant sr, $47,743
Sill, Tracy Michelle, office support assistant IV, $16.32/hr
Sills, Adam Wayne, research/lab technician, $13.80/hr
Silswal, Neerupma, fellow, post doctoral, $42,841
Silver, Antoine L, floor maint wkr, $13.84/hr

Silverberg, Ruth Ann, veterinary technician sr, $16.63/hr
Silverman, Jessica Clark, office support assistant IV, $14.90/hr
Silverman, Lewis Phillip, instructor, $51,695
Silverstein, Peter Steven, prof, asoc resrch, $60,000
Silvestre, Cora Andres, supv, lab, $67,225
Silvestri, Simone, prof, ast, $85,000
Silvey, Bethany Kaye, business support specialist sr, $20.42/hr
Silvey, Brian Ashley, prof, asoc, $64,934
Silvey, David W, business ops associate sr, $63,435
Silvey, Gina L, mgr, medical educ, $62,487
Silvey, Sarah Davie, office support assistant III, $12.42/hr
Silvey, Shelly C, media production director III, $54,048
Silvey, Sidney Ray, health physics technician I, $20.91/hr
Silvey, Stanley R, mgr broadcast operations, $62,000
Simek, Leonard Francis III, reactor operator sr, $30.26/hr
Simenson, Mark Herschel, hand therapist cert, $80,325
Simental, Monica, custodian lead, $14.03/hr
Simeone, Lorraine, mgr III business admin, $56,650
Simkin, Jenny Lynn, research/lab technician sr, $13.77/hr
Simmer-Beck, Melanie Lea, prof, asoc, $73,288
Simmerman, Joan Karen, revenue recovery spclst, $48,075
Simmerman, Randy G, telecom tech-princpl, $21.29/hr
Simmons-Gamble, Sandra Lee, office support asst IV, $14.70/hr
Simmons, Andrea Marie Johnson, office support asst III, $16.37/hr
Simmons, Angel Novel, prof, ast clincl, $86,523
Simmons, Carl Thomas, mental health tech, $12.20/hr
Simmons, Connie Louise, sterile processing tech, $18.31/hr
Simmons, Donald S, police captain, $67,710
Simmons, Jill Diane, pharmacist III, $128,835
Simmons, Juanita Marie, prof, asoc, $80,232
Simmons, Karla Jean, executive assistant, $22.36/hr
Simmons, Leslie Jane, executive assistant, $16.96/hr
Simmons, Malika Shante, prof, ast visiting, $62,650
Simmons, Renee L, human resources analyst sr, $58,870
Simmons, Robert A, asoc vice chancellor, $154,800
Simmons, Scott Herbert, dir II advancement, $99,337
Simmons, Thomas E, event assistant I, $7.55/hr
Simmons, William H, db programmer analyst-speclst, $53,194
Simmons, Yvonne D, office support assistant III, $11.64/hr
Simms, Earl C II, dir program/project operations, $79,500
Simms, E Wade, event assistant I, $7.50/hr
Simms, Glenda Juanita, office supervisor, $40,000
Simms, Jennifer Spearman, manager it, $64,032
Simoes, Eduardo J, professor, $280,908
Simon, Jessica Michelle, intern, $24,014
Simon, Karl Jesus Akil, instructor, clincl, $15,000
Simon, Keri D, exec director-wch, $154,977
Simon, Louise Josephine, nurse, staff II, $35.27/hr
Simon, Stephen David, prof, adjunct, $70,000
Simonds, Catherine Ann, sr mgr business admin, $65,801
Simonds, Susan Conrad, office support assistant IV, $14.57/hr
Simons, Alicia Maria, social worker, $54,337
Simons, Amy B, prof, ast/profl pract, $64,023
Simons, Cassandra Jo, nurse, staff I, $19.00/hr
Simons, Elizabeth V, grader, $52
Simons, John J, supv nursing acute care, $26.19/hr
Simonsen, Jon Christian, prof, ast, $81,325
Simonyi, Agnes, prof, asoc resrch, $60,260
Simpson, Allan Kenneth, human resources specialist III, $47,940
Simpson, Amanda Chinel, care team assoc-clinical, $14.00/hr
Simpson, Cassius Marcelles, temporary crafts service, $9.50/hr
Simpson, Gloria L, event assistant I, $8.40/hr
Simpson, John Charles, instructor, adjunct, $10,500
Simpson, Kristin Bauer, research specialist I, $32,944
Simpson, Lachelle Denise, educational pgm assoc I, $12.46/hr
Simpson, Rebecca G, 4-h spclst, $47,865
Simpson, Reynold, prof, asoc, $51,537
Simpson, Robert Alan, asoc dir program/project ops, $52,744
Simpson, Valerie Anne, hlth prgm spclst, $16.77/hr
Simpson, Vivian Jean, linen attd lead, $13.69/hr
Sims, Amanda Abston, grader, $100.00/hr
Sims, Charles Joseph, pharmacy tech, $10.85/hr
Sims, Cheryl L, custodian, $12.94/hr
Sims, Corey Steven, food svc wrkr I, $9.98/hr
Sims, Dona, custodian, $12.94/hr
Sims, Donna G, executive assistant, $25.86/hr
Sims, Gregory Garl, office support assistant IV, $14.50/hr
Sims, Jody Lynn, adjunct, $13,600
Sims, John R, food svc wrkr III, $13.21/hr

Sims, Mitzi A, surgical technl certified, $20.50/hr
Sims, Myisha T, library info specialist, $13.30/hr
Sims, Nathan Thomas, event assistant I, $7.85/hr
Sims, Rachelle Dawn, pat acct rep, $14.86/hr
Sims, Ryan Gabriel, system administrator-speclst, $46,530
Sims, Wendy L, professor, $108,191
Sinacore, Mary L, prof, ast teach, $70,138
Sinak, Levi Aaron, emrg med techn, $11.84/hr
Sindhwani, Vivek, prof, ast clincl dept, $250,000
Sinele, Alice S, nurse, staff, $31.47/hr
Singer, Dale, strat comm consultant, $57,087
Singer, Deborah Lenore, executive assistant, $20.67/hr
Singer, Nancy R, prof, asoc, $65,744
Singh, Amolak, professor, $340,742
Singh, Daulath, resident physician-1st yr, $49,025
Singh, Deepak Kumar, prof, ast, $78,780
Singh, Garima, resident physician-5th yr, $58,083
Singh, Jagkirat, resident physician-1st yr, $50,219
Singh, Kamlendra, prof, ast resrch, $61,002
Singh, Luv Kush, resident physician-3rd yr, $52,470
Singh, Niranjan Narain, prof, asoc clincl dept, $181,650
Singh, Priyanka, resident physician-4th yr, $54,425
Singh, Raghvendra, academic advisor, $35,500
Singh, Sunil Kumar, grader, $504
Singler, John Richard, prof, asoc, $71,912
Singleton, Jesse W, mgr csm operations, $55,225
Singleton, Stephanie A, office support assistant IV, $17.77/hr
Singley, Frances Joan, temporary professional, $27.64/hr
Sinha, Nishant RajIV, high school student, $7.50/hr
Sinha, Prashant RajIV, research/lab technician, $14.00/hr
Sinha, Sunilima, research specialist I, $33,400
Sinkler, Christopher S, research specialist I, $47,267
Sinn, Stephanie Carol, program/project supprt coor II, $59,166
Sinnott, Terrence Dean, custodian, $11.00/hr
Sipe, Daniel A, prof, asoc, $58,805
Sipe, Kim Wayne, cat scan technl (ct), $27.00/hr
Sipes, Cynthia Marie, business support specialist II, $14.95/hr
Sipocz, Ashley Elece, instructor, adjunct, $18,000
Sippel, Jeffrey, prof, asoc, $64,469
Sipple, Samantha Elaine, mental health professional, $36,000
Sireno, Lisa Marie, asoc dir business admin, $69,589
Sirigeere Prabhakar, Deepa, fellow, post doc clncl-yr2, $58,083
Sirridge, Jennifer McClear, teaching ast, $9,600
Sise, Daniel M, lecturer, $42,000
Sisemore, Elizabeth A, athletic trainer, $40,300
Sisk, Cynthia Michelle, nurse, staff I, $19.37/hr
Sisler, Bruce Wayne, med techl reg, $32.36/hr
Sisler, Jackie, office support assistant IV, $18.00/hr
Sisley, Mark, custodian, $13.23/hr
Sistrunk, Wendy, librarian III, $55,865
Sites, Robert William, professor, $98,231
Sites, Sandra D, program/project supprt coor I, $55,825
Sitton, Oliver Clifford III, prof, asoc, $105,113
Siva, Chokkalingam, prof, asoc clincl dept, $157,816
Sivanantharajah, Lovesha, fellow, post doctoral, $40,000
Sivaraman, Manjamalai, prof, asoc clincl dept, $166,400
Siyakwazi, Nomathemba, instructor, clincl, $15,375
Sizemore, Norma R, nurse, licensed prac, $18.37/hr
Skaff, D Andrew, resrch asoc, $43,858
Skaggs, Danny R, mech, bldg maint, $19.64/hr
Skarbek, Anita J, prof, ast clincl, $66,016
Skaria, Priya Elsa, resident physician-2nd yr, $50,810
Skeene, Jane L, business tech analyst-speclst, $53,841
Skeens, Stacy Rose, serv line spclst, $82,619
Skibiski, Katherine Elizabeth, physical therapist, $66,844
Skidmore, Max Joseph Jr, instructor, adjunct, $10,000
Skidmore, Max J, professor, $150,326
Skillern, Christopher Don, resident physician-1st yr, $50,219
Skillington, Charles Andrew, surgical technl certified, $16.76/hr
Skinner, Alexandra Michelle, hlth prgm ast, $12.50/hr
Skinner, Diane Kay, patient svc rep, $12.72/hr
Skinner, Jeremy B, prof, asoc clincl, $85,295
Skjei, Catherine, ast mgr hospitality services, $55,102
Skrabal, Harold Dean, pharmacist II, $60.00/hr
Skrabal, Scott Edward, temporary clerical, $9.00/hr
Skroh, Bart Allen, educational pgm associate I, $11.80/hr
Skubic, Marjorie, professor, $153,430
Skyberg, Jerod Alan, prof, ast, $93,745
Skyles, Beverly G, executive assistant, $19.40/hr

Skyles, Susan Amy, instructional designer-speclst, $50,732
Slack, Aniesa, resident physician-1st yr, $49,025
Slack, Cathy R, accountant I, $16.80/hr
Slade, Darryl Raymond, event assistant I, $7.55/hr
Slagle, Torria, high school student, $10.20/hr
Slama, Brandon G, practice manager, $69,345
Slansky, Barry, prof, ast adjunct, $27,000
Slapac, Alina, prof, asoc, $59,592
Slate, Donnie David Jr, building/mechanical maint I, $17.95/hr
Slater, Joseph V, sr farm manager, $79,311
Slates, Jerry, maint svc attd, $17.60/hr
Slaton, Robert Basil Jr, emrg med techn paramedic, $18.57/hr
Slaton, Lorah C, temporary technical, $10.00/hr
Slattery, Jennifer Marie, office support assistant IV, $14.50/hr
Slaughter, Asia Shameeka, tutor, $13.13/hr
Slaughter, Brett D, db programmer analyst-speclst, $54,621
Slaughter, David Wayne, db programmer analyst-expert, $59,726
Slaughter, Jack L, video comm admin-princpl, $74,376
Slaughter, James Richard, prof, asoc adjunct, $48,000
Slaughter, Joan Mitchell, nurse anesthetist, $147,900
Slaughter, Kathleen, nurse, staff II, $34.18/hr
Slaughter, Sharyl Elaine, pat acct rep, $15.42/hr
Slavit, Thomas Eli, custodian, $10.94/hr
Slight, Simon Howard, lab assistant, $13.76/hr
Slish, John J IV, business support specialist II, $16.82/hr
Slivka, Judd, prof, ast/profl pract, $61,660
Sloan, Joseph Caleb, student service coor II, $43,859
Slocum, Lee A, prof, asoc, $80,000
Slone, Austen Jameson, research/lab technician, $10.24/hr
Slowiak, Patricia Mae, office support assistant III, $12.66/hr
Slusarz, Anna, instructor, $18,000
Slutske, Wendy S, professor, $90,803
Smaistrla, Kathryn M, program/project supprt coor II, $39,000
Smale, Robert Leland, prof, asoc, $59,732
Small, Kimberly Sue, instructional developr-expert, $19.86/hr
Small, Laura Ann, reimbursement ast, $17.63/hr
Small, Natissia S, sr dir studnt supprt svcs, $98,818
Smalley, Dicky Dean, grader, $52
Smalley, Kristi D, director, $67,384
Smallwood, Julie Ann, care team assoc-clinical, $14.88/hr
Smarr, Janis R, ophthalmic techn cert, $19.71/hr
Smarr, Juanita Gayle, student support specialist sr, $20.18/hr
Smarr, Kristen E, dir I, strat communications, $100,470
Smeda, Reid J, professor, $102,630
Smedley, Georgia Ann, prof, asoc, $162,992
Smiley, Stefanie Marie, accountant I, $17.34/hr
Smirnova, Michelle Hannah, prof, ast, $56,000
Smith Bentley, Laqueta S, surgical techn certified, $19.47/hr
Smith II, Richard Dean, 4-h spclst, $42,861
Smith, Jimmy C Jr, bts carpenter, $20.23/hr
Smith-Frigerio, Sarah Michelle, academic advisor sr, $43,807
Smith-Parris, Penny Jane, prof, ast teach, $34,680
Smith, A Mark, prof, curators, $100,320
Smith, Aaron Brook, nurse, staff I, $19.37/hr
Smith, Agatha Faith, neurodiagnostic tech (non-reg), $18.35/hr
Smith, Alexander B, media production director I, $41,000
Smith, Alicia Gayle, rec/athletic specialist sr, $25.00/hr
Smith, Allen Lloyd, mts/refrigeration mech, $21.05/hr
Smith, Amanda M, business tech analyst-expert, $62,454
Smith, Amanda Nicole, patient svc rep, $13.06/hr
Smith, Amber Denise, instructor, adjunct, $2,400
Smith, Amy Elizabeth, student support specialist sr, $16.54/hr
Smith, Amy S, ast mgr hospitality services, $47,658
Smith, Andrew J, prof, asoc clincl, $103,000
Smith, Angel Danielle, db programmer analyst-entry, $39,600
Smith, Angelique Choene, nurse, licensed prac, $19.30/hr
Smith, Aquita Da'Neen, patient svc rep, $11.28/hr
Smith, Ariel Dae, nurse, licensed prac, $15.67/hr
Smith, Arthur Brian, db programmer analyst-princpl, $63,280
Smith, Ashlee Paige, sr mgr advancement, $47,543
Smith, Ashley Brie, sterile processing coord, $18.39/hr
Smith, Audrey R, nurse, staff II, $22.63/hr
Smith, Barbara B, museum paraprofessional sr, $19.51/hr
Smith, Becky M, prof, asoc clincl, $92,142
Smith, Belinda Ann, instructor, adjunct, $1,333
Smith, Beverly June, advancement associate II, $18.01/hr
Smith, Bradley Neil, prof, ast adjunct, $125.00/hr
Smith, Brenda Marie, instructor, adjunct, $4,200
Smith, Brendan Kyle, operations support tech II, $15.37/hr

Smith, Brian K, food svc wrkr II, $10.10/hr
Smith, Brian Keith, prof, ast, $74,430
Smith, Brian Q, head coach, $149,350
Smith, Brian W, mts/refrig mech-r, $19.21/hr
Smith, Bridget Kathleen, nurse, licensed prac, $16.45/hr
Smith, Brittany, office support assistant IV, $15.20/hr
Smith, Bruce D, mts/hvac, $22.50/hr
Smith, Bryant Keith, floor maint wkr, $13.84/hr
Smith, Byron L, custodian, $12.94/hr
Smith, Caleb Christian, student recruitment spclst, $14.96/hr
Smith, Carey Dale, mgr regulatory affairs, $97,469
Smith, Carl E, lab techn, persl svc-clin lab, $15.62/hr
Smith, Carol Jean, custodian, $13.23/hr
Smith, Cassandra Elaine, temporary technical, $28.85/hr
Smith, Charisse Laurelle, office support assistant III, $13.23/hr
Smith, Christa Lynn, executive assistant, $19.67/hr
Smith, Christine Ann, prof, ast adjunct, $9,600
Smith, Christopher R, psychologist, $71,580
Smith, Christy L, nurse, staff II, $29.47/hr
Smith, Connie S, circuit action analyst, $18.52/hr
Smith, Corliss J, office support assistant IV, $16.01/hr
Smith, Dale, grounds keeper-mrc, $11.11/hr
Smith, Dale A, csm operations supervisor, $44,669
Smith, Dale A, strat comm associate I, $41,518
Smith, Dan Alan, prof, ast teach, $50,000
Smith, Daniel C, nurse, staff II, $34.18/hr
Smith, Darius Jarod, athletic attd, $13.82/hr
Smith, Deana L, prof, asoc clincl, $74,953
Smith, Deanna J, nurse, staff now plus, $30.00/hr
Smith, Deanna Lee, student recruitment spclst, $16.60/hr
Smith, Deborah, prof, asoc, $74,371
Smith, Deborah L, nurse, staff II, $34.79/hr
Smith, Deborah S, central regstry-data coor sr, $25.93/hr
Smith, Debra L, radiation ther therapist, $34.94/hr
Smith, Delane Brianna, care team assoc-clinical, $12.08/hr
Smith, Dennis David, instructor, adjunct, $6,400
Smith, Dianne, professor, $85,927
Smith, Donna A, neurodiagnostic tech (reg), $22.80/hr
Smith, Donna Gail, nurse, licensed prac, $20.58/hr
Smith, Donna Marie, nurse, staff, $26.68/hr
Smith, Dustin Eric LeRoy, mover, $13.59/hr
Smith, Dustin W, nurse, staff II, $20.95/hr
Smith, Ebony S, business support specialist II, $19.49/hr
Smith, Elaina Grace, office support assistant IV, $15.29/hr
Smith, Elaine M, patient svc rep, $14.88/hr
Smith, Elizabeth L, sftware supprt analyst-princpl, $81,495
Smith, Emily Jo, student support specialist sr, $16.74/hr
Smith, Erica Ann, strat comm consultant, $45,000
Smith, Erin L, cat scan technl (ct), $27.54/hr
Smith, Evan S, instructor, extns, $63,137
Smith, George P, prof, curators, $101,000
Smith, Gregory Hurlin, chief info officer-campus, $148,250
Smith, Gwendelyn M, supv linen, $41,725
Smith, Harriet M, telecom it analyst-expert, $22.47/hr
Smith, Harrison Lee, resp therapist reg, $20.23/hr
Smith, Heather M, livestock spclst, $41,287
Smith, Herman Randolph, custodian, $12.94/hr
Smith, James A, grounds keeper III, $14.39/hr
Smith, James Alan, csm associate III, $23.63/hr
Smith, James Brian, resident physician-2nd yr, $50,810
Smith, James J, prof, ast visiting, $55,000
Smith, James L, managing engineer, $78,997
Smith, James R, floor care techn, $12.70/hr
Smith, Janice Marcy, instructor, clincl, $50,184
Smith, Jeffrey D, prof, asoc, $98,074
Smith, Jennifer Diane, office support assistant sr, $16.24/hr
Smith, Jennifer L, grounds keeper II, $14.39/hr
Smith, Jennifer L, staff nurse sr, $28.86/hr
Smith, Jennifer Leann, pat acct rep, $13.76/hr
Smith, Jennifer Leigh, office support assistant sr, $17.64/hr
Smith, Jessica, office support assistant IV, $16.30/hr
Smith, Joan Peters, csm professional II, $40,435
Smith, John Christopher, csm supervisor, $58,715
Smith, John Hillman, lecturer sr, $27,900
Smith, Jordan R, custodian, $13.23/hr
Smith, Joseph Andrew, steam plant opr I, $17.47/hr
Smith, Joseph D, professor, $163,087
Smith, Joseph L, instructor, adjunct, $4,200
Smith, Joshua T, academic advisor, $35,005

Smith, Karen M, instructor, adjunct, $7,845
Smith, Katharine Vogel, dean, ast, $101,724
Smith, Katherine J, nurse clinician, $65,700
Smith, Kathleen Alice, coor, service, $15.25/hr
Smith, Kathleen Ann, veterinary technician sr, $15.88/hr
Smith, Kathryn C, library info specialist sr, $14.95/hr
Smith, Kathryn Rexene, office support assistant III, $13.00/hr
Smith, Kathy A, educational pgm associate I, $15.49/hr
Smith, Kenneth D, patient svc rep, $13.02/hr
Smith, Kevin K, pharmacist III, $128,835
Smith, Kibby L, academic advisor, $35,901
Smith, Kimberley Kathleen, instructor, adjunct, $10,500
Smith, LaSadie R, custodian lead, $14.03/hr
Smith, Laura Lea, business support specialist sr, $25.51/hr
Smith, Laurence Douglas, professor, $173,519
Smith, Leanne M, supv pat accts, $46,582
Smith, Leeclair Everett, resp therapist reg, $30.30/hr
Smith, Leo Patrick, prof, ast adjunct, $22,000
Smith, Leonard Daryl, prof, ast teach, $81,448
Smith, Linda Katherine, nurse, licensed prac, $18.16/hr
Smith, Lisa Christine, serv line spclst, $74,318
Smith, Lisa M, food svc wrkr I, $9.60/hr
Smith, Lisa M, occl therapist, $69,143
Smith, Lua Julia, business tech analyst-entry, $34,916
Smith, Lucas Michael, grounds keeper, $12.12/hr
Smith, Lyndell S, office support assistant III, $13.00/hr
Smith, Margaret Katherine, bus support specialist II, $20.86/hr
Smith, Margaret Rose, research/lab technician, $10.24/hr
Smith, Marilyn Louise, prof, ast adjunct, $8,004
Smith, Marisa X, police sergeant, $20.04/hr
Smith, Marla J, dir clin ops & dir of nursing, $109,192
Smith, Marlene B, librarian II, $53,261
Smith, Marsha Anne, csm project manager, $79,010
Smith, Martha Ann, nurse, staff II, $39.23/hr
Smith, Martin S, bts carpenter, $20.23/hr
Smith, Marva, custodian, $13.36/hr
Smith, Mary E, office support assistant IV, $16.76/hr
Smith, Mary Ruth, office support assistant III, $16.14/hr
Smith, Matthew C, bts mason/tuckptr, $20.23/hr
Smith, Matthew J, prof, ast, $260,113
Smith, Matthew S, waiter/waitress, $13.22/hr
Smith, Megan Elizabeth, office support assistant III, $14.40/hr
Smith, Meredith Christian, head coach, $45,986
Smith, Michael Fielding, professor, $184,991
Smith, Micheal Stanley, instructor, adjunct, $18,000
Smith, Michele Marano, strat comm consultant, $51,506
Smith, Michele R, business support specialist II, $20.70/hr
Smith, Michele Renee, food svc wrkr II, $11.07/hr
Smith, Michelle L, business ops associate sr, $47,453
Smith, Michelle Lynn, educational prgm coor sr, $59,752
Smith, Mitchel Robert Lee, event assistant I, $8.50/hr
Smith, Nancy Ann, office support assistant IV, $16.73/hr
Smith, Niesha Theresa, supv outpatient svcs, $46,359
Smith, Nina Marie, custodian, $10.39/hr
Smith, Pamela, instructor, clincl, $54,649
Smith, Pamela, instructor, adjunct, $7,500
Smith, Pamela Ann, educational pgm associate I, $15.37/hr
Smith, Pamela Jeanette, prof, asoc, $96,041
Smith, Pamela S, nurse, staff II, $34.18/hr
Smith, Patricia A, practice manager, $66,279
Smith, Patricia K, business support specialist II, $18.36/hr
Smith, Patrick E, mgr III business admin, $68,340
Smith, Paul D, lecturer, $10,000
Smith, Paula L, manager II, $84,170
Smith, Paulette D, service rep III, $13.57/hr
Smith, Quinten Eugene, office support assistant IV, $13.65/hr
Smith, Rachel M, fin and acctg analyst sr, $60,270
Smith, Randall Darby, prof, profl practice, $129,952
Smith, Randi, custodian, $10.00/hr
Smith, Raymond L, bts painter, $20.23/hr
Smith, Rebecca, temporary professional, $9.00/hr
Smith, Rebecca Leann, educational pgm associate I, $14.23/hr
Smith, Rebecca Sue, event assistant I, $9.50/hr
Smith, Regina Kay, telecomm opr-h, $11.42/hr
Smith, Renae A, mgr II business admin, $57,651
Smith, Retha Carol, reimbursement ast-cert, $18.69/hr
Smith, Robert E, bts painter, $21.71/hr
Smith, Robert Harold, construction manager II, $30.00/hr
Smith, Robert R, physician ast, $123,714

Smith, Robert S, mts/electrician, $25.35/hr
Smith, Rodney D, asoc dir student support svcs, $67,626
Smith, Roma L, nurse, licensed prac sr, $20.45/hr
Smith, Rosalee Darlene, custodian, $10.00/hr
Smith, Ryan James, user interfce designer-entry, $42,000
Smith, Samantha C, temporary professional, $11.30/hr
Smith, Samantha Christine, office support assistant III, $11.92/hr
Smith, Sandra A, student support specialist I, $16.07/hr
Smith, Sarah Catherine, physical therapist, $35.00/hr
Smith, Sarah E, program/project supprt coor I, $20.19/hr
Smith, Savannah, care team assoc-clinical, $11.10/hr
Smith, Savannah Erin, veterinary technician, $14.00/hr
Smith, Sharon K, executive assistant sr, $55,968
Smith, Sharon R, student support specialist I, $12.98/hr
Smith, Shaun Aaron, event assistant I, $7.75/hr
Smith, Stephanie Kay, coor, reimbursement, $62,083
Smith, Steven Ray, user support analyst-spclst, $20.71/hr
Smith, Susan Renee, 4-h youth devlmnt educr, $35,894
Smith, Teresa Ann, food svc wrkr I, $9.98/hr
Smith, Terry, bts locksmith, $21.71/hr
Smith, Tisha Renee, nurse, staff II, $24.25/hr
Smith, Tracy Harold, mts/electrician, $21.05/hr
Smith, Tracy Renee, patient svc rep, $14.23/hr
Smith, Tracy Suzanne, instructor, adjunct, $6,300
Smith, Valerie Denae, nurse, staff I, $19.00/hr
Smith, Victoria Rose, office support assistant I, $9.05/hr
Smith, William B, environmental health prof II, $50,626
Smith, William Dwane, resp care clinical coor, $28.81/hr
Smith, Willie B, mech, bldg maint, $19.64/hr
Smithee, James David, bldg cntrl sys tech II, $22.49/hr
Smither, Erin M, manuscript specialist, $16,910
Smithmier Weeks, Mary L, office support assistant IV, $18.70/hr
Smitka, Linda A, strat comm associate II, $43,888
Smocks, Teresa M, business support specialist II, $16.05/hr
Smolanovich, Andrea L, strat comm associate I, $38,642
Smolderen, Kim, prof, ast, $85,000
Smolinski, Lauren Nicole, care team assoc-clinical, $11.10/hr
Smoot, Holly L, business support analyst sr, $22.25/hr
Smothers, Linda Sue, office support assistant IV, $16.01/hr
Smothers, Scotty L, resrch asoc, $61,440
Smotherson, Brittany N, mgr student support svcs, $31,305
Smyser, Mary E, asoc dir program/project ops, $51,587
Smythe, Helen Olivia, speech/lang pathologist, $35.00/hr
Snapp, Gerald E, state spclst, asoc, $61,345
Sneed, Dee Ann, office support assistant IV, $16.50/hr
Sneed, Lesley Haynes, prof, asoc, $90,171
Snell, James, prof, asoc, $93,715
Snell, June L, library info specialist, $14.91/hr
Snellen, Deborah Sue, dir program/project operations, $78,000
Snellen, Patricia Louise, cytotechnologist reg, $34.94/hr
Snellen, Troy V, payroll/cntrl proc spclst, $43,613
Snelson, Roy E, mts/plumber, $21.91/hr
Snelson, Vicky K, office support assistant IV, $15.21/hr
Snethen, Darcey Delynn, student support specialist I, $17.12/hr
Snider, Allen J, administrative consultant sr, $29,379
Snider, Jennifer Anne, nurse, staff I, $19.00/hr
Snider, Karrie Anne, resrch ast sr, $52,000
Snider, Kelly, mental health professional, $36,000
Snider, Laci Beth, nurse, licensed prac, $14.76/hr
Snipes, John David, custodian, $12.94/hr
Snitzer, Lauren A, resident physician-3rd yr, $53,763
Snoderly-Foster, Lisa Jo, lecturer, $15,000
Snodgrass, Angela Renea, custodian, $10.94/hr
Snodgrass, Brenda A, serv line spclst, $83,500
Snodgrass, Kelly L, care team assoc-clinical, $11.10/hr
Snodgrass, Patricia Louise, housing&envirn design spclst, $62,473
Snodgrass, Sarah Jean, office support assistant III, $11.47/hr
Snook, Amy Diane, office support assistant IV, $13.63/hr
Snow, Blaine, human resources specialist III, $46,318
Snow, Donald B, prof, asoc teach, $75,177
Snow, Eric David, physical therapist, $68,135
Snow, Joseph George, operations support tech I, $10.78/hr
Snow, LeAnne M, student support specialist I, $15.31/hr
Snow, Michelle Lee, nurse, staff II, $27.11/hr
Snow, Sandra Jean, office support assistant II, $10.34/hr
Snow, Sarah Nicole, office support assistant III, $12.88/hr
Snow, Stacy A, dir program/project operations, $71,497
Snow, William E, support systems admin-entry, $39,600
Snowden, Kimberly Elizabeth, surgical technl certified, $16.83/hr

Snyder-Rivas, Linley Anne, grader, $100.00/hr
Snyder, Alexander George, retail sales associate sr, $15.47/hr
Snyder, Andrew Michael, csm operations supervisor, $39,749
Snyder, Charles T, resident physician-4th yr, $55,804
Snyder, Devin Ditrolio, office support assistant III, $15.15/hr
Snyder, Jack E, lecturer, $18,000
Snyder, Jay Andrew, athletic attd, $15.20/hr
Snyder, Paula M, lecturer, $50,379
Snyder, Samuel R, student recruitment spclst, $16.85/hr
Snyder, Sharlene, business support specialist II, $18.71/hr
Sobba, Mary, extns professional, asoc, $67,568
Sobczak, Amanda Marie, pharmacy tech, $10.85/hr
Sobieck, Laura Jo, mgr student support svcs, $32,913
Sobule, Robert Marvin, emrg med techn, $12.88/hr
Socarides, Alexandra A, prof, asoc, $71,031
Socha, Matthew, resrch scientist/academic, $48,250
Soder, Aidan Leigh, prof, asoc, $56,346
Soest, Michele J, instructor, clincl, $84,000
Soey, Violet Darlean, nurse, staff per diem, $35.00/hr
Sohail, Umair, fellow, post doc clncl-yr2, $58,083
Sohal, Amanbir Singh, resident physician-2nd yr, $52,007
Sohal, Harjyot Singh, prof, asoc clincl dept, $265,140
Sohl, David Walter, program/project supprt coor II, $56,100
Sohl, Kristin Amanda Thomas, prof, asoc clincl dept, $150,537
Soisson, Leo, lecturer, $41,212
Sokoff, Michael Boyd, dir I, csm operations, $92,560
Sokolaski, Michael R, event assistant I, $7.65/hr
Solbrekken, Gary L, prof, asoc teach, $82,430
Solbrekken, Yvonne E, student service coor sr, $48,873
Soldan, Jill Marie, student support specialist II, $15.40/hr
Solis, Maryah Ann-Monique, event assistant I, $7.55/hr
Solomon, Ann Ryan, dir II advancement, $85,000
Solomon, Cameron Bernard, instructor, adjunct, $12,339
Solomon, John Bogy, mgr II business admin, $70,357
Solomon, Julie Kay, research/lab technician sr, $14.72/hr
Solomon, Ramon, mts/hvac, $24.13/hr
Solomon, Travis Edward, prof, teach, $107,625
Solomon, Val Rae A, accountant sr, $40,392
Solose, Jane M, professor, $74,160
Solovic-Roeder, Nancy J, lecturer, $35,368
Someili, Ali Mohammed A, resident physician-1st yr, $49,025
Somerville, Kristine A, strat comm associate I, $51,386
Sommer, Andrew James, mgr II business admin, $53,457
Sommer, Laurel E, prof, ast clincl, $39,984
Sommer, Mary A, office support assistant III, $11.97/hr
Sommer, Richard C, instructor, adjunct, $36,771
Sommerfeld-Sager, Jennifer Michelle, research/lab tech sr, $14.41/hr
Sommerfeldt, Corinna Jo, phlebotomist, $14.88/hr
Sommerjones, Judith Jean, office support assistant IV, $14.82/hr
Sommers, Randall J, lecturer, $33,104
Sommers, Whitney Leigh, office support assistant IV, $14.00/hr
Sommerville, Amanda Christine, res physician-2nd yr, $52,610
Sommerville, Ashley K, system support analyst-expert, $25.47/hr
Sommerville, Keith K, support systems admin-spclst, $46,512
Sommi, Roger W Jr, dean, asoc, $171,500
Sonah, Humira, fellow, post doctoral, $42,230
Sonderman, Barbara S, csm operations coordinator, $19.53/hr
Song, Hee Gyong, instructor, adjunct, $24,975
Song, Jingzhi, nurse, staff II, $31.58/hr
Song, Kim H, prof, asoc, $65,557
Song, Li, resrch asoc, $44,500
Song, Lihui, fellow, post doctoral, $24,000
Song, Lisa Zhao, prof, asoc, $152,228
Song, Michael, professor, $398,894
Song, Nianfu, resrch asoc, $45,895
Song, Qisheng, professor, $98,739
Song, Sejun, prof, asoc, $83,750
Song, Zhenwei, fellow, post doctoral, $35,000
Sonnenberg, Douglas Charles, temporary technical, $25.00/hr
Sontag, Harold Dean, csm operations supervisor, $26.20/hr
Sooter, Chad L, nurse, staff now III, $30.00/hr
Sopko, Matthew Douglas, instructor, adjunct, $21,000
Sorensen, Robert Lanford, emeritus, $27,000
Sorenson, Lily Ann, instructor, visiting, $48,000
Sorg, Shanna Kay, educational pgm associate I, $13.45/hr
Soria Lopez, Maria Del Mar, prof, ast, $57,126
Soria, Victor M, grader, $100.00/hr
Sorley, David Cole, prof, ast clincl dept, $200,000
Sorrell, Betty J, care team assoc-clinical, $14.32/hr

Sorrell, Deann, resp therapist reg, $26.85/hr
Sorrick, Jordan Wesley, nurse, staff II, $20.54/hr
Sorurbakhsh, Laila Fatemah, prof, ast visiting, $40,000
Sosa, Kayla Marais, grader, $6,400
Sossamon, Jefferson Dewey, strat comm associate I, $44,187
Soth McNett, Angela M, psychologist, $73,330
Sotir, Kelly Leanne, care team assoc-clinical, $11.10/hr
Sotiriou-Leventis, Chariklia, professor, $101,055
Soto, Christina M, pharmacy tech, $12.51/hr
Soucie, Kylee Rooney, business support specialist II, $15.11/hr
Soucie, Marilyn, program/project supprt coor I, $55,732
Souder, Kenneth Ray, nurse, staff stat, $24.37/hr
Souleymane Saley, Ali, sterile processing trainee, $12.20/hr
Souliere Staples, Jill E, office support assistant II, $12.50/hr
Soulli, Beth Kathleen, resident physician-4th yr, $54,425
Sousley, James O, mts/hvac lead, $25.35/hr
Southard, Audrey Kate, resident physician-2nd yr, $52,007
Souther, Matthew Edward, prof, ast, $180,000
Southerland, Joseph Ammon, academic advisor, $41,636
Southworth, Sarah Song, prof, ast, $63,000
Souza, Raquel Candida, nurse, staff I, $19.00/hr
Sovanski, Kari E, pat acct rep, $13.42/hr
Sowa, Grzegorz, prof, asoc, $98,548
Sowers, Stephen Edward III, high school student, $7.75/hr
Sowers, Jim Russell, professor, $226,842
Sowers, Linda Franz, instructor, $49,452
Spade, David A, prof, ast, $67,000
Spaeder, Nancy J, instructor, adjunct, $14,742
Spaeth, Amber Danielle, office support assistant IV, $15.01/hr
Spain, Jermaine Contrelle, custodian, $10.73/hr
Spain, Jimmy N, v provost, $182,492
Spaits, Gerald K, instructor, adjunct, $8,400
Spalding, Jonalyn Denise, child dev assistant, $8.08/hr
Spalding, Shawn W, police sergeant, $26.18/hr
Spalitto, Joseph P, prof, ast adjunct, $125.00/hr
Spang, Cheryl A, mgr III business admin, $74,751
Spano, Stacy Marie, office support assistant IV, $15.40/hr
Spanton, Derek B, event assistant I, $8.50/hr
Spare, Lucy M, office support assistant I, $10.00/hr
Sparkman-Barnes, Lynette Sheila, asoc dir student sup svcs, $61,000
Sparks, Louella Kay, 4-h spclst, $50,419
Sparks, Michael James, custodian, $10.69/hr
Sparlin, Don M, emeritus, $26,526
Spartan, Vanessa, instructor, adjunct, $23,004
Spate Smith, Laurie Elizabeth, instructor, adjunct, $4,800
Spate, Lee D, research specialist sr, $40,392
Spate, Vickie L, research lab manager, $41,957
Spates, Gloria Jean, custodian, $13.23/hr
Spaulding, Susan, service rep III, $15.77/hr
Spaur, Heather Sue, med records transcript, $14.29/hr
Speak, Adam Benjamin, instructor, adjunct, $9,000
Spear, David G, prof, ast adjunct, $36,809
Spears, Michael P, system support analyst-spcclst, $19.62/hr
Speck, Paul S Sr, prof, asoc, $100,826
Speck, Angela Karen, professor, $82,945
Speck, Angelique Denise, child dev assistant, $11.00/hr
Specker, Wennifer Irene, nurse, licensed prac, $17.33/hr
Speckhals, Laura Jean, occl therapist, $62,630
Speckhart, Daulton William, temporary technical, $8.30/hr
Speckman, Paul L, professor, $126,112
Speicher, Brian L, lecturer, $53,800
Speight, Sara Lynn, nurse, staff II, $24.27/hr
Spell, Dawn Marie, instructor, adjunct, $10,200
Spellman, Douglas L, csm project manager, $46.76/hr
Spellman, Kathryn Elizabeth, event assistant I, $7.55/hr
Spence, Ashley Yvonne, social worker, $45,080
Spence, Marcia L, professor, $63,581
Spence, Richard L, custodian, $12.94/hr
Spence, Sarah Ann, resrch asoc, $26,500
Spencer-Carver, Nancy Elaine, prof, asoc clincl, $73,397
Spencer-Morris, Laura Reese, media production dir I, $43,853
Spencer, Bailey Elizabeth, nurse, staff I, $19.00/hr
Spencer, Barbara Leeann, human resources assistant, $12.99/hr
Spencer, Bette L, pat acct rep, $15.66/hr
Spencer, Cheryl, supv, acute care nursing rnwp, $38.72/hr
Spencer, Christine R, lecturer, $61,800
Spencer, Hallie Elizabeth, editor II, $43,000
Spencer, Jeffrey W, system support analyst-expert, $26.23/hr
Spencer, John C, research consultant II, $42,146

Spencer, Mindy Marie, supv pat admiss, $42,228
Spencer, Paulette, prof, adjunct, $125.00/hr
Spencer, Stephanie Irene, mental health tech, $14.71/hr
Spene, Jennifer Louise, executive assistant, $19.71/hr
Spenner, Anne Hartung, vice chancellor, $177,472
Sperber, Jonathan, prof, curators, $124,893
Sperry, Kimberly Ann, nurse, staff II, $20.95/hr
Sperry, Morgan Leigh, prof, asoc clincl, $97,000
Spertus, John, professor, $110,000
Spielman, Susan Lynn, occl therapist, $53,389
Spiers, Donald E, professor, $102,184
Spiers, Margaret Jean, human resources manager sr, $66,650
Spies, Janet Alice, health records techn II, $12.21/hr
Spiess, Gretchen Elizabeth, temporary technical, $21.75/hr
Spilling, Christopher, professor, $116,343
Spindler, Christa D, educational pgm associate I, $14.13/hr
Spingola, Marc, prof, asoc teach, $64,700
Spiroff, Louise J, teaching ast, $13.00/hr
Spitzmiller, Gayle Y, office support assistant IV, $15.37/hr
Spollen, Linda Kay, emeritus, $56,794
Spollen, William George, programmer analyst-expert, $68,979
Sponamore, Gaye L, radiologic techl, $21.37/hr
Sponholtz, Scott Michael, sr ast dir studnt supprt svcs, $53,448
Spotswood, Julie Jolene, nurse, licensed prac, $21.07/hr
Spradley, Kyle J, strat comm associate I, $36,720
Sprague, Connie S, office support assistant III, $13.29/hr
Sprague, Debra J, program/project supprt coor II, $52,814
Sprick, David M, instructor, adjunct, $21,000
Springer, Gordon Kent, prof, asoc, $108,181
Springer, Peggie Ann, fin and acctg manager, $74,848
Sproat, Kori Lindsey, educational pgm assistant, $9.27/hr
Sprochi, Amanda K, librarian III, $49,400
Sprous, Karen Sue, lecturer, $25,710
Sprouse, Benjamin Allen, electronics technician III, $15.15/hr
Sprouse, Joanne M, office support assistant IV, $17.68/hr
Sprouse, Nina G, grader, $52
Spry, Dale L, serv coor clinics supp bldgs, $58,344
Spry, Dawn Louise, office support assistant IV, $15.00/hr
Spry, Dennis L, custodian, $12.94/hr
Spry, John Jeremy, powr plnt maint spclst III wld, $25.85/hr
Spry, Joshua, utility dist wrkr IV, $23.75/hr
Spry, Kala L, office support assistant IV, $14.02/hr
Spry, Tilford, supv engineering, $53,965
Spurgeon, Angela N, resident physician-6th yr, $60,415
Spurgin, Matthew W, clerk, operating room supply, $13.95/hr
Spurling, Carmen M, office support assistant IV, $16.66/hr
Spurling, Heather Suzanne, office support assistant III, $14.49/hr
Spurling, Shannon, network engineer-princpl, $73,242
Spurling, Teresa A, coor, service, $18.74/hr
Spurlock, David G, lecturer, $63,788
Squire, Peverill, professor, $177,496
Squires-Weber, Sara Jane, teaching ast, $13.00/hr
Squires, Jody J, dir program/project operations, $75,750
Squires, Julie Lynn, system support analyst-expert, $27.35/hr
Squires, Steven Wayne, distribution techn-mtls mgmt, $14.76/hr
Sredl, Darlene Rita, prof, teach, $74,238
Sreedharan, Vikram, fellow, post doctoral, $42,000
Srinivas, Shubra, resident physician-2nd yr, $52,610
Srinivasan, Hema, professor, $103,220
Sriram, Jayanthi Sanjeevi, fellow, post doctoral, $30,000
Srivastava, Rashmi, prof, asoc clincl dept, $161,823
St John, Alan A, sr dir program/project ops, $98,368
St Omer, Andrea R, pharm bus spclst - 340 b progm, $23.13/hr
St. John, Jane Ann, resrch asoc, $40,856
Staab, Ara Aidin, educational pgm associate I, $13.28/hr
Staab, Dianna S, executive assistant, $21.21/hr
Staab, Sherrlynn Ann, nurse, staff II, $45.00/hr
Staab, Sherrlynn Ann, proj mgr, appeals, $88,269
Staab, Sherrlynn Ann, pat admiss advisor, $30.56/hr
Stacey, Gary, prof, curators, $195,162
Stacey, Minviluz, resrch scientist/academic sr, $53,045
Stack, Jeffrey Francis, teaching ast, $13.00/hr
Stack, Joan E, research consultant, $54,220
Stackhouse, Robert Scott, prof, ast teach, $51,900
Stacy, James M Jr, editor sr, $46,512
Stacy, Carl Christopher, prof, ast clincl dept, $177,576
Stacy, Traci Jo, office support assistant IV, $14.00/hr
Stafford, Amanda Susanne, instructional designer-spclst, $50,400
Stafford, Rebecca Lea, business support specialist II, $22.11/hr

Stafford, Shauna Danielle, pat acct rep, $13.49/hr
Stafford, Stephanie S, telecom it analyst-speclst, $19.23/hr
Stageman, Lisa, student service coor I, $39,601
Stahl, Ted F, human resources specialist sr, $55,755
Stahlheber, Seth William, resrch anlyst, $32,400
Stahlman, Adam P, custodian, $13.21/hr
Stahlschmidt, Christine A, nurse, staff II rnwp, $34.42/hr
Stahnke, Amanda Michele, prof, ast clincl, $98,000
Stahr, Jason A, mgr event management, $74,298
Staiculescu, Ioana Claudia, research specialist I, $44,969
Staiger, Barbara Ann, dir III business admin, $95,771
Staley, Lynn M, prof, asoc teach, $40,809
Staley, Robert Eric, prof, adjunct, $36,000
Stallis, Victoria Renee, nurse, staff II, $22.24/hr
Stallmann, Judith I, professor, $129,048
Stam, Antonie, professor, $202,644
Stamate, Steven Lee, research/lab technician sr, $13.03/hr
Stambaugh, Michael C, prof, ast resrch, $65,426
Stammer, Andrew Wayne, nurse, staff II, $21.37/hr
Stamper, Christine, temporary clerical, $10.00/hr
Stamper, Tia Leanne, service rep III, $12.30/hr
Stampp, Erin Lind Hood, ast dir student support svcs, $46,950
Stamps, David Keith, prof, asoc adjunct, $18,000
Stamps, William T, research/lab technician, $12.00/hr
Stancel, Nancy Dietz, librarian IV, $83,900
Standifer, Walter S, instructor, clincl, $67,248
Stanek, Eldon Keith, emeritus, $46,000
Stanek, Jeremy L, resident physician-2nd yr, $52,007
Stanek, Megan Marjorie, extension asoc, $32,640
Staner, Derek Ross, prof, ast clincl dept, $255,000
Stanfield, Stanley P, custodian, $11.41/hr
Stanger, Albert Gerard, prof, ast teach, $48,593
Stanger, Kimberly K T, office support assistant IV, $18.53/hr
Stanis, Gregory J, dir I, human resources, $90,000
Stanley, Jeanne Elaine, prof, ast, $54,234
Stanley, Matthew D, system administrator-expert, $76,493
Stanley, Ronald Joe, prof, asoc, $91,470
Stanley, Sarah Margaret, prof, ast, $103,590
Stanley, Susan Nicole, strat comm associate II, $48,075
Stanley, Trisha Lee, grader, $52
Stannard, James Patrick, professor, $656,625
Stannard, Rebecca Faith Emiko, temporary clerical, $8.00/hr
Stansbeary, Sarah L, mngd care reimbursmt spclst, $60,501
Stansfield, John J, prof, asoc teach, $69,857
Stanton, Anne R, prof, asoc, $67,832
Stanton, Laura A, instructor, adjunct, $15,000
Stanton, Richard M, asoc dir program/project ops, $56,160
Stanton, Stephen, library info specialist sr, $14.95/hr
Staples, Costella D, office support assistant II, $14.00/hr
Stapleton, Erin Lea, serv line spclst, $67,810
Stapleton, Lynn Ellen, supv, food svc II-h, $38,606
Stapleton, Paula J, patient svc rep, $12.76/hr
Starbuck, Lacie Lee, nurse, staff per diem, $35.00/hr
Starbuck, Matthew Zane, animal caretaker-equine/food, $10.91/hr
Stark, Amy Elizabeth, nurse, staff II, $23.47/hr
Stark, Clara Luz, event assistant I, $8.00/hr
Stark, Danny A, resrch scientist/academic, $47,000
Stark, Daryn L, emrg med techn paramedic, $18.76/hr
Stark, Debra Sue, med techl reg, $29.43/hr
Stark, Moselle Marie, resident physician-2nd yr, $52,007
Stark, Myrna Lorraine, educational pgm associate I, $14.68/hr
Stark, Sarah Louise, emrg med techn paramedic, $19.22/hr
Starke, Kathy Lynn, nurse, staff II, $34.05/hr
Starke, Robert Edwin, nurse, staff now III, $30.00/hr
Starkey, Danielle Nicole, educational prgm coor sr, $56,500
Starkey, James P, carpenter, $21.87/hr
Starkey, Melvin, mech trades spclst (mts), $22.42/hr
Starks, Tonika R, human resources specialist I, $17.00/hr
Starr, Julie Ann, nurse, advanced practice, $80,197
Starr, Steven, instructor, clincl, $54,813
Stastny, Kenneth James, mgr finl plng & decision spt, $107,100
Staten, Brittany, child dev teacher sr, $25,000
Staudenmyer, Danielle Marie, dietitian, clincl, $47,894
Stauder, Rose M, pharmacist II, $119,304
Stavropoulos, Pericles, prof, asoc, $84,404
Stayton, Christopher M, library information assistant, $11.30/hr
Stealey, Josephine, professor, $81,207
Stearman, Melinda Joy, nurse, staff now III, $30.00/hr
Stebbins, Janet Marie, office support assistant III, $13.72/hr

Steck, Lara Noelle, physician ast, $84,115
Steckel, Dave A, asoc coach, $600,000
Steckmest, Robert, scientific photographer, $21.36/hr
Steding, Arianne, nurse, staff II rnwp, $21.37/hr
Stedman, Timothy Jon, asoc athletic director, $110,000
Steeby, Shaun Fay, fellow, post doc clncl-yr3, $60,415
Steeds, Craig Marshall, resident physician-5th yr, $56,120
Steel, Nikki Leigh, custodian, $10.94/hr
Steele, Beth A, instructor, adjunct, $13,500
Steele, Brian Douglas, student recruitment spclst sr, $23.07/hr
Steele, Megan Joy, resrch ast, $35,000
Steele, Nancy S, resrch asoc, $39,750
Steele, Precious Lashee, food svc wrkr I, $9.98/hr
Steele, Rachael Bode, dir II advancement, $89,355
Steele, Stacy Renee, nurse, staff II, $29.31/hr
Steele, Stephanie Marie, radiologic techl, $26.47/hr
Steelman, Rex Ned Jr, police officer, $17.93/hr
Steelman, Andrew James, nurse, staff I, $19.67/hr
Steelman, Sarah Hearne, prof, ast teach, $59,000
Steen, Brian C, emrg med techn paramedic, $17.74/hr
Steenbergen, Brendon G, dir II advancement, $86,700
Steenhusen, Kirk D, programmer analyst-speclst, $48,351
Steere, Leonard Andrew, network engineer-princpl, $75,234
Steevens, Barry Jerome, extension asoc, $40.00/hr
Steffen, Ann, prof, asoc, $87,374
Steffen, Mark Charles, chaplain, $49,387
Steffens, Brian L, administrative consultant II, $92,870
Steffens, Martha M, prof, profl practice, $119,119
Steffes, Terri Ann, asoc dir program/project ops, $50,000
Stegall, Dennis Glen, event assistant I, $10.00/hr
Steger, Karen E, office support assistant III, $12.41/hr
Stegmaier, Mary Ann, prof, ast, $75,000
Stegner, Daniel K, police sergeant, $20.85/hr
Stegner, Kenneth Gene, office support assistant II, $13.15/hr
Steigerwalt, Kristy Estelle, librarian II, $47,356
Steigman, Stephen, media production director I, $55,000
Stein, Linda, office support assistant IV, $19.28/hr
Stein, Sydney Renee, hospital lab tech, $12.46/hr
Stein, Thomas, prof, asoc, $60,536
Steinacker, Stephen Alan, system administrator-princpl, $63,228
Steinbach, Derek Evan, rec/athletic specialist, $13.23/hr
Steinbach, Marie Siobhan, mgr event services, $40,417
Steineman, JoAnne Christine, construction manager I, $58,250
Steiner, Judith Ann, research/lab technician ar, $15.00/hr
Steinhaus, Charles L, network engineer-princpl, $69,877
Steinhoff, Douglas Charles, instructor, $43,867
Steiniger, Mindy Marie, prof, ast, $68,150
Steinley, Douglas Lee, professor, $114,742
Steinmeier, Shannee Soo, program/project supprt coor II, $46,350
Steinmetz, Donna G, dir I, advancement, $78,142
Steinmetz, Jordan Cary, operations support tech I, $10.24/hr
Steinmetz, Pamela Lavonne, mgr student support svcs, $50,944
Steinwachs, Marie E, asoc dir program/project ops, $53,917
Steitz, Kirstin, office support assistant III, $12.57/hr
Stella, Salvatore Lucia, prof, ast, $88,868
Stellwagen, Carolyn Lee, retail sales assistant, $9.15/hr
Stelzer, Doug B, nurse anesthetist, $147,900
Stelzer, Henry Ellis, prof, asoc, $99,778
Stem, Jennifer Chase, occl therapist, $50,128
Stemmle, Jonathan T, prof, ast/profl pract, $66,506
Stemmons, Carolyn Eubanks, business ops associate II, $46,224
Stephan, Christina Lynn, asoc dir program/project ops, $60,000
Stephan, Lorene Lucille, prof, ast clincl, $77,500
Stephan, Shelby Lynn, nurse, licensed prac, $15.67/hr
Stephanchick, Shauna Lynn, prog/project supprt coor I, $37,500
Stephen, Mathew Lawrence, programmer analyst-speclst, $48,358
Stephen, Norma Virginia, finl counselor(eligibility), $15.61/hr
Stephens, Christopher A, temporary technical, $11.00/hr
Stephens, Cynthia Stotler, instructor, clincl, $25,000
Stephens, Donald, bts carpenter, $21.71/hr
Stephens, Kelly Ann, prof, ast clincl, $66,138
Stephens, Kristina M, nurse, licensed prac, $17.92/hr
Stephens, Lawrence R, temporary crafts service, $7.50/hr
Stephens, Mary Beth, nurse clinician, $67,855
Stephens, Pamela Ann, custodian, $10.94/hr
Stephens, Thomas M, prgm director, ast, $53,101
Stephens, Tom Ray, specialist, $43,708
Stephens, Vivian M, patient svc rep, $13.74/hr
Stephenson, Gloria Edd, account executive, $64,000

Stephenson, Morgan Beth, temporary clerical, $8.35/hr
Stephenson, Paul Jason, bts plasterer, $21.71/hr
Stephenson, Richard Wesley, chancellors prof, $40,759
Sterling, Antionette Glenda, program/proj supprt coor I, $42,623
Sterling, Eboni L, office support assistant III, $12.51/hr
Sterling, James, prof, profl practice, $118,320
Sterling, Kip Michael David Fritz, specialist, $10.00/hr
Sterling, Tammie L, custodian, $11.41/hr
Stern, Reuben Joseph, editor sr, $71,251
Sternadori, Richard Domintc, prog/proj supprt coor I, $42,517
Sternberg, Patricia M, academic advisor, $39,355
Sterne-Jackson, Tyler Lee, high school student, $7.50/hr
Sternecker, Aaron D, event assistant I, $7.55/hr
Stetzel, Eric C, tab techn III, $21.05/hr
Steuber, Carrie Leanne, mgr csm operations, $61,676
Stevens, Angela Lee, nurse, staff II wkend II, $27.83/hr
Stevens, Benjamin Robert, resident physician-1st yr, $50,219
Stevens, Cheryl Ann, office support assistant IV, $15.70/hr
Stevens, Christina Rena, office support assistant IV, $15.13/hr
Stevens, Crystal Shenell, custodian, $10.19/hr
Stevens, David J, business support specialist II, $17.43/hr
Stevens, Elfontay Deantray O, food svc wrkr I, $9.60/hr
Stevens, Joseph E, bindery opr II, $17.78/hr
Stevens, Liesl Schoengarth, physical therapist, $35.00/hr
Stevens, Lisa M, account executive, $6,000
Stevens, Lishia Jo, communications coordinator sr, $16.54/hr
Stevens, Peter F, founders professor, $30,584
Stevens, Tanisha Nicole, asoc dir program/project ops, $63,663
Stevens, Valerie E, student service coor sr, $48,985
Stevens, William Eugene, prof, extns, $112,506
Stevenson, Brittney Lynn, occl therapist, $57,925
Stevenson, Craig A, sr mgr external relations, $63,024
Stevenson, Cynthia Denise, bus support specialist II, $15.25/hr
Stevenson, Harry Band, nurse practitioner, $89,124
Stevenson, Julie W, program/project supprt coor I, $50,000
Stevenson, Patricia L, business support specialist II, $18.83/hr
Stever, Scott William, dir I, business admin, $123,194
Stevermer, James J, prof, clinical dept, $168,300
Stevinson, Cynthia A, temporary professional, $15.00/hr
Steward, Donna Kay, mgr volunteer & aux svcs, $73,798
Steward, Kevin R, maintenance supervisor, $51,312
Steward, Linda L, temporary professional, $11.30/hr
Steward, Nathaniel Issac, food svc wrkr II, $10.10/hr
Steward, Shiral D, health records techn II, $14.88/hr
Stewart, Rodney Dean Jr, police officer, $19.95/hr
Stewart Towns, Stephanie Lyn, bus support spec II, $15.85/hr
Stewart, Angela Kay, business support specialist sr, $22.06/hr
Stewart, Angela Ruth, prof, asoc clincl dept, $268,757
Stewart, Beverly Jean, asoc dir program/project ops, $82,896
Stewart, George, professor, $196,184
Stewart, James Edward, custodian, $12.72/hr
Stewart, Jason, forensic techn, $21.85/hr
Stewart, Jennifer Lynn, phys therapy ast, $19.92/hr
Stewart, John Andrew, lecturer, $15,000
Stewart, Kristine I, med techl reg, $30.36/hr
Stewart, Leanne, program/project supprt coor I, $47,736
Stewart, Mark Alan, sr dir program/project ops, $97,370
Stewart, Patricia W, administrative consultant II, $30,300
Stewart, Robert J, prof, ast resrch, $67,200
Stich, Roger William, professor, $117,564
Sticher, Kayln Lee, rec/athletic specialist sr, $39,600
Stichnote, Lynn K, dir II student support svcs, $96,254
Stichter, Janine Peck, professor, $124,579
Stickles, Sean Patrick, prof, ast clincl dept, $305,000
Stickney, Constance M, sr manager it, $80,997
Stidmon, LaJuana Jean, academic coor, $2,400
Stiefermann, Daniel, clinical nursing supvsr, $77,251
Stienbarger, Amber Marie, bus support specialist II, $16.82/hr
Stiers, Dan L, mts/pipefitter, $22.49/hr
Stiers, Julaine, physician, stu hlth, $114,564
Stifter, Daniel, instructor, adjunct, $10,500
Stilen, Patricia L, prgm director, $79,328
Still, Carol Denise, business support specialist II, $18.74/hr
Still, Lori Ann, nurse, staff now III, $30.00/hr
Stillwell, Elizabeth Erin, research specialist I, $29,545
Stillwell, Mark A, administrative consultant sr, $116,363
Stine, Keith, professor, $72,735
Stinson, Andrew Williams, instructor, adjunct, $9,000
Stinson, Melanie Jeanne, coor, service, $15.10/hr

Stiritz, Mary J, communications coordinator sr, $25.39/hr
Stites, Marcy E, instructor, adjunct, $24,975
Stites, Shannon R, office support assistant IV, $15.13/hr
Stivers, Jordan Leigh, nurse, staff II, $20.95/hr
Stoaks, Mary M, business support specialist II, $16.12/hr
Stober, Clintin P, prof, ast, $72,735
Stock, Jodee Marie, circuit action analyst, $16.79/hr
Stock, Leslie Marie, teaching ast, $13.00/hr
Stock, Phyllis A, office support assistant IV, $15.65/hr
Stockard, Jami Lynn, office support assistant IV, $14.00/hr
Stockard, Kevin A, fellow, post doctoral, $45,432
Stockard, Vivian Yates, patient svc rep, $13.24/hr
Stockert, Elliott D, bts carpenter, $23.55/hr
Stockett, Nancy L, office support assistant II, $12.05/hr
Stockhorst, Lisa Marie, office support assistant IV, $13.00/hr
Stockhorst, Lucas B, grounds keeper, $11.76/hr
Stocking, Lisa M, mammography technl, $30.36/hr
Stockman, Karmen Sue, human resources analyst sr, $62,500
Stockman, Willard Steven, mts/electrician, $22.50/hr
Stockstill, Jill R, food svc wrkr II, $11.83/hr
Stockton, Brandy M, business support specialist sr, $28.07/hr
Stockton, Christy Renee, mri technologist, $33.54/hr
Stockton, Terry James, radiologic techl, $18.59/hr
Stoddard, Elizabeth Roth, prof, asoc, $68,201
Stoecker, William Clayton, resident physician-1st yr, $50,219
Stoerker, Courtney L, office support assistant IV, $16.19/hr
Stoermer, Jessica Lynn, exercise physiologist, $20.77/hr
Stoermer, Robin L, office support assistant III, $13.33/hr
Stoffer, Cheri Lyn, med lab techn, $16.84/hr
Stofiel, Cynthia P, academic advisor, $43,173
Stogsdill, Herbert S, grounds keeper II, $14.96/hr
Stogsdill, Kelly J, mail carrier, $12.40/hr
Stohr, Donna Umbach, student service coor sr, $48,655
Stoker, Aaron M, prof, asoc resrch, $97,842
Stokes, Kenneth Leon, event assistant I, $7.55/hr
Stokes, Thomas J, office supervisor, $42,497
Stoll, Darci Elise, care team assoc-clinical, $11.10/hr
Stoll, Doris Ruth, office support assistant I, $11.49/hr
Stoll, Laura Kay, vice provost, $132,075
Stoll, Lori Jeannine, educational pgm associate I, $13.45/hr
Stoll, Megan Leigh Mudd, media producer sr, $40,000
Stoll, Randall Victor, dir III business admin, $117,200
Stoltz, Mary Helen, mgr external relations, $57,181
Stone II, Fred L, construction manager I, $52,354
Stone Underwood, Katherine Fera, library info asst, $11.30/hr
Stone-Bowers, Amy Jo, nurse advisor, telephone, $26.53/hr
Stone, Alexa Renee, temporary clerical, $10.85/hr
Stone, Amy Renee, nurse, staff I, $19.00/hr
Stone, Bethany, prof, asoc teach, $56,949
Stone, Craig Wilson, mts/electrician-ssd, $20.31/hr
Stone, D R, resident physician-4th yr, $58,265
Stone, Darin Lee, office support assistant III, $11.98/hr
Stone, David Glenn, technical trainer-expert, $45,724
Stone, Erik E, instructor, adjunct, $15,855
Stone, Glenda Fay, nurse, staff II, $27.70/hr
Stone, Jack W, library information assistant, $11.30/hr
Stone, Jennifer Yasu, supv, clinical-rehab svcs, $71,788
Stone, John Andrew, prof, ast clincl, $83,558
Stone, Joshua A, resident physician-4th yr, $54,425
Stone, Julianne, lecturer, $17,255
Stone, Katherine Grace Johnmeyer, instructor, $52
Stone, Marion Elizabeth, dir II student support svcs, $88,920
Stone, Matthew C, emrg med techn paramedic, $16.64/hr
Stone, Michelle Renee, supv, operating room nursing, $28.05/hr
Stone, Nancy J, professor, $101,485
Stone, Renee D, accountant I, $17.22/hr
Stone, Ruth Ann, nurse, staff II, $28.42/hr
Stone, Sandra Kay, pat acct rep, $17.10/hr
Stone, Sarah E, csm operations supervisor, $46,392
Stone, Scott H, temporary crafts service, $9.10/hr
Stone, Shannon L, ast vice chancellor, $97,963
Stone, Tanner James, grounds keeper, $12.12/hr
Stone, Tara L, student service coor I, $44,000
Stone, Terri L, business support specialist II, $20.24/hr
Stone, Tyler Thomas, fire protec/equip tech III, $20.75/hr
Stonecipher, Kimberly Marie, human resources spclst III, $42,186
Stoner, Christin Jennifer, nurse anesthetist, $141,000
Stoner, Joshua Douglas, ast athletic director, $90,100
Stoner, Steven C, prof, clincl, $150,000

Stoops, Janet L, research specialist I, $40,145
Storey, Pamela, instructor, lab, $45,768
Storm, C Todd, fin and acctg manager, $87,554
Storm, Douglas Wayne, stage services assistant sr, $16.00/hr
Storm, Susan L, docent, $10,000
Storman, Ashley N, student service coor II, $40,159
Stormont, Melissa, professor, $85,485
Stornello, Michael J, sr ast dir csm operations, $88,151
Story, Angela Renee, dir nursing svcs, $123,469
Story, John G, prof, asoc, $72,799
Story, John H, instructor, adjunct, $9,000
Stottle, Kathryn Diane, business support specialist II, $17.34/hr
Stottle, Matthew Garrett, business tech analyst-speclst, $55,000
Stout, Courtney Renee, nurse, staff II, $23.23/hr
Stout, Jessica Rae, resident physician-1st yr, $50,219
Stout, Karen Jane, db programmer analyst-expert, $58,704
Stout, Margee P, executive assistant, $21.95/hr
Stovall, Zachary Scott, advancement associate II, $16.79/hr
Stover, Eric Mason, grounds keeper II, $15.09/hr
Stowell, Justin Tyler, resident physician-2nd yr, $50,810
Stowers, Lester Samuel, prof, asoc teach, $39,052
Stoyanov, Alexandre, prof, ast resrch, $58,366
Straatman, Delinda Mary, serv line spclst, $95,000
Strack, Erin Rachel, instructor, adjunct, $6,300
Stracke, Eric, office support assistant II, $10.44/hr
Strain, Allen R, instructor, adjunct, $22,500
Strain, Ryan A, fellow, post doc clncl-yr4, $61,960
Strand, Connie Sue, nurse, licensed prac, $19.97/hr
Strand, Lauren Ashley, nurse, staff now III, $30.00/hr
Strange, Melissa Marie, resp therapist reg, $30.00/hr
Strasser, Kristen Marie Deppermann, res physician-5th yr, $56,120
Strassner, Keith D, dir III business admin, $138,829
Strathausen, Carsten, professor, $79,056
Strathman, Alan J, prof, teach, $84,534
Stratman, Christina M, office support assistant IV, $13.88/hr
Stratton, Mark D, office support assistant III, $12.65/hr
Straub, Jason H, food svc wrkr IV, $14.77/hr
Straub, Scott Michael, mts/pipefitter, $20.31/hr
Straube, Elizabeth Anne, nurse, staff II, $24.37/hr
Strauser, Lisa Anne, executive assistant, $20.04/hr
Straw, Melissa Marie Lock, patient svc rep, $12.76/hr
Strawn, Jessica Elaine, patient svc rep, $14.77/hr
Strawn, Kevin, electrician, high voltage, $27.26/hr
Strawn, Monica Paige, high school student, $8.50/hr
Strawn, Sterling Carole, office support assistant IV, $15.63/hr
Strawn, Tammy L, research specialist sr, $49,576
Streeter, Becky S, nurse, staff II, $34.73/hr
Streeter, Erin Nicole, nurse, licensed prac, $15.06/hr
Streeter, Kyle Craig, interventional technl (ir), $22.55/hr
Streeter, Laura Michele, student support specialist II, $20.00/hr
Streit, Mary Belle, research/lab technician, $13.37/hr
Streu, Lori Lynn, instructor, adjunct, $14,400
Strickland, Donna G, prof, asoc, $69,066
Strickland, Mona Marie, custodian, $12.90/hr
Strickler, Glenda R, office support assistant II, $10.56/hr
Strid, Deborah L, program/project supprt coor I, $39,413
Strid, Marc B, prgm director, $58,555
Stringer, Dorothy, business support specialist II, $18.43/hr
Strodtman, Debra Jo, nurse, licensed prac, $20.68/hr
Strodtman, Kayla Christine, nurse, staff per diem, $35.00/hr
Stroer, Dennis J, police officer, $20.88/hr
Stroer, Victoria Anne, business support specialist II, $24.63/hr
Strohbehn, Alisa Rae, business support specialist sr, $18.00/hr
Strohbehn, Austin L, resident physician-1st yr, $50,219
Strohschein, Lesley Ann, sr ast dir studnt supprt svcs, $52,400
Stroik, Thomas S, prof, curators, $110,009
Strom, Shyrle Yvonne, retail sales associate sr, $16.00/hr
Strong Helwig, Amber Diane, office support asst IV, $15.73/hr
Strong, Artesha Nicole, food svc wrkr I, $9.60/hr
Strong, Linda P, retail sales assistant sr, $13.48/hr
Strong, Marcia L, security officer, $11.60/hr
Strong, Michael H, instructor, adjunct, $25,600
Strong, Stacie Ilene, prof, asoc, $123,871
Strother, Jessica Lynne, nurse, staff II, $20.54/hr
Strother, Vonda K, office support assistant IV, $15.24/hr
Stroud, Dena Lou, med lab techn, $18.31/hr
Stroud, Tracy Ann, prof, asoc clincl dept, $159,607
Stroud, Tracy Ann, physician, $100.00/hr
Stroupe, Le Ann, strat comm manager, $56,588

Strubel, Courtney Elizabeth, fellow, $61,200
Struble, Struby Kathleen, student support specialist II, $17.63/hr
Struck, Steven D, health physics technician sr, $27.26/hr
Strumpf, Diane Christine, office support assistant IV, $14.50/hr
Stuart Simmons, Georgia, community dev spclst, $61,033
Stuart, Bette Crockett, library info specialist sr, $18.04/hr
Stuart, Michael, student support specialist I, $12.98/hr
Stubblefield, Gwendolyn, prof, ast adjunct, $34,200
Stubbs, Amy Marie, adjunct, $15,000
Stubbs, Andrew Louis, telecom tech-speclst, $15.18/hr
Stubbs, Bradley, grounds keeper lead, $15.84/hr
Stubbs, Heather Marie, office support assistant IV, $14.00/hr
Stubbs, Sue, prof, ast adjunct, $10,710
Stubbs, Wylie J, maintenance supervisor, $54,021
Stuber-Skipper, Joanne, social worker, $58,891
Stuby, Bill G, specialist, $62,192
Stuck Sr, David S, maint wrkr, prev, $16.28/hr
Stuck, Kelley Denise, asoc vice president, $196,946
Stuck, Kelly Ann, office support assistant III, $12.77/hr
Stuckel, Cara Christine, student support specialist I, $13.64/hr
Stuckenschneider, Steven Michael, rec/athletic spclst sr, $60,000
Stucky, Renee, prof, clincl, $123,055
Studer Logsdon, Mary, library information assistant, $11.30/hr
Studer, Robin B, nurse, staff II, $33.72/hr
Stuerke, Pamela S, prof, asoc, $137,629
Stueve, Wesley Duane, instructor, adjunct, $15,000
Stulgo, Sue, hris specialist-expert, $60,423
Stumbaugh, Geoffrey C, library information assistant, $11.30/hr
Stunkard, Kaitlyn Kristine, office support assistant III, $11.39/hr
Stuppy, Adam Joseph, resident physician-1st yr, $49,025
Sturgeon, James I, professor, $103,661
Sturgeon, Lisa M, office support assistant III, $15.15/hr
Sturgess, Kathy L, program/project supprt coor I, $28,560
Sturgill, Shelby Lynn, health records techn I, $9.64/hr
Sturgis, Timothy Fay, biological safety prof, $56,595
Sturguess, Gay Nell, office support assistant IV, $15.90/hr
Sturtevant, Amanda M, health records techn II, $12.35/hr
Stuteville, Robert Michael, bts painter, $21.23/hr
Stuth, Gretchen D, couns hlth/welfare/wellness sr, $30.00/hr
Stutte, Brenda, business ops associate II, $53,096
Stutts, Daniel S, prof, asoc, $79,774
Stutts, Diane B, ast dir student support svcs, $58,360
Stylianou, Antonis Pantakis, prof, ast, $75,000
Su, Jianbin, fellow, post doctoral, $22,500
Subasi, Musa, prof, ast, $183,070
Sublette, Mary Catherine, occl therapist, $35.00/hr
Subramanian, Krishna M, db programmer analyst-expert, $66,116
Subramanian, Rajalakshmi, chemist I, $35,913
Subramanian, Srikala, adjunct, $15,000
Sucher, Katherine Johanna, nurse, staff I, $19.00/hr
Suchman, Kelly Rogers, prof, ast adjunct, $125.00/hr
Sucre, Fernando Jose, strat comm associate II, $39,600
Sudduth, Sarah, adjunct, $15,000
Suedmeyer, Kevin Robert, med techl reg, $29.00/hr
Suess, Beth Marie, nurse, staff II, $34.18/hr
Suhre, Terry, prof, resrch, $65,602
Suits, Elizabeth K, temporary clerical, $9.50/hr
Sukys, Julija, prof, ast, $65,466
Sulgrove, Kristy Marie, research specialist I, $40,002
Sulko, Sara L, lecturer, $40,552
Sullins, Jesse F, bts painter, $19.59/hr
Sullivan, Christopher, psychologist, $56,978
Sullivan, Dan J, instructor, $52
Sullivan, Jeanne M, account executive, $62,684
Sullivan, Jeffrey Adam, teaching ast, $13.00/hr
Sullivan, Michael Joseph, system administrator-expert, $78,193
Sullivan, Renee M, prof, ast, $172,125
Sultan, Jelan Yehia, lab attd, $10.51/hr
Sultan, Wanda R, animal techn, ast lab, $13.19/hr
Sulzer, John Michael, police officer, $17.56/hr
Summerhays, Benjamin John, prof, ast/profl pract, $194,577
Summers, Carolyn Yvonne, nurse clinician, $71,934
Summers, Cynthia Lee, nurse, staff I, rnwp, $19.00/hr
Summers, Gerald F, prof, asoc, $83,820
Summers, Kevin L, business ops associate sr, $53,275
Summers, Lindsey Lane, temporary crafts service, $7.65/hr
Summers, Mary Lynn, business support specialist II, $17.88/hr
Summers, Max E, administrative consultant sr, $123,755
Summers, Robert Ray, mts/electrician, $21.05/hr

Summers, Russell Lynn, electronics technician sr, $23.59/hr
Summers, Susan Lynn, health records techn I, $12.96/hr
Summerville, Jade Evone, nursing ast, $12.08/hr
Sumners, Christy L, business support specialist sr, $18.62/hr
Sumowski, Heather Elaine, nurse, staff II rnwp, $20.84/hr
Sumpter, Laurie Christine Howard, nurse anesthetist, $147,900
Sun, Carlos Chung, prof, asoc, $102,140
Sun, Dongchu, professor, $177,054
Sun, Hongmin, prof, asoc, $91,681
Sun, Jianguo, professor, $147,814
Sun, Jing, business support specialist II, $23.89/hr
Sun, Lei, scholar, visiting, $24,000
Sun, Li, prof, ast, $113,322
Sun, Paula S, event assistant I, $7.55/hr
Sun, Shengxin, library information assistant, $11.40/hr
Sun, Yichang, research/lab technician sr, $18.63/hr
Sun, Yongpeng, fellow, post doctoral, $24,000
Sun, Zhe, prof, ast resrch, $77,320
Sundall, Jennifer, nurse, staff II rnwp, $28.52/hr
Sunderland, Tara K, serv line spclst, $68,793
Sundvold, Robert Allen, head coach, $84,335
Suni, Ellen Yankiver, dean, $209,650
Sunna, Ramez Sami, prof, asoc clincl dept, $264,120
Suo, Yuying, research specialist I, $45,603
Suppes, Galen, professor, $125,992
Surenler, Murat, food svc wrkr II, $10.10/hr
Suri Mohanram, Sharmila, resident physician-4th yr, $55,804
Surma, Tyler Jonathan, resident physician-1st yr, $50,219
Surprenant, Theresa, instructor, adjunct, $9,000
Sutch, Darren, operations support tech sr, $17.50/hr
Sutcliffe, Lucy Hortense, program/proj supprt coor sr, $51,379
Sutcliffe, Matthew Paul, lecturer, $15,000
Sutherland, Brandi Michelle, educational pgm assoc I, $13.00/hr
Sutherland, Logan Andrew, hospital security officer, $10.85/hr
Sutherland, Sharon Kay, educational pgm associate I, $13.45/hr
Sutovsky, Miriam, research specialist sr, $41,523
Sutovsky, Peter, professor, $121,025
Sutter, Catherine F, user support analyst-entry, $11.41/hr
Sutterby, Katie Jean, animal techn, $15.12/hr
Suttmoeller, Kevin Edward, prof, ast clincl dept, $160,059
Suttmoeller, Natalie R, nurse, clincl charge-rn, $34.18/hr
Sutton, Marvin Jr, custodian, $13.23/hr
Sutton, Arthur, custodian, $13.23/hr
Sutton, Brenda S, care team assoc-clinical, $13.40/hr
Sutton, Candice Yovonne, hospital lab tech, $14.01/hr
Sutton, Deborah Shockley, program/proj supprt coor I, $54,616
Sutton, John C, mech trades spclst (mts), $21.09/hr
Sutton, Jonni Kaye, office support assistant III, $13.45/hr
Sutton, Julie Darden, prof, ast, $62,000
Sutton, Melanie Kristin, instructor, clincl, $15,600
Svoma, Bohumil M, prof, ast, $70,000
Swadley, Kyle C, user support analyst-speclst, $19.28/hr
Swafford, Kent E, musical instrument technician, $26.24/hr
Swafford, Scott Cunnigham, prof, asoc profl practice, $63,487
Swaim, Amanda Michelle, office support assistant IV, $14.60/hr
Swaim, Carol L, office support assistant IV, $15.04/hr
Swain, Elaina Renee, temporary clerical, $10.00/hr
Swallow, Jennifer Lynn, office support assistant IV, $14.78/hr
Swallow, Joy D, professor, $99,351
Swan, Stephen R, nurse, staff II, $34.18/hr
Swanegan, Joseph M, dir II advancement, $68,614
Swanegan, Maria Theresa, student support spec sr, $17.15/hr
Swaney, Elaine K, event assistant I, $12.00/hr
Swaney, Rebecca Jan, prof, asoc clincl, $400.00/hr
Swanigan, Jesse C, lecturer sr, $21,000
Swank, Sara Elizabeth, nurse, staff II, $21.69/hr
Swanko Buenacasa, Dorothy Anne, office support asst IV, $14.00/hr
Swankoski, Lauren Marie, nurse, staff prn, $26.00/hr
Swanson, Blakely Rae, nurse, staff I, rnwp, $19.00/hr
Swanson, Heather Christine, executive assistant, $22.05/hr
Swanson, Mark Kenneth, prof, ast/profl pract, $66,422
Swanson, Nancee Jean, nurse, staff, $28.39/hr
Swanstrom, Todd Frederick, professor, $162,150
Swaringam, Elizabeth Ellen, office support asst IV, $13.14/hr
Swartwout, Jill Marie, asoc dir program/project ops, $63,085
Swartz, Amadi, social worker, $46,169
Swartz, Jessica Margaret, nurse, staff I, $19.00/hr
Swartz, John, instructor, adjunct, $16,200
Swartz, Morgan Kiino, student service coor sr, $50,225

Sweatt, Tosca R, sterile processing tech, $18.21/hr
Sweeney, Donald Charles II, prof, teach, $102,923
Sweeney, Anna Marie, student support specialist II, $16.99/hr
Sweeney, Heather Nicole, program/proj supprt coor I, $39,780
Sweeney, James Benjamin, ast coach, $74,000
Sweeney, Marion Elaine, prof, ast adjunct, $3,000
Sweet, Eric, prof, ast adjunct, $18,404
Sweet, Timothy J, supv radiology, $34.32/hr
Sweets, Laura Elizabeth, prof, asoc extns, $105,056
Sweetwood, Matthew Gerard, temporary crafts service, $9.50/hr
Sweezer, Claude, bts carpenter, $21.71/hr
Sweezer, Jackeline Jeneane, patient svc rep, $14.50/hr
Swenson, Amanda, prof, ast clincl dept, $147,900
Swenson, John, prof, asoc teach, $88,641
Swenson, Kristine, professor, $107,997
Swenson, Theresa Marie, nurse practitioner, $84,628
Swetz, Theodore F Jr, professor, $106,350
Swezy, Diana Lynn, instructor, adjunct, $8,325
Swick, Marly A, professor, $94,118
Swick, Mary L, office support assistant IV, $16.10/hr
Swierczek, Mark Bradley, nurse, staff I, $19.00/hr
Swift, Brian S, engineer II, $61,924
Swift, Theresa Mae, prof, ast teach, $68,728
Swilling, Robin Suzette, nurse anesthetist, $147,900
Swims, Pamela A, office support assistant IV, $19.57/hr
Swindell, Riley Everett, system support analyst-entry, $17.17/hr
Swindle, Lavonda L, educational pgm associate I, $13.45/hr
Swindle, Monica S, instructor, adjunct, $9,000
Swiney, Sharon Louise, patient svc rep, $13.47/hr
Swink, Douglas E, registrar, $87,451
Swisher, Chris L, sr mgr broadcast operations, $75,852
Switzer, Adrian, prof, ast teach, $45,000
Switzer, Jay A, professor, $193,276
Swofford, Sarah Jean, prof, asoc clincl dept, $155,856
Swope, Karen F, mgr III business admin, $73,440
Swope, Karen Godfrey, office support assistant III, $13.55/hr
Swope, Mary Alice, business support assistant II, $18.76/hr
Sword, Jean Therese, nurse, or/recovery-ch, $34.18/hr
Swyers, Sophia, student support specialist II, $15.00/hr
Syam, Niladri Baran, prof, asoc, $180,000
Sydow, Trenton Lane, reactor operator trainee II, $22.65/hr
Sykes Berry, Susan D, librarian III, $54,392
Sykes, Malory Collier, advancement officer, $46,284
Sykes, Sharvell Denise, model, $15.00/hr
Sykes, William Brett, ast coach, $40,400
Sykora, Michael T, operations support tech II, $13.24/hr
Sykuta, Michael E, prof, asoc, $93,400
Symington, Isaac McKim, event assistant I, $8.75/hr
Sypes, Ruth Yvonne, student support specialist I, $18.09/hr
Sypolt, Robin Michele, nurse, staff II rnwp, $26.03/hr
Szabo, Jamie Lynne, compliance manager sr, $70,008
Szabo, Lauren Christine, nurse, staff I, $19.00/hr
Szaj, Julie A, strat comm consultant, $49,870
Szekely, Eva Diana, professor, $73,777
Szpila, Joachim, temporary crafts service, $8.41/hr
Szucs, Joseph R, programmer analyst-expert, $61,751
Szy, Daniel Joseph, office support assistant III, $14.73/hr
Szy, Dusti Ann, teaching ast, $8,424
Szyhowski, Mary Lena, educational pgm associate I, $13.15/hr
Szymanski, Stella A, office support assistant IV, $16.89/hr
Ta, Vinam David Nguyen, instructional designer-spclst, $48,494
Tabanelli, Roberta, prof, asoc, $60,110
Tabler, Tanya Ruth, pharmacist II, $60.00/hr
Taborda, Romulo, care team assoc-clinical, $14.00/hr
Tacker, Allen Bernard, instructor, ast, $24.40/hr
Tackett, Mary L, ast registrar, $45,600
Tadinada, Bhanu Sateesh, programmer analyst-entry, $57,238
Tadych, Baadi, research/lab technician, $12.13/hr
Taft, Melinda S, clincl documnt spclst, $67,473
Taft, Raol J, prof, ast, $56,100
Tager, David Samuel, resident physician-4th yr, $55,804
Taggart, Cathryn Flaim, mgr purch-contract svcs, $78,036
Taggart, Jacob Ross, distribution techn-mtls mgmt, $15.48/hr
Taggart, Pamela L, office support assistant IV, $17.00/hr
Tague, David, research specialist sr, $46,800
Takahashi, T Nicole, program/project supprt coor sr, $74,298
Takeda, Shuichiro, prof, ast, $83,545
Talaat, Nizar Taha Ahmed, fellow, post doc clncl yr1, $55,804
Talbert, Andrew J, instructor, adjunct, $18,000

Talbert, Crystal Kay, reimbursement ast-cert, $18.69/hr
Talbott, Jeffrey D, mts/electrician-r, $20.87/hr
Talken, Brian J, nurse, staff II, $23.37/hr
Talley, Kyle Michael, temporary crafts service, $12.00/hr
Talley, William Ryan, temporary clerical, $10.35/hr
Tallmage, Allan E, coor, surg supply, $63,149
Tallmage, Anne Marie, surgical technl non cert, $24.64/hr
Talmage, Karen S, supv nursing acute care, $36.74/hr
Talton, Clay Dewayne Jr, mental health tech, $12.20/hr
Talton, Jimmy J, custodian, $12.94/hr
Tammeus, Lisen, ast vice chancellor, $122,000
Tan, Change Laura, prof, asoc, $72,966
Tan, Jinglu, director, $200,194
Tan, Kenneth Shu-Wen, resident physician-3rd yr, $53,763
Tan, Rachel, certif pharmacy techn, $16.27/hr
Tan, Teng-Kee, professor, $407,490
Tan, Victor E Y, professor, $78,255
Tanaka, Lanette E, prof, ast teach, $62,459
Tanaka, Tomoko, prof, ast, $218,484
Tandez, Julia Ann, nurse, staff per diem, $35.00/hr
Taneja, Harsh, prof, ast, $66,300
Tang, Fujian, fellow, post doctoral, $30,000
Tankersley-Bankhead, Elizabeth Ann, sr dir prog/proj ops, $86,491
Tann, John F, resident physician-1st yr, $50,219
Tanner Sr, Bobby Jay, farm wrkr II, $14.27/hr
Tanner, Douglas I, med techl reg, $30.10/hr
Tanner, John J, professor, $146,667
Tanner, Jonathan Luis, temporary clerical, $8.35/hr
Tanner, Miles A, research specialist sr, $55,048
Tanner, Steven Dwight, student support specialist II, $15.57/hr
Tansey, Patrick Michael, system support analyst-spclst, $23.73/hr
Tanzey, Kelly F, nurse, staff II rnwp, $20.95/hr
Tao, Xi, db programmer analyst-princpl, $72,360
Tapia, Sandie L, supv pat accts-up, $52,046
Tapia, Susan M, office support assistant IV, $15.08/hr
Tapp, Joan, nurse, licensed prac, $22.16/hr
Tapp, Tavair Dominque, office support assistant IV, $14.00/hr
Tappero, Ellen Paysinger, instructor, clincl, $31,775
Taqieddin, Salah A, prof, visiting, $86,667
Tardy, Garth L, library specialist, $33,825
Tariq, Syed Mohammad, prof, teach, $90,000
Tarkow, Theodore Alfred, dean, asoc, $147,223
Tarleton, Molly Malone, hlth prgm spclst, $22.40/hr
Tarr, James E, professor, $105,647
Tarr, Michael L, food svc wrkr IV, $12.19/hr
Tartiere, Jean-Gerald, teaching ast, $13.00/hr
Tarun, Tushar, resident physician-1st yr, $50,219
Tarwater, Douglas J, dir I, business admin, $111,367
Tarwater, Kristen Deane, prof, asoc clincl dept, $140,270
Tarwater, Kurtis Daniel, prof, ast clincl dept, $154,395
Tarwater, Steve Ross, custodian, $12.94/hr
Tascio, Elizabeth A, instructor, adjunct, $7,500
Taskov, Ivaylo Lybenov, custodian, $12.94/hr
Taskova, Tonka Hristozova, custodian, $12.94/hr
Tate-Kuhler, Denise Irene, technical trainer-princpl, $62,198
Tate, Deborah Joan, veterinary technician sr, $21.03/hr
Tate, John L, phys therapy ast, $24.57/hr
Tate, Kelley Nicole, supv, clinical-rehab svcs, $78,540
Tate, Kelly Jeanne, prof, ast teach, $41,610
Tate, Levi, event assistant I, $8.50/hr
Tate, Nia Marie, nurse, staff II, $21.37/hr
Tate, Ryan James, instructor, adjunct, $9,000
Tate, Valerie Gwenn, extns professional, ast, $47,552
Tatum, Paul E III, prof, asoc clincl dept, $161,058
Tatum, Aaron D, custodian, $12.94/hr
Tatum, Cheryl Jean, executive assistant, $20.22/hr
Tatum, Demaro Marquez, food svc wrkr I, $11.29/hr
Tatum, Demetrius J, event assistant I, $7.50/hr
Tatum, Joel, livestock spclst, $47,500
Tatum, Roqueshia Ronyea, surgical technl certified, $18.74/hr
Tatum, Steven R, care team assoc-suppt, $12.64/hr
Tatum, Teresa, business support specialist sr, $27.64/hr
Taub, Haskell, professor, $115,156
Taub, Maria Quiroz, instructor, ast, $16,568
Taube, Gregory, telecom tech-princpl, $20.17/hr
Taube, Kenneth Dwayne, mts/electronics, $21.05/hr
Taube, Nancy Ann, office support assistant IV, $17.78/hr
Tauber, Alyssa Carolyn, nurse, staff, $22.28/hr
Tauheed, Linwood F, prof, asoc, $77,745

Tauritz, Daniel R, prof, asoc, $95,407
Tauschek, Heidi Anna, instructor, adjunct, $9,000
Taussig, Lela Eunice, academic advisor, $27,933
Tavenner, Michelle Ann, nurse, staff II, $25.71/hr
Tayal, Aditi, resrch anlyst, $60,000
Tayloe, Judith Ann, executive assistant, $22.23/hr
Taylor, Amber E.B PhD, psychologist, $40.00/hr
Taylor-Braxton, Jacqueline Denise, custodian, $12.72/hr
Taylor-Stone, Erin Patricia, instructor, adjunct, $7,059
Taylor, Albert Lee, maintenance supervisor, $20.70/hr
Taylor, Alexys Marie, care team assoc-clinical, $11.10/hr
Taylor, Andrea Louise, lecturer, $30,000
Taylor, Andrea R, social worker asoc, $44,632
Taylor, Angelina Marie, nurse, staff II rnwp, $20.54/hr
Taylor, Ann R, dean, asoc, $114,693
Taylor, Caroles S, student support specialist sr, $21.63/hr
Taylor, Chelsea Elizabeth, human resources spclst II, $34,572
Taylor, Connie S, office support assistant IV, $13.52/hr
Taylor, Connie S, advancement associate II, $16.54/hr
Taylor, Deborah J, program/project supprt coor I, $56,082
Taylor, Debra Deann, office support assistant IV, $13.84/hr
Taylor, George Townsend, professor, $102,779
Taylor, Gregory Lee, instructor, adjunct, $4,200
Taylor, Holly L, veterinarian, residnt, $29,580
Taylor, Hope K, nurse, staff per diem, $35.00/hr
Taylor, James A, police officer, $18.69/hr
Taylor, Jean Nate', office support assistant III, $11.70/hr
Taylor, Jeremy F, prof, curators, $210,453
Taylor, Jessica Zabell, resrch ast, $32,811
Taylor, Jimmie E, research technical svcs supv, $23.70/hr
Taylor, Joyce Lee, educational pgm associate I, $13.54/hr
Taylor, Julia A, prof, ast resrch, $63,501
Taylor, Julie Blackwell, media producer I, $16.13/hr
Taylor, Karen, program/project supprt coor I, $34,916
Taylor, Katherine Ann, office support assistant III, $14.51/hr
Taylor, Kathleen E, nurse, staff II, $31.10/hr
Taylor, Kathleen Marie, instructor, clincl, $30,750
Taylor, Kelly Ann, academic coor, $2,400
Taylor, Kimberly Ann, instructor, ast, $19,386
Taylor, Kristen Hawkins, prof, ast, $100,776
Taylor, Kyle Matthew, stock clerk, $10.94/hr
Taylor, Lashaunda Denise, office support assistant III, $14.62/hr
Taylor, Laura S, museum professional I, $22.47/hr
Taylor, Lisa Lynnette, office support assistant IV, $15.59/hr
Taylor, Marilyn L, professor, $140,250
Taylor, Martha Jonel, nurse, staff, $29.41/hr
Taylor, Mary Catherine, instructor, adjunct, $7,500
Taylor, Matthew G, resident physician-7th yr, $63,475
Taylor, Matthew J, prof, asoc, $76,000
Taylor, Michael W, powr plnt maint spclst II, $23.75/hr
Taylor, Michele Renae, police officer, $18.84/hr
Taylor, Natalie Elaine, nurse, staff, $15.20/hr
Taylor, Natalie Nicole, office support assistant III, $13.29/hr
Taylor, Nathan Earl, mts/pipefitter, $24.13/hr
Taylor, Patricia Clare, patient svc rep, $14.70/hr
Taylor, Raleigh Jessup, office support assistant III, $13.75/hr
Taylor, Robert W, mgr III business admin, $82,000
Taylor, Ronald Kent, security officer, $11.08/hr
Taylor, Steven Rhees, resident physician-4th yr, $55,804
Taylor, Susan J, research specialist I, $19.15/hr
Taylor, Terrance James, prof, asoc, $74,350
Taylor, Timothy Starr, prof, adjunct, $10.00/hr
Taylor, Veronica Lorene, event assistant I, $7.50/hr
Taylor, Warren E, csm associate III, $20.79/hr
Taylor, Wayland Jason, emrg med techn, $13.69/hr
Taylor, William Michael, bldg cntrl sys techn I, $21.05/hr
Tchatalbachev, Vladislav Velizarov, res physician-5th yr, $61,683
Teague, Darlene K, instructor, adjunct, $3,300
Teague, Kristopher James, care team assoc-clinical, $12.57/hr
Tearney, Karalee H, retail sales associate sr, $18.13/hr
Teator, Jenny Marie, hlth prgm ast, $12.50/hr
Tebbe, Lori Ann, mgr, care coor, $100,880
Teclemariam, Ghennet Sebhatu, custodian, $10.00/hr
Tedesco, Patrick William, police sergeant, $19.47/hr
Teegarden, Joshua Blake, hospital security officer, $11.73/hr
Teegarden, Katelyn Marie, nurse, staff I, $19.00/hr
Teegarden, Tyten C, programmer analyst-speclst, $61,200
Teel, Cindy Kay, executive assistant, $26.27/hr
Teel, Paula Jean, business support specialist II, $22.78/hr

Teel, Rosemary Jean, med techl reg, $24.03/hr
Tegerdine, Madelyn Morgan, nurse, staff II rnwp, $20.54/hr
Tegerdine, Molly Elizabeth, specialist, $10.00/hr
Teixeiro Pernas, Maria Emma, prof, ast, $100,858
Tekie, Tesfasellassie Ghirmatzion, custodian, $10.00/hr
Telander, Abi Jean, office support assistant III, $12.96/hr
Tellier, Jacob Edward, resident physician-5th yr, $56,120
Tellman, Stefanie Alynn, occl therapist, $70,187
Temm, Wanda, prof, clincl, $94,150
Temmen, Diane, office support assistant III, $15.00/hr
Tempest-Browning, Lisa Jo, compliance specialist I, $18.50/hr
Temple, Deanna Sue, nurse, staff II, $26.94/hr
Temple, Kimberly Rae, nurse, staff II rnwp, $20.95/hr
Temple, Kristen M, asoc dir student support svcs, $93,983
Temple, Parker Bailey, temporary technical, $10.00/hr
Temple, Phillip C, mgr II csm operations, $50,000
Templeton, Brandy Nicole, nurse, staff now III, $30.00/hr
Tenholder, Jennifer Lynne, surgical technl certified, $24.40/hr
Tenkku Lepper, Leigh Ellen, prof, asoc resrch, $97,000
Tenkku, Rhonda, prof, ast teach, $55,478
Tennant, Kim, charge data analyst, $58,522
Tennill, Alethea L W, asoc dir program/project ops, $58,154
Tennill, Christopher Logan, seasonal farm ast, $8.93/hr
Tennill, Kimberly Diane, nurse, licensed prac, $15.06/hr
Tennill, Marcia, prof, ast adjunct, $8,004
Tennill, Virginia, business support specialist sr, $23.75/hr
Tennis, Geraldine L, office support assistant III, $14.15/hr
Tennison, Angela K, student service coor II, $60,844
Tennyson, William S, pat acct rep, $15.42/hr
Tenute, Holly J, office support assistant IV, $13.36/hr
TerBush, Jessica R, research specialist sr, $54,871
Terjung, Ronald L, prof, adjunct, $55,352
Terman, Mark, instructor, adjunct, $9,000
Terpack, Stephenie Cathereen, dental hygienist, $25.00/hr
Terrana, Patricia Marie, nurse, staff II, $30.81/hr
Terre, Lisa, prof, asoc, $69,891
Terrell, Jeremiah J, human dev spclst, $46,500
Terrell, Renee Denise, supv, house-mpc, $71,225
Terrell, Ureasta Arenda Edwards, student support spec II, $16.75/hr
Terrell, Valinda Diane, program/project supprt coor I, $28,560
Terrell, Whitney Sloan, prof, ast, $55,000
Terrill, Gretchen Mone Katherine, nurse, staff II rnwp, $21.37/hr
Terrill, John, asoc dir fin and acctg, $62,478
Terrock, Jennifer R, service rep III, $12.44/hr
Terry, Ashley Anne, patient svc rep, $11.97/hr
Terry, Catherine Heller, dir I, strat communications, $98,532
Terry, Christine E, asoc director, $69,020
Terry, Kimberly L, animal caretaker, $12.12/hr
Terry, Meagan Elizabeth, care team assoc-clinical, $12.08/hr
Terry, Rebecca S, student service coor II, $40,986
Terstriep-Herber, Tracy Lynn, instructor, adjunct, $18,000
Tesch, Amy Kristin, executive assistant, $17.25/hr
Teschan, Mary Ann, rec/athletic specialist sr, $20.00/hr
Teschner, Jessica A, nurse, staff now III, $30.00/hr
Tesfai, Kibreab, accountant sr, $43,849
Tesfai, Lily Kahsai, fellow, post doctoral, $37,500
Teson, Brea Ann, nurse, staff II, $23.33/hr
Teti, Michelle, prof, ast, $81,426
Tetrault, Lois Elaine, ultrasonographer, $34.94/hr
Tetro, Jeane M, office support assistant II, $12.50/hr
Tevault, Lezley Dawn, surgical technl certified, $16.66/hr
Tew, Patricia A, prof, ast clincl, $79,418
Tew, Patricia A, cat scan techncl (ct), $22.70/hr
Thacker, Rhonda, supv, lab, $69,221
Thaier, Christina Elizabeth, office support assistant IV, $13.71/hr
Thakkar, Mahesh Maganlal, prof, asoc, $101,543
Thakkar, Neela Patel, accountant sr, $46,046
Thal, Laura Katherine, research/lab technician, $15.00/hr
Thall, Jene Ann, pat acct rep, $16.30/hr
Thames, Angelica M, teaching ast, $13.00/hr
Tharakan, Ajit Kurien, prof, ast clincl dept, $421,232
Tharp, Darla L, resrch asoc, $45,315
Tharp, James K, human resources analyst sr, $52,135
Tharp, Steven Michael, prof, ast, $59,590
Tharpe, Nancy E, executive assistant, $23.30/hr
Thatcher, William Edward, bldg cntrl sys techn I, $21.05/hr
Thaxton, Mary Jane, executive assistant, $28.13/hr
Theberge, Nicole Maria, business support specialist II, $19.17/hr
Thein, David J, prof, ast clincl, $120,000

Theissen, Katie M, cook, $12.20/hr
Thelen, Jay J, prof, asoc, $115,824
Thelen, Joan McKenna Cartwri, resrch ast, $14,400
Theobald, Shawn Loren, healthcare admin fellow, $55,000
Theoharidis, Sherri Young, psychologist, $27,299
Thiagarajan, Ganesh, professor, $96,500
Thiel, Teresa, dean, asoc, $159,861
Thiele, Joshua Dalton, nurse, staff prn, $26.00/hr
Thiem, Laura, prof, ast clincl, $78,000
Thieman, Amy L, student service coor II, $44,680
Thiems, Grady E, resident physician-3rd yr, $52,470
Thienes, Jessica Lynn, nurse, staff I, $19.37/hr
Thies, Damian D, mts/electrician, $21.05/hr
Thies, Marjorie Joyce, planning & project spclst, $63,797
Thies, Paula K, ast registrar, $58,198
Thiessen, Aaron S, resident physician-2nd yr, $52,007
Thiessen, David L, asoc dir suprt svcs-mrc, $97,469
Thiessen, Sonya M, office support assistant IV, $15.82/hr
Thimgan, Matthew Scott, prof, ast, $66,250
Thiruvengadam, Magesh, fellow, post doctoral, $40,000
Thiry, Samantha Heather, temporary crafts service, $9.50/hr
Thoenen, Joan, compliance anlyst III, $69,252
Thoma, Crystal Jean, office support assistant III, $14.06/hr
Thomas, Amanda M, office support assistant III, $11.30/hr
Thomas, Andrew L, prof, ast resrch, $58,249
Thomas, Angela, cat scan technl (ct), $30.68/hr
Thomas, April Renee, nurse, licensed prac, $17.60/hr
Thomas, Brandon Scott, mts/electrician, $20.31/hr
Thomas, Brian R, grounds keeper II, $15.09/hr
Thomas, Carol D, tutor, $15.00/hr
Thomas, Caryn K, nurse, clincl charge-rn, $28.84/hr
Thomas, Cathy, prof, ast, $70,931
Thomas, Chancelor Tremaine, office support asst I, $10.00/hr
Thomas, Charles Randolph, prof, asoc teach, $89,035
Thomas, Colleen Deanna, grounds keeper, $12.55/hr
Thomas, Curtis Daniel, patient svc rep, $14.88/hr
Thomas, Daniel A, prof, ast, $54,780
Thomas, Deborah Byers, business support specialist II, $22.00/hr
Thomas, Dedra Raquel, family fincl edu spclst, $50,000
Thomas, Donna Marie, business support specialist II, $21.91/hr
Thomas, Edie Lynn, office support assistant IV, $13.30/hr
Thomas, Glenn Eldon, surgical technl certified, $17.18/hr
Thomas, Jacqueline Michelle, office support asst IV, $16.36/hr
Thomas, James Cleve, mail carrier sr, $16.64/hr
Thomas, James H, media production director I, $45,795
Thomas, Jeffery S, prof, asoc teach, $72,956
Thomas, Jeffrey E, dean, asoc, $154,200
Thomas, Jenna, couns hlth/welfare/wellness sr, $30.00/hr
Thomas, Jonathan Lee, prof, ast clincl dept, $201,917
Thomas, Jordan Matthew, research specialist sr, $41,500
Thomas, Joy, instructor, adjunct, $14,400
Thomas, Julie L, cat scan technl (ct), $30.74/hr
Thomas, Justin Daniel, animal caretaker, $11.76/hr
Thomas, Kami, dean, ast, $99,238
Thomas, Karl M, med techl reg, $28.31/hr
Thomas, Katie K, educational pgm associate I, $13.04/hr
Thomas, Kelly Bernice, educational pgm assistant, $17.81/hr
Thomas, Kenneth F, manuscript specialist sr, $44,296
Thomas, Kenneth P, professor, $70,024
Thomas, Letitia, resrch asoc, $64,974
Thomas, Mark E, dir rsrd II advancement, $94,006
Thomas, Matthew, csm associate sr, $32.81/hr
Thomas, Matthew E, construction manager II, $84,288
Thomas, Megan Brittany, food svc wrkr I, $11.29/hr
Thomas, Melanie Ann, business support specialist II, $16.83/hr
Thomas, Michelle Cameron, temporary professional, $11.30/hr
Thomas, Paul M, event assistant I, $12.00/hr
Thomas, Phyllis E, nurse, licensed prac, $21.18/hr
Thomas, Ranisha Marie, temporary crafts service, $8.16/hr
Thomas, Richard W, support systems admin-expert, $58,500
Thomas, Robert Lauren, nurse, staff II, $30.09/hr
Thomas, Ryan James, prof, ast, $65,924
Thomas, Samantha Kay, nurse, staff I, $19.00/hr
Thomas, Sandra L, nurse, staff now III, $30.00/hr
Thomas, Sharon G, instructor, clincl, $60,020
Thomas, Sheila D, business support specialist II, $17.75/hr
Thomas, Sherri Lee, office support assistant III, $12.75/hr
Thomas, Theresa Yvonne, custodian, $13.36/hr
Thomas, Tiffany Nicole, enrollment advisor, $15.25/hr

Thomas, Wally Linn, ast mgr pathology, $91,042
Thomas, William J, utility dist wrkr IV, $23.75/hr
Thomason, Trey Delmer, resident physician-4th yr, $56,225
Thomasson, Samantha Darlene, telecomm opr-h, $10.20/hr
Thombs, Lori Ann, prof, asoc, $101,130
Thompkins, Shannon Marie, instructor, adjunct, $3,200
Thompson, Scott William Jr, instructor, adjunct, $2,667
Thompson-Porter, Taureen Terrall, custodian, $10.39/hr
Thompson, Aaron Mathew, prof, ast, $71,500
Thompson, Allen L, professor, $86,917
Thompson, Anne Elizabeth, prof, ast adjunct, $11,520
Thompson, Blandin Michelle, lab tech, persl svc-clin lab, $14.98/hr
Thompson, Breanna Kaprice, telecomm opr-h, $9.64/hr
Thompson, Brenda Gail, nurse, licensed prac sr, $20.39/hr
Thompson, Bryan A, support systems admin-expert, $53,530
Thompson, Carolyn J, prof, asoc, $53,078
Thompson, Catherine, grader, $7,200
Thompson, Charlene Antoinette, executive assistant, $21.64/hr
Thompson, Chris Vincent, extns professional, asoc, $60,593
Thompson, Courtney Ann, office supervisor, $42,103
Thompson, Cynthia M, office support assistant IV, $14.69/hr
Thompson, Cynthia Marie, librarian II, $72,855
Thompson, Dana Cherise, office support assistant III, $12.00/hr
Thompson, Dana R, account executive, $6,000
Thompson, Daryl L, security analyst-speclst, $52,770
Thompson, David L, bts painter, $20.23/hr
Thompson, Derek W, strat comm associate II, $40,986
Thompson, Dewey William, asoc dir program/project ops, $73,828
Thompson, Donald Leo, professor, $148,026
Thompson, Donnie J, prof, asoc adjunct, $500.00/hr
Thompson, Elizabeth C, clinical educator, $61,089
Thompson, Emily Loren, lab assistant, $9.00/hr
Thompson, Greg A, maint svc attd-mrc, $14.86/hr
Thompson, Greig, museum paraprofessional sr, $22.14/hr
Thompson, Heidi Lyn, asoc dir strat communications, $135,000
Thompson, Jacqueline Louise, prof, ast, $45,000
Thompson, Jacqueline Noelle, interior designer, $46,920
Thompson, James E, professor, $260,724
Thompson, Jami Denise, business support specialist II, $18.03/hr
Thompson, Jeffrey J, prof, ast adjunct, $125.00/hr
Thompson, Jennifer L, pharmacist II, $112,000
Thompson, Jerry Dewayne, instructor, adjunct, $9,600
Thompson, Jody Jay, mgr path, tech & admin svcs, $108,000
Thompson, Joshua F, hospital security officer, $11.07/hr
Thompson, Kathleen, executive assistant, $25.53/hr
Thompson, Katie Lee, resident physician-3rd yr, $52,470
Thompson, Kelsey Leigh, occl therapist, $52,920
Thompson, Kirk M, strat comm associate II, $61,248
Thompson, Kristopher Lee Bennet, nurse, staff II rnwp, $25.88/hr
Thompson, Lauren Kennedy, nurse, staff II, $21.37/hr
Thompson, Lee David, prof, adjunct, $27,600
Thompson, Lisa Renee, executive assistant, $18.37/hr
Thompson, Lonnie Joseph, engineer II, $64,000
Thompson, Marie A, librarian II, $52,821
Thompson, Melva Rae, custodian, $12.94/hr
Thompson, Nathan L, research/lab technician, $12.00/hr
Thompson, Paul Edward, food svc wrkr II, $11.07/hr
Thompson, Ronald D, research consultant II, $61,583
Thompson, Ronald Lee, mail carrier, $14.14/hr
Thompson, Scott E, student health administrator, $92,310
Thompson, Shaylan A, care team assoc-suppt, $10.85/hr
Thompson, Sherry L, nurse, clincl charge-lpn, $22.09/hr
Thompson, Steven James, programmer analyst-expert, $58,917
Thompson, Susan, ast coach, $35.34/hr
Thompson, Teresa L, surgical technl certified, $25.13/hr
Thompson, Thomas F, mgr II business admin, $57,181
Thompson, Valerie Kay, stage services assistant lead, $20.60/hr
Thompson, Wilford C, event assistant I, $7.50/hr
Thompson, Wyatt Warren, prof, asoc, $117,662
Thompson, Yvonne, office support assistant II, $13.27/hr
Thomsen, Jamie Lee, pharmacy tech, $13.30/hr
Thomsen, Rene Michelle, office support assistant IV, $14.00/hr
Thomson, Nathaniel J, resident physician-2nd yr, $52,007
Thomure, Joyce A, event assistant I, $10.00/hr
Thomure, Matthew D, nurse, staff II, $20.95/hr
Thornburg, Kathy, emeritus, $14,653
Thorne, John Andrew, system support analyst-expert, $26.56/hr
Thorne, Pamela Katheryn, resrch ast, $69,733
Thornhill, Jennifer K, user support analyst-expert, $22.12/hr

Thornhill, Paula S, custodian, $12.94/hr
Thornton, Brenda L, operations support tech II, $15.29/hr
Thornton, Earlene Marie, mental health tech, $13.96/hr
Thornton, James Kariem, custodian, $12.94/hr
Thornton, Jerry Bennett, csm associate III, $29.93/hr
Thornton, Jessica Mercedes, prof, ast, $54,770
Thornton, Matthew L, sr ast dir csm operations, $67,000
Thornton, Roy Jay, genl stores attd, $12.48/hr
Thornton, Tamika Latrece, patient svc rep, $12.68/hr
Thoroughman, Keri Ann, coor, reimbursement, $56,723
Thorp, Victoria M, office support assistant III, $14.37/hr
Thorpe, Angres M, ast coach, $80,000
Thorpe, Anthony P, research specialist sr, $54,299
Thorson, Esther L, dean, asoc, $188,340
Thrasher, Deanna Elaine, nurse, licensed prac, $15.06/hr
Thrasher, Marcia Denise, social worker, $25.00/hr
Threlkeld, Larry Wayne, mgr csm operations, $45,000
Thullen, Lila Virginia Dodge, care coordinator, $28,688
Thullen, Matthew J, prof, ast, $74,542
Thunhorst, Lorie Sue, business support specialist II, $23.30/hr
Thunhorst, Philip, fire protec/equip tech III, $20.75/hr
Thurlow, Christine Brunmeier, instructor, adjunct, $7,200
Thurmaier, David Paul, prof, asoc, $60,000
Thurman, Denise A, patient svc rep, $13.02/hr
Thurman, Jessica Ryan, coor, service, $16.20/hr
Thurman, Meagan Renee, temporary technical, $9.00/hr
Thurman, Teresa Jean, service rep IV, $16.13/hr
Thurmond, John W, prof, asoc, $169,227
Thurmond, Mary Melinda, office support assistant IV, $20.41/hr
Thurnau, Dawn Louise, sr mgr external relations, $68,000
Thyfault, Jessica Ann Friberg, sr ast dir studnt supprt svcs, $59,915
Thyfault, John P, prof, asoc, $131,325
Tian, Yan, prof, asoc, $67,250
Tian, Yuchen, temporary technical, $9.73/hr
Tibaldi, Bryan Joseph, dir sports operations, $80,000
Tibbs, Gloria L, librarian III, $62,291
Tibbs, Roosevelt, custodian, $13.36/hr
Tice, Ronald G, prof, ast, $45,677
Ticgelaor, Jamie Lynn, physician ast, $117,000
Tichelkamp, Paul A, police officer, $17.93/hr
Tichenor, Andrew Lars, lecturer, $3,060
Tidwell, Tiffany Teneal, nurse anesthetist, $145,760
Tidwell, Tonya Jean, fellow, $55,804
Tiede-Lewis, Leann Marie, resrch asoc, $45,500
Tiefenthaler, Ryan Michael, office support assistant III, $11.75/hr
Tiemann, Emma Suzanne, model, $15.00/hr
Tifft, Sharleen Marie, optician ast, $11.73/hr
Tiggemann, Teri Nichole, surgical techn certified, $16.84/hr
Tigue, Tawanda Ann, custodian, $10.00/hr
Till, Debra E, compliance anlyst, $50,500
Tilley, Celeste Gunn, office support assistant II, $11.00/hr
Tillinger, Scott F, grounds keeper II, $14.39/hr
Tillman, James Edwards, custodian, $10.39/hr
Tillman, Mercedes Shantrell, bus support specialist II, $17.24/hr
Tillman, Teri L, educational pgm associate I, $14.49/hr
Tillman, Wilma Kay, office support assistant IV, $13.18/hr
Tilson-Mallett, Nancy R, adjunct, $15,000
Tima, Lori Lynn, specialist, $10.00/hr
Timbrook, Kayla Lynette, bus support specialist II, $14.95/hr
Timbrook, Regina Ann, nurse, staff, $24.29/hr
Timko, Joseph, care team assoc-clinical, $13.60/hr
Timko, Noah John, rehab therapy aide, $10.64/hr
Timmerman, Christine, dean, ast, $75,000
Timmerman, Randal J, powr plnt cntrl sys techn sr, $27.26/hr
Timmons, Elizabeth Anne, veterinary technician, $13.85/hr
Timms, Howard J, supv pipefitting-h, $55,058
Timms, Kathy L, professor, $113,067
Timothy, Richko, event assistant I, $7.85/hr
Timpe, Michael Christian, food svc wrkr I, $9.60/hr
Tindal, Donna Michelle, service rep IV, $14.45/hr
Tindal, Megan Marie, physician ast, $91,600
Tindall, Douglas Anthony, student recruitment spclst, $20.37/hr
Tindall, Shannon Margaret, ast vice chancellor, $126,063
Tinnon, Tracy Lynn, office support assistant IV, $14.94/hr
Tinsley, Mark W, ultrasonographer, $33.69/hr
Tinsley, Megan Rene, educational pgm associate I, $12.61/hr
Tipler, Teresa Ann, educational pgm associate I, $13.45/hr
Tippett, Dane Gordon, construction manager II, $76,250
Tipton-Montie, Carleton, care team assoc-clinical, $13.04/hr

Tipton, Adam, student support specialist II, $17.85/hr
Tipton, Angela Marie, physical therapist, $71,115
Tipton, Catherine Lyn, mgr II student support svcs, $54,124
Tipton, Christina Dawn, strat comm associate II, $48,858
Tipton, Frances K, nurse, licensed prac, $17.42/hr
Tipton, Matthew S, db programmer analyst-expert, $55,775
Tipton, Peter A, professor, $102,220
Tipton, Sally J, office support assistant III, $16.83/hr
Tira, Claire Cecile, central sterile assistant, $12.58/hr
Tisone, Thomas A, dir network affiliation, $157,000
Titus, Yarrow, research/lab technician, $14.00/hr
Tjaden, James R, lecturer, $16,200
Tobias, Carminia, office support assistant IV, $16.26/hr
Tobin, Doris E, ast mgr hospitality services, $40,911
Tobin, Lynn M, prof, asoc visiting, $60,000
Tobwala, Shakila Banu, scientist, $55,000
Tocco, Pamela Lynn, resrch ast, $9.00/hr
Todd, David Arnold III, research/lab technician, $11.25/hr
Todd, Alice Christine, office support assistant IV, $13.30/hr
Todd, Caroline S, business support specialist II, $15.15/hr
Todd, Dennise N, academic advisor, $37,681
Todd, Janeth J, nurse spclst, clincl, $89,643
Todd, Jessica Sue, serv line spclst, $77,541
Todd, Judy Louise, business ops associate II, $44,353
Todd, Kayla B, event assistant I, $7.75/hr
Todd, Robert Alexander, emrg med techn paramedic, $20.00/hr
Todd, Susan Ledawn, reimbursement ast-cert, $19.68/hr
Todd, Tatha Lynette, patient svc rep, $13.02/hr
Todd, Tiffany L, office support assistant III, $13.91/hr
Todd, Wendy, media producer II, $19.00/hr
Toebben, Cheryl Lynn, nurse, staff II, $35.46/hr
Toebben, Leon F, engineering technician II, $19.09/hr
Toedebusch, Brian W, resident physician-3rd yr, $53,763
Toedebusch, Cynthia M, business support analyst II, $20.08/hr
Toellner, Ann Lohman, dir II finance, $88,797
Tofle, Ruth Brent, professor, $136,223
Tohline, Andrew M, lecturer, $40,804
Toigo, Alan Michael, business support specialist sr, $20.86/hr
Toigo, Stephanie Christine, office support assistant II, $12.05/hr
Toivanen, Kati, dean, asoc, $120,260
Toland, Sonia Esther, interpreter, medical, $25.00/hr
Tolbert, Barbara Ann, library info specialist sr, $15.00/hr
Toler, Paul W, asoc vice chancellor, $151,980
Toler, Tracy Rene, nurse, staff II rnwp, $23.08/hr
Toliver, Carol Lynn, mgr bus dev & planning, $104,186
Toliver, Gary C, messenger, $10.35/hr
Toll, Marsha Jean, psychologist, $40.00/hr
Tolle, Christin Jane, enrollment advisor sr, $16.54/hr
Tolson, Aaron C, emrg med techn, $13.19/hr
Tolson, Leah Rachel, social worker, $53,716
Tolson, Pamela Paulette, coor, service, $15.96/hr
Tomlin, Deborah, custodian, $12.94/hr
Tomlin, Mauria Shermane, care team assoc-suppt, $10.85/hr
Tomlinson, Diana Leigh, coor, service, $15.90/hr
Tomlinson, James Leroy, professor, $129,183
Tomlinson, Kristoffer Ray, maint svc attd, $16.88/hr
Tompson, Robert V Jr, professor, $100,456
Tones, Lonnie James, custodian, $12.94/hr
Tontz, Elizabeth Marjorie, custodian, $10.39/hr
Tonyan, Stacey Jo, business support specialist II, $18.82/hr
Toohey, Michael, system administrator-expert, $56,226
Toole, Mark Ora, steam plant opr I, $19.00/hr
Toomey, Amanda Christine, technology resource coor, $45,600
Toomey, Annetta, student support specialist sr, $19.00/hr
Toomsen, Tyle Andsager, custodian, $10.39/hr
Tophinke, Megan Elizabeth, nurse, staff II, $20.54/hr
Topper, Richard Jr, custodian, $10.39/hr
Toprak, Ahmet, fellow, post doc clncl yr1, $50.00/hr
Toprak, Ahmet, fellow, post doc clncl-yr3, $60,415
Toral, Rosario, custodian, $12.94/hr
Torbert, Benjamin C, prof, asoc, $61,820
Torbett, Jim R, custodian mrc, $10.50/hr
Torgashov, Evgeniy, fellow, post doctoral, $60,000
Torkildsen, Laurie, intern, $25,500
Torres, Susana, custodian, $13.23/hr
Torres, Theresa Lynn, prof, asoc, $61,573
Torreyson, Carrie Ann, care coordinator, $60,473
Torrusio, Ann T, lecturer, $36,900
Tosee, Michael D, instructor, adjunct, $7,200

Tosh II, Paul A, prof, asoc, $60,488
Tosh-Mitchell, Debashree, resident physician-6th yr, $58,200
Tosh, Aneesh Kumar, prof, asoc clincl dept, $140,348
Toth, Katalin, fellow, post doctoral, $40,038
Totty, Katherine Marie, office support assistant III, $13.42/hr
Tougaw, Cassie Marie, nurse, licensed prac, $14.76/hr
Touliatos, Diane H, professor, $109,694
Touzeau, Karen E Cottledge, asoc vice chancellor, $170,344
Touzeau, Leslie E, research specialist I, $36,894
Tovar-Mendez, Alejandro, resrch scientist/academic, $50,265
Tovey, Jonathan C, resident physician-4th yr, $55,804
Towell, Pamela F, custodian, $10.69/hr
Towheed, Arooge, resident physician-1st yr, $49,025
Towne, Sarah J, office support assistant IV, $17.04/hr
Towner, Robbie Rosha, care team assoc-clinical, $12.32/hr
Townes, Malcolm Shabazz, mgr II business admin, $71,357
Townlain, Kimberly A, office support assistant IV, $15.60/hr
Townley, Ronald Lee Jr, clerk, stores, $13.63/hr
Towns, Diane Marie, office support assistant III, $11.53/hr
Townsend, Anna Pauline, custodian, $12.90/hr
Townsend, Dana Woodman, resrch ast, $10.00/hr
Townsend, Jennifer L, business support specialist II, $17.24/hr
Townsend, Martha A, professor, $84,043
Townsend, Sabresa Varasha, care team assoc-suppt, $13.37/hr
Townsend, Travas W, instructl technl, $54,419
Townsend, Ty, prof, ast adjunct, $7,575
Towsley, Matthew Shade, resident physician-5th yr, $56,120
Trabue, Tera L, nurse, registered-first ast, $28.66/hr
Trachtenberg, Ben Lev Winslade, prof, asoc, $110,984
Tracy-Smith, Emily Kathryn, research specialist sr, $40,102
Tracy, Daniel P, office support assistant IV, $13.70/hr
Tracy, Timothy R, physical therapist, $58,752
Trader, Barry Thomas, managing engineer, $100,773
Trader, Tammy D, support systems admin-princpl, $70,013
Trahan, Jessica L, coor athletic operations, $38,340
Traiger, Jeffrey Davis, sr dir studnt supprt svcs, $108,804
Trammell, Jeffrey Lee, nurse, staff II rnwp, $21.68/hr
Tran, Anh Nam, resrch asoc, $82,800
Tran, Phu T, physician, $159,655
Tran, Phu T, physician, $100.00/hr
Tran, Thu Hoang, student service coor I, $40,892
Tran, Thu Thi Thu, ultrasonographer, $30.69/hr
Tranel, Mark, academic dir, $112,538
Trantham, Angela Joenette, office support assistant IV, $18.54/hr
Traore-Gress, Rainatou Carole, business support spclst II, $18.75/hr
Trapani, Sandra L, prof, teach, $47,990
Tratchel, Jason, system administrator-princpl, $60,600
Traub, Sarah Marie, human dev spclst, $47,423
Trauterman, Barbara A, mgr II business admin, $55,890
Trauth, Kathleen M, prof, asoc, $103,090
Travis, Cynthia Diane, business support specialist sr, $20.60/hr
Travis, Frederick William, prof, ast, $70,000
Travis, Mark Douglas, prof, ast clincl dept, $255,000
Travlos, Benjamin John, temporary technical, $10.00/hr
Travlos, John S, system administrator-expert, $69,262
Travlos, Kalliope Marie, temporary technical, $8.25/hr
Travnichek, Rebecca J, extns professional, $61,391
Tray, Krystal Ann, supv, lab, $82,818
Trayford, Mary Ruth, dental auxiliary supervisor, $43,199
Treadway, Beauton Marie, office support assistant IV, $16.11/hr
Treadway, Richard J, painter, $21.15/hr
Trejo, Abigail L, nurse, staff II, $20.54/hr
Treloar, A Nathan, office support assistant IV, $13.73/hr
Treloar, Timothy Christophe, research/lab technician, $11.00/hr
Tremain, Janet Crandell, resrch ast sr, $24,000
Tremaine, Scarlett L, supv housekeeping, $38,044
Trent, Anne Obucina, ultrasonographer, $34.94/hr
Trent, Neil J, mgr rad technl/admin svcs-h, $128,835
Triatik, Rebecca L, student service coor II, $43,362
Tribble, Silvia C, nurse, staff II, $32.45/hr
Trice, Shameal, dental assistant II, $15.92/hr
Trice, Willie M, central sterile assistant, $11.85/hr
Trimble, Amanda Carroll, intern, $25,500
Trimble, Jessica Lynne, student recruitment spclst sr, $22.07/hr
Trindade, Vitor Manuel Correia, prof, asoc, $111,406
Trinkle, Karyn N, supv pat accts-up, $52,929
Trinklein, David Herbert, prof, asoc, $83,928
Triplett, Gregory É Jr, prof, asoc, $104,668
Triplett, Karen Kay, optician ast, $12.42/hr

Triplett, Richard Allen, floor maint wkr, $13.84/hr
Triplitt, Christopher Lynn, peoplesoft admin-expert, $75,000
Tripp, Bradley L, surgical technl certified, $18.50/hr
Tripp, Nicholas Dane, rehab therapy aide, $12.30/hr
Trish, Margaret E, librarian IV, $62,397
Tritschler, Lawren Marie, patient svc rep, $11.90/hr
Tritschler, Matthew Alan, floor care techn lead, $14.62/hr
Tritschler, Tracy Lynn, fin and acctg manager, $55,000
Trogdon, Timothy Lee, program/project supprt coor I, $25,000
Trom, Jennifer Lynn, fin and acctg specialist, $16.50/hr
Trombley, Ralph W, mts/electrician-r, $20.87/hr
Troppito, Charles C Jr, instructor, $42,000
Trotter, Carol W, prof, ast clincl, $12,752
Trotter, James Bruce, prof, ast clincl, $93,640
Troup, Jodi Rae, compliance manager sr, $48,645
Trout, Carlynn W, academic advisor, $37,931
Trout, Dennis E, prof, asoc, $81,894
Trout, Jacob Muir, high school student, $9.50/hr
Trout, Kenneth Ben, bts carpenter, $19.59/hr
Troutman, Charisse Renae, office support assistant IV, $16.50/hr
Troutwine, Alison Brown, executive assistant, $18.00/hr
Trowbridge, Jessica Lynn, care team assoc-clinical, $11.10/hr
Troy, Mary, professor, $67,433
Troyer, Matthew David, high school student, $8.00/hr
Troyer, Vickie Lynn, educational pgm assistant, $10.23/hr
Troyke, Lynelle Kathleen, office support assistant II, $10.34/hr
True, Cynthia Diane, resrch asoc, $57,087
Trueblood, Max Blair, resrch aide sr, $61,721
Trueblood, Michael T, prof, asoc adjunct, $20,475
Truesdell, David Lee, library info specialist, $15.15/hr
Truesdell, Jacqueline Kay, nurse, staff prn, $26.00/hr
Truitt, Kara Leann, office support assistant III, $11.67/hr
Trull, Timothy J, prof, curators, $166,991
Trulson, Jerry J, resident physician-5th yr, $58,083
Truman, Kevin Zane, dean, $254,100
Trumpold, Julia, instructor, adjunct, $8,100
Truss, Leslie Lee, custodian, $12.94/hr
Trussell, Jessica Lynn, human dev spclst, $45,187
Trust, Shannetrice Meria-Anne, custodian, $12.18/hr
Trusty, Whitney, resident physician-1st yr, $49,025
Tsai, Chia-Lin, research specialist I, $34,670
Tsai, Hailung, professor, $135,866
Tsai, Hui Hsien, instructional designer-spclst, $54,920
Tschirhart, David Bernard, user support analyst-spclst, $20.78/hr
Tse, Eliza, professor, $100,500
Tse, Yiuman, professor, $242,103
Tseng, Howard Jau-Haur, resident physician-1st yr, $50,219
Tsika, Richard W, professor, $118,580
Tsiklauri, Mikheil, prof, ast resrch, $50,337
Tsoi, Allanus Hakman, professor, $81,943
Tsuruta, Kaoru, research specialist I, $26,506
Tu, Junwu, prof, ast, $78,000
Tubbesing, Merribeth Ann, med techl reg, $28.30/hr
Tubbs, Arielle Kay, hospital lab tech, $12.71/hr
Tubbs, Mark E, prof, asoc, $66,572
Tucker, Beverly D, mental health professional, $56,923
Tucker, Gregory D, dir program/project operations, $80,000
Tucker, John Bernard, instructor, clincl, $21,075
Tucker, Kelsey Elise, nurse, staff I, $19.00/hr
Tucker, Kenrick L, police officer, $18.68/hr
Tucker, Lisa Diane, office support associate, $22.52/hr
Tucker, Naomi Erin, temporary crafts service, $9.50/hr
Tucker, Naomi Marie, student support specialist II, $15.50/hr
Tucker, Robert E, prof, adjunct, $12,750
Tucker, Wesley, extns professional, asoc, $57,537
Tucker, Zachary Edward, instructor, adjunct, $15,300
Tufts, Jennifer Marie, academic advisor, $47,500
Tuggle, Cheryl Ann, nurse, staff II, $30.00/hr
Tuggle, Mary Michelle, nurse, licensed prac, $18.89/hr
Tuggle, Molly A, educational pgm associate I, $13.45/hr
Tuggle, Teresa Suzanne, lecturer, $51,500
Tugushi, Molly Ann, office support assistant IV, $15.50/hr
Tukuli, Adama Roba, research/lab technician, $13.87/hr
Tuley, Suzan M, mgr III business admin, $81,508
Tulipana, Teresa, program/project supprt coor I, $50,000
Tuller, Erin Ragan, prof, ast clincl dept, $173,139
Tullock, Emily Marie, research/lab technician sr, $12.98/hr
Tullous, Tamara Danielle, high school student, $7.50/hr
Tummons, John D, specialist, $61,233

Tummons, Martha Elizabeth, strat comm associate sr, $55,657
Tun, Moe Phyu, resident physician-3rd yr, $52,470
Tunink, Jennifer Lynn, hlth prgm ast, $12.50/hr
Tunis, Jeanne C, nurse, staff II wkend II, $30.83/hr
Tunkuc, Yesim, prof, ast clincl, $88,434
Tupper, Jacob Norton, media producer I, $12.99/hr
Tupper, Stephen H, administrative consultant, $99,304
Turagam, Mohit K, fellow, post doc clncl yr1, $55,804
Turban, Daniel B, professor, $220,102
Turbush, Marilyn Tortocion, office support asst IV, $17.50/hr
Turbyeville, Sherry K, nurse, staff II, $34.18/hr
Turek, Christina Rose, food svc wrkr I, $9.60/hr
Turkmani, Danya, executive assistant, $19.23/hr
Turley, Danielle Nicole, program/project supprt coor I, $39,304
Turley, Samantha Jo, physical therapist, $62,220
Turley, Tony Albert, physical therapist, $59,928
Turnbull, Janet M, coor guest house-ef, $47,861
Turnbull, Jeffrey S, mech, bldg maint, $19.64/hr
Turnbull, John Jeffrey, student support specialist sr, $20.96/hr
Turnbull, Quentin Ray, mech, bldg maint, $19.25/hr
Turner, James Michael Jr, business tech analyst-princpl, $65,798
Turner-Malveaux, Deronda Wynette, supv sterile proc, $55,058
Turner, Blake R, event assistant I, $7.75/hr
Turner, Bobbie Jo, coor head injury svc, $40,129
Turner, Carla J, office support assistant IV, $15.51/hr
Turner, Carol Jane, library info specialist, $14.86/hr
Turner, Cathy Marie, office support assistant IV, $20.27/hr
Turner, Christina Kay, custodian, $10.39/hr
Turner, Christina Suzanne, instructor, adjunct, $7,059
Turner, Crystal D, compliance manager sr, $47,508
Turner, Danielle D, nurse, staff II, $24.90/hr
Turner, Darlene L, business support specialist II, $19.79/hr
Turner, Deann L, educational pgm associate I, $14.56/hr
Turner, Donna Jean, db programmer analyst-princpl, $74,271
Turner, Giedre Marit, research specialist sr, $40,580
Turner, Gladys A, custodian, $12.94/hr
Turner, Gwendolyn Yvonne, founders professor, $10,098
Turner, James T, bts carpenter, $21.71/hr
Turner, Jessica Dawn, emergency services rep, $14.88/hr
Turner, Karen M, program/project supprt coor I, $55,557
Turner, Laura L, human resources specialist I, $18.03/hr
Turner, Linda G, office support assistant IV, $19.57/hr
Turner, Linda R, mgr II business admin, $62,046
Turner, Linda Sue, dir program/project operations, $90,100
Turner, Michael D, lecturer, $37,638
Turner, Michael L, temporary crafts service, $9.10/hr
Turner, Nichole D, business ops associate I, $38,408
Turner, Pamela A, patient svc rep, $14.55/hr
Turner, Ramona Lynn, lab techn, persl svc-clin lab, $17.10/hr
Turner, Rhonda Diane, executive assistant, $23.80/hr
Turner, Sarah Y, business support specialist II, $21.78/hr
Turner, Sharon Yvonne, office support assistant III, $13.80/hr
Turner, Stephanie Nichole, care team assoc-clinical, $12.57/hr
Turner, Tammy Gale, fin and acctg manager, $56,311
Turner, Tammy L, nurse, licensed prac, $21.37/hr
Turner, Tracey Michelle, asoc dir program/project ops, $59,375
Turner, Tracy J, retail sales manager, $30,888
Turner, Victoria Lynn, coor, service, $15.08/hr
Turner, Wendy Anne, patient svc rep, $12.69/hr
Tutko, Kylie Erin, student recruitment spclst, $14.96/hr
Tutor, Brooke Nichole, resp therapist reg, $18.59/hr
Tuttle, Abigail Christine, fin and acctg manager sr, $83,554
Tuttle, Anna M, service rep IV, $16.13/hr
Tuttle, Dustin H, patient svc rep, $12.81/hr
Tuttle, Gabrielle Ellaine, library info specialist, $13.30/hr
Tuttle, Ronald Eugene, prof, asoc adjunct, $9,519
Twenter, Becky Sue, custodian, $12.94/hr
Twenter, Brian James, instructor, adjunct, $15,000
Twenter, Carla D, office support assistant III, $14.50/hr
Twenter, Carol Ann, mgr II business admin, $63,688
Twenter, Charles L, custodian, $12.94/hr
Twenter, Cynthia Rae, nurse, licensed prac, $18.92/hr
Twenter, Heidi Michelle, human resources specialist sr, $60,000
Twenter, Kathleen Margaret, nurse, licensed prac, $14.76/hr
Twenter, Marvin J, med techl reg, $26.94/hr
Twenter, Shance L, mover, $12.90/hr
Twenter, Shawn Aloysius, db programmer analyst-princpl, $68,470
Twenter, Vincent M, bts locksmith, $20.23/hr
Twillie, Kaylynn Nicole, office support assistant IV, $14.18/hr

Twillman, Nancy A, instructor, adjunct, $15,000
Twyman, Bridget Rae, mental health tech, $14.59/hr
Twyman, Nathan William, prof, ast, $105,000
Tyler, Lawson John Jr, engineer, resrch, $74,313
Tyler, Aurora Dawn, instructor, adjunct, $9,000
Tyler, Courtney Jo, med lab techn, $17.52/hr
Tyler, Dion Joseph, pharmacy intern first year, $12.00/hr
Tyler, Gary D, user support analyst-entry, $16.12/hr
Tyler, Krystal, fellow, post doctoral, $42,000
Tyler, Lindsey Leigh, media producer II, $14.95/hr
Tyler, Melvin C, vice chancellor, $184,185
Tyler, Vicki Kay, custodian, $11.41/hr
Tylski, Emily, resident physician-1st yr, $49,025
Tymoigne, Eric, prof, adjunct, $30,000
Tyner, Victoria B, db programmer analyst-expert, $56,263
Tynes, Donna J, event assistant I, $7.75/hr
Tyree, Steven Paul, nurse, staff I, $20.95/hr
Tyrer, Harry Wakeley Jr, professor, $109,030
Tyrer, Leslie Allan, office support assistant IV, $15.00/hr
Tyrrell, Marie Danette, educational pgm associate I, $13.11/hr
Tyrrell, Sarah Malia, prof, ast teach, $36,058
Tyson, Leslie Joan, nurse, staff II, $20.95/hr
Tzegay, Genet G, custodian, $10.00/hr
Tzou, Robert D, professor, $238,402
Ubinas, George Jesus, instructor, clincl, $100,000
Udani, Adriano Anthony A Jr, prof, ast, $67,347
Udawatta, Ranjith P, prof, asoc resrch, $74,263
Ueda, Keiko, prof, ast teach, $35,000
Ueki, Yasuyoshi, prof, asoc, $88,109
Uetrecht, Daniel Joseph, director it, $104,954
Uftring, Jennifer Lynne, patient svc rep, $11.73/hr
Ugarte, Michael, professor, $92,991
Uhlenhake, Molly A, adjunct, $15,000
Uhlmann, Jeffrey, prof, asoc, $94,232
Uhlmann, Scott K, ast vice president, $144,699
Uhlmann, Zachary Alberts, high school student, $10.00/hr
Ukatu, Ceisha Chinwe, resident physician-1st yr, $50,219
Ukpokodu, Omiunota Nelly, professor, $76,912
Ulam, Frederick Anthony, psychologist, $86,888
Ulbrich, Sherri Lynn, prof, ast clincl, $48,176
Ulery, Bret Daniel, prof, ast, $90,000
Ulery, Eva Schott, instructor, clincl, $75,000
Ullrich, Carsten Andreas, professor, $95,354
Ulrich, Catherine Louise, asoc dir program/project ops, $60,000
Ulrich, Cynthia Stephanie, executive assistant, $20.00/hr
Ulrich, Marilyn, office support assistant III, $17.00/hr
Ulrich, Theresa J, nurse, staff II, $36.29/hr
Umali, Arzelyn T, prgm mgr II studnt supprt svcs, $46,512
Umran, Kusai A, physician, $237,991
Unal, Ahmet, db programmer analyst-speclst, $50,902
Unal, Bonnie J, dir I, business admin, $69,745
Underwood, Alex Jordan, nurse, staff II, $20.54/hr
Underwood, Danielle Melissa, resrch ast sr, $32,136
Underwood, Edward, prof, asoc, $167,090
Underwood, Jennifer Ann, office support assistant IV, $20.22/hr
Underwood, Michael B, professor, $98,347
Underwood, Rosa Antoinette, instructor, clincl, $21,075
Underwood, William Lewis, prof, ast clincl dept, $200,000
Unger, Brent J, chair, asoc, $57,531
Unger, Jane Marie, hlthcre db prgmmr & anltcs adm, $70,616
Unger, Janet Leslie, office support assistant IV, $16.96/hr
Ungles, Bruce K, program/project supprt coor sr, $48,181
Ungles, Katherine N, office support assistant III, $17.94/hr
Union, Lisa Annie, custodian, $13.23/hr
Unni, Deepak Raveendran, resrch anlyst, $60,600
Unrath, Kathleen, prof, asoc, $78,631
Uong, Linette Lynn, retail sales associate sr, $15.47/hr
Upah, Jennifer R, prof, ast teach, $57,502
Updike, Heidi G, office support assistant IV, $16.32/hr
Upendran, Anandhi, temporary professional, $33.65/hr
Uphoff, Rodney J, professor, $227,798
Uppinghouse, Brad, research specialist I, $40,839
Upshaw, Adam K, lecturer, $23,874
Uptergrove, Adam D, nurse, staff II, $21.97/hr
Upton, Gary Lee, physician, stu hlth, $143,907
Upton, Kathy K, research specialist II, $27,874
Uranga, Ramona, custodian, $13.36/hr
Urban, Alex C, distribution techn-mtls mgmt, $12.22/hr
Urban, Karli Ross Echterling, prof, ast clincl dept, $137,700

Urban, Kerri L, strat comm associate II, $47,392
Urban, Michael A, prof, asoc, $92,253
Urdang, Liza Natalie, office support assistant IV, $17.08/hr
Urenda, Kimberly A, instructor, adjunct, $6,300
Uribe, Heriberto, custodian, $12.94/hr
Urie, Chelsea Lauren, care team assoc-clinical, $11.25/hr
Urkov, Samuel Aaron, nurse, staff I, rnwp, $19.00/hr
Urlacher, Lucy, musical instrument technician, $21.94/hr
Urton, David N, mech, auto, $19.23/hr
Usery, Carol Elaine, csm professional I, $45,732
Usery, Dennis E, grounds keeper II, $15.15/hr
Usery, Kevin Lee, grounds keeper II, $15.15/hr
Usman, Shoaib, prof, asoc, $93,008
Usui, Chikako, prof, asoc, $73,761
Utterback, Heather Noel, educational pgm assoc I, $13.31/hr
Utzmyers, Tracy Nicole, stage services assistant lead, $18.00/hr
Uwase, Nadege, executive assistant, $16.87/hr
Vacca, Joseph Lyle, instructor, $61,379
Vadali, Sirisha V, resident physician-1st yr, $50,219
Vaddi, Suman, resident physician-2nd yr, $52,007
Vadivelu, Hema, med techl reg, $26.49/hr
Vaidya, Naveen Kumar, prof, ast, $66,230
Vaill, Jerry Edward Jr, lecturer, $15,000
Valdivia, Corinne B, prof, asoc, $108,152
Valdovino, Anita, office support assistant IV, $15.52/hr
Vale, Joe Donald Jr, strat comm associate sr, $65,280
Valencia, Jayne Marie, activity aide, $13.50/hr
Valenti, Mary L, instructor, adjunct, $6,276
Valentine Fjone, Claudia A, prof, ast teach, $83,709
Valentine, Linda H, system administrator-princpl, $85,477
Valenzuela, Dalila, research/lab technician sr, $14.64/hr
Valiavska, Anna, student service coor II, $44,290
Vallambhatla, Kushal Kumar, programmer analyst-spclst, $53,560
Vallejo, Julian Alfredo, resrch ast, $32,000
Vallentyne, Peter L, professor, $164,530
Valleroy, Andrew Thomas, resident physician-2nd yr, $52,007
Valley, Michelle B, resp therapist reg, $20.92/hr
Valliyodan, Babu, resrch scientist/academic sr, $64,500
Vallot, Renee' Michelle, custodian, $10.94/hr
Valyear, Kenneth Franklin, fellow, post doctoral, $47,244
Van Aken, David C, prof, curator teach, $137,278
Van Ark, Robert E, powr plnt maint spclst III mw, $25.85/hr
Van Beek, Michael F, csm associate I, $20.66/hr
Van Cleave, Erika Sonja, food svc wrkr I, $9.60/hr
Van Dalsem, Kristyne Elizabeth, patient svc rep, $11.29/hr
Van Dam, Sara Fay, resident physician-3rd yr, $52,470
Van De Berg, Thomas J, forensic investigator, $28.01/hr
Van De Liefvoort, Appie H, professor, $112,361
Van De Mark, Michael R, prof, asoc, $86,629
Van Doren, Jessica Lynn, supv food svc I,-h, $33,293
Van Doren, Steven R, professor, $102,450
Van Dusseldorp, Rodger K, model, $17.00/hr
Van Dyke, James A, prof, asoc, $63,771
Van Eaton, Melinda Kaye, instructor, adjunct, $18,000
Van Garderen-Anderson, Delinda, prof, asoc, $78,590
Van Gessel, Christine Ann, fellow, post doctoral, $35,000
Van Hooser, Michael E, nurse, staff II, $20.95/hr
Van Hove, Elizabeth A, mgr, med staff affs & gme-umhc, $79,081
Van Hunnik, Pat M, sfty & emgncy prepdness coor, $54,138
Van Loo, Margaret J, nurse practitioner, $94,015
Van Morlan, Amie Margett, prof, ast clincl dept, $155,357
Van Ness, Christopher J, prof, ast resrch, $79,085
Van Ness, Forrest Lester, dir II university police, $95,500
Van Nice, Abbie Renee, waiter/waitress, $9.00/hr
Van Noy, Vicki D, business support specialist II, $19.51/hr
Van Pool, Christine I, prof, asoc, $59,872
Van Rhein, Stephanie Michelle, lecturer, $35,745
Van Stee, Stephanie K, prof, ast, $58,000
Van Trump, Richard Michael, resident physician-1st yr, $49,025
Van Uum, Elizabeth, ast vice chancellor, $187,419
Van Waes, Cheryl Ann, office support assistant IV, $18.25/hr
Van Wert, Paul David, lecturer, $48,410
Van Winkle, Velma Violet, education nurse, $78,374
Vanarsdale, Emily Ann, executive assistant sr, $62,105
Vanatta, Christina E, academic advisor sr, $48,338
Vance, Amy Michelle, nutrition spclst, $41,500
Vance, Cherilyn E, student support specialist I, $13.42/hr
Vance, GaeDene, nurse, staff II, $24.23/hr
Vance, Jason J, temporary professional, $15.30/hr
Vance, Marijean Louise, ast mgr hospitality services, $41,200
Vance, Nora L, service rep III, $12.58/hr
Vance, Wanda L, human resources specialist I, $16.42/hr
Vandagriff, Tyson C, resident physician-3rd yr, $53,763
Vandel, Jeffrey Todd, dir II csm operations, $105,060
Vandelicht, Virginia Lynn, asoc dir program/project ops, $57,292
Vandell, Caitlin Ann, speech/lang pathologist, $53,561
Vandeloecht, Harold B, agriculture associate II, $15.77/hr
Vandeloecht, Sharina Maxine, nurse, or/recovery-ch, $20.95/hr
Vandenberg, Brian Richard, professor, $97,573
VanDenBorn, John W, head coach, $58,000
Vander Ley, Brian L, prof, ast, $105,060
Vanderheyden, Joel Patrick, lecturer, $7,140
Vandermillion, Catherine Lacey, patient svc rep, $11.62/hr
Vandermolen, Sarah Ruth, nurse, staff II, $21.68/hr
VanDeVoorde, Tara K, human resources specialist sr, $58,055
VanDiggelen, Jacob Paul, operations support tech II, $11.30/hr
Vandike, James E, lecturer, $30,000
Vangel, Tracie Leigh, office support assistant IV, $14.93/hr
Vangilder, Larry D, instructor, $18,500
VanHorn, Jon David, prof, asoc, $71,122
Vanhove, Gregory A, system administrator-princpl, $68,515
Vanlandingham, Penny Dianne, health records techn II, $13.10/hr
Vanlerberghe, Deborah L, med techl reg, $29.71/hr
Vanloo, Tiffany Nicole, nurse, staff I, $19.00/hr
VanMarle, Kristy L, prof, ast, $69,106
Vannatta, Michelle Leigh, custodian, $11.41/hr
Vanpool, Todd Logan, prof, asoc, $65,780
Vansaghi, Thomas M, instructor, adjunct, $9,600
VanSciver, Allison Kate, media producer sr, $37,903
VanSciver, Edward H, teaching ast, $13.00/hr
VanSkike, Randy Rebel Jr, nurse, staff II, $21.37/hr
Vanskike, Katherine Paulette, ast mgr hospitality svcs, $42,007
Vanskike, Lyndle Ray, agriculture foreman, $23.50/hr
Vantassel, Desiree Marie, office support assistant III, $12.41/hr
Vantic, Sandra, educational pgm associate I, $12.87/hr
Vantine, Lucinda R, dir I, event services, $72,587
VanVo, Thanh, media producer I, $12.99/hr
Vanvoorden, Barbara, prof, asoc teach, $40,865
Vanvranken, Erika Lea, manuscript specialist, $35,000
Vardhanabhuti, Bongkosh, prof, ast, $65,367
Varela Giron, Alberto Enrique, prof, ast adjunct, $125.00/hr
Vargas, Ashley M, nurse, staff II, $20.95/hr
Vargas, Guadalupe Avrea, instructor, adjunct, $14,400
Varghese, Aaron Prasad, resident physician-1st yr, $49,025
Varghese, Ebby G, prof, ast clincl dept, $229,539
Vargo, Lyn E, prof, ast clincl, $58,853
Varner, Barbara L, trades helper, $10.78/hr
Varns, Curtis Wayne, instructor, adjunct, $9,000
Varvaro, John Anthony, patient svc rep, $11.29/hr
Vasconcelles, Erin Brooke, psychologist, $56,992
Vasko, Maria Vladimirovna, instructor, $42,894
Vasquez Encalada, Nataly Monserrath, fellow, post doc clncl
    yr 1, $55,804
Vasquez, Dondra F, custodian, $12.94/hr
Vassmer, Sara B, program/project supprt coor II, $53,333
Vasudevan, Archana, resident physician-1st yr, $50,219
Vatterott, Cathy, professor, $73,367
Vaughan, Gary F, animal caretaker, $12.55/hr
Vaughan, Vanessa Margaret, lab techn, persl svc-clin lab, $15.27/hr
Vaughn Ward, Crystal Dawn, sterile processing tech, $18.58/hr
Vaughn, Adrienne L, academic advisor, $37,878
Vaughn, Beverly Ann, executive assistant, $22.18/hr
Vaughn, David Jeremey, prof, adjunct, $11,700
Vaughn, Denise C, interventional technl (ir), $20.94/hr
Vaughn, Joseph Lesieur, mts/refrigeration mech, $21.05/hr
Vaughn, Katie Rochelle, head coach, $72,116
Vaughn, Latricia J, office support assistant III, $13.18/hr
Vaughn, Linda, office support assistant IV, $17.79/hr
Vaughn, Meredith Udell, press III, $20.77/hr
Vaughn, Michael Todd, db administrator-expert, $63,840
Vaughn, Paula Jean, surgical technl certified, $15.87/hr
Vaught, David R, prof, asoc teach, $78,170
Vaught, F Wayne, dean, $190,550
Vaught, Lawrence Allen, business support specialist II, $16.05/hr
Vaught, Raymond Fredrick, support systems admin-spclst, $55,000
Vavilin, Ilan, emrg med techn, $11.61/hr
Vawter, Linda Lee, lecturer, $41,450
Vazquez, Melissa Yazmin, child dev aide, $9.14/hr

Veach, Cathleen Anne, human resources specialist III, $54,432
Vedagiri, Anuradha, prof, ast/profl pract, $42,913
Vega, Abel, research specialist I, $35,755
Vega, Chastity Deann, surgical technl certified, $19.83/hr
Vega, Donna Kay, academic advisor, $16.71/hr
Vega, Margaret Grace, instructor, ast, $22,680
Vega, Matthew J, specialist, $40,921
Vega, Teresa Gale, business support specialist II, $17.59/hr
Veile, Steve Eric, instructor, adjunct, $9,000
Velagapudi, Poonam, fellow, post doc clncl-yr2, $58,083
Velazquez, Celso Raul, prof, asoc clncl dept, $203,991
Velders, Gary Stanley, mech trades spclst (mts), $22.42/hr
Velicer, Daniel James, prof, asoc adjunct, $40.00/hr
Veljkovich, Svetlana, sr ast dir studnt supprt svcs, $53,186
Vellai Badrdoss, Surya Prasath, fellow, post doctoral, $33,000
Vellema, Travis J, operations support tech sr, $18.39/hr
Vellema, William C, research engineering tech II, $28.40/hr
Velloff-Burris, Tara Marie, physician, stu hlth, $68.28/hr
Veltrop, Tonya Marie, student service coor sr, $53,685
Vena, Tammy Sue, office support assistant IV, $13.12/hr
Venkitachalam, Lakshmi, prof, ast, $83,000
Ventimiglia, Frances, office support assistant sr, $15.00/hr
Verano Camones, Katherine M, food svc wrkr II, $10.10/hr
Verbist, Daniel E, resident physician-2nd yr, $52,007
Verbitsky, Igor, prof, curators, $152,947
Verble, Steven H, police officer, $19.10/hr
Verhoff, Jade Nicole, surgical technl certified, $17.18/hr
Verkamp, Laura Elizabeth, instructor, adjunct, $9,000
Verma, Anju, resrch asoc, $41,096
Vermilion, Mary Rose, prof, ast adjunct, $10,500
Vernon, Kathryn Hazel, veterinary technician sr, $15.00/hr
Vernon, Kathy Ann, resrch asoc, $42,420
Verret, Sheryl Dawn, custodian, $11.41/hr
Verslues, Stephanie M, health records techn I, $10.93/hr
Vessell, Danna, technology resource director, $103,197
Vessell, Joann, food svc wrkr I, $9.60/hr
Vest, Teresa L, sr mgr business admin, $66,388
Vestal II, Robert D, pat acct rep, $14.15/hr
Vestal, Donna Steele, dir I, broadcast operations, $65,000
Vestal, Holly F, patient svc rep, $14.88/hr
Vetter-Smith, Molly J, prof, ast extns, $60,886
Vick, Angela, business support specialist II, $20.43/hr
Victor, Ernest Charles, fin and acctg manager, $73,144
Victor, Lisa Renae, mri technologist, $27.64/hr
Vie, Laura Leigh, instructor, adjunct, $4,800
Vieira Potter, Victoria Jeanne, prof, ast, $71,400
Vieira, Carter Behrens, student recruitment spclst, $15.25/hr
Vietti, Dana R, resident physician-3rd yr, $53,763
Vignale, Giovanni, prof, curators, $147,482
Vikulova, Yekaterina Eduardovna, programmer analyst-entry,
$40,400
Vilchez, Denise Azucena, resident physician-2nd yr, $50,810
Viley, David Foster, hospital security officer, $12.48/hr
Viley, Karen Gail, supv housekeeping, $37,502
Villamandos, Alberto, prof, asoc, $57,002
Villamil Monroy, Astrid Milena, prof, ast teach, $44,000
Villeda, Virgilio Alexander, resident physician-1st yr, $50,219
Vince, Louis Scott, nurse anesthetist, $147,900
Vincent-Masek, Shelly Renee, proj mgr, fac plng & sp anyls, $66,300
Vincent, Austin P, grader, $15.00/hr
Vincent, Deante M, pat acct rep, $14.24/hr
Vincent, Jean, resident physician-4th yr, $54,425
Vincenz, Felix Thaddeus, prof, ast resrch, $76,250
Viner, Tracie Lynn, nurse, staff II, $31.92/hr
Vines, Kelly Sue, program/project supprt coor I, $50,000
Vineyard, Megan Renee, emrg med techn, $11.61/hr
Vining, Elizabeth W, prof, ast teach, $57,989
Vining, Jennifer Hicks, med techl reg, $25.82/hr
Vinocour, Joshua W, asoc dir program/project ops, $63,085
Vinson, Daniel C, emeritus, $68,666
Vinyard, Kaylona Dazshanay, food svc wrkr III, $12.20/hr
Vinyard, Phillip K, practice manager, $84,660
Vinyard, Vashante, custodian, $10.94/hr
Vinzant, Lisa Thorn, instructor, adjunct, $10,800
Virden, Christina Lynn, librarian I, $13.08/hr
Virkler, Mark Robert, professor, $154,384
Visintainer, Sean David, librarian I, $41,602
Viswanathan, Deepa, resrch scientist/academic, $50,000
Vitiello, Massimiliano, prof, ast, $55,516

Viyanon, Suwit, programmer analyst-entry, $45,806
Vo, Tuoi Van, custodian, $10.39/hr
Voelkel, Lindsey Brooke, nurse, staff II, $21.37/hr
Voelker, Marsha Ann, prof, asoc, $72,250
Voelkl, Dawna Lynn, prof, ast teach, $97,566
Voeller, Teresa Snow, corp dir strtgc comm & med rel, $130,000
Vogan, Michael, fire protec/equip tech I, $12.55/hr
Vogan, Randall T, asoc dir fin and acctg, $96,000
Vogel, Christopher Thomas, resident physician-3rd yr, $52,470
Vogel, Gary Lee, prof, ast adjunct, $13,846
Vogel, Gary Ray, nurse, staff II, $34.18/hr
Vogel, Matthew S, prof, ast, $67,500
Vogel, Todd Rudolph, prof, asoc, $255,000
Vogel, Wendy Ann, office support assistant IV, $15.42/hr
Vogelsmeier, Amy, prof, asoc, $82,085
Vogelweid, Eric J, dir II finance, $104,864
Vogelweid, Mary Catherine, prof, asoc clncl, $108,421
Vogl, Jane Elizabeth, executive assistant sr, $49,059
Vogler, David L, mech trades spclst lead, $23.54/hr
Vogt, Michelle Lyn, mri technologist, $28.14/hr
Voight, Casey Glen, media producer sr, $46,761
Voigt-Catlin, Julia Dalenette, behavioral health prgm coor, $53,448
Voigt, Judy E, program/project supprt coor I, $31,471
Vojta, Agnes, lecturer, $36,434
Vojta, Steffen Thomas, professor, $99,183
Volgas, David Andrew, prof, asoc, $260,100
Volino, Brenda J, nurse, licensed prac, $18.46/hr
Volkart, Cory M, storage admin-expert, $64,086
Volkert, Wynn A, emeritus, $4,653
Volkmann, Derek Matthew, farm wrkr I, $10.57/hr
Volkmann, Dietrich Hans, prof, teach, $129,816
Volkmann, Jeremy M, system administrator-speclst, $52,437
Volle, Deana G, csm professional II, $43,631
Volle, Katina A, human resources specialist III, $52,187
Vollertsen, Jacob Lucas, mgr II business admin, $62,593
Vollmer, Dennis L, distribution techn-mtls mgmt, $14.79/hr
Vollmer, Katie J, program/project supprt coor I, $36,351
Vollmer, Kelsey Marie, care team assoc-clinical, $12.08/hr
Vollmer, Margaret Frances, finl counselor(eligibility), $15.87/hr
Vollrath, Candice M, food svc wrkr II, $11.83/hr
Vollrath, Christina M, dir nursing svcs, $128,520
Vollrath, Susan, office support assistant IV, $18.97/hr
Volner, Scott Lee, prof, ast adjunct, $8,043
Volz, Michael John, prof, ast teach, $45,581
Volz, Yong Zhang, prof, asoc, $80,594
Vomsaal, Frederick Stephen, prof, curators, $153,960
Von Engeln, Melody Ann, student support spec sr, $16.71/hr
von Schoenborn, Mary Leona, office support asst IV, $14.70/hr
Voney, Samantha A, executive assistant, $20.10/hr
Vonnahme, Elizabeth Miller, prof, asoc, $65,599
Vonnahme, Greg W, prof, ast, $56,100
vonStamwitz, Lisa Marie, staff nurse, $21.70/hr
Voon, James Kiun, resident physician-1st yr, $50,219
Voothuluru, Priyamvada, fellow, post doctoral, $43,384
Vopat, Thomas A, prof, asoc clncl, $96,929
Vorachack, Jennifer Renee, psychologist, $40.00/hr
Vorderstrasse, Valerie M, fellow, post doctoral, $39,000
Vore, Michelle Marie, executive assistant, $17.61/hr
Vornholt, Catherine Louise, teaching ast, $35,445
Vorst, Karen S, professor, $141,400
Vos, Tim P, prof, asoc, $79,140
Vosevich, Scott J, mech, auto cntrl, $22.42/hr
Voskoboynikova, Alla, prof, asoc teach, $41,620
Voss, Chad E, instructor, adjunct, $21,000
Voss, Kenneth L, director it, $114,762
Voss, Lynn K, mgr II business admin, $53,436
Voss, Sheila A, office support assistant IV, $13.83/hr
Votaw, Katheryn Lynn Blankmeyer, instructor, adjunct, $21,000
Vought, Thomas J Jr, research specialist II, $51,266
Voulov, Hristo Dimitrov, prof, asoc, $61,311
Voyles, Elizabeth Marie, office support assistant II, $13.00/hr
Vrabac, Daniel J, instructor, $60,000
Vroman, Amber Nicole, instructor, clncl, $28,800
Vroman, Kristine Noelle, office support assistant IV, $16.63/hr
Vu, Danh Cong, research/lab technician, $12.00/hr
Vu, Emily Hong-Nhi, high school student, $8.00/hr
Vu, Hai Truong, support systems admin-speclst, $45,600
Vuckovich, Steven Edward, supv food svc I,-h, $33,201
Vuong, Tri Dinh, resrch scientist/academic sr, $73,390

Waage, Brien R, enterprise architect, $93,907
Wachsmuth, Thomas Everett, police officer, $17.69/hr
Wachter, Lily Gurton, prof, ast, $60,819
Wack, Jayne Ann, project manager-speclst, $56,100
Wacker, Michael J, prof, asoc teach, $83,993
Waddell, Jennifer H, prof, asoc, $85,599
Waddell, David Michael, event assistant I, $7.55/hr
Waddill, George D, professor, $121,155
Wade, Austyn Patrice, nurse anesthetist, $109,320
Wade, D Dean, nurse, staff II rnwp, $27.15/hr
Wade, Davida Sue, service rep III, $13.69/hr
Wade, Heather Noelle, nurse practitioner, $36.77/hr
Wade, James M, tutor, $8.00/hr
Wade, Jason L, laborer II, $14.52/hr
Wade, Marcus Jerome, prof, ast clincl dept, $250,000
Wade, Orlando Todd, custodian, $13.36/hr
Wade, Robert Jon, office support assistant III, $13.86/hr
Wadhwa, Anant, resident physician-1st yr, $50,219
Wadsworth, Shawn Jeffery Eric, res physician-2nd yr, $50,810
Wagan, Prima M, administrative consultant, $67,805
Waggie, Aaron K, prof, ast adjunct, $54,131
Waggie, Aaron K, physician, $100.00/hr
Waggoner, Annalisha Dionne, custodian, $10.69/hr
Waggoner, Bruce Todd, manager it, $52,400
Waggoner, Rachel Gail, nurse, licensed prac, $18.01/hr
Waggoner, Sheena U, human resources assistant, $15.50/hr
Wagner, Vincent III, instructor, adjunct, $9,000
Wagner Mann, Colette Carol, prof, asoc teach, $79,722
Wagner, Algernon Demond, custodian, $12.94/hr
Wagner, Holly Helane, prof, ast, $58,000
Wagner, Jacob Aaron, prof, asoc, $71,555
Wagner, James Lee, temporary crafts service, $11.88/hr
Wagner, Judith A, instructor, clincl, $15,375
Wagner, Katherine C, office support assistant III, $13.22/hr
Wagner, Kristen Michelle, prof, ast, $61,025
Wagner, Paul Edward, library info specialist, $13.30/hr
Wagner, Sharra Marie, teaching ast, $31.80/hr
Wagner, Wende Lynn, business support specialist II, $14.95/hr
Wagnon, Samantha Jackson, nurse, staff I, $19.00/hr
Wagoner, Brenda D, office support assistant IV, $16.40/hr
Wagoner, James Bruce, custodian, $10.69/hr
Wagovich, Stacy Ann, prof, asoc, $93,158
Wagstaff, Jason, db programmer analyst-expert, $59,547
Wagster, Gary Dean, police officer, $17.50/hr
Wagster, Karen Ann, office support assistant IV, $15.14/hr
Waheed, Humza B, resident physician-3rd yr, $53,763
Wahl, James J, db programmer analyst-princpl, $74,271
Wahle, Jessica Mandy, nurse, staff II, $21.35/hr
Wahlman, Maude, professor, $114,456
Wahrenbrock, Mark D, sftware supprt analyst-expert, $51,898
Waibel, Janet A, exec ast to gen offcr, $69,791
Waid, Timothy R, prof, asoc teach, $90,145
Waint, Laurie, prgm director, $57,368
Wait, Linda L, business support specialist II, $19.09/hr
Wakefield, Douglas Sidney, professor, $227,354
Wakefield, Mark Richard, prof, asoc, $252,399
Walberg, Karen, office support assistant IV, $12.99/hr
Walch, Patricia Lee, nurse, licensed prac, $20.58/hr
Walden, Kimberly Kay, nurse, licensed prac sr, $18.31/hr
Walden, Rebecca Laferney, mgr III business admin, $67,028
Walden, Robin Lea, patient svc rep, $13.10/hr
Walden, Wendy Michelle, program/project supprt coor I, $34,400
Waldman, Steven Dee, prgm director, $82,000
Waldo, Allen James, specialist, $65,000
Waldron, Anna M, prof, ast clincl, $82,117
Walensky, Justin Ross, prof, ast, $81,392
Waliullah, Khalid I, resident physician-4th yr, $55,804
Walker de Felix, Judith, vice provost, $200,453
Walker, Martin W II, program/project supprt coor II, $83,849
Walker, Cliff Jr, mech trades spclst (mts), $24.45/hr
Walker-Williams, Brenda Gail, instructor, clincl, $49,661
Walker, Barbara Jean, office support assistant III, $12.89/hr
Walker, Bobbi Lynn, student support specialist I, $13.00/hr
Walker, Bobbi Sue, finance systems specialist III, $74,603
Walker, Brand, support systems admin-expert, $57,020
Walker, Cameron G, prof, ast adjunct, $125.00/hr
Walker, Carol Marie, med coding spclst-certified, $23.94/hr
Walker, David Lee, instructor, clincl, $75,748
Walker, Douglas, care team assoc-clinical, $15.22/hr

Walker, Dylan Nelson, mental health tech trainee, $9.27/hr
Walker, George Edward, custodian, $12.18/hr
Walker, James Michael, adjunct, $9,000
Walker, Janet, human resources specialist III, $50,225
Walker, Janet L, student service coor I, $42,100
Walker, Jayme Nathaniel, mri technologist, $34.43/hr
Walker, Jennifer Adams, accountant sr, $40,689
Walker, Jill Andrea, program/project supprt coor II, $50,000
Walker, John Charles, prof, curators, $191,695
Walker, Kelli Anne, ultrasonographer, $26.58/hr
Walker, Kim Reynee, student support specialist sr, $16.80/hr
Walker, Kristen Leigh Ann, office support assistant IV, $13.50/hr
Walker, Lucia Cristina, social worker, $38,998
Walker, Lynn Anthony, coor protocol svcs, $17.66/hr
Walker, Marcia Parish, business support specialist II, $17.56/hr
Walker, Mary P, dean, asoc, $155,330
Walker, Melissa Sue, scientist, $48,000
Walker, Naarah Beth, nurse, licensed prac, $17.17/hr
Walker, Nancy M, research specialist sr, $58,418
Walker, Robert S, prof, ast, $64,010
Walker, Robin Gene, program/project supprt coor sr, $67,259
Walker, Roger L, laborer II, $13.67/hr
Walker, Tabatha Renee, custodian, $10.94/hr
Walker, Tammy, custodian, $12.94/hr
Walker, Tiffany L, nurse practitioner, $91,127
Walker, William T, dean, $177,397
Walkonis, Janice Ruth, resrch asoc, $39,750
Wall, James Allen Jr, curator teach, $175,552
Wall, Drucilla M, prof, asoc teach, $40,355
Wall, Eamonn W, professor, $112,580
Wall, Judy Davis, professor, $184,207
Wall, Rebecca Pauline, product support rep-expert, $51,673
Wall, Timothy James, ast editor, $17.25/hr
Wallace, Austin Douglas Ed, seasonal farm ast, $8.93/hr
Wallace, David Lee, dir II student support svcs, $132,350
Wallace, Donna May, pat acct rep, $14.64/hr
Wallace, Doug, bts mason/tuckptr, $21.71/hr
Wallace, Douglas Craig, instructor, $12,000
Wallace, Douglas Keith, temporary crafts service, $18.12/hr
Wallace, Dustin P, instructor, adjunct, $15,000
Wallace, Dynessha Teashay, patient svc rep, $10.85/hr
Wallace, Kathleen S, instructor, adjunct, $9,600
Wallace, Lisa Allen, extns professional, $68,317
Wallace, Melissa Kay, pat acct rep, $14.66/hr
Wallace, Patricia A, child dev assistant, $10.60/hr
Wallace, Patricia Kay, extension asoc, $45,000
Wallace, Randy, custodian, $10.94/hr
Wallace, Sharon Marie, mgr student support svcs, $42,500
Wallace, Shawn Riley, academic advisor, $38,156
Wallace, Sue Ellen, asoc dir advancement, $82,500
Wallace, Susan Weston, event assistant I, $7.55/hr
Wallace, Teresa M, human resources assistant, $16.70/hr
Wallach, Barbara Price, prof, asoc, $55,975
Wallach, Emmanuelle Janet, instructor, adjunct, $42,000
Wallach, Virginia D, educational pgm assistant, $10.76/hr
Wallack, Fern Ann, nurse, staff per diem, $35.00/hr
Wallden, Grace Cathryn, care team assoc-clinical, $12.08/hr
Waller, Angela M, nurse clinician, $72,675
Waller, Erika McGraw, prof, ast clincl, $55,729
Waller, Jacob M, supv ambulance svcs, $17.60/hr
Waller, John Leroy, nurse, staff II, $27.18/hr
Waller, Joyce Marie, care team assoc-clinical, $11.32/hr
Waller, Leslie Ann, office support assistant IV, $13.17/hr
Waller, Susan S, prof, asoc, $57,557
Waller, Timothy Noel, ast mgr med rcds/data integ, $61,531
Wallman, Edward Albert, mts/pipefitter, $24.13/hr
Walls, Brandon Joseph, pat care techn, $12.18/hr
Walmer, Marcia J, instructor, clincl, $50,000
Walp, Tonille Jean, food svc wrkr II, $11.07/hr
Walquist, Macy Allyn, nurse, staff II, $20.95/hr
Walsh, Amber Dawn, resp therapist reg, $18.23/hr
Walsh, Amy Turlington, prof, ast visiting, $44,234
Walsh, Anne Elizabeth, instructor, adjunct, $5,000
Walsh, David B, library info specialist sr, $14.95/hr
Walsh, Jamie Michele, office support assistant III, $13.26/hr
Walsh, Karen Ann, office support assistant IV, $20.55/hr
Walsh, Kevin Raymond, security officer, $13.73/hr
Walsh, Michael E, temporary professional, $27.76/hr
Walsh, Nancy M, reimbursement ast-cert, $18.77/hr

Walsh, Samuel Peter, prof, ast, $77,063
Walstrom, Rebecca S, asoc dir program/project ops, $21.92/hr
Walter, August, user support analyst-expert, $18.71/hr
Walter, Beth Ann, dir I, business admin, $93,783
Walter, Jackie, fin and acctg manager, $78,109
Walter, Margaret Rose, prof, asoc profl practice, $60,414
Walter, Stephanie Paige, grader, $52
Walter, Susana Teresa, instructor, adjunct, $6,667
Walter, Wayne Leo, teaching ast, $13.00/hr
Walter, William D, resrch asoc, $71,650
Walters, Ashley Lyn, student service coor I, $34,750
Walters, Caroline Elizabeth, office support asst IV, $18.35/hr
Walters, Eric Michael, prof, ast resrch, $84,841
Walters, Garnett N, laborer II, $14.35/hr
Walters, Kimberly D, phlebotomist, $14.76/hr
Walters, Larry L, business support analyst II, $22.31/hr
Walters, Mary Edna, supv sterile processing, $54,633
Walters, Ralph Colin, grounds keeper, $12.18/hr
Walters, Ruth D, office support assistant III, $14.01/hr
Walters, Shirley J, student support specialist sr, $19.82/hr
Walters, Staci Gay, performace improvement prof, $66,279
Walterscheid, Kathryn, instructor, adjunct, $34,266
Walthall, Christine L, event assistant I, $9.50/hr
Walther, Mary Lou, custodian, $10.39/hr
Waltman, Anna C, mental health tech, $13.87/hr
Waltman, Donald D, event assistant I, $8.85/hr
Waltman, Janethel Lee, coor, care, $32.00/hr
Waltman, Ronda Leann, fin and acctg analyst sr, $51,651
Walton, Bailey L, compliance specialist I, $17.50/hr
Walton, Barbara J, nurse, licensed prac sr, $20.87/hr
Walton, Jacob Bastian, custodian, $10.94/hr
Walton, Leslie Marie, office support assistant IV, $15.96/hr
Walton, Norma Jean, office support assistant IV, $16.44/hr
Walton, Rosetta, custodian, $12.94/hr
Waltz, Wende S, db programmer analyst-princpl, $70,929
Walz, Catherine D, patient svc rep, $13.74/hr
Wambuguh, Loise Njambi, office support assistant II, $10.24/hr
Wampler, Daniel P, teaching ast, $8,424
Wampler, Janet Susan, strat comm associate II, $51,332
Wampler, Jennifer Egerer, dir II advancement, $86,700
Wampler, Margaret L, coor, care, $66,181
Wamser, Rachel Ann, psychologist, $60,000
Wan, Caixia, prof, ast, $82,820
Wan, Jinrong, resrch scientist/academic, $50,000
Wan, Kayan, psychologist, $71,500
Wan, Li, resrch scientist/academic, $50,000
Wan, Neng, research/lab technician sr, $17.59/hr
Wang, Cheng, prof, ast, $79,285
Wang, Derek Z, high school student, $8.00/hr
Wang, Fang, prof, ast teach, $59,740
Wang, Jee-Ching, prof, asoc, $88,000
Wang, Jialiang, prof, ast teach, $77,000
Wang, Jianmin, prof, asoc, $92,082
Wang, Jianping, prof, asoc, $87,379
Wang, Jianying, resrch asoc, $46,100
Wang, Juan, prof, ast teach, $40,400
Wang, Juexin, scholar, visiting, $19,200
Wang, Kun, fellow, post doctoral, $41,000
Wang, Le, programmer analyst-speclst, $48,294
Wang, Margaret, prof, ast clincl dept, $138,866
Wang, Meifang, supv, lab, $62,544
Wang, Michael Xia, prof, asoc clincl dept, $144,735
Wang, Qi, specialist, $10.00/hr
Wang, Qiang, professor, $278,901
Wang, Risheng, prof, ast, $70,000
Wang, Sheng, fellow, post doctoral, $35,000
Wang, Shu, scholar, visiting, $7,200
Wang, Songjie, fellow, post doctoral, $42,436
Wang, Tiannan, resident physician-1st yr, $50,219
Wang, Wei, fellow, post doctoral, $32,004
Wang, Wenjuan, fellow, post doctoral, $50,000
Wang, Xinghe, professor, $135,614
Wang, Xuemin, professor, $197,550
Wang, Ye, prof, ast, $53,044
Wang, Ying, resident physician-3rd yr, $53,763
Wang, Yong, resrch scientist/academic, $36,067
Wang, Yong, professor, $148,663
Wang, Yong Qin, fellow, post doctoral, $40,720

Wang, Ze, prof, asoc, $66,642
Wankel, Amber J, hlth prgm spclst, $20.20/hr
Wankum, Patricia Catherine, prof, asoc clincl dept, $271,502
Wann, Ashley Kaine, office support assistant III, $12.79/hr
Wapelhorst, Lynn M, asoc dir program/project ops, $50,000
Waqas, Muhammad, fellow, teaching, $48,000
Wara, AllisonMary, instructor, clincl, $45,000
Warchol, Danielle Nicole, student recruitment spclst sr, $18.22/hr
Ward, Derrick Anthony Jr, custodian, $10.73/hr
Ward-Bopp, Nicholas James, student support spec sr, $16.87/hr
Ward-Smith, Peggy A, prof, asoc, $93,478
Ward, Alyssa Brittany, instructor, adjunct, $9,000
Ward, Bobby Lavern, agriculture associate sr, $18.84/hr
Ward, Carol V, professor, $161,246
Ward, Ceresa J, coor staff dev tech & ops, $97,469
Ward, Dana S, prof, asoc clincl dept, $221,206
Ward, Darlene Joy, office support assistant II, $15.01/hr
Ward, Deborah H, librarian IV, $130,625
Ward, Emily Claire, research specialist sr, $45,476
Ward, Gary L, vice chancellor, $210,000
Ward, Jonathan Tyler, electronics technician I, $11.68/hr
Ward, Joyce Constance, office support assistant III, $11.30/hr
Ward, Kathryn J, nurse, staff II, $34.18/hr
Ward, Laura A, business support specialist II, $23.35/hr
Ward, Lisa Renee, patient svc rep, $11.17/hr
Ward, Monique Simone, office support assistant IV, $12.98/hr
Ward, Sidne Gail, prof, asoc, $159,467
Ward, Stephanie Renee, nurse, staff II rnwp, $20.54/hr
Wardenburg, Alana Michelle, tqip coordinator, $17.24/hr
Wardlow, Renette E, extns professional, $62,888
Warford-Perry, Janet Yvonne, human resources spec I, $14.96/hr
Warhol, Megan E, resident physician-1st yr, $50,219
Warhover, Thomas A, prof, asoc, $115,528
Waring, Deborah Anne, executive assistant, $19.60/hr
Waris, Robert G II, instructor, $60,000
Warm, Julie J, resrch asoc, $87,539
Warmund, Michele Renee, professor, $93,493
Warne-Griggs, Tara Rae, research project analyst sr, $43,697
Warner, Benjamin R, prof, ast, $59,058
Warner, Connor K, instructor, $47,000
Warner, Elizabeth Marie, educational pgm associate I, $13.22/hr
Warner, Melinda Ann, office support assistant III, $12.50/hr
Warner, Michelle Lee, lecturer, $9,000
Warner, Rikki Jo, office support assistant II, $13.39/hr
Warren, Brenda J, office support assistant IV, $16.85/hr
Warren, Christi, nurse, staff II, $30.10/hr
Warren, Gregory, maint svc attd, $17.78/hr
Warren, Gregory Loyd, custodian, $12.94/hr
Warren, Jennifer Doctolero, coor, service, $18.73/hr
Warren, Joshua M, lecturer, $6,000
Warren, Michael Anthony, instructor, adjunct, $2,400
Warren, Michele Frank, office support assistant III, $12.03/hr
Warren, Ranard, event assistant I, $7.65/hr
Warren, Valencia Dawn, custodian, $12.94/hr
Warren, William M, facilities supervisor, $66,504
Warrington-Dickerson, Barbara Charlene, nurse, staff II rnwp,
    $30.46/hr
Wartick, Judy Lynn, resrch asoc, $26,500
Warzak, Denise A, research/lab technician, $10.24/hr
Warzinik, Kelly Anne, extension asoc, $42,344
Wasden, Mitchell L, ceo chief oper offcr, $551,250
Washabaugh, Shana Dee, occl therapist, $35.00/hr
Washam, Terah Elizabeth, business support spec sr, $22.95/hr
Washburn, Brandi Lynn, office support assistant III, $11.75/hr
Washer, Glenn Alden, prof, asoc, $104,236
Washer, Karen Elizabeth, editor II, $28.84/hr
Washington, Aqua L, revenue recovery spclst, $45,000
Washington, Brian Thurman, trades helper, $10.78/hr
Washington, Daisy Marie, coor, service, $17.80/hr
Washington, Danielle Tameka, instructor, adjunct, $4,200
Washington, Donna Fern, office support assistant III, $15.73/hr
Washington, Duan Edward, event assistant I, $7.50/hr
Washington, Henry Lee, temporary technical, $20.00/hr
Washington, Karl Eugene, mail carrier, $14.85/hr
Washington, Karla Thomasson, prof, ast, $81,600
Washington, Kerry Tyrone, mental health tech, $13.46/hr
Washington, LaTasha M, operations support tech I, $11.27/hr
Washington, Lionel Lee, bts mason/tuckptr, $22.14/hr
Washington, Natasha K, custodian, $12.69/hr

Washington, Patrick Henry, ast coach, $282,000
Washington, Susan, office support assistant sr, $21.88/hr
Wasser, Megan Rose, nurse, staff I, $19.37/hr
Wassie, Almaz, custodian lead, $14.03/hr
Wassilak, Teresa Louise, fin and acctg specialist, $15.19/hr
Wassman, David W, office support assistant IV, $17.43/hr
Wassman, Rhonda F, telecom it analyst-princpl, $55,598
Wasson, Helen Rebecca, nurse, staff II, $20.95/hr
Wasson, Jillian Ann Woodford, intern, $22,783
Wasson, Kassie Marie, business support specialist II, $17.25/hr
Watanabe, Nicholas M, prof, ast teach, $66,096
Waterford, Henry Cecil Jr, office support assistant III, $12.48/hr
Waterman, Joseph Daniel, research lab supervisor, $54,101
Waterman, Lisa Ann, care coordinator, $68,289
Waterman, Matthew Wilbur, dir of surgical svcs, $165,548
Waters, Amy L, manuscript specialist, $38,145
Waters, Daphne Lawanne, health records techn I, $11.76/hr
Waters, James K, chemist sr, $84,543
Waters, Jason Nathaniel, instructor, adjunct, $19,200
Wathen, Monica Lynn, reimbursement ast-cert, $18.59/hr
Watkins-Parker, Shelley Elizabeth, mental health prof, $17.79/hr
Watkins, Barbara A, nurse, staff II, $32.78/hr
Watkins, Benjamin L, instructor, $19,305
Watkins, Catherine Joann, dir II research ops and plng, $60,000
Watkins, Debra A, office support assistant IV, $13.20/hr
Watkins, Elisa Ebony, lab techn, persl svc-clin lab, $13.21/hr
Watkins, Katherine Elizabeth, program/proj supprt coor I, $37,455
Watkins, Louis William Roy, maint svc attd, $16.12/hr
Watkins, Mary Ann, office support assistant III, $12.99/hr
Watkins, Scott R, hospital lab tech, $12.79/hr
Watkins, Steve E, professor, $104,570
Watkins, Terrence Jamel, instructor, adjunct, $4,200
Watkins, William H, powr plnt maint spclst II, $23.75/hr
Watkinson, Lisa Dawn, research specialist sr, $67,400
Watne, Davin Garth, lecturer, $38,620
Watring, Amy Sue, med coding spclst-certified, $20.08/hr
Watring, Jack William, dir II university police, $125,128
Watring, Jodie Lynn, office support assistant IV, $18.51/hr
Watsek, Anne Marie, nurse, staff I, $19.00/hr
Watson, Robert M Jr, professor, $106,806
Watson, Amy Regina, executive assistant sr, $49,440
Watson, Bonnie Elizabeth, tutor, $10.50/hr
Watson, Brett Alan, ast dir student support svcs, $46,000
Watson, Cameron Tyler, nurse, staff I, $19.00/hr
Watson, Darcy M, med techl reg, $29.56/hr
Watson, James, specialist, $10.00/hr
Watson, James Anthony, driver, $13.89/hr
Watson, Jennifer Lynn, office support assistant IV, $12.99/hr
Watson, Kevin E, utility dist wrkr I, $17.78/hr
Watson, Laurel B, prof, ast, $61,200
Watson, Linda A, temporary clerical, $10.60/hr
Watson, Linda M, office support assistant III, $11.91/hr
Watson, Lynette Sledge, specialist, $64,093
Watson, Meagan Caroline, nurse, staff II, $22.56/hr
Watson, Michael Paul, business support specialist II, $21.65/hr
Watson, Mike L, assoc director it, $105,635
Watson, Miles G, health physics technician I, $19.00/hr
Watson, Toiya Felicia, care team assoc-clinical, $14.88/hr
Watson, Walter Allen, maint svc attd, $17.78/hr
Watt, Laura DeVore, office support assistant II, $11.32/hr
Wattenbarger, Krystle Leigh, dietitian, clincl, $45,315
Watts, Gregory, construction manager II, $37.56/hr
Watts, Hannah Hessing, strat comm associate II, $45,695
Watts, Jennifer Lea, operations support tech I, $10.42/hr
Watts, Jeremy Lee, prof, ast resrch, $64,929
Watts, Josephine, child dev aide, $9.08/hr
Watts, Nykea Tamika, student support specialist I, $16.87/hr
Watts, Steven, professor, $128,302
Watts, Terri L, patient svc rep, $14.88/hr
Watts, Trent Alan, prof, assoc, $61,886
Wauthier, Dee Ann, mgr clinical services, $67,272
Wauthier, Gary J, csm professional I, $38,444
Wawrzyniak, Jude, csm project manager, $92,101
Wawrzyniak, Karen Elizabeth, office support asst III, $13.28/hr
Wax, Benjamin J, nurse, staff II, $23.00/hr
Way, Caitlin Rebecca, program/project supprt coor sr, $56,500
Way, Gordon Thomas, educational prgm coor sr, $56,500
Wayland, Patricia Kay, lecturer, $39,462
Wea, Darryl, facilities supervisor, $48,461

Weable, Jennifer Marie, supervisor it, $64,635
Weachter, Richard J Jr, prof, asoc clincl dept, $163,418
Weachter, Jean Gilmary, nurse, staff II, $34.18/hr
Weagley, Pamela N, professor, $86,597
Weagley, Robert O, prof, asoc, $115,835
Weakley, Melissa Ann, pat acct rep, $15.87/hr
Wear, Eugene C, mech, bldg maint, $19.64/hr
Weary, Patricia K, business support specialist II, $16.64/hr
Weatherford, Ted, fin and acctg manager sr, $88,780
Weatherholt, Nancy, prof, asoc, $95,554
Weathers, David Lee, steam plant opr II, $24.15/hr
Weathersby, Yolanda, dir I, student support svcs, $61,509
Weaver, David Stark, emrg med techn paramedic, $17.00/hr
Weaver, Deidra Marie, business support specialist sr, $23.08/hr
Weaver, Holly Marie, human resources specialist I, $21.37/hr
Weaver, James Roger, librarian II, $49,845
Weaver, Janet Lea, nurse, staff II, $34.18/hr
Weaver, Jeffrey, prof, adjunct, $8,220
Weaver, Jonathan William, system administrator-spclst, $54,000
Weaver, Lisa, program/project supprt coor sr, $60,000
Weaver, Rosie, office support assistant IV, $13.81/hr
Weaver, Sabrina Renee, office support assistant IV, $15.08/hr
Webb, James Otis II, business ops associate II, $50,396
Webb, Andrew, nurse, staff II, $33.84/hr
Webb, Denise Y, care team assoc-suppt, $13.78/hr
Webb, James Louis, instructor, adjunct, $12,000
Webb, Megan D, nutrition spclst, $42,369
Webb, Patricia Ann, office support assistant III, $11.53/hr
Webb, Rachel A, strat comm associate II, $42,630
Webb, Shonta D, tutor, $14.08/hr
Webb, Tenishia Nichole, custodian, $11.44/hr
Webb, Weldon D, dean, asoc, $158,898
Webber, David J, instructor, ast, $24.00/hr
Webber, Julia M, nurse, staff II, $34.36/hr
Webel, Corey M, prof, ast, $71,710
Webel, Richard R, prof, asoc clincl dept, $218,223
Weber, Alan Wayne, instructor, adjunct, $33,000
Weber, Alicia Michelle, nurse, staff I, rnwp, $19.00/hr
Weber, Andrea Kaye, nurse, licensed prac, $19.80/hr
Weber, Bridget R, veterinary technician sr, $16.32/hr
Weber, Crystal, community dev spclst, $46,770
Weber, Donna J, office support assistant IV, $17.46/hr
Weber, Kara Ann, food svc wrkr II, $10.10/hr
Weber, Kathryn R, instructor, adjunct, $21,000
Weber, Kenna L, interior designer sr, $59,813
Weber, Max, prof, ast adjunct, $125.00/hr
Weber, Paula B, professor, $110,743
Weber, Shawn Adrian, food svc wrkr I, $9.60/hr
Weber, Virginia K, distribution techn-mtls mgmt, $15.26/hr
Weber, Walter Kirk, prof, ast clincl, $90,244
Webster, Christina M, teaching ast, $27.00/hr
Webster, Christine L, instructor, adjunct, $12,300
Webster, Denise Darlene, pharmacy tech, $12.76/hr
Webster, Heather Dawn, office support assistant IV, $16.87/hr
Webster, James Nickels, instructor, $9,750
Webster, Savannah Theresa, child dev assistant, $13.40/hr
Webster, Stephanie Lynn, executive assistant, $20.01/hr
Wechsler, Barton J, dean, $196,496
Wechsler, Louise, mgr III business admin, $73,735
Weckenborg, Julie Christine, nurse, staff now III, $30.00/hr
Wecker, Christina Carol, patient svc rep, $13.49/hr
Weddle, Daniel B, prof, clincl, $81,000
Weddle, Lacey Ann, revenue cycle trainer, $47,448
Weddle, Stephanie R, educational pgm associate I, $14.09/hr
Weed, Adam L, db programmer analyst-expert, $68,359
Weed, Keli Woodard, instructor, adjunct, $12,000
Weekley, Lori Jean, nurse, staff II, $27.00/hr
Weeks, Carole L, nurse, licensed prac, $17.28/hr
Wefel, Heather Marie, library information assistant, $11.30/hr
Wegener, Duane S, temporary clerical, $10.60/hr
Wegener, William S, csm associate III, $28.07/hr
Wegmann, Martha Wurtsbaugh, advancement assoc I, $32,878
Wehmeier, Reta L, business support specialist II, $20.22/hr
Wehmeyer, Jayne Hartell, nurse, licensed prac, $19.78/hr
Wehmeyer, Patricia Lynn, business support spclst II, $20.50/hr
Wehmeyer, Randy J, mts/hvac, $22.50/hr
Wehner, Christine Erin, office support assistant IV, $14.93/hr
Wehner, Jessica T, nurse, staff II rnwp, $21.37/hr
Wehner, Kevin R, teaching ast, $13.00/hr

Wehrend, Jennifer Ann, resp therapist reg, $20.12/hr
Wehrend, Terry K, temporary clerical, $8.75/hr
Wehring, Susan Patricia, prof, ast teach, $68,680
Wehrman, Jodie Ann, pharmacist III, $124,584
Wehrman, Rebecca A, business support specialist II, $18.02/hr
Wei, Jun, prof, ast resrch, $28.85/hr
Wei, Mingzhen, prof, ast, $82,416
Wei, Shu Chuan Nicole, teaching ast, $13.00/hr
Wei, Xiaoying, research/lab technician sr, $15.91/hr
Wei, Xiuping, programmer analyst-expert, $62,142
Wei, Youfu, prof, asoc, $63,593
Weibel, Laurie Elyne, temporary professional, $11.30/hr
Weider, Kenneth, bts carpet installer, $21.71/hr
Weider, Rebecca Jean, nurse, licensed prac, $17.19/hr
Weidner, Nathan W, prof, ast, $66,116
Weidner, Theresa Bailey, office support assistant III, $12.13/hr
Weiher, Sharon Kay, pat acct rep, $14.12/hr
Weikert, Ben Spangler, specialist, $36,100
Weil, Virginia L, program/project supprt coor II, $24.81/hr
Weilandich, Candice M, nurse, staff II, $25.18/hr
Weilbaecher, Craig R, business ops associate sr, $56,650
Weilmuenster, Brenda M, health records techn II, $14.88/hr
Weimer, Brian, police captain, $84,276
Weimer, Margaret R, student service coor I, $37,533
Weinman, Matthew, model, $17.00/hr
Weinstein, Stephen H, prof, asoc, $249,072
Weir, Christina Fay, custodian, $12.94/hr
Weir, Dana Erin, mgr research activities, $63,572
Weir, Dionte Joshua, care team assoc-suppt, $10.64/hr
Weir, Jessica Leigh, retail sales associate sr, $15.47/hr
Weir, Joshua, resident physician-1st yr, $49,025
Weir, Joy L, reimbursement ast-cert, $18.59/hr
Weir, Robert B, office support associate, $23.41/hr
Weirich, Paul, prof, curators, $108,948
Weirich, Robert, professor, $146,761
Weis, Carol Thompson, office support assistant III, $17.21/hr
Weisbrook, Christa M, sr dir program/project ops, $107,433
Weise, Gwendolyn D'Anne, prof, asoc, $121,378
Weiseman, Martha F, med coding spclst-certified, $22.80/hr
Weiser, Abby B, enrollment advisor sr, $16.54/hr
Weiser, Scott F, user support analyst-speclst, $18.51/hr
Weisman, Gary A, professor, $170,838
Weisman, Pamela Michelle, wait service supervisor, $15.50/hr
Weisman, Sandra Hille, db programmer analyst-princpl, $76,110
Weisner, Morton A, event assistant I, $7.55/hr
Weiss, David Alan, lecturer, $15,000
Weiss, Jonathan Matthew, manager it, $74,836
Weiss, Mark R, nurse, staff I, $19.00/hr
Weitkemper, Jana Lea, business support specialist sr, $24.16/hr
Weitkemper, L A, nurse, staff II, $32.80/hr
Welbern, Vanessa R, resident physician-3rd yr, $52,470
Welborn, Donna L, telecomm opr-h, $13.69/hr
Welborn, Julie Ann, instructor, $13,467
Welborn, Julie Ann, coor, care, $32.00/hr
Welch, Amy Marlene, business ops associate sr, $50,016
Welch, Cynthia Louise, student recruitment spclst sr, $18.50/hr
Welch, Denise Lynn, business support specialist II, $16.65/hr
Welch, Larry, electrician, powr plant sr, $27.26/hr
Welch, Mandy Sue, prof, ast teach, $52,000
Welchert, Tammy Sue, lecturer, $52,498
Welcome, Suzanne E, prof, ast, $65,700
Weldin, Zachary Ellis, mts/hvac, $18.74/hr
Weldon, Bruce Craig, prof, clinical dept, $250,000
Weldon, Edward Arley, custodian, $11.41/hr
Welek, Frances A, nurse, staff II, $36.70/hr
Welker, Leslie D, mech, bldg maint, $19.64/hr
Welker, Margaret Rose, instructor, adjunct, $7,062
Welker, Shannon T, head coach, $128,750
Wellemeyer, Danielle Maureen, librarian I, $43,200
Weller, William Ross, high school student, $8.35/hr
Wellman, Joshua L, custodian, $10.69/hr
Wells-Glover, Linda, prof, asoc teach, $42,166
Wells, Amanda Renee, instructor, adjunct, $18,000
Wells, Christina E, professor, $198,698
Wells, Darcelle A, dir iv advancement, $129,800
Wells, Darlene Melody, food svc wrkr I, $9.60/hr
Wells, Edward D, grounds keeper II, $16.07/hr
Wells, J Robert, account manager, $35,209
Wells, Jack Cody, prof, asoc clincl dept, $160,450

Wells, Jessica Nicole, event assistant I, $8.50/hr
Wells, Johnnie Lee, driver, $11.58/hr
Wells, Kevin Dale, prof, asoc, $84,913
Wells, Linda M, dean, asoc, $154,200
Wells, Michael Thomas, custodian, $10.00/hr
Wells, Natalie C, nurse, licensed prac sr, $19.23/hr
Wells, Patricia L, staff dev spclst, $63,149
Wells, Raymond, garage attendant, $13.89/hr
Wells, Rhonda Sue, custodian, $12.94/hr
Wells, Rita Jo, mgr II business admin, $58,151
Wells, Samantha Ryan, office support assistant II, $11.00/hr
Wells, Shiela Marie, supv, operating room nursing, $31.16/hr
Wells, William Thomas, prof, asoc profl practice, $100,441
Wells, Zachary R, temporary crafts service, $12.00/hr
Welschmeyer, Krista Lee, office support assistant III, $11.51/hr
Welsh, Leann, reimbursement consultant, $48,562
Welshons, Wade Vincent, prof, asoc, $99,356
Welter, Beth A, office support assistant IV, $14.60/hr
Welty, Dwayne Phillip, data info spclst, $46,200
Wemhoff, Donna W, clincl documnt spclst, $37.66/hr
Wen, Dennis Y, prof, asoc clincl dept, $158,661
Wen, He, prof, ast, $142,100
Wen, Xuerong, prof, asoc, $72,192
Wendell, David Ellis, research/lab technician, $13.00/hr
Wendt, Angela L, program/project supprt coor I, $33,266
Weng, Jonathan Chun-Jen, system support analyst-princpl, $62,415
Wenger, Janice Kay, professor, $82,799
Wennerdahl, Laura Ann, veterinarian, residnt, $29,876
Wennihan, Gary, seasonal farm ast, $8.93/hr
Wense, Michael T, retail sales assistant sr, $11.32/hr
Wentz, Julie A, veterinarian, $82,000
Wenzel, Michael L, mgr csm operations, $49,229
Wenzel, Patricia A, library info specialist sr, $15.61/hr
Wepprich, Lauren Elizabeth, office support asst IV, $14.40/hr
Wermers, Joshua, resident physician-1st yr, $49,025
Werner, Amanda Lynne, educational pgm assistant, $9.50/hr
Werner, Cheri Nicole, nurse, staff II, $22.23/hr
Werner, Jeannie, office support assistant III, $15.23/hr
Werth, Dylan T, resident physician-3rd yr, $52,470
Werth, Katherine Ostermueller, nurse, staff II, $28.85/hr
Wertzberger, Daniel Joseph, animal caretaker-equine/food, $10.91/hr
Weru, Jane Samba Kididi, food svc wrkr II, $11.60/hr
Weru, Paul, mental health tech, $12.90/hr
Wesbury, Eric Steele, emrg med techn paramedic, $14.15/hr
Wescott, Anthony J, mts/hvac lead, $25.35/hr
Wescott, Peter, mts/hvac, $24.13/hr
Wescott, Sarah Jo, resident physician-2nd yr, $52,007
Wesley, Kenneth Ray, custodial supervisor, $34,500
Wesp, Julie A, resident physician-4th yr, $54,425
Wessel, Alexander Robert, resident physician-2nd yr, $52,007
Wesselmann, Andrew J, student support specialist I, $12.99/hr
Wesselmann, Dale Ray, bts painter, $20.23/hr
Wessing, Klarissa Elizabeth, radiologic techl, $19.24/hr
West, Althea Marie, prof, ast adjunct, $10,800
West, Amanda Louise, research/lab technician sr, $14.92/hr
West, David Lane, sr ast dir studnt supprt svcs, $53,328
West, Deborah Neet, nurse practitioner, $87,000
West, Deidra M, office support assistant IV, $17.60/hr
West, Elizabeth Ashley, pharmacy tech, $11.25/hr
West, Emily Ann, care team assoc-suppt, $10.64/hr
West, Jean M, instructor, adjunct, $9,000
West, Jennifer C, advancement associate sr, $42,572
West, Joshua David, intern, $16.66/hr
West, Kammeron Braun, seasonal farm ast, $8.93/hr
West, Kimali A, strat comm associate sr, $61,391
West, Linda D, office support assistant IV, $14.61/hr
West, Mary L, office support assistant II, $13.27/hr
West, Nancy M, director, $116,966
West, Rebecca Lynn, child dev specialist, $40,392
West, Ryan, support systems admin-entry, $39,600
Westbrook, Chartez D, temporary crafts service, $9.10/hr
Westbrook, Joann, human resources manager, $69,476
Westenberg, David J, prof, asoc, $73,171
Wester, Curtis, resp therapist reg, $27.47/hr
Wester, Jeremy Tyler, custodian, $10.00/hr
Westerfield, Mary C, lecturer, $40,102
Westergren, Hyekyeong, office support assistant III, $14.09/hr
Westermann, Paul, program/project supprt coor I, $43,773

Westermeyer, Frederick Alexander IV, sterile proc tech, $18.31/hr
Westermeyer, Lawrence W, dir institutional research, $137,000
Westfield, Teressa Lynn, strat comm associate sr, $50,490
Westgate, Steven Judson, prof, ast adjunct, $160,000
Westgren, Randall Edward, professor, $160,051
Westhoff, Jacob Thomas, fellow, post doctoral, $45,000
Westhoff, Laura, prof, asoc, $65,321
Westhoff, Patrick, professor, $161,725
Westhues, Brian J, mgr I, business admin, $43,000
Weston, Clayton A, custodian, bldg maint, $14.27/hr
Weston, Dana T, prof, asoc, $78,642
Weston, David, nurse, staff II, $30.62/hr
Weston, David Anthony, mail carrier sr, $15.90/hr
Weston, Katherine Amanda, prog/proj supprt coor II, $70,000
Weston, Mark Landon, temporary clerical, $8.75/hr
Weston, Michael D, serv line spclst, $68,793
Westvold-Justus, Pamela Anne, instructor, field, $38,912
Weter, Rick D, mts/pipefitter-mrc, $18.74/hr
Wetter, Paulette Suzanne, nurse, staff II rnwp, $33.73/hr
Wetzel, M Annice, prof, ast teach, $36,778
Wetzel, Nicholas James, stage services assistant, $14.00/hr
Wetzel, Shannon Lyndsay, student support spclst II, $20.84/hr
Wexler, Carlos, professor, $80,355
Weyenberg, Bruce R, clncl imprvmnt spclst, $63,464
Weyenberg, Christopher Ray, research/lab technician, $11.00/hr
Weyerich, Jason Christian, nurse, or/recovery-ch, $27.56/hr
Whalen, James P, lecturer sr, $18,600
Whalen, Melissa S, peoplesoft admin-entry, $73,214
Whalen, Timothy M, custodian, $12.94/hr
Whaley-Connell, Adam Tyler, prof, asoc, $4,813
Whaley, Katherine J, resident physician-3rd yr, $53,763
Wheatley, Holly Janelle, supv outpatient svcs, $46,500
Wheaton, Lindsey M, child dev assistant, $11.16/hr
Wheeler, Adrianna Lynn, academic advisor, $48,831
Wheeler, Alan, prof, asoc teach, $50,107
Wheeler, Amanda Gail, lab tech II-h, $14.66/hr
Wheeler, Carol Lynn, nurse, staff II, $31.55/hr
Wheeler, Jennifer Lea, office support assistant IV, $14.79/hr
Wheeler, Kaleb Jeffrey, care team assoc-clinical, $11.10/hr
Wheeler, Lesley Ann, instructor, adjunct, $15,000
Wheeler, Lisa Marie, patient svc rep, $13.55/hr
Wheeler, Marilyn Jill, medical coding spclst, $22.15/hr
Wheeler, Marvin E, boiler maint opr, $24.13/hr
Wheeler, Mary Kathleen, nurse, licensed prac sr, $18.09/hr
Wheeler, Matthew A, facilities supervisor, $39,600
Wheeler, Michael D, speech/lang pathologist, $71,261
Wheeler, Michelle Ann, speech/lang pathologist, $70,454
Wheeler, Schuyler Francis, programmer analyst-spclst, $51,538
Wheeling, Gregory Dean, account executive, $61,340
Whelan, Joseph E, fin and acctg specialist, $16.96/hr
Whelchel, Dorothy Daniel, prof, ast teach, $85,000
Whelove, Richard T, instructor, residnt, $53,247
Whistance, Jarrett Lea, resrch scientist/academic, $80,000
Whistance, Jeremy D, network engineer-princpl, $73,766
Whiston, Deborah Lynn, family fincl edu spclst, $73,778
Whitacre, Troy A, resp care clinical coor, $33.37/hr
Whitaker, Darius Marquell, student recruitment spclst sr, $18.36/hr
Whitaker, Raychel Genee, coor, service, $13.77/hr
Whitchurch, John J, engineer I, $60,698
White, Alexis Colbea, resident physician-2nd yr, $50,810
White, Amber M, instructor, adjunct, $8,400
White, Arthur Lynn, prof, asoc, $61,816
White, Ashley Jo-Ann, business support specialist sr, $17.75/hr
White, Benjamin M, student service coor I, $42,000
White, Caitlin Patricia, food svc wrkr I, $9.60/hr
White, Cinda S, engineering technician II, $18.20/hr
White, Connie L, prof, asoc, $129,944
White, Dana Michelle, patient advocate, $17.50/hr
White, DeOnna, business support specialist II, $15.40/hr
White, Donna Sue, office supervisor, $58,600
White, Elizabeth M, accountant sr, $44,880
White, Enola Riann, academic advisor, $43,000
White, Frank E, operations support tech II, $12.71/hr
White, Gina, nurse practitioner, $78,471
White, Jacob Daniel, environmental health tech II, $15.51/hr
White, Janice M, strat comm associate sr, $37,260
White, Jessica Dugger, office support assistant IV, $15.60/hr
White, Jon D, mgr env health and safety, $82,000
White, Jordan H, resident physician-2nd yr, $50,810

White, Joyce Ann, program/project supprt coor I, $29,751
White, Kamila Sheree Bruce, prof, asoc, $84,659
White, Karen B, nurse, staff per diem, $35.00/hr
White, Keisha Jewell, mental health tech, $14.10/hr
White, Kimberly Kay, nurse, licensed prac, $18.77/hr
White, Kristina Ann, security analyst-speclst, $54,736
White, Leanna G, business support specialist II, $19.48/hr
White, Leslea Diane, social worker, $48,280
White, Logan M, lab assistant, $10.00/hr
White, Megan Marie, business ops associate sr, $46,512
White, Melissa B, network engineer-expert, $60,514
White, Morgan Elizabeth, nurse, staff I, $19.00/hr
White, Nicholas L, student service coor I, $42,000
White, Pamela Anne, print services supervisor, $54,912
White, Patricia Ann, office support assistant IV, $16.00/hr
White, Rebecca Renee, pat acct rep, $14.49/hr
White, Richard A, prof, ast clincl dept, $255,029
White, Samantha J, executive assistant, $21.42/hr
White, Scott M, prof, ast clincl, $80,000
White, Shannon Hill, extns professional, ast, $65,975
White, Stacey Jo, instructor, adjunct, $17,100
White, Theodore Curtis, dean, $188,233
White, Tommi A, asoc director, $68,959
White, Tomoko, instructor, adjunct, $13,664
White, Violaine Lucienne, instructor, adjunct, $24,000
Whited, Linda Kathleen, program/project supprt coor I, $28,993
Whitefield, Philip D, vice provost, $181,947
Whiteford, Patricia Ann, custodian, $12.94/hr
Whitehead, Tanya, instructor, adjunct, $18,900
Whitehurse, Debra Jo, coor, reimbursement, $53,000
Whitehurse, Glenn E, custodian, $12.94/hr
Whitehurse, Jessica Swanson, program/proj supprt coor I, $41,000
Whiteid, Kristin Lee, nurse, staff II rnwp, $20.54/hr
Whiteley, Robin Lynn, business ops associate sr, $58,484
Whiteman, Drew William, temporary crafts service, $7.50/hr
Whitener, Katharine Joy, student recruitment spclst, $16.87/hr
Whites, Leeann, professor, $82,979
Whiteside, Brittney Chane', advancement coordinator, $45,000
Whitesides, Prudence, food svc wrkr II, $11.83/hr
Whithaus, Mark J, mgr research technical svcs, $96,484
Whithaus, Rhonda Kay, librarian III, $60,190
Whitley, Morrell DeAnre, student support spclst sr, $16.74/hr
Whitmarsh, Michael Ray, mts/pipefitter-mrc, $18.74/hr
Whitney, Carla Marie, ast registrar, $58,198
Whitney, James Edward, fellow, post doctoral, $45,000
Whitney, Kenneth W, bts painter, $20.23/hr
Whitney, Marlyn S, prof, asoc clincl, $120,256
Whitney, Rana Rachelle, nurse, staff II rnwp, $20.54/hr
Whitney, Stephen Dennis, prof, asoc, $61,396
Whitney, Terry M, temporary crafts service, $8.00/hr
Whitney, Vicki L, patient assistance spclst, $57,375
Whitsitt, Ellen Jolene, nurse, staff now III, $30.00/hr
Whitson, Heidi Allyn, food svc attd ii-mrc, $9.62/hr
Whitt, Joseph C, professor, $123,333
Whitt, Stevan P, prof, asoc clincl dept, $386,250
Whitter, Paul David Jr, scientist, certi-forensic drug, $72,422
Whittier, Joanna Blair, prof, ast resrch, $80,000
Whittington, Alan Geoffrey, professor, $119,500
Whitton, Shawn Michael, resident physician-4th yr, $55,804
Whitty, Jennifer R, media producer II, $17.65/hr
Whitworth, Gina L, business support specialist II, $19.62/hr
Whitworth, Kristin M, fellow, post doctoral, $47,039
Whorton, Sarah, media producer sr, $35,350
Whyte, Jeffrey John, resrch scientist/academic, $48,998
Whyte, Madelyn Tara, care team assoc-clinical, $12.08/hr
Whyte, Nicole J, executive assistant, $22.86/hr
Wickens, Michael T, research/lab technician, $14.00/hr
Wickham, Misty Dawn, nurse, staff II, $20.54/hr
Wickham, Sierra Nicole, patient svc rep, $11.70/hr
Wideman, Frank Lynn, naturl resrc engrg spclst, $69,568
Wideman, Stacey Hauschild, educational pgm assoc I, $13.07/hr
Widener, Allison Faith, customer service supervisor, $43,563
Widener, Becky Jo, temporary professional, $11.30/hr
Widhalm, Jack, high school student, $7.50/hr
Widhalm, Matthew Robert, high school student, $8.00/hr
Widner, James Lester, prof, teach, $76,714
Wieberg, Aaron Charles, programmer analyst-expert, $66,825
Wieberg, Jennifer Kristin, reimbursement ast, $17.84/hr
Wiebold, Jeremy W, programmer analyst-expert, $56,367

Wiebold, Suzanne B, human resources assistant, $14.00/hr
Wiebold, William J, professor, $129,605
Wiedemann, Denise Vasilas, dir prog/proj operations, $95,717
Wiederanders, Emily Joanne, pharmacy intern 3 yr, $15.00/hr
Wiederanders, Mark K, pharmacist III, $119,962
Wiederanders, Megan Elizabeth, care team assoc-clinical, $11.10/hr
Wiedmeyer, Charles E, prof, asoc, $114,308
Wiedmier, Carla Ann, dir iv advancement, $123,165
Wiedner, Beau Edwin, food svc wrkr I, $9.60/hr
Wiegand, Bryon R, professor, $96,347
Wiegel, Whitney J, busi spclst, agri, $49,231
Wiegenstein, Anna Louise B, clerk, oper room supply, $12.50/hr
Wielms, David Eugene, grounds keeper, $12.23/hr
Wielms, Debra Darlene, business support specialist II, $15.48/hr
Wiemer, Mary Susan, nurse spclst, clincl, $57,994
Wier, Aaron Paul, rec/athletic specialist, $12.98/hr
Wies, Kristin L, patient svc rep, $12.91/hr
Wies, Patsy Ann, nurse clinician, $61,637
Wies, Sarah Sue, social worker, $51,750
Wiese Fales, Janice Ann, editor sr, $56,148
Wiese, Jeffrey A, dean, ast, $111,000
Wiesner, Matthew A, nurse, licensed prac, $15.65/hr
Wiest, Aric Evan, resrch asoc, $49,400
Wiethop, Jeffrey David, operations support tech II, $11.30/hr
Wigger, John H, professor, $98,108
Wigger, Kelci Renee, ast coach, $34,340
Wigger, Melodie A, nurse, staff now II, $28.00/hr
Wiggins, Lauren Nichelle Dobbs, res physician-3rd yr, $53,763
Wiggins, Patricia G, educational pgm assistant, $11.73/hr
Wiggs, Jennifer Ann, teaching ast, $13.00/hr
Wight, Jared Winston, system administrator-expert, $57,750
Wight, Katherine Marie, office support assistant IV, $13.53/hr
Wiginton, Michelle Louise, student support spec sr, $20.00/hr
Wijnands, Bram, instructor, adjunct, $6,200
Wikle, Christopher K, professor, $142,713
Wiland, Eric G, prof, asoc, $66,339
Wilbanks, Cassie Lynn, nurse, licensed prac, $19.03/hr
Wilbanks, Karl J, custodian, $11.00/hr
Wilbanks, Megan Leigh Ann, bus support specialist II, $15.60/hr
Wilbur, James G, managing engineer, $78,044
Wilbur, Mary Ellen, nurse, staff II rnwp, $34.76/hr
Wilcox, Alice Irene, patient svc rep, $12.91/hr
Wilcox, Catherine M, event assistant I, $7.75/hr
Wilcox, Dale Lee, business svcs consultant sr, $66,144
Wilcox, Jeffrey Brian, museum professional II, $49,557
Wilcox, Kim, instructor, adjunct, $15,000
Wilcox, Lori Janae, director, $99,791
Wilcox, Robin Teresa, office support assistant III, $15.49/hr
Wilcox, Sammatha L, office support assistant IV, $13.25/hr
Wilcoxson, Linda M, pat acct rep, $14.32/hr
Wild, Alexander Harrington, lecturer, $12,000
Wilden, Ana Elizabeth, temporary clerical, $8.56/hr
Wilden, Peter A, prof, asoc, $94,639
Wilder, Leah Gaye, student recruitment spclst sr, $19.04/hr
Wilder, Michael C, reactor specialist, $82,000
Wilder, Roger M, instructor, adjunct, $8,800
Wilder, Stacy Lynn, research specialist sr, $26.40/hr
Wilding, Sarah Jane, lecturer, $9,910
Wilemski, Gerald, professor, $108,119
Wiles, Brandi Noel, nurse, staff II rnwp, $22.01/hr
Wiley, Michelle Lee, nurse, procedures, $30.73/hr
Wiley, Stephanie Ann, prof, ast resrch, $60,000
Wiley, Yolonda P, custodian, $13.36/hr
Wilgers, Tamara Michelle, dir III business admin, $93,649
Wilhelm Stanis, Sonja Ann, prof, asoc, $96,756
Wilhite, Haidera Damielle, mentor, $8.00/hr
Wilhite, Kiana A, administrative consultant, $70,000
Wilhite, Lisa Kay, temporary clerical, $10.50/hr
Wilhite, Melissa Anne, nurse, licensed prac, $17.00/hr
Wilhite, Melissa L, nurse, staff II, $30.62/hr
Wilhite, Natalie Martina, nurse, staff II, $20.54/hr
Wilhoit, Gloria J, nurse, staff prn, $26.00/hr
Wilke, Kristen M, student service coor II, $48,571
Wilke, Lisa Ann, food svc wrkr II, $10.10/hr
Wilkerson, Amanda Sue, sterile processing tech, $16.50/hr
Wilkerson, Cathy M, custodian, $10.94/hr
Wilkerson, Gary Lester, system administrator-expert, $67,683
Wilkerson, John David, temporary crafts service, $19.00/hr
Wilkerson, John Hiram, dir II student support svcs, $89,958

Wilkerson, Karen Denise, dir I, finance, $107,787
Wilkerson, Kathryn Elizabeth, charge data anlyst, $58,979
Wilkerson, Kelsey Elizabeth, bus support specialist II, $14.95/hr
Wilkerson, Mecca Mur Ray, clerk, diet, $9.74/hr
Wilkerson, Misty Larae, human resources specialist I, $17.51/hr
Wilkerson, Neva Jo, nurse, staff now I, $26.00/hr
Wilkerson, Robert C, 4-h youth devlmnt educr, $33,441
Wilkerson, Sarah R, cytotechnologist reg, $34.21/hr
Wilkerson, Wallace Dean, mgr csm operations, $58,161
Wilking, Bruce A, professor, $88,850
Wilking, Janet Braddock, prof, asoc, $68,200
Wilkins, Howard A Jr, system support analyst-expert, $27.95/hr
Wilkins, Barbara Jean, instructional designer-speclst, $51,485
Wilkins, Christine Michele, patient svc rep, $11.50/hr
Wilkins, Jordan M, fellow, post doctoral, $35,000
Wilkins, Marcus Owen, strat comm associate I, $36,134
Wilkins, Meika Rena, patient svc rep, $12.13/hr
Wilkinson, Gayle A, prof, asoc, $87,713
Wilkinson, Joann Frances, sr dir program/project ops, $90,000
Wilkinson, Kyle C, system support analyst-expert, $21.58/hr
Wilkinson, Lisa Lynn, clinical mgr, $106,435
Wilkinson, Megan Leigh, bus support specialist II, $15.25/hr
Wilkinson, Nancy M, mgr II student support svcs, $58,226
Wilkinson, Paulette, interior designer sr, $60,000
Wilkinson, Phillip Bruce, emrg med techn paramedic, $19.40/hr
Will, Matthew J, prof, asoc, $71,444
Will, Tarry Allen, hospital security officer, $12.21/hr
Willard, Adam R, academic advisor sr, $46,533
Willcox, Clair E Jr, asoc dir strat communications, $80,000
Willcox, Jennifer Lauren, instructor, clincl, $90,000
Willcoxon, Keith Joseph, cook, $12.64/hr
Wille, Melinda S, asoc dir program/project ops, $51,705
Willenburg, Christina Florence, care coordinator, $61,685
Willer, Jessica Paige, nurse, staff II rnwp, $20.95/hr
Willet, Katherine Gloor, resident physician-1st yr, $49,025
Willett, Ami Renee, office support assistant IV, $14.46/hr
Willett, Brie A, physician ast, $78,750
Willett, Dan L, professor, $71,553
Willett, Teresa Ann, polysomnograph techn reg, $24.27/hr
Williams, Fred III, prof, ast clincl, $102,780
Williams, Gerald G Jr, prof, adjunct, $20,475
Williams, Mark Douglas Jr, resp therapist reg, $19.93/hr
Williams-Dunbar, Kimberly Jenice, prog/proj supprt coor I, $35,232
Williams, Alayna Suzanne, nurse, staff, $21.53/hr
Williams, Amber Lynn, educational pgm associate I, $13.45/hr
Williams, Amy S, prof, ast clincl dept, $137,700
Williams, Asia M, academic advisor, $37,458
Williams, Barbara Diane, nurse, staff II, $32.31/hr
Williams, Benjamin J, instructor, $61,364
Williams, Brian J, prof, ast clincl, $89,162
Williams, Brittan Leigh, prgm mgr II studnt supprt svcs, $45,600
Williams, Bruce Allen, mts/electrician, $20.31/hr
Williams, Camille Denise, care team assoc-clinical, $11.10/hr
Williams, Carla Nicole, resrch asoc, $55,000
Williams, Carol L, office support assistant sr, $20.63/hr
Williams, Carol Louise, educational pgm associate I, $12.75/hr
Williams, Carole M, nurse, staff, $27.59/hr
Williams, Carrie Aletha, coor, service, $14.94/hr
Williams, Casey D, prof, ast clincl dept, $106,875
Williams, Catherine, program/project supprt coor I, $49,488
Williams, Catherine Marcella, office support asst III, $13.99/hr
Williams, Cazzie F, custodian, $10.00/hr
Williams, Charlene A, office support assistant I, $12.67/hr
Williams, Charles Blake, instructor, adjunct, $9,000
Williams, Charles M, db programmer analyst-expert, $53,000
Williams, Christina Ann, pat admiss advisor, $28.08/hr
Williams, Cody Jon, system support analyst-entry, $16.18/hr
Williams, Danielle Janae, nurse, licensed prac, $15.06/hr
Williams, Darnell B, library info specialist sr, $15.32/hr
Williams, Darrin M, support systems admin-expert, $53,448
Williams, Daryl W, care team assoc-suppt, $13.78/hr
Williams, Debra Ann, rehab therapy aide, $14.88/hr
Williams, Dee Conrad, patient svc rep, $13.67/hr
Williams, Derek Randolph, prof, asoc clincl, $93,969
Williams, Desiree' N, office support assistant III, $12.54/hr
Williams, Donctella, nurse, licensed prac, $20.95/hr
Williams, Dorothy M, nurse advisor, telephone, $30.91/hr
Williams, Douglas L, manager it, $53,448
Williams, Edie, clerk, unit, $14.88/hr

Williams, Erica Faith, office support assistant II, $10.24/hr
Williams, Erin R, support systems admin-speclst, $45,600
Williams, Florence Elizabeth, prof, ast adjunct, $16,008
Williams, Gary Michael, video comm admin-expert, $64,899
Williams, Gavin Hunter, temporary crafts service, $9.50/hr
Williams, Gloria D, custodian, $12.94/hr
Williams, Isha C, educational pgm associate I, $14.70/hr
Williams, J A, grounds keeper II, $15.09/hr
Williams, Jasmine, office support aide II, $11.06/hr
Williams, Jason Orlando, research lab supervisor, $48,865
Williams, Jerry Wayne, floor care techn lead, $13.34/hr
Williams, Jessica Marie, librarian I, $43,200
Williams, Joan D, office support assistant II, $10.44/hr
Williams, Joyce, interventional technl (ir), $30.36/hr
Williams, Julie, nurse, staff II rnwp, $28.94/hr
Williams, Julie C, educational pgm associate I, $14.72/hr
Williams, Kaminsky D, office support assistant II, $11.09/hr
Williams, Karen Beth, professor, $175,000
Williams, Katina R, office support assistant IV, $15.00/hr
Williams, Katy Farber, resident physician-3rd yr, $53,763
Williams, Kimberly Ann, care team assoc-clinical, $14.75/hr
Williams, Laron K, prof, ast, $75,137
Williams, Larry S, prof, ast/profl pract, $138,796
Williams, Lesa A, educational pgm associate I, $13.62/hr
Williams, Linder, program/project supprt coor II, $50,126
Williams, Lindsey R, prof, asoc, $53,623
Williams, Lucinda, library info specialist, $20.22/hr
Williams, Lutrissia Mariea, custodian, $12.94/hr
Williams, Mallory Alexandra, care team assoc-clinical, $12.08/hr
Williams, Mark Anthony, temporary technical, $9.25/hr
Williams, Marvin A, fin and acctg analyst sr, $60,030
Williams, Mary M, nurse, staff II, $34.18/hr
Williams, Maryann Theresa, office support asst III, $11.72/hr
Williams, Michelle Renee, food svc wrkr I, $9.60/hr
Williams, Nichole Jean, nurse, staff II, $22.01/hr
Williams, Paige Ashley, prof, asoc profl practice, $72,000
Williams, Pamela Lenice, rehab therapy aide, $13.21/hr
Williams, Paul, resident physician-1st yr, $49,025
Williams, Phillip Roy, health physics technician II, $20.60/hr
Williams, Rachel Michelle, custodian, $10.00/hr
Williams, Rajena Deniece, animal caretaker, $12.55/hr
Williams, Randi Elaine, office support assistant III, $13.39/hr
Williams, Richard Lee, prof, ast, $63,719
Williams, Sarah E, instructor, adjunct, $6,300
Williams, Sha Lai L, prof, ast, $62,800
Williams, Shaterrica L, nurse, licensed prac, $16.89/hr
Williams, Sheena S, office support assistant IV, $13.30/hr
Williams, Sherralyn, reimbursement consultant, $51,266
Williams, Stephanie Leann, strat comm manager, $55,000
Williams, Steven A, system support analyst-princpl, $63,160
Williams, Steven Tyler, research/lab technician, $10.24/hr
Williams, Tara Lynn, sterile processing tech, $14.09/hr
Williams, Terri Lynn, temporary professional, $12.00/hr
Williams, Terry Charles, prof, ast clincl, $87,167
Williams, Thomas C, prof, ast, $119,071
Williams, Thomas R, supv housekeeping, $36,572
Williams, Tiffany Shauntay, sr dir studnt supprt svcs, $85,280
Williams, Tina Marie, nurse advisor, telephone, $26.55/hr
Williams, Tracey Lee, food svc wrkr I, $9.60/hr
Williams, Tricia Ann, instructor, adjunct, $4,800
Williams, Troy Lee, athletic trainer, $40,000
Williams, Wendy S, temporary professional, $12.00/hr
Williamson, Handy Jr, V provost, $184,492
Williamson, Barbara, prof, asoc teach, $67,888
Williamson, Baye Garnette, fellow, post doctoral, $26,500
Williamson, Bryant S, stage services assistant lead, $18.00/hr
Williamson, Carolyn J, student service coor II, $40,392
Williamson, Harold Allen, V chancl health sciences, $386,863
Williamson, Jeanna Marie, pat acct rep, $15.25/hr
Williamson, Laura A, mgr advancement, $47,500
Williamson, Mary M, clinical mgr, $108,373
Williamson, Maryann, executive assistant, $21.23/hr
Williamson, Patricia Ann, nurse, staff II, $34.50/hr
Williamson, Tyler Robert, custodian, $12.18/hr
Williford, Sandra Jean, educational pgm associate I, $14.16/hr
Willingham, M Juanita, instructor, adjunct, $4,400
Willis Smith, Nancy M, prof, ast clincl, $75,276
Willis, Amanda Sue, service rep III, $12.30/hr
Willis, Barbara Gayle, student service coor II, $40,908

Willis, Bradley W, physical therapist, $65,040
Willis, Chesney Christine, speech/lang pathologist, $35.00/hr
Willis, Derrick Keith, resrch asoc, $77,014
Willis, John D, supervisor it, $60,002
Willis, Linda K, medical coding spclst, $20.82/hr
Willis, Linda Kay, student support specialist I, $14.06/hr
Willis, Patricia Diane, mgr II business admin, $57,175
Willis, Phyllis Ann, nurse anesthetist, $147,900
Willis, Wrainbeau Lynn, office support assistant III, $14.42/hr
Willits, Lynn, student service coor II, $45,000
Willmore, Theodore M, physician, $200.00/hr
Willouer, Jadon Bryce, custodian, $10.94/hr
Willoughby, Thomas Logan, media producer II, $15.00/hr
Willow Schomaker, Christina, office support asst IV, $15.45/hr
Wills, Barbara Jean, business support specialist sr, $20.89/hr
Wills, Martin, internet administrator-expert, $24.19/hr
Wills, Theodore E, prof, ast clincl, $62,549
Wills, William Noah, temporary crafts service, $9.75/hr
Willyard, Julie Kay, office support assistant III, $13.52/hr
Wilman, Richard, engineering technician II, $18.01/hr
Wilmarth, Paul, technical trainer-speclst, $43,699
Wilsdorf, Merilee Krueger, prof, asoc teach, $57,178
Wilsdorf, Nicholas Jon, temporary technical, $8.00/hr
Wilson, Charles R Jr, instructor, adjunct, $33,000
Wilson Kleekamp, Traci Lizzette, tutor, $10.00/hr
Wilson-Keenan, Nina Rose, student support spclst sr, $17.95/hr
Wilson-Tagoe, Veronica Nana, prof, teach, $88,434
Wilson, Ami N, instructor, adjunct, $9,000
Wilson, Amy Renee, psychologist, $42,488
Wilson, Anna, prof, ast teach, $94,000
Wilson, Ashley Kay, program/project supprt coor II, $41,580
Wilson, Barbara Eliza, prof, clincl, $75,220
Wilson, Barbara Jean, temporary crafts service, $14.00/hr
Wilson, Betty Ann, custodian, $12.94/hr
Wilson, Betty J, business support specialist II, $18.97/hr
Wilson, Betty Jo, compliance manager sr, $63,423
Wilson, Brent Darin, lecturer, $35,000
Wilson, Carla E Conway, athletic director, $150,000
Wilson, Carla M, temporary crafts service, $9.10/hr
Wilson, Christina Elise, office support assistant IV, $15.76/hr
Wilson, Christine Bartlow, db progrmer analyst-princpl, $70,685
Wilson, Christine Leanne, resident physician-1st yr, $50,219
Wilson, Christopher, prof, asoc teach, $39,052
Wilson, Christopher J, program/project supprt coor sr, $57,855
Wilson, Cody Lee, event assistant I, $8.00/hr
Wilson, Crystal Dawn, enrollment advisor sr, $17.69/hr
Wilson, Cynthia A, temporary clerical, $12.55/hr
Wilson, Danny D, operations support tech II, $12.53/hr
Wilson, David Alan, professor, $154,544
Wilson, Deborah Lee, office support assistant IV, $18.70/hr
Wilson, Dennis I, lecturer, $2,500
Wilson, Don C, prof, ast adjunct, $125.00/hr
Wilson, Donna Marie, office support assistant IV, $16.01/hr
Wilson, Dorothy A, nurse, licensed prac, $20.68/hr
Wilson, Elana M, research specialist I, $43,260
Wilson, Ellen Sherman, grader, $52
Wilson, Eric Luis, nurse anesthetist, $147,900
Wilson, Erin Kathleen, grader, $100.00/hr
Wilson, George D, retail sales associate sr, $19.01/hr
Wilson, Guy Christopher, technology resource mgr, $64,409
Wilson, James H, founders professor, $31,654
Wilson, Jarrod Scott, office support assistant III, $11.36/hr
Wilson, Jay Marsh, dir II advancement, $82,500
Wilson, Judy Ann, grounds keeper, $12.30/hr
Wilson, Justin D, animal techn, ast lab, $13.89/hr
Wilson, Kailey B, resident physician-1st yr, $50,219
Wilson, Karen Denise, student support specialist sr, $20.81/hr
Wilson, Kevin, asoc dir program/project ops, $78,718
Wilson, Kristen Marie, office support assistant III, $11.39/hr
Wilson, Kristian C, custodian, $12.94/hr
Wilson, Lisa Ruth, instructor, clincl, $79,000
Wilson, Lloyd Christopher, prof, asoc adjunct, $20,475
Wilson, Lois Kate, office support associate, $27.51/hr
Wilson, Margaret Elizabeth, office support assistant III, $12.22/hr
Wilson, Marion Virginia, emerg svcs educator, $51,000
Wilson, Mary Anne, food svc wrkr II, $11.60/hr
Wilson, Megan Jayne, resp therapist reg, $28.00/hr
Wilson, Michael Lee, coor life safety infrastr, $63,149
Wilson, Neal James, grader, $3,000

Wilson, Nichole Suzanne, nurse clinician, $72,668
Wilson, Ophelia, office support assistant II, $10.24/hr
Wilson, Patricia L, operations tech sr, $17.04/hr
Wilson, Peggy Jean, manager it, $66,110
Wilson, Philip Joseph, resident physician-2nd yr, $52,007
Wilson, Purificacion D, nurse, staff II, $34.18/hr
Wilson, Rachel A, prof, ast teach, $96,900
Wilson, Rachelle Loren, office support assistant III, $12.95/hr
Wilson, Richard A, prof, asoc, $61,125
Wilson, Robert Lee, coor head injury svc, $37,142
Wilson, Robert Mark, prof, asoc clncl, $88,430
Wilson, Roberta L, office support associate, $17.24/hr
Wilson, Ryan Bart, bldg cntrl sys techn III, $23.33/hr
Wilson, Ryan James, custodian, $10.00/hr
Wilson, Sandy Jean, fin and acctg manager, $66,500
Wilson, Sherlie S, office support assistant IV, $17.71/hr
Wilson, Steven J, powr plnt opr II, $28.70/hr
Wilson, Steven Lynn, bts mason/tuckptr, $22.14/hr
Wilson, Susan, vice chancellor, $130,000
Wilson, Teresa I, bindery opr III, $20.77/hr
Wilson, Terry J, prof, asoc teach, $50,103
Wilson, Theresa N, prgm mgr II studnt supprt svcs, $68,575
Wilson, Timothy James, psychologist, $40.00/hr
Wilson, Tonya L, bindery opr II, $17.78/hr
Wilson, Tracy L, mgr student support svcs, $50,600
Wilson, Virginia L, state spclst, asoc, $70,577
Wilson, William Brent, network engineer-princpl, $73,580
Wilson, William Robert, event assistant I, $7.50/hr
Wimmenauer, Lisa J, dir III business admin, $111,116
Wimmenauer, Michael A, fin and acctg manager, $60,213
Winans, Elizabeth Ann, prof, asoc clncl, $103,000
Winberg, Donna M, nurse, staff II, $34.61/hr
Winders, Christopher R, sr dir program/project ops, $95,844
Windett, Tina Yvonne, student service coor sr, $55,825
Windham, Linda Lou, lab assistant, $12.61/hr
Windmann, Jennifer Madeline, nurse, staff I, $19.00/hr
Windmiller, Debra A, nurse, procedures, $34.18/hr
Windsor, Lavecie Sue, nurse, staff II, $25.37/hr
Wineland, Christy M, asoc dir advancement, $62,426
Winfrey, David N, mgr csm operations, $57,549
Winfrey, Tammy Lynn, mgr III business admin, $61,850
Wingate, Terry L, lecturer, $100.00/hr
Wingert, Edmund Jarom, nurse anesthetist, $147,900
Wingert, Jared Ross, nurse anesthetist, $145,760
Wingert, Karen L, prof, asoc teach, $69,141
Wingert, Karen L, physical therapist, $37.28/hr
Wingler, Amber Leigh, reactor engineer, $48,646
Winholtz, Robert Andrew, prof, asoc, $85,969
Winiarz, Jeffrey G, prof, asoc, $70,002
Winingear, Rachel Marie, business support spec II, $19.20/hr
Winingear, Stevie Renee, office support assistant I, $8.89/hr
Winkel, Richard J, system administrator-expert, $71,168
Winkelman, Steven C, electrician, powr plant svc, $27.26/hr
Winkelmann, Susan E, prof, asoc clncl dept, $149,445
Winkler, Anne Elizabeth, professor, $105,436
Winkler, Bertha, preceptor, $8.69/hr
Winkler, Tammie A, business support specialist II, $17.85/hr
Winn, David Jackson, instructor, adjunct, $9,000
Winn, Hung N, professor, $487,800
Winn, Jeremy A, mts/machinist, $21.05/hr
Winn, Jessica L, fellow, post doc clncl yr1, $55,804
Winner, Priscilla Ann, office support assistant IV, $14.63/hr
Winningham, Peter Joel, resident physician-2nd yr, $50,810
Winschel, Amy Josephine, intern, $8.00/hr
Winscott, Kevin Andrew, event assistant I, $7.50/hr
Winslow, Denise Elaine, grader, $52
Winstead, Larissa Breelyn, student recruitment spclst, $14.96/hr
Winstead, Lisa L, office support assistant III, $11.47/hr
Winter, Caleb Scott, care team assoc-clinical, $11.10/hr
Winter, William Ernst, resrch asoc, $65,810
Winterbower, Angela Beth, coor phy suprt, $55,883
Winterbower, Todd H, program/project supprt coor I, $45,164
Winterburg, Nancy L, office support assistant IV, $18.03/hr
Winters, Amanda Lyn, rev cycle spclst, $47,122
Winters, Nathan Christopher, mgr student support svcs, $31,305
Winters, Steven C, asoc director it, $86,290
Winterwolf, Connor Douglas, food svc wrkr I, $9.60/hr
Winzer, Marie Antionett, support systems admin-spec, $45,600
Wion, Sarah Elizabeth, advancement associate II, $19.23/hr

Wipfler, Mark Stephen, mechl plant spclst, $19.63/hr
Wipke Tevis, Deidre D, prof, asoc, $83,897
Wiredu, Charles Kontor, fellow, post doc clncl yr1, $55,804
Wirkus, Anthony Aaron, coor athletic operations, $36,693
Wirt, Grace Zhang, custodian, $10.94/hr
Wirth, James B, extns professional, asoc, $61,031
Wisdom-Behounek, Jennifer R, prof, ast clincl dept, $142,800
Wisdom, Jason Dean, farm wrkr III, $16.47/hr
Wisdom, Michelle Marie, information security officer, $98,940
Wisdom, Russchelle L, house manager h, $70,649
Wise, Hester, lecturer, $24,482
Wise, Julian Michael, hospital security officer, $10.75/hr
Wise, Keely Karleen, program/project supprt coor I, $35,088
Wise, Kim Stuart, emeritus, $15,035
Wise, Lyndsay Brooke, occl therapist, $35.00/hr
Wise, Patti A, sftware supprt analyst-entry, $34,500
Wise, Rachel Kristene, editor II, $55,008
Wise, Ramsay B, grader, $100.00/hr
Wise, Rebecca Lynn, pat acct rep, $14.84/hr
Wise, Rhonda Renee, nurse, staff II, $33.37/hr
Wise, Rick J, dir I, csm operations, $93,233
Wise, Tracy Lynn, patient svc rep, $13.42/hr
Wiseman, Donald Eugene, csm project manager, $66,433
Wiseman, Judith, prof, teach, $85,500
Wiseman, Karla Jean, office support assistant IV, $18.05/hr
Wiseman, Le A, program/project supprt coor sr, $56,182
Wiser, Lauren C, office support assistant I, $11.15/hr
Wisman, Samuel C, teaching ast, $27.00/hr
Wisner, Clarissa Ann, research specialist sr, $56,942
Wisniewski, Dion James, emrg med techn, $13.48/hr
Wiss, David L, mechl plant spclst II, $20.89/hr
Wiss, Donna B, coor, reimbursement, $54,855
Wissmann, Mary Elizabeth, temporary professional, $22.30/hr
Withycombe, Amber Erin, dir advancemnt activities, $68,250
Witt, Doyle Thomas, resident physician-2nd yr, $50,810
Witt, Jacquelyn S, prof, asoc clincl, $87,579
Witt, Karen Paulik, librarian II, $47,111
Witte, Kacie Elizabeth, chargemaster spclst, $53,698
Witte, Peter Thomas, dean, $210,000
Wittenborn, Nancy S, staff development spclst, $56,297
Witter, David J, grader, $52
Witting, Nicole R, dir III business admin, $125,833
Wittman, Joseph L, temporary technical, $25.00/hr
Wittry, Mary Jo Rose, model, $15.00/hr
Witzman, Sean D, library info specialist sr, $14.95/hr
Wobbe, Janice M, office support assistant IV, $16.30/hr
Woehlke, Joshua Bruce, db programmer analyst-expert, $53,280
Woelfel, Stacey W, prof, asoc profl practice, $85,584
Woelk, Klaus Hubert, prof, asoc, $89,325
Wofford, Stephanie Kay, educational pgm associate I, $13.45/hr
Wohleber, Curt A, strat comm associate I, $46,057
Wohleber, Linda Peters, teaching ast, $13.00/hr
Wolf, Amanda Louise, educational pgm associate I, $13.45/hr
Wolf, Bradley E, police officer, $19.20/hr
Wolf, Christopher J, prof, ast clincl dept, $176,484
Wolf, Danica Suzanne, student service coor II, $42,264
Wolf, Jennifer Lee, resident physician-2nd yr, $51,134
Wolf, Kaitlin Elizabeth, safety monitor, $9.27/hr
Wolfe-Boyd, R Annamarie, student support spec II, $17.18/hr
Wolfe, Abigail E, intern, $23,000
Wolfe, Christopher Ryan, manager it, $69,745
Wolfe, Heidi Marie, instructor, adjunct, $25,650
Wolfe, John, parking lot attd, $12.58/hr
Wolfe, Karen R, patient svc rep, $13.81/hr
Wolfe, Kenneth Joseph, instructor, adjunct, $10,500
Wolfe, Laura Platt, resident physician-3rd yr, $52,470
Wolfe, Preston Noel, temporary clerical, $8.00/hr
Wolff, Christopher Ernest, retail sales manager, $53,702
Wolff, Jane C, instructor, adjunct, $13,200
Wolff, Sara M, business support specialist sr, $20.40/hr
Wolff, Tonya T, instructor, adjunct, $16,000
Wolfinbarger, Beverly, student support specialist sr, $16.71/hr
Wolfinbarger, David M, network engineer-expert, $65,000
Wolford, Kenneth A, security officer, $10.88/hr
Wolfrath, David A, mgr inpatient pharm clncl svcs, $139,259
Wolin, Christopher D, prof, ast teach, $45,715
Woltering, Michelle L, care team assoc-clinical, $13.72/hr
Woltkamp, Debra, anesthesia techn, $14.72/hr
Wolverson, Melinda Marie, technical trainer-expert, $47,497

Wolverton, Patricia A, business support specialist sr, $31.72/hr
Womack, William L Jr, physician, $200.00/hr
Womack, Abner Willis, emeritus, $50,409
Womack, April Renee, nurse, staff now III, $30.00/hr
Womack, Gavin Christopher, event assistant I, $11.00/hr
Wombles, Timothy Wayne, media producer I, $13.00/hr
Wombwell, Eric Anthony, prof, ast clincl, $99,000
Womer, Norman Keith, professor, $190,556
Won, JiYoung, communications assistant sr, $15.22/hr
Wondra, Alice, teaching ast, $13.00/hr
Wong, Chung Fun, prof, asoc, $69,120
Wong, Erwin Yen Hook, prof, asoc teach, $74,346
Wong, Ming, food svc wrkr III, $11.24/hr
Wongskhaluang, Jeff V, instructor, clincl, $100,000
Wood Harter, Joyce, nurse practitioner, $83,488
Wood IV, Chalmers Rieger, resident physician-2nd yr, $50,810
Wood Turley, Sharon, prof, ast teach, $72,200
Wood, Aaron Douglas, fellow, post doctoral, $48,000
Wood, Ann Marie, prof, ast teach, $45,788
Wood, Bondi Jo, grant writer sr, $30.89/hr
Wood, Darla Sue, educational pgm associate I, $13.58/hr
Wood, Deirdre Yvonne Manley, instructor, adjunct, $18,648
Wood, Donald Eugene, perfusionist sr, $141,450
Wood, Elizabeth Rae, veterinary technician sr, $15.69/hr
Wood, Henrietta Rix, prof, ast teach, $50,000
Wood, Jacqueline Edith, prof, asoc, $84,620
Wood, Jill Hermsen, dir II human resources, $92,400
Wood, John Gary, emrg med techn, $15.05/hr
Wood, Kelsey Marie, nurse, staff II rnwp, $22.22/hr
Wood, Lea Ashleigh, prof, ast teach, $72,000
Wood, Lisa Michelle, business support specialist II, $20.23/hr
Wood, Loretta M, nurse, licensed prac sr, $20.37/hr
Wood, Lori Leann, pat acct rep, $15.10/hr
Wood, Martha A, educational pgm associate I, $13.72/hr
Wood, Mary Jo, office support assistant III, $11.30/hr
Wood, Nichole Gale, office support assistant IV, $14.29/hr
Wood, Patricia Mae, educational pgm assistant, $12.48/hr
Wood, Phillip, professor, $105,190
Wood, Steve A, health physics technician II, $19.65/hr
Wood, Susan E, mental health tech, $13.85/hr
Woodall, Stachia Leigh, telecom it analyst-princpl, $53,448
Woodard, Debra J, prof, asoc teach, $54,935
Woodburn, Nathaniel J, histologic technl, $23.00/hr
Woodbury, Jack, csm operations supervisor, $50,368
Woodbury, Jacob Lee, temporary crafts service, $7.65/hr
Woodbury, Kay L, temporary professional, $11.30/hr
Wooden, Justin Ray, security officer, $14.00/hr
Wooden, Kevin Ray, utility dist wrkr IV, $23.75/hr
Woodhouse, Shawn, prof, asoc, $79,451
Woodley, Robert S, prof, ast adjunct, $22,500
Woodman, Brian James, office support assistant IV, $15.00/hr
Woodman, Ryan S, resident physician-3rd yr, $53,763
Woodruff, Douglas E, care team assoc-suppt, $13.37/hr
Woodruff, Emily Jean, nurse, staff I, $19.00/hr
Woods, Amanda Shay, office support assistant III, $13.50/hr
Woods, Bobbie Ayanna Louise, care team assoc-clinical, $11.10/hr
Woods, Bridget, custodian, $11.44/hr
Woods, Brittany Suzanne, service rep IV, $16.61/hr
Woods, Christine Michelle, social worker, $57,140
Woods, David Craig, police sergeant, $20.04/hr
Woods, Deborah Kaye, surgical technl certified, $23.01/hr
Woods, Demicco, instructor, adjunct, $1,000
Woods, Heather Rae, mental health tech, $11.73/hr
Woods, Jayne Tiana, prof, asoc adjunct, $6,000
Woods, Jennifer Nicole, nurse clinician, $56,244
Woods, John Paul, network engineer-speclst, $50,616
Woods, Kevin James, anesthesia techn, $14.15/hr
Woods, Kimberley Jo, reimbursement ast-cert, $20.25/hr
Woods, Kimberly, custodian, $10.94/hr
Woods, LaTanya Ann, office support assistant IV, $13.24/hr
Woods, Lucas Tyler, research specialist sr, $54,508
Woods, Mike, bts carpenter, $20.23/hr
Woods, Misty Sue, coor, service, $17.42/hr
Woods, Opal J, care team assoc-clinical, $15.08/hr
Woods, Rami J, research specialist I, $46,138
Woods, Samantha Marie, patient svc rep, $12.55/hr
Woods, Stephanie Lynn, instructor, visiting, $9,186
Woods, Tammy L, dental assistant II, $14.95/hr
Woods, Terry L, research specialist I, $33,225

Woods, William Jeffery, farm wrkr I, $12.12/hr
Woodson, Benjamin W, prof, ast, $55,000
Woodson, John Eric, program/project supprt coor sr, $58,098
Woodson, Joseph M, event assistant I, $9.50/hr
Woodson, Michael Anthony, system admin-princpl, $72,954
Woodson, Virginia Sue, business support specialist II, $17.11/hr
Woodward, Jason R, mts/electrician-r, $20.87/hr
Woody, James Chester, research/lab technician sr, $17.40/hr
Woody, Kaitlin E, office support assistant IV, $14.54/hr
Woody, Rhonda Jo, office support assistant III, $13.16/hr
Woody, Ronald D, engineering technician II, $15.23/hr
Wooldridge, Robert Dale, electronics technician II, $15.50/hr
Woolery, Daniel R, resident physician-2nd yr, $52,007
Woolery, Lee Ann, extns professional, asoc, $57,116
Woolf, Denise, resrch asoc, $48,001
Woolfolk, Hillary Elizabeth, nurse, licensed prac, $14.76/hr
Woolley, Emil G, program/project supprt coor I, $25.00/hr
Woolridge, Virgil W Jr, extns professional, asoc, $48,422
Woolridge, Glenda J, food svc wrkr III, $13.21/hr
Woolsey, Barbara J, instructor, adjunct, $9,900
Woolsey, Martin McClain, specialist, $10.00/hr
Wooten, Donald D, food svc wrkr III, $11.83/hr
Wootton, Maya L, care team assoc-suppt, $13.12/hr
Word, Deborah L, grader, $100.00/hr
Worden, John Wellington, sr dir program/project ops, $87,011
Worden, Shelley Jean, librarian II, $52,975
Workman, Jenny Lynn, human resources manager sr, $64,879
Workman, Mitchell J, temporary crafts service, $16.50/hr
Worley, Barbara A, office support assistant IV, $14.66/hr
Worley, Charles Robert, coor, surg supply, $51,000
Worley, Jillian Nicole, nurse, staff II, $22.24/hr
Worley, Karen Sue, dir I, strat communications, $112,173
Worley, Melanie Ann, temporary technical, $10.00/hr
Worley, Norma Jean, instructor, adjunct, $62.50/hr
Worley, Stefani Ann, med techl reg, $23.03/hr
Wormington, Ashley Michelle, event assistant I, $8.50/hr
Wormington, Denis Dee, instructor, clincl, $7,500
Worsey, Gillian M, prof, ast adjunct, $15,000
Worsey, Paul Nicholas, professor, $117,913
Worsowicz, Gregory M, prof, clinical dept, $404,427
Worsowicz, Peter Daniel, temporary clerical, $7.50/hr
Worstell, Susan Anjanette, office support assistant III, $14.47/hr
Worth, Corey Julius, custodian, $13.23/hr
Worthington, Ian, prof, curators, $82,802
Wortmann, Kelsey Marie, mentor, $12.00/hr
Wotawa, Michael J, student recruitment spclst, $17.95/hr
Wozniak, Katherine Jean, student service coor II, $49,781
Wray, Larry, professor, $54,909
Wray, Warren Kent, vice chancellor, $259,750
Wren, Georgia Gale, office support assistant IV, $15.54/hr
Wren, Traci J, mgr III business admin, $60,600
Wrench, Sylvia D, child dev assistant, $8.16/hr
Wright IV, William C, system support analyst-entry, $17.19/hr
Wright, Robert E Jr, athletic attd lead, $15.20/hr
Wright-Austin, Karren Denise, pat acct rep, $15.14/hr
Wright, Abbie C, prof, ast clincl dept, $238,000
Wright, Alecia K, media production director I, $50,659
Wright, Allen D, chemist II, $41,404
Wright, Cassidy Douglas, resident physician-3rd yr, $53,763
Wright, Cecilia Louise, high school student, $8.75/hr
Wright, Christopher J, research engineering tech I, $19.50/hr
Wright, Crystal Renae, care team assoc-clinical, $13.60/hr
Wright, Dale, dir iv advancement, $107,000
Wright, David Charles, bts carpenter, $18.12/hr
Wright, Deborah A, custodian, $12.94/hr
Wright, Deborah M, ast athletic director, $113,300
Wright, Deron A, custodian, $12.90/hr
Wright, Elena Victoria, db administrator-princpl, $65,499
Wright, Elizabeth Watson, research specialist I, $29,640
Wright, Emily Renee, health records techn II, $12.17/hr
Wright, Farroll Tim, emeritus, $27,360
Wright, Jamie Louise, couns hlth/welfare/wellness sr, $30.00/hr
Wright, Jasmin M, patient svc rep, $14.34/hr
Wright, Jeffrey Gene, programmer analyst-princpl, $68,141
Wright, Joshua C, physical therapist, $59,928
Wright, Kathleen Lyudmila, lab assistant, $8.50/hr
Wright, Kelli Kay, prgm director, ast, $62,000
Wright, Kristie Lynn, physical therapist, $46,113
Wright, Kristina Marie, prgm mgr II studnt supprt svcs, $50,194

Wright, Lisa Ann, lecturer, $100.00/hr
Wright, Lisa Marie, pat accts logic anlyst, $41,674
Wright, Maggie Leah, pat acct rep, $15.56/hr
Wright, Matthew Allen, certif pharmacy techn, $15.57/hr
Wright, Melissa Renae, animal caretaker, $12.55/hr
Wright, Michael David, prof, asoc, $63,090
Wright, Michele L, education nurse, $60,397
Wright, Michelle Selene, nurse, staff II, $22.59/hr
Wright, Nicole R, research specialist I, $41,117
Wright, Patti, prof, asoc, $65,099
Wright, Ray L, research specialist I, $36,161
Wright, Risa, teaching asst, $20,850
Wright, Ronald, prof, ast adjunct, $125.00/hr
Wright, Sara L, health records techn I, $11.68/hr
Wright, Sarah Gail, nurse, clincl charge-rn, $27.04/hr
Wright, Sarah Lynn, educational pgm assistant, $10.22/hr
Wright, Stacey Owsley, prgm director, $57,070
Wright, Susan P, food svc wrkr III, $13.21/hr
Wright, Tracy Lynn, coor, service, $17.10/hr
Wright, Tyrone Eugene, patient svc rep, $12.34/hr
Wright, Whitney Ann, practice manager, $68,228
Wright, William R, environmental enginrng tech sr, $16.54/hr
Wright, Yolanda E, event assistant I, $7.55/hr
Wrinkle, Jeremy David, advancement associate I, $16.82/hr
Wrisinger, Carli, strat comm associate II, $40,000
Wrobel, Jerzy Michal, professor, $90,783
Wrolstad, Jan L, asoc dir program/project ops, $62,115
Wronkiewicz, David J, prof, asoc, $88,530
Wu, Bin, professor, $113,938
Wu, Cheng Hsiao, professor, $89,327
Wu, Cheng-Shih, prof, ast adjunct, $27,000
Wu, Chun H, system administrator-speclst, $46,284
Wu, Jianbo, prof, ast resrch, $24,024
Wu, Jie, fellow, post doctoral, $30,000
Wu, Ying, prof, ast/profl pract, $51,765
Wu, Yuefeng, prof, ast, $75,793
Wu, Yuhsin Victoria, prof, ast clincl dept, $245,000
Wu, Yunna, programmer analyst-speclst, $52,803
Wu, Zihao, prof, ast clincl dept, $254,898
Wuest, Michael David, strat comm manager, $54,332
Wuger, Kimberly D, patient svc rep, $14.06/hr
Wulff, Kelly Suzanne, event assistant I, $10.00/hr
Wulff, Mary Louise, patient svc rep, $14.71/hr
Wulff, Melanie Dawn, office support associate, $16.81/hr
Wuller, Richard Johnston, rec/athletic associate sr, $30,000
Wundrack, Sara Lucinda, resp care clinical coor, $29.73/hr
Wung, Lynn M, prof, ast clincl dept, $113,144
Wunsch II, Donald C, professor, $145,200
Wyatt, Connie S, business ops associate sr, $52,604
Wyatt, Diane Renee, business support specialist II, $23.49/hr
Wyatt, Jared Clayton, temporary crafts service, $7.75/hr
Wyatt, Kerri Leigh, nurse, staff II, $29.26/hr
Wyatt, Matthew D, custodian lead, $11.98/hr
Wyatt, Michael Wayne, office support assistant IV, $15.22/hr
Wyatt, Richard Stephen, asoc vice chancellor, $193,703
Wyatt, Sheryl L, nurse, staff II, $29.53/hr
Wyatt, Stephanie Denise, mentor, $8.00/hr
Wyatt, Steve Allen, bts carpenter, $21.71/hr
Wyatt, Tommy Ray, bindery opr III, $20.77/hr
Wyble, Lori R, patient svc rep, $13.34/hr
Wybrant, Theresa Ann, compliance specialist II, $36,409
Wyckoff, Gerald Joseph, prof, asoc, $101,389
Wycoff, Donald E, fellow, post doctoral, $46,362
Wycoff, Linda Dianne, instructor, adjunct, $26,710
Wycoff, Wei G, research specialist sr, $65,489
Wylie, Cara M, program/project supprt coor sr, $55,676
Wyllie, Ellen Louise, student service coor II, $41,580
Wymer, Joshua S, maint svc attd, $17.78/hr
Wyss, Fred, food svc wrkr I, $11.29/hr
Xia, Chuan, fellow, post doctoral, $36,360
Xia, Jingyan, office support assistant IV, $14.84/hr
Xiao, Chengshan, professor, $117,136
Xiao, Hua, resrch scientist/academic, $38,436
Xiao, Zhiwei, mts/hvac, $24.13/hr
Xie, Hui, fin and acctg analyst sr, $43,156
Xie, Leike, fellow, post doctoral, $38,872
Xie, Yanxia, scholar, visiting, $19,200
Xie, Yixia, resrch asoc, $43,860
Xin, Ming, prof, asoc, $105,060

Xing, Yangchuan, professor, $119,590
Xiong, Keyu, director it, $91,690
Xiong, Xi, prof, ast, $77,167
Xochipa, Adolfo, custodian, $12.94/hr
Xu, Anjing, business support specialist II, $15.32/hr
Xu, Dong, professor, $218,409
Xu, Liang, business ops associate sr, $45,600
Xu, Tingsheng, resrch asoc, $61,200
Xu, Xianjin, fellow, post doctoral, $36,750
Xu, Xiaojun, resrch asoc, $39,204
Xu, Yu, academic advisor, $45,302
Xu, Yuanxi, resrch asoc, $38,189
Xu, Yun Sheng, prof, asoc resrch, $96,000
Xu, Zhi, prof, asoc, $75,284
Xue, Bing, resrch asoc, $38,000
Xufuris, Andreas K, db programmer analyst-expert, $52,746
Yabe, Shinichiro, fellow, post doctoral, $39,264
Yaeger, Sharon Sue, dir hosp finl svcs, $149,212
Yaglom, Hayley Danielle, office support assistant II, $15.00/hr
Yahuaca, Bernado I, resident physician-2nd yr, $52,007
Yakimo, Richard, prof, asoc teach, $74,700
Yalaoui, Shannyn Joliett, hr informatics spclst, $55,890
Yamilov, Alexey Georgiyevich, prof, asoc, $77,986
Yampara-Iquise, Helen, research specialist I, $39,736
Yan, Cheng, prof, ast teach, $60,000
Yan, Guirong, prof, ast, $84,500
Yan, Haojing, prof, ast, $83,608
Yan, Xuemin, professor, $230,560
Yancey, Christy Lynn, med office assistant, $13.33/hr
Yancey, William M, office support assistant IV, $15.50/hr
Yang, Fenghua, fellow, teaching, $48,000
Yang, Hsiao Tung, prof, resrch, $124,253
Yang, Li, office support assistant IV, $14.23/hr
Yang, Qiongying, lab assistant, $11.08/hr
Yang, Wan, prof, asoc, $83,328
Yang, Xiaodong, prof, ast, $82,616
Yang, Yan, research specialist sr, $53,206
Yang, Ying, resrch scientist/academic sr, $45,000
Yang, Zhongbo, resident physician-2nd yr, $52,007
Yanos, John, prof, asoc, $287,633
Yantko, Nicholas Tony, advancement coordinator, $45,000
Yao, Gang, professor, $123,061
Yao, Hong, resrch scientist/academic, $55,125
Yao, Rui, prof, asoc, $94,909
Yao, XiaoLan, prof, ast, $78,260
Yao, Xiaomei, resrch asoc, $38,160
Yarasi, Naveen Kumar Reddy, physician, $35,000
Yarbrough, Elizabeth Ann, nurse, staff now plus, $30.00/hr
Yardley, William Mark, custodian, $10.69/hr
Yarlagadda, Bharath, resident physician-1st yr, $50,219
Yarmer, Derek M, resident physician-3rd yr, $52,470
Yasbin, Ronald, dean, $205,766
Yasomanee, Jagodige Prithika, post doctoral asoc, $32,000
Yates Parker, Nancy L, business ops associate sr, $63,592
Yates, Benny Kay, program/project supprt coor sr, $59,039
Yates, Kimberly N, couns hlth/welfare/wellness sr, $30.00/hr
Yazell, Audrey Elizabeth, temporary crafts service, $9.00/hr
Ye, Shui Qing, professor, $75,000
Ye, Zhijian, fin and acctg consultant sr, $66,000
Yeager, Janet M, coor, service, $17.20/hr
Yeast, Carrie Elise, resident physician-3rd yr, $53,763
Yeggins, Shiree Shaunta, instructor, adjunct, $4,200
Yeggy, Todd A, lead mech trades spec, $21.91/hr
Yeh, Sherry Hsin-Ying, supv, operating room nursing, $30.98/hr
Yelenskiy, Mikhail, custodian, $12.72/hr
Yemane, Saba, db administrator-princpl, $76,652
Yentumi, Alexander Edward, tutor, $9.00/hr
Yerram, Preethi, prof, ast clincl dept, $151,000
Yerram, Sushma Reddy, resident physician-1st yr, $49,402
Yerrapu, Suresh R, db programmer analyst-princpl, $75,983
Yesis, Michaela Jean, snack bar attd, $11.15/hr
Yier, Lilian A, custodian, $10.94/hr
Yin, Da, scholar, visiting, $18,000
Yin, Dezhi, prof, ast, $133,289
Yin, Jun, fellow, post doctoral, $30,000
Yin, Xiaoyan, resrch scientist/academic sr, $67,615
Yin, Zhaozheng, prof, ast, $91,779
Yingling, Patsy, nurse, staff II, $34.99/hr
Yoakum, Nancy Katina, custodian, $11.41/hr

Yochum, Andrew Paul, system support analyst-spclst, $21.29/hr
Yocum, Peyton Danielle, child dev assistant, $8.16/hr
Yoder Kreger, Susan J, prof, teach, $47,163
Yoder, Allen E, animal techn, ast lab, $13.89/hr
Yoder, Marilyn, prof, asoc, $93,713
Yoebstl, Flora A, custodian lead, $11.98/hr
Yoest, Margaret Ann, nurse spclst, clncl, $78,780
Yohannes, Yordanos, prof, ast clincl dept, $200,000
Yonan, Michael E, prof, asoc, $65,275
Yong, Sarah Li-Jea, resident physician-2nd yr, $52,007
Yonkman, Carol Ann, emeritus, $23,003
Yoo, Hyo-Jin, lecturer sr, $9,000
Yoo, Ill Hoi, prof, asoc, $110,000
Yoon, Dongpil, prof, asoc, $66,946
Yord, William, instructor, adjunct, $15,000
York-Garesche, Jeanine Marie, lecturer, $6,120
York, Abigail Annalee, pharmacy tech, $10.64/hr
York, Ann M, nurse, staff II, $34.18/hr
York, Brenda S, instructor, ast, $31,671
York, Cheryl A, business support specialist II, $21.71/hr
York, Robert Dale, maintenance supervisor, $61,800
You, Seung Kwon, program/project supprt coor II, $59,115
Youan, Bi Botti Celestin, professor, $142,408
Youde, Jessica Ann, nurse, staff I, $19.00/hr
Youm, Ibrahima, post doctoral asoc, $23,340
Youmans, Laurel Diane, office support assistant IV, $16.30/hr
Young Sr, Roderick Edward, model, $15.00/hr
Young Walker, Laine M, prof, asoc clincl dept, $187,625
Young-Lewis, Quillian Michelle, nurse, staff II, $20.95/hr
Young, Ben E, lecturer, $33,892
Young, Cameron M, mts/hvac, $24.13/hr
Young, Christian Alwyn, office support assistant III, $14.39/hr
Young, Donell L, ast dir student support svcs, $60,632
Young, Holly M, business support specialist II, $20.17/hr
Young, James A, police officer, $19.10/hr
Young, Jason S, student support specialist II, $15.50/hr
Young, Jerry Charles, custodian lead, $13.96/hr
Young, Jessica Nicole, emrg med techn, $11.61/hr
Young, Jonathan Michael, business support spclst I, $16.17/hr
Young, Juliana Marie, nurse, licensed prac, $15.67/hr
Young, Karen Sue, health records techn II, $14.12/hr
Young, Kelcey S, temporary professional, $11.30/hr
Young, Kelly Marie, student support specialist sr, $16.87/hr
Young, Kimberly Crashon, sr dir research / inst prgms, $143,500
Young, Krista S, business ops associate I, $38,448
Young, Lauren Ruth, veterinarian, residnt, $26,000
Young, Letha J, police lieutenant, $46,976
Young, Levi Rex, retail sales manager, $47,083
Young, Maria Annette, student support specialist I, $15.00/hr
Young, Matthew William, retail sales assistant sr, $18.07/hr
Young, Megan L, research/lab technician ast, $16.20/hr
Young, Melina Elizabeth, mgr II business admin, $72,002
Young, Nancy Hastings, nurse, staff II, $29.24/hr
Young, Pamela Serena, instructor, clincl, $49,200
Young, Peggy K, fin and acctg manager sr, $67,248
Young, Relanda Denise, operations support tech I, $20.00/hr
Young, Robert David, support systems admin-entry, $42,024
Young, Ryan M, food svc wrkr III, $12.64/hr
Young, Ryan Patrick, head coach, $41,519
Young, Scott Michael, dir II student support svcs, $82,000
Young, Sherry E, office support assistant IV, $15.75/hr
Young, Steve M, custodian, $12.94/hr
Young, Steven Paul, resp therapist reg, $23.32/hr
Young, Tamara Lynn, office support associate, $25.36/hr
Youngblood, Paige Nicole, account executive, $25,467
Younger-Cotter, Casey Marie, program/proj supprt coor I, $28,000
Younger, Camelia R, nutrition spclst, $48,823
Younger, Dan, professor, $72,079
Younger, Edith S, coor nursing informatics, $81,224
Younger, Kelly M, educational pgm associate I, $12.77/hr
Younger, Melissa Townie Ann, nurse, staff I, $19.00/hr
Younger, Roger A, supervisor II, $69,032
Younger, Sarah Beth, prof, ast clincl dept, $196,320
Younger, Sarah E, mgr II business admin, $51,250
Younger, Theresa M, nurse, staff II, $30.47/hr
Younker, Thomas Dirk, prof, clinical dept, $250,000
Younkin, Adam D, temporary technical, $10.00/hr
Yount, Deann Jenifer Alexander, prof, ast adjunct, $13,950
Yount, Kyle Daniel, temporary technical, $10.00/hr

Yount, Logan Lloyd, nurse, staff II, $19.00/hr
Yount, Mark R, media producer II, $16.27/hr
Yount, Martha Shaw, reimbursement ast-cert, $18.23/hr
Yount, Michael Eric, nurse, procedures, $28.50/hr
Yousef, Hasan Abdulraheem Theeb, instructor, $43,404
Yousef, Ibraheem Fares Mohammad, res physician-3rd yr, $53,763
Yousef, Mohamad H, resident physician-2nd yr, $52,007
Yousuf, Mohammad, resident physician-2nd yr, $52,007
Youtsey, Angela, cat scan technl (ct), $30.36/hr
Youtsey, Roy Lee, event assistant I, $10.00/hr
Yowell, Linda S, certif pharmacy techn, $17.10/hr
Yu, Haiqing, fellow, post doctoral, $33,660
Yu, Jen Chieh, business tech analyst-princpl, $75,741
Yu, Mansoo, prof, asoc, $75,070
Yu, Ping, professor, $77,214
Yu, Qingsong, professor, $105,262
Yu, Wen-Bin, prof, asoc, $99,654
Yu, XiaoQiang, professor, $104,837
Yu, Ying-Chun, fellow, post doctoral, $30,000
Yuan, Ye, resrch scientist/academic, $42,000
Yucelen, Gulfem I, prof, ast resrch, $65,000
Yucelen, Tansel, prof, ast, $79,481
Yue, Yongping, research specialist sr, $61,316
Yun Fowler, Sue Jean, nurse, staff, $20.00/hr
Yund, Danielle Christine, care team assoc-clinical, $11.10/hr
Yung, Rachel L, coor, service, $17.10/hr
Yungbluth, Dennis C, research specialist I, $40,000
Yunker, John Anthony, instructor, adjunct, $7,386
Zablow, Lucy Ann, supv outpatient svcs, $55,058
Zach, Latesha May, student support specialist sr, $17.37/hr
Zachary, Iris, prof, ast resrch, $90,000
Zachary, Rudy, environmental health tech II, $15.47/hr
Zacher, Mary Jo, resp therapist reg, $31.72/hr
Zagar, Carol S, educational pgm associate I, $13.45/hr
Zagar, Eris A, nurse spclst, clincl, $86,369
Zaggy, Alan Peter, physician, $135.00/hr
Zaghouani, Fathia Kboubi, office support assistant IV, $15.09/hr
Zaghouani, Habib, professor, $215,772
Zahn, Patricia A, business svcs consultant sr, $72,821
Zahner, Jessica LaTisha, temporary professional, $11.30/hr
Zahringer, Kenneth A, resrch ast, $32,400
Zakeri, Ozra, peoplesoft admin-princpl, $84,270
Zakkour, Sam, fellow, post doctoral, $40,000
Zalcman, Amy Rachel, veterinarian, residnt, $26,000
Zalis, Aaron R, lecturer, $10,002
Zallaghi, Forough, resident physician-3rd yr, $52,470
Zalmai, Rana Sarwar, resrch ast, $28,000
Zamachaj, Melanie C, resrch ast, $39,791
Zamarripa, John Roy, powr plnt maint spclst II, $23.75/hr
Zambre, Ajit Prakash, resrch asoc, $48,000
Zane, Grant M, research specialist sr, $51,958
Zaner, Lora Denice, business support specialist II, $17.67/hr
Zaniletti, Isabella, prof, ast teach, $60,000
Zap, Patrice Ann, teaching ast, $13.00/hr
Zapata Arias, Sandra Patricia, educational pgm assoc I, $13.45/hr
Zapata, Maria Angelica, prof, ast, $70,700
Zarate, Richard, business spclst, $52,380
Zare, Alina, prof, ast, $97,678
Zars, Troy D, prof, asoc, $91,400
Zarucchi, Jeanne Morgan, professor, $74,421
Zavala, Usnise, custodian, $12.94/hr
Zawodniok, Maciej J, prof, asoc, $90,750
Zboray, Julie Anne, operations support tech sr, $21.00/hr
Zeff, Samford byron, media production director I, $50,000
Zeglis, Amanda Suzanne, resident physician-2nd yr, $52,007
Zeglis, Chad Parker, resident physician-2nd yr, $50,810
Zeiders, Katharine Ellen, prof, ast, $74,000
Zeilenga, Jeffrey R, ast vice chancellor, $169,115
Zeilman, Michelle R, instructor, adjunct, $14,118
Zeisler, Cathrine Marie, safety monitor, $9.27/hr
Zekry, Bassant, program/project supprt coor I, $37,916
Zelasko, Eric R, pat acct rep, $13.91/hr
Zeller, Carolyn J, temporary professional, $18.57/hr
Zeller, Michelle Renae, office support assistant IV, $13.93/hr
Zeller, Patrick Allen, resident physician-2nd yr, $50,810
Zellmer, David Lynn, program/project supprt coor II, $42,203
Zellner, Marian, ast mgr hospitality services, $42,919
Zembles, Shawn Lee, prof, ast clincl, $52,043
Zemke, John M, professor, $92,264

Zeng, Qiang, resident physician-3rd yr, $52,470
Zeng, Weiliang, fellow, post doctoral, $19.23/hr
Zeng, Yong, professor, $58,884
Zenitsky, Caleb D, av instal service tech-speclst, $14.96/hr
Zenner, Jean Anne, temporary professional, $12.00/hr
Zephir, Flore, professor, $116,806
Zerbolio, Carla Ann, service rep III, $13.77/hr
Zettler, Laura Reynolds, instructor, adjunct, $18,000
Zettwoch, Mary Beth, library info specialist sr, $21.00/hr
Zgonc, Donna L, care team assoc-clinical, $13.89/hr
Zgrabik, Stephen Lawrence, intern, $25,500
Zguta, Russell, professor, $152,070
Zhang, Bing, professor, $106,500
Zhang, Bingqi, prof, ast resrch, $65,000
Zhang, Fang, fin and acctg manager sr, $83,220
Zhang, Gaiyan, prof, asoc, $179,433
Zhang, Guoquan, prof, asoc, $110,780
Zhang, Hongxian, prof, ast, $110,000
Zhang, Huizhen, tutor, $13.00/hr
Zhang, Jennifer Jianfeng, research specialist sr, $31,680
Zhang, Keqing, research specialist I, $31,639
Zhang, Nannan, scholar, visiting, $20,400
Zhang, Ni, fellow, post doctoral, $39,264
Zhang, Qi, professor, $93,271
Zhang, Qiong, resrch asoc, $38,854
Zhang, Qiujuan, food svc wrkr II, $11.83/hr
Zhang, Shulei, fellow, post doctoral, $42,000
Zhang, Shuping, professor, $158,150
Zhang, Shuqun, professor, $120,050
Zhang, Tong, fellow, post doctoral, $36,720
Zhang, Xianyang, prof, ast, $85,850
Zhang, Xinyue, fellow, post doctoral, $35,800
Zhang, Xiuli, resrch scientist/academic, $45,651
Zhang, Yan, prof, ast resrch, $72,000
Zhang, Yanzhi, prof, ast, $65,820
Zhang, Yaojiang, prof, asoc resrch, $60,141
Zhang, Yun, prof, asoc teach, $49,129
Zhang, Yuwen, professor, $180,226
Zhang, Yuyan, program/project supprt coor I, $57,579
Zhang, Zhanyuan, prof, asoc resrch, $92,298
Zhao, Changzeng, research specialist I, $37,832
Zhao, Hong, resrch asoc, $36,613
Zhao, Junling, research/lab technician, $13.08/hr
Zhao, Qiuhong, prof, ast, $161,805
Zhao, Yunxin, professor, $128,446
Zheng, Yahong Rosa, prof, asoc, $93,620
Zheng, Yi-Min, research specialist sr, $56,700
Zheng, Yongjie, prof, ast, $83,640
Zhou, Caizhi, prof, ast, $88,663
Zhou, Jie, fellow, post doctoral, $28,000
Zhou, Liwen, research specialist I, $40,297
Zhou, Long, prof, distinguished, $101,550
Zhou, Mingyi, resrch asoc, $70,483
Zhou, Siyuan, instructional designer-expert, $58,000
Zhou, Xiao Li, accountant I, $17.65/hr
Zhou, Yuan, scholar, visiting, $24,000
Zhu, Da Ming, professor, $94,430
Zhu, Jiaying, scholar, visiting, $5,400
Zhu, Peizhen, prof, ast teach, $59,000
Zhuang, Xinhua, professor, $156,757
Zhukovsky, Mikhail Andreyevich, resrch scientist/academic, $45,000
Zhuo, Fu, librarian III, $51,237
Ziegler, Laura A, media production director I, $45,000
Ziegs, Beulah Grace, nurse, staff now III, $30.00/hr
Ziervogel, Deborah Ann, nurse, staff II rnwp, $30.43/hr
Zillig, Randy L, care team assoc-suppt, $13.37/hr
Zimbalist, Allison Marie, physical therapist, $32.62/hr
Zimmel, Peter T, prgm director, $105,649
Zimmer, Michael, bindery opr II, $17.78/hr
Zimmer, Randall L, research specialist sr, $46,211
Zimmerman, Christina M, bus support specialist II, $22.70/hr
Zimmerman, Christine Marie, instructor, clincl, $55,081
Zimmerman, Cynthia D, cardiovasc techn non inv, $18.17/hr
Zimmerman, Ian Daniel, prof, ast teach, $59,152
Zimmerman, Jeri Lou, business ops associate sr, $56,520
Zimmerman, Lynda A, extns professional, asoc, $57,621
Zimmerman, Rick S, professor, $177,187
Zimmerman, Stephanie Nicoll, temp professional, $15.00/hr
Zimmermann, Charlee Leann, nurse, staff prn, $26.00/hr

Zimmerschied, Alan D, powr plnt cntrl sys techn, $23.75/hr
Zimmerschied, Valerie Jo, nurse, staff II, $28.82/hr
Zimny, Stefanie Kay, nurse, staff II, $23.79/hr
Zinn, Wanda Marie, executive assistant, $17.21/hr
Zipf, Mindy Ann, nurse, staff II, $21.80/hr
Zipfel, Terry Lynn, safety communications operator, $13.48/hr
Ziskin, Rochelle, professor, $77,150
Zitsch, Robert P III, professor, $567,487
Zitsch, Whitley Grayson, event assistant I, $7.55/hr
Zluticky, Cynthia E, sr dir program/project ops, $91,989
Zoeller, Charles J Jr, mech, bldg maint, $21.15/hr
Zoeller, Lori A, business support specialist I, $15.17/hr
Zollar Jones, Gladys, student service coor I, $44,023
Zolman, Bethany Karlin, prof, asoc, $75,449
Zorsch, Susan, practice manager, $90,778
Zou, Bo, scholar, visiting, $38,000
Zou, Jing, sftware supprt analyst-speclst, $39,600
Zou, Shaoming, professor, $172,183
Zou, Xiaoqin, prof, asoc, $93,840
Zoughi, Reza, professor, $179,710
Zuber, Leah Christine, med techl reg, $23.43/hr
Zufall, Elisabeth Anna, office support assistant IV, $16.73/hr
Zulovich, Joseph M, prof, ast extns, $88,232
Zulovich, Joyce Ann, human resources specialist I, $15.41/hr
Zumalt, Kevin R, reactor operator trainee I, $16.07/hr
Zumsteg, Tamara, business support specialist II, $19.74/hr
Zumwalt, Andrew Mark, prof, ast extns, $66,405
Zumwalt, Daniel Paul, architect, hlth facilities, $72,675
Zumwalt, Kevin D, specialist, $74,271
Zumwalt, Kristin Joy, nursing ast, $12.08/hr
Zurowski, Susan, prof, asoc clincl dept, $241,176
Zwanziger, Duenda Kay, event assistant I, $7.75/hr
Zwanziger, Leonard Lee, event assistant I, $7.55/hr
Zweifel, Michael R, media producer II, $17.23/hr
Zweig, Steven C, professor, $294,693
Zwingle, Phillip, cat scan technl (ct), $28.29/hr
Zygmunt, Benjamin, manager it, $52,400
Zylstra, Alexandria C, instructor, $21,000
Zynda, James, audiologist, $69,768

Lincoln University

Jefferson City 65101

Rome, Kevin, president, $223,000
Abbott, Cole, supervisor of warehouse, $27,758
Abney, Timothy, asst athletic dir for academics & tennis coach, $55,682
Afrasiabi, Zahra, associate professor, $47,367
Ahuja, Sumangali, assistant professor of research, $64,087
Ajuzie, Emmanuel, associate professor of research, $67,048
Akers, Luke, academic advisor/ success coach, $39,140
Allen, Kayla, default management counselor, $35,288
Allute, Hamisi, technical support specialist, $37,529
Al-Qudah, Omar, post doctoral research associate, $34,500
Anderson, Felicia, regional educator, $42,940
Andrei, Adrian, associate professor, $47,214
Anunoby, Ogugua, professor, $64,639
Aruguete, Mara, professor, $59,743
Auboug, Reneesha, farm outreach worker, $29,355
Avery, Gina, secretary II, $26,500
Bah, Abdoulaye, professor, $69,049
Bailey, Carolyn, supervisor custodial services, $32,447
Balakumar, Sivanandan, professor, $69,850
Balasubramanian, Sunder, associate professor, $48,374
Baldwin, Christopher, utility laborer trades, $25,708
Ballard, Bruce, professor, $59,743
Bange, Julie, accountant II, $41,200
Bardot, Michael, professor, $59,722
Basinger, Lantie, building trade painter and motor pool, $37,834
Bax, Amy, research technician II, $41,200
Bayan, Maxim, assistant professor of research, $62,511
Bearnes, Constance, communications coordinator, $47,277
Beatty, Willie, facilities supervisor, $46,350
Beavers, Carol, o d s system administrator, $56,650
Belfiore, Marie, account clerk II, $28,300
Bellers, Jon-Yves, transcript processor, $25,215
Benne, Jennifer, professor, $59,743

Bennett-Smith, Laura, associate dir of development, $67,980
Bentlage, Garrett, police officer I, $34,007
Betts, Margo, custodian, $22,484
Bickel, Linda, dean, $105,167
Birk, Stefanie, assistant professor, $43,080
Bishop, Nahshon, small farm assistant, $36,246
Bitter, Mary, administrative assistant I, $36,480
Blau, Katrina, academic librarian, $46,156
Boeckmann, Christopher, organic program manager, $52,005
Bonham, Aron, dispatcher, $12,470
Borgwald, James, professor, $62,951
Borgwordt, Cindy, aquaculture fish specialist, $46,380
Bouras, David, associate professor, $58,556
Bowen, Mark, resident services director, $30,900
Boydston, Phillip, farm outreach worker, $29,613
Bradley, Ernest, program educator assistant II, $30,072
Broadnax, Anthony, assistant football coach, $31,986
Brower, Gregory, groundskeeper III, $31,803
Brown, Glenn, associate professor, $47,198
Brown, Jamere, coord of center of teaching / learning, $43,895
Brown, Sally, administrative assistant I, $28,840
Brown, Barbara, secretary II, $25,750
Brown, Curtis, custodian, $21,424
Brown, Steven, custodian, $21,424
Brownstein, Michael, learning specialist, $29,900
Bryant, Ithaca, library assistant II, $33,573
Buchanan, Larry, custodian/auxiliary, $21,424
Burgess, Eric, assistant professor, $63,036
Burkes, Felicia, secretary II, $25,750
Burrell, Elijah, assistant professor, $42,024
Busalacki, Aimee, associate professor, $47,198
Canada-Painter, Ruth, dir, center for career / academic support svcs, $62,764
Carr, Daniel, assistant athletic dir for media relations, $39,923
Carter, Catherine, coach, women's golf/compliance sec, $15,795
Carter-Curtiss, Janice, career services coordinator, $38,110
Cave, Laurie, custodian/auxiliary, $22,484
Chapel, Cynthia, professor, $62,951
Chowdhury, Manzoor, associate professor, $58,556
Chu, Bei, postdoctoral research assistant, $35,190
Clad, Michael, groundskeeper III, $26,644
Clark, Duwon, coord international student services, $40,000
Clark, Stephanie, instructor, $33,990
Clay, Robert, compliance & hazardous waste officer, $57,736
Clay, Paula, director, center for academic advising, $52,891
Clifford-Rathert, Charlotte, associate professor of extension & research, $62,673
Clifton, Richard, custodian, $23,566
Coffelt, Carl, groundskeeper I, $22,942
Coleman, Tyrone, admissions counselor, $35,271
Collier, Nicole, head women's basketball coach, $66,950
Collins, Marla, regional educator, $41,334
Connor, Kimberly, associate professor, $47,198
Coon, Myron, bowling center manager, $19,699
Cooper, Eric, recruiter/admission counselor, $37,080
Cordray, Ethan, academic librarian, $38,524
Cortez, Sean, warehouse clerk, $22,357
Covington, Ann, secretary II, $25,000
Crews, Alonzo, custodian, $21,424
Cross, Leslie, k j l u news director, $37,563
Crossnoe, Marshall, professor, $59,743
Crow, James, assistant professor, $21,839
Crowder, Annette, director of admissions, $57,783
Culberson, Vera, administrative assistant I, $27,810
Dahlstrom, Glenda, professor nursing, $72,501
Dalton, Richard, associate professor, $49,701
Davenport, Mary, secretary II, $24,547
Davis, Karen, regional educator, $45,176
Davis, Rosa, area educator, $36,246
Davis, Jennifer, community outreach worker, $29,098
Debord, Kurt, professor, $62,951
Demilia, Michael, baseball coach & event coordinator, $42,615
Demyers, George, area educator, $36,050
Deng, Daiyong, postdoctoral research associate, $35,190
Deornellis, Cynthia, organic/integrated farm system spclst, $42,024
Dickson, Michael, information technologist, $38,110
Dille, Kailey, academic advisor, $39,140
Dolan-Timpe, Marianne, research technician I, $31,930
Dollar, Patrice, regional coordinator, $50,314

Donner, Pamela, media center coordinator, $47,277
Doss, Khalilah, director of residential life, $57,680
Douglas, Darla, associate professor, $61,773
Downey, Michael, manager, k j l u, $59,291
Downey, Melinda, administrative assistant I, $31,518
Downey, Emily, secretary II, $23,072
Downing, Shirley, secretary II, $31,518
Driver, Bettye, grants-title III coordinator, $54,519
Dudenhoeffer, Gregory, research technician II, $46,175
Duhart, Danielle, custodian, $20,363
Duschack, Miranda, small farm specialist, $36,246
Dziadosz, Lynette, academic advisor/ success coach, $38,000
Eaton, Touria, assistant professor, $65,405
Edoho, Felix, professor, $84,795
Edwards, Jason, research technician I, $32,569
Egilla, Jonathan, assistant professor of research, $55,310
Eivazi, Frieda, professor research, $93,219
El-Dweik, Majed, associate professor, $47,198
El-Tayash, Youssef, assistant professor, $47,277
Emanuel, Audrey, nutrition program assistant, $29,098
English, Tanelle, custodian, $21,424
Enloe, Gloria, manager of j c t v, $48,507
Erb, Andrew, video conference technician, $40,658
Eveler, Mitchell, plumber, $45,946
Farrar, Rinalda, director of library services, $63,000
Ferguson, Cris, user support manager, $47,380
Flanary, Shawn, women's head bowling coach, $15,334
Flippin, Kellan, groundskeeper I, $22,484
Frank, Troy, assistant professor, $52,530
Frazier, Jane, associate professor, $47,214
Frederick, Mark, assistant football coach, $37,822
Freelin, Jeffrey, assistant professor, $21,937
Frost, Daniel, coach, men's golf, $15,795
Furey, Rachel, instructor, $37,053
Furr, Amber, accounting clerk II, $29,216
Galbreath, Craig, recruiter/admissions counselor, $39,140
Galbreath, Don, building trades supervisor, $36,794
Gamblin-Green, Michelle, asst professor/choir director, $43,285
Garrett, Stephen, farm outreach worker, $29,355
Garth, Jimmie, research technician II, $39,921
Gassner, Sheila, executive dir for facilities / planning, $81,370
Gates, Quentin, dispatcher, $25,688
Gedikoglu, Haluk, assistant professor of research, $60,935
Gerhard, Gilbert, chief operator/public access, $50,731
Gerling, Vicki, secretary II, $26,780
Ghinescu, Rodica, professor, $59,722
Goben, Erik, police officer 1, $34,007
Gohring, Allison, assistant professor, $43,260
Goodman, Thomas, systems administrator, $40,170
Goodman, Kandice, secretary II, $26,828
Gossett, Amy, professor, $59,722
Govang, Donald, assistant professor, $51,213
Graham, Carlos, campus and community liaison, $56,030
Gray, Marta, professor, $59,743
Green, Ashton, assistant football coach, $31,359
Greene, Debra, professor, $59,743
Greene, Javonna, assistant professor, $42,646
Greninger, Thomas, associate professor, $69,953
Griffin, Sandra, alumni projects specialists, $36,357
Groner, Caleb, corporal, $36,233
Grube, Jeffrey, instructor, $36,692
Gubbels, Thomas, associate professor, $47,198
Guerrant, Kristin, coord special programs & projects, $31,463
Haboub, Abdelmoula, assistant professor, $44,290
Hale, George, custodian, $19,281
Halim, Marion, regional coordinator, $48,708
Hanlin, Debra, administrative assistant II, $39,240
Hardwick, Samuel, assistant professor, $43,260
Hardy, Joe, compliance coordinator, $35,271
Harper, Rhonda, assistant professor/band director, $61,993
Harper, Wanda, associate registrar, $44,093
Harris, Kevin, chief information officer, $87,550
Hatef, Mansour, laboratory manager technician, $39,302
Headrick, Marilyn, professor, $65,830
Heermance, Noel, professor, $90,764
Heintz, Kelly, administrative assistant I, $26,280
Heise, David, assistant professor, $55,157
Heldenbrand, Lois, assistant professor, $52,530
Henderson, Michael, research facilities coordinator, $59,859

Henderson, Valerie, administrative assistant I, $30,166
Hendricks, Avila, professor, $59,743
Hendricks, Adrian, regional educator, $45,176
Hendricks, Andria, instructor, $36,750
Heyen, Anne, assistant professor, $43,080
Heyward, Leticia, academic success coordinator, $36,000
Hibbett, Cheryl, associate professor, $49,726
Hildreth, Brandon, director of continuing education, $51,500
Hilsenbeck, Heather, research technician II, $33,923
Hinde, Garry, dispatcher, $31,262
Hinton, Edward, academic advisor, $39,140
Hoelscher, Karen, advancement fiscal affairs specialist/internal
    auditor, $52,530
Hogg, Laurence, intake specialist 2, $34,429
Homann, Gary, associate professor, $47,214
Howard, Mary, medical assistant, $27,432
Hua, Bin, research technician II, $42,024
Huffer, Tisha, administrative assistant I, $32,321
Hunter, Adrienne, regional educator, $40,974
Hurst, Janet, farm outreach worker, $28,892
Hurtault, Rachel, instructor, $33,620
Hykes, Corey, learning management systems admin, $41,200
Ike, Roberto, professor, $64,918
Ikem, Abua, associate professor of research, $62,673
Jackson, Justin, instructor, $32,569
Jaegers, Lois, associate professor, $58,635
Jaster, Susan, farm outreach worker, $28,892
Jay, Jordan, professor, $62,919
Jenkins, Deborah, research assistant I, $39,365
Jenks, James, telecommunications administrator, $42,000
Johnson, Hwei-Yiing, associate professor of research, $64,087
Johnson, Michael, assoc band dir/associate professor, $62,688
Johnson, Walter, associate professor, $48,250
Johnson, Myca, student accounts cust service rep, $30,000
Johnson, Yvonne, financial services assistant/cashier, $22,520
Jones, Michael, head football coach, $80,000
Jones, Christopher, coord of annual giving & spec events, $47,380
Jones, Cynthia, payroll supervisor, $44,786
Jones, Cherryl, administrative assistant I, $36,504
Jude, Willie II, spec asst to the pres for fund raising, $85,000
Jungmeyer, Roger, professor, $67,634
Keeton, Kimberly, academic librarian, $45,969
Kemna, Betty, director of athletics, $80,000
Kempker, Julie, accounting clerk II, $29,216
Kent, Zandra, administrative assistant II, $30,900
Kern, James, professor, $59,722
Kidwell, Debra, director of purchasing, $58,938
Kirk, Steven, extension technician II, $40,974
Kliethermes, Kaitlyn, research technician I, $30,900
Koetting, Sandra, chief financial officer, $85,000
Kramer, Matthew, assistant farm manager, $41,200
Kremer, Martha, administrative assistant II, $31,518
Kremer-Coyne, Margaret, program assistant I, $22,063
Kronz, Matthew, regional educator, $36,852
Lael, Anita, associate professor, $47,198
Lane, Barbara, assistant professor, $52,951
Langendoerfer, Terry, information desk technologist, $36,050
Larry, Brittanie, recruiter/admissions counselor, $35,271
Lee, Keesoo, professor, $59,743
Lee, Bryant, assistant football coach, $32,640
Leslie, James, assistant professor, $42,024
Lilienfeld, Jane, professor, $67,549
Liu, Fengjing, assistant professor of research, $60,935
Lockhart, Jenny, instructor nursing, $37,080
Logan, James, associate professor, $61,409
Long, Janet, associate professor, $57,290
Long, Frances, nutrition program assistant, $29,098
Love, Shagonda, financial aid counselor, $32,569
Lucas, Patrick, boiler operator, $27,164
Luttrell, Alfred, access control specialist, $32,635
Luttrell, Jeanie, secretary II, $26,780
Luttrell, Parker, groundskeeper I, $22,484
Lynch, De'Recco, dir of orientation and new student svcs, $50,000
Manandhar, Roshan, postdoctoral research associate, $34,500
Mangold, Tammy, director of surgical technology, $61,986
Marcantonio, James, dir of human resource services, $67,310
Markway, Jeremia, farm manager, $52,005
Markway, Phillip, research technician II, $44,093
Martin, Angela, information technologist, $36,711

Martin, Darrell, research assistant I, $34,216
Martin, Jovaun, information desk technician, $23,690
Mason, Brian, custodian, $21,424
Matlock, Austin, head athletic trainer, $46,350
Matthews, Yvonne, instructor/state extension specialist, $53,618
Maxwell, Sheryl, program educator assistant, $37,336
McCord, Jennifer, assistant professor, $43,043
McGraw, Matthew, assistant professor, $42,886
McKinney, Dona, dir of sponsored research and grants, $65,920
McKnelly, Andrea, extension technician, $30,900
McSwain, Ann, associate professor, $60,584
Melloway, Janet, assistant professor, $43,075
Melloway, Barbara, secretary II, $25,728
Menning, Michael, police officer I, $34,007
Mersha Ayele, Zelalem, assistant research professor, $58,195
Meysami, Ahmad, assistant professor, $57,189
Middleton, David, farm outreach worker, $29,355
Miller, Amy, learning specialist, $29,900
Moeller, William, hvac technician, $35,526
Moeller, Douglas, farm assistant II, $29,896
Moffett, Joshua, media specialist, $33,990
Moore, Terry, assistant professor, $42,991
Morian, Christina, associate professor, $54,789
Morin, Cynthia, assistant professor, $42,679
Morrow, Elizabeth, registrar, $51,353
Morrow-Calvin, Teresa, administrative assistant I, $31,031
Moseley, John, men's basketball coach, $82,400
Moseley, Crystal, academic advisor, $39,140
Moton, Ramond, custodian, $20,363
Muenks, Katherine, budget officer, $53,268
Murray, Shashanta, database administrator, $46,350
Murray, Beth, assistant professor, $43,080
Myrick, Tara, resident services director, $30,900
Narens, Kathy, administrative assistant I, $28,720
Navarrete-Tindall, Nadia, assoc professor of extension, $63,036
Ndunguru, Grato, research technician 1, $29,870
Nelson, Billy, director of police department, $60,461
Nelson, Billy, learning specialist, $33,475
Nkongolo, Nsalambi, professor, $79,287
Nobles, Tammy, dir of student activities & greek life, $52,530
Nolte, Marabeth, dir, institutional research & assessment, $54,106
Nunn, Damon, corporal, $38,999
Nyaberi, David, assistant professor, $44,126
Nyirakabibi, Isabelle, research technician II, $39,921
O'Connor, Martha, extension technician 1, $30,900
O'Day, Sue, custodian, $23,566
O'Day, William, custodian, $23,566
Offord, Jerome, chief of staff, $105,060
Ogega, Nyankuru, information desk technician, $23,690
Omara-Alwala, Thomas, prof/research & investigation, $80,521
O'Neal, Montrice, athletics events coordinator, $28,840
Ortmeyer, Rose Ann, exec asst to the pres and curators, $72,000
Parker, Salona, bursar, $51,919
Pathan, Safiullah, assistant professor of research, $60,000
Patrick, Dean, custodian, $19,281
Paul, Kamalendu, prof state extension spec research, $91,282
Paumer, Peggy, administrative assistant II, $30,900
Payne, Ira, custodian, $23,566
Pearson, Virgil, resident services director, $26,265
Peck, Alyson, administrative assistant I, $27,316
Pendleton, Kelly, carpenter, $29,556
Petersen, Gregory, police officer I, $34,007
Pierce, James, farm outreach worker, $28,892
Pierson, Gregory, research engineer, $63,036
Pigford, Kevin, sergeant, $40,122
Pinero Ramirez, Jaime, assistant professor, $63,036
Porter, Samuel, boiler operator, $28,204
Potterton, Kelly, assistant professor, $42,230
Prettyman, Jessica, cashier, $22,520
Prettyman, Jeffrey, groundskeeper I, $22,484
Pritchard, Jill, news & development specialist, $28,393
Qian, Haiying, academic librarian, $45,969
Rackers, Steven, building service engineer, $42,972
Rainwater, Joyce, farm outreach worker, $28,892
Rankin, Debra, assistant professor, $43,532
Rant, William, associate professor, $71,939
Reed, Mary, research technician II, $35,535
Reid, Martin, auxiliary services coordinator, $41,200
Riggs-Butler, Tiara, secretary II, $26,476

Rivera, Jonathan, assistant professor, $43,260
Robertson, Ruth, professor, $62,951
Robinson, Alfred, dir of fin aid/student employment, $64,890
Robinson, Heather, program coordinator, $35,000
Robinson-Echols, Brenda, regional coordinator, $50,802
Rockers, Becki, administrative assistant I, $29,417
Roesner, Regina, accounts payable supervisor, $44,851
Rohrer, Laurence, associate professor, $47,214
Roling, Robert, assistant professor, $46,350
Romano, Michael, groundskeeper III, $24,939
Ross, Larry, professor, $59,743
Rossett, Wyoming, assistant professor, $45,268
Rothermich, Michael, supervisor of grounds, $40,974
Saha, Gouranga, professor, $59,743
Sale, Rachel, associate professor, $52,273
Salmons, Bryan, associate professor, $47,198
Saltzman, Nicole, assistant professor, $47,277
Sampson, Joylean, professor, $63,201
Schaefer, Joseph, instructor, $36,771
Schellman, Patrick, groundskeeper I, $24,648
Schleer, Mark, academic librarian, $41,426
Schlosser, Kelly, administrative assistant I, $28,059
Schnieders, Samuel, associate professor, $59,192
Schulte, Stacey, accountant II, $42,024
Scott, Michael, professor, $59,743
Scott, Tyanna, human resource coordinator, $47,408
Scott, Gerron, resident services director, $30,900
Scovill, Bruce, assistant professor, $42,024
Scroggins, Cynthia, program assistant II, $40,878
Seidner, Roxanne, research analyst I, $40,375
Semler, Brandon, assistant professor, $41,434
Sewell, Said, vice pres academic affairs / provost, $133,900
Shaeffer, Jordan, assistant athletic trainer, $33,620
Shanks, Bruce, assistant professor of research, $60,935
Sharma, Ajay, assistant professor research, $61,800
Shaw, Connie, assistant athletic director for operations, $39,140
Sheppard, Chio, director of male initiative, $51,500
Shinkut, Martins, professor, $62,656
Shoaf, Nicole, assistant professor, $41,818
Siegler, Julie, secretary II, $26,265
Simmons, Gary, police officer I, $34,007
Siriwardana, Nihal, professor, $59,743
Siriwardana, Sunethra, payroll clerk, $29,216
Sites, William, assistant professor, $45,268
Small, Paul, administrative assistant I, $26,677
Smith, James, mental health counselor, $46,350
Smith, Ailene, assistant track coach, $32,723
Smith, Nakeema, dispatcher, $12,470
Stacey, Nicole, head softball coach / concession coord, $42,230
Stallings, Donna, assistant professor, $41,028
Stallings, Roosevelt, audio visual technician, $30,900
Steck, Irasema, administrative assistant I, $30,320
Stegmann, John, buyer II, $45,000
Stephan, Kirsten, associate professor, $47,198
Stone, Sandra, assistant professor, $41,695
Sturdevant, Ruthi, dean, $105,167
Sullivan, Kellie, assistant professor, $42,848
Sutton, Dennis, police officer I, $34,007
Sykes, Tyrone, secretary II, $26,780
Tarka, Michael, research technician II, $36,050
Tate, James, custodian, $20,363
Teramoto, Yuki, multimedia specialist, $32,960
Tesfaye, Samson, professor of research, $79,287
Thomas, Victor, track coach, $67,263
Thomas, Shelby, assistant professor, $43,043
Thomas, Kevin, coord of living learning communities, $42,000
Thomas, Heinrich, strength and conditioning coach, $36,050
Thomas, Barbara, student health center office nurse, $31,552
Thomas, Davion, administrative assistant 1, $29,870
Thomas, Tytious, custodian, $21,424
Thompson, Karen, technical services coordinator, $46,350
Thompson, Cynthia, instructor/dir of simulation lab, $40,816
Thompson, Cindy, administrative assistant I, $30,468
Thompson, Regina, secretary II, $26,500
Todd, Kelli, financial aid counselor, $32,569
Todd, Connie, administrative assistant I, $30,708
Turner, Daniel, program director of k j l u, $37,573
Turner, Cashawn, groundskeeper I, $22,484
Vanzant, Anthony, assistant football coach, $31,986

Ward, Joseph, judicial affairs coordinator, $42,000
Warfield, Steve, system administrator, $38,500
Washington, Kimberly, custodian, $21,424
Welch, Linda, administrative assistant I, $30,236
Wells, Brittany, human resource associate, $36,050
Westbrooks, Jerry, financial aid counselor, $39,404
Westergaard, Tyrone, assistant professor, $58,043
Wetzel, James, associate professor of research, $62,673
White, Jerry, custodian, $21,424
White, Ylonda, custodian, $18,720
Wieberg, Lisa, instructor, $16,995
Wiggs, Alex, assistant women's basketball coach, $31,930
Wilbers, Luke, research technician II, $35,535
Williams, Gloria, assistant professor, $41,018
Williams, Cherilyn, graphic designer, $36,771
Williams, Bene, web designer/programmer, $36,771
Williams, Benecia, media assistant II, $28,961
Williams, Gail, secretary II, $27,295
Williams, Phyllis, administrative assistant I, $25,750
Wilson, Sylvia, director, alumni affairs, $56,650
Wilson, Michelle, instructor, $37,053
Wilson, Keverick, area educator, $36,454
Wilson, Edward, assistant men's basketball coach, $32,784
Wilson, Jacob, extension technician I, $31,518
Wilson, Lavaughn, communication coord / announcer, $30,517
Winkelmann, Jennifer, learning specialist, $28,272
Wollo, Wesseh, professor/research & investigator, $80,892
Wood, Rhonda, associate professor, $47,214
Woodruff, Kimberley, operations manager, $35,020
Woods, Gretchen, access and ability coordinator, $44,187
Woods, Amanda, admissions counselor, $35,271
Word, Deborah, associate professor, $51,727
Wright, Linda, facilities coordinator, $28,019
Wright, James, custodian, $21,424
Wulff, Joann, instructor, $16,064
Wuliji, Tumen, assistant professor of research, $64,087
Wurth, Tina, regional educator, $41,334
Yang, John, professor, $80,892
Yeager, Daniel, chief engineer, $64,881
York, Ernest, assistant professor, $62,736
Young, Misty, dir of public info / university relations, $60,023
Zambito, Peter, associate professor, $47,198
Zhang, Yongfang, postdoctoral research associate, $35,190
Zheng, Guolu, associate professor of research, $62,673

State Technical College of Missouri

One Technology Dr, Linn 65051

Claycomb, Don, president, $188,468
Ames, Amy, administrative assistant to the dean of academic and student affairs, $31,913
Anderson, Ashley, marketing / donor relations coord, $31,157
Anderson, Nadine, information technology specialist, $36,955
Andrei, Annamaria, instructor, $42,249
Ash-Schulte, Jessica, instructor, $37,976
Backes, Monica, bookstore assistant, $28,415
Barch, Amanda, enrollment mgmt assoc - events, $34,317
Barron, Briehan, department chair, $42,343
Bax, Jill, human resources coordinator, $38,709
Berhorst, Benjamin, department chair, $47,752
Berhorst, Shawn, lead instructor, $57,654
Berrey, Katherine, department chair, $51,029
Biere, Gary, instructor, $45,389
Boehm, William, instructor, $50,518
Bohl, Kathy, testing center coordinator/faculty support, $29,289
Boswell, Frances, data specialist, $25,143
Brandon, Jimmy, instructor, $44,108
Brandt, Elaine, registrar, $49,964
Branson, Mitchell, instructor, $33,982
Bruckerhoff, Tom, instructor, $53,029
Bryan, Elizabeth, instructor, $50,592
Clanton, Janet, associate dean of instruction, $64,965
Collins, Drew, instructor, $43,649
Cooper, Lyndell, instructor, $37,078
Cox, Chris, instructor, $39,471
Cox, Cynthia, const materials & safety institute coord, $59,548
Cox, Sandy, dir of management information services, $47,697

Crede, Brad, instructor, $55,473
DeBoeuf, Tony, department chair, $65,498
Deeken, Jordon, assistant to the registrar, $26,694
Dement, Lorinda, director of student support services, $37,477
Doede, Stephen, director of industry outreach, $52,731
Dummer, Dustin, instructor, $48,600
Dunn, Becky, instructor/ legislative liaison, $43,106
Edwards, Gregory, instructor, $37,000
Fast, Melva, instructor, $41,593
Fick, Christine, enrollment specialist ii, $29,783
Fick, Matt, instructor, $50,578
Fick, Tina, instructor, $52,637
Finlay, Jason, instructor, $46,997
Fowler, Matthew, lead instructor, $52,400
Franchini, Linda, instructor, $48,307
Franchini, Terry, instructor, $47,995
Franken, Desiree, academic support specialist, $33,017
Fredrick, Ed, department chair, $55,822
Gaines, Angela, instructor, $38,745
Geiger, Vince, department chair, $48,183
Gelven, Danny, instructor, $50,135
Gerloff, Logan, cont tech education lab tech & clerk, $24,960
Giessmann, Thomas, instructor, $50,650
Gillham, James, instructor, $40,777
Glascock, Chad, instructor, $40,295
Gove, Sue, administrative assistant to the president, $43,142
Grefrath, Aaron, activity center director, $50,379
Griffin, Dan, department chair, $57,497
Grosvenor, Robert, instructor, $72,400
Harlow, Gary, instructor, $62,122
Hart, Melissa, department chair, $60,847
Haslag, Donald, assistant dir of building & grounds, $28,691
Haslag, Roger, instructor, $57,360
Hatfield, Diane, accounts payable accountant, $33,746
Haulenbeek, Curtis, custodian - third shift, $22,000
Heckemeyer, Diane, department chair, $81,093
Helmering, James, resident manager, $31,500
Henley, James, admissions representative/military liaison, $39,183
Henley, Lori, academic support assistant, $33,583
Hernandez, Val, custodian, $24,095
Hoffmeyer, Jason, counselor/vocational resource educator, $46,569
Hollandsworth, Dwayne, mechanic/lab assistant, $41,338
Holtmeyer, Jeffrey, instructor, $42,991
Holtmeyer, Robert, housing custodian/custodian, $23,500
Honse, Edwin, lab assistant, $40,000
Hunolt, Sonja, instructor, $45,759
Hutcheson, Conrad, instructor, $37,500
Ittner, Joyce, program coordinator, $36,302
Jacobs, Jennifer, director of finanace, $78,403
Jacobs, Michelle, coord of bus and industry relations, $51,316
Jahnsen, Rheannon, enrollment specialist ii, $25,000
Johnson, Vicki, instructor, $60,747
Jones, Kelli, department chair, $45,555
Jose, Thomas, controller, $50,000
Kelley, Tammy, instructor, $44,505
Kinder, Bobby, instructor, $49,883
Klatt, Ryan, department chair, $51,403
Kliethermes, Aaron D, instructor, $55,013
Kliethermes, Aaron J, department chair, $55,267
Klouzek, Dana, lead instructor, $45,950
Koenigsfeld, Jamie, maintenance worker i, $25,080
Kremer, Janet, instructor, $39,545
Krimmel, Sandy, bookstore manager, $32,147
Kroll, Todd, tech services comp & telephone sup spec, $46,490
Lariosa, Pearl, department chair, $60,763
Lenger, Sheila, admissions representative, $35,293
Lloyd, Don, dean of information technology, $74,396
Luebbert, Sheila, curriculum support assistant, $31,163
Marden, Gregory, lab assistant, $28,173
Markway, Thomas, division chair, $65,675
Massey, Dwight, instructor, $56,734
Masso, Lorraine, instructor, $37,619
Mehmert, Rebecca, counselor, $37,000
Mihalevich, J Richard, dean of institutional research & planning, $74,399
Mitchell, Travis, custodian, $24,536
Moore, Amy, instructor, $39,445
Morfeld, Scott, admissions representative, $35,590
Muenks, Chris, department chair, $66,751

Neuner, Bernard, instructor, $44,763
Neuner, Lauren, accountant, $33,743
Neuner, Pat, lab assistant, $41,133
Neuner, Thomas, lab assistant, $37,402
Nevels, Gary, instructor, $62,218
Niekamp, Kenneth, instructor, $46,896
Nilges, Nicole, student activities director, $36,117
Parsons, Cheryl, administrative assistant for the advanced technology center, $27,632
Pemberton, Richard, associate dean of student affairs, $64,892
Peters, Scott, executive director of development, $54,639
Peterson, David, department chair, $68,217
Prater, Valerie, testing center coord/faculty support, $24,000
Probst, Cheryl, instructor, $46,130
Pruett, Matthew, instructional technology specialist/web programmer/analyst, $40,805
Pruett, Mike, director of technology services, $63,583
Rackers, Nick, instructor, $45,094
Radmacher, Eric, department chair, $47,158
Radmacher, Gary, instructor, $48,734
Ramsay, Daniel, lead instructor, $55,828
Relford, Jody, coordinator of academic records, $29,847
Rice, Kevin, instructor, $46,761
Rice, Randall, department chair, $44,740
Robinson, Brandi, information systems specialist, $48,500
Royston, Kelly, instructor, $52,919
Sadler, Michael, tool room aide, $17,490
Sallin, Dennis, director of building, grounds and safety, $33,879
Salmons, Sarah, instructor, $37,839
Schanzmeyer, Mark, lab assistant, $30,000
Scheulen, Kathleen, asst dean of enrollment management, $48,892
Scheulen, Stephanie, enrollment management associate - academic programs specialist, $34,317
Scheuler, Steve, instructor, $34,925
Schwartz, Gwen, financial services coordinator, $29,735
Schwartze, Thomas, department chair, $54,902
Schwinke, Vicki, dean of academic and student affairs, $76,650
Scott, Dana, instructor, $36,253
Senevey, Gary, lab assistant, $26,320
Shanks, Lindsey, administrative assistant to the associate dean of student affairs and career services director, $22,372
Sprenger, Nora, instructor, $47,703
Spurgeon, Kevin, department chair, $52,264
Stamp, Carol, library technician, $25,841
Stanek, George, instructor, $52,128
Stark, Misty, instructor, $50,000
Starke, Samantha, financial aid clerk, $26,000
Stout, Wanda, instructor, $42,331
Stumpf, Frances, director of library services, $55,079
Thompson, Ken, instructor/distance education coord, $40,450
Vaughan, Barbara, default prevention intervention specialist/financial aid specialist, $29,367
Vitela, Kathy, instructor, $53,888
Voss, Matt, instructor, $41,195
Voss, Shannon, lead instructor, $46,039
Wardell, Zak, instructor, $42,339
West, James, instructor, $46,106
White, Teresa, lead instructor, $51,030
Whithaus, Rebecca, director of financial aid, $49,925
Whitney, Glenda, career services director, $44,473
Wideman, Philip, instructor, $38,286
Wiley, Nancy, program manager, $42,970
Wolfe, Monica, employment/retention specialist, $30,301
Woods, Ross, admissions representative, $35,000
Yerian, Dawn, instructor, $36,741

Truman State University

100 E. Normal, Kirksville 63501

Paino, Troy D, president, $230,000
Acton, Timothy, groundskeeper, $26,497
Adams, Brian Phillip, temporary assistant professor, $42,330
Adams, Michael J, professor, $74,120
Afzal, Dawood, professor, $79,329
Ahmad, Hena, professor, $61,521
Ahrens, Lisa, production editor tsup, $34,000
Alberts, Kenneth Scott, professor, $65,168

Aleman, Lidice, temporary assistant professor, $43,000
Alexander, Natalie B, associate professor, $65,601
Alghalith, Nabil M, professor, $102,923
Allen, Lori B, secretary, $26,246
Allen, Stephen L, professor, $100,639
Anderson, Janet Linda, assoc dir-athletics, $55,988
Antal, Danny, system trades, $32,782
Anthes, Gina Sue, secretary, $24,221
Arabas, Jana Lu, temporary instructor-hes, $41,000
Arabas, Jeffrey R, dir-natatorium/tmp instr-hes, $48,344
Arias, Alcidean, asst dir-intl ed/study abroad, $37,500
Ashcraft, William Michael, professor, $65,321
Asher, Nancy L, coord-test & rpt/assoc bud off, $61,480
AuBuchon, Tim A, temporary assistant professor, $48,829
Aucutt, Mindy Joy, secretary, $21,799
Baker, Dean Putnam, driver, $28,835
Baker, Timothy Ethan, asst dir-physical plant, $65,556
Ball, Andrew, asst fb coach/tmp instr hes, $34,126
Ball, Douglas Lambourne, temp assistant professor, $43,191
Bame, Randall W, fa facilities mgr/temp pt instr, $38,259
Barcus, Timothy A, photographer/videographer, pr, $38,187
Barker, Shawna Patrice, secretary, $27,917
Barnes, Suzanne Monica, corp relations-major gifts officer, $52,000
Barrer, Joseph M, asst bskt coach/tmp instr hes, $38,500
Barron, Monica M, professor, $70,049
Bartlett, Jesse Broom, hvac technician, $29,232
Bates, Laura D, dir student involvement / campus activity, $47,989
Baughman, Russell G, professor, $84,064
Beane, Faith W, temporary assistant professor, $61,770
Beck, Jon A, professor, $89,970
Becker, Marc, professor, $59,566
Belanger, Jay P, professor, $79,208
Benevento, Joseph J, professor, $78,857
Bennett, Carol, asst dean-multicultural affairs, $55,000
Bergey, Margaret A, temporary instructor, $50,073
Berkowitz, Sheila L, certification analyst-education, $36,073
Best, Katie R, graphic designer, $33,778
Best, Mark Bradley, custodian-sub, $21,339
Bhatta, Dilli R, temporary assistant professor, $41,000
Billington, Terry Joe, building trades, $31,738
Bindner, Donald J, tmp visiting assistant professor, $58,495
Bird, Evonne C, temporary instructor, $43,934
Bird, H Michael, professor, $69,737
Blackstad, Richard B, machine operator, $24,367
Blades, J Anthony, blind/low vision specialist, $53,507
Blake, Lindsey Marie, secretary, $21,799
Blakely, Curt Ricky, associate professor, $56,338
Blakely, Shelynda Katherine, residence hall director, $24,000
Bloskovich, Diane G, coord of operations-advancement, $36,008
Blum, Michael W, professor, $101,044
Blurton, Gary W, custodian/housekeeper, $25,724
Bogeart, Lana Ruth, secretary, $26,330
Bohac, John W, professor, $67,742
Bolle, Michael Christopher, academic advisor-pt instr, $30,000
Bondy, Linda, secretary, $22,989
Bonzani, Patricia, custodian/housekeeper, $20,087
Boughton, Charles Michael, temporary instructor, $62,424
Boyd, Michelle D, trainer-head/tmp instr in hes, $48,948
Brammall, Kathryn M, professor, $78,579
Brandt, LaRoy, temporary assistant professor, $44,257
Brazier, Amy, secretary, $21,977
Breitenbach, Katherine, assistant professor, $56,500
Briney, Benjamin Ballow, coach - vb/tmp instr hes, $46,923
Brookhart, Dexter L, dps officer ii, $32,802
Brookhart, Steven, system trades, $25,912
Brown, Erin Maurine, coach - softball/tmp instr hes, $47,454
Buck, Angelia Kay, custodian/housekeeper, $22,738
Buckner, Brent, professor, $74,969
Bulen, Jay C, professor, $70,462
Bulen, Katalina, secretary, $26,246
Bump, Michael R, professor, $67,112
Bunch, Earl, groundskeeper, $22,404
Bunfill, Charles Stanley, manager-printing services, $44,477
Burden, Zachary Wade, residence hall director, $27,921
Burkett, Michael, building trades, $31,508
Burns, Julie Ann, financial aid counselor, $34,979
Cacioppo, Robert, professor, $81,823
Cagle, Wanda J, secretary, $29,566
Camara, Sana, professor, $65,498

Camarillo, Emmanuel, intrm see coordinator, $28,600
Cameron, David, system trades, $34,911
Cameron, Gary Michael, system trades, $32,782
Campbell, Mark R, professor, $66,145
Canfield, Jenna Marie, biology laboratory technician, $26,706
Cannon, Michael D, coach-soccer/temp instr hes, $45,302
Cannon-Breland, Michelle, stud education-support coord, $40,000
Capuano, Thomas M, professor, $78,539
Carnes, Joyce Elizabeth, housing app coord, admission, $28,464
Carreno Medina, Jose Clemente, assistant professor, $50,000
Carron, Angela Lynn, supervisor-accounts payable, $50,125
Carte, Pamela Rae, regional instructional facilitator, $56,086
Carter, Kenneth N, professor, $83,888
Cartwright, Debra K, professor, $98,911
Casady, Jeanie, temporary instructor, $40,000
Casey, Carlla, custodian/housekeeper, $22,404
Chambers, Bradley L, planned giving officer, $63,150
Chambers, Melody Lynn, director of admission, $69,815
Chan, David M, temporary assistant professor, $51,000
Chaudhary, Ankit, temporary assistant professor, $60,000
Chen, Xiaofen, professor, $70,423
Chrisman, Jeffrey, custodian/housekeeper, $19,398
Chrisman, Joshua, custodian/housekeeper, $19,398
Cianciola, Heather Shippen, temp assistant professor, $42,657
Cianciola, James David, associate professor, $53,034
Clark, Elizabeth M, intrm dean of social / cultural studies, $108,341
Clark, Janice L, professor, $64,060
Clark, Peggy J, secretary, $27,415
Cline, Adam L, asst athl trnr/tmp instr hes, $40,145
Cochran, Don Edward, coach - soccer/tmp instr hes, $38,518
Cochran, Paula S, professor, $79,406
Coggins, Janet I, staff accompanist, $30,930
Collett, Jacqueline, professor, $75,793
Collins, Chandrika Chaney, temporary instructor, $36,000
Collins, Myra June, regional math instructional facilitator, $58,866
Conner, David B, professor, $71,949
Conner, Kathy Jean, custodian/housekeeper, $26,225
Cook, Joyce Lynn, secretary, $27,207
Cook, Marsha K, secretary, $29,065
Cook, Sally Jane, professor, $64,245
Cooper, Cynthia L, professor, $76,837
Corrick, Michael R, building trades-key control, $35,099
Corrick, Molly Jo, custodian-sub, $21,339
Costa, Salvatore C, assistant professor, $71,785
Coughlin, Richard J, dean of library & museums, $122,772
Cox, Carolyn C, professor, $69,187
Cox, Carolyn Sue, secretary, $20,604
Cragg, Cheryl D, assistant comptroller, $55,692
Crist, Melanee Ann, asst dir international education, $50,000
Crook, Sharon J, custodian/housekeeper, $25,265
Crook, Terry E, custodian/housekeeper, $25,724
Cullity, Jocelyn, assistant professor, $49,000
D'Agostino, James, associate professor, $50,170
Dahl, Gretchen, secretary, $21,277
Damron-Martinez, Datha, associate professor, $89,279
Dare, Sherry L, sr teach learn tech specialist, $61,646
Dare-Halma, Ruth Sue, professor, $88,589
Daschke, Dereck M, professor, $57,984
Daughters, Anton T, assistant professor, $51,500
Davenport, Lorinda Kathleen, buyer, business office, $33,778
Davis, Adam Brooke, professor, $73,806
Davis, Alan Bruce, associate professor, $97,960
Davis, Alice Lucille, nurse practitioner, shc, $70,384
Davis, Andrea Wiedermann, temporary instructor, $48,690
Davis, Daniel Harroll, coach - baseball/tmp instr hes, $44,625
Davis, Eric Carl, asst payroll operations mgr, $26,601
Davis, John, asst fb coach/asst ath admin, $45,857
Davis, Ramona, secretary, $33,032
Davis, Ranee, secretary, $21,402
Deatherage, Narelle H, temporary assistant professor, $42,330
DeBlauw, Cassandra, asst athl trnr/tmp instr hes, $40,650
DeCock, Dean, professor, $63,982
DeLancey, Julia A, professor, $66,277
Delaney, Marie A, secretary, $25,808
Delmonico, Elizabeth Otten, professor, $80,879
Demers, Adam D, residence hall director, $25,080
Derezinski, Matthew, associate professor, $50,387
Derickson, Donald G, dps officer ii, $29,420
Detweiler, Paul W, custodian/housekeeper, $26,225

Di Stefano, Maria C, assoc provost/graduate dean, $107,570
Dierking, Rebecca Carolyn, assistant professor, $48,500
Doman, Danion Larry, professor, $57,865
Donahue, Roberta E, associate professor, $57,268
Dromey, Stacey, secretary, $21,799
Drury, Debra D, sp ed imprvmnt consultant rpdc, $56,450
Eagan, Amy Marie, coach - basktball/tmp inst hes, $63,240
Easley, Kevin L, professor, $85,591
Edgar, Julia D, assistant professor, $69,707
Edis, Taner, professor, $60,500
Edwards, Joyce, custodian/housekeeper, $26,225
Edwards, Margaret Emily, assistant professor, $50,000
Egley, Harold Arlen, temporary assistant professor, $40,800
Elam, John M, system trades, $29,232
Elam, Michael P, custodian/housekeeper, $25,724
Elam, Wanda K, custodian/housekeeper, $20,087
Elmlinger, Ilene G, associate professor, $56,000
Elschlager, Lori, health ins specialist/admin asst, $22,283
Elsea, Kathy Elaine, director of financial aid, $56,521
Elsea, Kelly, building trades, $28,021
Embree, Brenda S, secretary, $26,914
Engen, Deborah, secretary, $26,288
Erickson, Ronald Hartwick, temp assistant professor, $43,177
Ervin, Heather D, lab technician, $29,357
Escobar, Sergio, associate professor, $50,500
Fagan, Gary M, machine operator, $27,186
Falls, Vicki L, custodian/housekeeper, $25,724
Farley, Timothy, professor, $73,311
Fellows, Paul, associate professor, $107,493
Ferguson, Christopher, secretary, $21,402
Ferguson, Yuna Lee, assistant professor, $52,000
Fernandez, Marla Felice, supervisor-student accounts, $50,125
Fernando, Suren L, professor, $81,406
Festa, Roger, professor, $81,032
Fielden-Rechav, Laura Jane, professor, $63,949
Fine, Aaron L, professor, $60,818
Fisher, Robert O, building trades, $35,099
Foor, Alexander Gabriel, laboratory technician, $19,872
Fore, Stephanie Anne, professor, $66,145
Foster, Christopher G, coach - basketball/tmp instr hes, $67,000
Frevert, Kristin Nicole, counselor, ucs, $32,000
Frushour, Theodore Grayson, academic advisor/pt instr, $31,076
Fude, Donna Lynn, secretary, $32,218
Fuller, Amy L, temporary assistant professor, $43,177
Gall, Jeffrey L, professor, $69,474
Gambaiana, Mark Alan, vp for univ advancement, $142,906
Gardner, John, director-residence life, $57,587
Garlock, Sheila Jean, assistant professor, $54,282
Garth, David, professor, $64,169
Garvey, Alan J, professor, $79,876
Garzanelli, Melissa, secretary, $24,513
Gates, Kenny Lee, custodian/housekeeper, $25,724
George, Tyler, coordinator alumni relations, $28,000
Gering, Jonathan, dean-school of science & mathematics, $122,772
Gibson, Bethany, secretary, $26,998
Gilchrist, Lou Ann, dean of student affairs, $132,876
Gilchrist, Neil D, professor, $102,791
Gillette, David H, professor, $83,646
Gillette, Nathaniel Glenn, tmp intructional design, $43,013
Giovannini, Marianna, head acad advisor/pt instr, $69,905
Glaros, Dominique R, temporary assistant professor, $41,616
Glasgow, Dixie C, custodian/housekeeper, $22,738
Glaubitz, Lisa M, reference librarian, $50,000
Goggin, Michael Edward, professor, $72,231
Gokhale, Vayujeet, assistant professor, $53,500
Gooch, Janet L, dean-schl of health sciences & education, $121,571
Gooch, Judy M, payroll operations manager, $41,699
Gooch, Warren P, professor, $75,255
Goran, Lisa, assistant professor, $50,500
Gordy, Billi J, academic advisor, $27,600
Goyette, David Charles, temporary assistant professor, $45,100
Graham, Marcy J, head acad advisor/pt instr, $37,516
Gran, Charles L, associate professor, $49,826
Graves, Jill K, associate director-admission, $41,533
Graves, Kasey Dylan, system administrator-its, $47,776
Gray, Lori N, benefits coordinator, hr, $47,750
Green, John A, building trades, $32,990
Green, Rebecca A, temporary instructor, $43,500
Guffey, James M, professor, $81,559

Guffey, Susan A, temporary assistant professor, $63,185
Gunes, Itir, temporary assistant professor, $44,000
Hackney, Sharon K, media/curriculum librarian, $59,163
Hadwiger, Mariquit, associate professor, $67,571
Hadwiger, Stephen C, professor, $74,197
Hagerty, Randy, professor, $72,729
Hall, Laurie Rae, housing placement clerk, $24,221
Hamilton, Joe D, asst dir, ucs, $52,111
Hamilton, Susan Renee, secretary, $27,666
Hamlet, Daniel E, regional dir, sbtdc, $60,680
Hammerstrand, James William, temporary instructor, $43,191
Hanes, Coley L, groundskeeper, $23,469
Hanes, Julie A, technical support specialist, $42,700
Hanley, Mark Y, professor, $72,542
Hansen, Dean, secretary, $22,989
Hanson, Patricia Lynne, temporary instructor, $46,000
Hara, Masahiro, professor, $59,489
Hardesty, Leslie D, asst coach - track/tmp instr hes, $41,049
Harding, Jeanne M, dir field exper/tmp instr, $44,000
Harker, Christine Marie, professor, $64,036
Harrison, Keith E, professor, $99,443
Harrison, Rebecca R, professor, $75,528
Hass, Sarah A, director, upward bound, $51,000
Hatala, Mark, professor, $68,258
Hatfield, Charisse, records lead analyst-registrar, $27,630
Hayden, Jennifer, custodian/housekeeper, $20,087
Herleth, Sally Ann, ex dir hr/eeo & aa officer, $81,838
Herron, Margaret M, registrar, $65,052
Hessel, Jessica, asst coach - swim/tmp instr es, $23,040
Hettinger, Melinda J, secretary, $35,767
Higgins, Brenda C, dir shc & cs/asst prof, $89,432
Higgins, Cynthia Elaine, secretary, $23,239
Hill, Traci Ann, exec asst to the president, $65,031
Hines, Tina M, custodian/housekeeper, $25,265
Hintz, Ernst R, professor, $65,487
Holcomb, Jack Andrew, dir of center for acad excellence, $52,020
Holcomb, Melissa Jane Blagg, associate professor, $56,467
Holzmeier, Sara, dps sergeant i, $36,958
Hooper, Elisabeth A, associate professor, $61,921
Hopkins, Jeremy Allen, test associate, $20,880
Horvath, Michelle Renee, dir citiznshp & comm standards, $50,000
Howard, Dustin, network technician, its, $42,720
Howard, Eric J, professor, $81,230
Howard, Terrie Lynn, grants/foundation accountant, $37,719
Howd, Dawn Marie, assistant director-admission, $39,259
Howd, Walt R, network manager, $60,786
Hsieh, Ding-Hwa, professor, $61,521
Hudman, Stephen, associate professor, $53,480
Hudnall, David A, custodian/housekeeper, $25,724
Hueber, Thomas, professor, $72,849
Humphrey, Darla K, custodian/housekeeper, $24,597
Humphrey, Kara Jo, senior admission counselor, $31,220
Humphry, Timothy A, assistant professor, $51,000
Hunsaker, Charles R, dir of development-advancement, $62,161
Hurst, Jennifer R, associate professor, $55,000
Ikerd, Connie Sue, secretary, $36,143
Irwin, Kristen K, associate professor, $67,552
Jackson, Katherine L, associate professor, $93,711
Jackson, Lillian V, custodian/housekeeper, $26,225
Jacobs, Connie S Johnson, secretary, $32,635
Jacques, Marty L, building trades, $31,738
Janick-Buckner, Diane, professor, $74,969
Jaquez, Mario, custodian/housekeeper, $22,738
Jayne, Harry Martin, associate professor, $57,483
Jennings, Mark, associate professor, $52,369
Jennings, Melody, temporary instructor, $43,934
Jensen, Kelsey Anne, international admission coord, $30,600
Jereb, James A, professor, $64,853
Jesse, Jennifer G, professor, $57,984
Jewett, Margaret, intrm sales & mkt mgr-tsu press, $32,640
Johnson, Amber Lynn, professor, $57,732
Johnson, Judy H, temporary assistant professor, $52,541
Johnson, Pamela A, secretary, $27,207
Johnson, Roger J, custodian/housekeeper, $26,726
Jones, Gregory R, professor, $73,937
Jones, Jennifer Marie, temporary instructor, $37,740
Jones, John Y, assistant professor, $50,500
Jones, Margo Sue, secretary, $21,402
Jones, Robert, professor, $93,411

Jorn, Elizabeth, temporary instructor, $41,500
Jorn, Philip M, counselor, ucs, $37,561
Judd, James Frederick, dir of rpdc, $76,500
Jumper, M Shannon, professor, $73,706
Kaden, Stacey Renee, assistant professor, $120,000
Kallerud, Mauritz Royce, professor, $61,521
Kambli, Priya, professor, $58,599
Kearney, Thomas, asst coach - fb/tmp instr hes, $32,089
Kelley, Christopher P, temporary assistant professor, $40,000
Kelly, Peter S, professor, $62,389
Kelrick, Michael Ira, professor, $77,539
Kelsey, Curtis Michael, web developer ii, $57,120
Kennard, Rhoda R, secretary, $22,691
Kennedy, Kristin Denise, secretary, $27,770
Kennerk, Chad Allen, annual fund officer, advancement, $32,000
Kerby, Debra K, dean of school of business, $147,700
Kiefer, Mary Jane, secretary, $24,910
Killen, Brenda S, cash & credit card oper suprv, $29,942
Kim, Hyun-Joo, professor, $64,169
King, Adam C, assistant professor, $51,000
Kleine, Dawn Michelle, assistant professor, $50,000
Klingsmith, Shuan, facilities co-supervisor, $39,448
Klyukovski, Andrew Anatoliy, associate professor, $54,645
Kolenda, Miranda Ree, dir fit/well-rec cntr, $38,760
Kramer, Barbara, professor, $59,462
Krause, Donald W, associate professor, $53,108
Krebs, Jesse, associate professor, $49,887
Kreps, Clifton H, professor, $75,255
Kubin, Brian X, associate professor, $48,089
Kubus, Daniel Jacob, staff accompanist, $23,022
Kuhns, Todd Leron, emerging web tech specialist, $51,000
Kuntz, Billy R, farm manager, $34,536
LaGrassa, Susan L, professor, $73,998
Lambert, Susan, assistant professor, $57,000
Lamp, Brian D, professor, $66,881
Langendoerfer, Amanda Marie, special coll/arch-librarian, $53,500
Lay, Charles, driver, $24,680
Lay, Elizabeth J, secretary, $26,288
Lay, Sharon K, secretary, $28,459
Leaton, David S, dir writ cen/tmp instr, $47,457
Lecaque, Patrick, director of international education, $105,172
Lee, Lucy F, professor, $78,539
Lewis, Benjamin Aaron, temporary assistant professor, $50,000
Lewis, Melinda Sue, custodian/housekeeper, $22,404
Liao, Liyan, web developer, $50,844
Lile, Cella P, custodian/housekeeper, $24,597
Limestall, Susan M, dir of student rec center, $56,350
Lin, Jia-Yuan J, professor, $102,253
Lindevald, Ian M, professor, $76,692
Ling, Huping, professor, $72,542
Liss, Donna, chief information officer, $134,903
Lobert, Patrick, professor, $80,000
Lochbaum, Julie B, professor, $64,417
Locher, Morgan, asst athl trnr/tmp pt instr, $28,000
Lockhart, Carol A, reference librarian, $56,855
Loper, Kayla Renee, program advisor, $30,000
Lovegreen, Sara Stubbert, secretary, $21,799
Ludolph, Douglas E, building trades, $31,738
Lumsden, Clifford, system trades, $29,900
Luscier, Jason David, assistant professor, $51,000
Lusk, David, assoc dean-student affairs, $70,664
Ma, Zhong, associate professor, $54,895
Maag, Andrea Elaine, academic advisor/pt instr, $30,393
Macauley, Sylvia Victoria, professor, $59,566
Madsen, Thomas Tyler, athletic media relations asst, $29,600
Maggart, D Eileen, custodian/housekeeper, $22,404
Maggart, Melinda, custodian/housekeeper, $28,000
Maglio, Christopher, professor, $71,949
Magruder, Matthew Adam, senior admission counselor, $34,293
Maize, Debbie, custodian/housekeeper, $26,225
Maize, Tim J, co-supervisor-facilities, $40,101
Maldonado-Class, Joaquin, professor, $57,853
Mandell, Daniel, professor, $61,444
Manning, Ronald, dir llc-tmp asst prof, $59,495
Maples, William Eugene, systems analyst-its, $47,989
Marsh, Roger Scott, coord-mail & print services, $37,137
Marshall, Amanda Grace, secretary, $21,402
Marshall, Carol Ann, professor, $64,036
Marshall, Gregory Howard, web svcs integration mgr, $65,546

Martel, Danielle Marie, secretary, $21,799
Mason, Curtis Wayne, secretary, $21,799
Matteson, Pauline March, asst dir, univ career center, $39,899
Matthews, Robert E, associate professor, $73,778
Mayhew, Jerry, professor, $88,270
McAninch, Jeremy Kevin, secretary, $17,572
McClure, Sam J, professor, $69,089
McCormick, Deborah L, secretary, $31,174
McCormick, James M, associate professor, $57,791
McCurdy, David, professor, $77,539
McDow, Lisa Kay, secretary, $24,513
McDowell, Dana Gerald, rec center custodian, $31,571
McDuff, Elaine M, professor, $60,193
McGill, Rick Loren, intrm dir-intrmurl rec sports, $34,334
McGrew, Stephanie Ya-Net, prog coord/grant support, $24,336
McGurk, Daniel J, reference/elect resources libr, $50,000
McHenry, Gayla S, access ser supervisor - pml, $42,515
McKamie, David W, professor, $80,879
McKamie, Shirley, temporary instructor, $39,162
McKim, Kenneth, building trades supervisor, $44,790
McKim, Kristian D, grants & compliance specialist, $45,004
McKim, Louis Colman, building trades, $29,316
McLane-Iles, Betty L, professor, $81,264
McNabb, James Andrew, technical director, $89,518
Medlock-Klyukovski, Amanda Leigh, asst professor, $50,000
Meeker, Darren Shelby, admission counselor, $33,000
Melvin, Pamela Jan, assistant professor, $57,000
Mendez, Rosa Virginia, study abroad advisor, $31,000
Mickey, Patricia, temporary assistant professor, $48,093
Mielke, Robert E, professor, $78,539
Miles, Travis Lee, comm coord-public & alumni rel, $30,600
Miller, Cheryl J, custodian/housekeeper, $31,195
Miller, Elizabeth Anne, counselor, ucs, $30,500
Miller, Jill Eileen, positive behavior supp consult, $58,184
Miller, Ralph W, building trades, $32,990
Mills, Tim, its center manager, $57,054
Minch, Kevin M, assoc vp academic affairs / professor, $90,034
Miner, Wendy Sue, professor, $61,413
Minn, Shyn Chyn, temporary instructor, $47,317
Mitchell, Cinda L, secretary, $27,624
Mitchell, Jeanne M, temporary instructor, $51,041
Mohler, Chad H, professor, $59,566
Mohler, Sarah B, temporary assistant professor, $49,939
Monroe, Catherine Amanda, asst coach - sb/tmp instr, $24,476
Montgomery, Chad Edward, associate professor, $54,814
Moody, Anne Erwin, professor, $76,957
Moore, Brenda G, temporary instructor, $51,041
Moore, Diane M, secretary, $27,729
Moore, Julianna, professor, $75,123
Moore, Paula L, secretary, $32,635
Moore, Susan A, secretary, $25,223
Morin, Regina, assoc vp for enrollment mgt, $123,500
Morin, Shandra K, fin aid office asst/schol coor, $24,221
Morton, Jana L, secretary, $26,288
Morton, Jeffrey E, driver, $20,287
Motter, Leslie Susan, secretary, $19,589
Mourning, Talor Marie, residence hall director, $24,600
Mourning Byers, Kelly, secretary, $23,553
Muffley, Richard P, systems administrator, $53,324
Mullins, Judy M, comptroller, $114,731
Mun, Kyung Chun, professor, $98,793
Murphy, David G, professor, $75,255
Murphy, Kimberly L, purchasing supervisor, $43,476
Murray, Lori L, secretary, $27,958
Nash, John Paul, secretary, $18,024
Nash, Madeline S, coord facilities & processes, $35,726
Neitzke, John, professor, $93,071
Nelsen, William Lee, coord student life & development, $35,622
Nelson, Arletta Marie, admin asst vp admin/finc/plan, $32,640
Nelson, Doris Janie, custodian/housekeeper, $26,225
Nelson, Russell L, professor, $62,733
Nelson, Steven F, dps officer ii, $38,628
Nelson, Teak, associate professor, $57,000
Nesbitt, Gregg Douglas, coach - fb/asst ath admin, $86,380
Nesbitt, Kellen Christopher, asst coach - fb/asst ath admin, $45,857
Newcomer, Barbara A, secretary, $27,791
Ng, Lok, temporary assistant professor, $41,000
Nichting, Gay Annette, clinic nurse, shc, $24,516
Noel, Joshua, groundskeeper, $23,469

Nothdurft, Debra W, head acad advisor, $39,571
Nunan, Amy, lab manager, $53,800
Oberman, Elizabeth Anna, systems analyst-its, $59,029
O'Brien, John G, professor, $65,465
O'Donnell, James F, dean of school of arts and letters, $123,420
Ogden, Benjamin C, temporary assistant professor, $61,308
Olson, Janine Renea, custodian/housekeeper, $22,404
Olson, Terry L, professor, $83,646
Orel, Sara E, professor, $69,498
Orton, H Marie, professor, $61,752
Otero, Kathy F, assistant professor, $122,247
Outzen, Christopher, temporary instructor, $42,000
Owen, Allison J, secretary, $21,402
Padfield, James A, professor, $63,746
Page, William Brett, building trades, $31,090
Palmer, Sherri, professor, $71,894
Palmer, Terry, professor, $71,949
Palumbo, John Todd, professor, $78,702
Park, Yung-Hwal, assistant professor, $89,760
Parker, Paul E, professor, $75,255
Parks, Charles A, technical support specialist, $47,920
Partenheimer, David, professor, $78,539
Passe, Melissa, clinical supervisor in cmds, $49,453
Paulsen, Jed, asst coach - fb/asst ath admin, $38,259
Payne, Brian D, mover/laborer, $27,040
Pearce, Sherril A, secretary, $22,989
Peavler, Toby M, custodian/housekeeper, $25,724
Peel, Tasha, secretary, $22,989
Peeler, Steven DeBord, system trades, temp foreman, $42,491
Perez-Munoz, Carmen, assistant professor, $50,000
Perrachione, Beverly Ann, associate professor, $53,391
Perrachione, Gwen A, adademic computing spec-its, $48,465
Petersen, Steven Allen, asst to provost & vpaa, $55,000
Pflueger, Lloyd, professor, $69,190
Pigg, Blake, groundskeeper, $27,833
Pigg, Kelly Ann, secretary, $29,044
Pitaniello, Richard Henry, cataloging maint librarian, $44,217
Pites, Silvia E, professor, $75,123
Pollard, Stephen R, professor, $78,704
Porter, Charles P, system trades, $31,299
Powell, Kathleen M, executive secretary-provost vp, $35,467
Powelson, Stephanie Ann, professor, $70,650
Poyner, Barry Cole, professor, $72,542
Poyner, Catherine, temporary instructor, $59,004
Prendergast, Curran, assistant professor, $52,000
Prendergast, Jocelyn Stevens, assistant professor, $48,000
Presley, Adrien R, professor, $96,618
Pretre, Edward, coach - swim, $47,989
Preussner, Alanna, professor, $76,308
Prewitt, Tessa Elizabeth, secretary, $19,955
Price, Barbara J, professor, $66,881
Price, David Channing, temporary associate professor, $43,000
Price, Julia Elizabeth, admission counselor, $30,000
Primm, Jerrin Jay, groundskeeper, $23,469
Pultz, Janet Christina, mcnair program coordinator, $38,760
Pultz, Vaughan M, professor, $73,355
Quinn, John J, professor, $65,321
Ragas, Jason, custodian/housekeeper, $25,223
Ramberg, Peter, professor, $62,016
Ratliff, Tammy Lee, special education consultant, $50,000
Reardon, Lena Ann, secretary, $26,246
Rearick, Daisy R, reference/periodical librarian, $50,000
Rechtien, Michael, tech support specialist i, $42,929
Rector, David R, vp admin, finance & planning, $142,906
Redmon, Marsha Marie, secretary, $33,053
Reed, Steven RM, dps officer i, $28,272
Regan, Gracie Jeanette, temporary instructor, $38,500
Reschly, Steven D, professor, $66,200
Rhinesmith, Donna Lynn, professor, $76,859
Rhodes, Brittany L, international student advisor, $30,600
Rhodes, Darson L, assistant professor, $51,000
Rice, Marc, professor, $59,566
Richards, Andrea Greenlee, temporary instructor, $46,000
Richardson, Colton Boyd, admission counselor, $30,000
Richmond, Diane Elizabeth, dir, learning technology, $78,672
Richter, Gregory C, professor, $81,032
Rigby, Dana, secretary, $21,799
Riggle, Priscilla A, professor, $78,030
Riley, Carrie A, campus visit coordinator, $28,000

Robbins, Daniel L, groundskeeper, $29,190
Roberts, Tammy M, dir-administrative computing, $89,518
Robinson, Alison Rae, admission counselor, $30,000
Robinson, David Kent, professor, $75,135
Robinson, Dennis L, custodian/housekeeper, $23,177
Robinson, Heather, custodian/housekeeper, $22,404
Rodman, Melissa Ann, secretary, $26,288
Rogers, Edward Laurence, temporary instructor, $36,673
Rogers, Larry, system trades, $32,990
Rogers, Lenora, custodian/housekeeper, $23,949
Rogers, Lesley R, mover/warehouse foreman, $22,759
Rogers, Mark, custodian/housekeeper, $24,597
Romine, Janet I, head pub service/pml, $59,719
Rood, Deanna, web writer/editor, advancement, $43,860
Rooks, Aaron Scott, academic advisor/pt instr, $30,000
Rouse, Eldon, building trades, $28,021
Rudy, Michael Alan, assistant professor, $50,510
Ryan, Pamela J, professor, $68,199
Ryan, Philip Donal, associate professor, $65,095
Rybkowski, Ronald M, professor, $72,608
Safley, Ann, admission database supervisor, $41,350
Samiullah, Mohammad, professor, $81,351
Sandefur, Diane Elizabeth, secretary, $22,989
Sapp, Richard H, groundskeeper, $23,135
Sawani, Mustafa A, professor, $88,788
Sayre, Kimberly A, custodian/housekeeper, $26,225
Sayre, Larry W, groundskeeper, $23,469
Schmitz, Joyce F, secretary, $27,624
Schneider, Brandy Sue, assistant professor, $48,500
Schneider, Karl J, director of physical plant, $98,705
Schnetzler, Darin K, library technology specialist, $39,421
Schubert, Lillie Mae, custodian/housekeeper, $22,738
Schulte, George J, professor, $86,436
Schultz, Mark Eugene, univ architect/campus planner, $91,576
Schutter, David, coach - wrestling/asst ath admin, $42,778
Schwegler, Timothy M, head cc-track/tmp instr, $54,570
Scudder, Karen Elaine, chemistry technician, $39,463
Scuderi, Antonio, professor, $66,881
Sedinkin, Sergey L, temporary assistant professor, $42,000
Seidel, Linda, professor, $80,879
Seiffertt, John Edward, assistant professor, $70,000
Seipel, Michael, professor, $65,300
Self, John W, associate professor, $53,266
Sempertegui - Sosa, Carolina, temp assistant professor, $43,177
Sen, Astha, assistant professor, $46,000
Shafer, Donovan, system trades, $29,232
Shaffer, Fred B, professor, $88,283
Shapiro, Mary Beth, professor, $65,584
Shapiro, Paul, temporary associate professor, $51,000
Shaver, Jeremy E, system trades, $29,232
Shaw, Jason T, assistant professor, $57,000
Shears, Leon D, dps sergeant i, $36,958
Shelton, Brian Robert, groundskeeper, $23,469
Sherrow, Catherine S, secretary, $31,153
Shinn, George L, professor, $75,528
Shipman, Alice Dorothea, secretary, $22,989
Shook, Lori Ann, design project mgr/campus plan, $61,480
Shoop, Douglas, system trades, $25,912
Shoush, Caleb, secretary, $21,799
Shreves, Amanda, admission counselor, $30,000
Shwadlenak, Miranda Taylor, residence hall director, $24,000
Siewert, Gregg, professor, $72,542
Simmons, Stacy Michelle, counselor, ucs, $34,593
Sims, Julie Anne, secretary, $24,513
Sims, Shelby Rae, program advisor service/leader, $29,100
Smith, Carla D, associate professor, $60,893
Smith, Christopher J, dps officer ii, $27,750
Smith, Dana, professor, $61,444
Smith, Denise L, dir almni relat/spec gift officer, $55,109
Smith, Mark A, associate professor, $54,898
Smith, Michelle Mada, groundskeeper, $22,154
Smith, Randall, professor, $73,585
Smith, Steven Jay, professor, $81,559
Smith, Steven R, professor, $85,642
Smith-Mandell, Barbara, copy/acquisitions editor-tsup, $48,758
Snyder, Brian Scott, assistant professor, $52,042
Sparks, Richard A, system trades, $29,712
Speak, Jeri Leigh, secretary, $22,989
Speight, Aaron, digital projects librarian, $44,217

Sterup, Erika J, assistant dir-upward bound, $37,740
Stutsman, Angela, custodian/housekeeper, $22,404
Sung, Chein-Hsing, professor, $86,272
Surgener, Alyssa Jane, admission counselor, $30,000
Sweet, Sara Beth, secretary, $22,989
Swingle, Megan Aileen, residence hall director, $25,080
Tandez, Adam, asst coach - basketball/tmp intr, $36,720
Techau, Robert D, systems trades supervisor, $46,641
Tegtmeyer, Thomas J, temporary assistant professor, $42,657
Templeton, Heidi C, dir of public relations, $64,358
Tetlak, Alex E, temporary instructor, $40,331
Thatcher, Carol Lynne, professor, $65,608
Thomas, Bridget, professor, $61,521
Thomas, Susan L, executive vp & provost, $164,000
Thomas, Susan Marie, instructional designer ii, $53,321
Thrasher, Laura K, secretary, $29,002
Thurman, Sheila M, school resource specialist, $55,988
Tigner, Robert B, professor, $64,651
Titterington, Lauren Frances, admission coordinator, $32,640
Titus, Kimberly R, assistant registrar, $37,106
Tornatore, Matthew, professor, $68,718
Tran, Khang Duc, temporary assistant professor, $42,657
Treece, Diane M, rec center custodian, $22,989
Trendafilov, Rossen I, temporary assistant professor, $51,000
Tucker, Teresa Lyn, nurse practitioner-student health, $52,789
Tucker-Potter, Stacy M, manager of the annual fund, $45,000
Twining, Linda, professor, $81,899
Uchida, Shinya, temporary lecturer, $36,000
Valencia, Juan Carlos, associate professor, $55,484
Van Klootwyk, Lori Ann, school resource specialist, $55,988
Vanderhoof, Winston E, senior graphic designer, $71,245
Vazzana, Anthony, professor, $66,552
Vazzana, Dana, professor, $66,552
Veatch, Louis, system trades, $32,531
Velasco, Eduardo Sanchez, professor, $72,571
Vieker, Jonathan Matthew, academic advisor/pt instr, $30,100
Vittengl, Jeffrey, professor, $57,732
Vittengl, Karen Louise, professor, $59,446
Vorhees, Stachia Lynn, secretary, $24,513
Waddle, Bryan A, system trades, $32,990
Walston, Timothy D, associate professor, $55,050
Walter, Joetta Sue, special education consultant, $59,339
Walter, Kelly Winsco, assistant professor, $54,000
Wandel, Torbjorn, professor, $64,333
Ward, Mary A, admission counselor, $33,000
Wargo-Kearney, Megan Anne, asst coach - vb / asst ath admin, $30,608
Watson, Debra Ann, custodian/housekeeper, $26,225
Webber, Melanie Alta, custodian/housekeeper, $26,225
Wehner, Glenn R, professor, $81,274
Wehner, Vicky L, coord-disability services/rn, $44,520
Weidner, Ann M, secretary, $27,729
Weidner, Mark H, head acad advisor-pt instr, $44,477
Weisstein, Anton E, associate professor, $55,108
Welker, Jessica Marie, admission counselor, $30,000
Wells, Warren L, general counsel, $130,680
West, Sally, professor, $66,212
West, Teresa M, custodian-sub, $29,274
Western, Larry J, building trades, $31,738
Wheeler, Brenda K, associate professor, $56,467
Wheeler, Teresa J, manager pub/sr graph designer, $74,052
White, Kevin Earl, asst to the athletic director, $39,774
White, Norman, chief engineer, $55,988
White, Robin L, asst dir-financial aid, $41,538
Whittom, Chad Earl, interim director of public safety, $48,800
Wilbur, Wynne Martine, professor, $60,384
Williams, Cathy Sue, secretary, $19,335
Williams, Jaronda L, admission counselor, $30,000
Williams, Kathy, custodian/housekeeper, $26,225
Williams, Tina, custodian/housekeeper, $21,339
Williams, Tracy Ann, systems analyst-its, $53,668
Williams, Vanessa Janel, temporary instructor, $40,000
Wilson, Casey, custodian/housekeeper, $20,087
Winstead, Jack L, assistant professor, $117,300
Wodika, Alicia Brooke, temporary assistant professor, $41,000
Wodika, Benjamin R, temporary instructor, $37,740
Wohlers, Henry D, professor, $80,109
Wollmering, Gerald W, director of athletics, $93,330
Wood, Jacey Jean, secretary, $27,854

Woodcox, D Cole, professor, $75,617
Woods, Cynthia, prospect research officer, $34,971
Wriedt, Brandi Nicole, career coordinator, $33,293
Wriedt, Carolyn Jeanne, secretary, $32,802
Wuebker, LoraLane, dps officer i, $26,100
Wynn, Stephen Mark, head-tech serv & sys-library, $57,636
Xu, Ping, assistant professor, $48,000
Yakle, Danielle Nicole, temporary assistant professor, $41,000
Yaquinto, Marilyn, associate professor, $55,060
Yoder, Paul Leroy, associate professor, $52,942
Young, Candy C, professor, $83,877
Young, Jared Allen, tmp instr/cord sumr acdms, $36,000
Zhang, Lin, associate professor, $91,150
Zoumaras, Thomas, professor, $77,111

University of Central Missouri
Warrensburg 64093

Ambrose, Charles, president, $272,550
Aaberg, David, professor, $77,835
Abellan-Pagnani, Luisa, assistant professor, $45,844
Abner, Dalene, executive editor, $67,821
Abner, Melissa, assistant professor, $44,779
Adams, Katelyn, office professional II, $20,797
Adams, Robert, microcomputer/network spec II, $45,900
Adkins, Jeffrey, custodian, $23,775
Agueros, Eddy, manager, circulation/reserves, $30,115
Agueros, Mary, interim - supervisor, $20,800
Ahmadibasir, Mohammad, assistant professor, $60,000
Ake, Steven, dir, center for bus computing, $52,470
Alfino, Joseph, instructor, temporary, $35,058
Alkire, Margaret, associate dean, professor, $99,813
Allen, Patrick, landscape specialist I, $19,240
Allen, Russell, landscape specialist I, $18,720
Allen, Tammy, assistant professor, $52,681
Alpaugh, Micah, assistant professor, $53,935
Altis, Sherry, instructor, temporary, $35,058
Ament, Patrick, professor, $77,835
Ammon, Rebecca, landscape specialist I, $18,720
Ammon, Scott, assistant professor, $49,082
Anderson, Dawn, assistant professor, $72,726
Anderson, Gay, instructor, $44,894
Anderson, Johnny, custodian, $21,320
Anderson, Kathy, asst dir, internal relations, $80,000
Anderson, Nancy, financial aid counselor, $44,574
Anderson, Shawn, custodian, $21,320
Anderson, Susan, coach, women's softball, $59,458
Andrews, Kim, associate dean, professor, $127,037
Anthes, Kimberly, manager, operations, $41,631
Antrim, Patricia, dept chair, professor, $102,849
Aragon, Jamie, golf professional, $25,780
Arentsen, Elizabeth Ann, program asst, study abroad, $22,319
Armstrong, Brad, foreperson, custodial, $23,959
Armstrong, Tiffany, custodian, $18,880
Arnett, Dorothy, instructor, $37,906
Atkin, Phyllis, manager, accounting, $53,634
Atkins, Charlene, assistant professor, $45,844
Atkinson, Carol, professor, $77,835
Ayers, Daniel, event technology manager, $46,512
Azevedo, Christopher, professor, $95,800
Azevedo, Kari, academic coordinator, mocap, $49,776
Azimzadeh, Roya, assistant professor, $45,844
Babcock, David, associate professor, $62,756
Babrakzai, Sami, administrative assistant, $37,401
Bachman, Dale, professor, $89,500
Badger, Sujamanas, office professional III, $27,861
Baeth, Nicholas, associate professor, $62,917
Bailey, Larry, electrician II, $31,958
Bailey, Sarah, manager, operations, $54,522
Bailey, Sarah, assistant professor, $72,726
Baker, Kenneth, microcomputer/network spec II, $44,574
Baldwin, Ryan, materials handler, $18,880
Ballew, Nataliya, coord, business operations, $53,121
Bamman, Christopher, director, fpo, $105,080
Bancroft, William, school resource specialist, $52,426
Barabas, David, dir, ctr for print production, $84,252
Barker, Diana, office professional II, $25,418

Chenault, Scott, assistant professor, $44,000
Chiang, Chen-Fu, assistant professor, temp-es, $63,000
Chisom, Katherine, academic employment specialist, $42,292
Cho, Yeok-Il, associate professor, $65,257
Choi, Miyeon, instructor, temporary, $41,300
Christ, Sandra, office professional III, $29,470
Church, Tina, dir, grad school & int'l adm, $62,693
Ciafullo, Stephen, assistant professor, $48,051
Ciraulo, Darlene, associate professor, $62,756
Clawson, Julie, dept chair, professor, $105,160
Clear, Cathy, library assistant v, $32,219
Clemens, Charles, asst coach, football-def line, $49,168
Clemens, Marcia, administrative assistant, $33,296
Clements, Rachel, office professional iv, $24,420
Clevenger, Mary, outreach coordinator, $41,631
Clifford, Amber, associate professor, $62,159
Cline, Alan, system administrator III, $72,622
Clopton, James, assistant professor, $51,500
Clossin, George, network analyst I, $45,900
Clothier, Carrie, library assistant VI, $41,633
Cochran, Jonathan, network analyst I, $46,920
Cochran, Lori, assistant professor, $45,844
Coey, Candace, foreperson, custodial, $26,375
Cole, Abigail, development officer, $51,500
Cole, Richard, assistant director, $56,951
Collins, Robert, asst manager, facility service, $49,552
Combs, Deborah, administrative assistant, $47,201
Comer, Colin, director, police academy, $55,590
Comer, M, professor, $69,160
Conner, Harold, electrician II, $34,721
Conrad, Michelle, assistant professor, temporary, $53,935
Conrad-Brown, Rebecca, admissions representative, $36,788
Cooper, Curtis, professor, $104,272
Copus, Belinda, instructor, temporary, $43,000
Corbett, Galen, manager, property control, $46,037
Corkran, Dennis, carpenter II, $30,816
Courtwright, Kevin, foreperson, grounds, $29,537
Courtwright, Kimberly, office professional III, $27,172
Cowles, Janelle, professor, $77,835
Cox, Rachel, police officer, $34,838
Craig, David, applications manager, $69,386
Craig, Sarah, program administrator, $42,000
Craig, Sheryl, instructor, $41,772
Crain, Linda, positive behavior support, $49,587
Craioveanu, Mihaela, associate professor, $85,200
Creel, Charles, technical project manager, $57,218
Crews, Daniel, professor, $77,835
Crews, Rhonda, office professional iv, $33,652
Crooker, John, dir, institutional research, $126,480
Crookes, Kyle, coach, baseball, $65,000
Cruse, Kris, microcomputer/network spec I, $40,868
Cruse, Lydia, office professional III, $24,912
Cruz, Sandy, coord, distance learning, $44,574
Culp, John, coord, prog dev retention, $44,574
Culver, Robert, boiler technician II, $35,196
Cunconan, Debbie, instructor, $37,906
Cunconan, Terry, professor, $77,835
Cunningham, Debra, office professional II-, $19,446
Curtis, Deborah, provost/chief learning officer, $193,800
Curtis, John, assistant director, fpo, $81,600
Curtis, Kenneth, life safety technician II, $26,583
Curtis, Lauren, asst coach, softball, $31,212
Cust, Kenneth, professor, $77,835
Cutler, Christian, director, art gallery, $53,736
Dahlstrom, Charles, sr psychologist-, $70,530
Dahlstrom, Michelle, career counselor, $41,524
Dahman, Tami, custodian, $25,252
Daily, Tiffany, coord, communication programs, $40,096
Dake, Lori, manager, environmental health, $74,786
Daniels, Carmel, office professional iv, $31,528
Danley, Angela, assistant professor, $53,935
Davis, Charissa, asst dir, financial assistance, $55,497
Davis, Davie, dept chair, assoc professor, $69,714
Davis, Marian, associate professor, library, $68,107
Davis, Rose Ann, administrative assistant, $39,275
Day, Vanessa, help desk support spec II, $33,161
de Laurier, Michael, production engineer, $44,880
Dean, Kurtis, associate professor, $62,756
DeBoard, Donald, coord,ignition interlock progr, $36,016

DeJonge, Robert, professor, $81,163
Delap, James, program manager trans safety, $52,228
Delap, Susan, coord, business/fiscal ops, $44,492
Dempsey, Alice, accountant II, $32,437
Denham, Susan, office professional III, $32,033
Denne, Jennifer, office professional II-, $26,217
Depew, Victoria, assistant professor, $52,681
Desmond, Kathleen, professor, $83,276
Diaz, Paul, hvac III, $40,849
Dickerson, Lawrence, network analyst I, $45,900
Dieckman, Andrea, academic advisor, $38,478
Dierking, Elizabeth, instructor, temporary, $38,000
Diestel, Andrew, manager, technical services, $86,700
Ding, Dabin, assistant professor, temp-es, $63,000
Dinwiddie, Mollie, dean, $112,911
DioGuardi, Sherri, assistant professor, $55,000
Dixon, Ricki, director, human resources, $82,574
Docheff, Dennis, professor, $77,955
Donald, Susan, office professional II, $28,903
Doogs, Holly, assistant professor, $53,734
Dooley, Brenda, office professional III, $29,114
Dotson, Carmen, instructor, temporary, $35,058
Downing, Annette, database services manager, $77,361
Downing, Joyce, associate dean, professor, $105,496
Downing, Lucy, landscape specialist I, $21,320
Draisey, Tyler, athletic tickets oper coord, $38,003
Drake, Amanda, instructor, temporary, $41,245
Driskill, Jamie, system coordinator, $42,907
Drummond, Jason, vice president, advancement, $179,254
Dryden, Richard, coordinator, multimedia rooms, $47,957
Dubuque, David, system administrator I, $53,220
DuBuque, Ronald, head athletic trainer, $62,399
Duhamell, Daniel, asst director, residence life, $52,825
Duncan, Jacob, materials handler, $18,720
Duncan, Mona, administrative assistant, $36,067
Duncan, Tena, director, payroll services, $67,870
Dunn, Carol, instructor, temporary, $38,000
Durbin, Tracey, program manager sfst, $60,792
Dustin, Danielle, asst dir, res leadership, $48,222
Dustin, Randy, senior programmer/analyst, $51,690
Dutton, Jimmie, associate professor, library, $67,576
Dyer, Kandice, medical lab technician -, $27,405
Dyer, Kelly, manager, business applications, $44,641
Dyer, Nancy, office professional III, $32,386
Dzula, Wally, life safety technician I, $28,037
Eaden, Alan, microcomputer/network spec III, $49,980
Earles-Vollrath, Theresa, professor, $77,430
Eason, Cheryl, associate professor, $63,737
Eck, Matthew, associate professor, $62,756
Eckfeld, Kristina, interim site coordinator, wafb, $38,710
Edmondson, Kelly, instructor, temporary, $45,727
Elliott, Michael, instructor, temporary, $38,000
Elliott, Stanley, project facilitator, mic, $78,600
Ely, Joseph, associate professor, $62,756
Emily, Kathy, custodian, $20,280
Engle, Allan, director, tech support svcs, $85,000
Ensign, Justin, coach, wrestling, $44,640
Erickson, Julie, office professional III, $32,033
Espen, Brian, custodian, $21,320
Estep, Pamela, assistant professor, $53,552
Etter, Gregg, associate professor, $63,169
Ewart, Troy, aircraft mechanic II - a&p, $41,415
Ewing, David, manager, farm, $44,209
Ewing, David, associate professor, $65,874
Fahrmeier, Karen, coordinator of thrive-10mth, $41,817
Faja, Silvana, associate professor, $99,492
Farmer, DeeAnn, painter I, $20,197
Farr, William, custodian, $27,667
Farris, Mark, assistant professor, $53,935
Faubion, Scott, foreperson, custodial, $27,754
Faust, James, custodian, $18,720
Feeback, Susan, school resource specialist, $49,440
Fenley, J, professor, $77,835
Fenwick, Sherri, assistant professor, $53,579
Fernquist, Robert, professor, $77,835
Fiegenbaum, Karen, manager, circulation/reserves, $32,220
Fieth, Justina, financial aid counselor, $38,709
Fillinger, Adrianne, art & design manager, $50,000
Finkes, Wendy, accountant II, $37,747

Fischer, Lacey, office professional II, $34,689
Forbes, Steve, custodian, $18,720
Ford, Marilyn, office professional II, $21,840
Foree, Craig, microcomputer/network spec I, $42,840
Forth, Nancy, professor, $76,463
Foster, Karen, associate professor, $64,502
Foster, Michael, assistant professor, $45,844
Foster, William, custodian, $22,727
Fowler-Swarts, Rose, assistant professor, $53,564
Franklin, Joseph, help desk support spec II, $33,161
Freeman, Nicole, instructor, temporary, $35,689
Fritz, Shirley, instructor, $35,689
Fuhr, Brenda, academic advisor, $38,821
Fulcher, Barbara, office professional III, $27,624
Fulford, Mark, professor, $103,609
Fulk, Cynthia, custodian, $21,320
Fuller, Miriam, professor, $77,835
Fuller-St John, Adrianne, psychologist-9mth, $40,800
Furrey, Catherine, licensed practical nurse-, $28,473
Fussell, Maria, asst dir, student services, $51,612
Gage, Mary, special education coordinator, $46,344
Gai, James, professor, $77,835
Galley, Deborah, instructor, $49,452
Garrett, Angela, police officer, $42,844
Garrison, Carol, assistant professor, temporary, $51,565
Gasaway, Anthony, assistant professor, $46,750
Gauvin, Dawn, office professional iv, $26,333
Gee, Taylor, student services coordinator, $39,950
Geiger, Wendy, dept chair, professor, $96,571
Gelbach, Harry, custodian, $22,269
Gerdes, Daniel, professor, $77,835
Gerhart, Debra, coord, technical training, $47,957
Ghozzi, Kamel, associate professor, $62,806
Gibson, Matthew, custodian, $18,880
Gieselman, Nancy, administrative assistant, $32,726
Gill, James, carpenter II, $34,721
Gillespie, Robert, instructor, temporary, $35,058
Gillis, Delia, professor, $77,835
Gladfelter, Diana, instructor, $35,058
Gladfelter, Kristina, instructor, $35,689
Glasnapp, Pamela, instructor, $47,585
Glover, Janice, instructor, $38,076
Goad, Daryl, assistant professor, $53,935
Goavec, Della, professor, $77,835
Godard, Michael, dept chair, professor, $107,917
Godfrey, Denis, coordinator,airport operations, $38,709
Gole, Antje, customer service rep, $30,161
Gole, John, associate professor, $67,032
Gonzalez, Shelly, policy officer/paralegal, $52,214
Goodchild, Paul, assistant professor, $102,000
Goodwin, Steven, associate professor, $62,756
Gordon, Aqualus, assistant professor, $52,681
Gordon, Theresa, associate professor, $62,756
Goreham, Amber, director, career services, $61,812
Gotsch, Travis, custodian, $18,880
Gower, Dianne, office professional II, $27,557
Graham, James, vice prov & chief info officer, $128,775
Graham, Susan, office professional II, $33,561
Gravely, Page, office professional II, $20,197
Graves, Michael, assistant professor, $53,935
Grechus, Marilyn, professor, $77,835
Greene, Frances, accountant II, $31,076
Greene, Jeffrey, system coordinator, $44,574
Greife, Alice, dean, $138,736
Greife, Merle, office professional iv, $31,255
Greife, Michael, manager, news bureau, $41,631
Greinke, Russell, associate professor, $62,756
Grelle, Michael, vice prov, academic programs, $133,775
Grelle, Sheree, instructor, temporary, $38,000
Gremaud, Krystle, assistant professor, $44,779
Grieser, Sheila, instructor, $46,100
Griffin, Andrew, police sergeant, $46,677
Grigsby, Carl, associate professor, $62,756
Gross, Melanie, manager, client services, $79,050
Grote, Jon, landscape specialist III, $21,397
Gubele, Rosene, assistant professor, $53,935
Guin, John, assistant professor, $48,025
Guthrie, Mary Lee, prospect research manager, $60,000
Guy, Rebecca, book merchandiser, $22,520

Guyer, Ashley, research analyst, $41,883
Hadley, Steve, floorcrewperson, $19,635
Hafley, Jason, aircraft mechanic I - a&p, $29,121
Hafley, Samuel, environ/hazard materials coord, $58,344
Hakos, Gregory, visiting assistant professor, $53,935
Hall, Bonnie, senior programmer/analyst, $59,561
Hall, Franklin, bowling operations coordinator, $25,040
Hallis, Robert, associate professor, library, $80,018
Halsey, Beth, assistant director, fpo, $71,015
Hammons, Tonya, office professional II, $20,797
Haney, Kristee, assistant professor, $52,878
Haney, Matthew, instructor, temporary, $35,058
Hansen-Horn, Tricia, professor, $77,835
Hanson, Steven, hvac II, $27,204
Harmon, Harry, professor, $111,282
Harrington, Gwyndelon, office professional iv, $29,043
Harrison, Andrew, system administrator II, $58,000
Harrison, Peggy, accountant III, $43,868
Hartle, Jeffery, asst prof, temp-es, $45,844
Hartnett, Mary, assistant professor, $53,935
Haught, Aaron, foreperson, custodial, $21,730
Havnen, Mandy, student fin resource asst, $25,620
Havnen, Raymond, network analyst I, $44,920
Hawkins, Guy, network analyst II, $51,618
Hawkins, Wendy, library assistant v, $30,115
Hayes, Connie, custodian, $25,626
Hayes, Joseph, carpenter III, $35,291
Hayes, Linda, office professional I, $23,371
Hayward, Kevin, foreperson, set-ups, $20,780
Heapes, Thomas, associate professor, $62,239
Heater, Teresa, library assistant v, $39,685
Heath, Douglas, microcomputer/network spec I, $42,840
Hedglin, Stephanie, custodian, $18,720
Hellenthal, Ryan, asst coach, men's basketball, $56,112
Heming, Valerie, instructor/co-director, $50,194
Henson, Kerry, assistant professor, $93,500
Hentges, Julie, associate professor, $62,218
Herman, Diana, nurse practitioner-.8, $68,716
Herman, Richard, dept chair, professor, $99,319
Herod, Anna, programmer/analyst, $51,618
Herron, Michael, custodian, $18,880
Hewitt, Shellie, assistant director, $41,524
Hewlett, Demetrius, custodian, $18,880
Hiatt, Rosalie, clerk, central receiving, $25,938
Hibdon, Karen, manager, multipurpose building, $51,588
Hicks, Barbara, office professional iv, $31,730
Hicks, Kenneth, custodian, $18,720
Hicks, Steven, assistant professor, $56,712
Higgins, Regina, school improvement consultant, $55,200
Hinton, Jennifer, procurement specialist I, $34,170
Hirner, Anthony, assistant professor, $54,000
Hobson, Deborah, dir, union & meeting/conf serv, $85,048
Hodgins, David, custodian, $22,727
Hoel, Heather, dir, student & scholar svcs, $50,840
Hoeper, William, procurement specialist I, $37,332
Hoffman, Phil, director, broadcasting service, $100,000
Hoffmann, Joseph, athletics media relations asst, $36,067
Hoffmann, Sara, assistant professor, $51,564
Hogue, Laurel, interim director, int'l center, $78,500
Holbert, Scotti, office professional iv, $28,659
Holland, Jason, professor, $75,226
Holmes, Ronald, coach, bowling/asst coord even, $44,782
Holsten, Terry, carpenter II, $29,866
Homoly, Clarke, associate professor, $69,854
Honn, Darla, assistant professor, $120,000
Honomichl, Katherine, student services coordinator, $36,788
Honour, Eric, professor, $77,835
Hookey, Kyle, mechanic II, $29,866
Hoover, Dana, career counselor, $41,631
Horn, Adam, associate professor, $62,159
Horne-Popp, Laura, assistant professor, library, $58,000
Horta-Martinez, Cynthia, instructor, temp-es, $38,352
Houseworth, Matthew, assistant professor, $51,612
Howard, Dawn, library assistant v, $27,890
Howard, James, recreation center manager, $38,821
Howard, Sandra, custodian, $22,727
Howe, Mary, custodian, $18,880
Howery, Vickie, manager, accounts payable, $60,384
Hoyer, Pamela, assistant professor, $57,371

Hubbard, Patricia, office professional III, $30,954
Huff, Nichole, office professional III, $22,319
Huffman, Jeffrey, doj grant program coordinator, $57,332
Huffman, Joyce, coordinator, outreach, $45,481
Huffman, Monica, exec asst to the president, $94,718
Huffman, Teresa, administrative coordinator, $34,795
Huggans, Andrea, academic advisor, $38,478
Hughes, Brian, professor, $77,430
Hughes, Jerry, university director, athletics, $145,000
Hughes, Victoria, director of charter schools, $91,459
Hume, Nicole, membership & major gift ofc, $45,000
Humphrey, Penny, dir, central village-10mth, $30,540
Hutchinson, Sandra, professor, $77,835
Hwang, Hyeyeon, assistant professor, $53,935
Hynes, Mia, professor, $77,835
Ilu, Musa, associate professor, $62,756
Imboden, Jeffrey, manager, performing art series, $50,840
Ingham, Johnna, administrative assistant, $35,839
Irvine, Karl, electrician I, $28,037
Iske, Samuel, associate professor, $62,756
Israetel, Michael, assistant professor, $53,935
Jablonski, Joyce, professor, $77,835
Jackson, Mikayla, foreperson, custodial, $20,800
Jackson, Robert, coord, athletic promotions, $41,631
Jackson, Victoria, professor, $75,226
Jacobs, Katie, assistant professor, $53,935
Jacques-Nelson, Lisa, instructor, temporary, $38,760
James, Jason, instructor, temporary, $43,860
Janvrin, Kip, coach, track & cross country, $61,200
Jarboe, Joseph, coord, emerg preparedness - .8, $31,131
Jeffries, Chalice, instructor, temporary, $38,000
Jeffries, Michael, director, centralnet, $82,620
Jenkins, Sandra, instructor, $39,678
Jennings, Ernest, instructor, temporary, $46,000
Jennings, Heather, police officer, $34,838
Jennings, Jamie, coordinator, alumni events, $44,676
Jennings, Joseph, police officer, $34,820
Jennings, Sharon, academic advisor, $38,478
Jensen, Daniel, assistant professor, $78,625
Jeter, Matthew, asst coach, football, $76,269
Jockin, Colleen, assistant athletic trainer, $38,709
Johnson, Benjamin, associate professor, $62,756
Johnson, Marvin, carpenter II, $31,958
Johnson, Melanie, associate professor, $62,159
Johnson, Nathan, assistant coach, men's bb, $49,980
Johnson, Valery, coordinator, career developmnt, $40,096
Jones, Daniel, custodian, $18,880
Jones, Elaine, associate professor, $95,236
Jones, Kenda, office professional II, $23,040
Jones, Michael, parking lot attendant, $21,955
Jones, Philip, instructor, temporary, $41,772
Joyner, Dana, landscape specialist II, $20,280
Jurkowski, Odin, dept chair, professor, $99,706
Kacsor, Michael, athletic field maint coord, $50,000
Kahoe, Richard, associate professor, $55,065
Kaiser, Anthony, assistant professor, library, $58,579
Kalaitzidis, Archimidis, professor, $76,463
Kamal, Mustafa, professor, $107,643
Kane, Bert, carpenter II, $26,001
Karleskint, Douglas, coach, men's basketball, $122,400
Karlin, Angela, director, financial assistance, $73,280
Kelledes, Mary, financial aid counselor, $41,524
Keller, Harry, custodian, $18,880
Kelley, Sandra, outreach coordinator, $38,828
Kelley, Stephen, electrician I, $20,797
Kelly, Mary, associate professor, $62,806
Kelso, Brenda, office professional II, $26,521
Kemp, Arthur, associate professor, $73,405
Kennedy, John, web & media producer, $53,000
Kenney, Judy, transcript analyst, $38,823
Kenney, Russell, bindery technician, $35,954
Kennish, Laura, instructor, temporary, $35,058
Kerr, Julia, help desk support spec II, $31,103
Kerr, Robert, plumber I, $20,197
Kerr, Shantia, associate professor, $62,218
Kesh, Someswar, dept chair, professor, $127,067
Keys, Shelly, accountant I, $27,852
Kichiyev, Orazmuhammet, coord, student & scholar svcs, $33,048
Kidwaro, Fanson, dept chair, professor, $98,865

Kiger, Amy, director, vsap, $58,878
Killian, Virginia, assistant professor, $102,000
Kim, Chong, associate professor, $62,756
Kimble, Carlotta, associate professor, $62,159
King, Charles, custodian, $20,800
Kingsbury, Celia, professor, $77,430
Kippes, Raymond, system coordinator, $42,907
Kirby, William, laboratory technician, $41,631
Klein, Staci, custodian, $21,320
Kleitz, Beau, custodian, $18,720
Klimek, Janice, professor, $121,600
Knight, Carol, design specialist I, $46,308
Knipper, Michael, athletics media relations mgr, $50,000
Koch, Douglas, dept chair, assoc professor, $107,615
Koch, Gina, assistant professor, temporary, $60,000
Koehn, Jo, professor, $121,600
Koepke, Robert, supervisor, night maintenance, $35,700
Krahenbuhl, James, police officer, $31,206
Krahenbuhl, Jennifer, custodian, $18,720
Krause, Mark, life safety technician II, $31,958
Kreiner, David, dept chair, professor, $99,816
Kreisel, Betsy, interim V prov, enroll mgmt, $120,000
Kreke, Toni, controller, $91,800
Krewson, Kimberly, program assistant, $24,420
Krieger, Derrick, system administrator III, $71,400
Krisher, Edward, help desk support spec II, $33,161
Krizanich, Gary, instructor, $46,272
Krzesinski, Shirley, office professional III, $33,179
Kugler, Penny, assistant professor, $54,321
Kuhlman, Katherine, office professional III, $29,866
Kuhlman, Laura, custodian, $18,880
Kuhlmann, Robynn, assistant professor, $53,935
Kunkel, Jennifer, hr generalist, $46,084
Kupersmith, L, assistant professor, $50,374
Lacy, Richard, assistant professor, $49,048
Lafferty, Hayward, development officer, $51,500
LaGree, Mathew, admissions representative, $36,067
Lagud, Alishia, custodian, $18,720
Lagud, Philip, microcomputer/network spec III, $49,164
Lancaster, Amber, assistant professor, temporary, $46,080
Landkamer, Rebecca, senior programmer/analyst, $62,057
Lang, Christopher, admissions representative, $36,067
Lankford, Scott, associate professor, $66,912
Larsen, Jill, office professional II, $25,208
Lashlee, Robert, instructor, temp-es, $35,058
Lawrence, Brittany, student services coordinator, $37,400
Lawrence, Robert, professor, $77,430
Lawson, Joyce, hr generalist, $46,084
Lawson, Ray, supervisor, carpenter shop, $49,536
Laycox, Monty, instructor, temporary, $42,405
LeBlanc, Patricia, office professional I, $19,050
Lee, Jesse, electrician II, $31,958
Lee, John, custodian, $18,720
Lee, Woo-Young, associate professor, $62,159
Leicht, Kathleen, professor, $77,430
Lengfellner, Linda, instructor, temp-es, $42,840
Lenhart, Reid, admissions representative, $37,400
Leon Castro, Helga, international admissions spec, $36,067
Lestage, Bruce, boiler technician II, $29,866
Lewandowski, Joseph, dean, honors col & intl affair, $110,000
Lewis, Edwin, police sergeant, $50,005
Lewis, Julia, instructor, temporary, $35,058
Lewis, Robert, landscape specialist III, $20,197
Likcani, Adriatik, assistant professor, $53,935
Lindley, Daneh, custodian, $18,720
Lindley, Shawn, landscape specialist I, $21,320
Liu, Li, professor, $77,430
Loch, James, professor, $77,835
Loggins, Jodi, office professional III, $27,624
Loman, Karen, assistant professor, $52,681
Long, Brian, instructor/project coordinator, $55,080
Long, John, engineer III, $62,757
Louder, John, professor, $77,835
Love, Kirt, electrician II, $37,524
Love, Mark, associate professor, library, $68,107
Lovercamp, Kyle, associate professor, $62,746
Lubaroff, Scott, interim dept chair, professor, $100,950
Lucas, Dan, coord, breath alcohol programs, $33,000
Ludlam, Allison, office professional II, $28,247

Luechtefeld, Ray, assistant professor, $92,500
Luehrman, Michael, dept chair, professor, $101,304
Lui, Yui Man, assistant professor, temp-es, $63,000
Lund, Jessica, academic advisor, $41,631
Lund, Penny, office professional iv, $34,195
Lundervold, Duane, professor, $77,835
Lyle, Mark, plumber I, $28,037
Lynam, Linda, assistant professor, $54,000
Lyne, Rebecca, office professional III, $28,847
Lyons, Christina, financial aid counselor, $38,709
Ma, Qingxiong, associate professor, $99,492
Mackey, Bradley, manager, grounds, $70,500
Madden, Kimberly, transfer coordinator, $36,067
Madden, Rochelle, assistant professor, $47,544
Maham, Katherine, communications coordinator, $41,633
Mahir, Zaid, instructor, temporary, $41,245
Makara, Michael, assistant professor, $52,681
Malone, John, network analyst III, $62,009
Malta, John, assistant professor, $53,935
Maltas, Carla, associate professor, $62,756
Mandali, Swarna, professor, $82,212
Manley, Michael, mechanic III, $35,291
Mann, Keira, coord, career development, $41,524
Marcum, Kimberly, payroll specialist, $42,919
Marnholtz, Chad, manager harmon computer common, $36,788
Marsh, Hannah, instructor, temporary, $41,245
Marshall, Jacque, landscape specialist II, $21,320
Marshall, John, materials handler, $18,720
Martin, Barbara, professor, $77,835
Martin, Charles, professor, $76,463
Martinez, Richard, assistant professor, $49,065
Mason, Linwood, microcomputer/network spec II, $45,386
Massia, Karla, associate professor, library, $67,576
Massia, Victor, microcomputer/network spec I, $42,840
Mathews, Kathie, manager, copy center, $42,795
Mattson, Sheri, associate professor, $62,756
Matusiak, Randa, assistant professor, $55,000
Maxon, Misty, office professional III, $32,631
May, Amanda, certified flight instructor, $36,067
May, Sherry, custodian, $18,720
Mayeux, Donna, administrative assistant, $42,978
Mayfield, Barbara, dir, accessibility services, $66,265
McCandless, David, associate professor, $66,635
McClung, Roy, assistant coach, football, $68,605
McClure, Frances, system coordinator, $41,524
McClure, Kelly, nurse practitioner-, $66,300
McClure, Todd, assistant professor, temporary, $32,500
McCord, Mary, professor, $103,609
McCormack, David, manager, computer source, $45,839
McCormick, Kathryn, coord,tech enhanced instr desi, $58,422
McCoy, Ann, associate professor, $63,852
McGalliard, William, assistant professor, $61,812
McGathy, Steven, floor crew person, $21,957
McGirl, Stephanie, office professional II, $20,797
McGrath, Dorothy, mgr, tv & community programs, $53,159
McGrath, Heather, coordinator,chst academic advi, $30,594
McGraw, Cathy, instructor, temporary, $35,058
McKee, Rhonda, professor, $77,835
McLaughlin, Phoebe, professor, $77,835
McMenamin, John, assistant coach, football, $70,000
McNair, Chenelle, budget analyst, $47,940
McNeeley, Shara, library assistant iv, $29,044
McNeeley, Terry, instructional design spec I, $46,308
McNeil, Alice, office professional III, $27,621
McPherson, Lacole, assistant professor, temp-es, $50,000
McVey, Kevin, custodian, $21,320
McWilliams, Colene, academic advisor, $36,788
Mears, Bradley, professor, $76,463
Medaris, Linda, associate professor, library, $79,124
Meeks, Crystal, assistant athletic trainer, $49,000
Meisenheimer, Shannon, network analyst II, $53,220
Mends, Albion, instructor, temporary, $35,689
Meng, Ziyuan, assistant professor, temp-es, $63,000
Mercado, M, instructor, $37,848
Mercado-Mendez, Jose, dept chair, professor, $135,507
Merchant, Emily, administrative assistant, $38,823
Merrigan, John, vp, fin & chief oper officer, $151,286
Merrill, Sandra, professor, $77,835
Metcalf, Christina, custodian, $22,269

Metcalf, Daniel, lab technician, animals, $38,821
Metcalf, Erinn, instructor, temporary, $35,058
Metcalf, Matthew, supervisor, custodial, $28,489
Meyer, Amanda, licensed practical nurse-, $26,149
Milburn, Michael, custodian, $18,880
Milburn, Tia, book manager, $31,357
Millen, Christy, program & promotion producer, $41,631
Millen, Roy, production coordinator, $41,631
Miller, Ashley, associate professor, $62,159
Miller, Beth, asst director, residence life, $46,077
Miller, Laura, system coordinator, $49,914
Miller, Lisa, manager, ancillary accounting, $56,100
Miller, Michelle, library assistant iv, $27,620
Miller, Nathaniel, foreperson, custodial, $20,800
Minihan, Jane, assistant professor, $47,001
Mistele, Joy, senior major gifts officer, $66,975
Mitchell, Candice, custodian, $19,240
Mitchell, Christy, office professional iv, $28,681
Mitchell, Rachel, international admissions spec, $36,067
Mitchell, Robert, network analyst I, $46,002
Mitchell, Thomas, associate professor, $62,159
Mittelhauser, Jennifer, instructor, $36,574
Moeder, Brenda, dir, housing ops & facilities, $72,134
Moege, Gary, professor, $77,835
Mohn, Clifford, assistant professor, $55,242
Moley, Pauline, instructor, temporary, $44,000
Mollenkamp, Julie, professor, $77,835
Monetti, Raffaele, asst dean aviation/ex dir ap, $117,300
Montgomery, Gregory, instructor, temporary, $45,844
Montgomery, Nancy, associate professor, $69,326
Moore, Bettie, office professional III, $33,652
Moore, Cynthia, administrative assistant, $39,286
Moore, Dana, instructor, temporary, $35,058
Moore, Joseph, associate professor, $62,159
Moore, Marcella, office professional II, $24,597
Moran, Candice, psychologist-9mth, $40,800
Morris, Michael, custodian, $18,720
Morrison, Patricia, library assistant v, $38,023
Morse, Lisa, accountant I, $26,248
Moses, Emily, development officer, $51,500
Moussavi, Mina, instructor, $41,245
Muin, Michele, office professional III, $28,066
Mullen, James, carpenter I, $26,708
Mulligan, Linda, professor, $78,416
Mullins, Carol, custodian, $22,727
Mullins, Jennifer, instructor, temporary, $35,058
Mullins, Joseph, mgr, marketing application, $47,967
Murphy, Dean, maintenance planner, $47,847
Murphy, Jeffrey, asst director, media relations, $65,077
Mutzebaugh, Nathan, certified flight instructor, $36,067
Nance, Starlynn, assistant professor, $53,935
Napoleone, Tara, academic advisor, $37,400
Neal, Dee, office professional II-10 mth, $20,614
Neal, Jerry, professor, $77,835
Neal, Terry, warehouse clerk, $25,519
Nebeker, Dawn, library assistant iv, $27,621
Needham-Rives, Cheryl, instructor, $48,669
Neill, Rhonda, coordinator, vsap projects, $26,680
Nelson, Eric, associate professor, $98,790
Nelson, Gersham, dean, $139,883
Nelson, Gregory, landscape horticulturist, $35,933
Nestor, Kathleen, manager, mail services, $36,019
Neudigate, Michael, hvac III, $41,894
Newman, Shawna, senior marketing specialist, $41,310
Newsom, Eric, assistant professor, $53,935
Newsome, Kevin, engineer II, $39,484
Nguyen, Phong, associate professor, $62,756
Nicas, Kimberly, event coordinator I, $38,627
Nichols, Delilah, coord, military & veterans svc, $52,989
Nichols, Kristine, database technician III, $69,079
Nicholson, Michael, asst coach, women's basketball, $54,750
Nickens, Nicole, dept chair, professor, $98,524
Nicodemus, Wayne, dispatcher, $21,320
Nicoletti, Brandy, senior programmer/analyst, $59,160
Nielsen, Tracy, custodian, $21,320
Nieman, Terry, aircraft mechanic II - a&p, $55,037
Niemuth, Brian, recovery program coordinator, $42,565
Niesen, Melody, instructor, $35,058
Nikaido, Selene, associate professor, $62,756

Nimmer, Carole, director, testing services, $56,664
Nolan, Brian, manager, custodial services, $57,600
Noland, Deborah, office professional III, $28,006
Noland, Tina, custodian, $18,720
Noon, Steve, hvac I, $20,197
Nordyke, Alan, director, residence/greek life, $72,134
Nordyke, Ann, director, admissions, $72,192
Norris, Chance, supervisor, set-ups, $27,889
Norris, Trevor, microcomputer/network spec I, $42,141
Northup, Curt, mgr, marketing applications, $41,940
Norwood, Allison, assistant professor, $58,782
Norwood, Scott, associate professor, library, $68,107
Nuernberger, Jean, dept chair, assoc professor, $90,707
Nuernberger, Kathryn, assistant professor, $53,935
Oas, Denise, associate professor, $84,700
Obertino, James, associate professor, $68,912
Oetting, John, coordinator, cmms, $34,246
Oglesby, Rachel, office professional III, $24,520
O'Keefe, Karen, office professional II, $30,604
O'Keefe, Michael, coordinator, program services, $53,515
Olivares, Vidal, assistant professor, $61,812
Oller, Anna, professor, $77,430
Ollison, Troy, associate professor, $64,484
Olsen, Michael, assistant director, admissions, $46,161
Olson, Larry, plumber II, $26,601
Oltmanns, Ashton, instructor, temporary, $40,000
Opatrny, Christine, dept chair, professor, $126,946
Orcutt, Vicki, interim dir., central summit, $51,483
O'Reilly Sewell, Ellen, payroll specialist, $31,124
Orji, Cathleen, custodian, $18,720
Orr, Deborah, assistant professor, $54,672
Orr, James, associate professor, $62,806
Othic, Daniel, police sergeant, $55,415
Otten, Kaye, assistant professor, $52,681
Owens, Nicholas, custodian, $18,720
Pagnani, Alexander, assistant professor, $53,935
Palmer, Kyle, professor, $78,219
Pankratz, Caitlin, asst coach, volleyball, $42,907
Papasifakis, Michael, police sergeant, $50,022
Paravastu, Narasimha, assistant professor, $93,500
Park, Ikhyun, assistant professor, temp-es, $55,000
Parsons, AnJanell, office professional III, $27,172
Parvanov, Vencislav, assistant professor, $53,935
Patillo, Robert, custodian, $26,021
Patrick, Brian, manager, field services, $65,089
Patrick-Hammond, Patricia, mail clerk, $25,560
Pattison, Sarah, coordinator, study abroad, $36,067
Pattiz, Brian, research analyst, $44,506
Pauley, Constance, applications manager, $77,028
Paxton, Robert, boiler technician I, $20,197
Peck, Marlys, associate professor, $62,756
Pedersen, Kirk, coach, track & cross country, $61,200
Peirce, Dennis, system coordinator, $42,907
Peirce, Natalie, academic advisor, $39,372
Peltz, Jeffrey, professor, $75,226
Penland, Jerry, assistant professor, $68,914
Peppard, Amanda, custodian, $18,880
Pero, Justin, buyer, $30,161
Perrin, Billie, instructor, temporary, $40,000
Persing, Linda, office professional II, $27,000
Petentler, Charles, dir, international admissions, $63,074
Peterson, Frank, associate professor, $62,756
Petkovsek, Melissa, assistant professor, $55,000
Phillips, Angela, supervisor, receiving, $30,321
Pierce, Raymond, program manager, mms, $53,499
Pine, Janet, office professional III, $33,415
Pinkston, Timothy, asst dir, publishing & promo, $61,816
Pint, Jennifer, academic advisor, $51,633
Piontek, Philip, coach, volleyball, $63,660
Pitman, Kimari, coordinator, work control ctr, $30,285
Ploch, Jason, assistant professor, $54,000
Plummer, Darin, broadcast systems engineer, $51,858
Plummer, Kristen, administrative assistant, $41,624
Plummer, Paul, assistant professor, $64,362
Poe, Ashley, testing coordinator, $30,764
Poe, Brett, library assistant v, $27,890
Poe, Timothy, coach, golf director, $51,370
Polychronis, Paul, director, counseling center, $88,451
Popejoy, Steven, professor, $96,300

Popov, Georgi, associate professor, $74,164
Port, Christopher, coach,women's golf, $52,632
Porter, Joni, operations coordinator, $33,267
Powell-Brown, Dana, professor, $77,835
Price, Stephen, assistant professor, $53,935
Prindle, Jacob, police officer, $31,201
Pritchard, Rachelle, office professional iv, $26,001
Province, Keith, assistant professor, $63,929
Pryde, James, microcomputer/network spec III, $51,618
Pummill, Lea, library assistant v, $32,609
Pumure, Innocent, associate professor, $62,159
Putnam, Janice, academic policy coordinator, $103,240
Queen, Theresa, office professional II, $20,197
Quick, Stephen, director, aircraft maintenance, $68,340
Quigley, An, senior designer, $40,000
Quigley, Travis, data analyst, $41,633
Rabas, Jennifer, assistant director, vsap, $46,068
Racy, Michael, vp, legal, policy & strategy, $168,300
Ragland, Mary, associate professor, $55,810
Ragus, Elmer, instructor, temporary, $37,500
Ramanujan, Sam, professor, $107,643
Ramey, Gale, office professional II, $20,197
Rankin, Mark, professor, $81,313
Raub, Judith, support systems specialist, $36,788
Raveill, Jay, professor, $75,226
Rawashdeh, Mohammad, assistant professor, temp-es, $63,000
Ray, Larry, manager, contracts & cap devel, $65,617
Reddington, Frances, professor, $77,835
Reed, Donna, custodian, $18,720
Regelski, Linda, clinical care manager/lpn, $42,433
Reine, Judi, assistant director, $66,912
Reiter, Larry, director, $81,194
Reith Hutcherson, Amber, instructor, $35,689
Rennels, Arthur, department chair, assoc prof, $82,874
Reynolds, Gretchen, administrative assistant, $39,636
Rhoad, Scott, director, public safety, $80,390
Rhodes, Jessica, caseworker for thrive-10mth, $38,472
Richards, Alexander, assistant professor, $48,960
Richardson, Beverly, office professional II, $27,308
Richardson, Vivian, asst director, archives/museum, $41,631
Ridge, Darrell, floorcrewperson, $22,269
Ridge, Leslie, custodian, $18,880
Riggs, C, professor, $77,430
Riggs, Laura, office professional II, $25,418
Riley, Cheryl, professor/library services, $84,484
Ritter, G, administrative assistant, $36,197
Robbins, Allison, assistant professor, $53,935
Robbins, Brook, custodian, $18,720
Robbins, Lisa, assistant professor, $57,768
Roberts, Patricia, office professional III, $28,066
Robins, Jennifer, professor, $76,463
Robinson, Jeffrey, advancement/legal officer, $75,440
Rodchua, Suhansa, associate professor, $74,533
Rode, Matthew, custodian, $22,269
Roden, Stella, associate professor, $62,756
Rodewald, Teresa, custodian, $18,720
Rodriguez, Susanna, immigration & comm specialist, $24,420
Rogers, Christin, custodian, $18,960
Rogers, Jack, professor, $77,835
Rohr, Stuart, electronic access locksmith, $37,278
Rollins, Alethea, instructor, temp-es, $41,245
Rollins, Ronnie, assistant professor, $62,424
Roquet, Justina, academic advisor, $38,478
Rosario, Patricia, library assistant v, $27,890
Rosichelli, Marco, assistant professor, $53,935
Ross, Nathan, academic advisor, $38,760
Roth, Lexy, office professional II, $22,880
Roundtree, Matthew, microcomputer/network spec I, $42,840
Rowe, Mary, professor, $77,835
Ruleman, Alice, associate professor, library, $67,576
Runyan, Lisa, associate registrar, $50,840
Runyan, William, academic advisor, ce, $38,828
Runyon, William, asst chief flight instructor, $50,592
Russell, Ashley, custodian, $18,720
Russell, Barbara, accountant I, $29,117
Russell, Gene, manager, facility maintenance, $71,952
Russell, Henry, associate professor, $62,159
Rutland, John, associate professor, $62,756
Rutt, Beth, director, campus activities, $66,265

Rutt, Charles, director, university store, $83,352
Saadatmanesh, Majid, instructor, $58,000
Salas, Kristin, academic advisor, $38,760
Sampson, Ardith, accountant I, $27,881
Sarabia, Jonathan, dispatch supervisor, $27,290
Sarkar, Somnath, professor, $77,835
Sartwell, Karin, assistant professor, $51,565
Sattar, Haroon, associate professor, $66,207
Sauer, Aaron, associate professor, $73,835
Sawyer, Michael, associate professor, $62,756
Schawo, Donald, carpenter II, $35,933
Schelp, Suzanne, copyright specialist, $44,574
Schierenbeck, Daniel, dept chair, professor, $104,172
Schieszer, Fredrick, professor, temporary, $82,212
Schiltz, Phillip, boiler technician III, $41,846
Schleer, Paul, materials handler, $18,720
Schlueter, Mark, manager, network services, $83,640
Schmidt, Erich, programmer III, $45,900
Schmidt, Gary, police sergeant, $46,677
Schmidt, Lacey, coordinator, medical office, $29,284
Schmidt, Lisa, instructional design spec I, $52,567
Schmidt, Meghan, asst dir, new student programs, $44,937
Schnakenberg, Kathryn, coord, ctr for bus internships, $28,669
Schnakenberg, Linda, instructor, temporary, $35,058
Schneider, Lorri, custodian, $18,880
Schneider, Robert, custodian, $18,720
Schneider, Shelia, academic coordinator -trio sss, $40,708
Schreimann, Mary, accountant III, $50,412
Schroeder, Aaron, instructor, temporary, $37,000
Schroeder, Shannon, instructor, temporary, $35,802
Schroer, Scott, aircraft mechanic I - a&p, $36,150
Schubert, Michelle, major gifts officer, $52,078
Schueller, Kenneth, director & career counselor, $72,011
Schuetz, Steven, associate professor, $62,219
Schulz, Michelle, event coordinator I, $41,631
Schwepker, Charles, professor, $111,282
Scott, Laura, event coordinator I, $36,788
Scott, Shelby, instructor, $35,689
Seeley, Catherine, coordinator, $47,957
Seigfreid, Travis, inventory control lead, $28,601
Sekelsky, Michael, associate dean, professor, $109,673
Sentgeorge, Aaron, associate professor, $62,159
Sergent, Melinda, office professional II, $24,898
Sesser, George, professor, $77,835
Shaeffer, Betty, office professional II, $33,652
Shaffer, Tony, instructor, $36,573
Shanks, Tammy, communications coordinator, $41,633
Shapiro, Charles, associate professor, $69,843
Sharpe, Melonie, office professional II, $20,197
Shattuck, Cheryl, assistant professor, $51,500
Shattuck, Steven, assistant professor, $46,481
Shaver, Vicki, custodian, $20,280
Shaw, Justin, instructor, $41,245
Sheets, Cody, admissions representative, $36,067
Sherwood, Michael, custodian, $18,720
Shippy, Linda, cas consultant, $52,395
Sholl, Marcia, assistant professor, $51,565
Short, Douglas, assistant professor, $50,604
Shugart, Todd, skyhaven training scheduler, $27,997
Shull, Margaret, director, trio program, $59,262
Shumate, Tamara, academic advisor, $42,267
Shuster, George, landscape specialist III, $20,197
Shy, Terri, office professional III, $27,172
Silk, Jennifer, office professional iv, $27,994
Silvers, Diana, program assistant, $25,219
Simanowitz, Lindsey, instructor, temporary, $35,058
Sims, Adam, custodian, $19,270
Singh, Anshuman, assistant professor, $80,000
Skahan, Cynthia, library assistant v, $29,890
Skinner, Kelly, associate professor, $70,014
Slana, Robert, associate professor, $65,620
Slifer, David, coach, women's basketball, $80,578
Slobaszewski, John, assistant director, housing, $52,825
Smetana, Fredrick, microcomputer/network spec II, $50,499
Smith, Bruce, supervisor, garage, $47,036
Smith, Garrett, foreperson, set-ups, $20,797
Smith, Katherine, video operations coordinator, $36,067
Smith, Lisa, studentfinancial resource asst, $29,994
Smith, Nathan, custodian, $21,749

Smith, Rebecca, instructional specialist-mell, $54,374
Smith, Russell, library assistant v, $31,064
Smith, Scott, professor, $111,282
Smith, Shawn, coordinator, outreach, $44,574
Smith, Tana, graduate admissions specialist, $36,067
Smithson, Lindsey, cfm coord, nurs student serv, $37,200
Sneed, Kevin, asst dir, intramural & rec, $43,789
Soles, Larry, machinist II, $36,440
Sorell, Gregory, custodian, $22,269
Sowa, Michelle, office professional II, $28,033
Spader, Christine, academic advisor, $38,828
Sparks, Georgeanna, custodian, $18,720
Spence, Lagena, program manager research, $54,264
Spencer, Angela, custodian, $18,880
Spencer, James, instructor, temporary, $42,024
Sprenz, Thomas, accountant I, $24,960
Staab, James, professor, $77,835
Staat, Michael, police officer, $34,831
Stambersky, Damian, assistant coach, baseball, $40,000
Stanfield, Donna, custodian, $21,320
Stanford, Kelsey, buyer, $31,103
Stangel, Rhonda, assistant dir, student loans, $51,834
Stanley, Alan, microcomputer/network spec III, $51,618
Stanley, Kelley, custodian, $21,320
Stansberry, Nichole, custodian, $18,720
Stark, Kimberly, professor, $77,835
Steckel, Rebecca, asst director, health services, $58,842
Steinkruger, Jay, assistant professor, $53,935
Stephens, Dell, offset pressperson I, $33,836
Stephens, Joyce, lead accountant, $31,524
Stephens DeJonge, Julie, professor, $77,835
Stevens, Janet, office professional iv, $27,620
Stevens, Virdia, accountant II, $32,726
Stevenson, Susan, associate professor, $62,756
Stewart, Deanna, merchandiser, $25,439
Stewart, Karen, buyer, $31,103
Stewart, Keith, carpenter II, $30,816
Stewart, Kimberly, instructor, $48,506
Still, Jona, pack and ship clerk, $23,525
Stillman, Eugene, asst dir, multiculture affairs, $51,712
Stinson, Jessica, asst dir, res & greek life, $47,610
Stockdale, Jean, office professional II-, $22,504
Stockton, Susan, assistant professor, $53,936
Stokes, Tara, office professional II, $23,474
Stoneking, Shelia, foreperson, custodial, $27,322
Stowell, Randall, hvac II, $36,307
Stowell, Robin, supervisor, custodial, $27,289
Streck, Patrick, associate professor, $53,521
Streich, Gregory, department chair, professor, $100,643
Stringer, Amy, supervisor, custodial, $31,076
Stringer, Heather, office professional III, $26,620
Strohmeyer, H, professor, $77,835
Strohmeyer, Karen, electronic access locksmith, $37,286
Stuart, Parker, instructor, $41,245
Sturtevant, Thomas, facility supervisor, $28,543
Stykel, Eric, assistant professor, $52,681
Summers, Diana, accountant I, $29,117
Sundberg, Sara, professor, $76,463
Svoboda, James, coach, football, $128,775
Swope, Duard, engineer II, $47,738
Swope, Victoria, office professional iv, $31,422
Syler, Glenis, custodian, $18,880
Taft, Joshua, assistant professor, $53,935
Talebreza-May, Jon, assistant professor, $53,935
Tao, Jinhua, professor, $104,272
Taylor, Darlene, applications manager, $86,700
Taylor, James, associate professor, $62,806
Taylor, Jon, associate professor, $62,756
Taylor, Michelle, staff development specialist, $42,919
Tebbenkamp, Bryan, manager, photography/digital, $45,370
Tenbus, Eric, dept chair, professor, $100,863
Tenbus, Kristy, instructor, $35,689
Tenholder, Patricia, landscape specialist II, $19,320
Terrell, Robin, assistant to the provost, $63,454
Tessone, Elisabeth, library assistant v, $28,490
Teter, Sean, strength & conditioning coach, $44,480
Theobald, Lewis, coach-women's soccer/event cor, $61,200
Thomas, Douglas, professor, $77,835
Thomas, Jill, instructor, $35,058

Thomas, Karen, instructor, temporary, $35,658
Thomas, Matthew, professor, $77,835
Thomason, Scott, athletic fac coordinator, $43,000
Thomason, Shonda, academic & compliance coord, $43,701
Thompson, Robin, migrant identification special, $36,788
Tian, Songlin, professor, $104,272
Tian, Tian, assistant professor, $53,935
Tienken, Samantha, asst athletic trainer/instruct, $41,520
Tierney, Kathryn, coord, career devolpment, $40,096
Tilden, Colette, office professional iv, $30,348
Tomlinson, Joshua, coordinator, operations, $48,042
Tracy, Steven, mail clerk, $27,646
Trelow, Cheryl, asst director, human resources, $68,788
Tripp, Courtney, mgr, new media & communication, $55,000
Trobough, Debra, asst manager, accounts payable, $32,220
Trumpold, Julia, instructor, temp-es, $41,245
Turnbow, Deborah, director, sponsored programs, $69,360
Turner, Gregory, professor, $77,835
Turner, Tony, hvac III, $37,244
Turowski, Stanley, system administrator II, $57,613
Tye, Natalie, instructor, temporary, $38,000
Tyler, Noel, electrician II, $31,958
Ulmer, Jeffrey, associate professor, $68,605
Umphrey, Scott, senior programmer/analyst, $58,338
Underwood, Carlotta, hr generalist, $46,084
Underwood, Debbie, coord, financial services, $33,440
Underwood, Jeremy, assistant professor, $52,681
Urban, Lynn, dept chair, assoc prof, $85,766
Valdez, Rebecca, senior testing coordinator, $38,776
Vanderbout, Jennifer, asst vp, resources development, $93,451
VanSchenkhof, Matthew, assistant professor, $65,000
Vaughn, Charles, manager, support services, $45,900
Vaughn, William, professor, $77,835
Via, Traci, dir, alumni & constituent rel, $65,514
Vickers, Lucy, scholarships assistant, $27,912
Voland, Victoria, director, foster-knox, $44,574
von Schlemmer, Mark, assistant professor, $53,935
Voorhees, Frank, professor, $81,163
Vosieva, Dilafruz, instructor, $35,058
Wade, David, instructor, temporary, $41,245
Wagler, Candice, office professional II, $22,880
Wakou, Betty, assistant professor, $61,461
Waldram Cramer, Kelly, asst dir, mktg & promotions, $59,000
Wales, Barbara, professor, library, $84,484
Walker, Kenneth, maintenance worker, $24,139
Walker, Lorin, assistant professor, $92,500
Walker, Stephen, associate professor, library, $76,681
Walker, Tina, office professional III, $27,171
Walker, Vanessa, office professional II, $20,800
Wallace, Donald, professor, $77,835
Walters-Young, Paige, office professional II, $25,560
Wambull, Henry, professor, $76,463
Wang, Jun, instructor, temporary, $63,000
Wang, Lianwen, professor, $89,862
Ward, Diane, business operations manager, $41,524
Warner, Kathy, custodian, $21,320
Warness, Jennifer, custodian, $18,720
Washer, Barton, associate professor, $68,456
Watkins, Larae, instructor, temporary, $53,935
Weaver, Shannon, supervisor, custodial, $28,489
Weed, Rahila, associate professor, $62,756
Wehr, Martha, customer service rep/doc imag, $28,643
Weiland, Jeffrey, hvac II, $26,001
Weinmann, David, laboratory technician, $35,407
Weinmann, Ronda, office professional iv, $26,271
Welhoff, Claudia, help desk support spec II, $34,692
Welker, Joshua, assistant professor, library, $58,579
Wellman, Ashley, assistant professor, $55,000
Wellman, William, enrollment service coordinator, $39,474
Welsh, Catherine, laboratory technician, $42,487
Welsh, Robert, program manager breath alcohol, $60,622
Wenger, Alan, professor, $75,226
Werner, Corey, associate professor, $62,756
West, Krisana, academic advisor, $44,574
Westerhold, Joyce, library assistant v, $41,728
Westphal, Crystal, office professional II, $26,264
Westphal, Kyle, asst coach, football, $52,224
Wharton, Katelyn, instructor, $35,058
Whetzel, Jane, plumber II, $35,965

Whitby, William, shop & equipment room maint, $33,724
White, Becky, office professional iv, $35,481
White, Teresa, studentfinancial resource asst, $25,020
Whitehurst, Tammy, custodian, $21,320
Whiting, Cindy, custodian, $18,720
Wiggins, Andrea, program assistant, $26,223
Wiggins, Janet, instructor, $42,997
Wilbur, Richard, custodian, $24,224
Wildman, Wayne, office professional II, $25,418
Wilkins, J, accountant I, $31,564
Williams, Jeffrey, instructor, temporary, $50,000
Williams, Rodney, accountant III, ancillary, $52,511
Williams, Ruthann, assistant professor, $53,935
Wilson, John, professor, $77,835
Wilson, Melissa, coordinator, ctl, $40,005
Wilson, Scott, professor, $80,212
Wilson, Stephen, professor, $79,047
Wilt, Maureen, professor, $65,907
Winders, Andrew, event services technician, $39,484
Wirthwein, Carl, assistant director, union, $56,885
Wisker, David, applications manager, $62,609
Wong, Daniel, assistant professor, $64,575
Wood, Alice, custodian, $18,880
Woods, Brenda, instructor, $37,906
Woolen, Roderick, procurement specialist II, $41,412
Woolsey, Ronald, professor, $82,041
Woon, Jeanne, psychologist-, $54,995
Wright, Carissa, dispatcher, $21,320
Wright, Linda, senior programmer/analyst, $58,338
Wright, Michael, dean, college of education, $133,326
Wyss, Steven, foreperson, custodial setups, $23,120
Yancey, Amy, student services coordinator, $36,067
Yao, Yuankun, professor, $76,463
Yates, Robert, professor, $77,835
Yearns, S, library assistant v, $32,726
Yelton, Jeffrey, associate professor, $62,756
Yoder, Jefferson, hr generalist, $46,084
Youmans, Paul, certified flight instructor, $36,067
Young, Arthur, associate professor, $101,765
Young, Linda, electronic prepress technician, $32,640
Yousef, Mahmoud, professor, $104,272
Yue, Songqing, instructor, temporary, $55,000
Yue, Xiaodong, dept chair, professor, $134,718
Zabriskie, Alan, assistant professor, $53,935
Zelazek, John, assistant dean, professor, $104,132
Zellers, Sarah, associate professor, $62,756
Zey, John, professor, $86,197
Zey, Sarah, coord, student & scholar svcs, $27,289
Zhou, Chen, assistant professor, $53,935
Zimmer, Beverly, assistant professor, $56,355
Zupnick, Matthew, professor, $77,835

Northwest Missouri State University

Maryville 64468

Jasinski, John, president, $258,315
Abarr-Chandler, Leslie, coord: student orien/trans aff, $40,887
Abington, Casey, assistant professor, $76,398
Adam, Peter, assistant professor, $56,584
Adamson, Ronald, supply clerk/material handler, $32,668
Adkins, Joni, assistant professor, $75,625
Adwell, Michael, hardscape groundskeeper, $33,063
Akins, Robyn, instructor, $48,451
Alexander, Kristina, associate professor, $65,236
Allen, Jamison, assistant professor, $57,234
Allen, Michelle, lab technician, $35,499
Allen, Ricky, maintenance zone supervisor, $55,691
Allen, Stephanie, custodian, $25,072
Anderson, Ryan, softball coach/instructor, $50,684
Andrews, Jeffrey, pellet mill & recycling oper, $31,955
Antisdel, Aaron, custodian, $25,072
Archer, Robert, sportsfield groundskeeper, $27,090
Ashbaugh, Raymond, dairy herdsperson, $41,126
Asher, Kimberly, custodian, $25,072
Atkins, David, groundskeeper, $27,090
Badami, Charles, instructor, $47,116
Baker, Jill, instructor, $46,118

Baker, Lauren, secretary, $30,177
Baker, Matthew, vice president student affairs, $123,306
Baldwin, Rebecca, director/nwrpdc, $81,201
Bandi, Ajay, assistant professor, $71,196
Barber, Ashley, asst dir of admissions-mktg, $35,390
Barmann, Terrence, director of northwest-kc, $122,000
Barnett, Jerrold, professor, $86,759
Barr, Cathleen, secretary, $30,177
Barr, Rodney, senior instructor/chair, $55,948
Baudino, Frank, head librarian/asst professor, $57,684
Baumli, Jeremy, web application developer, $54,630
Beck, Shandy, multimedia & inst design spec, $42,926
Becker, Jameson, project custodian, $25,072
Bell, Richard, assistant professor, $71,196
Bellamy, Michael, professor, $74,640
Bennett, Paul, complex director, $27,939
Benson, Christine, professor/chair, $74,983
Benson, Joel, professor, $79,262
Beskid, Philip, instructor, $41,630
Best, Julie, academic advisor, $37,482
Biegelson, Daniel, instructor, $41,685
Bilbo, Katheryn, assistant professor, $54,224
Binette, Kori, instructor, $39,656
Binkley-Hopper, Meghaan, transcript specialist, $30,445
Birkenholz, Cheryl, pc specialist/help desk, $45,708
Bishop, Lisa, senior instructor, $56,577
Black, Richard, associate professor, $55,582
Blackford, Benjamin, assistant professor, $85,249
Blackman, Kenneth, admissions representative, $35,466
Bliley, Barbara, custodian, $25,072
Bliley, Steven, bricklayer tuck-pointer, $34,332
Boesdorfer, Albert, assoc director of maintenance, $86,105
Bond, Nola, vp of human resources, $113,098
Bond, Stancy, instructor, $41,685
Bostwick, Chad, linebackers coach/instr, $68,132
Bottiger, Shelby, admissions specialist, $33,840
Bowles, Brooke, acct clerk/scholarship coord, $38,242
Bowlin, Kelsey, instructor, $41,754
Bowman, Kirt, custodian, $25,072
Bracken, Raymond, custodian, $25,072
Bradley, Gina, university event coordinator, $41,268
Bradley, Jeff, senior instructor, $49,770
Bradshaw, Kathy, data specialist, $33,219
Brady, Brandy, info librarian/eresources mgmt, $53,100
Brady, Troy, general maintenance III, $49,601
Breckenridge, Martha, assistant professor, $51,162
Brown, Venus, membership dev/events coord, $40,320
Bryant, Steven, dir/multicultural stu success, $56,065
Bryant, Robert Jr, director of enrollment, $52,931
Buck, Nicole, assistant athletic trainer, $36,605
Bucy, Jack, carpenter/maintenance, $37,575
Bucy, Jennifer, financial analyst, $58,139
Bucy, Nikki, asst director/auxiliary serv, $47,357
Bulen, Casey, residential counselor, $25,766
Burchfield, Kendall, custodian, $25,072
Burnsides, Teresa, counselor/verification coord, $34,971
Butler, Loren, associate professor, $58,724
Byers, Angela, secretary, $30,177
Calfee, Kendel, pc technician, $42,707
Campbell, Alisha, assistant professor, $55,475
Campbell, James, assistant professor, $55,475
Capps, Lucinda, mail/copy center supervisor, $38,787
Carlyle, Timothy, director, senior unix admin, $78,785
Carmichael, LeAnne, lpn, $27,360
Carmichael, Terri, facility services coordinator, $47,205
Carr, John, admissions representative, $35,390
Carrick, Stacy, vice president of finance, $174,912
Carter, Jeremy, programmer, $52,676
Casey, Kimberly, assistant professor, $53,131
Ceperley, Michael, lieutenant, $61,200
Chakraborty, Himadri, associate professor, $60,773
Chandler, Wayne, associate professor, $56,279
Chappell, Crista, registrar services specialist, $29,448
Chappell, Steven, instructor, $50,712
Chavala, Girija, dir, administrative computing, $87,877
Chesnut, Leslie, groundskeeper, $32,288
Chesnut, Melissa, secretary, $29,790
Chloupek, Brett, assistant professor, $57,145
Chor, Steven, director/technician, telecomm, $70,445

Christensen, Summer, assistant professor, $55,523
Christian, Hannah, info librarian/digital lrning, $48,320
Clark, Judy, assistant professor, $75,625
Clayton, Brandon, secondary coach/instructor, $58,102
Clayton, Lathan, residential counselor, $25,090
Clements, Mark, assoc ad, internal operations, $54,012
Clements, Matthew, driver, $35,100
Cline, Keely, assistant professor, $54,124
Cline, Mary, custodian, $25,072
Cluff, Jerry, boiler operator, $42,226
Coalter, Terry, associate professor, $85,250
Cochenour, Jaclyn, asst dir ub/academic coord, $40,429
Coffey, John, news & sports prodcr/news dir, $49,590
Cole, Samantha, scholarship and outreach spec, $31,054
Coleman, Elizabeth, custodian, $25,072
Coleman, Paul, custodian/gym floor tech, $27,716
Collier, Benny, associate professor, $77,963
Collins, Jaime, office manager, $35,921
Collins, Mary, controller, $109,504
Collins, Tricia, receptionist/secretary, $30,177
Colvin, Lorraine, proj asst:prof learn community, $57,654
Colwell, Jason, trans fleet/sm engine mechanic, $36,225
Cordell, Deanne, data management coordinator, $36,465
Corson, Mark, professor/chair, $73,931
Craft, Mitzi, dir, corp & found relations, $79,007
Crater, Lisa, office manager, $35,921
Crawford, Ellen, secretary, $30,177
Creason, Michael, equipment/laundry manager, $31,652
Creason, Sarah, instructor, $44,458
Cross, Kathleen, custodian, $25,072
Cruz, Alex, data analyst, $39,289
Cullin, Amanda, communications & project coord, $44,856
Curphey, Avis, secretary, $30,177
Curry, Deborah, custodian, $25,072
Daggs, Joy, assistant professor, $51,281
Dakan, Linda, invoice/accounts payable clerk, $32,732
Davis, Ashley, assistant professor, $50,837
Davis, Kurt, hardscape groundskeeper, $33,718
Davis, Meghan, asst director/residential life, $47,392
Davis, Nathan, associate ad, administration, $38,542
Davis, Neal, director, student achievement, $45,487
Davison, Jerol, carpenter/maintenance, $42,508
Davison, Linda, counselor ub math/science, $36,286
Dennis, Cathy, instructor, $43,057
Devers, Bruce, hardscape groundskeeper, $33,064
Dewhirst, Robert, professor, $85,972
Dickey, Eric, assistant professor, $50,985
Dieringer, Gregg, professor, $77,101
Dimmitt, Elizabeth, instructor, $47,507
Dino, Deirdre, specialist, student involvemen, $35,921
Dixon, Kenneth, custodian, $25,072
Dorrel, Adam, head football coach/instructor, $143,947
Dorrel, Bryan, instructor, $46,269
Douglass, Monai, admissions representative, $35,390
Drake, Michelle, human resources generalist, $42,300
Drennen, Christopher, senior systems administrator, $59,087
Drews, Patricia, professor, $67,439
Duckworth, Omer, boiler operator, $42,003
Duff, Sara, coordinator, technical service, $59,784
Duffy, Zylpha, custodian, $25,072
Duis, Amber, graduate records specialist, $33,840
Dunnell, Rebecca, professor, $67,260
Durbin, Lori, senior instructor, $44,365
Durbin, Michael, complex director, $27,580
Ebrecht, John, athletic grounds supervisor, $42,232
Eckrich, Tara, transfer specialist, $36,054
Edmonds, Carole, associate professor, $54,364
Edwards, Carla, professor, $77,925
Ehlers, Donald, instructor, $47,507
Eiswert, James, associate professor, $66,371
Elston, Mary, assistant professor, $51,663
Erickson, Michelle, instructor, $55,824
Etherton, Kayla, academic advisor, $37,482
Euler, Russell, professor, $87,338
Evans, Rebecca, regional director, $70,910
Falke, Kathryn, academic success coach, $41,278
Farlow, Nancy, hm faculty: kindergarten, $46,720
Farnan, Clinton, custodian, $25,072
Farnan, Shantel, instructor, $43,706

Faustlin, Mellanie, custodian, $25,072
Feick, Terra, coordinator for access serv, $44,960
Ferguson, Jeffrey, associate professor, $70,215
Fey, Marshall, asst ad for media relations, $46,105
Field, Richard, associate professor, $60,360
Fink, Kurtis, associate professor, $67,882
Fisher, Andrew, director counseling, $46,545
Fisher, Brooke, executive secretary, $43,306
Flohr, Charles, offensive coordinator/instr, $76,203
Fodor, Laszlo, boiler operator, $42,003
Foley, Nancy, associate professor, $67,152
Foose, Alice, associate professor, $57,220
Foot, Jeffrey, dir international affairs/esl, $69,520
Ford, Elyssa, assistant professor, $53,204
Francis, Alisha, associate professor, $57,850
Francis, Sandra, p-t assistant loan coordinator, $17,235
Freeman, Virgil, associate professor, $65,236
Freemyer, Bryan, groundskeeper, $27,090
French, Kelli, executive secretary, $43,306
Fridell, Max, associate professor, $65,236
From, Karen, instructor, $45,731
Frueh, Judy, clinical supv/nurse practition, $61,545
Fulton, Robert, beef production technician, $38,060
Galbreath, Leslie, dean, academic & library serv, $105,443
Gallaher, John, associate professor, $56,279
Gallaher, Robin, assistant professor, $48,173
Gangala, Mayur, residential counselor, $25,090
Gard, Jessi, secretary, $30,177
Geller, Joseph, temperature control, $38,543
George, Garland, cataloging specialist, $32,630
George, Paul, custodian, $25,072
Gibson, Christopher, professor, $71,141
Gibson, Edward, coord/mlticultural stu success, $35,727
Giesken, Patricia, dispatcher, $27,579
Gilbert, Laura, admin specialist to president, $46,223
Gilley, Dawn, assistant professor, $59,209
Gordon, William, assistant professor/chair, $60,257
Goudge, Theodore, associate professor, $65,306
Grasty, Robert, pc specialist/notebooks, $50,776
Graves, Christopher, assistant professor, $51,162
Greeley, Ashley, bursar, $61,809
Green, Danton, sportsfield groundskeeper, $27,090
Green, Clarence Jr, chief of university police, $96,549
Greenlee, Dustin, pc technician, $37,543
Gregory, Jennee, proj asst: cont education, $58,106
Groomer, Jared, carpenter/cabinet maker, $39,813
Grow, Tamera, associate director/admissions, $52,051
Grudzinski, Michael, distance learning manager, $66,017
Guess, Linda, medical office manager, $35,921
Gustafson, Jon, dir of operations, moera/instr, $54,631
Gustafson, Teresa, development officer, $66,409
Guthrie, Kris, executive secretary, $43,306
Gutzmer, Sherry, custodian, $25,072
Gutzmer, Zach, custodial supervisor, $43,785
Haberyan, Kurt, professor, $79,285
Hackett, Nikki, office manager, $35,921
Haddock, Gregory, vice provost/dean grad school, $119,976
Haile, Brian, associate professor, $62,184
Hannigan, Cathie, office manager, $35,921
Hardee, Nancy, esl teacher, $45,021
Hardee, Tom, senior instructor, $43,147
Harderson, Joel, pc technician, $41,625
Hargrave, Diane, executive secretary, $43,306
Harper, Becky, custodian, $25,072
Harris, Rodney, director/station manager, $65,853
Hart, Jay, steamfitter/plumber, $35,638
Hart, Julia, asst director of library servs, $68,170
Haughey, Brandy, hm faculty: 2nd grade, $42,859
Haughey, Joseph, assistant professor, $50,837
Hawkins, Kevin, officer, $34,489
Hawley, Douglas, assistant professor, $71,196
Hefner, Andrew, custodian, $25,072
Hefner, James, custodian, $25,072
Heidendal, Egon, senior data analyst, $52,385
Heintz, Christina, instructor, $41,905
Heitman, Diana, associate bursar, $47,354
Heitman, Shannon, student payroll manager, $40,935
Heller, Ronald, material handler, $38,308
Hendrix, Ashlee, graphic designer, $39,568

Henggeler, Ashley, international affairs coord, $37,800
Henggeler, Susan, accounting manager, $50,283
Hernandez, John, coordinator, residential life, $35,635
Hesse, Brian, professor, $74,524
Hiatt, Rochelle, associate professor/chair, $59,007
Hicks, Jason, steamfitter/plumber, $40,675
Hill, Annette, service center supervisor, $39,328
Hilsabeck, David, custodian, $25,072
Hilsabeck, Grady, groundskeeper, $27,090
Hinson, James, director of student recreation, $52,828
Hobbs, Michael, professor/chair, $71,776
Hoffmann, Allison, senior instructor, $58,184
Hoffmann, Kori, director/student conduct & dev, $53,709
Hoffmeier, Justin, assistant professor, $55,384
Hoilett, Nigel, assistant professor, $56,412
Holley, Patricia, programming director, $49,590
Hollingsworth, Lynda, assistant professor, $50,751
Holtman, Keisha, admissions specialist, $33,840
Hoover, Alferd, floor care technician, $27,716
Hopkins, Lori, assoc ad, compliance/swa, $57,415
Hornickel, Mark, manager of communication, $60,780
Howell, Kathy, library circulation specialist, $31,606
Hoyt, Kyle, officer, $33,313
Hoza, Tracy, soccer coach/instructor, $45,221
Hull, Brooke, human resources specialist, $37,449
Hull, Michael, assistant professor, $55,953
Hull, Philip, international recruiter, $55,715
Hullinger, Kimberly, certification officer, $47,113
Hung, Ming-Chih, associate professor, $60,261
Hunt, Denise, custodian, $25,072
Husz, James, farm manager, $44,540
Immel, Patrick, associate professor, $56,713
Immel, Theresa, executive secretary, $43,306
Ingels, Marilyn, custodian, $25,072
Islam, Rafiq, professor, $77,799
Jackson, Jane, proj asst:schl impvmt & sp edu, $51,070
Jackson, Michael, senior systems administrator, $72,364
Jacobson, Cris, instructor, $43,184
Jerome, David, assistant professor, $52,491
Joachim, Bayo, professor, $75,060
Johnson, Aaron, associate professor, $59,756
Johnson, Carolyn, info librarian/asst professor, $61,995
Johnson, David, instructor, $62,409
Johnson, Jeremiah, driver, $35,100
Johnson, Kenna, director, talent dvlpment ctr, $62,372
Johnson, Matthew, senior instructor, $48,159
Johnson, Michael, vp university advancement, $142,463
Jones, Brenda, senior instructor, $56,577
Jones, Rego, instructor, $52,623
Jorandby, Stephanie, assistant professor, $54,224
Katsion, John, assistant professor, $52,614
Kegode, Redempta, p-t chemical safety manager, $37,203
Kelly, Alfred, professor, $102,262
Kelsey, Melinda, graphic designer, $40,135
Kemper, Ruth, risk mgmt/insurance specialist, $56,000
Kenkel, Cindy, assistant professor, $67,858
Kibler, Jacqueline, assistant professor, $54,124
Kiene, David, assistant professor, $58,068
King, Laura, hm faculty: 1st grade, $43,416
Kinman, Carma, executive secretary, $43,306
Kline, Heather, academic services assistant, $39,559
Kline, Travis, admissions representative, $35,466
Knowles, Mary, records specialist, $36,657
Kobbe, Lacy, customer support coordinator, $35,921
Kobialka, Gayla, assistant professor, $52,243
Koch, Courtney, counselor, $36,468
Konstantopoulos, Helen, esl teacher, $45,021
Korell, Debra, proj asst curr & instr, $53,044
Kramer, Ernest, professor, $75,548
Kreizinger, Joseph, associate professor/chair, $56,713
Kwon, Jamie, residential counselor, $26,153
Laber, Philip, professor, $81,281
Lacy, Jacqueline, instructor, $50,042
Lager, Robert, pellet mill operator/driver, $33,170
Lainhart, Colleen, office manager, $35,921
Lamer, Fred, assistant professor, $54,367
Lamer, Jacqueline, senior instructor, $48,460
Landhuis, Brad, asst dir/student advisement, $42,338
Lanier, Brian, professor, $67,260

Larson, James, associate professor, $68,686
Lawrence, Rebecca, ada/504 and title ix coord, $54,000
Leach-Steffens, Lauren, associate professor, $61,786
Lee, Lawrence, dir bus dvlp & tenant relation, $117,169
Lesley, Rhonda, director, pdc, $70,638
Lewis, Brenda, senior instructor, $43,147
Li, Na, assistant professor, $73,002
Lim, Chi Lo, associate professor, $85,250
Linville, Diana, instructor, $59,489
Little, Elizabeth, complex director, $27,580
Loe, Darin, baseball coach/instructor, $53,427
Loghry, Jacquelyn, asst dir/learning serv coord, $43,112
Long, Anne, human resources generalist, $42,300
Long, Justin, custodian, $25,072
Long, Laurie, development officer, $58,582
Long, Terry, professor, $69,566
Loomis, Jeffrey, professor, $76,290
Lorek, Scott, head cc & track coach/instr, $58,987
Lovett, Ann, executive secretary, $43,306
Ludwig, Stephen, assistant professor/chair, $90,840
Lugovskyy, Josephine, assistant professor, $72,553
Luke, Joyce, asst coord/field experience, $34,910
Lyons, Debra, proj asst: curr & instr pbs, $49,637
Machovsky, Kathryn, web content specialist, $44,145
Machovsky, Robert, dir alumni rel & annual giving, $66,833
Malkawi, Ahmed, professor, $76,274
Malm, Cheryl, associate professor, $65,180
Maly, Anthony, coord, student involvement, $36,895
Mandrick, Michael, pc specialist, $44,080
Mannasmith, Larry, admissions representative, $35,466
Mannasmith, Rhonda, administrative assistant, $43,306
Manning, Rick, custodian, $26,458
Manning, Susan, custodian, $25,072
Mardis, Lori, info librarian/asst professor, $58,544
Marta, Janet, professor, $96,656
Martin, Ann, director/purchasing, $83,156
Martin, Marsha, general project assistant, $41,340
Martin, Rolland, lib circulation & maint spec, $31,606
Martinez, Kristina, officer, $34,489
Mason, Andrea, hm faculty: 3rd/4th grades, $44,068
Mason, Elizabeth, office manager, $26,595
Mason, Samuel, underwriting sales associate, $32,441
Matheny, Salena, staff nurse/rn, $34,124
Mattock, Michael, counselor, $53,191
Mavity, Mary, faculty tech support asst/sec, $35,921
Mayes, Cynthia, admissions spec/intn'l spec, $33,840
Mayfield, Charles, director/financial assistance, $72,098
McAdams, Catherine, hm faculty: music/instructor, $33,874
McAliley, Lee, assistant professor, $55,475
McBride, Brooke, director, student involvement, $55,715
McBride, Michael, coord of peu assessment/ir, $55,715
McClintock, David, electrician, $37,590
McCollum, Benjamin, men's basketball coach/inst, $121,560
McCrary, Marla, office manager, $35,921
McCulloch, Carol, accounts receivable clerk, $32,003
McGhee, Jay, assistant professor, $55,475
McIntosh, LeDonna, hm faculty: part-time art, $21,273
McLain, Paula, sr human resources generalist, $54,551
McMahon, Kevin, driver, $37,608
McMahon, Thomas, custodian, $25,072
McNeese, Gina, instructor, $46,825
Meneely, Justin, maintenance zone supervisor, $50,328
Meneely, Rebecca, circu spec/inter loan & resv, $31,012
Merrill, David, sergeant, $48,600
Meyer, Alisa, office manager, $35,921
Meyer, Austin, assoc m-basketball coach/instr, $45,585
Meziani, Mohammed, associate professor, $58,259
Miller, Kyle, officer, $34,489
Miller, Merlin, dir of academic computing, $79,388
Miller, Michael, coordinator, residential life, $35,635
Mincy, Melissa, counselor/scholarhip coord, $34,971
Mollus, Doni, senior instructor, $59,108
Money, Karen, custodian, $25,072
Monk, Michael, custodian, $25,072
Montross, Gary, floor care technician, $27,716
Morin, Mark, custodian/gym floor tech, $27,716
Morley, Del, director/financial assistance, $72,098
Moser, Coy, custodian, $25,072
Moser, Robin, project custodian, $25,072

Mottaleb, Mohammad, analytical chemist, $57,030
Mottet, Timothy, provost, $192,470
Mozier, Steven, custodian, $25,072
Muhsam, Armin, professor, $69,616
Mullins, Callie, assistant professor, $57,823
Mulvaney, Debbie, custodian, $25,072
Murphy, Connie, secretary, $30,177
Murphy, Leslie, advertising/underwriting mgr, $44,750
Murphy, Tammy, custodian, $25,072
Murphy, William, tv/video engineer, $55,375
Musunuru, Naveen, assistant professor, $57,823
Myllykangas, Susan, associate professor, $59,653
Nally, Amy, asst dir, student involvement, $45,596
Neustadter, Roger, professor, $83,600
Newham, Amber, service response coordinator, $35,921
Nicholson, Cheryl, buyer ii, $40,742
Nickerson, Jeffrey, senior instructor, $58,184
Nickerson, Lisa, academic scheduling specialist, $30,771
Nickerson, Sue, executive secretary, $43,306
Nielson, Scott, assoc ad for external affairs, $58,582
Norman, Amber, residential counselor, $25,766
Northup, Michael, instructor, $55,824
Nuttall, Susanne, instructor, $49,497
Offutt, Samuel, instructor, $44,494
Olasz, Ildiko, assistant professor, $51,383
Olson, Anthony, professor, $68,176
Osborn, Joel, rec coach/recruit coord/instr, $58,102
Owens, Cindy, custodian, $25,072
Palacios Perez, Jose, lecturer, $38,007
Parker, Beth, custodian, $25,072
Parsons, William, grants coordinator, $60,664
Patet, Pradnya, assistant professor, $55,573
Penniston, Mary, director, institution research, $74,086
Perkins, Darren, chief engineer, $54,987
Peter, Rachel, staff nurse/rn, $33,619
Peters, Nicholas, assistant athletic trainer, $39,685
Peterson, Andy, assistant athletics director, $35,823
Peterson, Emily, asst cc & track coach/instr, $41,770
Phillips, Sheila, assistant professor, $52,243
Piel, Dixie, associate registrar, $49,497
Pitts, Jennifer, office manager, $35,921
Piveral, Joyce, dean of college edu & hum serv, $123,548
Pope, John, associate professor, $64,301
Poppa, Kirby, custodian, $25,072
Porterfield, Kurt, custodian, $25,072
Pratt-Hyatt, Jennifer, assistant professor, $55,940
Pregeant, Ashley, academic success coach, $41,278
Pulley, Alyssa, senior buyer, $44,441
Puriel-Foot, Jeaneth, research schlr/coord stdy abrd, $46,012
Quinlin, Joseph, strength & conditioning coach, $64,216
Quinlin, Kelly, head athletic trainer/instruct, $56,080
Raasch, Lisa, custodian, $25,072
Rabel Riley, Shelley, assistant professor, $55,953
Rand, Evan, asst dir, wellness services, $53,801
Rathje, Lonelle, exec dir, devpmnt/camp coord, $92,538
Rector, Joshua, hall director, $24,759
Redden, Christopher, hardscape & recycling supv, $47,486
Redden, Walter, student union event coord, $33,571
Redig, Robert, maintenance zone supervisor, $52,647
Redmond, Christopher, general maintenance i, $28,841
Redmond, Deborah, custodial supervisor, $44,291
Redmond, Steven, elevator tech/electrician, $47,210
Reno, Reginald, steamfitter/plumber, $41,667
Reusser, Janet, professor, $76,070
Rich, Gregory, assistant professor, $58,068
Richards, Mary, associate professor, $63,655
Richardson, David, associate professor, $61,987
Richardson, William, professor, $63,385
Riley, Tanya, coordinator of counseling, $34,878
Ringgold, Lola, custodian, $25,072
Roberts, Margie, collections supervisor, $40,280
Roberts, Rosemary, custodial supervisor, $44,291
Robinson, Stuart, assistant professor, $50,459
Robinson-Smith, Melanie, alumni & donor relations spec, $40,419
Rodrick, David, custodian, $25,072
Rogers, Michael, assistant professor, $78,012
Rolfes, Luke, instructor, $39,656
Romig, Kevin, assistant professor, $57,145
Rosewell, Mark, tennis coach/instructor, $64,671

Ross, Theophil, professor, $82,106
Roush, Marcy, senior instructor, $45,870
Ruehter, LaTessa, secretary, $29,790
Ruehter, Lisa, administrative assistant, $32,666
Rumpf, Cindy, p-t project asst: curr & instr, $25,705
Runde, Diane, it mgr oper, finance & hr, $67,746
Runyon, Darla, director, cite, $77,100
Rush, Douglas, driver, $38,406
Russell, Doug, assistant professor, $70,487
Ryan, Brenda, senior instructor, $43,147
Ryan, Kathleen, secretary, $30,177
Rytting, Jennifer, associate professor, $53,478
Sack, Jason, p-t cheer coach/facilities, $19,372
Sadek, Jawad, professor, $76,484
Salinas, April, mail/copy center clerk, $25,674
Samudzi, Cleopas, dean of academy, $108,000
Scadden, Sonny, capital program superintendent, $59,057
Scarbrough, Cindy, leet center faculty: director, $42,999
Schaffer, Karen, assistant professor, $56,584
Scheel, Jeremiah, asst women bsktball coach/inst, $40,964
Schenkel, Beverly, dean of enrollment management, $136,962
Schieber, Jennifer, custodian, $25,072
Schieber, Lawrence, floor care technician, $27,716
Schieber, Matthew, instructor, $59,489
Schneider, Joan, director/career services, $60,656
Schwienebart, Catherine, hm faculty: p-t teacher assoc, $37,076
Scott, James, driver, $37,221
Sebastian, Margaret, student development specialist, $33,100
Seeger, Victoria, assistant professor, $54,631
Seipel, Sandy, hm faculty: principal/instruct, $55,948
Shackelford, Lawrence, temperature control, $38,543
Shadinger, David, assistant professor, $51,859
Shannon, Pamela, associate professor, $55,936
Shaw, John, associate professor, $61,987
Sheil, Meghan, lc: early child teacher, $41,950
Shell, Cara, p-t school nurse, $19,377
Shepherd, Mary, professor, $71,198
Sherry, Donella, proj asst: curr & instr, $48,325
Sherry, Megan, transportation coordinator, $35,921
Shi, Tiebing, assistant professor, $94,534
Shields, Mary, hm faculty: resource teacher, $44,068
Shields, Scott, coordinator, residential life, $39,056
Shin, Kyoung-Ho, associate professor, $58,592
Sickman, David, custodian, $25,072
Sigman, Ronda, executive secretary, $43,306
Skoglund, Kirk, academic engagement coord, $41,375
Slagle, Lori, career services specialist, $31,791
Smith, Corey, sergeant, $48,600
Smith, Daniel, assistant professor, $51,236
Smith, Daniel, landscape zone supervisor, $44,500
Smith, Geoff, custodian, $25,072
Smith, Michael, women's basketball coach/inst, $78,489
Smith, Susan, administrative secretary, $31,148
Smith, Susan, instructor, $43,799
Snodderley, Judy, collections clerk, $32,847
Sonnenmoser, Richard, assistant professor, $51,383
Sons, Richard, officer, $33,812
Spainhower, Miles, director/auxiliary services, $81,017
Spears, Kathleen, assistant professor, $56,584
Spire, George, boiler operator, $42,226
Sportsman, John, steamfitter/plumber, $40,760
Spradling, Carol, associate professor, $79,512
Stafford, Elizabeth, residential counselor, $26,153
Standiford, Charles, boiler operator, $42,003
Stanley, Brandon, vp marketing & communication, $94,310
Staples, Jeremy, officer, $33,313
Steffens, Shirley, associate professor, $67,234
Stegall, Michael, boiler operator, $42,226
Stehlik, Lauren, coord, student involvement, $35,591
Steiner, Lori, fin offcr/exec dir adv servs, $87,119
Steiner, Michael, dean of college arts/science, $125,264
Steinman, Billy, hall director, $24,759
Steinman, Steven, complex director, $27,939
Steinmeyer, Michele, office manager, $35,921
Stephens, Diana, coord of it oper/enrollmt mgmt, $50,918
Sterling, Linda, associate professor, $56,271
Stobbe, Lisa, instructor, $39,985
Stokes, Stacey, career dev crd, emplr relation, $39,953
Stokes, Travis, mgr, landscape/sustainability, $58,332

Stone, Roger, custodian, $25,072
Stoner, Marjorie, loan coordinator/va rep, $41,436
Strauch, Jodell, assistant professor, $54,878
Strelluf, Christopher, assistant professor, $48,173
Strickland, Kathryn, asst professor/dir, athl bands, $50,458
Striplin, John, central receiving supervisor, $40,591
Stroburg, Carey, ag research technician, $38,599
Strueby, Beth, custodian, $25,072
Struthers, Lauren, proj asst: school improvement, $49,637
Sudhoff, Douglas, assistant professor, $54,878
Summa, Anna, medical secretary/receptionist, $30,177
Summa, Bernie, telecomm technician, $44,955
Sutton, Stephen, senior development officer, $68,404
Swafford, Brian, instructor, $40,890
Swalley, Rick, groundskeeper, $26,166
Swaney, Derick, pellet operator, $33,084
Sybert, Curtis, temperature control, $39,815
Symonds, Matthew, associate professor/chair, $57,681
Tapps, Tyler, assistant professor, $52,676
Tasi, Csilla, instructor, $41,905
Tavorn, Cassandra, trio director, $61,935
Taylor, Boyd, health educator, $45,585
Taylor, Michael, custodian, $25,072
Ternus, Dana, instructor, $44,212
Thompson, Patricia, assistant professor, $58,106
Thornsberry, Gretchen, assistant professor, $56,584
Thornsberry, Jeffry, associate professor, $59,931
Throener, Jody, residential life specialist, $34,829
Tiffany, John, transportation fleet mechanic, $41,265
Tjeersdma, Melvin, director of athletics, $132,354
Tobin, Malinda, instructor, $55,824
Tobin, Teri, textbook manager, $39,813
Todd, Kimberly, user consultant, $46,911
Toomey, Deborah, assistant professor, $94,534
Toomey, Richard, associate professor, $59,390
Town, Stephen, professor, $78,478
Trump, Pele, secretary, $30,177
Trussell, Matthew, sbtdc center director, $49,985
Tso, Kwok-Pong, lecturer, $41,343
Untiedt, Brenda, alumni rel/adv comm specialist, $48,839
Vandike, Gregory, swine production technician, $38,940
Vaught, Michelle, lc: early child teacher, $37,481
Veasey, Michele, instructor, $47,507
Veasey, Robert, dir, fitness & informal rec, $52,828
Verbick, Tabatha, user consultant, $47,185
Vest, Jessica, executive secretary/archivist, $43,306
Vetter, Rheba, associate professor, $58,724
Viau, John, sustainability coordinator, $43,765
Viau, Rose, director/residential life, $65,700
Vlieger, David, assistant professor, $52,679
Vogel, Karen, admissions specialist, $33,840
Vogel, Terri, registrar, $72,000
Von Behren, Belinda, proj asst: curr & instr pbs, $49,497
Von Behren, Suzanne, staff nurse/rn, $34,807
Von Holzen, Roger, vp information technology, $114,753
Voss, Robert, assistant professor, $50,838
Wake, Shawn, performance facilities manager, $42,541
Waldeier, Jeremy, associate director/admissions, $52,051
Walk, Barbara, payroll manager, $43,687
Walk, Scott, health/safety manager, $55,383
Walker, James, professor, $96,656
Walker, Matthew, assistant professor/chair, $53,756
Wall, Jennifer, assistant professor, $53,747
Wall, Timothy, associate professor, $65,236
Wallace, Connie, custodian, $25,072
Wallace, Deborah, custodian, $25,072
Walton, Nicole, primary care provider (n.p.), $54,702
Wanorie, Tekle, associate professor, $85,250
Ward, Crystal, manager; web services, $53,672
Warner, Craig, associate professor, $64,862
Warner, Patricia, instructor, $45,212
Washam, Amy, asst director, northwest-kc, $70,000
Welch, Mary, groundskeeper, $25,830
Welch, Rex, electrician, $32,752
Welch, Tammy, custodian, $25,072
Wessell, Ryan, associate professor, $56,271
Weuve, Eric, instructor, $51,845
White, Ellen, accounts receivable bookkeeper, $33,499
White, Jeremiah, general maintenance i, $29,418

Wiederholt, Joshua, hardscape groundskeeper, $26,676
Wiedmer, Stacey, counselor, $39,585
Wigger, Karen, proj asst: curr & instr pbs, $48,959
Wilcox, Kenton, instructor, $39,656
Williams, Anthony, officer, $34,489
Williams, Glenn, associate professor, $56,893
Wilmes, Amee, sr asst dir/fed & st programs, $47,524
Wilmes, Gerald, exec dir wellness services, $171,601
Wilmes, Judy, accounts payable supervisor, $39,527
Wilmes, Kelli, instructor, $44,572
Wilmes, Patricia, proj asst: curr & instr, $57,562
Wilson, Amy, teacher ed stud serv coord, $34,910
Wilson, Nathan, associate professor, $56,713
Withington, Melvin, p-t custodian, $12,536
Wittenburg, Alana, asst volleyball coach/instr, $32,344
Woerth, Amy, volleyball coach/instr, $52,271
Wolters, Angela, senior buyer, $46,605
Wood, Cynthia, purchasing manager, $52,589
Wood, Rahnl, associate professor, $90,840
Wood, Sue, assistant professor, $58,068
Woodard, Karen, assistant director of ubms, $38,941
Woodward, Bruce, boiler operator, $42,226
Workman, Denise, budget analyst, $58,139
Wray, Kurby, custodian, $25,072
Wright, Richard, def coord/asst hd coach/instr, $89,337
Wu, Yi-Hwa, associate professor, $60,261
Wyatt, Patricia, reference assistant, $39,971
Xiong, Wei, assistant professor, $71,196
Yocom, Erika, lc: early child teacher, $42,156
Yu, Han, assistant professor, $53,747
Zeliff, Nancy, professor, $83,689
Ziegler, Kimberly, brand manager, $52,777
Zweifel, Jolaine, computer specialist, $46,964
Zweifel, Thomas, assistant professor, $58,087

Southeast Missouri State University

Cape Girardeau 63701

Dobbins, Kenneth W, president emeritus, $235,009
Abu-Nada, Ali A, instructor, term, $40,525
Ackman, Douglas, maintenance custodian, $24,284
Adams, Janet J, instructor, $52,944
Adams, John G, network specialist, $44,604
Adams, Jordan A, security officer, $10,890
Adjei, Frederick A, instructor, $61,516
Adkins, Kathryn B, instructor, $41,204
Adkinson, Gregory A, director of development, $58,316
Agnew, Quentonia M, coord, employer relations-stl, $63,290
Aguinaga, Nancy J, associate professor, $67,298
Ahmed, Zahir, executive director, $99,846
Aide, Michael, chairperson, $95,425
Aitken, Jennifer M, iep instructional specialist, $34,574
Alberternst, Cheryl, instructor, $55,133
Aldridge, Amy J, advising & career specialist, $29,859
Alexander, Toni A, chairperson /assoc professor, $65,853
Alger, Alyssa, instructor, $44,000
Ali, Mohammed H, professor, $86,311
Allen, Maria R, spec educ reg tech asst coach, $51,269
Allender-Zivic, Jonathan E, lighting des/technical dir, $45,675
Alter, Aaron A, help desk & user services spt, $35,105
Alter, Curtis M, network specialist, $36,219
Althaus, Rickert R, professor, $69,568
Ambery, Mary E, associate professor, $58,356
Amer, Suhair M, associate professor, $79,398
Amick, Britne F, food and beverage manager, $34,855
Amick, Gail, admissions specialist, $30,699
Anand, Vijay, assistant professor, $96,214
Anderson, Floyd A, pipefitter/welder, $45,260
Anderson, Warren D, professor, $81,638
Angerer, Ashley E, asst athletic trainer, $34,760
Arnold, James P, asst coach, $50,000
Baffoni, Gabrielle J, assistant professor, $49,693
Bai, Kang, asst prov/inst res & acad asmt, $98,835
Bailey, Anthony L, network specialist, $42,648
Bailey, Deja T, coordinator, facilities & prog, $30,762
Baker, Candee E, instructor, $39,311
Baldwin, Christopher, assistant professor, $51,669

Ball, Jeremy, chairperson / professor, $78,000
Ball, Trent T, assoc dean of stud/dir of ret, $83,792
Balsmann, Cynthia C, textbook associate, $26,492
Baranovic, Kristopher N, instructional designer, $41,100
Barbatti, James H, assistant director, smc oper, $57,360
Barke, Brady L, interim director, athletics, $89,608
Barnes, Jeremy T, professor, $80,264
Barnes, Monica G, director, $50,670
Barrios, Francisco X, dean, $147,688
Barton, Ashley M, accountant, $39,466
Basinger, Nicholas J, public safety officer, $33,019
Batchelor, Angela K, mail processor journeyman, $22,942
Bawaneh, Khaled I, assistant professor, $69,060
Bays, Zachary T, admissions counselor i, $33,495
Beard, Deborah F, professor, $112,792
Beardslee, Christine E, administrative assistant, $23,893
Beasley, Roger A, network specialist, $33,272
Becker, Joyce D, director, ext & cont ed, $77,665
Beighley, Donn, instructor, $58,527
Below, Deborah L, vp enroll mgmt & stdnt succs, $154,789
Belvin, Kevin P, computer labs supervisor, $39,617
Benefield, Heather C, telephone specialist, $22,822
Bengtson, Jennifer, assistant professor, $49,955
Benn, Marissa K, custodial technician, $25,459
Benn, Treasa, mep journeyman, $44,241
Benton, Jean E, professor, $80,616
Bertrand, Lisa A, professor, $84,067
Beussink, Gloria E, speech & language pathologist, $63,926
Bieser, Steve R, head coach, $71,632
Bird, Daniel, custodial technician, $22,048
Birk, Angela L, accountant, $39,708
Birkman, Jamie S, administrative assistant, $27,484
Birks, Jaclyn J, hall director, $25,000
Bishop, Mary S, assistant dir online marketing, $56,794
Bittle, Janice L, administrative assistant, $22,822
Blanchard, Marsha L, director, kahec, $77,004
Bland, Xavier L, teacher/driver term, $25,516
Blaney, Amanda D, custodial technician, $23,691
Blankenship, Karl F, network systems engineer, $54,639
Blasdell, Raleigh, instructor, $41,627
Blaylock, Mark E, manager syst analyst/program, $67,885
Blaylock, Pamela J, administrative assistant, $25,812
Blechle, Michael A, mep apprentice, $39,894
Bloom, Carl N, instructor, $40,904
Blue, Sharon E, custodial technician, $24,939
Bluma, Maija, lab technician, $42,036
Blunt, Rachel A, asst athletic dir,comp & eligi, $57,474
Bodenheimer, M L, professor, $71,663
Bogantes, Christopher M, asst coach, $31,151
Bohannon, Raymond L, associate professor, $60,106
Bollinger II, Bobby, training coordinator, $36,219
Bomar, Becky J, administrative assistant, $23,893
Bond, Marcus R, professor, $73,508
Bonds, Luther R, public safety officer, $32,531
Boone, Rhonda J, administrative assistant, $26,001
Booth, Emily J, instructor, $45,061
Borgsmiller, Stephen J, director, sahec, $77,154
Bornstein, Allan J, professor, $89,696
Borst, David, telecom journeyman lead, $49,316
Bowen, Thomas R, groundskeeper, $30,076
Bowen, Wayne H, chairperson, $75,947
Bowers, Bryan E, instructor, $62,502
Boyce, Anthony G, custodial technician, $26,291
Boyd, Gregory H, professor, $82,889
Braden, Indi S, professor, $69,347
Bradley, Thomas I, sergeant, public safety, $43,317
Brandhorst, Scott R, instructor, $43,961
Branscum, Shelba Y, chairperson, $77,771
Brashear, Travis J, mep apprentice, $39,894
Brasso, Rebecka, assistant professor, $54,000
Bratberg, William D, associate professor, $58,887
Bratton, Lavetta M, administrative assistant, $26,704
Brazer, Jamie S, assistant behavior analyst, $53,579
Brethold, Jessica E, academic advisor, $33,555
Brickhaus, Margaret E, sr systems analyst/programmer, $62,236
Bridgeman, Maria J, assistant registrar, $39,534
Brockett, Kipley B, network specialist, $33,272
Brooks, Brandi O, assistant director, term, $48,357
Brown, Angela D, lead teacher, term - sahec cdc, $27,049

Brown, Jason C, operations director, $50,312
Brown, Michael J, custodial technician, $25,459
Brown-Haims, Marcia J, associate professor, $67,320
Browning, Tara J, iep instructional specialist, $36,925
Brubaker, James, assistant professor, $49,389
Brucker, Elizabeth A, director, business operations, $44,386
Brucker, Todd G, budget assistant, $32,094
Brucker, William C, locksmith, $41,475
Bruenderman, Jason J, library systems coordinator, $49,518
Bruenderman, Joyce, cashier supervisor, $33,302
Brune, Michelle L, professor, $70,601
Bruns, Diana L, professor, $77,440
Buchheit, Karen S, public safety officer, $35,835
Buchholz, Nicole C, asst coach, $30,884
Buck, Michael E, director, rec sports, $70,225
Buck, Tamara Z, associate professor, $61,482
Buerck, Andrea D, transcript specialist, $22,484
Buerck, Daphine D, hr specialist, $42,305
Buerck, Linda A, assistant director, $57,611
Buhs, Margaret L, assistant director, stu accts, $50,359
Burford, Lenny G, mgr, computer maint & network, $69,110
Burgard, Sharon L, coordinator, comm & social ser, $45,773
Burger, Joe R Jr, plumber journeyman, $44,449
Burke, Lindsay E, financial counselor, $36,356
Burleson, Marilyn L, instructor, $43,825
Burnette, Joy M, operations supervisor, $32,522
Burns, Andrea D, administrative assistant, $23,072
Burr, Jenna A, administrative assistant, $24,901
Burrow, Eric N, asst coach, $27,650
Burton, Rhoda L, custodial technician, $23,691
Buttry, Theresa L, administrative assistant, $29,935
Caile, Chelsea A, coordinator of se online prog, $48,166
Caldwell, James L, associate professor, $115,523
Callahan, Lindsey G, secretary, part time, $9,360
Cameron II, David, professor, $64,760
Campbell, John T Jr, instructor, $49,479
Campbell, Rhonda S, administrative assistant, $22,817
Campbell-Jones, Vera J, instructor, $60,046
Cannady, Alison M, administrative assistant, $23,893
Canoy, Jessie N, parent education coordinator, $31,174
Canoy, Rebecca A, senior adm asst, $31,449
Cardin, Donna L, administrative assistant, $23,893
Carter, Debra K, financial counselor, $36,356
Carter, Laura D, community mobilizer, $29,260
Carter, Lynn R, assistant dean of students, $62,417
Carter, Sally A, director, testing services, $52,432
Cauble, Dustin M, boiler plant manager, $58,235
Caudle-Antill, Julie A, science instructional spclst, $52,018
Centanni, Marsha, senior admin assistant, $30,297
Centanni, Nicholas A, iep instructional specialist, $35,898
Cerchio, Robert, assistant director, svpa, $83,001
Cervantes, Amber D, lead teacher, $26,390
Cesarz, Gary, instructor, $52,151
Chamberlain, Stephanie, professor, $73,640
Champine, James E, chairperson, $76,202
Chandler, John P, instructor, $41,669
Chapman, Megan B, research analyst, $40,759
Cherry, John W, professor, $109,061
Chiles, Patty J, administrative assistant, $26,299
Chisum, Misty M, instructor, $44,232
Cho, Hyeon J, assistant professor, $75,646
Choo, Yin Y, assistant professor, $52,799
Chou, Catherine, assistant professor, $50,656
Christensen, Brandon, professor, $68,278
Christian, Wade M, instructor, term, $36,000
Chronister, Dale E, administrative assistant, $26,704
Ciarniello, Janet E, senior administrative asst, $29,099
Claar, Robert L, plumber journeyman, $43,784
Clark, Christopher C, hall director, $25,468
Clark, Heidi L, instructor, $39,511
Clark, Henry L Jr, instructor, $40,171
Clark, Lisa B, instructor, $40,376
Clark, Marcia A, special education consultant, $52,018
Clark, Matthew H, custodial technician, $23,691
Clark, Tracie A, administrative assistant, $26,207
Clements, Eric L, professor, $75,947
Clifton, Tim W, groundskeeper, $30,180
Clubbs, Brooke H, instructor, $42,586
Cluney, Carrie L, administrative assistant, $25,633

Cobb, Michael L, professor, $82,121
Coffee, Melissia J, hr specialist, $43,064
Coffman, Meredith L, billing assistant, $25,711
Cohen, Joan Z, university legal counsel, term, $90,000
Colbert, Brittany L, library tech asst i, $22,822
Collins, Brian J, pc applications spclst, $51,000
Collins, Jacquelyn L, payroll technician, $27,635
Conger, Robert B, professor, $68,142
Contrino, Michelle, instructor, $47,298
Cook, James K, director, human resources, $120,035
Cook, Lowell A, hvac-r mechanic lead, $47,049
Cook, Martha J, assistant professor, $55,209
Coon, Ricky A Jr, asst coach, $46,100
Cooper, Anthony G, public safety officer, $35,835
Cooper, Cheryl A, financial aid prog specialist, $32,213
Cordes, Phillip S, hvac/refrig mech journeyman, $43,784
Cossey, Micheal R, supervisor, media services, $48,247
Cox, Janet B, senior adm asst, $29,456
Cox, Kristina M, executive assistant, $33,649
Cramer, Priya N, asst dir, int'l prog, $38,174
Crawford, Philip W, chairperson, $81,134
Criblez, Adam J, assistant professor, $46,748
Crisler, Rick, boiler plant technician i, $44,886
Crites, M J, director, public serv/publ, $69,110
Crocker, Daniel C, assistant professor, $46,749
Crumpecker, James E, head coach, $54,964
Crunkilton, Dhira D, associate professor, $62,627
Crutchfield, Chante E, asst coach, $45,000
Culbreath, Mishea D, academic advisor ii, $44,635
Cummings, Sara J, senior adm asst, $29,099
Cunningham, Sheri D, custodial technician lead, $28,267
Curtis, Dalton B Jr, professor, $95,551
Cwick, Gary J, professor, $82,661
Cwick, Simin L, chairperson, $79,247
Dalton, Margaret R, professor, $90,102
Daly, Daniel A, associate professor, $56,436
Daniel, Dana L, academic advisor (10 month), $38,091
Dannenmueller, Lance C, support service staff, $28,641
Davenport, Jon, assistant professor, $54,708
Davis, Heather J, media technician, $33,378
Davis, Kerry M, project & relief specialist, $25,459
Davis, Robbie J, instructor, $65,781
Davis, Susan A, assistant professor, $50,656
Davis, Tammy, instructor, $48,874
De Leon, Jesse, mell instructional specialist, $55,743
DeArman, Brooke A, int'l student counselor, $34,510
DeArman, Kevin L, driver/clinic assistant, $26,841
Decker, Edna, telecom journeyman tech, $46,716
Dedert, James R, custodial technician, $27,227
Dees, Sharon J, instructor, $46,745
Deiermann, Paul J, associate professor, $57,972
Deken, Bradley J, chairperson, $82,916
Delgado, Laura E, instructor, $46,538
Delph, Beverly A, administrative assistant, $26,309
Denlinger, Emily J, associate professor, $72,482
Devaney, Michael T, professor, $124,036
Devenport, Debbie, administrative assistant, $29,932
Dickson, Kevin E, professor, $108,487
Diebold, Emily L, lead teacher, $27,049
Dietl, Robert D, hvac/refrig mech journeyman, $44,449
Dimock, Chase F, instructor, $37,836
Dirnberger, Jyothi E, public safety officer, $35,835
Donley, Tara L, senior clerk, $26,069
Dow, Benjamin L III, professor, $115,312
Dudley, John D, instructor, $59,121
Dufek, James J, professor, $91,645
Duncan, Gwendolyn, coordinator, admin operations, $43,849
Dunn, Roxanne M, instructor, $50,242
Durow, Peter, assistant professor, $53,018
Easter, Beth A, professor, $69,142
Eckart, Gabriele, professor, $72,835
Eddleman, William R, professor, term, $192,625
Edgecombe, Philip A, instructor, $45,373
Edgerton, Sara A, professor, $80,907
Eisenhauer, Aaron B, digital image specialist, $42,097
Elfrink, Mark P, custodial technician, $25,459
Eller, Amanda S, coordinator, academic advising, $55,825
Eller, Ben L, project manager, $48,370
Ellermeier, Jeremy R, assistant professor, $54,000

Ely, Melvin E, warehouse worker journeyman, $39,873
Emmons, Donald L, carpenter lead, $44,075
Eom, Sean B, professor, $117,743
Ervin, Glenna S, administrative assistant, $23,338
Eskew, Torie L, administrative assistant, $22,817
Essmyer, Lisa D, instructor, $45,552
Essner, Cheryl L, assistant professor, $59,921
Essner, Christina M, assistant director, facilities, $39,070
Essner, James L, budget & enrollment analyst, $52,018
Evans, Beverly M, professor, $68,022
Evans, Lisa N, library technician, $23,898
Ewasko, Kristi B, head coach, $49,185
Faber, Anthony J, professor, $66,891
Farmer, Mary Ann, counselor I, $42,390
Farris, Judith L, instructor, $58,760
Farrish, Patricia S, instructor, $43,854
Farrow, Ellen M, manager, box office, $39,298
Farrow, Jeffrey, carpenter journeyman, $41,475
Farrow, Patrick L, project & relief specialist, $27,019
Fees, Kim M, associate director, res life, $57,855
Fehr, Christel D, instructor, $51,669
Figliolo, Carolyn S, associate dir, design & constr, $73,410
Fisher, Douglas B, area coordinator, $32,553
Fisher, Rita C, director,regional prof dev ctr, $83,230
Fluegge, Erin R, associate professor, $98,473
Forester, Daniel E, painter apprentice, $39,270
Foshee, Katie L, asst dir admsn/new stdt prog, $48,407
Fox, Benjamin M, co-head athletic trainer, $52,000
Francis, Joy L, senior adm asst, $27,635
Francis, Robert A, custodial technician, $23,691
Franklin, Chance C, program specialist, $35,525
Franklin, Stephen H, project & relief specialist, $27,435
Fraser-Smith, Kasey, coord,stu conduct/title ix inv, $40,160
Frazee, Chad L, custodial technician, $25,459
Fridley, Daryl E, associate professor, $57,614
Friedrich, Calvin K, project coordinator, $40,760
Friga, Jennifer M, administrative assistant, $24,933
Froemsdorf, Johannah T, iep instructional specialist, $35,898
Fruehwald, Robert D, professor, $75,730
Fulgham, Marc S, professor, $80,212
Fulkerson, W A, professor, $75,756
Fuller, Wade, custodial technician, $25,459
Gadberry, Jennifer M, instructor, $45,385
Gammon, Kenneita, custodial technician, $26,291
Gannon, Cynthia M, sr asso athl dir/sr women adm, $84,655
Garner, Linda R, assistant professor, $63,782
Garner, Sara L, instructor, $48,652
Garrett, James D, boiler plant technician ii, $43,201
Gasser, Alix S, asst dir for communications, $47,871
Gasser IV, George M, admissions counselor ii, $39,991
Gathman, Allen C, dean/dir of ctr scholarship, $133,950
Gause, Charles P, chairperson / professor, $83,076
Gean, Wilford D Jr, carpenter journeyman, $40,809
Gehring, Brian L, instructor, $53,721
Gentry, Autumn V, safety specialist, $47,675
Gerecke, Bonnie R, administrative assistant, $25,299
Gershuny, Pamela, professor, $94,934
Ghosh, Santaneel, associate professor, $76,781
Gill, Larry K, carpenter journeyman, $41,475
Gill, Richard C Jr, painter apprentice, $41,184
Gill, Tyler K, electrician, journeyman, $43,784
Glastetter, Brenda J, administrative assistant, $26,001
Glastetter, Gary W, custodial technician, $25,875
Glaus, Diane K, accounting assistant, $41,709
Glaus, Elizabeth A, manager, parking/transit/emerg, $57,371
Glaus, Jacob R, security officer, $10,890
Gleeson, Karen C, senior admin asst, $29,606
Glueck, Cara S, assistant dir, horizon prog, $42,447
Goeke, Christopher L, professor, $80,986
Gohn, George L, custodial technician, $25,459
Golightly, Nancie A, custodial technician, $23,691
Golike, Susan G, professor, $84,709
Gooden, Regina T, director, apple project, $30,414
Gordinier-Harkey, Cynthia L, instructor, $56,319
Gordon, Adam M, asst coach, $52,000
Gordon, Peter J, professor, $118,890
Gorman, William M III, director, show me center, $93,763
Gottlieb, Kelli, assistant professor, $50,656
Gottlieb, Sean M, instructor, $42,100

Gould, Creighton A, sergeant public safety, $45,054
Graham, Carla S, public safety dispatcher, $30,125
Graham, Melissa A, instructor, $42,131
Grantham, Kara R, project manager, $48,461
Graves, Joseph P, computer technician, $30,506
Gray, Clifton Jr, assistant director, telecom, $53,409
Gray, Jeremy J, public safety dispatcher, $27,682
Gray, Natallia, assistant professor, $75,731
Greable, Debra L, custodial technician lead, $29,515
Green, Gloria J, chairperson, $70,328
Green, Stephen D, public safety officer, $33,844
Gribler, Dawn R, adm asst, part time, $11,946
Griffin, Jeremy L, instructor, $49,693
Griffing, Aaron D, event services specialist, $23,307
Grissom, Angela M, senior adm asst, $31,711
Grogan, Torie N, dir, counslng & disability srv, $65,971
Grojean, Gretchen A, assistant dir, univ center, $45,773
Grotts, Allie S, instructor, $45,500
Grueneberg, Julia E, assistant registrar, $41,270
Guha, Bikiran, instructor, term, $44,000
Guiling, Shawn F, instructor, $43,961
Gullett, Kenneth R, lieutenant public safety, $51,180
Gunn, Sharon E, associate professor, $60,774
Hadler, Tom L, design project manager, $52,512
Hager, Joe L Jr, custodial technician lead, $29,099
Hahn, Lenell D, director, admissions, $79,812
Hahs, Ellen M, curator of education, $42,347
Halbert, Mitchell, boiler plant technician i, $44,782
Hale, Larry J, budget analyst, $51,297
Hale, Shelly L, senior research analyst, $45,000
Hall, Wayne, boiler plant technician i, $44,886
Ham, Kathy L, associate professor, $64,580
Ham, Kristin J, horticulturist, $40,227
Haman, Christopher W, library assistant III, $23,963
Haman, Shelia K, cashier, $21,166
Hamblin, Laurie K, instructor, $44,233
Hamilton, Leigh J, groundskeeper, $30,076
Hammock, Eric T, boiler plant technician ii, $43,201
Hampton, Edwin K, chairperson, $77,128
Han, Xue, assistant professor, $62,813
Hand, Joni M, assistant professor, $50,467
Haney, Peggy L, museum assistant, $29,412
Haney, Teresa A, asst director for recruitment, $52,018
Hankinson, Johnathon W, equipment manager, $31,527
Hargrove, Amanda S, administrative assistant, $23,893
Harmon, Jeff, exec dir of comm & mrktng, $119,643
Harper, Melissa G, financial aid prog specialist, $31,518
Harrington, Ashley B, administrative assistant, $22,880
Hartman, Kurt A, boiler plant technician ii, $42,744
Hase, Heath H, senior adm asst, $29,105
Haskell, Dale E, professor, $69,954
Hatcher, Laura, assistant professor, $50,656
Haug-Belvin, Theresa M, instructor, $43,561
Haupt, Martin L, equip operator journeyman, $42,744
Hayes, Ann, director, news bureau, $57,528
Hayes, Jonathan M, instructor, $37,836
Hayward, Albert W, associate professor, $63,949
Heath, Michael A, writing associate, $14,852
Heider, Jeremy D, associate professor, $65,981
Heischmidt, Kenneth, professor, $114,769
Heisserer, Carol A, asst director, acad advising, $61,915
Heitman, Linda K, professor, $88,736
Heizer, Carol A, executive assistant, $43,419
Hekmat, Susan L, special educ reg tech asst coa, $56,910
Helton, Francine A, data specialist ii, $27,016
Henckell, Mary M, director, user services, $72,703
Henderson, Byron T, lead teacher, $27,049
Hendricks, Lawrence S, sr systems analyst/programmer, $53,817
Hendrix, Marcia, clerk ii, $26,822
Hendrix, Robert G, boiler plant technician i, $44,886
Henry, Avery J, instructor, $42,500
Henry, Rashaun F, academic speclst, $39,228
Hepler, Brandy L, director, field & clinical exp, $52,020
Herbst, Cherie J, coordinator, $15,325
Heslinga, Amanda G, administrative assistant, $23,497
Heslinga, Ryan D, assistant registrar, $43,823
Heu, Benjamin L, professor, $69,020
Hicks, Cassandra M, financial aid coordinator, $48,221
Hicks, Shelby S, instructor, $47,810

Hicks, Stacey J, family specialist/trainer, $35,962
Hill, H Hamner, chairperson, $86,156
Hill, Margaret P, associate professor, $63,391
Hinkle, David, courier, $26,499
Hinkle, Sandra L, registrar, $74,663
Hirsch, Charles L, manager, central receiving, $51,850
Hoffman, Steven J, professor, $75,947
Hogan, Phyllis, custodial technician, $27,227
Holder, Sherry L, administrative assistant, $22,641
Holekamp, Paula G, financial aid prog specialist, $33,094
Holland, William P, vice president, adv & exec dir, $159,986
Hollerbach, Karie L, chairperson, $70,757
Holley, Natalie B, instructor, $40,018
Holman, Thomas R, professor, $68,492
Holshouser, Billie J, instructor, $42,824
Holzhauer, Debra J, associate professor, $59,304
Honza, Jeffrey M, director, sport information, $59,254
Hopkins, Brian K, graduation specialist, $23,816
Hopkins, Dustin L, network systems engineer ii, $55,913
Hopper, Laura L, behavior analyst, $62,152
Horst, Carol B, instructor, $43,961
Hosselkus, Erika, assistant professor, $47,232
Hotop, Tina S, academic advisor, $38,008
Howe, Lisa A, senior project manager, $68,317
Howell, Linda D, custodial technician, $23,691
Howell, Vicki, administrative assistant, $34,088
Huffman, Wilma, senior adm asst, $35,886
Huggins, Keith A, business dev associate, $41,534
Humphrey, Roberta L, associate professor, $112,473
Humrichouse, John, instructor, $41,080
Hunter, Joyce A, career counselor, $34,700
Hunter, Kyle D, media services technician, $40,574
Hutson, Helen, custodial technician, $25,875
Hutson, Patricia K, custodial technician, $25,875
Hwang, Seong Nam, assistant professor, $53,000
Ignacio, Michael A, intake specialist, $38,767
Ingram-Wilson, Kathryn J, instructor, $36,979
Irby, Michele C, director, campus life, $70,337
Jackson, Alex D, associate director of devel, $54,290
Jackson, Alice E, professor, $86,483
Jackson, Delois A, custodial technician, $26,291
Jackson, Ullanda A, accounting clerk, $21,925
Jacoby, Adam M, assistant professor, $55,133
Jacoby, Denise, instructor, term, $38,000
James, Twylla R, cataloguing associate, $44,439
Jansen, Ann M, prevention advocate, $36,166
Jeffery, India D, retention specialist, $46,161
Jenkins, Morris, dean, $137,202
Jenkins, Sherri L, senior adm asst, $36,652
Jerrolds, Elsie Audrey L, grant coordinator term prof, $45,470
Johnson, Brenda P, professor, $88,736
Johnson, Charles D, counselor III, $60,526
Johnson, Charles E, hall director, $26,232
Johnson, Gary, interim dean, $157,186
Johnson, Ryan J, head strength & cond coach, $46,414
Johnston, Deanna K, public safety officer, $33,019
Jones, Christopher C, smc operations staff journyman, $31,033
Jones, Crystal G, project coordinator ii, $49,735
Jones, Frederick C, professor, $76,639
Jones, Leslie I, professor, $58,877
Judd, Timothy M, professor, $73,577
Jung, Donald J, associate professor, $64,648
Justis, Ina M, accountant, $41,444
Kahler, Caroline A, chairperson, $69,786
Karnes, Jennifer A, box office manager, $32,985
Kashyap, Kumar G, lms programmer, $36,400
Kaufman, Crystal L, executive assistant, $40,535
Kaverman, Suzanne, senior adm asst, $31,593
Kehe, Rebecca A, asst dir, int'l prog, $39,005
Kelley, Gregory L, maintenance custodian, $25,848
Kelley, Nancy L, coordinator, public design, $44,236
Kendrick, Dena Susan, chairperson/assoc professor, $59,267
Kenney, Nicholas A, assistant professor, $47,616
Kent, Vickie S, custodial technician, $25,459
Keppner, Christopher A, boiler plant technician ii, $42,744
Keshtkar, Fazel, assistant professor, $72,470
Khalid, Tahsin, professor, $73,234
Kilburn, Michelle A, associate professor, $57,595
Killen, Leah C, head coach, $45,243

Kim, Jae Hee, assistant professor, $52,000
Kim, Kyoung T, assistant professor, $49,935
Kinder, Jessica L, buyer, $31,657
King, Alicia M, financial aid prog specialist, $30,295
King, Katrice M, lead teacher, $27,415
King, Micheal D, program technician, $28,395
King, Robert B, general mechanic journeyman, $40,227
Kinney, Norman E, associate professor, $61,623
Kinnison, Carl A, instructor, $44,623
Kisat, Courtney, assistant professor, $45,590
Kisner, Angela M, senior adm asst, $27,635
Kitchen, Carol A, senior adm asst, $30,965
Klaproth-Gentry, Judy D, sergeant, $43,749
Kleman, Adam M, asst coach, $25,050
Knoeppel-Holbert, Laura K, financial aid coordinator, $46,397
Koch, Daniel J, groundskeeper, $29,619
Koch, Shelby L, groundskeeper, $29,619
Kodish, Slavica, assistant professor, $53,123
Koeberl, Dennis E, gen mechanic journeyman lead, $42,827
Koelling, Matthew B, asst track & field coach, $28,557
Koenig, Tyson M, archival assistant, $42,361
Koeppel, Dan L, pc applications spclst, $59,822
Kraemer, John C, professor/dir ctr env analysis, $91,220
Krieger, Laura C, instructor, $43,561
Kubik, Joanna K, editor/production asst, $43,750
Kuehnel, Mark C, project & relief specialist, $26,187
Kunz, David A, professor, $118,819
Kuper, Stephanie A, instructional tech specialist, $52,018
Kurre, Jane E, textbook associate, $24,596
Kurzhals, Rebeccah L, assistant professor, $58,435
Kutsevalova, Natalya V, instructor, term, $38,000
Kyles, Tameka L, eap/outreach coordinator, term, $42,295
Lacey, Larry D, general mechanic journeyman, $40,019
Lacey, Peggy S, library assistant III, $23,955
Lacy, Jerry W, transit operations supervisor, $30,929
Ladwig, Christine A, assistant professor, $86,115
Lady, Phillip V, coordinator, mktg & promo, $45,048
Lagroone, Nicholas, director, basketball operations, $30,880
LaMantia, Kirsten N, assistant professor, $54,000
Lambert, Lea Anne, instructor, $47,810
Lambert, Verona M, director, student accounts, $75,562
Landgraf, Polly A, admissions specialist, $24,440
Lane, Ryan P, asst coach, $32,718
Langenfeld, Mark E, professor, $79,677
Langston, Mary S, coordinator, acquisitions, $48,332
Lashmet, Violet M, custodial technician, $26,291
Lauder, Daniel C, instructor, $62,660
Lawson, Andrew D, asst coach, $31,094
Lawson, Courtney J, academic advisor (10 month), $29,950
Lawson, Jeanette, administrative assistant, $26,704
Layton, Michael D, groundskeeper, $29,619
Lee, Jerry W, warehouse worker jrnyman, $39,977
Lee, Thomas C, supervisor, grnds/flt/ss, $56,737
Lee, Trudy G, director, planned gvng/endow, $91,950
Lee, Yvonne A, manager, accounts payable, $48,470
Lee-DiStefano, Debra K, professor, $68,766
Legrand, Nancy K, instructor, $47,848
Leible, Joyce M, custodial technician, $25,459
Lesch, Heather M, administrative assistant, $26,487
Lesch, Lisa A, custodial technician, $23,691
Lewis, Brenda S, accountant, $44,046
Lewis, Robert E, pc applications spclst, $44,728
Lichtenegger, Avelina, instructor, $38,255
Lightfoot, Sean M, house manager, $31,356
Lilly, Walt W, professor, $102,496
Lincoln, Alicia E, administrative assistant, $25,299
Lincoln, Amanda L, director of development, $69,618
Lincoln, Debbie, parent education coordinator, $31,179
Lindsey, Bradley K, maintenance custodian, term, $22,880
Lindy, Helen M, painter, journeyman, $41,184
Liu, Ziping, professor, $94,152
Livingston, Jessica R, cad supervisor, $40,766
Livingston, John R, carpenter lead, $44,075
Lockhart, Allison B, senior adm asst, $29,403
Lockhart, Floyd H, lms administrator, $45,924
Loenneke, Kristine A, financial aid coordinator, $45,945
Lohmann, Rebecca J, instructor, $56,514
Long, Rachel R, custodial technician pt, $11,024
Loos, Joyce L, administrative assistant, $30,076

Lorenz, Katie M, lead teacher, $27,861
Lott, Joni A, sr administrative assistant, $33,694
Louie, Kimberly K, assistant professor, $46,268
Lowell, Bryan M, mep apprentice, $39,894
Lowes, David W, groundskeeper, $29,619
Lowman, Samantha L, instructor, term, $36,000
Luehrs, Edgar H, sr systems analyst/programmer, $51,081
Luetkenhaus, Deana M, costume shop supervisor, $40,000
Luetkenhaus, Jeffrey M, production manager, $47,876
Lutes, Tara W, senior accountant, $49,293
Macke, Joyce A, sr systems analyst/programmer, $51,051
Madigan, Kimberly A, coordinator, acad prog, $53,294
Main, Brett E, senior adm asst, $29,099
Major, Terry L, supervisor, bldg maintenance, $64,609
Malone, Robin K, library assistant III, $27,890
Mangels, Darla J, secretary, $22,321
Mangels, Kathy M, vice president, $166,672
Mangels, Matthew W, media services technician, $44,207
Mardanov, Ismatilla T, professor, $105,430
Margrabe, Richard W, custodial technician, $24,523
Marietta, Anne B, associate professor, $60,060
Markham, Ervin R, custodial technician, $25,459
Marshall, Leisa L, chairperson, $113,881
Martin, Amanda D, co-head athletic trainer, $52,000
Martin, Christopher R, dir, corp & govt relations, $81,125
Martin, Jocelyn S, assistant professor, $52,951
Martin, Kenton R, public safety officer, $33,874
Martin, Matthew G, asst coach, $41,250
Massey, Brandon, boiler plant technician ii, $39,228
Masters, Mark E, warehouse worker jrnyman, $39,977
Mathis, Leshay A, admissions counselor i, term, $33,495
Matrisotto, Phillip L, network specialist, $37,697
Matthew, Cynthia J, pos beh supp reg tech coach, $51,269
Mattison, Christina R, senior buyer, $41,918
Matukewicz, Thomas M, head coach, $131,000
Matwijkiw, Bronik, instructor, $43,869
Mauk, Allan D, asst director, bus operations, $50,680
Mauk, William D, instructor, $53,352
Maxfield, Nicole D, assistant behavior analyst, $50,083
May, Sean, boiler plant tech ii, lead, $45,905
Mayberry, Kenneth D, lieutenant public safety, $53,429
Mayberry, Kevin C, energy manager, $65,781
Mayfield, Jaime M, administrative assistant, $25,705
Mayfield, Krista L, graphic arts specialist, $39,856
McAdams, Dana L, administrative assistant, $26,725
McAdams, Ron, network specialist ii, $47,912
McAlister, Leah R, arts resource cntr lib assoc, $45,370
McAlister, Victoria L, assistant professor, $45,590
McAllister, Charles D, vice provt/dean grad school, $133,963
McAllister, Cheryl A, associate professor, $57,735
McBride, Martha J, billing associate, $45,488
McBride, Marvin L, support service staff lead, $31,907
McBride, Nakisha, sr admin assistant, $27,635
McBroom, Ewelina S, assistant professor, $53,123
McBroom, Jeremy L, director, mil & vet services, $54,086
McCain, Brian, public safety officer, $34,721
McClard, Richard W, instructor, $52,384
McClellon, Lance M, support service staff, $28,641
McCollum, Dennis, oracle database administrator, $72,517
McCollum, Dixie G, instructor, $47,895
McCrite, Z J, gift processing specialist, $28,061
McDougall, Gerald S, interim provost, $220,137
McElderry, Cathy, chairperson / associate prof, $67,000
McElroy, Kim R, senior accounting clerk, $28,500
McEwen, James D, instructor, $39,803
McFerron, Alisa A, assistant dir for operations, $58,893
McGarr, Kia L, admissions specialist, $35,384
McGaugh, Janie D, administrative assistant, $27,068
McGill, James W, professor, $75,029
McGowan, Chris, dean, $144,632
McGraw, Jennifer C, communications specialist,term, $38,500
McHenry, Lawrence R, custodial technician, $25,875
McIntosh, Larry B, custodial technician, $23,691
McIntosh, Michael R, assistant professor, $47,500
McKee, Deborah A, senior adm asst, $30,790
McKenzie, William B, project & relief specialist, $26,187
McMeel, Kevin, instructor, $71,108
McMillan, Heather S, assistant professor, $93,497
McMurry, Belinda L, instructor, $55,905

McNeary, William W III, instructor, $39,311
McNeely, Carmen S, manager, operations, $54,460
McNew, Mary Shannon, instructor, $43,254
McVay, George B, instructor, $41,411
Meinke, Richard M, network systems engineer, $54,054
Meraz, Barbara J, site dir, sahec child dev cent, $42,905
Merget, Margarita E, instructor, $43,923
Mershon, Christina Y, assistant dir, ext & cont ed, $47,693
Messmer, Theresa A, senior adm asst, $31,621
Meyer, Angela D, director, facilities mgmt, $116,659
Michel, Leah M, academic advisor, $35,988
Miesner, Karen J, admissions specialist, $31,905
Miller, Amber D, customer svc specialist, $24,893
Miller, Christopher, hall director, $25,975
Miller, Elisabeth A, scheduling specialist, $28,886
Miller, Eugenia T, academic advisor ii, $41,300
Miller, Justin H, assistant professor, $53,123
Miller, Kathie A, instructor, $46,199
Miller, Rosalyn F, financial counselor, $37,447
Mills, Pamela A, instructor, $41,538
Mims, Bruce, professor, $92,680
Mims, Mary C, instructor, $38,779
Minton, Damian F, smc operation staff, $31,491
Mitchell, Angela G, assistant dir, facilities mgmt, $66,161
Mizicko, Shane J, professor, $63,248
Modglin, Bonnie L, operations specialist, $41,191
Moeser, John C, network specialist, $44,828
Monteiro-Leitner, Julieta, professor, $75,446
Moody, Ian C, public safety officer, $33,019
Moore, Charles C, asst coach, $60,000
Moore, Rebecca A, associate director, usyc, $40,759
Moore, Stafford L, support service staff, $28,641
Morgan, Jason D, public safety officer, $33,874
Morgan Theall, Rachel A, associate professor, $60,886
Morris, Amanda R, lead techer, $27,861
Morris, Tameika C, grants coordinator, $45,470
Morrow, Roger G, boiler plant technician i, $44,886
Mosley, Gladys F, program coordinator, $48,845
Mosley, James E, custodial technician, $25,875
Mruzik, Monica N, public safety dispatcher, $27,682
Mueller, Lori, instructor, $47,848
Mueller, Wesley J, professor, $83,744
Murray, Kelly M, library tech asst ii, $29,099
Murray, Megan W, coord, lead & involvement, $38,069
Murray, Stanley L, testing associate, $32,244
Myer, Karen J, library tech asst i, $26,001
Nacy, Philip K, professor, $55,309
Naeger, Joshua L, secretary, $10,967
Naugler, David R, professor, $101,398
Neighbors, Kasey G, smc oper staff journeyman, $31,699
Neighbors, Sheila, custodial technician, $24,523
Nelson, Heather M, head coach, $59,716
Nelson, Jennifer L, career counselor, $36,286
Nelson, Paul N, associate head coach, $32,571
Nelson, Stephen L, coordinator, campus-based prog, $46,595
Nesler, Carol L, instructor, $53,520
Nettelhorst, Stephen C, assistant professor, $54,000
Newell, Connie J, custodial technician, $23,691
Newman, James, assistant professor, $52,536
Newth, Joshua, instructor, $44,000
Nguyen, Cuong Peter X, museum director, $73,787
Nguyen, Nghia V, assistant professor, $53,189
Nichol, Deborah E, senior adm asst, $30,823
Nicholls, Gillian, assistant professor, $87,128
Nickell, Stephen M, instructor, $56,423
Nieveen-Phegley, Trishena A, associate professor, $56,298
Niswonger, Sarah E, financial aid coordinator, $47,940
Noe, Margaret A, professor, $87,891
Nolen, Eugene E, network systems engineer, $54,955
Nomi, Tomoaki, associate professor, $60,255
Northington, Dayna S, administrative assistant, $27,025
Noto, Quantella M, assistant professor, $56,940
Null, Linda K, mathematics consultant, $54,982
Odegard-Koester, Melissa A, associate professor, $61,624
Odhiambo, Millicent A, coordinator disability srvs, $45,341
Ogles, Jane R, manager, systems and research, $44,523
O'Kelly, Billy R Jr, custodial technician, $25,667
Okruch, Thomas M, project coordinator, $55,722
Oman, Peter, assistant professor, $48,203

Omran, Kimberly Suzann, assistant director, int'l prog, $41,197
O'Rourke, Ellen D, instructor, $52,356
Ortega, Tinea L, coord of academic programs, $49,086
Ostrenga, Barbara C, administrative assistant, $27,849
Overbey, Gail A, professor, $79,503
Overmann, Laurie W, instructor, $41,929
Owen, Jacob R, asst director of compliance, $35,220
Owens, Kelly A, administrative assistant, $24,143
Ozenkoski II, Glen J, financial counselor, $36,856
Painton, Marcus D, sr digital image specialist, $47,822
Palmer, Bobbi J, instructor, $69,847
Palmer, Casey D, admissions counselor i, $33,995
Palmer, Richard J, professor, $132,773
Park, Kang H, professor, $103,814
Parker, Cynthia L, online programs specialist, $36,915
Parker, Michael D, associate professor, $78,514
Parker, Tiffany, instructor, $49,644
Patrick, Michelle R, licensed clinical psychologist, $73,939
Patterson, Rekha, head coach, $94,000
Pavelka, Alicia A, lead teacher, $27,861
Pawielski, Vance S, secretary, $23,700
Payne, Whitney S, administrative assistant, $22,822
Peel, Marsha L, operations support technician, $32,863
Peel, Scott R, general mechanic journeyman, $40,227
Penca, Gabrielle M, project coordinator, $40,157
Peng, Jian, professor, $91,794
Penny, Terry, carpenter journeyman, $41,475
Pernell, Deshon A, public safety dispatcher, $27,002
Peterson, Hilary, assistant professor, $50,684
Pfeiffer, Carole L, instructor, $39,456
Pflueger, Pennie, instructor, $47,839
Phillips, Bradley, assistant professor, $61,081
Phillips, Christopher K, coord facility & event mgmt, $35,139
Phillips, James M, museum curator, $45,796
Phillips, Jerry D, telecom journeyman tech, $39,041
Phillips, Kimberly D, custodial technician, $24,523
Phillips, Marjorie A, writing associate, $36,432
Phillips, Sondra E, senior adm asst, $31,659
Pickens, Robert S, support service staff, $28,641
Pingel, Denise L, agriculturist/horticulturist, $49,136
Pogue, Christine C, parent education coordinator, $30,000
Pollina, Leslee K, chairperson, $80,202
Ponder, Sheri L, accounts payable technician, $35,343
Porter, Debra G, assistant professor, $54,185
Poteete, Sherard B, asst coach, $62,000
Powell, David V, associate professor, $59,366
Powell, Marion L, scene shop supervisor, $37,505
Powell, Salim H, asst coach, $26,728
Powers, Joshua E, instructor, $36,472
Powers, Leah E, operations manager, term, $37,555
Pracht, Carl J, professor, $68,671
Prater, Dwight A, resource 25 administrator, $52,474
Presson, Daniel S, assistant dir for transfer rec, $44,736
Price, Cynthia R, internet marketing specialist, $38,174
Price, David W, iep instructional specialist, $39,973
Primm, Angela L, library tech asst ii, $29,344
Prince, Aldwon G, custodial technician, $26,707
Probst, David K, chairperson, $103,422
Proffer, Matthew A, public safety officer, $34,721
Prost, Angela M, lead teacher, $26,390
Pruitt, Mary, custodial technician, $22,048
Pujol, Thomas J, chairperson, $85,330
Pullen, Stephanie L, custodial technician, $24,939
Pyle, Walter E Jr, gen mechanic journeyman lead, $42,619
Ragain, Christina, assistant professor, $52,682
Ramdial, Joel S, instructor, $45,000
Ramos, Adolfo, assistant professor, $49,176
Randen, Melissa G, program specialist, $30,295
Randolph, Tamela D, chairperson, $77,821
Raschke, Debrah K, professor, $73,640
Ray, Jayanti, professor, $76,946
Ray, Julie A, chairperson, $72,438
Ray, William, head coach, $132,000
Redburn, Mark D, head coach, $58,362
Redinger, Eric K, associate dir, rec sports, $49,811
Redman, Debra R, custodial technician, $25,875
Redmond, Willie, professor, $100,299
Rees, Penny S, administrative assistant, $25,988
Rees, Tyson D, carpenter journeyman, $40,809

Reilly-Sandoval, Arlene, assistant professor, $53,000
Reimann, Carol S, reading specialist, $59,292
Reinagel, Cheryl A, administrative assistant, $30,100
Renaud, Joyce R, instructor, $49,025
Renner, Christie A, executive assistant, $47,086
Reno, Desma R, assistant professor, $63,632
Reynolds, Martin C, associate professor, $64,255
Reynoso, Josafath, assistant professor, $47,500
Rhodes, Joel P, professor, $69,248
Rhodes, Lance A, asst coach, $25,800
Rhymer, Vickey, custodial technician, $26,291
Rice, Melvin A Jr, asst coach, $30,750
Richards, James D, director, public safety/transp, $81,723
Ricks, James E, professor, $80,515
Rider, Rebecca E, assistant director, $65,613
Rieger, Christopher B, associate professor, $54,808
Rivet, Cynthia A, custodial technician, $25,875
Rivet, Kenneth F Jr, boiler plant technician i, $44,782
Robert, Shanna M, project & relief specialist, $27,019
Roberts, Craig W, associate professor, $59,974
Roberts, Foster, assistant professor, $103,338
Robertson, John S, custodial technician, $24,523
Robertson, Kenneth, project & relief specialist, $25,667
Robins, James, instructor, $41,700
Robinson, Aaron J, smc operations staff journeyman, $28,641
Robinson, Bambi, assistant professor, $53,489
Rodgers, Michael L, professor, $81,134
Roeder, Catherine G, assistant professor, $62,214
Roehlk, Michael, hall director, $26,232
Rogers-Adkinson, Diana, dean, $141,074
Rose, Dennis J, custodial technician, $25,875
Rose, Jennifer S, asst dir, sports youth family, $43,176
Rosser, James H, asst coach, $66,625
Rowland, Mark A, instructor, $50,243
Rubach, Douglas W, hvac/refrig mech journeyman, $44,449
Rucker, Sonia, coordinator, inst equity & div, $75,000
Ruediger, Claudia, professor, $67,344
Rueseler, Kimberly A, infant lab teacher, $29,895
Rumfelt, Kathleen E, lead teacher, $26,390
Runde, Michael, asst coach, $25,800
Russell, Joshua J, digital image specialist, $39,836
Saia, Bryce T, football defense coordinator, $67,125
Sammut, William J, public safety officer, $33,812
Sander, Pamela J, controller, $98,108
Sander, Patricia, supervisor, data control, $31,054
Sanders, Hannah, assistant professor, $46,603
Sanders, Norma J, operations supervisor, $32,522
Sanderson, Jack L, boiler plant technician ii, $42,744
Sandoval, Natalie E, instructor, term, $40,525
Sansagraw, April L, senior adm asst, $29,099
Santoro-Williams, Lily A, assistant professor, $46,713
Sappington, Julie Y, professor, $80,864
Sautter, Alberta C, professor, $68,864
Savage, Alan M, ticket office manager, $32,180
Saverino, Nathaniel T, asst ad for external affairs, $57,294
Saylor, Kerri D, financial aid prog specialist, $33,906
Scaife, Jauwan M, asst coach, $35,000
Schabbing, Collin A, arc manager, $49,068
Schaefer, Timothy W, carpenter journeyman, $40,809
Schaffner, Steve B, director, music academy, $24,448
Scheibe, John S, professor, $93,613
Schenimann, Gary D, electrician lead, $47,049
Schetter, Sara J, instructor, term, $36,472
Schmid, Andrew J, web specialist, $38,301
Schmidt, Timothy A, associate professor, $54,098
Schmoll, Cynthia L, director, horizon day prog, $51,891
Schneider, Kyle R, instructor, $50,729
Schnur, Maxwell A, assistant technical director, $35,220
Schnurbusch, Ann N, instructor, $42,824
Schnurbusch, Brian K, director, telecommunications, $83,060
Schremp, Nancy J, administrative assistant, $24,960
Schrock, Ethan H, smc operations staff journeyman, $31,491
Schulz, Christy L, hr technician, $27,635
Schwartz, Andrew M, associate professor, $56,436
Schwieger, Dana C, professor, $114,519
Scott, Alicia D, instructor, $46,587
Scott, Deborah C, administrative assistant, $26,417
Scott, Sophia K, professor, $80,530
Seabaugh, Dana N, hr specialist, $43,064

Seabaugh, Lynda A, senior accountant, $49,293
Seabaugh, Patsy J, special programs facilitator, $30,888
Seesing, Beth A, financial counselor, $37,447
Sen, Sandipan S, associate professor, $107,823
Sentell, James E, instructor, $40,373
Severtson, Jamie M, assistant professor, $55,721
Sexton, Kevin P, instructor, $45,706
Shafaie, Shahrokh M, professor, $86,938
Sharp, Patty A, instructor, $41,799
Shaver, Joanna R, coord, uc, $40,447
Shaw, Kerry A, asst coach, $25,172
Shetley, Alyssa J, admissions counselor i, $34,332
Shirrell, David S, custodian technician, $25,459
Shirrell, Linda K, nurse, $35,221
Showalter, Ashley R, secretary, part time, $9,500
Sides, Anita S, field & clinical exp assit, $24,596
Sides, Diane, associate to the president, $93,791
Sides, Jason C, assistant professor, $50,500
Sidiropoulos, Efthymia M, administrative assistant, $25,799
Siebert, Mary S, testing associate, $34,611
Siegel, Dustin, assistant professor, $54,052
Sierman, Chad W, assistant director aquatics, $48,016
Simmons, Michael A, instructor, $39,623
Simon, Nicole M, project budget assistant, $27,635
Singh, Pradeep, professor, $78,431
Skinner, Bruce W, asst vp, stu succ & aux svcs, $119,003
Skinner, Kendra S, director,residence life, $73,815
Slattery, Annette R, instructor, $50,523
Slinkard, Michele A, iep instructional specialist, $37,706
Smart, Emily, instructor, $50,243
Smith, Arthur A, custodial technician, $23,691
Smith, Ciara C, admissions counselor i, $34,332
Smith, DeAnte, director of greek life, $55,139
Smith, George W, general mechanic journeyman, $40,123
Smith, Jennifer N, senior adm asst, $33,459
Smith, Katherine E, professor, $64,542
Smith, Kenneth E, custodial technician, $23,691
Smith, Lisa E, inventory assistant, $24,688
Smith, Miles A, asst coach, $26,172
Smith, Robin L, instructor, $41,411
Smith, Shonta M, associate professor, $57,070
Smith, Tiffiney D, spec ed compliance resource sp, $55,743
Smith, Travis, associate professor, $61,624
Smith, William J, apprentice proj & rel spec, $25,667
Snell, Jared P, electrician journeyman, $43,784
Snell, William E Jr, professor, $91,855
Sofo, Seidu, professor, $72,665
Speight, Larry D, instructor, $42,853
Spinks, Sean M, retention coordinator, term, $39,005
Squibb, Kevin, associate professor, $68,079
St John, Megan G, lead teacher, $27,861
Stader, David L, professor, $93,067
Standridge, Robin R, instructor, $51,180
Stapleton, James L, associate professor, $116,870
Starbuck, Sara J, associate professor, $62,577
Starke, Joseph R, painter lead, $43,888
Starr, Evan P, web specialist, $38,301
Steinnerd, Sarah J, manager, purchasing, $61,143
Stephens, Roger, river campus oper staff jnymn, $31,491
Stevens, DeeDee, financial aid prog specialist, $32,974
Stevenson, Melissa M, budget analyst, $48,658
Stevenson, Sean P, assistant dir,sports info, $40,123
Stidham, Laura J, custodial technician, $24,939
Stidham, Paula, custodial technician, $24,523
Stidham, Thomas L, custodial technician, $25,875
Stiegemeyer, Angela K, instructor, $48,701
Stilson, Kenneth L, chairperson, $84,803
Stinnett, Lorreen F, instructor, $54,052
Stinson, Leann K, hr technician, $29,949
Stovall, Sara A, teacher, horizon ctr, $27,872
Stover, Karen L, operations supervisor, $31,888
Stover, Tamara L, administrative assistant, $22,483
Strange, Alice J, professor, $77,585
Stricker, Kathryn L, lead teacher, $27,861
Stroder, Karie J, academic advisor ii, $44,599
Suedmeyer, Martha A, administrative assistant, $31,004
Suhr, Karl, associate professor, $59,709
Summary, Jennifer J, instructor, $41,436
Summary, Rebecca, chairperson, $103,659

Svenson, Sven E, associate professor, $61,798
Swartwout, Susan, professor, $78,706
Talbut, Mary H, senior instructional designer, $57,916
Talley, Brittany, educ & outreach coordinator, $41,509
Tansil, John, associate professor, $62,886
Tanz, Michele L, assistant professor, $61,800
Tapp, David B, director of outreach, term, $95,907
Tapp, Michele L, dir academic career advising, $69,512
Tatum, Jaclyn M, accounting clerk, $21,166
Tayie, Francis, assistant professor, $55,721
Taylor, Lauralee, assistant mgr, $46,420
Taylor, Michael S, professor, $67,321
Taylor, Steven M, coordinator, tutorial services, $46,805
Thiele, Nicholas J, director, crisp bec, $70,188
Thomas, Carmen L, program specialist, $30,402
Thompson, Cortney L, behavior analyst, $54,099
Thompson, Emmanuel, assistant professor, $64,187
Thompson, Jeremy F, writing associate, $9,724
Thompson, John R, painter journeyman, $40,622
Thompson, Paul, instructor, $47,839
Thornburgh, Caroline K, instructor, $39,311
Thorne, Scott, instructor, $52,978
Thurston, Judith C, instructor, $40,598
Ticer, Norman R, security officer, $9,360
Tiehes, Robert S, groundskeeper, $29,619
Tikoo, Mohan L, professor, $87,143
Timlin, Maureen T, associate professor, $61,624
Tipton, Julie A, instructor, $49,643
Todd, Eddy M, security officer, $23,028
Todd, Gloria A, hr technician, $27,635
Tong, Jingjing, assistant professor, $62,813
Totton, Walter, electrician journeyman, $44,345
Trendle, Kurt N, library assistant III, $11,700
Tripp, Eileen M, custodial technician, $25,875
Trost, Tina L, lead teacher, $27,827
TRUE, Robin D, contract compliance officer, $33,514
Tubbs, Chloe A, alum serv & events coordinator, $40,980
Tucker, Karen, academic advisor, $36,618
Tucker, Zachary W, media specialist, $43,371
Twidwell, Julie E, instructor, $51,669
Tyler, Gary W, mobile learn ctr specialist, $38,536
Tyler, Nicholas G, network specialist, $33,272
Tyler, Troy, mep journeyman, $44,345
Uchtman, Brooke E, instructor, $42,000
Underberg, Larry, professor, $64,857
Underdown, Linda R, administrative assistant, $23,100
Underwood, Tamara T, executive assistant, $39,694
Unterreiner, Stanley, plumber lead, $47,257
Ustinova, Irina P, professor, $64,586
Uzoaru, Darcy A, asst dir, oper & collections, $46,522
VanAmburg, Andrew D, custodial technician, $24,523
Vander Bol, Abbie J, events supervisor, $41,460
Vandeven, Alissa M, assistant dir, human resources, $66,507
Vangilder, Ed, elevator maint tech jrny, $46,820
Vangilder, Kathryn A, library assistant III, $11,875
VanPool, Larry K, senior adm asst, $27,622
Vanteddu, Gangaraju, associate professor, $100,123
Vargas, Pamela A, director, grant development, $72,145
Vargas-Aburto, Carlos, president, $270,000
Varnon, Anthony W, professor, $104,868
Vaughn, Charles H, lab technician, $42,546
Vaughn, Jolon M, instructor, $51,669
Vaughn, Laura M, adm asst, part time, $11,411
Veneziano, Carol, professor, $84,508
Vetter, Rebecca J, business manager, $46,816
Voelker, Patrick D, lab technician, $42,425
Voerg, Lloyd E, telecom journeyman tech, $46,716
Wade, John E, professor, $76,681
Wagganer, Jason D, associate professor, $60,382
Wagganer, Sara A, assistant dir,rec sports, $44,111
Walker, Amanda R, project manager, $45,769
Walker, Carrie M, administrative assistant, $22,310
Walker, Karen M, director, student fin serv, $82,845
Wallace, Kenneth W, support service staff, $29,099
Waller, Joshua T, sr systems analyst/programmer, $46,084
Wallhausen, Amy E, records specialist, $25,799
Wallhausen, Matthew, senior network specialist, $52,684
Wallhausen, Tre, manager, technical services, $73,928
Walling, Breanna L, director of iep, $57,433

Walling, Jeremy, professor, $72,496
Walters, Melanie L, instructor, $42,818
Walton, Candide, associate professor, $58,326
Wang, Haohao, professor, $70,302
Wang, Shaojun, professor, $85,597
Wang, Xiang-Sheng, assistant professor, $49,693
Wang-McGrath, Shu-Chuan, instructor, $41,436
Ward, Janice E, professor, $74,086
Warren, Christine, instructor, $46,069
Warren, Lisa A, custodial technician, $25,459
Waterman, Margaret A, professor, $90,353
Watkins, Paul J, professor, $78,143
Weathers, Julie D, associate professor, $67,608
Webb, Lisa C, coordinator, acad prog $53,294
Weber, Janet R, professor, $97,665
Weber, William L, professor, $103,659
Weiss, Jennifer L, coordinator, writing center, $40,470
Weiss, Laura, instructor, $36,000
Welker, Andrew K, fleet mechanic, $40,476
Welker, Michele L, consumer educator, $30,549
Welker, Susan M, library tech asst i, $23,893
Weller-Stilson, Rhonda C, associate dean & director, $102,163
Wellington, Roxanne, assistant professor, $46,603
Wells, Tonya L, assistant director, marketing, $61,081
Westrich, Mark A, mail specialist, $31,678
Wheeler, Keith S, assistant director, iep, $42,911
White, Brenda K, academic advisor ii, $39,005
White, Thomas A, broadcast engineer, $55,743
Whiteford Damerall, Alison P, assistant professor, $52,682
Whitener-Needling, Melanie S, reading first specialist, $55,253
Whitlow-Greenwood, Roseanna B, instructor, $49,504
Wiemers, Jon C, fb asst hc/offensive coord, $49,450
Wiemers, Sandy, academic srv/compliance assist, $33,555
Wight, Shauna S, assistant professor, $47,000
Wiginton, Thomas E III, equip operator journeyman, $42,536
Wilburn, Victor R, professor, $70,042
Wilde, David W, manager, computer systems, $73,188
Wilde, Susan T, director, budget, $93,055
Wiles, Judith A, chairperson, $111,032
Wilkerson, Kimberly A, sr administrative assistant, $29,099
Wilkins, Nicolas J, assistant professor, $57,976
Wilkinson, Linda C, executive assistant, $49,519
Williams, Amanda A, lead teacher, $27,827
Williams, Bartholomew P, assistant professor, $46,603
Williams, James C, admissions counselor ii, $39,991
Williams, Jodi L, secretary, $21,780
Williams, L G, chairperson, $79,643
Williams, Richard T, supervisor, help desk, $45,361
Williams, Susan B, custodial technician, $25,875
Williams, Violonda M, senior financial counselor, $43,166
Williford, Lonnie, custodial supervisor, $54,650
Willingham, J R, assistant professor, $59,630
Willingham, Patricia, associate professor, $63,350
Willmert, Philip C, coordinator of annual fund, $37,435
Wilson, Angela L, director of development, $73,621
Wilson, Jacqueline, assistant professor, $50,000
Windeknecht, Shelly M, project manager, $47,583
Winter, Stephanie M, asst coach, $31,905
Winters, Susan C, professor, $61,250
Wisker, Alexandria, area coordinator, $33,053
Wissmann, Deborah K, custodial technician, $25,875
Wissmann, Mark D, carpenter journeyman, $41,371
Wissmiller, Frances M, administrative assistant, $25,299
Wojdylo, Jerzy, associate professor, $59,567
Wolz, Jay F, director, alumni srvs, $64,873
Wood, Diane L, professor, $67,068
Woods, Amanda M, outreach coordinator, $37,207
Woods, Danny J, general manager, krcu, $64,685
Wormington, Christie L, administrative assistant, $22,484
Wright, Scott W, tech & resource ctr spvr, $62,799
Wu, Chen, assistant professor, $74,750
Wubbena, Christopher E, professor, $67,052
Wyckoff, Jack L, hvac-r mech jrnyman, $44,345
Xia, Yanping, associate professor, $70,598
Yankus, Julie A, head coach, $54,899
Yaskewich, David, assistant professor, $87,122
Yerington, C J, coord, career & planning assmt, $45,468
Yerington, Kari S, coor stud leadership/res exper, $42,863
Young, Gevonna D, senior adm asst, $29,459

Young, Jill P, instructor, $47,982
Young, Robyn A, senior adm asst, $34,310
Youngblood Ortiz, Alisha D, associate professor, $102,949
Yount, Matthew W, instructor, $42,673
Zalite, Valdis R, director, student support serv, $50,100
Zen, Deqi, professor, $76,543
Zerbe, Derek L, boiler plant technician ii, $43,201
Zhang, Xuesong, professor, $95,187
Zhang, Yumin, associate professor, $80,161
Zhong, Qin, sr systems analyst/programmer, $47,103
Zibluk, John B, professor, $76,419
Zou, Min, assistant professor, $50,622

Missouri State University
Springfield 65804

Smart, Clifton, president, $304,500
Abbey, Michael, public safety officer, $26,999
Abidogun, Jamaine, professor, $61,547
Abney, Julie, budget officer, $43,500
Ackerson, Amy, instructor, $50,070
Adams, David, assoc prof-library-12 mo appt, $85,676
Adams, Karen, executive assistant III, $32,876
Adams, Kathryn, clinical instructor, $51,765
Adams, Leigh, asst professor, $42,000
Adams, Lu, coordinator, mtn grove branch campus, $42,392
Adamson, Benjamin, asst dir athl comm, $35,574
Adamson, Reesha, assistant professor, $53,288
Adamson, Stanley, assoc professor, $101,947
Adinegara, Veronica, sr graphic designer-publications, $38,033
Adkins, Gilbert Jr, on-site outreach coordinator, $32,529
Adkison, Robert, administrative assistant I, $22,552
Admire, Glena, administrative assistant II, $28,243
Agee, Kevin, new media specialist, $32,500
Agee, William, electronics technician II, $60,303
Agnew, William, associate professor, $82,278
Ailor, Shannon, research administration specialist, $30,428
Aistrup, Vicki, admission evaluator, $28,243
Ajuwon, Paul, associate professor, $62,959
Akers, Leslie, administrative assistant II, $25,500
Alaimo, Ian, instructional tech support specialist, $56,733
Albaugh, Rickey, clinical assistant professor, $130,000
Albin, Craig, distinguished professor, $65,404
Aleshire, Donnie, maintenance general mechanic, $35,467
Allard, Ginger, library associate II, $34,759
Alldridge, Barbara, custodian I, $27,147
Allen, Jimmie, associate professor, $55,191
Allen, Linda, academic admin asst II, $31,438
Allen, Nancy, sr instructor, $46,183
Allen, Natalie, clinical instructor, $41,185
Allen, Rebecca, instructor nt 12/12, $40,487
Allen, Rose, assistant professor, $56,942
Allgeier, Shane, web programmer analyst/server, $41,412
Alsup, Jennifer, swmo ahec director, $57,088
Alsup-Egbers, Clydette, assoc prof 9/12, $65,078
Altena, Thomas, assoc professor, $57,924
Altic, Bruce, custodian I, $21,608
Amberg, Lucie, new media specialist, $34,510
Amberg, Richard III, assistant professor, $52,780
Amidon, Ethan, assistant professor, $62,000
Amundson, Lee, academic administrative assistant II, $27,419
Anderson, Angela, academic administrative assistant II, $32,811
Anderson, Angela, professor, $64,872
Anderson, Katie, academic records specialist, $21,183
Anderson, LaTrisha, admin specialist II, $19,208
Anderson, Rachel, entrepreneurial specialist, $45,000
Anderson, Rayanna, dir small bus tech dev ctr, $76,935
Anderson, Wayne, professor, $99,700
Anderson Cooper, Amy, accounting specialist, $29,119
Anderson-Ituarte, Julie, blindness skills specialist, $53,795
Aram, Roberta, professor, $69,732
Arendell, Telory, professor, $50,650
Arens, Joseph, enterprise system administrato, $57,264
Armstrong, Etta, admin asst II, $26,531
Armstrong, Joan, dir project access, $67,749
Arnold, Albert, programmer/analyst, $44,773
Arnold, Mark, lib sys adm-support speci, $58,294

Arnsmeyer, David, distributed user support specialist, $50,037
Arthaud, Tamara, department head, $98,541
Arthur, Sandra, executive assistant III, $35,516
Artman, Amy, instructor, $30,450
Asay, Nancy, senior instructor, $46,138
Ash, Karen, assistant director, $45,057
Ashcroft, Paul, associate professor, $123,051
Atkinson, Susan, athletic trainer, $37,168
Atwell, Jan, clinical instructor, $51,151
Aufdembrink, Amymarie, acad advisor, $37,741
Austin, Christopher, web designer, $36,960
Austin, Gayla, administrative spc II, $28,143
Avery, Calvin, distance learning engineer, $37,162
Axxe-Douglas, Shari, accounting technician, $28,243
Ayala, Priscilla, admission counselor for diversity outreach & recruitment, $31,210
Babington, April, academic administrative asst II, $26,838
Badovinac, Peter, assistant coach, $40,000
Baer, Claudia, accounting specialist, $29,327
Baggett, Holly, professor, $65,920
Bailey, Sandra, asst professor, $66,712
Bailey, Sherry, administrative spc II, $29,846
Baker, Anne, archivist, $46,707
Baker, James, vp rsrch & econ dev & int prog, $163,235
Baker, Rebecca, instructor, $43,394
Bakker, Klaas, professor, $77,779
Balasundaram, Clement, financial reporting & tech spc, $41,353
Balasundaram, Gautam, procurement card coordinator, $36,523
Baldwin, Jennifer, admissions evaluator, $28,243
Baldwin, Susan, instructor-nt, $45,754
Bales, Sandra, clinic assistant, $27,587
Balisle, Jessica, administrative spc II, $25,908
Ballard, Sheri, accountant, $36,540
Bampoe, Michel, asst dir of human resources-benefits, $49,735
Barakat, Terry, eli academic specialist, $39,341
Barber, Marlin, assistant professor, $51,765
Barber, Sarah, clinical assistant professor, $43,561
Barker, Angela, instructional tech suppor, $56,000
Barlowe, Jason, technology spc greenwood, $33,810
Barnes, Joshua, custodial specialist, $24,758
Barnes, Ruth, associate professor, $56,034
Barnett, Cynthia, dir campus recreation, $60,496
Barnette, Megan, admission evalutor, $28,246
Barnhart, Mary, custodian I, $21,397
Barnhart, Miles, professor, $80,818
Barnts, Kelly, administrative assistant II, $28,105
Barnwell, Melinda, patient services coordinator, $29,553
Barreau, Jacob, assistant coach, $33,300
Barreda, Albert, assistant professor, $67,000
Barrier, Tonya, professor, $98,206
Barrowclough, Gail, accounting specialist, $29,982
Barton, Sheila, project manager, $40,600
Bass, Randy, pharmacist, $105,193
Bass, Samuel, instructor, $37,826
Bassen, Krista, university facilities analyst/ais, $49,591
Bassett, Damon, sr instructor-nt, $45,577
Bassham, Donna, crd financial aid wp, $43,542
Basu Roy, Subhasree, assistant professor, $65,000
Bates, Dakota, admission counselor, $27,287
Baughman, Nelia, administrative assistant II, $27,995
Bauman, R, assoc professor, $60,068
Baumann, Denise, assoc dir res life housing & dining svcs, $63,391
Baumgartner, Vernon, custodian I, $31,128
Baumlin, James, distinguished professor, $84,806
Baumlin, Mary, professor, $69,936
Baynes, Leslie, associate professor, $42,364
Beach, Jeremy, radio communicaitons officer, $26,531
Beatty, Nick, instructor-nt, $33,792
Beck, Adam, equpment lending supervis, $33,857
Beck, Catherine, admininstrative spec III, $29,864
Becker, Brett, systems programmer wp, $57,496
Becker, Kelly, technology support spc wp, $46,811
Beckham, Tracy, asst program dir - nurse anesthesia, $140,000
Beckman, Daniel, associate dean, $76,800
Bee, Thomas, custodian I, $19,799
Behling, Pamela, administrative spc II, $30,259
Bell, Deana, custodian I - wp, $22,810
Bell, Elisabeth, clinical assistant professor, $60,955
Bell, Jonathan, residence hall director, $32,208

Bell, Kimberly, enrollment svcs systems c, $68,515
Bellis, James, asst to head, darr schl agr, stdt serv/pub affrs, $59,200
Belshoff, Richard, professor, $76,667
Bender, Timothy, professor, $85,738
Benford, Marilyn, custodian I, $21,427
Bennett, Drew, chancellor, west plains, $158,401
Bennett, Jessica, assistant professor, $41,000
Benson, Tara, assoc dir psu-dir student engagement, $60,047
Benton, Alan, centralized user supp spc, $54,628
Benton, Kimberly, accounting technician, $33,216
Berg, Susan, associate professor, $85,114
Berkwitz, Stephen, department head, $89,761
Berquist, Charlene, professor, $81,699
Berry, Jessica, assistant teacher, $20,934
Berry, Melissa, equal opportunity specialist, $51,765
Berry, Roberta, senior instructor, $39,824
Bess, Mitchell, library associate I, $28,777
Betz, Nathan, senior systems analyst, $68,920
Bhattacharyya, Gautam, assistant professor, $56,000
Biagioni, Richard, professor, $80,322
Biava, Christina, professor, $68,640
Biggs, Mark, interim associate dean, $97,672
Bigley, Louise, clinical instructor, $51,765
Bihlmeyer, James, professor, $63,101
Billington, Brandon, custodian I, $19,799
Bilyeu, Kristin, accountant, $36,540
Bingham, Bill, custodian I, $31,908
Bingham, Brent, custodian specialist, $26,902
Bird, Biff, systems-database analyst wp, $45,991
Bird, Donna, academic admin asst II, $31,874
Birdyshaw, Edward, assistant professor, $46,506
Birkes, Sheryl, administrative spc II, $31,745
Black, Alice, assoc professor, $60,596
Black, James, public safety officer, $26,999
Black, Troy, maintenance general mechanic, $40,596
Blackmon, W, department head, $98,749
Blacksher, Julie, human resources records technician, $30,051
Blackwood, Randall, exec dir athletic & enter, $103,984
Blades, Heather, assoc dir ctr for dispute reso, $38,332
Blades, Jeremy, microcomputer support administrator, $47,979
Blades, Melissa, academic administrative assistant I, $23,090
Blake, Michael, custodian I, $27,993
Blakemore, Rhonda, residence hall night host/hostess, $16,847
Blankenship, Melissa, assistant director, $33,130
Blansit, Amy, instructor, $40,000
Blanton, Patti, instructor, $36,864
Bledsoe, Nathaniel, postal technician II, $20,576
Blevins, Brian, custodian I, $30,110
Blevins, Brooks, professor, $76,222
Blevins, Sarah, custodian I, $22,154
Bloom, Scott, instructor nt, $42,240
Blunt, Sherry, res hall recpst 10/10, $23,062
Boaz, Ronald, dir jqh arena, hsc & psc, $62,524
Bobbitt-Boyce, Edith, clinical assistant professor, $59,885
Bodenhausen, Bradley, asst vp international prog/dir iltc, $95,000
Bodo, Bela, assoc professor, $42,746
Boehne, Tara, clinical assistant professor, $76,633
Boey, Jir, head music & media, library,
Boff, Rebecca, custodian I, $31,127
Bogart, John, human resource records te, $34,132
Bohn, Timothy, asst dir athl comm web & new m, $41,434
Bolin, Raymond, hvac-food svc equip mecha, $43,409
Bonds, Jim, custodial specialist, $35,409
Bonds, Nechell, director, $85,000
Bonebrake, Tara, instructor, $43,645
Bonner, Lisa, academic administrative assistant I, $23,129
Boon, Austin, academic advisor/retention specialist, $37,000
Borich, Lynn, instructor-nt, $38,813
Borneman, Dea, associate professor, $50,277
Bosch, Eric, distinguished professor, $89,079
Boslaugh, Benjamin, utilities manager, $59,662
Boulton-Funke, Adrienne, assistant professor, $50,000
Bourhis, John, professor, $91,442
Bowe, Laura, instructor, $37,083
Bowen, Misty, coordinator, $37,000
Bowen, Sheila, crd employee wellness programs, $66,600
Bowen, Tamra, payroll specialist, $36,000
Bowles, Christina, academic advisor, $34,621
Bowles, Elizabeth, research specialist II, $32,090

Bowman, Janet, admin asst II, $32,241
Boyce, Ronald, dir of track & field & cross country, $71,553
Boyd, Carmen, assistant professor, $48,135
Boyle, Megan, assistant professor, $52,500
Boyle, Michael, instructor nt, $40,320
Boys, Cathy, asst professor, $46,862
Braden, Steven, custodial services coordi, $44,704
Brady, Katherine, coordinator mba program, $55,825
Brahnam, S, professor, $118,283
Brandt, Kathryn, accounting technician, $28,852
Branson, Debra, assoc dir alumni relations, $52,780
Branton, Michelle, dir of developmental education, $52,980
Bray, William, department head, $118,713
Brazeal, LeAnn, assistant professor, $53,795
Breault, Donna, department head, $91,350
Breault, Rick, visiting professor, $55,825
Brennan, Kelly, executive assistant IV, $39,520
Breshears, Andrea, academic administrative assistant II, $26,553
Breshears, Rhonda, acad administrative assistant III, $29,385
Brewer, Kimberly, assistant teacher, $19,799
Brewer, Robert, head athletics coach, $50,581
Brewington, Cody, non-credit program coordinator, $35,219
Breyfogle, Bryan, professor, $68,192
Bridges, Cindy, coordinator, academic advisement, $45,675
Bridges, Kelly, administrative assistant II, $25,807
Bridges, Paul, maintenance general mechanic, $33,216
Bridges, Phillip, eli academic specialist, $39,341
Brinker, Heather, teacher, $26,411
Brinkerhoff, Kris, software support specialist wp, $46,154
Brinklow, Elaine, administrative spc II, $32,737
Brinson, Sabrina, professor, $70,755
Britton, Richard, custodian I, $21,397
Broaddus, Marilyn, instructor, $39,341
Brock, Timothy, assistant professor, $54,000
Brockman, Don, physician medical staff, $125,000
Brockman, Megan, accountant, $36,540
Brodeur, Amanda, assistant professor, $55,906
Brokaw, Dawn, administrative assistant II, $27,398
Brooks, Gerald, facilities manager, $54,913
Brower, Shawn, hvac mechanic, $33,216
Brown, Abby, admin assistant, $32,876
Brown, Billie, custodian I, $27,794
Brown, Candice, licensed practical nurse, $35,766
Brown, David, professor, $90,483
Brown, Edward, public safety officer - shift supervisor, $33,420
Brown, Jeffrey, env mgmt tech/recycling crd, $32,320
Brown, Kenneth, department head, $130,000
Brown, Mack, assistant coach, $40,000
Brown, Matthew, public safety officer, $26,531
Brown, Orville, associate dean, $93,380
Brown, Robert, instructor nt, $34,621
Brown, Susan, arena patron & event srvs crd, $26,001
Brown, Tara, registration & records assistant, $28,661
Brown, Traci, registered nurse, $41,807
Brown, William, technology support spc wp, $45,183
Broyles, Thora, preparatory math specialist, $37,444
Brummel, Sara, assoc professor, $56,034
Bryant, Stephanie, dean, $190,081
Bryson, Laurie, executive assistant I, $34,588
Buchanan, Erin, associate professor, $56,794
Bucher, Darrell, public safety officer, $34,954
Buckner, Margaret, professor, $74,286
Buckner, Sally, academic admin assistant II, $27,419
Bunn, Roger, instructor, $41,412
Burasco, Nico, videographer/editor,
Burch, Abby, instructor-nt, $40,779
Burge, Sara, instructor, $33,551
Burger, Elisabeth, admission counselor, $29,681
Burke, June, custodian I, $19,799
Burke, Martin, custodian I, $21,397
Burnett, Melissa, professor, $106,110
Burney, Larry, custodian I, $31,127
Burrell, Brenda, systems analyst, $52,311
Burton, Brian, assistant strength & conditioning coach, $33,495
Burton, Charles, custodian I, $22,486
Burton, Michael, professor, $71,168
Burton, Richard, instructor-nt, $38,621
Busby, Charles, internet specialist, $45,856
Busby, Cindy, academic administrative assistant II, $25,791

Busby, Cindy, executive asst IV, $51,244
Bushman, Barbara, professor, $87,064
Butler, Marcia, assistant professor, $54,925
Bynum, Sharon, lecturer, $34,000
Byrd, David, professor, $115,052
Byrd, Sandra, professor, $119,469
Cabrera Hurtado, Kelly, crd intntl leadership / training ctr, $35,525
Caddy, Cynthia, administrative specialist III, $34,260
Cadle, Lanette, assoc professor, $53,949
Cafagna, Marcus, professor, $58,194
Cahoj, Patricia, asst professor 12/12, $89,855
Cahoj, Richard, general buyer, $28,243
Cain, Mary, administrative spc II, $32,143
Caldwell, Cheryl, dir univ communications wp, $56,117
Caldwell, Kelly, custodian I, $19,799
Caldwell, Sarah, manager, accts payable & budgeting, $54,810
Calfano, Brian, associate professor, $46,403
Calico, Dean, custodian I, $25,744
Calihman, Matthew, associate professor, $56,509
Callahan, Kimberly, academic administrative asst II, $26,838
Callahan, Richard, department head, $132,001
Cameron, James, assoc professor, $55,895
Camp, Deanne, professor, $81,136
Camp, Susan, director of development & sales, $32,480
Campbell, Judith, academic admin asst II, $32,413
Campbell, Pamela, training specialist, $38,570
Canales, Roberto, associate professor, $95,497
Canella, John, public safety officer, $32,554
Capps, Steven, dir learning diagnostic clinic, $67,556
Caravella, David, operations coordinator fctl, $50,687
Carawan, Edwin, professor, $70,387
Cardenas, Carolyn, department head, $111,936
Cardin, Ashlea, assistant professor, $76,632
Cardwell, Lisa, clothing/soft goods inventory specialist, $32,320
Cardwell, Thomas, boiler fireman, $36,012
Carl, Teresa, executive assistant I, $35,067
Carney, Russell, professor, $88,970
Carr, Judy, assoc professor, $48,984
Carr, Sylvia, instructor-nt, $42,826
Carr, W, assistant professor, $61,915
Carrington, Terri, associate director, $52,780
Carroll, Michael, resource coordinator-mmp, $32,320
Carson, Edward, technical director, $39,909
Carson, Erin, academic records specialist, $27,699
Carson, Gay, administrative spc II, $29,523
Carter, Jonathan, web systems analyst, $52,837
Carter, Thomas, mgr programming & product, $67,394
Casada, Debra, custodian I, $26,484
Case, William, information technologies, $53,507
Casey, Lisa, professor, $63,797
Casey, Michael, professor,
Cash, Cody, instructor-nt, $30,450
Cashler, Jennifer, vivarium technician, $21,397
Cataldo, Monica, traffic coordinator, $33,399
Cates, Jared, career center data coordinator,
Cathey, Christie, assistant professor, $50,750
Caton, Barbara, asst professor, $55,514
Catron, Angela, residence hall receptionist, $21,369
Cemore Brigden, Joanna, assoc professor, $58,383
Chakraborty, Sapna, prog dir occupational therapy prog, $93,500
Chambers, Amanda, assistant professor, $51,765
Chambers, Jeffery, grounds foreman, $32,690
Champagne, Leslie, administrative spc II, $27,696
Champagne, Marcelle, systems analyst, $50,631
Chandler-Clayton, Cynthia, academic admin asst II, $30,892
Chang, Chih-Cheng, professor, $121,591
Chang, Ching-Wen, assoc professor, $60,900
Chapman, Carol, assistant professor, $52,800
Chapman, David, construction technician, $31,926
Chastain, William, hvac mechanic, $36,223
Chaston, Joel, distinguished professor, $70,875
Cheek, Julie, academic admin asst III, $35,253
Chen, Li-Ling, research specialist II, $31,834
Cheng, Yungchen, professor, $83,427
Chenoweth, Amelia, instructor, $42,000
Chesman, Jeremy, assoc professor 12/12, $63,713
Chester, Jarrad, coordinator of outdoor adventures, $32,000
Childress, Priscilla, coord parent & family programs, $43,500
Childs, Elaina, information specialist, $28,243

Chin, Jerry, professor, $115,000
Chin, Mary, senior instructor-nt, $49,179
Chism, Richard, public safety officer, $26,531
Choate, Edward, director, $101,015
Chorn, Gary, asst dir fac mgt, custodial, $56,821
Chorn, Malynda, stores clerk mechanical, $27,397
Christian, Donna, director internal audit & compliance, $96,425
Chuchiak, John, professor, $72,257
Claborn, David, associate professor, $74,962
Clark, Darryl, assistant professor, $49,048
Clark, Donald, custodial supervisor, $35,525
Clark, James, groundskeeper, $32,737
Clark, John, asst dir fac mgt, grounds, $52,821
Clark, Kaye, assistant teacher, $19,799
Clark, Kimberly, administrative assistant II, $28,243
Clark, Lisa, director of planned giving, $71,050
Clark, Ronald, assoc professor, $117,810
Clark, Sara, dir web & new media, $73,642
Claussen, Patty, financial aid counselor, $38,093
Clayton, Michael, assistant professor, $55,500
Clements, Melinda, res hall host/hostess, $21,701
Cleveland, Tracy, associate professor, $82,155
Cline, Andrew, assoc professor, $60,571
Cline, Cindy, registered nurse, $45,028
Cline, Lynn, professor 12/12, $92,512
Clouse, Nick, media systems technician, $36,242
Cobb, Barry, interim department head, $70,000
Cobban, Jean, administrative specialist III, $28,079
Cockrum, Angela, telecommunications system admin, $43,802
Cofer, James Sr, professor, $174,241
Cohen Ioannides, Mara, senior instructor, $41,733
Collier, Ellen, custodian I, $21,397
Collins, Alyssa, procurement/hr specialist, $35,721
Collins, CJ, systems-database analyst wp, $45,991
Collins, David, head athletics coach, $58,080
Collins, Kileene, administrative assistant II, $24,768
Collins, Peter, professor, $69,405
Colombo, Anne, instructor, $36,757
Coltharp, Allison, sr instructor-nt, $41,401
Combs, Cheryl, financial aid coord, stdt employment, $36,033
Combs, Christine, instructor-nt, $38,895
Combs, Julia, department head, $111,565
Combs, Theresa, records & registration assist, $28,243
Compton, Pamela, residence hall night host/hostess, $16,293
Conlon, Shannon, library associate II, $34,462
Connor, George, department head, $103,530
Cook, Caryn, academic admin assistant II, $24,959
Cook, Jeanne, department head, $100,672
Cook, Sherry, senior instructor-nt, $49,487
Cooksey, Floyd, custodian I, $25,318
Coombes, Andrew, academic advisor/retention spec, $31,500
Coombs, James, assoc professor, $58,458
Coones, Jacquelyn, director of development, $55,000
Cooper, Lisa, custodian I, $21,397
Coopwood, Kenneth, vp for diversity & inclusion, $118,273
Copeland, Karen, administrative spc II, $33,573
Copeland, Nancy, collector, $48,271
Corcoran, Deborah, senior instructor, $48,066
Cornelison, David, department head, $117,976
Cornelius, Sherri, executive assistant II, $29,993
Cornelius-White, Jeffrey, professor, $68,535
Cornell, Gary, warehouse & delivery clerk, $22,774
Coroleuski, Linda, academic administrative asst II, $25,814
Cortez, Willie, maintenance general mechanic, $30,533
Coughlin, Sean, asst coach, $60,000
Coulter, Ronald, department head, $132,001
Coulter, Terrie, administrative assistant II, $27,985
Coverston, Alicia, eli admissions specialist, $30,533
Cowden, Dennis, public safety officer, $35,076
Cox, Erica, cnas lab supervisor, $43,170
Cox, Jennifer, associate dir of facilities management, $67,542
Cox, Nora, instructor-nt, $37,683
Cox, Ronda, administrative spc I, $23,486
Crabtree, Mark, distributed user support specialist, $40,212
Crafts, Daniel, assoc professor, $69,175
Craig, Christopher, assoc provost-faculty & academic affairs, $135,169
Craig, Rebecca, financial aid counselor, $30,122
Crain, Susan, professor, $125,857

Creson, Michelle, financial aid technician, $30,036
Crews, Carrie, administrative assistant II, $31,865
Crews, Jennifer, dir of prosp mgmt & research, $51,355
Crockett, Jeffrey, public safety officer, $26,999
Crockett, Jonathan, construction technician, $29,972
Cron, Deborah, clinical assoc prof 12/12, $66,613
Crowder, Rebecca, instructor, $40,497
Cuebas, Dean, assoc professor, $55,935
Culbertson, Cory, custodian I, $19,799
Culver, Sandra, dir business advisement c, $53,954
Culver, Victoria, assistant director, student engagement, $34,108
Cummings, Valerie, dir marketing & promotions-access & outreach, $42,714
Cunningham, Denise, associate professor, $59,394
Cunningham, Kym, residence hall night host/hostess, $16,997
Curry, Matthew, dir case, $84,574
Curtis, Ginger, administrative specialist II, $26,831
Curtright, Lisa, executive assistant II, $29,760
Cutbirth, Suzanne, professional developer, $72,619
Czyzniejewski, Michael, assistant professor, $51,765
Daehn, Ann Marie, assistant professor, $51,765
Dake, Pamela, academic administrative assistant II, $26,321
Dale, Michal, instructor-nt, $37,965
Dallas, Melissa, professor, $109,555
Dalton, Benjamin, lab supervisor cnas, $29,000
Dalton, Kelly, senior accountant/analyst, $46,690
Dalton, Nicole, accounting technician, $27,767
Dalton, Tracy, senior instructor-nt, $41,223
Dane, Michelle, accounting technician, $27,287
Daniel, Carol, clinical instructor, $52,800
Daniel, Todd, instructor, $42,240
Daniels, Amy, accounting technician, $27,287
Daniels, Thomas, custodian I, $27,794
Daoust, Mario, asst professor, $53,105
Darabi, Rachelle, assoc prov stdt dev & pub affa, $129,642
Datema, Anna, executive assistant I, $34,778
Datema, Timothy, bookstore shipping & receiving/pawprints supervisor, $30,533
Dattero, Ronald, professor, $112,918
Daugherty, Timothy, professor, $90,721
Davidson, Bradley, centralized user support specialist, $40,530
Davis, Belinda, non-credit program coordinator, $38,033
Davis, Janet, academic administrative assistant I, $23,129
Davis, Kathy, dir advisement center, $69,103
Davis, Ronald, custodian II, $31,201
Davis, Ruth, public safety officer, $26,999
Davis, Sarah, administrative assistant II, $25,376
Day, Kaya, academic admin assistant II, $26,697
Day, Lori, senior admission evaluator, $31,095
Day, Michele, interim director, $61,068
Day, Patrick, coordinator of operations and systems, $73,971
De Azeredo Moura, Isabel, eli instruction specialist, $30,812
De la Hoz De la Hoz, Helena, visiting instructor, $33,000
DeBoef, Ryan, chief of staff & asst to pres for governmental relations, $137,025
DePaepe, Paris, professor, $75,839
DeWitt, Joyce, asst professor, $55,330
Deal, William, asst dir learning diag ct, $67,879
Debode, Jason, assistant professor, $110,000
Deckard, Shelly, executive assistant III, $34,287
Decker, James, eli academic specialist, $39,341
Dembele, Moussa, custodian I, $23,919
Denton, D, professor, $98,418
Denton, Melinda, assistant professor, $43,570
Depriest, Christopher, technical director theatr, $39,002
Derby, Norma, information specialist, $27,767
Derrick, Noel Jr, custodian I, $28,775
Derricks, Shannon, assistant director, $47,880
Dettmers, Crystal, administrative specialist II,
Devault, Guy, groundskeeper/arborist, $35,034
Dewberry, Jane, sr internal auditor, $66,320
Dicke, Thomas, professor, $71,411
Dickison, Lynn, senior enterprise systems administrator, $72,243
Dillon, Randy, professor, $80,789
Dimond, Jack, senior instructor, $42,746
Dion, Nancy, assistant professor, $84,758
Dionne, Dawn, food services manager, $32,200
Dirks-Ham, Chelsea, assistant coach, $32,252
Dixon, Kimberly, administrative assistant II, $26,058

Dixon, Richard II, custodian I, $22,790
Dixon, Stephanie, academic administrative assistant III, $28,079
Dixon, Tamarah, non-student part-time,
Dixon, Tammy, mental health clinician, $47,768
Dockery, Rachael, general counsel, $145,000
Dodge, Steven, department head, $105,130
Doennig, Eric, asst sports info dir, $36,652
Dogwiler, Toby, department head,
Dollar, Susan, professor, $83,411
Donelson, Randy, access control specialist, $35,395
Dong, Lifeng, associate professor, $61,788
Donham, Debra, administrative admin, $23,434
Donnellan, Debra, executive asst IV, $49,534
Donnelson, Nicki, public relations specialist, $35,566
Dotson, Brandy, custodian I, $20,934
Dotson, Seth, custodian I, $21,443
Douglas, Addie, custodian I, $30,355
Dover, Susan, graduate admissions evaluator, $32,703
Dowdy, David, professor, $75,243
Dowdy, Marcia, sr instructor-nt, $45,223
Downing, John, assoc professor, $65,354
Drennan, Sally, teacher, $28,243
Dressler, Howard, preventative maint coordinator, $38,361
Dreyer-Lude, Melanie, assistant professor, $51,000
Driskell, Russell, ranch hand, journagan ranch, $34,747
Driskell, Vickie, public relations specialist wp, $33,895
Dubinsky, Julie, assoc dir of hr, $70,171
Dubree, Kimberly, crd educational field experiences, $42,240
Dudash-Buskirk, Elizabeth, assoc professor, $59,194
Dudley, Larry, distributed user support spc, $51,197
Duitsman, Dalen, dir ozarks public health inst, $93,355
Duncan, Janice, dir greenwood lab school, $94,893
Dunlop, Vicki, asst professor, $52,851
Dunn, Kevin, assistant coach, $50,000
Dunn, William, vp for university advance, $145,795
Durden, Joni, academic admin asst III, $30,993
Durden, Karen, library associate I, $31,657
Durham, Paul, distinguished professor, $128,288
Dyer, Samuel Jr, assoc professor, $60,068
Eagleman, Laketa, admin asst II, $27,785
Earl, Melanie, dir annual funds, $56,413
East, Stephanie, senior pharmacy technician, $30,700
Easter, Lauren, asst dir campus recreation-rec sports, $33,966
Echols, Leslie, assistant professor, $54,500
Eckhardt, Brandon, asst dir of campus rec - aquatics, $33,792
Eddy, Glenda, executive assistant I, $27,480
Edgar, William Jr, clinical associate professor, $77,367
Edmond, Brian, senior systems analyst, $61,929
Edmondson, Elizabeth, administrative specialist III, $29,034
Edwards, Adam, groundskeeper, $22,686
Edwards, Christine, library associate I, $28,778
Edwards, Daniel, hvac mechanic, $39,964
Edwards, Mark, custodian I, $21,397
Edwards, Michael, crd, graduate admissions, $32,094
Egan, Michael, property control manager, $39,149
Egbert, Robert, professor, $98,740
Ehlers, Abigale, senior instructor, $45,095
Einhellig, Frank, provost/chancellor-mtn grove, $217,413
Eisenhauer, Isabel, assistant director, $60,780
Ekhause, Mary, postal technician I, $21,397
Ekstam, Keith, professor, $73,293
Elders, Vicki, admin spc I, $20,216
Eldred, Jannette, clinical instructor, $40,600
Ellickson, Mark, professor, $69,954
Elliott, Cindy, admin asst II, $26,531
Elliott, Elizabeth, academic administrative assistant I, $24,162
Elliott, Joshua, public safety officer, $27,527
Elliott, Robert, custodian wp, $22,827
Elliott, W, department head, $119,276
Ellis, Carol, course materials buyer, $31,269
Ellis, Christopher, instructor-nt, $38,417
Ellis, Deborah, administrative assistant II, $32,955
Ellis, Michael, professor, $69,837
Ellison, Margaret, custodian I, $23,638
Ellison, Tyrone, custodian I, $23,128
Elrod, Keri, crd fitness & athletic tr wp, $42,821
Embretson, Scott, customer service manager, $36,930
Emeric, Bruce, project manager-architect, $63,074
Emery, Jeremy, field & maint crew leader, $26,622

Emrie, Gail, academic advisor-program crd, $25,663
Endicott, Jordan, academic administrative assistant I, $17,302
Engler, Karen, clinical professor, $68,563
Englert, Andrew, patrol lieutenant, $44,000
Englis, Christie, academic admin assistant II, $33,384
English, Catherine, assistant professor, $50,750
Epperson, Tracey Jr, boiler fireman, $32,000
Erdman, Shawn, academic advisor, marketing & recruitment specialist, $34,000
Erfling, Dennis, maintenance electrician, $35,688
Erickson, Janet, library associate I, $34,302
Ernce, Keith, professor, $85,345
Espy, Brenda, admin asst IV, $37,287
Essel, Paul, sr accountant-analyst, $46,690
Estes, Rebecca, admin asst II, $26,531
Estrella, Ana, instructor, $37,788
Eth, Joe, programmer/analyst, $57,435
Ettinger, Lawrence, custodian wp, $27,250
Euglow, Todd Jr, career resources specialist, $38,570
Evans, Kelly, financial aid coordinator, $37,084
Evans, Kevin, professor, $67,245
Evans, Paul, asst coach, $56,987
Evans, Sarah, instructor-nt, $36,757
Evans, Vicki, accounting specialist, $34,203
Eversoll, Norwin, hvac mechanic, $39,964
Ewert, Debbie, telecommunications service coord, $61,478
Ewy, Timothy, centralized user support specialist, $40,530
Fairbairn, Candace, clinical faculty-instructor, $42,009
Faith, Jonathan, hvac mechanic, $32,955
Fallone, Melissa, asst professor, $51,184
Falls, Berlin II, custodian I, $31,908
Falls, Karen, custodian I, $30,905
Fan, Lori, executive director of alumni relations, $88,500
Fanetti, Matthew, professor, $70,772
Farmer, Jennifer, assistant teacher, $20,734
Farris, Kelli, asst director for co-curricular involvement, $34,621
Farris, Robin, clinic dir center city cnslg c, $44,858
Faucett, David, community planner, $35,688
Fearing, Cory, instructor, $41,032
Federman, Elizabeth, assistant professor, $60,268
Feeney, Sylvia, program dir nurse anesthesia, $155,295
Felicilda, Rhea, assistant professor, $59,136
Felker, Janice, academic administrative assistant II, $26,828
Ferber, Jason, videographer/editor, $33,550
Ferguson, Michael, foreman meyer alumni cent, $45,988
Ferguson, Suzann, career resources specialist, $41,080
Ferguson, Wendy, exec director development, $94,212
Fichter, Kathryn, assistant professor, $53,836
Fiedler, Scott, dir student svcs-cert officer, $65,078
Fife, Jordan, head athletics coach, $40,000
Finch, Ken, custodian I, $31,128
Finch, Kim, assistant professor, $55,459
Finch, Martha, assoc professor, $59,844
Fischer, Ashtyn, administrative assistant II, $25,891
Fischer, Donald, professor, $69,254
Fischer, Margaret, document & report specialist/adv, $30,044
Fischer, Scott, library associate I, $27,767
Fischer, Vicki, administrative spc II, $27,631
Fisher, Bradley, professor, $86,108
Fisher, Michael, production manager, $44,295
Fisk, Steven, groundskeeper, $29,669
Fitzgerald, Ivy, instructor, $40,000
Flanders, Janelle, instructor-nt, $40,072
Fletcher, Glenn, maintenance gen mechanic, $36,840
Flores, Tamara, administrative specialist II, $26,553
Flosi, Michael, programmer/analyst, $52,596
Follensbee, Billie, professor, $69,946
Ford, Luke Jr, public safety officer, $26,999
Foreman, Elizabeth, assistant professor, $55,000
Forester, Carol, administrative specialist II, $26,531
Forshee, Bryan, tech & const mgt lab tech, $43,170
Fortney, David, maintenance general mechanic, $29,762
Foster, Karen, administrative assistant IV, $35,912
Foster, Kurtis, english language instruction academic spec, $37,000
Foster, Lyle, instructor, $42,240
Foster, Micheal, assoc professor, $55,887
Foucart, Stephen, chief financial officer, $137,593
Foust, Billy, custodian I, $22,151
Fox, Corey, assistant professor, $110,000

Fox, Michael, telecommunications technician, $35,359
Fraczak, Jacek, associate professor, $56,259
Francka, Jacob Jr, maint general mechanic, $38,846
Francka, Samantha, marketing & web specialist, $36,960
Franklin, Keri, director of assessment, $85,869
Franklin, Rhonda, health information assist, $27,657
Franklin, Thomas, assoc professor, $70,343
Franks, Claudia, instructional specialist, $47,106
Frederick, Dana, instructor, $43,170
Frederick, Susan, associate head coach, $40,600
Frederick, Teresa, asst dir res life housing & dining - fac & op, $51,258
Freeman, Andrea, executive assistant III, $33,657
Freeman, Cynthia, instructor-nt, $39,697
Frevert, Brandon, assistant box office manager, $31,834
Frey, Jeremiah, head strength & conditioning coach, $46,340
Frietchen, Mark, project manager - prof engineer, $78,696
Fritz, Dean, public safety shift supervisor, $32,468
Frizell, Michael, dir stdt learning services, $59,416
Fuhrman, Ann, government document spc (, $42,682
Funderburk, Stacey, dir publications, $56,860
Furtak, Emily, library associate II, $31,523
Gagnon, Mollie, coordinator, $37,000
Galanes, Gloria, dean, $133,448
Gale, Crystal, assoc professor, $44,726
Gall, Elizabeth, instructor, $50,200
Gallaway, Julie, senior instructor, $49,048
Gallaway, Terrel, professor, $83,477
Gallion, Deborah, dir marketing & promotion, $59,126
Garbisch, Alisa, asst dir res life-student success initiatives, $47,000
Garcia, Josefina, sr accountant-analyst, $42,577
Gardner, Hobart, maintenance general mechanic, $29,944
Garg, Vinay, assoc professor, $90,069
Garland, Brett, assoc professor, $77,648
Garland, Diana, director of learning commons, $54,765
Garman, Stephen, financial aid counselor, $32,300
Garrad, Richard, professor, $79,422
Garrett, Filip, physician medical staff, $136,887
Garrison, Traci, clinical instructor, $64,960
Garrison-Kane, Linda, professor, $75,791
Gartin, Patrick, assoc professor, $78,319
Garton, Andrew, director of development, $55,000
Garton, Edwin, instructional tech support spc, $59,199
Gattis, Lyn, assoc professor, $56,301
Gebken, Richard, associate professor, $81,006
Geiger, Lacey, open-course coordinator, $33,495
George, Robert, public safety officer, $35,336
Gerasimchuk, Nikolay, professor, $70,397
Gholson, Martha, assoc professor, $50,420
Ghosh, Kartik, professor, $75,564
Gibbs, William, residence hall host/hostess, $16,847
Gibe, Sheri, university operator, $29,651
Giboney, Sharon, clinical assistant professor, $76,612
Gibson, Deana, academic admin asst III, $32,782
Gibson, Hugh, assoc professor, $60,761
Gibson, Kathryn, asst professor, $47,350
Gibson, Lisa, assoc dir international svs, $44,820
Gieselman-Holthaus, Tracie, library associate III, $33,551
Giles, Chelsey, assoc dir stdt financial, $58,933
Gillam, Kenneth, associate professor, $58,931
Gilsten, Heather, admin assistant II, $26,025
Girdley, Robert, grndskpr-gen maint worker wp, $29,959
Given, Mark, assoc professor, $58,672
Gladden, Monte, hvac mechanic, $43,448
Glaessgen, Tracey, asst director, first-year programs, $42,787
Glidewell, Elizabeth, research specialist II, $31,274
Glynn, Timothy, custodian I, $23,407
Gochenauer, Kristan, exec assistant to the president, $46,465
Goddard, Stacy, instructor, $36,960
Goeringer, Michael, clinical instructor, $41,412
Goerndt, Michael, asst professor, $32,452
Goin, Kelsey, eli special programs coordinator, $32,480
Goldade, Lois, admin asst II, $31,404
Golden, Mary, executive asst IV, $45,048
Gollhofer, Kami, health career coordinator, $38,000
Gomez-Sosa, Gabriela, head athletics coach, $39,916
Gong, Xiao'ou, china programs specialist coba, $42,240
Good, William, distributed user supp spc, $41,434
Goodman, Melissa, financial aid counselor, $31,834

Goodwin, Brenda, assistant professor, $52,438
Goodwin, David Jr, assoc professor, $58,496
Goodwin-Santo, Debra, admin specialist I, $24,785
Gordon, Grayson, campus web/database spc, wp, $51,047
Gordon, Nancy, assistant director fctl, $60,900
Goritschnig, Claus, public safety officer, $24,758
Gosselink, Carol, assoc professor, $62,576
Gouzie, Douglas, assoc professor, $60,639
Graham, Alexandra, writing specialist-wp, $37,281
Graham, Christy, executive asst III, $40,915
Graham, Phillip, copy center supervisor, $36,767
Grand, Melanie, asst professor, $60,941
Granger, Michele, professor, $81,656
Grant, Rebecca, administrative assistant II, $34,259
Graves, Carolyn, clinical instructor, $52,253
Gray, Emily, administrative assistant II, $27,581
Gray, Monica, administrative assistant II, $27,139
Greaser, Colin, equipment stores specialist, $25,542
Green, Aimee, coord, clinical education for resp care, $52,800
Green, Carol, business intelligence specialist, $37,010
Green, Geoffrey, membership coordinator-radio & tv, $27,925
Green, Marian, admin asst II, $28,467
Greene, Brian, assoc professor, $59,387
Greene, Janice, professor, $73,538
Greenfield, Robert, maintenance general mechanic, $30,533
Greim, Kevin, senior dir of athletics development, $70,918
Greiner, Douglas, dir counseling & testing, $69,194
Grevillius, Jeffrey, clothing/soft goods manag, $46,375
Grider, Jimmie, box office/business mgr, $44,858
Grier, Terry, admin asst II, $26,531
Griffin, Margie, executive assistant I, $29,448
Griffith, Alexes, custodian I, $20,576
Griffith, Cameron, instructor, $30,000
Griffith, Deborah, custodian I, $24,616
Grindstaff, Brian, experimental machinist, $45,221
Grosso, Karen, assistant dir of trio sss, $43,645
Groves, Fred, professor, $81,174
Gryder, Clella, licensed practical nurse, $34,902
Guinn, Kristina, immigration support coordinator, $40,194
Guo, Kanghui, professor, $82,433
Gutierrez, Melida, professor, $71,243
Guttin, Keith, head athletics coach, $88,419
Gutting, Edward, instructor-nt, $42,240
Gutzke, David, professor, $78,041
Gwynn, Ryan, custodian I, $20,576
Hachman, Shannon, administrative assistant II, $25,874
Hackeson, Michael, network analyst, $52,838
Hackney, James, associate professor 12/12, $91,031
Hackworth, Michel, manager,grants & cap proj acc, $54,821
Hader, William, distributed user supprt spc, $46,407
Haener, Lori, medical technologist, $41,125
Hagerman, Barron, enterprise systems adminis, $52,838
Haggard, Dana, assoc professor, $93,316
Haggard, Kelly, assoc professor, $122,234
Haik, Shellee, adm crd-acd adv, nurse anesthe, $31,522
Hail, Cynthia, professor, $79,983
Hains, Arthur, university marketing specialist, $58,665
Hale, Arnold, maintenance painter, $40,137
Hale, Beth, sr accountant/analyst, $42,578
Hale, Carole, academic admin assistant II, $33,086
Hall, Ann, accounting specialist, $29,403
Hall, Jamie, executive assistant III, $32,723
Hall, Lisa, assistant professor, $53,836
Hall, Milly, custodian wp, $22,827
Hallgren, Deanna, director cdc, $51,158
Hames, Jennifer, administrative assistant III, $30,159
Hamilton, Timmarie, program coordinator-mmp, $36,960
Hamm, Randall, professor, $64,663
Hamman, Bradley, systems analyst, $59,105
Hammers, Michael, utility locate coordinator, $41,323
Hammerschmidt, Melinda, instructor, $38,628
Hammond, Michael, senior instructor nt, $46,741
Hamon, Pascal, eli academic director, $50,000
Hamric, Randal, physician medical staff, $126,875
Hamwi, Georg, assistant professor, $107,291
Handley, Scott, assistant director, $45,307
Haney, Lisa, program manager mas, $37,300
Hankins, Amy, library associate II, $32,885
Hanley, Rodney, copy center/mail clerk, $21,397

Hansen, Anthony, residence hall director, $32,988
Hanson, Vicki, equity & compliance investigator, $31,059
Harbaugh, Adam, assistant professor, $54,871
Harbaugh, Rebecca, associate registrar, operations, $51,765
Hardie, Kimberly, administrative assistant III, $29,119
Hardin, Jonathan, laboratory & stores supervisor, $32,955
Harges, Mary, professor, $67,594
Haring, Katherine, enrollment & recruitment manager, $40,000
Harms, John, professor, $79,733
Harp, Patrick, computer operator, $33,760
Harper, Jonathan, assistant coach, $76,125
Harper, Kellie, head athletics coach, $160,000
Harper, Sharon, professor, $66,113
Harris, Marceda, academic records specialist, $28,511
Harris, Michael, visiting assistant professor, $45,675
Harris, Stephen, custodian foreman, $27,674
Harrison, Rebecca, accountant, $32,500
Harsen, Mark, coord of networking & telecom, $76,108
Harsha, Phillip, associate professor, $123,320
Hart, James, assistant professor, $45,067
Hartzler, Nathan, distributed user support specialist, $40,935
Harvey, Scott, director of news/content coordinator, $50,730
Harvey, Terrill, course materials buyer, $30,077
Haselden, Laura, administrative assistant I, $22,463
Haslam, Darryl, assoc professor, $63,684
Hass, Aida, assoc professor, $73,446
Hatch, Jerry, assoc professor, $58,745
Hatz, Kirsten, sr instructor-nt, $38,489
Hauff, Brian, project manager - architect, $69,365
Hausback, Jason, assistant professor, $51,765
Hauschildt, Mitchell, prevention rehab phys per, $45,367
Havel, John, professor, $83,906
Hawkins, Derrick, maintenance general mechanic, $30,051
Hawkins, Jordan, sr research scientist, $45,000
Hawkins, Ross, asst dir academic advisement ctr-transfer, $41,844
Hawkins, Thomas, custodian I, $20,576
Hayes, Frances, administrative spc II, $29,538
Haymans, Leonard III, maintenance gen mechanic, $30,533
Haynes, Tabitha, marketing & data comm specialist, $44,762
Haynes, Vickie, instructor, $39,697
Hays, Brian, distributed user support specialist, $48,804
Hays, David, professor, $64,057
Heath, Robert, physician medical staff, $136,810
Heaton, Brian, content mgt programmer/analyst, $62,106
Hedgpeth, Kent, instructor-nt, $43,310
Hein, Stephanie, department head, $112,101
Heinlein, Kurt, associate professor, $64,901
Heitger, Lester, professor, $128,622
Hellman, Andrea, instructor nt, $44,352
Hellman, Daniel, assoc professor, $54,129
Henary, Sara, assistant professor, $52,000
Hendershott, Dennis, warehouse & delivery cler, $25,130
Hendricks, Donovan, dir university communicat, $56,885
Hendrickson, Donald, system administrator, $40,828
Hendrickson, Nicole, instructor, $40,000
Henline, Jamie, membership crd - radio & tv, $31,575
Henne, Cassandra, clinical education crd - ahec, $32,736
Henry, Brian, maintenance foreman, $43,965
Henry, Kristina, assistant professor, $79,718
Henry, Leslie, groundskeeper, $32,748
Hensley, Ronald, supt of physical plant, wp, $55,877
Hensley, Teresa, accounting technician wp, $30,898
Henson, Jeremy, centralized user support specialist, $39,618
Henson, Pamela, sr instructor, $44,161
Hermans, Charles, professor, $109,484
Herr, Christopher, interim department head, $66,100
Herring, Ann, dir registration services, $45,050
Herring, Tara, laboratory supervisor cnas, $30,240
Heslip, Chris, warehouse & delivery clerk, $21,112
Hesse, Holly, head athletics coach, $70,216
Hetzler, Tona, department head, $107,325
Heyboer, Jill, professor, $63,797
Heywood, John, professor, $76,778
Hickey, Dennis, distinguished professor, $93,164
Hicks, Vickie, corporate relations specialist, $56,942
High, Brian, sr instructor nt-9 month appt, $42,552
High, Carrie, custodian I, $23,309
Hignite, Michael, interim department head, $95,861
Hill, Julie, asst dir psu-bldg svs & s, $39,667

Hill, Lindsay, instructor, $43,500
Hill, Patrick, studio shop maintenance s, $28,973
Hill, Sheryl, residence hall receptionist, $22,095
Hiller, Jokima, instructor, $50,000
Hinch, Steven, associate professor, $64,494
Hines, Christopher, assistant professor, $116,725
Hinman, Sarah, research specialist, $31,199
Hite, Brian, custodian I, $22,014
Hobbs, Lora, senior instructor, $46,273
Hoegeman, Catherine, assistant professor, $50,750
Hoelyfield, Dominiece, asst dir-crd lgbt student svcs, $40,381
Hoff, Nathan, assoc registrar-dgr prgrms & advs support, $55,993
Hoffmeyer, Joseph, energy management technician, $44,986
Hoggarth, Joshua, non-student part-time, $19,799
Holdt, Betty, custodian I, $26,484
Holdt, Don, custodian I, $26,484
Holland, Sharon, bookstore manager, $42,188
Holley, Catherine, administrative assistant II, $26,554
Holmer, Earl, senior instructor, $38,309
Holmer, Nancy, library associate II, $34,659
Holmes, Chad II, distributed user support specialist, $40,212
Holt, Shannon, assistant registrar-records & registration, $42,000
Homburg, Andrew, assistant professor, $52,800
Hong, Hye-Jung, associate professor, $51,450
Hoogestraat, Jane, professor, $69,929
Hook, Joi, accounting specialist, $27,397
Hooper, Madeleine, associate professor, $79,053
Hoover, Jerry, professor 12/12, $115,592
Hope, Kathryn, department head, $115,543
Hope, Marsha, information supv admissio, $33,422
Hopper, Donald, technology/supply buyer-technical support specialist, $33,499
Hopper, Tina-Maria, laboratory supervisor cnas, $35,362
Horeis, Nancy, academic admin asst II, $28,216
Horn, Debra, acad admin asst II, $25,807
Hornberger, Robert, asst vp enrollment mgmt/registrar, $83,901
Hornsby-Gutting, Angela, associate professor, $71,808
Horton, Tara, training coordinator sbtdc, $46,714
Horton, Leonard III, instructor, $47,705
Hough, David, dean, $151,235
Hough, Lyon, assistant professor, $54,810
Howard, Susanne, research specialist III, $38,033
Howell, Marcus, assoc professor, $52,100
Howerton, Phillip, associate professor, $48,092
Howerton, Victoria, coord testing / prior learning assesment, $33,000
Hu, Shouchuan, professor, $83,925
Huang, Shyang, professor, $71,704
Hubbard, Kevin, assistant professor, $81,200
Hubbell, Melody, assistant director of dev wp, $38,570
Huddleston, Carla, instructor, $49,653
Hudson, Danae, assoc professor, $31,737
Hudson, Michael, assoc professor, $73,800
Hudson, Nancy, accounting specialist, $32,572
Huelskamp, James, maintenance gen mechanic, $32,851
Huertas-Torres, Mariandine, teacher, $27,767
Huey, Paula, benefits specialist, $38,195
Huff, Jay, assistant director, $55,063
Huff, Jeffrey, asst professor, $45,067
Huff, Kristina, admin asst I, $23,648
Hufford, Lacey, teacher, $27,767
Hughes, Joseph, professor, $70,383
Hughes, Kevin, assoc professor, $55,620
Hughes, Myra, instructor-nt, $34,422
Hulett, Michelle, sr instructor-nt, $40,269
Hulgus, Joseph Jr, professor, $65,592
Humiston, John, maintenance painter, $34,692
Hummer, Carri, academic administrative assistant II, $26,930
Hunt, Anna, theatre scene shop sprv, $34,032
Hunt, Chastity, sr assoc dir athletics/swa, $92,704
Hunter, Anne Marie, assistant professor, $58,131
Hurst, Beth, professor, $80,915
Hurst, Judith, procurement technician, $27,247
Hurt, Timothy, centralized user support specialist, $41,433
Hutter, James, assoc professor, $65,019
Hwang, Chin-Feng, associate professor, $64,543
Hyde, William, groundskeeper/horticulturist, $36,455
Iantria, Linnea, instructor, $46,375
Ibach, Michael, groundskeeper, $23,530
Iman, Gary, instructor, $36,236

Ingle, Patricia, director of development, $65,000
Ioannides, Dimitri, professor, $23,086
Isackson, Abby, graphic designer-publications, $34,647
Jackson, Kenji, assistant coach, $40,000
Jackson-Brown, Grace, associate professor-library, $55,832
Jacobs, Phillip, custodial supply, delivery & storage foreman, $34,815
Jahnke, Tamera, dean, $140,932
Jamos, Abdullah, assistant professor, $55,825
Jay, Jon, custodial specialist, $24,728
Jenkins, Jay, distributed user supp spc, $51,678
Jenkins, Julie, instructor, $51,719
Jennings, Bryan, assistant professor, $53,856
Jennings, Mary, professor, $76,306
Jennings, Shannon, database analyst, $52,311
Jennings-Pineda, Joyce, asst professor, $45,972
Jensen, Donald Jr, custodial foreman, $33,167
Jensen, Jennifer, professional ed advisor/recruiter, $32,320
Jessee, Katy, academic advisor/retention specialist, $31,973
Jett, Melissa, crd of admissions wp, $42,821
Jochims, Lynda, accounting specialist, $28,227
John, Judith, professor, $67,545
John, Lacy, academic administrative assistant II, $26,846
Johns, Danny, custodian I, $21,397
Johns, Justin, mental health clinician/substance abuse, $39,341
Johnson, Alex, dir of comm involvement & service, $36,000
Johnson, Andrew, associate professor, $54,934
Johnson, Chalanda, administrative spc II, $30,395
Johnson, David, associate professor, $61,603
Johnson, Glen, technology support specialist, $45,643
Johnson, Hannah, residence hall night host/hostess, $16,293
Johnson, Janelle, distributed user support specialist, $41,388
Johnson, Julie, assoc professor, $63,788
Johnson, Laurie, custodian I, $30,905
Johnson, Mark, custodian I, $30,906
Johnson, Richard, professor, $99,803
Johnson, Sandra, admin spc III 10/10, $24,170
Johnson, Theresa, research specialist, $30,855
Johnson, Thomas, director, $83,000
Johnston, Ahren, asst professor, $107,291
Johnston, Jennifer, eli academic specialist, $41,599
Johnston, Tamara, administrative assistant II, $31,199
Jolivette, Catherine, assoc professor, $56,558
Jolley, Jan, department head, $89,761
Jones, Adena, assoc professor, $56,794
Jones, Adja, academic advisor-athletics achievement, $30,000
Jones, Barbara, dir special events coal, $47,788
Jones, Brian, custodial supply/delivery foreman, $31,200
Jones, Cheryl, professor, $58,014
Jones, Grant, business manager, $46,623
Jones, Jacqueline, accounting technician, $28,243
Jones, Jeffrey, assistant professor, $116,725
Jones, Kerri, academic advisor, $31,500
Jones, Lois, special ed compliance consultant, $52,538
Jones, Martin, assoc professor, $77,738
Jones, Matthew, electroni systems coordin, $35,049
Jones, Nadine, academic admin asst II, $29,051
Jones, Peggy, executive assistant IV, $46,375
Jones, Robert, interim department head, $86,150
Jones, Sandra, radio communications officer, $28,247
Jones, Sherry, administrative assistant II, $28,118
Jones, Steven, professor, $74,850
Jordan, Cathy, project manager - architect, $69,365
Jordan, Linda, dual credit coordinator, $32,094
Joswick, David, sr instructor-nt, $72,424
Joyce, Delores, project coordinator tup, $38,735
Jutla, Rajinder, professor, $68,738
Kaatz, James, assoc professor, $56,688
Kaf, Wafaa, professor, $83,369
Kamerer, Gwendolyn, medical assistant, $25,377
Kammerer, Joseph, director of dev wp, $51,975
Kane, Kevin, head athletics coach, $38,665
Kane, Thomas, professor, $74,183
Kaps, Martin, research prof 12/12, $86,894
Karanikas, Marianthe, assoc professor, $50,992
Karlen, Maria, energy manager, $52,028
Karuppan, Corinne, professor, $111,273
Katona, Paul, technical engineer, $54,993
Kaufman, Daniel, professor, $70,984
Kaula, Rajeev, professor, $102,818

Keene, Amy, sr admission evaluator, $31,562
Keeth, Jonathan, research technician II, $53,384
Keever, Amanda, accounting technician, $28,243
Keith, Nancy, professor, $107,540
Kekec, Susan, eli sevis specialist, $28,622
Keller, Anthony, assoc professor, $111,805
Keller, Carl Jr, associate professor, $121,717
Keller, Forrest, journeyman plumber, $39,942
Kellum, Mary, academic specialist, trio, $30,048
Keltner, Michael, instructor-nt, $36,349
Kemp, Matthew, maintenance general mechanic, $30,051
Kemp, Michael, maintenance general mechanic, $30,527
Kemp, Paula, distinguished professor, $99,988
Kendall, Carrie, administrative assistant II, $26,679
Kenneally, Maria, clinical assistant professor, $60,268
Kennedy, Kathleen, department head, $100,321
Kennedy, Robin, video comm administrator-pharmd, $50,750
Kenney, Phyllis, accounting technician, $30,121
Kent, Samantha, groundskeeper, $21,492
Kerley, Christina, accounting manager-wp, $48,162
Kerr, Jennifer, clinical assistant professor, $63,360
Ketchum-Brewer, Karmen, acad advisor/retention spec, $32,094
Kettering, Denise, dir advancement services, $75,927
Keuneke, Mark, custodian I, $24,039
Keys, Amanda, assistant professor, $52,000
Kidula, Iris, english language instruction specialist, $35,525
Kielhofner, Robert, director, $92,439
Kile, Thomas, dir operations, $50,975
Killian, Audrianna, asst director trio upward bound, $40,600
Killion, John, professor, $76,664
Kilmer, Shelby, professor, $78,715
Kim, Kyoungtae, assoc professor, $58,819
Kincaid, Brian, dir business incubator, $42,240
Kindhart, Richard, asst dir athletics for communi, $69,887
Kindle, Michael, telecommunications specialist, $69,040
King, Heather, director of scholarships, $54,698
King, Laura, administrative assistant II, $21,215
King, Sandra, advertising manager, $36,062
Kintner, Ellen, information specialist, $27,767
Kirkland-Ives, Mitzi, associate professor, $54,657
Kleeschulte, Melanie, visiting instructor, $36,540
Klem, Michael, coordinator business & support srvs, $50,657
Kliethermes, Sean, asst dir adms information, $48,092
Knackstedt, Konya, asst director-business operations, $33,800
Knapp, Timothy, professor, $81,127
Knepper, Charna, medical technologist, $42,985
Knight, Jack, professor, $78,546
Knight, Rachel, assistant general manager ksmu & opt, $73,489
Knowles, Amy, student teacher supervisor, $31,575
Kohnen, Angela, assistant professor, $51,765
Koo, Pedro, assoc professor, $56,675
Korn, Bradley, assistant coach, $86,445
Kostic, Bogdan, assistant professor, $50,730
Kostovic, Cedomir, professor, $76,513
Kovacs, Laszlo, professor, $80,867
Kramer, Justin, assistant coach, $40,000
Kuhlmeier, Sylvia, dir library srvs, $52,253
Kunkel, Allen, assoc vp econ dev & dir jvic, $123,254
Kwon, Seongchun, assistant professor, $39,000
Kyle, Jerri, sr instructor-nt, $40,305
Kyle, Laura, health information coordi, $34,979
LaBarr, Cameron, director of choral studies, $51,000
LaMontagne, Michael, visiting assistant professor, $48,000
LaPreze, Melody, asst professor, $85,596
Ladd, Ronda, res life facilities specialist, $31,948
Lair, Heath, technology support spc wp, $44,749
Lambert, Joshua, assoc prof-library-12 mo appt, $65,231
Lamouria, Lanya, assistant professor, $52,800
Lampe, James, professor, $138,662
Lancaster, Dennis, asst professor, $80,574
Landgraf, Tyler, athletic trainer, $39,668
Lane, Thomas, assoc vp for student life/dean of students,
Langston, Lisa, mental health clinicn <1fte, $36,224
Lanning, Brenda, senior procurement technician, $39,000
Lanpher, Larry, grounds equipment mech, $33,714
Larson, Deborah, assoc professor, $58,553
Lashley, Stephanie, sr dir donor relations / spec events, $60,290
Laswell, Kevin, custodian I, $24,225
Lathrop, Jonita, custodian I, $21,397

Lawrence, Idonna, licensed practical nurse, $35,766
Lawrence, Kristy, executive assistant IV, $37,427
Laws, Bethany, academic advisor/retention spc, $32,736
Lawson, Jeffrey, library associate I, $29,940
Leamy, Diane, senior instructor nt, $46,208
Leamy, Jonathan, head athletics coach, $53,989
Leas, Brian, classroom tech support admin, $40,000
Leasure, Stanley, associate professor, $88,530
Lee, Amanda, lead teacher, $33,764
Lee, Jason, network analyst, $52,838
Lee, Jonathan, centralized user support specialist, $40,931
Lee, Rose, executive assistant I, $27,973
Lehmann, Timothy, disability projects crd c, $34,263
Leibert, Don, assistant professor, $85,917
Leighton, Janet, academic admin assist II, $36,332
Leinweber, Ashley, assistant professor, $53,836
Leis, Sherry, program manager, fire science projects, $64,211
Lenahan, Debra, medical technologist, $42,787
Lescano, Brittany, academic advisor-retention spc, $32,736
Lesley, Caleb, residence hall director, $32,500
Lester, Sharon, administrative specialist II, $30,345
Letterman, Debbie, asst dir psu-event & meet, $37,179
Lewellen, Ashleigh, asst dir of campus rec-fac & oper, $35,018
Lewing, James, custodial foreman, $34,133
Lewis, Andrew, professor, $96,365
Lewis, Betty, international budget & fin mgr, $49,654
Lewis, Heather, instructor, $35,800
Lewis, Kiara, custodian I, $20,734
Liang, Yating, associate professor, $64,427
Libby, Cynthia, professor, $69,408
Lietz, Kevin, custodian I, $20,576
Liggett, Allan, clinical faculty-asst prof, $57,105
Ligon, Day, associate professor, $58,931
Lin, Shawn, web programmer/analyst, $50,347
Linder, Robert, director, $56,000
Lindsay, George, maintenance general mechanic, $40,127
Lindsay, Teresa, payroll manager, $63,360
Lines, Carrie, coordinator/aep program, $45,553
Lininger, M, executive assistant II, $32,883
Litle, Sandra, custodian I, $21,397
Little, Robert, professor, $62,188
Liu, Dandan, china operations specialist, $41,920
Liu, Hui, associate professor, $74,946
Llewellyn, John, professor, $76,033
Lo, Tsee, groundskeeper, $22,570
Lofton, Denise, benefits specialist, $38,195
Loge, Jana, plc project coordinator, $65,826
Lokie, Andrew Jr, dir, spc proj & editor e-journ, $84,520
Lombilla, Luis, sr instructor-nt, $39,319
Long, Sharon, head cashier, $44,231
Long, Shelia, field & maintenance worker, $23,126
Longcor, Tammy, telecommunications technician, $36,400
Lopez, Joyce, instructor-nt, $37,805
Lopinot, Neal, dir ctr for archeological rese, $73,646
Lopinot, Sharon, executive assistant II, $36,590
Lowe, Roberta, instructor-nt, $37,846
Lowery, Steven, public safety officer-shift supervisor, $35,155
Lucas, Patricia, software specialist, $41,815
Lueck, Eric, ranch hand, journagan ranch, $28,203
Lueck, Marty, journagan ranch manager, $68,640
Luellen, Heather, staff music dir-accompanist, $42,505
Lukas, Daniel, event & meeting services coord-psu, $27,453
Luo, Jun, associate professor, $59,491
Lusk, Paul, head athletics coach, $351,650
Lutz, David, professor, $84,625
Lyman, Sean, assoc professor, $52,270
Lyon, Eric, custodial supervisor, $30,051
MacDonald, Shauna, eli instruction specialist, $35,376
Macgregor, Cynthia, professor, $72,023
Madden, Bronwen, coordinator, sbtdc, $49,901
Madden, Etta, professor, $74,289
Maher, Sean, assistant professor, $53,500
Maier, Melissa, assistant professor, $51,765
Malam, Desiree, administrative specialist II, $26,893
Malarkey, Elizabeth, radio traffic crd & oper, $35,419
Malega, Ronald, assistant professor, $54,810
Maloney, Daniel, custodian I, $28,049
Mann, Kathy, academic specialist, trio, $30,825
Mantie-Kozlowski, Alana, assistant professor, $60,268

Maples, Carol, assoc professor, $54,949
Marcum, Andrew, distributed user support specialist, $41,434
Margavio, Geanie, assoc professor, $102,287
Margavio, Thomas, professor, $96,796
Marler, Travis, administrative specialist III, $28,243
Marlin-Hess, Maggie, assistant professor, $49,582
Marre, Ted Jr, custodian I, $20,934
Marrus, Malikah, clinical assistant professor, $59,200
Martin, Deborah, admin asst II, $29,207
Martin, Galen, associate director - campus recreation, $47,520
Martin, Jill, instructor-nt, $44,810
Martin, Judith, professor, $64,237
Martin, Robert, information security analyst, $52,838
Martindale, Susan, acad advisor, $39,316
Martinez, Blanca, instructor nt, $39,389
Martinez, Stephen, groundskeeper, $20,903
Martinez Hernandez, Edgar, academic records specialist,
Massey, Eddie, ranch hand, journagan ranch, $26,000
Massey, Michael, hvac mechanic, $43,532
Masterson, Gerald, professor, $79,697
Masterson, Julie, assoc provost / dean of the grad college, $134,500
Mathew, George, professor, $78,895
Mathis, S, department head, $108,182
Matlack, Joshua, eli instruction specialist, $30,812
Mattheis, Jon, construction technician, $29,972
Matthews, James, instructor-nt, $42,635
Matthews, Michael, physical plant foreman mt, $50,050
Matthews, Victor, dean, $139,766
Mattocks, Vicki, dir financial aid, $75,255
Maupin, Mary, writing specialist, $32,480
Mawhiney, Shannon, digital archivist, $40,569
May, Diane, asst professor, $55,438
Mayanovic, Robert, professor, $85,914
Mayers, Debra, assistant professor, $42,181
Mayes, Hillary, instructor, $50,918
Mays, Larry, instructor-nt, $35,923
McCallister, Sarah, department head, $105,239
McCart, Phillip, programmer/analyst, $57,157
McCart, Rachelle, academic administrative assistant II, $26,245
McCarthy, Belinda, professor, $184,560
McCarthy, Bernard, professor, $93,767
McCarty, Mark, printing service manager, $54,576
McClennen, Joan, professor, $78,219
McClure, Charles, vp administrative & info svcs, $146,830
McComb, Shawn, custodian I, $21,685
McCoy, Theresa, coord of mgmt information systems, $81,974
McCrory, Kenneth, instructional tech suppor, $60,644
McCrory, Sue, computers for learning cr, $44,929
McCroskey, Marilyn, professor 12/12, $87,129
McElwain, Jason, journeyman steamfitter, $41,671
McEowen, Lisa, library associate III, $37,291
McFadden, Robert, custodian I, $23,485
McFall, Catherine, accounting specialist, $33,366
McGauley, Larry, maintenance electrician, $42,808
McGee, Emily, administrative coordinator, $55,035
McGhee, Matthew, residence hall director, $32,500
McGinnis, Rachel, budget & contracts office, $57,879
McGownd, Lenord Jr, asst dir of res life, housing & dining srvs -
    business srvs, $56,896
McGowne, Sheila, administrative assistant II, $27,144
McIntyre, Stephen, professor, $65,920
McKee, Keri, director of development, $56,942
McKenzie, Geralyn, asst dir hr comp & info m, $60,908
McLean, Annice, sr instructor-nt, $44,790
McMahon, Katie, costume shop manager/draper, $31,667
McManus, Loren, enterprise systems administrator, $56,223
McManus, Mary, controller, $105,553
McMeekin, Barbara, manager, corporate support, $52,253
McMeley, Cynthia, instructor-nt, $39,697
McMellen, John, sr broadcast engineer - r, $39,536
McMurtrey, Shannon, senior instructor, $60,900
McTavish, James, project manager - professional engineer, $67,498
Meadows, Brenda, custodian I, $21,397
Meadows, William, professor, $64,515
Medley, Yvette, academic advisor/retention specialist, $33,551
Meek, Russell, instructor nt, $22,500
Mehany, Mohammed, assistant professor, $75,000
Meinert, David, associate dean, $168,961
Meints, Gary, associate professor, $58,812

Melton, Janelle, admin assistant II, $22,441
Melton, Shelly, academic administrative assistant II, $26,798
Mendenhall, Kathy, budget officer, $43,500
Mendez, Joanna, international admission coordinator, $35,500
Mendez, Samuel, custodian I, $24,211
Meraz, Juan, asst vp for multicultural serv, $74,542
Meredith, John, instructional designer, $53,856
Merrigan, Michael Jr, clinical assistant professor, $82,824
Metzger, Benjamin, asst dir admissons-office operations, $45,000
Meyer, Bradley, master control supervisor, $36,035
Meyer, James, professor, $67,022
Meyer, Jennifer, academic administrative assistant I, $23,132
Meyer, Judith, assoc professor, $61,195
Miao, Xin, assoc professor, $59,751
Michalczyk, Maria, assoc professor, $63,525
Michelfelder, Gary, assistant professor, $53,795
Mickus, Kevin, professor, $60,866
Miles, Kyla, licensed practical nurse, $35,766
Miller, Andrea, asst prof-12 mo appt-library, $48,675
Miller, Carol, distinguished professor, $114,586
Miller, Charles, eli instruction specialist, $30,812
Miller, F, professor, $71,191
Miller, Harriet, information spc supv-fin, $33,619
Miller, Kandi, custodian I, $21,397
Miller, Kathy, records supervisor, $38,612
Miller, Kyle, instructor, $41,412
Miller, Sandra, webmaster-univ advancement, $36,876
Miller, Shirley, accounting technician, $30,898
Mills, Nancy, admin asst III, $34,312
Mincey, Martha, curator-visual resources, $46,661
Mitchell, D, assoc professor, $64,082
Mitchell, David, professor, $80,942
Mitchell, Donald, custodian I, $21,397
Mitchell, Shirley, accountant, $42,697
Mitra, Mahua, professor, $86,334
Mitra, Saibal, professor, $74,305
Moats, Kyle, director of athletics, $160,302
Moentnish, Shirley, circ/shelving supervisor, $40,500
Moler, Leta, executive assistant IV, $39,807
Moncrief, Keith, custodian I, $29,346
Monkres, Lisa, administrative specialist II, $27,087
Monson, Tamicka, academic administrative assistant I, $23,129
Monzella, Harry, custodian I, $21,802
Moody, Bretticca, academic advisor/1st year exp coord, $37,000
Moore, David, chief engineer - tv, $68,943
Moore, Paula, eli special programs director, $47,705
Moore, Renee, professor, $60,106
Moore, Robert, assistant director, $42,000
Moore, Scott, operations assistant, basketball, $32,214
Moore, Teresa, assoc dir jqh arena, hsc & psc, $48,058
Moreno, Donald, custodian I, $28,830
Moreno, Ronald, custodian I, $31,351
Moreno, Sherry, custodian I, $26,862
Morgan, Connie, asst professor, $41,876
Morgan, Michelle, assistant professor, $53,856
Morris, Benjamin, boiler fireman, $35,956
Morris, Eric, asst professor, $58,080
Morris, Joseph, dir stdt orien,advise/reg, $49,266
Morris, Margaret, accounting specialist, $32,233
Morris, Matthew, assoc vp for ais, $100,321
Morris, Robert, assistant professor, $55,906
Morris, Taleyna, instructor, $35,525
Morrison, Jeffery, custodial supervisor, $30,000
Morrison, Kathleen, professor, $66,319
Morrison, Martin, instructor, $36,540
Morrissey, Dennis, journeyman plumber, $39,942
Morrissey, Jeff, chief information officer, $112,762
Morrissey, Sarah, administrative assistant II, $34,120
Morrissey, William, academic administrative asst II, $25,807
Morton, Carla, academic advisor-marketing, recruitment & retention, $36,720
Morton, Christian, assistant coach, $55,000
Moser, Linda, professor, $64,820
Moses, Duane, assoc professor, $80,853
Mosier, Robert, custodian I, $24,268
Mosier, Samantha, assistant professor, $54,000
Moskalski, Suzanne, academic administrative asst II, $27,502
Mosley, Debra, admin asst II, $26,531
Mostyn, Andrea, asst dir university commu, $42,904

Moyer, James, professor, $93,077
Muchnick, Amy, professor, $62,211
Muegge, Frederick, director of health & wellness, $140,670
Mullins, Marchalain, programmer/analyst, $52,905
Munoz Aliaga, Rut, network analyst, $51,797
Murphy, Jill, employment specialist, $43,446
Murphy, Michael, sr electronics technician, $63,923
Murphy, Richard Jr, groundskeeper, $33,208
Murphy, Stephanie, distance education & lab supervisor, $36,236
Murphy, Valerie, accounting technician, $36,524
Murray, Michael, professor, $66,357
Murray, Michael, professor, $68,371
Murray, Sarah, sr instructor-nt, $41,731
Murrell, Frankie, administrative spc II, $26,531
Murvin, Jennifer, sr instructor-nt, $36,088
Muse, Amanda, departmental academic advisor, $34,120
Mustion, Barbara, accounting technician wp, $34,543
Myers, Nancy, accounting manager, $64,543
Myhan, Kenneth, custodian I, $28,704
Nag, Nandita, laboratory supervisor, $31,465
Nagle, John, videographer/editor-marketing & comm, $36,400
Napier, Amanda, licensed practical nurse, $25,666
Neal, Karen, system administrator, $52,445
Neal, Tina, program coordinator, $38,895
Needham, Brad, custodian I, $23,910
Neely, Jeremy, instructor, $42,427
Nelsen, Janice, assoc professor, $57,924
Nelson, Diane, senior pharmacy technician, $30,700
Nelson, Eric, professor, $71,551
Nelson, Kirk, assistant coach, $29,361
Nelson, Nicole, research analyst, $42,000
Nelson, Walt, assoc professor, $94,115
Netzer, Kelly, groundskeeper, $22,531
Netzer, Shelley, scheduling coordinator, $33,601
Neumann, Richard, senior instructor-nt, $41,258
Neuschwander, Nathan, graphic designer, $40,389
Newman, Joan, admin asst II, $32,111
Newman, Mary, assoc professor, $66,043
Newton, Sean, assoc prof 12/12, $91,513
Nichols, Elvin, maintenance general mechanic, $36,713
Nichols, Larry, on-site outreach crd-joplin, $33,017
Nichols, Linda, accounting specialist, $36,995
Niell, Sherry, administrative specialist I, $24,086
Nino, Jose, custodian I, $23,919
Nixon, Salina, residence hall night host/hostess, $19,551
Nixon, Sarah, professor, $66,743
Noblin, Matthew, general buyer, $28,243
Noland, Michelle, assistant director-acia, $34,000
Norander, Per, sr instructor-nt, $48,964
Norander, Stephanie, associate professor, $58,397
Norat, Timothy, custodian I, $19,799
Norcross, Tyler, maintenance general mechanic,
Nordyke, Kathy, director, citizenship / service learning, $41,185
Norgren, Michelle, project director vesta, $75,230
Norris, Joye, associate provost for access & outreach, $133,056
Northrip, Donald, mgr bearpass card operations, $59,578
Northrip-Rivera, Angelia, senior instructor-nt, $39,761
Norton, Robert, professor, $85,590
Novik, Melinda, assoc professor, $55,826
Novotny, Daniela, instructor nt, $40,600
Nowell, Y, crd arts in the schools, $32,320
Nugent, Pauline, professor, $68,010
Nyden, Barbara, assistant professor, $46,506
O'Connell, Brenda, admin asst II, $32,367
O'Neal, Deborah, asst dir athletics business admin, $44,352
Oatman, David, professor, $81,377
Oconnor, Rhonda, library associate II, $32,341
Oden, Debra, professor, $109,986
Odneal, Clayton Jr, cellar technician, $33,050
Odneal, Marilyn, horticulture outreach advisor, $54,769
Oetting, Kristi, technical training & documentation administrator, $45,033
Oetting, Tara, clinical associate professor, $59,096
Olsen, Michelle, director institutional research, $90,229
Olsen, Reed, professor, $90,141
Olson, Stevan, professor, $106,229
Ondetti, Gabriel, associate professor, $60,269
Onyango, Benjamin, assoc professor, $64,480

Opfer, Barbara, admin assistant II, $26,531
Orr, Spencer, residence hall director, $30,812
Ortiz, Frank, custodial supervisor, $38,455
Orzek, Ann, mental health clinician, $60,896
Oshaughnessy, Megan, lead teacher, $33,764
Oswalt, Mary, clinic director comm sci, $83,283
Otte, Melissa, assistant teacher, $20,934
Overmyer, Allison, manager animal research facili, $39,893
Owen, Marc, assistant dir oewri, $51,765
Owrey, Savonna, clothing/soft goods specialist, $32,110
Oyeniyi, Bukola, assistant professor, $52,780
Ozbun, Marcus, academic advisor-athletics, $27,699
Pace, Glenn, instructor-nt, $43,676
Paddock, Joel, professor, $81,678
Palacios-Valladares, Indira, assistant professor, $51,765
Palmer, Christopher, maintenance general mechanic, $29,762
Panza, Juli, professional ed advisor, $40,320
Pardue, Mary, interim department head, $66,844
Parker, Cynthia, academic admin asst I, $25,868
Parker, Richard, professor, $114,719
Parker, Samuel, maintenance electrician, $45,027
Parnell, Patrick, director of international services, $54,810
Parrish, Erin, director, $71,050
Parrott, Neva, asst librarian, $46,983
Parsons, James, professor, $75,547
Patel, Rishi, sr research scientist, $67,225
Patterson, Jacquelene, academic administrative asst I, $23,129
Patterson, Kathryn, clinical assistant professor, $59,885
Patterson, Kim, administrative assistant II, $26,354
Patterson, Paula, assoc professor, $51,878
Patterson, Robert, professor, $80,061
Pattison, Matthew, res hall host/hostess, $27,255
Patton, Marciann, senior instructor, $46,685
Patton, Tracy, library associate III, $37,291
Paul, Richecard, public safety officer, $25,609
Pavlick, Laura, crd property control, $54,703
Pavlowsky, Robert, professor, $78,923
Paxton, Mark, professor, $70,279
Paxton, Miroslaba, admin specialist II, $26,531
Payne, Richard, assoc professor, $52,233
Peace, Robert, network analyst, $52,838
Pearce, Lori, event & meeting srvs crd, $28,446
Pearman, Cathy, department head, $98,201
Pecsok, Karen, admissions evaluator, $27,767
Pedersen, Johnna, jr research scientist-jvic, $52,607
Penkalski, James, director, $67,334
Penn, Barbara, administrative spc II, $30,319
Penn, Deborah, director, dual credit program, $34,207
Penner, Robert, public safety officer, $24,758
Perine, Elizabeth, assoc head coach, $40,600
Perkins, Amanda, assistant professor, $50,316
Perkins, Amy, band event coordinator, $35,958
Perkins, Gary Jr, custodian I, $21,397
Perkins, Sarah, professor, $75,412
Perry, Dennis, hvac-food svc equip machanic, $36,056
Perryman, Michael, energy mgt technician, $48,051
Pervukhin, Eric, professor, $78,407
Peters, Grant, professor, $68,403
Peters, Janet, administrative assistant II, $28,742
Peters, Thomas, dean, $115,954
Peterson, Dane, professor, $87,955
Peterson, Jacob, ranch hand, journagan ranch, $27,456
Peterson, Rachel, recruitment specialist wp, $33,895
Petkovic, Vickie, administrative assistant I, $21,527
Petr, Jeffrey, database analyst, $52,838
Pettijohn, Catherine, eli instruction specialist, $30,812
Pettus, David, distributed user support specialist, $53,150
Pfeil, Timothy, instructor, $38,306
Pham, Courtney, instructor-nt, $37,826
Phillips, Gary, assoc professor, $51,024
Phillips, Heather, health career coordinator, $39,000
Phillips, Raymond, stores clerk science/math, $31,660
Philpot, James, associate professor, $119,049
Piccolo, Diana, assoc professor, $59,032
Pickering, Judith, professional edu advisor, $41,006
Piekarski, Margaret, administrative spc III, $28,243
Piercy, Kevin, coordinator of user support, $73,333
Pierpoint, Sophie, director of development, $55,825
Pierson, Matthew, assistant professor, $71,756

Pinegar, Angela, asst dir advancement serv, $41,492
Pinnon, Alex, lecturer, $35,134
Pippenger, Ruby, material & inventory contro sp, $34,032
Piston, William, professor, $71,115
Plank, Angela, laboratory supervisor cnas, $47,378
Plaster, Daniel, public safety officer, $28,860
Plavchan, Peter, assistant professor, $57,000
Plymate, Lynda, professor, $75,009
Plymate, Thomas, department head, $102,378
Plymire, Carol, buyer, $43,087
Poindexter, Teri, graphic designer-publications, $35,012
Polking, Amanda, asst crd project success, $35,018
Polm, Michael, maintenance foreman, $43,296
Polyard, Brenda, dir univ/comm prog, wp, $54,767
Ponder, Sheila, library associate I, $34,302
Porter, Joshua, mba program academic advisor, $37,555
Potochnik, Robert, centralized user supp spc, $47,148
Poulette, Jacob, instructor, $37,443
Powell, Robin, academic admin asst II, $34,161
Poyraz, Serdar, visiting assistant professor, $40,600
Prather, Belva, professor 12/12, $89,219
Pratt, Francine, executive dir mrc/mp, $67,500
Pratt, Harold, equal opportunity officer, $80,574
Prescott, John, professor, $75,951
Presnell, Raymond, interim director, $46,591
Prewitt, Betty, custodian I, $21,397
Prewitt, Victor, telecommunications technician, $38,895
Price, Debra, visiting instructor, $40,376
Price, Melissa, coordinator of marketing, $47,269
Priest, Frank, associate professor, $47,257
Prince, Munir, assistant coach, $40,000
Proctor, Janene, research administration specialist, $41,396
Proctor, Lisa, professor, $84,271
Pruitt, Lindsey, licensed practical nurse, $25,666
Prussia, Celeste, research spc II, $30,181
Pszczolkowski, Maciej, associate research professor, $64,552
Puckett, Erica, administrative assistant II, $26,058
Pulley, Kathy, professor, $101,959
Pulleyking, Micki, senior instructor-nt, $47,256
Pulliam, Matthew, maintenance gen mechanic, $30,533
Pursley, Jennifer, instructor, $34,817
Putman, Mark, assoc professor, $53,184
Putzu, Vadim, assistant professor, $50,000
Pybas, Kevin, assoc professor, $59,322
Pyle, Connie, nursing coordinator, $59,126
Qiao, Yuhua, professor, $69,055
Qiu, Wenping, research professor, $74,682
Qiu, Xiaomin, assoc professor, $58,413
Quebbeman, Robert, professor, $74,724
Quinn, Justin, maintenance foreman, $43,296
Quinn, Nathaniel Jr, instructor, $45,675
Rabon, John, instructor, $41,412
Racer, Dana, sr academic records specialist, $31,576
Rader, John, dir online ed dev & policy, $81,770
Radier, George, academic advisor/retention specialist, $31,973
Ragan, Gay, professor, $68,307
Ragan, Kent, department head, $140,343
Ragsdale, Chansouk, library associate II, $37,384
Raines, Ashley, executive assistant IV, $37,959
Raines, Daniel, director of acad & stdt srvc-athletics, $49,228
Raines, Judy, accounting specialist, $29,981
Rainwater, Douglas, budget and financial mana, $60,117
Raleigh, Phillip, administrative specialist II, $27,081
Ramon, Michael, instructor, $42,447
Ramos, Duany, instructor, $35,000
Rasnake, Christina, asst strength & conditioning coach, $40,000
Ravenscraft, Julia, instructor nt, $20,000
Rawlings, Carol, custodial I, $20,934
Ray, Donna, custodian I, $29,955
Ray, Jack, asst director for arch research, $55,440
Rebaza-Vasquez, Jorge, associate dean, $67,940
Rector, Paula, sr instructor-nt, $45,813
Redburn, Angela, groundskeeper-gen maint worker, $24,788
Redd, Emmett, professor, $77,481
Reddick, Lindsey, graphic designer, $37,500
Reed, Jerilyn, wellness educator-student, $44,235
Reed, Jimmie, grndskpr-gen maint worker wp, $28,545
Reed, Michael, professor, $74,239
Reed, Ryan, co-curricular ombudsperson, $40,000

Reed, Tamara, sr internal auditor, $66,320
Rees, Christopher, enterprise system administrator, $62,885
Reeves, Stacie, residence hall receptionist, $18,872
Reichling, Susanna, library associate II, $31,066
Reid, Helen, dean, $143,907
Reid, Leslie, professor, $86,080
Reimer, Anthony, maintenance carpenter, $34,224
Reinert, John, asst crd educational field experiences, $26,400
Reinis, Austra, assoc professor, $59,294
Remley, Melissa, assistant professor, $60,900
Reynolds, Kristie, coordinator of casl special projects, $32,000
Rhea, Jason, grounds supervisor, $37,570
Rhodes, Joy, administrative specialist II, $25,646
Rhodes, Norman, custodian/equip maint specialist, $26,000
Ribas, Denise, custodial supervisor, $38,771
Rice, Stacy, instructional designer, $50,981
Richards, Byron, maintenance general mechanic, $33,208
Richards, David, assoc prof-library-12 mo appt, $76,928
Richardson, Timothy, residence hall host/hostess, $20,291
Richmond, Scott, assistant professor, $52,788
Richter, Mark, professor, $83,655
Ridinger, Rhonda, professor, $87,931
Rimal, Arbindra, professor, $74,707
Ringenberg, Thomas, visiting instructor, $35,000
Rios, Laura, academic admin asst II, $28,624
Roam, Kimberly, clinical instructor, $41,432
Robbins, Linda, instructor, $39,964
Roberts, Galen, custodial specialist, $30,431
Roberts, Hillary, senior instructor, $44,835
Roberts, Jenifer, asst professor, $63,806
Robertson, Jessica, professional education advisor, $31,274
Robinette, Stephen, assoc vp international program, $99,787
Robinson, Barbara, assoc prof 12/12, $95,250
Robinson, Jasmine, administrative assistant I, $24,129
Robinson, Melinda, instructor, $40,600
Robinson, Sally, administrative assistant II, $24,758
Robison, Holly, academic admin asst III, $32,451
Robison, Jane, exec dir, eli, $66,680
Robords, Susan, academic administrative assistant II, $26,519
Rockney, Andrea, professional developer, $45,675
Rockwell, Rae Ann, academic admin asst II, $26,214
Rodgers, David, maintenance gen mechanic, $30,533
Rodriguez de la Vega, Vanessa, assistant professor, $51,000
Rogers, Katy, custodian I, $23,198
Rogers, Lori, sr instructor, $36,953
Rogers, Mark, assoc professor, $60,065
Rogers, Michael, relief computer operator, $29,762
Rohall, David, department head, $100,000
Rohlman, Joseph, parking mechanic, $40,002
Roland, Alan, online systems spc cont e, $52,889
Rollinson, Paul, professor, $74,910
Romano, David, associate professor, $69,887
Rongali, Sharath, laboratory & stores supervisor, $36,355
Roop, Kristin, admission counselor, $31,210
Rose, Michelle, writer-editor, $35,155
Rosenkoetter, John, assoc professor, $64,153
Ross, Jaime, academic advisor/marketing, recruitment, $37,928
Rost, Ann, associate professor, $59,766
Rothschild, Philip, asst professor, $86,663
Rovey, Charles II, professor, $74,445
Rowe, Roberta, senior instructor, $41,484
Rowland, Daniel, dist learn media prod spc, $41,434
Rowland, Terry, project manager-architect, $69,365
Rozell, Elizabeth, associate dean, $168,961
Rude, Brian, asst copy center spvr, $25,096
Ruff-Hensley, Sheryl, acad administrative asst II, $33,661
Rugutt, Joseph, associate professor, $54,913
Ruhe, Richard, instructor, $51,958
Rund, Janice, executive asst I, $29,093
Runke, Gayle, asst professor, $53,686
Russell, Kristy, athletics equipment atten, $28,352
Russell, Regina, clinical instructor, $39,859
Russell, Terry, accounting technician, $29,207
Ruzicka, Francis, instrument control mech I, $47,414
Ryan, Ashley, study away advisor, $36,500
Ryburn, Karen, crd, trio student support services, $43,704
Ryder, Christina, instructor, $30,000
Sailors, Pamela, assoc dean, $109,427
Saitta, Alicia, regional admission counselor, $35,688

Sakidja, Ridwan, associate professor, $90,000
Salinas, Patti, department head, $101,500
Sallee, Neal, custodian I, $31,245
Saltzgaber, Grant, visiting instructor, $35,000
Sampson, Douglas, univ architect & dir of planning, design & construction, $92,439
Sampson, Loretta, systems analyst, $64,539
Sandefur, Diane, administrative spc II, $28,229
Sanders, Jason, public safety officer, $26,531
Santos, Theodore, custodian I, $20,934
Saquer, Jamil, assoc professor, $79,327
Sardeson, Jorel, public safety officer, $26,531
Sartin, Carl, distance learning engineer, $36,876
Satzinger, John, professor, $108,777
Saunders, Georgianna, assoc professor, $61,334
Savinske, Debra, clinical assistant professor, $62,229
Sawchak, Stephen, athl trainer-athl, med & rehab, $45,827
Saxon, Caryn, instructor-nt, $40,600
Scarlet, Freda, cataloger/ref librarian wp, $40,362
Schaefer, Allen, professor, $108,143
Schaefer, Weirong, sr instructor-nt, $42,507
Schanda, Jordan, sustainability coordinator, $30,812
Schehrer, Devin, asst dir of res life housing & dining srvs - ed & dev, $49,783
Schenk, Lynne, clinical instructor, $54,303
Scheve, Jesse, staff photographer, $32,480
Schick, G, department head, $117,976
Schilla, Travis, coordinator res, leadership development & program, $40,600
Schiller, Megan, research analyst, $38,895
Schlinder, Kelly, coordinator, $35,000
Schmalzbauer, John, assoc professor, $76,627
Schmedeke, Jeffrey, assistant director, $52,983
Schmelzle, George, professor, $117,299
Schmidt, Karl, director of development, $55,000
Schneider, Scott, director business & support services, $74,906
Schoneboom, Charles, groundskeeper, $22,065
Schotthofer, Melissa, instructor, $44,153
Schrader, Bonnie, administrative assistant II, $30,079
Schuldt, Amy, asst dir publications, $42,796
Schuldt, Richard, dist learn media prod crd, $48,220
Schull, Cynthia, dir acct & budgt, grants, $71,050
Schulte, Catherine, athletic trainer, $37,471
Schweiger, Jamie, academic advisor, $33,130
Schweiger, Paul, assistant professor, $53,836
Scott, Charles, assistant professor, $66,483
Scott, James, asst professor, $82,165
Scott, Karen, information specialist, $28,243
Scott, Michael, assistant coach, $32,934
Scott, Patrick, professor, $77,792
Scott, Robert, physician medical staff, $132,845
Scroggins, Michael, senior instructor, $46,913
Scroggins, Wesley, professor, $100,602
Seal, Stephen, asst dir greenwood labora, $55,923
Seale, Joyce, financial aid technician, $34,719
Seaman, Robert, custodial inventory/equip foreman, $36,351
Searles, Lisa, administrative assistant IV, $36,254
Secca, Phillip, sr graphic des access & outreach, $36,200
Sedaghat-Herati, Reza, professor, $78,689
Seever, Natalie, business process & reporting analyst, $51,000
Seibel, Craig, custodian I, $19,988
Seidel, Cody, administrative assistant II, $27,079
Self, Sharmistha, professor, $80,941
Self, William, access control specialist, $35,366
Sellers, Marie, accounting specialist, $31,095
Sellers, Todd, custodial supervisor, $33,497
Sells, Patrick, instructor-nt, $38,895
Senger, Steven, assistant professor, $53,000
Setzer, Shelby, visiting instructor, $34,000
Sevart, Jeanne, eli instruction specialist, $36,236
Severson, Jennifer, director of accounting & budgeting, $69,572
Sexton, Randall, professor, $113,763
Shadrick, Megan, assoc dir drc-access tech ctr, $42,723
Shaffer, Patricia, custodian I, $20,934
Shah, Kishor, professor, $76,609
Shain, Ralph, assoc professor, $55,725
Shand-Hawkins, Carolyn, instructor-nt, $36,028
Sharp, Keith, custodial eq rep & sp pro, $36,314
Sharum, Stephen, postal distribution clerk, $30,581

Shaw, Margaret, vp for marketing & communications, $135,000
Shea, Harry, instructor-nt, $38,792
Sheffield, Eric, professor, $68,144
Shepard, Jason, instructor, $28,420
Shepherd, John, convenience store supervisor, $32,094
Sheppard, Tessa, teacher,
Sherrill, Donna, senior instructor, $38,585
Shi, Yili, professor, $68,632
Shikles, Craig, custodial supply,del,&sto, $36,499
Shipley, Teresa, executive asst III, $36,298
Shirley, Corinne, instructor-nt, $36,757
Shirley, Deborah, accounting specialist, $34,942
Shively, Eric, distributed user support specialist, $40,931
Shoemaker, Amber, custodian I, $20,734
Shoptaugh, Carol, professor, $83,896
Shoumikhin, Andrei, instructor, $84,480
Siebert, Matthew, assistant professor, $53,836
Sikes, Scott, custodian I, $25,388
Sikonski, John, telecommunications technician - lead, $49,651
Sillyman, Wanda, postal services supervisor, $39,850
Silva-Galicia, Flor, receptionist, $23,649
Silvey, Jessica, executive assistant III, $35,516
Simmers, Christina, associate professor, $111,455
Simons, Vicki, administrative assistant I, $27,105
Simpson, Donald, assoc vp for enrollment manage, $111,982
Simpson, Wesley, clinical education coordinator, $33,000
Sims-Giddens, Susan, professor, $86,353
Singleton, Dorothy, accounting specialist, $31,525
Sisco, Richard Jr, workflow systems analyst, $51,390
Siscoe, Denita, vp for student affairs, $152,250
Sissel, Justin, farm operations manager, $35,633
Skalicky, Michele, morning show host-sr news, $35,966
Skeeters, Priscilla, course materials manager, $46,465
Skinner, Sophia, circ/shelving supv wp, $35,357
Slane, William, distributed user supp spc, $41,434
Slater, Lori, positive behavior support consultant,
Slattery, Dianne, professor, $96,403
Slattery, Kerry, assistant professor, $85,917
Slavens, Robert, custodian I, $19,799
Sliger, Ashley, contracts administrator, $32,000
Sligh, Matthew, assistant coach, $70,000
Smith, Allison, coordinator, housing assignments, $40,000
Smith, Andrew, construction foreman, $41,323
Smith, Anthony, master control operator, $24,002
Smith, Brenda, instructor, $40,482
Smith, Cara, instructor, $44,153
Smith, Cindy, director of respiratory care, $59,600
Smith, Deanna, on-site outreach coordinator, $33,700
Smith, Janis, accounting specialist, $27,883
Smith, Joshua, assoc professor, $61,976
Smith, Karen, executive assistant II, $30,341
Smith, Lloyd, professor, $87,757
Smith, Lucretia, clinical instructor, $59,012
Smith, Michele, assistant professor, $63,268
Smith, Tanya, buyer, $40,000
Smith, William, custodian I, $25,448
Smotherman, Rebecca, instructor, $42,000
Snider, Janet, admin asst II, $34,924
Snider, Stephen, senior database analyst, $67,439
Snider, William, maintenance general mechanic, $38,480
Sobel, Elizabeth, assoc professor, $56,369
Sottile, James, associate dean, $93,380
Spalding, Roger, network analyst, $59,094
Sparks, Andrew, programmer/analyst, $40,931
Spaulding, Cynthia, financial aid counselor, $31,300
Speer, Jason, distributed user support specialist, $40,931
Speer, Robert, sr research scientist, $49,048
Spencer, William, information security officer, $72,471
Spilken, Ryan, technical trainer, $40,212
Spinabella, Julie, admin crd-data & communications, $34,003
Spitzer, Chris, custodian I, $19,799
Stacey, Samantha, custodian I, $20,934
Stadler, Craig, hvac mechanic, $43,439
Stadler, Denise, residence hall receptionist, $27,785
Staeger, Roy, public safety trainer-invest, $30,533
Staeger-Wilson, Katheryne, dir disability resource ctr, $55,209
Stafford, Gary, career resources specialist, $41,032
Stafford, Gary, sr instructor-nt, $40,987
Stafford, Neal, head athletics coach, $31,044

Stagner, Kimberly, acad adv/retention spc co, $36,183
Stanley, Marianne, programmer/analyst, $54,380
Stanojevic, Vera, professor, $81,584
Stansbury, Sandra, custodian I, $19,799
Stanton, Dawn, residence hall receptionist, $17,804
Stanton, Rhonda, assistant professor, $52,780
Stanton, Shannon, asst box office manager, $35,270
Stanton, Tammy, academic admin assistant II, $25,814
Starr, Cathy, assistant professor, $59,200
Steckel, Dave, head athletics coach, $270,000
Steele, Lori, assistant director, dual credit, $25,413
Steele, Teresa, budget officer, $43,500
Steele, William, property control specialist, $29,538
Stefka, Joyce, executive asst II, $34,564
Steinle, Erich, associate dean, $59,658
Steinman, Christina, accountant, $36,000
Steinshouer, Linda, academic administrative asst II, $26,554
Stepanova, Maria, associate professor, $31,000
Stephens, Jill, software support specialist, $46,154
Stephens, Linda, asst dir hr employment &, $57,180
Stevens, Carol, accounting specialist, $30,030
Stevens, Darcy, recording arts educator, $41,958
Stevens, Jeffrey, public safety officer, $26,531
Stevens, Kevin, asst registrar-veteran student services, $42,000
Stevens, Linda, licensed practical nurse, $35,766
Stewart, Brenda, administrative assistant III, $29,932
Stewart, Byron, asst prof-12 mo appt-library, $71,868
Stewart, Gary, dir residence life housing & dining srvs, $84,057
Stewart, Joseph, sr fine arts producer, $37,016
Stewart, Marjorie, career resources specialist, $41,096
Stewart, Misty, coordinator of graduate recruitment, $33,265
Stewart, Tammy, asst prof-9 mo appt-library, $40,265
Stiles, Jackie, assistant coach, $77,359
Stipp, Timothy, budget officer, $43,500
Stock, Carla, accounting technician, $28,243
Stogsdill, Kelsey, public safety officer, $26,531
Stokes, Amy, assistant professor, $113,883
Stokes, Melissa, head athletics coach, $98,383
Stone, Lorene, professor, $106,333
Stonecipher, Alyssa, admission counselor, $29,682
Stopczynski, Stacey, accounting technician, $32,916
Storochuk, Allison, professor, $60,813
Stout, Michael, assoc professor, $57,000
Stout, Randy, field & maint crew leader, $28,872
Stout, Tracy, assoc prof-12 mo appt-library, $52,947
Stovall, Richard, employment specialist, $38,895
Stowe, Michael, senior instructor-nt, $43,504
Stranghoener, Michael, custodian I, $26,626
Street, Lisa, clinical assistant professor, $55,326
Street, Lori, membership mgr - radio & tv, $29,608
Strider, Angela, coordinator res life facilities & op, $44,660
Strong, Elizabeth, director, $55,127
Strong, Joe, distance learning engineer, $48,261
Strong, John, professor, $52,842
Strope, Kimberly, coordinator, $37,000
Stubbs, Ronnie, custodian I, $20,576
Stuppy, Joshua, senior network analyst, $67,161
Su, Shujun, professor, $69,255
Su, Wei-Han, professor, $62,343
Su, Yingcai, professor, $74,679
Sudbrock, Christine, instructor nt, $47,520
Sullivan, Jennifer, assistant coach, $82,215
Sullivan, John, guard manager, $25,309
Sullivan, Maxine, band coordinator, $29,005
Sullivan, Patrick, assistant professor, $55,000
Sun, Linda, instructor-nt, $35,126
Sun, Xingping, professor, $76,664
Surface, Janet, academic admin asst II, $31,121
Sutliff, Kristene, professor, $76,525
Suttmoeller, Michael, assistant professor, $62,000
Sutton, Tami, executive asst IV, $51,653
Sutton, Victoria, instructor-nt, $42,552
Swearingen, Andrew, centralized user supp spc, $41,434
Swearingen, Rebecca, associate professor, $73,171
Swift, Donald Jr, powerhouse foreman, $46,465
Swift, Kevin, senior instructor, $52,788
Swigert, Dwayne, library associate III, $37,300
Swindell, Lori, accountant, $37,271
Switzer, Jeffrey, boiler fireman, $40,118

Syler, Christopher, custodian I, $24,616
Syler, Melody, custodian I, $20,934
Talley, Jonathan, dir of adult non-trdtl stdt resources, $52,800
Tassin, Kerri, assistant professor, $116,725
Tate, Pamela, stdt support specialist, $36,116
Taylor, Darren, instructor-nt, $42,959
Taylor, Eric, videographer/editor, $30,812
Taylor, Lisa, paralegal, $44,895
Taylor, Rogers, crd student life & dev wp, $34,588
Teague, Kristy, academic admin assistant I, $23,386
Templeton, Kelly, managing director, $49,692
Templeton, Martha, acad admin asst II, $30,807
Terry, Jane, acad admin asst II, $29,705
Test, Joan, associate professor, $66,630
Thakur, Rajiv, assistant professor, $38,570
Thanomsing, Chulapol, instructional designer, $45,005
Tharp, Billy, public safety officer, $28,133
Theissen, Ryan, groundskeeper, $21,492
Thieman, Cynthia, prof ed advisor-recruiter, $35,155
Thimesch, Dianna, academic admin assistant II, $29,127
Thoenen, Seth, resnet administrator, $46,690
Thomas, Davey, custodian I, $31,020
Thomas, Joshua, radio communications officer, $26,531
Thomas, Kent, asst vp international programs-dir international recruiting, $96,425
Thomas, Steven, professor, $103,335
Thomas-Tate, Shurita, assistant professor, $60,193
Thompson, Chris, associate professor, $55,378
Thompson, Dian, asst box office manager, $36,736
Thompson, Dustin, project supervisor, $32,468
Thompson, Mark, custodial specialist, $35,165
Thompson, Nancy, administrative assistant II, $26,058
Thompson, Nathan, assistant coach, $50,000
Thurman, Robert, custodian I, $23,002
Tibbs, Bart, asst dir adms freshman cr, $49,195
Timson, Benjamin, professor, $79,023
Tinney, Robert, distributed user supp spc, $47,148
Tinsley, Tonia, assistant professor, $50,750
Tippin, Deborah, systems analyst, $52,838
Titus, Christy, acad admin asst I, $18,631
Tivener, Kristin, clinical instructor, $40,000
Todd, Danita, clinical instructor, $52,800
Tolleson, Melissa, admin asst II, $22,243
Tomasi, Thomas, assoc dean, $104,896
Totten, Linda, custodial foreman, $33,929
Totty, Angela, dean of student services, $84,000
Towell, Jay, asst professor, $41,420
Townsend, Steven, pressroom operator, $32,969
Travis, Brooks, distributed user supp spc, $41,434
Treese, Joe, journeyman plumber, $35,025
Trewatha, Pamela, professor, $73,202
Trewatha-Bach, Stacey, coord of pa special projects, $31,465
Trick, Abel, asst professor, $43,525
Trotter, Alisa, asst dir business advisem, $42,637
Tung, Katelyn, assistant teacher, $19,799
Turek, Stephanie, ods/edw database analyst, $52,838
Turk, Scott, database analyst, $52,838
Turner, John, senior instructor-nt, $44,150
Turner, Jon, assistant professor, $52,500
Turner, Pamela, admin asst IV, $36,298
Turner, Steve, custodian I, $21,397
Turner, Steven, vehicle & equipment mechanic, $30,533
Turner, Susan, grant development specialist, $39,341
Turner, Valerie, career resources specialist, $41,080
Twibell, Andrew, instructor, $45,675
Udan, Ryan, assistant professor, $53,500
Uffmann, Richard, assoc dir of taylor health, $52,712
Underhill, Nancy, groundskeeper/arborist, $27,604
Underlin, Nancy, academic admin assistant II, $30,387
Underwood, Judy, custodian I, $20,734
Underwood, Stacey, custodian I, $24,441
Underwood, Tabitha, exec dir-campus compact, $52,780
Uruakpa-Nweke, Florence, assistant professor, $58,500
Usukumah, Ime, assistant project manager, $40,600
Utley, Rose, professor, $72,349
Van Der Merwe, Sydney, assistant coach, $29,982
Van Huis, Robin, res hall recpst 10/10, $18,154
Van Landuyt, Cathryn, senior instructor-nt, $39,284
Van Ornum, Kimberly, instructor nt, $33,792

Van Riessen, Chad, assistant coach, $34,086
Van Someren, Thomas, senior programmer/analyst, $61,692
Vanderhoof, Glenna, senior instructor, $39,744
Vasquez, Yeni, identification & recruit spc, $32,590
Vassar, Travis, centralized user support specialist, $39,618
Vaughan, David, dir environmental managem, $72,607
Vaughan, Julie, budget officer, $43,500
Vaughan, Lori, residence hall receptionist, $21,215
Vaught, Linda, research coordinator, $43,818
Veach, Susan, administrative assistant II, $26,379
Verduzco, Mario, assistant coach, $100,000
Viau, Robroy, assistant project manager, $42,768
Viets, Paul, maintenance painter, $36,902
Vinton, Denise, instructor, $47,520
Visio, Michelle, assoc professor, $59,939
Vollmar, Kenneth, department head, $100,026
Vu, Duat, assoc professor, $55,907
Wade, Lisa, instructor-nt, $49,088
Wade, Lori, administrative spc II, $25,609
Wagner, Kimberly, assistant professor, $75,000
Wahl, Shawn, department head, $103,530
Wait, D, professor, $67,327
Walker, Clara, administrative assistant II, $28,952
Walker, Dwayne, visiting clinical instructor, $40,000
Walker, Elizabeth, assoc professor, $64,828
Walker, Grady, custodian I, $27,654
Walker, Jennifer, financial aid counselor, $32,320
Walker, Myrna, clinical faculty-instructor, $40,993
Walker, William, head athletics coach-wp, $52,293
Walker-Pacheco, Suzanne, professor, $66,897
Wall, Earl, parking-transit supervisor, $38,115
Wall, Laurie, registrar,
Wallace, J, instructor-nt, $35,525
Wallentine, Scott, assoc prof 12/12, $93,759
Walsh, Briana, assistant volleyball coach, $33,582
Walstrand, Gwen, professor, $62,331
Walters, Bradley, enterprise system administrator, $52,838
Walters, Heather, instructor-nt, $38,649
Wamsher, Zachary, maintenance general mechanic,
Wanekaya, Adam, assoc professor, $70,151
Wang, Jianjie, assistant professor, $55,968
Wang, Weiyan, assoc professor, $57,545
Wang, Yang, professor, $84,796
Wantland, Carisma, custodian I,
Ward, Dennis, custodian I, $31,316
Ward, Sandra, custodian I, $29,373
Ward, V, instructor-nt, $45,670
Wardell, Mary, physician medical staff, $133,240
Warner, Samantha, instructor, $45,000
Warnow, Cynthia, admin asst III, $30,688
Warren, Melissa, dir, interactive video & off-campus programs, $40,592
Washington, Johnny, professor, $84,444
Waters, Brenda, administrative assistant III, $34,621
Watson, Robert, professor, $71,877
Waugh, Douglas, chief radio engineer, $57,154
Weathermon, Danny, athletics equipment stores spc, $26,735
Weaver, Margaret, professor, $69,836
Webb, Gary, professor, $74,696
Webb, Joseph, farm operator, $24,167
Webb, Krista, technology support specialist, $41,434
Webb, Marion, food service coordinator, $20,734
Webb, Michael, preventative maintenance crd, $41,931
Webb, Susan, senior instructor 12/12, $50,538
Weber, Andrea, director of student conduct, $47,000
Weber, Donald Jr, director of plaster student union, $35,155
Weber, Mallory, head athletics coach, $35,525
Webster, Lauren, contract compliance manager, $49,582
Wedenoja, William, professor, $83,175
Weir, Cathie, instructor, $42,174
Welch, Granvill, custodian I, $21,465
Welch, Jacob, radio communications supervisor, $33,863
Welch, James, crd of web recruitment, $39,676
Welch, Laura, residence hall director, $32,988
Wells, Gary, maintenance foreman, $41,615
Wendel-Stevenson, Courtney, new media specialist, $33,130
Wessels, Emanuelle, assistant professor, $52,780
West, Bruce, professor, $74,085
West, Tracy, public safety officer, $26,531

Weter, Jennifer, sr pharmacy technician, $38,210
Wheeler, Jack, events crd jkhhpa, $37,143
Wheelis, Lori, custodian I, $20,734
Whipple, Tanya, senior instructor, $45,461
Whisenant, Brenda, senior computer operator, $44,662
Whisenhunt, Brooke, professor, $49,156
White, David, assoc professor, $54,406
White, Donald, sr broadcast engineer tv, $53,319
White, John, vip project coordinator, $30,825
White, Kevin, sr photographer, $39,334
White, Letitia, department head, $100,672
White, Timothy, assoc professor, $58,272
White, Victoria, financial aid counselor, $31,300
Whitmire, Laura, assoc director student engagement,
Whitten, Lori, administrative specialist II, $27,117
Whittington, Jessica, accounting technician, $27,039
Whittington, Kirk, laundry services repair t, $28,736
Wickham, Cameron, professor, $74,590
Wicks, Janet, invoicing specialist/clinique coordinator, $34,154
Wiechert, Raegan, asst prof-9 mo appt-library, $37,934
Wiedemann, Paula, head athletics coach, $52,293
Wienberg, Darren, academic advisor, $52,823
Wiggin, Sarah, assistant professor, $50,650
Wiggins, Jill, director, $70,000
Wilburn, Nicole, asst dir - education / development, $47,000
Wilcox, Joretta, clinical faculty-instructor, $41,387
Wiley, Tammy, general mgr ksmu & ozarks, $107,367
Wilhelm, Paula, asst dir hr emp dev & per, $59,171
Wilker, Karl, research professor-12 mon, $82,404
Willde, Karen, public safety parking ctrl att, $22,525
Williams, Deborah, library associate I, $28,777
Williams, Dixie, asst dir adms transfer crd, $45,000
Williams, John, dir sch of accountancy, $137,924
Williams, Joseph, instructor-nt, $43,170
Williams, Julia, academic admin asst II, $26,551
Williams, Kenneth, research technician I, $39,730
Williams, Sarah, assistant professor, $51,765
Williamson, Elizabeth, associate prof-12 month appt, $95,266
Willis, Steven, professor, $62,469
Wills, C, dir procurement, $75,771
Willson, Douglas, bursar, $68,384
Wilson, Brenda, custodial specialist, $24,758
Wilson, Daniel, professor, $70,898
Wilson, Kevin, testing technician, $29,088
Wilson, Lance, public safety officer, $25,609
Wilson, Laurie, executive assistant II, $32,555
Wilson, Ryan, centralized user support specialist, $40,530
Wilson, TaJuan, director trio programs, $60,290
Winborne, Joshua, administrative assistant II, $25,807
Wingo, Hannah, corp support rep-spc event crd, $36,975
Winkeler, Gregory, centralized user support specialist, $39,618
Winkler, Danny, instructional tech suppor, $57,635
Winslow, Jim Jr, reg admission counselor div outreach & recruit-ment, $34,510
Winstead, Cynthia, professor, $68,792
Wisdom, Barry, professor, $107,713
Wise, Brittany, coordinator psychology advisement, $33,000
Witkowski, Colette, department head, $105,099
Witt, Harrison, assistant professor, $51,000
Witte, Hugh, assoc professor, $120,615
Wittorff-Sandgren, Dorothy, comm development coord, $36,181
Wolf, Candice, assistant director alumni activities, $40,600
Wolf, Donald, maintenance general mechanic, $30,533
Wollard, Rick II, custodial I, $24,607
Wood, Gina, instructor, $41,566
Wood, Kelly, professor, $79,960
Wood, Mary, dir of public affairs support, $49,391
Wood, Michael, director first year progr, $48,799
Woodard, Rebecca, professor, $67,383
Wooden, Shannon, associate professor, $57,062
Woolsey, Mark, assessment learning outcomes consultant, $41,000
Worker, Dwight, clinical instructor, $80,000
Worman, Frederick, assistant professor, $51,765
Wray, Melinda, licensed practical nurse, $35,766
Wright, Amy, assistant teacher, $19,799
Wright, James, athletics equipment atten, $28,177
Wright, Jeremy, administrative assistant II, $25,871
Wright, Julie, admin asst II, $36,146
Wright, Matthew, assoc professor, $59,037

Wright, Thomas, custodial specialist, $31,986
Wrinkle, Cheryl, special ed improvement consultant, $45,675
Wrinkle, Cheryl, sr instructor, $57,317
Wu, Shuo-Sheng, geospatial information technician, $45,841
Wulff-Risner, Linda, assistant professor, $44,534
Wynn, Gerald, asst manager production tv, $49,297
Wynn, Jannette, custodian I, $19,799
Yadon, Carly, assistant professor, $52,788
Yarberry, Vonda, professor, $77,864
Yarckow-Brown, Ivy, senior instructor-nt, $44,331
Yates, Jonna, public safety officer, $24,758
Yates, Kyle, assoc dir athletics compliance, $54,284
Yeap, Emily, program coordinator, service learning, $32,000
Yin, Hongjun, library associate I, $29,721
Yoder, Larry, custodian I, $19,799
Yokeley, Marcus, assistant coach, $85,000
Yost, Nikki, accounting specialist, $20,825
Youn, Kay, assistant professor, $62,118
Young, Angela, assessment / learning outcomes consultant, $41,000
Young, Crystal, english lang institute academic spclst, $38,000
Young, Darren, technical support specialist, $41,702
Young Smith, Kelsie, foundation scholarship coord, $35,000
Younger, Arthur, research prof 12/12, $41,788
Yu, Hae Min, assistant professor, $52,500
Yu, Min, assistant professor, $51,765
Yurchak, David, sr buyer, $56,366
Zalewska-Duszek, Iwona, senior instructor, $43,704
Zay-Russell, Vickie, administrative specialist I, $26,056
Zhang, Peng, china operations specialist, $36,236
Zhang, Ying, assoc professor, $60,307
Zheng, Songfeng, assoc professor, $59,037
Zhou, QiongQiong, assistant professor, $54,810
Zhou, Xiaomin, financial tech support specialist, $36,383
Ziegler, Carol, military/veterans transition coordinator, $34,000
Zimmerman, David, assistant professor, $49,735
Zimmerman, Scott, associate professor, $67,859
Zordell-Reed, Marina, crd research administration, $54,347

Harris-Stowe State University

Springfield 65804

Warmack, Dwaun J, president, $219,170
Abbott, Mark K, professor, $68,714
Adams, Tommy F, instructor, $34,801
Adelani, Lateef A, dean of arts and sciences, $80,000
Akca, Zeynep K, associate professor, $57,348
Allen, Carla, assistant professor, $45,981
Anderson, Gladys, academic affairs admin, $36,575
Anderson, Reynaldo S, assoc professor, $54,507
Arbuthnot Jr, Robert L, advising, $31,415
Austin, Almaze' S, bursar, $46,874
Bailey, Benjale Jr, default prevention coordinator, $38,380
Bailey-Mosby, Keeva L, erp manager, $54,601
Baker, Shawn, assistant director of res life, $55,227
Balakrishna, Jayashree, professor, $68,714
Banks, Angelle, admissions counselor, $36,815
Barnes, David L, instructor, $40,319
Barsky, Shelley, buyer, $31,421
Bashir, Andreen, assistant professor, $48,823
Beach, Samuel, maintenance and receiving, $26,773
Bernard, Vicki, director of counseling, $53,166
Bostic, Heather M, director of sponsor programs, $69,318
Bowman, Kenneth G, instructor, $45,981
Brennan, Beverly B, instructor, $50,947
Brooks, Johnny L, maintenance, $23,004
Brooks, Wendell W, assistant professor, $48,823
Brown, Bettye, archivist, $36,893
Brown, Reynolda, director of enrollment management, $85,850
Brown, Thomas, instructor, $43,160
Busekrus, Mary C, president admin, $50,944
Byington, Ashley N, finaical aid counselor, $32,320
Byrd, Barbara A, teacher clay center, $21,953.44/hr
Calhoun, Josias J, intermurals, $26,270
Campbell, Brandon, finaical aid counselor, $35,350
Cannon, Thomas R, bus driver, $21,793
Carr, Gregory S, instructor, $43,160
Carter, Christopher L, library it support, $26,281

Christeson, Kevin E, grants/contracts support specialist, $48,629
Clay, Jasmine D, communication admin, $25,000
Clubbs, Tammy A, admissions data entry, $34,340
Coleman, Stephanie A, human resources specialist, $45,000
Colombo, Beverly K, rpdc consultatnt, $61,526
Cook, Chicana L, library it support, $35,019
Corbett, Jonathan, assistant professor, $45,981
Cruise, Hiram C, public safety officer, $24,642
Daily-Davis, Terry L, instructor, $43,160
Davis, Caandra K, public safety officer, $24,642
Davis, Jonetta, library admin, $25,189
De Araujo, Miguel F, admissions counselor, $34,512
Dee, Mary Ellen, staff accountant, $35,542
Dorsey, Donna L, accounts payable clerk, $31,000
Dyer, William E, b I analsyst, $56,642
Eisel, Joyce, assistant professor, $47,904
Essenpreis, Karen A, network tech, $47,515
Evans, Leonard, public safety officer, $24,642
Fogt, James D, vp of it services, $93,233
Fuller, Timothy, athletic coordinator, $25,250
Gardner, Derek J, maintenance, $22,058
Gentile, Denise L, library tech, $26,680
Gibson Jr, Michael A, admissions counselor, $34,512
Glast, Antonette L, public safety officer, $24,642
Granadillo, Lisette Y, senior program analysis, $64,431
Green, James E, director of financial aid, $70,700
Grice, Anne P, director of arc, $67,478
Griffin, William J, it helpdesk support, $41,527
Haden, Hana, equipment manager, $30,820
Hardy, Adolphus, instructor, $40,319
Harmon, Kiara, financial aid admin, $25,903
Harris, Jeffrey, media lab tech, $45,450
Hartwig, Scott, it assistant manager, $56,583
Harvey, Roslyn L, nurse, $54,060
Henry, Riquita M, assistant to the dean, $45,900
Herlihy, Timothy O, athletic trainer, $41,723
Higgs, Gary K, assistant professor, $45,981
Hightower, Marsha F, rpdc consultatnt, $30,000
Hilaire, Jourdan, assistant to res life coordinator, $30,300
Hocks, Richard, assistant professor, $48,823
Holland, Steven W, library research specialist, $34,974
Holloway, Leslie, dir of institutional advancement, $90,900
Huggins, Brian M, comptroller, $80,810
Hutcherson, Donald E, clay center admin, $30,300
Jackson, Indira S, teacher clay center, $31,428
Jarrett, Mariah D, accountant III, $30,300
Jefferson, Mildred, teacher clay center, $26,281
Jennaway, Lori S, assistant registar, $36,572
Johnson, Charlie, public safety officer, $24,642
Johnson, Tricia E, teacher clay center, $31,428
Johnson, Valerie, hr admin, $30,300
Jones, Charlene L, assistant dean of school, $45,981
Jones, Keyonna N, teacher clay center, $31,428
Jones, Veneesa M, arts and sciences admin, $33,792
Kamkwalala, Robert, assoc professor, $55,596
Kant, Sudarsan, assistant professor, $45,981
Kenyatta, Salim J, talent search coordinator, $34,511
Kerr, JohnDavid, assoc professor, $55,596
Kimbrough, Tammy, director of human resources, $70,700
Lalande, Emmanuel, dean of students success, $70,700
Latham, Eva N, teacher clay center, $25,252
Lenoir, Ida B, operations and reporting spec, $40,299
Lewis, Benny C, emerson faciltiy manager, $38,024
Lumsden, Kisha A, cashier, $23,193
MacDougal, John, assoc professor, $54,507
Marango, David O, lab tech, $28,927
Marcette, Jana D, assistant professor, $45,481
Mayo, Jamaal, director of athletics, $65,650
McClure, Michelle L, associate provost, $81,804
McElmurry-Green, Chauvette, registar, $52,233
McElroy, Walter, media lab tech, $37,499
McGilberry, Van, assist maintenance dir, $41,723
McKinney, Marva L, accounts payable clerk, $34,000
Menezes, David F, senior lan specialist, $44,544
Montgomery, Christine D, rpdc consultatnt, $71,610
Moore, Shamiya L, teacher clay center, $31,428
Moore, Stacy A, instructor, $43,784
Morrison, Robert C, media lab photograher, $41,723
Morrow, Barbara A, director of business services, $61,824

Ndoma-Ogar, Peter O, professor, $63,048
Negron, Catherine, asst director of student activities, $40,800
Noble, Barbara, director of library serv, $62,327
Norrington, Carol L, network support professional, $54,797
Norris, Tiffany T, admission admin, $27,250
OFallon, Heather E, verification specialist, $30,300
Onwumere, Remigius U, assistant professor, $57,348
Orea, Darrell E Jr, maintenance, $37,882
Orzel, Linda, library assistant, $37,882
Palazzolo, Steven J, maintenance, $36,996
Patton-Jordan, Jodi, director of clay center, $77,770
Pelster, Kristen, rpdc consultatnt, $107,000
Pernell Jr, Adolph, bus driver, $25,833
Perry, Ricky, sergant public safety, $25,630
Podleski, Ann, professor, $68,714
Poindexter, Clarice L, public safety admin, $30,643
Purham, Lorine, mailroom/copy center, $30,567
Richardson, Bertha M, rpdc consultatnt, $56,397
Robertson, Jeffrey, sergant public safety, $25,630
Robinson, Alice F, sponsor programs admin, $31,386
Robinson, Danyel S, teacher clay center, $30,300
Rogers, Nolan G, public safety officer, $24,642
Rothermel, Jeanne M, rpdc consultatnt, $61,526
Rugraff, Donald R, rpdc consultatnt, $96,606
Rushing, Tiffini P, advising, $31,415
Salaria, Aamir, assistant professor, $45,981
Sanders Jr, Richard, maintenance, $39,474
Schone, Christine M, librarian assistant, $25,755
Scott, Pier, public relations, $50,000
Smith, Cassandra, talent search admin, $25,693
Smith, Dwyane, provost, $108,585
Smith, Lucille, teacher ed admin, $23,203
Smoot, Diane, associate professor, $57,348
Speckman, Elizabeth R, advising, $31,415
Spence, Douglas A, instructor , $40,319
Sperry, Julie L, rpdc consultatnt, $116,038
Stewart, Marvin, instructor, $49,619
Sutherlin, Lea B, executive admin, $64,831
Sykes, Charles E, assistant dean of school, $62,565
Taylor, Twana M, registar admin, $26,281
Tiamiyu, Owolabi K, assistant professor, $61,297
Todoroff, Linda S, director of talent search, $53,591
Traber, Jason, senior advisor, $40,400
Turner, Jyhardis E, advising admin, $25,882
Turner, Karen D, it admin, $30,041
Turner, Tommie Y, director of nsf, $54,086
Ulak-Yilmaz, Yesim, teacher clay center, $30,906
Walls, Betty P, assistant professor, $57,176
Washington, Helen J, arc secertary, $25,590
Weatherford-Jacobs, Odesa M, interim dean teacher ed, $74,047
Weaver, Hattie K, instructor teacher ed, $64,445
Webb, Douglas E, maintenance, $29,664
Wesley, Rhonda S, title ix - hr, $35,000
Williams, Alfred, physical ed planning specialist, $42,000
Williams, Marilyn D, athletic secertary, $30,300
Williams, Scott B, public safety officer, $24,642
Yokley, Nakima L, outreach samsha, $41,208
Younas, Tahir M, it manager, $55,631
Zakery, Fatemeh, dean school of business, $143,012

Missouri Southern State University

Joplin 64801-1595

Marble, Alan, president, $183,917
Abrahams, Faustina, coord-fy advising/clinical c, $38,158
Abrahams, Nii, prof business admin, $93,961
Achey, Nathaniel, coord-network services, $51,337
Ackiss, David, prof english & philosophy, $71,092
Adamopoulos, Anthony, assoc prof psychology, $53,148
Adams, Charles, asst prof criminal justice, $47,986
Adams, Landon, director - student activities, $39,192
Adams, Meagan, coord - alumni relation, $36,235
Adongo, Jonathan, asst professor of economics, $68,005
Agee, Theresa, prof bus admin-accting, $96,299
Alexander, Charles, asst coach, defensive coord, $30,500
Allen, Brian, asst coach men's xc & track, $28,500
Almeter, Curtis, photographer (urm), $33,488

Appuhamy, Amila, asst prof mathematics, $49,024
Aranda, Katie, ets outreach specialist, $33,068
Archer, Marsi, prof chemical & phys sci/dh, $78,046
Arnold, Heather, director - aquatics & wellness, $29,940
Arwood, Michelle, financial accountant, $33,875
Atkinson, Addie, admin asst, physical plant, $24,960
Ayton, Grace, professor nursing, $83,802
Baker, Christine, admin asst, admissions, $21,359
Bankson, Dawn, admin asst school of business, $20,259
Barbosa, Karen, police officer, $32,186
Barry, Alla, assistant professor biology, $46,182
Bartholet, Francis, assoc prof ddet/eng tech, $62,373
Beeler, Sheri, professor kinesiology, $63,221
Behnke, Kandee, admin asst,teacher ed/honors, $21,966
Benfield, Steven, director - campus recreation, $45,395
Bennett, Angela, admin asst, criminal justice, $21,966
Bentley, Christine, assoc prof art/dh, $55,317
Berry, Jack, coordinator bsc events, $26,748
Berry, Lori, custodian, res./cj, days, $21,359
Bever, Megan, asst professor history, $43,800
Black, Robert, assoc prof/refer libr, $57,478
Blalock, Brenda, counselor - financial aid, $31,306
Blanton, Kelli, asst prof nursing, $49,694
Block, Beverly, prof bus admin-mktg/mgmt, $91,780
Blomgren, Peter, coord digital media tech, $38,072
Boman, Teresa, asst prof biology, $46,182
Boschee, Jeff, head men's basketball coach, $79,677
Boydston, Emily, secretary - school of business, $20,259
Boyer, Rita, admin assistant, music, $26,551
Bradshaw, Karen, dir-entrepreneurship ctr, $55,169
Bramwell, Nathaniel, coord, athletic facilities ops, $37,000
Branham, Bonnie, custodian, ummel, $20,259
Breidenstein, Desiree, admin asst dean sch business, $22,631
Broady, Kent, science lab technician, $28,908
Brown, Amber, admin asst to dean of a & s, $23,210
Brown, Barry, professor philosophy, $72,064
Brown, Deborah, prof/ interim dean of ed/psy, $110,649
Brown, Denice, academic records specialist, $31,369
Brown, Joey, prof english & philosophy, $65,677
Brown, Nicole, dir - career svcs, $47,665
Brownfield, Wesley, server tech, $30,254
Bruggeman, Jared, director of athletics, $92,773
Bruggeman, Maria, asst prof kinesiology, $43,720
Bryant, Elisa, development officer, $47,623
Bryant, Ward, assoc prof communications/dh, $55,052
Bucher, Frederick, assoc prof art, $55,317
Bullock, Heather, clinical counselor acad advisr, $33,593
Bunch, Srithawai, custodian, taylor, eve, $20,259
Burleson, Rachel, asst athletics dir-admin/comp, $47,721
Burnham, Jamie, women's xc/tf & pt equip mgr, $32,268
Burr, Karesa, athletics business manager, $31,679
Burrow, Lyndall, asst technical dir, $34,699
Buttle, Abigail, assistant registrar, $44,073
Callari, Klebon, academic records spec a-g, $31,369
Campbell, Scott, assoc prof international bus, $85,260
Capeci, James, asst prof/librarian/doc deliv, $45,853
Carmichael, Aaron, asst prof intl english prog, $40,600
Carr, Amber, pt mktg & outreach librarian, $24,000
Carter, Carolyn, custodian, taylor, $29,703
Centeno, Christina, training specialist, $30,764
Chmielewski, Melissa, asst softball coach, $30,000
Clark, Rhonda, asst prof of communications, $44,787
Clark, Willie, custodian, bsc, $20,259
Coffey, Randon, dir athletic mktg & corp sales, $38,759
Cole, Amy, professor psychology, $61,268
Cole, Kenneth, professor psychology, $69,552
Cole, Ranelle, early childhood teacher, $29,364
Collins, James, professor c.i.s, $91,781
Collins, Jimmie Jr, server tech - vm, $44,551
Collins, William, maintenance technician, $30,576
Coltharp, Jean, instructor of math, $38,500
Compton, Richard, custodian, music, evenings, $33,800
Comstock, S, assoc prof bus admin-accting, $97,857
Conklin, C, assoc prof kinesiology, $57,420
Coose, Jackie, carpenter supervisor, $45,947
Coose, Saowanee, custodian, health science, $20,759
Corcoran, Brian, admissions counselor, kc, $30,778
Corcoran, Chrys, asst prof nursing, $49,694
Corn, Robert, dir of alumni relations-ath, $88,985

Correll, Dallas, custodian, legg & platt, eve, $24,302
Corum, Kathrine, instructor dental hygiene, $44,660
Cotter, Cheryl, assoc prof music, $50,214
Courtney, Joyce, it - office manager, $39,703
Cowdin, Matthew, instr crim just/pol acad coord, $45,853
Cozens, Clara, assoc prof teacher ed, $53,365
Crabtree, Nancy, assoc prof ref librarian, $51,853
Cragin, E, prof bus admin-mktg/mgmt, $105,292
Craig, Susan, assoc prof teacher ed, $63,583
Creamer, Bradley, asst prof biology/int dh, $52,489
Critchfield, Sherri, senior systems analyst, $58,168
Cullers, Andrea, asst prof kineseology, $42,630
Cunningham, Anna, asst prof biology, $43,000
Curran, Kayla, library clerk, $20,759
Curtis, Amanda, learning mgmt systems admin, $29,364
Curtis, Carrie, asst prof mathematics, $39,689
Curtis, Charles, professor mathematics, $77,563
Cuttrell, Glenn, custodian, rec center, eve, $20,759
Dalbey, Robert, maintenance technician, $30,076
Damer, Sheila, coord - teacher education, $37,347
Danna, Valter, maintenance technician, $30,076
Darnell, Bryce, head coach baseball, $49,159
Davies, Michael, maintenance technician, $34,956
Dawson, Michelle, asst prof of mktg/mgmt, $51,783
Dawson, Ronnie, custodian, athletics, evening, $20,259
Day, Linda, hr payroll assistant, $26,000
Day, Peggy, asst prof teacher ed (tesol), $42,654
Delehanty, William, asst prof political science, $47,452
Dennis, Jennifer, prof biology & env hlth, $60,900
Derfelt, Joanna, assoc prof political science, $51,853
Diskin, Rebecca, dir - financial aid, $66,114
Doak, Joshua, dir - residence life, $48,456
Dobson, Cheryl, registrar, $58,735
Dodson, Gary, coord it user services, $33,009
Dodson, Jennifer, security technician, $29,096
Donelson, James, asst prof chemistry, $49,052
Douglas, Megan, instr bus admin-mktg/mgmt, $50,517
Douglas, Robin, coord testing services, $41,950
DuRossette, Brenda, data entry clerk, $21,359
Ducre, Michelle, development off - major gifts, $57,976
Dunagan, Bobby, painter, $28,244
Dunlop, James Jr, asst prof bus amin-mktg/mgmt, $57,027
Dworkin, Joy, dh/prof english & philosophy, $69,191
Ebert, Elizabeth, development bus mgr, $32,295
Edwards, Eric, central stores mangr, $33,800
Edwards, William Jr, professor teacher ed, $63,583
Eis, Linda, treasurer, $92,000
Eller, Christine, professor nursing, $66,583
Elliff Pound, Lee, dir - alumni, $62,009
Elliott, Karen, admin asst, psychology, $26,551
Ellis, Nancy, admin asst, communications, $22,781
Ennis, Elliot, asst prof chemistry, $50,118
Epperson, Melanie, admin asst, rec services, $26,551
Eriksen, Ashley, multimedia specialist, $30,805
Ernst, Jonathan, it software installer, $22,781
Espinosa, Michelle, instructor music, $37,000
Espinosa, Ricardo, assoc prof music, $58,000
Estes, Devon, asst prof art, $48,519
Evans, Kenneth, assistant football coach, $48,000
Faine, Gloria, professor teacher ed, $71,558
Faulstick, Dustin, asst prof of english and phil, $43,300
Fauss, Diana, asst professor nursing, $70,000
Ferdig, Kevin, dir - residence hall, $25,820
Fipps, Corey, asst football coach, $48,000
Fitzpatrick, Tina, sr coord of admissions ops, $41,921
Fletcher, Dale, maintenance technician, $43,971
Fletcher, Michael, prof biology & env hlth, $76,483
Fordham, Diana, instructional designer, $53,477
Forest, Leslie, student accounting specialist, $30,764
Forsythe, Melissa, admin asst, library, $21,966
Fort, Debra, academic skills specialist, $35,548
Francis, Shavonne, admin assistant, project stay, $22,781
Fraser, Sharon, default prev./sap counselor, $30,778
Fronzaglia, Brian, assoc prof music/dh, $60,000
Frossard, Robert, lead maintenance technician, $48,027
Fullerton, Darren, vp st affairs/ enrollment mgmt, $131,617
Funderburgh, Tosha, admin asst, career services, $20,259
Gallemore, Rebecca, assoc prof teacher ed, $51,811
Galve Rivera, Ruben, asst prof foreign lang-spanish, $43,000

Galvez Coronado, Amanda, custodian, reynolds, evenings, $20,259
Gandy, Alex, academic advisor, $30,778
Garner, Janine, payroll manager, $41,577
Garner, Jeffrey, instructor of accounting, $70,000
Garoutte, Michael, prof physical science, $78,046
Garrison, Dennis, skilled services, $33,169
Gibson, Jeff, dir - budget and operations, $95,690
Gilbert, Jeannie, coord-testing, academic adv, $36,259
Gilbert-Saunders, Lynell, assoc prof physical science, $59,412
Gilmore, Tracy, admin asst, cis/it, $26,615
Gish, Amanda, technical resource specialist, $34,123
Goettel, Donnie, advancement ser manager, $34,510
Gonzalez, Mayra, admin asst, financial aid, $21,966
Goodwin, Bryan, maint technician supervisor, $57,171
Gram, Kaitlin, interim dir intl english prog, $49,694
Gray, William, head coach softball, $47,986
Green, Billy, custodian, $33,800
Green II, Frederick, assistant professor of music, $42,325
Greenlee, George, prof english & philosophy, $65,677
Greer, Jill, assoc prof sociology, $57,532
Grimsley, Letitia, admin asst, dental hygiene, $21,966
Groesbeck, John, dean school of bus/kuhn chair, $141,267
Gubera, Conrad, prof sociology/soc sci, $77,405
Gullett, Craig, coord student services, $32,285
Hackett, Holly, asst prof psychology, $42,654
Hackett, Lorinda, assoc prof teacher ed, dh, $50,023
Hamilton, Christina, admin asst, bio/caps/math fac, $21,359
Hand, Linda, professor mathematics, $80,147
Harden, Chester, custodian, res hall/slc, days, $21,359
Harmon, Dennis, professor mathematics, $69,884
Harmon, Tara, custodian, justice ctr, eve, $20,259
Harrington, Robert, dir - physical plant, $96,000
Hartje, James Jr, it support spec, $33,822
Hayes, Brenda, admin asst, kinesiology, $22,781
Head, Jennifer, coord online academic adv, $42,584
Heaney, Michelle, admin asst, social science, $21,966
Heatherly, Raymond, custodian, $27,687
Heim, Mary, mktg & outreach clk - library, $21,966
Helms, Darren, custodial day supervisor, $34,024
Hempsmyer, Patricia, asst prof nursing, $49,694
Henson, Meghan, records assistant, $20,259
Herr, Dennis, professor c.i.s, $82,593
Heth, Robert, assoc professor bio & env hlth, $54,969
Hewett, Thomas, broadcast engineer, $43,453
Hicklin, Cherona, asst prof teacher ed, $43,720
Hicklin, Robin, dir - upward bound, $50,048
Hicks, Nathaniel, counselor, adm/campus visit c, $30,778
Higgins, Amber, systems coord - fin aid, $41,975
Hill, Sheryl, asst prof nursing, $54,302
Hinojoza, Amado, custodian, webster, evenings, $20,259
Hinojoza, Luz, custodian, rec center, $20,759
Hobbs, Jean, professor kinesiology/dh, $74,198
Hodson, Bradford, executive vice president, $155,000
Hoffman, Karen, admin assistant, athletics, $22,110
Holder, Patty, coord of student payments, $27,935
Holt, Melissa, custodian, reynolds, days, $21,966
Holtzman, Nicole, admin asst,foreign languages, $20,759
Hopkins, Coby, admin asst, bio/caps/math, $21,966
Hopkins, Stephanie, dir student success center, $47,665
Hopper, Randy, acad ser coord upward bound, $30,778
Hosp, Pamela, secretary - health center, $22,781
Hou, Sherman, dh/prof foreign languages, $73,584
Houk, Christopher, coord fire safety & env hlth, $33,364
Howarth, Michael, assoc prof english/dir of hon, $56,955
Howe, Elke, prof ind eng tech/dh, $72,502
Hubbard, Ronda, head coach, women's bsktb, $68,005
Huffman, Loreen, professor psychology, $69,552
Huffman, William, prof bus admin-accting, $95,007
Hughes, Alicia, bursar, $47,026
Hulderman, Michael, assoc prof crim just/inter dh, $70,035
Hunt, William, creative services director, $33,300
Jackson, Greg, academic support specialist, $32,285
Jackson, Vivian, asst prof nursing, $51,185
Jaros, Anne, professor theatre, $66,522
Jensen, Julia, title iv aid & compl counslr, $29,908
Jewsbury, Evan, dir - human resources, $77,000
Johnson, Denver, head football coach, $95,000
Johnson, Donna, assoc professor bio & env hlth, $54,969
Johnson, John, asst football coach, $30,000

Johnson, Kerry, prof mathematics/dept head, $69,884
Johnston, Nicole, cashier, $20,759
Jones, Cassandra, admissions comm specialist, $27,248
Jordan, Cynthia, admin asst,inst intl studies, $21,966
Jordan, Stephen, groundskeeper supervisor, $34,024
Jorgensen, Troy, conditioning coach, $43,406
Kearney, S, administrative asst, art, $31,013
Keller, Justin, univ police sergeant, $32,727
Keller, Kevin, asst prof intl english prog, $40,000
Kelley, Lisa, instructor distance dental hyg, $42,654
Kemm, Donna, director of accounting, $43,234
Kennedy, Kenneth, chief of campus police, $51,191
Kennedy, Michael, assoc professor bio & env hlth, $54,969
Kew, Robert, maintenance technician, $31,263
Killingsworth, Greg, carpenter, $38,500
Kilpatrick, James, assoc prof foreign language, $53,398
Kim, Hyunjung Jr, asst prof of communications, $48,659
Kimbrough, James, dir-educational talent search, $50,048
Kirkendall, Edward, counselor/academic advisor, $30,754
Klein, Timothy, assoc professor theatre, $48,104
Kneeland, Kenneth, custodian, crim jus, days, $21,966
Koch, Claudia, asst prof ind eng tech, $58,649
Koch, Whitney, counselor, admissions transfer, $28,813
Korth, Devin, central receiving coord, $28,886
Korvick, Lynda, assoc prof nursing/dh, $84,001
Kostan, Karen, assoc prof psychology, $51,037
Kumbier, William, prof english & philosophy, $73,979
Laird, Richard, professor mathematics, $69,884
Larson, Kelly, assoc prof communications, $57,230
Lathrom, Grant, assoc prof mathematics, $56,527
Lawson, Michael, prof biology & env hlth, $85,892
Leininger, Gregory, programmer/analyst, $40,970
Lemmons, Crystal, asst vp academic affairs, $101,530
Leslie, Emily, instructor distance dental hyg, $42,121
Lewis, Amber, counselor - financial aid, $30,778
Lewis, Caleb, simulation coordinator, $51,185
Li, Hong, librarian, technical services, $46,588
Lile, Ann, asst professor theatre, $42,014
Lile, James Jr, assoc professor theatre/dh, $59,784
Linder, J, professor nursing, $80,543
Lipira, Patsy, vp academic affairs, $138,626
Liso, Susana, asst prof foreign lang/spanish, $46,690
Lloyd, Mark, dean student engmt & retention, $70,383
Locher, David, prof social science, $68,849
Locher, Melissa, asst prof teacher ed, $41,251
Lovett, Sandra, grant writer, $43,227
Loyd, Dale, custodian, health science, eve, $21,966
Lyerla, Brett, asst dir univ relations & mktg, $48,517
MacDonald, Michael, custodian, tpac, eve, $31,013
Macomber, Jeffrey, professor music, $58,334
Madsen, Karen, asst prof nursing, $52,780
Marion, Terry, prof bus admin-mktg/mgmt, $91,571
Marsh, Daniel, prof physical science, $81,795
Marsh, James, asst prof engineering tech, $54,384
Martin, Marcus, telecom engineer, $39,546
Martinez, Frank, custodian, library, evenings, $21,966
Martinez, Vida, custodian, library, days, $26,016
Maskus, Justin, dir media relations athletics, $46,034
Mata, Kathryn, ath spec evnts/annual camp dir, $35,568
Mathes, Cassie, dir univ relations & marketing, $63,437
Matthews, Vincent, carpenter, $28,244
Mattix, Christi, instructor of accounting, $50,928
McDaniel, Brenda, academic aff project manager, $40,092
McDermid, Robert, professor psychology/dh, $77,022
McGrane, Wendy, associate prof/libr dir, $77,044
McKee, David, asst prof physical science, $49,735
McKenzie, Kyle, assistant professor art, $43,500
McKinney, Donald, groundskeeper, $22,781
McMain, Chloe, graphic designer, $30,254
McSpadden, Holly, prof english & philosophy, $65,677
Meeker, Scott, communications/new media spec, $37,051
Mehrens, Brian, technical-videographer, $36,528
Miller, Richard, prof/dean of arts and sci, $110,649
Mintert, Amber, assistant professor of art, $43,000
Mitchell, Ronald, dean of students, $79,976
Mitchell, T, custodian, young gym, days, $33,800
Mitts, Maryann, asst prof kinesiology, $58,827
Montee, Tani, admin asst,fye/acad outreach, $21,359
Moore, Darin, head athletic trainer, $46,743

Moorhouse, Brian, police officer, $30,160
Moos, Joseph, assoc prof intl bus, $90,710
Morley, Felicia, dl instl designr/mkting, $42,630
Moser, Bryce, custodian, billingsly, eve, $20,759
Moss, Michael, custodial rover, $23,982
Mouser, Rebecca, asst prof of english and phil, $43,300
Murphy, Mary, prof english & philosophy, $65,677
Musser, Lori, coord disability services, $45,553
Myers, Cindy, custodian, hearns, days, $21,966
Myers, Douglas, instr bus admin-mktg/mgmt, $53,027
Myers, Matthew, costumer, $39,924
Napier, John, head coach, women's volleyball, $53,287
Needham, Gregory, manager - bookstore, $48,556
Neely, Alyssa, office services printing clerk, $21,359
Newell, David, coord criminal justice sem, $41,975
Newsom, Bethany, scholarship counselor, $28,813
Nichols, Brian, assoc prof bus adm (fin/econ), $95,677
Nickle, Tonya, coord - student employment, $30,778
Nicoletti, Andrew, carpenter, $26,353
Nicoletti, Nicholas, assoc prof soc sci, $43,620
Nicoletti, Tony, automotive mechanic, $31,902
Noble, Lauren, asst volleyball coach, $26,732
Nodler, Charles Jr, prof, archivist librarian, $78,070
Noll, Kimberly, human resources coordinator, $28,808
Noller, Sherry, research associate, sbtdc, $30,772
Norvell, Christie, admin asst, rad/emt/resp, $21,966
O'Dell, Glenda, admin asst, st success ctr, $21,966
O'Neal, Gayle, library clerk, $22,781
Oakes, Jack, professor/chair - cis, $91,781
Odem, Sharon, admin asst to the president, $40,248
Ogle, Coeta, asst prof nursing, $49,000
Otero, Jason, software dev/prog analyst, $40,000
Outhouse, Michael, asst prof art, $45,573
Overdeer, Danny, professor teacher ed, $75,724
Owen, Timothy, dir - adm computing, $78,817
Owens, Christopher, campus card service ctr mgr, $43,234
Oxford, Marion, custodian, rover, evenings, $22,610
Parker, Mary, clincial counselor acad advisr, $35,147
Parrigon, Erin, asst mgr - bookstore, $30,780
Peine, Brett, instructor of emt, $53,317
Peine, Emalee, registered nurse, $50,668
Philibert, Nanette, assoc prof mktg/mgmt/dh, $85,059
Pickett, Jonathan, it security tech, $27,996
Pinet, William, assoc prof c.i.s, $74,593
Pishkur, Frank, assoc prof art, $55,317
Plucinski, Karen, prof biology & env hlth, $74,255
Pooley, Donna, library clerk, tech services, $21,966
Pooley, Jeffrey, mgr - procurements/its project, $59,938
Powell, Lauren, admin asst, acts, $21,966
Powell, Mike, carpenter, $26,353
Price, Michelle, admin assistant, teacher ed, $25,823
Pyle, Kevin, it software installer, $22,781
Quackenbush, Samantha, dir - residence hall, $25,820
Quade, Carol, adm asst-vp academic affairs, $31,700
Quinn, Dory, dir - project stay, $50,048
Randall, Ritchie, office services clerk, $20,759
Rawlins, Richard, prof bus admin-finance/econ, $103,979
Rearrick, Dianna, lead dispatcher, $21,966
Reed, Charles, custodian, webster, $26,551
Regnier, Helen, custodian, mccormick, $26,016
Regnier, Wesley, painter, $28,244
Ressel, Ronald, assoc women's bb coach, $48,212
Richardson, Linda, admin asst, rolla dental hyg, $21,966
Richeson, Penny, library clerk, $31,013
Rinner, Anna, asst prof biology, $45,500
Ritzman, Mary, admin asst, student services, $24,648
Roark, Brian, athletics fac caretaker, $22,759
Robertson, Anthony Sr, assoc prof teacher ed, $58,365
Robertson, Jerry, maintenance technician, $45,947
Robinson, Lisa, dir-small bus & tech dev ctr, $62,869
Rodgers, Michael, assoc prof english & phil, $49,619
Roettger, Vickie, prof biology & env hlth, $76,483
Rogers, Kimberly, asst prof dent hygiene, $47,154
Ross, Donald, senior broadcast engineer, $46,110
Routledge, Glenna, admin asst, upward bound/ets, $21,966
Routledge, Tristan, admissions counselor, $29,313
Russell, Mitzi, cashier, $21,966
Sandtorf, Elaine, office services clerk, $22,781
Sayles, James, oracle programmer/dba admin, $56,174

Schiavo, J, professor c.i.s, $82,160
Schiding, Bryan, head coach, men's xc & track, $52,145
Schiska, Alan, assoc prof radiology, $74,627
Schlink, Gerald, prof biology & env hlth, $85,940
Schmidt, Thomas, assoc professor marketing, $88,036
Schneider, Tara, master control switcher lll, $21,966
Schuster, Heather, coord of career services, $36,263
Scott, Trina, prof criminal justice, $69,756
Scrivner, Stacie, dh/asst prof dental hygiene, $56,453
Shafer, John, custodian,kuhn hall, $31,013
Sharlow, David, assoc prof music, $45,414
Shaw, Jennifer, counselor, admissions transfer, $30,778
Shearman, Lucinda, distance dental hyg instructor, $21,000
Shelton, Connie, admin asst, vp bus affairs, $38,500
Shufflin, Teresa, accounts payable specialist, $27,100
Skaggs, Derek, director of admissions, $71,498
Skibbe, Jeffrey, mgr - radio, $63,811
Slavings, Shanna, asst prof of communications, $43,720
Smith, Briana, mgr - student accounts, $30,264
Smith, Colleen, mobility engineer, $43,234
Smith, David, prof acct/dh of acct & finance, $95,007
Smith, Jennifer, custodial, health science, $21,966
Smith, Jill, asst prof bus admin-accting, $78,255
Smith, Leslie, asst prof foreign lang-spanish, $46,690
Smith, Ruth, counselor - financial aid, $30,778
Smith, Stephen, coord digital media content, $46,137
Smith, Stephen, assoc prof geog, $59,632
Smith, Susan, professor music, $63,822
Snell, Scott, director distance learning, $64,590
Snodgrass, Debra, asst prof music, $42,328
Spencer, Richard, assoc prof criminal justice, $58,362
Spencer, Terri, admin asst, theatre, $31,013
Spurlin, Brenda, admin assist,dean technology, $33,800
Spurlin, Jack Jr, assoc prof criminal justice, $58,362
Stadler, Albert, chief information officer, $83,176
Stafford, Cynthia, admin asst sikeston dent hyg, $21,966
Stanley, Rachel, asst director of honors, $38,570
Stebbins, Chad, prof/dir inst intl s, $83,908
Steddum, Kristine, admin assistant, english, $21,966
Stewart, Joseph, custodian, fine arts, day, $21,966
Stiles, Judy, general mgr, kgcs-tv, $56,066
Stockdale, Jason, network identity/dr technician, $32,285
Strait, Tia, dean school health sciences, $110,649
Strother, James, maintenance technician, $32,098
Sullivan, Olive, asst prof comm/chart advisor, $38,388
Summerfield, John, prof physical science, $79,788
Sundararajan, Jency, asst prof physical science, $49,000
Surber, Rae, switchboard operator, $26,551
Surber, Rodney, dir account development, $60,900
Surbrugg, Kenneth, sbtdc consultant, $49,544
Swadley, Janet, facilities drafter, $38,480
Swift, James, police officer, $32,186
Tackett, Howard Jr, police officer, $30,160
Talavera-Ibarra, Pedro, prof foreign languages-spanish, $77,652
Talley, Olive, admin asst, dean/edu, $33,800
Tappana, Nikki, director, child dev center, $35,525
Tarrant, Celeste, early childhood teacher-cdc, $27,941
Taubel, Gail, asst prof dist dental hygiene, $47,154
Teverow, Paul, prof of history/soc sci, $73,403
Thomas, Arleen, custodian, plaster, evenings, $21,966
Thomas, Jimmy, groundskeeper, $20,259
Thompson, Craig, intl student counselor, $29,313
Thompson, Cynthia, procure & budget office spec, $35,919
Thompson, Jeffrey, asst director admissions, $43,209
Thompson, Teresa, director first year experience, $46,690
Thornsbrough, Gary, custodian, blaine, days, $20,259
Thornton, Terri, admin assistant, nursing, $21,966
Toliver, Carl, prof english & philosophy, $63,764
Torix, Thaddaeus, inst of ems/clinical coord, $40,000
Tracy, Tina, records assistant, $21,966
Treat, Calvin, custodian, young gym, evenings, $21,966
Treat, Delores, custodian, plaster, days, $21,966
Treat, Thomas Jr, groundskeeper, $26,551
Tuck, Nicholas, asst baseball coach, $28,018
Tucker, Susan, asst prof psychology, $44,787
Tunnell, Leonard, assoc prof c.i.s, $74,489
Van De Mark, Janette, sr analyst & reporting spec, $44,517
Vandine, Julie, early childhood teacher, $29,364
Vann, Kyle, remote site technician, $39,097

Vavra, Patricia, asst prof/head wom track, $57,226
Vernon, T IV, prof bus admin-mktg/mgmt, $93,680
Vigil, Denise, records assistant (va), $22,781
Vlasin, Dianne, admin asst student activities, $21,784
Wagner, Steven, prof of history, $68,029
Wang, Xiaocan, assoc prof emg tech lib, $52,780
Watson, Rashad, football coach-assoc def coor, $38,080
Webb, Cynthia, fitness director, $32,285
Wells, Scott, prof biology & env hlth, $85,892
Wells-Lewis, N, dh/soc sci/prof sociology, $70,915
Wengert, Julie, director, academic outreach, $50,729
White, Jonathan, police officer, $30,160
White, Rhonda, asst prof dent hygiene, $48,026
Whitlock, Garrett, groundskeeper, $20,259
Willand, Jason, professor of biology, $45,500
Williams, Daniel, asst professor theatre, $42,014
Williams, Randy, painter, $42,078
Wilmoth, Judy, hr & workforce dev mgr, $43,640
Wilson, Jordan, professor of music, $42,300
Wilson, Kelly, director - acts, $66,426
Wise, Phillip, professor music, $63,822
Wiseman, Noel, coord multimedia, $41,597
Wood, Elisabeth, application eng - student mod, $49,694
Woolard, Alese, womens head soccer coach, $35,189
Workman, Stephanie, compliance coord - st records, $28,808
Yeboah-Forson, Albert, asst professor geophysics, $50,242
Yust, Robert, vp business affairs, $129,420
Zaidarhzauva, Lora, intl admissions coordinator, $33,875
Zamouski, Jared, ets outreach specialist, $33,068
Zolnierz, Melissa, asst prof biology, $45,000

Missouri Western State University

St. Joseph 64501

Vartabedian, Robert, president, $241,125
Adams, James, hvac/r technician, $31,141
Adkins, James, instructor, $58,000
Adkins, Kaye, professor, $66,189
Adkisson, Patricia, administrative assistant, $13,533
Adwell, Tara, associate exec director cfo foundation, $65,056
Agnew, Jessica, administrative assistant, $26,890
Allen, Sandra, collections specialist, $33,150
Anderson, Kevin, professor, $65,245
Andrews, Dana, instructor, $38,560
Andriano, Gregory, sr systems analyst/programmer, $63,415
Archdekin, Sybil, administrative assistant, $27,553
Arnold, William, math coordinator, $40,000
Baker, Dawn, administrative assistant, $27,846
Baker, Jason, professor, $74,866
Baker, Marilyn, director of financial aid, $86,350
Baldwin, Julie, associate professor, $57,596
Ball, Andrew, assistant coach (football), $37,086
Ball, Belinda, education psychologist wrdcc, $51,960
Balsamo, John, carpenter/cabinet maker, $33,676
Barnes, Clinton, locksmith, $35,392
Barnes, David, custodian, $25,798
Barnes, Susan, administrative support, asst, $20,211
Barta, Csengele, assistant professor, $51,414
Bartels, Cynthia, instructor, $49,735
Bashinski, Susan, associate professor, $63,196
Bausset Page, Ana, assistant professor, $50,257
Beahler, Debra, custodian, $22,191
Beard, Joel, assistant coach (football), $48,222
Becker, Deborah, assistant professor, $48,872
Beckett, Kim, administrative assistant, $29,581
Bell, Jason, university police officer, $37,732
Bell, Wesley, assistant coach (football), $55,137
Bensyl, Stacia, professor, $66,442
Berg, Sandi, administrative coordinator, $33,228
Bergland, Robert, professor, $72,894
Berry, Wonda, rec services/ facilities director, $58,458
Bidding, Robert, corporal, university police, $47,697
Bjelland, Mollie, assistant coach (softball), $25,500
Blacketer, Henry, custodian, $20,728
Bohon, Melissa, custodian, $21,352
Bond, Christopher, associate professor, $59,727
Bowen, Stacey, dir of center for success in math, $51,000

Bracciano, Susan, registrar, $69,570
Brock, Connie, executive associate to president, $48,960
Brooks, Evelyn, professor, $84,504
Brose, Carolyn, associate professor, $78,287
Brown, Harold, asst dean for health & wellness, $77,146
Brown, Ricky, application programmer, $55,161
Brown, Trevor, corporal, university police, $43,329
Browning, Shelle, administrative coordinator, $30,829
Bryant, Edith, dir student success & adv ctr, $59,976
Bryant, Jimmy, hardware/software technician, $45,103
Bucklein, Brian, assistant professor, $50,257
Buhman, Nathan, groundskeeper, $24,238
Burns, Jacqueline, librarian distance education, $50,389
Burton, Mark, hardware/software sup tech, sr, $47,599
Byer, Christa, marketing coordinator, $31,248
Cadden, Michael, professor, $75,646
Caldwell, Benjamin, professor, $71,789
Callow, Jennifer, assistant cataloging librarian, $38,760
Campbell, Christi, associate professor, $71,016
Campbell, Sabrina, custodian, $25,447
Carbin, Gregory, head coach (strength & condition), $36,720
Carbin, Marian, head coach (volleyball), $41,616
Carmichael, Blair, instructional designer, $39,015
Carter, Susan, professor, $64,905
Carviou, James, instructor, $41,616
Castilla-Ortiz, Eduardo, assistant professor, $52,187
Caswell, Angela, administrative coordinator, $31,141
Chambers, Judith, graduate records coordinator, $35,509
Charlton, Michael, associate professor, $55,357
Chevalier, Cary, professor, $74,612
Chiao, Michael, associate professor, $98,074
Choi, Paul, associate professor, $64,267
Church, William, assistant professor, $51,350
Claflin, M Susan, associate professor, $69,446
Clark, Linda, custodian, $25,915
Clark, Michael, university police officer, $34,203
Clary, Pam, assistant professor, $50,984
Collier, Isaiah, asst dean of student develop, $58,938
Coombs, Aaron, assistant coach (m basketball), $39,015
Coombs, Signe, assistant coach (volleyball), $24,969
Corder, Stephanie, associate professor, $69,293
Correa Torres, Minerva, executive admin associate, $36,348
Courington, John, professor, $90,682
Crain, Jeanie, professor, $95,527
Crawford, Tiffany, administrative assistant, $26,325
Criger, Cori, instructional technology director, $65,691
Crisler, Deborah, administrative assistant, $34,495
Crist, Teresa, administrative coordinator, $29,971
Cronk, Brian, professor, $91,315
Cross, Noel, administrative assistant, $38,590
Culp, Ryan, events, groundkeeper, $25,116
Cunningham, Jeffery, fa information system analyst, $38,872
Daffron, Dustin, academic computing technician, $36,426
Daffron, Jeanne, provost & vp academic affairs, $155,758
Daggett, Melissa, associate professor, $61,107
Dahanayake, Sunil, assistant professor, $105,060
Darrough, Craig, environmental safety coordinator, $52,629
Dasta, Stacey, collections specialist, $35,353
Davenport, Douglas, assoc provost for research & pla, $102,000
Dean, Mary, administrative coordinator, $38,161
Deatherage, Galen, custodian, $22,210
Deering, Susan, office coordinator, university police, $33,150
Deka, Teddi, professor, $66,766
Diaz, Michelle, acquisitions/collections mgt, $42,336
Dillon, Gregory, head coach (men's/women's golf), $41,616
Dockery, Mary, instructor, $35,373
Dodd, Regan, assistant professor, $49,272
Dolan, Marsha, professor, $72,163
Dowell, Jarrod, transcript evaluation coordinator, $29,835
Drake, Dawn, assistant professor, $49,272
Driggers, Sharon, telephone/technical serv coord, $42,840
Drubin, Tamara, accounting clerk, $26,403
Ducey, Michael, professor, $70,851
Dunn, Adriann, financial aid coordinator, $28,840
Eckdahl, Todd, professor, $82,907
Eckhoff, Daniel, bursar, $73,040
Edmisson, Robert, head coach (m basketball), $75,012
Edwards, Chad, head coach (wmn's soccer), $38,256
Edwards, Matthew, professor, $70,093

Edwards, Nicholeous, instructional designer, $40,185
Elifrits, Chad, interim director of diagnostic, $52,081
Elliott, Lisa, assistant professor, $51,000
Ellis, John, associate professor, $65,600
Ellis, Mark, mgr of its/app pro & data admi, $68,615
Ellis, Randy, print shop technician, $36,504
England, Benjamin, assistant professor, $47,940
Ertekin, Selcuk, assistant professor, $86,311
Esely, Jay, asso dir of ath external relat, $53,580
Esely, Pamela, administrative coordinator, $28,509
Euchner, Jonathan, assistant professor, $57,540
Evans, Claudine, instructor, $35,700
Evans, Derek, academic advisor, $40,686
Evans, Scott, custodian, $20,221
Everett, Cathy, cashier/billing clerk, $30,556
Exline, Jamie, residence hall director, $28,560
Fast, Kelly, assistant professor, $56,100
Fessler, Cale, vp, financial plan & administration, $133,951
Fisher, Stacy, data & communications coord, $38,780
Flaska, Thomas, instructional technologist, $40,055
Foley, Amy, fitness center coordinator, $47,304
Foley, Rebecca, associate professor, $57,442
Ford, Timothy, spec ed teacher, tm ldr wrdcc, $43,517
Fortune, Susan, custodian, leadwork, $23,029
Foster, Charlotte, assistant professor, $50,257
Foster, Jean, administrative assistant, $27,846
Foster, Roberta, admissions counselor, $31,000
Freemyer, Sara, administrative coordinator, $31,200
Frogge, Jessica, administrative coordinator, $29,503
Frye, Jana, assistant professor, $45,900
Ftizpatrick, Latoya, multicultural ed coordinator, $39,015
Fulton, Travis, university police officer, $36,036
Fuson, Eric, instructor, $38,580
Galloway, Jennifer, library asst, interlibrary lo, $27,748
Gammon, Kathy, accountant, $51,966
Gann, Catherine, academic advisor, $50,443
Garrison, Susan, ctr for academic success direct, $47,430
Garvey, Michael, academic computing technician, $36,426
Gawatz, Jennifer, administrative asst, support, $20,728
Gay, Nathan, assistant professor, $48,960
Gemmell, Cherie, administrative coordinator, $33,579
Gentry, Jerry, director of physical plant, $85,680
George, Gregory, mechanical supervisor, $46,672
Gerhart, Aron, instructor, $41,616
Glise, Tamara, administrative coordinator, $32,370
Gnuschke, Rodema, library technician, senior, $37,791
Godboldt, Suzanne, assistant professor, $53,556
Godfrey, Christopher, professor, $76,091
Graham, Michelle, adaptive technology specialist, $38,211
Graves, Rachel, development officer, $42,500
Gray, Nancy, administrative support, asst, $31,024
Greer, Martha, administrative assistant, $28,977
Gregory, John, administrative assistant, $27,358
Griffith, Brenda, administrative assistant, $29,562
Grimes, Judith, asso vp for sa & dean of stu, $98,373
Groner, Scott, athletic facilities coordinator, $26,500
Gunderson, Konrad, associate professor, $73,351
Guthery, Kelsey, admissions counselor, $32,182
Halloran, Michael, director of athletic facilities, $61,319
Hamzaee, Reza, professor, $99,307
Harding, Jerry, custodian, $23,400
Hardwick, Cosette, associate professor, $75,896
Hare, Carol, administrative assistant, $32,136
Hargis, Deborah, records clerk, $29,835
Harrah, Brian, building supervisor, $50,333
Harrelson, R Lee, associate professor, $58,357
Harris, Barbara, administrative assistant, $33,579
Harris, Crystal, associate professor, $70,398
Harris, David, associate professor, $55,357
Harris, Shawna, associate professor, $56,896
Harris, Teresa, associate professor, $60,630
Hartley, Sherri, accountant, fixed assets/grants, $45,366
Harton, Karma, secretary, hlth info/infroma mgt, $28,606
Hatch, Steven, assistant professor, $49,939
Hayes, Billie, custodian, $21,294
Hecker, Connie, assistant professor, $43,409
Heckman, Elizabeth, support staff coordinator, $26,988
Hegeman, Jennifer, associate professor, $60,494
Heier, Kent, asst dir/pub relations/market, $49,952

Heldenbrand, Dana, administrative coordinator, $29,074
Hennessy, Susan, professor, $70,492
Henry, Kelly, professor, $75,018
Hensley, Lisa, circulation coordinator, $32,097
Hepworth, Elise, associate professor, $56,100
Hepworth, Matthew, assistant professor, $48,960
Hewitt, John, intensive english specialist, $45,900
Hiley, Shauna, associate professor, $59,513
Hill, Kerri, payroll coordinator, $40,078
Hills, Jessica, sr financial aid coordinator, $40,721
Hinkle, Stena, administrative assistant, $40,969
Hinton, Jeffrey, assistant professor, $59,425
Hodge, Ronnie, plumber/fitter, $33,891
Hoffman, Travis, custodian, $21,177
Holt, Teresa, administrative assistant, $26,656
Holtz, Diane, public & alumni relations coord, $51,856
Hopper, John, carpenter, $36,504
Hriso, Peter, associate professor, $74,186
Huffman, Denece, assistant bursar, $48,583
Hughes, Brain, groundskeeper, $24,589
Hughes, Jane, speech pathologist wrdcc, $52,102
Hunt, Sarah, marketing coordinator, $37,791
Hunt, Marilyn, associate professor, $59,967
Irvine, Deborah, professor, $73,809
Jackson, Daniel, res hall resource officer, $33,715
Jacobs, Laura, administrative coordinator, $26,403
Jacobs, Roy, groundskeeper, $27,748
Jeney, Cynthia, associate professor, $57,995
Johnson, Adrienne, instructor, $41,616
Johnson, Britton, associate professor, $57,442
Johnson, Debra, administrative assistant, $38,922
Jones, David, groundskeeper, $28,294
Jones, Kendra, director campus printing services, $55,926
Kaasik, Ellen, residence hall director, $30,000
Kamali, Ali, professor, $73,799
Katchen, Meredith, instructor, $38,560
Katz, Joanne, professor, $81,590
Keller, Dennis, custodian supervisor, $36,000
Keller, Karen, graduate records coordinator, $39,780
Kelly, Jacob, instruc design, web & app pro, $52,795
Kelly, Kathy, administrative coordinator, $37,089
Kelly, Robin, asst to the chair, education, $41,089
Kendall, Heather, associate professor, $55,357
Kendig, Catherine, associate professor, $56,350
Kerner, Paul, hvac/r technician, $31,882
Kerns, Aurora, custodian, $25,915
Kibirige, Joachim, associate professor, $58,780
King, Christopher, events, groundskeeper, $24,238
King, Terry, hvac/r technician, $31,141
Kissock, Susan, associate professor, $57,578
Kissock, Timothy, risk manager, $72,679
Klassen, Steven, associate professor, $29,274
Klaus, Pamela, director for franchise program, $72,420
Kline, Gladys, administrative assistant, $31,648
Kluge, Brooksie, instructor, $34,680
Knight, Orrin, hvac/r technician, $32,370
Kobett, Kevin, custodian, $20,436
Kovacs, Melinda, assistant professor, $48,898
Kowich, Colleen, director of alumni relations, $47,759
Koy, Karen, associate professor, $58,635
Kraft, Justin, associate professor, $62,446
Kramer, Eric, asst dir of ath for ncaa compl, $43,696
Kramer, Melissa, application programmer/banner, $53,125
Krat Mathies, David, associate professor, $56,896
Kriewitz, Greg, instructor, $38,646
Kriley, Balise, athletic trainer, $46,765
Krueger, Wilbur, associate professor, $69,842
Kuechler, Patricia, conferences & spec prog direct, $45,579
Kunkel, Marianne, assistant professor, $47,940
Lance, Cindy, assistant professor, $47,940
Lance, Terry, accountant, $41,457
Lane, Michael, dean, craig school of business, $158,140
Lane, Peggy, professor, $105,060
Lau, Kathryn, administrative assistant, $27,397
Lawley, J Neil, assistant professor, $50,257
Lawson, Catherine, professor, $75,836
Lehman, Emily, administrative assistant, $26,403
Leland, Peggy, administrative assistant, $38,493
Lemanski, Jay, assistant professor, $49,272

Leslie, Susan, database specialist/foundation, $32,526
Lewis, Mark, professor, $106,034
Liao, Kathy, assistant professor, $48,450
Lindsteadt, Gregory, associate professor, $61,573
Lines, Janet, administrative assistant, support, $20,026
Lisenbee, Sherry, administrative assistant, $33,579
Loeffler, Anthony, assistant coach (baseball), $26,104
Loehr, Matthew, assistant professor, $51,000
Long, Bob, assistant professor, $59,851
Lorimor, Steven, associate professor, $58,472
Luke, Karen, administrative assistant, $33,579
Lund, Christina, administrative assistant, $28,411
Lundy, Shelly, administrative assistant, $27,846
Lutes, Jacob, custodian, $21,294
Luthans, Brett, professor, $79,538
Ma, Dalong, assistant professor, $86,700
Mabe, Mark, director of information tech, $101,780
Manning, Jeanie, director of developmental read, $43,735
Mapley, Gordon, dean, western institute, $143,730
Marash, Vincenza, counselor, diver & wmn's issues, $61,221
Marble, David, assistant professor, $54,100
Martens, Susan, assistant professor, $53,060
May, Lisa, administrative coordinator, $29,854
May, Nathanael, associate professor, $56,350
McCauley, Howard, dean of enrollment management, $103,254
McCumber, Sarah, information services librarian, $39,270
McCune, Lori, assistant professor, $48,898
McCutcheon, Nicholas, athletic media relations director, $35,700
McDonald, Jearl, degree audit coordinator, $36,738
McDonald, Jennifer, executive admin associate, $48,048
McGarrell, Andrew, catalog librarian, $52,895
McGaughy, Hassan, university police officer, $34,554
McGuffin, Kurt, director of athletics, $111,490
McIntire, David, assistant professor, $48,960
McKnight, Brett, student employment coordinator, $38,250
McLarren, Amy, asst director resident life, $38,383
McMahan, David, associate professor, $57,962
McMillian, Carey, asso vp for fin plan & admin, $94,837
McMurry, Patrick, professor, $86,524
McNeela, Rico, associate professor, $68,284
McQuirter, Kevin, video communications specialist, $40,422
McQuiston, Derin, custodian, $20,436
McWilliams, David, developmental math specialist, $42,639
Merritt, Karen, custodian, $22,210
Meyer, Shana, vp, student affairs, $131,272
Meyer, Yvonne, chief, university police, $66,300
Miller, Mary, administrative coordinator, $32,487
Miller, Misty, benefits coordinator, $40,551
Miller, Rhonda, custodian, $20,221
Miller, Timothy, assistant professor, $57,976
Mills, Louise, accounts payable clerk, $30,576
Mills, Toni, transcript evaluation coordinator, $32,038
Mills, Mark, associate professor, $56,723
Modlin, Susan, custodian, $24,004
Montee, Susan, assistant professor, $71,400
Moore, Michael, custodian, $20,221
Morsbach, Jill, assistant professor, $53,556
Moutray, Erin, financial aid coordinator, $30,108
Mulder, James, information services librarian, $49,670
Myers, Sue, mgr of its/-contracts, procrument/ts, $43,300
Nabors, Murray, dean, liberal arts & sciences, $142,095
Neeley, Kristen, asst director new student prog, $44,375
Neely, Levi, applications programmer, $41,644
Neidel, James, hvac/r technician, $36,153
Nesslage, Frederick, mgr of its/networks & pc supp, $74,764
Nix, Frederica, instructor, $38,560
Noah, David, electrician, $40,189
Noland, Judy, library asst, acquis/serials, $33,813
Nold, Laura, assistant professor, $13,260
Nold, Letha, chief accountant/dir of purchas, $53,580
Noyd, Jacob, operations engineer, $48,030
Noynaert, Evan, associate professor, $64,639
Nulph, Robert, assistant professor, $60,343
O'Connor, Kathleen, dean, professional studies, $128,593
Oakes, Natasha, asso dir of ath/senior wm admi, $59,160
Okapal, James, associate professor, $57,616
Otto, Alicia, administrative assistant, $28,606
Owens, Alexandra, content tutor coordinator, $39,700
Palmer, Anna, telephone/technical serv asst, $26,734

Parnell, Amy, executive admin associate, $38,239
Parnell, Leslie, accountant, student receivables, $41,535
Parsley, Bruce, painter, $32,116
Partridge, Gerald, head coach (football), $99,565
Payne, Peggy, asst director of admissions/re, $51,591
Pickett, Kent, assistant professor, $29,595
Pickman, Germain, vp, university advancement, $133,951
Poet, Jeffrey, professor, $71,436
Polsgrove, Crystal, assistant payroll coordinator, $29,659
Potter, Melanie, financial aid coordinator, $31,414
Potter, Steven, counselor, int'l student advisor, $56,185
Preshner, Sandra, administrative coordinator, $33,579
Prososki-Large, Kathy, hvac/r technician, $30,556
Qiao, Long, assistant professor, $52,442
Quedensley, Taylor, assistant professor, $48,960
Quenstedt-Moe, Gretchen, associate professor, $70,553
Quillin, Hiram, assistant professor, $50,257
Raffensperger, Maureen, professor, $97,342
Rahnat, Norhan, dir of international recruit/st serv, $69,360
Ray, Justin, academic computing technician, $36,426
Recob, Jon, groundskeeper, $42,100
Rhoad, Jonathan, associate professor, $57,540
Rice, Glenn, associate professor, $57,615
Riley, Jennifer, accountant, foundation, $37,763
Ritter, Michael, disability services coordinator, $43,180
Ritter, Michelle, web developer, $43,662
Rivera-Taupier, Miguel, assistant professor, $48,898
Roberts, Ian, professor, $66,460
Roberts, Nathan, director of residential life, $67,626
Rogers, Dennis, professor, $99,920
Root, Eric, groundskeeper, $28,294
Rops, Benjamin, articulation coordinator, $42,864
Rumpf, Hawley, procurement auditor/reimburs, $35,256
Russell, William, associate professor, $71,095
Saffell, Steven, institutional research analyst, $54,652
Sample, Victoria, central labs/lab coordinator, $51,966
Sanders, Sally, director of human resources, $84,164
Sands, Autumn, pr & marketing assistant, $29,425
Sapp, Laura, administrative assistant, $30,459
Schank, Tyson, asso dean of enrollment/dir adm, $66,585
Schartel Dunn, Stephanie, assistant professor, $55,000
Schindler, Carolyn, administrative coordinator, $34,105
Schneider, Julia, director of library, $101,615
Schottel, Sherilynn, mail systems manage, $33,462
Scott, Shelley, hr recruiting specialist, $37,167
Scroggs, Michael, technical operations coordinator, $47,456
Sharp, Tracy, associate registrar, $49,952
Shepherd, Daniel, assistant professor, $61,200
Sherlock, Jenny, executive admin associate, $35,529
Siebler, Kay, professor, $66,830
Silkett, Cheryl, custodian, $20,221
Skinner, Machelle, assistant professor, $51,000
Sloan, Jacob, residence hall director, $30,000
Sloan, Kelly, purchasing manager, $45,110
Small, Gerald, instructor, $37,454
Smilie, Kipton, assistant professor, $48,898
Smith, Deborah, administrative assistant, $29,386
Smith, Faye, professor, $104,861
Smith, Jeffrey, university police officer, $34,554
Smith, Michael, professor, $84,344
Smith, Montella, assistant professor, $50,979
Spalding, Marian, academic computing technician, $46,818
Spotts-Conrad, Cynthia, associate director of fa, $60,226
Stephens, Shawna, custodian, $20,221
Stevens, Daniel, academic advisor, $40,800
Stevens, Jenna, administrative coordinator, $28,782
Stewart, Corey, aux maintenance supervisor, $44,814
Stewart, Stephanie, assistant professor, $48,898
Stoll, Tara, video communications producer, $50,352
Stover, Jeff, assistant professor, $48,898
Stutterheim, Aaron, instructor, $39,332
Svojanovsky, Stanislav, assistant professor, $49,939
Sweiger, Jamie, asst director of admissions/opera, $55,067
Swope, Elliott, video communications specialist, $37,086
Tang, Shensheng, associate professor, $66,183
Tapia, John, professor, $90,329
Tarun, Prashant, associate professor, $89,603
Taylor, Alecia, administrative assistant, $30,010
Taylor, Edwin, assistant professor, $51,350

Taylor, Kay-Lynne, career develop center director, $56,244
Teal, Orion, assistant professor, $47,940
Terrick, Dawn, instructor, $42,859
Thomas, Melvin, custodian, $21,177
Thompson, Meri, asst developmental math spec, $36,835
Throckmorton, Todd, assistant coach (football), $54,945
Torres y Torres, Janelle, assistant professor, $52,442
Treat, Deborah, administrative assistant, $28,918
Trifan, Daniel, professor, $67,416
Trotter, Jennifer, head coach (softball), $63,081
Trotter, Reginald, assistant coach (football), $48,860
Turner, Stacy, special credit programs coord, $42,864
Tushaus, David, professor, $71,728
Tyler, Deatra, hr, information system analyst, $52,895
VanDyke, Steven, graphic design coordinator, $42,336
Vaughn, Deborah, administrative assistant, $15,229
Verduzco, Charles, head coach (baseball), $60,044
Vest, Sharon, special ed teacher, wrdcc, $36,720
Voight, Barbara, instructor, $47,129
Waggoner, Christina, academic advisor, $40,000
Walker, Dwania, financial aid coordinator, $28,840
Walsh, Kevin, remote campus computer tech, $38,493
Walton, Kristen, associate professor, $60,814
Wang, Bin, assistant professor, $86,700
Washburn, Christina, admissions counselor, $42,840
Waters, Gavin, associate professor, $57,622
Weddle, Kimberly, director of development, $65,280
Weeks, Annette, director ctr for entrepreneurs, $71,400
Weiberg, Brett, head coach (m basketball), $80,370
Weiberg, Kristy, instructor, $34,680
Wennihan, Deana, financial aid default coord, $35,626
Whipple, Matthew, applications/dual cr supp spec, $42,500
White, Jesse, graduate records coordinator, $29,737
Whitsell, John, grounds & events supervisor, $56,184
Widner, Vicky, custodian, $21,294
Wiebelt-Smith, Roger, assistant coach (w basketball), $42,864
Wilemin, Alex, assistant professor, $49,980
Wiley, Tamela, custodian, $20,221
Willenbrink, Robert, founding dean school of fine art, $126,928
Williams, Anna, custodian, $22,210
Williams, Jena, graphic design coordinator, $38,872
Williamson, Thomas, special assistant to the dean, $61,200
Willis, Jamie, west inst, office coordinator, $43,823
Willoughby, Eric, res hall resource officer, $33,715
Wilson, Angela, custodian, $20,221
Wilson, Kip, associate professor, $64,622
Wolfe, Michelle, administrative assistant, $29,484
Woodford, Jeffrey, assistant professor, $53,535
Woodruff, Pamela, custodian, $21,294
Yan, Biaoqiang, associate professor, $72,738
Yang, George, professor, $77,071
Yarnell, Robin, custodian, $23,283
Yeh, Pi-Ming, associate professor, $81,578
Young, Barbara, administrative, $33,579
Young, Mathew, mechanic, $31,414
Youtsey, William, hvac/r technician, $30,556
Zhang, Mei, associate professor, $57,934
Zhang, Zhao, professor, $66,904
Zhu, Jinwen, associate professor, $71,693
Ziemer, Christine, assistant professor, $48,898
Zuptich, Mark, fleet manager, $36,086

Department of Insurance, Financial Institutions & Professional Registration

PO Box 630, Jefferson City 65102

Huff, John M, state dept dir, $121,705
Abend, Melvin N, med cnslt, $59,988
Abernathy, Todd V, investigator II, $41,172
Adair, Russell B, insp (prof reg), $29,976
Adams, Debra F, board mbr, $6.25/hr
Adams, John, board mbr, $12.50/hr
Adams, William, insp, $6.25/hr
Adewale, Abiodun A, board mbr, $9.37/hr
Adrian, Julie A, insp (prof reg), $29,496
Ainsworth, Mallory, paralegal, $30,978
Alexander, M Kathleen, board mbr, $6.25/hr

Allen, Christy P, clerk, $18.15/hr
Allen, Robyn R, consumer complaint spec I, $36,204
Anderson, Timothy J, sr asst exam II, $52,476
Anderson-Weddle, Camille E, research analyst III, $40,380
Appleman, Jeffrey P, board mbr, $8.75/hr
Askeland, Paul E, sr mortgage exam III, $75,874
Astroth, Gregory J, bank exam II, $73,740
Atwell, Mariann B, board mbr, $6.25/hr
Aubert, Eric, board mbr, $6.25/hr
Avella, Gino A, trust sup, $83,319
Backer, Sheila R, consumer complaint spec II, $38,928
Backes, Carol S, processing technician I, $23,160
Badolato, Cristin M, consumer complaint spec II, $38,928
Baker, Adam, bank exam II, $64,479
Balas, Andrew T, fin exam III, $84,997
Baldree, Karen S, fin exam III, $75,725
Barnes, Jerald L, investigator II, $37,548
Barnett, Brian D, principal asst board/commisson, $64,381
Bax, Brittney N, sr asst bank exam, $49,534
Baysinger, Mary D, processing technician II, $26,652
Beauchamp, Vanessa A, principal asst board/comm, $61,148
Becker, Brian, bank exam II, $64,479
Becker, Sarah E, processing technician supv, $33,180
Beckman, Amy N, sr asst exam II, $52,476
Beffa, Kim, processing technician supv, $33,180
Behrens, Michael C, fin exam III, $75,725
Belt, Lesli A, fin exam spec, $72,271
Bequette, Jeanine L, board mbr, $6.25/hr
Bergman, Donna K, processing technician II, $26,652
Bergman, Michael J, investigator II, $41,172
Berra, Gideon H, tax auditor II, $38,928
Bestgen, Nicholas J, asst bank exam II, $45,077
Bilek, Barbara A, board mbr, $6.25/hr
Bird, Gary S, m c exam II, $61,257
Blake, Jordan, sr bank exam I, $69,596
Blount, Christopher T, sr cons credit exam I, $69,596
Blume, Jeffrey L, fin exam II, $54,504
Boczkiewicz, John M, exam-in-charge fin, $90,502
Boeckman, James J, clerk, $22.46/hr
Boessen, Sarah N, processing technician II, $26,652
Bognar, John L, board mbr, $6.25/hr
Bonnot, Kenneth J, div ofr, $99,990
Bosch, Christopher F, fin exam III, $75,725
Bossert, Lori L, board mbr, $6.25/hr
Boucher, James E, insp, $12.50/hr
Bowman, Elizabeth A, ins licensing tech II, $31,920
Bramblett, Linda, board mbr, $8.75/hr
Bramlett, Kevin S, sr cons credit exam III, $77,736
Branch, Tammy, snr Office support asst, $28,908
Brautigam, Melissa, sr ofc spt asst (steno), $29,412
Brester, Kimberly K, prof reg admstv coor, $41,172
Briscoe, Andrew W, special asst official & admstr, $76,255
Brockman, Roxanne M, sr ofc spt asst (keybrd), $33,636
Brodecker, Renate, board mbr, $8.75/hr
Brondel, Rita D, sr ofc spt asst (keybrd), $26,232
Brost, Kyle, board mbr, $6.25/hr
Bruce, Lori A, board mbr, $6.25/hr
Brueseke, Kevin P, fin exam, $52,178
Brush, Lisa A, real estate exam II, $35,568
Bryson, Emmett J, sr fin exam, $70,367
Buckman, Michael, asst bank exam, $42,555
Buechter, Leslie A, sr auditor, $44,304
Bullock, Abigail, clerk, $11.13/hr
Bullock, Debby, research analyst II, $36,888
Bureman, James E, board mbr, $6.25/hr
Burkemper, Ellen, board mbr, $8.75/hr
Burkhardt, Patricia S, designated principal asst dept, $39,915
Burlis, Tamara L, board mbr, $6.25/hr
Buschjost, Greg M, special asst prof, $34,340
Buschjost, Karen M, processing technician III, $32,052
Buschmann, Jeffery W, fin exam III, $63,635
Butler, Kristin, ins fin analyst II, $38,232
Calfee, June L, sr bank exam I, $69,596
Call, Janette L, board mbr, $6.25/hr
Camden, Archie, board mbr, $6.25/hr
Campbell, Michael P, supvsr of mortgage licensing, $85,850
Campbell, Tina, m c exam III, $73,117
Carder, Janet B, clerk, $12.18/hr
Cardwell, Susan E, fiscal & administrative mgr b1, $64,555

Carroll, Emily R, principal asst board/commisson, $59,433
Carroll, Jennifer M, consumer complaint spec I, $34,944
Cartee, Michelle, processing technician supv, $31,512
Carter, Jeffrey D, board mbr, $6.25/hr
Carver, Gary L, board mbr, $6.25/hr
Caskey, Aaron, insp, $12.50/hr
Chambly, Jessica R, sr ofc spt asst (keybrd), $26,232
Chapman, Bryan M, board mbr, $6.25/hr
Charlton, Toni M, ins fin analyst spec, $40,380
Church, Laura L, fin exam III, $63,635
Chute, Darrell E, investigation mgr b1, $54,129
Clarkston, Connie R, principal asst board/commisson, $76,266
Clarkston, Kallee R, clerk, $11.13/hr
Clemons, Regina, processing technician II, $26,652
Cline, Christopher C, designated principal asst dept, $63,529
Clubb, John T, m c exam III, $73,117
Coale-Brendel, Jennifer B, ofc spt asst (keybrd), $23,160
Cobb, Carmen M, prof reg admstv coor, $41,940
Coffman, Jane Q, processing technician II, $27,948
Colbert, Lisa J, sr bank exam III, $80,225
Coleman, Lori A, processing technician I, $24,264
Comensky, Mark, board mbr, $6.25/hr
Comer, M J, board mbr, $8.75/hr
Conde, Emily, prof reg admstv coor, $40,380
Conklin, Sidney W, investigator II, $37,548
Conner, Michele D, insp (prof reg), $29,004
Conrace, John, legal counsel, $50,000
Cook, Ryan S, board mbr, $8.75/hr
Cooper, Kourtney E, processing technician II, $27,084
Cooper, Sherry, board mbr, $9.37/hr
Coppedge, Andrew E, fin exam III, $75,725
Cottrell, Keith, assist trust exam II, $45,077
Couch, Carrie L, div dir, $79,285
Cox, Leann M, ins product analyst I, $32,052
Cozean, Nicole, board mbr, $6.25/hr
Cramm, Kelley, board mbr, $9.37/hr
Crawford, Robert J, board mbr, $6.25/hr
Crayden, Karen E, sr bank exam III, $76,784
Crider, Joseph L, sup of consumer credit, $90,031
Crow, Jacklyn J, board mbr, $8.75/hr
Crowe, Rachel N, research analyst III, $40,380
Crutchfield, Karen A, investigator II, $38,928
Cunningham, Thomas J, exam-in-charge fin, $90,502
Cupp, Gerald V, clerk, $60.84/hr
Curnutte, Cynthia S, board mbr, $6.25/hr
Custard, Gina L, workers compensation spec, $37,548
Dalbey, Rebekah, processing technician supv, $33,180
Daniels, Douglas R, fin exam III, $75,725
Danz, Jennifer R, exam-in-charge fin, $90,502
Davidson, Roger K, consumer complaint spec II, $40,380
Davis, Charles W, board mbr, $9.37/hr
Davis, Debra J, fiscal and administrative mngr, $54,072
Davis, Kent, insp, $12.50/hr
Davis, Peggy L, special prof, $55,550
Dawley, Kelley M, investigator II, $38,928
Dean, Bennie, pharmaceutical cnslt, $82,788
Dee, Jeanne, board mbr, $8.75/hr
Degroodt, Thomas O, principal asst board/commisson, $71,197
Denkler, Joseph M, principal asst board/commisson, $70,832
Denton, Vicki L, exam-in-charge fin, $90,502
Dickey, Jerald A, board mbr, $6.25/hr
Dino, Joseph, pharmaceutical cnslt, $82,788
Direnna, James D, board mbr, $6.25/hr
Dobbs, Kimberly M, fin exam III, $84,997
Doerhoff, Linda K, sr ofc spt asst (keybrd), $26,652
Doerhoff, Susan M, ins fin analyst II, $38,232
Doering, David A, chief exam, $96,859
Doggett, Deborah L, exam-in-charge fin, $90,502
Dohnal, Steven, insp (prof reg), $29,496
Doll, Robert G, insp, $12.50/hr
Donnell, John, board mbr, $6.25/hr
Donovan, Sarah M, processing technician II, $26,652
Douglass, Joseph A, sr bank exam I, $69,596
Dreier, Lorry L, sr bank exam II, $73,740
Dronberger, James, board mbr, $6.25/hr
Dudenhoeffer, Keith A, hr mgr b1, $52,109
Dudenhoeffer, Mark R, investigator III, $41,940
Duesing, Blaine A, board mbr, $6.25/hr
Duncan, Anna, procurement ofcr II, $43,488

Dunlap, Leslie, bank exam II, $64,479
Dunn, Becky A, clerk, $12.18/hr
Dutill, Joan M, ins regulatory mgr b2, $53,934
Eck, James, board mbr, $6.25/hr
Eddy, Barbara S, ins licensing tech II, $31,920
Eddy, Tanya S, ofc servs asst, $29,004
Edge, Regina, admin ofc spt asst, $29,976
Edmonson, Alicia N, investigator II, $38,928
Eggen, Casey S, insp, $12.50/hr
Eggen, Donald J, investigation mgr b1, $54,129
Eggen, Lori A, designated principal asst div, $36,219
Elder, Jaime R, consumer complaint spec I, $36,204
Emmerich, Lisa A, ins licensing tech I, $24,612
Engelmann, Linda A, board mbr, $6.25/hr
England, Donald R, board mbr, $6.25/hr
Engler, Andrew P, investigator II, $37,548
Erickson, Mary S, chief counsel, $89,385
Euler, Sharon K, legal counsel, $61,287
Even, Laura, report analyst, $35,514
Farris, Jodi M, designated principal asst div, $29,916
Feeler, Amy B, designated principal asst div, $29,916
Fehr, Noel, board mbr, $9.37/hr
Fennewald, Dana K, principal asst board/commisson, $58,816
Fennewald, Lauren J, ofc spt asst (keybrd), $24,264
Ferguson, Gregory H, sr bank exam II, $71,205
Ferguson, Janice, processing technician I, $25,824
Ferguson, Sylvia D, sr ofc spt asst (clerical), $28,452
Finklang, Kurt W, board mbr, $6.25/hr
Fischbach, Donald R, sr bank exam III, $85,717
Fisher, Andrea, processing technician II, $26,652
Fisher, Jill C, processing technician II, $26,652
Fisher, Joshua L, investigator II, $37,548
Fitzpatrick, Dennis A, investigator II, $37,548
Flett, Lori J, real estate exam II, $35,568
Flora, Timothy B, board mbr, $6.25/hr
Flowers, John M, board mbr, $9.37/hr
Fly, Adrienne A, board mbr, $6.25/hr
Foley, Dennis R, m c exam III, $73,117
Follis, Collin L, board mbr, $6.25/hr
Ford, Travis R, board mbr, $8.75/hr
Fox, Andrew J, designated principal asst div, $66,155
Fraker, Gary A, board mbr, $6.25/hr
Frala, Heather N, ins product analyst II, $33,744
France, Dean L, investigator II, $38,928
Freeman, Bradley D, board mbr, $6.25/hr
Freeman, Michael C, board mbr, $9.37/hr
Freihaut, Margaret M, board mbr, $6.25/hr
Freilich, Stewart M, sr counsel, $78,079
Frisbee, Jenny, board mbr, $6.25/hr
Frish, Barbara J, misc prof, $40.64/hr
Fritchey, Rob D, exam spec, $52,936
Fritchey, Victoria M, admin ofc spt asst, $10.00/hr
Friztlen, Thomas J, board mbr, $6.25/hr
Fulton, Angela, processing technician II, $26,232
Funk, Andrew K, info spt coor, $29,004
Funk, Debra A, registered nurse mgr b1, $66,726
Gale-Betzler, Lisa E, board mbr, $6.25/hr
Gallaher, James, sr counsel, $76,982
Galleano, Gerald L, insp, $12.50/hr
Galley, Deborah A, board mbr, $6.25/hr
Gammill, Tonya J, investigator II, $37,548
Garwood, Tammy C, processing technician I, $23,880
Gerling, Bradley M, research analyst II, $36,204
Gerlt, Kimberly, designated principal asst dept, $48,985
Gettemeier, Peggy R, board mbr, $6.25/hr
Giessing, Charles R, board mbr, $6.25/hr
Gill, Casey C, board mbr, $6.25/hr
Gillam, Collin C, ins fin analyst I, $35,568
Gilliam, Janice K, clerk, $12.18/hr
Gilpin, Kristi, paralegal, $33,180
Gingrich, Marcia C, board mbr, $6.25/hr
Glasgow, Brian, bank exam, $60,271
Glenski, Thomas M, pharmaceutical cnslt, $86,484
Golden, Diane C, board mbr, $6.25/hr
Gourley, David L, board mbr, $6.25/hr
Govero, Daniel L, board mbr, $9.37/hr
Graupman, Tara M, insp supv (prof reg), $33,744
Green, Lisa A, board mbr, $6.25/hr
Gregg, Charlotte A, sr ofc spt asst (keybrd), $26,652

Greiner, Karen A, board mbr, $6.25/hr
Grinston, Kimberly A, principal asst board/commisson, $69,611
Grobe, Aaron K, sr bank exam III, $82,169
Groose, Pamela V, principal asst board/commisson, $63,981
Gross, Angela J, designated principal asst div, $29,916
Gulino, Joseph, board mbr, $6.25/hr
Gulliford, Blake M, sr bank exam I, $69,596
Guthrie, Melanie J, board mbr, $6.25/hr
Haake, Mary A, pers clerk, $30,984
Hager, Shelley C, bank exam, $60,271
Haile, Jennifer N, m c exam III, $61,571
Hake, Brian W, sr bank exam I, $69,596
Hall, Lisa, processing technician I, $24,264
Hammers, Howard R, investigator II, $37,548
Hammond, Kenneth, investigation mgr b1, $54,129
Hansen, Cody, sr bank exam II, $73,740
Hansen, Katie N, sr asst exam II, $52,476
Harden, Carol A, mgr, $55,094
Hardman, Debra J, dpty div dir, $102,243
Harris, Boyd L, board mbr, $6.25/hr
Harris, Kayleigh G, asst bank exam II, $45,077
Hart, Mary L, board mbr, $6.25/hr
Hartnett, Robert N, board mbr, $9.37/hr
Hatfield, Rachel A, processing technician III, $29,976
Hauck, Leah N, processing technician II, $27,084
Hauptli, Ian D, legal counsel, $54,076
Hayes, Lori A, funeral establishment insp, $45,156
Hayes, Richard J, fin exam III, $75,725
Heckman, Judy M, sr ofc spt asst (keybrd), $26,652
Hedgpeth, John R, sr asst exam II, $52,476
Heidy, John W, investigator II, $21,744
Heimericks, Katelynn, pub info spec II, $36,204
Heimericks-Ash, Rita, m c exam III, $73,117
Heislen, Karen S, account clerk II, $26,232
Heislen, Michelle A, processing technician III, $29,976
Helm, Robert J, board mbr, $8.75/hr
Helton, Rebecca A, ins product analyst III, $41,940
Heming, Valerie A, board mbr, $6.25/hr
Hendrickson, Rochelle C, misc prof, $25.00/hr
Henke, Laura A, processing technician III, $29,976
Henningsen, Lisa A, fin exam spec, $82,631
Herin, Tad A, m c exam II, $52,000
Hernandez, Alice J, clerk, $19.80/hr
Herzing, Shelly L, m c exam III, $73,117
Hess, Karen P, board mbr, $8.75/hr
Hess, Sherry A, fiscal & administrative mgr b2, $64,555
Hesser, Julie G, m c exam III, $73,117
Hicks, Samantha H, designated principal asst div, $34,845
Hill, Thaddeous, consumer credit exam II, $64,479
Hillme, Twila G, board mbr, $9.37/hr
Hitt, Logan, processing technician I, $23,160
Hobart, Dale C, m c exam III, $73,117
Hodges, Michael L, board mbr, $6.25/hr
Hogan, Rosemary G, board mbr, $6.25/hr
Hogue, Frances A, board mbr, $6.25/hr
Hogue, Leslie H, investigator II, $37,548
Hollender, Jessica, asst mortgage exam, $42,555
Holloway, Michelle, real estate exam I, $30,984
Honse, Victoria A, processing technician I, $23,880
Hopfinger, William P, board mbr, $6.25/hr
Hopper, Kelly A, legal counsel, $54,000
Horman, Andrea J, sr bank exam I, $69,596
Horn, Dana M, asst bank exam II, $45,077
Horn, Susan M, ins licensing tech II, $31,920
House, Christopher, bank exam II, $64,479
Howard, Jean H, board mbr, $6.25/hr
Howard, Lou A, ins licensing tech I, $24,612
Hoyt, Amy, sr counsel, $76,679
Hruza, Carrie, board mbr, $6.25/hr
Hudson, Kimberly S, sr bank exam II, $73,740
Hudson, Legreta, board mbr, $6.25/hr
Hull, Micky L, rev exam, $81,305
Hunt, Becky A, sr bank exam III, $79,092
Intravia, Michael, insp, $12.50/hr
Jackson, Tracey, sr fin exam, $66,808
Jaegers, Lee A, investigator II, $41,172
James, Darick A, real estate exam I, $30,984
Janes, Jerry W, misc prof, $41.21/hr
Jenkins, Tamra B, investigator I, $31,512

Jennings, Randall T, ins fin analyst II, $41,940
Johannes, Ashley, processing technician I, $23,880
John, Martha K, board mbr, $9.37/hr
Johnson, Malcolm J, sr asst exam II, $52,476
Johnson, Mary J, investigation mgr b1, $52,520
Johnson, Sherrita, sr bank exam I, $69,596
Johnson, Taylor, clerk, $11.13/hr
Jolly, Gina, consumer credit exam II, $64,479
Jolly, Kathleen E, investigative consult, $27.51/hr
Jones, Kevin R, audit mgr-mkt conduct, $93,109
Jongerius, Nathan, sr asst cons credit exam, $49,534
Jordan, Darren D, m c exam III, $73,117
Jordan, Debra K, sr cons credit exam I, $69,596
Jordan, Robert P, exam-in-charge fin, $90,502
Jorgenson, Sarah B, budget analyst II, $38,928
Juergens, Rita J, processing technician III, $29,004
Kabler, Brent A, research analyst IV, $62,664
Kallenbach, Jami L, processing technician II, $27,504
Kaplan, Ross A, sr counsel, $57,000
Karns, Stacey L, board mbr, $6.25/hr
Kearns, Jeffrey, sr asst exam II, $52,476
Kearns, Tammy S, sr counsel, $57,000
Keeney, Douglas E, investigator I, $34,944
Kelly, James B, board mbr, $6.25/hr
Kemp, Randy D, m c exam III, $73,117
Kempf, Nathan R, consumer complaint spec II, $38,928
Kempker, Judy A, principal asst board/commisson, $66,725
Kenny, Stephen M, board mbr, $9.37/hr
Kessler, Loree V, principal asst board/commisson, $68,568
Kidder, Brigitte, fin exam asst II, $48,352
Kincannon, Christie A, chief counsel, $97,591
Kinder, Mark H, board mbr, $6.25/hr
Kindle, Wayne, board mbr, $8.75/hr
Klamet, Terrence G, board mbr, $8.75/hr
Kliethermes, Emily A, sr bank exam I, $69,596
Klimchak, Yaryna, pub info admstr, $43,488
Knopf, Darryl E, board mbr, $6.25/hr
Koelling, Laurie A, processing technician II, $27,948
Koelling, McKenzie, clerk, $11.13/hr
Koenigsfeld, Leslie R, processing technician II, $26,652
Koerkenmeier, Teresa M, exam-in-charge mc, $87,613
Koetting, Erika L, sr ofc spt asst (keybrd), $12.42/hr
Koonse, Steven K, fin exam III, $75,725
Kopp, Tamara W, sr counsel, $62,610
Korte, John S, exam-in-charge mc, $87,613
Krueger, Michelle L, legal counsel, $50,000
Lackey, David J, board mbr, $6.25/hr
Lager, Kevan, investigator II, $38,928
Lamb, Richard G, designated principal asst dept, $76,154
Lambert, Marion E, sr bank exam III, $79,092
Lampert, Benjamin A, board mbr, $6.25/hr
Landers, Kimberly S, paralegal, $31,277
Latimer, Kathryn M, paralegal, $31,277
Lauer, Karl K, insp, $12.50/hr
Lawrence, Scott A, insp, $12.50/hr
Le, Hai H, fin exam II, $57,570
Leapley, Nicholas G, sr bank exam III, $79,092
Lederer, Julie A, actuary, $131,300
Ledgerwood, Sarah E, chief counsel, $71,205
Lee, Brenda S, acct I, $36,888
Leggett, James D, exec I, $34,356
Lehman, Jodi L, investigator II, $37,548
Lehmen, Travis J, sr bank exam III, $79,569
Lennon, Patrick J, workers compensation spec, $39,624
Lentz, Brenda A, real estate exam I, $30,984
Lenzini, Tabatha L, processing technician II, $33,636
Lepper, Justin, clerk, $11.13/hr
Leung, William P, actuary, $141,400
Lewis, Cory, asst bank exam, $42,555
Lewis, Quinn C, investigation mgr b1, $54,129
Li, Meng, captive fin ex III, $63,635
Lightfoot, Sharon L, board mbr, $6.25/hr
Lilley, Elizabeth A, ins fin analyst II, $39,624
Lilly, Julia J, sr cons credit exam II, $71,607
Lindsay, Christina, board mbr, $6.25/hr
Liston, Amy M, m c exam III, $61,571
Litzsinger, Milton B, board mbr, $6.25/hr
Long, Martha B, exam-in-charge mc, $87,613
Lootens, Kyle R, fiscal & administrative mgr b2, $64,555

Lorts, Gary D, clerk, $18.37/hr
Lorts, Leanne M, pers ofcr I, $54,288
Luckenbach, Amanda J, fin exam III, $75,725
Luebbert, Hailey M, designated principal asst div, $34,845
Luebbert, Jennifer, investigator I, $32,628
Lueckenhoff, Danielle, clerk, $11.13/hr
Lueckenhoff, Timothy J, principal asst board/comm, $60,543
Luetkemeyer, Jeffrey L, dist sup, $95,673
Lyskowski, John C, board mbr, $6.25/hr
Maassen, Jeffrey T, rev exam, $85,345
Maddox, Kyle A, clerk, $10.63/hr
Maloney, Patrick, board mbr, $6.25/hr
Marcum, Samuel A, sr mortgage exam I, $69,596
Markwell, Kenneth E, board mbr, $6.25/hr
Marmion, Angela S, legal counsel, $58,299
Marshall, Pamela, board mbr, $6.25/hr
Marshall, Tess, asst bank exam II, $45,077
Martien, Brenda, board mbr, $6.25/hr
Martin, Grady S, div dir, $95,950
Martin, Joseph L, dpty div dir, $94,435
Marty, Terri R, board mbr, $8.75/hr
Mason, Pamela, processing technician II, $26,652
Massman, Brittney N, clerk, $11.13/hr
Massman, Gary L, sr ofc spt asst (clerical), $27,084
Massman, Krista, clerk, $11.13/hr
Massman, Matthew J, processing technician II, $26,232
Massman, Rodney P, legal counsel, $54,076
Maus, Nancy S, board mbr, $6.25/hr
Maxwell, Richard B, investigator II, $37,548
McAdams, James R, dpty state dept dir, $111,605
McConnell, George W, clerk, $39.17/hr
McCrary, Marvin G, investigator II, $38,928
McCray, Carrie, board mbr, $6.25/hr
McDaniel, Roxanne W, board mbr, $6.25/hr
McDowell, Margaret, investigator II, $36,204
McDowell, Randell R, investigator II, $38,928
McGhee, Kenneth, board mbr, $6.25/hr
McGregor, Fernando, board mbr, $6.25/hr
McIntyre, Brian, board mbr, $6.25/hr
McKay, Jill H, sr bank exam III, $81,305
McMullin, James W, investigator II, $39,624
McMullin, James W, insp, $12.50/hr
McNeely, Sara B, fin exam III, $63,635
McNeill, Nolan G, board mbr, $6.25/hr
McNiel, Johnny D, board mbr, $6.25/hr
Mealer, James E, chief mkt conduct exam, $96,145
Mealer, Mary G, ins regulatory mgr b2, $60,686
Meisel, Jennifer, processing technician I, $24,612
Menken, Jason L, clerk, $14.91/hr
Merchant, David, sr bank exam I, $69,596
Merritt, Penny, insp (prof reg), $29,004
Meyer, Andrew, bank exam II, $64,479
Meyer, Caitlin, clerk, $11.13/hr
Meyer, Jon R, m c exam III, $73,117
Meyers, Francis, legal counsel, $54,076
Miller, Andrea, pharmaceutical cnslt, $82,788
Miller, Eric, sr bank exam I, $69,596
Miller, Kathie, board mbr, $8.75/hr
Miller, Terrie L, processing technician II, $27,084
Mills, Shannon R, paralegal, $31,143
Milster, Karen J, fin exam III, $56,794
Minor, Ashley, processing technician I, $23,160
Mintert, James R, board mbr, $8.75/hr
Misko, Charles G, board mbr, $9.37/hr
Mitchell, Douglas E, board mbr, $6.25/hr
Molendorp, Julie A, board mbr, $6.25/hr
Monroe, Cynthia M, admin ofc spt asst, $33,180
Monroe, Monica L, processing technician II, $26,652
Morabito, Kristen, processing technician I, $23,880
Morgan, Jennifer, board mbr, $8.75/hr
Morice, Angela M, prof reg admstv coor, $41,940
Moroney, Kevin J, investigator II, $37,548
Morris, James R, m c exam III, $73,117
Morrow, Patricia A, processing technician III, $35,568
Mouser, Brandy M, board mbr, $8.75/hr
Munsterman, Laura B, acct I, $31,512
Murphy, Terry L, real estate edu spec, $34,944
Murray, Jason W, sr asst exam II, $52,476
Musopole, Ronald, ins fin analyst spec, $40,380

Nance, Mark A, audit mgr-fin exam, $96,297
Neal, Laura M, board mbr, $8.75/hr
Nehring, Leslie A, chief fin exam, $96,960
Nelson, Angela L, div dir, $96,496
Nelson, Carl D, board mbr, $8.75/hr
Nelson, Paige, clerk, $11.13/hr
Nelson, Robert A, misc prof, $35.00/hr
Nelson, Robert A, misc prof, $40.64/hr
Neubert, Peggy A, administrative sec, $38,160
Newberry, Kimberly, processing technician II, $27,084
Nichols, Jeff, investigator II, $36,204
Nicholson, Joseph A, board mbr, $8.75/hr
Nickel, Ted, sr cons credit exam I, $69,596
Nickens, Winfred O, audit mgr-mkt conduct, $93,109
Nicklas, Dawn, clerk, $60.00/hr
Nield, Cheryl C, sr counsel, $70,147
Niemeyer, Jeffrey D, real estate exam field spv, $37,548
Noren, Laura, board mbr, $6.25/hr
Nunn-Jones, Ann, board mbr, $6.25/hr
Nwasoria, Levi, exam-in-charge fin, $90,502
O'Neill, Daniel A, sr trust exam III, $75,874
Onstott, Charlotte R, consumer complain spec III, $40,380
O'Reilly, Nancy D, board mbr, $6.25/hr
O'Rourke, Leslie, administrative sec, $35,690
Orr, Patrice M, insp (prof reg), $30,984
Otto, Brenda M, ins regulatory mgr b1, $48,604
Otto, Brittany, processing technician II, $26,652
Otto, Nelson H, sr ofc spt asst (keybrd), $26,652
Overbey, Lillian E, ins regulatory mgr b1, $52,896
Padgett, Savannah, clerk, $11.13/hr
Parham, Rebecca L, sr asst exam II, $52,476
Parran, Anita K, board mbr, $6.25/hr
Pastorino, Judith E, board mbr, $6.25/hr
Patterson, Nathan, bank exam, $60,271
Payne, Karen, processing technician II, $17,647
Pemberton, Joan A, prof reg licensing/cert supv, $37,548
Pendergrass, Gary J, board mbr, $6.25/hr
Pendleton, Scott B, exam-in-charge mc, $87,613
Pennington, Emily E, fin exam II, $50,924
Peterson, Marc P, fin exam III, $75,725
Pfaender, John E, m c exam III, $73,117
Pfaff, Tracey R, investigator II, $37,548
Pfander, Michael B, board mbr, $6.25/hr
Philbert, Melissa A, processing technician I, $23,880
Phillips, Michael, board mbr, $6.25/hr
Pigg, Margaret, board mbr, $6.25/hr
Pitman, Tarlton E, board mbr, $6.25/hr
Pitts, David B, sr asst exam II, $52,476
Pitts, Garrett G, accounting spec I, $38,928
Placeway, Kerry L, investigator II, $37,548
Plaster, Nancy E, processing technician III, $32,052
Pleus, Laurie A, reins exam, $86,355
Plowman, John K, insp (prof reg), $29,976
Poggemeier, David A, board mbr, $6.25/hr
Pointer, Brittany L, processing technician III, $29,496
Polacek, Deborah, ofc spt asst (steno), $27,084
Polc, Deborah K, board mbr, $6.25/hr
Pollreisz, Tamara L, tax auditor II, $40,380
Popp, Michael, board mbr, $9.37/hr
Powell, Christopher B, insp, $12.50/hr
Powell, Teresa L, board mbr, $6.25/hr
Prenger, Donna K, processing technician III, $30,984
Prenger, Phyllis, processing technician II, $27,084
Prenger, Robert S, ins product analyst II, $37,548
Price, Leo, board mbr, $8.75/hr
Price-Land, Leata, board mbr, $8.75/hr
Puyear, J M, sr bank exam II, $73,740
Queen, Richard, insp (prof reg), $29,496
Quinlin, Kelly L, board mbr, $6.25/hr
Rachel, Mark J, legal counsel, $53,000
Rackers, Stacey S, pers ofcr, $44,069
Rademan, Brianne N, admin ofc spt asst, $30,984
Rademan, Melinda J, consumer complain spec III, $41,940
Ransdell, Melissa A, sr bank exam II, $73,740
Ray, Leann R, dist sup, $85,588
Rearden, James C, board mbr, $9.37/hr
Reeves, Scott A, fin exam II, $48,480
Rehagen, Darcie, acct II, $39,624
Rehagen, John F, designated principal asst div, $92,920

Reichard, Thomas M, principal asst board/commisson, $58,816
Reichart, Robert E, m c exam III, $73,117
Reinhard, James, board mbr, $6.25/hr
Relford, Randall H, board mbr, $6.25/hr
Renfrow, Robin J, budget analyst III, $45,156
Rhodes, Carol G, board mbr, $6.25/hr
Rice, Meshell, processing technician II, $27,948
Riley, Michael S, sr cons credit exam II, $71,205
Riley, Ryan C, sr bank exam I, $69,596
Rimel, Karen L, consumer complain spec III, $41,940
Rimiller, Sharlene A, board mbr, $6.25/hr
Rizzo, Anthony, insp, $12.50/hr
Roach, Gregory A, processing technician II, $27,084
Robertson, Ryan P, mortgage exam, $60,271
Robinett-Fogle, Rhonda A, investigator I, $34,944
Robinson, Sandra L, processing technician supv, $34,944
Rodgers, Teresa, board mbr, $6.25/hr
Rodriguez, Christie, board mbr, $8.75/hr
Roeback, Gregory, board mbr, $6.25/hr
Rohlfing, Christopher, board mbr, $6.25/hr
Rose, Jaron M, sr fin exam, $62,982
Rummerfield, Barbara A, ins product analyst II, $33,744
Rummerfield, Barbara E, ins product analyst II, $33,744
Rusatsi, Eric B, processing technician II, $26,232
Rushin, Jack, board mbr, $6.25/hr
Russell, Margaret J, board mbr, $6.25/hr
Rust, Randall L, planner II, $46,932
Rutherford, Shyra N, processing technician II, $26,652
Sadler, Elsie L, ins licensing tech I, $25,404
Saltzman, Terry, insp, $12.50/hr
Sample, Wyatt, exam-in-charge fin, $90,502
Sandbothe, Kimberly R, fiscal and administrative mngr, $53,303
Schappe, Sarah D, legal counsel, $58,299
Scheidt, Lori A, principal asst board/commisson, $81,205
Schlup, Alice N, sr ofc spt asst (keybrd), $27,051
Schmoeger, Shannon W, exam-in-charge fin, $90,502
Schrimpf, Jessica J, mgr, $48,166
Schulte, Shyra P, ins fin analyst spec, $41,172
Schultz, Ingeborg D, registered nurse mgr b1, $66,726
Schurman, Richard L, investigator II, $37,548
Schuster, Christina, processing technician I, $27,084
Schuster, Lisa A, pers analyst II, $40,380
Schwartzkopf, Dan W, sr bank exam II, $76,255
Scott, Kelly J, board mbr, $6.25/hr
Scrivner, Kade, sr asst bank exam, $48,572
Seabaugh, Carrie D, processing technician II, $13,326
Sebastian, Magen, processing technician II, $25,824
Sebastian, Sandra K, principal asst board/commisson, $66,933
Segura, Andrea, board mbr, $6.25/hr
Seyer, Cindy, board mbr, $6.25/hr
Shadowens, Michael, audit mgr-fin exam, $96,297
Shahlari, Stephen, fin exam II, $56,000
Sheehan, John J, board mbr, $8.75/hr
Sheffield, Frances M, designated principal asst div, $82,507
Sheftel, Matthew A, assist trust exam II, $45,077
Sheller, Hollie R, processing technician II, $27,084
Shimmens, Rhonda J, board mbr, $6.25/hr
Short, John R, investigator II, $37,548
Shotts, Robert S, board mbr, $9.37/hr
Siebert, Tammy L, prof reg admstv coor, $41,172
Skibiski, Kevin C, board mbr, $9.37/hr
Skidmore, Kenneth, special asst prof, $45,450
Skrade, Mark E, board mbr, $6.25/hr
Sloan, Sheri D, investigator II, $37,548
Smith, Chelsea L, asst mortgage exam II, $45,077
Smith, Danielle L, ofc spt asst (keybrd), $23,160
Smith, John M, dist sup, $95,904
Smithson, Claire, sr bank exam II, $73,740
Smittle, Linda K, clerk, $10.63/hr
Smittle, William D, med dir, $127,080
Snell, Mariea, board mbr, $6.25/hr
Snyder, Amy E, fin exam III, $75,725
Snyder, Nicholas A, sr asst exam II, $52,476
Sorrell, Sharon, board mbr, $8.75/hr
Speed, Alyson, board mbr, $6.25/hr
Springs, Kembra D, m c exam II, $48,840
Stamper, Richard A, fin exam III, $75,725
Stanford, Diane G, ins licensing tech II, $33,036
Stanley, Bart A, rev exam, $85,717

Stanley, Melissa S, ins product analyst I, $30,984
Stark, Valerie G, paralegal, $31,512
Steele Danner, Kathleen, div ofr, $110,000
Steen, Victoria L, processing technician II, $30,384
Stegeman, Ruth M, processing technician I, $25,824
Stephens, Linda S, insp (prof reg), $29,976
Stephenson, Shelly R, consumer complaint spec II, $38,928
Stevens, Elizabeth A, investigator II, $37,548
Steward, Neal P, sr bank exam II, $73,740
Stewart, Catherine J, investigator II, $39,624
Stingley, Scott V, sr asst bank exam, $49,534
Stocker, Michael W, insp, $12.50/hr
Storms, Derek M, sr asst mortgage exam II, $52,476
Story, William A, sr cons credit exam III, $80,765
Strate, Traci R, sr bank exam II, $71,205
Street, Connie J, admin ofc spt asst, $33,757
Streff, Todd, board mbr, $6.25/hr
Struemph, Tim, clerk, $11.13/hr
Stucky, Renee, board mbr, $6.25/hr
Stuecken, Noland R, tax auditor II, $43,488
Sullens, Kim, consumer complaint spec II, $38,928
Szturo, John, board mbr, $6.25/hr
Taber, Eric G, sr bank exam III, $79,569
Taggart, Christopher A, dist sup, $87,410
Tannehill, David, board mbr, $6.25/hr
Taylor, Gay, insp (prof reg), $29,004
Teitelbaum, Kevin, processing technician I, $23,160
Thomas, Ashley, exec I, $34,356
Thomas, David W, real estate exam II, $35,568
Thomas, Jeana E, mgr, $48,823
Thomas, Kathleen C, consumer complaint spec II, $38,928
Thomas, Megan, processing technician III, $29,004
Thompson, Lisa M, pharmaceutical cnslt, $82,788
Thompson, Marjorie G, investigator II, $38,928
Tomblinson, Brittany E, processing technician supv, $33,744
Tomka, Ramona, administrative sec, $43,794
Tomka, Rebecca A, processing technician II, $27,084
Torretta, Nina M, sr asst exam II, $52,476
Tougaw, Lindsay M, tax auditor II, $38,928
Townsend, Thomas M, legal counsel, $58,299
Trainer, Susan L, insp (prof reg), $29,496
Troop, Bernie R, fin exam III, $75,725
Tunks, Tim L, exam-in-charge fin, $90,502
Turner, Joy W, insp, $12.50/hr
Tuttle, Sherry L, exec II, $38,232
Tyree, Robert L, insp, $12.50/hr
Ushupun, Bunlue, exam-in-charge mc, $87,613
Van Fleet, Frank N, pharmaceutical cnslt, $82,788
Vanderfeltz, Don, board mbr, $6.25/hr
Vandersand, Daniel J, pharmaceutical cnslt, $82,788
Veit, Brian C, consumer credit exam, $60,271
Veltrop, Helen M, clerk, $11.35/hr
Vesely, Brian D, board mbr, $6.25/hr
Vickers, Michelle L, consumer complaint spec I, $34,944
Vinson, Julie A, dist sup, $87,410
Visser, Harry J, board mbr, $8.75/hr
Vitale, Rosemary, board mbr, $9.37/hr
Volkart, Carla, processing technician I, $24,264
Voss, William H, med cnslt, $59,988
Walk, Bart J, sr mortgage exam III, $79,092
Wallace, Kevin, board mbr, $6.25/hr
Wallace, Marla J, processing technician I, $26,652
Waller, Kimberly S, consumer complaint spec II, $38,928
Warden, Laura, processing technician I, $25,824
Warfield, Sherry L, processing technician I, $23,880
Washington, Jacquelynn V, consumer complaint spec I, $36,204
Watts, Edward J, sr fin exam, $66,807
Weaver, Craig L, ins fin analyst spec, $47,892
Weaver, Kevin E, chief fin exam, $94,435
Weddle, Eric J, investigator II, $37,548
Wedewer, Sandra K, board mbr, $8.75/hr
Wehmeyer, Shelly C, registered nurse - clin opers, $53,592
Welch, Sharon, account clerk II, $29,412
Weston, Brenda L, real estate exam field spv, $40,380
Whaley, Dana L, investigator II, $38,232
White, Molly L, ins regulatory mgr b1, $57,880
Wilde, Dawn M, investigator II, $39,624
Wilde, Jeanette M, processing technician supv, $38,232
Wildhaber, Lisa M, ins fin analyst spec, $46,932

Wilkinson, Guile P, insp, $12.50/hr
Willard, Elizabeth, exec I, $32,628
Williams, Paul, investigator II, $37,548
Willoughby, Todd W, fin exam spec, $80,121
Wilson, Donald L, m c exam III, $73,117
Wilson, Rhonda K, processing technician II, $25,824
Wilt, Vincil M, board mbr, $6.25/hr
Winchester, Kathleen, asst bank exam, $42,555
Wiseman, Susan E, sr bank exam III, $84,326
Wolken, Janet M, registered nurse mgr b1, $66,726
Wood, Barbara, pharmaceutical cnslt, $82,788
Wood, Rhonda J, board mbr, $6.25/hr
Woodruff, Ashley, sr accounting clerk, $28,596
Woolbright, Michael W, m c exam III, $73,117
Yetter, John, board mbr, $6.25/hr
Yoder, Lisa C, processing technician I, $23,508
Young, Christopher J, board mbr, $6.25/hr
Youngblood, Tina R, acct I, $30,420
Zagorac, Jennifer M, investigator II, $37,548
Zoellner, Karen A, ins product analyst III, $39,624

Department of Labor & Industrial Relations

3315 W. Truman Blvd, Jefferson City 65109

Abraham, Makita N, human rel ofcr I, $38,928
Adams, Jack K, claims exam, $34,944
Adams, Jennifer J, claims sup, $34,944
Adams, Mary E, sr ofc spt asst (keybrd), $27,504
Aduddell, Lori J, human rel ofcr II, $44,304
Albert, Andrew C, div dir, $65,533
Albertson, Teresa R, sr ofc spt asst (keybrd), $31,920
Allan-Estes, Tracey L, human rel ofcr I, $37,548
Allison, Krista M, claims spec II, $31,512
Allison, Shelly, mine safety instructor, $38,232
Alway, Kathleen M, claims spec II, $31,512
Anderson, Brian D, unemp ins auditor II, $34,356
Anderson, Karen M, human rel ofcr III, $51,096
Anderson, Stephanie L, occuptnl sfty & hlth cnslt II, $44,304
Andrews, Gloria J, exec II, $38,928
Angel, Eve B, sr ofc spt asst (keybrd), $25,032
Appleberry, Eyvalee, claims spec II, $31,512
Applegate, Ronette, ins fin analyst II, $36,204
Arnold, Mark S, unemp ins auditor II, $43,488
Arnold, Mary B, claims spec II, $31,512
Ashby, Sherri L, claims spec II, $31,512
Atchinson, Kimberly C, human rel ofcr I, $38,928
Atchison, Christopher E, contribs spec I, $29,004
Atwell, Chad A, workers' comp tech II, $27,228
Aubuchon, Denise E, labor & industrial rel mgr b1, $54,288
Auer, Michael T, appeals ref III, $57,744
Austin, Martha A, claims spec II, $40,380
Austin, Martina J, claims spec II, $31,512
Avery, James G, commissmbr, $106,626
Bachmann, Rebecca L, ins fin analyst II, $37,548
Backes, Elizabeth, clerk, $12.02/hr
Balke, Gayle M, contribs spec II, $31,512
Ballew, Katherine, contribs exam, $27,228
Banks, Betsy A, claims spec II, $31,512
Barker, Dorothy L, unemp ins auditor II, $34,356
Barlish, Barbara A, clerk, $27.17/hr
Barnhart, Gary, appeals ref III, $57,744
Barnhart, Marlene T, claims spec II, $41,172
Barocio, Sandra K, ofc spt asst (keybrd), $23,160
Barr, Robert A, labor & industrial rel mgr b1, $52,092
Barton, Juanita F, clerk, $13.90/hr
Bassmann, Donna K, labor & industrial rel mgr b1, $54,288
Bastian, Thomas A, designated principal asst dept, $61,105
Bauer, Amber R, admin ofc spt asst, $34,944
Bax, Betty M, clerk, $19.82/hr
Beller, Jeremy W, sr claims sup, $41,172
Bennett, Sara E, contribs sup, $35,568
Berendzen, Karen H, claims sup, $44,304
Berkstresser, Lisa A, claims exam, $27,228
Berner, John C, claims sup, $34,944

Bestgen, Amanda J, wkrs comp safety consult I, $40,380
Beuerlein, Annette D, claims spec II, $31,512
Beuerlein, Ron A, claims sup, $34,944
Bilyeu, Carol C, clerk, $12.03/hr
Biondolino, Amanda L, legal counsel, $46,814
Birge, Gwen N, contribs spec I, $30,984
Bittle, Sonja G, claims spec II, $31,512
Blair, Bruno K, claims spec II, $31,512
Blankenship, Lynn A, sr ofc spt asst (keybrd), $30,384
Bodenschatz, Dana L, court reporter II, $46,932
Boessen, Donna L, claims spec II, $32,628
Boessen, Joyce A, clerk, $12.03/hr
Bohanan, Donald C, claims spec II, $31,512
Bond-Ott, Karen S, admin ofc spt asst, $36,204
Bono, Mary E, human rel ofcr I, $45,156
Bonthu, Patricia J, claims sup, $34,944
Bookout, Lynn A, sr claims sup, $48,156
Boone, Jill M, admin ofc spt asst, $36,204
Boresi, Karla O, administrative law judge, $121,553
Boss, Joyce A, sr ofc spt asst (steno), $29,904
Bossom, Lura B, sr ofc spt asst (keybrd), $26,652
Boswell, Talisa R, workers' comp tech I, $25,032
Boyer, Mary C, claims spec II, $40,380
Boyer, Tashina J, claims spec II, $31,512
Brandes, Stacy C, court reporter II, $45,156
Braun, Roxanne, administrative analyst II, $46,068
Breeden, John P, workers' comp tech II, $27,228
Brenner, Russell W, investigator II, $40,380
Britton, Barbara A, claims spec II, $35,568
Brockes-Miller, Sarah K, contribs spec II, $31,512
Brockman, Jared L, labor & industrial rel mgr b1, $51,096
Brondel, Doris J, admin ofc spt asst, $36,888
Brotherton, Jeremy R, claims spec II, $31,512
Brown, Jacqueline E, ins fin analyst I, $30,984
Brownell, Karen K, claims spec II, $31,512
Brune, Amy M, sr contribs supv, $41,172
Brunnert, Debbie L, contribs spec II, $31,512
Bruno, Holly L, labor & industrial rel mgr b1, $46,932
Bulson, David T, sr contribs supv, $38,928
Bunch, Fonda B, sr claims sup, $46,932
Burkhardt, A J, appeals ref III, $57,744
Burton, Chad D, claims spec I, $29,976
Bushman, Sandilin, sr ofc spt asst (keybrd), $25,824
Butcher, Jason E, contribs spec I, $29,004
Butler, Christopher P, contribs exam, $26,400
Cain, Kenneth J, administrative law judge, $121,553
Calahan, Nancy J, contribs sup, $42,708
Caldwell, Kathryn A, claims spec II, $31,512
Caldwell, Therese M, claims sup, $36,204
Callier, Charles E, appeals ref III, $57,744
Campbell, Susan D, claims exam, $27,228
Cannada, Dennis R, contribs sup, $34,944
Cantrell, Charles E, mine safety instructor, $37,548
Carberry, Joseph K, appeals ref III, $57,744
Carl, Janet S, contribs spec II, $31,512
Carlisle, Suzette C, administrative law judge, $121,553
Carlyle, Tammy D, human rel ofcr II, $41,172
Carpenter, Barbara A, claims spec II, $33,744
Carpenter, Brandi M, sr ofc spt asst (keybrd), $25,824
Carroll, Michael A, claims spec II, $31,512
Cavender, Tammy M, labor & industrial rel mgr b3, $93,084
Chance, Scott H, claims spec II, $32,628
Chavez, Tyna K, workers' comp tech I, $25,032
Chick, Curtis F, commissmbr, $106,626
Childs, Lida D, sr contribs supv, $40,380
Chillington, Betty M, clerk, $12.03/hr
Chirlin, Aleksandra, appeals ref III, $57,744
Clark, Ruth A, clerk, $12.03/hr
Clark, Spencer A, designated principal asst div, $90,000
Cleveland, Robin W, unemp ins auditor II, $41,940
Cline, Jeanne M, contribs spec II, $31,512
Coatney, Shannon M, pub info spec II, $34,944
Cogshell, Eric R, claims sup, $44,304
Cohoon, Judith D, claims spec II, $31,512
Cole, Richard D, labor & industrial rel mgr b1, $52,092
Colli, Natalie P, claims sup, $34,944
Collins, Debra B, claims spec II, $31,512
Cones, William, unemp ins auditor I, $31,512
Conway, Christina L, unemp ins auditor II, $34,356

Coombs, James R, claims spec II, $31,512
Copeland, Judith A, unemp ins auditor II, $44,304
Coppay, Pamela A, appeals ref III, $61,332
Corcoran-Thompson, Kelly L, clerk, $12.12/hr
Cotten, Michelle M, admin ofc spt asst, $28,536
Cox, Daniel R, unemp ins auditor II, $34,356
Crader, Jennifer R, labor & industrial rel mgr b1, $42,708
Crames, Paul F, appeals ref III, $57,744
Crandall, Charles E, investigator II, $40,380
Creek, Robert A, labor & industrial rel mgr b1, $53,208
Crider, Joshua B, claims spec II, $31,512
Crider, Sherri L, claims exam, $27,228
Crockett, Rebecca L, claims spec II, $31,512
Cummings, Jennifer M, occuptnl sfty & hlth cnslt III, $49,128
Cunningham, Audrey C, fiscal & administrative mgr b1, $46,068
Cunningham, Curtis J, unemp ins auditor I, $31,512
Cunningham, Munai I, clerk, $13.95/hr
Curry, Patrick J, labor & industrial rel mgr b1, $42,708
Davidson, Amy B, pers clerk, $28,536
Davis, Patricia K, court reporter II, $45,156
Davis, Summer L, claims spec I, $29,976
Deloyola, Pamela J, claims spec II, $32,052
Denigan, Joseph E, administrative law judge, $121,553
Dickson, Jonathan C, occuptnl sfty & hlth cnslt II, $44,304
Dickson, Ronda L, unemp ins auditor II, $34,356
Dierkes, Robert J, chief administrative law judge, $126,553
Dillard, Cornell L, human rel ofcr II, $54,288
Dillon, William C, claims spec II, $31,512
Doan, William G, occuptnl sfty & hlth cnslt II, $48,156
Dobson, Lana K, claims spec II, $38,232
Dock, Kayla M, admin ofc spt asst, $30,984
Dodds, Janice, workers' comp tech II, $27,660
Doden, Stephen A, investigator III, $45,156
Doerhoff, Terry P, ofc servs coor, $44,304
Donahue, Joseph, clerk, $25.00/hr
Donnelly, Rebecca S, human rel ofcr I, $43,488
Dorge, Doris C, clerk, $12.03/hr
Dorson, Ernest C, clerk, $19.82/hr
Downs, Alan J, misc prof, $27.17/hr
Dozier, Linell, sr ofc spt asst (keybrd), $28,908
Dresel, Janet S, budget analyst II, $44,304
Drinkard, David R, claims spec II, $31,512
Duba, Stacy A, human rel ofcr I, $41,172
Duemmel, Michael E, labor & industrial rel mgr b1, $43,488
Duvall, Cheryl A, unemp ins auditor II, $34,356
Duvall, Gerald R, sr claims sup, $38,928
Dyer, Micheal D, appeals ref III, $57,744
Easley, Glenn E, mediator, $53,208
Eaton, Maryetta B, unemp ins auditor II, $34,356
Ebert, Kimberly R, unemp ins auditor II, $38,928
Edghill, Bridgette E, claims spec II, $29,976
Edmondson, Jeffrey L, labor & industrial rel mgr b3, $68,160
Edmondson, Lisa D, special asst ofc & clerical, $40,047
Edoho, Susan A, workers' comp tech I, $33,636
Edwards, Johnna J, unemp ins auditor II, $34,356
Edwards, Maridee F, appeals ref III, $58,908
Ehlers, Robert E, investigator II, $40,380
Eichelberger, Breanna L, occuptnl sfty & hlth cnslt II, $44,304
Ellis, Larhonda A, admin ofc spt asst, $29,976
Emery, Dyan, claims sup, $34,944
Ertmann, Jeanne B, unemp ins auditor III, $45,156
Esmail, Nasreen D, chief legal counsel, $110,406
Etz, Anice M, claims spec II, $32,052
Falter, Linda J, clerk, $12.03/hr
Farris, Liesel U, contribs spec II, $31,512
Farris, Teresa S, human rel ofcr I, $38,928
Faucett, Melissa R, claims spec II, $31,512
Feeney, Roberta L, court reporter II, $45,156
Fincher, Lisa M, claims spec II, $39,624
Fink, Amber S, labor & industrial rel mgr b2, $71,208
Fischer, Hannelore D, administrative law judge, $121,553
Fisher, Angela M, claims spec II, $31,512
Fisher, David E, labor & industrial rel mgr b1, $54,288
Fisher, Karen W, administrative law judge, $121,553
Forck, Rhonda K, sr ofc spt asst (keybrd), $31,920
Foresman, Pamela A, clerk, $12.02/hr
Fornkahl, Robert W, claims spec II, $31,512
Forrester, Heather E, claims spec II, $31,512
Forrester, Jeffrey R, claims sup, $43,488

Fortson, Rebecca J, labor & industrial rel mgr b1, $50,040
Fowler, Emily S, administrative law judge, $121,553
Frerking, Mark W, occuptnl sfty & hlth supv, $60,120
Fuller, Gerri R, claims spec II, $31,512
Fuller, Tracy G, claims spec I, $29,976
Gabriel, Christina M, human rel ofcr II, $45,156
Gage, Tiffany N, claims spec II, $31,512
Gallagher, Deanna K, claims spec II, $31,512
Garrison, Gaylord R, appeals ref III, $57,744
Gaskill, Kari A, ofc spt asst (keybrd), $23,160
Gaw, John D, clerk, $19.82/hr
George, Gregory T, appeals ref III, $57,744
Giger, Angela E, claims spec II, $31,512
Gilchrist, Melvin, human rel ofcr II, $46,932
Gillam, John F, investigator III, $40,380
Gillam, Rickey L, mine insp, $42,708
Gilleland, Moneen R, labor & industrial rel mgr b1, $54,288
Glavin, William J, claims spec I, $29,976
Gordy, Ira J, claims spec II, $31,512
Gowin, Sondra L, sr claims sup, $38,928
Graham, Angela S, claims spec I, $29,976
Gramblin, Linda, budget analyst III, $57,744
Grewe, Rodney K, unemp ins auditor II, $41,172
Grimm, Jill E, labor & industrial rel mgr b1, $56,520
Groner, Kurt P, claims spec II, $31,512
Gruen, Jerry A, claims spec I, $30,984
Gudde, Brenda C, claims exam, $29,976
Guthrie, Lucinda L, labor & industrial rel mgr b3, $83,479
Guy, Roseann, claims sup, $34,944
Guyton, Judy A, claims spec II, $38,928
Haarmann, Timothy A, claims spec II, $31,512
Hacker, Teri L, appeals ref III, $57,744
Hagenow, Angela, claims spec II, $31,512
Haines, Diana P, contribs spec II, $31,512
Hammen, Angela K, claims spec II, $31,512
Hand, Kristi M, contribs spec II, $31,512
Hankins, Matthew S, labor & industrial rel mgr b2, $71,208
Hanks, Danielle M, sr ofc spt asst (keybrd), $25,824
Harbison, Jan S, clerk, $12.03/hr
Harden, Rhonda S, claims spec II, $41,172
Hargus, Robert W, unemp ins auditor II, $39,624
Harms, Patricia A, unemp ins auditor II, $34,944
Harp, Alandra M, claims spec I, $29,976
Harp, Laura R, sr ofc spt asst (keybrd), $12,912
Harris, Brian D, claims spec II, $31,512
Harrison, Sara H, legal counsel, $48,985
Hart, Kathleen M, administrative law judge, $121,553
Harvey, Sheri L, labor & industrial rel mgr b1, $54,288
Haslag, Yvonne C, workers' comp tech supv, $41,940
Hathcoat, Greg L, claims spec II, $31,512
Haulenbeek, Maribeth R, account clerk II, $31,920
Haynes, Hardin T, legal counsel, $45,500
Hays, Dena G, human rel ofcr II, $46,932
Hazelton, Jeanine D, appeals ref III, $57,744
Healea, Shauna L, sr ofc spt asst (keybrd), $27,084
Heflin, Harl D, clerk, $21.72/hr
Hefner, Vicky G, claims spec II, $31,512
Heidbreder, Rosemary E, clerk, $12.03/hr
Helton, Cynthia I, contribs spec II, $31,512
Hendry, Guy R, claims spec II, $32,628
Hendry, Laura L, claims spec II, $31,512
Henke, Kay F, contribs sup, $34,944
Hentges, Brenda L, research analyst III, $48,156
Herigon, Dianne T, claims spec I, $29,976
Herigon, Jill R, account clerk II, $26,652
Herndon, Derese A, claims spec II, $31,512
Herring, Sandra S, human rel ofcr II, $44,304
Herrmann, Diane G, claims exam, $27,228
Hickey, Dewayne L, investigator III, $45,156
Hickey, John J, div dir, $128,553
Hickey, Ryan D, labor & industrial rel mgr b1, $46,932
Hicks, Donna A, unemp ins auditor II, $34,356
Hicks, Sheila K, claims spec II, $31,512
Hill, Helen M, claims exam, $28,104
Hill, Morgan M, claims spec II, $29,004
Hill, Tannyetta, claims spec II, $31,512
Hines, Chester, unemp ins auditor II, $34,356
Hinshaw, Helen M, claims spec I, $29,976
Hobbs, Michael L, clerk, $12.03/hr

Hoehn, Peter M, claims spec II, $36,888
Hoffman, Steven D, contribs spec I, $29,976
Hofmann, Pamela M, principal asst board/commisson, $67,468
Hogg, Karla S, special asst ofc & clerical, $53,285
Holder, Tami M, claims spec II, $31,512
Hollandsworth, G I, admin ofc spt asst, $28,536
Holmes, Catherine, occuptnl sfty & hlth cnslt III, $47,892
Holtmeyer, Marilyn S, clerk, $19.82/hr
Honse, Linda J, clerk, $12.02/hr
Hood, Jennifer K, claims spec I, $29,976
Hoogveld, Vicki J, sr ofc spt asst (keybrd), $31,920
Horton, Melissa M, claims spec II, $31,512
House, Robert H, chief administrative law judge, $126,553
Houseman, Karla J, sr ofc spt asst (keybrd), $25,824
Howard, Betty S, clerk, $16.52/hr
Howard, Timothy S, claims spec II, $31,512
Huber, David J, claims sup, $34,944
Hughes, Delia K, unemp ins auditor II, $34,356
Hughes, Leigh A, designated principal asst dept, $53,285
Hughes, Rodney W, claims spec II, $31,512
Humfeld, Holly A, unemp ins auditor II, $34,356
Hurd, Billie R, claims spec II, $31,512
Hurley, Lydia F, court reporter supv, $47,892
Ikerd, Jill R, claims spec II, $33,180
Imhoff, Jordan E, claims spec II, $31,512
Inlow, William H, wage & hour investigator II, $38,232
Inoue, Jason T, investigator II, $38,232
Jackson, Garrett L, claims spec I, $29,976
Jackson, Mandolin S, clerk, $12.00/hr
Jacob, Kenneth B, dpty state dept dir, $111,605
Janson, Colleen, unemp ins auditor II, $34,944
Jefferson, Dineika W, sr ofc spt asst (keybrd), $25,824
Jenkins, Bari J, unemp ins auditor I, $31,512
Jenkins, Christopher L, claims spec I, $29,976
Jenkins, Zachary C, investigator II, $41,940
Jessup, Ann M, claims spec II, $31,512
Jett, Jennifer, court reporter II, $49,128
Joens, Julie M, sr contribs supv, $48,156
Johnson, Alex D, claims spec II, $31,512
Johnson, David B, legal counsel, $70,000
Johnson, Lavonna R, claims spec II, $33,180
Jones, Annette, claims spec II, $31,512
Jones, Connie R, claims sup, $34,944
Jones, Danielle J, claims spec II, $31,512
Jones, David A, claims spec II, $31,512
Jones, Kerri J, claims spec II, $41,172
Jones, Lacrecia M, unemp ins auditor II, $34,356
Jones, Norma L, sr ofc spt asst (keybrd), $25,824
Jordan, Felicia Y, claims spec I, $29,976
Judd, James K, claims spec II, $31,512
Kampeter, Jean A, sr ofc spt asst (keybrd), $33,036
Karbinas, Linda S, claims spec II, $32,052
Kasten, Lawrence C, chief administrative law judge, $126,553
Kauflin, Michael E, investigator III, $40,380
Kaufman, Jerry A, claims spec I, $29,976
Keen, Jackie S, claims spec II, $32,052
Kemna, Glenda M, special asst ofc & clerical, $40,047
Kempker, Megan N, contribs spec II, $31,512
Kendrick, Dana M, claims spec II, $31,512
Kerr, Lynda S, claims sup, $34,356
Key, Casey, sr ofc spt asst (keybrd), $25,824
King, Deborah L, clerk, $12.03/hr
Kissinger, Brenda C, admin ofc spt asst, $33,180
Kixmiller, Carol A, clerk, $12.03/hr
Klein, Curtis P, investigator II, $40,380
Klein, Keri R, sr ofc spt asst (keybrd), $25,824
Klemme, Byron G, investigation mgr b2, $62,664
Kliethermes, Kathleen, admin ofc spt asst, $33,180
Kliethermes, Thomas F, claims spec I, $31,512
Klotz, Randall W, claims spec I, $29,976
Kmiec, Phyllis E, claims exam, $29,496
Knapp, Patricia L, research analyst I, $32,628
Knierim, Kalee D, account clerk II, $26,232
Koch, Tesa R, sr ofc spt asst (keybrd), $25,824
Koelling, Mary R, claims spec II, $31,512
Koetting, Carolyn J, sr ofc spt asst (keybrd), $32,472
Kohner, Edwin J, administrative law judge, $121,553
Komo, Martin N, wage & hour investigator III, $46,932
Kraus, Gwen A, admin ofc spt asst, $32,052

Krawat, Maria L, court reporter II, $49,128
Krekel, Eric N, hr mgr b2, $61,332
Kruse, Debbie J, clerk, $17.40/hr
Kueckelhan, Kaleb P, storekeeper I, $25,032
Kummerfeld, Emily L, contribs spec I, $29,004
Lambert, Kristy A, human rel ofcr III, $49,128
Landolt, Margaret D, administrative law judge, $121,553
Landon, Lisa A, admin ofc spt asst, $29,004
Lange, Katherine M, admin ofc spt asst, $37,548
Lange, Margaret M, court reporter supv, $53,208
Lanier, Destry A, sr ofc spt asst (keybrd), $25,824
Lansford, Betty J, clerk, $13.95/hr
Lark, Beverly J, claims spec II, $31,512
Larsen, John J, commisschair, $106,626
Latham, Jana M, wage & hour investigator II, $36,204
Latham-Jones, Dawn M, claims spec II, $34,356
Laughlin, Deborah A, contribs exam, $28,104
Lavery, Ryan L, claims spec II, $31,512
Lawley, Terry C, claims spec II, $43,488
Lawson, Jill R, claims spec II, $34,944
Lee, Margie, claims spec II, $31,512
Lee, Ronnell E, unemp ins auditor II, $42,708
Leishing, Faye R, claims spec II, $31,512
Leonard, Patrick A, clerk, $12.02/hr
Leonard, Rebecca L, clerk, $13.90/hr
Lepper, Janet M, labor & industrial rel mgr b3, $83,479
Lewis, Barbara K, acct III, $44,304
Lewis, Kathryn W, sr claims sup, $40,380
Lewis, Pamela J, claims spec I, $29,976
Limb, Susan J, claims spec II, $31,512
Lin, Cynthia G, contribs spec II, $31,512
Lindsey, John E, div dir, $75,940
Lindsey, Valerie L, sr claims sup, $46,068
Link, Debra L, ofc spt asst (keybrd), $23,160
Link, Julianna C, contribs spec II, $31,512
Livingston, Dawn R, court reporter II, $45,156
Loehr, Patricia A, labor & industrial rel mgr b1, $51,096
Loesch, Sue A, exec I, $41,940
Loethen, Michelle A, pers analyst II, $42,708
Logan, Marian L, claims spec II, $31,512
Logue, Debbie A, unemp ins auditor II, $34,356
Love, Carole A, sr ofc spt asst (keybrd), $25,824
Loveless-Guerrero, Renee D, info spt coor, $32,052
Luebbert, Casper A, claims spec II, $31,512
Luebbert, Jamie A, admin ofc spt asst, $35,568
Luebbert, Jessica L, claims spec II, $32,628
Lueckenhoff, Sharon F, clerk, $12.02/hr
Maassen, Betty C, ofc worker misc, $19.19/hr
Mahon, Victorine R, administrative law judge, $121,553
Mantle, Deborah L, claims spec I, $29,004
Mantle, Wanda L, clerk, $17.40/hr
Marcy, Jerome D, occuptnl sfty & hlth cnslt II, $44,304
Marston, Carolyn E, claims sup, $34,944
Martin, Brenda D, claims spec II, $31,512
Martin, Cynthia L, clerk, $12.00/hr
Martin, Margaret, contribs spec II, $31,512
Martin, Rocky L, contribs spec II, $31,512
Martin-Lee, Monica G, human rel ofcr III, $49,128
Massman, Jane, exec I, $39,624
Matanic, Bart A, legal counsel, $66,155
Mather, Sharon, contribs spec II, $31,512
May, Tracy E, designated principal asst div, $51,005
Mays, Ira W, claims sup, $36,204
McCaskill, Lisa Y, claims spec II, $31,512
McClain, Preston R, contribs sup, $34,944
McClure, Heather, workers' comp tech II, $27,228
McComb, Amanda F, claims sup, $34,944
McCubbin, Holly A, claims spec I, $29,976
McCubbin, Melissa S, graphic arts spec III, $39,624
McDaniel, Jacqueline A, unemp ins auditor III, $38,928
McDaniel, Lisa A, labor & industrial rel mgr b1, $51,096
McDonald, Lori L, claims spec II, $33,180
McDowell, Deborah H, claims exam, $27,228
Mcelroy Bradshaw, June D, training tech III, $58,908
McKenna, Ryan G, state dept dir, $121,705
McKeon, Paula A, chief administrative law judge, $126,553
McPherson, Sharman J, admin ofc spt asst, $32,628
McVey, Hugh M, designated principal asst div, $70,195
McVey, Joan A, sr ofc spt asst (keybrd), $25,824

McWilliams, Leah M, sr claims sup, $48,156
Mealy, Joanna K, clerk, $12.02/hr
Means, Betty D, sr claims sup, $48,156
Medley, Kimberly M, claims spec II, $31,512
Meiners, Lisa A, administrative law judge, $121,553
Mendez, Fernando H, mgmt analyst II es, $50,040
Meyer, Saundra S, court reporter II, $45,156
Miller, Dwight W, investigator III, $45,156
Miller, Richard W, investigator II, $40,380
Miller, Ronald J, labor & industrial rel mgr b3, $83,479
Milton, Desheila M, labor & industrial rel mgr b1, $49,128
Miner, Robert B, administrative law judge, $121,553
Mitchell, Breanna D, workers' comp tech II, $27,228
Moehle-Neff, Vicky, admin ofc spt asst, $28,536
Molden, Joann S, claims sup, $40,380
Montavy, Monica L, special asst ofc & clerical, $40,047
Montgomery, Gina A, sr ofc spt asst (keybrd), $27,504
Moomaw, Christy D, claims spec II, $31,512
Moomaw, Jason A, unemp ins auditor II, $34,356
Moore, Kevin W, investigator II, $40,380
Moore, Marian A, claims sup, $41,172
Morgan, Shanti S, claims spec II, $31,512
Morton, Alissa V, contribs spec II, $31,512
Moses, Mark A, investigator II, $40,380
Moses, Robin K, claims spec II, $33,180
Mueller, Michelle M, contribs spec II, $35,568
Mullins, Joshua W, sr ofc spt asst (keybrd), $26,652
Murphy, Erin E, contribs spec II, $31,512
Murphy, Marsha L, contribs exam, $27,228
Nangole, Paul F, human rel ofcr I, $37,548
Napolis, Kimberly S, claims spec II, $31,512
Nash, Jason L, contribs spec II, $31,512
Ndebesa, Bariyo J, unemp ins auditor II, $34,356
Neal, Martha D, appeals ref III, $57,744
Neises, Amber S, claims spec I, $29,976
Nelson, Casey O, occuptnl sfty & hlth cnslt II, $46,068
Nelson, Erin L, sr ofc spt asst (keybrd), $25,824
Newton, Stephanie L, claims spec II, $31,512
Nichols, Lorraine B, clerk, $14.58/hr
Nielsen, Jane E, contribs spec II, $32,052
Niemeyer, Robin M, sr ofc spt asst (keybrd), $26,652
Noble, Connie M, sr claims sup, $46,932
Noll, Charlotte L, sr ofc spt asst (keybrd), $25,824
Noonan, Patrick J, labor & industrial rel mgr b1, $53,208
North, Sarah M, occuptnl sfty & hlth cnslt III, $55,416
Notzke, Lori S, court reporter II, $49,128
Nuessle, Lela M, claims spec II, $31,512
Nunn, Kimberly N, claims sup, $34,944
Nunn, Mark E, sr claims sup, $38,928
Old, Terry G, info spt coor, $31,512
Oppy, Amanda M, contribs spec II, $31,512
Ott, Thomas W, appeals ref III, $57,744
Ottenad, John K, administrative law judge, $121,553
Overton, Stacey R, contribs spec I, $29,976
Owens, Scottie A, claims spec I, $29,004
Page, J S, claims spec II, $31,512
Painter, Nellie J, admin ofc spt asst, $33,180
Palmer, Brenda J, claims spec II, $31,512
Palmietto, Margaret M, chief administrative law judge, $126,553
Pampkin, Sandra T, claims sup, $33,180
Parks, Aaron D, claims spec I, $29,976
Patterson, Tammy D, procurement ofcr I, $36,888
Pearson, Lee M, claims spec II, $31,512
Pearson, Naomi L, sr ofc spt asst (keybrd), $33,636
Peeper, David T, exec I, $30,984
Pendleton, Natasha J, contribs spec II, $31,512
Pendleton, Nicholas J, unemp ins auditor I, $31,512
Peoples, Jeff D, claims spec II, $31,512
Perry, Joni L, claims spec II, $31,512
Peters, Margie M, special asst ofc & clerical, $53,285
Peterson, Cassie L, claims sup, $37,548
Pfeiffer, Dorothy M, contribs sup, $38,232
Pfund, Edward A, claims spec II, $31,512
Pinkston, James D, contribs spec II, $31,512
Pinkston, Jason D, labor & industrial rel mgr b1, $42,708
Pittsenbarger, Kelly G, claims spec II, $31,512
Poetker, Karen L, clerk, $12.03/hr
Poettgen, Susan K, mgmt analyst II es, $53,208
Porter, Nancy A, contribs sup, $34,944

Porter, Ron L, mgmt analyst II es, $37,548
Powers, Donna L, claims spec II, $33,180
Prenger, Glenda J, claims spec II, $41,172
Preston, Janella L, claims sup, $39,624
Prey, John D, sr contribs supv, $38,928
Price, Randy B, claims spec II, $31,512
Pritchett, Courtney E, workers' comp tech III, $32,628
Pritchett, Michael E, chief counsel, $97,077
Provencal, Guy J, unemp ins auditor II, $34,356
Prysock, Monica N, claims spec I, $29,004
Pudlowski, Thomas J, labor & industrial rel mgr b1, $46,932
Pulliam, Lafrancine, special asst ofc & clerical, $40,047
Qualls, Benjamin J, research analyst III, $48,156
Qualls, Matthew M, contribs exam, $28,536
Quintana, Rosamaria, claims spec II, $31,512
Rademan, Sharon A, contribs spec II, $33,744
Rains, Elizabeth, misc prof, $27.17/hr
Rakow, Danielle K, unemp ins auditor II, $34,356
Rebman, Lawrence G, administrative law judge, $121,553
Redding, Gene W, appeals ref III, $62,664
Reeder, Jeffery A, sr ofc spt asst (keybrd), $25,824
Rehmert, Denise M, contribs spec II, $34,356
Reifsteck, Judie M, contribs spec II, $32,628
Reimund, Daniel J, claims spec I, $29,976
Renicker, George M, clerk, $12.03/hr
Reynolds, Patricia J, unemp ins auditor I, $31,512
Reynolds, Sandra S, clerk, $13.95/hr
Rice, David L, unemp ins auditor II, $44,304
Rice, Rodney W, labor & industrial rel mgr b1, $54,288
Richardson, Judy L, court reporter II, $49,128
Richter, Christopher D, claims spec I, $29,976
Ridenhour, Rose M, sr ofc spt asst (keybrd), $25,824
Riechard, Ruth A, unemp ins auditor II, $34,944
Riley, Ninion S, legal counsel, $72,568
Rizzello, Dennis C, unemp ins auditor II, $41,172
Robbins, Gary L, administrative law judge, $121,553
Roberts, Lance L, investigator II, $40,380
Robertson, Sheila, claims spec II, $31,512
Robinson, Shamica A, unemp ins auditor II, $34,356
Rockers, Paul A, labor & industrial rel mgr b1, $65,364
Roderique, Renee L, unemp ins auditor III, $38,928
Rodriguez, Toni, claims sup, $44,304
Roe, Roy S, contribs spec II, $31,512
Roettgen, Jennifer, sr ofc spt asst (keybrd), $27,084
Rollins, Brittney M, sr ofc spt asst (keybrd), $25,032
Romero, Brenda K, contribs spec II, $32,052
Rose, Delores R, claims spec II, $31,512
Ross, Aaron G, claims spec II, $31,512
Roster, Melody J, claims spec II, $31,512
Roth, Russell A, unemp ins auditor II, $34,356
Rothove, Paul H, clerk, $23.15/hr
Rottmann, Karen M, court reporter II, $45,156
Ruhmann, Larry R, legal counsel, $72,568
Ruppel, Kathy V, clerk, $12.03/hr
Rush, Tonisha L, claims sup, $34,944
Russell, Amanda L, contribs spec II, $32,628
Russell, Scott L, investigator II, $40,380
Ryals, Madison H, sr ofc spt asst (keybrd), $25,824
Sams, Gwendolyn E, contribs spec I, $29,004
Sandberg, Sandra L, claims spec II, $31,512
Sanders, Janice M, claims spec II, $31,512
Sanders, Lori E, court reporter II, $49,128
Sarber, Deborah J, misc tech, $14.41/hr
Schaefer, Lee B, chief administrative law judge, $126,553
Scheulen, Donna K, pub info spec I, $32,052
Schmitz, Gloria J, procurement ofcr II, $54,288
Schmutzler, Barbara K, claims exam, $27,228
Schneider, Charmagne D, human rel ofcr I, $41,940
Schuman, Michelle, contribs spec I, $29,004
Schweer, Alice A, sr ofc spt asst (keybrd), $29,412
Scott, Crysta G, claims spec II, $31,512
Session, Dorothy S, pers analyst II, $43,488
Sevart, Mary C, claims spec II, $31,512
Shalley, Chet E, occuptnl sfty & hlth cnslt II, $44,304
Shanks, Donna S, sr contribs supv, $49,128
Sharp, Gerald F, claims sup, $36,204
Shaver, James W, claims spec II, $31,512
Shaw, Sandra I, admin ofc spt asst, $34,356
Sheppeck, Jesse L, occuptnl sfty & hlth supv, $53,208

Sherrell, Angela K, sr ofc spt asst (clerical), $32,472
Sherrill, Diana L, unemp ins auditor II, $34,356
Shoults, Robert, unemp ins auditor III, $38,928
Siedlik, Mark S, administrative law judge, $121,553
Simmons, Yvette, sr ofc spt asst (keybrd), $25,032
Simon, Lanae, claims spec II, $31,512
Sims, Aaron E, claims spec II, $31,512
Sisson, Carrie J, court reporter II, $49,128
Skain, James R, labor & industrial rel mgr b2, $71,100
Slaton, Beverlee A, claims spec II, $31,512
Smith, Ashley G, ofc spt asst (keybrd), $23,160
Smith, Melissa C, claims spec II, $31,512
Smith, Patricia K, claims sup, $36,888
Smith, Robin A, claims spec II, $31,512
Smith, Timothy W, investigator II, $46,068
Snider, Patricia L, court reporter II, $45,156
Sommerer, Abby L, contribs spec II, $32,628
Sommerer, Deidra M, contribs spec II, $31,512
Spears, Cheryl R, contribs spec II, $34,944
Spencer, Lois J, claims spec II, $31,512
Spicer, Jodi L, workers' comp tech II, $28,536
Spillars, Ann M, sr claims sup, $48,156
Stanley, Sara R, workers' comp tech I, $25,032
Stanton, Catherine I, human rel ofcr I, $38,928
Stark, Daniel A, labor & industrial rel mgr b3, $63,996
Stark, Vickie J, contribs sup, $34,944
Starke, Melissa A, claims spec II, $31,512
Stephan, Shirley J, clerk, $19.82/hr
Stewart, Rachel B, auditor II, $37,548
Stewart-Anderson, Beverly A, unemp ins auditor III, $38,928
Stimson, Scott E, labor & industrial rel mgr b1, $51,096
Stine, Linda A, claims spec II, $31,512
Stockton, Crystal L, unemp ins auditor II, $34,356
Storm, Jennifer S, sr claims sup, $38,928
Strange, Carl W, administrative law judge, $121,553
Strange, David V, clerk, $27.18/hr
Strange, David V, clerk, $13.90/hr
Stratman, Julie, auditor II, $37,548
Streeter, Roberta, sr ofc spt asst (keybrd), $29,412
Stretch, Carrie L, claims spec II, $31,512
Strickland, Diana M, special asst ofc & clerical, $40,047
Struemph, Cynthia J, labor & industrial rel mgr b2, $54,288
Sullens, Lila A, clerk, $10.84/hr
Sullentrup, Joshua T, contribs sup, $34,944
Sullivan, Rhonda L, claims spec II, $31,512
Summers, Melissa, claims exam, $27,228
Tackett, Daniel W, unemp ins auditor II, $34,356
Talley, David J, legal counsel, $59,999
Tarr, Tamera E, claims sup, $34,944
Taylor, Arlene R, pers ofcr I, $52,092
Taylor, Lisa E, sr ofc spt asst (keybrd), $27,504
Taylor, Willie J, designated principal asst dept, $62,317
Teal, Johnnie L, unemp ins auditor II, $34,356
Teeters, Katherine S, sr ofc spt asst (keybrd), $28,908
Temmen, Lana D, exec I, $35,568
Terpstra, Rita L, sr claims sup, $49,128
Terrill, Jamie L, clerk, $27.17/hr
Thiesen, Michael J, unemp ins auditor III, $45,156
Thomas, Christine M, acct I, $31,512
Thomas, Larry, claims spec I, $29,976
Thomas, Les E, labor & industrial rel mgr b3, $58,908
Thompson, Cheryl L, clerk, $12.03/hr
Thompson, Heather L, claims exam, $28,104
Thompson, Jaclyn M, contribs spec II, $31,512
Thompson, Nicole D, labor & industrial rel mgr b1, $52,092
Thompson, Shannon R, designated principal asst div, $47,892
Thorpe, Kevin J, claims spec II, $31,512
Thurston, Delores A, admin ofc spt asst, $28,536
Tiepelman, Melissa S, claims spec I, $29,976
Tilley, Maureen T, administrative law judge, $121,553
Tillman, Laura S, clerk, $12.12/hr
Tindle, Denise C, claims spec II, $31,512
Toebben, Sandra M, contribs spec II, $31,512
Tomlin, Shirley J, unemp ins auditor III, $34,356
Toombs, Dustin M, unemp ins auditor II, $34,356
Topps, Gail J, sr ofc spt asst (clerical), $27,948
Tortorello, Paul A, appeals ref III, $57,744
Townson, Betty J, claims spec II, $31,512
Trampp, Paula R, contribs spec II, $31,512

Travis, Christine M, claims spec II, $31,512
Tripp, Betty J, sr auditor, $42,708
Tritz, Deborah S, claims sup, $34,944
Troesser, Deborah L, clerk, $22.56/hr
Truitt, Sharon D, claims spec II, $34,356
Tsutsumi, Lauren M, claims spec II, $31,512
Turner, Kimberly, claims spec II, $31,512
Turner, Margie A, claims spec II, $35,568
Turpin, Kendra K, workers' comp tech II, $27,228
Tydings, Jess E, unemp ins auditor III, $38,928
Valdes, Anthony J, appeals ref II, $53,208
Vandelicht, Janet S, claims spec II, $31,512
Vandenburg, Luecinda, claims spec II, $31,512
Vanloo, Trent M, contribs spec II, $31,512
Vaughan, Anthony D, labor & industrial rel mgr b1, $48,113
Veltrop, Gerhard L, claims exam, $27,228
Venturella, Susan M, chief counsel, $87,365
Verhoff, Carol S, sr ofc spt asst (keybrd), $27,948
Vezeau, James F, appeals ref III, $62,664
Victorino, Connie R, claims spec II, $31,512
Viel, Juli M, unemp ins auditor II, $34,356
Volkart, Paula, claims spec II, $31,512
Vorwick, Patricia A, claims spec II, $31,512
Voss, Becky A, graphics spv, $51,096
Voss, Carl J, research analyst IV, $50,040
Voss, Rebecca A, fiscal & administrative mgr b3, $76,255
Wakeland, Bonnie M, clerk, $13.95/hr
Walker, Jessica L, administrative analyst II, $38,928
Walker, Kalan T, unemp ins auditor I, $32,628
Wall, Chelsey L, contribs spec I, $29,976
Walsh, Christine, claims spec II, $31,512
Walter, Charles R, claims spec II, $31,512
Walters, Brian M, claims spec II, $31,512
Wankum, Geralyn A, claims sup, $43,488
Wargo, Denice M, workers' comp tech II, $27,228
Warner, Patricia A, claims spec II, $38,232
Warren, Alisa J, div dir, $81,305
Warren, Vicki C, claims spec II, $31,512
Waterkotte, Stacy, court reporter II, $45,156
Watkins, William P, wage & hour investigator II, $41,172
Weatherly, Brenda R, sr claims sup, $46,068
Webb, Glen D, appeals ref III, $57,744
Webb, Jeffrey K, claims spec II, $31,512
Weber, Jeffrey S, contribs spec II, $31,512
Weems, Floreyne M, accounting spec II, $41,172
Wehmeyer, Kathleen M, clerk, $25.08/hr
Wehmeyer, Kathleen M, clerk, $12.03/hr
Weinlood, Sandra J, appeals ref III, $57,744
Welschmeyer, Lucille, clerk, $12.03/hr
Wenman, Linda J, administrative law judge, $121,553
Westergren, Chris J, claims spec II, $31,512
Weston, Shawn L, mine insp, $46,068
Whearty, Adam M, investigator II, $40,380
Wheeler, Patricia J, claims spec II, $31,512
Whiston, Michael J, claims sup, $34,944
Whitfield, Edith R, sr ofc spt asst (keybrd), $27,084
Whittle, Amber D, accounting spec I, $34,944
Wickham, Jennifer A, claims spec II, $31,512
Wieberg, Irene M, clerk, $12.03/hr
Wieberg, Linda K, clerk, $17.40/hr
Wieberg, Thomas T, claims spec I, $29,976
Wilbers, Linda S, training tech II, $45,156
Wilcox, Andrew P, appeals ref II, $52,092
Willard, Lisa R, admin ofc spt asst, $29,976
Williams, Ashlei M, claims spec II, $31,512
Williams, Candace D, labor & industrial rel mgr b1, $55,416
Williams, Erin D, contribs spec II, $33,744
Williams, Ginger A, sr ofc spt asst (keybrd), $29,412
Williams, Jacquelyn S, court reporter II, $45,156
Williams, Jannifer E, claims spec I, $29,004
Williams, Kelly A, human rel ofcr I, $39,624
Williams, Sharon M, contribs spec II, $40,380
Williamson, Robert L, claims spec II, $32,628
Willis, Sharon A, misc prof, $27.17/hr
Wilson, Amanda J, claims sup, $34,944
Wilson, Carmolisa J, sr ofc spt asst (keybrd), $25,824
Wilson, Carol E, claims spec II, $31,512
Wilson, Dina L, claims spec II, $31,512
Wilson, Joyce A, clerk, $12.03/hr

Wilson, Larry T, administrative law judge, $121,553
Winbush, Samara R, human rel ofcr I, $37,548
Wineland, Tina L, sr ofc spt asst (keybrd), $25,824
Wingate, Bettie J, claims spec II, $36,888
Wisdom, Jake D, claims spec II, $31,512
Wisdom, Jeremy D, claims spec II, $31,512
Wise, Patricia A, labor & industrial rel mgr b1, $53,208
Woemmel, Anita J, claims spec II, $32,628
Wolfe, Amanda L, sr contribs supv, $39,624
Wolfe, Bobbi G, claims spec II, $31,512
Wood, Cheryl A, claims spec II, $31,512
Wood, James D, appeals ref III, $61,332
Wood, Jill S, mgmt analyst III es, $42,708
Wood, Karen J, clerk, $12.03/hr
Worthington, Stacy M, claims spec II, $31,512
Wright, Elizabeth F, mgmt analyst II es, $40,380
Wright, Kari K, sr ofc spt asst (keybrd), $25,824
Young, Chastity S, designated principal asst dept, $76,255
Zerrer, David L, administrative law judge, $121,553

Department of Mental Health

1706 E. Elm, PO Box 687, Jefferson City 65102

Stringer, Mark G, state dept dir, $125,000
Abbott, Melvin E, ofc worker misc, $10,926
Abbott, Tina M, registered nurse sr, $71,587
Abdulameer, Nawfel, resident physician, $23,676
Abdullah, Nandiayesha, psychiatric technician I, $24,696
Abdulqader, Omeed M, registered nurse, $26,058
Abey, Sheila D, case mgr I dd, $31,512
Abissah-Agyare, Vivian, security aide I psy, $29,652
Abuawad, Hasan K, registered nurse, $28,374
Abuawad, Khaldoun K, psychiatric technician I, $22,728
Abuhadba, Martha, mental hlth mgr b2, $61,287
Acosta, Jennifer, registered nurse sr, $55,776
Acuna, Regina L, deval asst I, $23,352
Adair, Sarah, lpn II gen, $34,560
Adams, Aimee E, registered nurse sr, $61,836
Adams, Amos N, behavioral technician trne, $23,880
Adams, Ashley N, deval asst I, $24,036
Adams, Billy J, security aide I psy, $32,244
Adams, Gabriel A, deval asst I, $23,352
Adams, Rhiannon M, psychologist I, $65,364
Adams, Sheila A, registered nurse sr, $57,893
Adams, Takeela C, psychiatric technician I, $23,412
Adcock, Laura E, deval asst I, $27,252
Addington, James S, deval asst I, $22,728
Adebawore, Adeniyi, psychiatric technician I, $24,696
Adekanye-Sajo, Fadejogun U, deval asst II, $25,428
Adekoya, Pauline R, deval asst I, $23,352
Adetula, Yemisi A, deval asst I, $23,352
Adeusi, Michael, custodial worker I, $22,872
Adiele, Henry N, deval asst I, $26,400
Adu, Charles, security aide I psy, $32,244
Adusumilli, Narayana R, med dir, $145,380
Afeworki, Tesfalidet, registered nurse, $25,735
Afolayan, Abiola, deval asst I, $24,036
Agimassie, Gashaw, psychiatric technician I, $24,696
Aguinaldo, Jaime, med spec I, $129,552
Aguit, Deeno E, deval asst I, $24,036
Ahlert, Teresa M, security aide I psy, $29,652
Ahmad, Addae A, research analyst I, $32,628
Ahmad-Blake, Imanni D, security aide I psy, $31,620
Ahrens, Devon L, qual assurance spec mh, $40,380
Ainsworth, Shareen L, custodial worker II, $23,613
Ajayi, Paula, registered nurse sup, $81,266
Akanuligo, Jane C, custodial worker I, $10,632
Akers, Courtland J, psychiatric technician I, $22,728
Akers, Debra K, security aide I psy, $30,276
Akers, Loretta J, security aide II psy, $35,076
Akers, Mark A, habilitation spec II, $34,944
Akinade, John I, deval asst II, $25,584
Akinaw, Genet, registered nurse, $36,029
Akinloye, Folakemi A, registered nurse sr, $71,587
Akinyemi, Ajibola T, security aide I psy, $31,152
Akpaka, Opie K, deval asst I, $23,352
Akpan, Emmanuel U, deval asst I, $23,700

Akyerem, Isaac, security aide I psy, $32,244
Al Jabari, Rawya M, student intern, $20,936
Al Janabi, Sufian F, security aide I psy, $31,152
Alapbe, Stephen N, psychiatric technician I, $23,352
Albright, Brianne C, deval asst I, $23,352
Aldejanni, Salem, cook II, $23,880
Aldridge, Judy L, ofc spt asst (keybrd), $27,504
Aleem, Marilyn D, acct II, $44,304
Alemu, Paulos T, registered nurse, $28,375
Alexander, Alana F, lpn II gen, $40,404
Alexander, Bethany D, deval asst I, $23,412
Alexander, Bianca M, registered nurse, $28,374
Alexander, Jane M, mental hlth mgr b1, $52,081
Alexander, Joshua L, psychiatric technician I, $23,352
Alexander, Kelli L, deval asst II, $27,696
Alexander, Kryste J, deval asst I, $23,028
Alexander, Lasandra E, deval asst I, $22,728
Alexander, Lasonya, deval asst I, $23,076
Alexander, Regina M, deval asst II, $29,676
Alexander, Todd P, case mgr III dd, $37,548
Alford, Nichelle, deval asst II, $26,208
Al-Hamdi, Mohammad N, food serv helper I, $21,564
Aliyu, Morayo M, reimbursement ofcr I, $29,976
Al-Kurdi, Maryam E, security aide I psy, $31,620
Allard, Joylynn D, deval asst I, $22,404
Allar-Meine, Lynne E, designated principal asst div, $79,849
Allen, Amanda I, prog spec I mh, $38,928
Allen, Carla M, deval asst I, $24,036
Allen, Christopher E, deval asst III, $28,452
Allen, Heidi M, clin casework pract II, $37,548
Allen, James R, security aide II psy, $34,488
Allen, Jessica S, deval asst I, $23,352
Allen, Kelley A, security aide I psy, $30,276
Allen, Kendra R, deval asst I, $22,716
Allen, Kimberly L, account clerk II, $25,824
Allen, Kristan M, security aide I psy, $31,620
Allen, Michele C, case mgr II dd, $34,944
Allen, Rhonda K, admin ofc spt asst, $30,420
Allen, Ryann E, food serv helper I, $22,317
Allen, Velma L, food serv helper I, $20,664
Allen-Foster, Valerie J, nurse clinician/pract, $61,234
Allgier, Jason O, security aide I psy, $29,652
Allgier, Kathryn K, licensed prof cnslr II, $46,068
Alli, Fausat, registered nurse sup, $81,266
Allison, Kenneth W, deval asst I, $23,352
Allred, Derrick, storekeeper I, $25,824
Allred, Vincent, psychiatric technician II, $25,428
Allton, Jennifer S, case mgr I dd, $31,512
Almstrom, Jessica C, deval asst I, $22,728
Alston, Michelle E, deval asst I, $22,728
Althaus, Zachary T, activity aide II, $27,780
Alumbaugh, Amanda E, deval asst I, $22,728
Alumbaugh, Karley M, deval asst I, $22,728
Alumbaugh, Ross, deval asst I, $22,728
Alvers, Betty G, security aide II psy, $33,912
Amadi, Chris, psychiatric technician I, $24,696
Amado, Elia, security aide II psy, $35,112
Amajoyi, Damian C, clin casework asst II, $30,984
Aman, Assemian S, research analyst I, $32,628
Aman, Haphrat N, security aide I psy, $31,620
Amarine, Divine G, psychiatric technician I, $23,352
Amarteifio, Awula-Amerley, security aide I psy, $31,620
Amary, Jason I, qual assurance spec mh, $43,488
Amayo, Florence M, psychiatric technician I, $12,686
Ambacher, Nancy M, occup therapy asst, $32,947
Ameer, Aanisah J, psychiatric technician I, $23,352
Ament, Kyle T, investigator, $40.64/hr
Ament, Nathan C, security aide I psy, $31,620
Amiott, Jackie L, deval asst I, $22,728
Amor, Linda J, custodial worker I, $23,160
Amos, Robert, psychiatric technician I, $23,352
Amschler, Kevin L, recrtnal ther II, $36,204
Anderson, Adriene, lpn II gen, $31,832
Anderson, Antoinette, deval asst I, $22,716
Anderson, Ashley B, deval asst I, $23,352
Anderson, Danielle, psychiatric technician I, $24,072
Anderson, Donald R, security ofcr I, $25,824
Anderson, Elizabeth A, deval asst I, $23,352
Anderson, Michael B, institution supt, $82,077

Anderson, Michelle L, dev dis cmnty prog coord, $40,380
Anderson, Pier A, psychiatric technician I, $24,804
Anderson, Roderick A, custodial worker I, $20,664
Anderson, Sandra L, sr ofc spt asst (keybrd), $27,084
Anderson, Shawn, mental hlth mgr b3, $79,297
Anderson, Tiffany K, security aide I psy, $31,620
Anderson, Tiffany S, case mgr II dd, $34,944
Anderson, Vivian A, security aide I psy, $31,620
Anderson, William D, mental hlth mgr b1, $53,202
Anderson-Harper, Rosalyn, mental hlth mgr b3, $81,255
Anderson-Hawkins, Cheryl L, registered nurse sr, $54,720
Andre, Trina L, deval asst I, $25,224
Andres, Kelly M, custodial worker I, $20,664
Andrew, Kathrine M, security aide II psy, $32,760
Andrews, Brian, psychiatric technician I, $23,352
Andrews, Christopher D, security aide I psy, $29,208
Andrews, Katie, misc prof, $30,300
Andrews, Rhianna R, clin casework pract II, $41,172
Anthony, Kayla M, deval asst I, $22,728
Antley, Diana L, sr ofc spt asst (keybrd), $27,504
Anuforom, Chukwudi B, security aide I psy, $32,244
Anugwo, Nwanneka, deval asst I, $22,728
Anum, Joshua, security aide II psy, $34,488
Anunobi, Emeka P, security aide I psy, $32,244
Anyokwu, Okah J, consulting physician, $80.24/hr
Apperson, Gregory J, mental hlth mgr b2, $63,630
Applebee, Michelle L, security aide I psy, $32,244
Applegate, Benjamin E, security aide I psy, $29,208
Applewhite, Bessie L, psychiatric technician I, $23,352
Applewhite, Sharon, deval asst I, $24,396
Applewhite, Tomicka, deval asst I, $22,728
Aranda-Diaz, Lee A, deval asst I, $22,728
Arbogast, Katherine A, deval asst I, $22,728
Arcand, Gertrudes S, security aide I psy, $30,276
Archambo, Tamra L, registered nurse sup, $70,174
Ardenrieth, Keith E, psychiatric technician II, $25,428
Ardiansyah, Muhammad Ashari, security aide I psy, $31,152
Arellano, Nicole R, cosmetologist, $24,804
Armistead, Bridget A, registered nurse sr, $55,776
Armon, Kimberley R, cook I, $22,536
Arms, Angelina, deval asst I, $23,412
Armstead, Henri S, direct care aide, $13,698
Armstrong, Aletha, lpn II gen, $38,676
Armstrong, Christopher A, deval asst I, $23,352
Armstrong, Daniel W, deval asst I, $22,728
Armstrong, Krystal D, deval asst I, $22,728
Armstrong, Sandy M, registered nurse sr, $51,276
Arndt, Amanda M, deval asst I, $23,026
Arneson, Sandra J, qual assurance spec mh, $48,156
Arnett, Donald R, security aide I psy, $31,620
Arnett, Justin R, registered nurse mgr b3, $88,544
Arnett, Marsha E, behavioral technician, $27,696
Arni, Joyce J, deval asst I, $23,076
Arnold, Austin C, deval asst I, $24,036
Arnold, Laura K, food serv helper I, $10,880
Arnold, Lewis L, admin ofc spt asst, $44,981
Arnold, Loretta C, stores clerk, $24,264
Arnold, Sasha D, deval asst I, $22,728
Arnold, Tolbert C, deval asst I, $23,028
Aron, Mary, deval asst I, $23,412
Arrigal, Emily K, psychiatric technician I, $22,716
Arter, Amber N, registered nurse, $28,375
Arthur, Alisa S, dev dis cmnty prog coord, $46,932
Arthur, Curtisha, deval asst I, $23,352
Artis, Selena M, habilitation spec II, $34,944
Artman, Jamie L, music ther II, $36,888
Asche, Teri L, deval asst I, $22,728
Ashaolu, Sabrina V, lpn II gen, $40,404
Ashe, Amie J, food serv helper I, $10,332
Asher, Amanda G, psychiatric technician I, $23,352
Asher, Jessica S, sr ofc spt asst (keybrd), $25,824
Ashley, Michael, security aide I psy, $31,152
Ashlock, Cathi L, storekeeper I, $37,757
Ashton, Todd J, security aide II psy, $32,760
Asi, Junior V, security aide I psy, $32,244
Asidi, Augustine, deval asst I, $24,036
Asidi, Veronica E, registered nurse, $31,238
Asmerom, Semhar, psychiatric technician I, $24,696
Atkins, Aaron M, psychiatric technician I, $24,036

Atkins, Gregory R, custodial worker I, $20,664
Atkins, Lornette D, pers ofcr I, $48,156
Atkins, Rodney E, psychiatric technician II, $29,676
Atkinson, Andrew J, special asst official & admstr, $81,810
Atterberry, Betty H, registered nurse, $27.50/hr
Atterberry, Crystal D, food serv helper I, $20,664
Atterberry, Derek P, security aide I psy, $31,620
Aubuchon, Kristen N, ofc spt asst (keybrd), $22,536
Aubuchon, Sherri D, registered nurse sr, $60,796
Aubuchon, Steven R, lpn I gen, $35,736
Augustine, Donna M, mental hlth mgr b2, $60,111
Austin, Deitra L, deval asst I, $23,352
Austin, Jacqueline M, deval asst III, $31,008
Avance, Tangie R, deval asst I, $23,352
Avery, Debra K, activity aide III, $34,968
Avery, Ronny G, direct care aide, $31,920
Avery, Ross A, security aide II psy, $33,232
Aviles, Edward, registered nurse - clin opers, $69,996
Awodeyi, Comfort, deval asst I, $23,352
Awodeyi, Simon O, deval asst I, $23,352
Axmacher, Rebecca L, psychiatric technician I, $22,092
Ayers, Aurora, food serv helper I, $22,872
Ayidiya, Benedicta, deval asst I, $23,352
Ayuso, Mario T, security aide I psy, $29,832
Babcock, Michael G, security ofcr I, $25,824
Backer, Nathaniel Y, security aide I psy, $32,244
Bacon, Vicki L, ofc spt asst (clerical), $25,032
Bader, Lois A, security aide I psy, $30,276
Bader, Loralee D, psychiatric technician I, $23,352
Baer, Cheryl S, sr ofc spt asst (keybrd), $25,824
Baer, Jessica L, pers analyst I, $41,172
Bahati, Salome, psychiatric technician I, $23,352
Bahr, Anne M, music ther I, $33,180
Bailey, Amber L, deval asst I, $23,076
Bailey, Clifford R, deval asst I, $23,352
Bailey, Dwayne R, security aide I psy, $31,620
Bailey, Gerald D, sr ofc spt asst (keybrd), $25,824
Bailey, Marissa, deval asst I, $23,352
Bailey, Melissa A, cook II, $23,880
Bailey, Rachael, psychiatric technician II, $24,804
Bailey, Rebecca J, laundry worker I, $20,952
Bailey, Serena S, security aide I psy, $31,620
Bailey, Shelley A, registered nurse sr, $58,565
Bailey, Shylalea S, deval asst I, $24,036
Bailey, Veronica C, deval asst I, $22,728
Bailey, Willetta Y, deval asst I, $23,352
Baillie, Rachel J, registered nurse - clin opers, $59,340
Bain, Jasmine, deval asst I, $22,728
Bajramovic, Nedim, psychiatric technician I, $23,352
Baker, Amanda R, prog spec II mh, $46,068
Baker, Barbara S, case mgr II dd, $38,232
Baker, Christopher E, security aide I psy, $29,652
Baker, Christopher S, institution supt, $77,557
Baker, Janet L, lpn II gen, $30,396
Baker, Keira M, deval asst II, $25,428
Baker, Kimberly A, lpn II gen, $30,396
Baker, Michael K, psychiatric technician I, $23,352
Baker, Mondwell S, security aide I psy, $32,244
Baker, Raven L, deval asst I, $23,076
Baker, Regina M, security aide I psy, $30,276
Baker, Richard K, registered nurse sr, $58,565
Baker, Ronald E, security ofcr I, $25,824
Baker, Tamula S, psychiatric technician II, $24,804
Baker, Theresa M, deval asst II, $26,400
Baker, Tonia R, deval asst I, $22,728
Baker, Trina A, security aide I psy, $31,620
Baker Dukes, Deborah R, clerk, $10,926
Bakley, Calliope E, registered nurse, $36,029
Baldwin, Edward T, deval asst I, $22,728
Baldwin, Nicole M, ofc spt asst (keybrd), $12,702
Bales, Jason A, deval asst I, $22,728
Bales, Rebecca E, deval asst I, $22,728
Ball, Cindy L, dev dis cmnty spec, $41,172
Ballard-Rayl, Brin, prog spec II mh, $41,940
Ballentine, Kenneth W, deval asst I, $24,036
Ballew, Joshua D, supply mgr I, $31,512
Ballew, Ruth J, deval asst I, $26,400
Ballinger, Kim R, licensed prof cnslr II, $38,928
Baluka, Norah, security aide I psy, $29,652

Bankes, Jon D, security aide I psy, $29,652
Bannister, Janice M, registered nurse sr, $55,776
Barackman, Morgan L, direct care aide, $22,728
Barber, Tabitha A, security aide I psy, $29,208
Barber, Toni, custodial worker I, $20,664
Bareiss, Brittaney M, psychiatric technician I, $23,352
Barfield, Shay A, registered nurse sup, $65,291
Bargiel, Joseph M, security ofcr I, $25,824
Barham, Barry E, psychiatric technician I, $23,352
Bariana, Paula, registered nurse, $54,130
Barker, Mickey W, deval asst I, $22,728
Barks, Ruby J, food serv helper I, $10,332
Barkwell, Jessica R, lpn II gen, $36,710
Barlow, Sharon K, deval asst I, $24,036
Barnes, Darryl, deval asst I, $22,728
Barnes, David M, custodial worker I, $33,017
Barnes, Deirdre R, workshop spv I, $27,504
Barnes, Michael L, deval asst I, $23,352
Barnes, Rebecca C, registered nurse sr, $62,460
Barnes, Reyna Fe S, security aide I psy, $30,276
Barnett, Gena L, deval asst I, $26,004
Barnett, Jessica M, deval asst I, $22,404
Barnhart, Dawn M, resident physician, $83,876
Barnhart, Steven E, security aide I psy, $29,652
Barnhouse, Gary W, security aide II psy, $32,832
Barnhouse, Marcia L, food serv helper II, $21,864
Barnum, Nancy, deval asst II, $26,208
Barrett, Danielle L, deval asst I, $22,728
Barrie, Amadu, registered nurse sup, $81,266
Barron, Bruce E, security aide I psy, $29,652
Barron, Kathryn J, exec I, $35,568
Barry, Oumar, food serv helper I, $21,564
Barsh, Claudette, deval asst I, $24,432
Bartel, Donna V, ofc spt asst (keybrd), $23,160
Bartell, Richard L, hospital mgmt asst, $63,996
Bartlett, Travis A, security aide I psy, $31,152
Bartlett-Payne, Freda Y, sr ofc spt asst (keybrd), $25,824
Bartley, George C, security ofcr I, $27,948
Barton, Johnny W, registered nurse sr, $56,192
Barton, Lindell R, security ofcr II, $34,356
Barton, Mark A, psychiatric technician I, $23,352
Barton, Michelle L, food serv helper I, $20,664
Barton, Mikayla E, psychiatric technician I, $22,716
Barton, Patricia A, custodial worker II, $22,200
Bartram, Aaron N, psychiatric technician I, $22,092
Basler, Arthur A, registered nurse, $36,029
Basler, Mary A, security aide I psy, $29,652
Basler, Michael W, security aide I psy, $29,652
Bass, Louvenia, psychiatric technician I, $23,352
Bass, Mardell, deval asst II, $29,208
Bastain, Brooklynn M, registered nurse, $28,375
Bastean, Judith, misc prof, $24,000
Bastow, Rowann, deval asst I, $22,716
Batchelor, Jonathan M, childrens psy care spv, $26,652
Bateman, Steven J, security aide I psy, $31,152
Bates, Beverly S, motor veh driver, $24,612
Bates, David R, misc prof, $57,166
Bates, James A, security ofcr, $12,511
Bates, Tambra T, pers ofcr I, $45,156
Bateson, Nicole E, lpn II gen, $36,710
Battles, Ashley E, security aide II psy, $35,112
Bauer, Drew M, deval asst I, $22,728
Bauer, Jo A, ofc spt asst (keybrd), $26,232
Bauer, Molly A, psychiatric technician I, $23,352
Bax, Robert G, misc prof, $57,584
Baxter, Durward D, fiscal & administrative mgr b3, $72,765
Baylark, Laynetta M, deval asst I, $24,036
Bays, Melinda S, security aide I psy, $29,652
Bazin, Katherine M, prog spec II mh, $48,156
Beach, Steven W, psychiatric technician I, $23,352
Bean, Clifton, custodial worker I, $21,264
Bean, Dewayne J, psychiatric technician I, $23,352
Bean, Jolanda L, psychiatric technician I, $24,804
Bean, Viola, ofc worker misc, $16,644
Bean, Yvette Y, case mgr II dd, $34,944
Beard, Justin D, security aide I psy, $32,244
Beard, Rosalyn M, deval asst I, $22,728
Beard, Timothy, deval asst I, $22,728
Bearden, Judith A, deval asst I, $24,036

Beard-Kenner, Carol N, subs abuse cnslr II, $38,928
Beasley, Quentin, deval asst I, $23,352
Becker, Faye E, dining room spv, $23,880
Becker, Glonda D, lpn II gen, $32,220
Beckerdite, Mary E, licensed clin soc wkr, $42,708
Beckmann, Emilia, research analyst III, $48,156
Beckwith, Tara L, registered nurse, $28,375
Bedford, Albert, deval asst III, $27,708
Bedford, Susan D, lpn II gen, $37,390
Bedia, Annalie, registered nurse sup, $74,556
Bedsworth, Jennie, licensed clin soc wkr, $47,892
Beeler, James J, deval asst I, $26,208
Beene, Shante, psychiatric technician I, $22,728
Beerbower, Angelia D, deval asst I, $22,728
Beezley, Sheri E, registered nurse sr, $71,587
Belew, Donna M, admin ofc spt asst, $33,180
Belfield, Debra L, lpn II gen, $40,764
Belfield, Joshua L, security aide I psy, $30,276
Belken, Mary L, registered nurse, $59,645
Bell, Bertha A, deval asst I, $23,352
Bell, Catherine, case mgmt/assess spv, $47,892
Bell, Darren M, psychiatric technician I, $22,728
Bell, James W, security aide II psy, $35,076
Bell, Karla J, acct II, $36,204
Bell, Nicole, case mgr II dd, $34,944
Bell, Regina, pers analyst II, $41,940
Bell, Rosalind R, deval asst I, $23,352
Bellamy, Amy M, sr ofc spt asst (keybrd), $26,652
Bellatin, Anna Maria, psychologist II, $69,612
Bellew, Sara D, recrtnal ther I, $33,180
Bello, Musibau O, deval asst I, $23,352
Bello, Ramat, deval asst I, $22,728
Ben Naimah, Stephen C, security aide I psy, $32,244
Benavidez, Jade A, habilitation spec II, $34,944
Bench, Brian K, food serv helper I, $21,564
Bench, Daniel L, special asst prof, $105,000
Bender-Crice, Kristina L, unit prog spv mh, $38,928
Benedick, Sharon, vendor servs coor mh, $40,380
Benjamin, Michelle, registered nurse sup, $71,448
Bennett, Carrie M, psychiatric technician II, $25,584
Bennett, Christine M, security aide I psy, $30,276
Bennett, Dominique E, fiscal & administrative mgr b2, $60,600
Bennett, Evelyn I, deval asst I, $22,728
Bennett, Gary E, security aide I psy, $29,652
Bennett, Justin M, licensed clin soc wkr, $47,892
Bennett, Kevin S, security aide I psy, $32,244
Bennett, Terrana L, deval asst I, $22,728
Ben-Okoh, Lydia A, psychiatric technician I, $24,696
Benson, Anita K, psychiatric technician I, $23,352
Benson, Tracy M, sr ofc spt asst (keybrd), $25,824
Bentley, Erin M, assoc counsel, $61,105
Bentley, Tracy J, custodial worker II, $21,864
Benton, Pamela, direct care aide, $1,920
Bequette, Michelle L, security aide I psy, $29,652
Berdon, Jeff, deval asst I, $24,036
Berg, Ronald T, mental hlth mgr b1, $62,317
Berhorst, Dalonna J, acct I, $36,888
Berkholz, Christine A, sr ofc spt asst (keybrd), $27,504
Berlener, Nancy D, registered nurse, $26,675
Bermejo, Olga C, lpn II gen, $47,718
Bernhagen, Matthew E, registered nurse sr, $55,776
Bernhard, Richard P, registered nurse sr, $60,796
Bernstein, Julie B, clin casework pract II, $37,548
Berry, Andrew, deval asst II, $24,804
Berry, Aundra K, licensed clin soc wkr, $50,040
Berry, Donna L, clin casework pract II, $41,940
Berry, Edward L, security aide I psy, $36,984
Berry, Heather M, deval asst I, $24,036
Berry, Jarvis, deval asst I, $22,728
Berry, Mary C, psychiatric technician I, $22,728
Berry, Olga V, security aide I psy, $31,620
Bertels, Mark V, security aide I psy, $29,652
Berwaldt, Katelyn N, deval asst I, $22,728
Berwaldt, Teresa L, deval asst I, $26,400
Beshe, Marta, registered nurse, $25,734
Betrus, Justin T, cook I, $21,864
Bett, Reuben K, security aide I psy, $29,652
Bettis, Harold, food serv helper I, $21,564
Beussink, Pamela S, sr ofc spt asst (keybrd), $30,384

Bever, Julie L, dev dis cmnty prog coord, $39,624
Beverly, Marcia M, deval asst I, $22,728
Bevineau, Kenneth J, psychiatric technician I, $23,352
Bevly, Keisha, deval asst I, $26,400
Bias, Melanie S, vendor servs coor mh, $40,380
Bibbs, Bridgette L, case mgr II dd, $34,944
Bickel, Stacie L, mental hlth mgr b1, $57,744
Bickley, Laporsche C, psychiatric technician I, $23,352
Bieser, Lisa K, registered nurse sr, $51,552
Biggs, James A, deval asst II, $26,208
Biggs, Michael E, deval asst I, $23,028
Bikfasy, Craig P, case mgr II dd, $34,944
Biller, Dorae A, habilitation spec II, $36,204
Bills, Brenda K, deval asst I, $23,352
Binder, Kristi N, deval asst I, $22,728
Bins, Brett E, psychiatric technician I, $23,352
Birch, Bettie L, deval asst I, $23,352
Bird, Theresa C, psychiatric technician I, $22,728
Birkner, Rachelle N, licensed clin soc wkr, $47,892
Birkner, Vivian K, lpn II gen, $37,390
Bishop, Christopher F, psychiatric technician I, $23,352
Bishop, Susan M, institution supt, $77,556
Bitendelo, Ngombe Y, registered nurse, $28,375
Bizor, Phillip H, security ofcr I, $25,824
Black, Gail R, prog spec II mh, $44,304
Black, Jody, psychiatric technician I, $24,072
Black, John T, security aide II psy, $32,760
Black, Laurie L, licensed clin soc wkr, $47,892
Black, Lori A, deval asst I, $23,352
Black, Robert D, security aide I psy, $31,620
Black, Terry L, deval asst I, $23,352
Blackmon, Geraldine M, registered nurse, $58,769
Blackstad, Jennifer A, dev dis cmnty worker II, $37,548
Black-Underwood, Dakota L, deval asst I, $22,716
Blackwell, Talisha, dev dis cmnty worker II, $33,744
Blackwell, Terrell, deval asst I, $23,352
Blain, Elijah M, psychiatric technician I, $22,092
Blair, Julia M, phys ther III, $65,364
Blair, Sherrie S, security aide I psy, $29,652
Blake, Alan W, misc prof, $34,994
Blake, Jermaine, security aide I psy, $29,832
Blakeley, Dawn R, psychiatric technician I, $23,352
Blakely, Kayla N, deval asst I, $22,404
Blakley-Gorman, Mary R, pers ofcr I, $46,932
Bland, Cara L, habilitation spec II, $34,944
Bland, Whitney R, licensed clin soc wkr, $47,892
Blanke, Joseph E, activity aide III, $32,148
Blankenship, Wesley D, security aide I psy, $48,187
Blann, Kristy R, registered nurse sr, $51,552
Blanton, William C, security ofcr I, $29,412
Blaylock, Amy L, deval asst I, $25,428
Blaylock, Latonia M, psychiatric technician I, $23,412
Blevens, Adrian R, deval asst I, $26,004
Blind, Hildy B, case mgr II dd, $34,944
Blocker, Regina A, case mgr II dd, $33,744
Blum, Geraldine L, activity aide II, $24,804
Blume, Susan L, mental hlth mgr b2, $57,805
Blumer, Dusty J, security aide I psy, $29,652
Blumer, Gary D, security aide I psy, $29,652
Blumhorst, Donna K, deval asst I, $23,412
Blumhorst, Karen E, deval asst I, $27,876
Blunt, Jacqueline, admin ofc spt asst, $32,628
Bocanegra, Susan S, psychiatric technician I, $23,352
Bockenstedt, Bart G, special educ tchr III, $51,096
Boclair, Janice C, ofc spt asst (keybrd), $25,824
Bodenstedt, Ronald C, assoc psychologist II, $47,892
Bodunde, Oluwaseyi O, deval asst I, $23,412
Boeh, Andrea J, nutrition/dietary svcs mgr b1, $58,497
Boekemier, Timothy M, ofc spt asst (keybrd), $23,880
Bogan, Stephanie, deval asst I, $23,352
Bogart, Shelby L, deval asst I, $23,352
Bohnenkamp, John A, storekeeper II, $28,536
Bohnenkamp, Marvin H, dentist, $31,512
Bohnert, Martha M, misc prof, $10,504
Bohrer, Felicia K, psychiatric technician II, $26,400
Bolden, Lamira M, deval asst I, $26,004
Bolden, Van E, deval asst I, $23,412
Bolden, Yolanda L, deval asst II, $26,208
Bolser, Jerry A, reimbursement ofcr I, $29,976

Boltz, Debra J, psychiatric technician I, $23,352
Bomah-Swaray, Christiana, psychiatric technician I, $24,696
Bomar, Barbara E, sr ofc spt asst (keybrd), $25,824
Bomersbach, James R, psychological resident, $35,972
Bonnett, Karen A, deval asst I, $22,728
Bonnett, Kathryn, sr ofc spt asst (keybrd), $27,948
Bonte, Eugenie R, psychologist, $31,075
Bonwell, Tasha, psychiatric technician I, $24,696
Booher, Lynn M, stores clerk, $26,652
Booker, Sharon, deval asst I, $23,352
Boone, Andrea L, prog spec trainee mh, $36,888
Boone, Keonna L, pers clerk, $29,004
Booth, Jamie L, deval asst I, $22,728
Boots, Chanda N, ofc spt asst (keybrd), $25,404
Borghardt, Tabitha G, sr ofc spt asst (keybrd), $26,652
Borgstadt, Christy E, dining room spv, $23,880
Born, Thomas E, qual assurance spec mh, $47,892
Bosch, Mary, admin ofc spt asst, $30,984
Bosley, Ryan M, deval asst I, $22,404
Bostic, Tammy K, prog spec I mh, $32,304
Boswell, Mary A, deval asst I, $23,352
Boswell, Steven G, deval asst I, $23,352
Botbyl, Joshua A, psychiatric technician I, $22,728
Bounds, Jessica M, prog spec I mh, $38,928
Bouse, Sharon A, food serv helper I, $22,317
Boutros, Nashaat N, staff physician spec, $217,151
Bowden, James E, custodial worker I, $21,264
Bowdry, Danita I, direct care aide, $13.47/hr
Bowen, Kevin D, psychiatric technician I, $23,352
Bowers, Clara A, psychiatric technician I, $24,036
Bowles, Christina M, security aide I psy, $30,276
Bowles, Cleveland L, psychiatric technician I, $23,352
Bowles, Deborah K, security aide I psy, $30,276
Bowles, Glenda L, deval asst I, $26,004
Bowles, Kathy A, security aide I psy, $30,276
Bowman, Darin E, security aide I psy, $32,244
Bowman, Kathryn A, deval asst I, $23,352
Bowman, Susan K, mgmt analysis spec I, $39,624
Bowne, Daniel D, security aide I psy, $29,208
Bowser, Lakecia, deval asst I, $22,728
Bowyer, Amy L, activity aide II, $27,780
Boyd, Denise L, licensed clin soc wkr, $47,892
Boyd, Gwendolyn, registered nurse - clin opers, $69,996
Boyd, Larnice M, psychiatric technician I, $22,728
Boyd, Philip R, registered nurse sr, $58,140
Boyd, Phyllistine, deval asst I, $22,728
Boyd, Richard, activity aide I, $22,728
Boyd Shorter, Canee S, psychiatric technician I, $22,728
Boyd-Bostick, Toni T, case mgr II dd, $34,944
Boyer, Jamie L, registered nurse sr, $53,253
Boyer, Kelly M, dev dis cmnty spec, $43,488
Boyer, Linda L, deval asst II, $28,320
Boyes, Cynthia M, dev dis cmnty prog coord, $43,488
Boykin, Wayne L, security aide I psy, $29,652
Boyle, Constance, case mgmt/assess spv, $44,304
Boynton, Blaine J, habilitation spec II, $34,944
Bozich, Linda J, misc prof, $25,519
Bozich, Phillip, habilitation spv, $38,928
Braciszewski, Jennifer A, registered nurse sr, $55,776
Bracy, Dawn M, deval asst I, $26,628
Bradford, Dane W, security ofcr I, $25,824
Bradford, Dane W, security ofcr I, $38,174
Bradley, Angela T, security ofcr I, $25,824
Bradley, Breanna T, direct care aide, $12,353
Bradley, Darian L, security ofcr I, $26,652
Bradley, Daryl C, security aide II psy, $37,608
Bradley, Debbie D, security aide I psy, $29,652
Bradley, Earniecia M, deval asst I, $22,728
Bradley, Ethel M, habilitation spec II, $38,232
Bradley, Lesa D, behavioral technician supv, $31,531
Bradley, Leslie A, prog spec II mh, $41,940
Bradley, M Kevin, vendor servs coor mh, $38,928
Bradley-Sipes, Dorine M, deval asst III, $29,904
Bradshaw, Donald W, deval asst I, $24,036
Bradshaw, Kimberly A, deval asst I, $22,728
Bradshaw, Robert W, mental hlth mgr b2, $75,265
Brady, Heather M, sr ofc spt asst (keybrd), $27,504
Bragg, Rhonda L, registered nurse, $50,244
Braggs, Sandura, training tech II, $44,304

Brake, Rebecca E, direct care aide, $12.12/hr
Brammann, Trista M, security aide I psy, $32,244
Brammer, Ginger K, ofc servs asst, $30,984
Branch, Charles A, security aide I psy, $32,244
Brandon, Doris M, sr ofc spt asst (keybrd), $30,384
Brandon, Nathaniel T, deval asst III, $29,532
Brandt, Martina D, security aide I psy, $31,620
Brandt, Tacia L, security aide I psy, $31,776
Branham, Paul A, clin soc work spec, $45,156
Branigan, Shelly M, deval asst I, $22,728
Brannam, Matthew D, psychiatric technician I, $23,352
Branscomb, Cedric B, deval asst I, $26,628
Branson, Joyce M, deval asst I, $22,728
Branyon, Tiffany M, psychiatric technician I, $22,728
Brasser, Steven C, misc tech, $13,372
Brauner, Gretchen O, security aide I psy, $29,208
Bravo, Emily A, habilitation spec I, $33,744
Bray, Corey L, deval asst I, $23,076
Brazil, Lisa, clin soc work spec, $74,876
Bredehoeft, Shirlyn D, deval asst II, $25,584
Breece, Herbert C, registered nurse sr, $63,585
Breeland, Latonya R, deval asst I, $23,352
Breeland, Monique D, sr ofc spt asst (keybrd), $26,652
Breitbach, Michelle L, clin soc work spec, $49,128
Brennaman, Carol L, vendor servs coor mh, $40,380
Brenner, Angela, special asst official & admstr, $78,275
Brent, Joanna E, clin soc work spec, $49,128
Breshears, Lacey M, dev dis cmnty worker II, $34,944
Breshears, Zachary C, deval asst I, $23,028
Bress-Scroggins, Jean A, recrtnal ther II, $44,304
Brevik, Lilah R, dev dis cmnty worker II, $34,944
Brew, Dorris, printing/mail technician III, $39,685
Brew, Hyland, security ofcr I, $25,824
Brewah, Yeawah, deval asst II, $26,208
Brewer, Cherine G, deval asst I, $22,728
Brewer, Edward K, security aide I psy, $29,652
Brewer, Melinda R, custodial worker I, $22,317
Brewer, Melvin L, deval asst II, $28,776
Brewer, Patricia J, psychiatric technician I, $23,352
Bridges, Creasy, registered nurse sr, $58,415
Bridges, Sheila D, registered nurse sr, $56,526
Briggs, Karey B, lpn II gen, $36,086
Brightmon, Antonio D, deval asst II, $25,248
Brinkley, Kailey L, psychiatric technician I, $23,352
Brinkley, Marcus, deval asst I, $23,352
Brinkley, Travis W, deval asst II, $25,428
Briones Aguilar, Chris A, psychiatric technician I, $23,412
Brisby, Lakeshia, deval asst I, $23,352
Briscoe, Jayne H, account clerk II, $27,084
Brisendine-Smith, Lana K, dev dis cmnty worker II, $44,304
Briseno, Christine, custodial worker I, $10,932
Britton, John F, fire & safety spec, $38,928
Broadway, Brandy T, registered nurse, $28,375
Brobbey, Japheth D, security aide I psy, $32,244
Brocka, Eugenia C, pers clerk, $32,628
Brockes, Courtney B, registered nurse sr, $53,253
Brockmeier, Charles A, deval asst I, $22,728
Broege, Deborah L, deval asst III, $29,076
Brokaw, Jamie L, registered nurse sr, $65,676
Bronner, Diane, psychiatric technician I, $22,728
Brooks, Audrey L, misc prof, $30,882
Brooks, Bonnie L, deval asst I, $24,036
Brooks, Christhea L, psychiatric technician I, $22,728
Brooks, Clemeisha, deval asst I, $23,352
Brooks, Elizabeth K, deval asst I, $23,352
Brooks, Geraldine, deval asst I, $23,352
Brooks, Jarrett, psychiatric technician I, $23,352
Brooks, Jerry G, deval asst I, $23,352
Brooks, Jessica E, psychiatric technician I, $22,728
Brooks, John R, security aide I psy, $31,620
Brooks, Jonathan A, ofc spt asst (keybrd), $26,232
Brooks, Misty G, deval asst I, $22,728
Brooks, Valerie L, security aide I psy, $30,276
Brooks-Thompson, Regina A, deval asst I, $23,352
Brookter Schader, Tina M, custodial worker I, $22,317
Broomfield, Lisa K, mental hlth mgr b2, $60,125
Brotherton, Michael L, security aide I psy, $29,652
Browder, Zerlene, deval asst I, $24,072
Brower, Allison R, special educ tchr III, $45,156

Brower, Andrew R, security aide II psy, $32,208
Browers, Jill Y, psychiatric technician I, $22,728
Browers, Linda A, food serv helper I, $22,317
Brown, Aaronesha L, psychiatric technician I, $23,352
Brown, Adrienne, deval asst II, $24,804
Brown, Brian K, security ofcr II, $29,496
Brown, Catherine, deval asst I, $22,728
Brown, Catherine J, pers analyst I, $30,984
Brown, Channay, lpn, $18,631
Brown, Chris, custodial worker I, $20,664
Brown, Christina J, deval asst I, $22,728
Brown, Clarance R, workshop prog coor, $39,624
Brown, Darline Y, deval asst I, $23,352
Brown, Darris R, custodial work spv, $23,880
Brown, Deborah J, lpn II gen, $37,020
Brown, Denise R, registered nurse sup, $65,963
Brown, Derek E, resident physician, $52,995
Brown, Dustin M, security aide I psy, $32,244
Brown, Etay, deval asst I, $22,728
Brown, Glen D, deval asst I, $24,036
Brown, Jennifer E, psychiatric technician I, $24,072
Brown, Jennifer R, case mgr III dd, $41,172
Brown, Jerry, deval asst I, $22,716
Brown, Jerry E, laborer II, $26,232
Brown, John C, registered nurse - clin opers, $58,171
Brown, Juanita, food serv helper I, $20,664
Brown, Kay F, case mgr II dd, $34,944
Brown, Kay'la N, behavioral technician, $26,844
Brown, Kimberly, deval asst I, $22,728
Brown, Kori D, security aide I psy, $31,620
Brown, Koriann D, security aide I psy, $31,620
Brown, Laura R, dev dis cmnty worker II, $34,944
Brown, Marcia A, registered nurse, $30,882
Brown, Mark P, security aide II psy, $32,832
Brown, Mary R, dental hygienist, $41,940
Brown, Marylene, lpn II gen, $37,632
Brown, Matthew A, deval asst I, $24,036
Brown, Melissa M, deval asst I, $22,728
Brown, Michelle, mental hlth mgr b1, $51,070
Brown, Michelle M, dev dis cmnty prog coord, $40,380
Brown, Mistina M, deval asst I, $22,728
Brown, Nancy, case mgr II dd, $34,944
Brown, Phillip D, deval asst I, $22,728
Brown, Phillis L, ofc spt asst (keybrd), $23,880
Brown, Renee Y, cook I, $21,864
Brown, Rhonda M, mental hlth mgr b2, $60,524
Brown, Rinia M, storekeeper II, $28,104
Brown, Ronald M, food serv mgr I, $32,628
Brown, Ronnie D, security aide I psy, $33,912
Brown, Rosalind, ofc spt asst (keybrd), $25,404
Brown, Shanna R, registered nurse sup, $55,776
Brown, Shannon, security aide I psy, $31,620
Brown, Sharon M, deval asst I, $22,728
Brown, Shaunta R, childrens psy care spv, $27,504
Brown, Sheila L, dev dis cmnty worker II, $34,944
Brown, Shelly L, mental hlth mgr b1, $52,093
Brown, Stanley L, security aide III psy, $38,232
Brown, Tashekia, psychiatric technician I, $22,728
Brown, Terry L, deval asst I, $24,036
Brown, Timmy L, activity aide II, $27,780
Brownell, Kandrai F, deval asst I, $27,468
Brownell, Melody L, custodial worker II, $23,613
Browning, Brenda L, security aide I psy, $29,652
Browning, Lewis J, security aide I psy, $34,488
Brownlee, Hybrie J, direct care aide, $10.93/hr
Brownlee, James, deval asst II, $25,584
Broyles, Gladys B, case mgr III dd, $37,548
Bruce, David M, dev dis cmnty spec, $41,172
Bruce, Kelly A, storekeeper I, $25,824
Bruce, Stephen M, mgmt analysis spec II, $51,096
Brueshaber, John B, hlth info admin II, $54,288
Bruggeman, Mark D, training tech II, $41,172
Brumback, Heather L, psychiatric technician I, $22,716
Brundridge, Elisha D, deval asst I, $22,728
Bruns, Cathy M, misc prof, $29,504
Bruns, Michael J, licensed clin soc wkr, $43,103
Brunson, Tranesha S, habilitation spec I, $29,004
Bruton, Cheryl F, mental hlth mgr b2, $58,347
Bryan, Deborah D, staff physician, $137,245

Bryan, Lisa J, info technology spec II, $69,612
Bryant, Angeline, deval asst I, $24,804
Bryant, Donyell, pers analyst II, $48,857
Bryant, Elizabeth A, deval asst I, $24,072
Bryant, Enice, deval asst I, $23,352
Bryant, Kevin M, ch security ofcr, $42,708
Bryant, Sharon, deval asst I, $24,036
Bryant, Steven D, deval asst I, $23,352
Bryant-Hines, Brenda D, security aide I psy, $32,208
Bryson, Carol J, lpn II gen, $33,384
Bublitz, Vicki L, staff dev ofcr mh, $56,520
Buchanan, Autumn S, deval asst I, $22,728
Buchanan, Granita R, deval asst I, $22,092
Buchanan, Ronnie L, deval asst I, $23,352
Buck, Rosita D, deval asst II, $25,584
Buck Jaeger, Nancy S, security aide I psy, $31,620
Buckles, Lisa J, registered nurse sr, $55,776
Buckley, Jenifer N, mental hlth mgr b1, $48,150
Buckley, P S, misc prof, $31.15/hr
Buckman, Trudy J, fiscal & administrative mgr b1, $58,900
Buckner, Christopher L, food serv helper I, $20,664
Bufford, Antoine, cook III, $33,180
Buford, Angela B, mental hlth mgr b2, $75,261
Buhler, Karen L, ofc spt asst (keybrd), $23,160
Bullard, Danielle N, deval asst I, $24,036
Bullard, Kevin D, security aide I psy, $31,620
Bullard, Melanie L, dietary servs coor mh, $63,996
Bullock, Alicia M, psychiatric technician I, $23,352
Bullock, Donna A, ofc spt asst (keybrd), $24,612
Bunch, Tia, case mgr II dd, $34,944
Bundy, Melissa, special asst ofc & clerical, $40,061
Bunner, Bonny J, deval asst I, $22,728
Bunting, Breaha R, custodial worker I, $21,740
Bunton, Jill J, security ofcr I, $25,824
Buntyn, Deonte, deval asst I, $23,352
Buntyn, Erick, deval asst I, $23,352
Burbank, Jennylee E, typist, $10,804
Burbridge, Helen J, typist, $11,575
Burch, Carl E, security aide I psy, $32,244
Burch, Marilyn, psychiatric technician I, $23,412
Burcham, Kyle E, psychiatric technician I, $23,352
Burdick, Jerry A, deval asst I, $23,352
Burditt, Derrick C, deval asst III, $27,504
Burditt, Eric S, deval asst I, $22,728
Burditt, Jodie H, habilitation spec II, $34,944
Burgess, Mary L, registered nurse, $22,000
Burgess, Mauronda D, deval asst I, $26,844
Burgess, Megan, recrtnal ther I, $32,628
Burgett, Mary A, ofc spt asst (keybrd), $23,880
Burke, Roy M, security aide I psy, $32,226
Burks, Vanilla, custodial worker I, $21,264
Burlingame, Cherri L, deval asst I, $23,352
Burnes, Florence D, registered nurse sr, $62,460
Burnett, Kadesh B, dev dis cmnty spec, $40,380
Burnham, Kayla M, deval asst I, $23,352
Burnop, Vincent S, psychiatric technician I, $22,092
Burns, Danny R, storekeeper, $20,282
Burns, Jonathan D, acct I, $30,984
Burns, Lisa L, custodial worker I, $20,664
Burns, Valerie D, deval asst II, $27,024
Burrage, Latoya N, deval asst I, $22,728
Burrell, Jeffrey H, habilitation spec II, $34,944
Burrell, Misty D, deval asst I, $23,352
Burrow, Ernestine, lpn II gen, $40,404
Burton, Andrew G, psychiatric technician I, $22,728
Burton, Christina L, deval asst I, $27,252
Burton, Michael T, deval asst I, $22,728
Burton, Patricia J, registered nurse - clin opers, $74,556
Busbey, Sarah N, deval asst I, $22,728
Busby, Kelly, deval asst I, $23,700
Busch, Linda S, deval asst I, $24,072
Buschjost, Darlene F, sr ofc spt asst (keybrd), $28,452
Bush, Charlotte P, deval asst III, $35,472
Bushmoyer, Sherry L, admin ofc spt asst, $37,548
Bushnell, Deborah A, deval asst I, $24,804
Buskuehl, Linda L, clerk, $10,926
Buss, Melinda D, psychiatric technician II, $26,208
Bussen, Sarah D, deval asst I, $23,352
Butcher, Branden L, deval asst I, $22,728

Butcher, Donald P, account clerk II, $27,504
Butcher, Melissa J, acct I, $30,984
Butcher, Rebecca J, security aide I psy, $29,832
Butler, Carla L, sr ofc spt asst (clerical), $27,084
Butler, Jason L, deval asst I, $22,728
Butler, Jenai, food serv helper I, $20,664
Butler, Lavonda S, case mgr I dd, $32,628
Butler, Pamela D, ofc spt asst (keybrd), $26,232
Butler, Regina C, deval asst I, $31,776
Butler, Theresa I, security aide I psy, $29,652
Butner, Kelly S, psychiatric technician II, $27,696
Butterfield, Katie A, recrtnal ther I, $33,180
Butterfield, Krista R, psychiatric technician I, $22,716
Butterfield, Rachel L, psychiatric technician I, $22,728
Buttrey, Pamela S, security aide I psy, $29,832
Butzer, Daniel T, registered nurse sr, $73,393
Buxton, Levar E, deval asst III, $27,276
Buzzanga, Terra L, registered nurse mgr b3, $86,651
Bye, Kimberly S, psychological resident, $41,172
Byndom, Frederick, activity aide II, $25,224
Byndom, Sharod, psychiatric technician I, $23,352
Byram, Meleena K, sr ofc spt asst (keybrd), $13,116
Byrd, Carol, deval asst I, $23,352
Byrd, Deborah L, prog spec II mh, $46,068
Byrd, Jamie K, registered nurse sr, $58,565
Byrd, Keesha D, case mgr I dd, $32,628
Cable, Darcy M, deval asst I, $23,352
Cable, Dirk, housing dev ofcr II, $41,940
Cable, Suzanne, deval asst I, $22,728
Cafer, Jason E, staff physician spec, $210,818
Cahalan, Connie M, mental hlth mgr b3, $86,355
Cahill, Deborah A, acct II, $37,548
Cahill, Kiley M, deval asst I, $24,072
Cain, Marcia R, registered nurse, $27,794
Cain, Terry R, registered nurse sr, $56,976
Caldwell, Christopher D, account clerk II, $26,232
Caldwell, Rose M, deval asst II, $24,804
Caldwell, Windal, deval asst I, $23,352
Calender, Marjorie A, registered nurse, $30,627
Calhoun, Belinda E, admin ofc spt asst, $34,356
Calhoun, Damon J, deval asst I, $22,728
Calhoun, Joshua W, med admin, $205,535
Callen, Brenda L, hlth info tech I, $28,104
Callen, Shelby N, psychiatric technician I, $22,716
Calloway, Chelsie R, lpn, $16,470
Calvert, Beth L, case mgr II dd, $34,944
Calvert, Christine A, deval asst II, $27,696
Calvert, Myranda M, food serv helper I, $22,317
Cambre, Donna, case mgr III dd, $41,172
Cameron, Edith A, registered nurse sr, $52,608
Cameron, Melody L, registered nurse sr, $53,592
Cameron, Wendy S, deval asst I, $26,004
Camp, Debbie L, deval asst I, $24,072
Campanelli, Suzan K, registered nurse - clin opers, $66,504
Campbell, Dailey L, custodial worker I, $22,872
Campbell, Earlene D, deval asst II, $25,428
Campbell, Heather, ofc spt asst (keybrd), $23,508
Campbell, Janet, habilitation spec II, $35,966
Campbell, Julie A, activity aide III, $29,052
Campbell, Monica L, licensed clin soc wkr, $46,932
Campbell, Randa E, speech-language pathlgy ast II, $38,232
Campbell, Terry G, lpn II gen, $32,884
Campbell, William M, security aide II psy, $32,832
Canada, Tanya R, admin ofc spt asst, $28,104
Canfield, Ryan J, deval asst I, $24,036
Cann, Andrew, psychiatric technician I, $24,072
Cannell, Carl A, security aide I psy, $32,244
Cannon, Vivian, deval asst I, $22,728
Cannon-Herrick, Shelly A, habilitation spec II, $37,548
Canon, Cheryl D, psychologist I, $65,364
Canterbury, Keri, registered nurse, $54,766
Cantrell, Patricia E, deval asst I, $22,716
Capal, Raymond J, security aide I psy, $32,244
Caradine, Carla M, pers analyst II, $46,932
Caravella-Aguilar, Margaret A, psychiatric technician I, $28,584
Carbon, Martha J, deval asst II, $27,024
Carbon-Kemp, Candice D, deval asst I, $25,056
Carleton, Carolyn N, registered nurse sr, $53,253
Carlin, Mary S, direct care aide, $12.36/hr

Carney, Jill A, mental hlth mgr b2, $58,897
Caro, Joan M, sr ofc spt asst (steno), $31,416
Carpenter, Virginia K, mental hlth mgr b2, $70,494
Carr, Tijuana D, deval asst I, $24,036
Carr, Wylonda S, habilitation spec II, $35,568
Carrel, Cherry A, ofc spt asst (keybrd), $12,702
Carrel, Karlton C, lpn II gen, $37,020
Carrillo, Peter A, deval asst I, $23,352
Carroll, Aaronda, deval asst I, $23,352
Carroll, Earl S, dev dis cmnty spec, $41,940
Carroll, Julie A, registered nurse sr, $51,552
Carroll, Leonard P, security aide I psy, $30,276
Carroll, Megan R, deval asst I, $23,352
Carroll, Shaun L, psychiatric technician I, $23,352
Carron, David S, podiatrist, $9,212
Carr-Shaw, Leandra, dining room spv, $26,232
Carson, Tynisha, deval asst I, $22,728
Carstensen, Michael E, laundry worker II, $22,536
Carter, Candace R, deval asst I, $23,352
Carter, Jonathan L, prog spec trainee mh, $36,888
Carter, Marilyn, deval asst III, $27,276
Carter, Michael S, misc prof, $41,176
Carter, Patricia, special asst official & admstr, $96,960
Carter, Roshonda B, custodial worker I, $20,664
Carter, Shawniece M, deval asst I, $22,716
Carter, Shelby J, psychiatric technician I, $22,728
Carter, Tracie L, security aide I psy, $30,276
Cartwright, Lydia M, lpn II gen, $31,332
Cartwright, Stephanie D, deval asst I, $23,076
Caruthers, Andrew R, security aide I psy, $31,620
Carver, Jill A, custodial worker I, $21,760
Carver, Norman E, maint worker II, $30,420
Carver, Paul K, security aide I psy, $30,276
Carvin, Deanna, deval asst I, $22,728
Case, Heather N, deval asst I, $22,728
Case, James R, deval asst I, $23,412
Case, Karey L, research analyst III, $43,488
Case, Krystal K, deval asst I, $26,400
Case, Michael D, motor veh driver, $26,652
Case, Michael J, psychiatric technician I, $22,716
Case, Robin M, deval asst I, $23,412
Casey, Dana E, ofc spt asst (keybrd), $23,160
Casey, Georgia M, registered nurse, $28,375
Cash, Amy L, deval asst I, $22,728
Cash, Chelsie D, deval asst I, $22,716
Cashion, David W, security aide I psy, $29,652
Cason, Felicia M, acct I, $29,976
Cason, Helen M, registered nurse sr, $60,796
Cason, Kyle L, security aide I psy, $30,276
Cassel, Martha A, mental hlth mgr b1, $65,364
Cassidy, Camie C, reimbursement ofcr I, $29,976
Castillo, Victor M, acct I, $30,984
Caston, Donna J, deval asst I, $26,628
Catarinicchia, Mary G, security aide II psy, $35,076
Cato, Dinae A, registered nurse sr, $50,244
Catoire, Allison J, psychiatric technician I, $23,352
Caton, Amanda L, deval asst I, $23,352
Cattani, Stephanie L, cook II, $23,160
Causevic, Jelena, registered nurse sr, $52,608
Cavness, Trevor E, security ofcr I, $50,750
Cawelti, Gerald L, deval asst I, $22,728
Chailland, Jilian R, food serv helper I, $21,760
Chamberlain, Christopher R, security aide I psy, $29,652
Chamberlain, Khristian A, deval asst I, $24,036
Chamberlain, Ronald J, security aide I psy, $30,276
Chamberlin, Natalie N, qual assurance spec mh, $40,380
Chambers, Brittany N, security aide I psy, $29,652
Chambers, Jonaliza E, security aide I psy, $30,276
Chandler, Nicholas, psychiatric technician I, $23,352
Chapin, Deanna M, deval asst II, $25,428
Chapman, Gail L, security aide I psy, $32,244
Chapman, Joan E, food serv helper I, $10,332
Chapman, Tiara L, deval asst I, $23,352
Chapman, Valeri L, ofc spt asst (keybrd), $23,880
Charles, Nicole M, registered nurse sr, $54,766
Charleville, Janet K, account clerk II, $30,384
Charlton, Veronica S, deval asst II, $30,192
Chase, John, investigator I, $37,548
Chastain, Antonina J, licensed clin soc wkr, $49,128

Chavez, Kalin J, deval asst I, $22,728
Chazelle, Terri A, vendor servs coor mh, $40,380
Checkettschott, Kelly E, admin ofc spt asst, $28,104
Chen, Elizabeth, lpn I gen, $28,848
Chen, Michelle L, security aide I psy, $31,620
Chen, Tung W, direct care aide, $22.47/hr
Chen, Zhaoying, deval asst I, $24,072
Cheney-Salmons, Joyce R, food serv mgr I, $29,976
Chernich, Sarane M, ofc spt asst (keybrd), $23,880
Chernoff, Selbert G, med spec II, $140,494
Cherry, Lisa T, deval asst I, $23,076
Chesnut, Linda P, account clerk II, $30,384
Chester, Jerome D, registered nurse sr, $31,052
Chi, Ming B, resident physician, $30,882
Chidume, Scholastica, registered nurse, $59,665
Childress, Akilah T, deval asst I, $24,036
Childress, Marcus, custodial worker I, $20,664
Childress, Shanon L, deval asst III, $29,904
Childress, Warren R, deval asst I, $23,412
Chiles, Clayton J, motor veh driver, $27,084
Chilton, Lynzi T, security aide I psy, $30,276
Chilton, Vickie M, registered nurse sr, $53,253
Ching Sam, Eunice L, psychiatric technician I, $23,352
Chism, Deborah A, security aide II psy, $32,208
Chitty, Deanna M, psychiatric technician I, $23,352
Chitwood, Christopher J, deval asst III, $28,452
Chitwood, Jonathan W, registered nurse sr, $59,645
Chitwood, Millicent M, registered nurse sr, $59,645
Choat, Arlene, ofc spt asst (keybrd), $28,452
Cholak, Patricia D, case mgr I dd, $31,512
Chrisenberry, Krista K, deval asst I, $23,352
Chrisenberry, Niki R, deval asst I, $22,404
Christensen, Kelly E, deval asst I, $23,412
Christensen, Linda D, registered nurse, $36,029
Christensen, Renee D, habilitation spec II, $34,944
Christian, Janice L, admin ofc spt asst, $28,104
Christian, Kathleen S, custodial worker I, $20,664
Christian, Martin E, security ofcr II, $29,976
Christian, Rebecca L, qual assurance spec mh, $45,156
Christman, Jane H, data processor tech, $27,304
Christmas, Jacquelyn A, special asst official & admstr, $64,702
Chunn, Peggy D, custodial worker I, $20,664
Chunn, Trisha N, psychiatric technician I, $22,728
Cisewski, Crystal D, dev dis cmnty prog coord, $38,928
Clardy, Diana K, misc prof, $14,891
Clark Sr, Aaron R, psychiatric technician I, $23,352
Clark, Abigail D, psychiatric technician I, $23,352
Clark, Allan S, staff dev ofcr mh, $51,096
Clark, Debra M, case mgr I dd, $32,628
Clark, Denice J, security aide I psy, $30,276
Clark, Emergene, psychiatric technician I, $23,700
Clark, Frederica T, case mgr II dd, $34,944
Clark, John W, case mgr III dd, $37,548
Clark, Judy M, deval asst I, $22,728
Clark, Michael A, lpn, $18,631
Clark, Michael J, fiscal & administrative mgr b3, $72,765
Clark, Michael T, security ofcr, $18,631
Clark, Nancy, special educ tchr III, $47,892
Clark, Nancy J, registered nurse sr, $58,140
Clark, Patricia C, registered nurse sr, $59,645
Clark, Robert S, security aide I psy, $29,652
Clark, Shanique S, case mgr II dd, $34,944
Clark, Steven L, security aide II psy, $33,912
Clark, Tamera K, psychiatric technician II, $25,428
Clark-Murry, Jessica D, dining room spv, $23,880
Clatto, Nancy A, security ofcr I, $25,824
Clauser, Angelia R, stores clerk, $24,612
Clay, Alnedria, deval asst I, $22,728
Clay, Janice, registered nurse sup, $74,556
Claybon, Shuewonder L, psychiatric technician II, $25,428
Clayborne, Donna L, deval asst I, $22,728
Claypool, Lesa G, registered nurse - clin opers, $63,084
Clayton, Geraldine, nursing consult, $28,375
Clayton, Terry E, special educ tchr III, $45,156
Claywell, Andrew T, registered nurse sr, $59,645
Cleaveland, Machelle, licensed clin soc wkr, $51,096
Clement, Patty A, acct II, $41,172
Clemon, Jacqueline, psychiatric technician I, $23,352
Clemons, Charlean G, deval asst I, $27,252

Clemons, Danesha S, deval asst I, $22,092
Clemons, Jewel R, direct care aide, $11,140
Clemons, Jewel R, motor veh driver, $35,013
Clemons, Shaquilla L, psychiatric technician I, $22,728
Clervi, Eugene A, licensed clin soc wkr, $48,156
Click, Valda Y, security aide I psy, $30,276
Clifford, Kathye A, psychiatric technician II, $27,252
Clifton, Chad E, storekeeper I, $25,032
Cline, Tina M, registered nurse sup, $63,934
Clinton, Joseph W, custodial worker II, $23,613
Clopper, Stephanie D, activity aide III, $31,080
Clopper, Terry A, security ofcr III, $35,568
Clymer, Maricel S, custodial worker I, $20,148
Coats, Travis D, security aide I psy, $32,244
Cobb, Ella J, reimbursement ofcr I, $29,976
Coburn, Shannon L, deval asst I, $22,728
Cochran, Charity K, deval asst I, $22,728
Cochran, Dawn E, vendor servs coor mh, $40,380
Cochran, Ramona D, psychiatric technician I, $23,412
Coe, Mechelle R, childrens psy care spv, $27,504
Coen, Sara E, sr ofc spt asst (keybrd), $25,824
Coffee, Phyllis D, deval asst I, $23,772
Coffel, Cynthia M, psychiatric technician II, $25,428
Coffelt, Brandy N, exec I, $30,984
Coffelt, Jessica K, clin casework pract II, $37,548
Coffelt, Tina M, case mgr III dd, $41,172
Coffey, Gail L, ofc spt asst (steno), $27,084
Coffin, Amanda E, librarian I, $29,976
Cofield, Hilda S, subs abuse cnslr II, $38,232
Coggins, Joshua W, deval asst I, $23,352
Cogshell, Willie J, security aide I psy, $31,152
Cohen, Lorna, deval asst I, $23,352
Cohen, Shawna E, deval asst II, $27,252
Coil, Holly, hospital mgmt asst, $57,744
Coker, Amy M, investigator I, $41,940
Colborn, Stephanie A, deval asst I, $23,352
Cole, Aaron J, security aide I psy, $36,324
Cole, Curstie C, deval asst I, $22,728
Cole, Jamal A, security aide I psy, $31,620
Cole, Jamel M, deval asst I, $22,404
Cole, James A, direct care aide, $16.33/hr
Cole, Jennifer J, sr ofc spt asst (keybrd), $25,824
Cole, Julie, recrtnal ther II, $42,708
Cole, Kathryn A, deval asst II, $25,584
Cole, Leslie T, security aide I psy, $30,276
Cole, Marylynn M, recrtnal ther I, $32,628
Cole, Natalie E, food serv helper I, $20,664
Cole, Raymond Q, deval asst I, $26,004
Cole, Rodney, food serv helper II, $24,264
Cole, Ruth A, food serv helper I, $20,664
Cole, Sheena, deval asst I, $22,728
Cole, Shonte, deval asst I, $22,728
Cole, Stephen N, deval asst I, $22,728
Cole, Tequila, deval asst I, $22,728
Cole, Valerie L, speech-language pathlgy ast II, $39,624
Coleman, Alan D, deval asst I, $27,468
Coleman, Amy R, sr ofc spt asst (keybrd), $25,032
Coleman, Betty A, admin ofc spt asst, $33,744
Coleman, Brittany N, food serv helper I, $21,760
Coleman, Candace L, deval asst I, $23,352
Coleman, Donnie R, childrens psy care spv, $27,504
Coleman, Etienna, deval asst I, $23,352
Coleman, Ian P, psychiatric technician I, $23,352
Coleman, Miranda M, supply mgr I, $32,628
Coleman, Reve J, registered nurse mgr b1, $67,104
Coleman, Rhonda L, deval asst I, $23,352
Coleman, Sherniece, deval asst II, $24,804
Coley, Vanessa S, registered nurse, $28,375
Colley, Fred T, deval asst I, $23,352
Collier, Ashley M, deval asst I, $22,728
Collier, Cynthia D, psychiatric technician I, $22,728
Collier, Effinan U, hlth prog spec, $15,600
Collier, Lora A, security aide I psy, $30,276
Collier, Sherrie D, ofc spt asst (clerical), $22,536
Colling, Patricia A, admin ofc spt asst, $34,356
Collins, Brittany R, deval asst I, $22,728
Collins, Diana, deval asst I, $26,628
Collins, Jennie B, deval asst I, $26,400
Collins, Kala, deval asst I, $22,716

Collins, Linda F, psychiatric technician I, $23,412
Collins, M D, sr ofc spt asst (keybrd), $25,824
Collins, Mallarie P, psychiatric technician I, $22,716
Collins, Sonja L, registered nurse, $50,244
Collins, Tarren D, security aide I psy, $29,208
Collins, Yolanda A, mental hlth mgr b1, $56,055
Colloton, Cassie, habilitation spec II, $34,944
Colston, Ardella, hospital mgmt asst, $61,332
Colwick, Rachel I, licensed prof cnslr I, $36,204
Combs, Antonio, deval asst I, $23,352
Combs, Jessica N, dining room spv, $25,790
Combs, Michaila A, misc tech, $11,965
Compton, Stephanie J, psychiatric technician I, $22,728
Comstock, Charles, misc tech, $14,678
Conder, Jennifer A, lpn II gen, $38,022
Conkle, Taye, registered nurse, $36,083
Conklin, Jennifer M, food serv helper I, $20,664
Conklin, Larry D, custodial worker I, $20,664
Conley, Julia M, reimbursement ofcr I, $29,976
Conn, Kelly R, registered nurse sr, $51,552
Connell, Bryan C, fiscal & administrative mgr b2, $49,104
Connelly, Kevin, deval asst I, $23,352
Conner, Marie T, hlth care practnr(aprn)(pa), $74,040
Conners, Thelma R, security aide I psy, $30,276
Connor, Malisha L, food serv helper I, $20,148
Connors, Patricia A, behavior intvtn tech dd, $34,968
Contreras, Andrea L, psychiatric technician I, $23,352
Conway, Laura L, recrtnal ther II, $44,304
Conway, Sarah K, dev dis cmnty worker II, $34,944
Cooey, James M, deval asst I, $22,728
Cook, Chris A, security aide I psy, $31,620
Cook, Jennifer L, case mgr I dd, $31,512
Cook, Julie A, psychiatric technician I, $23,352
Cook, Julie A, sr ofc spt asst (keybrd), $25,824
Cook, Katelynn R, deval asst I, $22,728
Cook, Kimberly R, security aide I psy, $31,620
Cook, Maeve E, deval asst I, $23,028
Cook, Terri J, sr ofc spt asst (keybrd), $26,232
Cook, Timothy A, security aide II psy, $32,208
Cook, Wayne M, security aide I psy, $29,652
Cook, Wynetta D, training tech II, $40,380
Cooke, Stephen L, registered nurse sup, $71,947
Cookson, Trina L, mental hlth mgr b1, $52,093
Cooley, Charlotte, cook II, $25,824
Coones, Lori A, asst center dir admin, $61,332
Cooper, Alexandra J, dietitian I, $41,172
Cooper, Cary, work therapy spec II, $35,568
Cooper, Cheryl D, deval asst I, $22,404
Cooper, Edwin A, affordable housing cnslt mh, $55,416
Cooper, Jackie C, psychiatric technician II, $26,400
Cooper, Jason R, deval asst I, $22,728
Cooper, Jody, psychiatric technician I, $24,072
Cooper, Katrina, deval asst I, $23,352
Cooper, Kimberly, lpn II gen, $39,780
Cooper, Linda D, lpn II gen, $30,396
Cooper, Lisa A, psychiatric technician I, $23,352
Cooper, Matthew N, deval asst I, $23,352
Cooper, Nicole R, psychiatric technician I, $24,696
Cooper, Phyllis I, security aide II psy, $35,076
Cooper, Rita M, habilitation spv, $51,096
Cooper, Sharon, deval asst I, $23,352
Cope, James M, behavior intvtn tech dd, $31,080
Copeland, Amy M, affordable housing cnslt mh, $55,416
Copeland, Karen S, case mgr II dd, $34,944
Copeland, Lora L, dev dis cmnty spec, $36,204
Corbin, Leisa A, deval asst II, $29,208
Cordell, Stacey L, security aide I psy, $30,276
Cordray, Terri M, registered nurse mgr b2, $75,880
Cordrey, Katrina, security aide I psy, $31,152
Corkery, Christine A, case mgr II dd, $34,944
Cornell, Lee E, lpn II gen, $39,780
Cornine, Brittany N, deval asst I, $23,028
Cornine, Kelly S, deval asst I, $26,844
Corona, Jessica S, deval asst I, $22,728
Corp, Jennifer M, ofc spt asst (keybrd), $25,824
Corradino, Daniel O, security aide I psy, $29,652
Cortez, Linda, psychiatric technician I, $22,092
Corum, Diana M, acct I, $36,888
Corum, Ginger A, registered nurse sr, $63,585

Corwin, Mary J, assoc counsel, $59,085
Coskrey, Clarence W, food serv mgr I, $40,380
Coslet, David D, crpntr, $31,512
Cott, Lawrence S, direct care aide, $11,246
Cotter, Jared, deval asst I, $23,352
Cotton, Jeffrey D, mental hlth mgr b1, $52,093
Cotton, Latonya, custodial worker I, $20,664
Coughlin, Cynthia L, acct I, $30,984
Council, Maury R, registered nurse sr, $60,184
Countess, Michelle R, deval asst I, $22,728
Countess, Winifred M, deval asst I, $22,404
Counts, Chastity L, registered nurse, $54,720
Counts, Jeremy D, security aide I psy, $30,276
Coupland, Audrey, registered nurse, $36,029
Courter-Caldwell, Lisa D, habilitation spec II, $37,548
Courtney, Gregory P, security aide I psy, $29,652
Courtway, April R, registered nurse, $17,166
Courtway, Todd M, security ofcr I, $25,824
Cousett, Iesha, deval asst I, $23,352
Cousett, Mia, deval asst I, $23,412
Cove, Jeremy R, lpn II gen, $39,331
Cove, Sahra R, psychiatric technician I, $22,728
Cowhick, Lisa M, deval asst I, $25,428
Cowins, Joann, psychiatric technician I, $26,628
Cowper, Michael L, deval asst I, $22,728
Cox, Allison L, dev dis cmnty prog coord, $38,928
Cox, Caleb V, deval asst I, $22,716
Cox, Glenda C, deval asst II, $25,416
Cox, Jordan V, clin casework pract I, $35,568
Cox, Marie, asst center dir admin, $58,908
Cox, Mario L, deval asst I, $23,352
Cox, Stephanie, deval asst II, $24,072
Cox, Teresa A, psychiatric technician I, $23,352
Cox, Tonya R, deval asst I, $25,584
Coy, Tana E, habilitation spec II, $40,380
Crabb, Carissa J, licensed clin soc wkr, $46,068
Crabb, Jason A, recrtnal ther I, $36,204
Crabbe, Ralph J, psychological resident, $41,172
Crabdree, Anthony M, security aide II psy, $33,384
Crabdree, Ernest M, acad tchr III, $46,934
Crabill, Brendon S, security aide I psy, $31,152
Crable, Fatina L, deval asst I, $23,412
Craddock, Kyle V, deval asst II, $25,428
Craddock, Tyler E, psychiatric technician I, $23,352
Crader, Jennifer M, psychiatric technician I, $23,352
Crader, Tabatha S, custodial worker I, $22,317
Craft, Brandon V, psychiatric technician I, $22,728
Craft, Frances A, sr ofc spt asst (keybrd), $25,824
Crahan, Dorothy K, acct I, $36,888
Craig, Angela R, deval asst I, $23,352
Craig, George T, security aide II psy, $33,312
Craig, Judith K, case mgr III dd, $37,548
Craig, Margaret A, psychiatric technician I, $22,728
Craighead, Deborah L, behavioral technician, $27,696
Craighead, James L, security aide I psy, $31,620
Craighead, John L, security ofcr I, $25,824
Craighead, Vicki L, typist, $14,206
Craw, Dawn A, sr ofc spt asst (keybrd), $25,824
Crawford, Amy C, security aide I psy, $29,652
Crawford, Bobbi J, storekeeper I, $25,824
Crawford, Brandol C, deval asst II, $28,320
Crawford, Carlyn B, lpn II gen, $29,772
Crawford, Chester T, custodial worker I, $25,032
Crawford, Darielle D, psychiatric technician I, $23,352
Crawford, Darla A, registered nurse sup, $67,104
Crawford, Debbie A, registered nurse sr, $67,401
Crawford, Lutecia J, custodial worker I, $24,264
Crawford, Nancy S, mental hlth mgr b1, $53,202
Crawford, Starwyn M, case mgr III dd, $41,172
Crawford, Tara S, prog spec II mh, $48,156
Crawford, Uvetta R, clerk, $10,926
Crawford-Stephens, Samantha A, security ofcr, $12,353
Crawley, Arthur W, food serv helper I, $20,664
Crawley, Shantail M, psychiatric technician I, $22,728
Crenshaw, Lakeisha M, registered nurse sup, $71,448
Crews, Annette S, ofc spt asst (keybrd), $23,160
Crews, Kristen M, dietitian II, $46,932
Crews, Tammy J, deval asst I, $26,400
Cribb, Jean, acct I, $30,984

Crice, Jeremy L, security aide I psy, $29,652
Crider, Sara A, ofc spt asst (keybrd), $25,404
Crisp, Brian A, security ofcr II, $30,984
Crisp, Latonya C, registered nurse, $28,375
Crisp, Margaret A, registered nurse sup, $55,776
Crist, Jacqueline K, dev dis cmnty prog coord, $43,488
Crist, Laura M, mental hlth mgr b2, $63,723
Criswell, George T, security aide I psy, $29,652
Criswell, James D, ofc spt asst (keybrd), $22,536
Crites, Kadie E, registered nurse, $54,720
Crites, Misty V, ofc spt asst (keybrd), $22,536
Crites, Nicholas A, activity aide II, $27,780
Crocker, Barbara A, psychiatric technician I, $23,352
Crocker, Davey L, psychiatric technician I, $22,728
Croft, Leanthony, food serv helper I, $20,664
Cromwell, Ellian, psychiatric technician I, $25,428
Croney, Belva L, lpn I gen, $30,840
Cronk, Kassie L, recrtnal ther II, $36,888
Crosby, Sherita, ofc spt asst (keybrd), $25,032
Cross, Candace S, lpn, $35,736
Cross, Donald S, deval asst II, $26,608
Cross, Matthew D, psychologist I, $62,664
Cross, Neal E, deval asst I, $22,728
Cross, Roosevelt A, deval asst I, $22,728
Cross, Trenita M, ofc spt asst (keybrd), $23,880
Crossland, Julie, deval asst I, $24,804
Crouse-Johnson, Diana L, dev dis cmnty prog coord, $39,624
Crow, Miles C, deval asst II, $25,584
Crowder, Marshaundra, deval asst I, $23,352
Crowell, Brittany R, student intern, $20,936
Crowther, Donna J, clin soc work spec, $49,128
Crowther, Kathryn E, work therapy spec I, $24,612
Cruise, Heidi G, qual assurance spec mh, $43,488
Crum, Jesse L, prog spec II mh, $50,040
Crumby, Penny S, sr ofc spt asst (keybrd), $30,924
Crump, Melissa E, security aide I psy, $30,276
Crutchfield, Darlene L, lpn II gen, $30,216
Cruzen, Donna M, registered nurse sr, $55,360
Culver, Laura C, activity aide II, $26,844
Cummings, Audria C, deval asst II, $29,568
Cummings, Carmen L, registered nurse sr, $55,891
Cummings, Dena E, account clerk II, $25,824
Cummings, Jennifer, deval asst I, $23,352
Cundiff, Bridget A, security aide I psy, $31,620
Cundiff, Rita F, pers analyst II, $46,932
Cunningham, Barbara E, sr ofc spt asst (clerical), $25,824
Cunningham, Darlene D, registered nurse sr, $55,776
Cunningham, Etta M, deval asst I, $22,716
Cunningham, James D, human rel ofcr II, $44,304
Cunningham, Jeffrey W, psychiatric technician II, $26,208
Cunningham, Karla L, sr ofc spt asst (keybrd), $27,084
Curdt, Gregory D, security aide I psy, $32,244
Curdt, Henry J, psychiatric technician I, $23,352
Curdt, Kimberly F, pers clerk, $30,420
Cureton, Brent E, security aide I psy, $30,276
Curlett, Robert E, psychiatric technician I, $25,416
Curran, George D, supply mgr II, $36,888
Curran, Melissa M, psychiatric technician I, $23,352
Current, Cheryl L, deval asst III, $29,904
Current, Gail A, activity therapy coor, $62,664
Currier, Kathryn E, misc prof, $18,020
Curry, Ebonee L, deval asst I, $23,412
Curry, Kierra S, hlth info tech I, $36,204
Curry, Mary L, lpn II gen, $32,841
Curry, Neal P, deval asst II, $25,428
Curtis, Alicia M, security aide I psy, $31,620
Curtis, Andrea C, ofc spt asst (clerical), $22,536
Curtis, Ashley N, deval asst I, $22,728
Curtis, Craig A, activity aide III, $29,568
Cushshon, Shanorya T, deval asst I, $23,352
Cutts, Dionne M, registered nurse sr, $65,676
Daago, Elizabeth D, security aide II psy, $32,832
Dachs, Jennie A, habilitation spec II, $34,944
Dachs, Jimmy D, habilitation spec II, $37,548
Dady, Brenda M, habilitation spec II, $38,232
Dahmer, Donna C, registered nurse sr, $51,276
Dai, Weiping, registered nurse, $56,424
Dailey, David, deval asst I, $22,728
Dailey, Paula M, food serv helper I, $22,317

Dale, Alexandria D, ofc worker misc, $22,200
Dale, Dajah L, security aide I psy, $29,652
Dallas, Jessica A, misc prof, $22,647
Dalton, Andrea C, registered nurse, $28,375
Dalton, Deborah S, registered nurse sr, $51,552
Dambacher, Joyce A, ofc spt asst (clerical), $25,032
Dampier, Angel, deval asst I, $23,412
Dampier, Melvita, psychiatric technician I, $26,208
Danak, Shehnaaz S, licensed clin soc wkr, $48,156
Dancy, Chantel Y, registered nurse sr, $58,140
Dancy, Dakota T, psychiatric technician I, $23,412
Dandamudi, Babu R, consulting physician, $90,576
Dane, Tricia A, registered nurse sr, $54,720
Daniel, Celeste A, security aide I psy, $29,652
Daniel, Nathan, lpn II gen, $35,236
Daniel-Dim, Linda N, lpn, $16,470
Daniels, Ashley N, clin casework pract II, $47,892
Daniels, Vernette F, psychiatric technician I, $23,352
Dann, Chay A, security aide I psy, $30,276
Danner, James E, psychiatric technician I, $26,400
Dansberry, Tracy R, deval asst II, $28,776
Darby, Troy J, psychiatric technician I, $22,728
Darden Jr, Charles E, psychiatric technician I, $23,352
Darden, Sandra N, account clerk II, $26,232
Dark, Connie J, registered nurse sup, $74,556
Darling, Douglas B, clin casework pract II, $39,624
Darling, Tiana M, lpn II gen, $37,020
Darnall, Kelly J, hlth info admin II, $54,288
Darnel, Cindy M, acct I, $37,548
Darnell, Sherri L, food serv mgr II, $37,548
Daro, Catherine E, registered nurse mgr b2, $81,797
Darty, Ginger M, registered nurse, $34,653
Das, Jairam, staff physician spec, $205,648
Dashtaki, Zahra, subs abuse cnslr II, $42,708
Da-Silva, Manica, custodial worker I, $20,664
Daugherty, Amber L, assoc counsel, $55,000
Davenport, Alicia I, deval asst I, $22,728
Davidson, Amanda L, acct II, $38,928
Davidson, Anna L, psychiatric technician I, $22,728
Davidson, Douglas A, assoc psychologist II, $49,128
Davidson, Haley A, food serv helper I, $10,880
Davidson, Joseph W, dev dis cmnty worker II, $42,708
Davidson, Vicky D, mental hlth mgr b2, $77,176
Davie, Dena M, work therapy spec I, $27,948
Davie, Mykel S, security ofcr, $12,261
Davies, Rebecca F, security aide I psy, $33,912
Davis, Aaron S, psychiatric technician I, $24,036
Davis, Alisha D, deval asst I, $24,072
Davis, Amber D, clin casework pract II, $36,204
Davis, Angel L, deval asst I, $22,728
Davis, Angie S, deval asst I, $24,036
Davis, Arthur, deval asst I, $23,352
Davis, Bridgette, deval asst I, $23,076
Davis, Brittney G, food serv helper I, $20,664
Davis, Candyance T, security ofcr I, $25,824
Davis, Cathy J, registered nurse sr, $56,976
Davis, Crystal L, lpn II gen, $37,644
Davis, Cynthia, security ofcr I, $25,824
Davis, Dana R, deval asst I, $25,224
Davis, Dominique A, security aide I psy, $32,244
Davis, Donavon F, psychiatric technician I, $23,352
Davis, Doris F, deval asst I, $27,252
Davis, Doris G, deval asst I, $23,352
Davis, Duncan E, custodial worker I, $20,664
Davis, Emily J, registered nurse sup, $65,963
Davis, Erica A, qual assurance spec mh, $40,380
Davis, Gregory, deval asst I, $23,700
Davis, Gwendolyn G, sr ofc spt asst (keybrd), $26,232
Davis, Janine L, deval asst I, $26,004
Davis, Jannette C, psychiatric technician I, $23,352
Davis, Jatavia N, deval asst I, $23,352
Davis, Jeffrey L, deval asst I, $23,700
Davis, Jenecce F, ofc spt asst (keybrd), $23,160
Davis, Jodi D, case mgr I dd, $32,628
Davis, Joy E, psychiatric technician I, $23,352
Davis, Karen, case mgr III dd, $34,944
Davis, Kathleen, clin soc work spec, $54,288
Davis, Lashayla D, deval asst II, $25,428
Davis, Linda L, clerk, $33,036

Davis, Lisa A, deval asst I, $24,396
Davis, Lisa R, food serv helper I, $21,564
Davis, Mary S, deval asst I, $23,352
Davis, Melissa J, habilitation spec I, $33,744
Davis, Melody, pers clerk, $28,104
Davis, Mia A, deval asst I, $23,412
Davis, Mia G, psychiatric technician I, $23,412
Davis, Moriah L, psychiatric technician I, $22,728
Davis, Myron K, psychiatric technician I, $23,352
Davis, Nancy J, deval asst I, $22,728
Davis, Norman R, psychiatric technician I, $23,352
Davis, Ovella S, sr ofc spt asst (keybrd), $27,084
Davis, Rebekah S, security aide I psy, $29,652
Davis, Rita M, deval asst I, $22,728
Davis, Samantha N, custodial worker I, $20,664
Davis, Sandra G, qual assurance spec mh, $47,892
Davis, Sara A, psychiatric technician I, $23,352
Davis, Sarah J, deval asst I, $22,728
Davis, Shawn W, deval asst I, $23,412
Davis, Steven J, security aide I psy, $29,832
Davis, Suzanne, registered nurse sup, $71,478
Davis, Tammera K, dev dis cmnty spec, $36,204
Davis, Tasha R, sr ofc spt asst (keybrd), $27,948
Davis, Tekhirhy D, deval asst I, $23,352
Davis, Tina L, case mgr III dd, $37,548
Davis, Tyra, deval asst I, $23,352
Davis, Wendy D, special asst official & admstr, $83,325
Dawdy, Britni E, registered nurse sr, $55,361
Dawson, Kimberly M, security ofcr, $25,824
Dawson, Martha B, mental hlth mgr b2, $67,695
Day, Alvera D, childrens psy care spv, $26,652
Day, Dakota J, psychiatric technician I, $22,728
Day, Dana R, med spec II, $134,592
Day, Destiny R, deval asst I, $22,728
Day, Lori D, security aide I psy, $30,276
De Klein, Johan A, deval asst I, $23,352
De Martino, Margaret M, dietitian II, $22,152
Dean, Bobbie L, deval asst I, $22,728
Dean, Corneice, deval asst I, $23,700
Debose, Lois J, deval asst I, $24,036
Debrodie, Jennifer R, security aide I psy, $31,152
Deckard, Anita M, registered nurse sr, $56,192
Deckard, Carl J, deval asst I, $23,352
Decker, Jennifer M, security aide I psy, $31,620
Decker, Patricia A, acct I, $30,984
Declue, Hazel R, security aide I psy, $29,652
Dedman, Stuart W, habilitation spec II, $34,944
Deen, Unusa, security aide I psy, $31,620
Deforest, David S, occup ther II, $61,332
Degaris, John R, deval asst I, $23,352
Degaris, Pamela A, food serv helper I, $20,664
Degonia, Martha A, registered nurse - clin opers, $60,516
Degrant, Daeton H, cnslr in training, $33,744
Degroat, Leslie D, registered nurse - clin opers, $55,776
Dehaven, Joe' M, unit prog spv mh, $45,156
Delaney, Clarice M, food serv helper I, $20,664
Delaney, Gail, special educ tchr II, $48,156
Delia, Donna, licensed behavior analyst, $66,720
Dellenbaugh, Timothy, staff physician spec, $213,962
Dement, Barbara E, custodial worker I, $20,664
Demetrius, Kerry Ann N, security aide I psy, $31,620
Demis, Teresa A, admin ofc spt asst, $33,180
Denish, Lisa V, registered nurse sr, $56,976
Denlow, Ruth, occup ther II, $60,054
Dennis, Felicia A, deval asst I, $23,412
Dennis, Julian, deval asst I, $22,728
Dennis, Kristi L, registered nurse sr, $56,193
Dennis, Robert B, deval asst I, $22,404
Dennis-Castro, Yolanda M, case mgr II dd, $34,944
Dennison, Christine R, reimbursement ofcr I, $30,420
Denson, Angela, custodial worker I, $21,864
Denver, Kay A, tchr, $51,650
Deppeler, Kathleen E, habilitation spec II, $35,568
Depriest, Susan S, account clerk II, $27,948
Derboven, Tammy, acct II, $37,548
Derouchie, Kim M, registered nurse sup, $70,170
Deshay, Carlos M, deval asst I, $22,728
Despain, Jessica L, psychiatric technician I, $22,728
Despain, Penny G, sr ofc spt asst (keybrd), $25,824

Detienne, Geneva S, lpn II gen, $38,014
Detrempe, Russel H, mental hlth mgr b1, $65,358
Deville, Sherry L, security aide I psy, $32,244
Dewey, Jacee B, psychiatric technician I, $22,092
Dewitt, Donald E, account clerk II, $25,824
Dewitt, Tami M, deval asst II, $28,152
Dia, Alassane, cook II, $23,880
Diamond, Andra K, psychiatric technician I, $23,352
Dibiaso, Heidi K, special asst ofc & clerical, $54,663
Dickerson, Deanna R, licensed clin soc wkr, $47,892
Dickerson, Dorothy C, habilitation spv, $38,928
Dickerson, Francine P, lpn II gen, $37,020
Dickerson, Jennifer H, sr ofc spt asst (keybrd), $28,908
Dickerson, Joseph M, registered nurse sr, $61,451
Dickerson, Ronald D, custodial worker I, $22,317
Dickerson Crabtree, Jeanne M, custodial worker I, $22,200
Dickey, Becky, clerk, $10.30/hr
Dickey, O A, registered nurse sr, $51,276
Dickneite, Carol A, special asst ofc & clerical, $40,211
Dickson, Richard J, security ofcr I, $25,824
Dieckmann, Janet V, deval asst I, $22,728
Dilbeck, Kevin K, mental hlth mgr b1, $52,093
Dillard, Jacqueline M, custodial worker I, $20,664
Dillard, Sandra K, deval asst I, $22,728
Dillon, Christine R, psychiatric technician I, $22,728
Dillon, Deann R, food serv mgr I, $29,976
Dimmett, Alaine R, sr ofc spt asst (keybrd), $29,904
Dinehart, Susan C, registered nurse sr, $63,084
Ditmer, Bridgette A, deval asst I, $23,352
Dittmer, John M, deval asst I, $22,728
Divine, Allison, clin casework pract I, $34,944
Dixon, Carolyn, deval asst II, $28,152
Dixon, Jennifer L, ofc spt asst (keybrd), $25,404
Dixon, Karen R, account clerk II, $25,824
Dixon, Kimberly A, deval asst III, $29,412
Dixon, Tammy T, registered nurse sup, $95,478
Dixon, Teneisha, deval asst I, $23,352
Dixon-White, Sonja, deval asst I, $23,352
Dixson, Patrice M, deval asst I, $27,024
Djona, Mary, deval asst I, $23,352
Dobbins, Ashlie D, case mgr II dd, $34,944
Dobbs, Patricia A, sr ofc spt asst (keybrd), $25,824
Dodds, Mark L, security ofcr I, $27,084
Dodge, Margo M, deval asst I, $23,352
Dodolewa, Okonmiyo E, deval asst I, $23,412
Doebelin, Sharon J, ofc spt asst (keybrd), $24,612
Doersam, John E, security ofcr I, $28,452
Doherty, Cynthia A, case mgr II dd, $20,966
Dohogne, Philip T, edual aide, $10,154
Doisy, Richard P, med spec II, $140,110
Dollar, Rebecca L, case mgr III dd, $37,548
Dollins, Michael L, deval asst I, $23,352
Donald, Gloria A, deval asst III, $35,472
Donald, Willie J, deval asst II, $29,676
Donaldson, Judith A, security aide II psy, $32,832
Donaldson, Kim E, ofc worker misc, $15,441
Donelson, Barbara J, direct care aide, $8,850
Donovan, Nancy E, dev dis cmnty prog coord, $43,488
Donovan, Whitney, lpn II gen, $37,020
Donre, Radson, deval asst I, $24,036
Donson, Antoine, psychiatric technician I, $22,728
Donzo, Fatu A, deval asst I, $22,728
Dooley, Christina J, acct I, $30,984
Dooley, Tena K, sr ofc spt asst (keybrd), $25,824
Dore, Denise, registered nurse sr, $54,720
Dormuth, Barbara E, stores clerk, $25,824
Dorsey, Debra J, deval asst I, $22,728
Dorsey, Ruby L, psychiatric technician I, $22,728
Doss, Kenneth, activity aide II, $25,584
Doss, Shaunessy E, deval asst I, $23,352
Doss, Valerie A, security aide II psy, $31,776
Dotson, Karla M, exec I, $38,928
Dotson, Mark L, security aide I psy, $30,276
Dotson, Melanie D, registered nurse, $45,427
Doty, Theresa G, sr ofc spt asst (keybrd), $25,824
Dougherty, Linda M, activity aide II, $25,584
Douglas, Connie A, ofc spt asst (clerical), $22,536
Douglas, Cristal K, cook I, $21,864
Douglas, Janet E, account clerk II, $25,824

Douglas, Susan J, reimbursement ofcr I, $32,628
Douthit, Alice, deval asst I, $22,716
Dove, Marissa E, direct care aide, $535
Dover, Kathryn T, lpn II gen, $29,772
Dow, Timothy W, sr ofc spt asst (keybrd), $26,232
Dowd, Eddie R, psychiatric technician II, $25,428
Dowdy, Melissa K, ofc spt asst (keybrd), $23,880
Downard, Brandon L, lpn II gen, $40,648
Downs, Anthony C, psychiatric technician I, $23,352
Downs, Brenda K, deval asst I, $24,036
Downs, James E, deval asst I, $22,728
Downs, Jeremy W, deval asst I, $24,036
Downum, Ronda L, deval asst I, $23,352
Doyle, Cheri L, ofc spt asst (keybrd), $23,160
Doyle, Daniel D, deval asst I, $24,036
Doyle, Kelly F, deval asst I, $23,700
Doyle, Mary C, dev dis cmnty worker II, $36,204
Draffen, Joyce L, habilitation spec II, $38,232
Drake, Matthew A, case mgr II dd, $34,944
Drake, Richard D, deval asst I, $24,804
Dreher, Jessica D, psychiatric technician I, $24,072
Dreiman, Kimberly D, dev dis cmnty prog coord, $40,380
Drexelius, Anna M, music ther II, $36,204
Dreyer, Sandra L, nutrition/dietary svcs mgr b1, $58,905
Driggs, Lee A, deval asst III, $28,908
Drinkard, Jennifer J, ofc spt asst (keybrd), $23,880
Driskell, Catherine, psychiatric technician II, $25,428
Driver, Mary L, deval asst I, $23,352
Drumheller, Amber R, psychiatric technician I, $22,728
Drusch, Gerald S, reimbursement ofcr I, $32,628
Dryden, Jill E, security aide I psy, $31,620
Drye, Sherry K, registered nurse sr, $61,451
D'Souza, Mario E, case mgr II dd, $34,944
Dubose, Carl, resident physician, $51,318
Duckett, Pamela S, acct II, $49,128
Dudenhoeffer, Steven E, security aide I psy, $29,652
Dudley, William L, motor veh driver, $27,948
Duelley, Natasha R, deval asst I, $22,404
Duffy, Dani R, deval asst I, $23,412
Dugan-Wilson, Samantha R, psychological resident, $35,972
Duggal, Neeta, resident physician, $52,995
Duggan, Colin A, psychologist I, $68,160
Dugger, Tonia E, food serv helper II, $23,613
Dukovich, Eugenia D, psychiatric technician II, $28,152
Dumas, Kim R, psychiatric technician II, $29,747
Dumeh, Gertrude, security aide I psy, $31,152
Dummerth, Melinda G, prog spec trainee mh, $36,888
Dunbar, Carletta E, deval asst I, $24,036
Duncan, Bryan D, prog spec I mh, $38,928
Duncan, Carmin D, deval asst III, $27,504
Duncan, Connie J, habilitation spv, $43,488
Duncan, Joell D, mental hlth mgr b2, $64,790
Duncan, Joy R, ofc spt asst (keybrd), $23,160
Duncan, Mary E, deval asst I, $23,412
Dunfield, Wanda S, custodial worker I, $23,508
Dunham, Katrina C, registered nurse, $28,375
Dunkle, Elbert L, deval asst I, $24,804
Dunkle, Kalli L, deval asst I, $22,728
Dunkle, Tiffany M, deval asst I, $22,728
Dunlap, Amanda R, cook III, $28,104
Dunlap, Angel L, licensed behavior analyst, $66,720
Dunlap, Carol A, deval asst I, $26,004
Dunlap, David R, psychiatric technician I, $23,352
Dunlap, India, psychiatric technician I, $23,352
Dunlap, Tonya N, sr ofc spt asst (keybrd), $25,824
Dunlap, Wanda M, lpn II gen, $40,648
Dunn, Candice R, prog coord dmh dohss, $51,096
Dunn, Christopher A, security aide I psy, $31,152
Dunn, Debby L, registered nurse sr, $56,526
Dunn, Derrick D, psychiatric technician I, $23,352
Dunn, Jeffrey L, misc tech, $20,467
Dunn, Linda, registered nurse - clin opers, $74,556
Dunn, Reginald M, thrpst, $41,787
Dunscombe, Marilyn K, deval asst I, $22,728
Dupree, Brenda M, deval asst I, $23,352
Dupree, Dashaun S, psychiatric technician I, $24,696
Dupree, Misha M, deval asst I, $22,728
Duran, Angela, psychiatric technician I, $23,352
Duran, Cheryl L, security aide I psy, $29,832

Durbin, Ingrid R, registered nurse sr, $53,592
Durham, Glenda J, custodial worker I, $20,664
Durham, Kenneth A, security aide I psy, $31,620
Durham, Zoaca N, case mgr II dd, $34,944
Durigano, Christine M, security aide II psy, $34,488
Durigano, Felicia R, security aide I psy, $30,276
Durman, Sheila L, deval asst I, $23,352
Duron, Kelly M, psychologist I, $62,664
Durr, Ashley A, storekeeper I, $25,824
Dusheke, Tricia L, special asst ofc & clerical, $47,392
Duzan, Becky K, clerk, $10,930
Dyas, Elena C, deval asst I, $23,352
Dye, Lavonda I, deval asst I, $23,412
Dye, Vicki L, admin ofc spt asst, $28,552
Dykas, Thomas E, misc tech, $10,926
Dysart, Vivian J, deval asst I, $23,352
Eanes, Mesha Y, cook III, $32,052
Earl, Michael A, laborer II, $35,877
Earnst, Agnes C, security aide I psy, $30,660
Earvin, Angelic, deval asst I, $23,412
Easley, Zamika M, deval asst I, $23,352
Eason, Alfred T, mental hlth mgr b2, $67,695
Eason, Dorothy, custodial worker I, $20,664
Eason, Lynne, psychologist II, $69,612
Eason, Tidia, case mgmt/assess spv, $40,380
Easter, David L, security aide I psy, $29,652
Easter, David L, security aide I psy, $29,652
Easter, Joseph L, registered nurse mgr b1, $69,660
Easter, Julia L, security aide I psy, $29,652
Easter, Lesley A, activity aide II, $27,780
Easter, Ronald A, fiscal & administrative mgr b1, $58,900
Eastin, Lorena K, habilitation spec II, $38,928
Eastin, Zachary D, deval asst I, $22,728
Eastman, Elizabeth K, speech-language pathologist, $57,744
Eaton, A C, ofc spt asst (steno), $27,084
Eaton, Joan L, psychiatric technician II, $26,208
Eaton, Marsha L, deval asst I, $24,072
Eaves, Michelle M, psychiatric technician II, $26,208
Eberle, Susan R, dev dis cmnty worker II, $40,380
Ebersole, John K, research analyst III, $41,940
Ebling, Bernice L, lpn II gen, $32,844
Eckert, Lora J, registered nurse sr, $57,893
Eckhoff, Steven M, psychiatric technician I, $23,352
Eddins, Keisha A, deval asst II, $28,584
Eddy, Stephanie M, clin casework pract II, $37,548
Edegbe, Felicia, registered nurse sr, $60,796
Edeki, Stanley O, psychiatric technician I, $23,412
Edelen, Ami M, security aide II psy, $32,832
Edenburn, Joanna D, case mgr II dd, $34,944
Edgar, Barbara E, lpn II gen, $40,024
Edgar, Evelyn R, security aide I psy, $29,652
Edgar, Nikki L, cook I, $10,932
Edgar, Tyler L, psychiatric technician II, $26,208
Edgar-Wells, Cara, pers analyst II, $38,928
Edorh, Dossah, deval asst I, $23,352
Edson, Traci L, prog spec I mh, $38,928
Edward, Alfons, deval asst I, $23,352
Edwards, Carmel, case mgr II dd, $34,944
Edwards, Danielle M, psychiatric technician I, $22,728
Edwards, Elizabeth A, custodial worker I, $20,664
Edwards, Essie, deval asst I, $23,700
Edwards, Georganne A, med technologist II, $41,940
Edwards, Hollie K, security aide I psy, $31,620
Edwards, Melanie M, security aide I psy, $31,152
Edwards, Michael L, security aide I psy, $31,620
Edwards, Sandra E, security aide I psy, $30,276
Edwards, Steffani A, food serv helper I, $20,664
Edwards, Tyler J, psychiatric technician I, $22,728
Edwards, Waylon D, case mgr II dd, $34,944
Eftink, Crystal D, psychiatric technician I, $22,728
Egan, Lewis J, deval asst I, $23,352
Egbuniwe, Ebele, lpn, $16,470
Eggen, Cassandra K, security aide I psy, $32,244
Eiberger, Evangeline R, registered nurse, $27,794
Eichholz, Brian, cook I, $21,864
Eichholz, Randolph R, training tech II, $40,380
Eilts-Carothers, Natasha A, psychiatric technician I, $22,728
Eirls, Debbie A, registered nurse sr, $62,104
Eischeid, Joseph J, deval asst I, $22,728

Eisterhold, Heather R, principal asst board/commisson, $35,562
Ekeanya, Nora, resident physician, $51,318
Ekenwa, Sunday H, lpn, $16,470
Ekong, Enoabasi E, psychiatric technician I, $26,004
Elayer, Nan L, dev dis cmnty prog coord, $38,928
Elbert, Eddie, security ofcr I, $25,824
Elhosseiny, Ahmed M, psychiatric technician I, $24,024
Elijah, Lena M, deval asst I, $25,428
Elkins, David E, security ofcr I, $25,824
Elkins, David L, security aide I psy, $31,620
Elledge, Kelly R, case mgr III dd, $40,380
Ellermann, Shannon K, security aide I psy, $29,208
Ellermann, Stacy L, licensed clin soc wkr, $50,040
Elliff, Christine M, custodial worker I, $21,760
Ellifritz, Melissa R, psychiatric technician I, $22,092
Ellingsworth, Robert, housekeeper II, $44,304
Elliott, Johnny, security ofcr I, $25,824
Elliott, Johnny, direct care aide, $15.97/hr
Elliott, Patty J, deval asst III, $26,652
Elliott, Stacy, fire & safety spec, $20,582
Ellis, Asheldra, psychiatric technician I, $23,352
Ellis, Barbara J, security aide II psy, $34,488
Ellis, Carrie, ofc spt asst (keybrd), $23,880
Ellis, Dennis L, security aide I psy, $30,276
Ellis, Erica, psychiatric technician I, $25,428
Ellis, Jeffrey L, security aide I psy, $31,620
Ellis, Kaleathia I, deval asst I, $22,728
Ellis, Lisa F, mental hlth mgr b3, $72,311
Ellis, Patrice C, deval asst I, $23,352
Ellis, Tammy L, deval asst I, $23,076
Elmore, Carol A, sr ofc spt asst (keybrd), $25,824
Elmore, Jason P, dev dis cmnty spec, $36,888
Elmore, Jewel M, deval asst I, $26,004
Elmore-Lewis, Patricia A, ofc spt asst (clerical), $22,536
El-Ruwie, Nezar A, staff physician spec, $221,301
Elsea, Roger, reimbursement ofcr III, $41,172
Elser, Jordan S, psychiatric technician I, $23,352
Elson, Elizabeth A, sr ofc spt asst (steno), $30,384
Eltahir, Amged, staff physician, $105,290
Elwell, Donald L, deval asst I, $23,352
Emanuel, Gloria A, sr ofc spt asst (keybrd), $29,904
Embree, Jo A, security aide I psy, $29,652
Embree, Whitney B, security aide I psy, $30,276
Engel, Susan J, ofc spt asst (keybrd), $25,404
Engel, Tiffany D, deval asst I, $24,804
Engelhard, Cindy, sr ofc spt asst (keybrd), $25,824
England, Thomas A, security ofcr I, $28,908
Englander, Kurt E, registered nurse sr, $62,104
Englehart, Jay W, staff physician spec, $252,500
English, Byron C, psychologist II, $71,100
English, Geraldine K, misc prof, $8,275
English, Tina M, security aide I psy, $30,660
Eniade, Janet A, registered nurse sr, $54,769
Enke, Teri L, special asst ofc & clerical, $40,211
Enochs, Julie A, security ofcr I, $27,228
Enochs, William R, resident physician, $50,005
Enriquez, Jessica L, deval asst I, $23,700
Enwemeka, Grace O, case mgr II dd, $34,944
Epperson, Adrianne D, security aide I psy, $30,276
Epperson, Tony B, registered nurse sr, $61,095
Epple, Laurie D, dpty div dir, $95,950
Epple, Vickie L, mental hlth mgr b1, $59,896
Epps, Martina C, clerical sup, $25,824
Erby, Pamela J, habilitation spec II, $34,944
Erickson, Jaclin P, deval asst I, $23,412
Erickson, Marla L, deval asst I, $23,412
Erkiletian, Linda L, mental hlth mgr b2, $57,338
Ernest, Alpery, deval asst I, $24,036
Ernest, Lisa A, case mgmt/assess spv, $49,128
Ervin, Jessica L, recrtnal ther I, $32,628
Erwin, Autumn R, activity aide II, $27,780
Erwin, Harold S, deval asst III, $26,856
Erwin, Shannon R, security aide II psy, $34,488
Eskew, April N, deval asst I, $22,716
Eskew, Pamela G, deval asst I, $24,036
Espinosa-Bratten, Mayra, registered nurse, $27,794.00/hr
Esry, Connie L, exec I, $41,940
Esser, Angela E, edual aide, $10,826
Esser, Jerri D, psychiatric technician I, $22,728

Essmyer, Robin C, security aide I psy, $29,652
Estomagulang, Marvin B, psychiatric technician I, $22,716
Etheridge, Joe A, security aide I psy, $31,152
Ethridge, Jack C, deval asst I, $26,616
Ethridge, Jennifer M, deval asst I, $23,352
Etoh, Joseph C, security aide I psy, $30,276
Etoh, Maureen C, security aide I psy, $30,276
Etuk, Idongesit, deval asst I, $23,352
Evans, Amy M, dev dis cmnty spec, $38,232
Evans, Brenda L, security aide II psy, $35,112
Evans, Bruce A, custodial worker I, $20,148
Evans, Deborah S, acct I, $32,628
Evans, Diane, custodial worker I, $22,872
Evans, Donna E, dev dis cmnty worker II, $34,944
Evans, Evelyn L, deval asst I, $24,086
Evans, Ginger M, lpn II gen, $32,808
Evans, Ginger S, activity aide II, $25,584
Evans, Linda, psychiatric technician I, $24,696
Evans, Lucas J, behavioral technician, $27,696
Evans, Patricia R, deval asst I, $23,352
Evans, Rhiannon M, behavioral technician, $27,696
Evans, Richard A, registered nurse, $27,794
Evans, Samantha L, admin ofc spt asst, $28,104
Everett, Canda A, clin soc work spec, $44,304
Everett, Charissa R, deval asst I, $23,352
Everett, Julie, account clerk II, $27,084
Eversman, Kurt L, lpn II gen, $36,710
Eversman, Kyla, special asst prof, $79,285
Ewert, Lisa K, psychiatric technician I, $25,224
Ewharekuko, Omofodo, deval asst I, $22,716
Ewing, Melvin, laborer II, $23,160
Ewing, Stephanie L, deval asst II, $25,224
Eye, Karen L, security aide I psy, $30,276
Eye, Susan J, account clerk II, $25,824
Eze, Anuli G, registered nurse, $61,214
Ezell, Kathleen, clin soc work spv, $55,416
Ezzell, Orville, motor veh mech, $32,628
Fair, Jill, asst center dir admin, $58,908
Falcao-White, Andreia, psychiatric technician I, $24,696
Fall, Kevin L, psychological resident, $35,972
Faller, Kymalee A, deval asst II, $25,584
Faller, Robert, crpntr, $36,888
Falls, Alan C, habilitation spec II, $40,380
Falls, Dionna L, deval asst I, $23,352
Falls, Kassandra L, ofc spt asst (keybrd), $28,452
Falls, Laura C, food serv helper I, $20,952
Fann, Kerry T, locksmith, $36,204
Fanning, Rusty W, psychiatric technician II, $27,696
Fansher, Samantha A, acct I, $29,976
Farina, Laura L, deval asst I, $22,728
Farmer, Marvin D, security ofcr II, $27,228
Farmer, Melissa N, food serv helper I, $22,317
Farmer, Remedios F, deval asst I, $23,352
Farnan, Shelly J, psychologist I, $71,100
Farr, Bianca Y, mental hlth mgr b2, $61,105
Farr, Roxie A, deval asst I, $24,804
Farr, Tracy M, recrtnal ther II, $40,380
Farrah, Michael P, security aide I psy, $31,620
Farrell, Sharon, case mgr III dd, $38,928
Farrelly, Overia A, deval asst I, $22,404
Fasihuddin, Mohammed, staff physician spec, $195,750
Fast, Noelle E, cook III, $29,496
Faucett, Kimberly A, case mgr II dd, $34,944
Fauss, Tamra S, cnslr in training, $37,548
Favell, Demetrius D, psychiatric technician I, $23,352
Favell, Samantha, direct care aide, $10.93/hr
Favier, Heather L, security aide I psy, $30,276
Fawl, J B, fiscal & administrative mgr b2, $58,897
Fayne, Gloria D, deval asst I, $26,400
Featherstone, Kathleen, special asst official & admstr, $83,325
Fehr-Clark, Angela M, mental hlth mgr b2, $56,500
Feik, Elizabeth S, special educ tchr III, $46,068
Felchlia, Mark A, psychologist I, $65,364
Felix, Skyesha L, psychiatric technician I, $22,728
Felps, Brandon T, deval asst I, $22,092
Feltner, Heather N, registered nurse, $20,020
Felton, Lisa D, habilitation spec II, $34,944
Fennell, Henry L, deval asst I, $22,728
Fennewald, Laura J, sr ofc spt asst (keybrd), $25,824

Ferguson, Richard E, security aide I psy, $29,652
Fernandez, Theresa M, student intern, $20,936
Ferozi, Roya, security aide I psy, $32,244
Ferrell, Mia S, prog spec II mh, $43,488
Ferrell, Sheila P, mental hlth mgr b2, $61,287
Fetty, Valarie M, registered nurse, $54,766
Fewins, Reece W, ofc spt asst (keybrd), $23,160
Fiasco, Debra M, dev dis cmnty spec, $40,380
Fiedler, Vicky J, registered nurse sr, $51,276
Fields, Michele D, lpn II gen, $34,560
Fields, Sierra E, deval asst I, $22,404
Figur, Regis C, registered nurse sr, $55,891
Finch, Cassandra J, psychiatric technician II, $25,428
Finch, Tina M, deval asst II, $27,468
Finch, Yvonne, psychiatric technician II, $27,696
Fincher, Cynthia E, deval asst I, $22,728
Findlay, Ronda S, administrative asst, $16,470
Fink, Ruth A, licensed clin soc wkr, $47,892
Finnegan, Kimberly K, registered nurse sr, $60,796
Finney, Blake, deval asst I, $24,036
Finney, Sterling, deval asst I, $22,728
Firebaugh, Jonie L, cook I, $22,872
First, Anthony, deval asst I, $23,352
First, Pamela S, deval asst III, $30,528
Fischbeck, Suzanne M, registered nurse sr, $51,552
Fischer, Aaron J, psychiatric technician I, $22,728
Fischer, John D, reimbursement ofcr I, $30,420
Fischer, John W, security aide III psy, $41,940
Fischer, Mark V, security aide I psy, $30,276
Fischer, Mary B, sr ofc spt asst (keybrd), $29,904
Fishburn, Sherry L, security aide I psy, $32,244
Fisher, Crystal J, deval asst I, $24,036
Fisher, Ebony S, registered nurse mgr b3, $85,926
Fisher, Michelle A, deval asst I, $22,404
Fisher, Reba J, food serv helper I, $20,664
Fisher, Shantel L, deval asst I, $22,728
Fisher, Sharon, psychiatric technician I, $24,804
Fisher, Teri L, psychiatric technician II, $38,818
Fite, Karen S, deval asst III, $30,024
Fizer, George M, institution supt, $77,556
Fizer, Melanie D, deval asst II, $26,400
Flack, Judith A, registered nurse sup, $81,266
Flakes, Loretta T, psychiatric technician I, $22,728
Flanigan, Susan, special asst official & admstr, $78,780
Fleischman, Marjorie A, deval asst II, $25,428
Fleming, Jamel C, cook I, $21,864
Fleming, Tori, deval asst I, $23,352
Fletcher, Dion D, deval asst I, $24,036
Fletcher, Kevin R, mental hlth mgr b1, $51,092
Fletcher, Myron, deval asst II, $24,804
Fletcher, Rochelle P, qual assurance spec mh, $40,380
Fletcher, Stacy D, psychiatric technician I, $23,352
Flieger, April A, ofc spt asst (keybrd), $23,160
Flores, Cleta F, psychiatric technician I, $26,400
Flores, Hillary K, psychiatric technician I, $22,728
Flores, Justina V, deval asst I, $24,036
Flores, Rachel L, deval asst I, $24,036
Floretta, Sue M, sr ofc spt asst (keybrd), $29,412
Flowers, Faith E, lpn II gen, $41,462
Flowers, Lisa M, registered nurse sup, $84,560
Flowers, Stephanie L, dev dis cmnty worker II, $34,944
Floyd-Lee, Michelle, lpn II gen, $39,780
Fluger, Ian, psychologist II, $77,556
Flynn, Martha K, lpn II gen, $29,772
Flynn, Regina K, deval asst I, $22,728
Fofana, Alhaji, deval asst I, $23,352
Fofana, Fatu, deval asst I, $23,352
Fogarty, Bridget M, case mgr II dd, $34,944
Fogle, Kelsey J, deval asst I, $22,728
Foley, Kathryn L, deval asst I, $22,728
Fondren, Simonia, security ofcr II, $26,400
Fontaine, Keith, deval asst I, $22,092
Foose, Amy L, deval asst I, $26,004
Forbes, David A, misc tech, $13,372
Ford, Barrie C, case mgr II dd, $35,568
Ford, Cheryl L, deval asst III, $29,904
Ford, Ernest C, custodial worker I, $20,664
Ford, Gwendolyn A, psychiatric technician I, $22,728
Ford, Jerry, deval asst II, $25,428

Ford, Keenard J, deval asst I, $23,352
Ford, Marcia, institution supt, $82,077
Ford, Mary V, clin casework pract II, $38,232
Ford, Sandra, registered nurse, $28,375
Ford, Stephanie D, deval asst I, $22,728
Ford, Terry D, deval asst I, $24,036
Ford, Tifaan A, mental hlth mgr b1, $48,149
Forgy, Jessica E, registered nurse, $57,278
Forgy, Kirk R, security aide I psy, $36,336
Forkner, Jenelle R, deval asst I, $22,728
Fornah, Bai, deval asst I, $23,352
Fornelli, Natalie L, mental hlth mgr b2, $62,620
Forrest, Carmen L, registered nurse sr, $55,776
Forrest, Princess A, deval asst I, $23,412
Forsythe, Cynthia J, special asst ofc & clerical, $39,620
Forsythe, Daniel M, registered nurse sr, $51,552
Forsythe, Stephanie L, psychiatric technician I, $22,728
Forsythe, Terry L, security aide I psy, $30,276
Forte, Elisabeth L, direct care aide, $10.93/hr
Foster, Amanda L, deval asst I, $22,728
Foster, Amber D, registered nurse sup, $66,666
Foster, Carolyn S, registered nurse sr, $54,720
Foster, Christine M, registered nurse sup, $95,478
Foster, Danielle, deval asst I, $22,728
Foster, Michael T, psychiatric technician I, $22,728
Foster, Morgan E, registered nurse, $50,244
Foster, Nichole R, case mgr II dd, $34,944
Foster, Paige N, direct care aide, $12.36/hr
Foster, Renee, sr ofc spt asst (keybrd), $28,452
Foster, Stephanie, registered nurse sup, $67,104
Foster, Suzannah D, activity aide III, $27,696
Fowler, Tracy I, deval asst I, $22,728
Fowler, Trena J, activity therapy coor, $61,332
Fox, Alexander C, registered nurse, $41,676
Fox, Ashleigh D, licensed clin soc wkr, $50,040
Fox, Cheryl, security ofcr I, $25,824
Fox, Conor G, security aide I psy, $31,152
Fox, Delores A, security aide I psy, $29,208
Fox, Dhonnabel B, psychiatric technician I, $23,352
Fox, Heidi C, dev dis cmnty prog coord, $40,380
Fox, Kory L, motor veh driver, $23,880
Fox, Lori A, deval asst I, $22,728
Fox, Tina M, deval asst I, $23,352
France, Nicole A, psychiatric technician I, $23,352
Francis, Joshua D, unit prog spv mh, $45,156
Francis, Joshua L, deval asst I, $22,728
Francis, Lisa D, ofc spt asst (keybrd), $23,160
Francis, Sarah R, security aide I psy, $31,152
Franco Perez, Alberto D, deval asst I, $23,352
Frank, Denise A, occup therapy asst, $41,988
Frank, Margaret J, psychiatric technician I, $22,728
Franklin, Ashle M, psychiatric technician I, $23,352
Franklin, Brittany M, psychiatric technician I, $22,092
Franklin, Justin A, deval asst I, $22,404
Franklin, Karen J, occup therapy asst, $39,744
Franklin, Lori, prog spec II mh, $45,156
Franklin, Rachel A, deval asst I, $22,728
Frankovich, Sarah A, lpn II gen, $32,220
Frazier, Erica, habilitation spec II, $33,744
Frear, Jackie J, registered nurse sup, $64,380
Freed, John F, deval asst I, $23,352
Freeland, Brenda E, cook II, $25,404
Freeland, Jon L, behavioral technician trne, $23,880
Freeman, Angela C, deval asst I, $22,728
Freeman, Anthony, psychiatric technician I, $23,352
Freeman, Christine N, registered nurse sr, $58,565
Freeman, Doris S, psychiatric technician II, $37,417
Freeman, Jennifer S, registered nurse sr, $55,776
Freet, Michael R, security aide I psy, $34,488
French, James E, clin casework pract II, $37,548
French, Misty I, ofc spt asst (keybrd), $22,536
Frierson, Carolyn J, deval asst I, $22,728
Frieze, Lori A, recrtnal ther II, $41,940
Frisbey, Susan M, deval asst I, $23,076
Fritz, Larry D, security aide I psy, $35,112
Frock, Shanna L, deval asst I, $24,036
Frump, Jennifer L, custodial work spv, $27,504
Fry, Charles A, custodial worker I, $22,317
Fuentes, Esly I, deval asst I, $23,352

Fulks, Lynne R, special asst official & admstr, $73,225
Fullard, Michelle, deval asst I, $22,728
Fullard, Rakiesha A, deval asst I, $22,092
Fuller, Loretta M, registered nurse, $28,600
Fuller, Teonna, deval asst I, $22,728
Fuller, Whitney N, deval asst I, $23,412
Fulton, Gerald A, deval asst I, $24,804
Fulwood, Jean N, psychiatric technician II, $25,428
Furlong, Michelle L, food serv helper I, $22,317
Gaddie, Linda L, psychiatric technician I, $22,728
Gaddy, Brandon G, deval asst III, $26,652
Gaddy, Jordan W, deval asst I, $23,028
Gaddy, Kevin M, security aide I psy, $29,652
Gaddy, Tina L, deval asst I, $27,252
Gaebe, Janice L, behavioral technician trne, $23,880
Gaines, William, clerk, $16,644
Gaines, William, supply mgr I, $38,232
Gal, Pamela R, case mgr II dd, $39,624
Galbreath, Cassandra J, custodial worker II, $23,613
Galbreath, Charlotte Y, storekeeper I, $30,804
Galbreath, Ciarra N, security aide I psy, $30,276
Galbreath, Jeffrey T, workshop prog coor, $37,548
Galbreath, Thomas M, security aide I psy, $31,620
Galcatcher, Micheal D, security ofcr I, $25,824
Gale, Kasey L, psychiatric technician I, $23,352
Galegor, Deborah F, deval asst I, $22,728
Gall, Jason M, security aide I psy, $29,652
Gallagher, Carrie J, deval asst I, $23,412
Gallagher, Kathleen A, dev dis cmnty prog coord, $38,928
Galloway, Toyce L, deval asst II, $26,208
Galloway, Vana J, habilitation spec II, $42,708
Galucia, Melissa, case mgr III dd, $37,548
Galusha, Tammy L, registered nurse, $51,276
Gamet, Alice M, ofc spt asst (clerical), $22,536
Gammon, Michael T, recrtnal ther I, $33,180
Gammon, Sonya R, recrtnal ther I, $33,180
Gandhi, Jeramiah P, mental hlth mgr b2, $66,211
Gane, Elon J, deval asst I, $22,728
Gangel, April D, lpn, $16,470
Gann, Ericka M, security aide I psy, $30,276
Gant, Bertha, psychiatric technician I, $24,804
Gantt, Hursel J, account clerk II, $27,084
Gant-Wheeler, Kaleef O, psychiatric technician I, $24,696
Garber, Kelly J, psychiatric technician I, $23,352
Garcia, Patricia J, lpn II gen, $37,390
Gard, Lynn J, dev dis cmnty prog coord, $43,488
Gardner, Blythe N, lpn II gen, $32,844
Gardner, Kristie S, psychiatric technician I, $34,675
Gardner, Michael V, psychiatric technician I, $23,352
Gardner, Perla A, registered nurse sr, $55,776
Gardner, Tamara, deval asst I, $23,352
Garland, Regina R, activity aide II, $29,568
Garner, Jessica G, registered nurse sr, $60,184
Garner, Samantha L, deval asst I, $24,036
Garner, Steven H, deval asst II, $27,696
Garner, Sylvia H, deval asst I, $22,728
Garren, Morgan K, deval asst I, $22,728
Garrett, Anthony J, cook II, $23,880
Garrett, Christopher R, security aide I psy, $30,276
Garrett, Iva M, deval asst I, $22,728
Garrett, Patrick B, security aide I psy, $31,620
Garriott, Amanda L, security aide I psy, $29,652
Garriott, Jennifer L, storekeeper II, $28,104
Garriott, Kimberly D, custodial worker I, $20,664
Garriott, Tonya J, security aide I psy, $32,244
Garrison, Jessica, deval asst II, $24,804
Garton, Tyler S, deval asst I, $22,728
Garvin, Ann S, case mgr II dd, $40,380
Gary, Latisha, deval asst I, $22,728
Gassen, Amor T, deval asst I, $22,728
Gassen, Kyle W, habilitation spec II, $34,944
Gastel, Vicki M, deval asst I, $23,352
Gates, Dale L, deval asst I, $22,728
Gatson, Sara D, recrtnal ther I, $33,180
Gavirneni, Sridevi, staff physician spec, $130,083
Gayfield, Gail, deval asst I, $25,584
Gayler, Shahone L, ofc spt asst (keybrd), $23,880
Gayler, Susan L, activity aide II, $27,780
Gebhardt, Karla K, registered nurse sr, $51,276

Gebissa, Misrak, registered nurse sr, $63,373
Gee, Karen B, staff dev ofcr mh, $51,096
Geeson, Lynn R, special educ tchr III, $53,208
Gehlert, Gloria I, accounting spec III, $57,744
Geier, Denton W, deval asst I, $22,728
Geneyan, Jason J, security aide I psy, $31,620
George, Danotta L, deval asst I, $23,412
George, Donna S, custodial worker I, $20,664
George, Hallie S, deval asst I, $23,412
George, Kerri L, deval asst I, $26,400
George, Maggie R, housing dev ofcr I, $41,172
George, Michelle Y, deval asst II, $25,584
George, Raynell N, sr ofc spt asst (keybrd), $25,824
George, Sheila D, clin casework pract II, $41,172
Gerard, Travis W, security aide II psy, $33,312
German, Charolette R, sr ofc spt asst (keybrd), $27,504
Gholston, Ivy C, registered nurse, $56,976
Gholston, Paul C, deval asst II, $29,676
Giacometti, Kimberly A, pastoral cnslr, $41,804
Gibbons, Ashley L, psychiatric technician I, $23,352
Gibbs, Annetta L, deval asst I, $22,728
Gibbs, Dianne M, deval asst I, $22,728
Gibbs, Stephen A, registered nurse sup, $70,174
Giboney, Alecia G, security aide II psy, $32,208
Giboney, Imelda T, ofc spt asst (keybrd), $25,404
Giboney, Jeni L, activity aide II, $27,780
Giboney, Nancy J, hlth info admin II, $55,416
Gibson, Annette C, cook II, $23,880
Gibson, Bryan L, security aide I psy, $29,652
Gibson, Cynthia A, mental hlth mgr b1, $61,332
Gibson, Karla J, reimbursement ofcr I, $29,976
Gibson, Kasie L, food serv helper I, $22,317
Gibson, Leigh, special asst official & admstr, $39,725
Gibson, Michelle B, habilitation spec II, $34,944
Gibson, Tammy S, dev dis cmnty prog coord, $40,380
Gierer, Jennifer R, prog coord dmh dohss, $51,096
Gierer, Samuel, prog spec II mh, $41,940
Giessing, Doris E, registered nurse sr, $60,796
Giger, Andrea R, training tech II, $40,380
Gilbert, Christine D, dietitian III, $48,156
Gilbert, Randolph C, cook I, $41,905
Gilbert, Sherry L, pers clerk, $32,052
Gilkey, Terri L, deval asst I, $26,400
Gillam, Linda D, psychiatric technician II, $27,696
Gillenwater, Beverly L, ofc spt asst (keybrd), $34,483
Gillespie, Anita M, deval asst III, $29,532
Gillespie, Pamela D, deval asst I, $26,004
Gillespie, Patricia A, ofc worker misc, $10,814
Gillespie, Robert, registered nurse sr, $55,776
Gillespie, Robert, registered nurse, $36,029
Gillette, Larry D, security aide I psy, $36,984
Gilliam, Debra J, custodial worker I, $20,664
Gilliam, Donna J, deval asst I, $22,404
Gilliam, La'Sha M, deval asst I, $22,716
Gilliard, Kalli R, registered nurse sr, $60,780
Gillispie, Lancer S, cook II, $25,032
Gilltrap, Jua D, security aide II psy, $33,936
Gilltrap, Stephen G, security aide I psy, $30,276
Gilmer, Ginger R, deval asst I, $22,728
Gilmore, Brandon R, deval asst I, $22,728
Gilmore, Stacy L, security aide I psy, $29,208
Giovanetti, Scott, mental hlth mgr b2, $67,695
Gisi, Penny G, deval asst II, $24,804
Givens, Calvin, ofc spt asst (clerical), $24,612
Givens, Vershonna N, lpn II gen, $36,086
Giwa, Tad O, case mgr II dd, $34,944
Gjesvold, Darla M, proj spec, $20.70/hr
Glasco, Delilah A, deval asst I, $22,728
Glasper, Japaul C, deval asst I, $22,728
Glaspy, Margaret, security aide I psy, $30,276
Glass, Amanda L, security aide I psy, $32,244
Glass, Pamela C, psychiatric technician I, $24,804
Glaude, Jason C, security aide I psy, $32,244
Gleeson, Joseph T, security aide I psy, $32,244
Glenn, Danielle R, sr ofc spt asst (keybrd), $25,839
Glenn, Robin, recrtnal ther II, $36,204
Glidewell, Amara R, psychiatric technician I, $22,092
Glidewell, Tommy D, habilitation spec II, $42,708
Glore, Deana F, ofc spt asst (keybrd), $23,160

Glover, Joyce E, prog spec II mh, $41,940
Glover, Kit L, special asst official & admstr, $73,225
Gnade, Tammy J, psychiatric technician I, $22,092
Goans, Jenny L, deval asst I, $24,036
Gobeli, Joseph A, security aide I psy, $29,652
Goben, Tina R, security aide I psy, $31,620
Gober, Denise M, account clerk II, $27,504
Goche, Mary M, case mgr I dd, $31,512
Gochenouer, Yolanda L, deval asst I, $23,412
Godley, Angela N, security aide I psy, $32,244
Goebel, Jennifer A, admin ofc spt asst, $33,744
Goetz, Kimberley S, ofc spt asst (keybrd), $22,536
Goff, Edna, deval asst II, $25,428
Goff, Jeremy C, registered nurse, $49,497
Goforth, Cynthia D, deval asst I, $23,352
Goforth, Sherri D, psychiatric technician I, $23,352
Goforth, Stacy L, food serv helper II, $23,613
Gohil, Nimisha, case mgr II dd, $34,944
Gohring, Rickie L, special asst ofc & clerical, $40,211
Goines, April R, deval asst I, $25,428
Goins, Diana K, acct I, $30,984
Goldammer, Linda, admin ofc spt asst, $29,976
Goldstein, Richard G, mental hlth mgr b2, $65,046
Golian, Dana R, registered nurse sr, $54,720
Goligoski, Jerry T, security aide II psy, $34,488
Gomez, Angela A, dev dis cmnty prog coord, $43,488
Gomez, Linda, med lab tech, $31,080
Gonzalez, Carrisa M, dining room spv, $25,958
Good, Mary B, deval asst I, $24,036
Good, Roberta L, licensed clin soc wkr, $46,068
Good, Wendy S, ofc spt asst (keybrd), $12,516
Goode, Robin E, dev dis cmnty spec, $38,928
Gooden, Alberta R, deval asst I, $24,804
Goodlett, Brittany, deval asst I, $22,728
Goodman, Ashley R, deval asst I, $23,412
Goodman, Kimberly D, deval asst III, $28,908
Goodman, Sharie J, deval asst I, $22,728
Goodrich, Marvin, habilitation spec II, $35,568
Goodson, Lisa K, deval asst I, $22,728
Goodwin, James E, security aide I psy, $30,144
Goodwin, Stacey L, case mgmt/assess spv, $42,708
Goodwin, Tenniel, deval asst I, $23,352
Gordon, Bernadette M, activity aide III, $30,048
Gordon, James H, custodial worker I, $20,664
Gordon, Janet L, fiscal & administrative mgr b2, $72,529
Gordon, Randall L, security aide I psy, $35,712
Gorham, James D, deval asst I, $24,036
Goring, Barbara L, laundry worker I, $22,536
Gorman, Carol A, dev dis cmnty prog coord, $38,928
Gorman, Roger J, laborer I, $21,264
Gosal, Jagpal S, consulting physician, $28,361
Goskey, Kathy M, deval asst I, $22,404
Goslin, Richard G, security aide I psy, $32,208
Gosnell, Melissa A, lpn II gen, $31,872
Gosney, Joshua P, security aide I psy, $31,152
Gosoroski, Nancy L, deval asst I, $22,728
Goss, Ricky J Jr, psychiatric technician I, $23,352
Gossa, Kenean A, psychiatric technician I, $22,728
Gossett, Kelly C, licensed clin soc wkr, $50,040
Gossett, Wanda J, habilitation spec II, $36,900
Gossrau, Jerilynn J, licensed clin soc wkr, $53,208
Goth, Joshua, activity aide I, $24,072
Gottman, Tena L, mental hlth mgr b2, $63,985
Gougeon, Kathleen A, deval asst I, $23,352
Govro, David A, psychiatric technician II, $26,208
Govro, Douglas L, psychiatric technician I, $22,728
Gowdy, Richard N, special asst official & admstr, $112,000
Grabill, Connie C, prog spec I mh, $38,928
Grable, Diann L, habilitation spec II, $34,944
Grady, Billy D, security ofcr I, $25,824
Grady, Patricia L, prog spec I mh, $41,172
Graffam Fizer, Ashley A, dev dis cmnty spec, $36,888
Gragg, Edith M, account clerk II, $25,824
Graham, Amy M, registered nurse sr, $51,552
Graham, Bret C, habilitation spec II, $34,944
Graham, Dianna L, reimbursement ofcr I, $29,976
Graham, Doris L, phys thrpst asst, $39,744
Graham, Jessica, direct care aide, $22,728
Graham, Nicole, deval asst II, $25,584

Graham, Robert D, psychiatric technician I, $23,352
Graham-Pritt, Kristine B, registered nurse sr, $55,776
Graham-Royer, Bridget A, psychologist II, $69,612
Granger, Sharon Y, registered nurse sr, $56,976
Grant, Calvin G, deval asst I, $23,352
Grant, Ericka E, dev dis cmnty worker II, $33,744
Grant, Jessica G, prog spec I mh, $38,928
Grant, Maria C, habilitation spec II, $34,944
Grant, Trevor M, custodial worker I, $22,317
Grant, Viviene, security aide I psy, $31,620
Grant, Yvonne M, deval asst I, $22,728
Gratton, Michael R, security aide I psy, $30,276
Gravelle, Daniel C, security aide I psy, $31,620
Graves, Sharron N, deval asst I, $24,804
Graves, Terra R, clin casework pract II, $36,204
Graves, Velinda A, deval asst II, $25,584
Gray, Angela M, habilitation spec II, $34,944
Gray, Cindy L, registered nurse sr, $55,776
Gray, Joseph G, security aide I psy, $29,652
Gray, Mary K, habilitation spec II, $34,944
Gray, Rhonda R, food serv helper I, $22,317
Gray, Sarah M, case mgr II dd, $34,944
Gray, Scott W, registered nurse sr, $61,451
Gray, Willie J, security aide I psy, $31,620
Gray-Bickley, Shonda D, deval asst II, $28,152
Graybill, Gayle, lpn, $16,470
Greathouse, Dawn S, sr ofc spt asst (keybrd), $27,948
Grechus, Katherine M, security aide I psy, $29,832
Green, Angela C, security aide I psy, $31,620
Green, John B, security aide I psy, $31,620
Green, Khaleelah, case mgr II dd, $34,944
Green, Marlitia, deval asst I, $22,728
Green, Mellony C, security aide II psy, $34,488
Green, Miyoschi, ofc spt asst (keybrd), $23,880
Green, Robert D, case mgmt/assess spv, $40,380
Green, Sandra K, lpn II gen, $37,644
Green, Sarah A, admin ofc spt asst, $29,004
Green, Shontee, deval asst I, $22,728
Green, Tenika T, deval asst II, $24,804
Greenberry, Tyanna, deval asst II, $25,584
Greene, Janessa G, deval asst I, $23,352
Greenfield, Samantha L, security aide I psy, $29,652
Green-James, Freda, psychiatric technician II, $27,252
Greenlee, Belinda J, ofc spt asst (keybrd), $22,536
Greenlee, John E, registered nurse sr, $59,645
Greenstreet, Anita K, deval asst I, $23,352
Greer, Linda S, deval asst I, $26,628
Greer, Shelia D, food serv helper I, $20,664
Greer, Terry L, deval asst I, $23,352
Gregoroski, Leslie E, ofc spt asst (keybrd), $25,824
Gregory, Jessica, registered nurse sr, $55,776
Gremmel, Adam S, deval asst I, $24,804
Gress, Mary M, psychiatric technician I, $23,352
Grey, Ravel, security aide I psy, $31,620
Gribble, Lisa F, mental hlth mgr b2, $72,720
Grider, Martha J, activity aide I, $23,412
Grieshaber, Anita, admin ofc spt asst, $28,104
Griffin, Charleston, psychiatric technician I, $26,260
Griffin, Demon L, deval asst I, $22,728
Griffin, Kristin R, registered nurse, $54,766
Griffin, Michele J, deval asst I, $22,728
Griffin, Rene D, direct care aide, $7,228
Griffin, Sherri L, deval asst I, $22,728
Griffin, William J, psychiatric technician I, $22,728
Griffin, Willie C, psychiatric technician I, $23,352
Griffith, Cheryl L, security aide I psy, $31,620
Griffitt, Desiree Y, account clerk II, $25,824
Griffon, Kelly M, dev dis cmnty spec, $40,380
Griggs, Joseph R, habilitation spec II, $38,232
Griggs, Skylar N, food serv helper I, $20,664
Griggs, Teresa J, registered nurse sr, $54,720
Grigsby, Ginger K, case mgr II dd, $34,944
Grimes, Angela M, deval asst II, $25,584
Grimes, Billie G, deval asst I, $22,728
Grimes, Deedee J, deval asst I, $26,844
Grimmett, Jimmy W, security aide II psy, $35,112
Grimpo, Nichole L, deval asst I, $23,412
Grindley, Mary E, deval asst I, $22,728
Grissett, Stancy H, registered nurse, $28,375

Grobmyer, Sharon K, deval asst I, $22,404
Grogan, Asher G, psychiatric technician I, $22,092
Gromowski, Debra S, psychiatric technician I, $23,352
Grosch, Paula A, case mgr III dd, $37,548
Grothoff, Kristy J, fiscal & administrative mgr b2, $77,180
Groves, Delbert D, licensed clin soc wkr, $52,092
Grubbs, Anthony E, deval asst I, $23,352
Guest, Tammie L, sr ofc spt asst (keybrd), $26,652
Guffin, Katherine, deval asst I, $23,352
Guiden, Marvin C, stores clerk, $38,177
Guinn, Nathan C, deval asst I, $22,728
Gulley, Jennifer J, deval asst I, $24,034
Gulley, Pamela S, staff physician spec, $203,448
Gum, Virginia A, misc tech, $12,078
Gunn, Kenneth W, case mgr II dd, $36,204
Gunning, Paula C, case mgr II dd, $34,944
Gunter, Bailey M, deval asst I, $22,728
Gunter, Regina K, case mgr II dd, $41,172
Guthrie, Amber, lpn II gen, $30,396
Guynes, Danny L, psychiatric technician I, $23,352
Guzman, Francisco J, deval asst I, $23,352
Guzman, Juan H, direct care aide, $6,910
Gyamera, Anastacia A, security aide I psy, $32,244
Haake, Michael J, ofc servs coor, $47,892
Haas, Susan A, dev dis cmnty prog coord, $41,940
Hack, Marsha D, case mgr II dd, $34,944
Hackathorn, Cynthia L, psychologist II, $77,556
Hacker, Denise S, mental hlth mgr b1, $55,406
Hackney, Donna M, deval asst I, $23,076
Haddock, Makyla O, deval asst II, $25,428
Hader, Carol A, security aide I psy, $29,652
Hadley, Judy L, licensed clin soc wkr, $46,068
Hadley, Lakisha D, psychiatric technician I, $22,728
Hadlock, Cassandra R, deval asst I, $22,728
Hagar-Mace, Elizabeth, special asst prof, $71,205
Hagarty, Patricia A, cook II, $23,880
Hager, Elouise A, deval asst II, $27,696
Hager, Gregory A, deval asst I, $23,412
Hagerman, Devin M, motor veh driver, $26,232
Hagerman, Jordon T, deval asst I, $22,728
Hagler-Volner, Marcy A, designated principal asst div, $92,240
Hahn, Michael J, storekeeper II, $30,072
Hahn, Raymond E, security aide I psy, $30,276
Hahn, Sonya R, psychiatric technician I, $22,716
Hahne, Joseph W, misc prof, $13,372
Hahs, Erin L, clin soc work spv, $49,128
Haines, Terrell M, deval asst I, $23,700
Hains, Roberta L, mental hlth mgr b3, $71,094
Haislet, Linda M, activity aide II, $24,804
Halastanis, Brenda M, case mgr II dd, $34,944
Halbrook, Nancy D, cook I, $21,864
Halbrook, Stacie E, registered nurse sr, $53,253
Halcomb, Alice K, deval asst I, $27,252
Hale, Deanna, psychiatric technician I, $23,352
Hale, Kristi R, training tech II, $20,586
Hale, Stephanie F, sr ofc spt asst (keybrd), $25,824
Halici, Altan, registered nurse, $26,058
Hall, Barbara A, accounting spec III, $57,744
Hall, Becky A, registered nurse sr, $55,361
Hall, Earlene, ofc spt asst (keybrd), $24,264
Hall, Elizabeth N, deval asst I, $24,036
Hall, Joy C, food serv helper I, $22,317
Hall, Kimberly K, deval asst II, $25,584
Hall, Ladonna, case mgr I dd, $32,628
Hall, Michaelle R, registered nurse sr, $57,893
Hall, Robin L, psychiatric technician I, $24,072
Hall, Roseanna, deval asst I, $23,700
Hall, Shannon R, deval asst I, $23,412
Hall, Shelby L, deval asst I, $24,036
Haller, Ashley N, food serv helper I, $21,760
Halpin, Ronda K, custodial worker I, $10,332
Halterman, Justin L, deval asst I, $23,412
Halterman, Michele D, security aide I psy, $29,652
Halton, Brenda S, registered nurse sr, $54,720
Hamblin, Kay N, dev dis cmnty worker II, $34,944
Hamilton, Ashley, deval asst I, $22,716
Hamilton, Brandy, deval asst I, $22,728
Hamilton, Jacqueline, psychiatric technician I, $23,352
Hamilton, Jodi A, deval asst II, $25,584

Hamilton, Kareth T, security aide I psy, $30,276
Hamilton, Lori G, deval asst I, $23,352
Hamilton, Mary A, psychiatric technician I, $22,728
Hamilton, Michelle, dietitian III, $52,092
Hamilton, Samantha C, deval asst I, $22,728
Hamm, Roger D, motor veh driver, $24,264
Hammer, Linda M, thrpst, $20,434
Hammers, Pamelina M, psychiatric technician I, $22,728
Hammond, Dale G, lpn II gen, $37,390
Hammond, Tracy D, deval asst I, $26,628
Hammonds, Kizzy L, activity aide II, $25,224
Hamp, Tonya J, paralegal, $36,384
Hampton, Heidi, deval asst I, $13,002
Hampton, Savannah R, special asst prof, $45,156
Han, Bob, resident physician, $51,318
Hanaway, David P, resident physician, $50,005
Hanebrink, Cynthia L, habilitation spec II, $35,568
Haney, Alison A, dev dis cmnty spec, $48,156
Hanger, Shana L, unit prog spv mh, $38,928
Hann, Rebecca E, fiscal & administrative mgr b2, $63,375
Hansel, Staci A, vendor servs coor mh, $40,380
Hansen, Carol M, special educ tchr III, $47,892
Hansome, Jaurvoisier, deval asst I, $23,352
Hanson, James M, registered nurse sr, $58,140
Harbison, Henry J, psychiatric technician I, $22,716
Harden, Joy L, case mgr III dd, $37,548
Hardgrave, Kristin A, security aide I psy, $29,208
Hardimon, Lajunakie T, ofc spt asst (keybrd), $24,264
Hardin, Angela D, food serv helper I, $20,664
Hardin, Jerome D, deval asst I, $22,728
Hardin, Katina D, case mgr II dd, $34,944
Hardin, Kyle T, behavioral technician, $26,844
Hardin, Stacey L, security aide I psy, $29,652
Harding, Steve, deval asst I, $23,352
Hardman, Connie L, case mgr II dd, $34,944
Hardy, Amanda N, deval asst II, $25,584
Hargis, Marcy, mental hlth mgr b3, $71,205
Hargis, Richard R, unit prog spv mh, $41,172
Hargrave, Diane K, ofc worker misc, $19,783
Hargrave, Pamela S, deval asst I, $24,072
Hargreaves, Jennifer J, deval asst I, $22,728
Hargrove, Shawn A, deval asst II, $25,584
Harkrader, Marsha L, ofc spt asst (steno), $26,652
Harkrader, Shelli J, admin ofc spt asst, $28,536
Harl, Thomas C, security aide II psy, $32,208
Harlin, Jason A, deval asst III, $26,652
Harman, Brian L, psychiatric technician I, $22,716
Harman, Thomas J, deval asst I, $23,412
Harp, Lisa M, food serv helper I, $21,564
Harper, Ashlee D, deval asst I, $22,728
Harper, Kay Y, registered nurse, $59,645
Harper, Makeeda, deval asst I, $23,076
Harper, Mondrakus, deval asst II, $25,584
Harper, Tiffanie C, cook II, $23,880
Harrell, Dominick, vendor servs coor mh, $40,380
Harrell, Rhonda S, reimbursement ofcr I, $31,512
Harrelson, Karen, registered nurse sup, $70,174
Harrelson, Sharon K, psychiatric technician II, $27,876
Harriette, Josiah, security aide I psy, $31,620
Harriette, Jullia, security aide I psy, $30,276
Harriman, Bradley R, fire & safety spec, $39,624
Harrington, Archie J, ofc spt asst (keybrd), $26,232
Harrington, Lavail, security ofcr I, $25,824
Harrington-Wahlers, Rose M, security aide I psy, $30,276
Harris, Angela, psychiatric technician I, $23,352
Harris, Anthony L, deval asst II, $29,208
Harris, Brittney R, dev dis cmnty worker I, $32,628
Harris, C D, dev dis cmnty worker I, $31,512
Harris, Calvin L, deval asst I, $22,716
Harris, Catherine R, ofc spt asst (keybrd), $23,160
Harris, Charron M, deval asst I, $22,728
Harris, Cindy S, food serv helper I, $20,664
Harris, Cynthia K, storekeeper I, $25,840
Harris, Deborah C, deval asst II, $27,876
Harris, Denise, dining room spv, $23,880
Harris, Ebony, deval asst I, $23,352
Harris, Ellen A, registered nurse sr, $57,343
Harris, Kem D, motor veh mech, $32,052
Harris, Kimberly A, ofc spt asst (keybrd), $25,032

Harris, Larry, psychiatric technician I, $23,076
Harris, Laura M, fiscal & administrative mgr b1, $52,621
Harris, Lisa A, ofc spt asst (keybrd), $26,232
Harris, Lorenzo D, custodial worker I, $20,664
Harris, Malcolm J, deval asst I, $22,716
Harris, Marcia M, psychiatric technician I, $22,716
Harris, Marion, deval asst I, $23,412
Harris, Martha M, deval asst I, $26,004
Harris, Miceala, psychiatric technician I, $22,728
Harris, Rise C, deval asst II, $28,584
Harris, Ronnie A, food serv helper I, $21,564
Harris, Shaunte L, registered nurse sr, $58,140
Harris, Spencer R, deval asst I, $24,036
Harris, Tanya M, habilitation spec II, $34,944
Harris, Terry L, behavior intvtn tech dd, $28,152
Harris, Tony E, prog spec I mh, $51,096
Harris-Brekel, Donna, hr mgr b2, $67,309
Harris-McCraw, Lashonda M, deval asst I, $22,728
Harrison, Java D, lpn, $10,000
Harrison, Judieth J, registered nurse, $27.50/hr
Harrison, Marcia A, security aide I psy, $29,832
Harrison, Mary A, registered nurse, $28,600
Harrison, Pattie, habilitation spec II, $34,944
Harrison, Steven L, registered nurse, $8,250
Harshner, Stacey M, deval asst I, $22,728
Hart, Audrey N, deval asst I, $22,728
Hart, Lisa F, prog spec II mh, $41,940
Hart, Nelson C, lpn II gen, $37,644
Hart, Tina M, sr ofc spt asst (keybrd), $26,652
Hartfield, Tamara S, habilitation spec I, $29,976
Hartley, Steven R, mgmt analysis spec I, $51,096
Hartline, Carey M, deval asst I, $23,352
Hartline, Kelli A, vendor servs coor mh, $40,380
Hartman, John D, habilitation spec II, $40,380
Hartman, Lana F, special asst ofc & clerical, $40,211
Hartzler, Carrie S, ofc spt asst (keybrd), $23,160
Harvey, Amanda D, security aide I psy, $29,832
Harvey, Jennifer A, sr ofc spt asst (keybrd), $25,824
Harvey, Shalanda N, deval asst I, $23,076
Harwood, Clevelanda R, acct I, $32,628
Hash, Nicolle M, habilitation spec I, $29,976
Hashish, Hossam, security aide I psy, $31,152
Hass, Mark C, psychiatric technician I, $22,728
Hassell, Jacob O, food serv helper I, $20,664
Hassell, Julia E, security aide I psy, $32,208
Hasson, Carol M, dev dis cmnty worker II, $37,548
Hatton, Misty D, reimbursement ofcr I, $29,976
Haug, Daniel D, special asst official & admstr, $112,000
Haulcy, Demeitrus T, deval asst I, $24,036
Haupt, Mason, mgmt analysis spec I, $41,940
Haury, William E, deval asst I, $26,628
Hawkins, Alfred E, food serv helper I, $20,664
Hawkins, Christina D, security aide I psy, $30,276
Hawkins, Cynthia, psychiatric technician I, $28,372
Hawkins, Demetrius O, custodial worker I, $28,593
Hawkins, Gladys B, cook, $11,843
Hawkins, Kenneth, custodial worker I, $20,664
Hawkins, Margaret D, seamstress, $10,629
Hawkins, Shari N, deval asst I, $23,352
Hawkins, Sheilita, lpn II gen, $19,895
Hawkins, Tenisha R, psychiatric technician I, $24,072
Haws, Phillip C, deval asst I, $22,728
Hawthorne, Ann, sr ofc spt asst (keybrd), $30,924
Hawthorne, Chadwick S, security aide I psy, $29,208
Hawthorne, Tiffany A, habilitation spec II, $34,944
Hayden, Virginia, registered nurse sr, $55,776
Hayes, Carla M, deval asst I, $22,728
Hayes, Gayvell C, deval asst II, $28,776
Hayes, Heather N, qual assurance spec mh, $39,624
Hayes, Hertescene, psychiatric technician I, $25,428
Hayes, Javon N, deval asst I, $22,728
Hayes, Latrell P, pers analyst II, $40,380
Hayes, Metrius, deval asst I, $23,700
Hayes, Russell H, deval asst I, $23,352
Hayes, Shirley D, childrens psy care spv, $27,504
Hayes, Tess W, lpn II gen, $37,644
Hayes, Tonette, deval asst I, $22,716
Hayner, Rachel A, psychiatric technician I, $23,352
Haynes, Amy E, deval asst I, $23,028

Haynes, Frances M, deval asst I, $22,728
Haynes, Hope E, registered nurse sr, $56,526
Haynes, Nathan C, deval asst I, $22,728
Haynes, Stephanie D, deval asst I, $22,728
Hayreh, Davinder J, staff physician spec, $297,355
Hays, Jacob M, security aide I psy, $29,652
Hays, Trina L, licensed clin soc wkr, $47,892
Hays-Martin, Tonya L, librarian II, $37,548
Heard, Gary L, deval asst I, $22,728
Heard, Gwendolyn D, account clerk II, $28,452
Heard, James F, deval asst I, $22,716
Heard, Tonya, custodial worker I, $21,864
Hearod, Tamika, deval asst I, $22,728
Heath, Charla D, account clerk II, $25,824
Heath, Jetta R, registered nurse sr, $65,291
Heather, Sandra K, deval asst I, $26,844
Heathman, Ronald W, security ofcr II, $28,104
Heathman, Sharena J, registered nurse sr, $51,276
Heberlie, Sandra K, recrtnal ther II, $36,888
Hebron, Mimsy Y, case mgr II dd, $34,944
Heckadon, Philana L, deval asst I, $22,728
Hedges, Gail A, case mgmt/assess spv, $47,892
Hedrick, Anthony M, security aide I psy, $29,832
Hedrick, Melissa G, deval asst II, $24,804
Heflin, Linda M, domestic serv worker, $10,742
Hefner, Shelly M, qual assurance spec mh, $40,380
Hegarty, Lane C, recrtnal ther I, $32,628
Heimericks, Glenn L, security aide I psy, $30,276
Heimsoth, Michelle R, deval asst I, $22,728
Hein, Tabbitha N, deval asst I, $23,412
Heineken, Miranda M, deval asst I, $23,076
Heinemann, Ronald J, deval asst II, $25,584
Heinrich, Jasmine L, security ofcr I, $25,032
Heinrich, Steven M, security ofcr I, $44,221
Heinze, Mark C, dev dis cmnty prog coord, $47,892
Heinzer, Cheryl E, hr mgr b2, $67,309
Heisler, Kari A, deval asst I, $22,728
Heitert, Peggy A, acct I, $35,568
Held, Andrew M, security aide I psy, $32,244
Helena, Marilyn E, food serv helper I, $11,158
Heller, Malinda S, account clerk II, $25,824
Heller-Johnson, Ruth A, case mgmt/assess spv, $47,892
Helm, Marcus A, deval asst I, $22,404
Helm, Otis A, psychiatric technician II, $53,253
Helm, Thelma L, security aide I psy, $30,276
Helmick, Ileta J, registered nurse sup, $74,556
Helms, Kaleb A, psychiatric technician I, $22,716
Helton, Raven L, ofc spt asst (keybrd), $23,160
Helvey, Jason B, registered nurse sr, $59,645
Helwig, Larry L, registered nurse, $27.50/hr
Hemm, Luann M, ofc spt asst (keybrd), $26,652
Hemphill, Carneata D, deval asst I, $22,728
Henderson, Albert E, psychiatric technician I, $23,352
Henderson, Ambrose, psychiatric technician I, $23,352
Henderson, Ardella M, security aide I psy, $29,652
Henderson, Bryce D, security aide II psy, $33,312
Henderson, Charlene, psychiatric technician I, $22,728
Henderson, Clarence E, direct care aide, $9,530
Henderson, James L, dev dis cmnty prog coord, $51,096
Henderson, Jessica J, deval asst I, $23,412
Henderson, Juanequa, case mgr II dd, $34,944
Henderson, Kathleen D, food serv helper I, $10,332
Henderson, Nancy J, occup ther II, $31,332
Henderson, Samiyah, deval asst I, $22,728
Henderson, Shaneir, psychiatric technician I, $23,352
Hendricksmeyer, Richard T, registered nurse sr, $63,584
Hendrickson, Darrell W, misc prof, $40.64/hr
Henley, David C, psychiatric technician I, $23,352
Henley, Lisa, registered nurse sr, $55,776
Henley, Robert L, cook II, $27,504
Henneke, Susan L, acct I, $30,984
Hennes, Christina M, hlth info tech II, $35,568
Hennes, Kasey M, dev dis cmnty worker II, $34,944
Hennier, Gale A, budget analyst III, $49,128
Hennings, Kathleen, psychiatric technician I, $26,004
Henry, Cady L, deval asst I, $22,728
Henry, Deanna M, psychiatric technician I, $22,728
Henry, Phil R, custodial worker I, $22,628
Henry, Robert N, deval asst I, $22,728

Hensel, Shana G, registered nurse sr, $61,836
Hensley, Michelle L, habilitation spec II, $34,944
Hensley, Vicki R, ofc worker misc, $11.60/hr
Henson, Jason S, psychiatric technician I, $24,804
Henson, Zachary C, security aide I psy, $30,276
Herbert, Nancy A, therapy consult, $39,172
Herman, Andrew J, deval asst I, $22,728
Herman, Sarah E, motor veh driver, $25,824
Hermann, Julie A, habilitation spec II, $38,928
Hernandez, Brianna, deval asst I, $23,028
Hernandez, Jacqueline L, deval asst I, $22,404
Hernandez, Mauricio, deval asst I, $23,352
Hernandez, Yesenia Y, deval asst I, $23,352
Herrington, Geoffrey R, fire & safety spec, $41,172
Herron, Andrea C, deval asst I, $22,728
Herron, Dontrell C, deval asst I, $22,092
Herron, Osceola J, deval asst I, $24,036
Hertel, Michael, security ofcr I, $25,824
Herwig, Jessica N, sr ofc spt asst (keybrd), $25,824
Herwig, Joshua M, special asst prof, $87,500
Hess, Nikolos S, deval asst I, $23,352
Hess, Zachariah D, deval asst II, $24,804
Hessel, Anthony N, deval asst I, $22,728
Hettinger, Scotty R, misc tech, $13,372
Hetzel, Kathleen A, admin ofc spt asst, $33,744
Heusted, Patsy N, deval asst II, $28,776
Heuvelman, William M, fiscal consult, $31,534
Heyer, Janet M, qual assurance spec mh, $50,040
Hick, Stephen B, licensed clin soc wkr, $51,096
Hickerson, Brenda A, reimbursement ofcr I, $29,004
Hickman, Ginger L, habilitation spec II, $34,944
Hickman, Katinia A, mental hlth mgr b1, $54,286
Hickman, Nancy W, recrtnal ther II, $46,068
Hickman, Rebecca N, ofc spt asst (keybrd), $23,160
Hicks, Brandon S, deval asst I, $23,412
Hicks, Darrell D, deval asst I, $22,728
Hieb, Pamela, sr ofc spt asst (keybrd), $28,908
Higginbotham, Michael W, prog spec II mh, $46,068
Higgins, Brooke N, cnslr in training, $32,628
Higgins, Geneva, deval asst I, $23,352
Higgs, Kathy, dev dis cmnty worker II, $43,488
Higgs, Traci A, case mgr II dd, $34,944
Highley, Victoria A, security aide I psy, $30,276
Hill, Andrea P, deval asst I, $22,728
Hill, Anthony D, laborer I, $33,617
Hill, Barbara A, deval asst I, $23,352
Hill, Barry D, deval asst II, $26,208
Hill, Cassundra A, deval asst I, $26,652
Hill, Charlie H, custodial worker II, $21,864
Hill, Connie S, sr ofc spt asst (keybrd), $25,824
Hill, Jennifer S, ofc spt asst (keybrd), $22,536
Hill, Jodee B, deval asst I, $22,404
Hill, Joshua R, motor veh driver, $23,880
Hill, Lakeshia K, deval asst I, $23,352
Hill, Linda, lpn II gen, $34,560
Hill, Roger D, security aide I psy, $35,076
Hill, Sherry D, psychiatric technician II, $25,584
Hill, Sonja J, deval asst I, $23,352
Hill, Tommy L, psychiatric technician II, $26,400
Hill-Durham, Lisa J, registered nurse sr, $59,889
Hilliard, Jennifer A, psychiatric technician I, $23,352
Hilliard, Stephanie D, psychiatric technician I, $28,372
Hillyer, Julia A, special asst official & admstr, $87,365
Hilsenbeck, Lawrence L, security aide I psy, $31,620
Hilton, Lasommer D, ofc spt asst (keybrd), $23,160
Hinga, Alice W, deval asst I, $23,352
Hinkle, Chad L, workshop prog coor, $37,548
Hintch, Bella S, food serv helper I, $20,664
Hinton, Donald W, staff physician spec, $340,694
Hinz, Aaron, security ofcr I, $25,824
Hiranandani, Praveen, registered nurse sr, $55,776
Hires, Rachel A, deval asst I, $22,728
Hitchcock, Eric J, security aide I psy, $32,244
Hitchens, Jennifer D, psychiatric technician I, $23,076
Hitson, Diane J, clin soc work spec, $49,128
Hitzhusen, Mark B, psychiatric technician I, $23,412
Hixson, Gregory M, deval asst I, $23,352
Hobson, Bianca D, deval asst I, $23,352
Hobson, Kenya D, psychiatric technician I, $23,352

Hochstedler, Cynthia M, deval asst I, $26,004
Hocking, Terrance C, deval asst I, $23,352
Hockmeyer, Lonnie L, security aide I psy, $35,112
Hodges, Charlene, psychiatric technician II, $26,400
Hodges, Dodie E, dev dis cmnty spec, $36,888
Hodges, Elena A, deval asst II, $25,428
Hodges, Josephine, account clerk II, $25,824
Hodges, Shirley N, sr ofc spt asst (keybrd), $27,504
Hodges, Tiffany, deval asst I, $23,352
Hoefer, Cheryl J, registered nurse sr, $61,451
Hoefer, Leonna R, deval asst I, $22,728
Hoeflicker, Diane E, sr ofc spt asst (keybrd), $25,824
Hoehn, Joanne M, recrtnal ther I, $34,944
Hoeninger, Carl R, case mgr II dd, $34,944
Hoeppner, Deborah A, deval asst I, $22,728
Hoff, Floyd E, security aide I psy, $34,488
Hogan, Paul B, motor veh driver, $23,880
Hogan, Tamara L, lpn II gen, $38,352
Hohulin, Rebecca S, lpn II gen, $37,644
Hokamp, James, special educ tchr III, $49,128
Holder, Aleighia N, deval asst I, $22,716
Holder, Mary J, case mgr II dd, $34,944
Holder, Tonya D, habilitation spec II, $34,944
Holdman, Linda K, custodial worker I, $22,317
Holiday, Debra A, deval asst I, $24,804
Holland, Debbie A, case mgr II dd, $36,888
Holland, Tammy J, deval asst I, $23,412
Hollars, Julia, cook III, $28,536
Hollensteiner, Karen S, security aide I psy, $30,276
Holliday, Genise D, security aide I psy, $29,208
Holliday, Justin T, recrtnal ther II, $38,928
Holliday, Meredith J, security aide I psy, $31,620
Hollinger, Lori A, hr mgr b2, $67,309
Hollinger, Stephan P, security ofcr, $7,228
Hollingsworth, Misty, acct II, $37,548
Hollis, Darla P, sr ofc spt asst (steno), $33,036
Hollman, Deborah L, registered nurse sr, $52,608
Holloway, Brynn E, activity aide I, $35,111
Holm, Danielle J, lpn, $16,470
Holmes, Darlene A, deval asst I, $23,352
Holmes, Janet L, account clerk II, $25,824
Holmes, Marvin L, psychiatric technician I, $23,352
Holmes, Scott L, registered nurse sr, $63,373
Holmes, Shelia M, motor veh driver, $26,652
Holmes, Vickie, registered nurse sr, $64,681
Holmon, Jeronne D, food serv helper I, $20,952
Holmstrom, Jana, case mgr III dd, $37,548
Holt, Christopher K, workshop spv II, $29,850
Holt, James T, motor veh driver, $25,032
Holterman, Mary C, principal asst board/commisson, $40,211
Holzbierlein, Cynthia L, security aide I psy, $29,652
Holzendorf, Joseph, security ofcr I, $27,084
Honarmand, A L, case mgr II dd, $38,928
Hook, Lori M, custodial worker I, $24,702
Hooks, Falicia R, subs abuse cnslr II, $38,232
Hoots, Lakrista L, deval asst I, $22,716
Hoover, Tammy J, custodial worker I, $20,952
Hopkins, Mary, deval asst I, $23,352
Hoppe, Smile L, habilitation spec I, $29,976
Hopson, Ciara E, deval asst I, $22,728
Hopson, Renesha M, deval asst I, $22,728
Horine, Suzanne M, prog spec I mh, $38,928
Horn, Roy L, activity aide II, $24,804
Horn, Sherry L, sr ofc spt asst (keybrd), $25,824
Hornback, Linda G, deval asst I, $22,728
Hornburg, William A, ofc spt asst (keybrd), $26,652
Hornick, Leslie G, dietitian III, $50,040
Hornstra, Robijn K, staff physician spec, $203,449
Horstmeier, Carolyn J, ofc spt asst (keybrd), $12,912
Horton, Deborah K, food serv helper II, $23,880
Horton, Mary A, food serv helper I, $22,317
Horton, Melinda M, deval asst I, $23,352
Horton, Melissa J, lpn II gen, $36,086
Horton, Nenniccia M, registered nurse, $28,375
Horton, Shar-ron, custodial worker I, $24,612
Hose, William G, budget/plng analyst, $28,375
Hosenfelt, Sarah B, music ther II, $38,232
Hosking, Jarrod D, security aide I psy, $29,652
Hosler, Pamela J, dietitian III, $50,040

Hotop, Brandi N, case mgr II dd, $34,944
Hotop, Kaysie L, dietitian I, $41,172
Hotto, Mary, licensed clin soc wkr, $45,156
Houchins, Sandra L, ofc spt asst (keybrd), $25,032
Hounihan, Gayla M, lpn II gen, $37,644
House, Jeffrey E, custodial worker I, $21,564
Houston, Rebecca L, lpn II gen, $40,404
Houston, Tracy, psychiatric technician I, $23,412
Hovis, Heather L, deval asst I, $24,036
Howard, Cameron M, psychiatric technician I, $23,352
Howard, Catherine, security guard, $23,053
Howard, Coralicia, case mgr II dd, $34,944
Howard, Darryl, deval asst I, $22,728
Howard, Deon, deval asst II, $27,876
Howard, Francsen M, psychiatric technician I, $22,728
Howard, Jessica R, deval asst I, $22,728
Howard, Mechelle L, psychiatric technician I, $23,352
Howard, Sheri, food serv helper I, $22,317
Howard, Tina M, sr ofc spt asst (keybrd), $27,084
Howard, Vickie V, psychiatric technician I, $23,352
Howen, Milton W, storekeeper I, $27,504
Howery, Alyssa S, deval asst I, $24,036
Howley, Bonnie K, consulting physician, $29,511
Hoyle, Tracey M, account clerk II, $27,084
Hubbard, Anneliese C, case mgr II dd, $34,944
Hubbard, Carltez, deval asst I, $23,352
Hubbard, Debra S, sr ofc spt asst (steno), $30,384
Hubbard, Kathryn L, mental hlth mgr b2, $71,245
Huber, Kathleen, mental hlth mgr b2, $63,553
Hudhra, Xhovana, psychiatric technician I, $22,728
Hudnell-Littrell, Deborah M, ofc spt asst (keybrd), $23,880
Hudson, Andrea D, deval asst I, $24,036
Hudson, Desiray, deval asst I, $22,716
Hudson, Dominique A, deval asst I, $24,804
Hudson, Lorraine, psychiatric technician I, $22,728
Hudson, Niara, deval asst I, $23,352
Hudson, Rhonda, deval asst I, $23,412
Hudson, Ronald, deval asst I, $23,412
Hudson, Veronica Y, lpn II gen, $40,404
Huff, Bobby J, deval asst I, $27,876
Huff, Cheryl, admin ofc spt asst, $28,104
Huff, Ferlin L, psychiatric technician I, $22,728
Huff, Heather R, habilitation spec I, $33,744
Huff, Katherine J, deval asst I, $23,412
Huff, Lacey M, deval asst I, $23,352
Huff, Lisa D, security aide I psy, $29,652
Huff, Nichole R, psychiatric technician I, $23,352
Huffaker, Robyn R, custodial worker I, $20,664
Huffman, Marcia K, ofc spt asst (clerical), $15,775
Huffman, Shaunice N, clin casework asst I, $29,208
Huffman, Stacy R, registered nurse, $27,794
Huggins, Roger L, deval asst I, $22,728
Hughart, Justin L, direct care aide, $12,564
Hughes, Debra D, food serv helper I, $22,317
Hughes, Derek E, psychiatric technician I, $22,728
Hughes, Donna M, registered nurse, $31,200
Hughes, Donye H, deval asst I, $23,412
Hughes, Justin T, clin casework pract I, $34,944
Hughes, Lelia, acct II, $40,380
Hughes, Lora A, psychiatric technician II, $31,704
Hughes, Mechelle L, psychiatric technician I, $22,728
Hughes, Trenton L, food serv helper I, $16,531
Huhn, Leslie A, sr ofc spt asst (keybrd), $25,824
Huhn, Valerie D, special asst official & admstr, $112,000
Hulvey, William M, domestic serv worker, $11.41/hr
Humble, Debra A, registered nurse - clin opers, $56,976
Hummell, Christina L, registered nurse sr, $56,526
Hummer, Dorina G, registered nurse mgr b1, $70,174
Humphrey, Michelle L, prog spec II mh, $41,940
Humphrey, Montrice C, case mgr II dd, $34,944
Humphrey, Nick A, ofc spt asst (keybrd), $23,160
Humphrey, Zelma J, deval asst I, $27,876
Hunt, Jan L, unit prog spv mh, $40,346
Hunt, Patricia A, deval asst I, $23,700
Hunt, Sandra L, security aide I psy, $29,652
Hunt, Susan M, sr ofc spt asst (keybrd), $27,504
Hunter, Brittney N, psychiatric technician I, $22,728
Hunter, David R, staff physician spec, $233,461
Hunter, Haley N, deval asst I, $24,036

Hunter, Julian A, psychiatric technician I, $22,092
Hunter, Sarah E, clin casework pract II, $39,624
Huntington, Carolyn G, sr ofc spt asst (keybrd), $32,472
Huntspon, Monica, case mgmt/assess spv, $40,380
Hunyar, Amanda M, librarian I, $33,744
Huppe, Linda R, deval asst I, $22,728
Huppe, Michael E, deval asst III, $30,384
Hursman, Dana K, deval asst II, $27,696
Hursman, Monica K, ofc spt asst (keybrd), $23,160
Hurst, Denise, ofc spt asst (keybrd), $23,880
Hurt, Cody R, ofc spt asst (keybrd), $23,160
Hurt, Danielle N, psychiatric technician I, $23,352
Huse, Tammy L, registered nurse sr, $58,565
Huskey, Marva R, custodial worker I, $24,339
Huss, Bobby J, food serv helper II, $25,389
Huss, Georgia D, custodial worker I, $23,017
Hussey, Deborah L, special asst ofc & clerical, $35,350
Hutchason, Dawn M, custodial worker II, $21,564
Hutchason, Kenneth L, security aide I psy, $29,652
Hutchinson, Tonya A, licensed clin soc wkr, $43,488
Hutchison, Reva M, procurement ofcr II, $50,040
Hutson, Kevin W, deval asst I, $22,728
Hutt, Patrick M, psychiatric technician II, $24,804
Hutton, Winston G, food serv helper I, $20,664
Hyche, Teresa L, sr ofc spt asst (keybrd), $25,824
Hyder, Gean A, storekeeper II, $29,004
Hyman, Renee M, registered nurse sr, $53,253
Hymer, Josephine M, deval asst I, $26,400
Hymes-Houston, Wanda F, sr ofc spt asst (keybrd), $25,824
Hynes, Susan M, security aide I psy, $30,276
Hysten, Colby R, registered nurse, $50,750
Ibeh, Daniel A, psychiatric technician I, $24,696
Ibeh, Longinus, psychiatric technician I, $12,686
Ibeh, Margaret N, psychiatric technician I, $24,072
Ibekwe, Anselam, psychiatric technician I, $24,696
Ihenacho, Francis O, psychiatric technician I, $24,072
Ihlitskaya, Yuliya, registered nurse, $27.84/hr
Ijams, Dale C, deval asst I, $22,728
Ijioma, Ndubuisi, deval asst I, $23,352
Ikefuama, Fidelis, deval asst I, $23,412
Ikem, Ifeoma C, security aide I psy, $30,276
Ikpeama, Juliet E, psychiatric technician I, $24,696
Ikuegbuwa, Felicia, psychiatric technician II, $28,828
Ilu, Ladi M, deval asst I, $22,728
Imler, Kelly L, custodial worker I, $21,760
Imonitie, Prince, psychiatric technician I, $24,696
Ingalsbe, William J, security aide I psy, $32,244
Ingersoll, Kelli A, ofc spt asst (clerical), $24,264
Ingham, Anna M, habilitation spec II, $34,944
Ingoldsby, Steven E, locksmith, $29,976
Ingram, Amanda M, lpn, $20.80/hr
Ingram, Torian D, psychiatric technician I, $23,352
Ingrao, Roseann, security aide I psy, $29,652
Inman, Julie A, special asst official & admstr, $92,239
Insell, Brian I, security ofcr, $12,353
Inzunza, Anthony A, deval asst I, $24,036
Ipock-Ludiker, Crystal D, dev dis cmnty prog coord, $38,928
Iqbal, Adil S, security aide I psy, $31,152
Irby, Janis K, unit prog spv mh, $51,096
Irby, Patricia, registered nurse sr, $58,565
Irving, Nichole Y, account clerk II, $27,084
Irving, Pamela A, admin ofc spt asst, $32,628
Isaac, David O, lpn II gen, $32,292
Isaac, Shelia R, deval asst II, $27,252
Isaacson, Orna B, licensed clin soc wkr, $38,314
Isabel, Sharon G, registered nurse, $17,166
Isdell, Jennifer J, habilitation spec II, $34,944
Isherwood, Elizabeth A, case mgr I dd, $31,512
Ivester, Briana K, security aide I psy, $30,276
Ivicsics, Carolyn J, security aide I psy, $30,276
Izworski, Lori L, registered nurse sup, $78,315
Jabateh, Mamadee S, deval asst I, $24,036
Jackman, Thomas S, sr ofc spt asst (keybrd), $25,824
Jackmon, John R, housekeeper I, $34,356
Jackson, Antonio, security ofcr I, $25,824
Jackson, Brigitte D, lpn III gen, $34,560
Jackson, Cassie E, security aide I psy, $30,276
Jackson, Clester C, deval asst I, $24,036
Jackson, Dee A, work therapy spec II, $46,097

Jackson, Diane, deval asst I, $23,352
Jackson, Donald L, therapy aide, $13,052
Jackson, Eddis, sr ofc spt asst (keybrd), $27,948
Jackson, Edmonia, account clerk II, $25,824
Jackson, Ernest D, registered nurse mgr b2, $74,187
Jackson, Jacqueline, psychiatric technician I, $22,728
Jackson, James L, dpty state dept dir, $76,255
Jackson, Jenessa C, psychologist I, $66,720
Jackson, Karla D, acct II, $44,304
Jackson, Kayla M, security aide I psy, $30,276
Jackson, Kourion S, psychiatric technician I, $22,728
Jackson, Laura, psychiatric technician I, $23,700
Jackson, Leonard, registered nurse, $28,374
Jackson, Mallory M, deval asst I, $23,352
Jackson, Martha, security aide II psy, $33,912
Jackson, Mary J, psychiatric technician I, $23,352
Jackson, Mica, case mgr II dd, $34,944
Jackson, Nadine, deval asst I, $24,696
Jackson, Pamela C, registered nurse, $26,058
Jackson, Phyllis D, registered nurse, $28,375
Jackson, Rebecca M, registered nurse sr, $53,253
Jackson, Reiko M, deval asst I, $23,352
Jackson, Rosemary A, security aide I psy, $30,276
Jackson, Sheila D, lpn, $18,631
Jackson, Sherie M, security aide I psy, $29,832
Jackson, Susan R, lpn II gen, $36,086
Jackson, Tanisha, deval asst I, $23,352
Jackson, Tony L, recrtnal ther II, $46,932
Jacobe, Jennifer L, acct I, $30,984
Jacobe-Bradshaw, Nancy J, acct I, $32,628
Jacobs, Christopher K, deval asst I, $23,412
Jacobs, Veronica D, deval asst I, $22,728
Jacox, Ashley D, registered nurse sup, $78,567
Jacques, Bryon C, habilitation spec II, $39,624
Jager, Toni L, ofc spt asst (keybrd), $22,536
Jaidah, Selena, psychiatric technician I, $24,072
James, Eddie, direct care aide, $13,634.40/hr
James, Ginette G, ofc spt asst (keybrd), $25,032
James, Kim P, registered nurse sr, $55,776
James, Kyle A, security aide I psy, $30,276
James, Regina L, deval asst II, $27,696
James, Ruth A, deval asst I, $23,700
James, Ryan A, deval asst I, $24,396
James, Sean M, psychiatric technician I, $23,352
James, Sherrion, deval asst II, $24,804
Jamison, Felicia, deval asst I, $23,352
Jamison, Kimberly, deval asst I, $25,428
Jamison, Michael J, psychiatric technician I, $23,076
Jani, Piyushkumar, resident physician, $30,882
Jannaman, Cynthia H, registered nurse sup, $73,836
Janoch, Madeline P, direct care aide, $15,142.40/hr
Jansen, Cynthia J, sr ofc spt asst (keybrd), $25,824
Jansen, Katherine E, security aide I psy, $30,276
Jansen, Sharon F, security aide III psy, $36,204
Janson, Karen S, registered nurse sr, $51,552
Jaros, Angela M, psychiatric technician I, $22,728
Jarrett, Barbara A, acct II, $41,172
Jarrett, Jacqueline M, ofc spt asst (keybrd), $22,536
Jarrett, Kelly A, ofc spt asst (keybrd), $23,160
Jarvis, Shelly L, custodial worker I, $20,664
Jasensky, Christopher D, registered nurse, $55,891
Jauregui, Elizabeth, deval asst I, $23,412
Javois, Laurent D, special asst official & admstr, $92,240
Jaycox, Robin S, food serv helper I, $22,317
Jean-Baptiste, Micheline, custodial worker I, $20,664
Jefferson, Ronald L, deval asst I, $24,036
Jeffries, Toscha, psychiatric technician I, $24,072
Jenkins, Charlette L, deval asst I, $22,728
Jenkins, Charonda, psychiatric technician I, $23,352
Jenkins, Christy L, lpn II gen, $36,086
Jenkins, David A, deval asst I, $22,728
Jenkins, Felnena C, deval asst I, $23,352
Jenkins, Shirley A, psychiatric technician I, $22,728
Jenkins, Tamera L, sr ofc spt asst (keybrd), $25,824
Jenkins-McDermed, Jennifer A, dev dis cmnty prog coord, $45,156
Jennings, Angela D, registered nurse, $4,537
Jennings, Detricia L, deval asst I, $24,804
Jennings, Harolyn J, registered nurse, $28,375
Jennings, Jennifer A, deval asst I, $22,728

Jennings, Shantanya M, security aide I psy, $31,620
Jett, Laurinda D, ofc spt asst (keybrd), $26,652
Jett, Sedrick A, psychiatric technician I, $22,728
Jewell, Dylan S, deval asst I, $23,028
Jewell Burks, Erin, resident physician, $51,318
Jiao, Jianwei, resident physician, $51,318
Jloah, Melvin G, custodial worker I, $20,664
Jobe, Michelle L, sr ofc spt asst (keybrd), $33,636
Johns, Deidra A, security aide I psy, $30,276
Johns, Kelly C, unit prog spv mh, $38,928
Johnson, Alexander, psychiatric technician I, $23,352
Johnson, Alexis H, ofc spt asst (keybrd), $25,824
Johnson, Andrea M, deval asst I, $22,728
Johnson, Andrew C, psychiatric technician I, $24,696
Johnson, April A, deval asst I, $23,352
Johnson, Arlander J, security aide I psy, $31,620
Johnson, Barbara A, deval asst I, $23,700
Johnson, Benjamin, behavioral technician, $28,584
Johnson, Candice N, deval asst I, $22,404
Johnson, Carrie, deval asst II, $27,024
Johnson, Chelsea L, psychiatric technician I, $23,352
Johnson, Chelsey M, registered nurse sup, $97,791
Johnson, Cheryl C, lpn II gen, $29,772
Johnson, Christopher L, deval asst I, $24,036
Johnson, Clifford E, psychiatric technician I, $22,728
Johnson, Cody S, deval asst I, $22,728
Johnson, Crystal L, psychiatric technician I, $23,352
Johnson, Cynthia D, deval asst II, $27,696
Johnson, Deambre, account clerk I, $24,264
Johnson, Debra, deval asst I, $23,352
Johnson, Dorothy D, ofc spt asst (keybrd), $23,160
Johnson, Duane, deval asst I, $23,352
Johnson, Gina M, case mgr II dd, $34,944
Johnson, Gwen C, deval asst I, $22,728
Johnson, Iyaborde F, security aide I psy, $31,620
Johnson, Jackie, deval asst III, $27,708
Johnson, Jackie L, deval asst I, $26,400
Johnson, Jacquelyn, deval asst I, $23,352
Johnson, James N, deval asst I, $24,036
Johnson, James R, food serv mgr I, $40,380
Johnson, Janice L, sr ofc spt asst (keybrd), $28,452
Johnson, Jarohn C, psychiatric technician I, $22,728
Johnson, Jasmine B, psychiatric technician I, $23,352
Johnson, Jeffrey, misc tech, $11,336
Johnson, Jheria L, psychiatric technician I, $23,352
Johnson, John H, psychiatric technician I, $22,728
Johnson, Joyce A, deval asst I, $23,076
Johnson, Judy E, affordable housing cnslt mh, $52,092
Johnson, Katherine R, clin casework asst I, $30,144
Johnson, Kenneth R, security ofcr II, $32,628
Johnson, Kimberly D, deval asst I, $23,412
Johnson, Kinyotta, case mgr I dd, $32,628
Johnson, Kurtis F, registered nurse sr, $63,585
Johnson, Kylie S, psychiatric technician I, $22,716
Johnson, Laa, deval asst I, $23,352
Johnson, Lakesha A, deval asst I, $22,728
Johnson, Latanya D, psychiatric technician I, $24,696
Johnson, Lisa N, deval asst II, $26,208
Johnson, Lori B, admin ofc spt asst, $33,744
Johnson, Lorrie C, sr ofc spt asst (keybrd), $25,824
Johnson, Mae C, deval asst I, $23,352
Johnson, Marilyn J, hlth info admin II, $40,380
Johnson, Marissa E, food serv helper I, $22,317
Johnson, Michelle E, lpn II gen, $34,560
Johnson, Nick A, security aide II psy, $34,488
Johnson, Nikia, psychiatric technician I, $23,352
Johnson, Nikki S, registered nurse sr, $71,587
Johnson, Pamela P, deval asst I, $23,352
Johnson, Rachel R, custodial worker I, $20,664
Johnson, Renee, deval asst I, $23,352
Johnson, Richard L, motor veh driver, $27,084
Johnson, Rose M, qual assurance spec mh, $47,892
Johnson, Sara B, registered nurse mgr b2, $78,037
Johnson, Shanea M, registered nurse, $28,375
Johnson, Stacey D, deval asst I, $27,252
Johnson, Stevie, deval asst I, $23,700
Johnson, Theresa A, food serv helper I, $24,264
Johnson, Tonia I, registered nurse sup, $95,478
Johnson, Tramaine, psychiatric technician I, $23,352

Johnson, Valarie S, deval asst I, $23,352
Johnson, Vicki E, activity aide II, $24,072
Johnson, Victoria A, registered nurse sr, $54,720
Johnson, Wesley M, security aide I psy, $29,652
Johnson, William L, custodial work spv, $27,948
Johnston, J S, misc prof, $52.76/hr
Johnston, Karen E, cosmetologist, $25,584
Johnston, Melba J, psychiatric technician I, $23,412
Johnston, Melissa C, sr ofc spt asst (keybrd), $27,504
Johnston, Mindy M, registered nurse, $28,375
Johnston, Sandra K, direct care aide, $11.36/hr
Jolliff, Dbroski C Jr, deval asst I, $22,716
Jolliff, Lapaula L, psychiatric technician II, $30,048
Jolliff, Marsha L, deval asst I, $23,412
Jolly, Carlos D, deval asst I, $22,728
Jolly, Connie S, activity aide II, $24,804
Jolly, Mary C, edual aide, $12,353
Jolly, Sarah D, ofc spt asst (clerical), $10,932
Jonas, Lisa, prog spec II mh, $44,304
Jones, Amy D, fiscal & administrative mgr b2, $57,166
Jones, Aner, deval asst I, $22,728
Jones, Antonio D, activity aide II, $33,153
Jones, Arlene L, registered nurse sr, $61,836
Jones, Autumn M, direct care aide, $1,600
Jones, Ayshia L, deval asst I, $22,716
Jones, Barbara S, acct I, $30,984
Jones, Bonnie M, deval asst I, $22,728
Jones, Brandon S, security aide I psy, $31,620
Jones, Brandy J, food serv helper I, $10,074
Jones, Britney N, deval asst I, $23,352
Jones, Cassandra W, registered nurse sr, $63,585
Jones, Charles E, case mgr II dd, $34,944
Jones, Cherita, deval asst I, $23,352
Jones, Chris A, security aide I psy, $29,208
Jones, Cynthia, deval asst I, $23,352
Jones, Daymoneec M, psychiatric technician I, $23,352
Jones, Derick D, security aide I psy, $31,620
Jones, Devaughn D, case mgmt/assess spv, $40,380
Jones, Diana M, training tech II, $40,380
Jones, Earl, psychiatric technician I, $23,352
Jones, Earl T, security aide I psy, $32,244
Jones, Emma, deval asst I, $23,352
Jones, Eva, deval asst I, $23,352
Jones, Heather L, deval asst I, $23,352
Jones, Janice L, lpn II gen, $37,644
Jones, Jason P, mental hlth mgr b1, $53,206
Jones, Jennifer, cook I, $29,793
Jones, Jeremy L, deval asst I, $22,728
Jones, Joann, deval asst I, $23,352
Jones, Joycelyn M, lpn, $18,183
Jones, Juma L, deval asst I, $24,696
Jones, June, sr ofc spt asst (steno), $28,452
Jones, Justin D, security aide I psy, $29,652
Jones, Kara L, psychiatric technician I, $22,728
Jones, Keven S, security aide I psy, $31,152
Jones, Lanessia S, psychiatric technician I, $23,352
Jones, Larry A, registered nurse mgr b1, $69,651
Jones, Lendwood J, security ofcr I, $25,824
Jones, Lillian R, security aide I psy, $31,620
Jones, Linda D, sr ofc spt asst (keybrd), $25,824
Jones, Lisa D, case mgr II dd, $34,944
Jones, Marliessa G, deval asst III, $29,076
Jones, Martin W, deval asst I, $24,036
Jones, Mary E, custodial worker I, $20,664
Jones, Melissa, mental hlth mgr b2, $57,069
Jones, Moriam F, deval asst I, $23,352
Jones, Pamela J, deval asst I, $23,688
Jones, Quinika L, deval asst II, $24,804
Jones, Sarah, registered nurse - clin opers, $84,183
Jones, Steven L, deval asst I, $23,352
Jones, Tiffany, psychiatric technician I, $22,728
Jones, Tiffany A, admin ofc spt asst, $28,104
Jones, Valerie, deval asst I, $22,728
Jones, Yule, security aide I psy, $31,620
Jones Guilliams, Teresa D, deval asst I, $22,728
Jones-Laswell, Donna M, security aide I psy, $34,488
Jones-Morris, Sheronda L, psychiatric technician I, $23,352
Jordan, Hugh, deval asst I, $23,352

Jordan, Judy A, registered nurse, $36,029
Jordan, Karen, deval asst I, $23,412
Jordan, Phyllis, recrtnal ther I, $33,180
Jordan, Todd M, training tech II, $40,380
Journey, Elizabeth, deval asst I, $22,716
Jowers, Jeffery J, security aide I psy, $30,276
Joyner, Kayla D, psychiatric technician I, $23,352
Jozipovic, Svjetlana, lpn II gen, $39,780
Juarez, Brenda L, registered nurse sr, $58,565
Juhala, Steven A, deval asst I, $22,728
Julian, Coeta A, psychiatric technician I, $23,352
Junge, Sharon A, acct I, $35,568
Jungeblut, Ashley E, deval asst I, $22,728
Justice, Nativia, deval asst I, $22,728
Kabatra, Priscilla M, security aide I psy, $31,620
Kadic, Maja, security aide I psy, $31,620
Kain, Robert, deval asst I, $23,352
Kalu, Mindy E, lpn I gen, $33,384
Kalugina, Kateryna, research analyst III, $53,208
Kamanda, Victor, habilitation spec II, $34,944
Kamara, Abidu, security aide I psy, $32,244
Kamara, Gibrilla, deval asst I, $23,352
Kamara, Jallah, deval asst I, $23,352
Kamara, Vivian E, registered nurse sr, $58,565
Kamel, Mohamed, resident physician, $51,318
Kammerich, Justin R, custodial worker I, $21,760
Kamoni, Joseph, psychiatric technician I, $24,024
Kamp, Emily D, licensed clin soc wkr, $43,488
Kanneh, Mohammed F, custodial worker I, $20,664
Kappler, Sharon L, custodial worker I, $24,339
Karatela, Wajiha P, staff physician spec, $195,435
Kargbo, Kadiatu, deval asst I, $23,352
Karkue, Esther, deval asst II, $24,696
Karmi, Ki Ki, registered nurse, $28,375
Karoba, Purity W, psychiatric technician I, $24,696
Karr, Melinda A, food serv helper I, $20,148
Kastner, Rebecca M, student intern, $22,500
Kater, Tina A, unit prog spv mh, $38,928
Katzenberger, Kimberly L, lpn I gen, $38,104
Kaufman, Johna J, deval asst I, $23,076
Kaup, Mary B, recrtnal ther I, $32,628
Kaza, Ramarao, staff physician spec, $90,576
Kearns, Jennifer D, mental hlth mgr b2, $66,599
Keay, Deborah J, security aide I psy, $30,276
Keefer, Deborah, lpn II gen, $37,020
Keely, Derrick, housekeeper I, $29,004
Keen, Robert A, vendor servs coor mh, $40,380
Keenan, Joan D, prog spec I mh, $53,208
Keesee, Chad M, psychiatric technician I, $23,352
Keesee, Douglas A, storekeeper I, $25,824
Keeven, Diana L, registered nurse sr, $53,253
Keffer, Tina M, deval asst III, $30,528
Kegley, Anne D, registered nurse sr, $60,184
Keim, Ramona D, account clerk II, $25,824
Keipp, Tiffany, case mgr I dd, $31,512
Keirsey, Kimberly D, lpn II gen, $31,872
Keith, Brandon R, unit prog spv mh, $44,304
Keith, Melissa A, ofc spt asst (keybrd), $25,404
Keller, Daniel G, psychiatric technician I, $22,728
Keller, Julie L, deval asst I, $22,728
Kelley, Shevrick, behavior intvtn tech dd, $32,148
Kelley, Sonia, lpn II gen, $40,404
Kellum, Kimberly L, prog spec trainee mh, $36,888
Kelly, Betty A, lpn, $17,275
Kelly, Erica Y, lpn II gen, $37,020
Kelly, Jan M, case mgmt/assess spv, $51,096
Kelly, Judy L, recrtnal ther II, $39,624
Kelly, Paul K, deval asst I, $27,024
Kelly, Salem B, deval asst I, $22,092
Kelz, Scott R, deval asst I, $26,844
Kemery, Valerie M, dev dis cmnty worker II, $34,944
Kemp, Athena S, hospital mgmt asst, $64,026
Kemp, Beatrice B, ofc spt asst (keybrd), $28,452
Kemp, Briana T, food serv helper I, $22,317
Kemp, Kallin L, deval asst I, $24,036
Kemp, Karen M, psychiatric technician I, $23,352
Kemp, Marjorie K, pers analyst II, $39,624
Kemper, Jamika N, registered nurse sr, $62,104
Kempfer, Eric P, deval asst I, $23,352

Kempfer, Paula F, deval asst II, $27,876
Kendall, Earnest J, registered nurse, $36,029
Kendall, Krista D, psychiatric technician I, $24,696
Kendall, Mary L, registered nurse, $27,794
Kendor, Abraham T, deval asst I, $23,352
Kennedy, Derrick W, deval asst I, $24,036
Kennedy, Jauvle T, custodial worker I, $20,664
Kennedy, Jenna L, registered nurse, $50,750
Kennedy, Marjorie B, ofc spt asst (keybrd), $23,880
Kent, Angelia M, registered nurse, $28,375
Kerbel, George R, security aide I psy, $30,276
Kerns, Adam M, psychiatric technician II, $25,428
Kessel, Amy L, fiscal & administrative mgr b2, $57,166
Kessel, Royce A, dev dis cmnty prog coord, $41,172
Kesterson, Andrew L, lpn II gen, $32,844
Ketcherside, Daniel L, psychiatric technician I, $22,728
Ketcherside, Janet L, security aide I psy, $29,652
Ketcherside, Sandra K, security aide I psy, $30,276
Kettle, Jeffery T, security aide I psy, $29,652
Key, Angel F, security aide I psy, $31,620
Key, Anthony C, security ofcr I, $25,824
Keyser, Sandra L, dev dis cmnty worker II, $34,944
Khaliq, Sabeen, resident physician, $23,676
Khoo, Yit M, qual assurance spec mh, $48,156
Kibby, Ava, lpn II gen, $40,404
Kibler, Alexandra, clin casework pract II, $38,928
Kick, Robert F, storekeeper I, $26,232
Kidwell, Ronald D, psychiatric technician I, $22,092
Kieltyka, Jessica I, security aide I psy, $31,620
Kiely, Edward R, pastoral cnslr, $8,034
Kiernan, Edward J, case mgr II dd, $34,944
Kile, Jamie N, deval asst I, $22,404
Killday, Kevin M, psychiatric technician I, $22,092
Killian, George D, cnslr in training, $33,744
Killian, Rene M, clin casework pract II, $37,548
Kimble, Pamela R, psychiatric technician I, $23,352
Kimbro, Thomas G, area sub abuse trtmnt coor, $53,208
Kimbrow, Kimberly M, deval asst II, $25,428
Kincaid, Katie A, psychiatric technician I, $23,352
Kinder, Dana C, deval asst I, $23,412
Kinder, Haley J, deval asst I, $24,036
Kinder, Karen, registered nurse sr, $52,608
Kindle, Julia A, registered nurse sr, $67,959
King, Brittany M, mental hlth instructor, $29,004
King, Gavin D, deval asst I, $24,036
King, Greg, deval asst I, $27,468
King, Juanita M, deval asst III, $28,128
King, June, custodial worker II, $21,864
King, Karen A, ofc spt asst (clerical), $25,032
King, Latoya A, security aide I psy, $29,208
King, Latreice, food serv helper I, $20,664
King, Lisa R, custodial worker I, $22,317
King, Marchele A, ofc spt asst (clerical), $21,864
King, Penny L, qual assurance spec mh, $41,172
King, Simeon, resident physician, $50,005
King, Tina L, deval asst III, $30,384
King, Vesta C, habilitation spec II, $36,204
Kingsbury, David S, mental hlth mgr b2, $70,000
Kingsbury, Joseph S, mental hlth mgr b2, $59,158
Kingsley, Deborah S, food serv helper I, $22,317
Kingston, Ashley N, deval asst I, $24,036
Kingston, Pamela D, deval asst III, $27,276
Kinkead, Daniel R, dev dis cmnty spec, $37,548
Kinnard, Dameeka L, psychiatric technician I, $22,728
Kipkulei, Stanley K, registered nurse sr, $55,776
Kirahagazwe, Consolata B, security aide I psy, $31,620
Kirby, Sara L, deval asst I, $23,352
Kirkland, Josephine, psychiatric technician I, $22,728
Kirkman, Morris E, fire & safety spec, $41,940
Kirshner, Pamela L, account clerk II, $25,032
Kiso, Brandy M, deval asst I, $24,036
Kiso, Terrie L, deval asst I, $24,036
Kiso, Vanessa L, lpn II gen, $30,396
Kitchell, Brandon H, psychiatric technician I, $22,716
Kitchen, Preston, activity aide II, $32,148
Kitchen, Ricky R, security aide I psy, $29,652
Kitobo, Benjamin M, registered nurse sr, $59,645
Kiyee, James, security aide I psy, $31,620
Klamer, Kristin R, security aide I psy, $29,652

Klawuhn, Anita L, psychiatric technician II, $25,428
Klebba, Ricky L, fiscal & administrative mgr b3, $69,611
Klein, Michael R, nutrition/dietary svcs mgr b1, $59,428
Klein, Teresa L, registered nurse, $30,882
Kleinsorge, Kamber E, lpn II gen, $37,390
Kleoppel, Thomas E, deval asst I, $22,728
Klick, Curtis C, custodial worker I, $20,664
Klick, Katherine A, licensed clin soc wkr, $52,092
Kliethermes, Cynthia A, prog spec II mh, $44,304
Kline, Janet, registered nurse sup, $64,380
Kline, Jeffrey S, psychologist II, $77,626
Klingler, Michelle T, registered nurse sr, $71,587
Klingsmith, Rebecca K, acct I, $35,568
Knaebel, Suzanne R, accounting spec III, $57,744
Knapp, Annette M, security aide I psy, $29,208
Knifong, Tammy P, security aide I psy, $31,620
Knipp, Melissa K, mental hlth mgr b2, $70,559
Knoepflein, Susan G, registered nurse sup, $68,990
Knox, Dishon R, training tech II, $40,380
Knutson, Thomas J, resident physician, $54,969
Koca, Michael L, deval asst I, $23,352
Koch, Christina P, behavioral technician, $27,696
Koch, Norine, registered nurse sr, $65,676
Koch-Dunning, Misty L, dev dis cmnty worker II, $34,944
Kochis, Christina R, sr ofc spt asst (keybrd), $25,824
Kochis, Joseph S, registered nurse sr, $53,253
Koderick, Jarrod F, med lab tech, $26,844
Koderick, Karen R, psychiatric technician I, $23,352
Koenig, Emily E, designated principal asst dept, $74,235
Koenig, Robin L, mental hlth mgr b1, $55,406
Koenig, Ronald N, security aide I psy, $30,276
Koester, Brandon M, psychiatric technician I, $23,352
Kohler, Adam R, security aide II psy, $32,208
Kohler, Andrea P, security aide I psy, $29,652
Kohler, Mercedes N, deval asst I, $23,412
Kokelu, Gladys C, registered nurse sr, $71,587
Konneh, A F, case mgr II dd, $34,944
Kontor, Vincent O, security aide I psy, $24,244
Kopp, Tonya M, deval asst I, $22,728
Koppeis, Patricia K, special asst prof, $90,900
Koppeis, Richard D, pers ofcr I, $47,892
Kopriva, Megan, clin casework pract II, $37,548
Korman, Brenda M, ofc spt asst (keybrd), $23,160
Kornis, George D, deval asst I, $22,404
Koroma, Mohamed, deval asst I, $22,716
Kosia, Sao, deval asst I, $23,352
Kossman, Terri L, prog spec II mh, $46,068
Kouyate, Salimata, deval asst I, $23,352
Kovac, Carolyn, registered nurse, $36,029
Kowalewski, Kristina M, deval asst I, $22,728
Kramer, Bary A, licensed clin soc wkr, $46,932
Kramer, Janice A, licensed clin soc wkr, $31,130
Kramer, Nola D, dev dis cmnty worker II, $33,744
Krastanoff, Crystal M, cook I, $21,864
Kraus, Helen L, deval asst I, $22,728
Kreipe, John, psychiatric technician I, $22,728
Krekel, Mary A, ofc spt asst (keybrd), $27,084
Kremenak, Molly R, food serv helper I, $20,664
Kress, Samantha K, psychiatric technician I, $23,352
Kreyling, Vanessa J, security aide I psy, $29,652
Kroll, Andrea K, case mgr II dd, $34,944
Kronk, Rebecca L, lpn II gen, $39,366
Krummel, Sara E, clin casework pract II, $37,548
Kucharski, Elizabeth V, case mgr III dd, $37,548
Kuehner, Ryan M, recrtnal ther I, $33,744
Kurian, Nirmala, staff physician spec, $203,448
Kurrelmeyer, Elizabeth, phys thrpst asst, $36,324
Kurth, Janace K, ofc worker misc, $14,228
Kurz, Josephine B, mental hlth mgr b1, $45,000
Kuschell, Kayla E, psychiatric technician I, $22,728
Kwakye, Emmanuel, security aide I psy, $32,244
Kwentus, Crystal M, licensed prof cnslr II, $41,172
Kyllonen, David J, registered nurse sr, $51,552
La Breyere, John B, licensed prof cnslr II, $42,708
Labon, Jennifer N, case mgr II dd, $34,944
Labruyere, Kelly J, reimbursement ofcr I, $33,744
Lachance, Amy B, registered nurse mgr b1, $69,651
Lachance, Ruby, deval asst I, $22,716
Lackey, Andrew M, prog coord dmh dohss, $48,156

Lackey, David J, occup ther II, $63,996
Lacy, Tanja N, case mgr II dd, $34,944
Ladd, Norman D, recrtnal ther II, $36,888
Lagasse, Kandice D, dev dis cmnty worker II, $34,944
Lagore, Rebecca L, lpn II gen, $29,772
Lagrone, Marsha', food serv helper I, $20,664
Lagrone, Sheketa A, edual aide, $10,365
Lain, Tonda K, dev dis cmnty worker II, $42,708
Lake, Rebecca S, deval asst I, $22,404
Lake, Sarah L, deval asst I, $23,352
Lakebrink, Erin E, case mgr II dd, $34,944
Laks, Natarajan, staff physician spec, $106,272
Lamb, Ann M, lpn II gen, $32,364
Lamley, Tina L, recrtnal ther I, $38,928
Lammers, Rose M, deval asst I, $23,076
Lammert, Joseph, dev dis cmnty prog coord, $42,708
Lampe, Randall K, psychiatric technician I, $25,428
Lancaster, Dora L, security aide I psy, $29,208
Landis, Janae A, security aide I psy, $29,652
Lane, Brenda L, reimbursement ofcr I, $32,052
Lane, Catherine A, pers analyst II, $38,232
Lane, Jasmine D, psychiatric technician I, $22,728
Lane, Jennifer R, deval asst I, $22,092
Lane, Lori L, qual assurance spec mh, $43,488
Lane, Sue A, clin soc work spec, $48,156
Lane, Tricia L, security aide I psy, $30,276
Lanear, Martha, custodial worker I, $21,864
Laney, Kandance J, deval asst I, $27,252
Lange, Cindy L, dev dis cmnty spec, $36,204
Langum, Michelle R, ofc spt asst (keybrd), $22,536
Lanham, Deborah, reimbursement ofcr I, $30,984
Lansin, Ylynn L, deval asst I, $24,036
Lantz, Barbara A, nutrition/dietary svcs mgr b1, $56,510
Laramie-Petersen, Patricia A, case mgr II dd, $38,232
Larsen, Michael E, licensed clin soc wkr, $38,928
Lash, Shauna L, lpn II gen, $30,216
Lasley, Dorothy S, edual aide, $10,121
Laswell, Vernon L, security aide III psy, $38,928
Latty, Janet M, registered nurse sr, $66,505
Laubenstein, Jesse R, deval asst I, $22,728
Laurence, Kayla E, deval asst I, $22,404
Law, Amanda M, security ofcr I, $25,032
Law, Stacey J, dev dis cmnty spec, $36,888
Lawal, Ogunola, deval asst I, $23,352
Lawrence, Alecia D, lpn II gen, $36,086
Lawrence, Garrett, misc prof, $13,372
Lawrence, Kimberly G, case mgr II dd, $34,944
Laws, Darlene G, case mgr II dd, $34,944
Laws, Steven C, mental hlth mgr b1, $51,092
Lawson, Angel J, security aide II psy, $31,152
Lawson, Karen J, ofc spt asst (keybrd), $25,824
Lawson, Perry B, activity aide I, $27,780
Lawson, Sanette J, case mgr II dd, $34,944
Lay, Sarah K, ofc spt asst (keybrd), $23,880
Layton, Antoinette D, ofc spt asst (keybrd), $23,160
Layton, Jennie M, sr ofc spt asst (keybrd), $30,924
Leabig, Della, cook III, $29,496
Lean, Lana R, psychiatric technician II, $25,584
Lear, John, registered nurse sr, $60,796
Lease, Jacob, psychiatric technician I, $22,728
Lebrun, Alyssa B, deval asst I, $22,404
Lechner, Michelle D, clin soc work spv, $55,416
Lecure, Shelly D, special asst prof, $58,000
Ledbetter, Lisa M, deval asst I, $22,728
Ledbetter, Ross W, registered nurse, $48,043
Ledesma, Laura M, deval asst I, $22,728
Ledyard, Martha L, clin soc work spv, $56,520
Lee, Amanda R, security aide I psy, $29,652
Lee, Christopher, psychiatric technician I, $24,036
Lee, Demetria, psychiatric technician I, $23,700
Lee, Ellen K, security aide II psy, $38,352
Lee, Gwendolyn, deval asst I, $23,352
Lee, Jessica N, deval asst I, $22,092
Lee, Kim D, security aide I psy, $31,152
Lee, Mariah C, deval asst I, $23,352
Lee, Marsha N, security aide I psy, $32,760
Lee, Michelle D, deval asst II, $29,052
Lee, Shannon M, psychiatric technician I, $22,728
Lee, Shari E, cook I, $23,508

Lee, Sherry L, registered nurse mgr b3, $102,455
Lee, Tina J, special asst ofc & clerical, $37,497
Lee, Vickie, pers clerk, $34,356
Lee, Zandra S, deval asst I, $22,092
Leeker, Olivia A, psychologist I, $65,364
Leeper, Pamela L, work therapy spec II, $30,984
Lefkowitz, Heather L, custodial worker II, $23,613
Leflore, Kimberly L, deval asst II, $27,252
Leflore, Shaquita, deval asst I, $23,412
Legate, Beth, psychiatric technician I, $22,728
Leggett, Theresa M, case mgr II dd, $34,944
Leggins, Lenay M, psychiatric technician I, $23,352
Legrand, Angela D, psychiatric technician I, $24,696
Legrand, Mary J, registered nurse sr, $56,976
Lehmen, Bradley W, mgmt analysis spec II, $51,096
Lehr, Ann D, case mgr II dd, $34,944
Leigh, Ralph G, physician, $111,132
Leimkuehler, Robin L, psychiatric technician I, $24,804
Lele, Manisha M, staff physician spec, $297,355
Lemassi Kabiwa, Sarah N, security aide I psy, $31,152
Lemassi Lemassi, Jacques E, security aide I psy, $31,620
Lemoine, Erleine R, deval asst I, $22,728
Lenoir, Lagail M, ofc spt asst (keybrd), $24,612
Lenz, Martha A, deval asst I, $24,072
Leonard, Cody W, security aide I psy, $30,276
Leonard, Onita, deval asst I, $23,350
Leonard, Patricia S, admin ofc spt asst, $28,104
Leonard, Rachelle, psychiatric technician II, $32,148
Leonard, Russell L, registered nurse sr, $51,552
Lepage, Julia L, designated principal asst div, $81,305
Leslie, Abby E, psychiatric technician I, $23,352
Lester, Lisa R, psychiatric technician I, $24,804
Leuthen, Shannon L, sr ofc spt asst (keybrd), $25,032
Leuther, Heather N, sr ofc spt asst (keybrd), $27,504
Levall, Adrienne M, dietitian II, $44,304
Levin, Linda M, ofc spt asst (keybrd), $23,880
Levine, Sheryl J, licensed clin soc wkr, $45,156
Lewey, Jennifer H, rehab worker, $12,480
Lewis, Angela H, area sub abuse trtmnt coor, $53,208
Lewis, Brian, deval asst II, $24,804
Lewis, Dorshall N, qual assurance spec mh, $40,380
Lewis, Howard D, security aide I psy, $29,652
Lewis, Jairus, security aide I psy, $31,620
Lewis, Jeanette S, custodial work spv, $25,824
Lewis, Joe, custodial work spv, $25,824
Lewis, Juana V, security ofcr I, $25,824
Lewis, Kemar D, security aide I psy, $29,652
Lewis, Kenneth V, security aide I psy, $30,276
Lewis, Latonya L, registered nurse sr, $71,587
Lewis, Michael, registered nurse sr, $65,676
Lewis, Michael L, security aide I psy, $31,620
Lewis, Nikki L, acct I, $30,984
Lewis, Ramon, stores clerk, $22,872
Lewis, Sabrina V, food serv helper I, $20,148
Lewis, Tiana M, deval asst I, $24,036
Lewis, Wendy L, security aide I psy, $29,652
Lewis-Thomas, Beverly A, deval asst I, $23,076
Lezieanya, Uzoamaka, deval asst I, $23,352
Liberman, Marla B, psychologist II, $45,248
Liebich, David K, recrtnal ther I, $33,180
Liese, Jamie L, deval asst I, $22,728
Liggins, Frederick A, psychiatric technician I, $23,352
Liggins, Marshad, deval asst I, $23,352
Light, Sara E, case mgr I dd, $31,512
Lightfoot, Nancy J, ofc spt asst (clerical), $22,536
Lillich, Julie A, mental hlth mgr b2, $58,347
Lilly, Eric, registered nurse sr, $54,720
Lilly, Michelle A, psychiatric technician II, $28,152
Limbach, Lisa L, paralegal, $40,168
Limback, Denise L, registered nurse sr, $51,276
Limback, Donna S, account clerk II, $25,824
Lincoln, Richard S, security aide I psy, $29,652
Linden, Christina N, licensed clin soc wkr, $48,156
Lindley, Sherry L, registered nurse, $30,882
Lindman, Kasandra M, deval asst I, $22,728
Lindsey, Mary J, psychiatric technician I, $26,400
Lindstrom, Deborah M, lpn II gen, $29,772
Link, Michele R, lpn II gen, $40,024
Linn, James E, security aide I psy, $29,652

Linville, Cody G, deval asst I, $22,404
Lippert, Lisa K, deval asst I, $24,036
Lishock, Frances R, case mgr III dd, $37,548
Litterest, Cindy L, security aide I psy, $29,832
Little, Alfred W, cook I, $21,864
Little, Barbara A, deval asst II, $25,428
Little, George R, recrtnal ther I, $32,628
Littlejohn, Jessica R, psychiatric technician I, $23,352
Lloyd, Shelby L, deval asst I, $22,728
Lloyd, Vernon, deval asst II, $25,428
Locke, Diane M, food serv helper I, $22,317
Locke, Jimmie, dining room spv, $25,824
Lockett, Danyelle E, case mgr I dd, $32,628
Lockhart, Donna L, deval asst I, $26,400
Lockhart, Katherine E, deval asst I, $24,036
Lockhart, Kylene M, activity aide II, $25,584
Lockridge, Ada M, ofc worker misc, $10,926
Lockridge, Donnell, custodial worker I, $22,536
Lockwood, Jesse M, psychiatric technician I, $23,352
Lockwood, Kelly E, training tech II, $41,172
Loeb, Molly R, account clerk II, $27,084
Loeffel, Monica L, food serv helper I, $20,148
Loehr, Colleen T, staff physician spec, $203,448
Lofquest, Aaron L, deval asst I, $23,352
Loftis, Tracey R, unit prog spv mh, $41,940
Lofton, Natasha R, security ofcr II, $35,157
Logan, Angela J, case mgr III dd, $37,548
Logan, Dana I, registered nurse sr, $60,516
Logan, Helen E, pastoral cnslr, $50,041
Logan, Robert T, deval asst I, $22,728
Logwood-Jones, Brenda J, deval asst III, $32,472
Lohachart, Jirarat, registered nurse, $28,375
Lohsandt, Jill S, security aide I psy, $29,208
Lolley, Stephanie M, deval asst I, $22,728
Long, Colleen S, case mgmt/assess spv, $45,156
Long, Douglas E, prog coord dmh dohss, $62,664
Long, John W, fiscal & administrative mgr b2, $63,471
Long, Kendra D, dev dis cmnty worker II, $34,944
Long, Lisa L, deval asst I, $24,036
Long, Mary J, paralegal, $36,384
Long, Shirley, deval asst I, $23,352
Long, Tonya M, dentist, $63,024
Long, Travis C, custodial worker I, $22,317
Longmire, Clara D, custodial worker I, $23,160
Longmire, Shalanda L, deval asst II, $24,804
Longworth, Damon C, fiscal & administrative mgr b3, $76,514
Looney, Regina, deval asst I, $25,428
Lopez, John H, registered nurse sr, $57,893
Lopez, Megan E, deval asst I, $22,728
Lopez, Patty L, registered nurse sr, $53,592
Lord, Karen, custodial work spv, $26,205
Lorence, Margarita E, psychological resident, $50,000
Lortz, Terry D, custodial worker I, $22,317
Lotsu, Nora, security aide I psy, $31,620
Lotz, Charles M, pastoral cnslr, $37,651
Loucks, Andrea E, psychiatric technician II, $25,428
Loughridge, Mary E, sr ofc spt asst (keybrd), $25,824
Loukota, Holly L, psychiatric technician I, $22,092
Love, Duane D, security aide II psy, $38,256
Love, Ebony N, deval asst I, $22,728
Love, Jill N, food serv helper I, $20,664
Love, Kayla N, psychiatric technician I, $22,728
Love, Mae L, case mgr III dd, $40,380
Love, Stephanie J, activity aide II, $27,708
Love, Thomas, deval asst I, $22,728
Lovelace, Peggy A, psychiatric technician I, $24,696
Lovercamp, Mendy L, habilitation prog mgr, $45,156
Lowry, Eldora M, acct II, $43,488
Loyd, Donna, ofc spt asst (keybrd), $25,824
Loyd, Michael K, deval asst I, $23,352
Lozano, George D, unit prog spv mh, $42,708
Lucas, Anne V, registered nurse sr, $64,681
Lucas, Betty L, registered nurse, $36,029
Lucas, Chermeka B, deval asst I, $23,352
Lucas, Penny M, lpn, $18,631
Lucas, Sheila D, food serv helper I, $20,664
Lucht, Kimberlee L, deval asst I, $26,004
Lucy, Karen M, ofc spt asst (keybrd), $22,536
Ludewig, James J, music ther III, $41,172

Ludewig, Laura D, licensed clin soc wkr, $50,040
Luebbert, Anna L, mental hlth mgr b1, $60,125
Luebbert, Mary J, special asst ofc & clerical, $47,392
Luebbert, Trudy A, prog spec II mh, $41,940
Luebrecht, Jeffrey L, deval asst I, $27,876
Luechtefeld, Debra A, mental hlth mgr b3, $71,205
Lueckenhoff, Amanda B, registered nurse, $54,766
Lueckenhoff, Amanda P, behavioral technician trne, $23,880
Luehrs, Carolyn S, habilitation spec II, $34,944
Luellen, Donna, sr ofc spt asst (keybrd), $25,032
Lukowski, Laura L, licensed clin soc wkr, $47,892
Luna-Hill, Adrianna C, deval asst I, $23,076
Lundy, Christie J, special asst official & admstr, $70,000
Lunsford, Alexander D, psychiatric technician I, $23,352
Lusby, Melissa, pers analyst II, $36,888
Luss, Tenniell, deval asst I, $22,728
Luther, Amanda M, deval asst I, $22,728
Luther, Carla J, sr ofc spt asst (steno), $28,908
Luther, Donald L, cook II, $23,880
Luther, Rhonda J, deval asst I, $23,076
Luther, Ryan A, deval asst I, $22,728
Luye, Ellen M, psychiatric technician II, $25,584
Lyday, Travis, security aide I psy, $32,244
Lyell, Matthew S, deval asst I, $24,036
Lynn, Amy R, deval asst I, $24,072
Lynn, Janell D, unit prog spv mh, $38,928
Lynn, Karla J, deval asst III, $30,528
Lynn, Lorie M, registered nurse sr, $53,253
Lynn, Nancy J, security aide I psy, $29,652
Lynn, Vanessa J, music ther I, $32,628
Mabery, Kira J, ofc spt asst (keybrd), $23,160
Mabey, Amanda M, prog spec II mh, $41,940
Mabior, Mabior A, food serv helper I, $20,952
Mabry, Diana L, nursing consult, $28,375
Mace, Crystal A, clin casework asst II, $30,984
Mace, Steven L, security aide I psy, $30,276
Mach, Cheryl A, reimbursement ofcr II, $33,744
Machua, Lucy W, deval asst I, $22,092
Macinnes, Sandra K, case mgr II dd, $36,888
Mack, Angel D, security aide I psy, $29,832
Mack, Angelia M, registered nurse sup, $87,171
Mack, Danny J, security aide I psy, $29,652
Mackinnon, Misty D, security aide I psy, $29,832
Macklin, Precious, deval asst II, $27,024
Maddox, Cheryl K, registered nurse mgr b2, $82,279
Maddox, Marc C, mental hlth mgr b3, $79,297
Maddox, William H, security aide I psy, $33,312
Magee, Carla R, fiscal & administrative mgr b2, $62,726
Maggard, John P, assoc psychologist II, $49,128
Maggard, Lynn, mental hlth mgr b1, $52,081
Maguire, Sally A, hlth info admin I, $43,488
Mahanes, Jama A, mental hlth mgr b1, $52,015
Mahaney, Robert E, security aide I psy, $31,152
Mahaney, Robyne R, security aide I psy, $32,244
Mahil, Marsheena, deval asst I, $24,036
Mahler, Christine J, psychiatric technician I, $23,352
Mahone, Angela Y, admin ofc spt asst, $31,512
Mahone, Teajuana F, misc tech, $25,480
Mahoney, Ronda J, misc prof, $25,735
Mahr, Mallorie J, account clerk II, $27,084
Mahr, Michele A, case mgr III dd, $37,548
Mahr, Rhonda, custodial worker II, $21,564
Majok, Daniel, custodial worker I, $21,864
Major, Gary G, security aide I psy, $30,276
Major, Larry L, security aide II psy, $32,760
Malan, Darla K, pers ofcr II, $49,128
Malench, Elizabeth A, assoc counsel, $67,670
Malloyd, Christel, deval asst I, $22,728
Malone, Billie M, custodial worker I, $20,664
Maloy, Melissa R, deval asst I, $23,412
Mandala, Michael G, psychiatric technician I, $22,728
Mandracchia, Steven A, mental hlth mgr b2, $72,717
Manley, Eric D, custodial worker I, $22,317
Manley, Monica, registered nurse, $28,375
Mann, Christina A, workshop spv II, $29,850
Mann, Debra C, deval asst I, $22,728
Mann, Kari M, deval asst I, $23,412
Manning, Rayshun Y, case mgr II dd, $34,944
Mansell, Rose L, deval asst I, $22,728

Manus, Janet, special asst ofc & clerical, $41,659
Manville, Jodi R, mental hlth mgr b2, $58,000
Manyeh Kakpata, Susan K, registered nurse, $28,375
Mapes, Liberty, deval asst I, $22,728
Mapes, Matthew L, deval asst I, $23,076
Mapes, Tommy J, deval asst I, $23,028
Maple, Marlene E, behavior intvtn tech dd, $31,080
Maples, Peggy A, deval asst I, $25,428
Maragh, Tamar P, security aide I psy, $31,410
Maragh-Lawrence, Jacqueline S, registered nurse sr, $57,617
Marberry, Patricia M, ofc worker misc, $12,404
Marchese, Deborah A, deval asst I, $22,728
Marcum, Alexis L, deval asst I, $23,352
Marcum, Cheryl, prog spec II mh, $45,156
Marcum, Christopher R, deval asst I, $23,412
Mardini, Susan M, clin soc work spv, $51,096
Markt, Amanda D, mental hlth mgr b1, $53,592
Markway, Greg P, designated principal asst div, $84,083
Markworth, John D, laborer I, $21,264
Marler, Kimberly S, security aide I psy, $30,276
Marler, Ronda K, reimbursement ofcr I, $29,976
Marler-Baird, Kathryn J, registered nurse - clin opers, $68,532
Marriott, Linda K, psychiatric technician I, $23,352
Marsh, Dwight D, deval asst I, $23,352
Marshall, Dale A, special educ tchr I, $41,940
Marshall, Kashala D, deval asst I, $23,352
Marshall, Zameciah C, deval asst I, $22,728
Marston, Susan J, food serv helper I, $22,317
Martin, Albert, deval asst I, $22,728
Martin, Amanda M, sr ofc spt asst (keybrd), $25,824
Martin, Anthony A, security aide I psy, $31,152
Martin, Bonnie L, security aide II psy, $34,488
Martin, Bryanna G, mental hlth mgr b1, $54,282
Martin, Catherine J, account clerk II, $25,824
Martin, Darleen D, sr ofc spt asst (keybrd), $25,824
Martin, Ericka, case mgr III dd, $38,928
Martin, James E, fiscal & administrative mgr b3, $77,488
Martin, Kathy A, admin ofc spt asst, $34,944
Martin, Keri M, case mgmt/assess spv, $46,932
Martin, Lisa K, staff training & dev coor, $54,288
Martin, Mary K, deval asst I, $22,728
Martin, Mary Y, cook I, $21,864
Martin, Patricia J, security aide I psy, $29,832
Martin, Shaun E, security aide I psy, $32,244
Martin, Stella B, deval asst I, $22,404
Martin, Timothy A, custodial worker I, $20,664
Martin, Tyrone, food serv helper I, $20,664
Martinez, Francisco E, direct care aide, $9,389
Martinez, Joyce A, registered nurse, $7,150
Martinez, Mercedes D, deval asst I, $24,036
Martinez, Michelle D, deval asst I, $22,404
Martinez, Tammy L, reimbursement ofcr I, $29,976
Martin-Forman, Martha A, institution supt, $87,480
Marty, Thomas, case mgr II dd, $34,944
Maru, Wondwosen B, psychiatric technician I, $24,696
Marx, John J, deval asst I, $22,716
Marx, John S, security aide I psy, $30,276
Marx, Tammy R, security aide I psy, $30,276
Mason, Mae C, deval asst I, $26,004
Mason, Michelle D, deval asst II, $28,584
Mason, Tiara S, misc tech, $13,372
Massey, Dawn E, sr ofc spt asst (keybrd), $25,824
Massey, Kayla B, security aide I psy, $29,652
Massie, Anne M, activity aide III, $34,968
Massman, Linda C, sec, $19,701
Mathews, Adrian C, psychiatric technician I, $23,412
Mathews, Bonnie J, deval asst I, $22,728
Mathews, Jennifer, psychologist I, $60,120
Mathews, Julie A, hlth info tech I, $28,536
Mathews, Lisa M, psychologist I, $71,278
Mathis, Tracie R, psychiatric technician I, $22,728
Matlock, Trudy S, qual assurance spec mh, $42,708
Matter, Monzer, psychiatric technician I, $24,072
Matteson, Sandra J, ofc spt asst (keybrd), $25,824
Matthews, Annette L, habilitation spec I, $34,944
Matthews, Elizabeth R, registered nurse sr, $56,192
Matthews, Paige C, dev dis cmnty prog coord, $44,304
Matthews, Peter A, security ofcr I, $25,824
Matthews, Trameka L, deval asst I, $22,092

Mattingly, Charles F, dentist III, $96,504
Mattingly, Veronica L, ofc spt asst (keybrd), $26,232
Mauk, Tracy L, vendor servs coor mh, $40,380
Maupin, Dale A, deval asst I, $23,412
Maupin, Susan H, cook II, $23,880
Maxey, Tina L, psychiatric technician I, $22,728
Maxson, Joseph D, psychiatric technician I, $22,716
Maxwell, April Y, dpty div dir, $92,240
Maxwell, George B, childrens psy care spv, $26,652
Maxwell, Vida M, deval asst I, $22,728
Maxwell, Willie E, security aide III psy, $38,928
May, Ana Mae P, security aide I psy, $32,244
Mayberry, Ginger K, activity aide II, $24,804
Mayberry, Michael W, psychiatric technician II, $26,208
Mayberry, Titus S, dev dis cmnty spec, $37,548
Mayes, Veronica M, psychiatric technician I, $22,716
Mayfield, Brooke M, prog coord dmh dohss, $51,096
Mayo, Byron, psychiatric technician I, $22,728
Mayo, Paula D, psychiatric technician I, $23,352
Mays, Dianna N, lpn II gen, $36,086
Mayson, Linda A, sr ofc spt asst (keybrd), $25,824
Mc Vicar, Marissa J, case mgr II dd, $34,944
McAuley, Kristine, registered nurse, $54,766
McBaine, Debra S, misc prof, $40,768
McBride, Debra A, deval asst III, $28,128
McBride, Evelyn L, deval asst I, $22,728
McBride, Jamell, psychiatric technician I, $23,352
McBride, Keyona L, security aide I psy, $32,244
McBryan, Lois S, mental hlth mgr b1, $56,055
McCabe, Rick R, security aide II psy, $31,152
McCain, Felicia A, psychiatric technician I, $22,728
McCarrell, Vicki, dpty div dir, $96,455
McCarron, Brian D, security aide I psy, $29,652
McCarthy, Karen E, behavior intvtn tech dd, $29,568
McCarver-Boyer, Sheila G, housekeeper II, $34,356
McCauley, Darryl N, psychiatric technician I, $22,728
McCauley, Elizabeth A, therapy consult, $26,811
McCauslin, Debra, account clerk II, $25,824
McClain, Stevena D, deval asst II, $25,420
McClanahan, Carolyn D, licensed clin soc wkr, $47,892
McClanahan, Dawn M, psychiatric technician I, $22,728
McClellen, Lisa M, registered nurse, $58,769
McClendon, Leon Z, licensed clin soc wkr, $49,128
McClendon, Rachelle A, psychiatric technician I, $23,352
McCloud, Jarrett J, deval asst I, $24,036
McClure, Ashley, deval asst I, $22,728
McClure, Janet L, ofc spt asst (keybrd), $26,652
McCombs, Judith A, security aide I psy, $31,620
McConnaughey, Tara B, lpn II gen, $37,020
McConnell, Timothy L, acct I, $38,232
McCord, Cherri L, licensed prof cnslr I, $36,204
McCormack, Jan D, psychiatric technician I, $24,072
McCoy, Brooklyn D, security aide I psy, $31,620
McCoy, Tracey S, case mgr II dd, $37,548
McCoy, Wesley, cook II, $23,880
McCray, Bridgett F, psychiatric technician I, $18,182
McCray, Tionna S, deval asst III, $27,084
McCrorey, Merri E, security aide I psy, $29,652
McCulloch, Karla R, sr ofc spt asst (keybrd), $25,824
McCully, Frank, security aide I psy, $30,276
McCune, Joy L, registered nurse sr, $60,796
McCutcheon, Mary S, registered nurse sr, $58,415
McDaniel, Donna C, qual assurance spec mh, $40,380
McDaniel, Joan L, food serv helper I, $11,158
McDaniel, Latrice R, psychiatric technician I, $22,728
McDaniel, Timothy M, food serv helper I, $20,664
McDaniel, Traci J, psychiatric technician I, $22,728
McDonald, Debbie M, registered nurse sr, $63,585
McDonald, Deborah L, sr ofc spt asst (keybrd), $26,652
McDonald, Kelly R, special asst ofc & clerical, $47,392
McDonald, Syn, licensed behavior analyst, $66,720
McDonald, Terrie L, security aide I psy, $31,152
McDonald, Toyzella N, case mgr II dd, $34,944
McDowell, Sharon L, special asst prof, $36,204
McDowell, Taylor D, security aide I psy, $29,208
McDuffie, Debra F, dining room spv, $26,232
McElroy, Teresa K, deval asst I, $22,092
McEntee, Kathleen A, licensed prof cnslr II, $46,068
McFadden, Carol A, lpn II gen, $17,280

McFall, Jennifer R, psychiatric technician I, $22,728
McFarland, Jo, case mgr II dd, $34,944
McFarlane, Michael, investigator II, $46,932
McGaan, Dianne, deval asst I, $23,352
McGee, Penny, psychiatric technician I, $23,076
McGee-Morrow, Carolyn, psychiatric technician I, $24,696
McGeoghegan, Eileen, misc prof, $32,825
McGilberry, Wanda, pers clerk, $34,944
McGill, Cody B, deval asst I, $23,352
McGill, Jennifer, psychiatric technician I, $24,072
McGirt, Alicia A, psychiatric technician I, $23,352
McGirt, Janette M, domestic serv worker, $14.15/hr
McGirt, Janette M, ofc spt asst (keybrd), $27,084
McGlown, Teresa L, psychiatric technician I, $26,208
McGowan, Mary J, security aide I psy, $29,652
McGowen, Suzan J, pers clerk, $29,496
McGraw, Lynn M, registered nurse sr, $51,552
McGruder, Norvie M, deval asst I, $22,716
McGuire, Sarah A, deval asst II, $28,584
McInnis-Nash, Mayda L, acct I, $32,628
McIntosh, Jazmine, childrens psy care spv, $26,652
McIntosh, Jazmine, direct care aide, $15.56/hr
McIntyre, Brittney G, dev dis cmnty worker II, $34,944
McIntyre, Melissa K, lpn I gen, $33,384
McIntyre, Shanna, case mgr III dd, $41,172
McKee, Lauren M, case mgr II dd, $34,944
McKee, Patricia A, psychiatric technician I, $22,728
McKeller, Loretta D, sr ofc spt asst (keybrd), $25,824
McKelly, Daniel, psychiatric technician I, $22,728
McKenney, Sabrina L, psychiatric technician I, $23,352
McKenzie, Mikayla B, psychiatric technician I, $23,352
McKiddie, Jared T, psychiatric technician I, $24,696
McKifford, Jeannie L, mental hlth mgr b1, $55,065
McKifford, Mary A, qual assurance spec mh, $42,708
McKinley, Derrick F, security ofcr III, $29,496
McKinley, Dolores A, qual assurance spec mh, $38,928
McKinley, Marcus, psychiatric technician I, $24,696
McKinley-Cook, Lavonne M, sr ofc spt asst (keybrd), $27,948
McKinney, Derron L, security ofcr I, $25,824
McKinney, Jennifer, mgmt analysis spec II, $42,708
McKinney, Melissa M, pers clerk, $29,496
McKinney, Pamela A, motor veh driver, $24,264
McKissick, Jerilyn S, deval asst III, $30,528
McKnight, Annetta L, registered nurse sr, $59,340
McLanahan, Ariel L, deval asst I, $22,728
McLaughlin, Gina N, vendor servs coor mh, $40,380
McLean, Judith F, registered nurse sr, $65,676
McMackin, Bobby L, ofc spt asst (clerical), $25,032
McMahon, Cory J, misc prof, $12,854
McMahon, Heather A, psychologist I, $71,100
McManus, Thelma C, acct I, $31,512
McManus, Victoria S, clerk, $11,323
McMillan, Joshua D, registered nurse, $59,645
McMurray, Danny, psychiatric technician I, $23,352
McMurray, Lee C, assoc counsel, $63,863
McNeal, James C, deval asst I, $22,728
McNeal, Julliette M, registered nurse, $28,374
McNeese, Tramiya, deval asst I, $22,728
McNeil, Rosetta M, security aide I psy, $30,276
McNeil, Ruby D, deval asst II, $25,584
McNeill, Christie D, account clerk I, $21,864
McPherson, Robert, habilitation spec II, $34,944
McQueen, Alberta J, deval asst I, $22,728
McReynolds, Nancy L, registered nurse sr, $63,373
McSwain, Teresa, qual assurance spec mh, $40,380
McVay, Lee A, psychologist I, $71,208
Meckfessel, Dwight C, security aide I psy, $31,152
Medina, Amanda K, deval asst II, $24,804
Medina, J E, deval asst I, $23,028
Medley, Russell L, sr ofc spt asst (keybrd), $30,384
Medlock, Dana L, registered nurse sr, $58,140
Meehan, Claudia J, custodial worker I, $20,664
Meek, Cathy D, registered nurse sr, $55,776
Meier, Emily L, food serv helper I, $28,770
Mejia Campos, Carlos E, deval asst I, $23,412
Melcher, Shelly C, lpn II gen, $39,780
Melegrito, James P, registered nurse sr, $56,976
Melies, Lisa J, deval asst II, $27,876
Melton, Lori L, registered nurse, $48,043

Melton, Nickey L, custodial worker I, $22,317
Melton, Regina N, training tech II, $44,304
Menditto, Anthony A, mental hlth mgr b3, $82,792
Meng, Heather J, registered nurse, $50,244
Menning, Michelle L, deval asst I, $22,728
Mercer, Matthew P, dev dis cmnty worker I, $33,744
Merchant, Lisa A, edu asst II, $28,584
Merrill, Margaret F, psychiatric technician I, $23,352
Merrill, Michele L, fiscal & administrative mgr b2, $57,166
Merritt, Angela R, psychiatric technician I, $25,584
Merseal, Mikel, activity aide II, $24,804
Mesic, Medina, security aide I psy, $29,208
Messer, Glenda K, psychiatric technician I, $24,696
Messersmith, Jennifer, clin casework pract II, $37,548
Messick, Anna S, clin casework pract II, $42,708
Messinger, Kelly L, habilitation spec II, $34,944
Methner, Diane, registered nurse, $36,029
Metz, James H, deval asst I, $23,352
Metzinger, Kathie R, registered nurse - clin opers, $69,996
Metzler, Barbara K, sr ofc spt asst (clerical), $27,948
Meuth, Shirley A, ofc spt asst (keybrd), $23,880
Meyer, Amanda E, registered nurse sr, $32,843
Meyer, Barbara A, registered nurse sr, $55,776
Meyer, Gary W, security aide I psy, $29,652
Meyer, Melissa A, case mgr II dd, $20,966
Meyer, Sandra K, recrtnal ther III, $41,940
Meyer, Thomas J, storekeeper II, $35,320
Meyers, Mary E, deval asst I, $22,728
Mian, Humayun, resident physician, $49,515
Michael, Angel K, case mgr II dd, $34,944
Michael, Belinda K, deval asst I, $22,728
Michael, Robert L, security aide I psy, $31,620
Michaelis, Sarah E, therapy aide, $10,926
Michalek, Patricia A, security aide I psy, $31,152
Michalski, Merri R, sr ofc spt asst (keybrd), $27,948
Michel, Beth A, deval asst I, $23,352
Michel, Tabatha J, psychiatric technician I, $23,352
Middleton, Corey A, psychiatric technician I, $22,092
Midkiff, Kevin W, reimbursement ofcr III, $37,548
Miers, Eunice D, registered nurse sr, $57,893
Miles, Cheryl R, case mgr I dd, $32,628
Miles, Debra M, assoc counsel, $66,155
Miles, Lesley D, mental hlth mgr b1, $60,117
Miles, Sarah G, security aide I psy, $32,244
Miles, Shawn W, security aide I psy, $33,312
Miller, Ackeme J, custodial worker I, $22,317
Miller, Alicia V, deval asst I, $22,404
Miller, Amy M, misc prof, $25,828
Miller, Annamarie K, clin casework pract II, $37,548
Miller, Anthony T, deval asst I, $22,728
Miller, Austin W, deval asst I, $24,036
Miller, Bamby L, registered nurse - clin opers, $62,513
Miller, Bernice L, deval asst I, $26,400
Miller, Blanche E, security aide I psy, $31,620
Miller, Blaze E, deval asst I, $22,728
Miller, Bradley L, institution supt, $77,557
Miller, Carla D, deval asst I, $24,036
Miller, Christina M, case mgr II dd, $34,944
Miller, Dalton A, deval asst I, $22,728
Miller, David A, licensed prof cnslr II, $53,208
Miller, David L, cnslr in training, $32,628
Miller, Diane L, deval asst I, $24,036
Miller, Donyell D, deval asst II, $28,776
Miller, Faye, deval asst I, $25,428
Miller, Hannah M, deval asst I, $23,412
Miller, Howard W, psychiatric technician I, $22,716
Miller, Janice A, security aide I psy, $30,276
Miller, Jay F, security aide I psy, $33,312
Miller, Jean M, cook III, $29,976
Miller, Jeffrey, security aide I psy, $33,312
Miller, Jeffrey M, security ofcr I, $25,824
Miller, Jennifer L, lpn II gen, $30,708
Miller, Karen L, housekeeper I, $29,004
Miller, Karen S, recrtnal ther III, $49,128
Miller, Kimberly A, admin ofc spt asst, $29,004
Miller, Kimberly M, custodial worker I, $22,872
Miller, Kurtis L, security aide II psy, $35,112
Miller, Lavona L, registered nurse sr, $51,552
Miller, Leslie C, ofc spt asst (keybrd), $23,880

Miller, Linda K, mental hlth mgr b1, $65,364
Miller, Maggie N, deval asst I, $22,728
Miller, Phyllis R, sr ofc spt asst (keybrd), $26,652
Miller, Rachel A, vendor servs coor mh, $40,380
Miller, Richard D, deval asst I, $23,352
Miller, Ronald A, habilitation spec II, $42,708
Miller, Rosalie, security aide I psy, $30,276
Miller, Sharon J, direct care aide, $10,070
Miller, Shelly G, deval asst I, $26,844
Miller, Silva J, hr mgr b2, $67,309
Miller, Stephanie D, psychiatric technician I, $22,728
Miller, Suzette C, subs abuse cnslr II, $38,928
Miller, Tammy M, deval asst I, $22,728
Miller, Tressie M, security aide I psy, $29,652
Miller, Wade R, habilitation spec II, $34,944
Millican, Ashley, registered nurse, $25,735
Millikin, Jenifer L, registered nurse sr, $55,362
Milliron, Kristin S, habilitation spec II, $36,888
Milloy, Derwin, psychiatric technician I, $24,696
Mills, Cory J, security aide I psy, $29,208
Mills, Joneesha D, psychiatric technician I, $22,728
Mills, Jovan L, deval asst I, $24,036
Mills, Kelley A, stores clerk, $24,264
Mills, Sylvia K, psychiatric technician I, $24,036
Mills, Xeniphor L, security aide I psy, $32,244
Milton, Lakesha, deval asst II, $25,584
Mims, Linda K, area sub abuse trtmnt coor, $54,288
Minchin, Susan A, staff physician spec, $203,448
Miner, Adam C, psychiatric technician I, $22,728
Minion, Gethona, cosmetologist, $25,584
Minor, Brian, deval asst I, $22,728
Mireles, Roy L, security aide II psy, $37,632
Mischnick, Robin L, hlth info tech II, $39,944
Mistler, Ginger L, registered nurse sr, $51,276
Mitan, Carla A, fiscal & administrative mgr b2, $68,159
Mitchell, Alice L, registered nurse sup, $98,370
Mitchell, Andrew L, psychiatric technician I, $24,024
Mitchell, Angela, account clerk II, $27,504
Mitchell, Brandon M, deval asst I, $23,352
Mitchell, Carolyn A, storekeeper I, $25,824
Mitchell, David A, security aide II psy, $32,208
Mitchell, Dominique R, psychiatric technician II, $26,208
Mitchell, Donna C, custodial work spv, $27,948
Mitchell, Iona M, psychiatric technician I, $24,036
Mitchell, James M, motor veh driver, $24,612
Mitchell, James R, mental hlth mgr b2, $61,328
Mitchell, Jeffrey B, recrtnal ther II, $41,172
Mitchell, Johnathan S, deval asst II, $27,876
Mitchell, Johnna C, deval asst II, $25,584
Mitchell, Kenneth R, psychiatric technician I, $23,352
Mitchell, Marnique V, deval asst I, $23,352
Mitchell, Melody R, security aide I psy, $30,276
Mitchell, Teonna R, direct care aide, $10.93/hr
Mitchell, Thomas E, custodial worker I, $22,200
Mize, Geraldine F, cook III, $28,104
Modi, Anna, custodial worker I, $21,864
Moe, Kathleen C, case mgr II dd, $40,380
Moehrle, Katherine J, special asst ofc & clerical, $41,165
Moeller-Crow, Cynthia A, deval asst II, $25,584
Moellers, Serina D, dev dis cmnty prog coord, $38,928
Moffat, Rachelle M, qual assurance spec mh, $46,068
Moffatt, Yvonne, registered nurse mgr b2, $79,221
Mogan, Judith L, ofc spt asst (keybrd), $25,824
Mohlman, Brighid M, psychiatric technician I, $22,092
Mokry, Deborah A, registered nurse sup, $102,930
Mokwah, Joseph A, direct care aide, $22.47/hr
Molinaro, Elissa M, hlth info tech II, $37,548
Moll, Linda L, mental hlth mgr b3, $77,556
Moman, Jessica D, lpn II gen, $40,648
Momot, Robert A, security aide I psy, $29,652
Monaco, Elise T, dev dis cmnty worker I, $34,944
Monah, Evelyn, custodial worker I, $20,664
Monroe, Cortney L, security aide I psy, $30,276
Monroe, Robert L, custodial worker I, $22,317
Montano, Jack, deval asst II, $25,428
Montgomery, Bobbi L, ofc spt asst (clerical), $28,452
Montgomery, Dawn R, security aide I psy, $30,276
Montgomery, Dena L, custodial worker I, $20,664
Montgomery, Emma J, deval asst I, $24,036

Montgomery, Julianna P, registered nurse, $9,728
Montgomery, Leslie M, account clerk II, $27,084
Montgomery, William R, licensed prof cnslr II, $53,208
Montgomery-Adams, Latisha C, psychiatric tech I, $23,352
Moody, Patricia S, deval asst I, $23,412
Moon, Jennifer D, security aide I psy, $32,244
Moon, Jessica M, registered nurse, $45,427
Moon, Joseph, staff physician, $137,245
Moon, Joseph, staff physician spec, $203,449
Moon, Justin A, registered nurse, $45,427
Mooney, Barbara A, psychiatric technician I, $23,352
Mooneyham, Steven F, case mgr II dd, $34,944
Moore, Amanda, deval asst I, $23,352
Moore, Barbara E, deval asst II, $28,152
Moore, Brenda A, deval asst II, $28,152
Moore, Christie A, security ofcr I, $25,824
Moore, Christopher, registered nurse, $51,276
Moore, Courtney, security aide I psy, $29,652
Moore, Domiano, deval asst II, $25,428
Moore, Ellen C, clin casework pract II, $38,232
Moore, Erin, deval asst I, $23,352
Moore, Glenna J, pers clerk, $28,104
Moore, Kailey A, ofc worker misc, $10,783
Moore, Karen E, dev dis cmnty spec, $41,940
Moore, Karen M, acct II, $40,380
Moore, Kiara N, deval asst I, $23,352
Moore, Kristen L, recrtnal ther II, $39,624
Moore, Krystle I, lpn, $16,470
Moore, Laurice D, security aide I psy, $32,244
Moore, Linda, lpn II gen, $40,404
Moore, Linda S, security aide I psy, $31,620
Moore, Lisa, deval asst I, $24,396
Moore, Lisa A, food serv helper II, $21,864
Moore, Lucretia A, deval asst I, $23,352
Moore, Mark E, licensed prof cnslr I, $36,204
Moore, Melody M, psychiatric technician I, $22,728
Moore, Raymond J, psychiatric technician I, $23,352
Moore, Rita R, lpn II gen, $37,644
Moore, Robert, reimbursement ofcr II, $40,380
Moore, Rollyn, deval asst I, $23,352
Moore, Ronald W, registered nurse sr, $57,892
Moore, Stephanie L, fiscal & administrative mgr b2, $65,000
Moore, Tamara R, registered nurse sr, $65,676
Moore, Tessa M, deval asst I, $22,728
Moore, Tony L, clin soc work spv, $49,128
Moore, Yvonne M, prog spec I mh, $38,928
Moorehead, Willow, sr ofc spt asst (keybrd), $29,904
Mooring, Andrea D, deval asst III, $28,572
Morales, Raeann M, deval asst I, $23,700
Morales Rivera, Kevin N, deval asst I, $23,412
Moran, Gina C, registered nurse sr, $57,893
Moran, John M, dev dis cmnty worker II, $39,624
Moran, Robin R, registered nurse sr, $54,720
Moran, Tyjunna M, hlth info admin II, $40,380
Moranda, Monica A, security aide I psy, $30,276
Moreland, Leslie A, lpn, $16,470
Morera Arias, Diego A, security aide I psy, $31,620
Morgan, Brenda S, deval asst I, $24,804
Morgan, Debra S, account clerk II, $27,084
Morgan, Everett J, prog spec I mh, $38,928
Morgan, Heidi M, deval asst I, $22,728
Morgan, Jerome A, security aide I psy, $32,244
Morgan, Lisa D, deval asst II, $27,696
Morgan, Rachel K, cook I, $21,864
Morgan, Stephanie G, lpn II gen, $30,216
Morgan, Teresa L, registered nurse sr, $55,776
Morgan, Tiera, deval asst I, $22,728
Morgan, Tracy, deval asst I, $22,728
Morgan, Vandessa, deval asst I, $24,036
Morgan-Gillard, Shannon, psychologist I, $38,290
Morgenthaler, Michelle E, security aide I psy, $29,652
Moriarty, Susan, deval asst I, $22,728
Mornan, Jervis V, security aide I psy, $30,276
Morris, Antonio, workshop spv I, $27,504
Morris, Dean O, security aide I psy, $30,276
Morris, Kate, deval asst I, $22,728
Morris, Ladonna M, admin ofc spt asst, $34,356
Morris, Leah G, deval asst I, $22,728
Morris, Leah N, registered nurse sr, $56,976

Morris, Lisa L, security aide I psy, $29,208
Morris, Robby L, security aide III psy, $41,172
Morris, Sheri, phys thrpst asst, $41,988
Morris, Tara K, deval asst I, $22,092
Morris, Virgie F, habilitation spec II, $34,944
Morrison, Bruetta T, dev dis cmnty worker I, $33,744
Morrison, Kara D, deval asst I, $22,728
Morrison, Shelly D, security aide I psy, $31,620
Morrison, Stacey L, sr ofc spt asst (keybrd), $25,824
Morrow, Ashley M, deval asst I, $23,352
Morrow, Robin C, deval asst I, $22,728
Morrow, Shelly D, deval asst I, $26,628
Morrow, Teresa M, deval asst I, $25,428
Morse, Debra K, research worker, $16.80/hr
Mortell, Stacy R, lpn, $16,470
Morton, Audrey B, licensed prof cnslr II, $41,172
Morton, Cheryl L, custodial worker I, $22,536
Morton, Dustin S, registered nurse sr, $51,552
Morton, Melton R, custodial worker II, $21,864
Morts, Karen S, lpn II gen, $36,086
Mosby, Ashli L, recrtnal ther I, $32,628
Mosby, Cecilia, custodial work spv, $23,880
Mosby, Ladasha D, deval asst I, $22,716
Mosby, Lisa G, sr ofc spt asst (keybrd), $26,232
Moseley, Jessica N, deval asst I, $22,404
Moser, Nancy L, deval asst I, $26,400
Mosher, Karen S, deval asst I, $22,728
Mosier, Randy D, comm mntl hlth servs spv, $51,096
Mosquera, Martin A, deval asst I, $25,584
Moss, Anne M, registered nurse sup, $66,504
Moss, Jerri A, habilitation spec II, $38,661
Moss, John M, deval asst I, $23,352
Moss, Lekesha N, deval asst I, $22,728
Moss, Linda L, deval asst III, $29,412
Mosuro, Abisola O, deval asst I, $23,352
Motes, Tyler L, security aide I psy, $32,244
Motley, Dalton W, psychiatric technician I, $23,352
Moutria, Kristina N, ofc spt asst (keybrd), $23,880
Moyers, Donna S, ofc spt asst (steno), $27,084
Moyers, Paula S, lpn II gen, $40,648
Mozley, Kathryn M, recrtnal ther I, $38,928
Mua, Bracknell, deval asst I, $23,352
Mua, Joseph, prog spec II mh, $42,708
Mudd, James J, security aide I psy, $31,620
Muehlenbachs, Ilze, misc prof, $24,053
Mueller, Dallas C, psychiatric technician I, $22,728
Mueller, Jane E, case mgr II dd, $34,944
Mueller, Teresa, sr ofc spt asst (keybrd), $26,232
Mueller, Theresa, special asst prof, $105,000
Muex, Michael C, stores clerk, $22,872
Mullen, Kathleen M, registered nurse sr, $55,891
Mullen, Marceline R, registered nurse, $28,375
Mullen, Robert D, security aide I psy, $29,652
Mullins, Debra A, deval asst I, $25,584
Mullins, Kierra, deval asst I, $22,728
Mullins, Kimberly, deval asst I, $26,628
Mulnik, Barbara A, activity aide II, $28,152
Munkres, Brenda J, deval asst I, $22,728
Munoz, Coral A, psychologist I, $65,364
Munro, John S, staff physician, $136,909
Munson, Brian J, qual assurance spec mh, $45,156
Munsterman, Janet S, mental hlth mgr b2, $72,745
Munsterman, Troy E, dev dis cmnty spec, $41,940
Munthali, Grace G, registered nurse sup, $67,989
Murdock, Amy T, deval asst I, $27,252
Murney, Joanne, psychologist I, $68,160
Murphy, Brent A, mgmt analysis spec II, $42,708
Murphy, Daniel L, security aide I psy, $30,162
Murphy, Elise M, security aide I psy, $29,652
Murphy, Karen E, registered nurse sr, $60,795
Murphy, Sara L, pers ofcr II, $56,520
Murphy, Sean D, qual assurance spec mh, $46,068
Murphy, Sheila E, research analyst III, $48,156
Murphy, Sheryl L, security aide II psy, $34,488
Murray, Angela F, deval asst I, $23,352
Murray, John F, clin casework pract II, $37,548
Murray, Monica K, deval asst I, $23,352
Murray, Richard P, motor veh mech, $29,004
Murrell, Tanya D, custodial worker I, $22,317

Murry, Katherine S, training tech I, $40,380
Mwangi, Anne M, psychiatric technician I, $22,728
Mwangi, Wilson K, registered nurse, $52,287
Myers, Byron D, clin casework pract II, $41,172
Myers, Devin L, behavioral technician trne, $23,880
Myers, Harold G, reimbursement ofcr I, $29,976
Myers, Joi L, registered nurse mgr b1, $62,772
Myers, Michael J, admin ofc spt asst, $31,512
Myers, Mitchell L, psychiatric technician I, $22,092
Myers, Sarah K, deval asst II, $25,584
Myers, Trenton, resident physician, $30,882
Myrick, Stephen, case mgmt/assess spv, $45,156
Mysch, Melissa D, lpn, $20,800
Mzeru, Christopher R, security aide I psy, $31,620
Nadolski, Deborah E, registered nurse sr, $60,796
Nagus, Catherine E, qual assurance spec mh, $48,156
Najam, Seema, staff physician spec, $105,290
Nana Amoako, Emmanuel, security aide I psy, $31,152
Nandja, Seidou, deval asst I, $23,352
Napier-Kipngetich, Tyrica J, deval asst I, $23,412
Narancich, Frank J, custodial worker I, $23,289
Nash, Bonnie J, security aide I psy, $29,832
Nash, Nala R, sr ofc spt asst (keybrd), $27,948
Nash, Paul A, psychiatric technician I, $23,352
Nash, Rebecca L, psychiatric technician I, $17,046
Nausley, Brenda M, case mgr II dd, $34,944
Nave, Larry E, security ofcr I, $25,824
Ndeme, Akwo G, psychiatric technician I, $24,696
Neal, Christopher A, food serv helper I, $21,564
Needham, Christina B, lpn II gen, $40,648
Neely, Louvilla, food serv helper I, $23,508
Neely, Miesha T, psychiatric technician I, $23,412
Neely, Rosalyn D, custodial worker I, $20,664
Neff, Stacy L, staff physician spec, $221,301
Negm, Manatalla S, clin casework asst I, $29,208
Nehl, Jamie A, motor veh driver, $11,940
Neill, Dena K, registered nurse sr, $52,608
Nelson, Brandi L, deval asst I, $22,728
Nelson, Briana N, deval asst I, $23,352
Nelson, Cody J, security aide I psy, $29,208
Nelson, Deborah A, deval asst I, $22,728
Nelson, Elizabeth A, deval asst I, $22,404
Nelson, Jennifer A, music ther II, $39,624
Nelson, Julia A, deval asst I, $22,728
Nelson, Latasha, deval asst I, $22,728
Nelson, Marian K, storekeeper II, $30,420
Nelson, Melody L, deval asst II, $25,584
Nelson, Michael L, registered nurse sr, $60,796
Nelson, Michael N, direct care aide, $10.93/hr
Nelson, Nancy G, security aide I psy, $30,276
Nelson, Rhonda M, security aide I psy, $31,620
Nelson, Shawn A, security aide I psy, $29,652
Nelson, Thomas E, custodial worker I, $22,536
Nemeth, Diane E, ofc spt asst (clerical), $23,508
Neor, John, security aide I psy, $29,652
Neptune-Holmes, Charlene L, dev dis cmnty worker II, $34,944
Nettels, Thomas A, security ofcr I, $28,908
Neumeyer, Donna S, dev dis cmnty prog coord, $44,304
Neville, Andrea, dev dis cmnty prog coord, $40,380
Nevins, Brenda A, ofc spt asst (keybrd), $25,404
Newcomb, Robert L, painter, $39,624
Newcomb, Samantha M, deval asst I, $22,728
Newcomer, John, security ofcr I, $25,824
Newland, Leann N, recept, $11,486
Newland, Rosanne, sr ofc spt asst (keybrd), $28,452
Newman, Cristina L, security aide I psy, $31,620
Newman, Jacqueline P, psychiatric technician II, $30,048
Newman, Stephanie M, pers ofcr I, $45,156
Newsom, Barbara L, custodial worker I, $20,664
Newsom, Brittany C, lpn, $10,234
Newsom, Karin L, registered nurse sup, $59,645
Newsome, Jeffrey P, deval asst I, $24,432
Newson, Bieisha D, security aide I psy, $32,244
Newson, Sandra A, deval asst II, $29,676
Newson, Tandra L, deval asst I, $22,728
Newson-Cunningham, Kollier, psychiatric technician I, $23,352
Newton, Connie L, tchr, $51,470
Newton, Heidi, ofc spt asst (keybrd), $24,612
Newton, Kaelee A, direct care aide, $15.56/hr

Newton, Kaelee A, qual assurance spec mh, $41,940
Ngassi, Patricia E, clin casework pract II, $38,232
Nguyen, Giau S, direct care aide, $14.56/hr
Nguyen, Patricia L, security aide I psy, $30,276
Nichols, Juanita, lpn II gen, $37,020
Nichols, Melanie D, psychologist I, $60,120
Nichols, Raphael, motor veh driver, $24,612
Nicholson, Crunden J, deval asst I, $23,352
Nicholson, Jasmine M, lpn II gen, $37,644
Nicholson, Leroy, deval asst I, $23,352
Nicholson, Mardi S, registered nurse sr, $60,796
Nicka, John, registered nurse, $28,375
Nickelson, Lena F, registered nurse sr, $51,552
Nickerson, Deborah A, deval asst I, $23,352
Nickolaus, Charles F, prog coord dmh dohss, $51,096
Nikitin, Alexey, security aide I psy, $29,652
Nimmagadda, Praveen S, staff physician spec, $297,355
Nkwocha, Chinyere M, registered nurse, $16,500
Noble, Amanda L, licensed behavior analyst, $66,720
Nobles, Diane C, deval asst III, $27,084
Noel, George D, registered nurse, $36,029
Noel, Mindy J, reimbursement ofcr I, $29,976
Nokes, Lisa L, work therapy spec II, $28,104
Noland, Cheryl R, case mgr II dd, $34,944
Nolte, Linda D, sr ofc spt asst (steno), $33,036
Nolte, Sharon K, case mgr II dd, $34,944
Nolting, Jeffrey R, psychologist I, $71,208
Norbury, Rebecca D, special asst official & admstr, $92,240
Norem, Eric S, security ofcr I, $26,652
Norem, Karen L, psychiatric technician I, $22,728
Norfleet, Jermaine J, ofc spt asst (clerical), $31,437
Norman, Erica R, deval asst I, $23,352
Norman, John, psychiatric technician I, $22,728
Norrington, Dorothy J, case mgr I dd, $32,628
Norris, Kristine M, mental hlth mgr b2, $66,438
Norris, Lisa M, account clerk II, $25,824
Norris, Margie, sr ofc spt asst (keybrd), $26,232
Northcutt, Candace S, psychiatric technician I, $23,352
Norton, Jon W, custodial worker II, $24,264
Norval, Lori L, qual assurance spec mh, $49,128
Norwood, Dequoron J, deval asst I, $23,352
Nothaus, Lisa, misc prof, $33,503
Nougues, Jean W, security aide I psy, $30,276
Nowak, Jennifer B, licensed behavior analyst, $33,360
Noyes, Holly L, lpn II gen, $36,710
Noyes, Teresa, registered nurse, $50,244
Nozinor, Areon D, security ofcr I, $25,824
Nozinor, Vanessa S, special asst ofc & clerical, $46,902
Nshunju, Albert L, security aide I psy, $31,620
Null, Paula J, registered nurse sup, $65,676
Nunn, Dennis J, security ofcr I, $26,232
Nwamba, Gloria C, registered nurse, $27,795
Nwaneri, Chijioke A, lpn, $16,470
Nwaneri, Cletus E, registered nurse sr, $60,796
Nwaobasi, Stella A, deval asst I, $23,352
Nwasoria, Isabella, psychiatric technician I, $12,686
Nweke, Pauline, lpn II gen, $37,020
Nwinee, Pius, deval asst I, $22,728
Nwoke, Eunice, deval asst I, $23,352
Nwoke, Joel, deval asst I, $23,352
Nyatanga, David C, security aide I psy, $32,244
Nye, Holden B, security aide I psy, $29,832
Oakley, Marla D, exec II, $41,172
Obenauer, Nathalie S, lpn II gen, $40,648
Oberg, Mark O, motor veh mech, $38,928
Oberlag, David A, maint worker II, $31,512
Obi, Emelda, psychiatric technician II, $26,260
Obiebi, Oghenerue, deval asst II, $24,804
Obiebi, Sandra, registered nurse, $56,976
Obiesie, Chibuogwu, psychiatric technician II, $25,584
Obikwelu, Christian O, deval asst I, $22,716
O'Brien, Caitlin D, deval asst I, $22,728
O'Brien, Cheryl L, clin soc work spv, $51,096
O'Brien, Phyllis J, deval asst I, $23,352
Obryan, Julie A, registered nurse mgr b1, $67,104
O'Connor, Ann-Marie A, registered nurse sr, $63,585
O'Connor, Dawn M, registered nurse sr, $60,185
O'Connor, M D, deval asst I, $26,004
O'Connor, Whitney, clin casework pract II, $37,548

O'Day, Jennifer J, special asst official & admstr, $63,985
O'Dell, Andrew M, psychiatric technician I, $22,716
O'Dell, Bing, exec II, $37,548
O'Dell, Evelyn M, deval asst I, $22,728
O'Dell, Maranda L, lpn II gen, $30,396
O'Dell, Maura D, account clerk II, $25,032
Oden, Jameca, custodial worker I, $20,664
O'Donnell, Everett D, deval asst I, $22,728
Odoom, Mercy, registered nurse, $28,600
Odunleye, Carol R, hr mgr b1, $63,949
Ofori, Benjamin B, security aide I psy, $30,276
Ogbevoen, Joyce, deval asst I, $22,728
Ogunleye, Oluwakemi, deval asst I, $23,552
Oguntuase, Olajide, staff physician, $137,245
Ogwudile, Emeka J, registered nurse sr, $55,776
O'Hara, Carmen D, ofc spt asst (keybrd), $36,348
O'Hearne, Molly A, registered nurse sr, $59,340
Ohuonu, Stella I, habilitation spec II, $34,944
Ojukwu, George I, security ofcr I, $25,824
Ojukwu, Rita C, psychiatric technician I, $24,024
Okafor, Chika, registered nurse mgr b2, $77,276
Okafor, Francis U, registered nurse, $36,029
Okechukwu, Justina, deval asst I, $23,352
O'Keefe, Alice A, case mgr I dd, $32,628
Okeke, Chukwuemeka J, psychiatric technician I, $24,024
Okeke, Priscilla, case mgr II dd, $34,944
Okocha, Fidelia O, lpn II gen, $34,295
Okonkwo, Freeman, psychiatric technician I, $19,258
Okoro, Sussana, psychiatric technician I, $12,686
Okosi, Chineze, registered nurse sr, $71,587
Okpewho, Viola N, psychiatric technician I, $24,024
Okpodighe, Victor O, security aide I psy, $32,244
Okuneye, Michael A, registered nurse sr, $60,796
Oladimeji, Jacquelyn K, registered nurse sr, $60,796
Olaoye, Olusoji, case mgr II dd, $34,944
Olateru, Uche H, registered nurse, $28,375
Oledibe, Magdaline I, psychiatric technician I, $25,584
Olivarez, Jorge, security aide I psy, $29,652
Oliver, George A, physician, $57,789
Oliver, Joshua K, security aide I psy, $32,244
Oliver, Terry S, registered nurse sup, $55,979
Olivier, Nicole M, qual assurance spec mh, $38,928
Ollie-Young, Brenda, activity aide III, $28,152
Olodun, Bosede B, lpn II gen, $34,560
Oloh, Raphael, psychiatric technician I, $24,696
Olowojuni, Bosede J, deval asst I, $23,352
Olson, Diane M, registered nurse sr, $57,893
Olson, Robert M, security aide I psy, $31,620
Olson, Tamera K, ofc spt asst (keybrd), $23,880
Olson, Tracy M, registered nurse, $28,375
Olukotun, Abike O, psychiatric technician I, $24,696
Oluwadara, Bolanle, resident physician, $51,318
Oluwaseun, Iyabo H, registered nurse sr, $71,587
Oluyemi, Oladayo, lpn II gen, $40,404
O'Malley, Patrick N, case mgr II dd, $34,944
Omoloja, Aderosoye, deval asst I, $23,352
Omoniyi, Boboye, deval asst I, $23,352
Omoruyi, Patrick O, security aide I psy, $31,620
O'Neal, Stacey M, registered nurse, $28.60/hr
Onukogu, Anthonia O, deval asst II, $29,676
Onukogu, Samuel N, deval asst II, $28,776
Onwuemegbulem, Ray, direct care aide, $12.12/hr
Onyekwe, Ogochukwu, registered nurse, $36,029
Opara, Chukwuma G, security aide I psy, $15,810
Opara, Emmanuel, psychiatric technician I, $24,696
Oparaji, Stella C, registered nurse sr, $60,796
Opare, Michael, direct care aide, $22.47/hr
Orebiyi, Folasade A, deval asst I, $22,716
Orekoya, Oladipo O, deval asst I, $23,352
Orell, Dwana C, deval asst I, $22,728
Orf, Dustin D, case mgr III dd, $37,548
Orf, James A, registered nurse sr, $59,340
Organ, Regina J, psychiatric technician I, $23,352
Orjames, Susan M, psychiatric technician I, $22,728
O'Rourke, Daniel P, security aide I psy, $36,984
O'Rourke, Debbie L, behavioral technician, $28,584
Orr, Kelly, prog spec II mh, $41,940
Orr, Patricia A, habilitation spec II, $36,888
Ortbals, Crista M, psychologist I, $65,364

Osborn, Stacey R, deval asst I, $23,412
Osborne, Ashley, registered nurse, $28,375
Osborne, Heather D, licensed prof cnslr II, $38,928
Osborne, Kasie D, deval asst I, $22,728
Osborne-Bryant, Melisha M, deval asst I, $26,400
Osei-Mensah, Agatha, security aide I psy, $30,276
Osmanovic, Sihreta, security aide I psy, $29,652
Oster, James B, fiscal & administrative mgr b1, $63,985
Oster, Lauren E, lpn II gen, $40,648
Ostermann, Kathleen E, deval asst I, $23,028
O'Sullivan, Eileen, case mgr III dd, $43,488
Otter, Margina L, special asst ofc & clerical, $30,422
Otter, Stephanie M, deval asst I, $22,716
Ottmers, Loretta L, sr ofc spt asst (keybrd), $27,504
Ourth, Kelly S, case mgr II dd, $34,944
Overfelt, Debra E, registered nurse - clin opers, $91,478
Overkamp, Matthew C, direct care aide, $22.47/hr
Overstreet, Leah M, deval asst I, $22,728
Overton, Brittany N, deval asst I, $22,716
Overton, Sara J, deval asst I, $23,352
Overturf, Vicki, psychiatric technician I, $22,728
Ovwielefuoma, Ese, security aide I psy, $31,152
Owen, Elexa C, deval asst I, $22,728
Owens, Deloris, childrens psy care spv, $30,384
Owens, Judith A, account clerk II, $27,084
Owens, Lorrena, deval asst III, $29,904
Owens, Prishell V, deval asst II, $26,208
Owens, William D, security aide I psy, $31,620
Owensby, Debra L, deval asst II, $26,400
Owings, Janet K, registered nurse sr, $55,776
Owings, Mark, acct II, $47,892
Owolabi, Stephen F, deval asst I, $23,352
Owsley, Clint T, food serv helper I, $16,531
Pace, Janell L, storekeeper I, $25,032
Pacheco, Ruben, security aide I psy, $29,652
Page, Jacqueline R, registered nurse sr, $53,592
Paige, Heather N, security aide I psy, $31,620
Painter, Julie A, security aide I psy, $31,620
Pallangyo, Diana E, security aide I psy, $30,276
Palmer, Carlotta E, acct I, $29,976
Palmer, Ellen M, deval asst I, $22,728
Palmer, Rhonda E, clin casework pract I, $34,944
Palmer, Robert M, vendor servs coor mh, $40,380
Pangborn, Vickie S, deval asst II, $29,052
Panthi, Urmila, case mgr II dd, $34,944
Panus, Kim, registered nurse sr, $71,587
Pardee, Alicia L, psychological resident, $50,000
Parish, Lolita D, deval asst II, $24,804
Park, Inn T, staff physician, $69,764
Parker, Andrea M, psychiatric technician I, $22,728
Parker, Antione T, custodial worker I, $22,872
Parker, Darion J, deval asst I, $23,352
Parker, Kelsey K, clin casework pract II, $39,624
Parker, Lisa K, direct care aide, $5,228
Parker, Maria E, registered nurse sr, $60,184
Parker, Maria E, food serv helper I, $22,317
Parker, Mark D, food serv helper I, $20,664
Parker, Mary E, acct I, $29,976
Parker, Michele B, psychiatric technician I, $22,728
Parker, Quiana, registered nurse sr, $55,776
Parker, Tricia N, registered nurse sr, $52,608
Parkman, Katrina L, deval asst I, $22,404
Parks, Charles R, unit prog spv mh, $50,040
Parksel, Sylvia L, psychiatric technician II, $30,048
Parmley, Charles M, security aide I psy, $32,760
Parott, Wynetta D, deval asst I, $23,352
Parsa, Bruce, staff physician spec, $195,435
Parshall-Ross, Andra J, lpn I gen, $29,472
Parsons, Brenda A, registered nurse sup, $74,556
Parsons, Katherine D, sr ofc spt asst (keybrd), $31,920
Parsons, Rhonda L, ofc spt asst (keybrd), $22,536
Parsons, Sheila J, custodial worker I, $21,760
Partee, Astra L, lpn II gen, $36,086
Parungao, Agnes P, sr ofc spt asst (keybrd), $26,652
Parungao, Leonel D, security aide I psy, $32,244
Parwatikar, Sadashiv D, consulting physician, $41,434
Passawe, Mustapha, psychiatric technician II, $25,428
Pate, Gene R, psychiatric technician I, $23,352
Pate, Lynda D, deval asst I, $26,004

Patel, Kunal A, resident physician, $54,969
Patel, Maheshkumar K, staff physician spec, $203,449
Patel, Roopa, registered nurse sr, $56,976
Patrick, Tameka D, deval asst I, $23,352
Patterson, Brenda L, cook I, $21,864
Patterson, Freda M, licensed behavior analyst, $66,720
Patterson, Kacey A, registered nurse sr, $71,587
Patterson, Margaree, psychiatric technician II, $25,584
Patterson, Mary A, deval asst I, $24,804
Patterson, Melody A, registered nurse mgr b3, $85,926
Patton, Karen M, edual aide, $10,830
Patton, Martha A, acct I, $30,984
Patton, Penelope, case mgr II dd, $34,944
Patton, Richard D, acct II, $41,940
Patton, William L, deval asst I, $23,352
Paul, Angelia M, dev dis cmnty spec, $37,548
Paul, Joshua R, habilitation spec II, $34,944
Paul, Mattie R, account clerk II, $27,084
Paul, Nathaniel J, security aide I psy, $29,652
Paul, Richard, security ofcr I, $27,084
Paxton, Deborah D, lpn II gen, $32,884
Paxton, Kyle E, security aide II psy, $33,936
Payne, Jenny M, deval asst I, $24,036
Payne, Jimmie L, custodial worker I, $20,664
Payne, Kristen M, prog spec I mh, $38,928
Payne, Richard A, mental hlth mgr b2, $57,729
Payne, Sandra K, security aide I psy, $31,620
Payne, Sandra R, registered nurse sr, $71,587
Payne, Shelley M, deval asst I, $22,728
Payne, Tacoma, deval asst I, $23,352
Peabody, Deborah L, dev dis cmnty worker II, $37,548
Pearson, Crystal L, food serv helper I, $21,564
Pearson, Latarsha A, deval asst II, $26,208
Pearson, Mary M, registered nurse, $2,746
Pearson, Mila, deval asst I, $22,728
Peck, Katherine K, registered nurse sr, $64,680
Pedretti-Price, Susan L, lpn II gen, $39,780
Peebles, Jannet C, psychiatric technician I, $23,352
Peebles, Lachelle N, sr ofc spt asst (keybrd), $27,504
Peebles, Lucky, deval asst I, $22,728
Peek, Kyle C, security aide I psy, $31,152
Peet, Brittney N, deval asst I, $24,072
Pegues, Jazmine L, deval asst I, $23,028
Penberthy, Tammy L, psychiatric technician I, $22,716
Pendergras, Leta E, hlth info admin I, $60,274
Pendleton, Robin K, training tech I, $37,652
Peng, Chunxian, registered nurse, $56,192
Pennington, Barbara, deval asst I, $23,352
Pennington, Dana M, reimbursement ofcr I, $30,420
Peoples, Brandy S, psychological resident, $34,992
Peoples, Irhonia S, deval asst I, $24,036
Peppers, David B, licensed clin soc wkr, $47,892
Perdieu, Lorie A, misc tech, $13,372
Perez, Lindsay, registered nurse - clin opers, $74,556
Perez, Savannah C, deval asst I, $22,404
Perfater, Gaylene S, deval asst III, $26,652
Perkins, Benjamin, deval asst I, $22,728
Perkins, Janet, deval asst I, $23,352
Perkins, Jennifer L, psychiatric technician II, $24,804
Perkins, Lena M, deval asst I, $23,352
Perkins, Pascha L, activity aide II, $25,224
Perkins, Ruby, deval asst I, $23,352
Perks, Brandi N, deval asst I, $22,728
Perrine, Austin E, deval asst I, $22,404
Perry, Fonda J, mental hlth mgr b2, $68,498
Perry, Jasmine, deval asst II, $24,804
Perry, La'keisha J, psychiatric technician I, $23,352
Perry, Mark A, deval asst I, $23,352
Perry, Shatelle L, deval asst I, $22,404
Perry, Tammy S, lpn II gen, $30,384
Perry, Tanya L, psychiatric technician I, $24,036
Pestle, Karin H, recrtnal ther III, $47,892
Peterman, Karen, reimbursement ofcr I, $37,548
Peters, Amy D, case mgr II dd, $34,944
Peters, Kelsey L, recrtnal ther I, $31,512
Peters, Russell D, deval asst II, $29,052
Peters, Stacey J, acct I, $38,232
Peterson, Angel, deval asst I, $24,804
Peterson, Ashley M, deval asst I, $24,036

Peterson, Connie, cook I, $21,864
Peterson, Gregg A, food serv helper I, $23,160
Peterson, Jessica A, student intern, $23,500
Peterson, Rebecca L, security aide I psy, $29,652
Peterson, Sandra M, deval asst I, $24,804
Peterson, Wendy M, security aide II psy, $32,208
Petova, Anita, psychiatric technician I, $22,728
Petri, Jon P, activity therapy coor, $58,908
Pettus, Stephnie L, behavioral technician, $26,004
Petty, Carl S, security aide I psy, $31,620
Pettyjohn, Vina E, psychiatric technician II, $24,804
Peyla, Jeana R, security aide I psy, $31,620
Pfaus, Diane B, dev dis cmnty prog coord, $40,380
Pfeifer, Melanie L, security aide I psy, $29,652
Phelan, Linda K, registered nurse, $30,882
Phelps, Janice E, ofc spt asst (clerical), $22,536
Phillips, Arielle, deval asst I, $22,728
Phillips, Brenda L, ofc spt asst (keybrd), $26,232
Phillips, Deanna D, ofc spt asst (keybrd), $23,160
Phillips, Gwendolyn G, deval asst III, $26,652
Phillips, Jonathan C, deval asst I, $23,352
Phillips, Lydonna L, deval asst II, $25,428
Phillips, Monique A, habilitation spec II, $34,944
Phillips, Pamela R, pers analyst II, $37,548
Phillips, Sara L, psychiatric technician I, $23,352
Phillips, Steven C, security aide I psy, $29,208
Phinney, Sheryl L, case mgr II dd, $36,888
Phipps, Michelle, registered nurse sr, $65,676
Phoenix, Delores, psychiatric technician I, $23,352
Pickens, Kevin, psychiatric technician I, $23,352
Pickens, Marquita R, psychiatric technician I, $23,352
Pickering, Carol J, admin ofc spt asst, $29,496
Pidcock, James L, psychiatric technician I, $22,716
Piepenbrink, Mark A, habilitation spec II, $36,888
Piephoff, Tonya L, dpty div dir, $95,950
Pierce, Angela M, case mgr I dd, $31,512
Pierce, Douglas A, deval asst I, $22,728
Pierce, Gregory A, security aide II psy, $32,832
Pierce, Kathryn L, security aide I psy, $30,276
Pierce, Teddy D, ch security ofcr, $38,928
Pigg, Katherine, proj spec, $31,495
Pigg, Leisa D, cook II, $23,880
Piggee, Lyndon L, security aide I psy, $29,832
Pike, James L, psychiatric technician I, $25,428
Pike, Tanja M, deval asst I, $23,352
Piland, Ashlea A, deval asst I, $22,728
Piles, Monica A, habilitation spec II, $38,232
Pinet, Harvey L, security aide I psy, $30,276
Pinkerton, Wilma S, lpn II gen, $37,390
Pinkley, Corey L, security ofcr I, $27,948
Pinkley, Kyle C, registered nurse sr, $54,720
Pinkley, Kyndyl L, registered nurse sr, $25,776
Pinkley, Tabitha J, registered nurse sr, $61,451
Pinkston, Marilyn E, food serv helper I, $11,159
Pinnell, Terri A, dev dis cmnty worker II, $40,380
Pinson, Cheryl F, pers clerk, $28,104
Pippins-Topps, Jewelle L, psychiatric technician I, $22,728
Pirtle, Catherine R, sr ofc spt asst (keybrd), $25,824
Pisano, Nicholas J, psychiatric technician I, $22,816
Pitt, Karen E, pastoral cnslr, $52,015
Pitt, Matthew W, security aide I psy, $31,776
Pittman, Danel T, security aide I psy, $33,912
Pittman, Danniqua N, food serv helper I, $22,317
Pittman, Harold A, storekeeper I, $29,412
Pittman, Marneesha T, deval asst I, $22,716
Pittman, Porscha M, case mgr II dd, $34,944
Pittman, Shannon L, security aide II psy, $34,488
Pitts, Carme' M, behavioral technician trne, $23,160
Pitts, Joyce E, lpn II gen, $36,745
Pitts, Nancy A, hlth info admin I, $41,172
Pitts, Tammy L, lpn II gen, $30,708
Pitts, Travis L, deval asst I, $22,728
Plaggenberg, Rachel M, admin ofc spt asst, $33,180
Plate, Lesley D, special educ tchr III, $46,932
Plattner, Carol A, unit prog spv mh, $48,156
Pleasant, Rosie L, registered nurse, $28,375
Plopper, Julie K, registered nurse sr, $65,166
Plunkett, Destiny E, prog coord dmh dohss, $51,096
Pobst, Kimberly D, special asst prof, $41,172

Poe, Kimberly A, security aide I psy, $31,152
Pogue, Lorri R, ofc spt asst (keybrd), $23,160
Pointer, Joan, ofc spt asst (keybrd), $25,824
Pointer, Margaret, psychiatric technician I, $25,428
Pointer, Quantilla, deval asst I, $25,428
Polage, Claudia S, deval asst I, $23,412
Polanowski, Allen R, security aide I psy, $29,652
Polina, Mark A, sr ofc spt asst (clerical), $25,032
Politsch, Ray S, unit prog spv mh, $43,488
Polk, Jayson, deval asst I, $23,352
Polovina, Ilir, special asst prof, $101,000
Polston, Tamara, security aide I psy, $29,652
Ponton, John M, misc tech, $24,053
Poole, Bonnie E, research analyst III, $47,892
Pope, Chanel E, deval asst I, $24,072
Pope, Tamara L, registered nurse sr, $55,776
Popoola, Roseline O, deval asst I, $24,696
Popoola, Sunday O, deval asst II, $26,208
Popplewell, Lindley B, licensed clin soc wkr, $47,892
Porcelli, Mary L, acct I, $36,204
Portell, Jerry D, custodial worker I, $22,317
Portell, Penny L, registered nurse mgr b1, $66,180
Portell, Savannah D, deval asst I, $22,404
Porter, Anner L, clin casework asst II, $40,380
Porter, Channon M, deval asst III, $29,412
Porter, Chastity M, security aide I psy, $29,208
Porter, Lashea, deval asst I, $23,352
Porter, Lisa K, dev dis cmnty prog coord, $39,624
Porter, Lori A, reimbursement ofcr II, $36,204
Porter, Nathaniel D, deval asst I, $22,728
Porter-Scott, Kristy G, security aide II psy, $31,152
Post, Rebecca M, institution supt, $84,250
Poston, Amelia J, deval asst I, $22,728
Potash, Linda L, misc prof, $11,140
Potts, Bruce T, activity aide II, $27,780
Potts, Daniel D, security aide I psy, $29,208
Potts, Jarred C, activity aide II, $27,780
Potts, Kaitlyn N, lpn II gen, $34,295
Potts, Sonia M, deval asst III, $39,889
Poulette, Joshua A, music ther I, $33,180
Powell, Brenda, deval asst I, $23,352
Powell, David L, case mgr II dd, $34,944
Powell, Erica C, deval asst I, $23,412
Powell, George D, custodial worker I, $22,317
Powell, Holly M, deval asst I, $22,728
Powell, Jacqueline M, mental hlth mgr b2, $60,125
Powell, Regena A, psychiatric technician I, $22,728
Powell, Samantha L, deval asst I, $23,076
Powell, Valincia L, deval asst I, $22,716
Powell, Vonda K, dev dis cmnty spec, $37,548
Power, Michael R, security aide I psy, $31,620
Powers, Joyce, case mgmt/assess spv, $45,156
Poyner, Megan E, deval asst I, $23,352
Poynter, Heather D, cook I, $21,864
Poynter, Zenova M, account clerk II, $26,232
Pragman, Sandra L, deval asst I, $22,728
Pratt, Angela, dev dis cmnty spec, $36,204
Pratt, Patricia, mental hlth mgr b2, $70,999
Presberry, Larry D, security aide II psy, $35,112
Presberry, Nakeeta S, ofc spt asst (keybrd), $23,880
Presley, Melissa A, admin ofc spt asst, $32,052
Preston, Lynee R, deval asst I, $27,468
Pretz, Joshua N, registered nurse, $28,375
Prevallet, Lacey R, registered nurse sr, $25,776
Price, Alicia C, security aide I psy, $30,276
Price, Angela M, deval asst II, $25,428
Price, Antwon L, deval asst I, $23,352
Price, Bernice E, deval asst I, $24,072
Price, Jermayne A, deval asst I, $23,352
Price, Kenneth J, security aide II psy, $32,832
Price, Lena M, activity aide II, $25,224
Price, Leslie L, case mgmt/assess spv, $40,380
Price, Sharon A, dev dis cmnty worker II, $43,488
Price, Teresa A, unit prog spv mh, $42,708
Price-Suttee, Lisa A, mental hlth mgr b1, $52,093
Priefer, Douglas A, mgmt analysis spec I, $41,172
Priestly, Tawana S, deval asst I, $23,352
Primm, Sherita N, psychiatric technician I, $22,728
Principato, Sandra L, food serv helper I, $22,317

Prior, Tammy S, deval asst I, $22,728
Pritchard, Calvin L, unit prog spv mh, $53,208
Pritchard, Ronald Jr, deval asst I, $22,728
Pritchard, Stephany R, psychiatric technician I, $22,728
Pritchett, Edward S, security aide I psy, $30,726
Pritchett, Tamara M, acct I, $30,984
Prock, Donita J, case mgr II dd, $34,944
Proffer, Debra K, pers clerk, $30,984
Pruett, Connie G, deval asst I, $25,428
Pruitt, Rhonda L, deval asst I, $22,716
Pruitt, Sherry D, psychiatric technician II, $25,428
Pruitt, Terry R, security aide I psy, $32,244
Punzo, Cindy J, ofc worker misc, $14,350
Purkett, Sarah E, registered nurse sr, $53,253
Pursell, Sally, registered nurse sr, $59,340
Purtty, Kandice, registered nurse sr, $55,776
Pyatt, Angela R, ofc spt asst (keybrd), $23,880
Pyatt, Emily M, psychiatric technician I, $22,728
Pyatt, Shawna M, psychiatric technician II, $25,584
Pyle, Bailey, cnslr in training, $38,928
Quadri, Omar H, staff physician spec, $297,355
Qualls, Johnathon T, security aide I psy, $31,620
Qualls, Misty A, activity aide II, $25,428
Quarells, Selina R, deval asst II, $28,584
Quick, Tiffany R, deval asst I, $23,412
Quigley, Amanda G, lpn II gen, $32,364
Quigley, Jeffrey J, deval asst III, $28,908
Quinlan, William E, security ofcr I, $25,824
Quinn, Claretha, food serv helper II, $23,508
Quinn, Colleen, registered nurse sr, $60,796
Quintero, Danielle, rehab worker, $12,480
Rachel, Garlin, food serv helper I, $10,332
Raczkowski, Julie A, registered nurse, $27,794
Radden, Ann M, dietitian II, $23,955
Radford-Galbreath, Cassondra L, registered nurse sup, $63,373
Radionova, Nataliia G, deval asst I, $22,728
Radmanesh, Rebekah A, staff physician spec, $221,301
Ragan, Deborah L, security aide II psy, $33,384
Ragan, Wesley W, security aide II psy, $33,384
Ragsdale, Harriett A, sr ofc spt asst (keybrd), $27,948
Rainey, Heather C, deval asst I, $23,352
Rainey, Rickey, lpn II gen, $34,560
Rains, Ronald L, cook I, $21,564
Rains, Tina M, cook II, $23,160
Rakers, Allison E, registered nurse sr, $55,776
Ramesh, Sujatha, psychologist II, $69,612
Ramey, Heather A, prog spec II mh, $41,940
Ramirez, Amy M, special asst prof, $197,870
Ramirez, Katherine M, security aide I psy, $29,652
Ramlatchman, Edward C, lpn II gen, $36,360
Ramlatchman, Lana, registered nurse sup, $95,262
Ramos, Lisa, security aide I psy, $31,152
Rampola, Cathy R, psychiatric technician I, $26,628
Ramsel, Deena E, registered nurse sr, $54,766
Randazzo, Jan M, prog spec I mh, $38,928
Randle, Adrianna K, deval asst I, $23,352
Randle, Donna D, food serv helper II, $25,013
Rankin, Jared L, qual assurance spec mh, $41,172
Rapien, Shae L, deval asst I, $22,728
Rariden, Nancy E, registered nurse sr, $63,084
Rash, Dinna C, ofc spt asst (keybrd), $23,880
Rasheed, Mohammad A, staff physician spec, $283,305
Rasmussen, Janet M, registered nurse sr, $60,184
Rasmussen, Sandra S, deval asst I, $23,352
Ratcliffe, Brandy M, psychiatric technician I, $24,072
Ratliff, Patricia A, deval asst I, $22,728
Ratliff, Phyllis A, security aide II psy, $32,832
Ravindran, Prem, registered nurse sr, $64,681
Rawlings, Janice A, psychiatric technician I, $23,352
Rawlings, Mary L, ofc spt asst (keybrd), $23,160
Rawlins, Regina D, registered nurse sr, $56,526
Ray, Anthony, deval asst I, $22,728
Ray, Dwayne L, custodial worker I, $20,664
Ray, Tommelia, deval asst I, $23,352
Ray, Yolanda R, lpn II gen, $37,020
Rayborn, Judith A, case mgr II dd, $37,548
Rayford, Carolyn, deval asst I, $22,728
Raymond, Lily, psychologist I, $49,023
Raynes, Christine, typist, $13,137

Rea, Catherine L, habilitation spec II, $38,928
Reagan, Margaret M, case mgr II dd, $34,944
Reagan, Vivian E, security aide I psy, $31,284
Reary, Patricia A, sr ofc spt asst (keybrd), $29,904
Record, Emily K, therapy aide, $5,574
Rector, Donald W, deval asst I, $22,728
Rector, Ronald D, deval asst I, $25,584
Redburn, David M, deval asst I, $22,716
Redd, Deureka, deval asst I, $23,352
Redden, Lana J, psychiatric technician I, $22,728
Reddick, Cloudette, deval asst III, $29,412
Reddick, Ralph R, security aide I psy, $29,652
Reddy, Chandra S, consulting physician, $45,997
Reddy, Melissa A, registered nurse, $27,795
Reddy, Veera N, staff physician spec, $221,301
Redelfs, Kirk A, dev dis cmnty prog coord, $45,156
Redelsheimer, William F, psychiatric technician I, $23,352
Redhage, Lori A, deval asst I, $26,400
Reece, Miles C, physician, $104,940
Reed, Amanda J, psychiatric technician I, $22,716
Reed, Amber D, deval asst I, $23,076
Reed, Benjamin K, security aide I psy, $30,276
Reed, Bradley J, deval asst I, $22,728
Reed, Carmen F, deval asst I, $23,352
Reed, Catherine M, deval asst II, $24,804
Reed, Christina L, security aide I psy, $30,276
Reed, Dana L, security aide I psy, $29,208
Reed, Danielle E, psychiatric technician I, $23,352
Reed, Dominique D, psychiatric technician I, $22,728
Reed, Ira D, custodial worker II, $23,613
Reed, Jeffrey J, psychiatric technician I, $23,352
Reed, Kimberly P, voc rehab spec I, $34,944
Reed, Laura N, deval asst I, $22,404
Reed, Russell, registered nurse sr, $54,720
Reed-Lohmeyer, Peggy, mental hlth mgr b1, $61,327
Reese, Ashley, deval asst I, $22,728
Reeves, Deborah K, sr ofc spt asst (keybrd), $27,504
Reeves, Kenneth L, psychiatric technician I, $23,352
Reeves, Stephen C, fiscal consult, $75.00/hr
Rehak, Thomas E, misc prof, $51,714
Rehbein, Tamar M, pers clerk, $28,104
Rehkop, Samantha A, recrtnal ther I, $33,180
Reichel, Brittany L, security aide I psy, $32,244
Reid, Cassandra L, case mgr II dd, $34,944
Reiff, Holly J, mental hlth mgr b1, $52,081
Reilly, Kathleen J, case mgr II dd, $34,944
Reilmann, Lisa A, qual assurance spec mh, $41,940
Reinhart, Karen, habilitation spec II, $38,232
Reinkemeyer, David J, accounting analyst II, $44,304
Reissing, Stephany N, psychiatric technician II, $25,584
Reitinger, Debra, registered nurse sr, $71,587
Reitz, Nicole R, licensed clin soc wkr, $48,156
Reitz, Robert M, dpty div dir, $92,240
Reitz, Ronda Y, psychologist II, $69,612
Relford, Anthony E, storekeeper I, $25,032
Reliford, Rhonda L, deval asst I, $26,628
Rembecki, Mark S, mental hlth mgr b2, $61,520
Remlinger, Stephen, psychiatric technician I, $23,352
Remspecher, Mark J, hr mgr b2, $67,309
Rencher, Serena D, deval asst I, $26,004
Rennie, Rebekah L, psychiatric technician I, $22,716
Renno, Beth A, deval asst I, $26,004
Reno, Paula, deval asst I, $22,728
Rentfro, Jean F, prog spec II mh, $46,068
Rentfro, Sharon A, custodial worker II, $23,613
Reser, Jeffrey T, psychiatric technician I, $35,799
Resonno, Wanda R, security aide I psy, $31,620
Resz, Rossel J, deval asst I, $23,352
Reupke, Lolita, registered nurse sr, $60,796
Revelle, Carrie E, custodial worker I, $20,664
Revelle, Christopher I, registered nurse sr, $54,766
Revere, Stephanie A, dietitian II, $43,488
Rew, Melissa J, lpn II gen, $29,772
Rex, Jeffery W, security aide II psy, $32,760
Rey, Roque C, security aide II psy, $35,112
Reyburn, Kim I, sr ofc spt asst (keybrd), $28,452
Reyes, Randall C, dentist, $100.00/hr
Reynolds, Harvey R, security aide II psy, $32,208
Reynolds, James, staff physician spec, $359,635

Reynolds, James C, security aide I psy, $31,620
Reynolds, Lisa B, admin ofc spt asst, $33,744
Reynolds, Louise A, ofc spt asst (keybrd), $25,032
Reynolds, Sharon L, qual assurance spec mh, $51,096
Reynolds-Dickens, Sharon A, sr ofc spt asst (keybrd), $27,084
Rhinesmith, Greg S, storekeeper II, $30,420
Rhodes, Jonathan F, psychologist I, $69,612
Rhymes, Latosha, deval asst I, $23,352
Rhymes, Tyra, deval asst I, $23,352
Rhyne, Michael T Jr, account clerk II, $27,084
Rice, Dylan T, psychiatric technician I, $23,352
Rice, Gabrielle, deval asst I, $24,036
Rice, Kenna W, security aide II psy, $34,488
Rich, Anthony S, security aide I psy, $30,276
Rich, Tina K, deval asst I, $24,036
Richard-Smith, Armetia M, psychiatric technician II, $25,428
Richards, David J, security aide III psy, $36,204
Richards, Heather A, security aide I psy, $29,652
Richards, Lori A, pers analyst II, $43,488
Richards, Ronald W, deval asst II, $25,428
Richardson, Debra M, deval asst I, $26,628
Richardson, Deloris K, deval asst I, $22,728
Richardson, Gerald T, security aide I psy, $29,832
Richardson, Helen C, habilitation spec II, $34,944
Richardson, Jill K, exec I, $30,984
Richardson, Katherine L, security aide I psy, $31,776
Richardson, Marisa K, clin soc work spv, $51,096
Richardson, Nadine, psychiatric technician I, $23,352
Richardson, Teresea A, account clerk II, $25,824
Richeson, Laura D, registered nurse sup, $72,299
Richey-Arellin, Ileen, licensed clin soc wkr, $46,068
Richmond, Shada C, security aide I psy, $31,620
Richter, Julia M, recrtnal ther I, $38,928
Ricketts, Electa, psychiatric technician I, $24,696
Ricketts, Terri M, case mgr II dd, $34,944
Rickmar, Trenton M, psychiatric technician I, $22,728
Riddle, Eejuan, unit prog spv mh, $40,380
Riddle, Stacy, deval asst I, $23,076
Ridenhour, Jacqueline L, security aide I psy, $29,208
Ridinger, Megan N, deval asst I, $22,728
Rieke, Kimberly S, accounting analyst III, $53,208
Riekhof, Devon L, deval asst I, $23,412
Rife, Jedidiah S, deval asst I, $24,036
Riffe, Justin C, deval asst I, $23,076
Rigdon, Michael J, psychiatric technician I, $23,352
Riggins, Kimberly K, psychiatric technician I, $22,716
Riggins, Wendy, deval asst I, $22,716
Riggs, Kelly D, security aide I psy, $29,652
Riggs, Leslie F, deval asst I, $22,728
Riley, Brandi N, activity aide II, $27,780
Riley, Cheryl M, deval asst I, $22,728
Riley, Kevin T, training tech III, $50,040
Riley, Priscilla S, deval asst I, $22,728
Riley, Sharon K, deval asst I, $27,252
Riley, Tammy S, dev dis cmnty worker II, $34,944
Riley, Tracy A, sr ofc spt asst (keybrd), $25,824
Rimmer, Eric L, motor veh driver, $26,652
Rimmer, Sakeia M, ofc spt asst (keybrd), $23,880
Rinehart, Deborah A, custodial worker I, $22,317
Rinehart, Richard L, activity aide II, $27,780
Ring, Amy J, psychiatric technician I, $24,804
Ring, Jacqueline, licensed clin soc wkr, $47,892
Ring, Marie E, misc prof, $34,994
Ringo, Donna L, cook I, $21,864
Risch, Anita F, storekeeper I, $29,850
Risher, Tammy L, motor veh driver, $27,522
Ritch, Loretta B, deval asst I, $26,004
Ritchie, Stacey L, deval asst I, $26,844
Ritz, Cody A, deval asst I, $22,404
Rivera, Amy M, paralegal, $36,384
Rivers, Lavearn, food serv helper II, $22,200
Rivers, Leslie A, psychiatric technician I, $22,728
Rivers, Poala S, psychiatric technician I, $23,352
Rizvi, Syeda U, resident physician, $50,005
Roach, Charlotte A, food serv helper I, $930
Roach, Cynthia D, ofc spt asst (keybrd), $24,264
Roach, Gary L, motor veh driver, $23,880
Roach, Shaelin M, psychiatric technician I, $22,092
Robb, Kristina K, special asst ofc & clerical, $40,061

Robbins, Sharon B, psychologist II, $77,556
Robbins, Timothy P, recrtnal ther I, $33,744
Roberds, Evelyn L, psychiatric technician I, $22,728
Roberson, Charisisi E, deval asst I, $23,352
Robert, Christopher M, security aide II psy, $31,776
Roberts, Arville, custodial work spv I, $25,790
Roberts, B J, deval asst I, $24,036
Roberts, Ernest G, storekeeper II, $32,628
Roberts, Gwyndelyn, misc prof, $22,647
Roberts, John H, security aide I psy, $31,152
Roberts, Jonathan L, acad tchr III, $37,548
Roberts, Kenneth D, registered nurse sup, $64,380
Roberts, Linda K, dev dis cmnty spec, $40,380
Roberts, Nita L, ofc spt asst (keybrd), $26,232
Roberts, Rebecca R, activity aide II, $24,804
Roberts, Staci N, acct II, $40,380
Roberts, Stephen R, dev dis cmnty spec, $36,204
Robertson, Anthony B, psychiatric technician I, $22,092
Robertson, Christopher D, psychologist I, $65,364
Robertson, Darrell D, licensed clin soc wkr, $47,892
Robertson, Olivia A, food serv helper I, $20,664
Robertson, Tammy S, hlth info tech I, $28,104
Robertson, Tremone C, security aide I psy, $31,620
Robertson, Vivian, deval asst I, $23,352
Robertson, Vontella L, psychiatric technician I, $22,728
Robinett, Leaonna R, deval asst I, $23,352
Robinette, Jerry L, security ofcr I, $10,483
Robinson, Ashley, deval asst II, $24,696
Robinson, Avis D, deval asst II, $27,252
Robinson, Charles J, workshop spv I, $27,504
Robinson, Chelsee C, food serv helper I, $22,317
Robinson, Cheryle D, behavioral technician, $26,844
Robinson, Crystal, psychiatric technician I, $23,352
Robinson, Donald L, psychiatric technician I, $25,584
Robinson, Edith K, registered nurse sr, $56,192
Robinson, Frances L, food serv helper I, $22,317
Robinson, Kelly J, psychiatric technician I, $23,352
Robinson, Kierra B, security aide I psy, $31,152
Robinson, Kimberly D, food serv helper I, $20,664
Robinson, Marie, deval asst I, $26,400
Robinson, Michelle, deval asst I, $23,352
Robinson, Romanita D, deval asst II, $28,584
Robinson, Shawnda, deval asst I, $22,716
Robinson, Sigrid M, registered nurse, $28,600
Robinson, Tabatha L, registered nurse, $27,795
Robinson, Tina M, case mgr II dd, $34,944
Robinson, Wade D, psychiatric technician II, $25,428
Robison, Julie L, deval asst I, $26,844
Robison, Railean, psychiatric technician I, $22,728
Robison, Scott D, fiscal & administrative mgr b1, $51,094
Rockhill-Gray, Lori E, mental hlth mgr b1, $55,406
Roddel, Raymond B, food serv helper I, $20,664
Rodemeyer, Todd A, registered nurse sr, $54,720
Rodgers, Kenneth D, habilitation spec I, $31,512
Rodgers, Sharla J, clin casework asst II, $30,984
Rodgers, Teresa, special asst prof, $86,355
Rodgers, Thaddeus L, deval asst I, $24,036
Rodriguez, Belinda K, account clerk II, $25,032
Rodriguez, Cristobal A, mental hlth mgr b2, $55,106
Rodriguez, Donna A, prog spec II mh, $52,092
Rodriguez, Janine D, deval asst III, $27,504
Rodriguez, Maya M, ofc spt asst (keybrd), $23,880
Rodriguez, Michele D, sr ofc spt asst (keybrd), $27,948
Rodriguez-Miller, Michelle R, registered nurse, $48,043
Roebuck, Paulette, deval asst I, $25,428
Roedel, Megan N, mental hlth mgr b2, $65,363
Roemer, Sabrina A, ofc spt asst (keybrd), $23,880
Rofkahr, Tammy M, deval asst I, $22,716
Rogers, Brittney A, deval asst I, $23,352
Rogers, Kula, custodial worker I, $21,864
Rogers, Lakiya, deval asst I, $23,352
Rogers, Mary D, deval asst I, $25,428
Rogers, Mattie M, deval asst III, $27,084
Rogers, Myra L, deval asst I, $22,716
Rogers, Nina W, cook II, $25,032
Rogers, Sekani L, registered nurse sup, $58,170
Rogers, Terrance, storekeeper I, $27,948
Rogers, Todd A, registered nurse sr, $55,776
Rogers, Violet A, registered nurse, $5,500

Rohrer, David J, student intern, $22,500
Rojano, Julie, registered nurse sr, $65,676
Rokan, Brian S, custodial worker I, $20,664
Roll, Candice L, occup ther I, $53,208
Roll, Ronald R, custodial worker I, $22,317
Rolland, Barbara J, security aide I psy, $30,276
Rollett, Kristi L, acct I, $30,984
Rollins, Alexus, custodial worker I, $20,664
Romain-Tyson, Rosemarie A, med admin, $39,514
Romero, Timothy J, deval asst I, $24,036
Roney, John F, psychiatric technician I, $23,352
Rongey, Nancy F, registered nurse sr, $53,592
Root, Alisha G, deval asst I, $26,400
Root, Brenda D, exec I, $40,380
Root, Doris, acct, $12,865
Rorman, Teresa A, deval asst I, $23,352
Rosales, Yesenia, psychiatric technician I, $24,072
Rosario, Denise P, security aide I psy, $29,652
Roscher, Ruth E, registered nurse sr, $51,276
Rosco, Buddy, security aide I psy, $29,652
Rose, Christine R, registered nurse sr, $63,585
Rose, Harold B, clin casework pract I, $33,744
Rose, Musette L, case mgr II dd, $42,708
Rose, Yvonne M, acct II, $47,892
Rosenau, Mandy E, storekeeper I, $25,032
Rosenbum, Garret L, security aide II psy, $34,488
Rosenburg, Kimberly N, sr auditor, $41,940
Rosenfelder, Kimberly D, recrtnal ther I, $37,548
Rosenstengel, Amanda K, admin ofc spt asst, $36,302
Rosenstengel, Charlotte, misc tech, $17,597
Rosey, Dawn, clin casework pract II, $39,624
Ross, Aaron K, security aide II psy, $32,208
Ross, Angel A, lpn II gen, $35,736
Ross, Brandi C, psychiatric technician I, $22,728
Ross, Donald L, laborer II, $31,089
Ross, Jacob A, deval asst I, $23,028
Ross, Janet, deval asst II, $29,052
Ross, John, security ofcr I, $25,032
Ross, Judy M, deval asst II, $26,208
Rosser, Ilyn O, deval asst I, $23,352
Rost, Amy R, registered nurse, $27,794
Rost, Tosha L, security aide I psy, $32,244
Rotellini, Jowallace T, security ofcr I, $25,824
Roth, Georgia L, clin casework pract II, $37,548
Rothermich, Janice M, acct II, $43,488
Rothermich, Renee, research analyst IV, $56,520
Rothlisberger, John R, security aide I psy, $30,276
Rousan, Robert D, registered nurse sr, $51,552
Rouse, Amanda K, behavioral technician, $26,004
Rowden, Shannon K, vendor servs coor mh, $40,380
Rowe, Cindy S, psychiatric technician I, $23,352
Rowe, Mary B, registered nurse, $17,166
Rowell, Anthony T, security aide II psy, $34,488
Rowland, Franklin J, security aide II psy, $32,208
Rowlett, Else-Marie, psychiatric technician I, $23,412
Rowley, Angela M, activity aide II, $27,780
Roy, Charles, registered nurse, $27,795
Royer, Jade N, psychiatric technician I, $23,352
Royer, Russyl B, security ofcr I, $29,412
Rucker, Darlene, psychiatric technician I, $23,700
Rucker, Tiffiney R, psychiatric technician I, $23,700
Rud, Alan L, security aide II psy, $34,488
Rud, Charlotte J, custodial worker I, $21,760
Rud, Lucinda M, ofc spt asst (keybrd), $23,160
Rudder, Timothy J, mental hlth mgr b1, $58,640
Rudolph, Halen J, security aide I psy, $29,652
Rueter, Mallory L, psychiatric technician I, $22,728
Rulo, Anthony L Jr, psychiatric technician I, $23,412
Rulo, Karen L, deval asst I, $22,728
Rummel, Nettie A, habilitation spec II, $34,944
Rush, Theodis T, psychiatric technician I, $22,728
Russell, Carol A, pers clerk, $28,104
Russell, Christina A, storekeeper II, $27,660
Russell, Daniel C, pastoral cnslr, $49,658
Russell, Darryl K, cook II, $25,032
Russell, Jerry, security ofcr III, $34,944
Russell, Laura J, food serv helper I, $21,760
Russell, Loretta J, psychiatric technician I, $24,072
Russell, Richard R, security ofcr III, $34,944

Russell, Ronald, misc prof, $25,735
Russell, Sandra J, ofc spt asst (clerical), $21,864
Russell, Wanda L, mental hlth mgr b2, $66,155
Russo, Chastidy J, mental hlth mgr b1, $52,093
Rust, Robin, misc prof, $38.70/hr
Ruth, Deloris J, deval asst I, $23,352
Ryan, Melissa G, habilitation spec II, $41,940
Ryan, Phillip G, habilitation spec II, $40,380
Ryan, Shannon, dev dis cmnty worker II, $34,944
Rybar, Mary S, clerk, $15,838
Rye, Erin E, licensed clin soc wkr, $47,892
Ryland, Charles, psychiatric technician II, $25,584
Ryland, Charles C, psychiatric technician I, $23,352
Sabala, Jon D, mental hlth mgr b1, $61,105
Sachs, Danielle R, security aide I psy, $29,652
Sackett, Rozetta D, pers analyst II, $38,928
Sadler, Windy M, deval asst I, $25,428
Saffle, Courtney D, deval asst I, $23,352
Saffle, David W, security aide I psy, $34,488
Saggio, Elena C, psychiatric technician I, $23,352
Saggio, Zachary C, psychiatric technician I, $22,728
Sago, Rebecca J, hlth info admin II, $50,040
Sailer, Cassandra K, registered nurse sup, $79,826
Sails, Jackie Y, deval asst I, $23,352
Sain, Jamie M, deval asst I, $22,404
Sain, Sandra, registered nurse sup, $74,023
Saina, Reuben K, registered nurse, $28.60/hr
Saint Louis, Lola F, habilitation spec II, $38,928
Saladino, Janice N, deval asst I, $22,728
Salah, Safa, psychiatric technician I, $24,696
Salamone, Deidra L, psychological resident, $35,972
Salanic Alvarado, Enrique F, security aide I psy, $31,152
Salazar Rodriguez, Yazmin H, deval asst II, $25,428
Sales, Angela S, security aide I psy, $29,652
Salkil, Danielle M, deval asst I, $22,728
Salmeron, Daniel A, deval asst I, $23,412
Salmons, Angela F, admin ofc spt asst, $30,420
Salmons, Debra L, acct I, $35,568
Salmons, Dorothy A, storekeeper I, $25,824
Salmons, Edith V, security aide I psy, $36,336
Salmons, Ginger R, custodial work spv, $25,790
Salmons, Judy L, security aide I psy, $29,652
Salmons, Victoria A, cook I, $23,160
Salmons, Wade E, security aide I psy, $35,712
Salter, Richard S, security aide I psy, $30,276
Sams, Anna E, psychiatric technician I, $22,728
Samuels, Steven, deval asst III, $26,448
Sanchez, Andrew V, security aide II psy, $32,208
Sanchez, Bonnie J, custodial worker I, $22,317
Sanchez, Donna S, deval asst I, $22,404
Sander, Bobbie J, deval asst I, $22,728
Sander, Brittany D, deval asst II, $25,584
Sanders, Arthur, direct care aide, $13.11/hr
Sanders, Christy N, deval asst I, $23,352
Sanders, Crystal N, prog spec trainee mh, $36,888
Sanders, Karen M, registered nurse sr, $57,893
Sanders, Kevin S, psychologist II, $71,208
Sanders, Mary E, institution supt, $83,521
Sanders, Michael, psychiatric technician I, $24,696
Sanders, Tina, deval asst I, $23,412
Sanders, Tina G, deval asst I, $22,404
Sanderson, Bridget L, cook II, $23,880
Sandhu, Ravinder S, resident physician, $49,515
Sandlin, Carlissa, deval asst I, $23,352
Sanger, Avery L, qual assurance spec mh, $40,380
Sanna, Pamela K, ofc spt asst (keybrd), $26,652
Santiago, Joannah, registered nurse, $30,046
Sapone, Frank J, locksmith, $34,944
Sapone, Kimberly R, registered nurse sr, $51,276
Sapp, Samantha J, deval asst I, $22,404
Sargent, Christopher A, deval asst I, $22,728
Sarjo, Hawa, deval asst II, $25,428
Sarmiento-Tran, Rey Anthony, deval asst I, $23,352
Sartain, Karen M, lpn III gen, $36,396
Sartin, Erin L, clin casework pract II, $41,940
Sartin, Natalia V, psychiatric technician I, $23,412
Sassmann, Camila L, deval asst I, $22,404
Satterfield, Judy F, dev dis cmnty worker II, $38,928
Saunders, Xaviera S, deval asst I, $22,728

Sause, Deena G, dietitian III, $55,416
Savage, Bradley H, workshop spv II, $28,452
Savage, Kati R, security aide I psy, $31,620
Savala, Margo C, unit prog spv mh, $48,156
Sawyer, Arnetta, deval asst I, $22,716
Sawyer, Rebecca J, dev dis cmnty worker II, $38,928
Sawyer, Tommy D, psychiatric technician I, $26,400
Sayle, Sarah R, registered nurse, $54,766
Sayles, Patricia L, account clerk II, $29,412
Scalf, Sandra K, habilitation spec II, $34,944
Scanlan, Kimberlee A, psychiatric technician II, $25,428
Scarborough, Rebecca J, deval asst I, $22,728
Scarborough, Tracy L, deval asst II, $24,804
Scarlet, Kimberly J, ofc spt asst (keybrd), $24,612
Schaberg, Christine S, deval asst I, $22,728
Schader, Christopher S, security aide I psy, $32,244
Schaefer, Phyllis A, sr ofc spt asst (keybrd), $27,084
Schaeffer, Cheryl, speech pathologist, $48,269
Schaeffler, Courtney L, psychiatric technician I, $22,728
Schafer, Kathryn S, registered nurse - clin opers, $61,836
Schalamon, Dara L, ofc spt asst (clerical), $30,276
Schanda, Porcius W, security aide I psy, $29,652
Schanzmeyer, Gary A, fiscal & administrative mgr b2, $77,180
Schasteen, Kip V, deval asst II, $26,208
Scheers, Peter, mental hlth mgr b2, $62,651
Schenewerk, Mikaela L, deval asst I, $23,412
Schenk, Barbara J, vendor servs coor mh, $40,380
Scheper, Paulette T, registered nurse sr, $56,976
Scherer, Samuel J, case mgmt/assess spv, $40,380
Scherr, Renee J, registered nurse, $27.50/hr
Scheulen, Judith E, sr ofc spt asst (keybrd), $27,504
Schlegel, Cory J, dev dis cmnty prog coord, $38,928
Schlenker, Theodore G, deval asst I, $22,728
Schloman, Crystal I, deval asst I, $22,728
Schloman, Eric M, cook II, $23,880
Schlotter, Jennifer L, activity aide II, $27,780
Schlottog, Jill K, exec I, $38,232
Schlundt, Vanessa L, deval asst I, $22,092
Schlup, Karen J, deval asst I, $24,804
Schlup, Michelle R, budget analyst III, $47,892
Schmidt, Pamela J, special asst ofc & clerical, $40,211
Schmidt, Teresa S, account clerk II, $25,824
Schmitt, David E, institution supt, $87,480
Schnedler, Aleasha G, deval asst I, $22,728
Schneider, Amy L, acct I, $29,976
Schneider, Blake S, mental hlth mgr b1, $61,323
Schneider, Robert H, staff dev ofcr mh, $54,288
Schnidman, Robert E, psychologist II, $49,023
Schollmeyer, Vicki A, fiscal & administrative mgr b3, $77,180
Schondelmeyer, Sandra M, case mgr III dd, $41,172
Schoof, Vicki S, registered nurse, $27,794
Schort, Yvonne I, security aide I psy, $31,620
Schrader, Michael E, supply mgr I, $32,628
Schrag, Andrew A, deval asst II, $32,148
Schrum, Debbie M, account clerk II, $27,084
Schubert, Kenneth, direct care aide, $12.12/hr
Schuett, Tonya, deval asst I, $23,352
Schuldt, Anna M, sr ofc spt asst (keybrd), $25,824
Schulte, Elizabeth S, licensed clin soc wkr, $43,488
Schulte, Ronetta L, special asst ofc & clerical, $47,392
Schupp, Maureen E, licensed clin soc wkr, $52,092
Schuster, Rick D, security aide I psy, $32,244
Schuster, Veronica K, security aide I psy, $30,276
Schwalbe, Theresa M, registered nurse sr, $60,796
Schwent, Gregory A, psychiatric technician I, $22,728
Schwer, Harry L, registered nurse sr, $53,592
Scoggin, Ashley M, deval asst I, $23,352
Scoggin, Bradley K, psychiatric technician I, $23,352
Scoggin, Shawna N, security aide I psy, $29,208
Scoggin, Susan M, cook I, $21,864
Scoggins, Lynn P, security aide II psy, $38,256
Scoggins, Terry W, security aide I psy, $37,608
Scott, Catherine, deval asst I, $23,700
Scott, Christy, acct I, $41,172
Scott, David W, security ofcr I, $25,824
Scott, Heather J, qual assurance spec mh, $44,304
Scott, Jennifer R, deval asst I, $23,412
Scott, Karen D, food serv helper I, $22,317
Scott, Marion A, deval asst III, $27,084

Scott, Mollie L, cook I, $23,508
Scott, Passion, deval asst II, $25,428
Scott, Richard G, psychologist II, $74,304
Scott, Susan C, misc prof, $13,372
Scott, Susan D, habilitation spec II, $36,888
Scott, Tyanna, deval asst I, $22,728
Scoville, Juanita E, deval asst I, $26,400
Scroggins, Julie L, food serv helper I, $20,148
Scruggs, Basil, deval asst I, $22,728
Seal, Carmel L, qual assurance spec mh, $40,380
Seals, Erica D, deval asst I, $22,728
Seals, Lin A, sr ofc spt asst (keybrd), $25,824
Seals, Tyaira L, deval asst I, $23,412
Sebold, Karla J, account clerk II, $25,824
See, Eva J, registered nurse - clin opers, $61,740
Seelig, Jane W, licensed prof cnslr II, $34,551
Seely, Cathy M, admin ofc spt asst, $34,356
Segura, Alex M, psychiatric technician I, $22,716
Seitz, Elizabeth D, security aide I psy, $31,620
Seitz, Magen D, deval asst I, $22,728
Sekoni, Toyin G, registered nurse sr, $60,184
Selby, Penny E, deval asst I, $22,728
Sellars, Cynthia R, ofc spt asst (keybrd), $26,232
Selsor, Mun P, registered nurse sr, $54,766
Selvadurai, Paul N, consulting physician, $61,764.00/hr
Semar, Rebecca J, activity therapy coor, $58,908
Senneff, Sarah A, dietitian II, $46,932
Seran, Bruce, registered nurse sr, $60,796
Sergent, Lois L, qual assurance spec mh, $43,488
Sergio, Jessica A, psychologist I, $71,208
Sesay, Victor A, security aide I psy, $31,620
Sessler, Ashley A, lpn I gen, $31,248
Sessler, Melodey R, lpn II gen, $32,844
Sethi, Sanjiv, med admin, $230,926
Seton, Rachel A, deval asst I, $22,716
Sevier, Glennton, deval asst I, $24,036
Sexe, Robert B, med spec II, $107,374
Sexton, Kimberly K, psychiatric technician I, $24,036
Sexton, Melvona, pers clerk, $33,744
Sexton, Teresa I, mgmt analysis spec II, $42,708
Seye, Saer, cook I, $23,160
Seyer, Kenneth J, hearings ofcr, $59,085
Seymour, Carol J, deval asst I, $22,728
Shadden, Jimmy L, deval asst I, $23,352
Shadowens, Freida M, psychiatric technician I, $23,352
Shadwick, Lesia R, ofc spt asst (clerical), $22,536
Shadwick, Robert, security ofcr I, $25,824
Shafer, Glenna J, licensed clin soc wkr, $53,208
Shahid, Ayesha M, deval asst I, $22,716
Shannon, Kerri L, habilitation spec II, $39,624
Shannon, Matthew M, mental hlth mgr b2, $58,000
Shannon, Pamela K, habilitation spec II, $34,944
Shannon, Rahab W, registered nurse, $51,552
Shannon, Tina M, exec I, $30,984
Shaon, Brenda L, security aide I psy, $32,208
Sharma, Pooja, staff physician spec, $221,301
Sharman, Stephen D, deval asst I, $23,352
Sharp, Bobbie G, security aide I psy, $31,152
Sharp, Ineva K, security aide I psy, $29,652
Sharp, Jacqueline, psychiatric technician II, $29,676
Sharp, Sheila A, psychiatric technician I, $22,728
Shaw, Angela R, deval asst I, $23,352
Shaw, Brandon, deval asst I, $22,728
Shaw, Brynn C, direct care aide, $12.36/hr
Shaw, Joyce, deval asst I, $22,092
Shaw, Laverne, deval asst I, $23,352
Shaw, Sharae R, psychiatric technician I, $23,352
Shaw, Stirling A, fire & safety spec, $41,172
Shaw, Vicky S, security aide I psy, $30,276
Shaw, Winston M, cook II, $25,404
Shawhan, Julie, comm mntl hlth servs spv, $46,932
Shears, George M, security aide I psy, $31,152
Sheets, Tara M, mental hlth mgr b2, $66,739
Sheets, Timothy B, security aide I psy, $31,152
Sheikh, Shabnam N, med spec II, $62,328
Shelata, Jennifer R, cook II, $23,880
Shelden, William J, security aide I psy, $30,276
Sheley, Dayna G, sr ofc spt asst (keybrd), $29,412
Shelton, Brittany, deval asst I, $23,352

Shelton, De A, subs abuse cnslr III, $43,488
Shelton, Jerry, food serv helper II, $21,864
Shelton, Matthew B, security aide I psy, $31,620
Shelton, Nicole S, deval asst III, $26,652
Shelton, Sarah A, custodial worker I, $22,317
Shepard, Casey M, registered nurse, $17,166
Shepard, Karen L, reimbursement ofcr I, $36,888
Shepard, Randall L, psychiatric technician II, $25,584
Shepherd, Margaret J, special educ tchr III, $39,624
Sheppard, Onterio C, psychiatric technician I, $22,728
Shepperd, Marlon, deval asst I, $23,352
Sherdan-Chillers, Myra, lpn II gen, $39,780
Sheriff, Fatumata, psychiatric technician I, $22,728
Sherman, Beverly A, pers clerk, $28,104
Sherman, Gabrielle A, deval asst I, $23,352
Sherpa, Dawa P, security aide I psy, $31,620
Sherrell, Alan L, supply mgr II, $40,380
Sherrell, John K, deval asst I, $26,004
Sherrell, Keith S, motor veh driver, $23,880
Sherrill, John T, security aide I psy, $30,276
Sherrod, Manuel F, security ofcr III, $29,976
Sherrod, Marvin D, housekeeper II, $33,744
Shields, Crystal B, deval asst I, $23,352
Shields, Jackie H, account clerk II, $25,824
Shields, Mark R, special asst official & admstr, $78,511
Shilane, Lewis P, physician, $148,572
Shinuald-Herron, Gloria J, account clerk II, $27,084
Shipley, Darrell A, security aide II psy, $33,384
Shiraki, Anne M, music ther II, $36,204
Shireman, Eric E, habilitation spec II, $38,928
Shirley, Catherine L, storekeeper I, $27,084
Shirley, James M, storekeeper I, $25,824
Shirley, Kathy A, lpn II gen, $38,014
Shirley, Mary C, sr ofc spt asst (clerical), $33,636
Shockley, Ashley N, deval asst I, $23,352
Shoemate, Nicole M, prog spec II mh, $45,156
Shoki, Godfrey W, security aide I psy, $31,620
Short, Casey M, deval asst I, $23,028
Short, Dusty A, deval asst I, $23,028
Short, Kristy K, deval asst I, $22,728
Showers-Maynard, Crystal L, admin ofc spt asst, $37,548
Shrum, Redina L, psychiatric technician I, $23,352
Shryock, Sierra N, psychiatric technician I, $22,716
Shubert, Linda L, deval asst I, $22,728
Shumaker, Dustin E, dev dis cmnty worker II, $33,744
Shumate, Earl D, mental hlth mgr b2, $70,559
Shumpert, Pamela, sr ofc spt asst (keybrd), $27,504
Sickman, Deborah L, deval asst I, $24,036
Sidebottom, Megan R, dietitian III, $50,040
Sidebottom, Thomas J, security aide I psy, $31,620
Sides, Laura D, habilitation spec II, $39,624
Sidie, Rochelle A, registered nurse sr, $63,585
Siebeneck, Donna S, designated principal asst dept, $85,345
Siebeneck, Roberta L, procurement ofcr I, $41,172
Siefker, Patricia L, thrpst, $51,470
Siegel, Gail B, sr ofc spt asst (keybrd), $27,504
Siegel, Richard W, locksmith, $33,744
Siegel, Tammy L, ofc spt asst (keybrd), $25,404
Siegworth, Hope R, deval asst I, $22,728
Siemons, Mary, admin ofc spt asst, $30,420
Sierra, Lori G, account clerk I, $25,824
Sikes, Heather A, sr ofc spt asst (keybrd), $26,232
Sikes, Sherri L, lpn II gen, $35,736
Sikes, Tammy E, custodial work spv, $26,580
Silas, Felicia, lpn II gen, $34,560
Silas, Kala D, deval asst I, $22,728
Silkwood, Justin M, deval asst II, $25,584
Silkwood, Michael I, deval asst III, $28,452
Siller, Pamela, psychiatric technician I, $24,072
Silvey, Rachael M, deval asst I, $22,404
Silvey, Shane E, deval asst I, $22,728
Silvey, Shawn M, deval asst III, $30,384
Simes, Gail D, habilitation spec II, $35,568
Simmons, Alfreda, unit prog spv mh, $38,928
Simmons, Amanda M, deval asst I, $23,412
Simmons, Brandee, psychiatric technician I, $24,696
Simmons, Cathy A, case mgr II dd, $34,944
Simmons, Cheyenne C, deval asst I, $24,036
Simmons, Danielle, deval asst I, $23,352

Simmons, Reginald, food serv helper I, $20,664
Simmons, Jeanette M, institution supt, $83,521
Simmons, Jennifer J, deval asst I, $24,072
Simmons, Joseph W, security ofcr I, $25,824
Simmons, Kara M, deval asst I, $23,412
Simmons, Kecia M, case mgr II dd, $34,944
Simmons, Kristina D, vendor servs coor mh, $40,380
Simmons, Renita, psychiatric technician I, $24,072
Simmons, Ronnie D, deval asst I, $24,036
Simmons, Roosevelt, edu asst II, $24,804
Simmons, Scherob C, deval asst I, $23,352
Simmons, Shiril R, deval asst III, $26,652
Simmons, Thomas L, security aide I psy, $34,488
Simmons, Tonya L, deval asst I, $23,412
Simmons, Virginia D, security aide I psy, $30,276
Simmons, William H, security aide I psy, $29,652
Simms, Jeannette, storekeeper I, $26,652
Simms, Tina N, unit prog spv mh, $46,068
Simon, Ebony C, psychiatric technician I, $23,352
Simone, Sheela R, psychiatric technician I, $22,716
Simpson, Jeffery C, deval asst I, $24,804
Simpson, Nancy J, licensed prof cnslr II, $41,940
Simpson, Paul J, food serv helper I, $20,664
Simpson, Tammy E, psychiatric technician I, $22,716
Simpson, Thomas J, deval asst I, $22,728
Simrell, Orletta J, deval asst I, $22,716
Sims, Christopher J, security ofcr I, $25,824
Sims, Edward, custodial worker I, $20,664
Sims, Ida B, clerk, $10,926
Sims, Juanita, deval asst I, $23,352
Sims, Tricia N, voc rehab spec II, $44,304
Sinden, Gladys K, domestic serv worker, $11,866
Singleton, Dorothy, motor veh driver, $23,880
Singleton, Lisa M, lpn II gen, $40,648
Singleton, Raven S, psychiatric technician I, $23,352
Singleton, Tina R, sr ofc spt asst (keybrd), $27,084
Sinnett, Taylor S, deval asst I, $22,728
Sipes, Kenneth, clerk, $11,323
Sirikwa, Anna J, licensed clin soc wkr, $50,040
Sisney, Kevin L, deval asst III, $29,281
Sizemore, Lisa M, deval asst I, $22,728
Sjoblom, Beth, consulting physician, $24,072
Skid, Jonathan, food serv helper I, $21,864
Skinner, Dawn M, deval asst I, $25,584
Skinner, Shelly L, security aide I psy, $31,620
Skinner, Stacy A, account clerk II, $25,824
Skubal, Sara C, clin casework pract II, $37,548
Skyles, Connie S, account clerk II, $25,824
Slack, Carol S, deval asst I, $24,036
Slade, Ronda J, dental asst, $18,648
Slaughter, Brittany M, recrtnal ther I, $31,512
Slaughter, Christine, exec II, $42,708
Slaughter, Deaon E, deval asst I, $23,352
Slayden, Anthony, security ofcr II, $28,104
Slayton, Lonnie J, deval asst I, $23,352
Slayton, Martha K, case mgr II dd, $36,204
Sleper, Jaime D, registered nurse sr, $50,244
Slevin, Trintine L, security ofcr I, $25,824
Slivinski, Stacey D, registered nurse - clin opers, $64,380
Sloan, Kristy L, deval asst I, $23,352
Sloan, Shirley R, deval asst II, $25,428
Small, Ahijah, security aide I psy, $32,244
Small, Lashall M, psychiatric technician I, $24,696
Smallen, Tracy L, lpn II gen, $40,648
Smead, Sharon L, recrtnal ther II, $41,940
Smigell, Matthew J, registered nurse - clin opers, $63,084
Smiley, Tammy L, clin soc work spv, $57,744
Smith, Adam C, registered nurse, $50,244
Smith, Allen E, security aide I psy, $30,274
Smith, Amanda M, custodial worker I, $22,317
Smith, Ashley N, psychiatric technician I, $22,092
Smith, Austin L, psychiatric technician I, $22,092
Smith, Brenda J, dev dis cmnty prog coord, $43,488
Smith, Carlisha D, psychiatric technician I, $23,352
Smith, Chelsie L, security aide I psy, $31,620
Smith, Christy L, deval asst I, $23,412
Smith, Connie L, security aide I psy, $29,652
Smith, Corrine I, qual assurance spec mh, $40,380
Smith, Cynthia L, ofc spt asst (keybrd), $25,404

Smith, David, deval asst I, $23,352
Smith, David A, registered nurse, $50,244
Smith, Debra C, case mgr III dd, $41,172
Smith, Derek J, registered nurse sr, $54,720
Smith, Donna M, security aide I psy, $31,620
Smith, Erika, custodial worker I, $21,760
Smith, Esaw, psychiatric technician II, $30,672
Smith, Eva, psychiatric technician I, $23,700
Smith, Forrest H, fiscal & administrative mgr b3, $76,514
Smith, Gregory I, deval asst I, $26,628
Smith, Ingrid R, deval asst I, $27,024
Smith, Jacqueline M, cook III, $28,104
Smith, James L, security aide I psy, $31,620
Smith, Jane M, activity therapy coor, $66,720
Smith, Janis, licensed clin soc wkr, $46,068
Smith, Jenifer R, case mgr I dd, $32,628
Smith, Kay M, occup ther II, $62,664
Smith, Kristina J, dev dis cmnty spec, $37,548
Smith, Lakerra S, deval asst I, $22,728
Smith, Latoya S, deval asst II, $24,804
Smith, Leslie R, psychiatric technician I, $22,728
Smith, Lisa K, mental hlth mgr b2, $60,111
Smith, Lisa M, deval asst I, $22,728
Smith, Lisa M, registered nurse, $36,029
Smith, Lisbeth L, psychiatric technician I, $23,352
Smith, Martha M, special asst prof, $90,900
Smith, Marvin L, security ofcr I, $42,468
Smith, Megan E, security aide I psy, $31,620
Smith, Michelle A, registered nurse sr, $55,776
Smith, Michelle L, security aide I psy, $34,488
Smith, Molly J, psychiatric technician I, $23,352
Smith, Mona, investigator, $40.64/hr
Smith, Monica L, security aide I psy, $29,652
Smith, Nora A, deval asst I, $24,804
Smith, Paul, deval asst I, $23,352
Smith, Paul L, psychiatric technician I, $23,352
Smith, Phyllis M, ofc spt asst (keybrd), $25,824
Smith, Rachael J, deval asst I, $22,728
Smith, Randall C, proj spec, $26,112
Smith, Rebecca J, deval asst I, $24,036
Smith, Rhonda S, admin ofc spt asst, $30,420
Smith, Robin D, deval asst I, $23,352
Smith, Ronald B, security aide I psy, $31,620
Smith, Roslyn, psychiatric technician I, $22,728
Smith, Roxanna A, supply mgr I, $34,944
Smith, Ruth A, work therapy spec I, $24,612
Smith, Sammie D, registered nurse sr, $52,608
Smith, Shelia M, psychiatric technician I, $24,804
Smith, Sherry A, deval asst I, $25,428
Smith, Shirley A, security aide I psy, $31,152
Smith, Sophia L, deval asst I, $25,056
Smith, Susan E, dev dis cmnty prog coord, $38,928
Smith, Tigre N, registered nurse, $28,375
Smith, Tracy L, case mgr I dd, $31,512
Smith, Tracy Y, deval asst II, $26,208
Smith, Troy D, prog coord dmh dohss, $51,096
Smith, Vickie L, deval asst I, $23,352
Smyser, Melissa L, mental hlth mgr b2, $67,695
Snider, Andrew N, psychiatric technician I, $22,716
Snider, David, budget analyst III, $52,092
Snow, Jennifer M, deval asst I, $24,036
Snow, Juanita S, habilitation spec II, $36,888
Snow, Wendy I, qual assurance spec mh, $43,488
Snowden, Donald L, security ofcr I, $25,824
Snowden, Lajuana M, sr ofc spt asst (keybrd), $27,084
Snyder, Rita, sr ofc spt asst (keybrd), $25,824
Sohn, Robin G, security aide I psy, $29,652
Sommerville, Jennifer L, deval asst II, $25,584
Sooter, Mark W, edual aide, $10,826
Soptick, Amanda I, food serv helper I, $20,148
Sorgen, Kathy A, habilitation spec II, $36,888
Sou, Maumagaisiva, deval asst I, $23,028
Sousan, Anthony D, deval asst I, $23,352
Southard, Ashley N, deval asst I, $23,352
Souza, Karen L, soc servs sup, $25,022
Spann, Brittany, deval asst I, $23,352
Spann, Curtia J, deval asst I, $22,728
Spann, Jaaland K, ofc spt asst (keybrd), $23,160
Sparks, Claude W, security aide II psy, $35,112

Sparks, Dolores J, prog coord dmh dohss, $51,096
Sparks, John, security ofcr I, $25,824
Sparks, Nicole L, deval asst I, $22,728
Spears, Dewayne A, security aide I psy, $29,832
Spears, Regina K, ofc spt asst (keybrd), $29,904
Spence, Debbie A, food serv helper I, $22,317
Spence, Future M, psychiatric technician I, $25,428
Spence Bey, Teara, deval asst I, $22,728
Spencer, Ashley S, lpn II gen, $36,710
Spencer, Atilvia L, psychiatric technician I, $22,092
Spencer, Jameshia, special asst prof, $95,000
Spencer, Jameshia, registered nurse, $36,028
Spencer, Jarvis W, security aide I psy, $29,652
Spencer, Karen Y, deval asst I, $26,400
Sperry, Deborah D, deval asst I, $24,036
Spiller, Demetria, deval asst I, $23,352
Spire, Monica J, licensed clin soc wkr, $46,068
Spitler, Dennis E, recrtnal ther II, $41,172
Spitzmiller, Domitila, psychiatric technician I, $23,352
Spooner, David T, pastoral cnslr, $18,402
Spradley, Ralph E, registered nurse sr, $71,587
Spradling, Amber N, ofc spt asst (keybrd), $22,536
Spradling, Natalie N, case mgr II dd, $34,944
Spranaitis, Anthony H, clin soc work spec, $49,128
Springer, Valorie, cook II, $23,880
Springman, Rachael E, psychologist II, $69,612
Sprous, Thomas M, security aide I psy, $30,276
Sripal, Hungi P, physician, $124,775
Ssekasozi, Charles J, security aide I psy, $29,652
St John, Russlyn M, account clerk II, $27,084
Staats, Janice L, custodial work spv, $25,790
Staats, Karen S, custodial worker I, $22,872
Stacey, Michael L, clin casework pract I, $46,068
Stach, Michelle L, mental hlth mgr b3, $71,094
Stacy, Debra D, registered nurse sup, $73,143
Stacy, James F, pers ofcr I, $50,040
Stacy, Nelda L, food serv helper I, $20,664
Stafford, Karen A, cook III, $28,104
Stafford, Kimberly A, special asst ofc & clerical, $40,211
Stafford, Vanessa L, research analyst I, $32,052
Stagner, Sherri L, lpn II gen, $32,220
Stagner, Wanda S, custodial worker I, $33,016
Stahl, Paula, psychiatric technician II, $24,804
Stancil, Monica L, case mgr III dd, $37,548
Standford, Takesha C, deval asst II, $23,352
Standford, Teira, deval asst I, $22,728
Standiford, Gena N, psychiatric technician I, $23,352
Stanislaus, Angeline, med admin, $136,350
Stanley, Tona L, habilitation spec II, $33,744
Starke, Gary H, deval asst I, $26,004
Starling, Joyce A, security aide I psy, $29,208
Staten, Shawnda D, ofc spt asst (keybrd), $23,160
Stearns, Claude H, psychologist II, $77,556
Stearns, Sabrina M, deval asst I, $22,716
Steele, Charles G, deval asst I, $22,728
Steen, Etta M, deval asst II, $25,584
Steffenauer, Renee C, ofc spt asst (keybrd), $25,404
Steffens, Robert W, deval asst I, $22,728
Steffes, Patsy R, psychiatric technician I, $26,004
Stegall, Floyd J, food serv helper I, $11,159
Stegall, Kevin L, security ofcr I, $25,824
Steinc, Joseph R, security aide I psy, $32,244
Steingrubyhuddleston, erin E, licensed clin soc wkr, $43,488
Steinhoff, Mary E, registered nurse - clin opers, $69,996
Stemmerman, Paul P, registered nurse sr, $56,192
Stennis, Charlotte, deval asst I, $23,412
Stephan, Joshua C, security aide I psy, $31,620
Stephens, Danny G, security ofcr II, $27,228
Stephens, Jennifer L, deval asst I, $22,728
Stephens, Kaitlin C, psychiatric technician I, $22,716
Stevens, Amy E, mental hlth mgr b2, $67,695
Stevens, Ceri K, special asst ofc & clerical, $40,211
Stevens, Isaac W, security aide I psy, $31,620
Stevens, Julieann S, registered nurse - clin opers, $96,326
Stevens, Lisa A, sr ofc spt asst (keybrd), $28,908
Stevens, Michael W, lpn II gen, $40,764
Stevens, Nicholas, deval asst II, $25,584
Stevenson, Brittany Y, deval asst I, $22,728
Stevenson, Julie L, lpn II gen, $32,220

Stevenson, Kristin L, comm mntl hlth servs spv, $46,932
Steward, Debora D, deval asst I, $22,728
Steward, Kimberly J, motor veh driver, $24,612
Steward, Lachelle R, security aide I psy, $32,244
Stewart, Breonna R, psychiatric technician I, $23,352
Stewart, Dameisha, deval asst I, $23,352
Stewart, Deborah A, psychiatric technician II, $26,208
Stewart, Exie N, account clerk II, $27,084
Stewart, Karen D, deval asst I, $26,004
Stewart, Linda A, misc prof, $40.40/hr
Stewart, Micah J, security aide I psy, $29,652
Stewart, Pamella K, deval asst I, $22,728
Stewart, Sandra, deval asst I, $26,004
Stewart, Sarah A, psychiatric technician I, $22,728
Stewart, Sylvia, deval asst I, $23,700
Stickel, Teresa K, lpn II gen, $29,772
Stiefvater, Judith L, training tech III, $62,664
Stienkemeyer, Robert N, security ofcr I, $29,904
Still, Tara L, deval asst I, $23,412
Stinson, Calvin L, food serv helper II, $21,864
Stith, Milton, psychiatric technician I, $23,352
Stjohn, Linda, motor veh driver, $25,032
Stock, Kimberly S, mental hlth mgr b3, $86,355
Stock, Whitney L, recrtnal ther I, $32,628
Stockdale, Daniel L, psychiatric technician II, $26,208
Stocking, Jerry, psychiatric technician I, $23,352
Stockman, Linda D, lpn II gen, $40,404
Stockreef, Amber B, habilitation spec II, $34,944
Stoker, David M, security aide II psy, $34,488
Stoker, Jon J, security aide I psy, $32,244
Stokes, Ellis, deval asst I, $22,728
Stoll, Linda J, deval asst I, $22,728
Stone, Charles R, security aide III psy, $38,928
Stone, Lisa M, case mgr II dd, $34,944
Stone, Lorenne M, deval asst I, $23,076
Stone, Nettie R, food serv helper I, $20,664
Stoner, Gary L, licensed clin soc wkr, $48,156
Storms, Lori A, acct I, $37,548
Story, Carla J, acct I, $34,944
Stout, Connie C, deval asst II, $28,584
Stout-Wolford, Janet L, habilitation spec I, $29,004
Stowers, Vicki L, deval asst I, $22,728
Strahl, Agatha N, security aide I psy, $31,620
Strain, Daniel L, deval asst I, $22,728
Strain, Sherry R, deval asst I, $25,428
Strait, Joshua M, psychiatric technician I, $23,352
Stratton, Cari E, deval asst I, $22,728
Straughter, Bobbie J, food serv helper I, $20,664
Strauss, Joe R, supply mgr II, $46,068
Strautmann, Donna, account clerk II, $26,232
Strawn, Tina M, motor veh driver, $25,032
Strba, Suzanne M, psychological resident, $35,972
Street, Courtney A, deval asst I, $22,716
Street, Jennifer A, special asst ofc & clerical, $40,373
Street, Sarah J, psychiatric technician I, $23,352
Street, Valerie R, account clerk II, $28,452
Strickland, Cierra, deval asst I, $22,728
Strickland, Colette, special asst ofc & clerical, $40,361
Strickland, Helyn V, pastoral cnslr, $51,573
Strickland, Kim A, lpn II gen, $38,014
Strickland, Rhonda J, sr ofc spt asst (keybrd), $27,948
Stricklin, Aaron D, security aide I psy, $30,276
Stroud, Nathan G, deval asst I, $23,352
Strough, Angela M, recrtnal ther II, $38,928
Stroup, Beth M, nutrition/dietary svcs mgr b1, $58,905
Struchtemeyer, Glen R, deval asst I, $22,728
Stuart, Constance M, dining room spv, $25,790
Stuart, Janice G, custodial worker I, $22,317
Stuart, Jennifer J, food serv helper I, $22,317
Stubb, Sandra, licensed clin soc wkr, $46,932
Stubblefield, Sandra K, security aide I psy, $29,652
Stuckenschneider, Angela M, mental hlth mgr b2, $76,205
Stuckenschneider, John N, security aide I psy, $29,652
Sturgeon, Tiara L, deval asst I, $23,352
Stutes, Shawn K, registered nurse sr, $59,645
Stuve, Paul R, psychologist, $50.00/hr
Suaray, Mariatu, deval asst I, $23,352
Suarez, Marvin R, deval asst I, $24,036
Sucharski, Alana B, licensed prof cnslr II, $46,932

Sucharski, Wanda K, psychiatric technician II, $25,584
Suddith, Rose M, psychiatric technician I, $22,728
Sudmeyer, Arlene F, custodial worker I, $22,317
Suerig, Sarah E, sr ofc spt asst (keybrd), $27,084
Suess, Marla J, accounting analyst II, $44,304
Sulaiman, Bunmi, deval asst I, $23,352
Sulaiman, Omotola R, psychiatric technician I, $23,352
Sullentrup, Reba L, clin soc work spec, $55,416
Sullins, Laura, acct I, $32,628
Sullivan, Johnathon J, psychiatric technician I, $22,716
Sullivan, Kellie A, comm mntl hlth servs spv, $46,932
Sullivan, Richard L, deval asst I, $27,024
Summers, Barbara D, deval asst II, $26,400
Summers, Bobbi J, training tech II, $41,172
Summers, Brian K, deval asst I, $22,728
Summers, Hayley N, deval asst I, $22,728
Summers, Kermit H, deval asst II, $28,776
Summers, Niesha, deval asst I, $22,716
Summers, Shelly M, prog spec II mh, $50,040
Sumpter, Arnett E, deval asst I, $23,352
Sumpter, Judy F, acct II, $42,708
Sumpter, Sherry J, sr ofc spt asst (keybrd), $27,504
Sumpter, Terry D, maint worker, $12,906
Sundhausen, Tanner C, psychiatric technician I, $23,352
Surface, Christie L, special asst prof, $64,135
Surratt, Eleatha L, staff physician spec, $109,737
Suter, Jennifer M, licensed behavior analyst, $62,664
Sutherland, Melissa, mental hlth mgr b1, $55,406
Sutton, Tracy L, security aide I psy, $30,276
Swager, Judy E, deval asst I, $23,352
Swaim, Lauren N, lpn I gen, $31,710
Swain, Daryl E, deval asst I, $23,352
Swanigan, Mateka, deval asst I, $22,728
Swanson, Hayden T, deval asst I, $23,028
Swanson, Lisa W, psychologist II, $69,612
Swanson, Sandra J, registered nurse sr, $64,681
Swanson, Sandra K, security aide I psy, $29,652
Swarray, Tijan J, deval asst III, $27,276
Swart, Kimberly J, music ther III, $38,928
Swartwood, Kayla J, cook II, $23,880
Swartwood, Lesa K, sr ofc spt asst (keybrd), $28,908
Sweazea, Jamie L, custodial worker I, $20,664
Sweeney, Denise A, custodial worker II, $23,508
Sweeney, Lisa D, clin casework asst II, $36,204
Sweet, Melinda S, case mgr II dd, $34,944
Swerngin, Karen M, deval asst I, $22,728
Swift, Brenda E, investigator I, $30,984
Swift, Tyler C, deval asst I, $24,036
Swigart, Russel L, deval asst I, $22,404
Swigart, Shelby M, deval asst I, $22,404
Swinger, Nicole R, case mgr II dd, $34,944
Swinney, Alexandra C, subs abuse cnslr II, $36,888
Swinney, Charmaine A, deval asst I, $26,628
Swires, Tanya L, deval asst I, $24,036
Switzer, Brittany L, deval asst I, $22,728
Switzer, Sandra C, fiscal & administrative mgr b2, $71,201
Swoboda, Sandra A, registered nurse sr, $56,192
Swoboda, Shannon L, security aide I psy, $29,652
Swope, Terry L, security aide I psy, $31,152
Swuson, Betty J, misc prof, $17,224
Syed, Ahsan, staff physician spec, $203,448
Sykes, Meredith L, deval asst I, $23,412
Sykes, Rhonda, deval asst I, $27,024
Symonds, Donna K, account clerk II, $33,636
Szymankowski, Ronald, psychologist, $36,722
Tabales, Kimberly J, qual assurance spec mh, $47,892
Tabb, Carl L, deval asst II, $28,584
Tabb, Packkousky, registered nurse sup, $85,636
Tabor, Eric M, deval asst III, $28,128
Tackett, Adrian C, deval asst II, $25,584
Taha, Mande, deval asst I, $23,352
Talancon, Juliana E, habilitation spec I, $31,512
Talbott, Malinda L, deval asst I, $23,412
Tall, Dieynaba, custodial worker II, $21,864
Tanjim, Shakila, staff physician, $137,245
Tanksley, Joyce M, childrens psy care spv, $31,920
Tanksley, Linda J, registered nurse sr, $71,587
Tanner, Jennifer R, fiscal & administrative mgr b2, $56,520
Tannheimer, Bethany A, lpn II gen, $31,872

Tappana, Jessica L, licensed clin soc wkr, $47,892
Tappin, Latonya, storekeeper II, $28,104
Tarr, Patrick, deval asst I, $23,352
Tate, Boris A, ofc worker misc, $15,033
Taylor, Ateara F, deval asst I, $22,728
Taylor, Bonnie J, sr ofc spt asst (steno), $27,948
Taylor, Cathely L, deval asst I, $23,352
Taylor, Christina A, deval asst I, $25,584
Taylor, Christopher L, psychiatric technician I, $22,728
Taylor, Deborah B, unit prog spv mh, $44,304
Taylor, Derek E, security aide I psy, $30,276
Taylor, Dominque R, deval asst I, $22,728
Taylor, James A, dev dis cmnty worker I, $32,628
Taylor, Janice M, psychiatric technician II, $27,252
Taylor, Jennifer R, prog coord dmh dohss, $51,096
Taylor, Jessica L, deval asst I, $22,092
Taylor, Jodi N, mental hlth mgr b2, $60,125
Taylor, Kenneth J, deval asst I, $23,352
Taylor, Lazonya Q, psychiatric technician I, $22,728
Taylor, Leah M, security aide I psy, $32,244
Taylor, Marva D, deval asst III, $35,472
Taylor, Nicole R, security aide I psy, $31,620
Taylor, Prenness E, prog spec I mh, $38,928
Taylor, Ritchie, psychiatric technician I, $24,072
Taylor, Ronda L, deval asst I, $27,024
Taylor, Rozsharif D, security ofcr I, $25,824
Taylor, Sharon M, nutrition/dietary svcs mgr b1, $56,510
Taylor, Steven H, dev dis cmnty worker II, $41,172
Taylor, Tenisha N, custodial worker I, $20,664
Taylor, Tiffani D, deval asst I, $22,092
Taylor, Tiffany A, deval asst I, $22,728
Taylor, Tonia L, activity aide II, $25,584
Taylor, Victor D, security aide I psy, $29,208
Tebbe, Cynthia L, deval asst I, $27,252
Tebo, Diana C, sr auditor, $31,609
Tecle, Mebrahton A, psychiatric technician I, $23,352
Tedford, Orpha L, security aide I psy, $29,652
Tedford, Rebecca L, psychiatric technician I, $22,716
Teems, Paula S, psychiatric technician I, $22,728
Teepe, Vickie, licensed clin soc wkr, $51,096
Tegel, Helen J, case mgr I dd, $32,628
Telander, Randy L, psychologist I, $71,278
Templeton, Bruce L, deval asst III, $27,504
Teodorescu, Cristiana F, staff physician spec, $97,717
Terrell, Kim D, habilitation spec II, $38,928
Terrell, Torrance, deval asst I, $23,352
Terrill, Charles, psychiatric technician I, $22,728
Terrill, Crystal D, deval asst I, $23,412
Terrill, Tammy L, deval asst I, $23,412
Terry, Flowerie L, clin casework pract II, $46,932
Tesfai, Yodit, registered nurse, $28,375
Tesreau, William T, security aide II psy, $34,536
Teter, Stephanie D, security aide I psy, $31,620
Tetteh, Peace A, deval asst I, $24,036
Thackeray, Rita L, dietitian II, $46,932
Thaller, Jeffrey S, deval asst I, $26,004
Thaller, Mandy R, food serv helper I, $20,664
Thaman, Teresa K, prog spec II mh, $46,068
Tharp, Julie A, mental hlth mgr b2, $58,000
Tharp, Mari G, custodial worker I, $22,317
Theders, Christina, lpn II gen, $39,780
Theis, Kathrin A, case mgmt/assess spv, $40,380
Theobald, Lindsey J, psychiatric technician I, $11,364
Thibodeau, Christopher M, psychiatric technician II, $25,428
Thibon, Steven P, misc prof, $35,572
Thomas, Allandre D, psychiatric technician I, $23,352
Thomas, Ardell, ofc spt asst (keybrd), $24,264
Thomas, Bernadine, activity aide II, $25,224
Thomas, Bessie L, psychiatric technician II, $26,208
Thomas, Beverly A, ofc spt asst (keybrd), $23,880
Thomas, Brennan, deval asst I, $22,728
Thomas, Carleeta T, deval asst I, $22,728
Thomas, Charles R, security aide I psy, $30,276
Thomas, Cheryl L, deval asst I, $23,412
Thomas, Christine L, registered nurse sr, $57,893
Thomas, David M, acct II, $44,304
Thomas, Denise, assoc counsel, $85,000
Thomas, Denise R, comm mntl hlth servs spv, $46,932
Thomas, Derail J, security aide I psy, $30,276

Thomas, Elizabeth D, deval asst I, $23,412
Thomas, Keron P, food serv helper I, $20,664
Thomas, Lenarda L, psychiatric technician I, $22,728
Thomas, Linda F, security aide I psy, $29,652
Thomas, Lois O, proj spec, $36.42/hr
Thomas, Marcia F, account clerk II, $29,412
Thomas, Marie E, security aide I psy, $29,652
Thomas, Monica J, deval asst II, $26,400
Thomas, Nataka I, behavioral technician, $26,844
Thomas, Nichole D, registered nurse sr, $60,059
Thomas, Pamela C, deval asst I, $22,728
Thomas, Sharon J, deval asst I, $23,352
Thomas, Shirley A, deval asst I, $24,804
Thomas, Tammy D, assoc psychologist II, $49,128
Thomas, Toni, psychiatric technician I, $23,352
Thomas, Tyesha L, security aide I psy, $31,152
Thomas, Whitney E, deval asst I, $24,036
Thomason, Brenda S, deval asst I, $24,036
Thompson, Alexa L, prog spec II mh, $43,488
Thompson, Ashlea R, pers clerk, $33,180
Thompson, Brenda K, security aide I psy, $29,652
Thompson, Brenda L, pers analyst II, $45,156
Thompson, Brenda L, lpn II gen, $30,396
Thompson, Breshay, deval asst I, $23,352
Thompson, Burnadette, case mgr II dd, $34,944
Thompson, Carnetta J, mental hlth mgr b1, $59,913
Thompson, Carolyn L, deval asst II, $28,152
Thompson, Corryn N, case mgr II dd, $34,944
Thompson, Dakotta M, deval asst I, $24,036
Thompson, David B, procurement ofcr II, $47,892
Thompson, Debora R, security aide I psy, $32,244
Thompson, Dena M, registered nurse, $17,166
Thompson, Derek L, security aide II psy, $34,488
Thompson, Donna F, psychiatric technician I, $23,352
Thompson, Heath B, motor veh mech, $29,976
Thompson, James E, custodial worker II, $24,612
Thompson, Jessica M, deval asst I, $24,036
Thompson, Kamilah M, security aide I psy, $30,276
Thompson, Rebecca L, security aide I psy, $29,652
Thompson, Sharrie A, psychiatric technician I, $22,728
Thompson, Teremus J, psychiatric technician I, $24,036
Thomure, Roger C, reimbursement ofcr I, $38,232
Thorn, Dareth L, ofc spt asst (keybrd), $23,880
Thorn, Joseph M, psychiatric technician I, $23,352
Thornburgh, Marsha A, dev dis cmnty worker II, $34,944
Thornhill, Racheal C, security aide I psy, $32,244
Thornton, Wanda S, unit prog spv mh, $44,304
Thorp, Kirk W, security aide I psy, $30,276
Thorps-Wiley, Yolanda, cook II, $23,880
Threlkeld, Leah D, deval asst I, $23,352
Thumann, Kathryn T, mental hlth mgr b1, $61,323
Thurman, Benjamin B, security aide I psy, $30,276
Thurmon, Colleen T, hlth info tech II, $31,512
Thurow, Janet A, dev dis cmnty prog coord, $41,940
Thuston, Brindi K, psychiatric technician I, $22,728
Tibbs, Danny L, psychiatric technician II, $26,208
Tibebu, Meron L, registered nurse, $50,244
Tichenor, Angela L, deval asst I, $26,844
Tichenor, Michael L, direct care aide, $6,150
Tidwell, Laurie A, lpn I gen, $33,384
Tiefenauer, Donna G, activity aide II, $27,780
Tiefenbrun, Michael E, dev dis cmnty spec, $45,156
Tieman, Paul M, deval asst II, $25,584
Tiemann, Carl A, lpn II gen, $40,404
Tierney, Brenda K, deval asst I, $23,412
Tilley, Michelle L, security aide I psy, $29,832
Tillman, Brett E, storekeeper II, $29,496
Tillman, Meyosha S, psychiatric technician I, $23,352
Tillman, Sabrina, deval asst II, $27,252
Tillman-Roberts, Demetra, mental hlth mgr b2, $64,796
Tilson, Jennifer E, direct care aide, $22.47/hr
Timmermeyer, Sue I, ofc spt asst (keybrd), $23,508
Tindle, Ronda E, custodial worker I, $20,664
Tinker, Barbara E, case mgr II dd, $34,944
Tinker, Mark A, security aide I psy, $29,652
Tinker, Mary T, security aide I psy, $29,652
Tinnin, Christy A, registered nurse sr, $59,645
Tinsley, Doris J, psychiatric technician I, $23,352
Tipton, Kimberly, registered nurse sr, $56,191

Tittsworth, Deana M, deval asst I, $23,352
Tobias, Dexter, custodial worker I, $22,872
Todd, Brenda J, deval asst I, $22,728
Todd, Jeffrey D, cook I, $21,864
Todd, Travis, lpn II gen, $50,374
Todd, Yusef, security ofcr I, $25,824
Tolbert, Johnetta M, psychiatric technician I, $23,352
Tolle, Linda L, prog spec I mh, $44,304
Tolliver, Laquan M, psychiatric technician I, $23,352
Tolson, Tasca M, subs abuse cnslr II, $34,944
Toney, Reginal C, security ofcr I, $12,353
Tongay, Allison M, psychiatric technician I, $23,352
Tongay, Brittany N, psychiatric technician I, $23,352
Tonnar, Teresa A, deval asst II, $29,052
Tonnies, Frederick E, pharm, $41,250
Torbert, Marianne, registered nurse sr, $52,549
Torres, Alfa Z, registered nurse, $28,375
Totten, Ryan C, security aide I psy, $30,276
Totty, Alisha A, registered nurse, $51,276
Totty, Torty, deval asst II, $25,428
Tourtillott, Phyllis A, typist, $13,314
Towns, Harold L, deval asst I, $22,728
Townsend, Bernadine, deval asst I, $24,804
Townsend, Charles E, deval asst I, $24,036
Townsend, Christopher, cook III, $28,536
Townsend, John D, deval asst I, $23,352
Townsend, Latonia M, deval asst I, $22,728
Tracy, Lesa D, mental hlth mgr b2, $60,124
Trammell, David K, security aide I psy, $29,652
Tran, Henry T, custodial worker I, $21,864
Trandahl, Kristin T, psychiatric technician I, $24,072
Travis, Antoinette L, psychiatric technician II, $24,804
Travis, Heather R, registered nurse, $27,794
Travis, Jacquelyn L, deval asst I, $22,728
Travis, Kysha, deval asst I, $23,352
Travis, Mandy S, security aide I psy, $29,652
Traxler, Shelby, lpn II gen, $39,780
Trecker, Denise L, case mgr II dd, $34,944
Treece, Donald, ch security ofcr, $44,304
Treen, Vivian L, behavioral technician supv, $29,496
Tresler, Samantha L, deval asst I, $24,036
Triggs, Dion, custodial worker I, $20,664
Tripp, Christian D, security aide I psy, $29,652
Tripp, David A, security aide I psy, $30,144
Tripp, Janet E, deval asst I, $25,584
Tripp, Kerbie L, deval asst I, $23,076
Tripp, Stephen M, deval asst I, $22,728
Trisler, Annette L, activity aide II, $27,780
Troupe, Kimberly A, reimbursement ofcr II, $33,744
Trowbridge, Ryan A, security aide I psy, $29,652
TRUE, Kelsey M, dietitian I, $40,380
TRUE, Terrance, deval asst I, $22,728
Trujillo Linares, Willy A, deval asst I, $23,412
Trussel, Tanya R, account clerk II, $26,232
Tubbesing, Tara C, psychologist II, $77,556
Tuck, Michael R, direct care aide, $7,808
Tucker, Bruce A, security aide I psy, $31,152
Tucker, Collin R, psychiatric technician I, $22,092
Tucker, John B, registered nurse mgr b3, $88,544
Tucker, Lori A, security aide I psy, $29,652
Tucker, Stephenie L, hlth info tech I, $27,228
Tuggle, Cheryl N, case mgr II dd, $33,744
Tuinman-Campbell, Ayla G, deval asst I, $23,352
Tull, Mary E, lpn, $21,632
Tullis, Dena L, habilitation spec II, $35,568
Tulloch, Marlowe, training tech II, $42,708
Tulu, Eyrsalem G, security aide I psy, $32,244
Tune, Laverna S, registered nurse, $17,166
Tupper, Jeffrey L, activity aide II, $24,804
Turay, Joseph A, security aide I psy, $31,152
Turman, Keoysha, deval asst I, $22,728
Turnbull, Kurt R, deval asst I, $23,352
Turner, Beatrice A, security aide I psy, $31,620
Turner, Beth E, recrtnal ther II, $36,888
Turner, Betty J, deval asst I, $22,716
Turner, Dale F, security aide III psy, $43,332
Turner, Gregory B, security ofcr II, $29,496
Turner, Hope, mental hlth mgr b2, $62,664
Turner, James, psychiatric technician I, $24,696

Turner, James D, security ofcr, $12,353
Turner, Jeanne L, registered nurse sr, $53,253
Turner, Jennifer R, sr ofc spt asst (keybrd), $26,652
Turner, Lisa L, mental hlth mgr b1, $60,257
Turner, Loretta D, case mgmt/assess spv, $45,156
Turner, Marilyn A, misc tech, $23,503
Turner, Patrice, deval asst I, $23,352
Turner, Rhonda K, mental hlth mgr b1, $60,156
Turner, Sharon L, soc servs worker, $32,696
Turner, Susan, psychiatric technician II, $25,584
Turner, Virginia S, lpn II gen, $40,024
Tutt, James G, security aide I psy, $29,652
Tweedie, Sabrina A, deval asst I, $22,728
Twine, Charity, psychiatric technician I, $22,728
Tyler, Amber L, deval asst I, $23,352
Tyler, Byron A, deval asst I, $23,412
Tyler, Jordan W, deval asst I, $22,404
Tyler, Katherine A, registered nurse, $28,375
Tyler, Pamela M, lpn I gen, $30,216
Tyler, Ryan, deval asst I, $23,352
Tyler, Sarah M, deval asst I, $22,728
Ugbaja, Ngozika V, psychiatric technician I, $24,696
Ugweje, Edith C, registered nurse sr, $65,676
Ugwueke, Ann P, registered nurse, $56,192
Uhl, Travis J, deval asst I, $23,352
Uka, Bedriena, reimbursement ofcr I, $31,512
Umah, Ita E, security aide I psy, $32,244
Umana, Tammy S, lpn II gen, $31,740
Umfleet, Phyllis C, special asst prof, $61,884
Umfleet, Sheila J, prog spec I mh, $38,928
Umstead, Brandy, deval asst I, $23,352
Umwech, Gary K, deval asst I, $24,036
Underwood, Lisa J, custodial worker I, $21,760
Upchurch, Celena L, deval asst I, $24,072
Urena, Thomas R, deval asst I, $22,728
Urhahn, Kelly L, dev dis cmnty prog coord, $41,940
Usery, Lisa, psychiatric technician I, $22,728
Uthe, Donna L, psychiatric technician I, $22,728
Uwalaka, Regina O, registered nurse sr, $64,681
Uzomah, Bernadette C, psychiatric technician II, $27,076
Uzomah, Cynthia I, registered nurse sr, $56,976
Vaccaro, Michelle, case mgr II dd, $34,944
Valentine, Jamila E, sr ofc spt asst (keybrd), $26,232
Valenzuela, Kimberly S, lpn II gen, $38,952
Valiant, Charles E, deval asst I, $23,352
Valle, Susan E, training tech II, $42,708
Vamboi, Elsie T, habilitation spec II, $34,944
Van Leuven, Daniel E, registered nurse sup, $74,556
Van Winkle, Deloris A, ofc spt asst (keybrd), $25,824
Vanarsdale, Karla Y, deval asst II, $27,876
Vanarsdale, Leonard, stores clerk, $22,872
Vance, Abby, registered nurse - clin opers, $74,556
Vance, Arthur W, habilitation spec II, $34,944
Vance, Kristie D, registered nurse sup, $65,291
Vance, Laurel A, ofc spt asst (keybrd), $23,160
Vandenhoek, Kathryn L, security aide I psy, $32,832
Vandergriff, Amanda S, registered nurse - clin opers, $58,140
Vanderhook, Phyllis M, registered nurse sr, $55,361
Vanderklok, Mary C, licensed behavior analyst, $66,720
Vandiver, Taylor S, deval asst I, $22,728
Vangala, Sekhar, staff physician spec, $221,301
Vanhorn, Lola M, admin ofc spt asst, $33,744
Vannaman, Linda R, security ofcr I, $25,824
Vannorman, Leslie L, storekeeper, $11,866
Vantrease, Carla J, psychiatric technician I, $24,804
Varga, Veronica M, psychiatric technician I, $23,352
Varner, Emily, dietitian I, $40,380
Varney, Sampson, deval asst I, $22,728
Vasile, Alexandru L, staff physician spec, $219,474
Vatterott-Mori, Madeleine, psychologist, $32,696
Vaughan, Charles R, cook II, $23,880
Vaughn, Audrey M, food serv helper I, $24,702
Vaughn, Breann C, psychiatric technician I, $23,352
Vaughn, Marla Y, security aide II psy, $34,536
Vaughn, Melinda S, security aide I psy, $29,832
Vaughn, Raquel D, registered nurse, $48,888
Vaughn, Reggie G, security aide I psy, $31,152
Vaughn, Reva K, sr ofc spt asst (keybrd), $28,452
Vaughn, Ronald L, security aide I psy, $36,984

Vaughn, Terrence R, mental hlth instructor secur, $34,356
Vavak, Kami A, psychiatric technician I, $23,352
Veneziano, Paul R, licensed behavior analyst, $66,720
Ver Dught, Juliann E, therapy consult, $46,218
Verdught, Sawyer C, deval asst I, $22,404
Vesser, Janet E, deval asst I, $26,844
Vickers, Deborah A, deval asst I, $27,024
Videa, Victor, custodial worker I, $21,264
Viles, Arlene S, deval asst I, $24,036
Viles, Rhonda J, deval asst I, $26,844
Viles, Sharon R, deval asst I, $23,412
Viles, Teresa G, deval asst I, $22,728
Villafane, Terri L, qual assurance spec mh, $40,380
Villatoro, Elsa Y, habilitation spec II, $36,965
Villmer-Allen, Megan A, sr ofc spt asst (keybrd), $25,824
Vincenz, Felix T, misc administrative, $48,328
Vincenz, Meagan E, clin casework pract II, $37,548
Vincenz, Rachel M, direct care aide, $10.93/hr
Vineyard, Barbara A, fiscal & administrative mgr b2, $64,580
Vinson, Danielle M, psychiatric technician I, $23,352
Vinson, Joseph T, motor veh driver, $23,880
Vire, J V, misc prof, $40.64/hr
Visnovske, Brandi L, registered nurse, $17,166
Viviano, Allyson T, registered nurse sr, $51,552
Viviano, Jaime K, dev dis cmnty prog coord, $40,380
Vogel, Brett P, deval asst I, $24,036
Vogelsang, Chelsea M, activity aide II, $26,961
Vogl, Jane M, mental hlth mgr b2, $58,905
Volpe, Richard J, psychiatric technician I, $22,716
Vonderheide, Beth E, case mgr II dd, $34,944
Vorbeck, Cheryl A, psychiatric technician II, $25,428
Voss, Jodi A, qual assurance spec mh, $51,096
Voss, Susan, registered nurse mgr b2, $72,643
Waage, Mark D, security ofcr I, $27,504
Waddle, Jennifer, prog spec II mh, $41,940
Wade, Elain M, deval asst I, $26,004
Wade, Patricia E, registered nurse sup, $32,838
Wade, Willie I, deval asst I, $22,404
Wadlow, Angella N, qual assurance spec mh, $47,892
Wagan, Primitiva, med spec II, $134,592
Waggoner, Nicole L, security aide I psy, $29,652
Waggoner, Tara A, lpn II gen, $32,220
Waggoner, William M, dev dis cmnty prog coord, $41,940
Wagner, Jason R, security aide I psy, $32,244
Wagner, Mary, security aide I psy, $30,276
Wagner, Mikal R, deval asst II, $26,400
Wagner, Sharon K, mental hlth mgr b1, $73,785
Wagner, Susan K, registered nurse sr, $53,592
Wagner, Tammy L, deval asst I, $23,352
Wah, Beatrice, custodial worker I, $20,664
Wainright, Leslie K, security aide I psy, $34,488
Wainscott, Elizabeth D, dev dis cmnty spec, $37,548
Wainwright, Darren, security aide I psy, $30,276
Waithaka, Moses K, case mgr I dd, $32,628
Wakefield, Tamara R, security ofcr I, $25,824
Walden, John R, deval asst I, $24,036
Walden, Yvonne M, registered nurse, $36,029
Waldorf, Molly J, psychiatric technician I, $24,696
Wali, Mauritinia, behavior intvtn tech dd, $27,696
Walin, Elizabeth, psychiatric technician I, $24,072
Walker, Amanda M, registered nurse, $26,058
Walker, Chad L, deval asst I, $26,400
Walker, Chanel M, deval asst I, $22,716
Walker, Debra M, designated principal asst dept, $82,932
Walker, Duan M, motor veh driver, $27,948
Walker, Geneva, ofc spt asst (keybrd), $23,880
Walker, Gregory E, motor veh driver, $25,032
Walker, Gregory L, security aide I psy, $29,652
Walker, Gretchen M, motor veh driver, $24,612
Walker, Jeremiah, deval asst I, $23,352
Walker, Lisa M, ofc spt asst (keybrd), $23,160
Walker, Markus D, deval asst I, $23,352
Walker, Mary, psychiatric technician I, $23,700
Walker, Nadia L, deval asst I, $22,404
Walker, Nicholas G, security aide I psy, $29,652
Walker, Rose L, deval asst I, $23,352
Walker, Ruby D, registered nurse, $28,375
Walker, Tayna, psychiatric technician II, $24,804
Walker, Tony, deval asst II, $25,428

Walker Knight, Amber L, registered nurse sr, $61,095
Wallace, Glenda M, registered nurse, $17,166
Wallace, John M, security aide I psy, $32,244
Wallace, Larry D, security aide I psy, $29,652
Wallace, Pauline M, sr ofc spt asst (keybrd), $25,404
Wallace, Robin L, deval asst I, $24,036
Wallace, Rose M, deval asst I, $22,728
Wallen, Jill L, security aide I psy, $30,276
Wallen, Rhonda L, psychiatric technician I, $23,352
Waller, Jaime N, training tech II, $40,380
Waller, Jimmy M, psychiatric technician II, $26,208
Waller, Lisa J, training tech III, $53,208
Waller, Michelle C, lpn I gen, $35,736
Walsh, Kristen A, ofc spt asst (clerical), $22,536
Walsh, Laurel A, registered nurse sr, $60,516
Walters, Darlene, psychiatric technician I, $23,352
Walters, Sherdon T, security aide I psy, $29,652
Walton, Andrea L, registered nurse mgr b1, $67,512
Walton, Christy L, account clerk II, $27,084
Walton, Sandra, lpn II gen, $37,020
Walton, Sheila E, security aide I psy, $29,652
Wambayi, Naomi B, deval asst I, $23,352
Wampler, Clara E, security aide I psy, $30,276
Wampler, Kavina P, work therapy spec I, $24,612
Wandell, Artemia M, deval asst I, $22,728
Wandell, Scott W, deval asst I, $22,728
Wang, Xiaoshan, deval asst I, $24,072
Wangechi, Rahab, security aide I psy, $30,276
Wanko, Gary J, locksmith, $38,232
Wansing, Joseph W, security aide I psy, $30,276
Wansing, Kasandra L, deval asst I, $23,028
Ward, Brenda G, deval asst I, $27,876
Ward, Debra S, security aide I psy, $30,294
Ward, Denise R, deval asst I, $26,004
Ward, Edmond T, custodial worker I, $21,264
Ward, Eric J, deval asst I, $23,412
Ward, Jennifer R, security aide II psy, $34,488
Ward, Judith A, deval asst I, $23,352
Ward, Linda M, ofc spt asst (keybrd), $25,824
Ward, Lori J, registered nurse sr, $66,189
Ward, Nancy A, cosmetologist, $25,584
Ward, Sharon L, activity aide III, $30,065
Ward, Susan E, account clerk II, $25,824
Wardin, Colleen A, psychiatric technician I, $23,352
Ware, Latosha N, deval asst I, $23,028
Warfield, Teresa A, lpn II gen, $36,710
Warlick, Darlene R, deval asst I, $23,352
Warmack, Shertaurus T, prog spec trainee mh, $36,888
Warncke, Rachel E, security aide I psy, $29,652
Warner, Kenda L, habilitation prog mgr, $43,488
Warner, Michelle L, deval asst I, $22,728
Warr, Jasmine J, deval asst I, $23,352
Warren, Brenda C, deval asst I, $23,352
Warren, Dana L, food serv helper I, $20,664
Warren, Donna J, deval asst I, $23,352
Warren, Donna K, case mgmt/assess spv, $40,380
Warren, Dustin R, stores clerk, $21,864
Warren, Jerry R, psychiatric technician I, $22,728
Warren, Linda F, psychiatric technician I, $22,728
Warren, Lois L, special asst official & admstr, $87,365
Warren, Miranda S, mental hlth mgr b1, $56,507
Warren, Paris, deval asst I, $23,352
Warren, Selina L, deval asst I, $22,728
Washburn, Patricia A, registered nurse sr, $56,192
Washington, Antonnia M, lpn I gen, $36,360
Washington, Charlotte, psychiatric technician I, $23,352
Washington, Courtland F, deval asst I, $23,352
Washington, Crishna, deval asst I, $22,728
Washington, Jewell, typist, $12,383
Washington, La Queece, deval asst II, $26,208
Washington, Lindsey N, lpn II gen, $30,396
Washington, Lorenzo, activity aide III, $28,584
Washington, Selina R, dietitian II, $41,172
Washington, Shontay, deval asst I, $23,028
Washington, Zora L, deval asst I, $23,076
Waterman, Ashley D, deval asst I, $22,404
Waterman, Lena M, ofc spt asst (clerical), $21,864
Waterman, Tracy L, deval asst I, $24,036
Waters, Dara R, deval asst I, $22,728

Waters, Octavia, deval asst I, $23,352
Watkins, Bonnie, registered nurse sr, $66,189
Watkins, Lesley A, deval asst I, $22,092
Watkins, Regina A, case mgr II dd, $34,944
Watkins, Robert D, security ofcr II, $47,893
Watkins, Shawn M, registered nurse sr, $53,253
Watson, Bryant W, security aide I psy, $29,208
Watson, Jack D, psychiatric technician I, $23,076
Watson, Janet L, training tech II, $41,172
Watson, Richard Jr, activity aide II, $25,584
Watson, Sheila A, custodial worker I, $22,317
Watson, Stallone D, security aide I psy, $31,152
Watson, Valerie, psychiatric technician I, $25,416
Watson, Valerie R, deval asst I, $22,728
Watson, Vernell, deval asst I, $23,700
Watson-Gray, Dionne D, deval asst III, $27,948
Watts, Janet E, deval asst I, $26,400
Watts, Marva, lpn II gen, $38,352
Wayer, Laura S, institution supt, $88,650
Weaver, Angela L, psychiatric technician I, $26,004
Weaver, Deborah K, deval asst I, $23,352
Weaver, Gregory L, security aide I psy, $31,620
Weaver, Heather R, case mgr II dd, $33,744
Weaver, Joyce V, food serv helper I, $20,664
Weavers, Nichole L, security aide I psy, $31,152
Webb, Darnell J, deval asst I, $23,352
Webb, Diana M, deval asst II, $24,804
Webb, Sandra S, ofc spt asst (keybrd), $23,160
Webb, Sheila, lpn II gen, $39,780
Webb, Tara A, deval asst I, $22,728
Webb, Wardell, deval asst I, $23,352
Weber, Amanda S, ofc spt asst (clerical), $22,536
Weber, Mary S, security aide I psy, $29,208
Weber, Melinda A, licensed clin soc wkr, $47,892
Weber, Scott, pharm, $48,915
Webster, Debra A, deval asst I, $23,352
Webster, Randall A, deval asst III, $29,412
Weeks, Vanessa, deval asst I, $23,352
Wegener, Diane J, deval asst I, $22,728
Weger, Bethany J, mental hlth mgr b1, $50,500
Weinhold, Krystal N, registered nurse sr, $51,552
Weisenborn, Avarah L, registered nurse sr, $56,192
Weiser, Debra L, food serv helper I, $22,317
Weiser, Eric M, custodial worker I, $22,317
Weisman, Leo G, clin soc work spv, $55,416
Weiss, Kelley, registered nurse sr, $71,586
Welborn, Benjamin I, habilitation spec II, $34,944
Welborn, Jenna L, habilitation spec II, $34,944
Welch, Mary C, administrative asst, $35,672
Welch, Santonia T, registered nurse, $28,375
Welch, Shawn R, psychiatric technician I, $23,352
Welday, Biniam G, registered nurse sr, $60,796
Weldegiorgis, Aster, registered nurse, $36,029
Weldon, Corey J, psychiatric technician I, $22,092
Weldon, Jennifer L, clerk, $2,762
Welker, Robert E, deval asst I, $22,728
Wellman, Alicson S, deval asst I, $24,804
Wellman, Angela K, deval asst I, $24,804
Wellman, Connie S, deval asst II, $29,568
Wells, Brian L, deval asst I, $23,352
Wells, Deaun S, deval asst I, $23,352
Wells, Deborah A, psychiatric technician I, $25,428
Wells, Peggy A, lpn II gen, $36,396
Wells-McLarty, Cheryl A, psychiatric technician I, $26,628
Welsh, Brittany D, custodial worker II, $23,613
Welsh, Sandra L, sr ofc spt asst (keybrd), $27,948
Wemegah Atsangbe, Francis W, lpn II gen, $35,236
Wemhoff, Faith K, prog spec II mh, $43,488
Wenger, James L, security ofcr II, $27,228
Werdehausen, Stacey L, security aide II psy, $34,488
Werley, Glenda L, ofc spt asst (clerical), $22,536
Werner, Cynthia M, activity aide II, $27,780
Werner, Jacquelyn R, registered nurse sr, $62,104
Werner, Terri L, case mgmt/assess spv, $45,156
Werning, Sabine, deval asst III, $27,504
Werninger, Regina J, registered nurse, $26,058
Wesley, Stephen M, deval asst I, $22,728
Wessels, Juanita M, psychiatric technician I, $22,728
West, Arnita L, stores clerk, $24,264

West, Sheila R, deval asst II, $26,400
West, Valerie A, deval asst II, $27,876
Westbrook, Jennifer A, speech-language pathlgy ast II, $22,938
Westendorf, Deana M, lpn II gen, $30,396
Westfall, Heather L, deval asst I, $23,352
Westland, June E, registered nurse sr, $63,373
Westmoland, Delicia L, custodial worker I, $20,664
Westmoland, Jay C Jr, psychiatric technician I, $23,352
Weston, Laticia M, licensed clin soc wkr, $47,892
Wetzel, Terri L, licensed clin soc wkr, $50,040
Whalen, Danielle L, psychiatric technician I, $22,728
Whanger, Sally R, registered nurse sr, $63,585
Whanger, Sandra G, psychiatric technician I, $25,056
Wheeler, Dawn, case mgr III dd, $39,624
Wheeler, Nekisha R, case mgr I dd, $31,512
Wheeler, Ryan C, security aide I psy, $30,276
Wheeler, Timothy S, subs abuse cnslr II, $38,232
Wheelis, Zachary J, security aide I psy, $29,832
Wheetley, Pamela M, deval asst II, $27,024
Whelan, Maria T, registered nurse sr, $25,776
Whelan, Shari J, registered nurse - clin opers, $71,448
Whelen, Billie J, psychiatric technician I, $22,728
Whisennand, Joyce M, habilitation spec II, $40,380
Whisler, Virginia K, psychiatric technician I, $23,352
Whitaker, Deandre M, deval asst I, $23,412
Whitaker, Wayne L, food serv helper I, $20,664
White, Alicia J, deval asst III, $36,096
White, Amanda J, psychiatric technician I, $22,728
White, Amber D, deval asst I, $22,404
White, Andrew J, registered nurse sr, $60,184
White, Anthony D, food serv helper I, $22,317
White, Brett M, security aide I psy, $31,620
White, Cayci J, sr ofc spt asst (keybrd), $25,824
White, Charles B, psychiatric technician I, $26,004
White, Christine A, edual aide, $10,121
White, Christine D, deval asst I, $26,628
White, Christopher E, security aide II psy, $35,112
White, Crystal A, deval asst I, $23,352
White, David H, case mgr III dd, $37,548
White, Hope D, deval asst I, $25,584
White, Joel S, misc prof, $50,000
White, John E, deval asst II, $25,584
White, Jordan D, deval asst I, $24,036
White, Joyce A, food serv helper I, $20,664
White, Karen S, security aide II psy, $32,760
White, Kelly R, psychiatric technician I, $23,352
White, Markeshia, deval asst I, $22,728
White, Mary H, psychiatric technician I, $24,072
White, Melinda K, food serv helper I, $20,664
White, Natalie, deval asst I, $22,728
White, Rachel, activity aide III, $24,296
White, Raven R, direct care aide, $8,592
White, Regina, deval asst II, $25,428
White, Severos A, security ofcr I, $25,824
White, Shapan, psychiatric technician I, $24,696
White, Teresa A, habilitation spec II, $36,888
Whitehead, Antione T, deval asst I, $23,352
Whitehead, Jacob M, psychiatric technician I, $22,092
Whitehead, Jimmie, deval asst I, $22,728
Whitehead, Melissa A, registered nurse sr, $60,796
Whitehead, Michael L, psychiatric technician I, $22,728
Whitfield, Candace, case mgr II dd, $34,944
Whitfield, Darrius, deval asst I, $23,352
Whitfield, Robert A, food serv helper I, $22,200
Whitford, Cindy J, admin ofc spt asst, $29,496
Whitson, Ann M, habilitation spec II, $34,944
Whitt, Roena L, admin ofc spt asst, $37,548
Whittenberg, Audrey K, misc prof, $29,504
Whittington, George W, registered nurse sr, $53,592
Whittle, Mark A, storekeeper II, $29,412
Whittle, Sherri L, deval asst II, $26,208
Whittler, Karen S, custodial work spv, $23,160
Whitworth, Lisa M, deval asst I, $22,728
Whitworth, Lloyd E, security aide I psy, $30,276
Whitworth, Michelle M, registered nurse sup, $68,532
Wholf, Timothy W, special asst official & admstr, $86,500
Wickell, Joyce L, ofc worker misc, $16.04
Wicker, Holly A, cook II, $23,880
Wickham, Whitney D, security aide I psy, $29,652

Wieberg, Janet R, research analyst III, $54,288
Wieberg, Katherine, fiscal & administrative mgr b2, $70,000
Wieczorek, Katie A, case mgr II dd, $34,944
Wiedmaier, Danielle L, cosmetologist, $16,351
Wiedmer, Brently W, recrtnal ther II, $36,204
Wiedmier, Janelle R, acct I, $30,984
Wiegand, Linda, registered nurse sr, $58,140
Wieringa, Marjorie, sr ofc spt asst (keybrd), $27,084
Wieschhaus, Joseph C, security aide I psy, $30,276
Wieselthier, Arthur S, dentist III, $94,416
Wiggins, San, custodial worker I, $20,664
Wilburn, Mercedes C, vendor servs coor mh, $40,380
Wilckens, Christy M, custodial worker I, $20,664
Wilcox, William N, security aide I psy, $31,152
Wilcox-Bender, Jaymie, case mgr II dd, $36,888
Wilcoxson, Penny D, ofc spt asst (keybrd), $23,160
Wilcutt, Laura K, psychiatric technician I, $23,352
Wilde, Catherine B, special asst ofc & clerical, $43,211
Wilder, Sally A, deval asst I, $27,024
Wildhaber, Caroline M, sr ofc spt asst (keybrd), $26,232
Wildhaber-Bock, Nora, designated principal asst div, $86,355
Wildschuetz, Angela R, deval asst I, $23,412
Wiles, Susan D, registered nurse sr, $51,552
Wiley, Gloria L, custodial worker I, $22,536
Wiley, William H, security aide I psy, $29,652
Wilfong, Kourtney N, psychiatric technician I, $23,352
Wilhite, Jameka, deval asst I, $22,728
Wilhite, Kianna L, deval asst I, $22,716
Wilkins, Falby, deval asst I, $24,072
Wilkins, Linda L, admin ofc spt asst, $28,104
Wilkins, Toni L, psychiatric technician I, $22,728
Wilkinson, Desirea R, deval asst I, $22,404
Wilkinson, Jacqueline S, deval asst I, $22,404
Wilkinson, Krystal L, psychiatric technician I, $23,412
Wilkinson, Nancy A, ofc spt asst (keybrd), $25,824
Wilks, Madeline M, registered nurse, $28,375
Wilkson, Sara M, habilitation spec II, $38,232
Willbanks, Angela J, deval asst I, $22,728
Willenbrink, Barbara S, acct I, $36,204
Willenbrink, Joy M, music ther II, $38,232
Williams, Amanda L, psychiatric technician I, $25,224
Williams, Angela, cook I, $23,508
Williams, Antoine D, psychiatric technician I, $22,728
Williams, Brianna M, psychiatric technician I, $23,352
Williams, Candace E, case mgr II dd, $34,944
Williams, Carrie C, mental hlth mgr b2, $57,063
Williams, Cathy L, ofc spt asst (clerical), $22,536
Williams, Charita, psychiatric technician I, $22,728
Williams, Charnette R, deval asst I, $23,352
Williams, Charrell S, psychiatric technician I, $22,728
Williams, Christopher K, deval asst II, $29,208
Williams, Cindi J, deval asst I, $23,352
Williams, Darin L, deval asst I, $22,728
Williams, Deborah L, lpn II gen, $38,352
Williams, Doriano T Sr, psychiatric technician I, $23,352
Williams, Douglas R, nutrition/dietary svcs mgr b1, $53,196
Williams, Dwayne A, deval asst I, $23,028
Williams, Eric D, security ofcr I, $25,824
Williams, Ernestine, deval asst I, $23,352
Williams, Franklin D, psychiatric technician I, $23,352
Williams, Glenda L, deval asst I, $22,728
Williams, Gwendolyn A, psychiatric technician I, $26,680
Williams, Haley J, lpn I gen, $36,710
Williams, Jamie L, deval asst I, $23,352
Williams, Janie L, habilitation spec II, $33,744
Williams, Jasmine, deval asst I, $23,352
Williams, Keith A, registered nurse sr, $56,976
Williams, Kimberly S, custodial worker I, $20,664
Williams, Larry V, acct II, $38,928
Williams, Leslie A, deval asst III, $32,772
Williams, Linda K, workshop spv II, $28,908
Williams, Lori L, dev dis cmnty prog coord, $45,156
Williams, Marcia A, psychiatric technician I, $22,728
Williams, Martez J, deval asst I, $23,352
Williams, Nicole L, account clerk II, $25,824
Williams, Patrice L, acct I, $35,568
Williams, Perry L, security ofcr, $10,926
Williams, Regina K, case mgr II dd, $34,944
Williams, Roslin, deval asst I, $23,352

Williams, Scott, psychiatric technician I, $22,728
Williams, Shannon S, deval asst I, $24,036
Williams, Shantel, case mgr I dd, $31,512
Williams, Sherman L, psychiatric technician I, $22,728
Williams, Sherry, security ofcr I, $25,824
Williams, Stephanie L, food serv helper I, $16,531
Williams, Takohashi A, psychiatric technician I, $23,352
Williams, Tiffany, psychiatric technician I, $24,804
Williams, Toneia Q, lpn II gen, $40,404
Williams, Tonya S, custodial worker I, $22,872
Williams, Tracy V, deval asst I, $24,072
Williams, Vanessa, deval asst I, $24,036
Williams, Walter J, deval asst I, $22,728
Williams-Anthony, Marquinette D, ofc spt asst (clerical), $26,232
Williams-Center, Valarie, printing/mail technician II, $26,652
Williams-McIntyre, Jacqueline K, case mgr II dd, $34,944
Williamson, Barbara A, motor veh driver, $23,880
Williamson, Julie L, dev dis cmnty prog coord, $38,928
Williamson, Katherine R, deval asst I, $22,092
Williamson, Lisa A, special asst official & admstr, $83,325
Williamson, Nathaniel C, security aide I psy, $30,276
Williamson, Wanda J, deval asst II, $24,804
Willie, Mary C, licensed clin soc wkr, $50,040
Willingham, Jarod D, security aide II psy, $34,488
Willis, Barbara A, licensed clin soc wkr, $46,932
Willis, Johonda, registered nurse sr, $56,976
Willis, Melody K, registered nurse sr, $56,192
Willis, Sara, case mgr II dd, $34,944
Willoughby, Shauna D, sr ofc spt asst (keybrd), $25,824
Willoughby, Theo, custodial work spv, $23,880
Willoughby, Wanda, custodial worker I, $20,664
Wills, Amy M, mental hlth instructor secur, $34,944
Wills, Robert J, registered nurse, $24,960
Wills, Sarah M, registered nurse - clin opers, $67,104
Wilmot, Tara E, dietitian II, $47,892
Wilson, Angela J, deval asst II, $29,052
Wilson, Antonio, deval asst II, $25,428
Wilson, Brian T, special educ tchr II, $36,204
Wilson, Bruce L, psychologist I, $64,071
Wilson, Cheryl A, pers ofcr I, $48,156
Wilson, Dalton W, music ther II, $36,204
Wilson, Danyale J, deval asst I, $23,352
Wilson, Demetrius W, psychiatric technician I, $24,036
Wilson, Dena L, registered nurse mgr b2, $72,643
Wilson, Faith A, security aide I psy, $32,244
Wilson, Fedrick A, security aide I psy, $31,620
Wilson, Garrett L, registered nurse sup, $70,676
Wilson, Gayleah S, deval asst I, $23,352
Wilson, Gregory C, activity aide II, $27,780
Wilson, Irnez L, deval asst I, $24,036
Wilson, Lailin F, cert dental asst, $33,180
Wilson, Nancy A, custodial worker I, $22,536
Wilson, Nathan C, habilitation spec II, $34,944
Wilson, Pamela, psychiatric technician I, $24,804
Wilson, Patricia A, registered nurse sup, $58,140
Wilson, Rebekeh R, psychiatric technician I, $23,352
Wilson, Roy C, med admin, $230,647
Wilson, Sondra A, deval asst I, $22,404
Wilson, Timothy J, psychologist I, $63,996
Wimmer, April M, sr ofc spt asst (keybrd), $26,652
Wimmer, Jerry D, security aide I psy, $31,620
Wims, Tyrese R, food serv helper I, $10,327
Wininger, Jerry J, prog spec I mh, $38,928
Winjobi, Fatai A, lpn II gen, $38,014
Winn, Brandon L, deval asst I, $24,036
Winn, Kevin J, case mgr I dd, $31,512
Winn, Terrence J, deval asst I, $22,728
Winn, Tiera D, deval asst I, $23,028
Winston, Alletta J, psychiatric technician I, $22,728
Winston, Christine, psychiatric technician I, $24,036
Winston, Jasmyn S, case mgr II dd, $34,944
Winterbower, Debra J, food serv helper I, $22,536
Wintjen, Christine L, account clerk II, $25,824
Wisdom, Bonnie J, behavioral technician supv, $29,004
Wise, Carmen Y, ofc spt asst (keybrd), $24,612
Wise, Kiri K, deval asst I, $24,036
Wiseman, Janice B, custodial worker I, $22,872
Wiser, Alicia M, security aide I psy, $30,276
Wiser, Kendra L, psychiatric technician I, $22,716

Wiser, Marilyn A, food serv helper I, $11,159
Wiser, Matthew B, psychiatric technician I, $23,352
Wishom, Tracy Y, food serv helper I, $20,664
Wiskus, Richard J, workshop prog coor, $37,548
Witherspoon, Melantha J, licensed behavior analyst, $66,720
Witt, Edward L, custodial worker I, $20,664
Witte, Lisa D, ofc spt asst (keybrd), $23,880
Witte, Robin N, case mgr II dd, $38,232
Wofford, Ashley, clin casework pract I, $36,204
Wofford, Erica L, licensed clin soc wkr, $47,892
Wojcikiewicz, Stephanie, case mgr II dd, $17,472
Wolf, Darlene, deval asst I, $25,428
Wolf, Samantha W, deval asst II, $24,804
Wolfe, Jacqulyn A, psychiatric technician I, $23,352
Wolfe, Michelle L, food serv helper II, $23,613
Wolfe, Susan N, deval asst I, $24,036
Wolfgram, Edwin D, staff physician spec, $203,448
Wolk, Brandon J, work therapy spec II, $28,104
Womack, Amanda J, lpn II gen, $40,648
Womack, Denise M, security aide II psy, $33,384
Womack, Joseph D, security aide I psy, $32,208
Wondra, Terese A, behavior intvtn tech dd, $30,576
Wood, Andrea M, case mgr II dd, $34,944
Wood, Belva J, deval asst I, $22,728
Wood, Donna M, training tech I, $36,204
Wood, Gregory J, research analyst II, $36,888
Wood, Harlan H, security ofcr II, $27,228
Wood, Kerry L, case mgmt/assess spv, $40,380
Wood, Penny L, laundry worker I, $23,880
Wood, Todd C, dev dis cmnty prog coord, $40,380
Wood, Troy W, laborer II, $29,904
Wooden, Daniel J, deval asst I, $22,728
Woodley, Corine, registered nurse sr, $60,796
Woodruff, Lila G, psychiatric technician I, $23,352
Woods, Christopher, activity aide II, $24,804
Woods, Joy N, clin casework pract II, $37,548
Woods, Lori D, qual assurance spec mh, $40,380
Woods, Ronni R, ofc spt asst (keybrd), $22,536
Woodsmall, Michael T, pers ofcr II, $54,288
Woodward, Clive, misc prof, $53,773
Woolard, Samanthea M, psychiatric technician I, $22,092
Wooldridge, Krystal R, case mgr I dd, $32,628
Wooliver, Jeffrey C, stores clerk, $27,084
Woolsey, Brea M, security aide II psy, $34,488
Word, Denise L, deval asst I, $23,352
Word, Wanda F, cook II, $32,243
Workcuff, Skyy T, deval asst I, $23,028
Worley, Christie K, psychiatric technician I, $22,716
Worthen, Daniel B, licensed clin soc wkr, $52,092
Wren, Veldon C, security aide I psy, $30,276
Wrestler, Charlotte A, acct II, $38,928
Wright, Ciara N, deval asst I, $23,352
Wright, Delmar L, mental hlth instructor, $29,004
Wright, Donna, psychiatric technician I, $24,804
Wright, Janice N, registered nurse sr, $60,796
Wright, Janice R, deval asst II, $28,152
Wright, Jason A, deval asst I, $22,728
Wright, Kendall C, deval asst I, $22,728
Wright, Lisa F, psychiatric technician I, $22,728
Wright, Natasha A, deval asst III, $29,412
Wright, Norma Jean M, psychiatric technician I, $22,716
Wright, Phesa M, deval asst I, $26,844
Wright, Rikki J, dpty div dir, $96,455
Wright, Sandra M, psychiatric technician I, $23,412
Wright, Sarah E, registered nurse sr, $53,592
Wright, William B, deval asst I, $23,412
Wright-Robinson, Tiffany S, deval asst I, $25,584
Wrinkle, Julie M, acct I, $30,984
Wuesthoff, Michael F, security aide I psy, $30,276
Wulff, Thomas J, investigator I, $37,548
Wurth, Jessica L, psychiatric technician I, $23,352
Wyatt, Dustin E, registered nurse, $41,676
Wyatt, Karen E, security aide I psy, $29,652
Wyatt, Nicholas L, sr ofc spt asst (keybrd), $27,504
Wyble, Jennifer B, mental hlth mgr b1, $54,900
Wynn, Antonio, custodial worker I, $22,872
Wynn, James Z, security aide I psy, $29,652
Wyrick, Robyn D, deval asst I, $26,400
Wyrick, Sarah L, deval asst I, $23,412

Wyrick, Tara D, psychiatric technician I, $22,728
Wyrick, Thelma A, training consult, $28,823
Xiao, Ya L, custodial worker I, $22,317
Yahnig, Michelle R, misc prof, $25,735
Yansaneh, Salimatu I, security aide I psy, $32,244
Yarasi, Naveen K, staff physician spec, $203,448
Yarbro, Shanna A, dining room spv, $25,790
Yarbrough, Cynthia M, food serv helper I, $27,944
Yates, Elizabeth A, psychiatric technician I, $26,964
Yates, Paul A, security aide I psy, $30,276
Yates, Scott R, activity ther, $32,760
Yates, Tara, mental hlth mgr b1, $52,008
Ybarmea, Thomas, registered nurse sup, $74,556
Yeager, Eric S, security aide II psy, $32,832
Yelton, Terri L, mental hlth mgr b1, $52,093
Yeokum, Deborah G, accounting analyst II, $44,304
Yihdego, Abrehet, deval asst I, $23,412
Yimer, Ruth, registered nurse, $36,029
Yncierto O'Neal, Virginia, deval asst I, $23,412
Yokeley, Donald E, staff dev ofcr mh, $43,488
Yokeley, Kathy A, deval asst I, $230
Yokeley, Ruth A, deval asst I, $27,024
York, Loretta Z, lpn I gen, $35,736
York, Melodie I, mental hlth mgr b2, $67,695
Young, Alex, psychiatric technician I, $22,716
Young, Charlayne A, registered nurse sup, $92,754
Young, Danielle, deval asst I, $22,728
Young, Ebony, deval asst I, $22,728
Young, James J, deval asst II, $25,428
Young, Latoya L, psychiatric technician I, $22,728
Young, Loretha, direct care aide, $10.93/hr
Young, Melondy L, case mgr I dd, $32,628
Young, Ronald J, deval asst I, $22,728
Young, Scott A, psychiatric technician I, $22,728
Young, Shelly L, security aide I psy, $29,652
Young, Stephon R, deval asst I, $22,728
Young, Veronica E, psychiatric technician I, $22,728
Young-Walker, Laine M, med admin, $136,350
Yount, Cortney D, security aide I psy, $30,276
Yowell, Lincoln C, case mgr II dd, $34,944
Yuille, William B, security aide I psy, $32,244
Yundi, Constantine, psychiatric technician I, $24,696
Yurk, Sheila E, deval asst III, $28,128
Zadell, Jennifer C, ofc spt asst (keybrd), $23,880
Zajac, Wladyslawa, custodial worker I, $20,664
Zeih, Gloria L, deval asst I, $22,728
Zemon, Kevin A, psychiatric technician I, $22,728
Zeugin, Augustus R, psychiatric technician I, $22,728
Zhu, Hongbo, registered nurse sr, $59,645
Zhuang, Shimin, research analyst III, $42,708
Ziegelmeyer, Heather C, security aide I psy, $29,652
Ziegelmeyer, Michael D, security aide II psy, $32,208
Zieger, Janet E, registered nurse, $27,794
Zifcak, Cynthia, acct I, $30,984
Zimmer, Amanda G, security aide I psy, $31,152
Zimmerman, Amanda N, misc tech, $27,290
Zimmerman, Kasha R, security aide I psy, $29,652
Zimmerman, Ladonna L, clin soc work spv, $57,744
Zolla, Ann M, spv of vol servs, $33,453
Zornes, Kitreana N, deval asst I, $22,728
Zumbehl, Julianne M, security aide I psy, $31,152

Department of Natural Resources

1101 Riverside Dr, PO Box 176, Jefferson City 65102

Parker Pauley, Sara, state dept dir, $121,705
Abbott, Michael J, environ scientist, $51,096
Abdulkhaleq, Assem, environ engr II, $50,040
Abernathy, Laron G, seasonal aide, $8.05
Abernathy, Travis J, environ spec III, $41,940
Abrego, Anissa L, busser, $8.00/hr
Abrego, Anissa L, wait staff, $4.00/hr
Adam, Trisha, mgmt analysis spec II, $45,156
Adams, David S, environ engr II, $47,892
Adams, Justin M, natural resources mgr b1, $49,104
Adams, Lisa A, park maint wkr II, $26,652
Adams, Scott K, park maint wkr II, $26,652

Adams, Thomas, research analyst III, $42,708
Adkins, Cynthia L, admin ofc spt asst, $27,228
Adkisson, Kinsey R, tech asst I, $25,404
Adniskey, John E, seasonal aide, $10.33/hr
Agao, Daniel, busser, $8.00/hr
Agao, Daniel, wait staff, $4.00/hr
Akin, Phillip M, environ engr II, $47,892
Albrecht, Kevin, natural resources mgr b1, $51,096
Alexander, Alica C, geologist I, $37,548
Alexander, Jennifer A, designated principal asst dept, $47,712
Alexander, Ricky D, bldg const wkr I, $28,104
Alexander, Rita J, environ spec III, $41,940
Alhalabi, Maamoun, environ engr II, $49,128
Allee, Casandra L, ofc spt asst (keybrd), $25,032
Allee, Christi R, ofc spt asst (keybrd), $23,160
Allen, Brian, environ mgr b2, $66,395
Allen, Stacy, environ scientist, $48,156
Allison, David W, environ spec III, $45,156
Almond, Steven A, park maint wkr III, $32,628
Almond, Wesley K, park maint wkr III, $31,512
Alsharafi, Adel, environ engr II, $50,040
Amann, Michelle L, seasonal aide, $8.68/hr
Andary, Rebecca, busser, $8.00/hr
Andary, Rebecca, wait staff, $4.00/hr
Anderson, Christine A, seasonal aide, $8.05
Anderson, Douglas D, park maint wkr II, $29,904
Anderson, Gabrielle, sr ofc spt asst (keybrd), $25,824
Anderson, Genae, environ spec III, $40,380
Anderson, Jacqueline, busser, $8.00/hr
Anderson, Jacqueline, wait staff, $4.00/hr
Anderson, Kyle, chemist III, $40,380
Anderson, Patrick J, environ engr II, $47,892
Anderson, Teresa C, park maint wkr II, $28,452
Anderson, Thomas L, law enforce mgr b1, $51,096
Andrews, Brittany L, seasonal aide, $8.00/hr
Angelos, Adrienne, misc prof, $14.18/hr
Ankesheiln, Wade F, interpretive resource spec I, $15,496
Anthony, Eldon L, park maint wkr II, $28,452
Anthony, Jeremy L, bldg const wkr II, $32,052
Antonucci, Janet, seasonal aide, $10.00/hr
Antweiler, Lori L, chemist IV, $47,892
Antweiler, Michael B, laborer II, $23,160
Apel, Derek J, sr ofc spt asst (clerical), $25,824
Apel, Jessica, admin ofc spt asst, $28,104
Appelbaum, Andrew G, environ engr III, $58,908
Arant, Deborah, ofc spt asst (keybrd), $23,160
Archer, Connie, environ engr II, $47,892
Archer, Lawrence P, pub info coor, $49,128
Archer, Sheila D, park maint wkr II, $26,652
Ardrey, Brenda K, fiscal & administrative mgr b2, $54,163
Armstrong, Del B, mgmt analysis spec I, $37,548
Arney, Anita M, clerk, $14.14/hr
Arnold, Bill, natural resources mgr b1, $50,041
Arredondo, Zully Y, busser, $8.00/hr
Arredondo, Zully Y, wait staff, $4.00/hr
Arrigo, Benjamin E, seasonal aide, $8.47/hr
Atherton, Tiffanie, seasonal aide, $8.05
Aubuchon, Elizabeth A, environ spec III, $41,940
Audsley, Jackie M, wait staff, $4.00/hr
Audsley, Jackie M, busser, $8.00/hr
Ausberger, Teresa A, seasonal aide, $9.50/hr
Autry, Brick V, interpretive resource tech, $30,984
Ayers, Jeffrey D, natural resources mgr b1, $46,935
Bachle, Peter, geologist II, $41,940
Bacon, Robert R, hydrologist IV, $63,996
Baer, Lawrence J, environ spec III, $41,940
Bail, James R, seasonal aide, $8.70/hr
Bailey, Benjamin T, park maint wkr III, $30,420
Bailey, Kristin J, environ engr II, $47,892
Baker, Amy S, environ sup, $56,520
Baker, Everett C, environ engr IV, $69,612
Baker, Jackie D, environ mgr b2, $57,725
Baker, James F, seasonal aide, $10.00/hr
Baker, Michael P, park maint wkr II, $26,652
Baker, Ronald L, crpntr, $34,944
Baker, Stuart, special asst prof, $35,000
Baker, Wesley E, park maint wkr II, $26,652
Baker, Zachary D, seasonal aide, $9.50/hr
Balkenbush, Andrea M, planner IV, $68,160

Balkenbush, John A, law enforce mgr b2, $62,535
Ball, Robin, seasonal aide, $8.52/hr
Ball, Terry L, investigation mgr b1, $51,096
Bandelier, Stacy R, graphics spv, $40,380
Barbee, Carla R, admin ofc spt asst, $29,004
Barber, Darrell A, environ spec III, $45,156
Bardwell, Brenda K, fiscal & administrative mgr b1, $49,734
Bare, Andrew T, seasonal aide, $8.00/hr
Barlow, Galen D, park ranger, $41,940
Barlow, Joanna M, park/historic site spec III, $40,380
Barnes, Brett D, park ranger sergeant, $47,892
Barnes, Mary M, environ engr III, $55,416
Barnes, Richard, environ spec III, $47,892
Barnett, Clinton R, planner II, $40,380
Barnett, Jeanette A, research analyst III, $45,156
Barnhart, Edward S, park maint wkr III, $34,356
Barnhart, Rachel A, cultural resource pres I, $36,204
Bartels, Rachel A, seasonal aide, $8.05
Bartz, Brandon K, park ranger cpl, $41,940
Basham, Aaron P, environ engr II, $47,892
Basnett, Janice L, seasonal aide, $8.50/hr
Bassett, Gwenda J, environ spec III, $41,940
Bates, Courtney, seasonal aide, $8.00/hr
Bates, Hanna M, seasonal aide, $8.68/hr
Batts, Jared C, seasonal aide, $8.00/hr
Baughman, Josiah C, geologist II, $41,940
Baugus, Samuel, seasonal aide, $8.50/hr
Baumgartner, Scotty D, hydrologist IV, $56,520
Baumhoer, Brandon M, environ spec III, $41,940
Bax, Lori A, mgmt analysis spec I, $39,624
Bax, Sarah L, planner II, $41,940
Bax, Stacia M, environ sup, $52,092
Baxter, Kay A, sr ofc spt asst (keybrd), $28,908
Bayer, Brent W, designated principal asst div, $73,225
Baysinger, Bobbi S, seasonal aide, $8.90/hr
Bazal, Elizabeth, park/historic site spec II, $36,888
Beal, Mary K, seasonal aide, $8.00/hr
Bechtel, Cheri L, research analyst II, $36,888
Beck, Alexa S, seasonal aide, $8.05
Beckett, Michael D, natural resources mgr b1, $48,149
Becklenberg, Jessica R, admin ofc spt asst, $28,104
Becknell, Randy K, park/historic site spec III, $47,892
Begley, Jon L, environ spec III, $41,940
Belfiore, Donna S, sr ofc spt asst (keybrd), $25,824
Bell, Michael A, park maint wkr II, $26,652
Bell, Sherry, exec I, $32,628
Bender, Shilo A, seasonal aide, $13.41/hr
Benkowich, Carrie L, sr ofc spt asst (keybrd), $18,767
Bennett, Denver W, seasonal aide, $8.00/hr
Bennett, Sandra L, seasonal aide, $8.68/hr
Bennett, Therese L, ofc spt asst (keybrd), $11,263
Benoist, Charles M, seasonal aide, $10.20/hr
Bentley, Bonnie S, sr ofc spt asst (keybrd), $26,652
Bergthold, Brandy S, environ spec III, $41,940
Berhorst, Samantha M, admin ofc spt asst, $28,104
Bernabe, Brian V, admin ofc spt asst, $30,984
Bernat, Darren, environ spec III, $41,940
Bernhardt, Brenda K, sr ofc spt asst (keybrd), $25,824
Bertels, Keith A, environ mgr b2, $56,433
Berve, Trisha, exec I, $32,628
Besalke, Robert S, water spec III, $40,380
Besse-Morris, Dalton C, seasonal aide, $8.00/hr
Bessey, Hunter D, seasonal aide, $8.00/hr
Bethel, Bryan D, natural resources mgr b1, $43,485
Bethel, Edward H, environ spec III, $46,068
Beuer, Ralph D, seasonal aide, $9.65/hr
Bevfoden, Shawn A, seasonal aide, $8.66/hr
Beydler, Hylan L, pub info coor, $38,928
Beydler, Van E, pub info coor, $44,304
Beye, Deedra L, accounting analyst II, $38,928
Bibbs, Teri L, sr ofc spt asst (keybrd), $28,452
Binkley, Jeanne E, sr ofc spt asst (keybrd), $25,824
Binkley, Traci L, ofc spt asst (keybrd), $23,160
Birkeness, Eric M, seasonal aide, $8.00/hr
Birkhead, John W, seasonal aide, $8.00/hr
Bittle, Loretta A, mgmt analysis spec II, $41,172
Bitzer, Karen L, sr ofc spt asst (keybrd), $25,824
Black, Betty R, seasonal aide, $8.00/hr
Black, Corrin N, seasonal aide, $8.47/hr

Blackmore, Michele L, museum curator II, $40,380
Blair, Lancer T, seasonal aide, $8.90/hr
Blanc, Todd J, environ scientist, $53,208
Blankenship, Kenton W, seasonal aide, $8.91/hr
Blankenship, Sean D, seasonal aide, $8.00/hr
Blankenship, Tim, seasonal aide, $8.00/hr
Blanton, Charles D, seasonal aide, $8.00/hr
Bledsoe, Becky L, sr ofc spt asst (keybrd), $25,032
Bledsoe, William C, chemist III, $43,488
Bleich, Larry D, bldg const wkr II, $33,744
Blevins, Cara L, admin ofc spt asst, $28,104
Bleything, Connie, seasonal aide, $8.15/hr
Blodgett, Jonathan M, environ spec III, $41,940
Bloomer, Susan L, pub info spec II, $35,568
Blum, Joseph P, natural resources mgr b1, $48,149
Blume, Conrad J, environ engr II, $47,892
Blumhorst, Elizabeth, seasonal aide, $9.12/hr
Bobbitt, Laurie A, misc tech, $25.04
Bobbitt, Yvonne A, park/historic site spec II, $36,204
Bockstruck, Mark E, environ engr II, $47,892
Bodenstab, Chelsey M, sr ofc spt asst (keybrd), $25,824
Bodine, Larry D, capital imprvmts spec II, $50,040
Bodine, Marianne, interpretive resource spec II, $33,744
Boeckmann, Kurt D, special asst prof, $60,111
Boessen, John, environ engr II, $47,892
Bohs, George R, seasonal aide, $8.31/hr
Boland, Deanna L, budget analyst III, $49,128
Boldt, Christopher M, lab mgr b2, $61,339
Boldt, Jacob, misc tech, $14.18/hr
Bolling, Kevin D, natural resources mgr b1, $60,125
Bone, Fletcher N, geologist II, $41,940
Bonnell, Carl R, natural resources mgr b1, $48,149
Bonnell, William C, natural resources mgr b1, $52,091
Bonney, Jeffrey D, park/historic site spec II, $36,204
Bonney, Maria R, environ engr II, $47,892
Boone, Charles, misc tech, $14.18/hr
Boone, Steven M, environ sup, $57,744
Bopp, Dennis R, dpty div dir, $84,520
Boschert, Deborah G, misc tech, $22.15/hr
Boschert, James V, environ sup, $53,208
Boss, Travis W, water spec III, $40,380
Bost, Stephen H, interpretive resource spc III, $38,928
Bostic, Jackson L, environ mgr b3, $73,385
Bostick, Dwayne, park maint wkr III, $30,420
Boswell, Cecil E, tech asst III, $31,512
Bottomley, Brett, environ spec III, $41,940
Bouse, Natasha N, admin ofc spt asst, $28,104
Bowdish, Joseph A, environ sup, $53,208
Bowen, Dustin R, park maint wkr II, $26,652
Bowers, Mark A, park maint wkr II, $26,652
Bowman, Daryn R, seasonal aide, $8.50/hr
Boyd, Michael T, heavy equip oper, $32,628
Boyd, Michala M, seasonal aide, $8.00/hr
Boyer, Jessica, seasonal aide, $8.00/hr
Boyer, Nicole L, seasonal aide, $8.05
Boyster, Russell J, seasonal aide, $8.00/hr
Bozoian, Harry D, special asst prof, $102,064
Bozoian, Harry E, seasonal aide, $8.00/hr
Bradley, Elizabeth, seasonal aide, $8.68/hr
Bradley, Noah J, bldg const wkr II, $30,984
Brake, Colleen M, seasonal aide, $8.00/hr
Branch, Helen L, ofc spt asst (keybrd), $23,160
Branch, Lesley D, sr ofc spt asst (keybrd), $25,824
Brandt, April M, planner III, $47,892
Brandt, Debbie A, seasonal aide, $8.00/hr
Branson, Amanda, environ spec I, $29,976
Branson, Cecil L, seasonal aide, $11.00/hr
Branson, Kent D, environ engr I, $41,940
Braswell, Tammy J, sr ofc spt asst (keybrd), $27,948
Brawley, Justyn L, seasonal aide, $8.00/hr
Brennan, Kathleen A, seasonal aide, $9.75/hr
Brent, Kelley L, park opps & plng coord, $43,488
Bridges, Carey S, environ mgr b3, $73,225
Bridges, David L, geologist II, $41,940
Brigman, Daniel S, natural resources mgr b1, $41,927
Bristow, Ronald A, seasonal aide, $8.00/hr
Broadway, Rayna, environ scientist, $48,156
Brockman, Kayla D, busser, $8.00/hr
Brockman, Kayla D, wait staff, $4.00/hr

Brookshire, Cynthia, hydrologist IV, $61,332
Brouillette, Steven E, park maint wkr II, $19,984
Brown, Caleb Q, seasonal aide, $8.00/hr
Brown, Charles D, park maint wkr II, $25,824
Brown, Darrin J, park maint wkr III, $32,628
Brown, Freddie D, park maint wkr II, $28,908
Brown, Jeanne M, research analyst III, $41,172
Brown, Keith M, environ spec II, $36,204
Brown, Kristin L, seasonal aide, $10.00/hr
Brown, Linda K, seasonal aide, $8.52/hr
Brown, Linda S, exec I, $30,984
Brown, Melissa A, seasonal aide, $8.50/hr
Brown, Rebecca J, seasonal aide, $9.16/hr
Brown, Richard, environ spec III, $41,940
Brown, Robert F, seasonal aide, $8.65/hr
Brown, Wendy C, seasonal aide, $9.00/hr
Brown, Zach, misc tech, $14.18/hr
Brownawell, Daniel, environ spec III, $41,940
Browne, Cynthia J, park/historic site spec III, $38,928
Browning, Betsey, mgr, $40,384
Browning, Keith, park maint wkr III, $31,512
Bruemmer, Kurt A, environ spec II, $36,204
Brunnert, James A, environ sup, $56,520
Bruns, Laura M, seasonal aide, $8.00/hr
Bryan, Dana M, sr ofc spt asst (keybrd), $25,824
Bryan, Mary M, legal counsel, $68,175
Bryan, William J, designated principal asst div, $111,605
Bryant, Cherie, environ spec III, $41,940
Bryant, Evan T, environ scientist, $48,156
Bryant, Jacob D, park maint wkr II, $25,824
Bryant, Jillian N, seasonal aide, $8.90/hr
Bryant, Neva, sr ofc spt asst (keybrd), $25,032
Bryant, Todd D, park ranger cpl, $42,708
Bryant, Wyatt W, busser, $8.00/hr
Buchman, Elise M, sr ofc spt asst (keybrd), $25,032
Buchman, Susan L, seasonal aide, $9.36/hr
Buckland, Christopher D, planner III, $48,156
Buckler, Justin, environ spec III, $41,940
Budde, Brendon R, park maint wkr II, $26,652
Bueker, Melissa M, park opps & plng coord, $40,380
Buford, Ashley M, seasonal aide, $8.00/hr
Buford, Cammie S, seasonal aide, $8.00/hr
Buford, Candace, sr ofc spt asst (keybrd), $25,824
Buford, Sandra G, seasonal aide, $8.00/hr
Buie, Dakota C, seasonal aide, $8.00/hr
Buie, Douglas G, park ranger cpl, $42,708
Bull, Timothy W, environ sup, $49,128
Bullard, John, environ spec III, $41,940
Bullock, Teresa A, environ spec III, $41,940
Bungart, S Renee, pub info admstr, $62,664
Burch, Lisa M, seasonal aide, $8.11/hr
Burch, Peter L, environ spec II, $36,204
Burge, Russell A, natural resources mgr b1, $41,927
Burke, Amanda R, cultural resource pres II, $40,380
Burke, Emily A, interpretive resource tech, $21,746
Burkhart, Charles A, park maint wkr III, $31,512
Burkhart, Sadie J, seasonal aide, $8.50/hr
Burkholder, Blake R, seasonal aide, $8.00/hr
Burks, Lindsay R, interpretive resource spec I, $15,496
Burnsides, Linda, seasonal aide, $11.43/hr
Burrus, Justin N, tech asst IV, $34,944
Burtnett, Amanda R, seasonal aide, $8.00/hr
Burton, Lucy A, seasonal aide, $8.00/hr
Busch, Walter E, natural resources mgr b1, $48,149
Buschman, Alexander L, seasonal aide, $9.50/hr
Butcher, Tracy L, seasonal aide, $8.41/hr
Butler, Aristotle A, seasonal aide, $8.00/hr
Butler, Dustin R, seasonal aide, $8.00/hr
Butler, Gregory N, asst cook, $14.00/hr
Butterfield, Clifford M, seasonal aide, $8.00/hr
Buttig, David, environ engr II, $47,892
Bybee, Darcy, environ mgr b2, $57,633
Bynum-Banks, Lachae B, busser, $8.00/hr
Bynum-Banks, Lachae B, wait staff, $4.00/hr
Cady, Jonathan C, environ scientist, $53,208
Cage, Erica Y, sr auditor, $46,932
Cagle, Lori, ofc spt asst (keybrd), $22,536
Cain, Billy, seasonal aide, $8.00/hr
Cain, Pamela R, mgmt analysis spec II, $53,208

Caldwell, Gregory D, environ spec III, $49,128
Calloway, Caleb W, seasonal aide, $8.00/hr
Calvert, Deric L, environ spec III, $36,204
Cameron, Franklin B, seasonal aide, $8.05
Campbell, Beverly J, sr ofc spt asst (keybrd), $25,824
Campbell, Cecilia G, environ scientist, $50,040
Campbell, Kimberly J, sr ofc spt asst (keybrd), $25,824
Campbell, Robert D, sign maker I, $28,908
Campbell, Roxanna L, interpretive resource spc III, $38,928
Campbell, Shannon D, park maint wkr III, $30,420
Cannady, Christopher L, park ranger, $36,204
Cantrell, Caylen M, park maint wkr II, $26,652
Capell, Pia E, environ spec III, $42,334
Cardwell, Tony L, procurement ofcr I, $37,548
Carey, Daniel A, environ engr II, $50,040
Carletti, Matthew P, natural resources mgr b1, $45,163
Carlile, Cailie, environ engr II, $47,892
Carlson, Cayla, misc prof, $14.18/hr
Carlson, Lance H, arch II, $51,096
Carpenter, Emily T, environ engr II, $47,892
Carson, Victoria K, seasonal aide, $8.80/hr
Carter, Merle R, seasonal aide, $9.76/hr
Caruthers, Martha L, seasonal aide, $8.05
Case, Kimberly D, mgmt analysis spec II, $44,304
Cash, Vicki L, admin ofc spt asst, $29,004
Cather, Bryan S, seasonal aide, $9.32/hr
Caton, Maggie J, seasonal aide, $9.15/hr
Cea, Phanna L, environ sup, $51,096
Cecil, Rickie L, park maint wkr I, $25,824
Chamberlain, Patricia L, accounting spec III, $47,892
Chambers, Patricia L, interpretive resource spec II, $34,944
Champlain, Vickie S, sr ofc spt asst (keybrd), $27,504
Chancey, Kelly, seasonal aide, $8.00/hr
Chapman, Nikia, misc tech, $14.18/hr
Chapman, Patricia S, environ spec III, $43,488
Chapman, Samuel, seasonal aide, $8.00/hr
Charleville, Megan A, seasonal aide, $9.07
Charlton, Judith G, environ sup, $58,908
Chase, Kristine, cultural resource pres I, $36,204
Chastain, Lisa, museum curator coord, $45,156
Chavez-Newby, Debbie R, natural resources mgr b1, $46,062
Cheaney, Kevin, park maint wkr II, $26,652
Chevalier, Vickie L, seasonal aide, $8.00/hr
Chibnall, Timothy D, environ scientist, $61,332
Childs, Shari S, special asst prof, $50,500
Chilton, Taylor R, seasonal aide, $8.00/hr
Choudhury, Tarun, chemist III, $42,708
Chronister, Beverly J, seasonal aide, $8.05
Chronister, Jan E, environ spec III, $41,940
Chronister, John D, environ spec III, $41,940
Clark, Carol J, interpretive resource tech, $14,050
Clark, Margaret E, seasonal aide, $8.81/hr
Clark, Toni R, pers clerk, $29,496
Clarke, Allan G, environ spec III, $43,488
Clay, Robert A, design/develop/survey mgr b3, $67,954
Clifford, Timothy N, park maint wkr III, $34,356
Clubb, Carl J, seasonal aide, $9.91/hr
Cobb, Terry L, admin ofc spt asst, $31,512
Cochran, Jesse, environ sup, $51,096
Cody, Lori J, seasonal aide, $8.05
Coffer, Amanda L, environ engr I, $41,940
Cohen, Jacob D, bldg const wkr I, $29,004
Coker, Thomas T, seasonal aide, $8.05
Colatskie, Ronald M, natural resources steward, $40,380
Cole, Lauren, admin ofc spt asst, $29,004
Cole, Logan, environ spec III, $41,940
Cole, Nancy A, seasonal aide, $8.15/hr
Coleman, Steven L, seasonal aide, $9.50/hr
Collier, Andrea, designated principal asst div, $80,152
Collins, Emily, misc prof, $11.50/hr
Collins, Jessica L, environ spec I, $30,984
Collins, Lloyd F, seasonal aide, $8.05
Collins, Michael E, park maint wkr II, $26,652
Collins, William J, park maint wkr III, $30,420
Combs, Andrew S, environ spec III, $36,204
Combs, Cody M, seasonal aide, $8.00/hr
Combs, Greg, natural resources mgr b2, $61,339
Comer, Michael A, natural resources mgr b1, $50,045
Concannon, Rory P, seasonal aide, $8.56/hr

Conger, Patricia, sr ofc spt asst (keybrd), $27,504
Connell, James M, tractor trailer driver, $34,944
Conner, Garland D, park maint wkr II, $26,652
Conrath, Owen M, seasonal aide, $8.00/hr
Cook, Brittany N, seasonal aide, $8.05
Cook, Jonathan E, seasonal aide, $8.00/hr
Cooley, Charles B, seasonal aide, $8.00/hr
Coon, Adam J, mgmt analysis spec II, $45,156
Coon, Julie M, budget analyst III, $46,932
Coonce, Amanda G, interpretive resource tech, $29,004
Cooper, Kurtis, environ spec III, $41,940
Corcoran, Adam V, seasonal aide, $12.04
Corley, John, geologist I, $38,232
Cornell, Kelsey, environ spec I, $29,976
Corrigan, Leigh A, facilities opps mgr b2, $57,669
Cortner, Laura L, seasonal aide, $10.00/hr
Cortvrient, Alan, environ sup, $58,908
Cosgrove, Peter, special asst prof, $47,894
Cosner, Victoria L, natural resources mgr b1, $51,095
Couch, Mildred, seasonal aide, $8.00/hr
Council, Matthew, environ spec III, $42,708
Counihan, Sean M, environ spec III, $45,156
Counts, Danny J, park/historic site spec II, $36,204
Covington, Alicia M, seasonal aide, $10.00/hr
Cowen, Marissa, natural resources mgr b1, $41,932
Cox, Amber, ofc worker misc, $9.41/hr
Cox, Kelly R, seasonal aide, $8.68/hr
Cozad, Marletta L, tech asst II, $28,104
Crabtree, Chris D, natural resources steward, $40,380
Crabtree, Ronda Y, tech asst II, $27,660
Crafton, John B, seasonal aide, $8.16/hr
Craig, Melvina K, designated principal asst dept, $47,712
Crane, Michaela G, seasonal aide, $8.00/hr
Crannick, Jeffrey M, water spec III, $40,380
Crawford, Eric W, special asst prof, $70,680
Crawford, G Irene, environ mgr b3, $73,385
Crawford, Travis O, park maint wkr II, $26,652
Crawshaw, James A, environ spec I, $29,976
Creighton, Jacob M, seasonal aide, $8.00/hr
Crews, Courtney L, seasonal aide, $9.72/hr
Crews, Jeffrey A, geologist II, $41,940
Cripe, Donald B, environ sup, $49,128
Cripe, Rebecca, environ sup, $49,128
Crocker, Christopher E, natural resources mgr b2, $66,727
Crocker, Devin E, seasonal aide, $8.00/hr
Crocker, Jason M, environ spec III, $40,380
Crook, Jeffrey D, park maint wkr III, $32,628
Crouse, Linda K, sr ofc spt asst (keybrd), $25,032
Crow, Andrew, environ spec III, $41,940
Crow, Jason T, seasonal aide, $8.00/hr
Crowell, David A, seasonal aide, $9.72/hr
Cruse, Martha E, environ spec II, $36,204
Cruz-Ellison, Tammy S, seasonal aide, $8.00/hr
Cruzen, Jeffrey C, seasonal aide, $8.00/hr
Cullen, Robert M, seasonal aide, $8.96/hr
Culler, Mary E, environ spec III, $41,940
Culley, Shelly K, admin ofc spt asst, $28,104
Culp, Adam J, seasonal aide, $8.00/hr
Cunigan, Cedric, environ engr II, $47,892
Cunning, John D, natural resources mgr b2, $61,339
Cunningham, Michael A, environ sup, $51,096
Curran, John T, seasonal aide, $8.00/hr
Dachroeden, Charles A, environ mgr b1, $57,725
Dacila, Linda A, admin ofc spt asst, $28,104
Dagley, Donnie G, park maint wkr II, $26,652
Dalbom, Kaylyn J, seasonal aide, $8.00/hr
Dallas, Mary, sr auditor, $46,932
Danforth, Katie A, seasonal aide, $8.40/hr
Danforth, Kellie L, seasonal aide, $8.40/hr
Darnell, Brittany L, admin ofc spt asst, $27,228
Darr, Sarah E, misc prof, $11.50/hr
Daugherty, Daniel J, environ scientist, $54,288
Davenport, Ellen C, designated principal asst div, $39,697
Davidson, Kyle S, seasonal aide, $8.00/hr
Davies, Cynthia S, environ mgr b3, $73,385
Davis, Elizabeth E, seasonal aide, $8.05
Davis, Jane, environ spec III, $43,488
Davis, Justin G, geologist IV, $51,096
Davis, Matthew L, seasonal aide, $8.91/hr

Davis, Michael A, environ spec III, $41,940
Davis, Valerie, budget analyst III, $50,040
Dawson, Cody E, seasonal aide, $8.00/hr
Dayton, Christine, misc tech, $11.83/hr
Dayton, Hairl G, misc prof, $17.81/hr
De La Guerra, Mary L, admin ofc spt asst, $29,004
Deardeuff, Steven J, park maint wkr III, $31,512
Deaver, Courtney D, seasonal aide, $8.49/hr
Debold, Mitchel L, seasonal aide, $8.00/hr
Decelis, Matthew B, seasonal aide, $8.90/hr
Deckard, Rodney D, park maint wkr II, $19,984
Deeken, Deborah R, accounting spec II, $44,304
Deel, Judith, cultural resource pres II, $46,932
Degraffenreid, Shane G, park ranger, $37,548
Deidrick, Stephanie M, pub info admstr, $55,416
Delaney, Phillip M, seasonal aide, $8.00/hr
Denham, Abby L, seasonal aide, $10,560
Desmond, Barbara A, seasonal aide, $9.83/hr
Detweiler, Taylre, seasonal aide, $8.41/hr
Dewitt, Amanda S, admin ofc spt asst, $29,496
Dickerson, Dennis A, seasonal aide, $8.00/hr
Dickerson, Michael P, environ mgr b2, $57,633
Dickey, Joshua D, busser, $12.03
Dickey, Joshua D, wait staff, $4.00/hr
Dickey, Michael E, natural resources mgr b1, $52,091
Dickneite, Christa J, pers clerk, $27,228
Dickneite, Jason, environ engr II, $47,892
Dicks, Donald L, environ spec II, $51,096
Dieckow, Debra, environ spec III, $41,940
Diedriech, Michelle L, cultural resource pres II, $41,940
Digges, Paul E, seasonal aide, $9.45/hr
Digges, Wilma J, seasonal aide, $8.70/hr
Dillon, Kimberly, natural resources mgr b1, $46,062
Dixon, Laura M, graphic arts spec II, $29,004
Dkhili, Mohsen, environ sup, $56,520
Dobbs, Jr, seasonal aide, $9.36/hr
Dobson, Debra D, admin ofc spt asst, $29,004
Dodsworth, Jerry C, seasonal aide, $9.00/hr
Doerhoff, Joan M, environ sup, $51,096
Doggett, Theresa, planner II, $40,380
Dohmen, Anthony E, environ scientist, $54,288
Dolan, Francis J, environ engr III, $60,120
Dondlinger, Kristen A, seasonal aide, $8.00/hr
Donze, Mary M, planner III, $53,208
Doolen, Chad E, seasonal aide, $12.04
Doolen, Wanda S, natural resources mgr b1, $49,101
Dootson, Kelsey J, seasonal aide, $240
Dorsey, Lance W, environ mgr b1, $57,633
Doster, Branden, environ mgr b2, $67,850
Douglass, Eleanor L, seasonal aide, $8.35/hr
Dowd, Matthew H, seasonal aide, $8.47/hr
Dowdy, David, environ spec III, $42,708
Dowling, Sandra D, natural resources mgr b1, $46,926
Downs, Jerry, environ spec III, $41,940
Draine, Lucille, sr ofc spt asst (keybrd), $25,824
Drake, Tiffany, environ engr IV, $66,720
Dreher, Dalton W, seasonal aide, $8.11/hr
Dresner, Thomas G, park ranger, $36,204
Drilling, David, environ engr II, $47,892
Dubbert, Alison B, cultural resource pres II, $40,380
Dubbs, Steve A, seasonal aide, $10.00/hr
Ducharme, Charles B, hydrologist III, $49,128
Duckett, Heather, seasonal aide, $8.00/hr
Dudenhoeffer, Jennifer L, sr ofc spt asst (keybrd), $30,384
Dudenhoeffer, Nicole R, accounting spec I, $36,204
Dudley, David W, exec I, $32,052
Dudley, Teresa L, misc prof, $25.49/hr
Duewell, Bridget G, exec II, $36,204
Duffee, Meagan N, interpretive resource spec I, $30,984
Duggan, Robert M, seasonal aide, $8.00/hr
Duley, James W, misc prof, $19.06
Dumond, Gabriel, park/historic site spec III, $43,488
Durbin, Stephanie E, environ spec II, $36,204
Durham, Zackary C, seasonal aide, $8.00/hr
Durington, Jeff W, park maint wkr III, $32,052
Dwyer, Patrick J, environ sup, $54,288
Dyer, Cortney, exec II, $36,204
Dyer, Michael T, sign maker II, $33,744
Dysart, Cody M, park ranger, $37,548

Eagen, Tony J, bldg const wkr II, $32,052
Easley, Matthew A, seasonal aide, $8.00/hr
Eby, Nicole, environ sup, $51,096
Eddy, Jennifer R, hr mgr b2, $74,235
Edelman, Tandi L, environ engr II, $47,892
Edgar, Jon R, seasonal aide, $8.18/hr
Edwards, Charles R, maint worker II, $29,004
Edwards, Connie S, exec I, $32,628
Eichholz, Todd, environ mgr b2, $57,633
Eighmey, Carol R, exec dir, $87,073
Eiken, Timothy, planner III, $45,156
Eilerman, Neil, accounting spc I, $34,944
Eis, Joshua S, environ spec II, $36,204
Eisterhold, Cameron A, environ spec II, $36,204
Elam-Pyles, Dairan N, seasonal aide, $8.00/hr
Elder, Matt G, water spec III, $38,928
Elfrink, Neil M, geologist II, $46,932
El-Jayyousi, Jalal, environ engr IV, $68,160
Elkana, Michael A, environ spec II, $36,204
Ellebracht, Tammy, seasonal aide, $8.39/hr
Ellefsen, Steven, busser, $8.00/hr
Ellefsen, Steven, wait staff, $4.00/hr
Elliott, Matthew W, environ spec III, $41,940
Ellis, Daniel C, heavy equip oper, $29,004
Ellis, Rob D, park maint wkr III, $31,512
Ellis, Trevor C, geologist II, $41,940
Embree, Paul V, environ spec III, $41,940
Emory, Jennifer A, sr ofc spt asst (keybrd), $25,824
Enboden, Adam M, natural resources mgr b1, $49,104
Engeln, Joseph F, special asst prof, $74,802
Enloe, Christopher J, park ranger, $36,204
Erickson, David R, geologist II, $46,932
Erickson, Larry V, misc prof, $30.12/hr
Ernst, Joshua D, environ spec III, $41,940
Eschenbrenner, Holly E, seasonal aide, $8.96/hr
Espejo, Raissa E, environ spec III, $41,940
Evans, Geoffrey C, park ranger cpl, $41,940
Evans, Glennis L, environ spec III, $41,940
Evans, Joseph D, environ spec II, $36,204
Even, Angie L, park opps & plng coord, $44,304
Evers, Valerie G, designated principal asst dept, $54,663
Expose, Joshua, seasonal aide, $10.00/hr
Faerber, Nancy L, ofc worker misc, $17.10/hr
Fales, Calvin C, environ engr I, $43,488
Falls, Angela, environ spec II, $36,204
Fanska, William D, environ engr IV, $68,160
Farmer, Samantha N, seasonal aide, $8.00/hr
Farris, Brant J, environ spec III, $41,940
Farris, Tracy L, fiscal & administrative mgr b3, $69,999
Feeler, Steven S, dpty div dir, $84,520
Ferguson, Shannon A, seasonal aide, $8.00/hr
Ferree, Christopher A, park/historic site spec II, $36,204
Fester, Daniel W, planner III, $49,128
Fett, Karl F, environ mgr b2, $73,385
Fett, Walter, environ engr II, $47,892
Fick, Franklin J, environ spec III, $41,940
Ficken, Larry G, park maint wkr II, $26,652
Ficker, James J, park maint wkr III, $29,976
Ficker, Mary A, seasonal aide, $10.00/hr
Fields, Roderick, tech asst IV, $36,888
Filley, James A, seasonal aide, $8.50/hr
Fink, Don, natural resources mgr b1, $46,935
Finn, Clinton J, environ engr III, $55,416
Fitch, Charlene S, environ mgr b2, $61,241
Fitch, Christopher G, seasonal aide, $9.50/hr
Fitch, Jonathan L, design engr III, $69,612
Flannery, Jessica R, exec II, $36,204
Flannery, Terry A, seasonal aide, $8.00/hr
Flaton, Michael, planner I, $36,204
Flippin, Kathy S, environ mgr b2, $58,897
Flowers, Carlton S, environ engr II, $51,096
Fohey, Drake T, seasonal aide, $8.00/hr
Forbes, Randall, park maint wkr II, $26,652
Forbis, Shari J, admin ofc spt asst, $29,004
Forck, Keith B, environ engr III, $58,908
Ford, Pierce, seasonal aide, $8.00/hr
Forseth, David L, seasonal aide, $9.05
Foster, Albert C, seasonal aide, $8.56/hr
Foster, Dana L, special asst ofc & clerical, $47,713

Foster, John M, bldg const wkr II, $30,984
Foster, Richard L, seasonal aide, $8.47/hr
Fountain, Charles, seasonal aide, $8.25/hr
Fraga, John M, environ spec III, $47,892
Francis, Brant A, seasonal aide, $8.00/hr
Franke, Kenneth L, seasonal aide, $8.30/hr
Franklin, Dorothy E, environ mgr b3, $73,384
Franklin, Robert, facilities opps mgr b2, $47,559
Franklin, Yvonne M, environ engr II, $50,040
Franks, Taylor, seasonal aide, $8.00/hr
Franson, Raymond L, environ scientist, $48,156
Frazier, Guy R, environ sup, $56,520
Frederick, Shanea M, park maint wkr III, $29,976
Fredrick, Brian S, hydrologist II, $42,708
Fredrickson, Dawn K, natural resources mgr b1, $52,091
Fredrickson, Tucker, environ spec III, $42,708
Freeze, Megan K, seasonal aide, $8.00/hr
Freiheit, Bethany M, seasonal aide, $8.00/hr
Fritsche, Christopher R, interpretive resource spc III, $39,624
Fritz, Alex C, seasonal aide, $8.00/hr
Fritz, Jacob M, seasonal aide, $8.00/hr
Froemsdorf, Delphia A, seasonal aide, $8.00/hr
Froning, Dawn M, environ scientist, $57,744
Fry, Sheri, environ spec III, $42,708
Fuchs, Miranda J, busser, $8.00/hr
Fuchs, Miranda J, wait staff, $4.00/hr
Fuemmeler, Eric E, interpretive resource tech, $14,498
Fuhrman, Shawna, environ spec III, $41,940
Fuller, Janae A, natural resources mgr b1, $48,149
Gaddie, Satchel, environ spec III, $41,940
Gaddy, Samuel B, seasonal aide, $8.20/hr
Gale, Lori E, misc tech, $14.18/hr
Galvan, Delno R, park maint wkr II, $27,504
Gamel, David F, seasonal aide, $8.56/hr
Gann, Richard L, environ sup, $61,332
Ganz, Kyle J, geologist II, $41,940
Gardner, Terri L, interpretive resource spec II, $34,944
Garey, Carol K, planner III, $45,156
Garrett, Valerie J, environ scientist, $55,416
Garrison, Nancy M, park maint wkr II, $25,824
Garrison, Yancey P, park maint wkr III, $30,420
Gast, James A, natural resources mgr b1, $46,935
Gatlin, Jacquelin A, exec II, $36,204
Gearhart, Glen A, environ spec III, $46,932
Gensky, Henry E, seasonal aide, $9.12/hr
Gensler, Clifford D, seasonal aide, $9.41/hr
George, James R, seasonal aide, $10.00/hr
Gerard, Carla M, seasonal aide, $8.50/hr
Gerke, Terry K, seasonal aide, $8.00/hr
Gerling, Jodi M, fiscal & administrative mgr b2, $59,970
Gerlt, Caroline K, environ spec III, $41,940
Gerson, Laura M, environ spec II, $36,204
Getahun, Berhanu, environ engr II, $53,208
Giarratano, David J, environ sup, $56,520
Gibson, Alisha, sr ofc spt asst (keybrd), $25,824
Gibson, John C, environ sup, $53,208
Gideon, Kabriell, seasonal aide, $8.05
Gilbert, Steven C, maint worker II, $29,004
Gilham, Toby A, environ engr II, $47,892
Gillenwater, Jaden T, seasonal aide, $8.00/hr
Gillman, Joseph A, div dir, $91,082
Gilmore, David S, admin ofc spt asst, $29,004
Gilmore, Kelly J, seasonal aide, $8.00/hr
Gilstrap, Eric J, environ engr III, $58,908
Gilzow, Joy L, training tech II, $42,708
Gingrey, Rhonda S, seasonal aide, $8.47/hr
Giroir, Louis E, toxicologist, $58,908
Gittemeier, Morgan, misc tech, $14.18/hr
Glaskey, Thomas J, seasonal aide, $8.05
Glidewell, Kent A, seasonal aide, $10.00/hr
Glueck, Travis, environ spec III, $41,940
Goben, Scott E, seasonal aide, $8.00/hr
Godsy, Misty M, sr ofc spt asst (keybrd), $26,652
Goodin, Arthur L, environ sup, $51,096
Gordon, Lori A, designated principal asst div, $100,313
Gordon, Mark, graphic arts spec II, $29,004
Govero, Sharon G, seasonal aide, $8.47/hr
Gozia, Michael D, park ranger, $37,548
Grace, Emily A, environ spec II, $36,204

Gracz, Breanna D, seasonal aide, $9.05
Graessle, Nathaniel S, environ engr III, $55,416
Graf, Wayne J, environ sup, $60,120
Gramlich, Eric E, environ sup, $57,744
Grant, Andrea, admin ofc spt asst, $28,104
Grass, Diane L, seasonal aide, $14.18/hr
Gravatt, Madeleine L, seasonal aide, $8.37/hr
Graves, Benjamin J, seasonal aide, $8.90/hr
Graves, Catherine C, environ spec III, $45,156
Gray, Amanda J, exec I, $31,512
Green, David C, environ spec III, $42,708
Green, Ethan L, seasonal aide, $8.90/hr
Green, Joseph B, seasonal aide, $8.81/hr
Green, Lee A, sr ofc spt asst (keybrd), $25,824
Gregory, Dee A, environ spec III, $41,940
Gregory, Frederick E, natural resources mgr b1, $48,149
Gregory, Ronald, seasonal aide, $8.00/hr
Grellner, Connie J, admin ofc spt asst, $28,536
Gremard, Megan E, seasonal aide, $8.00/hr
Griffith, Janely E, environ engr I, $41,940
Griggs, Jim E, park/historic site spec III, $40,380
Grimes, Melinda L, busser, $8.00/hr
Grimes, Melinda L, wait staff, $4.00/hr
Groner, Darleen, environ engr IV, $68,160
Groner, Larry, fiscal & administrative mgr b1, $64,158
Groner, Wanda, fiscal & administrative mgr b3, $69,999
Grootens, Matthew A, environ spec I, $30,984
Grose, Michael J, environ engr II, $47,892
Grosvenor, Joshua L, environ engr II, $47,892
Grothoff, Natalie A, chemist III, $41,172
Groves, Ronda L, seasonal aide, $8.06
Gruhlke, Jamie A, sr ofc spt asst (keybrd), $20,667
Guenther, Mary S, seasonal aide, $8.80/hr
Guinn, Laura, environ spec III, $41,940
Gullic, David B, environ spec III, $48,156
Gurnow, Michael E, seasonal aide, $8.22/hr
Guthrie, Ferlin D, park maint wkr II, $26,652
Haag, Tracy A, environ engr II, $54,288
Haberl, Denise M, environ engr II, $47,892
Hackler, Pamilyn, environ scientist, $48,156
Hagans, Ralph L, supply mgr I, $32,628
Haines, Lee G, park maint wkr III, $31,512
Hale, Kendall, environ mgr b2, $65,256
Hall, Cynthia, interpretive resource coord, $42,708
Hall, Daniel M, seasonal aide, $8.50/hr
Hall, Deborah M, exec II, $34,944
Hall, Donald W, seasonal aide, $9.36/hr
Hall, Jeremy W, park maint wkr II, $26,652
Hall, Melissa A, park/historic site spec III, $38,928
Hall, Stephen M, environ mgr b2, $57,653
Hall, Wendell M, environ spec III, $50,040
Haller, Andrew, special asst prof, $35,855
Halterman-Wright, Tessa N, seasonal aide, $10.00/hr
Hampton, Ann R, seasonal aide, $8.80/hr
Hampton, Teresa A, seasonal aide, $8.00/hr
Hamzeh, Hani M, environ engr II, $53,208
Hand, Jeffrey G, park/historic site spec III, $38,928
Hannick, Marilyn, sr ofc spt asst (keybrd), $13,322
Hannon, Kenneth, environ spec III, $45,156
Hansen, Dennis D, misc tech, $24.56/hr
Hanson, Anika, seasonal aide, $8.00/hr
Happ, Erin N, seasonal aide, $8.00/hr
Harbin, Taylor W, interpretive resource spec I, $29,976
Harcourt, Mary E, seasonal aide, $8.69/hr
Hargiss, Garrett, seasonal aide, $8.68/hr
Hargraves, Wesley, environ spec III, $41,940
Harlow, Timothy E, arch III, $66,720
Harmon, Dylan M, seasonal aide, $8.00/hr
Harness, Ross J, seasonal aide, $8.25/hr
Harp, Vergial, natural resources mgr b1, $46,935
Harrel, Ellen, sr ofc spt asst (keybrd), $25,824
Harris, Bradley W, environ sup, $61,332
Harris, Carlton, environ spec III, $41,940
Harris, Cody G, seasonal aide, $8.00/hr
Harris, James R, environ spec III, $46,932
Harris, Marissa L, seasonal aide, $8.00/hr
Harris, Richard A, environ spec III, $45,156
Harris, Susan M, environ engr II, $46,068
Harris, Terry A, seasonal aide, $9.05

Harrison, Ashley D, environ spec I, $29,976
Harris-Schott, Holly K, seasonal aide, $8.90/hr
Hartley, Darrell, environ engr III, $55,416
Hartman, Lynn A, environ spec III, $41,940
Hartwig, John L, seasonal aide, $8.90/hr
Harvey, Rodney E, seasonal aide, $8.00/hr
Harwood, Charles M, environ spec III, $41,940
Haselwander, Airin J, geologist II, $41,940
Hasker, Anna, sr ofc spt asst (keybrd), $25,824
Hassler, Tawnya L, admin ofc spt asst, $32,628
Hastert, Sara K, seasonal aide, $8.10/hr
Hasty, Richard W, environ spec III, $36,204
Hatcher, Gregory E, seasonal aide, $9.00/hr
Hausman, Gregory, seasonal aide, $8.50/hr
Haverly, Zachary, misc tech, $14.18/hr
Hawk, Candy N, storekeeper I, $25,824
Hawkins, Riley M, seasonal aide, $8.90/hr
Hawkins, Ryan D, seasonal aide, $8.00/hr
Hawkins, Terry L, geologist III, $50,040
Hayes, Peter T, seasonal aide, $9.25/hr
Hays, Charles R, planner II, $51,096
Hays, Kerry P, natural resources mgr b1, $41,927
Head, Bethany, environ spec III, $41,940
Head, Charlton, asst cook, $10.65/hr
Head, Erin L, seasonal aide, $8.00/hr
Heaney, Denzil, park/historic site spec III, $40,380
Hearne, Sarah, environ spec III, $41,940
Heather, Mary L, seasonal aide, $8.00/hr
Heaton, Michael T, environ scientist, $52,092
Heberlie, Karl F, park maint wkr III, $30,984
Hebner, Gayle M, seasonal aide, $8.74/hr
Hebrank, Arthur W, natural resources mgr b1, $52,091
Heckenkamp, Susan M, environ engr IV, $66,720
Hedrick, David, bldg const wkr II, $33,180
Hedrick, Richard M, bldg const wkr II, $36,204
Heet, Cheryl A, sr ofc spt asst (keybrd), $25,824
Hefner, Helen M, seasonal aide, $8.00/hr
Hefner, Michael L, environ engr II, $51,096
Heimann, Howard D, seasonal aide, $8.90/hr
Heimbeaugh, Roy, capital imprvmts spec II, $50,040
Heimsoth, Christopher K, environ spec III, $41,940
Heine, Kurt W, environ spec I, $30,984
Heinemann, Shona L, seasonal aide, $8.47/hr
Heinrich, Debra, ofc spt asst (keybrd), $23,160
Heisler, Jacqueline E, sr ofc spt asst (keybrd), $29,904
Heisterberg, John, environ engr I, $41,940
Helgason, James, environ mgr b1, $57,725
Hellums, Denise M, seasonal aide, $8.81/hr
Helm, Meghan R, seasonal aide, $7,200
Helmig, Darlene M, environ sup, $51,096
Helming, Megan R, ofc spt asst (keybrd), $22,536
Helton, Charles S, park ranger sergeant, $42,708
Helton, Danny, park maint wkr III, $30,420
Helton, Dennis, sr ofc spt asst (keybrd), $25,824
Helwig, Zane, misc tech, $14.18/hr
Henderson, Christina Y, seasonal aide, $9.00/hr
Henderson, Justin W, seasonal aide, $8.90/hr
Henderson, Nathan M, seasonal aide, $8.25/hr
Hendrickson, Laura L, natural resources mgr b2, $63,905
Hendrix, Elaine M, seasonal aide, $8.00/hr
Henley, Carrie R, mgmt analysis spec II, $44,304
Hennen, Damon A, park maint wkr III, $34,356
Hennessy, Timothy, park maint wkr III, $27,084
Henrikson, Jan M, interpretive resource tech, $30,420
Henroid, Joshua B, park ranger sergeant, $47,892
Henry, Erin, environ spec II, $34,944
Henry, Vincent A, environ spec III, $41,940
Henson, Clay B, seasonal aide, $8.90/hr
Henson, Michael J, tech asst IV, $34,944
Herbst, Thomas G, geologist I, $36,204
Herigon, David, natural resources mgr b1, $50,045
Hermann, Alexander J, seasonal aide, $9.92/hr
Herring, Christopher L, seasonal aide, $8.00/hr
Hess, Alana L, environ engr III, $55,416
Hess, Kevin D, environ mgr b2, $57,725
Hess, Wanda J, seasonal aide, $8.89/hr
Hesse, Constance A, sr ofc spt asst (keybrd), $12,917
Heth, Rachel, environ spec III, $40,380
Hickman, Lullel H, park maint wkr III, $30,420

Hicks, Frederick J, risk mgmt spec II, $55,416
Higa, Samantha, busser, $8.00/hr
Higa, Samantha, wait staff, $4.00/hr
Higgerson, Elizabeth, seasonal aide, $9.09
Higgins, Jeff L, park maint wkr III, $34,356
Higgins, Susan J, environ spec III, $41,940
Hill, Barry L, park maint wkr III, $33,744
Hill, Braxton R, seasonal aide, $8.41/hr
Hill, Jasmin, misc tech, $14.18/hr
Hill, Joshua D, tech asst II, $28,104
Hill, Mason T, seasonal aide, $8.41/hr
Hill, Misty A, pers analyst II, $37,548
Hill, Roy L, park maint wkr II, $29,904
Hillis, Dustin D, seasonal aide, $9.50/hr
Hillis, Jeffrey J, environ spec II, $36,204
Hillygus, Patrick A, park maint wkr II, $26,652
Hilton, Vicki L, admin ofc spt asst, $29,004
Hinchey, Michael D, seasonal aide, $8.47/hr
Hindman, Jordan A, environ engr I, $43,488
Hinkle, Dale L, seasonal aide, $8.00/hr
Hinkson, Robert C, misc tech, $24.56/hr
Hirsch, Brian, misc prof, $14.18/hr
Hirsch, Larry B, fiscal & administrative mgr b2, $55,360
Hirschvogel, Lacey, environ spec II, $37,548
Hirtz, Katie, environ scientist, $46,068
Ho, Yun, seasonal aide, $3,600
Hoback-Reichl, Tammy R, accounting spec III, $47,892
Hobbs, Deborah, sr ofc spt asst (keybrd), $26,232
Hodgdon, Drew, environ spec III, $41,940
Hodges, Cheri L, ofc spt asst (keybrd), $23,160
Hodges, Mark, interpretive resource spec II, $26,208
Hoemann, Rachel E, interpretive resource tech, $29,004
Hoffmann, Kenneth W, seasonal aide, $8.25/hr
Hogan, Steven R, park ranger, $36,204
Hoggatt, Jennifer A, designated principal asst div, $60,111
Hohl, Eric L, tech asst III, $31,512
Hoisington, Dana M, interpretive resource spec II, $34,944
Hoke, John, environ mgr b2, $59,750
Hoke, Kimberly, environ mgr b2, $61,339
Holden, Nakeisha, seasonal aide, $10.00/hr
Hollman, Kurt R, hydrologist III, $49,128
Holmer, Katy, natural resources steward, $44,304
Holst, Elizabeth S, seasonal aide, $24.97/hr
Holtmeyer, Dianne G, misc prof, $21.27/hr
Holzschuh, Roarke D, environ spec III, $47,892
Honig, Scott F, environ engr III, $56,520
Hood, Walter, seasonal aide, $13.00/hr
Hoover, John P, law enforce mgr b3, $66,727
Hopke, Mary I, environ spec III, $45,156
Hopkins, Abby M, seasonal aide, $8.00/hr
Hopkins, Bryan T, planner IV, $65,364
Horan, Shauna L, sr ofc spt asst (keybrd), $25,824
Horstmann, Amanda F, environ spec II, $36,204
Horton, John, hydrologist III, $46,068
Hotard, Stephanie P, environ spec II, $36,204
Hou, Lei, environ engr III, $55,416
Hough, Cole E, environ spec I, $29,976
Hovis, Andrew A, seasonal aide, $8.00/hr
Hovis, Chad D, tech asst IV, $34,944
Hovis, Kimberly A, seasonal aide, $8.47/hr
Howard, Dolly C, admin ofc spt asst, $28,104
Howell, Corey E, seasonal aide, $8.00/hr
Howerton, Shelli R, seasonal aide, $9.00/hr
Howlett, Courtney D, seasonal aide, $8.06
Hoyle, Nancy J, admin ofc spt asst, $28,104
Hubert, Jamie, interpretive resource coord, $41,940
Huckstep, Gary S, environ mgr b2, $57,633
Hueffmeier, Michael E, bldg const wkr II, $33,180
Hufford, Joshua, environ spec I, $29,976
Hughes, Belinda, graphics spv, $42,708
Hultberg, Sharon A, natural resources mgr b1, $46,935
Hummel, Jonathan J, seasonal aide, $8.00/hr
Hummel, Mary, admin ofc spt asst, $28,104
Humphrey, Aidan, misc prof, $13.56/hr
Humphrey, Hannah K, environ mgr b2, $60,111
Humphrey, Harold, seasonal aide, $12.00/hr
Hunt, Brian L, park maint wkr II, $26,652
Hunter, Judy K, sr ofc spt asst (keybrd), $25,824
Huntley, Amanda J, seasonal aide, $9.00/hr

Huntley, Maryann R, seasonal aide, $8.50/hr
Hurd, Charles N, seasonal aide, $8.15/hr
Hurt, Derick W, seasonal aide, $9.50/hr
Hurt, Linda M, seasonal aide, $8.00/hr
Hutson, Vicki L, natural resources mgr b1, $48,149
Hutton, Shannondoah Y, sr ofc spt asst (keybrd), $25,824
Huxol, Katherine, environ engr III, $55,416
Hynes, Leah D, mgmt analysis spec II, $27,757
Ickes, Debbie S, accounting spec II, $42,708
Imhoff, Cindy, interpretive resource spec II, $34,944
Inman, Byron B, seasonal aide, $8.00/hr
Inman, Rebecca K, seasonal aide, $8.00/hr
Irwin, Michael, environ scientist, $46,068
Iski, Vicki N, seasonal aide, $8.68/hr
Jaafari, Maher, environ mgr b1, $61,210
Jabben, Steven L, park ranger, $37,548
Jackson, Dane G, seasonal aide, $8.00/hr
Jackson, Jeremiah S, geologist III, $41,940
Jackson, Stephen R, chemist III, $41,172
Jackson, Victoria S, interpretive resource spec II, $34,944
Jaco, Paul, park ranger cpl, $42,708
Jacobi, Laura G, seasonal aide, $9.16/hr
Jacobs, Brad, park maint wkr II, $26,652
Jacobs, Suzanne R, seasonal aide, $14.12/hr
Jacobsen, Laura A, seasonal aide, $8.00/hr
Jaegers, Bret M, misc prof, $11.13/hr
James, Diane R, administrative asst, $37,974
James, Joy M, seasonal aide, $12.04
Jameson, Brooke S, seasonal aide, $16.00/hr
Jannings, Mitchell F, seasonal aide, $8.47/hr
Jarman, Gregory A, environ spec III, $41,940
Jarvis, Judith, sr ofc spt asst (keybrd), $26,652
Jasper, Spencer R, domestic serv sup, $35,855
Jeffery, Paul W, designated principal asst div, $75,245
Jeffreys, Ronald D, park maint wkr II, $26,652
Jeffries, Rachel L, park opps & plng coord, $40,380
Johanson, Daryl W, seasonal aide, $8.00/hr
Johnson, Bern A, environ engr II, $48,156
Johnson, Clifford L, environ engr II, $50,040
Johnson, David I, park maint wkr II, $29,412
Johnson, Heather M, sr ofc spt asst (keybrd), $25,824
Johnson, Hunter M, seasonal aide, $8.00/hr
Johnson, John E, environ spec III, $46,932
Johnson, Kristy L, seasonal aide, $8.00/hr
Johnson, Leonard E, water spec III, $40,380
Johnson, Rebekah L, seasonal aide, $8.41/hr
Johnson, Reid N, park ranger sergeant, $47,892
Johnson, Trista N, seasonal aide, $8.50/hr
Johnson, Valarie G, ofc spt asst (keybrd), $23,160
Johnson-Foston, Decarlos E, seasonal aide, $8.50/hr
Johnston, Christopher M, park ranger, $37,548
Jones, Brenda D, seasonal aide, $9.25/hr
Jones, Catherine J, planner III, $48,156
Jones, Connie M, seasonal aide, $9.09
Jones, Darrell L, seasonal aide, $8.96/hr
Jones, Jacob C, seasonal aide, $8.00/hr
Jones, Kenneth W, park maint wkr III, $31,512
Jones, Kent L, seasonal aide, $8.47/hr
Jones, Loren C, seasonal aide, $8.47/hr
Jones, Peter J, seasonal aide, $8.10/hr
Jones, Takota, seasonal aide, $8.00/hr
Jones, Trey, seasonal aide, $8.00/hr
Jones, Virginia L, ofc spt asst (keybrd), $23,160
Jordan, Almetta L, natural resources mgr b1, $43,485
Jordan, Eddie, park ranger, $37,548
Judge, Evadene, interpretive resource tech, $21,746
Julius, Abigail, seasonal aide, $8.00/hr
Kaden, Scott, environ mgr b2, $59,990
Kantola, Matthew E, interpretive resource spec I, $30,984
Kapraun, Joshua R, seasonal aide, $8.68/hr
Karas, Ethan G, seasonal aide, $8.00/hr
Kateman, Robert D, seasonal aide, $10.33/hr
Katich Mudd, Julia M, legal counsel, $50,264
Kator, Martin L, environ scientist, $48,156
Keas, Ashley N, environ engr II, $47,892
Keely, Jacquelyn D, sr ofc spt asst (keybrd), $25,824
Keilholz, Lisa J, budget analyst II, $37,548
Keim, Emily R, seasonal aide, $8.00/hr
Keim, Tyler L, seasonal aide, $8.47/hr

Kelchner, Loretta L, ofc spt asst (keybrd), $23,160
Kellner, Quinn P, natural resources mgr b1, $48,132
Kelly, David B, natural resrcs mgr, band 3, $73,225
Kelly, Megan D, seasonal aide, $9.00/hr
Kempker, Jaymee L, chemist III, $40,380
Kempker, Paul A, heavy equip oper, $29,976
Kempker, Sheri K, park opps & plng spec II, $34,944
Kennon, Gralyn K, park maint wkr III, $29,976
Kennon, Krista D, sr ofc spt asst (keybrd), $27,504
Kerley, Tony L, environ spec III, $41,940
Kerr, Stephanie M, seasonal aide, $8.00/hr
Kesl, Abigail, misc tech, $14.18/hr
Keune, Jana C, interpretive resource spec I, $15,496
Kifer, Evan A, environ spec III, $43,488
Kilburn, James M, park maint wkr II, $19,984
Kimes, Richard E, seasonal aide, $8.47/hr
Kincade, Clint D, law enforce mgr b1, $53,196
King, Brittany, environ spec II, $36,204
King, Charles R, park/historic site spec II, $34,944
King, Coy, environ spec II, $36,204
Kinkhorst, Donald L, environ spec III, $43,488
Kirchner, Marlene F, research analyst II, $39,624
Kirk, Tyler P, seasonal aide, $8.00/hr
Kirkman, Jason D, water spec III, $40,380
Kirsch, Richard, chemist IV, $47,892
Kissel, Jennifer D, environ spec II, $36,204
Kissiar, Kyle W, seasonal aide, $8.00/hr
Kissiar, Ronald, seasonal aide, $8.00/hr
Kitchell, Joshua D, park ranger cpl, $41,940
Kitts, Jeremy, park maint wkr II, $26,652
Klaus, Mark A, water spec III, $42,708
Kliethermes, Carolyn M, fiscal & administrative mgr b1, $51,872
Kliethermes, Elizabeth, sr ofc spt asst (keybrd), $25,824
Kliethermes, Kirsten N, seasonal aide, $10.00/hr
Kliethermes, Matthew S, environ spec III, $41,940
Kliethermes-Cluck, Gloria, pers analyst III, $38,232
Knaebel, Dan R, environ spec III, $43,488
Knerr, Zachary W, seasonal aide, $9.50/hr
Knight, Matthew K, environ spec III, $41,940
Knox, Rebecca L, seasonal aide, $8.00/hr
Knudsen, John E, seasonal aide, $8.50/hr
Koch, Kelly M, seasonal aide, $8.90/hr
Koenig, Theodore J, environ spec III, $43,488
Kohl, Lydia D, seasonal aide, $8.00/hr
Kolb, Kathryn A, environ engr II, $47,892
Kommer, Erik A, seasonal aide, $9.71/hr
Koon, Kenneth, environ mgr b2, $58,897
Kotur, Donald R, environ engr II, $47,892
Kovac, Alex R, park/historic site spec II, $38,928
Kraisinger, David M, park maint wkr II, $26,652
Kraus, Nathan P, environ engr III, $55,416
Kremer, Karen, designated principal asst div, $39,664
Krieftmeyer, Allen B, park maint wkr III, $32,628
Kroes, Beth L, environ spec III, $41,940
Kroes, Gregory D, park ranger, $37,548
Kruse, Michael D, environ spec III, $41,940
Kuebler, Dustin M, environ scientist, $49,128
Kuessner, John C, seasonal aide, $24.00/hr
Kump-Mitchell, Christine M, environ engr III, $49,874
Kunce, James B, park/historic site spec III, $38,928
Kunkel, Mark A, park maint wkr III, $34,356
Kunkel, Montana B, seasonal aide, $9.15/hr
Kuttenkuler, Jeffrey W, environ spec III, $41,940
Laboube, Alan, crpntr, $33,744
Ladd, Hallie L, environ spec II, $36,204
Lako, David C, natural resources mgr b1, $46,935
Lalond, Troy E, water spec III, $40,380
Lamb, David, staff dir, $79,866
Lambert, Beth A, procurement ofcr I, $37,548
Lamons, Jennifer L, environ spec III, $41,940
Lamouria, Joshua J, bldg const wkr II, $32,052
Lancaster, Alan C, park/historic site spec III, $41,940
Lancaster, Nona L, fiscal & administrative mgr b2, $64,158
Landrith, Marcus G, seasonal aide, $8.00/hr
Lane, Ronald D, seasonal aide, $8.51/hr
Lang, Steven, environ engr III, $55,416
Lange, Misty D, research analyst II, $36,204
Langer, Devin R, seasonal aide, $9.91/hr
Largent, Timothy W, exec I, $32,628

Largura, Ryan A, environ spec II, $36,204
Laughlin, Janet C, fiscal & administrative mgr b1, $55,687
Lawman, Andrew W, park maint wkr III, $29,976
Laws, Joel A, park/historic site spec III, $38,928
Lawson, Emily, environ spec I, $29,976
Le, Thuy T, environ engr III, $55,416
Leath, Mark, environ engr III, $55,416
Ledbetter, Bradley K, environ sup, $53,208
Lee, Gordon J, seasonal aide, $8.15/hr
Lee, Joseph, park maint wkr II, $27,084
Lehman, Julia K, seasonal aide, $8.00/hr
Lehman, Larry J, environ mgr b2, $60,013
Lehman, Marilyn K, planner II, $41,172
Lemaster, Carla, sr ofc spt asst (keybrd), $25,824
Lepage, Cynthia J, environ engr III, $57,744
Lepper, Erin, environ engr II, $47,892
Leroy, Robert C, planner II, $40,380
Leroy, Thomas, park maint wkr III, $30,420
Lewis, Carlotta D, park opps & plng spec II, $41,172
Lewis, Kenneth E, seasonal aide, $8.05
Lewis, Lauren, environ spec II, $36,204
Lewis, Sally A, seasonal aide, $9.00/hr
Leytham, Bobby L, seasonal aide, $8.00/hr
Li, Yunfeng, environ engr I, $41,940
Libbert, Aaron, mgmt analysis spec I, $37,548
Libby, Ernest P, heavy equip oper, $36,204
Libby, Katherine M, seasonal aide, $9.91/hr
Licklider, Rachel, admin ofc spt asst, $28,104
Light, Anita L, sr ofc spt asst (keybrd), $27,504
Light, Benjamin A, seasonal aide, $8.90/hr
Lightfoot, Amanda J, seasonal aide, $8.05
Likely, Katlyn R, seasonal aide, $8.00/hr
Limback, Rusty, seasonal aide, $8.00/hr
Lindell, David J, park ranger, $37,548
Lister, Kenneth B, environ spec III, $41,940
Little, David, environ engr III, $55,416
Lloyd, Glenn D, civil engr dam safety, $58,908
Loaiza, Richard J, park ranger, $37,548
Locke, Matthew J, seasonal aide, $8.10/hr
Logan, Allen L, environ spec III, $41,940
Logan, Angelo G, arch III, $57,744
Long, Ashleigh B, seasonal aide, $8.00/hr
Looney, Heidi M, sr ofc spt asst (keybrd), $25,824
Looten, Judith L, admin ofc spt asst, $28,104
Lott, Carolyn J, seasonal aide, $8.90/hr
Loucks, Miles J, seasonal aide, $8.00/hr
Love, James N, park maint wkr II, $26,652
Love, Richard M, park/historic site spec III, $46,932
Love, Susan P, interpretive resource tech, $29,004
Loveall, Rhonda S, sr ofc spt asst (keybrd), $27,504
Lovelace, Shelby B, park maint wkr II, $26,652
Loveland, Karen L, tech asst II, $32,628
Lowe, Kaitlin J, seasonal aide, $9.00/hr
Lowrance, L A, seasonal aide, $9.00/hr
Lucas, Heather, environ spec II, $36,204
Luebbering, Cynthia M, fiscal & administrative mgr b3, $71,399
Luebbering, Geoffrey B, accounting spec III, $51,096
Luebbert, J, environ engr II, $47,892
Luebrecht, Marishka A, seasonal aide, $8.47/hr
Lueckenhoff, Curtis F, chemist IV, $52,092
Lutes, Patrick J, bldg const spv, $36,888
Luther, Laura, environ sup, $51,096
Luttrell, Claudia J, seasonal aide, $8.00/hr
Lynxwiler, Ryan C, seasonal aide, $8.91/hr
Lyon, Gregory T, environ spec II, $34,944
Lyskowski, Daniel H, legal counsel, $57,000
M Tsadik, Birhanu K, environ spec III, $46,932
Mabee, Randy B, seasonal aide, $10.00/hr
Mabrey, Kathleen M, exec I, $30,420
Maddux, Charles E, seasonal aide, $9.00/hr
Maddux, Michael, environ spec III, $41,940
Madonodo, Tapiwa F, admin ofc spt asst, $28,104
Madras, John J, staff dir, $79,866
Mahan, Levi A, seasonal aide, $8.00/hr
Mahar, Brooke M, interpretive resource spec II, $34,944
Maher, Christopher C, environ spec III, $41,940
Mahurin, Leon, park maint wkr II, $30,384
Maize, Leland, environ spec III, $41,940
Maki, John W, park maint wkr III, $31,512

Maki, Teresa, seasonal aide, $8.00/hr
Maliro, Patricia, environ sup, $51,096
Malorin, David, environ sup, $51,096
Maness, Anna M, seasonal aide, $8.68/hr
March, Wes D, environ spec III, $41,940
Marcum, Larry M, seasonal aide, $8.33/hr
Markowski, Thomas J, environ mgr b1, $57,725
Marrs, Hayden G, seasonal aide, $8.00/hr
Martin, Catherine D, account clerk II, $26,652
Martin, Jennifer, sr ofc spt asst (keybrd), $25,824
Martin, Joshua J, environ engr II, $47,892
Martin, Michael, environ sup, $51,096
Martin, Tiffani, pers analyst II, $41,940
Martin, Wayland M, seasonal aide, $9.16/hr
Martineau, Jacques P, water spec III, $40,380
Mason, Tracey J, geologist II, $41,940
Massey, Shawn C, environ spec I, $29,976
Massman, Denise J, procurement ofcr II, $45,156
Masterson, Nancy A, natural resources mgr b1, $53,196
Mathis, Nancy S, environ sup, $51,096
Mattes, Roy J, environ engr II, $52,092
Matthews, Diane L, mgmt analysis spec II, $42,708
Mattingly, Timothy C, environ spec III, $44,304
Matzenbacher, Craig C, park/historic site spec III, $39,624
Maus, Hannah C, seasonal aide, $8.00/hr
Maxson, Stanley D, seasonal aide, $9.41/hr
Mayberry, Foster, seasonal aide, $10.00/hr
Mayberry, Joseph R, seasonal aide, $8.00/hr
Mayfield, Benjamin G, park ranger, $37,548
Mayus, Andrea L, environ spec I, $30,984
McCain, Sandra L, park/historic site spec III, $43,488
McCann, Mark E, park maint wkr II, $25,824
McCarty, James K, natural resources mgr b2, $62,651
McClanahan, Andrew M, park ranger, $38,232
McCord, Sam, environ spec III, $44,304
McCurren, Brian, environ engr III, $57,744
McDaniel, Ashley D, environ spec III, $41,940
McDaniel, Lesley J, park/historic site spec III, $40,380
McDonald, Brenna E, geologist II, $41,940
McDonald, Linda A, sr ofc spt asst (keybrd), $27,504
McEwen, Jimmy R, seasonal aide, $8.90/hr
McFadden, Garry W, park maint wkr II, $19,984
McFarland, James M, seasonal aide, $8.68/hr
McGhee, Candice A, environ spec III, $46,068
McGhee, Valeta, ofc spt asst (keybrd), $16,205
McGlaughlin, Tempe M, hostess, $8.00/hr
McGlaughlin, Tempe M, wait staff, $4.00/hr
McIntosh, Steve A, environ mgr b2, $66,727
McKittrick, Paul D, seasonal aide, $8.00/hr
McLane, Robert S, occuptnl sfty & hlth cnslt III, $43,488
McMichael, Angela, fiscal & administrative mgr b2, $58,868
McMurphy, Danny J, seasonal aide, $8.00/hr
McNally, Melanie K, accounting spec II, $41,172
McNeal, Crystal, ofc spt asst (keybrd), $23,160
McNeil, Makayla C, seasonal aide, $8.00/hr
McNeill, Brooks A, environ spec III, $42,708
McPherson, Aimee, misc tech, $14.18/hr
McWilliams, Melissa K, tech asst II, $28,104
Mebruer, Linda S, admin ofc spt asst, $32,052
Medlock, Eric L, environ scientist, $48,156
Medlock, Vicki L, sr ofc spt asst (keybrd), $19,375
Meeker, David J, park maint wkr II, $25,824
Mefrakis, Refaat, design/develop/survey mgr b2, $68,170
Meinert, Dennis M, natural resources steward, $51,096
Melancon, Dennis R, bldg const wkr II, $33,180
Melancon, Mary E, park maint wkr II, $26,652
Mellerup, Randy, park maint wkr III, $31,512
Melsha, Donald L, seasonal aide, $8.81/hr
Meredith, Colleen F, staff dir, $73,225
Merrick, Nicholas D, seasonal aide, $8.50/hr
Merseal, Mikel, seasonal aide, $8.41/hr
Mertens, Janet P, fiscal & administrative mgr b2, $76,255
Meyer, Brian, park maint wkr II, $26,652
Meyer, Brian L, bldg const wkr II, $32,052
Meyer, Erin B, environ spec III, $41,940
Meyer, Jacob L, seasonal aide, $9.15/hr
Meyer, Timothy E, seasonal aide, $10.00/hr
Meyers, Leasue, environ engr II, $47,892
Meyers, Roger W, water spec III, $40,380

Michaelson, David L, environ sup, $53,208
Milberg, Lynn, environ mgr b1, $57,633
Miles, Joan K, sr ofc spt asst (keybrd), $12,917
Miller, Brian K, park/historic site spec II, $42,708
Miller, Christopher R, environ spec III, $41,940
Miller, Eddie, bldg const wkr II, $32,052
Miller, Elodia, seasonal aide, $8.81/hr
Miller, Eric G, seasonal aide, $8.00/hr
Miller, Jeffrey E, seasonal aide, $8.00/hr
Miller, Justin, seasonal aide, $8.00/hr
Miller, Lori K, sr ofc spt asst (keybrd), $25,824
Miller, Martin A, legal counsel, $88,880
Miller, Michael R, interpretive resource spc III, $37,548
Miller, Richard S, seasonal aide, $9.12/hr
Miller, Shelby, environ spec II, $36,204
Miller, Sidney A, seasonal aide, $8.78/hr
Miller, Suzette, seasonal aide, $8.00/hr
Miller, Wally D, environ spec III, $45,156
Miller, William H, seasonal aide, $8.96/hr
Mills, Susan, admin ofc spt asst, $28,104
Milne, Janna E, seasonal aide, $8.00/hr
Mitchell, Bradley A, geologist II, $41,940
Mitchell, Diane L, seasonal aide, $8.56/hr
Mitchell, Holly R, interpretive resource tech, $29,004
Mitchell, Kirk, environ spec III, $44,304
Mizell, Joseph M, seasonal aide, $8.00/hr
Moeller, Ronald C, misc prof, $26.47/hr
Mohammadi, Khosrow N, staff dir, $73,225
Mongler, Skyler, seasonal aide, $8.00/hr
Montgomery, Chelsi N, seasonal aide, $8.50/hr
Moore, Aaron L, park maint wkr III, $30,420
Moore, Ben L, environ engr III, $58,908
Moore, Kyra L, staff dir, $79,866
Moore, Linda S, sr ofc spt asst (keybrd), $25,824
Moore, Lorian D, seasonal aide, $8.68/hr
Moore, Penny S, admin ofc spt asst, $30,984
Moore, Roger W, park ranger, $38,232
Moore, Tina, admin ofc spt asst, $29,004
Morang, Lawrence A, seasonal aide, $9.11/hr
Moreau, Alan M, environ spec III, $41,940
Morgan, Andrew P, seasonal aide, $8.00/hr
Morgan, Anne D, environ spec III, $45,156
Morris, Amber D, seasonal aide, $8.00/hr
Morris, Paul H, environ sup, $54,288
Morrison, Judy R, environ spec I, $29,976
Morrow, Richard A, environ spec III, $41,940
Mortenson, Nicole K, sr ofc spt asst (keybrd), $25,824
Moss, Stephen, environ spec III, $41,940
Mueller, Michael J, environ sup, $54,288
Mueller, Paul E, environ spec III, $47,892
Mueller, Phillip L, seasonal aide, $9.00/hr
Mueller, Theresa A, exec II, $38,928
Muenks, Diane M, admin ofc spt asst, $29,004
Muenks, Shawn C, environ engr III, $55,416
Muessig, Dana M, hr mgr b2, $55,146
Mukhtar, Hashim K, environ spec III, $44,304
Mulhearn, Mary H, special asst prof, $70,000
Mullen, John E, environ spec III, $47,892
Mullich, Edward H, park maint wkr II, $19,984
Mulvany, Patrick, geologist IV, $58,908
Murphy, Mackenzie J, seasonal aide, $8.70/hr
Murphy, Rabahka K, sr ofc spt asst (keybrd), $25,824
Murrell, Raymond W, park maint wkr III, $33,180
Muschany, John D, natural resources mgr b1, $57,725
Musick, Ethan, environ spec I, $29,976
Mussey, Madalyn M, seasonal aide, $8.41/hr
Muzio, Peter M, environ spec III, $41,940
Myers, Hannah E, seasonal aide, $8.90/hr
Myers, Mary E, environ mgr b2, $57,724
Myers, Paul F, environ scientist, $49,128
Myers, Scott M, park maint wkr III, $29,496
Nacy, Kathleen M, budget analyst III, $49,128
Nagel, Christopher, staff dir, $73,225
Nahach, James, chemist III, $47,892
Nahach, Lisa, pub info spec II, $33,744
Natt, Dallas T, seasonal aide, $8.00/hr
Ndubuka, Chinwe I, environ sup, $49,128
Neal, Kenneth E, park/historic site spec II, $36,204
Neeley, Dana L, seasonal aide, $10.66/hr

Neeley, Sharon L, seasonal aide, $8.96/hr
Neer, Branden, park maint wkr II, $26,652
Nelson, Glenn R, sr ofc spt asst (keybrd), $14,456
Nelson, Kyle B, bldg const wkr I, $29,004
Nelson, Terry W, environ spec III, $41,940
Neubauer, Michelle, interpretive resource tech, $21,746
Neuman, Natasha R, seasonal aide, $8.41/hr
Neumann, Margaret E, exec I, $32,052
Newberry, James M, natural resources mgr b1, $51,096
Newberry, Traci A, environ sup, $54,288
Newby, Brian, environ scientist, $48,156
Newman, Larry A, park maint wkr III, $32,628
Newman, Melissa, designated principal asst div, $41,220
Nicastro, Carla, seasonal aide, $12.04
Nichols, John R, environ spec III, $41,940
Nichols, Melissa J, chemist III, $40,380
Nickell, Ann E, tech asst IV, $40,380
Nickelson, Benjamin T, pub info coor, $38,928
Nicolli, Melissa M, seasonal aide, $9.05
Nieman, Ashley, busser, $8.00/hr
Nieman, Ashley, wait staff, $4.00/hr
Niemeyer, Randy, environ sup, $56,520
Nihira, Maggie, environ spec III, $41,940
Nilges, Robert A, environ sup, $56,520
Nodine, Brian L, environ spec III, $44,304
Nolan, Pauline, ofc spt asst (keybrd), $23,160
Norcross, Seth, environ spec III, $41,940
Nordwald, Danny F, tech asst IV, $36,204
Norfleet, Alyce M, seasonal aide, $9.57/hr
Norfleet-Aiken, Miya M, seasonal aide, $10.00/hr
Norman, Randall S, park maint wkr III, $30,420
Nowack, Anna, environ spec III, $41,940
Noyes, Travis W, seasonal aide, $8.00/hr
Nuernberger, Logan P, park opps & plng spec I, $35,568
Nunn, Alexander B, seasonal aide, $8.30/hr
Nunn, Roy, seasonal aide, $9.71/hr
Nunn, William W, park maint wkr II, $30,384
Nussbaum, Richard A, environ mgr b2, $71,105
Nykodym, David, environ spec II, $36,204
Obenauer, Loretta J, seasonal aide, $9.16/hr
O'Dell, Johnny, environ spec III, $41,940
Oehring, Ciara R, environ spec II, $36,204
Oeltjen, Hannah D, seasonal aide, $8.05
Oesterly, Therese L, fiscal & administrative mgr b1, $59,611
Offu, David T, environ sup, $49,128
Offutt, Anna R, seasonal aide, $9.12/hr
Oglesby, Michelle E, environ spec III, $41,940
Ohnersorgen, Michael A, archaeologist, $38,928
O'Keefe, Christine M, environ spec III, $42,708
Oliphant, Echo L, seasonal aide, $8.00/hr
Olive, Vickie A, environ spec III, $44,304
Oliver, Sara E, ofc spt asst (keybrd), $23,160
Olson, James R, park maint wkr II, $26,652
Oneal, Ryan L, seasonal aide, $8.47/hr
O'Neil, Nathan J, environ sup, $49,128
Oravetz, Angela M, environ spec III, $41,940
Orazio, Anthony J, seasonal aide, $8.00/hr
Orbin, Jacob S, seasonal aide, $8.00/hr
Orf, Trenton J, seasonal aide, $8.00/hr
O'Rourke, Kyle, environ spec II, $36,204
Osborn, Mark W, environ spec III, $45,156
Ossenfort, Charles H, seasonal aide, $8.05
Otto, Erik, interpretive resource spec III, $39,624
Overbey, Tara K, admin ofc spt asst, $29,004
Overhoff, Malinda C, admin ofc spt asst, $31,512
Owens, Katherine E, museum curator II, $40,380
Owens, Sheila Y, admin ofc spt asst, $29,976
Owensby, Stephen D, seasonal aide, $8.47/hr
Pacheco, Rebeca V, exec II, $36,204
Paige, Adam J, environ spec II, $34,944
Paintner, Jerald J, park maint wkr III, $32,628
Palmer, Adria L, tech asst II, $28,104
Parker, Arvin C, seasonal aide, $8.00/hr
Parker, Linda K, seasonal aide, $8.00/hr
Parker, Matthew, geologist III, $51,096
Parker-Fullmer, Sarah A, mgmt analysis spec II, $41,940
Parmley, Jordan L, seasonal aide, $8.00/hr
Parris, Michael E, environ spec III, $46,932
Parrott, Tabatha L, sr ofc spt asst (keybrd), $25,824

Pate, John P, geologist II, $41,940
Patten, Orville H, seasonal aide, $11.80/hr
Patterson, Bernard D, seasonal aide, $8.90/hr
Patterson, Lavette, sr ofc spt asst (keybrd), $25,404
Patterson, Martha L, seasonal aide, $8.90/hr
Patterson, Tiffany J, natural resources mgr b1, $51,096
Pattinson, Kristen R, environ sup, $51,096
Patton, Michael L, park ranger cpl, $46,932
Pauley, Andrew C, seasonal aide, $8.00/hr
Pauley, Vanessa R, seasonal aide, $8.47/hr
Payne, Cody, seasonal aide, $8.00/hr
Payne, Jeremy, environ spec III, $41,940
Payne, Stan, environ engr II, $47,892
Payton, Laura L, exec I, $30,984
Pedigo, Kimberly E, park maint wkr II, $25,824
Pelikan, Daniel J, environ engr II, $47,892
Pellett, Jennifer L, environ spec III, $43,488
Peltz, Patrick K, environ spec III, $41,940
Pemberton, Angela L, mgmt analysis spec I, $41,940
Pennington, Bobbie, environ spec III, $41,940
Peoples, Elizabeth, seasonal aide, $8.50/hr
Perkins, Christopher, park ranger, $46,932
Perrigo, Penny L, admin ofc spt asst, $29,004
Perry, Kelsey, misc tech, $14.18/hr
Perry, Madelynn C, seasonal aide, $8.00/hr
Perry, Tamara, environ spec III, $42,708
Persell, Anna M, natural resources mgr b1, $46,062
Persinger, Ryan M, interpretive resource spec II, $34,944
Peters, Heather, environ scientist, $48,156
Peterson, William G, seasonal aide, $8.47/hr
Pfaff, Nicholas J, seasonal aide, $8.00/hr
Philipps, Michael D, special asst ofc & clerical, $32,320
Phillips, Gerald A, bldg const wkr II, $36,204
Phillips, Kara E, seasonal aide, $8.00/hr
Phipps, Andrew D, seasonal aide, $8.00/hr
Pickens, Elizabeth A, sr ofc spt asst (keybrd), $30,924
Pickerell, Whitney, accounting spec I, $34,944
Piepmeier-Goodwin, Dianne I, seasonal aide, $8.08
Pierce, Anthony, environ spec III, $41,940
Pierce, Daniel E, ofc worker misc, $13.66/hr
Pierce, Daniel W, park maint wkr II, $26,652
Pierce, Larry, environ mgr b2, $57,725
Pierce, Michael C, seasonal aide, $8.50/hr
Pigford, Desiree M, planner II, $40,380
Pine, Jamie M, accounting spec II, $40,380
Pinson, Edward J, environ spec III, $46,068
Plassmeyer, Christopher J, environ spec III, $41,940
Plassmeyer, James L, environ sup, $52,092
Plemmons, Eric L, seasonal aide, $8.00/hr
Plymell, Gary L, heavy equip oper, $29,496
Poehlman, Burton E, park maint wkr II, $26,652
Pogue, Diana J, seasonal aide, $8.60/hr
Pointer, Janet A, seasonal aide, $20.00/hr
Popoca, Reynaldo, seasonal aide, $10.00/hr
Porter, Emily, seasonal aide, $8.50/hr
Porth, Sutton M, seasonal aide, $8.00/hr
Post, Andrew S, seasonal aide, $8.00/hr
Potteiger, Troy, environ spec III, $41,940
Potter, Kimberly, sr ofc spt asst (keybrd), $25,824
Potter, Maria, natural resources mgr b1, $48,149
Potter, Pattrick M, investigation mgr b1, $51,096
Potthast, David H, environ spec III, $46,068
Powell, Christina M, dishwasher, $8.00/hr
Powell, Christina M, wait staff, $4.00/hr
Poynor, Joshua S, environ spec III, $43,488
Prather, Janice F, seasonal aide, $8.50/hr
Prawl, Toni M, natural resources mgr b2, $58,908
Prenger, Janet A, tech asst IV, $38,232
Prenger, Logan, seasonal aide, $8.00/hr
Prenger, Staci, mgmt analysis spec I, $44,304
President, Antwane, environ spec II, $36,204
Pretz, Richard E, environ sup, $57,744
Prewett, Jerry L, dpty div dir, $80,152
Price, Dakota P, seasonal aide, $8.90/hr
Price, Janet E, interpretive resource spc III, $39,624
Price, Peter, environ mgr b2, $58,897
Pringer, Sara, acct III, $43,488
Pritchett, Jesse W, seasonal aide, $8.00/hr
Prouhet, Elizabeth A, admin ofc spt asst, $29,004

Pupek, Mira N, seasonal aide, $9.91/hr
Pyatt, Charles E, seasonal aide, $12.04
Quinalty, Larry, seasonal aide, $9.88/hr
Rackers, Victor L, environ engr III, $55,416
Radcliffe, Christopher E, environ spec III, $41,940
Rader, Mark, environ mgr b2, $57,725
Ralph, Glynn A, park maint wkr II, $30,384
Ramsey, Theresa A, interpretive resource spc III, $38,928
Randolph, Kate J, seasonal aide, $8.00/hr
Randolph, Robert W, environ engr II, $51,096
Raney, Todd W, environ spec III, $44,304
Raney, Travis S, seasonal aide, $8.00/hr
Rangen, Kathleen L, environ spec III, $41,940
Rausch, Donna J, natural resources mgr b1, $41,927
Ray, Christopher, environ spec III, $41,940
Ray, Debra S, natural resources mgr b1, $46,935
Raymond, Randall E, misc prof, $30.76/hr
Rea, Donald W, environ engr II, $47,892
Reams, Drew A, seasonal aide, $8.00/hr
Recker, Lewis H, seasonal aide, $8.00/hr
Record, Douglas A, arch III, $63,996
Rector, Molly L, seasonal aide, $8.00/hr
Redden, Jeremy, environ spec III, $43,488
Reece, Ryan A, seasonal aide, $8.47/hr
Reed, Andrew J, environ spec III, $41,940
Reed, Billy B, tech asst IV, $37,548
Reed, Walter A, seasonal aide, $8.00/hr
Reed, Wilson K, park maint wkr III, $31,512
Reese, Adrianna R, seasonal aide, $8.25/hr
Reeves, Christopher D, seasonal aide, $9.11/hr
Reeves, Kenya S, seasonal aide, $8.70/hr
Rehard, James W, natural resources mgr b2, $61,339
Reich, Keaton V, seasonal aide, $8.68/hr
Reimer, Michelle, environ spec III, $41,940
Reinagel, Susan K, seasonal aide, $8.47/hr
Reinert, Diana L, environ spec III, $41,940
Reinhardt, Diane G, environ engr II, $38,322
Reinkemeyer, Alan J, environ mgr b3, $73,385
Renfro, John P, seasonal aide, $9.07
Resch, Abilene N, seasonal aide, $8.90/hr
Reynolds, David, park/historic site spec III, $38,928
Rhodes, Judith A, seasonal aide, $8.00/hr
Rice, Heidi R, environ spec III, $41,940
Richards, Amy L, admin ofc spt asst, $29,004
Richards, Randall W, bldg const wkr II, $34,356
Richardson, Betty F, seasonal aide, $8.68/hr
Richardson, Courtney, sr ofc spt asst (keybrd), $26,652
Richardson, Norman, park maint wkr II, $29,904
Richmond, Andrew P, pub info coor, $43,488
Richter, John K, tech asst I, $24,612
Ricketts, Harry M, environ spec III, $45,156
Ridder, Sarah G, seasonal aide, $8.68/hr
Rideout, Jennifer A, seasonal aide, $8.00/hr
Rielly, Patricia A, environ sup, $54,288
Rielly, Timothy J, environ mgr b3, $70,447
Riley, Mary A, seasonal aide, $8.68/hr
Ritzu, David J, seasonal aide, $9.45/hr
Rizo, Jaime L, environ spec II, $36,204
Robbins, Chelsea M, seasonal aide, $10.00/hr
Robbins, Michael P, seasonal aide, $8.90/hr
Roberto, Aarick, sr ofc spt asst (keybrd), $25,824
Roberts, Leonard C, park maint wkr II, $26,652
Roberts, Mitchell W, environ mgr b3, $73,385
Roberts, Sterling M, misc tech, $14.18/hr
Roberts, Wane, environ engr III, $55,416
Robertson, Carl G, environ sup, $57,744
Robertson, Jarrod J, environ spec III, $41,940
Robinett, Jacob R, environ engr II, $47,892
Robinett, Larry S, environ spec III, $42,708
Robinett, Terry E, seasonal aide, $9.91/hr
Robins, James M, park maint wkr II, $26,652
Robinson, Faith S, wait staff, $4.00/hr
Robinson, Faith S, busser, $8.00/hr
Robinson, Jeff S, natural resources mgr b1, $48,149
Robinson, Kennedy S, seasonal aide, $8.00/hr
Robinson, Lucas S, seasonal aide, $8.00/hr
Robinson, Valerie J, environ spec III, $41,940
Robson, Kelly, environ scientist, $50,040
Rodenberg, Darryl, misc tech, $14.18/hr
Roderick, Nola A, seasonal aide, $9.07
Roggensees, David P, natural resources mgr b1, $45,163
Rohr, Cary E, seasonal aide, $8.07
Rohrer, Kai J, seasonal aide, $8.47/hr
Rohter, Jacob E, tech asst III, $30,984
Rollins, Gary K, environ mgr b2, $57,724
Romans, Stephanie L, chemist II, $36,204
Rosania, Corinne, environ mgr b1, $55,504
Roscetti, Thomas R, environ engr III, $55,416
Rose, Nicholas B, seasonal aide, $8.47/hr
Rosewicz, Eric, seasonal aide, $8.41/hr
Ross, Ashton, ofc worker misc, $11.83/hr
Rost, Rebecca J, cultural resource pres II, $41,940
Roth, Amber M, seasonal aide, $8.00/hr
Roth, Megan R, busser, $8.00/hr
Roth, Megan R, wait staff, $4.00/hr
Roth, Tonya A, accounting spec II, $49,128
Rouse, Karen J, environ mgr b1, $56,427
Roussin, Glen D, environ spec II, $36,204
Routh, Franklin D, park ranger cpl, $46,068
Rowlett, Sheri, research analyst I, $29,976
Roy, Jessica A, seasonal aide, $9.41/hr
Ruble, Trevor J, seasonal aide, $8.47/hr
Ruby, David B, seasonal aide, $8.00/hr
Ruddy, Michael W, environ spec III, $44,304
Runyan, Mark A, fiscal & administrative mgr b2, $53,208
Rush, Janet L, sr ofc spt asst (keybrd), $25,824
Rush, Rachel D, environ spec II, $34,944
Rush, Ray L, bldg const wkr II, $36,204
Rusk, Douglas L, natural resources mgr b1, $56,510
Russell, Dakota, interpretive resource spec II, $34,944
Rustige, John S, environ engr III, $61,332
Sala, Catherine M, admin ofc spt asst, $29,976
Saldana, Mariah H, seasonal aide, $10.00/hr
Salzbrenner, Theresa, research analyst II, $36,204
Sampsell, Todd A, dpty state dept dir, $111,100
Samuels, Terryonna R, seasonal aide, $8.00/hr
Sanders, Aaron J, park maint wkr II, $26,652
Sanders, Garrett M, seasonal aide, $8.00/hr
Sanders, Kenda R, fiscal & administrative mgr b1, $46,935
Sanders, Maebel E, seasonal aide, $9.15/hr
Sanford, Kara J, seasonal aide, $8.00/hr
Sanning, Julia, sr ofc spt asst (keybrd), $25,824
Sapp, Benjamin R, environ spec II, $36,204
Sappington, Eric J, environ sup, $61,332
Sarver, Randy, environ spec III, $48,156
Savage, David R, park/historic site spec III, $38,928
Savage-Clarke, Kristi, environ spec III, $41,940
Schaben, Darlene, admin ofc spt asst, $33,744
Schaefer, Carson D, seasonal aide, $8.00/hr
Schaffer, Adam J, environ spec III, $41,940
Schaub, Robert, chemist III, $40,380
Scheel, Gary L, seasonal aide, $8.15/hr
Scheel, Patrick L, tech asst IV, $34,944
Schell, Sarah E, seasonal aide, $10.00/hr
Schell, Steven R, interpretive resource coord, $41,940
Scheperle, Melina S, admin ofc spt asst, $29,496
Schimmel, Kurt V, seasonal aide, $11.00/hr
Schlechte, Patricia, seasonal aide, $8.96/hr
Schlegel, Fred J, environ engr III, $55,416
Schmid, Aubree V, seasonal aide, $8.90/hr
Schmidt, Aaron, dpty div dir, $84,520
Schmidt, Connie S, natural resources mgr b1, $49,104
Schmidt, Taylor R, seasonal aide, $8.00/hr
Schmitz, Thomas J, seasonal aide, $8.00/hr
Schneider, Amy E, seasonal aide, $10.00/hr
Schneider, Edward D, misc prof, $24.06
Schneider, Rachel E, environ engr I, $41,940
Schoen, Sandra, tech asst I, $25,404
Schott, Edmund R, natural resources mgr b1, $43,485
Schott, Ryan A, environ engr II, $47,892
Schrimpf, Anne M, admin ofc spt asst, $31,512
Schroeder, Dennis J, chemist III, $42,708
Schroer, Erica R, accounting spec II, $38,928
Schubert, Terry W, seasonal aide, $12.04
Schuelke, Joy D, sr ofc spt asst (keybrd), $25,824
Schuermann, Robert T, seasonal aide, $9.36/hr
Schuette, Bruce M, seasonal aide, $10.16/hr
Schuler, Paul, seasonal aide, $8.00/hr

Schulte, Cari, admin ofc spt asst, $30,984
Schulte, Natalie A, seasonal aide, $8.25/hr
Schulte, Rosemarie, fiscal & administrative mgr b1, $53,207
Schultz, Abigail M, environ spec II, $34,944
Schuster, M Crew, environ spec III, $41,940
Schwartze, Tyler J, park opps & plng coord, $41,172
Schwarz, Rachael L, exec I, $32,052
Scoggins, Stephanie A, sr ofc spt asst (keybrd), $25,824
Scollan, Daniel, environ spec III, $41,940
Scott, Kyle, natural resources mgr b1, $45,163
Scott, Michael C, seasonal aide, $10,560
Seabaugh, Ryan W, environ engr II, $47,892
See, David, environ spec II, $36,204
Seeger, Cheryl M, geologist IV, $55,416
Segi, Candice, busser, $8.00/hr
Segi, Candice, wait staff, $4.00/hr
Semsch, Karen E, admin ofc spt asst, $30,984
Senecal, Diedre, seasonal aide, $8.25/hr
Senters, Andrew J, interpretive resource spc III, $38,928
Shackelford, Brandon C, seasonal aide, $8.00/hr
Shafer, Devan D, park maint wkr III, $29,004
Shannon, William, sr ofc spt asst (keybrd), $28,452
Sharma, Sushmita, environ engr III, $53,208
Shaw, Fred E, tech asst III, $31,512
Shaw, Terry L, park ranger, $37,548
Shearrer, Dennis J, seasonal aide, $8.47/hr
Shearrer, Eric L, park ranger, $38,232
Shearrer, Gary L, seasonal aide, $8.47/hr
Shearrer, Todd D, park ranger, $37,548
Shelton, Floyd R, park maint wkr II, $27,948
Shelton, Janet L, seasonal aide, $8.81/hr
Shelton, Kenneth R, park maint wkr II, $27,084
Shepherd, Sean Z, seasonal aide, $9.15/hr
Sherman, Warner D, environ engr III, $53,208
Sherrill, Darrin S, park maint wkr III, $29,496
Shields, Heather A, seasonal aide, $8.00/hr
Shinn, Jamie D, environ sup, $53,208
Shockley, Ashley R, account clerk II, $26,232
Short, Zachary R, park maint wkr II, $26,652
Shovlin, Frank, environ spec II, $35,568
Shumpert, Melba J, seasonal aide, $10.00/hr
Sidebottom, James, environ scientist, $48,156
Sieg, Jennifer L, pub info spec I, $19,812
Siemens, Michael A, geologist II, $46,932
Sifers, Rachel M, seasonal aide, $8.50/hr
Sifford, Amanda M, auditor II, $38,928
Sigman, Stephen C, park ranger, $37,548
Sillanpa, Daniel A, seasonal aide, $10.41/hr
Silvey, James D, seasonal aide, $8.00/hr
Simmerly, Donna R, seasonal aide, $8.00/hr
Simmons, Akeera L, ofc spt asst (keybrd), $23,160
Simmons, Blake W, misc tech, $11.83/hr
Simmons, Daniel M, seasonal aide, $9.50/hr
Simmons, Wesley R, environ spec III, $41,940
Simms, Keith A, seasonal aide, $9.68/hr
Simms, Richard, environ spec III, $41,940
Simon, Kara L, environ spec III, $41,940
Simon, Paul R, civil engr dam safety, $55,416
Simpson, Angel L, seasonal aide, $8.00/hr
Simpson, Benjamin, seasonal aide, $8.68/hr
Simpson, Robert D, design engr III, $60,120
Sims, Thomas W, environ sup, $56,520
Sitton, Steven D, park/historic site spec III, $40,380
Sitzes, Charles F, seasonal aide, $8.59/hr
Skaggs, Charles R, seasonal aide, $8.31/hr
Skaggs, Cynthia L, seasonal aide, $12.17/hr
Skouby, Daniel H, environ engr III, $55,416
Skrukrud, Robert G, seasonal aide, $8.90/hr
Slais, Daniel J, seasonal aide, $8.68/hr
Slechta, Larry J, environ spec III, $42,708
Smith, Andrea C, environ spec III, $41,940
Smith, Anthony D, park/historic site spec I, $32,628
Smith, Chad M, bldg const wkr I, $29,004
Smith, Christopher A, seasonal aide, $8.91/hr
Smith, Cynthia, environ engr III, $56,520
Smith, Dennis L, seasonal aide, $10.00/hr
Smith, Garrett T, seasonal aide, $8.50/hr
Smith, Ian P, seasonal aide, $8.00/hr
Smith, Karen L, sr ofc spt asst (keybrd), $25,824

Smith, Kenneth, natural resources mgr b1, $43,485
Smith, Kevin C, exec I, $31,512
Smith, Kevin G, park maint wkr III, $30,420
Smith, Lorisa S, planner III, $51,096
Smith, Mandy, sr ofc spt asst (keybrd), $26,652
Smith, Michael, environ spec III, $41,940
Smith, Tamlyn R, seasonal aide, $8.68/hr
Smith, Timothy R, interpretive resource coord, $41,940
Smith, Toni-Marie E, seasonal aide, $8.90/hr
Snellen, Gregory R, environ spec III, $41,940
Snow, Marissa S, seasonal aide, $8.00/hr
Soenksen, Michelle L, interpretive resource spc III, $38,928
Son, Vicky, sr ofc spt asst (keybrd), $25,824
Sons, Cynthia D, seasonal aide, $8.00/hr
Sons, Paul R, park maint wkr II, $27,084
Spears, Tami, designated principal asst dept, $47,712
Spenard, Curtis J, park maint wkr II, $28,908
Spence, Katy N, seasonal aide, $8.00/hr
Spencer, Jeffrey R, seasonal aide, $12.04
Splain, Rebecca, seasonal aide, $8.50/hr
Sporleder, Nicole M, sr ofc spt asst (keybrd), $15,500
Stack, Ryan P, civil engr dam safety, $55,416
Stackhouse, Cody A, dishwasher, $8.00/hr
Stamp, Vernon L, park maint wkr II, $26,652
Stamp, Vesper B, park maint wkr III, $31,512
Stanley, Seanmichael, environ spec II, $36,204
Stansfield, Anita, planner III, $41,172
Stansfield, Michael, environ engr III, $62,664
Starbuck, Edith A, geologist IV, $55,416
Stark, David E, park ranger, $38,232
Starkey, Molly A, geologist II, $41,940
Starks, Bryce T, seasonal aide, $8.00/hr
Stark-Ukaga, Cathy E, seasonal aide, $10.00/hr
Starr, Jeffrey A, planner III, $52,092
Staus, Karen E, admin ofc spt asst, $28,104
Steacy, Brent L, natural resources mgr b1, $48,149
Steding, Bruce E, park maint wkr III, $34,944
Steinman, Stacia, exec I, $32,628
Stephens, Connie R, admin ofc spt asst, $21,746
Stephens, Michael W, seasonal aide, $15.39/hr
Stephenson, Chad A, environ engr II, $46,068
Sterling, Marcia L, acct I, $30,984
Stevens, Ericka, seasonal aide, $8.00/hr
Stevens, Jeffrey, environ spec III, $46,068
Stevens, Linda W, seasonal aide, $8.77/hr
Stewart, Catherine E, seasonal aide, $8.25/hr
Stewart, Jonathan W, environ spec II, $37,548
Stier, Donald H, planner III, $51,096
Stinson, Dennis R, environ mgr b2, $58,897
Stinson, Judy M, env edu & info spec II, $41,940
Stith, Brian K, natural resources mgr b2, $61,339
Stith, Michael R, environ spec II, $36,204
Stivers, Andrew R, environ spec I, $29,976
Stock, Terrence C, environ spec III, $42,708
Stockman, Cathy J, sr ofc spt asst (keybrd), $25,824
Stockman, Tina M, exec I, $32,628
Stokes, Jean, sr ofc spt asst (keybrd), $25,824
Stonebarger, David L, seasonal aide, $9.00/hr
Stoner, Sherri, geologist IV, $51,096
Stout, Robert D, special asst prof, $68,165
Stover, Karrie A, seasonal aide, $9.91/hr
Strain, Karla M, interpretive resource spec II, $34,944
Straughan, Kevin R, seasonal aide, $8.00/hr
Stroh, Michael C, environ spec III, $27,690
Strolberg, Jeffrey G, park maint wkr II, $30,924
Stroud, Zachary M, seasonal aide, $8.00/hr
Stuart, Robert B, environ engr III, $62,664
Stuecken, Lisa, budget analyst III, $53,208
Sturgess, Steven W, principal asst board/commisson, $68,704
Suhler, Nicholaus C, seasonal aide, $8.00/hr
Sullivan, Russell G, environ sup, $51,096
Surber, Jennifer, environ spec III, $42,708
Sutter, Mary Ann E, misc prof, $24.06
Swank, Bradley D, environ spec III, $41,940
Swaringim, Katelyn A, seasonal aide, $8.00/hr
Swartz, Richard P, environ sup, $51,096
Sweaney, Brenda L, admin ofc spt asst, $29,004
Swearingen, Gary D, park maint wkr II, $26,652
Swee, Kendra B, interpretive resource coord, $43,488

Sweeney, Kathy L, seasonal aide, $8.47/hr
Swinney, Charles L, seasonal aide, $8.20/hr
Swofford, Steven E, capital imprvmts spec II, $50,040
Syphert, Nathaniel S, seasonal aide, $8.00/hr
Talkington, Patricia A, seasonal aide, $8.00/hr
Taylor, Gregory B, seasonal aide, $8.00/hr
Taylor, William B, seasonal aide, $8.90/hr
Teague, Russell A, park maint wkr II, $26,652
Tearney, Karalee K, seasonal aide, $8.88/hr
Tebbenkamp, Cody A, environ spec III, $43,488
Tedford, Billie, seasonal aide, $8.00/hr
Tellman, Christie, sr ofc spt asst (keybrd), $25,824
Tellman, Konnor P, seasonal aide, $10.50/hr
Tellman, Taris, seasonal aide, $12.00/hr
Templeton, Warren D, seasonal aide, $8.50/hr
Terrill, Amy M, seasonal aide, $8.90/hr
Terrill, Nicholas S, seasonal aide, $9.50/hr
Terry, Jennifer L, human rel ofcr I, $41,172
Teson, Larry J, environ spec III, $45,156
Tharp, Carter J, environ spec III, $45,156
Thevary, Teresa, environ spec I, $29,976
Thirkield, Deshaun A, seasonal aide, $8.00/hr
Thomas, Anna M, seasonal aide, $8.00/hr
Thomas, Bradley D, seasonal aide, $8.00/hr
Thomas, Chadd W, park maint wkr II, $26,652
Thomas, Clara F, busser, $8.00/hr
Thomas, Clara F, wait staff, $4.00/hr
Thomas, Malcolm, park maint wkr II, $27,948
Thomas, Melissa L, busser, $8.00/hr
Thomas, Melissa L, wait staff, $4.00/hr
Thomas, Wanda D, domestic serv sup, $38,855
Thomason, Teresa K, environ spec III, $46,932
Thomeczek, Kevin M, environ spec III, $41,940
Thompson, Alexis E, busser, $8.00/hr
Thompson, Alexis E, wait staff, $4.00/hr
Thompson, Douglas, environ spec III, $46,932
Thompson, Dwayne W, park maint wkr III, $31,512
Thompson, Jason R, seasonal aide, $8.00/hr
Thompson, Keegan M, arch II, $47,892
Thompson, Keith D, park maint wkr III, $31,512
Thompson, Ralph L, environ spec III, $45,156
Thompson, Sharon A, admin ofc spt asst, $29,004
Thornton, Michael R, environ spec III, $41,940
Thurmon, Ronald G, park maint wkr III, $30,420
Tiefenthaler, Cheryl L, admin ofc spt asst, $28,104
Timmons, Terry N, misc prof, $27.74/hr
Tippett Mosby, Leanne J, div dir, $104,011
Todey, Kimberly D, natural resources mgr b1, $51,096
Toebben, Tonya, admin ofc spt asst, $28,104
Tolbers, Allen H, seasonal aide, $10.00/hr
Tomlin, Kenneth P, environ spec III, $41,940
Tomlinson, Joshua C, seasonal aide, $8.00/hr
Toops, Jerry, natural resources mgr b1, $25,023
Torrence, Megan, environ engr II, $47,892
Totten, Scott B, misc prof, $45.71/hr
Townsend, Jordyn N, busser, $8.00/hr
Townsend, Jordyn N, wait staff, $4.00/hr
Trelow, Tammy K, seasonal aide, $8.47/hr
Treu, Deanna M, hr mgr b1, $58,747
Tripp, Eric M, environ spec I, $30,984
Tripp, Gary J, park maint wkr III, $31,512
Troutt, Eric C, environ spec II, $34,944
Trovillion, Alexander P, seasonal aide, $8.00/hr
Trunko, Joseph L, environ sup, $56,520
Tschirgi, Kimberly S, planner II, $46,068
Tucker, H Diane, interpretive resource spc III, $41,172
Turner, Leonard L, park maint wkr II, $29,904
Turner, Robert P, bldg const wkr II, $33,744
Turner, Tanya S, environ sup, $51,096
Turpin, Jack, bldg const wkr II, $33,180
Turpin, Tim, natural resources steward, $46,068
Tuttle, Matthew C, seasonal aide, $8.00/hr
Twining Gerdes, Emilie R, environ spec III, $41,940
Uhlenbrock, Thomas J, special asst prof, $86,355
Uhlig, David, environ engr II, $55,416
Upendram, Sreedhar, econ, $56,520
Utterback, Megan S, seasonal aide, $8.00/hr
Vale, Eugene R, interpretive resource spc III, $39,624
Valerien, Dawn M, seasonal aide, $8.39/hr

Van Black, Matthew C, seasonal aide, $8.00/hr
Van Dyke, Donald F, environ scientist, $54,288
Van Patten, Regina R, special analyst prof, $47,975
Van Woert, Amanda N, cultural resource pres II, $40,380
Vance, Karan P, sr ofc spt asst (keybrd), $29,412
Vandegriffe, Wendy L, accounting spec I, $36,204
Vander Veen, Joshua S, environ scientist, $48,156
Vanover, William K, sr ofc spt asst (keybrd), $25,824
Vansel, Roger D, park maint wkr II, $26,652
Vansickle, Kayla, seasonal aide, $8.00/hr
Vaughn, Allison J, natural resources steward, $41,940
Vaughn, Chelsea T, seasonal aide, $9.00/hr
Vaughn, Ronald L, bldg const wkr II, $29,976
Vavra, Patrick, environ spec III, $41,940
Veasman, Sara B, environ spec III, $41,940
Veenstra, Erik M, seasonal aide, $9.05
Veit, Christopher J, environ sup, $51,096
Vernon, Rebecca, research analyst II, $36,204
Verslues, Kimberly L, sr ofc spt asst (keybrd), $25,824
Vierrether, Christopher B, geologist IV, $55,416
Viers, Archie R, park maint wkr II, $27,504
Villeme, Kadi, seasonal aide, $14.18/hr
Vit, Wendy, environ mgr b2, $61,241
Vitello, Diane C, environ engr II, $47,892
Vitello, Matthew C, environ engr II, $47,892
Vitullo, Angelo, environ spec III, $41,940
Vladeff, Bruce, seasonal aide, $12.00/hr
Vogelsang, Betty J, seasonal aide, $9.75/hr
Voigt, Vicki, geologist II, $41,940
Vollmer, Betty L, seasonal aide, $8.39/hr
Volner, Teresa D, seasonal aide, $8.00/hr
Von Holten, Amy M, seasonal aide, $8.25/hr
Voss, Robert, environ spec III, $41,940
Vrabec, Adam M, environ spec III, $45,156
Wade, Jill S, environ engr III, $41,558
Wadlow, Kevin W, seasonal aide, $8.00/hr
Wagner, Loren N, seasonal aide, $8.00/hr
Wagoner, Marlene, sr ofc spt asst (keybrd), $26,232
Wainaina, Caroline N, environ spec III, $45,156
Wakefield, Carl K, environ spec III, $41,940
Wakefield, Dustin J, seasonal aide, $8.00/hr
Wakefield, Hillary, environ spec III, $31,455
Walchshauser, David L, environ spec III, $41,940
Walk, Nancy J, seasonal aide, $8.70/hr
Walker, David L, environ engr II, $50,040
Walker, Scott M, planner II, $40,380
Walker, Steven R, environ scientist, $50,040
Wallace, Donald W, seasonal aide, $9.07
Wallace, James L, laborer II, $23,160
Wallace, Jane S, seasonal aide, $8.74/hr
Wallace, Kimberly E, seasonal aide, $10.00/hr
Wallace, Lorrie M, admin ofc spt asst, $28,104
Wallace, Virginia K, planner III, $60,120
Walls, Sandra J, seasonal aide, $8.25/hr
Walsh, Daniel P, graphic arts spec II, $29,004
Walsh, Evelyn M, seasonal aide, $8.55/hr
Walther, Justin L, seasonal aide, $8.00/hr
Walton, Matthew C, seasonal aide, $8.00/hr
Walton, Scott A, park maint wkr II, $26,652
Waltrip, Scott, environ engr III, $58,908
Wandrey, Jacob A, seasonal aide, $8.00/hr
Wansing, Brenda, research analyst II, $36,204
Ward, Suzanne, environ spec I, $30,984
Ware, Abigail N, park maint wkr II, $26,652
Warnol, Jim L, bldg const wkr II, $33,180
Warren, Ronald E, seasonal aide, $8.05
Washburn, Eilayne P, planner III, $50,040
Washburn, Michael R, environ spec III, $41,940
Waters, Jacob K, environ spec III, $41,940
Watkins, Elizabeth R, arch II, $50,040
Watson, Kimberli R, seasonal aide, $8.00/hr
Watson, Michael C, heavy equip oper, $29,976
Wattenbarger, Brandon L, park maint wkr III, $29,976
Watts, Kristina M, environ spec II, $36,204
Weathers, Lora B, seasonal aide, $8.00/hr
Weaver, David E, heavy equip oper, $33,744
Weaver, Jennifer L, natural resources steward, $40,380
Weaver, Kevin M, park ranger, $38,928
Weaver, Mickel J, heavy equip oper, $30,420

Webb, Dustin, natural resources mgr b1, $51,096
Webb, Lawrence D, interpretive resource spc III, $38,928
Weber, Connie L, seasonal aide, $8.95/hr
Weber, Glendel S, seasonal aide, $9.50/hr
Webster, Christina J, ofc spt asst (keybrd), $16,895
Weckenborg, Colette M, fiscal & administrative mgr b1, $51,695
Weckenborg, Laverne M, account clerk II, $25,824
Weckenborg, Scott, environ spec III, $41,940
Wedemeyer, Daniel J, natural resources mgr b1, $50,045
Wedemeyer, Daniel P, environ spec II, $36,204
Wegrzyn, Linda G, environ sup, $49,128
Wehlermann, Abigail M, seasonal aide, $8.00/hr
Wehmeyer, Tyson, environ spec III, $41,940
Weible, Jayden D, seasonal aide, $8.00/hr
Weible, Steve E, land surv II, $47,892
Weidenbenner, Nicole, environ engr III, $55,416
Weis, Brent, environ spec II, $36,204
Weisbach, Jamie A, seasonal aide, $8.00/hr
Weisenborn, Fred W, tech asst IV, $41,172
Weisheyer, Kathryn A, seasonal aide, $8.00/hr
Welch, Dennis L, dishwasher, $8.00/hr
Weller, Michael, environ engr III, $55,416
Weller, Terry E, seasonal aide, $8.68/hr
Wellman, Crystal A, environ sup, $51,096
Wellman, Patricia J, seasonal aide, $8.90/hr
Wells, Larry, seasonal aide, $8.25/hr
Wesley, Frank A, planner III, $53,208
West, April L, tech asst IV, $35,568
West, Deloris M, seasonal aide, $8.55/hr
West, Ernest C, water spec III, $40,380
West, Megan C, seasonal aide, $8.50/hr
West, Taylor L, seasonal aide, $8.00/hr
West, Truman, seasonal aide, $8.47/hr
Westcott, Ernest, seasonal aide, $9.00/hr
Westhoff, Autumn N, seasonal aide, $8.15/hr
Westin, Karen S, environ spec II, $36,204
Westmoreland, Donald S, pub info admstr, $52,092
Wetherell, William, environ mgr b1, $57,650
Whipps, William W, environ sup, $51,096
White, Michael R, park maint wkr II, $26,652
White, Tina, environ sup, $51,096
White, Zachary T, seasonal aide, $8.47/hr
Whiteaker, Corey A, environ spec III, $41,940
Whited, Tristen, seasonal aide, $8.00/hr
Wieberg, Christopher G, environ mgr b2, $57,633
Wiggans, Sherry, exec II, $36,204
Wilbeck, Lee, interpretive resource coord, $43,488
Wilbers, Sharon K, ofc spt asst (keybrd), $22,536
Wilbur, Emily E, environ engr IV, $66,720
Wilcox, Brian, interpretive resource spc III, $38,928
Wilder, Valerie H, environ sup, $54,288
Wiles, Beverly A, research analyst II, $36,204
Wiles, Brandon N, environ spec II, $36,204
Wilhelm, Nancy, environ spec III, $41,940
Wilhite, Daniel B, park maint wkr III, $31,512
Wilkens, Kurt E, seasonal aide, $8.00/hr
Wilkerson, Josh L, environ spec III, $41,940
Wilkes, Emily, misc tech, $11.83/hr
Wilkes, Mari-Jo K, hr mgr b1, $51,984
Wilks, Rhonda L, sr ofc spt asst (keybrd), $29,412
Willeford, Brent E, environ engr III, $55,416
Williams, Dalton E, seasonal aide, $8.00/hr
Williams, Daronn, environ engr II, $47,892
Williams, John D, seasonal aide, $8.91/hr
Williams, Kathryn S, museum curator II, $41,172
Williams, Nancy L, seasonal aide, $9.12/hr
Williams, Terrie M, environ sup, $51,096
Williams, Thomas E, park maint wkr II, $28,908
Williams, Tina M, acct I, $29,976
Williamson, Jeff T, park maint wkr III, $29,976
Williamson, Karin F, seasonal aide, $9.00/hr
Williamson, Sarah E, seasonal aide, $8.91/hr
Williford, Danielle A, seasonal aide, $8.90/hr
Willoh, Donald A, special asst prof, $68,175
Willoh, Maureen K, training tech II, $42,708
Willoughby, Randall D, environ sup, $49,128
Wilson, Brock A, environ spec I, $30,984
Wilson, Chandler J, seasonal aide, $9.15/hr
Wilson, Clyde D, seasonal aide, $9.07/hr

Wilson, Ernest L, environ spec III, $41,940
Wilson, Tamela J, park/historic site spec III, $40,380
Wilson, Tammy L, mgmt analysis spec II, $45,156
Wilson, Wanda A, seasonal aide, $8.96/hr
Wilson, William G, environ mgr b2, $64,378
Winburn, Jack V, natural resources mgr b2, $61,339
Winchester, Kirstin M, seasonal aide, $8.00/hr
Windisch, Joseph R, seasonal aide, $8.96/hr
Winingear Jones, Melinda, sr ofc spt asst (keybrd), $25,824
Winkelman, Joann, seasonal aide, $12.04/hr
Winkelmann, Joseph, environ engr III, $57,744
Winslow, Dominic B, seasonal aide, $8.90/hr
Wisdom, Jered D, natural resources mgr b1, $41,927
Wiseman, Karla C, planner II, $45,156
Withington, Mary K, seasonal aide, $8.00/hr
Withington, William A, seasonal aide, $8.47/hr
Witthaus, David W, bldg const spv, $36,888
Wolf, Ashley L, seasonal aide, $8.50/hr
Wolf, Jason C, environ spec II, $36,204
Wolfe, Alycia C, chemist I, $31,512
Wolfe, Suzanne M, admin ofc spt asst, $28,104
Wolken, Cynthia K, planner III, $49,128
Wolverson, Shirley, environ spec III, $41,940
Womack, Michael P, environ spec I, $30,984
Wood, Christopher L, environ spec III, $41,940
Wood, Jennifer L, admin ofc spt asst, $29,004
Woods, Ebonee, special asst prof, $40,400
Woodward, Philip D, seasonal aide, $9.41/hr
Woodward, Thomas L, natural resources mgr b1, $48,149
Woody, Lana E, natural resources mgr b1, $45,163
Woolery, Anastacia E, seasonal aide, $8.00/hr
Wright, Erika L, seasonal aide, $9.00/hr
Wright, William C, seasonal aide, $8.05/hr
Wright-Aholt, Sarah, tech asst I, $24,612
Wyatt, Michael S, environ spec III, $41,940
Wymore, Sherie L, seasonal aide, $9.41/hr
Yacovazzi, Cassandra L, seasonal aide, $9.03/hr
Yaeger, Patricia A, seasonal aide, $9.68/hr
Yates, Jared D, seasonal aide, $8.00/hr
Yellets, Judith L, seasonal aide, $8.00/hr
Yoakum, Rodney T, seasonal aide, $8.47/hr
Yocum, Jared A, park maint wkr II, $26,652
Yoder, Sheila K, environ spec III, $31,450
York, Mallory F, seasonal aide, $8.50/hr
York, Rebecca J, seasonal aide, $11.00/hr
Young, Chia-Wei, environ engr III, $55,416
Young, Dustin P, park ranger sergeant, $43,488
Young, Glen J, geologist IV, $54,288
Young, Robert W, seasonal aide, $8.05/hr
Young, Summer N, designated principal asst div, $45,955
Yount, Arln E, park maint wkr II, $26,652
Yount, Marty R, bldg const wkr II, $33,180
Zachary, Muriel A, seasonal aide, $8.50/hr
Zamarripa, Ruben, environ sup, $56,520
Zdvorak, Christopher, misc tech, $14.18/hr
Zeaman, William S, environ sup, $51,096
Zeikle, Randy D, seasonal aide, $8.66/hr
Zewdie, Lemma, environ spec III, $41,940
Zimmerman, Tanner E, seasonal aide, $8.90/hr
Zimmerschied, Melissa D, seasonal aide, $8.90/hr
Zink, Linda K, admin ofc spt asst, $30,984
Zumalt, Terri J, chemist III, $41,172

Department of Public Safety

Truman State Office Bldg., PO Box 749, Jefferson City 65102

Roberts, Lane J, state dept dir, $121,716
Abbey, Marcie J, criminalist I, $41,940
Abel, William H, trooper 1st class, $66,516
Aberle, Pamela M, trnr/auditor III, $41,940
Abmeyer, Ronald O, commercial veh ofcr II, $43,488
Abramovitz, Dana M, nursing asst I, $24,900
Abrams, Amanda M, nursing asst I, $23,148
Acord, Matthew P, trooper, $42,612
Acosta, Brenda M, clin casework asst II, $32,628
Acree, James C, trooper 1st class, $55,644

Adamick, Joseph J, registered nurse sr, $53,592
Adams, Blaine L, sergeant, $75,588
Adams, Bradley W, garage supt, $45,156
Adams, Donald R, phys plant sup I, $43,488
Adams, Elan B, trooper 1st class, $54,024
Adams, Jackie, air depot maint spec II, $40,380
Adams, Jaime J, nursing asst I, $24,900
Adams, Michael D, trooper 1st class, $66,516
Adams, Terry J, cpl, $62,688
Adams, Tracy L, criminalist II, $46,932
Adams, Vance H, boiler/pressure vessel inspctr, $49,128
Adamson, Brandon W, cpl, $52,416
Adey, Alexis R, typist, $12.00/hr
Adkins, James S, chief technician, $67,716
Adler, Kimberly A, clerk-typist III, $28,908
Aegerter, Shaun, info technologist I, $32,052
Ahern, Ethan P, lt, $85,236
Ahern, Nathan C, lt, $85,236
Ahrens, Wallace V, lt, $85,236
Aiman, James, info technologist II, $34,944
Aiuppa, Heather M, nursing asst I, $23,856
Akers, Jason A, trooper 1st class, $46,536
Akrobetu, David F, comp info tech III, $45,156
Albers, Jason S, trooper 1st class, $49,392
Albin, John S, motor veh insp III, $33,180
Albus, William S, fire investigator, $41,940
Alcorn, Kyle E, probary trooper, $41,280
Alderson, Angela, exec I, $35,568
Aldrich, Ryan D, cve insp III, $36,204
Aleshire, Wilma E, lab evdnc tech II, $29,004
Alford, Melissa A, lpn, $21.00/hr
Alldridge, Pamela M, food serv helper II, $23,508
Allen, Jonathan, plumber, $29,976
Allen, Judy A, food serv helper I, $20,664
Allen, Kelly C, electronic gaming device coor, $51,096
Allen, Larry M, sergeant, $75,588
Allen, Margaret M, lab evdnc tech II, $29,004
Allen, Regina, maint worker I, $26,652
Allen, William, laborer II, $25,824
Allison-Mitchell, Yvonne M, vets serv ofcr, $31,512
Almond, Keith A, sergeant, $68,688
Alonzo, Cheryl A, fiscal & administrative mgr b2, $76,065
Alshati, Ahmad K, typist, $12.00/hr
Alshati, Ali J, typist, $12.00/hr
Alston-Smith, Virginia A, driver exam III, $31,512
Altermatt, Shawn D, cpl, $75,588
Alvarado, Jeffrey, food serv helper II, $23,160
Ambrose, Rachel L, sr ofc spt asst (keybrd), $27,948
Ambuehl, Jeffrey T, recrtnal ther I, $38,232
Amelunke, Melinda G, registered nurse sr, $51,552
Ames, Elmer L, maint worker II, $29,004
Ames, Teresa L, housekeeper I, $30,420
Amick, Tina A, info technology spec I, $63,996
Amighetti, Louis G, cpl, $60,840
Amistad, Divina R, activity aide II, $26,844
Amos, Lori M, registered nurse sup, $63,084
Amos, Paula L, misc prof, $17.23/hr
Amsinger, Janet L, fiscal&budgetary analyst III, $35,568
Anders, April M, cook II, $26,232
Anders, Brian M, cpl, $66,576
Anderson, Amber L, nursing asst II, $26,892
Anderson, Brian N, lt, $85,236
Anderson, Faith A, account clerk II, $32,472
Anderson, Franchon G, nursing asst I, $24,900
Anderson, Herbert, janitor, $8.16/hr
Anderson, Jaclyn M, nursing asst I, $24,900
Anderson, Nancy, janitor, $8.16/hr
Anderson, Richard L, trooper 1st class, $66,516
Anderson, Shane C, driver exam III, $31,512
Andre, Shirl L, registered nurse mgr b2, $82,248
Andreae, Alyssa L, registered nurse sr, $58,140
Andrews, Martha R, registered nurse, $27.00/hr
Andrews, Shelley M, registered nurse - clin opers, $72,984
Angle, Jacob P, sergeant, $75,588
Angrisani, Matthew T, trooper 1st class, $47,964
Angus, Gregory, maint worker I, $28,908
Anthony, Joanna J, custodial worker II, $23,880
Antill, Misty L, nursing asst I, $24,900
Aparicio, Javier, geographic info sys tech I, $30,984

Applebury, Dena R, asst chief oper, $56,784
Applebury, Jay D, automotive technician III, $37,548
Applegate, Michelle D, driver exam III, $31,512
Applewhite, Matthew, custodial worker I, $20,664
Appley, Sharon M, nursing asst II, $27,780
Araujo Zapien, Diana L, nursing asst I, $23,856
Arbuthnot, Christopher M, cpl, $59,064
Armistead, Joseph L, lt, $85,236
Armstrong, Andrew A, trooper 1st class, $62,688
Armstrong, Mitchell S, janitor, $8.16/hr
Arnold, Bryan G, sergeant, $75,588
Arnold, Debra R, food serv helper I, $21,264
Arnold, Jerry L, sergeant, $75,588
Arnold, Russell B, trooper 1st class, $62,688
Arnold, Stephen, janitor, $8.16/hr
Arsenault, Daniel J, trooper 1st class, $45,180
Arthur, Andy L III, nursing asst I, $23,148
Arvin, Carrie L, nursing asst II, $27,780
Ashby, Jason A, trooper 1st class, $46,536
Ashby, John S, sergeant, $75,588
Ashby, Marc R, trooper 1st class, $47,964
Ashby, Myla E, driver exam sprv, $36,888
Ashby, Timothy R, supply mgr I, $36,888
Ashcraft, Mark A, comp info tech spec II, $57,744
Asher, Megan K, laundry worker I, $22,200
Atkins, Monty D, cpl, $70,728
Atkinson, Edna A, nursing asst II, $28,224
Atkinson, Michael P, capitol police ofcr, $33,744
Atkinson, Neil R, cpl, $70,728
Atkinson, Rebbecca A, nursing asst I, $24,900
Aubuchon, Raymond L, vets serv ofcr, $29,976
Aubuchon, Robert J, trooper 1st class, $62,688
Austerman, Chester M, examination monitor, $17.73/hr
Austin, Mollye E, registered nurse sup, $68,532
Autenrieth, Michael G, trooper 1st class, $46,536
Autrey, Rainie L, technician I, $29,004
Aversman, Craig A, state vets cemetery worker, $27,948
Axelrod, David R, asst chief oper, $60,228
Axelrod, Denene C, driver exam III, $31,512
Ayala, Ariana (, therapy aide, $12.75/hr
Ayars, Christopher M, motor veh driver, $25,824
Ayars, Tara M, nursing asst I, $24,900
Aycock, Kristen A, nursing asst I, $23,148
Ayer, William A, agent (liquor ctrl), $40,380
Ayers, Richard L, cpl, $70,728
Ayers, Trudy, nursing asst II, $28,224
Aylward, Edward J, lt, $85,236
Ayres, Grant A, trooper, $42,612
Bach, Pamela J, custodial worker II, $23,508
Bachmann, Kathryn L, nursing asst I, $23,148
Backes, Theresa M, special asst-ofc & clerical, $50,208
Backues, Melissa A, info technologist IV, $52,092
Badgett, Trenton A, cpl, $70,728
Badresingh, Ryan C, comp info tech spec II, $57,744
Bagge, David T, planner III, $56,520
Bagley, David O, cvo sup I, $46,068
Baguio, Christopher S, domestic serv worker, $11.62/hr
Bahr, Ryan W, cpl, $66,576
Bailes, Shawn M, criminalist III, $57,744
Bailey, April S, registered nurse, $40.00/hr
Bailey, Wesley A, misc prof, $30.30/hr
Bain, Tabatha R, nursing asst I, $24,900
Bair, Jeffory A, lt, $85,236
Baird, Donette L, driver exam sprv, $37,548
Baird, Jeffrey S, cpl, $70,728
Baird, Jessica S, driver exam II, $29,976
Baker, Angela R, asst vets home admstr, $54,288
Baker, Bradley S, investigator II, $47,892
Baker, Bruce F, trooper 1st class, $66,516
Baker, Catherine P, chief oper, $62,016
Baker, Debra L, clerk, $9.69/hr
Baker, James L, comm technician I, $39,960
Baker, Karen K, dining room spv, $26,652
Baker, Michael J, criminalist sup, $65,364
Baker, Orry R, trooper, $43,872
Baker, Randi E, nursing asst I, $23,856
Baker, Ruth A, food serv helper I, $10,332
Baker, Sherry R, nursing asst I, $23,148
Baker, Todd, probary trooper, $41,280

Baldwin, Brittany A, criminalist III, $55,416
Baldwin, Katie L, nursing asst I, $23,856
Baldwin, Linda J, pers clerk, $30,420
Baldwin, Maria E, food serv helper I, $20,664
Ball, Steven M, bldg/gnds maint i temp, $9.69/hr
Ballard, Phyllis L, lpn III gen, $43,620
Ballard, Scott A, cpl, $62,688
Ballenger, Janice, nursing asst I, $24,900
Ballenger, Larry, security ofcr I, $26,652
Ballew, Kayle J, automotive technician III, $34,356
Ballinger, Joyce A, custodial worker I, $22,200
Bamvakais, Anthony, designated principal asst div, $82,578
Banasik, Daniel P, sergeant, $75,588
Barborek, Alan W, sergeant, $75,588
Barborek, Sonja Y, cook III, $24,612
Barbour, Donald R, sergeant, $75,588
Barbour, Olani K, nursing asst I, $24,900
Barclay, Charles M, trooper, $43,872
Bardwell, Cheryl S, driver exam - chief, $41,940
Barjenbruch, Peggy W, physician, $47,706
Barker, George, maint worker II, $29,976
Barks, Melvin A, fire insp, $35,568
Barlow, Britany R, nursing asst I, $23,856
Barlow, Jim R, cpl, $70,728
Barlow, Kevin, maint spv I, $38,928
Barnes, Amy M, technician III, $33,744
Barnes, Denise J, nursing asst I, $24,900
Barnes, Tonya C, nursing asst I, $24,900
Barnes, Wardell, cook II, $24,264
Barnett, Jerry R, state vets cemetery worker, $27,948
Barnett, Jessica R, direct care aide, $8.00/hr
Barnett, Kelly A, trooper 1st class, $47,964
Barnett, Vicki L, clerk, $9.69/hr
Barr, Katherine, exec I, $34,944
Barrett, Timothy A, trooper 1st class, $52,416
Barron, Jefferson E, motor veh insp III, $36,204
Barron, Mayela, probary trooper, $40,272
Bartel, Eric T, cpl, $70,728
Bartels, Codee R, nursing asst I, $23,148
Bartels, Kristina N, hlth prog aide, $11.50/hr
Bartels, Roland H, sergeant, $75,588
Barthelmass, Todd M, sergeant, $75,588
Bartle, Kimberly M, ofc spt asst (keybrd), $24,264
Bartlett, Dean A, cpl, $70,728
Barton, Edward L, fire insp, $35,568
Barton, Larry D, driver exam III, $31,512
Barton, Stacy R, mvi sup, $36,204
Bashor, Opal L, activity ther, $30,660
Basinger, Meghan E, clerk-typist III, $25,824
Basler, Sonna L, motor veh insp II, $29,976
Bassinson, Jeffrey K, vid prod spec II, $40,380
Bauer, David C, sergeant, $75,588
Bauer, Hillary K, nursing asst I, $24,900
Bauer, Julia, admin ofc spt asst, $28,104
Bauer, Travis S, automotive technician III, $34,356
Bauer, Zachary D, trooper 1st class, $46,536
Baughman, Joseph S, trooper 1st class, $54,024
Baughman-Pew, Tonie C, laundry worker I, $22,200
Baughn, James, pub safety mgr band 2, $67,464
Bauman, Clifford W, janitor, $6.97/hr
Bava, James M, trooper, $43,872
Bax, Kerry L, special asst-ofc & clerical, $41,664
Bax, Nicole D, comp info tech spec I, $51,096
Baxter, Charles G, state vets cemetery dir, $44,304
Baxter, Debbra M, miltry funeral hnrs team mbr, $27,084
Baxter, Trent A, trooper 1st class, $45,180
Bayer, Leigh D, criminalist III, $55,416
Bazzell, Christy D, nursing asst I, $23,148
Beal, Christopher J, fire investigator, $38,928
Beard, Bryan M, trooper 1st class, $50,904
Beard, Cynthia J, hlth info tech II, $34,356
Beard, Mark, security ofcr I, $27,084
Bearden, Bradley S, sergeant, $75,588
Beasley, Jodi V, nursing asst I, $24,900
Beasley, Lori A, nursing asst I, $24,900
Beasley, Morgan K, nursing asst I, $23,148
Beasley, Sally A, lpn III gen, $38,352
Beasley, Tracy L, custodial worker I, $20,664

Beaton, John B, asst chief oper, $68,412
Beatty, William D, bldg & grounds maint II, $24,612
Beaulieu, Melissa A, nursing asst I, $24,900
Bechaud, Kenneth R, probary trooper, $41,280
Beck, Colton J, probary trooper, $40,272
Beck, Matthew A, comp info tech spec II, $57,744
Beck, Mona L, laundry worker I, $20,664
Becker, Bruce A, cpl, $70,728
Becker, Daniel R, trooper, $42,612
Becker, Edward A, registered nurse sup, $63,084
Becker, Kimberly J, pub safety mgr band 1, $58,419
Becker, Matthew F, trnr/auditor III, $46,932
Beckett, Jimmy A, sergeant, $75,588
Beckley, Bryce, maint worker, $9.00/hr
Beckwith, Andrew M, trooper 1st class, $45,180
Beckwith, Mary M, hr mgr b1, $61,692
Bedford, Michele L, lpn III gen, $41,232
Beffa, David A, misc prof, $16.80/hr
Behrens, Paul M, cpl, $70,728
Belardo, Daren C, trooper 1st class, $46,536
Belcher, Jason N, cve insp sprv I, $38,928
Bell, Andrew J, sergeant, $70,932
Bell, Daniel J, pub info spec II, $41,940
Bell, Erica T, custodial worker I, $20,664
Bell, Melinda (, nursing asst II, $27,360
Bell, Miranda K, lpn III gen, $41,232
Bell, William L, investigator II, $49,128
Bell-Dawson, Racquel W, registered nurse sup, $67,104
Bellers, Jon-Yves, probary trooper, $40,272
Belote, Thomas L, cpl, $59,064
Belshe, Michael S, cpl, $70,728
Belt, Alexander A, criminalist III, $55,416
Belt, Jeffrey L, automotive technician III, $38,928
Belt, Mark P, motor veh insp III, $31,512
Bengston, Nicholas D, trooper 1st class, $49,392
Benhardt, Richard D, law enforce ofcr, $20.00/hr
Benne, Adam C, criminalist sup, $65,364
Benne, Catherine M, registered nurse sup, $65,676
Bennett, Alanong R, food serv helper I, $22,200
Bennett, George E, phys thrpst asst, $39,744
Bennett, James A, sergeant, $75,588
Bennett, Kaleb, janitor, $8.16/hr
Bennett, Lue Effie, nursing asst II, $28,224
Bennett, Mary E, lpn III gen, $39,072
Bennett, Sherry, custodial worker II, $23,880
Bennett, Sylvia J, exec I, $38,232
Benyo, Linda S, bldg/gnds maint i temp, $9.69/hr
Benzie, Maurice E, cpl, $70,728
Berck, Christopher W, lpn III gen, $33,948
Berendzen, Alan, const insp, $58,908
Berendzen, Bruce, misc tech, $18.75/hr
Berendzen, Theresa R, misc prof, $15.70/hr
Bergner, James A, firefighter, $38,232
Berhorst, Connie A, pub safety prog spec, $42,708
Berhorst, Loretta, ofc spt asst (keybrd), $23,880
Berkbigler, Vera K, food serv helper I, $10,332
Berney, Elizabeth M, cook I, $22,872
Bernhardt, Amber M, sr ofc spt asst (keybrd), $32,472
Bernhardt, Brent J, sergeant, $75,588
Bernier, Michael A, sergeant, $75,588
Berrey, Layne N, nursing asst I, $23,148
Berrey, Richard A, maint worker I, $26,652
Berry, John D, driver exam II, $29,976
Berry, Nicholas D, sergeant, $75,588
Berschauer, Jacqulyn R, lpn III gen, $41,976
Besemer, Steven C, planner III, $47,892
Bexten, Sandra L, comp info tech spec II, $57,744
Bible, Terry A, trooper 1st class, $66,516
Bickell, Danny A, trooper 1st class, $57,324
Bickers, Makenzie P, nursing asst I, $23,856
Bickings, Justin B, miltry funeral hnrs team mbr, $27,084
Biederman, Michelle N, auditor II, $50,040
Bielawski, Lisa A, qual ctrl clerk I, $25,824
Bielawski, Lori K, chief oper, $67,716
Bielawski, Mark A, lt, $85,236
Bielawski, Steve M, sergeant, $75,588
Bierer, Frederick D, sergeant, $70,932
Biermann, Drew A, electronic gaming device spec, $49,490
Biggs, Jennifer K, registered nurse sup, $63,084

Bigham, Scott R, section chief, $79,176
Billings, Geoffrey L, trooper 1st class, $66,516
Billings, Gregory Q, sergeant, $75,588
Bilyeu, Donald L, probary trooper, $41,280
Bird, Lisa L, driver exam III, $32,628
Bise, Dana G, ins clerk, $32,628
Bishop, Catherine M, trooper 1st class, $49,392
Bishop, Craig A, criminalist I, $40,380
Bishop, Cynthia A, technician III, $33,744
Bishop, Joann R, nursing asst I, $23,148
Bishop, Richard A, capitol police ofcr, $34,944
Bishop, Timothy P, supply mgr I, $35,568
Bivens, Deborah C, nursing asst I, $24,900
Black, Stuart D, sergeant, $75,588
Black, Thomas J, trooper 1st class, $46,536
Blackburn, Janna F, registered nurse sup, $65,676
Blackmon, Christopher R, trooper 1st class, $59,064
Blackmon, Shavette D, nursing asst I, $24,900
Blackston, Shawn M, probary trooper, $40,272
Blackwell, Erin E, clin casework pract I, $41,172
Blair, Bridgette N, lpn III gen, $39,780
Blair, Paula M, nursing asst II, $28,224
Blair, Tina M, pers clerk, $33,744
Blanc, Mary A, custodial worker I, $20,664
Blankenbeker, Benjamin J, cpl, $59,064
Blankenship, Darron F, sergeant, $75,588
Blankenship, Derek B, trooper 1st class, $47,964
Blankenship, Pamela S, nursing asst I, $24,900
Blatter, Lori A, special asst prof, $38,928
Blaylock, Edwin A, lt, $85,236
Blaylock, Kimberly A, nursing asst I, $24,900
Bledsoe, Shannon D, trooper 1st class, $66,516
Bleich, Julie M, laborer, $15.39/hr
Blessing, Joseph P, registered nurse sup, $64,380
Blevins, Douglas E, auditor I, $45,156
Bloomberg, Robert E, special asst prof, $58,488
Bloss, Keya S, nursing asst I, $24,900
Blum, Tracy M, nursing asst I, $24,900
Blunt, Alshon, trooper, $43,872
Blunt, Troy R, sergeant, $75,588
Blyzes, Christine E, nursing asst II, $28,224
Bock, Julie A, bldg & grounds maint I, $23,880
Bock, Lynn M, accounting spec II, $38,928
Bock, Sandra A, technician III, $33,744
Bodine, Alexander M, probary trooper, $40,272
Boeckman, Heather K, pers rec clerk II, $31,512
Boeckman, Mark A, clerk, $9.69/hr
Boeckman, Ryan L, comp info tech III, $45,156
Boeckmann, Arthur H, bldg/gnds maint i temp, $9.69/hr
Boeckmann, Helen A, typist, $9.69/hr
Boehmer, Jeffrey, maint worker II, $21,208
Bogart, Christine A, cpl, $70,728
Bogg, Deanne M, capitol police ofcr, $34,356
Bolden, Bernita R, nursing asst I, $24,900
Boley, Matthew O, planner II, $41,172
Bolinger, Stacey A, criminalist sup, $65,364
Bollier, Brian J, vets benefits claims rep, $32,628
Bolton, Logan M, trooper, $42,612
Bommel, Ronnie, sr ofc spt asst (keybrd), $27,084
Bonchonsky, Sean D, agent (liquor ctrl), $40,380
Bond, Nena L, nursing asst I, $23,856
Bonderer, Monica J, registered nurse - clin opers, $63,084
Bone, Carl W, cpl, $62,688
Boner, Tiffany A, lpn III gen, $41,232
Bonner, Cheryl D, fin auditor, $60,120
Bonner, Jeffrey G, comm oper III, $62,016
Bonner, Lisa C, nursing asst I, $23,148
Bonuchi, Dennis S, comm oper III, $56,784
Bonuchi, Marcy J, technician III, $33,744
Boone, Jennifer M, custodial worker I, $20,664
Bopp, Kyle S, comm technician I, $39,960
Borgfield, Betty S, custodial worker I, $20,664
Borgic, Aaron T, probary trooper, $41,280
Borgmeyer, Donald P, probary trooper, $41,280
Borgmeyer, Nicholas J, trooper 1st class, $47,964
Borlinghaus, Geoffrey L, sergeant, $75,588
Borman, Courtney M, acct II, $37,548
Bosnic, Adil, typist, $12.00/hr
Botfield, Robert B, trooper 1st class, $47,964

Bottcher, Cris E, registered nurse sr, $58,140
Bouse, Paula K, dining room spv, $25,404
Boutelle, Velvet N, lpn III gen, $37,020
Bowen, Donna A, sr ofc spt asst (keybrd), $29,412
Bowen, Whitney N, nursing asst I, $24,900
Bowen-Muenks, Christopher G, clerk, $9.69/hr
Bowers, Bridget, janitor, $8.16/hr
Bowland, Karen D, clerk-typist III, $29,904
Bowles, Charles A, cpl, $54,024
Bowles, Debbra A, registered nurse, $27.00/hr
Bowles, Jennifer C, nursing asst II, $27,780
Bowles, Tammy E, motor veh driver, $26,652
Bowling, Vickie Y, laundry worker I, $21,264
Bowman, Kelly L, comm oper III, $50,508
Bowman, Samatha K, therapy aide, $9.38/hr
Bowyer, Duffer, security ofcr I, $26,652
Boyd, Cynthia E, laundry worker I, $21,264
Boyd, Daniel L, cdl examination auditor, $36,888
Boyd, Stacey N, cook I, $22,200
Boyer, Nina, acct II, $41,940
Boyer, Patricia A, driver exam III, $31,512
Boyum, Stacia A, fiscal & budget analyst II, $29,976
Bozeman, Lillie, lpn, $30.00/hr
Bracken, Rebekah-Marie A, food serv helper I, $21,564
Bracken, Shirley A, typist, $9.69/hr
Bracker, Daniel S, lt, $85,236
Bracker, Michael S, cpl, $70,728
Brackett, Kent A, cpl, $70,728
Braden, Gary L, sergeant, $75,588
Bradford, Thomas M, examination monitor, $17.73/hr
Bradley, Charles E, comm oper III, $56,784
Bradley, Charles N, cpl, $70,728
Bradley, Jonathan D, probary trooper, $40,272
Bradley, Linda A, driver exam sprv, $36,204
Bradley, Michael L, probary trooper, $41,280
Bradley, Rebecca L, special asst prof, $48,768
Bradshaw, Cory W, trooper 1st class, $57,324
Brady, Cynthia J, elevatr/amusemt ride sfty insp, $41,172
Brady, Markita, nursing asst I, $23,856
Brakefield, Janet S, hlth prog aide, $13.00/hr
Brand, McDonald H, sergeant, $75,588
Brandt, Amanda L, exec I, $36,888
Brandt, Jodi E, comm oper I, $39,960
Brandt, Miranda, environ aide, $11.00/hr
Branham, Tammy R, food serv helper I, $21,264
Branham, Timothy D, nursing asst I, $24,900
Brannon, Ashley N, nursing asst I, $23,148
Branson, Melanie R, technician III, $33,744
Branson, Michelle P, special asst prof, $35,568
Branson, Roger D, technician III, $33,744
Branum, Ryne S, cve insp II, $33,744
Brashears, David, planner III, $58,908
Brashers, Elisabeth A, nursing asst II, $28,692
Brashers, Jimmy D, motor veh driver, $26,232
Bratcher, Priscilla A, custodial worker I, $22,200
Braun, Darin J, comp info tech trainee, $29,976
Braun, Holly R, nursing asst I, $23,856
Braun, Kevin L, asst chief technician, $50,508
Brauner, Pamela A, misc prof, $26.00/hr
Braunschweig, Bryan, comp info tech III, $45,156
Bray, Kelli L, lpn III gen, $41,232
Braynard, Dustin L, cpl, $54,024
Brazas, Shawn A, trooper 1st class, $50,904
Brazeal, Kass E, fire investigator, $38,928
Breen, Alanna J, nursing asst I, $23,148
Breen, Alma J, driver exam III, $31,512
Breitbach, Joshua R, trooper 1st class, $55,644
Bremer, William P, sergeant, $75,588
Brenneke, John G, bldg & grounds maint II, $24,612
Brenneke, Joseph W, misc prof, $15.70/hr
Brentano, Leona A, driver exam III, $31,512
Brenton, David S, trooper 1st class, $66,516
Bressman, Jack, groundskeeper I, $12,516
Brester, Jared R, clerk, $9.69/hr
Brester, William J, chief technician, $74,388
Brewer, Alice F, clin casework asst II, $34,944
Brewer, Ashley N, technician II, $30,984
Brewer, Stanley M, custodial worker I, $22,536
Bridges, Betty J, nursing asst I, $24,900

Bridges, Darren R, capitol police cpl, $37,548
Bridges, Justin B, capitol police ofcr, $33,744
Bridges, Robin K, food serv helper I, $20,664
Bridges, Sarah E, nursing asst I, $23,856
Briggs, Charlotte M, registered nurse sup, $65,676
Briggs, Jeffrey F, planner II, $41,172
Bright, Amanda G, nursing asst I, $24,900
Bright, Rick D, lab evdnc tech I, $27,228
Brinkley, Katrina K, lab evdnc tech I, $26,400
Brinkman, Charles E, elevatr/amusemt ride sfty insp, $43,488
Britt, Datrell M, nursing asst I, $23,856
Britt, Norman J, cpl, $70,728
Britton, Teresa M, registered nurse sup, $63,084
Brock, Bonita S, nursing asst I, $12,450
Brockman, Ronald J, pub safety mgr band 1, $54,604
Broniec, Mark G, cpl, $70,728
Broniec, Matthew J, sergeant, $75,588
Broniec, Michael E, cpl, $70,728
Brookins, Arrion S, nursing asst I, $24,900
Brookins, Kenetra S, nursing asst I, $23,148
Brooks, Anthony E, info technologist IV, $52,092
Brooks, Bret E, sergeant, $66,576
Brooks, Dawn M, cook I, $22,536
Brooks, Destiny R, therapy aide, $10.00/hr
Brooks, Justin K, trooper 1st class, $45,180
Brooks, Kawonza G, nursing asst I, $24,900
Brooks, Rhonda L, nursing asst I, $24,900
Brooks, Ronda L, nursing asst I, $24,900
Brooks, Sean C, criminalist III, $57,744
Brooks, Trinisia R, clin casework asst II, $36,888
Brookshier, Kathy A, nursing asst II, $28,224
Brookshire, Peggy L, admin ofc spt asst, $30,420
Broshuis, Patricia D, custodial worker I, $20,664
Brotherton, James, janitor, $8.16/hr
Broughton, Brooke M, storekeeper I, $25,824
Brown, Alina M, nursing asst I, $23,856
Brown, Amy, mil funeral hnrs area coor, $30,984
Brown, Caramel M, hlth prog aide, $16.00/hr
Brown, Catrina L, exec I, $30,984
Brown, Christina M, lpn III gen, $39,072
Brown, Christy J, lpn III gen, $43,620
Brown, Cora, nursing asst I, $24,900
Brown, Craig L, firefighter crew chief, $29,351
Brown, Cynthia S, driver exam sprv, $36,204
Brown, Danny, mil funeral hnrs team leader, $29,976
Brown, David H, cpl, $66,576
Brown, David M, firefighter crew chief, $31,933
Brown, Demetrius J, laundry worker I, $20,664
Brown, Donald, pub safety mgr band 1, $42,612
Brown, Donna M, custodial worker I, $20,664
Brown, Eric F, cpl, $60,840
Brown, Gloria J, nursing asst I, $24,900
Brown, Heather N, activity aide II, $26,400
Brown, James A, nursing asst I, $26,076
Brown, Jamie M, nursing asst II, $28,224
Brown, Kamillia L, trooper 1st class, $46,536
Brown, Kimberly K, laundry worker I, $23,508
Brown, Kristina J, nursing asst I, $23,148
Brown, Marcella D, ofc spt asst (clerical), $25,404
Brown, Nancy A, driver exam sprv, $36,204
Brown, Patricia D, nursing asst II, $28,224
Brown, Ray H, clerk, $26.52/hr
Brown, Ray H, driver exam sprv, $36,204
Brown, Regina C, motor veh insp III, $31,512
Brown, Russell, security ofcr I, $26,652
Brown, Schwana R, hlth prog aide, $16.00/hr
Brown, Shena R, clerk-typist III, $27,948
Brown, Travis L, trooper 1st class, $50,904
Brown, Yvonne R, lpn III gen, $41,232
Broxton, Ronald C, pub safety mgr band 2, $71,205
Broyles-Hofstetter, Jacqueline A, special asst prof, $35,855
Bruce, Kristopher R, driver, $11.59/hr
Bruce, Phil B, lpn III gen, $41,232
Brueggeman, Daniel, security ofcr III, $32,052
Bruemmer, Carla J, designated princ asst-div, $53,472
Bruemmer, Jennifer M, admin ofc spt asst, $29,976
Bruemmer, Rhonda C, clerk IV, $36,888
Brumble, Deborah, registered nurse - clin opers, $63,084
Brumble, Jason S, sergeant, $75,588

Bruns, Carolyn L, auditor II, $50,040
Bruns, Jennifer L, pub safety mgr band 1, $63,994
Brunzel, Derick L, cve insp III, $36,204
Bryan, Andrew L, cpl, $70,728
Bryan, Michael R, sergeant, $75,588
Bryan, Samantha L, qual ctrl clerk II, $29,904
Bryan, Zackery K, trooper 1st class, $52,416
Bryant, Angela M, nursing asst II, $27,360
Bryant, Jahlil A, food serv helper I, $20,148
Bryson, Kelley M, nursing asst I, $24,900
Bubach, Stacy L, processing technician II, $26,652
Buchheit, Samuel V, cpl, $59,064
Buckley, Ada M, cook II, $25,404
Buckner, Joshua D, bldg/gnds maint i temp, $9.69/hr
Buckner, Vincent H, technician I, $29,004
Buechter, Rebecca L, pers clerk, $37,548
Buff, Adam K, trooper 1st class, $66,516
Buhrmeister, Kenneth, janitor, $8.16/hr
Bullock, David, electrcn, $36,204
Bullock, Elizabeth A, domestic serv worker, $9.38/hr
Bullock, Shane M, fire insp, $35,568
Bumgardner, Patrick, maint worker II, $29,976
Burckhardt, Ryan A, lt, $85,236
Burgan, David L, planner III, $43,488
Burge, Karen C, crim intel analyst II, $36,204
Burgett, Ronald T, trooper 1st class, $62,688
Burgio, James, criminalist III, $55,416
Burgun, Stephen M, cpl, $54,024
Burk, Illa J, driver exam sprv, $36,204
Burke, Maureen, planner III, $51,096
Burkemper, Lori A, clerk IV, $33,744
Burks, Melinda, lab evdnc tech II, $29,004
Burlbaw, Ross, maint worker, $10.50/hr
Burlingame, Carla M, acct II, $40,380
Burnett, Jeffrey J, trooper, $42,612
Burnette, Harold D, tech spt mgr, $61,332
Burns, Jean A, telecommunicator, $31,512
Burns, Steven N, phys plant sup I, $23,533
Burns, Tracy R, domestic serv worker, $9.75/hr
Burr, Walter L, trooper 1st class, $66,516
Burrell, Elsie Z, nursing asst II, $27,360
Burris, Jessica, sr ofc spt asst (keybrd), $25,824
Burris, John E, dpty fire chief, $34,585
Burris, Joseph R, firefighter, $38,232
Burse, Shanisha L, nursing asst I, $24,900
Burton, Isis N, nursing asst I, $23,856
Burton, Julia M, recrtnal ther II, $40,380
Burton-Smith, Eniola T, lpn, $30.00/hr
Buscher, Lori, clerk, $9.69/hr
Buschjost, Adam L, driver exam II, $29,976
Buschjost, Chad A, duplicating equiper III, $33,180
Buschjost, Jason R, spec II, $36,204
Bush, Rebecca L, nursing asst I, $24,900
Bush, Tonya K, driver exam sprv, $38,232
Bush, William M, cpl, $70,728
Buthod, Blake A, clerk, $9.69/hr
Butler, Brandon L, probary trooper, $41,280
Butler, Freddie L, cpl, $70,728
Butner, Jonathan W, chief motor veh insp, $39,624
Butrum, Susan A, custodial worker I, $20,664
Butterfield, Cherron L, cook I, $23,508
Butterfield, Roselle M, typist, $9.69/hr
Buttram, Joslyn J, nursing asst I, $24,900
Buttram, Richard E, sergeant, $75,588
Bybee, Carolyn F, registered nurse - clin opers, $65,676
Bybee, Teresa M, account clerk III, $30,924
Byerly, Suzanne M, nursing asst I, $23,856
Byers, Franklin V, driver exam III, $31,512
Byington, David S, chief technician, $74,388
Byrd, Linda J, driver exam sprv, $39,624
Byrd, Tammy R, prog sup, $41,940
Byrnes, Robert B, cpl, $70,728
Cable, Rania D, hlth prog spec, $12.50/hr
Cade, Karen M, driver exam sprv, $36,204
Cahalan, Debbie L, cook I, $23,880
Cain, Patricia L, custodial worker I, $20,664
Caldwell, Barbara J, spv of vol servs, $31,512
Caldwell, Chester H, state vets cemetery worker, $27,948
Caldwell, Daniel E, sergeant, $75,588

Caldwell, Rondollune J, food serv helper I, $22,200
Caldwell, Tammy, admin ofc spt asst, $28,104
Calfee, Jeremy M, driver exam sprv, $36,204
Calhoon, Sarah, janitor, $8.16/hr
Call, Darren S, cpl, $70,728
Call, Jennifer J, spec II, $36,204
Callahan, Gerard G, sergeant, $75,588
Callahan, Hazel L, custodial worker II, $23,508
Callahan, Tabitha K, registered nurse sr, $51,552
Callen, Emie E, registered nurse, $51,276
Callihan, John P, comm oper III, $49,044
Calvert, Rodney L, cpl, $70,728
Calvillo, Alexander J, bldg/gnds maint i temp, $9.69/hr
Cameron, Danny W, state vets cemetery worker, $27,948
Cameron, Leslie M, ofc spt asst (keybrd), $25,824
Campbell, Brenda J, photographer, $29,004
Campbell, Charles E, maint worker II, $33,180
Campbell, Cynthia P, registered nurse - clin opers, $65,676
Campbell, David W, cpl, $70,728
Campbell, Emily D, direct care aide, $8.00/hr
Campbell, Gary L, motor veh insp III, $33,744
Campbell, James R, sergeant, $75,588
Campbell, Robin K, lpn III gen, $40,488
Campbell, Shawn M, cpl, $70,728
Canaday, Jennifer J, clerk IV, $31,512
Cannaday, Malia N, comm oper III, $44,928
Cannon, Eva L, activity ther, $35,076
Cannon, Leslie L, comm oper III, $51,996
Cantrell, Denise D, qual ctrl clerk II, $27,948
Cantrell, Rebecca S, nursing asst II, $28,224
Cantrell, William S, driver exam II, $29,976
Cape, Kyanna M, criminalist II, $46,932
Capps, Clinton R, trooper 1st class, $46,536
Capps, Nancy A, pub safety prog rep II, $36,204
Caraway, Sarah, exec I, $32,052
Cardenas, Kathryn D, paralegal, $38,045
Carel, Joshua M, automotive technician III, $34,356
Carel, Keith L, bldg/gnds maint i temp, $9.69/hr
Carello, Dominic R, trooper 1st class, $60,840
Carey, Shannon, admin ofc spt asst, $27,228
Carlock, Elisha M, technician II, $31,512
Carlyle, Harold S, cve sup II, $49,128
Carman, Stacie K, nursing asst I, $24,900
Carnagey, Derek B, trooper 1st class, $66,516
Carnelison, Alyssa R, hlth prog aide, $15.00/hr
Carpenter, Samuel D, trooper 1st class, $59,064
Carr, Bradley J, comp info tech spec II, $57,744
Carr, Caleb A, nursing asst I, $23,148
Carrell, Burke R, maint worker II, $30,420
Carrell, Gregory T, designated principal asst div, $68,916
Carrender, Marilyn C, clerk, $23.15/hr
Carroll, Patricia G, info technologist IV, $52,092
Carroll, Terry L, chief technician, $74,388
Carson, Michael E, sergeant, $75,588
Carter, Angela, sr ofc spt asst (steno), $30,384
Carter, Benjamin J, driver exam I, $29,004
Carter, Cabrina Y, nursing asst I, $24,900
Carter, Donald R, misc prof, $22.91/hr
Carter, Howard G, progmer/analyst mgr, $65,364
Carter, Howard G, comm technician I, $38,808
Carter, Maurice, driver exam II, $29,976
Carter, Patricia E, nursing asst I, $12,450
Carter, Quentin, maint spv I, $33,744
Carter, Tiffany L, registered nurse sr, $60,516
Carter, Veronica M, custodial worker I, $21,264
Cartwright, Alisha J, clerk-typist III, $27,948
Cartwright, Kevin, crpntr, $33,744
Carty, Emily A, nursing asst II, $27,780
Carver, Heidi M, planner II, $44,304
Cary, Michael L, trooper 1st class, $66,516
Case, Emily E, hlth prog aide, $12.00/hr
Casebeer, Jennifer L, electronic gaming device spec, $47,892
Casey, Crystal J, food serv helper I, $21,264
Casey, Stephanie N, food serv helper I, $21,264
Cashion, Carolyn S, lab evdnc tech II, $32,052
Casper, James T, trooper 1st class, $50,904
Casper, Rickey R, cvo sup II, $44,304
Cassil, Terry L, designated principal asst div, $71,201
Cassmeyer, Karen A, planner III, $43,488

Castor, Debra C, qual ctrl clerk II, $28,908
Cates, Tammy M, lpn III gen, $39,072
Caton, Dawn C, prob comm oper, $36,012
Caudle, Tony L, clerk, $26.52/hr
Caudle, Tony L, motor veh insp III, $31,512
Center, Erin M, staff artist III, $38,928
Cerroni, Christopher L, sergeant, $75,588
Chadwick, Jeanette M, clerk, $9.69/hr
Chambers, Gary, exec II, $38,232
Chambers, Robert E, custodial worker I, $20,148
Champagne, Donald D, state vets cemetery worker, $27,948
Chandler, Catherine F, bldg & grounds maint I, $23,880
Chanel, Chelsea N, acct II, $38,928
Chaney, Jonathan C, section chief, $79,176
Chapman, Catherine G, custodial worker I, $21,264
Chapman, Ricky J, trooper 1st class, $52,416
Chappell, Timothy M, commercial veh ofcr II, $44,304
Charrette, Thomas R, misc prof, $20.44/hr
Chase, Vonda R, nursing asst II, $27,360
Chatman, Cole P, trooper 1st class, $55,644
Chatman, Henry R Jr, custodial worker I, $20,148
Cheaney, Andrew F, cpl, $70,932
Cheney, Jeffrey, firefighter, $38,232
Chenoweth, Dale A, sergeant, $75,588
Cheshire, Deborah M, clerk, $25.25/hr
Cheung, Glenn E, maint spv I, $37,548
Chew, John E, pers ofcr I, $55,416
Chilcoat-Barron, Justin, firefighter, $38,232
Childers, Steven J, sergeant, $75,588
Childs, Percy S, driver exam III, $31,512
Chism, Calla L, nursing asst I, $23,856
Chisom, Sylvester, restorative aide, $28,584
Choate, Justin W, trooper 1st class, $59,064
Choate, Karen L, lab evdnc tech II, $32,052
Choate, William D, lt, $85,236
Choi, Sun N, custodial worker I, $20,664
Christensen, John E, cpl, $70,728
Christian, Christopher B, trooper 1st class, $46,536
Christian, Dwight L, motor veh insp III, $32,052
Christian, William, groundskeeper I, $23,880
Christlieb, Sonja A, vets serv ofcr, $29,976
Christman, Donna M, sr ofc spt asst (keybrd), $28,908
Christmas, Douglas S, trooper 1st class, $62,688
Christoffer, Tammy M, comm oper III, $49,044
Church, Patti J, registered nurse sup, $63,084
Cihal, Melissa D, technician I, $29,976
Cinotto, Dana S, typist, $9.69/hr
Clad, James A, misc prof, $15.70/hr
Clair, Christopher M, cpl, $70,728
Clamme, Janna K, motor veh insp III, $33,180
Clardy, Darewin L, lt, $85,236
Clark, Chad C, cpl, $59,064
Clark, Emily J, laundry worker II, $23,508
Clark, Jason P, sergeant, $75,588
Clark, Kyle, firefighter, $38,232
Clark, Lakisha T, nursing asst I, $24,900
Clark, Larry R, sergeant, $75,588
Clark, Marilyn M, driver exam III, $31,512
Clark, Sharon K, lpn III gen, $41,232
Clark, Tyrece L, nursing asst I, $23,148
Clarkston, Kimberly A, prog sup, $41,940
Clay, Teresa K, registered nurse, $32.00/hr
Claypool, Robert A, cook III, $25,824
Cleaveland, Karlee J, nursing asst I, $24,900
Clema, Debra S, driver exam sprv, $36,204
Clement, Ryan W, trooper 1st class, $46,536
Clemmons, Rebecca S, registered nurse sr, $58,140
Clemonds, Bruce T, special asst prof, $78,084
Clemons, Eric R, capitol police lt, $46,932
Cleveland, Jimmy L, chief technician, $74,388
Climer, David G, auditor I, $45,156
Cline, Anne M, laundry worker I, $20,664
Cline, Danny S, trnr/auditor III, $42,708
Close, Ashlie M, cve insp I, $29,004
Close, David A, probary trooper, $41,280
Clutter, Amanda K, sr ofc spt asst (keybrd), $32,472
Cluver, Jason J, sergeant, $75,588
Cluver, Jonathan A, cpl, $57,324
Coates, Diann M, cook III, $30,420

Coats, Stephen A, sergeant, $75,588
Cobb, Bonnie J, nursing asst I, $24,900
Cobb, Cheryl D, pub info spe III, $36,888
Cobb, John I, trooper, $43,872
Cobb, Kimberly D, custodial worker I, $20,664
Cobb, Randy G, chief cvo, $51,096
Cobb, Ronald G, nursing asst I, $24,900
Cochran, Ashton D, nursing asst I, $23,856
Cochran, Barbara A, mgmt analysis spec I, $40,380
Cochran, Kimberly M, stores clerk, $23,508
Cochrane, Shiloh L, motor veh insp II, $32,052
Cockrum, Nathan A, trooper, $43,872
Cody, Matthew J, sergeant, $75,588
Coffey, Bradley W, chief technician, $62,016
Coffey, Travis L, trooper 1st class, $49,392
Cogswell, Raymond, air depot maint spec II, $40,380
Cokenour, Mike, janitor, $8.16/hr
Coker, Branden S, comp info tech spec I, $50,040
Colbert, Charles R, sergeant, $75,588
Cole, Billy, trooper 1st class, $47,964
Cole, Charlesetta, laundry worker II, $23,880
Cole, Terri K, admin ofc spt asst, $32,052
Coleman, Amber R, nursing asst I, $23,148
Coleman, Bethany L, food serv mgr I, $33,744
Coleman, Michael W, trooper 1st class, $46,536
Colen, Brooke M, sr ofc spt asst (keybrd), $25,824
Coley, Vanessa S, registered nurse - clin opers, $69,996
Collier, Gaylan S, maint worker I, $30,384
Collier, Rheanne M, registered nurse sup, $59,340
Collins, Alonzo, direct care aide, $8.00/hr
Collins, Barbara A, trooper 1st class, $49,392
Collins, Derrick L, comm oper III, $47,628
Collins, James W, cpl, $59,064
Collins, Qwenteria P, nursing asst I, $23,148
Colman, Chris L, cvo sup I, $46,068
Colster, Laura M, nursing asst I, $23,856
Colwell, Charles, janitor, $8.16/hr
Colwell, Terry D, nursing asst I, $23,856
Colyott, Kevin E, training tech II, $43,488
Combs, Christopher B, custodial worker I, $20,664
Combs, Zackary, maint worker I, $28,908
Comer, Benjamin N, cpl, $62,688
Comer, Kyle W, prog mgr, $60,120
Compton, Michelle E, hlth prog spec, $12.35/hr
Conant, Stephen M, chief motor veh insp, $38,928
Conard, Beckie D, lpn III gen, $39,072
Cone, Brenda L, sergeant, $75,588
Conklin, Lisa K, custodial worker I, $20,664
Conklin, Sidney W, misc prof, $25.25/hr
Connally, Rhonda K, crim intel analyst I, $34,944
Conner, Rhonda K, registered nurse, $48,360
Conner, William S, comm oper III, $56,784
Conrad, Jonathan M, trooper 1st class, $49,392
Conrad, Joshua D, probary trooper, $41,280
Conway, Darla L, driver exam - chief, $38,928
Conway, James E, trooper 1st class, $50,904
Cook, Allen W, cve insp sprv I, $38,928
Cook, Amy M, driver exam II, $29,976
Cook, Christine A, cook I, $22,872
Cook, Craig A, trooper 1st class, $47,964
Cook, Eric A, prob comm technician, $36,012
Cook, Eyvone K, nursing asst II, $28,224
Cook, Janet L, housekeeper I, $29,496
Cook, Juliet, nursing asst II, $28,224
Cook, Loretta J, capitol police communs oper, $32,628
Cook, Matthew R, trooper 1st class, $50,904
Cook, Rachel A, nursing asst I, $23,856
Cook, Richard, security ofcr I, $26,652
Cook, Teresa J, capitol police ofcr, $32,628
Cook, Vickie R, special asst ofc & clerical, $49,824
Cook, Yvonne D, staff artist II, $33,744
Cooksey, James C, trooper 1st class, $50,904
Cool, Keenan J, trooper, $42,612
Cool, Stephen J, trooper 1st class, $46,536
Cooley, Carlton, food serv helper I, $20,148
Coon, Michele L, sergeant, $75,588
Cooper, Billie G, commercial veh ofcr II, $37,548
Cooper, Carol L, lpn III gen, $41,232
Cooper, Eric A, cpl, $70,728

Cooper, Johnnie, lpn III gen, $43,620
Cooper, Karen S, nursing asst I, $24,900
Cooper, Leroy J, nursing asst I, $24,900
Cooper, Randall K, cvo sup I, $41,172
Cooper, Todd M, asst chief oper, $62,016
Cooper, Vernon L, custodial worker I, $21,264
Cooper, William T, sergeant, $75,588
Cooseman, Pamela M, cdl exam, $33,744
Coots, Frank E, special asst prof, $58,596
Copas, Elizabeth H, comp info tech spec II, $57,744
Copeland, Kyle R, probary trooper, $41,280
Copeland, Natalie M, prob comm oper, $36,012
Copeland, Ronald A, sergeant, $75,588
Copley, Candace L, acct II, $41,940
Corcoran, Katie L, criminalist I, $41,940
Cordova, Terri L, nursing asst I, $23,148
Corn, Jared A, crim intel analyst II, $37,548
Cornett, Jason R, cpl, $70,728
Cornick, Helen C, direct care aide, $8.00/hr
Cornman, Eric D, cvo sup I, $41,172
Corrigan, James K, capitol police ofcr, $33,744
Cosey, Tumica L, driver exam sprv, $36,888
Costin, Eugenia A, registered nurse sr, $55,776
Cotter, Jack W, probary trooper, $41,280
Cottingham, Gregory E, mil funeral hnrs team leader, $29,976
Couch, Christopher A, cdl examination auditor, $36,204
Couch, Jennifer L, nursing asst I, $23,148
Couch, Stephanie D, nursing asst I, $23,856
Coulson, Jeffrey L, sergeant, $75,588
Coulson, Kristin D, lt, $85,236
Coulson, Shelby L, bldg/gnds maint i temp, $9.69/hr
Countryman, Chelsea M, account clerk III, $27,948
Countryman, Jennifer L, cook II, $23,160
Counts, Mark D, cve insp III, $36,204
Courtney, Bryan A, special asst prof, $86,376
Couts, Elaine M, cdl exam, $35,568
Coval, Angela M, trooper 1st class, $47,964
Cowan, Howard B, cpl, $70,728
Cowell, Roberta E, nursing asst II, $26,076
Cox, Amanda I, hlth prog aide, $16.00/hr
Cox, Amanda J, nursing asst I, $24,900
Cox, Isaac A, probary trooper, $41,280
Cox, James D, sergeant, $75,588
Cox, Kendra D, driver exam II, $29,976
Cox, Maghan N, clin casework asst II, $36,204
Cox, Pamela J, driver exam III, $31,512
Cox, Tabitha M, registered nurse sr, $50,244
Crabtree, Erica E, trooper, $43,872
Crabtree, Rita K, nursing asst I, $24,900
Crabtree, Steven H, cpl, $70,728
Crader, Linda M, laundry worker I, $22,536
Crafton, Dustin H, trooper 1st class, $57,324
Crafton, Jason W, criminalist III, $58,908
Crafton, Leamon E, technician I, $29,004
Crafton, Robert L, probary trooper, $41,280
Craig, Aaron S, trooper 1st class, $50,904
Craig, Cory W, sergeant, $75,588
Craig, Kelley J, restorative aide, $27,252
Craig, Robert J, maint worker I, $30,384
Craig, Timothy S, trooper 1st class, $50,904
Craigg, Maryann M, exec I, $36,888
Craighead, David L, cvo sup I, $46,932
Crandal, Laura M, criminalist III, $55,416
Crane, Meghan M, custodial worker I, $20,664
Crank, David W, cpl, $62,688
Crase, Michael D, comm oper III, $56,784
Cravens, Jeffrey A, sergeant, $70,932
Creach, Dalton K, bldg/gnds maint i temp, $9.69/hr
Creach, Kerry K, prog mgr, $60,120
Creasey, Keri K, recrtnal ther II, $41,172
Creasey, Robert C, trooper 1st class, $55,644
Creed, Michael R, nursing asst I, $23,148
Creed, Rodney D, maint worker II, $29,976
Crews, Lacey M, direct care aide, $8.00/hr
Crewse, Robert D, trooper 1st class, $59,064
Crewse, Stacy J, trooper 1st class, $62,688
Crites, Jason N, lt, $85,236
Crocfer, Cheryl A, fiscal & budget analyst II, $30,984
Crockett, Bradley L, trooper 1st class, $50,904

Croft, Travis S, sergeant, $62,688
Crose, William J, trooper 1st class, $66,516
Cross, Cynthia, nursing asst I, $24,900
Cross, Jason M, cpl, $57,324
Cross, Lisa M, hlth prog aide, $11.50/hr
Cross, Michael W, lt, $85,236
Cross, Roger D, div asst dir, $55,416
Crouch, Adam G, fire investigator, $38,928
Crouch, David M, cdl exam, $33,744
Crouch, Shannon W, sergeant, $75,588
Crowder, Brandy L, nursing asst II, $28,224
Crowder, Jason B, maint worker I, $30,384
Crowe, Leslie C, sergeant, $75,588
Crowe, Timothy E, sergeant, $75,588
Crowley, Amanda M, nursing asst I, $23,856
Crowley, Lisa R, baker I, $24,612
Crowther, Josiah N, misc prof, $13.50/hr
Cruise, Regina L, asst chief oper, $62,016
Crump, Donald L, sergeant, $75,588
Crump, Jerod J, trooper 1st class, $47,964
Crump, Lavonne, nursing asst II, $26,892
Crump, Mitzi A, comp info tech III, $45,156
Crutcher, Michael L, special asst prof, $35,000
Crutchfield, Tabitha D, trooper 1st class, $50,904
Cruz, Tami J, nursing asst I, $24,900
Cullifer, Kyle E, cvo sup I, $46,068
Culp, Billy J, nursing asst I, $23,148
Cummings, Caitlin J, nursing asst I, $23,148
Cummings, Deanna L, custodial worker I, $22,200
Cunningham, Jeffery S, trooper 1st class, $45,180
Cunningham, John T, trooper 1st class, $46,536
Cunningham, Laura, lpn III gen, $41,232
Cunningham, Michael A, sergeant, $75,588
Cunningham, Phyllis D, supply mgr I, $38,232
Cunningham, Ray L, janitor, $8.16/hr
Cunningham, Steven W, sergeant, $66,576
Curd, Sarah V, laundry worker I, $20,664
Cureton, Barbara A, custodial worker I, $20,664
Curl, Steve A, maint worker I, $29,904
Curless, Pauline L, nursing asst I, $24,900
Curnes, Gregory T, sergeant, $75,588
Curran, Scott, maint worker II, $30,420
Curry, Patricia L, nursing asst I, $23,856
Curtis, Rita M, nursing asst I, $24,900
Curtright, Joseph P, cve insp III, $36,204
Cutbirth, April L, registered nurse - clin opers, $65,676
Cutler, Chris M, automotive technician III, $37,548
Cyrus, John A, sergeant, $75,588
Cyrus, Reita D, clerk-typist III, $30,924
Czarnecki, Rhonda L, div asst dir, $58,908
Czerniewski, Zachary A, trooper 1st class, $45,180
Daise, Leland, maint worker II, $30,420
Dake, Jason D, comm oper III, $51,996
Dale, Alysia B, registered nurse sup, $59,340
Dale, Judy S, driver exam III, $33,180
Dale, Michael A, motor veh insp III, $31,512
Dalton, Daniel J, trooper, $43,872
Dalton, Samuel H, auditor I, $45,156
Daly, Jason C, trooper 1st class, $49,392
Daly, Tonia L, driver exam sprv, $36,888
Dancy, Liere R, trooper 1st class, $47,964
Dancy, Takira M, nursing asst II, $26,076
Dandamudi, Babu R, staff physician, $120.00/hr
Daniel, Brian L, lt, $85,236
Daniel, Deborah K, cve insp III, $36,204
Daniels, Christopher S, sergeant, $70,932
Daniels, Connie L, misc prof, $13.51/hr
Daniels, Gary T, probary trooper, $40,272
Daniels, Linda K, custodial worker I, $22,200
Danner, Stephen, div dir, $91,524
Darnel, Casey D, clerk, $9.69/hr
Darrah, Teresa L, driver exam II, $29,976
Dasta, Frank, environ spec III, $43,488
Daugherty, Tracy L, direct care aide, $9.00/hr
Daus, Vincent E, elevatr/amusemt ride sfty insp, $49,128
Davenport, Noel C, sergeant, $75,588
David, Viola, janitor, $8.16/hr
Davidson, Forest S, typist, $12.00/hr
Davidson, Gary D, sergeant, $75,588

Davidson, Joseph D, cpl, $60,840
Davidson, Rita F, lpn III gen, $37,020
Davidson, Sheri L, clerk-typist III, $30,924
Davidson, Teresa A, cve insp III, $36,204
Davies, Christopher T, sergeant, $66,576
Davis, Alyssa N, nursing asst I, $23,148
Davis, Brenda J, mvi analyst, $34,356
Davis, Cathryn L, trooper, $42,612
Davis, Charles E, technician III, $33,744
Davis, Christina M, nursing asst I, $23,856
Davis, Craig, heavy equip oper, $34,356
Davis, Daniel L, custodial worker II, $23,880
Davis, Deana L, nursing asst II, $28,224
Davis, Denise F, nursing asst I, $24,900
Davis, Gary D, criminalist III, $55,416
Davis, Howard, maint worker II, $30,420
Davis, Janet L, criminalist III, $55,416
Davis, Jauan D, activity aide II, $26,004
Davis, Joyce E, food serv helper I, $20,664
Davis, Justin L, comm oper I, $39,960
Davis, Kendra, nursing asst I, $23,856
Davis, Kimberly, cpl, $70,728
Davis, Kirk A, sergeant, $75,588
Davis, Krystalyn, trooper, $42,612
Davis, Melissa M, beautician, $15.00/hr
Davis, Noma A, misc prof, $20.85/hr
Davis, Paula L, registered nurse sup, $65,676
Davis, Paulette D, nursing asst I, $24,900
Davis, Price R, sergeant, $75,588
Davis, Renee, driver exam sprv, $36,204
Davis, Robert R, trooper 1st class, $46,536
Davis, Rodney E, qual ctrl clerk II, $29,904
Davis, Scott A, special asst prof, $60,600
Davis, Sharon A, food serv helper I, $20,664
Davis, Steve P, lt, $85,236
Davis, Steven, mil security ofcr I, $29,976
Davis, Theresa, trooper 1st class, $66,516
Davis, Tiffany T, pers clerk, $36,204
Davis-Brown, Rachel A, pers analyst II, $42,708
Davis-Hoagland, Holly C, clerk, $9.69/hr
Dawes, Robert W, elevatr/amusemt ride sfty insp, $44,304
Dawson, Bobbie, nursing asst I, $23,148
Dawson, Gregory, janitor, $8.16/hr
Dawson, Timothy D, comm oper III, $46,260
Day, Charles J, sergeant, $75,588
Day, Jeffrey T, trooper 1st class, $52,416
Dayringer, Michael J, cvo sup I, $41,940
Deason, Thomas D, trooper 1st class, $45,180
Debie, Lora L, ofc spt asst (clerical), $22,536
Debrodie, Rebecca S, exec II, $44,304
Deck, Tracy R, custodial worker I, $20,664
Decker, Jason L, sergeant, $64,584
Declue, Lance D, cpl, $62,688
Declue, Michael C, registered nurse mgr b2, $82,248
Decramer, Tye W, trooper 1st class, $46,536
Dedmon, Travis M, nursing asst I, $23,856
Deeds, Austin, typist, $12.00/hr
Dees, Shawn, janitor, $8.16/hr
Defer, Jessica L, driver exam sprv, $36,204
Degonia, Jessalin A, comm oper III, $47,628
Degraffenreid, Mark D, sergeant, $66,576
Dehaan, Blake R, trooper 1st class, $47,964
Deichman, Rhonda J, nursing asst I, $24,900
Dejager, Ashley N, nursing asst I, $24,900
Dejournett, Dylan L, trooper 1st class, $46,536
Delafuente, Stacey E, nursing asst I, $24,900
Delahunty, Jordan R, food serv helper I, $21,264
Delarber, Doris A, custodial worker II, $21,864
Delaurier, Steven D, domestic serv worker, $12.50/hr
Delgado, Jill L, pub safety mgr band 2, $69,720
Delgado, Lisa, registered nurse sr, $59,340
Dennis, Aaron, firefighter, $38,232
Dennis, James E, institution supt, $78,252
Dennis, Matthew L, driver exam II, $29,976
Denny, Lindsay J, exec II, $46,932
Denton, Thomas, air depot maint spec II, $40,380
Derousse, Amy E, registered nurse sup, $59,340
Derousse, Gaye A, cdl examination auditor, $36,204
Deshpande, Nikhil R, info technologist IV, $52,092

Dettenwanger, Blake A, trooper 1st class, $46,536
Devillez, Carlene R, nursing asst I, $23,148
Devore, Derek, custodial worker II, $23,880
Dewey, Chelsea M, nursing asst I, $23,148
Dewitt, David L, misc prof, $20.85/hr
Dewitt, Trisha L, nursing asst I, $23,148
Dexter, Diana, environ spec III, $43,488
Diaz, Eric D, probary trooper, $41,280
Dick, John W, sergeant, $75,588
Dickens, Greg C, fire insp, $35,568
Dickens, Marylyn A, trooper 1st class, $45,180
Dickens, Rebecca A, nursing asst I, $23,148
Dickneite, Kylie M, research analyst III, $48,156
Dicks, Teri L, driver exam sprv, $36,204
Dicus, Danial E, cpl, $70,728
Diehl, Todd E, fleet ctrl coord, $37,548
Dierenfeldt, Cindy M, criminalist III, $55,416
Diffee, Jamey R, cpl, $54,024
Dill, Andrew R, trooper 1st class, $66,516
Dillon, Adam V, cpl, $70,728
Dillon, Christine A, nursing asst II, $27,780
Dillon, Jared L, trooper, $43,872
Dillon, Jessica R, comm oper III, $51,996
Dinges, David C, sergeant, $62,688
Dinovi, Quinton L, trooper 1st class, $47,964
Dinwiddie, Kara R, probary trooper, $41,280
Distler, Andrew F, capital imprvmts spec II, $60,120
Ditzfeld, Mary L, nursing asst II, $28,224
Dixon, Carolyn S, nursing asst I, $24,900
Dlabach, Heather A, criminalist III, $55,416
Dochterman, Mark S, lt, $85,236
Dodd, Darylnisha T, nursing asst I, $23,772
Dodds, Carolyn S, food serv helper II, $24,264
Dodson, Benjamin R, trooper 1st class, $46,536
Dodson, Kimberlee A, sr ofc spt asst (steno), $29,412
Dodson, Shon E, trooper, $43,872
Doerhoff, Todd M, special agent (liquor ctrl), $47,892
Dolan, Mary, cook I, $23,508
Doll, Kyle M, bldg & grounds maint II, $24,612
Dollard, Chad M, trooper 1st class, $50,904
Dollens, Lori A, nursing asst II, $27,360
Dolweck, Brittany A, acct I, $29,976
Dometrorch, Shelly J, crim intel analyst II, $36,204
Donahue, Andrae D, lpn III gen, $35,148
Donnell, Steven A, cpl, $70,728
Doolittle, John B, electrcn, $23,977
Dopplick, Jennifer A, trooper 1st class, $46,536
Dorris, Daren L, maint worker II, $29,004
Dougan, Vernon C, capt, $93,120
Dougherty, Dolores M, nursing asst I, $23,856
Dougherty, Shawn M, cpl, $66,576
Douglas, Anita M, clerk-typist III, $27,948
Douglas, Brian D, chief technician, $74,388
Douglas, Donald, law enforce ofcr, $20.00/hr
Douglas, Eric B, comm oper III, $50,508
Douglas, Roiann L, clerk, $9.69/hr
Douglas, Rucell L, nursing asst I, $24,900
Douglass, Barbara F, lpn III gen, $43,620
Douthett, Reese E, trooper, $43,872
Dowd, Richard R, trooper 1st class, $66,516
Dowdell, Christopher, bldg & grounds maint I, $23,880
Dowell, Chelse Y, comp info tech III, $45,156
Dowell, Colby L, typist, $12.00/hr
Dowell, Meghan A, auditor I, $45,156
Downen, Cheryl J, custodial worker I, $22,200
Downey, Lori K, comm oper III, $55,128
Downey, Myron C, trooper 1st class, $66,516
Doyle, Jennifer L, processing technician I, $23,880
Doyle, John P, comp info tech III, $49,128
Doyle, Joshua B, trooper, $43,872
Doyle, Sandra, hr mgr b1, $65,363
Doza, Donald L, trooper 1st class, $66,516
Draffen, Medena M, registered nurse sup, $63,084
Drake, Jeanne G, laundry worker I, $22,200
Drenon, Christopher L, sergeant, $75,588
Dresel, Kay L, motor veh driver, $25,032
Driemeier, Harold L, sergeant, $75,588
Drum, Joseph, trooper 1st class, $66,516
Drummond, Brent J, sergeant, $70,932

Dubois, Gail A, acct II, $38,232
Dubois, Gregory A, sergeant, $75,588
Dubois, Rebekah J, nursing asst I, $23,856
Duby, Ashaley U, nursing asst I, $23,148
Duddleston, Daniel P, trooper, $43,872
Dudeck, Robert P, cpl, $54,024
Dudenhoeffer, Joan M, clerk, $12.60/hr
Dudley, Hailey M, direct care aide, $9.00/hr
Duensing, Lesa, lpn III gen, $41,232
Duffey, Donald H, automotive technician III, $38,928
Duffie, Dustin J, trooper 1st class, $46,536
Duke, Michael E, clerk, $26.52/hr
Duke, Michael E, asst garage supt, $41,172
Dulle, Bradley, mil funeral hnrs area supv, $36,204
Dunakey, Karah A, typist, $12.00/hr
Duncan, Charles, info technologist III, $42,708
Duncan, Deborah K, acct II, $37,548
Duncan, Kim S, laundry worker I, $20,148
Duncan, Ronald D, custodial worker I, $20,148
Dunfee, Cody G, sergeant, $62,688
Dungins, Marsha L, nursing asst I, $25,692
Dunlap, Patrick I, designated principal asst dept, $70,008
Dunlap, Rebecca L, driver exam III, $31,512
Dunmire, Joshua L, trooper, $43,872
Dunn, Jason T, fire investigator, $38,928
Dunn, Justin S, trooper 1st class, $50,904
Dunnavant, Christian S, nursing asst I, $23,148
Dunnigan, Suzette, examination monitor, $17.73/hr
Dunwiddie, Douglas R, div asst dir, $60,120
Dunworth, Shannon C, lpn III gen, $21.00/hr
Duppong, Clinton M, cpl, $70,728
Durbin, Cindy L, driver exam III, $31,512
Durham, Christopher M, comp info tech III, $50,040
Durham, Robert E, custodial worker I, $20,664
Durr, Brandon L, typist, $12.00/hr
Duvall, Ila R, comm oper III, $56,784
Duvall, Jake A, trooper 1st class, $45,180
Dye, Chandler, typist, $12.00/hr
Dye, Randy C, sergeant, $75,588
Dye, Steven R, cvo sup I, $46,932
Dykes, Zachary M, comm oper I, $39,960
Dyson, Gara E, clerk-typist III, $27,948
Eagan, Rebecca L, trooper 1st class, $66,516
Eagleson, Karen E, misc prof, $17.76/hr
Eaker, Jeffrey M, maint worker, $10.00/hr
Eakins, Ronald W, trooper 1st class, $66,516
Earl, Billie M, hlth prog aide, $16.00/hr
Early, Brittany L, nursing asst I, $23,856
Earney, David E, capt, $93,120
Easley, Kyle E, cpl, $57,324
Easter, Kathy A, typist, $13.90/hr
Eaton, Alexander B, registered nurse, $50,244
Eaton, Sandra M, cook II, $25,404
Eaton, Stephanie R, trooper 1st class, $47,964
Eberhard, Sarah L, major, $105,000
Ebersold, Keaton L, probary trooper, $41,280
Ebert, Enneth E, nursing asst I, $24,900
Ebert, Laura L, nursing asst II, $28,224
Ebright, Kristin N, nursing asst I, $23,148
Echaves, Melissa M, nursing asst I, $24,900
Echternacht, David F, cpl, $55,644
Eden, Deanna L, custodial worker I, $21,264
Eden, Michael K, trooper 1st class, $46,536
Edison, Betty J, nursing asst II, $30,144
Edson, Michele L, chief oper, $67,716
Edwards, Aliesha E, registered nurse sup, $65,676
Edwards, Aria A, laundry worker I, $22,200
Edwards, Billy J, const insp, $57,744
Edwards, Deanna R, exec I, $30,420
Edwards, Dewitt A, law enforce ofcr, $20.00/hr
Edwards, Diana, nursing asst I, $24,900
Edwards, Jeffrey S, vets serv ofcr, $29,004
Edwards, Nedeania R, nursing asst I, $23,148
Edwards, Sheila, registered nurse, $40.00/hr
Edwards, Travis, electronics tech, $32,628
Edwards, William, security ofcr I, $27,084
Eggen, James R, comp info tech III, $46,932
Eggers, Bobbie L, nursing asst I, $23,148
Ehsan, Salima B, food serv helper II, $22,536

Eichholz, Jamie L, clerk-typist III, $27,948
Eichholz, Jordan A, clerk, $9.69/hr
Eichholz, Margaret A, buyer II, $41,172
Eickhorst, Brenda M, technician III, $33,744
Eidson, Jon E, sergeant, $75,588
Eisenhauer, Amanda N, nursing asst I, $24,900
Eisterhold, Shelby R, bldg/gnds maint i temp, $9.69/hr
Elder, Heather J, spec II, $36,204
Elder, Lester D, capt, $93,120
Elder, Robert, laborer, $11.82/hr
Eldred, Joseph W, motor veh insp III, $31,512
Eldridge, Jill S, registered nurse sr, $51,552
Elfrink, Nelson D, lt, $85,236
Elgin, Tracey D, sr ofc spt asst (clerical), $28,908
Elkin, Charlene E, capitol police ofcr, $34,356
Elliott, Christine A, lpn III gen, $33,948
Elliott, David W, law enforce ofcr, $20.00/hr
Elliott, Deborah J, acct II, $39,624
Elliott, Logan S, sergeant, $66,576
Ellis, Cheyenne A, nursing asst I, $23,148
Ellis, Jeffrey J, motor veh insp II, $29,976
Ellison, Beth A, driver exam II, $29,976
Elliston, Trevor H, trooper 1st class, $46,536
Ellsworth, Johny L, sergeant, $68,688
Elwing, Joan D, registered nurse mgr b2, $75,228
Embrey, Kathleen, miltry funeral hnrs team mbr, $26,652
Emerson, Brett W, trooper 1st class, $54,024
Emo-Goodwin, Kimberly D, lpn III gen, $35,736
Enderle, Allison R, probary trooper, $41,280
Enderle, John M, lt, $85,236
Enderle, Sally L, driver exam III, $31,512
Endsley, Eric J, institution supt, $80,892
Engelhart, Aaron A, trooper, $43,872
Enloe, Jamie M, lpn, $20.00/hr
Ennis, Randi L, nursing asst I, $23,856
Enriquez, Brandy D, custodial worker I, $20,664
Enyart, Nikol, acct III, $40,380
Epperson, Tracy L, ofc spt asst (keybrd), $25,404
Epps, Darla D, cook II, $27,504
Epps, Deborah N, cook I, $17,154
Eravi, Melissa N, cook II, $23,160
Erb, Karen S, admin ofc spt asst, $32,628
Ernst, Mary E, lpn III gen, $40,488
Erpenbach, Todd E, trooper 1st class, $62,688
Esposito, Tiffony M, nursing asst I, $23,856
Esry, Chiqui J, nursing asst I, $24,900
Esry, Cordelia M, registered nurse, $31.83/hr
Estes, Ashley M, domestic serv worker, $9.75/hr
Estes, Clarence A, miltry funeral hnrs team mbr, $27,084
Estes, Jerry T, misc prof, $26.00/hr
Estes, Kelli C, sr ofc spt asst (keybrd), $27,084
Estes, Kelsey L, domestic serv worker, $9.38/hr
Estes, Raelene, driver exam III, $31,512
Estes, Virginia K, driver exam III, $34,356
Euans, Patrick B, asst chief oper, $62,016
Eubanks, Francis M, hlth prog aide, $11.00/hr
Eulinger, Kathey M, custodial worker I, $22,200
Eutsler, Christina D, food serv helper I, $21,264
Evans, Brooke N, registered nurse, $24.05/hr
Evans, Elisha, nursing asst I, $23,148
Evans, Myra, lpn III gen, $41,232
Evans, Ronald P, elevatr/amusemt ride sfty insp, $46,932
Evans, Shelia R, nursing asst I, $23,148
Evans, Sylvester, custodial worker I, $20,664
Evensen, Fred A, boiler/pressure vessel inspctr, $46,068
Evers, Beth A, pub safety prog rep II, $36,204
Ewers, Michael M, asst chief technician, $50,508
Ewigman, Lee C, trooper 1st class, $50,904
Ewing, Justin C, trooper, $43,872
Exner, Aaron J, criminalist II, $48,156
Ezell, Brenda J, institution supt, $77,676
Faber, Andrea A, registered nurse sup, $65,676
Faenger, Mary P, designated principal asst div, $89,400
Faherty, Tricia A, technician I, $30,420
Fain, Randy E, commercial veh ofcr II, $38,928
Fain, Randy E, clerk, $26.52/hr
Fairchild, Dana L, technician III, $36,888
Falchi, Laura, stores clerk, $23,508
Falk, Richard A, comp info tech III, $45,156

Fall, Allison J, driver exam III, $31,512
Falter, Leigh A, fiscal&budgetary analyst III, $33,180
Falterman, George H, sergeant, $75,588
Fariole, Jonathon D, trooper 1st class, $47,964
Farley, Jonna R, admin ofc spt asst, $32,628
Farmer, Brenda L, custodial worker I, $20,664
Farmer, Jim D, trooper 1st class, $59,064
Farmer, Lesa K, registered nurse sr, $50,244
Farr, Charles E, fire insp, $35,568
Farr, Edna E, sr ofc spt asst (keybrd), $32,472
Farr, Rachel L, auditor I, $45,156
Farr, Shirterra L, nursing asst I, $24,900
Farrales, Michael, air depot maint spec II, $40,380
Farrell, Angela K, driver exam II, $29,976
Farrell, Bridget H, nursing asst II, $27,360
Farrell, Jeffrey, crpntr, $33,744
Farris, Alexandra H, clerk, $9.69/hr
Farris, Connie L, comp info tech spec II, $57,744
Farris, Rebecca A, nursing asst I, $24,216
Farrow, Connie E, div asst dir, $55,416
Fechtig, Mark E, fire investigator, $38,928
Feeler, Brenda K, comp info tech III, $45,156
Feilner, Christopher D, prob comm oper, $37,392
Fellwock, Nicollette E, hlth prog aide, $11.00/hr
Feltrop, Adam J, asst garage supt, $38,928
Fender, Kevin L, sergeant, $75,588
Fender, Kyron M, nursing asst I, $23,856
Fennessey, Daniel P, clerk, $9.69/hr
Fennewald, Michael P, sergeant, $66,576
Ferguson, Brandon D, state vets cemetery worker, $27,948
Ferguson, David, air depot maint spec II, $40,380
Ferguson, Pamela E, misc prof, $17.40/hr
Ferrier, Stephen B, lt, $85,236
Fessenden, Douglas E, cpl, $57,324
Fessler, Reid T, cpl, $70,728
Fewell, Teresa J, asst chief oper, $68,412
Fichtner, Robinson R, commercial veh ofcr II, $39,624
Fick, Timothy C, trooper 1st class, $45,180
Fiddyment, Montanna R, lpn, $20.00/hr
Fidler, Megan D, activity ther, $31,152
Fields, Belma D, custodial worker I, $20,148
Fields, Donna F, motor veh insp III, $34,944
Fierge, Melanie A, registered nurse sup, $68,532
Fife, William, pub safety mgr band 2, $48,000
Figliolo, Brittney M, nursing asst I, $23,148
Filippi, Russell J, cpl, $70,728
Fines, Steven P, vets serv ofcr, $29,004
Finkemeier, Clint A, trooper, $43,872
Finnegan, Michael T, sergeant, $75,588
Finnigan, Shari L, nursing asst I, $24,900
Fischer, Joseph D, trooper 1st class, $66,516
Fischer, Joshua C, ofc spt asst (keybrd), $22,536
Fischer, Sharon K, nursing asst I, $24,900
Fish, Adam J, trooper, $43,872
Fish, Randall E, comm oper III, $62,016
Fisher, Felicia L, lpn III gen, $43,620
Fisher, Gregory G, vets serv ofcr, $31,512
Fisher, John P, capitol police cpl, $36,888
Fisher, Kevin M, sergeant, $75,588
Fisher, Lydia J, criminalist III, $55,416
Fisher, Matthew P, cpl, $59,064
Fisher, Stephen D, custodial worker I, $21,264
Fiske, Bruce D, lt, $85,236
Fitzgerald, David T, special asst prof, $70,008
Fitzgerald, Jeffery T, sergeant, $75,588
Fitzmaurice, Vernon J, nursing asst II, $27,780
Fizer, Lori A, lpn III gen, $41,232
Fizer, Lucille, nursing asst I, $24,900
Flannery, Allen R, cpl, $70,728
Flannigan, David A, capt, $93,120
Flannigan, Kathleen A, sr ofc spt asst (keybrd), $32,472
Flaugher, Jeffrey A, custodial worker II, $23,160
Fleener, Cynthia B, auditor I, $45,156
Fleetwood, Susanne R, criminalist sup, $65,364
Fleharty, Kristen D, nursing asst I, $23,856
Fleming, Gwendolyn A, nursing asst I, $26,076
Fletcher, Richard C, sergeant, $75,588
Fletcher, Samantha R, nursing asst I, $23,148
Fletcher, Virginia, mil funeral hnrs area coor, $30,984

Flickinger, Carla J, clerk IV, $36,204
Flippin, Amanda J, technician III, $33,744
Florea, Kelly J, electronic gaming device coor, $55,416
Florence, Carol A, nursing asst I, $23,148
Flores, Miriam E, sr ofc spt asst (keybrd), $25,824
Flowers, David J, lpn III gen, $41,976
Flowers, George C, custodial worker I, $20,664
Flowers, Kayla M, nursing asst I, $23,148
Flowers, Marisa L, sr ofc spt asst (keybrd), $27,948
Flowers, Traci L, nursing asst I, $23,148
Floyd, Ellen L, cve insp III, $36,204
Flye, Renee A, custodial worker I, $20,664
Flynn, Clinton R, commercial veh ofcr II, $38,928
Fogelbach, Rhonda L, acct, $25.00/hr
Fogler, Schawnn W, trooper 1st class, $66,516
Foley, Molly M, nursing asst II, $26,508
Foley, Troy M, motor veh insp III, $33,180
Follins, Elesha T, nursing asst I, $23,856
Folsom, Diana L, nursing asst I, $24,900
Fontana, Mark P, institution supt, $93,636
Fooks, Maria F, qual ctrl clerk II, $29,904
Forbis, Jay A, comp info tech III, $50,040
Forbis, Karen M, traffic safety analyst III, $37,548
Forbis, Michael L, comp info tech spv I, $51,096
Forbis, Nicole M, technician I, $29,004
Force, Steven J, trooper 1st class, $57,324
Forck, Carol, data entry oper, $15.00/hr
Forck, Christopher A, sergeant, $75,588
Forck, Elaine A, pers analyst II, $46,932
Forck, Pauline F, clerk, $9.69/hr
Ford, Jeanette L, clerk-typist III, $29,904
Ford, Pamela C, driver exam sprv, $36,204
Foreman, Amanda S, info technologist IV, $52,092
Forler, Mary K, trooper 1st class, $50,904
Formento, Carolyn S, clerk, $9.69/hr
Forst, Regenia K, driver exam III, $31,512
Forsythe, Brett A, trooper 1st class, $66,516
Foster, Brian D, sergeant, $62,688
Foster, Kellie L, comp info tech spec I, $50,040
Foster, Matthew B, trooper 1st class, $50,904
Foster, Steven N, sergeant, $66,576
Fouch, David L, trooper 1st class, $45,180
Fountain, Donald A, mvi sup, $43,488
Fountain, Lyndsey M, clerk-typist III, $27,948
Foust, Devin W, trooper 1st class, $46,536
Fowler, Ashley D, driver exam I, $29,004
Fowler, Brent J, cpl, $64,584
Fowler, Larry, clerk III, $27,948
Fowler, Nicole K, comm oper I, $39,960
Fox, William C, cpl, $66,576
Frager, Eric B, bldg & grounds maint II, $27,084
Frame, Cody C, trooper 1st class, $46,536
Francis, Charlea A, nursing asst II, $27,780
Frank, Anthony, groundskeeper I, $24,612
Frank, Charles J, bldg const wkr II, $38,232
Frank, Janice M, pers analyst II, $50,040
Franklin, Gregory L, driver exam I, $28,104
Franklin, Marcia T, cook I, $23,508
Franks, Angela D, designated principal asst div, $54,104
Franz, Sharon C, nursing asst I, $24,900
Frazer, Sherry L, lpn III gen, $39,072
Frazier, Linda R, special asst prof, $40,788
Frazier, Michael K, sergeant, $75,588
Frazier, Suzon L, custodial worker I, $22,200
Fredendall, Richard G, lt, $85,236
Freeman, Debra L, qual ctrl clerk II, $31,920
Freeman, Mark L, cpl, $70,728
Freeman, Matthew R, trooper, $42,612
Freeman-Buys, Rosemarie, lpn III gen, $40,488
French, Courtney M, nursing asst I, $23,148
French, James W, clerk, $9.69/hr
French, Kim M, registered nurse, $40.00/hr
Freppon, Douglas M, groundskeeper I, $25,824
Frerer, Michael L, bldg/gnds maint i temp, $9.69/hr
Freund-O'leary, Steffanie, nursing asst I, $23,856
Frey, Michelle L, trnr/auditor I, $36,204
Frie, Trina A, storekeeper I, $27,504
Friel, Melissa N, designated principal asst div, $80,151
Friend, Cathy B, restorative aide, $27,252

Friend, Kaylan S, clerk, $9.69/hr
Friend, Matthew, mil funeral hnrs team leader, $29,004
Friend, Willis W, motor veh insp III, $31,512
Friese, Darrel W, maint worker I, $26,652
Friese, Lisa R, cook II, $24,612
Friese, Margaret A, nursing asst II, $28,224
Friese-Cornelius, Priscilla C, nursing asst II, $28,224
Frigy, Mark A, trooper, $42,612
Frillman, Jerri S, nursing asst I, $24,900
Frisbie, Steven J, lt, $85,236
Frisch, Angela M, nursing asst II, $27,780
Fritzsche, Robin A, driver exam III, $31,512
Fry, Paula L, admin ofc spt asst, $32,628
Fry, Richard L, cvo sup II, $44,304
Frye, Charles, security guard, $23,880
Fugett, Jeffery D, sergeant, $75,588
Fugitt, Bruce R, driver exam II, $29,976
Fulkerson, Aimee N, cpl, $55,644
Fulkerson, Cody H, sergeant, $75,588
Fulton, Calvin G, stores clerk, $23,160
Funderburk, Matthew K, sergeant, $75,588
Funk, Delbert, mil security ofcr II, $32,628
Furlow, Cathlene M, lpn III gen, $20,244
Gabauer, Marcia K, nursing asst I, $23,856
Gabelsberger, Sandra M, fiscal & budget analyst I, $28,104
Gabriel, Danny, automotive technician III, $34,356
Gach, Christopher M, sergeant, $75,588
Gadberry, Andrew D, cpl, $57,324
Gaines, Fred, info technologist IV, $47,892
Gaines, Graydon L, trooper 1st class, $46,536
Gaines, Sherry A, custodial worker I, $20,664
Gaines, Timothy D, groundskeeper I, $25,032
Galaska, Spencer D, trooper 1st class, $47,964
Galate, Lora J, driver exam - chief, $43,488
Galatzer, Tracy M, domestic serv worker, $9.38/hr
Gall, Jamie L, nursing asst I, $23,148
Gallegos, Anthony J, nursing asst I, $24,900
Gamet, John M, driver, $11.59/hr
Gammill, Kayla E, nursing asst I, $23,148
Gammons, Brenda G, laundry worker I, $20,664
Gann, Linda C, nursing asst II, $27,780
Gann, Rebeca C, custodial worker I, $21,264
Ganschinietz, Karren A, nursing asst I, $24,900
Garbulski, Craig M, trooper 1st class, $66,516
Gard, Jo R, account clerk II, $27,948
Gardner, Quinn M, special asst prof, $53,033
Gardner, Tyson B, sergeant, $75,588
Garland, Joseph T, cvo sup I, $40,380
Garner, Cheryl A, qual ctrl clerk II, $28,908
Garner, Helen W, physician, $56,640
Garnett, Darin, vid prod spec II, $36,204
Garnett, Tiffany M, technician III, $33,744
Garrett, Barbara G, custodial worker I, $21,264
Garrett, Robert W, trooper 1st class, $55,644
Garrison, Evan T, criminalist sup, $69,604
Garrison, Timothy J, pub safety prog spec, $40,380
Gartner, Michael H, comm technician II, $41,148
Garton, Travis N, trooper 1st class, $57,324
Garzend Burnett, Sharon K, typist, $9.69/hr
Gassen, John P, cpl, $70,728
Gately, Allen N, maint worker I, $28,452
Gates, Stanley S, trooper 1st class, $66,516
Gaucin, Gregoria, nursing asst I, $24,900
Gaut, Karen E, fiscal & administrative mgr b2, $66,868
Gavin, Cynthia C, custodial worker I, $20,664
Gee, Diana F, lpn III gen, $37,680
Geeting, Mark, asst fire chief, $52,092
Geeting, Michael, firefighter, $41,940
Gehle, Larry L, clerk, $12.50/hr
Geier, Brian J, trooper 1st class, $62,688
Geiser, Lisa J, pub safety prog spec, $40,380
Geisinger, Kelly E, sr ofc spt asst (keybrd), $27,948
Geist, Dena R, driver exam - chief, $41,172
Gely, Sebastian H, special asst prof, $27,228
Gentges, Justin A, probary trooper, $40,272
Gentry, Mary H, nursing asst I, $23,856
Gentry, Renee S, driver exam sprv, $36,204
George, Anjanette L, comm oper III, $44,928

George, Anna C, barber, $15.00/hr
George, James W, trooper 1st class, $66,516
George, Margaret J, sr ofc spt asst (keybrd), $28,908
George, Robert, mil funeral hnrs area supv, $36,204
Gerbes, Lauren, account clerk II, $26,652
Gerhardt, Nicholas W, criminalist III, $69,604
Gerhart, Charles, capitol police ofcr, $33,744
Gering, Billie J, baker II, $25,032
Gerke, Ron S, accounting spec I, $41,172
Gerlach, Brenda V, planner III, $51,096
Germann, Bradley R, trooper 1st class, $55,644
Gerstenberger, Elaine K, vets serv ofcr, $29,004
Gertiser, James A, state vets cemetery worker, $27,948
Gertson, Jeffrey L, trooper 1st class, $66,516
Getman, Tyson C, automotive technician III, $34,356
Gettemeier, Stephen A, misc tech, $20.24/hr
Giacolone, Christopher S, probary trooper, $41,280
Gibbs, Billie, restorative aide, $27,696
Gibson, Angela J, comp info tech I, $34,944
Gibson, Brad D, criminalist sup, $68,165
Gibson, Cheryl A, lpn III gen, $41,232
Gibson, Eric W, mvi sup, $36,888
Gibson, Kordel L, trooper 1st class, $46,536
Gibson, Patsy I, food serv helper I, $22,536
Gibson, Ricky L, activity aide II, $28,584
Gibson, Russell R, trooper 1st class, $55,644
Gibson, Vicky I, nursing asst I, $24,900
Gilbert, Jessica L, nursing asst I, $23,856
Giles, Jeffrey, registered nurse, $40.00/hr
Gillette, William A, vets serv ofcr, $29,976
Gillig, Dalton J, typist, $12.00/hr
Gilliland, Christy M, domestic serv worker, $9.75/hr
Gilliland, John C, trooper 1st class, $52,416
Gilliland, Leslie A, nursing asst I, $12,450
Gilmore, Marilyn J, admin ofc spt asst, $30,420
Gilpin, David E, capitol police ofcr, $32,628
Gilstrap, Chelsy L, clerk-typist III, $28,908
Gilstrap, Patricia J, hlth prog aide, $12.00/hr
Ginel, Monique J, cdl examination auditor, $36,204
Gingerich, Jennifer M, cook I, $22,872
Gipson, David L, trooper 1st class, $45,180
Gisselbeck, Steven R, cpl, $70,728
Givens, Hannah E, hlth prog aide, $16.00/hr
Givens, Joel E, cpl, $57,324
Gladbach, Stacey L, nursing asst II, $27,360
Gladney, Sherril L, planner I, $34,944
Glaus, Brooke L, nursing asst I, $24,900
Glendenning, Jason H, sergeant, $75,588
Glenn, Sterling, miltry funeral hnrs team mbr, $25,824
Glick, David E, phys plant sup I, $41,940
Glidewell, Lisa R, lpn III gen, $41,232
Glueck, Ashley R, nursing asst I, $24,900
Goans, Jerry L, chief technician, $74,388
Goans, Joseph D, chief technician, $74,388
Goans, Kristy D, special asst prof, $35,364
Godsey, Luther V, div asst dir, $84,533
Goedecke, Leslie A, comm oper III, $49,044
Goeke, Nicholas J, pub safety mgr band 2, $63,125
Goeller, Abigayle R, criminalist I, $40,380
Goff, Chris, laborer I, $22,872
Goforth, Jennifer L, auditor I, $45,156
Goins, Carisa L, sergeant, $70,932
Gold, Jeanette A, custodial worker I, $21,264
Golden, Karissa A, nursing asst II, $25,692
Golden, Katherine M, lpn III gen, $39,072
Goldsberry, Dale A, motor veh insp III, $31,512
Golian, Pamela J, lpn III gen, $33,948
Gonzales, Angel D, clin casework asst II, $34,944
Goodall, David L, nursing asst I, $23,856
Goodings, Douglas R, training tech II, $42,708
Goodman, Debra J, housekeeper II, $39,624
Goodson, Matthew A, cpl, $54,024
Gooldy, Jan M, lpn III gen, $41,232
Goolsby, Travis I, trooper 1st class, $55,644
Gordanier, Richard D, clerk, $9.69/hr
Gordon, Kyndal L, commercial veh ofcr II, $39,624
Gordon, Suzanne K, pers clerk, $33,180
Gosney, Karla S, clerk, $9.69/hr
Goss, Janelle R, account clerk II, $27,084

Gottman, Erik A, lt, $85,236
Gove, Amanda L, clerk-typist III, $28,908
Gowens, Donna L, registered nurse sup, $69,996
Graham, Angela M, nursing asst I, $24,900
Graham, Brian Z, auditor II, $50,040
Graham, Bryan G, trooper 1st class, $66,516
Graham, Dana D, technician I, $30,420
Graham, Deborah S, technician III, $33,744
Graham, Michael K, custodial worker II, $23,880
Graham, Rhonda K, driver exam III, $31,512
Graham, Sharon, account clerk, $20.34/hr
Graham, Troy F, trooper 1st class, $50,904
Grant, Randy W, motor veh insp I, $29,004
Grant, Thomas L, custodial worker I, $20,664
Grant, William W, examination monitor, $16.22/hr
Graskewicz, Barry W, cpl, $70,728
Graslie, Eric J, trooper 1st class, $46,536
Grass, Erica L, trooper 1st class, $46,536
Grass, Stephen L, sergeant, $75,588
Graue, Jeffrey S, cpl, $70,728
Graver, Brittanie A, registered nurse sr, $54,720
Graves-Sampson, Malinda A, vets benefits claims rep, $32,628
Grawe, Tami L, custodial worker I, $20,664
Gray, Adam J, trooper 1st class, $46,536
Gray, Ashlie, nursing asst I, $23,148
Gray, Blake A, typist, $12.00/hr
Gray, Brenda L, registered nurse, $28.78/hr
Gray, Glenn, custodial worker I, $21,864
Gray, Randy C, laborer II, $25,824
Gray, Stephanie L, comm oper I, $38,808
Grayham, Rae P, nursing asst I, $23,148
Greatsinger, Charles D, capitol police ofcr, $32,628
Green, Amanda M, ofc spt asst (keybrd), $25,404
Green, Angela D, fin auditor, $51,096
Green, Beverly A, nursing asst I, $24,900
Green, Derek S, sergeant, $75,588
Green, Irene R, nursing asst I, $24,900
Green, Jason A, cpl, $70,728
Green, Kathleen M, criminalist III, $64,038
Green, Kevin D, mvi sup, $38,928
Green, Kyle A, cpl, $64,584
Green, Mark D, sergeant, $75,588
Green, Michelle M, traffic safety analyst III, $39,624
Green, Quinette L, trnr/auditor III, $44,304
Green, Robert O, probary trooper, $41,280
Green, Shannon L, nursing asst I, $24,900
Green, Shenika R, nursing asst I, $23,148
Greenan, Robert M, trooper 1st class, $60,840
Greenway, Phillip, janitor, $8.16/hr
Greenwood, Robert W, cook I, $22,872
Greer, Beverly J, laundry worker I, $22,200
Gregg, Cindy L, nursing asst I, $23,148
Gregg, Joann E, cook III, $31,512
Gregory, Bradford R, commercial veh ofcr II, $45,156
Gregory, Christopher R, probary trooper, $40,272
Gregory, Daniel A, mvi sup, $38,928
Gregory, Gerald L, cdl exam, $34,944
Gregory, Jason L, commercial veh ofcr II, $38,928
Gregory, Lalah M, comm oper III, $56,784
Gregory, Philip E, lt, $85,236
Greiner, Nicholas J, trooper 1st class, $50,904
Grewach, Edward J, chief counsel, $93,082
Grieme, Anne L, lpn III gen, $41,232
Griesinger, Annette M, acct II, $40,380
Griffin, Aaron K, trooper 1st class, $55,644
Griffin, Brandon C, trooper 1st class, $57,324
Griffin, Emma J, custodial worker I, $20,664
Griffin, Felicia D, account clerk I, $25,404
Griffin, Rosalyn A, registered nurse - clin opers, $68,532
Griffith, Dale, janitor, $8.16/hr
Griffith, Jonya L, processing technician I, $23,880
Griffith, Michael D, capitol police sergeant, $41,172
Griggs, Justin E, nursing asst I, $23,148
Griggs, Shawn M, sergeant, $62,688
Grimm, Kristen P, hlth prog aide, $11.50/hr
Grindstaff, Robert, janitor, $8.16/hr
Grissom, Eldon L, sergeant, $75,588
Gronemeyer, Gabriel T, driver exam III, $31,512
Groner, Paige E, typist, $12.00/hr

Grossman, Heather D, nursing asst I, $24,900
Grover, Phillip A, law enforce ofcr, $20.00/hr
Groves, Miranda L, clerk-typist II, $25,032
Groves, Steven A, motor veh insp III, $34,356
Groves, Steven D, asst chief oper, $68,412
Grubaugh, Philip B, trooper 1st class, $47,964
Gruben, Bryan C, sergeant, $75,588
Gruenberg, Sharlene L, auditor I, $43,488
Grueneberg, Debra J, exec II, $47,892
Gruer, Rhonda I, nursing asst I, $12,449
Guess, Sarah E, nursing asst I, $24,900
Guillermo, Lisa M, nursing asst I, $23,856
Guilliams, Herbert W, commercial veh ofcr II, $38,928
Gulick, Darlis F, driver exam II, $29,976
Gullett, Charles D, trooper 1st class, $47,964
Gumbs, Inelka D, food serv helper I, $20,664
Gunder, Amber R, nursing asst I, $23,772
Gundy, Gary E, trooper 1st class, $66,516
Gunnels, Thresa M, sr ofc spt asst (keybrd), $32,472
Gunnett, Loren R, driver exam I, $28,104
Guthrie, Aylia A, nursing asst I, $23,148
Guzan, Jennifer W, domestic serv worker, $9.38/hr
Gwaltney, Angela M, registered nurse - clin opers, $63,084
Gwinn, Jasmine L, nursing asst I, $23,148
Haarmann, Holly A, prog mgr, $60,120
Haas, Rene M, nursing asst II, $27,780
Hackett, Gregory T, trooper, $42,612
Hackman, Eric W, sergeant, $75,588
Haden, Curtis R, cpl, $70,728
Hadlock, Todd A, cpl, $70,728
Haeffner, Norma A, registered nurse sr, $60,516
Hafley, David, pub safety mgr band 1, $43,848
Hageman-Kieselhorst, Anne C, registered nurse sup, $67,104
Hagen, Gretchen A, misc tech, $12.69/hr
Hagen, Jeanna M, auditor I, $23,946
Hagen, Sherry L, lpn III gen, $41,232
Hager, Douglas R, comm oper III, $55,128
Hager, Melissa S, clerk-typist II, $25,032
Hagerty, Brian S, sergeant, $75,588
Haggard, Bradley E, institution supt, $78,252
Haggett, David B, sergeant, $75,588
Haggett, Landon J, trooper, $42,612
Hahn, Carolyn L, lpn III gen, $37,020
Hahn, Leslie V, pub safety mgr band 2, $64,054
Hainey, Joshua E, probary trooper, $41,280
Hains, Harold L, state vets cemetery worker, $27,948
Hair, Sheila, acct II, $41,940
Halavats, Jonna L, driver exam II, $29,976
Halbert, Brandy, planner III, $48,156
Haldiman, Marcia S, misc prof, $27.56/hr
Hale, April A, account clerk II, $28,452
Hale, Denise I, custodial worker I, $20,664
Haley, Trent J, trooper 1st class, $52,416
Halford, Matthew T, cpl, $62,688
Halford, Michael A, sergeant, $75,588
Halim, Michael K, probary trooper, $41,280
Hall, Anna M, nursing asst I, $23,856
Hall, Brady A, typist, $12.00/hr
Hall, Brandon A, trooper 1st class, $47,964
Hall, Brenda, nursing asst I, $24,900
Hall, Charity L, admin ofc spt asst, $28,104
Hall, Christina S, nursing asst I, $24,900
Hall, David A, capt, $93,120
Hall, Frankie L, nursing asst I, $24,900
Hall, Gregory N, commercial veh ofcr II, $38,928
Hall, John H, procurement ofcr II, $52,092
Hall, Joseph D, trooper 1st class, $46,536
Hall, Kevin E, special asst prof, $59,160
Hall, Kevin R, legal counsel, $76,260
Hall, Mary A, lpn III gen, $39,072
Hall, Michael A, chief technician, $74,388
Hall, Rachel M, nursing asst I, $23,148
Hall, Tasinee T, nursing asst I, $24,900
Hall, Thomas L, sergeant, $75,588
Hall, Tina G, cve insp III, $36,204
Hall, Tina M, processing technician I, $23,880
Halley, Jesse S, trooper, $43,872
Halsey, Monica, registered nurse sr, $60,516
Ham, Stephen M, motor veh insp III, $31,512

Hamblin, Donna K, pers clerk, $33,180
Hamblin, Melvin, janitor, $8.16/hr
Hamerle, Bryan, trooper 1st class, $45,180
Hamilton, Amber J, registered nurse sr, $51,552
Hamilton, John D, chief oper, $74,388
Hamlett, Christopher D, cpl, $54,024
Hammerling, Katherine L, trooper 1st class, $46,536
Hammerschmidt, Dawn A, lpn II gen, $32,808
Hammond, Jason W, info technologist IV, $52,092
Hampton, Jacqueline M, misc tech, $12.70/hr
Hampton, Kendall G, trooper 1st class, $66,516
Hampton, Michael, maint worker I, $29,904
Hampton, Valerie L, trnr/auditor III, $41,940
Hampton, Venita K, food serv helper I, $20,664
Hanavan, Cody R, electronic gaming device spec, $49,490
Hance, Llona C, motor veh insp III, $33,744
Handshy Feeler, Christy R, cdl exam, $33,744
Hane, Evan T, cpl, $52,416
Hanebrink, Terisa L, cook II, $24,264
Hannah, Michelle, sr ofc spt asst (clerical), $28,908
Hanrahan, Bobbi L, hlth prog aide, $12.00/hr
Hanrahan, Matthew J, trooper 1st class, $47,964
Hansen, Gregory A, trooper 1st class, $66,516
Hansen, Mallory A, driver exam I, $29,004
Harbison, Dale W, fire insp, $35,568
Hardester, Shelley L, cve insp III, $36,204
Hardimon, Hattie B, nursing asst I, $25,692
Hardin, Kimberly D, criminalist III, $55,416
Harding, Kenna J, nursing asst I, $23,856
Harding, Lacy J, nursing asst I, $24,900
Harding, Nina A, nursing asst I, $24,900
Hardy, Jacob R, trooper, $42,612
Hargis, Gaye L, driver exam III, $31,512
Hargis, William C, automotive tech sup, $36,204
Hargrove, Richard L, motor veh insp III, $31,512
Hargus, Michael D, lt, $85,236
Harker, Klarissa D, nursing asst I, $23,856
Harkrider, Carol J, licensed clin soc wkr, $44,304
Harlan, Christopher W, trooper 1st class, $66,516
Harlow, James C, misc prof, $34.84/hr
Harmon, Clifton G, driver exam III, $31,512
Harmon, Lysandra J, registered nurse sr, $51,552
Harmon, Patricia, custodial work spv, $26,232
Harmon, Travis L, probary trooper, $41,280
Harms, Patrick T, trooper 1st class, $46,536
Harper, Larry M, nursing asst I, $23,856
Harper, Mary M, nursing asst I, $23,856
Harper, Sharon K, examination monitor, $10.52/hr
Harper, Teresa A, nursing asst II, $27,780
Harpole, Tonya A, restorative aide, $28,152
Harrell, Brian N, sergeant, $75,588
Harrell, Christina M, nursing asst I, $24,900
Harrington, Kenneth, mgmt analysis spec I, $38,928
Harris, Brandon L, trooper, $42,612
Harris, Chris J, lt, $85,236
Harris, Clevon L, driver exam III, $31,512
Harris, Eric L, lpn III gen, $37,680
Harris, Eunice D, misc tech, $12.70/hr
Harris, Gregory, air depot maint spec II, $40,380
Harris, Jennifer L, nursing asst I, $24,900
Harris, Jessica A, nursing asst I, $24,900
Harris, Kellie, lpn III gen, $41,232
Harris, Kimberly K, nursing asst I, $24,900
Harris, Leena C, cdl exam, $33,744
Harris, Mable A, nursing asst I, $24,900
Harris, Marketa N, hlth prog aide, $16.00/hr
Harris, Schyler A, nursing asst I, $24,900
Harris, Stephanie, nursing asst I, $24,900
Harris, Tammy K, driver exam - chief, $38,928
Harris, Walter F, probary trooper, $40,272
Harrison, Aaron M, cpl, $70,728
Harrison, John M, trooper 1st class, $49,392
Harrison, Kimberly J, driver exam II, $29,976
Harrison, Thereasa J, driver exam II, $29,976
Harrison, William D, planner III, $49,128
Harrison, Zachary A, trooper 1st class, $50,904
Hart, Alan L, maint worker II, $30,984
Hart, Emily J, registered nurse sr, $58,140
Hart, Kendra R, hlth prog aide, $15.00/hr

Hartle, Emily A, nursing asst I, $23,148
Hartley, Tami J, nursing asst II, $27,780
Hartmann, Donald J, cve insp II, $33,744
Harvel, Nikki S, criminalist II, $48,156
Haseltine, Erin E, criminalist III, $57,744
Haslag, Darrin R, trooper 1st class, $50,904
Haslag, Heather M, pub safety mgr band 2, $61,692
Haslag, Theresa, maint worker, $12.24/hr
Hastings, Randall J, trooper 1st class, $49,392
Hatch, Niasia, account clerk II, $26,652
Hatcher, Charity N, nursing asst I, $23,856
Hatcher, William A, bldg/gnds maint i temp, $9.69/hr
Hatfield, Christopher J, cve insp II, $33,744
Hatheway, Merlin E, janitor, $8.16/hr
Haugen, Craig D, chief technician, $74,388
Haupt, Lynn M, account clerk II, $28,908
Haurdic, Alen, driver exam I, $28,104
Hauser, Wilma E, misc prof, $20.07/hr
Hausmann, Eileen M, hlth prog aide, $11.00/hr
Havens, Terry C, phys plant sup III, $46,932
Hawk, Lucinda A, nursing asst I, $23,856
Hawkins, Amy L, laundry worker I, $20,664
Hawkins, Earlene, registered nurse sr, $55,776
Hawkins, Laurie C, custodial worker I, $22,200
Hawkins, Michael W, nursing asst I, $24,900
Haws, Ward R, groundskeeper II, $30,384
Hay, Christine M, hlth prog aide, $12.00/hr
Hayes, Kari D, pers analyst II, $36,204
Hayes, Roger D, fire investigator, $38,928
Haymart, Germaine, typist, $9.69/hr
Haynes, Cathy A, institution supt, $77,676
Haynes, Clay D, custodial worker I, $20,664
Haynes, Julie A, lpn III gen, $18,512
Hayse, Malinda M, nursing asst I, $23,148
Hayward, Adam L, criminalist I, $41,940
Haywood, Kevin G, sergeant, $75,588
Hazel, Cherie A, nursing asst II, $28,224
Hazelwood, Perry C, cpl, $70,728
Hazlip, Jimmy, custodial worker I, $25,404
Heaper, Hope D, nursing asst I, $23,856
Heard, Roger M, misc prof, $35.06/hr
Hearn, Thomas J, driver exam II, $29,976
Hearring, Matthew W, cve insp I, $29,004
Heath, Cameron M, sergeant, $75,588
Heath, Cameron M, trooper 1st class, $46,536
Heath, Jeffrey L, sergeant, $75,588
Heberlein, Mark J, fire insp, $35,568
Heckenbach, Cynthia A, hlth prog spec, $13.00/hr
Heckman, Angela E, criminalist sup, $65,364
Heckman, Jeffrey A, comp info tech spec I, $50,040
Heckman, Lloyd E, housekeeper I, $31,512
Hedge, Richard S, driver exam II, $29,976
Hedlund, Mark W, trooper, $43,872
Hedrick, Cynthia K, nursing asst I, $24,900
Hedrick, Dianne, ofc spt asst (keybrd), $25,824
Hedrick, Donald M, sergeant, $75,588
Hedrick, Douglas J, sergeant, $75,588
Hedrick, James T, cpl, $70,728
Hees, Jason M, vets serv ofcr, $31,512
Heidbreder, Brenda L, pub safety mgr band 1, $61,328
Heidorn, Carmel, custodial worker I, $20,664
Heidorn, Matthew P, domestic serv worker, $11.62/hr
Heil, Chad A, trooper 1st class, $54,024
Heil, Danielle E, sergeant, $75,588
Heimsoth, Jonathan M, trooper 1st class, $45,180
Heinrich, Bradley M, comp info tech III, $43,488
Heinrich, Elizabeth A, clerk IV, $31,512
Heintz, Todd B, trooper 1st class, $54,024
Heislen, Karen A, crim intel analyst I, $30,984
Heitman, Sara L, fiscal & budget analyst I, $29,004
Heitmeyer, Eric L, boiler/pressure vessel inspctr, $43,488
Heits, Matthew R, cpl, $70,728
Helfers, Rodney J, cpl, $70,728
Helfrecht, Anthony C, cpl, $70,728
Helmig, Molly L, comm oper III, $44,928
Helms, Brandon D, cpl, $70,728
Helms, Lisa R, vets serv spv, $34,944
Hemmel, Jennifer L, auditor I, $41,940
Hemphill, Mary A, nursing asst I, $24,900

Hemphill-Bailey, Deanna, nursing asst I, $23,148
Hendershott, Timothy K, trooper 1st class, $47,964
Henderson, Damon D, nursing asst I, $23,148
Henderson, James L, fire inspection sup, $44,304
Henderson, Jennifer L, vets serv ofcr, $29,976
Henderson, Justin E, trooper 1st class, $59,064
Henderson, Karen T, nursing asst II, $27,780
Henderson, Malik A, major, $105,000
Henderson, Sandie J, nursing asst I, $24,900
Hendrick, Jeffrey A, driver exam II, $29,976
Hendricks, Debra L, statewide vol coor sema, $57,744
Hendricks, Tia L, registered nurse, $48,360
Hendrickson, Darrell W, misc prof, $55.17/hr
Hendrickson, Keith C, law enforce mgr b2, $66,868
Hendrix, Brett J, planner III, $47,892
Hendrix, Curtis A, maint worker I, $30,384
Hendrix, Grant H, cpl, $66,576
Hendrix, Jacob N, comp info tech spec I, $50,040
Henke, Brendan, clerk, $9.69/hr
Henke, Kyle, probary trooper, $41,280
Henley, David W, trooper, $42,612
Henman, Donna S, driver exam III, $31,512
Hennigh, Bradley, air depot maint spec I, $36,888
Henry, Andrew A, sergeant, $75,588
Henry, Darci S, recrtnal ther II, $43,488
Henry, John R, trooper 1st class, $47,964
Henry, Randall R, sergeant, $75,588
Henson, Anamarie A, nursing asst I, $23,148
Henson, Denise K, chief cvo, $52,092
Henson, Jessica N, nursing asst I, $24,900
Henson, Robert, maint worker, $10.92/hr
Henson, Thomas, air depot maint spec I, $36,888
Henton, Chereena T, nursing asst I, $23,856
Henton, Patricia A, trnr/auditor III, $41,940
Heppe, Dewey K, cpl, $70,728
Herbert, Michael, planner III, $54,288
Herigon, Charles M, comp info tech spec II, $57,744
Herigon, Jeffrey A, clerk III, $27,948
Herndon, Jason C, law enforce ofcr, $20.00/hr
Hert, Amanda J, nursing asst I, $26,508
Herzer, Jeffrey K, comm oper III, $62,016
Heskett, William E, automotive technician II, $33,180
Hesse, Jennifer R, registered nurse sup, $59,340
Hicks, Amanda, nursing asst I, $24,900
Hicks, Amanda M, qual ctrl clerk I, $25,032
Hicks, Coy R, food serv helper II, $23,160
Hicks, Darcy, exec I, $36,204
Hicks, Dorothy A, nursing asst II, $28,224
Hicks, Hanne D, lt, $85,236
Hicks, Mark W, cpl, $70,728
Hicks, Ralph W, sergeant, $75,588
Higgins, Diane L, criminalist III, $55,416
Highland, Charles, planner II, $38,928
Highley, Daniel C, trooper, $43,872
Hilburn, Travis W, trooper 1st class, $60,840
Hill, Bobbie D, nursing asst I, $24,900
Hill, Cristeta, lpn, $30.00/hr
Hill, Gregory L, comm oper III, $56,784
Hill, Lauren L, typist, $12.00/hr
Hill, Leilania S, food serv mgr I, $33,744
Hill, Paul E, storekeeper I, $27,504
Hill, Robert C, laborer II, $25,824
Hill, Wanda A, clerk-typist III, $31,416
Hillebrand, Sarah A, criminalist I, $41,940
Hillhouse, Christy D, driver exam III, $31,512
Hillhouse, Roger D, sergeant, $75,588
Hilliard, Benjamin R, cpl, $55,644
Hilliard, Jordan A, trooper 1st class, $46,536
Hilliard, Kelly M, driver exam I, $28,104
Hillyer, Brian T, trooper 1st class, $66,516
Hinkle, Brandy A, vets serv ofcr, $29,004
Hinson, Stacey L, technician II, $30,984
Hinz, Brandon L, maint worker, $15.00/hr
Hirtler, Rachel, mil security ofcr I, $29,004
Hitchcock, Travis W, sergeant, $75,588
Hitt, Adam M, trooper, $43,872
Hlavaty, Christina E, registered nurse sup, $65,676
Hobbs, Carole L, clerk-typist III, $30,924

Hobbs, Ethan T, probary trooper, $41,280
Hobbs, Joyce A, food serv helper I, $21,564
Hobson, Michael D, criminalist II, $46,932
Hodge, Gerard S, vets serv ofcr, $33,180
Hodge, Rose M, fiscal & administrative mgr b1, $46,068
Hodgen, Mathew E, progmer/analyst mgr, $61,332
Hodges, Matthew C, commercial veh ofcr II, $38,928
Hoehn, Robert E, sergeant, $75,588
Hoelscher, Robert L, automotive technician II, $33,180
Hoelscher, Sherry M, fiscal & administrative mgr b1, $62,520
Hoelscher, Thomas A, bldg & grounds maint supv, $30,924
Hoemann, Huntley H, trooper 1st class, $55,644
Hoerman, Elizabeth B, asst chief oper, $60,228
Hoerning, Patrick M, typist, $12.00/hr
Hoerschgen, Daniel G, misc prof, $16.80/hr
Hoey, Brian K, criminalist sup, $77,552
Hoey, Kristen L, criminalist III, $61,332
Hoff, Charles W, sergeant, $75,588
Hoffee, Imogene B, registered nurse sup, $69,996
Hoffman, Cherry M, registered nurse sr, $25,122
Hoffman, Dusty L, lt, $85,236
Hoffman, Philip D, sergeant, $75,588
Hoffman, Polly V, nursing asst I, $23,148
Hoffman, Ricky, firefighter crew chief, $46,068
Hoffman, Ronald W, clerk, $26.52/hr
Hoffman, Ronald W, motor veh insp III, $31,512
Hogan, Nicole L, nursing asst I, $23,148
Hogue, Charley A, sergeant, $75,588
Hohne, Karen S, driver exam III, $31,512
Hoke, Delores M, nursing asst I, $23,856
Holcomb, Brian D, sergeant, $75,588
Holcomb, Jay R, sergeant, $75,588
Holder, Steven A, sergeant, $75,588
Holee, Jacob L, clerk, $9.69/hr
Holland, Leigh A, nursing asst I, $23,856
Holle, Stacey L, direct care aide, $9.00/hr
Holley, Leslie, miltry funeral hnrs team mbr, $26,652
Holley-Davis, Diana E, nursing asst II, $28,224
Hollingsworth, Rebecca V, vets serv ofcr, $31,512
Hollis, Mason B, trooper 1st class, $52,416
Hollis, Thomas W, chief motor veh insp, $41,172
Hollmann, George J, mvi sup, $36,204
Hollmann, Mary A, driver exam III, $31,512
Hollmann, Tobin J, cpl, $59,064
Holloway, William, comp info tech III, $45,156
Holman, Bradley D, sergeant, $70,932
Holmes, Cora L, nursing asst I, $24,900
Holston, Taggart L, trooper, $43,872
Holterman, Mary F, ofc worker misc, $10.00/hr
Holtmeyer, Lindsey J, comp info tech spec II, $57,744
Holtmeyer, Nina D, qual ctrl clerk II, $30,924
Holzschuh, Coby G, cpl, $54,024
Honse, Michelle M, special asst prof, $68,842
Hood, Christine E, clin casework asst I, $32,760
Hoodenpyle, Kathryn E, criminalist I, $41,940
Hook, Elizabeth N, registered nurse sr, $54,720
Hooks, Laverne, custodial worker I, $20,148
Hooper, Charles, info technologist II, $36,204
Hooton, Roberta A, restorative aide, $27,252
Hoover, Karen M, criminalist III, $58,908
Hoover, Katie L, driver exam sprv, $36,204
Hoover, Kelly M, trooper 1st class, $47,964
Hoover, Rebecca L, nursing asst I, $26,076
Hoover, Shelly K, registered nurse sup, $63,084
Hoover, Teresa M, ofc spt asst (keybrd), $25,404
Hopkins, Brittni R, lpn III gen, $40,488
Horine, Stephanie A, criminalist III, $55,416
Horn, Michelle A, commercial veh ofcr II, $37,548
Hornecker, Brenda S, driver exam III, $34,356
Horrom, James M, electronic gaming device spec, $49,490
Horton, Chad, maint worker II, $29,976
Horton, David A, training tech II, $39,624
Horton, Gary S, sergeant, $75,588
Horton, Jamie, maint worker II, $29,976
Horton, Janice M, food serv helper I, $20,664
Horton-Jones, Kiwana E, registered nurse, $40.00/hr
Horvatin, Jill D, cook I, $23,508
Hoskins, Kathy G, food serv helper I, $22,200
Hoss, Jodi K, registered nurse sup, $65,676

Hoss, Tyler J, custodial worker I, $20,664
Hotz, John J, capt, $93,120
Hourani, Ghassan N, nursing asst I, $23,856
Hourihan, Timothy J, sergeant, $66,576
House, Kimberly D, trooper 1st class, $50,904
House, Stephen R, probary trooper, $40,272
Houston, Brian K, food serv helper I, $20,664
Houston, Bruce W, sergeant, $75,588
Howard, Gara N, sergeant, $75,588
Howard, Jason B, crim intel analyst II, $36,204
Howard-Beauford, Tia R, account clerk II, $27,948
Howe, Michael R, cve insp I, $29,004
Howe, Skylar K, nursing asst I, $23,148
Howell, Caleb W, lpn III gen, $37,680
Howell, David A, clerk, $26.52/hr
Howell, David A, driver exam sprv, $36,204
Howell, Jimmie C, cpl, $70,728
Howell, Judith A, misc prof, $20.85/hr
Howell, Wiley, geographic info sys spec, $49,128
Howery, Alexander K, trooper 1st class, $66,516
Howes, Pamela J, clerk, $9.69/hr
Hoxworth, Caroline R, custodial worker I, $20,664
Hoxworth, William D, nursing asst I, $23,148
Hoyer, Timothy R, phys plant sup I, $43,488
Hoyt, Junko, nursing asst I, $24,900
Hubbs, Chandra E, typist, $12.00/hr
Hubbs, Curtis W, trooper 1st class, $66,516
Huber, Barbara A, examination monitor, $10.52/hr
Huber, John G, sergeant, $75,588
Huber, Thomas, exec II, $38,232
Huckeby, Diane J, registered nurse sup, $59,340
Huckstep, Nicholas L, special agent (liquor ctrl), $42,708
Huddleston, Shannon W, info technologist IV, $52,092
Huddleston, Sheila I, training tech III, $46,068
Hudson, Cheryl K, driver exam sprv, $39,624
Hudson, Deborah A, nursing asst I, $23,856
Hudson, Erlinda M, custodial worker I, $21,264
Hudson, Jeremy E, nursing asst II, $27,780
Hudson, Steven L, vets benefits claims rep, $32,628
Huebotter, Alexa C, crim intel analyst I, $29,976
Hueffmeier, Carolyn, dining room spv, $26,232
Huff, Belinda K, trooper 1st class, $59,064
Huff, Jeffrey W, trooper 1st class, $47,964
Huff, Thaddeus W, chief technician, $60,228
Huffman, Buffy L, clin casework pract II, $37,548
Huffman, Dave A, trooper 1st class, $60,840
Huffman, Jeanie N, fiscal & budget analyst II, $29,976
Huffman, Sarah N, bldg & grounds maint I, $24,612
Hug, Erin C, comp info tech spec I, $50,040
Hugg, Joshua, miltry funeral hnrs team mbr, $26,652
Huggins, Kyle L, trooper, $42,612
Hughes, Amy L, cve insp III, $36,204
Hughes, Carly M, exec I, $35,568
Hughes, Casey M, misc tech, $25.00/hr
Hughes, David L, cpl, $70,728
Hughes, Demond L, dining room spv, $25,032
Hughes, Jesse, maint worker II, $30,420
Hughes, Johnny H, driver exam I, $28,104
Hughes, Keena A, nursing asst I, $24,900
Hughes, Lee E, probary trooper, $40,272
Hughes, Rosa L, nursing asst II, $28,224
Hughes, Scott G, phys plant sup III, $31,302
Huhn, Mark A, tech spt mgr, $65,364
Huhn, Theresa A, prog mgr, $60,120
Hukill, Darwin R, trooper 1st class, $66,516
Hull, Jane M, special asst-ofc & clerical, $41,664
Hull, Paige A, criminalist I, $40,380
Hull-Rost, Adrienne J, info analyst I, $25,032
Hulse, Jennifer L, clerk-typist III, $28,908
Hulse, Jon D, sergeant, $75,588
Hulsey, Brian J, cve insp I, $29,004
Humble, Emily L, comm oper III, $44,928
Hummel, James P, geographic info sys tech II, $37,548
Humphrey, Allison R, prob comm oper, $36,012
Humphrey, Jewelya A, nursing asst I, $23,148
Hunt, Bryan D, dpty div dir, $96,936
Hunt, Elizabeth S, clin casework asst II, $36,204
Hunt, Joan G, ofc worker misc, $12.00/hr
Hunt, Marilyn S, nursing asst II, $27,780

Hunt, Teri L, nursing asst II, $25,692
Hunter, Caroline L, bldg & grounds maint II, $24,612
Hunter, Chad M, trooper 1st class, $66,516
Hunter, Jerry W, trooper, $43,872
Hunter, Kevin J, sergeant, $75,588
Hurla, Glenn J, fire insp, $35,568
Hurst, Craig, firefighter, $38,232
Hurst, Erik L, sergeant, $75,588
Hurst, Jim M, misc prof, $16.36/hr
Hurt, Jason M, trooper 1st class, $47,964
Hurt, Todd L, designated principal asst dept, $63,432
Huskey, Adam S, trooper 1st class, $49,392
Hussey, Elizabeth A, sr ofc spt asst (keybrd), $27,504
Hutcheson, Tanya, exec I, $34,356
Hutchings, Jacob L, trooper, $43,872
Hutchison, Terri A, pub safety mgr band 1, $62,830
Huth, Patsy, data entry oper, $12.02/hr
Hutsell, Carolyn M, laundry worker I, $21,264
Hutson, Jessica K, lpn I gen, $32,220
Hutson, Kimberly J, crim intel analyst I, $30,984
Hutson, Shenita M, nursing asst I, $24,900
Hutson, Stacy L, nursing asst I, $23,856
Hutton, Ryan L, probary trooper, $41,280
Hutzler, Diana P, cpl, $59,064
Hux, Amanda L, driver exam II, $29,976
Hux, Shane M, cpl, $70,728
Hux, Tracy A, comm oper III, $46,260
Ice, Jeffrey A, trooper 1st class, $45,180
Ice, Ryan J, motor veh insp III, $31,512
Ickes, Peter W, comm technician II, $41,148
Idahosa, Osayoboyi M, nursing asst I, $23,148
Idom, Victoria R, nursing asst I, $23,148
Iman, Constance M, qual ctrl clerk II, $29,904
Iman, Raymond L, chaplain, $15.00/hr
Imdad, Riffat Y, physician, $56,640
Imhoff, Jonathan W, clerk, $9.69/hr
Ince, Helen S, registered nurse sr, $53,592
Ingram, Nicholas, ofc worker misc, $12.03/hr
Inman, Marcus, vets serv ofcr, $29,004
Inman, Mark G, capt, $93,120
Ireland, Hannah, nursing asst I, $23,148
Ishmael, Katie A, driver exam III, $31,512
Islam, Shamsun, nursing asst II, $28,224
Israel, Benjamin L, trooper 1st class, $66,516
Isringhausen, Dwade F, trooper 1st class, $46,536
Isringhausen, Dwell T, sergeant, $75,588
Isringhausen, Seth D, cpl, $60,840
Iven, Darla M, designated principal asst dept, $42,732
Iven, Donnetta M, admin ofc spt asst, $37,548
Iverson, Deborah R, driver exam II, $29,976
Ives, Leslie E, cook I, $22,200
Ivory, Easter, food serv helper I, $20,664
Jack, Sheila R, registered nurse sr, $53,592
Jackman, Erica L, nursing asst II, $27,780
Jackson, Alexander H, probary trooper, $41,280
Jackson, Demetria A, nursing asst I, $24,900
Jackson, Douglas J, probary trooper, $40,272
Jackson, Florence J, driver exam sprv, $36,204
Jackson, Gregory A, probary trooper, $41,280
Jackson, Jacquelynne E, registered nurse sup, $69,996
Jackson, Linda L, laundry worker I, $22,200
Jackson, Michael D, motor veh insp I, $28,104
Jackson, Raphael D, hlth prog aide, $16.00/hr
Jackson, Relnetta, nursing asst I, $23,148
Jackson, Sharissa, lpn III gen, $41,232
Jackson, Yolanda S, nursing asst I, $24,900
Jacobs, Sean D, automotive tech sup, $39,624
Jacobs, Tamra D, technician I, $29,004
Jacobs-Stokes, Leigh A, admin ofc spt asst, $32,052
Jadwin, Casey A, sergeant, $75,588
Jaegers, Cheryl A, typist, $14.60/hr
Jaggars, Tammy L, activity aide II, $27,252
Jakoubek, Katie E, driver exam I, $29,004
James, Austin M, probary trooper, $40,272
James, Carrie A, ins clerk, $32,628
James, Catherine A, nursing asst I, $24,900
James, Donna, food serv helper I, $20,664
James, Emily L, nursing asst I, $23,148
James, Raynalda H, nursing asst I, $23,856

James, Roni, custodial worker II, $11,940
James, Tarlice D, comm oper III, $51,996
James, Terry M, sergeant, $59,064
Jameson, Jacqui M, nursing asst I, $26,892
Jamison, Tracy J, capitol police sergeant, $40,380
Jamski, Edna M, food serv helper II, $23,508
Jannin, Neil V, trooper 1st class, $49,392
Jansen, Curtis P, automotive technician III, $34,356
Jansen, Daniel A, bldg & grounds maint II, $25,824
Jarman, Patricia L, cdl exam, $33,744
Jarrell, Stephen D, cpl, $70,728
Jarvis, Terry W, comp info tech spec I, $50,040
Jayaweera, Henry B, driver exam II, $29,976
Jeffers, Jennifer R, registered nurse mgr b2, $75,240
Jeffreys, Aaron M, trooper, $43,872
Jeffries, Misty R, comm oper II, $42,372
Jenkins, Basiel T, food serv helper I, $20,148
Jenkins, Gayla C, technician III, $33,744
Jenkins, Hailey B, nursing asst I, $23,856
Jenkins, Jerry L, mvi sup, $38,232
Jenkins, Ryan T, domestic serv worker, $9.75/hr
Jenkins, Tyler R, cpl, $60,840
Jenkins, Zachary L, typist, $12.00/hr
Jenner, Gabriel J, trooper 1st class, $46,536
Jennings, Bailey A, nursing asst I, $23,148
Jennings, Charles E, commercial veh ofcr II, $37,548
Jennings, Charles W, storekeeper I, $29,412
Jennings, Marie J, nursing asst I, $23,856
Jennings, Michael R, cook I, $21,264
Jennings, Peggy J, comp info tech III, $45,156
Jestes, Sharon A, motor veh driver, $26,232
Jestic, Levi, firefighter, $38,232
Jewell, Cynthia K, nursing asst II, $25,692
Jewell, Lisa J, registered nurse sup, $63,084
Jinkens, Dale O, lt, $85,236
Jobe, Cynthia L, nursing asst I, $25,284
Johler, Robert J, law enforce ofcr, $20.00/hr
John, Felicia R, food serv helper I, $20,664
John, Rebecca J, procurement ofcr I, $41,172
Johnmeyer, Alicia M, nursing asst I, $23,856
Johns, Christina A, comm oper II, $50,508
Johnson, Adam R, trooper 1st class, $49,392
Johnson, Amy K, cpl, $55,644
Johnson, Amye D, cpl, $54,024
Johnson, Andrew M, probary trooper, $40,272
Johnson, Bruce J, sergeant, $75,588
Johnson, Casey, firefighter, $36,888
Johnson, Charmaine G, cdl examination auditor, $36,204
Johnson, Christina M, driver exam sprv, $36,204
Johnson, Daniel E, fire investigator, $38,928
Johnson, Daniel J, trooper 1st class, $54,024
Johnson, David L, comp info tech III, $45,156
Johnson, David L, trooper 1st class, $49,392
Johnson, Gerald W, cvo sup II, $47,892
Johnson, Grant T, trooper 1st class, $52,416
Johnson, Harland, air depot maint spec III, $45,156
Johnson, Imani R, nursing asst I, $23,148
Johnson, Jackie B, colonel, $118,800
Johnson, James P, trooper 1st class, $59,064
Johnson, Jeffery D, sergeant, $70,932
Johnson, Jeffrey B, lt, $85,236
Johnson, Johannah, security guard, $23,880
Johnson, Judy C, cook I, $23,880
Johnson, Justin S, cpl, $62,688
Johnson, Kristy L, pers analyst II, $37,548
Johnson, Lakeisha S, hlth prog aide, $16.00/hr
Johnson, Lianne M, fire insp, $35,568
Johnson, Linda A, comp info tech spv II, $62,664
Johnson, Lois A, restorative aide, $27,696
Johnson, Loray, nursing asst I, $23,856
Johnson, Madeline R, nursing asst I, $23,148
Johnson, Marnice A, nursing asst I, $24,900
Johnson, Mary A, restorative aide, $28,584
Johnson, Megan L, nursing asst I, $24,900
Johnson, Neil K, sergeant, $75,588
Johnson, Pamela J, registered nurse sup, $69,996
Johnson, Pamela M, criminalist sup, $69,610
Johnson, Robert K, driver exam III, $33,180
Johnson, Ronald S, capt, $93,120

Johnson, Serita R, lpn III gen, $43,620
Johnson, Sharon D, driver exam III, $31,512
Johnson, Steven B, sergeant, $59,064
Johnson, Sylvia R, food serv helper I, $20,664
Johnson, Terri L, therapy aide, $10.00/hr
Johnson, Tina K, driver exam III, $31,512
Johnson, Tyler G, trooper, $43,872
Johnston, David L, cpl, $70,728
Johnston, Joseph R, trooper 1st class, $59,064
Johnston, Lisa, custodial worker II, $23,160
Johnston, Pamela M, clerk typist I, $22,872
Johnston, Rebecca, hlth prog rep II, $40,380
Jolliff, Bruce W, training tech II, $42,708
Jolly, Christopher S, capt, $93,120
Jones, Benjamin C, sergeant, $70,932
Jones, Breanna C, nursing asst I, $23,148
Jones, Brian E, lt, $85,236
Jones, Brittany L, domestic serv worker, $9.38/hr
Jones, Christine A, registered nurse sr, $51,552
Jones, Darin A, commercial veh ofcr II, $38,928
Jones, David A, trooper 1st class, $47,964
Jones, David E, auditor I, $45,156
Jones, Donald K, cpl, $59,064
Jones, Gary B, janitor, $8.16/hr
Jones, Gersene, sr ofc spt asst (keybrd), $28,908
Jones, Jacqueline M, nursing asst I, $23,148
Jones, Jennifer L, lpn III gen, $37,680
Jones, Jeremy M, criminalist sup, $65,364
Jones, Jill A, driver exam III, $31,512
Jones, Larry R, comp info tech spec II, $57,744
Jones, Leland R, comm oper III, $49,044
Jones, Marcel M, sergeant, $75,588
Jones, Martha J, nursing asst I, $24,900
Jones, Michael C, lpn I gen, $30,708
Jones, Michael W, sergeant, $75,588
Jones, Prota G, nursing asst I, $24,900
Jones, Reginald A, motor veh driver, $25,824
Jones, Robert L, hvac inst ctrls tech, $23,533
Jones, Ronald E, comp info tech III, $43,488
Jones, Rosalyn D, registered nurse, $40.00/hr
Jones, Sharon L, custodial work spv, $25,404
Jones, Shawna M, food serv helper I, $20,664
Jones, Staci N, food serv helper II, $21,864
Jones, Steven C, cpl, $70,728
Jones, Steven K, lpn I gen, $30,708
Jones, Verna M, food serv helper II, $22,200
Jordan, Cheyenne L, nursing asst I, $23,148
Jordan, Jade J, lpn II gen, $37,680
Joseph, Leslie A, registered nurse sup, $68,532
Joshlin, Ellen J, lpn III gen, $40,488
Joyce, Stefanie J, cve insp III, $36,204
Juergensmeyer, Keith C, bldg & grounds maint II, $25,824
Jungmeyer, Brandy N, pers analyst I, $36,888
Junkans, Paul, asst proj mgr, $30.30/hr
Just, Andrew A, custodial worker I, $22,200
Justice, Veronica I, laundry worker I, $21,264
Kaden, Shane M, cpl, $70,728
Kaempfe, Karlena R, criminalist II, $46,932
Kahler, Amanda J, trooper 1st class, $66,516
Kaiser, Keith W, trooper, $43,872
Kaltenbach, Dane A, law enforce ofcr, $20.00/hr
Kamler, Jamie E, domestic serv worker, $11.62/hr
Kammerer, James A, radiological sys maint supv, $41,940
Kampeter, Carol A, prog sup, $41,940
Kampeter, Sendera, acct I, $32,628
Kampeter, Shane, environ mgr b1, $56,172
Kampeter, Theresa L, qual ctrl clerk II, $28,908
Karizamimba, Taremba, probary trooper, $40,272
Karr, Nick A, cve insp III, $36,204
Karsten, Sandra K, lt colonel, $109,104
Kasischke, Kotter J, trooper 1st class, $62,688
Kasput, Vincent M, trooper 1st class, $46,536
Katz, Sherry L, nursing asst I, $23,148
Kauffman, Genevieve A, lpn III gen, $41,232
Kaufman, John E, nursing asst I, $24,900
Kaufman, Tammy L, nursing asst I, $24,900
Kauth, Michael E, sergeant, $75,588
Kay, Larry D, div dir, $105,408
Kayser, Kristin H, exec I, $35,568

Keathley, Jeremie L, cpl, $59,064
Keathley, Lonnie J, cpl, $70,728
Keehler, Cynthia D, nursing asst I, $24,900
Keen, Scotty, air depot maint spec III, $45,156
Keene, Thomas R, comm technician I, $38,808
Keeney, Matthew L, cpl, $70,728
Keilholz, Keith F, comp info tech spec II, $57,744
Keim, Eric J, sergeant, $75,588
Kelgard, Cyndi E, nursing asst I, $23,148
Keller-Machon, Beth, sr ofc spt asst (keybrd), $27,084
Kelley, Charles, exec I, $35,568
Kelley, Dennis S, commercial veh ofcr II, $43,488
Kelley, Kevin C, lt, $85,236
Kelley, Ronald L, trooper 1st class, $66,516
Kelly, Janie P, food serv helper I, $20,148
Kelly, Michael P, mvi sup, $36,888
Kelso, Angela B, lpn III gen, $39,072
Kemna, Diane E, acct II, $50,040
Kemna, Erin M, comp info tech spec II, $57,744
Kemp, Samuel L, planner II, $40,380
Kempke, Paul J, sergeant, $75,588
Kempker, Brian W, capitol police sergeant, $45,156
Kempker, Clayton, maint worker, $9.00/hr
Kempker, Dee A, admin ofc spt asst, $32,628
Kempker, Diana J, buyer 1, $39,624
Kempker, Gayla S, pub safety prog rep II, $37,548
Kempker, Karen S, info analyst II, $30,420
Kempker, Leshia J, pub safety mgr band 2, $67,670
Kempker, Lisa L, clerk IV, $33,744
Kempker, Michelle M, clerk-typist III, $27,948
Kempker, Nathan, environ spec III, $43,488
Kempker, Roger S, clerk, $9.69/hr
Kendall, Susan L, nursing asst II, $27,780
Kendrick, Sydney V, clerk-typist III, $27,948
Kennedy, Adam J, typist, $12.00/hr
Kennedy, Kevin, scale maint tech apprent, $34,944
Kennedy, Paul E, capt, $93,120
Kennedy, Taylor A, registered nurse, $50,244
Kenney, Donna, exec I, $35,568
Kennon, Jack D, security guard, $9.97/hr
Kennon, Michelle M, vets serv ofcr, $31,512
Kent, Tisha D, nursing asst I, $23,148
Kenyon, Joshua M, probary trooper, $41,280
Kern, Dennis R, phys plant sup I, $43,488
Kerner, Abigail J, prob comm oper, $36,012
Kerperin, Paul D, capt, $93,120
Kerr, Carolyn H, legal counsel, $71,205
Kerr, Julie A, lt, $85,236
Kerr, Karna N, clerk-typist III, $29,904
Kerwin, Linda K, sr ofc spt asst (keybrd), $32,472
Kessel, David A, administrative analyst III, $49,128
Kessler, Eric R, cpl, $59,064
Ketcham, Billy, storekeeper I, $27,948
Ketchem, Richard, security ofcr, $13.94/hr
Ketcherside, Mona L, clerk-typist III, $27,948
Kettenbach, Matthew G, trooper, $43,872
Kever, Linda L, technician III, $33,744
Keys, Kimberly K, driver exam II, $29,976
Kicker, Craig R, sergeant, $75,588
Kidwell, Caitlan L, technician I, $29,004
Kiehl, Frederick D, physician, $113,280
Kiekel, Ronald D, motor veh insp III, $31,512
Kieser, Timmy, firefighter crew chief, $43,488
Kiesling, Caroline L, special asst prof, $42,708
Kilby, Mark J, fire inspection sup, $41,940
Kimball, Paul M, cpl, $70,728
Kimble, Robert L, food serv helper I, $20,664
Kimes, Christopher A, trooper 1st class, $52,416
Kimmel, Malana L, ofc spt asst (keybrd), $25,404
Kinder, Jeffery R, sergeant, $75,588
Kindle, Gregory D, major, $105,000
Kindle, Keegan E, probary trooper, $40,272
King, Carol R, asst vets home admstr, $56,520
King, Charlotte E, food serv helper I, $20,148
King, Harold L, vets serv ofcr, $32,628
King, Kenneth W, driver exam III, $31,512
King, Leslie A, registered nurse sup, $65,676
King, Ronald D, telecommunicator, $37,548
King, Shelly R, food serv mgr I, $33,744

King, Terry S, ofc worker misc, $15.00/hr
King, Zernethia E, baker I, $23,508
Kings, Austin B, trooper 1st class, $46,536
Kinney, Adam M, trooper 1st class, $66,516
Kinsey, Keith A, cpl, $70,728
Kinsey, Macie J, typist, $9.69/hr
Kinslow, Charles L, driver exam II, $29,976
Kinyua, Genaro M, registered nurse, $40.00/hr
Kirby, Charles F, comm oper II, $42,372
Kirchhoff, Kristina I, pub safety prog rep II, $36,204
Kirchner, Lori A, spec II, $41,172
Kirk, Jessica R, restorative aide, $27,252
Kirkess, Tokeda A, custodial worker I, $20,664
Kirkwood, Mark D, nursing asst I, $23,856
Kirtley, Terry R, bldg & grounds maint II, $23,880
Kissinger, Douglas C, cpl, $70,728
Klass, Linda K, admin ofc spt asst, $31,512
Klausner, Lucinda R, crim intel analyst II, $37,548
Klebba, Michele J, technician III, $33,744
Kleffner, Victoria A, special asst-ofc & clerical, $41,040
Klempke, Ashley E, trooper 1st class, $46,536
Klempke, Megan N, clerk-typist II, $25,032
Kleyh, Dennis R, fire investigation sup, $46,068
Klier, Bruce L, sergeant, $75,588
Kliethermes, Dawn R, criminalist III, $55,416
Kliethermes, Jacob M, comp info tech spec II, $57,744
Kline, David J, cpl, $54,024
Kling, Daniel P, capitol police ofcr, $33,744
Kloppenborg, David N, spv of vol servs, $33,744
Klouzek, Nick D, scale maint tech, $39,624
Klug, Kevin A, clerk III, $26,232
Knight, Kyle L, trooper 1st class, $50,904
Knisley, Aimee S, driver exam sprv, $36,204
Knodell, Julia I, clerk-typist III, $27,084
Knoll, Beverly A, fiscal&budgetary analyst III, $36,888
Knotts, Angela M, soc servs worker, $29,208
Knouse, John S, janitor, $8.16/hr
Knowles, George F, lt, $85,236
Knox, Dale E, sergeant, $75,588
Knox, Deborah V, driver exam sprv, $37,548
Knox, Randy E, driver exam I, $28,104
Koch, Kathleen J, driver exam I, $28,104
Koch, Matthew B, sergeant, $70,932
Koch, Royce, crpntr, $29,976
Koch, Sherry, sr ofc spt asst (keybrd), $27,084
Koch, William R, cpl, $59,064
Koechner, Ruth S, clerk IV, $36,888
Koenigsfeld, Jeffrey S, technician II, $30,984
Koeppel, Alan W, maint worker, $15.00/hr
Koerber, Lynn A, misc prof, $15.70/hr
Koetting, Latisha A, spv of vol servs, $33,744
Koetting, Rochelle A, comp info tech spec I, $50,040
Kohl, Monika N, recrtnal ther II, $40,380
Kolieboi, Karen A, driver exam III, $31,512
Kollmer, Chris, maint worker II, $30,984
Koncor, Lacy J, comm oper I, $39,960
Koop, Aaron, air depot maint spec II, $40,380
Koopman, Dilniya, trnr/auditor III, $43,488
Kopec, Jennifer A, criminalist III, $57,744
Korando, Krysta A, nursing asst I, $23,148
Korte, Anastacia T, nursing asst I, $24,900
Kottwitz, Chris R, probary trooper, $41,280
Krajina, Armin, agent (liquor ctrl), $40,380
Kral, Katherine A, crim intel analyst II, $36,204
Kral, Zachary C, trooper 1st class, $47,964
Kraus, Gerald D, proj spec, $26.00/hr
Kreftmeyer, Kent M, cpl, $70,728
Krehbiel, Jason W, trooper 1st class, $66,516
Kriener, Alice A, misc tech, $14.00/hr
Krinke, Joseph K, automotive technician III, $37,548
Krinke, Rhonda G, comm oper III, $49,044
Kroeger, Gina B, driver exam sprv, $40,380
Kroeger, Micheale J, comp info tech spec II, $57,744
Kropp, Corey L, activity aide I, $25,224
Krumm, Sandra J, cook I, $23,880
Kuczka, Joseph A, probary trooper, $41,280
Kuechenmeister, Jacob P, law enforce ofcr, $20.00/hr
Kuechler, Dennis L, sergeant, $75,588
Kuessner, Jason C, trooper 1st class, $66,516

Kuhlmann, Patti B, registered nurse sr, $54,720
Kumpf, Barry A, sergeant, $75,588
Kuntz, Pauline F, misc prof, $14.15/hr
Kutrip, Joseph, maint worker II, $29,004
Kutzner, Chadwick S, cpl, $52,416
Kyle, Anne M, pub hlth sr nurse, $55,320
Kyle, Ronald D, sergeant, $75,588
Kyle, Tyler D, cve insp II, $33,744
Kyles, Gwenda L, nursing asst I, $23,148
Lacey, John A, cpl, $59,064
Lachance, April A, comm oper II, $41,148
Laclair, Amber N, nursing asst I, $23,856
Lacy, Justin E, trooper, $43,872
Lacy, Lafayette E, div dir, $84,758
Ladyman, Sarah M, motor veh insp III, $31,512
Laferney, Cecil E, misc tech, $15.15/hr
Lairmore, Louis B, trooper 1st class, $45,180
Lake, Lawrence, maint worker II, $29,976
Laks, Natarajan, staff physician, $100.00/hr
Lambert, Amanda K, sr ofc spt asst (keybrd), $32,472
Lambert, Lindsay M, criminalist III, $57,744
Lambert, Shelby S, nursing asst I, $11,574
Lambeth, Mindy M, trooper 1st class, $59,064
Lamoureux, Matthew J, probary trooper, $41,280
Lamy, Glenda E, cook III, $32,052
Lance, Scott M, sergeant, $64,584
Land, Carl R, sergeant, $75,588
Land, Clara E, crim intel analyst II, $36,204
Land, Lisa D, driver exam sprv, $36,204
Landers, Ashley G, hlth prog aide, $12.00/hr
Landers, Larry D, bldg & grounds maint supv, $32,472
Landi, Daniel A, trooper 1st class, $66,516
Lands, Madison M, nursing asst I, $23,148
Landwehr, Gregory S, training tech II, $39,624
Lane, Mary C, sr auditor, $53,208
Lang, Sherry A, registered nurse - clin opers, $72,984
Lange, Brian R, trooper 1st class, $55,644
Langsdale, Jacob T, trooper 1st class, $46,536
Laramore, Jody T, sergeant, $75,588
Largent, Garold L, vets serv ofcr, $31,512
Larimer, Robert P, comm oper III, $56,784
Larimore, Linda M, registered nurse sup, $65,676
Larison, Mary A, asst vets home admstr, $54,288
Larrison, Cindy, lpn III gen, $41,232
Larsen, Donald S, lt, $85,236
Lasater, Shelley A, nursing asst II, $26,076
Lashmet, William S, trooper 1st class, $55,644
Lasswell, Ana C, nursing asst II, $27,780
Latcham, Shena L, criminalist III, $57,744
Lathrom, Samuel B, fire insp, $35,568
Lattray, Ben, plumber, $32,628
Lauberth, Susan C, misc prof, $13.51/hr
Lauf, Douglas F, aircraft maint supervisr, $61,332
Laughlin, Christine M, chief acct, $58,908
Laughlin, William L, cpl, $62,688
Laves, Karen, misc prof, $21.50/hr
Lavin, Joseph E, nursing asst I, $24,900
Lawler, Brian C, trooper 1st class, $47,964
Lawmaster, Summer J, nursing asst II, $27,780
Lawrence, Abigail L, crim intel analyst I, $29,976
Lawrence, Dale S, criminalist sup, $71,105
Lawrence, Debra D, nursing asst I, $24,900
Lawrence, Jason E, cve insp III, $36,204
Lawrence, Lisa M, nursing asst II, $27,780
Lawrence, Rachel A, trooper 1st class, $46,536
Layman, Julie A, typist, $9.69/hr
Layton-Brinker, Lisa M, ofc worker misc, $10.00/hr
Leach, Christopher E, trooper, $43,872
Leach, James, air depot maint spec II, $40,380
Leachman, Donna M, nursing asst II, $28,224
Leake, Gina M, nursing asst I, $23,856
Leason, Arthur F, crim intel analyst II, $36,204
Leathers, Jeffry S, trooper 1st class, $50,904
Leathers, Mark L, driver exam III, $30,984
Lebeau, Lily M, typist, $12.79/hr
Leclaire, Ryan A, trooper 1st class, $49,392
Lecure, Brenda A, special asst-ofc & clerical, $41,040
Lecuru, Eric S, prop inventory ctrller, $37,548
Lecuru, Scott, custodial worker II, $23,160

Lee, Christopher M, lpn III gen, $37,680
Lee, David E, vets serv ofcr, $29,004
Lee, Jared C, typist, $12.00/hr
Lee, Michael W, trooper 1st class, $50,904
Lee, Sherry A, custodial worker I, $20,664
Lee, Terry W, cpl, $70,728
Lee, Tracy L, laundry worker I, $21,264
Leehy, Dawn M, electronic gaming device spec, $47,892
Leemasters, Justin D, trooper 1st class, $55,644
Leesmann, Janis A, clerk-typist III, $27,948
Leftwich, Gregory K, lt, $85,236
Leggett, Nicholas A, hlth prog aide, $12.00/hr
Lehman, Abigail J, criminalist III, $55,416
Lehman, John, environ spec II, $36,204
Lehmen, Bruce, energy spec III, $45,156
Lehmen, Randy J, automotive tech sup, $39,624
Lehmen, Tracy L, crim intel analyst II, $36,204
Leible, Ronald L, supply mgr I, $36,888
Leigers, Scott, info technologist III, $42,708
Leigh, Brenda J, restorative aide, $28,584
Leigh, Gerald D, comm oper III, $50,508
Leighty, Tucker J, typist, $12.00/hr
Leitman, David A, investigator II, $49,128
Leitman, Jacob D, nursing asst I, $24,900
Leitman, Kathleen A, driver exam III, $34,944
Leitman, Melissa L, nursing asst II, $27,360
Lejeune, Lonnie R, cpl, $70,728
Lemcool, Emily, firefighter, $38,232
Lemka, Alissa, domestic serv worker, $9.38/hr
Lemond, Martha S, fiscal & administrative mgr b2, $71,568
Lengyel, Dennis T, misc prof, $34.84/hr
Lennington, Ronnie W, cve insp III, $36,204
Lenoir, Mattie L, nursing asst I, $24,900
Lenox, Beverly L, activity ther, $28,296
Lentz, Ashley M, admin ofc spt asst, $29,004
Lenzy, Roy, mil funeral hnrs team leader, $29,976
Leon, Richard G, cve insp III, $36,204
Leonard, Patrick E, cpl, $70,728
Lepper, Amy L, special asst prof, $42,981
Lepper, Matthew J, criminalist sup, $65,364
Lesko, Keith A, arch consult, $33.21/hr
Leslie, Randi C, nursing asst I, $24,900
Lesmeister, Tasha A, nursing asst I, $24,900
Lester, Amy E, clerk, $9.69/hr
Levins, Patricia E, sr ofc spt asst (keybrd), $32,472
Lewis, Angela, nursing asst I, $23,148
Lewis, April D, comm oper III, $49,044
Lewis, Charlene V, nursing asst I, $25,692
Lewis, David J, storekeeper I, $32,472
Lewis, Eric D, pub safety mgr band 1, $50,964
Lewis, Erik P, maint worker, $10.92/hr
Lewis, Heidi J, qual ctrl clerk II, $29,904
Lewis, Jane A, nursing asst I, $23,148
Lewis, Jerry J, nursing asst I, $24,900
Lewis, Lori L, food serv helper I, $20,664
Lewis, Matthew J, trooper 1st class, $54,024
Lewis, Michael, supply mgr I, $32,628
Lewis, Roanna S, registered nurse, $27.00/hr
Lewis, Sharon M, nursing asst I, $24,900
Lewis, Sherry T, pers recs clerk III, $33,744
Lewis, Sirirat, nursing asst II, $27,780
Lewis, Susan A, custodial worker I, $20,664
Lewis, Tasha C, domestic serv worker, $9.75/hr
Lewis, Willis L, driver exam sprv, $37,548
Lewis, Zachary, janitor, $8.16/hr
Libbert, Amanda E, comp info tech spec I, $50,040
Libbert, Debra A, misc prof, $13.51/hr
Libbert, Leon J, automotive technician III, $38,928
Libbert, Lori M, comp info tech spec I, $50,040
Libertus, Jordan L, food serv helper I, $21,264
Lichay, Keith L, sergeant, $75,588
Lietz, Brittany, clerk, $9.69/hr
Light, Ashley R, nursing asst I, $24,900
Lightfield, Abby L, lpn II gen, $35,736
Liley, Angela L, custodial worker I, $22,200
Lilleman, Darrin K, sergeant, $75,588
Lilley, Tina J, nursing asst II, $28,224
Limbaugh, Patricia J, comm oper II, $41,148
Lincoln, Shannon R, nursing asst I, $24,900

Lindemann, Courtney L, food serv helper I, $20,664
Lindenbusch, Kevin J, motor veh insp II, $29,976
Linder, Collette D, emergency mgmnt coord, $46,068
Lindgren, Austin D, trooper 1st class, $47,964
Lindquist, Leon, custodial worker I, $10,782
Lindsay, Tommie, janitor, $8.16/hr
Linear, Kevin E, cpl, $70,728
Linegar, James M, trooper 1st class, $54,024
Lingle, Jackie L, nursing asst I, $24,900
Linhardt, Anthony J, info technology spec I, $52,092
Linhart, Paul, janitor, $8.16/hr
Linneman, Troy D, sergeant, $75,588
Lintner, Tonya L, custodial worker I, $22,200
Lipe, Judith A, nursing asst I, $23,148
Lisk, Brandie J, nursing asst II, $27,780
Little, Douglas P, sergeant, $75,588
Litton, Kaitlan, nursing asst I, $23,148
Litton, Letha L, restorative aide, $27,696
Littrell, Barbara M, trooper 1st class, $47,964
Lively, Bradley S, sergeant, $75,588
Livers, Jeanne V, comp info tech spec II, $57,744
Lloyd, Keri L, comm oper I, $39,960
Lock, Brenda K, clerk IV, $32,628
Lock, Nancy E, typist, $15.69/hr
Lockett, Louise, hlth prog spec, $16.00/hr
Loesch, Michael R, bldg & grounds maint I, $23,160
Logan, Jabrielle A, nursing asst I, $24,900
Logerman, Austin M, hlth prog aide, $11.50/hr
Logerman, Nicole E, nursing asst II, $27,360
Loggins, Ashea W, nursing asst II, $28,224
Lohner, Derek A, planner III, $51,096
Lomax, Ashley P, nursing asst I, $23,856
Lomedico, Matthew B, trooper 1st class, $55,644
Long, Bryan W, cpl, $54,024
Long, Carl T, maint spv I, $35,568
Long, Catherine A, misc prof, $22.50/hr
Long, James E, maint spv I, $38,232
Long, Josey J, trooper 1st class, $57,324
Long, Megan E, clerk-typist III, $27,948
Long, Paul C, trooper 1st class, $52,416
Long, Sean W, cpl, $60,840
Long, Stephanie, lpn III gen, $41,232
Longgrear, Barbara E, laundry worker I, $20,664
Looney, Melissa C, nursing asst II, $27,360
Looser, Jared P, electronic gaming device spec, $49,490
Lopane, Matthew A, sergeant, $75,588
Lord, Elizabeth E, nursing asst I, $24,900
Loring, Blaine M, trooper 1st class, $46,536
Loring, Garrett J, cpl, $55,644
Lorts, Doris A, clerk, $9.69/hr
Loughridge, Amanda L, admin ofc spt asst, $30,420
Louk-Denney, Stephany S, criminalist sup, $65,364
Love, Dominick D, comm oper II, $42,372
Love, Loritta M, nursing asst I, $24,900
Love, Marilyn, custodial worker I, $20,664
Love, Robert T, comp info tech spec II, $57,744
Lovejoy, Victoria A, emergency mgmnt spec, $38,928
Lovel, Holly M, pers clerk, $33,180
Lovelace, Brent W, prob comm oper, $37,392
Lovelace, Paula F, nursing asst I, $23,148
Lovelace, Russell A, nursing asst I, $23,148
Lovelace, Shelly L, lpn III gen, $40,488
Lovelace, Sheryl D, restorative aide, $28,152
Loveland, Jennifer L, nursing asst II, $26,892
Lovell, Shelley R, sr ofc spt asst (keybrd), $28,908
Lowary, James E, sergeant, $70,932
Lowe, David H, automotive technician III, $37,548
Lowe, Justin W, maint worker I, $30,384
Lowe, Lucas S, trooper 1st class, $46,536
Lowe, William W, sergeant, $75,588
Lowery, Linda G, registered nurse sup, $59,340
Lowry, William R, misc prof, $20.64/hr
Loyd, Tammy M, cosmetologist, $29,568
Lucas, Alexandria L, nursing asst I, $23,148
Lucas, Patsy M, cosmetologist, $27,252
Lucke, Sierra N, hlth prog spec, $12.35/hr
Ludwig, Catherine M, nursing asst I, $24,900
Ludwig, Van E, clerk, $26.52/hr
Ludwig, Van E, mvi sup, $40,380

Luebbering, Anthony G, marine mech, $37,548
Luebbering, Arthur L, comp info tech spec II, $57,744
Luebbering, Brent, groundskeeper II, $29,412
Luebbering, Patricia M, typist, $9.69/hr
Luebbers, Noelle M, bldg/gnds maint i temp, $9.69/hr
Luecke, Courtney E, clerk typist I, $23,508
Luecke, Lisa C, leasing/contracts coord, $37,548
Lueckenhoff, John H, cpl, $70,728
Lueckenhoff, Larry G, asst dir of ictd, $73,237
Lueckenhoff, Linda S, trnr/auditor III, $41,940
Lujan, John R, maint worker II, $32,052
Lukowski, Jason T, trooper, $43,872
Lumpkins, Carlos J, driver exam II, $29,976
Lund, Diane M, custodial worker I, $20,148
Lundy, Amelia D, nursing asst I, $23,856
Lunsford, Paula M, nursing asst I, $24,900
Lupardus, Glen D, emergency mgmnt coord, $44,304
Lusk, Brian J, prob comm oper, $37,392
Lusk, Elizabeth A, trooper 1st class, $54,024
Lute, James L, automotive technician III, $38,928
Lute, Karen L, crim intel analyst II, $37,548
Luteru, Mi-Re M, nursing asst I, $23,856
Lutjen, Steven L, sergeant, $75,588
Lutz, Misty A, nursing asst II, $27,780
Lutz, Parrish M, trooper 1st class, $49,392
Luyk, Pamela S, sr ofc spt asst (keybrd), $25,824
Luzenko, Walter J, trooper 1st class, $46,536
Lybarger, Cheryl S, designated principal asst div, $85,944
Lyle, Dustin L, cpl, $55,644
Lynch, Jonathon P, trooper 1st class, $60,840
Lynch, Michael D, sergeant, $75,588
Lyon, Randall B, cve insp I, $29,004
Lyon, Stevie, nursing asst I, $23,148
Macay, Mirna C, laundry worker I, $20,664
Macdonnell, Jeremy L, asst chief oper, $62,016
Mack, Eric L, domestic serv worker, $9.13/hr
Macke, Alicia A, ofc spt asst (keybrd), $23,160
Mackenzie, Robert K, research analyst I, $38,232
Maclaughlin, Lance M, capt, $93,120
Maddox, Nancy K, registered nurse - clin opers, $63,084
Maddux, Jamie L, clerk-typist III, $28,908
Madison, Davieonte L, nursing asst I, $23,148
Madison, Laquitta R, nursing asst I, $24,900
Madrid, Brittani N, nursing asst I, $24,900
Magee, Patricia K, sr ofc spt asst (keybrd), $25,404
Magers, Danny, custodial worker I, $21,564
Maggard, David R, state vets cemetery dir, $44,304
Maggard, Martha E, nursing asst I, $24,900
Maggard, Nia L, nursing asst I, $23,856
Maggard, Nicole S, activity aide II, $25,224
Magnan, Brian J, probary trooper, $41,280
Mahaffey, Judy M, registered nurse sup, $56,976
Mahaney, Tammy S, clerk-typist III, $28,908
Mahaney, Tanaya L, hlth prog aide, $11.50/hr
Mahl, Brittany D, hlth prog aide, $11.00/hr
Mahon, Patrick C, acct II, $38,232
Malam, Skylur B, typist, $12.00/hr
Mallery, Andrew A, sergeant, $75,588
Malmberg, Judy L, cook sup, $30,984
Malone, Barbara L, custodial worker I, $22,200
Malone, Carolyn L, registered nurse sup, $69,996
Malone, Michelle M, exec I, $36,204
Malone, Robert M, trooper 1st class, $50,904
Maloney, Trois L, sergeant, $66,576
Malugen, Kevin W, sergeant, $75,588
Malzner, Walter C, bldg & grounds maint supv, $29,904
Manahan, Maria L, nursing asst II, $26,892
Mangels, Wanda K, custodial worker I, $20,148
Manley, Brianna R, nursing asst I, $23,148
Manley, Elizabeth M, motor veh insp III, $32,052
Manley, Melissa L, nursing asst I, $23,856
Manning, Anna, nursing asst I, $23,856
Manning, Kristal L, nursing asst I, $23,148
Marbaker, Andrew W, criminalist I, $38,928
Marbaker, William E, div dir, $91,296
March, Nicholas W, trooper, $42,612
Marcott, Kali N, hlth prog aide, $12.00/hr
Marcott, Stephanie R, nursing asst I, $23,856
Maret, Kevin, miltry funeral hnrs team mbr, $26,652

Markes, Amanda L, nursing asst I, $23,856
Markway, Diane M, fiscal & administrative mgr b1, $57,731
Marlin, James C, cpl, $62,688
Marquart, Brian N, trooper, $42,612
Marquart, Kyle D, capt, $93,120
Marquart, Leann M, clerk typist I, $23,508
Marquez, Lorenzo, cve insp sprv I, $38,928
Marsch, Kenneth W, environ scientist, $49,128
Marsh, Tony D, bldg & grounds maint II, $27,084
Marshall, Karla D, admin ofc spt asst, $27,228
Marshall, Randi L, nursing asst II, $27,780
Martin, Adam D, probary trooper, $40,272
Martin, Amy N, nursing asst I, $23,856
Martin, Angela D, sr ofc spt asst (keybrd), $27,948
Martin, Angela S, sr ofc spt asst (keybrd), $27,948
Martin, Beth D, prob comm oper, $36,012
Martin, Bryant A, nursing asst I, $24,900
Martin, Cathy J, nursing asst I, $24,900
Martin, Charnyce N, food serv helper I, $21,564
Martin, Dawn S, lpn, $30.00/hr
Martin, Dean, pub safety mgr band 2, $63,125
Martin, Gregory P, sergeant, $75,588
Martin, Jackie A, comm technician III, $46,260
Martin, Jane M, cve insp III, $36,204
Martin, Michelle N, lpn III gen, $41,232
Martin, Paul D, state vets cemetery worker, $27,948
Martin, Roger D, chief oper, $67,716
Martin, Ronjayisha D, nursing asst I, $23,148
Martin, Terrell M, food serv helper I, $20,148
Martinez, Megan E, recrtnal ther II, $44,304
Marzigliano, Yashmeen N, nursing asst II, $28,224
Mason, Brent A, cpl, $70,728
Mason, Clinton S, trooper 1st class, $66,516
Mason, Derek A, trooper 1st class, $46,536
Mason, John L, trooper 1st class, $66,516
Mason, Mark C, cpl, $70,728
Massey, Barbara L, cook II, $23,880
Massey, John T, asst chief oper, $68,412
Massman, Carla K, acct II, $45,156
Massman, Nancy A, criminalist III, $55,416
Masso, Thomas, pub safety mgr band 1, $42,710
Mast, Ronny L, trooper 1st class, $66,516
Mast, Terry L, sergeant, $75,588
Masters, John P, trooper 1st class, $52,416
Masters, Martha A, ofc spt asst (keybrd), $26,232
Masterson, April D, technician II, $30,984
Mathes, Dennis D, cpl, $52,416
Mathes, Kevin W, bldg & grounds maint II, $24,612
Mathews, Nicholas W, cpl, $70,728
Mathis, Chad A, clerk, $9.69/hr
Mathis, Franklin K, bldg & grounds maint II, $28,452
Mathis, Tyler W, cdl exam, $33,744
Matney, Johnny W, fire investigator, $40,380
Matthews, John, proj mgr, $20.20/hr
Matthews, Jonathan M, nursing asst I, $23,148
Matthews, Robert K, maint worker II, $30,420
Mattingly, Jason M, sergeant, $68,688
Mattli, Jaclyn E, nursing asst I, $23,856
Mattox, Anthony J, sergeant, $75,588
Maudlin, Bradley E, cpl, $57,324
Maudlin, Jeffery D, trooper 1st class, $50,904
Maufas, Elaine S, custodial worker I, $20,664
Maxwell, Brenda L, food serv helper I, $20,664
May, Jonathan B, trooper 1st class, $66,516
May, Robert G, sergeant, $75,588
May, Robyn A, clerk typist I, $23,508
May, Vandy L, registered nurse, $25.00/hr
Mayer, Andrew J, trooper, $43,872
Mayfield, Jessica L, prob comm oper, $36,012
Mayhew, Jessica K, prog sup, $41,940
Mc Coy, De'lora, lpn III gen, $41,232
Mc Daniel, George C, food serv helper I, $20,148
Mc Garity, Kimberly G, nursing asst II, $26,076
Mc Ghee, Patricia L, registered nurse sr, $59,340
Mc Hugh, Karen, flood plain mgmnt ofcr, $46,068
Mc Lemore, Jasmine D, nursing asst I, $23,148
McAdams, Terrence G, special asst prof, $76,692
McAleenan, Kathleen A, licensed clin soc wkr, $46,932
McAtee, Adam G, cpl, $66,576

McBee, Mark W, maint worker, $15.00/hr
McBride, Donald J, trooper 1st class, $60,840
McBride, Lowell, maint spv II, $37,548
McBride, Timothy M, driver, $12.00/hr
McBride, Verland R, trooper 1st class, $66,516
McCalister, Marc A, sergeant, $75,588
McCall, Denise M, nursing asst I, $25,692
McCallister, David R, security ofcr I, $27,084
McCampbell, Victoria K, hlth info tech II, $31,512
McCann, David I, nursing asst I, $24,900
McCann, Robyn E, nursing asst I, $24,900
McCannon, Jamie A, asst vets home admstr, $54,288
McCarter, Joni G, special asst prof, $50,712
McCarthy, Leann P, pub info coor, $51,096
McCartney, Martha A, chief cvo, $51,096
McClaran, Christine M, cpl, $70,728
McClendon, Mark P, sergeant, $75,588
McClintock, Marieta M, restorative aide, $27,252
McClintock, Rachel M, food serv helper II, $21,564
McCluggage, Katherine E, accounting sup, $22.86/hr
McClure, James E, typist, $20.70/hr
McClure, Michael P, cpl, $70,728
McClurg, Jane M, cve insp sprv I, $38,928
McColl, Tina M, nursing asst II, $28,224
McCollum, Keverne L, lt, $85,236
McConkey, Quentin R, trooper, $43,872
McCormick, Dennis W, trooper 1st class, $50,904
McCormick, Katherine H, comm oper III, $47,628
McCormick, Meagan A, criminalist III, $55,416
McCormick, Robert V, cpl, $70,728
McCoy, Brandy J, hlth prog aide, $12.00/hr
McCoy, Caleb C, trooper, $43,872
McCoy, James W, maint worker II, $29,004
McCracken, Brenda G, lpn III gen, $41,976
McCracken, Monty L, bldg & grounds maint supv, $29,904
McCray, Evonne, cook II, $23,508
McCrory, Vanessa L, nursing asst II, $28,224
McCulley, Brenda D, nursing asst I, $23,856
McCullough, Jeffrey L, cpl, $70,728
McCullough, Justin L, lt, $85,236
McCune, Bobbie J, custodial worker I, $20,664
McCune, Stacey M, supply mgr I, $36,888
McCurdy, Jeremy R, cpl, $50,904
McCurdy, Nellie M, nursing asst I, $24,900
McCurley, David D, capitol police ofcr, $34,356
McDaniel, Debra J, sr ofc spt asst (keybrd), $31,920
McDaniel, Douglas M, sergeant, $75,588
McDaniel, Houston M, probary trooper, $41,280
McDaniel, Michele L, driver exam III, $34,356
McDaniel, Nogi H, trooper 1st class, $55,644
McDermott, Gretchen A, cook I, $22,872
McDonald, James E, capt, $93,120
McDonald, Joshua J, trooper 1st class, $52,416
McDonald, Natalie E, nursing asst II, $28,224
McDonald, Rickie G, bldg/gnds maint i temp, $9.69/hr
McDonell, Timothy E, phys plant sup II, $51,096
McDonnal, Samantha M, nursing asst I, $24,900
McDougal, Barbara A, paralegal, $53,582
McDowell, April M, nursing asst I, $23,856
McDowell, Bradley G, agent (liquor ctrl), $40,380
McDowell, Eric D, food serv helper II, $20,664
McDowell, Kimberly J, comm oper III, $51,996
McElhaney, Dana D, nursing asst II, $28,224
McElroy, Dennis R, vets serv spv, $36,204
McElroy, Shelly L, restorative aide, $28,584
McElyea, Terry, driver exam sprv, $36,204
McEntire, Preston A, security ofcr I, $26,652
McFarland, Dan, vets serv spv, $34,944
McFerren, James N, laundry worker I, $20,664
McGary, Dixie K, activity aide II, $27,252
McGary, Patsy J, laundry worker I, $20,664
McGary, Phillip R, maint worker I, $27,504
McGee, James, maint worker II, $30,420
McGhee, Anthony S, activity aide II, $27,696
McGhee, Stephen R, misc prof, $16.80/hr
McGinnis, Robert B, sergeant, $75,588
McGinnis, Tracy E, legal counsel, $97,476
McGivney, Kyle, trooper, $43,872
McGlothlin, Victoria L, nursing asst I, $23,148

McGowan, Colton H, probary trooper, $41,280
McGowan, Shannon L, section chief, $79,176
McGrail, Timothy P, pub safety mgr band 3, $92,383
McGuire, Michael E, bldg mgr I, $44,304
McHargue, Alison N, nursing asst I, $23,148
McHenry, Dixie V, telecommunicator, $30,984
McIntire, Catherine M, nursing asst I, $24,900
McIntosh, Caleb W, food serv helper II, $21,564
McIntyre, Brenda K, crim intel analyst I, $30,984
McIntyre, Mark, trooper 1st class, $66,516
McKay, Robert S, exec I, $34,356
McKinley, Julie C, nursing asst I, $24,900
McKinley, Patricia B, clerk, $9.69/hr
McKinney, Angela, restorative aide, $28,584
McKinney, Gregory R, capitol police ofcr, $32,628
McKinnon, Donald L, direct care aide, $8.00/hr
McKinnon, Lisa K, cook III, $28,536
McKinzie, Brenda S, sr ofc spt asst (keybrd), $32,472
McKnight, Mory C, trooper 1st class, $66,516
McLard, Kimberly G, nursing asst II, $28,224
McLaughlin, Bruce A, cpl, $70,728
McLean, John F, vets serv ofcr, $29,976
McManus, Matthias A, barber, $27,252
McMillan, Charles G, motor veh insp III, $33,744
McMurray, Sharon, sr ofc spt asst (keybrd), $28,908
McNair, Victoria, registered nurse, $40.00/hr
McNeal, Regina, nursing asst I, $24,900
McNeill, Bonnie C, misc prof, $23.15/hr
McPherson, Angela, cook III, $32,052
McPike, Douglas B, sergeant, $75,588
McQuerrey, Rickey I, trooper 1st class, $49,392
McReynolds, Earl S, bldg & grounds maint supv, $29,904
McReynolds, Louis G, cvo sup I, $40,380
McTheeney, Jason E, sergeant, $62,688
McWhorter, Julie K, laundry worker I, $20,664
McWilliams, Vincent L, cve insp I, $29,004
McWilliams, William C, mil funeral hnrs team leader, $29,976
Mead, Rachel E, hlth prog aide, $12.00/hr
Meade, Ronald V, cpl, $70,728
Means, Cole J, state vets cemetery worker, $27,948
Mears, Terry L, crim intel analyst II, $36,204
Mebruer, Terry G, mvi sup, $36,204
Mechlin, Penny C, registered nurse sr, $50,244
Medley, Audreanna M, nursing asst I, $23,148
Medlin, Adam S, typist, $12.00/hr
Mefford, Angela M, nursing asst II, $28,224
Mehl, Kristina M, criminalist III, $57,744
Mehling, Loretta J, nursing asst I, $24,900
Mehrhoff, Brenella, sr ofc spt asst (keybrd), $31,416
Mehrhoff, Donna, exec I, $34,944
Meisel, Mary A, misc prof, $29.48/hr
Mell, Robert, groundskeeper II, $29,412
Meller, Andrew, environ spec III, $43,488
Mendez, Christian J, probary trooper, $41,280
Mengwasser, Aaron M, bldg & grounds maint supv, $29,904
Mengwasser, Angela R, planner II, $41,172
Mengwasser, Chad J, crim intel analyst II, $36,888
Mengwasser, Rachel L, technician III, $33,744
Mensah, Trennette N, custodial worker I, $20,664
Menzimer, Jason, air depot maint spec II, $40,380
Meredith, Jean A, nursing asst II, $25,692
Merritt, Edward, custodial worker II, $23,880
Merseal, Kurt C, sergeant, $75,588
Mertens, Scott E, sergeant, $75,588
Mesias-Foster, Deloris K, nursing asst II, $28,224
Messersmith, Lara E, comm oper II, $42,372
Metteer, Ronald A, trooper 1st class, $55,644
Metzner, Dustin T, cpl, $59,064
Meyer, Ashton R, comm oper I, $39,960
Meyer, Charles C, sergeant, $75,588
Meyer, Douglas D, pub safety mgr band 2, $70,824
Meyer, Jeffrey A, cve insp sprv I, $39,624
Meyer, Jessica M, clerk IV, $30,420
Meyer, Justen E, clerk, $26.52/hr
Meyer, Justen E, automotive technician III, $36,204
Meyer, Michael V, misc prof, $21.71/hr
Meyer, Regina M, cultural resource pres II, $42,708
Meyer, Scott E, lt, $85,236
Meyer, Thomas W, trooper, $42,612

Meyer, Timothy J, asst chief oper, $68,412
Meyers, Dana N, food serv helper I, $20,664
Meyers, Larry D, driver exam III, $31,512
Meyers, Paul W, sergeant, $75,588
Michaels, Faron S, driver exam II, $29,976
Michajliczenko, Alexander H, cpl, $62,688
Michels, Adam J, trooper 1st class, $47,964
Michener, Levi B, probary trooper, $41,280
Middleton, Douglas S, crim intel analyst II, $36,204
Middleton, George R, driver exam III, $31,512
Middleton, Joey, phys plant sup I, $38,232
Miesner, Ronald J, lt, $85,236
Miles, Tyler R, clerk, $9.69/hr
Miller, Adam N, trooper 1st class, $52,416
Miller, Barbara L, custodial worker I, $22,200
Miller, Barry B, boiler/pressure vessel inspctr, $44,304
Miller, Brent A, div asst dir, $73,237
Miller, Brian K, driver exam - chief, $38,928
Miller, Christine J, therapy aide, $10.00/hr
Miller, Darlene, restorative aide, $28,584
Miller, Dayah C, therapy aide, $9.38/hr
Miller, Deborah S, cpl, $70,728
Miller, Diana C, typist, $9.69/hr
Miller, Hollie M, sr ofc spt asst (keybrd), $27,948
Miller, Jason D, trooper 1st class, $49,392
Miller, Jason F, laborer, $16.16/hr
Miller, Jeremy W, trooper 1st class, $45,180
Miller, Joella M, comm oper I, $39,960
Miller, Julie M, fiscal & administrative mgr b2, $75,552
Miller, Kevin B, sergeant, $75,588
Miller, Michael J, probary trooper, $41,280
Miller, Raymond S, cpl, $70,728
Miller, Robert, janitor, $8.16/hr
Miller, Robert S, criminalist II, $48,156
Miller, Scott A, comm oper I, $39,960
Miller, Scott A, cpl, $70,728
Miller, Sherman, nursing asst II, $28,224
Miller, Sherri D, lab evdnc tech II, $33,744
Miller, Sonya L, sr ofc spt asst (keybrd), $32,472
Miller, Wendell J, maint worker II, $32,052
Miller, Whitney J, driver exam I, $28,104
Millican, Roberta D, nursing asst I, $24,900
Mills, Darin S, storekeeper I, $27,948
Mills, Kevin L, sergeant, $75,588
Mills, Taylor R, nursing asst I, $23,148
Millsap, Jason P, trooper 1st class, $50,904
Milne, Dean H, trnr/auditor III, $43,488
Miner, Janell R, registered nurse, $28.78/hr
Minnick, Kimberly D, misc prof, $17.00/hr
Minor, Heather D, cook II, $23,880
Minter, Dina L, nursing asst I, $23,856
Minze, Paul D, law enforce mgr b1, $54,468
Miranda, Manuel D, cpl, $55,644
Mistler, Clinton R, trooper 1st class, $54,024
Mistler, Matthew H, trooper 1st class, $50,904
Mitchell, Donna K, nursing asst I, $24,900
Mitchell, Eunice M, custodial worker I, $20,664
Mitchell, Gail L, registered nurse sup, $59,340
Mitchell, Karri L, cdl exam, $33,744
Mitchell, Larry, misc tech, $12.42/hr
Mitchell, Loretta C, traffic safety analyst III, $36,204
Mitchell, Michael A, sergeant, $75,588
Mitchell, Nancy K, food serv helper II, $23,508
Mitchell, Randall L, firefighter crew chief, $49,128
Mitchell, Sarah E, motor veh insp II, $29,976
Mitchell, Sheri L, nursing asst I, $23,856
Mitchell, Stephen P, asst fire chief, $31,933
Mitchell, Thomas O, trooper 1st class, $60,840
Mitchell, Wendell L, trnr/auditor III, $46,932
Mitchem, Charlene E, exec I, $32,052
Mitchener, Michael E, electronic gaming device spec, $47,892
Mizer, Michael S, trooper 1st class, $46,536
Mobley, Carolyn L, misc prof, $15.39/hr
Mobley, Christy L, registered nurse sr, $55,776
Mobley, Michael L, sergeant, $75,588
Mock, Melissa K, registered nurse sup, $58,140
Moeller, Clay D, trooper 1st class, $54,024
Moffat, Kevin, trooper 1st class, $46,536
Mohammed, Virginia L, pub safety prog rep I, $30,984

Moll, Justin J, trooper 1st class, $46,536
Mollison, Jacqueline R, nursing asst I, $24,900
Monahan, Logan B, trooper 1st class, $52,416
Monds, Jeremy K, cve insp II, $33,744
Monk, Kay E, criminalist sup, $74,304
Monk, Shane R, sergeant, $75,588
Monroe, Debra J, spv of vol servs, $30,420
Monteer, Juanita R, processing technician supv, $32,628
Monteleone, Jennie L, registered nurse sup, $65,676
Montez, Kirsten G, nursing asst I, $23,148
Montgomery, Bryan W, trooper, $43,872
Montgomery, Keisha, admin ofc spt asst, $29,496
Montgomery, Ruth A, criminalist III, $60,120
Montpetit, Laurie J, nursing asst I, $23,856
Mooney, Nancy A, driver exam - chief, $39,624
Mooney, Seth, maint worker, $8.50/hr
Moore, Barbara J, nursing asst I, $23,856
Moore, Bradley D, sergeant, $75,588
Moore, Brent A, cpl, $60,840
Moore, Carla J, nursing asst I, $24,900
Moore, Dawn M, chief oper, $74,388
Moore, Deborah A, registered nurse sr, $51,552
Moore, Diana M, clerk, $25.00/hr
Moore, Donna K, pers analyst I, $39,624
Moore, Edwin, janitor, $8.16/hr
Moore, Gary L, prog spec, $26.00/hr
Moore, Henry W, sergeant, $75,588
Moore, Jacque R, registered nurse sr, $55,776
Moore, Linda A, lpn III gen, $37,020
Moore, Maria T, telecommunicator, $30,984
Moore, Michael, air depot maint spec II, $40,380
Moore, Michael S, maint worker I, $30,384
Moore, Michelle A, nursing asst II, $28,224
Moore, Rebecca J, clerk-typist III, $27,948
Moore, Richard W, lpn III gen, $37,020
Moore, Sean B, lt, $85,236
Moore, Shirley B, driver exam III, $31,512
Moore, Tianasha, nursing asst I, $23,148
Moran, Sheila A, nursing asst I, $24,900
Moravec, Gregory R, trooper 1st class, $47,964
Moreland, Clinton T, cpl, $70,728
Morey, Dustin N, trooper 1st class, $52,416
Morff, Mark D, bldg & grounds maint II, $24,612
Morff, Roger, misc prof, $15.60/hr
Morgan, Amanda R, nursing asst II, $27,360
Morgan, Denise A, admin ofc spt asst, $32,628
Morgan, Fred K, custodial worker I, $21,264
Morgan, Gregory G, sergeant, $75,588
Morgan, John C, nursing asst II, $28,224
Morgan, Robert L, driver exam II, $35,568
Morice, Matthew E, cpl, $59,064
Morre, Tammy A, designated principal asst div, $46,929
Morris, Kenna R, sr ofc spt asst (keybrd), $28,908
Morris, Kevin C, cpl, $66,576
Morris, Michael R, cvo sup I, $46,068
Morris, Tommy R, trooper 1st class, $50,904
Morrison, Philip W, lt, $85,236
Morris-Pulliam, Ebony B, nursing asst I, $11,574
Morrow, Leonard, training tech II, $40,380
Morrow, Lortha J, nursing asst I, $24,900
Morrow, Megan D, nursing asst I, $24,900
Morton, Debra G, telecommunicator, $33,180
Morton, Johnetta M, laundry worker II, $21,864
Moses, Edward N, misc prof, $14.88/hr
Mosher, Cassandra R, nursing asst I, $23,148
Mosher, Stacey L, cpl, $70,728
Mosley, Craig L, comp info tech II, $40,380
Mosley, Timothy V, trooper 1st class, $59,064
Motley, Angela C, driver exam III, $34,944
Mott, Jean A, nursing asst II, $27,780
Mounce, Christine, nursing asst I, $23,856
Moyer, Jessica L, comp info tech spec II, $57,744
Moyer, Sally L, food serv helper I, $21,264
Mpia, Comfort N, hlth prog aide, $16.00/hr
Muck, Bradley R, probary trooper, $41,280
Muehring, Jacob K, bldg/gnds maint i temp, $9.69/hr
Mueller, Dana J, driver exam sprv, $36,204
Mueller, Darren P, cpl, $70,728
Mueller, Eric L, trooper 1st class, $57,324

Mueller, Ethan B, trooper, $43,872
Mueller, Kurt E, sergeant, $75,588
Muenks, Leonard G, clerk, $9.69/hr
Muetzel, Mark T, clin casework asst II, $34,356
Mulkey, James A, sergeant, $75,588
Mullarkey, Gregory A, security ofcr I, $26,652
Mullins, Cynthia M, cook II, $25,404
Mullins, James H, driver exam II, $29,976
Mumba, Felix, nursing asst I, $23,148
Mungle, Jacqueline V, nursing asst I, $23,856
Munns, Shawana M, hlth prog aide, $16.00/hr
Munson, Marshall H, nursing asst I, $23,856
Murphey, Dale W, janitor, $8.16/hr
Murphy, Amy L, nursing asst II, $28,224
Murphy, Colby J, nursing asst II, $25,692
Murphy, Kathryn L, driver exam I, $29,004
Murphy, Kyle W, trooper 1st class, $50,904
Murphy, Norman A, capt, $93,120
Murphy, Timothy, driver exam sprv, $37,548
Murr, Melissa D, clerk-typist III, $28,908
Murray, Jason R, trnr/auditor IV, $49,128
Murrell, Michael D, maint worker I, $30,384
Murrell, Timothy W, trooper 1st class, $66,516
Murrell, Troy R, maint worker I, $28,908
Murrill, Michael D, trooper 1st class, $66,516
Musche, James L, sergeant, $75,588
Musche, Larry L, typist, $9.69/hr
Muschler, Lauren N, clerk-typist II, $25,032
Musyoki, Carrie J, lpn III gen, $20,616
Myers, Anna L, custodial worker II, $23,160
Myers, Crystal, maint worker, $10.98/hr
Myers, Dennis, janitor, $8.16/hr
Myers, Feryl S, cve insp III, $36,204
Myers, Jeffery B, cpl, $70,728
Myers, Jeffrey N, comp info tech spec II, $63,996
Myers, Jenny J, registered nurse - clin opers, $63,084
Myers, Jerrick W, probary trooper, $41,280
Myers, Phoebe, restorative aide, $27,696
Myers, Robert E, vets serv ofcr, $29,004
Myers, Roger A, cpl, $70,728
Myers, Sondra L, account clerk II, $27,948
Nabors, Joyce, registered nurse sr, $60,516
Nace, Dewayne S, sergeant, $75,588
Nagle, Peggy S, registered nurse sup, $63,084
Nail, Bradley L, cvo sup I, $40,380
Nalle, Rebecca S, custodial worker II, $23,880
Napoli, Cheryl L, exec II, $47,892
Nara, Jon A, prob comm technician, $37,392
Nash, Dakota L, probary trooper, $40,272
Nash, Daniel F, sergeant, $75,588
Nau, Marjorie E, nursing asst I, $23,856
Naumann, Pamela A, nursing asst I, $24,900
Naylor, Gretchen M, registered nurse sr, $51,552
Neal, Angela, environ spec III, $43,488
Nebel, Darla L, laundry worker I, $20,148
Neeley, Kevin R, trnr/auditor III, $41,940
Neff, Abbie L, nursing asst I, $24,900
Neff, Christopher J, auditor I, $45,156
Nehring, Laura M, investigator II, $47,892
Neidig, Sarah A, nursing asst I, $24,900
Neier, Dianna L, post prog coord, $34,356
Neisler, Jennifer, ofc spt asst (keybrd), $25,404
Nelson, Alicia D, clerk-typist II, $25,032
Nelson, Charles L, misc prof, $15.70/hr
Nelson, Chelsey B, probary trooper, $40,272
Nelson, Darrah J, comm oper I, $39,960
Nelson, David R, trooper 1st class, $66,516
Nelson, Larry K, cpl, $54,024
Nelson, Latricia C, lpn, $30.00/hr
Nelson, Mark C, comm oper III, $49,044
Nelson, Mary A, comm oper III, $50,508
Nelson, Scott L, sergeant, $75,588
Nelson, Tammy S, nursing asst II, $28,224
Nelson, Terry R, cpl, $70,728
Nelson, Todd A, pub safety mgr band 2, $67,670
Nelson, Vicki K, driver exam - chief, $38,928
Neurohr, Henry, boiler/pressure vessel inspctr, $38,928
Newberry, James O, custodial worker I, $21,264
Newberry, Janice L, nursing asst I, $24,900

Newberry, Nichelle E, hlth prog aide, $12.00/hr
Newell, Dorothy J, custodial worker I, $20,148
Newkirk, Faye A, cdl exam, $33,744
Newman, Kristi K, special asst-ofc & clerical, $41,664
Newman, Lance M, sergeant, $66,576
Newsom, David H, maint worker II, $33,180
Newsom, Larry S, comp info tech I, $34,944
Newsome, Justin D, lpn III gen, $41,232
Newson, Annette, nursing asst II, $28,224
Newton, Jeremy, tech asst IV, $40,380
Newton, Sherry M, laundry worker I, $20,664
Ngumoha, Morhans I, registered nurse sr, $60,516
Nichols, Deborah K, exec II, $38,232
Nichols, Jodi L, driver exam III, $31,512
Nichols, Tonya E, sr ofc spt asst (keybrd), $28,908
Nichols Dorsey, Juanita F, registered nurse sr, $53,592
Nicholson, Christopher R, asst chief oper, $58,476
Nickels, Randy G, state vets cemetery worker, $27,948
Niece, Mark D, state vets cemetery worker, $27,948
Niekamp, Willine E, typist, $9.69/hr
Nielsen, Melissa E, lpn II gen, $32,808
Nielsen, Randall W, electronic gaming device spec, $47,892
Nienhuis, Michelle T, training tech II, $38,928
Niewald, Cynthia A, clerk, $9.69/hr
Nilges, James N, comm technician II, $41,148
Nimley, Edna G, nursing asst I, $23,856
Nivens, Tara E, admin ofc spt asst, $35,568
Nix, Amie J, criminalist sup, $68,163
Noack, Jeffrey G, sergeant, $75,588
Noad, Simon, cook I, $22,536
Nolan, Debra K, misc prof, $25.25/hr
Nolan, Deirdre R, comm oper III, $44,928
Noland, Terri J, cvo sup II, $44,304
Nordin, Paula L, vets serv ofcr, $31,512
Norman, Byron, stores clerk, $25,824
Norman, Eric J, sergeant, $75,588
Norman, Megan R, nursing asst I, $12,449
Norment, Terry D, misc prof, $32.77/hr
Norris, Mitchell D, custodial worker I, $20,664
North, Chad J, cpl, $59,064
North, Robert J, trooper, $43,872
Norton, Christopher W, prob comm oper, $37,392
Norton, Timothy O, facilities opps mgr b3, $80,760
Nothum, Al P, sergeant, $75,588
Nott, Cheryl L, pub safety prog rep II, $36,204
Nott-Hopkins, Arthur M, vets serv ofcr, $29,004
Notz, Kevin P, fire insp, $37,548
Novotny, John R, asst chief oper, $62,016
Nowlin, Paula M, nursing asst I, $24,900
Nugent, James T, state vets cemetery dir, $42,708
Null, Anna D, nursing asst I, $23,148
Null, Candice M, custodial worker I, $20,664
Null, Jennifer L, driver exam II, $29,004
Nunnery, Miguel D, cve insp II, $33,744
Nussbaum, Sharon K, ofc spt asst (keybrd), $25,824
Nutt, Matthew K, special asst prof, $59,100
Obermann, Hannah L, nursing asst I, $24,900
Obert, Brenda J, nursing asst I, $23,856
Obert, Matthew D, probary trooper, $41,280
Obrien, Sheila A, custodial worker I, $20,664
O'Brien, Andrew J, trooper, $43,872
O'Brien, Tyler W, trooper, $42,612
O'Callaghan, Charles, mil security ofcr II, $36,204
O'Connell, Michael A, special asst prof, $81,336
O'Conner, Kimberly D, driver exam III, $31,512
O'Connor, Corey J, food serv helper II, $21,864
O'Connor, Mikayla D, nursing asst I, $23,856
O'Dell, Patrick A, fin auditor, $55,416
O'Dell, Richard M, firefighter, $38,232
O'Dell, Terrence L, fire insp, $36,204
Odle, Bradley D, cpl, $64,584
Odle, Melodie A, steno III, $29,904
Oehring, John N, bldg/gnds maint i temp, $9.69/hr
Oetting, Gary D, trooper 1st class, $66,516
Ogden, James D, cpl, $59,064
Oginni, Mojisola A, registered nurse, $40.00/hr
Olcott, Derek C, driver exam II, $29,976
Old, Susan B, registered nurse sup, $64,380
Olejniczak, Karen M, comm oper III, $50,508

Oliver, Teresa L, driver exam sprv, $38,232
Oliver, William E, cpl, $70,728
Oliveras, Debra A, criminalist sup, $74,304
Oliveras, John A, sergeant, $75,588
Oloughlin, Eugene, vets serv ofcr, $38,232
Olson, Eric T, capt, $93,120
O'Malley, Tammy J, lpn, $21.00/hr
Omoloja, Bolajoko, nursing asst II, $28,224
Onstott, Kevin W, capital imprvmts spec II, $60,120
Opel, David L, security ofcr I, $26,652
Orf, Marion E, lpn III gen, $43,620
Orf, Thomas G, fiscal & administrative mgr b2, $61,692
Oros, Cristian M, comp info tech spec II, $57,744
Orr, Sara A, dining room spv, $26,232
Orell, Katherina C, nursing asst I, $23,148
Ortiz, Brenda L, cook I, $22,872
Ortmeyer, Jim, planner II, $41,940
Osborn, Larry, plumber, $32,628
Osterloh, Deborah A, cook II, $26,232
O'Sullivan, Brian P, trooper 1st class, $66,516
Otey, Barbara J, registered nurse sup, $65,676
Ott, Mark A, sergeant, $75,588
Otto, Kelly J, planner II, $45,156
Otto, Sarah E, nursing asst I, $23,856
Oughton, Joseph D, sergeant, $60,840
Ousley, Adelita, nursing asst I, $23,148
Overstreet, Ella L, restorative aide, $27,252
Owen, Jeffery M, sergeant, $75,588
Owens, Benjamin A, probary trooper, $41,280
Owens, Brittney N, activity aide II, $26,400
Owens, Camris M, nursing asst I, $24,900
Owens, Jason P, cve insp I, $29,004
Owens, Joshua D, cpl, $55,644
Owens, Justin M, criminalist III, $57,744
Owens, Matthew W, trnr/auditor II, $38,928
Owens, Regina S, registered nurse sup, $63,084
Owens, Richard D, cpl, $66,576
Ownby, Briana R, nursing asst I, $23,148
Oxford, Sherri A, registered nurse - clin opers, $59,340
Pace, Jason M, sergeant, $75,588
Pace, Ryan W, trooper, $43,872
Paden, Gina L, exec I, $32,052
Paden, Susan E, spv of vol servs, $30,420
Padget, Robert N, electronic gaming device spec, $47,892
Page, Joanne S, sr ofc spt asst (keybrd), $25,404
Page, Raymond A, probary trooper, $40,272
Painton, Steven, janitor, $8.16/hr
Palmer, Dennis, maint worker I, $28,908
Palmer, Donald L, capitol police ofcr, $34,944
Palmer, Joseph S, trooper, $43,872
Palmer, Kerri L, nursing asst II, $26,076
Pankey, Barbara J, nursing asst II, $28,224
Pape, Elisha A, cpl, $50,904
Papen, Lisa L, qual ctrl clerk II, $31,920
Pappert, Charles S, capitol police ofcr, $33,744
Paraham, Martrez S, cook I, $22,200
Parden, Mary A, nursing asst I, $23,148
Pare, Julie M, registered nurse - clin opers, $63,084
Parker, Brandon M, trooper 1st class, $47,964
Parker, Malissa J, nursing asst I, $23,148
Parker, Matthew R, trooper, $42,612
Parks, James M, chief oper, $63,852
Parks, Justin K, comm oper III, $51,996
Parks, Michelle, pub safety prog rep II, $36,204
Parks, Tammy S, qual ctrl clerk II, $31,920
Parks, Terri A, food serv helper I, $21,264
Parr, Christopher L, trnr/auditor IV, $53,208
Parr, Robert J, sergeant, $64,584
Parraz, Krystal D, nursing asst I, $23,148
Parrish, Bobby L, fire insp, $35,568
Parrott, Bryan G, sergeant, $75,588
Parrott, Carmen M, clerk-typist III, $28,908
Parrott, Clark D, sergeant, $66,576
Paschal, Charlotte D, nursing asst I, $24,900
Pashia, Kenneth, maint worker II, $30,420
Passalacqua, Donna M, nursing asst II, $28,224
Patchett, Teresa M, restorative aide, $27,252
Pate, Mark A, cpl, $70,728
Patrick, Gloria J, nursing asst I, $23,856

Patterson, Kerry E, fiscal&budgetary analyst III, $35,568
Patterson, Morgan B, trooper 1st class, $47,964
Patterson, Nathan K, capitol police cpl, $37,548
Patterson, Ricky S, motor veh insp III, $31,512
Patterson, Sharon K, sr ofc spt asst (keybrd), $32,472
Patterson, Stanton M, cpl, $70,728
Patton, Christopher L, sergeant, $75,588
Patton, James D, trooper 1st class, $54,024
Patton, Jennifer L, comm oper III, $56,784
Pauley, Cathy F, acct II, $43,488
Paulsen, David A, trooper 1st class, $47,964
Paulus, Amanda M, criminalist I, $41,940
Paxton, Brandon, mil security ofcr I, $29,976
Paxton, Karen R, registered nurse sup, $63,084
Payden, Bernadette, nursing asst I, $23,856
Payne, Ginger D, nursing asst I, $24,900
Payne, Kalene M, clerk typist I, $22,872
Payne, Vera N, custodial worker II, $22,536
Payne, Wilhelmenia L, nursing asst I, $23,856
Peabody, Justin E, cpl, $59,064
Peak, Christopher W, custodial worker I, $22,536
Pearce, Steven G, firefighter, $26,762
Pearre, William, misc prof, $16.15/hr
Pearson, Brandon S, probary trooper, $41,280
Pearson, Carl R, laundry worker I, $20,664
Peart, Joseph T, cpl, $52,416
Peckman, Melissa L, nursing asst II, $27,780
Peebles, Amy L, criminalist III, $55,416
Peirce, Shannon L, trnr/auditor IV, $47,892
Pendergrass, Jessica D, nursing asst I, $23,856
Pendleton, Lynn M, technician II, $30,984
Pendleton, Stephanie C, soc servs worker, $25.00/hr
Penfield, Roberta S, nursing asst I, $24,900
Pengress, Jonathan W, probary trooper, $41,280
Penley, Jessica R, nursing asst I, $24,900
Pennino, Lisa, info technologist II, $34,944
Penrod, Eric C, trooper, $43,872
Perez, Claudia D, registered nurse sr, $59,340
Perez, Nicholas A, probary trooper, $41,280
Perkins, Britni L, driver exam III, $31,512
Perkins, David P, capt, $93,120
Perkins, Tabitha A, sr ofc spt asst (keybrd), $32,472
Perryman, Elizabeth E, nursing asst I, $23,856
Person, Joseph, maint spv II, $24,406
Peters, Brian R, trooper 1st class, $47,964
Peters, Jessica R, nursing asst I, $23,856
Peters, Logan J, comp info tech II, $40,380
Peters, Travis L, trooper 1st class, $45,180
Petersen, Deborah J, clerk, $9.69/hr
Peterson, Brandon, air depot maint spec II, $40,380
Peterson, Steven R, trooper 1st class, $66,516
Pethan, Mark W, planner III, $51,096
Petlansky, Michael A, sergeant, $70,932
Petre, Niki J, comm oper III, $51,996
Petty, Diane M, admin ofc spt asst, $29,976
Pew, Tammy M, lpn III gen, $41,232
Pewitt, Veronica M, nursing asst I, $24,900
Pezold, Paul R, therapy aide, $12.75/hr
Pfeifer, Douglas W, trooper 1st class, $49,392
Pfeifer, Jennifer, restorative aide, $27,696
Pfeiffer, Michelle E, technician II, $30,984
Phelps, Lisa M, food serv mgr I, $34,356
Phelps, Robert W, bldg & grounds maint II, $24,612
Phelps, Weston D, mil funeral hnrs team leader, $29,004
Phenix, Yevette N, nursing asst I, $23,856
Pherigo, Samuel R, planner III, $46,068
Phillips, Jeffrey M, driver exam III, $31,512
Phillips, Jesie C, cpl, $70,728
Phillips, Julia N, nursing asst I, $24,900
Phillips, Roger L, sergeant, $75,588
Philpott, Jason W, trooper 1st class, $49,392
Philpott, Mark A, trooper 1st class, $46,536
Phipps, James L, commercial veh ofcr II, $39,624
Piccinino, Justin D, trooper 1st class, $55,644
Pickard, Casey R, nursing asst I, $24,900
Pickens, Semetha, nursing asst I, $23,148
Pickett, Connie S, nursing asst I, $23,856
Pickett, Kaylee B, hlth prog aide, $12.00/hr
Piekutowski, Robert J, law enforce ofcr, $20.00/hr

Piepenbrink, Angela N, asst vets home admstr, $56,520
Pierce, Baylea M, therapy aide, $9.38/hr
Piercy, Anthony C, trooper 1st class, $66,516
Pierson, Paige O, typist, $12.00/hr
Pikey, Michelle L, registered nurse sr, $53,592
Pilkenton, Madelene R, domestic serv worker, $11.62/hr
Pingel, Debra J, restorative aide, $29,052
Pinson-Mitchell, Lititia A, nursing asst I, $24,900
Pipkin, Joel L, clin casework asst II, $37,548
Pipkin, Richard D, cpl, $70,728
Pismany, Ralph, vets serv spv, $36,204
Pithan, Joseph A, cpl, $70,728
Pitnick, Richard R, automotive technician III, $34,356
Pittman, Troy L, sergeant, $75,588
Pitts, Casey N, probary trooper, $40,272
Pitts, Debra D, driver exam sprv, $37,548
Pitts, Isaac, janitor, $8.16/hr
Pitts, Robert S, mvi sup, $36,888
Pitts, Steven, security ofcr I, $26,652
Pitts, Trayton T, cpl, $70,728
Plassmeyer, Tyler H, comp info tech III, $45,156
Plate, William J, investigator II, $37,548
Platt, John, geographic info sys tech II, $36,204
Pleasant, Charles L, trooper, $43,872
Plumley, William R, trooper 1st class, $55,644
Plunkett, Larry W, capt, $93,120
Plybon, John L, maint worker M, $33,180
Pobst, Rusty V, nursing asst I, $24,900
Poertner, Jan M, examination monitor, $17.73/hr
Pogue, Kristine L, nursing asst II, $28,224
Pohlmann, James G, laborer, $12.36/hr
Polacek, Joyce M, registered nurse sr, $53,592
Polen, Robert L, mvi sup, $36,204
Pollard, Lesa, acct II, $41,940
Pollard, Rebecca, administrative analyst II, $41,172
Pollard, Vernon A, food serv helper I, $21,264
Pollitt, Brian P, comm oper II, $41,148
Polodna, Martin T, sergeant, $75,588
Polson, Michael, mil security ofcr I, $34,356
Pond, Tyler D, probary trooper, $41,280
Ponder, Craig N, sergeant, $75,588
Ponder, Rocky L, chief oper, $74,388
Ponder, Rodney W, clerk, $9.69/hr
Ponder, Sheila R, traffic safety analyst III, $41,172
Popejoy, Sidney R, special asst-ofc & clerical, $84,533
Popplewell, Jamie M, nursing asst I, $24,900
Porter, Cary F, trooper 1st class, $52,416
Porter, Heather S, nursing asst II, $27,780
Porter, Nadia, miltry funeral hnrs team mbr, $26,652
Porter, Timothy A, agent (liquor ctrl), $40,380
Portillo, Erika D, sr ofc spt asst (keybrd), $29,412
Poteet, Keith A, custodial worker II, $25,032
Potocki, Jeremy M, cpl, $62,688
Potter, Cheryl A, laundry worker II, $23,880
Potter, Daniel R, custodial worker I, $20,664
Potter, Terry R, sergeant, $75,588
Potts, Opal M, hlth prog aide, $12.00/hr
Potts, Rhonda S, food serv helper I, $22,200
Poulson, Adam W, trooper 1st class, $59,064
Pound, Norman C, groundskeeper I, $26,232
Pounds, Dale B, sergeant, $62,688
Powell, Derrick R, cpl, $62,688
Powell, Raymond E, cve insp M, $33,744
Powell, Tina E, nursing asst I, $23,856
Powell, Zanita T, nursing asst I, $23,148
Power, Nancy L, nursing asst II, $25,284
Pragman, James A, sergeant, $75,588
Prater, Amber R, custodial worker I, $21,264
Prater, Jared O, probary trooper, $40,272
Pratt, Brooks A, trooper 1st class, $52,416
Pratt, Dale E, nursing asst I, $24,900
Preator, Allison N, nursing asst I, $23,856
Precht, Tamara R, lpn III gen, $37,020
Prenger, Alan J, pub safety mgr band 1, $54,282
Presby, Monica R, nursing asst I, $23,148
Presser, Eric W, asst chief oper, $55,128
Preston, Nicole, janitor, $12.24/hr
Prewitt, Jeffery L, cpl, $70,728
Price, Ada M, nursing asst I, $24,900

Price, Beth L, nursing asst I, $23,856
Price, Carol A, nursing asst II, $28,224
Price, Jessica M, laundry worker I, $20,664
Price, Marlowe T, nursing asst I, $23,148
Price, Paula J, comm oper III, $49,044
Price, Shawn L, sergeant, $75,588
Priest, Ashley N, comm oper II, $42,372
Primm, Chad D, trooper 1st class, $54,024
Primm, Gregory D, sergeant, $68,688
Prince, Caitlin E, food serv helper I, $21,264
Principato, David J, security ofcr I, $25,824
Pringer, Derrick, maint spv I, $35,568
Pringle, Malana S, processing technician II, $27,504
Pringle Stovall, Erin K, clerk, $9.69/hr
Prisk, Kyler J, typist, $12.00/hr
Pritzel, Scott E, cpl, $70,728
Procter, George, security ofcr I, $27,084
Proctor, Joseph T, capitol police cpl, $37,548
Proctor, Robert E, sergeant, $75,588
Profer, Nancy A, housekeeper I, $31,512
Propst, Kevin K, automotive technician III, $38,928
Propst, Thomas R, cpl, $70,728
Pruiett, Jon C, lt, $85,236
Pruitt, Alan J, custodial worker I, $20,148
Pruitt, Jr, activity ther, $30,144
Pruitt, Melinda J, asst vets home admstr, $54,288
Pruitt, Rhonda L, hlth prog aide, $16.00/hr
Pruitt, Stephanie P, food serv helper I, $20,148
Prussman, Greg M, cpl, $70,728
Pryor, Keilah S, registered nurse, $48,360
Puckett, Allyson R, account clerk II, $27,948
Pugh, Stassi M, nursing asst I, $23,148
Pullam, Michael L, driver exam II, $32,052
Pullen, Sherwin R, lpn, $30.00/hr
Pulley, Chase A, probary trooper, $41,280
Pulley, Timothy G, sergeant, $75,588
Pulliam, Michael R, lt, $85,236
Purnell, Conrad L, trooper 1st class, $46,536
Puryear, Carmen A, lpn III gen, $41,856
Push, Donna M, exec I, $39,624
Pyle, Tammy L, nursing asst I, $24,900
Qualls, John R, nursing asst II, $27,360
Quesenberry, John, janitor, $8.16/hr
Quick, Brian A, capitol police sergeant, $41,940
Quick, Sally J, pers analyst II, $42,708
Quigley, John T, misc tech, $15.70/hr
Quigley, Tamie L, special asst-ofc & clerical, $41,664
Quilty, Michael P, sergeant, $75,588
Quin, Barbara, exec II, $38,232
Quinlan, Michael L, staff physician, $43.48/hr
Quinn, Brian M, pub info admstr, $55,416
Quinn, Coleen L, nursing asst I, $23,856
Quinn, Jamaka S, cve insp sprv I, $38,928
Quinn, Lane P, cpl, $52,416
Quint, Lasandra D, telecommunicator, $30,984
Rackers, Jeffrey L, radiological sys maint tech, $41,940
Rademan, Tracy M, qual ctrl clerk II, $28,908
Rader, Larry M, motor veh insp III, $31,512
Raetz, John T, training tech II, $46,932
Rager, Pamela D, nursing asst I, $23,856
Ragle, Cassondra D, food serv helper I, $21,564
Rahm, Celestina, cook II, $23,880
Rainey, Dennis W, sergeant, $75,588
Rainey, Michael, custodial worker II, $12,306
Rains, Larry G, div dir, $81,552
Rains, Viviane L, institution supt, $77,676
Ramirez, Priscilla L, sr ofc spt asst (keybrd), $25,032
Ramos, Gianni N, nursing asst I, $23,148
Ramos, Jaime E, sr ofc spt asst (keybrd), $28,908
Ramsey, Christopher D, comm oper III, $62,016
Ramsey, Josey F, nursing asst I, $24,900
Ramsey, Tina M, trnr/auditor II, $38,928
Randall, Keith O, chief technician, $74,388
Randle, William A, criminalist sup, $68,172
Raney, Brian N, trooper 1st class, $60,840
Rapier, Kellen D, trooper 1st class, $45,180
Rapp, Hannah E, typist, $12.00/hr
Rasche, Robyn S, nursing asst I, $12,450
Rathbone, Angela N, food serv helper I, $21,264

Rauch, Rodney, air depot maint spec II, $40,380
Rawlings, Robert, mil security ofcr I, $29,976
Rawson, Levi E, trooper 1st class, $50,904
Rawson, Scott E, sergeant, $75,588
Ray, Amanda S, lpn III gen, $37,020
Ray, Jessica J, nursing asst II, $26,508
Ray, Larry L, trooper 1st class, $50,904
Rayfield, Anne M, driver exam III, $31,512
Rayfield, Samuel G, comm oper III, $46,260
Raymer, Timothy A, comp info tech spec II, $57,744
Razzaque, Naveed, consulting physician, $150.00/hr
Ream, Bradley D, sergeant, $75,588
Rearrick, Nicole R, nursing asst I, $23,148
Rector, James C, commercial veh ofcr II, $42,708
Redden, Letitia, ofc spt asst (keybrd), $26,652
Redel, Mary A, clerk IV, $32,628
Redmon, Mason E, comm oper II, $42,372
Redmond, Darius A, custodial worker I, $20,664
Reece, Cynthia A, registered nurse sup, $59,340
Reece, Gene E, boiler/pressure vessel inspctr, $49,128
Reece, Jeffrey D, prog mgr, $60,120
Reece, Rickey, mil security ofcr II, $33,744
Reed, Amy R, registered nurse, $27.00/hr
Reed, Brooklyn M, custodial worker I, $20,664
Reed, Dustin B, cpl, $59,064
Reed, Leonard S, trooper 1st class, $66,516
Reed, Madaline R, nursing asst I, $23,148
Reed, Michael K, special agent (liquor ctrl), $42,708
Reed, Teri L, comm oper III, $55,128
Rees, Raymond T, sergeant, $75,588
Reeves, Charlotte F, lpn III gen, $41,232
Reeves, George C, supply mgr I, $36,888
Reeves, Kelsey D, nursing asst II, $26,508
Rehagen, Gregory J, div asst dir, $53,208
Rehagen, James J, bldg/gnds maint i temp, $9.69/hr
Rehbein, Erica M, driver exam III, $31,512
Rehbein, Garold P, sr chief motor veh inspec, $43,488
Rehbock, Sarah E, nursing asst I, $24,900
Rehmeier, Brandy L, technician II, $30,984
Reichert, Craig W, trooper 1st class, $59,064
Reid, Mary A, technician III, $33,744
Reider, Jean M, sr ofc spt asst (keybrd), $29,904
Reimann, Darrin K, recrtnal ther II, $39,624
Reimund, Shaun C, custodial worker I, $20,664
Reinkemeyer, Bruce L, sergeant, $75,588
Reinkemeyer, Sandra, baker I, $24,612
Reinsch, Austin N, clerk, $9.69/hr
Reinsch, Paul J, lt, $85,236
Remillard, James W, capt, $93,120
Rencher, Erin, sr ofc spt asst (keybrd), $27,084
Renick, Jack D, misc tech, $20.44/hr
Renick, Joyce A, typist, $15.24/hr
Renick, Kyle W, bldg & grounds maint I, $23,160
Renken, Roger L, sergeant, $75,588
Renn, Amanda L, special asst-ofc & clerical, $53,203
Renna, Christopher A, comp info tech spec I, $50,040
Renshaw, Matthew R, sergeant, $75,588
Requa, Donna N, registered nurse sup, $59,340
Reuter, Dale R, trooper 1st class, $59,064
Revelle, Joel R, commercial veh ofcr II, $44,304
Reynolds, Amy E, lt, $85,236
Reynolds, Donna S, licensed clin soc wkr, $44,304
Reynolds, Eric M, trooper 1st class, $46,536
Reynolds, George D, laborer, $12.40/hr
Reynolds, Judy K, food serv helper II, $23,508
Reynolds, Kristen D, driver exam sprv, $36,204
Reynolds, Marcus S, cpl, $64,584
Reynolds, Rick D, electronic gaming device spec, $47,892
Reynolds, Robin L, ofc spt asst (keybrd), $25,824
Reynolds, Warren D, chief technician, $74,388
Reynoso, Esteban M, probary trooper, $40,272
Rhoades, Janettie A, nursing asst II, $27,780
Rhoades, Jeremy W, cve insp III, $36,204
Rhodes, Nicholle D, criminalist III, $55,416
Ribble, Donald C, maint worker II, $30,420
Rice, Adam S, trooper 1st class, $54,024
Rice, Ava M, nursing consult, $32.00/hr
Rice, Cole T, bldg/gnds maint i temp, $9.69/hr
Rice, David A, sergeant, $75,588

Rice, David S, cpl, $70,728
Rice, Jessica L, bldg & grounds maint II, $24,612
Rice, Matthew L, trooper 1st class, $54,024
Rice, Vince S, capt, $93,120
Richardet, Thomas, janitor, $8.16/hr
Richards, Katrice L, lpn, $30.00/hr
Richards, Lloyd G, motor veh insp III, $34,356
Richardson, Amber R, registered nurse, $51,552
Richardson, Dennis W, driver exam sprv, $36,204
Richardson, Glenease M, cook I, $22,200
Richardson, John C, trooper 1st class, $66,516
Richardson, Mark B, sergeant, $75,588
Richardson, Ryan C, trooper 1st class, $49,392
Richardson, Scott R, sergeant, $75,588
Richardson, Sterling P, trooper 1st class, $66,516
Richardson, Tamara A, driver exam sprv, $36,204
Richardson, Terry A, cpl, $70,728
Richardson, Yadira D, hlth prog aide, $16.00/hr
Richerson, Anthony M, trooper, $43,872
Richerson, Mark E, capt, $93,120
Ricketts, Raymond S, registered nurse sr, $60,516
Riddle, Ashley A, nursing asst I, $24,900
Riddle, Lori G, registered nurse - clin opers, $60,516
Ridenour, Terri L, nursing asst I, $23,148
Ridens, George E, capt, $93,120
Ridge, Jenna L, pub safety prog rep I, $30,984
Ridgway, Kristal F, nursing asst I, $24,900
Ridings, Katrina J, nursing asst II, $28,224
Riedl, Kimberly A, nursing asst I, $23,856
Riefle, Bobby L, trooper, $43,872
Riegel, Katie L, comp info tech spec II, $57,744
Rieke, Tyler A, pub safety mgr band 2, $61,692
Riggs, Gary W, sergeant, $75,588
Riggs, Jason E, sergeant, $75,588
Righter, Mary K, lpn III gen, $37,020
Righter, Rebecca A, nursing asst I, $24,900
Rikard, Danielle R, acct II, $47,892
Riley, Douglas W, trooper 1st class, $62,688
Riley, Gail F, sergeant, $75,588
Riley, Heather D, nursing asst I, $23,148
Riley, Jay K, cpl, $70,728
Riley, Kathy A, cook II, $23,880
Riley, Laken K, nursing asst II, $27,360
Riley, Matthew H, trooper, $42,612
Riley, Michael, law enforce ofcr, $20.00/hr
Riley, Stephen F, maint worker II, $33,180
Riley, Tina L, registered nurse sup, $59,340
Rimson, Josephine, nursing asst I, $24,900
Rinker-Lugo, Angela J, sr ofc spt asst (keybrd), $32,472
Riott, Jessica D, nursing asst I, $24,900
Ripperger, Daniel L, cpl, $70,728
Ripple, Myra J, driver exam III, $33,744
Ritchey, Mark L, research analyst II, $46,932
Ritchie, Michael D, miltry funeral hnrs team mbr, $27,084
Ritter, Terrance B, trooper 1st class, $52,416
Rivas, Marcos D, nursing asst I, $24,900
Rizo, Roberto A, trooper, $42,612
Roach, Jennifer L, clin soc work spv, $57,744
Roach, Sheri L, clin casework asst I, $32,760
Roberson, James L, comp info tech III, $45,156
Roberts, David P, sergeant, $75,588
Roberts, Gina R, sr ofc spt asst (keybrd), $30,384
Roberts, Johnathan R, trooper 1st class, $50,904
Roberts, Leslie E, nursing asst I, $23,856
Roberts, Lisa V, clerk, $9.69/hr
Roberts, Natalia A, lpn, $30.00/hr
Roberts, Terry R, driver exam II, $29,976
Roberts, Vicki L, cook II, $26,232
Robertson, Desri L, nursing asst I, $23,148
Robertson, Mackenzie R, hlth prog aide, $12.00/hr
Robertson, Roxanne L, lpn I gen, $35,148
Robinette, Patricia J, auditor II, $50,040
Robinson, Angela R, crim intel analyst II, $37,548
Robinson, Carla D, nursing asst II, $28,224
Robinson, Elizabeth A, food serv mgr, $31,512
Robinson, James W, cpl, $70,728
Robinson, Jamie D, state vets cemetery worker, $27,948
Robinson, Jr, laundry worker I, $20,148
Robinson, Kenneth M, sergeant, $75,588

Robinson, Lakresha S, nursing asst I, $23,148
Robinson, Linda R, nursing asst I, $26,076
Robinson, Lori A, driver exam I, $28,104
Robinson, Paige D, hlth prog aide, $16.00/hr
Robinson, William V, mil funeral hnrs team leader, $29,976
Robison, Amber D, mil security ofcr I, $29,976
Robitsch, Todd L, chief oper, $74,388
Roby, Tyler S, probary trooper, $40,272
Roddy, Carrie L, sergeant, $75,588
Rodenbaugh, Lisa L, sr ofc spt asst (keybrd), $27,948
Rodenberg, Eric C, trooper, $43,872
Rodenberg, Norman E, sergeant, $75,588
Rodgers, Betty J, comm oper III, $49,044
Rodgers, Jerry, security ofcr I, $25,824
Rodrigues, Anthony L, nursing asst I, $24,900
Rodriguez, Daniel, maint worker I, $29,904
Rodriguez, Emma T, custodial worker I, $20,664
Rodriguez, Jennifer A, driver exam II, $29,976
Rodrock, Donna S, cook II, $26,232
Roettger, Scott T, probary trooper, $41,280
Rogers, Adam J, food serv helper I, $21,264
Rogers, Casey R, cook II, $26,232
Rogers, Chelsa A, driver exam I, $28,104
Rogers, Derek E, trooper 1st class, $57,324
Rogers, Robert, bldg const wkr II, $34,356
Rogers, Shawna F, sr ofc spt asst (keybrd), $25,824
Rohan, Kaitlin M, agent (liquor ctrl), $40,380
Rohn, Thomas R, sergeant, $75,588
Rollins, John M, technician II, $30,984
Romero, Vicki L, special asst prof, $44,304
Romph, Eric S, div asst dir, $53,208
Ronald, Scott T, trooper 1st class, $47,964
Rongey, James J, sergeant, $75,588
Rooks, Troy J, laundry worker I, $20,148
Roop, Jared F, criminalist II, $48,156
Root, Barbara J, lpn III gen, $43,620
Root, Corey B, sergeant, $75,588
Rorie, James R, trooper 1st class, $50,904
Rose, Allen K, custodial worker I, $20,664
Rose, Gerald K, storekeeper I, $28,908
Rosemann, Georgia A, driver exam I, $29,004
Rosenow, Tracy M, sr ofc spt asst (keybrd), $27,948
Ross, Cliff, janitor, $8.16/hr
Ross, Nayomie M, nursing asst I, $23,856
Rossi, Charles L, maint worker II, $29,004
Roten, Michael, security ofcr II, $29,004
Roth, Lindell E, comm oper III, $56,784
Roth, Micah, miltry funeral hnrs team mbr, $26,652
Rothove, Robin L, criminalist sup, $74,304
Rourke, Kirk R, driver exam II, $29,976
Roussel, Samantha R, crim intel analyst II, $36,204
Rowbotham, Katy L, registered nurse sr, $54,720
Rowden, Amanda N, driver exam II, $29,976
Rowden, Blake C, probary trooper, $41,280
Rowe, Debra K, crim intel analyst II, $37,548
Rowe, James A, trooper, $43,872
Rowe, Kacie M, direct care aide, $9.00/hr
Rowe, Shane R, sergeant, $75,588
Rowland, Patricia L, lpn III gen, $37,020
Roy, Kenny, janitor, $8.16/hr
Royster, Christina M, driver exam III, $31,512
Ruckenbrod, Elyse J, trooper 1st class, $54,024
Rucker, Everett D, sergeant, $75,588
Rucker, Stacey A, prob comm oper, $37,392
Rudloff, Steven D, sergeant, $75,588
Ruettgers, Elizabeth A, clerk, $9.69/hr
Ruettgers, Tammy D, qual ctrl clerk II, $28,908
Rule, William C, cve insp III, $36,204
Rulo, Kimberly A, direct care aide, $8.00/hr
Rummans, Torlen L, food serv helper I, $20,148
Rupe, James, air depot maint spec I, $25,303
Rupp, Jacinta S, driver exam sprv, $36,888
Rush, Adam W, probary trooper, $40,272
Rush, Lawrence W, food serv helper I, $20,148
Rush-Jordan, Teolia D, ofc spt asst (keybrd), $23,160
Russell, Denise K, planner III, $51,096
Russell, Roger H, misc prof, $34.84/hr
Russell, Taylor J, maint worker I, $27,504
Rutland, Trudy S, registered nurse sr, $52,608

Rutledge, Kelsey J, trooper 1st class, $66,516
Ryerson, Ralph R, cpl, $70,728
Ryun, Beau M, trooper, $43,872
Ryun, Kathie A, cdl examination auditor, $36,204
Saberon, Democrito M, custodial worker I, $20,664
Saddler, Annie, nursing asst I, $24,900
Sale, Dwayne, storekeeper II, $32,052
Sale, Jo A, procurement ofcr I, $51,096
Salfrank, Steven M, cpl, $66,576
Sallee, Ricky D, maint spv I, $38,232
Salley, Tonya A, nursing asst II, $28,224
Salmon, Phillip A, probary trooper, $40,272
Salmond, Sarah J, lpn, $20.00/hr
Salmons, Bryan H, trooper 1st class, $59,064
Salmons, Rebecca L, technician III, $34,944
Salois, Rebecca S, nursing asst I, $23,856
Salter, Maria E, nursing asst I, $24,900
Samel, Julianne, clerk-typist III, $29,904
Sampietro, Jennifer D, typist, $9.69/hr
Samson, Jessica A, nursing asst I, $24,900
Samuels, Leslie S, design engr II, $52,092
Sanchez, Jose, info technologist II, $38,232
Sanchez, Jose, trooper, $42,612
Sanders, Brian C, commercial veh ofcr II, $38,928
Sanders, Daniel C, law enforce ofcr, $20.00/hr
Sanders, Jerry, environ spec III, $56,520
Sanders, Kenneth R, cpl, $62,688
Sanders, Lauren E, crim intel analyst I, $29,976
Sanders, Lowell W, trooper 1st class, $66,516
Sanders, Mary L, clerk, $10.52/hr
Sanders, Myra, nursing asst I, $24,900
Sanders, Richard J, sergeant, $75,588
Sanders, Robert A, cpl, $55,644
Sanders, Sharon L, registered nurse sr, $51,552
Sanders, Terry G, sergeant, $75,588
Sandgren, Siera, nursing asst I, $23,148
Sandifer, Diana K, registered nurse sr, $52,608
Sandoval, Antonio, trooper 1st class, $57,324
Sandridge, Shandon R, sr ofc spt asst (keybrd), $28,908
Sands, Carol M, nursing asst I, $24,900
Sanson, Brody R, cpl, $52,416
Sapp, Amanda F, trooper 1st class, $66,516
Sarakas, Phillip G, trooper 1st class, $60,840
Sargent, Chanele D, nursing asst I, $24,900
Sargent, Russ E, cpl, $70,728
Sater, David S, lt, $85,236
Satterfield, Shawn R, lt, $85,236
Sauer, James R, trooper 1st class, $59,064
Saultz, Chanda M, registered nurse mgr b2, $73,644
Saunders, Victoria, nursing asst I, $23,148
Savage, Robert C, cpl, $70,728
Saxby, Nathaniel S, technician II, $30,984
Scanlon, Jackson G, criminalist I, $38,928
Scerine, Julie A, sergeant, $75,588
Schabbing, Michele R, ofc spt asst (keybrd), $27,084
Schaben, Tonya M, comp info tech spec II, $57,744
Schaberg, Mark S, special agent (liquor ctrl), $45,156
Schack, David J, law enforce ofcr, $20.00/hr
Schad, David N, misc prof, $16.36/hr
Schafer, Robert W, cpl, $70,728
Schaffer, Nathaniel R, trooper 1st class, $46,536
Schanzmeyer, Preston P, clerk, $9.69/hr
Schaperclaus, Kevin P, aircraft maint spec, $47,892
Scharfenberg, Rebecca A, lpn, $18.00/hr
Scharnhorst, Debora J, registered nurse sr, $56,976
Schatz, Allison M, domestic serv worker, $9.75/hr
Schaub, Heidi K, registered nurse, $40.00/hr
Scheel, Dawn M, cook I, $22,872
Scheibeler, Janice D, comp info tech spec II, $57,744
Scheidt, Cynthia A, designated princ asst-div, $46,080
Schellhorn, Miles, firefighter, $38,232
Schellman, Richard H, misc prof, $17.40/hr
Schepers, Angela K, technician II, $30,984
Scheppers, Chris J, environ spec III, $43,488
Scherer, Victoria K, restorative technician, $30,576
Scheulen, Nancy A, crim intel analyst II, $36,204
Schicker, Mary Ellen, custodial work spv, $26,232
Schill, Scott R, dining room spv, $25,404
Schlarman, Rachel, mil funeral hnrs team leader, $29,004

Schlatt, Daniel R, maint worker I, $27,504
Schlemminger, Pamela D, cook III, $30,420
Schlief, Marcus L, probary trooper, $41,280
Schlosser, Patrick, groundskeeper I, $12,132
Schlueter, Rebecca L, clerk, $9.69/hr
Schlueter, Timothy R, div asst dir, $74,721
Schmid, Sandra A, registered nurse, $30.00/hr
Schmid, Sandra A, registered nurse, $30.00/hr
Schmidly, Ashley M, hlth prog aide, $11.00/hr
Schmidly, Janice, ofc spt asst (keybrd), $23,880
Schmidly, Ronald D, phys plant sup I, $42,708
Schmidly, Tonya M, registered nurse, $48,360
Schmidt, Jeffery A, chief technician, $60,228
Schmidt, Jessica R, nursing asst I, $24,900
Schmidt, Matthew R, sergeant, $62,688
Schmitt, Blake E, comp info tech I, $34,944
Schmitt, Jessica, nursing asst II, $28,224
Schmitz, Donald L, sergeant, $75,588
Schmutzler, Dale S, flood plain mgmnt ofcr, $52,092
Schmutzler, Kurt A, cpl, $59,064
Schnake, Marti S, custodial worker I, $21,264
Schneid, Ryan T, trooper, $43,872
Schneider, Todd D, comp info tech III, $45,156
Schnelten, Micah J, nursing asst I, $24,900
Schoene, Sandra K, misc tech, $16.22/hr
Schoeneberg, Corey J, capt, $93,120
Scholl, Lawrence, security ofcr III, $31,512
Schrader, Larry D, mvi analyst, $34,356
Schrage, Kyle A, trooper 1st class, $47,964
Schrage, Robert L, asst chief oper, $56,784
Schreiner, Carolyn, administrative sec, $13.50/hr
Schroeder, Joanne, telecommun analyst II, $39,624
Schubert, Daniel W, trooper 1st class, $66,516
Schuldies, Kelli E, criminalist III, $55,416
Schulte, Dennis B, progmer/analyst mgr, $61,332
Schulte, Jason E, comp info tech III, $45,156
Schulte, Kenneth J, sergeant, $75,588
Schulte, Mildred K, typist, $9.69/hr
Schulte, Tiffany, sr ofc spt asst (keybrd), $25,824
Schulte, Timothy W, environ mgr b2, $61,248
Schultz, Heather M, crim intel analyst II, $38,928
Schultz, Marquis C, ofc spt asst (keybrd), $23,880
Schultze, Robyn J, lpn III gen, $33,948
Schwalm, David L, sergeant, $75,588
Schwartz, Candace H, lab evdnc tech II, $29,004
Schwartz, Terrance C, maint worker II, $32,628
Schwarz, Caleb T, trooper 1st class, $45,180
Scism, Rex M, capt, $93,120
Scism, Rick E, cpl, $70,728
Scoggins, Michael L, cpl, $70,728
Scott, Brandi L, nursing asst I, $24,900
Scott, Christopher F, sergeant, $75,588
Scott, James E, nursing asst I, $23,148
Scott, Shaina E, restorative aide, $27,696
Scott, Thomas M, sergeant, $75,588
Scribner, Catherine A, acct I, $30,420
Scribner, Christina D, nursing asst I, $23,148
Scrivner, Stevens R, pub safety mgr band 2, $57,731
Scrogham, Clyde L, maint worker I, $27,504
Scronce, Mary E, laundry worker I, $20,664
Scruggs, Keith D, trooper, $42,612
Seabaugh, Kyle A, trooper 1st class, $49,392
Seals, Carolyn D, food serv helper I, $20,664
Seaman, Hope K, registered nurse sup, $63,084
Sears, Heath A, sergeant, $75,588
Sears, Spencer D, trooper, $42,612
Seaton, Pamela K, clerk, $9.69/hr
Seaton, Russell A, sergeant, $75,588
Seawood, Jaqueta T, lpn III gen, $43,620
Sebek, Kelly D, driver exam III, $31,512
Secrease, Connie L, ofc spt asst (keybrd), $25,404
Secrest, Michelle L, nursing asst I, $24,900
Seeley, Brenda F, food serv helper II, $21,864
Seevers, Daniel, phys plant sup I, $37,548
Seibert, William K, principal asst board/commisson, $96,000
Seiner, Rocky L, sergeant, $75,588
Sellars, Jacob R, trooper 1st class, $49,392
Sellers, John M, cpl, $70,728
Selsor, Valen F, trooper, $43,872

Senevey, Jordan, cook I, $23,508
Servais, Jared W, cpl, $55,644
Session, Gwenda, registered nurse, $40.00/hr
Settle, James R, pub safety mgr band 1, $49,128
Settle, Jessica L, training tech III, $46,068
Settle, Robbyn L, dining room spv, $23,160
Sevier, William B, sergeant, $75,588
Seymore, Barton M, cpl, $62,688
Shackelford, Phillip W, comp info tech III, $45,156
Shadowens, Dilbert, janitor, $8.16/hr
Shafer, Sarah J, nursing asst I, $23,148
Shaffer, Emilie A, technician I, $29,004
Shaffer, Patricia E, nursing asst II, $27,780
Shamblin, Brittney J, nursing asst I, $24,900
Shanika, Rhonda M, cpl, $70,728
Shank, Teresa R, criminalist III, $55,416
Shanks, Brettany E, nursing asst I, $24,900
Shannon, Christopher K, cpl, $70,728
Shannon, Sandy L, nursing asst I, $23,856
Sharp, Alicia C, nursing asst I, $23,148
Sharp, Andrew H, vets serv spv, $34,944
Sharp, Joshua D, cve insp III, $36,204
Sharp, Tammy L, restorative aide, $27,696
Shatto, Jamie D, lpn III gen, $41,232
Shaul, Christopher A, housekeeper I, $30,420
Shaul, Russell W, cpl, $70,728
Shaver, Richard P, state vets cemetery worker, $27,948
Shaw, Matthew W, law enforce ofcr, $20.00/hr
Shaw, Robert H, custodial worker I, $20,664
Shawhan, Meagan R, clerk-typist III, $27,948
Shawhan, Timothy A, bldg & grounds maint I, $23,160
Sheehan, Thomas A, law enforce ofcr, $20.00/hr
Sheehy, Donald R, bldg & grounds maint II, $27,504
Sheehy, Larry J, cvo sup I, $46,932
Sheets, Cynthia, nursing asst I, $24,900
Shell, Kendra L, comm oper III, $50,508
Shelledy, Kathelyn A, clerk-typist III, $29,904
Shelton, Ginger A, restorative aide, $26,844
Shelton, Gleta L, mvi sup, $36,204
Shelton, Linda, exec I, $34,356
Shepard, Danielle R, comm oper III, $44,928
Shepard, Patricia A, lpn III gen, $41,232
Shepherd, Scott R, clerk, $9.69/hr
Shepperd, Marilyn S, dining room spv, $25,032
Sherlock, Jennifer J, driver exam II, $29,976
Sherlock, Terressa M, exec II, $44,304
Sherman, Calvin R, cve insp III, $36,204
Sherman, Roger A, cpl, $70,728
Sherod, Marsalis, probary trooper, $40,272
Sherrill, Jean L, registered nurse mgr b2, $73,644
Shewey, Kenneth L, cvo sup I, $41,940
Shibley, Alex J, trooper, $42,612
Shibley, Alyxandria L, criminalist I, $41,940
Shier, Shelby T, nursing asst I, $24,900
Shike, Renee M, nursing asst II, $26,076
Shikles, Dale P, misc prof, $27.75/hr
Shikles, Derek T, trooper 1st class, $45,180
Shikles, Roger D, sergeant, $75,588
Shinkle, Jeffrey B, comm oper III, $44,928
Shinkle, Nathan J, cpl, $70,728
Shipers, Scott A, capt, $93,120
Shirley, Jay A, cpl, $70,728
Shirley, Johnathan P, nursing asst I, $24,900
Shively, Sharon A, cdl exam, $33,744
Shoemaker, Felton R, fire insp, $35,568
Shoemaker, Vicky L, nursing asst I, $24,900
Shoop, Timmy D, sergeant, $75,588
Shoun, Kemp A, major, $105,000
Shoush, Ronda K, clerk IV, $32,628
Shreves, Roland R, law enforce ofcr, $20.00/hr
Shull, Charla, security ofcr III, $32,052
Shupe, Tyler L, probary trooper, $41,280
Shy-Doney, Ashley N, driver exam I, $29,004
Siasoco, Amber L, clin casework pract I, $37,548
Sickels, Dewayne R, cdl exam, $33,744
Sickman, Susan K, admin ofc spt asst, $32,052
Sides, Joanna D, criminalist III, $57,744
Siebeneck, Carla J, fiscal&budgetary analyst III, $33,180
Siebeneck, Charles, ofc servs asst, $33,180

Siegfried, Doug E, cpl, $62,688
Siegler, Logan M, special asst prof, $35,868
Siercks, Brian R, probary trooper, $40,272
Sieren, Bernadette C, pers recs clerk III, $33,744
Sigman, Darren E, trooper 1st class, $66,516
Sigman, Randal C, food serv helper I, $21,264
Sigman, Teresa M, pers clerk, $33,180
Sills, Michael L, bldg const wkr II, $32,052
Silva, Artemio, nursing asst I, $23,148
Silverthorn, Bryan S, cpl, $54,024
Simmons, Amanda S, nursing asst I, $23,856
Simmons, James A, maint worker II, $29,496
Simmons, James D, misc serv, $30.00/hr
Simmons, Scott W, sergeant, $75,588
Simokaitis, Austin, maint worker, $10.00/hr
Simonton, June E, admin ofc spt asst, $29,976
Simpson, John F, vets serv ofcr, $29,004
Simpson, Kathryn Y, comm oper III, $62,016
Sims, Brian C, driver exam III, $31,512
Sims, Charquese A, nursing asst I, $23,148
Sims, Cody, firefighter, $38,232
Sims, Jamila A, hlth prog aide, $16.00/hr
Sims, Jeffrey R, chief cvo, $46,932
Sims, Thomas G, cpl, $70,728
Sims, Virginia J, driver exam III, $31,512
Sims, William S, lt, $85,236
Sinden, Cassidy M, comm oper III, $46,260
Sing, Tonya M, driver exam I, $29,004
Singer, John L, maint worker I, $29,904
Singleton, Alexis S, nursing asst I, $23,148
Singleton, Judy E, nursing asst I, $24,900
Singleton, Meghan C, cook sup, $27,228
Sitton, Shannon S, probary trooper, $41,280
Sizer, Scotty L, sergeant, $75,588
Skabialka, Matthew, miltry funeral hnrs team mbr, $25,824
Skaggs, Beth E, food serv helper I, $21,264
Skaggs, Billy, janitor, $8.16/hr
Skaggs, Rollie B, cpl, $70,728
Skidmore, John J, driver exam clerk III, $29,965
Skiles, Lacey, qual ctrl clerk I, $25,824
Skillman, Joseph, maint worker, $10.92/hr
Skinner, Altemese, nursing asst II, $28,224
Skinner, Melissa L, research analyst II, $44,304
Skoglund, Shawn P, lt, $85,236
Skora, John, laborer, $12.40/hr
Skouby, Dakota D, nursing asst I, $23,856
Skyles, Theresa M, domestic serv worker, $9.13/hr
Slaughter, Michael G, cpl, $70,728
Sloan, Gary S, trooper, $43,872
Sloan, Leslie C, planner III, $47,892
Sloan, Melita L, typist, $9.69/hr
Slover, John D, pers ofcr I, $48,156
Slover, Valerie L, ofc spt asst (keybrd), $25,404
Smart, Adrean J, qual ctrl clerk II, $29,904
Smelser, Emily N, criminalist III, $57,744
Smelser, Natasha F, nursing asst I, $24,900
Smiles, Brandy J, nursing asst I, $23,856
Smith, Adam D, trooper 1st class, $46,536
Smith, Alicia L, prob comm oper, $37,392
Smith, Amanda K, lpn II gen, $31,740
Smith, Ashlie E, hlth prog aide, $15.00/hr
Smith, Beulah V, food serv mgr I, $36,204
Smith, Bruce G, asst chief oper, $68,412
Smith, Caitlin B, food serv helper I, $20,664
Smith, Carolyn J, food serv helper II, $22,872
Smith, Conda S, laundry worker I, $20,664
Smith, Daniel L, trooper 1st class, $46,536
Smith, Daniel W, bldg/gnds maint i temp, $9.69/hr
Smith, David L, maint spv I, $38,232
Smith, David M, trooper 1st class, $46,536
Smith, Dennis S, bldg & grounds maint supv, $29,904
Smith, Gregory, firefighter, $38,232
Smith, Gregory D, sergeant, $75,588
Smith, Gregory K, major, $105,000
Smith, Harold E, sergeant, $75,588
Smith, Jacob A, comm oper III, $44,928
Smith, Jacqueline J, hlth prog aide, $16.00/hr
Smith, James K, mil security ofcr I, $29,976
Smith, Jamie L, nursing asst I, $24,900

Smith, Jared E, probary trooper, $40,272
Smith, Jessica L, nursing asst I, $23,148
Smith, Karen J, food serv helper I, $20,664
Smith, Karen L, registered nurse sup, $56,976
Smith, Karen R, driver exam sprv, $36,888
Smith, Kerri L, prob comm oper, $37,392
Smith, Margie E, lpn III gen, $40,488
Smith, Mary L, admin ofc spt asst, $29,976
Smith, Michael D, phys plant sup I, $43,488
Smith, Michael E, const insp, $57,744
Smith, Nellie J, lpn III gen, $37,020
Smith, Nicholas A, trooper 1st class, $46,536
Smith, Patti R, ofc servs asst, $35,568
Smith, Perry L, sergeant, $75,588
Smith, Rachael M, clerk, $9.69/hr
Smith, Ronda D, domestic serv worker, $9.38/hr
Smith, Ryan S, cpl, $60,840
Smith, Shannon E, therapy aide, $10.49/hr
Smith, Sharla K, food serv helper I, $22,200
Smith, Sharon K, nursing asst I, $24,900
Smith, Sylvia I, exec I, $34,944
Smith, Tammy L, sr ofc spt asst (keybrd), $28,908
Smith, Theodore A, info technology supv, $63,996
Smith, Tiffany N, nursing asst I, $23,148
Smith, Toni, criminalist II, $46,932
Smith, Travon C, probary trooper, $40,272
Smith, Trisha D, ofc spt asst (keybrd), $25,824
Smith, Vonda K, chief cvo, $52,092
Smith, William B, pub safety mgr band 1, $50,304
Smithee, Jeffrey R, maint worker II, $29,004
Smithee, Stacie J, licensed clin soc wkr, $42,708
Smotherman, Dale R, cvo sup I, $40,380
Snapp, Debra F, registered nurse, $28.00/hr
Snell, Kimberly S, sr ofc spt asst (keybrd), $28,908
Snider, Bruce D, trnr/auditor III, $49,128
Snider, Christa K, registered nurse sr, $51,552
Snider, Jeff P, maint worker I, $26,652
Snider, Marty D, state vets cemetery worker, $27,948
Snodgrass, Andrea K, nursing asst I, $24,900
Snodgrass, Christina M, investigator III, $40,380
Snodgrass, Jamie L, criminalist III, $55,416
Snook, Kelly E, ofc worker misc, $10.00/hr
Snyder, Aaron A, maint worker II, $32,052
Snyder, Cherie, acct I, $34,944
Sokoloff, Stephen P, designated principal asst dept, $111,624
Soldan, Matthew L, comp info tech spec III, $57,744
Solovic, Raymond W, maint worker II, $29,004
Soncrant, Tamela, admin ofc spt asst, $29,976
Soole, Justin M, food serv helper I, $21,264
Sorbello-Amelunke, Melinda S, registered nurse sr, $51,552
Soules, Kristen N, criminalist III, $55,416
Spain, Jayson R, trooper 1st class, $49,392
Spain, Letisha R, nursing asst II, $27,780
Spain, Steven M, trooper 1st class, $50,904
Spangler, Cindy R, sr ofc spt asst (keybrd), $32,472
Spargo, Lisa J, driver exam I, $29,004
Sparkman, Cecile J, restorative aide, $26,400
Sparks, Alan D, comp info tech III, $45,156
Sparks, Debra L, clerk, $12.60/hr
Spencer, Naykia M, driver exam II, $29,976
Spire, Jeffery D, cpl, $70,728
Spoor, Amy L, ofc spt asst (keybrd), $25,404
Spradlin, Barbara S, motor veh driver, $25,824
Spradlin, Justin S, law enforce ofcr, $20.00/hr
Spradling, Martha E, activity ther, $30,660
Spratt, Jeremy S, pub safety mgr band 2, $61,692
Sprenger, Sharon E, info technology spec I, $63,996
Spring, Daniel A, cpl, $62,688
Springston, Lisa M, cve insp II, $33,744
Sprous, Anna M, restorative aide, $28,584
Spurgeon, David D, sergeant, $75,588
Spurgeon, Linda M, soc servs worker, $23.00/hr
Spurling, Nora L, restorative aide, $28,152
Stacks, Eric R, cpl, $70,728
Stacy, Jaclyn E, clerk typist I, $22,872
Stacye, Donna M, acct II, $40,380
Stafford, Eva A, comp info tech spv I, $51,096
Stafford, Melissa A, admin ofc spt asst, $27,228
Stafford, Stacey, janitor, $8.16/hr

Stahl, Evalena D, lpn III gen, $41,232
Stallcup, Chase A, trooper 1st class, $50,904
Stallcup, Jordan L, cdl exam, $33,744
Stallsworth, Melanie A, prob comm oper, $37,392
Stamps, Mark R, sergeant, $75,588
Standhardt, Felicia R, nursing asst I, $23,856
Stanfield, Becky L, bldg/gnds maint i temp, $9.69/hr
Stanford, Kelvin E, custodial worker I, $20,664
Stanley, Tammy D, nursing asst II, $27,780
Staples, Tonie M, registered nurse - clin opers, $74,556
Stark, Diane L, examination monitor, $16.22/hr
Stark, Ladonna M, lpn III gen, $37,020
Stark, Robert L, trooper, $43,872
Starke, Brenda L, clerk IV, $33,744
Starks, Austin C, typist, $12.00/hr
Starmer, Mark L, trooper 1st class, $50,904
Starnes, Aaron M, trooper, $43,872
Statun, Mark D, motor veh insp III, $31,512
Stauffer, Clara L, laundry worker I, $22,200
Stauffer, Cory M, trooper 1st class, $49,392
Steele, Chi-Chi N, driver exam sprv, $37,548
Steele, Elaine J, typist, $13.24/hr
Steen, Christina C, clin casework asst II, $31,512
Steen, Lorie L, spv of vol servs, $33,744
Steenrod, Dianna L, nursing asst II, $26,508
Steeples, Maria, registered nurse, $40.00/hr
Stefanus, Christine M, driver exam III, $34,356
Stegeman, Cynthia A, exec I, $34,944
Stegeman, Lynn M, special asst-ofc & clerical, $41,040
Stegeman, Michelle L, traffic safety analyst III, $36,204
Stegeman, Troy D, sergeant, $66,576
Steinman, Brandyn N, clerk, $26.52/hr
Steinman, Brandyn N, driver exam II, $29,976
Stephan, Charles A, comp info tech III, $45,156
Stephens, Emily D, nursing asst I, $23,856
Stephens, Hannah R, clerk, $9.69/hr
Stephens, Melissa R, pub safety prog spec, $46,932
Stephens, Stacy W, nursing asst I, $24,900
Sterling, Richard C, prob comm technician, $37,392
Sterman, David W, special asst technician, $46,980
Sterner, Robbie L, fire investigator, $38,928
Stevens, Darin A, comm oper II, $42,372
Stevens, Diane M, typist, $9.69/hr
Stevens, Holly R, probary trooper, $41,280
Stevens, Thomas J, cpl, $70,728
Stevenson, Grace E, nursing asst II, $27,780
Stevenson, Patricia A, nursing asst I, $24,900
Stevenson, Patrick B, registered nurse mgr b2, $75,900
Stewart, Bonnie K, account clerk II, $25,824
Stewart, Carl, air depot maint spec II, $40,380
Stewart, Donald L, groundskeeper I, $23,880
Stewart, Jefferson D, vets serv ofcr, $32,628
Stewart, Jeremy S, sergeant, $75,588
Stewart, Richard A, trooper 1st class, $66,516
Stewart, Tyler D, trooper 1st class, $59,064
Stiefel, Marcy G, criminalist sup, $65,364
Stiefermann, Mark C, clerk, $9.69/hr
Stiefermann, Thomas B, pub safety mgr band 2, $63,125
Stigall, Anna M, clerk, $9.69/hr
Stiles, Theresa S, prog spec, $25.00/hr
Stillwell, Robin, maint worker II, $35,568
Stimpson, Lilli R, nursing asst I, $23,856
Stinson, Darian B, criminalist III, $55,416
Stitz, Clarence B, misc prof, $34.84/hr
Stockton, Gary W, mvi sup, $36,204
Stoelting, Jeremy S, sergeant, $75,588
Stoffregen, Fred J, cpl, $70,728
Stokes, Alison D, clerk-typist III, $27,948
Stone, James F, clerk, $26.52/hr
Stone, James F, cvo sup II, $44,304
Stone, Nichole L, nursing asst I, $23,148
Stone, Nicole M, clin casework asst II, $31,512
Stoneberger, Scott, fire investigator, $40,380
Storey, Jennifer D, comm spec, $30,984
Stortz, Denny D, comm oper III, $47,628
Stosberg, Collin M, sergeant, $75,588
Stout, Geoffery, firefighter, $38,232
Stout, Jordan M, prob comm oper, $37,392
Stovall, Donna F, buyer II, $41,172

Strait, Melissa, sr ofc spt asst (keybrd), $27,084
Stratman, Nicole, driver exam sprv, $36,204
Stratton, Clark N, lt, $85,236
Strauss, Marlene E, nursing asst I, $24,900
Streeter, Leo A, driver exam III, $31,512
Stricker, Dianne P, account clerk III, $34,250
Stricklan, Steven J, maint worker I, $28,452
Strickland, Arthur, security ofcr I, $26,652
Striegel, David K, capt, $93,120
Stroder, Anjelica, nursing asst I, $24,900
Stroder, Matthew W, custodial worker II, $22,872
Strope, Roger D, section chief, $81,516
Stroud, Saundra A, admin ofc spt asst, $36,888
Struemph, Nancy J, misc prof, $20.91/hr
Stuart, Cort A, sergeant, $75,588
Stuart, Wade E, sergeant, $75,588
Stucker, Donald B, mil security ofcr I, $32,052
Stuefer, Kimberly A, planner III, $45,156
Stults, Tyler N, driver exam I, $29,004
Sturtz, David M, bldg & grounds maint II, $27,084
Sublette, Patrick D, cpl, $55,644
Suddarth, Austin, janitor, $8.16/hr
Sudduth, Susan A, pub safety mgr band 1, $61,692
Suhr, Darryl C, sergeant, $75,588
Suling, Scott M, cvo sup I, $46,068
Suling, Wyatt D, clerk, $9.69/hr
Sullivan, Alan R, sergeant, $75,588
Sullivan, Brad S, fire insp, $35,568
Sullivan, Byron W, spec II, $36,204
Sullivan, Christopher J, trooper 1st class, $49,392
Sullivan, Derek K, trooper 1st class, $52,416
Sullivan, Loren, maint worker, $10.92/hr
Sullivan, Patricia A, registered nurse sup, $68,532
Sullivan, Steven W, state vets cemetery worker, $27,948
Summers, Jessica M, nursing asst I, $23,148
Summers, Joshua R, trooper 1st class, $47,964
Summers, Kevin J, clerk, $26.52/hr
Summers, Kevin J, cve insp III, $36,204
Summers, Lesli D, nursing asst I, $24,900
Summers, Michael E, comm oper III, $51,996
Summers, Nicholas W, probary trooper, $40,272
Sumner, Christina A, probary trooper, $41,280
Surface, William J, trooper 1st class, $66,516
Sutherland, Kelsey R, hlth prog aide, $12.00/hr
Sutton, Alysa R, nursing asst I, $23,856
Sutton, Kewonna R, nursing asst I, $24,900
Svardal, Doreen L, comm oper III, $56,784
Swain, Michelle K, nursing asst I, $23,856
Swanson, Abby L, driver exam I, $29,004
Swartz, Gary C, sergeant, $75,588
Swearengin, Kenneth, pub safety mgr band 1, $44,340
Swearingin, Andrew B, sergeant, $75,588
Sweeney, Joycelyn J, licensed clin soc wkr, $44,304
Sweeney, Nicole L, cook I, $22,200
Sweet, Randall L, fire investigator, $41,940
Sweet, Robert J, technician I, $29,004
Swinford, Melissa A, asst chief oper, $55,128
Swisher, Ruth E, crim intel analyst II, $36,204
Switlik, Jessica D, nursing asst I, $23,856
Swizdor, Toni L, vets serv ofcr, $29,004
Swope, Sherry S, activity aide II, $25,584
Sybert, Justin T, phys plant sup I, $43,488
Sybert, Kit, phys plant sup III, $48,156
Sykes, Cameron, maint worker, $10.00/hr
Sykes, Patrick, firefighter, $38,232
Tackett, Michael D, sergeant, $75,588
Taddeucci, Kimberly A, designated principal asst div, $96,444
Taibi, Carl A, cpl, $62,688
Talbert, Ricky L, chief cvo, $50,040
Talbert, Stephanie D, nursing asst II, $27,780
Talburt, Shayne K, trooper 1st class, $50,904
Talburt, Wayne E, lt, $85,236
Talik, Bonnie K, sergeant, $75,588
Talken, Daniel L, bldg/gnds maint i temp, $9.69/hr
Talken, Jamie L, pub info spec I, $39,624
Talken, Jill, principal asst board/commisson, $58,116
Talli, Victoria R, lpn, $21.00/hr
Tantype, Sharon M, nursing asst II, $28,224
Tapella, Betty J, lpn III gen, $41,232

Tappel, Ann L, ofc worker misc, $16.66/hr
Tappendorf, Brett D, trooper 1st class, $47,964
Tate, Ebony D, hlth prog aide, $16.00/hr
Tate, Malynda L, food serv helper I, $20,148
Tate, Thomas C, driver exam II, $29,976
Tatlow, Steve, planner II, $41,172
Tatum, Jonna K, driver exam II, $29,976
Tatum, Steven M, driver exam III, $31,512
Taube, Darrell J, acct III, $46,932
Taube, Kaitlin C, typist, $9.69/hr
Taube, Rebecca S, special asst-ofc & clerical, $41,040
Tauber, Demond, sergeant, $75,588
Taylor, Cameron J, clerk-typist III, $27,948
Taylor, Catherine R, licensed clin soc wkr, $46,932
Taylor, David B, vets serv ofcr, $29,976
Taylor, Desmonique D, nursing asst I, $23,148
Taylor, Dorothy E, lt, $85,236
Taylor, Jacqueline C, asst vets home admstr, $63,996
Taylor, Jessica S, hlth prog aide, $16.00/hr
Taylor, Karen L, driver exam clerk III, $31,416
Taylor, Michelle L, clerk-typist III, $27,948
Taylor, Paula J, nursing asst I, $24,900
Taylor, Roberta, restorative aide, $28,584
Taylor, Sean W, registered nurse sr, $59,340
Taylor, Shontel D, clin casework asst II, $35,568
Taylor, Steven G, fire insp, $35,568
Taylor, Tiffany N, typist, $24,612
Teague, Brock A, trooper 1st class, $45,180
Tell, Jamilla R, nursing asst I, $23,148
Temme, Jennifer, mil funeral hnrs area coor, $29,976
Templemire, Travis D, trooper 1st class, $50,904
Terry, Christopher L, supply mgr II, $34,944
Terry, Jodey M, lpn III gen, $37,020
Terry, Robert L, food serv mgr I, $38,928
Tesch, Annette G, comm oper I, $39,960
Tesch, Gregory K, trooper 1st class, $50,904
Tesch, Katie A, prob comm oper, $36,012
Teske, Laura, special asst prof, $35,855
Tharp, Melodie A, auditor II, $50,040
Thayer, Michael A, misc tech, $30.69/hr
Theobald, Robert L, bldg const wkr II, $32,052
Thering, Sandra K, nursing asst II, $28,224
Theser, Jenny L, nursing asst II, $27,780
Thessen, Stanley, environ mgr b1, $56,172
Thiele, Cynthia L, hlth info tech II, $33,744
Thomae, Laura L, nursing asst I, $23,148
Thoman, Bruce E, trooper 1st class, $47,964
Thomas, Alisha D, prog sup, $41,940
Thomas, Cortney M, hlth prog aide, $11.50/hr
Thomas, De Vonta T, nursing asst I, $23,856
Thomas, Jack T, trooper, $43,872
Thomas, Jarrod S, trooper 1st class, $59,064
Thomas, Jeffrey D, auditor I, $43,488
Thomas, Julie A, custodial worker I, $22,200
Thomas, Kevin, miltry funeral hnrs team mbr, $26,652
Thomas, Nathan D, nursing asst I, $24,900
Thomas, Ryan, student worker, $10.10/hr
Thomas, Shabrail L, nursing asst I, $23,148
Thomas, Wonetta J, food serv helper II, $21,264
Thomason, Jack A, marine mech, $37,548
Thompson, Barbara J, lpn III gen, $41,232
Thompson, Caroline R, technician III, $33,744
Thompson, Dallas R, trooper 1st class, $59,064
Thompson, Dawn M, driver exam sprv, $36,204
Thompson, Elizabeth R, admin ofc spt asst, $29,976
Thompson, Jared J, probary trooper, $40,272
Thompson, Jeffrey H, sergeant, $75,588
Thompson, John, law enforce ofcr, $20.00/hr
Thompson, Keegan N, nursing asst I, $23,148
Thompson, Larry, phys plant sup II, $38,928
Thompson, Lisa J, cdl exam, $33,744
Thompson, Lisa M, nursing asst I, $24,900
Thompson, Marilyn J, driver exam sprv, $36,204
Thompson, Nina L, activity aide II, $27,252
Thompson, Ryan S, sergeant, $66,576
Thompson, Steven K, cvo sup II, $44,304
Thompson, Susan M, custodial worker I, $20,148
Thompson, William A, custodial worker II, $23,880
Thornburg, Lori A, acct I, $32,628

Thornhill, Danny G, cpl, $66,576
Thorpe, Ok Sun N, nursing asst I, $12,449
Thowe, Rachel M, clerk-typist III, $27,084
Thurman, Donald T, pub safety prog spec, $40,380
Thurman, Jane, sr ofc spt asst (keybrd), $28,908
Thurman, Kevin T, comp info tech III, $45,156
Thurman, Leroy, heavy equip oper, $34,356
Thurmon, Barbara A, cook II, $24,264
Thurmond, Holli L, nursing asst I, $23,148
Thurston, Amanda L, custodial worker I, $20,664
Thurston, Leslie D, lt, $85,236
Thurston, Tammara T, nursing asst I, $23,856
Thuss, James E, trooper 1st class, $66,516
Tidd, Angelina R, comm oper III, $44,928
Tierney, Colby W, trooper 1st class, $45,180
Tiggs, Colette, lpn III gen, $43,620
Tillman, Roxanne A, clin casework asst II, $37,548
Tillmon, Bobbie A, custodial worker I, $20,664
Tilson, Linda F, registered nurse sr, $59,340
Times, Gala D, nursing asst II, $28,224
Times, Tanika N, nursing asst I, $24,900
Timmons, Myneia C, cook I, $21,864
Timmons, Timya C, nursing asst I, $24,900
Tinder, Heather A, laundry worker I, $20,664
Tinnin, Timothy R, sergeant, $75,588
Tipton, Denice D, info analyst II, $28,104
Tipton, Wayne, security guard, $23,880
Titsworth, Sharon C, registered nurse sr, $59,340
Tittle, James L, laundry worker I, $20,664
Toal, Jeffrey M, sergeant, $70,932
Todd, Brittany R, nursing asst I, $24,900
Todd, Dennis J, supply mgr I, $34,356
Todd, Dusty J, maint worker I, $28,908
Todd, Gary, environ aide, $17.40/hr
Todd, Virginia, exec II, $23,533
Todd-Williams, Ariane, lpn III gen, $39,072
Toebben, Jerry A, clerk, $9.69/hr
Toler, Michelle R, nursing asst I, $24,900
Toler, Misti A, hlth prog aide, $12.00/hr
Toler, Tamara R, lpn III gen, $39,072
Tompkins, Suzzie R, auditor I, $45,156
Toms, Diane R, cdl exam, $38,232
Toney, Amber B, hlth prog aide, $11.50/hr
Tooley, Alicia Y, registered nurse sr, $54,720
Torbeck, Arthur G, trooper 1st class, $59,064
Tortonesi, Pheadra A, nursing asst I, $23,148
Totten, Mandy A, registered nurse sr, $53,592
Toupous, Pamela A, nursing asst I, $23,856
Tourney, Andrew O, lt, $85,236
Towe, Benjamen L, cve insp III, $36,204
Townlian, James, storekeeper II, $31,512
Towns, Jeffrey A, chief motor veh insp, $38,928
Trachsel, Amy L, auditor I, $45,156
Tracy, Cleo L, motor veh driver, $26,232
Tracy, Maria S, registered nurse sr, $58,140
Tracy, Sierra D, nursing asst I, $24,900
Trammell, Jason B, sergeant, $75,588
Trankle, Kayla A, cook II, $24,264
Trapani, Rebecca S, training tech II, $41,940
Travis, Janice D, planner III, $47,892
Trent, Carita L, sr ofc spt asst (keybrd), $28,908
Trentham, Effie L, nursing asst I, $24,900
Trevillion, Jewell C, housekeeper I, $32,052
Trickel, Arielle L, nursing asst II, $26,508
Trojan, Iii, custodial worker I, $20,664
Trower, Tiffany D, nursing asst I, $24,900
Troxell, Carissa G, nursing asst I, $23,856
Truman, Barbara J, sr ofc spt asst (keybrd), $29,412
Tubbs, Casey O, cpl, $70,728
Tuck, Sam W, trnr/auditor III, $44,304
Tucker, Corey W, cpl, $70,728
Tull, Seann G, capitol police sergeant, $41,940
Tull, William B, fire investigator, $38,928
Tura, Riza M, nursing asst I, $24,900
Turlington, Michael T, cpl, $70,728
Turnbeaugh, Kevin J, comm oper III, $62,016
Turnbough, Sandra W, custodial worker I, $20,664
Turner, Alysha L, nursing asst I, $11,928
Turner, Annette R, pub safety prog rep I, $40,380

Turner, Ashley L, custodial worker I, $22,200
Turner, Carol L, nursing asst I, $23,856
Turner, Christopher M, cpl, $55,644
Turner, Darren E, driver exam III, $31,512
Turner, Justin W, trooper 1st class, $52,416
Turner, Kati I, activity aide II, $27,252
Turner, Larry A, cpl, $54,024
Turner, Michael A, capt, $93,120
Turpin, Amber E, storekeeper I, $27,084
Twehous, John W, bldg & grounds maint II, $12,306
Twehous, Julie, cook I, $23,508
Twenter, Wilbert M, heavy equip oper, $24,406
Tye, Patricia S, sr ofc spt asst (keybrd), $25,824
Tyler, Bobbi J, comm oper III, $53,544
Tyler, Crystal J, nursing asst II, $28,224
Tyler, Ralicia A, trooper 1st class, $47,964
Tyree, Lisa, environ spec III, $43,488
Tyrrell, Evan L, trooper 1st class, $55,644
Ullrich, Heather M, nursing asst I, $23,148
Ulm, Gregory T, trooper, $42,612
Umfleet, Julie D, food serv helper I, $20,664
Umphry, Garry L, cve insp III, $36,204
Upchurch, Angel J, nursing asst I, $24,900
Urban, Anthony W, cvo sup I, $41,172
Urban, Dawn R, sr ofc spt asst (keybrd), $27,504
Urban, Luann K, clerk-typist III, $27,948
Ussary, Bradly D, sergeant, $75,588
Utley, Tina L, pub safety prog spec, $40,380
Utterback, Casey E, sergeant, $66,576
Utz, Joshua C, cpl, $62,688
Van Housen, Lateasha Y, driver exam I, $29,976
Van Meter, Joseph M, trooper 1st class, $46,536
Van Tress, Jeffrey L, sergeant, $75,588
Van Tress, Laura L, driver exam III, $33,744
Vanaalsburg, Brent, miltry funeral hnrs team mbr, $27,084
Vance, Madison, pers analyst I, $32,052
Vance, Tobi A, mvi sup, $38,928
Vandegriff, Jana M, fiscal&budgetary analyst III, $34,356
Vandegriff, Lori A, pers recs clerk III, $34,944
Vanderhoof, Judith L, hlth info tech II, $33,744
Vandermark, David A, mvi sup, $36,204
Vandeusen, Jessica L, registered nurse sup, $59,340
Vangeison, Nathan J, direct care aide, $9.00/hr
Vannada, Ricky L, trooper 1st class, $55,644
Vanscoy, Randy L, comm technician I, $39,960
Vanwinkle, Evan M, trooper 1st class, $47,964
Vasquez, Denny, maint worker II, $29,976
Vaughan, Erica M, criminalist I, $38,928
Vaughan, Robert A, sergeant, $75,588
Vaughan, Ryan D, trooper 1st class, $55,644
Vaughn, Anthony C, trooper 1st class, $46,536
Vaught, Kyle J, technician III, $33,744
Vaught, Michael A, clerk, $9.69/hr
Veasman, Joseph A, cpl, $59,064
Veit, James, bldg const wkr II, $34,356
Veit, Shelby R, spec I, $30,984
Velleri, Teddie L, state vets cemetery dir, $44,304
Verbrugge, Michael K, driver exam sprv, $36,204
Verdone, Charles P, cpl, $52,416
Verhoff, Linda M, typist, $9.69/hr
Vermillion, James T, sergeant, $75,588
Vernon, Brian W, sergeant, $75,588
Vesser, Trisha B, food serv helper I, $21,264
Vette, Darcy D, cvo sup I, $40,380
Vick, Benita D, cdl exam, $33,744
Vick, Norman J, laundry worker I, $20,664
Victorian, Erin J, registered nurse, $50,244
Viessman, Lauren, typist, $12.00/hr
Viken, Chad A, registered nurse sup, $63,084
Vilchez-Gago, Elida M, domestic serv worker, $9.75/hr
Villagomez, Tanya, laundry worker I, $20,664
Villanueva, Emilio J, probary trooper, $41,280
Villanueva, Juan O, capt, $93,120
Vineyard, Katherine M, driver exam II, $29,976
Vinson, Hannah L, comp info tech spec I, $52,092
Vinyard, Elisa, consulting physician, $59.58/hr
Virgin, Ashley J, pub safety prog rep I, $30,984
Virgin, Kevin C, capitol police cpl, $36,888
Vislay, Gretchen L, misc prof, $22.15/hr

Vislay, Jacob H, probary trooper, $41,280
Vislay, Luke, major, $105,000
Vitale, Deborah S, clerk, $9.69/hr
Vitale, Jeffrey N, lt, $85,236
Vivas, Alexander R, trooper 1st class, $50,904
Viveiros, Sandra M, registered nurse, $27.00/hr
Vogt, Leann M, licensed clin soc wkr, $42,708
Volkart, Collin M, vets serv ofcr, $29,004
Volkmer, Eric K, sergeant, $75,588
Volkmer, Paul V, trooper 1st class, $47,964
Vollmer, Mandy M, cook I, $23,880
Voltmer, Michael, mil security ofcr I, $30,984
Vondracek, Kristie N, nursing asst I, $23,148
Vonholt, Cathy L, vets serv ofcr, $31,512
Von-Thun, Tena M, clerk-typist III, $28,908
Voorhis, Debbie L, nursing asst I, $24,900
Voris, Michele, air depot maint spec II, $40,380
Voss, Ann E, sr auditor, $53,208
Voss, Gregory, pub safety mgr band 2, $63,125
Vredenburg, John, maint worker II, $30,984
Wade, Ellice R, clerk, $9.69/hr
Wade, Keith A, vets serv ofcr, $17,986
Wade, Timothy E, chief motor veh insp, $38,928
Wages, Jessica M, sr ofc spt asst (keybrd), $27,948
Wagganer, Patricia D, clerk-typist III, $29,904
Wagler, Corinna A, direct care aide, $8.00/hr
Wagner, Christina A, comm oper III, $44,928
Wagner, Jay, bldg const wkr II, $30,984
Wagoner, Jeffrey S, sergeant, $75,588
Wahlert, Loren, phys plant sup II, $41,940
Waid, Frances L, technician II, $30,984
Wakefield, Christopher C, probary trooper, $41,280
Wakefield, Pamela S, lab evdnc tech II, $29,496
Waldron, Cynthia A, lpn I gen, $15,870
Waldron, Michelle E, criminalist III, $57,744
Wales, Dillon F, probary trooper, $41,280
Walkenhorst, Christopher D, laundry worker I, $20,664
Walker, Beth A, criminalist sup, $65,364
Walker, Derek L, probary trooper, $41,280
Walker, Dominick J, trooper 1st class, $66,516
Walker, Eddie J, sergeant, $75,588
Walker, Gail A, registered nurse sr, $58,140
Walker, Kent M, capitol police lt, $45,156
Walker, Richard A, trooper 1st class, $62,688
Walker, Ronald L, special asst prof, $98,483
Walker, Teresa R, nursing asst I, $24,900
Wall, John D, lt, $85,236
Wall, Julia A, driver exam - chief, $41,172
Wall, Laurie C, chief oper, $74,388
Wallace, Angela M, acct III, $52,092
Wallace, Brian G, driver exam I, $28,104
Wallace, Kimberly S, nursing asst I, $23,148
Wallace, Nathan D, trooper 1st class, $49,392
Wallace, Teresa L, lab evdnc tech II, $29,004
Wallain, Gary, maint mpv II, $37,548
Walley, Thomas R, cpl, $70,728
Walotka, Elizabeth M, nursing asst I, $24,900
Walsh, Lori A, custodial worker I, $20,148
Walters, Kenneth D, cpl, $70,728
Walters, Sandra K, acct II, $38,928
Walton, Chad W, trooper 1st class, $60,840
Walz, Matthew C, capt, $93,120
Wang, Zachary S, trooper 1st class, $46,536
Wann, Karen S, restorative aide, $27,696
Wansing, Don J, clerk, $9.69/hr
Wansing, Drew M, comp info tech III, $45,156
Ward, Allen L, vets serv ofcr, $29,004
Ward, Andrew B, trooper 1st class, $54,024
Ward, Brittany N, nursing asst I, $23,148
Ward, Gary, bldg & grounds maint II, $24,612
Ward, Glen D, sergeant, $75,588
Ward, Jennifer C, cdl exam, $33,744
Ward, Kindel C, trooper 1st class, $62,688
Ward, Leeta, registered nurse sup, $69,996
Ward, Mark D, cpl, $70,728
Ware, Belinda A, registered nurse, $27.00/hr
Ware, Rochelle, hlth prog aide, $16.00/hr
Warner, Jamie M, food serv helper I, $22,200
Warnol, Kenneth S, state vets cemetery worker, $27,948

Warren, April L, comm oper III, $62,016
Warren, David F, criminalist III, $55,416
Warren, Dawn L, designated principal asst div, $86,703
Warren, Everett E, driver exam sprv, $36,888
Warren, Gary, janitor, $8.16/hr
Warren, Ivy A, trooper 1st class, $66,516
Warren, John S, cpl, $70,728
Warren, Kevin B, state vets cemetery worker, $27,948
Warren, Melba C, driver exam III, $31,512
Warren, Saundra L, lpn III gen, $43,620
Washabaugh, Steven J, trooper 1st class, $47,964
Wasmer, Michelle R, registered nurse sup, $59,340
Waterman, Kris A, pub safety prog rep I, $30,984
Waterman, Virginia L, nursing asst II, $27,780
Waters, Kevin R, cpl, $60,840
Watkins, April S, crim intel analyst II, $36,204
Watson, Chichota R, driver exam III, $33,180
Watson, Christopher W, sergeant, $75,588
Watson, Helen, data entry oper, $12.04/hr
Watson, Justin D, trooper 1st class, $66,516
Watson, Lashunta N, nursing asst II, $28,224
Watson, Lawrence E, pub safety mgr band 1, $58,402
Watson, Michael W, lt, $85,236
Watson, Randall, hr mgr b1, $54,864
Watson, Ricky L, sergeant, $70,932
Watson, Scott R, vets serv ofcr, $29,976
Watson, Shannon S, food serv helper I, $22,200
Watson, Sharnitha M, nursing asst I, $23,148
Watson, Shinita R, nursing asst I, $24,900
Watson, Todd P, trooper 1st class, $66,516
Watson, Yolanda D, food serv helper I, $20,664
Watt, Corey D, custodial worker I, $20,664
Watterson, Ashley B, prob comm oper, $36,012
Weadon, Jeremy L, sergeant, $75,588
Weadon, Joseph M, sergeant, $75,588
Weakley, Michael T, trooper 1st class, $50,904
Webb, Adam J, trooper 1st class, $52,416
Webb, Colin C, typist, $12.00/hr
Webb, Deborah J, nursing asst II, $27,780
Weber, Deryk A, probary trooper, $40,272
Weddington, Angela M, driver exam - chief, $38,928
Weddington, Nicole, nursing asst I, $24,900
Weddle, Greg A, cpl, $70,728
Weeden, Demetrice C, driver exam III, $31,512
Wehmeier, Richard, custodial worker II, $23,880
Weinkein, Gene J, maint spv II, $29,352
Weinkein, Rhonda G, typist, $9.69/hr
Weirich, Shanna M, clerk-typist III, $28,908
Weisacosky, Jason C, sergeant, $75,588
Weisacosky, Pennie S, comm oper III, $56,784
Weiseman, Michael D, chief oper, $74,388
Weissinger, Kelly S, motor veh insp III, $33,744
Welch, William C, trnr/auditor III, $42,708
Welker, David W, probary trooper, $41,280
Wells, David A, vets serv ofcr, $29,004
Wells, Paul R, trooper 1st class, $47,964
Welschmeyer, Kelly A, acct II, $44,304
Welschmeyer, Shawn J, bldg & grounds maint II, $24,612
Wenderski, Tena D, nursing asst I, $23,856
Wendt, Amber L, nursing asst I, $23,148
Wendt, Miranda R, nursing asst I, $23,856
Wendt, Rose L, nursing asst I, $24,900
Wendt, Traci L, nursing asst I, $23,856
Wensel, Geoffrey N, probary trooper, $41,280
Werner, April D, registered nurse sr, $51,552
Wessel, Katherine, laundry worker I, $20,664
West, Gerry L, cpl, $62,688
West, Jerry C, lt, $85,236
West, John J, trooper 1st class, $50,904
West, Madonna A, cook III, $32,628
West, Robert C, cpl, $66,576
West, Samantha L, food serv helper I, $22,200
West, Tekesha, nursing asst I, $23,856
Westcott, Connie J, steno III, $29,904
Westerhoff, Roger M, cve insp III, $36,204
Westmoreland, Emily M, probary trooper, $41,280
Weston, Julie A, comm oper II, $42,372
Weston, June A, nursing asst I, $23,856
Wetstein, Max A, misc tech, $12.70/hr

Wetzel, Debra L, lpn III gen, $43,620
Wever, Theresa L, registered nurse sr, $58,140
Wever, Timothy L, misc prof, $20.85/hr
Weyrauch, Elizabeth A, pub safety mgr band 1, $51,096
Wheat, Michael D, electronic gaming device spec, $46,068
Wheatley, Pamela D, restorative aide, $26,844
Wheeler, Carol S, sr ofc spt asst (keybrd), $25,824
Wheeler, John D, cpl, $70,728
Wheeler, Samantha D, nursing asst I, $23,148
Wheetley, Juston R, cpl, $59,064
Whelan, Heather R, sr ofc spt asst (keybrd), $25,824
Whetsten, Ronald, air depot maint spec II, $40,380
Whipple, Maranda M, nursing asst I, $24,900
Whisenton, Terrance, mil funeral hnrs team leader, $29,976
White, Brandon M, sergeant, $70,932
White, Brenda R, registered nurse sup, $59,340
White, James D, bldg & grounds maint II, $24,612
White, James E, motor veh insp III, $31,512
White, Jeffrey L, sergeant, $75,588
White, Jeffrey L, clerk, $26.52/hr
White, Joshua L, trooper 1st class, $62,688
White, Justin D, clerk-typist III, $27,948
White, Lakeisha A, custodial worker I, $20,664
White, Lorna Y, driver exam sprv, $37,548
White, Maggie, fin auditor, $63,996
White, Michael A, probary trooper, $41,280
White, Michael J, maint worker II, $33,180
White, Rebecca J, food serv helper I, $20,664
White, Ryan D, cpl, $60,240
White, Scott B, cpl, $55,644
White, Steven C, designated princ asst-div, $73,237
Whited, Jared L, cve insp II, $33,744
Whitehead, Alexander W, cpl, $70,728
Whitehead, Grace, hlth prog spec, $16.00/hr
Whitfield, James S, mil funeral hnrs area supv, $36,204
Whiting, Jennifer M, driver exam sprv, $36,204
Whitlock, Vernon, trooper 1st class, $66,516
Whitt, Alexis L, nursing asst I, $23,148
Whitt, Jason J, sergeant, $75,588
Whitt, Kenyatta D, nursing asst I, $23,772
Whittington, Brandon S, cve insp III, $36,204
Whittle, Barbara E, pub safety mgr band 1, $55,867
Whittler, Roger D, capt, $93,120
Whittom, Adam E, comm oper III, $47,628
Whorton, Christy S, nursing asst I, $24,900
Widener, Donna K, therapy aide, $10.00/hr
Wieberg, Janice, misc prof, $15.00/hr
Wiedemann, Warren W, sergeant, $75,588
Wiegand, Joyce L, technician III, $33,744
Wiggins, Jeanette M, processing technician III, $29,004
Wiggins, Michelle D, nursing asst I, $23,856
Wiggins, Terryn S, nursing asst II, $28,224
Wightman, Tonya L, nursing asst I, $24,900
Wilbers, Jennifer E, fiscal & administrative mgr b2, $76,065
Wilcox, Glenda M, licensed clin soc wkr, $44,304
Wilde, Christopher S, comp info tech I, $36,204
Wilde, Clara J, clerk, $9.69/hr
Wilde, James E, cpl, $70,728
Wilde, Nanilehua O, driver exam II, $29,976
Wildhaber, Chikako O, crim intel analyst II, $36,204
Wildhaber, Lisa, security ofcr I, $26,652
Wilding, Melissa C, pub info spec II, $44,304
Wiley, Vince P, cve insp II, $33,744
Wilhoit, Eric S, designated principal asst div, $76,065
Wilhoit, Mark A, sergeant, $75,588
Wilhoit, Ryan J, cpl, $59,064
Wilhoit, Steven V, lt, $85,236
Wilkerson, Rebecca M, custodial worker I, $20,148
Wilkins, Robert R, trooper 1st class, $66,516
Wilkinson, Alice I, nursing asst II, $27,780
Wilkinson, Melissa D, nursing asst I, $24,900
Willeford, Michele J, nursing asst I, $24,900
Willhite, Carol A, acct II, $39,624
Williams, Alice D, cook I, $22,200
Williams, Allison K, clerk-typist III, $28,908
Williams, Angela C, restorative technician, $30,048
Williams, Arik, security guard, $23,880
Williams, Chelsea R, nursing asst I, $24,900
Williams, Cocoa M, nursing asst I, $11,929

Williams, Dana J, sr ofc spt asst (keybrd), $29,412
Williams, Danny L, examination monitor, $15.15/hr
Williams, Dorine D, nursing asst I, $24,900
Williams, Edward, stores clerk, $25,824
Williams, Ericka R, laundry worker I, $21,564
Williams, Glyn, groundskeeper I, $23,880
Williams, Grant N, sergeant, $66,576
Williams, Jarom L, nursing asst I, $24,900
Williams, Joseph J, driver exam III, $31,512
Williams, Joshua E, trooper 1st class, $45,180
Williams, Justin, mil security ofcr I, $29,976
Williams, Kenneth G, commercial veh ofcr II, $44,304
Williams, Lacey A, driver exam I, $28,104
Williams, Lashundra R, nursing asst I, $24,900
Williams, Leonard C, custodial worker I, $20,664
Williams, Lindsay M, asst chief oper, $62,016
Williams, Michael M, trooper 1st class, $49,392
Williams, Peggy L, sr ofc spt asst (keybrd), $28,908
Williams, Rebecca L, registered nurse sup, $59,340
Williams, Robert O, vets serv ofcr, $29,976
Williams, Roger S, sergeant, $75,588
Williams, Ronald W, nursing asst I, $24,900
Williams, Ronald W, firefighter, $28,267
Williams, Travis L, sergeant, $75,588
Williams, Tycee M, cpl, $59,064
Williams, Verlyn, nursing asst I, $24,900
Williams, Violet L, direct care aide, $10.50/hr
Williams, Wayne R, bldg & grounds maint II, $24,612
Willis, Amber D, procurement ofcr II, $48,156
Willis, Cynthia D, nursing asst I, $24,900
Willis, Erica M, nursing asst I, $24,900
Willis, Jerry E, security guard, $16,786
Willis, Richard L, state vets cemetery worker, $27,948
Willoughby, Deborah, clerk IV, $32,628
Wilmes, Brook L, hlth prog aide, $12.00/hr
Wilmont, Kyle D, cpl, $70,728
Wilson, Anastasia M, sr ofc spt asst (keybrd), $28,908
Wilson, Cheryl L, nursing asst II, $26,892
Wilson, Christopher E, sergeant, $75,588
Wilson, Denzil, maint worker, $9.00/hr
Wilson, Dorothy J, cook I, $22,200
Wilson, Ethan N, trooper, $42,612
Wilson, James A, cpl, $62,688
Wilson, John E, bldg & grounds maint I, $23,880
Wilson, Jonathan T, trooper 1st class, $50,904
Wilson, Katie L, lpn III gen, $35,148
Wilson, Leslie A, trooper 1st class, $66,516
Wilson, Melissa S, recrtnal ther II, $41,940
Wilson, Phillip, janitor, $8.16/hr
Wilson, Sharia N, domestic serv worker, $9.75/hr
Wilson, Thad M, sergeant, $75,588
Wilson, Tina M, nursing asst I, $24,900
Wilson, Woodrow W, nursing asst I, $23,148
Wilson-Lagermann, Shelly L, driver exam III, $31,512
Wilt, Curtis B, trooper 1st class, $55,644
Wilt, James E, capt, $93,120
Winder, Mark A, cpl, $70,728
Windham, Donald J, sergeant, $75,588
Windle, Rodger R, fire investigation sup, $47,892
Windle, Russel A, comm oper III, $56,784
Winkelman, Kathy A, activity ther, $29,208
Winkler, Mark A, planner III, $53,208
Winkler, Michael, facilities opps mgr b2, $66,000
Winkler, Nathan L, motor veh insp III, $31,512
Winn, Jeffery A, lpn III gen, $43,620
Winn, Suzanne M, account clerk II, $28,452
Winn, Terrell L, probary trooper, $40,272
Winter, Christopher A, trooper 1st class, $59,064
Wirths, Curtis W, sergeant, $75,588
Wise, Marisa L, crim intel analyst II, $36,204
Wiseman, Martin L, trooper 1st class, $66,516
Wishon, Rachel M, food serv helper I, $20,664
Withers, Alexandria N, ofc spt asst (keybrd), $22,872
Withers, Lois J, nursing asst I, $25,284
Witherspoon, Brandon M, domestic serv worker, $9.13/hr
Witt, Emily A, typist, $12.00/hr
Woehr, Lori L, qual ctrl clerk II, $29,904
Wogan, Megan E, technician I, $29,004
Wohler, Daniel D, trooper 1st class, $47,964

Wohnoutka, Daniel P, sergeant, $75,588
Woirhaye, Debbie J, registered nurse mgr b2, $75,240
Wolf, Robert F, capt, $93,120
Wolken, Becky A, admin ofc spt asst, $37,548
Wolken, Gail A, pers ofcr I, $50,040
Wood, Jeffery A, motor veh insp III, $31,512
Wood, Lela A, asst chief oper, $63,852
Wood, Lori L, comm oper II, $42,372
Wood, Rondia J, driver exam III, $31,512
Wood, Ryan A, cpl, $54,024
Wood, William J, trooper, $43,872
Woodall, Marlene R, housekeeper I, $31,512
Woodcock, Carla J, nursing asst II, $28,224
Woodruff, Wanda F, driver exam III, $33,744
Woods, Andrew L, trooper 1st class, $49,392
Woods, Leslie R, spec I, $30,984
Woods, Patricia A, registered nurse sr, $59,340
Woods, Patrick J, info security ofcr, $62,664
Woods, Tiffany A, registered nurse sr, $55,776
Woods, Tiffany L, trooper, $43,872
Woods, Travis R, motor veh driver, $26,232
Woolridge, Sheila M, lpn III gen, $43,620
Woolsey, Christina A, nursing asst I, $23,856
Woolsey, David W, environ spec III, $43,488
Wooten, Randy D, maint spv I, $38,232
Workman, Courtney E, criminalist III, $57,744
Workman, Michael S, criminalist III, $57,744
Wormington, Diana K, lpn III gen, $37,020
Wormsley, Monica M, barber, $15.00/hr
Worthley, Jason M, trooper 1st class, $55,644
Wortley, Joshua, janitor, $8.16/hr
Wray, Darrin, groundskeeper II, $29,412
Wright, Allen J, motor veh insp III, $32,628
Wright, Charles M, trooper 1st class, $45,180
Wright, Fay, lpn III gen, $43,620
Wright, George B, trooper 1st class, $49,392
Wright, Tyler R, trooper, $43,872
Wrinkles, Nikki T, account clerk II, $25,032
Wunderlich, Blake D, trooper, $43,872
Wunderlich, Daniel M, prob comm oper, $37,392
Wyatt, Bonnie K, lpn, $21.00/hr
Wyatt, Daniel L, bldg & grounds maint II, $24,612
Wyatt, Donald D, driver exam I, $29,004
Wyatt, Steven C, food serv helper II, $21,864
Wyckoff, Jason L, criminalist sup, $65,364
Wyss, Michael F, cpl, $70,728
Yates, Nancy A, ofc spt asst (keybrd), $25,404
Yeager, Christopher C, pub safety prog rep II, $36,204
Yeast, Beverly A, lpn III gen, $37,020
Yendes, Matthew G, trooper, $43,872
Yingling, Daniel A, trooper 1st class, $46,536
Yoakum, Teresa A, cook II, $27,084
Yoder, Matthew J, trooper 1st class, $49,392
Yoor, Bruce M, registered nurse sr, $56,976
Yordt, Katherine J, nursing asst I, $23,148
York, Katie P, comm oper III, $50,508
Youmans, Vanessa N, lpn III gen, $41,232
Young, Chelsea M, nursing asst I, $24,900
Young, Elicia R, nursing asst I, $23,148
Young, Galen R, driver exam sprv, $38,232
Young, Kelley S, sergeant, $75,588
Young, Mark, maint spv I, $35,568
Young, Matthew R, trooper 1st class, $55,644
Young, Robin L, sr ofc spt asst (keybrd), $20,420
Young, Sandra, food serv mgr I, $35,568
Young, Steve A, cve insp III, $36,204
Young, Thomas E, cpl, $60,840
Young, Tyrone D, food serv helper I, $20,664
Youngermann, Alice J, nursing asst I, $24,900
Yount, Ruth A, food serv helper I, $20,664
Yount, Suzanne D, restorative technician, $30,048
Youtsey, Angel R, nursing asst II, $26,892
Zacher, Todd A, sergeant, $75,588
Zeilenga, Cassie L, recrtnal ther II, $37,548
Zeilinger, Rhonda L, lab evdnc tech II, $29,004
Zeller, Jennifer J, lab evdnc tech I, $27,228
Zeller, William R, trooper 1st class, $59,064
Zeman, Alexander, hvac inst ctrls tech, $30,984
Ziegler, Thomas B, sergeant, $75,588

Ziegler, Travis N, probary trooper, $41,280
Zieres, William F, law enforce mgr b2, $60,649
Zimmerman, Tyler G, trooper, $43,872
Zink, Karen E, lpn III gen, $39,072
Zumsteg, Bryan D, driver exam II, $29,976
Zvolanek, Michael S, trnr/auditor III, $45,156
Zyla, Lauren N, ofc worker misc, $10.00/hr

Department of Revenue

*Truman State Office Bldg., PO Box 860, Jefferson City
65102*

Ray, Nia V, state dept dir, $121,705
Adair, Andrea M, rvnue processing tech I, $23,880
Adamik, Laura M, rvnue processing tech I, $23,880
Adams, Rachel N, rvnue processing tech I, $23,880
Adams, Reginald T, lottery sales rep, $34,944
Adams, Tempie A, rvnue processing tech II, $30,924
Adkins, Beth A, info technologist IV, $45,156
Agniel, Jana L, special asst ofc & clerical, $41,717
Ahlers, Stephen J, rvnue mgr, band 1, $52,019
Ahrens, Katherine J, rvnue processing tech I, $23,880
Akers, Andrew S, lottery sales rep, $36,204
Albrecht, Shelby L, rvnue processing tech I, $23,880
Alexander, Lester F, photographic-machine oper, $23,160
Alexander, Lorie K, management analysis specialist I, $37,548
Allen, Chandreka N, sr counsel, $54,168
Allen, Kyle C, tel info oper I rev, $23,880
Allen, Paula B, lottery cust serv rep, $13,752
Allison, Joel M, rvnue mgr, band 3, $75,000
Allison, Kristie L, admin analyst I, $29,976
Amego, Daniel S, rvnue processing tech IV, $36,204
Andersen, Cedric B, sr auditor, $40,380
Anderson, Debbie D, rvnue processing tech I, $23,880
Anderson, Randy, printing/mail technician I, $25,032
Anderson, Trayce D, tax auditor I, $37,548
Andrews, Tabitha M, rvnue processing tech III, $29,004
Aragon, Ethan J, rvnue processing tech III, $29,004
Arand, Michael C, investigator III, $54,288
Arisgado, Alona P, rvnue processing tech I, $23,880
Armour, Lynn C, rvnue section supv, $36,204
Arnold, Bryce J, mgmt analysis spec I, $37,548
Asberry, Joyce A, rvnue processing tech II, $29,904
Ash, Charlene B, rvnue processing tech IV, $33,744
Atchison, Kathryn L, rvnue processing tech I, $23,880
Atkisson, Brenda A, rvnue processing tech I, $23,880
Ausmus, Mark D, assoc counsel, $47,348
Avery, Patricia, rvnue field servs coor, $42,708
Backman, Sandra L, tel info oper I rev, $23,880
Bade, Daniel W, rvnue section supv, $38,232
Baker, Corey D, legal counsel, $43,474
Baker, Samantha J, rvnue processing tech I, $23,880
Baker, Sherron R, rvnue processing tech II, $26,232
Baker, Tammy J, rvnue processing tech II, $29,412
Baker, Wendy L, pub info coor, $47,892
Baldwin, Mary L, rvnue processing tech I, $23,880
Barbano, Karen S, rvnue field servs coor, $36,204
Barber, Adelaida Q, rvnue processing tech II, $26,652
Barge, Tammy A, tax auditor I, $37,548
Barnes, Melinda K, rvnue section supv, $36,204
Barnes, Sarah D, rvnue processing tech II, $26,232
Barnett, Kimberly D, rvnue processing tech II, $26,232
Barnhart, Wendy C, rvnue processing tech II, $26,652
Bartley, Carolyn S, rvnue processing tech II, $27,504
Bastion, Misty D, rvnue processing tech II, $26,652
Bateman, Kevin E, rvnue processing tech II, $26,232
Bauer, Helen M, rvnue processing tech II, $26,232
Bauer, Lindsay J, tax collection tech I, $23,880
Bax, Ashley R, rvnue processing tech III, $29,004
Bax, Debra A, tax collection tech III, $29,004
Bax, Denise, rvnue processing tech II, $26,652
Bax, Glenn D, ofc spt asst (keybrd), $26,232
Bax, Michelle L, rvnue processing tech II, $26,232
Beaumaster, Amanda M, tax collection tech III, $29,004
Beazley, Heather M, mgmt analysis spec I, $37,548
Bechel, Sonja M, graphic arts spec III, $42,708
Bechtel, Elizabeth A, account clerk II, $26,232

Beck, Justin A, tax auditor I, $37,548
Bedsworth, Chanda N, rvnue processing tech III, $29,004
Beenders, Tonya L, lottery mgr b3, $83,325
Bell, Amanda R, taxpayer services sup, $36,204
Bell, Felicia A, rvnue processing tech II, $26,652
Bellinger, Mark J, rvnue processing tech I, $23,880
Bemboom, Jackie, div dir, $86,359
Bentlage, Casey S, printing/mail technician I, $25,032
Bentley, Shannon E, tax collection tech I, $23,880
Benton, April M, rvnue processing tech I, $23,880
Berezowski, Joseph M, appraiser II, $39,624
Berger, Michelle L, admin ofc spt asst, $36,888
Berhorst, Darlene A, ofc spt asst (keybrd), $23,508
Bernskoetter, Dana G, rvnue processing tech II, $28,908
Bertalott, Timothy, tax audit supv, $62,664
Bestgen, Danny R, exec I, $41,940
Bestgen, Mary E, sr ofc spt asst (keybrd), $27,948
Bethune, Andrea L, rvnue processing tech I, $23,880
Betley, Laura R, out-state audit pers, $64,068
Bexten, Delores L, div dir, $81,309
Beyer, Timothy A, appraiser III, $46,932
Biehl, Janet L, out-state audit pers, $39,206
Bieri, Anne, rvnue processing tech I, $23,880
Binkley, Ronda S, rvnue processing tech II, $29,412
Bishop, Jessica C, rvnue processing tech I, $23,880
Blankenship, Heather L, rvnue processing tech II, $26,232
Blankenship, Jeffrey F, comp opps spv II, $50,040
Blankenship, Melissa D, accounting spec II, $55,416
Blankenship, Teri K, tax collection tech III, $29,004
Blazich, Grace, out-state audit pers, $60,935
Blazich, John A, out-state audit pers, $67,641
Block, Georgia C, special asst ofc & clerical, $49,385
Bloomer, Warren G, rvnue processing tech II, $26,652
Blythe, Deborah, rvnue processing tech III, $29,004
Bock, Patricia A, sr ofc spt asst (steno), $31,416
Boeckmann, Kalynn M, rvnue processing tech I, $23,880
Bohannan, Jessica L, rvnue processing tech I, $23,880
Bohl, Keith P, rvnue mgr, band 1, $61,889
Bohl, Nathan P, printing/mail technician I, $25,032
Bollinger, Justin L, rvnue processing tech II, $26,232
Bolzenius, Eric J, tax auditor II, $40,380
Bonnot, Joyce A, rvnue processing tech II, $27,084
Borgmeyer, Lucinda A, printing/mail technician I, $25,824
Borgmeyer, Patricia M, rvnue processing tech I, $23,880
Borgmeyer, Stephanie L, rvnue processing tech II, $26,232
Borth, Richard E, rvnue processing tech I, $23,880
Bosch, Cheryl L, rvnue mgr, band 1, $50,000
Bouse, Brandy K, tax auditor I, $37,548
Bownds, Emily, tax auditor I, $37,548
Boyster, Dustin J, rvnue processing tech III, $29,004
Bradley, Stephanie N, lottery sales rep, $36,204
Brake, Heidi L, tax collection tech I, $23,880
Branstetter, Christopher J, compoper II, $29,004
Brauner, Connie S, rvnue processing tech I, $23,880
Brauner, Darrell G, rvnue processing tech II, $27,084
Brester, Bradley J, rvnue mgr, band 2, $68,068
Brewer, Janet M, sr ofc spt asst (keybrd), $26,232
Brewer, Kim L, rvnue processing tech II, $35,472
Bright, Deanna M, sr counsel, $54,168
Brinkley, Donald L, info technology spec I, $58,908
Briones, Jennifer R, rvnue processing tech II, $26,652
Brooks, Amanda L, tax collection tech I, $23,880
Brown, Diana L, tax auditor I, $37,548
Brown, Jessica L, rvnue processing tech I, $23,880
Brown, Sherry L, rvnue processing tech II, $30,924
Browner, Pamela J, lottery mgr b1, $51,199
Brownfield, Emily N, tax collection tech II, $26,232
Broyles, Melissa M, rvnue section supv, $36,204
Bruce, Cindy G, rvnue field servs coor, $40,380
Bruemmer, Allison, info technology spec II, $74,304
Brunner, Paul D, rvnue field servs coor, $40,380
Bruns, Tina S, rvnue processing tech II, $27,084
Buechter, Michelle L, tax collection tech I, $23,880
Buechter, Summer D, account clerk II, $25,824
Buehrle, David G, investigator II, $37,548
Bunder, Michael L, tax auditor I, $37,548
Bunting, Carisa L, rvnue processing tech II, $26,652
Burks, Patricia E, account clerk II, $26,232
Burlingame, Gary P, supply mgr I, $37,548

Burnett, Lori A, exec II, $43,488
Burns, Brittany M, fiscal & administrative mgr b1, $48,396
Burrus-Gustafson, Ginni R, lottery sales rep, $34,944
Burton, William E, lottery mgr b1, $59,996
Buschjost, Mary L, acct I, $30,984
Buschman, Janet S, rvnue processing tech II, $26,232
Bush, Sandra R, rvnue processing tech II, $27,084
Bushko, Rachelle L, rvnue mgr, band 1, $54,040
Butler, Michelle R, rvnue section supv, $36,204
Butts, Deanna L, rvnue processing tech II, $30,384
Byrd, Sonya K, rvnue processing tech II, $27,084
Cady, Tina M, tax collection tech I, $23,880
Caldwell, Stephen A, rvnue processing tech II, $26,232
Callahan, Victor E, commissmbr, $106,620
Calvert, Gene V, compoper III, $34,944
Camden, Suzanne L, lottery inside sales rep, $29,976
Campbell, Angela K, printing/mail technician I, $25,032
Campbell, Jordan E, ofc spt asst (keybrd), $23,160
Canole, Rashell D, rvnue processing tech I, $23,880
Carel, Ashley K, lottery mgr b1, $63,125
Carmack, Heather L, lottery sales rep, $36,888
Carnahan, Dawn T, lottery sales rep, $34,944
Carpenter, Desiree C, rvnue processing tech III, $29,496
Carrender, Kathleen P, rvnue processing tech II, $26,652
Carrender, Lori A, account clerk II, $27,948
Carroll, Bridget E, rvnue processing tech II, $26,652
Carter, Crystal A, rvnue section supv, $36,204
Carter, Rhonda J, appraiser II, $39,624
Carter, Ross C, research mgr b1, $61,254
Carter, Tiffany S, rvnue processing tech I, $23,880
Cartmill, Julie, rvnue processing tech II, $27,084
Carvel, Ashley C, rvnue processing tech I, $23,880
Carver, Adriane K, tax auditor I, $39,624
Carwile, Brittany A, rvnue processing tech I, $23,880
Cassidy, Neshaelondia L, rvnue processing tech I, $23,880
Cassmeyer, Peggy M, rvnue mgr, band 1, $49,394
Castleman, Chad A, info technologist II, $43,488
Cavender, Mike A, lottery mgr b2, $63,652
Chambers, Austin B, investigator II, $41,172
Chambers, Kimberly D, rvnue processing tech II, $28,452
Chambers, Marilyn B, rvnue mgr, band 1, $49,118
Chambers, Marita K, rvnue processing tech II, $26,232
Chambly, Leon G, tax collection tech I, $23,880
Cheek, Cece B, tax collection tech III, $29,004
Chen, Tung Y, investigator III, $45,156
Chen, Yanling, out-state audit pers, $43,850
Chenault, James A, sr counsel, $60,988
Chesnut, Thresa S, printing/mail technician I, $25,032
Childress, Jennifer G, rvnue mgr, band 2, $62,655
Chilton, Katherine J, lottery sales coord, $46,932
Christenson, Jeffrey, appraiser II, $40,380
Clark, Jonni L, rvnue processing tech II, $26,232
Clark, Matthew, tax audit supv, $52,092
Clark, Stacy R, lottery sales coord, $50,040
Clark, William S, rvnue processing tech III, $32,052
Clutter, Justin D, administrative analyst III, $40,380
Coale, Toko S, rvnue processing tech II, $26,652
Coker, Aubrey J, sr ofc spt asst (keybrd), $25,824
Cole, Rodney L, appraiser sup, $53,208
Colen, Matthew Z, rvnue processing tech I, $23,880
Collier, Gershon B, div dir, $86,287
Conley, Carla J, appeals ref I, $38,928
Conley, Ronald E, rvnue processing tech II, $26,652
Conner, Amanda C, rvnue processing tech III, $29,004
Connor, Matthew D, administrative analyst III, $40,380
Conol, Kathleen B, rvnue processing tech II, $26,652
Conway, Joseph E, out-state audit pers, $40,505
Conway, Stephen, legal counsel, $43,474
Cook, Kaitlyn L, sr ofc spt asst (keybrd), $25,824
Cooper, Nicole C, administrative analyst I, $29,976
Cordry, Patricia A, sr ofc spt asst (clerical), $29,412
Cowles, Brandon E, investigator II, $37,548
Cox, Joseph M, sr counsel, $54,168
Cox, Kevin L, investigation mgr b3, $64,382
Cox, Kim M, rvnue processing tech I, $23,880
Cox, Naomi J, rvnue processing tech II, $26,652
Crader, Mary T, rvnue processing tech II, $26,652
Crocker, Ashley D, rvnue processing tech I, $23,880
Crockett, Laurel J, tax collection tech I, $23,880

Crosby, Ryan C, rvnue processing tech II, $26,232
Cross, Denise A, printing/mail technician II, $27,948
Crownover, Andrea L, rvnue processing tech I, $23,880
Crowson, Joseph B, info technologist IV, $48,156
Crull, Karen T, rvnue processing tech I, $26,232
Crutchfield, Amanda N, rvnue processing tech II, $26,232
Curry, Tara R, administrative analyst I, $29,976
Dam, James F, investigator II, $37,548
Daniell, Monica L, tax auditor I, $37,548
Davenport, Brittany L, investigator II, $41,172
Davidson, Mary K, account clerk II, $27,948
Davis, Brenda A, facilities opps mgr b2, $58,874
Davis, Bruce E, commisschair, $106,620
Davis, Michael Y, rvnue mgr, band 2, $65,000
Davis, Sheila L, rvnue processing tech III, $30,420
Dearixon, Norma S, rvnue mgr, band 1, $50,000
Deelo, Alysha B, rvnue processing tech II, $26,652
Delehant, Brandy M, rvnue processing tech I, $23,880
Dellino, Deanna J, rvnue processing tech I, $23,880
Denich, Daphne G, sr ofc spt asst (keybrd), $25,824
Dickneite, Bryan K, rvnue processing tech I, $23,880
Dickneite, Jamie L, printing/mail technician II, $27,948
Dickneite, Janice, rvnue processing tech II, $26,232
Dinolfo, Joseph A, mgmt analysis spec I, $37,548
Dippold, Wendy M, account clerk II, $26,232
Distler, Patricia A, rvnue processing tech II, $26,652
Dixon, Maurice L, rvnue processing tech II, $26,232
Dobbs, Kenneth L, rvnue processing tech II, $26,232
Dobbs, Stephanie M, tel info oper I rev, $23,880
Dodson, Tamara L, pers analyst I, $34,356
Doerhoff, Roger G, rvnue processing tech I, $25,404
Donaldson, Hilary A, assess rep II tax comm, $36,888
Donnici, John M, tax audit supv, $49,128
Doron, Amanda R, rvnue processing tech I, $23,880
Doss, Angela M, rvnue section supv, $36,204
Doss, Cynthia L, rvnue mgr, band 1, $50,000
Doucette, Amy B, printing/mail technician I, $25,032
Downs, Amberly K, tax auditor I, $37,548
Drake, Shelly R, acct I, $34,356
Drapiza, Angie M, account clerk II, $26,232
Dreste, Sheri L, acct I, $30,984
Druml, Stella M, account clerk II, $26,232
Dudenhoeffer, Karen A, rvnue mgr, band 1, $53,312
Dudenhoeffer, Linda M, rvnue processing tech III, $29,004
Dunavan, Stephanie D, tax auditor II, $40,380
Dunbar, Megan N, rvnue processing tech I, $23,880
Duncan, Marcie A, rvnue processing tech II, $26,652
Duncan, Michelle J, tax collection tech II, $26,232
Dyhouse, Rose M, rvnue processing tech II, $26,232
Eads, Julie A, mgmt analysis spec I, $37,548
Edvall, Rebecca K, rvnue processing tech II, $26,232
Edwards, Angela C, rvnue section supv, $36,204
Edwards, Vicky L, rvnue section supv, $36,204
Eggen, Jakeb P, rvnue processing tech II, $26,232
Eggen, Maureen A, rvnue processing tech I, $23,880
Ehrhardt, Jennifer S, investigator I, $34,356
Eichholz, Amy, exec I, $31,512
Eiken, Susan H, investigator II, $41,940
Eilers, Cassandra L, tax collection tech II, $26,232
Elliott, Janette M, tax commissmgr, band 3, $66,264
Ellis-Johnston, Camelia D, tax auditor I, $37,548
Endsley, Jennifer J, rvnue processing tech I, $23,880
Engelbrecht, Vicki N, rvnue section supv, $36,204
Enriquez, Sheila, lottery cust serv rep, $26,232
Espinales, Vannesa J, rvnue processing tech I, $23,880
Etter, Phoebe M, rvnue processing tech I, $27,084
Evans, Amber D, sr ofc spt asst (keybrd), $25,824
Everett, Andrew T, ofc spt asst (clerical), $22,536
Evers, Cheryl D, rvnue processing tech III, $29,976
Evers, Jason A, rvnue processing tech III, $29,004
Evers, Kimberly A, info technologist III, $46,932
Fallert, Mark H, appraiser II, $40,380
Falls, Carolyn R, tax audit supv, $63,996
Farley, Sharon L, sr ofc spt asst (keybrd), $25,824
Farris, Jennifer L, rvnue processing tech III, $29,004
Farris, Madalyn M, rvnue processing tech I, $23,880
Farrow, Sherrice S, rvnue processing tech II, $26,232
Fehr, Christopher R, assoc counsel, $47,348
Fehr, Rhonda L, lottery mgr b1, $48,240

Felleti, Linda D, rvnue processing tech II, $26,652
Ferguson, Dana L, lottery sales rep, $36,204
Findley, Amber L, tax collection tech I, $23,880
Finley, Frank C, pub info coor, $57,736
Fischer, Teresa R, rvnue processing tech II, $28,908
Fisher, Rachel C, tax collection tech I, $23,880
Fisher, Tracey L, rvnue processing tech I, $23,880
Fitzgerald, Michelle, lottery sales rep, $34,944
Fitzpatrick, Shannon L, rvnue processing tech II, $26,652
Flaugher, Shanna M, rvnue processing tech II, $27,504
Fleming, Kay L, lottery sales rep, $34,944
Fletcher, Jason M, tax audit supv, $52,092
Forbes, Rachelle W, tax audit supv, $49,128
Forbis, David W, photographic-machine oper, $26,232
Forck, Teri A, rvnue processing tech I, $23,880
Ford, Elizabeth J, tax collection tech I, $23,880
Forrester, Susan B, rvnue processing tech II, $26,232
Fortner, Jonathan D'auna, rvnue processing tech III, $29,004
Fortson, Dustin J, rvnue processing tech II, $26,652
Fossett, Fawn L, exec I, $34,944
Foster, Mary D, rvnue processing tech II, $26,232
Fouts, Leighann M, tax collection tech III, $29,004
Fowler, Lance J, lottery sales rep, $34,944
Fowler, Lisa M, rvnue processing tech II, $29,904
Francis, Robert E, rvnue processing tech I, $23,880
Frank, Ruth A, rvnue processing tech II, $26,232
Frank, Wanda M, rvnue section supv, $36,204
Franklin, Alisa G, rvnue processing tech II, $26,652
Franklin, Sandra, sr ofc spt asst (keybrd), $25,824
Fraser, Kelly C, tax auditor III, $34,790
Frazer, Sheena M, tax audit supv, $49,128
Frazier, Mary K, rvnue processing tech II, $26,232
French, Russell W, lottery sales rep, $34,944
Frerking, Brenda K, ofc spt asst (keybrd), $23,508
Freudenberg, Roger L, managing counsel, $68,300
Friend, Kevin J, investigator II, $37,548
Fryer, Michael R, investigator II, $37,548
Gainey, Debra A, rvnue processing tech II, $30,384
Gaither, Melissa J, tax auditor II, $40,380
Galbraith, James C, legal counsel, $43,474
Galm, Alicia M, tax audit supv, $49,128
Gammon, Nancy L, tax auditor III, $43,488
Garavaglia, Joe M, tax auditor II, $40,380
Garay, Maureen M, out-state audit pers, $33,995
Gardner, Juanita J, rvnue mgr, band 2, $72,768
Garrett, Mina S, tax audit supv, $50,040
Garro, David S, rvnue mgr, band 1, $52,000
Gast, E. K, rvnue mgr, band 1, $50,000
Gaverth, Jessica M, lottery cust serv rep, $26,232
Gehlert, Allis K, rvnue processing tech I, $23,880
Gehlert, Tucker L, rvnue processing tech I, $23,880
Gehlert, Zachariah C, photographic-machine oper, $23,160
Gehrke, Judy, fiscal & administrative mgr b3, $91,260
Geiser, John, rvnue processing tech I, $23,880
Gerges, Rahan R, tax audit supv, $49,128
Gerlach, Megan E, tax auditor I, $37,548
Gibson, Cathy L, rvnue processing tech III, $29,496
Gibson, Nancy J, appraiser I, $36,204
Gilbert, Jason E, labor spv, $30,384
Gill, Robert A, compoper III, $36,888
Gill, Sharon L, lottery sales coord, $46,932
Gillam-Rogers, Connie A, rvnue mgr, band 2, $62,655
Gillispie, Karen, account clerk II, $27,948
Gilmore, Brandon D, tax auditor I, $37,548
Gilmore, Michael T, info technology spec II, $66,720
Gilmore, Richard K, sr ofc spt asst (clerical), $25,824
Ginther, Steven A, managing counsel, $68,300
Gleba, Michelle L, designated principal asst dept, $62,118
Glick, Justin N, investigator III, $54,288
Glover, Abigail L, rvnue processing tech II, $27,504
Goedde, Susan T, lottery mgr b2, $61,548
Goff, Jamie L, rvnue processing tech II, $26,232
Gonder, Gary J, div dir, $97,632
Gooch, Charles L, managing counsel, $68,300
Goode, Heather N, tax collection tech I, $23,880
Gordon, Bridgitt C, lottery cust serv rep, $26,232
Gorman, Karen A, rvnue section supv, $36,204
Gorman, Kimberly E, rvnue processing tech I, $23,880
Gosda, Donna R, rvnue processing tech II, $26,652

Goss, Eva D, mgmt analysis spec I, $37,548
Graham, Linda G, rvnue processing tech II, $26,232
Graham, Toby M, rvnue processing tech II, $26,652
Greenwood, Robert L, rvnue processing tech II, $26,652
Gregg, Denise K, rvnue processing tech II, $28,908
Grothoff, Charlotte L, rvnue processing tech III, $30,384
Grothoff, Stacy R, rvnue processing tech I, $23,880
Guinn, Presal L, auditor II, $39,624
Gunter, Earl D, storekeeper II, $28,104
Gutierrez, Jessica D, rvnue processing tech I, $23,880
Hader, Tiffany D, rvnue processing tech I, $23,880
Hafner-Reed, Steven D, rvnue processing tech IV, $32,628
Hagenhoff, Deborah M, rvnue processing tech II, $27,504
Hagenhoff, Melody S, rvnue processing tech I, $23,880
Hagens, Kyra, tax auditor I, $37,548
Hagerman, Bradley T, sr ofc spt asst (clerical), $27,504
Hahn, Natalie N, lottery sales rep, $34,944
Hairston, D'auna M, tax auditor I, $37,548
Halbert, Christine M, lottery sales rep, $42,708
Halbert, Vicki L, rvnue processing tech II, $26,652
Halbrook, Anthony T, gen ofc asst, $21,864
Halbrook, Donna K, rvnue processing tech I, $23,880
Hale, Joshua W, printing/mail technician II, $27,948
Haller, Amber R, rvnue processing tech I, $23,880
Hallford, Nicole A, mgmt analysis spec I, $37,548
Hamburg, Mandy S, rvnue processing tech II, $26,652
Hamer, Schnequka R, tax auditor I, $37,548
Hamilton, Leah M, lottery sales coord, $49,128
Hammer, Sharron M, rvnue processing tech I, $23,880
Hammond, Laura L, rvnue processing tech III, $29,004
Haner, Philip, printing/mail technician II, $30,384
Haney, Chelsea P, rvnue processing tech I, $23,880
Hankins, Sara R, rvnue processing tech II, $26,232
Harrell, Melissa J, rvnue processing tech I, $23,880
Harrell, Michael L, sr ofc spt asst (clerical), $25,032
Harris, Michael E, legislative coord, $47,892
Harris, Roman M, storekeeper II, $28,104
Harrison, Steve R, rvnue field servs coor, $40,380
Hartman, Christina A, mgmt analysis spec I, $41,172
Hartman, Frances E, tax auditor I, $37,548
Hartness, Melissa R, rvnue section supv, $36,204
Harvey, Linda J, admin ofc spt asst, $30,420
Haslag, Deborah S, paralegal, $35,572
Hatcher, Karan A, rvnue processing tech II, $27,948
Haugen, Brenda L, lottery security spec, $61,332
Hayden, Michelle R, rvnue processing tech III, $29,004
Hayes, Kelley J, administrative analyst II, $34,944
Haymart, Laci J, tax collection tech II, $26,232
Hazelbaker, Jana M, tax auditor III, $41,674
Healy, Matthew G, out-state audit pers, $76,537
Heard, Mary T, rvnue field servs coor, $36,204
Hedrick, Mariah C, rvnue processing tech I, $23,880
Hees, Cathy, rvnue processing tech II, $27,948
Hees, Nicole M, rvnue processing tech I, $23,880
Heeter, Lindsey E, special asst official & admstr, $61,109
Heinz, Catherine M, lottery inside sales rep, $33,744
Heislen, Shannon L, rvnue processing tech I, $23,880
Helmig, Danielle M, rvnue processing tech I, $23,880
Helton, Amanda A, rvnue processing tech I, $23,880
Hemmel, Aaron R, lottery sales rep, $36,888
Henderson, Brenda K, rvnue processing tech II, $26,232
Henderson, Michael C, rvnue processing tech III, $38,232
Henley, Gaiya G, rvnue processing tech III, $29,004
Henry, Diana M, rvnue processing tech II, $30,384
Henry, Johanna N, rvnue processing tech II, $26,652
Henry, Michael C, tax auditor II, $40,380
Hensiek, Norma L, rvnue mgr, band 2, $65,653
Henson, Rebecca S, rvnue processing tech III, $29,004
Hentges, Amelia M, rvnue processing tech III, $29,004
Hentges, Shirley M, rvnue processing tech II, $26,232
Herigon, Cathy M, rvnue mgr, band 2, $66,660
Herigon, Lindsey K, rvnue processing tech I, $23,880
Herron, Clay J, account clerk II, $26,232
Hershey, Cathie J, pub info coor, $46,932
Higgins, Brooke N, lottery sales rep, $34,944
Higgins, Crystyll G, tax collection tech III, $29,004
Hilgert, Jessica B, tax collection tech I, $23,880
Hill, Nicholas A, lottery cust serv rep, $26,232
Hillstrom, Victoria J, hr mgr b1, $63,423

Hite, Chelsea M, rvnue processing tech III, $29,004
Hixson, Larry W, tax commissmgr, band 2, $58,896
Hlavacek, Ryan J, tax collection tech I, $23,880
Hodges, Pamela S, rvnue processing tech I, $23,880
Hoellering, Angela M, ofc spt asst (clerical), $22,536
Hoellering, Cheyenne R, ofc spt asst (keybrd), $23,160
Hoelscher, Jennifer R, rvnue processing tech II, $26,232
Hoelscher, Leann R, rvnue processing tech II, $26,652
Hoffman, Lisa A, tax auditor I, $37,548
Hofmann, Clair A, rvnue processing tech I, $23,880
Hofstetter, Jill M, rvnue processing tech II, $28,908
Hogue, Erica R, rvnue processing tech I, $23,880
Holden, Brian D, appraiser II, $39,624
Holder, Jessica L, rvnue processing tech I, $23,880
Holland, Jessica R, rvnue processing tech I, $23,880
Holliday, Lindsey N, rvnue processing tech III, $29,004
Hollingsworth, Taylor E, rvnue processing tech I, $23,880
Hollis, Eden A, lottery inside sales supv, $37,548
Hollstein, Lena M, lottery sales rep, $34,944
Holman, Randy B, commissmbr, $106,620
Holt, Lexi A, admin ofc spt asst, $28,104
Holt, Wanda K, rvnue processing tech II, $26,652
Holtmeyer, Diana J, lottery inside sales rep, $33,744
Holtmeyer, Jamie A, tax collection tech I, $23,880
Holtschneider, Nancy D, fiscal & administrative mgr b3, $70,700
Holzem, Mark W, info technologist IV, $48,156
Honse, Dana M, rvnue processing tech I, $23,880
Hoover, Sara C, rvnue processing tech I, $23,880
Horstman, Kelly L, rvnue mgr, band 1, $48,769
Horton, Nichole A, rvnue processing tech I, $23,880
Hoskins, Steven E, rvnue mgr, band 2, $66,660
Hostetler, Sarah R, printing/mail technician I, $25,032
Houdek, Thomas A, assoc counsel, $47,348
Houston, Cayce L, rvnue section supv, $36,204
Houston, Robert R, printing/mail technician IV, $35,568
Hukeljic, Amila, tax auditor II, $40,380
Humphrey, Nicholas R, investigation mgr b3, $69,481
Hunger, Chelsi L, rvnue processing tech I, $23,880
Hunter, Susan M, rvnue processing tech II, $26,652
Huntley, Martell J, investigator II, $40,380
Hurd, Leslie R, rvnue processing tech I, $23,880
Hurst, Daniel G, rvnue processing tech I, $33,180
Hurt, Anthony J, rvnue processing tech II, $26,232
Husting, Maximus A, lottery inside sales rep, $28,104
Huston, Crystal M, rvnue processing tech I, $23,880
Huston, Scott L, rvnue processing tech II, $26,232
Hutinger, James D, storekeeper I, $26,232
Hutson, Edward L, mgmt analysis spec I, $37,548
Hyde, Randi J, rvnue processing tech I, $23,880
Ichrist, Alicia A, taxpayer servs supv, $36,204
Iven, Holly J, lottery cust serv rep, $26,232
Iveson, Herbert T, div dir, $105,408
Jacobs, Stacey M, exec I, $41,172
Jaegers, Kelsey L, rvnue processing tech I, $23,880
Jeffers, Kayla A, taxpayer servs supv, $36,204
Jeffrey, Dorothy L, rvnue processing tech II, $26,232
Jeffries, Stephanie G, tel info oper I rev, $23,880
Jenkins, Robert L, tel info oper II rev, $27,084
Jennings, Elizabeth D, lottery sales rep, $40,380
Jennings, Gwendolyn D, rvnue processing tech I, $23,880
Jensen, Daniel J, compoper I, $28,908
Jerozal, Caryn E, rvnue processing tech I, $23,880
Jett, Roxanne M, rvnue processing tech III, $30,984
Johns, Julie M, tax audit supv, $54,288
Johnson, Darlea R, rvnue processing tech II, $26,652
Johnson, Dolores M, rvnue processing tech I, $23,880
Johnson, Ricky S, lottery mgr b2, $62,414
Johnson, Roberta L, sr hearings ofcr, $54,576
Jones, Christopher R, investigator III, $45,156
Jones, Donald R, auditor II, $39,624
Jones, Dwight, facilities opps mgr b1, $58,875
Jones, Jennifer A, admin ofc spt asst, $34,944
Jones, Jessica B, rvnue processing tech II, $26,232
Jones, Linda A, rvnue processing tech II, $26,232
Jones, Michael C, tax auditor II, $43,488
Jones, Rachel M, appellate counsel, $46,868
Jones, Robin M, special asst paraprof, $54,113
Jones, Sarah B, tax audit supv, $49,128
Jones-Henry, Jennifer S, rvnue processing tech II, $26,232

Jordan, Carol L, account clerk II, $25,824
Jordan, Dustin W, tax auditor II, $40,380
Judge, Crystal D, rvnue processing tech I, $23,880
Jung, Thomas L, rvnue processing tech II, $26,652
Kadam, Shilpa V, info technology spec II, $66,720
Kaiser, Linda C, rvnue processing tech II, $27,084
Kallmeyer, Kelley R, rvnue processing tech II, $26,652
Kandlbinder, Brittany M, rvnue processing tech I, $23,880
Keeling, Lisa A, rvnue section supv, $36,204
Keeney, Karen S, rvnue processing tech III, $29,004
Keeney, Lori L, rvnue processing tech II, $26,232
Keeran, Chelsey R, rvnue processing tech I, $23,880
Keilholz, Trisha E, rvnue processing tech I, $23,880
Kellogg, Mary F, rvnue processing tech III, $29,004
Kelly, Connie M, rvnue processing tech I, $23,880
Kelly, Ta'sha P, rvnue processing tech II, $26,232
Kelly, Taylor M, rvnue processing tech II, $26,232
Kemp, Alicia M, tax collection tech I, $23,880
Kemp, Alicia R, rvnue processing tech I, $23,880
Kemp, Emily D, rvnue processing tech I, $26,652
Kemp, Jeri L, rvnue processing tech II, $27,948
Kemp, Lindsay J, rvnue processing tech I, $23,880
Kempker, Crystal D, rvnue processing tech I, $23,880
Kempker, Josh, lottery inside sales rep, $29,004
Kempker, Sarah N, tax collection tech III, $29,004
Kempker, Tiffany N, account clerk II, $26,232
Kempker Miller, Shyanne R, rvnue processing tech I, $23,880
Kennedy, Daniel J, legal counsel, $43,474
Kern, Gary W, appraiser II, $36,888
Kersten, Jacquelyn A, lottery sales rep, $34,944
Kever, Jenna M, rvnue processing tech III, $29,004
Kever, Kimberly M, rvnue processing tech III, $29,004
Key, Darrin V, appraiser sup, $52,092
Kibort, Kenne A, investigator II, $40,380
Kilson, Nina A, rvnue processing tech I, $23,880
Kincaid, Vivian, sr ofc spt asst (keybrd), $26,232
King, Cynthia M, rvnue processing tech II, $26,652
King, Larry E, investigator III, $45,156
King, Stacey A, rvnue section supv, $36,204
Kingery, Connie J, rvnue processing tech II, $26,232
Kinney, Chelsey D, rvnue processing tech I, $23,880
Kiral, Melody A, rvnue processing tech I, $23,880
Kirkweg, Mary K, rvnue processing tech II, $26,232
Kirkweg, Matthew W, rvnue processing tech I, $23,880
Kirsch, Nicole L, rvnue processing tech I, $23,880
Kisling, Michael S, gen counsel - div, $71,209
Kiss, Ilona O, tel info oper I rev, $23,880
Klebba, Angie M, admin ofc spt asst, $37,548
Klebba, Trenton J, exec I, $31,512
Kleffner, Danielle M, rvnue processing tech II, $27,504
Kleffner, Debra N, rvnue processing tech II, $26,652
Kleffner, Marlene S, rvnue processing tech IV, $32,628
Klick, Jennifer L, rvnue processing tech III, $29,004
Kliethermes, Kayla D, rvnue processing tech II, $26,232
Klindt, Nathan J, lottery sales rep, $34,944
Klindworth, Shelby L, rvnue processing tech I, $23,880
Klug, Amanda R, rvnue processing tech I, $26,232
Knipp, Amanda M, admin ofc spt asst, $28,104
Kohl, Erin K, administrative analyst III, $40,380
Kohls, Carol A, tax auditor II, $40,380
Kolb, Mitchell A, maint spv II, $44,304
Kottwitz, Heather A, rvnue processing tech II, $26,232
Krachey, Lisa J, rvnue processing tech I, $23,880
Kraft, Kandyce G, acct III, $41,172
Krause, Jacob J, rvnue processing tech II, $26,232
Kremer, Jennifer E, rvnue processing tech II, $26,232
Kremer, Sandra K, rvnue processing tech III, $31,512
Kriegshauser, Dylan T, misc tech, $10.00/hr
Kroeger, Steven O, info technology supv, $75,948
Kueffer, Zachary P, printing/mail technician II, $27,948
Kuensting, Charles J, printing/mail technician I, $25,032
Kuensting - Lochhead, carol S, training tech I, $36,204
Kulp, Stanley J, info technologist III, $49,128
Kuo, Grace, tax auditor II, $40,380
Kyle, James A, assess rep II tax comm, $40,380
Lacross, Amanda C, investigator II, $41,172
Lafaver, Beverly L, sr counsel, $55,287
Laffoon, Monty A, printing/mail technician I, $25,032
Lagemann, Stanley S, out-state audit pers, $71,283

Laks, Yamini A, managing counsel, $65,650
Lane, Gerald E, tax auditor III, $49,128
Languell, Alice K, rvnue processing tech III, $29,004
Languell, Alicia J, rvnue processing tech I, $23,880
Latham, James M, storekeeper II, $28,104
Laughlin, Jane A, sr counsel, $60,604
Laughlin, Jerry L, fiscal & administrative mgr b1, $60,752
Lauvstad, Sue E, assess rep II tax comm, $36,888
Lawless, Appolnia S, rvnue processing tech I, $23,880
Lawrence, Darrell K, lottery sales coord, $46,932
Lawson, Heather A, rvnue processing tech I, $23,880
Lazo, Donald J, out-state audit pers, $69,513
Leary, Scott J, rvnue mgr, band 2, $75,249
Lee, Brianna N, rvnue processing tech II, $26,232
Lee, Tammy C, rvnue processing tech II, $26,652
Lehnhoff, Brenda K, tax collection tech II, $26,232
Leininger, Theresa A, rvnue mgr, band 1, $60,000
Lepper, Deann M, acct II, $42,708
Letcher, Amber M, sr ofc spt asst (keybrd), $27,948
Lewis, Adrienne N, tax audit supv, $49,128
Lewis, Janice S, lottery sales coord, $46,932
Lewis, Jocelyn M, tax auditor III, $43,488
Lewis, Maya, rvnue processing tech II, $26,652
Lewis, Mikala F, rvnue processing tech I, $23,880
Lewis, Sherry L, rvnue processing tech II, $26,232
Li, Jingbin, out-state audit pers, $43,850
Libbert, Katlyn M, printing/mail technician I, $25,032
Liberty, Matthew F, tax auditor I, $37,548
Licklider, Kathy, rvnue section supv, $41,172
Lieneke, Julie L, rvnue processing tech I, $26,232
Liles, Kacey A, rvnue processing tech II, $29,412
Lindsay, Samantha M, admin ofc spt asst, $28,104
Ling, Eunice, out-state audit pers, $40,505
Linsenbardt, Mary B, special asst prof, $23.93/hr
Linville, Jeffrey, tax auditor I, $37,548
Lissant, Susan L, sr counsel, $54,168
Lister, Amy R, research analyst III, $51,096
Lister, Kelly J, rvnue processing tech I, $23,880
Lister, Sherry L, rvnue processing tech II, $29,412
Livingston, Carrie M, tax auditor II, $40,380
Loar, Wilson G, motor veh driver, $26,232
Loehner, Brittany N, mgmt analysis spec I, $41,172
Loethen, Douglas H, mgmt analysis spec II, $41,940
Loethen, Rosina R, rvnue processing tech I, $23,880
Loethen, Shelby R, rvnue processing tech I, $23,880
Longoria, Vanessa M, lottery sales rep, $34,944
Lopez, Sarah L, tax auditor I, $37,548
Ludlow, Denise M, exec I, $41,940
Ludy, James O, rvnue processing tech I, $23,880
Luebbering, Jayne M, rvnue processing tech II, $27,084
Luecke, Sheila N, rvnue processing tech I, $23,880
Lueckenotte, Janel E, rvnue mgr, band 2, $62,655
Luetkemeyer, Melissa S, rvnue processing tech II, $28,908
Luetkemeyer, Tyler A, pub info coor, $38,928
Luttrell, Brittany R, rvnue processing tech II, $26,232
Lutz, Kimberly J, legal counsel, $43,474
Lyman, Thomas R, lottery sales rep, $34,944
Ma, Alison S, out-state audit pers, $50,795
Madson, David C, exec I, $38,928
Mantle, Kathy M, rvnue mgr, band 3, $71,209
Maples, Dwayne L, rvnue mgr, band 2, $62,507
Martin, Deann, rvnue processing tech III, $29,004
Martin, Jamie L, rvnue processing tech II, $26,232
Martin, Karen L, account clerk II, $26,232
Martin, Spencer A, assoc counsel, $47,348
Martin, Tiffany J, tax collection tech II, $26,232
Martinez, Elia, out-state audit pers, $57,388
Mason, Ashley C, administrative analyst I, $29,976
Matheson, Kathleen R, rvnue section supv, $36,204
Mathews, Jennifer L, rvnue processing tech II, $26,652
Mathias, Timothy A, investigator II, $37,548
Mathney, Debbra S, rvnue processing tech II, $26,232
Matzes, Virginia J, tax collection tech I, $23,880
Maxwell, Lana S, rvnue field servs coor, $40,380
McCarrell, Craig B, lottery sales rep, $34,944
McCarty, John D, tax audit rev spec, $55,416
McCray, Estelle M, tax auditor III, $43,488
McDaniel, Eric W, rvnue processing tech II, $26,232
McDonald, Heather A, rvnue processing tech II, $26,232

McKay, Nancy E, tax auditor III, $43,488
McKee, Lisa R, rvnue processing tech II, $26,652
McKinney, Kady J, mgmt analysis spec I, $37,548
McKinney, Teresa A, rvnue processing tech I, $23,880
McKinnon, Kara A, rvnue processing tech I, $23,880
McLain, Amy M, rvnue field servs coor, $36,204
McLaughlin, David W, lottery sales coord, $50,040
McLellan, Kierra S, rvnue processing tech I, $23,880
McNail, Michael G, tax collection tech I, $23,880
Mealy, Jessica S, rvnue processing tech I, $23,880
Mealy, Michelle D, acct II, $46,068
Mecum, Brenda G, tax auditor III, $49,128
Meier, Cynthia E, investigator II, $37,548
Mello, Theressa A, rvnue processing tech I, $23,880
Merancis, Kephen D, rvnue processing tech II, $26,232
Merrill, Anthony V, tax auditor I, $37,548
Mertens, Tammy J, rvnue processing tech II, $27,948
Mertens, Tammy J, rvnue processing tech II, $27,504
Mesa, Theresa L, sr ofc spt asst (keybrd), $27,504
Messersmith, Jessica, ofc spt asst (keybrd), $23,160
Metcalf, Celeste, designated principal asst dept, $100,495
Meyer, Bobbi J, rvnue processing tech II, $27,084
Meyer, Carla S, tel info oper II rev, $26,652
Meyer, David E, sr ofc spt asst (clerical), $30,924
Meyer, Jocelyn G, rvnue processing tech II, $26,232
Meyer, Le A, rvnue processing tech II, $26,652
Mickelis, Dinah J, rvnue processing tech II, $27,084
Mickelis, Donna J, ofc spt asst (clerical), $25,404
Miller, Annette L, rvnue processing tech II, $26,232
Miller, Dale W, div dir, $87,369
Miller, Eva J, rvnue processing tech II, $26,652
Miller, Gary M, rvnue processing tech II, $26,232
Miller, Jeffrey A, investigation mgr b1, $56,964
Miller, Lori A, tax audit supv, $49,128
Miller, Lydia J, rvnue processing tech I, $23,880
Miller, Melissa L, rvnue processing tech III, $29,004
Miller, Shelly M, tax audit supv, $52,092
Mills, James D, lottery sales rep, $42,708
Mitchell, Marvel D, appraiser II, $36,204
Mitchell, Stephanie R, tax auditor III, $43,488
Mitchem, Teryn R, tax collection tech I, $23,880
Mollenkamp, John R, dpty state dept dir, $111,609
Monaghan, Maureen M, chief counsel, $66,264
Monteer, Michael L, motor veh driver, $26,232
Moore, Connie S, rvnue processing tech II, $26,652
Moraitis, Geracimo C, out-state audit pers, $63,777
Moreau, Sheryl L, sr counsel, $27.68/hr
Morff, Charlene M, rvnue processing tech II, $26,652
Mormann, Beverly J, rvnue processing tech I, $23,880
Mormann, Caleasa D, rvnue processing tech I, $23,880
Morrow, Katelyn K, account clerk II, $26,232
Morrow, Lesa J, rvnue mgr, band 3, $81,309
Moses, Kenneth E, admin ofc spt asst, $29,496
Mosley, Heather A, rvnue processing tech II, $26,652
Moss, Barbara D, sr ofc spt asst (keybrd), $27,948
Moss, John B, clerk, $9.93/hr
Moss, Stephanie A, lottery sales rep, $34,944
Mueller, Lora G, rvnue processing tech II, $26,232
Mugera, Tonny, tax auditor I, $39,624
Muldrow, Stephanie A, lottery mgr b2, $61,200
Murphy, Colleen E, rvnue processing tech II, $26,652
Murray, Michael L, managing counsel, $68,300
Myers, Alicia M, ofc spt asst (keybrd), $27,084
Myers, Kimberly J, mgmt analysis spec I, $37,548
Myers, Michael K, appraiser II, $38,928
Nalagan, Alvin N, lottery sales rep, $36,204
Nations, Pamela S, rvnue processing tech II, $26,232
Neal, Jeannette, tax auditor II, $41,940
Neeley, Jennifer R, tax collection tech I, $23,880
Neff, Clark E, lottery inside sales rep, $29,976
Nelp, James M, human rel ofcr II, $41,940
Nelson, Dana S, rvnue processing tech II, $27,084
Nelson, Edwin D, lottery sales rep, $35,568
Nelson, Lana R, tel info oper I rev, $23,880
Nelson, Malinda K, lottery sales rep, $41,172
Nentwig, Kevin J, rvnue processing tech III, $29,004
Nesbit, Rachel L, tax collection tech I, $23,880
Neuman, Casey J, administrative analyst II, $34,944
Newbrough, Amanda L, rvnue processing tech I, $23,880

Newman, Deniece M, investigator II, $37,548
Nguyen, Jason V, tax auditor II, $40,380
Nichols, Timothy D, mgmt analysis spec II, $49,128
Nickens, Damian R, rvnue processing tech I, $23,880
Niekamp, Evelyn A, ofc spt asst (keybrd), $23,508
Nielsen, Robert K, out-state audit pers, $89,672
Nielson, Garrett J, tax auditor II, $40,380
Niemann, Abby L, rvnue processing tech II, $26,652
Niere, Laura M, rvnue processing tech I, $23,880
Niermeyer, William T, lottery inside sales rep, $30,984
Nilges, Gail A, rvnue processing tech II, $33,036
Nilges, Preston H, misc tech, $10.00/hr
Norris, Angela J, tax collection tech I, $23,880
Nwaobasi, Emmanuel O, tax auditor III, $43,488
O'Brien, Angela K, account clerk II, $27,084
Ochs, Heather N, rvnue processing tech II, $26,232
O'Connell, Dana K, rvnue processing tech II, $27,084
Odarczenko, Stephen W, out-state audit pers, $43,850
Oghenejobo, Allen, tax auditor III, $44,304
Olenick, Kathleen A, out-state audit pers, $61,617
Oliver, Jessica R, rvnue processing tech I, $23,880
Oliver, Marcia A, rvnue processing tech I, $23,880
Orcutt, Heather N, tax collection tech I, $23,880
Ordway, Lisa R, rvnue processing tech II, $26,232
Orengo Cortes, Lauren E, tax auditor II, $42,708
Orick, Hannah L, rvnue processing tech II, $26,652
Osborn, Haylei B, rvnue processing tech I, $23,880
Otto, Carolyn S, rvnue processing tech II, $27,948
Otto, Crista R, rvnue processing tech II, $26,232
Otto, Ronald L, rvnue processing tech II, $27,948
Otto, Ruth R, rvnue mgr, band 3, $70,708
Otto, Sharon A, rvnue processing tech II, $27,084
Owen, Jared C, rvnue processing tech I, $23,880
Owen, Jessica L, rvnue processing tech I, $23,880
Owen, Sarah B, rvnue processing tech I, $23,880
Owens, Karen M, admin ofc spt asst, $29,976
Pace, Von P, lottery sales rep, $36,204
Paneitz, Stephen M, rvnue field servs coor, $36,204
Parker, Alice M, sr ofc spt asst (steno), $34,224
Parla, Amra, tax audit supv, $49,128
Patterson, Taylor M, rvnue processing tech I, $23,880
Pattyson, John J, rvnue processing tech I, $23,880
Payne, Jasmine R, tax auditor I, $37,548
Payne, Kwannesha S, tax collection tech I, $23,880
Payne, Sheri D, sr ofc spt asst (clerical), $25,824
Pearson, Dena K, rvnue processing tech II, $26,652
Pearson, Jessica T, rvnue processing tech I, $23,880
Pearson, Laura K, photographic-machine oper, $23,160
Pearson, Tiphanie K, rvnue processing tech I, $23,880
Peck, Robert D, appraiser sup, $57,744
Perkins, Craig B, tax auditor III, $48,156
Pessetto, Virginia K, account clerk II, $26,232
Petershagen, Ladonna, rvnue processing tech III, $29,004
Peterson, Ruth A, rvnue processing tech III, $29,004
Pfantz, Nikki L, admin ofc spt asst, $29,976
Pfefferkorn, Kelly A, tax auditor I, $39,624
Pfenenger, Jennifer O, rvnue section supv, $36,204
Phan, Minh H, rvnue processing tech I, $23,880
Phillips, Desiree S, rvnue processing tech II, $27,084
Phillips, Kelly M, rvnue processing tech IV, $32,628
Phillips, Terry J, rvnue processing tech I, $28,452
Phillips, Tracy D, rvnue processing tech II, $26,652
Pierce, Kathryn A, rvnue processing tech II, $26,232
Pierson, Brian C, lottery security spec, $53,208
Plaggenberg, Joseph G, gen counsel - div, $55,000
Pointer, Kelly J, rvnue processing tech I, $23,880
Polly, Rita F, rvnue processing tech II, $26,232
Porter, Monica D, mgmt analysis spec I, $37,548
Porter, Scott E, printing/mail technician I, $25,032
Powell, Judi, lottery sales rep, $41,940
Pratt, Lisa M, rvnue processing tech I, $23,880
Predmore, Christina L, rvnue mgr, band 1, $48,929
Prenger, Amy L, rvnue processing tech I, $23,880
Prenger, Emily J, rvnue processing tech III, $29,004
Prenger, Natasha M, rvnue processing tech III, $29,004
Preston, William B, designated principal asst div, $71,266
Prince, Michael, lottery sales rep, $34,944
Pritchard, Jan, sr counsel, $54,168
Propst, Vicki J, rvnue processing tech III, $30,984

Pyatt, Sherrie B, admin ofc spt asst, $28,104
Questar, Vicki, rvnue processing tech II, $26,652
Quinn, Donna J, rvnue processing tech II, $28,908
Quinn, Russell E, planner III, $46,068
Rackers, Cynthia L, rvnue processing tech II, $26,232
Rackers, Darrell W, rvnue processing tech III, $30,420
Rackers, Joyce M, rvnue processing tech III, $29,004
Rackers, Karen M, rvnue section supv, $36,204
Rackers, Nicholas J, rvnue processing tech II, $26,652
Rademann, Megan A, auditor I, $37,548
Rader, Dawn M, rvnue processing tech III, $29,004
Rains, Amanda J, rvnue processing tech II, $26,232
Rains, Rose I, rvnue processing tech II, $26,652
Ralston, Mary C, admin ofc spt asst, $28,104
Rapier, James W, rvnue processing tech II, $26,652
Ratcliff, Daniel R, training tech I, $36,204
Ray, J R, rvnue field servs coor, $36,204
Rebert, Thomas A, rvnue field servs coor, $41,172
Reed, Amy N, rvnue processing tech III, $29,004
Reed, Brenda J, printing/mail technician I, $25,032
Reichel, Melody S, mgmt analysis spec I, $46,068
Reid, Patrick D, lottery security spec, $49,128
Reimund, Jason M, rvnue processing tech III, $29,004
Reinhardt, Elizabeth A, rvnue processing tech III, $29,004
Reininger, Barbara M, tax auditor III, $42,566
Reinkemeyer, Craig A, printing/mail cust svc rep, $38,232
Reinkemeyer, Marcella B, clerk, $9.93/hr
Reppond, Ramona L, lottery sales rep, $36,888
Reynolds, Andrew T, rvnue processing tech I, $23,880
Reynolds, Kimberly H, out-state audit pers, $48,951
Rhame, Brian D, designated principal asst div, $81,305
Rice, Ronetta L, rvnue processing tech I, $23,880
Richards, Charles E, tax collection tech I, $23,880
Richter, Toni L, printing/mail technician II, $27,948
Ridenhour, Millicent L, rvnue section supv, $36,204
Ridenhour, Tanner K, rvnue processing tech III, $29,004
Riley, Dana S, rvnue processing tech II, $26,232
Riley, Stephen F, investigator II, $40,380
Riney, Danielle L, rvnue processing tech I, $23,880
Rippstein, Victoria A, rvnue processing tech II, $26,232
Ritter, Mark E, lottery sales coord, $46,932
Roark, Angeline A, rvnue processing tech II, $27,084
Roark, Nicole L, rvnue processing tech I, $23,880
Roark, Vanessa M, rvnue processing tech I, $23,880
Robertson, Tracy, rvnue mgr, band 1, $49,108
Robinett, Amanda L, rvnue processing tech I, $23,880
Robinett, Darlene M, hr mgr b2, $58,874
Robinett, Gerald W, rvnue section supv, $36,204
Robinett, Maria A, rvnue processing tech III, $29,496
Robinson, Joseph M, rvnue processing tech I, $23,880
Robinson, Victoria A, rvnue processing tech I, $23,880
Robinson Brown, Sarah O, tax collection tech I, $23,880
Roe, Daniel W, assess rep I tax comm, $36,204
Roe, Donna L, acct I, $30,984
Rogers, Darla M, gen ofc asst, $21,864
Rogers, Kelly J, rvnue section supv, $36,204
Rogers, Melissa A, tax collection tech I, $23,880
Rogers, Travis A, rvnue processing tech I, $23,160
Rollins, Nancy J, lottery mgr b3, $81,529
Rose, Gloria J, sr counsel, $60,206
Rosemann, Heather M, rvnue section supv, $36,204
Rosenthal, Wayne A, tax audit supv, $65,364
Ross, Laura L, rvnue processing tech I, $23,880
Rost, Casey L, rvnue processing tech I, $23,880
Roth, Todd A, investigator II, $37,548
Rowden, Tina M, lottery cust serv rep, $30,924
Ruettgers, Julie A, fiscal & administrative mgr b2, $58,874
Rugen, Chris A, ofc spt asst (clerical), $22,872
Rumsey, Stacey L, tax auditor III, $47,892
Runyan, Joshua L, pers analyst I, $34,356
Rus, Jeanette M, tax auditor III, $43,488
Rush, Lindsay K, admin ofc spt asst, $31,512
Russell, Heather M, tel info oper I rev, $23,880
Russell, Kimberly A, rvnue mgr, band 1, $58,588
Russell, Kimberly D, tax auditor I, $37,548
Russell, Susan L, rvnue processing tech II, $26,232
Rustemeyer, Heather L, rvnue processing tech II, $26,232
Rutledge, Christin M, rvnue section supv, $36,204
Ryan, Charles A, rvnue processing tech I, $23,880

Ryan, Lora R, rvnue processing tech III, $29,004
Sajol, Tessie N, rvnue processing tech II, $26,652
Sallas, Marina O, out-state audit pers, $50,795
Sallee, Sabrina A, rvnue processing tech I, $23,880
Sanchez, Molly E, rvnue processing tech I, $23,880
Sandbothe, Connie E, tel info oper II rev, $26,652
Sander, Chiou-Sheue C, tax audit supv, $53,208
Sanders, Anthony W, rvnue processing tech II, $26,232
Sanders, Jessica E, rvnue processing tech II, $26,652
Sanders, Maria A, sr counsel, $54,168
Sanders, Toni L, tax collection tech II, $26,232
Sandweg, Christopher S, lottery sales rep, $34,944
Sanford, Alissa K, photographic-machine oper, $23,160
Santiago Wolfe, Jose L, tax collection tech I, $23,880
Saunders, Kelsey L, rvnue processing tech II, $26,652
Schad, Rosella, appraisal spec, $58,908
Schaefer, Connie J, rvnue processing tech II, $27,948
Schaffer, Susan D, account clerk II, $26,232
Schenewerk, Kimberly J, rvnue processing tech II, $27,504
Scheperle, Cathy C, special asst ofc & clerical, $46,868
Scheperle, Gregory, printing/mail technician I, $25,032
Schepers, Christina A, pers clerk, $30,984
Scheppers, Julie L, special asst official & admstr, $51,290
Scheulen, Alice M, sr ofc spt asst (steno), $32,472
Scheve-Reardon, May E, principal asst board/comm, $115,064
Schilling, Tyson W, lottery sales rep, $34,944
Schilpp, Julia M, rvnue processing tech IV, $32,628
Schlottog, Rachel G, rvnue processing tech II, $26,232
Schlueter, Stacy M, lottery sales rep, $37,548
Schlupp, Victoria J, rvnue processing tech III, $29,004
Schmidt, Hsing-Ying L, rvnue processing tech II, $26,232
Schmidt, Jeffrey D, tax commissmgr, band 2, $58,896
Schmidt, Mary N, tax auditor I, $37,548
Schnieders, Melissa A, tax collection tech I, $23,880
Schnieders, Pete J, lottery mgr b2, $61,200
Schnur, John S, ofc spt asst (keybrd), $23,160
Schoen, Connie, rvnue processing tech II, $26,652
Schollmeyer, Heather R, rvnue mgr, band 1, $48,929
Schollmeyer, Ronald E, exec II, $36,204
Schoonover, Terry A, exec I, $33,744
Schrader, Kelly R, rvnue processing tech II, $26,232
Schroeder, Kenneth L, out-state audit pers, $43,608
Schroeder, William C, sr ofc spt asst (clerical), $27,948
Schulte, Julie A, rvnue processing tech III, $29,976
Schulte, Skylar T, rvnue processing tech I, $23,880
Schulte, Stacy K, sr ofc spt asst (keybrd), $25,824
Schuster, Linda A, rvnue processing tech II, $27,084
Schuster, Lisa G, rvnue section supv, $36,204
Schwermer, Mary J, tax collection tech III, $29,976
Scoles, Karen L, tax audit supv, $49,128
Scott, Lauren P, rvnue processing tech I, $23,880
Scott, Lois M, tax auditor III, $43,488
Scott, Melissa A, rvnue processing tech II, $26,232
Scott, Travis M, rvnue processing tech III, $29,004
Sebastian, Jeremy D, administrative analyst I, $29,976
Sellnow, Theresa M, rvnue processing tech I, $23,880
Seneker, Lawrence D, designated principal asst div, $76,259
Servidio, Nicholas, out-state audit pers, $67,641
Shanks, Phyllis R, rvnue processing tech II, $27,948
Shanks, Robbyn K, rvnue processing tech II, $27,948
Sharp, Gabrielle M, rvnue processing tech II, $26,232
Sharp, Linda L, tax audit supv, $55,416
Sheahan, Amy L, rvnue processing tech II, $27,084
Shelton, Christina L, rvnue processing tech II, $26,652
Shepherd, Stephen M, rvnue processing tech II, $26,232
Sherwood, Deanna L, rvnue processing tech II, $29,004
Shewmaker, Joshua W, administrative analyst I, $29,976
Shields, Heather J, administrative analyst I, $29,976
Shields, Kristina L, acct II, $36,204
Shirley, Brent D, rvnue processing tech II, $29,412
Shively, John E, lottery sales rep, $36,204
Shiverdecker, Courtney M, fiscal & admin mgr b1, $48,396
Shockley, Amanda C, rvnue processing tech III, $29,004
Shore, Cheryl R, tax auditor III, $38,314
Shull, Faith L, rvnue processing tech I, $23,880
Sides, Matthew J, tax auditor I, $37,548
Silkwood, Crystal A, rvnue field servs coor, $36,204
Silver, Verna J, appraiser II, $36,888
Silvermintz, Marshall A, tax auditor III, $56,520

Sims, Reginald, info technologist IV, $52,092
Singleton, Aaron L, ofc spt asst (keybrd), $23,160
Singleton, Kandi S, administrative analyst II, $34,944
Sipchen, Michael A, tax auditor I, $37,548
Sivert, Laura A, training tech I, $36,204
Skaggs, Elizabeth A, rvnue processing tech II, $26,652
Skelton, Melanie K, rvnue processing tech II, $27,948
Skouby, Jean M, account clerk II, $26,652
Slawson, Benjamin C, assoc counsel, $47,348
Slayton, Stacy A, rvnue processing tech II, $26,652
Slight, Ryan B, tax auditor I, $37,548
Sloan, Jennifer S, rvnue processing tech I, $23,880
Slusser, Lori L, tax collection tech I, $23,880
Smith, Adam N, rvnue processing tech III, $29,004
Smith, Amanda F, rvnue processing tech I, $23,880
Smith, Brandon M, rvnue processing tech I, $23,880
Smith, Donavin J, rvnue processing tech I, $23,880
Smith, Mark T, rvnue processing tech II, $26,232
Smith, Nicholas J, tax auditor I, $37,548
Smith, Philip G, designated principal asst div, $86,287
Smith, Rita A, rvnue processing tech II, $26,652
Smithson, Daniel R, investigator II, $40,380
Sneller, Janice M, rvnue processing tech I, $27,948
Snodgrass, Leeann M, rvnue processing tech III, $29,004
Soendker, Alyssa R, designated principal asst div, $47,886
Solindas, Kristopher N, research analyst II, $38,232
Southard, Karana B, mgmt analysis spec I, $37,548
Spencer, Mary C, rvnue processing tech II, $27,084
Spradlin, James L, sr counsel, $54,168
Sprouse, Debra L, sr ofc spt asst (steno), $27,948
Spurlock, Benjamin, printing/mail technician I, $25,032
Stafford, Kristina L, rvnue processing tech I, $23,880
Stanco, Dawn M, out-state audit pers, $48,400
Stark, Laura M, exec I, $37,548
Starke, Michelle L, administrative analyst I, $34,944
Stayton, Tammy L, sr ofc spt asst (keybrd), $27,084
Steelman, Debra K, printing/mail technician I, $25,032
Steelman, Phyllis A, rvnue processing tech II, $26,652
Stegeman, Cindy L, admin ofc spt asst, $32,052
Stegeman, Sarah J, admin ofc spt asst, $29,004
Stegeman, Susan M, tax collection tech I, $23,880
Steinman, Rebecca A, tax audit supv, $49,128
Stephens, Jill M, rvnue processing tech III, $29,004
Stephenson, Tanner J, rvnue processing tech I, $23,880
Stevens, Stephanie K, assess rep II tax comm, $39,624
Stevison, Thomas P, lottery sales rep, $35,568
Stewart, Mariya J, rvnue processing tech II, $26,232
Stieferman, Connor J, pub info coor, $38,232
Stilson, Dawn M, rvnue processing tech I, $23,880
Stobbart, Christina A, sr ofc spt asst (keybrd), $25,824
Stockman, Matthew C, rvnue mgr, band 1, $48,396
Stockman, Rebecca L, rvnue processing tech III, $29,004
Stone, Jacqueline R, lottery sales rep, $34,944
Strain, Stephanie R, sr ofc spt asst (keybrd), $29,904
Strobel, Silvana M, rvnue processing tech II, $26,652
Strope, Ruth A, rvnue processing tech II, $27,948
Stroup, Cheryl L, rvnue processing tech II, $26,232
Stroup, Gary L, appraiser sup, $53,208
Struemph, Mark J, photographic-machine oper, $23,160
Struemph, Virginia B, rvnue processing tech I, $25,404
Stuckenschneider, Don, rvnue processing tech II, $34,224
Stuecken, Mary K, graphic arts spec II, $37,548
Stuecken, Roger T, ofc spt asst (clerical), $24,612
Sullivan, Shelly R, tax auditor III, $52,092
Sullivan, Stephen P, sr counsel, $57,578
Summerford, Dana S, rvnue processing tech II, $26,652
Summers, Samantha J, rvnue processing tech I, $23,880
Sumpter, Cristine M, rvnue processing tech III, $29,004
Sundermeyer, Sharon K, rvnue processing tech II, $28,908
Surface, Sue A, rvnue processing tech I, $23,880
Suthoff, Tracy A, special asst ofc & clerical, $46,201
Swalwell, Jamie M, mgmt analysis spec I, $37,548
Swan, Cecille L, rvnue mgr, band 2, $65,387
Swensen, Jenny L, tax auditor III, $43,488
Sydenstricker, Jana, rvnue processing tech I, $23,880
Syvokozova, Olena, tax auditor II, $40,380
Tabor, Darrell L, investigator II, $40,380
Talken, Paul A, lottery sales rep, $38,232
Talleur, Joanne M, rvnue processing tech II, $29,904

Tambke, Dalton J, rvnue processing tech I, $23,880
Tanoh, Jakaya E, tax collection tech I, $23,880
Taube, Tabatha A, tax collection tech II, $26,232
Taube, Wendy A, rvnue processing tech II, $28,908
Taylor, Michael J, tax auditor I, $37,548
Terry, Brian K, rvnue field servs coor, $36,204
Terry, Deanna M, tax collection tech I, $23,880
Tesfai, Petros, account clerk II, $26,232
Teter, Jessica A, rvnue processing tech I, $23,880
Theising, Peter J, sr ofc spt asst (clerical), $25,824
Thoenen, Donna, acct II, $41,172
Thoenen, Joseph R, printing/mail technician II, $30,384
Thomas, Andrew, compoper III, $34,944
Thompson, Deborah J, rvnue processing tech III, $29,004
Thompson, Judith A, rvnue section supv, $38,928
Thompson, Karla S, rvnue processing tech I, $25,404
Thompson, Nichole A, rvnue processing tech II, $26,232
Thompson, Shyanne N, rvnue processing tech I, $23,880
Tinsley, Dana L, tax audit supv, $57,744
Tipton, Corey J, rvnue processing tech I, $23,880
Toebben, Abigail R, rvnue processing tech I, $23,880
Toebben, Angel R, sr ofc spt asst (keybrd), $25,824
Toebben, Tonya S, rvnue processing tech II, $26,652
Tomaselli, Salvatore, out-state audit pers, $67,641
Townsend-Sinkfield, April R, tax auditor III, $43,488
Tremaine, Shawn D, storekeeper I, $26,232
Trepanier, Christina M, rvnue processing tech II, $26,652
Treu, John J, sr hearings ofcr, $50,520
Troutman, Barbara J, mgmt analysis spec I, $37,548
Turner, Bessie R, exec II, $36,204
Turner, Brad, lottery inside sales rep, $29,976
Turner, Kim L, rvnue processing tech II, $27,504
Twehus, Samantha R, rvnue processing tech I, $23,880
Twyman, Kelly K, rvnue processing tech I, $23,880
Tyree, Jennifer L, rvnue processing tech II, $26,232
Uptegrove, Ashley N, rvnue processing tech II, $26,232
Utter, Jennifer A, rvnue mgr, band 1, $43,613
Valle, Jeffrey L, appraiser II, $40,380
Vandegriffe, Cally A, rvnue processing tech I, $23,880
Vandeloecht, Jessica M, rvnue processing tech II, $26,652
Vanzant, John R, lottery sales rep, $39,624
Vaughan, Alexis L, rvnue processing tech II, $26,232
Veit, Dawn R, legal counsel, $43,474
Veit, Kenneth A, info technologist IV, $50,040
Verhoff, Ashlie M, account clerk II, $26,232
Vernon, Deborah A, rvnue processing tech II, $26,652
Vieth, Eric W, mgmt analysis spec I, $37,548
Vieth, Gwendolyn L, ch acct, $55,416
Vincent, Patricia E, designated principal asst dept, $86,000
Vitale, Desiree J, legal counsel, $48,989
Vittetoe, Devin M, rvnue processing tech I, $23,880
Vogt, Melanie, sr ofc spt asst (keybrd), $25,824
Voss, Lucy M, rvnue processing tech II, $26,232
Vowels, Lillian T, rvnue processing tech I, $23,880
Vuichard, Ray L, tax auditor III, $51,096
Vuilcott, Kristin J, lottery mgr b1, $48,240
Wagner, Kristy M, rvnue processing tech I, $23,880
Waite, Peggy L, rvnue processing tech II, $27,504
Wakeman, Pamela L, rvnue processing tech I, $24,264
Walden, Amanda L, rvnue processing tech I, $23,880
Walden, Brittany N, rvnue processing tech II, $26,232
Walker, Pamela A, rvnue processing tech II, $26,652
Wallendorf, Laura J, mgmt analysis spec I, $38,232
Walters, Jamie L, photographic-machine oper, $26,232
Wankum, Cassandra M, principal asst board/commisson, $62,064
Ward, Cynthia J, rvnue processing tech I, $23,880
Warden, Jona L, rvnue processing tech I, $23,880
Warren, Christa M, account clerk II, $25,824
Wasser, Brooklyn S, rvnue section supv, $36,204
Wasser, Casey A, legislative coord, $56,520
Waterman, Laura L, tax auditor I, $37,548
Watson, Beverly S, rvnue processing tech I, $23,880
Watson, Latosha A, rvnue processing tech I, $23,880
Watts, Mary E, rvnue processing tech II, $26,232
Watts, Patricia L, rvnue section supv, $36,204
Webb, Daniel P, exec II, $35,568
Webb, Rebecca J, rvnue processing tech IV, $32,628
Weber, Mark S, exec I, $34,944
Webster, Donna J, rvnue processing tech II, $26,652
Wehmeir, Larissa D, rvnue processing tech II, $27,504

Weider, Derek J, tax collection tech I, $23,880
Wekenborg, Rebecca B, paralegal, $28,325
Weldesselasie, Meheret K, rvnue processing tech II, $26,652
Weller, Carol J, acct II, $36,204
Wells, Darren L, rvnue processing tech II, $26,652
Wells, John H, pub info coor, $46,932
Wells, Larry C, lottery sales rep, $38,232
Wells, Samuel I, rvnue section supv, $36,204
Werdehausen, Glenda C, rvnue processing tech II, $28,452
Werdehausen, Katy M, mgmt analysis spec II, $41,940
Werner, Carmela A, rvnue processing tech II, $27,504
Westcott, Erica L, rvnue processing tech I, $23,880
Westfall, Anita K, admin ofc spt asst, $30,984
Whaley, Elizabeth A, special asst official & admstr, $51,290
Whaley, Matthew K, rvnue processing tech I, $23,880
White, David E, tax auditor I, $39,624
White, Jervonna T, tax collection tech I, $23,880
White, Raymond S, lottery mgr b1, $59,776
White, Susan M, rvnue section supv, $36,888
Whitson, Zachary A, rvnue processing tech I, $23,880
Wieberg, Bethany N, sr ofc spt asst (keybrd), $25,824
Wieberg, Deann N, admin ofc spt asst, $28,104
Wieberg, Lisa A, rvnue processing tech II, $26,652
Wieberg, Roxanne E, tax collection tech I, $23,880
Wilbers, Adam L, mgmt analysis spec I, $37,548
Wilde, Melinda K, lottery inside sales supv, $37,548
Wilde, Renee T, training tech III, $45,156
Wiler, Lisa M, special asst ofc & clerical, $36,812
Wiles, Curtis L, rvnue processing tech II, $26,232
Wiles, Rachel A, pers ofcr I, $41,172
Wilhelm, James, lottery sales rep, $41,940
Wilk, Lisa M, rvnue processing tech I, $23,880
Williams, Amy L, acct I, $30,984
Williams, Darryl L, admin ofc spt asst, $27,228
Williams, Deborah L, rvnue processing tech II, $27,084
Williams, Gregory D, designated principal asst div, $42,711
Williams, Jeanne D, rvnue processing tech I, $23,880
Williams, Joyce L, tax auditor III, $50,040
Williams, Linda, rvnue processing tech II, $28,908
Williams, Marlene M, rvnue processing tech II, $26,652
Williams, Mercedes G, admin ofc spt asst, $32,052
Williams, Nathan, photographic-machine oper, $23,160
Willis, Casandra J, rvnue section supv, $36,204
Willis, Cynthia L, tax collection tech I, $23,880
Willmeno, Ruby M, rvnue processing tech II, $26,232
Wilson, Sue A, lottery mgr b1, $48,949
Wilson, Tamra L, tax collection tech I, $23,880
Wingrath, Gregory A, rvnue processing tech II, $28,452
Winkert, Mary K, tax auditor III, $47,892
Wisch, Gina M, mgmt analysis spec II, $45,156
Wolf, Nora M, tax auditor I, $37,548
Wolfe, Brianna K, rvnue processing tech I, $23,880
Wolfe, Denise J, rvnue processing tech III, $29,004
Wolfe, Joshua E, tax collection tech I, $23,880
Woll, Regina A, tax audit supv, $63,996
Won, Jacqui C, rvnue processing tech II, $26,652
Wood, Jacklyn L, admin ofc spt asst, $31,512
Wood, Tonya D, rvnue processing tech II, $26,652
Wood, Victoria M, admin ofc spt asst, $34,356
Woods, Melissa A, ofc spt asst (keybrd), $23,160
Woody, Karen L, rvnue processing tech III, $29,976
Woolard, Debra F, rvnue processing tech II, $28,452
Woolery, William R, rvnue processing tech II, $27,084
Workman, Brandie D, rvnue processing tech I, $23,880
Wright, Donald C, rvnue field servs coor, $36,204
Wright, Donald W, tax collection tech I, $23,880
Wright, Jessie L, tax collection tech I, $23,880
Wright, Michele R, sr ofc spt asst (keybrd), $25,824
Wright, Randall Z, appraisal spec, $57,744
Wulff, Cara M, rvnue processing tech I, $23,880
Yancy, Holly E, rvnue processing tech I, $23,880
Yarnell, Bethany M, tax collection tech I, $23,880
Yates, Julieanna N, tax audit supv, $49,128
Zachar, Nicole R, sr ofc spt asst (keybrd), $25,824
Zan, Tongbin, tax auditor II, $40,380
Zanone, David, designated principal asst div, $54,039
Zaring, Esta K, rvnue mgr, band 1, $46,969
Zeng, Wanwen, out-state audit pers, $43,850
Zordel, Emily R, tax collection tech I, $23,880
Zuniga, Martin A, designated principal asst div, $63,453

Department of Social Services

PO Box 1527, Jefferson City 65102

Kinkade, Brian D, state dept dir, $121,704
Abbey, Mary L, fam spt elig spc, $29,976
Abbott, Kimberly J, youth fac mgr I, $41,940
Abby, Anton L, youth spec II, $31,512
Abell, Jessica L, special educ tchr I, $30,984
Abmeyer, Gary W, fam spt elig spc, $29,976
Abmeyer, Troy, fam spt elig spc, $29,976
Abuzahra, Tammy S, corres & info spec I, $34,944
Acres, Gloria D, mgmt analysis spec II, $44,304
Adair, Deborah K, children's serv worker III, $41,940
Adams, Aletha E, fam spt elig spc, $30,984
Adams, Allison M, fam spt elig spc, $29,976
Adams, Amanda R, prog dev spec, $40,380
Adams, Ashley L, children's serv worker II, $34,356
Adams, Ashley N, children's serv worker I, $30,984
Adams, Betty J, corres & info spec I, $35,568
Adams, Candace, children's serv worker III, $35,568
Adams, Casey M, youth spec II, $31,512
Adams, Cheryl L, admin ofc spt asst, $28,536
Adams, Dakota, fam spt elig spc, $29,976
Adams, Dawn, child spt enforce spv, $38,232
Adams, Dorothy M, youth spec I, $29,496
Adams, Jeff L, soc servs mgr, band 1, $54,288
Adams, Jennifer D, children's serv worker II, $34,356
Adams, Karla M, children's serv worker II, $34,356
Adams, Kenneth C, clerk, $9.69/hr
Adams, Lillian E, child spt spec, $33,744
Adams, Lindsey R, children's serv worker II, $34,356
Adams, Lissa M, children's serv worker II, $34,356
Adams, Loretta, children's serv worker III, $40,380
Adams, Lynn E, youth spec II, $33,180
Adams, Mary S, youth spec II, $31,512
Adams, Phylis I, cook II, $23,160
Adams, Shelly A, special asst ofc & clerical, $45,876
Adams, Susan M, fam spt elig spc, $29,976
Adams, Tammy L, children's serv worker III, $40,380
Adamson, Sheila S, medicaid technician, $32,628
Adeyemo, Sherri O, fam spt elig spc, $29,976
Adkins, Jacqueline S, acad tchr III, $37,548
Adkins, Kathy L, registered nurse, $42,420
Adkins, Steven, children's serv worker II, $34,356
Adkirson, Shauna M, child spt spec, $29,976
Adkison, Regina J, ofc spt asst (keybrd), $22,536
Agee, Natalie D, corres & info spec I, $34,944
Ainsworth, Michele A, soc servs worker, $17.07/hr
Ainsworth, Michele A, prog dev spec, $43,488
Aitch, Michael J, children's serv worker III, $35,568
Ajibola, Johnson A, youth spec II, $32,628
Akright, Debra A, serv coor yth srvcs, $42,708
Albin, James F, youth group leader, $32,628
Albrecht, Angela M, fam spt elig spc, $32,052
Alcala, Jennifer I, fam spt elig spc, $29,976
Alejandro, Marilyn D, children's serv worker II, $32,628
Aleshire, Tabitha L, children's serv spec, $37,548
Alexander, Angela, youth spec II, $31,512
Alexander, Brian K, children's serv worker II, $34,356
Alexander, Donald A, youth spec II, $31,512
Alexander, Katherine L, corres & info spec I, $34,944
Alexander, Kathern S, children's serv worker III, $36,888
Alexander, Sharon L, ofc spt asst (keybrd), $22,536
Alexander, Sybil Y, corres & info spec I, $34,944
Alford, Lisa R, children's serv worker II, $34,356
Alfred, Janelle M, children's serv worker I, $29,976
Ali, Shahenda I, children's serv worker I, $29,976
Allan, Cornell L, youth spec II, $30,984
Allchin, Patricia M, children's serv spv, $38,232
Allee, Gayle L, ofc spt asst (keybrd), $23,160
Allen, Amy K, children's serv worker II, $34,356
Allen, Amy M, fam spt elig spc, $29,976
Allen, Brandi J, children's serv spv, $34,944
Allen, Brandy N, fam spt elig spc, $29,976
Allen, Christopher, youth spec II, $31,512
Allen, Cleveland E, soc servs mgr, band 1, $48,156
Allen, Courtney L, human rel ofcr I, $37,548
Allen, Dacia, fam spt elig spc, $29,976

Allen, Delores A, ofc spt asst (keybrd), $11,940
Allen, Eboney J, fam spt elig spc, $29,976
Allen, Heather D, children's serv worker II, $34,356
Allen, India L, fam spt elig spc, $31,512
Allen, Keith, corres & info spec I, $34,944
Allen, Letrisa D, children's serv worker II, $34,356
Allen, Marie H, fam spt elig spc, $33,180
Allen, Martha L, youth spec II, $29,976
Allen, Matthew A, youth spec I, $29,004
Allen, Misty M, children's serv worker III, $36,888
Allen, Nancy S, fam spt elig spc, $29,976
Allen, Natalie N, special asst prof, $47,856
Allen, Nuru S, acad tchr III, $37,548
Allen, Patricia L, fam spt elig spv, $36,888
Allen, Reston G, corres & info spec I, $34,944
Allen, Scotty L, legal counsel, $73,164
Allen, Suzan D, child spt spec, $29,976
Allen, Suzanne J, lpn II gen, $29,772
Allen Cash, Felicia K, fam spt elig spc, $29,004
Allen-Price, Elizabeth, child spt spec, $29,976
Allgire, Susan M, children's serv worker II, $34,356
Allison, Harry W, children's serv worker II, $40,380
Allmon, Theresa L, fam spt elig spc, $34,356
Alonzo, Kristina M, child spt spec, $29,976
Alotta, Samuel P, account clerk I, $22,536
Alston, Erica D, children's serv worker III, $41,172
Alston, Pamela M, soc servs mgr, band 1, $52,092
Altmansberger, Alan W, fam spt elig spc, $29,976
Alu, Jessica S, children's serv worker III, $36,888
Amayo, Deborah L, ofc spt asst (keybrd), $23,160
Ambus, Lisa, ofc spt asst (keybrd), $26,652
Amelunke, Christy L, serv coor spv yth srvcs, $43,488
Amend, Allison A, pers clerk, $29,496
Amend, Tammy M, medicaid unit spv, $45,156
Ames-Rolufs, Pamela J, child spt enforce spv, $35,568
Amos, Heather D, fam spt elig spc, $29,976
Amunrud, Debra, child spt spec, $29,976
Anderson, Anjelica M, youth spec II, $30,984
Anderson, Anna M, children's serv worker II, $34,356
Anderson, Cheryl A, ofc spt asst (keybrd), $23,160
Anderson, Elizabeth, child spt spec, $29,976
Anderson, Florence N, ofc spt asst (keybrd), $23,160
Anderson, James, children's serv worker II, $34,356
Anderson, James C, youth spec II, $30,984
Anderson, Janet E, fam spt elig spc, $30,420
Anderson, Jessi L, children's serv worker II, $34,356
Anderson, Joel E, div dir, $93,228
Anderson, Joel Edward, legal counsel, $46,008
Anderson, Jolene D, children's serv worker III, $41,940
Anderson, Jonathen L, special asst prof, $49,128
Anderson, Linda L, fam spt elig spc, $33,744
Anderson, Mary B, children's serv worker II, $33,744
Anderson, Morgan L, children's serv worker II, $32,628
Anderson-Bond, Sheranda, ofc spt asst (keybrd), $22,536
Andrews, April L, sr ofc spt asst (keybrd), $25,824
Andrews, Bertha L, children's serv spv, $48,156
Andrews, Carla C, ofc spt asst (keybrd), $23,160
Andrews, Carolyn S, fam spt elig spc, $33,744
Andrews, Glenda M, children's serv worker III, $38,232
Andrews, Jerry L, soc servs mgr, band 1, $41,940
Andrews, Stacey E, children's serv worker III, $36,888
Andula, Corinna S, sr ofc spt asst (keybrd), $25,032
Angle, Jeanie M, ofc spt asst (keybrd), $23,160
Anglin, Angela M, fam spt elig spc, $29,976
Anthofer, Robert P, serv coor yth srvcs, $33,744
Anthony, Lorne A, serv coor II yth srvcs, $41,172
Anthony, Mary J, children's serv worker III, $35,568
Apgar, Janet R, clerical servs spv fs, $32,628
Aponte-Sanchez, Carla L, sr ofc spt asst (keybrd), $25,032
Appiah, Christabel A, children's serv worker I, $30,984
Appleby, Tana L, children's serv worker III, $35,568
Archer, Linda M, medicaid clerk, $30,420
Ardison, Kyla M, children's serv worker II, $34,356
Arens, Alexandra, children's serv spv, $38,232
Arias, Maricela, soc servs aide, $11.13/hr
Arkle, Richard S, fam spt elig spc, $29,976
Arl, Carolyn, prog dev spec, $46,068
Armenta, Martha J, fam spt elig spc, $29,976
Armes, Samuel A, youth spec II, $31,512

Armistead, Daniel J, children's serv worker I, $29,976
Armistead, Teri L, special asst prof, $64,176
Armstead, Tenia M, child spt spec, $29,976
Armstrong, Darcy, children's serv worker II, $34,356
Armstrong, Noralyn A, child spt spec, $32,052
Armstrong, Robert S, youth spec II, $29,976
Armstrong, Sherri V, children's serv worker II, $32,628
Arnaud, Margaret J, fam spt elig spc, $17,472
Arndt, Courtney M, children's serv worker II, $34,356
Arnold, Angela M, fam spt elig spc, $29,976
Arnold, Dixie R, ofc spt asst (keybrd), $24,264
Arnold, Elizabeth A, children's serv spv, $38,232
Arnold, Janice L, admin ofc spt asst, $30,984
Arnold, Mallory N, fam spt elig spv, $34,944
Arnold, Michael R, serv coor yth srvcs, $34,944
Arrington, Amber N, children's serv worker II, $34,356
Arterbery, Rebecca, fam spt elig spc, $35,568
Ary, Robin, fam spt elig spc, $29,976
Asbury, Mari L, children's serv worker II, $33,744
Ashby, Christie, fam spt elig spv, $35,568
Ashcraft, Kathryn S, youth spec II, $31,512
Ashcraft, Mable L, fam spt elig spc, $33,180
Asher, Genny S, sr voc rehab cnslr f/t blind, $38,928
Asher, Kristopher K, youth spec II, $31,512
Asher, Sharon L, children's serv worker III, $36,888
Ashford, Ariadne K, child spt spec, $29,976
Ashley, Linda L, child spt enforce spv, $38,928
Ashley, Nicole L, medicaid pharmaceutical tech, $32,628
Ast, Megan L, children's serv worker III, $36,888
Atchley, Misty A, children's serv worker I, $30,984
Atherton, Jean M, youth fac mgr II, $41,940
Athy, Lawrence, child spt spec, $31,512
Atkins, Gladys, ofc spt asst (keybrd), $25,824
Atkins, Heather N, prog dev spec, $40,380
Atkins, Rhonda L, ofc spt asst (keybrd), $23,160
Atkinson, Chandelle N, soc servs aide, $11.13/hr
Atkinson, Rikki J, youth spec II, $29,976
Atkinson, William J, youth spec II, $30,984
Atteberry, Sue A, medicaid technician, $32,628
Aubuchon, Daniel G, acad tchr III, $36,204
Aubuchon, Teresa A, fam spt elig spv, $36,888
Aubuchon, Thomas J, children's serv spv, $39,624
Audsley, Chris E, children's serv worker I, $30,984
Aufdenberg, Jessica M, children's serv worker III, $35,568
August, Stephanie A, training tech III, $50,040
Aulbur, Ashley D, mgmt analysis spec II, $46,068
Aupiu, Tanya S, fam spt elig spc, $29,976
Austin, James M, serv coor yth srvcs, $34,356
Austin, Wendy E, special asst prof, $69,852
Aux-Tinee, Michael J, fam spt elig spc, $29,976
Aversman, Tamara J, corres & info spec I, $34,944
Avery, Callie L, fam spt elig spc, $29,976
Avery, Scotilda S, children's serv worker II, $32,628
Ayala, Corina L, children's serv worker III, $35,568
Ayers, Rebecca R, children's serv worker II, $44,304
Ayers, Rufus A, soc servs mgr, band 1, $41,940
Babbitt, Nancy L, children's serv worker I, $29,976
Babington, Laura L, children's serv worker III, $35,568
Babor, Collette R, child spt spec, $29,976
Bachali, Holly E, children's serv worker I, $29,976
Baclesse, Kevin E, facilities opps mgr b1, $45,228
Baer, Christina M, children's serv worker I, $29,976
Baer-Hoehn, Dana A, child spt spec, $29,976
Bafford, Jennifer A, fam spt elig spv, $34,944
Bagin, Maureen A, fam spt elig spc, $14,988
Bagnull, Gary, mgmt analysis spec II, $41,940
Bailey, Andrew L, fam spt elig spc, $29,976
Bailey, Brian L, investigator III, $46,932
Bailey, Cynthia A, fam spt elig spc, $29,976
Bailey, Debby A, ofc spt asst (keybrd), $25,404
Bailey, Evonna L, corres & info spec I, $38,232
Bailey, Heather L, children's serv worker I, $29,976
Bailey, Mary, fam spt elig spc, $29,976
Bailey, Ryan C, investigator III, $41,940
Bailey, Sharole, child spt spec, $31,512
Bailiff, Rebecca L, special educ tchr III, $37,548
Bain, Marilyn, sr ofc spt asst (keybrd), $25,824
Baiotto, Leah A, children's serv worker I, $30,984
Bakeman, James R, fam spt elig spc, $33,180

Baker, Amanda L, admin ofc spt asst, $33,744
Baker, Carol, sr ofc spt asst (keybrd), $25,824
Baker, Debra K, ofc spt asst (keybrd), $24,264
Baker, Jacob K, youth spec II, $31,512
Baker, Kevin B, youth spec II, $31,512
Baker, Lisa R, rehab asst rehab srvs for blnd, $26,652
Baker, Michelle A, fam spt elig spc, $29,976
Baker, Tasha, soc servs mgr, band 1, $50,040
Balassone, Amy D, fam spt elig spc, $29,976
Baldner, Tiffani N, children's serv spv, $39,624
Baldridge, Michelle K, children's serv spv, $45,156
Baldus, Patricia J, fam spt elig spv, $36,204
Baldwin, Christina M, exec I, $30,984
Baldwin, James L, youth fac mgr I, $41,172
Baldwin, Wanda, ofc spt asst (keybrd), $23,160
Bales, Amy, sr ofc spt asst (keybrd), $25,824
Bales, Juanita M, fam spt elig spc, $30,984
Bales, Melissa L, ofc spt asst (keybrd), $23,160
Balke, Pamela A, fam spt elig spc, $30,420
Ball, Diana, fam spt elig spc, $29,976
Ballantyne, Rebecca A, children's serv worker II, $32,628
Ballard, Crystal A, children's serv worker I, $29,976
Ballard, James M, hearings ofcr, $39,648
Ballard, Pamela S, human rel ofcr I, $38,928
Ballard, Sarah J, children's serv spec, $41,940
Ballay, Melissa F, children's serv worker III, $41,940
Ballenger, Carrie, ofc spt asst (keybrd), $23,160
Ballew, Keri D, medicaid spec, $37,548
Ballinger, Jewelquelle S, children's serv worker II, $32,628
Ballmann, Jennifer A, youth fac mgr I, $38,928
Balser, Mary J, fam spt elig spc, $34,356
Banister, Brandon T, youth spec II, $31,512
Banks, Gabrielle A, children's serv worker II, $34,356
Banks, Natashia N, fam spt elig spc, $29,976
Banks, Patricia M, children's serv worker II, $34,356
Banks, Richard E, soc servs aide, $11.13/hr
Banks, Teangela M, children's serv worker I, $30,984
Banks, Tiffany N, fam spt elig spc, $29,976
Banning, Amy L, children's serv worker III, $36,888
Barbeau, Jessica N, youth spec II, $29,976
Barbee, Dwayne, youth spec II, $30,984
Barbour, Lindsey R, children's serv worker II, $32,628
Barbre, Kathleen B, cook III, $28,536
Barchak, Alex, youth spec II, $31,512
Bardle, Richard G, corres & info spec I, $37,548
Barker, Julie A, fam spt elig spc, $34,356
Barker, Sherri L, child spt spec, $33,180
Barks, Sarah M, serv coor yth srvcs, $34,356
Barnard, Nicole R, children's serv worker II, $34,356
Barnes, Adam W, youth spec II, $31,512
Barnes, Catherine A, fam spt elig spc, $29,976
Barnes, Julie S, fam spt elig spc, $29,976
Barnes, Lawrence E, acad tchr III, $36,204
Barnes, Sandra J, registered nurse mgr b2, $60,811
Barnes, Stanley W, soc servs aide, $11.13/hr
Barnes, Tammy L, children's serv spec, $47,892
Barnett, Donald N, children's serv worker I, $29,976
Barnett, Krista A, investigator III, $40,380
Barnett, Rachel L, fam spt elig spc, $29,976
Barnhart, Maryanne P, children's serv worker I, $29,976
Barnhart, Melissa, child spt spec, $29,976
Barnhill, Brett D, youth spec II, $31,512
Barnhouse, Linda S, fam spt elig spc, $29,976
Barr, Elizabeth D, children's serv worker II, $32,628
Barr, Janine R, fam spt elig spc, $29,976
Barrett, Evan J, children's serv worker II, $34,356
Barrett, Janet L, children's serv worker II, $38,232
Barrett, Stephanie, fam spt elig spc, $29,976
Barrett, Timothy B, investigator III, $41,940
Barringhaus, Jamie S, ofc spt asst (keybrd), $23,160
Barron, Lisa, fam spt elig spc, $29,976
Barron, Scott R, serv coor yth srvcs, $42,708
Barry, Angela Y, fam spt elig spc, $29,976
Barry, Heather E, children's serv spv, $41,172
Barry, Laura J, fam spt elig spc, $29,976
Barsby, Sharon K, exec I, $29,976
Bartelli, Bruce D, child spt spec, $33,744
Bartels, Barbara A, child spt spec, $34,356
Bartig, Marguerita L, acad tchr III, $36,204

Barton, Gisele, rehab asst rehab srvs for blnd, $27,948
Barton, Laurie J, fam spt elig spc, $35,568
Bash, April D, children's serv worker II, $32,628
Bashford, Ruth B, fam spt elig spc, $29,976
Bashore, Sarah J, prog dev spec, $40,380
Baskar, Muthu, fam spt elig spc, $29,976
Basler, Sarah, children's serv spv, $39,624
Basnett, Pamela J, admin ofc spt asst, $29,976
Bass, Margie A, fam spt elig spc, $29,976
Bassett, Malinda R, admin ofc spt asst, $28,104
Bateman, Rebecca L, child spt spec, $31,512
Bates, Ashley L, registered nurse - clin opers, $52,608
Bates, Jessica L, sr ofc spt asst (keybrd), $25,032
Bates, Lisa O, child spt spec, $29,976
Bates, Nicole R, corres & info spec I, $34,944
Bates, Sabrina J, child spt spec, $29,976
Bates, Tammy R, children's serv spv, $41,172
Batey, Amy D, fam spt elig spv, $34,944
Bathon, James, fam spt elig spc, $29,976
Batson, Jennifer A, children's serv worker II, $34,356
Bauer, Marsha G, ofc spt asst (keybrd), $23,160
Baughman, Gary E, mgmt analysis spec II, $41,940
Baughman, Linda L, children's serv worker III, $40,380
Baumann, Scott A, fam spt elig spc, $29,976
Baumgartner, Kassondra L, ofc spt asst (keybrd), $23,160
Bax, Jennifer E, soc servs mngr, band 2, $49,128
Bayless, Charity D, corres & info spec I, $33,744
Bayless, Fairelyn K, fam spt elig spc, $29,976
Bayless, Jodie L, investigator III, $41,940
Bayless-Shaw, Melissa D, children's serv worker II, $34,356
Baynum, Rebecca J, children's serv worker I, $31,512
Bazzell, Vonita C, fam spt elig spc, $29,976
Beaird, David, children's serv worker II, $34,356
Beakley, Corrine W, special asst prof, $67,476
Beal, Douglas W, misc prof, $34,344
Beamer, Brenda D, fam spt elig spc, $29,976
Bean, Eric D, children's serv worker II, $33,744
Bean, Jordan L, children's serv worker I, $30,984
Beard, Leslie G, corres & info spec I, $34,944
Beard, Susan L, fam spt elig spc, $33,180
Beard, Taylor D, children's serv worker III, $36,888
Bearden, Katherine D, children's serv worker III, $36,888
Beardslee, Elizabeth A, youth group leader, $34,356
Becerril, Esteban R, youth spec II, $29,976
Bechtold, John, children's serv worker II, $36,888
Beck, Jennifer, fam spt elig spc, $29,976
Beck, Larry M, telecommun analyst IV, $54,288
Beck, Sandra K, ofc spt asst (keybrd), $27,504
Beck, Stephanie M, reg cnslt resid lcsng unit, $49,128
Becker, Brenda S, special asst ofc & clerical, $45,540
Becker, Laura, fam spt elig spc, $31,512
Becker, Phyllis, div dir, $98,784
Becker, Sarah, medicaid technician, $32,628
Becker, Timothy J, youth spec II, $35,568
Beckett, Anna M, soc servs mgr, band 1, $50,040
Beckett, Joanna M, children's serv worker III, $36,888
Beckett, Kathryn, sr ofc spt asst (keybrd), $25,824
Beckett, Thelma K, training tech II, $40,380
Beckley, Shelley E, children's serv worker II, $34,356
Beckman, Vicki L, ofc spt asst (keybrd), $23,160
Bedell, Ashley A, fam spt elig spc, $29,976
Bedsworth, Donna L, children's serv spv, $46,932
Beeks, Kelly D, ofc spt asst (keybrd), $23,880
Beeler, Robin R, medicaid unit spv, $41,940
Beem, Gwendolyn J, fam spt elig spv, $36,888
Beem, Joni D, children's serv worker III, $40,380
Beemer, Earl J, child spt spec, $29,976
Beeson, Edna E, fam spt elig spc, $32,052
Beetsma, Michael, children's serv spv, $39,624
Behymer, Carol A, fam spt elig spc, $29,976
Beiseman, Kindra, child spt spec, $29,976
Beisser, Kelly N, children's serv worker II, $32,628
Beistel, Brenda K, sr ofc spt asst (keybrd), $28,908
Belanger, Thomas J, children's serv worker I, $30,984
Belaska, Penelope J, corres & info spec I, $35,568
Belin, Sarah B, youth spec II, $30,984
Belk, Jan L, child spt enforce spv, $38,928
Bell, Jennifer C, fam spt elig spc, $29,976
Bell, Julie L, child spt spec, $29,976

Bell, Katherine A, fam spt elig spc, $33,180
Bell, Leona R, fam spt elig spc, $29,976
Bell, Lori K, child spt spec, $31,512
Bell, Marc R, special educ tchr III, $40,380
Bell, Marva, ofc spt asst (keybrd), $23,880
Bell, Miranda G, children's serv worker II, $33,744
Bell, Tasha M, youth spec II, $30,984
Bell, Theresa A, fam spt elig spv, $34,944
Bell, Victoria E, children's serv worker II, $33,744
Bellamy, Becky, corres & info spec I, $34,944
Belt, Cheryl L, medicaid spec, $37,548
Belt, Christina M, fam spt elig spc, $29,976
Belton, Gwendolyn E, soc servs mgr, band 1, $41,940
Bemberger, Kent L, child spt spec, $29,976
Benbow, Tiffany J, youth spec II, $29,976
Bench, Denise, fam spt elig spc, $29,976
Bender, Ashley, corres & info spec I, $34,944
Benitez, Maria N, youth spec II, $31,512
Benna, Carol A, soc servs mgr, band 1, $42,708
Benne, Joy E, procurement ofcr II, $45,156
Bennett, Ann M, corres & info spec I, $38,232
Bennett, Brenda M, children's serv worker II, $42,708
Bennett, Carol S, children's serv worker II, $34,356
Bennett, Cassandra, ofc spt asst (keybrd), $24,264
Bennett, Diane L, fam spt elig spc, $35,568
Bennett, Mary E, soc servs aide, $11.13/hr
Bennett, Melissa A, children's serv worker III, $39,624
Bennett, Mitchell L, soc servs mgr, band 1, $48,156
Bennett-Williams, Kelsey L, fam spt elig spv, $34,944
Benson, Aloni D, youth spec II, $31,512
Benson, Barbara J, children's serv worker II, $38,928
Benson, Chanel C, youth spec I, $28,104
Benson, Dorothy M, acad tchr III, $37,548
Benson, Mary A, rehab asst rehab srvs for blnd, $31,920
Bentinganan, Vernon M, youth spec II, $31,512
Bentley, Barbara L, cook II, $23,880
Bentley, Ellen D, fam spt elig spc, $34,356
Bentley, Kyle, training tech II, $40,380
Bentley, Rebecca J, fam spt elig spc, $31,512
Bentley, Shawn E, children's serv spv, $41,172
Bentz, Billie J, registered nurse, $44,904
Benz, Vicki J, medicaid pharmaceutical tech, $32,628
Bergman, Nikki A, youth group leader, $34,356
Bergmann, Lisa, child spt spec, $32,628
Berhorst, Jennifer, children's serv spv, $39,624
Berkemeyer, Heather J, rehab asst rehab srvs for blnd, $26,652
Berls, Lisa, ofc spt asst (keybrd), $29,412
Berney, Kristine L, case analyst, $32,628
Berney, Pamela G, special asst prof, $40,380
Bernier, Dana L, medicaid spec, $37,548
Bernskoetter, Marvin B, fiscal & administrative mgr b1, $56,520
Berry, Beverly G, fam spt elig spc, $29,976
Berry, Charlotte T, sr ofc spt asst (keybrd), $28,452
Berry, Greg J, children's serv worker III, $36,888
Berry, James, hearings ofcr, $52,032
Berry, Janis E, child spt spec, $33,180
Berry, Jennifer D, children's serv worker I, $29,976
Berry, Madeline D, children's serv worker II, $34,356
Bertelson, Christine A, special asst prof, $101,000
Beseda, Nicole M, children's serv spv, $39,624
Bess, Billie J, children's serv worker II, $33,180
Bess, Crystal R, fam spt elig spv, $35,568
Bess, Dawn O, children's serv worker I, $29,976
Best, Laura A, fam spt elig spc, $31,512
Best, Robert R, fam spt elig spc, $30,420
Bethea, Megan E, children's serv worker I, $29,976
Bethel, Kelly R, children's serv worker III, $35,568
Bethmann, Tess, children's serv spv, $39,624
Bettinger, Kathryn A, fam spt elig spc, $29,976
Bettis, Julie L, youth group leader, $34,356
Bevelle, Saraha L, fam spt elig spc, $30,984
Bewley, Bruce E, child spt spec, $29,976
Bey, Caitlin D, special educ tchr II, $34,944
Beyer, Brandi L, children's serv spv, $38,232
Bialczyk, Danica, medicaid clerk, $27,660
Bialczyk, Garret L, sr auditor, $40,380
Bibb, Raymond T, child spt spec, $32,052
Bible, Julie M, ofc spt asst (keybrd), $23,160
Bickerstaff, Dionne A, ofc spt asst (keybrd), $23,160

Bielawski, Theresa E, children's serv spec, $46,932
Bieri, Kristen M, children's serv worker II, $34,356
Bieri, Tina M, child spt spec, $33,180
Biester, Kyla D, children's serv worker II, $32,628
Bigge, David B, soc servs mgr, band 1, $41,940
Bigge, Julie A, fam spt elig spc, $34,944
Biggs, Lesa D, fam spt elig spc, $33,180
Bigham, Braden D, youth spec II, $29,976
Bilbrough, Nichole L, children's serv spv, $39,624
Billings, Desiree, fam spt elig spc, $29,976
Billingslea, Denise M, youth spec II, $32,052
Billington, Rita, fam spt elig spc, $29,976
Binder, Angelia M, fam spt elig spc, $29,976
Binder, Kristen M, children's serv worker II, $34,356
Bingaman, Lucas C, cook II, $23,880
Binkley, Mary V, youth spec II, $31,512
Binkley, Theresa L, children's serv worker I, $30,984
Binowitz, Lisa J, children's serv worker II, $38,928
Bird, Brandi N, children's serv worker II, $34,356
Bird, Richard D, children's serv spv, $39,624
Birdsong, Crystal, ofc spt asst (keybrd), $23,160
Bisacca, Adam M, youth spec II, $30,984
Bisacca, Cynthia L, soc servs mgr, band 1, $48,156
Bise, Tammy J, children's serv worker I, $29,976
Bisges, Johanna M, reg fam spec, $37,548
Bishop, Helen S, area supv bus entprs blind, $36,204
Biskie, Darlene, fam spt elig spc, $29,976
Bitterman, Cindy L, admin ofc spt asst, $28,536
Black, Ashley T, children's serv worker II, $34,356
Black, Crystle, fam spt elig spc, $29,976
Black, Nakisha A, youth spec II, $31,512
Black, Pamela J, fam spt elig spv, $34,944
Black, Rodney A, youth fac mgr II, $40,380
Black, Shae D, child spt spec, $29,976
Black, Tamara G, youth spec II, $31,512
Black, Valerie M, children's serv worker I, $30,984
Blackburn, Beth A, fam spt elig spc, $29,976
Blackwell, Emory B, children's serv worker III, $36,888
Blackwell, Katherine A, youth spec II, $31,512
Blackwell, Kelly A, youth spec II, $31,512
Blair, Chelsea L, administrative analyst I, $34,944
Blair, Heather M, children's serv worker III, $36,888
Blair, Mason A, children's serv worker II, $34,356
Blake, Brett S, youth spec II, $33,180
Blake, Christopher L, children's serv worker II, $34,356
Blake, Letitia A, fam spt elig spc, $29,976
Blake, Siegfried, fam spt elig spc, $33,180
Blake, Sydney D, children's serv worker I, $30,984
Bland, Aaron A, fam spt elig spc, $29,976
Bland, Judith A, fam spt elig spc, $29,976
Blandford, Katherine M, special educ tchr III, $38,928
Blanks, Terry D, youth spec I, $29,004
Blase, Tracy H, prog dev spec, $44,304
Blattner, Lori J, reg fam spec, $40,380
Blaylock, Amanda R, children's serv worker II, $34,356
Bledsoe, Jennifer, fam spt elig spv, $33,744
Bledsoe, Lisa R, youth spec II, $31,512
Bledsoe, Shellie R, fam spt elig spv, $34,944
Blevins, Jody M, children's serv worker II, $34,356
Bliss, Benjamin, fam spt elig spc, $29,976
Bliss, Cassandra, fam spt elig spc, $29,976
Bliss, Gary A, youth group leader, $34,356
Blissett, Laura A, corres & info spec I, $34,944
Block, Joyce A, child spt spec, $34,356
Blockton, Victoria, fam spt elig spc, $29,976
Blomberg, Kourtney J, investigator I, $30,984
Blount, Tina D, child spt spec, $31,512
Blum, Regina L, fam spt elig spc, $34,356
Blume, Jeffery L, youth spec II, $31,512
Blunt, Sheila, fam spt elig spc, $29,976
Blyze, Bernadette R, fam spt elig spc, $29,976
Boatright, Meghan K, children's serv worker III, $36,888
Bockman, Ann M, children's serv spec, $43,488
Boclair, Shannette M, children's serv worker II, $34,356
Bode, Zachary R, youth spec II, $31,512
Bodenstein, Peggy L, fam spt elig spc, $29,976
Bodine, Branden L, youth spec II, $31,512
Bodinson, Krista K, serv coor yth srvcs, $38,928
Boeckman, Karla D, soc servs mgr, band 1, $41,940

Boehm, Agnes, medicaid unit spv, $47,892
Bogacki, Robert M, youth spec II, $33,180
Bogart, Jodene D, mgmt analysis spec II, $46,932
Bogdanoff, Carrie S, children's serv worker I, $30,984
Bohanan, Curtis B, investigator II, $41,940
Bohnarczyk, Joyce E, fam spt elig spc, $29,976
Bolden, Lela M, cook III, $28,104
Boles, Elaine N, acad tchr III, $37,548
Bolin, Ashley, fam spt elig spc, $29,976
Bolin, Eleanor S, special educ tchr III, $42,708
Bolin, Kimberly, children's serv spv, $39,624
Bollig, Trina K, ofc spt asst (keybrd), $23,160
Bollinger, Constance, fam spt elig spc, $34,944
Bollinger, Dena, ofc spt asst (keybrd), $23,160
Bollinger, Jacqueline C, corres & info spec I, $34,944
Bollinger, Jodi, children's serv worker II, $34,356
Bollinger, Peggy J, child spt spec, $34,944
Bollinger, Sherry L, children's serv worker I, $30,984
Bolt, Michael A, fam spt elig spc, $29,976
Bommarito, Lesley R, children's serv worker II, $33,744
Bond, Andrew J, designated principal asst div, $83,424
Bond, Carrie, children's serv worker II, $34,356
Bond, Janel M, youth spec II, $31,512
Bone, Debra L, fam spt elig spc, $33,180
Bone, Julie C, fam spt elig spc, $30,984
Bonner, Rachel, children's serv spec, $40,380
Bonner, Vivian E, fam spt elig spc, $29,976
Bono, Gabriel D, children's serv worker II, $34,356
Booher, Anthony C, soc servs aide, $11.13/hr
Booher, Christopher T, children's serv spec, $37,548
Booher, Jennifer S, staff training & dev coor, $51,096
Book, Jeanette F, prog dev spec, $40,380
Bookout, Alisa, sr ofc spt asst (keybrd), $25,824
Bookout, Laura M, youth spec II, $31,512
Boone, Elliott J, fam spt elig spc, $29,976
Boone, Kimberly A, acct I, $30,984
Booth, Francine, youth spec II, $31,512
Boothe, Richard L, youth spec II, $31,512
Bortka, Lee E, serv coor II yth srvcs, $41,940
Borts, Amanda, ofc spt asst (keybrd), $23,160
Bortvit, Lean, fam spt elig spc, $29,976
Bosch, Kathleen E, admin ofc spt asst, $29,496
Bosman, Beverly A, exec I, $32,052
Boston, Lynatte K, fam spt elig spc, $29,976
Boswell, Maria C, youth spec II, $35,568
Boswell, Violet B, fam spt elig spv, $34,944
Botkin, Rachel A, youth spec I, $28,104
Bottcher, Diane M, ofc spt asst (keybrd), $27,084
Bottorff, Kimberly A, ofc spt asst (keybrd), $23,160
Bouchard, Deanne, children's serv worker III, $36,888
Boulch, Michael P, youth spec II, $31,512
Bounds, Donald R, youth spec II, $31,512
Bouse, Cindy, fam spt elig spc, $29,976
Bouse, Wendy C, children's serv worker II, $34,356
Bowdry, Mannie S, youth spec II, $36,888
Bowen, Jonathan A, youth spec II, $31,512
Bowen, Louise M, exec I, $30,984
Bowen, Robyn R, children's serv worker I, $29,976
Bowens, Latonya N, voc rehab cslr f/t blin, $36,204
Bowling, Barbara, fam spt elig spc, $29,976
Bowling, Bridget, fam spt elig spc, $29,976
Bowman, Jeremy L, case analyst, $32,628
Bowman, Julie A, corres & info spec I, $34,944
Bowman, Rebecca A, children's serv worker II, $33,744
Bowman, Stephani D, fam spt elig spc, $29,976
Bowman, Tisha R, prog dev spec, $42,708
Box, Lawana J, admin ofc spt asst, $30,420
Boxberger, Gina R, legal counsel, $73,164
Boyd, Ashley R, fam spt elig spc, $29,976
Boyd, Bradley R, fiscal & administrative mgr b1, $49,128
Boyd, Catherine L, children's serv worker III, $37,548
Boyd, Halbert, children's serv worker II, $34,356
Boyd, Kevin G, youth spec II, $31,512
Boyd, Larentz E, youth spec II, $31,512
Boyd, Maranda A, corres & info spec I, $34,944
Boyd, Ramona L, rehab asst rehab srvs for blnd, $26,652
Boyd, Sarah A, youth spec II, $31,512
Boyd, Shawn H, soc servs mgr, band 1, $51,312
Boydston, Tina D, children's serv worker III, $35,568

Boyer, Angela M, children's serv worker I, $29,976
Boyer, Gayleen C, fam spt elig spc, $30,984
Boyette, Robin M, fam spt elig spc, $34,944
Boyles, Justin D, children's serv worker II, $32,628
Boyles, Larry J, children's serv worker II, $34,356
Boyt, Joelena L, serv coor yth srvcs, $33,744
Boyt, Ricky D, serv coor yth srvcs, $33,744
Bozeman, Carol A, child spt spec, $33,744
Bracken, Holly M, fam spt elig spc, $29,976
Brackins, Jordan E, youth spec II, $31,512
Bracy, Denise M, fam spt elig spc, $29,976
Bradbury, Diane, youth group leader, $34,356
Bradford, Ann M, fam spt elig spc, $29,976
Bradford, Marianne E, fam spt elig spc, $29,976
Bradford, Sheritha L, fam spt elig spv, $34,944
Bradley, Brianna L, ofc spt asst (keybrd), $22,536
Bradley, Debbie L, medicaid spec, $41,172
Bradley, Krista L, youth spec I, $29,004
Bradley, Larry A, youth spec II, $31,512
Bradley, Lola M, sr ofc spt asst (keybrd), $29,412
Bradley, Patricia A, fam spt elig spc, $33,744
Bradley, Tiffany R, fam spt elig spc, $29,976
Bradshaw, Barbara E, child spt spec, $29,976
Brady, Gina G, case analyst, $32,628
Brady, Mary Ellen, child spt spec, $33,744
Brady, Tiffaney M, youth spec II, $29,976
Brake, Barbara, soc servs worker, $17.07/hr
Braker, Trent A, children's serv worker III, $35,568
Brame, Sandra F, sr ofc spt asst (keybrd), $25,824
Brame, Teresa S, children's serv worker III, $40,380
Bramlett, Alfreida D, admin ofc spt asst, $30,984
Branch, Kristina L, children's serv worker II, $34,356
Brand, Denise A, prog dev spec, $42,708
Brandes, Margaret, child spt spec, $34,944
Branham, Stacy D, corres & info spec I, $33,744
Branscom, Casaundra F, children's serv worker I, $29,976
Branson, Joseph C, serv coor spv yth srvcs, $40,380
Branson, Larry R, soc servs mngr, band 2, $50,424
Branstetter, Katherine A, fam spt elig spv, $34,944
Brashears, Nickole, fam spt elig spc, $29,976
Bratcher, Monica, child spt spec, $29,004
Braun, Barbara A, fam spt elig spc, $30,420
Bravo, Rigoberto, youth spec II, $31,512
Brazzle, Betty J, fam spt elig spc, $29,976
Breaux, Juliet D, soc servs mngr, band 2, $71,100
Breeden, Debbie L, ofc spt asst (keybrd), $23,160
Breeden, Debra K, cook II, $23,880
Breeden, Diane, child spt spec, $35,568
Breinig, Brenda L, children's serv worker II, $34,356
Brendler, Pamela, children's serv worker III, $36,888
Breneman, Nancy J, child spt enforce spv, $38,928
Brenner, Misty, child spt spec, $29,976
Brent, Shawn R, mgmt analysis spec I, $37,548
Breuer, Nikki M, children's serv worker II, $34,356
Brewer, Heather, fam spt elig spc, $29,976
Brewer, Tynia D, fam spt elig spc, $29,976
Brewington, Dana G, fam spt elig spc, $29,976
Bridges, Judy, fam spt elig spc, $29,976
Briggs, Andrea D, children's serv worker II, $34,356
Briggs, Carlos L, youth group leader, $34,356
Bright, Tisha D, youth spec II, $30,984
Brightman, James A, hearings ofcr, $58,464
Brightwell, Melissa A, fam spt elig spc, $33,180
Briguglio-Mays, Antoinette R, prog dev spec, $40,380
Brimer, Shawn H, fam spt elig spc, $29,976
Briner, Hannah M, children's serv worker I, $29,976
Brinkley, Becky L, child spt spec, $29,976
Brinkley, Joshua A, children's serv worker II, $34,356
Brinkley, Lori R, ofc spt asst (keybrd), $24,264
Brinkley, Tina, fam spt elig spc, $33,180
Brinkman, Rene L, children's serv prog mgr, $40,380
Brinkmann, James D, soc servs mgr, band 1, $48,156
Briscoe, Vianne E, fam spt elig spc, $32,052
Brite, Anthony M, fiscal & administrative mgr b2, $63,996
Britt, Travis S, auditor I, $33,744
Brittain, Carol L, children's serv worker III, $35,568
Brittman, Ladonna F, fam spt elig spc, $29,976
Broadbent, Amanda, ofc spt asst (keybrd), $23,160
Broadbent, Rebecca L, youth spec II, $29,976

Broadus, Kierei K, children's serv worker II, $32,628
Brock, Katrina R, corres & info spec I, $34,944
Brock, Lisa C, children's serv worker II, $37,548
Brock, Susan L, fam spt elig spc, $29,976
Brockman, Deanna S, child spt enforce spv, $34,944
Broderick, Theresa A, children's serv spv, $40,380
Brodie, Linda, ofc spt asst (keybrd), $25,824
Brondel, Terri E, corres & info spec I, $36,204
Broniec, Carrie L, soc servs mgr, band 1, $47,892
Brooke, Mica A, child spt spec, $29,976
Brooke, Susan A, child spt enforce spv, $38,928
Brookfield, Lawaune D, youth spec II, $31,512
Brookreson, Steven W, youth spec II, $32,052
Brooks, Angela C, fam spt elig spc, $29,976
Brooks, Austin S, reg fam spec, $37,548
Brooks, Elizabeth, reg cnslt resid lcsng unit, $41,940
Brooks, Kendra, children's serv worker II, $34,356
Brooks, Melissia J, child spt spec, $29,976
Brooks, Robin R, children's serv spv, $39,624
Brooks, Tina M, fam spt elig spc, $29,976
Brooks, Tracie L, children's serv worker III, $36,888
Brothers, Brenda B, sr ofc spt asst (keybrd), $25,824
Brouder, John F, fam spt elig spc, $34,944
Broussard, Danielle, child spt spec, $29,976
Brower, Betty L, children's serv spv, $45,156
Brower, Lori L, child spt spec, $29,976
Brown, Anastasia, fam spt elig spc, $29,976
Brown, Andrea R, corres & info spec I, $34,944
Brown, Ariel R, fam spt elig spc, $29,976
Brown, Barbara M, fam spt elig spc, $29,976
Brown, Bianca N, youth spec II, $29,976
Brown, Cabot A, youth spec I, $29,496
Brown, Carral A, fam spt elig spc, $30,984
Brown, Cathy E, fam spt elig spc, $29,976
Brown, Christine M, soc servs mgr, band 1, $47,892
Brown, Christine M, child spt spec, $33,180
Brown, Constance R, children's serv worker I, $30,984
Brown, Cornelious, youth spec II, $33,744
Brown, Curtis L, youth spec II, $31,512
Brown, Gretchen, fam spt elig spc, $29,976
Brown, Hannah A, ofc spt asst (keybrd), $25,824
Brown, Idelia R, fam spt elig spc, $29,976
Brown, James, serv coor yth srvcs, $33,744
Brown, Jane E, fam spt elig spc, $29,976
Brown, Jeanine R, training tech II, $45,156
Brown, Jennifer R, children's serv worker II, $34,356
Brown, Joann B, sr ofc spt asst (keybrd), $27,084
Brown, Kelsey M, children's serv worker III, $36,888
Brown, Lajuanna M, corres & info spec I, $34,944
Brown, Lawrence E, youth spec II, $30,984
Brown, Lora K, research analyst III, $46,932
Brown, Lorena J, admin ofc spt asst, $28,536
Brown, Marilou R, fam spt elig spc, $29,976
Brown, Marjorie S, fam spt elig spc, $29,976
Brown, Mecha T, children's serv worker II, $34,356
Brown, Megan D, youth spec II, $30,984
Brown, Michele L, case analyst, $32,628
Brown, Michelle, soc servs mgr, band 1, $41,940
Brown, Michelle L, children's serv worker I, $29,976
Brown, Randa, fam spt elig spc, $29,976
Brown, Roberta S, child spt spec, $29,976
Brown, Sandra D, soc servs mgr, band 1, $41,940
Brown, Sandra S, children's serv spv, $39,624
Brown, Sheila, fam spt elig spc, $34,356
Brown, Sherry, fam spt elig spc, $29,976
Brown, Tanya L, ofc spt asst (keybrd), $23,160
Brown, Tassica L, children's serv worker III, $35,568
Brown, Terrolon S, soc servs mgr, band 1, $50,040
Brown, Vanessa, fam spt elig spc, $29,976
Brown, Vera J, prog dev spec, $42,708
Brown, Vincent M, acad tchr III, $36,204
Brown, Virginia, fam spt elig spc, $29,976
Brown-Hawkins, Debra L, child spt spec, $33,180
Browning, Amber, children's serv worker II, $34,356
Browning, Gabriel A, children's serv worker II, $34,356
Browning, Jane, child spt enforce spv, $38,232
Brown-Long, Marti D, children's serv worker III, $38,232
Bruce, Debra J, admin ofc spt asst, $29,976
Bruce, Lisa A, edu sup, $46,932

Bruce, Megan G, children's serv worker III, $36,888
Brueggemann, Barbara A, fam spt elig spc, $29,976
Bruemmer, Karrie L, child spt spec, $17,178
Bruffett, Zane L, youth spec II, $31,512
Brundage, Teresa L, acct I, $30,984
Bruner, Kristi L, fam spt elig spc, $29,976
Bruning, Paul D, youth spec II, $31,512
Brunner, Jennifer L, child spt spec, $29,976
Bruns, Devin H, children's serv worker II, $34,356
Bryan, Sarah E, children's serv worker III, $36,888
Bryant, Alexandra M, children's serv worker II, $34,356
Bryant, Aracelli J, fam spt elig spc, $32,052
Bryant, Breanna N, ofc spt asst (keybrd), $22,536
Bryant, Kenneth W, fam spt elig spc, $29,976
Bryant, Monica D, children's serv spv, $39,624
Bryant, Phyllis J, ofc spt asst (keybrd), $24,264
Bryant, Wendy A, fam spt elig spv, $34,944
Bryce, Michael R, youth group leader, $34,356
Bryson, Craig P, fam spt elig spc, $34,944
Bryson, Norma, fam spt elig spc, $29,976
Bubalo, Julia, child spt spec, $29,976
Buchanan-Reid, Annitta C, fam spt elig spc, $29,976
Bucher, Sara A, children's serv spv, $39,624
Buchheit, Joshua S, soc servs aide, $11.13/hr
Buchmeier, Nancy L, soc servs mgr, band 1, $45,156
Buck, Martha L, fam spt elig spc, $29,976
Buckallew, Emily R, children's serv worker III, $35,568
Buckles, Carol A, child spt spec, $34,356
Buckner, Naomi M, fam spt elig spc, $29,976
Buddemeyer, Gail M, fam spt elig spc, $29,976
Budnik, Marjorie J, children's serv spv, $39,624
Buechter, Carol A, exec I, $36,888
Buechter, Jeanne L, medicaid spec, $43,488
Buenaflor, Sunshine B, youth spec II, $31,512
Buersmeyer, Melody A, child spt spec, $29,976
Buettgenbach, Tiffany, area supv bus entprs blind, $36,204
Buffa, Henry A, youth spec II, $30,984
Buholt, Rose M, corres & info spec I, $36,204
Buhr, Karen J, acct II, $38,232
Bukaty, Grace F, fam spt elig spc, $29,976
Bullard, Kaitlyn L, hearings ofcr, $38,928
Bullock, Patricia, fam spt elig spv, $34,944
Bullock, Sharmain A, case analyst, $32,628
Bulluck, Kimberley S, fam spt elig spc, $33,180
Bunch, Brenda, fam spt elig spc, $30,984
Bundy, Nancy L, prog dev spec, $52,092
Bundy, Susan E, soc servs mgr, band 1, $46,812
Buntin, Sabrina M, fam spt elig spc, $29,976
Burbridge, Laura B, children's serv worker III, $36,888
Burch, Julia A, rehab tchr for the blind, $39,624
Burch, Penelope C, children's serv worker II, $34,356
Burchard, Michael D, youth group leader, $34,356
Burger, Karen J, medicaid spec, $37,548
Burgess, Justin C, youth spec I, $28,104
Burk, Amy L, child spt spec, $29,976
Burk, Devon P, youth spec II, $31,512
Burke, John M, youth spec II, $33,180
Burke, Shirley A, fam spt elig spv, $34,944
Burkhead, Tileta, fam spt elig spc, $29,976
Burkholder, Melinda A, fam spt elig spc, $30,984
Burks, Cindy L, special asst prof, $71,208
Burlingham, Teresa M, children's serv worker I, $30,984
Burnau, Alice A, fam spt elig spc, $29,976
Burnett, Amy L, children's serv spv, $38,232
Burnett, Peter F, acad tchr III, $37,548
Burnett, Shane A, youth spec II, $35,568
Burnham, Kimberly, medicaid spec, $37,548
Burns, Debbie J, soc servs mgr, band 1, $41,940
Burns, Geralyn M, fam spt elig spc, $29,976
Burrell, Eva B, ofc spt asst (keybrd), $23,880
Burrell, Pamela D, fam spt eligblty prg mg, $43,488
Burris, Pamela L, sr ofc spt asst (keybrd), $25,824
Burrow, Gina R, fam spt elig spc, $29,976
Burrow, Jill, fam spt elig spc, $29,976
Burton, Evelyn J, fam spt elig spc, $29,976
Burton, Nancy S, fam spt elig spc, $29,976
Burtrum, Kalisha D, children's serv worker II, $33,744
Bush, Clarissa V, investigator I, $30,984
Bush, Jackie L, soc servs aide, $11.13/hr

Bush, Kristy L, children's serv worker III, $35,568
Bushner, Lori A, registered nurse - clin opers, $54,720
Bushong, Marlie D, children's serv worker II, $34,356
Busken, Mark P, youth spec II, $31,512
Bussard, Anna M, case analyst, $31,512
Bussard, Kimberly, fam spt elig spc, $29,976
Busse, Linda, fam spt elig spc, $29,976
Bussone, Julie M, procurement ofcr II, $45,156
Butcher, Bridget A, fam spt elig spc, $29,976
Butler, Abbie L, fam spt elig spc, $35,568
Butler, Jackie L, ofc spt asst (keybrd), $23,160
Butler, Regina, fam spt elig spc, $29,976
Butler, Sally A, ofc spt asst (keybrd), $23,160
Butler, Viola J, acad tchr III, $37,548
Butts, Rebecca, account clerk II, $25,824
Bwashi, Adonis, youth spec I, $29,004
Bybee, Sara A, soc servs aide, $11.13/hr
Bynum, Lynn R, fam spt elig spc, $32,628
Byous, G. R, fam spt elig spc, $33,744
Byrd, Anthony, youth spec II, $33,180
Byrd, Genine Y, child spt spec, $29,976
Byrd, Keyana Q, children's serv worker II, $34,356
Byrne, Rebekah C, children's serv worker I, $30,984
Caddell, Justin W, youth spec II, $31,512
Caddell, Sheila R, cook II, $23,880
Cahalan, Thomas V, youth spec II, $31,512
Cain, Melissa V, exec I, $33,744
Cain, Robert B, soc servs mgr, band 1, $45,156
Calahan, John H, ofc spt asst (keybrd), $23,160
Caldwell, Patrick E, fam spt elig spv, $35,568
Caldwell, Tori M, children's serv worker I, $29,976
Caldwell, Travis K, youth spec II, $31,512
Caldwell, Veronica K, children's serv worker I, $29,976
Caldwell-Shelby, Belinda K, sr voc rehab cnslr f/t blind, $38,928
Calhoun, Jennifer R, fam spt elig spc, $29,976
Calhoun, Marsha L, children's serv worker III, $36,888
Calhoun, Vicki L, sr ofc spt asst (keybrd), $27,948
Callahan, Donna C, serv coor yth srvcs, $33,744
Callahan, Hillary N, children's serv worker III, $36,888
Callahan, Lori A, fam spt elig spc, $29,976
Callahan, Peni, child spt spec, $33,744
Callier, Sandra D, children's serv worker II, $34,356
Callihan, Bradley E, children's serv worker I, $32,628
Callihan, Victoria A, ofc spt asst (keybrd), $22,536
Calloway, Stephen M, special asst prof, $120,000
Calvert, Holly A, children's serv spv, $43,488
Calvert, Karen R, lpn II gen, $29,772
Camacho, Sherry M, children's serv worker II, $33,744
Cameron, Brooklyn M, fam spt elig spc, $29,976
Cameron, Karen J, fam spt elig spc, $29,976
Cameron, Matthew T, children's serv worker II, $34,356
Campbell, Cara R, children's serv worker II, $34,356
Campbell, Darwin L, misc tech, $20.00/hr
Campbell, Glenda L, fam spt elig spc, $34,356
Campbell, Gregory M, training tech II, $48,156
Campbell, Jana L, children's serv worker II, $32,628
Campbell, Jessica L, children's serv worker III, $36,888
Campbell, Kimberly S, youth spec II, $29,976
Campbell, Marjorie, ofc spt asst (keybrd), $23,160
Campbell, Melissa A, fam spt elig spv, $39,624
Campbell, Sharon L, cook III, $28,104
Campbell, Tonya S, children's serv worker II, $32,628
Campbell, Zachary C, youth spec I, $28,104
Camper, Kimberly S, children's serv worker I, $30,984
Canaday, Frances M, children's serv worker I, $29,976
Canania, Cheryl L, fam spt elig spc, $29,976
Cancel-Rodriguez, Eileen, children's serv worker II, $32,628
Candie, Karen A, children's serv spec, $42,708
Cannoles, Donelda S, cook II, $23,880
Cannon, Carol D, ofc spt asst (keybrd), $25,824
Cannon, Heather S, fam spt elig spc, $29,976
Cantrell, Brandi G, fam spt elig spc, $29,976
Cantrell, Douglas L, youth spec II, $32,052
Cantrell, Kenneth S, soc servs aide, $11.13/hr
Cantrell, Rachel N, children's serv worker II, $34,356
Cantwell, Bruce A, children's serv worker II, $34,356
Capes, James M, soc servs aide, $11.13/hr
Capps, David W, children's serv worker III, $36,888
Capps, Jennifer L, child spt spec, $31,512

Capriglione, Trisha M, fam spt elig spc, $29,976
Carantza, Debra T, child spt spec, $32,052
Cardin, Watha J, sr ofc spt asst (keybrd), $27,504
Cardona, Arlene, fam spt elig spc, $29,976
Cardoza, Gabrielle M, children's serv worker II, $34,356
Cardwell, James D, serv coor yth srvcs, $33,744
Carey, Brooke L, children's serv worker II, $34,356
Carey, Linda S, child spt spec, $30,984
Carlock, Golena, children's serv worker II, $34,356
Carney, James R, soc servs mngr, band 2, $75,948
Carpenter, Alyce M, children's serv spv, $44,304
Carpenter, Karla R, exec I, $30,984
Carpenter, Mary E, children's serv prog mgr, $48,156
Carpenter, Twyla M, ofc spt asst (keybrd), $23,160
Carr, Diamond V, youth spec II, $30,984
Carr, Dianne M, ofc spt asst (keybrd), $23,160
Carr, Donald D, soc servs mgr, band 1, $52,092
Carr, Sauda, fam spt elig spc, $29,976
Carriker, Edmond W, youth spec II, $31,512
Carriker, Sara A, children's serv worker II, $34,356
Carrington, Dana R, special asst prof, $45,456
Carroll, Anthony D, youth spec I, $29,004
Carroll, Brittani P, youth spec II, $30,984
Carroll, Jennifer L, fam spt elig spc, $29,976
Carson, Angela L, children's serv spv, $39,624
Carson, Wanda D, children's serv worker II, $32,628
Carsten, Brenda S, sr ofc spt asst (keybrd), $25,824
Carter, Alex R, fam spt elig spc, $29,004
Carter, Ann T, ofc spt asst (keybrd), $23,160
Carter, Brandi L, child spt spec, $29,976
Carter, Caitlin D, youth spec II, $30,984
Carter, Christine, fam spt elig spc, $29,976
Carter, Donna J, fam spt elig spc, $29,976
Carter, Jandra D, misc prof, $35.35/hr
Carter, Jessica L, fam spt elig spc, $29,976
Carter, Kathleen M, children's serv worker III, $36,888
Carter, Kelli M, children's serv worker II, $34,356
Carter, Megan E, youth spec II, $31,512
Carter, Rebecca J, child spt spec, $29,976
Carter, Rosalie, children's serv spv, $47,892
Carter, Tamara S, sr ofc spt asst (keybrd), $25,824
Carter, Virginia, fiscal & administrative mgr b1, $49,128
Cartwright, Morgan A, fam spt elig spc, $29,976
Carver, Carolyn, child spt spec, $33,744
Carver, Vickie S, fam spt elig spc, $29,976
Casad, Cameron M, legal counsel, $40,356
Case, Adam C, fam spt elig spv, $34,944
Case, Charles F, auditor II, $37,548
Caselman, Lacey M, fam spt elig spc, $29,976
Casey, Brandon J, fam spt elig spc, $29,976
Cash, Lisa D, fam spt elig spc, $29,976
Cassity, Diane M, child spt spec, $33,180
Cassmeyer, Elizabeth F, special educ tchr III, $37,548
Castanedo, Jennifer M, fam spt elig spc, $29,976
Casteel, Celesta J, medicaid clerk, $27,228
Castlebury, Christina I, fam spt elig spc, $29,976
Castor, Jami L, corres & info spec I, $34,944
Castorena, Delores M, youth spec II, $30,984
Castro, Terri A, lpn II gen, $29,772
Cathcart, Deanna K, fam spt elig spc, $29,976
Cathcart, Deborah, children's serv worker III, $36,888
Cato, Clifford N, youth spec I, $28,104
Catron, Grace B, fam spt elig spv, $34,944
Cauble, Rachel, fam spt elig spv, $33,744
Causbie, Ashley L, youth spec I, $28,104
Causey, Rhonda K, fam spt elig spc, $35,568
Cavin, David S, fam spt elig spc, $29,976
Cawdron, Kathryn A, rehab tchr for the blind, $34,944
Ceasor, Bernard, fam spt elig spv, $34,944
Cecil, Starla J, case analyst, $34,944
Ceplina, Melissa, fam spt elig spc, $29,976
Cepowski, Bertina, ofc spt asst (keybrd), $23,160
Cermak, Blythe S, fam spt elig spc, $29,976
Chadek, Kristi A, ofc spt asst (keybrd), $24,264
Chailland, Greg A, soc servs mngr, band 2, $61,332
Chalfant, Angela K, corres & info spec I, $34,944
Chalmers, Albert C, fam spt elig spc, $29,976
Chamberlain, Melody K, fam spt elig spc, $34,356
Chamberlain, Vallorie, fam spt elig spc, $31,512

Chambers, Becky M, youth group leader, $34,356
Chambers, Gia L, youth spec II, $32,628
Chamma, Barbara J, sr ofc spt asst (keybrd), $25,824
Chamma, Maher S, fiscal & administrative mgr b1, $43,488
Chance, Janice F, children's serv worker III, $41,940
Chandler, Brittney R, children's serv worker II, $34,356
Chandler, Jeanne M, fam spt elig spc, $34,356
Chandler, Joyce A, auditor I, $34,944
Chandler, Matthew W, librarian I, $29,976
Chaney, Laura M, child spt spec, $35,568
Channel, Latasha, children's serv worker III, $35,568
Chapin, Courtney R, hearings ofcr, $40,356
Chapman, Ashlee C, youth spec I, $28,104
Chapman, Donna K, youth spec II, $34,944
Chapman, Grant A, prog dev spec, $41,940
Chapman, Jason D, children's serv worker II, $34,356
Chapman, Jeannie, fam spt elig spc, $29,976
Chapman, Nygia C, fam spt elig spc, $29,976
Chappell, Annalee, children's serv worker II, $34,356
Charles, Brandi N, fam spt elig spc, $29,976
Charles, Renee' B, fam spt elig spc, $38,232
Charles, Shelia J, fam spt elig spv, $34,944
Charleville, Cheri Y, fam spt elig spc, $29,976
Chase, Nicholas I, fam spt elig spc, $29,976
Chastain, Rebecca A, ofc spt asst (keybrd), $26,232
Chatat, Jesse, youth spec I, $29,004
Chatman, Beckie L, corres & info spec I, $34,944
Chavis, Daryl, soc servs aide, $11.13/hr
Cheatham, C'ara L, children's serv worker II, $32,628
Cheek, Kalah C, youth spec I, $28,104
Cheek, Krista L, children's serv worker II, $32,628
Cheers, Danielle A, children's serv worker II, $34,356
Cherry, Paula M, children's serv prog mgr, $47,892
Chestnut, Dena D, children's serv worker II, $34,356
Childress, Gerald M, case analyst, $32,628
Childress, Richard J, legal counsel, $60,456
Childress, Tammy, fiscal & administrative mgr b2, $61,584
Childs, Alisha R, ofc spt asst (keybrd), $23,508
Chilton, Kristy, children's serv worker III, $36,888
Chism, Jennifer L, soc servs mgr, band 1, $43,488
Chism, Lara V, children's serv spv, $39,624
Chorice, Hayley C, youth spec II, $31,512
Chrisman, Elizabeth J, youth spec II, $31,512
Chrisman, Jeremy W, fam spt elig spv, $34,944
Christian, Amanda L, children's serv worker II, $34,356
Christian, Eileen, legal counsel, $52,920
Christian, John R, child spt spec, $29,976
Christian, Maryetta M, children's serv worker III, $38,232
Chrysostome, Ermise A, corres & info spec I, $34,944
Chumbley, Mary A, fam spt elig spc, $33,744
Chwascinski, Monica, children's serv worker II, $34,356
Cibulka, Barbara E, ofc spt asst (keybrd), $23,160
Cindrich, Angela S, serv coor yth srvcs, $33,744
Cizewski Baird, Nena, children's serv worker II, $34,356
Clancy, Tina, children's serv worker II, $34,356
Clapper, Ellen C, prog dev spec, $40,380
Clardy, Donna R, medicaid technician, $32,628
Clark, Claudia F, child spt enforce spv, $36,204
Clark, Courtney L, fam spt elig spc, $29,976
Clark, David D, youth spec II, $31,512
Clark, Deana L, special educ tchr III, $40,380
Clark, Denise L, ofc spt asst (keybrd), $23,160
Clark, Deyishia L, youth spec I, $29,004
Clark, Domenique T, children's serv worker II, $32,628
Clark, Freda M, fam spt elig spv, $36,888
Clark, Funtasia D, children's serv worker III, $35,568
Clark, H. W, soc servs mgr, band 1, $56,520
Clark, Jazmine M, youth spec II, $29,976
Clark, Kelly L, children's serv worker I, $29,976
Clark, Kristian R, children's serv worker II, $34,356
Clark, Lizabeth, child spt spec, $29,976
Clark, Lizzie, admin ofc spt asst, $29,004
Clark, Mary E, children's serv worker III, $41,172
Clark, Rosalind, fam spt elig spc, $29,976
Clark, Rose M, child spt spec, $29,976
Clark, Stacey D, youth spec II, $31,512
Clark, Suzanne W, corres & info spec I, $34,944
Clark, Tiffany E, children's serv worker III, $35,568
Clark, Tisha A, corres & info spec I, $33,744

Clark, Tonita S, children's serv worker II, $34,356
Clarkston, Renee B, children's serv worker III, $36,888
Clarridge, Amy E, children's serv spv, $39,624
Clay, Mary A, child spt spec, $29,976
Claycomb, Kimberly A, children's serv worker II, $34,356
Clayton, Martel J, youth group leader, $34,356
Cleek, Susan N, children's serv worker II, $33,744
Clement, Christy L, children's serv spv, $39,624
Clemons, Janet J, fam spt elig spc, $29,976
Clemons, Nancy A, fam spt elig spc, $33,180
Clemons, Rainier G, fam spt elig spc, $29,976
Clemons, Rebecca, fam spt elig spc, $29,976
Clemons, Sharon M, fam spt elig spc, $29,976
Clenney, Joseph W, youth group leader, $34,356
Cleveland, Margaret M, corres & info spec I, $36,888
Clevenger, Brady, sr voc rehab cnslr f/t blind, $38,928
Clifton, Lorena, fam spt elig spc, $29,976
Cline, Marye K, child spt spec, $29,976
Clingman, Brittany S, children's serv worker II, $32,628
Clinkenbeard, Johnna L, special educ tchr III, $38,928
Clinton, Heather, fam spt elig spc, $29,976
Clites, Kelley M, fam spt elig spc, $29,976
Cloninger, Mona, fam spt elig spc, $29,976
Close, Amy D, fam spt elig spc, $29,976
Cloutier, Tonia K, fam spt elig spc, $29,976
Cloyd, Kimberly K, youth spec II, $31,512
Clubb, Rebekah D, children's serv worker III, $35,568
Clyburn, Travis L, children's serv worker II, $34,356
Clyde, Michelle A, children's serv worker I, $30,984
Coates, Mitzi J, fam spt elig spc, $29,976
Cobb, Belinda G, ofc spt asst (keybrd), $23,160
Cobb, Callie L, corres & info spec I, $34,944
Cobb, Cory G, corres & info spec I, $34,944
Cobb, Holly A, ofc spt asst (keybrd), $23,508
Cobb, Ronnie L, corres & info spec I, $34,944
Cobbins, Andre D, children's serv worker II, $32,628
Coble, Tiffany L, children's serv worker I, $30,984
Cochran, Joy L, ofc spt asst (keybrd), $23,160
Cockrum, Janice K, cook II, $23,880
Cody, Brian D, cook III, $28,104
Cody, Nicholas T, youth fac mgr II, $40,380
Coe, Rebecca A, children's serv worker III, $36,888
Coffelt, Rebecca A, admin ofc spt asst, $28,536
Coffey, Karoline J, fam spt elig spc, $29,976
Coffey, Kasey A, children's serv worker II, $34,356
Coffey, Laura M, children's serv worker II, $33,180
Coffman, Marian L, youth spec II, $31,512
Coffman, Paula J, sr ofc spt asst (keybrd), $26,652
Coggeshall, Amanda E, children's serv worker II, $34,356
Cohan, Kevin M, youth spec II, $31,512
Coker, Anastasia E, children's serv worker II, $34,356
Colbert, Donna L, admin ofc spt asst, $33,180
Cole, Janet I, sr ofc spt asst (keybrd), $29,412
Cole, Margaret R, child spt spec, $31,512
Coleman, Crystal M, hearings ofcr, $45,132
Coleman, James A, youth group leader, $32,628
Coleman, Linda A, ofc spt asst (keybrd), $24,264
Coleman, Maida J, special asst prof, $121,200
Coleman, Shannon M, cook II, $23,880
Coleman, Sophia L, child spt spec, $32,628
Coleman, Staci N, children's serv spv, $41,172
Coleman, Tammy R, fam spt elig spc, $29,976
Coleman-Lobster, Edith M, ofc spt asst (keybrd), $25,404
Coley, Kara V, children's serv worker I, $30,984
Collamore, Jamie, ofc spt asst (keybrd), $23,160
Collida, Gina M, children's serv worker I, $29,976
Collier, Christopher C, youth spec II, $33,180
Collier, Courtney L, dpty div dir, $83,424
Collier, Darrick, youth spec II, $31,512
Collier, Linda F, child spt spec, $33,744
Collier, Terrance, children's serv worker II, $34,356
Collins, Christine E, fam spt elig spc, $29,976
Collins, Christy M, soc servs mgr, band 1, $52,092
Collins, Cynthia M, children's serv spec, $38,928
Collins, Dalyn P, children's serv worker I, $30,984
Collins, Daphane V, fam spt elig spc, $29,976
Collins, Frederica D, child spt spec, $29,976
Collins, Leon, corres & info spec I, $34,944
Collins, Lynette M, fam spt elig spc, $29,976

Collins, Roberta, fam spt elig spc, $29,976
Collins, Stacey E, children's serv worker I, $30,984
Collins, Tamara A, children's serv spv, $39,624
Collins, Tammy A, ofc spt asst (keybrd), $25,032
Collins, Yvette R, soc servs mgr, band 1, $41,940
Colvin, Carmon M, sr ofc spt asst (keybrd), $25,824
Comer, Jason E, soc servs mgr, band 1, $41,940
Comick, Doris, fam spt elig spc, $29,976
Compton, Rebecca L, fam spt elig spv, $34,944
Conboy, Tamara, children's serv spv, $40,380
Conboy-Renuard, Tracy A, youth spec II, $31,512
Coney, Sharon D, ofc spt asst (keybrd), $22,536
Conlee, Lea A, children's serv worker II, $34,356
Connell, Kelly A, medicaid spec, $37,548
Connell, Kimberly D, children's serv worker I, $29,976
Connelly, Alisa K, children's serv worker II, $34,356
Conner, Caitlin M, children's serv worker II, $34,356
Conner, Lori, fam spt elig spc, $29,976
Conner, Mary E, ofc spt asst (keybrd), $23,160
Conner, Melissa D, children's serv worker III, $36,888
Conner, Theresa D, fam spt elig spv, $42,708
Conway, Nichole M, special asst official & admstr, $50,040
Cook, Andre L, investigator II, $41,940
Cook, Ashley J, child spt spec, $29,976
Cook, Becky S, child spt spec, $33,180
Cook, Jennifer D, fam spt elig spc, $30,984
Cook, Joanie B, special asst ofc & clerical, $34,908
Cook, Katherine M, fam spt elig spc, $29,976
Cook, Keir S, youth spec II, $31,512
Cook, Leann M, children's serv spec, $46,068
Cook, Samantha N, soc servs mngr, band 2, $63,996
Cook, Scott A, fam spt elig spc, $29,976
Cook, Shelia, child spt spec, $29,976
Cook, Sherry R, fam spt elig spc, $33,744
Cook, Spring S, children's serv spv, $39,624
Cook, Teresa J, fam spt elig spc, $33,180
Cooley, Julia L, medicaid technician, $32,628
Cooley, Taunya J, serv coor yth srvcs, $38,232
Cooper, Clifton D, youth spec II, $31,512
Cooper, Diane M, children's serv spv, $45,156
Cooper, Janet L, fam spt elig spc, $30,984
Cooper, Melody D, fam spt elig spc, $33,744
Cooper, Shelia Y, soc servs mgr, band 1, $41,940
Cooper, Tanya R, corres & info spec I, $34,944
Coots, Brenda L, youth spec II, $37,548
Corbett, Christian M, children's serv worker II, $34,356
Corbin, Patricia G, ofc spt asst (keybrd), $25,404
Corcimiglia, Angela D, children's serv worker III, $39,624
Cordonnier, Michelle R, fam spt elig spv, $34,944
Corey, Phyllis C, fam spt elig spc, $29,976
Corley, Danielle N, soc servs mgr, band 1, $52,092
Cornelison, Penny S, ofc spt asst (keybrd), $23,160
Cornelius, Mary B, children's serv worker III, $36,888
Corpening, Candy S, fam spt elig spc, $31,512
Corrales, Donna L, child spt spec, $33,180
Cortvrient, Stephanie M, exec I, $29,976
Cosgrove, Jennifer, child spt spec, $29,976
Costerison, Brandon L, special asst prof, $42,744
Cotton, Gina L, fam spt elig spc, $32,628
Cotton, Renee A, fam spt elig spc, $34,356
Coulter, Heather M, fam spt elig spc, $29,976
Council, Jessica M, fam spt elig spc, $29,976
Counts, Deanna N, children's serv spv, $39,624
Counts, Kathleen M, admin ofc spt asst, $35,568
Court, Steven, fam spt elig spc, $33,180
Courtwright, Melvin E, hearings ofcr, $53,088
Cousins, Roland C, youth group leader, $32,628
Couts, Michael K, child spt enforce spv, $38,928
Cowan, Margie N, youth spec II, $31,512
Cowdry, Margaret E, fam spt elig spv, $38,232
Cox, Angela R, ofc spt asst (keybrd), $26,652
Cox, Ashli D, children's serv worker II, $34,356
Cox, Beth A, fam spt elig spv, $39,624
Cox, Casey L, children's serv worker III, $35,568
Cox, Derrick P, storekeeper I, $25,824
Cox, Jacqueline H, child spt spec, $29,976
Cox, Martha J, fam spt elig spv, $36,888
Cox, Melissa K, fam spt elig spc, $32,052
Cox, Sheena M, youth spec II, $31,512

Cox, Sheryl, special educ tchr III, $40,380
Cox, Tamara D, sr ofc spt asst (keybrd), $25,824
Coy, Danielle M, children's serv worker I, $29,976
Coyle, Sabra, ofc spt asst (keybrd), $23,160
Crader, Priscilla M, special educ tchr III, $38,928
Craft, Jessica M, sr ofc spt asst (keybrd), $25,032
Craft, Leonna L, children's serv worker I, $29,976
Craft, Thomas R, storekeeper I, $25,032
Craig, Donna R, ofc spt asst (keybrd), $24,612
Craig, Harold W, fam spt elig spc, $29,976
Craig, Kathryn, ofc spt asst (keybrd), $23,160
Craig, Trisha A, children's serv worker III, $35,568
Craig, Valerie, children's serv worker II, $34,356
Craighead, Deborah, ofc spt asst (keybrd), $23,160
Crain, Christina J, children's serv worker I, $31,512
Crain, Kenneth R, exec I, $30,984
Crane, Delia M, youth spec II, $31,512
Crane, Hollie C, children's serv worker III, $35,568
Crape-Williams, Bonita, fam spt elig spc, $29,976
Cravens, Heidi M, youth group leader, $34,944
Cravens-Purl, Crystal G, children's serv worker I, $29,976
Crawford, Deanna L, ofc spt asst (keybrd), $25,032
Crawford, Deardra E, youth group leader, $35,568
Crawford, Deborah L, fam spt elig spc, $33,180
Crawford, Kayla J, children's serv worker III, $38,232
Crawford, Lisa J, children's serv prog mgr, $43,488
Crawford, Ryan M, youth spec II, $30,984
Crawford, Susan K, sr ofc spt asst (steno), $15,192
Creason, Lindsay M, children's serv worker II, $34,356
Creek, Melissa A, prog dev spec, $40,380
Creekmore, Andrea R, child spt spec, $29,976
Creel, Thomas F, children's serv worker II, $33,744
Creson, John, soc servs mngr, band 2, $71,100
Cresswell, Janna S, ofc spt asst (keybrd), $23,160
Crews, Christine L, fam spt elig spc, $29,976
Crews, Sandra B, sr ofc spt asst (keybrd), $25,824
Crigler, Sue A, youth group leader, $34,356
Crimm, Sharkura K, fam spt elig spc, $30,420
Crisel, Myshena A, children's serv worker III, $36,888
Crist, Carole, children's serv spec, $44,304
Criswell, Erika F, fam spt elig spv, $34,944
Crites, Carol A, sr ofc spt asst (keybrd), $25,824
Crites, Vanita, fam spt elig spc, $31,512
Crocker, Beth K, corres & info spec I, $38,928
Crocker, Kathleen R, fam spt elig spc, $29,976
Crocker, Lisa C, soc servs mgr, band 1, $41,940
Crocker, Nancy J, soc servs mgr, band 1, $52,092
Crocker, Tara, children's serv spec, $37,548
Crone, Dennis J, child spt spec, $33,744
Cronin, Katherine C, sr voc rehab cnslr f/t blind, $38,928
Cropp, Rhonda, child spt spec, $33,180
Cross, Anthony J, hearings ofcr, $40,356
Cross, Rosanna, corres & info spec I, $34,944
Crossno, Gary E, soc servs aide, $11.13/hr
Crouch, Tamra J, child spt spec, $34,944
Crow, Lisa A, soc servs mgr, band 1, $43,488
Crowder, Charlotte M, ofc spt asst (keybrd), $23,160
Crowe, Christina, fam spt elig spc, $29,976
Crowe, Lacy M, fam spt elig spc, $29,976
Crowe, Sara, children's serv worker III, $36,888
Crowley, Rhonda J, ofc spt asst (keybrd), $23,160
Crowley, Sarah Y, fam spt elig spc, $29,976
Crowther, Glenn B, youth spec II, $29,976
Crull, Jennifer L, prog dev spec, $40,380
Crumer, Tiffany M, children's serv worker II, $34,356
Crump, Schylon L, fam spt elig spc, $29,976
Crunk, Coleen, sr ofc spt asst (keybrd), $25,824
Crusoe, Stephanie E, training tech II, $45,156
Crutcher, Terri A, children's serv spv, $45,156
Crutchfield, Aaron M, youth spec II, $31,512
Cruz, Kathryn D, children's serv worker II, $34,356
Cryts, Brenda, fam spt elig spc, $29,976
Culbertson, Dixie S, child spt spec, $31,512
Cullen, Heather M, youth spec II, $30,984
Cullen, Stephanie, children's serv worker I, $29,976
Cullers, Kelly D, soc servs mgr, band 1, $41,940
Culp, Stephanie, ofc spt asst (keybrd), $23,160
Culton, Sheila L, fam spt elig spc, $29,976
Cumings, Robin L, fam spt elig spc, $29,976

Cummings, Norvell, fam spt elig spc, $29,976
Cumpton, Kayla D, children's serv worker I, $30,984
Cumpton, Patricia A, ofc spt asst (keybrd), $23,160
Cunningham, Alyssa B, serv coor yth srvcs, $33,744
Cunningham, Christel M, children's serv worker III, $35,568
Cunningham, Cliff A, children's serv worker I, $29,976
Cunningham, Darla S, fam spt elig spv, $38,232
Cunningham, Jolene, child spt spec, $32,628
Cunningham, Melinda J, lpn II gen, $29,772
Cupples, Julie, child spt spec, $29,976
Cuppy, Tara G, child spt spec, $29,976
Curns, Akeem Q, children's serv worker I, $29,976
Curnutte, Christie M, children's serv worker II, $34,356
Curran, Melissa L, children's serv worker II, $34,356
Curran, Susan F, fam spt elig spc, $29,976
Currie, Krystal F, children's serv worker I, $29,976
Curry, Anita, ofc spt asst (keybrd), $24,264
Curry, Catheren M, children's serv worker I, $29,976
Curry, Elizabeth M, fam spt elig spv, $36,204
Curry, Esther R, ofc spt asst (keybrd), $23,160
Curry, Larue, fam spt elig spc, $29,976
Curry, Michelle L, soc servs mgr, band 1, $41,940
Curry, Rachelle D, soc servs mgr, band 1, $41,940
Curry, Ruth E, child spt spec, $29,976
Curtis, Jacqueline I, exec I, $32,628
Curtis, Leanna J, fam spt elig spc, $29,976
Curtis, Marcia, fam spt elig spc, $29,976
Curtis, Shana D, children's serv worker I, $30,984
Curtis, Tiffany N, youth spec II, $31,512
Custer, Cathy J, ofc spt asst (keybrd), $23,160
Custer, David R, soc servs mgr, band 1, $48,156
Cusumano, Ken D, corres & info spec I, $34,944
Cutler, Elizabeth N, child spt spec, $29,976
Cutler, Grada A, children's serv worker II, $35,568
Cypret, Terri, ofc spt asst (keybrd), $23,160
Czeschin, Ashley N, children's serv worker II, $34,356
Czuczejko, Jennifer S, children's serv worker III, $36,888
Dabney, Alfreda, fam spt elig spc, $34,356
Daen, Tania, children's serv worker II, $34,356
Dagenais, Kelly A, soc servs aide, $11.13/hr
Dahler, Lindsey N, medicaid pharmaceutical tech, $32,628
Dahn, Sherry D, child spt spec, $33,744
Dake, Mary L, child spt spec, $33,180
Dake, Stephanie A, medicaid technician, $32,628
Dake, Tina, administrative analyst II, $34,944
Dale, Dorothy J, child spt spec, $35,568
Dale, Karen S, cmnty svs coord-youth srvs, $43,488
Dale, Sandy, fam spt elig spc, $29,976
Dale, Susan A, children's serv worker III, $35,568
Dalessandro, Stephen A, prog dev spec, $40,380
Dalton, Dan J, soc servs mgr, band 1, $41,940
Dame, Opal S, children's serv worker III, $36,888
Damitz, Dana K, fam spt elig spc, $33,180
Damron, Arlene S, fiscal & administrative mgr b1, $50,916
D'angelo, Tecla, child spt spec, $32,628
Daniel, Ruby, ofc spt asst (steno), $29,904
Daniel Powell, Marty L, children's serv worker III, $40,380
Daniele, Patricia L, ofc spt asst (keybrd), $22,536
Daniels, Amber M, youth spec II, $30,984
Daniels, Freida L, ofc spt asst (keybrd), $23,508
Daniels, Karen F, fam spt elig spc, $29,976
Daniels, Ronda L, corres & info spec I, $39,624
Darby, Karen R, children's spec for the blind, $36,204
Darnell, Delbert D, youth spec II, $34,944
Daro, Cynthia J, cook III, $28,104
Daro, Terri L, sr ofc spt asst (keybrd), $28,908
Daskalakis, Alexander N, legal counsel, $43,000
Davenport, Chad D, youth fac mgr II, $40,380
Davenport, Ellen R, sr ofc spt asst (keybrd), $26,652
Davenport, Sara R, soc servs mngr, band 2, $63,996
Davidson, Nicole M, children's serv worker II, $34,356
Davidson, Shirley, sr ofc spt asst (keybrd), $25,032
Davies, Ann M, fam spt elig spc, $29,976
Davila, Amy N, children's serv worker II, $33,180
Davis, Abby L, children's serv worker II, $34,356
Davis, Amber, fam spt elig spc, $29,976
Davis, Anita R, fam spt elig spc, $29,976
Davis, Ashton R, children's serv worker I, $30,984
Davis, Bobbie L, fam spt elig spc, $33,180

Davis, Brandy K, fam spt elig spc, $29,976
Davis, Brittany, child spt spec, $29,976
Davis, Chad R, voc rehab cslr f/t blin, $34,944
Davis, Cherrie K, children's serv worker II, $33,180
Davis, Christina K, fiscal & administrative mgr b2, $61,584
Davis, Corrina A, fam spt elig spc, $29,976
Davis, Deanna J, youth spec II, $31,512
Davis, Debora L, fam spt elig spc, $29,976
Davis, Dee A, soc servs mgr, band 1, $47,892
Davis, Deneen, child spt spec, $29,976
Davis, Donnell R, youth spec II, $32,052
Davis, Ebonie S, reg fam spec, $36,204
Davis, Edith, child spt spec, $32,052
Davis, Elaine, ofc spt asst (keybrd), $24,264
Davis, Erica, fam spt elig spc, $29,976
Davis, Faydreia D, child spt enforce spv, $35,568
Davis, Heather L, youth spec II, $31,512
Davis, Jennifer, children's serv spv, $39,624
Davis, Jessica, children's serv worker III, $36,888
Davis, Jina D, case analyst, $32,628
Davis, Joshua F, youth spec II, $29,976
Davis, Julie C, children's serv worker II, $34,356
Davis, Kelly M, youth spec II, $30,984
Davis, Ki-Yonna L, youth group leader, $34,356
Davis, Kolin J, mgmt analysis spec I, $38,928
Davis, Kyle D, fam spt elig spc, $29,976
Davis, Lakeitha J, fam spt elig spc, $29,976
Davis, Latanya Y, corres & info spec I, $33,744
Davis, Laura A, fam spt elig spc, $34,944
Davis, Lucille, child spt spec, $29,976
Davis, Nicole L, children's serv spv, $39,624
Davis, Rick L, children's serv spec, $49,128
Davis, Rochelle L, admin ofc spt asst, $29,496
Davis, Ryan L, youth spec II, $29,976
Davis, Ryan W, fam spt elig spc, $29,976
Davis, Sandra R, fam spt elig spv, $38,232
Davis, Shana M, children's serv worker III, $35,568
Davis, Sherry L, investigator II, $37,548
Davis, Shomica L, children's serv worker II, $34,356
Davis, Shonnisha D, children's serv worker I, $29,976
Davis, Stacey J, youth spec II, $29,976
Davis, Stacy L, corres & info spec I, $34,944
Davis, Steven L, fam spt elig spc, $29,976
Davis, Summer D, ofc spt asst (keybrd), $23,160
Davis, Tausha J, child spt spec, $29,976
Davis, Timothy J, children's serv worker I, $29,976
Davis, Tonette, fam spt elig spc, $30,984
Davis, Tracey, fam spt elig spc, $29,976
Davis, Yolanda L, children's serv worker II, $34,356
Davolt, Shelly A, exec I, $30,984
Dawes, Angela M, children's serv worker II, $32,628
Dawkins, Karen L, fam spt elig spc, $29,976
Dawson, Conni L, children's serv worker II, $35,568
Dawson, Marianne A, soc servs mgr, band 1, $52,092
Dawson, Meghan L, children's serv worker I, $29,976
Dawson, Regina V, exec I, $30,984
Day, Mallory A, children's serv worker I, $29,976
Day, Molly E, soc servs aide, $11.13/hr
Day, Stephanie R, children's serv worker II, $34,356
Day, Steve D, child spt spec, $33,744
Days, Joann H, child spt spec, $29,976
De La Rocha, Carolina D, medicaid pharmaceutical tech, $32,628
Deaguero, Janet K, fam spt elig spc, $32,628
Dean, Thomas L, children's serv worker II, $32,628
Dearing-Buehrer, Kellie D, children's serv spv, $45,156
Deason, Glenda R, soc servs mgr, band 1, $49,128
Deason, Sarah B, fam spt elig spc, $29,976
Deatherage, Amber M, fam spt elig spc, $29,976
Debold, Kristin D, children's serv worker I, $29,976
Deckard, Crystal M, children's serv spv, $41,172
Deckard, Julie, sr ofc spt asst (keybrd), $27,084
Decker, Kathleen M, youth spec II, $30,984
Decker, Timothy J, div dir, $98,784
Declue, Robert D, soc servs mgr, band 1, $49,128
Dee, Jennifer L, child spt spec, $16,590
Defreece, Mary S, fam spt elig spc, $32,628
Degaris, Donna L, special educ tchr III, $40,380
Degeare, Cynthia L, fam spt elig spc, $29,976
Degeare, Sheila A, corres & info spec I, $34,944

Degonia, Leola D, children's serv worker I, $29,976
Degonia, Tammy R, fam spt elig spc, $31,512
Degraw, Amy D, children's serv worker II, $34,356
Dehart, Johnna G, children's serv worker II, $34,356
Deimeke, Gwen M, edu sup, $46,068
Deken, Margaret A, fam spt elig spv, $38,232
Del Percio, Marc M, fam spt elig spc, $29,976
Delana, Janet S, fam spt elig spc, $33,180
Delaney, Charles, children's serv worker II, $34,356
Delap, Shannon P, children's serv worker I, $31,512
Delcour, Candi, children's serv worker I, $29,976
Delfino, Megan, children's serv worker I, $30,984
Deluca, Crystal J, serv coor yth srvcs, $33,744
Demasters, Cheryl S, ofc spt asst (keybrd), $23,160
Dempsey, David, fam spt elig spc, $29,976
Dempsey, Mary V, soc servs mgr, band 1, $46,932
Dempster, Teri A, child spt spec, $30,984
Demsko, Ethan G, sr ofc spt asst (keybrd), $25,824
Demsko, Lauren E, ofc spt asst (keybrd), $22,536
Demyers, Mary A, youth spec II, $31,512
Denham, Amanda, children's serv worker II, $34,356
Denk, Rhonda L, fam spt elig spv, $34,944
Denman, Shirlene K, children's serv worker III, $36,888
Dennis, Angela R, sr ofc spt asst (keybrd), $27,948
Dennis, Gwinn A, children's serv worker II, $34,356
Dennis, Kim A, child spt spec, $32,052
Dennis, Lucinda P, fam spt elig spc, $29,976
Dennison, Theresa L, children's serv worker II, $34,356
Dent, William T, special asst prof, $71,208
Denti, Debra A, child spt spec, $29,976
Denton, Martha J, child spt spec, $30,984
Depew, Sandy, children's serv worker II, $34,356
Derousse, Rebecca D, cook II, $11,940
Derra, Erika L, acad tchr III, $41,172
Deshazo, Cherie J, fam spt elig spv, $38,232
Deskins, Heather K, child spt spec, $30,984
Desravines, Sheevenson M, children's serv worker II, $34,356
Detienne, Christine N, mgmt analysis spec II, $48,156
Dettmann, Gladys G, account clerk II, $25,032
Devries, Arthur D, children's serv spec, $44,304
Dewein, Kathryn M, psychologist I, $66,720
Dewesplore, Leslie A, child spt spec, $29,976
Dial, Beth, fam spt elig spc, $29,976
Dicicco, Summer D, fam spt elig spc, $29,976
Dick, Anginette, exec II, $37,548
Dickensheet, Katherine A, children's serv spv, $39,624
Dickerson, Leesa M, fam spt elig spc, $29,976
Dickey, Deborah L, corres & info spec I, $34,944
Dickey, Shelby J, children's serv worker I, $29,976
Dickinson, Mary P, children's serv worker III, $36,888
Dickson, Sarah E, children's serv worker I, $29,976
Dicus, Crystal N, children's serv worker II, $34,356
Dicus, Katie, ofc spt asst (keybrd), $22,536
Diebal, Donna S, youth spec II, $31,512
Dieckmeyer, Jim R, fam spt elig spc, $33,180
Diekemper, Jenny L, children's serv worker II, $32,628
Diemler, Stephen C, mgmt analysis spec II, $46,932
Diercks, Charlie C, ofc spt asst (keybrd), $22,536
Dierker, Karen S, fam spt elig spc, $29,976
Dierker, Stephanie I, children's serv spv, $41,172
Dierkes, David L, fam spt elig spc, $29,976
Dietrich, Martha L, children's serv worker II, $34,356
Diffenderfer, Samantha K, children's serv worker II, $32,628
Diffey, John M, reg fam spec, $37,548
Diggs, Edward D, youth spec II, $29,976
Diggs, Mellisa K, ofc spt asst (keybrd), $23,160
Dill, Samantha J, children's serv worker II, $32,628
Dillon, Erica, fam spt elig spc, $29,976
Dillon, Michelle R, children's serv worker II, $34,356
Dillon, Tammy L, admin ofc spt asst, $28,536
Dillon, Wendy M, fam spt elig spc, $32,052
Dimaggio, Frank V, hearings ofcr, $42,708
Dimmock, Cheryl, ofc spt asst (keybrd), $25,032
Dinwiddie, Kathryn M, medicaid unit spv, $46,932
Dinwiddie, Kimberly D, children's serv worker III, $35,568
Dinwiddie, Mary D, fam spt elig spc, $34,944
Dippold, Melinda K, children's serv worker II, $33,180
Dishman, Pamela J, sr ofc spt asst (keybrd), $27,948
Distler, Julie D, registered nurse - clin opers, $56,976

Dittmann, Megan L, legal counsel, $52,500
Dixon, Javon, youth spec II, $31,512
Dixon, Kathleen, ofc spt asst (keybrd), $23,160
Dixon, Michelle L, children's serv spec, $39,624
Dixon, Rickey L, youth spec II, $35,568
Dixon, Ronald L, youth spec II, $31,512
Dixon, Shane M, youth spec II, $30,984
Dixson, Suzette, fam spt elig spc, $29,976
Dlouhy, Rhonda S, soc servs mgr, band 1, $52,104
Dobbins, Desirae L, fam spt elig spc, $29,976
Dobbs, Rebecca, child spt spec, $29,976
Dobson, Angela D, fam spt elig spc, $32,628
Docherty, Sheila L, children's serv worker II, $34,356
Dockery, Brianna, children's serv worker III, $35,568
Dockett, Angela, children's serv prog mgr, $47,892
Dodge, April S, children's serv spv, $39,624
Dodson, Brenda K, corres & info spec I, $38,232
Dodson, Terri, fam spt elig spc, $29,976
Dodson, Tommy W, fam spt elig spv, $34,944
Doerr, Darren K, fam spt elig spc, $29,976
Dolan, Lucinda K, children's serv worker III, $38,928
Dolce, Heather A, special asst prof, $39,900
Dolezal, Shelby L, children's serv worker I, $30,984
Dollins, Angela M, youth spec II, $30,984
Dominique, Jennifer L, child spt spec, $29,976
Donnell, Natalie N, children's serv worker I, $30,984
Donnelly, Amanda N, children's serv spv, $37,548
Donovan, Rita L, child spt spec, $29,976
Donson, Angel, children's serv worker III, $35,568
Donze, Lisa A, exec II, $36,204
Dooley, Barbara J, child spt spec, $29,976
Dooley, Ryan P, investigator II, $37,548
Dopuch, David A, soc servs mgr, band 1, $50,040
Doran, Pamela J, youth spec II, $31,512
Dorris, Garry L, children's serv spv, $39,624
Dortch, Roy D, outdoor rehab cnslr I, $34,944
Dotson, Autry A, fam spt elig spc, $34,356
Douglas, Brittney E, children's serv worker II, $34,356
Douglas, Deborah J, fam spt elig spc, $29,976
Douglas, Janet L, prog dev spec, $40,380
Douglas, Johnny, child spt spec, $33,180
Douglas, Stephanie L, fam spt elig spc, $33,180
Douglas, Tamara O, youth spec I, $28,104
Douglas, Virginia, fam spt elig spc, $29,976
Douglass, Amber D, youth spec II, $29,976
Dove, Diane K, fam spt elig spc, $35,568
Dove, Mary L, fam spt elig spc, $34,356
Dowd, Kimberly, special asst prof, $49,440
Dowell, Verline, youth spec II, $31,512
Downey, Laura E, fam spt elig spc, $29,976
Doxley, Ivy C, training tech II, $41,940
Doyle, Kimberly A, fam spt elig spc, $29,976
Doyle, Susan E, soc servs mgr, band 1, $47,892
Draisey, Brandon T, children's serv worker II, $32,628
Drake, Gwendolyn, child spt spec, $33,744
Drake, Pamela S, children's serv worker III, $35,568
Drane, Deborah, fam spt elig spc, $29,976
Draper, Patricia K, children's serv worker III, $36,888
Draude, James F, soc servs aide, $11.13/hr
Drayton, Phyllis L, fam spt elig spc, $33,180
Dresner, Jessica E, designated principal asst dept, $83,424
Driskell, Kathleen L, corres & info spec I, $34,944
Driver, Dena D, children's serv spec, $49,128
Driver, Rhonda A, dpty div dir, $153,216
Dubois, Jennifer, fam spt elig spc, $29,976
Dubois, Natalie, sr ofc spt asst (keybrd), $25,824
Dubose, James R, youth group leader, $34,356
Ducich, Valynda M, child spt spec, $29,976
Duddy, Nichole M, children's serv worker II, $34,356
Dudenhoeffer, Meghan J, child spt spec, $29,976
Dudley, Tyler Y, youth spec I, $28,104
Duemmel, Traci L, ofc spt asst (keybrd), $23,160
Duenne, Christopher R, children's serv worker II, $33,744
Duewell, Carissa A, medicaid spec, $37,548
Duffin, Tammy L, youth spec II, $31,512
Dugan, Allison M, ofc spt asst (steno), $27,504
Dugan, Frances D, child spt enforce spv, $35,568
Duis, Bryce N, children's serv worker III, $35,568
Duke, Cindy L, fam spt elig spc, $29,976

Duke, Jansen D, children's serv worker III, $36,888
Dumala, Therese, ofc spt asst (keybrd), $22,536
Dumers, Deana A, sr ofc spt asst (keybrd), $32,472
Duncan, Cheryl E, fam spt elig spc, $29,976
Duncan, Karen S, child spt enforce spv, $40,380
Duncan, Lindsey A, children's serv worker I, $30,984
Dunford, Diane K, fam spt elig spc, $32,628
Dunham, Shannon, fam spt elig spc, $29,976
Dunkin, Michael A, youth spec II, $31,512
Dunkle, Patricia, youth spec II, $33,744
Dunlap, Angela L, sr ofc spt asst (keybrd), $28,452
Dunn, Amy J, children's serv worker II, $34,944
Dunn, Jennifer, fam spt elig spc, $29,976
Dunn, Marcia R, children's serv worker I, $29,976
Dunn, Monty S, fam spt elig spc, $30,984
Dunnegan, Marcia A, prog dev spec, $45,156
Dunning, Cynthia L, fam spt elig spc, $29,976
Dunston, Corey M, youth spec II, $29,004
Dunwoody, Rachael L, prog dev spec, $40,380
Dupree, Gwendolyn W, children's serv spv, $39,624
Durland, Rachael R, children's serv worker III, $35,568
Durran, Amanda, fam spt elig spv, $34,944
Dusky, Ronette, lpn II gen, $31,248
Dutcher, Hayley A, fam spt elig spv, $34,944
Duym, Deirdre L, children's serv worker I, $30,984
Dydell, Aisha M, serv coor yth srvcs, $33,744
Dyer, Audrey L, children's serv worker II, $33,744
Dyer, Cathy J, children's serv worker II, $34,356
Dyer, Lauren M, hearings ofcr, $41,940
Dyer, Shelby L, children's serv worker I, $30,984
Dykes, Deborah J, fam spt elig spc, $29,976
Dykes, Jeff L, fam spt elig spc, $29,976
Dykstra, Anita D, ofc spt asst (keybrd), $26,232
Dyle, Timothy R, fam spt elig spc, $29,976
Ealey, Raymond E, reg cnslt resid lcsng unit, $52,092
Earley, Angela M, youth spec II, $31,512
Easter, Burke E, youth spec II, $31,512
Easter, Richard B, child spt spec, $29,976
Easterhouse, Leslie A, acad tchr III, $37,548
Eaton, Karla O, fam spt elig spc, $34,944
Eaves, Courtney E, ofc spt asst (keybrd), $23,160
Ebersold, Logan D, youth spec II, $31,512
Ebert, Alaina J, children's serv worker II, $33,180
Ebling, Shannon M, fam spt elig spc, $29,976
Ebling, Tracy L, corres & info spec I, $35,568
Ebrecht, Chandra N, children's serv worker II, $32,628
Ebrite, Deann, soc servs mgr, band 1, $41,940
Echelberry, Adrienne L, children's serv worker I, $29,976
Eck, Cheryl A, ofc spt asst (keybrd), $23,160
Eckert, Jessica A, children's serv worker I, $29,976
Eckert, Tiffany L, children's serv worker I, $29,976
Eckhoff, Jennifer L, children's serv worker III, $36,204
Eddings, Alexander S, youth spec I, $28,104
Eddings, Letisha N, child spt spec, $29,976
Eddy, Jason L, mgmt analysis spec I, $37,548
Eddy, Paula D, corres & info spec I, $34,944
Ederer, Stacey L, soc servs mgr, band 1, $56,064
Edgar, Leeanna C, fam spt elig spc, $34,356
Edgeller, Carol A, fam spt elig spc, $34,356
Edgeston, Karen, corres & info spec I, $35,568
Edgin, Melissa L, fam spt elig spc, $29,976
Edmond, Michele D, ofc spt asst (keybrd), $23,160
Edmonds, Melinda E, fam spt elig spc, $29,976
Edwards, Chanee S, children's serv worker I, $29,976
Edwards, Christopher L, youth spec II, $31,512
Edwards, Claudia M, fam spt elig spc, $33,180
Edwards, Debbie M, fam spt elig spc, $30,984
Edwards, Jennifer A, child spt spec, $29,976
Edwards, Kenneth L, medicaid technician, $32,628
Edwards, Yulonda N, fam spt elig spc, $29,976
Eggebrecht, Jon W, youth group leader, $34,356
Eggers, Teri A, fam spt elig spc, $34,944
Eggert, Iva A, corres & info spec I, $34,356
Ehlers, Kelsey M, children's serv worker I, $29,976
Ehrhardt, Amy B, children's serv worker II, $35,568
Ehrhardt, Ellen A, research analyst III, $44,304
Eikerman, Patricia D, fam spt elig spc, $32,628
Eisenberg, Deborah A, fam spt elig spc, $33,744
Eissinger, Richard E, child spt enforce spv, $33,744

Elam, Jessica, ofc spt asst (keybrd), $23,160
Elam, Linda M, soc servs mgr, band 1, $41,940
Eldred, Joseph P, youth spec II, $31,512
Eldridge-Phillips, Markelia S, children's serv worker III, $36,888
Eldringhoff, Jennifer L, acad tchr III, $37,548
Eleby, Kenyatta L, children's serv worker II, $34,356
Elfrink, Brooke K, children's serv worker II, $33,180
Elge, Elizabeth V, children's serv worker I, $30,984
Elicke, Jeanelle C, children's serv worker I, $29,976
Ellard, Judith L, ofc spt asst (keybrd), $25,032
Eller, Elizabeth M, children's serv worker II, $35,568
Ellington, Mark E, youth spec II, $31,512
Elliott, Mary J, child spt spec, $29,976
Elliott, Pam, ofc spt asst (keybrd), $23,160
Elliott, Sherry S, sr ofc spt asst (steno), $26,652
Elliott, Tonya S, corres & info spec I, $34,944
Elliott, Twilla, ofc spt asst (keybrd), $23,160
Ellis, Felicia R, fam spt elig spc, $29,976
Ellison, Debra L, fam spt elig spc, $29,976
Ellison, Megan L, fam spt elig spc, $29,976
Ellsworth, Alyssa M, children's serv worker III, $35,568
Elmore, Allyssa L, children's serv worker II, $32,628
Elrod, Dirk B, procurement ofcr II, $52,092
Elsenraat, Chelsey M, children's serv worker I, $29,976
Elwood, Nathan, student intern, $14.65/hr
Emehiser, Roger E, ofc spt asst (keybrd), $23,160
Emerick, Scott A, fam spt elig spc, $29,976
Emery, Sherri M, fam spt elig spc, $29,976
Emmons, Jennifer N, children's serv spv, $39,624
Endicott, Victoria L, child spt spec, $29,976
Engel, Thomas F, fam spt elig spc, $36,888
Engelbrecht, Kristy K, fam spt elig spc, $29,976
Engelbrecht, Roseann, medicaid spec, $46,932
Engelhardt, Velvet A, fam spt elig spc, $29,976
Engelhart, Rose M, child spt spec, $33,744
Englert, Sherry A, acad tchr III, $37,548
English, Belinda J, corres & info spec I, $34,944
Enloe, Shannon E, fam spt elig spc, $29,976
Ent, Cherie D, children's serv worker II, $34,356
Entrikin, Marilyn A, ofc spt asst (keybrd), $23,160
Epley, Crystal R, children's serv spv, $39,624
Epley, Lori D, children's serv spv, $39,624
Epperson, Courtney N, fam spt elig spc, $29,976
Epperson, Lisa L, clerical servs spv fs, $32,628
Epperson, Paula, children's serv worker I, $30,984
Epple, Kenneth J, special educ tchr III, $44,304
Erb, Angela R, serv coor spv yth srvcs, $43,488
Erickson, Jeri R, child spt spec, $29,976
Erwin, Melissa A, soc servs sup, $37,548
Escobar, Brittany N, children's serv worker I, $29,976
Eshenroder, Barbara A, children's serv spec, $51,096
Eshenroder, Linda A, child spt spec, $29,976
Essary, Bonita J, corres & info spec I, $33,744
Essary, Michelle D, fam spt elig spv, $37,548
Essenpries, Tiffany L, children's serv spec, $37,548
Eston, Pauletta F, fam spt elig spc, $30,984
Etter, Lisa A, children's serv worker II, $34,356
Euler, Kaleeah, hearings ofcr, $43,500
Eustace, Hilary L, children's serv worker I, $29,976
Evans, Anita C, ofc spt asst (keybrd), $23,160
Evans, Anita G, soc servs aide, $11.13/hr
Evans, Anita G, cook II, $11,940
Evans, Christine J, youth spec I, $29,004
Evans, Cynthia M, fam spt elig spc, $29,976
Evans, David A, fam spt elig spv, $34,944
Evans, Hannah E, youth spec II, $31,512
Evans, Kim R, dpty div dir, $83,424
Evans, Lisa, sr ofc spt asst (keybrd), $25,824
Evans, Marilyn A, children's serv worker III, $37,548
Evans, Rocky E, fam spt elig spc, $40,380
Evans, Susan J, children's serv spv, $48,156
Evans, Terry, youth spec II, $31,512
Evans, Terry M, youth spec II, $31,512
Evans, Tiffany L, fam spt elig spc, $29,976
Evans, Toni L, children's serv spv, $39,624
Eveland, Cody T, youth spec II, $30,984
Everett, Lori A, investigator II, $37,548
Everette, Glenda M, fam spt elig spc, $29,976
Everitt, Lisa, child spt spec, $30,420

Evers, Cynthia A, medicaid spec, $37,548
Evers, Heather E, exec I, $30,984
Evers, Joann D, account clerk II, $29,412
Ewald, Beverly F, fam spt elig spc, $29,976
Ewing, Shannon R, child spt spec, $31,512
Ezell, Melissa S, children's serv worker III, $36,888
Fahs, Jennifer A, children's serv worker II, $34,356
Fairbanks, Amanda L, children's serv worker III, $36,888
Fairchild, Angela D, children's serv worker II, $34,356
Fall, Cora, fam spt elig spc, $29,976
Falls, Linda M, soc servs worker, $17.07/hr
Fancher, Angela K, fam spt elig spc, $31,512
Farley, Kathleen E, fam spt elig spc, $29,976
Farmar, Renee M, children's serv spec, $46,068
Farmer, Charlie L, fam spt elig spc, $29,976
Farmer, Samantha R, children's serv spv, $39,624
Farmer, Sean T, children's serv worker I, $30,984
Farrar, Patricia, child spt enforce spv, $34,944
Farris, Donna, soc servs mgr, band 1, $41,940
Farris, Jan D, children's serv worker II, $34,356
Farris, Marilyn F, fam spt elig spc, $29,976
Farthing, Samantha L, fiscal & administrative mgr b1, $49,440
Faucett, Seth L, serv coor yth srvcs, $33,744
Faust, Kevin R, special asst official & admstr, $83,424
Favors, Tionna M, children's serv worker II, $32,628
Fazenbaker, Camilla S, fam spt elig spc, $29,976
Fechtig, Barbara A, corres & info spec I, $34,944
Fehring, Kelsey L, fam spt elig spc, $29,976
Feldman, Jill D, child spt spec, $29,976
Fels, Susan L, children's serv worker III, $35,568
Fennewald, Dan D, children's serv worker II, $34,356
Fennewald, Lauren R, sr ofc spt asst (keybrd), $25,032
Fenske, Donna M, soc servs mgr, band 1, $42,708
Fenske, Laura M, fam spt elig spc, $30,420
Fenster, Paul S, fam spt elig spc, $34,356
Fenton, Regina, children's serv worker III, $35,568
Ferenczi, Zseraldina K, children's serv worker II, $34,356
Ferguson, Brian J, fam spt elig spc, $29,976
Ferguson, Charlecia, corres & info spec I, $34,944
Ferguson, Haley M, children's serv worker I, $29,976
Ferrari, Richard S, investigator III, $41,940
Ferreira, Ronni D, soc servs aide, $11.13/hr
Ferrell, Andrea L, ofc spt asst (keybrd), $23,160
Ferrell, Mark K, soc servs mgr, band 1, $41,940
Fible, Cheryl L, youth spec I, $29,496
Fick, Wilma, prog dev spec, $46,932
Fiddler, Kimberly, children's serv worker II, $34,356
Fields, Chondeice D, serv coor yth srvcs, $37,548
Fields, Cynthia E, child spt spec, $33,744
Fields, Valerie V, children's serv prog mgr, $48,156
Fifer, Judi L, acct III, $41,940
Figueroa, Santana M, children's serv worker I, $30,984
Finafrock, Lesley L, fam spt elig spc, $29,976
Fincher, Jill N, children's serv spv, $39,624
Fincher, Leslie A, soc servs mgr, band 1, $44,304
Fincher, Lindsey R, children's serv worker II, $34,356
Findley, Kara M, fam spt elig spc, $29,976
Findley, Kelsey J, children's serv worker III, $36,888
Findling, Laurie A, prog dev spec, $40,380
Finklang, Shelby D, youth spec II, $31,512
Finley, Julia S, child spt spec, $31,512
Finley, Lisa Y, children's serv worker III, $36,888
Finley, Timothy D, children's serv spv, $41,172
Finney, D'oreal N, child spt spec, $29,976
Firth, Nicole A, children's serv worker II, $33,744
Fischer, Edward R, children's serv worker II, $34,356
Fischer, Kenneth J, fam spt elig spc, $33,180
Fischer, Melissa N, child spt spec, $29,976
Fischer, Natalie D, children's serv spv, $39,624
Fischer, Tracy D, children's serv worker II, $34,356
Fischer, Walt, special asst prof, $62,316
Fish, Tamara L, children's serv worker I, $29,976
Fishel, Deana, child spt spec, $29,976
Fisher, Alana, children's serv worker III, $35,568
Fisher, Amber K, lpn II gen, $29,772
Fisher, Casey B, youth group leader, $34,356
Fisher, Debra K, fam spt elig spc, $32,628
Fisher, Landon N, children's serv worker II, $34,356
Fisher, Sybil D, children's serv worker II, $34,356

Fisher, Tanya G, children's serv worker II, $34,356
Fisher, Theresa M, children's serv spv, $39,624
Fisher, Walter H, soc servs aide, $11.13/hr
Fitzgerald, Jessica E, children's serv worker III, $35,568
Fitzgerald, Kathryn S, children's serv worker III, $36,888
Fitzmaurice, Patricia S, fam spt elig spc, $29,976
Fitzpatrick, Brian K, youth spec II, $31,512
Flanigan, Christopher A, youth spec II, $35,568
Flaugher, Krista G, ofc spt asst (keybrd), $23,160
Flaugher, Natasha N, children's serv worker III, $35,568
Fleischer, Bruce A, children's serv worker II, $34,356
Fleming, Melissa A, youth spec II, $31,512
Flemons, Dominic T, fam spt elig spc, $29,976
Flenthrope, Gary D, children's serv spv, $39,624
Flesher, Susan L, fam spt elig spc, $36,204
Fletcher, Deborah L, prog dev spec, $40,380
Fletcher, Denise, child spt spec, $29,976
Fletcher, Sarah E, children's serv worker III, $36,888
Flint, Devree, youth spec II, $31,512
Flood, Amanda L, children's serv worker I, $30,984
Flores, Jessica C, youth spec II, $31,512
Florian, Lisa D, child spt spec, $29,976
Flowers, Jason L, fam spt elig spc, $29,976
Flowers, Sherry M, youth spec II, $31,512
Flynn, Michael N, training tech II, $40,380
Fobbs, Angela, fam spt elig spc, $29,976
Foerstel, Douglas L, cook III, $28,104
Foerster, Laura A, soc servs mgr, band 1, $47,052
Foerster, Thomas J, children's serv worker III, $36,888
Folks, Shari D, children's serv worker II, $34,356
Follins, Wynetta, cook III, $28,104
Fontenot, Lakeysha R, children's serv worker III, $36,888
Foote, Stephanie S, children's serv spv, $37,548
Forbeck, Sarah M, youth spec I, $28,104
Forbes, Judy K, acad tchr III, $37,548
Forbes, Lisa R, ofc spt asst (steno), $25,824
Forbis-Bonnot, Nancy L, fiscal & administrative mgr b2, $70,560
Forck, Lisa, mgmt analysis spec II, $43,488
Forck, Sharon A, acct II, $43,488
Ford, April M, fam spt elig spv, $34,944
Ford, Bethany, corres & info spec I, $34,944
Ford, Heather D, soc servs mgr, band 1, $60,624
Ford, Jason M, training tech II, $43,488
Ford, Johnny, child spt spec, $29,976
Ford, Rebecca S, child spt enforce spv, $34,944
Ford, Roni S, child spt spec, $29,976
Foree, Alicia A, fam spt elig spc, $29,976
Forkner, Janet R, fam spt elig spc, $33,180
Forrester, Beth A, youth spec II, $31,512
Forshee, Gary R, special educ tchr III, $40,380
Forsythe, David S, cook II, $23,880
Forth, Robert J, reg fam spec, $37,548
Forthofer, Madonna, children's serv spv, $39,624
Fortner, Chad M, youth spec II, $29,976
Fortson, Rodney L, acct III, $41,940
Foster, Erica D, child spt spec, $29,976
Foster, Jacqueline L, exec I, $32,052
Foster, Jasmin, children's serv worker II, $34,356
Foster, Lindsey M, children's serv worker III, $35,568
Foster, Pamela K, sr ofc spt asst (keybrd), $25,824
Foster, Pamela K, fam spt elig spc, $29,976
Foster, Stephanie, ofc spt asst (keybrd), $23,160
Foulks, Teresa J, children's serv spv, $41,172
Fountain, Donetta J, child spt spec, $33,744
Foust, Logan R, youth spec II, $31,512
Fouts, Allison K, legal counsel, $40,356
Fowler, Lori, fam spt elig spc, $29,976
Fowler, Marie A, fam spt elig spc, $29,976
Fowler, Shanna M, children's serv worker III, $36,888
Fowler, Stephanie S, soc servs mngr, band 2, $61,332
Fowler, Stephen R, youth spec II, $31,512
Fox, Donna J, admin ofc spt asst, $27,660
Fox, Emma-Jane E, fam spt elig spc, $32,052
Fox, Melissa, child spt spec, $29,976
Fox, Meridithe E, fam spt elig spv, $34,944
Fox, Romena J, children's serv worker III, $35,568
Fox, Suzanne M, youth spec II, $31,512
Frakes, Brenda R, children's serv worker II, $34,356
Frakes, Brion L, youth spec I, $28,104

Frala-Cooper, Jamie Q, child spt spec, $29,976
Fraley, Wendy D, admin ofc spt asst, $27,228
France, Bethany K, youth spec II, $29,976
Francis, Adrienne L, corres & info spec I, $34,944
Francis, David, youth fac mgr I, $38,928
Francis, Mary L, youth spec II, $31,512
Francis, Natasha R, fam spt elig spc, $29,976
Francis, Sheri K, fam spt elig spc, $29,976
Frank, Kevin J, youth spec II, $31,512
Frank, Kimberly A, special educ tchr III, $44,304
Frank, Mona R, children's serv spv, $41,172
Franke, Andrea J, fam spt elig spc, $29,976
Frank-Jones, Richard N, children's serv worker II, $34,356
Franklin, Charles, children's serv worker III, $36,888
Franklin, Christina, children's serv worker I, $30,984
Franklin, Renae, sr ofc spt asst (keybrd), $26,652
Franklin, Robbin K, fam spt elig spv, $38,232
Franks, Karen R, fam spt elig spc, $34,356
Frankum, Cassie D, children's serv worker I, $30,984
Fraser, Dana, edu sup, $46,932
Frasier, Stephanie, children's serv worker II, $33,744
Frazier, Sophia N, fam spt elig spc, $29,976
Frederick, Cory L, acad tchr III, $36,204
Frederick Gaudette, Amy J, children's serv worker III, $38,232
Fredrick, Bonita A, cook II, $23,880
Fredrick, Shannon M, children's serv worker I, $29,976
Freeman, Angela B, training tech II, $44,304
Freeman, Donna L, fam spt elig spc, $29,004
Freeman, Jennifer R, fam spt elig spc, $29,976
Freeman, Joshua E, youth spec II, $31,512
Freeman, Sherri, children's serv spec, $42,708
Freitas, Tracy, child spt spec, $29,976
French, Cynthia E, fam spt elig spc, $34,356
French, Dennis, soc servs mgr, band 1, $43,488
French, Holly, child spt spec, $31,512
French, Janet M, children's serv worker II, $33,180
French, Michael E, soc servs aide, $11.13/hr
Frenking, Tiffany R, training tech II, $40,380
Frey, Roberta S, fam spt elig spc, $34,356
Friend, Kaleb L, youth spec II, $30,984
Fritts, Teresa L, fam spt elig spc, $29,976
Fritz, Darlene M, training tech III, $46,932
Fritz, Kathleen, sr ofc spt asst (keybrd), $25,824
Fritz, Margaret J, children's serv worker II, $38,928
Frost, Rene M, child spt spec, $29,976
Frueh, Stacie A, soc servs mgr, band 1, $52,092
Fry, Janna L, special educ tchr III, $45,156
Fry, Jessica D, children's serv worker II, $32,628
Frye, Brenda, fam spt elig spc, $29,976
Frye, Deborah L, children's serv worker III, $36,888
Frye, Kelly L, children's serv spec, $41,940
Fryer, Wayne B, child spt spec, $33,744
Fuemmeler, Kendra E, children's serv spec, $40,380
Fugate, Hannah M, ofc spt asst (keybrd), $23,160
Fulks, Amanda L, medicaid spec, $36,204
Fulks, Christina L, youth spec II, $31,512
Fuller, Dawn, children's serv worker III, $35,568
Fuller, Ethel M, children's serv worker II, $34,356
Fuller, Juanita M, child spt spec, $31,512
Fuller, Lisa M, hearings ofcr, $52,032
Fuller, Tina, medicaid clerk, $28,104
Fuller, Tresa, sr ofc spt asst (keybrd), $25,824
Fullerton, Jennifer, children's serv worker I, $30,984
Fulton, Alfred L, youth spec II, $31,512
Fulton, Janalynn F, child spt spec, $33,744
Fulton, Martina M, fam spt elig spc, $29,976
Funk, Terry L, fam spt elig spv, $39,624
Furch, William, youth spec II, $31,512
Gadberry, Rhonda S, children's serv worker II, $32,628
Gaddy, Melissa A, sr ofc spt asst (keybrd), $25,824
Gadt, Nicole L, children's serv worker II, $34,356
Gagliarducci, Anna M, children's serv worker III, $35,568
Gaines, Chastity T, children's serv worker I, $30,984
Gaines, Earlene, special educ tchr III, $38,928
Gaines, Sally A, prog dev spec, $44,304
Gaither, Abigail, fam spt elig spc, $29,976
Gaither, Jewel D, fam spt elig spc, $29,976
Galeazzi, Jessica F, children's serv worker II, $34,356
Gallagher, Robert L, youth spec I, $28,104

Gallamore, Jamie L, children's serv worker II, $32,628
Gallant, Jeanette, fam spt elig spv, $34,944
Gallant, Zena, children's serv worker II, $34,356
Gallaway, Heather M, fam spt elig spc, $29,976
Gallinger, Chadwick J, serv coor yth srvcs, $32,628
Galloway, Brandy, ofc spt asst (keybrd), $23,160
Gamarsh, Kayce E, children's serv worker II, $32,628
Gamble, Ashlee M, children's serv worker I, $30,984
Gamblin, Anita, ofc spt asst (keybrd), $23,160
Gamblin-Hurn, Carla, ofc spt asst (keybrd), $23,160
Gammill, E.r., fam spt elig spc, $29,976
Gammon, Becky J, children's serv worker I, $29,976
Gant, Kay F, child spt spec, $33,744
Gant, Marcia L, child spt spec, $29,976
Garavaglia, Michael L, youth spec I, $28,104
Garcia, Carlos A, youth spec II, $29,976
Gardner, Danielle R, children's serv worker I, $29,976
Gardner, David S, investigator II, $39,624
Gardner, Desiree N, children's serv worker II, $32,628
Gardner, Erica J, fam spt elig spc, $29,976
Gardner, Kathleen M, children's serv worker III, $35,568
Gardner, Kelly, pers analyst II, $41,940
Gardner, Patricia C, child spt spec, $32,052
Gardner, Toni E, fam spt elig spc, $29,976
Garfield, Avory D, youth fac mgr II, $38,928
Gargano, Adrienne M, ofc spt asst (keybrd), $23,160
Garland, Melody C, children's serv spv, $45,156
Garms, Carolyn C, child spt spec, $33,180
Garner, Paula, child spt spec, $33,180
Garrels, Mikayla J, reg fam spec, $37,548
Garrett, Robin M, fam spt elig spc, $29,976
Garrett, Rodney L, training tech II, $45,156
Garrett, Tammy M, fam spt elig spc, $29,976
Garrett, Towana F, fam spt elig spc, $29,976
Garrett, Trisha R, children's serv worker II, $32,628
Garrison, Karen L, fam spt elig spc, $32,052
Garrity, Brian M, soc servs mgr, band 1, $56,280
Garrity, Michael, fam spt elig spc, $29,976
Garrity, Molly, fam spt elig spv, $34,944
Garver, Penny L, special educ tchr III, $41,172
Gary, Valerie M, fam spt elig spc, $29,976
Gates, Alisha L, children's serv worker II, $34,356
Gautier, Nathan W, children's serv worker II, $32,628
Gavin, Amy N, corres & info spec I, $34,944
Gayer, Jean A, children's serv worker II, $34,356
Gbologe, Olusegun S, fam spt elig spc, $29,976
Gbomina, Mercy H, children's serv worker I, $29,976
Geatley, Sara D, fam spt elig spc, $29,976
Gebelin, Miranda M, children's serv worker III, $35,568
Geddie, Mary C, children's serv worker II, $33,744
Gee, Cheryl A, child spt enforce spv, $38,928
Geer, Joseph L, youth spec I, $29,004
Geier, Lana L, children's serv worker II, $34,356
Geiser, Debra S, fam spt elig spc, $35,568
Genaro, Rachael A, children's serv worker II, $32,628
Gentges, Jana L, child spt spec, $33,180
Gentry, Jennifer L, children's serv worker III, $35,568
Gentry, Kristin D, soc servs mgr, band 1, $41,940
George, Cliff W, children's serv worker I, $29,976
George, Karen R, children's serv worker II, $34,356
George, Wendy M, children's serv spv, $42,708
Georges, Brandon, fam spt elig spc, $29,004
Georgie, Cindy S, youth spec II, $30,984
Gerard, Debra L, soc servs aide, $11.13/hr
Gerber, Carolyn F, soc servs mgr, band 1, $47,052
Gerding, Kathleen J, children's serv spv, $39,624
Gerding, Shirley A, fam spt elig spc, $30,984
Gerlach, James M, fam spt elig spc, $29,976
Gerland, Betty T, youth spec II, $31,512
Germain, Vernon B, serv coor yth srvcs, $43,488
Gernander, Erik C, medicaid technician, $32,628
Gerstenberger, Kari J, fam spt elig spc, $29,976
Gesch, Danielle N, corres & info spec I, $33,744
Gesch, Ryan L, mgmt analysis spec II, $41,940
Gettemeyer, Kevin L, hearings ofcr, $43,500
Gettys, Angie K, corres & info spec I, $38,232
Ghant, Clarissa M, fam spt elig spc, $29,976
Gholson, Cheryl K, corres & info spec I, $34,944
Giarratano, Caryn D, child spt spec, $29,976

Gibbon, Amanda, medicaid spec, $37,548
Gibbon, Terri C, case analyst, $32,628
Gibbons, Ashley, children's serv worker I, $29,976
Gibbons, Lisa R, youth spec II, $31,512
Gibbs, Kourtney, child spt spec, $29,004
Gibler, Debbie A, medicaid spec, $37,548
Gibson, Christoff B, corres & info spec I, $33,744
Gibson, Cynthia L, prog dev spec, $46,068
Gibson, Diana L, child spt spec, $33,744
Gibson, Elva M, lpn II gen, $29,772
Gibson, Kristina L, admin ofc spt asst, $28,104
Gibson, Margaret J, div dir, $104,838
Gibson, Stacie L, medicaid spec, $37,548
Gibson, Tony D, youth spec II, $31,512
Gibson-Kelly, Amy J, fam spt elig spc, $29,976
Giesler, Stephanie L, fam spt elig spc, $29,976
Giffin, Faith L, youth spec II, $32,052
Gifford, Anthony, fam spt elig spc, $29,976
Gilbert, Ann M, child spt spec, $29,976
Gilbert, Anne E, prog dev spec, $40,380
Gilbert, Cynthia A, fam spt elig spc, $29,976
Gilbert, Iris V, fam spt elig spc, $32,628
Gilbert, Tammy L, ofc spt asst (keybrd), $23,160
Gilden, Gissella R, edu asst II, $13,848
Gildersleeve, Megan K, child spt spec, $29,976
Gile, Mahala E, ofc spt asst (keybrd), $25,824
Gill, Katina L, children's serv worker II, $34,356
Gillam, Brandi L, children's serv worker II, $33,180
Gillam, Lindsey M, fam spt elig spc, $29,976
Gillam, Lorie B, fam spt elig spc, $33,180
Gillespie, Jennifer S, children's serv spv, $39,624
Gillespie, Martha M, legal counsel, $39,648
Gilliam, Kristy J, children's serv worker II, $34,356
Gilliland, Kristian P, children's serv worker I, $29,976
Gillis, Laron, child spt enforce spv, $38,928
Gilman, Chelsea A, soc servs aide, $11.13/hr
Gilmer, Charma L, fam spt elig spc, $29,976
Gilmore, Casey L, children's serv worker II, $34,356
Gilmore, Diann, pers analyst II, $39,624
Gilmore, Ilea M, admin ofc spt asst, $28,536
Gilmore, Sharon M, children's serv worker II, $34,356
Gilmore, Tanisha, children's serv worker I, $30,984
Gilpin, Richard D, medicaid clerk, $30,420
Gilzow, Carla R, soc servs mgr, band 1, $52,092
Gimlin, Misti M, youth fac mgr II, $40,380
Ginger, Sylvia, fam spt elig spc, $29,976
Ginwright, John B, dpty div dir, $83,424
Gipson, Gordon W, youth spec II, $34,944
Gish, Darla K, ofc spt asst (keybrd), $25,404
Gish, Rick E, cook II, $23,880
Gitchos, Milo A, investigator II, $38,928
Givans, Fallon R, serv coor yth srvcs, $33,744
Given, Patricia J, fam spt elig spc, $29,976
Givens, Joshua B, children's serv worker I, $29,976
Gladney, Harriett E, fam spt elig spc, $29,976
Glaser, Jason R, special educ tchr III, $46,068
Glass, Charleen G, child spt spec, $29,976
Glass, Jessica, ofc spt asst (keybrd), $23,160
Glastetter, Courtney A, children's serv worker II, $34,356
Glastetter, Mary B, child spt spec, $32,052
Glawson, Carrie E, children's serv spv, $39,624
Glenn, Dylan E, children's serv worker I, $29,976
Glenn, James L, youth spec II, $31,512
Glenn, Jeanelle D, corres & info spec I, $35,568
Glore, Brandon L, fam spt elig spc, $29,976
Glore, Katie, fam spt elig spc, $29,976
Glore, Nicholas A, fam spt elig spc, $29,976
Glore, Sabrina D, fam spt elig spc, $29,976
Glover, Deanna E, child spt spec, $31,512
Glueck, Therese M, sr ofc spt asst (keybrd), $28,452
Godier, Steven W, training tech II, $40,380
Goebel, Charlotte H, children's serv worker I, $29,976
Goebel, Marti J, ofc spt asst (keybrd), $22,536
Goeller, Deborah A, ofc servs coor, $41,940
Goetz, David, fam spt elig spc, $29,976
Goewert, Patricia A, soc servs aide, $11.13/hr
Goforth, Dorinda L, fam spt elig spc, $29,976
Goins, Tara E, children's serv spv, $38,232
Gold, Lori M, fam spt elig spv, $38,232

Golden, Ashley R, children's serv worker III, $36,888
Golden, Caitlyn E, youth spec II, $30,984
Goldenhersh, Rachel L, children's serv worker I, $30,984
Goldsby, Ricky L, fam spt elig spc, $29,976
Goldthrite, Megan, sr ofc spt asst (keybrd), $25,032
Goliday, Tressa, fam spt elig spc, $34,944
Gomera, Elisa I, fam spt elig spc, $29,976
Gomez, Angel O, cook III, $28,104
Gomez, Illa, children's serv worker I, $29,976
Gonder, Katherine O, children's serv worker II, $34,356
Gonzales, Amber M, fam spt elig spc, $29,976
Gonzales, Unique M, children's serv worker II, $32,628
Gonzalez, Valerie A, ofc spt asst (keybrd), $23,160
Gooch, Charlotte R, soc servs mgr, band 1, $52,092
Gooch, Christie D, sr ofc spt asst (keybrd), $25,824
Goodeluinas, Lara M, ofc spt asst (keybrd), $23,160
Gooden, Eileen T, fam spt elig spc, $29,976
Gooden, Shanese J, fam spt elig spc, $29,976
Gooden, Telecia, youth spec II, $31,512
Goodloe, Monteshia, children's serv spv, $39,624
Goodman, Lisa K, cook III, $28,104
Goodrich, Jacqueline L, admin ofc spt asst, $28,104
Goodrich, Kylee S, exec II, $34,944
Goodrich, Tamela R, fam spt elig spc, $34,356
Goods, Vickie L, fam spt elig spc, $29,004
Goodson, Goldie E, children's serv worker II, $34,356
Goolsby, Antonio T, youth spec II, $31,512
Goosby-Gaines, Shivonne L, children's serv worker II, $35,568
Goosens, Donald A, sr voc rehab cnslr f/t blind, $38,928
Gordon, Valerie A, child spt spec, $30,420
Gori, David L, youth spec II, $32,628
Gorman, Kristie, fam spt elig spc, $29,976
Gorman, Mary E, soc servs mgr, band 1, $53,208
Gorney, Bethany C, pers clerk, $28,104
Gose, Kimberly S, child spt spec, $29,976
Gosney, Kimberly D, serv coor yth srvcs, $36,888
Gosney, Michael R, soc servs aide, $11.13/hr
Gosney, Samantha B, children's serv worker II, $34,356
Goss, Bosalyn J, youth spec II, $31,512
Goss, Robin J, ofc spt asst (keybrd), $23,160
Gott, Grace M, fam spt elig spc, $33,180
Gott, Sherril A, soc servs mgr, band 1, $41,940
Gottfried-Caulk, Edmund, children's serv worker III, $36,888
Goude, Rachel A, children's serv worker II, $33,744
Govan, Linda S, children's serv worker II, $33,180
Gowen, Amie R, children's serv worker III, $36,888
Gozia, Erin R, fam spt elig spc, $29,976
Grabanski, Chloe N, youth spec II, $30,984
Grace, William R, youth spec II, $31,512
Graham, Barbara A, children's serv spv, $41,172
Graham, Jessica N, fam spt elig spc, $29,976
Graham, Kimberly N, children's serv spv, $39,624
Graham, Michelle L, fam spt elig spc, $29,976
Graham, Nikki N, medicaid technician, $16,314
Grant, Kailey E, children's serv spv, $39,624
Graves, Carol, fam spt elig spc, $29,976
Graves, Kapree, misc tech, $12.12/hr
Graves, Nikki R, youth spec II, $30,984
Graves, Robin D, youth fac mgr II, $40,380
Grawe, Kari L, sr ofc spt asst (keybrd), $25,824
Gray, Barbara S, misc tech, $28.00/hr
Gray, Emily R, sr ofc spt asst (keybrd), $25,824
Gray, Erica L, fam spt elig spc, $29,976
Gray, Frank W, youth group leader, $34,356
Gray, Glenn A, child spt spec, $29,976
Gray, Kenneth L, motor veh driver, $25,824
Gray, Ladea N, fam spt elig spc, $29,976
Gray, Melissa A, children's serv worker II, $34,356
Gray, Michael W, investigator III, $41,940
Gray, Patricia L, children's serv spv, $39,624
Gray, Paul A, reg fam spec, $37,548
Gray, Ron M, soc servs mgr, band 1, $49,128
Gray, Sarah E, children's serv worker I, $30,984
Gray, Scott S, mgmt analysis spec I, $36,204
Gray, Shawn M, children's serv worker II, $34,356
Gray, Sheila M, sr ofc spt asst (keybrd), $28,452
Gray, Sondra H, children's serv worker II, $33,744
Gray, Theresa M, children's serv spv, $41,172
Gray, Tiffaney, ofc spt asst (keybrd), $23,160

Gray, Vaneeta D, special educ tchr III, $38,928
Grebe, Linda C, children's serv spv, $46,932
Grebner, Kimberly A, investigator III, $41,940
Green, Betty J, child spt spec, $30,420
Green, Beverly D, youth spec II, $31,512
Green, Christine A, children's serv worker I, $29,976
Green, Debbie L, fam spt elig spc, $34,356
Green, Debra, account clerk II, $25,824
Green, Kristen A, case analyst, $32,628
Green, Laura B, children's serv spv, $39,624
Green, Melissa D, pers clerk, $28,104
Green, Michelle A, children's serv worker II, $34,356
Green, Ollie M, legal counsel, $55,000
Green, Paula, fam spt elig spc, $29,976
Green, Samantha E, child spt spec, $29,976
Green, Twana D, sr ofc spt asst (keybrd), $29,412
Greene, Larry D, youth spec I, $29,004
Greene, Nina M, youth spec II, $29,976
Greene, Rachel, fam spt elig spc, $29,976
Greenup, Lori A, children's serv spv, $39,624
Greer, Joshua E, youth spec I, $28,104
Gregg, Amy E, edu sup, $52,092
Gregg, Robin K, fam spt elig spc, $33,180
Gregory, Bonita G, soc servs mgr, band 1, $47,052
Gregory, Ty'rese M, children's serv worker II, $34,356
Greninger, Jason, fam spt elig spc, $29,976
Gretlein, David, area supv bus entprs blind, $36,204
Grewe, Angie L, fam spt elig spc, $29,976
Grewe, Helen R, fam spt elig spc, $29,976
Grider, Lakita D, youth spec II, $30,984
Grider, Linda E, fam spt elig spc, $32,052
Grider, Pamela A, fam spt elig spc, $33,180
Grieshaber, Douglas L, training tech III, $46,068
Griest, Glenda S, children's serv spv, $39,624
Griffin, Amber L, children's serv worker I, $32,052
Griffin, Ashlee J, sr ofc spt asst (keybrd), $25,824
Griffin, B. J, children's serv worker III, $40,380
Griffin, David D, youth spec II, $32,052
Griffin, Jennifer, child spt spec, $29,976
Griffin, Karen S, ofc spt asst (keybrd), $25,032
Griffin, Megan L, children's serv worker II, $34,356
Griffin, Steve, youth spec II, $31,512
Griffin, Susan E, fam spt elig spc, $29,976
Griffin, Travis, fam spt elig spc, $29,976
Griffy-Hundley, Raynera B, children's serv worker III, $35,568
Griggs, Norma N, ofc spt asst (keybrd), $12,702
Griggs, Susanne, ofc spt asst (keybrd), $23,160
Grimes, Carol A, fam spt elig spc, $32,052
Grimes, Emanuel M, youth spec II, $31,512
Grimes, Lorri K, children's serv spv, $39,624
Grimes, Melissa M, fam spt elig spc, $29,976
Grimm, Amy, child spt spec, $29,976
Grimm, Loruhanah K, ofc spt asst (keybrd), $23,160
Grinston, Cassandra S, children's serv worker II, $34,356
Grisaffe, George C, youth spec II, $31,512
Grissom, Deborah K, fam spt elig spc, $29,976
Grob, Carl L, children's serv worker II, $38,928
Groce, Peter M, fiscal & administrative mgr b2, $65,364
Grosvenor, Susan L, fam spt elig spc, $29,976
Grotjohn, Lindsey D, children's serv worker II, $32,628
Groves, Toni, ofc spt asst (keybrd), $25,824
Groves, William G, soc servs mgr, band 1, $49,128
Grubbs, Cloyce D, soc servs mgr, band 1, $44,304
Gruhala, Brenda M, children's serv worker III, $36,888
Grund, Nicole J, soc servs sup, $37,548
Grunow, Kayla A, fam spt elig spc, $29,004
Gruschka, Brigitte U, fam spt elig spc, $29,976
Guffey, Valerie S, children's serv spv, $39,624
Guill, Rachel D, fam spt elig spc, $29,976
Guinn, Brehan J, children's serv worker II, $33,744
Gulick, Amanda L, children's serv worker III, $35,568
Gulley, John S, youth spec II, $31,512
Gunnels, Jennifer A, children's serv spec, $38,928
Gunter, Michelle L, children's serv spv, $41,172
Gunter, Tammy J, children's serv spec, $38,928
Gunter, Vicky, cook II, $23,880
Gurley, Donald L, children's serv worker III, $43,488
Gutchen, Mark, legal counsel, $75,252
Guthrie, Karrie L, children's serv worker II, $34,356

Gutierrez, Janeris A, children's serv worker III, $36,888
Gutierrez, Luis, youth spec II, $30,984
Guzman, Saira E, children's serv worker II, $32,628
Haas, Allen A, prog dev spec, $40,380
Haas, Lesa E, fam spt elig spc, $30,984
Hacker, Pamela J, soc servs aide, $11.13/hr
Hackett, Kimberly H, edu sup, $46,932
Hackett, Kristina M, fam spt elig spc, $29,976
Hackmann, Darin, designated principal asst div, $90,396
Hackney, Alyssa L, children's serv worker II, $34,356
Haddon, Vicki K, child spt enforce spv, $38,232
Hadley, Joy L, investigator II, $36,204
Hadley-Boatman, Jacqueline T, misc tech, $40,000
Haesemeyer, Samantha C, children's serv worker I, $29,976
Hafer, William E, soc servs mgr, band 1, $47,052
Hagen, Rebecca L, soc servs mgr, band 1, $41,940
Hagenhoff, Lori A, child spt spec, $32,628
Hagerty, Renee P, children's serv worker I, $30,984
Hague, Denise A, children's serv worker II, $36,888
Haigler, Kenneth E, staff training & dev coor, $61,332
Halderman, Roxanna M, medicaid spec, $37,548
Hale, Christine A, children's serv worker II, $34,356
Hale, Jimmie S, child spt spec, $31,512
Hale, Travis, acad tchr III, $36,204
Hale, Virginia M, ofc spt asst (keybrd), $23,160
Halfmann, Kassandra L, children's serv worker I, $29,976
Hall, Alan, fam spt elig spc, $29,976
Hall, Annette L, youth spec II, $29,976
Hall, Becky J, children's serv spv, $39,624
Hall, Blaire E, youth spec I, $28,104
Hall, Christie L, ofc spt asst (keybrd), $23,160
Hall, Christopher S, children's serv worker II, $34,356
Hall, Edwin D, edu sup, $41,940
Hall, Holly, children's serv worker II, $34,356
Hall, Kimberley R, fam spt elig spc, $31,512
Hall, Lauren A, children's serv worker III, $36,888
Hall, Lora J, children's serv worker II, $34,356
Hall, Mary J, fam spt elig spc, $29,976
Hall, Rhonda D, fam spt elig spc, $29,976
Hall, Sarah E, fam spt elig spc, $33,180
Hall, Sheree D, youth fac mgr II, $42,708
Hall, Thomas J, youth spec II, $30,984
Hall, Tracey T, fam spt elig spc, $29,976
Hallam, Cynthia A, children's serv worker III, $41,940
Halzel, Gerrilee N, sr ofc spt asst (keybrd), $25,032
Hambrick, Shannon J, youth spec II, $31,512
Hamel, Kathryn, children's serv worker II, $33,744
Hamilton, Brian J, hearings ofcr, $43,500
Hamilton, Brianne M, serv coor yth srvcs, $33,744
Hamilton, Cynthia J, fam spt elig spc, $34,356
Hamilton, Deanna L, child spt spec, $30,984
Hamilton, Genevra, children's serv worker III, $36,888
Hamilton, Rebecca J, children's serv worker III, $38,232
Hamilton, Seanetta, fam spt eligblty prg mg, $38,928
Hamilton, Sharon S, fam spt elig spc, $34,356
Hamilton, Steven W, prog dev spec, $45,156
Hamilton, Tramondre A, youth group leader, $34,356
Hamilton, Valerie O, fam spt elig spc, $29,976
Hamlett, Chastity L, fam spt elig spc, $29,976
Hamm, Emilie, fam spt elig spc, $29,976
Hammack, Ronnie W, youth spec I, $29,496
Hammer, Carli G, children's serv worker I, $30,984
Hammond, Carolyn, fam spt elig spc, $29,976
Hammond, Kristin N, youth spec II, $31,512
Hammond, Lillie K, fam spt elig spc, $29,976
Hammons, Cassandra L, children's serv worker III, $19,116
Hamner, Rovene, soc servs mgr, band 1, $46,068
Hamp, Jamesha D, youth spec II, $30,984
Hamptiol, Roman D, corres & info spec I, $34,944
Hampton, Aubrey L, children's serv worker III, $36,888
Hampton, Dealia F, soc servs aide, $11.13/hr
Hampton, Dorothy A, sr ofc spt asst (keybrd), $25,824
Hampton, Mary A, child spt spec, $29,976
Hampton, Richard M, fam spt elig spc, $29,976
Hampton, Shelley R, soc servs mgr, band 1, $40,380
Hamre, Stacey N, soc servs mgr, band 1, $48,156
Hams, Shantel N, fam spt elig spc, $29,976
Hanaway, Sandra, ofc spt asst (keybrd), $23,160
Hancock, Amber M, children's serv worker I, $30,984

Hancock, Joseph P, mgmt analysis spec II, $46,068
Hancock, Marlene L, acad tchr III, $37,548
Hanes, Deborah D, cook II, $23,880
Haney, Christy M, corres & info spec I, $34,944
Haney, Jennifer R, ofc spt asst (keybrd), $23,160
Haney, Roger D, children's serv worker I, $29,976
Hanger, Melanie, children's serv worker I, $29,976
Hankins, Kelli B, children's serv worker I, $29,976
Hankins, Misty D, children's serv spv, $39,624
Hankins, Peggy L, special educ tchr III, $46,068
Hanks, Heather E, fam spt elig spc, $29,976
Hanlin, Nicole M, rehab tchr for the blind, $34,944
Hannaford, Adam N, child spt spec, $29,976
Hannaman, Jessica D, youth spec II, $29,976
Hanner, Ursula B, fam spt elig spc, $29,976
Hansen, Craig C, children's serv worker III, $36,888
Hansen, Mary J, children's serv worker II, $34,356
Hanshaw, Glenda L, fam spt elig spc, $30,420
Hanten, Susan R, fam spt elig spc, $29,976
Harbison, Kelly D, sr ofc spt asst (keybrd), $27,504
Hardberger, Tracey K, children's serv spv, $41,172
Harden, David N, fam spt elig spc, $29,976
Harden, Tammy S, child spt spec, $29,976
Hardesty, Stephanie K, children's serv spv, $45,156
Hardin, Teresa, children's serv worker II, $36,888
Harding, James M, ofc spt asst (keybrd), $23,160
Hardrick, Dollie, child spt spec, $29,004
Hardwick, Rebecca J, child spt spec, $29,976
Hardy, Jon J, youth spec II, $30,984
Hardy, Marika R, ofc spt asst (keybrd), $23,508
Hardy, Stephanie D, ofc spt asst (keybrd), $23,160
Hare, Dena L, acct II, $37,548
Hargate, Sherry L, sr ofc spt asst (steno), $27,948
Hargis, Jamie L, children's serv worker II, $34,356
Hargrove, Denita E, serv coor yth srvcs, $34,356
Harman, Robert L, children's serv worker I, $29,976
Harmon, Bradley D, children's serv worker II, $34,356
Harmon, Crystalyn H, children's serv worker I, $30,984
Harmon, Cynthia D, fam spt elig spc, $29,976
Harmon, James, children's serv spv, $38,232
Harmon, Janel L, fam spt elig spc, $29,976
Harmon, Sanford L, fam spt elig spc, $29,976
Harmon, Tammy, fam spt elig spc, $29,976
Harmon-Ward, Regina Y, ofc spt asst (keybrd), $25,824
Harness, Carole S, special educ tchr III, $40,380
Harness, Penny L, registered nurse, $45,732
Harold, Artelia V, children's serv worker II, $34,356
Harp, Elaina A, children's serv spv, $38,232
Harper, Brian K, hearings ofcr, $50,040
Harper, Paul E, soc servs aide, $11.13/hr
Harper, Tiffany N, children's serv worker I, $29,976
Harpham, Debra M, sr ofc spt asst (keybrd), $25,824
Harpole, John H, children's serv worker III, $36,888
Harrell, Monica J, fam spt elig spc, $29,976
Harrell, Rhonda J, sr ofc spt asst (keybrd), $25,824
Harrill, Jill E, children's serv worker III, $41,940
Harris, Angela M, rehab asst rehab srvs for blnd, $26,652
Harris, Ashley J, children's serv worker II, $32,628
Harris, Ashley N, ofc spt asst (keybrd), $23,160
Harris, Barbara J, fam spt elig spc, $29,976
Harris, Beverly A, rehab asst rehab srvs for blnd, $26,652
Harris, Courtney M, sr ofc spt asst (keybrd), $26,652
Harris, Daneshea, fam spt elig spc, $29,976
Harris, Daniella E, ofc spt asst (keybrd), $22,536
Harris, David B, children's serv spv, $39,624
Harris, Diana L, fam spt elig spc, $32,628
Harris, Doris A, ofc spt asst (keybrd), $23,508
Harris, Hannah, children's serv worker I, $30,984
Harris, James R, children's serv spv, $39,624
Harris, Joan E, child spt spec, $29,976
Harris, Julie A, soc servs mgr, band 1, $56,064
Harris, Leslie L, children's serv worker II, $34,356
Harris, Lisa A, corres & info spec I, $34,944
Harris, Lisa J, youth spec II, $31,512
Harris, Lisa M, child spt spec, $29,976
Harris, Lori A, acct I, $30,984
Harris, Marva L, child spt spec, $29,976
Harris, Melisalyn M, children's serv worker II, $34,356
Harris, Pamela L, corres & info spec I, $34,944

Harris, Pearlynn M, exec I, $29,976
Harris, Ramona L, children's serv spv, $39,624
Harris, Renee M, children's serv worker II, $34,356
Harris, Rita M, ofc spt asst (keybrd), $28,452
Harris, Roger L, fam spt elig spv, $34,944
Harris, Sherry A, child spt enforce spv, $38,928
Harris, Theresa A, children's serv spv, $46,932
Harris, Tiffany R, youth spec I, $29,004
Harris-Miller, Betty J, fam spt elig spc, $33,180
Harrison, Donna F, ofc spt asst (keybrd), $25,824
Harrison, Richard F, edu sup, $43,488
Harrison, Teresa D, fam spt elig spv, $38,232
Harriss, Sharon M, ofc spt asst (keybrd), $25,824
Hart, Barbara J, account clerk II, $25,032
Hart, Cheryl, ofc spt asst (keybrd), $23,160
Hart, Gerald F, serv coor yth srvcs, $33,744
Hart, Jennifer A, children's serv worker II, $34,356
Hart, Julie A, fam spt elig spc, $29,976
Hart, Lilliane M, fam spt elig spc, $29,976
Hartgrave, Jill A, children's serv worker II, $34,356
Hartman, James L, serv coor yth srvcs, $36,888
Hartmann, Elizabeth S, children's serv spv, $39,624
Hartsfield, David, child spt spec, $29,004
Hartsfield, Tara N, training tech I, $36,204
Hartupee, Pamela J, child spt spec, $29,976
Hartzell, John F, youth spec II, $35,568
Hartzler, Kathryn A, children's serv worker II, $32,628
Harvey, Brandi, ofc spt asst (keybrd), $23,160
Harvey, Markitia S, serv coor yth srvcs, $35,568
Harvey, Michael R, child spt spec, $29,976
Harvey, Travis R, youth spec II, $31,512
Hashbarger, Ann C, child spt spec, $29,976
Haskins, Brenda K, ofc spt asst (steno), $27,084
Haslag, Andrew J, fiscal & administrative mgr b2, $62,664
Haslag, Frances L, exec II, $34,944
Hassos, Christopher J, cook II, $23,880
Hastings, Natasha J, legal counsel, $42,708
Hastings, Tammy, fam spt elig spc, $29,976
Hasty, David D, youth spec I, $29,496
Hatcher, Amanda L, children's serv worker II, $34,356
Hatcher, Karinne D, children's serv worker II, $34,356
Hatcher, Tina S, corres & info spec I, $36,204
Hatches, James A, fam spt elig spc, $29,976
Hatfield, Cathy A, fam spt elig spc, $29,976
Hathcock, Robert E, children's serv worker I, $29,976
Hatheway, Rick A, youth spec II, $31,512
Haus, Angela C, children's serv worker II, $34,356
Haus, Linda B, mgmt analysis spec II, $46,068
Hausel, Abbie C, fam spt elig spc, $29,976
Haviland, Judith A, children's serv worker II, $34,356
Hawk, Jessica D, investigator II, $36,204
Hawkins, Ashley C, children's serv worker I, $29,976
Hawkins, Carla D, fam spt elig spv, $35,568
Hawkins, John S, serv coor yth srvcs, $33,744
Hawkins, Julie A, cmnty svs coord-youth srvs, $41,940
Hawkins, Kelly, children's serv worker II, $34,356
Hawkins, Kevin D, youth spec II, $30,984
Hawkins, Laura, child spt spec, $30,420
Hawthorne, Jennifer, youth spec II, $29,976
Hayden, Patricia A, youth group leader, $34,356
Hayden, Patricia J, ofc spt asst (keybrd), $26,652
Haye-Mitchell, Angelee S, admin ofc spt asst, $28,104
Hayes, Ana B, youth spec II, $31,512
Hayes, Betty, fam spt elig spc, $29,976
Hayes, Dawn E, sr ofc spt asst (steno), $27,948
Hayes, Jessica T, youth spec II, $30,984
Hayes, Lindsey J, children's serv worker II, $34,356
Hayes, Rhonda C, youth group leader, $34,356
Hayes, Tonia D, cook II, $23,880
Haynes, Camille M, youth spec II, $29,976
Haynes, Ellen K, legal counsel, $55,548
Haynes, James T, children's serv spv, $39,624
Haynes, Marietta A, child spt spec, $29,976
Haynes, Michelle, children's serv worker III, $36,888
Haynes, Pretalia V, fam spt elig spc, $30,984
Haynes, Sabre M, fam spt elig spc, $29,976
Haynes, Terri J, child spt spec, $29,976
Haynie, Terry L, fam spt elig spc, $29,976
Hays, Onalee, fam spt elig spc, $29,976

Hayter-Sirls, Sa'raia, children's serv worker I, $29,976
Hayward, Linda M, fam spt elig spc, $29,976
Head, Daryl J, children's serv worker I, $30,984
Heard, Lashawndra, fam spt elig spc, $29,976
Heath, Robert A, soc servs aide, $11.13/hr
Heavilin, Sara J, youth spec I, $29,004
Heckadon, Denise L, fam spt elig spc, $34,356
Heckemeyer, Janet M, misc prof, $50.50/hr
Heckerman, Connie K, admin ofc spt asst, $31,512
Heckman, Linda S, children's serv worker II, $34,356
Hedrick, Adrienna D, account clerk II, $25,824
Heeb, Tamma R, fam spt elig spc, $29,976
Hefner, Geoffry L, fam spt elig spc, $29,976
Hegerfeld, Rhonda K, medicaid technician, $32,628
Hegwood, Bernice F, fam spt elig spc, $34,944
Heidbreder, Lisa A, fam spt elig spc, $29,976
Heidrick, Vera B, fam spt elig spc, $29,976
Heimbeaugh, Tamara, sr ofc spt asst (keybrd), $33,036
Heimericks, Jennifer K, prog dev spec, $40,380
Heine, Alice M, prog dev spec, $40,380
Heine, Erin L, medicaid clerk, $27,660
Heinzl, William J, investigator II, $38,232
Heldenbrand, Deborah L, soc servs mgr, band 1, $41,940
Helfrich, Audrey A, soc servs mgr, band 1, $49,128
Helle, Lisa D, child spt enforce spv, $39,624
Heller, William G, child spt enforce spv, $38,928
Hellerich, Andrea L, soc servs aide, $11.13/hr
Helm, Susan J, ofc spt asst (keybrd), $25,404
Helms, Barbara D, corres & info spec I, $34,944
Helms, Brittany O, children's serv worker I, $30,984
Helms, Harvey B, mgmt analysis spec II, $48,156
Helms, Mary L, fam spt elig spc, $29,976
Helms, Peggy S, ofc spt asst (keybrd), $23,880
Helms, Rosalyn A, ofc spt asst (keybrd), $22,536
Helton, Shawna L, youth fac mgr I, $37,548
Hemme, Jeff T, cmnty svs coord-youth srvs, $40,380
Hemphill, Alicia M, child spt enforce spv, $34,944
Henderson, Elizabeth F, child spt spec, $29,976
Henderson, Eric S, ofc spt asst (keybrd), $23,160
Henderson, Evelyn T, corres & info spec I, $34,944
Henderson, Janet M, child spt spec, $29,976
Henderson, Vickie E, cook III, $30,984
Henderson-Orton, Lisa A, child spt spec, $33,744
Hendrick, Chiquita J, special educ tchr III, $41,172
Hendrix, Pamela F, medicaid spec, $39,624
Hendrix, Tasha N, youth spec II, $30,984
Henfling, Verna D, sr ofc spt asst (keybrd), $27,504
Henley, Debra S, medicaid spec, $39,624
Henley, Roxanne L, youth spec II, $30,984
Henry, Amy E, children's serv worker I, $30,984
Henry, Candace M, fam spt elig spc, $31,512
Henry, Carla M, fiscal & administrative mgr b1, $47,544
Henry, Cyntha, fam spt elig spc, $29,976
Henry, Deborah A, sr ofc spt asst (keybrd), $25,824
Henry, Durias T, youth spec II, $29,976
Henry, John E, fam spt elig spc, $34,356
Henry, Samuel A, youth spec II, $30,984
Henry, Susan D, fam spt elig spc, $29,976
Henry, Vanessa, fam spt elig spc, $29,976
Hensley, Ashley, fam spt elig spc, $29,976
Hensley, Phyllis D, sr ofc spt asst (keybrd), $25,824
Henson, Lodi G, prog dev spec, $52,092
Henson, Tanna, child spt spec, $33,180
Herbert, Victoria R, children's serv worker I, $29,976
Hercules, Christina B, corres & info spec I, $34,944
Hering, Raymond, corres & info spec I, $34,944
Herkelman, Kenneth, case analyst, $36,204
Hern, Holly M, prog dev spec, $40,380
Hernandez, Jessica D, children's serv worker II, $33,744
Hernandez, Jose L, youth spec II, $30,984
Hernandez, Shelby K, children's serv worker I, $29,976
Hernandez Pimentel, Melissa J, special asst prof, $55,548
Hernandez-Johnson, Paula V, legal counsel, $51,192
Herrera, Sarah, children's serv worker III, $36,888
Herring, Debra K, fam spt elig spv, $36,888
Herring, Sandra K, fam spt elig spc, $29,976
Hersh, Stephanie A, serv coor spv yth srvcs, $39,624
Herzog, Pamela R, children's serv worker III, $36,888
Hess, Ceann Y, children's serv spv, $43,488

Hess, Jean F, fam spt elig spv, $38,232
Hess, John W, child spt enforce spv, $34,944
Heusted, Leslie A, children's serv spv, $38,928
Hewitt, Deborah L, children's serv worker II, $34,356
Hiatt, Kimberly O, child spt spec, $29,976
Hibbler, Sharon, child spt spec, $34,944
Hibner, Angela D, corres & info spec I, $34,944
Hickey, Stephanie, corres & info spec I, $34,944
Hickman, Jacqueline K, medicaid unit spv, $45,156
Hickman, Jamie J, child spt spec, $29,004
Hickman, Patricia A, fam spt elig spv, $38,232
Hickman, Rachel J, case analyst, $32,628
Hickman, Vanessa M, fam spt elig spc, $29,976
Hicks, Brian H, youth fac mgr II, $40,380
Hicks, Janice, children's serv worker II, $38,232
Hicks, Jeremy L, children's serv worker II, $34,356
Hicks, Korbin L, soc servs aide, $11.13/hr
Hicks, Lindel D, youth spec II, $31,512
Hicks, Mark D, youth group leader, $36,204
Hicks, Sawnie, ofc spt asst (keybrd), $23,160
Hicks, Sheila L, soc servs mgr, band 1, $41,940
Hicks, Stephen B, youth fac mgr II, $40,380
Hickson, Sabrina D, soc servs aide, $11.13/hr
Higdon, Crystal R, soc servs aide, $11.13/hr
Higginbotham, Ronda, child spt enforce spv, $38,928
Higgins, Elizabeth S, children's serv worker I, $29,976
Higgins, Katherine S, youth spec II, $31,512
Higgins, Mary S, misc tech, $12.59/hr
Hiles, Joshua S, youth spec II, $33,180
Hiles, Kristie J, fam spt elig spc, $29,976
Hilgert, April L, sr ofc spt asst (keybrd), $25,824
Hill, Annetta J, children's serv worker II, $34,356
Hill, Antoinette J, admin ofc spt asst, $28,536
Hill, Cassie E, children's serv worker II, $34,356
Hill, Charles D, fam spt elig spc, $29,976
Hill, Denesia G, fam spt elig spc, $32,628
Hill, Elijah D, fam spt elig spv, $35,568
Hill, Janice R, fam spt elig spc, $29,976
Hill, Joann, fam spt elig spc, $31,512
Hill, John D, fam spt elig spv, $34,944
Hill, Lydia A, fam spt elig spc, $30,984
Hill, Mary, children's serv worker II, $34,356
Hill, Maurine R, investigator III, $44,304
Hill, Rebecca L, youth spec II, $31,512
Hill, Renee M, fam spt elig spc, $29,976
Hillen, Kathleen S, acct I, $30,984
Hillhouse-Murphy, Gayla, fam spt elig spv, $36,888
Hilliard, David W, child spt spec, $29,976
Hillman, Allison, children's serv worker II, $34,356
Hillsman-Tilden, Susanna, children's serv worker II, $34,356
Hilton, Michelle A, prog dev spec, $41,172
Hindman, Anita J, fam spt elig spc, $36,204
Hines, Ashley C, children's serv worker II, $32,628
Hines, Kathy J, ofc spt asst (keybrd), $24,264
Hines, Laura L, child spt enforce spv, $40,380
Hines, Sue A, children's serv worker III, $38,232
Hinkle, Kimberly S, fam spt elig spc, $29,976
Hinrichsen, Betsy A, youth spec II, $29,976
Hinten, Jessica, children's serv worker III, $36,888
Hinton, Randall, children's serv worker II, $33,744
Hinz, Jennifer, hearings ofcr, $38,928
Hinzpeter, Gary H, soc servs mngr, band 2, $61,332
Hipkins, Kirsten M, serv coor yth srvcs, $32,628
Hippauf, Logan A, ofc spt asst (keybrd), $22,536
Hirstein, Courtney L, children's serv worker III, $35,568
Hise, Amy, fam spt elig spc, $29,976
Hise, Samina C, children's serv worker II, $32,628
Hite, Timothy M, children's serv worker II, $34,356
Hlavaty, Macy L, fam spt elig spc, $29,976
Hoag, Laina P, fam spt elig spc, $29,976
Hoch, Karen L, child spt spec, $29,976
Hocker, Amanda M, fam spt elig spc, $29,004
Hockman, Ronald, soc servs aide, $11.13/hr
Hodel, Kathryn A, children's serv worker III, $36,888
Hodge, Kelli, children's serv worker III, $36,888
Hodge, Vickie, sr ofc spt asst (keybrd), $26,652
Hodges, Ashlee C, children's serv worker I, $29,976
Hodges, Nicole S, reg fam spec, $37,548
Hodson, Melanie A, child spt spec, $29,976

Hoefer, Teresa L, child spt enforce spv, $40,380
Hoeflicker, Raschel R, children's serv worker II, $34,356
Hoeing, Mary L, children's serv spv, $39,624
Hoelscher, Angela M, mgmt analysis spec II, $48,156
Hoenshell, Renee D, children's serv worker II, $34,356
Hofacre, Robin L, soc servs aide, $11.13/hr
Hoff, Robin A, investigator II, $37,548
Hoffman, Jeffrey J, corres & info spec I, $34,944
Hoffman, Leone D, ofc spt asst (keybrd), $13,326
Hoffmann, Carrie, children's serv spv, $39,624
Hoffmann, Rachel M, corres & info spec II, $42,708
Hoffmeyer, Connie J, child spt spec, $29,976
Hogan, Janet L, fam spt elig spc, $33,180
Hogan, Michael K, fam spt elig spc, $29,976
Hogan, Tia A, children's serv spv, $39,624
Hogenmiller, Carrie L, fam spt elig spc, $29,976
Hogle, Rebecca A, children's serv worker II, $34,356
Hogrefe, Rachel J, procurement ofcr I, $37,548
Hogue, Debra A, fam spt elig spc, $30,984
Hogue, Donna M, special asst ofc & clerical, $35,350
Hogue, Monica R, special asst prof, $69,852
Hohensee, Gina, fam spt elig spc, $29,976
Hohensee, Melody, fam spt elig spc, $29,976
Holcomb, Cassie D, children's serv worker I, $29,976
Holcomb, Marissa A, children's serv worker I, $30,984
Holcomb, Stacy R, children's serv worker III, $36,888
Hold, Karrie, fam spt elig spc, $29,976
Holden, Ebony V, youth spec II, $31,512
Holdmeier, Nicole C, children's serv spv, $39,624
Holenda, Michele L, children's serv spv, $39,624
Holifield, Teresa J, ofc spt asst (keybrd), $23,160
Holiway, Joseph S, children's serv worker I, $29,976
Holiway, Michelle L, children's serv worker I, $29,976
Hollar, Brenda S, soc servs mgr, band 1, $52,092
Hollensbe, Joan E, youth spec II, $29,976
Hollensteiner, Nicole B, children's serv worker II, $34,356
Holliday, De'nel, soc servs mgr, band 1, $49,128
Holliday, Rebecca K, corres & info spec I, $34,944
Hollies, Anita, youth spec II, $31,512
Holliman, Shana M, fam spt elig spc, $29,976
Holliman, Shawn, children's serv worker II, $34,356
Hollingsworth, Adella M, children's serv worker I, $29,976
Hollingsworth, Lucas M, children's serv worker II, $34,356
Hollis, Melanie L, children's serv spv, $39,624
Hollis-Siebeneck, Michele L, fam spt elig spc, $29,976
Hollomon, Trina A, fam spt elig spv, $38,928
Holloway, Jeana J, corres & info spec I, $34,944
Holloway, Rebecca L, fam spt elig spc, $29,976
Holloway, Sharon L, soc servs mgr, band 1, $41,940
Holman, Lori D, youth spec II, $31,512
Holman, Zephera L, corres & info spec I, $34,944
Holmes, Charles R, children's serv worker II, $34,356
Holmes, Charlia, fam spt elig spc, $29,976
Holmes, Jana K, children's serv worker II, $33,180
Holmes, Judith A, acad tchr III, $18,774
Holmes, Keva V, children's serv worker II, $34,356
Holmes, Marghita, ofc spt asst (keybrd), $23,880
Holmes, Patricia S, corres & info spec I, $34,944
Holmes, Shanon L, case analyst, $32,628
Holmes, Sheila K, serv coor yth srvcs, $36,888
Holt, Carol R, ofc spt asst (keybrd), $23,160
Holt, Jamie L, youth spec II, $31,512
Holt, Marian, child spt enforce spv, $40,380
Holt, Michele L, ofc spt asst (keybrd), $23,160
Holt, Rebecca S, children's serv spec, $46,932
Holtmeyer, Dorothy J, sr ofc spt asst (keybrd), $25,824
Holton, Mooreen L, child spt spec, $34,944
Holton, Stacie L, fam spt elig spc, $29,976
Holzschuh, Susan K, children's serv worker III, $36,888
Holzwarth, Lori A, special educ tchr III, $42,708
Homan, Vicki L, youth spec II, $31,512
Homann, Guy M, serv coor yth srvcs, $33,744
Hommes, Kurt D, corres & info spec I, $39,624
Honeycutt, Joe C, fam spt elig spc, $29,976
Hood, Shante D, fam spt elig spc, $29,976
Hood, Travis, fam spt elig spc, $29,976
Hook, Emily A, children's serv worker I, $30,984
Hooks, Anika R, ofc spt asst (keybrd), $26,232
Hooper, Anne G, fam spt elig spc, $30,984

Hootman, David E, fam spt elig spc, $29,976
Hootselle, Chizuru A, child spt spec, $29,976
Hoover, Debra A, child spt spec, $33,744
Hopkins, Debra M, fam spt elig spc, $29,976
Hopkins, Kathleen D, fam spt elig spv, $35,568
Hopper, Robyn L, children's serv worker II, $34,356
Horlacher, Paul, child spt enforce spv, $36,888
Horner, Kim R, sr ofc spt asst (keybrd), $26,652
Horstmann, Andrea P, children's serv worker II, $34,356
Horton, Carlene K, fam spt elig spc, $31,512
Horton, Deoneisha D, youth spec II, $29,976
Hosna, Lee A, children's serv worker II, $34,356
Hoteling, Tracy M, children's serv worker II, $36,888
Houchens, Bernadette B, sr ofc spt asst (keybrd), $25,824
Houdek, Theodore C, legal counsel, $46,920
Hough, Jana M, fam spt elig spc, $34,356
Houltzhouser, Brenda K, fam spt elig spc, $34,356
House, Annette G, special asst prof, $69,852
House, Brookelyette K, ofc spt asst (keybrd), $23,160
House, Crystal M, fam spt elig spc, $29,976
House, Deanna L, child spt spec, $29,976
House, Jill N, fam spt elig spc, $29,976
House, Karen L, children's serv spv, $43,488
House, Marlice J, children's serv worker II, $34,356
Houser, Rita F, child spt spec, $33,744
Howard, Cynthia, ofc spt asst (keybrd), $25,032
Howard, Rolacia Y, medicaid clerk, $27,228
Howard, Tina L, fam spt elig spc, $33,180
Howard, Tracey L, children's serv worker I, $30,984
Howard, Valerie S, special asst prof, $50,040
Howard, Vicky L, fam spt elig spc, $29,976
Howe, Jordan D, children's serv worker II, $32,628
Howell, Betty A, cook II, $23,880
Howell, Cheri P, fam spt elig spc, $34,356
Howell, Heather, case analyst, $32,628
Howell, Jamal A, youth spec II, $31,512
Howells, Marina E, soc servs aide, $11.13/hr
Howery, Jeremy N, youth spec II, $31,512
Howser, Jacqueline D, sr ofc spt asst (keybrd), $25,824
Hoyt, Keri J, corres & info spec I, $34,944
Hubbard, Muriel D, ofc spt asst (keybrd), $24,612
Huber, Tracey E, children's serv worker II, $34,356
Huddleston, Aaron S, reg fam spec, $38,232
Huddleston, Kelsey L, children's serv worker I, $29,976
Huddleston, Robert B, children's serv worker I, $30,984
Hudnell, Idella M, children's serv worker II, $32,628
Hudson, Amanda K, children's serv worker I, $29,976
Hudson, Cynthia A, hr mgr b1, $55,416
Hudson, Elizabeth Y, children's serv worker II, $34,356
Hudson, Wilda, sr ofc spt asst (keybrd), $25,824
Huebner, Julie A, sr voc rehab cnslr f/t blind, $38,928
Huesgen, Carmen, ofc spt asst (keybrd), $22,536
Hueste, Lisa A, fiscal & administrative mgr b2, $67,488
Huettenmueller, Eric R, youth spec I, $28,104
Huey, Gale J, sr ofc spt asst (keybrd), $25,824
Huey, Wendy J, fam spt elig spc, $29,976
Huff, Chris W, children's serv spv, $44,304
Huff, Stephanie A, fam spt elig spc, $29,976
Hug, Bridget A, dpty div dir, $73,164
Hug, Bryan G, human rel ofcr II, $41,172
Hug, Christina M, admin ofc spt asst, $28,104
Hughes, Bernadette, child spt spec, $29,976
Hughes, Conchita A, youth spec II, $33,744
Hughes, Gwendolyn M, acad tchr III, $37,548
Hughes, Howard, youth spec II, $30,984
Hughes, Jennifer K, fam spt elig spc, $29,976
Hughes, Susan M, corres & info spec I, $38,928
Hughes, Timothy R, youth spec I, $28,104
Hughlett, Jennifer, child spt spec, $29,976
Huling, Sonya D, children's serv worker II, $34,356
Hull, Angela M, fam spt elig spc, $32,628
Hull, Megan L, corres & info spec I, $34,944
Hulsey, Justin M, youth spec I, $29,004
Hume, Loran P, soc servs aide, $11.13/hr
Hume, Michael L, soc servs mgr, band 1, $46,932
Hummer, Melanie J, ofc spt asst (keybrd), $23,160
Humphrey, Ashley J, sr ofc spt asst (keybrd), $25,032
Humphrey, Julie A, fam spt elig spv, $38,232
Humphrey, Latasha, fam spt elig spc, $29,976

Humphrey, Sheila L, youth spec II, $31,512
Humphrey, Stacia L, prog dev spec, $41,940
Hunnius, Shawna L, child spt spec, $29,976
Hunt, Deidre L, fam spt elig spc, $29,976
Hunt, Donna S, fam spt elig spc, $29,976
Hunt, Gregory S, prog dev spec, $40,380
Hunt, Jennifer, special educ tchr III, $37,548
Hunt, Kelsea S, children's serv worker II, $34,356
Hunt, Kenneth W, fam spt elig spc, $29,976
Hunt, Matthew J, youth group leader, $34,356
Hunt, Sherry L, fam spt elig spc, $29,976
Hunt, Stephanie G, corres & info spec I, $34,944
Hunter, Brooke M, fam spt elig spv, $34,944
Hunter, Detrice L, fam spt elig spc, $29,976
Hunter, Jennifer L, special asst prof, $42,708
Hunter, Joyce E, child spt spec, $29,976
Huntington, Darla S, fam spt elig spc, $29,976
Hurrell, Jeanne M, child spt enforce spv, $38,928
Hurst, Emily M, children's serv worker III, $35,568
Hurst, Tammy R, fam spt elig spc, $29,976
Hurt, Gloria A, corres & info spec I, $34,944
Hurt, Victoria, children's serv worker II, $34,356
Huse, Diana B, children's serv worker II, $37,548
Huskey, Crystal, children's serv worker I, $29,976
Husong, Paul M, fam spt elig spv, $34,944
Hutchcraft, Preston E, fam spt elig spc, $32,628
Hutchison, Dana L, children's serv spv, $39,624
Hutchison, Floyd J, youth spec II, $32,052
Hutchison, Julie M, youth spec II, $31,512
Hutchison, Lynnann K, youth spec II, $29,976
Hutson, Angela C, corres & info spec I, $34,944
Hutson, Sharon, children's serv worker II, $34,356
Hwang, Elizabeth, children's serv worker II, $34,356
Hyerstay, Sharyl K, child spt spec, $29,976
Hyman, Jody L, children's serv worker I, $31,512
Ibrahim, Ashraf N, ofc spt asst (keybrd), $23,880
Ice, Terry L, registered nurse, $42,420
Igo, Katie R, soc servs mgr, band 1, $41,940
Ikemeier, Jeffrey L, fam spt elig spc, $29,976
Ikemeier, Paulette J, fam spt elig spc, $35,568
Iler, Jamie L, exec I, $30,984
Imbrogno, Marsha L, children's serv worker I, $30,984
Imhoff, Donna K, fiscal & administrative mgr b1, $52,020
Impey, James E, legal counsel, $69,264
Ingenthron, Christina M, children's serv worker I, $29,976
Ingle, Keri, children's serv spec, $37,548
Ingram, Andrea L, fam spt elig spc, $32,052
Ingram, Dan, youth spec II, $31,512
Ingram, Jennifer L, corres & info spec I, $34,944
Ingram, Tracy K, children's serv worker II, $32,628
Inman, Jamie J, mgmt analysis spec II, $41,940
Innes, Stephanie L, children's serv worker III, $34,356
Irons, Donna M, ofc spt asst (keybrd), $25,824
Irvin, Jennifer, fam spt elig spc, $29,976
Irwin, Bion, fam spt elig spc, $29,976
Irwin, Chad E, soc servs mgr, band 1, $48,156
Isaacson, Mary K, fam spt elig spv, $34,944
Isaacson, Teresa P, youth group leader, $34,356
Isbell, Autumn M, youth spec II, $29,976
Isgrig, Donna L, children's serv worker III, $35,568
Isom, Cynthia B, sr ofc spt asst (keybrd), $25,824
Isom, Karen K, ofc spt asst (keybrd), $23,160
Isom, Kendah A, fam spt elig spc, $29,976
Ives, Jennifer A, fam spt elig spc, $33,180
Ivie, Erin K, children's serv worker III, $36,888
Ivory, Sheila J, ofc spt asst (keybrd), $24,264
Jack, Stephanie J, fam spt elig spc, $29,976
Jackson, Aisha, ofc spt asst (keybrd), $23,160
Jackson, Alesha R, fam spt elig spc, $29,976
Jackson, Bridget A, fam spt elig spc, $29,976
Jackson, Bridget K, investigator II, $37,548
Jackson, Christina A, ofc spt asst (keybrd), $23,160
Jackson, David G, prog dev spec, $42,708
Jackson, Erma L, sr ofc spt asst (keybrd), $28,452
Jackson, Gary W, fam spt elig spc, $29,976
Jackson, Gloria, fam spt elig spc, $33,180
Jackson, Gwynnette, fam spt elig spc, $29,976
Jackson, Jacob A, youth spec II, $29,976
Jackson, Janet N, ofc spt asst (keybrd), $23,160

Jackson, Jenae S, youth spec II, $31,512
Jackson, Jennifer J, acad tchr I, $29,004
Jackson, Jennifer L, children's serv spv, $38,232
Jackson, Kelly R, children's serv worker II, $34,356
Jackson, Lajuana J, child spt spec, $29,976
Jackson, Latasha O, sr ofc spt asst (keybrd), $25,824
Jackson, Laura A, child spt spec, $29,976
Jackson, Maison G, youth group leader, $32,628
Jackson, Mary E, child spt spec, $33,744
Jackson, Michael S, youth spec II, $31,512
Jackson, Nakita S, children's serv worker I, $29,976
Jackson, Sarah N, children's serv worker II, $33,744
Jackson, Shanieka, child spt spec, $29,976
Jackson, Tamara I, sr ofc spt asst (keybrd), $25,032
Jackson, Todd A, cook II, $23,880
Jackson, Trinece L, youth spec II, $29,976
Jaco, Rachel, child spt spec, $29,976
Jacobs, Gina M, designated principal asst div, $83,424
Jacoway, Lashonda, children's serv worker II, $32,628
Jacques, Rex A, children's serv worker II, $34,356
Jaegers, Janelle P, fiscal & administrative mgr b2, $61,584
Jaegers, Jeriane M, soc servs mnngr, band 2, $61,332
Jagels, Ricky J, youth spec II, $31,512
Jahnke, Robert, serv coor spv yth srvcs, $43,488
Jamerson, Linda D, medicaid clerk, $30,420
Jamerson, Maggie M, ofc spt asst (keybrd), $23,160
James, Callie M, fam spt elig spc, $29,976
James, Christina M, children's serv worker I, $31,512
James, Donna, child spt spec, $31,512
James, Gwendolyn, fam spt elig spv, $34,944
James, Jennifer L, fam spt elig spc, $29,976
James, Lori, special asst ofc & clerical, $42,708
James, Rosa, corres & info spec I, $34,944
James, Sandra J, cook II, $23,880
James, Shirley J, fam spt elig spc, $32,052
James, Tammy T, children's serv spv, $38,232
Jameson, Corey J, special educ tchr I, $32,628
Jamison, Brenda S, medicaid technician, $32,628
Jamison, Kathleen B, children's serv worker II, $34,356
Jamison, Nicole, children's serv worker II, $34,356
Jamison, Vernon R, soc servs aide, $11.13/hr
Janish, Ashlie N, youth spec II, $29,976
Jansen, Vanessa H, children's serv worker III, $36,888
Jarrett, Jessica E, children's serv worker I, $29,976
Jarrett, Jessica J, lpn II gen, $29,772
Jarrett, Moriah J, children's serv spv, $39,624
Jarvis, Jerrod D, youth spec II, $30,420
Javan, Ryan A, youth group leader, $34,356
Jay, Morgan L, youth spec II, $33,180
Jaycox, Michael L, child spt enforce spv, $40,380
Jefferson, Amber C, children's serv worker II, $32,628
Jefferson, Sonja C, soc servs mgr, band 1, $47,892
Jeffery, Veta L, special asst prof, $69,690
Jeffries, Janis J, fam spt elig spc, $29,976
Jeffries, Lisa R, fam spt elig spc, $34,356
Jenkins, Danny W, children's serv worker II, $37,548
Jenkins, Julie, registered nurse sr, $46,560
Jenkins, Latresa M, children's serv worker II, $34,356
Jenkins, Melvin L, investigator III, $43,488
Jenkins, Suttan D, sr ofc spt asst (keybrd), $29,412
Jenkins- Reese, Traynette A, soc servs mgr, band 1, $47,892
Jenks, Christina M, fiscal & administrative mgr b1, $50,040
Jennings, Amy E, children's serv worker II, $34,356
Jennings, John M, youth spec II, $31,512
Jennings, Kathy J, soc servs aide, $11.13/hr
Jennings, Leah J, fam spt elig spc, $29,976
Jennings, Timothy D, soc servs aide, $11.13/hr
Jensen, Lori J, children's serv worker I, $30,984
Jensen, Roberta E, child spt spec, $29,976
Jensen, Robin V, fam spt elig spc, $29,976
Jerabek, Laura L, children's serv worker I, $29,976
Jester, Lori, children's serv spv, $39,624
Jett, Rosemary, children's serv worker II, $36,888
Jett, Toleda D, corres & info spec I, $36,204
Jewell, Darlene G, fam spt elig spc, $29,976
Jewell, James L, hearings ofcr, $38,928
Jiles, Kysha D, youth spec II, $29,976
Jobe, Melonie S, admin ofc spt asst, $32,052
Joedicke, Erica M, fam spt elig spc, $29,976

Johns, Janet M, child spt spec, $33,180
Johns, Stacy A, children's serv spec, $46,932
Johnson, Alice M, rehab asst rehab srvs for blnd, $26,652
Johnson, Amy M, child spt spec, $33,180
Johnson, Barbara S, children's serv spv, $45,156
Johnson, Brandy L, fam spt elig spc, $29,976
Johnson, Brittney L, ofc spt asst (keybrd), $23,160
Johnson, Carie D, fam spt elig spc, $34,944
Johnson, Carletta, child spt spec, $29,976
Johnson, Cherie L, sr ofc spt asst (keybrd), $25,824
Johnson, Cheryl S, ofc spt asst (keybrd), $26,232
Johnson, Cory, fam spt elig spc, $29,976
Johnson, Cynthia G, children's serv worker II, $34,356
Johnson, Daniel C, case analyst, $32,628
Johnson, Deyanna J, children's serv worker I, $30,984
Johnson, Edward A, youth spec II, $31,512
Johnson, Elaine R, fam spt elig spv, $35,568
Johnson, Elizabeth M, children's serv worker III, $35,568
Johnson, Gail J, admin ofc spt asst, $30,420
Johnson, Ginger L, fam spt elig spv, $35,568
Johnson, Holly N, children's serv worker III, $36,888
Johnson, J'shon Q, youth spec II, $30,984
Johnson, Jacqueline A, fam spt elig spc, $29,976
Johnson, Jeffery A, youth spec II, $31,512
Johnson, Jodi A, fam spt elig spc, $29,976
Johnson, Kelsie R, ofc spt asst (keybrd), $23,160
Johnson, Kerry L, children's serv worker II, $33,180
Johnson, Kiara D, children's serv worker II, $34,356
Johnson, Kimberly, soc servs mngr, band 2, $50,040
Johnson, Lorna J, fam spt elig spc, $34,356
Johnson, Mary K, youth spec II, $31,512
Johnson, Michael L, youth spec II, $30,984
Johnson, Myeesha R, youth spec II, $30,420
Johnson, Myer A, fam spt elig spc, $29,976
Johnson, Myrtis, child spt spec, $29,976
Johnson, Nancy J, fam spt elig spc, $29,976
Johnson, Nancy P, fam spt elig spc, $29,976
Johnson, Octavia L, youth group leader, $35,568
Johnson, Patricia A, medicaid technician, $31,512
Johnson, Peggy L, soc servs mgr, band 1, $50,040
Johnson, Ruby L, children's serv worker II, $34,356
Johnson, Saundra D, ofc spt asst (keybrd), $22,536
Johnson, Sherry L, children's serv spv, $39,624
Johnson, Soraya Q, corres & info spec I, $38,928
Johnson, Susan G, children's serv worker II, $38,928
Johnson, Tanjala O, children's serv worker II, $35,568
Johnson, Teresa A, corres & info spec I, $34,944
Johnson, Terrico D, children's serv worker I, $30,984
Johnson, Tiffanie M, fam spt elig spc, $29,976
Johnson, Tiffany C, child spt spec, $33,180
Johnson, Traci L, children's serv worker II, $34,356
Johnson, Tynee J, children's serv spv, $39,624
Johnson, Vickie E, fam spt elig spc, $29,976
Johnson-Jackson, Charlotte, fam spt elig spc, $33,744
Johnson-Roy, Shannon M, fam spt elig spc, $33,180
Johnston, Angela, child spt spec, $32,628
Johnston, Angela M, corres & info spec I, $34,944
Johnston, Dan A, children's serv spec, $38,928
Johnston, Darla R, children's serv worker II, $34,356
Johnston, Kendal N, children's serv worker III, $36,888
Johnston, Linda K, fam spt elig spc, $32,052
Johnston, Misty, ofc spt asst (keybrd), $23,160
Johnston, Steven B, soc servs mgr, band 1, $50,040
Johnwell, Esa, children's serv worker I, $29,976
Jokerst, Nykina C, special educ tchr III, $38,928
Jolly, Glenda S, ofc spt asst (keybrd), $23,160
Jones, Addie, child spt spec, $31,512
Jones, Alanna B, admin ofc spt asst, $27,660
Jones, Amy B, fam spt elig spc, $30,420
Jones, Bonita M, children's serv worker I, $30,984
Jones, Brian K, children's serv worker I, $29,976
Jones, Bridget A, prog dev spec, $45,156
Jones, Bridgette D, children's serv worker III, $36,888
Jones, Cassandra M, corres & info spec I, $34,944
Jones, Cassandra S, fam spt elig spc, $29,976
Jones, Chateau L, children's serv spv, $39,624
Jones, Christal D, serv coor yth srvcs, $33,744
Jones, Dana Z, soc servs mgr, band 1, $51,312
Jones, Daniel A, children's serv worker I, $29,976

Jones, Debra L, fam spt elig spc, $29,976
Jones, Denise A, fam spt elig spc, $29,976
Jones, Diana L, special asst ofc & clerical, $45,876
Jones, Dwayne A, youth spec II, $31,512
Jones, Eric B, ofc spt asst (keybrd), $26,652
Jones, Eric L, children's serv worker II, $35,568
Jones, Eva J, sr ofc spt asst (keybrd), $25,824
Jones, Gwendolyn Y, child spt spec, $29,976
Jones, Hallie M, admin ofc spt asst, $36,204
Jones, Heather P, soc servs mgr, band 1, $50,040
Jones, Helen D, special asst prof, $68,160
Jones, Janica R, children's serv worker III, $35,568
Jones, Jason Z, fam spt elig spc, $29,976
Jones, Jessica L, children's serv worker I, $29,976
Jones, Johanna L, fam spt elig spc, $29,976
Jones, Karen J, children's serv spv, $46,932
Jones, Keisha, fam spt elig spc, $29,976
Jones, Kimberly L, children's serv worker II, $34,356
Jones, Kimberly L, fam spt elig spc, $29,976
Jones, Larry D, children's serv worker II, $34,356
Jones, Marcelius C, youth spec I, $28,104
Jones, Mary J, ofc spt asst (keybrd), $23,160
Jones, Matthew E, youth spec II, $35,568
Jones, Meghan E, children's serv worker I, $29,976
Jones, Melanie, fam spt elig spc, $29,976
Jones, Michael S, youth spec II, $31,512
Jones, Nicole E, children's serv worker I, $30,984
Jones, Nicole M, children's serv worker II, $34,356
Jones, Pamela, sr ofc spt asst (keybrd), $25,824
Jones, Rebecca S, children's serv worker II, $34,356
Jones, Robert E, youth spec II, $31,512
Jones, Robyn L, rehab tchr for the blind, $33,744
Jones, Sherron A, fam spt elig spv, $34,944
Jones, Sherwin T, youth spec II, $29,976
Jones, Sue A, fam spt elig spc, $29,976
Jones, Taletha P, fam spt elig spc, $29,976
Jones, Winetta A, child spt spec, $34,944
Jones-Smith, Patricia, fam spt elig spc, $29,976
Jordan, Dedrie J, children's serv worker II, $34,356
Jordan, Grace, sr voc rehab cnslr f/t blind, $37,548
Jordan, Janice K, ofc spt asst (keybrd), $24,264
Jordan, Lacritia N, fam spt elig spc, $29,976
Jordan, Lynette M, youth spec II, $33,180
Jordan, Michael C, fam spt elig spc, $35,568
Jordan, Pamela J, children's serv worker III, $35,568
Joseph, Brenda S, sr ofc spt asst (keybrd), $25,824
Joyce, Stephen J, serv coor yth srvcs, $34,356
Judd, Amanda K, children's serv worker II, $34,356
Judd, Amber N, youth group leader, $34,356
Juergens, Julie A, special asst prof, $60,684
Julian, Donna, ofc spt asst (keybrd), $23,160
Juliette, Jeremy M, children's serv worker II, $32,628
Julius, Megan M, children's serv worker II, $34,356
Jung, Karen S, fam spt elig spc, $30,984
Justice, Jacqueline J, youth spec II, $29,976
Justman, Jana L, youth spec II, $30,984
Kacena, Jay O, special educ tchr III, $45,156
Kafer, Shelly A, fam spt elig spc, $29,976
Kagarice, Tamara, child spt spec, $29,976
Kahler, Janie L, fam spt elig spc, $29,976
Kalthoff, John M, soc servs worker, $17.07/hr
Kalz, Geraldine M, ofc spt asst (keybrd), $25,824
Kamara, Iyesatu M, soc servs mgr, band 1, $51,096
Kanel, Darlene M, fam spt elig spc, $29,976
Karle, Timothy S, fiscal & administrative mgr b2, $67,488
Kates, Felicia A, soc servs aide, $11.13/hr
Kattelmann, Julie M, ofc spt asst (keybrd), $23,160
Kattich, Katina, children's serv worker I, $30,984
Kaufman, Benjamen M, children's serv worker II, $34,356
Kavan, Sharmon, corres & info spec I, $34,944
Kaye, Georgia C, fam spt elig spc, $29,976
Kaylor, Stacy, child spt spec, $29,976
Kean, Barbara A, admin ofc spt asst, $30,420
Kean, Tammy S, case analyst, $34,356
Kearbey, Jason L, children's serv spec, $40,380
Kearbey, Kimberly B, fam spt elig spc, $29,976
Kearney, Jana I, training tech III, $46,932
Keating, Tammy, child spt spec, $33,180
Kee, Patricia R, fam spt elig spc, $33,180

Kee, Thressa E, children's serv worker III, $36,888
Keebler, Carol L, sr ofc spt asst (keybrd), $25,824
Keener, Denise R, ofc spt asst (keybrd), $23,160
Keeth, Stevie L, children's serv worker II, $34,356
Keeton, Adam M, youth spec II, $30,984
Keeven, Patrick A, youth spec II, $31,512
Kehrer, Paige N, children's serv worker I, $29,976
Kehrer, Robert A, fam spt elig spc, $29,976
Keiser, David F, youth spec II, $31,512
Keith, Vanessa, ofc spt asst (keybrd), $24,264
Keithley, April D, ofc spt asst (keybrd), $23,160
Keithley-Crawford, Treva, ofc spt asst (keybrd), $23,160
Kelch, Kathy J, corres & info spec I, $38,232
Kellams, Dawn, child spt spec, $31,512
Kelleh, Fatuma B, children's serv worker I, $30,984
Kellerman, Ashley J, ofc spt asst (keybrd), $22,536
Keller-Shamet, Sabine, youth spec II, $31,512
Kelley, Jodi, children's serv worker III, $36,888
Kelley, Krystal, sr ofc spt asst (keybrd), $25,824
Kelley, Kurt, youth fac mgr II, $40,380
Kelley, Maryke M, reg fam spec, $37,548
Kellim, Phyllis A, children's serv worker II, $38,232
Kellison, Charlotte K, children's serv worker III, $36,888
Kelly, Brandi A, youth spec I, $28,104
Kelly, Danielle A, youth spec II, $31,512
Kelly, George W, children's serv worker II, $38,928
Kelly, Gwendolyn P, corres & info spec I, $33,744
Kelly, Paula, child spt spec, $33,180
Kelly, Theresa, corres & info spec II, $40,380
Kelm, Daphne, fam spt elig spv, $38,232
Kemna, Dana L, sr auditor, $41,940
Kemp, Christie, children's serv worker III, $36,888
Kemp, Emily G, children's serv worker II, $34,356
Kempker, Christy L, hr mgr b2, $64,715
Kempker, Jessica M, acct I, $30,984
Kempker, Sandy K, acct III, $42,708
Kenady, Vickie L, rehab tchr for the blind, $33,744
Kenaga, Bridget, children's serv worker III, $36,888
Kendrick, Gail J, ofc spt asst (keybrd), $13,116
Kendrick, Jennifer R, corres & info spec I, $36,204
Kendrick, Kyle E, soc servs mgr, band 1, $52,092
Kenedy, Lori C, fam spt elig spc, $31,512
Kennedy, Brenda K, coor prev of blindness, $46,932
Kennedy, Crystal D, children's serv worker III, $35,568
Kennedy, Jane J, prog dev spec, $48,156
Kennedy, Richard, youth spec II, $31,512
Kennedy, Rodney E, youth group leader, $34,356
Kennedy, Terrence M, children's serv worker II, $32,628
Kennedy, Wayne, children's serv worker II, $33,744
Kenner, Andrew T, youth spec II, $30,984
Kenniston, Blanca E, rehab asst rehab srvs for blnd, $26,652
Kenny, Lacy K, youth spec II, $30,984
Kenny, Melissa L, children's serv spv, $39,624
Kent, Nathan C, soc servs mgr, band 1, $41,940
Kent, Stacey L, children's serv prog mgr, $42,708
Keown, Rodney W, youth spec II, $31,512
Kepler, Elizabeth R, children's serv worker II, $34,356
Kerns, Vanessa J, fam spt elig spc, $29,976
Kersey, Candi L, children's serv worker II, $32,628
Kesel, Heather D, corres & info spec I, $34,944
Kessler, Mitzi A, training tech II, $41,940
Kessler, Ronald, fam spt elig spc, $29,976
Ketchum, Janice, fam spt elig spc, $29,976
Keyes, James A, children's serv spv, $38,232
Keys, Tanya, special asst prof, $69,852
Kidd, Sue P, serv coor spv yth srvcs, $40,380
Kiefer, Kathryn C, children's serv worker II, $34,356
Kientzy, Katie M, fam spt elig spc, $29,976
Kiger, Michele A, children's serv worker II, $34,356
Kiley, Mary K, sr ofc spt asst (keybrd), $28,908
Kilgore, Braid D, youth group leader, $34,356
Kilpatric, Shelley A, fam spt elig spc, $29,976
Kim, Angela, children's serv spv, $39,624
Kimberling, Tobi A, youth spec II, $30,984
Kimlinger, Brittany, child spt spec, $29,976
Kimmel, Tiffany R, children's serv worker I, $30,984
Kimsey, Christopher R, soc servs mgr, band 1, $41,940
Kinder, Debra A, youth spec II, $34,944
Kinder, Julie A, children's serv spv, $38,232

Kinder, Teresa M, medicaid technician, $31,512
Kindle, Monica S, youth group leader, $34,356
Kiner, Cole, fam spt elig spc, $29,976
King, Athisha R, children's serv spv, $39,624
King, Carissa J, corres & info spec I, $34,944
King, Cederick, corres & info spec I, $33,744
King, Cheryle J, fam spt elig spc, $36,888
King, Damon Q, fam spt elig spc, $33,180
King, Donna R, fam spt eligblty prg mg, $38,928
King, Dusty J, ofc spt asst (keybrd), $23,160
King, Heidi A, children's serv worker III, $35,568
King, Jean M, cook II, $23,880
King, Jennifer D, prog dev spec, $40,380
King, Kelly E, children's serv worker III, $35,568
King, Laura R, corres & info spec I, $34,944
King, Lauren J, children's serv worker III, $36,888
King, Lynn R, investigator I, $35,568
King, Marquess L, serv coor yth srvcs, $34,944
King, Meghann M, ofc spt asst (keybrd), $23,160
King, Roerica E, children's serv worker II, $33,744
King, Sarah, sr ofc spt asst (keybrd), $25,824
King, Susan D, medicaid spec, $37,548
Kinne, Paula M, ofc spt asst (keybrd), $23,160
Kinney, Amber C, sr ofc spt asst (keybrd), $25,824
Kinney, Lesa M, fam spt elig spc, $29,976
Kinsey, Erin K, child spt spec, $29,976
Kintz, Lorie J, fam spt elig spc, $29,976
Kinzinger, Corinne M, fam spt elig spc, $29,976
Kipper-Dunbar, Renee' A, fam spt elig spc, $31,512
Kirby, Rose M, fam spt elig spc, $29,976
Kirchner, Charlene, corres & info spec I, $34,944
Kirchner, Sheri L, child spt spec, $29,976
Kirk, Carolyn S, training tech II, $45,156
Kirkland, Belinda C, children's serv worker II, $34,356
Kirkland, Britnay F, children's serv worker III, $35,568
Kirkland, Donna, child spt spec, $29,976
Kirkover, Marjorie R, children's serv worker I, $29,976
Kirksey, William B, youth spec I, $29,004
Kirkweg, Lisa B, medicaid clerk, $28,536
Kirn, Jennifer A, children's serv worker II, $34,356
Kirsch, Donna M, misc tech, $12.59/hr
Kissinger, Steve, child spt enforce spv, $38,928
Kistler, Scott A, corres & info spec I, $41,940
Kitchen, Helener, fam spt elig spc, $34,356
Kithcart, James N, special educ tchr III, $40,380
Kitsmiller, Linda L, fam spt elig spc, $29,976
Kivett, Michael, child spt enforce spv, $40,380
Kixmiller, Jennifer L, rehab tchr for the blind, $34,944
Kleeschulte, Dawn E, children's serv worker II, $32,628
Kleffner, Judith A, hr mgr b2, $71,208
Kleffner, Shayla R, children's serv worker II, $34,356
Kleiboeker, Robyn L, children's serv worker II, $33,744
Kleinheider, Kristina R, medicaid technician, $32,628
Kleinheider, Michelle I, medicaid clerk, $28,536
Kleinhenz, Jon A, fam spt elig spc, $29,976
Kleinschmidt, Lisa, ofc spt asst (keybrd), $23,160
Klemme, Jennifer R, youth group leader, $34,356
Klepzig, Terri L, acad tchr III, $37,548
Kley, Heather M, child spt spec, $33,180
Kliegel, Kassidy, ofc spt asst (keybrd), $23,160
Kliegel, Nicole P, exec I, $30,984
Kliethermes, Barbara A, mgmt analysis spec II, $47,892
Kliethermes, Catherine A, exec I, $33,180
Kliethermes, Holly A, auditor II, $37,548
Kliethermes, Mary C, child plcmnt coor (ss), $45,156
Kline, Shereen C, auditor II, $38,928
Kling, Timothy G, physician, $119,976
Klingaman, Heather, fam spt elig spc, $29,976
Klingler, Daniel B, ofc spt asst (keybrd), $23,160
Kloess, Dana L, training tech II, $42,708
Klohr, Michelle A, children's serv spv, $42,708
Klopfer, David T, children's serv worker II, $33,180
Kloppenborg, Lisa J, sr ofc spt asst (keybrd), $25,404
Klote, Cathy E, ofc spt asst (keybrd), $23,160
Kluesner, Dana C, children's serv worker II, $34,356
Klumpe, Diana M, children's serv worker III, $35,568
Klusman, Arlina A, serv coor yth srvcs, $33,744
Kluttz, Christopher D, youth spec II, $31,512
Knackstedt, Tracey W, fam spt elig spc, $32,628

Knapp, Derek D, acad tchr III, $37,548
Knapp, Kari L, children's serv worker II, $32,628
Knat, Brenda S, admin ofc spt asst, $28,104
Knierim, Terisa B, child spt spec, $29,976
Knight, Bonita, fam spt elig spc, $29,976
Knight, Candida, children's serv worker II, $34,356
Knipker, Sandra M, mgmt analysis spec II, $43,488
Knipp, Lisa M, prog dev spec, $40,380
Knipp, Marla D, special asst ofc & clerical, $45,780
Knittig, Raymond P, area supv bus entprs blind, $38,232
Knopf, Kimberly S, acct I, $30,984
Knox, Krystin C, children's serv worker II, $34,356
Knuckles, Shellie C, children's serv worker III, $35,568
Knudsen, Katherine M, children's serv worker II, $34,356
Knudson, Michaela M, fam spt elig spc, $29,976
Knutson, Marla, child spt enforce spv, $34,944
Koch, Danny L, youth spec II, $31,512
Koch, Lindsay N, sr ofc spt asst (keybrd), $25,824
Koch, Lisa L, mgmt analysis spec II, $46,932
Koch, Melissa, fam spt elig spc, $29,976
Koch, Wm. M, soc servs mgr, band 1, $47,892
Koeller, Sherri A, fam spt elig spc, $33,744
Koenig, Lois A, fam spt elig spc, $29,976
Koenigsfeld, Konnie, children's serv worker II, $34,356
Koester, Tiffany N, children's serv worker III, $35,568
Kohl, Broc, ofc servs coor, $41,940
Kohl, Dana K, exec I, $30,984
Kohm, Diane M, children's serv worker II, $33,744
Kohn, Gale O, ofc spt asst (keybrd), $25,032
Kolaga, Kent, children's spec for the blind, $34,944
Kolb, Alicia M, fiscal & administrative mgr b2, $63,996
Kolb, Tialisa L, child spt enforce spv, $38,928
Kolden, Joshua, fam spt elig spc, $29,976
Kolkebeck, Edward W, hearings ofcr, $40,356
Kollanda, Kelly A, children's serv worker II, $34,356
Kolosik, Linda S, fam spt elig spc, $34,356
Koons, Andrew M, corres & info spec I, $34,944
Korenberg, Karen R, budget analyst III, $45,156
Kormann, Pamela J, pers clerk, $33,180
Korte, Caitlin L, case analyst, $32,628
Koser, Ed R, children's serv worker II, $32,628
Kovich, Julie, fam spt elig spc, $38,232
Kowalski, Heather L, children's serv worker I, $29,976
Kowalski, Tania, fam spt elig spc, $29,976
Kozak, Linda, fam spt elig spc, $29,976
Krachey, Darcie M, corres & info spec I, $33,744
Krajina, Aida, children's serv worker II, $34,356
Kramer, Christina, ofc spt asst (keybrd), $25,824
Kramer, Steven T, administrative analyst I, $29,976
Kramer, Tracey A, children's serv worker III, $41,940
Kramme, Marilyn, fam spt elig spc, $33,180
Krantz, Jessica M, children's serv worker II, $34,356
Krapf, Larry A, fam spt elig spc, $34,944
Kraus, Tracey A, children's serv worker I, $29,976
Krawl, Lana M, fam spt elig spv, $34,944
Kreisler, Jacob O, fam spt elig spc, $29,976
Kreisler, James O, soc servs mgr, band 1, $41,940
Kremer, Glenda A, soc servs mngr, band 2, $62,748
Kretzer, Kelly L, fam spt elig spc, $31,512
Krigbaum, Jennifer C, fam spt elig spc, $29,976
Kroninger, Andrea L, children's serv worker II, $32,628
Kruse, Lisa A, children's serv worker II, $34,356
Krystoff, Cheryl, fam spt elig spc, $30,984
Kuda, Kathy R, ofc spt asst (keybrd), $25,824
Kuehn, Dana L, children's serv spv, $39,624
Kuennen, Shirley K, fam spt elig spc, $29,976
Kuhl, Kelly, children's serv worker II, $32,628
Kuhn, Abigail T, children's serv worker I, $30,984
Kuhn, Joan C, prog dev spec, $40,380
Kuhnel, Erika L, cook II, $23,880
Kuntz, Nancy J, admin ofc spt asst, $31,512
Kuper, Daniel T, serv coor yth srvcs, $33,744
Kurutz, Audrea B, ofc servs coor, $41,940
Kuyper, Autumn M, children's serv worker I, $29,976
Kyriazis, Amy, serv coor yth srvcs, $33,744
Kyser, Charles, fam spt elig spc, $29,976
La Piana, Vonda K, corres & info spec I, $34,944
La Velle, Jennifer L, children's serv spv, $43,488
La Venture, Mark W, fam spt elig spc, $32,628

La Violette, Paulette D, child spt spec, $29,976
Labella, Brenda I, fiscal & administrative mgr b2, $59,220
Labella, Joseph R, soc servs mngr, band 2, $61,332
Labonte-Thomas, Sadonya L, children's serv spec, $38,928
Labrado, Rachel M, sr voc rehab cnslr f/t blind, $49,128
Lacaze, Holly C, children's serv worker II, $32,628
Lacorte, Mary J, corres & info spec I, $34,944
Lacy, Stacey L, ofc spt asst (keybrd), $25,032
Lafevers, Hunter B, children's serv worker II, $32,628
Lafrenz, Jennifer S, children's serv worker II, $34,356
Lager, Victoria J, soc servs mgr, band 1, $41,940
Laird-Allen, Michelle, children's serv worker III, $36,888
Lake, Kristi L, fam spt elig spc, $29,976
Lakey, Lane E, soc servs mngr, band 2, $61,332
Lamb, Jessie C, children's serv worker I, $30,984
Lamb, Nita A, child spt spec, $33,744
Lamb, Ruth A, budget analyst III, $45,156
Lambe, Ashley, fam spt elig spc, $29,976
Lamberson, Steven J, fam spt elig spc, $29,976
Lambert, Alan, mgmt analysis spec II, $41,940
Lambert, April K, training tech II, $40,380
Lambert, Brittany N, children's serv worker I, $29,976
Lambert, Yolonda T, ofc spt asst (keybrd), $23,160
Lame, Cody L, youth spec II, $31,512
Lamm, Theresa D, special asst ofc & clerical, $31,044
Lamon-Ladd, Odette, children's serv worker II, $34,356
Lamons, Dennis M, training tech II, $40,380
Lampher, Tamera R, youth spec I, $29,496
Lampkin-Page, Christine, fam spt elig spv, $35,568
Lampley, Harold, child spt spec, $29,976
Lampley, Sabrina A, legal counsel, $39,648
Lance, Sarah R, ofc spt asst (keybrd), $23,160
Land, Heather M, children's serv worker I, $31,512
Landers, Sandra E, fam spt elig spc, $33,744
Landi, Lynne R, children's serv worker II, $34,356
Landolt, Lucas C, fam spt elig spc, $34,944
Lane, Brian P, investigator III, $41,940
Lane, Kathleen E, rehab asst rehab srvs for blnd, $30,384
Lane, Pamela L, fam spt elig spv, $39,624
Laneman, Christine M, child spt spec, $32,628
Lanfersieck, Katie A, child spt spec, $29,976
Lang, Antoinette, ofc spt asst (keybrd), $22,536
Langford, Elaine, special educ tchr III, $43,488
Langford, Teresa R, children's serv spv, $42,708
Langston, Ida K, fam spt elig spc, $29,976
Langston, Jon, youth spec II, $31,512
Langum, Ricky K, youth spec II, $31,512
Lanier, Myrna L, children's serv worker II, $32,628
Lanigan, David C, investigation mgr b1, $52,092
Lankerd, Bonnie J, fam spt elig spc, $29,976
Lankford, Sarah J, special educ tchr III, $40,380
Lankford, Scott A, fam spt elig spc, $29,976
Lapointe, Anisa C, children's serv worker II, $34,356
Lappi, Ashley, children's serv worker I, $30,984
Lara, Joy J, fam spt elig spc, $29,976
Larimer, Julie R, outdoor rehab cnslr I, $34,944
Lark, Amanda J, corres & info spec I, $34,944
Larry, Donna M, clerical servs spv fs, $36,888
Larson, Christie, fam spt elig spc, $29,976
Larson, Matthew T, youth group leader, $34,356
Larue, Macey L, fam spt elig spc, $29,004
Lasky, Jewelia A, children's serv worker II, $34,356
Lassabe, Susan L, fam spt elig spc, $29,976
Latham, Anna M, youth spec I, $28,104
Latimer, Alvina, child spt spec, $31,512
Latta, Jessica B, soc servs sup, $37,548
Lattimore, Keita L, fam spt elig spc, $29,976
Laughlin, Cheryl L, medicaid spec, $42,708
Laughlin, Jan-Michael, children's serv worker II, $34,356
Laughman, Konrad, children's serv worker II, $34,356
Lauver, Jeanette A, child spt spec, $31,512
Laux, Heather M, admin ofc spt asst, $28,536
Lawless, Lisa M, child spt spec, $31,512
Lawrence, Joanne, fam spt elig spc, $29,976
Lawrence, Sue Anne, fam spt elig spc, $29,976
Lawshea, Lynda E, fam spt elig spc, $33,744
Lawson-Frazier, Annette, fam spt elig spc, $30,984
Lawson-Johnson, Vickie, training tech III, $48,156

Lay, Joann, fam spt eligblty prg mg, $39,624
Layman, Christopher B, children's serv worker II, $34,356
Le Fors-Jemes, Dawn R, children's serv worker II, $35,568
Leach, Ashley, child spt spec, $29,976
Leamon, Patricia L, sr ofc spt asst (steno), $28,908
Leard, Scott M, youth spec II, $31,512
Leason, Leanne D, soc servs mgr, band 1, $57,168
Leblanc, Janice L, ofc spt asst (keybrd), $24,612
Lech, Cindy K, child spt enforce spv, $38,928
Lechliter, Susan, reg fam spec, $37,548
Leclaire, Carrie G, children's serv worker II, $34,356
Ledbetter, Earlene, child spt spec, $33,180
Ledford, Tiffany N, children's serv worker II, $33,744
Lee, Barbara, fam spt elig spv, $34,944
Lee, Denim J, youth spec II, $31,512
Lee, Denise, fam spt elig spc, $29,976
Lee, Denise K, case analyst, $32,628
Lee, Jakara D, children's serv worker I, $30,984
Lee, Judy L, ofc spt asst (keybrd), $25,032
Lee, Kevin I, corres & info spec I, $34,944
Lee, Michael B, corres & info spec I, $34,944
Lee, Mindy C, medicaid technician, $16,314
Lee, Rebecca K, children's serv worker III, $35,568
Lee, Shanylrica N, children's serv worker II, $34,356
Lee, Terri A, children's serv spv, $39,624
Lee Moore, Glenda K, child spt spec, $33,180
Leeker, Holli N, children's serv worker II, $34,356
Leffler, Deborah, ofc spt asst (keybrd), $25,824
Leggett, Nicole, ofc spt asst (keybrd), $23,160
Legrand, Nicole A, children's serv worker I, $29,976
Lehman, Amy V, special asst ofc & clerical, $33,180
Lehman, Diana L, training tech I, $41,172
Lehmann, Elaine L, child spt spec, $32,628
Lehto, Joshua J, sr ofc spt asst (keybrd), $25,032
Leible, Lynn M, sr ofc spt asst (keybrd), $28,908
Leigers, Patty, child spt spec, $29,976
Leigh, Nicole R, fam spt elig spc, $29,976
Leikam, Robin J, soc servs mgr, band 1, $49,128
Leivian, Gail E, soc servs worker, $17.07/hr
Lemaster, Kimberly J, children's serv spv, $37,548
Lemons, Rebecca L, children's serv spv, $38,232
Lenger, Cindy, medicaid spec, $41,172
Lenihan, Shauna, children's serv worker I, $30,984
Lennan, Carla J, fam spt elig spc, $29,976
Lent, Mindy T, children's serv spv, $39,624
Lenz, Michael P, youth spec II, $33,180
Leonhard, Anna L, fam spt elig spc, $29,976
Leos, Bethany, children's serv worker I, $29,976
Lepski, Kevin C, hearings ofcr, $46,920
Lercher, Tammy L, children's serv worker II, $36,888
Leslie, Jennifer, ofc spt asst (keybrd), $23,160
Lesniak, Cassady C, children's serv worker II, $32,628
Lester, Imelda, fam spt elig spc, $29,976
Lester, Julie M, dpty div dir, $83,424
Lester, Roderick, fam spt elig spv, $34,944
Lett, Melissa L, children's serv worker II, $18,774
Letterman, Tom L, corres & info spec I, $34,944
Leuschen, Dale, child spt spec, $32,052
Leuthauser, Melissa N, child spt spec, $29,976
Levalley, Maya, children's serv worker II, $33,180
Levsen, Tyler J, legal counsel, $40,356
Lewellen, Denise E, fam spt elig spc, $29,976
Lewey, David A, children's serv worker I, $30,984
Lewey, Mary B, training tech II, $43,488
Lewis, Beverley J, fam spt elig spc, $29,976
Lewis, Bobbie, children's serv worker II, $32,628
Lewis, Bonnie G, fam spt elig spc, $29,976
Lewis, Charlene M, fam spt elig spc, $29,976
Lewis, Debra, fam spt elig spc, $35,568
Lewis, Jill A, children's serv spv, $41,940
Lewis, Jo A, children's serv worker I, $30,984
Lewis, John M, soc servs aide, $11.13/hr
Lewis, Julie A, children's serv worker II, $34,356
Lewis, Paul G, rehab tchr for the blind, $34,944
Lewis, Ronnetta, youth spec II, $31,512
Lewis, Sequoia W, children's serv worker II, $32,628
Lewis, Terry D, fam spt elig spc, $29,976
Lewis, Tiffany N, children's serv worker II, $34,356
Lewis-Johnson, Diana, children's serv worker III, $35,568

Lewis-Shrout, Angela M, fam spt elig spc, $29,976
Lewis-Somersall, Yvonne W, youth group leader, $35,568
Lewsader, Holly L, children's serv worker II, $34,356
Libey, Wendy C, training tech II, $40,380
Lichtenwalter, Phillip L, fam spt elig spc, $29,976
Liebig, Patricia A, rehab asst rehab srvs for blnd, $26,652
Lightwine, Scott J, youth spec II, $30,984
Like, Bryan M, youth group leader, $32,628
Lilleman, Kelly R, fam spt elig spc, $31,512
Lillis, Cathleen M, children's serv worker III, $38,232
Liming, Rhonda B, children's serv spv, $41,172
Limpus, Rachel L, children's serv spv, $39,624
Lindemeyer, Matthew R, investigator III, $40,380
Linder, Charles, child spt enforce spv, $38,928
Linders, Brittany, ofc spt asst (keybrd), $23,160
Lindgren, Christopher D, youth spec II, $29,976
Lindquist, Deborah S, special asst ofc & clerical, $37,380
Lindsay, Michelle, children's serv worker II, $34,356
Lindsey, Adrienne A, reg fam spec, $37,548
Lindsey, Mandy L, children's serv spv, $38,232
Lindsey, Richard R, youth spec II, $31,512
Lindsey, Tawanna S, fam spt elig spc, $29,976
Linenfelser, Sara J, soc servs mgr, band 1, $52,092
Linkous, Joshua J, special educ tchr III, $40,380
Linneman, Heidi A, children's serv worker I, $30,984
Lipshield, Deborah L, accounting spec II, $41,940
Lites, Ayesha S, children's serv worker III, $35,568
Little, Paige E, children's serv worker II, $33,744
Littleton, Andrea A, children's serv worker II, $36,204
Littleton, Debbie L, fam spt elig spc, $29,976
Litton, Janice F, ofc spt asst (keybrd), $13,116
Littrell, Kellie L, children's serv worker I, $32,052
Livesay, Cheri D, fam spt elig spv, $34,944
Livingston, Kimberly S, children's serv worker III, $36,888
Livingston, Summer E, youth spec II, $31,512
Lloyd, Bryan, legal counsel, $43,500
Lloyd, Rebecca M, children's serv worker II, $34,356
Lloyd, Ruth E, ofc spt asst (keybrd), $23,160
Lloyd, Sandra L, child spt spec, $29,976
Lockett, Ayrica S, children's serv worker I, $29,976
Lockett, Brittney N, children's serv worker II, $32,628
Lockett, Tasean R, children's serv worker II, $34,356
Lockhart, Karen, child spt spec, $29,976
Lockhart, Karen, fam spt elig spv, $34,944
Lockman, Elizabeth L, fam spt elig spc, $29,976
Lodholz, Robyn L, fam spt elig spc, $32,628
Loesch, Diana K, sr voc rehab cnslr f/t blind, $40,380
Loethen, Jeannie, admin ofc spt asst, $28,536
Lofton, Josephine A, fam spt elig spc, $29,976
Lofton-Barbee, Laverne, fam spt elig spc, $34,356
Logan, Frank R, youth spec II, $29,976
Logan, Icy L, fam spt elig spc, $29,976
Logan, Justin C, mgmt analysis spec I, $38,928
Logan, Rebecca L, soc servs mngr, band 2, $50,040
Logan, Tammy, fam spt elig spc, $29,976
Logsdon, Deitra L, soc servs mgr, band 1, $47,052
Lohaus, Angela B, child spt spec, $29,976
Lohnes, Joshua W, training tech II, $41,940
Loibl, Jennifer, children's serv spv, $39,624
Lomax, Eugena N, soc servs mgr, band 1, $49,128
Long, D. M, fam spt elig spc, $33,180
Long, Erica L, children's serv worker II, $34,356
Long, Gregory A, youth group leader, $39,624
Long, Holly N, corres & info spec I, $34,944
Long, Judy D, child spt spec, $33,180
Long, Justin M, procurement ofcr I, $37,548
Long, Kerry K, children's serv spv, $46,068
Long, Kimberly L, youth spec II, $31,512
Long, Mitchell T, youth spec II, $35,568
Long, Trichia R, soc servs mgr, band 1, $49,128
Long, Whitney, children's serv worker III, $35,568
Longan, Devora A, exec I, $30,984
Longing, Eric, fam spt elig spc, $29,976
Longwell, Tessa L, registered nurse sr, $44,904
Looker, Deidra M, voc tchr III, $37,548
Looney, Roxie L, children's serv worker II, $32,628
Loos, Gary M, child spt spec, $33,744
Lopez, Jennifer M, fam spt elig spc, $29,976
Lorenz, Dylan R, children's serv worker II, $34,356

Lott, Connie F, fam spt elig spc, $32,052
Lotts, Arletra D, ofc spt asst (keybrd), $23,160
Louis, Danielle M, children's serv spv, $38,232
Love, Allison Y, fam spt elig spc, $29,976
Love, Dana M, soc servs aide, $11.13/hr
Love, Deborah L, youth spec II, $32,052
Love, Lashai M, fam spt elig spc, $29,976
Love, Lewanna, child spt spec, $30,984
Love, Melissa J, children's serv worker III, $36,888
Love, Pamela S, sr ofc spt asst (keybrd), $25,824
Loveall, Jennifer M, admin ofc spt asst, $32,052
Lovelace, Jessica D, children's serv worker II, $34,356
Lovings, Jillan M, fam spt elig spc, $29,976
Lowe, Connie V, children's serv worker II, $34,356
Lowe, Deedra, fam spt elig spc, $29,976
Lowe, Edmund E, youth spec II, $31,512
Lowe, Gary A, children's serv worker II, $34,356
Lowe, Katrina K, rehab asst rehab srvs for blnd, $28,908
Lowe, Kelli S, children's serv spv, $39,624
Lowe, Kelly, sr ofc spt asst (keybrd), $25,824
Lowe, Laura A, fam spt elig spc, $29,976
Lowe, Tara, fam spt elig spc, $29,976
Lowe, Tracy J, youth spec II, $31,512
Lowery, Jo M, children's serv worker III, $35,568
Lowry, Jessica D, children's serv worker II, $34,356
Lowry, Meghan N, children's serv spv, $39,624
Loyd, April S, fam spt elig spc, $29,976
Loza, Anthony P, soc servs aide, $11.13/hr
Luaders, Daniel T, youth spec II, $31,512
Luber, Kendra N, children's serv worker II, $32,628
Lucio, Magdalene M, soc servs worker, $17.07/hr
Ludlam, James E, dpty div dir, $88,884
Ludwig, Angela E, fam spt elig spc, $33,180
Ludwig, Heather A, children's serv worker II, $34,356
Ludwig, Mary L, medicaid spec, $40,380
Luebbering, Alicia M, exec I, $30,984
Luebbering, Elyssa A, admin ofc spt asst, $32,052
Luebbering, Jacob P, fiscal & administrative mgr b2, $59,220
Luebbering, Kevin M, legal counsel, $40,356
Luebbering, Patrick, div dir, $93,228
Luebbert, Donna M, registered nurse sr, $46,560
Lujan, Apiphanie J, children's serv worker I, $29,976
Luman, Brandy J, children's serv worker II, $33,180
Luna, Terri E, fam spt eligblty prg mg, $43,488
Lundberg, Laurie A, children's serv worker I, $29,976
Lundt, Robyn R, legal counsel, $58,464
Lundy, Stephanie L, special educ tchr III, $40,380
Luney, Wanda F, child spt spec, $29,976
Lunn, Emily, fam spt elig spc, $29,976
Lurten, Candy J, soc servs mgr, band 1, $41,940
Lusk, Carol J, child spt spec, $32,052
Lusk, Jeremy S, fam spt elig spc, $29,976
Luster, Karema Y, children's serv worker II, $34,356
Lutes, Karen M, children's serv spv, $39,624
Lutes, Sandra A, fam spt elig spc, $33,180
Luthy, Sydney S, ofc spt asst (keybrd), $23,160
Luttrull, Kimberly B, children's serv worker III, $35,568
Lutz, Elizabeth L, fam spt elig spc, $30,984
Ly, Brittany R, children's serv worker II, $34,356
Lyerla, Nicole S, children's serv worker II, $34,356
Lynch, Julie A, corres & info spec I, $34,944
Lynch, Rita A, rehab tchr for the blind, $34,944
Lynn, Heather J, soc servs mgr, band 1, $44,100
Lynn, Rachael N, children's serv worker I, $29,976
Lyons, Clayson C, special educ tchr III, $40,380
Lyons, Devon L, children's serv worker I, $30,984
Lyster, Hannah J, youth spec II, $29,976
Lytton, Rebecca L, registered nurse sr, $50,244
Maahs, Hanz E, youth spec II, $31,512
Maben, John P, child spt spec, $33,744
Mabrey, Glenda M, child spt spec, $33,180
Macan, Kimberly M, fam spt elig spc, $29,976
Macdonald, Andrea, fam spt elig spc, $29,976
Macias, Kami S, prog dev spec, $41,940
Macios, Stuart L, serv coor yth srvcs, $34,944
Mack, Triauna D, fam spt elig spc, $29,976
Macrelli, Amanda L, children's serv worker III, $36,888
Madden, Sarah G, legal counsel, $68,688
Maddox, Sonya F, child spt enforce spv, $34,944

Madison, Deborah S, fam spt elig spc, $29,976
Madison, Erica M, soc servs mgr, band 1, $49,128
Madison-Lapsley, Michelle D, children's serv worker II, $34,356
Madonna, Karen M, admin ofc spt asst, $31,512
Magers, Jennifer A, children's serv worker II, $34,356
Magers, Loree A, corres & info spec I, $34,944
Magers, Ryan C, youth fac mgr I, $38,928
Maggard, Jerry D, corres & info spec I, $34,944
Magill, Stephanie D, children's serv worker II, $34,356
Magruder, Cortney R, fam spt elig spc, $29,976
Mahan, Victoria L, youth spec II, $31,512
Mahdi, Ahmad, special asst prof, $45,984
Mahoney, Kara K, children's serv worker II, $34,356
Malan, Angel D, children's serv worker I, $30,984
Malcolm, Darla, child spt spec, $33,744
Malecki, Madeline E, fam spt elig spc, $29,976
Mallett, Linda L, corres & info spec I, $34,944
Malone, Erica C, youth fac mgr II, $38,928
Malone, Hallie M, prog dev spec, $44,304
Malone, Joel B, fam spt elig spc, $29,976
Malone, Mike L, children's serv worker III, $35,568
Malone, Rebecca S, child spt spec, $29,976
Malott, Leta J, children's serv worker III, $41,940
Malotte, Bradley J, soc servs aide, $11.13/hr
Manasco, Brenda, asst spv business entprs blind, $40,380
Manczuk, Jeremy D, youth spec II, $30,984
Manda, Melissa M, hearings ofcr, $50,040
Mandell, Mark, child spt spec, $33,180
Mandina, Amy E, corres & info spec I, $38,928
Maness, Freda M, medicaid technician, $32,628
Maness, Rhonda K, medicaid technician, $32,628
Maney, Victoria, prog dev spec, $40,380
Manier, Callie J, fam spt elig spc, $29,976
Manis, Esther, ofc spt asst (keybrd), $23,160
Manley, Marcia L, child spt spec, $33,744
Manley, Pamela D, fam spt elig spc, $33,180
Mann, Brenna M, children's serv spv, $39,624
Mann, Dorothy, child spt spec, $33,744
Manning, April D, fam spt elig spc, $31,512
Manning, Flennord T, soc servs aide, $11.13/hr
Mannon, Shamyia, fam spt elig spc, $29,976
Mansfield, Connie R, children's serv worker III, $35,568
Mansfield, Jeremy, serv coor spv yth srvcs, $38,928
Mansfield, Kelly J, serv coor yth srvcs, $34,944
Manson, Sherry, ofc spt asst (keybrd), $23,160
Mantia, Jessica M, fam spt elig spc, $29,976
Marable, Reuben, serv coor yth srvcs, $33,744
Marchese, Cheryl J, child spt spec, $31,512
Marcinek, Dayna M, children's serv worker II, $34,356
Marcolla, Christy L, fam spt elig spc, $29,976
Marcou, Elefteria C, children's serv prog mgr, $47,892
Marcus, Laura A, children's serv worker II, $34,356
Marino, Gina M, children's serv worker II, $32,628
Marino-Johnson, Natalie R, children's serv spv, $41,172
Mark, Debby N, fam spt elig spc, $29,976
Markland, Beverly, fam spt elig spc, $30,984
Markland, Mary T, children's serv worker II, $34,356
Markusic, Jacquelynn P, soc servs mgr, band 1, $47,052
Markway, Tina M, special asst ofc & clerical, $35,304
Marler, Linda A, fam spt elig spc, $32,052
Marler, Melinda, children's serv worker II, $34,356
Marley, Alicia E, fam spt elig spc, $29,976
Marley, Danielle R, children's serv worker II, $32,628
Marlin, Van M, child spt spec, $29,976
Marquart, Elexis M, children's serv worker II, $32,628
Marquette, Joyce M, registered nurse sr, $51,276
Marquez, Kristin L, youth spec II, $29,976
Marsh, Babbette M, child spt enforce spv, $38,928
Marsh, Rachael A, children's serv worker III, $36,888
Marshall, Janice L, children's serv worker II, $34,356
Marshall, Tammy L, ofc spt asst (keybrd), $23,160
Marshall, Teressa A, sr ofc spt asst (keybrd), $28,452
Martellaro, Kay E, misc prof, $25.25/hr
Martin, Aigner Y, children's serv worker II, $34,356
Martin, Amy L, soc servs mgr, band 1, $52,092
Martin, Angela J, youth group leader, $34,356
Martin, Celestine, fam spt elig spc, $29,976
Martin, Charles R, children's serv worker II, $33,744
Martin, Christopher E, children's serv worker II, $33,744

Martin, Eric A, legal counsel, $50,376
Martin, Eric D, special asst prof, $87,876
Martin, John K, youth spec II, $33,180
Martin, Kristy L, corres & info spec I, $34,944
Martin, Linda K, fam spt elig spc, $32,628
Martin, Nicole L, mgmt analysis spec II, $41,940
Martin, Nicole L, children's serv prog mgr, $40,380
Martin, Philip A, fam spt elig spc, $29,976
Martin, Rachel D, children's serv spv, $38,232
Martin, Ryan B, children's serv prog mgr, $40,380
Martin, Shawnanna R, child spt spec, $29,976
Martin, Stacy J, soc servs mgr, band 1, $41,940
Martin, Stefanie R, soc servs mgr, band 1, $41,940
Martin, Teresa M, children's serv worker I, $30,984
Martin, Willie T, youth spec II, $31,512
Martindale, Kerry D, youth spec II, $31,512
Martinez, Jasmine D, children's serv worker III, $35,568
Martin-Watson, Paige L, children's serv prog mgr, $49,128
Martley, Taya L, fam spt elig spc, $34,356
Maryman, Lisa G, ofc spt asst (keybrd), $23,160
Maschger, Gretchen N, corres & info spec II, $42,708
Masek, Lori, prog dev spec, $46,068
Mash, Blake N, children's serv worker II, $32,628
Mash, Rhonda J, children's serv spv, $46,932
Maskell, Kelly M, ofc spt asst (keybrd), $23,160
Mason, Al Taurus, outdoor rehab cnslr I, $34,944
Mason, Kristopher, fam spt elig spc, $29,976
Mason, Ruth A, fam spt elig spc, $29,976
Masoner, Michelle L, corres & info spec I, $34,944
Massey, Elizabeth S, children's serv worker I, $29,976
Massey, Mary, fam spt elig spc, $29,976
Massie, Kimberly, children's serv spv, $39,624
Massman, Janet M, medicaid spec, $37,548
Massman, Melissa A, fiscal & administrative mgr b1, $50,040
Massman, Richard A, child spt enforce spv, $39,624
Masterson, Christie M, auditor I, $33,744
Masterson, Lauren, children's serv spv, $39,624
Masulit, Dely E, children's serv worker II, $34,356
Matfield, Jennifer, children's serv worker III, $35,568
Matherly, Michelle L, children's serv worker II, $34,356
Mathews, Janet, sr ofc spt asst (keybrd), $25,824
Mathews, Stacey M, children's serv worker II, $36,888
Mathis, Karen L, fam spt elig spv, $36,888
Matney, Deana L, sr ofc spt asst (keybrd), $25,824
Matson, Kristin L, ofc spt asst (keybrd), $12,132
Matthews, David S, youth spec II, $31,512
Matthews, Lorraine L, fam spt elig spc, $31,512
Matthews, Michael A, legal counsel, $41,136
Matthews, Paula A, children's serv worker I, $30,984
Matthews, Rachel, children's serv worker III, $36,888
Matthews, Ruth A, children's serv worker I, $29,976
Matthiesen, Julie R, fam spt elig spc, $29,976
Mattoon, Kylee R, children's serv worker II, $32,628
Mattox, Emily C, fam spt elig spc, $30,984
Maue, Cammie J, children's serv worker II, $34,356
Maugeri, Joseph N, fam spt elig spc, $32,628
Maulsby, April L, children's serv worker I, $29,976
Maupin, Daphne R, admin ofc spt asst, $35,568
Maupin, Jessie F, sr ofc spt asst (keybrd), $25,824
Mauzy, Kathleen A, children's serv worker II, $34,356
Maxwell, Pinkie, children's serv spec, $38,928
Maxwell, Sandra, ofc spt asst (keybrd), $23,160
Maxwell, Shannon N, children's serv worker III, $35,568
Maxwell, Susan A, special educ tchr III, $40,380
Maxwell, Tiffany N, fam spt elig spc, $29,976
May, Amanda C, fam spt elig spc, $29,976
May, Crystal L, fam spt elig spc, $29,976
May, Mary P, ofc spt asst (keybrd), $23,160
Mayberry, Brianna, fam spt elig spc, $29,976
Mayer, Charles, ofc servs coor, $41,940
Mayer, Nicole L, fam spt elig spc, $29,976
Mayes, Rachel M, fam spt elig spc, $29,976
Mayes, Windy E, children's serv spv, $39,624
Maynard, David A, children's serv worker II, $32,628
Maynie, John J, children's serv worker II, $34,356
Mayo, Michele J, fam spt elig spc, $29,976
Mays, Rockael M, youth group leader, $34,356
Mayse, Steven K, youth group leader, $34,356
Maze, Reina C, children's serv worker II, $33,744

Mazzocchio, Joseph P, child spt spec, $29,976
Mazzocchio, Kimberly K, soc servs mngr, band 2, $65,412
McAdoo, Anna M, children's serv spv, $41,172
McAllister, Karen E, admin ofc spt asst, $28,104
McAnally, Jennifer N, fam spt elig spc, $31,512
McAninch, Linda S, children's serv worker II, $42,708
McAvoy, Lisa M, fam spt elig spc, $29,976
McCain, Norita A, fam spt elig spc, $29,976
McCain, Tracy, fam spt elig spc, $29,976
McCall, Kandi A, ofc spt asst (keybrd), $23,160
McCall, Tammy E, children's serv spec, $43,488
McCandless, Barbara N, children's serv worker II, $34,356
McCandless, Mary K, procurement ofcr II, $46,068
McCann, Christopher A, children's serv worker II, $32,628
McCarley, Brian S, soc servs mgr, band 1, $43,488
McCarty, Shelby R, sr ofc spt asst (keybrd), $25,824
McCarver, John E, soc servs mgr, band 1, $52,092
McClaran, Traci L, soc servs mgr, band 1, $41,940
McCleary, Mary E, special asst prof, $61,104
McClellan, Kenna, children's serv worker III, $36,888
McClellan, Melissa S, fam spt elig spc, $29,976
McClellan, Terrance D, youth spec II, $31,512
McClention, Patricia D, youth group leader, $34,356
McCleskey, Brenda, fam spt elig spv, $34,944
McClurkin, Brenda L, fam spt elig spc, $29,976
McCoin, Debra I, soc servs mgr, band 1, $47,052
McCoin, Melissa M, sr auditor, $41,940
McCollough, Patsy M, exec II, $33,180
McComas, Alexis S, medicaid spec, $37,548
McConnell, Angela K, ofc spt asst (keybrd), $23,160
McConnell, Mallory S, fam spt elig spc, $29,976
McConnell, Rebecca I, ofc spt asst (keybrd), $23,160
McCool, April L, serv coor yth srvcs, $35,568
McCormack, Tessa I, children's serv worker I, $30,984
McCormick, Audrey E, legal counsel, $43,500
McCoun, Brenda K, youth spec II, $32,052
McCoy, Ashley N, children's serv worker I, $30,984
McCoy, Brooke N, children's serv worker II, $34,356
McCoy, Diana R, ofc spt asst (keybrd), $25,404
McCoy, Elise M, children's serv worker I, $29,976
McCoy, Gina, child spt spec, $29,976
McCoy, Ricky N, children's serv worker III, $36,888
McCoy, Robin V, fam spt elig spc, $29,976
McCoy, Timothy L, youth spec II, $33,180
McCracken, Paula R, children's serv worker II, $35,568
McCraven, Kathern R, youth spec II, $29,976
McCreary, Angelica, youth spec II, $31,512
McCrite, Reagan, fam spt elig spc, $29,004
McCubbin, Janet, exec II, $36,204
McCubbin, Kenneth N, sr ofc spt asst (keybrd), $25,824
McCubbins, Heather N, youth spec II, $29,004
McCubbins, Sarah R, children's serv worker III, $36,888
McCullah, Nina, ofc spt asst (keybrd), $23,160
McCullen, Fran E, soc servs aide, $11.13/hr
McCully, Tony B, youth spec II, $31,512
McCune, Kyle D, serv coor yth srvcs, $37,548
McCush, Donna J, admin ofc spt asst, $28,104
McDaniel, Amy J, fam spt elig spc, $32,052
McDaniel, Christina K, fam spt elig spc, $29,976
McDaniel, Leanna, fam spt elig spv, $34,944
McDaniel, Logan T, children's serv worker I, $29,976
McDermit, Randall D, prog dev spec, $46,068
McDermott, Blain O, youth fac mgr I, $38,928
McDonald, Erica, children's serv worker II, $34,356
McDonald, Jacqulyn, fam spt elig spc, $29,976
McDonald, Julie L, special educ tchr III, $38,928
McDonald, Kaitlin R, children's serv worker II, $34,356
McDonald, Lisa M, children's serv spv, $39,624
McDonald, Theresa R, fiscal & administrative mgr b2, $73,164
McDonald, Wade S, fiscal & administrative mgr b1, $52,092
McDonough, Angela M, fam spt elig spc, $30,984
McDougal, Anikeh, child spt spec, $29,976
McDowell, Donald B, children's serv worker II, $34,356
McElwee, Cindy L, children's serv worker II, $34,356
McEowen, Anne M, special asst prof, $61,104
McFadden, Michael J, youth spec II, $30,984
McFarland, John P, fam spt elig spc, $29,976
McFarland, Matthew W, children's serv worker II, $34,356
McGee, April L, fam spt elig spv, $34,944

McGee, Kandice V, children's serv worker I, $29,976
McGeough, Julie A, fam spt elig spc, $29,976
McGhaw, Nancy E, fam spt elig spc, $29,976
McGhee, Brandi P, youth spec II, $29,976
McGhee, Jaime D, children's serv worker II, $34,356
McGhee, Renese L, children's serv worker II, $34,356
McGhee, Tomorrow F, children's serv worker II, $37,548
McGhee, Vicki A, fam spt elig spv, $39,624
McGinn, Heather, ofc spt asst (keybrd), $23,160
McGinnis, Carol S, child spt spec, $29,976
McGinnis, Kimberlie D, corres & info spec I, $34,944
McGinnis, Samantha R, children's serv wurker I, $29,976
McGinnis, Sherrie L, fam spt elig spc, $29,976
McGlone, Emily G, fam spt elig spc, $29,976
McGough, Patricia A, sr ofc spt asst (keybrd), $25,824
McGowan, Tisha A, special asst prof, $71,100
McGuire, Emerson F, special asst prof, $69,680
McGuire, Ginger E, fam spt elig spc, $29,976
McGuire, Joyce A, fam spt elig spc, $29,976
McGuire, Malcolm, children's serv worker I, $31,512
McIntosh, Sydney L, youth spec I, $28,104
McIntyre, Jennifer, children's serv worker II, $34,356
McIntyre, Stephanie L, fam spt elig spc, $29,976
McKechan, Valerie P, children's serv worker II, $38,232
McKee, Lori J, mgmt analysis spec II, $45,156
McKee, Valerie E, corres & info spec I, $34,944
McKenna, Katherine L, case analyst, $32,628
McKenzie, Becky, ofc spt asst (keybrd), $23,160
McKenzie, Cathy D, medicaid spec, $37,548
McKenzie, Jennifer R, children's serv spec, $42,708
McKenzie, Lauren L, youth spec II, $29,976
McKenzie, Phoelica S, children's serv spec, $42,708
McKenzie, Rachael, children's serv worker III, $35,568
McKenzie, Teresa A, children's serv spv, $41,172
McKerracher, Joshua M, youth group leader, $34,356
McKim, Mary R, misc tech, $12.59/hr
McKinley, Tammy S, children's serv worker I, $31,512
McKinney, Ladonna R, youth spec II, $29,976
McKinney, Michelle, lpn II gen, $29,772
McLallen, Rikki B, children's serv worker II, $34,356
McMahon, Margaret, fam spt elig spc, $29,976
McMahon-Hughes, Mary-Anne A, children's serv worker II, $34,356
McMickle, Pamela G, rehab tchr for the blind, $34,944
McMillan, Debora J, child spt spec, $33,744
McMillian, Darryce N, youth spec II, $31,512
McMullin, Amanda B, fam spt elig spc, $29,976
McMurphy, Sherry L, child spt enforce spv, $36,204
McMurtrey, Cynthia K, special educ tchr III, $38,928
McNail, Crystal L, registered nurse - clin opers, $56,976
McNamee, Jane, ofc spt asst (keybrd), $23,160
McNeal, Rochelle L, fam spt elig spc, $29,976
McNeel, Angela L, child spt spec, $29,976
McNeely, Denekia R, children's serv worker II, $34,356
McNeely, Tasha M, fam spt elig spc, $29,976
McNeil, Vernon L, youth spec II, $31,512
McNew, Karen R, children's serv worker III, $36,888
McNulty, Phillip, youth spec II, $31,512
McNutt, Deanna K, fam spt elig spc, $29,976
McPeeks, Debra K, fam spt elig spc, $29,976
McPheeters, Ellen H, admin ofc spt asst, $32,052
McQuaide, Mary B, exec I, $36,888
McReynolds, Jonathan M, youth group leader, $32,628
McTeer, Jenna B, registered nurse - clin opers, $54,720
McTeer, Matthew J, prog dev spec, $40,380
McVay, Ashton L, child spt spec, $29,976
McVey, Kimberly P, children's serv worker II, $34,356
McWherter-Weldele, Michele L, fam spt elig spc, $29,976
McWhirter, Michele J, children's serv worker II, $36,888
McWhorter, Stacy L, soc servs aide, $11.13/hr
Meadows, Robin D, reg cnslt resid lcsng unit, $45,156
Meads, Dana B, fam spt elig spc, $34,356
Mealy, Aaron D, sr ofc spt asst (keybrd), $25,824
Mease, Traci E, children's serv worker II, $32,628
Medley, Deana, children's serv worker II, $34,356
Medlin, Amanda, children's serv worker II, $34,356
Medrow, Tonya S, recrtn ofcr II, $37,548
Meek, Amy K, children's serv worker II, $34,356
Meek, Gary L, fiscal & administrative mgr b1, $47,892

Meeker, Frances A, fam spt elig spc, $33,180
Meeks, Idrissa M, fam spt elig spc, $29,976
Mehmert, Eric T, ofc spt asst (keybrd), $23,160
Meiler, Nancy L, child spt enforce spv, $34,944
Meister, Ashley F, child spt spec, $29,976
Meixner, Elizabeth C, children's serv worker II, $33,744
Melbo, Rebecca, fam spt elig spc, $29,976
Melby, Catherine, fam spt elig spc, $33,180
Meller, Deborah L, special asst ofc & clerical, $49,908
Meloy, Dawn, children's serv spv, $39,624
Meloy, Jeannie M, children's serv worker III, $36,888
Melton, Susie, corres & info spec I, $34,944
Menconi, Sonya L, children's serv spv, $38,232
Menczer, Barbara, child spt spec, $33,180
Menhennet, Erin, medicaid spec, $37,548
Menning, Jana, children's serv worker II, $34,356
Meo, Jeanette E, sr ofc spt asst (keybrd), $25,824
Mercer, Carolyn S, child spt spec, $29,976
Mercer, Susan M, fam spt elig spc, $30,984
Meredith, Jennifer, fam spt elig spc, $32,052
Merrell, Mark C, fam spt elig spc, $34,356
Merrill, Pamela J, admin ofc spt asst, $28,104
Merriman, Frances A, fam spt elig spv, $36,888
Merriman, Tammy L, sr ofc spt asst (keybrd), $28,908
Merritt, Barbara J, fam spt elig spc, $29,976
Merritt, Liza, sr ofc spt asst (keybrd), $26,232
Mersman, Glynis J, fam spt elig spv, $40,380
Mertz, Caylin M, children's serv worker II, $34,356
Meske, Lindsey, fam spt elig spc, $29,976
Messer, Joyce M, account clerk II, $25,824
Messier, Wendy, fam spt elig spv, $34,944
Metcalf, Kelley A, fam spt elig spc, $29,976
Metcalfe-Davis, Kathy D, fam spt elig spc, $35,568
Metelski, Adam L, youth spec II, $29,976
Mettlach, Taylor L, soc servs aide, $11.13/hr
Meyer, Carl F, sr auditor, $40,380
Meyer, Donn F, child spt spec, $33,744
Meyer, Jennifer L, child spt spec, $29,976
Meyer, Karen S, hr mgr b3, $81,036
Meyer, Louis C, fam spt elig spc, $29,976
Meyer, Melissa R, ofc spt asst (keybrd), $24,264
Meyer, Rachel D, children's serv worker I, $29,976
Meyer, Todd M, special asst prof, $71,100
Meyer, William R, prog dev spec, $44,304
Meyr, Gerald L, legal counsel, $50,376
Michael, Jonna L, fam spt elig spc, $29,976
Michael, Patty L, youth spec II, $31,512
Michel, Catherine E, fam spt elig spc, $29,976
Middick, Cori A, children's serv worker II, $34,356
Middleton, Samantha J, youth spec II, $30,984
Midgett, Tanya A, prog dev spec, $40,380
Midyett, Linda S, child spt spec, $30,420
Mier, John R, prog dev spec, $48,156
Mier, Karen L, fam spt elig spc, $31,512
Mikel, Bonnie R, fam spt elig spc, $29,976
Mikrut, Lucille M, fam spt elig spc, $29,976
Milburn, Steven B, soc servs mngr, band 2, $61,332
Miles, Julie A, children's serv spec, $38,232
Miles, Naomi J, children's serv worker II, $34,356
Miller, Amanda L, children's serv worker I, $29,976
Miller, Andrew J, youth spec II, $31,512
Miller, Annie L, sr ofc spt asst (keybrd), $25,824
Miller, Bethany D, fam spt elig spc, $29,976
Miller, Chris R, designated principal asst div, $83,424
Miller, Christina J, fam spt elig spc, $29,976
Miller, Cody R, children's serv worker I, $29,976
Miller, Cyndie, fam spt elig spc, $29,976
Miller, Cynthia L, fam spt elig spc, $30,420
Miller, David L, youth spec II, $31,512
Miller, David L, child spt enforce spv, $38,232
Miller, Deborah M, ofc spt asst (keybrd), $23,160
Miller, Deneene L, fam spt elig spc, $29,976
Miller, Denise A, sr ofc spt asst (keybrd), $25,032
Miller, Gabriel H, outdoor rehab cnslr I, $39,624
Miller, Heather E, children's serv worker II, $34,356
Miller, Jacquelyn D, children's serv worker III, $38,232
Miller, Janet S, children's serv worker II, $38,232
Miller, Jennifer, children's serv worker IV, $38,928
Miller, Judy L, ofc spt asst (keybrd), $23,160

Miller, Kathleen E, children's serv worker II, $34,356
Miller, Kelly M, medicaid technician, $32,628
Miller, Kenneth W, corres & info spec I, $34,944
Miller, Kristin M, corres & info spec I, $34,944
Miller, Kristina A, fam spt elig spc, $29,976
Miller, Laura M, corres & info spec I, $34,944
Miller, Leslie J, fam spt elig spc, $30,984
Miller, Linda J, fam spt elig spc, $36,888
Miller, Lindsay D, children's serv worker III, $35,568
Miller, Lindsey R, fam spt elig spc, $29,976
Miller, Maureen L, corres & info spec I, $44,304
Miller, Michael A, voc tchr III, $41,940
Miller, Nancy L, fam spt elig spc, $32,628
Miller, Pamela E, fam spt elig spc, $30,984
Miller, Peter J, youth spec II, $36,888
Miller, Shannon N, fam spt elig spc, $29,976
Miller, Shari L, soc servs worker, $17.07/hr
Miller, Sharry A, soc servs mgr, band 1, $41,940
Miller, Shasta M, children's serv spec, $38,928
Miller, Sheila K, children's serv worker II, $34,356
Miller, Susan M, fam spt elig spc, $29,976
Miller, Travis J, youth spec II, $31,512
Miller, Zeze O, prog dev spec, $45,156
Milligan, Barbara J, sr ofc spt asst (keybrd), $25,824
Mills, Martha A, soc servs mgr, band 1, $41,940
Mills, Rebekah A, children's serv worker I, $29,976
Mills, Terri A, prog dev spec, $43,488
Milward, Mary F, fam spt elig spc, $33,180
Minnis, Haley J, ofc spt asst (keybrd), $23,160
Minnis, Jennifer A, children's serv worker III, $35,568
Minor, Sharon, fam spt elig spc, $29,976
Minter, Patricia A, corres & info spec I, $34,944
Minx, Bette A, fam spt elig spc, $33,180
Mirabito, John W, case analyst, $38,928
Miranda, Jennifer L, children's serv worker I, $29,976
Miskell, Cathy L, fam spt elig spv, $34,944
Misuraca, Melanie E, fam spt elig spc, $29,976
Mitchell, Ann E, children's serv spv, $44,304
Mitchell, Antonio D, youth spec II, $31,512
Mitchell, Bobbie L, sr ofc spt asst (clerical), $26,652
Mitchell, Donna, ofc spt asst (keybrd), $23,160
Mitchell, Heather L, child spt spec, $31,512
Mitchell, Lamont P, youth spec II, $33,744
Mitchell, Laura, children's serv worker II, $34,356
Mitchell, Laura E, children's serv spv, $39,624
Mitchell, Lynnette E, youth spec II, $31,512
Mitchell, Marisa, fam spt elig spc, $29,976
Mitchell, Mary E, children's serv worker II, $32,628
Mitchell, Nicole M, children's serv worker I, $29,976
Mitchell, Rhonda A, fam spt elig spc, $29,976
Mitchell, Sharon, fam spt elig spc, $29,976
Mitchell, Timothy B, training tech II, $43,488
Mitchem, Alicia, prog dev spec, $40,380
Mitchem, Essence L, youth spec II, $30,984
Mize, Diana E, fam spt elig spc, $33,180
Mizer, Sharon K, children's serv worker III, $36,888
Moeckli, Andrew J, cmnty svs coord-youth srvs, $41,172
Moeckli, Lorrie M, youth spec II, $32,052
Moeller, Sandra, child spt spec, $35,568
Moffatt, Andrea V, ofc spt asst (keybrd), $23,160
Moller, Sherry L, children's serv spec, $41,940
Mollette, Holly J, child spt spec, $29,976
Monat, Christopher, child spt spec, $29,976
Monda, Monea, child spt spec, $29,976
Monfee, Leesa K, fam spt elig spc, $30,984
Monnig-Jones, Camille M, special educ tchr I, $30,984
Monrotus, Anna M, children's serv worker II, $34,356
Montemayor, Lisette, sr ofc spt asst (keybrd), $25,824
Montes, Anthea R, children's serv worker I, $30,984
Montgomery, Maureen T, fam spt elig spc, $29,976
Montgomery, Saundra J, fam spt elig spc, $29,976
Montgomery, Scott B, mgmt analysis spec II, $46,068
Montiel, Crystal R, children's serv worker II, $34,356
Montrel-Smith, Courtenay A, fam spt elig spc, $29,976
Moody, Patrick D, fam spt eligblty prg mg, $43,488
Moon, Amy, children's serv worker II, $34,356
Mooney, Angela M, fam spt elig spc, $32,052
Mooney, Lizabeth E, children's serv worker I, $29,976
Mooney, Tonya F, children's serv worker II, $34,356

Mooneyham, Jonna J, children's serv worker III, $36,888
Moore, Angela D, ofc spt asst (keybrd), $25,032
Moore, Angie M, children's serv worker II, $34,356
Moore, Brandon J, acad tchr II, $34,944
Moore, Brenda J, soc servs mgr, band 1, $41,940
Moore, Crissy M, children's serv worker III, $36,888
Moore, Donnetta L, ofc spt asst (keybrd), $23,160
Moore, Enya-Otecka R, corres & info spec I, $34,944
Moore, Eric L, youth spec II, $31,512
Moore, Erin R, children's serv worker II, $34,356
Moore, Ethel D, soc servs aide, $11.13/hr
Moore, Evan, youth spec II, $30,984
Moore, Janet R, exec I, $37,548
Moore, Kari A, fam spt elig spc, $35,568
Moore, Kathryn M, ofc spt asst (keybrd), $23,160
Moore, L. Deenee, fam spt elig spc, $29,976
Moore, Leona, fam spt elig spc, $29,976
Moore, Margaret M, fam spt elig spc, $30,984
Moore, Mary P, children's serv worker III, $35,568
Moore, Peyton S, children's serv worker II, $34,356
Moore, Ramona C, acad tchr III, $18,774
Moore, Rynetta D, children's serv worker I, $30,984
Moore, Sarah K, fam spt elig spc, $29,976
Moore, Sean, children's serv worker III, $35,568
Moore, Sharon, fam spt elig spc, $29,976
Moore, Stacey J, child spt spec, $30,420
Moore, Suzanne R, soc servs aide, $11.13/hr
Moore, Tiffany R, soc servs mgr, band 1, $50,040
Moore, Tonzeal D, printing/mail technician IV, $30,984
Moore-Black, Tova J, fam spt elig spc, $36,888
Moppin, Jennifer L, fam spt elig spc, $29,976
Morales, Victoria, ofc spt asst (keybrd), $23,160
Morff, Cynthia L, misc prof, $28.28/hr
Morford, Christina L, corres & info spec I, $34,944
Morgan, Angela M, child spt enforce spv, $38,232
Morgan, Cathy, corres & info spec I, $34,944
Morgan, Cheryl M, investigator II, $38,928
Morgan, Debra J, fam spt elig spc, $32,628
Morgan, Jennifer A, children's serv worker III, $35,568
Morgan, Kimberly D, medicaid prog rel rep, $40,380
Morgan, Ladonna V, fam spt elig spv, $34,944
Morgan, Monica D, children's serv worker III, $36,888
Morgan, Thomas J, youth spec II, $36,888
Moriarity, Timothy T, investigator II, $41,940
Morlock, Tina B, mgmt analysis spec II, $48,156
Morning, John G, youth group leader, $34,356
Moroni, Sharon, special educ tchr III, $40,380
Morrill, Alexander P, youth spec II, $29,976
Morris, Angela B, corres & info spec I, $35,568
Morris, Christopher B, youth spec II, $31,512
Morris, Constance L, child spt spec, $31,512
Morris, Debra J, child spt spec, $30,420
Morris, Jacqueline M, children's serv worker II, $33,744
Morris, Kelly R, children's serv spv, $39,624
Morris, Krista V, corres & info spec I, $34,944
Morris, Matthew E, soc servs mgr, band 1, $57,744
Morris, Melissa A, children's serv worker I, $30,984
Morris, Nakisha, ofc spt asst (keybrd), $23,160
Morris, Nancy K, child spt spec, $31,512
Morris, Rebecca A, child spt spec, $29,976
Morris, Sarah K, fam spt elig spc, $29,976
Morris, Tamara, child spt spec, $29,976
Morris, Timothy, fam spt elig spc, $29,976
Morris, Wendy E, fam spt elig spc, $29,976
Morrison, Kathy D, fam spt elig spc, $29,976
Morrison, Mary A, procurement ofcr I, $37,548
Morrison, Nicholas J, children's serv worker II, $33,744
Morrison, Penny R, ofc spt asst (keybrd), $23,160
Morris-Wiley, Kaya T, fam spt elig spc, $29,976
Morrow, Angela M, fam spt elig spc, $31,512
Morrow, Jacqueline M, child spt spec, $29,976
Morrow, John Q, serv coor spv yth srvcs, $42,708
Morrow, Keri K, children's serv spv, $39,624
Morrow, Kerry, fam spt elig spc, $29,976
Morrow - Kempf, Kerensa, training tech II, $40,380
Mosby, Angela D, children's serv worker II, $34,356
Moser, Megan A, children's serv worker III, $35,568
Moses, Melanie, fam spt elig spc, $29,976
Mosher, Randy P, medicaid unit spv, $48,156

Mosier, Janice L, fam spt elig spc, $33,180
Mosley, Freddie, youth spec II, $31,512
Moss, Jennifer A, children's serv worker spv, $42,708
Moss, Teri L, fam spt elig spc, $34,356
Mote, Kathleen J, medicaid spec, $36,204
Motzkus, Sheila, fam spt elig spc, $29,976
Moulder, Julie J, children's serv prog mgr, $41,940
Mount, Amy, children's serv worker II, $34,356
Mowery, Dawn M, fam spt elig spc, $29,976
Mowry, Earnie L, child spt spec, $29,976
Moyers, Caroline S, children's serv spv, $38,232
Moyers, Jane E, ofc spt asst (keybrd), $25,824
Mueller, Amanda J, child spt enforce spv, $34,944
Mueller, Christy, fam spt elig spc, $29,976
Mueller, Susan J, acad tchr III, $37,548
Mueller, Toni E, children's serv worker II, $33,180
Muenks, Amy J, exec I, $30,984
Muhammad, Salim A, youth spec II, $31,512
Muirhead, Amanda D, fam spt elig spc, $29,976
Mulac, Priscilla M, training tech II, $46,932
Mulholland, Tamara J, ofc spt asst (keybrd), $22,536
Mullen, Melissa K, fam spt elig spc, $29,976
Mullings, Mary E, fam spt elig spc, $32,052
Mullins, Angela M, soc servs mgr, band 1, $51,312
Mullins, Barbara D, youth spec II, $30,420
Mulvany, Brian K, rehab tchr for the blind, $38,928
Munckton, Marilyn K, fam spt elig spv, $39,624
Munkholm, Anna E, youth spec II, $30,984
Munoz, Lisa C, fam spt elig spc, $29,976
Muns, Jacqueline M, fam spt elig spc, $29,976
Murdick, Colin, investigator II, $41,940
Murdock, Robert C, voc tchr III, $37,548
Murph, Renita J, fam spt elig spc, $29,976
Murphey, Joan E, ofc spt asst (keybrd), $26,652
Murphy, Joseph A, youth spec II, $31,512
Murphy, Kathleen A, youth spec I, $29,004
Murphy, Marady, children's serv worker I, $29,976
Murphy, Melanie, ofc spt asst (keybrd), $25,404
Murphy, Mikaila M, children's serv worker II, $34,356
Murphy, Penny K, misc tech, $12.59/hr
Murphy, Sandra A, sr ofc spt asst (keybrd), $25,824
Murphy, Teresa R, sr ofc spt asst (keybrd), $26,652
Murphy-Johnson, Andrea K, fam spt elig spc, $29,976
Murray, Alicia, ofc spt asst (keybrd), $23,160
Murray, Barbara L, fam spt elig spc, $34,356
Murray, Cody M, children's serv worker II, $34,356
Murray, Darisha, ofc spt asst (keybrd), $22,536
Murray, Debra, prog dev spec, $41,940
Murray, Emalie A, children's serv worker II, $33,744
Murray, Fusun E, fam spt elig spv, $36,888
Murray, Kathleen A, prog dev spec, $47,892
Murray, Tobie L, children's serv worker II, $33,744
Murrell, Elissa M, children's serv worker II, $34,356
Murrell, Theresa, research analyst I, $34,944
Murrie-Robinson, Stephen, youth spec II, $31,512
Murry, Melissa R, fam spt elig spc, $29,976
Muschany, Glenda, ofc spt asst (keybrd), $23,160
Musgrave, Ashley L, children's serv worker II, $34,356
Musser, Amanda D, children's serv worker I, $30,984
Muttschall, Elizabeth H, fam spt elig spc, $29,976
Muzaffar, Samar, special asst prof, $167,160
Myers, Carly E, children's serv worker II, $34,356
Myers, Meaghan P, hearings ofcr, $38,928
Myers, Michelle L, children's serv worker II, $33,744
Myers, Nicole M, ofc spt asst (keybrd), $23,160
Myers, Pamela D, sr ofc spt asst (keybrd), $25,824
Myers, Patsy N, fam spt elig spc, $29,976
Myers, Samantha R, child spt spec, $29,976
Myler, Amy R, soc servs aide, $11.13/hr
Nacy, Morgan D, child spt spec, $29,976
Naddaf, Lindsey K, fam spt elig spc, $29,976
Naffa, Bonnie R, fam spt elig spc, $35,568
Nahler, Candice, children's serv spv, $39,624
Nall, Rebecca, ofc spt asst (keybrd), $23,160
Nalley, Martha J, corres & info spec I, $34,944
Nance, Carley P, children's serv worker I, $29,976
Nance, Julia E, soc servs mgr, band 1, $52,092
Nance, Ronda K, children's serv worker III, $41,172
Nanchal, Rekha, soc servs mgr, band 1, $48,156

Napier, Jessica A, children's serv worker I, $29,976
Napier, Mary, fam spt elig spc, $29,976
Nardi, Racheal E, medicaid spec, $37,548
Nash, Loren A, children's serv worker II, $34,356
Nastave, Ashley B, children's serv worker I, $29,976
Nations, Justin, children's serv spv, $39,624
Nations, Meredith L, fam spt elig spc, $29,976
Nations, Stephanie, fam spt elig spc, $29,976
Navarro, Mary, ofc spt asst (keybrd), $24,264
Neace, Amanda, children's serv worker III, $36,888
Neal, Bonnie J, children's serv spec, $53,208
Neal, Donna M, fam spt elig spc, $35,568
Neal, Jacquline L, ofc spt asst (keybrd), $23,160
Neal, Jennifer, corres & info spec I, $33,744
Neal, Marcus T, youth spec II, $31,512
Neal, Melanie K, sr ofc spt asst (steno), $28,908
Neal, Nina, fam spt elig spc, $29,976
Neal, Rose K, youth spec II, $31,512
Neasby-Miller, Kelly J, children's serv worker II, $34,356
Neblock, Patricia L, children's serv worker I, $30,984
Needham, Charity A, children's serv worker II, $33,744
Needy, Miranda L, account clerk II, $25,824
Neeley, Dalana D, sr ofc spt asst (keybrd), $25,824
Neeley, Susan K, corres & info spec I, $18,102
Neely, Brittany J, fam spt elig spc, $29,976
Nelp, Cynthia M, ofc spt asst (keybrd), $29,412
Nelson, Andrea M, soc servs aide, $11.13/hr
Nelson, Bernard M, youth spec I, $28,104
Nelson, Craig A, serv coor yth srvcs, $34,356
Nelson, Crystal J, fam spt elig spc, $29,976
Nelson, Dmitric B, soc servs aide, $11.13/hr
Nelson, Linda M, ofc spt asst (keybrd), $23,160
Nelson, Lisa, child spt spec, $31,512
Nelson, Sandra K, misc prof, $30.54/hr
Nelson, Sheila R, children's serv worker II, $38,928
Nelson, Tennille R, fam spt elig spc, $29,976
Nelson, Tracy A, sr ofc spt asst (keybrd), $25,824
Nentwig, Cheryl A, acct II, $44,304
Nepote, Valerie K, child spt spec, $30,984
Nettleton, Gayla, child spt spec, $29,976
Nettleton, Patricia E, children's serv worker II, $34,356
Nettleton, Todd A, children's serv worker II, $35,568
Neugent, Dana'l R, children's serv worker II, $34,356
Neuhalfen, Rebecca, children's serv spec, $40,380
Neumann, Kimberly S, fam spt elig spc, $32,628
Nevills, Tanika M, fam spt elig spc, $29,976
Newberry, Carlos, soc servs mgr, band 1, $47,892
Newby, Michelle A, fam spt elig spc, $29,976
Newell, Kathleen, child spt spec, $16,872
Newell, Sheila, children's serv worker III, $35,568
Newham, Cara L, fam spt elig spv, $34,944
Newkirk, Rachel, children's serv worker II, $34,356
Newman, Amber L, fam spt elig spc, $29,976
Newman, Katherine L, children's serv worker I, $29,976
Newman, Sharon K, soc servs aide, $11.13/hr
Newton, Tamara F, acad tchr II, $34,944
Newton, Terrill B, exec I, $30,984
Nibarger, Janet L, fam spt elig spc, $34,356
Nibert, Ryan J, serv coor yth srvcs, $33,744
Nicholls, Steven R, youth group leader, $34,356
Nichols, Alexandria C, youth spec I, $28,104
Nichols, Caleigh R, children's serv worker II, $34,356
Nichols, Donna M, soc servs mgr, band 1, $58,908
Nichols, Judy K, fam spt elig spc, $30,420
Nichols, Linda M, corres & info spec I, $36,204
Nichols, Melody L, prog dev spec, $40,380
Nichols, Toni M, admin ofc spt asst, $28,536
Nicholson, Britanie J, fam spt elig spc, $29,976
Nicholson, Stephanie, children's serv worker III, $35,568
Nickelson, Karen, ofc spt asst (keybrd), $23,160
Nicks, Brooke A, children's serv worker II, $34,356
Nicks, Greta F, youth group leader, $34,356
Nicosia, Emily J, children's serv spv, $39,624
Niebling, Cynthia M, fam spt elig spc, $29,976
Niekamp, Martha J, info spt coor, $30,420
Nielsen, Mercedez M, youth spec I, $28,104
Nieman, Kimberly, ofc spt asst (keybrd), $23,160
Niemeyer, Dawn, children's serv worker II, $34,356
Nierman, Wanda J, soc servs mgr, band 1, $41,940

Niethe, Veronica L, fam spt elig spc, $29,976
Nikodym, Nanci M, soc servs mngr, band 2, $50,040
Niner, Patricia A, soc servs mgr, band 1, $41,940
Nixon, Tyrone R, youth spec II, $31,512
Nkweti, Delphine K, children's serv worker I, $30,984
Nnedu, Nnamdi C, hearings ofcr, $38,928
Noakes, Jaquetta, fam spt elig spc, $29,976
Nobis, Deanna K, children's serv spv, $52,092
Noce, Melissa A, child spt spec, $31,512
Noel, Clarissa M, special educ tchr III, $38,928
Nolan, Laura I, child spt spec, $29,976
Nolan, Lourie J, youth spec II, $33,180
Nolan, Michelle A, children's serv worker II, $35,568
Nolan, Robin G, prog dev spec, $42,708
Nolting, Karen E, admin ofc spt asst, $28,536
Nolting, Sherry A, exec I, $30,984
Nong, Melessa, fam spt elig spc, $29,976
Noonan, Julie A, fam spt elig spc, $29,976
Nootbaar, Dorothy A, fam spt elig spc, $29,976
Norbury, Susan G, fam spt elig spc, $30,984
Nord, Sarah, ofc spt asst (keybrd), $11,580
Norden, Robin L, ofc spt asst (keybrd), $24,264
Norell, Garrett K, soc servs mgr, band 1, $47,052
Norman, Donald, youth group leader, $34,356
Norman, Janet S, corres & info spec I, $36,204
Norris, Laura, children's serv spv, $39,624
Norris, Quintin L, ofc spt asst (keybrd), $23,508
Norship-Haney, Susan, children's serv worker II, $34,356
Norton, Kristy R, fam spt elig spc, $32,052
Norwood, Leslie N, fam spt elig spc, $29,976
Nott, Kimberly, exec I, $30,984
Null, Leevona D, children's serv worker II, $34,356
Nunn, Rhonda, child spt spec, $29,976
Nurnberg, Tony, children's serv worker III, $36,888
Nyatanga, Kassandra L, child spt spec, $29,976
Oaker, Tamara D, corres & info spec I, $34,944
Oaks, Barbara M, corres & info spec I, $34,944
Oberhaus, Michael E, youth fac mgr II, $40,380
Oberkirsch, Kirsten M, children's serv worker I, $30,984
Oberlag, Michelle R, soc servs mgr, band 1, $47,052
Obiesie, Emmanuel, child spt spec, $31,512
O'Brien, Bonita S, child spt spec, $29,976
O'Brien, Joseph R, corres & info spec I, $39,624
Oda, Sharhonda C, fam spt elig spc, $29,976
Odom, Kimberly A, fam spt elig spc, $29,976
Odom, Shannon C, fam spt elig spc, $29,976
O'Donnell, Brittney L, children's serv worker II, $34,356
Odum, Scott A, dpty div dir, $83,424
Oelke, Jessica J, children's serv worker I, $29,976
Oelschlaeger, Kayla S, youth spec I, $29,004
Oelzen, Karin L, children's serv spv, $40,380
Oesterreicher, Linda L, youth spec I, $28,104
Oestreich, Amy L, ofc spt asst (keybrd), $23,160
Oetting, Jill L, fam spt elig spc, $33,180
Offutt, Aimee, children's serv spv, $39,624
Offutt, Patricia A, fam spt elig spc, $29,976
Ogden, Pamela S, fam spt elig spc, $29,976
Ogle, Cathleen J, children's serv worker II, $38,928
Ogle, Juanita J, cook III, $28,536
O'Hara, Kimberly S, soc servs mgr, band 1, $47,892
O'Hara, Tracy D, registered nurse, $42,420
Ohmes, Daniel J, children's serv worker III, $36,888
Okeke, Ebenezer C, ofc spt asst (keybrd), $26,652
Okojie, Isaac E, youth spec I, $29,004
Olatunji, Olayinka, special educ tchr III, $38,928
Oldsen, Kathleen E, children's serv worker II, $33,744
Olin, Amanda J, youth spec II, $33,180
Olson, Gloria J, soc servs mgr, band 1, $65,364
Olson, Sheri J, corres & info spec I, $38,232
O'Neal, Amanda K, children's serv spv, $39,624
O'Neal, Elizabeth N, children's serv worker I, $30,984
O'Neal, Michelle A, ofc spt asst (keybrd), $23,160
Ononye, Anthony, fam spt elig spv, $35,568
Openlander, John R, children's serv worker II, $34,356
Oppermann, Mark G, hearings ofcr, $51,012
O'Quinn, Diane L, ofc spt asst (keybrd), $23,160
Ordway, Nancy P, children's serv worker II, $34,356
O'Rear, Darren G, serv coor yth srvcs, $37,548
Orebiyi, Oluwatoyin, child spt spec, $29,976

Orebiyi, Oluyinka A, fam spt elig spc, $29,976
Orf, Nichole L, children's serv spv, $39,624
Orlando, Faith E, special educ tchr III, $38,928
Orlando, Paula, youth fac mgr II, $42,708
Orourke, Kelly H, children's serv worker III, $36,888
Orozco, Carrie S, fam spt elig spc, $29,976
Orr, Michele E, corres & info spec I, $36,888
Ortega, Cindy L, children's serv worker III, $36,888
Osborn, Debra K, soc servs aide, $11.13/hr
Osborn, Jennifer, children's serv worker I, $30,984
Osborne-Smith, Marion L, youth group leader, $34,356
O'Shea, Brian W, ofc spt asst (keybrd), $29,412
O'Shea, Chelsea, children's serv worker III, $35,568
O'Shea, Debra K, fam spt elig spv, $36,204
Ostermeyer, Christine C, children's serv worker II, $32,628
Otis, Alisha G, children's serv spv, $45,156
Ott, Shanna, fam spt elig spc, $29,976
Otting, Therena K, sr ofc spt asst (keybrd), $25,824
Otto, Lisa A, fam spt elig spc, $34,356
Otwell, Alicia A, outdoor rehab cnslr I, $36,204
Otwell, Rick W, youth fac mgr II, $40,380
Overby, Lisa G, acad tchr III, $37,548
Overmann, Regina E, medicaid prog rel rep, $38,928
Overstreet, Danielle D, children's serv worker II, $34,356
Overton, Desiree' D, fam spt elig spc, $29,976
Overton, Donny W, youth spec II, $33,180
Overton, Hans E, youth spec II, $31,512
Overton, Norma L, children's serv worker I, $29,976
Overton, William A, youth spec II, $31,512
Owczarek, Elizabeth K, hearings ofcr, $41,940
Owens, Barbara J, fam spt elig spc, $30,984
Owens, Gregory, child spt spec, $33,180
Owens, Michelle, sr ofc spt asst (keybrd), $25,032
Owens, Susan L, sr ofc spt asst (keybrd), $26,652
Owings, Cynthia M, ofc spt asst (keybrd), $25,824
Pace, Carla R, sr ofc spt asst (keybrd), $25,824
Pace, Julie A, medicaid spec, $37,548
Pacheco, Natalie C, fam spt elig spv, $34,944
Pack, Connie L, mobility spec for the blind, $39,624
Paden, Deanna L, children's serv worker II, $32,628
Paffrath, Caleb A, children's serv worker II, $32,628
Page, Elizabeth A, children's serv spv, $39,624
Page, Jessica C, children's serv worker I, $34,356
Page, Saundra, ofc spt asst (keybrd), $23,160
Painter, Brenda L, fam spt elig spc, $29,976
Painter, Colby T, fam spt elig spc, $29,976
Painter, Kristen D, fam spt elig spc, $29,976
Pajazetovic, Kadika, children's serv worker I, $29,976
Palmer, Brandi N, children's serv worker II, $33,744
Palmer, Elizabeth M, children's serv worker III, $35,568
Palmer, George M, children's serv worker II, $33,744
Palmer, Kimberly, children's serv worker II, $34,356
Palmer, Susan L, child spt spec, $33,744
Palmer-McHone, Christina M, children's serv worker I, $29,976
Papalotzi-Ahuactzi, Alexandria L, children's serv worker I, $29,976
Papavlasopoulos, Panagiotis K, children's serv worker II, $34,356
Pappert, Douglas A, mobility spec for the blind, $43,488
Pappert, Kirra S, children's serv worker II, $34,356
Parham-Carruthers, Diera A, children's serv worker II, $34,356
Paris, Brittany L, children's serv worker III, $35,568
Parish, Donna M, corres & info spec I, $34,944
Parish-Nunley, Ethel M, children's serv worker III, $36,888
Park, Angela G, medicaid spec, $37,548
Parker, Alisha N, children's serv worker II, $34,356
Parker, Barbara J, fam spt elig spc, $30,984
Parker, Clifton D, investigator II, $37,548
Parker, Jennifer, corres & info spec I, $34,944
Parker, Jermaine D, soc servs aide, $11.13/hr
Parker, Kathy D, child spt spec, $29,976
Parker, Kimberly J, ofc spt asst (keybrd), $23,160
Parker, Laquita M, ofc spt asst (keybrd), $23,160
Parker, Marcia E, child spt enforce spv, $38,232
Parker, Melodie, youth spec II, $31,512
Parker, Patricia J, children's serv worker III, $35,568
Parker, Rebecca F, corres & info spec I, $33,744
Parker, Rhonda, corres & info spec I, $34,944
Parker, Sherry L, fam spt elig spc, $30,984
Parkins, Marisa, children's serv worker III, $36,888

Parks, Joseph J, div dir, $205,536
Parks, Rebecca, children's serv worker I, $30,984
Parks, Tandra M, children's serv worker II, $34,356
Parlette, Shawna L, fam spt elig spv, $34,944
Parr, Jennifer, children's serv worker I, $30,984
Parr, Susan L, youth spec I, $29,004
Parra, Eric V, serv coor yth srvcs, $33,744
Parrigon, Justin D, youth spec II, $31,512
Parrin-Hathaway, Elizabeth, children's serv worker III, $36,888
Parris, Brandi L, soc servs mgr, band 1, $47,052
Parris, Keith B, serv coor yth srvcs, $33,744
Parrish, Colissa M, fam spt elig spc, $29,976
Parrish, Tara D, children's serv worker I, $34,356
Parrish, Taylar G, children's serv worker II, $32,628
Parrott, Caitlin, children's serv worker I, $29,976
Parson, Scott W, youth spec II, $31,512
Parsons, Michael, sr ofc spt asst (keybrd), $25,824
Parsons, Vicki L, admin ofc spt asst, $28,104
Partney, Andrea N, children's serv worker III, $35,568
Paruszkiewicz, Janet L, children's serv worker II, $34,356
Parvin, Dawn M, soc servs mgr, band 1, $41,940
Paschal, Amaryllis C, child spt spec, $30,984
Pashia, Dione F, fam spt elig spv, $34,944
Passley, Jordan C, children's serv worker II, $32,628
Pate, Stephanie G, children's serv worker III, $35,568
Patel, Ami B, special asst prof, $67,488
Patrick, Amanda L, children's serv worker III, $36,888
Patrick, Carrie T, children's serv worker III, $35,568
Patrick, Chamone L, youth spec II, $30,984
Patrick, Dorthella J, children's serv worker II, $34,356
Patrick, Kaleena R, children's serv worker II, $34,356
Patterson, Kristin I, youth spec I, $29,004
Patterson, Marissa J, youth spec II, $29,976
Patterson, Tara D, children's serv worker I, $30,984
Patterson, Whitney D, children's serv worker II, $34,356
Patton, Brittany A, youth spec II, $29,976
Patton, Jennifer R, children's serv worker I, $29,976
Patton, Lisa A, child spt spec, $29,976
Patton, Ruthie, fam spt elig spc, $29,976
Patton, Shirley M, children's serv worker II, $34,356
Patton, William G, soc servs mngr, band 2, $74,304
Pattrin, Kristen D, special asst official & admstr, $83,424
Paul, Lea E, child spt spec, $16,872
Paul, Mary L, children's serv worker II, $34,356
Paule, Tyler D, youth spec II, $34,356
Paull, Haylee R, children's serv worker I, $29,976
Paulsmeyer, Pamela C, fam spt elig spc, $30,420
Pavlica, Kate M, children's serv worker II, $32,628
Payne, Julie A, fam spt elig spv, $41,940
Payne, Katherine R, sr ofc spt asst (keybrd), $25,824
Paynes, Deena R, fam spt elig spc, $29,976
Payton, Letitia, ofc spt asst (keybrd), $23,508
Pearson, Anne M, fam spt elig spc, $29,976
Pearson, Kimberly, fam spt elig spc, $37,548
Pearson, Ronald J, soc servs aide, $11.13/hr
Pease, Teresa A, child spt spec, $30,984
Peavler, Helen R, fam spt elig spc, $29,976
Peckman, Walter A, children's serv worker II, $34,356
Pedersen, Jens, fam spt elig spc, $29,976
Pedersen, Sabra M, youth spec II, $30,984
Peebles, Byron R, cmnty svs coord-youth srvs, $40,380
Peebles, Sharon, admin ofc spt asst, $28,104
Peek, Mark E, prog dev spec, $45,156
Peeples, Scott A, children's serv worker II, $34,356
Pehle, Dawn M, account clerk II, $25,032
Pehle, John A, investigation mgr b1, $48,156
Pellersels, Janice E, children's serv worker III, $35,568
Peltzer, Jeanna L, fam spt elig spc, $35,568
Pemberton, Brandon M, sr ofc spt asst (keybrd), $25,824
Pemberton, Jami M, fam spt elig spc, $29,976
Pemberton, Kasey, ofc spt asst (keybrd), $23,160
Pembrick, Shana N, fam spt elig spc, $31,512
Pendergrass, Ann Marie, child spt spec, $29,976
Pendleton, Karen T, medicaid spec, $37,548
Pendleton, Lillian L, corres & info spec I, $34,944
Pendleton, Megan R, ofc spt asst (keybrd), $23,160
Peniston, Leah E, children's serv worker II, $34,356
Penn, Jeanarae, fam spt elig spc, $29,976
Pennington, Deborah, fam spt elig spc, $29,976

Pennington, Rhonda, children's serv worker II, $34,356
Penry, Sharon L, child spt spec, $33,744
Perdue, Diane M, ofc spt asst (keybrd), $25,824
Perkins, Andrewniquis G, youth spec II, $30,984
Perkins, Ann, exec I, $30,984
Perkins, Beatrice, sr ofc spt asst (keybrd), $25,824
Perkins, Courtney R, children's serv spv, $37,548
Perkins, Dana B, soc servs mgr, band 1, $47,052
Perkins, Jason J, children's serv spv, $43,488
Perkins, Kimberly R, youth spec II, $32,052
Perkins, Marquita A, fam spt elig spv, $34,944
Perpitch-Harvey, Stephen R, corres & info spec II, $40,380
Perr, Penny L, sr voc rehab cnslr f/t blind, $43,488
Perry, Jennifer D, children's serv spv, $39,624
Perry, Joey B, children's serv worker II, $34,356
Perry, Sheryl, ofc spt asst (keybrd), $23,160
Perry-Hall, Nicole J, case analyst, $32,628
Perryman, Donna S, corres & info spec I, $34,944
Perryman, Heather M, ofc spt asst (keybrd), $23,160
Persall, Christina L, sr ofc spt asst (keybrd), $27,948
Peters, Alexandria J, youth spec I, $28,104
Peters, Angela E, child spt spec, $29,976
Peters, Angela M, children's serv worker II, $34,356
Peters, Arthea, fam spt elig spc, $29,976
Peters, Rachelle, youth spec II, $37,548
Petersen, Gennifer L, child spt enforce spv, $33,744
Peterson, Mila M, children's serv worker II, $34,356
Peterson, Nina A, fam spt elig spv, $36,888
Peterson, Susan E, youth spec II, $31,512
Peterson, Tara, fam spt elig spc, $29,976
Peterson, Zanetta L, children's serv spv, $39,624
Petree, Holli M, exec I, $30,984
Petschonek, Amy K, sr ofc spt asst (keybrd), $28,908
Pettey, Patricia, serv coor yth srvcs, $36,888
Pettiford, Sharron M, children's serv worker II, $32,628
Pettit, Tracy D, child spt enforce spv, $35,568
Petty, Lynda A, admin ofc spt asst, $28,536
Pevehouse, Danielle T, soc servs worker, $17.07/hr
Pfaff, Gregory F, fam spt elig spc, $29,976
Pfalzgraf, Elizabeth D, children's serv spv, $39,624
Pfeffer, Sandra A, fam spt elig spc, $29,976
Pfefferkorn, Abby J, rehab tchr for the blind, $34,944
Pfeifer, Mark, fam spt elig spc, $29,976
Pfeiffer, Nikki M, children's serv worker I, $30,984
Pfeifly, Deborah L, child spt spec, $29,976
Pfyl, Gabrielle K, children's serv worker I, $29,976
Phares, Katie L, serv coor yth srvcs, $33,744
Phelps, Lucy R, fam spt elig spc, $29,976
Philbert, Jaime M, prog dev spec, $40,380
Philbert, Julie K, soc servs mgr, band 1, $56,520
Philbert, Mary A, medicaid technician, $32,628
Phillips, Dawn M, soc servs mgr, band 1, $47,052
Phillips, Edward M, youth spec II, $30,984
Phillips, Emilie N, reg fam spec, $37,548
Phillips, Eric R, youth spec II, $31,512
Phillips, Gwendolyn, soc servs mgr, band 1, $41,940
Phillips, Janice M, sr ofc spt asst (keybrd), $28,452
Phillips, Linda M, fam spt elig spc, $34,356
Phillips, Marguerite A, youth spec II, $36,204
Phillips, Susan L, rehab tchr for the blind, $41,940
Phillips, Tricia L, soc servs mngr, band 2, $61,332
Phillips, Vernon A, youth spec II, $33,744
Philpot, Othello, acad tchr III, $39,624
Piacentini, Ashlee E, youth spec II, $30,420
Piburn, Lisa A, fam spt elig spc, $33,180
Piccinini, Carol A, youth spec II, $32,628
Pickens, Elisia, fam spt elig spc, $29,976
Pickens, Natashia J, fam spt elig spc, $29,976
Pickerell, Sherri R, fam spt elig spc, $29,976
Piel, Kelly, fam spt elig spc, $29,976
Pierce, Dawn D, fam spt elig spc, $29,976
Pierce, Kelly N, fam spt elig spc, $29,976
Pierce, Lindy G, sr voc rehab cnslr f/t blind, $38,928
Pierre, Alain J, children's serv worker I, $29,976
Pierson, Elizabeth A, children's serv prog mgr, $51,096
Piffins, Darlene A, child spt spec, $29,976
Pigg, Karen M, special asst ofc & clerical, $45,780
Pigg, Nicole A, soc servs mgr, band 1, $47,052
Pikes, Edward, youth group leader, $38,232

Pilny, Brenda A, fam spt elig spv, $37,548
Pine, Carol L, youth spec II, $30,984
Pingel, Jill M, children's serv spv, $39,624
Pinkley, Thomas S, youth group leader, $34,356
Pinney, Jamie R, training tech II, $41,172
Piper, Dustin A, children's serv worker II, $32,628
Pippert, Barbee, child spt spec, $29,976
Pippin, Nina J, fam spt elig spc, $29,976
Pitera, Susan L, children's serv worker I, $31,512
Pitford, Mitzie J, child spt spec, $29,976
Pitney, Beth A, fam spt elig spc, $29,976
Pittman, Mary A, fam spt elig spv, $34,944
Pitts, Sheryl M, fam spt elig spc, $29,976
Pitzen, Michael A, soc servs mngr, band 2, $71,100
Plaggenburg, Gretchen G, children's serv spv, $41,172
Plank, Linda K, child spt spec, $29,976
Plate, Brian J, fam spt elig spc, $33,744
Platz, Rachel, children's serv worker I, $29,976
Platzer, Cynthia L, children's serv worker III, $41,940
Platzer, Kurt, corres & info spec I, $36,888
Pleimann, Julie M, children's serv worker III, $36,888
Pleus, Matthew C, fam spt elig spc, $29,976
Ploesser, Kelly R, children's serv worker III, $38,232
Plumlee, Matthew W, children's serv worker II, $32,628
Plungkhen, Kathaleeya, legal counsel, $50,376
Pobst, Diane L, ofc spt asst (keybrd), $23,880
Poe, Terrance L, youth spec II, $31,512
Poertner, Destiny L, children's serv worker I, $29,976
Poese, Bobbie J, children's serv worker II, $34,356
Pogue, Savannah, children's serv worker III, $35,568
Pointer, Cari A, children's serv spec, $40,380
Pokorny, Donald P, designated principal asst div, $83,424
Politte, Margaret, ofc spt asst (keybrd), $23,508
Polk, Lorraine J, ofc spt asst (keybrd), $23,160
Pollard, Connie, children's serv worker III, $36,888
Pollard, Rachel M, ofc spt asst (keybrd), $23,160
Pollock, Scott D, fam spt elig spv, $38,232
Pollreisz, Brenda, sr ofc spt asst (keybrd), $25,824
Polly, Elizabeth, child spt spec, $29,976
Polonskaya, Angela N, children's serv worker I, $29,976
Polson, Karla A, soc servs mgr, band 1, $42,708
Polston, Sonia C, children's serv worker II, $32,628
Pool, Tammy, fam spt elig spc, $29,976
Poole, Laci, fam spt elig spc, $29,976
Popa, Mihai, mgmt analysis spec II, $41,940
Pope, Lisa D, ofc spt asst (keybrd), $24,612
Pope-Farabee, Tracey L, child spt spec, $33,744
Porch, Kimberly J, corres & info spec I, $34,944
Portell, Cindy L, sr ofc spt asst (keybrd), $27,948
Porter, Brenda G, children's serv worker II, $32,628
Porter, Kendra L, case analyst, $31,512
Porter, Leslie A, child spt spec, $32,628
Porter, Nathan A, children's serv worker II, $34,356
Porter, Robin R, children's serv worker II, $36,204
Porter, Rodney W, youth group leader, $34,356
Porter, Tara J, children's serv worker III, $36,888
Portis, Lashonda D, children's serv worker II, $32,628
Posala, Emily T, youth spec II, $30,984
Posey, Teri T, fam spt elig spc, $29,976
Potter, Annora L, children's serv worker II, $34,356
Potter, Blake A, fam spt elig spc, $29,976
Potter, Christine V, children's serv spv, $39,624
Pough, Cynthia D, youth spec I, $28,104
Powell, Carla R, fam spt elig spc, $34,356
Powell, Cathryn L, fam spt elig spc, $29,976
Powell, Lisa A, corres & info spec I, $34,944
Powell, Roxann F, children's serv spv, $39,624
Powell, Stacey, ofc spt asst (keybrd), $23,160
Powell, Stephanie T, fam spt elig spc, $29,976
Powers, Jessica L, fam spt elig spc, $29,976
Powers, Kathleen, hearings ofcr, $38,928
Powers, Robert B, acad tchr III, $37,548
Powers, Terence P, children's serv spec, $45,156
Prater, Elizabeth D, corres & info spec I, $34,944
Prather-Rhoads, Donna J, child spt spec, $30,420
Pratt, Heather R, fam spt elig spv, $34,944
Pratt, Malcolm E, fam spt elig spc, $29,976
Pratt, Stephanie L, serv coor yth srvcs, $35,568
Prebianca, Yolanda L, child spt spec, $34,944

Premer, Kayla, children's serv worker II, $34,356
Prenger, Jodi M, sr ofc spt asst (keybrd), $25,824
Prenger, Sarah B, medicaid pharmaceutical tech, $32,628
Pressley, Tanella S, sr ofc spt asst (keybrd), $26,232
Preston, Shelby L, fam spt elig spv, $34,944
Preston, Tamara J, children's serv worker II, $34,356
Price, Deyone R, ofc spt asst (keybrd), $24,264
Price, Jennifer R, fam spt elig spc, $29,976
Price, Tara E, training tech II, $41,940
Price, Tracy D, fam spt elig spc, $29,976
Prichard, Melissa L, fam spt elig spc, $29,976
Prifogle, Angela L, youth spec II, $31,512
Prifogle, Roy D, youth spec II, $31,512
Prince, Carole L, fam spt elig spc, $30,984
Pritchett, Marybeth, fam spt elig spv, $34,944
Pritzel, Marla J, soc servs mgr, band 1, $52,092
Privett, Rodger W, fam spt elig spc, $29,976
Privott, Shannon F, children's serv worker II, $34,356
Proctor, Kennard F, soc servs mgr, band 1, $48,156
Proctor, Lucinda M, exec I, $30,984
Proffitt, Staci D, children's serv worker I, $29,976
Proper, Anita, fam spt elig spc, $29,976
Provancha, Cheri L, children's serv worker II, $32,628
Pruessner, Anthony L, youth spec II, $31,512
Pruett, Thomas A, special educ tchr III, $38,928
Pry, Laraine A, child spt spec, $33,744
Pry, Regina L, children's serv worker III, $38,232
Przybylowski, John V, youth spec II, $31,512
Psomas, Michelle L, children's serv spv, $38,232
Puchta, Nita N, children's serv worker III, $43,488
Puckett, Sandra S, children's serv spv, $39,624
Puentes, Barbara J, fam spt elig spv, $36,888
Pueppke, Tammy L, fam spt elig spc, $29,976
Pulliam, Henry J, youth spec II, $31,512
Pullins, Nehemiah J, youth spec II, $31,512
Purdy, Larry R, soc servs aide, $11.13/hr
Puryear, Scott W, youth spec II, $31,512
Pyatt, Kimberly M, children's serv worker II, $33,744
Pyle, James, youth spec I, $29,004
Pyron, Haley J, ofc spt asst (keybrd), $23,160
Quargnenti, Anne E, fam spt elig spc, $29,976
Queensland, Jennifer R, children's serv worker III, $36,888
Quigley, Marcia J, sr ofc spt asst (keybrd), $28,452
Quinn, Charles E, fam spt elig spc, $29,976
Quinn, Jonathan J, fam spt elig spc, $29,976
Quinn, Katherine A, children's serv worker II, $34,356
Quisenberry, Heather N, children's serv worker II, $34,356
Raby, Jill, children's serv worker II, $34,356
Rackers, Lisa A, soc servs mgr, band 1, $41,940
Radcliff, Lindsey, children's serv worker II, $34,356
Rademan, Amy L, medicaid spec, $37,548
Rademan, Rebecca C, admin ofc spt asst, $28,104
Rader, Brenda L, child spt enforce spv, $34,944
Rader, Emily C, children's serv worker II, $32,628
Rader, Michael A, serv coor yth srvcs, $33,744
Rader, Nancy L, fam spt elig spc, $33,180
Radford-Kapp, Barbara A, fam spt elig spc, $29,976
Radney, Heather E, children's serv worker III, $35,568
Ragan, Amy L, fam spt elig spc, $29,976
Ragan, Sarah R, children's serv worker II, $34,356
Ragus, Danyale R, fam spt elig spc, $29,976
Raines, Nancy M, children's serv worker II, $34,356
Rainey, Jacinda L, soc servs mgr, band 1, $55,000
Rainey, Lynn M, children's serv worker III, $35,568
Rains, Julie A, misc tech, $12.59/hr
Rainwater, Angela, sr ofc spt asst (keybrd), $26,652
Rainwater, Cynthia L, child spt spec, $33,744
Ralls, Candace M, child spt enforce spv, $40,380
Ralph, Ashley, children's serv worker II, $35,568
Ralph, Joni L, children's serv spec, $40,380
Rames, Rainbow, ofc spt asst (keybrd), $23,160
Ramos, Phyllis C, children's serv spv, $39,624
Ramsey, Cara M, children's serv spv, $38,232
Ramsey, Rodney V, children's serv worker II, $34,356
Randall, Aleesa K, children's serv worker I, $29,976
Randall, Judy K, children's serv worker II, $33,744
Randall, Sharon, ofc spt asst (keybrd), $11,580
Randell, Maria R, children's serv worker II, $33,744
Randle, Marge, misc prof, $30.54/hr

Randle, Pamela D, fam spt elig spc, $29,976
Randle, Vicky E, child spt spec, $33,744
Randol, Nancy A, child spt spec, $29,976
Randolph, Barbara D, ofc spt asst (keybrd), $23,160
Randolph, Lindsey R, fam spt elig spc, $29,976
Randolph, Lisa Y, soc servs mgr, band 1, $48,156
Raney, Kristin, ofc spt asst (keybrd), $23,160
Raney, Trisha, fam spt elig spc, $29,976
Range, Erin, ofc spt asst (keybrd), $23,160
Rangel, William G, misc tech, $20.00/hr
Rankin, Walter M, youth spec II, $31,512
Rantz, Amanda E, fam spt elig spc, $29,976
Rapp, Susan M, fam spt elig spc, $33,180
Rappold, Courtney R, children's serv worker I, $29,976
Rasmussen, Brianne N, medicaid clerk, $27,660
Rathert, Deborah K, special asst prof, $76,260
Ratliff, Jacqueline N, children's serv worker I, $30,984
Ratliff, Janet L, fam spt elig spc, $34,356
Rau, John D, youth spec II, $34,356
Rauh, Barbara J, children's serv worker III, $36,888
Rawlings, Melissa L, youth spec I, $28,104
Ray, Alexis L, children's serv worker II, $33,744
Ray, Andrea J, children's serv worker II, $34,356
Ray, Charles J, cmnty svs coord-youth srvs, $37,548
Ray, Cynthia J, youth group leader, $34,356
Ray, Kimberly A, fam spt elig spc, $32,628
Ray, Kristy E, ofc spt asst (keybrd), $23,160
Ray, Lori E, ofc spt asst (keybrd), $23,160
Ray, Sharon A, soc servs mgr, band 1, $41,940
Ray, Steve E, youth spec II, $31,512
Rayhart, Tracey, fam spt elig spc, $29,976
Rayle, Rhonda K, sr ofc spt asst (keybrd), $25,824
Rea, Connie L, sr ofc spt asst (keybrd), $25,824
Read, Vance T, soc servs mgr, band 1, $49,128
Read Julian, Tabitha D, children's serv spv, $44,304
Reagan, Katie L, fam spt elig spc, $29,976
Reasor-West, Elfreda N, special educ tchr II, $36,204
Reavey, Timothy A, fam spt elig spc, $29,976
Reavis, Lana F, ofc spt asst (keybrd), $23,508
Rebello, Lisa M, child spt spec, $29,976
Reber, Lori M, rehab tchr for the blind, $34,944
Reckling, Rebecca J, fam spt elig spc, $29,976
Recob, Luella K, fam spt elig spv, $41,172
Record, Brenda K, admin ofc spt asst, $33,744
Rector, Brenda, ofc spt asst (keybrd), $23,160
Rector, Cynthia, administrative analyst I, $29,496
Rector, Dawn M, children's serv spec, $41,940
Redfearn, Marcie J, fam spt elig spc, $29,976
Redmon, Lisa J, children's serv worker III, $36,888
Redmond, Adrianne M, fam spt elig spc, $30,984
Reece, Celestine, fam spt elig spc, $29,976
Reece, Mary T, ofc spt asst (keybrd), $25,404
Reed, Ashley N, youth spec II, $31,512
Reed, Charles E, youth spec II, $31,512
Reed, Craig E, soc servs mgr, band 1, $52,092
Reed, Dalene R, children's serv worker II, $34,356
Reed, Deneen, admin ofc spt asst, $28,536
Reed, Jamie L, youth spec II, $32,628
Reed, Jennifer C, fam spt elig spc, $33,180
Reed, Kristina, fam spt elig spc, $29,976
Reed, Kyle W, guidance cnslr I, $33,744
Reed, Latoshia L, fam spt elig spc, $29,976
Reed, Lawonda M, fam spt elig spc, $29,976
Reed, Leanne E, children's serv worker II, $38,232
Reed, Lindsay, ofc spt asst (keybrd), $23,160
Reed, Loreen D, medicaid spec, $42,708
Reed, Lucinda, fam spt elig spc, $29,976
Reed, Malinda, admin ofc spt asst, $28,536
Reed, Mariah B, children's serv worker II, $34,356
Reed, Michelle M, children's serv worker II, $34,356
Reed, Regina A, corres & info spec I, $36,888
Reed, Roxanne F, fam spt elig spv, $34,944
Reed, Teri L, children's serv worker III, $36,888
Reed, Tina M, fam spt elig spc, $29,976
Reed, Vicki M, guidance cnslr II, $42,708
Reed, Whitney L, children's serv worker II, $32,628
Reeder, Christine E, children's serv worker II, $34,356
Reemes, Monica A, serv coor yth srvcs, $38,232
Reese, Timothy M, fam spt elig spc, $29,976

Reeves, Catherine M, fam spt elig spc, $29,976
Reeves, Joan M, child spt spec, $33,744
Reeves, Linda L, fam spt elig spc, $29,976
Reid, Lisa A, fam spt elig spc, $29,976
Reid, Nancy L, prog dev spec, $40,380
Reifschneider, Erica L, fam spt elig spc, $29,976
Reimer, Brittany C, children's serv worker II, $34,356
Reindel, Yvonne C, ofc spt asst (keybrd), $25,824
Reinkemeyer, Dawn M, child spt spec, $29,976
Reisig, Stacey R, special educ tchr III, $40,380
Reker, Brooke A, children's serv worker I, $29,976
Remelius, Patricia A, soc servs aide, $11.13/hr
Renaud, Carolyn A, ofc spt asst (keybrd), $26,652
Renaud, Kimberly, children's serv worker II, $34,356
Renn, Mark K, ofc spt asst (keybrd), $23,160
Renner, Jennifer A, child spt spec, $32,052
Renner, Mary K, children's serv worker III, $36,888
Repp, Margy A, prog dev spec, $40,380
Respress, Marel C, youth spec II, $31,512
Ressel, April L, children's serv spv, $39,624
Reutter, Lisa M, exec I, $29,976
Reynolds, Deborah S, soc servs mgr, band 1, $41,940
Reynolds, Dena D, fam spt elig spc, $33,180
Reynolds, Karen L, sr ofc spt asst (keybrd), $25,824
Reynolds, Patricia D, fam spt elig spc, $34,356
Reynolds, Rhonda A, ofc spt asst (keybrd), $23,160
Reynolds, Rodney, children's serv worker II, $34,356
Reynolds, Zarrin-Taj, acad tchr III, $37,548
Rhoads, Robyn, fam spt elig spv, $36,204
Rhodes, Carolyn M, fam spt elig spv, $36,888
Rhodes, Danny J, mgmt analysis spec II, $49,128
Rhodes, Jean, child spt enforce spv, $34,944
Rhodes, Tara T, children's serv worker II, $32,628
Rice, Bobbie J, sr ofc spt asst (keybrd), $25,824
Rice, Kathy L, child spt spec, $29,976
Rice, Nicole A, children's serv spv, $41,172
Rice, Rayna S, medicaid unit spv, $41,940
Rice, Reginald J, youth spec II, $31,512
Rich, Wendy L, child spt enforce spv, $34,944
Richard, David, youth spec II, $31,512
Richards, Christine M, fam spt elig spc, $31,512
Richards, Lajuana M, child spt spec, $29,976
Richards, Shannon J, fam spt elig spc, $29,976
Richards, Sharon M, fam spt elig spc, $32,052
Richards, Susan I, youth spec II, $31,512
Richardson, Alisha L, children's serv worker III, $36,888
Richardson, Angela M, case analyst, $36,888
Richardson, Christina M, children's serv worker I, $30,984
Richardson, Jamel R, youth group leader, $32,628
Richardson, John M, child spt spec, $36,204
Richardson, Krista, corres & info spec I, $34,944
Richardson, Regina A, ofc spt asst (keybrd), $23,160
Richardson, Sherry A, fam spt elig spc, $32,628
Richardson, Thomas S, fam spt elig spc, $29,976
Richardson, William L, prog dev spec, $40,380
Richey, Branden J, youth spec II, $31,512
Richey, Debbie, ofc spt asst (keybrd), $23,160
Richie, Yolanda M, admin ofc spt asst, $32,628
Richmond, Burtina K, fam spt elig spc, $35,568
Richmond, Charles D, children's serv worker II, $34,356
Richter, Jennifer B, reg cnslt resid lcsng unit, $45,156
Richter, Rosalind R, case analyst, $32,628
Rickey, Ashley N, fam spt elig spc, $29,976
Ricks, Ashley A, children's serv worker II, $34,356
Rickstrew, Sheree A, sr ofc spt asst (keybrd), $29,412
Riddle, Bennie L, clerical servs spv fs, $32,628
Ridenour, Dena, exec I, $30,984
Ridgell, Kimshon, children's serv worker II, $34,356
Ridgway, Nancy J, fam spt elig spc, $31,512
Ridley, Rekeena, fam spt elig spc, $29,976
Riegel, Ann M, child spt spec, $31,512
Riehn, Holly L, child spt spec, $33,744
Riehn, Susan L, special educ tchr III, $46,068
Rienks, Noah, children's serv spv, $38,232
Ries, Ruthann J, ofc spt asst (keybrd), $28,452
Rigdon, Helen R, ofc spt asst (keybrd), $23,160
Riggs, Kristen A, auditor II, $37,548
Rigsby, Rosella R, lpn II gen, $29,772
Rikard, Kaliann M, youth spec II, $30,984

Riles, Demarco S, fam spt elig spc, $29,976
Riley, Angee R, corres & info spec I, $34,944
Riley, Laverna R, soc servs mngr, band 2, $50,040
Riley, Onnalee, children's serv worker II, $36,888
Riley, Patrick L, children's serv worker II, $32,628
Riley, Sally L, soc servs worker, $17.07/hr
Rimmer, Christina J, fam spt elig spv, $34,944
Rimson-Hope, Hermione L, case analyst, $36,204
Rinck, Jennifer M, soc servs aide, $11.13/hr
Rinehart, Susan J, children's serv worker I, $30,984
Riner, Amanda S, fam spt elig spv, $34,944
Riney, Leslie J, soc servs mgr, band 1, $41,940
Rishmawi, Khalil S, mobility spec for the blind, $43,488
Rising, Dawn M, soc servs mgr, band 1, $41,940
Ritchie, Kendra R, children's serv worker I, $30,984
Ritter, Belinda J, serv coor yth srvcs, $33,744
Ritter, Nancy L, fam spt elig spc, $33,744
Rittmayer, Carol A, child spt spec, $33,744
Ritz, Michelle D, children's serv worker II, $34,356
Ritzo, Jan E, fam spt elig spc, $33,180
Rivera, Francisca, children's serv worker II, $34,356
Rivera, Heather M, youth spec II, $31,512
Rivera, Ramon I, acad tchr I, $30,420
Rizzuto, Debbie A, child spt spec, $30,420
Roark, Craig A, medicaid technician, $32,628
Roark, Laurie E, child spt spec, $30,420
Roark, Lisa L, ofc spt asst (keybrd), $23,160
Roaseau, Mark, special asst prof, $116,664
Robards, Dana, fam spt elig spc, $29,976
Robb, Amy L, child spt spec, $29,976
Robbins, Brenda E, fam spt elig spc, $32,628
Robbins, Brittany A, children's serv worker II, $34,356
Robbins, Patricia A, sr ofc spt asst (keybrd), $28,452
Robbins, Ralund M, fam spt elig spc, $29,976
Roberson, Allison M, ofc spt asst (keybrd), $23,160
Robert, Lorie L, child spt spec, $34,356
Roberto, Lydia M, corres & info spec I, $34,944
Roberts, Amber E, fam spt elig spc, $29,976
Roberts, Carol J, ofc spt asst (keybrd), $26,232
Roberts, Christopher M, children's serv worker II, $34,356
Roberts, Debra, ofc spt asst (keybrd), $26,652
Roberts, Erica L, child spt spec, $29,976
Roberts, Erica S, children's serv worker II, $34,356
Roberts, Erin L, corres & info spec I, $34,944
Roberts, Jennifer L, soc servs mgr, band 1, $52,092
Roberts, Karen R, ofc spt asst (keybrd), $23,160
Roberts, Kimberly L, children's serv worker II, $34,356
Roberts, Laresa A, children's serv worker II, $34,356
Roberts, Lisa A, child spt spec, $30,420
Roberts, Marlene, youth spec II, $32,052
Roberts, Maureen, case analyst, $33,744
Roberts, Michael J, children's serv worker II, $38,928
Roberts, Michele, fam spt elig spc, $29,976
Roberts, Michelle J, children's serv spv, $39,624
Roberts, Myron M, corres & info spec I, $36,204
Roberts, Steve C, youth spec II, $31,512
Roberts, Tasia J, administrative analyst I, $34,356
Robertson, Betty D, children's serv worker III, $36,888
Robertson, Betty J, fam spt elig spc, $29,976
Robertson, Bridget A, fam spt elig spv, $38,232
Robertson, Chad D, children's serv worker II, $34,356
Robertson, Cristle L, child spt spec, $29,976
Robertson, Houston K, fam spt elig spc, $29,976
Robertson, Melissa A, fam spt elig spc, $29,976
Robertson, Staci L, child spt spec, $33,744
Robertson, Tracy C, child spt spec, $16,026
Roberts-Smith, Elizabeth A, fam spt elig spv, $34,944
Robinson, Amber G, children's serv worker II, $34,356
Robinson, Angela J, fam spt elig spc, $29,976
Robinson, Crystal V, case analyst, $32,628
Robinson, Daniel G, youth spec II, $31,512
Robinson, Jacqueline, ofc spt asst (keybrd), $25,824
Robinson, Justina M, children's serv spec, $40,380
Robinson, Lashonda K, children's serv worker I, $29,976
Robinson, Latreece L, youth spec II, $29,976
Robinson, Linda K, child spt spec, $33,180
Robinson, Margaret M, children's serv spv, $45,156
Robinson, Mary B, cook II, $23,880
Robinson, Patricia L, children's serv worker I, $29,976

Robinson, Renee, sr ofc spt asst (steno), $27,084
Robinson, Richard E, youth spec II, $30,984
Robinson, Tameka D, fam spt elig spc, $29,976
Robinson, Tavonna L, fam spt elig spc, $29,976
Robinson, Trace L, youth spec I, $28,104
Robison, Alison, pers ofcr I, $43,488
Robison, James, child spt spec, $29,976
Robison, John, child spt spec, $30,420
Robison, Micah D, fam spt elig spc, $29,976
Robison, Paula, fam spt elig spc, $29,976
Robison, Susan L, special asst prof, $67,332
Roby, Stephanie, exec I, $29,976
Rochester, Katie M, youth spec II, $30,984
Rockhold, Timothy D, children's serv worker II, $34,356
Roderick, Jennifer R, children's serv worker II, $34,356
Roderick, Keith A, fiscal & administrative mgr b2, $61,332
Rodgers, Erica D, youth spec I, $29,496
Rodgers, Julie D, fam spt elig spc, $29,976
Rodgers, Lisa L, fam spt elig spc, $29,976
Rodgers, Peggy L, ofc spt asst (keybrd), $24,264
Rodgers, Regina L, sr ofc spt asst (keybrd), $25,824
Rodgers, Rochelle R, children's serv spv, $39,624
Rodriguez, Dan E, children's serv worker III, $36,888
Rodriguez, Jean C, soc servs mgr, band 1, $47,052
Rodriguez, John D, youth fac mgr II, $40,380
Rodriguez, Tina M, youth spec II, $31,512
Roe, Holly M, fam spt elig spc, $29,976
Roesle, Deanne, youth spec II, $35,568
Roettgen, Stephanie L, admin ofc spt asst, $32,628
Roetto, Debra J, children's serv worker III, $36,888
Rogalski, Chester J, youth spec II, $35,568
Rogers, Amanda D, children's serv worker III, $36,888
Rogers, Angela G, soc servs mgr, band 1, $50,040
Rogers, Ashley R, youth spec II, $31,512
Rogers, Asia N, child spt spec, $29,976
Rogers, Bruce W, children's serv worker II, $34,356
Rogers, Charity D, acct I, $30,984
Rogers, Jon C, youth group leader, $34,356
Rogers, Leslye C, children's serv worker III, $36,888
Rogers, Lorena M, corres & info spec I, $34,944
Rogers, Paola R, serv coor yth srvcs, $33,744
Rogers, Ronnie J, youth spec II, $33,180
Rogers, Sarah E, training tech II, $43,488
Rogers, Tasha R, children's serv spec, $40,380
Rogers, Vanessa D, fam spt elig spc, $29,976
Rohr, Chad D, rehab tchr for the blind, $33,744
Rohwedder, Judy, child spt spec, $29,004
Rojas, Rose M, youth spec II, $31,512
Rojas Fast, Natalie R, children's serv worker II, $34,356
Roling, Diane M, medicaid spec, $41,172
Rolle, Bobby L, youth spec II, $31,512
Rolph, Danielle L, youth fac mgr II, $40,380
Rone, Rodney K, youth spec II, $34,944
Rooks, Rise D, fam spt elig spc, $33,180
Rooney, Linda A, ofc spt asst (keybrd), $23,160
Rooney, Tamara L, fam spt elig spv, $36,888
Roper, April L, fam spt elig spc, $29,976
Rose, Janet F, fam spt elig spv, $37,548
Rose, Karen A, ofc spt asst (keybrd), $23,160
Rose, Kimberly L, soc servs mgr, band 1, $47,892
Rosenbaum, Jenniffer L, child spt spec, $29,976
Rosenberger, Mari A, children's serv worker I, $29,976
Ross, Cecelia Y, serv coor yth srvcs, $33,744
Ross, Clint M, children's serv worker II, $34,356
Ross, Deanna L, fam spt elig spc, $29,976
Ross, Debra J, fam spt elig spc, $32,628
Ross, Gwen, ofc spt asst (keybrd), $23,160
Ross, Kacie L, youth spec II, $29,976
Ross, Kelly D, serv coor yth srvcs, $36,888
Ross, Kimberly D, child spt spec, $33,744
Ross, Merris A, children's serv worker II, $33,744
Ross, Quiana P, youth spec II, $31,512
Ross, Tracey A, children's serv worker II, $34,356
Ross, Victoria, sr ofc spt asst (keybrd), $25,824
Roth, Carolyn J, training tech II, $43,488
Roth, Chelsea R, children's serv worker I, $29,976
Roth, Mary Ellen, ofc spt asst (keybrd), $26,232
Rothermich, Heather M, child spt spec, $29,976
Rouse, Melissa A, children's serv worker III, $36,888

Roussan, Marilyn Y, children's serv worker II, $34,356
Routon, Ashley, ofc spt asst (keybrd), $23,160
Rowden, Amy E, children's serv spec, $38,928
Rowden, Rosemary, edu asst II, $12,402
Rowden, Sharon L, child spt spec, $29,976
Rowden, Winifred F, fam spt elig spc, $33,180
Rowe, Danielle S, corres & info spec I, $33,744
Rowe, Mary E, child spt spec, $29,976
Rowe, Virginia K, fam spt elig spc, $33,180
Rowland, Joann, fam spt elig spc, $29,976
Rowsey, Hannah M, soc servs aide, $11.13/hr
Roy, Annie M, ofc spt asst (keybrd), $23,160
Royse-Keefe, Donna T, fiscal & administrative mgr b1, $42,744
Rozell-Killion, Amy J, children's serv worker III, $36,888
Rubich, Joncey, children's serv worker II, $34,356
Ruble, Cammie, children's serv worker III, $36,888
Ruble, Kelly A, children's serv spv, $39,624
Rucker, Rebecca L, fiscal & administrative mgr b2, $63,996
Rude, Michael A, youth spec II, $31,512
Ruder, Linda A, sr ofc spt asst (keybrd), $31,920
Rudisill, Nicole I, children's serv worker II, $34,356
Rudloff, Allison J, children's serv worker III, $36,888
Ruemker, Stephanie M, youth group leader, $33,744
Rueweler Pogue, Christina A, fam spt elig spc, $29,976
Ruffen, Tammie L, fam spt elig spc, $29,976
Ruiz, Marsha A, ofc spt asst (keybrd), $23,160
Rule, Andrea J, admin ofc spt asst, $31,512
Rummens, Tyler, fam spt elig spc, $29,976
Runyan, Nicolas D, fam spt elig spc, $29,004
Rupard, Lisa R, child spt spec, $29,976
Ruppert, Jamie D, children's serv worker II, $34,356
Rush, Daniel J, medicaid spec, $36,204
Rush, Darlene M, ofc spt asst (keybrd), $29,904
Rush, Jodi R, mgmt analysis spec II, $41,940
Rusher, Patricia L, fam spt elig spc, $30,984
Rushing, Laura A, youth group leader, $33,744
Rusk, Susan J, soc servs mgr, band 1, $52,092
Russell, Andrea, child spt spec, $29,976
Russell, Judy A, youth spec II, $35,568
Russell, Lisa D, fam spt elig spv, $36,888
Russell, Shianne, ofc spt asst (keybrd), $23,160
Ruth, Paul M, fiscal & administrative mgr b1, $50,040
Rutherford, Regina, child spt spec, $35,568
Rutherford, Stacy J, fam spt elig spc, $30,984
Rutledge, Jeanine M, sr ofc spt asst (keybrd), $25,824
Rutledge, Travis R, youth spec II, $29,976
Rutledge-Clarke, Robin L, children's serv worker I, $29,976
Ryan, Heather, children's serv worker III, $35,568
Ryan, Scott C, youth spec II, $31,512
Ryder, Dawn, prog dev spec, $40,380
Ryno, Randall G, children's serv worker III, $36,888
Saddler, Terry G, ofc spt asst (keybrd), $23,160
Saint, Racheal A, ofc spt asst (keybrd), $23,160
Sajid, Nargis, children's serv worker I, $30,984
Salas, Amanda L, children's serv worker III, $38,232
Salas, Jamie M, admin ofc spt asst, $28,536
Salisbury, Diane L, soc servs mgr, band 1, $47,880
Salisbury, Julie A, fam spt elig spc, $33,180
Salmons, Darla S, corres & info spec I, $34,944
Salter, Kimberly, fam spt elig spc, $29,976
Saltzman, Elizabeth A, fam spt elig spc, $29,976
Saltzmann, Cindy, child spt spec, $29,976
Salyer, Daniel C, acad tchr I, $29,976
Samons, Andrea D, ofc spt asst (keybrd), $24,264
Sample, Michelle C, fam spt elig spc, $29,976
Samuelson, Ryan A, misc tech, $20.00/hr.00/hr
San Paolo, Joanna L, children's serv worker II, $32,628
Sanchez, Glenda A, fam spt elig spc, $29,976
Sanchez, Ignacio L, youth spec II, $31,512
Sandage, Cally A, youth spec II, $31,512
Sandberg, Elaine, fam spt elig spc, $29,976
Sandbothe, Lois L, medicaid unit spv, $46,932
Sanders, Crystal, children's serv worker I, $29,976
Sanders, Denna A, soc servs aide, $11.13/hr
Sanders, Ferman O, youth spec II, $31,512
Sanders, Katherine H, youth spec II, $31,512
Sanders, Kristin M, children's serv worker II, $34,356
Sanders, Lauri, fam spt elig spc, $29,976
Sanders, Paul M, prog dev spec, $38,928

Sanders, Tonya, fam spt elig spc, $29,976
Sandridge, Deanna, children's serv spv, $39,624
Sands, Martha A, soc servs mgr, band 1, $50,040
Sandstoe, Angela A, ofc spt asst (keybrd), $23,160
Sansoucie, Sheila J, prog dev spec, $42,708
Sappenfield, Denise M, medicaid spec, $37,548
Sardis, Readic, human rel ofcr II, $42,708
Sargent, Benita, fam spt elig spv, $36,204
Sargent, Thel, soc servs aide, $11.13/hr
Sartin, Daphne D, fam spt elig spc, $29,976
Sartor, Brenda E, soc servs mgr, band 1, $51,312
Satterfield, Elizabeth V, children's serv spv, $39,624
Satterlee, Lana S, fam spt elig spc, $29,976
Sauerbrunn, Patty K, child spt spec, $34,356
Saunders, Jamella D, serv coor yth srvcs, $33,744
Savage, Cecelia D, sr ofc spt asst (keybrd), $25,824
Savage, Katherine M, fam spt elig spc, $29,976
Savage, Shawn E, children's serv worker II, $32,628
Savage, Susan K, dpty div dir, $83,424
Sawkins, Phillip D, youth spec II, $31,512
Sawyers, Cassie, fam spt elig spv, $34,944
Sawyers, Della, sr ofc spt asst (keybrd), $25,824
Sawyers, Marlene K, fam spt elig spv, $38,232
Sax, Jason L, serv coor spv yth srvcs, $38,928
Saxon, Gus M, youth spec II, $31,512
Sayer, Sarah E, children's serv worker III, $36,888
Saylor, John D, fam spt elig spc, $29,976
Saylor, Scott L, reg fam spec, $38,928
Sayre, Andrea, children's serv worker II, $34,356
Scails, Gregory L, acad tchr III, $36,204
Scalf, Derek M, youth spec II, $31,512
Scalise, Erica G, children's serv worker II, $32,628
Schaaf, Patty, ofc spt asst (keybrd), $23,160
Schachtele, Karen J, children's serv spv, $41,940
Schaefer, Marjorie, ofc spt asst (keybrd), $25,824
Schaefer, Mary P, child spt spec, $34,356
Schaeffer, Hal O, fam spt elig spv, $34,944
Schaeffer, Robert C, soc servs aide, $11.13/hr
Schafer, Melissa K, children's serv worker II, $34,356
Schaller, Debra A, child spt enforce adm, $43,488
Schartz, Crystal L, corres & info spec I, $34,944
Schatzler, Tanya L, child spt spec, $29,976
Schauer, Joann, fiscal & administrative mgr b1, $49,440
Scheiper, Mark, child spt enforce spv, $38,928
Schellman, Jennifer E, child spt spec, $29,976
Schenck, Katie, children's serv worker III, $35,568
Schenewerk, Jason R, special educ tchr III, $38,928
Schenewerk, Rhonda G, medicaid prog rel rep, $43,488
Schenk, Lance L, fam spt elig spc, $29,976
Scherer, Jody C, children's serv spec, $41,940
Schiwitz, Janet S, child spt spec, $29,976
Schlueter, Kathleen G, children's serv worker II, $34,356
Schmidly, Gregory D, youth spec II, $31,512
Schmidt, Ashley D, children's serv worker II, $32,628
Schmidt, Gena M, children's serv worker III, $36,888
Schmidt, Heather N, youth spec I, $28,104
Schmidt, Jerie D, children's serv worker II, $32,628
Schmidt, Kelly A, children's serv worker II, $34,356
Schmidt, Linda M, ofc spt asst (keybrd), $29,412
Schmitt, Ronda A, exec I, $36,204
Schmitt, Theresa, sr ofc spt asst (keybrd), $30,384
Schmitz, Rachael D, medicaid spec, $37,548
Schmitz, Rochelle L, children's serv worker III, $35,568
Schnakenberg, Jamie R, cook III, $28,104
Schneider, Christina L, children's serv worker III, $36,888
Schneider, Debra L, fam spt elig spc, $29,976
Schneider, John B, misc prof, $24.06/hr
Schneider, Kasey A, children's serv worker II, $34,356
Schneider, Kelly S, registered nurse - clin opers, $54,720
Schneider, Mary C, case analyst, $32,052
Schneider, Rebecca J, medicaid pharmaceutical tech, $34,356
Schnelle, Steve A, rehab tchr for the blind, $34,944
Schnieders, Deborah S, admin ofc spt asst, $30,984
Schnieders, Jonathan L, accounting spec I, $36,204
Schnieders, Lisa G, acct III, $41,940
Schnoebelen, Laura E, prog dev spec, $44,304
Schnur, Joyce F, child spt spec, $34,944
Schoeneck, Elizabeth A, children's serv worker II, $33,744
Schoenig, Daniel P, sr voc rehab cnslr f/t blind, $38,928

Scholz, Diana L, children's serv worker III, $36,888
Scholz, Emily S, soc servs mgr, band 1, $52,152
Schrader, Joanne M, youth spec II, $31,512
Schrimpf, Kristine E, mgmt analysis spec II, $41,940
Schrimpf-Mueller, Stephanee A, children's serv worker II, $17,178
Schrock, Nicole, children's serv worker III, $35,568
Schrock, Penny R, hr mgr b1, $58,908
Schrock, Renee L, fam spt elig spc, $31,512
Schroeder, Emily J, children's serv worker I, $32,052
Schroeder, Lisa M, prog dev spec, $44,304
Schroepfer, Cassandra L, fam spt elig spc, $29,976
Schroer, Kathleen S, medicaid technician, $32,628
Schroer, Linda S, medicaid technician, $33,180
Schroeter, Michelle M, case analyst, $32,628
Schroeter, Trisha, child spt spec, $29,976
Schrunk, Jennifer M, children's serv worker II, $34,356
Schubert, Ashlee A, children's serv spv, $38,232
Schuemann, Shana E, child spt spec, $29,976
Schuitema, Andrea L, corres & info spec I, $34,944
Schulte, Elizabeth A, edu asst II, $24,804
Schultz, Laura M, children's serv worker III, $36,888
Schultz, Mary J, children's serv spv, $39,624
Schultz, Rhonda, ofc spt asst (keybrd), $23,160
Schuster-Lackey, Melissa R, children's serv worker III, $35,568
Schutte, Melissa, child spt spec, $29,976
Schwach, Elisabeth A, children's serv spec, $44,304
Schwarm, Rebecca K, ofc spt asst (keybrd), $22,536
Schweigert, Anthony G, fam spt elig spc, $29,976
Schweigert, Jeanna A, special educ tchr III, $38,928
Scimeca, Katheryn M, fam spt elig spc, $31,512
Scism, Stephanie, children's serv worker I, $30,984
Scism, Victoria D, children's serv worker I, $29,976
Scott, Barbara A, child spt spec, $30,420
Scott, Beverly A, fam spt elig spc, $29,976
Scott, Cathy M, fam spt elig spc, $32,628
Scott, Daytron A, fam spt elig spc, $29,976
Scott, Donna S, child spt spec, $29,976
Scott, Jama B, children's serv worker III, $35,568
Scott, Mary S, ofc spt asst (keybrd), $23,160
Scott, Nakisha, fam spt elig spc, $29,976
Scott, Natonya Y, fam spt elig spc, $29,976
Scott, Patty L, children's serv spv, $38,232
Scott, Sarah B, children's serv worker III, $36,888
Scott, Sharonda M, fam spt elig spc, $29,976
Scott, Susan J, child spt spec, $33,180
Scott, Tammy D, children's serv worker II, $34,356
Scudder, Rebecca M, soc servs mgr, band 1, $44,304
Seabaugh, Elizabeth D, fam spt elig spv, $36,888
Seabaugh, Molly E, children's serv worker I, $30,984
Seabourne, Gary L, misc prof, $25.49/hr
Seahorn, Myra L, ofc spt asst (keybrd), $23,160
Searcy, Jeri N, fam spt elig spc, $29,976
Searcy, Marilyn S, ofc spt asst (keybrd), $23,160
Seaton, Charis L, ofc spt asst (keybrd), $22,536
Seaton, Gary, sr ofc spt asst (keybrd), $25,824
Seaver, Sara E, pers analyst II, $41,940
Seay, Ashley E, children's serv worker III, $36,888
Sebastian, Jong H, fam spt elig spc, $29,976
Sebree, Tiatay M, fam spt elig spc, $29,976
Seek, Jennifer M, sr ofc spt asst (keybrd), $25,824
Seeley, Beverly M, fam spt elig spc, $29,976
Seiling, Steven M, children's serv worker II, $34,356
Sekscinski, Kortney M, children's serv worker II, $34,356
Sekscinski, Monica S, child plcmnt coor (ss), $42,708
Selby, Kimberly, children's serv spv, $39,624
Self, Kimberly A, fam spt elig spc, $29,976
Self, Roxanne, acct I, $32,628
Self, Valerie S, fam spt elig spc, $32,052
Sell, Glenda G, medicaid spec, $37,548
Sellers, Lindsay R, soc servs aide, $11.13/hr
Sellers, Melanie A, child spt spec, $29,976
Senf, Christy D, fam spt elig spc, $29,976
Sentman, Haley, fam spt elig spc, $29,976
Sessions, Sara E, children's serv worker II, $34,356
Setzkorn, William R, children's serv worker II, $34,356
Severino, Frank M, acad tchr III, $37,548
Sewer, Emanuel W, fam spt elig spc, $29,976
Shaeffer, Elizabeth A, children's serv spv, $41,172
Shaeffer, Elizabeth A, misc tech, $12.59/hr

Shafer, Gregory A, area supv bus entprs blind, $36,204
Shaffer, Glenda R, child spt spec, $29,976
Shahangian, Tara M, sr ofc spt asst (keybrd), $25,824
Shaiffer, Crystal A, fam spt elig spc, $29,976
Shalley, Pamela L, ofc spt asst (keybrd), $23,160
Shamily, Patricia D, ofc spt asst (keybrd), $25,032
Shanks, Darren W, youth spec II, $29,976
Shanks, Glenda L, ofc spt asst (keybrd), $26,232
Shanks, Mandy S, ofc spt asst (keybrd), $23,160
Shannon, Karen M, soc servs aide, $11.13/hr
Shannon, Nadine B, fam spt elig spc, $33,744
Shannon, Nicole D, case analyst, $33,744
Shannon, Randy L, fam spt elig spc, $29,976
Shaon, Matthew L, serv coor yth srvcs, $33,744
Sharkey, Meghann E, youth spec II, $29,976
Sharon, Cassie L, fam spt elig spc, $29,976
Sharp, George, children's serv worker II, $34,356
Sharp, Melissa, ofc spt asst (keybrd), $23,160
Sharp, Rebecca A, fam spt elig spc, $29,976
Sharpe, Asia R, children's serv worker I, $30,984
Sharr, Elizabeth M, children's serv spec, $38,928
Sharr, Ronald J, mgmt analysis spec II, $45,156
Sharwarko, John M, child spt enforce spv, $34,944
Sharwarko, Judith G, child spt spec II, $33,180
Shatto, Jerry L, outdoor rehab cnslr II, $45,156
Shaver, Angela B, fam spt elig spc, $31,512
Shaw, Angela R, children's serv worker I, $29,976
Shaw, Paula K, soc servs mngr, band 2, $71,100
Shaw, Sara B, fam spt elig spc, $29,976
Shaw, Tina, child spt spec, $29,976
Shearrer, Sarah, ofc spt asst (keybrd), $23,160
Shekon, Phyllis E, ofc spt asst (keybrd), $23,160
Shelby, Cheryl G, child spt spec, $33,744
Shelby, Marietta D, child spt spec, $31,512
Shelby, Myles, serv coor yth srvcs, $33,744
Shelton, Angela S, fam spt elig spc, $29,976
Shelton, Christina A, children's serv worker II, $33,744
Shelton, Daniel L, youth spec II, $31,512
Shelton, Joy K, youth group leader, $34,356
Shelton, Margaret E, child spt spec, $33,180
Shelton, Mary A, sr ofc spt asst (steno), $29,412
Shelton, Mockia, children's serv worker III, $36,888
Shelton, Sara L, children's serv worker I, $30,984
Shelton, Susan A, soc servs worker, $19.70/hr
Shelton, Sylvia L, acad tchr III, $37,548
Shelton, Tabatha N, children's serv worker I, $30,984
Shepard, Beverly J, fam spt elig spc, $31,512
Shepard, Denise M, ofc spt asst (keybrd), $23,160
Shepard, Jennifer L, children's serv worker I, $29,976
Shepherd, Robert H, children's serv worker II, $36,888
Sheppard, Shakina L, youth spec II, $30,984
Sherbo, Kateri L, soc servs mgr, band 1, $44,304
Sherman, Dawn M, fam spt elig spc, $29,976
Sherrill, Amanda P, fam spt elig spc, $29,976
Sherwood, Keta, fam spt elig spc, $29,976
Shields, Debbie A, ofc spt asst (keybrd), $23,160
Shields, Mari B, fam spt elig spc, $32,628
Shields, Nikita R, children's serv worker II, $32,628
Shields, Rebecca J, soc servs mgr, band 1, $41,940
Shiflett, Melissa I, corres & info spec I, $33,744
Shinn, Anne E, fam spt elig spc, $29,976
Shinn, Catherine A, fam spt elig spc, $33,180
Shipley, Sandra, fam spt elig spc, $29,976
Shipman, Brenda L, prog dev spec, $40,380
Shipman, William A, serv coor yth srvcs, $33,744
Shirk, Karen S, ofc spt asst (keybrd), $11,580
Shirley, Mary E, child spt spec, $29,976
Shively, Melissa D, fam spt elig spc, $29,976
Shivers, Lisa A, fam spt elig spc, $34,356
Shivley, Peggy L, registered nurse sr, $50,244
Shoats, Carmen N, ofc spt asst (keybrd), $22,536
Shockley, Alice L, hearings ofcr, $53,088
Shockley, Steven W, youth spec II, $34,356
Shoemaker, Shane, fam spt elig spc, $29,976
Shoemyer, Patricia M, youth spec II, $31,512
Shollenberger, Gloria D, youth spec II, $31,512
Shollenberger, Marcus A, youth spec II, $31,512
Shoop, Dena E, fam spt elig spc, $34,356
Short, Elizabeth A, medicaid spec, $39,624

Short, Miranda, youth spec I, $28,104
Short, Stacy D, fam spt elig spc, $29,976
Short, Stephen C, acad tchr III, $37,548
Shoults, Bernadette S, rehab asst rehab srvs for blnd, $26,652
Shouse, Deborah A, ofc spt asst (keybrd), $26,232
Shriver, Connor S, soc servs aide, $11.13/hr
Shrum, Juanita M, exec II, $38,232
Shuck, Jeanne M, fam spt elig spc, $30,984
Shumake, Carolyn A, fam spt elig spc, $29,976
Shumpert, Kelly, ofc spt asst (keybrd), $23,160
Shupert, Nelda R, fam spt elig spc, $33,744
Shuster, Gina M, fam spt elig spc, $33,180
Shymanski, Kathryn C, serv coor yth srvcs, $33,744
Siacotos, Sara, ofc spt asst (keybrd), $23,160
Siars, Paulette K, fam spt elig spc, $29,976
Siebert, Jessica N, investigator I, $30,984
Siegler, Carol S, fam spt elig spc, $29,976
Siercks, Samantha J, children's serv worker I, $29,976
Sievers, Larry A, fam spt elig spc, $33,180
Sifferman, Loretta C, children's serv worker I, $29,976
Sigg, Tracy L, mgmt analysis spec II, $41,940
Siglar, Brooke E, children's serv worker II, $34,356
Sigman, Timothy E, youth spec II, $31,512
Signars, Tommy J, serv coor yth srvcs, $33,744
Sikes, Leo C, children's serv worker II, $33,744
Sikorski, Edith A, fam spt elig spc, $29,976
Sillas, Alma S, sr ofc spt asst (keybrd), $27,504
Silver, Jessica M, investigator II, $37,548
Silverstein, Sharon T, job dev spec for the blind, $41,940
Silveus, Stacey L, fam spt elig spc, $31,512
Silvey, Cara, fam spt elig spc, $29,976
Silvey, Joseph A, youth spec II, $30,420
Simmerock, Brooke, children's serv spv, $39,624
Simmoneau, Linda L, prog dev spec, $39,624
Simmons, Alice M, fam spt elig spc, $33,744
Simmons, Jill, children's serv spv, $39,624
Simmons, Julie M, sr ofc spt asst (keybrd), $25,032
Simmons, Kathy A, medicaid technician, $32,628
Simmons, Rex, youth spec II, $31,512
Simmons, Sandra K, child spt spec, $32,628
Simms, Kelley D, fam spt elig spc, $29,976
Simms, Stacey C, child spt spec, $29,976
Simons, Derrick D, youth spec II, $31,512
Simpson, Amy M, fam spt elig spc, $29,976
Simpson, Lasha D, children's serv worker II, $34,356
Simpson, Renee J, fam spt elig spc, $29,976
Simpson, Shannon, child spt spec, $29,976
Sims, Catherine A, children's serv spec, $41,940
Sims, Karen, legal counsel, $47,808
Sims, Tiffany K, fam spt elig spc, $29,976
Simshauser, Rachel E, children's serv worker III, $36,888
Sinclair, Sabrina, fam spt elig spc, $29,976
Sinden, Dianne K, fiscal & administrative mgr b1, $50,040
Singleton, Francesca H, fam spt elig spv, $36,888
Sirdoreus, Catherine H, fam spt elig spc, $29,976
Sirdoreus, Valerie A, fam spt elig spc, $29,976
Sisco, Rose, fam spt elig spc, $33,180
Sisk, Dave E, acad tchr III, $37,548
Sita, Jenna T, corres & info spec I, $34,944
Sitts, Tiffany, children's serv worker III, $36,888
Sjostrand, Megan M, children's serv worker II, $34,356
Skelton, Norma J, soc servs mgr, band 1, $47,892
Skidmore, Leslie L, sr ofc spt asst (keybrd), $25,824
Skinner, Gaylene, children's serv worker II, $34,356
Slane, Amie L, ofc spt asst (keybrd), $23,160
Slater, Michael E, fam spt elig spc, $33,180
Slater, Pauline A, fam spt elig spc, $29,976
Slater, Samantha L, children's serv worker II, $32,628
Slater, Stephanie, children's serv worker III, $36,888
Slaughter, Audrey C, ofc spt asst (keybrd), $23,160
Slaughter, Ronald, youth spec II, $31,512
Slinkard, Ryan M, children's serv worker II, $34,356
Sloan, Anajanette R, children's serv worker III, $36,888
Slocum, Julie A, children's serv spv, $43,488
Slover, Jacquelyn S, special educ tchr III, $37,548
Slover, Timothy D, training tech II, $42,708
Small, Bradley M, children's serv worker II, $34,356
Smalley, Andrea, children's serv worker III, $35,568
Smart, Clarissa D, youth spec II, $31,512

Smart, Kenneth G, youth spec II, $31,512
Smiles, Marilyn, fam spt elig spc, $29,976
Smiley, Janet, serv coor spv yth srvcs, $47,892
Smith, Abigail J, children's serv worker III, $35,568
Smith, Alan, corres & info spec I, $33,744
Smith, Alicia M, children's serv worker III, $36,888
Smith, Alison, children's serv spv, $39,624
Smith, Allison M, fam spt elig spc, $29,976
Smith, Amber J, youth spec II, $31,512
Smith, Amber N, children's serv worker II, $32,628
Smith, Anastasia D, soc servs aide, $11.13/hr
Smith, Angela D, children's serv worker I, $30,984
Smith, Angela M, fam spt elig spc, $34,356
Smith, Antoinette, fam spt elig spc, $29,976
Smith, Autumn L, youth spec I, $28,104
Smith, Bennetta D, fam spt elig spc, $29,976
Smith, Beverly K, admin ofc spt asst, $32,052
Smith, Brandi L, children's serv worker I, $29,976
Smith, Calita, fam spt elig spc, $30,984
Smith, Cindy, admin ofc spt asst, $32,628
Smith, Deborah A, fam spt elig spc, $29,976
Smith, Deborah M, sr ofc spt asst (keybrd), $25,824
Smith, Denise G, children's serv spv, $42,708
Smith, Ebony M, fam spt elig spc, $29,976
Smith, Elaine I, children's serv prog mgr, $47,892
Smith, Elaine L, ofc spt asst (keybrd), $25,824
Smith, Felawn, youth spec I, $29,004
Smith, Gina L, children's serv worker III, $38,232
Smith, Jacqueline A, fam spt elig spc, $29,976
Smith, James L, acad tchr III, $37,548
Smith, Jessica M, child spt spec, $29,004
Smith, Johnna A, sr ofc spt asst (keybrd), $25,824
Smith, Judy Y, fam spt elig spc, $29,976
Smith, Julie M, registered nurse sr, $46,560
Smith, Karen S, ofc spt asst (keybrd), $27,084
Smith, Karen T, children's serv worker II, $34,356
Smith, Karla G, children's serv worker III, $41,940
Smith, Katie E, youth spec II, $31,512
Smith, Kristen N, fam spt elig spc, $29,976
Smith, Lachandra Y, fam spt elig spc, $29,976
Smith, Laurie G, child spt spec, $31,512
Smith, Lisa E, prog dev spec, $40,380
Smith, Margaret A, hlth prog rep II, $38,928
Smith, Mariah N, children's serv worker I, $30,984
Smith, Marilyn, children's serv spv, $39,624
Smith, Marjorie K, prog dev spec, $41,172
Smith, Mary Lou A, children's serv worker III, $35,568
Smith, Megan, children's serv worker III, $35,568
Smith, Megan, fam spt elig spc, $29,976
Smith, Megan N, children's serv worker III, $35,568
Smith, Norman D, acad tchr III, $37,548
Smith, Pamela D, training tech III, $45,156
Smith, Pamela K, soc servs mgr, band 1, $61,332
Smith, Precious S, children's serv worker II, $34,356
Smith, Romon, ofc spt asst (keybrd), $22,536
Smith, Sara, children's serv spec, $41,940
Smith, Sarah, corres & info spec I, $34,944
Smith, Scott R, special asst prof, $47,892
Smith, Shalanda J, hearings ofcr, $39,648
Smith, Shartina A, soc servs mgr, band 1, $41,940
Smith, Shelley E, corres & info spec I, $36,888
Smith, Sherita E, children's serv worker II, $32,628
Smith, Sherry L, soc servs mgr, band 1, $47,052
Smith, Sherry L, child spt spec, $33,180
Smith, Taylor W, youth spec I, $28,104
Smith, Tekeia N, fam spt elig spc, $29,976
Smith, Timothy L, youth spec II, $31,512
Smith, Tisa M, children's serv worker II, $37,548
Smith, Tonya L, fam spt elig spc, $29,976
Smith, Tracy J, ofc spt asst (keybrd), $25,824
Smith, Travis W, soc servs mgr, band 1, $48,156
Smith, Tricia A, prog dev spec, $40,380
Smith, Ursula D, youth fac mgr I, $38,928
Smith, Vicki G, fam spt elig spc, $29,976
Smith, Vickie L, ofc spt asst (keybrd), $23,160
Smith, Vicky L, child spt spec, $29,976
Smith, Wanda J, children's serv worker II, $32,628
Smith Shepherd, Jetona L, fam spt elig spc, $34,356
Smither, Phyllis P, sr ofc spt asst (keybrd), $25,824

Smithers, Saronya M, ofc spt asst (keybrd), $23,160
Smithey, Robert S, youth spec I, $28,104
Smith-Gonzales, Linda M, admin ofc spt asst, $28,536
Smith-Vandergriff, Michelle, children's serv worker II, $34,356
Smolke, Melissa J, fam spt elig spc, $30,420
Smoote, Annette, fam spt elig spc, $29,976
Smulders, Debra N, child spt spec, $33,744
Smyser, Alexa A, children's serv worker II, $32,628
Sneed, Madeline C, children's serv worker II, $34,356
Sneed, Shaune R, youth spec II, $31,512
Sneller, Cassie R, child spt spec, $29,004
Sneller, Toni, medicaid pharmaceutical tech, $32,628
Snider, Angelica J, youth spec II, $30,984
Snider, Contrina, children's serv worker I, $29,976
Snider, Susan A, fam spt elig spc, $29,976
Snodgrass, Dawn R, fam spt elig spc, $32,628
Snodgrass, Dustin J, youth spec II, $33,180
Snook, Karen, child spt spec, $36,204
Snow, Ebony M, youth group leader, $34,356
Snowbarger, Theron S, fam spt elig spc, $29,976
Snyder, Aubrey L, medicaid spec, $37,548
Snyder, Cindy, child spt spec, $31,512
Snyder, Rachel L, children's serv spv, $39,624
Snyder, Robert M, medicaid clerk, $28,104
Snyder, Susan E, children's serv worker II, $37,548
Soendker, Racheal E, fam spt elig spv, $34,944
Sokolic, Pamela L, fam spt elig spv, $34,944
Solomon, Johnna R, fam spt elig spc, $29,976
Solomon, Paul A, prog dev spec, $38,928
Solomon, Stuart, fam spt elig spc, $29,976
Soltero, Mary K, ofc spt asst (steno), $27,504
Sommer, Cindy S, child spt spec, $29,976
Sommers, Linda J, admin ofc spt asst, $28,104
Sorbie, Laura K, fam spt elig spc, $29,976
Sorenson, Linda K, sr ofc spt asst (keybrd), $25,824
Soria, Tamara D, soc servs aide, $11.13/hr
Soule, Naomi, soc servs mgr, band 1, $51,096
Soulier, Mandi, fam spt elig spc, $29,976
South, Laura J, children's serv worker III, $36,888
South, William L, fam spt elig spv, $36,888
Southard, Ginger, ofc spt asst (keybrd), $23,160
Southard, Joyce D, fam spt elig spc, $29,976
Souza, Deborah S, fam spt elig spc, $29,976
Sowers, Wendy M, children's serv spv, $39,624
Spaid, Amanda, fam spt elig spc, $29,976
Spalding, Barbara S, ofc spt asst (keybrd), $25,824
Spalding, Lynn M, fam spt elig spc, $34,944
Spaller, Wendy G, child spt spec, $29,976
Spanley, Samantha R, children's serv worker I, $29,976
Sparkling, Montine, children's serv worker II, $34,356
Sparks, Jeanne, corres & info spec I, $34,944
Sparks, Laura L, fam spt elig spv, $34,944
Sparks, Mary A, child spt spec, $29,976
Spaulding, Lillian D, fam spt elig spc, $29,976
Speakes, Jennifer J, fam spt elig spc, $29,976
Speakes, Kelly J, children's serv worker II, $34,356
Spearman, Angela T, children's serv worker I, $30,984
Spears, Derek J, youth spec II, $31,512
Spears, Timothy W, youth spec I, $28,104
Spellmeyer, Kenneth, children's serv worker II, $34,356
Spells, Diana L, children's serv worker II, $33,744
Spence, Rita D, children's serv worker II, $34,356
Spencer, Kirsten N, children's serv worker II, $33,744
Spencer, Oret C, soc servs aide, $11.13/hr
Spencer, Stacy A, fam spt elig spc, $29,976
Sperry, Megan N, fam spt elig spc, $29,976
Spicer, Denise Y, youth spec II, $31,512
Spies, Vernon J, youth spec II, $31,512
Spinks, Francine E, training tech II, $40,380
Spinks, Patryce N, fam spt elig spc, $29,976
Spitzer, Brett, children's serv worker II, $34,356
Spivey, Carl F, child spt spec, $29,976
Sponder, Andrea E, children's serv worker II, $33,180
Sponsler, Nancy R, soc servs mgr, band 1, $41,940
Spraggins, Olainki F, children's serv spec, $41,172
Spraggs, Freddie S, research analyst IV, $55,416
Spraggs, Freddie S, soc servs worker, $17.07/hr
Sprague, Cynthia M, fam spt elig spc, $29,976
Spray, Deanna, child spt enforce spv, $40,380

Sprenger, Kimberley B, special asst prof, $76,050
Springer, Justin C, youth group leader, $34,356
Sprofera, Anthony M, ofc spt asst (keybrd), $23,160
Spruiell, Jason C, soc servs mgr, band 1, $48,156
Spry, Robyn D, soc servs mgr, band 1, $46,068
Spurgeon, Deanna M, fam spt elig spc, $29,976
Spurgin, Tory S, children's serv worker II, $34,356
Spurling, Tamara, ofc spt asst (keybrd), $23,160
Srader, Regina, sr ofc spt asst (steno), $29,904
St Julien, Michael A, soc servs mngr, band 2, $61,332
Staab, Heather D, children's serv worker II, $34,356
Stacy, Linda K, fam spt elig spv, $35,568
Stacy, Lori L, fam spt elig spc, $30,984
Staehle, Shellana R, medicaid clerk, $28,536
Stafford, Cindy L, ofc spt asst (keybrd), $23,160
Stafford, Jennifer M, children's serv worker II, $33,180
Stagner, Lisa A, ofc spt asst (keybrd), $23,160
Stahlman, Katrina, fam spt elig spc, $29,976
Staley, Crystal, children's serv worker II, $34,356
Stallings, Shellie R, serv coor yth srvcs, $38,928
Stallman, Margaret A, soc servs mgr, band 1, $41,940
Stallo, Sarah M, children's serv spv, $39,624
Stallo, Shaunna E, children's serv worker II, $34,356
Stallworth, Jacob K, youth fac mgr II, $40,380
Stamburski, Nathan B, prog dev spec, $40,380
Stamps, Pamela A, fam spt elig spv, $36,888
Stankovich, Alexis N, children's serv worker I, $29,976
Staples, Nathan R, children's serv worker III, $35,568
Stapleton, Sherry L, fam spt elig spc, $31,512
Stark, Amanda G, sr ofc spt asst (keybrd), $25,824
Stark, Jeremy D, fam spt elig spc, $29,976
Stark, Jonathan P, youth spec II, $31,512
Stark, Stacy R, youth group leader, $34,356
Starke, Sabrina K, fam spt elig spc, $29,976
Starks, Stacy I, cook III, $28,104
Starling, Charles, youth spec II, $30,984
Starr, Julie L, children's serv spec, $46,068
Starr, Mark W, fam spt elig spc, $33,180
Stasiak, Kelli L, ofc spt asst (keybrd), $22,536
Statler, Jeana M, children's serv spv, $39,624
Stayton, Monique, fam spt elig spc, $29,976
Steele, Christine E, children's serv spv, $39,624
Steele, Lisa L, fam spt elig spc, $29,976
Steele, Robert, sr ofc spt asst (keybrd), $25,824
Steele, Thomas I, fam spt elig spc, $33,180
Steen, Rhonda L, corres & info spec I, $40,380
Steen, Tiffany, fam spt elig spc, $29,976
Steers, Barbara, sr ofc spt asst (keybrd), $25,824
Steffens, Neal W, special educ tchr III, $41,172
Stegall, Marsha R, fam spt elig spc, $29,976
Stegemann, Frances E, medicaid spec, $39,624
Steidley, Jennifer R, children's serv worker I, $29,976
Steinhauser, Beth A, fam spt elig spc, $32,628
Steinman, Mary J, ofc spt asst (keybrd), $25,032
Steinmeyer, John D, prog dev spec, $49,128
Stephan, David K, corres & info spec I, $36,888
Stephan, Virginia M, special educ tchr III, $40,380
Stephen, Johnnie, children's serv worker I, $29,976
Stephens, Connie, fam spt elig spc, $29,976
Stephens, Douglas R, admin ofc spt asst, $27,228
Stephens, Karen F, child spt spec, $29,976
Stephens, Karen S, ofc spt asst (keybrd), $25,824
Stephens, Michele I, fam spt elig spc, $29,976
Stephenson, Jessica R, children's serv worker II, $34,356
Stephenson, Shirley J, children's serv worker II, $38,232
Stepleton, Aaron L, youth spec II, $31,512
Sterling, Kimberly D, children's serv worker II, $34,356
Sterling, Willie M, ofc spt asst (keybrd), $23,160
Sterling Wagner, Marina, sr ofc spt asst (keybrd), $25,824
Stetina, Jeremy W, children's serv worker II, $34,356
Stetson, Pamela F, account clerk II, $25,824
Steuck, Maria F, soc servs aide, $11.13/hr
Steva, Tracy A, fam spt elig spc, $34,356
Stevens, Cartha M, fam spt elig spc, $32,628
Stevens, Jennifer, child spt spec, $29,004
Stevens, Joyce M, registered nurse sr, $51,552
Stevens, Paul R, children's serv worker II, $37,548
Stevenson, Kimberly S, children's serv worker II, $18,102
Stevenson, Kristen A, children's serv worker I, $29,976

Steward, Jennifer M, fam spt elig spv, $34,944
Stewart, Amber E, children's serv worker II, $32,628
Stewart, Gregory L, fam spt elig spv, $34,944
Stewart, Ricky W, soc servs mgr, band 1, $48,156
Stewart, Robert A, youth spec II, $31,512
Stewart, Sharon Y, children's serv spv, $45,156
Stewart, Sherry R, ofc spt asst (keybrd), $23,160
Stewart, Stacy L, fam spt elig spc, $33,180
Stewart, Tambra L, fam spt elig spc, $29,976
Stidham, Heather, children's serv worker II, $34,356
Stiles, Sara J, children's serv spv, $39,624
Stilley, Angela, fam spt elig spc, $29,976
Stillions, Violet B, children's serv worker II, $37,548
Stillman, Shelly, children's serv spec, $37,548
Stimage, Tiffany N, youth spec II, $31,512
Stinebaker, Marjorie A, corres & info spec I, $36,204
Stith, Debra J, ofc spt asst (keybrd), $23,160
Stith, Jerry E, child spt spec, $31,512
Stock, Sara J, sr ofc spt asst (keybrd), $25,824
Stockman, Connie J, fam spt elig spv, $39,624
Stockman, Kimberly S, pers ofcr I, $40,380
Stoff, Cory, investigator III, $41,940
Stoffregen, Rodney A, fam spt elig spc, $29,976
Stokes, Jenny L, child spt spec, $29,976
Stolle, Phillip R, youth spec II, $31,512
Stone, Connie J, ofc spt asst (keybrd), $26,232
Stone, Cynthia A, children's serv spec, $42,708
Stone, Natalie, children's serv worker II, $34,356
Stoneberger, Victoria, children's serv spec, $43,488
Stonefield, Elizabeth R, children's serv prog mgr, $46,068
Stoner, Klarissa L, children's serv worker II, $34,356
Stonestreet, Heather D, ofc spt asst (keybrd), $23,160
Storey, Pamela A, medicaid technician, $32,628
Storm, Michael L, children's serv worker III, $36,888
Stotler, Ambra, medicaid spec, $37,548
Stotler, Holly S, children's serv spv, $37,548
Stotler, Roxanne, sr ofc spt asst (keybrd), $25,824
Stotts, Jennifer L, children's serv worker III, $36,888
Stouder, Brian D, children's serv worker II, $33,744
Stoufer, Krista L, children's serv worker III, $35,568
Stout, Christopher W, prog dev spec, $40,380
Stout, Janice S, soc servs mgr, band 1, $41,940
Stovall, Casie M, children's serv worker III, $36,888
Stovall, Cassandra, ofc spt asst (keybrd), $23,508
Stover, Sandra L, special educ tchr III, $19,464
Stow, Sandra, fam spt elig spc, $29,976
Stowers, Gara D, fam spt elig spv, $38,928
Stranahan, Mary M, fam spt elig spc, $29,976
Strassburg, Theodora L, legal counsel, $44,292
Strathman, Brandon M, corres & info spec I, $34,944
Stratman, Victoria, fam spt elig spc, $29,976
Stratton, Cathy, fam spt elig spc, $29,976
Stratton, Christopher S, hearings ofcr, $41,940
Straub, Shamita R, children's serv worker II, $34,356
Strawn, Lance D, serv coor yth srvcs, $33,744
Street, Paula L, fam spt elig spc, $30,984
Street-Bogue, Denise L, sr ofc spt asst (keybrd), $25,824
Strickland, Tarlise D, youth spec II, $31,512
Stricklin, Robert S, acad tchr I, $29,976
Stricklin, Stacia L, children's serv worker II, $34,356
Stripp, Suzan L, fam spt elig spc, $29,976
Strobel, Kathleen M, prog dev spec, $40,380
Strode, Brooke L, children's serv worker II, $34,356
Strohm, Kate E, children's serv worker III, $36,888
Strong, Aviane D, child spt spec, $29,976
Strong, Jennifer R, sr ofc spt asst (keybrd), $25,824
Strong, Lisa R, children's serv worker II, $34,356
Stroot, Vickie L, child spt enforce spv, $33,744
Strope, Kathleen A, fam spt elig spc, $29,976
Struemph, Beverly J, hr mgr b2, $71,208
Struemph, Michele D, special asst prof, $57,168
Strunk, Elizabeth A, children's serv worker III, $40,380
Stuart, Karin E, children's serv worker III, $35,568
Stuart, Katherine A, children's serv spv, $39,624
Stubblefield, Candice M, youth spec II, $29,976
Stubblefield, Tracey E, fam spt elig spc, $34,356
Stuckey, Carol J, child spt spec, $29,976
Stuerke, Joan L, special educ tchr III, $39,624
Stull, Ashley K, children's serv worker III, $35,568

Sturghill, Patricia, ofc spt asst (keybrd), $27,084
Stuve, Paul R, special asst prof, $116,664
Suber, Cedric D, youth spec I, $29,004
Sucher, Vince J, youth spec II, $31,512
Suh, Ra, children's serv worker II, $32,628
Sullens, Sarah K, prog dev spec, $40,380
Sullins, Hailey A, fam spt elig spc, $29,976
Sullivan, Darlene A, child spt enforce spv, $39,624
Sullivan, Diane T, ofc spt asst (keybrd), $23,508
Sullivan, Elizabeth M, soc servs mgr, band 1, $47,892
Sullivan, Megan R, children's serv worker II, $33,744
Sullivan, Sheila M, fam spt elig spc, $29,976
Sullivan, William M, serv coor yth srvcs, $33,744
Summerhill, Kristiann, children's serv prog mgr, $43,488
Summerlin, Vanessa A, fam spt elig spc, $30,420
Summers, Annette, pers analyst II, $41,940
Summers, Deanna, prog dev spec, $40,380
Supakit, Christie L, child spt spec, $33,744
Sutcliffe, Deborah L, children's serv worker II, $38,232
Sutherland, Ray M, acad tchr III, $37,548
Sutherland, Toni G, prog dev spec, $40,380
Sutter, Connie M, sr auditor, $42,708
Sutton, Darlene, child spt enforce spv, $36,204
Sutton, Debra K, children's serv spec, $44,304
Sutton, Harvetta M, ofc spt asst (keybrd), $23,160
Sutton, Rebecca C, children's serv worker II, $34,356
Swanks, Michele D, acad tchr III, $37,548
Swanz, David J, child spt spec, $29,976
Swarnes, Angela D, special asst prof, $69,852
Swart, Jeffrey J, serv coor yth srvcs, $39,624
Swartz, Tyler S, youth spec II, $31,512
Sweeney, Chester A, youth spec II, $31,512
Sweney, Alicia E, youth spec II, $31,512
Swift, Pamela S, ofc spt asst (keybrd), $23,160
Swilley, Beverly J, fam spt elig spc, $29,976
Swindle, Laura S, child spt spec, $33,744
Switzer, Sharron K, child spt enforce spv, $34,944
Swoboda, Bailey A, children's serv worker III, $35,568
Swoboda, Julie A, corres & info spec I, $36,204
Swofford, Charlotte M, fam spt elig spc, $34,356
Swopes, Hannah B, children's serv spv, $39,624
Swopes, Ruth, fam spt elig spc, $29,976
Sybouts, Donna, special asst ofc & clerical, $49,968
Sykes, Cecilia, child spt spec, $29,976
Szabados, Michelle L, ofc spt asst (keybrd), $23,160
Taber, Dana L, fam spt elig spc, $33,180
Tabor, Elizabeth D, fam spt elig spc, $31,512
Tabor, Gayla A, ofc spt asst (keybrd), $23,160
Tackett, Lisa D, sr ofc spt asst (keybrd), $25,824
Tadrick, Theresa, children's serv worker II, $34,356
Talamantez, Doris A, fam spt elig spc, $31,512
Talken, Sandra L, medicaid spec, $37,548
Talley, Colleen K, children's serv worker II, $34,356
Talley, Rhonda M, children's serv worker III, $37,548
Talley, Sylvia D, pers analyst II, $40,380
Tamburro, Michelle, sr ofc spt asst (keybrd), $25,824
Tannehill, Sheila A, fiscal & administrative mgr b2, $70,560
Tannlund, Chris J, soc servs mgr, band 1, $41,940
Tappana, Mary E, child spt enforce spv, $34,944
Tarkington, Brandy J, children's serv worker II, $33,744
Tarkington, Crendy S, sr voc rehab cnslr f/t blind, $38,928
Tate, Benjamin F, youth spec II, $31,512
Tate, Laura M, fam spt elig spc, $34,944
Tate, Mary K, youth spec II, $30,984
Tate, William A, children's serv worker II, $32,628
Tatom, Shawn M, children's serv worker III, $40,380
Tattershall, Elizabeth, prog dev spec, $41,940
Tavener, Bradley D, youth group leader, $32,628
Taylor, Anthoney J, youth spec II, $29,976
Taylor, Ashley K, youth spec I, $28,104
Taylor, Brandy, fam spt elig spc, $29,976
Taylor, Cathy E, fam spt elig spc, $32,628
Taylor, Christine A, children's serv worker II, $34,356
Taylor, Cynthia A, child spt spec, $29,976
Taylor, Cynthia K, fam spt elig spc, $34,944
Taylor, Djuana S, fam spt elig spc, $34,356
Taylor, Donald L, youth spec II, $29,976
Taylor, Emily D, soc servs aide, $11.13/hr
Taylor, Eric J, fam spt elig spc, $29,976

Taylor, Francine C, child spt spec, $31,512
Taylor, James D, youth spec II, $31,512
Taylor, Jeffrey, outdoor rehab cnslr I, $36,204
Taylor, Jennifer K, fam spt elig spc, $29,976
Taylor, Jillian E, children's serv spv, $39,624
Taylor, Joshua D, youth spec II, $30,984
Taylor, Linette M, child spt spec, $29,976
Taylor, Melinda, fam spt elig spc, $29,976
Taylor, Melinda G, children's serv worker II, $34,356
Taylor, Minden L, youth spec I, $28,104
Taylor, Nancy, fam spt elig spc, $29,976
Taylor, Paula R, cook III, $29,496
Taylor, Raquel J, youth spec II, $31,512
Taylor, Robin A, sr ofc spt asst (keybrd), $25,824
Taylor, Valerie, soc servs mgr, band 1, $47,892
Taylor-Amos, Susan A, reg cnslt resid lcsng unit, $46,068
Taylor-Foster, Debora K, children's serv worker III, $41,172
Teer, Marvin O, legal counsel, $111,100
Tejan, Omar B, research analyst III, $48,156
Telker, Stephanie D, youth spec II, $31,512
Temme, Donna L, child spt spec, $32,628
Temple, Brianne N, ofc spt asst (keybrd), $22,536
Templeton, Christin H, investigator II, $41,940
Templeton, Sondra K, children's serv worker II, $34,356
Tennell, Khalilah N, children's serv worker II, $34,356
Tennis, Leah A, child spt enforce spv, $38,232
Ternak, Anthony G, child spt spec, $33,180
Terrazas, Cynthia M, children's serv spv, $39,624
Terry, Angela R, prog dev spec, $40,380
Terry, Gina C, fam spt elig spc, $33,180
Terry, Jeffrey R, child spt spec, $32,628
Terry, Kytrell M, children's serv worker I, $29,976
Teson, Sandra L, youth spec II, $31,512
Testerman, Mary C, ofc spt asst (keybrd), $23,160
Tharp, Karen E, rehab tchr for the blind, $38,928
Thaxton, Latasha, youth group leader, $34,356
Theberge, Matthew A, ofc spt asst (keybrd), $23,160
Theurer, Melva J, corres & info spec I, $34,944
Thiede, Rachael S, fam spt elig spc, $29,976
Thiesen, Pamela, corres & info spec I, $34,944
Thirkield, Nicole L, special educ tchr III, $38,928
Thoenen, Mary E, sr ofc spt asst (steno), $29,904
Thomas, Alexander S, children's serv worker II, $34,356
Thomas, Alicia A, children's serv worker II, $34,356
Thomas, Bobbie J, children's serv spec, $38,928
Thomas, Carol B, youth spec II, $31,512
Thomas, Carolyn, ofc spt asst (keybrd), $25,824
Thomas, Chaunte F, child spt spec, $29,976
Thomas, Cheryl R, fam spt elig spc, $33,744
Thomas, Cindy K, ofc spt asst (keybrd), $23,160
Thomas, David C, children's serv spv, $39,624
Thomas, Deborah D, ofc spt asst (keybrd), $24,264
Thomas, Jacqueline F, children's serv worker II, $38,928
Thomas, Janet S, fam spt elig spc, $33,180
Thomas, Jason K, training tech II, $40,380
Thomas, Jennifer A, children's serv worker II, $35,568
Thomas, Johnny C, youth spec II, $31,512
Thomas, Kathleen M, fam spt elig spc, $29,976
Thomas, Leandrea D, children's serv worker II, $33,180
Thomas, Margarette S, fam spt elig spv, $35,568
Thomas, Melodie L, fam spt elig spc, $32,628
Thomas, Michele L, corres & info spec II, $38,928
Thomas, Orlando A, soc servs mgr, band 1, $43,488
Thomas, Patricia L, youth spec II, $31,512
Thomas, Ray-Buck L, youth spec II, $31,512
Thomas, Ruby J, special educ tchr III, $45,156
Thomas, Sara F, youth spec II, $30,984
Thomas, Sarah E, children's serv prog mgr, $41,940
Thomas, Sarah M, children's serv worker III, $35,568
Thomas, Taishaun, ofc spt asst (keybrd), $23,160
Thomas, Tanydria S, child spt spec, $29,976
Thomas, Teresa J, fam spt elig spc, $34,356
Thomas, Tiffani N, fam spt elig spc, $29,976
Thomas, Tondaling L, fam spt elig spc, $32,052
Thomas, Tywana L, sr ofc spt asst (keybrd), $28,452
Thomas, William R, fam spt elig spc, $29,976
Thomas-Weaver, Cynthia, admin ofc spt asst, $29,496
Thomlinson, Samantha, soc servs sup, $37,548
Thompson, Alexandria, children's serv worker I, $30,984

Thompson, Cari, corres & info spec I, $34,944
Thompson, Carolyn G, children's serv worker I, $29,976
Thompson, Debra A, fam spt elig spv, $38,232
Thompson, Francis, fam spt elig spc, $29,976
Thompson, Gina, youth fac mgr II, $40,380
Thompson, Ginger L, acct I, $32,628
Thompson, Jessica B, soc servs aide, $11.13/hr
Thompson, Julie L, fam spt elig spc, $29,976
Thompson, Kathy S, serv coor yth srvcs, $37,548
Thompson, Kerre L, exec I, $30,984
Thompson, Kristina K, prog dev spec, $40,380
Thompson, Paula J, corres & info spec I, $34,944
Thompson, Shaun T, acad tchr III, $37,548
Thompson, Shawn L, children's serv worker II, $34,356
Thompson, Stacy L, children's serv worker II, $35,568
Thompson, Taunya M, children's serv worker III, $36,888
Thoms, Sarah D, children's serv worker I, $30,984
Thornburg, Lisa B, youth spec II, $31,512
Thornburgh, Robert E, children's serv worker II, $34,356
Thornton, Lakisha S, youth spec I, $28,104
Thornton, Rafael O, fam spt elig spc, $29,976
Thorpe, Christopher E, youth spec II, $31,512
Thrasher, Stacey J, acad tchr III, $37,548
Threlkeld, Marsha G, sr ofc spt asst (keybrd), $25,404
Thurman, Ashley L, ofc spt asst (keybrd), $23,160
Thurman, Teresa, fam spt elig spc, $29,976
Thurmond, Lisa C, ofc spt asst (keybrd), $26,232
Tice, Tammy, corres & info spec I, $35,568
Tidball, Jennifer R, dpty state dept dir, $110,244
Tiemann, Jeffrey, investigator II, $36,204
Tietsort, Elizabeth, children's serv spv, $39,624
Tiffany, Joseph B, children's serv worker III, $35,568
Tilford, Jacqueline J, misc prof, $30.00/hr
Tilley, Sarah M, children's serv worker II, $34,356
Tillman, Daylon, child spt spec, $29,004
Tillman, Kathy S, fam spt elig spc, $29,976
Tillman, Kerri, children's serv worker I, $30,984
Tilton Faucett, Mary F, children's serv spec, $41,940
Tilus, Ryan P, youth spec II, $29,976
Tindell, Amber L, serv coor yth srvcs, $33,744
Tinker, Patricia, ofc spt asst (keybrd), $23,160
Tinkle, Linda D, fam spt elig spc, $29,976
Tinnin, Sharron, soc servs mgr, band 1, $42,708
Tintera, Lisbeth, children's serv worker III, $35,568
Tisdale, Linda, sr ofc spt asst (keybrd), $26,652
Titius, Michelle K, children's serv worker III, $35,568
Tlamka, Timothy N, youth spec II, $30,984
Tobias, Arlise C, fam spt elig spc, $29,976
Todaro, Kathryn M, youth group leader, $33,744
Todaro, Kayla M, children's serv worker III, $36,888
Todd, Angela L, children's serv spv, $41,172
Todd, Chasity L, special educ tchr III, $40,380
Todd, Ed W, children's serv spv, $39,624
Todt, Nathaniel A, soc servs aide, $11.13/hr
Toler, Sara J, fam spt elig spc, $29,976
Tolley, Devon L, youth spec II, $31,512
Tomaw, Kimberly M, children's serv worker I, $30,984
Tomczak, Mark C, children's serv spv, $46,932
Tomlin, Jerome E, youth spec II, $31,512
Tomlin, Kenneth, motor veh driver, $25,032
Tomlin, Reginald J, youth fac mgr I, $38,928
Tomlin, Yolanda R, youth spec II, $31,512
Tomlinson, Grace E, children's serv worker III, $41,172
Tomlinson, Ryan L, youth spec I, $28,104
Tomlinson, Stephan, special asst prof, $65,652
Tonis, Angela J, fam spt elig spc, $29,976
Toppins, Rebecca S, fam spt elig spv, $36,888
Tornay, Beverly J, fam spt elig spc, $29,976
Torrance, Octavia R, ofc spt asst (keybrd), $23,160
Torrence, Vicki D, fam spt elig spc, $29,976
Torres, Shannon R, soc servs mgr, band 1, $47,052
Totten, Dana L, fam spt elig spc, $29,976
Tourtillott, Jeffery, youth spec II, $31,512
Toussaint, Jennifer A, child spt enforce spv, $34,944
Towles, Nina, children's serv worker II, $34,356
Townes, Adrian N, youth spec II, $31,512
Townsend, Emily A, children's serv worker II, $34,356
Townsend, Holly B, youth spec II, $30,984
Townsend, Michael W, youth spec II, $31,512

Tracy, Anna L, fam spt elig spv, $38,232
Tracy, Matthew, fam spt elig spc, $29,976
Tracy, Sabrina J, soc servs aide, $11.13/hr
Trader, Donna L, child spt spec, $33,180
Trail-Brown, Susan E, fam spt elig spv, $36,888
Tran, Hien V, fam spt elig spc, $33,180
Traner, Gail A, fam spt elig spc, $29,976
Trapani, Shay D, children's serv worker II, $34,356
Trapp, Audrey L, fam spt elig spc, $34,356
Trapp, Jessica, child spt spec, $29,004
Trass, Arthur I, youth fac mgr II, $41,940
Traver, Michael R, research analyst III, $48,156
Traver, Rachel E, misc prof, $35.00/hr
Treece, Pamela J, fam spt elig spc, $29,976
Tremain, Annie L, hr mgr b2, $71,208
Trenholm, Amy R, children's serv worker II, $34,356
Trigg, Alicia N, children's serv worker II, $34,356
Trimble, Julie A, prog dev spec, $41,172
Trimble, Shelby A, children's serv worker II, $34,356
Trimm, Angie L, children's serv worker II, $34,356
Triplett, Jennifer, sr ofc spt asst (keybrd), $25,824
Triplett, Jenny, fam spt elig spc, $29,976
Triplett, Vanessa, child spt enforce spv, $36,204
Tripp, Kimberly A, corres & info spec I, $34,944
Troncin, Shelley R, children's serv worker II, $34,356
Trotter, Kelley J, ofc spt asst (keybrd), $25,824
Troutman, Linda J, fam spt elig spc, $33,180
Troutman, Stephanie, fam spt elig spc, $29,976
Troxel, Corinne J, fam spt elig spc, $29,976
Troxell, Deborah L, corres & info spec I, $38,232
Truska-Elders, Rosalie N, children's serv worker I, $29,976
Trusty, Candy, fam spt elig spc, $29,976
Tucker, Ashley C, youth spec II, $30,984
Tucker, Brenda L, child spt spec, $32,628
Tucker, Christina L, fam spt elig spc, $29,976
Tucker, Debra L, training tech III, $46,932
Tucker, Kathleen M, child spt spec, $29,976
Tucker, Shannon J, fam spt elig spc, $29,976
Tucker, Steven B, child spt spec, $33,744
Tucker, Sue E, children's serv worker III, $41,940
Tullock, Melissa R, ofc spt asst (keybrd), $22,536
Tune, Paula, fam spt elig spc, $29,976
Tunnell, Karen, fam spt elig spc, $29,976
Tunnell, Lora D, fam spt elig spc, $29,976
Turley, Cletus R, ofc spt asst (keybrd), $25,404
Turman, Diamon N, children's serv worker II, $34,356
Turnbough, Amy N, children's serv worker II, $34,356
Turnbough, Bruce A, fam spt elig spc, $29,976
Turnbough, Dawn, children's serv spec, $45,156
Turnbough, Jamie L, children's serv worker II, $34,356
Turner, Amanda F, children's serv worker II, $33,744
Turner, Andrew K, youth spec II, $30,984
Turner, Angela M, children's serv worker I, $29,976
Turner, Ashli, children's serv worker II, $34,356
Turner, Brandy K, children's serv worker I, $29,976
Turner, Cathy J, investigator II, $43,488
Turner, Cynthia, fam spt elig spc, $29,976
Turner, Delphine D, children's serv worker II, $38,928
Turner, Jacqueline M, child spt spec, $29,976
Turner, Julie A, children's serv worker II, $33,744
Turner, Karen K, fam spt elig spc, $33,180
Turner, Kelli J, serv coor yth srvcs, $37,548
Turner, Lena, youth spec II, $30,984
Turner, Mary L, child spt enforce spv, $38,232
Turner, Melissa C, children's serv spv, $39,624
Turner, Melissa L, fam spt elig spc, $29,976
Turner, Renee, sr ofc spt asst (keybrd), $25,824
Turner, Renee, fam spt elig spc, $29,976
Turner, Samuel D, soc servs aide, $11.13/hr
Turner, Sylvia E, child spt spec, $31,512
Turner, Tina, sr ofc spt asst (keybrd), $28,452
Turner, Vicki B, soc servs mgr, band 1, $44,304
Turner, Whitney R, children's serv worker II, $32,628
Turpen, Angela M, sr ofc spt asst (keybrd), $25,824
Tutt, Kathy S, fam spt elig spc, $30,984
Twardowski, Carolyn B, ofc spt asst (clerical), $22,536
Twellman, Lacey J, youth spec II, $29,976
Twenter, Nancy A, ofc spt asst (keybrd), $12,132
Twitty, Jacqueline M, youth group leader, $34,356

Tyes, Marsha D, lpn II gen, $29,772
Tyo, Molly, children's serv worker I, $30,984
Tyus, Alisa D, serv coor yth srvcs, $36,888
Uchtman, Amanda K, ofc spt asst (keybrd), $23,160
Ueligger, Kayla D, children's serv worker II, $34,356
Uffmann, James W, misc prof, $45.26/hr
Uhrhan, Whitney, children's serv worker III, $36,888
Ukena, Xiomara E, soc servs aide, $11.13/hr
Uketui, Ikenna J, youth spec II, $31,512
Ulen, Lesley B, children's serv worker II, $34,356
Underwood, Jordan, youth spec II, $31,512
Underwood, Ralph, child spt spec, $29,976
Underwood, Trena M, fam spt elig spc, $34,944
Union, Lori, lpn II gen, $29,772
Unruh, Elizabeth D, children's serv worker II, $34,356
Upton, Donna R, case analyst, $32,628
Ursery, Letitia G, fam spt elig spv, $39,624
Uthe, Suzanne N, fam spt elig spc, $29,976
Utley, James A, serv coor yth srvcs, $38,232
Valbracht, Kimberly, children's serv spv, $39,624
Valentine, Amber J, children's serv spec, $37,548
Valentine, Carolyn D, fam spt elig spc, $34,356
Valentine, Jonathan S, fam spt elig spc, $34,356
Valentine, Waridi T, fam spt elig spc, $29,976
Valley, Michael J, investigator II, $41,940
Van Norman, James M, youth spec II, $30,984
Van Rhein, Carol S, voc rehab cslr f/t blin, $36,204
Vanausdoll, Julie, child spt spec, $31,512
Vance, Daisy M, children's serv worker III, $38,232
Vance, Daisy M, misc tech, $12.59/hr
Vandeloecht, Tammy, child spt spec, $29,976
Vandergriff, Linda K, fam spt eligblty prg mg, $41,940
Vanderpool, Jilla K, fam spt elig spc, $29,976
Vandillen, Gerard, fam spt elig spc, $29,976
Vandiver, Celestial F, children's serv worker II, $34,356
Vandiver, Lori M, fam spt elig spv, $38,232
Vandiver, Victoria C, youth spec II, $29,976
Vanmeter, Karen, children's serv worker III, $35,568
Vansickel, Stephanie, fam spt elig spc, $29,976
Vanskike, Amy E, fam spt elig spc, $30,420
Vanzandt, Nakicia D, fam spt elig spv, $34,944
Varner, Jenny L, children's serv worker II, $34,356
Varner, Malorie L, children's serv worker II, $32,628
Varner, Theresa L, children's serv worker III, $35,568
Varvaryuk, Valentina V, fam spt elig spc, $29,976
Vasquez, Ashlee K, youth spec I, $28,104
Vaughan, Charlotte I, serv coor yth srvcs, $36,888
Vaughan, Linda, fam spt elig spc, $29,976
Vaughn, Curtis R, youth fac mgr II, $40,380
Vaughn, Joshua A, serv coor yth srvcs, $33,744
Vazquez, Xavier E, youth spec I, $29,004
Vedenhaupt, Adrianne, children's serv spv, $38,232
Veit, Rebecca J, research mgr b2, $61,332
Velez, Eric W, children's serv worker I, $29,976
Velleux, Peter A, youth spec II, $31,512
Veltrop, Lisa M, sr ofc spt asst (keybrd), $25,824
Venable, Windy, child spt spec, $29,976
Vercellone, Benjamin J, mobility spec for the blind, $36,204
Verhelle, Catherine R, fam spt elig spc, $29,976
Vernon, Stacey R, special educ tchr III, $41,172
Vernor, Angela P, fam spt elig spc, $29,976
Vert, Barbara A, fam spt elig spc, $30,984
Vestal, Amy M, fam spt elig spc, $31,512
Vestal, Sharon K, sr ofc spt asst (keybrd), $33,036
Veth, Robert H, admin ofc spt asst, $32,052
Vice, Christina E, child spt spec, $29,004
Vickers, Lynnette R, corres & info spec I, $34,944
Viehman, Jill C, fam spt elig spc, $29,976
Viers, Christine E, children's serv worker II, $34,356
Viers, Kathy R, ofc spt asst (keybrd), $23,160
Vieth, Michelle L, investigator II, $18,774
Vining, Rachael E, soc servs sup, $38,232
Vinson, Stephanie L, children's serv worker II, $32,628
Visser, Quenten S, outdoor rehab cnslr I, $34,944
Voegtle, Ladonna J, fam spt elig spc, $29,976
Vogel, Christina R, youth spec II, $31,512
Vogel, Sherry L, youth spec II, $31,512
Vogelbaugh, Cynthia M, soc servs aide, $11.13/hr
Vogeler, Megan A, children's serv worker II, $34,356

Vogliardo, Brenda L, youth spec II, $31,512
Vogliardo, Carl J, youth spec II, $31,512
Vogt, Jerelyn R, exec I, $30,984
Vogt, Kathy A, admin ofc spt asst, $29,976
Volkart, Jamie G, fam spt elig spc, $29,976
Voltmer, Marla J, corres & info spec I, $34,944
Von David, Kimberly A, children's serv worker II, $38,232
Von Der Bruegge, Shawn F, prog dev spec, $44,304
Vonallmen, Claire E, children's serv spv, $39,624
Vonallmen, Jake F, children's serv worker III, $38,232
Vorwark, Valerie, fam spt elig spc, $29,976
Voss, Julie A, medicaid technician, $32,628
Votra, Dawne M, case analyst, $32,628
Vulic, Dragan, children's serv worker II, $34,356
Waddell, Laurren M, youth spec II, $30,984
Wade, Cathy S, fiscal & administrative mgr b1, $49,128
Wade, Debra J, special educ tchr III, $38,928
Wade, Shonda L, fam spt elig spv, $34,944
Waganer, Shelly D, fam spt elig spc, $29,976
Wagers, Katherine R, soc servs worker, $17.07/hr
Wages, Dianna E, children's serv worker III, $35,568
Waggoner, Suzanne D, fam spt elig spc, $32,628
Wagner, Douglas E, soc servs aide, $11.13/hr
Wagner, Jon T, legal counsel, $51,192
Wagner, William T, outdoor rehab cnslr I, $37,548
Wagoner, Dave M, child spt spec, $33,180
Waide, Rhonda K, children's serv spv, $39,624
Wainscott, Anna D, pers ofcr I, $43,488
Waite, Billie, legal counsel, $72,792
Waite, Kylee, children's serv spv, $39,624
Waldram, Kathryn M, ofc spt asst (keybrd), $26,652
Waldron, Amity D, children's serv spv, $38,232
Waldron, Jacob M, fam spt elig spc, $29,976
Waldron, Kimberly B, children's spec for the blind, $34,944
Waldusky, Amanda M, budget analyst II, $37,548
Walker, Aletrice J, fam spt elig spc, $31,512
Walker, Aza O, youth spec II, $31,512
Walker, Brianne L, children's serv worker I, $29,976
Walker, Camille S, children's serv worker III, $35,568
Walker, Catherine A, child spt spec, $31,512
Walker, Christina M, children's serv worker II, $32,628
Walker, Cynthia A, fam spt elig spc, $33,180
Walker, Dale, acct I, $30,984
Walker, Jacobi, fam spt elig spv, $34,944
Walker, Kristine A, fam spt elig spc, $29,976
Walker, Ray S, youth spec II, $31,512
Walker, Ronald M, youth spec II, $29,976
Walker, Sherika, fam spt elig spc, $29,976
Walker, Sonja C, case analyst, $32,628
Walker, Twyla N, corres & info spec I, $34,944
Wallace, Cole M, youth spec II, $31,512
Wallace, Evelyn E, children's serv spv, $39,624
Wallace, Marsha, fam spt elig spc, $29,976
Wallace, Rick L, children's serv worker III, $39,624
Wallace, Sandra M, fam spt elig spc, $29,976
Wallace, Susan D, fam spt elig spc, $34,356
Wallace, Vonda I, soc servs mgr, band 1, $52,092
Wallace, Vonda L, ofc spt asst (keybrd), $23,880
Waller, Diane, fam spt elig spc, $29,976
Waller, Gale M, children's serv spv, $43,488
Waller, Kenneth, child spt spec, $33,744
Walls, Samantha L, child spt enforce spv, $38,928
Walsh, Jeremy G, fam spt elig spc, $29,976
Walsh, Sean A, sr auditor, $41,940
Waltenbaugh, Virginia L, youth spec II, $30,984
Walters, Brook M, child spt spec, $29,976
Walters, Kathy A, sr ofc spt asst (keybrd), $32,472
Walters, Sandra K, ofc spt asst (keybrd), $23,160
Walton, Hannah E, fam spt elig spc, $29,976
Walton, Victoria L, children's serv worker II, $34,356
Waltz, Eric J, youth spec II, $31,512
Walworth, Michele L, child spt spec, $33,744
Wamarema, Bernard M, children's serv worker I, $29,976
Wamble, Tammy J, child spt spec, $29,976
Wampler, Anna M, child spt spec, $29,976
Wandrey, Yvette A, soc servs mgr, band 1, $50,040
Wankum, Adam J, ofc servs coor, $41,940
Warbington, Deloria S, fam spt elig spc, $29,976
Ward, Carol A, ofc spt asst (keybrd), $23,508

Ward, Debra A, fam spt elig spc, $33,180
Ward, Gail A, children's serv worker II, $34,356
Ward, Jason, fam spt elig spc, $29,976
Ward, Kristen, fam spt elig spc, $29,976
Ward, Kristina E, children's serv worker II, $34,356
Ward, Lauren G, youth spec I, $28,104
Ward, Marsha L, ofc spt asst (steno), $23,880
Ward, Maxine, admin ofc spt asst, $31,512
Ward, Roxann L, children's serv worker I, $30,984
Ward, Susan A, child spt spec, $29,976
Ward, Tracy D, children's serv worker III, $35,568
Ware, Angela M, youth spec II, $29,976
Ware, Lee E, youth spec II, $35,568
Warmack, Carlotta M, children's serv worker II, $34,356
Warman, Sidney L, ofc spt asst (keybrd), $25,824
Warner, Andrew, outdoor rehab cnslr I, $36,204
Warner, Nicholas E, children's serv worker II, $34,356
Warren, Danielle L, children's serv spv, $39,624
Warren, Julie A, misc prof, $20.44/hr
Warren, Lenetta V, ofc spt asst (keybrd), $23,160
Warren, Marie, fam spt elig spc, $29,976
Warren, Richard J, fam spt eligblty prg mg, $42,708
Warren, Sandra K, ofc spt asst (keybrd), $25,824
Warren, Terry L, children's serv worker I, $30,984
Warren-Crain, Cherana L, sr ofc spt asst (keybrd), $25,032
Washburn, Delaney R, youth spec II, $30,984
Washburn, Ronald D, fam spt elig spc, $29,976
Washington, Antoinette M, ofc spt asst (keybrd), $23,880
Washington, Donna M, fam spt elig spc, $29,976
Washington, Dorothy A, corres & info spec I, $34,944
Washington, Eunice, fam spt elig spc, $29,976
Washington, Kerensa, youth spec II, $31,512
Washington, Marsellis D, children's serv worker I, $29,976
Washington, Shantrena, children's serv spv, $39,624
Washington, Shauntrae R, fam spt elig spc, $29,976
Washington, Sylvia A, ofc spt asst (keybrd), $24,264
Washington, Yashica N, children's serv worker II, $34,356
Wassenhove, Lisa K, children's serv worker I, $29,976
Waters, Leslie A, ofc spt asst (keybrd), $23,160
Wathen, Jamie A, children's serv worker II, $32,628
Watkins, Alicia, child spt spec, $31,512
Watkins, Angela M, children's serv worker III, $35,568
Watkins, Elizabeth, child spt spec, $29,976
Watkins, Keith, ofc spt asst (keybrd), $23,160
Watkins, Lauren A, children's serv worker II, $34,356
Watkins, Linda S, fam spt elig spc, $29,976
Watkins, Sarah, children's serv worker II, $32,628
Watkins, Sheri A, children's serv worker II, $34,356
Watson, Antonia L, corres & info spec I, $34,944
Watson, Danny G, soc servs mgr, band 1, $40,380
Watson, Denise L, serv coor spv yth srvcs, $44,304
Watson, Donnette, ofc spt asst (keybrd), $27,084
Watson, Esther J, fam spt elig spc, $32,052
Watson, Jasmine D, ofc spt asst (keybrd), $23,160
Watson, Linda, sr ofc spt asst (keybrd), $25,824
Watson, Lynn E, youth spec II, $31,512
Watson, Nikki, children's serv worker I, $30,984
Watson, Stephanie J, children's serv worker II, $34,356
Watson, Waymon F, serv coor yth srvcs, $39,624
Watts, Alva Y, special educ tchr III, $42,708
Watts, Rena M, prog dev spec, $40,380
Weagley, Lisa A, fam spt elig spc, $29,976
Weakland, Kelcy M, medicaid clerk, $28,104
Wealot, William S, acad tchr III, $37,548
Wears, Christi L, admin ofc spt asst, $28,536
Weatherly, Luann, fam spt elig spv, $41,172
Weathers, Sandra R, fam spt elig spc, $29,976
Weaver, Ashley N, children's serv worker II, $34,356
Weaver, Judy D, child spt spec, $32,052
Weaver, Linda A, children's serv worker II, $34,356
Weaver, Melyssa, children's serv worker II, $35,568
Weaver, Phyllis L, soc servs mgr, band 1, $41,940
Webb, Ashley N, youth spec II, $31,512
Webb, Carla L, soc servs mngr, band 2, $61,332
Webb, Christie M, child spt spec, $29,976
Webb, Christie S, rehab asst rehab srvs for blnd, $30,384
Webb, Deanna M, sr ofc spt asst (keybrd), $27,948
Webb, Germell K, fam spt elig spc, $30,984
Webb, Kenneth M, acad tchr III, $38,928

Webb, Melody A, soc servs mngr, band 2, $50,040
Webb, Rhonda G, registered nurse sr, $58,140
Webb, Ricky, fam spt elig spc, $29,976
Webber, Zachary T, children's serv worker I, $30,984
Webb-Ward, Karen A, ofc spt asst (keybrd), $24,612
Weber, Betty J, children's serv spv, $39,624
Weber, Marilyn S, sr ofc spt asst (keybrd), $32,472
Weber, Regina K, mgmt analysis spec I, $40,380
Weber, Sarah E, special educ tchr III, $40,380
Weber Vaught, Bonita, soc servs mgr, band 1, $50,040
Webster, Holly G, fam spt elig spc, $29,976
Webster, Kenya, ofc spt asst (keybrd), $23,160
Webster, Legetta, corres & info spec I, $34,944
Webster, Perry R, children's serv worker II, $32,628
Weddle, Nancy, medicaid technician, $31,512
Weding, Christian, fam spt elig spc, $29,976
Weekley, Darla L, medicaid unit spv, $46,932
Weeks, Ann R, children's serv worker II, $34,356
Weems, Susan E, ofc spt asst (keybrd), $23,160
Wegner, Renee D, children's serv worker II, $34,356
Wehmeier, Lynn M, prog dev spec, $40,380
Wehmeier, Shauna-Renae, children's serv worker III, $35,568
Wehr, Genessa, ofc spt asst (keybrd), $23,160
Weibel, Crystal M, children's serv worker II, $34,356
Weidenbenner, Steven A, serv coor yth srvcs, $34,944
Weimholt, Vicky L, misc prof, $35.35/hr
Weinrich, Denise, fam spt elig spc, $29,976
Weisbrod, Harold B, fam spt elig spc, $29,976
Weiss, Sharon P, fam spt elig spc, $29,976
Weitzel, Jeff, youth spec II, $35,568
Welborn, Marsha, case analyst, $32,628
Welch, Daniel V, children's serv worker II, $34,356
Welch, Gwen, training tech II, $40,380
Welch, Jesse R, child spt enforce spv, $34,944
Welch, Luella J, ofc spt asst (keybrd), $25,824
Welch, Melissa, ofc spt asst (keybrd), $24,264
Welch, Patricia, sr ofc spt asst (keybrd), $25,824
Welch, Tammy R, child spt spec, $29,976
Welchert, Jennifer L, children's serv spv, $39,624
Welker, Mildred, fam spt elig spv, $34,944
Weller, Steven M, youth group leader, $34,356
Wellington, Whitney A, children's serv worker II, $34,356
Wells, Andrew S, child spt spec, $29,976
Wells, Joyce A, ofc spt asst (keybrd), $23,160
Wells, Judy M, child spt spec, $30,420
Wells, Rachel, fam spt elig spc, $29,976
Wells, Sheri D, hearings ofcr, $43,500
Wells, Tisha L, children's serv spv, $39,624
Welly, Sarah M, children's serv worker II, $34,356
Welsh, Janet L, fam spt elig spv, $37,548
Welty, Lola K, fam spt elig spc, $29,976
Wendel, Rani L, serv coor II yth srvcs, $41,940
Wendler, Sonya A, fam spt elig spc, $29,976
Wenger, Crystal D, children's serv spec, $37,548
Werdehausen, Cynthia J, medicaid spec, $37,548
Wesley, Shelvin J, youth spec II, $31,512
Wessels, Elizabeth R, children's serv worker II, $34,356
West, Brenda K, fam spt elig spv, $36,888
West, Brian, soc servs mgr, band 1, $51,312
West, Dana J, fam spt elig spc, $30,984
West, Hannah E, children's serv worker II, $34,356
West, Jordan R, youth spec II, $31,512
West, Lisa A, fam spt elig spc, $32,628
West, Roxanne, fam spt elig spc, $29,976
West, Sallie M, soc servs mgr, band 1, $47,052
West, Shemika N, children's serv worker II, $34,356
West, Susan, telecommun analyst II, $42,708
West, Terry J, children's serv worker I, $29,976
West, Victor, fam spt elig spc, $29,976
West, Yolanda R, children's serv spec, $43,488
Westerkamp, Patricia L, children's serv worker II, $34,356
Westfall, Teara O, children's serv worker II, $34,356
Westmoreland, Teresa C, fam spt elig spc, $31,512
Weston, Juria A, fam spt elig spc, $29,976
Weston, Leslie J, fam spt elig spc, $31,512
Westphal, Sheila M, fam spt elig spv, $34,944
Westrater, Ashley L, account clerk II, $25,032
Wettengel, Bobby D, rehab tchr for the blind, $35,568
Whaley, Laurie A, youth spec II, $31,512

Whaley, Sherry D, fam spt elig spc, $29,976
Whaley, Theresa M, children's serv worker III, $38,232
Wharton, Racheal C, children's serv spv, $39,624
Wheeler, Barbara J, ofc spt asst (keybrd), $25,824
Wheeler, Jeanette K, fam spt elig spc, $29,976
Wheeler, Mari L, children's serv worker II, $34,356
Wheeler, Pamela F, medicaid spec, $37,548
Wheeler, Pamela S, special educ tchr III, $38,928
Wheeler, Randy A, fam spt elig spc, $30,984
Wheeler, Sharon K, fam spt elig spc, $29,976
Wheeler, Sharon M, children's serv worker II, $18,774
Wheelis, Krystal M, children's serv spv, $39,624
Wheelock, Lori A, children's serv worker III, $40,380
Wheetley, Amanda D, sr ofc spt asst (keybrd), $25,824
Whisenand, Ernest E, children's serv worker II, $34,356
Whitaker, Sarah B, fam spt elig spc, $29,976
Whitaker, Shandy K, child spt spec, $29,976
Whitchurch, Ronald F, children's serv worker III, $36,888
White, Ashley B, children's serv worker II, $34,356
White, Charry C, pers clerk, $32,628
White, Christopher A, child spt spec, $29,976
White, Elizabeth K, children's serv worker II, $34,356
White, Jazmine L, youth spec II, $31,512
White, Jennifer, child spt spec, $34,944
White, Lakeisha M, youth spec II, $29,976
White, Mary A, case analyst, $35,568
White, Michele A, children's serv worker II, $34,356
White, Paula R, children's serv spec, $44,304
White, Ricky, corres & info spec I, $34,944
White, Sara, fam spt elig spc, $29,976
White, Stephanie L, corres & info spec I, $34,944
White, Stephanie L, soc servs mgr, band 1, $47,892
White, Suzanne M, sr ofc spt asst (keybrd), $27,948
White, Tamara L, fam spt elig spc, $34,356
White, Wendy B, fam spt elig spc, $32,628
Whited, Courtney A, children's serv spec, $40,380
White-Davis, Leon J, youth spec II, $31,512
Whitehead, Heather C, child spt spec, $30,984
Whitehead, Nathan L, children's serv worker II, $35,568
Whitener, Christopher R, prog dev spec, $38,928
Whiteside, Mary B, fam spt elig spc, $33,744
Whiteside, Seandale L, youth spec I, $28,104
Whitmore, Joann, corres & info spec I, $34,356
Whitney, Christopher C, fam spt elig spc, $29,976
Whitney, Rhonda L, soc servs mgr, band 1, $43,488
Whitten, Derek T, children's serv worker II, $34,356
Whittico, James M, consulting physician, $22,668
Whittier, Alfreda L, fam spt elig spc, $29,976
Whittington, Paul D, children's serv worker I, $29,976
Whittle, Janet L, corres & info spec I, $34,944
Wichmer, Jennifer E, children's serv worker II, $34,356
Wickern, Eric S, corres & info spec I, $34,944
Wickern, Jolon J, soc servs mngr, band 2, $61,332
Wickstrum, Rachel N, hearings ofcr, $38,928
Wideman, Jody L, fam spt elig spc, $31,512
Widner, Tammy L, fam spt elig spc, $29,976
Wieand, Wanda J, fam spt elig spc, $34,356
Wieberg, Joyce E, exec II, $44,304
Wieberg, Robert, pers analyst II, $46,068
Wiedeman, Donald L, fam spt elig spv, $38,232
Wiedeman, Frances E, fam spt elig spv, $36,888
Wiederholt, Tyann L, children's serv worker I, $30,984
Wiegard, Tina A, child spt spec, $29,976
Wiese, Sheila R, fam spt elig spc, $29,976
Wiggins, Susan M, children's serv worker II, $34,356
Wigton, Tiffany M, children's serv worker III, $35,568
Wilber, Christina, fam spt elig spc, $34,356
Wilbers, Amanda M, serv coor yth srvcs, $33,744
Wilburn, Lora A, children's serv spv, $47,892
Wilcox, James R, children's serv worker II, $34,356
Wilcox, Robert E, soc servs aide, $11.13/hr
Wilcox-Bauer, Kara B, prog dev spec, $43,488
Wilcoxson, Kathleen S, pub info admstr, $52,092
Wilde, Lori J, pers clerk, $28,104
Wilde, Sidney J, registered nurse - clin opers, $60,516
Wildhaber, Stefanie L, sr ofc spt asst (keybrd), $25,824
Wilfong, Susan K, children's serv worker III, $40,380
Wilhite, Shirley J, corres & info spec I, $34,944
Wilken, Tara A, children's serv worker II, $32,628

Wilkerson, Marla, child spt spec, $31,512
Wilkerson, Robin D, children's serv worker II, $34,356
Wilkerson, Stephanie L, soc servs mgr, band 1, $43,488
Wilkes, Carmen G, corres & info spec I, $34,944
Wilkes, Jeannie, children's serv worker II, $35,568
Wilkes, Latoya L, children's serv worker III, $39,624
Wilkin, Joshua W, children's serv worker II, $34,356
Wilkins, Gloria, youth fac mgr II, $40,380
Wilks, Stephen J, children's serv worker III, $35,568
Williams, Ada P, children's serv worker I, $29,976
Williams, Adrienne, children's serv spec, $41,940
Williams, Amanda E, children's serv spv, $39,624
Williams, Angela D, fam spt elig spc, $29,976
Williams, Angelia, fam spt elig spc, $29,976
Williams, Avis D, prog dev spec, $42,708
Williams, Bertha V, cook II, $24,264
Williams, Bethdaly M, children's serv worker I, $29,976
Williams, Beverly E, children's serv worker III, $38,928
Williams, Brandy, children's serv worker II, $34,356
Williams, Brenda F, fam spt elig spc, $29,976
Williams, Brian J, cook II, $23,880
Williams, Cameron J, youth spec II, $30,984
Williams, Christian N, child spt spec, $29,976
Williams, Constance V, child spt enforce spv, $40,380
Williams, Danielle C, children's serv worker III, $34,944
Williams, Dixie L, sr ofc spt asst (keybrd), $27,084
Williams, Durema A, fam spt elig spc, $30,984
Williams, Edward A, youth spec II, $31,512
Williams, Harold L, fam spt elig spc, $30,984
Williams, Jamie L, children's serv spec, $45,156
Williams, Janet K, soc servs mgr, band 1, $41,940
Williams, Janis A, fam spt elig spc, $29,976
Williams, Jocelyn M, fam spt elig spc, $31,512
Williams, John L, youth group leader, $35,568
Williams, Johnisha, children's serv worker II, $34,356
Williams, Joseph C, soc servs mgr, band 1, $40,380
Williams, Joyce A, fam spt elig spc, $29,976
Williams, Karla A, fam spt elig spc, $29,976
Williams, Kimmie A, child spt enforce spv, $38,232
Williams, La Carla A, children's serv worker II, $34,356
Williams, Lancelot, ofc spt asst (keybrd), $23,160
Williams, Marci K, children's serv worker III, $35,568
Williams, Marlo D, soc servs mgr, band 1, $49,128
Williams, Matthew, prog dev spec, $52,092
Williams, Michele J, sr ofc spt asst (keybrd), $25,824
Williams, Pamela M, ofc spt asst (keybrd), $23,160
Williams, Priscilla M, children's serv worker I, $29,976
Williams, Roy B, acad tchr III, $37,548
Williams, Ryan A, youth spec II, $31,512
Williams, Sonja C, soc servs mngr, band 2, $71,100
Williams, Steven J, youth spec II, $31,512
Williams, Stormy R, children's serv worker I, $30,984
Williams, Tammy, fam spt elig spc, $29,976
Williams, Tammy J, sr ofc spt asst (steno), $27,948
Williams, Teresa A, children's serv worker III, $35,568
Williams, Tonya R, children's serv worker II, $38,928
Williams, Traci M, soc servs mgr, band 1, $50,040
Williams, Tracy M, administrative analyst I, $29,976
Williams, Wa-Kim J, fam spt elig spc, $30,984
Williams-Cooper, Deborah A, ofc spt asst (keybrd), $23,160
Williamson, Brenda M, ofc spt asst (steno), $27,084
Williamson, Bryce C, fam spt elig spv, $38,928
Williamson, Jerlyn L, children's serv worker II, $32,628
Williamson, Jessica L, ofc spt asst (keybrd), $26,232
Williamson, Mary L, fam spt elig spc, $29,976
Williamson, Steven B, serv coor yth srvcs, $37,548
Williamson, Yvonne, fam spt elig spc, $29,976
Williams-Samuel, Lashawna, child spt spec, $29,004
Willis, Fatina L, fam spt elig spc, $29,004
Willis, Jennifer L, children's serv worker III, $36,888
Willis, Kenya E, children's serv spv, $39,624
Willis, Marianne K, child spt spec, $33,744
Willis, Sandra A, children's serv spv, $38,232
Wills, Carla D, fam spt elig spc, $29,976
Wills, Tamara M, child spt enforce spv, $34,944
Willson, Marshelle M, child spt spec, $34,356
Willyard, Sarah L, children's serv worker III, $36,888
Wilmes, Cynthia M, corres & info spec I, $36,888
Wilmes, Shalene G, fam spt elig spc, $29,976

Wilmore, Kim, fam spt elig spc, $29,976
Wilner, Aeriel, soc servs mgr, band 1, $46,068
Wilson, Alan L, soc servs mgr, band 1, $49,128
Wilson, Angela B, soc servs mgr, band 1, $49,128
Wilson, Anna L, children's serv worker I, $32,052
Wilson, Ashley L, soc servs mgr, band 1, $50,040
Wilson, Brian O, children's serv worker III, $41,940
Wilson, Charli A, fam spt elig spc, $29,976
Wilson, Crystal, ofc spt asst (keybrd), $23,160
Wilson, Crystal L, prog dev spec, $41,940
Wilson, Deborah E, sr ofc spt asst (keybrd), $25,824
Wilson, Donna, fam spt elig spc, $29,976
Wilson, Donna M, fam spt elig spc, $29,976
Wilson, Dustin L, children's serv worker II, $34,356
Wilson, Dustin L, fam spt elig spc, $29,976
Wilson, Garry W, youth spec I, $28,104
Wilson, Jessica, fam spt elig spc, $29,976
Wilson, Joni M, children's serv worker II, $17,784
Wilson, Karen J, fam spt elig spc, $34,356
Wilson, Kathryn, special asst technician, $39,624
Wilson, Kelly R, corres & info spec I, $34,944
Wilson, Krystale C, youth spec I, $28,104
Wilson, Larry R, corres & info spec I, $34,944
Wilson, Latonji D, youth fac mgr I, $38,928
Wilson, Lora N, youth spec II, $31,512
Wilson, Lori J, corres & info spec I, $34,944
Wilson, Megan K, children's serv worker I, $30,984
Wilson, Melissa A, children's serv worker III, $36,888
Wilson, Melissa M, children's serv worker II, $34,356
Wilson, Monica M, child spt spec, $29,976
Wilson, Nicole L, youth spec II, $31,512
Wilson, Philip R, youth spec II, $30,984
Wilson, Rachel D, ofc spt asst (keybrd), $23,160
Wilson, Renee J, children's serv worker II, $34,356
Wilson, Rita A, soc servs mgr, band 1, $41,940
Wilson, Ryan B, fam spt elig spc, $29,976
Wilson, Stacia N, children's serv worker II, $34,356
Wilson, Susan J, special educ tchr III, $43,488
Wilson, Susan M, children's serv worker II, $32,628
Wilson, Tami Jo, corres & info spec I, $34,944
Wilson, Tara A, youth spec I, $29,004
Wilson, Vicky A, ofc spt asst (keybrd), $23,160
Wilson, Virginia D, ofc spt asst (keybrd), $22,536
Wilson, Wanda F, prog dev spec, $41,172
Wilson, Whitney B, children's serv worker II, $34,356
Winchester, Mark A, special asst prof, $45,456
Windau, Ryan A, youth spec I, $28,104
Winder, Cheryl L, corres & info spec I, $36,204
Winder, Denissa E, sr ofc spt asst (keybrd), $25,824
Windon, Vicki L, children's serv worker I, $29,976
Wineland, Amber J, children's serv worker I, $30,984
Winfrey, Karen A, youth fac mgr I, $41,940
Wing, Brian K, youth spec II, $30,984
Wininger, Margaret L, child spt enforce spv, $33,744
Wininger-Watson, Cindy S, prog dev spec, $43,488
Winkelmann, Sean M, youth spec II, $31,512
Winkler, Kelly M, soc servs aide, $11.13/hr
Winkler, Nicole M, ofc spt asst (keybrd), $23,160
Winn, Dinah A, youth spec II, $31,512
Winstead, Mamie L, children's serv worker III, $38,232
Winston, Lacresha D, youth spec II, $31,512
Winter, Christina M, children's serv worker I, $30,984
Winters, David W, fam spt elig spc, $30,984
Wirsig, Marty J, children's serv worker II, $34,356
Wisdom, Dennis B, acad tchr III, $39,624
Wisdom, Mary R, fam spt elig spc, $33,180
Wise, Anna M, hr mgr b2, $62,664
Wise, Betty, children's serv worker I, $29,976
Wise, Stephanie J, youth spec II, $30,984
Wiseman, Paige A, ofc spt asst (keybrd), $23,160
Wiseman, Wendy G, ofc spt asst (keybrd), $23,160
Witherspoon, Aaron D, corres & info spec I, $34,944
Witherspoon, Cynthia, ofc spt asst (keybrd), $23,160
Witt, Eric R, fam spt elig spc, $29,976
Witt, Janelle, fam spt elig spc, $29,976
Witten, Kimberly, children's serv spv, $39,624
Witthaus, Casey M, youth spec II, $31,512
Witthaus, Ronna A, children's serv worker II, $34,356
Wittman, Shannon M, children's serv spec, $37,548

Woelfel, Rebecca, designated principal asst dept, $76,260
Wofford, Amber S, children's serv worker II, $34,356
Wohlberg, Hillary F, children's serv worker II, $32,628
Woldanski, Florence J, exec I, $30,984
Wolf, Melissa D, prog dev spec, $40,380
Wolf, Pamela M, fam spt elig spc, $29,976
Wolfe, Jared M, fam spt elig spc, $29,976
Wolfe, Melissa D, prog dev spec, $40,380
Wolfe, Stacy E, ofc spt asst (keybrd), $25,824
Wolfe, Tina M, fam spt elig spc, $31,512
Wolfe, Valarie K, youth spec II, $31,512
Wolford, Anny N, children's serv worker II, $34,356
Wolters, Barret J, investigator III, $48,156
Wolters, William D, medicaid technician, $33,180
Womble, Kellie R, corres & info spec I, $34,944
Womble, Michelle L, fam spt elig spc, $29,976
Wonderly, Shannon N, children's serv worker II, $34,356
Wood, Cathy L, soc servs mgr, band 1, $41,940
Wood, Christina, fiscal & administrative mgr b2, $68,160
Wood, Deanna L, medicaid clerk, $28,536
Wood, Elizabeth M, fam spt elig spc, $29,976
Wood, Jennifer M, child spt spec, $33,180
Wood, Jenorey R, children's serv worker III, $35,568
Wood, Karen, child spt spec, $33,180
Wood, Lacinda A, fam spt elig spc, $29,976
Wood, Rhonda H, medicaid clerk, $28,536
Wood, Sally A, child spt spec, $33,744
Wood, Sheila L, prog dev spec, $41,172
Wood, Sheila L, soc servs worker, $17.07/hr
Wood, Tracey, ofc spt asst (keybrd), $23,160
Wood, Tyler, children's serv worker III, $36,888
Woodcock, Daniel J, fam spt elig spv, $34,944
Woodcock, Tina L, corres & info spec I, $34,944
Wooden, Angela, children's serv worker II, $32,628
Woodring, Rachael L, fam spt elig spc, $29,976
Woodruff, Barbara J, fam spt elig spc, $31,512
Woodruff, Jessica L, children's serv spv, $38,232
Woods, Andrea J, fam spt elig spc, $29,976
Woods, Ardene, child spt spec, $31,512
Woods, Debra L, fam spt elig spv, $38,232
Woods, Lorrie L, lpn II gen, $29,772
Woods, Maxine, fam spt elig spc, $29,976
Woods, Rachele L, children's serv worker III, $36,888
Woodson, Lenise A, corres & info spec I, $34,944
Woodson, Lisa R, training tech II, $44,304
Woodson, Rebecca J, children's serv worker III, $36,888
Woodward, Rebecca A, child spt spec, $29,976
Woodward, Theresa L, children's serv spv, $39,624
Woodworth, Terri L, ofc spt asst (keybrd), $23,160
Woody, Amy M, children's serv worker II, $34,356
Woody, Darla L, children's serv worker I, $30,984
Woolverton, Michelle K, children's serv prog mgr, $45,156
Woosencraft, Gregory T, youth group leader, $34,356
Worden, Marcella S, ofc spt asst (keybrd), $27,084
Workineh, Genene, acct I, $30,984
Workman, Sheila A, fam spt elig spc, $34,356
Worsley, Laura A, mgmt analysis spec II, $41,940
Wortham, Rhonda R, children's serv worker II, $34,356
Worthington, Karen, acad tchr III, $37,548
Wray, Deneen, ofc spt asst (keybrd), $24,612
Wray, Wanda F, fam spt elig spc, $29,976
Wren, Jennifer A, youth spec II, $31,512
Wrenfrow, Sharon, fam spt elig spc, $29,976
Wright, Diana, child spt spec, $29,976
Wright, Ellen S, fam spt elig spc, $33,180
Wright, Hannah D, admin ofc spt asst, $28,104
Wright, James M, cook II, $23,160
Wright, Kia J, fam spt elig spv, $34,944
Wright, Mona G, youth spec I, $28,104
Wright, Robert, fam spt elig spc, $29,976
Wright, Stacy J, fiscal & administrative mgr b2, $67,476
Wright, Wesley C, youth spec I, $28,104
Wroblewski, Claire, children's serv worker I, $29,976
Wucher, Linda C, children's serv prog mgr, $49,128
Wurth, Kristen L, children's serv worker I, $29,976
Wyatt, Andrew L, sr auditor, $41,940
Wyatt, Candace D, youth spec I, $29,004
Wyatt, Deborah L, fam spt elig spc, $29,976
Wyatt, Geraldine R, serv coor yth srvcs, $36,204

Department of Transportation

100 W. Capitol, PO Box 270, Jefferson City 65102

Allgier, Joseph P, sr maint worker, $35,856
Allinson, Curtis C, sr info syss technologist, $57,756
Allison, James R, trans planner, $39,876
Allison, John L, maint sup, $47,736
Allmeroth, Rebecca D, state maint engr, $103,944
Allred, Daniel D, materials insp, $41,316
Allred, David E, sr maint worker, $35,220
Allsbury, Richard R, rail safety spec, $47,736
Alstat, Joshua G, const intern, $13.85/hr
Alston, George D, sr maint worker, $35,220
Alter, James E, sr traffic syss oper, $46,044
Amatey, Dawn M, int motor carrier agent, $30,120
Amburn, Stephen M, const insp, $47,736
Amelunke, Jeffrey T, maint sup, $45,192
Amerson, Kenndrix V, maint worker, $29,064
Amidei, Lawrence J, sr equip technician, $42,072
Amos, David R, sr engnring profess-tpt/sspd, $24.80/hr
Amos, Elmer J, maint crew leader, $39,156
Amthor, Cory D, sr maint worker, $33,996
Anderson, Austin M, transp enfrcmnt investigator, $37,800
Anderson, Brandon M, empl dev specialis, $39,876
Anderson, Bryce M, maint crew leader, $39,156
Anderson, Clem, maint sup, $45,192
Anderson, David C, maint worker, $29,064
Anderson, Derek R, sr const insp, $52,596
Anderson, Gregory J, transp proj dsgnr, $79,596
Anderson, Jeffery M, sr maint worker, $34,596
Anderson, Jerry L, maint crew leader, $36,504
Anderson, Justin L, maint sup, $45,192
Anderson, Katherine B, sr const insp, $57,756
Anderson, Loyde D, sr fac opps crew wo, $35,220
Anderson, Lynn M, sr const insp, $55,620
Anderson, Michelle, traffic intern, $11.64/hr
Anderson, Robert L, sr maint worker, $37,800
Anderson, Roger L, sr maint worker, $39,156
Anderson, Ronald D, sr maint worker, $34,596
Anderson, Ryan D, maint worker, $29,064
Anderson, Telisa M, maint crew leader, $36,504
Andrews, Betty A, sr design technician, $36,504
Andrews, Rhonette C, sr ofc asst, $27,612
Anglen, Aaron A, sr historic preserve speci, $52,596
Anglin, Anthony F, maint worker, $29,064
Anspach, Kelley L, sr maint worker, $38,472
Apperson, Darren L, maint sup, $46,044
Arbuckle, James R, sr maint worker, $36,504
Archer, Anthony D, electrcn, $37,800
Archer, Brenda K, sr maint worker, $37,800
Arment, Chad L, maint crew leader, $37,140
Armour, Cary C, sr const insp, $52,596
Armstrong, Charles A, electrcn, $40,608
Armstrong, Shawn D, intermed maint wrkr, $31,164
Armstrong, Stacy A, sr roadside mgmt special, $61,092
Arnall, Benjamin A, maint crew leader, $36,504
Arnall, Richard J, maint supt, $57,756
Arnett, Michael J, sr maint worker, $34,596
Arney, William G, sr maint worker-tpt, $21.27/hr
Arnold, Daniel T, sr const insp, $61,092
Arnold, Darrel L, sr maint worker, $34,596
Arnold, John T, maint sup, $45,192
Arnold, Kimberly A, sr maint worker, $34,596
Arnold, Micheal P, sr maint worker, $35,220
Arounpradith, Anousone, structural proj mgr, $73,788
Arthaud, Kevin T, sr empl dev specia, $47,736
Arthur, Lyron S, mkt analysis coord, $56,676
Asahi, Jamey, maint crew leader, $36,504
Ash, John D, maint worker, $29,064
Ashby, Michael P, maint worker, $29,064
Asher, Andrew J, maint worker, $29,064
Asher, Donald R, maint crew leader, $40,608
Ashley, Kevin L, maint worker, $29,064
Ashley, Renita, sr maint worker, $34,596
Ashley, Stephen W, sr maint worker, $35,856
Atha, Joel H, maint worker, $29,064
Atha, Megan R, cert appraiser, $50,676
Atkins, Craig N, sr maint worker, $34,596
Atkinson, Michele A, structural proj mgr, $71,016
Atkisson, Stephen E, maint crew leader, $36,504
Atteberry, Michael R, sr maint worker, $34,596
Auala, Elquin L, transp proj dsgnr, $68,364

Aubuchon, Jason G, sr const insp, $50,676
Aufdenberg, Mark H, roadside mgr, $49,752
Aulbur, Randall E, dist maint engr, $72,372
Austin, Dennis S, sr maint worker, $37,800
Austin Rashid, Stephanie A, interm gen serv spec, $42,072
Autrey, Daniel J, sr maint worker, $36,504
Avers, John A, land surv, $48,828
Avery, Antwinette, sr info syss technologist, $46,884
Avery, Bret R, sr maint worker, $34,596
Axtell, Eric C, materials insp, $40,608
Aylor, Dillon L, intermed equip tech, $36,504
Ayres, Lawrence L, sr historic preserve speci, $56,676
Bachman, Kristi A, trans proj mgr, $64,632
Bachman, Scott E, asst to the dist engr, $76,596
Backes, Douglas A, sr admin profressional-tpt, $27.49/hr
Backes, Sherry L, sr fin servs speciali, $51,624
Backues, Kelly J, sr organizational perf analyst, $47,736
Backus, David P, sr design technician, $37,800
Bagley, Kurt T, sr maint worker, $34,596
Bagwill, Kristen B, empl dev mgr, $54,600
Bahr, David T, sr maint worker, $33,996
Bailey, Amy K, sr inf syss technician, $37,140
Bailey, Bryan S, rt of way mgr, $67,092
Bailey, Cedrick, maint worker, $29,064
Bailey, Eric F, maint worker, $29,064
Bailey, Howard L, maint crew leader, $36,504
Bailey, Jeffrey L, sr maint worker-tpt, $20.58/hr
Bailey, Keith J, sr info syss technologist, $54,600
Bailey, Lanette E, maint worker, $29,064
Bailey, Richard V, fac opps crew worke, $28,584
Bailey, Warren D, sr maint worker, $36,504
Bailie, Joseph W, maint worker, $29,064
Bain, Christopher D, sr maint worker, $36,504
Baird, Jeffery P, sr traffic studies special, $56,676
Baker, Brian P, seasonal maint worker, $12.44/hr
Baker, Christopher D, maint sup, $48,828
Baker, Curtiss P, sr maint worker, $34,596
Baker, Donald L, maint worker, $29,064
Baker, Frank R, maint crew leader, $37,800
Baker, Jeffrey J, maint worker, $29,064
Baker, Michael N, info sys technology spec, $65,856
Baker, Nathan A, equip technician, $33,996
Baker, Randy J, sr maint worker, $35,220
Baker, Russell L, maint worker, $29,064
Baker, Tammy L, sr procurement agent, $47,736
Balark, Devon, maint worker, $29,064
Baldridge, Roxanna R, spt servs mgr, $59,928
Baldwin, Brandi J, dist utilities engr, $61,092
Baldwin, Chad E, inter const insp, $44,400
Baldwin, Jason G, sr maint worker, $35,220
Baldwin, Mica A, exec asst, $32,280
Bales, Anthony W, intermed maint wrkr, $31,164
Bales, Bruce E, sr maint worker, $34,596
Balestreri, Jason M, sr hwy dsgnr, $54,600
Balfour, Rahsaan M, motorist assistance oper, $33,996
Ball, Cheryl R, admin of freight & waterways, $81,108
Ball, Megan K, const intern, $12.47/hr
Ball, Susan M, sr const insp, $62,232
Ballew, Casey B, sr maint worker, $34,596
Ballew, Randy J, sr maint worker, $37,140
Baltz, Rebecca J, dist engr, $103,944
Bandermann, Geoffery R, maint worker, $29,064
Banes, Brent C, maint crew leader, $36,504
Banes, Scott R, maint sup, $45,192
Baney, Arein D, intermed maint wrkr, $31,164
Baquet, Brock D, maint worker, $29,064
Barbarick, Chase N, const intern, $13.14/hr
Barbee, John E, info syss technologist, $38,472
Barber, Billy J, sr maint worker, $34,596
Barber, Kellen M, intermed maint wrkr, $31,164
Barchus, Clifford W, maint worker, $29,064
Barger, Chad A, sr maint worker, $33,996
Barker, Dale L, intermed maint wrkr, $31,164
Barker, Kory J, maint worker, $29,064
Barker, Ronnie W, maint worker, $29,064
Barnard, Thomas M, land surv in training, $39,876
Barnes, Adam J, sr trns enfrcemnt investigator, $45,192
Barnes, Bruce A, maint crew leader, $36,504
Barnes, James T, maint crew leader, $38,472

Barnes, Jay P, sr maint worker, $35,856
Barnes, Jonathan M, rt of way mgr, $64,632
Barnes, Kenneth E, sr info syss technologist, $48,828
Barnett, Dalvin P, intermed equip tech, $36,504
Barnett, John B, maint worker, $29,064
Barnett, Kenneth E, sr materials technician, $39,876
Barnett, Kimberly S, sr fin servs tech, $43,608
Barnett, Ryan, transp enfrcmnt investigator, $39,156
Barnfield, Chris W, sr const technician, $37,800
Barnhouse, Jeff, sr maint worker, $37,140
Barnum, Douglas K, maint crew leader, $36,504
Barrett, Albert L, maint worker, $29,064
Barrett, Deborah A, sr ofc asst, $34,596
Barrows, Heather, sr hwy dsgnr, $53,580
Barrows, William B, sr hwy dsgnr, $62,232
Barry, Susan E, dist plng mgr, $71,016
Bartel, Dewey W, sr maint worker, $35,220
Bartley, William P, intermed maint wrkr, $30,624
Barton, Joshua R, maint worker, $29,064
Barton, Tommy W, maint worker, $29,064
Barton, Wilber L, sr maint worker, $35,856
Bartz, Roddy L, maint crew leader, $36,504
Basham, Douglas H, sr maint worker, $42,816
Basham, Jason R, asst maint sup, $45,192
Bashore, Adam R, maint worker, $29,064
Basinger, Monte R, maint crew leader, $36,504
Basler, William D, inter const insp, $45,192
Bass, Anthony D, maint worker, $29,064
Bass, Linda G, sr r/w spec, $51,624
Bassett, Daniel E, sr maint worker, $37,140
Bateman, Jeffrey R, sr maint worker, $33,996
Batenhorst, Thomas P, dist plng mgr, $82,692
Bates, Steve B, sr chemist, $53,580
Bates, William A, sr maint worker, $33,996
Bathgate, Jeffrey L, sr maint worker, $34,596
Bathgate, William D, maint worker, $29,064
Battle, Alfred C, asst maint sup, $40,608
Bauer, Christopher A, sr materials technician, $36,504
Bauer, David R, sr const insp, $62,232
Bauer, Kathryn E, maint worker, $29,064
Bauer, Leroy E, maint sup, $46,884
Bauer, Patrick J, maint crew leader, $37,140
Baugher, Blake E, maint worker, $29,064
Bauknecht, Karlee A, const insp, $45,192
Baum, Dawndy J, sr hwy dsgnr, $52,596
Bauman, Steven G, sr info syss technologist, $55,620
Baumann, Mark A, sr maint worker, $34,596
Baumli, Richard G, sr maint worker, $33,996
Bax, Dana L, sr motor carrier agent, $34,596
Bax, Darrell J, sr fac opps spe, $46,884
Bax, Joseph M, dist land survey mgr, $56,676
Bax, Michael J, sr equip technician, $42,072
Bax, Monica R, sr fin servs speciali, $49,752
Bax, Rachel L, hr intern, $11.84/hr
Baxter, Michael E, ast dist constr & mater en, $68,364
Bayan Wilson, Lorene N, cert appraiser, $52,596
Bays, Ricky D, maint crew leader, $37,800
Beagle, William S, sr maint worker, $35,220
Bearce, Lee, sr safety ofcr, $51,624
Beard, Shelby L, sr maint worker, $34,596
Beasley, David A, asst maint sup, $40,608
Beattie, James V, sr hwy dsgnr, $53,580
Beauregard, Michael L, maint worker, $29,064
Becerra, James P, sr traffic spec, $44,400
Bechel, Robert D, sr auditor, $56,676
Beck, Cherie, sr info syss technologist, $46,884
Beck, Connor J, const intern, $13.36/hr
Beck, David N, intermed maint wrkr, $31,164
Beck, Kenneth W, sr maint worker, $34,596
Beck, Michael S, asst maint sup, $40,608
Beckemeier, Karl W, materials insp, $47,736
Becker, Jennifer L, sr hwy dsgnr, $55,620
Becker, Robert G, asst dist maint engr, $65,856
Beckmann, Jessica L, bridge intern, $13.14/hr
Beckwith, Debra M, sr structural technician, $36,504
Bedard, Loraine B, const technician, $28,584
Bedsworth, Lynn A, legal asst, $30,120
Bedwell, Danny L, sr materials insp, $50,676
Beebe, Jim, motorist assistance oper, $39,156

Beerly, Brenda S, sr maint worker, $34,596
Beets, Terry J, intermed equip tech, $35,856
Beganovic, Denis, sr trans planner, $47,736
Begley, Simon M, maint sup, $45,192
Behl, Danny D, int tr studies spec, $54,600
Belanger, David A, central ofc gen serv mg, $54,600
Belcavitch, Jeremy A, motorist assistance oper, $35,856
Belcher, Steven J, traffic spec, $39,876
Belding, Michael P, maint worker, $29,064
Bell, David E, sr maint worker, $34,596
Bell, Jason A, maint sup, $46,044
Bellamy, Troy M, maint worker, $29,064
Belle, Sonja R, hr spec, $38,472
Belote, Melanie P, hwy dsgnr, $46,044
Belt, Bethany M, exec asst, $32,280
Belt, Michael W, maint supt, $54,600
Benfield, Edward D, sr maint worker, $34,596
Benham, Donald G, sr fin servs tech, $44,400
Bennett, Anthony W, sr maint worker, $35,220
Bennett, Linda J, sr maint worker, $33,396
Bennett, Richard E, traffic liaison engr, $81,108
Bennett, Sheldon C, sr engnring profess-tpt/sspd, $28.53/hr
Bennett, Todd L, chem lab dir, $67,092
Bentley, James B, sr const insp, $51,624
Benton, Craig S, sr equip technician, $42,072
Bequette, Christopher A, maint worker, $29,064
Berger, Michael A, sr maint worker, $35,220
Bergman, Barry M, sr engnring profess-tpt/sspd, $35.54/hr
Berhorst, Elizabeth L, sr design technician, $36,504
Berhorst, Gina M, sr data report analyst, $47,736
Bernard, Ryan K, sr chemist, $46,884
Bernardino, Eric J, maint worker, $29,064
Bernsen, William F, sr maint worker, $34,596
Bernskoetter, Eric G, inf syss proj mgr, $57,756
Berry, Chris E, trans proj mgr, $69,672
Berry, Deidre K, exec asst, $37,140
Berry, Holli M, sr hr spec, $46,884
Berry, Matthew C, maint crew leader, $36,504
Berry, Wilber L, maint crew leader, $36,504
Besaw, Jeffrey M, sr maint worker, $33,996
Bessard, Floyd, motorist assistance oper, $34,596
Bestgen, Jay, asst state co and ma engr, $87,540
Beverlin, Carey D, sr maint worker, $34,596
Bevier, Henry R, sr traffic studies special, $54,600
Bickel, John P, sr electrcn, $50,676
Biegel, Darin L, equip technician superviso, $49,752
Biegel, Shawn P, sr maint worker, $36,504
Biele, Jacqueline L, exec asst, $39,876
Biesemeyer, Mark L, trans prog mgr, $59,928
Bigley, Denis G, int engring professnl-tpt, $28.84/hr
Bigsby, Douglas E, maint worker, $29,064
Bilyeu, Jonathon J, fac opps crew worke, $13.12/hr
Binger, Janice L, maint sup, $46,044
Binkley, Amy K, inf syss proj mgr, $55,620
Biondo, Anthony J, fin servs intern, $11.24/hr
Bird, Shane L, transp enfrcmnt investigator, $39,876
Biri, Michael W, maint worker, $29,064
Birke, Kenneth A, maint crew leader, $36,504
Birmingham, Harold C, maint worker, $29,064
Bishop, David L, sr maint worker, $34,596
Bishop, Samuel R, sr maint worker, $34,596
Bishop, Thomas J, sr maint worker, $35,220
Bittick, Beth J, inter const insp, $44,400
Bixler, Karen A, sr ofc asst, $26,244
Black, Barbara R, sr auditor, $47,736
Black, Brian E, maint crew leader, $36,504
Black, Jonathan S, intermed maint wrkr, $31,164
Black, Kenneth A, sr electrcn, $48,828
Black, Melissa R, comm mgr, $58,836
Black, Michael T, maint worker, $29,064
Black, Ricky L, land surv, $51,624
Blackburn, James F, asst to the resident engi, $71,016
Blackburn, Shane A, materials insp, $42,072
Blades, John L, sr equip technician, $49,752
Blair, Robby D, maint sup, $53,580
Blair, Thomas K, asst dist engr, $85,884
Blake, Howard C, maint crew leader, $43,608
Blakely, Thomas J, maint worker, $29,064
Blalock, David S, transp proj dsgnr, $61,092

Blalock, Rachel R, sr administrative technician, $36,504
Blalock, Randy G, maint worker, $29,064
Blanchard, James M, sr maint worker, $39,156
Blanchard, James R, sr maint worker, $34,596
Bland, Andrea L, sr risk mgmt technic, $38,472
Bland, Randy L, sr maint worker, $34,596
Blankenship, Amy B, fin servs mgr, $55,620
Blankenship, F L, sr traffic technician, $37,140
Blankenship, James E, sr maint worker, $34,596
Blankenship, Kevin W, sr maint worker, $35,220
Blankenship, Lester E, maint worker, $29,064
Blankenship, Terry D, maint crew leader, $36,504
Blattner, Michael E, sr const insp, $54,600
Blecha, Kenneth W, sr maint worker, $34,596
Bledsoe, Billy D, maint sup, $50,676
Bledsoe, Gregory D, maint worker, $29,064
Bledsoe, James D, sr maint worker, $36,504
Bledsoe, Raymond L, maint sup, $50,676
Blender, Christopher M, transp enfrcmnt investigator, $37,800
Blevins, Blake L, maint worker, $29,064
Blevins, Robert G, sr equip technician, $45,192
Blincoe, Ryan J, intermed maint wrkr, $31,164
Blixt, Patrick M, maint worker, $29,064
Block, Douglas O, sr electrcn, $42,816
Blomberg, Jason M, pavement engr, $62,232
Blundell, David K, maint sup, $45,192
Blunt, Kent J, int tr studies spec, $48,828
Blythe, David R, maint crew leader, $40,608
Bock, Kathy A, exec asst, $32,280
Bock, Micheal R, sr traffic studies special, $57,756
Bock, Shirley K, fin servs mgr, $55,620
Bodart, James E, int traffic spec-tpt, $23.88/hr
Boenisch, Paul C, sr hwy dsgnr, $67,092
Boessen, Cheryl L, lead info syss technologist, $59,928
Boessen, Jessica L, investigator, $37,800
Bogan, Elgin D, sr maint worker, $35,220
Bogeart, Brady A, safety intern, $11.24/hr
Bogeart, Mark G, sr maint worker, $36,504
Boggs, Dustin A, maint worker, $29,064
Boggs, Joseph N, asst maint sup, $40,608
Bohannon, Dennis, sr const technician, $39,876
Bohlen, Theotis L, maint worker, $29,064
Bohler, Jeffrey A, trans proj mgr, $76,596
Bohon, Kenton D, maint supt, $51,624
Bokel, Linda W, trans proj mgr, $78,060
Boland, Adam D, intermed maint wrkr, $31,164
Bolden, Michelle L, const proj ofc asst, $36,504
Boling, R K, equip technician superviso, $47,736
Bollinger, Dale E, sr maint worker, $34,596
Bollinger, Matthew B, maint worker, $29,064
Bollinger, Paul J, sr maint worker, $39,876
Bollinger, Ronald L, maint crew leader, $42,816
Bollinger, Seth Z, sr const insp, $56,676
Bolser, Michael W, maint worker, $29,064
Bond, Michael L, sr maint worker, $34,596
Bond, Travis D, sr info syss technologist, $48,828
Bonine, James P, cert appraiser, $52,596
Bonner, Jason M, intermed maint wrkr, $31,164
Bonner, William E, intermed maint wrkr, $30,624
Bonnot, Angela S, sr motor carrier agent, $39,156
Booher, Kenneth S, maint worker, $29,064
Booher, Robert J, motorist assistance oper, $35,220
Bookhart, Ikeshia L, maint worker, $29,064
Books, Edward F, sr structural dsgnr, $72,372
Booth, Barry L, sr r/w spec, $49,752
Boothe, Kevin M, inter const insp, $50,676
Bordeleau, Jacqueline R, sr const insp, $58,836
Borders, Chantelle A, maint worker, $29,064
Borders, Johnny D, maint worker, $31,164
Borgmann, Douglas A, sr maint worker, $35,220
Bosley, James L, asst maint sup, $43,608
Boswell, Lindsey M, sr rt of way technician, $32,832
Bottcher, Brian A, maint crew leader, $42,816
Boultinghouse, Lee R, intermed maint wrkr, $31,164
Boulware, Donald L, sr maint worker, $37,140
Bouse, Donald K, maint crew leader, $37,800
Bouvier, Jeffery R, sr maint worker, $34,596
Bowen, Michael A, maint worker, $29,064
Bowen, Nathan E, motor assistance shift supv, $39,876

Bowen, Tona L, fin servs administrat, $63,408
Bower, David A, sr r/w spec, $48,828
Bowers, Dennis A, maint crew leader, $42,072
Bowers, Eric E, sr electrcn, $42,816
Bowers, Timothy L, sr maint worker, $34,596
Bowles, Bradley A, sr maint worker, $34,596
Bowling, Danny J, sr maint worker, $37,140
Bowman, Andrew J, inter const insp, $47,736
Bowman, C J, sr maint worker, $34,596
Bowman, Michael A, inter const tech, $32,280
Bowman, Patrick E, land surv, $46,044
Boyd, Andy R, sr maint worker, $36,504
Boyd, Randy S, seasonal maint worker, $12.44/hr
Boyd, Ryan L, maint crew leader, $39,156
Boyer, Donald J, sr maint worker, $37,140
Boyer, Joseph L, maint crew leader, $36,504
Boyer, Scott W, gen servs mgr, $57,756
Boyher, Branden M, maint worker, $29,064
Boyles, Marion L, sr maint worker, $39,876
Boyster, Tony L, maint crew leader, $37,140
Bozarth, Michael L, maint crew leader, $39,156
Brackett, McKenzie J, maint worker, $29,064
Brackman, Chase M, safety intern, $11.84/hr
Braden, Andrew L, maint worker, $30,624
Braden, John L, sr traffic spec, $44,400
Brader, Roger A, sr materials technician, $37,800
Bradford, James L, maint sup, $46,044
Bradley, Jacob R, sr maint worker, $34,596
Bradley, Stephen D, intermed maint wrkr, $31,164
Bradshaw, Anthony M, intermed maint wrkr, $33,396
Bradshaw, Caleb D, sr const insp, $54,600
Bradshaw, Debra L, motor carrier compliance supv, $45,192
Bradshaw, Kenneth A, maint worker, $29,064
Brady, Dennis E, sr const insp, $55,620
Bragg, Derek A, intermed maint wrkr, $31,164
Brake, Bradley S, land surv, $43,608
Braman, Rodney A, sr gen servs techni, $32,280
Brammer, Garry E, sr electrcn, $44,400
Branch, Kevin R, sr maint worker, $37,140
Branch, Travis L, intermed maint wrkr, $31,164
Brandel, Matthew R, intermed maint wrkr, $31,164
Brandenburger, James M, maint worker, $29,064
Brandes, Charles W, sr maint worker, $38,472
Brandon, Adleana, seasonal maint worker, $12.44/hr
Brandon, Michael J, transp proj dsgnr, $62,232
Brandt, Dale S, fac opps sup, $53,580
Branson, Douglas F, maint crew leader, $37,800
Branson, Joyce A, sr maint worker, $34,596
Branson, Paul, core drill asst, $27,156
Brant, Tyler J, maint worker, $29,064
Brassfield, Ryan W, const intern, $11.64/hr
Braswell, Darlene M, maint crew leader, $36,504
Braun, Brenda M, sr plng technician, $36,504
Braun, Deirdre E, hwy dsgnr, $46,044
Smith, Megan E, transp enfrcmnt investigator, $37,800
Brauner, Ian M, equip technician intern, $10.56/hr
Brauner, Matthew J, sys mgmt spec, $37,800
Brawner, Kevin J, maint crew leader, $39,156
Breckner, Glenn E, maint crew leader, $42,816
Breeding, Scott W, materials testing spec, $42,816
Brejnik, Rodney J, sr equip technician, $46,884
Brelsford, Scott L, urban traffic sup, $54,600
Brendel, John W, sr const insp, $64,632
Brendel, Robert C, special projs coord, $75,180
Brenner, Thomas K, maint sup, $46,044
Brenner, Timmy W, sr maint worker, $34,596
Brewer, Cullen C, maint crew leader, $45,192
Brewer, Jon W, land surv in training, $39,876
Brewington, Maria T, design technician, $31,164
Brewster, William E, intermed equip tech, $35,856
Bricker, Douglas W, intermed maint wrkr, $31,164
Brickhaus, Thomas J, maint crew leader, $36,504
Bridge, Mark R, inter maint technician, $32,832
Bridgewater, Harley J, maint worker, $29,064
Brietzke, Rebecca L, hr spec, $37,800
Briggs, Kevin L, maint crew leader, $46,044
Bright, Claude L, sr maint worker, $34,596
Brimer, Nicholas D, maint worker, $29,064
Brink, Roger A, sr const technician, $37,800

Brittain, Tracy L, const proj ofc asst, $31,164
Broaddus, Aaron L, sr maint worker, $35,220
Brobst, Ryan D, sr const insp, $50,676
Brock, April L, sr rt of way technician, $43,608
Brock, Christopher T, sr equip technician, $45,192
Brockhaus, George I, sr maint worker, $35,220
Broeker, Roberta L, interim dir of transporta, $173,472
Brokes, Rick D, maint crew leader, $37,140
Bromley, David L, electrcn asst, $32,280
Brondel, Bruce G, intermed maint wrkr, $31,164
Bronenkant, Scott D, sr maint worker, $34,596
Bronson, Cedric I, maint worker, $29,064
Bronson, Lori K, exec asst, $32,832
Brookman, Loren D, intermed maint wrkr, $31,164
Brooks, Billy R, sr maint worker, $34,596
Brooks, Buck H, wetland coord, $59,928
Brooks, James W, intermed maint wrkr, $31,164
Brooks, Lawrence R, ast dist constr & mater en, $64,632
Brooks, Melody B, sr hr technic, $35,220
Brooks, Ralph L, maint sup, $45,192
Brooks, Russell A, const insp, $47,736
Brooks, Trent A, sr maint worker, $34,596
Brooks, Trent A, dist traffic engr, $78,060
Brooks, Wendy L, dist const liaison, $56,676
Brooks-Walton, Geraldine, bus syst supp spec, $46,884
Brooks-White, Beverly S, maint worker, $29,064
Brose, Martin A, sr engring professnl-tpt, $27.49/hr
Brower, Layton E, sr maint worker, $35,220
Brown, Adam S, sr asst counsel, $71,448
Brown, Ashlin E, seasonal maint worker, $12.44/hr
Brown, Beth A, dist final plans & rep proc, $47,736
Brown, Chad O, sr maint worker, $37,800
Brown, Charles B, sr pavement spec, $59,928
Brown, Christopher D, sr equip technician, $40,608
Brown, Claude A, maint crew leader, $39,156
Brown, David, sr equip technician, $42,816
Brown, David A, sr materials insp, $54,600
Brown, Dennis W, sr maint worker, $35,220
Brown, Henry C, intermed maint wrkr, $31,164
Brown, Jason A, maint crew leader, $37,800
Brown, Jimmy L, intermed maint wrkr, $31,164
Brown, Kyle L, lead info syss technologist, $58,836
Brown, Mark R, sr info syss technologist, $55,620
Brown, Nathan H, sr survey technician, $37,140
Brown, Robert A, intermed maint wrkr, $30,624
Brown, Stephen E, sr traffic spec, $53,580
Brown, Todd A, maint sup, $45,192
Brown, Tommy R, maint crew leader, $37,800
Brownell, Lydia B, sr geotech spec, $56,676
Brownell, Sidney C, sr hwy dsgnr, $52,596
Broyles, Stephen R, maint worker, $29,064
Brucks, Dennis H, const & materials liaison engr, $84,288
Bruffett, Timothy M, maint worker, $29,064
Brumagin, Daniel S, maint supt, $50,676
Brumbaugh, Hunter D, seasonal maint worker, $12.44/hr
Brumble, Charles K, intermed maint wrkr, $31,164
Brumitt, Helen L, sr fin servs tech, $37,140
Brune, Mathew D, bridge inspection crew leader, $38,472
Bruner, Jonathan L, int tr studies spec, $49,752
Brunjes, David M, inter const insp, $47,736
Brunk, Andrew G, intermed maint wrkr, $31,164
Brunk, Bradley L, transp proj dsgnr, $64,632
Brunnert, Jenny A, info syss technologist, $39,156
Bruns, Margaret A, sr hwy dsgnr, $56,676
Bryan, Joshua L, maint worker, $29,064
Bryan, Paul R, asst maint sup, $47,736
Bryant, Amy M, sr pavement spec, $56,676
Bryant, Steven E, maint sup, $52,596
Bryant, Tawanda, sr traffic syss oper, $34,596
Bryson, Bruce J, maint sup, $49,752
Buchanan, Gideon W, sr maint worker, $34,596
Buck, John S, inter const insp, $45,192
Buck, Raymond L, motorist assistance oper, $33,996
Buckley, Dennis K, sr maint worker, $36,504
Buckner, Cody A, intermed maint wrkr, $31,164
Buckner, Gregory E, sr maint worker, $36,504
Buczek, Kristin E, sr pavement spec, $51,624
Buddemeyer, Anita R, sr info syss technologist, $47,736
Buechter, Susan C, sr administrative technician, $40,608

Bueker, George F, sr maint worker, $37,800
Bummer, Jacob T, maint worker, $29,064
Bunch, Cody D, maint worker, $29,064
Bunch, Donald V, sr supply agent, $35,220
Bunch, Gloria J, sr procurement agent, $51,624
Bundgard, Timothy R, maint supt, $50,676
Bunton, Glenn C, sr maint worker, $34,596
Burbridge, Arron W, maint crew leader, $36,504
Burch, Barbara L, sr data report analyst, $57,756
Burcham, Matthew L, sr envirnmental spec, $56,676
Burchell, Michael E, sr maint worker, $35,220
Burchell, Randy L, intermed maint wrkr, $31,164
Burdick, Jonathan W, sr maint worker, $34,596
Burditt, Kevin C, asst maint sup, $40,608
Burger, Brian R, resident engr, $67,092
Burgess, James C, trans proj mgr, $81,108
Burgess, Todd J, sr electrcn, $42,816
Burgess, Tommy J, sr maint worker, $35,856
Burgett, Craig L, motorist assistance oper, $39,156
Burgett, Jerome M, sr maint worker, $34,596
Burkett, Patrick L, maint worker, $29,064
Burkhart, Shawndra E, sr survey technician, $35,856
Burkhead, Brandon J, seasonal maint worker, $12.44/hr
Burks, Joshua T, maint supt, $50,676
Burlbaw, Eric S, inter const insp, $44,400
Burnett, Krista L, sr materials insp, $61,092
Burnett, Otis W, sr maint worker, $33,996
Burns, Jeffery R, sr hwy dsgnr, $55,620
Burns, Jerry L, sr maint worker, $34,596
Burns, Jessica M, materials insp, $43,608
Burns, Kellen C, int comm spec, $42,072
Burns, Michael T, sr equip technician, $45,192
Burns, Travis A, maint sup, $46,884
Burnworth, William B, traffic intern, $13.36/hr
Burris, Glendon P, maint sup, $45,192
Burris, Ronnie E, sr maint worker, $35,220
Burroughs, Mark R, sr maint worker, $35,220
Burrow, Anthony T, sr equip technician, $48,828
Burson, Michael D, sr maint worker, $35,220
Burton, Chad A, maint crew leader, $38,472
Burton, Charles D, sr maint worker, $34,596
Burton, Corey D, sr maint worker, $33,396
Burton, Javal L, hr mgr, $55,620
Burton, Kenneth C, inter hwy dsgnr, $51,624
Buscher, Mark R, maint supt, $54,600
Buschjost, Kacey L, sys mgmt spec, $37,800
Buschjost, Shawn J, sr electrcn, $42,816
Buschman, Debra J, exec asst, $32,832
Buschman, James M, sr maint worker, $34,596
Buschmann, Stephanie A, sr fin servs speciali, $49,752
Bushko, Stephen J, sr multimedia servs spe, $39,156
Busse, Homer C, dist land survey mgr, $56,676
Butcher, Darrel D, sr procurement agent, $51,624
Butler, Brenda A, maint crew leader, $37,140
Butler, Jake C, traffic studies spec, $46,044
Butler, Paul O, sr maint worker, $34,596
Butler, Ronald L, maint worker, $29,064
Butler, Stephen P, maint sup, $45,192
Butner, Jennifer A, sr hr spec, $49,752
Butner, Jody A, sr maint worker, $36,504
Butterworth, Sally A, intermed maint wrkr, $31,680
Buxton, Curtis A, maint crew leader, $37,800
Buzzard, Dwayne L, sr maint worker, $34,596
Buzzell, Bruce D, sr design technician, $46,044
Byes, Lee O, maint crew leader, $39,156
Byrd, Albert J, sr admin profressional-tpt, $23.24/hr
Byrd, Brandon E, maint crew leader, $36,504
Byrd, Christopher D, seasonal maint worker, $12.44/hr
Byrge, Jeffrey S, sr maint worker, $37,800
Caffey, Jeffrey D, maint crew leader, $36,504
Cagle, Patricia M, inter const tech, $33,396
Cagle, Troy L, maint crew leader, $36,504
Cain, Barbara L, sr design technician, $19.86/hr
Cain, Mark P, sr maint worker, $33,396
Cain, Phil C, sr maint worker, $38,472
Calandro, Christopher V, sr const insp, $59,928
Caldwell, Christopher B, hwy dsgnr, $43,608
Caldwell, John H, sr maint worker, $35,220
Caldwell, Joseph, sr maint worker, $37,140

Caldwell, Sherwin A, electrcn asst, $32,280
Caley, Ian R, seasonal maint worker, $12.44/hr
Calhoon, Ronnie W, sr const technician, $43,608
Calhoun, Samuel L, maint worker, $29,064
Callahan, James J, electrcn asst, $32,280
Calton, Dennis, maint crew leader, $37,800
Calvas, Lewis K, asst maint sup, $40,608
Calvin, Ronald D, maint supt, $50,676
Camden, Joseph K, maint worker, $29,064
Camden, Lisa A, sr const technician, $37,800
Camenisch, David E, sr maint worker, $35,220
Cameron, Benjamin C, sr maint worker, $33,996
Campbell, Brandon D, traffic opps engr, $63,408
Campbell, Brent L, sr maint worker, $35,220
Campbell, Craig E, sr fac opps spe, $40,608
Campbell, David A, sr materials technician, $36,504
Campbell, Jeffery R, sr estimator, $63,408
Campbell, John E, sr maint worker, $34,596
Campbell, Laura A, sr maint technician, $36,504
Campbell, Orville D, sr maint worker, $37,800
Campbell, Rachel A, historic preserve speciali, $37,800
Campbell, Richard L, sr equip technician, $46,044
Campbell, Scott W, sr maint worker, $36,504
Campbell, Steven V, dist const & materials eng, $76,596
Campos, Carlos A, maint worker, $29,064
Canady, Torrey D, motorist assistance oper, $35,856
Cano, Anthony G, bridge inspection intern, $11.64/hr
Canole, Matthew G, sr maint worker, $33,396
Cantrell, Randy L, sr maint worker, $33,996
Capeder, Jacob D, inter const insp, $51,624
Capehart, Susan L, info sys technology spec, $62,232
Capell, David W, rt of way spec, $41,316
Capra, Nicholas J, maint sup, $48,828
Carder, Bryce E, seasonal maint worker, $12.44/hr
Carey, Joshua C, gis spec, $37,800
Carey Gerhardt, Rita F, exec asst, $33,396
Caringer, Travis W, maint worker, $29,064
Carlisle, Tanya M, sr administrative technician, $40,608
Carmack, Kenneth W, bridge insp, $54,600
Carnahan, Casey L, sr const insp, $56,676
Carpenter, Kenneth R, intermed maint wrkr, $31,164
Carr, Aaron T, maint crew leader, $36,504
Carr, James E, int engring professnl-tpt, $23.88/hr
Carr, Jordan B, maint worker, $29,064
Carriger, Kimberly L, sr auditor, $47,736
Carriker, Jim A, maint sup, $45,192
Carroll, Arney L, maint worker, $29,064
Carroll, Darrin L, sr maint worker, $34,596
Carroll, Louise, sr cust serv rep, $40,608
Carroll, Matthew J, sr maint worker, $33,996
Carron, John P, electrcn, $37,800
Carson, Jon R. sr maint worker, $34,596
Carsten, Christopher D, inter const insp, $48,828
Cartee, Aaron G, sr maint worker, $34,596
Carter, Charles W, maint crew leader, $37,140
Carter, Deborah K, sr maint worker, $34,596
Carter, Joseph A, int gis spec, $42,072
Carter, Kyle C, maint worker, $29,064
Carter, Melena A, sr fin servs speciali, $47,736
Carter, Quentin D, intermed maint wrkr, $31,164
Carter, Tia J, electrcn asst, $32,280
Carusa, Anthony W, maint sup, $45,192
Carver, Larry W, sr gen servs spec, $51,624
Cary, Glen D, sr materials technician, $37,800
Casas, Erik, sr maint worker, $34,596
Casey, John W, sr maint worker, $39,156
Casey, John W, sr const insp, $51,624
Cash, Annette N, int motor carrier agent, $30,120
Cash, Eric T, maint crew leader, $36,504
Cash, Michael E, maint worker, $29,064
Cassmeyer, Allen R, asst maint sup, $40,608
Castillo, Jonathan A, const insp, $42,816
Castillo, Ventura, maint worker, $29,064
Castro, Michael J, dist const & materials eng, $73,788
Catanzaro, Kevin L, intermed maint wrkr, $31,164
Catching, Michael W, maint crew leader, $36,504
Cate, Aaron J, sr maint worker, $37,800
Caudle, Tommy D, info syss sup, $62,232
Cauldwell, Shelly L, sr administrative technician, $38,472

Causey, Travis G, intermed maint wrkr, $31,164
Cauwenbergh, John S, asst chief counsel - admin, $117,816
Cavanah, Amy L, legal sec, $28,584
Cernea, Susan E, sr administrative technician, $33,396
Cervantes, Jose M, maint crew leader, $37,140
Cervas, Michael A, maint worker, $29,064
Chadd, Ron W, maint crew leader, $37,140
Chadwick, Joseph H, maint sup, $45,192
Chaffin, Sonja K, maint worker, $29,064
Chaidez, Pedro D, asst maint sup, $40,608
Chalmers, Tomikia L, exec asst, $33,996
Chamberlin, Andrew L, intermed maint wrkr, $31,164
Chamberlin, Luke E, inter const insp, $51,624
Chambers, Aaron M, gen servs spec, $37,800
Chambers, Jeffrey T, inter const insp, $51,624
Chambers, Lonnie D, maint supt, $53,580
Chambers, Vance A, inter hwy dsgnr, $51,624
Chandler, Carroll E, investigator, $37,800
Chandler, Keith A, maint crew leader, $36,504
Chapman, Gregory R, resident engr, $64,632
Chapman, Harley J, sr maint worker, $33,396
Chapman, Joshua C, intermed maint wrkr, $31,164
Chappell, William R, sr const insp, $50,676
Charles, Cody J, asst equip technician, $28,584
Chase, Kimberly A, maint worker, $29,064
Chasteen, Michael P, sr hwy dsgnr, $54,600
Chavez, Manuel J, sr trans planner, $56,676
Chesnut, Stanley D, sr maint worker, $37,140
Chew, Fred T, asst maint sup, $40,608
Chidester, Shannon R, maint sup, $45,192
Childress, Tammy S, sr fin servs tech, $33,396
Chitwood, Tommie L, maint crew leader, $38,472
Chojnacki, Timothy M, maint liaision engr, $76,596
Choudhury, Anup K, int info syss technologist, $42,072
Christenson, Michael A, sr maint worker, $34,596
Christian, Kevin L, sr maint worker, $34,596
Christie, Brenda E, sr procurement agent, $47,736
Christy-Kerns, Marisa M, sr comm spec, $48,828
Chumbley, Bradley L, motorist assistance oper, $33,996
Churchill, Cody M, maint worker, $29,064
Ciolli, Ian U, electrcn, $37,800
Cissell, David M, maint crew leader, $46,884
Claiborn, Marty R, sr maint worker, $33,996
Clark, Alex R, maint worker, $30,120
Clark, Alvin L, intermed maint wrkr, $31,164
Clark, Anita M, sr hwy dsgnr, $54,600
Clark, Arthur, sr maint worker-tpt, $18.07/hr
Clark, Bradley D, maint worker, $29,064
Clark, Curtis W, maint sup, $48,828
Clark, Daniel W, maint worker, $29,064
Clark, Donald D, maint crew leader, $36,504
Clark, Douglas, sr maint worker, $35,220
Clark, Jeremy L, sr materials technician, $40,608
Clark, Jonathan D, maint worker, $29,064
Clark, Kevin C, sr electrcn, $42,816
Clark, Mark L, sr maint worker, $36,504
Clark, Nathaniel S, const intern, $13.36/hr
Clark, Norman L, sr maint worker, $34,596
Clark, Scott E, maint crew leader, $39,156
Clark, Scotty K, sr maint worker, $33,996
Clark, Serita J, sr maint worker, $34,596
Clark, Steven E, sr materials technician, $38,472
Clarkston, Gregory P, sr organizational perf analyst, $53,580
Claspill, Joshua S, sr maint worker, $36,504
Claycomb, Scott E, sr maint worker, $34,596
Claypool, Carmen M, motor carrier compliance supv, $45,192
Clayton, Michelle A, sr auditor, $51,624
Clem, Roland C, dist info systm mgr, $58,836
Clement, Doyle D, sr maint worker, $36,504
Clements, Johnathan D, maint worker, $29,064
Clemons, Steven A, sr maint worker, $34,596
Clevenger, Michael D, sr maint worker, $35,220
Clevenger, Robert D, seasonal maint worker, $12.44/hr
Clevenger, Steven B, sr maint worker, $37,800
Cline, Bedford E, sr maint worker, $35,220
Cline, Nicholas J, maint worker, $29,064
Cline, Sandra J, sr fin servs tech, $40,608
Closser, Samuel L, sr maint worker, $33,996
Clubb, Jason R, maint worker, $29,064

Clutts, Tamara R, lead info syss technologist, $59,928
Coats, Levi J, maint worker, $29,064
Cockrum, Scot D, sr maint worker, $34,596
Coffer, Lloyd D, maint crew leader, $37,140
Coffey, Gregory A, sr maint worker, $35,220
Coffey, Joseph E, motorist assistance oper, $39,156
Coffey, Randall K, cert appraiser, $53,580
Coffin, Dewayne D, sr maint worker, $35,856
Cohill, Anthony J, maint crew leader, $36,504
Colatrella, Thomas M, sr maint worker, $37,800
Colbert, Brandon D, const intern, $14.59/hr
Colbert, Levi T, sr maint worker, $34,596
Colbert, Rodney J, equip technician superviso, $50,676
Cole, Clinton R, sr maint worker, $36,504
Cole, Donnetta A, sr civil rights spec, $49,752
Cole, Edward L, sr maint worker, $43,608
Cole, Glenn D, maint crew leader, $36,504
Cole, Lorri A, sr fin servs speciali, $47,736
Cole, Robert D, sr maint worker, $37,140
Cole, Steve A, sr maint worker, $34,596
Cole, Thomas W, maint worker, $29,064
Coleman, Cynthia J, sr r/w spec, $56,676
Coleman, Jeffrey L, sr electrcn, $42,816
Coleman, Paul T, const technician, $28,584
Coleman, Vincent T, maint crew leader, $44,400
Colf, David H, maint sup, $45,192
Collier, James D, traffic sup, $53,580
Collier, Jeremy B, maint sup, $45,192
Collins, Billy J, sr maint worker, $35,220
Collins, Dillan L, maint worker, $29,064
Collins, Erin E, sr const technician, $37,800
Collins, Jason T, research analyst, $46,044
Collins, Joseph P, maint crew leader, $38,472
Collins, Kemmy M, inter const insp, $44,400
Collins, Terry R, sr maint worker, $34,596
Collins, Thomas R, historic preserve speciali, $37,800
Collins, Willard E, sr maint worker, $37,800
Collison, James D, maint sup, $45,192
Collyott, Stephen M, sr const insp, $51,624
Cologna, Leo, traffic opps engr, $69,672
Colonna, James D, intermed maint wrkr, $32,832
Colter, Ashley M, survey intern, $11.64/hr
Combs, Ronald D, sr maint worker, $35,220
Compas, Craig D, dist traffic engr, $72,372
Compton, Douglas R, sr maint worker, $32,832
Compton, Michele L, sr comm spec, $49,752
Conard, Joshua M, intermed maint wrkr, $31,164
Condron, Darren E, sr const insp, $51,624
Conley, Joseph V, intermed maint wrkr, $31,164
Conley, Melissa A, paralegal, $37,800
Connell, James D, sr traffic spec, $44,400
Conner, Barbara J, sr cust serv rep, $32,832
Conner, Gabriel C, intermed equip tech, $35,856
Conner, Linda K, sr rt of way technician, $37,800
Conner, Nathan R, sr const insp, $55,620
Conover, Timothy K, sr maint worker, $35,856
Contreras, Adam J, sr maint worker, $33,996
Conway, Danny S, maint worker, $30,120
Conway, Jeffrey M, sr maint worker, $33,996
Cook, Bernard D, sr maint worker, $37,140
Cook, Brad L, maint crew leader, $39,156
Cook, Danny W, sr maint worker, $34,596
Cook, Darrell R, sr hwy dsgnr, $55,620
Cook, Donald S, sr maint worker, $33,996
Cook, Jerry G, maint worker, $29,064
Cook, Kevin W, sr maint worker, $35,220
Cook, Kurtis G, sr maint worker, $35,220
Cook, Lisa G, sr administrative technician, $38,472
Cook, Nichol M, sr maint worker, $39,156
Cook, Randy R, sr info syss technologist, $51,624
Cook, Ronald L, maint sup, $45,192
Cook, Timothy O, maint worker, $29,064
Cook, Tony F, maint worker, $29,064
Cooksey, Jonathon, materials intern, $13.36/hr
Cooksey, Raphael D, maint worker, $29,064
Cookson, Alvin D, sr maint worker, $33,996
Cooley, Derek A, sr maint worker, $33,996
Cooley, Luke L, maint crew leader, $36,504
Coonce, Mark A, intermed equip tech, $37,140

Cooper, Donald T, maint crew leader, $44,400
Cooper, Dustin H, sr maint worker, $34,596
Cooper, Joseph T, sr fac opps spe, $44,400
Cooper, Shelly L, int info syss technologist, $42,072
Cooper, Steven E, sr maint worker, $36,504
Cooper, William L, equip technician, $33,396
Copeland, Gary R, maint sup, $45,192
Copeland, Gregory R, inter materials tech, $32,832
Copeland, Heather M, sr const insp, $55,620
Copeland, Jim, land survey coord, $56,676
Copeland, Stephanie D, mc investigations administratr, $69,672
Coppinger, Kristina T, intermed safety ofcr, $42,072
Cora, Marion S, sr const technician, $37,800
Corbett, Charles H, intermed maint wrkr, $31,164
Corbett, Steven M, sr hwy dsgnr, $55,620
Corbin, David S, sr maint worker, $39,876
Corbin, Donna M, inter const tech, $33,396
Corbin, Mark L, maint crew leader, $39,876
Corcoran, Glenn J, intermed maint wrkr, $31,164
Corl, Michael S, sr equip technician, $49,752
Corley, Michael G, sr maint worker, $36,504
Cornelison, Joshua A, intermed maint wrkr, $31,164
Cornine, Kimberly A, const proj ofc asst, $28,104
Correnti, Nicholas M, transp proj dsgnr, $61,092
Corum, Carolyn S, sr motor carrier agent, $42,816
Cosentino, Nicholas A, inter const insp, $47,736
Cossey, Derek R, maint worker, $29,064
Cota, Rogelio, motorist assistance oper, $33,996
Cotter, Gregory A, sr maint worker, $34,596
Cottey, Tyson C, maint worker, $29,064
Cotton, Jimmy D, sr maint worker, $34,596
Couch, Debra L, asst rt of way mngr-certifi, $61,092
Couffer, Jimmy J, sr const technician, $37,800
Coward, Charles D, sr maint worker, $37,140
Cowger, James A, sr maint worker, $33,996
Cowherd, Delmar S, sr maint worker, $35,220
Cox, Benjy L, sr maint worker, $35,220
Cox, Christopher A, maint crew leader, $35,856
Cox, Donald M, sr maint worker, $36,504
Cox, Jack R, motorist assistance oper, $33,996
Cox, James A, sr rr safety insp, $42,816
Cox, Sally L, dist utilities engr, $64,632
Cox, Thomas H, maint worker, $29,064
Cox, Timothy R, sr const insp, $57,756
Crabb, Ricky L, sr maint worker, $34,596
Cracraft, Brandon L, sr const insp, $53,580
Crader, Timothy R, maint crew leader, $39,156
Crafton, Travis L, sr maint worker, $37,140
Craig, Bryan K, sr maint worker, $33,996
Craig, Caleb D, maint worker, $29,064
Craig, Lisa M, sr maint worker, $33,996
Crain, Dustin W, sr maint worker, $34,596
Cranford, Terrance W, maint worker, $29,064
Crannick, Michael S, sr maint worker, $35,856
Crawford, Amy B, area engr, $64,632
Crawford, Andrew W, structural technician, $28,584
Crawford, Bobby J, intermed maint wrkr, $31,164
Crawford, Lloyd D, maint crew leader, $36,504
Crawford, Steven D, sr maint worker, $34,596
Crawford, Trenton B, sr structural dsgnr, $53,580
Creamer, Robert L, sr const technician, $38,472
Creech, Kyle E, motorist assistance oper, $33,996
Creech, Mason R, maint worker, $29,064
Creek, Richard E, sr maint worker-tpt, $15.65/hr
Creek, Wayne L, sr maint worker, $34,596
Crego, Dennis H, sr hr spec, $46,884
Crenshaw, William H, sr const technician, $39,156
Cretzmeyer, William C, sr maint worker, $35,220
Crews, Richard W, asst maint sup, $46,884
Crewse, Lloyd D, maint crew leader, $40,608
Crewse, Steven D, sr maint worker, $35,220
Criddle, Enos W, dist sfty & hlth mgr, $56,676
Cridlebaugh, Joe L, sr maint worker, $34,596
Crisp, Donnie A, sr maint worker, $35,220
Crites, Donald W, sr traffic studies special, $56,676
Crites, Roy A, sr maint worker, $39,156
Croarkin, Mark E, dist maint engr, $72,372
Crocker, Beckwith S, sr adminstrative techn-tpt, $16.22/hr
Crocker, Christopher S, sr const insp, $56,676

Cronin, Danny G, sr maint worker-tpt, $21.92/hr
Crookshanks, Douglas J, sr maint worker, $37,140
Cross, Corey E, maint crew leader, $36,504
Crossman, Errol D, intermed maint wrkr, $31,164
Crow, Robert D, sr maint worker, $34,596
Crowder, Daniel E, sr maint worker, $36,504
Crowe, Douglas O, maint worker, $29,064
Crowley, Melissa A, sr cust serv rep, $32,832
Crudgington, Michael J, sr const technician, $36,504
Crull, Charles L, sr maint worker-tpt, $20.89/hr
Crum, Joe D, sr maint worker, $39,876
Crump, Sally E, sr fin servs tech, $43,608
Crusha, Anthony J, maint worker, $29,064
Crusoe, Gloria M, maint worker, $29,064
Cryer, Karla L, maint crew leader, $45,192
Culver, Deanna J, sr administrative technician, $38,472
Cunningham, Kent J, maint crew leader, $37,140
Cunningham, Larry T, intermed equip tech, $37,800
Cunningham, Michael G, sr maint worker, $34,596
Cunningham, Robert L, maint sup, $49,752
Cuquet, Chip F, maint worker, $29,064
Cureton, Shannon W, sr maint worker, $34,596
Curl, Roger D, intermed maint wrkr, $32,280
Curlile, Melanie L, intermed safety ofcr, $42,072
Curnutt, Craig P, sr const technician, $37,800
Curnutt, John C, maint worker, $29,064
Curran, Bryan J, transp enfrcmnt investigator, $37,800
Currey, Tracy L, sr maint worker, $35,220
Currie, Trina T, maint worker, $29,064
Curtis, Benjamin E, maint worker, $29,064
Curtis, Charles W, maint worker, $31,680
Curtis, Christopher D, maint crew leader, $36,504
Curtit, Eric J, admin of rrs, $72,372
Cutler, Dustin L, intermed maint wrkr, $31,164
Czeschin, Dustin A, maint worker, $29,064
Dahmm, Charles W, maint worker, $29,064
Dailey, Stoney J, sr maint worker, $35,220
Dailey, Trenton L, maint worker, $29,064
Dale, Darin D, sr maint worker, $35,856
Dalton, Marcus G, maint crew leader, $36,504
Dame, William C, sr maint worker, $36,504
Dames, Alphonse F, maint supt, $50,676
Damron, Charles G, sr maint worker, $35,220
Daniel, Brandon D, sr traffic spec, $45,192
Daniel, Chad E, bridge rating & invent engr, $69,672
Daniel, Shelie A, area engr, $71,016
Daniels, Andrew L, intermed maint wrkr, $32,280
Daniels, Christopher E, sr maint worker, $34,596
Daniels, Dale R, sr maint worker, $36,504
Daniels, Derrick L, maint worker, $29,064
Daniels, Karen L, sr historic preserv spec-nss, $53,580
Dao, Quyet T, sr materials insp, $53,580
Darden, Linda J, sr row spec-tpt, $24.12/hr
Darley, Valinda J, sr fin servs tech, $39,876
Dassrath, Elisha C, fin servs spec, $37,800
Daulton, Matthew B, sr const insp, $54,600
Dauma, Tanya R, sr gen servs spec, $51,624
Davault, L L, sr fin servs speciali, $49,752
Dave, Gary T, maint worker, $29,064
Davenport, Byron W, sr const insp, $50,676
Davenport, Carol J, sr ofc asst, $17.86/hr
Davenport, Karl D, rt of way mgr, $73,788
Davidson, Bret E, geologist, $63,408
Davidson, George F, seasonal maint worker, $12.44/hr
Davidson, Kevin J, maint sup, $48,828
Davidson, Robert N, sr const insp, $52,596
Davis, Adam L, maint worker, $29,064
Davis, Alfred E, maint crew leader, $36,504
Davis, Austin T, maint worker, $29,064
Davis, Caleb S, maint worker, $29,064
Davis, Chad W, equip technician, $32,280
Davis, Dale M, sr maint worker, $42,816
Davis, Eugene E, sr maint worker, $34,596
Davis, George H, geologist, $62,232
Davis, Jackie L, administrative technician-tpt, $15.94/hr
Davis, James E, sr info syss technologist, $52,596
Davis, James R, maint crew leader, $36,504
Davis, James R, sr maint worker, $34,596
Davis, Jeffrey S, sr maint worker, $41,316

Davis, Kevin S, maint crew leader, $36,504
Davis, Manuel, intermed maint wrkr, $31,164
Davis, Matthew J, sr hr spec, $52,596
Davis, Michael S, sr maint worker, $36,504
Davis, Mitchell A, sr equip technician, $44,400
Davis, Paul A, maint worker, $29,064
Davis, Phillip D, traffic syss sup, $40,608
Davis, Robert R, asst maint sup, $40,608
Davis, Rodney J, sr maint worker, $34,596
Davison, Jeremy S, sr maint worker, $35,220
Dawes, Cory D, maint worker, $29,064
Dawson, Christina J, sr maint worker, $35,220
Dawson, Keith P, sr electrcn, $42,816
Dawson, Tony D, sr maint worker, $35,220
Day, Allen W, sr maint worker, $35,856
Day, Dennis E, maint sup, $45,192
Day, John C, maint crew leader, $36,504
Deardeuff, Ethan J, const insp, $45,192
Deardeuff, Robert P, sr maint worker, $35,220
Deatherage, Jay P, maint worker, $29,064
Deaton, Mary K, sr traffic technician, $42,072
Debrock, Wayne B, sr maint worker, $34,596
Debrot, Michael W, sr electrcn, $46,044
Decker, Kody P, maint worker, $29,064
Declue, Susan D, sr gen servs techni, $34,596
Dee, Charles R, maint worker, $29,064
Deen, Ronald A, sr maint worker, $33,996
Degraffenreid, Gary D, core drill asst, $27,156
Degroat, William L, sr const technician, $36,504
Deken, Adam J, sr maint worker, $35,220
Delameter, Jordan T, sr maint worker, $34,596
Delcour, Clayton D, maint worker, $29,064
Demann, James M, sr electrcn, $44,400
Demery, Randy L, sr maint worker, $37,140
Dempsay, Rick, maint worker, $29,064
Dempsey, Keith A, sr traffic technician, $37,800
Demshar, Donald D, sr traffic spec, $48,828
Denby, Christopher A, maint worker, $29,064
Denkler, Brandon R, inter benefits spec, $42,072
Denkler, Megan J, transp mgt syss admin, $59,928
Denkler, Paul T, pavement engr, $59,928
Denmark, Sheila G, maint crew leader, $37,140
Denning, Betty J, sr administrative technician, $32,832
Dennis, Jeffrey J, sr const insp, $50,676
Denson, Boyd L, sr structural dsgnr, $61,092
Dent, Jo A, sr envirnmental spec, $48,828
Denton, Eric J, sr maint worker, $35,220
Deornellis, Benjamin M, seasonal maint worker, $12.44/hr
Deppe, Brian D, sr maint worker, $33,996
Depue, Garrett W, sr traffic studies special, $56,676
Derboven, Charles E, sr maint worker, $35,856
Derrow, Andrea J, maint worker, $29,064
Desch, Karl F, sr equip technician, $42,072
Deters, Daniel J, sr equip technician, $40,608
Deters, Robert R, maint sup, $45,192
Detienne, Richard L, sr maint worker, $34,596
Dettling, Todd A, sr maint worker, $35,220
Devaul, Colby B, maint crew leader, $37,140
Devonshire, Leroy G, sr maint worker, $33,996
Dewall, Thomas J, sr equip technician, $49,752
Deweese, Dale E, sr fac opps spe, $46,044
Dewey, Brian G, sr const insp, $57,756
Dewitt, Garland L, sr maint worker, $39,876
Dickerson, David L, maint worker, $29,064
Dickinson, John P, maint crew leader, $36,504
Dickmeier, Loren G, maint crew leader, $40,608
Dickneite, Haley N, design intern, $12.47/hr
Dickneite, Norbert T, sr maint worker, $36,504
Dickneite, Stephen G, intermed maint wrkr, $31,164
Dickson, James R, transp plng coord, $64,632
Dickson, Larry H, seasonal maint worker, $12.44/hr
Didriksen, Kelly L, exec asst, $33,396
Diebal, Jeremy A, sr maint worker, $33,996
Dierkens, Adam W, sr maint worker, $34,596
Dietrich, Philip A, sr const insp, $56,676
Dietzel, John A, sr hwy dsgnr, $51,624
Diggins, Rodney L, sr maint worker, $36,504
Dille, Dwayne P, sr maint worker, $37,140
Dillon, Dustin M, seasonal maint worker, $12.44/hr

Dingman, Ryan M, inter const insp, $44,400
Dinsmore, John K, sr maint worker, $37,140
Dipley, Donald R, sr maint worker, $35,220
Dishman, James J, lead info syss technologist, $55,620
Distler, Aaron J, sr outdoor advertising perm sp, $42,072
Distler, Melvin L, land surv in training, $39,876
Dittmer, Andrew D, maint crew leader, $36,504
Divanbeigi, Davar, sr traffic studies special, $68,364
Divine, Christopher J, sr maint worker, $34,596
Divine, Russell M, maint crew leader, $38,472
Dixon, Donald K, maint worker, $29,064
Dobbs, Lucas C, maint crew leader, $36,504
Dobnikar, Andrew L, maint crew leader, $37,140
Dobson, Steve E, intermed maint wrkr, $31,164
Dockins, Matthew M, sr maint worker, $33,396
Dodd, Robert A, dist info systm mgr, $61,092
Dodd, Robert B, sr maint worker, $35,220
Doerhoff, Marjorie C, lead info syss technologist, $55,620
Dolejsi, Charles F, bridge insp, $57,756
Domzalski, Richard A, resident engr, $79,596
Donahoe, Michael A, core drill oper, $39,876
Donahue, Angela N, const insp, $47,736
Donahue, John P, const & materials liaison engr, $78,060
Donovan, Peter M, asst chief counsel-proj devel, $117,816
Dooley, James C, maint worker, $29,064
Dooley, Scott D, maint crew leader, $35,856
Dorenkamp, Dustin J, transp proj dsgnr, $62,232
Dorenkamp, Julianne E, sr fin servs tech, $39,876
Dorko, Kimberly A, maint worker, $29,064
Dorner, Randy W, sr maint worker, $34,596
Dorrel, Bryan S, maint crew leader, $43,608
Dorris, Arlene K, sr plng technician, $38,472
Dorris, Joseph L, sr maint worker, $35,220
Dorrough, Jaime M, mcs sys & training analyst, $39,876
Doss, Blaine M, sr info syss technologist, $49,752
Doss, Dakota L, maint worker, $29,064
Dotson, Joseph L, traffic sup, $54,600
Doty, Janet L, sr gen servs spec, $47,736
Dougherty, Brian L, maint crew leader, $35,856
Douglas, Holly R, hwy dsgnr, $47,736
Douglas, Karen B, motor carrier technician, $30,120
Douty, Michael W, maint crew leader, $37,140
Dow, James K, maint worker, $29,064
Dowden, Curtis L, sr materials insp, $52,596
Dowdy, Darius W, asst to the resident engi, $64,632
Downey, Angela I, sr hr spec, $49,752
Downing, George T, sr maint worker, $39,876
Downing, Jeffery L, sr traffic studies special, $55,620
Downs, Ashley N, historic preserve intern, $12.25/hr
Doyel, Tonya R, sr motor carrier agent, $34,596
Doyle, Gerri A, sr trans planner, $51,624
Drace, Preston V, sr maint worker, $39,876
Draffen, Christopher L, asst maint sup, $40,608
Drake, David L, sr const insp, $52,596
Drake, Jeffery S, sr maint worker, $34,596
Drebes, Donald E, sr maint worker, $35,220
Drebes, Toshia M, sr hwy dsgnr, $56,676
Drecktrah, Bryce A, seasonal maint worker, $12.44/hr
Dreher, Richard E, intermed maint wrkr, $30,624
Drennan, Mary K, sr info syss technologist, $48,828
Drennon, Mark S, maint crew leader, $35,856
Drew, Timothy A, maint crew leader, $39,156
Drinkard, Charlotte M, sr plng technician, $39,876
Driskell, Kyle S, sr maint worker, $33,996
Driver, Christopher W, intermed maint wrkr, $30,624
Drury, Freddie R, maint sup, $45,192
Dry, Terry S, sr maint worker, $42,072
Duclos, Donald E, motorist assistance oper, $42,072
Ducote, Brian A, electrcn, $37,800
Dudenhoeffer, Brenda M, sr risk mgmt technic, $42,072
Dudenhoeffer, Cody A, inter structural technician, $32,280
Dudley, Douglas L, maint worker, $29,064
Dudley, John P, sr maint worker, $33,996
Dudley, Seth W, maint worker, $29,064
Dudley, William R, maint worker, $29,064
Duffner, Christopher E, sr const insp, $52,596
Dugan, Josh M, sr design technician, $36,504
Duggan, Donald J, intermed maint wrkr, $31,164
Duke, Danny L, maint sup, $45,192

Duke, Umo B, traffic intern, $13.85/hr
Dukes, Allen L, maint crew leader-tpt, $19.55/hr
Duley, Andrew P, maint worker, $29,064
Dumas, Zachariah E, const mgmt intern, $11.24/hr
Dumey, Doris M, exec asst, $33,996
Dunakey, Curtis R, maint crew leader, $41,316
Duncan, Craig A, sr maint worker, $33,996
Duncan, Dan, maint crew leader, $36,504
Duncan, George B, maint sup, $45,192
Duncan, James R, sr equip technician, $42,816
Duncan, Monica H, sr trans planner, $48,828
Dunham, Shane A, sr maint worker, $35,856
Dunivin, Bradley A, maint worker, $29,064
Dunker, Clyde E, sr maint worker, $34,596
Dunkle, Jesse A, maint crew leader, $36,504
Dunlap, Kevin S, maint worker, $29,064
Dunlap, Mitchell A, intermed maint wrkr, $31,164
Dunn, Donald, sr maint worker, $35,220
Dunn, Jason A, const intern, $13.36/hr
Dunn, William J, strctural prelim & rev engr, $73,788
Dunnaway, Cynthia A, ast dist constr & mater en, $63,408
Dupree, Daniel A, intermed maint wrkr, $31,164
Durham, Douglas E, sr maint worker, $35,856
Durnell, Zane W, intermed maint wrkr, $31,164
Durossette, Jesse D, maint crew leader, $36,504
Durrington, Clint R, maint sup, $45,192
Dusenberg, Michael W, trans proj mgr, $76,596
Duvall, Keith A, sr maint worker, $34,596
Dwight, Justin B, sr const insp, $50,676
Dydell, Amber M, sr ofc asst, $25,812
Dydell, Rye'll M, gen laborer, $11.37/hr
Dye, Brian P, sr const technician, $37,140
Dye, Randy G, maint worker, $29,064
Dye, Shari R, dist sfty & hlth mgr, $57,756
Dzurick, Cindy L, sr const insp, $50,676
Eads, Harold R, maint crew leader, $36,504
Eagles, Denise R, sr maint worker, $33,996
Eagles, James A, sr maint worker, $39,876
Ealey, Steven M, br inspection crew sup, $45,192
Earls, David J, sr info syss technologist, $49,752
Earls, Jesse L, maint sup, $46,044
Earls, Teddy J, sr const insp, $50,676
Earnheart, Scotty D, sr equip technician, $43,608
Easley, Randall E, maint crew leader, $36,504
Easter, Randy N, sr maint worker, $43,608
Eastman, John A, sr motor carrier agent, $43,608
Ebker, Lyndon D, sr maint worker-tpt, $19.43/hr
Ebker, Ryan A, maint worker, $29,064
Echols, Bradley T, maint crew leader, $36,504
Eckhoff, Dustin D, maint crew leader, $39,876
Eckhoff, Kristopher M, sr maint worker, $35,220
Edde, Ryan L, intermed equip tech, $35,856
Edelman, Ross H, maint worker, $29,064
Eden, Angela I, sr comm spec, $54,600
Edgar, Donald W, maint sup, $52,596
Edgar, Randall L, maint crew leader, $36,504
Edgmond, Nikkolas J, const intern, $14.59/hr
Edmiston, James M, seasonal maint worker, $12.44/hr
Edmonds, Shawn E, sr maint worker, $36,504
Edmondson, Dana R, sr design technician, $45,192
Edwards, James G, dist info systm mgr, $56,676
Edwards, Richard L, fac opps crew worke, $28,584
Effland, Ronald E, non-motorized transp engr, $76,596
Eggemeyer, Kevin L, traffic sup, $52,596
Eggemeyer, Ruth A, lead info syss technologist, $59,928
Eidson, Clint D, sr maint worker, $35,220
Eidson, Jason E, maint crew leader, $37,800
Eivins, James R, maint crew leader, $37,140
Elam, Curtis L, sr const insp, $50,676
Elder, Charles E, maint worker, $29,064
Elder, William T, sr maint worker, $35,220
Eldred, Danielle H, asst counsel, $51,924
Elias, Michael J, sr maint worker, $33,996
Elijah, Richard A, maint sup, $46,884
Eliuk, Damon J, trans planner, $39,876
Elkin, Lydia A, intermed mt worker-tpt, $18.50/hr
Ellen, Laura S, trans plng specia, $61,092
Elliott, Chance A, maint worker, $29,064
Elliott, John K, sr const insp, $56,676

Elliott, Keith W, maint sup, $46,044
Elliott, Martin D, sr maint worker, $35,856
Elliott, Nicholas L, maint crew leader, $37,140
Elliott, Tara L, sr hr spec, $47,736
Elliott, Wayne V, sr structural dsgnr, $63,408
Elliott, William A, sr maint worker, $34,596
Elliott, Yvonne M, comm mgr, $59,928
Ellis, Dameon K, sr maint worker, $33,996
Ellis, Todd M, sr const technician, $36,504
Ellison, Marisa L, comm worker, $62,232
Ellsworth, Andrew J, sr r/w spec, $55,620
Elmore, Craig A, dist final plans & rep proc, $40,608
Elrick, Steven R, inter materials insp, $44,400
Elseman, Jesse S, bridge inspection technician, $47,736
Embree, Darrin G, maint sup, $45,192
Embrey, Chad S, sr maint worker, $34,596
Emery, Darrell W, maint sup, $45,192
Emig, Kirk A, maint worker, $29,064
Ena, Oja E, maint worker, $29,064
Endraske, Christopher M, land survey sup, $47,736
Engel, Shayne, sr maint worker, $38,472
Engelage, Victor K, sr maint worker, $34,596
Engelbrecht, Christopher R, dist sfty & hlth mgr, $57,756
Engelbrecht, Steven W, dist plng mgr, $81,108
Engelhart, Nancy J, sr ofc asst, $33,996
Engemann, Chad D, inter const tech, $33,996
Ennes, Corey A, sr equip technician, $40,608
Ennes, Jennifer S, sr fin servs speciali, $47,736
Epperson, Dale A, sr maint worker, $34,596
Epperson, Darin R, sr maint worker, $36,504
Epperson, Dennis C, sr maint worker, $34,596
Epperson, Shawn M, sr maint worker, $34,596
Eppright, David W, maint sup, $45,192
Epps, Kentrell I, maint worker, $29,064
Ernst, Scott A, equip technician superviso, $45,192
Erwin, Clinton D, sr maint worker, $36,504
Erwin, Maria A, sr motor carrier agent, $34,596
Espey, Daniel R, sr maint worker, $34,596
Esser, Gerald D, sr maint worker, $33,996
Essien, Kereidung E, administrative technician, $28,584
Essner, Donald J, sr electrcn, $45,192
Estes, Jason L, maint crew leader, $37,140
Estes, Jonathan E, sr maint worker, $37,140
Estes, Lance J, sr maint worker, $35,220
Estopare, Roger T, sr const technician, $37,800
Etter, Robert W, intermed maint wrkr, $31,164
Ettinger, Ronald D, sr maint worker, $42,816
Eutsler, Dalton C, maint worker, $29,064
Eutsler, Mitchell, traffic intern, $12.47/hr
Evans, Billy J, sr maint worker, $34,596
Evans, James L, maint worker, $29,064
Evans, Johnathan E, sr maint worker, $33,996
Evans, Justin T, intermed maint wrkr, $31,164
Evans, Kenneth R, sr maint worker, $38,472
Evans, Kevin L, sr const insp, $55,620
Evans, Larry A, maint sup, $51,624
Evans, Michael P, maint worker, $29,064
Evans, Richard M, sr maint worker, $33,996
Evans, Zachary G, maint technician, $13.74/hr
Even, Douglas L, sr equip technician, $42,816
Evenden, Jason D, resident engr, $64,632
Evers, Christopher N, lead field acquisition tech, $42,072
Evers, Christy L, sr multimodal oper spec, $47,736
Evers, Curtis D, sr field acquisition techn, $40,608
Evers, Gregory C, inter fld acquisition tech, $32,280
Evers, Paula A, sr risk mgmt spec, $48,828
Evers, Thomas J, dist design engr, $72,372
Everts, Clifford D, maint crew leader, $36,504
Ewalt, Anthony R, sr maint worker, $34,596
Ewert, Jesse L, maint worker, $29,064
Ewigman, Michael J, asst maint sup, $49,752
Ewing, Randal J, sr maint worker, $35,220
Ewing, Randall L, maint crew leader, $35,856
Ezzell, Kendra M, hr mgr, $59,928
Fackler, Ervin H, asst dist maint & traff engine, $76,596
Faenger, Sheree A, sr maint worker, $33,996
Fagerstone, Nathan V, materials intern, $13.14/hr
Fagre, Justin E, sr maint worker, $35,220
Falter, Ruth M, intermed is technician, $35,856

Fankhauser, David G, sr maint worker, $35,220
Farley, Robert P, maint crew leader, $36,504
Farley, Wyatt C, maint worker, $29,064
Farmer, Teresa J, sr fin servs speciali, $51,624
Farr, Ada M, sr maint worker, $34,596
Farr, Maurice L, maint crew leader, $36,504
Farr, Robey L, sr equip technician, $49,752
Farrar, Cynthia M, inter const insp, $44,400
Farrell, Aaron J, seasonal maint worker, $12.44/hr
Farrington, Carla R, sr maint worker, $35,856
Farris, Thomas H, sr hwy dsgnr, $56,676
Farrow, Ken C, sr core drill asst, $34,596
Fassler, Ryan D, maint worker, $29,064
Fast, Jimmy S, maint worker, $29,064
Fearon, Rhapsody A, transp enfrcmnt investigator, $37,800
Fee, Jessica L, intermed maint wrkr, $31,164
Feeler, Christopher J, sr equip technician, $43,608
Feeney, James W, maint crew leader, $36,504
Feilbach, Bridget D, sr fin servs tech, $33,996
Feller, Teri D, maint sup, $48,828
Fellows, Thomas F, sr maint worker, $43,608
Felty, Daniel W, historic preserve speciali, $39,156
Fender, Nathan L, maint worker, $29,064
Fennessey, Thomas W, geotech engr, $69,672
Fennewald, Denise A, exec asst, $33,996
Fennewald, Leslie N, sr info syss technologist, $63,408
Fennewald, Richard L, equip technician superviso, $47,736
Fenton, Randall R, sr maint worker, $36,504
Fergison, Jamie I, exec asst, $32,280
Ferguson, Bryan J, land surv, $50,676
Ferguson, Candy R, seasonal maint worker, $12.44/hr
Ferguson, Gary, sr electrcn, $46,884
Ferguson, Jason A, sr const insp, $50,676
Ferguson, Lori S, sr traffic syss oper, $36,504
Ferguson, Lynn M, int info syss technologist, $43,608
Ferguson, Michael E, sr maint worker, $33,996
Ferkel, Donna C, hr mgr, $56,676
Ferkel, Philip J, sr maint worker-tpt, $19.78/hr
Ferrell, Keith J, sr structural engr, $68,364
Fichtel, Derek F, ast dist constr & mater en, $61,092
Fick, Ashley M, gen servs technician, $28,584
Fickle, Ernest F, sr design technician, $39,876
Fielder, Hal K, intermed maint wrkr, $30,624
Fields, Daniel R, intermed maint wrkr, $31,164
Fields, Terry A, sr materials insp, $50,676
Filley, Phyllis A, const proj ofc asst, $32,832
Finch, Jennifer L, sr maint worker, $34,596
Finch, Jerad A, maint crew leader, $36,504
Finley, Larry D, sr maint worker, $34,596
Finley, Misty M, inter trans planner, $46,884
Finley, Terri L, sr sys mgmt specialis, $54,600
Fipps, Tanya A, cert appraiser, $49,752
Firebaugh, Albert E, maint worker, $29,064
Fischer, Brent P, comp liaison, design, $53,580
Fischer, Kyle W, maint sup, $46,044
Fischer, Shaire L, const proj ofc asst, $31,680
Fischer, Travis J, maint sup, $45,192
Fish, Duane M, sr equip technician, $42,072
Fisher, Angela L, cert appraiser, $49,752
Fisher, Christopher W, sr maint worker, $33,996
Fisher, Craig A, maint crew leader, $36,504
Fisher, Mark C, trans proj mgr, $75,180
Fisher, Monte D, maint sup, $51,624
Fisher, Russell L, maint crew leader, $36,504
Fisher, Russell T, maint crew leader, $37,800
Fisher, Travis G, maint worker, $29,064
Fiske, James R, sr maint worker, $34,596
Fiske, Tabitha S, const insp, $46,044
Fissell, Donna M, sr traffic technician, $37,800
Fitch, Elliott L, intermed maint wrkr, $31,164
Fitzpatrick, Delbert J, sr maint worker, $34,596
Fitzpatrick, Roger K, maint crew leader, $37,800
Flake, Michael S, maint crew leader, $39,876
Flandermeyer, Ricky A, maint worker, $29,064
Flanigan, Ryan T, motorist assistance oper, $33,996
Fleak, Robert D, sr maint worker, $35,220
Fleming, Andrew C, maint worker, $29,064
Fleming, Belinda F, comm dir, $97,128.01/hr
Flesch, Mary A, business syst spt mgr, $54,600

Fletcher, Austin L, maint worker, $29,064
Fletcher, Donald E, asst maint sup, $40,608
Fletcher, Eric D, sr electrcn, $42,816
Fletcher, Shane A, transp enfrcmnt investigator, $37,800
Flickinger, Troy S, sr field acquisition techn, $36,504
Flint, Jared W, intermed maint wrkr, $31,164
Flora, Janique M, materials insp, $40,608
Flores, Amy M, ofc asst, $22,608
Flores, Glenn E, sr maint worker, $34,596
Flory, Tony D, maint worker, $29,064
Fluchel, Jeffrey S, sr equip technician, $49,752
Flynn, Steven R, const technician, $31,164
Fodge, Carrie E, sr traffic syss oper, $34,596
Foley, Douglas E, intermed safety ofcr, $47,736
Foley, Lyle E, sr maint worker, $35,856
Follett, Robert W, sr electrcn, $50,676
Fontaine, Nathan C, sr motor carrier agent, $33,996
Fontana, Mary Sue, sr fin servs speciali, $27.77/hr
Foppe, Michael F, maint supt, $50,676
Forand, Dana, asst equip technician, $28,584
Forck, Laurie A, sr risk mgmt technic, $43,608
Forck, Rory C, risk mgmt spec, $37,800
Ford, Clinton D, maint sup, $45,192
Ford, Ellis O, intermed maint wrkr, $31,164
Ford, Timothy C, equip technician superviso, $46,044
Forde, Randall L, sr maint worker, $35,220
Fordyce, Jerad L, maint worker, $29,064
Forrest, Anthony E, sr design technician, $37,800
Forson, Michael L, sr maint worker, $36,504
Fort, John E, sr maint worker, $37,140
Fortner, Glenn B, maint sup, $50,676
Foster, Caleb P, maint crew leader, $36,504
Foster, Debra S, sr cust serv rep, $43,608
Foster, Eric E, sr r/w spec, $48,828
Foster, Gerald E, sr risk mgmt spec, $64,632
Foster, Leonard D, sr fabrication technician, $54,600
Fountain, Randy A, sr maint worker, $33,996
Fourman, Deron A, maint worker, $29,064
Fouts, David P, lead info syss technologist, $54,600
Fowler, Carlos L, asst maint sup, $40,608
Fowler, Richard W, sr maint worker, $35,220
Fox, Dan M, sr const technician, $41,316
Fox, Kevin G, sr const insp, $52,596
Fox, Theodore E, sr const insp, $54,600
Fraley, Nicholas J, sr maint worker, $33,996
Frame, Johnathan C, sr maint worker, $34,596
Francis, Karlheinz R, sr maint worker, $34,596
Francis, Kimberly K, int hr speclst, $43,608
Frank, Allen J, maint sup, $46,044
Frank, Cortez D, maint crew leader, $35,856
Frank, Devin M, resource mgmt analyst, $37,800
Frank, Marjorie A, exec asst, $42,816
Frank, Michael D, estimator-tpt, $29.63/hr
Frank, Steven J, sr hwy dsgnr, $56,676
Franke, Dean D, structural proj mgr, $72,372
Franke, Judith M, sr procurement agent, $49,752
Franklin, Matthew L, const insp, $47,736
Franks, Geoffrey M, sr hwy dsgnr, $55,620
Frasher, Albert C, maint crew leader, $38,472
Frazier, Brian K, sr const technician, $37,800
Frazier, Edward M, sr maint worker, $34,596
Frazier, Michael S, asst maint sup, $40,608
Frazier, Robert L, sr maint worker, $33,996
Frazier, Tyler C, hwy dsgnr, $43,608
Fredrick, Jeffrey A, maint worker, $29,064
Fredrick, Rick D, core drill oper, $45,192
Freed, Bradley C, design intern, $11.64/hr
Freed, James D, maint worker, $29,064
Freeman, Angela D, info syss sup, $58,836
Freeman, Kendall L, maint crew leader, $39,156
Freeman, Matthew, maint worker, $29,064
Freeman, Rodney L, materials technician, $28,584
Freeman, William L, maint crew leader, $42,072
Freese, Ronald F, maint crew leader, $46,884
Freeze, James R, sr maint worker, $35,856
Freeze, Kevin P, sr maint worker, $33,996
Freie, Mark E, intermed maint wrkr, $31,164
French, David M, sr maint worker, $33,996
French, Thomas E, intermed equip tech, $35,856

Frerking, Darryl W, maint crew leader, $37,800
Frese, Rob A, sr traffic studies special, $55,620
Fretwell, Mark E, structural dsgnr, $46,044
Friederich, Zachary R, materials intern, $13.36/hr
Friedli, Tyler W, maint crew leader, $36,504
Friedrich, Allen E, sr const insp, $61,092
Fries, Scott W, maint worker, $29,064
Fritchey, Dennis L, sr maint worker, $36,504
Fritz, Lawrence W, br inspection crew sup, $46,884
Frizzell, Michael W, sr const insp, $56,676
Fry, Dean D, dist final plans & rep proc, $40,608
Fuemmeler, Charles A, maint crew leader, $36,504
Fuhro, Paula B, sr ofc asst, $28,104
Fulks, Michael A, sr maint worker, $34,596
Fuller, James A, intermed maint wrkr, $31,164
Fuller, Rodney B, sr maint worker, $33,996
Fuller, William C, sr maint worker, $42,816
Fullington, James W, intermed maint wrkr, $31,164
Fulton, Jessie C, sr maint worker, $35,856
Fuqua, Virgena A, sr bldg cstdn, $24,540
Furr, Jeremy E, sr maint worker, $34,596
Gabathuler, John W, sr maint worker, $42,816
Gabel, Jeffrey S, materials insp, $46,884
Gabelsberger, Richard A, structural analyst, $45,192
Gabler, William F, hwy dsgnr, $47,736
Gabriel, Marilyn M, dist final plans & rep proc, $42,072
Gahagan, John E, sr info syss technologist, $50,676
Gaines, Charles H, maint crew leader, $45,192
Gaiser, Robert M, intermed maint wrkr, $31,164
Galen, Stephen W, maint worker, $29,064
Gallagher, Deborah L, inter const tech, $33,996
Gallagher, Timothy J, asst equip technician, $28,584
Gallagher, William D, sr maint worker, $34,596
Gallatin, Timothy M, maint crew leader, $36,504
Gamache, Cynthia M, sr info syss technologist, $48,828
Gambaro, Anthony J, sr const insp, $54,600
Gamblin, Bryce D, sr administrative counsel, $71,448
Gander, Jeffery L, resident engr, $71,016
Gander, Russell L, sr maint worker, $34,596
Gandy, Archie R, sr maint worker, $35,220
Garcia, Herberto F, sr maint worker, $34,596
Garcia, Richard, sr maint worker, $37,140
Gardner, Jackie W, sr maint worker, $35,220
Gardner, Jeff J, incident mgmt coordinatr, $51,624
Garner, Douglas R, maint crew leader, $42,072
Garner, John W, sr maint worker, $35,220
Garner, Rockey L, maint crew leader, $42,816
Garnett, Amy K, sr fin servs speciali, $53,580
Garrett, Darrin G, sr maint worker, $34,596
Garrett, Marc B, sr maint worker, $37,140
Garrett, Stephen L, intermed maint wrkr, $31,164
Garrison, John N, intermed maint wrkr, $31,164
Garrison, Randy L, sr maint worker, $38,472
Gartner, Kenneth W, sr paralegal, $47,736
Garver, Bradley S, maint worker, $29,064
Gasama, Sheku A, equip technician, $32,280
Gaskins, Steven M, maint worker, $29,064
Gassen, Ronald W, intermed maint wrkr, $32,280
Gater, Kiana J, design intern, $11.64/hr
Gates, Andrew M, sr comm spec, $47,736
Gates, Bradford A, maint supt, $55,620
Gates, Tony J, maint sup, $46,884
Gathings, Alton P, maint worker, $29,064
Gaudette, Addisen W, seasonal maint worker, $12.44/hr
Gaul, Richard A, sr maint worker, $34,596
Gaunt, Corey A, materials intern, $13.85/hr
Gayman, Matthew D, asst maint sup, $43,608
Gebhards, Raymond L, maint crew leader, $39,156
Gedris, Bentley M, hwy dsgnr, $46,044
Gehringer, Ellen H, hr mgr, $63,408
Gehrke, Tyler E, maint worker, $29,064
Geiger, Matthew D, bridge insp, $50,676
Geisendorfer, Jody B, asst maint sup, $41,316
Geldmacher, Kevin M, inter const insp, $44,400
Gentry, Donald R, sr info syss technologist, $56,676
Gentry, Keith A, maint supt, $56,676
Gentry, Richard P, maint worker, $29,064
Geohagan, Douglas J, maint crew leader, $37,140
George, Jerome D, sr traffic spec, $45,192

Georges, Stephen A, sr hwy dsgnr, $53,580
Gerke, Christopher E, sr maint worker, $33,996
Gerke, Donna J, sr maint worker, $35,856
Gerlemann, Gary J, sr maint worker, $39,156
Gerlemann, Richard L, sr equip technician, $42,072
Germann, Daniel P, sr maint worker, $34,596
Gerstenecker, Danielle K, traffic intern, $13.36/hr
Gettemeier, Kathy L, maint sup, $47,736
Gholson, Randy R, sr maint worker, $40,608
Gibbons, Nicholas J, inter const insp, $47,736
Gibbs, Lonnie G, sr maint worker, $35,220
Gibson, David W, maint worker, $29,064
Gibson, Jeremy G, sr equip technician, $45,192
Gibson, Joe T, sr maint worker, $34,596
Gibson, Ronald T, maint supt, $54,600
Gieck, Janis M, sr cust serv rep, $36,504
Giedinghagen, Gregory K, intermed maint wrkr, $31,164
Giesken, Jason A, sr maint worker, $35,220
Giesken, Karen L, const proj ofc asst, $28,104
Giffin, Philip E, inter const insp, $44,400
Gilgour, Caleb C, sr maint worker, $35,220
Gillaspie, Robert L, sr enginerring tech-tpt/ss, $21.92/hr
Gillespie, Garrett D, equip technician superviso, $49,752
Gillespie, Gloria J, sr fin servs speciali, $47,736
Gillespie, James R, resident engr, $71,016
Gillespie, Marvin L, maint supt, $58,836
Gillette, Brandon A, sr maint worker, $35,220
Gillette, Walter L, seasonal maint worker, $12.44/hr
Gilliland, Randy A, sr civil rights spec, $50,676
Gillispie, Dustin G, maint worker, $29,064
Gillmore, Lisa M, sr motor carrier agent, $35,856
Gilmore, Harry F, lead info syss technologist, $55,620
Gilmore, Trina L, maint worker, $29,064
Gilpatrick, Joshua R, intermed maint wrkr, $31,164
Gilpin, Jamie L, maint worker, $29,064
Gilreath, Kevin E, maint worker, $29,064
Gimse, William A, maint sup, $46,884
Girgin, Aydogan L, sr const insp, $52,596
Girth, Ronald D, sr maint worker, $36,504
Givens, Marcus H, maint worker, $29,064
Glaser, Douglas D, maint crew leader, $37,800
Glaser, Randall S, transp proj dsgnr, $79,056
Glasgow, Timothy R, sr maint worker, $34,596
Glastetter, Gary L, sr maint worker, $33,996
Glastetter, Heather K, cust serv rep, $30,102
Glastetter, Sherry L, rt of way mgr, $73,788
Glenn, Dale W, core drill supt, $55,620
Glenn, Trey M, maint worker, $29,064
Glosemeyer, Carla E, maint crew leader, $36,504
Glover, Amy R, sr paralegal, $47,736
Glover, Kenny, sr info syss technologist, $56,676
Gluzman, Yan W, sr traffic studies special, $59,928
Goble, Billy C, maint worker, $29,064
Goddard, Everett D, sr maint worker, $35,856
Goeller, Christopher G, sr fac opps crew wo, $37,800
Goessmann, Gary S, geologist, $69,672
Goetz, Brittany A, organizational perf ana, $39,156
Goetz, Deloris K, maint sup, $45,192
Goff, Daniel L, sr maint worker, $34,596
Goff, Lucille F, materials testing sup, $45,192
Gohring, Charles E, asst motor carrier serv direct, $76,596
Goins, Douglas A, maint crew leader, $35,856
Golden, Brenda K, sr maint worker, $35,220
Golden, Kevin W, sr maint worker-tpt, $19.78/hr
Golden, Sharon E, asst human resource dir, $92,688
Goldsmith, Clinton M, maint worker, $29,064
Golian, Keith A, maint crew leader, $37,140
Golson, Audra S, sr civil rights spec, $46,884
Golson, Jerome F, sr materials technician, $36,504
Golston, Nettie J, sr ofc asst, $29,592
Gonzales, Louis C, maint worker, $29,064
Good, Kyle A, intermed maint wrkr, $31,164
Goodall, Brian K, sr electrcn, $44,400
Goodall, Donald W, sr maint worker, $35,220
Goodall, Thomas A, maint worker, $29,064
Goodman, Jerry G, bridge maint superintend, $59,928
Goodrich, James A, airplane pilot, $54,600
Goodrich, John S, intermed maint wrkr, $31,164
Goodwyn, Tyler G, sr hwy dsgnr, $54,600

Gordon, Charles D, sr maint worker, $36,504
Gordon, Dave, sr hwy dsgnr, $52,596
Gordon, Timothy D, maint worker, $29,064
Gordon Roberts, Kim I, sr cust serv rep, $42,816
Gosnell, Derek C, maint worker, $29,064
Goss, Garry L, maint supt, $50,676
Gosseen, Deryl F, sr maint worker, $35,220
Goth, Darrell B, sr const insp, $54,600
Gott, Bradley R, maint crew leader, $36,504
Gott, Derrick J, maint sup, $45,192
Gott, Mark R, intermed equip tech, $35,856
Gottman, James E, maint sup, $45,192
Gough, Diana M, sr maint worker, $34,596
Gough, Karin A, sr maint worker, $33,996
Gough, Paula A, dist engr, $103,944
Gowe, Dave, intermed maint wrkr, $31,164
Gower, Gregory A, intermed maint wrkr, $31,164
Grable, David E, sr maint worker, $42,816
Grace-Beasley, Melinda K, asst chief counsel-human rsrcs, $113,340
Grady, Timothy, maint crew leader, $35,856
Graesser, Artur S, traffic intern, $12.47/hr
Graessle, Lauren, structural dsgnr, $46,044
Graf, Douglas E, sr equip technician, $40,608
Graham, Christopher A, sr const insp, $55,620
Graham, Edward A, sr maint worker, $34,596
Graham, Janet K, sr structural technician, $17.55/hr
Graham, Joshua A, intermed maint wrkr, $31,164
Graham, Paul M, sr traffic spec, $43,608
Graham, Stephanie D, environ spec-ss, $37,800
Grame, Thomas W, intermed maint wrkr, $31,164
Grana, John V, resident engr, $71,016
Grandstaff, Brent L, sr maint worker, $38,472
Grannemann, Sherry K, sr plng technician, $46,884
Grant, Jason R, sr maint worker, $34,596
Grapes-Bess, Mindy D, sr traffic technician-nss, $36,504
Gray, Charles P, sr maint worker, $35,220
Gray, Cory M, maint crew leader, $36,504
Gray, Jason E, intermed maint wrkr, $31,164
Gray, Scott D, maint supt, $51,624
Gray, William T, sr maint worker, $34,596
Grayson, Kyle E, sr envirnmental spec, $47,736
Graziano, Tina M, sr administrative technician, $39,156
Green, Arthur J, maint crew leader, $37,800
Green, Chad D, sr cadd spt spec, $47,736
Green, Christopher D, motorist assistance oper, $35,220
Green, Evelyn H, maint worker, $29,064
Green, Harley J, maint crew leader, $41,316
Green, Jason C, sr maint worker, $33,996
Green, Logan M, maint worker, $29,064
Green, Mark R, sr traffic studies special, $56,676
Green, Randon D, const insp, $46,044
Green, Richard J, sr maint worker, $34,596
Green, Robert B, trans proj mgr, $75,180
Green, Robin L, inter materials insp, $44,400
Green, Ron L, sr maint worker, $35,220
Green, Stephanie L, sr administrative technician, $35,856
Green, Steven M, intermed maint wrkr, $31,164
Green, Timothy P, equip technician superviso, $49,752
Green, Zachariah, intermed maint wrkr, $30,624
Greenfield, Dennis J, sr equip technician, $40,608
Greeno, Davin G, motor carrier proj mgr, $55,620
Greenstreet, Todd E, maint sup, $47,736
Greenwood, Brianne L, sr historic preserve speci, $47,736
Greer, Lori L, field materials engr, $59,928
Greer, Lyndell L, sr maint worker, $35,856
Gregg, David M, sr fin servs tech, $33,996
Gregg, Thomas C, land surv, $49,752
Gregory, Bryan S, aviation opps mgr, $59,928
Gregory, Darnell K, intermed maint wrkr, $31,164
Gregory, Deborah E, sr fin servs speciali, $52,596
Gregory, Tamara S, sr r/w spec, $49,752
Greig, Eric S, sr maint worker, $33,996
Gremaud, James R, trans proj mgr, $81,108
Greufe, Robert J, sr maint worker, $34,596
Grgurich, Clint A, sr maint worker, $33,996
Gribble, Kurt E, structural liaison engr, $82,692
Gricher, Ronald R, motorist assistance oper, $39,876
Griep, Kevin D, sr gen servs spec, $50,676

Griffaw, Russell A, sr survey technician, $37,140
Griffin, Billy L, hwy dsgnr, $39,876
Griffin, Pamela G, sr hr spec, $53,580
Griffin, William J, sr maint worker, $40,608
Griffith, James B, sr maint worker, $34,596
Griffith, Kyle C, equip technician intern, $10.87/hr
Griffitt, Leslie A, const proj ofc asst, $29,592
Grigsby, Johnny D, maint sup, $50,676
Grimes, Cheryl M, sr const technician, $37,800
Grimm, Andrew J, bridge inventory analyst, $36,504
Gripka, Donald B, resident engr, $64,632
Groenda, Janet F, sr hr spec, $47,736
Groes, Candy D, sr fin servs speciali, $49,752
Groff, Aaron J, sr hwy dsgnr, $57,756
Grogan, Kerry P, sr maint worker, $34,596
Gronniger, Anthony C, intermed maint wrkr, $31,164
Groose, Loren C, sr maint worker, $33,996
Gross, Stanley R, land survey sup, $46,884
Grossman, Curtis R, maint sup, $45,192
Grosvenor, Todd M, special projs coord, $69,672
Grote, Anthony G, asst maint sup, $41,316
Grote, Randy W, sr maint worker, $34,596
Grothoff, Darryl E, sr printing technician, $40,608
Grothoff, Tina L, sr cust serv rep, $37,800
Gruber, Erin L, transp proj dsgnr, $65,856
Gruenloh, Lambert F, sr maint worker, $42,072
Gruenloh, Travis M, maint crew leader, $36,504
Grundvig, Terri C, seasonal maint worker, $12.44/hr
Guerin, Billy E, sr maint worker, $35,220
Guerin, David W, sr maint worker, $35,220
Guerrero, Steven M, intermed maint wrkr, $31,164
Guess, Gary D, sr maint worker, $35,220
Guess, Lance L, maint worker, $29,064
Guffey, Michael E, sr maint worker, $33,996
Guillen, Juan P, sr maint worker, $35,220
Gundel, Joe D, intermed maint wrkr, $31,164
Gunnels, Johnny R, sr maint worker, $34,596
Gunter, Travis L, const insp, $44,400
Gust, Jonathan A, sr maint worker, $34,596
Hackman, Dylan J, hwy dsgnr, $45,192
Haddix, Zachary B, seasonal maint worker, $12.44/hr
Haden-Stiles, Julie A, sr hwy dsgnr, $54,600
Haeffner, Brian A, area engr, $76,596
Hageman, Kevin W, maint sup, $45,192
Hagemeyer, David J, bridge inspection engr, $64,632
Hagen, Dennis A, sr maint worker, $34,596
Hagen, Michael H, maint crew leader, $36,504
Hagenhoff, Sandra K, sr fin servs tech, $39,876
Hager, Garrett L, design intern, $13.85/hr
Hager, James F, maint supt, $50,676
Hager, Mark S, sr maint worker, $33,996
Haggard, Joseph H, sr const insp, $56,676
Hagston, Nicolette S, fac opps crew worke, $13.12/hr
Hahn, Benjamin J, seasonal maint worker, $12.44/hr
Hahn, Doug E, sr maint worker, $33,996
Hahn, Eric R, sr equip technician, $40,608
Hailey, Marcus L, asst equip technician, $32,280
Haines, Glenn D, maint crew leader, $39,876
Hake, Donald R, sr maint worker, $34,596
Hake, James C, sr maint worker, $34,596
Hake, Jeramy D, sr equip technician, $40,608
Hake, Patrick J, sr estimator, $58,836
Halamar, Frank M, maint crew leader, $37,800
Halbert, Jeffrey L, maint sup, $46,884
Halbert, Michael S, maint crew leader, $36,504
Hale, Charles E, maint worker, $29,064
Hale, Marlene O, intermed maint wrkr, $31,680
Hale, Ryan T, sr hwy dsgnr, $56,676
Halford, Ashley L, empl benefits mgr, $55,620
Halford, Brent S, maint crew leader, $43,608
Hall, Brian K, sr maint worker, $35,220
Hall, Donald L, sr maint technician, $37,140
Hall, Garry L, sr maint worker, $38,472
Hall, Jennifer J, outdoor advertising spec, $47,736
Hall, Johnny L, sr equip technician, $42,072
Hall, Kelly A, maint crew leader, $37,800
Hall, Les H, maint worker, $29,064
Hall, Marcus D, motorist assistance oper, $35,856
Hall, Marion T, registered arch, $55.00/hr

Hall, Michael L, sr maint worker, $35,220
Hall, Shirley T, airport proj technician, $43,608
Hall, Timothy K, motorist assistance oper, $35,220
Halley, Roger P, sr maint worker, $38,472
Halton, Russell W, sr auditor, $50,676
Ham, Mark S, sr maint worker, $35,220
Hamelink, Darin R, area engr, $67,092
Hamilton, Billy D, sr maint worker, $34,596
Hamilton, John W, intermed maint wrkr, $30,624
Hamilton, Nevin B, maint crew leader, $36,504
Hamilton, Philip E, fac opps sup, $47,736
Hamlin, David K, sr maint worker, $34,596
Hamm, Rick G, maint crew leader, $36,504
Hampson, Seth A, maint worker, $29,064
Hampton, Amy A, hr technician, $28,584
Hampton, Herman, maint worker, $29,064
Hancock, Mark S, asst maint sup, $42,072
Hancock, Paul D, maint crew leader, $35,856
Haner, Kevin M, sr equip technician, $44,400
Haney, Jacob T, maint worker, $29,064
Haney, Jerry D, sr maint worker, $33,996
Hanke, Nicole D, const intern, $13.36/hr
Hanks, Andrew C, aviation progs mgr, $65,856
Hanks, Gretchen F, sr hwy dsgnr, $50,676
Hanna, David N, electrcn asst, $32,280
Hannar, Christina L, maint sup, $48,828
Hannar, Jess J, sr maint worker, $34,596
Hansen, Bradley H, intermed maint wrkr, $33,396
Harangozo, Keith M, inter const tech, $33,396
Harbian, Melissa N, legal ofc mgr, $46,884
Harbin, Jake R, sr maint worker, $34,596
Hardie, Laurie J, sr maint worker, $35,220
Hardy, David L, motorist assistance oper, $40,608
Hardy, Dustin J, sr equip technician, $42,816
Hardy, Jeffrey J, dist design engr, $82,692
Hardy, Terry L, intermed maint wrkr, $31,164
Harfst, Dale G, sr fac opps crew wo, $32,280
Hargrave, Robert J, sr const technician, $37,800
Hargrove, James M, sr maint worker, $35,220
Hargus, Craig R, maint worker, $29,064
Harlan, Pamela J, sec to the commission, $67,092
Harlan, Stuart A, lead info syss technologist, $56,676
Harman, Paul S, sr structural dsgnr, $61,092
Harmon, Carolyn S, sr hr technic, $42,072
Harmon, Donald N, intermed maint wrkr, $31,164
Harmon, Donald W, sr maint worker-tpt, $14.59/hr
Harmon, Jason M, maint crew leader, $36,504
Harms, Derek J, intermed maint wrkr, $31,164
Harms, Michael D, structural liaison engr, $84,288
Harpenau, Rodney J, trans enforce investi supv, $49,752
Harper, Bart D, sr const insp, $63,408
Harper, Devin M, sr maint worker, $33,996
Harper, Jennifer L, research engr, $62,232
Harper, Ryan A, maint worker, $29,064
Harreld, David E, maint worker, $29,064
Harris, Brandon S, transp enfrcmnt investigator, $37,800
Harris, Brenda K, sr r/w spec, $51,624
Harris, Cade R, seasonal maint worker, $12.44/hr
Harris, Caleb M, maint crew leader, $36,504
Harris, Charles G, maint worker, $29,064
Harris, Clint, intermed maint wrkr, $31,164
Harris, Erica M, fin servs spec, $37,800
Harris, Jason B, sr maint worker, $34,596
Harris, Lindsay M, sr traffic studies special, $56,676
Harris, Lindsey L, interm fin serv speciali, $42,072
Harris, Malcolm R, sr maint worker, $33,396
Harris, Mark L, inter materials insp, $49,752
Harris, Michael A, intermed maint wrkr, $31,164
Harris, Michael K, sr hwy dsgnr, $50,676
Harris, Michael W, maint crew leader, $39,876
Harris, William J, sr maint worker, $39,156
Harris, Zachary L, maint worker, $29,064
Harris-Turner, Judy M, const proj ofc asst, $36,504
Hart, Gary D, sr const insp, $50,676
Hart, Onas E, maint crew leader, $37,140
Hart-Hopkins, Elizabeth L, maint crew leader, $36,504
Hartman, David J, maint worker, $29,064
Hartman, Heath E, sr const insp, $50,676
Hartman, Randall E, asst to the dist engr, $82,692

Hartman, Vernon J, sr fabrication technician, $62,232
Hartnagel, Bryan A, structural resource mgr, $79,596
Hartung, Sammy L, traffic spec, $39,876
Hartwig, Keith A, maint supt, $56,676
Harvel, Bruce A, geologist, $68,364
Harvey, Bobbie M, administrative technician, $28,584
Harvey, Darrin E, sr maint worker, $37,140
Harvey, Jason G, sr equip technician, $42,816
Harvey, Kathryn P, asst chief engr, $126,204
Harvey, Kerry A, sr maint worker, $34,596
Hasanovic, Nevzeta, sr traffic studies special, $55,620
Haskew, James K, sr maint worker, $33,996
Haskins, Jarren M, seasonal maint worker, $12.44/hr
Haslag, Allan C, sr maint worker, $37,140
Haslag, Dawn T, sr traffic technician-nss, $39,876
Haslag, Diane M, info syss sup, $61,092
Haslag, Patrick J, intermed design technicn, $32,280
Hassinger, Edward W, chief engr, $138,648
Hasson, Owen W, incident mgmt coordinatr, $55,620
Hastings, Daniel J, sr r/w spec, $49,752
Hastings, Spencer L, maint worker, $29,064
Hatch, Gregory P, sr maint worker, $33,996
Hathaway, Kurtis K, inter const insp, $44,400
Hathcock, Mark D, sr maint worker, $36,504
Hauser, Rodney W, sr maint worker, $34,596
Hawken, Gregory D, maint worker, $29,064
Hawkins, Charles L, electrcn, $40,608
Hawkins, Earl D, maint worker, $29,064
Hawkins, Jeremy P, sr maint worker, $34,596
Hawkins, Kevin E, maint worker, $29,064
Hawkins, Martin W, maint sup, $45,192
Hawkins, Robert J, maint supt, $50,676
Hawkins, William A, intermed maint wrkr, $31,164
Hawkins, Willie C, sr survey technician, $41,316
Hay, Brent D, sr trns enfrcemnt investigator, $46,044
Hayden, Ena M, sr materials insp, $51,624
Hayden, John D, equip tech spt spec, $49,752
Hayes, James R, land surv, $51,624
Haynes, Amanda J, exec asst, $32,280
Hays, Bradley E, inter const insp, $45,192
Hays, Timothy A, sr materials insp, $52,596
Hays, Timothy L, asst maint sup, $40,608
Hayslett, Carl A, seasonal maint worker, $12.44/hr
Hazlett, Timothy A, structural dsgnr, $46,044
Heath, Jason E, intermed maint wrkr, $31,164
Heathman, Alan G, motor assistance shift supv, $40,608
Heavin, Kevin L, sr maint worker, $35,220
Heavin, Stephen N, maint sup, $50,676
Hecht, Kory E, sr maint worker, $33,996
Heck, David B, sr const insp, $56,676
Heck, Eric T, materials insp, $46,044
Heckendorn, Richard K, sr maint worker, $37,800
Heckert, Stacy R, sr outdoor advertising perm sp, $42,816
Heckman, Bryan J, sr multimodal oper spec, $51,624
Heckman, Dennis W, state bridge engr, $103,944
Hedrick, Brody D, maint crew leader, $35,856
Heerboth, Bruce M, sr info syss technologist, $50,676
Heeter, Mari L, sr r/w spec, $51,624
Hefner, Tammy M, resident engr, $65,856
Heidlage, Dennis G, sr equip technician, $42,816
Heinlein, Matthew J, sr maint worker, $34,596
Heintz, Allison M, sr risk mgmt technic, $32,280
Heitmann, Jacob L, sr maint worker, $35,220
Held, Steven H, intermed maint wrkr, $30,624
Hellebusch, Tim A, resident engr, $69,672
Helton, Stephen D, sr electrcn, $49,752
Hemme, David P, sr maint worker, $34,596
Henderson, Dale M, structural hydraulics engr, $73,788
Henderson, Eli T, intermed maint wrkr, $31,164
Henderson, Michael E, trans plng specia, $57,756
Henderson, Wayne H, sr equip technician, $42,816
Hendricks, Robert E, asst maint sup, $42,072
Hendricks-Brown, April J, sr civil rights spec, $51,624
Hendrix, Bradley J, maint crew leader, $36,504
Hendrix, Shaun L, sr maint worker, $34,596
Hendrix, Steven C, maint worker, $29,064
Henke, Joseph E, sr maint worker, $35,220
Henke, Paul J, maint crew leader, $38,472
Henley, Kenneth W, sr maint worker, $37,140

Henningfeld, Edward J, maint worker, $29,064
Henry, Billy J, intermed maint wrkr, $31,164
Henry, David W, maint crew leader, $37,800
Henry, Randy W, sr maint worker, $35,220
Hensen, Kelly R, maint sup, $46,884
Hensley, Michael L, sr maint worker, $37,800
Henson, Benjamin R, sr maint worker, $33,996
Henson, Brandon W, sr maint worker, $34,596
Henson, Brian W, maint crew leader, $36,504
Henson, Christofer F, motorist assistance oper, $33,996
Henson, David E, sr maint worker, $34,596
Henson, Eric J, maint crew leader, $39,156
Henson, James D, asst maint sup, $40,608
Henson, Jerome C, maint sup, $50,676
Henson, Lester E, asst maint sup, $40,608
Henson, Robert W, sr structural technician, $36,504
Hentges, Valerie A, int environ spec-ss, $45,192
Herbst, David L, sr equip technician, $46,884
Herd, Rodney D, motorist assistance oper, $34,596
Herigon, Julie A, auditor, $37,800
Hernandez, Francisco G, sr maint worker, $33,996
Herndon, Steve E, intermed maint wrkr, $31,164
Heronemus, Seth M, design intern, $12.47/hr
Herrera, Olmedo, multimedia servs spec, $32,280
Herron, Dustin W, sr equip technician, $46,044
Hertel, Michael D, maint worker, $29,064
Heryford, Ryan A, intermed maint wrkr, $31,164
Herzog, David L, asst maint sup, $40,608
Hess, Edward J, dist bridge engr, $79,596
Hess, Paula A, sr maint worker, $34,596
Hessenflow, Chad L, sr maint technician, $36,504
Heuring, Danny R, sr maint worker, $37,140
Heussner, Haden A, maint worker, $29,064
Hibdon, Timothy R, maint crew leader, $38,472
Hibler, Austin D, ast dist constr & mater en, $63,408
Hickey, Kimberly A, hr mgr, $62,232
Hickman, Darrel L, maint crew leader, $42,072
Hicks, Bret A, maint supt, $52,596
Hicks, Johnny W, sr fac opps spe, $41,316
Hicks, Michele E, sr hwy dsgnr, $53,580
Hiebert, Charles M, asst comm dir, $76,596
Higgs, Mark P, sr maint worker, $33,396
Hilburn-Thomas, Kimberly D, sr traffic spec, $45,192
Hilchen, Paul E, geotech engr, $62,232
Hildenbrand, Wade D, inter const insp, $54,600
Hill, Charles L, sr maint worker, $34,596
Hill, Deborah L, audit mgr, $62,232
Hill, Devin R, sr ofc asst, $25,380
Hill, Garrett R, seasonal maint worker, $12.44/hr
Hill, Gregory B, maint crew leader, $36,504
Hill, Mark A, maint worker, $29,064
Hill, Mark O, sr maint worker-tpt, $18.74/hr
Hill, Scott W, maint crew leader, $36,504
Hill, Taylor D, sr hwy dsgnr, $52,596
Hill, Terry, sr maint worker, $33,996
Hill, Timothy D, sr maint worker, $33,996
Hill, Timothy J, maint worker, $29,064
Hillis, Douglas L, sr maint worker, $42,072
Hillis, Jeffrey P, sr maint worker, $37,140
Hillner, Garland L, trans proj mgr, $84,288
Hills, Donald A, asst to the resident engi, $59,928
Hills, Justin W, maint sup, $46,884
Hills, Timothy E, sr maint worker, $34,596
Hilsabeck, Michael D, sr maint worker, $33,996
Hilt, Donald R, sr fin servs tech, $37,140
Hilte, Monty D, sr maint worker, $35,856
Hindman, Randall, sr trns enfrcemnt investigator, $44,400
Hinnah, Nicholas J, maint worker, $29,064
Hinson, Jennifer L, dist maint & traffic engin, $81,108
Hinton, Gregory S, sr maint worker, $35,220
Hinton, Joseph D, gen servs mgr, $57,756
Hird, Virginia A, sr maint worker, $36,504
Hitt, Randy C, const & materials liaison engr, $90,948
Hixson, Dennis P, traffic sup, $47,736
Hixson, Katherine A, sr design technician, $37,140
Hixson, Kristi, sr gen servs spec, $49,752
Hoback, Dennis H, sr maint worker, $33,996
Hochlan, Jessica N, int comm spec, $42,072
Hochlan, Tiesun T, motorist assistance oper, $33,996

Hochstatter, David L, intermed maint wrkr, $30,624
Hodges, Jeremy L, commrcial mtr veh prog mgr, $55,620
Hodges, Michael W, dist utilities engr, $64,632
Hodges, Nicole E, cust serv rep, $9.27/hr
Hodges, Tommy R, sr maint worker, $39,876
Hodgson, Kerry W, maint sup, $46,044
Hoecker, Angela S, sr trans planner, $49,752
Hoecker, Joni H, sr risk mgmt technic, $32,832
Hoecker, Tara L, seasonal maint worker, $12.44/hr
Hoeller, Donna J, materials testing spec, $46,044
Hoellering, Dale J, sr maint worker, $34,596
Hoelscher, Stanley P, sr fin servs speciali, $50,676
Hoener, Kenneth F, maint worker, $29,064
Hoener, Stacy A, sr fin servs tech, $32,832
Hoepker, Cody D, maint worker, $29,064
Hoer, Michael P, sr info syss technologist, $47,736
Hoernig, Steven D, traffic opps engr, $64,632
Hof, Brian E, sr equip technician, $44,400
Hoff, Jeannie M, sr traffic studies special-nss, $55,620
Hoffman, Adam C, sr hr technic, $32,280
Hoffman, Steven E, maint worker, $29,064
Hoffman-Everhart, Lisa M, exec asst, $32,280
Hoffmann, Robert C, maint sup, $49,752
Hofmann, Aaron D, inter structural technician, $32,280
Hogan, Deborah L, hr mgr, $59,928
Hografe, Robert K, maint worker, $29,064
Hografe, Steven P, maint worker, $29,064
Hogsett, Roy D, gen servs mgr, $57,756
Hohe, Marc W, sr const technician, $36,504
Hohowski, Christopher J, sr traffic studies special, $27.77/hr
Hoke, Sammie L, sr maint worker-tpt, $18.22/hr
Holcomb, Quentin G, sr maint worker, $34,596
Holcomb, Trevor E, maint worker, $29,064
Holdeman, Craig A, transp proj dsgnr, $64,632
Holder, Joshua L, intermed equip tech, $35,856
Holdmeier, James H, maint crew leader, $36,504
Holdt, Charlene M, final plans rever, $48,828
Holem, Joann R, risk mgmt technician, $28,584
Holland, Barbara E, sr hr technic, $44,400
Holland, Curtis W, sr maint worker, $34,596
Holland, Thomas M, sr maint worker, $33,996
Hollmann, David B, sr traffic studies special, $54,600
Hollmann, Gabrielle S, intermed maint wrkr, $31,164
Hollon, Francis S, sr maint worker, $34,596
Holloway, Michael R, sr hr spec, $51,624
Holloway, Stephen M, sr traffic spec, $46,044
Holmes, Aaron J, intermed maint wrkr, $31,164
Holmes, Billy L, sr maint worker, $35,220
Holmes, Glenn M, intermed maint wrkr, $31,680
Holmes, Marcus D, inter sys mgmt specia, $42,072
Holmes, Morgan T, traffic intern, $11.64/hr
Holt, Brian N, resident engr, $67,092
Holt, James R, sr maint worker, $35,220
Holtmeyer, Gary J, sr litigation counsel, $74,208
Holtsclaw, Brent M, sr maint worker, $33,996
Holtsclaw, Jerica L, design liaison engr, $71,016
Honerkamp, Chad L, maint worker, $29,064
Honeycutt, Dirk R, maint sup, $45,192
Honich, Thomas R, sign & marking engr, $64,632
Honse, Zachary Q, materials insp, $39,876
Hood, Douglas J, fin servs administrat, $64,632
Hood, Nicole A, asst state design engin, $81,108
Hood, Richard W, equip technician, $32,280
Hooper, Alan D, maint sup, $45,192
Hopper, Denise, dist final plans & rep proc, $40,608
Hopper, Jeremy W, fac opps sup, $45,192
Horan, Joseph F, sr field acquisition techn, $36,504
Horbyk, Kristopher A, sr maint worker, $33,996
Horn, Gregory J, dist engr, $110,496
Horn, Linda S, comm coord, $68,364
Horner Gonzalez, Kathryn E, inter const insp, $51,624
Horst, Barry D, dist design engr, $84,288
Horstmann, Gabriel C, sr maint worker, $33,996
Horstmann, Gary O, equip technician - tpt, $23.00/hr
Hortness, Brian W, sr maint worker, $33,996
Horvatic, Ryan P, sr maint worker, $34,596
Hoskins, Randall S, sr gis spec, $47,736
Houchins, Charles R, sr maint worker, $37,800
Houchins, Curtis W, maint sup, $45,192

House, Forrest D, sr maint worker, $37,800
House, Lowell C, sr maint worker, $36,504
House, Reginald B, land survey sup, $56,676
Housewright, Jared C, maint crew leader, $36,504
Houston, Percy L, motor assistance shift supv, $45,192
Howard, Carla J, sr materials insp, $52,596
Howard, Jerry L, intermed maint wrkr, $31,164
Howard, Joseph W, seasonal maint worker, $12.44/hr
Howard, Kent, maint sup, $47,736
Howe, Amanda M, sr maint worker, $34,596
Howell, James A, sr maint worker, $34,596
Howell, Steven R, sr const insp, $52,596
Howerton, Scott D, intermed maint wrkr, $31,164
Howlett, Donald R, sr maint worker, $34,596
Hoyer, Darrell J, maint crew leader, $36,504
Hoyt, Dustin R, const insp, $46,044
Hubbard, Charles R, sr maint worker, $34,596
Hubbard, Christopher A, motor carrier proj mgr, $55,620
Hubbs, Melissa A, sr hr spec, $25.76/hr
Huber, David L, sr maint worker, $35,220
Huber, James W, maint crew leader, $36,504
Huber, John J, sr maint worker, $34,596
Huchteman, Kris A, maint worker, $29,064
Huckaby, Russel C, sr const insp, $52,596
Huckstep, Crystal G, sr maint worker, $34,596
Huddleston, Justin D, sr maint worker, $33,996
Hudnut, Curtis R, maint worker, $29,064
Hudson, Brandon M, maint worker, $29,064
Hudson, Taylor L, traffic intern, $12.47/hr
Hudson, Travis L, maint worker, $29,064
Huey, Aaron S, hwy dsgnr, $47,736
Huff, Josiah S, comp science intern, $13.36/hr
Huff, Robert L, maint worker, $29,064
Huff, Shannon D, maint worker, $29,064
Huffman, Deborah J, trans proj mgr, $33.50/hr
Huffner, Brian L, sr maint worker, $35,220
Hugenberg, Aaron B, bridge insp, $55,620
Hughes, Brenda S, maint crew leader, $40,608
Hughes, Brenten W, maint worker, $29,064
Hughes, Johnny A, sr const insp, $57,756
Hughes, Matthew L, maint crew leader, $36,504
Hughes, Matthias W, const insp, $46,884
Hughes, Troy E, rr projs mgr, $69,672
Huhmann, Thomas W, sr maint worker, $33,996
Huitt, Darin J, asst maint sup, $42,072
Hulbert, Stephen L, bridge inspection crew leader, $38,472
Hulet, Cameron M, maint worker, $29,064
Hulett, Brian S, sr maint worker, $33,996
Hulett, Michael D, sr maint worker, $35,856
Hull, Allen L, sr maint worker, $34,596
Hull, Nathan E, sr electrcn, $42,816
Hulmes, Maria E, intermed maint wrkr, $31,164
Humeida, Arij Y, hwy dsgnr, $43,608
Humphrey, Arlis D, maint crew leader, $37,800
Humphrey, Beth A, sr maint worker, $34,596
Humphrey, Brent D, sr maint worker, $35,856
Humphrey, Phyllis D, sr maint worker, $34,596
Humphrey, Terry L, intermed maint wrkr, $31,164
Hunolt, Robert J, sr maint worker, $34,596
Hunt, Angela N, const insp, $44,400
Hunt, Austin P, maint worker, $29,064
Hunt, Nathan P, maint sup, $46,884
Hunter, Jacob A, maint worker, $29,064
Hunter, Jason E, maint worker, $29,064
Huntsman, Andrew I, sr maint worker, $33,996
Hunziger, Edward R, sr maint worker, $39,156
Hurst, Michael E, sr electrcn, $42,816
Hurt, Larry D, maint crew leader, $39,156
Huseynov, Parviz G, sr trns enfrcemnt investigator, $42,072
Huskey, Lindell G, resident engr, $81,108
Huskey, Mitchell R, sr materials insp, $51,624
Huskey, Paul W, fac opps sup, $49,752
Huskey, Tim A, maint sup, $45,192
Hutto, Dale L, sr maint worker, $34,596
Hyde, Richard A, maint crew leader, $39,876
Hyle, David R, maint crew leader, $42,816
Hynes, Rachelle K, sr r/w spec, $48,828
Iddings, William D, sr maint worker, $43,608
Idel, Larry S, seasonal maint worker, $12.44/hr

Iles, Brian K, resident engr, $67,092
Ilgenfritz, Matthew, asst maint sup, $43,608
Imhoff, Paul J, compensation mgr, $65,856
Imhoff, Terry R, resident engr, $71,016
Ingersoll, Kenneth E, sr maint worker, $37,140
Inglish, Charles L, maint crew leader, $39,876
Ingrum, Eric V, sr const technician, $39,876
Inlow, Randy W, sr maint worker, $39,156
Inman, Douglas S, sr maint worker, $34,596
Inman, Shannon W, sr materials insp, $53,580
Inman, Timothy S, sr maint worker, $40,608
Intaratip, Ploisongsaeng, traffic studies spec, $47,736
Ipock, Randall W, maint supt, $50,676
Irizarry Rivera, Cesar A, sr maint worker, $33,996
Ivie, Danny R, sr maint worker, $34,596
Ivy, Susan E, transp proj dsgnr, $62,232
Jackson, Artemus J, maint worker, $29,064
Jackson, Brian P, maint worker, $29,064
Jackson, Carl G, maint crew leader, $37,800
Jackson, Colin, maint worker, $29,064
Jackson, David E, intermed maint wrkr, $31,164
Jackson, Edward L, maint worker, $29,064
Jackson, Jeremy W, maint sup, $45,192
Jackson, Kelly M, sr comm spec, $47,736
Jackson, Levi, maint worker, $29,064
Jackson, Rebecca L, central ofc gen serv mg, $63,408
Jackson, Robert L, maint worker, $29,064
Jackson, Timothy A, standards spec, $68,364
Jacobs, Alicia D, fin servs technician, $28,584
Jacobs, Mary A, sr plng technician, $42,072
Jacobsen, Keith M, sr supply agent, $37,800
Jacobson, Larry W, resident engr, $67,092
Jacobson, Roberta L, claims administration mgr, $57,756
Jaeger, Aaron D, transp proj dsgnr, $59,928
Jaegers, Deborah K, sr exec asst, $41,316
Jaegers, Joyce A, sr hr technic, $33,996
Jaegers, Kevin A, structural spec, $42,072
Jaegers, Tawnya R, fin servs technician, $29,592
Jaegers, Valerie J, lead info syss technologist, $54,600
James, Alan W, maint worker, $29,064
James, Christopher A, sr equip technician, $40,608
James, Danny R, maint sup, $45,192
James, Dwayne E, maint worker, $31,164
James, James J, sr maint worker, $37,800
James, Kevin C, asst dist engr, $82,692
James, Nathaniel, maint worker, $29,064
Jamison, James A, maint worker, $29,064
Jamison, Kristine A, rr opps mgr, $57,756
Janssens, Albert L, sr const insp, $57,756
Jansson, Matthew N, resident engr, $71,016
Jantosik, Stephen J, land surv, $43,608
Jany, Robert J, transp proj dsgnr, $62,232
Jarquio, Jason L, survey intern, $13.36/hr
Jarrell, Jeffrey D, maint sup, $48,828
Jefferson, Courtney G, intermed maint wrkr, $31,164
Jeffery, Stephen B, sr const insp, $52,596
Jeffreys, Larry D, sr equip technician, $42,072
Jeffries, Amity R, inter risk mgt spec, $42,072
Jeffries, Graig L, motorist assistance oper, $34,596
Jeffries, Justin B, maint crew leader, $36,504
Jenkins, Dustin R, maint crew leader, $36,504
Jenkins, Keith J, sr maint worker, $35,220
Jenkins, Tina M, sr maint worker, $34,596
Jennings, Cody R, intermed maint wrkr, $31,164
Jennings, Karen L, sr maint worker, $37,140
Jennings, Nathan L, maint worker, $29,064
Jernigan, Jerrod B, sr const insp, $56,676
Jett, Desley L, summer maint laborer, $9.27/hr
Jett, Nathan C, sr maint worker-tpt, $23.88/hr
Jewsbury, James A, maint sup, $50,676
Jobson, Jeremy C, maint worker, $29,064
Joedicke, Lawrence A, fac opps spec, $35,856
Joens, Jeffery S, sr materials spec, $52,596
John, Jeena, sr hwy dsgnr, $55,620
Johner, Thomas J, sr maint worker, $32,832
Johns, Billy L, maint crew leader, $37,140
Johns, Kevin E, sr maint worker, $35,220
Johnson, Anthony D, maint worker, $29,064
Johnson, Bradley W, intermed maint wrkr, $32,280

Johnson, Bryan L, maint worker, $29,064
Johnson, Casey S, sr maint worker, $34,596
Johnson, Darrin W, intermed equip tech, $35,856
Johnson, David L, maint sup, $45,192
Johnson, David T, maint worker, $29,064
Johnson, Diana L, inter const insp, $46,044
Johnson, Duane N, sr maint worker, $34,596
Johnson, Harold D, intermed maint wrkr, $31,164
Johnson, Jamie L, const insp, $44,400
Johnson, Jay F, maint crew leader, $36,504
Johnson, Jeffrey M, dist maint engr, $84,288
Johnson, Jermyn, sr materials technician, $37,800
Johnson, Johnny W, sr maint worker-tpt, $15.89/hr
Johnson, Jonathon P, maint worker, $29,064
Johnson, Justin M, maint worker, $29,064
Johnson, Karen L, const proj ofc asst, $36,504
Johnson, Kevin D, sr electrcn, $42,816
Johnson, Kyle B, maint crew leader, $37,800
Johnson, Larry D, sr maint worker, $33,996
Johnson, Larry D, sr maint worker, $41,316
Johnson, Larry T, maint sup, $45,192
Johnson, Leon, intermed maint wrkr, $33,996
Johnson, Marcia N, int comm spec, $42,072
Johnson, Markl T, sr comm spec, $53,580
Johnson, Matthew K, maint crew leader, $36,504
Johnson, Michael A, sr survey technician, $46,884
Johnson, Michael T, sr maint worker, $33,996
Johnson, Randolph T, electrcn asst, $32,280
Johnson, Randy L, traffic center mgr, $76,596
Johnson, Raymond C, sr equip technician, $44,400
Johnson, Robert D, motorist assistance oper, $39,876
Johnson, Rocky J, sr maint worker, $35,856
Johnson, Sara M, sr const technician, $36,504
Johnson, Shannon D, maint crew leader, $36,504
Johnson, Shannon D, sr electrcn, $44,400
Johnson, Shawn M, intermed maint wrkr, $31,164
Johnson, Stanley C, asst dist maint engr, $78,060
Johnson, Stephen D, sr proj rever, $58,836
Johnson, Stowe K, int environ spec-ss, $46,884
Johnson, Tyler, const intern, $13.36/hr
Johnson, William W, sr const insp, $57,756
Johnston, Robert L, sr maint worker, $34,596
Johnston, Sonya A, sr traffic spec, $45,192
Jolley, Wayne D, maint crew leader, $37,140
Jolliffe, Kenneth R, sr maint worker, $34,596
Jolly, Krystal, int tr studies spec, $47,736
Jones, Aaron J, sr const technician, $36,504
Jones, Angelia Y, sr maint worker, $35,220
Jones, Brandon L, sr survey technician, $35,856
Jones, Brent A, sr maint worker, $37,140
Jones, Brent R, sr maint worker, $37,140
Jones, Brian J, sr maint worker, $33,996
Jones, Clinton D, sr maint worker, $35,220
Jones, Cyle M, asst equip technician, $28,584
Jones, Delton R, maint sup, $45,192
Jones, Donald W, sr printing technician, $40,608
Jones, Douglas E, sr const insp, $53,580
Jones, Gary E, sr maint worker, $39,156
Jones, Harold L, sr maint worker, $33,996
Jones, Jeffrey W, sr maint worker, $33,996
Jones, Jennifer J, sr trans planner, $51,624
Jones, Joe H, maint sup, $46,884
Jones, John C, intermed maint wrkr, $31,164
Jones, Joseph A, design technician, $28,584
Jones, Joshua C, maint worker, $29,064
Jones, Kolton R, maint worker, $29,064
Jones, Larry D, sr maint worker, $35,220
Jones, Lee E, sr maint worker, $35,220
Jones, Leslie A, administrative technician, $38,472
Jones, Levi M, sr const technician, $38,472
Jones, Matthew A, rt of way spec, $37,800
Jones, Monnie T, sr maint worker, $33,996
Jones, Phillip M, intermed maint wrkr, $34,596
Jones, Randy W, maint crew leader, $42,816
Jones, Richard R, sr maint worker-tpt, $18.98/hr
Jones, Rickie, sr supply agent, $37,140
Jones, Ronald L, sr maint worker, $34,596
Jones, Scott D, hwy safety prog admin, $64,632
Jones, Ted, maint worker, $29,064

Jones, Travis N, maint supt, $51,624
Jones, Tyrone, maint worker, $29,064
Jones, Willie J, sr maint worker, $35,220
Jordan, Jody L, interm gen serv spec, $42,072
Jordan, Kristina L, maint crew leader, $39,156
Jordan, Patrick T, maint intern, $13.36/hr
Jordon, Lonnie K, maint crew leader, $46,044
Jorgensen, Jennifer L, sr exec asst, $38,472
Jovich, Stanley J, asst maint sup, $40,608
Judah, Thomas C, sr maint worker, $39,876
Judd, Michael R, sr maint worker, $33,996
Judon, Lashawna M, sr maint worker, $35,220
Juliana, Nathan M, sr traffic spec, $43,608
Julien, Malissa S, cert appraiser, $59,928
Jump, Sandra L, const proj ofc asst, $29,064
Jungmeyer, Matthew A, const technician, $28,584
Kadric, Aziz, inter materials insp, $51,624
Kaercher, David L, fac opps spec, $35,856
Kaimann, Vince G, asst to the resident engi, $62,232
Kaiser, Dana L, sr exec asst, $39,876
Kaiser, Eric J, maint sup, $45,192
Kaiser, Jeffrey R, sr maint worker, $36,504
Kaiser, Stacy M, sr hr spec, $49,752
Kallenbach, Cristifer D, tr communication spec, $42,816
Kampeter, Jeremy M, constr mangmnt syss adminis, $62,232
Karlin, Christopher J, const insp, $46,044
Karney, Adam W, intermed maint wrkr, $31,164
Karr, Adam S, maint worker, $29,064
Kassebaum, Katherine H, sr hr technic, $32,280
Kassen, Debra L, maint worker, $29,064
Kauffman, James L, sr maint worker, $35,220
Kaut, Eric W, sr r/w spec, $47,736
Kautz, Richard E, intermed maint wrkr, $31,164
Kavanaugh, James M, sr maint worker, $34,596
Kay, Daniel W, sr maint worker, $33,396
Keating, Henry C, maint worker, $29,064
Keehn, Terry J, sr electrcn, $42,816
Keel, Jerry W, maint worker, $29,064
Keen, Lincoln W, sr materials insp, $56,676
Keena, Paul L, sr equip technician, $47,736
Keeney, Jacob A, maint sup, $45,192
Keeven, Jeffery A, maint crew leader, $37,140
Keim, Matthew F, sr maint worker, $34,596
Lowramce, Michael C, maint worker, $29,064
Keith, Michael J, sr maint worker, $34,596
Kelemen, John M, sr equip technician, $44,400
Kell, Lee A, trans proj mgr, $76,596
Kellar, Sean K, dist traffic engr, $71,016
Keller, Kevin W, sr maint worker, $33,996
Keller, Patrick J, sr equip technician, $41,316
Kelley, Austin W, asst equip technician, $28,584
Kelley, Bradley W, sr info syss technologist, $48,828
Kelley, Matthew E, sr maint worker, $35,220
Kelley, Michelle L, sr cust serv rep, $33,996
Kelley, Richard A, sr maint worker, $33,396
Kellison, Lisa M, sr cust serv rep, $32,832
Kellner, Shannon M, resident engr, $64,632
Kelly, Christopher A, sr const insp, $56,676
Kelly, Gregory S, design intern, $11.64/hr
Kelly, Jeffrey R, maint worker, $29,064
Kelly, Patrick K, sr maint worker, $35,220
Kemmett, Douglas G, sr maint worker, $34,596
Kemna, Aaron C, sr structural engr, $62,232
Kemna, Darren J, sr structural dsgnr, $58,836
Kemp, Samuel D, sr maint worker, $37,800
Kemper, Jonathan, sr maint worker, $34,596
Kemper, Toby J, sr const insp, $53,580
Kempf, Margaret M, bridge intern, $13.36/hr
Kempker, Darren L, sr supply agent, $33,396
Kempker, Roy D, maint sup, $45,192
Kempker, Suzette C, fin servs administrat, $69,672
Kennedy, Joshua L, seasonal maint worker, $12.44/hr
Kennedy, Michael T, int info syss technologist, $42,072
Kenney, John T, sr maint worker, $34,596
Kennicott, Bethanie K, inter hwy dsgnr, $47,736
Kensinger, Gregory T, sr maint worker, $38,472
Kenslow, Calvin T, electrcn asst, $32,280
Kent, Kenton J, intermed maint wrkr, $31,164
Kerby, Jacob D, sr maint worker, $39,156

Kern, Richard D, sr maint worker, $33,996
Kertz, Dustin A, sr maint worker, $35,220
Key, Cody, asst maint sup, $40,608
Kidder, Matthew R, intermed maint wrkr, $31,164
Kidwell, Brian N, asst dist engr, $92,688
Kidwell, Henry C, maint worker, $29,064
Kiefer, Matthew J, trans enforce investi supv, $47,736
Kier, James D, equip technician superviso, $50,676
Kiesling, Kevin M, sr empl dev specia, $46,884
Kiger, Kolt A, maint worker, $29,064
Killen, Andrew R, const intern, $9.84/hr
Killen, Keith A, trans proj mgr, $68,364
Killian, Joseph L, trans planner, $39,876
Killion, Matthew D, area engr, $67,092
Kincaid, Aaron S, employment mgr, $55,620
Kincaid, Paul M, fac opps spec, $35,856
King, Chad D, sr maint worker, $36,504
King, Gary D, maint crew leader, $39,156
King, Gena K, sr maint worker, $34,596
King, Giles W, sr maint worker, $34,596
King, Jason W, maint worker, $29,064
King, Jeffrey S, maint sup, $48,828
King, John W, sr maint worker, $35,220
King, Michael T, sr const insp, $56,676
King, Nathan G, inter const insp, $44,400
King, Ronald D, sr const insp, $50,676
King, Sylvester, maint worker, $29,064
King, Todd N, maint crew leader, $41,316
Kingery, Richard S, dist bridge engr, $68,364
Kinnison, Johnnie L, sr maint worker, $35,220
Kirschman, Eric A, intermed equip tech, $35,856
Kiser, Jeffery J, maint crew leader, $38,472
Kish, Robert A, sr maint worker, $37,140
Kissner, August J, maint worker, $29,064
Kistner-Munson, Cody B, gen laborer, $11.37/hr
Klaus, Donald E, sr maint worker, $38,472
Kleffner, Douglas R, sr maint worker, $36,504
Kleffner, Leann G, sr motor carrier agent, $34,596
Klein, Robert J, equip technician, $32,280
Klein, Russell N, sr const insp, $56,676
Kleinschmit, Sarah K, field materials engr, $59,928
Kliethermes, Alan D, sr equip technician, $42,816
Kliethermes, Carol S, sr fin servs speciali, $55,620
Kliethermes, David W, sr maint worker, $34,596
Kliethermes, Duane L, dist final plans & rep proc, $57,756
Kliethermes, Jerry D, spt servs mgr, $59,928
Kliethermes, Keith J, structural analyst, $48,828
Kliethermes, Mandy A, inter sys mgmt specia, $42,072
Kliethermes, Michelle L, sr hr spec, $46,884
Kliethermes, Ryan J, sr maint worker, $34,596
Kling, Marisa J, sr motor carrier agent, $34,596
Klocke, Darrell, sr maint worker, $43,608
Kloeppel, Shelley J, sr supply agent, $39,156
Knackstedt, Seth A, maint worker, $29,064
Knapp, Christopher S, trans proj mgr, $68,364
Kneib, Ryan M, const insp, $45,192
Knerr, Caleb J, environ spec-ss, $37,800
Knickerbocker, Jon M, asst maint sup, $47,736
Knierim, Darrell S, inter trans planner, $45,192
Knight, Nikki R, intermed maint wrkr, $33,996
Knight, Richard R, maint crew leader, $39,876
Knipp, Dion J, admin of transit, $69,672
Knobloch, Ronald, sr maint worker, $33,996
Knudsen, Michaelene A, hr dir, $108,084
Koch, Brad W, sr maint worker, $35,220
Koch, Cheyenne L, sr fin servs tech, $32,832
Koch, Daniel L, sr equip technician, $42,072
Koch, Kevin J, sr const insp, $54,600
Koch, Timothy L, maint sup, $45,192
Koch, Vernon H, traffic opps sup, $55,620
Koenig, David M, bridge mgmt engr, $81,108
Koenig, John W, rgnal counsel, $101,904
Koenig, Larry K, maint crew leader, $44,400
Koenig, Matthew T, sr maint worker, $36,504
Koenig, Robin R, maint crew leader, $40,608
Koester, Ted S, sr structural dsgnr, $56,676
Koestner, Russell A, sr info syss technologist, $50,676
Koestner, Travis D, asst dist engr, $85,884
Koetting, Beverly A, sr plng technician, $42,816

Kogen, Regina, transp proj dsgnr, $63,408
Kohler, Debra A, sr design technician, $37,800
Kolb, Curt D, sr r/w spec, $49,752
Kolberg, Harry F, maint worker, $29,064
Koll, Richard L, maint crew leader, $43,608
Komnick, Kelsey A, transp proj dsgnr, $59,928
Koochak-Yazdi, Shahid R, sr maint worker, $33,396
Kooman, Carrie L, const proj ofc asst, $34,596
Kopinski, Eric T, stormwater compliance coordina, $57,756
Kopp, Dennis H, sr maint worker, $34,596
Koppitz, Matthew J, const insp, $47,736
Korman, Matthew R, sr maint worker, $33,996
Kottwitz, Leann K, sr gen servs spec, $50,676
Kraft, Fredrick J, sr maint worker, $34,596
Kraft, Paul W, sr equip technician, $48,828
Kramer, Preston L, area engr, $67,092
Kramme, Shane A, maint worker, $29,064
Krapf, Eric F, trans proj mgr, $71,016
Kratky, Jack C, const insp, $39,876
Kraus, Adam R, sr trns enfrcemnt investigator, $42,072
Kraus, Brett W, traffic intern, $13.36/hr
Kraus, Deborah L, sr fin servs speciali, $64,632
Kraus, Jennifer L, sr chemist, $46,884
Kraus, Matthew W, const insp, $46,044
Kreisel, Melissa N, sr r/w spec, $49,752
Kremer, Cindy L, hwy dsgnr, $39,876
Krenning, Dennis P, resident engr, $69,672
Krenning, Teresa A, traffic opps engr, $72,372
Krieg, Kenneth J, maint crew leader, $39,876
Krodinger, Steven S, asst maint sup, $39,876
Kroner, Jeffery W, sr pavement spec, $55,620
Kruessel, Glenn W, sr maint worker, $35,220
Kruger, Jared R, intermed equip tech, $36,504
Krull, Phillip A, maint crew leader, $40,608
Krummel, Mary L, const proj ofc asst, $35,856
Kruse, Lisa L, sr administrative technician, $33,996
Kuder, Danny R, maint crew leader, $36,504
Kuelker, David C, materials insp, $46,044
Kuhlman, John L, sr traffic spec, $49,752
Kuk, Kenneth M, sr maint worker, $33,996
Kumberg, Justin J, sr maint worker, $35,220
Kuntz, Lisa L, area engr, $65,856
Kunze, Cody W, electrcn, $37,800
Kunze, David W, maint crew leader, $36,504
Kurich, Amanda L, traffic intern, $13.36/hr
Kurtz, Kelly F, maint crew leader, $40,608
Kusilek, Shannon D, dist plng mgr, $69,672
Labelle, Ryan J, seasonal maint worker, $12.44/hr
Lacey, William W, maint supt, $51,624
Lackman, Jason T, maint crew leader, $36,504
Lackman, Matthew J, sr sys mgmt specialis, $47,736
Rackers, Melissa R, bridge inventory analyst, $46,044
Lacroix, Richard D, sr traffic syss oper, $34,596
Lacy, Daniel W, maint sup, $45,192
Lacy, Shamar D, maint worker, $29,064
Ladyman, David A, sr maint worker, $34,596
Lafave, Aaron, structural dsgnr, $46,044
Lafaver, Damon L, sr info syss technologist, $49,752
Laffoon, Sam J, intermed maint wrkr, $31,164
Lager, Anthony E, maint crew leader, $41,316
Lair, Gary J, sr rr safety insp, $44,400
Lake, Kyle T, maint worker, $29,064
Lake, Samuel R, intermed maint wrkr, $31,164
Lake, Timmy E, sr maint worker, $42,072
Lake, Tonya E, sr maint worker, $34,596
Lakey, Matthew L, sr equip technician, $40,608
Laks, Michael J, sr electrcn, $46,044
Lalla, Richard T, sr electrcn, $42,816
Lalumondiere, Shawn B, maint sup, $46,044
Lamar, Dwayne A, sr maint worker, $33,996
Lamb, Roger A, sr fac opps spe, $48,828
Lamberson, Julie R, sr chemist, $50,676
Lamberson, Sheri J, sr geotech spec, $53,580
Lambert, Brian P, maint sup, $45,192
Lambert, Jeffrey K, trans plng specia, $67,092
Lambert, Nicholas R, maint crew leader, $36,504
Lambertson, Marty R, maint crew leader, $36,504
Lambeth, Douglas E, maint worker, $29,064
Lambrecht, Paula R, of counsel-tpt, $55.00/hr

Lamons, Gerald D, sr maint worker, $33,996
Lamons, Holden D, hwy dsgnr, $44,400
Lamons, Randy D, const insp, $44,400
Lamp, Nathan D, sr maint worker, $33,996
Lancaster, Nancy M, sr gen servs techni, $37,800
Lance, Jason D, sr maint worker, $34,596
Land, James E, maint worker, $29,064
Landes, Mitchell E, sr maint worker, $34,596
Landon, Ronald K, maint worker, $29,064
Landvik, Michael T, transp plng coord, $55,620
Lane, Allen C, fac opps sup, $45,192
Lane, Anthony T, maint worker, $29,064
Lane, George B, sr maint worker, $34,596
Lane, Karen R, sr const insp, $50,676
Laney, Ronald T, sr equip technician, $49,752
Langa, John N, const intern, $12.47/hr
Lange, Brian D, sr const insp, $56,676
Lankford, Danielle N, risk mgmt technician, $29,064
Lanpher, Patrick S, maint worker, $29,064
Lansford, Robert K, sr maint worker, $35,856
Laplante, John C, sr maint worker, $33,996
Lappe, Jeffery P, sr traffic spec, $43,608
Lara, Rojelio A, maint worker, $29,064
Larimore, Kimberly A, sr hr spec, $25.29/hr
Larimore, Michael D, lead info syss technologist, $58,836
Larose, Robin K, sr maint worker, $33,996
Larson, Edward A, intermed maint wrkr, $31,164
Lasley, Micah J, maint worker, $29,064
Latchaw, Herbert L, sr maint worker, $34,596
Lauer, Micah E, sr maint worker, $34,596
Laughlin, James M, off-sys plans rever, $51,624
Laughlin, Tyler G, intermed safety ofcr, $46,884
Laughlin, Tyler R, chemist Intern, $12.47/hr
Lavender, Brian E, sr traffic technician, $36,504
Lawrence, Dustin D, sr maint worker, $33,996
Lawrence, James L, sr maint worker, $34,596
Lawrence, Melinda A, const proj ofc asst, $28,584
Lawrence, Robert R, maint crew leader, $41,316
Lawson, Donielle M, sr hr spec, $47,736
Lawson, Keith D, maint crew leader, $36,504
Layman, Rodney C, maint crew leader, $37,800
Lea, Randall D, maint crew leader, $37,800
Leach, Charles D, sr maint worker, $35,220
Leach, James L, sr maint worker, $34,596
Leach, Michael D, intermed maint wrkr, $31,164
Leader, Joe A, sr maint worker, $36,504
Leader, Travis R, maint crew leader, $37,140
Leake, Craig S, asst maint sup, $40,608
Leake, Gayle E, sr maint worker, $33,996
Leake, Jeffrey D, maint crew leader, $37,140
Lear, Tyler L, maint worker, $29,064
Leaton, Robert A, maint worker, $29,064
Leavy, Nathan D, maint worker, $29,064
Lebeau, Jeannemarie, sr trans planner, $51,624
Leblanc, Mollie D, asst to the dist engr, $78,060
Lecure, Kara L, fin servs technician, $29,592
Lecure, Philip J, sr maint worker, $39,876
Ledgerwood, David R, sr maint worker, $33,996
Ledgerwood, William D, maint sup, $45,192
Lee, Alexis K, design intern, $12.47/hr
Lee, Dena R, intermed maint wrkr, $31,680
Lee, Keith E, sr maint worker, $34,596
Lee, Kevin A, sr equip technician, $42,816
Lee, Michael J, maint worker, $29,064
Lee, Timothy A, maint crew leader, $42,072
Lee, Tony D, maint worker, $29,064
Lee, Zachary R, const intern, $13.36/hr
Leeks, Christopher B, sr maint worker, $33,396
Leeper, Trevor W, maint crew leader, $37,800
Lee-Williams, Bertha M, sr plng technician, $38,472
Lefarth, Patrick R, maint worker, $29,064
Lefholz, Martin P, sr electrcn, $42,816
Lehmann, Robert D, maint crew leader, $37,140
Leible, Jeffrey L, maint sup, $45,192
Leicher, David O, maint crew leader, $40,608
Leingang, Elizabeth C, plng intern, $14.59/hr
Lemaster, Lisa A, sr govt rel spec, $51,624
Lemley, Benjamin J, electrcn asst, $32,280
Lemmon, Joe D, maint sup, $46,044

Lemon, Stephanie A, sr materials technician, $37,140
Lemongelli, Patricia L, dist const & materials eng, $79,596
Lemons, Kevin L, sr maint worker, $34,596
Lenon, Rebecca S, const proj ofc asst, $27,156
Leonard, Bradley A, fac opps sup, $56,676
Leonard, David R, sr maint worker, $34,596
Lepage, Kyle D, sr multimodal oper spec, $50,676
Lepper, Derek F, sr const insp, $54,600
Lesmeister, Kourtney L, intermed maint wrkr, $30,624
Lesmeister, Robert E, maint worker, $29,064
Lester, Gregory S, sr maint worker, $34,596
Lewandowski, Nicholas G, hwy dsgnr, $46,044
Lewis, Carolyn D, const proj ofc asst, $30,624
Lewis, Clinton F, sr equip technician, $41,316
Lewis, Harvey D, maint sup, $51,624
Lewis, Holly, motorist assistance oper, $16.63/hr
Lewis, Jeffrey W, maint crew leader, $44,400
Lewis, Jerry A, maint crew leader, $39,876
Lewis, Jerry L, sr const technician, $37,800
Lewis, John C, resident engr, $75,180
Lewis, Lawrence W, maint crew leader, $37,140
Lewis, Lynn R, sr survey technician, $41,316
Lewis, Marc E, dist info systm mgr, $55,620
Lewis, Michael J, maint sup, $46,044
Lewis, Shelly K, sr fabrication technician, $53,580
Lewis, William A, sr equip technician, $40,608
Liao, Tao, const insp, $48,828
Libbert, Janice A, exec asst, $32,280
Libbert, Ryan J, transp proj dsgnr, $59,928
Libbert, Trevor L, sr materials technician, $36,504
Libby, Michael D, sr maint worker, $35,220
Libeer, Jacob B, const intern, $13.14/hr
Licklider, Christopher B, sr maint worker, $34,596
Liebhart, David J, sr const insp, $51,624
Lightfoot, Joseph E, maint worker, $29,064
Lightner, Michael R, intermed maint wrkr, $31,164
Liles, Martin W, dist maint & traffic engin, $79,596
Lim, Marecar A, design intern, $13.36/hr
Limbaugh, Steve B, sr maint worker, $35,856
Linam, Lewis A, sr maint worker, $35,220
Lincoln, Martin D, resident engr, $67,092
Lindbloom, David L, sr maint worker, $41,316
Lindeman, Timothy J, sr maint worker, $39,156
Lindemann, Clyde J, maint worker, $29,064
Lindquist, Virginia L, sr bldg cstdn, $12.84/hr
Lindsay, Ernest E, electrcn asst, $32,280
Lindsay, Tyler R, sr structural dsgnr, $56,676
Lindsey, Sheanna L, maint worker, $29,064
Linhart, Robert W, sr maint worker, $35,856
Link, Dylan C, const insp, $46,044
Linneman, Bradley C, maint worker, $29,064
Linthacum, Joeann A, maint worker, $29,064
Lipper, Deborah F, sr maint worker, $37,140
Lipper, Linley J, sr maint worker, $37,140
Lippold, Larry J, const intern, $14.59/hr
Lipsey, Charlotte D, const proj ofc asst, $35,856
Little, Kirsty A, const insp, $47,736
Littleton, Ryan M, sr maint worker, $35,220
Litzau, Michael J, sr const insp, $50,676
Livesay, Robin L, sr const insp, $54,600
Livingston, Charles J, maint worker, $29,064
Livingston, Deron S, maint crew leader, $37,140
Lizenbee, Larry W, sr maint worker, $37,140
Lockard, Robert E, sr maint worker, $37,140
Lockett, Steven H, sr traffic studies special, $58,836
Loe, Derek R, sr maint worker, $33,396
Loesing, Mark E, maint worker, $29,064
Loethen, Clinton M, int info syss technologist, $42,072
Loftin, Paul R, interm gen serv spec, $42,072
Logan, Darby D, sr trans planner, $50,676
Logsden, Douglas F, sr maint worker, $34,596
Logsdon, Charles D, sr maint worker, $35,220
Lohman, Tonya R, area engr, $68,364
Lohsandt, James R, sr const insp, $52,596
Lollar, Clayton F, sr maint worker, $34,596
Lombeida, Andres F, maint worker, $30,624
Long, Andrew K, const insp, $41,316
Long, Brian K, maint crew leader, $43,608
Long, David R, inter const insp, $44,400

Long, Dustin M, maint worker, $29,064
Long, Forrest L, sr maint worker, $37,140
Long, Heath A, maint worker, $29,064
Long, James A, sr maint worker, $34,596
Long, Jeffery D, sr maint worker, $33,996
Long, Keith E, sr traffic spec, $44,400
Long, Kenneth R, sr maint worker, $33,996
Long, Kevin W, sr maint worker, $33,996
Long, Robert W, asst maint sup, $40,608
Long, William L, sr maint worker, $35,220
Longoria, Maria T, sr hwy dsgnr, $50,676
Loomer, Gerald E, maint worker, $29,064
Loomis, Bruce L, maint worker, $29,064
Lootens, Joyce A, sr ofc asst-tpt, $16.06/hr
Lopez, Sergio, maint worker, $29,064
Lord, Bryan J, maint worker, $29,064
Lorenz, Jeffrey A, sr maint worker, $35,220
Lorigan, Michael A, sr maint worker, $34,596
Loughridge, Lucas R, sr fac opps spe, $40,608
Lovan, Marsha A, const proj ofc asst, $33,996
Lovatt, Raymond J, maint worker, $29,064
Love, Michael J, sr maint worker, $33,996
Love, Paul M, maint worker, $29,064
Love, Russ A, sr const insp, $53,580
Loveland, Bobby C, sr maint worker, $35,220
Lovins, Joseph C, maint worker, $29,064
Lowe, Roscoe D, maint worker, $29,064
Lowery, Ethan S, equip technician, $32,280
Lowrance, Todd W, maint crew leader, $36,504
Lucas, Kelly D, rt of way dir, $99,072
Lucas, Mario A, maint worker, $29,064
Lucas, Rose A, sr civil rights spec, $47,736
Luck, Rhonda A, structural spec, $42,072
Ludens, Steven H, maint crew leader, $36,504
Ludiker, Allan J, trans proj mgr, $73,788
Ludwick, Gary L, maint crew leader, $39,156
Ludwig, Amy M, admin of aviation, $69,672
Luebbering, Julie A, gen servs technician, $32,832
Luebbert, Michelle M, sr ofc asst, $13.51/hr
Luebrecht, Patrick W, sr maint worker, $38,472
Luecke, Brook E, benefits spec, $37,800
Luecke, Dean M, sr maint worker, $34,596
Lueckenhoff, Jason H, comp science intern, $13.36/hr
Lueckenhoff, Marc J, structural dsgnr, $46,044
Lueckenotto, Pamela S, mc investigations spec, $48,828
Lule, Francisco C, sr maint worker, $33,996
Lunatto, Mark L, intermed maint wrkr, $30,624
Lunceford, Josiah T, seasonal maint worker, $12.44/hr
Lund, Darrin G, sr equip technician, $42,072
Lundry, Franklin P, sr maint worker, $34,596
Lunsford, Darin M, maint crew leader, $37,800
Lurtz, Nicholas E, maint crew leader, $35,856
Lutgen, William J, maint crew leader, $35,856
Luther, James D, sr const insp, $50,676
Luther, Lynelle S, asst to the resident engi, $76,596
Luther, William E, maint crew leader, $39,876
Luttrell, Gari L, sr paralegal, $47,736
Luttrell, Jason D, sr maint worker, $35,220
Luttrull, Christopher A, maint worker, $29,064
Lutz, Glen M, sr maint worker, $35,220
Lybarger, David L, sr maint worker, $35,856
Lynch, Kenneth L, sr electrcn, $45,192
Lynch, R Daniel P, maint crew leader, $36,504
Lynch, Robert T, area engr, $79,596
Lyon, Gregory T, sr maint worker, $34,596
Lyon, Richard O, sr equip technician, $42,816
Lyons, Scott G, sr maint worker, $34,596
Lyston, Gerald C, maint crew leader, $36,504
Lytton, Kevin B, asst maint sup, $42,816
Maasen, Leon J, sr maint worker, $39,876
Maassen, Eric V, inter const insp, $51,624
Mabery, Eric L, sr maint worker, $33,396
Mabury, Jeffrey C, maint sup, $45,192
Mac, Bernie J, sr const insp, $61,092
Mace, Travis A, asst maint sup, $42,816
Mack, Kelvin R, materials insp, $41,316
Mackay, Joann B, sr inf syss technician, $36,504
Mackey, John R, maint worker, $29,064
Mackey, Owen J, maint worker, $29,064

Mackey, Rebecca A, sr materials technician, $37,800
Mackley, Cathy J, maint crew leader, $39,156
Maddox, Donald A, maint crew leader, $36,504
Maddox, Ellissha N, sr maint worker, $34,596
Maddox, Hubert R, sr const insp, $68,364
Maddux, Keith M, sr maint worker, $36,504
Madison, Donna M, sr risk mgmt spec, $54,600
Madison, Helen C, sr design technician, $48,828
Madrigal, Nabor L, intermed maint wrkr, $31,164
Madsen, Jeffery S, sr const insp, $73,788
Maedel, John R, sr enginerring tech-tpt/ss, $17.07/hr
Magers, Christopher G, maint worker, $29,064
Maggard, Chance R, maint worker, $29,064
Magruder, Aaron R, sr equip technician, $44,400
Magruder, Christopher L, sr maint worker, $33,996
Magruder, Judith L, sr fin servs speciali, $51,624
Mahurin, Jeremy R, electrcn, $37,800
Mahurin, Michael R, sr maint worker, $34,596
Mais, Mark A, transp proj dsgnr, $67,092
Majors, Rocky D, sr equip technician, $45,192
Malan, Levi C, maint worker, $29,064
Malkowski, Norman L, sr equip technician, $49,752
Mallett, William J, sr equip technician, $45,192
Mallicoat, Michael E, maint crew leader, $36,504
Ryan, Beth L, asst counsel, $48,012
Malone, Debra A, cert appraiser, $57,756
Malone, Matthew B, sr const insp, $62,232
Maloney, Jon B, sr maint worker, $36,504
Malott, Claude D, maint sup, $45,192
Maninga, Erik J, area engr, $72,372
Mankey, Carl D, sr maint worker, $33,996
Mann, Roger L, sr const insp, $50,676
Manning, Donnie E, sr maint worker-tpt, $18.53/hr
Manthey, Jeffrey A, sr maint worker, $33,996
Manula, Grant D, inter const insp, $51,624
Manzke, Robert J, dist design liaison, $53,580
Mao, Haiying, lead info syss technologist, $54,600
Maples, Kathrine N, maint worker, $29,064
Marbough, Michael T, sr maint worker, $34,596
March, Cory C, maint crew leader, $37,140
March, Dustin L, maint worker, $29,064
March, Gale E, sr hwy dsgnr, $55,620
Marino, Sarah F, gen servs spec, $37,800
Marion, Bradley S, motor carrier servs directr, $103,944
Marion, Michael L, sr electrcn, $42,816
Markham, Steven T, sr const insp, $50,676
Markiewicz, Andrew R, land survey sup, $50,676
Markl, Mathew S, sr motor carrier servs asst, $27,612
Markway, Thomas J, resident engr, $76,596
Marler, Christopher J, maint sup, $46,044
Marnell, Catherine M, intermed paralegal, $42,072
Maroney, Brian L, maint worker, $29,064
Marriott, Michael W, sr const insp, $56,676
Marsden, Magdalena K, const proj ofc asst, $27,156
Marsden, Rhonda L, sr maint worker, $37,140
Marshall, Barbara K, sr trans planner, $50,676
Marshall, Kate M, const insp, $46,884
Marshall, Kristina L, sr maint worker, $35,220
Marshall, Robert S, sr materials spec, $55,620
Marshall, William K, sr maint worker-tpt, $21.92/hr
Martel, Samuel C, const intern, $13.14/hr
Martens, Rochelle A, const proj ofc asst, $33,396
Marti, Kevin K, transp proj dsgnr, $64,632
Martin, Anthony R, sr maint worker, $35,856
Martin, Christie R, sr auditor, $47,736
Martin, Cindy L, sr maint worker, $34,596
Martin, Douglas C, sr maint worker, $35,220
Martin, Erin N, fin servs spec, $37,800
Martin, James R, sr hwy dsgnr, $55,620
Martin, Jared W, fin servs spec, $37,800
Martin, Jimmie D, maint crew leader, $36,504
Martin, Joseph A, sr maint worker, $37,140
Martin, Keith D, sr hwy dsgnr, $65,856
Martin, Larry W, seasonal maint worker, $12.44/hr
Martin, Lawrence D, maint worker, $29,064
Martin, Rodney M, maint crew leader, $43,608
Martin, Steven L, sr equip technician, $42,816
Martin, Teresa G, sr ofc asst, $30,624
Martinez, Alejandro, sr traffic studies special, $52,596

Maryniak, Brian C, maint worker, $29,064
Marzuco, Anthony C, const insp, $39,876
Mason, Joseph S, maint crew leader, $36,504
Mason, Robert H, sr auditor, $47,736
Massey, Corey J, inter const tech, $36,504
Massey, David R, sr maint worker, $34,596
Massman, Robert J, materials testing sup, $47,736
Masson, Brian L, maint crew leader, $36,504
Masters, Aaron M, intermed maint wrkr, $31,164
Masterson, Pamela K, sr r/w spec, $50,676
Matheis, Stephen C, sr maint worker, $43,608
Mathes, Jamie R, sr maint worker, $33,396
Mathew, Thankam, sr hwy dsgnr, $54,600
Mathews, Dennis R, sr maint worker, $35,856
Mathews, Johnny C, maint supt, $52,596
Mathews, Kenneth L, sr core drill asst, $36,504
Mathis, Brenda L, motor carrier technician, $28,584
Mathis, Paul A, sr maint worker, $35,220
Matias, James C, maint worker, $29,064
Matlock, Sean L, trans proj mgr, $73,788
Matter, Matthew C, sr maint worker, $40,608
Matthews, David P, maint worker, $29,064
Matthews, Roger A, sr traffic spec, $52,596
Matthews, Todd W, sr const insp, $52,596
Mattli, David M, lead info syss technologist, $54,600
Mattox, Carl R, electrcn asst, $32,280
Mauzy, Kelly M, trans planner, $40,608
Maxwell, Leroy H, seasonal maint worker, $12.44/hr
May, Michael A, sr const insp, $50,676
Mayer, Carl R, intermed maint wrkr, $31,164
Mayes, Jeffrey D, maint worker, $29,064
Mayes, Melanie D, asst maint sup, $40,608
Maynard, Micheal D, maint crew leader, $37,140
Mayo, Charles C, sr maint worker, $33,996
Mays, Alexis, sr maint worker, $34,596
Mays, Chad A, sr const technician, $37,800
Mays, Dirk E, sr maint worker, $42,816
Mays, Jeffrey D, maint sup, $45,192
Mays, John C, seasonal maint worker, $12.44/hr
Mazdra, Gary A, sr maint worker, $34,596
Mazur, Dennis J, sr maint worker, $36,504
McAdams, Grant F, const intern, $11.64/hr
McAntire, Dennis A, intermed maint wrkr, $31,164
McBride, Bradford A, maint worker, $29,064
McCallister, Roger L, sr maint worker, $35,220
McCameron, Kenneth L, sr maint worker, $34,596
McCarthy, Joe, seasonal maint worker, $12.44/hr
McCarty, Payden J, intermed equip tech, $36,504
McCauley, Andrew U, land surv in training, $39,876
McClain, Brenda N, sr maint worker, $34,596
McClain, Britt S, sr materials insp, $58,836
McClain, Richard A, sr maint worker, $34,596
McClanahan, Shawn A, electrcn, $37,800
McClary, Robert E, maint worker, $29,064
McClaskey, Brandon L, maint worker, $29,064
McClellan, Stephen E, sr survey technician, $37,140
McCloskey, Thomas G, sr hwy dsgnr, $54,600
McClure, David M, sr maint worker, $32,832
McCollum, James M, sr const insp, $55,620
McCollum, Steven L, sr maint worker, $35,220
McConkey, Warren E, maint sup, $47,736
McCord, Reid T, maint worker, $29,064
McCormick, Michael T, roadside mgr, $46,044
McCourt, Christopher W, maint worker, $29,064
McCoy, Gene G, int comm spec, $42,072
McCoy, Henry L, sr fac opps crew wo, $32,832
McCoy, Mark A, maint supt, $56,676
McCrite, Audrey S, fin servs spec, $37,800
McDaniel, David A, sr traffic technician, $36,504
McDaniel, Lisa M, intermed maint wrkr, $30,624
McDaniel, Randall L, land surv in training, $41,316
McDiarmid, Jimmy D, asst to the resident engi, $78,060
McDonald, Jacob W, maint worker, $29,064
McDonald, Malcolm S, seasonal maint worker, $12.44/hr
McDowell, Gregory, asst maint sup, $39,876
McDowell, John O, maint crew leader, $42,072
McElhaney, Dustin T, sr maint worker, $35,220
McElhaney, Robert L, sr maint worker, $35,856
McElroy, Garen L, inter const insp, $47,736

McElwaine, Victoria L, exec asst, $35,220
McEuen, David J, bridge loc & layout dsgnr, $64,632
McFadden, Charles E, sr maint worker, $35,220
McFadden, Larry K, motorist assistance oper, $34,596
McFarlin, Brian G, seasonal maint worker, $12.44/hr
McGartland, Kevin G, sr const insp, $61,092
McGaughey, Timothy G, sr maint worker, $34,596
McGaughy, Anthony J, asst dist engr, $89,244
McGilvray, Karen A, sr rt of way technician, $37,800
McGinnis, James R, sr maint worker, $38,472
McGlone, Christopher W, sr maint worker, $33,996
McGlothlin, Kevin L, maint crew leader, $39,876
McGoldrick, David M, maint crew leader, $39,876
McGowan, Brent A, sr maint worker, $36,504
McGrath, John R, inter const tech, $32,280
McGrath, Michael E, area engr, $81,108
McGregor, Lairyn P, comm intern, $11.24/hr
McGregor, Sherri L, spt servs mgr, $59,928
McGuire, Barbie K, sr maint worker, $34,596
McHaffie, Billy L, sr maint worker, $35,220
McIntyre, Mark A, maint worker, $29,064
McKean, Laurel A, asst dist engr, $87,540
McKee, Jason E, sr r/w spec, $48,828
McKee, Robin D, sr fin servs speciali, $50,676
McKee, Scott A, sr hwy dsgnr, $65,856
McKee, Shawn D, inter fld acquisition tech, $35,856
McKenzie, Tommy L, sr maint worker, $33,996
Resler, Ashley, comm intern, $11.24/hr
McKinley, Stacey A, sr ofc asst, $26,700
McKinney, Keith B, sr maint worker, $35,220
McKinney, Randy L, inter const insp, $44,400
McKnight, David P, sr maint worker, $33,396
McKown, Richard K, sr maint worker, $38,472
McLain, Kevin W, geotech dir, $71,016
McLarry, Gary A, dist sfty & hlth mgr, $57,756
McLaughlin, Scott W, maint sup, $45,192
McLaughlin, William M, sr hwy dsgnr, $63,408
McLelland, Kendra, sr gis spec, $47,736
McManus, Teresa M, sr traffic technician, $42,072
McMichael, Jimmy D, maint worker, $29,064
McMichael, Matthew B, sr trans planner, $56,676
McMillan, Stacy L, structural liaison engr, $75,180
McMillian, Brian L, maint sup, $45,192
McMurray, Bree K, sr envirnmental spec-ss, $52,596
McNees, Venesa R, intermed maint wrkr, $31,164
McNeil, Stuart R, sr hwy dsgnr, $54,600
McNeill, Andrew J, sr procurement agent, $49,752
McNeill, Joseph B, sr hwy dsgnr, $50,676
McNew, Heath L, sr traffic technician, $38,472
McNulty, Sean P, const intern, $13.36/hr
McPeak, Ethan W, const insp, $47,736
McPeters, Westly P, sr const technician, $36,504
McQuay, Juanita, paralegal, $37,800
McQueen, David E, sr maint worker, $35,220
McRae, Adam S, inter materials insp, $44,400
McRoy, Dallas L, sr equip technician, $42,072
McWhorter, Myles W, const technician, $28,584
Meador, Pamela J, maint crew leader, $36,504
Means, Ross L, maint worker, $29,064
Medley, Christopher R, sr electrcn, $44,400
Medley, Shay H, sr hr technic, $35,856
Medsker, Donald B, sr maint worker, $35,220
Meeks, Bennetez J, sr maint technician, $37,140
Meese, Lucas K, maint crew leader, $36,504
Meese, Nicholas L, sr equip technician, $41,316
Mehaffy, Kevin T, traffic syss sup, $39,876
Meier, Margaret E, sr risk mgmt spec, $58,836
Meinhardt, Michael T, asst maint sup, $45,192
Meinkoth, Michael C, historic preserve mgr, $65,856
Meintz, Dalton A, maint worker, $29,064
Meisenheimer, Nicholas R, maint crew leader, $36,504
Meissen, Matthew C, maint worker, $29,064
Meister, Eric F, lead info syss technologist, $59,928
Meister, Victoria V, const insp, $43,608
Meller, Cyrus B, hwy dsgnr, $45,192
Melton, Chadley S, intermed maint wrkr, $31,164
Melton, David L, maint worker, $29,064
Melton, Dylan C, intermed maint wrkr, $31,164
Melton, Jedidiah C, intermed maint wrkr, $31,164

Melton, Scotty D, dist sfty & hlth mgr, $55,620
Mendenhall, Wesley G, intermed maint wrkr, $31,164
Meneely, Tammy K, const proj ofc asst, $33,396
Mengwasser, James F, sr maint worker, $35,220
Menke, Bernard W, maint sup, $54,600
Menz, Corey A, sr maint worker, $35,220
Meredith, Benjamin C, maint crew leader, $36,504
Merriman, Robert D, sr maint worker, $41,316
Merritt, Cindy L, sr hwy dsgnr, $56,676
Merritt, Harold D, sr maint worker, $35,856
Merritt, Robert L, maint sup, $45,192
Merryman, Brent, land surv in training, $39,876
Merson, Robert J, inter const tech, $32,280
Mertens, Kelly B, trans data analyst, $46,884
Messner, Richard L, sr maint worker, $36,504
Mettes, Pamela S, intermed maint wrkr, $35,220
Mettlach, Patrick J, sr maint worker, $35,220
Meyer, Andrew L, dist const & materials eng, $76,596
Meyer, Bradley N, maint sup, $49,752
Meyer, Daren L, sr maint worker, $34,596
Meyer, David J, maint worker, $35,220
Meyer, Donald E, sr info syss technologist, $51,624
Meyer, Jason W, sr maint worker, $34,596
Meyer, Michael J, sr historic preserve speci, $53,580
Meyer, Richard K, sr equip technician, $43,608
Meyerhoff, Michael R, field materials engr, $61,092
Meystrik, Stephen A, special projs coord, $68,364
Mezinis, Gregory, sr electrcn, $44,400
Middendorf, Anthony G, maint crew leader, $36,504
Middendorf, Cheri M, sr sys mgmt specialis, $50,676
Middleton, James A, sr engring professnl-tpt, $37.16/hr
Middleton, Michael C, dist maint engr, $76,596
Middleton, Nicholas T, maint crew leader, $37,800
Migletz, James P, const intern, $12.47/hr
Milbauer, Roy A, sr maint worker, $34,596
Miles, James E, maint worker, $29,064
Miley, Brian A, sr maint worker, $37,140
Milford, Rodney L, maint crew leader, $37,800
Miller, Alan D, geotech engr, $63,408
Miller, Burt J, intermed maint wrkr, $31,164
Miller, Clayton J, maint worker, $29,064
Miller, Correy A, asst maint sup, $41,316
Miller, Curtis A, intermed maint wrkr, $31,164
Miller, Davis W, maint worker, $29,064
Miller, Dawn M, maint crew leader, $37,140
Miller, Donald E, sr maint worker, $34,596
Miller, Frank O, dist plng mgr, $67,092
Miller, Glen C, sr maint worker, $36,504
Miller, Gregg B, sr maint worker, $33,996
Miller, Jason A, sr maint worker, $36,504
Miller, Jeffrey W, equip technician superviso, $49,752
Miller, John P, traffic liaison engr, $72,372
Miller, Karen S, organizational perf spe, $55,620
Miller, Karrie A, intermed maint wrkr, $31,164
Miller, Luke A, trans planner, $39,876
Miller, Lynette, sr maint worker, $36,504
Miller, Marshall D, sr maint worker, $34,596
Miller, Mary B, dist const & materials eng, $71,016
Miller, Michael E, asst is dir, $99,072
Miller, Michael F, sr maint worker, $33,996
Miller, R T, maint liaision engr, $69,672
Miller, Ray N, motorist assistance oper, $33,996
Miller, Robert R, intermed maint wrkr, $31,164
Miller, Rodney G, sr maint worker, $35,220
Miller, Ryan D, maint crew leader, $37,140
Miller, Scott D, sr maint worker, $35,220
Miller, Stephen D, land surv, $46,044
Miller, Terry A, sr maint worker, $37,800
Miller, Timothy L, sr maint worker, $34,596
Miller, Todd E, sr maint worker, $37,800
Miller, William K, sr maint worker-tpt, $16.06/hr
Milligan, Michael E, sr maint worker, $34,596
Millikan, Morgan L, maint worker, $29,064
Mills, Jody L, sr fin servs tech, $35,220
Milton, Amanda C, maint worker, $29,064
Milton, Ronald M, const technician, $28,584
Minear, Johnnie G, maint crew leader, $44,400
Minear, Kevin E, sr hwy dsgnr, $52,596
Minnick, Troy A, sr maint worker, $34,596

Minnick, Valerie L, sr outdoor advertising tec, $39,876
Minnis, Keith A, sr maint worker, $35,220
Minor, Caroline J, maint worker, $29,064
Miron, Mark D, seasonal maint worker, $12.44/hr
Mitchell, Alexa B, cadd servs engr, $69,672
Mitchell, Anthony L, intermed maint wrkr, $31,164
Mitchell, Darius P, maint worker, $29,064
Mitchell, Dennis W, sr maint worker, $37,800
Mitchell, Ida S, sr hr spec, $47,736
Mitchell, Jerome L, asst maint sup, $40,608
Mitchell, John D, int comm spec, $42,072
Mittag, Dustin N, maint crew leader, $37,800
Mize, Ronald H, traffic sup, $47,736
Moeller, Donna M, sr ofc asst-tpt, $12.20/hr
Moellering, Mark J, intermed maint wrkr, $31,164
Moffett, Gary L, sr maint worker, $35,220
Moffitt, Jacob L, maint worker, $29,064
Molinaro, Joseph J, sr traffic studies special, $58,836
Momphard, Kenneth W, maint worker, $29,064
Mondaine, Roderick Q, sr maint worker, $37,800
Monroe, Ryan C, intermed equip tech, $35,856
Monroe, Sharon M, sr exec asst to the direc, $50,676
Monsalvo, Mariano, sr maint worker, $33,996
Montes-de-Oca, Thomas, trans proj mgr, $81,108
Montgomery, Edward A, maint sup, $52,596
Montgomery, Mark A, sr equip technician, $46,044
Montgomery, Michael K, intermed maint wrkr, $32,832
Moody, Edmund T, sr structural dsgnr, $65,856
Moon, Michael K, sr maint worker, $38,472
Mooney, Michael C, sr hwy dsgnr, $51,624
Moore, Catherine M, exec asst, $35,856
Moore, Christopher A, sr const insp, $50,676
Moore, Cody J, seasonal maint worker, $12.44/hr
Moore, David M, maint worker, $29,064
Moore, Donald C, sr maint worker, $35,220
Moore, Hal D, maint crew leader, $38,472
Moore, Jay W, sr resource mgt analyst, $64,632
Moore, John L, sr maint worker, $34,596
Moore, Johnny S, sr const technician, $37,800
Moore, Joseph G, sr pavement spec, $50,676
Moore, Kevin T, sr geotech spec, $54,600
Moore, Loren E, maint crew leader, $37,140
Moore, Michael R, sr maint worker, $33,396
Moore, Richard W, environ complnc mgr, $56,676
Moore, Rick A, sr maint worker, $35,220
Moore, Rod A, maint sup, $52,596
Moore, Shonta, sr fin servs tech, $32,832
Moore, Thomas W, sr maint worker, $37,140
Moore, Wesley K, trans proj mgr, $68,364
Moots, Bryan N, sr hwy dsgnr, $54,600
Moppin, Matthew D, sr maint worker, $33,996
Moreland, Scott L, maint worker, $29,064
Morey, Joseph B, sr maint worker, $33,396
Morff, Jason P, sr electrcn, $43,608
Morgan, Brett W, sr maint worker, $34,596
Morgan, Christopher K, asst to the resident engi, $62,232
Morgan, Gregory L, motor assistance shift supv, $46,884
Morgan, Kevin T, maint worker, $29,064
Morgan, Page A, sr const insp, $50,676
Morgan, Randall M, sr maint worker, $35,220
Morgan, Richard C, sr maint worker, $33,996
Morgan, Shawn G, sr maint worker, $37,140
Morgan, Terry M, sr const insp, $52,596
Morgan, Timothy R, lead info syss technologist, $55,620
Moriarty, Andrew M, transp enfrcmnt investigator, $37,800
Moriarty, Justin R, sr maint worker, $33,996
Morris, Brenda J, fin servs dir, $103,944
Morris, Casey D, sr maint worker, $33,996
Morris, David L, sr maint worker, $34,596
Morris, Deon C, intermed maint wrkr, $31,164
Morris, Helen M, sr maint worker, $35,220
Morris, James C, sr maint worker, $35,220
Morris, John P, sr maint worker, $41,316
Morris, Mark L, maint crew leader, $36,504
Morris, Marvin M, asst to the resident engi, $64,632
Morris, Randy S, sr traffic studies special, $61,092
Morris, Ricardo A, info syss technologist, $37,800
Morris, Theodie Jr, sr maint worker, $40,608
Morrison, Catherine V, sr multimedia servs spe, $39,156

Morrison, Connie S, transp enfrcmnt investigator, $41,316
Morrow, Lerita, maint worker, $29,064
Morton, Katherine L, sr trns enfrcemnt investigator, $42,816
Morton, Lesli M, seasonal maint worker, $12.44/hr
Morton, Thomas R, maint worker, $29,064
Moses, Ronald W, sr maint worker, $34,596
Mosley, Carl W, sr maint worker, $34,596
Moss, Bruce H, sr engring tech-tpt, $20.14/hr
Moss, Julian B, maint worker, $29,064
Moss, Nathan A, sr design technician, $39,156
Moten, Esther E, sr administrative technician, $36,504
Mothersbaugh, Eric L, sr const insp, $52,596
Mothersbaugh, Stephen K, maint crew leader, $42,816
Mott, Gidget J, trans proj mgr, $64,632
Motti, Joshua M, const insp, $46,044
Mount, Teresa M, sr procurement agent, $48,828
Moyers, Cody R, maint crew leader, $36,504
Muck, Randall, sr equip technician, $45,192
Mudd, Mike L, sr maint worker, $40,608
Muehlbach, James P, sr hwy dsgnr, $64,632
Muehlenkamp, Edward J, sr hwy dsgnr, $63,408
Mueller, Andrew T, asst dist engr, $87,540
Mueller, Arthur R, sr maint worker, $42,072
Mullen, Joseph D, asst maint sup, $40,608
Mulligan, Kevin M, sr const insp, $54,600
Mullings, Bradley G, sr const technician, $38,472
Mullings, Michelle F, exec asst, $32,832
Mullins, Alfred V, intermed maint wrkr, $30,624
Mullins, Douglas K, maint supt, $50,676
Mullins, Kevin L, sr maint worker, $33,996
Mulnik, Joseph V, electrcn intern, $13.36/hr
Mummert, Steven W, sr maint worker, $34,596
Munck, Kirsten A, asst to the resident engi, $68,364
Muratovic, Almedin, sr maint worker, $33,996
Mure, Leroy A, maint worker, $29,064
Murphy, Adam M, bridge inspection intern, $13.85/hr
Murphy, Dennis M, motorist assistance oper, $35,856
Murphy, John P, intermed maint wrkr, $31,164
Murphy, Kathy M, lead info syss technologist, $63,408
Murphy, Leah S, const insp, $46,044
Murphy, Tyler A, maint worker, $29,064
Murr, Jarod A, sr traffic spec, $44,400
Murray, Aaron C, maint worker, $29,064
Murray, Bradley J, maint worker, $29,064
Murray, Phyllis J, maint crew leader, $39,156
Murray, Raymond A, core drill oper, $40,608
Murray, Richard J, sr maint worker, $34,596
Murray, Terry K, sr maint worker, $34,596
Murrell, Bruce A, sr maint worker, $36,504
Murry, Jennifer S, sr hr spec, $47,736
Musick, Joyce R, outdoor advertising mgr, $57,756
Musser, David E, sprving bridge inspection en, $78,060
Mussulman, James D, sr maint worker, $36,504
Myers, David L, sr materials insp, $50,676
Myers, Larry E, sr maint worker, $43,608
Myers, Nicholas J, seasonal maint worker, $12.44/hr
Myers, Randy D, maint crew leader, $36,504
Myers, Roy A, maint worker, $29,064
Myers, Todd A, sr maint worker, $34,596
Myers, Troy D, sr maint worker, $36,504
Myles, Shirlyn A, cmnty liaison, $48,828
Nachtweih, Thomas C, sr maint worker, $35,220
Nailling, Terry S, maint crew leader, $36,504
Nanneman, Jennifer D, sr fin servs tech, $35,220
Nanneman, Larry J, land surv, $46,044
Nash, Amy S, sr hwy dsgnr, $59,928
Nash, Justin W, sr maint worker, $34,596
Nauman, Blake R, sr maint worker, $35,220
Naumann, Stephan A, sr maint worker, $34,596
Navarro, Sarah L, sr structural dsgnr, $55,620
Nave, Taylor J, maint worker, $29,064
Naylor, Deborah J, asst maint sup, $40,608
Naylor, Sandra K, sr fin servs tech, $34,596
Neal, James D, maint crew leader, $37,800
Neal, John A, sr maint worker, $34,596
Needham, Sharon R, sr hwy dsgnr, $50,676
Neff, Melissa A, sr design technician, $36,504
Neisen, Julie L, sr fin servs speciali, $49,752
Nell, Thomas H, intermed maint wrkr, $31,164

Nelp, Jennifer L, exec asst, $33,996
Nelson, Akera L, maint crew leader, $39,156
Nelson, Bryant K, sr equip technician, $42,816
Nelson, Cortez R, sr maint worker, $34,596
Nelson, Daniel W, sr maint worker, $35,220
Nelson, Jonathan A, traffic mngmnt & opp eng, $62,232
Nelson, Julie K, sr maint worker, $36,504
Nelson, Justin E, sr maint worker, $34,596
Nelson, Kent W, fabrication opps engr, $81,108
Nelson, Kevin L, maint worker, $29,064
Nelson, Simmual J, sr maint worker, $33,996
Nemec, Glennon R, sr electrcn, $45,192
Nerea, Belay K, inter structural dsgnr, $48,828
Nerini, Kenneth W, sr maint worker, $33,996
Ness, Steven D, sr maint worker, $35,220
Nester, Danielle L, sr engring professnl-tpt, $29.38/hr
Nett, Scott J, sr hwy dsgnr, $50,676
Neuman, Chad N, maint worker, $29,064
Neuman, Justin M, maint crew leader, $36,504
Nevels, Lawrence W, maint crew leader, $36,504
New, Kenneth L, sr maint worker, $35,220
Newberry, Bradley J, sr const technician, $46,884
Newcomb, Steven J, sr maint worker, $34,596
Newland, Teresa M, sr maint worker, $37,140
Newman, Bobby J, land surv, $44,400
Newton, Brett D, maint crew leader, $37,140
Newton, Christopher S, maint worker, $30,624
Ngugi, Simon K, const insp, $44,400
Nguyen, Khoa V, sr equip technician, $42,816
Nguyen, Phillip H, materials intern, $13.85/hr
Nichols, Anthony J, sr maint worker, $34,596
Nichols, Bruce A, sr maint worker, $36,504
Nichols, Charles A, sr maint worker, $34,596
Nichols, Dannie B, seasonal maint worker, $12.44/hr
Nichols, Emmett E, lead field acquisition tech, $42,816
Nichols, Mark A, sr maint worker, $34,596
Nichols, Scott M, interm fin serv speciali, $44,400
Nickens, Rudolph W, equal op & diversity dir, $92,772
Nickle, Brian D, maint worker, $29,064
Niec, Daniel C, dist engr, $108,084
Niederhelm, Amy M, sr govt rel spec, $47,736
Niederhelm, Samuel J, sr estimator, $55,620
Niekamp, Kelly R, audit mgr, $55,620
Niemeyer, Jeffrey G, const insp, $45,192
Niemeyer, Roy K, maint sup, $45,192
Nijmeh, Nedal A, const intern, $13.36/hr
Nilges, Jerry W, sr engring professnl-tpt, $26.98/hr
Nilges, Kerry P, sr maint worker, $37,140
Nilges, Shawn M, sr maint worker, $34,596
Nixon, Teresa M, sr traffic spec, $45,192
Noakes, Douglas C, sr maint worker, $34,596
Noble, Billie G, maint crew leader, $36,504
Noble, John Z, sr maint worker, $34,596
Noblitt, Lovell S, maint sup, $47,736
Noe, Clinton E, maint worker, $29,064
Noe, Kory M, maint worker, $29,064
Noel, Melanie R, sr fin servs tech, $32,832
Noeth, Schuyler F, inter hwy dsgnr, $47,736
Nolan, Timothy A, maint worker, $29,064
Noland, Jared E, sr equip technician, $43,608
Noland, Jerad R, dist design engr, $72,372
Nold, Adam C, sr maint worker, $33,396
Nold, Eric B, sr maint worker, $34,596
Nolting, Robbie C, maint crew leader, $42,072
Noriega, Miguel A, sr electrcn, $42,816
Norman, Angela L, hr spec, $40,608
Norman, Cindy L, sr gen servs techni, $37,800
Norman, Noel C, sr maint worker, $34,596
Norment, Dane W, info syss technologst, $37,800
Norris, Derrick J, sr maint worker, $36,504
Norris, Jamie L, maint crew leader, $36,504
Norris, Jason W, sr maint worker, $39,156
Norris, Shirley J, trans proj mgr, $82,692
Norsworthy, Leslie K, interm gen serv spec, $42,072
Norton, Nathan R, maint worker, $29,064
Novak, Kevin R, sr maint worker, $35,220
Novinger, Bartholomew C, sr maint worker, $35,220
Novinger, Becky L, maint sup, $45,192
Noyes, William D, sr procurement agent, $51,624

Nugent, Pamela L, sr design technician, $38,472
Null, Reggie W, sr maint worker, $33,996
Nunley, Louis, sr const insp, $52,596
Nunn, Tommy L, sr risk mgmt technic, $35,856
Oakes, Eric A, maint crew leader, $36,504
O'Banion, Robert W, intermed maint wrkr, $31,164
Obermann, Thomas G, sr maint worker, $34,596
O'Connell, Alicia C, sr asst counsel, $59,172
O'Connor, Andrew M, const insp, $47,736
O'Connor, Britni L, intermed auditor, $42,072
O'Connor, David M, dist bridge engr, $79,596
O'Connor, Jaylyn A, hr mgr, $56,676
O'Connor, Robert G, sr structural engr, $63,408
O'Daniell, Russel J, transp proj dsgnr, $68,364
Oder, Alex J, maint worker, $29,064
Odom, David R, asst maint sup, $40,608
Oesch, Daniel J, field materials engr, $61,092
Ogden, Luther W, maint worker, $29,064
Ogle, John R, sr maint worker, $33,996
Ohlms, John P, sr traffic technician, $48,828
Okenfuss, Brian G, area engr, $64,632
Olalekan, Adeyemi A, automation liaison analyst, $40,608
Olbrey, Richard W, maint worker, $29,064
Oligschlaeger, Timothy M, inter hwy dsgnr, $47,736
Oliver, Danielle N, sr risk mgmt technic, $32,280
Oliver, David K, sr info syss technologist, $56,676
Oliver, Elizabeth M, intermed auditor, $42,072
Oliver, Scott A, sr maint worker, $33,396
Olson, Derek A, dist traffic engr, $69,672
Olson, Sue E, sr cartographer, $39,156
Olubogun, Jeanne M, dist traffic engr, $76,596
O'Maley, Dana A, sr rt of way technician, $36,504
O'Neal, Bobby D, sr maint worker, $34,596
O'Neal, Brian C, sr maint worker, $35,220
Ordonia, Christopher J, sr maint worker, $35,220
Ordway, David P, cert appraiser, $62,232
Orf, Nathan B, maint crew leader, $37,800
O'Rourke, Patrick J, sr r/w spec, $53,580
Orozco-Stillman, Gina R, sr const insp, $53,580
Orr, Pamela L, sr motor carrier agent, $35,856
Orr, Richard W, dist utilities engr, $71,016
Orr, Stewart W, sr maint worker, $33,996
Ortner, John D, rt of way mgr, $67,092
Osborn, Destinee N, maint worker, $29,064
Osborn, James D, sr electrcn, $45,192
Osborne, David W, intermed maint wrkr, $31,164
Osburn, Thomas D, sr maint worker, $34,596
Oser, Eugene W, maint crew leader, $37,140
Osman, Zachary A, hwy dsgnr, $47,736
Oswalt, Eddy D, maint crew leader, $39,156
Otis, Leaann, sr maint technician, $37,800
Ott, Tim J, maint crew leader, $36,504
Otte, Heath J, maint supt, $50,676
Otto, Angelia J, sr administrative technician, $33,396
Otto, Travis J, equip technician superviso, $45,192
Overbey, Gary K, sr core drill asst, $37,800
Overkamp, Jeremy J, sr equip technician, $42,816
Overstreet, Bryan L, sr maint worker, $35,220
Overstreet, Travis M, maint sup, $45,192
Owen, George W, sr maint worker, $35,220
Owen, Thomas W, inter const insp, $44,400
Owens, Brian K, maint worker, $29,064
Owens, Cedrick C, sr traffic studies special, $55,620
Owens, Gary H, maint crew leader, $44,400
Owens, Gregory, traffic opps engr, $72,372
Owens, Justin E, sr electrcn, $42,816
Owens, Robert D, sr maint worker, $34,596
Owens, Steven D, sr maint worker, $36,504
Ownbey, Jeffrey D, exec asst, $32,280
Oxenhandler, Sally S, comm mgr, $59,928
Ozbun, Bryan C, maint sup, $45,192
Padgett, Jeffery B, risk and benefits mgt dir, $99,072
Page, Gregory A, sr maint worker, $34,596
Page, Roger D, sr maint worker, $43,608
Pagel, Guy T, sr maint worker, $36,504
Paige, Maurice T, maint worker, $29,064
Painter, Dennis I, maint worker, $29,064
Palm, Josshe I, hwy dsgnr, $46,044
Palmer, Kenneth E, maint worker, $29,064

Palmer, Lori K, sr traffic technician, $40,608
Pankau, Colby J, seasonal maint worker, $12.44/hr
Pardoe, Matthew D, maint crew leader, $36,504
Pardue, Dee A, sr gen servs techni, $33,996
Parker, Michael D, sr maint worker, $34,596
Parker, Millicent I, interm multimodal oper special, $42,072
Parker, Pamela O, sr hr spec, $52,596
Parker, Paul G, intermed maint wrkr, $30,624
Parker, Terri L, rgnal counsel, $101,904
Parkes, Glen L, sr maint worker, $37,140
Parks, Johnnie J, sr equip technician, $49,752
Parks, Lawrence, electrcn, $37,800
Parmenter, John C, sr maint worker, $39,156
Parrett, Adam L, sr maint worker, $34,596
Parrigon, Glenn W, sr maint worker, $37,140
Parrish, Brian C, maint worker, $29,064
Parrish, Shawn D, sr hwy dsgnr, $51,624
Parson, Douglas B, sr equip technician, $42,816
Parsons, Marcus D, sr equip technician, $42,816
Parsons, Ronald D, maint worker, $29,064
Partin, Shannon E, maint crew leader, $36,504
Pash, Bryan K, sr maint worker, $34,596
Pasley, Elizabeth A, sr fin servs tech, $39,876
Patel, Suresh P, sr structural engr, $63,408
Patrick, Darrell L, sr info syss technologist, $47,736
Patrick, David L, sr maint worker, $33,996
Patten, Bethany A, sr risk mgmt technic, $41,316
Patterson, Brianna L, historic preserve intern, $10.88/hr
Patterson, John R, maint crew leader, $36,504
Patterson, Lawrence W, maint worker, $29,064
Patterson, Patrick W, maint worker, $29,064
Patterson, Randy L, maint crew leader, $37,800
Patterson, Richard S, safety and claims mgr, $55,620
Patton, Douglas K, maint sup, $45,192
Paul, Shane C, intermed maint wrkr, $30,624
Payne, James E, sr maint worker, $33,996
Payne, Jeffrey E, sr maint worker, $38,472
Payne, Jeffrey T, mc investigations spec, $55,620
Payne, Jodie A, sr risk mgmt technic, $32,832
Peak, Phillip E, maint worker, $29,064
Pearce, Regina L, sr traffic technician, $37,800
Pearcy, Ryan J, sr hwy dsgnr, $54,600
Pearson, Travis A, maint sup, $45,192
Peavler, Alvin E, sr fac opps spe, $40,608
Peck, Aaron B, ast dist constr & mater en, $59,928
Peck, Alyson M, automation liaison analyst, $39,876
Peck, Kevin B, sr maint worker, $33,996
Peel, Raymond O, intermed maint wrkr, $31,680
Pefferman, Brad T, maint crew leader, $36,504
Pegelow, Curtis R, sr maint worker, $41,316
Pehle, Keith L, maint sup, $45,192
Pelton, John L, traffic intern, $12.47/hr
Pemberton, Aaron W, motorist assistance oper, $34,596
Pemberton, Jason D, sr maint worker, $35,220
Pemberton, Jesse J, maint worker, $29,064
Penner, Russell A, const insp, $46,044
Pennington, Carl D, sr maint worker, $37,140
Pennington, Marvin E, sr maint worker, $34,596
Pennington, Travis W, intermed equip tech, $37,140
Pennock, Brian P, sr maint worker, $34,596
Peper, Christine A, int info syss technologist, $44,400
Perkins, David A, electrcn, $37,800
Perkins, Kevin S, maint worker, $30,624
Perkins, Melvin L, sr maint worker, $34,596
Perkins, Oliver S, sr maint worker, $34,596
Perriman, Brandon J, const intern, $13.14/hr
Perry, Brian K, sr maint worker, $34,596
Perry, Danny W, sr equip technician, $40,608
Persinger, Richard L, sr maint worker, $35,220
Peters, Amie D, info syss sup, $68,364
Peters, Jeffery R, maint sup, $51,624
Peters, Kevin R, sr maint worker, $34,596
Peters, Kristen N, rt of way spec, $37,800
Peters, Maria K, dist utilities engr, $65,856
Petersen, Glen P, sr hwy dsgnr, $57,756
Peterson, Charlie R, maint sup, $48,828
Peterson, Dennis P, sr motor carrier agent, $34,596
Peterson, Emily V, const intern, $12.47/hr
Peterson, Ronald L, const insp, $39,876

Peterson, Travis L, sr maint worker, $35,220
Petrich, Donna R, sr hwy dsgnr, $56,676
Petrus, Calvin J, const insp, $46,884
Pettig, Douglas A, sr const insp, $51,624
Pettit, Gary E, intermed maint wrkr, $30,624
Pettit, Kristy L, sr fin servs speciali, $49,752
Pettus, Bruce C, incident mgmt coordinatr, $55,620
Pettus, Corey M, sr maint worker, $33,996
Peyton, David L, sr hwy dsgnr, $54,600
Pfeffer, Douglas P, maint worker, $29,064
Pfeffer, Mark D, sr hwy dsgnr, $50,676
Pflum, James J, asst to the resident engi, $61,092
Phelps, Barry L, sr maint worker, $34,596
Phelps, Jason A, sr maint worker, $33,996
Phillips, Bryan K, sr maint worker, $34,596
Phillips, Carl L, maint worker, $29,064
Phillips, Evan D, maint crew leader, $36,504
Phillips, Robert K, maint worker, $29,064
Phillips, Stephen D, maint crew leader, $36,504
Phillips, Travis W, maint worker, $29,064
Philpot, Jessie B, dist land survey mgr, $61,092
Phipps, Connie S, sr risk mgmt technic, $39,156
Phipps, Jeffery R, sr electrcn, $42,816
Pickering, Christopher A, sr maint worker, $33,996
Pickering, Mark A, maint crew leader, $37,140
Pickett, James R, bridge inspection crew mbr, $30,120
Pickett, Staci L, sr fin servs tech, $32,832
Pickett, Timothy C, transp proj dsgnr, $61,092
Pierce, Daniel S, sr survey technician, $42,816
Pierce, Larry D, sr maint worker, $38,472
Pierce, Pennie S, maint worker, $29,064
Pierson, Phillip R, traffic studies spec, $46,884
Pietrzak, Nancy A, sr maint worker, $39,876
Pigg, Keith E, materials testing sup, $49,752
Pike, Steven F, spt servs mgr, $63,408
Pilcher, Richard R, sr hwy dsgnr, $63,408
Pilcher, Ryan R, info syss technologist, $37,800
Pillow, Chad M, sr maint worker, $36,504
Pine, Dennis N, sr maint worker, $35,220
Pinel, Mallorie K, maint worker, $29,064
Pinet, Kevin M, maint worker, $29,064
Pingel, Tyson P, maint worker, $29,064
Pinkston, Dustin L, maint worker, $29,064
Pinson, Joseph D, maint crew leader, $36,504
Piper, Michael J, sr maint worker, $34,596
Pippin, Timothy E, sr maint worker, $34,596
Pitchford, Burt, sr const insp, $68,364
Pittman, Jeffery S, maint sup, $50,676
Pitts, Kevin R, asst maint sup, $41,316
Pitts, Tamara M, sr const insp, $51,624
Pitts, Thomas L, const insp, $47,736
Plassmeyer, Cody C, int info syss technologist, $42,072
Plassmeyer, Jacob A, comp science intern, $12.47/hr
Plassmeyer, Mary H, lead info syss technologist, $59,928
Plaster, Christopher P, sr maint worker, $35,220
Plaster, Ronald E, maint crew leader, $41,316
Pletka, James S, maint worker, $30,120
Plott, Kevin R, sr const insp, $56,676
Plunk, George L, maint crew leader, $36,504
Pobst, Glenn A, maint worker, $29,064
Poe, Gavin T, sr maint worker, $33,996
Poe, Gregory M, intermed maint wrkr, $31,164
Pogue, Patricia L, maint sup, $47,736
Pogue, Timmy R, maint crew leader, $37,800
Poindexter, Mark, intermed maint wrkr, $31,164
Poke, Michael A, maint worker, $29,064
Polen, Cristi L, motorist assistance oper, $38,472
Polen, Linda K, maint crew leader, $42,816
Politte, William K, cadd spt analyst, $58,836
Pollard, Blake E, summer maint laborer, $9.27/hr
Pollard, Jesse D, maint worker, $29,064
Polodna, Charles R, sr maint worker, $34,596
Polston, Andrew M, maint worker, $29,064
Polston, David A, sr trns enfrcemnt investigator, $42,816
Ponder, James A, maint worker, $29,064
Poole, Ivory E, maint worker, $29,064
Poor, Robert L, sr maint worker, $34,596
Porter, Grady I, traffic studies spec, $47,736
Porter, Harold L, intermed maint wrkr, $31,164

Porter, Richard W, maint worker, $29,064
Porter, Timmy M, maint crew leader, $36,504
Porter, Timothy J, sr maint worker, $36,504
Porter, Treasa A, sr materials technician, $37,800
Porter, William C, sr maint worker, $36,504
Porting, Carl J, sr equip technician, $44,400
Porting, Theodore L, intermed equip tech, $35,856
Post, Erich R, intermed maint wrkr, $31,164
Potter, Mary E, maint worker, $29,064
Potts, Felicia D, intermed maint wrkr, $31,164
Potts, Randall D, transp proj dsgnr, $64,632
Powell, Audrey D, paralegal, $37,800
Powell, David M, asst maint sup, $46,884
Powell, Michael D, sr materials insp, $53,580
Powell, Nancy A, traffic syss sup, $42,072
Powell, Richard E, sr maint worker, $39,876
Powell, Tanya M, sr motor carrier agent, $35,856
Powers, Thomas M, sr const technician, $36,504
Poynter, David A, maint worker, $29,064
Prapaisilp, Arisa, sr traffic studies special, $55,620
Pratt, Robin L, const proj ofc asst, $35,220
Pratt, Tresa J, maint crew leader, $39,876
Prenger, Jennifer R, interm fin serv speciali, $42,072
Prenger, Joanie M, sr fin servs speciali, $47,736
Prenger, Michael J, motor carrier compliance supv, $49,752
Presley, Eugene, maint crew leader, $37,140
Presson, Justin C, sr maint worker, $36,504
Prewitt, Ronald C, sr maint worker, $35,220
Price, Brennen L, sr maint worker, $35,220
Price, David R, sr maint worker, $35,220
Price, Erick B, maint crew leader, $36,504
Price, Gregory J, maint sup, $49,752
Price, Michael W, land surv, $52,596
Priest, Dustin C, const intern, $13.85/hr
Priest, Zachary J, maint worker, $29,064
Prilwetz, Charles N, maint worker, $29,064
Pringer, Randy M, lead info syss technologist, $55,620
Pritchett, John L, sr maint worker-tpt, $22.44/hr
Prock, David L, sr const insp, $54,600
Proctor, Brian E, sr maint worker, $34,596
Propst, Cathy A, inf syss proj mgr, $56,676
Pruett, Raymond J, sr maint worker, $35,220
Prussman, Curtis V, maint crew leader, $39,156
Pryor, Carol J, info syss technician, $30,120
Pryor, Marion L, sr maint worker, $35,220
Puckett, Bradley R, seasonal maint worker, $12.44/hr
Puett, Earl R, maint crew leader, $38,472
Pugh, David A, sr maint worker, $34,596
Puhr, Jodie L, transp proj dsgnr, $62,232
Pullen, Nathaniel B, intermed maint wrkr, $31,164
Pulliam, Audie A, resident engr, $71,016
Pulliam, Brandon P, intermed maint wrkr, $31,164
Purcell, Amos P, sr maint worker, $35,220
Purdy, Michael J, sr maint worker, $36,504
Pursley, Charles R, design liaison engr, $85,884
Pyatt, Edward T, maint crew leader, $37,140
Pyatt, Ronnie G, sr maint worker, $35,220
Pycke, Jeffrey R, sr equip technician, $42,816
Pyles, Jason M, maint worker, $29,064
Qualls, Jamie L, sr maint worker, $38,472
Querry, Bryan D, maint crew leader, $36,504
Quick, Rusty L, maint crew leader, $36,504
Quinton, Kurtis D, maint worker, $29,064
Racer, Pamela S, sr maint worker, $36,504
Rackers, Bruce A, sr maint worker, $34,596
Rackers, Eileen H, state traffic&hwy safty engr, $103,944
Rackers, Janelle M, info sys technology spec, $67,092
Rackers, Mary M, sr r/w spec, $49,752
Radford, Larry J, maint worker, $29,592
Rafa, Tudor, sr electrcn, $49,752
Ragan, Daniel R, maint crew leader, $37,140
Ragan, Douglas P, sr maint worker, $42,072
Ragan, Gary M, sr maint worker, $36,504
Ragland, Danielle J, intermed maint wrkr, $31,164
Ragland, Thomas C, sr maint worker, $34,596
Ragsdale, Nathaniel M, sr maint worker, $34,596
Raines, Jonathon R, maint crew leader, $36,504
Rainey, Homer W, sr maint worker, $34,596
Rainey, Warren D, maint crew leader, $37,800

Rains, Mark S, maint worker, $29,064
Rains, Terry L, maint worker, $29,064
Raithel, Amanda E, lead info syss technologist, $54,600
Raithel, Kevin J, br inspection crew sup, $50,676
Ralovo, Erin C, sr traffic studies special, $50,676
Ralston, Robert D, maint sup, $53,580
Ramirez, Donald M, sr maint worker, $35,856
Ramirez, Ricardo R, sr maint worker, $39,876
Ramos, Carsen K, maint worker, $29,064
Ramsbottom, Charles A, sr survey technician, $39,156
Ramsey, Eric G, dist sfty & hlth mgr, $55,620
Ramsey, Eric R, maint crew leader, $36,504
Ramsour, Kerry R, maint worker, $29,064
Randolph, Edwin G, sr maint worker, $34,596
Raney, James A, sr design technician, $38,472
Rankin, Matthew J, motorist assistance oper, $33,996
Rankin, Ralph M, sr proj rever, $68,364
Rath, Janet R, sr maint worker, $35,220
Ratliff, Warren L, sr fac opps spe, $41,316
Ray, Buddy L, sr maint worker, $33,996
Ray, Clarence L, sr maint worker, $35,220
Ray, Jacob D, traffic opps engr, $63,408
Ray, Kelly F, special projs coord, $64,632
Ray, Robert P, sr maint worker, $35,220
Raybourn, Lisa G, const insp, $39,876
Rayfield, Jeremy M, maint worker, $29,064
Reagan, Brian F, tranport sys analysis engr, $73,788
Reavis, James A, maint worker, $29,064
Reavis, James D, sr maint worker, $36,504
Reber, James D, maint worker, $29,064
Redden, Jeffrey S, sr equip technician, $44,400
Redding, Mark A, sr maint worker, $35,220
Redel, Dennis J, of counsel-tpt, $40.09/hr
Redel, Sheldon L, sr procurement agent, $47,736
Redhage, Christine M, resident engr, $67,092
Redline, Christopher G, asst dist engr, $87,540
Reeb, Cheryl D, inter materials insp, $44,400
Reed, Elizabeth A, sr hr spec, $49,752
Reed, Harry C, intermed maint wrkr, $31,164
Reed, Jeffrey D, maint worker, $29,064
Reed, John R, intermed maint wrkr, $31,164
Reed, Lola J, sr maint worker, $35,220
Reed, Nathan B, sr const insp, $50,676
Reed, Robert S, sr maint worker, $36,504
Reed, Steven G, sr maint worker, $34,596
Reed, Virgil T, inter const insp, $44,400
Reeder, Michael R, sr maint worker, $36,504
Reedy, Jarrett A, asst maint sup, $40,608
Reedy, Steven R, sr const technician, $37,800
Reel, Vincent E, maint supt, $57,756
Reents, Eric B, sr const insp, $52,596
Reese, Stacy M, dist design engr, $75,180
Reese, Travis C, sr maint worker, $34,596
Reeser, Newell R, int tr studies spec, $49,752
Reeser, Robert B, long range trans plng co, $75,180
Reeter, Jacob A, const intern, $12.47/hr
Reeves, Douglas J, sr maint worker, $37,140
Reeves, James A, seasonal maint worker, $12.44/hr
Reeves, John R, sr maint worker, $35,220
Piper, Clover S, intermed paralegal, $42,072
Regelsperger, Cale L, maint worker, $29,064
Reger, Roger W, sr materials insp, $51,624
Rehkop, Ron A, sr maint worker, $34,596
Reichart, Francis J, environ chemist, $58,836
Reid, Kim R, rgnal counsel, $101,904
Reidlinger, William C, sr fac opps crew wo, $33,996
Reimler, Nicholas B, materials insp, $46,044
Reinhardt, David H, sr survey technician, $37,140
Reinkemeyer, Ashley M, comp aided drft supprt eng, $61,092
Reinkemeyer, Karen M, sr gen servs spec, $51,624
Reliford, Fredrico B, sr maint worker, $37,800
Remick, Justin T, seasonal maint worker, $12.44/hr
Renfro, Aaron L, sr equip technician, $40,608
Renfro, Jack C, const intern, $13.14/hr
Renick, Larry W, intermed maint wrkr, $34,596
Rennick, Craig E, sr const technician, $37,800
Rentel, Russell D, sr equip technician, $42,816
Resa, John W, maint crew leader, $36,504
Ressel, Cindy G, exec asst, $33,996

Resz, Caleb S, maint worker, $29,064
Reynolds, Cory S, sr rr safety insp, $49,752
Reynolds, Donald E, sr maint worker, $36,504
Reynolds, Joshua M, maint crew leader, $35,856
Reynolds, Joyce M, sr hwy dsgnr, $59,928
Reynolds, Kenneth D, sr maint worker, $36,504
Reynolds, Mark L, sr maint worker, $34,596
Reynolds, Ronald W, sr maint worker, $36,504
Rhoades, Tammie S, sr maint worker, $37,800
Rhodelander, Terry G, maint worker, $29,064
Rhodes, Charles M, intermed maint wrkr, $31,680
Rhodes, Kenneth R, maint worker, $31,164
Rhodes, Kevin D, maint crew leader, $39,156
Rhodes, Robert C, dist utilities engr, $68,364
Rhodus, Ashley M, maint worker, $29,064
Rhorer, Alvin F, sr info syss technologist, $57,756
Rhoten, Lucas A, maint worker, $29,064
Rice, Clayton, sr maint worker, $34,596
Rice, Donald R, maint worker, $29,064
Rice, John M, sr maint worker, $33,996
Rice, Nathaniel W, maint worker, $29,064
Rice, Randy J, sr materials insp, $52,596
Rich, Amanda L, sr traffic studies special, $53,580
Rich, George A, intermed maint wrkr, $31,164
Richardson, Alvin R, sr maint worker, $35,220
Richardson, Britney L, hr spec, $38,472
Richardson, Charles R, maint worker, $29,064
Richardson, Justin R, sr trns enfrcemnt investigator, $42,072
Richardson, Kenneth D, maint worker, $29,064
Richmond, Nicholas D, maint crew leader, $36,504
Richter, Kimberly C, sr motor carrier agent, $34,596
Richter, Pamela F, sr plng technician, $43,608
Richter, Robert D, maint worker, $29,064
Rickabaugh, Deanne P, motor carrier proj mgr, $58,836
Rickard, Angela R, mcs sys & training analyst, $39,876
Rickard, Deborah S, gen servs dir, $103,944
Ricker, Gary D, sr maint worker, $35,856
Rickerson, Curtis H, bridge inspection crew leader, $42,072
Rickman, Joseph C, dist traffic engr, $82,692
Ricks, Carol A, inter admin prof-tpt, $23.00/hr
Riddle, Anthony T, sr maint worker, $33,396
Riddle, Robert T, const intern, $12.47/hr
Rideout, Robert C, maint crew leader, $36,504
Ridings, Michael G, sr maint worker, $34,596
Ridnour, Roseanna M, int info syss technologist, $45,192
Rieder, Aaron M, sr const insp, $50,676
Riegel, Jennifer A, sr design technician, $37,800
Riegle, Jeffery C, sr maint worker, $38,472
Rightnowar, Steven W, maint sup, $45,192
Riley, Adam S, sr hwy dsgnr, $49,752
Riley, Gary L, sr maint worker, $42,072
Riley, Johnathan A, sr maint worker, $34,596
Riley, Michael D, sr maint worker, $35,856
Riley, Reid N, asst to the resident engi, $63,408
Riley, Robert D, maint worker, $29,064
Riley, Sandra K, auditor, $42,816
Rinehart, Damon S, sr maint worker, $35,220
Rinehart, Michael E, area engr, $75,180
Riney, Christopher L, sr engring professnl-tpt, $27.25/hr
Riney, Samone C, ofc asst, $22,608
Ring, Elizabeth R, info syss dir, $103,944
Ringeisen, Susan R, sr maint worker, $34,596
Rinne, Martin L, sr maint worker, $36,504
Rispoli, Catherine L, rt of way mgr, $64,632
Rissler, David J, maint worker, $29,064
Ritoch, Christopher J, sr plng technician, $40,608
Rivers, Kelly B, intermed maint wrkr, $31,164
Rix, Susan R, maint worker, $29,064
Roach, Charles R, maint supt, $54,600
Roach, Daniel L, maint sup, $54,600
Roadruck, Connie J, sr admin profressional-tpt, $23.24/hr
Roark, Ardita, sr administrative counsel, $71,448
Roark, Justin L, sr trns enfrcemnt investigator, $42,816
Roark, Natalie R, dist design engr, $71,016
Roark, Susan A, sr motor carrier agent, $34,596
Robbins, John L, intermed maint wrkr, $31,164
Robbins, Leslie A, intermed maint wrkr, $32,832
Roberts, Bradley A, sr maint worker, $33,996

Roberts, Donald R, maint worker, $29,064
Roberts, Jake A, maint worker, $29,064
Roberts, John M, sr maint worker, $33,996
Roberts, Lonny P, maint crew leader, $39,156
Roberts, Melissa A, maint crew leader, $37,140
Roberts, Michael A, sr fac opps spe, $45,192
Roberts, Todd A, sr maint worker, $40,608
Roberts, Warren F, sr engring professnl-tpt, $32.87/hr
Robertson, Gregg D, maint crew leader, $44,400
Robertson, Jeffrey L, maint sup, $50,676
Robertson, Marissa V, sr comm spec, $47,736
Robertson, Rodney A, maint worker, $29,064
Robey, Dewayne B, traffic sup, $53,580
Robinett, Grady C, intermed maint wrkr, $32,280
Robins, Chase V, sr maint worker, $33,996
Robinson, Alvin T, emergency maint equip operat, $15.00/hr
Robinson, Charles R, sr structural technician, $37,800
Robinson, Connie P, sr administrative technician, $38,472
Robinson, Dana B, maint sup, $45,192
Robinson, James D, sr equip technician, $42,816
Robinson, Jason D, maint worker, $29,064
Robinson, Michael L, sr maint worker, $34,596
Robinson, Patrick L, sr structural technician, $38,472
Rocchio, John A, intermed maint wrkr, $31,164
Rocchio, Joseph A, sr electrcn, $42,816
Roche, Nathan W, info syss technologist, $37,800
Rodenbaugh, Macy J, dist const & materials eng, $76,596
Rodgers, Steven T, sr maint worker, $37,140
Rodriguez, Deborah M, sr maint worker, $35,220
Rodriguez, Jaime A, maint worker, $29,064
Rodriguez, Jose A, traffic opps engr, $59,928
Roeger, Daniel J, sr const insp, $51,624
Roegge, Diane R, environ chemist, $59,928
Roeseler, Joan M, trans plng specia, $63,408
Roethemeier, Dennis R, maint sup, $48,828
Roewe, Donna J, div admin spt sup, $44,400
Rogers, Billy J, audits & investigations dir, $99,072
Rogers, Cayce G, const technician, $28,584
Rogers, Chaseton D, intermed maint wrkr, $31,164
Rogers, Cody L, sr equip technician, $40,608
Rogers, David R, maint worker, $29,064
Rogers, Dwayne N, sr maint worker, $36,504
Rogers, Jacqueline S, sr sys mgmt specialis, $50,676
Rogers, Jeff A, sr equip technician, $49,752
Rogers, Kelly G, maint worker, $29,064
Rogers, Matthew V, intermed equip tech, $35,856
Rogers, Michael G, sr electrcn, $42,816
Rogers, Robert G, intermed maint wrkr, $31,164
Rogers, Scott D, sr equip technician, $45,192
Rogers, Tony, electrcn asst, $32,280
Rohner, Matthew R, intermed maint wrkr, $31,164
Rohr, Larry F, dist utilities engr, $72,372
Roland, Darrius V, seasonal maint worker, $12.44/hr
Roland, Suzanne, const proj ofc asst, $35,220
Rolf, Michael L, maint worker, $29,064
Rollins, Joshua B, sr maint worker, $35,220
Romine, Jeremy M, sr equip technician, $40,608
Romine, Rodger D, sr equip technician, $40,608
Roop, David C, sr equip technician, $42,816
Rose, Charles D, sr maint worker, $34,596
Rose, Melissa D, sr const insp, $55,620
Rosenbohm, Danny J, gen servs mgr, $61,092
Rosenthal, Brian M, sr hwy dsgnr, $55,620
Ross, Arthur M, sr maint worker, $40,608
Ross, Bryan J, sr multimodal oper spec, $50,676
Ross, Ericka R, int tr studies spec, $49,752
Ross, Kevin L, maint sup, $47,736
Ross, Myranda M, legal sec, $28,584
Ross, Neal T, maint crew leader, $39,156
Ross, Terry M, land surv, $52,596
Rosser, George E, sr maint worker, $33,396
Rost, Austin M, seasonal maint worker, $12.44/hr
Roth, Alex D, maint worker, $29,064
Roth, Bryan J, intermed maint wrkr, $31,164
Roth, Kelly J, sr trns enfrcemnt investigator, $43,608
Roth, Paul G, sr maint worker, $36,504
Roth, Todd L, fac opps sup, $53,580
Rother, Robert W, maint crew leader, $39,156
Rothermich, Larry D, sr const insp, $50,676

Rothove, Ronald H, sr equip technician, $42,072
Roth-Roffy, Brian, const insp, $47,736
Rothschild, Kenneth L, sr maint worker, $39,876
Rotter, April C, intermed equip tech, $35,856
Rottinghaus, Erin E, hwy dsgnr, $46,044
Rottman, Justin L, sr maint worker, $34,596
Rounkles, Todd W, maint sup, $46,044
Roush, Dorothy J, sr paralegal, $49,752
Roush, Roy A, sr maint worker, $33,396
Routh, Jamie A, sr maint worker, $34,596
Rowden, Glen J, sr maint worker, $33,396
Rowden, Paul D, maint worker, $29,064
Rowe, Travis J, const insp, $47,736
Rowland, Jan A, maint crew leader, $36,504
Rudd, Ricky, maint worker, $29,064
Ruedrich, David W, maint worker, $29,064
Ruffus, Phillip M, sr pavement spec, $52,596
Ruga, Janet M, lead info syss technologist, $63,408
Rugen, Amy R, sr auditor, $47,736
Ruggeri, Jeanette K, sr traffic studies special, $54,600
Rumfelt, Bradley J, asst maint sup, $40,608
Runquist, Kristina L, sr maint worker, $35,220
Runyon, Brandon, sr maint worker, $36,504
Rupe, Joshua L, intermed maint wrkr, $30,624
Ruppel, Lucas J, maint crew leader, $36,504
Ruscha, Duane M, maint worker, $29,064
Ruser, Linda J, sr maint worker, $35,220
Rush, Keith F, asst maint sup, $40,608
Russell, Amy N, sr maint worker, $36,504
Russell, Jason D, sr equip technician, $43,608
Russell, John, maint sup, $46,044
Russell, Richard J, maint supt, $52,596
Russell, Wendell D, maint worker, $29,064
Ruth, Janet M, automation liaison analyst, $40,608
Rutledge, Christian B, asst dist engr, $82,692
Rutledge, Thomas E, maint crew leader, $40,608
Rutledge, Tyson R, sr maint worker, $37,140
Ryan, Randy L, sr maint worker, $34,596
Saey, Jason D, sr asst counsel, $71,448
Saiko, Donald T, trans proj mgr, $71,016
Saleny, Roger L, maint worker, $29,064
Salfrank, Michael A, maint worker, $29,064
Samuel, Kevin D, intermed maint wrkr, $30,624
Sanders, Diania D, sr maint worker, $34,596
Sanders, Gary E, maint crew leader, $39,156
Sanders, Gregory E, struct dev & spt engr, $78,060
Sanders, John L, resident engr, $67,092
Sanders, Krista M, sr maint worker, $33,996
Sanders, Mike L, sr traffic spec, $45,192
Sanders, Richard W, maint crew leader, $38,472
Sanders, Robert C, sr maint worker, $33,996
Sanders, Terry L, maint crew leader, $37,140
Sanders, Tracie, sr maint worker, $34,596
Sanders, Travis M, sr maint worker, $34,596
Sandgren, Douglas K, maint crew leader, $37,140
Sandifer, Philip E, sr const insp, $63,408
Sanning, Steven A, sr field acquisition techn, $39,876
Sanny, Cody G, maint crew leader, $36,504
Sappington, David A, sr maint worker, $35,856
Sardeson, Doug L, sr maint worker, $38,472
Sardigal, Jennifer L, inter const insp, $49,752
Sartin, Jamie L, maint sup, $45,192
Saucier, Jeannette M, lead info syss technologist, $26.74/hr
Sauer, Heather A, intermed maint wrkr, $31,164
Sauerwein, Mark A, sr engring professnl-tpt, $28.29/hr
Saulberry, Charles A, hr intern, $9.84/hr
Saunders, Glenda L, sr risk mgmt technic, $38,472
Savageau, Daniel W, sr hwy dsgnr, $54,600
Saville, Dale L, seasonal maint worker, $12.44/hr
Sawyer, Danny R, sr fac opps spe, $42,816
Sawyer, Jessica B, sr outdoor advertising perm sp, $47,736
Sawyer, Norman L, maint crew leader, $43,608
Sawyers, Ronnie D, sr maint worker, $34,596
Scales, David M, maint worker, $29,064
Scales, Dustin R, comp science intern, $13.36/hr
Scarbrough, Freddy D, sr maint worker, $40,608
Schaefer, James W, sr maint worker, $36,504
Schaefer, John J, sr maint worker, $34,596
Schaefer, John J, sr traffic studies special, $61,092

Schaefer, Jordan L, historic preserve intern, $10.88/hr
Schaeffer, Benjamin J, maint worker, $29,064
Schaeffer, Christopher L, intermed equip tech, $35,856
Schafer, Samuel E, sr electrcn, $42,816
Schaffer, Jamie J, sr maint worker, $34,596
Schaffner, Nikolas E, sr hwy dsgnr, $55,620
Schall, Mark W, dist info systm mgr, $58,836
Schaller, Beth A, area engr, $69,672
Schaperclaus, Jason P, sr maint worker, $34,596
Scharnhorst, William W, maint crew leader, $36,504
Schatzer, Nicholas L, const insp, $41,316
Schauer, Joshua D, sr maint worker, $33,996
Schenk, Curtis D, sr hwy dsgnr, $56,676
Scheperle, Debbie A, sr ofc asst, $28,104
Scheperle, Larry E, rail safety spec, $47,736
Scheperle, Melissa A, sr envirnmental spec-ss, $52,596
Schepers, Beverly J, sr fin servs speciali, $58,836
Scherer, Gerard L, sr electrcn, $42,816
Scherer, Gilbert W, maint sup, $45,192
Scherrer, Jessie D, sr maint worker, $34,596
Schey, Victor I, seasonal maint worker, $12.44/hr
Schiller, Michael D, sr equip technician, $41,316
Schilling, Travis L, sr hwy dsgnr, $54,600
Schlater, Gary D, sr const insp, $50,676
Schleicher, John C, maint crew leader, $43,608
Schlereth, Kevin E, maint worker, $29,064
Schlichting, Neil D, sr maint worker-tpt, $27.25/hr
Schloman, Betty L, administrative technician-tpt, $15.94/hr
Schlosser, Gary V, sr maint worker, $34,596
Schlotzhauer, Alec R, bridge intern, $13.85/hr
Schmauch, Brynn E, sr design technician, $37,140
Schmauch, Lisa C, sr ofc asst, $12.20/hr
Schmidt, Andrew J, const intern, $12.47/hr
Schmidt, Ivan W, standards spec, $50,676
Schmidt, Joseph T, sr maint worker, $35,220
Schmidt, Reagan, sr ofc asst, $25,380
Schmitt, Jeffrey E, maint crew leader, $37,140
Schmitz, Donna H, sr fin servs tech, $43,608
Schmitz, Melissa, outdoor advert permit spec, $37,800
Schmitz, Shaun W, sr supply agent, $37,140
Schmitz, Tina K, sr ofc asst, $31,164
Schnakenberg, Michael, maint worker, $29,064
Schnaufer, Billy R, sr maint worker, $35,220
Schneider, Daniel W, maint worker, $29,064
Schneider, Jon W, maint crew leader, $37,140
Schneider, Maurice J, intermed maint wrkr, $31,164
Schneider, Michael F, sr maint worker, $34,596
Schneider, Richard R, maint supt, $54,600
Schneidewind, Randy M, sr maint worker, $42,072
Schnell, Bill J, asst dist engr, $85,884
Schnoebelen, Derek, const intern, $12.47/hr
Schoemehl, Christan M, const intern, $11.64/hr
Scholl, Anthony M, maint crew leader, $36,504
Scholz, Christine E, maint crew leader, $36,504
Schomaker, Richard W, int info syss technologist, $42,072
Schooler, Houston H, trans enforce investi supv, $47,736
Schoonover, Pleasant W, seasonal maint worker, $12.44/hr
Schopp, Dennis D, sr maint worker, $33,996
Schrader, Brandon S, const intern, $11.64/hr
Schrader, Drew L, const insp, $47,736
Schrautemeier, Rick L, sr materials technician, $39,876
Schreimann, Brandon K, maint sup, $45,192
Schroeder, Jay R, sr structural engr, $64,632
Schroeder, Timothy J, trans proj mgr, $76,596
Schroeder, Timothy P, sr maint worker, $36,504
Schroeter, Eric E, state design engr, $103,944
Schroyer, Charles D, maint supt, $55,620
Schuber, Molly K, sr maint worker, $34,596
Schubert, Gabriel L, structural spec, $40,608
Schulte, Brent T, materials testing spec, $40,608
Schulte, Daniel E, sr maint worker, $35,220
Schulte, Joseph B, sr materials insp, $51,624
Schulte, Norma L, info syss sup, $67,092
Schultheiss, Matthew P, sr survey technician, $35,856
Schumann, Charles H, sr design technician, $41,316
Schupp, Michael J, area engr, $71,016
Schwab, Jerrett D, materials insp, $43,608
Schwab, Robert E, sr auditor, $57,756
Schwandtner, Christian O, design mgt syss administrat, $64,632

Schwartz, Daniel L, maint crew leader, $36,504
Schwendemann, Michael R, maint crew leader, $37,800
Schwent, Carl J, sr equip technician, $46,884
Scott, Charolette W, maint crew leader, $36,504
Scott, Christopher E, maint crew leader, $37,800
Scott, Dane L, sr maint worker, $33,996
Scott, Danny R, maint crew leader, $36,504
Scott, Jonathan F, intermed maint wrkr, $31,164
Scott, Joshua J, sr hwy dsgnr, $57,756
Scott, Nicole A, sr materials technician, $36,504
Scott, Shannon D, int motor carrier agent, $30,120
Scott, Steven E, inter traffic technician, $32,280
Scott, Tim F, sr maint worker, $35,220
Scott, William L, sr maint worker, $34,596
Scrivens, David A, asst dist maint & traff engine, $67,092
Scroggie, Tanner W, seasonal maint worker, $12.44/hr
Seabaugh, Debra L, sr const technician, $37,800
Seabaugh, Laura D, comm spec, $37,800
Sealock, Ryan L, electrcn, $37,800
Sears, Dustin M, sr const technician, $36,504
Sears, Jason W, asst maint sup, $40,608
See, Clayton T, maint worker, $29,064
Seeley, Roger E, maint worker, $29,064
Sefton, Brian L, sr investigator, $47,736
Seiler, Andrew B, sr trans planner, $51,624
Seiler, Matthew C, asst dist engr, $90,948
Sen, Trisha, pavement spec, $47,736
Senevey, Marisa M, lead info syss technologist, $59,928
Sensabaugh, Donald R, maint worker, $29,064
Sentman, William L, maint sup, $48,828
Sercu, Randall L, maint worker, $29,064
Severs, Dwayne C, sr const technician, $37,800
Seward, Daniel R, maint worker, $29,064
Seyer, Chester M, maint worker, $29,064
Seymore, Mary K, sr ofc asst, $30,624
Shabazz, Omar M, const intern, $11.64/hr
Shaddox, Shea N, sr maint worker, $33,996
Shafer, Clint J, maint sup, $46,884
Shafer, Jason E, asst dist maint engr, $65,856
Shafer, Jason M, asst dist maint engr, $63,408
Shahan, David L, sr maint worker, $38,472
Shamet, Kenneth A, sr structural dsgnr, $61,092
Shaneberger, Mitchell T, const insp, $46,884
Shaner, Johnathon G, maint worker, $29,064
Shank, Raymond B, sr traffic studies special-nss, $49,752
Shanks, Brandon D, const technician, $28,584
Shanks, Christopher M, bridge loc & layout dsgnr, $59,928
Shanks, Michael J, maint crew leader, $36,504
Shanks, Terry R, maint crew leader, $36,504
Shannon, James E, sr traffic studies special, $54,600
Sharp, Charles E, sr maint worker, $40,608
Sharp, Eric E, maint worker, $29,064
Sharp, James W, sr const insp, $54,600
Sharp, Randel D, sr maint worker, $38,472
Shaver, Raymond J, maint worker, $29,064
Shaver, Wayne L, maint sup, $46,884
Shaw, Aaron E, maint worker, $29,064
Shaw, Carla A, sr maint worker, $35,220
Shaw, Joyce E, const proj ofc asst, $30,624
Shaw, Robert M, sr const insp, $54,600
Shaw, Timothy M, maint crew leader-tpt, $18.98/hr
Shawn, Al, sr structural dsgnr, $57,756
Shea, Mike W, maint liaision engr, $79,596
Shears, Lester R, sr maint worker, $41,316
Shefferd, Dennis A, maint crew leader-tpt, $20.89/hr
Sheldon, Kevin L, sr maint worker, $33,996
Shelton, Mark E, dist engr, $103,944
Shelton, Stephen R, rt of way mgr, $67,092
Shelton, Steven C, motorist assistance oper, $33,996
Shelton, Taylor N, const intern, $11.64/hr
Shepherd, Brady S, sr maint worker, $33,996
Shepherd, Casey M, gen laborer, $11.37/hr
Shepherd, David C, intermed maint wrkr, $31,164
Sherman, Kirk W, sr const technician, $36,504
Shields, Harry H, maint worker, $29,064
Shields, Lonnie R, sr supply agent, $32,280
Shields, Michael L, sr maint worker, $36,504
Shields, Stanley D, sr maint worker, $35,220
Shikles, Kathleen A, exec asst, $43,608

Shimbo, Seiji, materials insp, $45,192
Shineman, Stephen T, maint crew leader, $36,504
Shipers, Richard G, sr maint worker, $34,596
Shipley, Christopher S, maint sup, $45,192
Shipley, Regina R, transp proj dsgnr, $61,092
Shipley, Richard W, trans proj mgr, $65,856
Shipman, Kelly L, sr maint worker, $34,596
Shirley, Mike, sr maint worker, $35,220
Shockley, Scot A, sr maint worker, $34,596
Shoemaker, Danny G, sr maint worker, $37,140
Shoemaker, Roy A, spt servs mgr, $57,756
Sholl, Christopher M, maint supt, $50,676
Shoop, Ethan J, maint worker, $29,064
Shores, John D, sr electrcn, $42,816
Shouse, David W, maint worker, $29,064
Shrubb, Mary E, sr hr technic, $35,220
Shrum, Tom W, sr const insp, $50,676
Shryock, Michelle D, intermed maint wrkr, $32,280
Shubert, Daniel J, maint worker, $29,064
Shulse, Christopher D, sr envirnmental spec-ss, $51,624
Shunamon, Terry L, sr br inspection crew mbr, $35,856
Sickendick, Danny L, sr trans planner, $56,676
Siddens, Blaine K, sr equip technician, $44,400
Sideboard, Yergana O, maint worker, $29,064
Sidebottom, Mark A, sr structural technician, $37,140
Siebeneck, Todd M, sr materials insp, $51,624
Sierra, Ismael C, maint crew leader, $36,504
Sifford, Sue A, sr risk mgmt technic, $35,220
Sifford, William S, maint sup, $46,884
Sikes, Thomas P, sr equip technician, $45,192
Siler, Todd W, sr maint worker, $35,220
Silkwood, Mark E, maint sup, $46,884
Sill, Curt R, maint crew leader, $39,876
Silver, Jonathan M, sr const insp, $56,676
Silvester, David T, dist engr, $103,944
Silvey, Michael R, maint crew leader, $36,504
Simcosky, Kevin D, sr maint worker, $34,596
Simmerman, David G, sr maint worker, $33,996
Simmons, Brice M, safety ofcr, $39,156
Simmons, Chris M, maint worker, $29,064
Simmons, Craig A, maint worker, $29,064
Simmons, Cynthia R, sr hwy dsgnr, $54,600
Simmons, David J, trans proj mgr, $64,632
Simmons, David V, sr fac opps spe, $44,400
Simmons, James P, sr maint worker, $33,996
Simmons, Jeff L, sr maint worker, $35,220
Simmons, Ricky L, sr const insp, $52,596
Simmons, Robert D, asst maint sup, $40,608
Simmons, William L, maint worker, $29,064
Simon, Mark D, geologist, $59,928
Simpher, Janice F, const proj ofc asst, $33,996
Simpson, Brandon C, proj rever, $45,192
Simpson, Curtiss J, structural spec, $40,608
Simpson, Frederick R, maint crew leader, $40,608
Simpson, Jimmy L, sr maint worker, $39,876
Sims, David A, sr maint worker, $35,220
Sims, Keith A, sr maint worker, $35,220
Sims, Timothy E, sr const insp, $50,676
Sims, William J, maint sup, $47,736
Sinclair, John A, gen servs mgr, $57,756
Sipes, Diane M, dist sfty & hlth mgr, $55,620
Sirb, Joshua P, fac opps crew worke, $13.12/hr
Sisk, Kenneth R, seasonal maint worker, $12.44/hr
Sisson, Kenneth E, sr inf syss technician, $36,504
Sisson, Mark D, sr maint worker, $34,596
Sisson, Thomas D, maint sup, $45,192
Skaggs, Randy K, sr maint worker, $34,596
Skain, Patrick M, traffic studies spec, $45,192
Skeen, Donna J, exec asst, $39,156
Skelton, Richard D, maint sup, $45,192
Skinner, Jesse J, dist maint engr, $72,372
Skirvin, Richard G, sr maint worker, $34,596
Skoglund, Shannon P, sr hwy dsgnr, $51,624
Skorseth, Craig T, sr hwy dsgnr, $55,620
Skyles, Richard E, sr maint worker, $33,996
Slagle, Troy D, dist design engr, $85,884
Slater, Amanda J, seasonal maint worker, $12.44/hr
Slater, Bobby R, maint sup, $45,192
Slaughter, Marcus B, maint supt, $54,600

Slaughter, Mary E, cert appraiser, $54,600
Sloan, Dennis N, maint worker, $29,064
Sloan, Dwight R, asst maint sup, $39,876
Sloan, Sandra, sr administrative technician, $32,832
Slone, James M, sr litigation counsel, $75,624
Slusher, Bradley A, sr maint worker, $34,596
Small, Christopher J, intermed equip tech, $37,140
Smalley, Jonathon E, maint worker, $29,064
Smiley, Brian N, sr maint worker, $34,596
Smith, Anastasia M, sr hwy dsgnr, $54,600
Smith, Andrew J, sr hwy dsgnr, $55,620
Smith, Brandon E, maint worker, $29,064
Smith, Bruce, sr maint worker, $36,504
Smith, Bryan T, maint worker, $29,064
Smith, Carolyn A, sr maint technician, $41,316
Smith, Chadwick A, sr equip technician, $42,816
Smith, Charles M, sr maint worker, $35,220
Smith, Christopher A, intermed maint wrkr, $31,164
Smith, Christopher L, sr maint worker, $34,596
Smith, Clinton W, seasonal maint worker, $12.44/hr
Smith, Daniel J, traffic mngmnt & opp eng, $64,632
Smith, Daniel M, structural proj mgr, $72,372
Smith, Danny R, sr maint worker, $39,876
Smith, Daryl K, maint worker, $29,064
Smith, David L, maint worker, $29,064
Smith, Donald D, maint worker, $29,064
Smith, Donald L, sr maint worker, $36,504
Smith, Eddie M, maint sup, $45,192
Smith, Eric S, inter const tech, $32,280
Smith, Gerri L, const proj ofc asst, $33,996
Smith, Gregory D, asst maint sup, $40,608
Smith, Griffin T, asst dist maint engr, $61,092
Smith, Hal D, sr maint worker, $35,220
Smith, James E, design liaison engr, $84,288
Smith, James N, rail safety spec, $48,828
Smith, Jason A, maint crew leader, $36,504
Smith, Jay L, asst chief counsel-risk mngmnt, $117,816
Smith, Jennifer A, const proj ofc asst, $31,680
Smith, Jerry W, maint sup, $46,884
Smith, Jimmy D, sr equip technician, $39,156
Smith, John E, sr maint worker, $34,596
Smith, John T, sr maint worker, $34,596
Smith, Joseph L, const insp, $44,400
Smith, Juli A, const proj ofc asst, $30,120
Smith, Keith L, standards spec, $62,232
Smith, Kelly B, sr equip technician, $46,044
Smith, Kim D, maint crew leader, $40,608
Smith, Larry D, maint worker, $29,064
Smith, Lucy S, int br inspection crew mbr, $35,220
Smith, Lynn W, sr const insp, $50,676
Smith, Mark A, sr electrcn, $42,816
Smith, Michael L, rt of way spec, $37,800
Smith, Michael L, maint sup, $45,192
Smith, Michael S, comp liaison, design, $53,580
Smith, Montrez D, maint worker, $29,064
Smith, Nicole I, maint crew leader, $37,800
Smith, Oscar L, maint crew leader, $36,504
Smith, Philip R, sr maint worker, $34,596
Smith, Rickey D, maint crew leader, $39,156
Smith, Scott A, sr fac opps crew wo, $32,280
Smith, Scott C, sr cust serv rep, $32,832
Smith, Scott K, maint worker, $29,064
Smith, Scottie L, maint crew leader, $41,316
Smith, Shaun A, sr maint worker, $33,996
Smith, Stephen J, sr gen servs techni, $34,596
Smith, Stephen W, maint supt, $53,580
Smith, Steven L, sr maint worker, $42,072
Smith, Todd A, maint crew leader, $39,876
Smith, Tommy E, sr maint worker, $39,876
Smith, Weston K, sr maint worker, $42,816
Smith, Zachary P, const intern, $12.47/hr
Smitherman, Sim T, maint crew leader, $37,140
Smothers, Eric W, intermed maint wrkr, $31,164
Snelling, Scott L, sr const insp, $50,676
Snider, Marie D, sr maint worker, $35,220
Snider, Ronald K, sr maint worker, $39,156
Snider, Stanley S, maint crew leader, $40,608
Sniffen, Nicole L, traffic intern, $13.36/hr
Snodgrass, William J, sr maint worker, $34,596

Snook, Jay D, fac opps crew worke, $13.12/hr
Snorgrass, Anthony W, motorist assistance oper, $34,596
Snow, Cody B, const insp, $47,736
Snow, Von B, maint crew leader, $36,504
Snyder, James W, sr maint worker, $35,220
Solari, Anthony P, maint worker, $29,064
Sommerhauser, Karsten M, trans proj mgr, $71,016
Sonner, Matthew W, fac opps sup, $45,192
Soots, Cody A, survey intern, $11.64/hr
Sorensen, Monty J, sr maint worker, $34,596
Spanberger, Michael A, const insp, $46,884
Sparks, Donald J, maint crew leader, $37,140
Speak, Crystal D, sr maint worker, $35,220
Spears, Christopher S, dist land survey mgr, $56,676
Spears, James T, seasonal maint worker, $12.44/hr
Spencer, Donald E, traffic syss sup, $44,400
Spencer, Tara N, exec asst, $33,396
Sperry, Matthew L, maint crew leader, $36,504
Spire, Stephen P, motorist assistance oper, $35,856
Sportsman, Christopher S, maint worker, $29,064
Spradling, Jeffrey W, maint worker, $29,064
Sprigg, John P, const insp, $41,316
Sprock, Mark E, sr maint worker, $43,608
Sprogoe, Cheryl L, sr gen servs spec, $49,752
Squire, Wesley E, sr maint worker, $35,220
St Gemme, Robert W, sr const insp, $53,580
St John, Brenda K, sr info syss technologist, $47,736
Stacy, Clinton T, seasonal maint worker, $12.44/hr
Staeger, Tonya J, cust serv rep, $28,584
Staffen, Daniel L, maint crew leader, $35,856
Stafford, Roy J, maint crew leader, $36,504
Staley, Bruce E, sr maint worker, $38,472
Stalker, Warren R, sr electrcn, $43,608
Stallings, Tammy J, sr maint worker, $38,472
Stamper, Howard M, intermed maint wrkr, $31,164
Stampley, Quentin J, hwy dsgnr, $44,400
Stanback, Travis, maint crew leader, $37,800
Stanbery, Matthew D, seasonal maint worker, $12.44/hr
Standley, Donald I, maint crew leader, $41,316
Standley, Phillip E, sr maint worker, $34,596
Stanfield, Brett L, maint worker, $29,064
Stanfill, Daniel E, intermed maint wrkr, $32,280
Stanley, Darren L, maint worker, $29,064
Stannard, Edward A, sr survey technician, $37,140
Stansbury, Richard L, sr maint worker, $34,596
Staples, Levi G, maint worker, $29,064
Stapleton, Darryl K, maint worker, $29,064
Starchman, Richard E, sr maint worker, $34,596
Stark, Alistair P, motorist assistance oper, $37,140
Stark, Carie D, sr info syss technologist, $47,736
Stark, Cheyanne R, sr hr technic, $32,280
Starke, Karen A, sr info syss technologist, $52,596
Starke, Rickey J, sr maint worker, $40,608
Staufenbiel, Robert J, intermed maint wrkr, $31,164
Stauffer, Marcus R, sr maint worker, $34,596
Stavenau, Dawn M, sr ofc asst, $25,380
Steeby, Lisa M, maint worker, $29,064
Steele, Nicole L, sr design technician, $37,800
Stegeman, Curtis W, bridge inspection tech-tpt, $26.74/hr
Stegner, Barbara J, dist final plans & rep proc, $45,192
Steiger, Jill M, traffic opps sup, $50,676
Steinbruegge, Luke A, sr maint worker, $32,832
Steiner, Kevin K, inter const insp, $44,400
Steinman, Eva M, trans planner, $39,876
Stennis, Willie M, motorist assistance oper, $39,876
Stephen, Wesley C, dist plng mgr, $68,364
Stephens, Blake E, bridge intern, $14.59/hr
Stephens, Christina L, sr procurement agent, $47,736
Stephens, Scott D, dist bridge engr, $69,672
Stephens, Shawn M, inter const tech, $32,832
Stephenson, Scot A, sr maint worker, $34,596
Stern, Kurt J, intermed maint wrkr, $31,164
Sterrett, Paul R, sr asst counsel, $78,552
Stervinou, Gregory L, resident engr, $68,364
Steuber, Matthew G, const insp, $47,736
Steuck, Galen M, asst maint sup, $41,316
Stevens, Gary M, sr maint worker, $34,596
Stevenson, David A, bridge loc & layout dsgnr, $67,092
Steward, David R, intermed maint wrkr, $31,164

Stewart, Arthur D, sr maint worker, $34,596
Stewart, Bruce R, maint worker, $29,064
Stewart, Charlotte M, const proj ofc asst, $34,596
Stewart, James D, transp enfrcmnt investigator, $40,608
Stewart, Jason W, sr traffic spec, $46,884
Stewart, Jeff E, roadside mgr, $45,192
Stewart, Nora L, sr maint worker, $36,504
Stewart, Richard W, asst maint sup, $40,608
Stewart, Thomas K, asst maint sup, $40,608
Stidham, Aubrey W, sr maint worker, $34,596
Stiens, Terry R, sr maint worker, $34,596
Still, Jeffrey T, traffic syss sup, $40,608
Still, Lukas D, seasonal maint worker, $12.44/hr
Stock, Nathan A, maint intern, $13.36/hr
Stockdall, Samuel R, maint crew leader, $39,156
Stockman, Jennifer M, interm fin serv speciali, $42,072
Stockman, Morgan B, geology intern, $13.36/hr
Stockton, Douglas M, maint crew leader, $36,504
Stoddard, Roy D, maint crew leader, $44,400
Stone, Craig E, seasonal maint worker, $12.44/hr
Stone, Richard L, sr maint worker, $34,596
Stone, Travis E, maint worker, $29,064
Stone, William A, research admin, $78,060
Stoner, Jackie D, sr const technician, $39,876
Stoops, Andrea N, sr fin servs tech, $32,280
Stotlemeyer, Julie C, traffic liaison engr, $72,372
Stotlemeyer, Scott B, asst state bridge engr, $87,540
Stotts, Tracee D, sr const insp, $55,620
Stout, Arthur M, asst maint sup, $39,876
Stout, Joshua J, asst const tech, $25,380
Stout, Wesley O, hr spec, $37,800
Stout, Zachary K, sr maint worker, $34,596
Stovall-Taylor, Danica D, estimate and rev engr, $64,632
Strain, Ray, sr maint worker, $34,596
Strand, Laurence D, maint worker, $29,064
Stranghoner, William A, sr maint worker, $36,504
Stratman, Thomas P, sr hwy dsgnr, $57,756
Stratton, Steven D, maint crew leader, $45,192
Street, Jerod M, maint crew leader, $36,504
Stringer, Derek E, equip technician, $32,280
Strong, Andrew, sr maint worker, $35,856
Strong, Benjamin J, intermed equip tech, $35,856
Strong, Brian M, sr maint worker, $36,504
Strong, Jeffrey L, sr maint worker, $33,996
Strong, Stewart C, ofc asst, $11.80/hr
Strong, Todd G, sr const insp, $55,620
Stroyan, Christina R, sr traffic technician, $37,140
Strube, Kenneth D, maint supt, $55,620
Strube, Kent A, sr maint worker, $33,996
Struemph, Douglas G, fld acquisition coord, $53,580
Stuart, Deborah, spt servs mgr, $56,676
Stuckenschneider, Chris A, sr equip technician, $42,072
Studeny, Allan W, maint worker, $29,064
Studt, Rex G, int engineering prof-tpt/sspd, $21.13/hr
Stuedle, Bradley R, maint worker, $29,064
Stuedle, Melissa A, sr civil rights spec, $49,752
Stuettger, Shawn A, asst maint sup, $40,608
Stumberg, John H, sr maint worker, $35,856
Stump, Travis S, sr structural dsgnr, $56,676
Stumpe, Darla J, sr sys mgmt specialis, $51,624
Stumpe, Melinda S, int info syss technologist, $46,044
Stupps, Lisa A, transp proj dsgnr, $68,364
Sublette, Christine D, sr ofc asst, $35,220
Sudheimer, Benjamin A, intermed equip tech, $35,856
Suellentrop, Jefre M, sr maint worker-tpt, $21.92/hr
Suiter, Darryl E, maint worker, $29,064
Suling, Patricia A, mcs sys & training analyst, $40,608
Sullentrup, James W, maint sup, $46,044
Sullivan, Brandon K, maint worker, $29,064
Sullivan, Caleb R, intermed maint wrkr, $31,164
Sullivan, Charles A, resident engr, $78,060
Sullivan, Thomas J, sr maint worker, $35,220
Summa, Stacy R, asst rt of way mngr-certifi, $62,232
Summers-Harmon, Susan M, sr traffic studies special, $55,620
Sumowski, Stefan, sr equip technician, $50,676
Sunde, Gregory G, sr engring professnl-tpt, $35.54/hr
Sundell, Justin P, sr maint worker, $33,396
Sundermeyer, Mendy J, rt of way liaison, $64,632
Surface, Chanta D, sr maint worker, $34,596

Surface, Cynthia L, sr ofc asst, $30,624
Surface, Julie A, sr motor carrier agent, $35,220
Susnic, James R, sr const insp, $56,676
Susnic, Lise G, sr const insp, $55,620
Sutton, Angela D, sr civil rights spec, $47,736
Sutton, Cole J, const technician, $33,396
Sutton, Randall E, maint crew leader, $40,608
Sutton, Timothy M, sr maint worker, $34,596
Swafford, Mark A, sr maint worker, $35,220
Swan, Brent E, sr const insp, $54,600
Swanigan, Randy E, sr roadside mgmt special, $55,620
Swearingin, Mike A, sr maint worker, $35,220
Sweem, Cody S, maint worker, $29,064
Sweet, Craig E, sr maint worker, $38,472
Swierk, Richard G, sr maint worker, $36,504
Swift, Earl E, sr maint worker, $35,220
Swindle, Daryl L, sr maint worker, $43,608
Swing, Jordan V, hwy dsgnr, $47,736
Swisher, Matthew G, sr maint worker, $34,596
Switzer, Christopher R, maint sup, $46,044
Switzer, Craig A, sr hwy dsgnr, $56,676
Swofford, Matthew S, sr maint worker, $34,596
Tackett, Lori A, gen servs spec, $37,800
Taegtmeyer, Thomas N, sr const insp, $54,600
Talken, Matthew V, sr rr safety insp, $43,608
Talley, Terry J, sr maint worker, $34,596
Tallman, Curtis L, sr equip technician, $42,816
Tappin, Kevin J, seasonal maint worker, $12.44/hr
Tarr, Steven L, sr traffic spec, $51,624
Tarrant, Marsha D, sr gen servs techni, $37,140
Tate, Tommy J, sr maint worker, $39,156
Tatum, Harold R, sr maint worker, $33,996
Taurone, Sandra J, sr maint technician, $37,140
Taylor, Dave B, sr traffic studies special, $62,232
Taylor, David E, intermed safety ofcr, $46,884
Taylor, David L, sr maint worker, $36,504
Taylor, Freddie L, sr maint worker, $41,316
Taylor, James A, sr safety ofcr, $49,752
Taylor, Jeffrey P, dist land survey mgr, $55,620
Taylor, Llans E, innovations engr, $76,596
Taylor, Timothy A, sr risk mgmt spec, $52,596
Taylor, Timothy K, sr const technician, $37,800
Taylor, Travis B, maint worker, $29,064
Teagarden, Richard S, sr maint worker, $41,316
Teague, Braxton E, maint worker, $29,064
Teague, Terrence L, maint worker, $29,064
Teasley, Stephanie J, sr auditor, $50,676
Tedder, Kayla M, risk mgmt technician, $28,584
Teegardin, Johnny L, resident engr, $67,092
Teel, Chris A, sr const insp, $56,676
Teel, Jason E, maint crew leader, $36,504
Teel, Michael E, transp mgt sys admin, $68,364
Teel, Michelle L, multimodal opratns dir, $103,944
Temmen, Kim E, sr fin servs tech, $38,472
Temple, Angela L, sr hr spec, $47,736
Templer, James A, sr hwy dsgnr, $63,408
Tennis, Justin G, maint worker, $29,064
Terbrak, Donald L, sr maint worker, $35,220
Terrett, Michael L, sr maint worker, $35,220
Terrill, Elvin W, sr maint worker, $34,596
Terry, Dustin L, intermed maint wrkr, $31,164
Terry, Toni F, sr gen servs techni, $37,140
Tesreau, Travis D, sr historic preserve speci, $48,828
Teter, Christina M, const contract administ, $42,072
Teter, Michael L, sr maint worker, $35,220
Teter, Robert W, maint crew leader, $41,316
Teter, Scott A, sr maint worker, $36,504
Teter, Stephen L, sr equip technician, $42,072
Teter, Travis J, maint crew leader, $36,504
Thatch, Demarcus N, sr maint worker, $33,996
Thiemann, Travis D, land surv, $44,400
Thieret, Nicole S, comm mgr, $57,756
Thieret, Todd J, sr maint worker, $42,816
Thoenen, Allen C, sr maint worker, $36,504
Thoenen, Kevin M, environ chemist, $57,756
Thomas, Bertrian L, sr maint worker-tpt, $17.54/hr
Thomas, Clark E, maint crew leader, $36,504
Thomas, Dale L, intermed maint wrkr, $31,164
Thomas, Donald J, maint worker, $29,064

Thomas, Donald R, maint crew leader, $36,504
Thomas, Douglas R, sr const insp, $62,232
Thomas, Easaw, sr materials insp, $52,596
Thomas, Jennifer A, trans proj mgr, $63,408
Thomas, Kenneth V, sr maint worker, $38,472
Thomas, Kennth D, sr maint worker, $33,996
Thomas, Stacy W, maint crew leader, $36,504
Thomas, Tania B, exec asst, $32,280
Thomas, William R, sr maint worker, $37,800
Thomason, Ronald F, sr maint worker, $35,220
Thompson, Adam W, sr maint worker, $34,596
Thompson, David S, maint sup, $45,192
Thompson, Eric G, sr r/w spec, $49,752
Thompson, Jeremy S, intermed maint wrkr, $31,164
Thompson, Mark E, sr info syss technologist, $57,756
Thompson, Phillip R, sr const insp, $50,676
Thompson, Rebecca G, asst counsel, $51,924
Thompson, Rhonda M, sr info syss technologist, $47,736
Thompson, Russell D, sr maint worker, $32,832
Thompson, Shawn M, sr equip technician, $39,876
Thompson, Waldo W, sr maint worker, $35,220
Thornton, Timothy N, sr maint worker, $34,596
Thornton, Warren L, maint worker, $29,064
Thorp, William D, sr maint worker, $35,220
Thorpe, Max K, maint worker, $29,064
Thorpe, Steven J, sr maint worker, $41,316
Thrasher, Johnathan T, maint worker, $29,064
Thrasher, Leslie S, maint crew leader, $36,504
Throener, Mark A, sr hwy dsgnr, $55,620
Throndson, Holly B, sr r/w spec, $49,752
Thurman, Andy W, sr maint worker, $34,596
Thurman, Marion D, maint sup, $45,192
Thurman, Tina R, motor carrier compliance supv, $45,192
Thurston, Darren S, sr maint worker, $37,140
Tibbetts, Paul R, maint worker, $29,064
Tiemeyer, Richard L, chief counsel, $127,056
Tillery, Lionel L, supply ofc asst, $25,380
Tilley, James B, maint worker, $29,064
Tillitt, Clinton W, sr maint worker, $34,596
Tillman, Shawn R, maint crew leader, $36,504
Tincknell, Victor, const insp, $39,876
Tiner, Daniel S, hr spec, $37,800
Tinker, Kevin L, sr const insp, $61,092
Tinkle, Donald W, sr maint worker, $38,472
Tinnon, Monte W, sr maint worker, $35,220
Tipton, Kimberly J, sr info syss technologist, $51,624
Tobias, Matthew A, inter const insp, $49,752
Tocco, Kennith W, maint worker, $29,064
Todd, Brian A, sr const insp, $52,596
Todd, Michael C, safety ofcr, $37,800
Todd, Ricardo N, sr geotech spec, $50,676
Toler, Charles E, intermed equip tech, $35,856
Tolivar, Gary D, sr fac opps spe, $42,072
Tollison, Paul R, maint worker, $29,064
Tombleson, David R, sr maint worker, $34,596
Tomson, Travis A, land surv in training, $39,876
Tooley, Travis W, sr maint worker, $33,996
Torner, Billie J, sr maint worker, $35,220
Tornow, Patty L, maint worker, $29,064
Tourney, Michael J, sr maint worker, $36,504
Tourtillott, Lucas K, sr equip technician, $42,816
Towne, Demetrios X, intermed maint wrkr, $31,164
Townsend, Gary S, maint supt, $50,676
Townsend, Jonathon M, maint crew leader, $36,504
Trabue, Timothy M, maint worker, $29,064
Trainor, Kimberly M, transp proj dsgnr, $62,232
Trammell, Herschel D, sr maint worker, $37,140
Trampe, Alan L, dist bridge engr, $78,060
Trautman, Brett S, phys lab dir, $71,016
Travis, Laurie A, inter hwy dsgnr, $44,400
Traw, Jacky D, gen servs mgr, $57,756
Treasure, Albezza C, hr spec, $37,800
Treat, Donald G, maint crew leader, $36,504
Trepanier, Lewis E, sr maint worker, $36,504
Triebel, Jud W, maint crew leader, $36,504
Triplett, James E, sr maint worker, $33,996
Tripp, Kathy J, sr gen servs spec, $50,676
Tripp, Robert W, sr maint worker, $34,596
Trivette, Donald J, sr maint worker, $36,504

Troesser, Christopher P, sr equip technician, $42,816
Troester, Donald D, sr maint worker, $37,140
Trotter, Louis C, sr maint worker, $37,140
Trout, Jimmy D, maint crew leader, $40,608
Troutwine, Tyson N, sr maint worker, $33,996
Trower, Ricky E, sr maint worker, $39,876
Trupiano, Eric F, inter const insp, $51,624
Truskoski, Mark E, asst maint sup, $45,192
Tubbesing, Lee R, investigator, $37,800
Tucker, Benjamin S, intermed maint wrkr, $31,164
Tucker, Billie D, sr const insp, $54,600
Tucker, Billy R, intermed maint wrkr, $31,164
Tucker, Daniel, maint supt, $50,676
Tucker, Myrna R, transp mgt sys admin, $67,092
Tuerck, Andrew J, asst to the resident engi, $62,232
Tuley, Tate A, maint crew leader, $36,504
Tummons, Kelly R, sr maint worker, $34,596
Tune, Brian D, sr equip technician, $43,608
Turner, Andrew P, maint worker, $29,064
Turner, Dekota L, seasonal maint worker, $12.44/hr
Turner, Eric J, sr traffic studies special, $56,676
Turner, Gary D, maint worker, $29,064
Turner, Joseph D, sr traffic studies special, $55,620
Turner, Kevin M, sr maint worker, $34,596
Turner, Michael V, electrcn asst, $32,280
Turner, Patrick S, sr electrcn, $44,400
Turner, Paul D, maint worker, $29,064
Turner, Ronald E, intermed maint wrkr, $31,164
Turner, Thomas M, sr maint worker, $35,220
Tuter, Patrick L, const insp, $46,044
Tutt, John E, maint supt, $57,756
Tuttle, Kenneth A, core drill sup, $47,736
Twellmann, Amy M, asst dist maint engr, $64,632
Twenter, Noel G, sr maint worker, $33,996
Twyman, David G, maint crew leader, $37,800
Tyler, Herman L, maint worker, $29,064
Tyler, Todd N, sr fin servs speciali, $50,676
Uebelhart, Brent G, materials intern, $13.36/hr
Um, Virak I, motorist assistance oper, $35,856
Umfleet, Brian W, traffic opps engr, $68,364
Underwood, Aaron L, equip technician superviso, $46,884
Unger, Joseph L, sr rr safety insp, $43,608
Unglesbee, Sean E, sr maint worker, $35,220
Unruh, Gayle A, environ & hist presv mgr, $76,596
Untiedt, Brian J, traffic opps engr, $62,232
Uptegrove, Richard S, sr const insp, $50,676
Urban, Jarrod E, maint worker, $29,064
Uti, Henry C, sr electrcn, $49,752
Utrecht, Aaron J, sr gen servs spec, $47,736
Utz, Jason T, maint sup, $46,044
Vader, Leonard A, environ chemist, $62,232
Valadez, Paul D, asst maint sup, $40,608
Valdez, Gilbert, sr electrcn, $42,816
Valentin, Milton, maint crew leader, $36,504
Valentine, Robert D, maint sup, $45,192
Van Dyne, William W, maint sup, $45,192
Van Horn, Gregory D, asst maint sup, $42,072
Van Loon, Greggory D, const intern, $13.36/hr
Van Patten, Gregory B, const insp, $45,192
Van Winkle, John C, sr hwy dsgnr, $57,756
Van Wye, Joy L, maint worker, $35,220
Vanbibber, Paul, sr maint worker, $34,596
Vance, Curtis E, sr maint worker, $33,996
Vance, Franklin T, sr const insp, $53,580
Vance, Steven J, sr gis spec, $46,884
Vandelicht, John D, maint crew leader, $45,192
Vandelicht, Randall W, sr electrcn, $42,816
Vandeloecht, Phillip L, maint worker, $29,064
Vanderfeltz, Jason R, bid & contract serv engr, $75,180
Vandiver, Jerad L, sr maint worker, $33,996
Vangennip, Richard A, sr maint worker, $34,596
Vanloo, Derek A, sr gen servs spec, $46,884
Vanzandt, Thomas J, seasonal maint worker, $12.44/hr
Varner, Jonathan C, materials spec, $47,736
Varvera, Ronald J, sr maint worker, $34,596
Vaughan, Jenna L, exec asst, $32,280
Vaughn, Julia F, sr traffic technician, $36,504
Vaughn, Robert, sr maint worker, $35,856
Vaughn, Samuel S, sr maint worker, $34,596

Vaught, Clayton D, maint crew leader, $36,504
Veasman, James L, intermed maint wrkr, $31,164
Veasman, Tom, sr gen servs spec, $58,836
Veltrop, Karyn M, sr fin servs tech, $35,856
Verdun, Joshua, const insp, $47,736
Vermillion, Jackie D, sr const insp, $50,676
Vermillion, Samantha E, electrcn asst, $32,280
Versemann, James H, maint worker, $29,064
Verslues, Jeffrey A, sr survey technician, $39,156
Vest, Randy J, maint crew leader, $36,504
Viayra, Michael R, maint worker, $29,064
Vicich, John P, maint worker, $29,064
Vierling, William E, const intern, $13.36/hr
Viers, Shane I, sr const insp, $58,836
Vieth, Lisa A, statewide incident response co, $65,856
Vincent, Sandra J, sr hr spec, $47,736
Vinson, Debra L, sr gen servs techni, $43,608
Voegele, Michelle A, area engr, $64,632
Vogel, Jerry W, sr maint worker, $34,596
Vogel, Roy S, sr maint worker, $37,140
Vogt, Stephen D, sr maint worker, $33,996
Volkart, Bruce D, sr maint worker, $37,140
Volkart, Misty L, investigation mgr, $62,232
Vollet, Kevin J, cadd spt analyst, $61,092
Voltmer, Andrew R, sr maint worker, $33,996
Vomund, Chance T, maint worker, $29,064
Vomund, Janette M, multimodal opps speciali, $37,800
Vonburg, James S, sr maint worker, $35,220
Voss, Eva R, sr trans planner, $57,756
Voss, Jon G, resident engr, $69,672
Voss, Kenneth L, local progs admin, $85,884
Voyles, Brandon S, const insp, $45,192
Wachter, Jeffery A, transp proj dsgnr, $68,364
Waddle, Wesley J, maint worker, $29,064
Wade, Michael B, sr trns enfrcemnt investigator, $44,400
Waelder, Joshua D, maint crew leader, $36,504
Wagner, James W, maint worker, $29,064
Wagner, Judy A, area engr, $71,016
Wagner, Justin G, sr traffic studies special, $54,600
Wagner, Larry A, sr maint worker, $35,220
Wake, Michael L, sr traffic studies special, $52,596
Waldron, Randy W, sr electrcn, $47,736
Walker, Jonathon L, seasonal maint worker, $12.44/hr
Walker, Oni E, sr ofc asst, $25,380
Walker, Rebel J, sr maint worker, $36,504
Walker, Roger W, maint crew leader, $36,504
Walker, Steve I, sr maint worker, $33,996
Walker, Terry J, asst maint sup, $42,072
Walker, Wayne A, maint worker, $29,064
Walker, Will, transp proj dsgnr, $63,408
Walker, Zachary S, resident engr, $65,856
Walkup, Steven G, sr maint worker, $36,504
Wallace, Brian D, sr maint worker, $39,876
Wallace, Brison J, sr maint worker, $36,504
Wallace, Donald R, sr electrcn, $44,400
Wallace, Lori A, sr maint worker, $34,596
Wallace, Tammy S, sr comm spec, $54,600
Waller, Darian C, maint worker, $29,064
Wallick, Wesley C, land surv, $48,828
Walsh, Michael T, maint crew leader, $36,504
Walsh, Rebecca S, sr cust serv rep, $37,140
Walter, Crystal, sr fin servs tech, $32,280
Walter, Debra J, sr maint worker, $35,220
Walters, Steven R, sr maint worker, $35,220
Walters, Todd L, info syss sup, $63,408
Walters, Tyler R, electrcn asst, $32,280
Walton, Edith R, exec asst, $32,832
Walton, Jason I, maint crew leader, $37,140
Wang, Chunlei, sr hwy dsgnr, $63,408
Wankum, Allen J, sr fac opps spe, $40,608
Warbritton, Kenyon R, maint liaision engr, $87,540
Ward, Christopher E, inter const insp, $44,400
Ward, Marisela, sr hwy dsgnr, $59,928
Ward, Scott D, outdoor advert permit spec, $40,608
Ward, Stephen A, maint crew leader, $35,856
Warden, David W, sr maint worker, $34,596
Wardlow, Robin D, sr maint worker, $35,220
Ward-Melton, Ryan P, sr maint worker, $34,596
Ware, Jay A, sr engring tech-tpt/sspd, $20.23/hr

Warfield, Matthew T, maint worker, $29,064
Waris, Pamela P, sr traffic syss oper, $35,856
Warlick, Curtis L, maint worker, $29,064
Warmouth, David L, sr maint worker, $34,596
Warner, Ethan C, maint worker, $29,064
Warren, Gary P, sr design technician, $37,800
Warren, Kyle W, sr maint worker, $33,996
Warren, Michael S, sr const insp, $50,676
Warren, Robin L, sr gen servs spec, $51,624
Warren, Torionto M, maint worker, $29,064
Warren, Tyler B, maint worker, $29,064
Warren, Weston M, maint worker, $29,064
Wash, Albert E, motorist assistance oper, $33,996
Washausen, Scott J, resident engr, $72,372
Washington, David B, sr const technician, $37,800
Wassman, Alexander L, sr traffic studies special, $52,596
Wasson, Scott L, maint crew leader, $36,504
Waterbury, Kurt M, maint worker, $29,064
Waterman, David L, sr maint worker, $36,504
Waters, Andrew L, maint worker, $29,064
Waters, Mitchell D, maint worker, $29,064
Waters, Timothy A, sr maint worker, $37,140
Waters-Hamblin, Megan L, sr administrative counsel, $71,448
Watkins, Brad E, sr const insp, $51,624
Watkins, Brett N, maint worker, $29,064
Watkins, Eddie, int tr studies spec, $47,736
Watkins, Machelle B, trans plng dir, $103,944
Watson, Adam K, dist utilities engr, $68,364
Watson, Brady M, sr const technician, $36,504
Watson, Dale L, sr equip technician, $40,608
Watson, Jeffrey A, maint crew leader, $36,504
Watson, Joseph B, sr maint worker, $39,156
Watson, Paul R, sr maint worker, $33,996
Watson, Robert J, maint crew leader, $36,504
Watson, Tyson K, land surv in training, $39,876
Watterson, Ryan M, sr maint worker, $34,596
Watts, Gary J, maint worker, $29,064
Watts, Ronald L, dist design liaison, $56,676
Weakland, Lori A, sr ofc asst, $27,156
Weaver, Austin J, sr maint worker, $34,596
Weaver, Barry W, maint sup, $48,828
Weaver, Daniel D, sr const technician, $37,140
Weaver, Donald L, maint crew leader, $39,876
Weaver, Jacob M, sr maint worker, $33,996
Weaver, Randy W, sr maint worker, $35,220
Webb, Wesley W, intermed maint wrkr, $30,624
Webber, Joseph W, sr maint worker, $34,596
Weber, Dianna L, lead info syss technologist, $59,928
Weber, Donald G, sr maint worker, $34,596
Weber, Robert A, sr maint worker, $36,504
Weber, Stanley E, maint crew leader, $36,504
Webster, Christopher L, maint worker, $29,064
Weddle, Harley D, intermed maint wrkr, $31,164
Wegener, Kevin W, sr inspection crew mbr, $38,472
Wehmeyer, Bradley S, sr maint worker, $34,596
Wehner, Daniel J, motorist assistance oper, $33,996
Wehrman, Larry G, sr maint worker, $42,072
Weigel, Darren L, sr maint worker, $34,596
Weigum, Christopher R, maint worker, $29,064
Weikel, Christopher V, traffic sup, $51,624
Weimar, Daniel N, maint worker, $29,064
Weiser, Lyle D, sr maint worker, $34,596
Weisman, Russell M, sr historic preserve speci, $55,620
Wekenborg, Hannah L, fin servs technician, $29,592
Welch, Rodney A, maint supt, $50,676
Welling, George F, comp science intern, $12.47/hr
Wells, Billy R, maint crew leader, $38,472
Wells, Brenda C, mcs sys & training analyst, $40,608
Wells, Larry D, sr maint worker, $39,876
Wells, Vicki L, sr plng technician, $41,316
Welschmeyer, Andrew M, sr maint worker, $34,596
Welsh, Larry L, sr equip technician, $39,876
Welter, Coleen R, gen servs mgr, $58,836
Welton, Gill B, sr const insp, $52,596
Weno, Colby J, maint worker, $29,064
Werdehausen, Jeremiah J, maint crew leader, $36,504
Werner, Timothy M, intermed maint wrkr, $31,164
Werner, Wendy R, fin servs spec, $37,800
Werths, Davin D, sr maint worker, $33,996

Wesley, Darryl D, maint worker, $29,064
Wesley, Javon T, seasonal maint worker, $12.44/hr
Wessel, Joshua J, maint crew leader, $41,316
West, Chris M, sr maint worker, $37,800
West, Christopher A, sr hwy dsgnr, $53,580
West, Christopher A, intermed equip tech, $35,856
West, Jeannie P, sr maint worker, $39,876
West, Robert M, gen laborer, $11.37/hr
West, Ryan L, maint sup, $46,044
Westfaul, Jami J, maint worker, $29,064
Westhoff, Jim P, sr equip technician, $42,072
Wethington, Dean A, sr maint worker, $34,596
Whaley, James F, transp mgt sys admin, $65,856
Wharton, Benjamin H, maint sup, $48,828
Wheatley, Becky L, inter const insp, $46,884
Wheatley, William G, sr maint worker, $36,504
Wheeler, Danny J, sr maint worker, $43,608
Wheeler, Edward L, sr maint worker, $33,996
Whelchel, Vanessa E, maint worker, $29,064
Whitaker, Celine A, sr fin servs tech, $35,856
Whitaker, Patrick M, transp proj dsgnr, $67,092
White, Andre T, maint worker, $29,064
White, Barry O, maint crew leader, $36,504
White, Cepeda, maint worker, $29,064
White, Charles A, maint crew leader, $39,156
White, David D, sr hwy dsgnr, $51,624
White, Douglas L, maint sup, $46,884
White, Jackie E, sr maint worker, $33,996
White, Jason D, sr const insp, $52,596
White, Jason E, maint worker, $29,064
White, Jody R, sr maint worker, $34,596
White, Johnny D, sr maint worker, $33,996
White, Ricky G, sr maint worker, $34,596
White, Robert L, seasonal maint worker, $12.44/hr
White, Shaunda A, comm spec, $37,800
White, Sherita C, sr cust serv rep, $37,140
White, Thomas C, sr maint worker, $34,596
White, Tommy G, maint crew leader, $37,140
Whiteaker, Frances M, sr maint worker, $34,596
White-Cronin, Tina M, sr traffic syss oper, $41,316
Whitehead, Patrick E, sr maint worker, $33,996
Whiteman, Duane M, maint crew leader, $45,192
Whitfield, William R, hwy safety dir, $92,772
Whitley, Kelly C, sr maint worker, $34,596
Whitmore, Kyle B, maint worker, $29,064
Whitsitt, James L, intermed equip tech, $37,800
Whittaker, Delmar E, inter const tech, $37,140
Whittaker, Michael S, sr equip technician, $43,608
Whittle, Rodney D, intermed maint wrkr, $31,164
Whyde, Randy A, fac opps spec, $35,856
Wich, Kenneth F, maint crew leader, $36,504
Wichern, Don G, dist engr, $103,944
Wieberg, Carol S, sr administrative technician, $42,072
Wieberg, Leroy H, sr info syss tech, $37,140
Wieberg, Leslie A, sr materials technician, $41,316
Wieberg, Raymond B, maint crew leader, $38,472
Wiechens, Joshua G, motorist assistance oper, $33,996
Wiedmaier, Nicholas D, maint worker, $29,064
Wies, Travis L, sr maint worker, $35,220
Wiggans, Nathan L, maint worker, $29,064
Wiggins, Charles, maint crew leader, $42,816
Wilbers, Donna A, sr motor carrier agent, $42,816
Wilbers, Melissa A, design spt engr, $63,408
Wilbers, Paula J, lead info syss technologist, $58,836
Wilbers, Yvonne M, sr trans planner, $50,676
Wilcox, Jamale V, sr maint worker, $39,876
Wilcox, William J, maint crew leader, $48,828
Wilde, Fredrick J, land surv, $44,400
Wilde, Mark M, equip tech spt spec, $47,736
Wilde, Sunshine E, resource mgmt spec, $55,620
Wilder, Andrew L, const insp, $47,736
Wilder, William J, sr envirnmental spec-ss, $52,596
Wildhaber, Kevin R, sr maint worker, $35,220
Wiles, David K, inter const insp, $48,828
Wiles, Jonathan W, info syss technologist, $37,800
Wiles, Rodney L, sr const insp, $52,596
Wiley, Shannon D, intermed maint wrkr, $31,164
Wilfong, Andrew C, maint worker, $29,064
Wilfong, Travis G, asst maint sup, $40,608

Wilhelm, Gregory A, sr engring professnl-tpt, $31.70/hr
Wilhelm, Rachel L, transp proj dsgnr, $75,180
Wilhite, Stephen J, maint worker, $29,064
Wilhoit, Claire A, structural spec, $42,072
Wilk, Steven S, transp enfrcmnt investigator, $37,800
Wilken, Darren M, sr maint worker, $36,504
Wilkerson, Christina L, fin servs mgr, $55,620
Wilkerson, Jason L, intermed maint wrkr, $31,680
Wilkerson, Matthew D, sr const insp, $53,580
Wilkerson, Susan L, exec asst, $32,280
Wilkerson, Thomas F, sr gis spec, $47,736
Wilkinson, John D, intermed maint wrkr, $31,164
Wilkinson, Renate A, plng & progming engr, $82,692
Wilks, Doug H, sr equip technician, $49,752
Willard, Kenneth L, sr maint worker, $32,832
Willard, Matthew G, sr const insp, $52,596
Willett, Robert J, sr electrcn, $42,816
Williams, Adam J, intermed maint wrkr, $31,164
Williams, Angela D, emergency maint equip operat, $15.00/hr
Williams, Betherny J, sr const insp, $54,600
Williams, Brenda K, sr fin servs tech, $37,800
Williams, Brian K, sr proj dev special, $54,600
Williams, Christopher L, maint sup, $45,192
Williams, Danny, sr maint worker, $37,800
Williams, Donald D, maint crew leader, $37,800
Williams, Freddie J, sr maint worker, $34,596
Williams, James W, maint supt, $50,676
Williams, Jason M, trans proj mgr, $71,016
Williams, Jeffrey B, maint worker, $29,064
Williams, Jennifer K, comm mgr, $54,600
Williams, Jesse C, maint crew leader, $45,192
Williams, Kevin D, sr maint worker, $36,504
Williams, Kevin E, land surv in training, $49,752
Williams, Kevin L, maint worker, $29,064
Williams, Lee Q, sr electrcn, $42,816
Williams, Phillip J, sr maint worker, $35,220
Williams, Scott D, seasonal maint worker, $12.44/hr
Williams, T J, maint sup, $45,192
Williams, Timothy G, maint crew leader, $36,504
Williams, Timothy S, maint crew leader, $36,504
Williamson, Daron M, sr equip technician, $41,316
Williford, Andrew R, sr traffic studies special-nss, $61,092
Willing, Matthew, sr maint worker, $37,140
Willis, Jason R, sr maint worker, $35,220
Willis, Justin C, maint worker, $29,064
Willis, Robert A, sr equip technician, $43,608
Willis, Steven E, sr traffic technician, $37,800
Willis, Wendell D, sr maint worker, $34,596
Willman, Lance, sr maint worker, $35,856
Wills, Charles M, roadside mgr, $49,752
Willson, Danny D, sr maint worker, $34,596
Wilmes, Andrew N, maint worker, $29,064
Wilmes, Leonard J, maint crew leader, $37,140
Wilson, Amy L, info syss sup, $64,632
Wilson, Charles E, sr maint worker, $35,220
Wilson, Cody A, trans enforce investi supv, $49,752
Wilson, Daniel L, urban traffic sup, $49,752
Wilson, Darryl W, sr maint worker, $41,316
Wilson, Duston W, inter const insp, $44,400
Wilson, Edwin L, maint crew leader, $36,504
Wilson, Jacob A, sr hwy dsgnr, $56,676
Wilson, James A, maint crew leader, $37,140
Wilson, Jeff L, sr chemist, $46,884
Wilson, Jeffrey A, sr maint worker, $35,220
Wilson, John E, maint worker, $29,064
Wilson, Kelly S, sr trans planner, $48,828
Wilson, Larry E, maint sup, $45,192
Wilson, Larry L, intermed maint wrkr, $31,164
Wilson, Loyd C, sr maint worker, $34,596
Wilson, Mary M, sr r/w spec, $49,752
Wilson, Melanie L, sr fin servs tech, $18.83/hr
Wilson, Michael E, sr maint worker, $33,396
Wilson, Phillip A, sr electrcn, $46,044
Wilson, Phillip P, sr survey technician, $42,816
Wilson, Rebecca N, sr const insp, $55,620
Wilson, Regina R, central ofc gen serv mg, $62,232
Wilson, Richard G, seasonal maint worker, $12.44/hr
Wilson, Ronald D, sr maint worker, $35,220
Wilson, Ronald D, maint crew leader, $38,472

Wilson, Terry W, bridge inspection technician, $55,620
Wilson, Tracy K, intermed maint wrkr, $31,164
Wilson, Troy A, sr maint worker, $36,504
Wimmer, Tammy L, sr ofc asst, $30,120
Wims, Fred L, sr maint worker, $33,396
Winch, Kyle J, sr maint worker, $33,996
Windsor, Kaitlin E, const intern, $11.64/hr
Windsor, Kenneth L, intermed maint wrkr, $32,280
Winemiller, Joshua L, seasonal maint worker, $12.44/hr
Winge, Bruce R, maint worker, $29,064
Wink, Ann M, sr maint worker, $35,220
Winkelman, Justin L, seasonal maint worker, $12.44/hr
Winkle, Jason L, sr maint worker, $34,596
Winkler, Clara M, electrcn asst, $37,140
Winkler, Daniel G, sr maint worker, $36,504
Winkler, Gary R, sr electrcn, $42,816
Winkler, Robert O, maint crew leader-tpt, $19.21/hr
Winn, Frankie L, intermed maint wrkr, $31,164
Winningham, Mark E, maint sup, $46,884
Winship, David B, maint crew leader, $36,504
Winston, Tobias D, maint worker, $29,064
Winters, Brian K, sr maint worker, $35,220
Wion, Mikia W, seasonal maint worker, $12.44/hr
Wischmeier, Jimmy D, sr maint worker, $34,596
Wischmeier, Larry K, maint sup, $47,736
Wisdom, Jeffrey E, sr design technician, $37,800
Wise, Brad D, sr r/w spec, $52,596
Wisham, Lashanda R, info syss sup, $58,836
Withington, Jeffrey L, sr maint worker, $34,596
Witkowski, Scott D, intermed maint wrkr, $31,164
Witt, Gregory W, maint worker, $29,064
Witt, Jason D, sr maint worker, $34,596
Wolf, Justin A, transp proj dsgnr, $64,632
Wolfe, Alvin L, sr supply agent, $38,472
Wolfe, Jeffrey S, sr info syss technologist, $48,828
Wolff, Jeffrey S, sr maint worker, $34,596
Wolfinbarger, Mickie M, sr maint worker, $36,504
Wolk, Tyler J, const insp, $46,044
Wolken, Carrie J, sr sys mgmt specialis, $47,736
Wolken, Gabriel G, off-sys plans rever, $51,624
Wolken, John M, materials intern, $11.64/hr
Wombwell, Travis M, dist bridge engr, $73,788
Wommack, Thomas A, maint worker, $29,064
Wood, Adam A, int tr studies spec, $51,624
Wood, Anthony C, sr maint worker, $35,856
Wood, Carson B, electrcn, $37,800
Wood, Clay S, sr equip technician, $41,316
Wood, Craig A, sr const insp, $51,624
Wood, David E, sr maint worker, $42,816
Wood, Gregory S, rt of way liaison, $67,092
Wood, Jason C, sr maint worker, $33,396
Wood, John S, sr equip technician, $42,816
Wood, Michael L, maint crew leader, $36,504
Wood, Norma K, spt servs mgr, $65,856
Wood, Patrick R, comm spec, $37,800
Wood, Ray L, sr envirnmental spec-ss, $49,752
Wood, Spencer B, maint worker, $29,064
Wood, Stephen P, motorist assistance oper, $33,996
Wood, Wade P, maint crew leader, $36,504
Woodall, Jesse R, maint worker, $29,064
Wooden, Philip B, intermed maint wrkr, $31,164
Woodruff, Johnny W, sr maint worker, $39,876
Woods, Danny A, roadside mgr, $52,596
Woods, David L, maint worker, $29,064
Woods, Kirby F, sr const insp, $53,580
Woods, Lester, external civil rights dir, $92,772
Woods, Patrick M, sr maint worker, $33,996
Woods, Tommy E, sr maint worker, $43,608
Woody, Amanda N, empl dev specialis, $37,800

Woody, Danny C, sr maint worker, $34,596
Woody, George W, sr maint worker, $35,856
Woolard, Earl V, sr maint worker, $33,396
Wooldridge, John B, maint worker, $29,064
Woolsey, Curt D, sr hwy dsgnr, $59,928
Woolstenhulme, Timothy S, maint crew leader, $36,504
Workes, Michael B, maint crew leader, $38,472
Worley, Jason M, sr maint worker, $36,504
Worthington, Kent D, sr const insp, $50,676
Wortmann, Mark A, maint crew leader, $36,504
Wren, Kevin J, lead info syss technologist, $54,600
Wright, Bruce L, sr const technician, $38,472
Wright, Dale D, maint sup, $45,192
Wright, Jack S, rail safety spec, $49,752
Wright, James R, resident engr, $64,632
Wright, Keith A, maint crew leader, $36,504
Wright, Milton N, maint sup, $51,624
Wright, Robin L, sr maint worker, $37,140
Wulff, John V, seasonal maint worker, $12.44/hr
Wunderlich, James K, governmental rel directo, $92,772
Wunderlich, Sheryl A, sr design technician, $36,504
Wuthnow, Quentin R, sr maint worker, $33,996
Wyant, Mitch D, intermed maint wrkr, $31,164
Wyckoff, Joseph C, gen laborer, $11.37/hr
Wyman, David L, area engr, $67,092
Wyrick, Laurie E, sr engring professnl-tpt, $31.94/hr
Wyrick, Steven R, sr materials insp, $52,596
Wyss, Linda G, sr motor carrier agent, $41,316
Yagelowich, John P, materials intern, $13.14/hr
Yager, Kelly C, maint crew leader, $37,140
Yamnitz, Steven W, sr maint worker, $34,596
Yarber, Jerry K, maint crew leader, $37,140
Yarnell, David R, maint crew leader, $37,800
Yarnell, Russell D, sr maint worker, $42,816
Yates, Scott J, sr maint worker, $33,996
Yeager, Christopher J, lead info syss technologist, $55,620
Yeager, Joshua, int motor carrier agent, $30,120
Yearns, Ivy D, sr maint worker, $35,220
Yeomans, Karen D, area engr, $73,788
Yimer, Ahimed, sr equip technician, $41,316
Yin, Juan, transp proj dsgnr, $63,408
Yost, Rodney G, maint sup, $46,044
Young, Anthony M, sr maint worker, $35,220
Young, Curtis L, sr maint worker, $35,220
Young, Donald G, sr maint worker, $34,596
Young, Douglas K, fac opps sup, $49,752
Young, James C, electrcn asst, $14.90/hr
Young, Roseann, intermed maint wrkr, $31,164
Young, Tammy J, maint worker, $29,064
Young, Trent P, maint crew leader, $36,504
Youngblood, Glen H, electrcn, $39,156
Youngblood, Kirk M, maint sup, $45,192
Younger, Clint A, sr maint worker, $34,596
Youse, Lissie L, comm spec, $37,800
Zeigenbein, Douglas C, maint crew leader, $39,156
Zeiger, Teresa L, sr cust serv rep, $37,800
Zentz, Adam L, bridge insp, $59,928
Zhang, Siyang, gis intern, $13.36/hr
Zibert, Julie A, sr trans planner, $51,624
Zickefoose, Chad E, transp proj dsgnr, $71,016
Ziegler, Brian S, sr equip technician, $50,676
Ziegler, David M, materials insp, $44,400
Zimmer, Ashley N, motor carrier agent, $27,156
Zimmerman, Benjamin R, maint worker, $29,064
Zona, Tim R, sr const insp, $50,676
Zurn, Charles C, equip technician superviso, $46,044
Zuroweste, Janet E, sr maint worker, $35,220
Zuroweste, Ralph A, sr maint worker, $38,472
Zwilling, Laura, legal sec, $28,584

CHAPTER 11

INDEX

Cypresses at Big Oak Tree State Park
Photo Courtesy of Missouri State Archives

Index

D

E

I

J

T

U

V

W

Z